It's my future.

Education. Career. Life.

It's my road.

MyRoad.com invites you to chart a personal roadmap to your future with the most comprehensive and integrated solution for education and career planning. Get started today at MyRoad.com.

In Partnership With
PETERSON'S
THOMSON LEARNING

MYROAD.COM
Explore Your Destiny

PETERSON'S 2001

4 Year Colleges

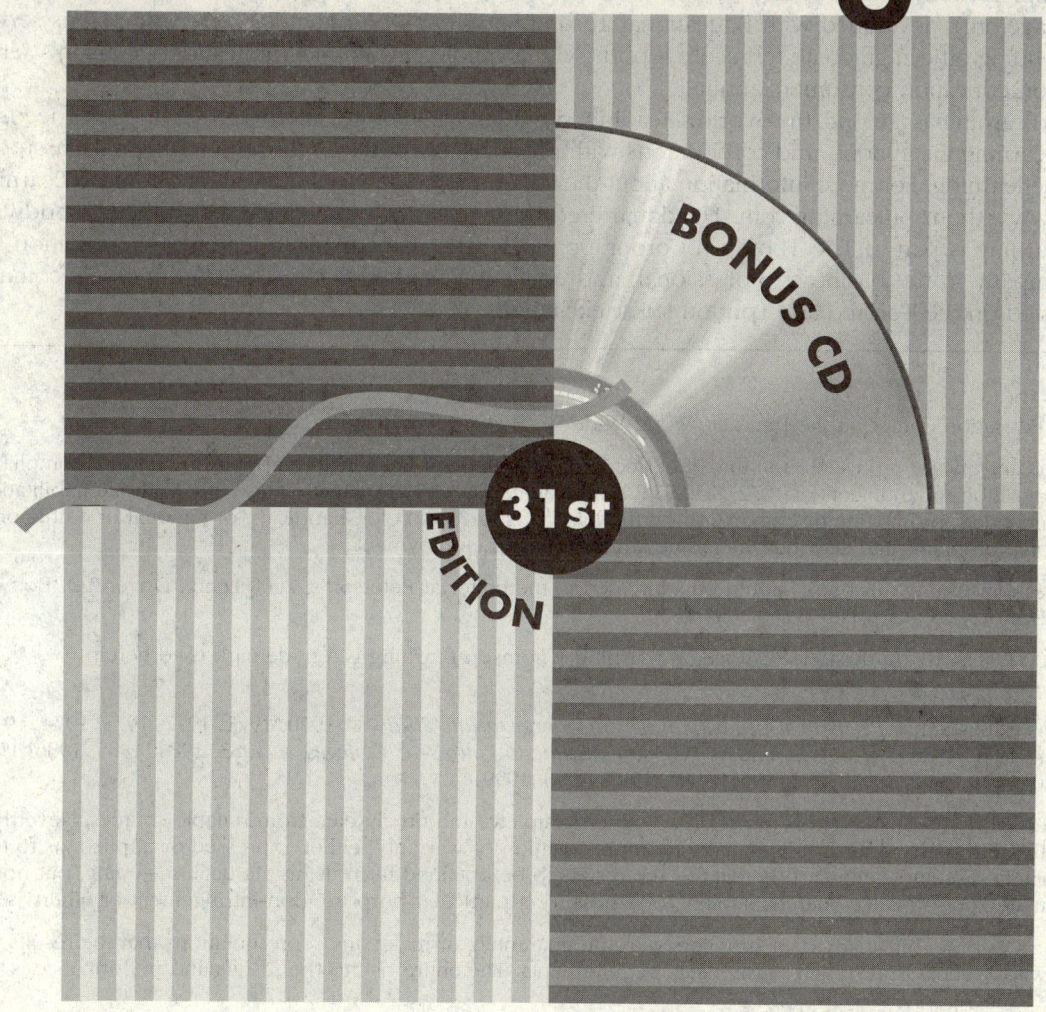

31st EDITION

BONUS CD

"The #1 Bestselling College Guide" —*Publishers Weekly*

The only guide endorsed by the College Parents of America

Peterson's
Thomson Learning

Australia • Canada • Denmark • Japan • Mexico • New Zealand • Philippines
Puerto Rico • Singapore • Spain • United Kingdom • United States

About Peterson's

Founded in 1966, Peterson's, a division of Thomson Learning, is the nation's largest and most respected provider of lifelong learning online resources, software, reference guides, and books. The Education Supersite[SM] at petersons.com—the Web's most heavily traveled education resource—has searchable databases and interactive tools for contacting U.S.-accredited institutions and programs. CollegeQuest[SM] (CollegeQuest.com) offers a complete solution for every step of the college decision-making process. GradAdvantage[TM] (GradAdvantage.org), developed with Educational Testing Service, is the only electronic admissions service capable of sending official graduate test score reports with a candidate's online application. Peterson's serves over 55 million education consumers annually.

Thomson Learning is among the world's leading providers of lifelong learning, serving the needs of individuals, learning institutions, and corporations with products and services for both traditional classrooms and for online learning. For more information about the products and services offered by Thomson Learning, please visit www.thomsonlearning.com. Headquartered in Stamford, Connecticut, with offices worldwide, Thomson Learning is part of The Thomson Corporation (www.thomson.com), a leading e-information and solutions company in the business, professional, and education marketplaces. The Corporation's common shares are listed on the Toronto and London stock exchanges.

Visit Peterson's Education Center on the Internet (World Wide Web) at www.petersons.com

The colleges and universities represented in this book recognize that federal laws, where applicable, require compliance with Title IX (Education Amendments of 1972), Title VII (Civil Rights Act of 1964), and Section 504 of the Rehabilitation Act of 1973 as amended, prohibiting discrimination on the basis of sex, race, color, handicap, or national or ethnic origin in their educational programs and activities, including admissions and employment.

Editorial inquiries concerning this book should be addressed to the editor at Peterson's, 2000 Lenox Drive, P.O. Box 67005, Lawrenceville, New Jersey 08648 (609-896-1800).

Copyright © 2000 Peterson's, a division of Thomson Learning. Thomson Learning is a trademark used herein under license.

Previous editions published as *Peterson's Annual Guide to Undergraduate Study*, © 1970, 1971, 1972, 1973, 1974, 1975, 1976, 1977, 1978, 1979, 1980, 1981, 1982, and as *Peterson's Guide to Four-Year Colleges*, © 1983, 1984, 1985, 1986, 1987, 1988, 1989, 1990, 1991, 1992, 1993, 1994, 1995, 1996, 1997, 1998, 1999

Peterson's makes every reasonable effort to obtain accurate, complete, and timely data from reliable sources. Nevertheless, Peterson's and the third-party data suppliers make no representation or warranty, either expressed or implied, as to the accuracy, timeliness, or completeness of the data or the results to be obtained from using the data, including, but not limited to, its quality, performance, merchantability, or fitness for a particular purpose, non-infringement or otherwise.

Neither Peterson's nor the third-party data suppliers warrant, guarantee, or make any representations that the results from using the data will be successful or will satisfy users' requirements. The entire risk to the results and performance is assumed by the user.

All rights reserved. No part of this book may be reproduced, stored in a retrieval system, or transmitted, in any form or by any means—electronic, mechanical, photocopying, recording, or otherwise—except for citations of data for scholarly or reference purposes with full acknowledgment of title, edition, and publisher and written notification to Peterson's prior to such use.

For permission to use material from this text or product, contact us by
- Web: www.thomsonrights.com
- Phone: 1-800-730-2214
- Fax: 1-800-730-2215

ISSN 0894-9336
ISBN 0-7689-0377-7

Printed in the United States of America

10 9 8 7 6 5 4 3 2 1

CONTENTS

College Countdown Calendar	v
What's in Our Guide	1
A New Way to Target Colleges	3
Making Your Top-Ten College List: How This Guide Can Help	11
Surviving Standardized Tests	21
Preparing to Get In	23
Paying for College: Financial Aid Basics	27
What International Students Need to Know About Admission to U.S. Colleges & Universities	31
Using the Internet in Your College Quest	35
The Military and Higher Education	37
The Military as a Source of Financial Aid	39
The Army ROTC Program	43
Army ROTC Colleges and Universities	49
College Profiles and Special Announcements	53
Quick-Reference College Search Indexes	941
Entrance Difficulty Index	943
Cost Ranges Index	951
Majors Index	959
1999–2000 Changes in Institutions	1103
Alphabetical Index	1105
Geographic Index of In-Depth Descriptions	1117
In-Depth Descriptions of the Colleges	1123

College Countdown
CALENDAR

This practical month-by-month calendar is designed to help you stay on top of the process of applying to college. For most students, the process begins in September of the junior year and ends in June of the senior year. You may want to begin considering financial aid options, reviewing your academic schedule, and attending college fairs before your junior year.

JUNIOR YEAR

September
- Check with your counselor to make sure your course credits will meet college requirements.
- Be sure you are involved in one or two extracurricular activities.
- Begin building your own online college admissions and applications file in your Personal Organizer at http://www.CollegeQuest.com.

October
- Register for and take the PSAT.

November
- Strive to get the best grades you can. Now, a serious effort will provide you with the most options during your application process.

December
- Get involved in a community service activity.
- Begin to read newspapers and a weekly news magazine and keep updated on college news at http://www.CollegeQuest.com.
- Buy *SAT Success* or *ACT Success* and begin to study for the tests.

January
- With your school counselor, decide when to take the ACT, SAT I, and SAT II Subject Tests (and which Subject Tests to take).
- Keep your grades up!

February
- Plan a challenging schedule of classes for your senior year.
- Think about which teachers you will ask to write recommendations.
- Check http://www.nacac.com/fairs.html for schedules and locations of college fairs.

March
- Register for the tests you will take this spring (ACT, SAT I, and SAT II).
- Meet with your school counselor to discuss college choices.
- Review your transcript and test scores with your counselor to determine how competitive your range of choices should be.
- Use CollegeQuest.com on the Web to do initial college research.
- Develop a preliminary list of 15 to 20 colleges and universities and search for information on them.
- Start scheduling campus visits. When school is in session (but never during final exams) is the best time. Summers are OK but will not show you what the college is really like. If possible, save your top college choices for the fall. Be aware, however, that fall is the busiest visit season, and you will need advance planning. (Don't forget to write thank-you letters to your interviewers.)

April
- Take any standardized tests you have registered for.
- In your CollegeQuest Personal Organizer, create a list of your potential college choices and begin to record personal and academic information that can be later transferred to your college applications.

May
- Plan college visits and make appointments.
- Structure your summer plans to include advanced academic work, travel, volunteer work, or a job. See GreatSummerJobs.com for help.
- Confirm your academic schedule for the fall.

Summer
- In your Personal Organizer at CollegeQuest.com, begin working on your application essays.
- Write to any colleges on your list that do not accept the Common or Universal Applications to request application forms.
- Buy the latest edition of *Peterson's Guide to Four-Year Colleges*.

Peterson's Guide to Four-Year Colleges 2000   www.petersons.com

SENIOR YEAR

September
- Register for the ACT, SAT I, and SAT II, as necessary.
- Check with your school counselor for the fall visiting schedule of college reps.
- Ask appropriate teachers if they would write recommendations for you (don't forget to write thank-you letters when they accept).
- Meet with your counselor to compile your final list of colleges.

October
- Mail or send early applications electronically after carefully checking them to be sure they are neat and completely filled out.
- Photocopy or print extra copies of your applications to use as a backup.
- Take the tests you have registered for.
- Don't be late! Keep track of all deadlines for transcripts, recommendations, etc.

November
- Be sure that you have requested your ACT and SAT scores be sent to your colleges of choice.
- Complete and submit all applications. Use CollegeQuest eApply to fill out one application that is accepted at more than 1,200 colleges. This makes it easier for you to apply to several colleges at once. The eApply feature houses the Universal Application, the Common Application, and other custom college applications. Print or photocopy an extra copy for your records.

December
- Take any necessary ACT, SAT I, and SAT II tests.
- Meet with your counselor to verify that all is in order and that transcripts are out to colleges.

January
- Prepare the Free Application for Federal Student Aid (FAFSA), available at http://www.fafsa.ed.gov or through your school counseling office. An estimated income tax statement (which can be corrected later) can be used. The sooner you apply for financial aid, the better your chances.

February
- Send in your FAFSA via the Web or U.S. mail.
- Be sure your midyear report has gone out to the colleges to which you've applied.
- Let your colleges know of any new honors or accomplishments that were not in your original application.

March
- Register for any Advanced Placement (AP) tests you might take.
- Be sure you have received a FAFSA acknowledgment.

April
- Review the acceptances and financial aid offers you receive.
- Go back to visit one or two of your top-choice colleges.
- Notify your college of choice that you have accepted its offer (and send in a deposit by May 1).
- Notify the colleges you have chosen not to attend of your decision.

May
- Take AP tests.

June
- Graduate! Congratulations and best of luck.

Adapted from *Get Organized* by Edward B. Fiske and Phyllis Steinbrecher (Peterson's).

WHAT'S IN OUR GUIDE

Peterson's gives students and parents the most comprehensive, up-to-date information on undergraduate institutions in the United States and Canada. The data published in *Peterson's Guide to Four-Year Colleges* are researched each year by Peterson's. The information is furnished by the colleges and is completely accurate and current.

This guide also features up-to-date advice and tips, such as how to consider the factors that truly make a difference in your college search process, understand the application process, and file for financial aid. If you seem to be getting more, not less, anxious about choosing and getting into the right college, *Peterson's Guide to Four-Year Colleges* provides just the right help. It gives you the knowledge you need to make important college decisions and to approach the admissions process without fear.

Opportunities abound for students, and this guide can help you find what you want in a number of ways:

- If you have certain criteria in mind, turn to the easy-to-use College Yellow Pages. In these quick-reference indexes, you can look up a particular feature—entrance difficulty level, cost range, or the major you're interested in—and immediately find the colleges that meet your criteria. (A separate list in the Army ROTC section shows which colleges offer this option.)

- For good advice, just turn the page. Robert Zemsky, Director of the world-famous Institute for Research on Higher Education, reports on the first truly meaningful college choice consumer guide, a system featured last year in *Time* magazine that rates colleges on how well they fulfill twenty-one specific categories of need for their graduates. This new research and data will allow students to meaningfully compare college choices in light of their own specific requirements and see how well each college has answered the same requirements for its own graduates; *Making Your Top-Ten College List: How This Guide Can Help* explains some of the key factors you need to consider in the college search process and how to locate this information in the individual college profiles; *Surviving Standardized Tests* describes the most frequently used tests and lists test dates for 2000–01; *Preparing to Get In* provides advice on how best to approach the applying phase of the process; *Paying for College: Financial Aid Basics* gives you the essential information on how to meet your educational expenses; *What International Students Need to Know About Admission to U.S. Colleges & Universities* is a basic guide with helpful tips to college admissions for non–U.S. citizens and can also be helpful to U.S. citizens; and *Using the Internet in Your College Quest* explains college searching on the World Wide Web. For information about the military's incredible financial aid deal, see the section titled *The Military and Higher Education* on page 0.

- For information about particular colleges, turn to the section called *College Profiles and Special Announcements* on page 53. In this section, our unparalleled college descriptions are arranged alphabetically by state. They provide a complete picture of need-to-know information about every accredited four-year college—from admission to graduation, including current expenses, financial aid, and campus safety. All the information you need at hand to apply is placed together at the conclusion of each college profile. In addition, for almost 1,000 colleges, two-page narrative descriptions appear in the *In-Depth Descriptions of the Colleges* section, in the back of the book. These descriptions are written by admissions deans and provide great detail about each college. They are edited to provide a consistent format across entries for your ease of comparison.

Welcome to the world of well-informed college decisions—courtesy of Peterson's.

- For help with the overall application process, turn to the back of the book, where you will find your bonus CD-ROM. The CD includes full-length SAT and ACT practice tests, and direct access to CollegeQuest on the World Wide Web, where you can set up your own personal college search file, search for and compare colleges using various criteria, find scholarships, and complete and submit one application that is accepted at more than 1,200 colleges.

Peterson's publishes a full line of resources to help you and your family with any information you need to guide you through the admissions process. Peterson's publications can be found at your local bookstore, library, and high school guidance office. CollegeQuest.com from Peterson's combines these resources and more in an interactive center that helps with every aspect of the college choice and application process.

Colleges will be pleased to know that Peterson's helped you in your selection. Admissions staff members are more than happy to answer questions, address specific problems, and help in any way they can. CollegeQuest's Ask the Experts forum allows you to ask admissions and financial aid experts about any college concerns. Answers to students' questions are posted on a regular basis and archived for everyone to read. The staff at Peterson's wishes you great success in your college search.

A New Way to Target Colleges

Whether you are a teenager or parent, you are well aware that choosing a college is serious business. On the surface, the process may seem relatively simple. Within several months, your task is to narrow the choice of colleges and universities to a manageable few, submit applications, and pick a school to attend from those that send acceptance letters.

Beneath the surface, it's not so simple. The college selection process can be quite nerve-racking. Choosing a college is often the first major decision that many teenagers have to make. Many applicants and their parents are going through this for the first time, which creates an even more intimidating situation. Fortunately, a great deal of support is available. Be prepared to sift through a lot of information in the form of brochures, Web sites, videos, catalogues, and advice. You will receive a great deal of advice. Some people will warn you that this is the most critical decision you'll ever make. Others will cheerfully tell you not to worry because you can always change your mind. Parents, aunts, teachers, friends-everyone will have opinions. Everyone will want to be helpful. A seemingly endless stream of people praising the virtues of their alma maters probably will visit you in your high school. At home, you'll have piles of written information from admissions offices to read. In addition, there are publications that attempt to rank institutions in order to help make the choice easier. However, these rankings lack precision because the rankers are constantly changing the formula. Needless to say, rankings are not a viable tool to use in choosing a college or university and could very easily lead you down the wrong path.

Once your applications are submitted, it is the institution's turn to go to work and your turn to wait. An admissions committee reads your essays, letters of recommendation, and transcripts. They deliberate about whether you could make a special contribution to the institution by playing in the orchestra or on the basketball team. They take into consideration whether members of your family are graduates of their institution. Then they will render judgment. If you are one of the lucky ones, you will get a thick envelope on or about March 1. Otherwise, you will get a thin letter which contains a short but nicely written message wishing you good luck at some other college or university.

YOU ARE A CONSUMER

Let's back up and look at this quick overview about getting into college from another viewpoint. You probably never realized that higher education is a business that makes approximately $150 billion a year. While it's true that colleges and universities are devoted to teaching and scholarly research, simulta-

A New Way to Target Colleges

neously they are enterprises that require revenues—the tuition you will pay. Even the most famous, most prestigious, and best endowed colleges and universities depend on tuition to pay their faculty, operate their facilities, and field their sports teams. Without students, there is no revenue and no institution!

What does this make you? A learner and a consumer; a student and a customer. Because you are buying something that is expensive, you must know what you want and be able to distinguish between a high-quality product and one that does not measure up to your standards. You are the consumer, and as such, the range and quality of products available to you—in this case colleges—is primarily dependent on how good a shopper you are. Good shoppers are informed, observant, and ready to look elsewhere if they are not offered the level of quality they expect at the tuition they can afford. Once you understand that the admissions process is also a market process, you will have more standards by which to choose a college.

WOULD YOU BUY AN EXPENSIVE ITEM WITHOUT THE BEST INFORMATION AVAILABLE?

You are buying a product that many people want and one which is getting more expensive each year. There's no question that the demand for higher education is rising along with tuition rates. Your stakes in the process are rising, too. You need unbiased information so that you can meaningfully compare institutions and be equipped to obtain the best education that is available within your budgetary and other constraints.

Being a smart consumer requires comparison shopping. Suppose you were buying your dream car. Obviously, a college education has more lasting value than a car; however, you can use the same principles when shopping for either. First, you would zero in on what you really wanted in a car. You would talk to other car buyers in order to put your criteria in perspective with theirs—what were they looking for, and how did their objectives compare with your own? Second, you'd talk to recent buyers who had driven their new cars for a while to see if their standards were met.

Now apply the consumer scenario of buying an expensive car to buying a college education. Wouldn't it be nice to know how recent graduates felt about how their alma maters met their expectations? In fact, by talking to graduates from many institutions you will get a good idea of how colleges measure up to certain attributes. For example, suppose a college claims to produce many engineers and you find that a high percentage of the graduates are engineers. If you were considering engineering as a career, this college could be one to choose. Conversely, if a low percentage of graduates indicate that they have strong religious values, you may not want to consider that school if religion is important to you.

The first step in the process is to determine what is important to you. What do you want to get out of a college education? What values are important to you? What career are you considering? What skills do you see yourself using on the job? By determining your expectations and characteristics, you can make a well-informed decision when choosing a college.

WHAT IS IMPORTANT TO TEENAGERS IN GENERAL?

Dr. Robert Zemsky, along with his colleagues Susan Shaman and Ann Duffield of the University of Pennsylvania's Institute for Research on Higher Education, have been developing a methodology to compare colleges and universities by gathering data on the experiences of college students six years after their graduation. The findings from these surveys can make a big difference in how you compare colleges. You will see how this works later, but first, let's look at teenagers today.

Dr. Zemsky surveyed teenagers currently in high school about their expectations for the future. Seven thousand teens responded to his survey *What Internet-Savvy, College-Bound Teenagers Think About College*. The data indicated what teenagers expect from college and the workplace and what they value. For example, as you can see in Figure 1, friendship and financial security are the top two values that are most important to the teens that responded to the survey. You can obtain a copy of this research report at **www.petersons.com/teensurvey**.

How closely do your values coincide with what these teens said? How do their values put into perspective the things that matter to you? Wouldn't you want your college experience to reflect your values before making such a big commitment of time and money?

A New Way to Target Colleges

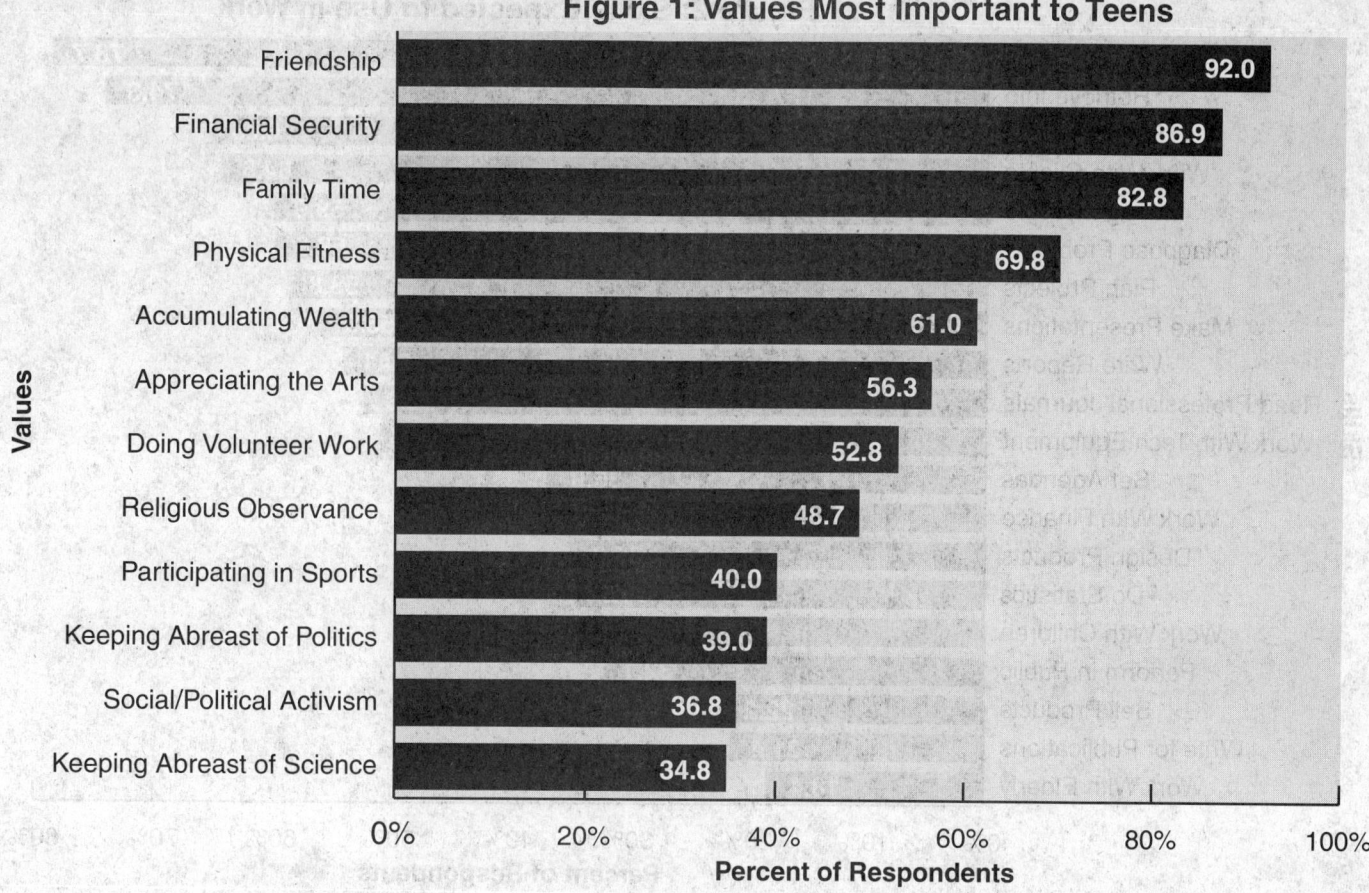

Source: *What Internet-Savvy, College-Bound Teenagers Think About College,* Peterson's (www.petersons.com/teensurvey).

The data also showed what skills teens expect to use once they graduate from college and enter the workplace. The responses indicate that teenagers show a keen awareness that the skills they acquire must be usable in a rapidly changing world (see Figure 2). Being able to set priorities, retrieve and interpret data, and work with people topped their lists. Is this what you think you'll need to be successful once you graduate? Finding out will establish how a college can further your goals. Will it offer courses and programs to help you gain and develop the skills you will need in the career of your choice? The answers to the questions you ask yourself will play an important part in the selection of a college or university. You will be able to match the values and expectations that are important to you to colleges and universities.

THE ULTIMATE COLLEGE CONSUMER GUIDE—RECENT GRADS

In conjunction with the National Center for Postsecondary Improvement and Peterson's, Dr. Zemsky is conducting ongoing research of recent graduates from colleges and universities. Similar to people who have purchased new cars, these graduates were the consumers of the product you want to buy. They have been using the education they received in the workplace and their daily lives.

In order to accumulate pertinent data that is useful for college applicants, graduates were asked survey questions that fell into five general categories:

- PERSONAL VALUES-values that are important to graduates now
- ABILITIES-complex tasks graduates feel confident performing

A New Way to Target Colleges

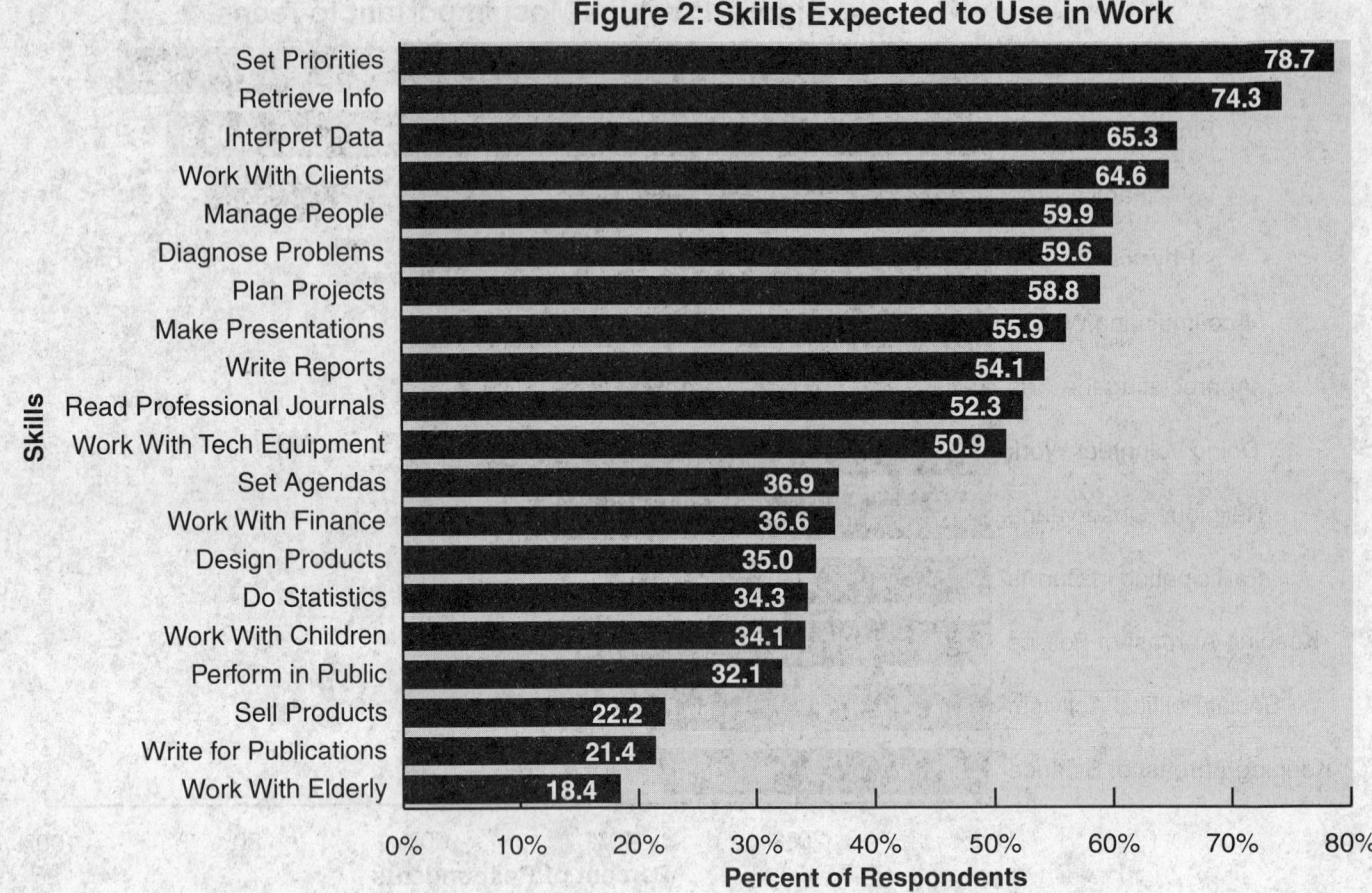

Source: *What Internet-Savvy, College-Bound Teenagers Think About College,* Peterson's (www.petersons.com/teensurvey).

- OCCUPATION-current occupations and annual incomes
- WORK SKILLS-job skills graduates are using
- LIFELONG LEARNING-how much to they like to learn and continue to learn

As the data is gathered and analyzed, it begins to show how institutions measure up to preparing and building values in their students. As you can see in Figure 3, the five categories are divided into twenty-four attributes. Around the perimeter of the target are the attributes. For example, community/civic, cultural, religious, and friends/family make up the personal values category. The data shows how institutions measure up to the attributes. If a high percentage of the graduates exhibit an attribute, the college hits the bull's-eye in terms of that attribute. The lower the percentage, the further the institution will be from the bull's-eye, with regard to that attribute.

The research results provide powerful consumer information you can use in your search for a college. By determining what is important to you, you can compare your desires and expectations to the attributes of the colleges on your list. In other words, you can determine how your bull's-eyes stack up against the institution's bull's-eyes.

If two thirds or more of the graduates possess a particular attribute, that institution hit the bull's-eye. If less than two thirds of the responses indicated that an institution possessed an attribute, it hit the middle ring of the target. The institution landed on the outer rim of the target if less than one third of the responses indicated that the attribute applied to the institution. In the initial data collection, all of the institutions hit the bull's-eye on the attribute of friends and family. If you refer back to the survey about what teens said

A New Way to Target Colleges

Figure 3

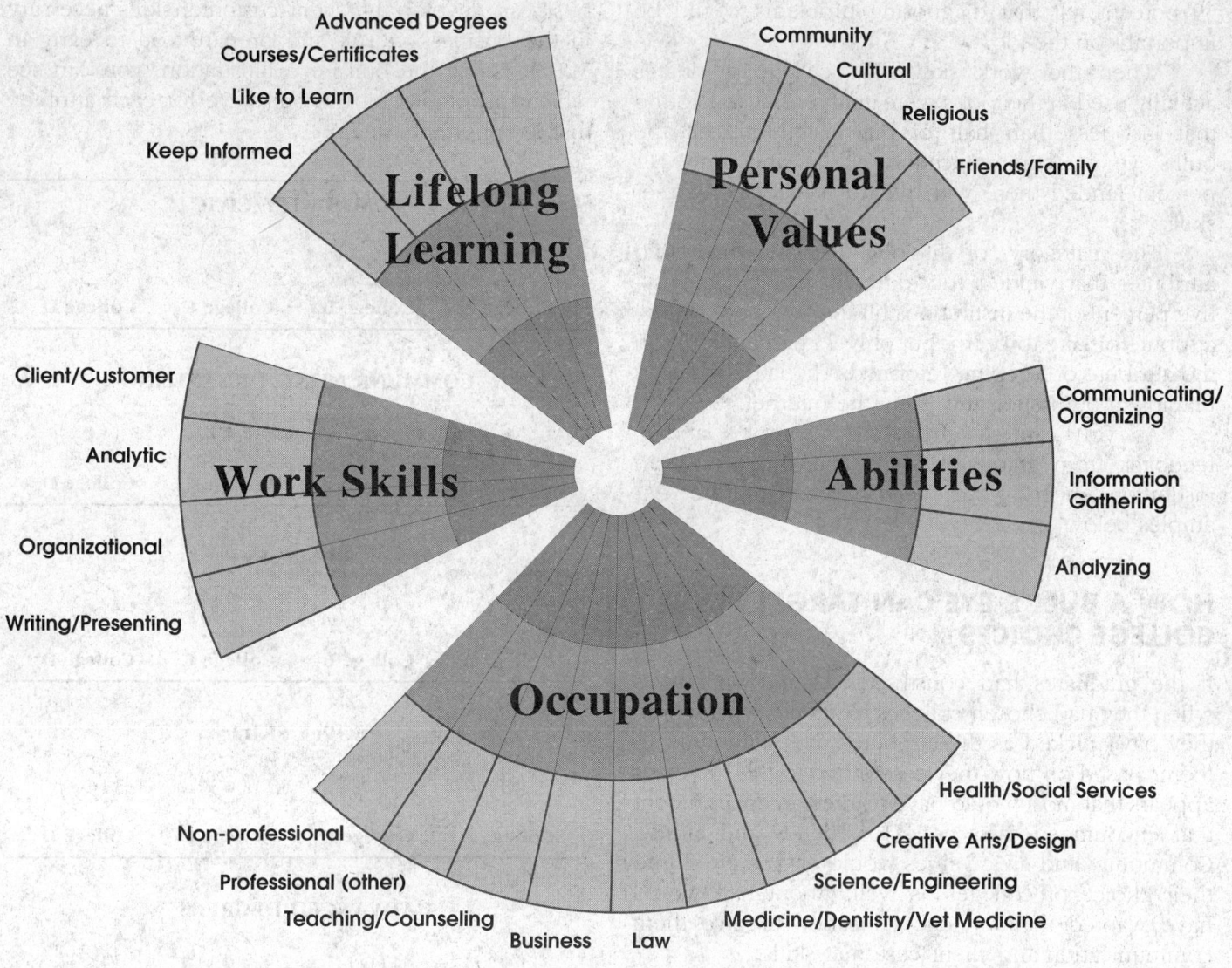

they value most, you'll see that friendship tops their list, too. From this, it can be assumed that a common personal value among teens and graduates are the relationships they have with friends and family.

In another example, institutions were assessed on the attributes of community/civic, cultural, and religious in the category of personal values. Of these, 93 percent of the institutions hit the middle ring on community and cultural attributes, whereas only 4 percent hit the bull's-eye. When it came to religion, none hit the bull's-eye. Fifty-six percent landed on the middle ring, while 44 percent landed on the outer rim of the target.

There are some similarities between the values of teens and the personal values of college graduates. Almost 53 percent of the teen respondents said that volunteer work matters to them, which closely matches the mid-range scores that community values held for college graduates.

In the abilities category, 98 percent of the institutions hit the bull's-eye for the attribute of communicating/organizing. Conversely, only 20 percent of the institutions hit the bull's-eye for problem

A New Way to Target Colleges

solving. Most of the teen respondents said they expect to set priorities when they reach the workplace, and 59 percent felt that diagnosing problems would be important on the job.

When the work skills that college graduates actually used in their jobs were analyzed, it was found that just less than half of the institutions hit the bull's-eye in communication skills, and only 11 percent landed there with regard to client/customer skills.

The category of lifelong learning had two attributes that yielded very different results. Seventy-five percent of the institutions hit the bull's-eye on the attribute of Like to Learn, but only 23 percent hit it on the attribute of Keeping Informed. The latter includes reading about issues and using the Internet.

As you can see from the examples above, feedback from graduates helps you assess how an institution meets your needs. Look at the examples below.

HOW A BULL'S-EYE CAN TARGET YOUR COLLEGE CHOICES

If the graduates had constructed their own targets when they had chosen colleges to attend, what would they have picked as the attributes most important to them? Based on how they responded to the survey, it appears that most would have wanted an environment that encouraged their need for friends and family. Community and civic values would have figured into their choice of colleges as well. About half would have wanted their college education to give them communication and client/customer skills.

They didn't have the benefit of knowing how to target attributes when they were making their decisions, but you do. You can determine your own list of attributes and use them to compare the colleges on your list. Let's examine how you would go about this.

Suppose that you are interested primarily in private liberal arts colleges and considering a career in business. You come from a family that has encouraged you to do volunteer work in the community, so you want your college years to strengthen your community and civic values. Imagine that you have narrowed your choices to four colleges and wish to compare what their graduates report against the attributes you have chosen for your bull's-eye. You want a college to foster an environment that encourages your community values, build your ability to communicate and organize, give you what is required for a career in business, develop the client/customer skills necessary in the business world, and prepare you to earn an M.B.A. Using the bull's-eye illustration, you can see which institutions hit the bull's-eye for each attribute that is important you.

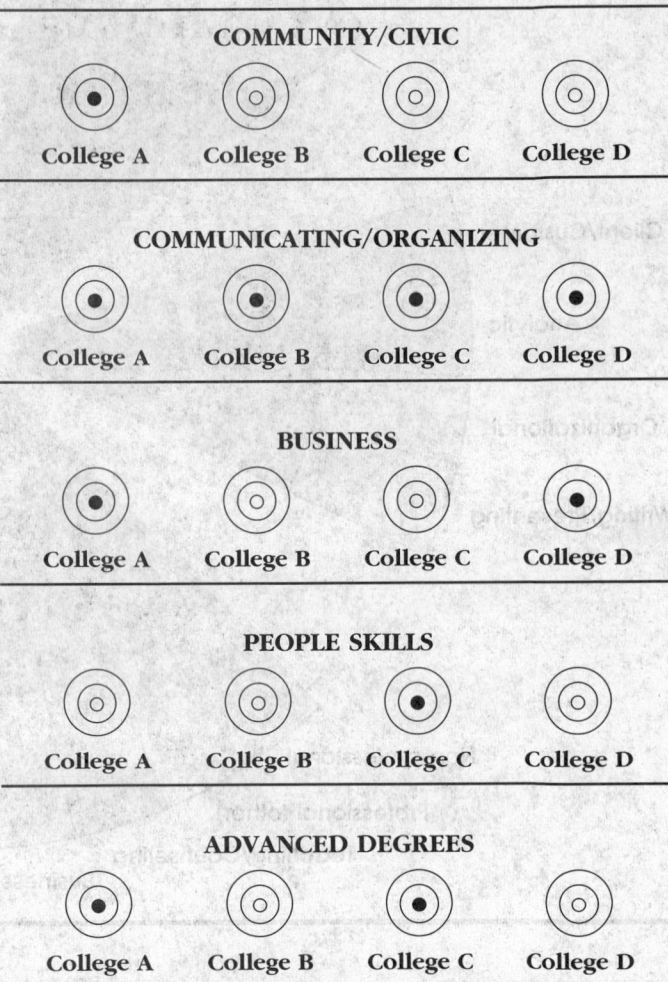

How did your four liberal arts colleges compare? On four of the five attributes you chose as important, College A hit the bull's-eye. If your personal ranking of the institutions was a simple score card reporting who got the most bull's-eyes, then College A was the clear winner.

Unfortunately, real-world choices are seldom that clear-cut. In any major decision, there are many facets to consider. It looks like the graduates of College A reported that people skills are not very significant. If people skills are important to you, this is a reason to pause and look again at the targets.

A New Way to Target Colleges

What about College C? It has a bull's-eye in communicating/organizing, advanced degrees, and client/customer skills, but not in community/civic or business occupations. You would find that this college was particularly good in providing its graduates the work skills they used on the job. Do not choose from these comparisons alone! You must visit the college to get the feel of the campus and talk with students and faculty members.

Here's another example that compares the same four liberal arts colleges. This time we'll rate them as if you were interested in a career in a science field.

LIBERAL ARTS COLLEGES COMPARED FROM A SCIENCE STUDENT'S PERSPECTIVE

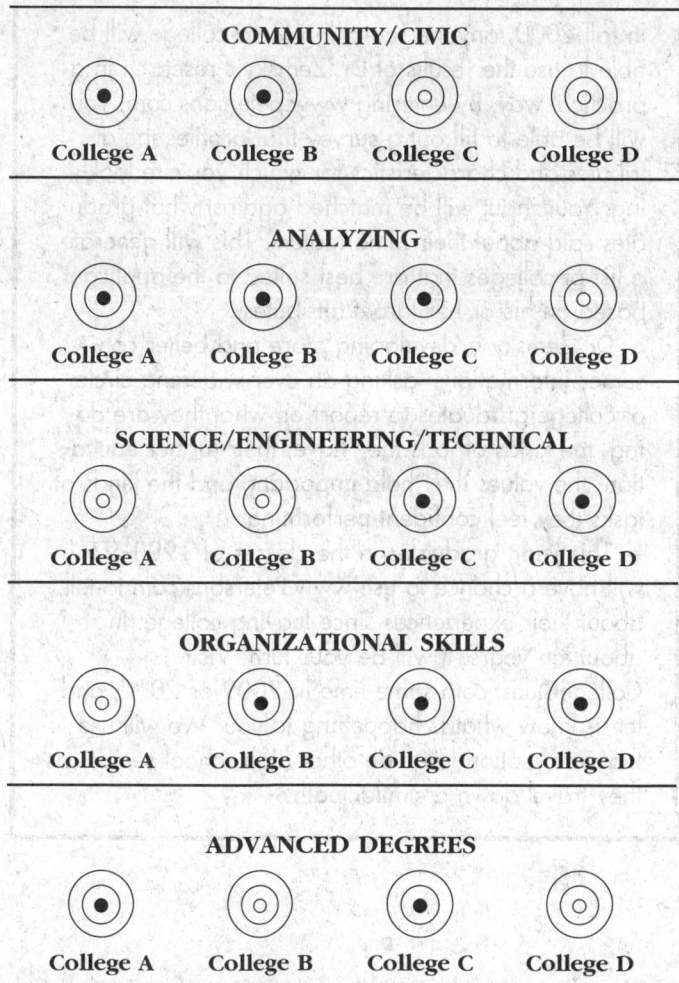

Remember, these are the same colleges as in the first example. Given that these colleges are being compared by a science student, the top rated choice now probably would be College C with four bull's-eyes. However, there are some other factors to consider. Perhaps College A's graduates were not as concentrated in the sciences as in some other colleges. You might extend your search to other liberal arts colleges that scored a bull's-eye for scientific occupations, or you might find that the graduates of this institution go on to advanced degrees and use science and technical skills on the job. On the other hand, you may want to attend a college that specializes in science and engineering education only. Again, the purpose of the comparisons is not to let a chart make the decision for you but to help you think through what you really want.

SOME OTHER ATTRIBUTES TO ADD TO YOUR TARGET: PRICE, LOCATION, AND SIZE

Up to now, nothing has been said about the factors that applicants often think about first when choosing a college: price, location, and size. Without realizing it, you may have pared down your college choices with these prerequisites in mind. For example, you might want to attend a less costly institution. The cost of tuition is usually an enormous part of choosing a college.

You may have decided that you will begin comparing the possibilities of institutions within a 200-mile radius of your home. Other students might decide that they definitely want to be within a specific region near the ocean or in the mountains.

Size is usually a primary consideration for many students as well. Coming from large high schools, some students want the closeness of relationships and class size that smaller colleges offer, or it could be the other way around—they would like the variety of options found at a large university.

PUBLIC UNIVERSITIES COMPARED FOR A SCIENCE STUDENT

COMMUNITY/CIVIC

University A   University B   University C   University D

Peterson's Guide to Four-Year Colleges 2001   www.petersons.com   9

A New Way to Target Colleges

ANALYZING

University A University B University C University D

SCIENCE/ENGINEERING/TECHNICAL

University A University B University C University D

ORGANIZATIONAL SKILLS

University A University B University C University D

ADVANCED DEGREES

University A University B University C University D

In this illustration, the institution with the most bull's-eyes is University B. For this set of ratings criteria, University B has as many bull's-eyes as the best of the liberal arts colleges. The public university's most glaring weakness is probably the fact that relatively few of its graduates go on to advanced degrees.

These three graphics give you a basic idea about how you can make a more informed choice. Knowing how the graduates of a particular college or university turn out is important. Armed with this information, you can more easily imagine yourself as a graduate of that institution. Getting information about the colleges and universities that is meaningful to you ensures that you won't have to use someone else's definition of quality. You should use criteria that constitutes your best institution and then apply those standards to the colleges and universities you are considering.

This is not to suggest that you should rely on charts or scores to determine which college or university you should attend. Knowing what college-bound teens want and what recent graduates got out of their degrees can help you to think about your needs and expectations. It will also give you the basis for formulating insightful questions to ask of others. You will be able to put into perspective the advice of your parents, teachers, and guidance counselors and ask pertinent questions of those who are still in college or have already graduated. You will know what to look for when you visit campuses to gather firsthand information. Good luck in your search.

In fall 2000, anyone searching for a college will be able to use the results of Dr. Zemsky's research in a practical way. By entering www.petersons.com, you will be able to fill out a survey that profiles the attributes and characteristics for which you are looking. Your input will be matched against what graduates said about their alma maters. This will generate a list of colleges that are best suited to the applicant based on his or her target attributes.

Dr. Zemsky is developing more and better consumer information—asking an ever widening circle of college graduates to report on what they are doing, the kinds of jobs they have, their further education, the values they hold important, and the kinds of tasks they feel confident performing.

This year, graduates in the classes of 1993–97 will have a chance to use www.Petersons.com to tell about their experiences since leaving college. In about ten years, it will be your turn. Visit CollegeQuest.com some time in 2009 or 2010, and let us know what is happening to you. We will use that information to guide other high school seniors as they travel down a similar path.

MAKING YOUR TOP TEN COLLEGE LIST:

How This Guide Can Help

By using all the information in the various sections of this guide, you will find the colleges worthy of the most important top ten list on the planet--yours.

The first thing you will need to do is decide what type of institution of higher learning you want to attend. Each of the more than 1,700 colleges and universities in the United States is as unique as the people applying to it. Although listening to the voices around you can make it sound as though there are only a few elite schools worth attending, this simply is not true. By considering some of the following criteria, you will soon find that the large pool of interesting colleges has been narrowed to a more reasonable number.

1. Size and Category. Schools come in all shapes and sizes, from tiny rural colleges of 400 students to massive state university systems serving 100,000 students or more. If you are coming from a small high school, a college with 3,500 students may seem large to you. If you are currently attending a high school with 3,000 students, selecting a college of a similar size may not feel like a new enough experience. Some students coming from very large impersonal high schools are looking for a place where they will be recognized from the beginning and offered a more personal approach. If you don't have a clue about what size might feel right to you, try visiting a couple of nearby colleges of varying sizes. You do not have to be seriously interested in them; just feel what impact the number of students on campus has on you.

Large Universities. Large universities offer a wide range of educational, athletic, and social experiences. Universities offer a full scope of undergraduate majors and award master's and doctoral degrees as well. Universities are usually composed of several smaller colleges. Depending on your interest in a major field or area of study, you would likely apply to a specific college within the university. Each college has the flexibility to set its own standards for admission, which may differ from the overall average of the university. For example, a student applying to a university's College of Arts and Sciences might need a minimum GPA of 3.2 and a minimum SAT I score of 1200. Another, applying to the College of Engineering, may find that a minimum GPA of 3.8 and SAT I score of 1280 are the standards. The colleges within a university system also set their own course requirements for earning a degree.

Universities may be public or private. Some large private universities, such as Harvard, Yale, Princeton, University of Pennsylvania, New York University, Northwestern, and Stanford, are well-known for their high entrance standards, the excellence of their education, and the success rates of their graduates. These institutions place a great deal of emphasis on research and compete aggressively for grants from the federal government to fund these projects. Large public universities, such as the State University of New York (SUNY) System, University of Michigan, University of Texas, University of Illinois, University of Washington, and University of North Carolina, also support excellent educational programs, compete for and win research funding, and have successful graduates. Public universities usually offer substantially lower tuition

Making Your Top Ten College List: How This Guide Can Help

rates to in-state students, although their tuitions to out-of-state residents are often comparable to private institutions.

At many large universities, sports play a major role on campus. Athletics can dominate the calendar and set the tone year-round at some schools. Alumni travel from far and wide to attend their alma mater's football or basketball games, and the campus, and frequently the entire town, grinds to a halt when there is a home game. Athletes are heroes and dominate campus social life.

What are some other features of life on a university campus? Every kind of club imaginable, from literature to bioengineering and chorus to politics, can be found on most college campuses. You will be able to play the intramural version of almost every sport in which the university fields interscholastic teams and join fraternities, sororities, and groups dedicated to social action. You can become a member of a band, an orchestra, or perhaps a chamber music group or work on the newspaper, the literary magazine, and the Web site. The list can go on and on. You may want to try out a new interest or two or pursue what you have always been interested in and make like-minded friends along the way.

Take a look at the size of the classrooms in the larger universities and envision yourself sitting in that atmosphere. Would this offer a learning environment that would benefit you?

Liberal Arts Colleges. If you have considered large universities and come to the conclusion that all that action could be a distraction, a small liberal arts college might be right for you. Ideally tucked away on a picture-perfect campus, a liberal arts college generally has fewer than 5,000 students. The mission of most liberal arts schools is learning for the sake of learning, with a strong emphasis on creating lifelong learners who will be able to apply their education to any number of careers. This contrasts with objectives of the profession-based preparation of specialized colleges.

Liberal arts colleges cannot offer the breadth of courses provided by the large universities. As a result, liberal arts colleges try to create a niche for themselves. For instance, a college may place its emphasis on its humanities departments, whose professors are all well-known published authors and international presenters in their areas of expertise. A college may highlight its science departments by providing state-of-the-art facilities where undergraduates conduct research side by side with top-notch professors and copublish their findings in the most prestigious scientific journals in the country. The personal approach is very important at liberal arts colleges. Whether in advisement, course selection, athletic programs tailored to students' interests, or dinner with the department head at her home, liberal arts colleges emphasize that they get to know their students.

If they are so perfect, why doesn't everyone choose a liberal arts college? Well, the small size limits options. Fewer people may mean less diversity. The fact that many of these colleges encourage a study-abroad option (a student elects to spend a semester or a year studying in another country) reduces the number of students on campus even further. Some liberal arts colleges have a certain reputation that does not appeal to some students. You should ask yourself questions about the campus life that most appeals to you. Will you fit in with the campus culture? Will the small size mean that you go through your social options quickly? Check out the activities listed on the Student Center bulletin board. Does the student body look diverse enough for you? Will what is happening keep you busy and interested? Do the students have input into decision making? Do they create the social climate of the school?

Small Universities. Smaller universities, often combine stringent admissions policies, handpicked faculty members, and attractive scholarship packages. These institutions generally have undergraduate enrollments of about 4,000 students. Some are more famous for their graduate and professional schools, but have established strong undergraduate colleges. Smaller universities balance the great majors options of large universities with a smaller campus community. They offer choices but not to the same extent as large universities. On the other hand, by limiting admissions and enrollment, they manage to cultivate some of the characteristics of a liberal arts college. Like a liberal arts college, a small university may emphasize a particular program and go out of its way to draw strong candidates in a specific area, such as premed, to its campus. Universities such as Johns Hopkins University, University of Notre Dame, Vanderbilt University, Washington University in St. Louis, and Wesleyan University in Connecticut are a few examples of this category.

Specialized Colleges. Another alternative to the liberal arts college or to the large university is the technical or otherwise specialized college. Their goal is to offer a specialized and saturated experience in a particular field of study. Such an institution might limit its course offerings to engineering and science, the performing or fine arts, or business. Schools such as the California Institute of Technology, Carnegie Mellon University, Massachusetts Institute of Technology, and Rensselaer Polytechnic Institute concentrate on attracting the finest math and science students in the country. At other schools, like Bentley College in Massachusetts or Bryant College in Rhode Island, students eat, sleep, and breathe business. These institutions are purists at heart and strong believers in the necessity of focused, specialized study to produce excellence in their graduates' achievements. If you are certain about your chosen path in life and want to immerse yourself in subjects such as math, music, or business to be best prepared for a particular kind of career, you will fit right in.

Religious Colleges. Many private colleges have religious origins, and many of these have become secular institutions with virtually no trace of their religious roots. Others remain dedicated to a religious way of education.

What sets religious colleges apart is the way they combine faith, learning, and student life. Faculty members and administrators are hired with faith as a criterion as much as their academic credentials.

Student life is organized according to the tenets and understandings of the college's religious faith. A prospective student looking for a faith-structured education might feel comfortable at a college affiliated with a different but similar denomination within a religious category. For example, the Council for Christian Colleges and Universities, which sponsors *Peterson's Christian Colleges and Universities* guide, encompasses thirty-four different Protestant denominations. Students who belong to one church likely would feel comfortable at most colleges in the group, regardless of the fact that they may be affiliated with a different church.

Single-Gender Colleges. There are strong arguments that being able to pursue one's education without the distraction, competition, and stress caused by the presence of the opposite sex helps a student evolve a stronger sense of her or his self-worth; achieve more academically; have a more fulfilling, less pressured social life; and achieve more later in life. For various historic, social, and psychological reasons, there are many more all-women than all-men colleges. A strict single-sex environment is rare. Even though the undergraduate day college adheres to an all-female or all-male admissions policy, coeducational evening classes or graduate programs and coordinate facilities and classes shared with nearby coed or opposite-sex institutions can result in a good number of students of the opposite sex being found on campus. Women's colleges, such as Scripps College, Smith College, Sweet Briar College, and Wellesley College, pride themselves on turning out leaders. If you want to concentrate on your studies and hone your leadership qualities, a single-gender school might be an option.

2. Location. Location and distance from home are two other important considerations. If you have always lived in the suburbs, choosing an urban campus can be an adventure, but after a week of the urban experience, will you long for a grassy campus and open space? On the other hand, if you choose a college in a rural area, will you run screaming into the Student Center some night looking for noise, lights, and people? The location—urban, rural, or suburban—can directly affect how easy or how difficult adjusting to college life will be for you.

Don't forget to factor in distance from home. Everyone going off to college wants to think he or she won't be homesick, but sometimes it's nice to get a home-cooked meal or to do the laundry in a place that does not require quarters. Even your kid sister may seem like less of a nuisance after a couple of months away.

Here are some questions you might ask yourself as you go through the selection process: In what part of the country do I want to be? How far away from home do I want to be? What is the cost of returning home? Do I need to be close to a city? How close? How large of a city? Would city life distract me? Would I concentrate better in a setting that is more rural or more suburban?

In the state-by-state College Profiles and Special Announcements, which begin on page 55, you'll find state maps in the College Profiles that indicate the location of each college within the state. In every college profile, the third bulleted highlight indicates if a campus is located in an urban, suburban, small-town, or rural area. In the In-Depth Descriptions of the Colleges section, the second paragraph of each college description provides a description of the college's location.

3. Entrance Difficulty. Many students will look at a college's entrance difficulty as an indicator of whether or not they will be admitted. For instance, if you have an excellent academic record, you might wish to *primarily* consider those colleges that are highly competitive. Although entrance difficulty does not translate directly to quality of education, it indicates which colleges are attracting large numbers of high-achieving students. A high-achieving student body usually translates into prestige for the college and its graduates. Prestige has some advantages but should definitely be viewed as a secondary factor that might tip the scales when all the other important factors are equal. Never base your decision on prestige alone!

The other principle to keep in mind in using this factor is to not sell yourself short. If everything else tells you that a college might be right for you, but your numbers just miss that college's average range, apply there anyway. Your numbers—grades and test scores—are undeniably important in the admissions decision, but there are other considerations. First, lower grades in honors or AP courses will impress colleges more than top grades in regular-track courses because they demonstrate that you are the kind of student willing to accept challenges. Second, admissions directors are looking for different qualities in students that can be combined to create a multifaceted class. For example, if you did poorly in your freshman and sophomore years but made a great improvement in your grades in later years, this usually will impress a college. If you are likely to contribute to your class because of your special personal qualities, a strong sense of commitment and purpose, unusual and valuable experiences, or special interests and talents, these factors can outweigh numbers that are weaker than average. Nevertheless, be practical. Overreach yourself in a few applications, but put the bulk of your effort into gaining admission to colleges where you have a realistic chance for admission.

To narrow your list using entrance difficulty as a criterion, consult the Entrance Difficulty Index on page 943. This index groups colleges by their own assessment of their entrance difficulty level according to the following categories: most difficult, very difficult, moderately difficult, minimally difficult, and noncompetitive.

4. The Price of an Education. The price tag for higher education continues to rise, and it has become an increasingly important factor for people. While it is necessary to consider your family's resources when choosing a list of colleges to which you might apply, never eliminate a college solely because of cost. There are many ways to pay for college, including loans, and a college education will never depreciate in value like other purchases. It is an investment in yourself and will pay back the expense many times over in your lifetime. You may be able to obtain the necessary financial aid to allow you to enroll in your higher-priced college of choice. (For more information on financial aid and how to obtain it, refer to the *College Money Handbook*.) For a quick look at college costs—with and without room and board—consult the Cost Ranges Index on page 951. This index groups colleges according to the cost ranges in which they fall. In addition, you will find detailed expense information in the individual college profiles.

5. Majors. In addition to all of the other factors that might influence your selection, certainly one of the most important is whether a college offers a program in your academic area of interest. An easy way to find which colleges offer your major is by referring to the Majors Index on page 1102. To see which majors a particular institution offers, consult CollegeQuest.com, where online college profiles tell you about the majors and athletic programs available at specific colleges.

CRITERIA FOR INCLUSION IN THIS BOOK

The term four-year college is the commonly used designation for institutions that grant the baccalaureate. Four years is the normal duration to earn this degree, although some bachelor's degree programs may be completed in three years, others require five years, and part-time programs may take considerably longer. Upper-level institutions offer only the junior and senior years and accept only students with two years of college-level credit. Therefore, four-year college is a conventional term that accurately describes most of the institutions included in this guide but should not be taken literally in all cases.

To be included in this guide, an institution must have full accreditation or candidate for accreditation (preaccreditation) status by an institutional or specialized accrediting body recognized by the U.S. Department of Education or the Council for Higher Education Accreditation (CHEA). Institutional accrediting bodies, which review each institution as a whole, are as follows: the six regional associations of schools and colleges (Middle States, New England, North Central, Northwest, Southern, and Western), each of which is responsible for a specified portion of the United States and its territories; the Accrediting Association of Bible Colleges (AABC); the Accrediting Council for Independent Colleges and Schools (ACICS); the Accrediting Commission for Career Schools and Colleges of Technology (ACCSCT); the Distance Education and Training Council (DETC); the American Academy for Liberal Education; the Council on Occupational Education; and the Transnational Association of Christian Colleges and Schools (TRACS). Program registration by the New York State Board of Regents is considered to be the equivalent of institutional accreditation, since the board requires that all programs offered by an institution meet its standards before recognition is granted. A Canadian institution must be chartered and authorized to grant degrees by the provincial government, affiliated with a chartered institution, or accredited by a recognized U.S. accrediting body. This guide also includes institutions outside the United States that are accredited by these U.S. accrediting bodies. There are recognized specialized accrediting bodies in more than forty different fields, each of which is authorized to accredit specific programs in its particular field. For specialized institutions that offer programs in one field only, we designate this to be the equivalent of institutional accreditation. A full explanation of the accrediting process and complete information on recognized accrediting bodies can be found online at http://www.chea.org.

RESEARCH PROCEDURES

The data contained in the college indexes and college profiles were researched between fall 1999 and spring 2000 through *Peterson's Annual Survey of Undergraduate Institutions*. Questionnaires were sent to the more than 2,000 colleges and universities that met the criteria for inclusion outlined above. All data included in this edition have been submitted by officials (usually admissions and financial aid officers, registrars, or institutional research personnel) at the colleges themselves. In addition, many of the institutions that submitted data were contacted directly by the Peterson's research staff to verify unusual figures, resolve discrepancies, and obtain additional data. All usable information received in time for publication has been included. The omission of any particular item from an index or profile listing signifies that the information is either not applicable to that institution or not available. Because of Peterson's comprehensive editorial review and because all material comes directly from college officials, we believe that the information presented in this guide is accurate. You should check with a specific college or university at the time of application to verify such figures as tuition and fees, which may have changed since the publication of this volume.

ENTRANCE DIFFICULTY INDEX

This index groups colleges by their own assessment of their entrance difficulty level. The five levels of entrance difficulty, as defined on page 17, are based on the percentage of applicants who were accepted for fall 1999 freshman admission (in the case of upper-level colleges, for entering-class admission) and on the high school class rank and standardized test scores of the accepted freshmen who actually enrolled in fall 1999. The colleges were asked to select the level, according to the guidelines, that most closely corresponds to their entrance difficulty in order to assist prospective students in assessing their chances for admission. Canadian colleges, specialized schools of art and music, upper-level colleges, and other institutions for

Making Your Top Ten College List: How This Guide Can Help

which high school class rank or standardized test scores do not apply as admission criteria were asked to select the level that best indicates their entrance difficulty as compared to other institutions of the same type that use similar admission criteria.

COST RANGES INDEX

In this index, colleges are listed by name and location within eleven minimum-cost ranges: less than $2000, $2000–$3999, $4000–$5999, $6000–$7999, $8000–$9999, $10,000–$11,999, $12,000–$13,999, $14,000–$15,999, $16,000–$17,999, $18,000–$19,999, and $20,000 and over. Costs are based on the total of full-time tuition, mandatory fees, and room and board for the 2000–01 academic year (or estimated for the 2000–01 academic year) or for the 1999–2000 academic year if 2000–01 figures were not yet available. Within each range, colleges that do not offer room and board or offer room only are listed separately from colleges that offer both room and board. For colleges that do not offer room and board, an estimate of living expenses should be added to the minimum figure given in order to make realistic comparisons with other colleges. For institutions that have different tuition rates for different categories of students or types of programs, the lowest rate is represented. Institutions that have all students enrolled part-time are not listed in this index.

MAJORS INDEX

This index presents more than 700 undergraduate fields of study that are currently offered most widely according to the colleges' responses on *Peterson's Annual Survey of Undergraduate Institutions*. The majors appear in alphabetical order, each followed by an alphabetical list of the schools that offer a bachelor's-level program in that field. (Liberal Arts and Studies indicates a general program with no specified major.) For an index of associate degree programs offered at four-year colleges, see *Peterson's Guide to Two-Year Colleges*.

The terms used for the majors are those of the U.S. Department of Education Classification of Instructional Programs (CIPs). Many institutions, however, use different terms. Readers should visit http://www.petersons.com in order to contact a college and ask for its catalog or refer to the In-Depth Description in this book for the school's exact terminology. In addition, although the term major is used in this guide, some colleges may use other terms, such as concentration, program of study, or field.

COLLEGE PROFILES AND SPECIAL ANNOUNCEMENTS

The college profiles contain basic data in capsule form for quick review and comparison. The following outline of the profile format shows the section headings and the items that each section covers. Any item that does not apply to a particular college or for which no information was supplied is omitted from that college's profile. Special Announcements, which appear in the profiles just below the bulleted highlights, have been written by those colleges that wished to supplement the profile data with additional information.

CollegeQuest.com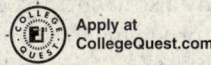

The CollegeQuest icon beside a college's name in the profile section indicates that the college participates in the application function of Peterson's CollegeQuest. CollegeQuest is a revolutionary Internet site that, among other services, streamlines the task of applying to college. The eApply function of CollegeQuest allows a student to fill out one application that is accepted at more than 1,200 colleges and universities. This makes it easier to apply to several colleges at once. The eApply feature hosts the Universal Application, the Common Application, and other custom college applications. Direct access to CollegeQuest on the World Wide Web is included in the bonus CD that comes with this guide and is also directly accessible at http://www.CollegeQuest.com.

Bulleted Highlights

The bulleted highlights feature important information for quick reference and comparison. The number of *possible* bulleted highlights that an ideal profile would have if all questions were answered in a timely manner are represented below. However, not every institution provides all of the information necessary to fill out every bulleted line. In such instances, the line will not appear.

First bullet

Institutional control: Private institutions are designated as independent (nonprofit), proprietary (profit-making), or independent, with a specific religious denomination or affiliation. Nondenominational or interdenominational religious orientation is possible and would be indicated.

Public institutions are designated by the source of funding. Designations include federal, state, province, commonwealth (Puerto Rico), territory (U.S. territories), county, district (an educational administrative unit often having boundaries different from units of local government), city, state and local (local may refer to county, district, or city), or state-related (funded primarily by the state but administratively autonomous).

Institutional type: Each institution is classified as one of the following:

Primarily two-year college: Awards baccalaureate degrees, but the vast majority of students are enrolled in two-year programs.

Four-year college: Awards baccalaureate degrees; may also award associate degrees; does not award graduate (postbaccalaureate) degrees.

Five-year college: Awards a five-year baccalaureate in a professional field such as architecture or pharmacy; does not award graduate degrees.

Making Your Top Ten College List: How This Guide Can Help

Upper-level institution: Awards baccalaureate degrees, but entering students must have at least two years of previous college-level credit; may also offer graduate degrees.

Comprehensive institution: Awards baccalaureate degrees; may also award associate degrees; offers graduate degree programs, primarily at the master's, specialist's, or professional level, although one or two doctoral programs may be offered.

University: Offers four years of undergraduate work plus graduate degrees through the doctorate in more than two academic or professional fields.

Founding date: If the year an institution was chartered differs from the year when instruction actually began, the earlier date is given.

Second bullet

Degrees: This names the full range of levels of certificates, diplomas, and degrees, including prebaccalaureate, graduate, and professional, that are offered by this institution.

Associate degree: Normally requires at least two but fewer than four years of full-time college work or its equivalent.

Bachelor's degree (baccalaureate): Requires at least four years but not more than five years of full-time college-level work or its equivalent. This includes all bachelor's degrees in which the normal four years of work are completed in three years and bachelor's degrees conferred in a five-year cooperative (work-study plan) program. A cooperative plan provides for alternate class attendance and employment in business, industry, or government. This allows students to combine actual work experience with their college studies.

Master's degree: Requires the successful completion of a program of study of at least the full-time equivalent of one but not more than two years of work beyond the bachelor's degree.

Doctoral degree (doctorate): The highest degree in graduate study. The doctoral degree classification includes Doctor of Education, Doctor of Juridical Science, Doctor of Public Health, and the Doctor of Philosophy in any nonprofessional field.

First professional degree: The first postbaccalaureate degree in one of the following fields: chiropractic (DC, DCM), dentistry (DDS, DMD), medicine (MD), optometry (OD), osteopathic medicine (DO), rabbinical and Talmudic studies (MHL, Rav), pharmacy (BPharm, PharmD), podiatry (PodD, DP, DPM), veterinary medicine (DVM), law (JD), or divinity/ministry (BD, MDiv).

First professional certificate (postdegree): Requires completion of an organized program of study after completion of the first professional degree. Examples are refresher courses or additional units of study in a specialty or subspecialty.

Post-master's certificate: Requires completion of an organized program of study of 24 credit hours beyond the master's degree but does not meet the requirements of academic degrees at the doctoral level.

Third bullet

Setting: Schools are designated as *urban* (located within a major city), *suburban* (a residential area within commuting distance of a major city), *small-town* (a small but compactly settled area not within commuting distance of a major city), or *rural* (a remote and sparsely populated area). The phrase *easy access to . . .* indicates that the campus is within an hour's drive of the nearest major metropolitan area that has a population greater than 500,000.

Fourth bullet

Student body: An institution is coed (coeducational—admits men and women), primarily (80 percent or more) women, primarily men, women only, or men only.

Undergraduate students: Represents the number of full-time and part-time students enrolled in undergraduate degree programs as of fall 1999. The percentage of full-time undergraduates and the percentages of men and women are given.

Fifth bullet

Entrance level: See guidelines in the box below.

Percent of applicants admitted: The percentage of applicants who were granted admission.

Sixth bullet

Student-faculty ratio: The school's estimate of the ratio of matriculated undergraduate students to faculty members teaching undergraduate courses.

Seventh bullet

Percent who graduate in six years or less: Shows the percentage of first-time, full-time bachelor's (or equivalent) degree-seeking students, minus those ineligible to graduate for various reasons, entering in summer and fall 1993 who graduated by August 31, 1999.

Eighth bullet

Tuition and fees: Costs are given for the 2000–01 academic year (or estimated for the 2000–01 academic year) or for the 1999–2000 academic year if 2000–01 figures were not yet available.

Ninth bullet

Average financial aid package: The amount of scholarships, grants, work-study payments, or loans in the institutionally administered financial aid package divided by the number of students who received any financial aid. Amounts used to pay the officially designated Expected Family Contribution (EFC), such as PLUS or other alternative loans, are excluded from the amounts reported.

Average indebtedness: The average per-borrower indebtedness of the last graduating undergraduate class from amounts borrowed at this institution through any loan programs, excluding parent loans.

Making Your Top Ten College List: How This Guide Can Help

Endowment: The total dollar value of donations to the institution or the multicampus educational system of which the institution is a part.

Special Announcements

These messages have been written by those colleges that wished to supplement the profile data with additional, timely, important information.

College Profile

In the first line, any coordinate institutions or system affiliations are indicated. An institution that has separate colleges or campuses for men and women but shares facilities and courses it is termed a coordinate institution. A formal administrative grouping of institutions, either private or public, of which the college is a part, or the name of a single institution with which the college is administratively affiliated is a system.

Students

Undergraduates: For fall 1999, the number of full- and part-time degree-seeking undergraduate students is listed. This list provides the number of states and U.S. territories, including the District of Columbia and Puerto Rico (or, for Canadian institutions, provinces and territories), and other countries from which undergraduates come.

THE FIVE LEVELS OF ENTRANCE DIFFICULTY

1. **Most difficult:** More than 75 percent of the current freshmen were in the top 10 percent of their high school class and scored above 1310 on the SAT I (verbal and mathematical combined) or above 29 on the ACT (composite); about 30 percent or fewer of the applicants to this class were accepted.
2. **Very difficult:** More than 50 percent of the current freshmen were in the top 10 percent of their high school class and scored above 1230 on the SAT I or above 26 on the ACT; about 60 percent or fewer of the applicants were accepted.
3. **Moderately difficult:** More than 75 percent of the current freshmen were in the top half of their high school class and scored above 1010 on the SAT I or above 18 on the ACT; about 85 percent or fewer of the applicants were accepted.
4. **Minimally difficult:** Most current freshmen were not in the top half of their high school class and scored somewhat below 1010 on the SAT I or below 18 on the ACT; up to 95 percent of the applicants were accepted.
5. **Noncompetitive:** Virtually all applicants were accepted regardless of high school rank or test scores. Many public institutions are required to admit all state residents.

Graduate: Number of graduate students attending the institution in professional programs and in other graduate programs.

Educational spending per undergraduate 1999–2000: Dollar value of average expenditure per full-time (or equivalent) student for all instructional divisions of an institution. Includes general academic instruction, academic remediation, adult education, tutoring, and vocational and technical instruction. Expenditures for academic administration are not included.

Graduate students: Number of graduate students attending the institution.

Most frequently chosen baccalaureate fields: The percentages of undergraduates pursuing degree programs in the following fields of study: agriculture, architecture, area and ethnic studies, biological and life sciences, business management and administrative services, communications and journalism, computer and information sciences, education, engineering and applied sciences, English language/literature/letters, fine arts, foreign language and literature, health professions and related sciences, interdisciplinary studies, liberal arts/general studies, library and information studies, mathematics, military science, natural resource sciences, performing arts, philosophy, physical sciences, predentistry, prelaw, premed, pre–veterinary science, psychology, social sciences, theology/religion, and vocational and home economics.

Undergraduate breakdown: Percentages are given of undergraduates who are from out of state, living on campus, age 25 or older, transfer students, international students, African American, Asian American/Pacific Islander, Hispanic American, and Native American (these are the ethnic designations equivalent to those used by the U.S. Department of Education).

Faculty

The total number of faculty members and the percentage of full-time faculty members as of fall 1999 and the percentage of full-time faculty members who hold doctoral/first professional/terminal degrees.

Expenses

If provided by the institution, a one-time required fee is listed. Costs are given for the 2000–01 academic year (or estimated for the 2000–01 academic year) or for the 1999–2000 academic year if 2000–01 figures were not yet available. Annual expenses may be expressed as a comprehensive fee (including full-time tuition, mandatory fees, and college room and board) or as separate figures for full-time tuition, fees, room and board, or room only. For public institutions where tuition differs according to residence, separate figures are given for area or state residents and for nonresidents. Part-time tuition is expressed in terms of a per-unit rate (per credit, per semester hour, etc.) as specified by the institution.

The tuition structure at some institutions is complex in that freshmen and sophomores may be charged a different

Making Your Top Ten College List: How This Guide Can Help

rate from that for juniors and seniors, a professional or vocational division may have a different fee structure from the liberal arts division of the same institution, or part-time tuition may be prorated on a sliding scale according to the number of credit hours taken. Tuition and fees may vary according to academic program, campus/location, class time (day, evening, weekend), course/credit load, course level, degree level, reciprocity agreements, and student level. Room and board charges are reported as an average for one academic year and may vary according to the board plan selected, campus/location, type of housing facility, or student level. If no college-owned or -operated housing facilities are offered, the phrase *college housing not available* will appear in the Housing section of the College Life paragraph.

Tuition payment plans that may be offered to undergraduates include tuition prepayment, installment, and deferred payment. A tuition prepayment plan gives a student the option of locking in the current tuition rate for the entire term of enrollment by paying the full amount in advance rather than year by year. Colleges that offer such a prepayment plan may also help the student to arrange financing.

The availability of full or partial undergraduate tuition waivers to minority students, children of alumni, employees or their children, adult students, and senior citizens may be listed.

Library
This section lists the name of the main library, the number of other libraries on campus, the libraries' operating expenditures for 1999–2000, and the number of titles and current serial subscriptions.

College Life
Housing: The institution's policy about whether students are permitted to live off campus or are required to live on campus for a specified period; whether freshmen-only, coed, single-sex, cooperative, and disabled student housing options are available. The phrase *college housing not available* indicates that no college-owned or -operated housing facilities are provided for undergraduates and that noncommuting students must arrange for their own accommodations.

Social organizations: The types of social organizations (national and local fraternities and sororities, eating clubs, etc.), and the percentages of eligible undergraduate men and women who are members of these groups.

Campus Security: Campus safety measures, including 24-hour emergency response devices (telephones and alarms) and patrols by trained security personnel, student patrols, late-night transport/escort service, and controlled dormitory access (key, security card, etc.).

After Graduation
This section lists the number of organizations, corporations, government agencies, and nonprofit organizations that recruited on campus during the 1998–99 academic year and the percentage of students in the class of 1999 that had job offers within six months of graduation.

Graduate education: Lists the percentage of students who went directly to graduate and professional schools. Percentages are given for those pursuing study in the fields of arts and sciences, business, dentistry, education, engineering, law, medicine, theology, and veterinary medicine.

Application Profile

Freshmen
Figures are given for the number of students who applied for fall 1999 admission, the number of those who were admitted, and the number who enrolled. The number of 1999 freshmen who were National Merit Scholars, National Black Merit Scholars, Westinghouse recipients, class presidents, valedictorians, and student government officers is shown. Freshman statistics include the average high school GPA; the percentage of freshmen who took the SAT I and received verbal and math scores above 500 as well as the percentage of freshmen taking the ACT who received a composite score of 18 or higher; the percentages of freshmen from the top 10 percent, top quarter, and top half of their secondary school classes; and the percentage of 1998 freshmen (or, for upper-level institutions, entering students) who returned for the fall 1999 term.

Application
Application and admission options include the following:

eApply at www.CollegeQuest.com: Provides access to Peterson's Universal Application, the NASSP (National Association of Secondary School Principals) Common Application, and the State University of New York (SUNY) System common application. More than 1,200 colleges and universities accept one or more of these applications as an official application to their institution.

Common Application: Private colleges who are members of the Common Application Group and accept the NASSP Common Application.

Electronic Application: A disk or online version of a paper application form that can be transferred directly into an institution's student records system.

Early admission: Highly qualified students may matriculate before graduating from high school.

Early action plan: An admission plan that allows students to apply and be notified of an admission decision well in advance of the regular notification dates. If accepted, the candidate is not committed to enroll; students may reply to the offer under the college's regular reply policy.

Early decision plan: A plan that permits students to apply and be notified of an admission decision (and financial aid offer, if applicable) well in advance of the regular notification date. Applicants agree to accept an offer of admission and to withdraw their applications from other colleges. Candidates who are not accepted under early decision are automatically considered with the regular applicant pool, without prejudice.

Deferred entrance: The practice of permitting accepted students to postpone enrollment, usually for a period of one academic term or year.

Open admission: Admission policy under which virtually all secondary school graduates or students with GED equivalency diplomas are admitted without regard to academic record, test scores, or other qualifications.

Preference: First consideration is given to qualified applicants from specified geographical, religious, or other groups based on institutional support or control.

Application fee: The fee required with an application is noted. This is typically nonrefundable, although under certain specified conditions it may be waived or returned.

Requirements: Other application requirements are grouped into three categories: required for all, required for some, and recommended. They may include an essay, standardized test scores, a high school transcript, a minimum high school grade point average (expressed as a number on a scale of 0 to 4.0, where 4.0 equals A, 3.0 equals B, etc.), letters of recommendation, an interview on campus or with local alumni, and, for certain types of schools or programs, special requirements such as a musical audition or an art portfolio.

Standardized Tests

The most commonly required standardized tests are ACT, SAT I, and SAT II Subject Tests, including the SAT II: Writing Test (see *Surviving Standardized Tests*). These and other standardized tests may be used for selective admission, as a basis for counseling or course placement, or for both purposes. This section notes if a test is used for admission or placement.

In addition to the ACT and SAT I, the following standardized entrance and placement examinations are referred to by their initials:

ABLE: Adult Basic Learning Examination
ACT ASSET: ACT Assessment of Skills for Successful Entry and Transfer
ACT PEP: ACT Proficiency Examination Program
CAT: California Achievement Tests
CELT: Comprehensive English Language Test
CPAt: Career Programs Assessment
CPT: Computerized Placement Test
DAT: Differential Aptitude Test
LSAT: Law School Admission Test
MAPS: Multiple Assessment Program Service
MCAT: Medical College Admission Test
MMPI: Minnesota Multiphasic Personality Inventory
OAT: Optometry Admission Test
PAA: Prueba de Aptitude Académica (Spanish-language version of the SAT I)
PCAT: Pharmacy College Admission Test
PSAT: Preliminary SAT
SCAT: Scholastic College Aptitude Test
SRA: Scientific Research Association (administers verbal, arithmetical, and achievement tests)
TABE: Test of Adult Basic Education
TASP: Texas Academic Skills Program
TOEFL: Test of English as a Foreign Language (for international students whose native language is not English)
WPCT: Washington Pre-College Test

Significant Dates

Admission application deadlines and dates for notification of acceptance or rejection are given either as specific dates or as *rolling* and *continuous*. Rolling means that applications are processed as they are received, and qualified students are accepted as long as there are openings. Continuous means that applicants are notified of acceptance or rejection as applications are processed up until the date indicated or the actual beginning of classes. The application deadline and the notification date for nonresidents are given if they differ from the dates for state residents. Early decision and early action application deadlines and notification dates are also indicated when relevant.

A college's financial aid application deadline may be given as a specific date or as a priority date, meaning that students are encouraged to apply by that date in order to have the best chance of obtaining aid.

Admission Office Contact

The name, title, and telephone number of the person to contact for application information are given at the end of the profile. The admission office address is listed. Toll-free telephone numbers may also be included. The admission office fax number and e-mail address, if available, are listed, provided the school wanted them printed for use by prospective students.

If a college admissions video or electronic viewbook is available, it is noted here.

Additional Information

Each college that has an In-Depth Description in the guide will have a cross-reference appended to the profile, referring you directly to that In-Depth Description.

SURVIVING STANDARDIZED TESTS

DON'T FORGET TO . . .
- Take the SAT or ACT before application deadlines
- Note that test registration deadlines precede test dates by about six weeks
- Practice your test-taking skills with *Peterson's SAT Success* and *Peterson's ACT Success* (both available with software)
- Contact the College Board or American College Testing, Inc., in advance if you need special accommodations when taking tests

WHAT ARE STANDARDIZED TESTS?

Colleges and universities in the United States use tests to help evaluate applicants' readiness for admission or to place them in appropriate courses. The tests that are most frequently used by colleges are the ACT Assessment of American College Testing, Inc., and the College Board's SAT. The tests are offered at designated testing centers located at high schools and colleges throughout the United States and U.S. territories and at testing centers in various countries throughout the world. The ACT Assessment test and the SAT tests are each taken by more than a million students each year.

Both services offer, upon request, special accommodations for students with documented visual, hearing, physical, or learning disabilities. Examples of special accommodations include tests in Braille or large print and such aids as a reader, recorder, magnifying glass, or sign language interpreter. Additional testing time may be allowed in some instances. Contact the appropriate testing program or your guidance counselor for details on how to request special accommodations.

Here is a brief description of each testing program.

College Board SAT Program

The SAT Program consists of the SAT I Reasoning Test and the SAT II Subject Tests. The SAT I is a 3-hour test, primarily multiple-choice, that measures verbal and mathematical abilities. The verbal sections test vocabulary, verbal reasoning, and critical reading skills. Emphasis is placed on reading passages, which are 400–850 words in length. Some reading passages are paired; the second opposes, supports, or in some way complements the point of view expressed in the first. The mathematics sections test a student's ability to solve problems involving arithmetic, algebra, and geometry. They include questions that require students to produce their own responses rather than choose from four or five answer choices. Students may use calculators on the SAT I mathematics sections.

The SAT II Subject Tests are 1-hour tests, primarily multiple-choice, in specific subjects that measure students' knowledge of these subjects and their ability to apply that knowledge. Tests offered include Writing, Literature, American History, World History, Mathematics Level IC, Mathematics Level IIC, Biology (General), Biology E/M (Ecological/Molecular), Chemistry, Physics, French, German, Modern Hebrew, Italian, Latin, and Spanish as well as Foreign Language Tests with Listening in Chinese, French, German, Japanese, Korean, Spanish, and English Proficiency (ELPT). The Mathematics Level IC and IIC tests require the use of a scientific calculator.

SAT scores are sent automatically to each student who has taken the test. Students may request that the scores be reported to their high schools or to the colleges to which they are applying. If they choose the Score Choice Option, students may review their SAT II Subject Test scores and decide whether they want them to appear on their cumulative score record.

ACT Assessment Program

The ACT Assessment Program is a comprehensive data collection, processing, and reporting service designed to assist in educational and career planning. The ACT Assessment instrument consists of four academic tests, taken under timed conditions, and a Student Profile Section and Interest Inventory, completed when students register for the ACT.

The academic tests cover four areas—English, mathematics, reading, and science reasoning. They are designed

Surviving Standardized Tests

to assess the student's educational development and readiness to handle college-level work. The minimum standard score is 1, the maximum is 36, and the national average is 21.

The Student Profile Section requests information about each student's admission and enrollment plans, academic and out-of-class high school achievements and aspirations, and high school course work. The student is also asked to supply biographical data and self-reported high school grades in the four subject-matter areas covered by the academic tests.

ACT has a number of career planning services, including the ACT Interest Inventory, which is designed to measure six major dimensions of student interests. Results are used to compare the student's interests with those of college-bound students who later majored in each of a wide variety of areas. Inventory results are also used to help students compare their work-activity preferences with work activities that characterize twenty-three "job families."

Because the information resulting from the ACT Assessment Program is used in a variety of educational settings, American College Testing, Inc., prepares three reports for each student: the Student Report, the High School Report, and the College Report. The Student Report normally is sent to the student's high school, except after the June test date, when it is sent directly to the student's home address. The College Report is sent to the colleges the student designates.

Early in the school year, American College Testing, Inc., sends to high schools across the country registration packets containing all the information a student needs to register for the ACT Assessment. High school guidance offices also receive a supply of *Preparing for the ACT Assessment,* a booklet that contains a complete practice test, an answer key, and general information about preparing for the test. You may also be interested in *Peterson's ACT Success* (with practice software).

Contact your secondary school counselor for full information about the SAT and ACT programs.

ACT

September 23, 2000
October 28, 2000
December 9, 2000
February 10, 2001
April 7, 2001
June 9, 2001

All test dates fall on a Saturday. The September test is available only in Arizona, California, Florida, Georgia, Illinois, Indiana, Maryland, Nevada, North Carolina, Pennsylvania, South Carolina, Texas, and Washington. The February test date is not available in New York. Tests are also given on the Sundays following the Saturday test dates for students who cannot take the test on Saturday because of religious reasons. The basic ACT registration fee for 1999–2000 was $22 ($25 in Florida).

SAT

October 14, 2000 (SAT I and SAT II)
November 4, 2000 (SAT I, SAT II, and Language Tests with Listening*)
December 2, 2000 (SAT I and SAT II)
January 27, 2001 (SAT I and SAT II)
March 31, 2001 (SAT I only)
May 5, 2001 (SAT I and SAT II)
June 2, 2001 (SAT I and SAT II)

For the 1999–2000 academic year, the basic fee for the SAT I Reasoning Test was $10.50 plus a $13 basic registration and reporting fee. The basic fee for the SAT II Subject Tests was $11 for the Writing Test, $8 for the Language Tests with Listening, and $6 for all other Subject Tests. Students can take up to three SAT II Subject Tests on a single date, and a $13 basic registration and reporting fee should be added for each test date. Tests are also given on the Sundays following the Saturday test dates for students who cannot take the test on Saturday because of religious reasons. Fee waivers are available to juniors and seniors who cannot afford test fees.

*Language Tests with Listening (including ELPT) are offered only on this date and only at some test centers. See the Registration Bulletin for details.

Preparing to Get In . . .

Once you have successfully pared down your original list of potential colleges to the top five or ten choices, it's time to start the actual application process. Rule number one for this stage of the game is to get organized. If you take the time up front to familiarize yourself with what's required of you, putting the pieces in place will be far less intimidating.

The words "applying yourself" have several important meanings in the college application process. One meaning refers to the fact that you need to keep focused during this important time in your life, keep your priorities straight, and know the dates that your applications are due so that you can apply on time. The phrase might also refer to the person who is really responsible for your application--you.

You are the only person who should compile your college application. You need to take ownership of this process. The intervention of others should be for advisement only. The guidance counselor is not responsible for completing your applications, and your parents shouldn't be typing them. College applications must be completed in addition to your normal workload at school, college visits, and SAT or ACT testing.

STANDARDIZED TESTS

In all likelihood, you will take the SAT I, the ACT, or both tests sometime during your junior year of high school and, perhaps, again in your senior year if you are trying to improve your scores. For detailed information on the SAT and ACT Programs, including 2000–01 test dates, see page 17.

THE APPLICATION

The application is your way of introducing yourself to a college admissions office. As with any introduction, you should try to make a good first impression. The first thing you should do in presenting your application is to find out what the college or university needs from you. Read the application carefully to find out the application fee and deadline, required standardized tests, number of essays, interview requirements, and anything else you can do or submit to help improve your chances for acceptance.

Completing college applications yourself helps you learn more about the schools to which you are applying. The information a college asks for in its application can tell you much about the school. State university applications often tell you how they are going to view their applicants. Usually, they select students based on GPAs and test scores. Colleges that request an interview, ask you to respond to a few open-ended questions, or require an essay are interested in a more personal approach to the application process and may be looking for a different type of student than a state school.

Most colleges have an individual paper application form, but at CollegeQuest.com, the eApply function allows you to fill out one application that is accepted at more than 1,200 institutions. This makes it easier for you to apply to several colleges at once. The eApply feature houses the Universal Application, the Common Application, and other custom college applications. Using a standardized application lets you concentrate on being organized and writing good essays.

FOLLOW THESE TIPS WHEN FILLING OUT YOUR APPLICATION:

1. **Start early!** You can use your Personal Organizer at CollegeQuest.com any time.
2. **Follow the directions to the letter.** You don't want to be in a position to ask an admissions officer for exceptions due to your inattentiveness.
3. **Make a photocopy** of the application and work through a rough draft before you actually fill out the application copy to be submitted.
4. **Proofread all parts of your application,** including your essay. Again, the final product indicates to the admissions staff how meticulous and careful you are in your work.
5. **Submit your application as early as possible,** provided all of the pieces are available. If there is a problem with your application, this will allow you to work through it with the admissions staff in plenty of time. If you wait until the last minute, it not only takes away that cushion but also reflects poorly on your sense of priorities.

Preparing to Get In...

In addition to submitting the actual application, there are several other items that are commonly required. You will be responsible for ensuring that your standardized test scores and your high school transcript arrive at the colleges you apply to. Most colleges will ask that you submit teacher recommendations as well. Select teachers who know you and your abilities well and allow them plenty of time to complete the recommendations. When all portions of the application have been completed and sent in, whether electronically or by mail, make sure you follow up with the college to ensure their receipt.

THE APPLICATION ESSAY

Whereas the other portions of your application—your transcript, test scores, and involvement in extracurricular activities—are a reflection of what you've accomplished up to this point, your application essay is an opportunity to present yourself in the here and now. The essay shows your originality and verbal skills and is very important. Test scores and grades may represent your academic results, but your essay shows how you approach a topic or problem and express your opinion.

Admissions officers, particularly those at small or mid-size colleges, use the essay to determine how you, as a student, will fit into life at that college. What makes a good impression? Colleges are looking for enthusiasm, maturity, creativity, the ability to communicate, talent, and leadership. Colleges are looking for an honest representation of who you are and what you think; that won't necessarily be found in the facts and figures in your records.

Some colleges may request one essay or a combination of essays and short-answer topics to learn more about who you are and how well you can communicate your thoughts. Common essay topics cover such simple themes as writing about yourself and your experiences or why you want to attend that particular school. Other colleges will ask that you show your imaginative or creative side by writing about a favorite author, for instance, or commenting on a hypothetical situation. In such cases, they will be looking at your thought processes and your level of creativity.

Regardless of what the questions are, make sure you set aside enough time to write the essay, revise it, and revise it *again*. Always answer the question that is being asked, making sure that you are specific, clear, and true to your personality. Enlist the help of reviewers who know you well—friends, parents, teachers—since they are likely to be the most honest and will keep you on track in the presentation of your true self.

THE PERSONAL INTERVIEW

Although it is relatively rare that a personal interview is actually required, many colleges recommend that you take this opportunity for a face-to-face discussion with a member of the admissions staff. Read through the application materials to determine whether or not a college places great emphasis on the interview. If they strongly recommend that you have one, it may work against you to forego it.

In contrast to a group interview and some alumni interviews, which are intended to provide information about a college, the personal interview is viewed both as an information session and as further evaluation of your skills and strengths. You will meet with a member of the admissions staff who will be assessing your personal qualities, high school preparation, and your capacity to contribute to undergraduate life at the institution. On average, these meetings last about 45 minutes—a relatively short amount of time in which to gather information and leave the desired impression—so here are some suggestions on how to make the most of it.

1. **Scheduling Your Visit.** Generally, students choose to visit campuses in the summer or fall of their senior year. Both times have their advantages. A summer visit, when the campus is not in session, generally allows for a less hectic visit and interview. Visiting in the fall, on the other hand, provides the opportunity to see what campus life is like in full swing. If you choose the fall, consider arranging an overnight trip so that you can stay in one of the college dormitories. At the very least, you should make your way around campus to take part in classes, athletic events, and social activities. Always make an appointment and avoid scheduling more than two college interviews on any given day. Multiple interviews in a single day hinder your chances of making a good impression, and your impressions of the colleges will blur into each other as you hurriedly make your way from place to place.

2. **Preparation.** Know the basics about the college before going for your interview. Read the college viewbook or catalog in addition to this guide. You will be better prepared to ask questions that are not answered in the literature and that will give you a better understanding of what the college has to offer. You should also spend some time thinking about your strengths and weaknesses and, in particular, what you are looking for in a college education. You will find that as you get a few interviews under your belt, they will get easier. You might consider starting with a college that is not a top contender on your list, where the stakes are not as high.

3. **Asking Questions.** Inevitably, your interviewer will ask you, "Do you have any questions?" Not having one may suggest that you're unprepared or, even worse, not interested. When you do ask questions, make sure that they are ones that matter to you and that have a bearing on your decision about whether or not to attend. The questions that you ask will give the interviewer some insight into your personality and priorities. Avoid asking questions that can be answered in the college literature—again, a sign of unpreparedness. Although the interviewer will undoubtedly pose questions to you, the interview should not be viewed merely as a question-and-answer session. If a conversation evolves out of a particular question, so much the better. Your interviewer can learn a great deal about you from how you sustain a conversation. Similarly, you will be able to glean a great deal about the college in a conversational format.

Preparing to Get In...

4. **Separate the Interview from the Interviewer.** Many students base their feelings about a college solely on their impressions of the interviewer. Try not to characterize a college based only on your personal reaction, however, since your impressions can be skewed by whether you and your interviewer hit it off. Pay lots of attention to everything else that you see, hear, and learn about a college. Once on campus, you may never see your interviewer again.

In the end, remember to relax and be yourself. Don't drink jitters-producing caffeinated beverages prior to the interview, and suppress nervous fidgets like leg-wagging, finger-drumming, or bracelet-jangling. Your interviewer will expect you to be somewhat nervous, which will relieve some of the pressure. Consider this an opportunity to put forth your best effort and to enhance everything that the college knows about you up to this point.

THE FINAL DECISION

Once you have received your acceptance letters, it is time to go back and look at the whole picture. Provided you received more than one acceptance, you are now in a position to compare your options. The best way to do this is to compare your original list of important college-ranking criteria with what you've discovered about each college along the way. In addition, you and your family will need to factor in the financial aid component, which is discussed in detail on the following pages. You will need to look beyond these cost issues and the quantifiable pros and cons of each college, however, and know that you have a good feeling about your final choice. Before sending off your acceptance letter, you need to feel confident that the college will feel like home for the next four years. Once the choice is made, the only hard part will be waiting for an entire summer before heading off to college!

Paying for College: Financial Aid Basics

A college education is expensive: more than $100,000 for four years at some of the higher-priced colleges and universities and more than $50,000 even at many lower-cost, state-supported colleges. Figuring out how you and your family will come up with the necessary funds to pay for your education requires planning, perseverance, and learning as much as you can about the options available.

For most families, paying the total cost of a student's college education out of savings is not possible. Obviously, the more your family has saved, the better off you will be and the less you will need to earn and borrow. But paying for college should not be looked at merely as a four-year financial commitment. Some of the money you need will likely come from funds that you and your parents have managed to save, and some will come from a portion of your or your parents' current income. Some will come from future earnings, through loans you or your parents will pay off later, but if this is not enough, the rest of the expenses will be met through financial aid programs.

HOW FINANCIAL AID IS AWARDED

When you apply for aid, your family's financial situation is analyzed using a government-approved formula called the Federal Methodology. The result of this is the amount you and your family are expected to contribute toward your college expenses, called your Expected Family Contribution or EFC. (The chart on page 24 will give you an approximate idea of your family's EFC.) If this is equal to or more than the cost at a particular college, then, of course, you have no need for additional funds. However, even if you don't have financial need, you may still qualify for aid since there are many grants, scholarships, and loans that do not consider financial need.

If the cost of your education is greater than your EFC, then you will likely qualify for assistance, possibly enough to meet the full cost. Here's the formula:

$$\begin{array}{r} \text{Total Cost of Attendance} \\ - \text{ Expected Family Contribution} \\ \hline = \text{Financial Need} \end{array}$$

The EFC remains constant, but your need will vary according to the costs of attending a given college.

SOURCES OF FINANCIAL AID

The largest single source of aid is the federal government, which awards some $46 billion to more than 8½ million students each year. The next largest source of financial aid is the college and university community. Institutions award an estimated $8 billion to students each year. Some of this aid is awarded to students who have a demonstrated need based on either the Federal Methodology or on another formula, the Institutional Methodology, which is used by some colleges to award their own funds in conjunction with federal aid. Aid not based on need is called merit aid and is usually awarded for a student's academic performance or specific talents or abilities or to attract the students a college most wants to enroll.

Another large source of financial aid is state government. All fifty states offer grant aid, most of which is need-based. Most state programs award aid only to students attending college in that state.

Other sources of financial aid include private agencies, foundations, corporations, clubs, fraternal and service organizations, civic associations, unions, and religious groups that award grants, scholarships, and low-interest loans. Some employers provide tuition reimbursement benefits for employees.

More information about these different sources of aid is available from high school guidance offices, public libraries, college financial aid offices, and directly from the sponsoring organizations. In addition, Peterson's *College Money Handbook* and *Scholarships, Grants & Prizes* give detailed information on private and college aid.

APPLYING FOR FINANCIAL AID

Every student must complete the Free Application for Federal Student Aid (FAFSA) to be considered for federal aid. The

Paying for College: Financial Aid Basics

FAFSA is available in your high school guidance office, many public libraries, or directly from the U.S. Department of Education.

Students also can apply for federal student aid over the Internet using the interactive FAFSA on the Web. FAFSA on the Web can be accessed at http://www.fafsa.ed.gov. It can be used with any computer, including Macintosh and UNIX.

To award their own funds, many colleges require a second application, the Financial Aid PROFILE. The PROFILE asks additional questions that some colleges and awarding agencies feel provide a more accurate assessment of the family's ability to pay for college. It is up to the college to decide whether it will use only the FAFSA or both the FAFSA and the Financial Aid PROFILE. The college profiles in the book will tell you which form is required.

If Every College You're Applying to for Fall 2001 Requires Just the FAFSA
. . . then it's pretty simple: Complete the FAFSA sometime after January 1, 2001, being certain to send it in before any college-imposed deadlines. (You are not permitted to send in the 2001–02 FAFSA before January 1, 2001, which should not pose a problem because most college application deadlines are in February or March.) It is best if you wait until you have all your financial records for the previous year available, but if that is not possible, you can use estimated numbers.

After you send in your FAFSA, either on paper or electronically, you'll receive a Student Aid Report (SAR) in the mail that reviews the information you reported and contains your EFC. If you used estimated numbers to complete the FAFSA, you may have to resubmit the SAR with any corrections to the data. The college(s) you have designated on the FAFSA will receive the information you reported and will use that data to make their decision. In many instances, the colleges you've applied to will ask you to send copies of your and your parents' income tax returns for 2000 plus any other documents needed to verify the information you reported.

If a College Requires the PROFILE

Step 1: Register for the Financial Aid PROFILE in the fall of your senior year in high school.
Registering for the Financial Aid PROFILE begins the financial aid process. You register by calling the College Scholarship Service at 800-778-6888 and providing basic demographic information, a list of colleges to which you are applying, and your credit card number to pay for the service. College-Quest.com is a great starting place for registration and other financial aid assistance.

Registration packets with a list of the colleges requiring the PROFILE are available in most high school guidance offices.

There is a fee for using the Financial Aid PROFILE application ($22 for the first college and $16 for each additional college). You must pay for the service by credit card when you register. If you do not have a credit card, you will be billed.

Step 2: Fill out your customized Financial Aid PROFILE.
A few weeks after you register, you'll receive in the mail a customized financial aid application that you can use to apply for institutional aid at the colleges you've designated as well as from some private scholarship programs, like the National Merit Scholarship. (Note: if you've waited until winter and a college's financial aid application deadline is approaching, you can get overnight delivery by paying an extra fee.) The PROFILE contains all the questions necessary to calculate your EFC plus the questions that the colleges and organizations you've designated require you to answer. Your individualized packet will also contain a customized cover letter instructing you what to do and informing you about deadlines and requirements for the colleges and programs you designated when you registered for the PROFILE, codes that indicate which colleges wanted which additional questions, and supplemental forms (if any of the colleges to which you are applying require them—e.g., the Business/Farm Supplement for students whose parents own their own business or the Divorced/Separated Parents' Statement).

Make sure you submit your PROFILE by the earliest deadline listed. Two to four weeks after you do so, you will receive an acknowledgment of receipt and a report estimating your EFC (only the FAFSA can be used to get an official EFC) and another calculated family contribution using the second formula, the Institutional Methodology, that uses the additional data elements you provided in your PROFILE.

FINANCIAL AID PROGRAMS

There are three types of financial aid: scholarships (also known as grants or gift aid), loans, and student employment. Scholarships and grants are outright gifts and do not have to be repaid. Loans must be repaid, usually after graduation; the amount you have to pay back is the total you've borrowed plus an interest charge. Student employment is a job arranged for you during the academic year, usually on campus. Loans and student employment programs are generally referred to as self-help aid.

The federal government has two large grant programs—the Federal Pell Grant and the Federal Supplemental Educational Opportunity Grant; a student employment program called Federal Work-Study; and several loan programs, including two for parents of undergraduate students.

The Subsidized FFEL Stafford Loan, the Subsidized Direct Stafford Loan, and the Federal Perkins Loan are all need-based, government-subsidized loans. Students who borrow under these programs do not have to pay interest on the loan until after they graduate or leave school. The Unsubsidized FFEL Stafford Loan, Unsubsidized Direct Stafford Loan, and the parent loan programs are not awarded based on need, and borrowers are responsible for interest even while the student is in school.

After you've submitted your financial aid application, and usually when you've been accepted for admission, each college will send you a letter containing your financial aid award. Most award letters show estimated college costs, how

Paying for College: Financial Aid Basics

much you and your family are expected to contribute, and the amount and types of aid you have been awarded. Most students are awarded aid from a combination of sources and programs; hence, your award is often called a "package."

IF YOU DON'T QUALIFY FOR NEED-BASED AID

If you are not eligible for need-based aid, you can still find ways to lessen the burden on your parents.

There are three sources to look into. First is the search for merit scholarships that you can start at the initial stages of your application process. Private scholarships are given for special skills and talents (see Peterson's *Scholarships, Grants & Prizes*). College merit awards are becoming increasingly important as more and more colleges award these grants to students they especially want to attract. As a result, applying to a college at which your qualifications put you at the top of the entering class may give you a larger merit award.

The second source of aid for those not qualifying for need-based assistance is employment during the summer and the academic year. The student employment office at your college should be able to help you locate a school-year job. Many colleges and local businesses have vacancies remaining even after they have hired students who are receiving work-study financial aid.

The third source is borrowing through the Unsubsidized Stafford Loan programs, which are open to all students. The terms and conditions are similar to the subsidized loans. The biggest difference is that the borrower is responsible for the interest while still in college, although most lenders permit students to delay paying the interest right away and add the accrued interest to the total amount owed.

After you've contributed what you can through scholarships, working, and borrowing, your parents will be expected to meet their share of the college bill, that is, the Expected Family Contribution. Many colleges offer monthly payment plans that spread the cost over the academic year. If the monthly payments are too high, parents can borrow through the Federal Parent Loan for Undergraduate Students (PLUS), through one of the many private education loan programs available, or through home equity loans and lines of credit. Families seeking assistance in financing college expenses might also seek the advice of professional financial advisers and tax consultants.

For more information about financing a college education, see Peterson's *Insider's Guide to Paying for College*.

Paying for College: Financial Aid Basics

HOW IS YOUR FAMILY CONTRIBUTION CALCULATED?

Approximate Expected Family Contribution for 2000–01

ASSETS	FAMILY SIZE	$20,000	30,000	40,000	50,000	60,000	70,000	80,000	90,000	100,000
$20,000	3	$220	2,100	3,200	5,400	8,700	11,800	14,800	17,600	20,400
	4	0	1,400	2,000	4,000	7,400	10,500	13,400	15,900	19,300
	5	0	300	1,300	3,000	6,200	9,300	12,200	15,100	18,100
	6	0	0	600	2,100	5,000	7,800	10,800	13,700	16,600
$30,000	3	$220	2,100	3,200	5,400	8,700	11,800	14,800	17,600	20,400
	4	0	1,400	2,000	4,000	7,400	10,500	13,400	15,900	19,300
	5	0	300	1,300	3,000	6,200	9,300	12,200	15,100	18,100
	6	0	0	600	2,100	5,000	7,800	10,800	13,700	16,600
$40,000	3	$220	2,200	3,300	5,600	8,900	11,900	14,900	14,700	21,700
	4	0	1,500	2,100	4,100	7,500	10,700	13,600	16,000	20,400
	5	0	400	1,400	3,100	6,300	9,400	12,300	15,200	18,100
	6	0	0	600	2,200	5,100	8,000	11,000	13,900	16,700
$50,000	3	$600	2,500	3,800	6,200	9,500	12,500	15,500	18,300	21,200
	4	0	1,800	2,400	4,600	8,200	11,300	14,200	16,700	20,000
	5	0	600	1,600	3,500	6,900	10,000	12,900	15,700	18,700
	6	0	0	900	2,500	5,700	8,600	11,600	14,500	17,300
$60,000	3	$800	2,900	4,200	6,700	10,100	13,100	16,000	18,900	21,800
	4	140	2,000	2,700	5,100	8,700	11,900	14,800	17,600	20,600
	5	0	900	1,900	3,900	7,500	10,600	13,500	16,300	19,300
	6	0	0	1,200	2,900	6,300	9,200	12,200	15,100	17,900
$80,000	3	$1,400	3,500	5,100	7,800	11,000	14,200	17,100	20,000	22,900
	4	600	2,600	3,400	6,100	9,800	12,900	15,700	18,300	21,600
	5	0	1,400	2,500	4,800	8,600	11,700	14,600	17,400	20,400
	6	0	300	1,700	3,600	7,300	10,200	13,200	16,000	19,100
$100,000	3	$1,800	4,400	6,100	8,900	12,300	15,300	18,200	21,100	24,000
	4	1,200	3,300	4,200	7,200	10,900	14,000	16,800	15,400	22,700
	5	100	1,900	3,200	5,800	9,700	12,800	15,600	18,500	21,500
	6	0	900	2,300	4,400	8,400	11,400	14,400	17,200	20,100
$120,000	3	$2,500	5,300	7,300	10,100	13,400	16,300	19,300	22,300	25,100
	4	1,700	4,100	5,100	8,400	12,100	15,200	18,000	20,600	23,900
	5	600	2,500	4,000	6,900	10,800	13,900	16,600	19,600	22,600
	6	250	1,400	2,900	5,400	9,600	12,500	15,500	18,300	21,200
$140,000	3	$3,200	6,500	8,400	11,200	14,500	17,400	20,400	23,300	26,200
	4	2,300	5,100	6,200	9,500	13,200	16,200	19,100	21,700	25,000
	5	1,200	3,200	4,900	8,100	11,900	15,100	17,900	20,800	23,800
	6	800	1,900	3,700	6,500	10,700	13,600	16,500	19,400	22,400

What International Students Need to Know About Admission to U.S. Colleges and Universities

by Kitty M. Villa

Selecting an institution and securing admission require a significant investment of time and effort.

There are two principles to remember about admission to a university in the United States. First, applying is almost never a one-time request for admission but an ongoing process that may involve several exchanges of information between applicant and institution. "Admission process" or "application process" means that a "yes" or "no" is usually not immediate, and requests for additional information are to be expected. To successfully manage this process, you must be prepared to send additional information when requested and then wait for replies. You need a thoughtful balance of persistence to communicate regularly and effectively with your selected universities and patience to endure what can be a very long process.

The second principle involves a marketplace analogy. The most successful applicants are alert to opportunities to create a positive impression that sets them apart from other applicants. They are able to market themselves to their target. Marketing works both ways. Institutions are also trying to attract the highest-quality student that they can. The admissions process presents you with the opportunity to analyze your strengths and weaknesses as a student and to look for ways to present yourself in the most marketable manner.

BEGINNING THE APPLICATION PROCESS: SELECTING INSTITUTIONS

With more than 3,000 institutions of higher education in the U.S., how do you begin to narrow your choice to the best institutions for you? There are many factors to consider, and you must ultimately decide which factors are most important to you.

Location

You may spend several years studying in the U.S. Do you prefer an urban or rural campus? Large or small metropolitan area? If you need to live on campus, will you be unhappy at a university where most students commute from off-campus housing? How do you feel about extremely hot summers or cold winters? Eliminating institutions that do not match your preferences in terms of location will narrow your choices.

Recommendations from Friends, Professors, or Others

There are valid academic reasons to consider the recommendations of people who know you well and have firsthand knowledge about particular institutions. Friends and contacts may be able to provide you with "inside information" about the campus or its academic programs to which published sources have no access. You should carefully balance anecdotal information with your own research and your own impressions. Still, current and former students, professors, and others may provide excellent information during the application process.

Your Own Academic and Career Goals

Consideration of your academic goals is more complex than it may seem at first glance. All institutions do not offer the same academic programs. This guide identifies those institutions that offer your desired field of study. The application form usually provides a definitive listing of the academic programs offered by an institution. A course catalog describes the degree program and all the courses offered. In addition to printed sources, there is a tremendous amount of institutional information available through the Internet and the World Wide Web. Program descriptions, even course descriptions and course syllabi, are often available to peruse via computer.

You may be interested in the rankings of either the university or of a program of study. Rankings are interesting,

What International Students Need to Know About Admission to U.S. Colleges and Universities

Keep in mind, however, that rankings usually assume that quality is quantifiable. Rankings are usually based on presumptions about how data relate to quality that are likely to be unproven. It is important to carefully consider the source and the criteria of any ranking information before believing and acting upon it.

Your Own Educational Background

You may be concerned about interpretation of your educational credentials, since your country's degree nomenclature and the grading scale may differ from those in the U.S. Universities use reference books about educational systems of other countries to guide them in understanding specific educational credentials. Generally, these credentials are interpreted by each institution, and there is not a single interpretation that applies to every institution. The lack of uniformity is good news for most students, since it means that students from a wide variety of educational backgrounds can find a U.S. university appropriate to their needs.

To choose an appropriate institution, you can and should do an informal self-evaluation of your educational background. This self-analysis involves three important questions:

How Many Years of Study Have You Completed?

Completion of secondary school with at least twelve total years of education usually qualifies students to apply for undergraduate (bachelor's) degree programs. Completion of a university degree program that involves at least sixteen years of total education qualifies one to apply for admission to graduate (master's) degree programs in the U.S.

Does the Education That You Have Completed in Your Country Provide Access to Further Study in the U.S.?

Consider the kind of institution where you completed your previous studies. If educational opportunities in your country are limited, it may be necessary to investigate many U.S. institutions and programs in order to find a match.

Are Your Previous Marks or Grades Excellent, Average, or Poor?

Your educational record influences your choice of U.S. institutions. If your grades are average or poor, it may be advisable to apply to several institutions with minimally difficult or noncompetitive entrance levels.

YOU are one of the best sources of information about the level and quality of your previous studies. Awareness of your educational assets and liabilities will serve you well throughout the application process.

SECOND STEP—PLANNING AND ASSEMBLING THE APPLICATION

Planning and assembling a university application can be compared to the construction of a building. First, you must start with a solid foundation, the application form itself. The application form usually contains a wealth of useful information, such as deadlines, fees, and degree programs available at that institution. To build a solid application, it is best to obtain the application form well in advance.

How to Obtain the Application Form

Traditionally, a request for an application form is made in writing. Some institutions still follow this old style. Many institutions now accept requests for application forms by e-mail, fax, or telephone. Increasingly, universities use and accept one application form that needs to be completed only once and then can be sent to several institutions. In this book, universities that accept the Universal Application, Common Application, or other custom college forms that are available at the Internet site http://www.CollegeQuest.com have a special symbol beside their names. Some of these institutions will accept the application form over the Internet.

Application forms may also be available at a U.S. educational advising center associated with the American Embassy or Consulate in your country. These centers are excellent resources for international students and provide information about standardized test administration, scholarships, and other matters to students interested in study in the U.S. Your local U.S. Embassy or Consulate can guide you to the nearest educational advising center.

Completing the Application Form

Whether sent by mail or electronically, the application form must be neat and thoroughly filled out. Parts of the application may not seem to apply to you or your situation. If you are unsure, do your best to answer the question. If you must leave it blank or have questions, write notes on the form where you have questions or concerns.

Remember that this is a process. You provide information, and your proposed university then requests clarification and further information. If you have questions, it is better to initiate the entire process by submitting the application form rather than asking questions before you apply. The university will be better able to respond to you after it has your application. Always complete as much as you can. Do not permit uncertainty about the completion of the application form requirements to cause unnecessary delays.

What Are the Key Components of a Complete Application?

Institutional requirements vary, but the standard components of a complete application include:

- Transcript
- Required standardized examination scores
- Letters of recommendation
- Letter of financial support
- Application fee

Transcript

A complete academic record or transcript includes all courses completed, grades earned, and degrees awarded. Most universities require an official transcript directly sent from the school or university. In many other countries, however, the practice is to issue official transcripts and degree certificates directly to the student. If you have only one official copy of your transcript, it may be a challenge to get additional certified copies that are acceptable to U.S. universities. Some institutions will issue additional official copies for application purposes.

If your institution does not provide this service, you may have to seek an alternate source of certification. As a last resort, you may send a photocopy of your official transcript, explain that you have only one original, and ask the university for advice on how to deal with this situation.

Standardized Examinations

Arranging to take the examinations and earning the required scores seem to cause the most anxiety for international students.

The university application form usually indicates which examinations are required. The standardized examination required most often for undergraduate admission is the Test of English as a Foreign Language (TOEFL). In most countries, TOEFL has changed from a paper-and-pencil test to a computer-based test. Institutions may also require the SAT I of undergraduate applicants. Some institutions also require the Test of Spoken English (TSE). These standardized examinations are administered by the Educational Testing Service (ETS).

These examinations are offered in almost every country of the world. It is advisable to begin planning for standardized examinations at least six months prior to the application deadline of your desired institutions. Test centers fill up quickly, so it is important to register as soon as possible. Information about the examinations is available at U.S. educational advising centers associated with embassies or consulates.

Questions about test formats, locations, dates, and registration may be addressed to TOEFL/TSE Services–Princeton, P.O. Box 6151, Princeton, New Jersey 08541-6151, or to ETS's Web sites: http://www.ets.org or http://www.toefl.org. ETS's telephone number is 609-771-7100, and the fax number is 609-771-7500.

Most universities require that the original test scores, not a student copy, be sent directly by the testing service. When you register for the test, be sure to indicate that the testing service should send the test scores directly to your proposed universities.

Minimum Score Requirements

You should usually begin your application process before you receive your test scores. Delaying submission of your application until the test scores arrive may cause you to miss deadlines and negatively effect the outcome of your application. If you want to know your scores in order to assess your chances of admission to an institution with rigorous admission standards, you should take the tests early.

Many universities in the U.S. set minimum required scores on the TOEFL or on other standardized examinations. Test scores are an important factor, but most institutions also consider a number of other factors in their consideration of a candidate for admission.

Evidence of Financial Support

Evidence of financial support is required to issue immigration documents to admitted students. This is part of a complete application package but usually plays no role in determining admission. Most institutions make admissions decisions without regard to the source and amount of financial support.

Letters of Recommendation

Most institutions require one or more letters of recommendation. The best letters are written by former professors, employers, or others who can comment on your academic achievements or professional potential.

Some universities provide a special form for the letters of recommendation. If possible, use the forms provided. If you are applying to a large number of universities, however, or if your recommenders are not available to complete several forms, it may be necessary for you to duplicate a general recommendation letter.

Application Fee

Most universities also require an application fee, ranging from $25 to $100, which must be paid to initiate consideration of the application.

THIRD STEP—DISTINGUISH YOUR APPLICATION

To distinguish your application—to market yourself successfully—is ultimately the most important part of the application process. As you select your prospective universities, you begin to analyze your strengths and weaknesses as a prospective student. As you complete your application, you should strive to create a positive impression and set yourself apart from other applicants, to highlight your assets and bring these qualities to the attention of the appropriate university administrators and professors. Applying early is a very easy way to distinguish your application.

Deadline or Guideline?

The application deadline is the last date that an application for a given semester will be accepted. Often, the application will specify that all required documents and information be submitted before the deadline date. To meet the deadlines, start the application process early. This also gives you more time to take—and perhaps retake and improve—the required standardized tests.

Admissions deliberations may take several weeks or months. In the meantime, most institutions accept additional information, including improved test scores, after the posted deadline.

Even if your application is initially rejected, you may be able to provide additional information to change the decision. You can request reconsideration based on additional information, such as improved test scores, strong letters of recommendation, or information about your rank in class. Applying early allows more time to improve your application. Also, some students may decide not to accept their offers of admission, leaving room for offers to students on a waiting list. Reconsideration of the admission decisions can occur well beyond the application deadline.

Think of the deadline as a guideline rather than an impermeable barrier. Many factors—the strength of the application, the student's research interests, the number of spaces available at the proposed institution—can override the enforcement of an application deadline. So, if you lack a test score or transcript by the official deadline, you may still be able to apply and be accepted.

Statement of Purpose

The statement of purpose is your first and perhaps best opportunity to present yourself as an excellent candidate for admission. Whether or not a personal history essay or statement of purpose is required, always include a carefully written statement of purpose with your applications. A compelling statement of purpose does not have to be lengthy, but it should include some basic components.

In the first paragraph or two, introduce yourself and describe your previous educational background. This is your opportunity to describe any facet of your educational system that you wish to emphasize. Perhaps you attended a highly ranked secondary school or university in your home country. Mention the name and any noteworthy characteristics of the secondary school or university from which you graduated. Explain the grading scale used at your university. Do not forget to mention your rank in your graduating class and any honors you may have received. This is not the time to be modest.

In the second part of the statement of purpose, describe your current academic interests and goals. It is very important to describe in some detail your specific study or career interests. Think about how these will fit into those of the institution to which you are applying, and mention the reasons why you have selected that institution.

Finally, describe your long-term goals. When you finish your program of study, what do you plan to do next? If you already have a job offer or a career plan, describe it. Give some thought to ways to demonstrate that the opportunity for you to study in the U.S. will ultimately benefit others.

Use Personal Contacts When Possible

Appropriate and judicious use of your own network of contacts can be very helpful. Friends, former professors, former students of your selected institutions, and others may be willing to advise you during the application process and to provide you with introductions to key administrators or professors. If suggested, you may wish to contact certain professors or administrators by mail, telephone, or e-mail. Even a personal visit to discuss your interest in the institution may be appropriate. Whatever your choice of communication, try to make the encounter pleasant and personal. Your goal is to make a positive impression, not to rush the admission decision.

There is no single right way to be admitted to U.S. universities. The same characteristics that make the educational choice in the U.S. so difficult—the number of institutions and the variety of programs of study—are the same attributes that allow so many international students to find the right institution in the U.S.

Kitty M. Villa is Assistant Director, International Office, at the University of Texas at Austin.

USING THE INTERNET
in Your College Quest

The Internet is everywhere these days. It is almost impossible to look through a magazine or view a commercial without observing the ubiquitous *please visit us on the Web at www-dot-com*.

The Internet enables users to communicate with others all over the planet. One segment of the Internet, called the World Wide Web, handles the majority of all electronic activity. To access the Web, users need a computer equipped with a modem, access to the Internet, and browser software. You can obtain access to the Internet by using your modem to call an *Internet Service Provider*, or ISP. An ISP maintains one or more computer *servers* that will connect you with almost any computer server in the world. ISPs often provide a variety of information in addition to Internet access. *Browsers* are programs that decipher the information your computer receives from the Internet into a form you can read on your monitor screen. Popular browsers include Netscape Navigator (www.netscape.com) and Microsoft Internet Explorer (www.microsoft.com).

USING THE WORLD WIDE WEB IN YOUR COLLEGE QUEST

The World Wide Web can be of great assistance for soon-to-be college students in gathering information about colleges. There are hundreds of worthwhile Web sites that are ready to help guide you through the various aspects of the college choice process. There are Web sites designed to help you prepare for, select, apply for, and finance a college education. Some sites require that you pay a service fee before you access their information, but most offer their information for free.

Almost all colleges and universities maintain Web sites, which often devote a large amount of space to admissions information for prospective students. You will find many other interesting tidbits about the colleges on these sites, including virtual campus tours, weather conditions, newspaper articles on school issues, *chat rooms* where you can interact with other Web surfers, students' personal home pages, and live images of the main quad captured by the campus Web camera.

As you surf the sea of information available on the Internet, keep in mind that Web sites can vary greatly in appearance and quality. While some sites are attractive, easy to navigate, and home to plentiful amounts of useful information, others are unimaginative and complex. Make a habit of identifying the thrust and purpose of the sites you visit in order to utilize each of them most effectively. Upon arriving at a Web site, determine the source. Who put the Web site together and why? Is the Web site easy to navigate? Can you find the kind of information you need? There is nothing more frustrating than spending 30 minutes at a particular site and learning nothing that will help you. Use the capability of most Web browsers known as "bookmarking" to capture the addresses of sites that provide the most information in the most user-friendly manner.

CollegeQuest

Did you know there's one place you can go to get help with every aspect of the college choice and application process? That place is CollegeQuest, and you can find it at www.CollegeQuest.com.

You can search through Peterson's complete college database to find the colleges that best fit your needs and then view in-depth profiles, or you can do a side-by-side comparison of selected colleges. If you need help finding colleges, ask CollegeQuest's Personal Counselor to narrow your search to the schools that fit you best. Want to spend four years in a bustling city or in a more suburban area? What about housing? Do you want to live in a single-sex or coed dorm? These are just a few of the questions that the Personal Counselor will help you explore.

CollegeQuest also helps students understand and prepare for standardized tests. The site offers test dates, helpful test-taking tips, and full-length, downloadable practice tests for the SAT and ACT. In addition, this section provides tips and sample questions for the TOEFL.

Attending college is very expensive. That is why CollegeQuest provides an extensive financial aid section that explains aid in terms that are easy to understand. This part of the site helps you organize your financial materials, estimate how much your family will have to contribute to college bills, and figure out how to budget your expenses and possibly lower the monthly cost of attending college. You can tell CollegeQuest about your financial situation, your personal characteristics, and your college choices, and it will provide results tailored to your individual needs. CollegeQuest also offers an extensive scholarship search that features more than 850,000 awards. Once you input your personal data, the program will give you information about the need-based and merit scholarships for which you qualify.

You can also read daily campus news articles and feature articles that address many facets of college preparation—including tips on summer jobs, choosing the right classes, and more. Students who have specific questions can go to CollegeQuest's Advice Center. This forum allows you to ask admissions and financial aid experts about any college concerns. Answers to students' questions are posted on a regular basis and archived for everyone to read.

eApply at CollegeQuest

In an effort to provide you with more convenient ways to apply, many colleges accept common applications. Once you are ready to apply, you can use CollegeQuest eApply to fill out one application that is accepted at more than 1,200 colleges. This makes it easier for you to apply to several colleges at once. The eApply feature houses the Universal Application and the Common Application.

CollegeQuest also offers a personal organizer that acts like a virtual filing cabinet, monitoring your applications in progress. It helps you build and maintain your list of potential colleges. You can enter personal and academic information into the organizer, and it will be transferred into any online applications that you open on CollegeQuest. This reduces the amount of time you have to spend repeatedly entering information, and it also reduces the risk of errors. Once you have completed your applications, you can then print and mail them, or, if the colleges accept electronic applications, you can submit your applications electronically through CollegeQuest's secure connection. An Application Manager helps monitor your applications and gives you a checklist of important steps to complete along the way.

CHECK OUT ALL RESOURCES

There are a number of other Web sites that are well worth a look if you have time. The U.S. Department of Education (www.ed.gov/pubs/Prepare) provides a no-nonsense informational brochure on how to prepare for, select, and apply to college. The College Board (www.collegeboard.org) provides online registration for the SAT. The National Association for College Admission Counseling (www.nacac.com/fairs.html) lists dates and locations for many of the college fairs held across the country. If you need more information, be sure to check out Resources for Students at petersons.com (www.petersons.com/resources), where you'll find links to research reports, professional association Web sites, announcements from schools and colleges, and more.

There is ample information on the Internet to help you become a more informed person when it comes to the college choice process. Exploring the resources listed above or venturing out on your own into cyberspace should not be a substitute for discussing your college plans with the experts. Don't forget the importance of talking things over with your guidance counselor at school and with your parents at home before you make any big decisions.

Choosing a college is an involved and complicated process. The tools available to you on the Internet can help you to be more productive in this process, should you choose to use them. Well, what are you waiting for? Fire up the computer—your future alma mater may just be a mouse click away.

The Military And Higher Education

The first part of this section offers an overview of the opportunities that exist today for students who wish to explore the possibility of financing their higher education by participating in ROTC or attending a service academy. This information is provided in order to help students and families make well-informed decisions about this important investment. The second part of this section presents, in the Army's own words and photos, a detailed description of one military financial aid option—the Army ROTC Program.

The Military as a Source of Financial Aid

One of the major problems facing families today is how to come up with the money to meet college expenses. Many people are unaware that the military is a source of financial aid. Its focus, however, is quite different from that of other sources: military financial aid programs do not consider need but are either a payment for training or a reward for service. This large source of money (about $1 billion each year) can prove quite helpful in assisting a wide range of students. The military financial aid programs are by far the largest source of college money that is not based on need.

HOW THE MILITARY PROVIDES FINANCIAL AID

One form of military financial aid is college money for officer candidates: tuition assistance and monthly pay in return for the student's promise to serve as an officer in the Army, Navy, Air Force, Marine Corps, Coast Guard, or Merchant Marine. Most of this money is awarded to high school seniors who go directly to college. The main benefits are reduced or free tuition and $100 to $150 per month if the student is enrolled in the Reserve Officers' Training Corps (ROTC) Scholarship Program or free tuition, room and board, and $500 per month if the student is enrolled at one of the service academies. ROTC units are located on college campuses and provide military training for a few hours a week. The five service academies (West Point, Annapolis, the Air Force Academy, the Coast Guard Academy, and the Merchant Marine Academy) are military establishments that combine education and training for the armed forces. For those already in college, financial aid is obtainable through ROTC scholarships for enrolled students or special commissioning programs.

By participating in ROTC, attending a service academy, or enrolling in a special program for military commissioning, a student not only can become an officer but also can become eligible for financial aid, thus turning the dream of an affordable college education into a reality. The military trains students to become officers and pays them to learn at the same time. (A detailed look at one such program, that of the Army ROTC, appears following this article.)

IS OFFICER TRAINING RIGHT FOR YOU?

Military scholarship programs exist largely to provide money to college students as they go through officer training, and, in return, the military receives from the students a commitment to serve in the armed forces. The military's goal is to produce, through this method of attracting outstanding young men and women, "entry-level" officers who are well educated both academically and in the workings of the military itself. Obviously, you would not be the ideal candidate for one of these programs if you had moral or religious reservations about serving your country as a military officer. You also should not apply if the program's main appeal for you is the money. The financial benefits may be very important, but their attraction should be balanced by genuine feelings on your part that you will seriously consider becoming an officer, you will undertake military training with a positive attitude, and you will be flexible and open-minded about your plans. Applicants are typically young men or women who are willing to serve at least four or five years as officers in exchange for four years of a good education at little or no cost.

First: Are You the Military Type?

At the outset, it is essential that you determine whether or not you are cut out to be in the military. Take a personal inventory: What are you like? How do you relate to others? What kind of organization do you want to be part of?

- Do you consider yourself intelligent, well-rounded, energetic, organized, and somewhat athletic? Are you a serious student with good grades in precollege courses and an aptitude for science and math?
- Are you outgoing? Does leadership appeal to you? Do you work well with others, both in groups and in one-on-one situations? Can you willingly take direction from others?
- Can you exist in a structured and disciplined environment? Do you have strong feelings of patriotism? Are you willing to defend your country in a time of war?
- If "yes" is your answer to most of these questions, you are the type of individual the military services are interested in. Even more important, you may be the type of person who can be comfortable with the military's lifestyle. Although there are many different types of military officers—from the quiet intellectual to the extroverted athlete—the average officer usually conforms to a set of general characteristics: a mixture of certain personal traits and a willingness to be part of and contribute to a large and very structured organization.

Second: What Kind of Military Training Might Be Appropriate for You?

If your personal inventory revealed you to be at least somewhat the "military type," your next step is to see which of the programs offered by the different services is best for you.

The Military as a Source of Financial Aid

Now ask yourself which of the following most closely describes your feelings at present.

1. I have firsthand knowledge of military service. I can picture myself as an officer, perhaps even a career officer. I have experience with discipline, both in taking and in giving orders. I plan to major in science or engineering while I'm in college. Obtaining a top-quality education at very low cost is very important to me.
2. Service in the military is of interest to me. I don't have much direct experience, but I'm willing to learn more. I'm not sure whether I'm ready to immerse myself completely in a military environment as a college student. I've done well in math and science, but I may decide to major in another field. I can look forward to the prospect of four years of service as an officer before deciding whether to stay on. A tuition scholarship is appealing, and it would widen the range of colleges that are within my reach.
3. I don't have a negative attitude toward the military, but it's not something I know much about. I might be interested in giving it a look. Studying math and science may not be for me; my interests are probably in other areas. I'm concerned about paying for college, but my parents could help me for at least one or two years.
4. I don't think I'm the military type, but actually I haven't thought that much about it. I doubt if I would go for the discipline. Certainly, I wouldn't want to commit to anything until I've been in college for a few years and can see my choices more clearly. I might be able to see myself serving in the military—if I could get duty that matches my academic interests. I could use a scholarship, but I plan to seek financial aid through other sources.

When you've determined which of the foregoing paragraphs mostly closely describes your attitude toward military service, review the following items, the numbers of which generally relate to the numbers above.

1. Think seriously about competing for an appointment to a service academy. (You must be nominated by an official source, usually your congressional representative. Each member of Congress has a set number of nominees he or she can recommend for admission. Neither political influence nor a personal relationship with the member of Congress is necessary.)
2. Plan to enter the national ROTC four-year scholarship competition.
3. Join an ROTC unit in college and see what the military is like. Scholarship opportunities are available if you decide to stay on.
4. Don't get involved with a military program yet, but keep the service in mind for possible entrance after two years of college.
5. It should go without saying that it's best to avoid extreme discrepancies between the two lists. For example, if description number 4 applies, a military academy or even the four-year scholarship is probably not right for you. It would be far wiser to choose item three or four. Later on, after you are enrolled in college, you might find that certain aspects of the military complement your academic interests and that the military lifestyle is something you can adapt to. If, on the other hand, description number 1 suits you, it will be worth your while to pursue either the ROTC scholarship or service academy option when you graduate from high school. If you are this far along in your thinking about a possible future in the military, you can take advantage of both the financial benefits the services offer and the head start you will get toward a possible military career by trying for an officer training program.

Preparation While in High School

Enrolling in a precollege program while you're attending high school will improve your chances of winning a four-year ROTC scholarship or receiving an appointment to a service academy. For the most part, the services don't require that you take specific subjects (the exceptions are the Coast Guard Academy and the Merchant Marine Academy). Nonetheless, the Army, Navy, Air Force, and Marine Corps all stress the importance of a good high school curriculum. They suggest the following: 4 years of English, 4 years of math (through calculus), 2 years of a foreign language, 2 years of laboratory science, and 1 year of American history.

Being an active member of your school and community is also important, as is holding leadership positions in sports and/or other extracurricular activities. If your high school has a Junior ROTC unit, join the detachment; doing so could improve your chances of being selected for an ROTC scholarship or admitted to a service academy.

Standardized Tests

For entrance into the academies and most other colleges, be prepared to take the SAT I or ACT, used by college admission offices as one of the measures of a prospective college student's academic potential. For more details, see Surviving Standardized Tests.

Who Is a Successful Candidate?

A fictional though typical winner of a four-year ROTC scholarship or an appointment to a service academy exhibits certain kinds of characteristics. That person (whom we will call John Doe):

- Follows a curriculum that includes 4 years of English, 4 years of math, 3 or 4 years of a foreign language, 2 years of laboratory science, and 2 years of history—with some of the courses at the honors level. John maintains a B+ average and ranks in the top 15 percent of his class. On the SAT I, he received scores of 610 verbal and 640 math (based on original, rather than recentered, scores). (Had he taken the ACT, his composite score would have been 28.)
- Is a member of the National Honor Society. He holds an office in student government and is a candidate for Boys State. John has a leadership position on the student newspaper and is a member of both the debate panel and math club. He is active in varsity athletics and is cocaptain of the basketball team.
- Is one of the top all-around students in his class and makes a positive contribution to both his school and

community. He is described as intelligent, industrious, well-organized, self-confident, concerned, and emotionally mature.
- The services believe and expect that a person with John Doe's abilities and traits will do well in college—in both academic and military training—and will also have great potential to become a productive officer after graduation.

Facts About the Officer Training Programs

Officer Pay and Benefits. As a military officer, you will be paid the standard rate for all members of the armed forces of your rank and length of service. In addition to your salary, significant fringe benefits include free medical care and a generous retirement plan.

The Difference Between a Regular and a Reserve Officer. Officer training programs offer Regular and Reserve commissions. However, all initial commissions after September 30, 1996, have been Reserve only. You should be aware of the difference between the two designations.

When commissioned as a Regular officer, you are on a career path in the military. In the event that you choose not to serve at least twenty years, you must write a letter asking if you can resign your commission. Such requests are normally accepted once you have completed your minimum service obligation. If you plan to make the military your career, it is a definite advantage to be a Regular officer.

As a Reserve officer, you contract for a specific term, for example, four years of active duty in the case of an ROTC scholarship. Nearly all Air Force ROTC second lieutenants are in this category, along with about 85 percent of Army ROTC graduates. If you want to remain on active duty after your initial obligation, you must request to sign on for a second term.

There is another category of Reserve officer—those who are assigned to the Reserve Forces rather than to active duty. About 50 percent of the officers who are commissioned through the Army ROTC are given orders to the National Guard or Army Reserve. After attending the Basic Course for six months, these officers join the Reserve Forces to finish their obligated service as "weekend warriors." In this case, the time commitment is 7½ years in the Reserve, the first 5½ years involving drills one weekend per month and two weeks of active duty per year. During the last two years of obligated service, these officers are transferred to inactive Reserve status, in which drills are not required.

Women Officers. Virtually all of the officer training programs are open to women. With the exception of differences in height and weight standards and lower minimums on the physical fitness test, the eligibility rules, benefits, and obligations are the same for both genders. When it comes to duty assignments, however, there is a notable difference between men and women. Depending on the branch of the service, this law restricts the types of jobs women can choose. Other than the limits imposed by certain combat restrictions for women, the position of women within the military has improved considerably in the past ten years. There are variations among the services, but overall, women make up between 8 and 20 percent of the officers, and they are gradually but steadily moving into the higher-ranking positions.

Medical Requirements. Candidates for an ROTC scholarship must pass a medical examination. You need take only one physical, even if you apply for more than one type of scholarship. Medical standards vary considerably and can be quite complicated. Nevertheless, it is worth having an idea of the general medical requirements at the outset, particularly the eyesight and height and weight rules. Keep in mind, too, that medical standards change periodically, and some of them may be waived under certain conditions. (Service academy medical requirements for the Army and Navy/Marine Corps are the same as the ROTC requirements; the Air Force requirements are also the same except that flight training has its own height and vision standards; and the Coast Guard and Merchant Marine medical requirements are similar to Naval ROTC, except that eyesight standards for the Merchant Marine are more lenient.)

THE ROTC PROGRAMS

The predominant way for a college student to become a military officer is through the Reserve Officers' Training Corps program. ROTC is offered by the Army, Navy, and Air Force, while students taking the Marine Corps option participate in Naval ROTC. (The Coast Guard and Merchant Marine do not sponsor ROTC programs.)

Each service that has an ROTC program signs an agreement with a number of colleges to host a unit on their campuses. Each of these units has a commanding officer supervising a staff of active-duty officers and enlisted servicemembers who conduct the military training of cadets and midshipmen. This instruction includes regular class periods in which military science is taught as well as longer drill sessions in which students concentrate on developing leadership qualities through participation in military formations, physical fitness routines, and field exercises.

It is not necessary for you to attend a college that hosts a unit to participate in ROTC. You may attend any of the approved colleges that have a cross-enrollment contract and participate in ROTC at the host institution, provided you are accepted into the unit and you are able to arrange your schedule so that you have time to commute to the ROTC classes and drill sessions. (The Army also has extension centers—small branches of host colleges that provide an additional way to participate in Army ROTC.)

As a member of an ROTC unit, you are a part-time cadet or midshipman. You are required to wear a uniform and adhere to military discipline when you attend an ROTC class or drill, but not at other times. Since this involvement averages only about 4 hours per week, most of the time you will enjoy the same lifestyle as a typical college student. You must realize, however, that while you are an undergraduate, you are being trained to become an officer when you graduate. You therefore will have a number of obligations and responsibilities your classmates do not face. Nevertheless, the part-time nature of your military training is the major difference be-

The Military as a Source of Financial Aid

tween participating in ROTC and enrolling at a service academy, where you are in a military environment 24 hours a day.

In each ROTC unit there are two types of student—scholarship and nonscholarship. Although the focus of this section is on military programs that provide tuition aid, it should be pointed out that you may join an ROTC unit after you get to college even if you don't receive a scholarship. You take the same ROTC courses as a scholarship student, and you may major in nearly any subject. You can drop out at any time prior to the start of your junior year. If you continue, you will be paid $200 per month for your last two years of college and be required to attend a summer training session between your junior and senior years. Upon graduation, you will be commissioned as a second lieutenant or ensign. For the Army, your minimum active-duty obligation is six months; four years if you are in the Air Force or Navy.

The major source of scholarships is the four-year tuition scholarship program. Four-year scholarships are awarded to high school seniors on the basis of a national competition. Each year, more than 4,000 winners are selected (roughly 2,000 Army, 1,300 Navy, and 1,300 Air Force) from about 25,000 applicants. Recipients of four-year Army, Air Force, and Naval ROTC scholarships may attend either a host college or approved cross-enrollment college. In return for an Army ROTC scholarship, you must serve eight years in the Active Army, Army Reserve, or Army National Guard or a combination thereof. For scholarships from other services, four years' active duty service is required. After you accept the scholarship, you have a one-year grace period before you incur a military obligation. Prior to beginning your sophomore year, you may simply withdraw from the program. If you drop out after that time, you may be permitted to leave without penalty, ordered to active duty as an enlisted servicemember, or required to repay the financial aid you have received. The military will choose one of these three options, depending on the circumstances of your withdrawal.

Should you decide to try for a four-year ROTC scholarship, it is important that you apply to a college to which you can bring an ROTC scholarship. Because there is always the possibility you may not be accepted at your first choice, it is a good idea to apply to more than one college with an ROTC affiliation. In the case of Army and Air Force ROTC scholarships, both of which may require you to major in a specified area, you also need to be admitted to the particular program for which the scholarship is offered. For example, if you win an Air Force ROTC scholarship designated for an engineering major, you must be accepted into the engineering program as well as to the college as a whole.

While the majority of new ROTC scholarships are four-year awards given to high school seniors, each service sets aside scholarships for students who are already enrolled in college and want to try for this kind of military financial aid for their last two or three years. These in-college scholarships are a rapidly growing area within the ROTC program, since the services are finding they can do a better job of selecting officer candidates after observing one or two years of college performance. Of further interest to applicants is the fact that for some of the services, the selection rate is quite a bit higher for the two- and three-year awards than it is for the four-year scholarship. For example, in a recent year, Air Force ROTC accepted 37 percent of its candidates for four-year awards and 63 percent of its candidates for two- and three-year awards. Most of these in-college scholarships are given to students who join an ROTC unit without a scholarship and then decide to try for a tuition grant. Since a cadet or midshipman takes the same ROTC courses whether on scholarship or not, it makes good sense for those who are not receiving aid to apply for an in-college award.

Even if you have not been a member of an ROTC unit during your first two years in college, it is possible to receive a two-year scholarship, provided you apply by the spring of your sophomore year. If you win a two-year scholarship, you will go to a military summer camp where you will receive training equivalent to the first two years of ROTC courses. You then join the ROTC unit for your junior and senior years. (There are also limited opportunities for non-ROTC members to try for a three-year in-college scholarship; interested students should check with an ROTC unit.)

You may be married and still receive an ROTC scholarship (you may not be married in the service academies). The benefits are the same regardless of whether you are married or single.

In summary, there are four ways to participate in ROTC: as a winner of a four-year scholarship (or, in some cases, a three-year award) for high school seniors; as a recipient of a two- or three-year scholarship for ROTC members who are not initially on scholarship; by receiving an in-college scholarship (usually for two years) designated for students who have not yet joined an ROTC unit; or as a nonscholarship student.

This section, adapted from *How the Military Will Help You Pay for College: The High School Student's Guide to ROTC, the Academies, and Special Programs,* second edition, by Don M. Betterton (Peterson's), has provided an overview of the options available if you choose to turn to the military as a source of financial aid. One such option, Army ROTC, is discussed in detail in the following pages.

The Army ROTC Program

Through Army ROTC, a student can become an officer while pursuing a regular college degree.

WHAT IS ROTC?

Army ROTC is a college program that enables students not only to graduate with a degree in their chosen college majors but also to receive officers' commissions in the U.S. Army, the Army National Guard, or the Army Reserve.

ROTC courses are like any other college elective. And most college students can try ROTC for a year without incurring any military service obligation.

ROTC cadets are eligible for numerous financial benefits, including scholarships worth in some cases more than $60,000.

ROTC graduates have the opportunity to serve full time as officers in the active Army or serve part time in the Army National Guard or Reserve while pursuing regular civilian careers or continuing their education.

Students at hundreds of colleges and universities nationwide have access to Army ROTC programs, and about 40,000 students participate each year.

WHAT ARE THE BENEFITS OF ARMY ROTC?

Army ROTC helps ensure a young person's success in college and in life. It is "The Smartest College Course You Can Take."

ROTC builds confidence and teaches the planning and time-management skills needed to succeed in college and the leadership, management, and motivational skills critical to success in life. These skills are not just taught in class. ROTC cadets can practice them in special ROTC activities and summer training. ROTC classes last just a few hours a week and at most colleges fulfill elective requirements.

Army ROTC provides a competitive edge that will be of value in either a military or a civilian career. In fact, many civilian employers place a premium on the skills and experience gained through ROTC.

WHAT TYPES OF FINANCIAL BENEFITS ARE AVAILABLE?

In the face of today's growing college costs, Army ROTC offers merit-based scholarships that can help pay tuition and on-campus educational expenses.

Juniors and seniors in ROTC, plus certain other ROTC cadets, receive allowances of up to $2000 each school year and are paid to attend a special summer camp.

Students who enroll in Army ROTC at college and who also join the National Guard or Army Reserve are eligible for other financial benefits. For more information, students should contact the Professor of Military Science at the college they plan to attend.

The Army ROTC Program

Army ROTC provides the leadership and management training that will help make students a success in college and in life.

WHAT IS THE COMMITMENT?

College freshmen can try Army ROTC without making any commitment to join the Army. That commitment does not usually come until the junior year.

When students graduate with officers' commissions, they can serve in the active Army, the Army National Guard, the Army Reserve, or a combination for a total of eight years.

In the active Army, they serve full time as Army officers. In the Guard or Reserve, they serve part time, generally one weekend a month and two weeks during the summer, while pursuing their chosen civilian careers.

THE FOUR-YEAR PROGRAM

Army ROTC is traditionally a four-year college program consisting of a two-year Basic Course and a two-year Advanced Course.

The Basic Course is usually taken during a college student's freshman and sophomore years. The subjects taught cover such areas as management principles, military history and tactics, leadership development, communication skills, first aid, land navigation, and rappelling.

Most students incur no military obligation by participating in the Basic Course, and all necessary ROTC textbooks, materials, and uniforms are furnished without cost.

After completing the Basic Course, only students who have demonstrated leadership potential and who meet scholastic, physical, and moral standards are eligible to enroll in the Advanced Course.

The Advanced Course is normally taken during a college student's junior and senior years. Instruction includes further training in leadership, organization theory, management, military tactics, strategic thinking, and professional ethics.

ROTC cadets in the Advanced Course attend a paid Advanced Camp during the summer between their junior and senior years. This camp further permits cadets to put into practice the principles and theories they have learned in the classroom. It also exposes them to Army life in a tactical and field environment.

All ROTC cadets in the Advanced Course receive an allowance of up to $2000 each school year and are paid to attend Advanced Camp. They are also furnished, without cost, all necessary ROTC textbooks, materials, and uniforms.

Before entering the Advanced Course, ROTC cadets must sign contracts that certify an understanding of their future Army service obligation, which is for eight years. This obligation may be fulfilled through various combinations of full-time active duty and part-time reserve forces duty depending upon a cadet's personal preference and the needs of the Army at the time of commissioning.

ROTC cadets selected for reserve forces duty actually serve on active duty for three to six months before they join a National Guard or Army Reserve unit. This is so that they can attend an Officer Basic Course to receive additional Army training. Reserve officers generally serve part time in the National Guard or Army Reserve while they pursue regular full-time civilian careers.

See page 48 for details on how to learn more about the Army ROTC four-year program.

More than 20 percent of all current ROTC cadets are women.

The Army ROTC Program

THE TWO-YEAR PROGRAM

Students can also be commissioned after only two years of ROTC instruction.

This program is open to students who did not take Army ROTC during their first two years of college. Two-year program cadets include community and junior college graduates who have transferred to a four-year institution, graduate students, high school students planning to attend a Military Junior College, veterans, and members of the National Guard or the Army Reserve.

Students can take advantage of the two-year program by successfully completing a paid Basic Camp (usually attended between the sophomore and junior years of college) and entering the Advanced Course.

Veterans and members of the National Guard and Army Reserve do not have to attend Basic Camp since their prior military service serves as the prerequisite for entering the Advanced Course.

Students interested in the two-year ROTC program should contact the nearest on-campus Army ROTC office for information before the end of the sophomore year of college.

EXTRACURRICULAR ACTIVITIES

Like regular college students, ROTC cadets participate in a wide variety of social, educational, professional, and athletic activities. Most of these activities are sponsored by the colleges hosting Army ROTC, but some are sponsored by ROTC itself.

Ranger Challenge is sponsored by Army ROTC and includes competition in patrolling, marksmanship, rope-bridge building, and a 10-kilometer run. Each ROTC unit fields a Ranger Challenge team that competes against teams from ROTC units at other colleges and universities.

These and other challenging activities offer leadership opportunities that increase self-confidence.

THE SCHOLARSHIP PROGRAM

Army ROTC offers valuable four-year scholarships to students entering college as freshmen and two- or three-year scholarships to students with two or three years remaining toward their bachelor's degrees.

These scholarships may pay thousands of dollars toward college tuition and required educational fees. In addition, they provide a specified amount for textbooks, supplies, and equipment. Each scholarship recipient also receives a personal allowance of up to $2000 for each school year the scholarship is in effect.

Army ROTC scholarships are merit scholarships awarded on a competitive basis. Selection is based on high school or college grades, SAT or ACT scores, personal recommendations, physical fitness, athletic and extracurricular activities, leadership potential, a personal interview, and other criteria as prescribed by regulation.

Many of these scholarships are specifically targeted to students pursuing degrees in engineering, nursing, the physical sciences, or other technical programs.

Army ROTC scholarship winners who fail to complete the ROTC program or do not accept commissions as Army officers will be required to pay back the amount of their scholarships or serve as enlisted soldiers in the Army. This provision is binding for three- and four-year scholarship winners when they enter the sophomore year and for two-year scholarship winners when they enter the junior year.

Completed applications for four-year Army ROTC scholarships must be postmarked by November 15 of a high school student's senior year. Applications for two- and three-

All ROTC units offer instruction in some type of adventure training, including rappelling, orienteering, mountaineering, or white-water rafting.

The Army ROTC Program

year scholarships are usually due by March of a college student's freshman and sophomore years. Since special application forms and procedures are required, interested students should contact Army ROTC for information well before these deadlines.

ARMY NURSE CORPS

Army ROTC offers two-, three-, and four-year scholarships to qualified students who are seeking bachelor's degrees in nursing. Most of these scholarships must be used at certain nursing programs affiliated with ROTC. These programs are called Partnership in Nursing Education (PNE) programs. Army ROTC nurse candidates join the Army Nurse Corps upon graduation from an accredited nursing program, successful completion of a state board examination, and commissioning as Army officers.

The management training provided through Army ROTC is just as important to a nursing career as it is to any other career, and nursing students enrolled in Army ROTC can receive special nursing leadership experiences.

In lieu of attending the regular ROTC Advanced Camp, ROTC nursing cadets attend the ROTC Nurse Summer Training Program (NSTP). NSTP allows ROTC nurse cadets to develop both leadership and nursing skills. It introduces the cadets to the Army Medical Department and the roles and responsibilities of an Army Nurse Corps officer. NSTP cadets report to Army hospitals for clinical training under the supervision of Army Nurse Corps office "preceptors." These professionals work one-on-one with the cadets throughout the training, which concentrates on "hands-on" experiences in areas like medical-surgical wards and intensive care units.

The Army also provides Army nurses specialty training. Army nurses can apply for clinical specialty courses in such areas as obstetrics/gynecology, critical care, perioperative, and psychiatric health nursing. They can also become nurse anesthetists.

In addition to training, the Army offers nurses many unique benefits. Army nurses serve around the world, get thirty days paid vacation from the start of their career, and don't lose seniority when changing geographical areas or specialties.

Students seeking a bachelor's degree in nursing are especially encouraged to enroll in Army ROTC.

OPPORTUNITIES FOR SCIENCE OR ENGINEERING STUDENTS

Army scientists designed America's first earth satellite, developed the first operational computer, and devised innovative production methods for transistors and titanium, among other scientific discoveries. All this was accomplished by giving priority to scientific knowledge and investing in students who put their scientific skills to work while serving the nation.

As Army officers, students have exciting opportunities to be a part of world-class science from the very beginning of their careers. The Army also provides many students fully funded graduate tuition programs for approved courses of study. No matter which scientific or technical course of college study students choose, the Army offers them a chance to gain technical skills and leadership experience sooner and in more fields than any other employer.

THE SIMULTANEOUS MEMBERSHIP PROGRAM

The Simultaneous Membership Program (SMP) allows students to attend college, participate in Army ROTC, serve part time in the Army National Guard or Army Reserve, and receive generous Army benefits.

Eligible students who desire to attend one of the historically black colleges or universities (HBCU) that host Army ROTC may apply for an ROTC four-year HBCU Scholarship.

The Army ROTC Program

SMP cadets receive their Guard or Reserve pay; G.I. Bill benefits, if eligible; and a monthly ROTC allowance. In many states, Guard and Reserve members are eligible for additional state benefits. In some states, this includes free tuition at state-supported colleges and universities.

OPPORTUNITIES FOR VETERANS

Veterans who attend college can enroll in Army ROTC and participate in the two-year program. Their prior military service could fulfill the requirements for the Basic Course, so they could start ROTC in the Advanced Course.

In addition to the Veterans Administration benefits to which they are already entitled, veterans in ROTC receive the ROTC allowance of up to $1500 each school year and may apply for ROTC scholarships.

Army ROTC—Leadership Excellence Starts Here.

Soldiers who have two years of active duty may be eligible for an Army ROTC scholarship. These "Green-to-Gold" scholarships allow selected soldiers to be released from the Army in order to attend college. Interested soldiers should contact the nearest on-campus Army ROTC office or their installation Education Offices for details.

WHAT DOES BECOMING AN ARMY OFFICER MEAN?

Army officers are leaders, thinkers, doers, and decision makers, proudly serving their country in a role that is vital to the national defense. They are required to have traits such as courage, confidence, integrity, and self-discipline.

In the Army, ROTC graduates start out as Second Lieutenants. Most become eligible for promotion and new job assignments at regular intervals.

In addition to their pay, they qualify for excellent medical, educational, and retirement benefits as well as other entitlements.

In the active Army, ROTC graduates have the opportunity to serve on Army posts located across the nation as well as abroad. In the Army National Guard or Army Reserve, they are able to serve close to where they live and work.

ADDITIONAL INFORMATION

To get more information about Army ROTC and any of the specific programs described above, students should call 800-USA-ROTC (toll-free) or contact the Professor of Military Science at a college hosting Army ROTC. Students can also write: College Army ROTC, QUEST Center, Attn: Department PG99, P.O. Box 3279, Warminster, Pennsylvania 18974-9872. Information about Army ROTC is also available on the World Wide Web at www.armyrotc.com.

Army ROTC Colleges and Universities

Army ROTC is offered at the colleges and universities listed below. Students at other institutions can often take ROTC at a nearby college campus; note that affiliated schools may cross state boundaries. The four-digit code that follows each institution name should be used to identify the college when seeking further information.

ALABAMA
†• Alabama Agricultural and Mechanical University, Normal (1002)
■ Auburn University, Auburn (1009)
‡ Auburn University at Montgomery, Montgomery (8310)
‡ Jacksonville State University, Jacksonville (1020)
○ Marion Military Institute, Marion (1026)
■• Tuskegee University, Tuskegee (1050)
■ University of Alabama, Tuscaloosa (1051)
■ University of Alabama at Birmingham, Birmingham (1052)
‡ University of North Alabama, Florence (1016)
■ University of South Alabama, Mobile (1057)
  University of West Florida, Pensacola, FL (3955)

ALASKA
† University of Alaska Fairbanks, Fairbanks (1063)

ARIZONA
■ Arizona State University, Tempe (1081)
■ Northern Arizona University, Flagstaff (1082)
■ University of Arizona, Tucson (1083)

ARKANSAS
■ Arkansas State University, State University (1090)
■ University of Arkansas, Fayetteville (1108)
‡• University of Arkansas at Pine Bluff, Pine Bluff (1086)
‡ University of Central Arkansas, Conway (1092)

CALIFORNIA
† California Polytechnic State University, San Luis Obispo (1143)
■ California State University, Fresno (1147)
† Claremont-McKenna College, Claremont (1168)
    († Harvey Mudd College, Scripps College, Pitzer College) (1171)
    † California State University Fullerton (1137)
■ San Diego State University, San Diego (1151)
† Santa Clara University, Santa Clara (1326)
‡ University of California, Berkeley (1312)
† University of California, Davis (1313)
■ University of California, Los Angeles (1315)
† University of California, Santa Barbara (1320)
‡ University of San Francisco, San Francisco (1325)
■ University of Southern California, Los Angeles (1328)

COLORADO
† Colorado State University, Fort Collins (1350)
† University of Colorado at Boulder, Boulder (1370)
† University of Colorado at Colorado Springs, Colorado Springs (4509)

CONNECTICUT
■ University of Connecticut, Storrs (29013)

DELAWARE
■ University of Delaware, Newark (1431)

DISTRICT OF COLUMBIA
‡ Georgetown University, Washington (1445)
■• Howard University, Washington (1448)

FLORIDA
† Embry-Riddle Aeronautical University, Daytona (1479)
■• Florida Agricultural and Mechanical University, Tallahassee (1480)
  Florida International University, Miami (9635)
† Florida Institute of Technology, Melbourne (1469)
  Florida Southern College, Lakeland (1488)
‡ Florida State University, Tallahassee (1489)
■ University of Central Florida, Orlando (3954)
■ University of Florida, Gainesville (1535)
■ University of South Florida, Tampa (1537)
  University of Tampa, Tampa (1538)

GEORGIA
  Augusta State University, Augusta (1552)
‡ Columbus State University, Columbus (1561)
†• Fort Valley State University, Fort Valley (1566)
† Georgia Institute of Technology, Atlanta (1569)
○ Georgia Military College, Milledgeville (1571)
■ Georgia Southern University, Statesboro (1572)
‡ Georgia State University, Atlanta (1574)
‡* North Georgia College, Dahlonega (1585)
† University of Georgia, Athens (1598)

GUAM
  University of Guam, Mangilao (3935)

HAWAII
■ University of Hawaii, Honolulu (1610)

IDAHO
‡ Boise State University, Boise (1616)
† University of Idaho, Moscow (1626)

ILLINOIS
  Eastern Illinois University, Charleston (1674)
  Illinois State University, Normal (1692)
■ Northern Illinois University, DeKalb (1737)
† Southern Illinois University Carbondale, Carbondale (1758)
  Southern Illinois University Edwardsville, Edwardsville (1759)
■ University of Illinois at Chicago, Chicago (1776)
‡ University of Illinois at Urbana-Champaign, Champaign (1775)
  Western Illinois University, Macomb (1780)
  Wheaton College, Wheaton (1781)

INDIANA
‡ Ball State University, Muncie (1786)
‡ Indiana University Bloomington, Bloomington (1809)
■ Indiana University-Purdue University Indianapolis, Indianapolis (1813)
■ Purdue University, West Lafayette (1825)
† Rose-Hulman Institute of Technology, Terre Haute (1830)
† University of Notre Dame, Notre Dame (1840)

IOWA
† Iowa State University of Science and Technology, Ames (1869)
■ University of Iowa, Iowa City (1892)
  University of Northern Iowa, Cedar Falls (1890)

KANSAS
† Kansas State University, Manhattan (1928)
■ Pittsburgh State University, Pittsburg (1926)
■ University of Kansas, Lawrence (1948)

---

* Military College or University
○ Military Junior College
• Historically Black College/University
† Accredited engineering
‡ Accredited nursing
■ Accredited both engineering and nursing

Peterson's Guide to Four-Year Colleges 2001   www.petersons.com

Army ROTC Colleges and Universities

KENTUCKY
- ‡ Eastern Kentucky University, Richmond (1963)
- Morehead State University, Morehead (1976)
- ■ University of Kentucky, Lexington (1989)
- ■ University of Louisville, Louisville (1999)
- ■ Western Kentucky University, Bowling Green (2002)

LOUISIANA
- ‡• Grambling State University, Grambling (2006)
- † Louisiana State University and Agricultural and Mechanical College, Baton Rouge (2010)
- ‡ Northwestern State University of Louisiana, Natchitoches (2021)
- ‡• Southern University and Agricultural and Mechanical College, Baton Rouge (9636)
- † Tulane University, New Orleans (2029)

MAINE
- ■ University of Maine, Orono (2053)

MARYLAND
- Bowie State College, Bowie (2062)
- ■ Johns Hopkins University, Baltimore (2077)
- † Loyola College in Maryland, Baltimore (2078)
- • Morgan State University, Baltimore (2083)
- Western Maryland College, Westminster (2109)

MASSACHUSETTS
- † Boston University, Boston (2130)
- † Massachusetts Institute of Technology, Cambridge (2178)
- ■ Northeastern University, Boston (2199)
- ■ University of Massachusetts, Amherst (2221)
- † Worcester Polytechnic Institute, Worcester (2233)

MICHIGAN
- Central Michigan University, Mount Pleasant (2243)
- ‡ Eastern Michigan University, Ypsilanti (2259)
- ■ Michigan State University, East Lansing (2290)
- † Michigan Technological University, Houghton (2292)
- ‡ Northern Michigan University, Marquette (2301)
- ■ University of Michigan, Ann Arbor (9092)
- † Western Michigan University, Kalamazoo (2330)

MINNESOTA
- ■ Minnesota State University, Mankato, Mankato (2360)
- St. John's University, Collegeville (2379)
- ■ University of Minnesota, Minneapolis (3969)

MISSISSIPPI
- ‡• Alcorn State University, Lorman (2396)
- • Jackson State University, Jackson (2410)
- † Mississippi State University, Mississippi State (2423)
- † University of Mississippi, University (2440)
- ■ University of Southern Mississippi, Hattiesburg (2441)

MISSOURI
- ‡ Central Missouri State University, Warrensburg (2454)
- ○ Kemper Military School and College, Boonville (2475)
- • Lincoln University, Jefferson City (2479)
- Missouri Western State College, St. Joseph (2490)
- Southwest Missouri State University, Springfield (2503)
- ‡ Truman State University, Kirksville (2495)
- ■ University of Missouri-Columbia, Columbia (2516)
- † University of Missouri-Rolla, Rolla (2517)
- † Washington University in St. Louis, St. Louis (2520)
- ○ Wentworth Military Academy and Junior College, Lexington (2522)

MONTANA
- ■ Montana State University, Bozeman (2532)
- University of Montana, Missoula (2536)

NEBRASKA
- ‡ Creighton University, Omaha (2542)
- ■ University of Nebraska, Lincoln (2565)

NEVADA
- ■ University of Nevada, Reno (2568)

NEW HAMPSHIRE
- ■ University of New Hampshire, Durham (2589)

NEW JERSEY
- ■ Princeton University, Princeton (2627)
- † Rutgers, The State University of New Jersey, New Brunswick (6964)
- ‡ Seton Hall University, South Orange (2632)

NEW MEXICO
- ○ New Mexico Military Institute, Roswell (2656)
- ■ New Mexico State University, Las Cruces (2657)

NEW YORK
- Canisius College, Buffalo (2681)
- † Clarkson University, Potsdam (2699)
- † Cornell University, Ithaca (2711)
- Fordham University, Bronx (2722)
- † Hofstra University, Hempstead (2732)
- † Niagara University, Niagara (2788)
- † Rochester Institute of Technology, Rochester (2806)
- St. Bonaventure University, St. Bonaventure (2817)
- St. John's University, Jamaica (2823)
- Siena College, Loudonville (2816)
- State University of New York College at Brockport, Brockport (2841)
- ■ Syracuse University, Syracuse (2882)

NORTH CAROLINA
- Appalachian State University, Boone (2906)
- Campbell University, Buies Creek (2913)
- ■ Duke University, Durham (2920)
- ‡ East Carolina University, Greenville (2923)
- Elizabeth City State University, Elizabeth City (2926)
- ■• North Carolina Agricultural and Technical State University, Greensboro (2905)
- † North Carolina State University at Raleigh, Raleigh (2972)
- • St. Augustine's College, Raleigh (2968)
- ■ University of North Carolina at Chapel Hill (2974)
- ■ University of North Carolina at Charlotte, Charlotte (2975)
- Wake Forest University, Winston-Salem (2978)

NORTH DAKOTA
- † North Dakota State University, Fargo (9265)
- ■ University of North Dakota, Grand Forks (3005)

OHIO
- ‡ Bowling Green State University, Bowling Green (3018)
- ‡ Capital University, Columbus (3023)
- • Central State University, Wilberforce (3026)
- John Carroll University, Cleveland (3050)
- ‡ Kent University, Kent (3051)
- ■ Ohio State University, Columbus (6883)
- † Ohio University, Athens (3100)
- ■ University of Akron, Akron (3123)
- ■ University of Cincinnati, Cincinnati (3125)
- † University of Dayton, Dayton (3127)
- ■ University of Toledo, Toledo (3131)
- ‡ Wright State University, Dayton (9168)
- Xavier University, Cincinnati (3144)

OKLAHOMA
- Cameron University, Lawton (3150)
- † Oklahoma State University, Stillwater (3170)
- ‡ University of Central Oklahoma, Edmond (3152)
- ■ University of Oklahoma, Norman (3184)

OREGON
- † Oregon State University, Corvallis (3210)
- University of Oregon, Eugene (3223)
- ■ University of Portland, Portland (3224)

PENNSYLVANIA
- † Bucknell University, Lewisburg (3238)
- Dickinson College, Carlisle (3253)
- † Drexel University, Philadelphia (3256)
- Edinboro University of Pennsylvania, Edinboro (3321)
- ■ Gannon University, Erie (3266)
- ‡ Indiana University of Pennsylvania, Indiana (8810)
- † Lehigh University, Bethlehem (3289)
- Lock Haven University of Pennsylvania, Lock Haven (3323)
- ■ Pennsylvania State University, University Park Campus, University Park (6965)
- Shippensburg University of Pennsylvania, Shippensburg (3326)
- ‡ Slippery Rock University of Pennsylvania, Slippery Rock (3327)

---

* Military College or University
○ Military Junior College
• Historically Black College/University
† Accredited engineering
‡ Accredited nursing
■ Accredited both engineering and nursing

Army ROTC Colleges and Universities

‡ Temple University, Pennsylvania (3371)
■ University of Pennsylvania, Philadelphia (3378)
■ University of Pittsburgh, Pittsburgh (3379)
‡ University of Scranton, Scranton (3384)
○ Valley Forge Military Academy and Junior College, Wayne (3386)
■ Widener University, Chester (3313)

PUERTO RICO
■ University of Puerto Rico, Mayaguez (3944)
University of Puerto Rico, Rio Piedras Campus, Rio Piedras (7108)

RHODE ISLAND
Providence College, Providence (3406)
■ University of Rhode Island, Kingston (3414)

SOUTH CAROLINA
†* The Citadel, Charleston (3423)
■ Clemson University, Clemson (3425)
Furman University, Greenville (3434)
Presbyterian College, Clinton (3445)
● South Carolina State University, Orangeburg (3446)
■ University of South Carolina, Columbia (3448)
Wofford College, Spartanburg (3457)

SOUTH DAKOTA
† South Dakota School of Mines and Technology, Rapid City (3470)
■ South Dakota State University, Brookings (3471)
University of South Dakota, Vermillion (10300)

TENNESSEE
‡ Austin Peay State University, Clarksville (3478)
‡ Carson-Newman College, Jefferson City (3481)
■ East Tennessee State University, Johnson City (3487)
‡ Middle Tennessee State University, Murfreesboro (3510)
■ Tennessee Technological University, Cookeville (3523)
■ The University of Memphis, Memphis (3509)
■ University of Tennessee, Knoxville, Knoxville (3530)
† University of Tennessee at Martin, Martin (3531)
■ Vanderbilt University, Nashville (3535)

TEXAS
■● Prairie View Agricultural and Mechanical University, Prairie View (3630)
† St. Mary's University of San Antonio, San Antonio (3623)
Sam Houston State University, Huntsville (3606)
Southwest Texas State University, Canyon (3615)
‡ Stephen F. Austin State University, Nacogdoches (3624)
Tarleton State University, Stephenville (3631)
† Texas Agricultural and Mechanical University, College Station (10366)
† Texas Agricultural and Mechanical University, Kingsville (3639)
‡ Texas Christian University, Fort Worth (3636)
■ Texas Tech University, Lubbock (3644)

† University of Houston, Houston (3652)
■ University of Texas at Arlington, Arlington (3656)
■ University of Texas at Austin, Austin (3658)
■ University of Texas at El Paso, El Paso (3661)
‡ University of Texas-Pan American, Edinburg (3599)
■ University of Texas at San Antonio, San Antonio (10115)

UTAH
■ Brigham Young University, Provo (3670)
■ University of Utah, Salt Lake City (3675)
‡ Weber State University, Ogden (3680)

VERMONT
■* Norwich University, Northfield (3692)
■ University of Vermont, Burlington (3696)

VIRGINIA
College of William and Mary, Williamsburg (3705)
George Mason University, Fairfax (3749)
‡● Hampton University, Hampton (3714)
‡ James Madison University, Harrisonburg (3721)
‡● Norfolk State University, Norfolk (3765)
■ Old Dominion University, Norfolk (3728)
University of Richmond, Richmond (3744)
■ University of Virginia, Charlottesville (6968)
†* Virginia Military Institute, Lexington (3753)
† Virginia Polytechnic Institute and State University, Blacksburg (3754)
● Virginia State University, Petersburg (3764)

WASHINGTON
Central Washington University, Ellensburg (3771)
■ Eastern Washington University, Cheney (3775)
■ Gonzaga University, Spokane (3778)
■ Seattle University, Seattle (3790)
■ University of Washington, Seattle (3798)
■ Washington State University, Pullman (3800)

WEST VIRGINIA
‡ Marshall University, Huntington (3815)
● West Virginia State College, Institute (3826)
■ West Virginia University, Morgantown (3827)

WISCONSIN
■ Marquette University, Milwaukee (3863)
University of Wisconsin-LaCrosse, LaCrosse (3919)
■ University of Wisconsin-Madison, Madison (3895)
‡ University of Wisconsin-Oshkosh, Oshkosh (9630)
University of Wisconsin-Stevens Point, Stevens Point (3924)

WYOMING
■ University of Wyoming, Laramie (3932)

---

* Military College or University
○ Military Junior College
● Historically Black College/University
† Accredited engineering
‡ Accredited nursing
■ Accredited both engineering and nursing

Army ROTC Colleges and Universities

Becoming an Army officer is an exciting opportunity. And the best part is that, through Army ROTC, a student can become an officer while pursuing a regular college degree.

There are many ways to obtain a scholarship application or simply more information about Army ROTC:
1. Contact the Professor of Military Science at one of the colleges or universities listed on the previous pages.
2. Write to: College Army ROTC
   QUEST Center
   Attn: Department PG99
   P.O. Box 3279
   Warminster, PA 18974-9872
3. Call 800-USA-ROTC (toll-free).
4. Call the Army ROTC Advisor nearest you

Blue Grass	502-624-4457/1870
Delaware Valley	609-562-4074
Florida	941-680-4235/800-283-4235
Georgia	912-352-3080/692-8544
Guam/Pacific	808-956-7766/888-456-1444
Mid-Atlantic	703-805-4040/800-253-5729
Midwest	847-266-3105
New England	800-431-4781
North Central	719-526-6879
Northwest	253-967-6272
Ohio Valley	573-596-0114
Puerto Rico	787-833-0054
South Central	210-221-0618/0634
Southeastern	910-396-8408/3774
Southern	256-955-7577
Southwest	831-242-7818/7726

5. Check out Army ROTC on the World Wide Web: http://www.armyrotc.com

---

* Military College or University
o Military Junior College
• Historically Black College/University
† Accredited engineering
‡ Accredited nursing
■ Accredited both engineering and nursing

College Profiles AND SPECIAL ANNOUNCEMENTS

This section contains detailed factual profiles of colleges, covering such items as background facts, enrollment figures, faculty size, admission and graduation requirements, expenses, financing, special programs, career services, housing, campus life and student services, sports (including athletic scholarships), majors and degrees, and whom to contact for more information. In addition, there are special announcements from college administrators about new programs or special events. The data in each of these profiles, collected from fall 1998 to spring 1999, come solely from Peterson's Annual Survey of Undergraduate Institutions, which was sent to deans or admission officers at each institution. The profiles are organized state by state and arranged alphabetically within those sections by the official names of the institutions.

ALABAMA

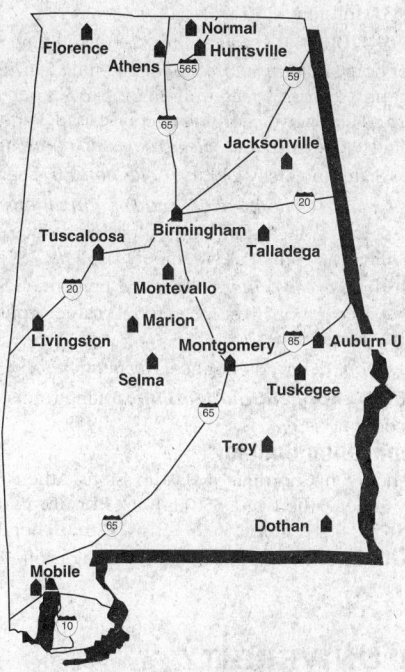

ALABAMA AGRICULTURAL AND MECHANICAL UNIVERSITY
Normal, Alabama

- **State-supported**, university, founded 1875
- **Degrees** bachelor's, master's, doctoral, and post-master's certificates
- **Suburban** 2,001-acre campus
- **Coed**, 4,332 undergraduate students, 92% full-time, 51% women, 49% men
- **Minimally difficult** entrance level, 33% of applicants were admitted
- **22:1** student-to-undergraduate faculty ratio
- **37% graduate** in 6 years or less
- **$2732 tuition** and fees (in-state); $4664 (out-of-state)
- **$4978 average financial aid** package, $17,021 average indebtedness upon graduation, $25 million endowment

AAMU is a dynamic and progressive multicultural institution with a strong commitment to academic excellence. Some 100 programs are offered through 6 schools. The School of Graduate Studies offers the MS, MBA, MSW, MEd, MURP, EdS, and PhD degrees. Serving approximately 5,500 students, the research institution ably meets the challenges launched by the nation's 2nd-largest research park in Huntsville, Alabama, and the world beyond. Moreover, AAMU students placed on *USA Today*'s Academic First Team in 1997 and 1998. Scholarships are available in academics, athletics, music, and theater.

Students *Undergraduates:* 3,976 full-time, 356 part-time. Students come from 39 states and territories, 13 other countries. *The most frequently chosen baccalaureate fields are:* business/marketing, biological/life sciences, education. *Graduate:* 1,165 in graduate degree programs.

From out-of-state	52%	Reside on campus	45%
Age 25 or older	9%	Transferred in	5%
International students	4%	African Americans	89%
Asian Americans/Pacific Islanders	0.3%	Hispanic Americans	0.3%
Native Americans	0.3%		

Faculty 286 (85% full-time), 81% with terminal degrees.
Expenses (2000–2001) *Tuition, state resident:* full-time $2332; part-time $119 per semester hour. *Tuition, nonresident:* full-time $4264; part-time $219 per semester hour. *Required fees:* full-time $400. Part-time tuition and fees vary according to course load. *College room and board:* $2678. Room and board charges vary according to housing facility. *Payment plan:* deferred payment. *Waivers:* minority students and employees or children of employees.

Library J. F. Drake Learning Resources Center. *Operations spending 1999–2000:* $1.8 million. *Collection:* 506,396 titles, 2,439 serial subscriptions, 32,617 audiovisual materials.

College life *Housing:* on-campus residence required through sophomore year. *Options:* men-only, women-only, disabled students. *Social organizations:* national fraternities, national sororities, local fraternities, local sororities; 50% of eligible men and 50% of eligible women are members. *Most popular organizations:* University Voices Gospel Choir, university choir and band, elementary/early childhood club, National Alliance of Business Students, fraternities/sororities.

Campus security 24-hour patrols, late-night transport-escort service, controlled dormitory access.

After graduation 530 organizations recruited on campus 1997–98. 60% of class of 1998 had job offers within 6 months. *Career center:* 5 full-time personnel. Services include job fairs, resume preparation, resume referral, career counseling, careers library, job bank, job interviews. *Graduate education:* 42% of class of 1999 went directly to graduate and professional school: 20% graduate arts and sciences, 15% education, 10% business, 2% engineering.

Freshmen 3,376 applied, 1,098 admitted, 1,121 enrolled. 21 National Merit Scholars.

Average high school GPA	2.5	SAT verbal scores above 500	N/R
SAT math scores above 500	N/R	ACT above 18	45%
1998 freshmen returning in 1999	67%		

Application *Options:* Common Application, electronic application, deferred entrance. *Application fee:* $10. *Required:* high school transcript; minimum 2.0 GPA. *Recommended:* 1 letter of recommendation.

Standardized tests *Admission: Recommended:* ACT.

Significant dates *Application deadlines:* rolling (freshmen), rolling (transfers). *Financial aid deadline priority date:* 3/17.

Freshman Application Contact
Mr. Antonio Boyle, Director of Admissions, Alabama Agricultural and Mechanical University, PO Box 908, Normal, AL 35762. **Phone:** 256-851-5245. **Toll-free phone:** 800-553-0816. **Fax:** 256-851-9747. **E-mail:** aboyle@asnaam.aamu.edu

Visit CollegeQuest.com for information on majors offered and athletics. College video and electronic viewbook available at CollegeQuest.com.

ALABAMA STATE UNIVERSITY
Montgomery, Alabama

- **State-supported**, comprehensive, founded 1867
- **Degrees** associate, bachelor's, and master's
- **Urban** 114-acre campus
- **Coed**, 4,588 undergraduate students, 88% full-time, 55% women, 45% men
- **Minimally difficult** entrance level, 68% of applicants were admitted
- **18:1** student-to-undergraduate faculty ratio
- **18% graduate** in 6 years or less
- **$2520 tuition** and fees (in-state); $5040 (out-of-state)
- **$7788 average financial aid** package, $10.5 million endowment

Part of Alabama Commission on Higher Education.
Students *Undergraduates:* 4,023 full-time, 565 part-time. Students come from 37 states and territories, 16 other countries. *The most frequently chosen baccalaureate fields are:* business/marketing, biological/life sciences, education. *Graduate:* 981 in graduate degree programs.

From out-of-state	28%	Reside on campus	43%
Age 25 or older	16%	Transferred in	4%

Faculty 362 (59% full-time).
Expenses (1999–2000) *Tuition, state resident:* full-time $2520; part-time $105 per credit hour. *Tuition, nonresident:* full-time $5040; part-time $210 per credit hour. Full-time tuition and fees vary according to course load, degree level, and student level. Part-time tuition and fees vary according to course load, degree level, and student level. *College room and board:* $3700.

Alabama

Alabama State University (continued)
Room and board charges vary according to housing facility. *Payment plans:* installment, deferred payment. *Waivers:* employees or children of employees.
Library Levi Watkins Learning Center. *Operations spending 1999–2000:* $1.6 million. *Collection:* 383,649 titles, 1,270 serial subscriptions, 42,047 audiovisual materials.
College life *Housing: Options:* men-only, women-only. *Social organizations:* national fraternities, national sororities; 2% of eligible men and 2% of eligible women are members. *Most popular organizations:* Student Orientation Services Leaders, Voices of Praise Gospel Choir, Student Government Association, university bands, Commuter Student Association.
Campus security 24-hour emergency response devices and patrols, late-night transport-escort service, self-defense education, well-lit campus.
After graduation 235 organizations recruited on campus 1997–98. *Career center:* 4 full-time personnel. Services include job fairs, resume preparation, interview workshops, resume referral, career counseling, job interviews. *Graduate education:* 50% of class of 1999 went directly to graduate and professional school.
Freshmen 5,816 applied, 3,968 admitted, 1,203 enrolled.

Average high school GPA	2.62	SAT verbal scores above 500	16%
SAT math scores above 500	11%	ACT above 18	26%
1998 freshmen returning in 1999	41%		

Application *Options:* early admission, deferred entrance. *Application fee:* $0. *Required:* high school transcript; minimum 2.0 GPA.
Standardized tests *Admission: Required:* SAT I or ACT.
Significant dates *Application deadlines:* 7/30 (freshmen), 7/30 (transfers). *Financial aid deadline priority date:* 5/1.
Freshman Application Contact
Mrs. Danielle Kennedy-Lamar, Director of Admissions and Recruitment, Alabama State University, PO Box 271, Montgomery, AL 36101-0271. **Phone:** 334-229-4291. **Toll-free phone:** 800-253-5037. **Fax:** 334-229-4984. **E-mail:** dcrump@asunet.alasu.edu
Visit CollegeQuest.com for information on majors offered and athletics. College video available at CollegeQuest.com.

THE AMERICAN INSTITUTE FOR COMPUTER SCIENCES
Birmingham, Alabama

Admissions Office Contact
The American Institute for Computer Sciences, 2101 Magnolia Avenue, Suite 207, Birmingham, AL 35205. **Toll-free phone:** 800-767-AICS. **Fax:** 205-328-2229.

ANDREW JACKSON UNIVERSITY
Birmingham, Alabama

Admissions Office Contact
Andrew Jackson University, 10 Old Montgomery Highway, Birmingham, AL 35209. **Fax:** 205-871-9294.

ATHENS STATE UNIVERSITY
Athens, Alabama

- **State-supported**, upper-level, founded 1822
- **Degree** bachelor's
- **Small-town** 45-acre campus
- **Coed**, 2,790 undergraduate students, 42% full-time, 64% women, 36% men
- **Noncompetitive** entrance level, 100% of applicants were admitted
- **17:1** student-to-undergraduate faculty ratio
- **$2400 tuition** and fees (in-state); $4736 (out-of-state)

Students *Undergraduates:* 1,177 full-time, 1,613 part-time. Students come from 5 states and territories. *The most frequently chosen baccalaureate fields are:* business/marketing, education, protective services/public administration.

Transferred in	24%	African Americans	11%
Asian Americans/Pacific Islanders	1%	Hispanic Americans	0.4%
Native Americans	2%		

Faculty 156 (53% full-time).
Expenses (1999–2000) *Tuition, state resident:* full-time $2336; part-time $73 per semester hour. *Tuition, nonresident:* full-time $4672; part-time $146 per semester hour. *Required fees:* full-time $64; $2 per semester hour. Full-time tuition and fees vary according to course load. Part-time tuition and fees vary according to course load. *College room and board:* room only: $840.
Library Athens State University Library. *Collection:* 307 serial subscriptions.
College life *Housing: Option:* coed. *Social organizations:* national fraternities, national sororities, local fraternities, local sororities; 14% of eligible men and 19% of eligible women are members.
After graduation *Career center:* 4 full-time personnel. Services include job fairs, resume preparation, resume referral, career counseling, careers library, job bank, job interviews.
Application *Option:* deferred entrance. *Application fee:* $30.
Significant dates *Application deadline:* rolling (transfers). *Financial aid deadline:* continuous.
Freshman Application Contact
Ms. Necedah Henderson, Coordinator of Admissions, Athens State University, 300 North Beaty Street, Athens, AL 35611-1902. **Phone:** 256-233-8217. **Toll-free phone:** 800-522-0272. **Fax:** 256-233-8164. **E-mail:** henden@athens.edu
Visit CollegeQuest.com for information on majors offered and athletics.

AUBURN UNIVERSITY
Auburn, Alabama

- **State-supported**, university, founded 1856
- **Degrees** bachelor's, master's, doctoral, first professional, and post-master's certificates
- **Small-town** 1,875-acre campus
- **Coed**, 18,616 undergraduate students, 92% full-time, 48% women, 52% men
- **Moderately difficult** entrance level, 88% of applicants were admitted
- **16:1** student-to-undergraduate faculty ratio
- **66% graduate** in 6 years or less
- **$2955 tuition** and fees (in-state); $8745 (out-of-state)

Students *Undergraduates:* 17,171 full-time, 1,445 part-time. Students come from 53 states and territories, 51 other countries. *The most frequently chosen baccalaureate fields are:* business/marketing, education, engineering/engineering technologies. *Graduate:* 658 in professional programs, 2,793 in other graduate degree programs.

From out-of-state	31%	Reside on campus	16%
Age 25 or older	6%	Transferred in	7%
International students	1%	African Americans	7%
Asian Americans/Pacific Islanders	1%	Hispanic Americans	1%
Native Americans	1%		

Faculty 1,255 (91% full-time), 90% with terminal degrees.
Expenses (1999–2000) *Tuition, state resident:* full-time $2895; part-time $80 per credit. *Tuition, nonresident:* full-time $8685; part-time $240 per credit. *Required fees:* full-time $60. Full-time tuition and fees vary according to program. Part-time tuition and fees vary according to program. Room and board charges vary according to housing facility. Part-time mandatory fees per term: $165 for state residents, $495 for nonresidents. *Waivers:* children of alumni and employees or children of employees.
Library R. B. Draughon Library plus 2 others. *Collection:* 2.4 million titles, 19,410 serial subscriptions.
College life *Social organizations:* national fraternities, national sororities; 17% of eligible men and 27% of eligible women are members. *Most popular organizations:* student government association, university program council, IMPACT, Panhellenic Council, Interfraternity Council.
Campus security 24-hour emergency response devices and patrols, late-night transport-escort service, controlled dormitory access.
After graduation 75 organizations recruited on campus 1997–98. 75% of class of 1998 had job offers within 6 months. *Career center:* 19 full-time, 3

Alabama

part-time personnel. Services include job fairs, resume preparation, resume referral, career counseling, careers library, job bank, job interviews. **Graduate education:** 35% of class of 1999 went directly to graduate and professional school: 9% business, 6% medicine, 5% education, 5% graduate arts and sciences, 4% engineering, 3% law, 2% veterinary medicine, 1% dentistry.

Freshmen 10,542 applied, 9,264 admitted, 3,692 enrolled. 34 National Merit Scholars.

Average high school GPA	3.08	SAT verbal scores above 500	71%
SAT math scores above 500	75%	ACT above 18	96%
From top 10% of their h.s. class	24%	From top quarter	54%
From top half	81%	1998 freshmen returning in 1999	81%

Application *Options:* early admission, deferred entrance. *Preference* given to state residents, children of alumni. *Application fee:* $25. *Required:* high school transcript; minimum 2.0 GPA. *Required for some:* minimum 3.0 GPA.
Standardized tests *Admission: Required:* SAT I or ACT.
Significant dates *Application deadlines:* 9/1 (freshmen), 9/1 (transfers). *Financial aid deadline priority date:* 4/15.
Freshman Application Contact
Dr. John Fletcher, Acting Assistant Vice President of Enrollment Management, Auburn University, 202 Mary Martin Hall, Auburn University, AL 36849-0001. **Phone:** 334-844-4080. **Toll-free phone:** 800-AUBURN9. **E-mail:** admissions@mail.auburn.edu

Visit CollegeQuest.com for information on majors offered and athletics. College video available at CollegeQuest.com.

■ *See page 1204 for a narrative description.*

AUBURN UNIVERSITY MONTGOMERY
Montgomery, Alabama

- **State-supported**, comprehensive, founded 1967
- **Degrees** bachelor's, master's, and doctoral
- **Suburban** 500-acre campus
- **Coed**, 4,400 undergraduate students, 68% full-time, 63% women, 37% men
- **Moderately difficult** entrance level, 99% of applicants were admitted
- **18:1 student-to-undergraduate faculty ratio**
- **$2577 tuition** and fees (in-state); $7731 (out-of-state)
- **$19.9 million endowment**

Part of Auburn University.
Students *Undergraduates:* 2,986 full-time, 1,414 part-time. Students come from 34 states and territories, 21 other countries. *The most frequently chosen baccalaureate fields are:* business/marketing, biological/life sciences, education. *Graduate:* 815 in graduate degree programs.

From out-of-state	4%	Reside on campus	16%
Age 25 or older	30%	Transferred in	10%
International students	1%	African Americans	31%
Asian Americans/Pacific Islanders	2%	Hispanic Americans	1%
Native Americans	0.4%		

Faculty 329 (58% full-time), 46% with terminal degrees.
Expenses (1999–2000) *One-time required fee:* $25. *Tuition, state resident:* full-time $2577; part-time $59 per quarter hour. *Tuition, nonresident:* full-time $7731; part-time $177 per quarter hour. Full-time tuition and fees vary according to course load. *College room and board:* room only: $2010. *Payment plan:* deferred payment. *Waivers:* employees or children of employees.
Library Auburn University Montgomery Library. *Operations spending 1999–2000:* $1.7 million. *Collection:* 273,947 titles, 1,480 serial subscriptions, 1,441 audiovisual materials.
College life *Housing: Options:* coed, disabled students. *Social organizations:* national fraternities, national sororities; 5% of eligible men and 4% of eligible women are members. *Most popular organizations:* Student Government Association, Baptist campus ministries, International Student Association, African-American Student Alliance.
Campus security 24-hour emergency response devices and patrols, student patrols, late-night transport-escort service.
After graduation 250 organizations recruited on campus 1997–98. *Career center:* 2 full-time personnel. Services include job fairs, resume preparation,

interview workshops, resume referral, career/interest testing, career counseling, careers library, job bank, job interviews, co-op placement.

Freshmen 914 applied, 904 admitted, 863 enrolled.

SAT verbal scores above 500	54%	SAT math scores above 500	43%
ACT above 18	69%		

Application *Options:* eApply at www.CollegeQuest.com, electronic application, early admission, deferred entrance. *Application fee:* $25. *Required:* high school transcript.
Standardized tests *Admission: Required:* SAT I or ACT.
Significant dates *Application deadlines:* 7/29 (freshmen), 7/29 (transfers). *Financial aid deadline priority date:* 3/15.
Freshman Application Contact
Ms. Michele Moore, Assistant Director, Admissions, Auburn University Montgomery, PO Box 244023, Montgomery, AL 36124-4023. **Phone:** 334-244-3621. **Toll-free phone:** 800-227-2649. **Fax:** 334-244-3795. **E-mail:** auminfo@mickey.aum.edu

Visit CollegeQuest.com for information on majors offered and athletics. College video and electronic viewbook available at CollegeQuest.com.

BIRMINGHAM-SOUTHERN COLLEGE
Birmingham, Alabama

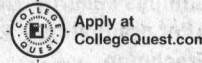

- **Independent Methodist**, comprehensive, founded 1856
- **Degrees** bachelor's and master's
- **Urban** 196-acre campus
- **Coed**, 1,442 undergraduate students, 94% full-time, 60% women, 40% men
- **Moderately difficult** entrance level, 95% of applicants were admitted
- **13:1 student-to-undergraduate faculty ratio**
- **$15,498 tuition** and fees
- **$8521 average financial aid** package, $13,226 average indebtedness upon graduation, $127 million endowment

Birmingham-Southern is a nationally ranked institution noted for an outstanding record of job placement and graduate admission to medical, law, and professional schools as well as for the Mentor Program, service learning, leadership development, and international programs. *U.S. News & World Report*, *Money* magazine, and *National Review* have also recognized Southern, which has 1 of 2 Phi Beta Kappa chapters in Alabama.

Students *Undergraduates:* 1,362 full-time, 80 part-time. Students come from 28 states and territories. *The most frequently chosen baccalaureate fields are:* business/marketing, English, interdisciplinary studies. *Graduate:* 75 in graduate degree programs.

From out-of-state	23%	Age 25 or older	1%
Transferred in	4%	International students	1%
African Americans	12%	Asian Americans/Pacific Islanders	4%
Hispanic Americans	0.3%	Native Americans	1%

Faculty 131 (73% full-time), 68% with terminal degrees.
Expenses (1999–2000) *Comprehensive fee:* $20,958 includes full-time tuition ($15,170), mandatory fees ($328), and room and board ($5460). *College room only:* $2800. Full-time tuition and fees vary according to class time and course load. Room and board charges vary according to board plan and housing facility. *Part-time tuition:* $632 per credit. *Part-time fees:* $114 per term part-time. Part-time tuition and fees vary according to class time and course load. *Payment plan:* installment. *Waivers:* children of alumni and employees or children of employees.
Library Charles Andrew Rush Learning Center/N. E. Miles Library. *Operations spending 1999–2000:* $916,174. *Collection:* 270,296 titles, 1,032 serial subscriptions.
College life *Housing:* on-campus residence required through senior year. *Options:* men-only, women-only. *Social organizations:* national fraternities, national sororities; 62% of eligible men and 65% of eligible women are members. *Most popular organizations:* Southern Volunteer Services, Student Conservancy, Greek organizations, Residence Hall Association.
Campus security 24-hour emergency response devices and patrols, late-night transport-escort service, controlled dormitory access.
After graduation 29 organizations recruited on campus 1997–98. *Career center:* 2 full-time personnel. Services include job fairs, resume preparation,

Alabama

Birmingham-Southern College (continued)
interview workshops, resume referral, career/interest testing, career counseling, careers library, job bank, job interviews. **Graduate education:** 39% of class of 1999 went directly to graduate and professional school: 13% graduate arts and sciences, 8% business, 7% medicine, 3% dentistry, 3% education, 3% law, 2% theology.

Freshmen 867 applied, 825 admitted, 337 enrolled. 13 National Merit Scholars, 11 valedictorians.

Average high school GPA	3.22	SAT verbal scores above 500	87%
SAT math scores above 500	83%	ACT above 18	100%
From top 10% of their h.s. class	34%	From top quarter	60%
From top half	89%	1998 freshmen returning in 1999	80%

Application *Options:* eApply at www.CollegeQuest.com, Common Application, electronic application, early admission, early action, deferred entrance. *Application fee:* $25. *Required:* essay or personal statement; high school transcript; minimum 2.0 GPA; 1 letter of recommendation. *Required for some:* interview.

Standardized tests *Admission: Required:* SAT I or ACT.

Significant dates *Application deadlines:* rolling (freshmen), rolling (transfers). *Early action:* 12/1. *Notification:* 12/15 (early action). **Financial aid deadline priority date:** 3/1.

Freshman Application Contact
Ms. DeeDee Barnes Bruns, Dean of Admission and Financial Aid, Birmingham-Southern College, Box 549008, Birmingham, AL 35254. **Phone:** 205-226-4696. **Toll-free phone:** 800-523-5793. **Fax:** 205-226-3074. **E-mail:** admissions@bsc.edu

Visit CollegeQuest.com for information on majors offered and athletics. College video available at CollegeQuest.com.

■ *See page 1278 for a narrative description.*

CONCORDIA COLLEGE
Selma, Alabama

- **Independent Lutheran**, 4-year, founded 1922
- **Degrees** associate and bachelor's
- **Small-town** 22-acre campus with easy access to Birmingham
- **Coed**
- **Noncompetitive** entrance level
- **$5642 tuition** and fees

Expenses (1999–2000) *Comprehensive fee:* $8542 includes full-time tuition ($5600), mandatory fees ($42), and room and board ($2900). *College room only:* $1500. Room and board charges vary according to board plan and housing facility. *Part-time tuition:* $195 per credit. *Part-time fees:* $21 per term part-time.

Application *Option:* deferred entrance. *Application fee:* $10. *Required:* high school transcript; minimum 2.0 GPA.

Standardized tests *Placement: Required:* ACT

Admissions Office Contact
Concordia College, 1804 Green Street, PO Box 1329, Selma, AL 36701. **Fax:** 334-874-3728.

Visit CollegeQuest.com for information on athletics.

DRAUGHONS JUNIOR COLLEGE
Alabama—See South College

FAULKNER UNIVERSITY
Montgomery, Alabama

- **Independent**, comprehensive, founded 1942, affiliated with Church of Christ
- **Degrees** associate, bachelor's, master's, and first professional
- **Urban** 75-acre campus
- **Coed**, 2,199 undergraduate students, 71% full-time, 60% women, 40% men
- **Moderately difficult** entrance level, 37% of applicants were admitted
- **20:1** student-to-undergraduate faculty ratio

- **16.7% graduate** in 6 years or less
- **$7500 tuition** and fees
- **$6650 average financial aid** package, $18,000 average indebtedness upon graduation, $9.7 million endowment

Students *Undergraduates:* 1,572 full-time, 627 part-time. Students come from 22 states and territories, 3 other countries. *The most frequently chosen baccalaureate fields are:* (pre)law, business/marketing, education. **Graduate:** 363 in professional programs, 50 in other graduate degree programs.

From out-of-state	10%	Reside on campus	59%
Age 25 or older	53%	Transferred in	3%
International students	0.3%	African Americans	37%
Asian Americans/Pacific Islanders	0.3%	Hispanic Americans	1%
Native Americans	0.5%		

Faculty 57 (96% full-time), 63% with terminal degrees.

Expenses (1999–2000) *Comprehensive fee:* $11,490 includes full-time tuition ($7500) and room and board ($3990). *College room only:* $1900. Full-time tuition and fees vary according to program. Room and board charges vary according to board plan and housing facility. *Part-time tuition:* $250 per semester hour. Part-time tuition and fees vary according to program. *Payment plans:* installment, deferred payment. *Waivers:* adult students and employees or children of employees.

Library Gus Nichols Library plus 2 others. *Operations spending 1999–2000:* $647,034. *Collection:* 92,000 titles, 1,153 serial subscriptions, 179 audiovisual materials.

College life *Housing:* on-campus residence required through junior year. *Options:* coed, men-only, women-only. *Social organizations:* local fraternities, local sororities; 53% of eligible men and 49% of eligible women are members. *Most popular organizations:* social clubs, student government, Ambassadors, Thespians, Acappella Chorus.

Campus security 24-hour patrols, late-night transport-escort service.

After graduation *Career center:* Services include career counseling.

Freshmen 495 applied, 181 admitted, 397 enrolled.

SAT verbal scores above 500	N/R	SAT math scores above 500	N/R
ACT above 18	N/R	1998 freshmen returning in 1999	58%

Application *Options:* eApply at www.CollegeQuest.com, Common Application, electronic application, early admission, deferred entrance. *Application fee:* $10. *Required:* high school transcript; minimum 2.0 GPA; 2 letters of recommendation. *Recommended:* interview.

Standardized tests *Admission: Required:* SAT I or ACT.

Significant dates *Application deadlines:* rolling (freshmen), rolling (transfers). **Financial aid deadline priority date:** 5/1.

Freshman Application Contact
Mr. Keith Mock, Director of Admissions, Faulkner University, 5345 Atlanta Highway, Montgomery, AL 36109. **Phone:** 334-386-7200. **Toll-free phone:** 800-879-9816. **Fax:** 334-260-6137. **E-mail:** admissions@faulkner.edu

Visit CollegeQuest.com for information on majors offered and athletics. College video available at CollegeQuest.com.

HERZING COLLEGE
Birmingham, Alabama

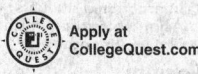

- **Proprietary**, primarily 2-year, founded 1965
- **Degrees** associate and bachelor's (bachelor's degree in computer information systems and electronics engineering technology only)
- **Urban** campus
- **Coed**, 470 undergraduate students
- **Minimally difficult** entrance level

Part of Herzing Institutes, Inc.

Faculty 18 (67% full-time).

Admissions Office Contact
Herzing College, 280 West Valley Avenue, Birmingham, AL 35209. **Fax:** 205-916-2807.

Visit CollegeQuest.com for information on majors offered and athletics. College video available at CollegeQuest.com.

Alabama

HUNTINGDON COLLEGE
Montgomery, Alabama

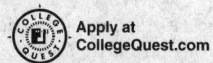

- **Independent United Methodist**, 4-year, founded 1854
- **Degrees** associate and bachelor's
- **Suburban** 58-acre campus with easy access to Birmingham
- **Coed**, 700 undergraduate students, 88% full-time, 62% women, 38% men
- **Moderately difficult** entrance level, 78% of applicants were admitted
- **12:1 student-to-undergraduate faculty ratio**
- **39.05% graduate** in 6 years or less
- **$11,910 tuition** and fees
- **$10,541 average financial aid** package, $15,262 average indebtedness upon graduation, $37.4 million endowment

Students *Undergraduates:* 616 full-time, 84 part-time. Students come from 24 states and territories, 12 other countries. *The most frequently chosen baccalaureate fields are:* business/marketing, English, visual/performing arts.

From out-of-state	34%	Reside on campus	73%
Age 25 or older	12%	Transferred in	5%
International students	4%	African Americans	7%
Asian Americans/Pacific Islanders	2%	Hispanic Americans	0.3%
Native Americans	1%		

Faculty 71 (65% full-time), 63% with terminal degrees.

Expenses (2000–2001) *Comprehensive fee:* $17,650 includes full-time tuition ($11,000), mandatory fees ($910), and room and board ($5740). Full-time tuition and fees vary according to class time and reciprocity agreements. Room and board charges vary according to housing facility. *Part-time tuition:* $390 per semester hour. Part-time tuition and fees vary according to class time and course load. *Payment plan:* deferred payment. *Waivers:* employees or children of employees.

Library Houghton Memorial Library. *Operations spending 1999–2000:* $320,440. *Collection:* 100,481 titles, 370 serial subscriptions, 1,214 audiovisual materials.

College life *Housing:* on-campus residence required through senior year. *Option:* coed. *Social organizations:* national fraternities, national sororities; 26% of eligible men and 27% of eligible women are members. *Most popular organizations:* College Programs Council, United Student Alliance, Voluntary Action Center, Circle K, SALT (Students Actively Learning the Truth).

Campus security 24-hour emergency response devices and patrols, late-night transport-escort service, controlled dormitory access.

After graduation 56% of class of 1998 had job offers within 6 months. *Career center:* 2 full-time personnel. Services include job fairs, resume preparation, interview workshops, resume referral, career/interest testing, career counseling, careers library, job bank, job interviews.

Freshmen 690 applied, 540 admitted, 163 enrolled. 12 valedictorians.

Average high school GPA	3.37	SAT verbal scores above 500	80%
SAT math scores above 500	65%	ACT above 18	97%
From top 10% of their h.s. class	34%	From top quarter	63%
From top half	88%	1998 freshmen returning in 1999	75%

Application *Options:* eApply at www.CollegeQuest.com, Common Application, electronic application, early admission, deferred entrance. *Application fee:* $25. *Required:* high school transcript; minimum 2.25 GPA. *Required for some:* essay or personal statement; 2 letters of recommendation; interview. *Recommended:* 3 letters of recommendation.

Standardized tests *Admission: Required:* SAT I or ACT.

Significant dates *Application deadlines:* rolling (freshmen), rolling (transfers). *Financial aid deadline priority date:* 4/15.

Freshman Application Contact
Ms. Suellen Ofe, Vice President for Enrollment Management, Huntingdon College, 1500 East Fairview Avenue, Montgomery, AL 36106. **Phone:** 334-833-4515. **Toll-free phone:** 800-763-0313. **Fax:** 334-833-4347. **E-mail:** admiss@huntington.edu

Visit CollegeQuest.com for information on majors offered and athletics. Electronic viewbook available at CollegeQuest.com.

- *See page 1810 for a narrative description.*

INTERNATIONAL BIBLE COLLEGE
Florence, Alabama

- **Independent**, 4-year, founded 1971, affiliated with Church of Christ
- **Degrees** associate and bachelor's
- **Small-town** 43-acre campus
- **Coed**, 135 undergraduate students, 45% full-time, 24% women, 76% men
- **Noncompetitive** entrance level, 85% of applicants were admitted
- **$5492 tuition** and fees
- **$3 million endowment**

Students *Undergraduates:* 61 full-time, 74 part-time. Students come from 20 states and territories, 5 other countries. *The most frequently chosen baccalaureate field is:* philosophy.

From out-of-state	60%	Reside on campus	19%
Age 25 or older	65%	Transferred in	6%
International students	4%	African Americans	11%
Asian Americans/Pacific Islanders	1%	Hispanic Americans	3%

Faculty 15 (60% full-time).

Expenses (1999–2000) *Tuition:* full-time $5012; part-time $179 per semester hour. *Required fees:* full-time $480; $20 per semester hour. *College room only:* $1200. *Payment plans:* installment, deferred payment. *Waivers:* employees or children of employees.

Library Overton Memorial Library. *Collection:* 18,474 titles, 260 serial subscriptions.

College life *Most popular organizations:* missions club, preachers club, Student Government Association.

After graduation *Career center:* Services include resume referral, career counseling, job interviews. *Graduate education:* 1% of class of 1999 went directly to graduate and professional school.

Freshmen 89 applied, 76 admitted, 16 enrolled.

SAT verbal scores above 500	N/R	SAT math scores above 500	N/R
ACT above 18	N/R		

Application *Options:* early admission, deferred entrance. *Preference* given to applicants interested in preaching in Churches of Christ. *Required:* high school transcript; 3 letters of recommendation. *Recommended:* interview.

Standardized tests *Placement: Recommended:* ACT.

Significant dates *Application deadlines:* rolling (freshmen), rolling (transfers). *Notification:* continuous until 7/1 (freshmen). *Financial aid deadline priority date:* 6/1.

Freshman Application Contact
Mr. Jim Collins, Director of Enrollment Services, International Bible College, PO Box IBC, Florence, AL 35630-0050. **Phone:** 256-766-6610 Ext. 26. **Toll-free phone:** 800-367-3565.

Visit CollegeQuest.com for information on majors offered and athletics. College video available at CollegeQuest.com.

JACKSONVILLE STATE UNIVERSITY
Jacksonville, Alabama

- **State-supported**, comprehensive, founded 1883
- **Degrees** bachelor's and master's
- **Small-town** 345-acre campus with easy access to Birmingham
- **Coed**, 6,599 undergraduate students, 79% full-time, 57% women, 43% men
- **Minimally difficult** entrance level, 53% of applicants were admitted
- **22:1 student-to-undergraduate faculty ratio**
- **32% graduate** in 6 years or less
- **$2440 tuition** and fees (in-state); $4880 (out-of-state)

Students *Undergraduates:* 5,246 full-time, 1,353 part-time. Students come from 40 states and territories, 74 other countries. *The most frequently chosen baccalaureate fields are:* business/marketing, education, protective services/public administration. *Graduate:* 1,288 in graduate degree programs.

Peterson's Guide to Four-Year Colleges 2001 · www.petersons.com

Alabama

Jacksonville State University (continued)

From out-of-state	10%	Reside on campus	20%
Age 25 or older	25%	Transferred in	11%
International students	2%	African Americans	18%
Asian Americans/Pacific Islanders	1%	Hispanic Americans	1%
Native Americans	1%		

Faculty 362 (72% full-time), 40% with terminal degrees.
Expenses (1999–2000) *One-time required fee:* $10. *Tuition, state resident:* full-time $2440; part-time $102 per semester hour. *Tuition, nonresident:* full-time $4880; part-time $204 per semester hour. Full-time tuition and fees vary according to course load and reciprocity agreements. Part-time tuition and fees vary according to course load and reciprocity agreements. *College room and board:* $3080; room only: $1150. Room and board charges vary according to board plan and housing facility. *Waivers:* senior citizens and employees or children of employees.
Library Houston Cole Library. *Operations spending 1999–2000:* $2.2 million. *Collection:* 411,044 titles, 4,791 serial subscriptions, 31,380 audiovisual materials.
College life *Housing: Options:* coed, men-only, women-only, disabled students. *Social organizations:* national fraternities, national sororities; 10% of eligible men and 10% of eligible women are members. *Most popular organizations:* Student Government Association, archaeology club, campus fellowship clubs, computer science club, biology club.
Campus security 24-hour emergency response devices and patrols, student patrols, late-night transport-escort service, night security officer in female residence halls.
After graduation 120 organizations recruited on campus 1997–98. *Career center:* 8 full-time, 2 part-time personnel. Services include job fairs, resume preparation, interview workshops, resume referral, career/interest testing, career counseling, careers library, job bank, job interviews.
Freshmen 2,037 applied, 1,076 admitted, 1,069 enrolled.

Average high school GPA	3.11	SAT verbal scores above 500	N/R
SAT math scores above 500	N/R	ACT above 18	N/R
1998 freshmen returning in 1999	60%		

Application *Options:* eApply at www.CollegeQuest.com, early admission, deferred entrance. *Application fee:* $20. *Required:* high school transcript.
Standardized tests *Admission: Required:* SAT I or ACT.
Significant dates *Application deadlines:* rolling (freshmen), rolling (transfers). *Financial aid deadline priority date:* 3/15.
Freshman Application Contact
Ms. Martha Mitchell, Freshman Admission and Recruiting, Jacksonville State University, 700 Pelham Road North, Jacksonville, AL 36265. **Phone:** 256-782-5363. **Toll-free phone:** 800-231-5291. **Fax:** 256-782-5291. **E-mail:** kcambron@jsucc.edu
Visit CollegeQuest.com for information on majors offered and athletics. College video available at CollegeQuest.com.

JUDSON COLLEGE
Marion, Alabama

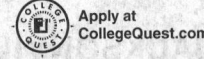
Apply at CollegeQuest.com

- **Independent Baptist**, 4-year, founded 1838
- **Degree** bachelor's
- **Rural** 80-acre campus with easy access to Birmingham
- **Women** only, 292 undergraduate students, 90% full-time
- **Moderately difficult** entrance level, 81% of applicants were admitted
- **10:1** student-to-undergraduate faculty ratio
- **36% graduate** in 6 years or less
- **$7640 tuition** and fees
- **$8764 average financial aid** package, $12,085 average indebtedness upon graduation, $13.6 million endowment

Students *Undergraduates:* 262 full-time, 30 part-time. Students come from 19 states and territories, 4 other countries. *The most frequently chosen baccalaureate fields are:* business/marketing, education, psychology.

From out-of-state	12%	Reside on campus	89%
Age 25 or older	8%	Transferred in	5%
International students	2%	African Americans	13%
Asian Americans/Pacific Islanders	1%		

Faculty 40 (88% full-time), 63% with terminal degrees.
Expenses (2000–2001, estimated) *One-time required fee:* $195. *Comprehensive fee:* $12,240 includes full-time tuition ($7400), mandatory fees ($240), and room and board ($4600). Full-time tuition and fees vary according to course load. *Part-time tuition:* $216 per semester hour. *Part-time fees:* $75 per term. Part-time tuition and fees vary according to course load. *Payment plan:* installment. *Waivers:* employees or children of employees.
Library Bowling Library. *Operations spending 1999–2000:* $162,795. *Collection:* 68,120 titles, 397 serial subscriptions, 6,372 audiovisual materials.
College life *Housing:* on-campus residence required through senior year. *Option:* women-only. *Most popular organizations:* Student Government Association, Campus Ministries, Judson Ambassadors, science club, SIFE (Students in Free Enterprise).
Campus security 24-hour emergency response devices and patrols, late-night transport-escort service, controlled dormitory access.
After graduation 72% of class of 1998 had job offers within 6 months. *Career center:* 1 full-time personnel. Services include job fairs, resume preparation, interview workshops, resume referral, career/interest testing, career counseling, careers library, job bank. *Graduate education:* 21% of class of 1999 went directly to graduate and professional school: 13% graduate arts and sciences, 8% education.
Freshmen 243 applied, 196 admitted, 79 enrolled. 2 valedictorians.

Average high school GPA	3.14	SAT verbal scores above 500	93%
SAT math scores above 500	50%	ACT above 18	93%
From top 10% of their h.s. class	22%	From top quarter	52%
From top half	69%	1998 freshmen returning in 1999	57%

Application *Options:* eApply at www.CollegeQuest.com, Common Application, electronic application, early admission, deferred entrance. *Application fee:* $25. *Required:* high school transcript; minimum 2.0 GPA; 2 letters of recommendation; interview.
Standardized tests *Admission: Required:* SAT I or ACT.
Significant dates *Application deadlines:* rolling (freshmen), rolling (transfers). *Financial aid deadline priority date:* 3/1.
Freshman Application Contact
Mrs. Charlotte Clements, Director of Admissions, Judson College, PO Box 120, Marion, AL 36756. **Phone:** 334-683-5110 Ext. 110. **Toll-free phone:** 800-447-9472. **Fax:** 334-683-5158. **E-mail:** admissions@future.judson.edu
Visit CollegeQuest.com for information on majors offered and athletics. Electronic viewbook available at CollegeQuest.com.

MILES COLLEGE
Birmingham, Alabama

- **Independent Christian Methodist Episcopal**, 4-year, founded 1905
- **Degree** bachelor's
- **Small-town** 35-acre campus
- **Coed**
- **Noncompetitive** entrance level
- **$4630 tuition** and fees

Expenses (1999–2000) *Comprehensive fee:* $7570 includes full-time tuition ($4280), mandatory fees ($350), and room and board ($2940). Room and board charges vary according to housing facility. *Part-time tuition:* $180 per semester hour.
College life *Social organizations:* national fraternities, national sororities, local fraternities, local sororities; 18% of eligible men and 22% of eligible women are members. *Most popular organizations:* Choir, Education Club, Business Club.
Campus security 24-hour emergency response devices and patrols.
Application *Application fee:* $25. *Required:* high school transcript. *Recommended:* letters of recommendation.
Standardized tests *Placement: Required:* SAT I or ACT
Admissions Office Contact
Miles College, PO Box 3800, Birmingham, AL 35208.
Visit CollegeQuest.com for information on athletics. College video available at CollegeQuest.com.

OAKWOOD COLLEGE
Huntsville, Alabama

- **Independent Seventh-day Adventist**, 4-year, founded 1896
- **Degrees** associate and bachelor's

- **1,200-acre** campus
- **Coed**, 1,736 undergraduate students, 88% full-time, 56% women, 44% men
- **Minimally difficult** entrance level, 47% of applicants were admitted
- **18:1 student-to-undergraduate faculty ratio**
- **26% graduate** in 6 years or less
- **$9058 tuition** and fees

Students *Undergraduates:* 1,523 full-time, 213 part-time. Students come from 39 states and territories, 22 other countries. *The most frequently chosen baccalaureate fields are:* biological/life sciences, business/marketing, education.

From out-of-state	67%	Reside on campus	56%
Age 25 or older	15%	International students	13%
African Americans	79%	Asian Americans/Pacific Islanders	0.2%
Hispanic Americans	1%	Native Americans	0.2%

Faculty 159 (62% full-time).

Expenses (2000–2001) *Comprehensive fee:* $14,350 includes full-time tuition ($8820), mandatory fees ($238), and room and board ($5292). Room and board charges vary according to board plan and housing facility. *Part-time tuition:* $350 per credit hour. *Part-time fees:* $119 per term part-time. Part-time tuition and fees vary according to course load. *Payment plan:* installment. *Waivers:* employees or children of employees.

Library Eva B. Dykes Library. *Collection:* 125,302 titles, 650 serial subscriptions, 4,816 audiovisual materials.

College life *Housing:* on-campus residence required in freshman year. *Options:* men-only, women-only. *Most popular organization:* United Student Movement.

Campus security 24-hour patrols, student patrols, late-night transport-escort service.

After graduation 100 organizations recruited on campus 1997–98. *Career center:* 2 full-time personnel. Services include job fairs, resume preparation, resume referral, career counseling, careers library, job bank, job interviews.

Freshmen 986 applied, 467 admitted, 407 enrolled.

Average high school GPA	2.88	SAT verbal scores above 500	38%
SAT math scores above 500	20%	ACT above 18	58%
From top 10% of their h.s. class	10%	From top quarter	24%
From top half	52%	1998 freshmen returning in 1999	67%

Application *Option:* deferred entrance. *Application fee:* $20. *Required:* high school transcript; letters of recommendation.

Standardized tests *Placement: Recommended:* SAT I or ACT.

Significant dates *Application deadlines:* rolling (freshmen), rolling (transfers). *Financial aid deadline priority date:* 3/1.

Freshman Application Contact
Mr. Fred Pullins, Director of Enrollment Management, Oakwood College, 7000 Adventist Boulevard, Huntsville, AL 35810. **Phone:** 256-726-7354. **Toll-free phone:** 800-824-5312. **Fax:** 256-726-7404. **E-mail:** admission@oakwood.edu

Visit CollegeQuest.com for information on majors offered and athletics. College video and electronic viewbook available at CollegeQuest.com.

SAMFORD UNIVERSITY
Birmingham, Alabama

- **Independent Baptist**, university, founded 1841
- **Degrees** associate, bachelor's, master's, doctoral, first professional, post-master's, and postbachelor's certificates
- **Suburban** 180-acre campus
- **Coed**, 2,815 undergraduate students, 94% full-time, 62% women, 38% men
- **Moderately difficult** entrance level, 88% of applicants were admitted
- **14:1 student-to-undergraduate faculty ratio**
- **65.3% graduate** in 6 years or less
- **$10,300 tuition** and fees
- **$8748 average financial aid** package, $14,228 average indebtedness upon graduation, $243.3 million endowment

A Samford education is carefully crafted to provide personal empowerment, academic and career competency, social and civic responsibility, and ethical and spiritual strength. It is built around broadening international awareness and the development of transferable skills, such as computer familiarity in every academic major, to keep Samford graduates on the leading edge in a constantly changing career environment.

Students *Undergraduates:* 2,645 full-time, 170 part-time. Students come from 39 states and territories, 25 other countries. *The most frequently chosen baccalaureate fields are:* business/marketing, education, health professions and related sciences. *Graduate:* 1,184 in professional programs, 455 in other graduate degree programs.

From out-of-state	56%	Reside on campus	70%
Age 25 or older	3%	Transferred in	3%
International students	1%	African Americans	5%
Asian Americans/Pacific Islanders	1%	Hispanic Americans	1%
Native Americans	0.4%		

Faculty 391 (62% full-time), 67% with terminal degrees.

Expenses (1999–2000) *Comprehensive fee:* $14,860 includes full-time tuition ($10,300) and room and board ($4560). *College room only:* $2236. Room and board charges vary according to board plan and housing facility. *Part-time tuition:* $341 per semester hour. Part-time tuition and fees vary according to course load. *Waivers:* employees or children of employees.

Library Harwell G. Davis Library plus 3 others. *Operations spending 1999–2000:* $3.1 million. *Collection:* 844,250 titles, 5,387 serial subscriptions, 4,488 audiovisual materials.

College life *Housing:* on-campus residence required through sophomore year. *Options:* men-only, women-only, disabled students. *Social organizations:* national fraternities, national sororities; 42% of eligible men and 48% of eligible women are members. *Most popular organizations:* student ministries, Interfraternity Council, student government, student bar, Panhellenic Council.

Campus security 24-hour emergency response devices and patrols, student patrols, late-night transport-escort service, controlled dormitory access.

After graduation 65 organizations recruited on campus 1997–98. *Career center:* 4 full-time, 1 part-time personnel. Services include job fairs, resume preparation, interview workshops, resume referral, career/interest testing, career counseling, careers library, job bank, job interviews.

Freshmen 1,974 applied, 1,738 admitted, 675 enrolled. 5 National Merit Scholars, 31 class presidents, 35 valedictorians, 43 student government officers.

Average high school GPA	3.6	SAT verbal scores above 500	85%
SAT math scores above 500	80%	ACT above 18	99%
From top 10% of their h.s. class	38%	From top quarter	69%
From top half	91%	1998 freshmen returning in 1999	80%

Application *Options:* Common Application, early admission, deferred entrance. *Application fee:* $25. *Required:* essay or personal statement; high school transcript; 2 letters of recommendation. *Recommended:* interview.

Standardized tests *Admission: Required:* SAT I or ACT.

Significant dates *Application deadline:* rolling (transfers). *Financial aid deadline priority date:* 3/1.

Freshman Application Contact
Mr. Phil Kimrey, Dean of Admissions and Financial Aid, Samford University, 800 Lakeshore Drive, Samford Hall, Birmingham, AL 35229-0002. **Phone:** 205-726-3673. **Toll-free phone:** 800-888-7218. **Fax:** 205-726-2171. **E-mail:** seberry@samford.edu

Visit CollegeQuest.com for information on majors offered and athletics.

- *See page 2442 for a narrative description.*

SOUTH COLLEGE
Montgomery, Alabama

- **Proprietary**, primarily 2-year, founded 1887
- **Degrees** associate and bachelor's
- **Urban** 1-acre campus
- **Coed**, primarily women, 207 undergraduate students, 54% full-time, 84% women, 16% men
- **Minimally difficult** entrance level

Faculty 32 (22% full-time).

Admissions Office Contact
South College, 122 Commercer Street, Montgomery, AL 36104-2538. **Fax:** 334-262-7326.

Alabama

South College (continued)
Visit CollegeQuest.com for information on majors offered and athletics.

SOUTHEAST COLLEGE OF TECHNOLOGY
Mobile, Alabama

Admissions Office Contact
Southeast College of Technology, 828 Downtowner Loop West, Mobile, AL 36609-5404.

SOUTHEASTERN BIBLE COLLEGE
Birmingham, Alabama

- **Independent nondenominational**, 4-year, founded 1935
- **Degrees** associate and bachelor's
- **Suburban** 10-acre campus
- **Coed**
- **Moderately difficult** entrance level
- **$5740 tuition** and fees

Expenses (1999–2000) *Comprehensive fee:* $8980 includes full-time tuition ($5740) and room and board ($3240). *Part-time tuition:* $205 per semester hour.
College life on-campus residence required through senior year. *Most popular organizations:* Student Council, Student Missions Fellowship, chorale, cheerleading.
Campus security 24-hour emergency response devices, student patrols.
Application *Options:* Common Application, deferred entrance. *Application fee:* $20. *Required:* essay or personal statement; high school transcript; minimum 2.0 GPA; 3 letters of recommendation. *Required for some:* interview.
Standardized tests *Admission: Required:* SAT I or ACT.
Admissions Office Contact
Southeastern Bible College, 3001 Highway 280 East, Birmingham, AL 35243-4181. **Fax:** 205-970-9207.
Visit CollegeQuest.com for information on athletics. College video available at CollegeQuest.com.

SOUTHERN CHRISTIAN UNIVERSITY
Montgomery, Alabama

- **Independent**, comprehensive, founded 1967, affiliated with Church of Christ
- **Degrees** bachelor's, master's, doctoral, and first professional
- **Urban** 9-acre campus
- **Coed**, 97 undergraduate students
- **Minimally difficult** entrance level
- **$8830 tuition** and fees

Students *Undergraduates:* Students come from 30 states and territories.
Age 25 or older	90%	African Americans	24%
Asian Americans/Pacific Islanders	2%	Hispanic Americans	6%

Faculty 24 (75% full-time).
Expenses (1999–2000) *Tuition:* full-time $8280; part-time $230 per semester hour. *Required fees:* full-time $550; $275 per term part-time.
Library Southern Christian University Library. *Collection:* 73,000 titles, 500 serial subscriptions.
College life *Housing:* college housing not available.
Freshmen
SAT verbal scores above 500	N/R	SAT math scores above 500	N/R
ACT above 18	N/R	1998 freshmen returning in 1999	85%

Application *Option:* Common Application. *Application fee:* $35. *Required:* high school transcript; 2 letters of recommendation.
Significant dates *Application deadlines:* rolling (freshmen), rolling (transfers). *Financial aid deadline:* continuous.

Freshman Application Contact
Mr. Gilbert Sanford, Director of Admissions, Southern Christian University, 1200 Taylor Road, Montgomery, AL 36117. **Phone:** 334-277-2277 Ext. 212. **Toll-free phone:** 800-351-4040. **E-mail:** scuniversity@mindspring.com
Visit CollegeQuest.com for information on majors offered and athletics. College video available at CollegeQuest.com.

SPRING HILL COLLEGE
Mobile, Alabama

- **Independent Roman Catholic (Jesuit)**, comprehensive, founded 1830
- **Degrees** associate, bachelor's, master's, and postbachelor's certificates
- **Suburban** 500-acre campus
- **Coed**, 1,153 undergraduate students, 86% full-time, 60% women, 40% men
- **Moderately difficult** entrance level, 89% of applicants were admitted
- **13:1 student-to-undergraduate faculty ratio**
- **58% graduate** in 6 years or less
- **$16,254 tuition** and fees
- **$14,654 average financial aid** package, $34.4 million endowment

Students *Undergraduates:* 986 full-time, 167 part-time. Students come from 37 states and territories, 11 other countries. *The most frequently chosen baccalaureate fields are:* business/marketing, communications/communication technologies, psychology. *Graduate:* 272 in graduate degree programs.
From out-of-state	45%	Reside on campus	58%
Age 25 or older	20%	Transferred in	4%
International students	2%	African Americans	14%
Asian Americans/Pacific Islanders	1%	Hispanic Americans	3%
Native Americans	1%		

Faculty 125 (52% full-time), 62% with terminal degrees.
Expenses (2000–2001) *Comprehensive fee:* $22,022 includes full-time tuition ($15,254), mandatory fees ($1000), and room and board ($5768). *College room only:* $2992. Room and board charges vary according to board plan and housing facility. *Part-time tuition:* $565 per semester hour. *Part-time fees:* $32 per semester hour; $10 per term part-time. *Payment plan:* deferred payment. *Waivers:* employees or children of employees.
Library Thomas Byrne Memorial Library. *Collection:* 88,100 titles, 1,324 serial subscriptions, 336 audiovisual materials.
College life *Housing:* on-campus residence required through junior year. *Options:* coed, men-only, women-only. *Social organizations:* national fraternities, national sororities, local fraternities; 27% of eligible men and 30% of eligible women are members. *Most popular organizations:* Circle K, Habitat for Humanity, Public Relations Council of America.
Campus security 24-hour emergency response devices and patrols, late-night transport-escort service, controlled dormitory access.
After graduation 8 organizations recruited on campus 1997–98. 30% of class of 1998 had job offers within 6 months. *Career center:* 1 full-time personnel. Services include job fairs, resume preparation, resume referral, career/interest testing, career counseling, careers library, job bank, job interviews.
Freshmen 974 applied, 864 admitted, 310 enrolled. 9 valedictorians.
Average high school GPA	3.3	SAT verbal scores above 500	75%
SAT math scores above 500	74%	ACT above 18	94%
From top 10% of their h.s. class	33%	From top quarter	57%
From top half	81%	1998 freshmen returning in 1999	78%

Application *Options:* early admission, deferred entrance. *Application fee:* $25. *Required:* high school transcript; 1 letter of recommendation. *Recommended:* essay or personal statement; minimum 2.0 GPA; interview.
Standardized tests *Admission: Required:* SAT I or ACT.
Significant dates *Application deadlines:* 7/31 (freshmen), rolling (transfers). *Financial aid deadline priority date:* 3/1.
Freshman Application Contact
Mr. Steven Pochard, Dean of Enrollment Management, Spring Hill College, 4000 Dauphin Street, Mobile, AL 36608-1791. **Phone:** 334-380-3030. **Toll-free phone:** 800-SHC-6704. **Fax:** 334-460-2186. **E-mail:** admit@shc.edu
Visit CollegeQuest.com for information on majors offered and athletics.

Alabama

STILLMAN COLLEGE
Tuscaloosa, Alabama

- **Independent**, 4-year, founded 1876, affiliated with Presbyterian Church (U.S.A.)
- **Degree** bachelor's
- **Urban** 100-acre campus with easy access to Birmingham
- **Coed**, 1,458 undergraduate students
- **Minimally difficult** entrance level, 50% of applicants were admitted
- **17:1 student-to-undergraduate faculty ratio**
- **39% graduate** in 6 years or less
- **$5880 tuition** and fees
- **$23.6 million endowment**

Students *Undergraduates:* Students come from 27 states and territories, 8 other countries. *The most frequently chosen baccalaureate fields are:* business/marketing, education, trade and industry.

From out-of-state	19%	Reside on campus	75%
Age 25 or older	19%	International students	0.1%
African Americans	96%	Asian Americans/Pacific Islanders	1%

Faculty 86 (60% full-time).
Expenses (1999–2000) *Comprehensive fee:* $9644 includes full-time tuition ($5570), mandatory fees ($310), and room and board ($3764). Room and board charges vary according to board plan and housing facility. *Part-time tuition:* $245 per semester hour. *Part-time fees:* $51 per term part-time. *Payment plan:* installment. *Waivers:* employees or children of employees.
Library Shepard's Library. *Collection:* 390 serial subscriptions, 3,534 audiovisual materials.
College life *Housing: Options:* men-only, women-only. *Social organizations:* national fraternities, national sororities, local fraternities. *Most popular organizations:* Student Government Association, Pre-Alumni United Negro College Fund, Christian Student Association.
Campus security 24-hour patrols.
After graduation *Career center:* 6 full-time personnel. Services include job fairs, resume preparation, resume referral, career counseling, job bank, job interviews.
Freshmen 2,591 applied, 1,291 admitted.

Average high school GPA	2.6	SAT verbal scores above 500	N/R
SAT math scores above 500	N/R	ACT above 18	40%
From top 10% of their h.s. class	18%	From top quarter	48%
From top half	78%	1998 freshmen returning in 1999	82%

Application *Options:* early admission, deferred entrance. *Application fee:* $15. *Required:* high school transcript. *Required for some:* letters of recommendation. *Recommended:* essay or personal statement; interview.
Standardized tests *Admission: Required:* SAT I or ACT.
Significant dates *Application deadlines:* rolling (freshmen), rolling (transfers). *Financial aid deadline priority date:* 4/1.
Freshman Application Contact
Mr. Mason Bonner, Director of Admissions, Stillman College, P.O. Box 1430, 3600 Stillman Boulevard, Tuscaloosa, AL 35403. **Phone:** 205-366-8817. **Toll-free phone:** 800-841-5722. **Fax:** 205-366-8996.
Visit CollegeQuest.com for information on majors offered and athletics.

TALLADEGA COLLEGE
Talladega, Alabama

- **Independent**, 4-year, founded 1867
- **Degree** bachelor's
- **Small-town** 130-acre campus with easy access to Birmingham
- **Coed**, 455 undergraduate students, 97% full-time, 61% women, 39% men
- **Minimally difficult** entrance level, 22% of applicants were admitted
- **9:1 student-to-undergraduate faculty ratio**
- **$5873 tuition** and fees
- **$7.2 million endowment**

Students *Undergraduates:* 443 full-time, 12 part-time. Students come from 29 states and territories. *The most frequently chosen baccalaureate fields are:* biological/life sciences, business/marketing, social sciences and history.

From out-of-state	44%	Reside on campus	77%
Age 25 or older	13%	Transferred in	6%
International students	0.2%	African Americans	97%
Hispanic Americans	1%		

Faculty 51 (78% full-time), 100% with terminal degrees.
Expenses (1999–2000) *Comprehensive fee:* $8837 includes full-time tuition ($5666), mandatory fees ($207), and room and board ($2964). *College room only:* $1424. Full-time tuition and fees vary according to student level. *Part-time tuition:* $236 per credit hour. *Part-time fees:* $104 per term part-time. Part-time tuition and fees vary according to course load and student level. *Payment plan:* installment. *Waivers:* employees or children of employees.
Library Savery Library. *Operations spending 1999–2000:* $246,326. *Collection:* 117,000 titles, 88 serial subscriptions, 300 audiovisual materials.
College life *Housing: Options:* men-only, women-only. *Social organizations:* national fraternities, national sororities; 1% of eligible men and 3% of eligible women are members. *Most popular organizations:* Student Government Association, Crimson Ambassadors, Greek letter organizations, academic major clubs, religious based organizations.
Campus security 24-hour patrols, late-night transport-escort service, campus police.
After graduation 17 organizations recruited on campus 1997–98. *Career center:* 1 full-time personnel. Services include job fairs, resume preparation, resume referral, career counseling, careers library, job bank, job interviews.
Freshmen 1,098 applied, 239 admitted, 79 enrolled.

Average high school GPA	2.7	SAT verbal scores above 500	N/R
SAT math scores above 500	N/R	ACT above 18	34%
1998 freshmen returning in 1999	61%		

Application *Options:* Common Application, electronic application, deferred entrance. *Application fee:* $25. *Required:* essay or personal statement; high school transcript; minimum 2.0 GPA; 1 letter of recommendation.
Standardized tests *Admission: Required:* SAT I or ACT.
Significant dates *Application deadlines:* 4/1 (freshmen), rolling (transfers). *Financial aid deadline:* 6/30. *Priority date:* 5/1.
Freshman Application Contact
Mrs. Bernee Long, Director of Admissions, Talladega College, 627 West Battle Street, Talladega, AL 35160. **Phone:** 256-761-6219. **Toll-free phone:** 800-762-2168 (in-state); 800-633-2440 (out-of-state). **Fax:** 256-362-2268. **E-mail:** be21long@talladega.edu
Visit CollegeQuest.com for information on majors offered and athletics. College video and electronic viewbook available at CollegeQuest.com.

- *See page 2590 for a narrative description.*

TROY STATE UNIVERSITY
Troy, Alabama

Apply at CollegeQuest.com

- **State-supported**, comprehensive, founded 1887
- **Degrees** associate, bachelor's, and master's
- **Small-town** 577-acre campus
- **Coed**, 4,544 undergraduate students, 85% full-time, 60% women, 40% men
- **Moderately difficult** entrance level, 74% of applicants were admitted
- **21:1 student-to-undergraduate faculty ratio**
- **43% graduate** in 6 years or less
- **$2900 tuition** and fees (in-state); $5560 (out-of-state)

Part of Troy State University System.
Students *Undergraduates:* 3,841 full-time, 703 part-time. Students come from 41 states and territories, 33 other countries. *The most frequently chosen baccalaureate fields are:* business/marketing, education, protective services/public administration. *Graduate:* 1,571 in graduate degree programs.

From out-of-state	14%	Reside on campus	30%
Transferred in	11%	International students	3%
African Americans	22%	Asian Americans/Pacific Islanders	1%
Hispanic Americans	1%	Native Americans	1%

Faculty 391 (54% full-time).
Expenses (1999–2000) *Tuition, state resident:* full-time $2660; part-time $110 per credit hour. *Tuition, nonresident:* full-time $5320; part-time $220

Alabama

Troy State University (continued)
per credit hour. *Required fees:* full-time $240; $10 per credit hour. *College room and board:* $3854; room only: $1970. Room and board charges vary according to board plan and housing facility. *Payment plan:* installment. *Waivers:* employees or children of employees.

Library Wallace Library. *Collection:* 239,382 titles, 3,742 serial subscriptions, 7,592 audiovisual materials.

College life *Housing:* on-campus residence required in freshman year. *Options:* coed, men-only, women-only. *Social organizations:* national fraternities, national sororities; 20% of eligible men and 20% of eligible women are members. *Most popular organizations:* University Band, University Choir, yearbook, Union Board.

Campus security 24-hour patrols, student patrols, late-night transport-escort service, controlled dormitory access.

After graduation *Career center:* 3 full-time, 4 part-time personnel. Services include job fairs, resume preparation, interview workshops, resume referral, career/interest testing, career counseling, careers library, job bank, job interviews.

Freshmen 1,951 applied, 1,437 admitted, 733 enrolled.
SAT verbal scores above 500	N/R	SAT math scores above 500	N/R
ACT above 18	75%	1998 freshmen returning in 1999	72%

Application *Options:* eApply at www.CollegeQuest.com, deferred entrance. *Application fee:* $20. *Required:* high school transcript. *Recommended:* interview.

Standardized tests *Admission: Required:* SAT I or ACT.

Significant dates *Application deadlines:* rolling (freshmen), rolling (transfers). *Financial aid deadline priority date:* 5/1.

Freshman Application Contact
Mr. Buddy Starling, Dean of Enrollment Services, Troy State University, Adams Administration Building, Room 134, Troy, AL 36082. **Phone:** 334-670-3179. **Toll-free phone:** 800-551-9716. **Fax:** 334-670-3815. **E-mail:** bstarling@trojan.troyst.edu

Visit CollegeQuest.com for information on majors offered and athletics. College video available at CollegeQuest.com.

■ *See page 2650 for a narrative description.*

TROY STATE UNIVERSITY DOTHAN
Dothan, Alabama

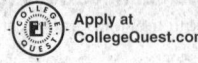
Apply at CollegeQuest.com

- **State-supported**, comprehensive, founded 1961
- **Degrees** associate, bachelor's, master's, and post-master's certificates
- **Small-town** 250-acre campus
- **Coed**, 1,479 undergraduate students, 51% full-time, 63% women, 37% men
- **Minimally difficult** entrance level, 77% of applicants were admitted
- **22:1** student-to-undergraduate faculty ratio
- **$2832 tuition** and fees (in-state); $5712 (out-of-state)

Part of Troy State University System.
Students *Undergraduates:* 756 full-time, 723 part-time. Students come from 10 states and territories. *Graduate:* 446 in graduate degree programs.

Age 25 or older	77%	Transferred in	22%
International students	0.1%	African Americans	15%
Asian Americans/Pacific Islanders	1%	Hispanic Americans	2%
Native Americans	1%		

Faculty 207.

Expenses (1999–2000) *Tuition, state resident:* full-time $2760; part-time $115 per semester hour. *Tuition, nonresident:* full-time $5640; part-time $230 per semester hour. *Required fees:* full-time $72; $3 per semester hour. *Payment plan:* installment. *Waivers:* senior citizens and employees or children of employees.

Library *Operations spending 1999–2000:* $565,493. *Collection:* 87,500 titles, 697 serial subscriptions.

College life *Housing:* college housing not available. *Most popular organizations:* creative writing club, American Marketing Association, Alpha Upsilon Alpha, Gamma Beta Phi, Delta Mu Delta.

Campus security 24-hour patrols.

After graduation 75 organizations recruited on campus 1997–98. *Career center:* 1 full-time, 2 part-time personnel. Services include job fairs, resume preparation, resume referral, career counseling, careers library, job bank, job interviews.

Freshmen 77 applied, 59 admitted, 47 enrolled.
Average high school GPA	2.94	SAT verbal scores above 500	N/R
SAT math scores above 500	N/R	ACT above 18	100%
1998 freshmen returning in 1999	65%		

Application *Options:* eApply at www.CollegeQuest.com, Common Application, electronic application, deferred entrance. *Application fee:* $20. *Required:* high school transcript; minimum 2.0 GPA. *Recommended:* minimum 3.0 GPA.

Standardized tests *Admission: Required for some:* SAT I or ACT.

Significant dates *Application deadlines:* rolling (freshmen), rolling (transfers). *Financial aid deadline priority date:* 5/1.

Freshman Application Contact
Mr. Bob Willis, Director of Enrollment Services, Troy State University Dothan, PO Box 8368, Dothan, AL 36304-0368. **Phone:** 334-983-6556 Ext. 205. **Fax:** 334-983-6322. **E-mail:** bwillis@tsud.edu

Visit CollegeQuest.com for information on majors offered and athletics.

TROY STATE UNIVERSITY MONTGOMERY
Montgomery, Alabama

- **State-supported**, comprehensive, founded 1965
- **Degrees** associate, bachelor's, and master's
- **Urban** 6-acre campus
- **Coed**, 2,619 undergraduate students, 33% full-time, 62% women, 38% men
- **Noncompetitive** entrance level, 95% of applicants were admitted
- **$2460 tuition** and fees (in-state); $4890 (out-of-state)

Part of Troy State University System.
Students *Undergraduates:* 873 full-time, 1,746 part-time. Students come from 10 states and territories. *Graduate:* 564 in graduate degree programs.

From out-of-state	1%	Age 25 or older	63%
African Americans	40%	Asian Americans/Pacific Islanders	1%
Hispanic Americans	2%	Native Americans	1%

Faculty 179 (19% full-time).

Expenses (1999–2000) *Tuition, state resident:* full-time $2430; part-time $58 per quarter hour. *Tuition, nonresident:* full-time $4860; part-time $116 per quarter hour. *Required fees:* full-time $30; $10 per term part-time. *Payment plan:* deferred payment. *Waivers:* employees or children of employees.

Library Troy State University Montgomery Library plus 1 other. *Operations spending 1999–2000:* $198,631. *Collection:* 44,169 titles, 481 serial subscriptions, 9,068 audiovisual materials.

College life *Housing:* college housing not available.

Campus security 24-hour emergency response devices, late-night transport-escort service, evening patrols by security.

After graduation 5 organizations recruited on campus 1997–98. *Career center:* 1 part-time personnel. Services include resume preparation, resume referral, career counseling, careers library, job bank, job interviews.

Freshmen 943 applied, 896 admitted, 169 enrolled.
SAT verbal scores above 500	N/R	SAT math scores above 500	N/R
ACT above 18	N/R		

Application *Options:* electronic application, early admission. *Application fee:* $15. *Required:* high school transcript; minimum 2.0 GPA.

Standardized tests *Placement: Recommended:* SAT I or ACT.

Significant dates *Application deadlines:* rolling (freshmen), rolling (transfers). *Financial aid deadline priority date:* 5/1.

Freshman Application Contact
Mr. Frank Hrabe, Director of Enrollment Management, Troy State University Montgomery, PO Drawer 4419, Montgomery, AL 36103-4419. **Phone:** 334-241-9506. **Toll-free phone:** 800-355-TSUM.

Visit CollegeQuest.com for information on majors offered and athletics.

Alabama

TUSKEGEE UNIVERSITY
Tuskegee, Alabama

- **Independent**, comprehensive, founded 1881
- **Degrees** bachelor's, master's, and first professional
- **Small-town** 4,390-acre campus
- **Coed**, 2,616 undergraduate students, 96% full-time, 59% women, 41% men
- **Moderately difficult** entrance level, 66% of applicants were admitted
- **13:1 student-to-undergraduate faculty ratio**
- **43.3% graduate** in 6 years or less
- **$9690 tuition** and fees

Students *Undergraduates:* 2,510 full-time, 106 part-time. Students come from 41 states and territories, 30 other countries. *The most frequently chosen baccalaureate fields are:* business/marketing, engineering/engineering technologies, health professions and related sciences. *Graduate:* 224 in professional programs, 169 in other graduate degree programs.

From out-of-state	71%	Reside on campus	63%
Age 25 or older	1%	Transferred in	2%
International students	2%	African Americans	98%
Hispanic Americans	0.04%		

Faculty 262 (88% full-time), 72% with terminal degrees.
Expenses (1999–2000) *Comprehensive fee:* $14,790 includes full-time tuition ($9500), mandatory fees ($190), and room and board ($5100). *Part-time tuition:* $384 per credit. *Part-time fees:* $95 per term part-time. Part-time tuition and fees vary according to course load. *Payment plan:* installment. *Waivers:* employees or children of employees.
Library Hollis B. Frissell Library plus 3 others. *Operations spending 1999–2000:* $1.1 million. *Collection:* 623,824 titles, 81,157 serial subscriptions.
College life On-campus residence required through sophomore year. *Social organizations:* national fraternities, national sororities; 7% of eligible men and 8% of eligible women are members.
Campus security 24-hour emergency response devices and patrols, late-night transport-escort service.
After graduation 350 organizations recruited on campus 1997–98. *Career center:* 1 full-time, 3 part-time personnel. Services include job fairs, resume preparation, career counseling. *Graduate education:* 21% of class of 1999 went directly to graduate and professional school: 9% graduate arts and sciences, 4% medicine, 3% business, 3% engineering, 1% law, 1% veterinary medicine.
Freshmen 2,378 applied, 1,559 admitted, 694 enrolled.

Average high school GPA	3.0	SAT verbal scores above 500	N/R
SAT math scores above 500	N/R	ACT above 18	N/R
From top 10% of their h.s. class	17%	From top quarter	44%
From top half	82%	1998 freshmen returning in 1999	71%

Application *Option:* early admission. *Application fee:* $25. *Required:* high school transcript; minimum 2.0 GPA.
Standardized tests *Admission: Required:* SAT I or ACT.
Significant dates *Application deadlines:* 4/15 (freshmen), 4/15 (transfers). *Financial aid deadline priority date:* 3/31.
Freshman Application Contact
Mr. William E. Mathis, Admissions, Tuskegee University, 102 Old Administration Building, Tuskegee, AL 36088. **Phone:** 334-727-8500. **Toll-free phone:** 800-622-6531.
Visit CollegeQuest.com for information on majors offered and athletics. College video available at CollegeQuest.com.

■ *See page 2656 for a narrative description.*

THE UNIVERSITY OF ALABAMA
Tuscaloosa, Alabama

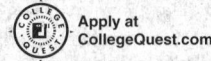
Apply at CollegeQuest.com

- **State-supported**, university, founded 1831
- **Degrees** bachelor's, master's, doctoral, first professional, and post-master's certificates
- **Suburban** 1,000-acre campus with easy access to Birmingham
- **Coed**, 14,357 undergraduate students, 90% full-time, 52% women, 48% men
- **Moderately difficult** entrance level, 89% of applicants were admitted
- **18:1 student-to-undergraduate faculty ratio**
- **58.6% graduate** in 6 years or less
- **$2872 tuition** and fees (in-state); $7722 (out-of-state)
- **$3866 average financial aid** package, $18,994 average indebtedness upon graduation, $287.9 million endowment

Part of University of Alabama System.
Students *Undergraduates:* 12,976 full-time, 1,381 part-time. Students come from 52 states and territories, 83 other countries. *The most frequently chosen baccalaureate fields are:* business/marketing, communications/communication technologies, education. *Graduate:* 626 in professional programs, 3,473 in other graduate degree programs.

From out-of-state	19%	Reside on campus	30%
Age 25 or older	12%	Transferred in	9%
International students	2%	African Americans	14%
Asian Americans/Pacific Islanders	1%	Hispanic Americans	1%
Native Americans	1%		

Faculty 1,022 (83% full-time), 84% with terminal degrees.
Expenses (1999–2000) *Tuition, state resident:* full-time $2872; part-time $614 per course. *Tuition, nonresident:* full-time $7722; part-time $1241 per course. Full-time tuition and fees vary according to course load. Part-time tuition and fees vary according to course load. *College room and board:* $4154; room only: $2454. Room and board charges vary according to board plan and housing facility. *Payment plans:* installment, deferred payment. *Waivers:* employees or children of employees.
Library Amelia Gayle Gorgas Library plus 8 others. *Operations spending 1999–2000:* $9.6 million. *Collection:* 1.4 million titles, 17,984 serial subscriptions, 473,432 audiovisual materials.
College life *Housing: Options:* coed, men-only, women-only, disabled students. *Social organizations:* national fraternities, national sororities; 15% of eligible men and 18% of eligible women are members. *Most popular organizations:* Coordinating Council of Student Organizations, Residence Hall Association, International Student Association, Circle K, African-American Association.
Campus security 24-hour emergency response devices and patrols, student patrols, late-night transport-escort service, controlled dormitory access, crime prevention programs, community police protection.
After graduation 525 organizations recruited on campus 1997–98. 55% of class of 1998 had job offers within 6 months. *Career center:* 15 full-time personnel. Services include job fairs, resume preparation, interview workshops, resume referral, career/interest testing, career counseling, careers library, job bank, job interviews. *Major awards:* 3 Fulbright Scholars.
Freshmen 7,433 applied, 6,650 admitted, 2,720 enrolled. 41 National Merit Scholars.

Average high school GPA	3.22	SAT verbal scores above 500	70%
SAT math scores above 500	68%	ACT above 18	96%
From top 10% of their h.s. class	26%	From top quarter	55%
From top half	82%	1998 freshmen returning in 1999	80%

Application *Options:* eApply at www.CollegeQuest.com, electronic application, early admission, deferred entrance. *Application fee:* $25. *Required:* high school transcript; minimum 2.0 GPA. *Required for some:* interview.
Standardized tests *Admission: Required:* SAT I or ACT.
Significant dates *Application deadlines:* 8/15 (freshmen), rolling (transfers). *Financial aid deadline priority date:* 3/1.
Freshman Application Contact
Dr. Lisa B. Harris, Director of Admissions and Financial Aid, The University of Alabama, Box 870132, Tuscaloosa, AL 35487-0132. **Phone:** 205-348-5666. **Toll-free phone:** 800-933-BAMA. **Fax:** 205-348-9046.
Visit CollegeQuest.com for information on majors offered and athletics. College video and electronic viewbook available at CollegeQuest.com.

THE UNIVERSITY OF ALABAMA AT BIRMINGHAM
Birmingham, Alabama

- **State-supported**, university, founded 1969
- **Degrees** bachelor's, master's, doctoral, first professional, post-master's, and postbachelor's certificates
- **Urban** 265-acre campus

Alabama

The University of Alabama at Birmingham (continued)
- **Coed**, 9,532 undergraduate students, 70% full-time, 59% women, 41% men
- **Moderately difficult** entrance level, 89% of applicants were admitted
- **18:1 student-to-undergraduate faculty ratio**
- **30.3% graduate** in 6 years or less
- **$3240 tuition** and fees (in-state); $5970 (out-of-state)
- **$15,459 average indebtedness** upon graduation, $234 million endowment

Part of University of Alabama System.

Students *Undergraduates:* 6,714 full-time, 2,818 part-time. Students come from 36 states and territories, 73 other countries. *The most frequently chosen baccalaureate fields are:* business/marketing, education, health professions and related sciences. *Graduate:* 1,004 in professional programs, 3,674 in other graduate degree programs.

From out-of-state	3%	Reside on campus	11%
Age 25 or older	33%	Transferred in	10%
International students	3%	African Americans	27%
Asian Americans/Pacific Islanders	3%	Hispanic Americans	1%
Native Americans	0.3%		

Faculty 788 (88% full-time), 91% with terminal degrees.

Expenses (1999–2000) *Tuition, state resident:* full-time $2730; part-time $91 per hour. *Tuition, nonresident:* full-time $5460; part-time $182 per hour. *Required fees:* full-time $510; $13 per hour; $40 per term part-time. Full-time tuition and fees vary according to course load and program. Part-time tuition and fees vary according to course load and program. *College room and board:* room only: $2438. Room and board charges vary according to housing facility. *Waivers:* employees or children of employees.

Library Mervyn Sterne Library plus 1 other. *Operations spending 1999–2000:* $8.6 million. *Collection:* 5,288 serial subscriptions, 37,366 audiovisual materials.

College life *Housing: Options:* coed, women-only. *Social organizations:* national fraternities, national sororities; 6% of eligible men and 6% of eligible women are members. *Most popular organizations:* campus ministries, service-oriented groups, sports affiliated groups.

Campus security 24-hour emergency response devices and patrols, late-night transport-escort service, controlled dormitory access.

After graduation 100 organizations recruited on campus 1997–98. *Career center:* 7 full-time personnel. Services include job fairs, resume preparation, resume referral, career counseling, careers library, job bank, job interviews. *Graduate education:* 15% of class of 1999 went directly to graduate and professional school. *Major awards:* 1 Rhodes scholar.

Freshmen 2,915 applied, 2,590 admitted, 1,233 enrolled. 9 National Merit Scholars.

SAT verbal scores above 500	N/R	SAT math scores above 500	N/R
ACT above 18	88%	From top 10% of their h.s. class	24%
From top quarter	48%	From top half	75%
1998 freshmen returning in 1999	74%		

Application *Options:* early admission, deferred entrance. *Application fee:* $25. *Required:* high school transcript; minimum 2.0 GPA.

Standardized tests *Admission: Required:* SAT I or ACT.

Significant dates *Application deadlines:* 8/1 (freshmen), 8/31 (transfers). *Financial aid deadline priority date:* 5/1.

Freshman Application Contact
Ms. Chenise Ryan, Director of Undergraduate Admissions, The University of Alabama at Birmingham, Office of Undergraduate Admissions, 260 HUC, 1530 3rd Avenue south, Birmingham, AL 35294-1150. **Phone:** 205-934-8221. **Toll-free phone:** 800-421-8743. **Fax:** 205-975-7114. **E-mail:** UndergradAdmit@uab.edu

Visit CollegeQuest.com for information on majors offered and athletics. College video available at CollegeQuest.com.

■ *See page 2684 for a narrative description.*

THE UNIVERSITY OF ALABAMA IN HUNTSVILLE
Huntsville, Alabama

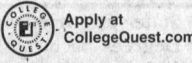 Apply at CollegeQuest.com

- **State-supported**, university, founded 1950
- **Degrees** bachelor's, master's, doctoral, post-master's, and postbachelor's certificates
- **Suburban** 376-acre campus
- **Coed**, 4,526 undergraduate students, 65% full-time, 52% women, 48% men
- **Moderately difficult** entrance level, 92% of applicants were admitted
- **14:1 student-to-undergraduate faculty ratio**
- **35% graduate** in 6 years or less
- **$3112 tuition** and fees (in-state); $6516 (out-of-state)
- **$6145 average financial aid** package, $15,146 average indebtedness upon graduation, $19.3 million endowment

Part of University of Alabama System.

Students *Undergraduates:* 2,953 full-time, 1,573 part-time. Students come from 49 states and territories, 66 other countries. *The most frequently chosen baccalaureate fields are:* engineering/engineering technologies, business/marketing, health professions and related sciences. *Graduate:* 1,361 in graduate degree programs.

From out-of-state	10%	Reside on campus	13%
Age 25 or older	32%	Transferred in	13%
International students	4%	African Americans	15%
Asian Americans/Pacific Islanders	4%	Hispanic Americans	2%
Native Americans	2%		

Faculty 421 (66% full-time), 60% with terminal degrees.

Expenses (1999–2000) *Tuition, state resident:* full-time $3112; part-time $698 per term. *Tuition, nonresident:* full-time $6516; part-time $1458 per term. Full-time tuition and fees vary according to course load. Part-time tuition and fees vary according to course load. *College room and board:* $3780; room only: $2780. Room and board charges vary according to board plan and housing facility. *Payment plan:* deferred payment. *Waivers:* employees or children of employees.

Library University of Alabama in Huntsville Library. *Operations spending 1999–2000:* $2.3 million. *Collection:* 2,687 serial subscriptions, 9,563 audio-visual materials.

College life *Housing: Option:* coed. *Social organizations:* national fraternities, national sororities; 6% of eligible men and 5% of eligible women are members. *Most popular organizations:* Student Government Association, Association for Campus Entertainment, Circle K International, Anointed Voices, Institute of Electrical and Electronic Engineers.

Campus security 24-hour emergency response devices and patrols, late-night transport-escort service, controlled dormitory access.

After graduation 310 organizations recruited on campus 1997–98. *Career center:* 3 full-time, 1 part-time personnel. Services include job fairs, resume preparation, interview workshops, resume referral, career/interest testing, career counseling, careers library, job bank, job interviews. *Graduate education:* 15% of class of 1999 went directly to graduate and professional school: 9% graduate arts and sciences, 3% engineering, 2% business, 1% law, 1% medicine.

Freshmen 1,100 applied, 1,013 admitted, 574 enrolled. 2 National Merit Scholars, 1 valedictorian.

Average high school GPA	3.3	SAT verbal scores above 500	84%
SAT math scores above 500	82%	ACT above 18	98%
From top 10% of their h.s. class	32%	From top quarter	62%
From top half	86%	1998 freshmen returning in 1999	77%

Application *Options:* eApply at www.CollegeQuest.com, Common Application, electronic application, early admission, deferred entrance. *Application fee:* $20. *Required:* high school transcript.

Standardized tests *Admission: Required:* SAT I or ACT.

Significant dates *Application deadlines:* 8/15 (freshmen), 8/15 (transfers). *Financial aid deadline priority date:* 4/1.

Freshman Application Contact
Ms. Sabrina Williams, Associate Director of Admissions, The University of Alabama in Huntsville, 301 Sparkman Drive, Huntsville, AL 35899. **Phone:** 256-890-6070. **Toll-free phone:** 800-UAH-CALL. **Fax:** 256-890-6073. **E-mail:** admitme@email.uah.edu

Visit CollegeQuest.com for information on majors offered and athletics. Electronic viewbook available at CollegeQuest.com.

■ *See page 2686 for a narrative description.*

Alabama

UNIVERSITY OF MOBILE
Mobile, Alabama

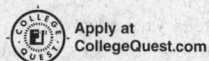

- **Independent Southern Baptist**, comprehensive, founded 1961
- **Degrees** associate, bachelor's, and master's
- **Suburban** 830-acre campus
- **Coed**, 1,565 undergraduate students, 84% full-time, 68% women, 32% men
- **Moderately difficult** entrance level, 98% of applicants were admitted
- **17:1 student-to-undergraduate faculty ratio**
- **$7830 tuition** and fees
- **$8250 average financial aid** package, $14,000 average indebtedness upon graduation, $5.8 million endowment

Students *Undergraduates:* 1,317 full-time, 248 part-time. Students come from 26 states and territories, 23 other countries. *The most frequently chosen baccalaureate fields are:* business/marketing, education, health professions and related sciences. *Graduate:* 206 in graduate degree programs.

Reside on campus	20%	Age 25 or older	22%
Transferred in	28%	International students	2%
African Americans	19%	Asian Americans/Pacific Islanders	0.3%
Hispanic Americans	1%	Native Americans	1%

Faculty 159 (59% full-time), 45% with terminal degrees.

Expenses (1999–2000) *Comprehensive fee:* $12,110 includes full-time tuition ($7710), mandatory fees ($120), and room and board ($4280). Full-time tuition and fees vary according to course load. Room and board charges vary according to board plan. *Part-time tuition:* $257 per semester hour. *Part-time fees:* $15 per term part-time. Part-time tuition and fees vary according to course load. *Payment plan:* installment. *Waivers:* employees or children of employees.

Library J. L. Bedsole Library plus 2 others. *Operations spending 1999–2000:* $378,879. *Collection:* 81,881 titles, 758 serial subscriptions, 2,116 audiovisual materials.

College life *Housing: Options:* men-only, women-only, disabled students. *Most popular organizations:* Campus Activity Board, Baptist Campus Ministry, Student Government Association, Fellowship of Christian Athletes.

Campus security 24-hour emergency response devices and patrols.

After graduation 79 organizations recruited on campus 1997–98. *Career center:* 1 full-time, 1 part-time personnel. Services include job fairs, resume preparation, resume referral, career counseling, careers library, job bank, job interviews.

Freshmen 471 applied, 460 admitted, 251 enrolled.

| SAT verbal scores above 500 | N/R | SAT math scores above 500 | N/R |
| ACT above 18 | 90% | | |

Application *Options:* eApply at www.CollegeQuest.com, Common Application, early admission, early action, deferred entrance. *Application fee:* $30. *Required:* high school transcript; minimum 2.0 GPA. *Required for some:* interview.

Standardized tests *Admission: Required:* SAT I or ACT.

Significant dates *Application deadlines:* rolling (freshmen), rolling (transfers). *Early action:* 11/1. *Notification:* 11/15 (early action). *Financial aid deadline priority date:* 3/21.

Freshman Application Contact
Mr. Brian Boyle, Director of Admissions, University of Mobile, PO Box 13220, Mobile, AL 36663-0220. **Phone:** 334-442-2287. **Toll-free phone:** 800-946-7267. **Fax:** 334-675-6329. **E-mail:** adminfo@umobile.edu

Visit CollegeQuest.com for information on majors offered and athletics. College video available at CollegeQuest.com.

UNIVERSITY OF MONTEVALLO
Montevallo, Alabama

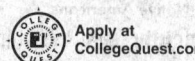

- **State-supported**, comprehensive, founded 1896
- **Degrees** bachelor's, master's, and post-master's certificates
- **Small-town** 106-acre campus with easy access to Birmingham
- **Coed**, 2,653 undergraduate students, 90% full-time, 67% women, 33% men
- **Moderately difficult** entrance level, 82% of applicants were admitted
- **$3290 tuition** and fees (in-state); $6440 (out-of-state)
- **$10.3 million endowment**

Students *Undergraduates:* 2,395 full-time, 258 part-time. Students come from 22 states and territories, 26 other countries. *Graduate:* 456 in graduate degree programs.

From out-of-state	5%	Reside on campus	33%
Age 25 or older	16%	Transferred in	29%
International students	2%	African Americans	14%
Asian Americans/Pacific Islanders	0.3%	Hispanic Americans	1%
Native Americans	1%		

Expenses (1999–2000) *Tuition, state resident:* full-time $3150; part-time $105 per semester hour. *Tuition, nonresident:* full-time $6300; part-time $210 per semester hour. *Required fees:* full-time $140; $35 per term part-time. Full-time tuition and fees vary according to course load. Part-time tuition and fees vary according to course load. *College room and board:* $3354; room only: $2144. Room and board charges vary according to board plan and housing facility. *Payment plan:* deferred payment. *Waivers:* senior citizens and employees or children of employees.

Library Carmichael Library. *Operations spending 1999–2000:* $810,521. *Collection:* 240,911 titles, 880 serial subscriptions, 6,308 audiovisual materials.

College life *Housing:* on-campus residence required in freshman year. *Options:* coed, men-only, women-only. *Social organizations:* national fraternities, national sororities; 23% of eligible men and 23% of eligible women are members. *Most popular organizations:* Golden Key, Student Government Association, University Programming Council, Campus Ministries, African-American Association.

Campus security 24-hour emergency response devices and patrols, late-night transport-escort service, controlled dormitory access.

After graduation 130 organizations recruited on campus 1997–98. *Career center:* 2 full-time, 1 part-time personnel. Services include job fairs, resume preparation, resume referral, career counseling, careers library, job bank, job interviews.

Freshmen 1,237 applied, 1,016 admitted, 538 enrolled. 54 valedictorians.

Average high school GPA	3.22	SAT verbal scores above 500	N/R
SAT math scores above 500	N/R	ACT above 18	89%
From top 10% of their h.s. class	18%	From top quarter	52%
From top half	86%	1998 freshmen returning in 1999	68%

Application *Options:* eApply at www.CollegeQuest.com, Common Application, electronic application, early admission. *Application fee:* $25. *Required:* high school transcript; minimum 2.0 GPA. *Recommended:* interview.

Standardized tests *Admission: Required:* SAT I or ACT.

Significant dates *Application deadlines:* 8/1 (freshmen), rolling (transfers). *Financial aid deadline priority date:* 4/15.

Freshman Application Contact
Mr. William C. Cannon, Director of Admissions, University of Montevallo, Station #6030, Montevallo, AL 35115. **Phone:** 205-665-6030. **Toll-free phone:** 800-292-4349. **E-mail:** admissions@um.montevallo.edu

Visit CollegeQuest.com for information on majors offered and athletics. Electronic viewbook available at CollegeQuest.com.

- See page 2780 for a narrative description.

UNIVERSITY OF NORTH ALABAMA
Florence, Alabama

- **State-supported**, comprehensive, founded 1830
- **Degrees** bachelor's and master's
- **Urban** 125-acre campus
- **Coed**, 5,099 undergraduate students, 85% full-time, 59% women, 41% men
- **Minimally difficult** entrance level, 53% of applicants were admitted
- **22:1 student-to-undergraduate faculty ratio**
- **40.6% graduate** in 6 years or less
- **$2512 tuition** and fees (in-state); $4744 (out-of-state)
- **$16,466 average indebtedness** upon graduation, $4.6 million endowment

Part of Alabama Commission on Higher Education.

Students *Undergraduates:* 4,346 full-time, 753 part-time. Students come from 29 states and territories. *The most frequently chosen baccalaureate fields*

Alabama

University of North Alabama (continued)
are: business/marketing, education, health professions and related sciences.
Graduate: 706 in graduate degree programs.

From out-of-state	16%	Reside on campus	19%
Age 25 or older	21%	Transferred in	11%
International students	0.02%	African Americans	11%
Asian Americans/Pacific Islanders	1%	Hispanic Americans	1%
Native Americans	2%		

Faculty 310 (65% full-time).
Expenses (1999–2000) *Tuition, state resident:* full-time $2232; part-time $93 per semester hour. *Tuition, nonresident:* full-time $4464; part-time $186 per semester hour. *Required fees:* full-time $280; $13 per semester hour; $26 per term part-time. Part-time tuition and fees vary according to course load. *College room and board:* $3672. *Waivers:* employees or children of employees.
Library Collier Library. *Operations spending 1999–2000:* $2.1 million. *Collection:* 328,456 titles, 1,962 serial subscriptions, 8,020 audiovisual materials.
College life *Housing: Options:* coed, men-only, women-only. *Social organizations:* national fraternities, national sororities; 4% of eligible men and 5% of eligible women are members. *Most popular organizations:* Student Government Association, University Program Council, Baptist Campus Ministries, Physical Education Majors Club, Residence Hall Association.
Campus security 24-hour emergency response devices and patrols.
After graduation *Career center:* 2 full-time personnel. Services include job fairs, resume preparation, resume referral, career counseling, careers library, job bank, job interviews.
Freshmen 1,524 applied, 809 admitted, 809 enrolled.

| SAT verbal scores above 500 | 43% | SAT math scores above 500 | 33% |
| ACT above 18 | 80% | 1998 freshmen returning in 1999 | 55% |

Application *Options:* early admission, deferred entrance. *Application fee:* $25. *Required:* high school transcript.
Standardized tests *Admission: Required:* SAT I or ACT.
Significant dates *Application deadlines:* rolling (freshmen), rolling (transfers). *Financial aid deadline priority date:* 4/1.
Freshman Application Contact
Mrs. Kim O. Mauldin, Director of Admissions, University of North Alabama, Office of Admissions, Box 5011, Florence, AL 35632-0001. **Phone:** 256-765-4680. **Toll-free phone:** 800-TALKUNA. **Fax:** 256-765-4329. **E-mail:** admis1@unanov.una.edu
Visit CollegeQuest.com for information on majors offered and athletics. College video and electronic viewbook available at CollegeQuest.com.

UNIVERSITY OF SOUTH ALABAMA
Mobile, Alabama

- **State-supported**, university, founded 1963
- **Degrees** bachelor's, master's, doctoral, and first professional
- **Suburban** 1,215-acre campus
- **Coed**, 8,816 undergraduate students, 65% full-time, 58% women, 42% men
- **Moderately difficult** entrance level, 94% of applicants were admitted
- **22:1** student-to-undergraduate faculty ratio
- **30.5% graduate** in 6 years or less
- **$2670 tuition** and fees (in-state); $5340 (out-of-state)

Students *Undergraduates:* 5,701 full-time, 3,115 part-time. Students come from 42 states and territories, 95 other countries. *The most frequently chosen baccalaureate fields are:* business/marketing, education, health professions and related sciences. *Graduate:* 257 in professional programs, 1,899 in other graduate degree programs.

From out-of-state	16%	Reside on campus	20%
Age 25 or older	29%	Transferred in	11%
International students	5%	African Americans	15%
Asian Americans/Pacific Islanders	3%	Hispanic Americans	1%
Native Americans	1%		

Faculty 917 (75% full-time), 60% with terminal degrees.
Expenses (2000–2001) *Tuition, state resident:* full-time $2670; part-time $89 per semester hour. *Tuition, nonresident:* full-time $5340; part-time $178 per semester hour. *Required fees:* $90 per term part-time. Full-time tuition and fees vary according to course level, course load, and program. Part-time tuition and fees vary according to course level, course load, and program. *College room and board:* $3114; room only: $1604. Room and board charges vary according to board plan and student level. *Waivers:* employees or children of employees.
Library University Library plus 1 other. *Operations spending 1999–2000:* $4.6 million. *Collection:* 578,615 titles, 3,981 serial subscriptions, 13,349 audiovisual materials.
College life *Housing: Option:* coed. *Social organizations:* national fraternities, national sororities; 8% of eligible men and 6% of eligible women are members. *Most popular organizations:* Student Government Association, Black Student Union, Nontraditional Student Committee.
Campus security 24-hour emergency response devices and patrols, late-night transport-escort service.
After graduation 362 organizations recruited on campus 1997–98. 63% of class of 1998 had job offers within 6 months. *Career center:* 7 full-time, 10 part-time personnel. Services include job fairs, resume preparation, interview workshops, resume referral, career counseling, careers library, job bank, job interviews, co-op placement. *Graduate education:* 13% of class of 1999 went directly to graduate and professional school.
Freshmen 2,457 applied, 2,298 admitted, 1,210 enrolled.

Average high school GPA	3.2	SAT verbal scores above 500	N/R
SAT math scores above 500	N/R	ACT above 18	97%
From top half of their h.s. class	87%	1998 freshmen returning in 1999	66%

Application *Option:* early admission. *Preference* given to state residents in certain allied health programs. *Application fee:* $25. *Required:* high school transcript. *Recommended:* minimum 2.0 GPA.
Standardized tests *Admission: Required:* SAT I or ACT.
Significant dates *Application deadlines:* 8/10 (freshmen), 8/10 (transfers). *Notification:* continuous until 8/10 (freshmen). **Financial aid deadline:** continuous.
Freshman Application Contact
Ms. Norma Pepperhorst, Acting Director of Admissions, University of South Alabama, 307 University Boulevard, Mobile, AL 36688-0002. **Phone:** 334-460-6141. **Toll-free phone:** 800-872-5247. **Fax:** 334-460-7023. **E-mail:** admiss@jaguar1.usouthal.edu
Visit CollegeQuest.com for information on majors offered and athletics. College video available at CollegeQuest.com.

THE UNIVERSITY OF WEST ALABAMA
Livingston, Alabama

- **State-supported**, comprehensive, founded 1835
- **Degrees** associate, bachelor's, and master's
- **Small-town** 595-acre campus
- **Coed**, 1,666 undergraduate students, 91% full-time, 57% women, 43% men
- **Minimally difficult** entrance level, 68% of applicants were admitted
- **19:1** student-to-undergraduate faculty ratio
- **$2688 tuition** and fees (in-state); $4968 (out-of-state)
- **$357,926 endowment**

Students *Undergraduates:* 1,520 full-time, 146 part-time. Students come from 21 states and territories, 9 other countries. *The most frequently chosen baccalaureate fields are:* business/marketing, education, social sciences and history. *Graduate:* 299 in graduate degree programs.

From out-of-state	20%	Reside on campus	35%
Age 25 or older	14%	Transferred in	11%
International students	1%	African Americans	37%
Asian Americans/Pacific Islanders	0.2%	Hispanic Americans	1%
Native Americans	0.5%		

Faculty 115 (94% full-time), 51% with terminal degrees.
Expenses (1999–2000) *Tuition, state resident:* full-time $2280; part-time $95 per semester hour. *Tuition, nonresident:* full-time $4560; part-time $190 per semester hour. *Required fees:* full-time $408; $55 per term part-time. Part-time tuition and fees vary according to course load. *College room and board:* $2740; room only: $1110. Room and board charges vary according to board plan and housing facility. *Payment plan:* deferred payment. *Waivers:* employees or children of employees.

Library Julia Tutwiler Library. *Operations spending 1999–2000:* $362,175. *Collection:* 140,141 titles, 4,000 serial subscriptions, 1,813 audiovisual materials.
College life *Housing:* on-campus residence required through sophomore year. *Options:* coed, men-only, women-only. *Social organizations:* national fraternities, national sororities; 10% of eligible men and 10% of eligible women are members. *Most popular organization:* Campus Outreach.
Campus security 24-hour patrols.
After graduation 28 organizations recruited on campus 1997–98. *Career center:* 4 full-time personnel. Services include job fairs, resume preparation, interview workshops, resume referral, career/interest testing, career counseling, careers library, job interviews. *Graduate education:* 10% of class of 1999 went directly to graduate and professional school: 7% education, 1% business, 1% law, 1% medicine.
Freshmen 955 applied, 652 admitted, 327 enrolled.

SAT verbal scores above 500	N/R
ACT above 18	62%
SAT math scores above 500	N/R
1998 freshmen returning in 1999	61%

Application *Options:* eApply at www.CollegeQuest.com, Common Application, electronic application, early admission, deferred entrance. *Application fee:* $20. *Required:* high school transcript; minimum 2.0 GPA.
Standardized tests *Admission: Required:* SAT I or ACT.
Significant dates *Application deadlines:* rolling (freshmen), rolling (transfers). *Financial aid deadline:* continuous.
Freshman Application Contact
Dr. Ervin L. Wood, Vice President for Student Affairs, The University of West Alabama, Livingston, AL 35470. **Phone:** 205-652-9661 Ext. 352. **Toll-free phone:** 800-621-7742 (in-state); 800-621-8044 (out-of-state).
Visit CollegeQuest.com for information on majors offered and athletics. College video available at CollegeQuest.com.

VIRGINIA COLLEGE AT BIRMINGHAM
Birmingham, Alabama

- **Proprietary**, 4-year, founded 1989
- **Degrees** associate and bachelor's
- **Urban** 1-acre campus
- **Coed**
- **Moderately difficult** entrance level
- **$7000 tuition** and fees

Expenses (1999–2000) *Tuition:* full-time $7000; part-time $175 per quarter hour. Full-time tuition and fees vary according to program. Part-time tuition and fees vary according to program.
Institutional Web site http://www.vc.edu/
College life *Housing:* college housing not available. *Social organizations:* local fraternities, local sororities.
Application *Required:* high school transcript.
Standardized tests *Admission: Required:* CPAt.
Admissions Office Contact
Virginia College at Birmingham, 65 Bagby Drive, Birmingham, AL 35209. **Fax:** 205-802-1597.
Visit CollegeQuest.com for information on athletics.

ALASKA

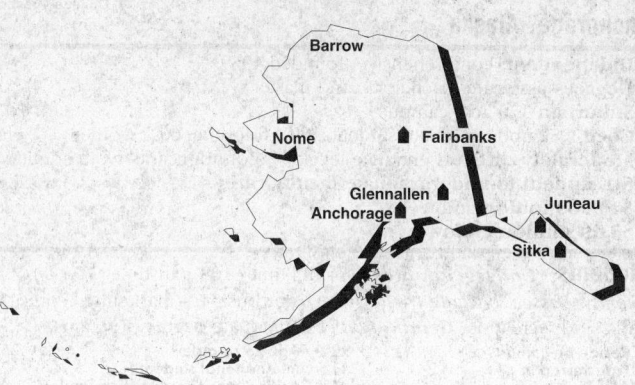

ALASKA BIBLE COLLEGE
Glennallen, Alaska

- **Independent nondenominational**, 4-year, founded 1966
- **Degrees** associate and bachelor's
- **Rural** 80-acre campus
- **Coed**, 35 undergraduate students, 74% full-time, 37% women, 63% men
- **Minimally difficult** entrance level, 78% of applicants were admitted
- **5:1 student-to-undergraduate faculty ratio**
- **50% graduate** in 6 years or less
- **$4750 tuition** and fees
- **$12,600 endowment**

Students *Undergraduates:* 26 full-time, 9 part-time. Students come from 16 states and territories. *The most frequently chosen baccalaureate field is:* philosophy.

From out-of-state	51%	Reside on campus	77%
Age 25 or older	40%	Transferred in	20%
Asian Americans/Pacific Islanders	3%	Native Americans	14%

Faculty 11 (36% full-time), 73% with terminal degrees.
Expenses (2000–2001) *Comprehensive fee:* $8650 includes full-time tuition ($4750) and room and board ($3900). *Part-time tuition:* $200 per credit. *Payment plan:* installment. *Waivers:* employees or children of employees.
Library Alaska Bible College Library Center. *Operations spending 1999–2000:* $8080. *Collection:* 26,895 titles, 217 serial subscriptions, 108 audiovisual materials.
College life *Housing:* on-campus residence required through sophomore year. *Option:* coed.
Campus security 24-hour emergency response devices, campus curfew enforced.
Freshmen 9 applied, 7 admitted, 8 enrolled.

Average high school GPA	2.83	SAT verbal scores above 500	N/R
SAT math scores above 500	N/R	ACT above 18	N/R
1998 freshmen returning in 1999	50%		

Application *Option:* deferred entrance. *Application fee:* $25. *Required:* essay or personal statement; high school transcript; minimum 2.0 GPA; 2 letters of recommendation; health form.
Significant dates *Application deadlines:* 8/1 (freshmen), 8/1 (transfers). *Notification:* 8/15 (freshmen). *Financial aid deadline:* 8/5. *Priority date:* 5/31.
Freshman Application Contact
Ms. Jackie Colwell, Admissions Officer, Alaska Bible College, Box 289, Glennallen, AK 99588-0289. **Phone:** 907-822-3201. **Toll-free phone:** 800-478-7884. **Fax:** 907-822-5027. **E-mail:** info@akbible.edu
Visit CollegeQuest.com for information on majors offered and athletics. College video available at CollegeQuest.com.

Alaska

ALASKA PACIFIC UNIVERSITY
Anchorage, Alaska

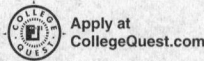
Apply at CollegeQuest.com

- **Independent**, comprehensive, founded 1959
- **Degrees** associate, bachelor's, and master's
- **Suburban** 170-acre campus
- **Coed**, 352 undergraduate students, 69% full-time, 60% women, 40% men
- **Moderately difficult** entrance level, 39% of applicants were admitted
- **8:1 student-to-undergraduate faculty ratio**
- **$10,068 tuition** and fees
- **$31.9 million endowment**

Students *Undergraduates:* 244 full-time, 108 part-time. *The most frequently chosen baccalaureate fields are:* business/marketing, education, parks and recreation. *Graduate:* 171 in graduate degree programs.

Reside on campus	22%	Age 25 or older	26%
Transferred in	11%	International students	2%
African Americans	6%	Asian Americans/Pacific Islanders	4%
Hispanic Americans	5%	Native Americans	14%

Faculty 35 (86% full-time), 71% with terminal degrees.
Expenses (1999–2000) *Comprehensive fee:* $15,158 includes full-time tuition ($9988), mandatory fees ($80), and room and board ($5090). Full-time tuition and fees vary according to program. Room and board charges vary according to board plan and housing facility. *Part-time tuition:* $412 per semester hour. *Part-time fees:* $40 per term part-time. Part-time tuition and fees vary according to program. Additional tuition for nonresidents: $1964 full-time, $86 per semester hour part-time. *Payment plan:* deferred payment. *Waivers:* employees or children of employees.
Library Consortium Library. *Operations spending 1999–2000:* $95,000. *Collection:* 676,745 titles, 3,842 serial subscriptions.
College life *Housing: Option:* coed. *Most popular organizations:* environmental club, Student Government Association, Nordic Ski Club, Student Organization of Native Americans, drama club.
Campus security 24-hour emergency response devices.
After graduation *Career center:* 1 full-time personnel. Services include resume preparation, career counseling, job bank, job interviews.
Freshmen 89 applied, 35 admitted, 34 enrolled.

SAT verbal scores above 500	67%	SAT math scores above 500	57%
ACT above 18	72%	1998 freshmen returning in 1999	48%

Application *Options:* eApply at www.CollegeQuest.com, electronic application, early decision, deferred entrance. *Application fee:* $25. *Required:* essay or personal statement; high school transcript; minimum 2.0 GPA; 2 letters of recommendation. *Required for some:* interview.
Standardized tests *Admission: Required:* SAT I or ACT.
Significant dates *Application deadlines:* 2/1 (freshmen), 2/1 (transfers). *Early decision:* 1/1. *Notification:* 3/15 (freshmen), 1/15 (early decision). *Financial aid deadline priority date:* 3/15.
Freshman Application Contact
Mr. Dale Montague, Director of Admissions, Alaska Pacific University, 4101 University Drive, Anchorage, AK 99508-4672. **Phone:** 907-564-8248. **Toll-free phone:** 800-252-7528. **Fax:** 907-564-8317. **E-mail:** admissions@alaskapacific.edu
Visit CollegeQuest.com for information on majors offered and athletics. Electronic viewbook available at CollegeQuest.com.

SHELDON JACKSON COLLEGE
Sitka, Alaska

Apply at CollegeQuest.com

- **Independent**, 4-year, founded 1878, affiliated with Presbyterian Church (U.S.A.)
- **Degree** bachelor's
- **Small-town** 320-acre campus
- **Coed**, 204 undergraduate students, 87% full-time, 57% women, 43% men
- **Noncompetitive** entrance level, 100% of applicants were admitted
- **$7250 tuition** and fees
- **$4.8 million endowment**

Students *Undergraduates:* 177 full-time, 27 part-time. Students come from 25 states and territories, 2 other countries. *The most frequently chosen baccalaureate fields are:* education, liberal arts/general studies, natural resources/environmental science.

From out-of-state	66%	Reside on campus	80%
Age 25 or older	68%	Transferred in	20%

Faculty 47 (47% full-time).
Expenses (2000–2001, estimated) *Tuition:* full-time $7250. Room and board charges vary according to housing facility. *Payment plan:* installment. *Waivers:* children of alumni and employees or children of employees.
Library Stratton Library. *Operations spending 1999–2000:* $139,752. *Collection:* 100,000 titles, 300 serial subscriptions.
College life *Housing:* on-campus residence required through sophomore year. *Option:* coed. *Most popular organizations:* Aquatic Resources Club, Culture Club, Social Justice Club, Bible Club, Rod and Gun Club.
Campus security 24-hour patrols, controlled dormitory access.
Freshmen 80 applied, 80 admitted, 52 enrolled. 4 student government officers.

Average high school GPA	2.71	SAT verbal scores above 500	N/R
SAT math scores above 500	N/R	ACT above 18	N/R
1998 freshmen returning in 1999	60%		

Application *Options:* eApply at www.CollegeQuest.com, Common Application, electronic application, deferred entrance. *Preference* given to Alaska natives. *Application fee:* $25. *Required:* high school transcript. *Required for some:* essay or personal statement. *Recommended:* minimum 2.0 GPA.
Significant dates *Application deadlines:* 7/15 (freshmen), 7/15 (transfers). *Financial aid deadline priority date:* 3/1.
Freshman Application Contact
Mr. John Schafer, Dean of Enrollment, Sheldon Jackson College, 801 Lincoln Street, Sitka, AK 99835. **Phone:** 907-747-5221. **Toll-free phone:** 800-478-5220 (in-state); 800-949-5220 (out-of-state). **Fax:** 907-747-5212. **E-mail:** yukonjohn@sj-alaska.com
Visit CollegeQuest.com for information on majors offered and athletics. Electronic viewbook available at CollegeQuest.com.

UNIVERSITY OF ALASKA ANCHORAGE
Anchorage, Alaska

- **State-supported**, comprehensive, founded 1954
- **Degrees** associate, bachelor's, and master's
- **Urban** 428-acre campus
- **Coed**
- **Noncompetitive** entrance level

Part of University of Alaska System.
Institutional Web site http://www.uaa.alaska.edu/
College life *Housing: Option:* coed. *Most popular organizations:* accounting club, African-American Students Association, Association of Latin-American Spanish Students, Inter-Varsity Christian Fellowship, Student Nurses Association.
Campus security 24-hour emergency response devices and patrols, student patrols, late-night transport-escort service, controlled dormitory access.
Application *Options:* Common Application, early admission, deferred entrance. *Application fee:* $35. *Required:* minimum 2.0 GPA. *Required for some:* high school transcript.
Standardized tests *Placement: Required for some:* SAT I or ACT, ACT ASSET.
Admissions Office Contact
University of Alaska Anchorage, Administration Building, Room 176, Anchorage, AK 99508-8060. **Fax:** 907-786-4888.
Visit CollegeQuest.com for information on athletics. College video available at CollegeQuest.com.

- *See page 2688 for a narrative description.*

UNIVERSITY OF ALASKA FAIRBANKS
Fairbanks, Alaska

- **State-supported**, university, founded 1917
- **Degrees** associate, bachelor's, master's, and doctoral

Alaska

- **Small-town** 2,250-acre campus
- **Coed**, 3,991 undergraduate students, 74% full-time, 56% women, 44% men
- **Moderately difficult** entrance level, 90% of applicants were admitted
- **$3412 tuition** and fees (in-state); $8332 (out-of-state)

UAF is America's premier institution of northern scholarship, discovery, and adventure. Located in Interior Alaska, a land of rivers, forests, mountains, wildlife, and the Northern Lights, the University is known for research in arctic phenomena, including global climate change. The 2,250-acre campus boasts state-of-the-art classrooms, laboratories, recreational facilities, and residence halls.

Part of University of Alaska System.

Students *Undergraduates:* 2,962 full-time, 1,029 part-time. *The most frequently chosen baccalaureate fields are:* education, engineering/engineering technologies, protective services/public administration. *Graduate:* 740 in graduate degree programs.

From out-of-state	14%	Reside on campus	26%
Age 25 or older	39%	Transferred in	12%
International students	2%	African Americans	4%
Asian Americans/Pacific Islanders	3%	Hispanic Americans	3%
Native Americans	16%		

Faculty 697 (67% full-time).

Expenses (2000–2001) *Tuition, state resident:* full-time $2460; part-time $77 per credit. *Tuition, nonresident:* full-time $7380; part-time $241 per credit. *Required fees:* full-time $952. Full-time tuition and fees vary according to course level, course load, program, reciprocity agreements, and student level. Part-time tuition and fees vary according to course level, course load, program, and reciprocity agreements. *College room and board:* $4150; room only: $2150. Room and board charges vary according to board plan, housing facility, and location. *Payment plan:* deferred payment. *Waivers:* children of alumni, senior citizens, and employees or children of employees.

Library Rasmuson Library plus 8 others. *Collection:* 1 million titles, 6,233 serial subscriptions.

College life *Housing: Options:* coed, disabled students. *Social organizations:* national fraternities, national sororities; 1% of eligible men and 1% of eligible women are members. *Most popular organizations:* Associated Students of Business, North Star Chinese Association, Golden Key National Honor Society, Alaska Alpine Club, University Contra Dancers.

Campus security 24-hour emergency response devices and patrols, student patrols, late-night transport-escort service, controlled dormitory access, ID check at door of residence halls, crime prevention and safety workshops.

After graduation 62% of class of 1998 had job offers within 6 months. *Career center:* 4 full-time, 2 part-time personnel. Services include job fairs, resume preparation, interview workshops, resume referral, career/interest testing, career counseling, careers library, job bank, job interviews. *Graduate education:* 20% of class of 1999 went directly to graduate and professional school: 2% business, 1% law, 1% medicine.

Freshmen 1,301 applied, 1,166 admitted, 790 enrolled.

Average high school GPA	3.01	SAT verbal scores above 500	61%
SAT math scores above 500	55%	ACT above 18	76%
From top 10% of their h.s. class	9%	From top quarter	30%
From top half	63%		

Application *Options:* electronic application, early admission, deferred entrance. *Application fee:* $35. *Required:* high school transcript; minimum 2.0 GPA.

Standardized tests *Admission: Required:* SAT I or ACT.

Significant dates *Application deadlines:* 8/1 (freshmen), 8/1 (transfers). *Notification:* continuous until 8/15 (freshmen). *Financial aid deadline priority date:* 6/1.

Freshman Application Contact

Ms. Nancy Dix, Admissions Counselor, University of Alaska Fairbanks, PO Box 757480, Fairbanks, AK 99775. **Phone:** 907-474-7500. **Toll-free phone:** 800-478-1823. **Fax:** 907-474-5379.

Visit CollegeQuest.com for information on majors offered and athletics.

- *See page 2690 for a narrative description.*

UNIVERSITY OF ALASKA SOUTHEAST
Juneau, Alaska

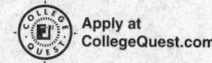

- **State-supported**, comprehensive, founded 1972
- **Degrees** associate, bachelor's, and master's
- **Small-town** 198-acre campus
- **Coed**
- **Noncompetitive** entrance level

Part of University of Alaska System.

Institutional Web site http://www.jun.alaska.edu/

College life *Housing: Option:* coed. *Most popular organization:* Native Student club.

Campus security 24-hour emergency response devices and patrols, late-night transport-escort service, controlled dormitory access.

Application *Options:* eApply at www.CollegeQuest.com, Common Application, early admission, deferred entrance. *Application fee:* $35. *Required:* high school transcript; minimum 2.0 GPA. *Required for some:* essay or personal statement.

Standardized tests *Placement: Recommended:* SAT I or ACT.

Admissions Office Contact

University of Alaska Southeast, 11120 Glacier Highway, Juneau, AK 99801-8625. **Fax:** 907-465-6365. **E-mail:** jyuas@acadi.alaska.edu

Visit CollegeQuest.com for information on athletics. Electronic viewbook available at CollegeQuest.com.

- *See page 2692 for a narrative description.*

ARIZONA

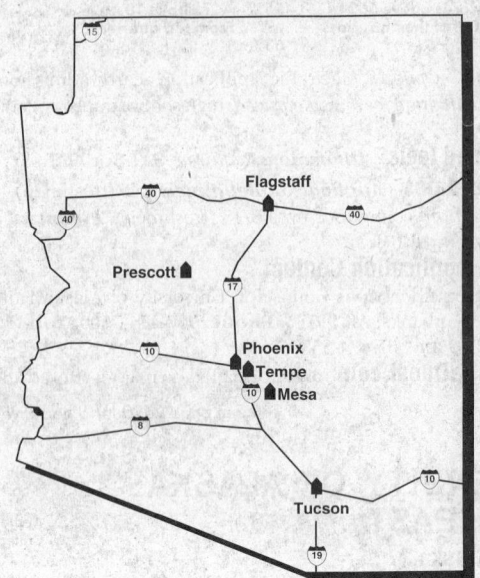

AL COLLINS GRAPHIC DESIGN SCHOOL
Tempe, Arizona

Part of Career Education Corporation.
Students *Undergraduates:* Students come from 49 states and territories.

Age 25 or older	26%	African Americans	7%
Asian Americans/Pacific Islanders	3%	Hispanic Americans	18%
Native Americans	4%		

Faculty 70 (86% full-time), 11% with terminal degrees.
Expenses (1999–2000) *One-time required fee:* $100. *Tuition:* part-time $18,800 per degree program. Full-time tuition and fees vary according to program. *Payment plans:* tuition prepayment, installment, deferred payment. *Waivers:* employees or children of employees.
Library Al Collins Graphic Design School Library. *Operations spending 1999–2000:* $60,000. *Collection:* 1,000 titles.
College life *Housing: Options:* coed, cooperative, disabled students.
After graduation 30 organizations recruited on campus 1997–98. 92% of class of 1998 had job offers within 6 months. *Career center:* 4 full-time personnel. Services include job fairs, resume preparation, interview workshops, resume referral, career counseling, careers library, job bank, job interviews.
Freshmen 3,540 applied, 1,423 admitted.

SAT verbal scores above 500	N/R	SAT math scores above 500	N/R
ACT above 18	N/R	1998 freshmen returning in 1999	100%

Application *Options:* Common Application, early admission, deferred entrance. *Required:* essay or personal statement; high school transcript; interview.
Standardized tests *Admission: Recommended:* SAT I or ACT.
Significant dates *Application deadlines:* rolling (freshmen), rolling (transfers). *Financial aid deadline:* continuous.
Freshman Application Contact
Mr. Jeff Marcus, Vice President of Marketing, Al Collins Graphic Design School, 1140 South Priest, Tempe, AZ 85281. **Phone:** 480-966-3000 Ext. 121. **Toll-free phone:** 800-876-7070. **Fax:** 602-966-2599. **E-mail:** jen@alcollins.com
Visit CollegeQuest.com for information on majors offered and athletics. College video available at CollegeQuest.com.

AMERICAN INDIAN COLLEGE OF THE ASSEMBLIES OF GOD, INC.
Phoenix, Arizona

- **Independent**, 4-year, founded 1957, affiliated with Assemblies of God
- **Degrees** associate and bachelor's
- **Urban** 10-acre campus
- **Coed**, 76 undergraduate students, 89% full-time, 58% women, 42% men
- **Minimally difficult** entrance level, 64% of applicants were admitted
- **4:1 student-to-undergraduate faculty ratio**
- **61.5% graduate** in 6 years or less
- **$3400 tuition** and fees

Students *Undergraduates:* 68 full-time, 8 part-time. Students come from 8 states and territories, 1 other country. *The most frequently chosen baccalaureate fields are:* education, philosophy.

From out-of-state	32%	Age 25 or older	42%
Transferred in	12%	International students	1%
African Americans	1%	Hispanic Americans	11%
Native Americans	75%		

Faculty 21 (67% full-time), 100% with terminal degrees.
Expenses (1999–2000) *Comprehensive fee:* $6550 includes full-time tuition ($3000), mandatory fees ($400), and room and board ($3150). Full-time tuition and fees vary according to course load. *Part-time tuition:* $125 per semester hour.
Library Cummings Memorial Library. *Collection:* 13,000 titles, 120 serial subscriptions.
College life On-campus residence required through senior year. *Most popular organizations:* Missions Fellowship, Associated Student Body, yearbook.
Campus security Student patrols.
After graduation *Career center:* Services include career counseling.
Freshmen 44 applied, 28 admitted, 11 enrolled.

SAT verbal scores above 500	N/R	SAT math scores above 500	N/R
ACT above 18	N/R	1998 freshmen returning in 1999	50%

Application *Preference* given to members of Assemblies of God and other evangelical churches. *Application fee:* $0. *Required:* high school transcript; 1 letter of recommendation. *Recommended:* essay or personal statement; interview.
Standardized tests *Admission: Required:* SAT I or ACT.
Significant dates *Application deadlines:* 8/15 (freshmen), 8/15 (transfers). *Financial aid deadline priority date:* 4/1.
Freshman Application Contact
Ms. Sandy Ticeahkie, Admissions Coordinator, American Indian College of the Assemblies of God, Inc., 10020 North 15th Avenue, Phoenix, AZ 85021. **Phone:** 602-944-3335 Ext. 227. **Toll-free phone:** 800-933-3828. **E-mail:** aicadm@juno.com
Visit CollegeQuest.com for information on majors offered and athletics.

ARIZONA STATE UNIVERSITY
Tempe, Arizona

- **State-supported**, university, founded 1885
- **Degrees** bachelor's, master's, doctoral, first professional, post-master's, and postbachelor's certificates
- **Suburban** 814-acre campus with easy access to Phoenix
- **Coed**, 32,927 undergraduate students, 80% full-time, 53% women, 47% men
- **Moderately difficult** entrance level, 80% of applicants were admitted
- **21:1 student-to-undergraduate faculty ratio**
- **46.7% graduate** in 6 years or less
- **$2261 tuition** and fees (in-state); $9413 (out-of-state)
- **$6794 average financial aid** package, $17,385 average indebtedness upon graduation, $202 million endowment

Nationally recognized academic programs, an outstanding faculty, Research I and Truman institution designations, state-of-the-art facilities, and a beautiful Southwest setting make Arizona State University one of the leading public universities in the nation. With 3 campuses and 94 undergraduate majors to

Arizona

choose from, ASU students are offered challenging academic programs combined with a rewarding college experience. In addition, ASU's exceptional Honors College provides a distinctive opportunity for students to live and learn in a community devoted to academic excellence and personal achievement.

Part of Arizona State University.

Students *Undergraduates:* 26,348 full-time, 6,579 part-time. Students come from 52 states and territories, 102 other countries. *The most frequently chosen baccalaureate fields are:* business/marketing, communications/communication technologies, social sciences and history. *Graduate:* 461 in professional programs, 9,806 in other graduate degree programs.

From out-of-state	23%	Reside on campus	15%
Age 25 or older	21%	Transferred in	11%
International students	4%	African Americans	3%
Asian Americans/Pacific Islanders	5%	Hispanic Americans	11%
Native Americans	2%		

Faculty 1,747 (95% full-time), 83% with terminal degrees.

Expenses (1999–2000) *Tuition, state resident:* full-time $2188; part-time $115 per credit. *Tuition, nonresident:* full-time $9340; part-time $389 per credit. *Required fees:* full-time $73; $18 per term part-time. *College room and board:* $5010; room only: $3010. Room and board charges vary according to board plan and housing facility. *Waivers:* employees or children of employees.

Library Hayden Library plus 4 others. *Operations spending 1999–2000:* $17.5 million. *Collection:* 2.3 million titles, 34,042 serial subscriptions, 1.1 million audiovisual materials.

College life *Housing: Options:* coed, men-only, women-only, disabled students. *Social organizations:* national fraternities, national sororities, NPHC fraternities and sororities; 8% of eligible men and 6% of eligible women are members. *Most popular organizations:* ski club, outing club, Students Against Discrimination (SAD).

Campus security 24-hour emergency response devices and patrols, late-night transport-escort service.

After graduation 550 organizations recruited on campus 1997–98. *Career center:* 18 full-time, 4 part-time personnel. Services include job fairs, resume preparation, resume referral, career counseling, careers library, job bank, job interviews. *Major awards:* 4 Fulbright Scholars.

Freshmen 17,082 applied, 13,620 admitted, 5,868 enrolled. 132 National Merit Scholars.

Average high school GPA	3.36	SAT verbal scores above 500	72%
SAT math scores above 500	74%	ACT above 18	94%
From top 10% of their h.s. class	30%	From top quarter	57%
From top half	85%	1998 freshmen returning in 1999	75%

Application *Option:* early action. *Application fee:* $40 for nonresidents. *Required:* high school transcript; minimum 3.0 GPA.

Standardized tests *Admission: Required:* SAT I or ACT.

Significant dates *Application deadlines:* rolling (freshmen), rolling (transfers). *Early action:* 11/1. *Notification:* 12/1 (early action). *Financial aid deadline priority date:* 3/1.

Freshman Application Contact
Mr. Timothy J. Desch, Director of Undergraduate Admissions, Arizona State University, Box 870112, Tempe, AZ 85287-0112. **Phone:** 480-965-7788. **Fax:** 482-965-1608. **E-mail:** ugradadm@asuvm.inre.asau.edu

Visit CollegeQuest.com for information on majors offered and athletics. College video and electronic viewbook available at CollegeQuest.com.

■ *See page 1182 for a narrative description.*

ARIZONA STATE UNIVERSITY EAST
Mesa, Arizona

- **State-supported**, comprehensive, founded 1995
- **Degrees** bachelor's and master's
- **Suburban** 600-acre campus with easy access to Phoenix
- **Coed**, 857 undergraduate students, 42% full-time, 32% women, 68% men
- **Moderately difficult** entrance level, 81% of applicants were admitted
- **11:1 student-to-undergraduate faculty ratio**
- **$2211 tuition** and fees (in-state); $9363 (out-of-state)
- **$7125 average financial aid** package, $3.3 million endowment

Part of Arizona State University.

Students *Undergraduates:* 358 full-time, 499 part-time. Students come from 36 states and territories, 27 other countries. *The most frequently chosen baccalaureate fields are:* agriculture, engineering/engineering technologies. *Graduate:* 361 in graduate degree programs.

From out-of-state	8%	Reside on campus	13%
Age 25 or older	52%	Transferred in	12%
International students	3%	African Americans	3%
Asian Americans/Pacific Islanders	5%	Hispanic Americans	10%
Native Americans	2%		

Faculty 57 (95% full-time), 84% with terminal degrees.

Expenses (1999–2000) *Tuition, state resident:* full-time $2188; part-time $115 per semester hour. *Tuition, nonresident:* full-time $9340; part-time $389 per semester hour. *Required fees:* full-time $23; $13 per term part-time. Full-time tuition and fees vary according to location. Part-time tuition and fees vary according to course load and location. *College room and board:* room only: $2440. Room and board charges vary according to housing facility. *Waivers:* employees or children of employees.

Library ASU East Library plus 1 other. *Operations spending 1999–2000:* $353,000. *Collection:* 3.1 million titles.

College life *Housing: Options:* coed, disabled students. *Social organizations:* national fraternities, national sororities. *Most popular organizations:* Aero Devils (American Association of Airport Executives), Aero Management Tech—Student Advisory Committee, ASU Precision Flight Team, National Agri-Marketing Association, Society of Manufacturing Engineers.

Campus security 24-hour emergency response devices and patrols, late-night transport-escort service, controlled dormitory access.

After graduation 25 organizations recruited on campus 1997–98. *Career center:* Services include job fairs, resume preparation, interview workshops, resume referral, career/interest testing, career counseling, careers library, job bank, job interviews.

Freshmen 206 applied, 166 admitted, 86 enrolled.

| SAT verbal scores above 500 | N/R | SAT math scores above 500 | N/R |
| ACT above 18 | N/R | 1998 freshmen returning in 1999 | 0% |

Application *Options:* Common Application, electronic application. *Application fee:* $40. *Required:* high school transcript. *Recommended:* minimum 3.0 GPA.

Standardized tests *Admission: Recommended:* SAT I or ACT.

Significant dates *Application deadlines:* rolling (freshmen), rolling (transfers). *Financial aid deadline priority date:* 3/1.

Freshman Application Contact
Ms. Carmen Prado, Student Recruitment/Retention Specialist, Arizona State University East, Undergraduate Admissions, Arizona State University, PO Box 870112, Tempe, AZ 85287-0112. **Phone:** 480-727-1165. **Fax:** 480-727-1008.

Visit CollegeQuest.com for information on majors offered and athletics. College video and electronic viewbook available at CollegeQuest.com.

ARIZONA STATE UNIVERSITY WEST
Phoenix, Arizona

- **State-supported**, upper-level, founded 1984
- **Degrees** bachelor's, master's, and postbachelor's certificates
- **Urban** 300-acre campus
- **Coed**, 3,371 undergraduate students, 51% full-time, 69% women, 31% men
- **Moderately difficult** entrance level, 92% of applicants were admitted
- **10:1 student-to-undergraduate faculty ratio**
- **$2191 tuition** and fees (in-state); $9413 (out-of-state)

Part of Arizona State University.

Students *Undergraduates:* 1,723 full-time, 1,648 part-time. Students come from 17 states and territories. *The most frequently chosen baccalaureate fields are:* business/marketing, education, social sciences and history. *Graduate:* 1,206 in graduate degree programs.

From out-of-state	1%	Age 25 or older	59%
Transferred in	25%	International students	1%
African Americans	4%	Asian Americans/Pacific Islanders	3%
Hispanic Americans	14%	Native Americans	2%

Faculty 321 (63% full-time), 64% with terminal degrees.

Expenses (1999–2000) *Tuition, state resident:* full-time $2118; part-time $115 per credit hour. *Tuition, nonresident:* full-time $9340; part-time $389

Arizona

Arizona State University West (continued)
per credit hour. *Required fees:* full-time $73; $18 per term part-time. Part-time tuition and fees vary according to course load. *Payment plan:* installment. *Waivers:* employees or children of employees.
Library ASU West Library. *Operations spending 1999–2000:* $3.4 million. *Collection:* 293,740 titles, 3,549 serial subscriptions, 23,618 audiovisual materials.
College life *Housing:* college housing not available. *Most popular organizations:* justice studies club, American Marketing Association West, Beta Alpha Psi Accounting Honor Society, Communication Club of ASU West, outdoor recreation club.
Campus security 24-hour emergency response devices and patrols, student patrols, late-night transport-escort service.
After graduation 112 organizations recruited on campus 1997–98. *Career center:* 4 full-time, 2 part-time personnel. Services include job fairs, resume preparation, interview workshops, resume referral, career counseling, careers library, job bank, job interviews.
Application *Options:* Common Application, electronic application, deferred entrance. *Application fee:* $0.
Standardized tests *Admission: Required for some:* SAT I or ACT.
Significant dates *Application deadline:* rolling (transfers). *Financial aid deadline:* continuous.
Freshman Application Contact
Ms. B.J. Hart, Coordinator of Admissions, Arizona State University West, 4701 West Thunderbird Road, PO Box 37100, Phoenix, AZ 85069-7100. **Phone:** 602-543-9378.
Visit CollegeQuest.com for information on majors offered and athletics.

THE ART INSTITUTE OF PHOENIX
Phoenix, Arizona

- **Proprietary**, 4-year, founded 1995
- **Degrees** associate and bachelor's
- **Suburban** campus
- **Coed**, primarily men, 900 undergraduate students
- **Minimally difficult** entrance level
- **$15,420 tuition** and fees

Part of The Art Institutes.
Students *Undergraduates:* Students come from 18 states and territories, 8 other countries.

From out-of-state	25%	Reside on campus	20%
Age 25 or older	25%		

Faculty 47 (28% full-time).
Expenses (1999–2000) *One-time required fee:* $100. *Tuition:* full-time $15,420; part-time $257 per credit. Full-time tuition and fees vary according to course load, degree level, and program. Part-time tuition and fees vary according to degree level and program. *College room only:* $4302. Room and board charges vary according to housing facility. *Payment plans:* guaranteed tuition, installment, deferred payment. *Waivers:* employees or children of employees.
Library Resource Center. *Collection:* 1,900 titles, 110 serial subscriptions.
College life *Housing: Options:* men-only, women-only.
Campus security 24-hour emergency response devices, controlled dormitory access, security guard during open hours.
After graduation 2 organizations recruited on campus 1997–98. 91% of class of 1998 had job offers within 6 months. *Career center:* 3 full-time, 1 part-time personnel. Services include job fairs, resume preparation, resume referral, career counseling, careers library, job bank, job interviews.
Freshmen

Average high school GPA	2.75	SAT verbal scores above 500	N/R
SAT math scores above 500	N/R	ACT above 18	N/R
From top 10% of their h.s. class	12%	From top quarter	18%
From top half	70%		

Application *Option:* Common Application. *Application fee:* $50. *Required:* essay or personal statement; high school transcript; interview. *Recommended:* minimum 2.0 GPA.
Standardized tests *Placement: Recommended:* SAT I or ACT.

Significant dates *Application deadline:* rolling (freshmen). *Financial aid deadline:* continuous.
Freshman Application Contact
Ms. Janet Scott, Director of Admissions, The Art Institute of Phoenix, 2233 West Dunlap Avenue, Phoenix, AZ 85021-2859. **Phone:** 602-678-4300 Ext. 114. **Toll-free phone:** 800-474-2479 Ext. 114. **Fax:** 602-997-0191. **E-mail:** scottj@aii.edu
Visit CollegeQuest.com for information on majors offered and athletics. College video available at CollegeQuest.com.

CHAPARRAL COLLEGE
Tucson, Arizona

- **Proprietary**, primarily 2-year, founded 1972
- **Degrees** associate and bachelor's (bachelor's degree in business administration only)
- **Suburban** campus with easy access to Phoenix
- **Coed**, 383 undergraduate students, 100% full-time, 66% women, 34% men
- **Noncompetitive** entrance level
- **25:1** student-to-undergraduate faculty ratio
- **$6485 tuition** and fees

Faculty 44 (25% full-time), 14% with terminal degrees.
Admissions Office Contact
Chaparral College, 4585 East Speedway, No 204, Tucson, AZ 85712. **Fax:** 520-325-0108.
Visit CollegeQuest.com for information on majors offered and athletics.

DEVRY INSTITUTE OF TECHNOLOGY
Phoenix, Arizona

- **Proprietary**, 4-year, founded 1967
- **Degrees** associate and bachelor's
- **Urban** 18-acre campus
- **Coed**, 3,664 undergraduate students, 79% full-time, 24% women, 76% men
- **Minimally difficult** entrance level, 64% of applicants were admitted
- **33:1** student-to-undergraduate faculty ratio
- **$7778 tuition** and fees

Part of DeVry, Inc.
Students *Undergraduates:* 2,902 full-time, 762 part-time. Students come from 42 states and territories, 7 other countries. *The most frequently chosen baccalaureate fields are:* computer/information sciences, business/marketing, engineering/engineering technologies.

From out-of-state	37%	Age 25 or older	42%
Transferred in	7%	International students	1%
African Americans	6%	Asian Americans/Pacific Islanders	6%
Hispanic Americans	13%	Native Americans	4%

Faculty 113 (72% full-time).
Expenses (1999–2000) *Tuition:* full-time $7778; part-time $290 per credit hour. Part-time tuition and fees vary according to class time and course load. *Payment plans:* installment, deferred payment. *Waivers:* employees or children of employees.
Library Learning Resource Center. *Collection:* 14,780 titles, 95 serial subscriptions.
College life *Housing:* college housing not available. *Most popular organizations:* American Production and Inventory Control Society, board and ski club, travel club, Data Processing Management Association, Institute of Electronic and Electrical Engineers.
Campus security Late-night transport-escort service, trained security personnel on duty.
After graduation 98% of class of 1998 had job offers within 6 months. *Career center:* 8 full-time, 5 part-time personnel. Services include job fairs, resume preparation, resume referral, career counseling, careers library, job bank, job interviews.
Freshmen 1,886 applied, 1,216 admitted, 1,069 enrolled.

SAT verbal scores above 500	N/R	SAT math scores above 500	N/R
ACT above 18	N/R	1998 freshmen returning in 1999	49%

Arizona

Application *Options:* electronic application, deferred entrance. *Application fee:* $25. *Required:* high school transcript; interview.
Standardized tests *Admission: Required:* Computerized Placement Test. *Recommended:* SAT I or ACT.
Significant dates *Application deadlines:* rolling (freshmen), rolling (transfers). *Financial aid deadline:* continuous.
Freshman Application Contact
Mr. Raymond Toledo, Director of Admissions, DeVry Institute of Technology, 2149 West Dunlap, Phoenix, AZ 85021-2995. **Phone:** 602-870-9201 Ext. 451. **Toll-free phone:** 800-528-0250. **E-mail:** webadmin@devry-phx.edu
Visit CollegeQuest.com for information on majors offered and athletics.

EMBRY-RIDDLE AERONAUTICAL UNIVERSITY
Prescott, Arizona

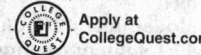

- **Independent**, 4-year, founded 1978
- **Degree** bachelor's
- **Small-town** 547-acre campus
- **Coed**, primarily men, 1,583 undergraduate students, 91% full-time, 16% women, 84% men
- **Moderately difficult** entrance level, 80% of applicants were admitted
- **21:1 student-to-undergraduate faculty ratio**
- **46.2% graduate** in 6 years or less
- **$11,020 tuition** and fees
- **$5198 average financial aid** package, $17,125 average indebtedness upon graduation, $31.7 million endowment

Students *Undergraduates:* 1,445 full-time, 138 part-time. Students come from 51 states and territories, 32 other countries. *The most frequently chosen baccalaureate fields are:* engineering/engineering technologies, computer/information sciences, trade and industry.

From out-of-state	66%	Reside on campus	47%
Age 25 or older	12%	Transferred in	9%
International students	4%	African Americans	1%
Asian Americans/Pacific Islanders	5%	Hispanic Americans	4%
Native Americans	1%		

Faculty 94 (65% full-time), 51% with terminal degrees.
Expenses (2000–2001) *Comprehensive fee:* $15,446 includes full-time tuition ($10,700), mandatory fees ($320), and room and board ($4426). *College room only:* $2646. Full-time tuition and fees vary according to course load and program. Room and board charges vary according to board plan, housing facility, and location. Part-time tuition and fees vary according to course load and program. *Waivers:* employees or children of employees.
Library ERAU—Prescott Campus Library. *Operations spending 1999–2000:* $1.9 million. *Collection:* 27,790 titles.
College life *Housing:* on-campus residence required in freshman year. *Options:* coed, men-only, disabled students. *Social organizations:* national fraternities, national sororities; 83% of eligible men and 96% of eligible women are members. *Most popular organizations:* Hawaii Club, Strike Eagles, American Institute of Aeronautics and Astronautics (AIAA), Sigma Pi, Arnold Air Society.
Campus security 24-hour emergency response devices and patrols, student patrols, late-night transport-escort service.
After graduation 51 organizations recruited on campus 1997–98. 95% of class of 1998 had job offers within 6 months. *Career center:* 2 full-time, 9 part-time personnel. Services include job fairs, resume preparation, interview workshops, resume referral, career/interest testing, career counseling, careers library, job bank, job interviews. *Graduate education:* 10% of class of 1999 went directly to graduate and professional school.
Freshmen 1,119 applied, 900 admitted, 313 enrolled.

Average high school GPA	3.31	SAT verbal scores above 500	74%
SAT math scores above 500	84%	ACT above 18	96%
From top 10% of their h.s. class	14%	From top quarter	44%
From top half	80%	1998 freshmen returning in 1999	80%

Application *Options:* eApply at www.CollegeQuest.com, Common Application, electronic application, early admission, early decision, deferred entrance. *Application fee:* $30. *Required:* high school transcript; minimum 2.0 GPA. *Required for some:* minimum 3.0 GPA; medical examination for flight students. *Recommended:* essay or personal statement; letters of recommendation; interview.
Standardized tests *Admission: Required:* SAT I or ACT.
Significant dates *Application deadlines:* rolling (freshmen), rolling (transfers). *Early decision:* 12/1. *Notification:* 12/15 (early decision). *Financial aid deadline:* 6/30. *Priority date:* 4/15.
Freshman Application Contact
Bill Thompson, Director of Admissions, Embry-Riddle Aeronautical University, 3200 Willow Creek Road, Prescott, AZ 86301. **Phone:** 520-708-6692. **Toll-free phone:** 800-888-3728. **Fax:** 520-708-6606. **E-mail:** admit@pc.erau.edu
Visit CollegeQuest.com for information on majors offered and athletics. Electronic viewbook available at CollegeQuest.com.

■ *See page 1628 for a narrative description.*

GRAND CANYON UNIVERSITY
Phoenix, Arizona

- **Independent Southern Baptist**, comprehensive, founded 1949
- **Degrees** bachelor's and master's
- **Suburban** 90-acre campus
- **Coed**, 1,534 undergraduate students, 81% full-time, 65% women, 35% men
- **Moderately difficult** entrance level
- **15:1 student-to-undergraduate faculty ratio**
- **49% graduate** in 6 years or less
- **$8380 tuition** and fees
- **$8068 average financial aid** package, $4.9 million endowment

Grand Canyon University is among a very select group included in the *Student's Guide to America's 100 Best College Buys*. *U.S. News & World Report* continues to rank Grand Canyon in the top Western liberal arts colleges. In addition, Grand Canyon is included in the Honor Roll for Character Building Colleges.

Students *Undergraduates:* 1,243 full-time, 291 part-time. Students come from 40 states and territories, 14 other countries. *The most frequently chosen baccalaureate fields are:* biological/life sciences, education, psychology. *Graduate:* 1,457 in graduate degree programs.

From out-of-state	19%	Reside on campus	30%
Age 25 or older	28%	Transferred in	16%
International students	3%	African Americans	5%
Asian Americans/Pacific Islanders	2%	Hispanic Americans	8%
Native Americans	2%		

Faculty 189 (50% full-time), 80% with terminal degrees.
Expenses (1999–2000) *Comprehensive fee:* $12,626 includes full-time tuition ($7680), mandatory fees ($700), and room and board ($4246). Full-time tuition and fees vary according to course load. Room and board charges vary according to board plan and housing facility. *Part-time tuition:* $320 per semester hour. *Part-time fees:* $6 per semester hour. Part-time tuition and fees vary according to course load. *Payment plan:* installment. *Waivers:* employees or children of employees.
Library Fleming Library. *Operations spending 1999–2000:* $258,654. *Collection:* 1,256 serial subscriptions, 4,404 audiovisual materials.
College life *Housing:* on-campus residence required through sophomore year. *Options:* men-only, women-only.
Campus security 24-hour emergency response devices and patrols, student patrols, late-night transport-escort service, controlled dormitory access.
After graduation 50 organizations recruited on campus 1997–98. 67% of class of 1998 had job offers within 6 months. *Career center:* 1 full-time, 1 part-time personnel. Services include resume referral, job interviews.
Freshmen 242 enrolled. 1 National Merit Scholar, 10 valedictorians.

Average high school GPA	3.44	SAT verbal scores above 500	55%
SAT math scores above 500	48%	ACT above 18	88%
From top 10% of their h.s. class	29%	From top quarter	57%
From top half	79%	1998 freshmen returning in 1999	73%

Application *Options:* early admission, deferred entrance. *Application fee:* $25. *Required:* high school transcript; minimum 3.0 GPA. *Required for some:* essay or personal statement; 3 letters of recommendation; interview. *Recommended:* minimum 3.0 GPA.

Arizona

Grand Canyon University *(continued)*

Standardized tests *Admission: Required:* SAT I or ACT.

Significant dates *Application deadlines:* rolling (freshmen), rolling (transfers). *Notification:* continuous until 9/1 (freshmen). *Financial aid deadline:* continuous.

Freshman Application Contact
Mrs. April Chapman, Director of Admissions, Grand Canyon University, 3300 West Camelback Road, PO Box 11097, Phoenix, AZ 86017-3030. **Phone:** 602-589-2855 Ext. 2811. **Toll-free phone:** 800-800-9776. **Fax:** 602-589-2580. **E-mail:** admiss@grand-canyon.edu

Visit CollegeQuest.com for information on majors offered and athletics.

■ *See page 1736 for a narrative description.*

INTERNATIONAL BAPTIST COLLEGE
Tempe, Arizona

- **Independent Baptist**, comprehensive, founded 1980
- **Degrees** associate, bachelor's, master's, and doctoral
- **Suburban** 12-acre campus with easy access to Phoenix
- **Coed**, 53 undergraduate students
- **$4350 tuition** and fees

Students

African Americans	6%	Asian Americans/Pacific Islanders	4%
Hispanic Americans	8%		

Expenses (1999–2000) *Comprehensive fee:* $7350 includes full-time tuition ($4000), mandatory fees ($350), and room and board ($3000). *Part-time tuition:* $150 per semester hour. *Part-time fees:* $8 per semester hour.

Freshmen

SAT verbal scores above 500	N/R	SAT math scores above 500	N/R
ACT above 18	N/R		

Application *Options:* Common Application, early admission. *Application fee:* $25. *Required:* essay or personal statement; 3 letters of recommendation. *Recommended:* high school transcript.

Standardized tests *Admission: Recommended:* SAT I and SAT II or ACT.

Significant dates *Financial aid deadline:* continuous.

Freshman Application Contact
Dr. Stanley Bushey, Administrative Services Director, International Baptist College, 2150 East Southern Avenue, Tempe, AZ 85282. **Phone:** 480-838-7070. **Toll-free phone:** 800-422-4858. **Fax:** 602-838-5432.

Visit CollegeQuest.com for information on majors offered and athletics.

ITT TECHNICAL INSTITUTE
Phoenix, Arizona

- **Proprietary**, primarily 2-year, founded 1972
- **Degrees** associate and bachelor's
- **Urban** 2-acre campus
- **Coed**, 400 undergraduate students, 100% full-time, 16% women, 84% men
- **Minimally difficult** entrance level

Part of ITT Educational Services, Inc.

Faculty 22 (91% full-time).

Admissions Office Contact
ITT Technical Institute, 4837 East McDowell Road, Phoenix, AZ 85008-4292. **Toll-free phone:** 800-879-4881. **Fax:** 602-267-8727.

Visit CollegeQuest.com for information on majors offered and athletics.

METROPOLITAN COLLEGE OF COURT REPORTING
Phoenix, Arizona

- **Private**, 4-year, founded 1991
- **Degrees** associate and bachelor's
- **Suburban** 1-acre campus
- **Coed**

College life *Housing:* college housing not available.

Application *Options:* early admission, deferred entrance. *Application fee:* $50. *Required:* high school transcript; interview.

Admissions Office Contact
Metropolitan College of Court Reporting, 4640 East Elwood Street, Suite 12, Phoenix, AZ 85040. **Fax:** 602-894-8999.

Visit CollegeQuest.com for information on athletics.

NORTHERN ARIZONA UNIVERSITY
Flagstaff, Arizona

- **State-supported**, university, founded 1899
- **Degrees** bachelor's, master's, and doctoral
- **Small-town** 730-acre campus
- **Coed**, 13,686 undergraduate students, 86% full-time, 58% women, 42% men
- **Moderately difficult** entrance level, 82% of applicants were admitted
- **17:1** student-to-undergraduate faculty ratio
- **39.4% graduate** in 6 years or less
- **$2262 tuition** and fees (in-state); $8378 (out-of-state)

Students *Undergraduates:* 11,790 full-time, 1,896 part-time. Students come from 55 states and territories, 54 other countries. *The most frequently chosen baccalaureate fields are:* business/marketing, education, liberal arts/general studies. *Graduate:* 6,034 in graduate degree programs.

From out-of-state	19%	Reside on campus	53%
Age 25 or older	21%	International students	1%
African Americans	1%	Asian Americans/Pacific Islanders	2%
Hispanic Americans	9%	Native Americans	7%

Faculty 1,077 (64% full-time).

Expenses (1999–2000) *Tuition, state resident:* full-time $2188; part-time $115 per semester hour. *Tuition, nonresident:* full-time $8304; part-time $346 per semester hour. *Required fees:* full-time $74; $37 per term part-time. Part-time tuition and fees vary according to course load. *College room and board:* $3682; room only: $1832. Room and board charges vary according to board plan and housing facility. *Waivers:* employees or children of employees.

Library Cline Library. *Collection:* 6,253 serial subscriptions, 28,535 audio-visual materials.

College life *Housing: Options:* coed, men-only, women-only, disabled students. *Social organizations:* national fraternities, national sororities; 10% of eligible men and 5% of eligible women are members.

Campus security 24-hour emergency response devices and patrols, late-night transport-escort service, controlled dormitory access.

After graduation 400 organizations recruited on campus 1997–98. *Career center:* 7 full-time, 6 part-time personnel. Services include job fairs, resume preparation, interview workshops, resume referral, career/interest testing, career counseling, careers library, job bank, job interviews.

Freshmen 7,109 applied, 5,794 admitted, 2,249 enrolled. 14 National Merit Scholars.

Average high school GPA	3.4	SAT verbal scores above 500	59%
SAT math scores above 500	60%	ACT above 18	89%
From top 10% of their h.s. class	23%	From top quarter	47%
From top half	83%	1998 freshmen returning in 1999	70%

Application *Options:* electronic application, deferred entrance. *Application fee:* $40. *Required:* high school transcript. *Required for some:* essay or personal statement; letters of recommendation; interview. *Recommended:* minimum 3.0 GPA.

Standardized tests *Admission: Required:* SAT I or ACT.

Significant dates *Application deadlines:* rolling (freshmen), rolling (transfers). *Financial aid deadline priority date:* 2/14.

Freshman Application Contact
Ms. Molly Munger, Director of Admissions, Northern Arizona University, PO Box 4084, Flagstaff, AZ 86011. **Phone:** 520-523-5511. **Toll-free phone:** 888-MORE-NAU. **Fax:** 520-523-6023. **E-mail:** undergraduate.admissions@nau.edu

Visit CollegeQuest.com for information on majors offered and athletics. College video and electronic viewbook available at CollegeQuest.com.

■ *See page 2182 for a narrative description.*

Arizona

PRESCOTT COLLEGE
Prescott, Arizona

- **Independent**, comprehensive, founded 1966
- **Degrees** bachelor's and master's
- **Small-town** campus
- **Coed**
- **Moderately difficult** entrance level
- **$13,450 tuition** and fees

Expenses (1999–2000) *Tuition:* full-time $12,350; part-time $2100 per term. *Required fees:* full-time $1100; $110 per year part-time. Full-time tuition and fees vary according to course load and program. Part-time tuition and fees vary according to course load and program.
Institutional Web site http://www.prescott.edu/
College life *Housing:* college housing not available. *Most popular organizations:* Student Union, Amnesty International, Student Environmental Network.
Application *Option:* deferred entrance. *Application fee:* $45. *Required:* essay or personal statement; high school transcript; 2 letters of recommendation. *Required for some:* interview.
Admissions Office Contact
Prescott College, 220 Grove Avenue, Prescott, AZ 86301-2990. **Toll-free phone:** 800-628-6364. **Fax:** 520-776-5252. **E-mail:** rdpadmissions@prescott.edu
Visit CollegeQuest.com for information on athletics. College video available at CollegeQuest.com.

■ *See page 2290 for a narrative description.*

SOUTHWESTERN COLLEGE
Phoenix, Arizona

- **Independent Conservative Baptist**, 4-year, founded 1960
- **Degrees** associate and bachelor's
- **Urban** 19-acre campus
- **Coed**
- **Minimally difficult** entrance level
- **$7640 tuition** and fees

Expenses (1999–2000) *Comprehensive fee:* $10,580 includes full-time tuition ($7400), mandatory fees ($240), and room and board ($2940). *College room only:* $2100. Full-time tuition and fees vary according to program. *Part-time tuition:* $315 per credit. *Part-time fees:* $120 per term part-time. Part-time tuition and fees vary according to program.
Institutional Web site http://www.southwesterncollege.edu/
College life *Housing:* on-campus residence required through senior year. *Options:* men-only, women-only.
Campus security Controlled dormitory access.
Application *Option:* deferred entrance. *Application fee:* $25. *Required:* essay or personal statement; high school transcript; minimum 2.0 GPA; 2 letters of recommendation.
Standardized tests *Admission: Required:* SAT I and SAT II or ACT.
Admissions Office Contact
Southwestern College, 2625 East Cactus Road, Phoenix, AZ 85032-7042. **Toll-free phone:** 800-247-2697. **E-mail:** admissions@southwesterncollege.edu
Visit CollegeQuest.com for information on athletics.

UNIVERSITY OF ADVANCING COMPUTER TECHNOLOGY
Tempe, Arizona

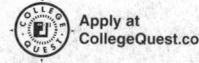
Apply at CollegeQuest.com

- **Proprietary**, comprehensive, founded 1983
- **Degrees** associate, bachelor's, and master's
- **Urban** campus
- **Coed**, 1,055 undergraduate students, 100% full-time, 19% women, 81% men

Students

African Americans	3%	Asian Americans/Pacific Islanders	3%
Hispanic Americans	13%	Native Americans	2%

Library University of Advancing Computer Technology Library.
College life *Housing:* college housing not available.
Campus security 24-hour patrols.
After graduation 90% of class of 1998 had job offers within 6 months. *Career center:* 2 full-time personnel. Services include resume referral, job bank, job interviews.
Freshmen 459 admitted.

SAT verbal scores above 500	N/R	SAT math scores above 500	N/R
ACT above 18	N/R		

Application *Option:* eApply at www.CollegeQuest.com. *Required:* high school transcript; interview. *Recommended:* essay or personal statement.
Standardized tests *Admission: Required:* SAT I or ACT. *Required for some:* Wonderlic aptitude test.
Significant dates *Financial aid deadline:* continuous.
Freshman Application Contact
Mr. Dominic Pistillo, President, University of Advancing Computer Technology, 2625 West Baseline Road, Tempe, AZ 85283-1042. **Phone:** 602-383-8228. **Toll-free phone:** 800-658-5744. **Fax:** 602-383-8222. **E-mail:** admissions@uact.edu
Visit CollegeQuest.com for information on majors offered and athletics. College video available at CollegeQuest.com.

■ *See page 2680 for a narrative description.*

THE UNIVERSITY OF ARIZONA
Tucson, Arizona

- **State-supported**, university, founded 1885
- **Degrees** bachelor's, master's, doctoral, and first professional
- **Urban** 351-acre campus
- **Coed**, 25,356 undergraduate students, 85% full-time, 53% women, 47% men
- **Moderately difficult** entrance level, 84% of applicants were admitted
- **18:1 student-to-undergraduate faculty ratio**
- **53% graduate** in 6 years or less
- **$2264 tuition** and fees (in-state); $9416 (out-of-state)
- **$8808 average financial aid** package, $17,143 average indebtedness upon graduation, $150 million endowment

Students *Undergraduates:* 21,450 full-time, 3,906 part-time. Students come from 55 states and territories, 126 other countries. *The most frequently chosen baccalaureate fields are:* business/marketing, biological/life sciences, social sciences and history. *Graduate:* 1,122 in professional programs, 6,946 in other graduate degree programs.

From out-of-state	29%	Reside on campus	20%
Age 25 or older	17%	Transferred in	8%
International students	4%	African Americans	3%
Asian Americans/Pacific Islanders	5%	Hispanic Americans	14%
Native Americans	2%		

Faculty 1,383 (97% full-time), 97% with terminal degrees.
Expenses (1999–2000) *Tuition, state resident:* full-time $2264; part-time $115 per unit. *Tuition, nonresident:* full-time $9416; part-time $389 per unit. *Required fees:* $7 per unit. Part-time tuition and fees vary according to course load. *College room and board:* $5548. Room and board charges vary according to board plan and housing facility. *Waivers:* minority students and employees or children of employees.
Library University of Arizona Main Library plus 5 others. *Operations spending 1999–2000:* $21.1 million. *Collection:* 4 million titles, 18,961 serial subscriptions.
College life *Housing: Options:* coed, men-only, women-only. *Social organizations:* national fraternities, national sororities, local fraternities, local sororities; 15% of eligible men and 15% of eligible women are members. *Most popular organization:* Student Government Association.
Campus security 24-hour patrols, student patrols, late-night transport-escort service, emergency telephones.

Peterson's Guide to Four-Year Colleges 2001   www.petersons.com   77

Arizona

The University of Arizona (continued)

After graduation *Career center:* 12 full-time personnel. Services include job fairs, resume preparation, resume referral, career counseling, careers library, job bank, job interviews.

Freshmen 17,700 applied, 14,868 admitted, 5,365 enrolled. 54 National Merit Scholars, 105 valedictorians.

Average high school GPA	3.33	SAT verbal scores above 500	70%
SAT math scores above 500	73%	ACT above 18	92%
From top 10% of their h.s. class	32%	From top quarter	59%
From top half	86%	1998 freshmen returning in 1999	77%

Application *Options:* electronic application, early admission, deferred entrance. *Preference* given to state residents. *Application fee:* $40 for nonresidents. *Required:* high school transcript. *Required for some:* minimum 3.0 GPA; letters of recommendation; interview.

Standardized tests *Admission: Required:* SAT I or ACT.

Significant dates *Application deadlines:* 4/1 (freshmen), 5/1 (transfers). *Notification:* continuous until 8/1 (freshmen). **Financial aid deadline priority date:** 3/1.

Freshman Application Contact
Ms. Lori Goldman, Director of Admissions, The University of Arizona, PO Box 210040, Tucson, AZ 85721-0040. **Phone:** 520-621-3237. **Fax:** 520-621-9799. **E-mail:** appinfo@arizona.edu

Visit CollegeQuest.com for information on majors offered and athletics. College video and electronic viewbook available at CollegeQuest.com.

UNIVERSITY OF PHOENIX
Phoenix, Arizona

- **Proprietary**, comprehensive, founded 1976
- **Degrees** associate, bachelor's, master's, doctoral, post-master's, postbachelor's, and first professional certificates (courses conducted at 54 campuses in 13 states with significant enrollment reflected in profile)
- **Urban** campus
- **Coed**, 46,473 undergraduate students, 100% full-time, 56% women, 44% men
- **Noncompetitive** entrance level
- **13:1 student-to-undergraduate faculty ratio**
- **$7200 tuition** and fees

Students *Undergraduates:* 46,473 full-time. Students come from 52 states and territories, 21 other countries. *The most frequently chosen baccalaureate fields are:* business/marketing, health professions and related sciences. *Graduate:* 20,061 in graduate degree programs.

Age 25 or older	86%	African Americans	13%
Asian Americans/Pacific Islanders	6%	Hispanic Americans	18%
Native Americans	2%		

Faculty 6,771 (2% full-time), 13% with terminal degrees.

Expenses (1999–2000) *Tuition:* full-time $7200; part-time $240 per credit. Full-time tuition and fees vary according to location and program. *Payment plan:* deferred payment. *Waivers:* employees or children of employees.

Library Learning Resource Center. *Operations spending 1999–2000:* $962,000.

College life *Housing:* college housing not available.

Campus security 24-hour patrols, late-night transport-escort service.

Freshmen 466 enrolled.

SAT verbal scores above 500	N/R	SAT math scores above 500	N/R
ACT above 18	N/R		

Application *Option:* deferred entrance. *Application fee:* $50. *Required:* 2 years of work experience. *Required for some:* high school transcript.

Significant dates *Application deadlines:* rolling (freshmen), rolling (transfers).

Freshman Application Contact
Ms. Beth Barilla, Director of Admissions, University of Phoenix, 4615 East Elwood Street, Phoenix, AZ 85040. **Phone:** 480-927-0099 Ext. 1216. **E-mail:** beth.barilla@apollogrp.edu

Visit CollegeQuest.com for information on majors offered and athletics.

WESTERN INTERNATIONAL UNIVERSITY
Phoenix, Arizona

- **Proprietary**, comprehensive, founded 1978
- **Degrees** associate, bachelor's, and master's
- **Urban** 4-acre campus
- **Coed**
- **Moderately difficult** entrance level
- **$7136 tuition** and fees

Expenses (1999–2000) *One-time required fee:* $50. *Tuition:* full-time $7136; part-time $223 per credit hour. Full-time tuition and fees vary according to location. Part-time tuition and fees vary according to course load and location.

Institutional Web site http://www.wintu.edu/

College life *Housing:* college housing not available. *Most popular organizations:* Delta Mu Delta, Student Association, International Student Organization.

Campus security 24-hour emergency response devices and patrols, late-night transport-escort service.

Application *Option:* deferred entrance. *Application fee:* $50. *Required:* high school transcript; minimum 2.5 GPA; interview. *Required for some:* 3 letters of recommendation. *Recommended:* 3 letters of recommendation.

Admissions Office Contact
Western International University, 9215 North Black Canyon Highway, Phoenix, AZ 85021-2718.

Visit CollegeQuest.com for information on athletics.

ARKANSAS

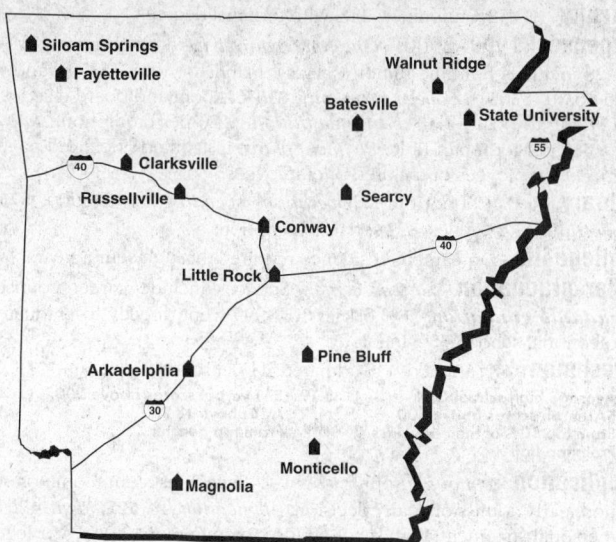

ARKANSAS BAPTIST COLLEGE
Little Rock, Arkansas

- **Independent Baptist**, 4-year, founded 1884
- **Degrees** associate and bachelor's
- **Urban** campus
- **Coed**
- **Noncompetitive** entrance level
- **$2200 tuition** and fees

Faculty 23 (52% full-time).
Expenses (1999–2000) *Comprehensive fee:* $5200 includes full-time tuition ($2200) and room and board ($3000). *Part-time tuition:* $89 per semester hour.
After graduation *Career center:* Services include career counseling.
Freshmen

SAT verbal scores above 500	N/R	SAT math scores above 500	N/R
ACT above 18	N/R		

Application *Option:* deferred entrance. *Required:* high school transcript.
Significant dates *Application deadline:* rolling (freshmen). *Financial aid deadline priority date:* 4/15.
Freshman Application Contact
Mrs. Annie Hightower, Registrar, Arkansas Baptist College, 1600 Bishop Street, Little Rock, AR 72202-6067. **Phone:** 501-374-7856 Ext. 19.
Visit CollegeQuest.com for information on majors offered and athletics.

ARKANSAS STATE UNIVERSITY
Jonesboro, Arkansas

- **State-supported**, comprehensive, founded 1909
- **Degrees** associate, bachelor's, master's, doctoral, and post-master's certificates
- **Small-town** 900-acre campus with easy access to Memphis
- **Coed**, 9,398 undergraduate students, 79% full-time, 58% women, 42% men
- **Moderately difficult** entrance level, 76% of applicants were admitted
- **19:1 student-to-undergraduate faculty ratio**
- **28% graduate** in 6 years or less
- **$2972 tuition** and fees (in-state); $6644 (out-of-state)
- **$2300 average financial aid** package, $12,500 average indebtedness upon graduation, $11 million endowment

Arkansas State University is a premier institution of higher education in the mid-South. Located in Jonesboro (northeast Arkansas), the University offers its 10,000 students degrees that range from the associate to the doctoral levels.

Students can participate in any of the 160 student organizations. The University also offers a low student-faculty ratio and competitive tuition rates.

Students *Undergraduates:* 7,448 full-time, 1,950 part-time. Students come from 45 states and territories, 43 other countries. *The most frequently chosen baccalaureate fields are:* business/marketing, education, health professions and related sciences. *Graduate:* 1,063 in graduate degree programs.

From out-of-state	11%	Reside on campus	20%
Age 25 or older	22%	Transferred in	10%
International students	2%	African Americans	12%
Asian Americans/Pacific Islanders	1%	Hispanic Americans	1%
Native Americans	0.2%		

Faculty 540 (78% full-time), 57% with terminal degrees.
Expenses (1999–2000) *Tuition, state resident:* full-time $2352; part-time $98 per credit hour. *Tuition, nonresident:* full-time $6024; part-time $251 per credit hour. *Required fees:* full-time $620; $19 per credit hour; $15 per term part-time. Full-time tuition and fees vary according to class time, course level, course load, degree level, location, and reciprocity agreements. Part-time tuition and fees vary according to class time, course load, degree level, location, and reciprocity agreements. *College room and board:* $3020. Room and board charges vary according to board plan and housing facility. *Payment plan:* installment. *Waivers:* children of alumni, senior citizens, and employees or children of employees.
Library Dean B. Ellis Library. *Operations spending 1999–2000:* $2.6 million. *Collection:* 539,370 titles, 2,326 serial subscriptions, 6,094 audiovisual materials.
College life *Housing:* on-campus residence required through sophomore year. *Options:* coed, men-only, women-only. *Social organizations:* national fraternities, national sororities; 12% of eligible men and 12% of eligible women are members. *Most popular organizations:* Student Government Association, Greek organizations, intramurals, academic clubs, minority/international organizations.
Campus security 24-hour emergency response devices and patrols.
After graduation 227 organizations recruited on campus 1997–98. *Career center:* 5 full-time, 1 part-time personnel. Services include job fairs, resume preparation, interview workshops, resume referral, career/interest testing, career counseling, careers library, job bank, job interviews.
Freshmen 2,713 applied, 2,056 admitted, 1,714 enrolled.

Average high school GPA	3.22	SAT verbal scores above 500	N/R
SAT math scores above 500	N/R	ACT above 18	82%
1998 freshmen returning in 1999	66%		

Application *Options:* early admission, deferred entrance. *Application fee:* $15. *Required:* high school transcript; minimum 2.0 GPA; proof of immunization.
Standardized tests *Admission:* Required: SAT I, ACT or ACT ASSET.
Significant dates *Financial aid deadline priority date:* 2/15.
Freshman Application Contact
Ms. Paula James, Director of Admissions, Arkansas State University, PO Box 1630, State University, AR 72467. **Phone:** 870-972-3024. **Toll-free phone:** 800-382-3030 (in-state); 800-643-0080 (out-of-state). **Fax:** 870-972-2090. **E-mail:** admissions@chickasaw.astate.edu
Visit CollegeQuest.com for information on majors offered and athletics. College video available at CollegeQuest.com.

- *See page 1184 for a narrative description.*

ARKANSAS TECH UNIVERSITY
Russellville, Arkansas

- **State-supported**, comprehensive, founded 1909
- **Degrees** associate, bachelor's, and master's
- **Small-town** 517-acre campus
- **Coed**, 4,576 undergraduate students, 83% full-time, 52% women, 48% men
- **Minimally difficult** entrance level, 80% of applicants were admitted
- **18:1 student-to-undergraduate faculty ratio**
- **36% graduate** in 6 years or less
- **$2462 tuition** and fees (in-state); $4814 (out-of-state)
- **$4145 average financial aid** package, $15,849 average indebtedness upon graduation, $6.6 million endowment

Arkansas

Arkansas Tech University *(continued)*

Students *Undergraduates:* 3,801 full-time, 775 part-time. Students come from 29 states and territories, 35 other countries. *The most frequently chosen baccalaureate fields are:* business/marketing, education, health professions and related sciences. *Graduate:* 264 in graduate degree programs.

From out-of-state	5%	Reside on campus	21%
Age 25 or older	23%	Transferred in	9%
International students	3%	African Americans	4%
Asian Americans/Pacific Islanders	1%	Hispanic Americans	1%
Native Americans	1%		

Faculty 286 (67% full-time).

Expenses (1999–2000) *Tuition, state resident:* full-time $2352; part-time $104 per semester hour. *Tuition, nonresident:* full-time $4704; part-time $208 per semester hour. *Required fees:* full-time $110; $30 per term part-time. Full-time tuition and fees vary according to location. Part-time tuition and fees vary according to location. *College room and board:* $3222. Room and board charges vary according to board plan and housing facility. *Payment plan:* deferred payment. *Waivers:* senior citizens and employees or children of employees.

Library Tomlinson Library. *Operations spending 1999–2000:* $668,910. *Collection:* 223,057 titles, 1,298 serial subscriptions, 13 audiovisual materials.

College life *Housing:* on-campus residence required through sophomore year. *Options:* coed, men-only, women-only, disabled students. *Social organizations:* national fraternities, national sororities, local fraternities, local sororities. *Most popular organizations:* student government association, Student Activities Board, Wesley Foundation, Chi Alpha, Baptist Student Union.

Campus security 24-hour patrols, controlled dormitory access.

After graduation 64 organizations recruited on campus 1997–98. 91% of class of 1998 had job offers within 6 months. *Career center:* 2 full-time, 4 part-time personnel. Services include job fairs, resume preparation, resume referral, career/interest testing, career counseling, careers library, job bank, job interviews.

Freshmen 2,035 applied, 1,637 admitted, 1,149 enrolled. 65 valedictorians.

Average high school GPA	3.2	SAT verbal scores above 500	N/R
SAT math scores above 500	N/R	ACT above 18	84%
From top 10% of their h.s. class	66%	From top quarter	86%
From top half	97%	1998 freshmen returning in 1999	65%

Application *Options:* electronic application, early admission, deferred entrance. *Application fee:* $0. *Required:* high school transcript; minimum 2.0 GPA. *Required for some:* 2 letters of recommendation; interview.

Standardized tests *Admission: Required:* SAT I or ACT, SAT II: Writing Test. *Required for some:* ACT COMPASS.

Significant dates *Application deadlines:* 9/15 (freshmen), 9/15 (transfers). *Financial aid deadline priority date:* 4/15.

Freshman Application Contact Ms. Shauna Donnell, Director of Enrollment Management, Arkansas Tech University, L.L. "DOC" Bryan Student Services Building, Suite 141, Russellville, AR 72801-2222. **Phone:** 501-968-0404. **Toll-free phone:** 800-582-6953. **Fax:** 501-964-0522. **E-mail:** tech.enroll@mail.atu.edu

Visit CollegeQuest.com for information on majors offered and athletics. College video available at CollegeQuest.com.

CENTRAL BAPTIST COLLEGE
Conway, Arkansas

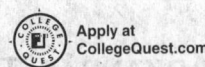 Apply at CollegeQuest.com

- **Independent Baptist**, 4-year, founded 1952
- **Degrees** associate and bachelor's
- **Small-town** 11-acre campus
- **Coed**, 312 undergraduate students, 94% full-time, 44% women, 56% men
- **Minimally difficult** entrance level, 84% of applicants were admitted
- **17:1 student-to-undergraduate faculty ratio**
- **60% graduate** in 6 years or less
- **$5794 tuition** and fees
- **$165,293 endowment**

Students *Undergraduates:* 294 full-time, 18 part-time. Students come from 15 states and territories, 8 other countries. *The most frequently chosen baccalaureate field is:* philosophy.

From out-of-state	16%	Reside on campus	40%
Age 25 or older	11%	Transferred in	7%
International students	2%	African Americans	5%
Asian Americans/Pacific Islanders	1%	Native Americans	0.3%

Faculty 31 (52% full-time), 23% with terminal degrees.

Expenses (1999–2000) *One-time required fee:* $20. *Comprehensive fee:* $9428 includes full-time tuition ($5424), mandatory fees ($370), and room and board ($3634). *College room only:* $1076. Room and board charges vary according to board plan. *Part-time tuition:* $226 per credit hour. *Part-time fees:* $85 per term part-time. *Payment plans:* installment, deferred payment. *Waivers:* employees or children of employees.

Library J. E. Cobb Library. *Operations spending 1999–2000:* $75,647. *Collection:* 43,232 titles, 322 serial subscriptions.

College life On-campus residence required through senior year.

After graduation *Career center:* Services include career counseling. *Graduate education:* 38% of class of 1999 went directly to graduate and professional school: 38% theology.

Freshmen 177 applied, 148 admitted, 117 enrolled.

Average high school GPA	3.19	SAT verbal scores above 500	N/R
SAT math scores above 500	N/R	ACT above 18	70%
From top 10% of their h.s. class	17%	From top quarter	41%
From top half	71%		

Application *Options:* eApply at www.CollegeQuest.com, Common Application, early admission, early decision. *Application fee:* $25. *Required:* essay or personal statement; high school transcript; minimum 2.0 GPA; 2 letters of recommendation.

Standardized tests *Admission: Required:* ACT.

Significant dates *Application deadlines:* 8/15 (freshmen), 8/15 (transfers). *Financial aid deadline priority date:* 7/1.

Freshman Application Contact Mr. Eric Etchison, Director of Admissions, Central Baptist College, 1501 College Avenue, Conway, AR 72032-6470. **Phone:** 501-329-6872 Ext. 167. **Toll-free phone:** 800-205-6872. **E-mail:** eetchison@admin.cbc.edu

Visit CollegeQuest.com for information on majors offered and athletics.

HARDING UNIVERSITY
Searcy, Arkansas

 Apply at CollegeQuest.com

- **Independent**, comprehensive, founded 1924, affiliated with Church of Christ
- **Degrees** bachelor's and master's
- **Small-town** 200-acre campus with easy access to Little Rock
- **Coed**, 3,752 undergraduate students, 94% full-time, 55% women, 45% men
- **Moderately difficult** entrance level, 80% of applicants were admitted
- **17:1 student-to-undergraduate faculty ratio**
- **56% graduate** in 6 years or less
- **$8472 tuition** and fees
- **$8349 average financial aid** package, $22,420 average indebtedness upon graduation, $74.6 million endowment

Located in the beautiful foothills of the Ozark Mountains, Harding is one of America's more highly regarded private universities. At Harding, students build lifetime friendships and, upon graduation, are highly recruited. Harding's Christian environment and challenging academic program develop students who can compete and succeed.

Students *Undergraduates:* 3,530 full-time, 222 part-time. Students come from 50 states and territories, 34 other countries. *The most frequently chosen baccalaureate fields are:* business/marketing, education, health professions and related sciences. *Graduate:* 224 in graduate degree programs.

From out-of-state	74%	Reside on campus	84%
Age 25 or older	7%	Transferred in	5%
International students	4%	African Americans	4%
Asian Americans/Pacific Islanders	1%	Hispanic Americans	1%
Native Americans	1%		

Faculty 266 (76% full-time), 61% with terminal degrees.

Expenses (1999–2000) *Comprehensive fee:* $12,722 includes full-time tuition ($8272), mandatory fees ($200), and room and board ($4250). *College room only:* $1998. Room and board charges vary according to board plan and housing facility. *Part-time tuition:* $258 per semester hour. *Part-time fees:* $10 per semester hour. Part-time tuition and fees vary according to course load. *Payment plans:* tuition prepayment, installment. *Waivers:* senior citizens and employees or children of employees.

Library Brackett Library plus 1 other. *Operations spending 1999–2000:* $1.2 million. *Collection:* 489,291 titles, 1,330 serial subscriptions, 2,797 audiovisual materials.

College life *Housing:* on-campus residence required through senior year. *Options:* men-only, women-only. *Social organizations:* local fraternities, local sororities; 56% of eligible men and 46% of eligible women are members. *Most popular organizations:* University Singers, RENEW–environmental group, JOY, concert choir, Omicron Delta Kappa.

Campus security 24-hour emergency response devices and patrols.

After graduation 240 organizations recruited on campus 1997–98. 90% of class of 1998 had job offers within 6 months. *Career center:* 2 full-time, 9 part-time personnel. Services include job fairs, resume preparation, resume referral, career counseling, careers library, job bank, job interviews. *Graduate education:* 25% of class of 1999 went directly to graduate and professional school: 9% education, 7% graduate arts and sciences, 3% business, 2% medicine, 2% theology, 1% dentistry, 1% law.

Freshmen 1,552 applied, 1,241 admitted, 940 enrolled. 13 National Merit Scholars, 45 valedictorians.

Average high school GPA	3.3	SAT verbal scores above 500	N/R
SAT math scores above 500	N/R	ACT above 18	90%
From top 10% of their h.s. class	35%	From top quarter	60%
From top half	87%	1998 freshmen returning in 1999	76%

Application *Options:* eApply at www.CollegeQuest.com, Common Application, electronic application, early admission, deferred entrance. *Application fee:* $25. *Required:* high school transcript; 2 letters of recommendation; interview.

Standardized tests *Admission: Required:* SAT I or ACT.

Significant dates *Application deadlines:* 7/1 (freshmen), 7/1 (transfers). *Financial aid deadline:* continuous.

Freshman Application Contact
Mr. Mike Williams, Assistant Vice President of Admissions, Harding University, Box 11255, Searcy, AR 72149-0001. **Phone:** 501-279-4407. **Toll-free phone:** 800-477-4407. **Fax:** 501-279-4865. **E-mail:** admissions@harding.edu

Visit CollegeQuest.com for information on majors offered and athletics. College video available at CollegeQuest.com.

■ *See page 1764 for a narrative description.*

HENDERSON STATE UNIVERSITY
Arkadelphia, Arkansas

- **State-supported**, comprehensive, founded 1890
- **Degrees** associate, bachelor's, and master's
- **Small-town** 135-acre campus with easy access to Little Rock
- **Coed**, 2,982 undergraduate students, 89% full-time, 55% women, 45% men
- **Moderately difficult** entrance level, 93% of applicants were admitted
- **16:1 student-to-undergraduate faculty ratio**
- **$2488 tuition** and fees (in-state); $4768 (out-of-state)
- **$5426 average financial aid** package, $13,000 average indebtedness upon graduation, $5.2 million endowment

Students *Undergraduates:* 2,658 full-time, 324 part-time. Students come from 31 states and territories, 30 other countries. *The most frequently chosen baccalaureate fields are:* business/marketing, education, social sciences and history. *Graduate:* 386 in graduate degree programs.

From out-of-state	9%	Reside on campus	28%
Age 25 or older	18%	Transferred in	10%
International students	2%	African Americans	15%
Asian Americans/Pacific Islanders	0.5%	Hispanic Americans	1%
Native Americans	1%		

Faculty 227 (63% full-time), 53% with terminal degrees.

Expenses (1999–2000) *One-time required fee:* $20. *Tuition, state resident:* full-time $2280; part-time $95 per semester hour. *Tuition, nonresident:* full-time $4560; part-time $190 per semester hour. *Required fees:* full-time $208; $2 per semester hour; $50 per term part-time. Full-time tuition and fees vary according to course load. Part-time tuition and fees vary according to course load. *College room and board:* $2976. Room and board charges vary according to board plan and housing facility. *Waivers:* senior citizens and employees or children of employees.

Library Huie Library. *Operations spending 1999–2000:* $969,813. *Collection:* 209,509 titles, 1,525 serial subscriptions, 17,703 audiovisual materials.

College life *Housing:* on-campus residence required in freshman year. *Options:* coed, men-only, women-only. *Social organizations:* national fraternities, national sororities; 11% of eligible men and 13% of eligible women are members. *Most popular organizations:* Heart and Key, Student Government Association, Residence Hall Association.

Campus security 24-hour patrols, controlled dormitory access.

After graduation 80 organizations recruited on campus 1997–98. *Career center:* 2 full-time personnel. Services include job fairs, resume preparation, interview workshops, resume referral, career/interest testing, career counseling, job bank, job interviews.

Freshmen 1,171 applied, 1,089 admitted, 568 enrolled.

Average high school GPA	3.23	SAT verbal scores above 500	46%
SAT math scores above 500	77%	ACT above 18	92%
From top 10% of their h.s. class	17%	From top quarter	44%
From top half	80%	1998 freshmen returning in 1999	67%

Application *Options:* electronic application, deferred entrance. *Application fee:* $0. *Required:* high school transcript. *Required for some:* essay or personal statement; 3 letters of recommendation. *Recommended:* minimum 2.5 GPA.

Standardized tests *Admission: Required:* SAT I or ACT. *Recommended:* ACT.

Significant dates *Application deadlines:* rolling (freshmen), rolling (transfers). *Financial aid deadline:* 6/1.

Freshman Application Contact
Ms. Vikita Hardwrick, Director of University Relations/Admissions, Henderson State University, 1100 Henderson Street, PO Box 7560, Arkadelphia, AR 71999-0001. **Phone:** 870-230-5028. **Toll-free phone:** 800-228-7333. **Fax:** 870-230-5144. **E-mail:** lancask@hsu.edu

Visit CollegeQuest.com for information on majors offered and athletics.

HENDRIX COLLEGE
Conway, Arkansas

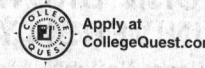

- **Independent United Methodist**, 4-year, founded 1876
- **Degree** bachelor's
- **Suburban** 158-acre campus
- **Coed**, 1,143 undergraduate students, 98% full-time, 54% women, 46% men
- **Very difficult** entrance level, 88% of applicants were admitted
- **14:1 student-to-undergraduate faculty ratio**
- **58% graduate** in 6 years or less
- **$11,615 tuition** and fees
- **$11,601 average financial aid** package, $123.4 million endowment

Students *Undergraduates:* 1,123 full-time, 20 part-time. Students come from 39 states and territories, 10 other countries. *The most frequently chosen baccalaureate fields are:* biological/life sciences, psychology, social sciences and history. *Graduate:* 4 in graduate degree programs.

From out-of-state	32%	Reside on campus	78%
Age 25 or older	0.01%	Transferred in	3%
International students	1%	African Americans	5%
Asian Americans/Pacific Islanders	4%	Hispanic Americans	2%
Native Americans	1%		

Faculty 86 (93% full-time), 99% with terminal degrees.

Expenses (1999–2000) *Comprehensive fee:* $16,030 includes full-time tuition ($11,440), mandatory fees ($175), and room and board ($4415). Room and board charges vary according to housing facility. *Part-time tuition:* $1270 per course. *Part-time fees:* $15 per term part-time. Additional part-time mandatory fees per term: $55 for fall term, $35 for winter and spring terms. *Payment plan:* installment. *Waivers:* employees or children of employees.

Library Olin C. and Marjorie H. Bailey Library. *Operations spending 1999–2000:* $766,579. *Collection:* 146,294 titles, 704 serial subscriptions, 4,965 audiovisual materials.

Arkansas

Hendrix College (continued)

College life *Housing:* on-campus residence required through senior year. *Options:* coed, men-only, women-only. *Most popular organizations:* Volunteer Action Center, Sophomore Council, Young Democrats, Big Buddy, Social Committee.

Campus security 24-hour emergency response devices and patrols, late-night transport-escort service, controlled dormitory access.

After graduation 76 organizations recruited on campus 1997–98. 61% of class of 1998 had job offers within 6 months. *Career center:* 2 full-time personnel. Services include job fairs, resume preparation, interview workshops, resume referral, career/interest testing, career counseling, careers library, job bank, job interviews.

Freshmen 962 applied, 844 admitted, 369 enrolled. 24 National Merit Scholars, 27 valedictorians.

Average high school GPA	3.7	SAT verbal scores above 500	95%
SAT math scores above 500	93%	ACT above 18	100%
From top 10% of their h.s. class	45%	From top quarter	75%
From top half	94%	1998 freshmen returning in 1999	86%

Application *Options:* eApply at www.CollegeQuest.com, Common Application, electronic application, early admission, deferred entrance. *Application fee:* $25. *Required:* essay or personal statement; high school transcript. *Required for some:* 1 letter of recommendation; interview.

Standardized tests *Admission: Required:* SAT I or ACT.

Significant dates *Application deadlines:* rolling (freshmen), rolling (transfers). *Financial aid deadline priority date:* 2/16.

Freshman Application Contact
Mr. Rock Jones, Vice President for Enrollment, Hendrix College, 1600 Washington Avenue, Conway, AR 72032. **Phone:** 501-450-1362. **Toll-free phone:** 800-277-9017. **Fax:** 501-450-3843. **E-mail:** adm@hendrix.edu

Visit CollegeQuest.com for information on majors offered and athletics. Electronic viewbook available at CollegeQuest.com.

■ *See page 1782 for a narrative description.*

JOHN BROWN UNIVERSITY
Siloam Springs, Arkansas

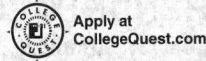
Apply at CollegeQuest.com

- **Independent interdenominational**, comprehensive, founded 1919
- **Degrees** associate, bachelor's, and master's
- **Small-town** 200-acre campus
- **Coed**, 1,368 undergraduate students, 97% full-time, 51% women, 49% men
- **Moderately difficult** entrance level, 80% of applicants were admitted
- **16:1 student-to-undergraduate faculty ratio**
- **47% graduate** in 6 years or less
- **$11,492 tuition** and fees
- **$9323 average financial aid** package, $12,260 average indebtedness upon graduation, $37.3 million endowment

Students *Undergraduates:* 1,324 full-time, 44 part-time. Students come from 43 states and territories, 33 other countries. *The most frequently chosen baccalaureate fields are:* business/marketing, education, philosophy. *Graduate:* 96 in graduate degree programs.

From out-of-state	68%	Reside on campus	69%
Age 25 or older	24%	Transferred in	6%
International students	9%	African Americans	1%
Asian Americans/Pacific Islanders	1%	Hispanic Americans	2%
Native Americans	1%		

Faculty 102 (75% full-time).

Expenses (2000–2001) *Comprehensive fee:* $15,970 includes full-time tuition ($11,022), mandatory fees ($470), and room and board ($4478). Room and board charges vary according to board plan and housing facility. Part-time tuition and fees vary according to course load and program. *Payment plan:* installment. *Waivers:* minority students, adult students, senior citizens, and employees or children of employees.

Library Arutunoff Learning Resource Center plus 4 others. *Operations spending 1999–2000:* $433,171. *Collection:* 93,190 titles, 1,580 serial subscriptions, 8,310 audiovisual materials.

College life *Housing:* on-campus residence required through junior year. *Options:* coed, men-only, women-only. *Most popular organizations:* Student Government Association, Student Ministries Organization, Student Missionary Fellowship, African Heritage Fellowship.

Campus security 24-hour emergency response devices and patrols, late-night transport-escort service.

After graduation 50 organizations recruited on campus 1997–98. 84% of class of 1998 had job offers within 6 months. *Career center:* 2 full-time personnel. Services include job fairs, resume preparation, career counseling, careers library, job bank. *Graduate education:* 28% of class of 1999 went directly to graduate and professional school: 11% business, 9% education, 2% law, 2% theology, 1% dentistry, 1% engineering, 1% graduate arts and sciences, 1% medicine.

Freshmen 629 applied, 502 admitted, 271 enrolled. 2 National Merit Scholars, 11 class presidents, 21 valedictorians, 42 student government officers.

Average high school GPA	3.49	SAT verbal scores above 500	76%
SAT math scores above 500	80%	ACT above 18	93%
From top 10% of their h.s. class	24%	From top quarter	45%
From top half	96%	1998 freshmen returning in 1999	80%

Application *Options:* eApply at www.CollegeQuest.com, Common Application, deferred entrance. *Application fee:* $25. *Required:* essay or personal statement; high school transcript; minimum 3.0 GPA; 2 letters of recommendation. *Recommended:* interview.

Standardized tests *Admission: Required:* SAT I or ACT.

Significant dates *Application deadlines:* 3/1 (freshmen), 3/1 (transfers). *Notification:* 5/1 (freshmen). *Financial aid deadline priority date:* 3/1.

Freshman Application Contact
Ms. Karyn Byrne, Application Coordinator, John Brown University, 200 West University Street, Siloam Springs, AR 72761-2121. **Phone:** 501-524-7454. **Toll-free phone:** 877-JBU-INFO. **Fax:** 501-524-9548. **E-mail:** jbuinfo@acc.jbu.edu

Visit CollegeQuest.com for information on majors offered and athletics. College video available at CollegeQuest.com.

■ *See page 1842 for a narrative description.*

LYON COLLEGE
Batesville, Arkansas

Apply at CollegeQuest.com

- **Independent Presbyterian**, 4-year, founded 1872
- **Degree** bachelor's
- **Small-town** 136-acre campus
- **Coed**, 462 undergraduate students, 90% full-time, 58% women, 42% men
- **Very difficult** entrance level, 81% of applicants were admitted
- **10:1 student-to-undergraduate faculty ratio**
- **45.7% graduate** in 6 years or less
- **$10,622 tuition** and fees
- **$11,633 average financial aid** package, $13,610 average indebtedness upon graduation, $53.8 million endowment

The University, ideally located between Palm Beach and Fort Lauderdale, enrolls approximately 2,000 students. The faculty-student ratio of 1:19 provides an academic environment in which the well-being and development of the individual are assured. The University currently hosts students from 38 states and 73 nations, creating a community in which each student is provided with a rich multicultural experience and global awareness.

Students *Undergraduates:* 416 full-time, 46 part-time. Students come from 22 states and territories, 21 other countries. *The most frequently chosen baccalaureate fields are:* biological/life sciences, English, social sciences and history.

From out-of-state	17%	Reside on campus	80%
Age 25 or older	11%	Transferred in	6%
International students	7%	African Americans	4%
Asian Americans/Pacific Islanders	1%	Hispanic Americans	1%
Native Americans	1%		

Faculty 54 (78% full-time), 72% with terminal degrees.

Expenses (1999–2000) *One-time required fee:* $200. *Comprehensive fee:* $15,325 includes full-time tuition ($10,272), mandatory fees ($350), and room and board ($4703). *College room only:* $1935. *Part-time tuition:* $82 per credit hour. Part-time tuition and fees vary according to course load. *Payment plan:* installment. *Waivers:* employees or children of employees.

Library Mabee-Simpson Library. *Operations spending 1999–2000:* $443,772. *Collection:* 138,674 titles, 964 serial subscriptions, 4,344 audiovisual materials.
College life *Housing:* on-campus residence required through senior year. *Options:* men-only, women-only. *Social organizations:* national fraternities, national sororities, local sororities; 19% of eligible men and 34% of eligible women are members. *Most popular organizations:* Lyon Ambassadors, Baptist Student Union, student activities council, student government association, P.A.R.T.Y. (alcohol education).
Campus security 24-hour patrols, late-night transport-escort service.
After graduation 5 organizations recruited on campus 1997–98. 48% of class of 1998 had job offers within 6 months. *Career center:* 2 part-time personnel. Services include job fairs, resume preparation, career counseling, careers library, job bank. *Graduate education:* 27% of class of 1999 went directly to graduate and professional school: 7% medicine, 6% graduate arts and sciences, 5% law, 2% education, 1% business, 1% dentistry, 1% engineering, 1% theology.
Freshmen 470 applied, 380 admitted, 145 enrolled. 16 valedictorians.

Average high school GPA	3.72	SAT verbal scores above 500	62%
SAT math scores above 500	71%	ACT above 18	100%
From top 10% of their h.s. class	43%	From top quarter	79%
From top half	97%	1998 freshmen returning in 1999	74%

Application *Options:* eApply at www.CollegeQuest.com, electronic application, early admission, deferred entrance. *Application fee:* $25. *Required:* essay or personal statement; high school transcript; 1 letter of recommendation. *Recommended:* minimum 2.25 GPA; interview.
Standardized tests *Admission: Required:* SAT I or ACT.
Significant dates *Application deadlines:* rolling (freshmen), rolling (transfers). *Financial aid deadline priority date:* 2/15.
Freshman Application Contact
Ms. Kristine Penix, Director of Admissions, Lyon College, PO Box 2317, Batesville, AR 72503-2317. **Phone:** 870-698-4250. **Toll-free phone:** 800-423-2542. **Fax:** 870-698-4622. **E-mail:** admissions@lyon.edu
Visit CollegeQuest.com for information on majors offered and athletics. College video and electronic viewbook available at CollegeQuest.com.

OUACHITA BAPTIST UNIVERSITY
Arkadelphia, Arkansas

- **Independent Baptist**, 4-year, founded 1886
- **Degrees** associate and bachelor's
- **Small-town** 84-acre campus with easy access to Little Rock
- **Coed**, 1,638 undergraduate students, 94% full-time, 55% women, 45% men
- **Moderately difficult** entrance level, 71% of applicants were admitted
- **13:1 student-to-undergraduate faculty ratio**
- **51.7% graduate** in 6 years or less
- **$9010 tuition** and fees
- **$10,614 average financial aid** package, $13,865 average indebtedness upon graduation, $40.6 million endowment

Students *Undergraduates:* 1,538 full-time, 100 part-time. Students come from 36 states and territories, 58 other countries. *The most frequently chosen baccalaureate fields are:* education, business/marketing, philosophy.

From out-of-state	44%	Reside on campus	83%
Age 25 or older	4%	Transferred in	3%
International students	4%	African Americans	4%
Asian Americans/Pacific Islanders	0.4%	Hispanic Americans	1%
Native Americans	0.4%		

Faculty 147 (70% full-time), 50% with terminal degrees.
Expenses (1999–2000) *Comprehensive fee:* $12,460 includes full-time tuition ($8850), mandatory fees ($160), and room and board ($3450). Room and board charges vary according to board plan and housing facility. *Part-time tuition:* $260 per semester hour. *Payment plan:* installment. *Waivers:* employees or children of employees.
Library Riley–Hickinbotham Library plus 1 other. *Operations spending 1999–2000:* $587,639. *Collection:* 119,437 titles, 1,862 serial subscriptions, 8,043 audiovisual materials.
College life *Housing:* on-campus residence required through senior year. *Options:* men-only, women-only. *Social organizations:* local fraternities, local sororities; 20% of eligible men and 25% of eligible women are members. *Most popular organizations:* Phi Beta Lambda, SELF, Student Education Association, Student Foundation, International Club.
Campus security 24-hour emergency response devices and patrols, controlled dormitory access.
After graduation 20 organizations recruited on campus 1997–98. 60% of class of 1998 had job offers within 6 months. *Career center:* 1 full-time, 2 part-time personnel. Services include job fairs, resume preparation, interview workshops, resume referral, career/interest testing, career counseling, careers library, job interviews. *Graduate education:* 10% of class of 1999 went directly to graduate and professional school.
Freshmen 931 applied, 665 admitted, 448 enrolled. 3 National Merit Scholars, 15 valedictorians.

Average high school GPA	3.47	SAT verbal scores above 500	73%
SAT math scores above 500	70%	ACT above 18	95%
From top 10% of their h.s. class	31%	From top quarter	64%
From top half	88%	1998 freshmen returning in 1999	75%

Application *Options:* early admission, deferred entrance. *Application fee:* $25. *Required:* high school transcript; minimum 2.5 GPA. *Recommended:* interview.
Standardized tests *Admission: Required:* SAT I or ACT.
Significant dates *Application deadlines:* 8/15 (freshmen), 8/15 (transfers). *Financial aid deadline:* 6/1. *Priority date:* 2/15.
Freshman Application Contact
Mrs. Rebecca Jones, Director of Admissions Counseling, Ouachita Baptist University, 410 Ouachita Street, Arkadelphia, AR 71998-0001. **Phone:** 870-245-5110. **Toll-free phone:** 800-342-5628. **Fax:** 870-245-5500. **E-mail:** jonesj@sigma.obu.edu
Visit CollegeQuest.com for information on majors offered and athletics. College video available at CollegeQuest.com.

PHILANDER SMITH COLLEGE
Little Rock, Arkansas

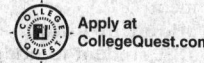

- **Independent United Methodist**, 4-year, founded 1877
- **Degree** bachelor's
- **Urban** 25-acre campus
- **Coed**, 932 undergraduate students, 74% full-time, 61% women, 39% men
- **Noncompetitive** entrance level, 100% of applicants were admitted
- **16:1 student-to-undergraduate faculty ratio**
- **18.4% graduate** in 6 years or less
- **$3808 tuition** and fees
- **$5 million endowment**

Students *Undergraduates:* 692 full-time, 240 part-time. Students come from 13 states and territories, 18 other countries. *The most frequently chosen baccalaureate fields are:* business/marketing, psychology, social sciences and history.

From out-of-state	8%	Reside on campus	17%
Age 25 or older	33%	Transferred in	9%
International students	4%	African Americans	95%

Faculty 70 (57% full-time), 51% with terminal degrees.
Expenses (1999–2000) *Comprehensive fee:* $6554 includes full-time tuition ($3616), mandatory fees ($192), and room and board ($2746). *College room only:* $1334. Full-time tuition and fees vary according to class time, course load, location, and program. *Part-time tuition:* $140 per credit. *Part-time fees:* $5 per credit. Part-time tuition and fees vary according to class time and course load. *Payment plans:* installment, deferred payment. *Waivers:* employees or children of employees.
Library M. L. Harris Library. *Operations spending 1999–2000:* $95,552. *Collection:* 60,000 titles, 280 serial subscriptions, 196 audiovisual materials.
College life *Housing:* on-campus residence required in freshman year. *Options:* men-only, women-only. *Social organizations:* national fraternities, national sororities; 8% of eligible men and 8% of eligible women are members. *Most popular organizations:* Student Government Association, Pre-Alumni Council, Student Christian, Delta Sigma Theta Sorority, Inc.
Campus security 24-hour patrols.
After graduation 78 organizations recruited on campus 1997–98. *Career center:* 2 full-time personnel. Services include job fairs, resume preparation,

Arkansas

Philander Smith College (continued)
resume referral, career counseling, careers library, job interviews. ***Graduate education:*** 8% of class of 1999 went directly to graduate and professional school.

Freshmen 339 applied, 339 admitted, 170 enrolled.

Average high school GPA	2.42	SAT verbal scores above 500	0%
SAT math scores above 500	0%	ACT above 18	24%
From top 10% of their h.s. class	4%	From top quarter	23%
From top half	55%	1998 freshmen returning in 1999	61%

Application *Options:* eApply at www.CollegeQuest.com, Common Application, electronic application, deferred entrance. *Application fee:* $10. *Required:* high school transcript.
Standardized tests *Placement: Required:* SAT I or ACT
Significant dates *Application deadlines:* rolling (freshmen), rolling (transfers). *Financial aid deadline priority date:* 4/15.
Freshman Application Contact
Mrs. Arnella Hayes, Admission Officer, Philander Smith College, 812 West 13th Street, Little Rock, AR 72202-3718. **Phone:** 501-370-5310. **Toll-free phone:** 800-446-6772. **Fax:** 501-370-5225. **E-mail:** admissions@philander.edu
Visit CollegeQuest.com for information on majors offered and athletics. College video and electronic viewbook available at CollegeQuest.com.

SOUTHERN ARKANSAS UNIVERSITY—MAGNOLIA
Magnolia, Arkansas

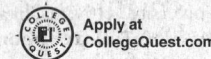

- **State-supported**, comprehensive, founded 1909
- **Degrees** associate, bachelor's, and master's
- **Small-town** 781-acre campus
- **Coed**, 2,465 undergraduate students, 91% full-time, 55% women, 45% men
- **Minimally difficult** entrance level, 92% of applicants were admitted
- **18:1 student-to-undergraduate faculty ratio**
- **$2232 tuition** and fees (in-state); $3360 (out-of-state)
- **$5047 average financial aid** package, $9259 average indebtedness upon graduation, $14 million endowment

Part of Southern Arkansas University System.
Students *Undergraduates:* 2,240 full-time, 225 part-time. Students come from 28 states and territories, 33 other countries. *The most frequently chosen baccalaureate fields are:* business/marketing, education, psychology. *Graduate:* 269 in graduate degree programs.

From out-of-state	23%	Reside on campus	33%
Age 25 or older	22%	Transferred in	5%
International students	5%	African Americans	22%
Asian Americans/Pacific Islanders	0.3%	Hispanic Americans	1%
Native Americans	1%		

Faculty 161 (74% full-time), 50% with terminal degrees.
Expenses (1999–2000) *Tuition, state resident:* full-time $2112; part-time $88 per credit hour. *Tuition, nonresident:* full-time $3240; part-time $135 per credit hour. *Required fees:* full-time $120; $4 per credit hour. Full-time tuition and fees vary according to course load. Part-time tuition and fees vary according to course load. *College room and board:* $2800. *Payment plans:* installment, deferred payment. *Waivers:* children of alumni, senior citizens, and employees or children of employees.
Library Magale Library. *Operations spending 1999–2000:* $754,645. *Collection:* 146,367 titles, 992 serial subscriptions, 7,611 audiovisual materials.
College life *Housing:* on-campus residence required through junior year. *Options:* men-only, women-only. *Social organizations:* national fraternities, national sororities; 13% of eligible men and 13% of eligible women are members. *Most popular organizations:* Student Government Association, IMPACT.
Campus security 24-hour emergency response devices, late-night transport-escort service, controlled dormitory access.
After graduation 65 organizations recruited on campus 1997–98. *Career center:* 1 full-time, 4 part-time personnel. Services include job fairs, resume preparation, interview workshops, resume referral, career counseling, careers library, job bank, job interviews.

Freshmen 977 applied, 901 admitted, 566 enrolled.

Average high school GPA	3.17	SAT verbal scores above 500	N/R
SAT math scores above 500	N/R	ACT above 18	78%
From top 10% of their h.s. class	12%	From top quarter	41%
From top half	74%	1998 freshmen returning in 1999	60%

Application *Options:* eApply at www.CollegeQuest.com, Common Application, early admission, deferred entrance. *Required:* high school transcript; ACT score of 19 or above, rank in upper 25% of high school class.
Standardized tests *Admission: Required:* ACT.
Significant dates *Application deadlines:* 8/15 (freshmen), 8/15 (transfers). *Financial aid deadline priority date:* 7/1.
Freshman Application Contact
Mr. James E. Whittington, Director of Admissions, Southern Arkansas University–Magnolia, PO Box 9382, Magnolia, AR 71754-9382. **Phone:** 870-235-4040. **Fax:** 870-235-5005. **E-mail:** adsonny@saumag.edu
Visit CollegeQuest.com for information on majors offered and athletics.

UNIVERSITY OF ARKANSAS
Fayetteville, Arkansas

- **State-supported**, university, founded 1871
- **Degrees** bachelor's, master's, doctoral, and first professional
- **Suburban** 420-acre campus
- **Coed**, 11,978 undergraduate students, 87% full-time, 49% women, 51% men
- **Moderately difficult** entrance level, 88% of applicants were admitted
- **15:1 student-to-undergraduate faculty ratio**
- **43.3% graduate** in 6 years or less
- **$3334 tuition** and fees (in-state); $8318 (out-of-state)
- **$7191 average financial aid** package, $14,910 average indebtedness upon graduation, $220 million endowment

Part of University of Arkansas System.
Students *Undergraduates:* 10,441 full-time, 1,537 part-time. Students come from 50 states and territories, 106 other countries. *The most frequently chosen baccalaureate fields are:* business/marketing, engineering/engineering technologies, trade and industry. *Graduate:* 377 in professional programs, 2,550 in other graduate degree programs.

From out-of-state	9%	Reside on campus	23%
Age 25 or older	10%	Transferred in	9%
International students	3%	African Americans	7%
Asian Americans/Pacific Islanders	3%	Hispanic Americans	1%
Native Americans	2%		

Faculty 857 (93% full-time), 87% with terminal degrees.
Expenses (1999–2000) *Tuition, state resident:* full-time $2800; part-time $100 per credit hour. *Tuition, nonresident:* full-time $7784; part-time $278 per credit hour. *Required fees:* full-time $534. Full-time tuition and fees vary according to course load, degree level, program, and student level. Part-time tuition and fees vary according to course load, degree level, program, and student level. *College room and board:* $4225. Room and board charges vary according to board plan and housing facility. *Payment plan:* installment. *Waivers:* senior citizens and employees or children of employees.
Library David W. Mullins Library plus 5 others. *Operations spending 1999–2000:* $6 million. *Collection:* 643,468 titles, 15,431 serial subscriptions, 26,673 audiovisual materials.
College life *Housing:* on-campus residence required in freshman year. *Option:* coed. *Social organizations:* national fraternities, national sororities; 15% of eligible men and 20% of eligible women are members. *Most popular organizations:* University Programs, Arkansas Booster Club, Associated Student Government, Black Students Association, Alpha Phi Omega.
Campus security 24-hour emergency response devices and patrols, student patrols, late-night transport-escort service, controlled dormitory access, RAD (Rape Aggression Defense program).
After graduation 200 organizations recruited on campus 1997–98. *Career center:* 11 full-time, 3 part-time personnel. Services include job fairs, resume preparation, resume referral, career counseling, careers library, job bank, job interviews. *Major awards:* 2 Fulbright Scholars.
Freshmen 4,452 applied, 3,907 admitted, 2,268 enrolled. 38 National Merit Scholars, 166 valedictorians.

Arkansas

Average high school GPA	3.51	SAT verbal scores above 500	77%
SAT math scores above 500	83%	ACT above 18	96%
From top 10% of their h.s. class	36%	From top quarter	66%
From top half	90%	1998 freshmen returning in 1999	74%

Application *Options:* eApply at www.CollegeQuest.com, electronic application, early admission, early action. *Application fee:* $30. *Required:* essay or personal statement; high school transcript. *Required for some:* essay or personal statement; high school transcript; interview. *Recommended:* minimum 3.0 GPA; 1 letter of recommendation.

Standardized tests *Admission: Required:* SAT I or ACT.

Significant dates *Application deadlines:* 2/15 (freshmen), 8/15 (transfers). *Early action:* 11/15. *Notification:* 12/15 (early action). **Financial aid deadline priority date:** 3/15.

Freshman Application Contact
Ms. Maribeth Lynes, Director of Undergraduate Recruitment, University of Arkansas, 200 Silas H. Hunt Hall, Fayetteville, AR 72701-1201. **Phone:** 501-575-5346. **Toll-free phone:** 800-377-8632. **Fax:** 501-575-7515. **E-mail:** uafadmis@comp.uark.edu

Visit CollegeQuest.com for information on majors offered and athletics. College video and electronic viewbook available at CollegeQuest.com.

■ *See page 2694 for a narrative description.*

UNIVERSITY OF ARKANSAS AT LITTLE ROCK
Little Rock, Arkansas

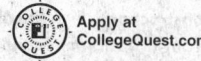

Apply at CollegeQuest.com

- **State-supported**, university, founded 1927
- **Degrees** associate, bachelor's, master's, doctoral, first professional, and postbachelor's certificates
- **Urban** 150-acre campus
- **Coed**, 8,383 undergraduate students
- **Minimally difficult** entrance level, 62% of applicants were admitted
- **$2820 tuition** and fees (in-state); $6636 (out-of-state)
- **$7.6 million endowment**

Part of University of Arkansas System.

Students *Undergraduates:* Students come from 45 states and territories, 43 other countries.

From out-of-state	4%	Reside on campus	3%
Age 25 or older	35%		

Faculty 701 (53% full-time).

Expenses (1999–2000) *Tuition, state resident:* full-time $2424; part-time $101 per credit hour. *Tuition, nonresident:* full-time $6240; part-time $260 per credit hour. *Required fees:* full-time $396; $16 per credit hour. *College room and board:* room only: $2500. Room and board charges vary according to housing facility. *Payment plan:* deferred payment. *Waivers:* senior citizens and employees or children of employees.

Library Ottenheimer Library plus 1 other. *Operations spending 1999–2000:* $2.7 million. *Collection:* 3,998 serial subscriptions.

College life *Housing: Option:* coed. *Social organizations:* national fraternities, national sororities; 2% of eligible men and 2% of eligible women are members.

Campus security 24-hour emergency response devices, student patrols, late-night transport-escort service.

After graduation *Career center:* 5 full-time personnel. Services include job fairs, resume preparation, career counseling, careers library, job bank, job interviews.

Freshmen 2,048 applied, 1,269 admitted.

SAT verbal scores above 500	N/R	SAT math scores above 500	N/R
ACT above 18	N/R	1998 freshmen returning in 1999	63%

Application *Options:* eApply at www.CollegeQuest.com, early admission, deferred entrance. *Application fee:* $0. *Required:* high school transcript; minimum 2.5 GPA; proof of immunization.

Standardized tests *Placement: Required:* SAT I or ACT

Significant dates *Application deadlines:* rolling (freshmen), rolling (transfers).

Freshman Application Contact
Office of Admissions and Records, University of Arkansas at Little Rock, 2801 South University Avenue, Little Rock, AR 72204-1099. **Phone:** 501-569-3127. **Toll-free phone:** 800-482-8892. **Fax:** 501-569-8915. **E-mail:** dspine@ualr.edu

Visit CollegeQuest.com for information on majors offered and athletics. College video available at CollegeQuest.com.

UNIVERSITY OF ARKANSAS AT MONTICELLO
Monticello, Arkansas

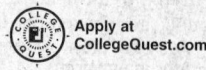

Apply at CollegeQuest.com

- **State-supported**, comprehensive, founded 1909
- **Degrees** associate, bachelor's, and master's
- **Small-town** 400-acre campus
- **Coed**, 2,094 undergraduate students
- **Noncompetitive** entrance level, 57% of applicants were admitted
- **17:1 student-to-undergraduate faculty ratio**
- **26% graduate** in 6 years or less
- **$2530 tuition** and fees (in-state); $5290 (out-of-state)

Part of University of Arkansas System.

Students *Undergraduates:* Students come from 20 states and territories, 2 other countries. *The most frequently chosen baccalaureate fields are:* business/marketing, agriculture, education.

From out-of-state	9%	Reside on campus	25%
Age 25 or older	22%	International students	0.1%
African Americans	22%	Asian Americans/Pacific Islanders	1%
Hispanic Americans	2%	Native Americans	1%

Faculty 136 (82% full-time).

Expenses (1999–2000) *Tuition, state resident:* full-time $2100; part-time $70 per hour. *Tuition, nonresident:* full-time $4860; part-time $162 per hour. *Required fees:* full-time $430; $14 per hour; $5 per term part-time. Full-time tuition and fees vary according to reciprocity agreements. Part-time tuition and fees vary according to reciprocity agreements. *College room and board:* $2580. Room and board charges vary according to board plan and housing facility. *Waivers:* senior citizens and employees or children of employees.

Library *Collection:* 126,229 titles, 862 serial subscriptions.

College life *Housing: Options:* men-only, women-only. *Social organizations:* national fraternities, national sororities; 20% of eligible men and 22% of eligible women are members.

Campus security 24-hour emergency response devices and patrols.

After graduation *Career center:* Services include career counseling.

Freshmen 994 applied, 567 admitted.

SAT verbal scores above 500	N/R	SAT math scores above 500	N/R
ACT above 18	N/R	1998 freshmen returning in 1999	55%

Application *Options:* eApply at www.CollegeQuest.com, early admission, deferred entrance. *Application fee:* $0. *Required:* high school transcript; proof of immunization.

Standardized tests *Placement: Required:* SAT I or ACT. *Recommended:* ACT.

Significant dates *Application deadlines:* 8/1 (freshmen), 8/1 (transfers). *Financial aid deadline:* continuous.

Freshman Application Contact
Mary Whiting, Director of Admissions, University of Arkansas at Monticello, PO Box 3600, Monticello, AR 71656. **Phone:** 870-460-1026. **Toll-free phone:** 800-844-1826. **Fax:** 870-460-1321. **E-mail:** admissions@uamont.edu

Visit CollegeQuest.com for information on majors offered and athletics. College video available at CollegeQuest.com.

UNIVERSITY OF ARKANSAS AT PINE BLUFF
Pine Bluff, Arkansas

- **State-supported**, comprehensive, founded 1873
- **Degrees** associate, bachelor's, and master's
- **Urban** 327-acre campus

Arkansas

University of Arkansas at Pine Bluff (continued)
- **Coed**, 2,863 undergraduate students, 90% full-time, 55% women, 45% men
- **Minimally difficult** entrance level, 71% of applicants were admitted
- **15:1 student-to-undergraduate faculty ratio**
- **25% graduate** in 6 years or less
- **$2620 tuition** and fees (in-state); $5322 (out-of-state)

Part of University of Arkansas System.

Students *Undergraduates:* 2,587 full-time, 276 part-time. Students come from 32 states and territories, 5 other countries. *The most frequently chosen baccalaureate fields are:* business/marketing, education, protective services/public administration. *Graduate:* 66 in graduate degree programs.

Age 25 or older	17%	International students	1%
African Americans	95%	Asian Americans/Pacific Islanders	0.2%
Hispanic Americans	0.2%	Native Americans	0.04%

Faculty 226 (77% full-time), 42% with terminal degrees.

Expenses (1999–2000) *One-time required fee:* $25. Tuition, state resident: full-time $2058; part-time $74 per semester hour. *Tuition, nonresident:* full-time $4760; part-time $170 per semester hour. *Required fees:* full-time $562; $14 per semester hour; $48 per term part-time. Full-time tuition and fees vary according to course load. Part-time tuition and fees vary according to course load. *College room and board:* $3940. Room and board charges vary according to board plan and housing facility. *Payment plan:* installment. *Waivers:* senior citizens and employees or children of employees.

Library *Collection:* 236,219 titles, 914 serial subscriptions.

College life *Housing: Option:* coed. *Social organizations:* national fraternities, national sororities, local fraternities, local sororities; 6% of eligible men and 6% of eligible women are members. *Most popular organizations:* Pre Alumni, Honors College, Alpha Kappa Alpha Sorority.

Campus security 24-hour emergency response devices.

After graduation 205 organizations recruited on campus 1997–98. 53% of class of 1998 had job offers within 6 months. *Career center:* 4 full-time personnel. Services include job fairs, resume preparation, resume referral, career counseling, careers library, job bank, job interviews. *Graduate education:* 15% of class of 1999 went directly to graduate and professional school.

Freshmen 1,550 applied, 1,108 admitted, 705 enrolled.

SAT verbal scores above 500	25%	SAT math scores above 500	25%
ACT above 18	30%	1998 freshmen returning in 1999	70%

Application *Options:* early admission, deferred entrance. *Required:* high school transcript; minimum 2.0 GPA.

Standardized tests *Placement: Required:* ACT

Significant dates *Application deadline:* 8/1 (freshmen). *Notification:* 8/10 (freshmen). *Financial aid deadline priority date:* 4/15.

Freshman Application Contact
Ms. Kwurly M. Floyd-Tate, Director of Admissions and Academic Records, University of Arkansas at Pine Bluff, UAPB Box 17, 1200 University Drive, Pine Bluff, AR 71601-2799. **Phone:** 870-543-8487. **Toll-free phone:** 800-264-6585. **Fax:** 870-543-2021.

Visit CollegeQuest.com for information on majors offered and athletics.

UNIVERSITY OF ARKANSAS FOR MEDICAL SCIENCES
Little Rock, Arkansas

- **State-supported**, upper-level, founded 1879
- **Degrees** associate, bachelor's, master's, doctoral, and first professional (bachelor's degree is upper-level)
- **Urban** 5-acre campus
- **Coed**, 549 undergraduate students
- **Very difficult** entrance level
- **$22.1 million endowment**

Part of University of Arkansas System.

Students

Age 25 or older	42%

Library Medical Sciences Library. *Operations spending 1999–2000:* $2.6 million. *Collection:* 183,975 titles, 1,567 serial subscriptions.

College life *Housing: Option:* coed.

Campus security 24-hour emergency response devices and patrols, late-night transport-escort service, controlled dormitory access.

Freshman Application Contact
Mr. Paul Carter, Assistant to the Vice Chancellor for Academic Affairs, University of Arkansas for Medical Sciences, 4301 West Markham-Slot 601, Little Rock, AR 72205-7199. **Phone:** 501-686-5454.

Visit CollegeQuest.com for information on majors offered and athletics.

UNIVERSITY OF CENTRAL ARKANSAS
Conway, Arkansas

- **State-supported**, comprehensive, founded 1907
- **Degrees** associate, bachelor's, master's, doctoral, and post-master's certificates
- **Small-town** 365-acre campus
- **Coed**, 7,800 undergraduate students, 88% full-time, 61% women, 39% men
- **Moderately difficult** entrance level, 62% of applicants were admitted
- **18:1 student-to-undergraduate faculty ratio**
- **34% graduate** in 6 years or less
- **$3402 tuition** and fees (in-state); $6144 (out-of-state)

UCA is a multipurpose university with Colleges of Business Administration, Education, Liberal Arts, Health and Applied Sciences, Fine Arts and Communication, and Natural Sciences and Mathematics. More than $100 million in construction, diversification of faculty, and a developing international program are major recent advancements. On-campus housing is available for 2,000 students.

Students *Undergraduates:* 6,852 full-time, 948 part-time. Students come from 36 states and territories, 51 other countries. *The most frequently chosen baccalaureate fields are:* business/marketing, education, health professions and related sciences. *Graduate:* 1,015 in graduate degree programs.

From out-of-state	4%	Reside on campus	22%
Age 25 or older	14%	Transferred in	7%
International students	3%	African Americans	13%
Asian Americans/Pacific Islanders	1%	Hispanic Americans	1%
Native Americans	1%		

Faculty 496 (76% full-time), 57% with terminal degrees.

Expenses (2000–2001) *Tuition, state resident:* full-time $2856; part-time $119 per credit hour. *Tuition, nonresident:* full-time $5598; part-time $234 per credit hour. *Required fees:* full-time $546; $20 per credit hour; $29 per term part-time. Part-time tuition and fees vary according to course load. *College room and board:* $3290; room only: $1860. Room and board charges vary according to board plan and housing facility. *Payment plan:* installment. *Waivers:* senior citizens and employees or children of employees.

Library Torreyson Library. *Operations spending 1999–2000:* $2.2 million. *Collection:* 414,709 titles, 2,561 serial subscriptions.

College life *Housing:* on-campus residence required in freshman year. *Options:* coed, men-only, women-only. *Social organizations:* national fraternities, national sororities; 10% of eligible men and 10% of eligible women are members. *Most popular organizations:* Student Government Association, Royal Rooters, student orientation staff, Ambassadors.

Campus security 24-hour emergency response devices and patrols, student patrols, late-night transport-escort service, controlled dormitory access, security personnel at entrances during evening hours.

After graduation 50 organizations recruited on campus 1997–98. *Career center:* 5 full-time, 7 part-time personnel. Services include job fairs, resume preparation, interview workshops, resume referral, career/interest testing, career counseling, careers library, job bank, job interviews.

Freshmen 3,689 applied, 2,300 admitted, 1,837 enrolled.

Average high school GPA	3.1	SAT verbal scores above 500	N/R
SAT math scores above 500	N/R	ACT above 18	93%
From top 10% of their h.s. class	27%	From top quarter	56%
From top half	82%	1998 freshmen returning in 1999	65%

Application *Options:* electronic application, early admission, deferred entrance. *Required:* high school transcript. *Required for some:* minimum 2.75 GPA.

Standardized tests *Admission: Required:* SAT I or ACT.

Significant dates *Application deadlines:* rolling (freshmen), rolling (transfers). *Financial aid deadline priority date:* 2/15.
Freshman Application Contact
Mr. Joe F. Darling, Director of Admissions, University of Central Arkansas, 201 Donaghey Avenue, Conway, AR 72035-0001. **Phone:** 501-450-5145. **Toll-free phone:** 800-243-8245. **Fax:** 501-450-5228. **E-mail:** admisson@ecom.uca.edu
Visit CollegeQuest.com for information on majors offered and athletics. College video available at CollegeQuest.com.

■ *See page 2704 for a narrative description.*

UNIVERSITY OF THE OZARKS
Clarksville, Arkansas

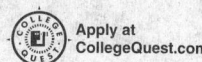

- **Independent Presbyterian**, 4-year, founded 1834
- **Degrees** associate and bachelor's
- **Small-town** 56-acre campus with easy access to Little Rock
- **Coed**, 596 undergraduate students, 93% full-time, 50% women, 50% men
- **Moderately difficult** entrance level, 78% of applicants were admitted
- **15:1** student-to-undergraduate faculty ratio
- **27.5% graduate** in 6 years or less
- **$8530 tuition** and fees
- **$9295 average financial aid** package, $15,000 average indebtedness upon graduation, $71,700 endowment

Students *Undergraduates:* Students come from 18 states and territories, 14 other countries. *The most frequently chosen baccalaureate fields are:* biological/life sciences, education, liberal arts/general studies.

From out-of-state	33%	Reside on campus	95%
Age 25 or older	6%	International students	14%
African Americans	2%	Asian Americans/Pacific Islanders	0.2%
Hispanic Americans	2%	Native Americans	3%

Faculty 46 (72% full-time), 63% with terminal degrees.
Expenses (1999–2000) *Comprehensive fee:* $12,454 includes full-time tuition ($8290), mandatory fees ($240), and room and board ($3924). *Part-time tuition:* $350 per semester hour. Part-time tuition and fees vary according to course load. *Payment plan:* installment. *Waivers:* employees or children of employees.
Library Robson Library plus 1 other. *Operations spending 1999–2000:* $147,107. *Collection:* 96,128 titles, 624 serial subscriptions, 3,370 audiovisual materials.
College life *Housing:* on-campus residence required through junior year. *Options:* coed, men-only, women-only. *Most popular organizations:* Beta Sigma Kappa, planet club, SGA, Student Foundation Board, Baptist Student Union.
Campus security 24-hour emergency response devices, late-night transport-escort service.
After graduation 26 organizations recruited on campus 1997–98. 9% of class of 1998 had job offers within 6 months. *Career center:* 1 full-time, 1 part-time personnel. Services include job fairs, resume preparation, interview workshops, resume referral, career/interest testing, career counseling, careers library, job bank, job interviews. *Graduate education:* 20% of class of 1999 went directly to graduate and professional school.
Freshmen 376 applied, 294 admitted. 3 National Merit Scholars, 19 valedictorians.

Average high school GPA	3.36	SAT verbal scores above 500	N/R
SAT math scores above 500	N/R	ACT above 18	91%
From top 10% of their h.s. class	38%	From top quarter	53%
From top half	96%	1998 freshmen returning in 1999	77%

Application *Options:* eApply at www.CollegeQuest.com, electronic application, deferred entrance. *Application fee:* $10. *Required:* essay or personal statement; high school transcript; minimum 2.0 GPA. *Required for some:* letters of recommendation; interview.
Standardized tests *Admission: Required:* SAT I or ACT.
Significant dates *Application deadlines:* rolling (freshmen), 8/15 (transfers). *Financial aid deadline priority date:* 2/15.
Freshman Application Contact
Mr. James D. Decker, Director of Admissions, University of the Ozarks, 415 North College Avenue, Clarksville, AR 72830-2880. **Phone:** 501-979-1209. **Toll-free phone:** 800-264-8636. **Fax:** 501-979-1355. **E-mail:** admiss@ozarks.edu
Visit CollegeQuest.com for information on majors offered and athletics.

WILLIAMS BAPTIST COLLEGE
Walnut Ridge, Arkansas

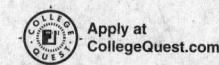

- **Independent Southern Baptist**, 4-year, founded 1941
- **Degrees** associate and bachelor's
- **Rural** 186-acre campus
- **Coed**, 614 undergraduate students, 80% full-time, 57% women, 43% men
- **Minimally difficult** entrance level, 80% of applicants were admitted
- **16:1** student-to-undergraduate faculty ratio
- **$6270 tuition** and fees
- **$15,450 average indebtedness** upon graduation, $3.2 million endowment

Williams Baptist College is a 4-year, liberal arts college affiliated with the Arkansas Baptist State Convention located in Walnut Ridge, Arkansas. The College offers more than 22 academic programs with an average class size of 17 and is one of the least expensive private colleges in the US. Williams, a member of the NAIA, fields varsity teams in 7 sports. Telephone: 800-722-4434 (toll-free); World Wide Web: http://www.wbcoll.edu

Students *Undergraduates:* 489 full-time, 125 part-time. Students come from 14 states and territories, 6 other countries. *The most frequently chosen baccalaureate fields are:* education, philosophy, psychology.

From out-of-state	22%	Reside on campus	62%
Age 25 or older	20%	Transferred in	8%
International students	3%	African Americans	3%
Asian Americans/Pacific Islanders	0.2%	Hispanic Americans	1%
Native Americans	1%		

Faculty 45 (64% full-time), 33% with terminal degrees.
Expenses (1999–2000) *Comprehensive fee:* $9470 includes full-time tuition ($6000), mandatory fees ($270), and room and board ($3200). *Part-time tuition:* $250 per hour. *Part-time fees:* $135 per term part-time. Part-time tuition and fees vary according to course load. *Payment plan:* installment. *Waivers:* senior citizens and employees or children of employees.
Library Felix Goodson Library. *Collection:* 57,321 titles, 284 serial subscriptions.
College life *Housing:* on-campus residence required through senior year. *Options:* men-only, women-only. *Most popular organizations:* Campus Ministries, Fellowship of Christian Athletes, international club, Alpha Psi Omega.
Campus security 24-hour emergency response devices, student patrols.
After graduation *Career center:* 2 part-time personnel. Services include job fairs, resume preparation, career counseling, job bank.
Freshmen 516 applied, 411 admitted, 160 enrolled.

Average high school GPA	3.2	SAT verbal scores above 500	N/R
SAT math scores above 500	N/R	ACT above 18	81%
From top 10% of their h.s. class	20%	From top quarter	40%
From top half	80%	1998 freshmen returning in 1999	51%

Application *Options:* eApply at www.CollegeQuest.com, early admission, deferred entrance. *Application fee:* $20. *Required:* high school transcript; minimum 2.25 GPA. *Recommended:* essay or personal statement; interview.
Standardized tests *Admission: Required:* SAT I or ACT.
Significant dates *Application deadlines:* rolling (freshmen), rolling (transfers). *Financial aid deadline:* continuous.
Freshman Application Contact
Ms. Angela Flippo, Director of Admissions, Williams Baptist College, PO Box 3665, Walnut Ridge, AR 72476. **Phone:** 870-886-6741 Ext. 127. **Toll-free phone:** 800-722-4434. **E-mail:** admissions@wbcoll.edu
Visit CollegeQuest.com for information on majors offered and athletics. College video available at CollegeQuest.com.

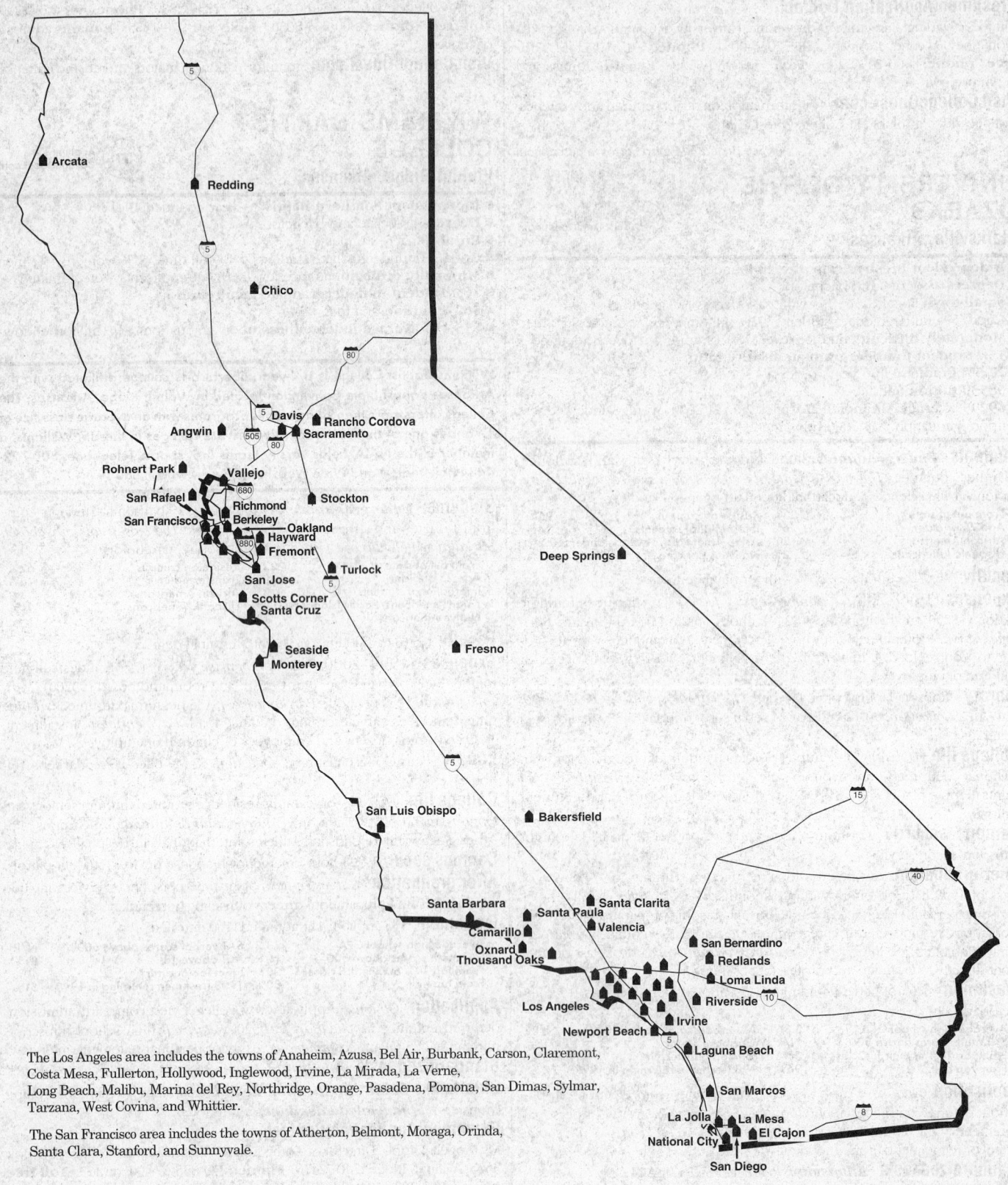

California

ACADEMY OF ART COLLEGE
San Francisco, California

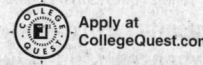 Apply at CollegeQuest.com

- **Proprietary**, comprehensive, founded 1929
- **Degrees** associate, bachelor's, and master's
- **Urban** 3-acre campus
- **Coed**, 4,723 undergraduate students, 59% full-time, 41% women, 59% men
- **Noncompetitive** entrance level, 74% of applicants were admitted
- **15:1 student-to-undergraduate faculty ratio**
- **48% graduate** in 6 years or less
- **$10,860 tuition** and fees

Students *Undergraduates:* 2,794 full-time, 1,929 part-time. Students come from 41 states and territories, 52 other countries. *The most frequently chosen baccalaureate field is:* visual/performing arts. *Graduate:* 651 in graduate degree programs.

From out-of-state	37%	Reside on campus	6%
Age 25 or older	39%	Transferred in	15%
International students	26%	African Americans	4%
Asian Americans/Pacific Islanders	16%	Hispanic Americans	9%
Native Americans	1%		

Faculty 600 (17% full-time), 10% with terminal degrees.
Expenses (1999–2000) *Tuition:* full-time $10,860; part-time $450 per unit. *Required fees:* $30 per term part-time. *College room only:* $6000. Room and board charges vary according to housing facility. *Payment plan:* installment.
Library Academy of Art College Library. *Operations spending 1999–2000:* $500,000. *Collection:* 18,573 titles, 276 serial subscriptions, 87,175 audiovisual materials.
College life *Housing:* Option: coed. *Most popular organizations:* Circle of Nations, advertising club, Western Art Directors Club, Pinoy and Pinay Artists Club, Taiwanese Student Association.
Campus security Late-night transport-escort service, ID check at all buildings.
After graduation 84% of class of 1998 had job offers within 6 months. *Career center:* 2 full-time, 1 part-time personnel. Services include resume preparation, career counseling, careers library, job bank, job interviews. *Graduate education:* 13% of class of 1999 went directly to graduate and professional school: 13% graduate arts and sciences.
Freshmen 1,656 applied, 1,227 admitted, 383 enrolled.

Average high school GPA	2.6	SAT verbal scores above 500	N/R
SAT math scores above 500	N/R	ACT above 18	N/R
From top half of their h.s. class	80%	1998 freshmen returning in 1999	82%

Application *Options:* eApply at www.CollegeQuest.com, Common Application, early admission, deferred entrance. *Application fee:* $100. *Required:* high school transcript. *Recommended:* minimum 2.0 GPA; interview; portfolio.
Significant dates *Application deadlines:* rolling (freshmen), rolling (transfers). *Financial aid deadline priority date:* 3/2.
Freshman Application Contact
Mr. Ron Bunn, Director of Admissions, Academy of Art College, 79 New Montgomery Street, San Francisco, CA 94105. **Phone:** 415-263-4127. **Toll-free phone:** 800-544-ARTS. **Fax:** 415-263-4130. **E-mail:** info@academyart.edu
Visit CollegeQuest.com for information on majors offered and athletics. College video available at CollegeQuest.com.

- *See page 1126 for a narrative description.*

THE ADVERTISING ARTS COLLEGE
San Diego, California

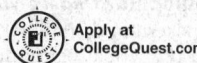 Apply at CollegeQuest.com

- **Proprietary**, 4-year, founded 1981
- **Degrees** associate and bachelor's
- **Urban** campus
- **Coed**, 250 undergraduate students, 100% full-time, 54% women, 46% men
- **Minimally difficult** entrance level, 85% of applicants were admitted
- **28:1 student-to-undergraduate faculty ratio**
- **$9550 tuition** and fees

Students *Undergraduates:* 250 full-time. Students come from 10 states and territories, 7 other countries.

Age 25 or older	10%

Faculty 21 (43% full-time), 19% with terminal degrees.
Expenses (1999–2000) *Tuition:* full-time $9550. Full-time tuition and fees vary according to program and student level. *Payment plans:* tuition prepayment, installment.
Library The Advertising Arts College Library plus 1 other. *Collection:* 906 titles, 17 serial subscriptions.
College life *Housing:* college housing not available. *Most popular organizations:* Advertising Club, Communicating Art Club.
Campus security 24-hour emergency response devices.
After graduation 100% of class of 1998 had job offers within 6 months. *Career center:* 1 full-time personnel. Services include resume preparation, resume referral, career counseling, job bank, job interviews.
Freshmen 200 applied, 170 admitted, 160 enrolled.

Average high school GPA	2.6	SAT verbal scores above 500	N/R
SAT math scores above 500	N/R	ACT above 18	N/R
1998 freshmen returning in 1999	85%		

Application *Options:* eApply at www.CollegeQuest.com, Common Application, deferred entrance. *Application fee:* $30. *Required:* essay or personal statement; high school transcript.
Significant dates *Application deadlines:* rolling (freshmen), rolling (transfers). *Financial aid deadline:* continuous.
Freshman Application Contact
Ms. Tracy Myers, Vice President and Director of Admissions, The Advertising Arts College, 10025 Mesa Rim Road, San Diego, CA 92121. **Phone:** 858-546-0602. **E-mail:** info@taac.edu
Visit CollegeQuest.com for information on majors offered and athletics.

THE AMERICAN COLLEGE
California—See American InterContinental University

AMERICAN INTERCONTINENTAL UNIVERSITY
Los Angeles, California

- **Proprietary**, comprehensive, founded 1982
- **Degrees** associate, bachelor's, and master's
- **Urban** campus
- **Coed**, 601 undergraduate students
- **Noncompetitive** entrance level
- **$11,850 tuition** and fees

Students *Undergraduates:* Students come from 42 other countries.

Age 25 or older	3%	International students	56%
African Americans	8%	Asian Americans/Pacific Islanders	6%
Hispanic Americans	7%	Native Americans	0.3%

Faculty 47 (49% full-time).
Expenses (1999–2000) *Tuition:* full-time $11,850; part-time $1315 per course. Full-time tuition and fees vary according to location. Part-time tuition and fees vary according to location. *College room only:* $4245. *Payment plans:* installment, deferred payment. *Waivers:* employees or children of employees.
Library *Operations spending 1999–2000:* $175,000. *Collection:* 20,000 titles, 228 serial subscriptions.
College life *Housing:* Options: coed, men-only, women-only.
After graduation *Career center:* 2 full-time personnel. Services include job fairs, resume preparation, resume referral, career counseling, careers library, job interviews.
Freshmen

SAT verbal scores above 500	N/R	SAT math scores above 500	N/R
ACT above 18	N/R		

Peterson's Guide to Four-Year Colleges 2001   www.petersons.com

California

American InterContinental University *(continued)*

Application *Options:* early admission, deferred entrance. *Application fee:* $35. *Required:* essay or personal statement; high school transcript; 2 letters of recommendation; interview.

Significant dates *Application deadlines:* rolling (freshmen), rolling (transfers). *Financial aid deadline:* continuous.

Freshman Application Contact
Mr. Eric Thompson, Director of Admissions, American InterContinental University, 12655 West Jefferson Boulevard, Los Angeles, CA 90066. **Phone:** 310-302-2482. **Fax:** 310-302-2001.

Visit CollegeQuest.com for information on majors offered and athletics. College video available at CollegeQuest.com.

ANTIOCH SOUTHERN CALIFORNIA/LOS ANGELES
Marina del Rey, California

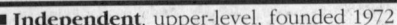

- **Independent**, upper-level, founded 1972
- **Degrees** bachelor's, master's, post-master's, and postbachelor's certificates
- **Urban** 1-acre campus with easy access to Los Angeles
- **Coed**, 184 undergraduate students, 36% full-time, 77% women, 23% men
- **Moderately difficult** entrance level, 78% of applicants were admitted
- **$10,650 tuition** and fees

Part of Antioch University.

Students *Undergraduates:* 66 full-time, 118 part-time. Students come from 2 states and territories. *Graduate:* 384 in graduate degree programs.

Age 25 or older	95%	African Americans	22%
Asian Americans/Pacific Islanders	3%	Hispanic Americans	8%
Native Americans	1%		

Expenses (2000–2001) *Tuition:* full-time $10,650; part-time $355 per unit. Full-time tuition and fees vary according to course load. Part-time tuition and fees vary according to course load. *Payment plan:* installment. *Waivers:* minority students, senior citizens, and employees or children of employees.

College life *Housing:* college housing not available.

Campus security 24-hour emergency response devices, late-night transport-escort service.

Application *Options:* eApply at www.CollegeQuest.com, deferred entrance. *Application fee:* $60.

Significant dates *Application deadline:* 8/4 (transfers). *Notification:* continuous until 10/1 (transfers).

Freshman Application Contact
Mr. Scott Russell, Director of Admissions, Antioch Southern California/Los Angeles, 13274 Fiji Way, Marina del Rey, CA 90292-7092. **Phone:** 310-578-1080. **Toll-free phone:** 800-7ANTIOCH. **Fax:** 310-822-4824. **E-mail:** admissions@antiochla.edu

Visit CollegeQuest.com for information on majors offered and athletics. Electronic viewbook available at CollegeQuest.com.

ANTIOCH SOUTHERN CALIFORNIA/ SANTA BARBARA
Santa Barbara, California

- **Independent**, upper-level, founded 1977
- **Degrees** bachelor's and master's
- **Small-town** campus with easy access to Los Angeles
- **Coed**, 95 undergraduate students, 43% full-time, 73% women, 27% men
- **Minimally difficult** entrance level
- **$9750 tuition** and fees
- **$16.8 million endowment**

Part of Antioch University.

Students *Undergraduates:* 41 full-time, 54 part-time. *The most frequently chosen baccalaureate field is:* liberal arts/general studies. *Graduate:* 152 in graduate degree programs.

Age 25 or older	95%	African Americans	2%
Asian Americans/Pacific Islanders	3%	Hispanic Americans	14%

Faculty 49 (20% full-time).

Expenses (1999–2000) *Tuition:* full-time $9750; part-time $325 per quarter hour. Part-time tuition and fees vary according to course load. *Payment plan:* installment. *Waivers:* employees or children of employees.

Library *Operations spending 1999–2000:* $33,205.

College life *Housing:* college housing not available.

Campus security Late-night transport-escort service.

After graduation *Graduate education:* 32% of class of 1999 went directly to graduate and professional school.

Application *Options:* Common Application, deferred entrance. *Application fee:* $60.

Significant dates *Application deadline:* rolling (transfers). *Financial aid deadline:* continuous.

Freshman Application Contact
Mrs. Carol Flores, Director of Admissions, Antioch Southern California/Santa Barbara, 801 Garden Street, Santa Barbara, CA 93101-1580. **Phone:** 805-962-8179 Ext. 113. **Fax:** 805-962-4786. **E-mail:** cflores@antiochsb.edu

Visit CollegeQuest.com for information on majors offered and athletics.

ARMSTRONG UNIVERSITY
Oakland, California

- **Independent**, comprehensive, founded 1918
- **Degrees** associate, bachelor's, and master's
- **Urban** campus with easy access to San Francisco
- **Coed**
- **Moderately difficult** entrance level

Institutional Web site http://www.armstrong-u.edu/

College life *Housing:* college housing not available. *Most popular organization:* Associated Students of Armstrong University.

Campus security 24-hour emergency response devices, student patrols, patrols by trained security personnel during daytime hours.

Application *Options:* Common Application, deferred entrance. *Application fee:* $50. *Required:* high school transcript; minimum 2.0 GPA. *Recommended:* essay or personal statement; letters of recommendation.

Admissions Office Contact
Armstrong University, 1608 Webster Street, Oakland, CA 94612. **Fax:** 510-835-8935. **E-mail:** info@armstrong-u.edu

Visit CollegeQuest.com for information on athletics. Electronic viewbook available at CollegeQuest.com.

- *See page 1186 for a narrative description.*

ART CENTER COLLEGE OF DESIGN
Pasadena, California

- **Independent**, comprehensive, founded 1930
- **Degrees** bachelor's and master's
- **Suburban** 175-acre campus with easy access to Los Angeles
- **Coed**, 1,345 undergraduate students, 100% full-time, 39% women, 61% men
- **Very difficult** entrance level, 65% of applicants were admitted
- **9:1** student-to-undergraduate faculty ratio
- **$18,890 tuition** and fees
- **$15,460 average financial aid** package, $16.9 million endowment

Students *Undergraduates:* 1,345 full-time. Students come from 38 states and territories, 51 other countries. *The most frequently chosen baccalaureate field is:* visual/performing arts. *Graduate:* 93 in graduate degree programs.

From out-of-state	31%	Age 25 or older	65%
Transferred in	2%	International students	20%
African Americans	1%	Asian Americans/Pacific Islanders	28%
Hispanic Americans	10%	Native Americans	1%

Faculty 362 (20% full-time).

Expenses (1999–2000) *Tuition:* full-time $18,890. *Payment plan:* installment. *Waivers:* employees or children of employees.

California

Library James LeMont Fogg Library. *Operations spending 1999–2000:* $630,747. *Collection:* 73,595 titles, 385 serial subscriptions, 5,265 audiovisual materials.

College life *Housing:* college housing not available. *Most popular organizations:* Contraste, Chroma, Women's Alliance, Korean Student Alliance, Industrial Design Society Student Chapter.

Campus security 24-hour patrols.

After graduation 200 organizations recruited on campus 1997–98. 94% of class of 1998 had job offers within 6 months. *Career center:* 3 full-time personnel. Services include resume preparation, resume referral, career counseling, careers library, job bank, job interviews.

Freshmen 1,148 applied, 741 admitted, 33 enrolled.

Average high school GPA	3.1	SAT verbal scores above 500	N/R
SAT math scores above 500	N/R	ACT above 18	N/R
1998 freshmen returning in 1999	89%		

Application *Option:* deferred entrance. *Application fee:* $45. *Required:* essay or personal statement; high school transcript; portfolio. *Recommended:* minimum 3.0 GPA; interview.

Standardized tests *Admission:* Required for some: SAT I or ACT.

Significant dates *Application deadlines:* rolling (freshmen), rolling (transfers). *Financial aid deadline priority date:* 3/1.

Freshman Application Contact
Ms. Kit Baron, Vice President, Student Services, Art Center College of Design, 1700 Lida Street, Pasadena, CA 91103-1999. **Phone:** 626-396-2373. **Fax:** 626-795-0578. **E-mail:** admissions@artcenter.edu

Visit CollegeQuest.com for information on majors offered and athletics. College video available at CollegeQuest.com.

ART INSTITUTE OF SOUTHERN CALIFORNIA
Laguna Beach, California

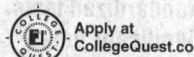
Apply at CollegeQuest.com

- **Independent**, 4-year, founded 1962
- **Degree** bachelor's
- **Small-town** 9-acre campus with easy access to Los Angeles
- **Coed**, 244 undergraduate students
- **Moderately difficult** entrance level
- **10:1** student-to-undergraduate faculty ratio
- **$13,600 tuition** and fees
- **$525,000 endowment**

AISC hosts an annual Open House/Portfolio Review to introduce prospective students and their families to the school. Individuals may schedule personal tours/portfolio reviews by contacting Anthony Padilla, Dean of Admissions, or Susan DeRosa, Assistant Dean of Admissions. Campus hours: Monday–Friday, 9 a.m.–5 p.m.

Students *Undergraduates:* Students come from 20 states and territories, 16 other countries.

| From out-of-state | 26% | Age 25 or older | 30% |

Faculty 52 (19% full-time).

Expenses (2000–2001, estimated) *Tuition:* full-time $13,400; part-time $560 per unit. *Required fees:* full-time $200. *Payment plan:* installment. *Waivers:* employees or children of employees.

Library Ruth Salyer Library plus 1 other. *Operations spending 1999–2000:* $50,665. *Collection:* 15,000 titles, 90 serial subscriptions.

College life *Housing:* college housing not available.

Campus security 24-hour emergency response devices.

After graduation 10 organizations recruited on campus 1997–98. 88% of class of 1998 had job offers within 6 months. *Career center:* 2 full-time personnel. Services include career counseling.

Freshmen 220 applied, 120 admitted. 2 National Merit Scholars, 4 class presidents, 2 valedictorians, 16 student government officers.

Average high school GPA	3.1	SAT verbal scores above 500	88%
SAT math scores above 500	80%	ACT above 18	100%
1998 freshmen returning in 1999	88%		

Application *Options:* eApply at www.CollegeQuest.com, Common Application, electronic application. *Application fee:* $35. *Required:* essay or personal statement; high school transcript; minimum 3.0 GPA; 1 letter of recommendation; interview; portfolio. *Recommended:* minimum 3.5 GPA.

Standardized tests *Admission:* Required: SAT I or ACT.

Significant dates *Application deadlines:* 3/2 (freshmen), 4/2 (transfers). *Notification:* 5/1 (freshmen).

Freshman Application Contact
Mr. Anthony Padilla, Dean of Admissions, Art Institute of Southern California, 2222 Laguna Canyon Road, Laguna Beach, CA 92651-1136. **Phone:** 949-376-6000 Ext. 232. **Toll-free phone:** 800-255-0762. **Fax:** 949-376-6009. **E-mail:** admissions@aisc.edu

Visit CollegeQuest.com for information on majors offered and athletics. College video and electronic viewbook available at CollegeQuest.com.

■ *See page 1194 for a narrative description.*

ART INSTITUTES INTERNATIONAL AT SAN FRANCISCO
San Francisco, California

- **Independent**, 4-year, founded 1939
- **Degrees** associate and bachelor's
- **Urban** campus
- **Coed**, 215 undergraduate students, 91% full-time, 41% women, 59% men
- **Moderately difficult** entrance level, 97% of applicants were admitted
- **12:1** student-to-undergraduate faculty ratio
- **$14,160 tuition** and fees

Part of Educational Management Corporation.

Students *Undergraduates:* 195 full-time, 20 part-time. *The most frequently chosen baccalaureate field is:* visual/performing arts.

International students	4%	African Americans	6%
Asian Americans/Pacific Islanders	20%	Hispanic Americans	18%
Native Americans	0.5%		

Faculty 30 (17% full-time).

Expenses (1999–2000) *Tuition:* full-time $14,160; part-time $295 per quarter hour. Full-time tuition and fees vary according to course load. Part-time tuition and fees vary according to course load. College housing is available through the California Culinary Academy. *Payment plans:* guaranteed tuition, installment. *Waivers:* employees or children of employees.

College life *Housing:* college housing not available.

Campus security 24-hour emergency response devices.

After graduation *Career center:* Services include resume preparation, career counseling, job interviews.

Freshmen 171 applied, 166 admitted, 69 enrolled.

| SAT verbal scores above 500 | N/R | SAT math scores above 500 | N/R |
| ACT above 18 | N/R | | |

Application *Options:* Common Application, deferred entrance. *Application fee:* $50. *Required:* essay or personal statement; high school transcript. *Recommended:* minimum 2.0 GPA; 2 letters of recommendation; interview.

Significant dates *Application deadlines:* rolling (freshmen), rolling (transfers). *Financial aid deadline priority date:* 3/2.

Freshman Application Contact
Ms. Donna Scott, Acting Director of Admissions, Art Institutes International at San Francisco, 1170 Market Street, San Francisco, CA 94102-4908. **Phone:** 415-865-0198. **Toll-free phone:** 888-493-3261. **Fax:** 415-863-6344.

Visit CollegeQuest.com for information on majors offered and athletics.

AZUSA PACIFIC UNIVERSITY
Azusa, California

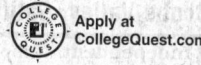
Apply at CollegeQuest.com

- **Independent nondenominational**, comprehensive, founded 1899
- **Degrees** bachelor's, master's, doctoral, and first professional
- **Small-town** 60-acre campus with easy access to Los Angeles

California

Azusa Pacific University (continued)
- **Coed**, 3,092 undergraduate students, 96% full-time, 63% women, 37% men
- **Moderately difficult** entrance level, 80% of applicants were admitted
- **15:1 student-to-undergraduate faculty ratio**
- **52% graduate** in 6 years or less
- **$14,727 tuition** and fees
- **$6859 average financial aid** package, $18.7 million endowment

At Azusa Pacific, a Christian liberal arts university, students are challenged academically, participate in dynamic leadership experiences, and utilize the latest technology, gaining the skills needed to reach their goals. Located 26 miles northeast of Los Angeles, APU offers 34 undergraduate majors, 19 master's programs, 3 doctoral programs, and extensive credential and certificate programs.

Students *Undergraduates:* 2,972 full-time, 120 part-time. Students come from 52 other countries. *The most frequently chosen baccalaureate fields are:* business/marketing, health professions and related sciences, liberal arts/general studies. *Graduate:* 106 in professional programs, 2,784 in other graduate degree programs.

From out-of-state	26%	Reside on campus	62%
Age 25 or older	19%	Transferred in	8%
International students	3%	African Americans	4%
Asian Americans/Pacific Islanders	6%	Hispanic Americans	13%
Native Americans	1%		

Faculty 590 (32% full-time).
Expenses (1999–2000) *Comprehensive fee:* $19,607 includes full-time tuition ($14,630), mandatory fees ($97), and room and board ($4880). *College room only:* $2380. *Part-time tuition:* $600 per unit. *Part-time fees:* $35 per term part-time. Part-time tuition and fees vary according to course load. *Payment plan:* installment. *Waivers:* employees or children of employees.
Library Marshburn Memorial Library plus 2 others. *Operations spending 1999–2000:* $1.3 million. *Collection:* 147,377 titles, 1,411 serial subscriptions.
College life *Most popular organizations:* community service groups, choir, Outreach ministries groups, Habitat for Humanity.
Campus security 24-hour emergency response devices and patrols, student patrols, late-night transport-escort service, controlled dormitory access.
After graduation 150 organizations recruited on campus 1997–98. *Career center:* 3 full-time, 3 part-time personnel. Services include job fairs, resume preparation, career counseling, careers library, job interviews.
Freshmen 1,967 applied, 1,578 admitted, 680 enrolled.

Average high school GPA	3.57	SAT verbal scores above 500	66%
SAT math scores above 500	61%	ACT above 18	100%
From top quarter of their h.s. class	49%	From top half	76%

Application *Options:* eApply at www.CollegeQuest.com, deferred entrance. *Application fee:* $45. *Required:* essay or personal statement; high school transcript; minimum 2.5 GPA; 2 letters of recommendation. *Required for some:* interview.
Standardized tests *Admission: Required:* SAT I or ACT.
Significant dates *Application deadlines:* 7/1 (freshmen), 7/1 (transfers). *Financial aid deadline:* 8/1. *Priority date:* 3/2.
Freshman Application Contact
Mrs. Deana Porterfield, Dean of Admissions, Azusa Pacific University, 901 East Alosta Avenue, PO Box 7000, Azusa, CA 91702-7000. **Phone:** 626-812-3016. **Toll-free phone:** 800-TALK-APU. **E-mail:** admissions@apu.edu
Visit CollegeQuest.com for information on majors offered and athletics. College video available at CollegeQuest.com.

- *See page 1216 for a narrative description.*

BETHANY COLLEGE OF THE ASSEMBLIES OF GOD
Scotts Valley, California

- **Independent**, comprehensive, founded 1919, affiliated with Assemblies of God
- **Degrees** associate, bachelor's, and master's
- **Small-town** 40-acre campus with easy access to San Francisco and San Jose
- **Coed**, 511 undergraduate students, 84% full-time, 62% women, 38% men
- **Minimally difficult** entrance level, 87% of applicants were admitted
- **$10,280 tuition** and fees

Students *Undergraduates:* Students come from 21 states and territories. *Graduate:* 42 in graduate degree programs.

Age 25 or older	48%	International students	2%
African Americans	6%	Asian Americans/Pacific Islanders	5%
Hispanic Americans	13%	Native Americans	1%

Faculty 81 (30% full-time).
Expenses (1999–2000) *Comprehensive fee:* $14,860 includes full-time tuition ($9800), mandatory fees ($480), and room and board ($4580). *College room only:* $2080. Room and board charges vary according to board plan. *Part-time tuition:* $410 per credit hour. *Part-time fees:* $235 per term part-time.
Library Wilson Library. *Collection:* 59,453 titles, 858 serial subscriptions.
College life On-campus residence required through junior year.
Campus security 24-hour emergency response devices, student patrols, controlled dormitory access.
After graduation *Career center:* 1 part-time personnel. Services include resume preparation, career counseling, careers library.
Freshmen 228 applied, 199 admitted.

Average high school GPA	3.1	SAT verbal scores above 500	53%
SAT math scores above 500	50%	ACT above 18	N/R
From top 10% of their h.s. class	16%	From top quarter	59%
From top half	75%	1998 freshmen returning in 1999	76%

Application *Options:* early admission, deferred entrance. *Preference* given to members of Assemblies of God and other evangelical churches. *Application fee:* $35. *Required:* essay or personal statement; high school transcript; minimum 2.0 GPA; 3 letters of recommendation; interview.
Standardized tests *Admission: Required:* SAT I or ACT.
Significant dates *Application deadlines:* 7/1 (freshmen), 7/1 (transfers). *Notification:* continuous until 7/1 (freshmen). *Financial aid deadline priority date:* 3/2.
Freshman Application Contact
Ms. Deborah Sain, Director of Admissions, Bethany College of the Assemblies of God, 800 Bethany Drive, Scotts Valley, CA 95066-2820. **Phone:** 831-438-3800 Ext. 1400. **Toll-free phone:** 800-843-9410. **Fax:** 831-438-4517. **E-mail:** info@bethany.edu
Visit CollegeQuest.com for information on majors offered and athletics. Electronic viewbook available at CollegeQuest.com.

BETHESDA CHRISTIAN UNIVERSITY
Anaheim, California

- **Independent**, comprehensive, founded 1978, affiliated with Full Gospel World Mission
- **Degrees** bachelor's and master's
- **63 undergraduate students, 86% full-time, 71% women, 29% men**
- **77% of applicants were admitted**
- **9:1 student-to-undergraduate faculty ratio**
- **57% graduate** in 6 years or less
- **$4170 tuition** and fees
- **$3 million endowment**

Students *Undergraduates:* 54 full-time, 9 part-time. Students come from 55 states and territories, 4 other countries. *The most frequently chosen baccalaureate fields are:* education, philosophy. *Graduate:* 43 in graduate degree programs.

Age 25 or older	0.04%	Transferred in	48%

Faculty 20 (25% full-time), 25% with terminal degrees.
Expenses (1999–2000) *Tuition:* full-time 4000; part-time 120 per credit. *Required fees:* full-time 170; 60 per term part-time. Part-time tuition and fees vary according to program. *Payment plans:* installment, deferred payment. *Waivers:* minority students and employees or children of employees.
Library *Operations spending 1999–2000:* $39,862.
College life *Housing:* college housing not available. *Most popular organizations:* Student Council, Soccer Team.
Campus security Student patrols, late-night transport-escort service, 24-hour security monitor.

California

After graduation *Graduate education:* 55% of class of 1999 went directly to graduate and professional school.
Freshmen 57 applied, 44 admitted, 24 enrolled.

Average high school GPA	2.98	SAT verbal scores above 500	N/R
SAT math scores above 500	N/R	ACT above 18	N/R
From top 10% of their h.s. class	0.4%	From top quarter	28%
From top half	0.4%	1998 freshmen returning in 1999	36%

Application *Application fee:* 25. *Required:* essay or personal statement; high school transcript; 3 letters of recommendation; interview; 2 photographs.
Significant dates *Application deadlines:* 8/27 (freshmen), 8/27 (transfers). *Notification:* 8/13 (freshmen).
Freshman Application Contact
Ms. Haein Hong, Admissions & Registrar, Bethesda Christian University, 730 N. Euclid Street, Anaheim, CA 92801. **Phone:** 714-517-1945. **Fax:** 714-517-1948. **E-mail:** admin@bcu.edu
Visit CollegeQuest.com for information on majors offered and athletics.

■ *See page 1272 for a narrative description.*

BIOLA UNIVERSITY
La Mirada, California

- **Independent interdenominational**, university, founded 1908
- **Degrees** bachelor's, master's, and doctoral
- **Suburban** 95-acre campus with easy access to Los Angeles
- **Coed**, 2,564 undergraduate students, 92% full-time, 63% women, 37% men
- **Moderately difficult** entrance level, 84% of applicants were admitted
- **18:1 student-to-undergraduate faculty ratio**
- **56% graduate** in 6 years or less
- **$15,914 tuition** and fees
- **$12,882 average financial aid** package, $19,521 average indebtedness upon graduation, $12.1 million endowment

Students *Undergraduates:* 2,351 full-time, 213 part-time. Students come from 41 states and territories, 40 other countries. *The most frequently chosen baccalaureate fields are:* business/marketing, communications/communication technologies, philosophy. *Graduate:* 1,308 in graduate degree programs.

From out-of-state	21%	Reside on campus	69%
Age 25 or older	19%	Transferred in	7%
International students	5%	African Americans	4%
Asian Americans/Pacific Islanders	10%	Hispanic Americans	9%
Native Americans	1%		

Faculty 298 (52% full-time), 68% with terminal degrees.
Expenses (1999–2000) *Comprehensive fee:* $21,053 includes full-time tuition ($15,914) and room and board ($5139). *College room only:* $2707. Full-time tuition and fees vary according to program. Room and board charges vary according to board plan and housing facility. *Part-time tuition:* $663 per unit. Part-time tuition and fees vary according to course load and program. *Payment plan:* installment. *Waivers:* employees or children of employees.
Library Rose Memorial Library. *Operations spending 1999–2000:* $1 million. *Collection:* 259,285 titles, 1,175 serial subscriptions, 9,650 audiovisual materials.
College life *Housing:* on-campus residence required through junior year. *Options:* men-only, women-only. *Most popular organizations:* Biola Korean Student Association, Brothers and Sisters in Christ, Biola Accounting Society, Maharlika (Filipino Club), SOUL (seeking out unity and love).
Campus security 24-hour emergency response devices and patrols, student patrols, late-night transport-escort service, controlled dormitory access, access gates to roads through the middle of campus.
After graduation 75 organizations recruited on campus 1997–98. 50% of class of 1998 had job offers within 6 months. *Career center:* 1 full-time, 2 part-time personnel. Services include job fairs, resume preparation, resume referral, career/interest testing, career counseling, careers library, job bank, job interviews. *Graduate education:* 21% of class of 1999 went directly to graduate and professional school.
Freshmen 1,501 applied, 1,263 admitted, 565 enrolled.

Average high school GPA	3.52	SAT verbal scores above 500	80%
SAT math scores above 500	75%	ACT above 18	95%

Application *Options:* eApply at www.CollegeQuest.com, Common Application, electronic application, early admission, deferred entrance. *Application fee:* $45. *Required:* essay or personal statement; high school transcript; 2 letters of recommendation; interview. *Recommended:* minimum 2.8 GPA.
Standardized tests *Admission: Required:* SAT I or ACT.
Significant dates *Application deadlines:* 6/1 (freshmen), 6/1 (transfers). *Financial aid deadline priority date:* 3/2.
Freshman Application Contact
Mr. Greg Vaughan, Director of Enrollment Management, Biola University, 13800 Biola Avenue, La Mirada, CA 90639-0001. **Phone:** 562-903-4752. **Toll-free phone:** 800-652-4652. **Fax:** 562-903-4709. **E-mail:** admissions@biola.edu
Visit CollegeQuest.com for information on majors offered and athletics. College video and electronic viewbook available at CollegeQuest.com.

■ *See page 1276 for a narrative description.*

BROOKS INSTITUTE OF PHOTOGRAPHY
Santa Barbara, California

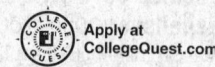

- **Proprietary**, comprehensive, founded 1945
- **Degrees** bachelor's and master's
- **Suburban** 25-acre campus
- **Coed**, 469 undergraduate students, 100% full-time, 42% women, 58% men
- **Moderately difficult** entrance level
- **10:1 student-to-undergraduate faculty ratio**
- **$16,260 tuition** and fees

Students *Undergraduates:* 469 full-time. Students come from 27 states and territories, 22 other countries. *Graduate:* 64 in graduate degree programs.

Age 25 or older	36%	Transferred in	12%
International students	15%	African Americans	0.4%
Asian Americans/Pacific Islanders	3%	Hispanic Americans	3%
Native Americans	0.4%		

Faculty 39 (49% full-time).
Expenses (1999–2000) *Tuition:* full-time $15,750. *Required fees:* full-time $510. *Payment plans:* installment, deferred payment.
Library Brooks Institute of Photography Library. *Collection:* 6,500 titles, 128 serial subscriptions.
College life *Housing:* college housing not available.
Campus security Campus closed after 11:30 p.m.
After graduation 83% of class of 1998 had job offers within 6 months. *Career center:* 1 part-time personnel. Services include resume preparation, career counseling, job bank.
Freshmen 36 enrolled.

SAT verbal scores above 500	N/R	SAT math scores above 500	N/R
ACT above 18	N/R	1998 freshmen returning in 1999	84%

Application *Options:* eApply at www.CollegeQuest.com, deferred entrance. *Application fee:* $35. *Required:* essay or personal statement; high school transcript; minimum 3.0 GPA; 15 semester hours of college credit. *Recommended:* interview.
Significant dates *Application deadlines:* rolling (freshmen), rolling (transfers). *Financial aid deadline priority date:* 3/2.
Freshman Application Contact
Ms. Inge B. Kautzmann, Director of Admissions, Brooks Institute of Photography, 801 Alston Road, Santa Barbara, CA 93108-2399. **Phone:** 805-966-3888 Ext. 4601. **Fax:** 805-564-1475. **E-mail:** admissions@brooks.edu
Visit CollegeQuest.com for information on majors offered and athletics. College video and electronic viewbook available at CollegeQuest.com.

CALIFORNIA BAPTIST UNIVERSITY
Riverside, California

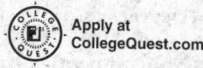

- **Independent Southern Baptist**, comprehensive, founded 1950
- **Degrees** bachelor's and master's

Peterson's Guide to Four-Year Colleges 2001   www.petersons.com

California

California Baptist University (continued)
- **Suburban** 75-acre campus with easy access to Los Angeles
- **Coed**, 1,616 undergraduate students, 81% full-time, 60% women, 40% men
- **Minimally difficult** entrance level, 80% of applicants were admitted
- **19:1 student-to-undergraduate faculty ratio**
- **50% graduate** in 6 years or less
- **$10,682 tuition** and fees
- **$9100 average financial aid** package, $15,800 average indebtedness upon graduation, $4.9 million endowment

Students *Undergraduates:* 1,314 full-time, 302 part-time. Students come from 24 states and territories. *The most frequently chosen baccalaureate fields are:* education, liberal arts/general studies, psychology. *Graduate:* 440 in graduate degree programs.

From out-of-state	28%	Reside on campus	37%
Age 25 or older	32%	Transferred in	9%
International students	0.1%	African Americans	2%
Asian Americans/Pacific Islanders	3%	Hispanic Americans	7%
Native Americans	0.5%		

Faculty 164 (48% full-time), 60% with terminal degrees.
Expenses (2000–2001) *One-time required fee:* $140. *Comprehensive fee:* $15,648 includes full-time tuition ($10,062), mandatory fees ($620), and room and board ($4966). *College room only:* $2250. Full-time tuition and fees vary according to program. Room and board charges vary according to board plan and housing facility. *Part-time tuition:* $387 per unit. *Part-time fees:* $50 per term part-time. Part-time tuition and fees vary according to course load. *Payment plans:* installment, deferred payment. *Waivers:* employees or children of employees.
Library Annie Gabriel Library. *Operations spending 1999–2000:* $589,981. *Collection:* 62,743 titles, 434 serial subscriptions, 797 audiovisual materials.
College life *Housing: Options:* men-only, women-only. *Most popular organizations:* Christian Student Organization, Student Senate, FOCUS, Fellowship of Christian Athletes, multi-cultural club.
Campus security 24-hour emergency response devices and patrols, student patrols, late-night transport-escort service, controlled dormitory access.
After graduation 15 organizations recruited on campus 1997–98. *Career center:* 1 full-time, 1 part-time personnel. Services include job fairs, resume preparation, interview workshops, resume referral, career/interest testing, career counseling, careers library, job bank, job interviews, software programs.
Freshmen 504 applied, 401 admitted, 226 enrolled. 3 National Merit Scholars, 2 class presidents, 5 valedictorians, 19 student government officers.

Average high school GPA	3.3	SAT verbal scores above 500	30%
SAT math scores above 500	27%	ACT above 18	55%
From top half of their h.s. class	57%	1998 freshmen returning in 1999	82%

Application *Options:* eApply at www.CollegeQuest.com, Common Application, early admission, early action, deferred entrance. *Application fee:* $30. *Required:* essay or personal statement; high school transcript; minimum 2.5 GPA; 2 letters of recommendation. *Recommended:* interview.
Standardized tests *Admission: Required:* SAT I or ACT.
Significant dates *Application deadlines:* 8/1 (freshmen), 8/1 (transfers). *Notification:* continuous until 9/1 (freshmen). *Financial aid deadline priority date:* 3/2.
Freshman Application Contact
Mr. Doug Wible, Dean of Admissions, California Baptist University, , 8432 Magnolia Avenue, Riverside, CA 92504-3297. **Phone:** 909-343-4212. **Toll-free phone:** 877-228-8866. **Fax:** 909-351-1808. **E-mail:** admissions@calbaptist.edu
Visit CollegeQuest.com for information on majors offered and athletics.

CALIFORNIA CHRISTIAN COLLEGE
Fresno, California

- **Independent religious**, 4-year
- **Degrees** associate and bachelor's
- **Coed**, 99 undergraduate students, 74% full-time, 37% women, 63% men
- **Noncompetitive** entrance level
- **8:1 student-to-undergraduate faculty ratio**
- **$3450 tuition** and fees

Students *Undergraduates:* 73 full-time, 26 part-time. Students come from 2 states and territories. *The most frequently chosen baccalaureate field is:* philosophy.

African Americans	25%	Hispanic Americans	7%
Native Americans	3%		

Faculty 11, 18% with terminal degrees.
Expenses (1999–2000) *One-time required fee:* $15. *Comprehensive fee:* $6210 includes full-time tuition ($3220), mandatory fees ($230), and room and board ($2760). Full-time tuition and fees vary according to course load. Room and board charges vary according to board plan. *Part-time tuition:* $115 per credit. *Part-time fees:* $75 per term part-time. Part-time tuition and fees vary according to course load. *Payment plan:* installment. *Waivers:* employees or children of employees.
College life *Housing:* on-campus residence required in freshman year. *Options:* men-only, women-only.
Freshmen 14 enrolled.

SAT verbal scores above 500	N/R	SAT math scores above 500	N/R
ACT above 18	N/R		

Application *Application fee:* $40. *Required:* essay or personal statement; 3 letters of recommendation; interview; statement of faith, moral/ethical statement. *Required for some:* high school transcript.
Standardized tests *Admission: Recommended:* SAT I and SAT II or ACT.
Significant dates *Application deadlines:* rolling (freshmen), rolling (transfers).
Freshman Application Contact
Mrs. Pamela Hatwig, Registrar, California Christian College, 4881 East University Avenue, Fresno, CA 93703. **Phone:** 559-251-4215. **E-mail:** cccfresno@aol.com
Visit CollegeQuest.com for information on majors offered and athletics.

CALIFORNIA COLLEGE FOR HEALTH SCIENCES
National City, California

- **Proprietary**, comprehensive, founded 1978
- **Degrees** associate, bachelor's, and master's (offers primarily external degree programs)
- **Urban** 2-acre campus with easy access to San Diego
- **Coed**
- **Noncompetitive** entrance level

Students *Undergraduates:* Students come from 52 states and territories, 15 other countries. *Graduate:* 2,075 in graduate degree programs.

From out-of-state	90%	Age 25 or older	85%

Faculty 17 (35% full-time).
College life *Housing:* college housing not available.
Freshmen

SAT verbal scores above 500	N/R	SAT math scores above 500	N/R
ACT above 18	N/R	1998 freshmen returning in 1999	85%

Application *Option:* deferred entrance. *Application fee:* $35. *Required:* high school transcript. *Required for some:* essay or personal statement; employment in a health science field. *Recommended:* essay or personal statement; employment in a health science field.
Significant dates *Application deadlines:* rolling (freshmen), rolling (transfers). *Financial aid deadline priority date:* 9/1.
Freshman Application Contact
Ms. Marita Gubbe, Registrar, Director of Admissions, California College for Health Sciences, 222 West 24th Street, National City, CA 91950-6605. **Phone:** 619-477-4800 Ext. 320. **Toll-free phone:** 800-221-7374. **Fax:** 619-477-4360. **E-mail:** admissions@cchs.edu
Visit CollegeQuest.com for information on majors offered and athletics.

CALIFORNIA COLLEGE OF ARTS AND CRAFTS
San Francisco, California

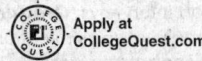

- **Independent**, comprehensive, founded 1907
- **Degrees** bachelor's and master's

- **Urban** 4-acre campus
- **Coed**, 1,004 undergraduate students, 92% full-time, 60% women, 40% men
- **Moderately difficult** entrance level, 73% of applicants were admitted
- **10:1 student-to-undergraduate faculty ratio**
- **$18,368 tuition** and fees
- **$13,089 average financial aid** package, $22,500 average indebtedness upon graduation, $15.1 million endowment

CCAC is the only regionally accredited school of art, architecture, and design on the West Coast, distinguished by the interdisciplinary nature and breadth of its programs in fine art, design, and architecture taught by a faculty of active professionals. Current initiatives include expansion of architecture and design programs in a new San Francisco facility, and new graduate programs in design, visual studies, and writing.

Students *Undergraduates:* 919 full-time, 85 part-time. Students come from 40 states and territories, 23 other countries. *The most frequently chosen baccalaureate fields are:* architecture, visual/performing arts. *Graduate:* 69 in graduate degree programs.

From out-of-state	19%	Reside on campus	9%
Age 25 or older	50%	Transferred in	17%
International students	10%	African Americans	2%
Asian Americans/Pacific Islanders	13%	Hispanic Americans	7%
Native Americans	1%		

Faculty 293 (12% full-time), 50% with terminal degrees.
Expenses (1999–2000) *Comprehensive fee:* $24,226 includes full-time tuition ($18,188), mandatory fees ($180), and room and board ($5858). *College room only:* $3500. Full-time tuition and fees vary according to course load. Room and board charges vary according to housing facility. *Part-time tuition:* $758 per unit. *Part-time fees:* $90 per term part-time. Part-time tuition and fees vary according to course load. *Payment plans:* installment, deferred payment. *Waivers:* employees or children of employees.
Library Meyer Library plus 1 other. *Operations spending 1999–2000:* $425,189. *Collection:* 35,000 titles, 216 serial subscriptions, 400 audiovisual materials.
College life *Housing: Option:* coed. *Social organizations:* President's Circle. *Most popular organizations:* American Institute of Architecture Students, American Institute of Graphic Arts, Student Chapter, Women's Caucus for the Arts, International Student Club, Artists That Are Queer.
Campus security 24-hour emergency response devices and patrols, late-night transport-escort service.
After graduation 10% of class of 1998 had job offers within 6 months. *Career center:* 1 part-time personnel. Services include resume preparation, interview workshops, career/interest testing, career counseling, careers library, job bank, portfolio development, career workshops. *Major awards:* 1 Fulbright Scholar.
Freshmen 363 applied, 264 admitted, 99 enrolled.

Average high school GPA	3.08	SAT verbal scores above 500	62%
SAT math scores above 500	54%	ACT above 18	57%
1998 freshmen returning in 1999	68%		

Application *Options:* eApply at www.CollegeQuest.com, deferred entrance. *Application fee:* $30. *Required:* essay or personal statement; high school transcript; minimum 2.0 GPA; 2 letters of recommendation; portfolio. *Required for some:* interview. *Recommended:* interview.
Standardized tests *Admission: Recommended:* SAT I or ACT.
Significant dates *Application deadlines:* rolling (freshmen), rolling (transfers). *Financial aid deadline priority date:* 3/2.
Freshman Application Contact
Ms. Annie McGeudy, Director of Admissions, California College of Arts and Crafts, 1111 Eighth Street at 16th and Wisconsin, San Francisco, CA 94107. **Phone:** 415-703-9523 Ext. 9532. **Toll-free phone:** 800-447-1ART. **Fax:** 415-703-9539. **E-mail:** enroll@ccac-art.edu
Visit CollegeQuest.com for information on majors offered and athletics.

- *See page 1334 for a narrative description.*

CALIFORNIA INSTITUTE OF INTEGRAL STUDIES
San Francisco, California

- **Independent**, upper-level, founded 1968
- **Degrees** bachelor's, master's, and doctoral
- **Coed**
- **$14,010 tuition** and fees

Expenses (1999–2000) *Tuition:* full-time $13,740; part-time $370 per unit. *Required fees:* full-time $270. Full-time tuition and fees vary according to degree level. Part-time tuition and fees vary according to degree level. *Payment plan:* deferred payment.
College life *Most popular organization:* Student Alliance.
Significant dates *Financial aid deadline priority date:* 6/15.
Freshman Application Contact
Ms. Beth Bremer, Admissions Officer, California Institute of Integral Studies, 1453 Mission Street, San Francisco, CA 94103. **Phone:** 415-575-6151. **Fax:** 415-575-1264.
Visit CollegeQuest.com for information on majors offered and athletics.

CALIFORNIA INSTITUTE OF TECHNOLOGY
Pasadena, California

- **Independent**, university, founded 1891
- **Degrees** bachelor's, master's, and doctoral
- **Suburban** 124-acre campus with easy access to Los Angeles
- **Coed**, 907 undergraduate students, 100% full-time, 30% women, 70% men
- **Most difficult** entrance level, 18% of applicants were admitted
- **3:1 student-to-undergraduate faculty ratio**
- **85% graduate** in 6 years or less
- **$19,959 tuition** and fees
- **$17,833 average financial aid** package, $11,573 average indebtedness upon graduation, $1.2 billion endowment

Academics—with a focus on math, science, and engineering—in a research environment characterize Caltech. The core curriculum emphasizes the fundamentals of each of the sciences plus study in the humanities and social sciences. Caltech values and encourages study and research across disciplines. A renowned faculty and facilities, including the Jet Propulsion Laboratory, contribute to Caltech's reputation as one of the world's major research centers.

Students *Undergraduates:* 907 full-time. Students come from 39 states and territories, 33 other countries. *The most frequently chosen baccalaureate fields are:* engineering/engineering technologies, biological/life sciences, physical sciences. *Graduate:* 982 in graduate degree programs.

From out-of-state	57%	Reside on campus	86%
Transferred in	2%	International students	9%
African Americans	1%	Asian Americans/Pacific Islanders	24%
Hispanic Americans	5%	Native Americans	0.2%

Faculty 337 (88% full-time), 100% with terminal degrees.
Expenses (2000–2001) *Comprehensive fee:* $26,139 includes full-time tuition ($19,743), mandatory fees ($216), and room and board ($6180). *Payment plans:* installment, deferred payment. *Waivers:* employees or children of employees.
Library Millikan Library plus 10 others. *Operations spending 1999–2000:* $5.3 million. *Collection:* 550,325 titles, 3,449 serial subscriptions.
College life *Housing:* on-campus residence required in freshman year. *Option:* coed. *Most popular organizations:* ASCIT, entrepreneur's club, instrumental music groups, glee club, Theater Arts at Cal Tech.
Campus security 24-hour emergency response devices and patrols, late-night transport-escort service.
After graduation 176 organizations recruited on campus 1997–98. *Career center:* 5 full-time, 1 part-time personnel. Services include job fairs, resume preparation, resume referral, career counseling, careers library, job bank, job interviews.
Freshmen 2,894 applied, 520 admitted, 234 enrolled. 58 National Merit Scholars, 4 Westinghouse recipients, 93 valedictorians.

California

California Institute of Technology (continued)

| SAT verbal scores above 500 | 100% | SAT math scores above 500 | 100% |
| ACT above 18 | N/R | 1998 freshmen returning in 1999 | 96% |

Application *Options:* early admission, early action, deferred entrance. *Application fee:* $40. *Required:* essay or personal statement; high school transcript; 3 letters of recommendation.

Standardized tests *Admission: Required:* SAT I, SAT II Subject Tests, SAT II: Writing Test, SAT II Subject Test in math and either physics, chemistry, or biology.

Significant dates *Application deadlines:* 1/1 (freshmen), 3/1 (transfers). *Early action:* 11/1. *Notification:* 4/1 (freshmen), 12/30 (early action). *Financial aid deadline priority date:* 1/15.

Freshman Application Contact
Ms. Charlene Liebau, Director of Admissions, California Institute of Technology, 1200 East California Boulevard, Pasadena, CA 91125-0001. **Phone:** 626-395-6341. **Toll-free phone:** 800-568-8324. **Fax:** 626-683-3026. **E-mail:** ugadmissions@caltech.edu

Visit CollegeQuest.com for information on majors offered and athletics. Electronic viewbook available at CollegeQuest.com.

■ *See page 1336 for a narrative description.*

CALIFORNIA INSTITUTE OF THE ARTS
Valencia, California

■ **Independent**, comprehensive, founded 1961
■ **Degrees** bachelor's, master's, and postbachelor's certificates
■ **Suburban** 60-acre campus with easy access to Los Angeles
■ **Coed**, 804 undergraduate students, 98% full-time, 44% women, 56% men
■ **Very difficult** entrance level, 40% of applicants were admitted
■ **7:1 student-to-undergraduate faculty ratio**
■ **$19,950 tuition** and fees
■ **$17,674 average financial aid** package, $24,873 average indebtedness upon graduation, $86.1 million endowment

Students *Undergraduates:* 791 full-time, 13 part-time. Students come from 46 states and territories, 41 other countries. *The most frequently chosen baccalaureate field is:* visual/performing arts. *Graduate:* 420 in graduate degree programs.

From out-of-state	55%	Reside on campus	40%
Age 25 or older	18%	Transferred in	12%
International students	10%	African Americans	5%
Asian Americans/Pacific Islanders	9%	Hispanic Americans	9%
Native Americans	2%		

Faculty 274 (45% full-time).

Expenses (2000–2001) *Comprehensive fee:* $25,100 includes full-time tuition ($19,750), mandatory fees ($200), and room and board ($5150). *College room only:* $3000. Room and board charges vary according to housing facility. *Waivers:* employees or children of employees.

Library Main library plus 1 other. *Operations spending 1999–2000:* $1.1 million. *Collection:* 95,973 titles, 613 serial subscriptions, 20,611 audiovisual materials.

College life *Housing: Options:* coed, disabled students.

Campus security 24-hour emergency response devices and patrols, late-night transport-escort service, controlled dormitory access.

After graduation 50 organizations recruited on campus 1997–98. *Career center:* 1 full-time, 1 part-time personnel. Services include job fairs, resume preparation, resume referral, career counseling, careers library, job bank, job interviews. *Graduate education:* 25% of class of 1999 went directly to graduate and professional school; 25% graduate arts and sciences. *Major awards:* 1 Fulbright Scholar.

Freshmen 1,271 applied, 503 admitted, 146 enrolled.

| SAT verbal scores above 500 | N/R | SAT math scores above 500 | N/R |
| ACT above 18 | N/R | 1998 freshmen returning in 1999 | 86% |

Application *Option:* deferred entrance. *Application fee:* $60. *Required:* essay or personal statement; high school transcript; portfolio or audition. *Required for some:* letters of recommendation; interview.

Significant dates *Application deadlines:* rolling (freshmen), rolling (transfers). *Financial aid deadline priority date:* 3/2.

Freshman Application Contact
Mr. Kenneth Young, Director of Admissions, California Institute of the Arts, 24700 McBean Parkway, Valencia, CA 91355-2340. **Phone:** 661-253-7863. **Toll-free phone:** 800-292-ARTS (in-state); 800-545-ARTS (out-of-state). **E-mail:** admiss@calarts.edu

Visit CollegeQuest.com for information on majors offered and athletics. College video available at CollegeQuest.com.

■ *See page 1338 for a narrative description.*

CALIFORNIA LUTHERAN UNIVERSITY
Thousand Oaks, California

Apply at CollegeQuest.com

■ **Independent Lutheran**, comprehensive, founded 1959
■ **Degrees** bachelor's and master's
■ **Suburban** 290-acre campus with easy access to Los Angeles
■ **Coed**, 1,750 undergraduate students
■ **Moderately difficult** entrance level, 77% of applicants were admitted
■ **15:1 student-to-undergraduate faculty ratio**
■ **$16,200 tuition** and fees
■ **$12,175 average financial aid** package, $14,500 average indebtedness upon graduation, $15.4 million endowment

California Lutheran University's commitment to the use of new technology in and out of the classroom was acknowledged by the 1996 CAUSE Award for Excellence in Campus Networking. CLUnet is available in every classroom, residence hall, and office on campus. Students can see why CLU is a leader in information technology in education by visiting CLUnet at http://www.clunet.edu.

Students *Undergraduates:* Students come from 30 states and territories, 21 other countries.

Reside on campus	63%	Age 25 or older	6%
International students	5%	African Americans	2%
Asian Americans/Pacific Islanders	2%	Hispanic Americans	13%
Native Americans	3%		

Faculty 209 (49% full-time).

Expenses (1999–2000) *Comprehensive fee:* $22,440 includes full-time tuition ($16,020), mandatory fees ($180), and room and board ($6240). *College room only:* $3040. Room and board charges vary according to board plan. *Part-time tuition:* $535 per unit. *Payment plan:* installment. *Waivers:* employees or children of employees.

Library Pearson Library. *Operations spending 1999–2000:* $231,703. *Collection:* 114,275 titles, 605 serial subscriptions.

College life *Housing:* on-campus residence required through junior year. *Option:* coed. *Most popular organizations:* Associated Students of CLU, music and drama clubs, Rotaract.

Campus security 24-hour emergency response devices and patrols, late-night transport-escort service, controlled dormitory access.

After graduation 45 organizations recruited on campus 1997–98. *Career center:* 2 full-time, 1 part-time personnel. Services include job fairs, resume preparation, interview workshops, resume referral, career/interest testing, career counseling, careers library, job bank, job interviews.

Freshmen 902 applied, 693 admitted.

Average high school GPA	3.49	SAT verbal scores above 500	69%
SAT math scores above 500	73%	ACT above 18	97%
From top 10% of their h.s. class	27%	From top quarter	55%
From top half	85%	1998 freshmen returning in 1999	84%

Application *Options:* eApply at www.CollegeQuest.com, electronic application, deferred entrance. *Application fee:* $45. *Required:* essay or personal statement; high school transcript; minimum 2.75 GPA; 1 letter of recommendation. *Recommended:* minimum 3.0 GPA; interview.

Standardized tests *Admission: Required:* SAT I or ACT.

Significant dates *Application deadlines:* 6/1 (freshmen), 6/1 (transfers). *Notification:* continuous until 6/15 (freshmen). *Financial aid deadline priority date:* 3/1.

Freshman Application Contact
Mr. Marc D. Meredith, Director of Admission, California Lutheran University, Office of Admission, #1350, Thousand Oaks, CA 91360. **Phone:** 805-493-3135. **Toll-free phone:** 877-278-3678. **Fax:** 805-493-3114. **E-mail:** cluadm@clunet.edu

California

Visit CollegeQuest.com for information on majors offered and athletics. Electronic viewbook available at CollegeQuest.com.

■ *See page 1340 for a narrative description.*

CALIFORNIA MARITIME ACADEMY
Vallejo, California

- **State-supported**, 4-year, founded 1929
- **Degree** bachelor's
- **Suburban** 67-acre campus with easy access to San Francisco
- **Coed**, primarily men, 495 undergraduate students
- **Moderately difficult** entrance level, 76% of applicants were admitted
- **17:1 student-to-undergraduate faculty ratio**
- **$9158 tuition and fees (out-of-state)**

Part of California State University System.

Students *Undergraduates:* Students come from 27 states and territories, 3 other countries.

Age 25 or older	31%

Faculty 39 (69% full-time).

Expenses (2000–2001) *One-time required fee:* $3700. *Tuition, area resident:* full-time $1428. *Tuition, nonresident:* full-time $7380. *Required fees:* full-time $1778. *College room and board:* $5750; room only: $2500. Room and board charges vary according to board plan and housing facility. *Payment plan:* installment.

Library Hugh Gallagher Library plus 1 other. *Collection:* 28,377 titles, 273 serial subscriptions, 241 audiovisual materials.

College life *Housing:* on-campus residence required through senior year. *Option:* coed. *Most popular organizations:* propeller club, dive club, drill team.

Campus security 24-hour patrols, student patrols.

After graduation 32 organizations recruited on campus 1997–98. 90% of class of 1998 had job offers within 6 months. *Career center:* 2 full-time personnel. Services include resume preparation, resume referral, career counseling, careers library, job bank, job interviews. *Graduate education:* 1% of class of 1999 went directly to graduate and professional school: 1% business.

Freshmen 384 applied, 292 admitted.

Average high school GPA	3.09	SAT verbal scores above 500	N/R
SAT math scores above 500	N/R	ACT above 18	N/R
From top 10% of their h.s. class	10%	From top quarter	24%
From top half	65%	1998 freshmen returning in 1999	76%

Application *Option:* electronic application. *Application fee:* $55. *Required:* high school transcript; 1 letter of recommendation.

Standardized tests *Admission: Required:* SAT I or ACT.

Significant dates *Application deadlines:* rolling (freshmen), rolling (transfers). *Financial aid deadline priority date:* 3/2.

Freshman Application Contact
Ms. Patricia Beitter, Admissions Counselor, California Maritime Academy, PO Box 1392, Vallejo, CA 94590-0644. **Phone:** 707-654-1333. **Toll-free phone:** 800-561-1945. **Fax:** 707-648-4204. **E-mail:** enroll@csum.edu

Visit CollegeQuest.com for information on majors offered and athletics.

CALIFORNIA NATIONAL UNIVERSITY FOR ADVANCED STUDIES
North Hills, California

Admissions Office Contact
California National University for Advanced Studies, 16909 Parthenia Street, North Hills, CA 91343. **Fax:** 818-830-2418.

CALIFORNIA POLYTECHNIC STATE UNIVERSITY, SAN LUIS OBISPO
San Luis Obispo, California

- **State-supported**, comprehensive, founded 1901
- **Degrees** bachelor's and master's
- **Small-town** 6,000-acre campus
- **Coed**, 15,406 undergraduate students, 93% full-time, 44% women, 56% men
- **Moderately difficult** entrance level, 42% of applicants were admitted
- **20:1 student-to-undergraduate faculty ratio**
- **59% graduate** in 6 years or less
- **$2210 tuition** and fees (in-state); $8114 (out-of-state)
- **$6527 average financial aid** package, $17,340 average indebtedness upon graduation, $2.7 million endowment

Part of California State University System.

Students *Undergraduates:* 14,376 full-time, 1,030 part-time. Students come from 48 states and territories, 41 other countries. *The most frequently chosen baccalaureate fields are:* agriculture, business/marketing, engineering/engineering technologies. *Graduate:* 967 in graduate degree programs.

From out-of-state	3%	Reside on campus	17%
Age 25 or older	10%	Transferred in	6%
International students	1%	African Americans	1%
Asian Americans/Pacific Islanders	11%	Hispanic Americans	11%
Native Americans	1%		

Faculty 1,107 (60% full-time), 70% with terminal degrees.

Expenses (1999–2000) *Tuition, state resident:* full-time $0. *Tuition, nonresident:* full-time $5904; part-time $164 per unit. *Required fees:* full-time $2210. Full-time tuition and fees vary according to course load. Part-time tuition and fees vary according to course load. *College room and board:* $5553; room only: $2781. Room and board charges vary according to board plan. *Payment plan:* installment. *Waivers:* senior citizens and employees or children of employees.

Library Kennedy Library. *Operations spending 1999–2000:* $4.6 million. *Collection:* 621,062 titles, 4,917 serial subscriptions, 84,209 audiovisual materials.

College life *Housing:* Options: coed, men-only, women-only. *Social organizations:* national fraternities, national sororities, local fraternities, local sororities; 11% of eligible men and 7% of eligible women are members. *Most popular organizations:* ski club, American Marketing Association, Rose Float Club, MECHA, Society of Women Engineers.

Campus security 24-hour emergency response devices and patrols, student patrols, late-night transport-escort service, controlled dormitory access.

After graduation 630 organizations recruited on campus 1997–98. 90% of class of 1998 had job offers within 6 months. *Career center:* 15 full-time, 3 part-time personnel. Services include job fairs, resume preparation, resume referral, career counseling, careers library, job bank, job interviews. *Graduate education:* 15% of class of 1999 went directly to graduate and professional school.

Freshmen 15,407 applied, 6,473 admitted, 2,716 enrolled.

Average high school GPA	3.61	SAT verbal scores above 500	82%
SAT math scores above 500	89%	ACT above 18	95%
From top 10% of their h.s. class	36%	From top quarter	73%
From top half	95%	1998 freshmen returning in 1999	87%

Application *Options:* electronic application, early admission, early decision. *Application fee:* $55. *Required:* high school transcript.

Standardized tests *Admission: Required:* SAT I or ACT.

Significant dates *Application deadlines:* 11/30 (freshmen), 11/30 (transfers). *Early decision:* 10/31. *Notification:* 3/15 (freshmen), 12/15 (early decision). *Financial aid deadline priority date:* 3/2.

Freshman Application Contact
Mr. James Maraviglia, Director of Admissions and Evaluations, California Polytechnic State University, San Luis Obispo, San Luis Obispo, CA 93407. **Phone:** 805-756-2311. **E-mail:** admprosp@calpoly.edu

Visit CollegeQuest.com for information on majors offered and athletics. College video and electronic viewbook available at CollegeQuest.com.

CALIFORNIA STATE POLYTECHNIC UNIVERSITY, POMONA
Pomona, California

- **State-supported**, comprehensive, founded 1938
- **Degrees** bachelor's and master's
- **Urban** 1,400-acre campus with easy access to Los Angeles
- **Coed**, 15,894 undergraduate students, 80% full-time, 43% women, 57% men

California

California State Polytechnic University, Pomona (continued)
- **Moderately difficult** entrance level, 71% of applicants were admitted
- **19:1 student-to-undergraduate faculty ratio**
- **$1875 tuition** and fees (in-state); $9747 (out-of-state)
- **$6889 average financial aid** package, $12,248 average indebtedness upon graduation, $96,000 endowment

Part of California State University System.

Students *Undergraduates:* 12,729 full-time, 3,165 part-time. Students come from 52 states and territories, 54 other countries. *The most frequently chosen baccalaureate fields are:* business/marketing, computer/information sciences, engineering/engineering technologies. *Graduate:* 1,935 in graduate degree programs.

From out-of-state	2%	Reside on campus	3%
Age 25 or older	25%	Transferred in	8%
International students	5%	African Americans	3%
Asian Americans/Pacific Islanders	35%	Hispanic Americans	22%
Native Americans	1%		

Faculty 1,113 (58% full-time), 53% with terminal degrees.

Expenses (1999–2000) *Tuition, state resident:* full-time $0. *Tuition, nonresident:* full-time $7872; part-time $164 per unit. *Required fees:* full-time $1875; $389 per term part-time. Part-time tuition and fees vary according to course load. *College room and board:* $6278. Room and board charges vary according to board plan and housing facility. *Payment plan:* installment. *Waivers:* senior citizens and employees or children of employees.

Library University Library. *Collection:* 410,257 titles, 19,085 audiovisual materials.

College life *Housing: Option:* coed. *Social organizations:* national fraternities, national sororities, local fraternities, local sororities, coed fraternity; 1% of eligible men and 1% of eligible women are members. *Most popular organizations:* Rose float club, Ridge Runners Ski Club, Barkada (Asian club), American Marketing Association, Cal Poly Society of Accountants.

Campus security 24-hour emergency response devices and patrols, student patrols, late-night transport-escort service, video camera surveillance.

After graduation 261 organizations recruited on campus 1997–98. *Career center:* 10 full-time, 2 part-time personnel. Services include job fairs, resume preparation, interview workshops, career/interest testing, career counseling, careers library, job bank, job interviews.

Freshmen 9,174 applied, 6,479 admitted, 2,661 enrolled.

Average high school GPA	3.26	SAT verbal scores above 500	43%
SAT math scores above 500	63%	ACT above 18	73%
1998 freshmen returning in 1999	76%		

Application *Options:* electronic application, early admission. *Application fee:* $55. *Required:* high school transcript; minimum 2.0 GPA.

Standardized tests *Admission: Required:* SAT I or ACT.

Significant dates *Application deadlines:* rolling (freshmen), rolling (transfers). *Financial aid deadline priority date:* 3/2.

Freshman Application Contact
Ms. Rose M. Smith, Director of Admissions, California State Polytechnic University, Pomona, 3801 West Temple Avenue, Pomona, CA 91768. **Phone:** 909-869-2000 Ext. 3423. **Fax:** 909-869-4529. **E-mail:** cppadmit@csupomona.edu

Visit CollegeQuest.com for information on majors offered and athletics. College video available at CollegeQuest.com.

- *See page 1342 for a narrative description.*

CALIFORNIA STATE UNIVERSITY, BAKERSFIELD
Bakersfield, California

- **State-supported**, comprehensive, founded 1970
- **Degrees** bachelor's and master's
- **Urban** 575-acre campus
- **Coed**
- **Moderately difficult** entrance level
- **$1875 tuition** and fees (in-state); $9255 (out-of-state)

Part of California State University System.

Expenses (1999–2000) *Tuition, state resident:* full-time $0. *Tuition, nonresident:* full-time $7380; part-time $164 per unit. *Required fees:* full-time $1875; $415 per term part-time. *College room and board:* $4345.

Institutional Web site http://www.csubak.edu/

College life *Housing: Option:* coed. *Social organizations:* national fraternities, national sororities; 2% of eligible men and 2% of eligible women are members. *Most popular organizations:* MECHA, LUPE, STAAR, Psi Chi, art club.

Campus security 24-hour emergency response devices and patrols, late-night transport-escort service.

Application *Options:* electronic application, early admission, deferred entrance. *Preference* given to state residents. *Application fee:* $55. *Required:* high school transcript.

Standardized tests *Admission: Required:* SAT I or ACT. *Recommended:* SAT II Subject Tests.

Admissions Office Contact
California State University, Bakersfield, 9001 Stockdale Highway, Bakersfield, CA 93311-1099. **Toll-free phone:** 800-788-2782. **Fax:** 661-664-3188.

Visit CollegeQuest.com for information on athletics.

CALIFORNIA STATE UNIVERSITY, CHICO
Chico, California

- **State-supported**, comprehensive, founded 1887
- **Degrees** bachelor's, master's, and postbachelor's certificates
- **Small-town** 119-acre campus
- **Coed**, 13,397 undergraduate students, 91% full-time, 54% women, 46% men
- **Moderately difficult** entrance level, 80% of applicants were admitted
- **19:1 student-to-undergraduate faculty ratio**
- **51.3% graduate** in 6 years or less
- **$1994 tuition** and fees (in-state); $9374 (out-of-state)
- **$16.9 million endowment**

Part of California State University System.

Students *Undergraduates:* 12,129 full-time, 1,268 part-time. Students come from 40 states and territories, 47 other countries. *The most frequently chosen baccalaureate fields are:* business/marketing, liberal arts/general studies, social sciences and history. *Graduate:* 1,864 in graduate degree programs.

From out-of-state	1%	Reside on campus	13%
Age 25 or older	17%	Transferred in	11%
International students	2%	African Americans	2%
Asian Americans/Pacific Islanders	4%	Hispanic Americans	10%
Native Americans	2%		

Faculty 961, 63% with terminal degrees.

Expenses (1999–2000) *Tuition, state resident:* full-time $0. *Tuition, nonresident:* full-time $7380; part-time $246 per unit. *Required fees:* full-time $1994; $697 per term part-time. Full-time tuition and fees vary according to course load. Part-time tuition and fees vary according to course load. *College room and board:* $5860; room only: $3728. *Payment plan:* deferred payment. *Waivers:* senior citizens and employees or children of employees.

Library Meriam Library. *Operations spending 1999–2000:* $5.5 million. *Collection:* 614,747 titles, 4,040 serial subscriptions, 17,733 audiovisual materials.

College life *Housing: Options:* coed, disabled students. *Social organizations:* national fraternities, national sororities, local fraternities, local sororities; 4% of eligible men and 5% of eligible women are members. *Most popular organizations:* Gold Key Honor Society, The Edge, Student Chapter of the California Teacher's Association, Linux User's Group, Newman Center.

Campus security 24-hour emergency response devices and patrols, student patrols, late-night transport-escort service, controlled dormitory access, crime prevention workshops, RAD self-defense Program, Chico Safe Rides.

After graduation 250 organizations recruited on campus 1997–98. 30% of class of 1998 had job offers within 6 months. *Career center:* 7 full-time personnel. Services include job fairs, resume preparation, interview workshops, resume referral, career/interest testing, career counseling, careers library, job bank, job interviews. *Graduate education:* 25% of class of 1999 went directly to graduate and professional school.

California

Freshmen 6,827 applied, 5,448 admitted, 2,052 enrolled.

Average high school GPA	3.12	SAT verbal scores above 500	50%
SAT math scores above 500	57%	ACT above 18	82%
From top 10% of their h.s. class	35%	From top quarter	76%
From top half	100%	1998 freshmen returning in 1999	83%

Application *Options:* Common Application, electronic application, deferred entrance. *Application fee:* $55. *Required:* high school transcript.
Standardized tests *Admission: Required:* SAT I or ACT.
Significant dates *Application deadline:* 11/30 (freshmen). *Notification:* 3/1 (freshmen). *Financial aid deadline priority date:* 3/2.
Freshman Application Contact
Ms. Linda MacMichael, Director of Admissions, California State University, Chico, 400 West First Street, Chico, CA 95929-0722. **Phone:** 530-898-4428. **Toll-free phone:** 800-542-4426. **Fax:** 530-898-6456. **E-mail:** info@csuchico.edu
Visit CollegeQuest.com for information on majors offered and athletics. College video and electronic viewbook available at CollegeQuest.com.

CALIFORNIA STATE UNIVERSITY, DOMINGUEZ HILLS
Carson, California

- **State-supported**, comprehensive, founded 1960
- **Degrees** bachelor's and master's
- **Urban** 350-acre campus with easy access to Los Angeles
- **Coed**, 7,683 undergraduate students, 60% full-time, 71% women, 29% men
- **Moderately difficult** entrance level, 77% of applicants were admitted
- **21:1 student-to-undergraduate faculty ratio**
- **29.4% graduate** in 6 years or less
- **$1730 tuition** and fees (in-state); $9110 (out-of-state)

Part of California State University System.
Students *Undergraduates:* 4,612 full-time, 3,071 part-time. Students come from 33 states and territories, 55 other countries. *The most frequently chosen baccalaureate fields are:* business/marketing, health professions and related sciences, liberal arts/general studies. *Graduate:* 4,841 in graduate degree programs.

From out-of-state	4%	Age 25 or older	55%
Transferred in	16%	International students	2%
African Americans	30%	Asian Americans/Pacific Islanders	10%
Hispanic Americans	30%	Native Americans	1%

Faculty 679 (46% full-time), 54% with terminal degrees.
Expenses (1999–2000) *One-time required fee:* $5. *Tuition:* part-time $246 per unit. *Required fees:* full-time $1730; $565 per term. Part-time tuition and fees vary according to course load. *College room only:* $3436. Room and board charges vary according to housing facility. *Waivers:* employees or children of employees.
Library Leo F. Cain Educational Resource Center. *Collection:* 432,827 titles.
College life *Housing: Option:* coed. *Social organizations:* national fraternities, national sororities.
Campus security Late-night transport-escort service.
After graduation *Career center:* Services include job fairs, resume preparation, career counseling.
Freshmen 2,215 applied, 1,709 admitted, 490 enrolled.

SAT verbal scores above 500	N/R	SAT math scores above 500	N/R
ACT above 18	N/R	1998 freshmen returning in 1999	73%

Application *Options:* electronic application, early admission. *Preference* given to state residents. *Application fee:* $55. *Required:* high school transcript.
Standardized tests *Admission: Required for some:* SAT I or ACT.
Significant dates *Application deadlines:* rolling (freshmen), rolling (transfers). *Financial aid deadline priority date:* 3/2.
Freshman Application Contact
Information Center, California State University, Dominguez Hills, 1000 East Victoria Street, Carson, CA 90747-0001. **Phone:** 310-516-3696.
Visit CollegeQuest.com for information on majors offered and athletics.

CALIFORNIA STATE UNIVERSITY, FRESNO
Fresno, California

- **State-supported**, comprehensive, founded 1911
- **Degrees** bachelor's, master's, and doctoral
- **Urban** 1,410-acre campus
- **Coed**, 14,767 undergraduate students, 82% full-time, 56% women, 44% men
- **Moderately difficult** entrance level, 68% of applicants were admitted
- **17:1 student-to-undergraduate faculty ratio**
- **91% graduate** in 6 years or less
- **$1746 tuition** and fees (in-state); $10,872 (out-of-state)
- **$6065 average financial aid** package, $13,557 average indebtedness upon graduation, $45.9 million endowment

Part of California State University System.
Students *Undergraduates:* 12,175 full-time, 2,592 part-time. Students come from 43 states and territories, 64 other countries. *The most frequently chosen baccalaureate fields are:* business/marketing, health professions and related sciences, liberal arts/general studies. *Graduate:* 3,558 in graduate degree programs.

From out-of-state	1%	Reside on campus	7%
Age 25 or older	25%	Transferred in	12%
International students	2%	African Americans	6%
Asian Americans/Pacific Islanders	12%	Hispanic Americans	29%
Native Americans	1%		

Faculty 1,110 (59% full-time).
Expenses (2000–2001, estimated) *Tuition, state resident:* full-time $0. *Tuition, nonresident:* full-time $9126; part-time $246 per unit. *Required fees:* full-time $1746; $573. *College room and board:* $5816. Room and board charges vary according to board plan and housing facility. *Waivers:* senior citizens and employees or children of employees.
Library Henry Madden Library. *Operations spending 1999–2000:* $5.5 million. *Collection:* 1.6 million titles, 2,673 serial subscriptions, 210,402 audiovisual materials.
College life *Housing: Option:* coed. *Social organizations:* national fraternities, national sororities, local fraternities, local sororities; 42% of eligible men and 58% of eligible women are members.
Campus security 24-hour emergency response devices and patrols, late-night transport-escort service, controlled dormitory access.
After graduation 580 organizations recruited on campus 1997–98. *Career center:* 11 full-time personnel. Services include job fairs, resume preparation, interview workshops, resume referral, career/interest testing, career counseling, careers library, job bank, job interviews, cooperative education employment services.
Freshmen 5,884 applied, 4,000 admitted, 1,742 enrolled.

Average high school GPA	3.23	SAT verbal scores above 500	34%
SAT math scores above 500	39%	ACT above 18	61%
From top half of their h.s. class	100%	1998 freshmen returning in 1999	82%

Application *Option:* electronic application. *Preference* given to state residents. *Application fee:* $55. *Required:* high school transcript.
Standardized tests *Admission: Required:* SAT I or ACT.
Significant dates *Application deadlines:* 7/30 (freshmen), 7/30 (transfers). *Notification:* 11/15 (freshmen). *Financial aid deadline priority date:* 3/1.
Freshman Application Contact
Ms. Vivian Franco, Director, California State University, Fresno, 5150 North Maple Avenue, M/S JA 57, Fresno, CA 93740-8026. **Phone:** 559-278-2261. **Fax:** 559-278-4715. **E-mail:** donna_mills@csufresno.edu
Visit CollegeQuest.com for information on majors offered and athletics.

CALIFORNIA STATE UNIVERSITY, FULLERTON
Fullerton, California

- **State-supported**, comprehensive, founded 1957
- **Degrees** bachelor's and master's
- **Suburban** 225-acre campus with easy access to Los Angeles

California

California State University, Fullerton (continued)
- **Coed**, 22,449 undergraduate students, 70% full-time, 58% women, 42% men
- **Moderately difficult** entrance level, 69% of applicants were admitted
- **22:1 student-to-undergraduate faculty ratio**
- **$1869 tuition** and fees (in-state); $9249 (out-of-state)

Part of California State University System.

Students *Undergraduates:* Students come from 38 states and territories, 78 other countries. *Graduate:* 4,718 in graduate degree programs.

From out-of-state	1%	Reside on campus	2%
Age 25 or older	29%	International students	4%
African Americans	3%	Asian Americans/Pacific Islanders	25%
Hispanic Americans	23%	Native Americans	1%

Faculty 1,711 (39% full-time).

Expenses (1999–2000) *Tuition, state resident:* full-time $0. *Tuition, nonresident:* full-time $7380; part-time $246 per unit. *Required fees:* full-time $1869; $620 per term part-time. *College room and board:* room only: $3672. *Waivers:* minority students and employees or children of employees.

Library California State University, Fullerton Library. *Collection:* 654,790 titles, 2,455 serial subscriptions.

College life *Housing: Option:* coed. *Social organizations:* national fraternities, national sororities, local fraternities, local sororities; 9% of eligible men and 8% of eligible women are members.

Campus security 24-hour emergency response devices and patrols, student patrols, late-night transport-escort service.

After graduation *Career center:* 17 full-time, 3 part-time personnel. Services include job fairs, resume preparation, resume referral, career counseling, careers library, job bank, job interviews.

Freshmen 10,451 applied, 7,251 admitted.

Average high school GPA	3.2	SAT verbal scores above 500	39%
SAT math scores above 500	49%	ACT above 18	69%

Application *Options:* Common Application, early admission. *Preference* given to state residents. *Application fee:* $55. *Required:* high school transcript; minimum 2.0 GPA.

Standardized tests *Admission: Required:* SAT I or ACT.

Significant dates *Application deadlines:* rolling (freshmen), rolling (transfers). *Financial aid deadline priority date:* 3/2.

Freshman Application Contact
Ms. Nancy J. Dority, Admissions Director, California State University, Fullerton, Office of Admissions and Records, PO Box 6900, Fullerton, CA 92834-6900. **Phone:** 714-278-2370.

Visit CollegeQuest.com for information on majors offered and athletics.

CALIFORNIA STATE UNIVERSITY, HAYWARD
Hayward, California

- **State-supported**, comprehensive, founded 1957
- **Degrees** bachelor's, master's, post-master's, and postbachelor's certificates
- **Suburban** 343-acre campus with easy access to San Francisco and San Jose
- **Coed**, 9,364 undergraduate students, 75% full-time, 64% women, 36% men
- **Moderately difficult** entrance level, 57% of applicants were admitted
- **21:1 student-to-undergraduate faculty ratio**
- **38% graduate** in 6 years or less
- **$1683 tuition** and fees (in-state); $9063 (out-of-state)
- **$5743 average financial aid** package, $4.7 million endowment

Part of California State University System.

Students *Undergraduates:* 7,067 full-time, 2,297 part-time. Students come from 50 states and territories, 65 other countries. *The most frequently chosen baccalaureate fields are:* business/marketing, liberal arts/general studies, social sciences and history. *Graduate:* 3,303 in graduate degree programs.

Reside on campus	4%	Age 25 or older	35%
Transferred in	14%	International students	4%
African Americans	13%	Asian Americans/Pacific Islanders	27%
Hispanic Americans	13%	Native Americans	1%

Faculty 761 (47% full-time), 57% with terminal degrees.

Expenses (1999–2000) *Tuition, state resident:* full-time $0. *Tuition, nonresident:* full-time $7380; part-time $164 per unit. *Required fees:* full-time $1683; $361 per term part-time. Full-time tuition and fees vary according to course load. Part-time tuition and fees vary according to course load. *College room and board:* room only: $3100. *Payment plan:* installment. *Waivers:* senior citizens and employees or children of employees.

Library California State University, Hayward Library plus 1 other. *Operations spending 1999–2000:* $3.5 million. *Collection:* 850,000 titles, 2,086 serial subscriptions.

College life *Housing: Option:* coed. *Social organizations:* national fraternities, national sororities, local sororities. *Most popular organizations:* Vietnamese Student Association, Accounting Association, Philipino-American Students Association, Movimiento Estudiantil Chicano, Hayward Orientation Team.

Campus security 24-hour emergency response devices and patrols, late-night transport-escort service.

After graduation 285 organizations recruited on campus 1997–98. *Career center:* 12 full-time, 5 part-time personnel. Services include job fairs, resume preparation, resume referral, career counseling, careers library, job bank, job interviews.

Freshmen 3,224 applied, 1,853 admitted, 737 enrolled.

Average high school GPA	3.09	SAT verbal scores above 500	N/R
SAT math scores above 500	N/R	ACT above 18	N/R
1998 freshmen returning in 1999	75%		

Application *Options:* electronic application, deferred entrance. *Application fee:* $55. *Required:* high school transcript.

Standardized tests *Admission: Required for some:* SAT I or ACT.

Significant dates *Application deadlines:* 9/10 (freshmen), 9/10 (transfers). *Financial aid deadline priority date:* 3/2.

Freshman Application Contact
Ms. Susan Lakis, Associate Director of Admissions, California State University, Hayward, 25800 Carlos Bee Boulevard, Hayward, CA 94542-3035. **Phone:** 510-885-3248. **Fax:** 510-885-3816. **E-mail:** adminfo@csuhayward.edu

Visit CollegeQuest.com for information on majors offered and athletics. Electronic viewbook available at CollegeQuest.com.

CALIFORNIA STATE UNIVERSITY, LONG BEACH
Long Beach, California

- **State-supported**, comprehensive, founded 1949
- **Degrees** bachelor's and master's
- **Suburban** 320-acre campus with easy access to Los Angeles
- **Coed**, 24,109 undergraduate students, 76% full-time, 58% women, 42% men
- **Moderately difficult** entrance level, 81% of applicants were admitted
- **20:1 student-to-undergraduate faculty ratio**
- **33% graduate** in 6 years or less
- **$9082 tuition and fees (out-of-state)**
- **$6812 average financial aid** package, $18.6 million endowment

Part of California State University System.

Students *Undergraduates:* 18,359 full-time, 5,750 part-time. Students come from 43 states and territories, 98 other countries. *The most frequently chosen baccalaureate fields are:* business/marketing, psychology, social sciences and history. *Graduate:* 5,902 in graduate degree programs.

From out-of-state	5%	Reside on campus	8%
Age 25 or older	29%	Transferred in	13%
International students	5%	African Americans	7%
Asian Americans/Pacific Islanders	23%	Hispanic Americans	22%
Native Americans	1%		

Faculty 1,702 (56% full-time), 56% with terminal degrees.

Expenses (1999–2000) *Tuition, nonresident:* full-time $7380; part-time $246 per unit. *Required fees:* full-time $1702; $551 per term part-time. Full-time tuition and fees vary according to program. Part-time tuition and fees vary according to course load and program. *College room and board:* $5400. Room and board charges vary according to board plan. *Payment plan:* installment. *Waivers:* senior citizens and employees or children of employees.

Library University Library. *Operations spending 1999–2000:* $7 million. *Collection:* 781,111 titles, 5,424 serial subscriptions, 68,354 audiovisual materials.

College life *Housing: Option:* coed. *Social organizations:* national fraternities, national sororities, local fraternities, local sororities; 15% of eligible men and 7% of eligible women are members.

Campus security 24-hour emergency response devices and patrols, student patrols, late-night transport-escort service.

After graduation 300 organizations recruited on campus 1997–98. *Career center:* 13 full-time, 1 part-time personnel. Services include job fairs, resume preparation, interview workshops, resume referral, career/interest testing, career counseling, careers library, job bank, job interviews.

Freshmen 12,591 applied, 10,223 admitted, 3,476 enrolled.

Average high school GPA	3.18	SAT verbal scores above 500	40%
SAT math scores above 500	49%	ACT above 18	N/R
From top half of their h.s. class	96%	1998 freshmen returning in 1999	83%

Application *Option:* electronic application. *Application fee:* $55. *Required:* high school transcript.

Standardized tests *Admission: Required for some:* SAT I or ACT.

Significant dates *Application deadlines:* 11/30 (freshmen), 11/30 (transfers). *Notification:* continuous until 8/31 (freshmen). *Financial aid deadline priority date:* 3/2.

Freshman Application Contact
Mr. Thomas Enders, Director of Enrollment Services, California State University, Long Beach, Brotman Hall, 1250 Bellflower Boulevard, Long Beach, CA 90840. **Phone:** 562-985-4641.

Visit CollegeQuest.com for information on majors offered and athletics. College video and electronic viewbook available at CollegeQuest.com.

CALIFORNIA STATE UNIVERSITY, LOS ANGELES
Los Angeles, California

- **State-supported**, comprehensive, founded 1947
- **Degrees** bachelor's, master's, and doctoral
- **Urban** 173-acre campus
- **Coed**, 13,732 undergraduate students, 71% full-time, 59% women, 41% men
- **Moderately difficult** entrance level, 52% of applicants were admitted
- **$1722 tuition** and fees (in-state); $7626 (out-of-state)
- **$6950 average financial aid** package, $16 million endowment

Part of California State University System.

Students *Undergraduates:* 9,816 full-time, 3,916 part-time. Students come from 25 states and territories. *The most frequently chosen baccalaureate fields are:* business/marketing, education, protective services/public administration. *Graduate:* 6,051 in graduate degree programs.

From out-of-state	4%	Transferred in	9%
International students	4%	African Americans	8%
Asian Americans/Pacific Islanders	21%	Hispanic Americans	48%
Native Americans	0.4%		

Faculty 1,118 (61% full-time).

Expenses (1999–2000) *Tuition, state resident:* full-time $0. *Tuition, nonresident:* full-time $5904; part-time $164 per unit. *Required fees:* full-time $1722; $373 per term part-time. Part-time tuition and fees vary according to course load. *College room and board:* room only: $2979. *Waivers:* employees or children of employees.

Library John K. Kennedy Memorial Library. *Operations spending 1999–2000:* $4.3 million. *Collection:* 1.9 million titles, 2,357 serial subscriptions, 4,309 audiovisual materials.

College life *Housing: Option:* coed. *Social organizations:* national fraternities, national sororities, local fraternities, local sororities; 3% of eligible men and 2% of eligible women are members.

Campus security 24-hour emergency response devices, student patrols, late-night transport-escort service.

After graduation *Career center:* 10 full-time, 1 part-time personnel. Services include job fairs, resume preparation, interview workshops, career/interest testing, career counseling, careers library, job bank, job interviews.

Freshmen 7,283 applied, 3,801 admitted, 1,246 enrolled.

| SAT verbal scores above 500 | N/R | SAT math scores above 500 | N/R |
| ACT above 18 | N/R | | |

Application *Options:* Common Application, electronic application, early admission. *Application fee:* $55. *Required:* high school transcript.

Standardized tests *Admission: Required:* SAT I or ACT.

Significant dates *Application deadlines:* 6/15 (freshmen), 6/15 (transfers). *Financial aid deadline priority date:* 3/2.

Freshman Application Contact
Mr. George Bachmann, Associate Director of Admissions and University Outreach, California State University, Los Angeles, 5151 State University Drive, Los Angeles, CA 90032-8530. **Phone:** 323-343-3131. **Fax:** 323-343-2670. **E-mail:** jslanin@calstatela.edu

Visit CollegeQuest.com for information on majors offered and athletics.

CALIFORNIA STATE UNIVERSITY, MONTEREY BAY
Seaside, California

- **State-supported**, comprehensive, founded 1994
- **Degrees** bachelor's, master's, and postbachelor's certificates
- **1,500-acre** campus with easy access to San Jose
- **Coed**, 1,992 undergraduate students, 90% full-time, 60% women, 40% men
- **Minimally difficult** entrance level, 52% of applicants were admitted
- **$1893 tuition** and fees (in-state); $9521 (out-of-state)

Students *Undergraduates: The most frequently chosen baccalaureate fields are:* liberal arts/general studies, communications/communication technologies, natural resources/environmental science. *Graduate:* 275 in graduate degree programs.

Reside on campus	65%	Age 25 or older	25%
International students	1%	African Americans	4%
Asian Americans/Pacific Islanders	7%	Hispanic Americans	25%
Native Americans	1%		

Expenses (1999–2000) *Tuition, state resident:* full-time $0. *Tuition, nonresident:* full-time $7628; part-time $246 per credit. *Required fees:* full-time $1893; $632 per term part-time. *College room and board:* $4100. Room and board charges vary according to housing facility. *Payment plan:* installment. *Waivers:* senior citizens.

College life *Housing:* on-campus residence required through sophomore year. *Options:* men-only, women-only, disabled students. *Most popular organization:* MECHA.

Campus security 24-hour emergency response devices and patrols, student patrols, late-night transport-escort service, controlled dormitory access.

Freshmen 1,796 applied, 928 admitted.

Average high school GPA	3.11	SAT verbal scores above 500	N/R
SAT math scores above 500	N/R	ACT above 18	N/R
1998 freshmen returning in 1999	85%		

Application *Option:* deferred entrance. *Application fee:* $55. *Required:* high school transcript; minimum 2.0 GPA.

Standardized tests *Admission: Required:* SAT I or ACT.

Significant dates *Application deadlines:* rolling (freshmen), rolling (transfers).

Freshman Application Contact
Ms. Beth Appenzeller, Director of Admissions and Records, California State University, Monterey Bay, 100 Campus Center, Seaside, CA 93955-8001. **Phone:** 831-582-3518. **Fax:** 831-582-3540. **E-mail:** student.info@monterey.edu

Visit CollegeQuest.com for information on majors offered and athletics.

CALIFORNIA STATE UNIVERSITY, NORTHRIDGE
Northridge, California

- **State-supported**, comprehensive, founded 1958
- **Degrees** bachelor's and master's

California

California State University, Northridge (continued)
- **Urban** 353-acre campus with easy access to Los Angeles
- **Coed**, 21,560 undergraduate students, 75% full-time, 58% women, 42% men
- **Moderately difficult** entrance level, 80% of applicants were admitted
- **$1814 tuition** and fees (in-state); $9532 (out-of-state)
- **$7736 average financial aid** package, $12,147 average indebtedness upon graduation, $25.6 million endowment

Part of California State University System.

Students *Undergraduates:* Students come from 45 states and territories, 120 other countries. *Graduate:* 6,387 in graduate degree programs.

From out-of-state	3%	Age 25 or older	32%
International students	3%	African Americans	9%
Asian Americans/Pacific Islanders	14%	Hispanic Americans	25%
Native Americans	1%		

Faculty 1,564 (53% full-time).

Expenses (1999–2000) *Tuition, state resident:* full-time $0. *Tuition, nonresident:* full-time $7718; part-time $246 per unit. *Required fees:* full-time $1814; $607 per term part-time. *College room and board:* $5865; room only: $3540. Room and board charges vary according to housing facility. *Waivers:* senior citizens and employees or children of employees.

Library Oviatt Library. *Operations spending 1999–2000:* $7.1 million. *Collection:* 1.2 million titles, 2,754 serial subscriptions.

College life *Housing: Option:* coed. *Social organizations:* national fraternities, national sororities; 6% of eligible men and 4% of eligible women are members.

Campus security 24-hour emergency response devices, late-night transport-escort service.

After graduation *Career center:* 14 full-time personnel. Services include job fairs, resume preparation, resume referral, career counseling, careers library, job interviews.

Freshmen 9,227 applied, 7,350 admitted.

| Average high school GPA | 3.06 | SAT verbal scores above 500 | N/R |
| SAT math scores above 500 | N/R | ACT above 18 | N/R |

Application *Options:* electronic application, early admission, early action. Preference given to state residents for business administration, engineering, computer science, economics programs. *Application fee:* $55. *Required:* high school transcript.

Standardized tests *Admission: Recommended:* SAT I or ACT.

Significant dates *Application deadlines:* 11/30 (freshmen), rolling (transfers). *Early action:* 8/30. *Notification:* 9/30 (early action). *Financial aid deadline priority date:* 3/2.

Freshman Application Contact
Ms. Mary Baxton, Associate Director of Admissions and Records, California State University, Northridge, 18111 Nordhoff Street, Northridge, CA 91330-8207. **Phone:** 818-677-3777. **Fax:** 818-677-3766. **E-mail:** admissions.records@csun.edu

Visit CollegeQuest.com for information on majors offered and athletics.

CALIFORNIA STATE UNIVERSITY, SACRAMENTO
Sacramento, California

- **State-supported**, comprehensive, founded 1947
- **Degrees** bachelor's and master's
- **Urban** 288-acre campus
- **Coed**, 19,343 undergraduate students, 75% full-time, 56% women, 44% men
- **Moderately difficult** entrance level, 41% of applicants were admitted
- **21:1** student-to-undergraduate faculty ratio
- **$1867 tuition** and fees (in-state); $9247 (out-of-state)

Part of California State University System.

Students *Undergraduates:* 14,454 full-time, 4,889 part-time. Students come from 45 states and territories, 77 other countries. *The most frequently chosen baccalaureate fields are:* business/marketing, protective services/public administration, social sciences and history. *Graduate:* 5,187 in graduate degree programs.

From out-of-state	3%	Reside on campus	3%
Age 25 or older	32%	Transferred in	16%
International students	2%	African Americans	7%
Asian Americans/Pacific Islanders	18%	Hispanic Americans	13%
Native Americans	1%		

Faculty 1,446 (57% full-time), 54% with terminal degrees.

Expenses (2000–2001) *Tuition, state resident:* full-time $0. *Tuition, nonresident:* full-time $7380; part-time $246 per unit. *Required fees:* full-time $1867; $634 per term part-time. *College room and board:* $5510; room only: $3312. Room and board charges vary according to board plan. *Payment plan:* installment. *Waivers:* senior citizens and employees or children of employees.

Library California State University, Sacramento Library. *Collection:* 1.1 million titles, 4,754 serial subscriptions.

College life *Housing: Option:* coed. *Social organizations:* national fraternities, national sororities, local fraternities, local sororities; 7% of eligible men and 5% of eligible women are members. *Most popular organizations:* ski club, American Marketing Association, Society for Advancement of Management, Accounting Society, Human Resources Management Association.

Campus security 24-hour emergency response devices and patrols, student patrols, late-night transport-escort service, controlled dormitory access.

After graduation 287 organizations recruited on campus 1997–98. 73% of class of 1998 had job offers within 6 months. *Career center:* 10 full-time, 1 part-time personnel. Services include job fairs, resume preparation, resume referral, career counseling, careers library, job bank, job interviews. *Major awards:* 2 Fulbright Scholars.

Freshmen 7,004 applied, 2,893 admitted, 1,836 enrolled.

Average high school GPA	3.21	SAT verbal scores above 500	41%
SAT math scores above 500	50%	ACT above 18	71%
1998 freshmen returning in 1999	75%		

Application *Options:* electronic application, deferred entrance. *Application fee:* $55. *Required:* high school transcript; minimum 2.0 GPA.

Standardized tests *Admission: Required for some:* SAT I or ACT.

Significant dates *Application deadline:* 8/1 (transfers). *Financial aid deadline priority date:* 3/2.

Freshman Application Contact
Ms. Doris Tormes, Director of University Outreach Services, California State University, Sacramento, 6000 J Street, Sacramento, CA 95819-6048. **Phone:** 916-278-7362. **E-mail:** glasmirel@csus.edu

Visit CollegeQuest.com for information on majors offered and athletics.

CALIFORNIA STATE UNIVERSITY, SAN BERNARDINO
San Bernardino, California

- **State-supported**, comprehensive, founded 1965
- **Degrees** bachelor's and master's
- **Suburban** 430-acre campus with easy access to Los Angeles
- **Coed**, 9,471 undergraduate students, 80% full-time, 62% women, 38% men
- **Moderately difficult** entrance level

Part of California State University System.

Students *Undergraduates:* 7,544 full-time, 1,927 part-time. Students come from 31 states and territories, 84 other countries. *Graduate:* 3,809 in graduate degree programs.

| Reside on campus | 3% | Age 25 or older | 38% |

Faculty 571 (74% full-time).

Library Pfau Library. *Collection:* 466,000 titles, 2,350 serial subscriptions.

College life *Housing: Option:* coed. *Social organizations:* national fraternities, national sororities, local fraternities, local sororities.

Campus security 24-hour emergency response devices and patrols, student patrols, late-night transport-escort service, residence staff on call 24-hours.

After graduation *Career center:* 4 full-time personnel. Services include job fairs, resume preparation, resume referral, career counseling, careers library, job bank, job interviews.

Freshmen 943 enrolled.

| SAT verbal scores above 500 | N/R | SAT math scores above 500 | N/R |
| ACT above 18 | N/R | | |

Application *Option:* early admission. *Application fee:* $55. *Required:* high school transcript.

Standardized tests *Admission: Required for some:* SAT I or ACT.

Significant dates *Application deadlines:* rolling (freshmen), rolling (transfers). *Financial aid deadline priority date:* 3/2.

Freshman Application Contact
Ms. Cynthia Shum, Admissions Counselor, California State University, San Bernardino, 5500 University Parkway, San Bernardino, CA 92407-2397. **Phone:** 909-880-5212.

Visit CollegeQuest.com for information on majors offered and athletics.

CALIFORNIA STATE UNIVERSITY, SAN MARCOS
San Marcos, California

- **State-supported**, comprehensive, founded 1990
- **Degrees** bachelor's and master's
- **Suburban** 302-acre campus with easy access to San Diego
- **Coed**, 4,103 undergraduate students, 64% full-time, 65% women, 35% men
- **Moderately difficult** entrance level, 65% of applicants were admitted
- **$1694 tuition** and fees (in-state); $7598 (out-of-state)
- **$4700 average financial aid** package, $11,293 average indebtedness upon graduation, $5.9 million endowment

Part of California State University System.

Students *Undergraduates:* 2,610 full-time, 1,493 part-time. *Graduate:* 922 in graduate degree programs.

From out-of-state	2%	Reside on campus	2%
Age 25 or older	46%	Transferred in	22%
International students	2%	African Americans	3%
Asian Americans/Pacific Islanders	9%	Hispanic Americans	18%
Native Americans	2%		

Faculty 330 (51% full-time).

Expenses (1999–2000) *One-time required fee:* $5. *Tuition, state resident:* full-time $0. *Tuition, nonresident:* full-time $5904; part-time $246 per unit. *Required fees:* full-time $1694; $537 per term part-time. Part-time tuition and fees vary according to course load. *College room and board:* room only: $3924. Room and board charges vary according to housing facility. *Waivers:* senior citizens and employees or children of employees.

Library Library and Information Services. *Operations spending 1999–2000:* $2.7 million. *Collection:* 126,080 titles, 1,916 serial subscriptions, 6,621 audiovisual materials.

College life *Housing: Options:* men-only, women-only, disabled students. *Social organizations:* national fraternities, national sororities; 3% of eligible men and 2% of eligible women are members. *Most popular organizations:* accounting club, liberal studies club, MECHA, Sigma IOTA Epsilon.

Campus security 24-hour patrols, student patrols, late-night transport-escort service.

After graduation 120 organizations recruited on campus 1997–98. *Career center:* 8 full-time personnel. Services include job fairs, resume preparation, interview workshops, resume referral, career/interest testing, career counseling, careers library, job bank, job interviews.

Freshmen 1,408 applied, 919 admitted, 362 enrolled.

| SAT verbal scores above 500 | N/R | SAT math scores above 500 | N/R |
| ACT above 18 | N/R | 1998 freshmen returning in 1999 | 68% |

Application *Option:* electronic application. *Application fee:* $55. *Required:* high school transcript; minimum 3.0 GPA.

Standardized tests *Admission: Required for some:* SAT I or ACT.

Significant dates *Application deadlines:* rolling (freshmen), rolling (transfers). *Financial aid deadline priority date:* 3/2.

Freshman Application Contact
Ms. Terrie Rodriguez, Director of Admissions, California State University, San Marcos, San Marcos, CA 92096. **Phone:** 760-750-4848. **Fax:** 760-750-4030. **E-mail:** how_apply@mailhost1.csusm.edu

Visit CollegeQuest.com for information on majors offered and athletics.

CALIFORNIA STATE UNIVERSITY, STANISLAUS
Turlock, California

- **State-supported**, comprehensive, founded 1957
- **Degrees** bachelor's and master's
- **Small-town** 220-acre campus
- **Coed**, 5,048 undergraduate students, 70% full-time, 64% women, 36% men
- **Moderately difficult** entrance level, 76% of applicants were admitted
- **18:1 student-to-undergraduate faculty ratio**
- **41.7% graduate** in 6 years or less
- **$1877 tuition** and fees (in-state); $11,134 (out-of-state)

Part of California State University System.

Students *Undergraduates:* 3,538 full-time, 1,510 part-time. Students come from 28 states and territories. *The most frequently chosen baccalaureate fields are:* business/marketing, liberal arts/general studies, social sciences and history. *Graduate:* 1,441 in graduate degree programs.

From out-of-state	1%	Reside on campus	5%
Age 25 or older	35%	Transferred in	89%
International students	1%	African Americans	3%
Asian Americans/Pacific Islanders	8%	Hispanic Americans	25%
Native Americans	1%		

Faculty 423 (63% full-time), 59% with terminal degrees.

Expenses (2000–2001, estimated) *Tuition, state resident:* full-time $0. *Tuition, nonresident:* full-time $9257. *Required fees:* full-time $1877; $518 per term part-time. *College room and board:* $6480; room only: $3541. Room and board charges vary according to board plan and housing facility. *Waivers:* senior citizens.

Library Vasche Library. *Operations spending 1999–2000:* $781,000. *Collection:* 323,118 titles, 2,063 serial subscriptions, 2,210 audiovisual materials.

College life *Housing: Option:* coed. *Social organizations:* national fraternities, national sororities, local fraternities, local sororities; 4% of eligible men and 4% of eligible women are members. *Most popular organizations:* Phi Sigma Sigma sorority, Alpha Xi Delta sorority, SnoBord-em Club, Theta Chi fraternity, MECHA.

Campus security 24-hour emergency response devices and patrols, student patrols, late-night transport-escort service, controlled dormitory access.

After graduation 200 organizations recruited on campus 1997–98. 68% of class of 1998 had job offers within 6 months. *Career center:* 9 full-time, 3 part-time personnel. Services include job fairs, resume preparation, interview workshops, career/interest testing, career counseling, careers library, job interviews.

Freshmen 2,961 applied, 2,255 admitted, 535 enrolled.

Average high school GPA	3.3	SAT verbal scores above 500	42%
SAT math scores above 500	44%	ACT above 18	70%
1998 freshmen returning in 1999	81%		

Application *Options:* Common Application, electronic application, early admission, deferred entrance. *Application fee:* $55. *Required:* high school transcript.

Standardized tests *Admission: Required for some:* SAT I or ACT.

Significant dates *Application deadlines:* 6/30 (freshmen), 6/30 (transfers). *Financial aid deadline priority date:* 3/2.

Freshman Application Contact
Admissions Office, California State University, Stanislaus, Enrollment Services, 801 West Monte Vista Avenue, Turlock, CA 95382. **Phone:** 209-667-3070. **Toll-free phone:** 800-300-7420. **Fax:** 209-667-3333. **E-mail:** outreach@toto.csustan.edu

Visit CollegeQuest.com for information on majors offered and athletics. College video available at CollegeQuest.com.

CHAPMAN UNIVERSITY
Orange, California

- **Independent**, comprehensive, founded 1861, affiliated with Christian Church (Disciples of Christ)

California

Chapman University (continued)
- **Degrees** bachelor's, master's, and first professional
- **Suburban** 42-acre campus with easy access to Los Angeles
- **Coed**, 2,591 undergraduate students, 90% full-time, 56% women, 44% men
- **Moderately difficult** entrance level, 58% of applicants were admitted
- **13:1 student-to-undergraduate faculty ratio**
- **$20,994 tuition** and fees
- **$18,054 average financial aid** package, $18,893 average indebtedness upon graduation, $61 million endowment

Students *Undergraduates:* 2,331 full-time, 260 part-time. Students come from 38 states and territories, 29 other countries. *Graduate:* 188 in professional programs, 1,115 in other graduate degree programs.

Reside on campus	38%	Age 25 or older	15%
Transferred in	10%	International students	3%
African Americans	4%	Asian Americans/Pacific Islanders	8%
Hispanic Americans	23%	Native Americans	1%

Faculty 397 (51% full-time).
Expenses (2000–2001, estimated) *Comprehensive fee:* $28,614 includes full-time tuition ($20,724), mandatory fees ($270), and room and board ($7620). Room and board charges vary according to board plan and housing facility. *Part-time tuition:* $645 per credit. *Part-time fees:* $30 per term part-time. Part-time tuition and fees vary according to course load. *Payment plans:* tuition prepayment, installment, deferred payment. *Waivers:* children of alumni and employees or children of employees.
Library Thurmond Clarke Memorial Library plus 1 other. *Operations spending 1999–2000:* $1.5 million. *Collection:* 203,915 titles, 2,121 serial subscriptions, 3,350 audiovisual materials.
College life *Housing:* on-campus residence required in freshman year. *Option:* coed. *Social organizations:* national fraternities, national sororities; 10% of eligible men and 15% of eligible women are members. *Most popular organizations:* Associated Students, Disciples on Campus, Gamma Beta Phi honor society, Panhellenic Council, Interfraternity Council.
Campus security 24-hour emergency response devices and patrols, late-night transport-escort service, full safety education program.
After graduation 70 organizations recruited on campus 1997–98. *Career center:* 4 full-time personnel. Services include job fairs, resume preparation, interview workshops, resume referral, career/interest testing, career counseling, careers library, job bank, job interviews.
Freshmen 2,303 applied, 1,331 admitted, 562 enrolled. 2 class presidents, 7 valedictorians, 121 student government officers.

Average high school GPA	3.51	SAT verbal scores above 500	83%
SAT math scores above 500	87%	ACT above 18	98%
From top 10% of their h.s. class	33%	From top quarter	65%
From top half	90%	1998 freshmen returning in 1999	84%

Application *Options:* Common Application, electronic application, early admission, early action, deferred entrance. *Application fee:* $30. *Required:* essay or personal statement; high school transcript; minimum 2.5 GPA; 1 letter of recommendation. *Recommended:* minimum 3.0 GPA; interview.
Standardized tests *Admission: Required:* SAT I or ACT. *Recommended:* SAT II Subject Tests.
Significant dates *Application deadlines:* 1/31 (freshmen), 3/15 (transfers). *Early action:* 11/30. *Notification:* 12/21 (early action). **Financial aid deadline priority date:** 3/1.
Freshman Application Contact
Mr. Michael O. Drummy, Associate Dean for Enrollment Services and Chief Admission Officer, Chapman University, One University Drive, Orange, CA 92866. **Phone:** 714-997-6711. **Toll-free phone:** 888-CUAPPLY. **Fax:** 714-997-6713. **E-mail:** admit@chapman.edu
Visit CollegeQuest.com for information on majors offered and athletics. Electronic viewbook available at CollegeQuest.com.

■ *See page 1404 for a narrative description.*

CHARLES R. DREW UNIVERSITY OF MEDICINE AND SCIENCE
Los Angeles, California

- **Independent**, comprehensive, founded 1966
- **Degrees** associate, bachelor's, master's, and doctoral
- **Coed**
- **Moderately difficult** entrance level
- **$8400 tuition** and fees

Expenses (1999–2000) *One-time required fee:* $100. *Tuition:* full-time $8400; part-time $200 per unit. Full-time tuition and fees vary according to course load.
Institutional Web site http://www.cdrewu.edu/
College life *Housing:* college housing not available.
Application *Application fee:* $35. *Required:* essay or personal statement; high school transcript; minimum 2.0 GPA; 3 letters of recommendation; interview.
Standardized tests *Admission: Required:* SAT I or ACT.
Admissions Office Contact
Charles R. Drew University of Medicine and Science, 1731 East 120th Street, Los Angeles, CA 90059.
Visit CollegeQuest.com for information on athletics. College video available at CollegeQuest.com.

CHRISTIAN HERITAGE COLLEGE
El Cajon, California

- **Independent nondenominational**, 4-year, founded 1970
- **Degree** bachelor's
- **Suburban** 32-acre campus with easy access to San Diego
- **Coed**
- **Moderately difficult** entrance level
- **$10,840 tuition** and fees

Expenses (1999–2000) *Comprehensive fee:* $15,565 includes full-time tuition ($10,840) and room and board ($4725). Full-time tuition and fees vary according to class time, course load, and program. Room and board charges vary according to housing facility. *Part-time tuition:* $365 per unit. Part-time tuition and fees vary according to class time, course load, and program.
Institutional Web site http://www.christianheritage.edu/
College life on-campus residence required through senior year. *Most popular organizations:* Senate, missions club, aviators club, S.I.F.E.
Campus security 24-hour emergency response devices and patrols.
Application *Option:* deferred entrance. *Application fee:* $25. *Required:* essay or personal statement; high school transcript; 2 letters of recommendation. *Recommended:* minimum 2.25 GPA; interview.
Standardized tests *Admission: Required:* SAT I or ACT.
Admissions Office Contact
Christian Heritage College, 2100 Greenfield Drive, El Cajon, CA 92019-1157.
Toll-free phone: 800-676-2242. **Fax:** 619-440-0209. **E-mail:** chcadm@adm.christianheritage.edu
Visit CollegeQuest.com for information on athletics. College video available at CollegeQuest.com.

CLAREMONT MCKENNA COLLEGE
Claremont, California

- **Independent**, 4-year, founded 1946
- **Degree** bachelor's
- **Small-town** 50-acre campus with easy access to Los Angeles
- **Coed**, 1,016 undergraduate students, 99% full-time, 44% women, 56% men
- **Very difficult** entrance level, 28% of applicants were admitted
- **8:1 student-to-undergraduate faculty ratio**
- **84% graduate** in 6 years or less
- **$20,760 tuition** and fees
- **$18,980 average financial aid** package, $16,266 average indebtedness upon graduation, $392.8 million endowment

Claremont McKenna College (CMC) offers a traditional liberal arts education with a twist: within the context of a liberal arts curriculum, CMC focuses on educating students for leadership in public policy and public affairs. CMC's

California

enrollment of 1,000 students ensures that students receive a personalized educational experience. However, as one of the Claremont Colleges, CMC provides its students with the academic, intellectual, social, and athletic resources typical of a medium-sized university.

Part of The Claremont Colleges Consortium.

Students *Undergraduates:* 1,013 full-time, 3 part-time. Students come from 40 states and territories, 22 other countries. *The most frequently chosen baccalaureate fields are:* interdisciplinary studies, psychology, social sciences and history.

From out-of-state	37%	Reside on campus	97%
Age 25 or older	1%	Transferred in	3%
International students	3%	African Americans	4%
Asian Americans/Pacific Islanders	17%	Hispanic Americans	13%
Native Americans	0.2%		

Faculty 139 (86% full-time), 100% with terminal degrees.

Expenses (1999–2000) *Comprehensive fee:* $27,820 includes full-time tuition ($20,600), mandatory fees ($160), and room and board ($7060). Room and board charges vary according to board plan and housing facility. *Part-time tuition:* $3433 per course. *Payment plan:* installment. *Waivers:* employees or children of employees.

Library Honnold Library plus 3 others. *Operations spending 1999–2000:* $2.3 million. *Collection:* 2 million titles, 6,028 serial subscriptions, 606 audiovisual materials.

College life *Housing:* on-campus residence required in freshman year. *Option:* coed. *Most popular organizations:* student government, Debate/Forensics Club, newspaper, Volunteer Student Admission Committee, Civitas (community service club).

Campus security 24-hour emergency response devices and patrols, student patrols, late-night transport-escort service, controlled dormitory access.

After graduation 100 organizations recruited on campus 1997–98. 64% of class of 1998 had job offers within 6 months. *Career center:* 4 full-time, 1 part-time personnel. Services include job fairs, resume preparation, resume referral, career/interest testing, career counseling, careers library, job bank, job interviews. **Graduate education:** 24% of class of 1999 went directly to graduate and professional school: 11% law, 6% graduate arts and sciences, 2% business, 2% medicine, 1% education, 1% engineering, 1% veterinary medicine. **Major awards:** 1 Fulbright Scholar.

Freshmen 2,827 applied, 785 admitted, 252 enrolled. 19 National Merit Scholars, 3 class presidents, 27 valedictorians, 31 student government officers.

Average high school GPA	3.87	SAT verbal scores above 500	100%
SAT math scores above 500	100%	ACT above 18	N/R
From top 10% of their h.s. class	78%	From top quarter	98%
From top half	100%	1998 freshmen returning in 1999	96%

Application *Options:* eApply at www.CollegeQuest.com, Common Application, electronic application, early admission, early decision, deferred entrance. *Application fee:* $50. *Required:* essay or personal statement; high school transcript; minimum 3.0 GPA; 2 letters of recommendation. *Recommended:* interview.

Standardized tests *Admission: Required:* SAT I or ACT. *Recommended:* SAT II Subject Tests.

Significant dates *Application deadlines:* 1/15 (freshmen), 4/1 (transfers). *Early decision:* 11/15. *Notification:* 4/1 (freshmen), 12/15 (early decision). *Financial aid deadline:* 2/1.

Freshman Application Contact
Mr. Richard C. Vos, Vice President/Dean of Admission and Financial Aid, Claremont McKenna College, 890 Columbia Avenue, Claremont, CA 91711. **Phone:** 909-621-8088. **E-mail:** admission@mckenna.edu
Visit CollegeQuest.com for information on majors offered and athletics.

■ *See page 1424 for a narrative description.*

CLEVELAND CHIROPRACTIC COLLEGE OF LOS ANGELES
Los Angeles, California

Admissions Office Contact
Cleveland Chiropractic College of Los Angeles, 590 North Vermont Avenue, Los Angeles, CA 90004-2196. **Toll-free phone:** 800-446-CCLA. **Fax:** 323-660-5387.

COGSWELL POLYTECHNICAL COLLEGE
Sunnyvale, California

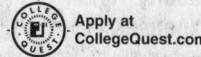
Apply at CollegeQuest.com

- **Independent**, 4-year, founded 1887
- **Degree** bachelor's
- **Suburban** 2-acre campus with easy access to San Francisco and San Jose
- **Coed**, 500 undergraduate students, 55% full-time, 13% women, 87% men
- **Moderately difficult** entrance level, 85% of applicants were admitted
- **$8420** tuition and fees
- **$3737 average financial aid** package, $22,345 average indebtedness upon graduation, $6.8 million endowment

Cogswell students have a rare opportunity to develop engineering and creative skills. Students in the music engineering and computer imaging programs produce television/radio commercials, create demo tapes for local music schools, and execute product designs and multimedia concepts for outside agencies. Students in the engineering programs participate in local design competition and assist local companies in software development and programming code.

Students *Undergraduates:* 273 full-time, 227 part-time. Students come from 20 states and territories.

From out-of-state	9%	Reside on campus	9%
Age 25 or older	50%	Transferred in	13%
African Americans	2%	Asian Americans/Pacific Islanders	17%
Hispanic Americans	5%	Native Americans	1%

Faculty 76 (24% full-time).

Expenses (2000–2001) *Tuition:* full-time $8400; part-time $350 per unit. *Required fees:* full-time $20; $10 per term part-time. Full-time tuition and fees vary according to course load. Part-time tuition and fees vary according to course load. *Payment plan:* deferred payment. *Waivers:* employees or children of employees.

Library Cogswell College Library. *Operations spending 1999–2000:* $77,625. *Collection:* 11,257 titles, 102 serial subscriptions, 359 audiovisual materials.

College life *Housing: Options:* men-only, women-only. *Most popular organization:* ASB.

Campus security 24-hour emergency response devices.

After graduation 6 organizations recruited on campus 1997–98. *Career center:* 1 part-time personnel. Services include resume preparation, resume referral, career counseling, careers library, job interviews. **Graduate education:** 2% of class of 1999 went directly to graduate and professional school: 2% engineering.

Freshmen 88 applied, 75 admitted, 30 enrolled.

SAT verbal scores above 500	N/R	SAT math scores above 500	N/R
ACT above 18	N/R	From top 10% of their h.s. class	20%
From top quarter	30%	From top half	100%
1998 freshmen returning in 1999	64%		

Application *Options:* eApply at www.CollegeQuest.com, Common Application, deferred entrance. *Application fee:* $50. *Required:* essay or personal statement; high school transcript; minimum 2.5 GPA. *Required for some:* letters of recommendation; interview; portfolio.

Standardized tests *Admission: Recommended:* SAT I and SAT II or ACT.

Significant dates *Application deadlines:* 6/1 (freshmen), 6/1 (transfers). *Financial aid deadline:* continuous.

Freshman Application Contact
Mr. Paul A. Schreivogel, Dean of Recruitment and Marketing, Cogswell Polytechnical College, 1175 Bordeaux Drive, Sunnyvale, CA 94089. **Phone:** 408-541-0100 Ext. 112. **Toll-free phone:** 800-264-7955. **Fax:** 408-747-0764. **E-mail:** admin@cogswell.edu
Visit CollegeQuest.com for information on majors offered and athletics.

■ *See page 1444 for a narrative description.*

COLEMAN COLLEGE
La Mesa, California

Students *Undergraduates:* 739 full-time, 305 part-time. Students come from 19 states and territories. *Graduate:* 16 in graduate degree programs.

Peterson's Guide to Four-Year Colleges 2001 www.petersons.com 105

California

Coleman College (continued)

From out-of-state 1% Age 25 or older 68%

Faculty 101.

Expenses (1999–2000) *Tuition:* part-time $130 per unit. Tuition per degree: $13,260 for associate degree, $23,400 for bachelor's degree. *Payment plans:* guaranteed tuition, installment. *Waivers:* employees or children of employees.

Library Coleman College LaMesa Library. *Operations spending 1999–2000:* $6000. *Collection:* 66,800 titles, 69 serial subscriptions.

College life *Housing:* college housing not available.

Campus security 24-hour emergency response devices and patrols, late-night transport-escort service.

After graduation 83% of class of 1998 had job offers within 6 months. *Career center:* 3 full-time, 1 part-time personnel. Services include job fairs, resume preparation, interview workshops, resume referral, career counseling, job bank, job interviews.

Freshmen 332 enrolled.

| SAT verbal scores above 500 | N/R | SAT math scores above 500 | N/R |
| ACT above 18 | N/R | 1998 freshmen returning in 1999 | 88% |

Application *Options:* Common Application, deferred entrance. *Required:* high school transcript; interview.

Significant dates *Application deadlines:* rolling (freshmen), rolling (transfers). *Financial aid deadline:* continuous.

Freshman Application Contact
Admissions Department, Coleman College, 7380 Parkway Drive, La Mesa, CA 91942-1532. **Phone:** 619-465-3990. **Fax:** 619-465-0162. **E-mail:** jschafer@cts.com

Visit CollegeQuest.com for information on majors offered and athletics.

COLLEGE OF NOTRE DAME
Belmont, California

 Apply at CollegeQuest.com

- **Independent Roman Catholic**, comprehensive, founded 1851
- **Degrees** bachelor's and master's
- **Suburban** 80-acre campus with easy access to San Francisco
- **Coed**, 961 undergraduate students
- **Moderately difficult** entrance level, 79% of applicants were admitted
- **15:1 student-to-undergraduate faculty ratio**
- **$16,850 tuition** and fees
- **$5.9 million endowment**

Students *Undergraduates:* Students come from 18 states and territories, 19 other countries.

Age 25 or older	46%	International students	9%
African Americans	5%	Asian Americans/Pacific Islanders	12%
Hispanic Americans	15%	Native Americans	0.4%

Faculty 194 (33% full-time), 42% with terminal degrees.

Expenses (2000–2001, estimated) *Comprehensive fee:* $24,710 includes full-time tuition ($16,850) and room and board ($7860). Room and board charges vary according to board plan and housing facility. *Payment plan:* installment. *Waivers:* employees or children of employees.

Library College of Notre Dame Library. *Operations spending 1999–2000:* $568,320. *Collection:* 726 serial subscriptions, 8,314 audiovisual materials.

College life *Housing:* Options: coed, men-only, women-only. *Most popular organizations:* Associated Students of College of Notre Dame, Social Events Club, Social Action Club, Alianza Latina, Hawaiian Club.

Campus security 24-hour emergency response devices and patrols, late-night transport-escort service, controlled dormitory access.

After graduation 10 organizations recruited on campus 1997–98. *Career center:* 1 full-time, 2 part-time personnel. Services include job fairs, resume preparation, resume referral, career counseling, careers library, job bank, job interviews. *Graduate education:* 11% of class of 1999 went directly to graduate and professional school: 5% graduate arts and sciences, 4% business, 1% law, 1% medicine.

Freshmen 529 applied, 417 admitted. 7 class presidents, 15 student government officers.

Average high school GPA	3.3	SAT verbal scores above 500	43%
SAT math scores above 500	40%	ACT above 18	N/R
From top 10% of their h.s. class	14%	From top quarter	32%
From top half	69%	1998 freshmen returning in 1999	74%

Application *Options:* eApply at www.CollegeQuest.com, deferred entrance. *Application fee:* $35. *Required:* essay or personal statement; high school transcript; 1 letter of recommendation. *Required for some:* interview.

Standardized tests *Admission:* Required: SAT I or ACT.

Significant dates *Application deadlines:* rolling (freshmen), rolling (transfers). *Financial aid deadline priority date:* 3/2.

Freshman Application Contact
Ms. Susan Solomon, Associate Director of Admission, College of Notre Dame, 1500 Ralston Avenue, Belmont, CA 94002-1997. **Phone:** 650-508-3607. **Toll-free phone:** 800-263-0545. **Fax:** 650-637-0493. **E-mail:** admiss@cnd.edu

Visit CollegeQuest.com for information on majors offered and athletics. College video available at CollegeQuest.com.

■ *See page 1466 for a narrative description.*

COLUMBIA COLLEGE–HOLLYWOOD
Tarzana, California

- **Independent**, 4-year, founded 1952
- **Degrees** associate and bachelor's
- **Urban** 1-acre campus
- **Coed**, 144 undergraduate students, 97% full-time, 21% women, 79% men
- **Minimally difficult** entrance level, 88% of applicants were admitted
- **39% graduate** in 6 years or less
- **$10,725 tuition** and fees

Students *Undergraduates:* 140 full-time, 4 part-time. Students come from 21 states and territories, 17 other countries.

Age 25 or older	35%	International students	33%
African Americans	9%	Asian Americans/Pacific Islanders	4%
Hispanic Americans	7%		

Expenses (1999–2000) *One-time required fee:* $75. *Tuition:* full-time $10,500; part-time $3000 per term. *Required fees:* full-time $225; $75 per term part-time. *Payment plan:* installment.

Library Joseph E. Blath Memorial Library. *Collection:* 5,500 titles, 23 serial subscriptions, 220 audiovisual materials.

College life *Housing:* college housing not available.

Campus security Late-night transport-escort service.

After graduation *Career center:* Services include career counseling. *Graduate education:* 8% of class of 1999 went directly to graduate and professional school: 8% graduate arts and sciences.

Freshmen 32 applied, 28 admitted, 23 enrolled.

Average high school GPA	3.3	SAT verbal scores above 500	N/R
SAT math scores above 500	N/R	ACT above 18	N/R
From top 10% of their h.s. class	8%	From top quarter	23%
From top half	44%	1998 freshmen returning in 1999	83%

Application *Options:* early action, deferred entrance. *Application fee:* $50. *Required:* essay or personal statement; high school transcript; minimum 2.0 GPA; 2 letters of recommendation; interview.

Standardized tests *Admission:* Recommended: SAT I.

Significant dates *Application deadline:* rolling (freshmen). *Early action:* 1/15. *Notification:* continuous until 9/1 (freshmen), 2/15 (early action). *Financial aid deadline priority date:* 2/24.

Freshman Application Contact
Ms. Jacqueline Rossman, Admissions Director, Columbia College–Hollywood, 18618 Oxnard Street, Tarzana, CA 91356. **Phone:** 818-345-8414. **Fax:** 818-345-9053. **E-mail:** cchadfin@columbiacollege.edu

Visit CollegeQuest.com for information on majors offered and athletics.

■ *See page 1508 for a narrative description.*

CONCORDIA UNIVERSITY
Irvine, California

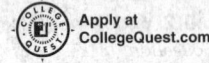 Apply at CollegeQuest.com

- **Independent**, comprehensive, founded 1972, affiliated with Lutheran Church–Missouri Synod

California

- **Degrees** bachelor's and master's
- **Suburban** 70-acre campus with easy access to Los Angeles
- **Coed**, 723 undergraduate students, 98% full-time, 64% women, 36% men
- **Moderately difficult** entrance level, 28% of applicants were admitted
- **18:1 student-to-undergraduate faculty ratio**
- **$15,700 tuition** and fees
- **$8000 average financial aid** package, $16,000 average indebtedness upon graduation, $3.8 million endowment

Students *Undergraduates:* 708 full-time, 15 part-time. Students come from 24 states and territories, 7 other countries. *The most frequently chosen baccalaureate fields are:* business/marketing, education, philosophy. **Graduate:** 125 in graduate degree programs.

From out-of-state	13%	Reside on campus	68%
Age 25 or older	8%	Transferred in	17%
International students	4%	African Americans	4%
Asian Americans/Pacific Islanders	5%	Hispanic Americans	8%
Native Americans	1%		

Faculty 78 (42% full-time), 49% with terminal degrees.

Expenses (2000–2001) *Comprehensive fee:* $20,990 includes full-time tuition ($15,700) and room and board ($5290). *College room only:* $3300. Room and board charges vary according to board plan. *Part-time tuition:* $480 per unit. *Payment plan:* installment. *Waivers:* employees or children of employees.

Library Concordia University Library. *Operations spending 1999–2000:* $430,000. *Collection:* 100,000 titles, 3,743 audiovisual materials.

College life *Housing:* on-campus residence required through senior year. *Options:* men-only, women-only. *Most popular organizations:* Student Senate, Fellowship of Christian Athletes, Student Life Board, intramurals, outreach.

Campus security 24-hour emergency response devices and patrols, student patrols, late-night transport-escort service.

After graduation 37 organizations recruited on campus 1997–98. *Career center:* 1 full-time, 6 part-time personnel. Services include job fairs, resume preparation, interview workshops, career/interest testing, career counseling, careers library, job bank, job interviews, graduate school workshop.

Freshmen 691 applied, 193 admitted, 193 enrolled.

Average high school GPA	3.3	SAT verbal scores above 500	52%
SAT math scores above 500	46%	ACT above 18	78%
From top 10% of their h.s. class	12%	From top quarter	36%
From top half	67%	1998 freshmen returning in 1999	73%

Application *Options:* eApply at www.CollegeQuest.com, Common Application, electronic application, deferred entrance. *Application fee:* $40. *Required:* high school transcript; 1 letter of recommendation. *Recommended:* minimum 2.8 GPA; interview.

Standardized tests *Admission: Required:* SAT I or ACT.

Significant dates *Application deadlines:* rolling (freshmen), rolling (transfers). *Notification:* continuous until 7/1 (freshmen). *Financial aid deadline:* 6/30. *Priority date:* 3/2.

Freshman Application Contact
Mr. Gary R. McDaniel, Vice President of Enrollment Services, Concordia University, , 153 Concordia West, Irvine, CA 92612-3299. **Phone:** 949-854-8002 Ext. 1108. **Toll-free phone:** 800-229-1200. **Fax:** 949-854-6894. **E-mail:** admission@cui.edu

Visit CollegeQuest.com for information on majors offered and athletics. College video and electronic viewbook available at CollegeQuest.com.

DESIGN INSTITUTE OF SAN DIEGO
San Diego, California

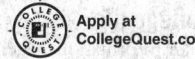
Apply at CollegeQuest.com

- **Proprietary**, 4-year, founded 1977
- **Degree** bachelor's
- **Urban** campus
- **Coed**, 261 undergraduate students
- **Noncompetitive** entrance level
- **$10,200 tuition** and fees

Students *Undergraduates:* Students come from 10 states and territories, 15 other countries.

Age 25 or older	70%

Faculty 41 (5% full-time).

Expenses (1999–2000) *Tuition:* full-time $10,200; part-time $425 per credit. *Payment plan:* installment.

Library *Collection:* 5,000 titles, 90 serial subscriptions.

College life *Housing:* college housing not available. *Most popular organizations:* American Society of Interior Designers, International Interior Designers Association, Illuminating Electrical Society.

After graduation 100% of class of 1998 had job offers within 6 months. *Career center:* Services include resume preparation, career counseling.

Freshmen

Average high school GPA	2.5	SAT verbal scores above 500	N/R
SAT math scores above 500	N/R	ACT above 18	N/R
1998 freshmen returning in 1999	87%		

Application *Option:* eApply at www.CollegeQuest.com. *Application fee:* $25. *Required:* high school transcript; minimum 2.0 GPA. *Recommended:* interview.

Significant dates *Application deadlines:* rolling (freshmen), rolling (transfers). *Financial aid deadline:* continuous.

Freshman Application Contact
Ms. Paula Parrish, Director of Admissions, Design Institute of San Diego, 8555 Commerce Avenue, San Diego, CA 92121-2685. **Phone:** 619-566-1200. **Toll-free phone:** 800-619-4DESIGN. **Fax:** 619-566-2711.

Visit CollegeQuest.com for information on majors offered and athletics.

- *See page 1576 for a narrative description.*

DEVRY INSTITUTE OF TECHNOLOGY
Fremont, California

- **Proprietary**, 4-year, founded 1998
- **Degrees** associate and bachelor's
- **Suburban** 17-acre campus with easy access to San Francisco
- **Coed**, 1,417 undergraduate students, 74% full-time, 24% women, 76% men
- **Minimally difficult** entrance level, 54% of applicants were admitted
- **32:1 student-to-undergraduate faculty ratio**
- **$8776 tuition** and fees

Part of DeVry, Inc.

Students *Undergraduates:* 1,052 full-time, 365 part-time. Students come from 16 states and territories, 10 other countries.

From out-of-state	5%	Age 25 or older	32%
Transferred in	6%	International students	1%
African Americans	9%	Asian Americans/Pacific Islanders	42%
Hispanic Americans	17%	Native Americans	1%

Faculty 44 (68% full-time).

Expenses (1999–2000) *Tuition:* full-time $8776; part-time $325 per credit hour. Part-time tuition and fees vary according to class time and course load. *Payment plans:* installment, deferred payment. *Waivers:* employees or children of employees.

Library Learning Resource Center.

College life *Housing:* college housing not available. *Most popular organizations:* Linux, Women Network, Routing, IEEE, soccer.

Campus security 24-hour emergency response devices and patrols, late-night transport-escort service.

Freshmen 945 applied, 514 admitted, 606 enrolled.

SAT verbal scores above 500	N/R	SAT math scores above 500	N/R
ACT above 18	N/R	1998 freshmen returning in 1999	52%

Application *Options:* electronic application, deferred entrance. *Application fee:* $25. *Required:* high school transcript; interview.

Standardized tests *Admission: Required:* Computerized Placement Test. *Recommended:* SAT I or ACT.

Significant dates *Application deadlines:* rolling (freshmen), rolling (transfers). *Financial aid deadline:* continuous.

Freshman Application Contact
Ms. Denise Sandoval, Director of Admissions, DeVry Institute of Technology, 6600 Dumbarton Circle, Fremont, CA 94555. **Phone:** 510-574-1100. **Toll-free phone:** 888-393-3879. **Fax:** 510-742-0868.

California

DeVry Institute of Technology (continued)

Visit CollegeQuest.com for information on majors offered and athletics.

DEVRY INSTITUTE OF TECHNOLOGY
Long Beach, California

- **Proprietary**, 4-year, founded 1984
- **Degrees** associate and bachelor's
- **Urban** 23-acre campus with easy access to Los Angeles
- **Coed**, 2,616 undergraduate students, 73% full-time, 28% women, 72% men
- **Minimally difficult** entrance level, 62% of applicants were admitted
- **24:1 student-to-undergraduate faculty ratio**
- **$7778 tuition** and fees

Part of DeVry, Inc.

Students *Undergraduates:* 1,921 full-time, 695 part-time. Students come from 27 states and territories, 13 other countries. *The most frequently chosen baccalaureate fields are:* business/marketing, computer/information sciences, engineering/engineering technologies.

From out-of-state	4%	Age 25 or older	48%
Transferred in	0.1%	International students	2%
African Americans	16%	Asian Americans/Pacific Islanders	26%
Hispanic Americans	24%	Native Americans	1%

Faculty 109 (27% full-time).

Expenses (1999–2000) *Tuition:* full-time $7778; part-time $290 per credit hour. Part-time tuition and fees vary according to class time and course load. *Payment plan:* installment. *Waivers:* employees or children of employees.

Library Learning Resource Center. *Collection:* 6,420 titles, 74 serial subscriptions.

College life *Housing:* college housing not available. *Most popular organizations:* Associated Student Body, Society of Hispanic Professional Engineers, National Society of Black Engineers, Institute of Electronics, United Islands.

Campus security 24-hour emergency response devices and patrols, late-night transport-escort service, motion detectors, closed hours.

After graduation 95% of class of 1998 had job offers within 6 months. *Career center:* 5 full-time personnel. Services include job fairs, resume preparation, resume referral, career counseling, careers library, job bank, job interviews.

Freshmen 1,040 applied, 644 admitted, 783 enrolled.

SAT verbal scores above 500	N/R	SAT math scores above 500	N/R
ACT above 18	N/R	1998 freshmen returning in 1999	55%

Application *Options:* electronic application, deferred entrance. *Application fee:* $25. *Required:* high school transcript; interview.

Standardized tests *Admission: Required:* Computerized Placement Test. *Recommended:* SAT I or ACT.

Significant dates *Application deadlines:* rolling (freshmen), rolling (transfers). *Financial aid deadline:* continuous.

Freshman Application Contact
Ms. Elaine Francisco, Director of Admissions, DeVry Institute of Technology, 3880 Kilroy Airport, Long Beach, CA 90806. **Phone:** 562-427-4162. **Toll-free phone:** 800-597-0444.

Visit CollegeQuest.com for information on majors offered and athletics.

DEVRY INSTITUTE OF TECHNOLOGY
Pomona, California

- **Proprietary**, 4-year, founded 1983
- **Degrees** associate and bachelor's
- **Urban** 15-acre campus with easy access to Los Angeles
- **Coed**, 3,491 undergraduate students, 71% full-time, 27% women, 73% men
- **Minimally difficult** entrance level, 62% of applicants were admitted
- **23:1 student-to-undergraduate faculty ratio**
- **$7778 tuition** and fees

Part of DeVry Inc.

Students *Undergraduates:* 2,466 full-time, 1,025 part-time. Students come from 24 states and territories, 17 other countries. *The most frequently chosen baccalaureate fields are:* business/marketing, computer/information sciences, engineering/engineering technologies.

From out-of-state	3%	Age 25 or older	44%
Transferred in	0.03%	International students	1%
African Americans	8%	Asian Americans/Pacific Islanders	31%
Hispanic Americans	28%	Native Americans	1%

Faculty 152 (32% full-time).

Expenses (1999–2000) *One-time required fee:* $670. *Tuition:* full-time $7778; part-time $290 per credit hour. Part-time tuition and fees vary according to class time and course load. *Payment plans:* installment, deferred payment. *Waivers:* employees or children of employees.

Library Learning Resource Center. *Collection:* 9,016 titles, 70 serial subscriptions.

College life *Housing:* college housing not available. *Most popular organizations:* Associated Student Body, International Club, National Society of Black Engineers, Filipino-American Student Business Association, Sigma Beta Delta.

Campus security 24-hour emergency response devices, late-night transport-escort service.

After graduation 96% of class of 1998 had job offers within 6 months. *Career center:* 10 full-time personnel. Services include job fairs, resume preparation, resume referral, career counseling, careers library, job bank, job interviews.

Freshmen 1,195 applied, 735 admitted, 934 enrolled.

SAT verbal scores above 500	N/R	SAT math scores above 500	N/R
ACT above 18	N/R	1998 freshmen returning in 1999	54%

Application *Options:* electronic application, deferred entrance. *Application fee:* $25. *Required:* high school transcript; interview.

Standardized tests *Admission: Required:* CPT. *Recommended:* SAT I or ACT.

Significant dates *Application deadlines:* rolling (freshmen), rolling (transfers). *Financial aid deadline:* continuous.

Freshman Application Contact
Mr. Byron Chung, Director of Admissions, DeVry Institute of Technology, 901 Corporate Center Drive, Pomona, CA 91768-2642. **Phone:** 909-622-9800. **Toll-free phone:** 800-243-3660. **Fax:** 909-623-5666.

Visit CollegeQuest.com for information on majors offered and athletics.

DEVRY INSTITUTE OF TECHNOLOGY
West Hills, California

- **Proprietary**, 4-year, founded 1999
- **Degrees** associate and bachelor's
- **Coed**, 364 undergraduate students, 61% full-time, 22% women, 78% men
- **61% of applicants were admitted**
- **$7778 tuition** and fees

Part of DeVry, Inc.

Students *Undergraduates:* 223 full-time, 141 part-time. Students come from 2 states and territories.

Age 25 or older	45%	Transferred in	0.3%
African Americans	5%	Asian Americans/Pacific Islanders	21%
Hispanic Americans	23%	Native Americans	1%

Expenses (1999–2000) *Tuition:* full-time 7778; part-time 290 per credit hour. Part-time tuition and fees vary according to class time and course load. *Payment plan:* installment. *Waivers:* employees or children of employees.

College life *Most popular organizations:* Associated Student Body, Computer Information Systems/Telecommunication Association, Accounting and Business Student Association, Filipino Student Association, Institute of Electronics and Electrical Engineers.

Campus security 24-hour emergency response devices and patrols, late-night transport-escort service.

Freshmen 791 applied, 483 admitted, 331 enrolled.

SAT verbal scores above 500	N/R	SAT math scores above 500	N/R
ACT above 18	N/R		

Application *Application fee:* 25. *Required:* high school transcript; interview.

California

Standardized tests *Admission: Recommended:* SAT I or ACT.
Significant dates *Application deadlines:* rolling (freshmen), rolling (transfers). *Financial aid deadline:* continuous.
Freshman Application Contact
Ms. Kathy Courtney, New Student Coordinator, DeVry Institute of Technology, 22801 Roscoe Boulevard, West Hills, CA 91304. **Phone:** 818-932-3001.
Visit CollegeQuest.com for information on majors offered and athletics.

DOMINICAN SCHOOL OF PHILOSOPHY AND THEOLOGY
Berkeley, California

- **Independent Roman Catholic**, upper-level, founded 1932
- **Degrees** bachelor's, master's, and first professional
- **Urban** campus with easy access to San Francisco
- **Coed**
- **Moderately difficult** entrance level
- **$7850 tuition** and fees

Expenses (1999–2000) *Tuition:* full-time $7800; part-time $325 per credit. *Required fees:* full-time $50; $50 per year part-time.
Institutional Web site http://www.dspt.edu/
College life *Housing: Option:* coed. *Most popular organization:* DSPT Associated Students.
Campus security Late-night transport-escort service.
Application *Option:* deferred entrance. *Application fee:* $30.
Admissions Office Contact
Dominican School of Philosophy and Theology, 2401 Ridge Road, Berkeley, CA 94709-1295. **E-mail:** rsconnolly@aol.com
Visit CollegeQuest.com for information on athletics.

DOMINICAN UNIVERSITY OF CALIFORNIA
San Rafael, California

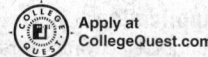

- **Independent**, comprehensive, founded 1890, affiliated with Roman Catholic Church
- **Degrees** bachelor's, master's, and postbachelor's certificates
- **Suburban** 80-acre campus with easy access to San Francisco
- **Coed**, 974 undergraduate students, 59% full-time, 81% women, 19% men
- **Moderately difficult** entrance level, 87% of applicants were admitted
- **12:1 student-to-undergraduate faculty ratio**
- **54.5% graduate** in 6 years or less
- **$16,844 tuition** and fees
- **$16,216 average financial aid** package, $11.1 million endowment

Students *Undergraduates:* 579 full-time, 395 part-time. Students come from 15 states and territories, 15 other countries. *The most frequently chosen baccalaureate fields are:* business/marketing, health professions and related sciences, psychology. *Graduate:* 447 in graduate degree programs.

From out-of-state	3%	Reside on campus	20%
Age 25 or older	54%	Transferred in	11%
International students	3%	African Americans	7%
Asian Americans/Pacific Islanders	11%	Hispanic Americans	9%
Native Americans	1%		

Faculty 205 (23% full-time), 37% with terminal degrees.
Expenses (1999–2000) *Comprehensive fee:* $24,364 includes full-time tuition ($16,512), mandatory fees ($332), and room and board ($7520). Full-time tuition and fees vary according to program. Room and board charges vary according to board plan. *Part-time tuition:* $688 per unit. *Part-time fees:* $166 per term part-time. Part-time tuition and fees vary according to program. *Payment plan:* installment. *Waivers:* employees or children of employees.
Library Archbishop Alemany Library plus 1 other. *Operations spending 1999–2000:* $510,410. *Collection:* 97,508 titles, 423 serial subscriptions, 532 audiovisual materials.

College life *Housing: Option:* coed. *Most popular organizations:* Amnesty International, Humans Interested in Psychology Club, science club, art club, multicultural club.
Campus security 24-hour patrols, late-night transport-escort service, controlled dormitory access.
After graduation 11 organizations recruited on campus 1997–98. 70% of class of 1998 had job offers within 6 months. *Career center:* 1 full-time personnel. Services include job fairs, resume preparation, interview workshops, career/interest testing, career counseling, careers library, job bank.
Freshmen 290 applied, 252 admitted, 114 enrolled.

Average high school GPA	3.17	SAT verbal scores above 500	59%
SAT math scores above 500	48%	ACT above 18	N/R
From top 10% of their h.s. class	15%	From top quarter	50%
From top half	77%	1998 freshmen returning in 1999	74%

Application *Options:* eApply at www.CollegeQuest.com, Common Application, electronic application, early admission, deferred entrance. *Application fee:* $40. *Required:* essay or personal statement; high school transcript; minimum 2.5 GPA; 1 letter of recommendation. *Required for some:* interview.
Standardized tests *Admission: Required:* SAT I or ACT. *Recommended:* SAT II Subject Tests.
Significant dates *Application deadlines:* rolling (freshmen), rolling (transfers). *Notification:* continuous until 8/15 (freshmen). *Financial aid deadline priority date:* 3/2.
Freshman Application Contact
Ms. Kris Thornton, Director of Freshman Admissions, Dominican University of California, 50 Acacia Avenue, San Rafael, CA 94901-2298. **Phone:** 415-257-1338. **Toll-free phone:** 888-323-6763. **Fax:** 415-485-3214. **E-mail:** enroll@dominican.edu
Visit CollegeQuest.com for information on majors offered and athletics. College video available at CollegeQuest.com.

■ *See page 1584 for a narrative description.*

EMMANUEL BIBLE COLLEGE
Pasadena, California

- **Independent**, 4-year, affiliated with Church of the Nazarene
- **Degrees** associate and bachelor's
- **10 undergraduate students**, 30% full-time, 30% women, 70% men
- **100% of applicants were admitted**
- **10:1 student-to-undergraduate faculty ratio**
- **4% graduate** in 6 years or less
- **$48,000 tuition** and fees
- **$51,000 endowment**

Students *Undergraduates:* 3 full-time, 7 part-time. Students come from 2 other countries. *The most frequently chosen baccalaureate field is:* philosophy.

From out-of-state	10%	Age 25 or older	100%
Transferred in	20%		

Faculty 6 (17% full-time), 67% with terminal degrees.
Expenses (1999–2000) *Tuition:* full-time 48,000; part-time 100 per quarter hour. Part-time tuition and fees vary according to course load. *Payment plan:* installment.
Library *Operations spending 1999–2000:* $800.
College life *Housing:* college housing not available. *Most popular organizations:* Student Council, Drama.
Campus security 24-hour emergency response devices and patrols.
Freshmen 10 applied, 10 admitted, 10 enrolled.

SAT verbal scores above 500	N/R	SAT math scores above 500	N/R
ACT above 18	N/R	1998 freshmen returning in 1999	90%

Application *Option:* eApply at www.CollegeQuest.com. *Application fee:* $25. *Required:* essay or personal statement; high school transcript; interview; Christian commitment. *Recommended:* letters of recommendation.
Significant dates *Application deadline:* 9/15 (freshmen). *Notification:* continuous until 8/31 (freshmen).
Freshman Application Contact
Mr. Yeghia Babikian, Director, Emmanuel Bible College, 1605 East Elizabeth Street, Pasadena, CA 91104. **Phone:** 626-791-2575. **Fax:** 626-398-2424.

Peterson's Guide to Four-Year Colleges 2001   www.petersons.com

California

Emmanuel Bible College (continued)
Visit CollegeQuest.com for information on majors offered and athletics.

FRESNO PACIFIC UNIVERSITY
Fresno, California

- **Independent**, comprehensive, founded 1944, affiliated with Mennonite Brethren Church
- **Degrees** associate, bachelor's, and master's
- **Suburban** 42-acre campus
- **Coed**, 872 undergraduate students, 93% full-time, 64% women, 36% men
- **Moderately difficult** entrance level, 83% of applicants were admitted
- **15:1 student-to-undergraduate faculty ratio**
- **63% graduate** in 6 years or less
- **$14,248 tuition** and fees
- **$15,556 average financial aid** package, $5 million endowment

Students *Undergraduates:* 811 full-time, 61 part-time. Students come from 14 states and territories, 12 other countries. *The most frequently chosen baccalaureate fields are:* business/marketing, education, philosophy. *Graduate:* 802 in graduate degree programs.

From out-of-state	3%	Reside on campus	55%
Age 25 or older	26%	Transferred in	15%
International students	4%	African Americans	4%
Asian Americans/Pacific Islanders	4%	Hispanic Americans	17%
Native Americans	2%		

Faculty 123 (62% full-time).
Expenses (2000–2001) *Comprehensive fee:* $18,668 includes full-time tuition ($13,950), mandatory fees ($298), and room and board ($4420). *College room only:* $2000. Room and board charges vary according to board plan and housing facility. *Part-time tuition:* $495 per unit. *Part-time fees:* $89 per term part-time. *Payment plan:* installment. *Waivers:* senior citizens and employees or children of employees.
Library Hiebert Library. *Operations spending 1999–2000:* $565,181. *Collection:* 148,000 titles, 2,000 serial subscriptions, 6,000 audiovisual materials.
College life *Housing:* on-campus residence required through sophomore year. *Options:* men-only, women-only. *Most popular organizations:* international club, kid's club, Amigos Unidos, Slavic club, women's soccer club.
Campus security 24-hour emergency response devices and patrols, student patrols, late-night transport-escort service, controlled dormitory access.
After graduation 7 organizations recruited on campus 1997–98. 30% of class of 1998 had job offers within 6 months. *Career center:* 1 full-time personnel. Services include resume preparation, interview workshops, resume referral, career/interest testing, career counseling, careers library, job bank, job interviews.
Freshmen 400 applied, 330 admitted, 168 enrolled.

Average high school GPA	3.52	SAT verbal scores above 500	49%
SAT math scores above 500	50%	ACT above 18	N/R
1998 freshmen returning in 1999	81%		

Application *Options:* electronic application, early admission, deferred entrance. *Application fee:* $30. *Required:* essay or personal statement; high school transcript; 1 letter of recommendation. *Required for some:* interview.
Standardized tests *Admission: Required:* SAT I or ACT.
Significant dates *Application deadlines:* rolling (freshmen), rolling (transfers). *Notification:* continuous until 7/31 (freshmen). **Financial aid deadline priority date:** 3/2.
Freshman Application Contact
Mr. Jon Endicott, Director of Admissions, Fresno Pacific University, 1717 South Chestnut Avenue, Fresno, CA 93702-4709. **Phone:** 559-453-2039. **Toll-free phone:** 800-660-6089. **Fax:** 559-453-2007. **E-mail:** ugadmis@fresno.edu

Visit CollegeQuest.com for information on majors offered and athletics. College video available at CollegeQuest.com.

- *See page 1698 for a narrative description.*

GOLDEN GATE UNIVERSITY
San Francisco, California

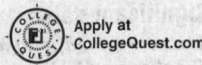

- **Independent**, university, founded 1853
- **Degrees** associate, bachelor's, master's, doctoral, and first professional
- **Urban** campus
- **Coed**, 1,222 undergraduate students, 27% full-time, 59% women, 41% men
- **Moderately difficult** entrance level, 97% of applicants were admitted
- **59% graduate** in 6 years or less
- **$8592 tuition** and fees
- **$11.3 million endowment**

Students *Undergraduates:* 332 full-time, 890 part-time. Students come from 66 other countries. *The most frequently chosen baccalaureate fields are:* business/marketing, computer/information sciences, trade and industry. *Graduate:* 555 in professional programs, 3,522 in other graduate degree programs.

From out-of-state	5%	Age 25 or older	80%
Transferred in	13%	International students	18%
African Americans	10%	Asian Americans/Pacific Islanders	14%
Hispanic Americans	9%	Native Americans	0.2%

Faculty 846 (11% full-time), 13% with terminal degrees.
Expenses (1999–2000) *Tuition:* full-time $8592; part-time $1074 per course. Full-time tuition and fees vary according to course level, location, and program. Part-time tuition and fees vary according to course level, location, and program. *Payment plan:* installment. *Waivers:* employees or children of employees.
Library Golden Gate University Library plus 1 other. *Operations spending 1999–2000:* $1 million. *Collection:* 79,204 titles, 3,335 serial subscriptions.
College life *Housing:* college housing not available.
Campus security Late-night transport-escort service.
After graduation *Career center:* 4 full-time personnel. Services include job fairs, career counseling.
Freshmen 66 applied, 64 admitted, 19 enrolled.

SAT verbal scores above 500	N/R	SAT math scores above 500	N/R
ACT above 18	N/R	1998 freshmen returning in 1999	80%

Application *Options:* eApply at www.CollegeQuest.com, Common Application, electronic application, deferred entrance. *Application fee:* $55. *Required:* high school transcript; minimum 2.0 GPA. *Required for some:* minimum 3.2 GPA; interview. *Recommended:* essay or personal statement; minimum 3.0 GPA.
Standardized tests *Admission: Recommended:* SAT I.
Significant dates *Application deadlines:* rolling (freshmen), rolling (transfers). *Financial aid deadline:* continuous.
Freshman Application Contact
Enrollment Services, Golden Gate University, 536 Mission Street, San Francisco, CA 94105-2968. **Phone:** 415-442-7800. **Toll-free phone:** 800-448-4968. **Fax:** 415-442-7807. **E-mail:** info@ggu.edu

Visit CollegeQuest.com for information on majors offered and athletics.

HARVEY MUDD COLLEGE
Claremont, California

- **Independent**, comprehensive, founded 1955
- **Degrees** bachelor's and master's
- **Suburban** 33-acre campus with easy access to Los Angeles
- **Coed**, 695 undergraduate students, 100% full-time, 26% women, 74% men
- **Most difficult** entrance level, 33% of applicants were admitted
- **9:1 student-to-undergraduate faculty ratio**
- **78% graduate** in 6 years or less
- **$22,083 tuition** and fees
- **$17,616 average financial aid** package, $17,544 average indebtedness upon graduation, $163.6 million endowment

Part of The Claremont Colleges Consortium.
Students *Undergraduates:* 695 full-time. Students come from 43 states and territories, 15 other countries. *The most frequently chosen baccalaureate*

California

fields are: engineering/engineering technologies, computer/information sciences, protective services/public administration. **Graduate:** 6 in graduate degree programs.

From out-of-state	54%	Reside on campus	96%
Age 25 or older	1%	Transferred in	1%
International students	3%	African Americans	1%
Asian Americans/Pacific Islanders	23%	Hispanic Americans	4%
Native Americans	0.3%		

Faculty 78 (96% full-time), 100% with terminal degrees.
Expenses (1999–2000) *Comprehensive fee:* $30,100 includes full-time tuition ($21,584), mandatory fees ($499), and room and board ($8017). *College room only:* $4077. Room and board charges vary according to board plan. *Part-time tuition:* $674 per credit hour. *Part-time fees:* $499 per year part-time. *Payment plan:* installment. *Waivers:* employees or children of employees.
Library Honnold Library plus 1 other. *Operations spending 1999–2000:* $886,506. *Collection:* 1.4 million titles, 4,321 serial subscriptions, 606 audiovisual materials.
College life *Housing:* on-campus residence required in freshman year. *Option:* coed. *Most popular organizations:* Delta "H" Outdoor Club, Etc. Players—Drama Club, club sports, Jazz Orchestra, Women's Forum.
Campus security 24-hour emergency response devices and patrols, late-night transport-escort service.
After graduation 72 organizations recruited on campus 1997–98. 90% of class of 1998 had job offers within 6 months. *Career center:* 2 full-time personnel. Services include job fairs, resume preparation, resume referral, career counseling, careers library, job bank, job interviews. *Graduate education:* 36% of class of 1999 went directly to graduate and professional school. *Major awards:* 1 Rhodes scholar.
Freshmen 1,642 applied, 535 admitted, 170 enrolled. 39 National Merit Scholars, 24 valedictorians.

SAT verbal scores above 500	100%	SAT math scores above 500	100%
ACT above 18	N/R	From top 10% of their h.s. class	87%
From top quarter	95%	From top half	100%
1998 freshmen returning in 1999	96%		

Application *Options:* eApply at www.CollegeQuest.com, Common Application, electronic application, early decision, deferred entrance. *Application fee:* $50. *Required:* essay or personal statement; high school transcript; 3 letters of recommendation. *Recommended:* interview.
Standardized tests *Admission: Required:* SAT I, SAT II Subject Tests, SAT II: Writing Test, SAT II Subject Test in math, third SAT II Subject Test.
Significant dates *Application deadlines:* 1/15 (freshmen), 5/1 (transfers). *Early decision:* 11/15. *Notification:* 4/1 (freshmen), 1/15 (early decision). *Financial aid deadline:* 2/1.
Freshman Application Contact
Mr. Deren Finks, Vice President, Dean of Admissions and Financial Aid, Harvey Mudd College, 301 East 12th Street, Claremont, CA 91711-5994. **Phone:** 909-621-8011. **Fax:** 909-621-8360. **E-mail:** admission@hmc.edu
Visit CollegeQuest.com for information on majors offered and athletics. Electronic viewbook available at CollegeQuest.com.

■ *See page 1774 for a narrative description.*

HOLY NAMES COLLEGE
Oakland, California

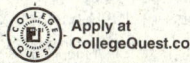 Apply at CollegeQuest.com

■ **Independent Roman Catholic**, comprehensive, founded 1868
■ **Degrees** bachelor's, master's, and postbachelor's certificates
■ **Urban** 60-acre campus with easy access to San Francisco
■ **Coed**, primarily women, 591 undergraduate students, 37% full-time, 82% women, 18% men
■ **Moderately difficult** entrance level, 75% of applicants were admitted
■ **12:1** student-to-undergraduate faculty ratio
■ **37% graduate** in 6 years or less
■ **$15,070 tuition** and fees
■ **$16,000 average financial aid** package, $16,324 average indebtedness upon graduation, $6.4 million endowment

Students *Undergraduates:* 219 full-time, 372 part-time. Students come from 7 states and territories, 9 other countries. *The most frequently chosen baccalaureate fields are:* business/marketing, health professions and related sciences, liberal arts/general studies. **Graduate:** 338 in graduate degree programs.

Reside on campus	52%	Age 25 or older	70%
Transferred in	18%	International students	4%
African Americans	30%	Asian Americans/Pacific Islanders	9%
Hispanic Americans	14%	Native Americans	1%

Faculty 122 (40% full-time).
Expenses (2000–2001) *Comprehensive fee:* $21,470 includes full-time tuition ($14,950), mandatory fees ($120), and room and board ($6400). Full-time tuition and fees vary according to course load. Room and board charges vary according to housing facility. *Part-time tuition:* $295 per unit. *Part-time fees:* $60 per term part-time. Part-time tuition and fees vary according to class time and location. *Payment plans:* installment, deferred payment. *Waivers:* employees or children of employees.
Library Cushing Library. *Operations spending 1999–2000:* $198,572. *Collection:* 110,455 titles, 457 serial subscriptions, 4,315 audiovisual materials.
College life *Housing:* Options: coed, women-only. *Most popular organizations:* Phi Kappa Delta Speech Club, AASU, Global Outlook, The Drama Club, Asian Pacific Club.
Campus security 24-hour emergency response devices, late-night transport-escort service, controlled dormitory access, electronically operated main gate.
After graduation 75 organizations recruited on campus 1997–98. *Career center:* 1 full-time, 1 part-time personnel. Services include job fairs, resume preparation, interview workshops, career/interest testing, career counseling, careers library, job bank, job interviews, career and life planning course.
Freshmen 161 applied, 121 admitted, 57 enrolled.

Average high school GPA	3.16	SAT verbal scores above 500	55%
SAT math scores above 500	43%	ACT above 18	N/R
From top 10% of their h.s. class	14%	From top quarter	40%
From top half	80%	1998 freshmen returning in 1999	81%

Application *Options:* eApply at www.CollegeQuest.com, Common Application, electronic application, deferred entrance. *Application fee:* $35. *Required:* essay or personal statement; high school transcript; 1 letter of recommendation.
Standardized tests *Admission: Required:* SAT I or ACT.
Significant dates *Application deadlines:* 6/1 (freshmen), 8/1 (transfers). *Financial aid deadline priority date:* 3/2.
Freshman Application Contact
Ms. Jo Ann Berridge, Dean of Undergraduate Admission, Holy Names College, Admission Office, Oakland, CA 94619. **Phone:** 510-436-1321. **Toll-free phone:** 800-430-1321. **Fax:** 510-436-1325. **E-mail:** admissions@admin.hnc.edu
Visit CollegeQuest.com for information on majors offered and athletics. College video available at CollegeQuest.com.

HOPE INTERNATIONAL UNIVERSITY
Fullerton, California

■ **Independent**, comprehensive, founded 1928, affiliated with Christian Churches and Churches of Christ
■ **Degrees** associate, bachelor's, and master's
■ **Suburban** 16-acre campus with easy access to Los Angeles
■ **Coed**, 706 undergraduate students, 78% full-time, 57% women, 43% men
■ **Moderately difficult** entrance level, 49% of applicants were admitted
■ **17:1** student-to-undergraduate faculty ratio
■ **$11,220 tuition** and fees
■ **$1.9 million endowment**

Students *Undergraduates:* 553 full-time, 153 part-time. Students come from 24 states and territories, 24 other countries. **Graduate:** 178 in graduate degree programs.

From out-of-state	31%	Reside on campus	36%
Age 25 or older	36%	Transferred in	14%
International students	7%	African Americans	5%
Asian Americans/Pacific Islanders	4%	Hispanic Americans	16%
Native Americans	1%		

Faculty 32 (78% full-time).
Expenses (1999–2000) *One-time required fee:* $200. *Comprehensive fee:* $15,720 includes full-time tuition ($10,980), mandatory fees ($240), and room and board ($4500). Room and board charges vary according to board

California

Hope International University (continued)
plan and housing facility. *Part-time tuition:* $407 per unit. *Part-time fees:* $240 per year part-time. Part-time tuition and fees vary according to course load. *Payment plan:* installment. *Waivers:* senior citizens and employees or children of employees.

Library Hurst Memorial Library. *Operations spending 1999–2000:* $246,780. *Collection:* 72,000 titles, 468 serial subscriptions.

College life *Housing:* on-campus residence required through sophomore year. *Options:* men-only, women-only.

Campus security 24-hour emergency response devices, student patrols.

After graduation 30% of class of 1998 had job offers within 6 months. *Career center:* 2 part-time personnel. Services include job fairs, resume preparation, interview workshops. *Graduate education:* 40% of class of 1999 went directly to graduate and professional school: 10% business, 10% education, 10% graduate arts and sciences, 10% theology.

Freshmen 381 applied, 186 admitted, 112 enrolled.

Average high school GPA	3.07	SAT verbal scores above 500	53%
SAT math scores above 500	58%	ACT above 18	89%
From top 10% of their h.s. class	4%	From top quarter	25%
From top half	30%	1998 freshmen returning in 1999	63%

Application *Options:* early admission, deferred entrance. *Application fee:* $30. *Required:* essay or personal statement; high school transcript; minimum 2.5 GPA; 2 letters of recommendation. *Required for some:* interview.

Standardized tests *Admission: Required:* SAT I or ACT.

Significant dates *Application deadlines:* 5/1 (freshmen), 5/1 (transfers). *Notification:* continuous until 7/1 (freshmen). *Financial aid deadline priority date:* 3/1.

Freshman Application Contact
Ms. Cheryl Lynn Edmond, Assistant Director, Admissions, Hope International University, 2500 East Nutwood Avenue, Fullerton, CA 92831-3138. **Phone:** 714-879-3901 Ext. 2225. **Toll-free phone:** 800-762-1294 Ext. 2235. **Fax:** 714-526-0231. **E-mail:** twinston@hiu.edu

Visit CollegeQuest.com for information on majors offered and athletics. College video available at CollegeQuest.com.

HUMBOLDT STATE UNIVERSITY
Arcata, California

- **State-supported**, comprehensive, founded 1913
- **Degrees** bachelor's and master's
- **Rural** 161-acre campus
- **Coed**, 6,426 undergraduate students, 90% full-time, 54% women, 46% men
- **Moderately difficult** entrance level, 80% of applicants were admitted
- **18:1 student-to-undergraduate faculty ratio**
- **46.7% graduate** in 6 years or less
- **$1861 tuition** and fees (in-state); $7765 (out-of-state)
- **$6794 average financial aid** package, $14,000 average indebtedness upon graduation, $16.4 million endowment

Part of California State University System.

Students *Undergraduates:* 5,812 full-time, 614 part-time. Students come from 46 states and territories, 23 other countries. *The most frequently chosen baccalaureate fields are:* interdisciplinary studies, natural resources/environmental science, social sciences and history. *Graduate:* 975 in graduate degree programs.

From out-of-state	3%	Reside on campus	18%
Age 25 or older	26%	Transferred in	15%
International students	0.5%	African Americans	2%
Asian Americans/Pacific Islanders	3%	Hispanic Americans	8%
Native Americans	3%		

Faculty 542 (58% full-time), 52% with terminal degrees.

Expenses (2000–2001, estimated) *Tuition, state resident:* full-time $0. *Tuition, nonresident:* full-time $5904. *Required fees:* full-time $1861; $629 per term part-time. *College room and board:* $5845; room only: $3366. Room and board charges vary according to board plan and housing facility. *Payment plan:* installment. *Waivers:* senior citizens and employees or children of employees.

Library *Operations spending 1999–2000:* $2.1 million. *Collection:* 3,169 serial subscriptions.

College life *Housing: Option:* coed. *Social organizations:* national fraternities, national sororities, local sororities; 1% of eligible men and 1% of eligible women are members. *Most popular organizations:* student radio station, Student Environmental Action Coalition, Youth Educational Services, Ballet Folklorico, International Student Union.

Campus security 24-hour emergency response devices and patrols, late-night transport-escort service, controlled dormitory access.

After graduation 67 organizations recruited on campus 1997–98. *Career center:* 8 full-time, 4 part-time personnel. Services include job fairs, resume preparation, interview workshops, career/interest testing, career counseling, careers library, job bank, job interviews.

Freshmen 3,298 applied, 2,645 admitted, 760 enrolled.

Average high school GPA	3.2	SAT verbal scores above 500	69%
SAT math scores above 500	63%	ACT above 18	85%
1998 freshmen returning in 1999	74%		

Application *Option:* electronic application. *Preference* given to state residents. *Application fee:* $55. *Required:* high school transcript; minimum 2.0 GPA.

Standardized tests *Admission: Required for some:* SAT I or ACT.

Significant dates *Application deadlines:* rolling (freshmen), 11/30 (transfers). *Financial aid deadline priority date:* 3/2.

Freshman Application Contact
Mr. Jeffery Savage, Office of Admissions and School Relations, Humboldt State University, 1 Harpst Street, Arcata, CA 95521-8299. **Phone:** 707-826-4402. **Fax:** 707-826-6194. **E-mail:** hsuinfo@laurel.humboldt.edu

Visit CollegeQuest.com for information on majors offered and athletics. College video and electronic viewbook available at CollegeQuest.com.

HUMPHREYS COLLEGE
Stockton, California

- **Independent**, comprehensive, founded 1896
- **Degrees** associate, bachelor's, and first professional
- **Suburban** 10-acre campus with easy access to San Francisco
- **Coed**, 597 undergraduate students
- **Noncompetitive** entrance level
- **$6804 tuition** and fees

Students *Undergraduates:* Students come from 3 states and territories, 4 other countries.

Reside on campus	6%	Age 25 or older	70%

Faculty 70 (31% full-time).

Expenses (1999–2000) *Tuition:* full-time $6804; part-time $162 per unit. Part-time tuition and fees vary according to course load. *College room only:* $2075. *Payment plans:* tuition prepayment, installment. *Waivers:* employees or children of employees.

Library Humphreys College Library plus 1 other. *Operations spending 1999–2000:* $66,952. *Collection:* 20,500 titles, 115 serial subscriptions.

College life *Housing: Option:* coed. *Most popular organizations:* Business Club, Paralegal Club, Student Council, Collegiate Secretaries International.

Campus security 24-hour patrols, late-night transport-escort service.

After graduation 25 organizations recruited on campus 1997–98. 60% of class of 1998 had job offers within 6 months. *Career center:* 1 full-time, 1 part-time personnel. Services include resume preparation, resume referral, career counseling, careers library, job bank, job interviews.

Freshmen

SAT verbal scores above 500	N/R	SAT math scores above 500	N/R
ACT above 18	N/R	1998 freshmen returning in 1999	50%

Application *Options:* early admission, deferred entrance. *Application fee:* $20. *Required:* high school transcript; minimum 2.0 GPA. *Required for some:* letters of recommendation. *Recommended:* interview.

Standardized tests *Placement: Recommended:* SAT I and SAT II or ACT. *Required for some:* SAT I and SAT II or ACT.

Significant dates *Application deadlines:* rolling (freshmen), rolling (transfers). *Financial aid deadline:* 6/30. *Priority date:* 1/1.

California

Freshman Application Contact
Ms. Wilma Okamoto Vaughn, Dean of Administration, Humphreys College, 6650 Inglewood Avenue, Stockton, CA 95207-3896. **Phone:** 209-478-0800. **Fax:** 209-478-8721.

Visit CollegeQuest.com for information on majors offered and athletics.

INSTITUTE OF COMPUTER TECHNOLOGY
Los Angeles, California

- **Proprietary**, 4-year, founded 1981
- **Degrees** associate and bachelor's
- **Urban** campus
- **Coed**, 231 undergraduate students, 100% full-time, 48% women, 52% men
- **Noncompetitive** entrance level

Students *Undergraduates:* Students come from 4 other countries.
Age 25 or older 94%

Library Main library plus 1 other. *Collection:* 2,000 titles.
College life *Housing:* college housing not available.
Campus security 24-hour patrols.
After graduation 6 organizations recruited on campus 1997–98. 98% of class of 1998 had job offers within 6 months. *Career center:* 1 full-time personnel. Services include job fairs, resume preparation, resume referral, career counseling, job interviews.

Freshmen
SAT verbal scores above 500   N/R   SAT math scores above 500   N/R
ACT above 18   N/R

Application *Option:* Common Application. *Application fee:* $75. *Required:* high school transcript; interview.
Standardized tests *Admission: Required:* CPAt.
Significant dates *Financial aid deadline:* continuous.
Freshman Application Contact
Mr. Bud Hutchins, Director of Admissions, Institute of Computer Technology, 3200 Wilshire Boulevard, # 400, Los Angeles, CA 90010-1308. **Phone:** 213-838-8300.

Visit CollegeQuest.com for information on majors offered and athletics.

INTERIOR DESIGNERS INSTITUTE
Newport Beach, California

Admissions Office Contact
Interior Designers Institute, 1061 Camelback Road, Newport Beach, CA 92660.

ITT TECHNICAL INSTITUTE
Anaheim, California

- **Proprietary**, primarily 2-year, founded 1982
- **Degrees** associate and bachelor's
- **Suburban** 5-acre campus with easy access to Los Angeles
- **Coed**
- **Minimally difficult** entrance level
- $9190 tuition and fees

Part of ITT Educational Services, Inc.
Admissions Office Contact
ITT Technical Institute, 525 North Muller Street, Anaheim, CA 92801-9938.
Visit CollegeQuest.com for information on majors offered and athletics.
College video available at CollegeQuest.com.

ITT TECHNICAL INSTITUTE
Hayward, California

- **Proprietary**, primarily 2-year, founded 1994
- **Degrees** associate and bachelor's
- **Minimally difficult** entrance level
- $9190 tuition and fees

Part of ITT Educational Services, Inc.
Admissions Office Contact
ITT Technical Institute, 3979 Trust Way, Hayward, CA 94545.
Visit CollegeQuest.com for information on majors offered and athletics.
College video available at CollegeQuest.com.

ITT TECHNICAL INSTITUTE
Oxnard, California

- **Proprietary**, primarily 2-year, founded 1993
- **Degrees** associate and bachelor's
- **Urban** campus with easy access to Los Angeles
- **Coed**, 708 undergraduate students, 100% full-time, 10% women, 90% men
- **Minimally difficult** entrance level

Part of ITT Educational Services, Inc.
Faculty 22 (73% full-time).
Admissions Office Contact
ITT Technical Institute, 2051 Solar Drive, Suite 150, Oxnard, CA 93030. **Toll-free phone:** 800-530-1582 Ext. 112. **Fax:** 805-988-1813.
Visit CollegeQuest.com for information on majors offered and athletics.
College video available at CollegeQuest.com.

ITT TECHNICAL INSTITUTE
Rancho Cordova, California

- **Proprietary**, primarily 2-year, founded 1954
- **Degrees** associate and bachelor's
- **Urban** 5-acre campus
- **Coed**
- **Minimally difficult** entrance level
- $9190 tuition and fees

Part of ITT Educational Services, Inc.
Admissions Office Contact
ITT Technical Institute, 10863 Gold Center Drive, Rancho Cordova, CA 95670-6034. **Toll-free phone:** 800-488-8466. **Fax:** 916-366-9225.
Visit CollegeQuest.com for information on majors offered and athletics.
College video available at CollegeQuest.com.

ITT TECHNICAL INSTITUTE
San Bernardino, California

- **Proprietary**, primarily 2-year, founded 1987
- **Degrees** associate and bachelor's
- **Urban** campus with easy access to Los Angeles
- **Coed**
- **Minimally difficult** entrance level

Part of ITT Educational Services, Inc.
Admissions Office Contact
ITT Technical Institute, 630 East Brier Drive, Suite 150, San Bernardino, CA 92408-2800. **Toll-free phone:** 800-942-0088. **Fax:** 909-888-6970.
Visit CollegeQuest.com for information on majors offered and athletics.
College video available at CollegeQuest.com.

ITT TECHNICAL INSTITUTE
San Diego, California

- **Proprietary**, primarily 2-year, founded 1981
- **Degrees** associate and bachelor's
- **Suburban** campus
- **Coed**
- **Minimally difficult** entrance level
- $9190 tuition and fees

Part of ITT Educational Services, Inc.

California

ITT Technical Institute (continued)
Admissions Office Contact
ITT Technical Institute, 9680 Granite Ridge Drive, San Diego, CA 92123. **Fax:** 619-462-9418.

Visit CollegeQuest.com for information on majors offered and athletics. College video available at CollegeQuest.com.

ITT TECHNICAL INSTITUTE
Sylmar, California

- **Proprietary**, primarily 2-year, founded 1982
- **Degrees** associate and bachelor's
- **Urban** campus with easy access to Los Angeles
- **Coed**
- **Minimally difficult** entrance level
- **$9190 tuition** and fees

Part of ITT Educational Services, Inc.
Admissions Office Contact
ITT Technical Institute, 12669 Encinitas Avenue, Sylmar, CA 91342-3664. **Toll-free phone:** 800-363-2086.

Visit CollegeQuest.com for information on majors offered and athletics. College video available at CollegeQuest.com.

ITT TECHNICAL INSTITUTE
West Covina, California

- **Proprietary**, primarily 2-year, founded 1982
- **Degrees** associate and bachelor's
- **Suburban** 4-acre campus with easy access to Los Angeles
- **Coed**
- **Minimally difficult** entrance level
- **$9190 tuition** and fees

Part of ITT Educational Services, Inc.
Admissions Office Contact
ITT Technical Institute, 1530 West Cameron Avenue, West Covina, CA 91790-2711. **Fax:** 626-960-8681.

Visit CollegeQuest.com for information on majors offered and athletics. College video available at CollegeQuest.com.

JOHN F. KENNEDY UNIVERSITY
Orinda, California

- **Independent**, comprehensive, founded 1964
- **Degrees** bachelor's, master's, doctoral, first professional, post-master's, and postbachelor's certificates
- **Suburban** 14-acre campus with easy access to San Francisco
- **Coed**, 207 undergraduate students, 10% full-time, 77% women, 23% men
- **Noncompetitive** entrance level
- **12:1 student-to-undergraduate faculty ratio**
- **$10,251 tuition** and fees

Students *Undergraduates:* 20 full-time, 187 part-time. *The most frequently chosen baccalaureate fields are:* business/marketing, liberal arts/general studies, psychology. *Graduate:* 318 in professional programs, 1,074 in other graduate degree programs.

Age 25 or older	93%	African Americans	13%
Asian Americans/Pacific Islanders	3%	Hispanic Americans	9%
Native Americans	1%		

Faculty 798 (4% full-time), 48% with terminal degrees.
Expenses (1999–2000) *Tuition:* full-time $10,215; part-time $227 per quarter hour. *Required fees:* full-time $36; $9 per term part-time. *Waivers:* employees or children of employees.
Library Robert M. Fisher Library. *Collection:* 87,746 titles, 946 serial subscriptions, 1,631 audiovisual materials.
College life *Housing:* college housing not available.
Campus security Late-night transport-escort service.

After graduation *Career center:* 1 full-time, 6 part-time personnel. Services include resume preparation, career counseling, careers library, job bank.
Freshmen

SAT verbal scores above 500	N/R	SAT math scores above 500	N/R
ACT above 18	N/R		

Application *Options:* Common Application, deferred entrance. *Application fee:* $50.
Significant dates *Application deadline:* rolling (transfers). *Financial aid deadline priority date:* 3/2.
Freshman Application Contact
Ms. Ellena Bloedorn, Director of Admissions and Records, John F. Kennedy University, 12 Altarinda Road, Orinda, CA 94563-2689. **Phone:** 925-258-2213. **Fax:** 925-254-6964.

Visit CollegeQuest.com for information on majors offered and athletics.

LA SIERRA UNIVERSITY
Riverside, California

- **Independent Seventh-day Adventist**, comprehensive, founded 1922
- **Degrees** associate, bachelor's, master's, doctoral, and post-master's certificates
- **Suburban** 630-acre campus with easy access to Los Angeles
- **Coed**, 1,215 undergraduate students, 94% full-time, 54% women, 46% men
- **Minimally difficult** entrance level, 74% of applicants were admitted
- **$14,910 tuition** and fees
- **$8.6 million endowment**

Students *Undergraduates:* 1,137 full-time, 78 part-time. Students come from 34 states and territories, 51 other countries. *The most frequently chosen baccalaureate fields are:* biological/life sciences, business/marketing, liberal arts/general studies. *Graduate:* 149 in graduate degree programs.

From out-of-state	17%	Reside on campus	41%
Age 25 or older	14%	Transferred in	15%
International students	13%	African Americans	7%
Asian Americans/Pacific Islanders	22%	Hispanic Americans	19%
Native Americans	1%		

Expenses (1999–2000) *Comprehensive fee:* $19,101 includes full-time tuition ($14,580), mandatory fees ($330), and room and board ($4191). Full-time tuition and fees vary according to course load. Room and board charges vary according to board plan and housing facility. *Part-time tuition:* $405 per unit. Part-time tuition and fees vary according to course load. *Payment plan:* installment. *Waivers:* employees or children of employees.
Library University Library plus 1 other. *Operations spending 1999–2000:* $925,981. *Collection:* 238,369 titles, 1,585 serial subscriptions.
College life *Housing:* on-campus residence required through senior year. *Options:* men-only, women-only. *Most popular organizations:* Student Association of LSU, Korean Student Association, Students In Free Enterprise (SIFE), Olé Club, Black Student Association.
Campus security 24-hour emergency response devices and patrols, student patrols, late-night transport-escort service.
After graduation 40 organizations recruited on campus 1997–98. 35% of class of 1998 had job offers within 6 months. *Career center:* 3 part-time personnel. Services include job fairs, resume preparation, interview workshops, resume referral, career/interest testing, career counseling, careers library, job bank, job interviews.
Freshmen 644 applied, 474 admitted, 465 enrolled.

Average high school GPA	3.25	SAT verbal scores above 500	50%
SAT math scores above 500	51%	ACT above 18	64%
From top 10% of their h.s. class	14%	From top quarter	34%
From top half	68%	1998 freshmen returning in 1999	55%

Application Preference given to Seventh-day Adventists. *Application fee:* $30. *Required:* high school transcript; minimum 2.5 GPA; 2 letters of recommendation. *Required for some:* interview.
Standardized tests *Placement: Required:* SAT I or ACT. *Required for some:* SAT II: Writing Test.
Significant dates *Application deadlines:* rolling (freshmen), rolling (transfers).

California

Freshman Application Contact
Dr. Tom Smith, Vice President for Enrollment Services, La Sierra University, 4700 Pierce Street, Riverside, CA 92515-8247. **Phone:** 909-785-2432. **Toll-free phone:** 800-874-5587. **Fax:** 909-785-2901. **E-mail:** ivy@polaris.lasierra.edu

Visit CollegeQuest.com for information on majors offered and athletics.

LEE COLLEGE AT THE UNIVERSITY OF JUDAISM
California—See University of Judaism

LIFE BIBLE COLLEGE
San Dimas, California

Apply at CollegeQuest.com

- **Independent**, 4-year, founded 1923, affiliated with International Church of the Foursquare Gospel
- **Degrees** associate and bachelor's
- **Suburban** 9-acre campus with easy access to Los Angeles
- **Coed**, 501 undergraduate students, 78% full-time, 51% women, 49% men
- **Minimally difficult** entrance level, 93% of applicants were admitted
- **21:1 student-to-undergraduate faculty ratio**
- **47% graduate** in 6 years or less
- **$5625 tuition** and fees
- **$5205 average financial aid** package, $5218 average indebtedness upon graduation, $1.8 million endowment

Students *Undergraduates:* 389 full-time, 112 part-time. Students come from 32 states and territories. *The most frequently chosen baccalaureate field is:* philosophy.

From out-of-state	48%	Reside on campus	54%
Age 25 or older	23%	Transferred in	13%
International students	1%	African Americans	3%
Asian Americans/Pacific Islanders	5%	Hispanic Americans	11%
Native Americans	0.4%		

Faculty 31 (48% full-time), 19% with terminal degrees.
Expenses (2000–2001) *Comprehensive fee:* $8725 includes full-time tuition ($5375), mandatory fees ($250), and room and board ($3100). *Part-time tuition:* $175 per semester hour. Part-time tuition and fees vary according to course load. *Payment plan:* installment. *Waivers:* employees or children of employees.
Library LIFE Alumni Library. *Operations spending 1999–2000:* $111,191. *Collection:* 29,518 titles, 254 serial subscriptions.
College life *Housing:* on-campus residence required in freshman year. *Options:* men-only, women-only. *Most popular organizations:* choir, chorale, Youth for Christ.
Campus security 24-hour emergency response devices, part-time security personnel.
After graduation 80 organizations recruited on campus 1997–98. 90% of class of 1998 had job offers within 6 months. *Career center:* 1 full-time, 1 part-time personnel. Services include resume preparation, career counseling, careers library, job bank, job interviews. *Graduate education:* 15% of class of 1999 went directly to graduate and professional school: 10% theology, 5% education.
Freshmen 90 applied, 84 admitted, 79 enrolled.

Average high school GPA	3.14	SAT verbal scores above 500	65%
SAT math scores above 500	16%	ACT above 18	83%
From top 10% of their h.s. class	0%	From top quarter	5%
From top half	43%	1998 freshmen returning in 1999	74%

Application *Options:* eApply at www.CollegeQuest.com, Common Application, electronic application, deferred entrance. *Application fee:* $35. *Required:* essay or personal statement; high school transcript; minimum 2.0 GPA; 3 letters of recommendation; Christian testimony.
Standardized tests *Admission: Required:* SAT I or ACT. *Recommended:* SAT II: Writing Test.
Significant dates *Application deadlines:* 7/1 (freshmen), 7/1 (transfers). *Financial aid deadline priority date:* 7/15.

Freshman Application Contact
Mrs. Linda Hibdon, Admissions Director, LIFE Bible College, 1100 Covina Boulevard, San Dimas, CA 91773-3298. **Phone:** 909-599-5433 Ext. 303. **Toll-free phone:** 800-356-0001. **Fax:** 909-599-6690. **E-mail:** adm@lifebible.edu

Visit CollegeQuest.com for information on majors offered and athletics.

LINCOLN UNIVERSITY
Oakland, California

- **Independent**, comprehensive, founded 1919
- **Degrees** bachelor's and master's
- **Urban** 2-acre campus
- **Coed**, 109 undergraduate students, 100% full-time, 35% women, 65% men
- **Minimally difficult** entrance level
- **$6015 tuition** and fees

Students *Undergraduates:* 109 full-time. Students come from 37 other countries. *The most frequently chosen baccalaureate field is:* computer/information sciences. *Graduate:* 100 in graduate degree programs.

Age 25 or older	58%	International students	95%

Faculty 35 (23% full-time).
Expenses (1999–2000) *Tuition:* full-time $5760. *Required fees:* full-time $255. Full-time tuition and fees vary according to program. *Payment plan:* deferred payment. *Waivers:* employees or children of employees.
Library Lincoln Library. *Collection:* 17,532 titles, 642 serial subscriptions.
College life *Housing:* college housing not available.
Campus security 24-hour emergency response devices.
After graduation 79% of class of 1998 had job offers within 6 months. *Career center:* 1 full-time personnel. Services include job fairs, resume preparation, career counseling.
Freshmen 18 enrolled.

SAT verbal scores above 500	N/R	SAT math scores above 500	N/R
ACT above 18	N/R		

Application *Option:* deferred entrance. *Application fee:* $50. *Required:* high school transcript; minimum 2.0 GPA. *Required for some:* essay or personal statement; letters of recommendation; interview.
Standardized tests *Placement: Required:* Michigan English Language Assessment Battery
Significant dates *Application deadlines:* 8/31 (freshmen), 8/31 (transfers).
Freshman Application Contact
Ms. Vivian Xu, Admissions Officer, Lincoln University, 401 15th Street, Oakland, CA 94612. **Phone:** 415-221-1212 Ext. 115. **Fax:** 510-628-8026.
Visit CollegeQuest.com for information on majors offered and athletics.

LOMA LINDA UNIVERSITY
Loma Linda, California

- **Independent Seventh-day Adventist**, university, founded 1905
- **Degrees** associate, bachelor's, master's, doctoral, first professional, post-master's, and postbachelor's certificates
- **Small-town** campus with easy access to Los Angeles
- **Coed**, 1,272 undergraduate students, 79% full-time, 70% women, 30% men
- **$14,220 tuition** and fees

Students *Undergraduates:* Students come from 49 states and territories. *Graduate:* 1,034 in professional programs, 1,277 in other graduate degree programs.

From out-of-state	25%	Age 25 or older	46%
African Americans	4%	Asian Americans/Pacific Islanders	24%
Hispanic Americans	17%	Native Americans	0.4%

Faculty 1,290 (77% full-time).
Expenses (1999–2000) *Tuition:* full-time $14,220. Full-time tuition and fees vary according to course load, degree level, and program. Part-time tuition and fees vary according to course load, degree level, and program.

California

Loma Linda University (continued)
College room only: $1983. Room and board charges vary according to housing facility. *Part-time tuition per unit:* $395 for 1 to 6 units, $237 for 7 to 11 units.
Library Del E. Webb Memorial Library. *Collection:* 304,152 titles, 1,145 serial subscriptions.
College life *Housing:* on-campus residence required through senior year. *Options:* men-only, women-only. *Most popular organizations:* Students for International Mission Services, Students Computing Organization.
Campus security 24-hour emergency response devices and patrols, late-night transport-escort service.
Freshmen

| SAT verbal scores above 500 | N/R | SAT math scores above 500 | N/R |
| ACT above 18 | N/R | | |

Application *Option:* Common Application. *Application fee:* $50.
Significant dates *Financial aid deadline priority date:* 3/2.
Freshman Application Contact
Dr. Cyril Connelly, Director of Marketing, Loma Linda University, Loma Linda, CA 92350. **Phone:** 909-824-4792.
Visit CollegeQuest.com for information on majors offered and athletics.

LOUISE SALINGER ACADEMY OF FASHION
California—See Art Institutes International at San Francisco

LOYOLA MARYMOUNT UNIVERSITY
Los Angeles, California

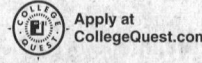
Apply at CollegeQuest.com

- **Independent Roman Catholic**, comprehensive, founded 1911
- **Degrees** bachelor's, master's, and first professional
- **Suburban** 128-acre campus
- **Coed**, 4,567 undergraduate students, 94% full-time, 58% women, 42% men
- **Moderately difficult** entrance level, 62% of applicants were admitted
- **13:1 student-to-undergraduate faculty ratio**
- **$19,225 tuition** and fees

Students *Undergraduates:* 4,303 full-time, 264 part-time. Students come from 50 states and territories, 76 other countries. *Graduate:* 1,344 in professional programs, 1,234 in other graduate degree programs.

From out-of-state	17%	Reside on campus	51%
Age 25 or older	7%	Transferred in	7%
African Americans	7%	Asian Americans/Pacific Islanders	14%
Hispanic Americans	20%	Native Americans	1%

Faculty 599 (58% full-time), 38% with terminal degrees.
Expenses (2000–2001) *Comprehensive fee:* $26,833 includes full-time tuition ($19,100), mandatory fees ($125), and room and board ($7608). *College room only:* $4328. Full-time tuition and fees vary according to course load. Room and board charges vary according to board plan and housing facility. *Part-time tuition:* $795 per unit. *Part-time fees:* $2 per unit; $14 per term part-time. Part-time tuition and fees vary according to course load. *Payment plan:* installment. *Waivers:* employees or children of employees.
Library Charles von der Ahe Library plus 1 other. *Collection:* 487,232 titles, 9,505 serial subscriptions.
College life *Housing:* Option: coed. *Social organizations:* national fraternities, national sororities; 13% of eligible men and 11% of eligible women are members. *Most popular organization:* service clubs.
Campus security 24-hour emergency response devices and patrols, late-night transport-escort service, controlled dormitory access.
After graduation 80 organizations recruited on campus 1997–98. *Career center:* 4 full-time personnel. Services include job fairs, resume preparation, resume referral, career counseling, careers library, job interviews. *Major awards:* 1 Fulbright Scholar.

Freshmen 6,341 applied, 3,959 admitted, 1,024 enrolled.

Average high school GPA	3.29	SAT verbal scores above 500	84%
SAT math scores above 500	83%	ACT above 18	N/R
From top 10% of their h.s. class	28%	From top quarter	50%
From top half	85%	1998 freshmen returning in 1999	3%

Application *Options:* eApply at www.CollegeQuest.com, electronic application, early admission, deferred entrance. *Application fee:* $40. *Required:* essay or personal statement; high school transcript; 1 letter of recommendation. *Recommended:* interview.
Standardized tests *Admission: Required:* SAT I or ACT.
Significant dates *Application deadlines:* 2/1 (freshmen), 7/1 (transfers). *Financial aid deadline priority date:* 2/15.
Freshman Application Contact
Mr. Matthew X. Fissinger, Director of Admissions, Loyola Marymount University, 7900 Loyola Boulevard, Los Angeles, CA 90045-8366. **Phone:** 310-338-2750. **Toll-free phone:** 800-LMU-INFO. **Fax:** 310-338-2797. **E-mail:** admissns@lmumail.lmu.edu
Visit CollegeQuest.com for information on majors offered and athletics. College video available at CollegeQuest.com.

■ *See page 1954 for a narrative description.*

THE MASTER'S COLLEGE AND SEMINARY
Santa Clarita, California

- **Independent nondenominational**, comprehensive, founded 1927
- **Degrees** bachelor's, master's, and first professional
- **Suburban** 110-acre campus with easy access to Los Angeles
- **Coed**
- **Moderately difficult** entrance level
- **$13,400 tuition** and fees

Expenses (1999–2000) *Comprehensive fee:* $18,700 includes full-time tuition ($13,200), mandatory fees ($200), and room and board ($5300). *College room only:* $3000. Full-time tuition and fees vary according to course load. Room and board charges vary according to board plan. *Part-time tuition:* $550 per unit. *Part-time fees:* $100 per term part-time. Part-time tuition and fees vary according to course load.
Institutional Web site http://www.masters.edu/
College life *Housing:* on-campus residence required through sophomore year. *Options:* men-only, women-only.
Campus security 24-hour patrols.
Application *Options:* early action, deferred entrance. *Application fee:* $35. *Required:* essay or personal statement; high school transcript; minimum 2.5 GPA; 2 letters of recommendation; interview.
Standardized tests *Admission: Required:* SAT I or ACT.
Admissions Office Contact
The Master's College and Seminary, 21726 Placerita Canyon Road, Santa Clarita, CA 91321-1200. **Toll-free phone:** 800-568-6248. **E-mail:** enrollment@masters.edu
Visit CollegeQuest.com for information on athletics. College video available at CollegeQuest.com.

MENLO COLLEGE
Atherton, California

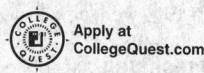
Apply at CollegeQuest.com

- **Independent**, 4-year, founded 1927
- **Degree** bachelor's
- **Small-town** 45-acre campus with easy access to San Francisco
- **Coed**, 626 undergraduate students, 78% full-time, 45% women, 55% men
- **Minimally difficult** entrance level, 79% of applicants were admitted
- **19:1 student-to-undergraduate faculty ratio**
- **28% graduate** in 6 years or less
- **$16,800 tuition** and fees
- **$14,482 average financial aid** package, $4 million endowment

Students *Undergraduates:* 486 full-time, 140 part-time. Students come from 18 states and territories, 17 other countries.

California

From out-of-state	17%	Reside on campus	66%
Age 25 or older	22%	Transferred in	16%
International students	7%	African Americans	8%
Asian Americans/Pacific Islanders	15%	Hispanic Americans	9%
Native Americans	0.5%		

Faculty 59 (36% full-time).
Expenses (1999–2000) *One-time required fee:* $300. *Comprehensive fee:* $23,600 includes full-time tuition ($16,800) and room and board ($6800). Room and board charges vary according to housing facility. *Part-time tuition:* $700 per unit. Part-time tuition and fees vary according to course load. *Payment plan:* installment. *Waivers:* employees or children of employees.
Library Bowman Library. *Operations spending 1999–2000:* $173,181. *Collection:* 55,000 titles, 350 serial subscriptions.
College life *Housing:* on-campus residence required through sophomore year. *Option:* coed. *Social organizations:* Wine Tasting and Protocol Club; 5% of eligible men and 5% of eligible women are members. *Most popular organizations:* International Club, Residence Hall Association, French Club, Media Network, Hawaiian Club.
Campus security 24-hour emergency response devices and patrols.
After graduation *Career center:* 1 full-time personnel. Services include job fairs, resume preparation, resume referral, career counseling, careers library, job bank, job interviews.
Freshmen 404 applied, 320 admitted, 128 enrolled.

Average high school GPA	3.0	SAT verbal scores above 500	N/R
SAT math scores above 500	N/R	ACT above 18	N/R
From top 10% of their h.s. class	5%	From top quarter	27%
From top half	63%	1998 freshmen returning in 1999	61%

Application *Options:* eApply at www.CollegeQuest.com, electronic application, deferred entrance. *Application fee:* $40. *Required:* essay or personal statement; high school transcript; minimum 3.0 GPA; 1 letter of recommendation. *Recommended:* interview.
Standardized tests *Admission: Required:* SAT I or ACT.
Significant dates *Application deadlines:* rolling (freshmen), rolling (transfers). *Financial aid deadline:* continuous.
Freshman Application Contact
Dr. Greg Smith, Director of Admissions, Menlo College, 1000 El Camino Real, Atherton, CA 94027-4301. **Phone:** 650-833-3305. **Toll-free phone:** 800-556-3656. **Fax:** 650-617-2395. **E-mail:** admissions@menlo.edu
Visit CollegeQuest.com for information on majors offered and athletics. College video and electronic viewbook available at CollegeQuest.com.

■ *See page 2038 for a narrative description.*

MILLS COLLEGE
Oakland, California

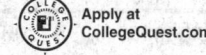 Apply at CollegeQuest.com

■ **Independent**, comprehensive, founded 1852
■ **Degrees** bachelor's, master's, and doctoral
■ **Urban** 135-acre campus with easy access to San Francisco
■ **Women** only, 727 undergraduate students, 94% full-time
■ **Moderately difficult** entrance level, 78% of applicants were admitted
■ **11:1 student-to-undergraduate faculty ratio**
■ **$17,852 tuition** and fees
■ **$18,246 average financial aid** package, $17,083 average indebtedness upon graduation, $177.9 million endowment

Why Mills? Why a women's college? Because since half of the College's professors are women (not the case at coeducational institutions), students have successful role models in every field. And all of Mills' undergraduate resources are committed to women. When women graduate from Mills, they know they can succeed. That confidence makes all the difference.

Students *Undergraduates:* 680 full-time, 47 part-time. Students come from 39 states and territories, 10 other countries. *The most frequently chosen baccalaureate fields are:* interdisciplinary studies, social sciences and history, visual/performing arts. *Graduate:* 395 in graduate degree programs.

From out-of-state	20%	Reside on campus	53%
Transferred in	13%	International students	0.4%
African Americans	7%	Asian Americans/Pacific Islanders	8%
Hispanic Americans	7%	Native Americans	1%

Faculty 177 (46% full-time).

Expenses (1999–2000) *Comprehensive fee:* $25,148 includes full-time tuition ($17,250), mandatory fees ($602), and room and board ($7296). Room and board charges vary according to board plan and housing facility. *Part-time tuition:* $2690 per course. *Part-time fees:* $301 per term part-time. *Payment plan:* installment. *Waivers:* employees or children of employees.
Library F. W. Olin Library plus 1 other. *Operations spending 1999–2000:* $1.1 million. *Collection:* 189,814 titles, 2,029 serial subscriptions, 6,046 audio-visual materials.
College life *Housing: Options:* women-only, cooperative. *Most popular organizations:* class organizations, MECHA, ASA (Asian Sisterhood Alliance), Mills Environmental Organization, BWC (Black Women's Collective).
Campus security 24-hour emergency response devices and patrols, late-night transport-escort service, controlled dormitory access.
After graduation 17 organizations recruited on campus 1997–98. *Career center:* 3 full-time personnel. Services include resume preparation, resume referral, career counseling, careers library, job bank, job interviews.
Freshmen 461 applied, 360 admitted, 116 enrolled.

Average high school GPA	3.52	SAT verbal scores above 500	85%
SAT math scores above 500	75%	ACT above 18	N/R
From top 10% of their h.s. class	35%	From top quarter	64%
From top half	96%	1998 freshmen returning in 1999	77%

Application *Options:* eApply at www.CollegeQuest.com, Common Application, early action, deferred entrance. *Application fee:* $40. *Required:* high school transcript; 3 letters of recommendation; essay or graded paper. *Recommended:* interview.
Standardized tests *Admission: Required:* SAT I or ACT. *Recommended:* SAT II Subject Tests.
Significant dates *Application deadlines:* 2/15 (freshmen), 3/2 (transfers). *Early action:* 11/15. *Notification:* 3/30 (freshmen), 12/30 (early action). *Financial aid deadline priority date:* 2/15.
Freshman Application Contact
Avis Hinkson, Dean of Admission, Mills College, 5000 MacArthur Boulevard, Oakland, CA 94613-1000. **Phone:** 510-430-2135. **Toll-free phone:** 800-87-MILLS. **Fax:** 510-430-3314. **E-mail:** admission@mills.edu
Visit CollegeQuest.com for information on majors offered and athletics. College video available at CollegeQuest.com.

■ *See page 2062 for a narrative description.*

MONTEREY INSTITUTE OF INTERNATIONAL STUDIES
Monterey, California

■ **Independent**, upper-level, founded 1955
■ **Degrees** bachelor's and master's
■ **Small-town** 5-acre campus
■ **Coed**, 20 undergraduate students, 100% full-time, 60% women, 40% men
■ **Moderately difficult** entrance level, 80% of applicants were admitted
■ **10:1 student-to-undergraduate faculty ratio**
■ **$19,500 tuition** and fees

Students *Undergraduates:* Students come from 10 states and territories, 6 other countries. *Graduate:* 635 in graduate degree programs.

From out-of-state	50%	Age 25 or older	15%
International students	30%		

Faculty 170 (49% full-time), 100% with terminal degrees.
Expenses (2000–2001) *Tuition:* full-time $19,500; part-time $820 per credit. *Payment plan:* installment. *Waivers:* employees or children of employees.
Library Barnet J. Segal Library. *Collection:* 68,000 titles, 556 serial subscriptions, 15 audiovisual materials.
College life *Housing:* college housing not available. *Most popular organizations:* Green Planet Club, Amnesty International, Spanish Club, Japan Forum, Chinese Student Association.
Campus security 24-hour patrols.
After graduation 85 organizations recruited on campus 1997–98. 90% of class of 1998 had job offers within 6 months. *Career center:* 5 full-time

California

Monterey Institute of International Studies (continued)
personnel. Services include job fairs, resume preparation, resume referral, career counseling, careers library, job bank, job interviews. *Major awards:* 1 Fulbright Scholar.
Application *Options:* electronic application, deferred entrance. *Application fee:* $50.
Significant dates *Application deadline:* 8/15 (transfers). *Financial aid deadline priority date:* 3/15.
Freshman Application Contact
Ms. Berta Aug, Director of Recruiting and Admissions, Monterey Institute of International Studies, 425 Van Buren Street, Monterey, CA 93940. **Phone:** 831-647-4123. **Toll-free phone:** 800-824-7235. **Fax:** 831-647-6405. **E-mail:** admit@miis.edu
Visit CollegeQuest.com for information on majors offered and athletics.

MOUNT ST. MARY'S COLLEGE
Los Angeles, California

- **Independent Roman Catholic**, comprehensive, founded 1925
- **Degrees** associate, bachelor's, and master's
- **Suburban** 71-acre campus
- **Coed,** primarily women, 1,753 undergraduate students, 69% full-time, 94% women, 6% men
- **Moderately difficult** entrance level, 44% of applicants were admitted
- **15:1** student-to-undergraduate faculty ratio
- **$17,328** tuition and fees
- **$46.9 million** endowment

Students *Undergraduates:* 1,206 full-time, 547 part-time. Students come from 21 states and territories, 3 other countries. *The most frequently chosen baccalaureate fields are:* health professions and related sciences, biological/life sciences, liberal arts/general studies. *Graduate:* 313 in graduate degree programs.

From out-of-state	4%	Age 25 or older	16%
Transferred in	12%	International students	0.2%
African Americans	12%	Asian Americans/Pacific Islanders	18%
Hispanic Americans	40%	Native Americans	1%

Faculty 260 (35% full-time), 32% with terminal degrees.
Expenses (1999–2000) *Comprehensive fee:* $23,962 includes full-time tuition ($16,776), mandatory fees ($552), and room and board ($6634). Full-time tuition and fees vary according to program. Room and board charges vary according to housing facility. *Part-time tuition:* $722 per unit. *Part-time fees:* $56 per term part-time. Part-time tuition and fees vary according to program. *Payment plan:* deferred payment. *Waivers:* employees or children of employees.
Library Charles Williard Coe Memorial Library. *Operations spending 1999–2000:* $1 million. *Collection:* 140,000 titles, 690 serial subscriptions.
College life *Social organizations:* national sororities, local sororities; 6% of women are members. *Most popular organizations:* Latinas Unidas, student government, Pi Theta Mu, Kappa Delta Chi, Student Ambassadors.
Campus security 24-hour patrols, controlled dormitory access.
After graduation 65% of class of 1998 had job offers within 6 months. *Career center:* 1 full-time personnel. Services include job fairs, resume preparation, career counseling, careers library, job bank. *Graduate education:* 30% of class of 1999 went directly to graduate and professional school.
Freshmen 480 applied, 211 admitted, 320 enrolled.

Average high school GPA	3.51	SAT verbal scores above 500	65%
SAT math scores above 500	52%	ACT above 18	93%
From top 10% of their h.s. class	19%	From top quarter	57%
From top half	89%	1998 freshmen returning in 1999	85%

Application *Options:* electronic application, deferred entrance. *Application fee:* $35. *Required:* essay or personal statement; high school transcript; minimum 2.0 GPA; 1 letter of recommendation. *Recommended:* minimum 3.0 GPA; interview.
Standardized tests *Admission: Required:* SAT I or ACT.
Significant dates *Application deadlines:* rolling (freshmen), rolling (transfers). *Financial aid deadline priority date:* 3/2.

Freshman Application Contact
Ms. Katy Murphy, Executive Director of Admissions and Financial Aid, Mount St. Mary's College, 12001 Chalon Road, Los Angeles, CA 90049-1599. **Phone:** 310-954-4252. **Toll-free phone:** 800-999-9893. **E-mail:** admissions@msmc.la.edu
Visit CollegeQuest.com for information on majors offered and athletics.

■ *See page 2120 for a narrative description.*

MT. SIERRA COLLEGE
Monrovia, California

Admissions Office Contact
Mt. Sierra College, 101 East Huntington Drive, Monrovia, CA 91016.

MUSICIANS INSTITUTE
Hollywood, California

- **Proprietary**, 4-year, founded 1976
- **Degrees** associate and bachelor's
- **Coed**
- **Minimally difficult** entrance level
- **$12,000** tuition and fees

Expenses (1999–2000) *Tuition:* full-time $12,000; part-time $200 per credit.
College life *Housing:* college housing not available.
Application *Application fee:* $100.
Admissions Office Contact
Musicians Institute, 1655 North McCadden Place, Hollywood, CA 90028. **Toll-free phone:** 800-255-PLAY. **Fax:** 323-462-6978.
Visit CollegeQuest.com for information on athletics.

THE NATIONAL HISPANIC UNIVERSITY
San Jose, California

- **Independent**, 4-year, founded 1981
- **Degrees** associate, bachelor's, and postbachelor's certificates
- **Urban** 1-acre campus
- **Coed**
- **Minimally difficult** entrance level
- **$3100** tuition and fees

Expenses (1999–2000) *Tuition:* full-time $3000; part-time $125 per unit. *Required fees:* full-time $100; $50 per term part-time.
College life *Housing:* college housing not available. *Most popular organization:* Teatro De Los Pobres.
Campus security 24-hour emergency response devices and patrols.
Application *Options:* Common Application, electronic application. *Application fee:* $50. *Required:* high school transcript; letters of recommendation; interview. *Recommended:* essay or personal statement.
Standardized tests *Admission: Recommended:* SAT I and SAT II or ACT, SAT II: Writing Test.
Admissions Office Contact
The National Hispanic University, 14271 Story Road, San Jose, CA 95127-3823.
Visit CollegeQuest.com for information on athletics. College video and electronic viewbook available at CollegeQuest.com.

NATIONAL UNIVERSITY
La Jolla, California

- **Independent**, comprehensive, founded 1971
- **Degrees** associate, bachelor's, master's, and postbachelor's certificates
- **Urban** 15-acre campus
- **Coed**, 5,071 undergraduate students, 52% full-time, 52% women, 48% men

California

- **Noncompetitive** entrance level, 100% of applicants were admitted
- **20:1 student-to-undergraduate faculty ratio**
- **$7485 tuition** and fees
- **$120.1 million endowment**

Students *Undergraduates:* 2,659 full-time, 2,412 part-time. Students come from 64 other countries. *The most frequently chosen baccalaureate fields are:* business/marketing, interdisciplinary studies, psychology. **Graduate:** 11,993 in graduate degree programs.

Age 25 or older	85%	Transferred in	52%
International students	2%	African Americans	14%
Asian Americans/Pacific Islanders	9%	Hispanic Americans	17%
Native Americans	1%		

Faculty 764 (14% full-time), 53% with terminal degrees.
Expenses (1999–2000) *Tuition:* full-time $7425; part-time $825 per course. *Required fees:* full-time $60; $60 per year part-time. Full-time tuition and fees vary according to course load. Part-time tuition and fees vary according to course load.
Library Central Library. *Operations spending 1999–2000:* $3 million. *Collection:* 176,329 titles, 3,857 serial subscriptions, 4,173 audiovisual materials.
College life *Housing:* college housing not available.
Campus security 24-hour emergency response devices and patrols, late-night transport-escort service.
Freshmen 1,245 applied, 1,245 admitted, 1,245 enrolled.

| SAT verbal scores above 500 | N/R | SAT math scores above 500 | N/R |
| ACT above 18 | N/R | | |

Application *Option:* deferred entrance. *Application fee:* $60. *Required:* high school transcript; interview. *Required for some:* essay or personal statement.
Significant dates *Application deadlines:* rolling (freshmen), rolling (transfers). *Financial aid deadline:* continuous.
Freshman Application Contact
Ms. Nancy Rohland, Director of Enrollment Management, National University, 11255 North Torrey Pines Road, La Jolla, CA 92037. **Phone:** 858-642-8180. **Toll-free phone:** 800-628-8648. **Fax:** 858-563-7395. **E-mail:** nrohland@nu.edu
Visit CollegeQuest.com for information on majors offered and athletics.

NEW COLLEGE OF CALIFORNIA
San Francisco, California

- **Independent**, comprehensive, founded 1971
- **Degrees** bachelor's, master's, and first professional certificates
- **Urban** campus
- **Coed**
- **Noncompetitive** entrance level
- **$8850 tuition** and fees

Expenses (1999–2000) *Tuition:* full-time $8750; part-time $375 per unit. *Required fees:* full-time $100; $50 per term part-time. Full-time tuition and fees vary according to program. Part-time tuition and fees vary according to course load and program.
Institutional Web site http://www.newcollege.edu/
College life *Housing:* college housing not available.
Campus security Trained security personnel.
Application *Option:* deferred entrance. *Application fee:* $40. *Required:* essay or personal statement; high school transcript. *Required for some:* 2 letters of recommendation. *Recommended:* interview.
Admissions Office Contact
New College of California, 50 Fell Street, San Francisco, CA 94102-5206. **Toll-free phone:** 888-437-3460. **Fax:** 415-865-2636. **E-mail:** cmesposito@ncgate.newcollege.edu
Visit CollegeQuest.com for information on athletics.

▪ *See page 2144 for a narrative description.*

NEWSCHOOL OF ARCHITECTURE
San Diego, California

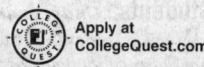

- **Proprietary**, comprehensive, founded 1980
- **Degrees** associate, bachelor's, master's, and first professional
- **Urban** campus
- **Coed**
- **Minimally difficult** entrance level
- **$15,909 tuition** and fees

Expenses (1999–2000) *Comprehensive fee:* $21,909 includes full-time tuition ($15,750), mandatory fees ($159), and room and board ($6000). Full-time tuition and fees vary according to course load. *Part-time tuition:* $350 per quarter hour. *Part-time fees:* $53 per term part-time.
Institutional Web site http://www.newschoolarch.edu/
College life *Housing: Option:* coed. *Most popular organization:* American Institute of Architects-Student Chapter.
Campus security 24-hour emergency response devices, controlled dormitory access.
Application *Option:* eApply at www.CollegeQuest.com. *Application fee:* $25. *Required:* essay or personal statement; high school transcript; minimum 2.5 GPA; interview. *Recommended:* letters of recommendation.
Admissions Office Contact
Newschool of Architecture, 1249 F Street, San Diego, CA 92101-6634. **E-mail:** admissions@newschoolarch.edu
Visit CollegeQuest.com for information on athletics. College video available at CollegeQuest.com.

NORTHWESTERN POLYTECHNIC UNIVERSITY
Fremont, California

- **Independent**, comprehensive, founded 1984
- **Degrees** bachelor's, master's, and doctoral
- **Urban** 2-acre campus with easy access to San Francisco and San Jose
- **Coed**
- **$9405 tuition** and fees

Expenses (1999–2000) *Tuition:* full-time $9000; part-time $250 per credit. *Required fees:* full-time $405; $135 per term part-time. Full-time tuition and fees vary according to course load. Part-time tuition and fees vary according to course load.
Institutional Web site http://www.npu.edu/
College life *Housing: Option:* coed.
Campus security Late-night transport-escort service.
Application *Application fee:* $50. *Required:* high school transcript.
Standardized tests *Admission: Required:* SAT I, SAT II Subject Tests.
Admissions Office Contact
Northwestern Polytechnic University, 117 Fourier Avenue, Fremont, CA 94539-7482. **Fax:** 510-657-8975. **E-mail:** npuadm@upu2.upu.edu
Visit CollegeQuest.com for information on athletics.

OCCIDENTAL COLLEGE
Los Angeles, California

- **Independent**, comprehensive, founded 1887
- **Degrees** bachelor's and master's
- **Urban** 120-acre campus
- **Coed**, 1,541 undergraduate students, 99% full-time, 57% women, 43% men
- **Very difficult** entrance level, 60% of applicants were admitted
- **11:1 student-to-undergraduate faculty ratio**
- **78.4% graduate** in 6 years or less
- **$23,850 tuition** and fees
- **$23,869 average financial aid** package, $14,049 average indebtedness upon graduation, $260 million endowment

Peterson's Guide to Four-Year Colleges 2001   www.petersons.com

California

Occidental College (continued)

Students *Undergraduates:* 1,527 full-time, 14 part-time. Students come from 47 states and territories, 45 other countries. *The most frequently chosen baccalaureate fields are:* biological/life sciences, social sciences and history, visual/performing arts. *Graduate:* 33 in graduate degree programs.

From out-of-state	40%	Reside on campus	79%
Age 25 or older	2%	Transferred in	4%
International students	3%	African Americans	6%
Asian Americans/Pacific Islanders	20%	Hispanic Americans	14%
Native Americans	1%		

Faculty 188 (73% full-time), 82% with terminal degrees.

Expenses (2000–2001, estimated) *Comprehensive fee:* $30,730 includes full-time tuition ($23,532), mandatory fees ($318), and room and board ($6880). *College room only:* $2924. Room and board charges vary according to board plan and housing facility. *Part-time tuition:* $980 per unit. *Payment plans:* tuition prepayment, installment. *Waivers:* employees or children of employees.

Library Mary Norton Clapp Library plus 2 others. *Operations spending 1999–2000:* $1.9 million. *Collection:* 475,641 titles, 2,100 serial subscriptions.

College life *Housing:* on-campus residence required in freshman year. *Options:* coed, women-only. *Social organizations:* national fraternities, local sororities; 11% of eligible men and 6% of eligible women are members. *Most popular organizations:* Asian-Pacific Islander Alliance, community service, Inter-faith Student Council, Black Student Alliance, MECHA/ALAS.

Campus security 24-hour emergency response devices and patrols, student patrols, late-night transport-escort service, controlled dormitory access, community police services.

After graduation 62 organizations recruited on campus 1997–98. 63% of class of 1998 had job offers within 6 months. *Career center:* 2 full-time personnel. Services include job fairs, resume preparation, resume referral, career/interest testing, career counseling, careers library, job bank, job interviews, graduate/professional school fairs. *Graduate education:* 30% of class of 1999 went directly to graduate and professional school: 23% graduate arts and sciences, 3% law, 3% medicine, 1% dentistry.

Freshmen 3,002 applied, 1,799 admitted, 411 enrolled. 9 valedictorians.

SAT verbal scores above 500	89%	SAT math scores above 500	91%
ACT above 18	N/R	From top 10% of their h.s. class	44%
From top quarter	75%	From top half	93%
1998 freshmen returning in 1999	87%		

Application *Options:* eApply at www.CollegeQuest.com, Common Application, early admission, early decision, deferred entrance. *Application fee:* $50. *Required:* essay or personal statement; high school transcript; 2 letters of recommendation. *Recommended:* interview.

Standardized tests *Admission: Required:* SAT I or ACT. *Recommended:* SAT II Subject Tests, SAT II: Writing Test.

Significant dates *Application deadlines:* 1/15 (freshmen), 3/15 (transfers). *Early decision:* 11/15. *Notification:* 4/1 (freshmen), 12/15 (early decision). *Financial aid deadline priority date:* 2/1.

Freshman Application Contact
Mr. Mark Hatch, Director of Admission, Occidental College, Halo Campus Road, Los Angeles, CA 90041-3392. **Phone:** 323-259-2700. **Toll-free phone:** 800-825-5262. **Fax:** 323-341-4875. **E-mail:** admission@oxy.edu

Visit CollegeQuest.com for information on majors offered and athletics.

OTIS COLLEGE OF ART AND DESIGN
Los Angeles, California

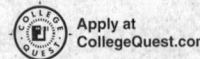
Apply at CollegeQuest.com

- **Independent**, comprehensive, founded 1918
- **Degrees** bachelor's and master's
- **Urban** 5-acre campus
- **Coed**, 811 undergraduate students, 97% full-time, 60% women, 40% men
- **Moderately difficult** entrance level, 68% of applicants were admitted
- **10:1 student-to-undergraduate faculty ratio**
- **39% graduate** in 6 years or less
- **$19,294 tuition** and fees

Students *Undergraduates:* 784 full-time, 27 part-time. Students come from 42 states and territories, 23 other countries. *The most frequently chosen baccalaureate fields are:* architecture, visual/performing arts. *Graduate:* 23 in graduate degree programs.

Age 25 or older	22%	Transferred in	18%
International students	13%	African Americans	4%
Asian Americans/Pacific Islanders	26%	Hispanic Americans	13%
Native Americans	1%		

Faculty 192 (11% full-time).

Expenses (2000–2001) *Tuition:* full-time $18,894; part-time $630 per credit. *Required fees:* full-time $400. *Payment plan:* installment. *Waivers:* employees or children of employees.

Library Millard Sheets Library. *Collection:* 27,000 titles, 154 serial subscriptions.

College life *Housing:* college housing not available. *Most popular organizations:* student council, international students organization, Otis Students in Service (OASIS).

Campus security 24-hour patrols.

After graduation 70% of class of 1998 had job offers within 6 months. *Career center:* 2 full-time personnel. Services include resume preparation, career counseling, job bank.

Freshmen 456 applied, 312 admitted, 121 enrolled.

Average high school GPA	2.92	SAT verbal scores above 500	N/R
SAT math scores above 500	N/R	ACT above 18	N/R

Application *Options:* eApply at www.CollegeQuest.com, Common Application, electronic application, early admission, deferred entrance. *Application fee:* $50. *Required:* essay or personal statement; high school transcript; minimum 2.5 GPA; portfolio, 1 assigned art exercise. *Required for some:* minimum 3.0 GPA; interview. *Recommended:* 2 letters of recommendation.

Standardized tests *Admission: Required for some:* SAT I or ACT.

Significant dates *Application deadlines:* rolling (freshmen), rolling (transfers). *Financial aid deadline priority date:* 2/15.

Freshman Application Contact
Mr. Michael Fuller, Assistant Vice President of Enrollment Management, Otis College of Art and Design, 9045 Lincoln Boulevard, Los Angeles, CA 90045-9785. **Phone:** 310-665-6800. **Toll-free phone:** 800-527-OTIS. **Fax:** 310-665-6805. **E-mail:** otisart@otisart.edu

Visit CollegeQuest.com for information on majors offered and athletics. College video available at CollegeQuest.com.

■ *See page 2228 for a narrative description.*

PACIFIC OAKS COLLEGE
Pasadena, California

- **Independent**, upper-level, founded 1945
- **Degrees** bachelor's, master's, and post-master's certificates
- **Small-town** 2-acre campus with easy access to Los Angeles
- **Coed**, primarily women, 253 undergraduate students, 4% full-time, 94% women, 6% men
- **8:1 student-to-undergraduate faculty ratio**
- **$12,060 tuition** and fees
- **$20,000 average indebtedness** upon graduation, $3 million endowment

Students *Undergraduates:* 9 full-time, 244 part-time. Students come from 17 states and territories. *The most frequently chosen baccalaureate field is:* social sciences and history. *Graduate:* 580 in graduate degree programs.

From out-of-state	7%	Age 25 or older	89%
Transferred in	22%	International students	0.4%
African Americans	9%	Asian Americans/Pacific Islanders	6%
Hispanic Americans	24%	Native Americans	2%

Faculty 81 (31% full-time), 17% with terminal degrees.

Expenses (1999–2000) *Tuition:* full-time $12,000; part-time $500 per unit. *Required fees:* full-time $60; $30 per term part-time. Full-time tuition and fees vary according to program. *Payment plan:* installment. *Waivers:* employees or children of employees.

Library Andrew Norman Library. *Operations spending 1999–2000:* $183,023. *Collection:* 16,350 titles, 101 serial subscriptions, 161 audiovisual materials.

College life *Housing:* college housing not available. *Most popular organizations:* Community Alliance, Men's Support Group, Latina/o Support Group.

California

Application *Option:* deferred entrance. *Application fee:* $55.
Significant dates *Application deadline:* 7/1 (transfers). *Notification:* continuous until 9/1 (transfers). **Financial aid deadline priority date:** 4/15.
Freshman Application Contact
Ms. Marsha Franker, Director of Admissions, Pacific Oaks College, Admissions Office, Pacific Oaks College, 5 Westmoreland Place, Pasadena, CA 91103. **Phone:** 626-397-1349. **Toll-free phone:** 800-684-0900. **Fax:** 626-397-1317. **E-mail:** admissions@pacificoaks.edu
Visit CollegeQuest.com for information on majors offered and athletics.

PACIFIC STATES UNIVERSITY
Los Angeles, California

- **Independent**, comprehensive, founded 1928
- **Degrees** bachelor's and master's
- **Urban** 1-acre campus
- **Coed**
- **Minimally difficult** entrance level

Institutional Web site http://www.psuca.edu/
College life *Housing:* college housing not available.
Campus security Patrols by trained security personnel during campus hours.
Application *Options:* Common Application, electronic application, early admission, deferred entrance. *Application fee:* $50. *Required:* essay or personal statement; high school transcript.
Admissions Office Contact
Pacific States University, 1516 South Western Avenue, Los Angeles, CA 90006. **Toll-free phone:** 888-200-0383. **Fax:** 323-731-7276. **E-mail:** admission@psuca.edu
Visit CollegeQuest.com for information on athletics.

PACIFIC UNION COLLEGE
Angwin, California

Apply at CollegeQuest.com

- **Independent Seventh-day Adventist**, comprehensive, founded 1882
- **Degrees** associate, bachelor's, and master's
- **Rural** 200-acre campus with easy access to San Francisco
- **Coed**, 1,623 undergraduate students, 90% full-time, 55% women, 45% men
- **Moderately difficult** entrance level, 44% of applicants were admitted
- **12:1** student-to-undergraduate faculty ratio
- **$14,475 tuition** and fees

Students *Undergraduates:* 1,457 full-time, 166 part-time. Students come from 41 states and territories, 13 other countries. *The most frequently chosen baccalaureate fields are:* business/marketing, engineering/engineering technologies, health professions and related sciences. *Graduate:* 2 in graduate degree programs.

From out-of-state	19%	Reside on campus	65%
Age 25 or older	13%	Transferred in	10%
International students	13%	African Americans	4%
Asian Americans/Pacific Islanders	15%	Hispanic Americans	8%
Native Americans	0.4%		

Faculty 114 (88% full-time), 46% with terminal degrees.
Expenses (1999–2000) *Comprehensive fee:* $18,900 includes full-time tuition ($14,475) and room and board ($4425). *College room only:* $2655. *Part-time tuition:* $418 per credit. *Payment plans:* guaranteed tuition, installment, deferred payment. *Waivers:* senior citizens and employees or children of employees.
Library W. E. Nelson Memorial Library. *Operations spending 1999–2000:* $640,346. *Collection:* 240,213 titles, 925 serial subscriptions, 53,582 audiovisual materials.
College life *Housing:* on-campus residence required through senior year. *Options:* men-only, women-only.
Campus security 24-hour emergency response devices and patrols, late-night transport-escort service.

After graduation *Career center:* 3 full-time, 1 part-time personnel. Services include job fairs, career/interest testing, career counseling, careers library.
Freshmen 858 applied, 374 admitted, 378 enrolled.

SAT verbal scores above 500	N/R	SAT math scores above 500	N/R
ACT above 18	71%	From top quarter of their h.s. class	51%
From top half	85%		

Application *Options:* eApply at www.CollegeQuest.com, electronic application, deferred entrance. *Application fee:* $30. *Required:* high school transcript; minimum 2.3 GPA; 3 letters of recommendation.
Standardized tests *Placement: Required:* SAT I and SAT II or ACT
Significant dates *Application deadlines:* rolling (freshmen), rolling (transfers). **Financial aid deadline priority date:** 3/2.
Freshman Application Contact
Mr. Al Trace, Director of Enrollment Services, Pacific Union College, Enrollment Services, Angwin, CA 94508-9707. **Phone:** 800-862-7080. **Toll-free phone:** 800-862-7080. **Fax:** 707-965-6432. **E-mail:** enroll@puc.edu
Visit CollegeQuest.com for information on majors offered and athletics. College video available at CollegeQuest.com.

PATTEN COLLEGE
Oakland, California

- **Independent interdenominational**, comprehensive, founded 1944
- **Degrees** associate, bachelor's, master's, and postbachelor's certificates
- **Urban** 5-acre campus with easy access to San Francisco
- **Coed**, 635 undergraduate students, 45% full-time, 39% women, 61% men
- **Noncompetitive** entrance level, 68% of applicants were admitted
- **16:1** student-to-undergraduate faculty ratio
- **$7992 tuition** and fees
- **$262,120 endowment**

Students *Undergraduates:* 286 full-time, 349 part-time. Students come from 12 states and territories. *The most frequently chosen baccalaureate fields are:* business/marketing, liberal arts/general studies, philosophy.

From out-of-state	5%	Reside on campus	15%
Age 25 or older	59%	International students	0.5%
African Americans	22%	Asian Americans/Pacific Islanders	23%
Hispanic Americans	12%		

Faculty 58 (28% full-time).
Expenses (2000–2001, estimated) *Comprehensive fee:* $11,460 includes full-time tuition ($7968), mandatory fees ($24), and room and board ($3468). *College room only:* $2468. Full-time tuition and fees vary according to course load. *Part-time tuition:* $332 per unit. *Part-time fees:* $24 per year. *Payment plan:* installment. *Waivers:* employees or children of employees.
Library Patten Library. *Operations spending 1999–2000:* $89,808. *Collection:* 35,000 titles, 250 serial subscriptions.
College life *Housing: Option:* coed. *Most popular organizations:* student council, Patten College Chorus, Patten Symphonette.
Campus security 24-hour emergency response devices, student patrols, late-night transport-escort service.
After graduation 15 organizations recruited on campus 1997-98. 60% of class of 1998 had job offers within 6 months. *Career center:* 1 full-time, 1 part-time personnel. Services include job fairs, resume preparation, career counseling, job bank, job interviews. *Graduate education:* 80% of class of 1999 went directly to graduate and professional school: 60% theology, 10% education, 5% business, 5% graduate arts and sciences.
Freshmen 66 applied, 45 admitted, 27 enrolled. 7 National Merit Scholars, 5 class presidents, 1 valedictorian, 6 student government officers.

Average high school GPA	2.8	SAT verbal scores above 500	N/R
SAT math scores above 500	N/R	ACT above 18	N/R
From top 10% of their h.s. class	13%	From top quarter	35%
From top half	52%	1998 freshmen returning in 1999	70%

Application *Options:* early admission, deferred entrance. *Application fee:* $30. *Required:* essay or personal statement; high school transcript; minimum 2.5 GPA; 2 letters of recommendation. *Recommended:* interview.
Standardized tests *Admission: Required:* SAT I or ACT.
Significant dates *Application deadlines:* 3/31 (freshmen), rolling (transfers). **Financial aid deadline priority date:** 5/31.

Peterson's Guide to Four-Year Colleges 2001   www.petersons.com

California

Patten College (continued)
Freshman Application Contact
Ms. Inez Bailey, Director of Admissions, Patten College, 2433 Coolidge Avenue, Oakland, CA 94601-2699. **Phone:** 510-533-8500 Ext. 765. **Fax:** 510-534-8564.
Visit CollegeQuest.com for information on majors offered and athletics. College video available at CollegeQuest.com.

PEPPERDINE UNIVERSITY
Malibu, California

- **Independent**, university, founded 1937, affiliated with Church of Christ
- **Degrees** bachelor's, master's, doctoral, and first professional (the university is organized into five colleges: Seaver, the School of Law, the School of Business and Management, the School of Public Policy, and the Graduate School of Education and Psychology. Seaver College is the undergraduate, residential, liberal arts school of the University and is committed to providing education of outstanding academic quality with particular attention to Christian values)
- **Small-town** 830-acre campus with easy access to Los Angeles
- **Coed**, 3,230 undergraduate students, 91% full-time, 60% women, 40% men
- **Very difficult** entrance level, 32% of applicants were admitted
- **13:1** student-to-undergraduate faculty ratio
- **$23,070 tuition** and fees

Students *Undergraduates:* Students come from 51 states and territories, 70 other countries. *The most frequently chosen baccalaureate fields are:* business/marketing, communications/communication technologies, liberal arts/general studies. *Graduate:* 4,655 in graduate degree programs.

Reside on campus	48%	Age 25 or older	4%
International students	8%	African Americans	5%
Asian Americans/Pacific Islanders	6%	Hispanic Americans	8%
Native Americans	1%		

Faculty 315 (53% full-time), 100% with terminal degrees.
Expenses (1999–2000) *Comprehensive fee:* $30,080 includes full-time tuition ($23,000), mandatory fees ($70), and room and board ($7010). *College room only:* $4440. Room and board charges vary according to housing facility. *Part-time tuition:* $720 per unit. *Payment plans:* tuition prepayment, installment, deferred payment. *Waivers:* employees or children of employees.
Library Payson Library plus 2 others. *Collection:* 515,238 titles, 3,882 serial subscriptions.
College life *Housing:* on-campus residence required through sophomore year. *Options:* men-only, women-only. *Social organizations:* national fraternities, national sororities; 25% of eligible men and 25% of eligible women are members. *Most popular organizations:* Student Government Association, Black Student Union, International Club, Alpha Chi Honor Society, Golden Key Honor Society.
Campus security 24-hour emergency response devices and patrols, student patrols, late-night transport-escort service, front gate security, 24-hour security in residence halls, controlled access, crime prevention programs.
After graduation 78 organizations recruited on campus 1997–98. 40% of class of 1998 had job offers within 6 months. *Career center:* 3 full-time, 8 part-time personnel. Services include job fairs, resume preparation, interview workshops, career counseling, careers library, job interviews. *Graduate education:* 63% of class of 1999 went directly to graduate and professional school.
Freshmen 4,652 applied, 1,489 admitted.

Average high school GPA	3.79	SAT verbal scores above 500	97%
SAT math scores above 500	96%	ACT above 18	99%
1998 freshmen returning in 1999	88%		

Application *Options:* electronic application, early action. *Application fee:* $55. *Required:* essay or personal statement; high school transcript; 2 letters of recommendation. *Recommended:* interview.
Standardized tests *Admission: Required:* SAT I or ACT.
Significant dates *Application deadlines:* 1/15 (freshmen), 1/15 (transfers). *Early action:* 11/15. *Notification:* 4/1 (freshmen), 12/15 (early action). *Financial aid deadline:* 4/1. *Priority date:* 1/15.

Freshman Application Contact
Mr. Paul A. Long, Dean of Admission, Pepperdine University, 24255 Pacific Coast Highway, Malibu, CA 90263-0002. **Phone:** 310-456-4392. **Fax:** 310-456-4861. **E-mail:** admission-seaver@pepperdine.edu
Visit CollegeQuest.com for information on majors offered and athletics. College video and electronic viewbook available at CollegeQuest.com.

■ *See page 2260 for a narrative description.*

PITZER COLLEGE
Claremont, California

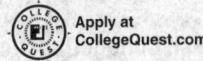
Apply at CollegeQuest.com

- **Independent**, 4-year, founded 1963
- **Degree** bachelor's
- **Suburban** 35-acre campus with easy access to Los Angeles
- **Coed**, 930 undergraduate students, 92% full-time, 64% women, 36% men
- **Moderately difficult** entrance level, 72% of applicants were admitted
- **12:1** student-to-undergraduate faculty ratio
- **68% graduate** in 6 years or less
- **$24,096 tuition** and fees
- **$22,648 average financial aid** package, $20,530 average indebtedness upon graduation, $38.5 million endowment

Part of The Claremont Colleges Consortium.
Students *Undergraduates:* 856 full-time, 74 part-time. Students come from 29 states and territories, 6 other countries. *The most frequently chosen baccalaureate fields are:* psychology, social sciences and history, visual/performing arts.

From out-of-state	41%	Reside on campus	75%
Age 25 or older	10%	Transferred in	6%
International students	5%	African Americans	5%
Asian Americans/Pacific Islanders	11%	Hispanic Americans	14%
Native Americans	1%		

Faculty 74 (78% full-time).
Expenses (1999–2000) *Comprehensive fee:* $30,386 includes full-time tuition ($21,520), mandatory fees ($2576), and room and board ($6290). *College room only:* $4124. Full-time tuition and fees vary according to course load. Room and board charges vary according to board plan. *Part-time tuition:* $2690 per course. *Part-time fees:* $298 per course; $96 per term part-time. Part-time tuition and fees vary according to course load. *Payment plans:* installment, deferred payment. *Waivers:* employees or children of employees.
Library Honnold Library plus 1 other. *Operations spending 1999–2000:* $719,000. *Collection:* 1.4 million titles, 4,321 serial subscriptions, 606 audio-visual materials.
College life *Housing:* on-campus residence required through junior year. *Options:* coed, cooperative, disabled students. *Most popular organizations:* Pitzer activities, Student Senate, The Other Side, Without A Box, Residence Hall Association.
Campus security 24-hour emergency response devices and patrols, late-night transport-escort service, controlled dormitory access.
After graduation 50 organizations recruited on campus 1997–98. 75% of class of 1998 had job offers within 6 months. *Career center:* 1 full-time, 5 part-time personnel. Services include job fairs, resume preparation, interview workshops, resume referral, career/interest testing, career counseling, careers library, job bank, job interviews. *Major awards:* 2 Fulbright Scholars.
Freshmen 1,716 applied, 1,234 admitted, 246 enrolled.

Average high school GPA	3.55	SAT verbal scores above 500	86%
SAT math scores above 500	83%	ACT above 18	96%
From top 10% of their h.s. class	34%	From top quarter	65%
From top half	89%	1998 freshmen returning in 1999	79%

Application *Options:* eApply at www.CollegeQuest.com, Common Application, electronic application, early admission, early action, deferred entrance. *Application fee:* $40. *Required:* essay or personal statement; high school transcript; 2 letters of recommendation. *Recommended:* interview.
Standardized tests *Admission: Required:* SAT I or ACT. *Recommended:* SAT II Subject Tests, SAT II: Writing Test.
Significant dates *Application deadlines:* 2/1 (freshmen), 4/15 (transfers). *Early action:* 12/1. *Notification:* 4/1 (freshmen), 1/1 (early action). *Financial aid deadline:* 2/1.

California

Freshman Application Contact
Dr. Arnaldo Rodriguez, Vice President for Admission and Financial Aid, Pitzer College, 1050 North Mills Avenue, Claremont, CA 91711-6101. **Phone:** 909-621-8129. **Toll-free phone:** 800-748-9371. **Fax:** 909-621-8770. **E-mail:** admission@pitzer.edu

Visit CollegeQuest.com for information on majors offered and athletics.

▪ *See page 2272 for a narrative description.*

POINT LOMA NAZARENE UNIVERSITY
San Diego, California

- **Independent Nazarene**, comprehensive, founded 1902
- **Degrees** bachelor's, master's, post-master's, and postbachelor's certificates
- **Suburban** 88-acre campus
- **Coed**, 2,343 undergraduate students, 96% full-time, 61% women, 39% men
- **Moderately difficult** entrance level, 78% of applicants were admitted
- **16:1 student-to-undergraduate faculty ratio**
- **60% graduate** in 6 years or less
- **$13,626 tuition** and fees

Students *Undergraduates:* 2,254 full-time, 89 part-time. Students come from 34 states and territories, 21 other countries. *The most frequently chosen baccalaureate fields are:* business/marketing, education, liberal arts/general studies. *Graduate:* 361 in graduate degree programs.

From out-of-state	22%	Reside on campus	66%
Age 25 or older	6%	Transferred in	8%
International students	1%	African Americans	2%
Asian Americans/Pacific Islanders	4%	Hispanic Americans	7%
Native Americans	1%		

Faculty 257 (55% full-time), 42% with terminal degrees.
Expenses (1999–2000) *Comprehensive fee:* $19,106 includes full-time tuition ($13,186), mandatory fees ($440), and room and board ($5480). Full-time tuition and fees vary according to course load. Room and board charges vary according to board plan. *Part-time tuition:* $549 per unit. *Part-time fees:* $15 per unit. Part-time tuition and fees vary according to course load and student level. *Payment plan:* installment. *Waivers:* senior citizens and employees or children of employees.
Library Ryan Library. *Operations spending 1999–2000:* $303,354. *Collection:* 120,991 titles.
College life *Housing:* on-campus residence required through junior year. *Options:* men-only, women-only. *Social organizations:* national sororities, local fraternities, local sororities; 3% of eligible men and 5% of eligible women are members. *Most popular organizations:* Cai Delta Psi, Psi Omega Theta, SNAPL (nurses association), Chi Beta Sigma.
Campus security 24-hour patrols, student patrols, late-night transport-escort service.
After graduation 100 organizations recruited on campus 1997–98. *Career center:* 1 full-time personnel. Services include job fairs, resume preparation, interview workshops, resume referral, career/interest testing, career counseling, careers library, job bank, job interviews.
Freshmen 1,681 applied, 1,303 admitted, 554 enrolled. 19 valedictorians.

Average high school GPA	3.65	SAT verbal scores above 500	67%
SAT math scores above 500	68%	ACT above 18	94%
From top 10% of their h.s. class	33%	From top quarter	66%
From top half	91%	1998 freshmen returning in 1999	76%

Application *Options:* early action, deferred entrance. *Application fee:* $20. *Required:* essay or personal statement; high school transcript; minimum 2.8 GPA; 2 letters of recommendation. *Required for some:* interview.
Standardized tests *Admission: Required:* SAT I or ACT. *Recommended:* SAT I.
Significant dates *Application deadlines:* 3/1 (freshmen), rolling (transfers). *Early action:* 12/1. *Notification:* 1/15 (early action). *Financial aid deadline priority date:* 3/15.

Freshman Application Contact
Mr. Scott Schoemaker, Director of Admissions, Point Loma Nazarene University, 3900 Lomaland Drive, San Diego, CA 92106-2899. **Phone:** 619-849-2225. **Fax:** 619-849-2579. **E-mail:** discover@ptloma.edu

Visit CollegeQuest.com for information on majors offered and athletics. College video available at CollegeQuest.com.

POMONA COLLEGE
Claremont, California

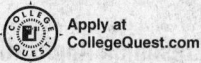
Apply at CollegeQuest.com

- **Independent**, 4-year, founded 1887
- **Degree** bachelor's
- **Suburban** 140-acre campus with easy access to Los Angeles
- **Coed**, 1,530 undergraduate students, 100% full-time, 47% women, 53% men
- **Most difficult** entrance level, 32% of applicants were admitted
- **9:1 student-to-undergraduate faculty ratio**
- **88.2% graduate** in 6 years or less
- **$23,170 tuition** and fees
- **$22,032 average financial aid** package, $15,800 average indebtedness upon graduation, $759.5 million endowment

Pomona is one of the nation's premier liberal arts colleges. Its widely diverse student body enjoys a broad range of resources and opportunities that are among the strongest of any comparable-size college. Pomona is the founding member of the Claremont Colleges, offering the benefits of a university setting with the advantages of a small college.

Part of The Claremont Colleges Consortium.

Students *Undergraduates:* 1,530 full-time. Students come from 49 states and territories. *The most frequently chosen baccalaureate fields are:* biological/life sciences, physical sciences, social sciences and history.

From out-of-state	61%	Reside on campus	95%
Age 25 or older	1%	Transferred in	1%
International students	2%	African Americans	4%
Asian Americans/Pacific Islanders	18%	Hispanic Americans	10%
Native Americans	1%		

Faculty 178 (87% full-time), 95% with terminal degrees.
Expenses (1999–2000) *Comprehensive fee:* $30,920 includes full-time tuition ($22,940), mandatory fees ($230), and room and board ($7750). Room and board charges vary according to board plan. *Part-time tuition:* $3830 per course. *Payment plan:* installment. *Waivers:* employees or children of employees.
Library Honnold Library plus 3 others. *Operations spending 1999–2000:* $2.2 million. *Collection:* 1.9 million titles, 5,967 serial subscriptions.
College life *Housing:* on-campus residence required in freshman year. *Option:* coed. *Social organizations:* local fraternities, local coed fraternities; 6% of men are members. *Most popular organizations:* student newspaper, student government, music organizations, service organizations, intramural sports.
Campus security 24-hour emergency response devices and patrols, late-night transport-escort service, controlled dormitory access.
After graduation 165 organizations recruited on campus 1997–98. 60% of class of 1998 had job offers within 6 months. *Career center:* 4 full-time, 1 part-time personnel. Services include job fairs, resume preparation, interview workshops, resume referral, career/interest testing, career counseling, careers library, job bank, job interviews. *Graduate education:* 33% of class of 1999 went directly to graduate and professional school: 17% graduate arts and sciences, 9% law, 9% medicine. *Major awards:* 5 Fulbright Scholars.
Freshmen 3,612 applied, 1,147 admitted, 390 enrolled. 41 National Merit Scholars, 6 class presidents, 32 valedictorians, 59 student government officers.

SAT verbal scores above 500	100%	SAT math scores above 500	100%
ACT above 18	100%	From top 10% of their h.s. class	80%
From top quarter	96%	From top half	100%
1998 freshmen returning in 1999	98%		

Application *Options:* eApply at www.CollegeQuest.com, Common Application, electronic application, early admission, early decision, deferred entrance. *Application fee:* $55. *Required:* essay or personal statement; high school transcript; 2 letters of recommendation. *Recommended:* minimum 3.0 GPA; interview; portfolio or tapes for art and performing arts programs.
Standardized tests *Admission: Required:* SAT I and SAT II or ACT, 3 SAT II Subject Tests (including SAT II Writing Test).
Significant dates *Application deadlines:* 1/1 (freshmen), 3/15 (transfers). *Early decision:* 11/15 (for plan 1), 12/28 (for plan 2). *Notification:* 4/10 (freshmen), 12/15 (early decision plan 1), 2/15 (early decision plan 2). *Financial aid deadline:* 2/1.

Peterson's Guide to Four-Year Colleges 2001 www.petersons.com 123

California

Pomona College (continued)
Freshman Application Contact
Mr. Bruce Poch, Vice President and Dean of Admissions, Pomona College, 333 North College Way, Claremont, CA 91711. **Phone:** 909-621-8134. **Fax:** 909-621-8403. **E-mail:** admissions@pomona.edu

Visit CollegeQuest.com for information on majors offered and athletics.

■ *See page 2282 for a narrative description.*

ST. JOHN'S SEMINARY COLLEGE
Camarillo, California

- **Independent Roman Catholic**, 4-year, founded 1939
- **Degree** bachelor's
- **Suburban** 100-acre campus with easy access to Los Angeles
- **Men** only, 84 undergraduate students, 100% full-time
- **Moderately difficult** entrance level, 84% of applicants were admitted
- **3:1** student-to-undergraduate faculty ratio
- **63% graduate** in 6 years or less
- **$7555 tuition** and fees

Students *Undergraduates:* 84 full-time. Students come from 5 states and territories. *The most frequently chosen baccalaureate fields are:* English, foreign language/literature, philosophy.

From out-of-state	11%	Reside on campus	95%
Age 25 or older	44%	Transferred in	31%
Asian Americans/Pacific Islanders	36%	Hispanic Americans	45%

Faculty 36 (61% full-time), 39% with terminal degrees.
Expenses (1999–2000) *Comprehensive fee:* $11,555 includes full-time tuition ($7270), mandatory fees ($285), and room and board ($4000). *Payment plans:* installment, deferred payment.
Library Carrie Estelle Doheney Library plus 1 other. *Collection:* 74,000 titles, 142 serial subscriptions.
College life *Housing:* on-campus residence required through senior year. *Option:* men-only. *Most popular organizations:* La Hermandad, Vietnamese Club, Forensics Club, Pacifica Club, choir.
Campus security Late night and front gate security.
After graduation *Graduate education:* 33% of class of 1999 went directly to graduate and professional school: 33% theology.
Freshmen 31 applied, 26 admitted, 2 enrolled.

Average high school GPA	2.78	SAT verbal scores above 500	N/R
SAT math scores above 500	N/R	ACT above 18	N/R
From top 10% of their h.s. class	25%	From top quarter	40%
From top half	75%	1998 freshmen returning in 1999	89%

Application Preference given to Roman Catholics. *Application fee:* $40. *Required:* essay or personal statement; high school transcript; 2 letters of recommendation; interview; intention of studying for Roman Catholic priesthood.
Standardized tests *Admission: Recommended:* SAT I or ACT.
Significant dates *Application deadlines:* 7/15 (freshmen), 7/15 (transfers). *Notification:* continuous until 8/20 (freshmen).
Freshman Application Contact
Rev. Gary Landry CM, Director of Admissions, St. John's Seminary College, 5118 Seminary Road, Camarillo, CA 93012-2599. **Phone:** 805-482-4697 Ext. 206. **Fax:** 805-987-5097.

Visit CollegeQuest.com for information on majors offered and athletics.

SAINT MARY'S COLLEGE OF CALIFORNIA
Moraga, California

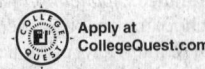
Apply at CollegeQuest.com

- **Independent Roman Catholic**, comprehensive, founded 1863
- **Degrees** bachelor's, master's, and doctoral
- **Suburban** 420-acre campus with easy access to San Francisco
- **Coed**, 2,860 undergraduate students, 80% full-time, 61% women, 39% men
- **Moderately difficult** entrance level, 85% of applicants were admitted
- **13:1** student-to-undergraduate faculty ratio
- **66.5% graduate** in 6 years or less
- **$17,475 tuition** and fees
- **$18,886 average financial aid** package, $16,500 average indebtedness upon graduation, $63.6 million endowment

Students *Undergraduates:* 2,285 full-time, 575 part-time. Students come from 31 states and territories, 14 other countries. *The most frequently chosen baccalaureate fields are:* business/marketing, health professions and related sciences, social sciences and history. *Graduate:* 1,200 in graduate degree programs.

From out-of-state	11%	Reside on campus	63%
Age 25 or older	3%	Transferred in	5%
International students	3%	African Americans	6%
Asian Americans/Pacific Islanders	8%	Hispanic Americans	13%
Native Americans	1%		

Faculty 456 (38% full-time).
Expenses (1999–2000) *Comprehensive fee:* $24,845 includes full-time tuition ($17,340), mandatory fees ($135), and room and board ($7370). *College room only:* $4020. Room and board charges vary according to board plan and housing facility. *Part-time tuition:* $2167 per course. *Payment plans:* tuition prepayment, installment. *Waivers:* employees or children of employees.
Library St. Albert Hall plus 1 other. *Operations spending 1999–2000:* $1.3 million. *Collection:* 149,200 titles, 1,069 serial subscriptions.
College life *Housing: Options:* coed, women-only, disabled students. *Most popular organizations:* MECHA, Student Alumni Association, Black Student Union, Intervarsity Christian Fellowship, Asian Pacific America Student Association.
Campus security 24-hour emergency response devices and patrols, late-night transport-escort service.
After graduation 132 organizations recruited on campus 1997-98. *Career center:* 4 full-time, 1 part-time personnel. Services include job fairs, resume preparation, interview workshops, career/interest testing, career counseling, careers library, job bank, job interviews. *Graduate education:* 28% of class of 1999 went directly to graduate and professional school.
Freshmen 2,830 applied, 2,419 admitted, 706 enrolled.

Average high school GPA	3.38	SAT verbal scores above 500	75%
SAT math scores above 500	75%	ACT above 18	N/R
1998 freshmen returning in 1999	82%		

Application *Options:* eApply at www.CollegeQuest.com, Common Application, electronic application, early action, deferred entrance. *Application fee:* $35. *Required:* essay or personal statement; high school transcript; minimum 2.0 GPA; 1 letter of recommendation. *Required for some:* minimum 3.0 GPA; interview. *Recommended:* minimum 3.0 GPA.
Standardized tests *Admission: Required:* SAT I or ACT.
Significant dates *Application deadlines:* 2/1 (freshmen), 7/1 (transfers). *Early action:* 11/30. *Notification:* 1/15 (early action). **Financial aid deadline priority date:** 3/2.
Freshman Application Contact
Ms. Dorothy Benjamin, Director of Admissions, Saint Mary's College of California, PO Box 4800, Moraga, CA 94556-4800. **Phone:** 925-631-4224. **Toll-free phone:** 800-800-4SMC. **Fax:** 925-376-7193. **E-mail:** smcadmit@stmarys-ca.edu

Visit CollegeQuest.com for information on majors offered and athletics.

■ *See page 2412 for a narrative description.*

SAMUEL MERRITT COLLEGE
Oakland, California

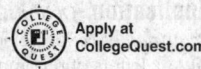
Apply at CollegeQuest.com

- **Independent**, comprehensive, founded 1909
- **Degrees** bachelor's, master's, and post-master's certificates (bachelor's degree offered jointly with Saint Mary's College of California)
- **Urban** 1-acre campus with easy access to San Francisco
- **Coed**, primarily women
- **Moderately difficult** entrance level
- **$16,425 tuition** and fees

California

Expenses (1999–2000) *Tuition:* full-time $16,360; part-time $686 per unit. *Required fees:* full-time $65; $32 per term part-time. Full-time tuition and fees vary according to program. Part-time tuition and fees vary according to program. *College room only:* $3510.
Institutional Web site http://www.samuelmerritt.edu/
College life *Housing:* Option: coed. *Most popular organizations:* Multicultural Group, California Nursing Students Association, Student Body Association.
Campus security 24-hour emergency response devices and patrols, late-night transport-escort service, controlled dormitory access, 24-hour controlled access.
Application *Options:* eApply at www.CollegeQuest.com, Common Application, deferred entrance. *Application fee:* $35. *Required:* essay or personal statement; high school transcript; minimum 2.5 GPA; 1 letter of recommendation. *Required for some:* interview.
Standardized tests *Admission: Required:* SAT I or ACT.
Admissions Office Contact
Samuel Merritt College, 370 Hawthorne Avenue, Oakland, CA 94609-3108. **Toll-free phone:** 800-607-MERRITT. **Fax:** 510-869-6525. **E-mail:** admission@samuelmerritt.edu
Visit CollegeQuest.com for information on athletics. College video available at CollegeQuest.com.

SAN DIEGO STATE UNIVERSITY
San Diego, California

- **State-supported**, university, founded 1897
- **Degrees** bachelor's, master's, and doctoral
- **Urban** 300-acre campus
- **Coed**, 25,631 undergraduate students, 77% full-time, 56% women, 44% men
- **Moderately difficult** entrance level, 60% of applicants were admitted
- **37% graduate** in 6 years or less
- **$9156 tuition and fees (out-of-state)**
- **$7300 average financial aid** package, $13,600 average indebtedness upon graduation, $84.2 million endowment

Part of California State University System.
Students *Undergraduates:* 19,737 full-time, 5,894 part-time. Students come from 68 other countries. *The most frequently chosen baccalaureate fields are:* business/marketing, psychology, social sciences and history. *Graduate:* 5,782 in graduate degree programs.

From out-of-state	2%	Reside on campus	12%
Age 25 or older	22%	Transferred in	10%
International students	2%	African Americans	5%
Asian Americans/Pacific Islanders	15%	Hispanic Americans	21%
Native Americans	1%		

Faculty 1,781 (53% full-time).
Expenses (2000–2001) *Tuition, nonresident:* full-time $7380; part-time $246 per unit. *Required fees:* full-time $1776; $612 per term part-time. *College room and board:* $7110; room only: $3413. Room and board charges vary according to board plan and housing facility. *Payment plan:* installment. *Waivers:* senior citizens and employees or children of employees.
Library Malcolm A. Love Library. *Operations spending 1999–2000:* $9.1 million. *Collection:* 5,381 serial subscriptions, 456,004 audiovisual materials.
College life *Housing:* Options: coed, disabled students. *Social organizations:* national fraternities, national sororities, local fraternities, local sororities; 9% of eligible men and 7% of eligible women are members. *Most popular organizations:* American Marketing Association, Associated Students, Student Accounting Society, Residence Hall Association, MECHA.
Campus security 24-hour emergency response devices and patrols, student patrols, late-night transport-escort service.
After graduation 748 organizations recruited on campus 1997–98. *Career center:* 19 full-time personnel. Services include job fairs, resume preparation, resume referral, career counseling, careers library, job bank, job interviews. *Graduate education:* 2% of class of 1999 went directly to graduate and professional school.

Freshmen 19,350 applied, 11,632 admitted, 3,813 enrolled.

Average high school GPA	3.33	SAT verbal scores above 500	54%
SAT math scores above 500	62%	ACT above 18	83%
1998 freshmen returning in 1999	73%		

Application *Options:* electronic application, early action. *Application fee:* $55. *Required:* high school transcript; minimum 2.0 GPA.
Standardized tests *Admission: Required:* SAT I or ACT.
Significant dates *Application deadlines:* 11/30 (freshmen), rolling (transfers). *Early action:* 11/30. *Notification:* 3/15 (freshmen), 1/15 (early action). *Financial aid deadline:* continuous.
Freshman Application Contact
Admissions and Records Office, San Diego State University, 5500 Campanile Drive, San Diego, CA 92182. **Phone:** 619-594-6871.
Visit CollegeQuest.com for information on majors offered and athletics.

SAN FRANCISCO ART INSTITUTE
San Francisco, California

- **Independent**, comprehensive, founded 1871
- **Degrees** bachelor's, master's, and postbachelor's certificates
- **Urban** 3-acre campus
- **Coed**, 473 undergraduate students, 88% full-time, 47% women, 53% men
- **Moderately difficult** entrance level, 69% of applicants were admitted
- **12:1 student-to-undergraduate faculty ratio**
- **16% graduate** in 6 years or less
- **$19,300 tuition** and fees
- **$21,084 average financial aid** package, $8.3 million endowment

The Interdisciplinary Core Program offers students with no previous college experience an intensive introduction to the visual arts. A structured program of studio practice and academic study, the Core Program also provides sufficient flexibility for the individual creative freedom for which SFAI has long been known. Most important, the program allows young artists to share their experiences and ideas with their peers.

Students *Undergraduates:* 418 full-time, 55 part-time. Students come from 24 states and territories, 18 other countries. *The most frequently chosen baccalaureate field is:* visual/performing arts. *Graduate:* 124 in graduate degree programs.

From out-of-state	33%	Age 25 or older	44%
Transferred in	28%	International students	8%
African Americans	3%	Asian Americans/Pacific Islanders	4%
Hispanic Americans	10%	Native Americans	1%

Faculty 122 (31% full-time).
Expenses (1999–2000) *Tuition:* full-time $19,300; part-time $804 per semester hour. *Payment plan:* installment. *Waivers:* employees or children of employees.
Library Anne Bremer Memorial Library. *Collection:* 29,000 titles, 210 serial subscriptions, 1,400 audiovisual materials.
College life *Housing:* college housing not available. *Most popular organization:* Student Senate.
Campus security 24-hour patrols, security cameras.
After graduation *Career center:* 2 full-time personnel. Services include resume preparation, career counseling, careers library, job bank.
Freshmen 193 applied, 133 admitted, 40 enrolled.

SAT verbal scores above 500	N/R	SAT math scores above 500	N/R
ACT above 18	N/R	1998 freshmen returning in 1999	24%

Application *Option:* deferred entrance. *Application fee:* $50. *Required:* essay or personal statement; high school transcript; portfolio. *Recommended:* interview.
Standardized tests *Admission: Required:* SAT I or ACT.
Significant dates *Application deadlines:* 9/1 (freshmen), rolling (transfers). *Notification:* continuous until 4/15 (freshmen). *Financial aid deadline priority date:* 3/1.
Freshman Application Contact
Mr. Tim Robison, Vice President of Enrollment Services, San Francisco Art Institute, 800 Chestnut Street, San Francisco, CA 94133. **Phone:** 415-771-7020. **Toll-free phone:** 800-345-SFAI. **E-mail:** admissions@cdmweb.sfai.edu

California

San Francisco Art Institute (continued)
Visit CollegeQuest.com for information on majors offered and athletics. College video available at CollegeQuest.com.

■ *See page 2444 for a narrative description.*

SAN FRANCISCO CONSERVATORY OF MUSIC
San Francisco, California

- **Independent**, comprehensive, founded 1917
- **Degrees** bachelor's, master's, and post-master's certificates
- **Urban** 2-acre campus
- **Coed**, 131 undergraduate students, 98% full-time, 54% women, 46% men
- **Moderately difficult** entrance level, 64% of applicants were admitted
- **6:1 student-to-undergraduate faculty ratio**
- **82% graduate** in 6 years or less
- **$18,670 tuition** and fees
- **$12,281 average financial aid** package, $17,582 average indebtedness upon graduation, $27.2 million endowment

Students *Undergraduates:* 128 full-time, 3 part-time. Students come from 25 states and territories, 14 other countries. *The most frequently chosen baccalaureate field is:* visual/performing arts. *Graduate:* 107 in graduate degree programs.

From out-of-state	35%	Age 25 or older	12%
Transferred in	18%	International students	17%
African Americans	2%	Asian Americans/Pacific Islanders	15%
Hispanic Americans	8%		

Faculty 70 (37% full-time), 21% with terminal degrees.
Expenses (1999–2000) *Tuition:* full-time $18,400; part-time $820 per semester hour. *Required fees:* full-time $270; $135 per term part-time. Part-time tuition and fees vary according to course load. *Payment plan:* installment. *Waivers:* employees or children of employees.
Library Conservatory Library. *Operations spending 1999–2000:* $148,600. *Collection:* 33,574 titles, 78 serial subscriptions.
College life *Housing:* college housing not available.
Campus security Late-night transport-escort service.
After graduation *Graduate education:* 50% of class of 1999 went directly to graduate and professional school: 45% graduate arts and sciences, 5% education.
Freshmen 95 applied, 61 admitted, 21 enrolled.

Average high school GPA	3.34	SAT verbal scores above 500	67%
SAT math scores above 500	58%	ACT above 18	100%

Application *Option:* early admission. *Application fee:* $60. *Required:* high school transcript; 2 letters of recommendation; audition.
Standardized tests *Admission: Required:* SAT I or ACT. *Recommended:* SAT I.
Significant dates *Application deadlines:* 3/1 (freshmen), 3/1 (transfers). *Financial aid deadline priority date:* 3/1.
Freshman Application Contact
Ms. Joan Gordon, Admissions Officer, San Francisco Conservatory of Music, 1201 Ortega Street, San Francisco, CA 94122-4411. **Phone:** 415-759-3431. **Fax:** 415-759-3499. **E-mail:** jog@sfcm.edu
Visit CollegeQuest.com for information on majors offered and athletics.

SAN FRANCISCO STATE UNIVERSITY
San Francisco, California

- **State-supported**, comprehensive, founded 1899
- **Degrees** bachelor's and master's
- **Urban** 90-acre campus
- **Coed**, 21,138 undergraduate students, 71% full-time, 59% women, 41% men
- **Moderately difficult** entrance level, 73% of applicants were admitted
- **34.8% graduate** in 6 years or less
- **$1826 tuition** and fees (in-state); $7730 (out-of-state)
- **$6759 average financial aid** package, $12,000 average indebtedness upon graduation, $3.6 million endowment

Part of California State University System.
Students *Undergraduates:* 14,934 full-time, 6,204 part-time. Students come from 48 states and territories, 113 other countries. *The most frequently chosen baccalaureate fields are:* business/marketing, social sciences and history, visual/performing arts. *Graduate:* 6,563 in graduate degree programs.

From out-of-state	1%	Reside on campus	5%
Age 25 or older	33%	Transferred in	16%
International students	6%	African Americans	7%
Asian Americans/Pacific Islanders	33%	Hispanic Americans	13%
Native Americans	1%		

Faculty 1,627 (48% full-time), 48% with terminal degrees.
Expenses (1999–2000) *Tuition, state resident:* full-time $0. *Tuition, nonresident:* full-time $5904; part-time $246 per unit. *Required fees:* full-time $1826; $613 per term part-time. *College room and board:* $7380. Room and board charges vary according to board plan and housing facility. *Payment plans:* installment, deferred payment. *Waivers:* employees or children of employees.
Library J. Paul Leonard Library plus 2 others. *Operations spending 1999–2000:* $8.2 million. *Collection:* 876,022 titles, 6,065 serial subscriptions.
College life *Housing: Options:* coed, disabled students. *Social organizations:* national fraternities, national sororities, local fraternities, local sororities; 1% of eligible men and 1% of eligible women are members. *Most popular organizations:* African Student Union, Asian Student Union, Laraza Student Organization, Filipino Collegial Endeavor, Sigma Sigma Sigma.
Campus security 24-hour emergency response devices and patrols, student patrols, late-night transport-escort service, controlled dormitory access.
After graduation 50 organizations recruited on campus 1997–98. *Career center:* 9 full-time, 6 part-time personnel. Services include job fairs, resume preparation, career counseling, careers library, job bank, job interviews. *Major awards:* 1 Fulbright Scholar.
Freshmen 10,547 applied, 7,752 admitted, 2,101 enrolled.

Average high school GPA	3.1	SAT verbal scores above 500	44%
SAT math scores above 500	47%	ACT above 18	66%
1998 freshmen returning in 1999	78%		

Application *Options:* Common Application, early admission. *Application fee:* $55. *Required:* high school transcript.
Standardized tests *Admission: Required for some:* SAT I or ACT.
Significant dates *Application deadline:* 8/1 (freshmen). *Financial aid deadline priority date:* 3/2.
Freshman Application Contact
Ms. Patricia Wade, Admissions Officer, San Francisco State University, Administration 154, San Francisco, CA 94132. **Phone:** 415-338-2037. **E-mail:** ugadmit@sfsu.edu
Visit CollegeQuest.com for information on majors offered and athletics.

SAN JOSE CHRISTIAN COLLEGE
San Jose, California

- **Independent nondenominational**, 4-year, founded 1939
- **Degrees** associate and bachelor's
- **Urban** 9-acre campus
- **Coed**, 372 undergraduate students, 63% full-time, 43% women, 57% men
- **Noncompetitive** entrance level, 42% of applicants were admitted
- **12:1 student-to-undergraduate faculty ratio**
- **$6660 tuition** and fees

Students *Undergraduates:* 236 full-time, 136 part-time. Students come from 7 states and territories, 7 other countries. *The most frequently chosen baccalaureate field is:* philosophy.

Reside on campus	25%	Age 25 or older	63%
International students	15%	African Americans	8%
Asian Americans/Pacific Islanders	13%	Hispanic Americans	10%
Native Americans	1%		

Faculty 93 (11% full-time), 11% with terminal degrees.
Expenses (1999–2000) *Comprehensive fee:* $11,436 includes full-time tuition ($6660) and room and board ($4776). Full-time tuition and fees vary according to program. Room and board charges vary according to board plan. *Part-time tuition:* $185 per quarter hour. Part-time tuition and fees vary according to program. *Payment plan:* deferred payment. *Waivers:* employees or children of employees.

Library San Jose Christian College Memorial Library. *Collection:* 31,689 titles, 157 serial subscriptions.
College life *Housing:* on-campus residence required through sophomore year. *Options:* men-only, women-only. *Most popular organizations:* missions club, student leadership, drama team, music ensemble.
Campus security Student patrols, late-night transport-escort service, day and evening patrols by trained security personnel.
After graduation 16 organizations recruited on campus 1997–98. *Career center:* Services include resume preparation, career/interest testing, career counseling, job interviews.
Freshmen 199 applied, 83 admitted, 31 enrolled.

Average high school GPA	2.2	SAT verbal scores above 500	38%
SAT math scores above 500	35%	ACT above 18	35%
From top 10% of their h.s. class	15%	From top quarter	19%
From top half	33%	1998 freshmen returning in 1999	62%

Application *Option:* deferred entrance. *Application fee:* $30. *Required:* essay or personal statement; high school transcript; minimum 2.0 GPA; 2 letters of recommendation; letter of introduction.
Standardized tests *Admission: Required:* SAT I or ACT.
Significant dates *Application deadlines:* 8/1 (freshmen), 8/1 (transfers). *Financial aid deadline priority date:* 6/1.
Freshman Application Contact
Ms. Stephany Haskins, Admissions Counselor, San Jose Christian College, 790 South Twelfth Street, San Jose, CA 95112-2381. **Phone:** 408-278-4333. **Toll-free phone:** 800-355-7522. **Fax:** 408-293-7352. **E-mail:** rjones@sjchristian.edu
Visit CollegeQuest.com for information on majors offered and athletics. College video available at CollegeQuest.com.

SAN JOSE STATE UNIVERSITY
San Jose, California

- **State-supported**, comprehensive, founded 1857
- **Degrees** bachelor's and master's
- **Urban** 104-acre campus
- **Coed**, 20,732 undergraduate students, 69% full-time, 51% women, 49% men
- **Moderately difficult** entrance level, 72% of applicants were admitted
- **38.5% graduate** in 6 years or less
- **$1939 tuition** and fees (in-state); $7843 (out-of-state)
- **$6999 average financial aid** package, $9981 average indebtedness upon graduation, $2.4 million endowment

Part of California State University System.
Students *Undergraduates:* 14,374 full-time, 6,358 part-time. Students come from 45 states and territories, 129 other countries. *Graduate:* 6,205 in graduate degree programs.

From out-of-state	1%	Reside on campus	10%
Age 25 or older	35%	Transferred in	13%
International students	4%	African Americans	4%
Asian Americans/Pacific Islanders	39%	Hispanic Americans	15%
Native Americans	1%		

Expenses (1999–2000) *Tuition, state resident:* full-time $0. *Tuition, nonresident:* full-time $5904; part-time $246 per unit. *Required fees:* full-time $1939; $654 per term part-time. Part-time tuition and fees vary according to course load. *College room and board:* $6248; room only: $3552. Room and board charges vary according to board plan. *Waivers:* senior citizens and employees or children of employees.
Library Robert D. Clark Library plus 1 other. *Operations spending 1999–2000:* $6.8 million. *Collection:* 1.1 million titles, 2,504 serial subscriptions, 37,146 audiovisual materials.
College life *Housing: Option:* coed. *Social organizations:* national fraternities, national sororities, local fraternities, local sororities; 6% of eligible men and 3% of eligible women are members.
Campus security 24-hour emergency response devices and patrols, student patrols, late-night transport-escort service.
After graduation 250 organizations recruited on campus 1997–98. 81% of class of 1998 had job offers within 6 months. *Career center:* 16 full-time, 1 part-time personnel. Services include job fairs, resume preparation, interview workshops, resume referral, career/interest testing, career counseling, careers library, job bank, job interviews.

Freshmen 10,275 applied, 7,434 admitted, 2,388 enrolled.

Average high school GPA	3.13	SAT verbal scores above 500	41%
SAT math scores above 500	56%	ACT above 18	68%

Application *Options:* Common Application, electronic application. *Preference* given to state residents. *Application fee:* $55. *Required:* high school transcript.
Standardized tests *Admission: Required for some:* SAT I or ACT.
Significant dates *Application deadlines:* rolling (freshmen), rolling (transfers). *Financial aid deadline priority date:* 3/2.
Freshman Application Contact
Mr. John Bradbury, Interim Director of Admissions, San Jose State University, One Washington Square, San Jose, CA 95192-0001. **Phone:** 408-924-2000. **Fax:** 408-924-2050.
Visit CollegeQuest.com for information on majors offered and athletics.

SANTA CLARA UNIVERSITY
Santa Clara, California

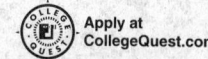
Apply at CollegeQuest.com

- **Independent Roman Catholic (Jesuit)**, university, founded 1851
- **Degrees** bachelor's, master's, doctoral, first professional, post-master's, and postbachelor's certificates
- **Suburban** 104-acre campus with easy access to San Francisco and San Jose
- **Coed**, 4,461 undergraduate students, 97% full-time, 54% women, 46% men
- **Moderately difficult** entrance level, 70% of applicants were admitted
- **15:1 student-to-undergraduate faculty ratio**
- **80.9% graduate** in 6 years or less
- **$19,311 tuition** and fees
- **$381.7 million endowment**

Students *Undergraduates:* 4,321 full-time, 140 part-time. *The most frequently chosen baccalaureate fields are:* business/marketing, engineering/engineering technologies, social sciences and history. *Graduate:* 907 in professional programs, 2,286 in other graduate degree programs.

Reside on campus	41%	Age 25 or older	3%
Transferred in	4%	International students	3%
African Americans	2%	Asian Americans/Pacific Islanders	19%
Hispanic Americans	13%	Native Americans	1%

Faculty 435 (80% full-time).
Expenses (1999–2000) *Comprehensive fee:* $26,955 includes full-time tuition ($19,311) and room and board ($7644). *College room only:* $4828. Full-time tuition and fees vary according to program and student level. Room and board charges vary according to board plan and housing facility. *Part-time tuition:* $2088 per course. Part-time tuition and fees vary according to course load and student level. *Payment plans:* tuition prepayment, installment, deferred payment. *Waivers:* employees or children of employees.
Library Orradre Library plus 1 other. *Operations spending 1999–2000:* $3.4 million. *Collection:* 454,470 titles, 8,611 serial subscriptions, 7,693 audiovisual materials.
College life *Housing: Option:* coed. *Social organizations:* national fraternities, national sororities, local fraternities, local sororities; 13% of eligible men and 14% of eligible women are members. *Most popular organizations:* Santa Clara Community Action Program, Associated Students, Activities Programming Board, Multicultural Programming Board, Residence Hall Association.
Campus security 24-hour emergency response devices and patrols, late-night transport-escort service, controlled dormitory access.
After graduation 300 organizations recruited on campus 1997–98. 63% of class of 1998 had job offers within 6 months. *Career center:* 7 full-time, 3 part-time personnel. Services include job fairs, resume preparation, interview workshops, resume referral, career/interest testing, career counseling, careers library, job bank, job interviews.
Freshmen 5,562 applied, 3,868 admitted, 1,103 enrolled. 1 National Merit Scholar, 42 valedictorians, 101 student government officers.

California

Santa Clara University (continued)

Average high school GPA	3.51	SAT verbal scores above 500	91%
SAT math scores above 500	93%	ACT above 18	N/R
From top 10% of their h.s. class	37%	From top quarter	71%
From top half	95%	1998 freshmen returning in 1999	90%

Application *Options:* eApply at www.CollegeQuest.com, Common Application, electronic application, deferred entrance. *Application fee:* $50. *Required:* essay or personal statement; high school transcript; 1 letter of recommendation. *Recommended:* interview.

Standardized tests *Admission: Required:* SAT I or ACT.

Significant dates *Application deadlines:* 1/15 (freshmen), 5/15 (transfers). *Notification:* continuous until 4/1 (freshmen). *Financial aid deadline priority date:* 2/1.

Freshman Application Contact
Sr. Annette Schmeling, Dean of Undergraduate Admissions, Santa Clara University, 500 El Camino Real, Santa Clara, CA 95053. **Phone:** 408-554-4700. **Fax:** 408-554-5255. **E-mail:** ugadmissions@scu.edu

Visit CollegeQuest.com for information on majors offered and athletics. College video and electronic viewbook available at CollegeQuest.com.

■ *See page 2446 for a narrative description.*

SCRIPPS COLLEGE
Claremont, California

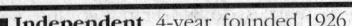

Apply at CollegeQuest.com

- **Independent**, 4-year, founded 1926
- **Degrees** bachelor's and postbachelor's certificates
- **Suburban** 30-acre campus with easy access to Los Angeles
- **Women** only, 769 undergraduate students, 99% full-time
- **Very difficult** entrance level, 70% of applicants were admitted
- **12:1** student-to-undergraduate faculty ratio
- **70% graduate** in 6 years or less
- **$21,130 tuition** and fees
- **$19,799 average financial aid** package, $18,278 average indebtedness upon graduation, $167.2 million endowment

Part of The Claremont Colleges Consortium.

Students *Undergraduates:* 764 full-time, 5 part-time. Students come from 41 states and territories, 19 other countries. *The most frequently chosen baccalaureate fields are:* social sciences and history, interdisciplinary studies, visual/performing arts. *Graduate:* 17 in graduate degree programs.

From out-of-state	50%	Reside on campus	85%
Age 25 or older	3%	Transferred in	1%
International students	2%	African Americans	3%
Asian Americans/Pacific Islanders	15%	Hispanic Americans	6%
Native Americans	1%		

Faculty 85 (67% full-time), 84% with terminal degrees.

Expenses (1999–2000) *Comprehensive fee:* $29,000 includes full-time tuition ($21,000), mandatory fees ($130), and room and board ($7870). *College room only:* $4170. Full-time tuition and fees vary according to program. Room and board charges vary according to board plan. *Part-time tuition:* $2625 per course. *Part-time fees:* $130 per year part-time. Part-time tuition and fees vary according to program. *Payment plan:* installment. *Waivers:* employees or children of employees.

Library Honnold Library plus 4 others. *Operations spending 1999–2000:* $588,362. *Collection:* 2 million titles, 4,113 serial subscriptions, 606 audiovisual materials.

College life *Housing:* on-campus residence required in freshman year. *Option:* women-only. *Most popular organizations:* college council, Asian/Black/Latina Clubs, National Organization for Women, Sexual Assault Task Force, Family.

Campus security 24-hour emergency response devices and patrols, late-night transport-escort service, controlled dormitory access.

After graduation 200 organizations recruited on campus 1997–98. 69% of class of 1998 had job offers within 6 months. *Career center:* 4 full-time personnel. Services include job fairs, resume preparation, interview workshops, resume referral, career/interest testing, career counseling, careers library, job bank, job interviews. *Graduate education:* 30% of class of 1999 went directly to graduate and professional school.

Freshmen 1,063 applied, 749 admitted, 212 enrolled. 1 National Merit Scholar, 10 valedictorians.

Average high school GPA	3.67	SAT verbal scores above 500	96%
SAT math scores above 500	97%	ACT above 18	100%
From top 10% of their h.s. class	48%	From top quarter	83%
From top half	98%	1998 freshmen returning in 1999	88%

Application *Options:* eApply at www.CollegeQuest.com, Common Application, electronic application, early admission, early decision, deferred entrance. *Application fee:* $50. *Required:* essay or personal statement; high school transcript; 3 letters of recommendation; graded writing sample. *Recommended:* minimum 3.0 GPA; interview.

Standardized tests *Admission: Required:* SAT I or ACT.

Significant dates *Application deadlines:* 2/1 (freshmen), 4/1 (transfers). *Early decision:* 11/1 (for plan 1), 1/1 (for plan 2). *Notification:* 4/1 (freshmen), 12/1 (early decision plan 1), 2/1 (early decision plan 2). *Financial aid deadline priority date:* 11/15.

Freshman Application Contact
Ms. Patricia F. Goldsmith, Dean of Admission and Financial Aid, Scripps College, 1030 Columbia Avenue, Claremont, CA 91711-3948. **Phone:** 909-621-8149. **Toll-free phone:** 800-770-1333. **Fax:** 909-621-8323. **E-mail:** admofc@ad.scrippscol.edu

Visit CollegeQuest.com for information on majors offered and athletics.

■ *See page 2464 for a narrative description.*

SHASTA BIBLE COLLEGE
Redding, California

Apply at CollegeQuest.com

- **Independent nondenominational**, 4-year, founded 1971
- **Degrees** associate and bachelor's
- **Small-town** 25-acre campus
- **Coed**, 212 undergraduate students, 21% full-time, 63% women, 37% men
- **14:1** student-to-undergraduate faculty ratio
- **91% graduate** in 6 years or less
- **$4830 tuition** and fees
- **$1.1 million endowment**

Students *Undergraduates:* 45 full-time, 167 part-time. Students come from 7 states and territories, 2 other countries.

From out-of-state	3%	Age 25 or older	10%
International students	1%	Asian Americans/Pacific Islanders	0.5%

Faculty 20 (30% full-time), 40% with terminal degrees.

Expenses (1999–2000) *Tuition:* full-time $4650; part-time $155 per credit. *Required fees:* full-time $180; $70 per term part-time. Full-time tuition and fees vary according to course load. *College room only:* $1350. Room and board charges vary according to housing facility. *Payment plan:* deferred payment. *Waivers:* minority students, children of alumni, and employees or children of employees.

College life *Housing: Options:* men-only, women-only.

After graduation *Graduate education:* 37% of class of 1999 went directly to graduate and professional school: 21% education, 16% theology.

Freshmen 12 enrolled.

Average high school GPA	2.95	SAT verbal scores above 500	N/R
SAT math scores above 500	N/R	ACT above 18	N/R
1998 freshmen returning in 1999	58%		

Application *Option:* eApply at www.CollegeQuest.com. *Application fee:* $30. *Required:* essay or personal statement; high school transcript; 4 letters of recommendation.

Significant dates *Financial aid deadline:* continuous.

Freshman Application Contact
Ms. Dawn Rodriguez, Registrar, Shasta Bible College, 2980 Hartnell Avenue, Redding, CA 96002. **Phone:** 530-221-4275. **Toll-free phone:** 800-800-45BC (in-state); 800-800-6929 (out-of-state). **E-mail:** ggunn@shasta.edu

Visit CollegeQuest.com for information on majors offered and athletics.

SIMPSON COLLEGE AND GRADUATE SCHOOL
Redding, California

- **Independent**, comprehensive, founded 1921, affiliated with The Christian and Missionary Alliance

- **Degrees** associate, bachelor's, and master's
- **Suburban** 60-acre campus
- **Coed**, 966 undergraduate students, 96% full-time, 64% women, 36% men
- **Moderately difficult** entrance level, 55% of applicants were admitted
- **17:1 student-to-undergraduate faculty ratio**
- **$10,540 tuition** and fees
- **$10,815 average financial aid** package, $2.4 million endowment

Students *Undergraduates:* 928 full-time, 38 part-time. Students come from 28 states and territories, 7 other countries. *The most frequently chosen baccalaureate fields are:* liberal arts/general studies, business/marketing, psychology. *Graduate:* 215 in graduate degree programs.

From out-of-state	25%	Reside on campus	91%
Transferred in	10%	International students	1%
African Americans	0.4%	Asian Americans/Pacific Islanders	4%
Hispanic Americans	5%	Native Americans	1%

Faculty 86 (48% full-time), 43% with terminal degrees.

Expenses (1999–2000) *One-time required fee:* $60. *Comprehensive fee:* $15,220 includes full-time tuition ($9400), mandatory fees ($1140), and room and board ($4680). Room and board charges vary according to board plan. *Part-time tuition:* $400 per credit. *Part-time fees:* $25 per credit. *Payment plan:* installment. *Waivers:* employees or children of employees.

Library Start-Kilgour Memorial Library. *Operations spending 1999–2000:* $209,993. *Collection:* 66,103 titles, 316 serial subscriptions, 1,139 audiovisual materials.

College life *Housing:* on-campus residence required through junior year. *Options:* men-only, women-only, disabled students. *Social organizations:* men's and women's associations; 60% of eligible men and 50% of eligible women are members. *Most popular organizations:* Student Senate, Missions Committee, psychology club, drama club, Spiritual Action Committee.

Campus security 24-hour emergency response devices, student patrols, controlled dormitory access, late night security patrols by trained personnel.

After graduation *Career center:* 1 full-time personnel. Services include job fairs, resume preparation, interview workshops, career/interest testing, career counseling, job bank.

Freshmen 885 applied, 488 admitted, 191 enrolled.

Average high school GPA	3.33	SAT verbal scores above 500	65%
SAT math scores above 500	53%	ACT above 18	86%
From top 10% of their h.s. class	16%	From top quarter	44%
From top half	76%	1998 freshmen returning in 1999	65%

Application *Options:* electronic application, deferred entrance. *Application fee:* $20. *Required:* essay or personal statement; high school transcript; minimum 2 GPA; 2 letters of recommendation; Christian commitment. *Required for some:* interview.

Standardized tests *Admission: Required:* SAT I or ACT.

Significant dates *Application deadlines:* rolling (freshmen), rolling (transfers). *Financial aid deadline priority date:* 3/2.

Freshman Application Contact
Mrs. Beth Spencer, Administrative Assistant to Vice President for Enrollment, Simpson College and Graduate School, 2211 College View Drive, Redding, CA 96003-8606. **Phone:** 530-224-5606 Ext. 2602. **Toll-free phone:** 800-598-2493. **Fax:** 530-224-5608. **E-mail:** admissions@simpsonca.edu

Visit CollegeQuest.com for information on majors offered and athletics. Electronic viewbook available at CollegeQuest.com.

SONOMA STATE UNIVERSITY
Rohnert Park, California

- **State-supported**, comprehensive, founded 1960
- **Degrees** bachelor's and master's
- **Small-town** 220-acre campus with easy access to San Francisco
- **Coed**, 5,845 undergraduate students, 84% full-time, 65% women, 35% men
- **Moderately difficult** entrance level, 80% of applicants were admitted
- **20:1 student-to-undergraduate faculty ratio**
- **45% graduate** in 6 years or less
- **$7878 tuition and fees (out-of-state)**
- **$8520 average financial aid** package, $26.2 million endowment

Part of California State University System.

Students *Undergraduates:* 4,890 full-time, 955 part-time. Students come from 33 states and territories, 34 other countries. *The most frequently chosen baccalaureate fields are:* business/marketing, psychology, social sciences and history. *Graduate:* 1,235 in graduate degree programs.

From out-of-state	2%	Reside on campus	21%
Age 25 or older	26%	Transferred in	14%
International students	1%	African Americans	2%
Asian Americans/Pacific Islanders	5%	Hispanic Americans	10%
Native Americans	1%		

Faculty 516 (51% full-time), 71% with terminal degrees.

Expenses (1999–2000) *Tuition, nonresident:* full-time $5904; part-time $246 per unit. *Required fees:* full-time $1974; $687 per term part-time. Part-time tuition and fees vary according to course load. *College room and board:* $6217; room only: $4092. Room and board charges vary according to board plan and housing facility. *Payment plan:* deferred payment. *Waivers:* employees or children of employees.

Library Ruben Salazar Library. *Operations spending 1999–2000:* $2.9 million. *Collection:* 521,053 titles, 2,087 serial subscriptions, 7,572 audiovisual materials.

College life *Housing: Options:* coed, women-only. *Social organizations:* national fraternities, national sororities; 6% of eligible men and 5% of eligible women are members. *Most popular organizations:* Accounting Forum, Sonoma Earth Action, Re-Entry Student Association, La-Crosse Club, Inter-varsity Christian Fellowship.

Campus security 24-hour emergency response devices and patrols, student patrols, late-night transport-escort service.

After graduation 55 organizations recruited on campus 1997–98. *Career center:* 3 full-time personnel. Services include job fairs, resume preparation, resume referral, career counseling, careers library, job bank, job interviews.

Freshmen 4,122 applied, 3,303 admitted, 860 enrolled.

Average high school GPA	3.23	SAT verbal scores above 500	62%
SAT math scores above 500	61%	ACT above 18	N/R
From top 10% of their h.s. class	14%	From top quarter	45%
From top half	84%	1998 freshmen returning in 1999	78%

Application *Options:* electronic application, early admission, early action. *Application fee:* $55. *Required:* high school transcript.

Standardized tests *Admission: Required:* SAT I or ACT.

Significant dates *Application deadlines:* 1/31 (freshmen), 1/31 (transfers). *Early action:* 11/1. *Financial aid deadline priority date:* 1/31.

Freshman Application Contact
Mrs. Margo Axsom, Registrar, Sonoma State University, 1801 East Cotati Avenue, Rohnert Park, CA 94928-3609. **Phone:** 707-664-3129. **E-mail:** admitme@sonoma.edu

Visit CollegeQuest.com for information on majors offered and athletics.

SOUTHERN CALIFORNIA BIBLE COLLEGE & SEMINARY
El Cajon, California

Admissions Office Contact
Southern California Bible College & Seminary, 2075 East Madison Avenue, El Cajon, CA 92019. **Fax:** 619-442-4510.

SOUTHERN CALIFORNIA COLLEGE
California—See Vanguard University of Southern California

SOUTHERN CALIFORNIA INSTITUTE OF ARCHITECTURE
Los Angeles, California

- **Independent**, comprehensive, founded 1972
- **Degrees** bachelor's and master's
- **Urban** campus
- **Coed**
- **Moderately difficult** entrance level

California

Southern California Institute of Architecture *(continued)*
Institutional Web site http://www.sciarc.edu/
College life *Housing:* college housing not available. *Most popular organizations:* student council, academic council.
Campus security 24-hour emergency response devices and patrols.
Application *Option:* deferred entrance. *Application fee:* $60. *Required:* essay or personal statement; high school transcript; minimum 2.0 GPA; 3 letters of recommendation; charette, portfolio. *Recommended:* interview.
Standardized tests *Admission: Required:* SAT I or ACT.
Admissions Office Contact
Southern California Institute of Architecture, 5454 Beethoven Street, Los Angeles, CA 90066-7017. **Fax:** 310-829-7518. **E-mail:** admissions@sciarc.edu
Visit CollegeQuest.com for information on athletics.

■ *See page 2506 for a narrative description.*

STANFORD UNIVERSITY
Stanford, California

- **Independent**, university, founded 1891
- **Degrees** bachelor's, master's, doctoral, and first professional
- **Suburban** 8,180-acre campus with easy access to San Francisco
- **Coed**, 6,404 undergraduate students, 100% full-time, 49% women, 51% men
- **Most difficult** entrance level, 15% of applicants were admitted
- **8:1 student-to-undergraduate faculty ratio**
- **$23,058 tuition** and fees
- **$20,926 average financial aid** package, $15,892 average indebtedness upon graduation, $6.2 billion endowment

Students *Undergraduates:* 6,404 full-time. Students come from 52 states and territories, 55 other countries. *The most frequently chosen baccalaureate fields are:* engineering/engineering technologies, interdisciplinary studies, social sciences and history. *Graduate:* 1,030 in professional programs, 9,269 in other graduate degree programs.

From out-of-state	56%	Reside on campus	94%
Age 25 or older	1%	Transferred in	0.3%
International students	5%	African Americans	9%
Asian Americans/Pacific Islanders	24%	Hispanic Americans	11%
Native Americans	1%		

Faculty 1,640 (98% full-time), 98% with terminal degrees.
Expenses (1999–2000) *One-time required fee:* $275. *Comprehensive fee:* $30,939 includes full-time tuition ($23,058) and room and board ($7881). Room and board charges vary according to board plan and housing facility. *Payment plans:* installment, deferred payment.
Library Green Library plus 17 others. *Operations spending 1999–2000:* $65.5 million. *Collection:* 44,504 serial subscriptions, 1.3 million audiovisual materials.
College life *Housing:* on-campus residence required in freshman year. *Options:* coed, women-only, cooperative, disabled students. *Social organizations:* national fraternities, national sororities, eating clubs. *Most popular organizations:* Ram's Head (theatre club), Axe committee (athletic support), Business Association of Stanford Engineering Students, Asian American Student Association, Stanford Daily.
Campus security 24-hour emergency response devices and patrols, late-night transport-escort service, controlled dormitory access.
After graduation 450 organizations recruited on campus 1997–98. *Career center:* 15 full-time, 9 part-time personnel. Services include job fairs, resume preparation, resume referral, career counseling, careers library, job bank, job interviews. *Major awards:* 2 Marshall, 8 Fulbright Scholars.
Freshmen 17,919 applied, 2,689 admitted, 1,749 enrolled. 4 Westinghouse recipients.

Average high school GPA	3.9	SAT verbal scores above 500	100%
SAT math scores above 500	100%	ACT above 18	100%
From top 10% of their h.s. class	88%	From top quarter	98%
From top half	100%	1998 freshmen returning in 1999	99%

Application *Options:* early admission, early decision, deferred entrance. *Application fee:* $60. *Required:* essay or personal statement; high school transcript; 2 letters of recommendation.
Standardized tests *Admission: Required:* SAT I or ACT. *Recommended:* SAT II Subject Tests, SAT II: Writing Test.
Significant dates *Application deadlines:* 12/15 (freshmen), 3/15 (transfers). *Early decision:* 11/1. *Notification:* 4/1 (freshmen), 12/15 (early decision). *Financial aid deadline priority date:* 2/1.
Freshman Application Contact
Mr. Robert M. Kinnally, Dean of Undergraduate Admissions and Financial Aid, Stanford University, Stanford, CA 94305-9991. **Phone:** 650-723-2091. **Fax:** 650-725-2846. **E-mail:** undergrad.admissions@forsythe.stanford.edu
Visit CollegeQuest.com for information on majors offered and athletics. College video available at CollegeQuest.com.

■ *See page 2530 for a narrative description.*

THOMAS AQUINAS COLLEGE
Santa Paula, California

- **Independent Roman Catholic**, 4-year, founded 1971
- **Degree** bachelor's
- **Rural** 170-acre campus with easy access to Los Angeles
- **Coed**, 267 undergraduate students, 100% full-time, 41% women, 59% men
- **Very difficult** entrance level, 81% of applicants were admitted
- **11:1 student-to-undergraduate faculty ratio**
- **75% graduate** in 6 years or less
- **$14,900 tuition** and fees

Students *Undergraduates:* 267 full-time. Students come from 35 states and territories, 5 other countries. *The most frequently chosen baccalaureate field is:* liberal arts/general studies.

From out-of-state	63%	Reside on campus	98%
Age 25 or older	6%	International students	9%
African Americans	0.4%	Asian Americans/Pacific Islanders	2%
Hispanic Americans	9%		

Faculty 26 (92% full-time), 77% with terminal degrees.
Expenses (1999–2000) *Comprehensive fee:* $19,200 includes full-time tuition ($14,900) and room and board ($4300). *Payment plan:* installment.
Library St. Bernardine Library. *Operations spending 1999–2000:* $417. *Collection:* 45,000 titles, 48 serial subscriptions, 2,000 audiovisual materials.
College life *Housing:* on-campus residence required through senior year. *Options:* men-only, women-only. *Most popular organizations:* choir, Legion of Mary, drama club, prison ministry, pro-life ministry.
Campus security 24-hour emergency response devices, student patrols, weekend security patrol.
After graduation 4 organizations recruited on campus 1997–98. 62% of class of 1998 had job offers within 6 months. *Career center:* 2 part-time personnel. Services include job fairs, resume preparation, career/interest testing, career counseling, job bank. *Graduate education:* 9% of class of 1999 went directly to graduate and professional school: 7% theology, 2% graduate arts and sciences.
Freshmen 151 applied, 123 admitted, 86 enrolled. 1 National Merit Scholar, 2 valedictorians.

Average high school GPA	3.66	SAT verbal scores above 500	100%
SAT math scores above 500	97%	ACT above 18	100%
From top 10% of their h.s. class	48%	From top quarter	70%
From top half	93%	1998 freshmen returning in 1999	74%

Application *Options:* Common Application, early admission, deferred entrance. *Application fee:* $0. *Required:* essay or personal statement; high school transcript; 3 letters of recommendation. *Required for some:* interview. *Recommended:* minimum 2.0 GPA.
Standardized tests *Admission: Required:* SAT I or ACT.
Significant dates *Application deadline:* rolling (freshmen). *Financial aid deadline:* continuous.
Freshman Application Contact
Mr. Thomas J. Susanka Jr., Director of Admissions, Thomas Aquinas College, 10000 North Ojai Road, Santa Paula, CA 93060-9980. **Phone:** 805-525-4417 Ext. 361. **Toll-free phone:** 800-634-9797. **Fax:** 805-525-0620. **E-mail:** admissions@thomasaquinas.edu
Visit CollegeQuest.com for information on majors offered and athletics. College video available at CollegeQuest.com.

California

UNITED STATES INTERNATIONAL UNIVERSITY
San Diego, California

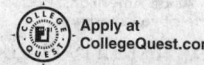
Apply at CollegeQuest.com

- **Independent**, university, founded 1952
- **Degrees** bachelor's, master's, and doctoral
- **Suburban** 200-acre campus
- **Coed**, 451 undergraduate students, 94% full-time, 57% women, 43% men
- **Moderately difficult** entrance level, 78% of applicants were admitted
- **19:1 student-to-undergraduate faculty ratio**
- **$13,611 tuition** and fees
- **$11,659 average financial aid** package, $16,210 average indebtedness upon graduation, $175,000 endowment

Students *Undergraduates:* 425 full-time, 26 part-time. Students come from 7 states and territories, 64 other countries. *The most frequently chosen baccalaureate fields are:* business/marketing, liberal arts/general studies, social sciences and history. *Graduate:* 853 in graduate degree programs.

From out-of-state	6%	Reside on campus	30%
Age 25 or older	21%	Transferred in	22%
International students	34%	African Americans	8%
Asian Americans/Pacific Islanders	7%	Hispanic Americans	18%
Native Americans	1%		

Faculty 146 (31% full-time).

Expenses (2000–2001, estimated) *Comprehensive fee:* $19,386 includes full-time tuition ($13,200), mandatory fees ($411), and room and board ($5775). Full-time tuition and fees vary according to course load and location. Room and board charges vary according to board plan. *Part-time tuition:* $320 per unit. *Part-time fees:* $117 per term part-time. Part-time tuition and fees vary according to course load and location. *Payment plans:* installment, deferred payment. *Waivers:* employees or children of employees.

Library Walter Library. *Operations spending 1999–2000:* $535,000. *Collection:* 152,860 titles, 788 serial subscriptions.

College life *Housing:* on-campus residence required in freshman year. *Options:* coed, men-only, women-only. *Most popular organizations:* residence hall association, Pacific Islanders club, student council, Rotaract, Sigma Iota Epsilon.

Campus security 24-hour patrols.

After graduation *Career center:* 5 full-time, 1 part-time personnel. Services include job fairs, resume preparation, career counseling, careers library.

Freshmen 578 applied, 450 admitted, 110 enrolled.

Average high school GPA	2.88	SAT verbal scores above 500	34%
SAT math scores above 500	36%	ACT above 18	75%
1998 freshmen returning in 1999	67%		

Application *Options:* eApply at www.CollegeQuest.com, Common Application, deferred entrance. *Application fee:* $40. *Required:* high school transcript; minimum 2.0 GPA. *Recommended:* minimum 3.0 GPA.

Standardized tests *Admission: Required:* SAT I or ACT.

Significant dates *Application deadlines:* rolling (freshmen), rolling (transfers). *Financial aid deadline priority date:* 3/2.

Freshman Application Contact
Ms. Susan Topham, Director of Admissions, United States International University, 10455 Pomerado Road, San Diego, CA 92131-1799. **Phone:** 858-635-4772. **Fax:** 858-635-4739. **E-mail:** admissions@usiu.edu

Visit CollegeQuest.com for information on majors offered and athletics. College video available at CollegeQuest.com.

UNIVERSITY OF CALIFORNIA, BERKELEY
Berkeley, California

- **State-supported**, university, founded 1868
- **Degrees** bachelor's, master's, doctoral, and first professional
- **Urban** 1,232-acre campus with easy access to San Francisco
- **Coed**, 22,259 undergraduate students, 93% full-time, 50% women, 50% men
- **Very difficult** entrance level, 27% of applicants were admitted
- **17:1 student-to-undergraduate faculty ratio**
- **83% graduate** in 6 years or less
- **$4046 tuition** and fees (in-state); $13,850 (out-of-state)
- **$11,330 average financial aid** package, $1.4 billion endowment

Part of University of California System.

Students *Undergraduates:* 20,614 full-time, 1,645 part-time. Students come from 53 states and territories, 100 other countries. *Graduate:* 1,080 in professional programs, 7,670 in other graduate degree programs.

From out-of-state	10%	Reside on campus	25%
Transferred in	7%	International students	4%
African Americans	5%	Asian Americans/Pacific Islanders	41%
Hispanic Americans	11%	Native Americans	1%

Faculty 1,438, 93% with terminal degrees.

Expenses (1999–2000) *Tuition, state resident:* full-time $0. *Tuition, nonresident:* full-time $9804. *Required fees:* full-time $4046. *College room and board:* $8266. Room and board charges vary according to housing facility. *Payment plan:* installment.

Library Doe Library plus 30 others. *Operations spending 1999–2000:* $6.5 million. *Collection:* 8.4 million titles, 83,000 serial subscriptions.

College life *Housing:* on-campus residence required in freshman year. *Options:* coed, men-only, women-only. *Social organizations:* national fraternities, national sororities, local fraternities, local sororities; 10% of eligible men and 10% of eligible women are members.

Campus security 24-hour emergency response devices and patrols, late-night transport-escort service, controlled dormitory access, Office of Emergency Preparedness.

After graduation 600 organizations recruited on campus 1997–98. *Career center:* 30 full-time, 30 part-time personnel. Services include job fairs, resume preparation, interview workshops, career counseling, careers library, job bank, job interviews. *Major awards:* 28 Fulbright Scholars.

Freshmen 31,108 applied, 8,444 admitted, 3,727 enrolled. 184 National Merit Scholars.

Average high school GPA	3.9	SAT verbal scores above 500	91%
SAT math scores above 500	95%	ACT above 18	N/R
From top 10% of their h.s. class	96%	From top half	100%
1998 freshmen returning in 1999	94%		

Application *Option:* electronic application. Preference given to state residents. *Application fee:* $40. *Required:* essay or personal statement; high school transcript; minimum 3.3 GPA for California residents; 3.4 for all others.

Standardized tests *Admission: Required:* SAT II Subject Tests, SAT II: Writing Test.

Significant dates *Application deadlines:* 11/30 (freshmen), 11/30 (transfers). *Notification:* 3/31 (freshmen). *Financial aid deadline priority date:* 3/2.

Freshman Application Contact
Pre-Admission Advising, Office of Undergraduate Admission and Relations With Schools, University of California, Berkeley, Berkeley, CA 94720-1500. **Phone:** 510-642-3175. **Fax:** 510-642-7333. **E-mail:** ouars@uclink.berkeley.edu

Visit CollegeQuest.com for information on majors offered and athletics. Electronic viewbook available at CollegeQuest.com.

UNIVERSITY OF CALIFORNIA, DAVIS
Davis, California

- **State-supported**, university, founded 1905
- **Degrees** bachelor's, master's, doctoral, first professional, and postbachelor's certificates
- **Suburban** 5,993-acre campus with easy access to San Francisco
- **Coed**, 19,393 undergraduate students, 89% full-time, 56% women, 44% men
- **Very difficult** entrance level, 62% of applicants were admitted
- **$4214 tuition** and fees (in-state); $14,536 (out-of-state)
- **$9651 average financial aid** package, $223.5 million endowment

Part of University of California System.

Students *Undergraduates:* 17,285 full-time, 2,108 part-time. Students come from 48 states and territories, 117 other countries. *The most frequently chosen baccalaureate fields are:* biological/life sciences, psychology, social sciences and history. *Graduate:* 1,330 in professional programs, 4,245 in other graduate degree programs.

Peterson's Guide to Four-Year Colleges 2001 www.petersons.com 131

California

University of California, Davis (continued)

From out-of-state	3%	Reside on campus	25%
Age 25 or older	7%	International students	1%
African Americans	3%	Asian Americans/Pacific Islanders	35%
Hispanic Americans	10%	Native Americans	1%

Faculty 1,602 (86% full-time).

Expenses (1999–2000) *Tuition, state resident:* full-time $0. *Tuition, nonresident:* full-time $10,322; part-time $1596 per term. *Required fees:* full-time $4214; $903 per term part-time. *College room and board:* $7012. Room and board charges vary according to board plan and housing facility. *Waivers:* employees or children of employees.

Library Peter J. Shields Library plus 5 others. *Operations spending 1999–2000:* $17.7 million. *Collection:* 2.9 million titles, 45,665 serial subscriptions.

College life *Housing: Options:* coed, men-only, women-only. *Social organizations:* national fraternities, national sororities, state fraternities and sororities; 6% of eligible men and 7% of eligible women are members. *Most popular organizations:* Filipino Student Organization, Vietnamese Student Association, Jewish Student Union, Alpha Phi Omega.

Campus security 24-hour emergency response devices and patrols, student patrols, late-night transport-escort service, controlled dormitory access, rape prevention programs.

After graduation 91% of class of 1998 had job offers within 6 months. *Career center:* 18 full-time, 8 part-time personnel. Services include job fairs, resume preparation, resume referral, career counseling, careers library, job bank, job interviews. *Graduate education:* 41% of class of 1999 went directly to graduate and professional school: 17% graduate arts and sciences, 7% medicine, 6% education, 6% law, 3% engineering, 3% veterinary medicine, 1% business, 1% dentistry. *Major awards:* 3 Fulbright Scholars.

Freshmen 23,126 applied, 14,369 admitted, 3,819 enrolled. 16 National Merit Scholars.

Average high school GPA	3.73	SAT verbal scores above 500	81%
SAT math scores above 500	89%	ACT above 18	93%
1998 freshmen returning in 1999	89%		

Application *Options:* electronic application, deferred entrance. *Preference* given to state residents for certain programs. *Application fee:* $40. *Required:* essay or personal statement; high school transcript.

Standardized tests *Admission: Required:* SAT I and SAT II or ACT, SAT II: Writing Test.

Significant dates *Application deadlines:* 11/30 (freshmen), 11/30 (transfers). *Notification:* continuous until 5/15 (freshmen). *Financial aid deadline priority date:* 3/2.

Freshman Application Contact
Dr. Gary Tudor, Director of Undergraduate Admissions, University of California, Davis, Undergraduate Admission and Outreach Services, 175 Mrak Hall, Davis, CA 95616. **Phone:** 530-752-2971. **Fax:** 530-752-6363. **E-mail:** thinkucd@ucdavis.edu

Visit CollegeQuest.com for information on majors offered and athletics. College video available at CollegeQuest.com.

UNIVERSITY OF CALIFORNIA, IRVINE
Irvine, California

- **State-supported**, university, founded 1965
- **Degrees** bachelor's, master's, doctoral, and first professional
- **Suburban** 1,489-acre campus with easy access to Los Angeles
- **Coed**, 15,235 undergraduate students, 95% full-time, 53% women, 47% men
- **Moderately difficult** entrance level, 60% of applicants were admitted
- **74.1% graduate** in 6 years or less
- **$3,871 tuition** and fees (in-state); $13,675 (out-of-state)
- **$11,254 average financial aid** package, $13,199 average indebtedness upon graduation, $103.6 million endowment

Part of University of California System.

Students *Undergraduates:* 14,516 full-time, 719 part-time. Students come from 35 states and territories, 34 other countries. *The most frequently chosen baccalaureate fields are:* biological/life sciences, interdisciplinary studies, social sciences and history. *Graduate:* 381 in professional programs, 3,533 in other graduate degree programs.

From out-of-state	2%	Reside on campus	32%
Age 25 or older	6%	Transferred in	7%
International students	2%	African Americans	2%
Asian Americans/Pacific Islanders	56%	Hispanic Americans	11%
Native Americans	0.4%		

Expenses (1999–2000) *Tuition, state resident:* full-time $0. *Tuition, nonresident:* full-time $9804; part-time $2475 per term. *Required fees:* full-time $3,870; $779 per term part-time. *College room and board:* $6407. Room and board charges vary according to board plan and housing facility. *Payment plan:* installment.

Library Main Library plus 1 other. *Collection:* 2.3 million titles, 18,187 serial subscriptions, 87,375 audiovisual materials.

College life *Housing: Options:* coed, men-only, women-only, disabled students. *Social organizations:* national fraternities, national sororities, local fraternities, local sororities; 7% of eligible men and 7% of eligible women are members.

Campus security 24-hour emergency response devices and patrols, late-night transport-escort service.

After graduation *Career center:* 16 full-time personnel. Services include job fairs, resume preparation, career counseling, careers library, job bank, job interviews. *Major awards:* 3 Fulbright Scholars.

Freshmen 22,157 applied, 13,311 admitted, 3,629 enrolled.

Average high school GPA	3.63	SAT verbal scores above 500	78%
SAT math scores above 500	91%	ACT above 18	N/R
From top 10% of their h.s. class	90%	From top quarter	100%
From top half	100%	1998 freshmen returning in 1999	91%

Application *Option:* electronic application. *Application fee:* $40. *Required:* essay or personal statement; high school transcript.

Standardized tests *Admission: Required:* SAT I or ACT, SAT II Subject Tests, SAT II: Writing Test.

Significant dates *Application deadlines:* 11/30 (freshmen), 11/30 (transfers). *Notification:* 3/1 (freshmen). *Financial aid deadline priority date:* 3/2.

Freshman Application Contact
Dr. Susan Wilbur, Director of Admissions, University of California, Irvine, Office of Admissions and Relations with Schools, 204 Administration, Irvine, CA 92697-1075. **Phone:** 949-824-6701. **E-mail:** wnn.uci.edu/uci/admissions

Visit CollegeQuest.com for information on majors offered and athletics.

UNIVERSITY OF CALIFORNIA, LOS ANGELES
Los Angeles, California

- **State-supported**, university, founded 1919
- **Degrees** bachelor's, master's, doctoral, and first professional
- **Urban** 419-acre campus
- **Coed**, 24,668 undergraduate students, 95% full-time, 55% women, 45% men
- **Very difficult** entrance level, 29% of applicants were admitted
- **18:1 student-to-undergraduate faculty ratio**
- **78% graduate** in 6 years or less
- **$3698 tuition** and fees (in-state); $13,872 (out-of-state)
- **$8596 average financial aid** package, $1.3 billion endowment

Part of University of California System.

Students *Undergraduates:* 23,483 full-time, 1,185 part-time. Students come from 50 states and territories, 100 other countries. *The most frequently chosen baccalaureate fields are:* psychology, biological/life sciences, social sciences and history. *Graduate:* 1,833 in professional programs, 9,849 in other graduate degree programs.

From out-of-state	3%	Reside on campus	31%
Age 25 or older	8%	Transferred in	9%
International students	3%	African Americans	5%
Asian Americans/Pacific Islanders	37%	Hispanic Americans	15%
Native Americans	1%		

Faculty 3,435.

Expenses (1999–2000) *Tuition, state resident:* full-time $0. *Tuition, nonresident:* full-time $10,174. *Required fees:* full-time $3698. *College room and board:* $7692. Room and board charges vary according to board plan and housing facility.

California

Library University Research Library plus 13 others. *Collection:* 5.9 million titles, 94,748 serial subscriptions, 4.6 million audiovisual materials.
College life *Housing: Options:* coed, cooperative. *Social organizations:* national fraternities, national sororities, local fraternities, local sororities; 11% of eligible men and 9% of eligible women are members. *Most popular organizations:* Student Alumni Association, student government, Rally Committee.
Campus security 24-hour emergency response devices, student patrols, late-night transport-escort service.
After graduation 1,400 organizations recruited on campus 1997–98. *Career center:* 41 full-time, 16 part-time personnel. Services include job fairs, resume preparation, interview workshops, resume referral, career/interest testing, career counseling, careers library, job bank, job interviews. *Graduate education:* 33% of class of 1999 went directly to graduate and professional school. *Major awards:* 15 Fulbright Scholars.
Freshmen 35,681 applied, 10,299 admitted, 3,751 enrolled. 73 National Merit Scholars.

SAT verbal scores above 500	92%	SAT math scores above 500	95%
ACT above 18	98%	1998 freshmen returning in 1999	97%

Application *Option:* electronic application. *Preference* given to California residents. *Application fee:* $40. *Required:* essay or personal statement; high school transcript. *Recommended:* minimum 3.5 GPA.
Standardized tests *Admission: Required:* SAT I or ACT, SAT II: Writing Test, SAT II Subject Test in math, third SAT II Subject Test.
Significant dates *Application deadlines:* 11/30 (freshmen), 11/30 (transfers). *Financial aid deadline priority date:* 3/2.
Freshman Application Contact
Dr. Rae Lee Siporin, Director of Undergraduate Admissions, University of California, Los Angeles, 405 Hilgard Avenue, Los Angeles, CA 90095. **Phone:** 310-825-3101. **E-mail:** ugadm@saonet.ucla.edu
Visit CollegeQuest.com for information on majors offered and athletics. Electronic viewbook available at CollegeQuest.com.

UNIVERSITY OF CALIFORNIA, RIVERSIDE
Riverside, California

- **State-supported**, university, founded 1954
- **Degrees** bachelor's, master's, and doctoral
- **Urban** 1,200-acre campus with easy access to Los Angeles
- **Coed**, 10,120 undergraduate students, 96% full-time, 54% women, 46% men
- **Very difficult** entrance level, 84% of applicants were admitted
- **19:1 student-to-undergraduate faculty ratio**
- **68% graduate** in 6 years or less
- **$4126 tuition** and fees (in-state); $13,930 (out-of-state)
- **$8997 average financial aid** package, $34.7 million endowment

University of California, Riverside, combines the comprehensive excellence of the nation's finest public university with the individual attention of a small campus. Small class sizes and faculty interaction contribute to favorable graduation rates. The vast majority of incoming freshmen graduate in 4 years or fewer. Extensive support services and activities ensure students' academic success and personal enjoyment. Ample housing and financial aid are available.

Part of University of California System.
Students *Undergraduates:* 9,712 full-time, 408 part-time. Students come from 49 states and territories, 45 other countries. *The most frequently chosen baccalaureate fields are:* business/marketing, biological/life sciences, social sciences and history. *Graduate:* 50 in professional programs, 1,430 in other graduate degree programs.

From out-of-state	1%	Reside on campus	30%
Age 25 or older	8%	Transferred in	7%
International students	2%	African Americans	5%
Asian Americans/Pacific Islanders	41%	Hispanic Americans	21%
Native Americans	0.5%		

Faculty 637 (72% full-time), 98% with terminal degrees.
Expenses (1999–2000) *Tuition, state resident:* full-time $0. *Tuition, nonresident:* full-time $9804. *Required fees:* full-time $4126. *College room and board:* $6579. Room and board charges vary according to board plan and housing facility. *Payment plans:* installment, deferred payment.
Library Tomas Rivera Library plus 6 others. *Operations spending 1999–2000:* $11.1 million. *Collection:* 1.9 million titles, 12,800 serial subscriptions, 18,233 audiovisual materials.
College life *Housing: Option:* coed. *Social organizations:* national fraternities, national sororities, local fraternities, local sororities, coed fraternities; 5% of eligible men and 7% of eligible women are members. *Most popular organizations:* Associated Students, UCR Ambassadors, Community Service/Human Corps Program, BEAR FACTS Student Orientation.
Campus security 24-hour emergency response devices and patrols, student patrols, late-night transport-escort service, controlled dormitory access.
After graduation 165 organizations recruited on campus 1997–98. 54% of class of 1998 had job offers within 6 months. *Career center:* 16 full-time, 2 part-time personnel. Services include job fairs, resume preparation, interview workshops, resume referral, career/interest testing, career counseling, careers library, job bank, job interviews. *Graduate education:* 41% of class of 1999 went directly to graduate and professional school. *Major awards:* 1 Fulbright Scholar.
Freshmen 16,316 applied, 13,766 admitted, 2,721 enrolled.

Average high school GPA	3.54	SAT verbal scores above 500	54%
SAT math scores above 500	70%	ACT above 18	77%
From top 10% of their h.s. class	94%	1998 freshmen returning in 1999	86%

Application *Options:* electronic application, early admission. *Application fee:* $40. *Required:* essay or personal statement; high school transcript; minimum 2.82 GPA.
Standardized tests *Admission: Required:* SAT I or ACT, SAT II: Writing Test.
Significant dates *Application deadlines:* 11/30 (freshmen), rolling (transfers). *Financial aid deadline priority date:* 3/2.
Freshman Application Contact
Ms. Laurie Nelson, Director of Undergraduate Admission, University of California, Riverside, 1138 Hinderaker Hall, Riverside, CA 92521-0102. **Phone:** 909-787-3411. **Fax:** 909-787-6344. **E-mail:** discover@pop.ucr.edu
Visit CollegeQuest.com for information on majors offered and athletics. College video and electronic viewbook available at CollegeQuest.com.

■ *See page 2702 for a narrative description.*

UNIVERSITY OF CALIFORNIA, SAN DIEGO
La Jolla, California

- **State-supported**, university, founded 1959
- **Degrees** bachelor's, master's, doctoral, and first professional
- **Suburban** 1,976-acre campus with easy access to San Diego
- **Coed**, 16,230 undergraduate students
- **Very difficult** entrance level, 41% of applicants were admitted
- **$3849 tuition** and fees (in-state); $14,023 (out-of-state)
- **$9205 average financial aid** package, $11,000 average indebtedness upon graduation, $1.2 billion endowment

Part of University of California System.
Students *Undergraduates:* Students come from 70 other countries.

From out-of-state	2%	Reside on campus	34%
Age 25 or older	8%	African Americans	2%
Asian Americans/Pacific Islanders	35%	Hispanic Americans	10%
Native Americans	1%		

Faculty 1,465.
Expenses (1999–2000) *Tuition, state resident:* full-time $0. *Tuition, nonresident:* full-time $10,174. *Required fees:* full-time $3849. *College room and board:* $7134. Room and board charges vary according to board plan. *Payment plan:* deferred payment.
Library Geisel Library plus 6 others. *Operations spending 1999–2000:* $20.5 million. *Collection:* 2.5 million titles, 23,421 serial subscriptions, 78,130 audiovisual materials.
College life *Housing: Options:* coed, disabled students. *Social organizations:* national fraternities, national sororities; 10% of eligible men and 10% of eligible women are members. *Most popular organizations:* Radically Inclined Snow Ski Club, Interfraternity Council, MECHA (Movimiento Estudiantil Chicano de Aztlan).

California

University of California, San Diego (continued)

Campus security 24-hour emergency response devices, late-night transport-escort service, crime prevention programs.

After graduation 4,249 organizations recruited on campus 1997–98. 85% of class of 1998 had job offers within 6 months. *Career center:* 22 full-time, 2 part-time personnel. Services include job fairs, resume preparation, resume referral, career counseling, careers library, job bank, job interviews. *Graduate education:* 35% of class of 1999 went directly to graduate and professional school. *Major awards:* 5 Fulbright Scholars.

Freshmen 32,539 applied, 13,249 admitted.

Average high school GPA	3.98	SAT verbal scores above 500	N/R
SAT math scores above 500	N/R	ACT above 18	N/R
From top 10% of their h.s. class	95%	1998 freshmen returning in 1999	93%

Application *Preference* given to state residents. *Application fee:* $40. *Required:* essay or personal statement; high school transcript; minimum 3.3 GPA. *Required for some:* minimum 3.4 GPA.

Standardized tests *Admission: Required:* SAT I or ACT, 3 SAT II Subject Tests (including SAT II: Writing Test).

Significant dates *Application deadlines:* 11/30 (freshmen), 11/30 (transfers). *Notification:* 3/15 (freshmen). *Financial aid deadline priority date:* 3/2.

Freshman Application Contact
Mr. Tim Johnston, Associate Director of Admissions and Outreach, University of California, San Diego, 9500 Gilman Drive, 0337, La Jolla, CA 92093-0337.
Phone: 858-534-4831. **E-mail:** admissionsinfo@ucsd.edu

Visit CollegeQuest.com for information on majors offered and athletics.

UNIVERSITY OF CALIFORNIA, SANTA BARBARA

Santa Barbara, California

- **State-supported**, university, founded 1909
- **Degrees** bachelor's, master's, and doctoral
- **Suburban** 989-acre campus
- **Coed**, 17,685 undergraduate students, 97% full-time, 54% women, 46% men
- **Very difficult** entrance level, 53% of applicants were admitted
- **70% graduate** in 6 years or less
- **$3844 tuition** and fees (in-state); $14,018 (out-of-state)

Part of University of California System.

Students *Undergraduates:* 17,075 full-time, 610 part-time. Students come from 48 states and territories, 35 other countries. *The most frequently chosen baccalaureate fields are:* business/marketing, biological/life sciences, social sciences and history. *Graduate:* 2,357 in graduate degree programs.

From out-of-state	4%	Reside on campus	23%
Age 25 or older	5%	Transferred in	7%
International students	1%	African Americans	2%
Asian Americans/Pacific Islanders	15%	Hispanic Americans	14%
Native Americans	1%		

Expenses (1999–2000) *Tuition, state resident:* full-time $0. *Tuition, nonresident:* full-time $10,174. *Required fees:* full-time $3844. *College room and board:* $7156. Room and board charges vary according to housing facility. *Waivers:* employees or children of employees.

Library Davidson Library. *Collection:* 2.4 million titles, 18,100 serial subscriptions, 90,900 audiovisual materials.

College life *Housing: Options:* coed, cooperative. *Social organizations:* national fraternities, national sororities, local fraternities, local sororities; 8% of eligible men and 10% of eligible women are members.

Campus security 24-hour emergency response devices, late-night transport-escort service.

After graduation 56% of class of 1998 had job offers within 6 months. *Career center:* 38 full-time, 2 part-time personnel. Services include job fairs, resume preparation, interview workshops, resume referral, career/interest testing, career counseling, careers library, job bank, job interviews. *Graduate education:* 24% of class of 1999 went directly to graduate and professional school. *Major awards:* 6 Fulbright Scholars.

Freshmen 26,931 applied, 14,375 admitted, 3,781 enrolled.

Average high school GPA	3.69	SAT verbal scores above 500	84%
SAT math scores above 500	89%	ACT above 18	N/R
1998 freshmen returning in 1999	89%		

Application *Options:* electronic application, early admission. *Application fee:* $40. *Required:* essay or personal statement; high school transcript. *Required for some:* interview.

Standardized tests *Admission: Required:* SAT I or ACT, SAT II Subject Tests.

Significant dates *Application deadlines:* 11/30 (freshmen), 11/30 (transfers). *Notification:* 3/15 (freshmen). *Financial aid deadline:* 5/31. *Priority date:* 3/2.

Freshman Application Contact
Mr. William Villa, Director of Admissions/Relations with Schools, University of California, Santa Barbara, Santa Barbara, CA 93106. **Phone:** 805-893-2485. **E-mail:** appinfo@sa.ucsb.edu

Visit CollegeQuest.com for information on majors offered and athletics. College video available at CollegeQuest.com.

UNIVERSITY OF CALIFORNIA, SANTA CRUZ

Santa Cruz, California

- **State-supported**, university, founded 1965
- **Degrees** bachelor's, master's, and doctoral
- **Small-town** 2,000-acre campus with easy access to San Francisco and San Jose
- **Coed**, 10,228 undergraduate students, 94% full-time, 57% women, 43% men
- **Very difficult** entrance level, 79% of applicants were admitted
- **61.9% graduate** in 6 years or less
- **$4377 tuition** and fees (in-state); $14,699 (out-of-state)
- **$9749 average financial aid** package, $57.8 million endowment

Part of University of California System.

Students *Undergraduates:* 9,659 full-time, 569 part-time. Students come from 48 states and territories, 62 other countries. *Graduate:* 1,033 in graduate degree programs.

Reside on campus	50%	Age 25 or older	10%
Transferred in	8%	International students	1%
African Americans	2%	Asian Americans/Pacific Islanders	14%
Hispanic Americans	13%	Native Americans	1%

Expenses (1999–2000) *Tuition, state resident:* full-time $0. *Tuition, nonresident:* full-time $10,322. *Required fees:* full-time $4377. *College room and board:* $7337. Room and board charges vary according to board plan and housing facility. *Payment plans:* installment, deferred payment. *Waivers:* senior citizens.

Library McHenry Library plus 9 others. *Operations spending 1999–2000:* $9.2 million. *Collection:* 1.2 million titles, 10,004 serial subscriptions, 500,000 audiovisual materials.

College life *Housing: Options:* coed, men-only, women-only. *Social organizations:* national fraternities, national sororities, local fraternities, local sororities; 1% of eligible men and 1% of eligible women are members. *Most popular organizations:* Asian Pacific Islander Student Alliance, African/Black Student Alliance, Movimiento Estudiantil Chicano de Aztlan, Students Alliance of North American Indians, Estudiantes Para Salud del Pueblo.

Campus security 24-hour emergency response devices and patrols, late-night transport-escort service, controlled dormitory access, evening main gate security.

After graduation 237 organizations recruited on campus 1997–98. *Career center:* 9 full-time, 2 part-time personnel. Services include job fairs, resume preparation, interview workshops, resume referral, career/interest testing, career counseling, careers library, job bank, job interviews. *Major awards:* 5 Fulbright Scholars.

Freshmen 13,931 applied, 11,027 admitted, 2,365 enrolled.

Average high school GPA	3.53	SAT verbal scores above 500	81%
SAT math scores above 500	84%	ACT above 18	91%
From top 10% of their h.s. class	96%	1998 freshmen returning in 1999	80%

Application *Option:* electronic application. *Preference* given to qualified state residents. *Application fee:* $40. *Required:* essay or personal statement; high school transcript.

Standardized tests *Admission: Required:* SAT I or ACT, SAT II: Writing Test.
Significant dates *Application deadlines:* 11/30 (freshmen), 11/30 (transfers). *Notification:* 3/1 (freshmen). *Financial aid deadline priority date:* 3/2.
Freshman Application Contact
Mr. J. Michael Thompson, Associate Vice Chancellor, Outreach, Admissions, and Student Academic Services, University of California, Santa Cruz, Admissions Office, Cook House, Santa Cruz, CA 95064. **Phone:** 831-459-4008. **Fax:** 831-459-4452. **E-mail:** admissions@cats.ucsc.edu
Visit CollegeQuest.com for information on majors offered and athletics. College video available at CollegeQuest.com.

UNIVERSITY OF JUDAISM
Bel Air, California

- **Independent Jewish**, comprehensive, founded 1947
- **Degrees** bachelor's and master's
- **Suburban** 28-acre campus with easy access to Los Angeles
- **Coed**, 102 undergraduate students
- **Moderately difficult** entrance level, 91% of applicants were admitted
- **6:1 student-to-undergraduate faculty ratio**
- **61% graduate** in 6 years or less
- **$18,250 average financial aid** package, $12,448 average indebtedness upon graduation, $18.6 million endowment

Students *Undergraduates:* Students come from 23 states and territories, 2 other countries. *The most frequently chosen baccalaureate fields are:* area/ethnic studies, biological/life sciences, English.

From out-of-state	40%	Reside on campus	60%
Age 25 or older	13%	International students	2%
African Americans	2%	Hispanic Americans	3%
Native Americans	1%		

Faculty 91 (21% full-time), 42% with terminal degrees.
Library Ostrow Library. *Operations spending 1999–2000:* $284,000. *Collection:* 105,000 titles, 400 serial subscriptions.
College life *Housing:* on-campus residence required through junior year. *Option:* coed. *Most popular organizations:* ASUJC, Graduate Student Association, Resident Life Council, College Urban Fellows, UJ Chorale.
Campus security 24-hour emergency response devices and patrols, controlled dormitory access.
After graduation *Career center:* 1 part-time personnel. Services include resume preparation, career counseling. *Graduate education:* 85% of class of 1999 went directly to graduate and professional school: 50% graduate arts and sciences, 10% business, 10% education, 10% law, 5% medicine.
Freshmen 58 applied, 53 admitted.

Average high school GPA	3.4	SAT verbal scores above 500	63%
SAT math scores above 500	69%	ACT above 18	100%
From top 10% of their h.s. class	22%	From top quarter	28%
From top half	50%	1998 freshmen returning in 1999	58%

Application *Options:* early decision, deferred entrance. *Application fee:* $35. *Required:* essay or personal statement; high school transcript; 2 letters of recommendation. *Required for some:* interview. *Recommended:* minimum 3.2 GPA; interview.
Standardized tests *Admission: Required:* SAT I or ACT.
Significant dates *Application deadlines:* 1/31 (freshmen), 4/15 (transfers). *Early decision:* 11/15. *Notification:* 12/15 (early decision). *Financial aid deadline priority date:* 3/2.
Freshman Application Contact
Mr. Richard Scaffidi, Dean of Admissions, University of Judaism, 15600 Mulholland Drive, Bel Air, CA 90077. **Phone:** 310-476-9777 Ext. 250. **Toll-free phone:** 888-853-6763. **Fax:** 310-471-3657. **E-mail:** admissions@uj.edu
Visit CollegeQuest.com for information on majors offered and athletics.

■ *See page 2740 for a narrative description.*

UNIVERSITY OF LA VERNE
La Verne, California

- **Independent**, university, founded 1891
- **Degrees** associate, bachelor's, master's, doctoral, first professional, and post-master's certificates (also offers continuing education program with significant enrollment not reflected in profile)
- **Suburban** 26-acre campus with easy access to Los Angeles
- **Coed**, 1,292 undergraduate students, 96% full-time, 59% women, 41% men
- **Moderately difficult** entrance level, 75% of applicants were admitted
- **50% graduate** in 6 years or less
- **$16,860 tuition** and fees
- **$14,792 average financial aid** package, $30.5 million endowment

Students at the University of La Verne, a small liberal arts college that takes pride in offering personalized education, are encouraged to apply the theoretical concepts taught in the classroom to real-world settings, often through internships. The core curriculum emphasizes a multicultural world view, which is evident in the diversity of the campus community. The University also has a special history of serving students who are the first in their families to attend college; a large portion of this group come from the Latino/Hispanic community.

Students *Undergraduates:* 1,246 full-time, 46 part-time. Students come from 14 states and territories, 16 other countries. *The most frequently chosen baccalaureate fields are:* business/marketing, education, social sciences and history. *Graduate:* 180 in professional programs, 1,475 in other graduate degree programs.

From out-of-state	6%	Reside on campus	30%
Age 25 or older	6%	Transferred in	10%
International students	2%	African Americans	10%
Asian Americans/Pacific Islanders	7%	Hispanic Americans	34%
Native Americans	1%		

Faculty 120 full-time.
Expenses (2000–2001) *One-time required fee:* $110. *Tuition:* full-time $16,800; part-time $525 per unit. *Required fees:* full-time $60; $30 per term part-time. Full-time tuition and fees vary according to course load, degree level, location, and program. Part-time tuition and fees vary according to course load, degree level, location, and program. Room and board charges vary according to board plan, housing facility, and location. *Payment plans:* installment, deferred payment. *Waivers:* adult students and employees or children of employees.
Library Wilson Library plus 1 other. *Operations spending 1999–2000:* $1 million. *Collection:* 200,000 titles, 2,000 serial subscriptions.
College life *Housing: Options:* coed, women-only. *Social organizations:* national fraternities, national sororities, local sororities; 9% of eligible men and 13% of eligible women are members. *Most popular organizations:* Latino Student Forum (LSF), Interfraternity/Sorority Council, African-American Student Association (AASA), ASF (Associated Students Federation), Alpha Kappa Psi.
Campus security 24-hour emergency response devices and patrols, late-night transport-escort service, controlled dormitory access, whistle program.
After graduation 51 organizations recruited on campus 1997–98. *Career center:* 2 full-time, 1 part-time personnel. Services include job fairs, resume preparation, interview workshops, career/interest testing, career counseling, careers library, job bank, job interviews.
Freshmen 1,269 applied, 957 admitted, 321 enrolled.

Average high school GPA	3.3	SAT verbal scores above 500	39%
SAT math scores above 500	42%	ACT above 18	87%
1998 freshmen returning in 1999	81%		

Application *Options:* Common Application, electronic application, deferred entrance. *Application fee:* $35. *Required:* essay or personal statement; high school transcript; minimum 2.6 GPA; 2 letters of recommendation. *Recommended:* minimum 3.3 GPA; interview.
Standardized tests *Admission: Required:* SAT I or ACT.
Significant dates *Application deadlines:* rolling (freshmen), rolling (transfers). *Financial aid deadline:* continuous.
Freshman Application Contact
Ms. Lisa Meyer, Director of Admissions, University of La Verne, 1950 Third Street, La Verne, CA 91750. **Phone:** 909-593-3511 Ext. 4032. **Toll-free phone:** 800-876-4858. **Fax:** 909-593-0965. **E-mail:** admissions@ulv.edu
Visit CollegeQuest.com for information on majors offered and athletics. College video available at CollegeQuest.com.

■ *See page 2742 for a narrative description.*

California

UNIVERSITY OF REDLANDS
Redlands, California

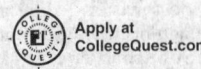
Apply at CollegeQuest.com

- **Independent**, comprehensive, founded 1907
- **Degrees** bachelor's, master's, post-master's, and postbachelor's certificates
- **Small-town** 140-acre campus with easy access to Los Angeles
- **Coed**, 1,653 undergraduate students, 99% full-time, 55% women, 45% men
- **Moderately difficult** entrance level, 80% of applicants were admitted
- **13:1** student-to-undergraduate faculty ratio
- **62.7% graduate** in 6 years or less
- **$19,811 tuition** and fees
- **$18,959 average financial aid** package, $22,072 average indebtedness upon graduation, $78.7 million endowment

Students *Undergraduates:* 1,631 full-time, 22 part-time. Students come from 43 states and territories, 29 other countries. *The most frequently chosen baccalaureate fields are:* business/marketing, interdisciplinary studies, social sciences and history. *Graduate:* 67 in graduate degree programs.

From out-of-state	31%	Reside on campus	73%
Age 25 or older	3%	Transferred in	7%
International students	3%	African Americans	3%
Asian Americans/Pacific Islanders	7%	Hispanic Americans	12%
Native Americans	1%		

Faculty 186 (64% full-time), 61% with terminal degrees.

Expenses (1999–2000) *One-time required fee:* $140. *Comprehensive fee:* $27,179 includes full-time tuition ($19,490), mandatory fees ($321), and room and board ($7368). Room and board charges vary according to board plan and housing facility. *Part-time tuition:* $609 per credit. *Part-time fees:* $40 per term part-time. Part-time tuition and fees vary according to course load. *Payment plan:* installment. *Waivers:* employees or children of employees.

Library Armacost Library. *Operations spending 1999–2000:* $1.3 million. *Collection:* 264,385 titles, 8,435 audiovisual materials.

College life *Housing:* on-campus residence required through junior year. *Options:* coed, men-only, women-only. *Social organizations:* local fraternities, local sororities; 18% of eligible men and 20% of eligible women are members. *Most popular organizations:* Associated Students of the University of Redlands, Greek system, service organizations, cultural organizations, social awareness groups.

Campus security 24-hour emergency response devices and patrols, student patrols, late-night transport-escort service, controlled dormitory access, safety whistles.

After graduation 25 organizations recruited on campus 1997–98. 40% of class of 1998 had job offers within 6 months. *Career center:* 3 full-time personnel. Services include job fairs, resume preparation, interview workshops, resume referral, career/interest testing, career counseling, careers library, job bank, job interviews. *Graduate education:* 30% of class of 1999 went directly to graduate and professional school: 3% business, 2% education, 1% law.

Freshmen 1,975 applied, 1,581 admitted, 474 enrolled. 5 National Merit Scholars.

Average high school GPA	3.46	SAT verbal scores above 500	76%
SAT math scores above 500	79%	ACT above 18	96%
1998 freshmen returning in 1999	79%		

Application *Options:* eApply at www.CollegeQuest.com, Common Application, electronic application, early admission, deferred entrance. *Application fee:* $40. *Required:* essay or personal statement; high school transcript; 2 letters of recommendation. *Recommended:* interview.

Standardized tests *Admission: Required:* SAT I or ACT.

Significant dates *Application deadlines:* 2/1 (freshmen), rolling (transfers). *Financial aid deadline priority date:* 2/15.

Freshman Application Contact
Mr. Paul Driscoll, Dean of Admissions, University of Redlands, PO Box 3080, Redlands, CA 92373-0999. **Phone:** 909-335-4074. **Toll-free phone:** 800-455-5064. **Fax:** 909-335-4089. **E-mail:** admissions@uor.edu

Visit CollegeQuest.com for information on majors offered and athletics. College video available at CollegeQuest.com.

■ *See page 2810 for a narrative description.*

UNIVERSITY OF SAN DIEGO
San Diego, California

- **Independent Roman Catholic**, university, founded 1949
- **Degrees** bachelor's, master's, doctoral, and first professional
- **Urban** 180-acre campus
- **Coed**, 4,623 undergraduate students, 96% full-time, 58% women, 42% men
- **Moderately difficult** entrance level, 52% of applicants were admitted
- **18:1** student-to-undergraduate faculty ratio
- **$19,128 tuition** and fees
- **$14,958 average financial aid** package, $23,100 average indebtedness upon graduation, $96.7 million endowment

Students *Undergraduates:* 4,442 full-time, 181 part-time. Students come from 50 states and territories, 57 other countries. *Graduate:* 1,118 in professional programs, 1,117 in other graduate degree programs.

From out-of-state	43%	Reside on campus	48%
Age 25 or older	11%	Transferred in	8%
International students	4%	African Americans	2%
Asian Americans/Pacific Islanders	7%	Hispanic Americans	14%
Native Americans	1%		

Faculty 606 (49% full-time), 70% with terminal degrees.

Expenses (2000–2001) *Comprehensive fee:* $27,568 includes full-time tuition ($19,020), mandatory fees ($108), and room and board ($8440). *College room only:* $4400. Room and board charges vary according to board plan and housing facility. *Part-time tuition:* $660 per unit. *Part-time fees:* $19 per term part-time. Part-time tuition and fees vary according to course load. *Payment plan:* installment. *Waivers:* employees or children of employees.

Library Helen K. and James S. Copley Library plus 1 other. *Operations spending 1999–2000:* $5.1 million. *Collection:* 500,000 titles, 2,600 serial subscriptions, 14,000 audiovisual materials.

College life *Housing:* on-campus residence required in freshman year. *Options:* coed, men-only, women-only, disabled students. *Social organizations:* national fraternities, national sororities; 20% of eligible men and 20% of eligible women are members. *Most popular organizations:* Greek organizations, International Student Organization, Student Alumni Association.

Campus security 24-hour emergency response devices and patrols, student patrols, late-night transport-escort service, controlled dormitory access, escort service.

After graduation 105 organizations recruited on campus 1997–98. 96% of class of 1998 had job offers within 6 months. *Career center:* 4 full-time, 2 part-time personnel. Services include job fairs, resume preparation, interview workshops, resume referral, career/interest testing, career counseling, careers library, job bank, job interviews. *Graduate education:* 40% of class of 1999 went directly to graduate and professional school.

Freshmen 6,291 applied, 3,286 admitted, 992 enrolled. 31 valedictorians.

Average high school GPA	3.71	SAT verbal scores above 500	89%
SAT math scores above 500	93%	ACT above 18	100%
From top 10% of their h.s. class	50%	From top quarter	87%
From top half	99%	1998 freshmen returning in 1999	91%

Application *Options:* electronic application, early admission, early action, deferred entrance. *Application fee:* $55. *Required:* essay or personal statement; high school transcript; 1 letter of recommendation.

Standardized tests *Admission: Required:* SAT I or ACT. *Recommended:* SAT II: Writing Test.

Significant dates *Application deadlines:* 1/5 (freshmen), 3/1 (transfers). *Early action:* 12/1. *Notification:* 4/15 (freshmen), 1/31 (early action). *Financial aid deadline priority date:* 2/20.

Freshman Application Contact
Mr. Stephen Pultz, Director of Undergraduate Admissions, University of San Diego, 5998 Alcala Park, San Diego, CA 92110. **Phone:** 619-260-4506. **Toll-free phone:** 800-248-4873 Ext. 4506. **E-mail:** admissions@is.acusd.edu

Visit CollegeQuest.com for information on majors offered and athletics. Electronic viewbook available at CollegeQuest.com.

■ *See page 2824 for a narrative description.*

California

UNIVERSITY OF SAN FRANCISCO
San Francisco, California

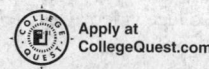
Apply at CollegeQuest.com

- **Independent Roman Catholic (Jesuit)**, university, founded 1855
- **Degrees** bachelor's, master's, doctoral, first professional, and post-master's certificates
- **Urban** 55-acre campus
- **Coed**, 4,447 undergraduate students, 96% full-time, 62% women, 38% men
- **Moderately difficult** entrance level, 80% of applicants were admitted
- **13:1 student-to-undergraduate faculty ratio**
- **65% graduate** in 6 years or less
- **$19,060 tuition** and fees
- **$15,159 average financial aid** package, $22,238 average indebtedness upon graduation, $145 million endowment

Students *Undergraduates:* 4,288 full-time, 159 part-time. Students come from 52 states and territories, 71 other countries. *The most frequently chosen baccalaureate fields are:* business/marketing, health professions and related sciences, interdisciplinary studies. *Graduate:* 614 in professional programs, 2,611 in other graduate degree programs.

From out-of-state	19%	Reside on campus	37%
Age 25 or older	9%	Transferred in	7%
International students	8%	African Americans	5%
Asian Americans/Pacific Islanders	22%	Hispanic Americans	10%
Native Americans	1%		

Faculty 716 (44% full-time).

Expenses (2000–2001) *Comprehensive fee:* $27,302 includes full-time tuition ($18,860), mandatory fees ($200), and room and board ($8242). *College room only:* $5112. Room and board charges vary according to board plan and housing facility. *Part-time tuition:* $689 per unit. *Part-time fees:* $200 per year part-time. *Payment plan:* installment. *Waivers:* employees or children of employees.

Library Gleeson Library plus 2 others. *Operations spending 1999–2000:* $3.3 million. *Collection:* 755,000 titles, 2,706 serial subscriptions, 1,730 audiovisual materials.

College life *Housing:* on-campus residence required through sophomore year. *Options:* coed, women-only. *Social organizations:* national fraternities, national sororities, local fraternities, local sororities; 12% of eligible men and 7% of eligible women are members. *Most popular organizations:* Student Leadership, Student Media, College Players.

Campus security 24-hour emergency response devices and patrols, late-night transport-escort service, controlled dormitory access.

After graduation 111 organizations recruited on campus 1997–98. *Career center:* 6 full-time personnel. Services include job fairs, resume preparation, resume referral, career counseling, careers library, job bank, job interviews. *Graduate education:* 42% of class of 1999 went directly to graduate and professional school: 16% graduate arts and sciences, 15% business, 6% medicine, 5% law.

Freshmen 3,504 applied, 2,805 admitted, 762 enrolled.

Average high school GPA	3.33	SAT verbal scores above 500	68%
SAT math scores above 500	68%	ACT above 18	93%
From top 10% of their h.s. class	21%	From top quarter	52%
From top half	82%	1998 freshmen returning in 1999	84%

Application *Options:* eApply at www.CollegeQuest.com, Common Application, electronic application, early action, deferred entrance. *Application fee:* $45. *Required:* essay or personal statement; high school transcript; minimum 2.8 GPA; 1 letter of recommendation. *Required for some:* interview. *Recommended:* minimum 3.0 GPA.

Standardized tests *Admission: Required:* SAT I or ACT.

Significant dates *Application deadlines:* 2/1 (freshmen), rolling (transfers). *Early action:* 12/1. *Notification:* continuous until 8/15 (freshmen), 1/15 (early action). *Financial aid deadline priority date:* 2/15.

Freshman Application Contact
Mr. William Henley, Director of Admissions, University of San Francisco, Office of Admissions, 2130 Fulton Street, San Francisco, CA 94117-1080. **Phone:** 415-422-6563. **Toll-free phone:** 800-CALL USF. **Fax:** 415-422-2217. **E-mail:** admissions@usfca.edu

Visit CollegeQuest.com for information on majors offered and athletics. College video and electronic viewbook available at CollegeQuest.com.

■ *See page 2826 for a narrative description.*

UNIVERSITY OF SOUTHERN CALIFORNIA
Los Angeles, California

- **Independent**, university, founded 1880
- **Degrees** bachelor's, master's, doctoral, first professional, and post-master's certificates
- **Urban** 155-acre campus
- **Coed**, 15,218 undergraduate students, 95% full-time, 49% women, 51% men
- **Very difficult** entrance level, 36% of applicants were admitted
- **13:1 student-to-undergraduate faculty ratio**
- **70.33% graduate** in 6 years or less
- **$22,636 tuition** and fees

Hailed for linking a powerful educational community with a diverse city and neighborhood, USC is the largest private university in the west. USC students benefit from a creative research and teaching menu, freely choosing majors and minors from demanding traditional liberal arts and science programs and 17 respected professional schools. Living in Southern California gives students a comprehensive academic, civilizing, and hands-on experience.

Students *Undergraduates:* 14,447 full-time, 771 part-time. Students come from 52 states and territories. *Graduate:* 2,661 in professional programs, 10,525 in other graduate degree programs.

From out-of-state	31%	Age 25 or older	9%
Transferred in	9%	International students	8%
African Americans	6%	Asian Americans/Pacific Islanders	23%
Hispanic Americans	14%	Native Americans	1%

Expenses (1999–2000) *Comprehensive fee:* $29,918 includes full-time tuition ($22,198), mandatory fees ($438), and room and board ($7282). Room and board charges vary according to board plan and housing facility. *Part-time tuition:* $748 per unit. *Part-time fees:* $219 per term part-time. Part-time tuition and fees vary according to course load. *Payment plans:* tuition prepayment, installment. *Waivers:* employees or children of employees.

Library Doheny Memorial Library plus 17 others. *Operations spending 1999–2000:* $33.1 million. *Collection:* 3.3 million titles, 27,000 serial subscriptions.

College life *Housing: Options:* coed, cooperative, disabled students. *Social organizations:* national fraternities, national sororities, local fraternities, local sororities; 20% of eligible men and 20% of eligible women are members. *Most popular organizations:* joint educational project, International Student Assembly, University Residential Student Community, Troy Camp, Latino Business Student Association.

Campus security 24-hour emergency response devices and patrols, student patrols, late-night transport-escort service, controlled dormitory access.

After graduation 500 organizations recruited on campus 1997–98. 85% of class of 1998 had job offers within 6 months. *Career center:* 9 full-time, 20 part-time personnel. Services include job fairs, resume preparation, resume referral, career/interest testing, career counseling, careers library, job bank, job interviews. *Major awards:* 1 Marshall, 2 Fulbright Scholars.

Freshmen 24,626 applied, 8,904 admitted, 2,980 enrolled. 127 National Merit Scholars.

Average high school GPA	3.8	SAT verbal scores above 500	97%
SAT math scores above 500	98%	ACT above 18	100%
1998 freshmen returning in 1999	96%		

Application *Options:* electronic application, early admission, deferred entrance. *Application fee:* $55. *Required:* essay or personal statement; high school transcript. *Required for some:* letters of recommendation. *Recommended:* letters of recommendation; interview.

Standardized tests *Admission: Required:* SAT I or ACT. *Recommended:* SAT II Subject Tests.

Significant dates *Application deadlines:* 1/10 (freshmen), 3/1 (transfers). *Notification:* 4/1 (freshmen).

Freshman Application Contact
Mr. Joseph Allen, Vice Provost for Enrollment, University of Southern California, University Park Campus, Los Angeles, CA 90089. **Phone:** 213-740-1111. **Fax:** 213-740-6364.

Visit CollegeQuest.com for information on majors offered and athletics. College video available at CollegeQuest.com.

■ *See page 2832 for a narrative description.*

California

UNIVERSITY OF THE PACIFIC
Stockton, California

Apply at CollegeQuest.com

- **Independent**, university, founded 1851
- **Degrees** bachelor's, master's, doctoral, and first professional
- **Suburban** 175-acre campus with easy access to Sacramento
- **Coed**, 2,937 undergraduate students, 97% full-time, 58% women, 42% men
- **Moderately difficult** entrance level, 82% of applicants were admitted
- **14:1 student-to-undergraduate faculty ratio**
- **63.1% graduate** in 6 years or less
- **$20,725 tuition** and fees
- **$95.1 million endowment**

Comprehensive is the best word to describe the University of the Pacific. The integration of liberal arts and sciences with professional study provides undergraduate students with a wealth of academic opportunities in a personally supportive community. Located halfway between the San Francisco Bay and the Sierra Nevada mountains, Pacific offers its students a wide variety of educational, cultural, recreational, and social opportunities.

Students *Undergraduates:* 2,848 full-time, 89 part-time. Students come from 45 states and territories, 50 other countries. *The most frequently chosen baccalaureate fields are:* biological/life sciences, business/marketing, social sciences and history. *Graduate:* 2,109 in professional programs, 587 in other graduate degree programs.

Reside on campus	58%	Age 25 or older	5%
Transferred in	15%	International students	5%
African Americans	3%	Asian Americans/Pacific Islanders	25%
Hispanic Americans	10%	Native Americans	1%

Faculty 599 (62% full-time).
Expenses (2000–2001) *One-time required fee:* $100. *Comprehensive fee:* $27,103 includes full-time tuition ($20,350), mandatory fees ($375), and room and board ($6378). Room and board charges vary according to board plan and housing facility. *Payment plan:* deferred payment. *Waivers:* employees or children of employees.
Library Holt Memorial Library plus 1 other. *Operations spending 1999–2000:* $5 million. *Collection:* 689,733 titles, 2,674 serial subscriptions.
College life *Housing:* on-campus residence required through sophomore year. *Option:* coed. *Social organizations:* national fraternities, national sororities, local fraternities; 18% of eligible men and 22% of eligible women are members. *Most popular organizations:* social sororities and fraternities, student government, cultural organizations, marketing club, Model United Nations.
Campus security 24-hour emergency response devices and patrols, late-night transport-escort service, controlled dormitory access.
After graduation 80 organizations recruited on campus 1997–98. *Career center:* 4 full-time, 1 part-time personnel. Services include job fairs, resume preparation, interview workshops, resume referral, career/interest testing, career counseling, careers library, job bank, job interviews. *Graduate education:* 30% of class of 1999 went directly to graduate and professional school.
Freshmen 2,831 applied, 2,312 admitted, 746 enrolled. 1 Westinghouse recipient.

Average high school GPA	3.42	SAT verbal scores above 500	69%
SAT math scores above 500	77%	ACT above 18	92%
From top 10% of their h.s. class	37%	From top quarter	75%
From top half	90%	1998 freshmen returning in 1999	87%

Application *Options:* eApply at www.CollegeQuest.com, Common Application, electronic application, early admission, early action, deferred entrance. *Application fee:* $50. *Required:* essay or personal statement; high school transcript; minimum 2.5 GPA; 1 letter of recommendation. *Required for some:* audition for music program. *Recommended:* minimum 3.0 GPA; interview.
Standardized tests *Admission: Required:* SAT I or ACT.
Significant dates *Application deadlines:* 2/15 (freshmen), 2/15 (transfers). *Early action:* 12/15. *Notification:* 1/15 (early action).
Freshman Application Contact
Ms. Janet Dial, Associate Dean of Admissions, University of the Pacific, 3601 Pacific Avenue, Stockton, CA 95211-0197. **Phone:** 209-946-2211. **Toll-free phone:** 800-959-2867. **Fax:** 209-946-2413. **E-mail:** admissions@uop.edu

Visit CollegeQuest.com for information on majors offered and athletics. College video available at CollegeQuest.com.

■ *See page 2848 for a narrative description.*

UNIVERSITY OF WEST LOS ANGELES
Inglewood, California

- **Independent**, upper-level, founded 1966
- **Degrees** bachelor's and first professional
- **Suburban** 2-acre campus with easy access to Los Angeles
- **Coed**, 84 undergraduate students, 25% full-time, 71% women, 29% men
- **Minimally difficult** entrance level
- **$6030 tuition** and fees
- **$457,745 endowment**

Students *Undergraduates:* 21 full-time, 63 part-time. *The most frequently chosen baccalaureate field is:* (pre)law. *Graduate:* 295 in professional programs.
Age 25 or older 90% Transferred in 60%
Faculty 29 (3% full-time), 100% with terminal degrees.
Expenses (1999–2000) *Tuition:* full-time $5670; part-time $210 per unit. *Required fees:* full-time $360; $120 per term part-time. *Payment plan:* installment. *Waivers:* employees or children of employees.
Library Kelton Library. *Operations spending 1999–2000:* $376,007. *Collection:* 33,000 titles, 250 serial subscriptions.
College life *Housing:* college housing not available. *Most popular organizations:* Black Law Students Association, American Trial Lawyers Association, Asian Pacific American Law Students Association, Toastmasters.
Campus security Late-night transport-escort service.
After graduation *Career center:* 1 full-time personnel. Services include resume preparation, resume referral, career counseling, careers library, job bank. *Graduate education:* 10% of class of 1999 went directly to graduate and professional school: 8% law.
Application *Option:* deferred entrance. *Application fee:* $45.
Significant dates *Application deadline:* rolling (transfers).
Freshman Application Contact
Ms. Yvonne Alwag, Admissions Counselor, University of West Los Angeles, School of Paralegal Studies, 1155 West Arbor Vitae Street, Inglewood, CA 90301-2902. **Phone:** 310-342-5287. **Fax:** 310-313-2124. **E-mail:** paralegaladmissions@uwla.edu
Visit CollegeQuest.com for information on majors offered and athletics.

■ *See page 2860 for a narrative description.*

VANGUARD UNIVERSITY OF SOUTHERN CALIFORNIA
Costa Mesa, California

- **Independent**, comprehensive, founded 1920, affiliated with Assemblies of God
- **Degrees** bachelor's and master's
- **Suburban** 38-acre campus with easy access to Los Angeles
- **Coed**, 1,282 undergraduate students, 80% full-time, 62% women, 38% men
- **Moderately difficult** entrance level, 90% of applicants were admitted
- **16:1 student-to-undergraduate faculty ratio**
- **$13,778 tuition** and fees
- **$4.5 million endowment**

Vanguard University offers a number of majors that prepare students to work in cross-cultural applications: international business (with an anthropology minor), Spanish, cultural anthropology, sociology, and religion, with a concentration in intercultural and urban studies. In addition, the southern California region provides a wealth of intercultural experiences.

Students *Undergraduates:* 1,025 full-time, 257 part-time. Students come from 39 states and territories. *The most frequently chosen baccalaureate fields are:* business/marketing, liberal arts/general studies, philosophy. *Graduate:*

California

151 in graduate degree programs.

From out-of-state	24%	Reside on campus	65%
Age 25 or older	23%	Transferred in	9%
International students	1%	African Americans	5%
Asian Americans/Pacific Islanders	4%	Hispanic Americans	10%
Native Americans	0.4%		

Faculty 140 (41% full-time), 49% with terminal degrees.

Expenses (2000–2001, estimated) *Comprehensive fee:* $18,838 includes full-time tuition ($13,230), mandatory fees ($548), and room and board ($5060). *College room only:* $2820. Room and board charges vary according to board plan and housing facility. *Part-time tuition:* $514 per unit. *Payment plan:* installment. *Waivers:* employees or children of employees.

Library O. Cope Budge Library. *Collection:* 121,000 titles, 825 serial subscriptions.

College life *Housing:* on-campus residence required through senior year. *Options:* men-only, women-only. *Most popular organization:* student ministries.

Campus security 24-hour emergency response devices and patrols, late-night transport-escort service.

After graduation *Career center:* Services include job fairs, resume preparation, interview workshops, career counseling, job interviews.

Freshmen 582 applied, 524 admitted, 330 enrolled. 1 National Merit Scholar, 5 valedictorians.

Average high school GPA	3.36	SAT verbal scores above 500	56%
SAT math scores above 500	48%	ACT above 18	N/R
From top 10% of their h.s. class	17%	From top quarter	41%
From top half	76%	1998 freshmen returning in 1999	71%

Application *Options:* Common Application, electronic application, deferred entrance. *Preference* given to Christians. *Application fee:* $30. *Required:* essay or personal statement; high school transcript; minimum 2.5 GPA; 1 letter of recommendation. *Required for some:* interview.

Standardized tests *Admission: Required:* SAT I or ACT.

Significant dates *Application deadlines:* rolling (freshmen), rolling (transfers). *Notification:* continuous until 8/31 (freshmen). *Financial aid deadline priority date:* 3/2.

Freshman Application Contact
Ms. Jessica Mireles, Associate Director of Admissions, Vanguard University of Southern California, 55 Fair Drive, Costa Mesa, CA 92626-6597. **Phone:** 714-556-3610 Ext. 327. **Toll-free phone:** 800-722-6279. **Fax:** 714-668-6194.

Visit CollegeQuest.com for information on majors offered and athletics. College video available at CollegeQuest.com.

■ *See page 2880 for a narrative description.*

WESTMONT COLLEGE
Santa Barbara, California

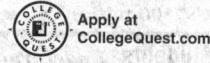
Apply at CollegeQuest.com

- **Independent nondenominational**, 4-year, founded 1937
- **Degree** bachelor's
- **Suburban** 133-acre campus with easy access to Los Angeles
- **Coed**, 1,323 undergraduate students, 99% full-time, 61% women, 39% men
- **Moderately difficult** entrance level, 71% of applicants were admitted
- **14:1 student-to-undergraduate faculty ratio**
- **60.7% graduate** in 6 years or less
- **$20,965 tuition** and fees
- **$15,299 average financial aid** package, $18,319 average indebtedness upon graduation, $13.6 million endowment

Students *Undergraduates:* 1,319 full-time, 4 part-time. Students come from 41 states and territories, 12 other countries. *The most frequently chosen baccalaureate fields are:* biological/life sciences, liberal arts/general studies, social sciences and history. *Graduate:* 12 in graduate degree programs.

From out-of-state	31%	Reside on campus	90%
Age 25 or older	2%	Transferred in	5%
International students	1%	African Americans	1%
Asian Americans/Pacific Islanders	4%	Hispanic Americans	8%
Native Americans	2%		

Faculty 139 (61% full-time).

Expenses (2000–2001) *Comprehensive fee:* $28,033 includes full-time tuition ($20,379), mandatory fees ($586), and room and board ($7068).

College room only: $4104. Room and board charges vary according to board plan. *Payment plans:* installment, deferred payment. *Waivers:* employees or children of employees.

Library Roger John Voskuyl Library. *Operations spending 1999–2000:* $728,054. *Collection:* 158,332 titles, 29,218 serial subscriptions, 8,531 audio-visual materials.

College life *Housing: Options:* coed, disabled students. *Most popular organizations:* Christian Concerns, student government, Leadership Development, Music and Theater Ensembles, intramural athletics.

Campus security 24-hour emergency response devices and patrols, late-night transport-escort service, controlled dormitory access.

After graduation 66 organizations recruited on campus 1997–98. *Career center:* 4 full-time, 1 part-time personnel. Services include job fairs, resume preparation, resume referral, career/interest testing, career counseling, careers library, job bank, job interviews.

Freshmen 1,292 applied, 918 admitted, 318 enrolled. 7 National Merit Scholars, 50 class presidents, 50 valedictorians, 176 student government officers.

Average high school GPA	3.64	SAT verbal scores above 500	92%
SAT math scores above 500	90%	ACT above 18	99%
From top 10% of their h.s. class	43%	From top quarter	73%
From top half	96%	1998 freshmen returning in 1999	84%

Application *Options:* eApply at www.CollegeQuest.com, Common Application, electronic application, early admission, early action, deferred entrance. *Application fee:* $40. *Required:* essay or personal statement; high school transcript. *Required for some:* letters of recommendation; interview. *Recommended:* minimum 3.0 GPA; letters of recommendation; interview.

Standardized tests *Admission: Required:* SAT I or ACT.

Significant dates *Application deadlines:* 3/1 (freshmen), 4/1 (transfers). *Early action:* 12/1. *Notification:* 3/15 (freshmen), 1/15 (early action). *Financial aid deadline:* 3/2. *Priority date:* 3/1.

Freshman Application Contact
Mrs. Joyce Luy, Director of Admissions, Westmont College, 955 La Paz Road, Santa Barbara, CA 93108. **Phone:** 805-565-6200 Ext. 6005. **Toll-free phone:** 800-777-9011. **Fax:** 805-565-6234. **E-mail:** admissions@westmont.edu

Visit CollegeQuest.com for information on majors offered and athletics. College video available at CollegeQuest.com.

■ *See page 2968 for a narrative description.*

WHITTIER COLLEGE
Whittier, California

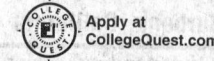
Apply at CollegeQuest.com

- **Independent**, comprehensive, founded 1887
- **Degrees** bachelor's, master's, and first professional
- **Suburban** 95-acre campus with easy access to Los Angeles
- **Coed**, 1,296 undergraduate students, 98% full-time, 56% women, 44% men
- **Moderately difficult** entrance level, 92% of applicants were admitted
- **12:1 student-to-undergraduate faculty ratio**
- **$20,128 tuition** and fees
- **$17,150 average financial aid** package, $51.4 million endowment

Students *Undergraduates:* 1,276 full-time, 20 part-time. Students come from 33 states and territories, 20 other countries. *The most frequently chosen baccalaureate fields are:* business/marketing, biological/life sciences, interdisciplinary studies. *Graduate:* 657 in professional programs, 250 in other graduate degree programs.

From out-of-state	27%	Reside on campus	60%
Age 25 or older	7%	Transferred in	7%
International students	4%	African Americans	5%
Asian Americans/Pacific Islanders	8%	Hispanic Americans	26%
Native Americans	1%		

Faculty 133 (72% full-time).

Expenses (1999–2000) *Comprehensive fee:* $26,864 includes full-time tuition ($19,828), mandatory fees ($300), and room and board ($6736). *College room only:* $3694. Room and board charges vary according to board plan and housing facility. *Part-time tuition:* $720 per credit. *Payment plan:* installment. *Waivers:* children of alumni and employees or children of employees.

Library Bonnie Bell Wardman Library plus 1 other. *Operations spending 1999–2000:* $3.2 million. *Collection:* 225,337 titles, 1,357 serial subscriptions.

California

Whittier College (continued)

College life *Housing:* on-campus residence required through junior year. *Options:* coed, women-only. *Social organizations:* local fraternities, local sororities; 15% of eligible men and 15% of eligible women are members. *Most popular organizations:* Hispanic Students Association, Hawaiian Islander Club, choir, Asian Students Association, Students Organized for Multicultural Awareness.

Campus security 24-hour patrols, late-night transport-escort service, controlled dormitory access.

After graduation 25 organizations recruited on campus 1997–98. 61% of class of 1998 had job offers within 6 months. *Career center:* 2 full-time, 1 part-time personnel. Services include job fairs, resume preparation, resume referral, career counseling, careers library, job bank, job interviews. *Graduate education:* 22% of class of 1999 went directly to graduate and professional school: 10% education, 5% graduate arts and sciences, 2% law, 1% business, 1% dentistry, 1% medicine, 1% theology, 1% veterinary medicine.

Freshmen 1,345 applied, 1,233 admitted, 381 enrolled. 4 valedictorians.

Average high school GPA	3.12	
SAT verbal scores above 500		62%
SAT math scores above 500	66%	
ACT above 18		93%
From top 10% of their h.s. class	25%	
From top quarter		59%
From top half	84%	
1998 freshmen returning in 1999		74%

Application *Options:* eApply at www.CollegeQuest.com, Common Application, electronic application, early action, deferred entrance. *Application fee:* $35. *Required:* essay or personal statement; high school transcript; minimum 2.0 GPA; 2 letters of recommendation. *Required for some:* minimum 3.5 GPA. *Recommended:* minimum 2.5 GPA; interview.

Standardized tests *Admission:* Required: SAT I or ACT. Recommended: SAT II Subject Tests.

Significant dates *Application deadlines:* rolling (freshmen), rolling (transfers). *Early action:* 12/1. *Notification:* 12/31 (early action). *Financial aid deadline:* 3/2. Priority date: 2/1.

Freshman Application Contact
Ms. Urmi Kar, Dean of Enrollment, Whittier College, 13406 E Philadelphia Street, PO Box 634, Whittier, CA 90608-0634. **Phone:** 562-907-4238. **Fax:** 562-907-4870. **E-mail:** admission@whittier.edu

Visit CollegeQuest.com for information on majors offered and athletics.

■ *See page 2986 for a narrative description.*

WOODBURY UNIVERSITY
Burbank, California

- **Independent**, comprehensive, founded 1884
- **Degrees** bachelor's and master's
- **Suburban** 23-acre campus with easy access to Los Angeles
- **Coed**, 1,021 undergraduate students, 78% full-time, 54% women, 46% men
- **Moderately difficult** entrance level, 93% of applicants were admitted
- **12:1 student-to-undergraduate faculty ratio**
- **55% graduate** in 6 years or less
- **$16,710 tuition** and fees
- **$14,150 average financial aid** package, $4.8 million endowment

Students *Undergraduates:* 792 full-time, 229 part-time. Students come from 31 other countries. *The most frequently chosen baccalaureate fields are:* architecture, business/marketing, visual/performing arts. *Graduate:* 173 in graduate degree programs.

Reside on campus	16%	Age 25 or older	36%
Transferred in	19%	International students	7%
African Americans	7%	Asian Americans/Pacific Islanders	19%
Hispanic Americans	30%	Native Americans	0.5%

Faculty 208 (15% full-time), 52% with terminal degrees.

Expenses (1999–2000) *One-time required fee:* $950. *Comprehensive fee:* $22,700 includes full-time tuition ($16,590), mandatory fees ($120), and room and board ($5990). *College room only:* $3390. Full-time tuition and fees vary according to program. Room and board charges vary according to board plan and housing facility. *Part-time tuition:* $540 per unit. *Part-time fees:* $135 per term part-time. Part-time tuition and fees vary according to class time and program. *Payment plans:* installment, deferred payment. *Waivers:* employees or children of employees.

Library Los Angeles Times Library. *Operations spending 1999–2000:* $618,887. *Collection:* 66,156 titles, 1,435 serial subscriptions, 14,752 audiovisual materials.

College life *Housing:* Option: coed. *Social organizations:* national fraternities, national sororities, local fraternities, local sororities; 30% of eligible men and 30% of eligible women are members. *Most popular organizations:* Associated Student Government, Fashion Guild, American Institute of Architecture Students, Delta Sigma Phi, Reliving Intercultural Experiences (RICE).

Campus security Late-night transport-escort service, controlled dormitory access.

After graduation 60 organizations recruited on campus 1997–98. 84% of class of 1998 had job offers within 6 months. *Career center:* 1 full-time personnel. Services include job fairs, resume preparation, interview workshops, resume referral, career/interest testing, career counseling, careers library, job bank, job interviews.

Freshmen 455 applied, 424 admitted, 136 enrolled.

Average high school GPA	3.2	
SAT verbal scores above 500		36%
SAT math scores above 500	31%	
ACT above 18		N/R
From top 10% of their h.s. class	5%	
From top quarter		40%
From top half	80%	
1998 freshmen returning in 1999		83%

Application *Option:* deferred entrance. *Application fee:* $30. *Required:* essay or personal statement; high school transcript; minimum 2.0 GPA; 2 letters of recommendation. *Required for some:* portfolio. *Recommended:* minimum 3.0 GPA; interview.

Standardized tests *Admission:* Required: SAT I or ACT.

Significant dates *Application deadlines:* rolling (freshmen), rolling (transfers). *Financial aid deadline priority date:* 3/2.

Freshman Application Contact
Mr. Don St. Clair, Vice-President of Enrollment Planning, Woodbury University, 7500 Glenoaks Boulevard, Burbank, CA 91504-1099. **Phone:** 818-767-0888. **Toll-free phone:** 800-784-WOOD. **Fax:** 818-504-9320. **E-mail:** admissions@vaxb.woodbury.edu

Visit CollegeQuest.com for information on majors offered and athletics.

■ *See page 3016 for a narrative description.*

YESHIVA OHR ELCHONON CHABAD/ WEST COAST TALMUDICAL SEMINARY
Los Angeles, California

- **Independent Jewish**, 4-year, founded 1953
- **Degree** bachelor's
- **Urban** 4-acre campus
- **Men** only, 56 undergraduate students, 100% full-time
- **Moderately difficult** entrance level
- **$7500 tuition** and fees

Students *Undergraduates:* Students come from 6 states and territories, 5 other countries. *The most frequently chosen baccalaureate field is:* philosophy.

Reside on campus	100%	International students	7%
Asian Americans/Pacific Islanders	7%		

Faculty 5 (100% full-time).

Expenses (1999–2000) *Comprehensive fee:* $11,500 includes full-time tuition ($7500) and room and board ($4000). *Payment plan:* installment. *Waivers:* employees or children of employees.

Library Yeshiva Ohr Elchonon Chabad Library plus 3 others. *Collection:* 12,000 titles, 200 serial subscriptions.

College life On-campus residence required through senior year.

Campus security 24-hour emergency response devices, student patrols.

Freshmen 1 class president, 2 valedictorians, 4 student government officers.

Average high school GPA	3.1	
SAT verbal scores above 500		N/R
SAT math scores above 500	N/R	
ACT above 18		N/R
From top 10% of their h.s. class	20%	
From top quarter		30%
From top half	50%	

Application *Options:* Common Application, early admission, deferred entrance. *Preference* given to applicants with religious commitment. *Application fee:* $0. *Required:* high school transcript; minimum 2.0 GPA; interview; oral examination. *Required for some:* letters of recommendation. *Recommended:* letters of recommendation.

Significant dates *Application deadlines:* rolling (freshmen), rolling (transfers).

Freshman Application Contact
Rabbi Ezra Binyomin Schochet, Dean, Yeshiva Ohr Elchonon Chabad/West Coast Talmudical Seminary, 7215 Waring Avenue, Los Angeles, CA 90046-7660. **Phone:** 213-937-3763.

Visit CollegeQuest.com for information on majors offered and athletics.

COLORADO

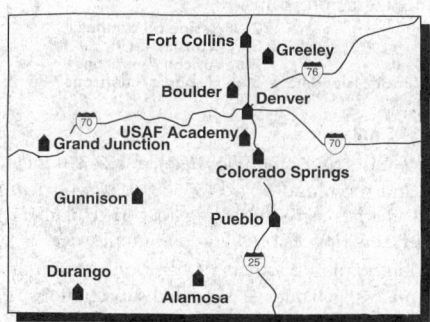

The Denver area includes the towns of Englewood, Greenwood Village, Lakewood, Golden, and Aurora.

ADAMS STATE COLLEGE
Alamosa, Colorado

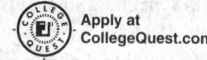 Apply at CollegeQuest.com

- **State-supported**, comprehensive, founded 1921
- **Degrees** associate, bachelor's, and master's
- **Small-town** 90-acre campus
- **Coed**, 1,968 undergraduate students, 88% full-time, 58% women, 42% men
- **Moderately difficult** entrance level, 93% of applicants were admitted
- **18:1** student-to-undergraduate faculty ratio
- **34% graduate** in 6 years or less
- **$2092 tuition** and fees (in-state); $6302 (out-of-state)
- **$6.4 million** endowment

Part of State Colleges in Colorado.

Students *Undergraduates:* 1,726 full-time, 242 part-time. Students come from 46 states and territories, 4 other countries. *The most frequently chosen baccalaureate fields are:* business/marketing, liberal arts/general studies, social sciences and history. *Graduate:* 487 in graduate degree programs.

From out-of-state	20%	Reside on campus	45%
Age 25 or older	18%	Transferred in	6%
International students	0.3%	African Americans	3%
Asian Americans/Pacific Islanders	2%	Hispanic Americans	28%
Native Americans	2%		

Faculty 141 (65% full-time).

Expenses (1999–2000) *Tuition, state resident:* full-time $1530; part-time $77 per semester hour. *Tuition, nonresident:* full-time $5740; part-time $287 per semester hour. *Required fees:* full-time $562; $21 per semester hour. Full-time tuition and fees vary according to reciprocity agreements. Part-time tuition and fees vary according to course load. *College room and board:* $5080; room only: $2580. Room and board charges vary according to board plan and housing facility. *Payment plans:* installment, deferred payment. *Waivers:* employees or children of employees.

Library Nielsen Library. *Operations spending 1999–2000:* $539,637. *Collection:* 146,154 titles, 1,005 serial subscriptions, 2,090 audiovisual materials.

College life *Housing:* on-campus residence required through sophomore year. *Options:* coed, women-only. *Most popular organizations:* student government, Student Ambassadors, Program Council, Circle K, Tri Beta.

Campus security 24-hour emergency response devices and patrols, student patrols, late-night transport-escort service, controlled dormitory access.

After graduation 103 organizations recruited on campus 1997–98. *Career center:* 1 full-time, 5 part-time personnel. Services include job fairs, resume preparation, career counseling. *Graduate education:* 21% of class of 1999 went directly to graduate and professional school: 7% business, 5% graduate arts and sciences, 4% medicine, 4% veterinary medicine, 1% law.

Freshmen 1,743 applied, 1,626 admitted, 580 enrolled.

Average high school GPA	3.09	SAT verbal scores above 500	57%
SAT math scores above 500	57%	ACT above 18	76%
From top 10% of their h.s. class	13%	From top quarter	41%
From top half	75%	1998 freshmen returning in 1999	58%

Application *Options:* eApply at www.CollegeQuest.com, Common Application, electronic application, early admission, deferred entrance. *Application fee:* $25. *Required:* high school transcript; minimum 2.0 GPA. *Required for some:* essay or personal statement; letters of recommendation; interview.

Standardized tests *Admission:* Required: SAT I or ACT.

Significant dates *Application deadlines:* 8/1 (freshmen), 8/1 (transfers). *Financial aid deadline priority date:* 4/15.

Freshman Application Contact
Ms. Lori Lee Laske, Assistant Director of Admissions, Adams State College, 208 Edgemont Boulevard, Alamosa, CO 81102. **Phone:** 719-587-7712. **Toll-free phone:** 800-824-6494. **Fax:** 719-587-7522. **E-mail:** ascadmit@adams.edu

Visit CollegeQuest.com for information on majors offered and athletics. Electronic viewbook available at CollegeQuest.com.

■ *See page 1130 for a narrative description.*

THE ART INSTITUTE OF COLORADO
Denver, Colorado

- **Proprietary**, 4-year, founded 1952
- **Degrees** associate and bachelor's
- **Urban** campus
- **Coed**, 1,977 undergraduate students
- **Minimally difficult** entrance level, 99% of applicants were admitted
- **20:1** student-to-undergraduate faculty ratio
- **$12,480 tuition** and fees

Part of Education Management Corporation.

Students *Undergraduates:* Students come from 49 states and territories.

From out-of-state	50%	Reside on campus	9%
Age 25 or older	28%	African Americans	3%
Asian Americans/Pacific Islanders	4%	Hispanic Americans	6%
Native Americans	1%		

Faculty 129 (34% full-time).

Expenses (2000–2001) *Comprehensive fee:* $18,480 includes full-time tuition ($12,480) and room and board ($6000). Full-time tuition and fees vary according to course load, degree level, and program. Room and board charges vary according to board plan, housing facility, and location. *Part-time tuition:* $260 per credit. Part-time tuition and fees vary according to course load and program. *Payment plans:* guaranteed tuition, installment. *Waivers:* employees or children of employees.

Library Colorado Institute of Art Learning Resource Center. *Operations spending 1999–2000:* $130,394. *Collection:* 10,483 titles, 200 serial subscriptions.

College life *Housing:* Option: coed. *Most popular organizations:* Culinary Student Forum, Computer Animation Club, Student Chapter—American Society of Interior Designers.

Campus security 24-hour emergency response devices.

After graduation 160 organizations recruited on campus 1997–98. 87% of class of 1998 had job offers within 6 months. *Career center:* 9 full-time personnel. Services include job fairs, resume preparation, resume referral, career counseling, job bank, job interviews.

Freshmen 996 applied, 990 admitted.

SAT verbal scores above 500	N/R	SAT math scores above 500	N/R
ACT above 18	N/R	1998 freshmen returning in 1999	65%

Application *Options:* early admission, deferred entrance. *Application fee:* $50. *Required:* essay or personal statement; high school transcript; interview.

Significant dates *Application deadlines:* rolling (freshmen), rolling (transfers). *Financial aid deadline:* continuous.

Colorado

The Art Institute of Colorado (continued)
Freshman Application Contact
Ms. Barbara Browning, Vice President and Director of Admissions, The Art Institute of Colorado, 1200 Lincoln Street, Denver, CO 80203-2903. **Phone:** 303-837-0825 Ext. 520. **Toll-free phone:** 800-275-2420. **Fax:** 303-860-8520. **E-mail:** houstonj@aii.edu
Visit CollegeQuest.com for information on majors offered and athletics. College video available at CollegeQuest.com.

COLORADO CHRISTIAN UNIVERSITY
Lakewood, Colorado

- **Independent interdenominational**, comprehensive, founded 1914
- **Degrees** associate, bachelor's, and master's
- **Suburban** 26-acre campus with easy access to Denver
- **Coed**, 1,654 undergraduate students, 67% full-time, 55% women, 45% men
- **Moderately difficult** entrance level, 74% of applicants were admitted
- **12:1 student-to-undergraduate faculty ratio**
- **30% graduate** in 6 years or less
- **$10,790 tuition** and fees
- **$9274 average financial aid** package, $5.3 million endowment

Students *Undergraduates:* 1,105 full-time, 549 part-time. Students come from 40 states and territories, 20 other countries. *The most frequently chosen baccalaureate fields are:* business/marketing, education, philosophy. **Graduate:** 240 in graduate degree programs.

From out-of-state	20%	Age 25 or older	50%
International students	1%	African Americans	6%
Asian Americans/Pacific Islanders	1%	Hispanic Americans	5%
Native Americans	1%		

Faculty 245 (20% full-time).
Expenses (1999–2000) *Comprehensive fee:* $15,950 includes full-time tuition ($9960), mandatory fees ($830), and room and board ($5160). *College room only:* $2960. Room and board charges vary according to board plan. *Part-time tuition:* $415 per semester hour. Part-time tuition and fees vary according to program. *Payment plan:* installment. *Waivers:* employees or children of employees.
Library Colorado Christian University Library. *Collection:* 56,000 titles, 1,600 serial subscriptions, 2,542 audiovisual materials.
College life On-campus residence required in freshman year.
Campus security 24-hour emergency response devices and patrols.
After graduation *Career center:* 1 full-time personnel. Services include resume preparation, career counseling, careers library, job bank.
Freshmen 780 applied, 577 admitted, 214 enrolled. 1 National Merit Scholar.

SAT verbal scores above 500	N/R	SAT math scores above 500	N/R
ACT above 18	N/R	1998 freshmen returning in 1999	53%

Application *Options:* Common Application, deferred entrance. *Application fee:* $40. *Required:* essay or personal statement; high school transcript; minimum 2.0 GPA; 2 letters of recommendation. *Required for some:* 3 letters of recommendation; interview.
Standardized tests *Admission: Required:* SAT I or ACT.
Significant dates *Application deadline:* rolling (freshmen). *Financial aid deadline priority date:* 3/15.
Freshman Application Contact
Ms. Kay Myrick, Director of Admissions, Colorado Christian University, 180 South Garrison Street, Lakewood, CO 80226-7499. **Phone:** 303-963-3203. **Toll-free phone:** 800-44-FAITH. **Fax:** 303-238-2191. **E-mail:** admissions@ccu.edu
Visit CollegeQuest.com for information on majors offered and athletics. College video available at CollegeQuest.com.

- *See page 1496 for a narrative description.*

THE COLORADO COLLEGE
Colorado Springs, Colorado

 Apply at CollegeQuest.com

- **Independent**, comprehensive, founded 1874
- **Degrees** bachelor's and master's (master's degree in education only)
- **Urban** 90-acre campus with easy access to Denver
- **Coed**, 1,929 undergraduate students, 100% full-time, 55% women, 45% men
- **Very difficult** entrance level, 55% of applicants were admitted
- **11:1 student-to-undergraduate faculty ratio**
- **79% graduate** in 6 years or less
- **$21,822 tuition** and fees
- **$18,764 average financial aid** package, $13,418 average indebtedness upon graduation, $332.5 million endowment

Founded in 1874, Colorado College is a private, 4-year, coeducational college. Its 90-acre campus is located in downtown Colorado Springs (metro population 452,415) on the front range of the Rocky Mountains, 70 miles south of Denver. It employs an innovative one-course-at-a-time approach (the Block Plan) in structuring its traditional liberal arts and sciences curriculum.

Students *Undergraduates:* 1,929 full-time. Students come from 50 states and territories, 31 other countries. *The most frequently chosen baccalaureate fields are:* biological/life sciences, English, social sciences and history. **Graduate:** 23 in graduate degree programs.

From out-of-state	72%	Reside on campus	66%
Age 25 or older	0.3%	Transferred in	3%
International students	2%	African Americans	2%
Asian Americans/Pacific Islanders	3%	Hispanic Americans	6%
Native Americans	1%		

Faculty 166 (100% full-time).
Expenses (1999–2000) *Comprehensive fee:* $27,390 includes full-time tuition ($21,822) and room and board ($5568). *College room only:* $2984. Room and board charges vary according to board plan. *Payment plan:* installment. *Waivers:* employees or children of employees.
Library Tutt Library plus 2 others. *Operations spending 1999–2000:* $862,957. *Collection:* 650,000 titles, 2,312 serial subscriptions, 4,309 audiovisual materials.
College life *Housing:* on-campus residence required through junior year. *Options:* coed, men-only, women-only. *Social organizations:* national fraternities, national sororities; 13% of eligible men and 18% of eligible women are members. *Most popular organizations:* Community Service Center, student government, arts and crafts organizations, Outdoor Recreation Committee, theater workshop.
Campus security 24-hour emergency response devices and patrols, late-night transport-escort service, controlled dormitory access, whistle program.
After graduation 68 organizations recruited on campus 1997–98. *Career center:* 4 full-time, 1 part-time personnel. Services include resume preparation, interview workshops, resume referral, career/interest testing, career counseling, careers library, job bank, job interviews.
Freshmen 3,644 applied, 2,008 admitted, 483 enrolled. 22 National Merit Scholars, 38 valedictorians, 35 student government officers.

Average high school GPA	3.8	SAT verbal scores above 500	96%
SAT math scores above 500	97%	ACT above 18	100%
From top 10% of their h.s. class	42%	From top quarter	84%
From top half	98%	1998 freshmen returning in 1999	93%

Application *Options:* eApply at www.CollegeQuest.com, Common Application, electronic application, early action, deferred entrance. *Application fee:* $40. *Required:* essay or personal statement; high school transcript; 3 letters of recommendation.
Standardized tests *Admission: Required:* SAT I or ACT.
Significant dates *Application deadlines:* 1/15 (freshmen), 4/1 (transfers). *Early action:* 11/15. *Notification:* 4/1 (freshmen), 1/1 (early action). *Financial aid deadline:* 2/15.
Freshman Application Contact
Mr. Terrance K. Swenson, Dean of Admission and Financial Aid, The Colorado College, 14 East Cache la Poudre, 900 Block North Cascade, West, Colorado Springs, CO 80903-3294. **Phone:** 719-389-6344. **Toll-free phone:** 800-542-7214. **Fax:** 719-389-6282. **E-mail:** admission@coloradocollege.edu
Visit CollegeQuest.com for information on majors offered and athletics. College video and electronic viewbook available at CollegeQuest.com.

- *See page 1498 for a narrative description.*

Colorado

THE COLORADO INSTITUTE OF ART
Colorado—See The Art Institute of Colorado

COLORADO SCHOOL OF MINES
Golden, Colorado

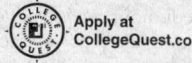 Apply at CollegeQuest.com

- **State-supported**, university, founded 1874
- **Degrees** bachelor's, master's, and doctoral
- **Small-town** 373-acre campus with easy access to Denver
- **Coed**, 2,473 undergraduate students, 96% full-time, 24% women, 76% men
- **Very difficult** entrance level, 76% of applicants were admitted
- **16:1** student-to-undergraduate faculty ratio
- **55% graduate** in 6 years or less
- **$5211 tuition** and fees (in-state); $15,311 (out-of-state)
- **$10,195 average financial aid** package, $17,500 average indebtedness upon graduation, $104.8 million endowment

Students *Undergraduates:* 2,374 full-time, 99 part-time. Students come from 51 states and territories, 28 other countries. *The most frequently chosen baccalaureate fields are:* engineering/engineering technologies, mathematics, physical sciences. *Graduate:* 729 in graduate degree programs.

From out-of-state	21%	Reside on campus	25%
Age 25 or older	2%	Transferred in	4%
International students	4%	African Americans	1%
Asian Americans/Pacific Islanders	5%	Hispanic Americans	7%
Native Americans	1%		

Faculty 268 (71% full-time), 85% with terminal degrees.
Expenses (1999–2000) *Tuition, state resident:* full-time $4616; part-time $154 per semester hour. *Tuition, nonresident:* full-time $14,716; part-time $491 per semester hour. *Required fees:* full-time $595. Part-time tuition and fees vary according to course load. *College room and board:* $4920. Room and board charges vary according to board plan and housing facility. *Payment plan:* installment.
Library Arthur Lakes Library. Operations spending 1999–2000: $1.9 million. *Collection:* 260,000 titles, 2,000 serial subscriptions, 48 audiovisual materials.
College life *Housing: Option:* coed. *Social organizations:* national fraternities, national sororities; 20% of eligible men and 20% of eligible women are members. *Most popular organizations:* Interfraternity Council, Residence Hall Association, Society of Women Engineers, Panhellenic Council, American Institute of Chemical Engineers.
Campus security 24-hour emergency response devices and patrols.
After graduation 169 organizations recruited on campus 1997–98. 85% of class of 1998 had job offers within 6 months. *Career center:* 3 full-time, 1 part-time personnel. Services include job fairs, resume preparation, resume referral, career counseling, careers library, job bank, job interviews. *Graduate education:* 15% of class of 1999 went directly to graduate and professional school: 11% engineering, 1% business, 1% graduate arts and sciences, 1% law, 1% medicine.
Freshmen 1,984 applied, 1,502 admitted, 566 enrolled. 77 class presidents, 77 valedictorians, 232 student government officers.

Average high school GPA	3.8	SAT verbal scores above 500	87%
SAT math scores above 500	99%	ACT above 18	100%
From top 10% of their h.s. class	57%	From top quarter	91%
From top half	100%	1998 freshmen returning in 1999	88%

Application *Options:* eApply at www.CollegeQuest.com, electronic application, deferred entrance. *Application fee:* $25. *Required:* high school transcript. *Required for some:* essay or personal statement; letters of recommendation; interview. *Recommended:* rank in upper one-third of high school class.
Standardized tests *Admission: Required:* SAT I or ACT.
Significant dates *Application deadlines:* 6/1 (freshmen), 7/1 (transfers). *Financial aid deadline priority date:* 3/1.
Freshman Application Contact
Mr. Bill Young, Director of Enrollment Management, Colorado School of Mines, Weaver Towers-1811 Elm Street, Golden, CO 80401-1842. **Phone:** 303-273-3227. **Toll-free phone:** 800-446-9488. **Fax:** 303-273-3509. **E-mail:** admit@mines.edu

Visit CollegeQuest.com for information on majors offered and athletics.

COLORADO STATE UNIVERSITY
Fort Collins, Colorado

- **State-supported**, university, founded 1870
- **Degrees** bachelor's, master's, doctoral, and first professional
- **Urban** 666-acre campus with easy access to Denver
- **Coed**, 18,483 undergraduate students, 90% full-time, 52% women, 48% men
- **Moderately difficult** entrance level, 77% of applicants were admitted
- **20:1** student-to-undergraduate faculty ratio
- **$3062 tuition** and fees (in-state); $10,748 (out-of-state)
- **$6929 average financial aid** package, $14,253 average indebtedness upon graduation, $84.3 million endowment

Part of Colorado State University System.
Students *Undergraduates:* 16,584 full-time, 1,899 part-time. Students come from 55 states and territories, 49 other countries. *The most frequently chosen baccalaureate fields are:* business/marketing, agriculture, engineering/engineering technologies. *Graduate:* 530 in professional programs, 3,452 in other graduate degree programs.

From out-of-state	20%	Reside on campus	30%
Age 25 or older	13%	Transferred in	10%
International students	1%	African Americans	2%
Asian Americans/Pacific Islanders	3%	Hispanic Americans	6%
Native Americans	1%		

Faculty 979 (100% full-time), 92% with terminal degrees.
Expenses (1999–2000) *Tuition, state resident:* full-time $2340; part-time $130 per credit. *Tuition, nonresident:* full-time $10,026; part-time $557 per credit. *Required fees:* full-time $722; $130 per credit; $32 per term part-time. Full-time tuition and fees vary according to program. Part-time tuition and fees vary according to course load and program. *College room and board:* $5200. Room and board charges vary according to board plan and housing facility. *Payment plan:* installment. *Waivers:* employees or children of employees.
Library William E. Morgan Library plus 3 others. *Collection:* 1.1 million titles, 21,255 serial subscriptions, 9,226 audiovisual materials.
College life *Housing:* on-campus residence required in freshman year. *Option:* coed. *Social organizations:* national fraternities, national sororities, local fraternities, local sororities; 11% of eligible men and 12% of eligible women are members. *Most popular organizations:* Associated Students of Colorado State University, fraternities/sororities, Campus Crusades for Christ, Office of Community Services, Colorado Public Interest Research Group.
Campus security 24-hour emergency response devices and patrols, student patrols, late-night transport-escort service, controlled dormitory access.
After graduation 501 organizations recruited on campus 1997–98. *Career center:* 19 full-time, 27 part-time personnel. Services include job fairs, resume preparation, interview workshops, resume referral, career/interest testing, career counseling, careers library, job bank, job interviews.
Freshmen 10,465 applied, 8,104 admitted, 3,137 enrolled. 14 National Merit Scholars, 100 valedictorians.

Average high school GPA	3.5	SAT verbal scores above 500	77%
SAT math scores above 500	79%	ACT above 18	99%
From top 10% of their h.s. class	25%	From top quarter	58%
From top half	92%	1998 freshmen returning in 1999	82%

Application *Options:* electronic application, deferred entrance. *Application fee:* $30. *Required:* high school transcript. *Recommended:* essay or personal statement; letters of recommendation.
Standardized tests *Admission: Required:* SAT I or ACT.
Significant dates *Application deadlines:* 7/1 (freshmen), 7/1 (transfers). *Financial aid deadline priority date:* 3/1.
Freshman Application Contact
Ms. Mary Ontiveros, Director of Admissions, Colorado State University, Spruce Hall, Fort Collins, CO 80523-0015. **Phone:** 970-491-6909. **Fax:** 970-491-7799. **E-mail:** admissions@vines.colostate.edu
Visit CollegeQuest.com for information on majors offered and athletics. College video available at CollegeQuest.com.

- *See page 1500 for a narrative description.*

Colorado

COLORADO TECHNICAL UNIVERSITY
Colorado Springs, Colorado

- **Proprietary**, comprehensive, founded 1965
- **Degrees** associate, bachelor's, master's, and doctoral
- **Suburban** 14-acre campus with easy access to Denver
- **Coed**, 1,067 undergraduate students, 56% full-time, 24% women, 76% men
- **Moderately difficult** entrance level
- **25:1** student-to-undergraduate faculty ratio
- **$6108 tuition** and fees

Students *Undergraduates:* 595 full-time, 472 part-time. Students come from 7 other countries. *The most frequently chosen baccalaureate fields are:* computer/information sciences, engineering/engineering technologies. **Graduate:** 640 in graduate degree programs.

Age 25 or older	78%	Transferred in	10%
International students	1%	African Americans	8%
Asian Americans/Pacific Islanders	3%	Hispanic Americans	1%
Native Americans	0.5%		

Faculty 114 (25% full-time), 37% with terminal degrees.
Expenses (1999–2000) *One-time required fee:* $100. *Tuition:* full-time $5940; part-time $165 per quarter hour. *Required fees:* full-time $168; $56 per term part-time. Part-time tuition and fees vary according to course load. *Payment plan:* installment. *Waivers:* employees or children of employees.
Library Resource Center. *Operations spending 1999–2000:* $397,745. *Collection:* 14,200 titles, 340 serial subscriptions.
College life *Housing:* college housing not available. *Most popular organizations:* Institute of Electrical and Electronics Engineers, Society of Logistic Engineers, Association of Computing Machinery, Society of Women Engineers, Phi Beta Lambda.
Campus security 24-hour emergency response devices, late-night transport-escort service.
After graduation 62 organizations recruited on campus 1997–98. 96% of class of 1998 had job offers within 6 months. *Career center:* 1 full-time personnel. Services include job fairs, resume preparation, resume referral, career counseling, careers library, job bank, job interviews.
Freshmen 358 enrolled.

Average high school GPA	3.45	SAT verbal scores above 500	50%
SAT math scores above 500	63%	ACT above 18	N/R
From top 10% of their h.s. class	20%	From top quarter	30%
From top half	50%	1998 freshmen returning in 1999	51%

Application *Option:* deferred entrance. *Application fee:* $50. *Required for some:* essay or personal statement; high school transcript. *Recommended:* minimum 3.0 GPA; interview.
Standardized tests *Admission: Recommended:* SAT I or ACT. *Required for some:* ACT ASSET tests in English and math.
Significant dates *Application deadlines:* rolling (freshmen), rolling (transfers). *Financial aid deadline:* continuous.
Freshman Application Contact
Mr. Bill Somners, Admissions Manager, Colorado Technical University, 4435 North Chestnut Street, Colorado Springs, CO 80907-3896. **Phone:** 719-598-0200. **E-mail:** cotechcs@iex.net
Visit CollegeQuest.com for information on majors offered and athletics. College video available at CollegeQuest.com.

COLORADO TECHNICAL UNIVERSITY DENVER CAMPUS
Greenwood Village, Colorado

- **Proprietary**, comprehensive, founded 1965
- **Degrees** associate, bachelor's, master's, and doctoral
- **Urban** 1-acre campus with easy access to Denver
- **Coed**, 202 undergraduate students, 31% full-time, 21% women, 79% men
- **Minimally difficult** entrance level, 65% of applicants were admitted
- **15:1** student-to-undergraduate faculty ratio
- **$6108 tuition** and fees

Part of Whitman Education Group.
Students *Undergraduates:* 63 full-time, 139 part-time. Students come from 12 states and territories. **Graduate:** 93 in graduate degree programs.

Age 25 or older	60%	Transferred in	43%
International students	1%	African Americans	11%
Asian Americans/Pacific Islanders	7%	Hispanic Americans	7%
Native Americans	0.5%		

Faculty 46 (13% full-time), 41% with terminal degrees.
Expenses (1999–2000) *Tuition:* full-time $5940; part-time $165 per credit hour. *Required fees:* full-time $168; $56 per term part-time. Full-time tuition and fees vary according to course load. *Payment plans:* installment, deferred payment.
Library Colorado Technical University Resource Center. *Operations spending 1999–2000:* $35,000. *Collection:* 2,262 serial subscriptions, 15 audiovisual materials.
College life *Housing:* college housing not available. *Most popular organization:* Association of Information Technology Professionals.
Campus security 24-hour emergency response devices and patrols.
After graduation 4 organizations recruited on campus 1997–98. *Career center:* Services include job fairs, career counseling, careers library, job bank.
Freshmen 23 applied, 15 admitted, 2 enrolled.

Average high school GPA	2.5	SAT verbal scores above 500	N/R
SAT math scores above 500	N/R	ACT above 18	N/R
1998 freshmen returning in 1999	80%		

Application *Option:* deferred entrance. *Application fee:* $50. *Required:* high school transcript; interview.
Standardized tests *Admission: Recommended:* SAT I, ACT, SAT I and SAT II or ACT.
Significant dates *Application deadlines:* 10/2 (freshmen), rolling (transfers). *Financial aid deadline:* continuous.
Freshman Application Contact
Ms. Rufina Butler, Admissions Manager, Colorado Technical University Denver Campus, 5775 DTC Boulevard, Suite 100, Greenwood Village, CO 80111. **Phone:** 303-694-6600 Ext. 130. **E-mail:** ctudenver@coloradotech.edu
Visit CollegeQuest.com for information on majors offered and athletics. College video and electronic viewbook available at CollegeQuest.com.

COMMONWEALTH INTERNATIONAL UNIVERSITY
Colorado—See Education America–Denver Campus

DENVER INSTITUTE OF TECHNOLOGY
Colorado—See Westwood College of Technology

DENVER TECHNICAL COLLEGE
Denver, Colorado

- **Proprietary**, comprehensive, founded 1945
- **Degrees** associate, bachelor's, and master's
- **Urban** 1-acre campus
- **Coed**
- **Moderately difficult** entrance level
- **$7600 tuition** and fees

Expenses (1999–2000) *Tuition:* full-time $7600; part-time $100 per quarter hour. Full-time tuition and fees vary according to degree level and program. Part-time tuition and fees vary according to degree level and program.
Institutional Web site http://www.dtc.edu/
College life *Housing:* college housing not available.
Campus security Late-night transport-escort service.
Application *Option:* deferred entrance. *Application fee:* $30. *Required:* high school transcript; interview.
Standardized tests *Admission: Required:* TABE.
Admissions Office Contact
Denver Technical College, 925 South Niagara Street, Denver, CO 80224-1658.
Visit CollegeQuest.com for information on athletics.

Colorado

DENVER TECHNICAL COLLEGE AT COLORADO SPRINGS
Colorado Springs, Colorado

- **Proprietary**, 4-year, founded 1945
- **Degrees** associate and bachelor's
- **Urban** 3-acre campus with easy access to Denver
- **Coed**
- **Noncompetitive** entrance level

Institutional Web site http://www.dtc.edu/
College life *Housing:* college housing not available.
Campus security 24-hour patrols, late-night transport-escort service.
Application *Application fee:* $30. *Required:* high school transcript. *Required for some:* essay or personal statement; interview.
Standardized tests *Placement: Required:* TABE, Wonderlic aptitude test
Admissions Office Contact
Denver Technical College at Colorado Springs, 225 South Union Boulevard, Colorado Springs, CO 80910. **Fax:** 719-632-1909.
Visit CollegeQuest.com for information on athletics.

EDUCATION AMERICA– DENVER CAMPUS
Denver, Colorado

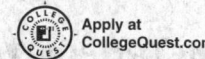

- **Proprietary**, 4-year
- **Degrees** associate and bachelor's
- **Suburban** 1-acre campus
- **Coed**
- **Noncompetitive** entrance level

Part of Education America Inc.
College life *Housing:* college housing not available.
Application *Options:* eApply at www.CollegeQuest.com, Common Application, early admission, deferred entrance. *Application fee:* $50.
Admissions Office Contact
Education America–Denver Campus, 7350 North Broadway, Denver, CO 80221. **Toll-free phone:** 800-999-5181. **Fax:** 303-426-0641.
Visit CollegeQuest.com for information on athletics.

FORT LEWIS COLLEGE
Durango, Colorado

- **State-supported**, 4-year, founded 1911
- **Degree** bachelor's
- **Small-town** 350-acre campus
- **Coed**, 4,357 undergraduate students, 90% full-time, 48% women, 52% men
- **Moderately difficult** entrance level
- **19:1** student-to-undergraduate faculty ratio
- **25% graduate** in 6 years or less
- **$2219 tuition** and fees (in-state); $8671 (out-of-state)
- **$4550 average financial aid** package, $13,432 average indebtedness upon graduation, $11.1 million endowment

Part of Colorado State University System.
Students *Undergraduates:* Students come from 50 states and territories, 14 other countries. *The most frequently chosen baccalaureate fields are:* business/marketing, English, social sciences and history.

From out-of-state	33%	Reside on campus	35%
Age 25 or older	20%	International students	1%
African Americans	1%	Asian Americans/Pacific Islanders	1%
Hispanic Americans	4%	Native Americans	15%

Faculty 244 (70% full-time).
Expenses (1999–2000) *One-time required fee:* $45. *Tuition, state resident:* full-time $1676; part-time $102 per credit hour. *Tuition, nonresident:* full-time $8128; part-time $506 per credit hour. *Required fees:* full-time $543; $51 per term part-time. Full-time tuition and fees vary according to reciprocity agreements. Part-time tuition and fees vary according to course load. *College room and board:* $4452; *room only:* $2270. Room and board charges vary according to board plan and housing facility. *Waivers:* minority students and employees or children of employees.
Library John F. Reed Library. *Operations spending 1999–2000:* $1.4 million. *Collection:* 189,265 titles, 2,742 serial subscriptions, 3,600 audiovisual materials.
College life *Housing:* on-campus residence required in freshman year. *Option:* coed. *Most popular organizations:* business club, AISES (American Indian Science and Engineering Club), sociology club, chemistry club, computer science club.
Campus security 24-hour emergency response devices and patrols, late-night transport-escort service.
After graduation 50 organizations recruited on campus 1997–98. 75% of class of 1998 had job offers within 6 months. *Career center:* 2 full-time personnel. Services include job fairs, resume preparation, interview workshops, resume referral, career/interest testing, career counseling, careers library, job bank, job interviews. *Graduate education:* 20% of class of 1999 went directly to graduate and professional school.
Freshmen

Average high school GPA	2.85	SAT verbal scores above 500	45%
SAT math scores above 500	47%	ACT above 18	73%
From top 10% of their h.s. class	17%	From top quarter	30%
From top half	47%	1998 freshmen returning in 1999	57%

Application *Options:* eApply at www.CollegeQuest.com, electronic application, deferred entrance. *Application fee:* $20. *Required:* high school transcript; minimum 2.0 GPA. *Recommended:* essay or personal statement; letters of recommendation.
Standardized tests *Admission: Required:* SAT I or ACT.
Significant dates *Application deadlines:* 8/1 (freshmen), 8/1 (transfers). *Financial aid deadline priority date:* 2/15.
Freshman Application Contact
Mr. Harlan Steinle, Vice President of Admission, Fort Lewis College, 1000 Rim Drive, Durango, CO 81301-3999. **Phone:** 970-247-7184. **Fax:** 970-247-7179. **E-mail:** steinle_h@fortlewis.edu
Visit CollegeQuest.com for information on majors offered and athletics. College video and electronic viewbook available at CollegeQuest.com.

INTERNATIONAL UNIVERSITY
Colorado—See Jones International University

ITT TECHNICAL INSTITUTE
Thornton, Colorado

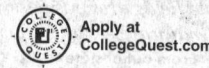

- **Proprietary**, primarily 2-year, founded 1984
- **Degrees** associate and bachelor's
- **Suburban** 2-acre campus with easy access to Denver
- **Coed**
- **Minimally difficult** entrance level
- **$9190 tuition** and fees

Part of ITT Educational Services, Inc.
Admissions Office Contact
ITT Technical Institute, 500 East 84th Avenue, Suite B12, Thornton, CO 80229. **Toll-free phone:** 800-395-4488. **Fax:** 303-288-8166.
Visit CollegeQuest.com for information on majors offered and athletics. College video available at CollegeQuest.com.

JONES INTERNATIONAL UNIVERSITY
Englewood, Colorado

- **Independent**, upper-level, founded 1995
- **Degrees** bachelor's and master's
- **Coed**, 18 undergraduate students, 100% full-time, 50% women, 50% men
- **Noncompetitive** entrance level
- **$3750 tuition** and fees

Colorado

Jones International University (continued)
- **$5 million endowment**

As the first fully online accredited university, Jones International University (JIU) offers credit and noncredit courses, and certificate and undergraduate and graduate degree programs completely online. To learn more about JIU's content-rich, highly focused programs, visit the Web site (www.jonesinternational.edu) or call 800-811-5663 (toll-free).

Students *Undergraduates:* The most frequently chosen baccalaureate field is: business/marketing. *Graduate:* 96 in graduate degree programs.

From out-of-state	99%	Age 25 or older	100%
African Americans	11%		

Faculty 38 (3% full-time).
Expenses (1999–2000) *Tuition:* full-time $3600; part-time $600 per course. *Required fees:* full-time $150; $25 per course. *Payment plan:* guaranteed tuition.
College life *Housing:* college housing not available.
Application *Options:* Common Application, electronic application, deferred entrance. *Application fee:* $75.
Significant dates *Application deadline:* rolling (transfers).
Freshman Application Contact
Ms. Gloria Brown, Admissions Coordinator, Jones International University, 9697 East Mineral Avenue, Englewood, CO 80112. **Phone:** 303-784-8048. **Toll-free phone:** 800-811-5663. **Fax:** 303-784-8547. **E-mail:** info@international.edu
Visit CollegeQuest.com for information on majors offered and athletics. Electronic viewbook available at CollegeQuest.com.

MESA STATE COLLEGE
Grand Junction, Colorado

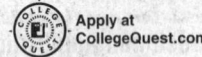 Apply at CollegeQuest.com

- **State-supported**, comprehensive, founded 1925
- **Degrees** associate, bachelor's, and master's
- **Small-town** 42-acre campus
- **Coed**, 4,845 undergraduate students, 77% full-time, 55% women, 45% men
- **Minimally difficult** entrance level, 94% of applicants were admitted
- **19:1 student-to-undergraduate faculty ratio**
- **63% graduate** in 6 years or less
- **$2123 tuition** and fees (in-state); $6512 (out-of-state)

Part of State Colleges in Colorado.
Students *Undergraduates:* 3,723 full-time, 1,122 part-time. Students come from 46 states and territories. *The most frequently chosen baccalaureate fields are:* business/marketing, psychology, social sciences and history. *Graduate:* 40 in graduate degree programs.

From out-of-state	9%	Reside on campus	18%
Age 25 or older	31%	Transferred in	7%
International students	1%	African Americans	1%
Asian Americans/Pacific Islanders	1%	Hispanic Americans	7%
Native Americans	1%		

Faculty 301 (68% full-time), 60% with terminal degrees.
Expenses (1999–2000) *Tuition, state resident:* full-time $1577; part-time $79 per credit hour. *Tuition, nonresident:* full-time $5966; part-time $298 per credit hour. *Required fees:* full-time $546; $26 per credit hour. Full-time tuition and fees vary according to course load. *College room and board:* $5048; room only: $2438. Room and board charges vary according to board plan and housing facility. *Waivers:* senior citizens and employees or children of employees.
Library John U. Tomlinson Library. *Operations spending 1999–2000:* $1.3 million. *Collection:* 329,681 titles, 1,010 serial subscriptions, 25,578 audiovisual materials.
College life *Housing:* on-campus residence required through sophomore year. *Option:* coed. *Most popular organizations:* Environmental Club, Student Body Association, KMSA Radio Station, Rodeo Club, Campus Residents Association.
Campus security 24-hour emergency response devices and patrols, late-night transport-escort service, controlled dormitory access.

After graduation 65 organizations recruited on campus 1997–98. *Career center:* 2 full-time, 3 part-time personnel. Services include job fairs, resume preparation, career/interest testing, career counseling, job interviews.
Freshmen 1,940 applied, 1,823 admitted, 1,044 enrolled.

Average high school GPA	3.2	SAT verbal scores above 500	50%
SAT math scores above 500	51%	ACT above 18	77%
From top 10% of their h.s. class	18%	From top quarter	32%
From top half	70%	1998 freshmen returning in 1999	60%

Application *Options:* eApply at www.CollegeQuest.com, Common Application, early admission, deferred entrance. *Application fee:* $30. *Required:* high school transcript; minimum 2.0 GPA. *Required for some:* 1 letter of recommendation; interview.
Standardized tests *Admission: Required:* SAT I or ACT.
Significant dates *Application deadlines:* 8/15 (freshmen), 8/15 (transfers). *Financial aid deadline priority date:* 3/1.
Freshman Application Contact
Mr. Mike Poll, Associate Director, Admissions and Recruitment, Mesa State College, PO Box 2647, Grand Junction, CO 81502-2647. **Phone:** 970-248-1875. **Toll-free phone:** 800-982-MESA. **Fax:** 970-248-1973. **E-mail:** admissions@mesastate.edu
Visit CollegeQuest.com for information on majors offered and athletics. College video available at CollegeQuest.com.

METROPOLITAN STATE COLLEGE OF DENVER
Denver, Colorado

- **State-supported**, 4-year, founded 1963
- **Degree** bachelor's
- **Urban** 175-acre campus
- **Coed**, 16,399 undergraduate students, 56% full-time, 57% women, 43% men
- **Minimally difficult** entrance level, 86% of applicants were admitted
- **20:1 student-to-undergraduate faculty ratio**
- **19.8% graduate** in 6 years or less
- **$2112 tuition** and fees (in-state); $7433 (out-of-state)
- **$6299 average financial aid** package, $23,000 average indebtedness upon graduation, $1.3 million endowment

Part of State Colleges in Colorado.
Students *Undergraduates:* 9,181 full-time, 7,218 part-time. Students come from 35 states and territories, 125 other countries. *The most frequently chosen baccalaureate fields are:* business/marketing, protective services/public administration, social sciences and history.

From out-of-state	2%	Age 25 or older	46%
Transferred in	9%	International students	1%
African Americans	6%	Asian Americans/Pacific Islanders	4%
Hispanic Americans	13%	Native Americans	1%

Faculty 1,033 (37% full-time).
Expenses (1999–2000) *Tuition, state resident:* full-time $1718; part-time $72 per semester hour. *Tuition, nonresident:* full-time $7039; part-time $293 per semester hour. *Required fees:* full-time $394; $103 per term part-time. Full-time tuition and fees vary according to course load and location. Part-time tuition and fees vary according to course load and location. *Payment plan:* deferred payment. *Waivers:* senior citizens.
Library Auraria Library. *Operations spending 1999–2000:* $3.1 million. *Collection:* 790,173 titles, 4,690 serial subscriptions.
College life *Housing:* college housing not available. *Most popular organizations:* Political Science Association, Accounting Students Organization, Christian Students Organization, LGBTA, Golden Key National Honor Society.
Campus security 24-hour emergency response devices and patrols, late-night transport-escort service.
After graduation *Career center:* 4 full-time personnel. Services include job fairs, resume preparation, interview workshops, resume referral, career/interest testing, career counseling, careers library, job bank, job interviews.

Freshmen 3,331 applied, 2,880 admitted, 1,807 enrolled.

SAT verbal scores above 500	39%	SAT math scores above 500	39%
ACT above 18	67%	From top 10% of their h.s. class	6%
From top quarter	8%	From top half	38%
1998 freshmen returning in 1999	58%		

Application *Options:* Common Application, deferred entrance. *Application fee:* $25. *Required:* high school transcript. *Required for some:* essay or personal statement; letters of recommendation. *Recommended:* minimum 2.0 GPA.

Standardized tests *Admission: Required for some:* SAT I or ACT.

Significant dates *Application deadlines:* 8/1 (freshmen), rolling (transfers). *Financial aid deadline priority date:* 2/15.

Freshman Application Contact
Ms. Miriam Tapia, Assistant Director, Metropolitan State College of Denver, PO Box 173362, Campus Box 16, Denver, CO 80217-3362. **Phone:** 303-556-2615. **Fax:** 303-556-6345.

Visit CollegeQuest.com for information on majors offered and athletics. College video available at CollegeQuest.com.

NAROPA UNIVERSITY
Boulder, Colorado

- **Independent**, comprehensive, founded 1974
- **Degrees** bachelor's, master's, and post-master's certificates
- **Urban** 4-acre campus with easy access to Denver
- **Coed**, 377 undergraduate students, 80% full-time, 66% women, 34% men
- **Moderately difficult** entrance level, 73% of applicants were admitted
- **12:1** student-to-undergraduate faculty ratio
- **$12,867 tuition** and fees
- **$19,816 average indebtedness** upon graduation, $2.6 million endowment

Students *Undergraduates:* 301 full-time, 76 part-time. Students come from 39 states and territories, 10 other countries. *The most frequently chosen baccalaureate fields are:* psychology, natural resources/environmental science, visual/performing arts. *Graduate:* 589 in graduate degree programs.

From out-of-state	47%	Age 25 or older	37%
Transferred in	30%	International students	5%
African Americans	0.3%	Asian Americans/Pacific Islanders	2%
Hispanic Americans	2%	Native Americans	1%

Faculty 201 (18% full-time).

Expenses (1999–2000) *Tuition:* full-time $12,300; part-time $410 per semester hour. *Required fees:* full-time $567; $284 per term part-time. Full-time tuition and fees vary according to course load. Part-time tuition and fees vary according to course load. *Payment plans:* tuition prepayment, installment, deferred payment. *Waivers:* employees or children of employees.

Library Allen Ginsberg Library. *Operations spending 1999–2000:* $94,760. *Collection:* 29,700 titles, 109 serial subscriptions, 11,916 audiovisual materials.

College life *Housing: Option:* coed. *Most popular organizations:* Student Union of Naropa (SUN), Garuda Theater, Student Union for Ethnic Inclusion, Diversity Awareness Working Group, Students for a Free Tibet.

After graduation *Career center:* 1 part-time personnel. Services include job fairs, resume preparation, career counseling, careers library, job bank.

Freshmen 67 applied, 49 admitted, 93 enrolled.

SAT verbal scores above 500	N/R	SAT math scores above 500	N/R
ACT above 18	N/R		

Application *Option:* deferred entrance. *Application fee:* $35. *Required:* essay or personal statement; high school transcript; 2 letters of recommendation; interview.

Significant dates *Application deadlines:* rolling (freshmen), rolling (transfers). *Financial aid deadline priority date:* 3/1.

Freshman Application Contact
Mr. Andrew Lopuszynski, Admissions Counselor, Naropa University, 2130 Arapahoe Avenue, Boulder, CO 80302-6697. **Phone:** 303-546-3511. **Toll-free phone:** 800-772-0410. **Fax:** 303-444-0410. **E-mail:** admissions@naropa.edu

Visit CollegeQuest.com for information on majors offered and athletics. Electronic viewbook available at CollegeQuest.com.

- *See page 2130 for a narrative description.*

NATIONAL AMERICAN UNIVERSITY
Colorado Springs, Colorado

- **Proprietary**, 4-year, founded 1941
- **Degrees** associate and bachelor's
- **Suburban** 1-acre campus with easy access to Denver
- **Coed**
- **Noncompetitive** entrance level

College life *Housing:* college housing not available.

Campus security Late-night transport-escort service.

Application *Option:* deferred entrance. *Application fee:* $25. *Required:* high school transcript; interview.

Standardized tests *Placement: Required for some:* ACT.

Admissions Office Contact
National American University, 2577 North Chelton Road, Colorado Springs, CO 80909. **Toll-free phone:** 888-471-4781. **Fax:** 719-471-4751. **E-mail:** nau@clsp.uswest.net

Visit CollegeQuest.com for information on athletics.

NATIONAL AMERICAN UNIVERSITY
Denver, Colorado

- **Proprietary**, 4-year, founded 1974
- **Degrees** associate and bachelor's
- **Urban** campus
- **Coed**
- **Noncompetitive** entrance level
- **$8880 tuition** and fees

Part of National College.

Expenses (1999–2000) *One-time required fee:* $50. *Tuition:* full-time $8880; part-time $185 per credit.

College life *Housing:* college housing not available.

Application *Option:* deferred entrance. *Application fee:* $25. *Required:* high school transcript.

Standardized tests *Placement: Recommended:* SAT I or ACT.

Admissions Office Contact
National American University, 1325 South Colorado Blvd, Suite 100, Denver, CO 80222. **Fax:** 303-758-6810.

Visit CollegeQuest.com for information on athletics.

NAZARENE BIBLE COLLEGE
Colorado Springs, Colorado

- **Independent**, 4-year, founded 1967, affiliated with Church of the Nazarene
- **Degrees** associate and bachelor's
- **Urban** 64-acre campus with easy access to Denver
- **Coed**, 462 undergraduate students, 44% full-time, 29% women, 71% men
- **Noncompetitive** entrance level, 100% of applicants were admitted
- **16:1** student-to-undergraduate faculty ratio
- **29% graduate** in 6 years or less
- **$5760 tuition** and fees

Students *Undergraduates:* 201 full-time, 261 part-time. Students come from 47 states and territories, 5 other countries. *The most frequently chosen baccalaureate field is:* philosophy.

Age 25 or older	90%	International students	2%
African Americans	3%	Asian Americans/Pacific Islanders	2%
Hispanic Americans	2%	Native Americans	0.4%

Faculty 33 (42% full-time), 55% with terminal degrees.

Expenses (1999–2000) *Tuition:* full-time $5550; part-time $110 per quarter hour. *Required fees:* full-time $210; $10 per term part-time. *Waivers:* employees or children of employees.

Library Trimble Library. *Collection:* 50,358 titles, 180 serial subscriptions.

College life *Housing:* college housing not available.

Campus security Student patrols.

Colorado

Nazarene Bible College (continued)

After graduation *Career center:* Services include career counseling.

Freshmen 20 applied, 20 admitted, 41 enrolled.

| SAT verbal scores above 500 | N/R | SAT math scores above 500 | N/R |
| ACT above 18 | N/R | 1998 freshmen returning in 1999 | 89% |

Application *Options:* Common Application, deferred entrance. *Application fee:* $20. *Required:* high school transcript; 2 letters of recommendation.

Significant dates *Application deadlines:* 8/31 (freshmen), 8/31 (transfers). *Financial aid deadline:* continuous.

Freshman Application Contact
Dr. David Phillips, Director of Admissions/Public Relations, Nazarene Bible College, 1111 Academy Park Loop, Colorado Springs, CO 80910-3704. **Phone:** 719-596-5110 Ext. 167. **Toll-free phone:** 800-873-3873. **Fax:** 719-550-9437.

Visit CollegeQuest.com for information on majors offered and athletics. College video available at CollegeQuest.com.

PLATT COLLEGE
Aurora, Colorado

- **Proprietary**, primarily 2-year, founded 1986
- **Degrees** associate and bachelor's
- **Suburban** campus
- **Coed**, 190 undergraduate students
- **Noncompetitive** entrance level

Faculty 19 (74% full-time).

Admissions Office Contact
Platt College, 3100 South Parker Road, Suite 200, Aurora, CO 80014-3141.

Visit CollegeQuest.com for information on majors offered and athletics.

REGIS UNIVERSITY
Denver, Colorado

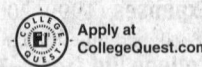 Apply at CollegeQuest.com

- **Independent Roman Catholic (Jesuit)**, comprehensive, founded 1877
- **Degrees** bachelor's and master's
- **Suburban** 90-acre campus
- **Coed**, 1,022 undergraduate students
- **Moderately difficult** entrance level, 84% of applicants were admitted
- **44% graduate** in 6 years or less
- **$16,670 tuition** and fees
- **$15,602 average financial aid** package, $24.2 million endowment

The Regis Guarantee ensures that entering freshmen will graduate in 4 years—or take the additional course work at no charge. The Learn and Earn Program offers every new freshman the opportunity to work on campus to gain valuable experience and money to help defray expenses. These programs, and its 123-year history of offering high-quality, value-oriented Jesuit education, make Regis a leader in the Rocky Mountain region.

Students *Undergraduates:* Students come from 40 states and territories, 11 other countries.

From out-of-state	39%	Age 25 or older	7%
International students	3%	African Americans	2%
Asian Americans/Pacific Islanders	3%	Hispanic Americans	8%
Native Americans	0.5%		

Faculty 108 (63% full-time).

Expenses (1999–2000) *Comprehensive fee:* $23,370 includes full-time tuition ($16,500), mandatory fees ($170), and room and board ($6700). *College room only:* $3900. Room and board charges vary according to board plan and housing facility. *Part-time tuition:* $515 per semester hour. *Part-time fees:* $60 per term part-time. *Payment plan:* deferred payment. *Waivers:* adult students, senior citizens, and employees or children of employees.

Library Dayton Memorial Library. *Operations spending 1999–2000:* $1.6 million. *Collection:* 430,514 titles, 7,850 serial subscriptions, 104,887 audiovisual materials.

College life *Housing:* on-campus residence required in freshman year. *Option:* coed. *Most popular organizations:* Programming Activities Council, hall governing boards, Student Executive Board, Regis Outdoor Club, Rugby Club.

Campus security 24-hour emergency response devices and patrols, student patrols, late-night transport-escort service, controlled dormitory access.

After graduation 50 organizations recruited on campus 1997–98. 90% of class of 1998 had job offers within 6 months. *Career center:* 2 full-time, 2 part-time personnel. Services include job fairs, resume preparation, interview workshops, resume referral, career/interest testing, career counseling, careers library, job bank, job interviews. *Graduate education:* 15% of class of 1999 went directly to graduate and professional school.

Freshmen 1,327 applied, 1,117 admitted. 3 class presidents, 8 valedictorians, 1 student government officer.

Average high school GPA	3.12	SAT verbal scores above 500	73%
SAT math scores above 500	66%	ACT above 18	97%
From top 10% of their h.s. class	21%	From top quarter	47%
From top half	70%	1998 freshmen returning in 1999	79%

Application *Options:* eApply at www.CollegeQuest.com, Common Application, deferred entrance. *Application fee:* $40. *Required:* essay or personal statement; high school transcript; minimum 2.2 GPA; 1 letter of recommendation. *Required for some:* 2 letters of recommendation; interview.

Standardized tests *Admission: Required:* SAT I or ACT. *Recommended:* SAT II Subject Tests.

Significant dates *Application deadlines:* 8/15 (freshmen), 8/15 (transfers). *Financial aid deadline priority date:* 3/5.

Freshman Application Contact
Director of Admissions, Regis University, 3333 Regis Boulevard, Denver, CO 80221-1099. **Phone:** 303-458-4900. **Toll-free phone:** 800-388-2366 Ext. 4900. **Fax:** 303-964-5534. **E-mail:** regisadm@regis.edu

Visit CollegeQuest.com for information on majors offered and athletics. College video available at CollegeQuest.com.

■ *See page 2320 for a narrative description.*

ROCKY MOUNTAIN COLLEGE OF ART & DESIGN
Denver, Colorado

- **Proprietary**, 4-year, founded 1963
- **Degree** bachelor's
- **Urban** 1-acre campus
- **Coed**, 394 undergraduate students, 79% full-time, 46% women, 54% men
- **Moderately difficult** entrance level, 93% of applicants were admitted
- **$15,510 tuition** and fees

Students *Undergraduates:* 310 full-time, 84 part-time. Students come from 32 states and territories, 5 other countries.

| Age 25 or older | 35% | Transferred in | 13% |

Faculty 51 (16% full-time).

Expenses (1999–2000) *Tuition:* full-time $15,480; part-time $430 per credit. *Required fees:* full-time $30; $15 per term part-time. *Payment plan:* installment. *Waivers:* employees or children of employees.

Library Rocky Mountain College of Art and Design Library. *Collection:* 6,287 titles, 65 serial subscriptions.

College life *Housing:* college housing not available.

After graduation 20 organizations recruited on campus 1997–98. 87% of class of 1998 had job offers within 6 months. *Career center:* 1 full-time personnel. Services include job fairs, resume preparation, interview workshops, career counseling, careers library, job bank, job interviews. *Graduate education:* 3% of class of 1999 went directly to graduate and professional school: 3% graduate arts and sciences.

Freshmen 99 applied, 92 admitted, 80 enrolled.

| SAT verbal scores above 500 | N/R | SAT math scores above 500 | N/R |
| ACT above 18 | N/R | | |

Application *Options:* Common Application, deferred entrance. *Application fee:* $50. *Required:* essay or personal statement; high school transcript; minimum 2.0 GPA. *Recommended:* 1 letter of recommendation; interview; portfolio.

Standardized tests *Admission: Required for some:* SAT I and SAT II or ACT.

Significant dates *Application deadlines:* rolling (freshmen), rolling (transfers). *Financial aid deadline priority date:* 3/1.

Colorado

Freshman Application Contact
Ms. Amy Williams, Assistant Director of Admissions, Rocky Mountain College of Art & Design, 6875 East Evans Avenue, Denver, CO 80224-2329. **Phone:** 303-753-6046. **Toll-free phone:** 800-888-ARTS. **Fax:** 303-759-4970. **E-mail:** admit@rmcad.edu
Visit CollegeQuest.com for information on majors offered and athletics.

TEIKYO LORETTO HEIGHTS UNIVERSITY
Denver, Colorado

Admissions Office Contact
Teikyo Loretto Heights University, 3001 South Federal Boulevard, Denver, CO 80236-2711.

UNITED STATES AIR FORCE ACADEMY
Colorado Springs, Colorado

- **Federally supported**, 4-year, founded 1954
- **Degree** bachelor's
- **Suburban** 18,000-acre campus with easy access to Denver
- **Coed**, 4,161 undergraduate students, 100% full-time, 16% women, 84% men
- **Most difficult** entrance level, 20% of applicants were admitted
- **7:1** student-to-undergraduate faculty ratio
- **79.5% graduate** in 6 years or less
- **$0 comprehensive fee**

Students *Undergraduates:* 4,161 full-time. Students come from 54 states and territories, 22 other countries. *The most frequently chosen baccalaureate fields are:* engineering/engineering technologies, business/marketing, social sciences and history.

From out-of-state	95%	Reside on campus	100%
International students	1%	African Americans	5%
Asian Americans/Pacific Islanders	4%	Hispanic Americans	7%
Native Americans	1%		

Faculty 531 (100% full-time), 50% with terminal degrees.
Expenses (2000–2001) Tuition, room and board, and medical and dental care are provided by the U.S. government. Each cadet receives a salary from which to pay for uniforms, supplies, and personal expenses. Entering freshmen are required to deposit $2500 to defray the initial cost of uniforms and equipment.
Library United States Air Force Academy Library plus 2 others. *Collection:* 445,379 titles, 1,693 serial subscriptions, 4,458 audiovisual materials.
College life *Housing:* on-campus residence required through senior year. *Option:* coed. *Most popular organizations:* cadet ski club, choir, scuba club, aviation club, Drum and Bugle Corps.
Campus security 24-hour emergency response devices and patrols, late-night transport-escort service, self-defense education, well-lit campus.
After graduation 1 organization recruited on campus 1997–98. 100% of class of 1998 had job offers within 6 months. *Career center:* Services include careers library. *Major awards:* 1 Marshall scholar.
Freshmen 8,828 applied, 1,762 admitted, 1,282 enrolled. 175 National Merit Scholars, 159 class presidents, 106 valedictorians, 490 student government officers.

Average high school GPA	3.8	SAT verbal scores above 500	99%
SAT math scores above 500	100%	ACT above 18	N/R
From top 10% of their h.s. class	52%	From top quarter	86%
From top half	98%	1998 freshmen returning in 1999	89%

Application *Application fee:* $0. *Required:* essay or personal statement; high school transcript; interview; authorized nomination.
Standardized tests *Admission: Required:* SAT I or ACT.
Significant dates *Application deadlines:* 1/31 (freshmen), 1/31 (transfers). *Notification:* continuous until 5/15 (freshmen).
Freshman Application Contact
Mr. Rolland Stoneman, Associate Director of Admissions/Selections, United States Air Force Academy, HQ USAFA/RR 2304 Cadet Drive, Suite 200, USAF Academy, CO 80840-5025. **Phone:** 719-333-2520. **Toll-free phone:** 800-443-9266. **Fax:** 719-333-3012. **E-mail:** rr_webmail@usafa.af.mil

Visit CollegeQuest.com for information on majors offered and athletics. College video available at CollegeQuest.com.

■ *See page 2664 for a narrative description.*

UNIVERSITY OF COLORADO AT BOULDER
Boulder, Colorado

- **State-supported**, university, founded 1876
- **Degrees** bachelor's, master's, doctoral, and first professional
- **Suburban** 600-acre campus with easy access to Denver
- **Coed**, 21,781 undergraduate students, 92% full-time, 48% women, 52% men
- **Moderately difficult** entrance level, 85% of applicants were admitted
- **14:1** student-to-undergraduate faculty ratio
- **64% graduate** in 6 years or less
- **$3118 tuition** and fees (in-state); $15,898 (out-of-state)
- **$8470 average financial aid** package, $16,422 average indebtedness upon graduation, $161.3 million endowment

Part of University of Colorado System.
Students *Undergraduates:* 19,967 full-time, 1,814 part-time. Students come from 56 states and territories, 88 other countries. *The most frequently chosen baccalaureate fields are:* business/marketing, communications/communication technologies, social sciences and history. *Graduate:* 492 in professional programs, 5,221 in other graduate degree programs.

From out-of-state	31%	Reside on campus	26%
Age 25 or older	9%	Transferred in	6%
International students	2%	African Americans	2%
Asian Americans/Pacific Islanders	6%	Hispanic Americans	5%
Native Americans	1%		

Faculty 1,276 (89% full-time), 86% with terminal degrees.
Expenses (1999–2000) *One-time required fee:* $35. *Tuition, state resident:* full-time $2444; part-time $148 per credit. *Tuition, nonresident:* full-time $15,224. *Required fees:* full-time $674; $215 per term part-time. Full-time tuition and fees vary according to program. Part-time tuition and fees vary according to course load and program. *College room and board:* $5202; room only: $2728. Room and board charges vary according to board plan, housing facility, and location. *Payment plan:* deferred payment. *Waivers:* senior citizens.
Library Norlin Library plus 6 others. *Operations spending 1999–2000:* $16.2 million. *Collection:* 2.9 million titles, 25,300 serial subscriptions, 57,656 audiovisual materials.
College life *Housing:* on-campus residence required in freshman year. *Options:* coed, disabled students. *Social organizations:* national fraternities, national sororities, local sororities; 10% of eligible men and 13% of eligible women are members. *Most popular organizations:* University of Colorado Student Union (student government), ski and snowboard club, Environmental Center, AIESEC, Program Council.
Campus security 24-hour emergency response devices and patrols, student patrols, late-night transport-escort service, university police department.
After graduation 582 organizations recruited on campus 1997–98. *Career center:* 16 full-time, 6 part-time personnel. Services include job fairs, resume preparation, interview workshops, resume referral, career/interest testing, career counseling, careers library, job bank, job interviews. *Graduate education:* 18% of class of 1999 went directly to graduate and professional school: 6% graduate arts and sciences, 5% medicine, 3% engineering, 2% law, 1% business, 1% education. *Major awards:* 2 Fulbright Scholars.
Freshmen 14,617 applied, 12,386 admitted, 4,596 enrolled. 135 valedictorians.

Average high school GPA	3.41	SAT verbal scores above 500	85%
SAT math scores above 500	87%	ACT above 18	98%
From top 10% of their h.s. class	24%	From top quarter	57%
From top half	91%	1998 freshmen returning in 1999	84%

Application *Options:* electronic application, deferred entrance. *Preference* given to state residents. *Application fee:* $40. *Required:* essay or personal statement; high school transcript; minimum 2.0 GPA. *Required for some:* audition for music program. *Recommended:* minimum 3.0 GPA; letters of recommendation.

Colorado

University of Colorado at Boulder (continued)
Standardized tests *Admission: Required:* SAT I or ACT.
Significant dates *Application deadlines:* 2/15 (freshmen), 4/1 (transfers). *Notification:* continuous until 5/1 (freshmen). ***Financial aid deadline priority date:*** 4/1.
Freshman Application Contact
Admission Counselor, University of Colorado at Boulder, Campus Box 30, Boulder, CO 80309-0030. **Phone:** 303-492-6301. **Fax:** 303-492-7115. **E-mail:** apply@colorado.edu
Visit CollegeQuest.com for information on majors offered and athletics.

■ *See page 2714 for a narrative description.*

UNIVERSITY OF COLORADO AT COLORADO SPRINGS
Colorado Springs, Colorado

- **State-supported**, comprehensive, founded 1965
- **Degrees** bachelor's, master's, and doctoral
- **Suburban** 400-acre campus with easy access to Denver
- **Coed**, 4,776 undergraduate students, 74% full-time, 60% women, 40% men
- **Moderately difficult** entrance level, 78% of applicants were admitted
- **16:1 student-to-undergraduate faculty ratio**
- **28% graduate** in 6 years or less
- **$3191 tuition** and fees (in-state); $11,561 (out-of-state)
- **$5787 average financial aid** package, $15,067 average indebtedness upon graduation, $14.5 million endowment

Part of University of Colorado System.
Students *Undergraduates:* 3,533 full-time, 1,243 part-time. Students come from 44 states and territories, 26 other countries. *The most frequently chosen baccalaureate fields are:* business/marketing, communications/communication technologies, psychology. **Graduate:** 1,658 in graduate degree programs.

From out-of-state	14%	Reside on campus	12%
Age 25 or older	34%	International students	1%
African Americans	4%	Asian Americans/Pacific Islanders	6%
Hispanic Americans	9%	Native Americans	1%

Faculty 404 (51% full-time), 47% with terminal degrees.
Expenses (1999–2000) *One-time required fee:* $25. *Tuition, state resident:* full-time $2820; part-time $94 per credit. *Tuition, nonresident:* full-time $11,190; part-time $373 per credit. *Required fees:* full-time $371; $12 per credit; $371 per term part-time. Full-time tuition and fees vary according to program and student level. Part-time tuition and fees vary according to program and student level. *College room and board:* $5683. Room and board charges vary according to board plan and housing facility. *Payment plan:* deferred payment. *Waivers:* employees or children of employees.
Library University of Colorado at Colorado Springs Kraemer Family Library. *Operations spending 1999–2000:* $1.8 million. *Collection:* 361,280 titles, 2,205 serial subscriptions, 3,309 audiovisual materials.
College life *Housing: Options:* coed, men-only, women-only. *Social organizations:* local sororities; 1% of women are members. *Most popular organizations:* Business Club, Science Club, Ski Club, United Students of Color, psychology club.
Campus security 24-hour emergency response devices and patrols, student patrols, late-night transport-escort service, controlled dormitory access.
After graduation 106 organizations recruited on campus 1997–98. *Career center:* 1 part-time personnel. Services include job fairs, resume referral, career counseling, job bank.
Freshmen 1,989 applied, 1,548 admitted, 619 enrolled.

Average high school GPA	3.36	SAT verbal scores above 500	68%
SAT math scores above 500	71%	ACT above 18	90%
From top 10% of their h.s. class	12%	From top quarter	46%
From top half	76%	1998 freshmen returning in 1999	65%

Application *Options:* eApply at www.CollegeQuest.com, electronic application. *Preference* given to state residents. *Application fee:* $45. *Required:* high school transcript.
Standardized tests *Admission: Required:* SAT I or ACT.
Significant dates *Application deadlines:* 7/1 (freshmen), 7/1 (transfers). ***Financial aid deadline priority date:*** 4/1.
Freshman Application Contact
Mr. James Tidwell, Assistant Admissions Director, University of Colorado at Colorado Springs, PO Box 7150, Colorado Springs, CO 80933-7150. **Phone:** 719-262-3383. **Toll-free phone:** 800-990-8227 Ext. 3383. **E-mail:** admrec@mail.uccs.edu
Visit CollegeQuest.com for information on majors offered and athletics. Electronic viewbook available at CollegeQuest.com.

UNIVERSITY OF COLORADO AT DENVER
Denver, Colorado

- **State-supported**, university, founded 1912
- **Degrees** bachelor's, master's, and doctoral
- **Urban** 171-acre campus
- **Coed**, 5,993 undergraduate students, 63% full-time, 54% women, 46% men
- **Moderately difficult** entrance level, 76% of applicants were admitted
- **14:1 student-to-undergraduate faculty ratio**
- **34% graduate** in 6 years or less
- **$2418 tuition** and fees (in-state); $11,544 (out-of-state)
- **$5268 average financial aid** package, $15,275 average indebtedness upon graduation, $9.2 million endowment

Part of University of Colorado System.
Students *Undergraduates:* 3,788 full-time, 2,205 part-time. Students come from 36 states and territories, 57 other countries. *The most frequently chosen baccalaureate fields are:* business/marketing, psychology, social sciences and history. **Graduate:** 5,721 in graduate degree programs.

From out-of-state	3%	Age 25 or older	42%
Transferred in	16%	International students	4%
African Americans	5%	Asian Americans/Pacific Islanders	10%
Hispanic Americans	12%	Native Americans	2%

Faculty 803 (60% full-time).
Expenses (1999–2000) *One-time required fee:* $25. *Tuition, state resident:* full-time $2068; part-time $126 per semester hour. *Tuition, nonresident:* full-time $11,194; part-time $672 per semester hour. *Required fees:* full-time $350; $3 per semester hour; $130 per term part-time. Full-time tuition and fees vary according to program. Part-time tuition and fees vary according to course load and program. *Payment plans:* installment, deferred payment. *Waivers:* employees or children of employees.
Library Auraria Library. *Operations spending 1999–2000:* $6 million. *Collection:* 553,821 titles, 4,690 serial subscriptions.
College life *Housing:* college housing not available. *Most popular organizations:* American Marketing Club, Psi Chi Honor Society, Model United Nations, Pre-Health Careers Club, Snow Bashers.
Campus security 24-hour emergency response devices and patrols, student patrols, late-night transport-escort service.
After graduation 35 organizations recruited on campus 1997–98. *Career center:* 11 full-time, 9 part-time personnel. Services include job fairs, resume preparation, resume referral, career/interest testing, career counseling, careers library, job bank, job interviews.
Freshmen 1,122 applied, 855 admitted, 454 enrolled.

Average high school GPA	3.29	SAT verbal scores above 500	62%
SAT math scores above 500	67%	ACT above 18	83%
From top 10% of their h.s. class	18%	From top quarter	57%
From top half	84%	1998 freshmen returning in 1999	73%

Application *Options:* Common Application, electronic application, deferred entrance. *Application fee:* $40. *Required:* high school transcript; minimum 2.5 GPA.
Standardized tests *Admission: Required:* SAT I or ACT.
Significant dates *Application deadlines:* 7/22 (freshmen), 7/22 (transfers). ***Financial aid deadline priority date:*** 3/1.
Freshman Application Contact
Ms. Alice Holman, Associate Director of Admissions, University of Colorado at Denver, PO Box 173364, Campus Box 167, Denver, CO 80217-3364. **Phone:** 303-556-2275. **Fax:** 303-556-4838. **E-mail:** admissions@castle.cudenver.edu
Visit CollegeQuest.com for information on majors offered and athletics.

Colorado

UNIVERSITY OF COLORADO HEALTH SCIENCES CENTER
Denver, Colorado

- **State-supported**, upper-level, founded 1883
- **Degrees** bachelor's, master's, doctoral, first professional, post-master's, and first professional certificates
- **Urban** 40-acre campus
- **Coed**, 513 undergraduate students, 100% full-time, 80% women, 20% men
- **Moderately difficult** entrance level, 31% of applicants were admitted
- **$6276 tuition** and fees (in-state); $17,429 (out-of-state)
- **$103.6 million endowment**

Part of University of Colorado System.

Students *Undergraduates: The most frequently chosen baccalaureate field is:* health professions and related sciences.

From out-of-state	9%	International students	1%
African Americans	4%	Asian Americans/Pacific Islanders	15%
Hispanic Americans	8%	Native Americans	1%

Faculty 1,700.

Expenses (1999–2000) *Tuition, state resident:* full-time $6101; part-time $151 per credit hour. *Tuition, nonresident:* full-time $17,254; part-time $514 per credit hour. *Required fees:* full-time $175. Full-time tuition and fees vary according to course level and program. Part-time tuition and fees vary according to course level and program. *Payment plans:* installment, deferred payment.

Library Denison Library plus 1 other. *Operations spending 1999–2000:* $2.8 million. *Collection:* 250,000 titles, 1,650 serial subscriptions.

College life *Housing:* college housing not available.

Campus security 24-hour patrols, late-night transport-escort service.

After graduation *Career center:* Services include career counseling.

Application Preference given to state residents.

Significant dates *Application deadline:* 7/1 (transfers). *Financial aid deadline priority date:* 3/15.

Freshman Application Contact
Dr. David P. Sorenson, Director of Admissions, University of Colorado Health Sciences Center, 4200 East Ninth Avenue, Denver, CO 80262. **Phone:** 303-315-7676. **Fax:** 303-315-3358. **E-mail:** stuserv@mongo.uchsc.edu

Visit CollegeQuest.com for information on majors offered and athletics.

UNIVERSITY OF DENVER
Denver, Colorado

Apply at CollegeQuest.com

- **Independent**, university, founded 1864
- **Degrees** bachelor's, master's, doctoral, first professional, and first professional certificates
- **Suburban** 125-acre campus
- **Coed**, 3,715 undergraduate students, 86% full-time, 58% women, 42% men
- **Moderately difficult** entrance level, 82% of applicants were admitted
- **13:1 student-to-undergraduate faculty ratio**
- **67.75% graduate** in 6 years or less
- **$19,440 tuition** and fees
- **$137.2 million endowment**

Students *Undergraduates:* 3,200 full-time, 515 part-time. Students come from 52 states and territories, 54 other countries. *The most frequently chosen baccalaureate fields are:* business/marketing, communications/communication technologies, social sciences and history. *Graduate:* 1,020 in professional programs, 4,363 in other graduate degree programs.

From out-of-state	56%	Reside on campus	41%
Age 25 or older	16%	Transferred in	6%
International students	6%	African Americans	4%
Asian Americans/Pacific Islanders	5%	Hispanic Americans	6%
Native Americans	1%		

Faculty 835 (48% full-time).

Expenses (1999–2000) *Comprehensive fee:* $25,605 includes full-time tuition ($18,936), mandatory fees ($504), and room and board ($6165). Full-time tuition and fees vary according to class time, course load, and program. Room and board charges vary according to board plan and housing facility. *Part-time tuition:* $526 per quarter hour. *Part-time fees:* $54 per quarter hour. Part-time tuition and fees vary according to class time, course load, and program. *Payment plan:* deferred payment. *Waivers:* employees or children of employees.

Library Penrose Library. *Operations spending 1999–2000:* $5.9 million. *Collection:* 1.2 million titles, 5,788 serial subscriptions, 1,736 audiovisual materials.

College life *Housing:* on-campus residence required through sophomore year. *Option:* coed. *Social organizations:* national fraternities, national sororities; 24% of eligible men and 23% of eligible women are members. *Most popular organizations:* student government, club sports council, Denver University Programming Board, International Student Organization, Residence Hall Association.

Campus security 24-hour emergency response devices and patrols; late-night transport-escort service, controlled dormitory access, 24-hour locked residence hall entrances.

After graduation 242 organizations recruited on campus 1997–98. 67% of class of 1998 had job offers within 6 months. *Career center:* 9 full-time, 1 part-time personnel. Services include job fairs, resume preparation, interview workshops, resume referral, career/interest testing, career counseling, careers library, job bank, job interviews. *Graduate education:* 24% of class of 1999 went directly to graduate and professional school. *Major awards:* 3 Fulbright Scholars.

Freshmen 3,303 applied, 2,710 admitted, 834 enrolled.

Average high school GPA	3.41	SAT verbal scores above 500	81%
SAT math scores above 500	79%	ACT above 18	95%
From top 10% of their h.s. class	32%	From top quarter	57%
From top half	85%	1998 freshmen returning in 1999	84%

Application *Options:* eApply at www.CollegeQuest.com, Common Application, electronic application, early admission, deferred entrance. *Application fee:* $45. *Required:* essay or personal statement; high school transcript; 2 letters of recommendation. *Recommended:* minimum 2.0 GPA; interview.

Standardized tests *Admission: Required:* SAT I or ACT.

Significant dates *Application deadlines:* rolling (freshmen), rolling (transfers).

Freshman Application Contact
Mr. Morris Price, Associate Dean of Admission, University of Denver, University Park, Denver, CO 80208. **Phone:** 303-871-3373. **Toll-free phone:** 800-525-9495. **Fax:** 303-871-3301. **E-mail:** admission@du.edu

Visit CollegeQuest.com for information on majors offered and athletics. College video and electronic viewbook available at CollegeQuest.com.

UNIVERSITY OF NORTHERN COLORADO
Greeley, Colorado

- **State-supported**, university, founded 1890
- **Degrees** bachelor's, master's, and doctoral
- **Suburban** 240-acre campus with easy access to Denver
- **Coed**, 9,080 undergraduate students, 93% full-time, 59% women, 41% men
- **Moderately difficult** entrance level, 81% of applicants were admitted
- **21:1 student-to-undergraduate faculty ratio**
- **41.7% graduate** in 6 years or less
- **$2754 tuition** and fees (in-state); $9737 (out-of-state)

Students *Undergraduates:* 8,440 full-time, 640 part-time. Students come from 50 states and territories, 51 other countries. *The most frequently chosen baccalaureate fields are:* business/marketing, parks and recreation, social sciences and history. *Graduate:* 2,092 in graduate degree programs.

From out-of-state	12%	Reside on campus	31%
Age 25 or older	9%	Transferred in	9%
International students	1%	African Americans	2%
Asian Americans/Pacific Islanders	5%	Hispanic Americans	8%
Native Americans	1%		

Faculty 572 (74% full-time).

Expenses (1999–2000) *Tuition, state resident:* full-time $2014; part-time $112 per hour. *Tuition, nonresident:* full-time $8997; part-time $500 per hour. *Required fees:* full-time $740; $38 per hour. Full-time tuition and fees vary according to course load. *College room and board:* $4796; room only: $2286.

Peterson's Guide to Four-Year Colleges 2001   www.petersons.com   151

Colorado

University of Northern Colorado *(continued)*
Room and board charges vary according to board plan and housing facility. *Payment plan:* deferred payment. *Waivers:* employees or children of employees.
Library James A. Michener Library plus 2 others. *Operations spending 1999–2000:* $3.7 million. *Collection:* 711,965 titles, 3,219 serial subscriptions, 40,224 audiovisual materials.
College life *Housing:* on-campus residence required in freshman year. *Options:* coed, women-only. *Social organizations:* national fraternities, national sororities; 5% of eligible men and 4% of eligible women are members.
Campus security 24-hour emergency response devices and patrols, student patrols, late-night transport-escort service, controlled dormitory access.
After graduation 385 organizations recruited on campus 1997–98. 84% of class of 1998 had job offers within 6 months. *Career center:* 9 full-time, 6 part-time personnel. Services include job fairs, resume preparation, interview workshops, resume referral, career/interest testing, career counseling, careers library, job bank, job interviews. *Graduate education:* 11% of class of 1999 went directly to graduate and professional school.
Freshmen 6,964 applied, 5,662 admitted, 2,177 enrolled. 34 valedictorians.

Average high school GPA	3.18	SAT verbal scores above 500	57%
SAT math scores above 500	57%	ACT above 18	90%
From top 10% of their h.s. class	12%	From top quarter	35%
From top half	72%	1998 freshmen returning in 1999	67%

Application *Options:* Common Application, electronic application, early admission, deferred entrance. *Application fee:* $30. *Required:* high school transcript; minimum 2.8 GPA. *Required for some:* interview.
Standardized tests *Admission: Required:* SAT I or ACT.
Significant dates *Application deadlines:* rolling (freshmen), rolling (transfers). *Financial aid deadline priority date:* 3/1.
Freshman Application Contact
Mr. Gary O. Gullickson, Director of Admissions, University of Northern Colorado, Greeley, CO 80639. **Phone:** 970-351-2881. **E-mail:** unc@mail.unco.edu
Visit CollegeQuest.com for information on majors offered and athletics. College video available at CollegeQuest.com.

UNIVERSITY OF SOUTHERN COLORADO
Pueblo, Colorado

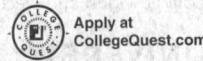 Apply at CollegeQuest.com

- **State-supported**, comprehensive, founded 1933
- **Degrees** bachelor's and master's
- **Suburban** 275-acre campus with easy access to Colorado Springs
- **Coed**, 4,167 undergraduate students, 80% full-time, 56% women, 44% men
- **Moderately difficult** entrance level, 84% of applicants were admitted
- **17:1 student-to-undergraduate faculty ratio**
- **25% graduate** in 6 years or less
- **$2307 tuition** and fees (in-state); $8947 (out-of-state)
- **$3850 average financial aid** package, $2.3 million endowment

Part of Colorado State University System.
Students *Undergraduates:* 3,334 full-time, 833 part-time. Students come from 44 states and territories, 37 other countries. *The most frequently chosen baccalaureate fields are:* business/marketing, engineering/engineering technologies, social sciences and history. *Graduate:* 669 in graduate degree programs.

Reside on campus	18%	Age 25 or older	35%
Transferred in	9%	International students	4%
African Americans	4%	Asian Americans/Pacific Islanders	2%
Hispanic Americans	26%	Native Americans	1%

Faculty 264 (63% full-time).
Expenses (1999–2000) *Tuition, state resident:* full-time $1808; part-time $90 per semester hour. *Tuition, nonresident:* full-time $8448; part-time $422 per semester hour. *Required fees:* full-time $499; $23 per semester hour. Full-time tuition and fees vary according to reciprocity agreements. Part-time tuition and fees vary according to reciprocity agreements. *College room and board:* $4768; room only: $2088. Room and board charges vary according to board plan and housing facility. *Payment plans:* installment, deferred payment. *Waivers:* senior citizens and employees or children of employees.
Library University of Southern Colorado Library. *Operations spending 1999–2000:* $1.1 million. *Collection:* 270,761 titles, 1,327 serial subscriptions, 16,862 audiovisual materials.
College life *Housing:* on-campus residence required in freshman year. *Option:* coed. *Social organizations:* national fraternities, national sororities, local fraternities, local sororities; 2% of eligible men and 1% of eligible women are members. *Most popular organizations:* Belmont Residence Hall Association, Associate Student Government, Hawaii Club, Medical Science Society, Student Social Worker's Association.
Campus security 24-hour emergency response devices and patrols, late-night transport-escort service, controlled dormitory access.
After graduation 97 organizations recruited on campus 1997–98. *Career center:* 3 full-time, 3 part-time personnel. Services include job fairs, resume preparation, interview workshops, resume referral, career/interest testing, career counseling, careers library, job bank, job interviews. *Graduate education:* 12% of class of 1999 went directly to graduate and professional school: 4% graduate arts and sciences, 2% business, 2% medicine, 1% dentistry, 1% engineering, 1% law, 1% veterinary medicine.
Freshmen 1,843 applied, 1,541 admitted, 646 enrolled.

Average high school GPA	3.08	SAT verbal scores above 500	49%
SAT math scores above 500	45%	ACT above 18	70%
From top 10% of their h.s. class	13%	From top quarter	34%
From top half	68%		

Application *Options:* eApply at www.CollegeQuest.com, Common Application, electronic application, deferred entrance. *Application fee:* $25. *Required:* high school transcript. *Required for some:* essay or personal statement; letters of recommendation.
Standardized tests *Admission: Required:* SAT I or ACT.
Significant dates *Application deadlines:* rolling (freshmen), rolling (transfers). *Financial aid deadline priority date:* 3/15.
Freshman Application Contact
Ms. Christie Kangas, Director of Admissions, University of Southern Colorado, 2200 Bonforte Boulevard, Pueblo, CO 81001-4901. **Phone:** 719-549-2461. **Toll-free phone:** 877-872-9653. **Fax:** 719-549-2419. **E-mail:** info@uscolo.edu
Visit CollegeQuest.com for information on majors offered and athletics. College video available at CollegeQuest.com.

WESTERN STATE COLLEGE OF COLORADO
Gunnison, Colorado

- **State-supported**, 4-year, founded 1901
- **Degree** bachelor's
- **Small-town** 381-acre campus
- **Coed**, 2,425 undergraduate students, 91% full-time, 41% women, 59% men
- **Moderately difficult** entrance level, 90% of applicants were admitted
- **18:1 student-to-undergraduate faculty ratio**
- **22.5% graduate** in 6 years or less
- **$2208 tuition** and fees (in-state); $7720 (out-of-state)
- **$9880 average financial aid** package, $12,500 average indebtedness upon graduation, $2.6 million endowment

Western is home to about 2,500 students pursuing undergraduate degrees in a range of liberal arts and science areas and compatible professional disciplines. Small classes afford students tremendous amounts of hands-on instruction from professors. The residential setting in the midst of the Rocky Mountains gives them ample opportunity for campus involvement and spectacular recreational activities. Visit the Western Web site at http://www.western.edu/welcome.html.

Part of State Colleges in Colorado.
Students *Undergraduates:* 2,212 full-time, 213 part-time. Students come from 49 states and territories. *The most frequently chosen baccalaureate fields are:* business/marketing, parks and recreation, social sciences and history.

Colorado

From out-of-state	29%	Reside on campus	41%
Age 25 or older	13%	Transferred in	9%
African Americans	1%	Asian Americans/Pacific Islanders	1%
Hispanic Americans	4%	Native Americans	1%

Faculty 150 (77% full-time).
Expenses (1999–2000) *Tuition, state resident:* full-time $1516; part-time $76 per credit. *Tuition, nonresident:* full-time $7028; part-time $351 per credit. *Required fees:* full-time $692; $23 per credit; $64 per term part-time. Full-time tuition and fees vary according to course load. Part-time tuition and fees vary according to course load. *College room and board:* $4890; room only: $2650. Room and board charges vary according to board plan and housing facility. *Payment plans:* installment, deferred payment. *Waivers:* senior citizens and employees or children of employees.
Library Savage Library. *Operations spending 1999–2000:* $704,573. *Collection:* 156,266 titles, 854 serial subscriptions, 4,537 audiovisual materials.
College life *Housing:* on-campus residence required in freshman year. *Options:* coed, men-only, women-only. *Social organizations:* national fraternities, local fraternities, local sororities. *Most popular organizations:* Mountain Search and Rescue Team, student government association, Rodeo Club, Wilderness Pursuits.
Campus security 24-hour emergency response devices and patrols, student patrols, late-night transport-escort service, controlled dormitory access.
After graduation 45 organizations recruited on campus 1997–98. 96% of class of 1998 had job offers within 6 months. *Career center:* 1 full-time, 1 part-time personnel. Services include job fairs, resume preparation, interview workshops, resume referral, career/interest testing, career counseling, careers library, job bank, job interviews. *Graduate education:* 12% of class of 1999 went directly to graduate and professional school.
Freshmen 1,596 applied, 1,436 admitted, 576 enrolled. 11 valedictorians.

Average high school GPA	2.95	SAT verbal scores above 500	52%
SAT math scores above 500	48%	ACT above 18	68%
From top 10% of their h.s. class	9%	From top quarter	22%
From top half	58%	1998 freshmen returning in 1999	56%

Application *Options:* Common Application, deferred entrance. *Application fee:* $25. *Required:* high school transcript. *Required for some:* essay or personal statement; 2 letters of recommendation; interview. *Recommended:* minimum 2.5 GPA.
Standardized tests *Admission: Required:* SAT I or ACT.
Significant dates *Application deadlines:* rolling (freshmen), rolling (transfers). *Financial aid deadline priority date:* 4/1.
Freshman Application Contact
Ms. Tonya Van Hee, Assistant Director, Western State College of Colorado, 600 North Adams Street, Gunnison, CO 81231. **Phone:** 970-943-2119. **Toll-free phone:** 800-876-5309. **Fax:** 970-943-7069. **E-mail:** discover@western.edu
Visit CollegeQuest.com for information on majors offered and athletics. College video and electronic viewbook available at CollegeQuest.com.

■ *See page 2958 for a narrative description.*

WESTWOOD COLLEGE OF TECHNOLOGY
Denver, Colorado

■ **Proprietary**, 4-year, founded 1953
■ **Degrees** associate and bachelor's
■ **Suburban** 11-acre campus
■ **Coed**, 1,925 undergraduate students, 54% full-time, 23% women, 77% men
■ **Moderately difficult** entrance level, 79% of applicants were admitted
■ **17:1 student-to-undergraduate faculty ratio**
■ **$8919 tuition** and fees

Students *Undergraduates:* 1,034 full-time, 891 part-time. Students come from 14 states and territories.

Age 25 or older 25%

Faculty 69, 7% with terminal degrees.
Expenses (1999–2000) *One-time required fee:* $50. *Tuition:* full-time $8919; part-time $388 per credit hour. Full-time tuition and fees vary according to course load, degree level, and program. Part-time tuition and fees vary according to course load, degree level, and program. *Payment plans:* installment, deferred payment. *Waivers:* employees or children of employees.
Library DIT Library. *Operations spending 1999–2000:* $26,950. *Collection:* 2,500 titles, 90 serial subscriptions.
College life *Housing:* college housing not available. *Most popular organizations:* student government, athletic club, American Institute of Graphic Arts, social club.
Campus security 24-hour emergency response devices.
After graduation 150 organizations recruited on campus 1997–98. 98% of class of 1998 had job offers within 6 months. *Career center:* 5 full-time personnel. Services include job fairs, resume preparation, resume referral, career/interest testing, career counseling, job bank, job interviews, career newspaper.
Freshmen 1,027 applied, 812 admitted, 719 enrolled.

| SAT verbal scores above 500 | N/R | SAT math scores above 500 | N/R |
| ACT above 18 | N/R | 1998 freshmen returning in 1999 | 22% |

Application *Option:* deferred entrance. *Application fee:* $100. *Required for some:* high school transcript. *Recommended:* interview.
Standardized tests *Admission: Required for some:* CPAt.
Significant dates *Application deadlines:* rolling (freshmen), rolling (transfers). *Financial aid deadline:* continuous.
Freshman Application Contact
Ms. Louisa Duley, New Student Coordinator, Westwood College of Technology, 7350 North Broadway, Denver, CO 80221-3653. **Phone:** 303-650-5050 Ext. 329. **Toll-free phone:** 800-992-5050. **Fax:** 303-426-1832.
Visit CollegeQuest.com for information on majors offered and athletics. College video available at CollegeQuest.com.

YESHIVA TORAS CHAIM TALMUDICAL SEMINARY
Denver, Colorado

Admissions Office Contact
Yeshiva Toras Chaim Talmudical Seminary, 1400 Quitman Street, Denver, CO 80204-1415. **Fax:** 303-623-5949.

Connecticut

CONNECTICUT

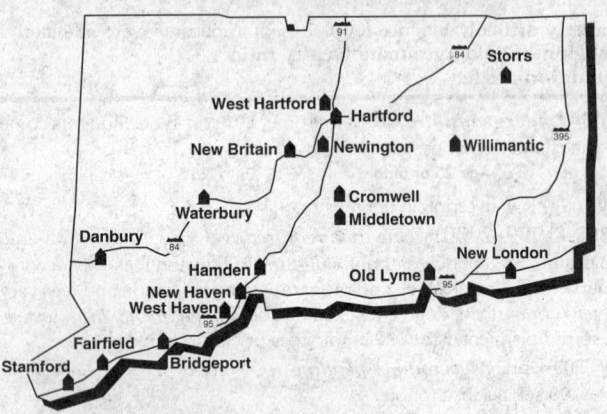

ALBERTUS MAGNUS COLLEGE
New Haven, Connecticut

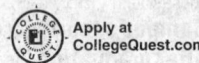 Apply at CollegeQuest.com

- **Independent Roman Catholic**, comprehensive, founded 1925
- **Degrees** associate, bachelor's, and master's
- **Suburban** 55-acre campus with easy access to New York City and Hartford
- **Coed**, 1,720 undergraduate students
- **Moderately difficult** entrance level, 92% of applicants were admitted
- **$14,343 tuition** and fees
- **$8000 average financial aid** package, $3.4 million endowment

Celebrating 75 years of liberal arts education, Albertus Magnus College is well known for its psychology and business programs as well as 46 other fields of study. The College offers extensive facilities and services, including a strong internship program and career planning. Students can visit the Web site at http://www.albertus.edu.

Students *Undergraduates:* Students come from 11 states and territories, 1 other country.

From out-of-state	2%	Reside on campus	60%
Age 25 or older	71%		

Expenses (1999–2000) *Comprehensive fee:* $20,855 includes full-time tuition ($13,908), mandatory fees ($435), and room and board ($6512). *Part-time tuition:* $1,738 per course. *Part-time fees:* $15 per term part-time. Part-time tuition and fees vary according to class time. *Payment plan:* installment. *Waivers:* senior citizens and employees or children of employees.

Library Rosary Hall. *Operations spending 1999–2000:* $221,593. *Collection:* 538 serial subscriptions, 817 audiovisual materials.

College life *Housing:* Options: coed, women-only. *Most popular organizations:* Student Government Association, College Drama, Minority Student Union.

Campus security 24-hour emergency response devices and patrols, late-night transport-escort service, controlled dormitory access.

After graduation 15 organizations recruited on campus 1997–98. *Career center:* 1 full-time personnel. Services include job fairs, resume preparation, resume referral, career counseling, careers library, job bank, job interviews.

Freshmen 310 applied, 286 admitted. 2 class presidents, 5 valedictorians, 12 student government officers.

Average high school GPA	2.87	SAT verbal scores above 500	50%
SAT math scores above 500	44%	ACT above 18	N/R
From top 10% of their h.s. class	16%	From top quarter	42%
From top half	64%	1998 freshmen returning in 1999	88%

Application *Options:* eApply at www.CollegeQuest.com, deferred entrance. *Application fee:* $35. *Required:* high school transcript; 1 letter of recommendation. *Required for some:* minimum 2.0 GPA. *Recommended:* minimum 2.0 GPA; interview.

Standardized tests *Admission: Required:* SAT I or ACT. *Recommended:* SAT II Subject Tests, SAT II: Writing Test.

Significant dates *Application deadlines:* rolling (freshmen), rolling (transfers). *Financial aid deadline priority date:* 2/15.

Freshman Application Contact
Ms. Allison Rowett-Sewell, Assistant Director of Admissions, Albertus Magnus College, 700 Prospect Street, New Haven, CT 06511-1189. **Phone:** 203-773-8501. **Toll-free phone:** 800-578-9160. **Fax:** 203-785-8652. **E-mail:** admissions@albertus.edu

Visit CollegeQuest.com for information on majors offered and athletics.

■ *See page 1142 for a narrative description.*

BETH BENJAMIN ACADEMY OF CONNECTICUT
Stamford, Connecticut

Admissions Office Contact
Beth Benjamin Academy of Connecticut, 132 Prospect Street, Stamford, CT 06901-1202.

CENTRAL CONNECTICUT STATE UNIVERSITY
New Britain, Connecticut

- **State-supported**, comprehensive, founded 1849
- **Degrees** bachelor's and master's
- **Suburban** 294-acre campus
- **Coed**, 9,264 undergraduate students
- **Moderately difficult** entrance level, 74% of applicants were admitted
- **16:1** student-to-undergraduate faculty ratio
- **45% graduate** in 6 years or less
- **$3772 tuition** and fees (in-state); $8384 (out-of-state)

Part of Connecticut State University System.

Students *Undergraduates:* Students come from 31 states and territories, 41 other countries. *The most frequently chosen baccalaureate fields are:* business/marketing, psychology, social sciences and history.

Reside on campus	31%	Age 25 or older	27%
International students	1%	African Americans	8%
Asian Americans/Pacific Islanders	3%	Hispanic Americans	6%
Native Americans	0.4%		

Faculty 829 (46% full-time), 38% with terminal degrees.

Expenses (1999–2000) *Tuition, state resident:* full-time $2062; part-time $160 per credit hour. *Tuition, nonresident:* full-time $6674; part-time $160 per credit hour. *Required fees:* full-time $1710; $43 per term part-time. Full-time tuition and fees vary according to class time, course level, and reciprocity agreements. Part-time tuition and fees vary according to class time and course level. *College room and board:* $5652. Room and board charges vary according to board plan. *Payment plans:* installment, deferred payment. *Waivers:* senior citizens and employees or children of employees.

Library Burritt Library plus 1 other. *Operations spending 1999–2000:* $3.8 million. *Collection:* 592,060 titles, 2,946 serial subscriptions, 4,402 audiovisual materials.

College life *Housing:* Option: coed. *Social organizations:* national fraternities, national sororities, local fraternities, local sororities; 1% of eligible men and 1% of eligible women are members. *Most popular organizations:* Inter-residence Council, student radio station, Program Council, Outing Club, NAACP.

Campus security 24-hour emergency response devices and patrols, student patrols, late-night transport-escort service.

After graduation 55 organizations recruited on campus 1997–98. 90% of class of 1998 had job offers within 6 months. *Career center:* 10 full-time, 2 part-time personnel. Services include job fairs, resume preparation, resume referral, career counseling, careers library, job bank, job interviews. **Graduate education:** 28% of class of 1999 went directly to graduate and professional school: 17% graduate arts and sciences, 6% education, 4% business, 1% engineering.

Freshmen 4,096 applied, 3,025 admitted.

SAT verbal scores above 500	40%	SAT math scores above 500	40%
ACT above 18	N/R	From top 10% of their h.s. class	4%
From top quarter	11%	From top half	31%
1998 freshmen returning in 1999	72%		

Application *Options:* Common Application, electronic application. *Application fee:* $40. *Required:* high school transcript; minimum 2.0 GPA. *Required for some:* interview. *Recommended:* minimum 3.0 GPA; 1 letter of recommendation.

Standardized tests *Admission: Required:* SAT I.

Significant dates *Application deadlines:* 5/1 (freshmen), 5/1 (transfers). *Notification:* continuous until 7/1 (freshmen). **Financial aid deadline:** 9/24. *Priority date:* 4/22.

Freshman Application Contact
Ms. Myrna Garcia-Bowen, Director of Admissions, Central Connecticut State University, 1615 Stanley Street, New Britain, CT 06050-4010. **Phone:** 860-832-2285. **Toll-free phone:** 800-755-2278. **Fax:** 860-832-2522. **E-mail:** admissions@ccsu.edu

Visit CollegeQuest.com for information on majors offered and athletics. College video available at CollegeQuest.com.

■ *See page 1394 for a narrative description.*

CHARTER OAK STATE COLLEGE
New Britain, Connecticut

- $155,725 endowment

Students *Undergraduates:* 1,429 part-time. Students come from 46 states and territories. *The most frequently chosen baccalaureate field is:* liberal arts/general studies.

From out-of-state	28%	Age 25 or older	98%
Transferred in	22%	International students	0.1%
African Americans	7%	Asian Americans/Pacific Islanders	2%
Hispanic Americans	4%	Native Americans	0.5%

Faculty 67, 90% with terminal degrees.

Expenses (1999–2000) Yearly fee of $318-$500 for state residents, $453-698 for nonresidents. *Payment plan:* installment.

College life *Housing:* college housing not available.

Campus security 24-hour emergency response devices.

Freshmen

SAT verbal scores above 500	N/R	SAT math scores above 500	N/R
ACT above 18	N/R		

Application *Options:* electronic application, deferred entrance. *Application fee:* $40.

Significant dates *Application deadline:* rolling (transfers). **Financial aid deadline:** continuous.

Freshman Application Contact
Mr. Harry White, Dean of Enrollment Management, Charter Oak State College, 55 Paul Manafort Drive, New Britain, CT 06053-2142. **Phone:** 860-832-3863. **Fax:** 860-832-3999. **E-mail:** info@mail.cocs.edu

Visit CollegeQuest.com for information on majors offered and athletics. Electronic viewbook available at CollegeQuest.com.

CONNECTICUT COLLEGE
New London, Connecticut

 Apply at CollegeQuest.com

- **Independent**, comprehensive, founded 1911
- **Degrees** bachelor's and master's
- **Suburban** 702-acre campus
- **Coed**, 1,645 undergraduate students, 97% full-time, 57% women, 43% men
- **Very difficult** entrance level, 39% of applicants were admitted
- **11:1 student-to-undergraduate faculty ratio**
- **$30,595 comprehensive fee**
- **$21,186 average financial aid** package, $17,280 average indebtedness upon graduation, $145.4 million endowment

Students *Undergraduates:* 1,603 full-time, 42 part-time. Students come from 38 states and territories, 51 other countries. *Graduate:* 56 in graduate degree programs.

From out-of-state	75%	Reside on campus	96%
Age 25 or older	3%	Transferred in	2%
International students	8%	African Americans	4%
Asian Americans/Pacific Islanders	2%	Hispanic Americans	3%
Native Americans	0.3%		

Faculty 177 (89% full-time), 75% with terminal degrees.

Expenses (1999–2000) Comprehensive fee: $30,595. *Part-time tuition:* $695 per course. Part-time tuition and fees vary according to program. *Payment plan:* installment. *Waivers:* employees or children of employees.

Library Charles Shain Library plus 1 other. *Collection:* 938,566 titles, 2,357 serial subscriptions, 142,303 audiovisual materials.

College life *Housing:* on-campus residence required through senior year. *Options:* coed, cooperative, disabled students. *Most popular organizations:* Student Government Association, Student Advisory Council, unity clubs, sports clubs, student radio station.

Campus security 24-hour emergency response devices and patrols, late-night transport-escort service, controlled dormitory access.

After graduation 84 organizations recruited on campus 1997-98. *Career center:* 8 full-time, 1 part-time personnel. Services include job fairs, resume preparation, resume referral, career counseling, careers library, job bank, job interviews.

Freshmen 3,700 applied, 1,454 admitted, 477 enrolled. 2 National Merit Scholars, 11 valedictorians.

SAT verbal scores above 500	97%	SAT math scores above 500	95%
ACT above 18	100%	From top 10% of their h.s. class	56%
From top quarter	92%	From top half	99%
1998 freshmen returning in 1999	91%		

Application *Options:* eApply at www.CollegeQuest.com, Common Application, early decision, deferred entrance. *Application fee:* $50. *Required:* essay or personal statement; high school transcript; minimum 2.0 GPA; 2 letters of recommendation. *Recommended:* interview.

Standardized tests *Admission: Required:* ACT or 3 SAT II Subject Tests (including SAT II: Writing Test). *Recommended:* SAT I.

Significant dates *Application deadlines:* 1/15 (freshmen), 4/1 (transfers). *Early decision:* 11/15. *Notification:* 4/1 (freshmen), 12/15 (early decision). **Financial aid deadline:** 1/15.

Freshman Application Contact
Mr. Lee A. Coffin, Dean of Admissions, Connecticut College, 270 Mohegan Avenue, New London, CT 06320-4196. **Phone:** 860-439-2202. **Fax:** 860-439-4301. **E-mail:** admit@conncoll.edu

Visit CollegeQuest.com for information on majors offered and athletics.

■ *See page 1530 for a narrative description.*

EASTERN CONNECTICUT STATE UNIVERSITY
Willimantic, Connecticut

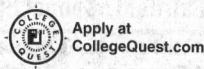 Apply at CollegeQuest.com

- **State-supported**, comprehensive, founded 1889
- **Degrees** associate, bachelor's, and master's
- **Small-town** 178-acre campus
- **Coed**, 4,286 undergraduate students, 80% full-time, 56% women, 44% men
- **Moderately difficult** entrance level, 79% of applicants were admitted
- **16:1 student-to-undergraduate faculty ratio**
- **34.5% graduate** in 6 years or less
- **$4146 tuition** and fees (in-state); $8938 (out-of-state)
- **$5165 average financial aid** package, $10,200 average indebtedness upon graduation, $60,000 endowment

Part of Connecticut State University System.

Students *Undergraduates:* 3,428 full-time, 858 part-time. Students come from 23 states and territories, 25 other countries. *The most frequently chosen baccalaureate fields are:* psychology, business/marketing, social sciences and history. *Graduate:* 314 in graduate degree programs.

From out-of-state	6%	Reside on campus	41%
Age 25 or older	27%	Transferred in	7%
International students	2%	African Americans	8%
Asian Americans/Pacific Islanders	1%	Hispanic Americans	4%
Native Americans	1%		

Faculty 342 (47% full-time), 48% with terminal degrees.

Connecticut

Eastern Connecticut State University (continued)

Expenses (1999–2000) *Tuition, state resident:* full-time $2142; part-time $149 per credit hour. *Tuition, nonresident:* full-time $6934; part-time $149 per credit hour. *Required fees:* full-time $2004; $40 per term part-time. Full-time tuition and fees vary according to reciprocity agreements. *College room and board:* $5850; room only: $3232. Room and board charges vary according to board plan and housing facility. *Payment plans:* installment, deferred payment. *Waivers:* senior citizens.

Library J. Eugene Smith Library. *Collection:* 201,907 titles, 2,269 serial subscriptions, 2,514 audiovisual materials.

College life *Housing: Options:* coed, women-only. *Most popular organizations:* Nubian Society, Organization of Latin American Students, International Student Organization, West Indian Student Society.

Campus security 24-hour patrols, student patrols, late-night transport-escort service, controlled dormitory access.

After graduation 103 organizations recruited on campus 1997–98. 74% of class of 1998 had job offers within 6 months. *Career center:* 4 full-time, 3 part-time personnel. Services include job fairs, resume preparation, resume referral, career counseling, careers library, job bank, job interviews. *Graduate education:* 30% of class of 1999 went directly to graduate and professional school.

Freshmen 2,775 applied, 2,188 admitted, 932 enrolled.

SAT verbal scores above 500	42%	SAT math scores above 500	35%
ACT above 18	N/R	From top 10% of their h.s. class	3%
From top quarter	13%	From top half	33%
1998 freshmen returning in 1999	72%		

Application *Options:* eApply at www.CollegeQuest.com, Common Application, electronic application, early admission, deferred entrance. *Application fee:* $40. *Required:* high school transcript. *Required for some:* interview. *Recommended:* essay or personal statement; letters of recommendation; rank in upper 50% of high school class.

Standardized tests *Admission: Required:* SAT I or ACT.

Significant dates *Application deadline:* rolling (transfers). *Financial aid deadline:* 3/15.

Freshman Application Contact
Ms. Kimberly Crone, Director of Admissions and Enrollment Management, Eastern Connecticut State University, 83 Windham street, Willimantic, CT 06336. **Phone:** 860-465-5286. **Toll-free phone:** 877-353-3278. **E-mail:** admissions@ecsu.ctstateu.edu

Visit CollegeQuest.com *for information on majors offered and athletics.*

■ *See page 1602 for a narrative description.*

FAIRFIELD UNIVERSITY
Fairfield, Connecticut

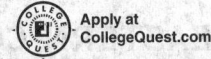
Apply at CollegeQuest.com

- **Independent Roman Catholic (Jesuit)**, comprehensive, founded 1942
- **Degrees** bachelor's, master's, and post-master's certificates
- **Suburban** 200-acre campus with easy access to New York City
- **Coed**, 4,064 undergraduate students, 79% full-time, 53% women, 47% men
- **Moderately difficult** entrance level, 61% of applicants were admitted
- **13:1 student-to-undergraduate faculty ratio**
- **81% graduate** in 6 years or less
- **$20,435 tuition** and fees
- **$14,460 average financial aid** package, $18,765 average indebtedness upon graduation, $91 million endowment

Students *Undergraduates:* 3,228 full-time, 836 part-time. Students come from 34 states and territories, 34 other countries. *The most frequently chosen baccalaureate fields are:* business/marketing, English, social sciences and history. *Graduate:* 1,063 in graduate degree programs.

From out-of-state	73%	Reside on campus	75%
Age 25 or older	1%	Transferred in	1%
International students	2%	African Americans	3%
Asian Americans/Pacific Islanders	3%	Hispanic Americans	4%
Native Americans	0.1%		

Faculty 463 (45% full-time), 42% with terminal degrees.

Expenses (1999–2000) *Comprehensive fee:* $27,815 includes full-time tuition ($20,000), mandatory fees ($435), and room and board ($7380). Room and board charges vary according to board plan and housing facility. *Part-time tuition:* $310 per credit. *Part-time fees:* $25 per term part-time. Part-time tuition and fees vary according to course load. *Payment plan:* installment. *Waivers:* employees or children of employees.

Library Nyselius Library. *Operations spending 1999–2000:* $1.7 million. *Collection:* 482,475 titles, 1,881 serial subscriptions, 11,045 audiovisual materials.

College life *Housing:* on-campus residence required through senior year. *Options:* coed, disabled students. *Most popular organizations:* student government, Glee Club, drama club, multicultural organizations, Mission Volunteers.

Campus security 24-hour emergency response devices and patrols, late-night transport-escort service, controlled dormitory access, bicycle patrols by security staff.

After graduation 130 organizations recruited on campus 1997–98. 72% of class of 1998 had job offers within 6 months. *Career center:* 5 full-time, 1 part-time personnel. Services include job fairs, resume preparation, interview workshops, resume referral, career/interest testing, career counseling, careers library, job bank, job interviews. *Graduate education:* 18% of class of 1999 went directly to graduate and professional school: 5% graduate arts and sciences, 5% law, 5% medicine, 3% education. *Major awards:* 4 Fulbright Scholars.

Freshmen 6,457 applied, 3,966 admitted, 837 enrolled. 13 National Merit Scholars, 26 class presidents, 5 valedictorians, 26 student government officers.

Average high school GPA	3.3	SAT verbal scores above 500	89%
SAT math scores above 500	92%	ACT above 18	N/R
From top 10% of their h.s. class	22%	From top quarter	65%
From top half	93%	1998 freshmen returning in 1999	89%

Application *Options:* eApply at www.CollegeQuest.com, Common Application, early admission, early decision, deferred entrance. *Application fee:* $50. *Required:* high school transcript; minimum 3.0 GPA; 1 letter of recommendation; rank in upper 40% of high school class. *Recommended:* interview.

Standardized tests *Admission: Required:* SAT I or ACT. *Recommended:* SAT II Subject Tests.

Significant dates *Application deadlines:* 2/1 (freshmen), 6/1 (transfers). *Early decision:* 11/15. *Notification:* 4/1 (freshmen), 12/25 (early decision). *Financial aid deadline priority date:* 2/15.

Freshman Application Contact
Ms. Mary Spiegel, Director of Admission, Fairfield University, 1073 North Benson Road, Fairfield, CT 06430-5195. **Phone:** 203-254-4100. **Fax:** 203-254-4199. **E-mail:** admis@fair1.fairfield.edu

Visit CollegeQuest.com *for information on majors offered and athletics.* College video available at CollegeQuest.com.

HARTFORD COLLEGE FOR WOMEN
Hartford, Connecticut

- **Independent**, 4-year, founded 1933
- **Degrees** associate, bachelor's, and postbachelor's certificates (offers only evening and weekend programs)
- **Suburban** 13-acre campus
- **Women** only
- **Moderately difficult** entrance level
- **$18,920 tuition** and fees

Expenses (1999–2000) *Comprehensive fee:* $26,518 includes full-time tuition ($17,910), mandatory fees ($1010), and room and board ($7598). *College room only:* $4710. Room and board charges vary according to board plan. *Part-time tuition:* $280 per credit. *Part-time fees:* $110 per year part-time. Part-time tuition and fees vary according to class time and program.

College life *Most popular organizations:* student government, yearbook.

Campus security 24-hour patrols, late-night transport-escort service.

Application *Options:* Common Application, deferred entrance. *Application fee:* $35. *Required:* essay or personal statement; high school transcript. *Recommended:* interview.

Standardized tests *Admission: Required:* SAT I. *Recommended:* SAT II Subject Tests.

Connecticut

Admissions Office Contact
Hartford College for Women, 1265 Asylum Avenue, Hartford, CT 06105-2299. **Toll-free phone:** 800-582-6118. **Fax:** 860-233-5493. **E-mail:** arogers@mail.hartford.edu
Visit CollegeQuest.com for information on athletics. College video available at CollegeQuest.com.

■ *See page 1768 for a narrative description.*

HOLY APOSTLES COLLEGE AND SEMINARY
Cromwell, Connecticut

- **Independent Roman Catholic**, comprehensive, founded 1956
- **Degrees** associate, bachelor's, master's, and first professional
- **Small-town** campus
- **Coed**
- **Noncompetitive** entrance level
- **$5630 tuition** and fees

Expenses (1999–2000) *Comprehensive fee:* $11,560 includes full-time tuition ($5550), mandatory fees ($80), and room and board ($5930). Full-time tuition and fees vary according to program. *Part-time tuition:* $185 per credit hour. Part-time tuition and fees vary according to program.
Institutional Web site http://www.holy-apostles.org/
College life on-campus residence required through senior year.
Campus security 24-hour emergency response devices and patrols.
Application *Options:* Common Application, deferred entrance. *Application fee:* $50. *Required:* high school transcript; interview. *Required for some:* letters of recommendation.
Admissions Office Contact
Holy Apostles College and Seminary, 33 Prospect Hill Road, Cromwell, CT 06416-2005. **Toll-free phone:** 800-330-7272. **Fax:** 860-632-0176. **E-mail:** holy_apostles@msn.com
Visit CollegeQuest.com for information on athletics.

LYME ACADEMY OF FINE ARTS
Old Lyme, Connecticut

- **Independent**, 4-year, founded 1976
- **Degree** bachelor's
- **Small-town** 3-acre campus
- **Coed**, 75 undergraduate students, 67% full-time, 56% women, 44% men
- **Moderately difficult** entrance level, 100% of applicants were admitted
- **6:1 student-to-undergraduate faculty ratio**
- **$10,550 tuition** and fees
- **$1.1 million endowment**

Students *Undergraduates:* 50 full-time, 25 part-time. Students come from 16 states and territories. *The most frequently chosen baccalaureate field is:* visual/performing arts.

From out-of-state	50%	Age 25 or older	53%
Transferred in	16%	African Americans	3%
Asian Americans/Pacific Islanders	1%	Hispanic Americans	4%
Native Americans	1%		

Faculty 19 (37% full-time), 42% with terminal degrees.
Expenses (1999–2000) *Tuition:* full-time $10,500; part-time $438 per credit. *Required fees:* full-time $50; $45 per term part-time. *Payment plan:* installment. *Waivers:* employees or children of employees.
Library Nancy Kriebly Library. *Operations spending 1999–2000:* $80,736. *Collection:* 5,875 titles, 50 serial subscriptions.
College life *Housing:* college housing not available. *Most popular organization:* Student Association.
After graduation *Graduate education:* 10% of class of 1999 went directly to graduate and professional school.
Freshmen 15 applied, 15 admitted, 8 enrolled.

Average high school GPA	3.3	SAT verbal scores above 500	N/R
SAT math scores above 500	N/R	ACT above 18	N/R
From top quarter of their h.s. class	1%	From top half	1%

Application *Option:* deferred entrance. *Application fee:* $35. *Required:* essay or personal statement; high school transcript; 2 letters of recommendation; portfolio. *Required for some:* interview. *Recommended:* minimum 2.0 GPA.
Standardized tests *Admission: Recommended:* SAT I.
Significant dates *Application deadlines:* rolling (freshmen), rolling (transfers). *Financial aid deadline:* 3/15.
Freshman Application Contact
Mr. Christopher S. Rose, Associate Dean of Enrollment Management, Lyme Academy of Fine Arts, 84 Lyme Street, Old Lyme, CT 06371. **Phone:** 860-434-5232 Ext. 122. **Fax:** 860-434-8725. **E-mail:** admissions@lymeacademy.edu
Visit CollegeQuest.com for information on majors offered and athletics.

MITCHELL COLLEGE
New London, Connecticut

- **Independent**, primarily 2-year, founded 1938
- **Degrees** associate and bachelor's
- **Suburban** 67-acre campus with easy access to Hartford and Providence
- **Coed**, 537 undergraduate students, 89% full-time, 48% women, 52% men
- **Minimally difficult** entrance level
- **14:1 student-to-undergraduate faculty ratio**
- **$14,860 tuition** and fees

Faculty 71 (28% full-time), 18% with terminal degrees.
Admissions Office Contact
Mitchell College, 437 Pequot Avenue, New London, CT 06320-4498. **Toll-free phone:** 800-443-2811. **Fax:** 860-444-1209. **E-mail:** admissions@mitchell.edu
Visit CollegeQuest.com for information on majors offered and athletics. College video and electronic viewbook available at CollegeQuest.com.

■ *See page 2072 for a narrative description.*

PAIER COLLEGE OF ART, INC.
Hamden, Connecticut

- **Proprietary**, 4-year, founded 1946
- **Degrees** associate and bachelor's
- **Suburban** 3-acre campus with easy access to New York City
- **Coed**, 229 undergraduate students, 64% full-time, 54% women, 46% men
- **Minimally difficult** entrance level, 83% of applicants were admitted
- **5:1 student-to-undergraduate faculty ratio**
- **40% graduate** in 6 years or less
- **$10,835 tuition** and fees

Students *Undergraduates:* 146 full-time, 83 part-time. Students come from 5 states and territories, 2 other countries. *The most frequently chosen baccalaureate field is:* visual/performing arts.

From out-of-state	2%	Age 25 or older	25%
Transferred in	6%		

Faculty 43 (26% full-time), 5% with terminal degrees.
Expenses (1999–2000) *Tuition:* full-time $10,500; part-time $335 per semester hour. *Required fees:* full-time $335; $33 per term part-time. Full-time tuition and fees vary according to course load, degree level, and program. Part-time tuition and fees vary according to course load, degree level, and program. *Payment plan:* installment. *Waivers:* senior citizens and employees or children of employees.
Library Adele K. Paier Memorial Library. *Operations spending 1999–2000:* $41,865. *Collection:* 11,515 titles, 69 serial subscriptions, 66,136 audiovisual materials.
College life *Housing:* college housing not available. *Most popular organization:* student council.
Campus security Evening patrols by security.
After graduation 4 organizations recruited on campus 1997–98. 65% of class of 1998 had job offers within 6 months. *Career center:* 1 full-time, 1 part-time personnel. Services include job fairs, resume preparation, interview workshops, resume referral, career counseling, careers library, job bank, job

Peterson's Guide to Four-Year Colleges 2001   www.petersons.com   157

Connecticut

Paier College of Art, Inc. (continued)
interviews. **Graduate education:** 1% of class of 1999 went directly to graduate and professional school: 1% graduate arts and sciences.

Freshmen 153 applied, 127 admitted, 63 enrolled.

SAT verbal scores above 500	38%	SAT math scores above 500	27%
ACT above 18	N/R	From top 10% of their h.s. class	2%
From top quarter	7%	From top half	44%
1998 freshmen returning in 1999	78%		

Application *Options:* eApply at www.CollegeQuest.com, deferred entrance. *Application fee:* $25. *Required:* high school transcript; 1 letter of recommendation; interview; portfolio. *Recommended:* essay or personal statement.

Standardized tests *Admission: Required:* SAT I or ACT.

Significant dates *Application deadlines:* rolling (freshmen), rolling (transfers). *Financial aid deadline priority date:* 4/15.

Freshman Application Contact
Ms. Lynn Pascale, Secretary to Admissions, Paier College of Art, Inc., 20 Gorham Avenue, Hamden, CT 06514-3902. **Phone:** 203-287-3031. **E-mail:** info@paierart.com

Visit CollegeQuest.com for information on majors offered and athletics. College video and electronic viewbook available at CollegeQuest.com.

■ *See page 2240 for a narrative description.*

QUINNIPIAC UNIVERSITY
Hamden, Connecticut

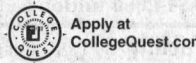 Apply at CollegeQuest.com

- **Independent**, comprehensive, founded 1929
- **Degrees** bachelor's, master's, and first professional
- **Suburban** 300-acre campus with easy access to Hartford
- **Coed**, 4,341 undergraduate students, 93% full-time, 65% women, 35% men
- **Moderately difficult** entrance level, 70% of applicants were admitted
- **16:1 student-to-undergraduate faculty ratio**
- **70% graduate** in 6 years or less
- **$17,780 tuition** and fees
- **$10,947 average financial aid** package, $13,177 average indebtedness upon graduation, $53.9 million endowment

The $7-million Lender School of Business Center features local area network classrooms, satellite service, and the Ed McMahon Center for Mass Communications, 1 of the most advanced in higher education. The communications facilities include TV and radio studios, print journalism and desktop publishing laboratories, a news technology center, and audio and video equipment. The center establishes national recognition for the undergraduate and graduate mass communication and business programs.

Students *Undergraduates:* 4,018 full-time, 323 part-time. Students come from 27 states and territories, 17 other countries. *The most frequently chosen baccalaureate fields are:* business/marketing, health professions and related sciences, liberal arts/general studies. *Graduate:* 785 in professional programs, 749 in other graduate degree programs.

From out-of-state	70%	Reside on campus	70%
Age 25 or older	10%	Transferred in	3%
International students	1%	African Americans	2%
Asian Americans/Pacific Islanders	2%	Hispanic Americans	3%
Native Americans	0.4%		

Faculty 404 (63% full-time).

Expenses (2000–2001) *Comprehensive fee:* $25,955 includes full-time tuition ($17,000), mandatory fees ($780), and room and board ($8175). Room and board charges vary according to board plan and housing facility. *Part-time tuition:* $420 per semester hour. *Part-time fees:* $75 per course. Part-time tuition and fees vary according to course load. *Payment plan:* installment. *Waivers:* senior citizens and employees or children of employees.

Library Quinnipiac Library plus 1 other. *Operations spending 1999–2000:* $3.1 million. *Collection:* 285,000 titles, 4,400 serial subscriptions.

College life *Housing: Option:* coed. *Social organizations:* national fraternities, national sororities, local sororities; 5% of eligible men and 7% of eligible women are members. *Most popular organizations:* Student Government, Greek organizations, Social Programming Board, drama club, student newspaper.

Campus security 24-hour emergency response devices and patrols, late-night transport-escort service, controlled dormitory access.

After graduation 125 organizations recruited on campus 1997–98. 84% of class of 1998 had job offers within 6 months. *Career center:* 9 full-time personnel. Services include job fairs, resume preparation, interview workshops, resume referral, career counseling, careers library, job bank, job interviews. **Graduate education:** 21% of class of 1999 went directly to graduate and professional school: 7% business, 4% medicine, 3% graduate arts and sciences, 3% law, 2% education, 1% dentistry, 1% veterinary medicine.

Freshmen 6,495 applied, 4,520 admitted, 1,164 enrolled. 30 valedictorians.

Average high school GPA	3.1	SAT verbal scores above 500	67%
SAT math scores above 500	72%	ACT above 18	91%
From top 10% of their h.s. class	24%	From top quarter	55%
From top half	90%	1998 freshmen returning in 1999	84%

Application *Options:* eApply at www.CollegeQuest.com, Common Application, electronic application, early admission, deferred entrance. *Application fee:* $45. *Required:* essay or personal statement; high school transcript; 1 letter of recommendation. *Required for some:* minimum 3.0 GPA. *Recommended:* minimum 2.5 GPA; interview.

Standardized tests *Admission: Required:* SAT I or ACT.

Significant dates *Application deadlines:* 2/15 (freshmen), rolling (transfers). *Notification:* continuous until 8/1 (freshmen). *Financial aid deadline priority date:* 3/1.

Freshman Application Contact
Ms. Joan Isaac-Mohr, Vice President and Dean of Admissions, Quinnipiac University, 275 Mount Carmel Avenue, Hamden, CT 06518-1940. **Phone:** 203-582-8600. **Toll-free phone:** 800-462-1944. **Fax:** 203-281-8906. **E-mail:** admissions@quinnipiac.edu

Visit CollegeQuest.com for information on majors offered and athletics. College video available at CollegeQuest.com.

■ *See page 2304 for a narrative description.*

SACRED HEART UNIVERSITY
Fairfield, Connecticut

 Apply at CollegeQuest.com

- **Independent Roman Catholic**, comprehensive, founded 1963
- **Degrees** associate, bachelor's, master's, and post-master's certificates (also offers part-time program with significant enrollment not reflected in profile)
- **Suburban** 56-acre campus with easy access to New York City
- **Coed**, 3,786 undergraduate students, 64% full-time, 62% women, 38% men
- **Moderately difficult** entrance level, 82% of applicants were admitted
- **17:1 student-to-undergraduate faculty ratio**
- **$14,720 tuition** and fees
- **$10,887 average financial aid** package, $16,880 average indebtedness upon graduation, $22.6 million endowment

Students *Undergraduates:* 2,415 full-time, 1,371 part-time. Students come from 27 states and territories, 50 other countries. *The most frequently chosen baccalaureate fields are:* business/marketing, protective services/public administration, psychology. *Graduate:* 1,608 in graduate degree programs.

From out-of-state	63%	Reside on campus	68%
Age 25 or older	1%	Transferred in	4%
International students	2%	African Americans	7%
Asian Americans/Pacific Islanders	2%	Hispanic Americans	5%
Native Americans	0.3%		

Faculty 449 (32% full-time), 50% with terminal degrees.

Expenses (1999–2000) *Comprehensive fee:* $21,920 includes full-time tuition ($14,670), mandatory fees ($50), and room and board ($7200). *College room only:* $5130. Room and board charges vary according to board plan. *Part-time tuition:* $305 per credit. *Part-time fees:* $58 per term part-time. *Payment plans:* installment, deferred payment. *Waivers:* senior citizens and employees or children of employees.

Library Ryan-Matura Library. *Operations spending 1999–2000:* $882,321. *Collection:* 127,079 titles, 1,711 serial subscriptions, 11,534 audiovisual materials.

Connecticut

College life *Housing: Options:* coed, disabled students. *Social organizations:* local fraternities, local sororities. *Most popular organizations:* student government association, recreational clubs, Campus Ministry, multicultural clubs.
Campus security 24-hour emergency response devices and patrols, late-night transport-escort service, controlled dormitory access, campus housing has sprinklers and fire alarms.
After graduation 100 organizations recruited on campus 1997–98. 67% of class of 1998 had job offers within 6 months. *Career center:* 4 full-time personnel. Services include job fairs, resume preparation, resume referral, career counseling, careers library, job bank, job interviews. *Graduate education:* 40% of class of 1999 went directly to graduate and professional school: 11% graduate arts and sciences, 10% education, 9% business, 7% medicine, 3% law.
Freshmen 3,152 applied, 2,579 admitted, 755 enrolled. 2 National Merit Scholars, 26 class presidents, 2 valedictorians, 128 student government officers.

Average high school GPA	3.2	SAT verbal scores above 500	60%
SAT math scores above 500	57%	ACT above 18	N/R
From top 10% of their h.s. class	25%	From top quarter	37%
From top half	77%	1998 freshmen returning in 1999	76%

Application *Options:* eApply at www.CollegeQuest.com, Common Application, electronic application, early admission, early decision, deferred entrance. *Application fee:* $45. *Required:* essay or personal statement; high school transcript; minimum 3.0 GPA; 2 letters of recommendation. *Recommended:* minimum 3.2 GPA; interview.
Standardized tests *Admission: Required:* SAT I or ACT.
Significant dates *Application deadlines:* rolling (freshmen), rolling (transfers). *Early decision:* 10/1 (for plan 1), 12/1 (for plan 2). *Notification:* 10/15 (early decision plan 1), 12/15 (early decision plan 2). *Financial aid deadline priority date:* 2/15.
Freshman Application Contact
Ms. Karen N. Guastelle, Dean of Undergraduate Admissions, Sacred Heart University, 5151 Park Avenue, Fairfield, CT 06432-1000. **Phone:** 203-371-7880. **Fax:** 203-371-7889. **E-mail:** enroll@sacredheart.edu
Visit CollegeQuest.com for information on majors offered and athletics.

■ *See page 2364 for a narrative description.*

SAINT JOSEPH COLLEGE
West Hartford, Connecticut

Apply at CollegeQuest.com

- **Independent Roman Catholic**, comprehensive, founded 1932
- **Degrees** bachelor's and master's
- **Suburban** 84-acre campus with easy access to Hartford
- **Women** only, 951 undergraduate students, 68% full-time
- **Moderately difficult** entrance level, 87% of applicants were admitted
- **12:1 student-to-undergraduate faculty ratio**
- **55% graduate** in 6 years or less
- **$16,150 tuition** and fees
- **$14,452 average financial aid** package, $7541 average indebtedness upon graduation, $13 million endowment

Saint Joseph College provides outstanding academic, professional, and leadership opportunities for women. More than 25 majors are accompanied by internships locally or abroad. Success in every program springs from the liberal arts and sciences curriculum and active mentoring by faculty members, advisers, and alumnae. This mentoring guides students directly into postgraduate business, professional, and academic communities. Students serve on every College committee, from strategic planning to Web site development, and, like the founding Sisters of Mercy, they perform community service around the world.

Students *Undergraduates:* 650 full-time, 301 part-time. Students come from 14 states and territories. *The most frequently chosen baccalaureate fields are:* health professions and related sciences, education, protective services/public administration. *Graduate:* 626 in graduate degree programs.

From out-of-state	6%	Reside on campus	45%
Age 25 or older	26%	Transferred in	9%
African Americans	10%	Asian Americans/Pacific Islanders	2%
Hispanic Americans	5%	Native Americans	0.3%

Faculty 85 (89% full-time), 89% with terminal degrees.
Expenses (1999–2000) *Comprehensive fee:* $22,760 includes full-time tuition ($15,900), mandatory fees ($250), and room and board ($6610). *College room only:* $3110. Room and board charges vary according to board plan. *Part-time tuition:* $405 per credit. *Part-time fees:* $25 per credit. *Payment plan:* installment. *Waivers:* senior citizens and employees or children of employees.
Library Pope Pius XII Library plus 1 other. *Operations spending 1999–2000:* $506,694. *Collection:* 133,500 titles, 624 serial subscriptions, 1,315 audiovisual materials.
College life *Social organizations:* 20% of eligible undergrads are members. *Most popular organizations:* Student Government Association, Student Nurse Association, psychology club, SJC choir, business society.
Campus security 24-hour emergency response devices and patrols, late-night transport-escort service, controlled dormitory access.
After graduation 53 organizations recruited on campus 1997–98. 63% of class of 1998 had job offers within 6 months. *Career center:* 1 full-time, 2 part-time personnel. Services include job fairs, resume preparation, interview workshops, career/interest testing, career counseling, careers library, job bank, job interviews.
Freshmen 369 applied, 322 admitted, 147 enrolled.

SAT verbal scores above 500	N/R	SAT math scores above 500	4%
ACT above 18	N/R	From top 10% of their h.s. class	21%
From top quarter	46%	From top half	79%
1998 freshmen returning in 1999	72%		

Application *Options:* eApply at www.CollegeQuest.com, electronic application, early admission, early decision, early action, deferred entrance. *Application fee:* $35. *Required:* essay or personal statement; high school transcript; minimum 2.5 GPA; 1 letter of recommendation. *Recommended:* interview.
Standardized tests *Admission: Required:* SAT I or ACT.
Significant dates *Application deadlines:* 5/1 (freshmen), 7/1 (transfers). *Early decision:* 11/15, 11/15. *Notification:* continuous until 6/14 (freshmen), 12/15 (early decision), 12/15 (early action). *Financial aid deadline priority date:* 2/15.
Freshman Application Contact
Ms. Kelly Crowley, Director of Admissions, Saint Joseph College, 1678 Asylum Avenue, West Hartford, CT 06117-2700. **Phone:** 860-231-5216. **Toll-free phone:** 800-285-6565. **Fax:** 860-233-5695. **E-mail:** admissions@mercy.sjc.edu
Visit CollegeQuest.com for information on majors offered and athletics. College video available at CollegeQuest.com.

■ *See page 2388 for a narrative description.*

SOUTHERN CONNECTICUT STATE UNIVERSITY
New Haven, Connecticut

Apply at CollegeQuest.com

- **State-supported**, comprehensive, founded 1893
- **Degrees** associate, bachelor's, master's, and post-master's certificates
- **Urban** 168-acre campus with easy access to New York City
- **Coed**
- **Moderately difficult** entrance level
- **$3773 tuition** and fees (in-state); $9451 (out-of-state)

Part of Connecticut State University System.
Expenses (1999–2000) *Tuition, state resident:* full-time $2124; part-time $166 per credit. *Tuition, nonresident:* full-time $7802; part-time $166 per credit. *Required fees:* full-time $1649; $45 per term part-time. Full-time tuition and fees vary according to reciprocity agreements. *College room and board:* $5825; room only: $3115. Room and board charges vary according to housing facility.
Institutional Web site http://www.southernct.edu/
College life *Housing: Option:* coed. *Social organizations:* national fraternities, national sororities, local sororities; 1% of eligible men and 1% of eligible women are members. *Most popular organizations:* People to People, Pre-Law Society, Accounting Society, Crescent Players, Black Student Union.

Connecticut

Southern Connecticut State University *(continued)*

Campus security 24-hour emergency response devices and patrols, late-night transport-escort service, controlled dormitory access.
Application *Options:* eApply at www.CollegeQuest.com, Common Application, electronic application, deferred entrance. *Application fee:* $40. *Required:* essay or personal statement; high school transcript. *Recommended:* letters of recommendation.
Standardized tests *Admission: Required:* SAT I.
Admissions Office Contact
Southern Connecticut State University, Admissions House, New Haven, CT 06515-1202. **Fax:** 203-392-5727. **E-mail:** adminfo@scsu.ctstateu.edu
Visit CollegeQuest.com for information on athletics.

■ *See page 2508 for a narrative description.*

TEIKYO POST UNIVERSITY
Waterbury, Connecticut

 Apply at CollegeQuest.com

- **Independent**, 4-year, founded 1890
- **Degrees** associate and bachelor's
- **Suburban** 70-acre campus with easy access to Hartford
- **Coed**, 1,289 undergraduate students, 47% full-time, 66% women, 34% men
- **Minimally difficult** entrance level, 82% of applicants were admitted
- **15:1 student-to-undergraduate faculty ratio**
- **37% graduate** in 6 years or less
- **$13,400 tuition** and fees
- **$10,639 average financial aid** package, $4.6 million endowment

Western Connecticut's only 4-year, private, accredited, coeducational, residential liberal arts and business university. This globally focused university is known for its comprehensive and affordable education, lively study-abroad program, and ideal environment for learning and growth, where students experience large-university academics in a small, collegial atmosphere.

Students *Undergraduates:* 600 full-time, 689 part-time. Students come from 12 states and territories, 19 other countries. *The most frequently chosen baccalaureate fields are:* business/marketing, liberal arts/general studies, psychology.

From out-of-state	12%	Reside on campus	46%
Age 25 or older	51%	Transferred in	3%
International students	6%	African Americans	12%
Asian Americans/Pacific Islanders	6%	Hispanic Americans	5%
Native Americans	0.4%		

Faculty 24 full-time.
Expenses (1999–2000) *Comprehensive fee:* $19,300 includes full-time tuition ($13,125), mandatory fees ($275), and room and board ($5900). *Part-time tuition:* $440 per credit. Part-time tuition and fees vary according to class time and course load. *Payment plans:* installment, deferred payment. *Waivers:* minority students, senior citizens, and employees or children of employees.
Library Trauriq Library and Resource Center. *Operations spending 1999–2000:* $310,113. *Collection:* 83,966 titles, 586 serial subscriptions, 586 audiovisual materials.
College life *Housing:* on-campus residence required in freshman year. *Option:* coed. *Most popular organizations:* Black Student Union, international club, Residence Hall Council, Student Government Association, Program Board.
Campus security 24-hour emergency response devices and patrols, late-night transport-escort service.
After graduation 71 organizations recruited on campus 1997–98. 82% of class of 1998 had job offers within 6 months. *Career center:* 1 full-time, 1 part-time personnel. Services include job fairs, resume preparation, resume referral, career counseling, careers library, job bank, job interviews. *Graduate education:* 10% of class of 1999 went directly to graduate and professional school: 6% business, 2% graduate arts and sciences.

Freshmen 657 applied, 541 admitted, 188 enrolled.

Average high school GPA	2.15	SAT verbal scores above 500	18%
SAT math scores above 500	16%	ACT above 18	N/R
From top 10% of their h.s. class	8%	From top quarter	27%
From top half	39%	1998 freshmen returning in 1999	82%

Application *Options:* eApply at www.CollegeQuest.com, Common Application, electronic application, deferred entrance. *Application fee:* $40. *Required:* high school transcript; 1 letter of recommendation. *Recommended:* essay or personal statement; interview.
Standardized tests *Admission: Required:* SAT I.
Significant dates *Application deadlines:* rolling (freshmen), rolling (transfers). *Notification:* continuous until 9/1 (freshmen). *Financial aid deadline priority date:* 3/1.
Freshman Application Contact
Mr. Scott Ouellette, Senior Assistant Director of Admissions, Teikyo Post University, PO Box 2540, Waterbury, CT 06723. **Phone:** 203-596-4520. **Toll-free phone:** 800-345-2562. **Fax:** 203-756-5810. **E-mail:** tpuadmiss@teikyopost.edu
Visit CollegeQuest.com for information on majors offered and athletics. Electronic viewbook available at CollegeQuest.com.

■ *See page 2594 for a narrative description.*

TRINITY COLLEGE
Hartford, Connecticut

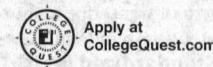 Apply at CollegeQuest.com

- **Independent**, comprehensive, founded 1823
- **Degrees** bachelor's and master's
- **Urban** 100-acre campus
- **Coed**, 2,112 undergraduate students, 92% full-time, 48% women, 52% men
- **Very difficult** entrance level, 40% of applicants were admitted
- **10:1 student-to-undergraduate faculty ratio**
- **82% graduate** in 6 years or less
- **$24,490 tuition** and fees
- **$22,495 average financial aid** package, $13,761 average indebtedness upon graduation, $334 million endowment

Students *Undergraduates:* 1,953 full-time, 159 part-time. Students come from 44 states and territories, 29 other countries. *The most frequently chosen baccalaureate fields are:* biological/life sciences, English, social sciences and history. *Graduate:* 202 in graduate degree programs.

From out-of-state	76%	Reside on campus	96%
Age 25 or older	7%	Transferred in	1%
International students	2%	African Americans	6%
Asian Americans/Pacific Islanders	5%	Hispanic Americans	5%
Native Americans	0.1%		

Faculty 257 (65% full-time), 77% with terminal degrees.
Expenses (1999–2000) *One-time required fee:* $25. *Comprehensive fee:* $31,380 includes full-time tuition ($23,730), mandatory fees ($760), and room and board ($6890). *College room only:* $4150. Room and board charges vary according to board plan. *Part-time tuition:* $7910 per term. Part-time tuition and fees vary according to program. *Payment plan:* installment. *Waivers:* adult students and employees or children of employees.
Library Trinity College Library plus 2 others. *Operations spending 1999–2000:* $4 million. *Collection:* 941,010 titles, 3,126 serial subscriptions, 22,936 audiovisual materials.
College life *Housing: Options:* coed, disabled students. *Social organizations:* coed fraternities; 19% of eligible men and 19% of eligible women are members. *Most popular organizations:* community outreach, Habitat for Humanity, Trinity College Activities Council, student government, Multi-Cultural Affairs Committee.
Campus security 24-hour emergency response devices and patrols, late-night transport-escort service, controlled dormitory access.
After graduation 261 organizations recruited on campus 1997–98. 75% of class of 1998 had job offers within 6 months. *Career center:* 7 full-time personnel. Services include job fairs, resume preparation, interview workshops, resume referral, career/interest testing, career counseling, careers library, job bank, job interviews. *Graduate education:* 14% of class of 1999 went directly to graduate and professional school.

Freshmen 4,648 applied, 1,855 admitted, 566 enrolled.

SAT verbal scores above 500	97%	SAT math scores above 500	94%
ACT above 18	100%	From top 10% of their h.s. class	51%
From top quarter	82%	From top half	98%
1998 freshmen returning in 1999	92%		

Application *Options:* eApply at www.CollegeQuest.com, Common Application, electronic application, early admission, early decision, deferred entrance. *Application fee:* $50. *Required:* essay or personal statement; high school transcript; 3 letters of recommendation. *Recommended:* interview.

Standardized tests *Admission: Required:* SAT I and SAT II or ACT, SAT II: Writing Test.

Significant dates *Application deadlines:* 1/15 (freshmen), 4/1 (transfers). *Early decision:* 11/15 (for plan 1), 2/1 (for plan 2). *Notification:* 4/1 (freshmen), 12/15 (early decision plan 1), 2/28 (early decision plan 2). *Financial aid deadline:* 3/1. *Priority date:* 2/1.

Freshman Application Contact
Mr. Larry Dow, Dean of Admissions and Financial Aid, Trinity College, 300 Summit Street, Hartford, CT 06106-3100. **Phone:** 860-297-2180. **Fax:** 860-297-2287. **E-mail:** admissions.office@trincoll.edu

Visit CollegeQuest.com for information on majors offered and athletics. Electronic viewbook available at CollegeQuest.com.

■ *See page 2640 for a narrative description.*

UNITED STATES COAST GUARD ACADEMY
New London, Connecticut

- **Federally supported**, 4-year, founded 1876
- **Degree** bachelor's
- **Suburban** 110-acre campus
- **Coed**, 838 undergraduate students, 100% full-time, 29% women, 71% men
- **Very difficult** entrance level, 6% of applicants were admitted
- **7:1 student-to-undergraduate faculty ratio**
- **$0 comprehensive fee**

Students *Undergraduates:* 838 full-time. Students come from 50 states and territories, 6 other countries. *The most frequently chosen baccalaureate fields are:* (pre)law, business/marketing, engineering/engineering technologies.

From out-of-state	91%	Reside on campus	100%
International students	2%	African Americans	5%
Asian Americans/Pacific Islanders	5%	Hispanic Americans	6%
Native Americans	1%		

Faculty 114 (98% full-time), 39% with terminal degrees.

Expenses (1999–2000) Tuition, room and board, and medical and dental care are provided by the U.S. government. Each cadet receives a salary from which to pay for uniforms, supplies, and personal expenses. Entering freshmen are required to deposit $3000 to defray the initial cost of uniforms and equipment.

Library *Collection:* 150,000 titles, 1,690 serial subscriptions.

College life *Housing:* on-campus residence required through senior year. *Option:* coed.

Campus security 24-hour patrols, student patrols.

Freshmen 5,457 applied, 326 admitted, 264 enrolled. 27 class presidents, 9 valedictorians, 60 student government officers.

Average high school GPA	3.67	SAT verbal scores above 500	99%
SAT math scores above 500	100%	ACT above 18	100%
From top 10% of their h.s. class	44%	From top quarter	78%
From top half	100%	1998 freshmen returning in 1999	83%

Application *Option:* early action. *Application fee:* $0. *Required:* essay or personal statement; high school transcript; 3 letters of recommendation. *Required for some:* interview.

Standardized tests *Admission: Required:* SAT I or ACT.

Significant dates *Application deadline:* 12/15 (freshmen). *Early action:* 11/1. *Notification:* 12/15 (early action).

Freshman Application Contact
Capt. R. W. Thorne, Director of Admissions, United States Coast Guard Academy, 31 Mohegan Avenue, New London, CT 06320-4195. **Phone:** 860-444-8500. **Toll-free phone:** 800-883-8724. **Fax:** 860-444-8289. **E-mail:** admissions@cga.uscg.mil

Visit CollegeQuest.com for information on majors offered and athletics. College video and electronic viewbook available at CollegeQuest.com.

■ *See page 2666 for a narrative description.*

UNIVERSITY OF BRIDGEPORT
Bridgeport, Connecticut

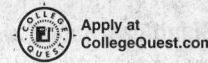
Apply at CollegeQuest.com

- **Independent**, comprehensive, founded 1927
- **Degrees** associate, bachelor's, master's, doctoral, first professional, and post-master's certificates
- **Urban** 86-acre campus with easy access to New York City
- **Coed**, 1,212 undergraduate students, 78% full-time, 53% women, 47% men
- **Moderately difficult** entrance level, 78% of applicants were admitted
- **12:1 student-to-undergraduate faculty ratio**
- **17% graduate** in 6 years or less
- **$14,641 tuition** and fees

The University of Bridgeport offers scholarships and grants to students, including the Challenge Grant (up to $3000), Academic Grant (up to $6000), Academic Scholarship (up to $10,000), and Academic Excellence and Leadership Scholarship (up to $20,770). All awards are renewable for 4 years, based on satisfactory academic achievement and good standing. Students may also be eligible for financial aid in addition to a scholarship or grant. Telephone: 800-EXCEL-UB (toll-free); Web site: www.bridgeport.edu.

Students *Undergraduates:* 941 full-time, 271 part-time. Students come from 29 states and territories, 67 other countries. *The most frequently chosen baccalaureate fields are:* business/marketing, home economics/vocational home economics, protective services/public administration. *Graduate:* 242 in professional programs, 1,232 in other graduate degree programs.

From out-of-state	37%	Reside on campus	47%
Age 25 or older	29%	Transferred in	7%
International students	42%	African Americans	17%
Asian Americans/Pacific Islanders	5%	Hispanic Americans	8%
Native Americans	0.2%		

Faculty 340 (28% full-time).

Expenses (1999–2000) *Comprehensive fee:* $21,611 includes full-time tuition ($13,800), mandatory fees ($841), and room and board ($6970). *College room only:* $3780. Full-time tuition and fees vary according to program. Room and board charges vary according to board plan. *Part-time tuition:* $330 per credit. *Part-time fees:* $50 per term part-time. Part-time tuition and fees vary according to program. *Payment plans:* installment, deferred payment. *Waivers:* senior citizens and employees or children of employees.

Library Wahlstrom Library. *Operations spending 1999–2000:* $940,128. *Collection:* 272,430 titles, 2,117 serial subscriptions, 5,485 audiovisual materials.

College life *Housing:* on-campus residence required through sophomore year. *Option:* coed. *Social organizations:* national sororities, local fraternities, local sororities; 1% of eligible men and 2% of eligible women are members. *Most popular organizations:* student congress, international relations club, Black Students Alliance, scuba club, Japanese Student Association.

Campus security 24-hour emergency response devices and patrols, student patrols, late-night transport-escort service.

After graduation *Career center:* 1 full-time personnel. Services include job fairs, resume preparation, resume referral, career/interest testing, career counseling, careers library, job bank, job interviews. *Graduate education:* 15% of class of 1999 went directly to graduate and professional school: 5% business, 3% engineering, 2% graduate arts and sciences, 2% law, 1% dentistry, 1% medicine, 1% veterinary medicine.

Freshmen 1,732 applied, 1,354 admitted, 195 enrolled. 2 valedictorians.

Average high school GPA	2.86	SAT verbal scores above 500	37%
SAT math scores above 500	41%	ACT above 18	N/R
From top 10% of their h.s. class	10%	From top quarter	30%
From top half	61%	1998 freshmen returning in 1999	78%

Application *Options:* eApply at www.CollegeQuest.com, electronic application, early admission, early action, deferred entrance. *Application fee:* $40.

Connecticut

University of Bridgeport (continued)
Required: essay or personal statement; high school transcript; minimum 2.0 GPA. *Required for some:* interview; portfolio, audition. *Recommended:* 1 letter of recommendation; interview.
Standardized tests *Admission: Required:* SAT I or ACT. *Required for some:* SAT II Subject Tests.
Significant dates *Application deadlines:* 4/1 (freshmen), rolling (transfers). *Early action:* 1/1. *Notification:* continuous until 8/1 (freshmen), 1/15 (early action). *Financial aid deadline priority date:* 4/15.
Freshman Application Contact
Joseph Marrone, Director of Undergraduate Admissions, University of Bridgeport, 380 University Avenue, Bridgeport, CT 06601. **Phone:** 203-576-4552. **Toll-free phone:** 800-EXCEL-UB (in-state); 800-243-9496 (out-of-state). **Fax:** 203-576-4941. **E-mail:** admit@bridgeport.edu
Visit CollegeQuest.com for information on majors offered and athletics. College video available at CollegeQuest.com.

■ *See page 2698 for a narrative description.*

UNIVERSITY OF CONNECTICUT
Storrs, Connecticut

- **State-supported**, university, founded 1881
- **Degrees** associate, bachelor's, master's, doctoral, first professional, and post-master's certificates
- **Rural** 4,178-acre campus
- **Coed**, 11,987 undergraduate students, 95% full-time, 53% women, 47% men
- **Moderately difficult** entrance level, 70% of applicants were admitted
- **15:1 student-to-undergraduate faculty ratio**
- **66% graduate** in 6 years or less
- **$5404 tuition** and fees (in-state); $13,922 (out-of-state)
- **$6904 average financial aid** package, $16,598 average indebtedness upon graduation, $180.8 million endowment

Recognized for its excellent academic programs, knowledgeable professors, and top-notch athletics, UConn has also been called a "top value" and a "best buy." A top-rated research university, UConn is currently in the midst of a historic building program called UCONN 2000, a nationally unprecedented 10-year, $1-billion program to renew, rebuild, and enhance UConn campuses for the next century.

Students *Undergraduates:* 11,411 full-time, 576 part-time. Students come from 51 states and territories, 45 other countries. *The most frequently chosen baccalaureate fields are:* business/marketing, health professions and related sciences, social sciences and history. *Graduate:* 637 in professional programs, 5,863 in other graduate degree programs.

From out-of-state	19%	Reside on campus	69%
Age 25 or older	6%	Transferred in	4%
International students	1%	African Americans	5%
Asian Americans/Pacific Islanders	6%	Hispanic Americans	4%
Native Americans	0.3%		

Faculty 1,075 (97% full-time), 94% with terminal degrees.
Expenses (1999-2000) *Tuition, state resident:* full-time $4158; part-time $173 per credit. *Tuition, nonresident:* full-time $12,676; part-time $528 per credit. *Required fees:* full-time $1246; $117 per credit. Part-time tuition and fees vary according to course load. *College room and board:* $5694; room only: $2894. Room and board charges vary according to board plan and housing facility. *Payment plans:* installment, deferred payment. *Waivers:* employees or children of employees.
Library Homer Babbidge Library plus 3 others. *Operations spending 1999-2000:* $37.5 million. *Collection:* 2.2 million titles, 13,132 serial subscriptions, 28,658 audiovisual materials.
College life *Housing: Options:* coed, men-only, women-only. *Social organizations:* national fraternities, national sororities, local fraternities, local sororities; 9% of eligible men and 4% of eligible women are members.
Campus security 24-hour emergency response devices, late-night transport-escort service.
After graduation 330 organizations recruited on campus 1997-98. 71% of class of 1998 had job offers within 6 months. *Career center:* 14 full-time

personnel. Services include job fairs, resume preparation, interview workshops, resume referral, career/interest testing, career counseling, careers library, job bank, job interviews. *Graduate education:* 11% of class of 1999 went directly to graduate and professional school.
Freshmen 11,781 applied, 8,269 admitted, 2,956 enrolled. 12 National Merit Scholars, 26 valedictorians.

SAT verbal scores above 500	82%	SAT math scores above 500	84%
ACT above 18	N/R	From top 10% of their h.s. class	20%
From top quarter	58%	From top half	95%
1998 freshmen returning in 1999	86%		

Application *Options:* eApply at www.CollegeQuest.com, Common Application, early admission, early action, deferred entrance. *Application fee:* $50. *Required:* essay or personal statement; high school transcript. *Recommended:* 1 letter of recommendation.
Standardized tests *Admission: Required:* SAT I or ACT.
Significant dates *Application deadlines:* 3/1 (freshmen), 5/1 (transfers). *Financial aid deadline priority date:* 3/1.
Freshman Application Contact
Mr. Brian Usher, Associate Director of Admissions, University of Connecticut, 2131 Hillside Road, U-88, Storrs, CT 06269-3088. **Phone:** 860-486-3137. **Fax:** 860-486-1476. **E-mail:** beahusky@uconnvm.uconn.edu
Visit CollegeQuest.com for information on majors offered and athletics.

■ *See page 2716 for a narrative description.*

UNIVERSITY OF HARTFORD
West Hartford, Connecticut

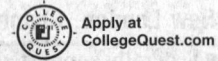

- **Independent**, comprehensive, founded 1877
- **Degrees** associate, bachelor's, master's, and doctoral
- **Suburban** 320-acre campus with easy access to Hartford
- **Coed**, 5,030 undergraduate students, 82% full-time, 53% women, 47% men
- **Moderately difficult** entrance level, 72% of applicants were admitted
- **13:1 student-to-undergraduate faculty ratio**
- **51.25% graduate** in 6 years or less
- **$19,696 tuition** and fees
- **$14,715 average financial aid** package, $72.5 million endowment

Students *Undergraduates:* 4,144 full-time, 886 part-time. Students come from 44 states and territories, 54 other countries. *The most frequently chosen baccalaureate fields are:* health professions and related sciences, business/marketing, visual/performing arts. *Graduate:* 1,542 in graduate degree programs.

From out-of-state	60%	Reside on campus	64%
Age 25 or older	14%	Transferred in	5%
International students	4%	African Americans	8%
Asian Americans/Pacific Islanders	2%	Hispanic Americans	4%
Native Americans	0.1%		

Faculty 618 (50% full-time).
Expenses (2000-2001) *Comprehensive fee:* $27,536 includes full-time tuition ($18,626), mandatory fees ($1070), and room and board ($7840). *College room only:* $4836. Room and board charges vary according to board plan and housing facility. *Part-time tuition:* $285 per credit. *Part-time fees:* $110 per term part-time. Part-time tuition and fees vary according to course load. *Payment plans:* tuition prepayment, installment. *Waivers:* senior citizens and employees or children of employees.
Library Mortenson Library. *Operations spending 1999-2000:* $2 million. *Collection:* 522,640 titles, 2,089 serial subscriptions.
College life *Housing: Options:* coed, disabled students. *Social organizations:* national fraternities, national sororities; 17% of eligible men and 21% of eligible women are members. *Most popular organizations:* Program Council, Brothers and Sisters United, Hillel, Student Government Association, Residence Hall Association.
Campus security 24-hour emergency response devices and patrols, late-night transport-escort service, controlled dormitory access, bicycle patrols.
After graduation *Career center:* 6 full-time, 1 part-time personnel. Services include resume preparation, career counseling, careers library, job interviews. *Graduate education:* 22% of class of 1999 went directly to graduate and professional school.

Connecticut

Freshmen 7,979 applied, 5,777 admitted, 1,410 enrolled.

SAT verbal scores above 500	62%	SAT math scores above 500	64%
ACT above 18	90%	From top 10% of their h.s. class	10%
From top quarter	33%	From top half	67%
1998 freshmen returning in 1999	74%		

Application *Options:* eApply at www.CollegeQuest.com, Common Application, electronic application, early admission, deferred entrance. *Application fee:* $35. *Required:* high school transcript. *Required for some:* essay or personal statement. *Recommended:* 2 letters of recommendation; interview.

Standardized tests *Admission: Required:* SAT I or ACT.

Significant dates *Application deadlines:* rolling (freshmen), rolling (transfers). *Financial aid deadline priority date:* 2/1.

Freshman Application Contact
Mr. Richard Zeiser, Dean of Admissions, University of Hartford, 200 Bloomfield Avenue, West Hartford, CT 06117-1599. **Phone:** 860-768-4296. **Toll-free phone:** 800-947-4303. **Fax:** 860-768-4961. **E-mail:** admission@uhavax.hartford.edu

Visit CollegeQuest.com for information on majors offered and athletics. College video and electronic viewbook available at CollegeQuest.com.

■ *See page 2732 for a narrative description.*

UNIVERSITY OF NEW HAVEN
West Haven, Connecticut

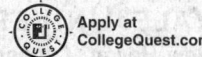

- **Independent**, university, founded 1920
- **Degrees** associate, bachelor's, master's, doctoral, post-master's, and postbachelor's certificates
- **Suburban** 78-acre campus with easy access to Hartford
- **Coed**, 2,496 undergraduate students, 60% full-time, 38% women, 62% men
- **Moderately difficult** entrance level, 78% of applicants were admitted
- **11:1 student-to-undergraduate faculty ratio**
- **37.1% graduate** in 6 years or less
- **$14,550 tuition** and fees
- **$12,800 average financial aid** package, $15,500 average indebtedness upon graduation, $5 million endowment

The University of New Haven is a comprehensive, independent, coeducational institution offering undergraduate and graduate degrees in arts and sciences, business, engineering, hotel/restaurant, tourism and dietetics administration, and public safety and professional studies. Small classes, close student-faculty relationships, and preparation for successful careers in today's competitive global marketplace are the hallmarks of a UNH education.

Students *Undergraduates:* 1,491 full-time, 1,005 part-time. Students come from 28 states and territories, 56 other countries. *The most frequently chosen baccalaureate fields are:* business/marketing, engineering/engineering technologies, protective services/public administration. *Graduate:* 1,878 in graduate degree programs.

From out-of-state	22%	Reside on campus	31%
Age 25 or older	36%	Transferred in	11%
International students	6%	African Americans	10%
Asian Americans/Pacific Islanders	2%	Hispanic Americans	5%
Native Americans	0.4%		

Faculty 207 (77% full-time).

Expenses (1999–2000) *Comprehensive fee:* $21,110 includes full-time tuition ($14,250), mandatory fees ($300), and room and board ($6560). Full-time tuition and fees vary according to program. Room and board charges vary according to board plan and housing facility. *Part-time tuition:* $270 per credit hour. *Part-time fees:* $10 per term part-time. Part-time tuition and fees vary according to class time, location, and program. *Payment plans:* installment, deferred payment. *Waivers:* senior citizens and employees or children of employees.

Library Marvin K. Peterson Library. *Operations spending 1999–2000:* $1 million. *Collection:* 535,381 titles, 223 audiovisual materials.

College life *Housing: Option:* coed. *Social organizations:* national fraternities, local fraternities, local sororities; 2% of eligible men and 3% of eligible women are members. *Most popular organizations:* Inter Fraternity/Sorority Council, WNHU (radio station), USGA (Undergraduate Student Government Association), American Criminal Justice Association, Black Student Union.

Campus security 24-hour emergency response devices and patrols, late-night transport-escort service, escort service, vehicle, bicycle and foot patrols, crime prevention programs.

After graduation *Career center:* 3 full-time, 1 part-time personnel. Services include job fairs, resume preparation, resume referral, career counseling, careers library, job bank, job interviews.

Freshmen 1,932 applied, 1,516 admitted, 417 enrolled. 20 class presidents, 3 valedictorians, 50 student government officers.

Average high school GPA	2.74	SAT verbal scores above 500	39%
SAT math scores above 500	36%	ACT above 18	N/R
1998 freshmen returning in 1999	70%		

Application *Options:* eApply at www.CollegeQuest.com, Common Application, deferred entrance. *Application fee:* $25. *Required:* high school transcript. *Recommended:* essay or personal statement; minimum 2.75 GPA; 3 letters of recommendation; interview.

Standardized tests *Admission: Required for some:* SAT I or ACT.

Significant dates *Application deadlines:* rolling (freshmen), rolling (transfers). *Financial aid deadline priority date:* 3/1.

Freshman Application Contact
Mr. Patrick Quinn, Director of Admissions, University of New Haven, 300 Orange Avenue, West Haven, CT 06516. **Phone:** 203-932-7469. **Toll-free phone:** 800-DIAL-UNH. **Fax:** 203-937-0756. **E-mail:** adminfo@charger.newhaven.edu

Visit CollegeQuest.com for information on majors offered and athletics. College video available at CollegeQuest.com.

■ *See page 2790 for a narrative description.*

WESLEYAN UNIVERSITY
Middletown, Connecticut

- **Independent**, university, founded 1831
- **Degrees** bachelor's, master's, doctoral, and post-master's certificates
- **Small-town** 120-acre campus
- **Coed**, 2,734 undergraduate students, 99.9% full-time, 52% women, 48% men
- **Most difficult** entrance level, 29% of applicants were admitted
- **9:1 student-to-undergraduate faculty ratio**
- **88% graduate** in 6 years or less
- **$25,120 tuition** and fees
- **$21,135 average financial aid** package, $24,430 average indebtedness upon graduation, $530.3 million endowment

Students *Undergraduates:* 2,732 full-time, 2 part-time. Students come from 51 states and territories, 35 other countries. *The most frequently chosen baccalaureate fields are:* psychology, English, social sciences and history. *Graduate:* 442 in graduate degree programs.

From out-of-state	91%	Reside on campus	93%
Transferred in	3%	International students	5%
African Americans	9%	Asian Americans/Pacific Islanders	7%
Hispanic Americans	6%	Native Americans	0.2%

Faculty 329 (85% full-time).

Expenses (2000–2001) *Comprehensive fee:* $31,630 includes full-time tuition ($24,330), mandatory fees ($790), and room and board ($6510). *College room only:* $3860. Full-time tuition and fees vary according to program. Room and board charges vary according to board plan and housing facility. Part-time tuition and fees vary according to program. *Payment plan:* installment. *Waivers:* employees or children of employees.

Library Olin Memorial Library plus 3 others. *Operations spending 1999–2000:* $4.7 million. *Collection:* 1.2 million titles, 3,166 serial subscriptions.

College life *Housing:* on-campus residence required in freshman year. *Option:* coed. *Social organizations:* national fraternities, national sororities, local fraternities, eating clubs; 4% of eligible men and 3% of eligible women are members. *Most popular organizations:* community service, Students of Color groups, theater- student and faculty productions, campus publications, intramurals.

Campus security 24-hour emergency response devices and patrols, student patrols, late-night transport-escort service, controlled dormitory access.

After graduation 180 organizations recruited on campus 1997–98. 70% of class of 1998 had job offers within 6 months. *Career center:* 5 full-time, 4

Connecticut

Wesleyan University *(continued)*
part-time personnel. Services include job fairs, resume preparation, interview workshops, resume referral, career/interest testing, career counseling, careers library, job bank, job interviews. *Graduate education:* 13% of class of 1999 went directly to graduate and professional school: 7% graduate arts and sciences, 3% medicine, 2% law, 1% business. *Major awards:* 6 Fulbright Scholars.

Freshmen 6,402 applied, 1,856 admitted, 732 enrolled. 247 National Merit Scholars, 80 class presidents, 212 valedictorians.

SAT verbal scores above 500	98%	SAT math scores above 500	98%
ACT above 18	N/R	From top 10% of their h.s. class	70%
From top quarter	90%	From top half	99%
1998 freshmen returning in 1999	95%		

Application *Options:* eApply at www.CollegeQuest.com, Common Application, electronic application, early admission, early decision, deferred entrance. *Application fee:* $55. *Required:* essay or personal statement; high school transcript; 3 letters of recommendation. *Recommended:* interview.

Standardized tests *Admission: Required:* SAT I and SAT II or ACT, SAT II: Writing Test.

Significant dates *Application deadlines:* 1/1 (freshmen), 3/15 (transfers). *Early decision:* 11/15 (for plan 1), 1/1 (for plan 2). *Notification:* 4/15 (freshmen), 12/15 (early decision plan 1), 2/20 (early decision plan 2). *Financial aid deadline:* 2/1.

Freshman Application Contact
Mrs. Nancy Hargrave Meislahn, Dean of Admissions and Financial Aid, Wesleyan University, Stewart M Reid House, Middletown, CT 06459-0265. **Phone:** 860-685-3000. **Fax:** 860-685-3001. **E-mail:** admissions@wesleyan.edu

Visit CollegeQuest.com for information on majors offered and athletics.

■ *See page 2938 for a narrative description.*

WESTERN CONNECTICUT STATE UNIVERSITY
Danbury, Connecticut

- **State-supported**, comprehensive, founded 1903
- **Degrees** associate, bachelor's, and master's
- **Urban** 340-acre campus with easy access to New York City
- **Coed**, 4,174 undergraduate students, 74% full-time, 55% women, 45% men
- **Moderately difficult** entrance level, 69% of applicants were admitted
- **15:1** student-to-undergraduate faculty ratio
- **44% graduate** in 6 years or less
- **$3758 tuition** and fees (in-state); $9298 (out-of-state)

Part of Connecticut State University System.

Students *Undergraduates:* 3,098 full-time, 1,076 part-time. Students come from 15 states and territories, 27 other countries. *The most frequently chosen baccalaureate fields are:* business/marketing, education, protective services/public administration. *Graduate:* 931 in graduate degree programs.

From out-of-state	10%	Age 25 or older	24%
Transferred in	9%	International students	1%
African Americans	6%	Asian Americans/Pacific Islanders	3%
Hispanic Americans	6%	Native Americans	0.3%

Faculty 328 (54% full-time).

Expenses (1999–2000) *Tuition, state resident:* full-time $2062; part-time $154 per semester hour. *Tuition, nonresident:* full-time $7602; part-time $154 per semester hour. *Required fees:* full-time $1696; $30 per term part-time. Full-time tuition and fees vary according to reciprocity agreements. *College room and board:* $5434; room only: $3750. Room and board charges vary according to housing facility. *Waivers:* senior citizens and employees or children of employees.

Library Ruth Haas Library plus 1 other. *Collection:* 261,328 titles, 2,538 serial subscriptions, 10,846 audiovisual materials.

College life *Housing:* Options: coed, women-only. *Social organizations:* national fraternities, national sororities, local sororities; 7% of eligible men and 5% of eligible women are members.

Campus security 24-hour emergency response devices and patrols, student patrols, late-night transport-escort service, controlled dormitory access.

After graduation *Career center:* 4 full-time personnel. Services include job fairs, resume preparation, interview workshops, resume referral, career/interest testing, career counseling, careers library, job bank. *Graduate education:* 20% of class of 1999 went directly to graduate and professional school: 6% graduate arts and sciences, 5% education, 3% business, 2% law.

Freshmen 2,369 applied, 1,643 admitted, 811 enrolled.

SAT verbal scores above 500	40%	SAT math scores above 500	38%
ACT above 18	N/R	From top 10% of their h.s. class	4%
From top quarter	15%	From top half	46%
1998 freshmen returning in 1999	63%		

Application *Options:* Common Application, electronic application, early admission, deferred entrance. *Preference* given to state residents. *Application fee:* $40. *Required:* high school transcript. *Required for some:* interview. *Recommended:* essay or personal statement; letters of recommendation.

Standardized tests *Admission: Required:* SAT I or ACT.

Significant dates *Application deadlines:* 5/1 (freshmen), 7/1 (transfers). *Financial aid deadline:* 4/15. *Priority date:* 3/15.

Freshman Application Contact
Mr. William Hawkins, Director of Admissions and Financial Aid, Western Connecticut State University, Undergraduate Admissions Office, 181 White Street, Danbury, CT 06810. **Phone:** 203-837-9000. **Toll-free phone:** 877-837-9278. **Fax:** 203-837-8320. **E-mail:** weasil@wcsu.edu

Visit CollegeQuest.com for information on majors offered and athletics. College video available at CollegeQuest.com.

YALE UNIVERSITY
New Haven, Connecticut

- **Independent**, university, founded 1701
- **Degrees** bachelor's, master's, doctoral, and first professional
- **Urban** 200-acre campus with easy access to New York City
- **Coed**, 5,294 undergraduate students, 99% full-time, 50% women, 50% men
- **Most difficult** entrance level, 16% of applicants were admitted
- **$24,500 tuition** and fees
- **$6.6 billion endowment**

Students *Undergraduates:* 5,273 full-time, 21 part-time. Students come from 55 states and territories, 74 other countries. *Graduate:* 1,226 in professional programs, 4,366 in other graduate degree programs.

From out-of-state	90%	Reside on campus	86%
Age 25 or older	1%	International students	6%
African Americans	7%	Asian Americans/Pacific Islanders	16%
Hispanic Americans	6%	Native Americans	1%

Expenses (1999–2000) *Comprehensive fee:* $31,940 includes full-time tuition ($24,500) and room and board ($7440). *College room only:* $4070. *Payment plan:* installment. *Waivers:* employees or children of employees.

Library Sterling Memorial Library plus 20 others. *Operations spending 1999–2000:* $16.4 million. *Collection:* 10.8 million titles, 57,377 serial subscriptions.

College life *Housing:* on-campus residence required through sophomore year. *Option:* coed. *Social organizations:* national fraternities, national sororities. *Most popular organizations:* community service, intramural sports, theater productions, music groups, campus publications.

Campus security 24-hour emergency response devices and patrols, late-night transport-escort service, controlled dormitory access.

After graduation 62% of class of 1998 had job offers within 6 months. *Career center:* 13 full-time, 20 part-time personnel. Services include resume preparation, interview workshops, resume referral, career counseling, careers library, job interviews. *Major awards:* 3 Rhodes, 20 Fulbright Scholars.

Freshmen 13,270 applied, 2,135 admitted, 1,296 enrolled. 2 Westinghouse recipients.

SAT verbal scores above 500	N/R	SAT math scores above 500	N/R
ACT above 18	N/R	From top 10% of their h.s. class	95%
1998 freshmen returning in 1999	98%		

Application *Options:* electronic application, early admission, early decision, deferred entrance. *Application fee:* $65. *Required:* essay or personal statement; high school transcript; 3 letters of recommendation. *Recommended:* interview.

Standardized tests *Admission: Required:* SAT I and SAT II or ACT.

Significant dates *Application deadlines:* 12/31 (freshmen), 3/1 (transfers). *Early decision:* 11/1. *Notification:* 4/1 (freshmen), 12/15 (early decision). *Financial aid deadline priority date:* 2/1.

Freshman Application Contact
Admissions Director, Yale University, PO Box 208234, New Haven, CT 06520-8324. **Phone:** 203-432-9300. **Fax:** 203-432-9392. **E-mail:** undergraduate.admissions@yale.edu

Visit CollegeQuest.com for information on majors offered and athletics. College video and electronic viewbook available at CollegeQuest.com.

DELAWARE

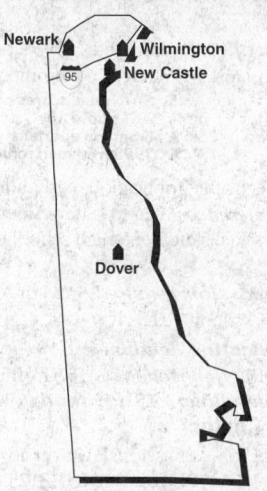

DELAWARE STATE UNIVERSITY
Dover, Delaware

- **State-supported**, comprehensive, founded 1891
- **Degrees** bachelor's and master's
- **Small-town** 400-acre campus
- **Coed**, 2,910 undergraduate students, 78% full-time, 59% women, 41% men
- **Moderately difficult** entrance level
- **13:1 student-to-undergraduate faculty ratio**
- **$3256 tuition** and fees (in-state); $7248 (out-of-state)
- **$5745 average financial aid** package, $12.3 million endowment

Part of Delaware Higher Education Commission.
Students *Undergraduates:* 2,272 full-time, 638 part-time. Students come from 33 states and territories. *The most frequently chosen baccalaureate fields are:* business/marketing, education, protective services/public administration. *Graduate:* 249 in graduate degree programs.

From out-of-state	47%	Reside on campus	46%
Age 25 or older	19%	Transferred in	5%
International students	4%	African Americans	77%
Asian Americans/Pacific Islanders	1%	Hispanic Americans	2%
Native Americans	0.2%		

Faculty 261 (70% full-time).
Expenses (1999–2000) *Tuition, state resident:* full-time $3096; part-time $129 per credit hour. *Tuition, nonresident:* full-time $7088; part-time $295 per credit hour. *Required fees:* full-time $160; $40 per term part-time. *College room and board:* $4880. Room and board charges vary according to housing facility. *Payment plans:* installment, deferred payment. *Waivers:* senior citizens and employees or children of employees.
Library William C. Jason Library. *Operations spending 1999–2000:* $1.3 million. *Collection:* 194,977 titles, 3,058 serial subscriptions.
College life *Social organizations:* national fraternities, national sororities; 50% of eligible men and 50% of eligible women are members. *Most popular organizations:* NAACP, Women's Senate, Men's Council.
Campus security 24-hour emergency response devices and patrols, student patrols, late-night transport-escort service, controlled dormitory access.
After graduation 246 organizations recruited on campus 1997–98. 20% of class of 1998 had job offers within 6 months. *Career center:* 3 full-time personnel. Services include job fairs, resume preparation, career/interest

Connecticut–Delaware

testing, career counseling, careers library, job bank, job interviews. *Graduate education:* 15% of class of 1999 went directly to graduate and professional school: 8% business, 6% graduate arts and sciences, 1% law.
Freshmen 684 enrolled.

Average high school GPA	2.62	SAT verbal scores above 500	N/R
SAT math scores above 500	N/R	ACT above 18	N/R
From top 10% of their h.s. class	5%	From top quarter	17%
From top half	52%	1998 freshmen returning in 1999	68%

Application *Options:* Common Application, early admission. *Preference* given to state residents. *Application fee:* $10. *Required:* high school transcript; minimum 2.0 GPA; 2 letters of recommendation. *Recommended:* interview.
Standardized tests *Admission:* Required: SAT I or ACT.
Significant dates *Application deadlines:* 6/1 (freshmen), 6/1 (transfers). *Financial aid deadline priority date:* 1/15.
Freshman Application Contact
Mr. Jethro C. Williams, Director of Admissions, Delaware State University, 1200 North Dupont Highway, Dover, DE 19901. **Phone:** 302-857-6353. **Fax:** 302-739-5309. **E-mail:** dadmiss@dsc.edu

Visit CollegeQuest.com for information on majors offered and athletics.

GOLDEY-BEACOM COLLEGE
Wilmington, Delaware

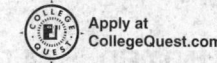
Apply at CollegeQuest.com

- **Independent**, comprehensive, founded 1886
- **Degrees** associate, bachelor's, and master's
- **Suburban** 27-acre campus with easy access to Philadelphia
- **Coed**, 1,248 undergraduate students, 56% full-time, 65% women, 35% men
- **Moderately difficult** entrance level, 84% of applicants were admitted
- **28:1 student-to-undergraduate faculty ratio**
- **$9398 tuition** and fees
- **$1.7 million endowment**

Goldey-Beacom is a small, private, nationally accredited college offering challenging undergraduate degrees in business as well as a master's in business administration. The College is known for dedicated faculty members, small class size, and individual attention and is recognized regionally as a leader in the business field. Apartment-style housing is available on the safe, suburban campus located 15 minutes from downtown Wilmington.

Students *Undergraduates:* 693 full-time, 555 part-time. Students come from 15 states and territories, 50 other countries. *Graduate:* 149 in graduate degree programs.

From out-of-state	50%	Reside on campus	16%
Age 25 or older	43%	Transferred in	4%

Faculty 49 (51% full-time), 43% with terminal degrees.
Expenses (2000–2001) *Tuition:* full-time $9248; part-time $272 per credit. *Required fees:* full-time $150; $5 per credit. *College room only:* $3490. *Payment plans:* installment, deferred payment. *Waivers:* employees or children of employees.
Library J. Wilbur Hirons Library. *Operations spending 1999–2000:* $120,352. *Collection:* 29,700 titles, 817 serial subscriptions.
College life *Housing: Option:* coed. *Social organizations:* national fraternities, national sororities; 10% of eligible men and 10% of eligible women are members. *Most popular organizations:* marketing/management association, Circle K International, data processing management association, GBC singers.
Campus security 24-hour emergency response devices.
After graduation 65 organizations recruited on campus 1997–98. 95% of class of 1998 had job offers within 6 months. *Career center:* 1 full-time personnel. Services include job fairs, resume preparation, resume referral, career counseling, careers library, job bank, job interviews. *Graduate education:* 5% of class of 1999 went directly to graduate and professional school: 4% business, 1% law.

Delaware

Goldey-Beacom College (continued)

Freshmen 684 applied, 574 admitted, 330 enrolled.

Average high school GPA	2.97	SAT verbal scores above 500	33%
SAT math scores above 500	32%	ACT above 18	N/R
From top 10% of their h.s. class	10%	From top quarter	30%
From top half	73%	1998 freshmen returning in 1999	70%

Application *Options:* eApply at www.CollegeQuest.com, Common Application, electronic application, early admission, deferred entrance. *Application fee:* $30. *Required:* high school transcript; minimum 2.0 GPA. *Required for some:* 1 letter of recommendation; interview.

Standardized tests *Admission: Required:* SAT I. *Required for some:* DTLS, DTMS.

Significant dates *Application deadlines:* rolling (freshmen), rolling (transfers). *Notification:* continuous until 8/15 (freshmen). *Financial aid deadline priority date:* 4/1.

Freshman Application Contact
Mr. Kevin M. McIntyre, Dean of Admissions, Goldey-Beacom College, 4701 Limestone Road, Wilmington, DE 19808-1999. **Phone:** 302-998-8814 Ext. 266. **Toll-free phone:** 800-833-4877. **Fax:** 302-996-5408. **E-mail:** mcintyrk@goldey.gbc.edu

Visit CollegeQuest.com for information on majors offered and athletics. College video available at CollegeQuest.com.

UNITED STATES OPEN UNIVERSITY
Wilmington, Delaware

Admissions Office Contact
United States Open University, 901 Market Street, Wilmington, DE 19801. **Toll-free phone:** 800-232-7705. **Fax:** 302-429-5953.

UNIVERSITY OF DELAWARE
Newark, Delaware

- **State-related**, university, founded 1743
- **Degrees** associate, bachelor's, master's, and doctoral
- **Small-town** 1,000-acre campus with easy access to Philadelphia and Baltimore
- **Coed**, 15,463 undergraduate students, 92% full-time, 59% women, 41% men
- **Moderately difficult** entrance level, 63% of applicants were admitted
- **13:1 student-to-undergraduate faculty ratio**
- **70% graduate** in 6 years or less
- **$4858 tuition** and fees (in-state); $13,228 (out-of-state)
- **$8200 average financial aid** package, $14,000 average indebtedness upon graduation, $777.4 million endowment

Students *Undergraduates:* 14,287 full-time, 1,176 part-time. Students come from 50 states and territories, 100 other countries. *The most frequently chosen baccalaureate fields are:* business/marketing, education, social sciences and history. *Graduate:* 3,108 in graduate degree programs.

From out-of-state	60%	Reside on campus	53%
Age 25 or older	7%	Transferred in	3%
International students	1%	African Americans	6%
Asian Americans/Pacific Islanders	3%	Hispanic Americans	2%
Native Americans	0.3%		

Faculty 1,215 (82% full-time), 79% with terminal degrees.

Expenses (1999–2000) *Tuition, state resident:* full-time $4380; part-time $183 per credit hour. *Tuition, nonresident:* full-time $12,750; part-time $531 per credit hour. *Required fees:* full-time $478; $15 per term part-time. *College room and board:* $5132; room only: $2810. Room and board charges vary according to housing facility. *Payment plans:* tuition prepayment, installment. *Waivers:* senior citizens and employees or children of employees.

Library Hugh Morris Library plus 3 others. *Operations spending 1999–2000:* $12.7 million. *Collection:* 12,220 serial subscriptions, 6,200 audiovisual materials.

College life *Housing:* on-campus residence required in freshman year. *Options:* coed, women-only, disabled students. *Social organizations:* national fraternities, national sororities, local sororities; 13% of eligible men and 15% of eligible women are members. *Most popular organizations:* Panhellenic Association, Hillel, Interfraternity Council, Resident Student Association, Business Student Association.

Campus security 24-hour emergency response devices and patrols, student patrols, late-night transport-escort service, controlled dormitory access.

After graduation 330 organizations recruited on campus 1997–98. 73% of class of 1998 had job offers within 6 months. *Career center:* 9 full-time, 3 part-time personnel. Services include job fairs, resume preparation, interview workshops, resume referral, career/interest testing, career counseling, careers library, job bank, job interviews. *Graduate education:* 18% of class of 1999 went directly to graduate and professional school: 10% graduate arts and sciences, 4% law, 3% business, 1% dentistry, 1% engineering, 1% medicine, 1% veterinary medicine.

Freshmen 14,107 applied, 8,891 admitted, 3,503 enrolled. 17 National Merit Scholars, 40 valedictorians, 759 student government officers.

Average high school GPA	3.5	SAT verbal scores above 500	84%
SAT math scores above 500	86%	ACT above 18	96%
From top 10% of their h.s. class	26%	From top quarter	62%
From top half	94%	1998 freshmen returning in 1999	87%

Application *Options:* electronic application, early admission, early decision, deferred entrance. *Preference* given to state residents. *Application fee:* $45. *Required:* essay or personal statement; high school transcript; 1 letter of recommendation.

Standardized tests *Admission: Required:* SAT I or ACT. *Recommended:* SAT II Subject Tests, SAT II: Writing Test.

Significant dates *Application deadlines:* 2/15 (freshmen), 5/1 (transfers). *Early decision:* 11/15. *Notification:* 3/15 (freshmen), 12/15 (early decision). *Financial aid deadline:* 3/15. Priority date: 2/1.

Freshman Application Contact
Mr. Larry Griffith, Director of Admissions, University of Delaware, 116 Hullihen Hall, Newark, DE 19716. **Phone:** 302-831-8123. **Fax:** 302-831-6905. **E-mail:** admissions@udel.edu

Visit CollegeQuest.com for information on majors offered and athletics. Electronic viewbook available at CollegeQuest.com.

WESLEY COLLEGE
Dover, Delaware

- **Independent United Methodist**, comprehensive, founded 1873
- **Degrees** associate, bachelor's, master's, and postbachelor's certificates
- **Small-town** 20-acre campus
- **Coed**, 1,401 undergraduate students, 74% full-time, 52% women, 48% men
- **Moderately difficult** entrance level, 37% of applicants were admitted
- **19:1 student-to-undergraduate faculty ratio**
- **51.4% graduate** in 6 years or less
- **$11,919 tuition** and fees
- **$5 million endowment**

Students *Undergraduates:* 1,039 full-time, 362 part-time. Students come from 15 states and territories, 9 other countries. *The most frequently chosen baccalaureate fields are:* business/marketing, education, psychology. *Graduate:* 93 in graduate degree programs.

From out-of-state	62%	Reside on campus	62%
Age 25 or older	14%	Transferred in	14%
International students	2%	African Americans	18%
Asian Americans/Pacific Islanders	1%	Hispanic Americans	2%

Faculty 77 (65% full-time), 56% with terminal degrees.

Expenses (2000–2001) *Comprehensive fee:* $16,937 includes full-time tuition ($11,314), mandatory fees ($605), and room and board ($5018). *College room only:* $2572. Full-time tuition and fees vary according to class time and program. Room and board charges vary according to board plan. *Part-time tuition:* $471 per credit hour. *Part-time fees:* $10 per term part-time. *Payment plan:* installment. *Waivers:* senior citizens and employees or children of employees.

Library Robert H. Parker Library. *Operations spending 1999–2000:* $230,400. *Collection:* 72,000 titles, 400 serial subscriptions, 1,814 audiovisual materials.

College life *Housing:* on-campus residence required in freshman year. *Options:* coed, men-only, women-only. *Social organizations:* national fraternities, national sororities, local fraternities, local sororities; 20% of eligible men and 20% of eligible women are members. *Most popular organizations:* Student Activity Board, Student Government Association, National Coeducation Community Service Organization.

Campus security 24-hour patrols, controlled dormitory access.

After graduation 36 organizations recruited on campus 1997–98. *Career center:* 1 full-time personnel. Services include job fairs, resume preparation, interview workshops, resume referral, career/interest testing, career counseling, careers library, job bank, job interviews.

Freshmen 1,587 applied, 591 admitted, 689 enrolled.

Average high school GPA	2.75	SAT verbal scores above 500	32%
SAT math scores above 500	28%	ACT above 18	N/R
From top 10% of their h.s. class	6%	From top quarter	12%
From top half	64%	1998 freshmen returning in 1999	70%

Application *Options:* Common Application, early admission, early decision, deferred entrance. *Application fee:* $20. *Required:* essay or personal statement; high school transcript; minimum 2.2 GPA; 1 letter of recommendation. *Recommended:* interview.

Standardized tests *Placement: Required:* SAT I or ACT

Significant dates *Application deadlines:* rolling (freshmen), rolling (transfers). *Early decision:* 11/15. *Notification:* 12/1 (early decision). **Financial aid deadline priority date:** 4/15.

Freshman Application Contact Mr. Art Jacobs, Director of Admissions, Wesley College, 120 North State Street, Dover, DE 19901-3875. **Phone:** 302-736-2400. **Toll-free phone:** 800-937-5398. **Fax:** 302-736-2301. **E-mail:** admissions@mail.wesley.edu

Visit CollegeQuest.com for information on majors offered and athletics. College video available at CollegeQuest.com.

■ *See page 2940 for a narrative description.*

WILMINGTON COLLEGE
New Castle, Delaware

- **Independent**, comprehensive, founded 1967
- **Degrees** associate, bachelor's, master's, doctoral, post-master's, and postbachelor's certificates
- **Suburban** 17-acre campus with easy access to Philadelphia
- **Coed**, 3,560 undergraduate students, 36% full-time, 74% women, 26% men
- **Noncompetitive** entrance level, 99% of applicants were admitted
- **18:1 student-to-undergraduate faculty ratio**
- **$6110 tuition** and fees
- **$15 million endowment**

Wilmington College is a small career-oriented college that specializes in offering a personal learning atmosphere to every student. Wilmington College encourages applications from students who, in its judgment, show promise of academic achievement regardless of past performance. Applications are reviewed and accepted on a continuous basis. Freshmen and transfer students are admitted to the fall, spring, and summer terms.

Students *Undergraduates:* 1,279 full-time, 2,281 part-time. Students come from 7 states and territories.

| Age 25 or older | 51% |

Faculty 584 (8% full-time).

Expenses (1999–2000) *Tuition:* full-time $6060; part-time $202 per credit hour. *Required fees:* full-time $50; $25 per term part-time. Full-time tuition and fees vary according to degree level and location. Part-time tuition and fees vary according to degree level and location. *Payment plan:* installment. *Waivers:* employees or children of employees.

Library Robert C. and Dorothy M. Peoples Library plus 1 other. *Collection:* 111,000 titles, 500 serial subscriptions, 6,795 audiovisual materials.

College life *Housing:* college housing not available.

Campus security 24-hour emergency response devices and patrols, late-night transport-escort service.

After graduation 5 organizations recruited on campus 1997–98. *Career center:* Services include job fairs, resume preparation, resume referral, careers library, job interviews.

Freshmen 738 applied, 733 admitted, 958 enrolled.

Average high school GPA	2.5	SAT verbal scores above 500	N/R
SAT math scores above 500	N/R	ACT above 18	N/R
1998 freshmen returning in 1999	85%		

Application *Options:* early admission, deferred entrance. *Application fee:* $25. *Required:* high school transcript. *Recommended:* letters of recommendation; interview.

Standardized tests *Placement: Recommended:* SAT I or ACT.

Significant dates *Application deadlines:* rolling (freshmen), rolling (transfers).

Freshman Application Contact Dr. JoAnn Ciuffetelli, Assistant Director of Admissions, Wilmington College, 320 DuPont Highway, New Castle, DE 19720-6491. **Phone:** 302-328-9407 Ext. 104. **Toll-free phone:** 877-967-5464. **Fax:** 302-328-5902. **E-mail:** jciuf@wilm.coll.edu

Visit CollegeQuest.com for information on majors offered and athletics. College video available at CollegeQuest.com.

■ *See page 3006 for a narrative description.*

DISTRICT OF COLUMBIA

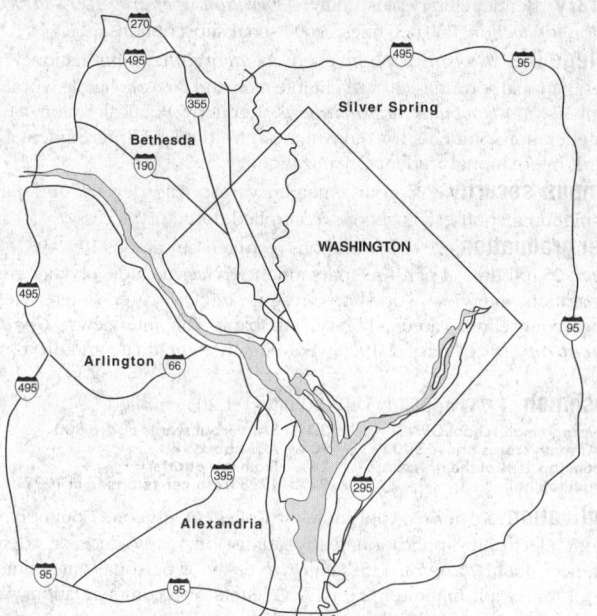

AMERICAN INTERCONTINENTAL UNIVERSITY
Washington, District of Columbia

Admissions Office Contact American InterContinental University, Suite 1C, 1776 G Street NW, Washington, DC 20006. **Toll-free phone:** 800-295-9989. **Fax:** 202-478-6201.

AMERICAN UNIVERSITY
Washington, District of Columbia

Apply at CollegeQuest.com

- **Independent Methodist**, university, founded 1893
- **Degrees** associate, bachelor's, master's, doctoral, and first professional
- **Suburban** 77-acre campus with easy access to Baltimore
- **Coed**, 5,161 undergraduate students, 91% full-time, 61% women, 39% men
- **Moderately difficult** entrance level, 72% of applicants were admitted
- **14:1 student-to-undergraduate faculty ratio**
- **67.2% graduate** in 6 years or less
- **$21,399 tuition** and fees
- **$19,470 average financial aid** package, $132 million endowment

District of Columbia

American University (continued)
American University is for students who want to understand and influence how the world works. American's unique curriculum, location in Washington, D.C., and emphasis on the practical application of knowledge prepare students to be major contributors in their fields. AU's students come from all 50 states and 150 countries.

Students *Undergraduates:* 4,707 full-time, 454 part-time. Students come from 53 states and territories, 130 other countries. *The most frequently chosen baccalaureate fields are:* business/marketing, communications/communication technologies, social sciences and history. *Graduate:* 1,313 in professional programs, 4,048 in other graduate degree programs.

From out-of-state	85%	Reside on campus	57%
Age 25 or older	7%	Transferred in	7%
International students	13%	African Americans	7%
Asian Americans/Pacific Islanders	3%	Hispanic Americans	5%
Native Americans	0.4%		

Faculty 463 full-time.

Expenses (2000–2001) *Comprehensive fee:* $29,791 includes full-time tuition ($21,144), mandatory fees ($255), and room and board ($8392). *College room only:* $5370. Room and board charges vary according to board plan and housing facility. *Payment plans:* tuition prepayment, installment, deferred payment. *Waivers:* senior citizens and employees or children of employees.

Library Bender Library plus 1 other. *Operations spending 1999–2000:* $8.4 million. *Collection:* 700,000 titles, 3,600 serial subscriptions.

College life *Housing:* Option: coed. *Social organizations:* national fraternities, national sororities; 20% of eligible men and 25% of eligible women are members. *Most popular organizations:* Kennedy Political Union, Student Confederation, Students for the American Volunteer Effort, Student Union Board, International Student Organization.

Campus security 24-hour emergency response devices and patrols, late-night transport-escort service, controlled dormitory access.

After graduation 200 organizations recruited on campus 1997–98. *Career center:* 25 full-time, 4 part-time personnel. Services include job fairs, resume preparation, interview workshops, resume referral, career/interest testing, career counseling, careers library, job bank, job interviews. *Graduate education:* 50% of class of 1999 went directly to graduate and professional school.

Freshmen 7,754 applied, 5,603 admitted, 1,203 enrolled.

Average high school GPA	3.19	SAT verbal scores above 500	93%
SAT math scores above 500	90%	ACT above 18	99%
From top 10% of their h.s. class	24%	From top quarter	61%
From top half	92%	1998 freshmen returning in 1999	85%

Application *Options:* eApply at www.CollegeQuest.com, Common Application, electronic application, early admission, early decision, deferred entrance. *Application fee:* $45. *Required:* essay or personal statement; high school transcript; minimum 2.0 GPA; 3 letters of recommendation; writing sample. *Recommended:* minimum 3.0 GPA; interview.

Standardized tests *Admission: Required:* SAT I or ACT. *Recommended:* SAT II Subject Tests.

Significant dates *Application deadlines:* 2/1 (freshmen), 7/1 (transfers). *Early decision:* 11/15. *Notification:* 4/1 (freshmen), 12/31 (early decision). *Financial aid deadline priority date:* 3/1.

Freshman Application Contact
Ms. Sharon Alson, Director of Admissions, American University, 4400 Massachusetts Avenue, NW, Washington, DC 20016-8001. **Phone:** 202-885-6000. **Fax:** 202-885-6014. **E-mail:** afa@american.edu

Visit CollegeQuest.com for information on majors offered and athletics. College video available at CollegeQuest.com.

■ *See page 1164 for a narrative description.*

THE CATHOLIC UNIVERSITY OF AMERICA
Washington, District of Columbia

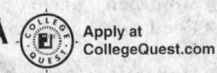
Apply at CollegeQuest.com

- **Independent**, university, founded 1887, affiliated with Roman Catholic Church
- **Degrees** bachelor's, master's, doctoral, first professional, and post-master's certificates
- **Urban** 144-acre campus
- **Coed**, 2,494 undergraduate students, 92% full-time, 54% women, 46% men
- **Moderately difficult** entrance level, 88% of applicants were admitted
- **10:1 student-to-undergraduate faculty ratio**
- **$18,972 tuition** and fees

Students *Undergraduates:* 2,304 full-time, 190 part-time. Students come from 50 states and territories, 48 other countries. *The most frequently chosen baccalaureate fields are:* architecture, engineering/engineering technologies, social sciences and history. *Graduate:* 975 in professional programs, 2,065 in other graduate degree programs.

From out-of-state	94%	Reside on campus	59%
Age 25 or older	9%	Transferred in	3%
International students	5%	African Americans	8%
Asian Americans/Pacific Islanders	5%	Hispanic Americans	5%
Native Americans	0.3%		

Faculty 649 (56% full-time).

Expenses (1999–2000) *One-time required fee:* $126. *Comprehensive fee:* $26,737 includes full-time tuition ($18,200), mandatory fees ($772), and room and board ($7765). *College room only:* $4285. Full-time tuition and fees vary according to program. Room and board charges vary according to board plan and housing facility. *Part-time tuition:* $700 per credit. *Part-time fees:* $194 per term part-time. *Payment plans:* installment, deferred payment. *Waivers:* employees or children of employees.

Library Mullen Library plus 7 others. *Operations spending 1999–2000:* $6 million. *Collection:* 1.4 million titles, 10,945 serial subscriptions, 35,080 audiovisual materials.

College life *Housing:* on-campus residence required through sophomore year. *Options:* coed, men-only, women-only. *Social organizations:* national fraternities, national sororities, local sororities; 1% of eligible men and 1% of eligible women are members. *Most popular organizations:* CUA Rowing Association, Cardinal Yearbook, College Republicans, Habitat for Humanity.

Campus security 24-hour emergency response devices and patrols, late-night transport-escort service, controlled dormitory access, controlled access of academic buildings.

After graduation 160 organizations recruited on campus 1997–98. 88% of class of 1998 had job offers within 6 months. *Career center:* 5 full-time personnel. Services include job fairs, resume preparation, resume referral, career counseling, careers library, job bank, job interviews. *Graduate education:* 33% of class of 1999 went directly to graduate and professional school: 10% graduate arts and sciences, 7% engineering, 6% law, 4% medicine, 3% education, 2% business, 1% dentistry.

Freshmen 2,604 applied, 2,295 admitted, 797 enrolled.

Average high school GPA	3.3	SAT verbal scores above 500	86%
SAT math scores above 500	83%	ACT above 18	93%
From top 10% of their h.s. class	27%	From top quarter	56%
From top half	88%	1998 freshmen returning in 1999	85%

Application *Options:* eApply at www.CollegeQuest.com, Common Application, early admission, early action, deferred entrance. *Application fee:* $55. *Required:* essay or personal statement; high school transcript; 1 letter of recommendation.

Standardized tests *Admission: Required:* SAT I or ACT. *Recommended:* SAT II Subject Tests, SAT II: Writing Test.

Significant dates *Application deadlines:* 2/15 (freshmen), 5/1 (transfers). *Early action:* 11/15. *Notification:* 4/15 (freshmen), 12/15 (early action). *Financial aid deadline priority date:* 2/1.

Freshman Application Contact
Mr. John Dolan, Dean of Enrollment Management, The Catholic University of America, Cardinal Station Post Office, Washington, DC 20064. **Phone:** 202-319-5305. **Toll-free phone:** 800-673-2772. **Fax:** 202-319-6533. **E-mail:** cua-admissions@cua.edu

Visit CollegeQuest.com for information on majors offered and athletics. College video and electronic viewbook available at CollegeQuest.com.

■ *See page 1382 for a narrative description.*

District of Columbia

THE CORCORAN COLLEGE OF ART AND DESIGN
Washington, District of Columbia

- **Independent**, 4-year, founded 1890
- **Degree** bachelor's
- **Urban** 7-acre campus
- **Coed**, 292 undergraduate students, 99% full-time, 66% women, 34% men
- **Moderately difficult** entrance level, 58% of applicants were admitted
- **8:1 student-to-undergraduate faculty ratio**
- **44% graduate** in 6 years or less
- **$14,140 tuition** and fees
- **$7670 average financial aid** package, $29.5 million endowment

Students *Undergraduates:* 289 full-time, 3 part-time. Students come from 20 states and territories, 14 other countries. *The most frequently chosen baccalaureate field is:* visual/performing arts.

From out-of-state	86%	Age 25 or older	24%
Transferred in	18%	International students	13%
African Americans	8%	Asian Americans/Pacific Islanders	8%
Hispanic Americans	7%	Native Americans	0.3%

Faculty 35 (83% full-time), 60% with terminal degrees.

Expenses (1999–2000) *Tuition:* full-time $14,110; part-time $366 per credit. *Required fees:* full-time $30. Part-time tuition and fees vary according to course load. *Payment plan:* installment. *Waivers:* employees or children of employees.

Library Corcoran School of Art Library. *Operations spending 1999–2000:* $160,000. *Collection:* 20,518 titles, 148 serial subscriptions, 45,175 audiovisual materials.

College life *Housing:* college housing not available. *Most popular organization:* Student Government Association.

Campus security 24-hour patrols, ID check at all entrances.

After graduation *Career center:* 1 part-time personnel. Services include job fairs, resume preparation, interview workshops, resume referral, career counseling, careers library, job bank, job interviews.

Freshmen 227 applied, 132 admitted, 44 enrolled.

Average high school GPA	2.94	SAT verbal scores above 500	61%
SAT math scores above 500	42%	ACT above 18	67%
From top 10% of their h.s. class	16%	From top quarter	26%
From top half	74%	1998 freshmen returning in 1999	65%

Application *Options:* early admission, deferred entrance. *Application fee:* $30. *Required:* high school transcript; minimum 2.5 GPA; portfolio. *Required for some:* essay or personal statement; 2 letters of recommendation; interview. *Recommended:* essay or personal statement; minimum 3.0 GPA; 2 letters of recommendation; interview.

Standardized tests *Admission: Required:* SAT I or ACT.

Significant dates *Application deadlines:* rolling (freshmen), rolling (transfers). *Financial aid deadline priority date:* 3/15.

Freshman Application Contact
Ms. Anne E. Bowman, Director of Admissions, The Corcoran College of Art and Design, 500 17th Street, NW, Washington, DC 20006-4804. **Phone:** 202-639-1814. **Toll-free phone:** 888-CORCORAN. **E-mail:** admofc@corcoran.org

Visit CollegeQuest.com for information on majors offered and athletics.

GALLAUDET UNIVERSITY
Washington, District of Columbia

- **Independent**, university, founded 1864
- **Degrees** bachelor's, master's, and doctoral (all undergraduate programs open primarily to hearing-impaired)
- **Urban** 99-acre campus
- **Coed**, 1,190 undergraduate students, 86% full-time, 54% women, 46% men
- **Moderately difficult** entrance level, 75% of applicants were admitted
- **6:1 student-to-undergraduate faculty ratio**
- **24% graduate** in 6 years or less
- **$7180 tuition** and fees
- **$127.8 million endowment**

Students *Undergraduates:* 1,026 full-time, 164 part-time. Students come from 51 states and territories, 58 other countries. *The most frequently chosen baccalaureate fields are:* biological/life sciences, education, protective services/public administration. *Graduate:* 417 in graduate degree programs.

From out-of-state	99%	Reside on campus	62%
Age 25 or older	20%	Transferred in	6%
International students	11%	African Americans	10%
Asian Americans/Pacific Islanders	4%	Hispanic Americans	6%
Native Americans	1%		

Faculty 227 (100% full-time).

Expenses (1999–2000) *One-time required fee:* $10. *Comprehensive fee:* $14,310 includes full-time tuition ($6870), mandatory fees ($310), and room and board ($7130). *College room only:* $4070. Room and board charges vary according to board plan. *Part-time tuition:* $344 per credit hour. *Payment plan:* installment. *Waivers:* employees or children of employees.

Library Merrill Learning Center. *Operations spending 1999–2000:* $1.6 million. *Collection:* 159,142 titles, 1,649 serial subscriptions, 188,130 audiovisual materials.

College life *Housing: Option:* coed. *Social organizations:* national fraternities, national sororities, local fraternities, local sororities.

Campus security 24-hour emergency response devices and patrols, late-night transport-escort service.

After graduation *Career center:* 15 full-time personnel. Services include job fairs, resume preparation, resume referral, career counseling, careers library, job bank, job interviews. *Graduate education:* 25% of class of 1999 went directly to graduate and professional school. *Major awards:* 3 Fulbright Scholars.

Freshmen 642 applied, 479 admitted, 253 enrolled.

SAT verbal scores above 500	N/R	SAT math scores above 500	N/R
ACT above 18	N/R	1998 freshmen returning in 1999	63%

Application *Options:* early admission, deferred entrance. *Application fee:* $35. *Required:* high school transcript; 1 letter of recommendation; audiogram. *Required for some:* interview. *Recommended:* essay or personal statement.

Standardized tests *Admission: Required:* Stanford Achievement Test. *Recommended:* SAT I or ACT.

Significant dates *Application deadlines:* 7/1 (freshmen), 5/15 (transfers). *Financial aid deadline priority date:* 8/15.

Freshman Application Contact
Ms. Deborah E. DeStefano, Director of Admissions, Gallaudet University, 800 Florida Avenue, NE, Washington, DC 20002-3625. **Phone:** 202-651-5750. **Toll-free phone:** 800-995-0550. **Fax:** 202-651-5774. **E-mail:** admissions@gallua.gallaudet.edu

Visit CollegeQuest.com for information on majors offered and athletics. College video and electronic viewbook available at CollegeQuest.com.

GEORGETOWN UNIVERSITY
Washington, District of Columbia

- **Independent Roman Catholic (Jesuit)**, university, founded 1789
- **Degrees** bachelor's, master's, doctoral, and first professional
- **Urban** 110-acre campus
- **Coed**, 6,089 undergraduate students, 98% full-time, 54% women, 46% men
- **Most difficult** entrance level, 23% of applicants were admitted
- **12:1 student-to-undergraduate faculty ratio**
- **90.2% graduate** in 6 years or less
- **$23,295 tuition** and fees
- **$19,048 average financial aid** package, $19,016 average indebtedness upon graduation, $704 million endowment

The School of Nursing offers a program committed to values and education in the Jesuit tradition. Opportunities for study include the Bachelor or Science degree in nursing or health studies. Students at the School of Nursing have a chance to study abroad as well as at some of the nation's most prestigious health-care centers.

Students *Undergraduates:* 5,937 full-time, 152 part-time. Students come from 52 states and territories, 84 other countries. *The most frequently chosen baccalaureate fields are:* business/marketing, English, social sciences and history. *Graduate:* 2,721 in professional programs, 3,416 in other graduate

District of Columbia

Georgetown University (continued)
degree programs.

From out-of-state	99%	Reside on campus	67%
Age 25 or older	4%	Transferred in	4%
International students	7%	African Americans	6%
Asian Americans/Pacific Islanders	9%	Hispanic Americans	6%
Native Americans	0.2%		

Faculty 1,074 (58% full-time).
Expenses (1999–2000) *Comprehensive fee:* $31,988 includes full-time tuition ($23,088), mandatory fees ($207), and room and board ($8693). *College room only:* $5605. Room and board charges vary according to board plan and housing facility. *Part-time tuition:* $962 per credit hour. Part-time tuition and fees vary according to course load. *Payment plans:* installment, deferred payment. *Waivers:* employees or children of employees.
Library Lauinger Library plus 6 others. *Operations spending 1999–2000:* $17.1 million. *Collection:* 2.4 million titles, 27,379 serial subscriptions, 150,206 audiovisual materials.
College life *Housing:* on-campus residence required through sophomore year. *Options:* coed, disabled students. *Most popular organizations:* university choir, Mask and Bauble, student newspaper, international relations, Young Democrats/Republicans.
Campus security 24-hour emergency response devices and patrols, late-night transport-escort service, controlled dormitory access.
After graduation 327 organizations recruited on campus 1997–98. 75% of class of 1998 had job offers within 6 months. *Career center:* 16 full-time, 4 part-time personnel. Services include job fairs, resume preparation, interview workshops, career/interest testing, career counseling, careers library, job bank, job interviews, career network database, networking events on campus. *Graduate education:* 20% of class of 1999 went directly to graduate and professional school: 7% graduate arts and sciences, 6% law, 6% medicine, 1% business.
Freshmen 13,244 applied, 3,024 admitted, 1,498 enrolled. 1 Westinghouse recipient, 60 class presidents, 114 valedictorians, 221 student government officers.

SAT verbal scores above 500	97%	SAT math scores above 500	98%
ACT above 18	99%	From top 10% of their h.s. class	78%
From top quarter	94%	From top half	99%
1998 freshmen returning in 1999	97%		

Application *Options:* electronic application, early admission, early action, deferred entrance. *Application fee:* $50. *Required:* essay or personal statement; high school transcript; 2 letters of recommendation; interview.
Standardized tests *Admission: Required:* SAT I or ACT. *Recommended:* SAT II Subject Tests, SAT II: Writing Test.
Significant dates *Application deadlines:* 1/10 (freshmen), 3/1 (transfers). *Early action:* 11/1. *Notification:* 4/1 (freshmen), 12/15 (early action). *Financial aid deadline priority date:* 2/1.
Freshman Application Contact
Mr. Charles A. Deacon, Dean of Undergraduate Admissions, Georgetown University, 37th and O Street, NW, Washington, DC 20057. **Phone:** 202-687-3600. **Fax:** 202-687-6660.
Visit CollegeQuest.com for information on majors offered and athletics.

■ *See page 1714 for a narrative description.*

THE GEORGE WASHINGTON UNIVERSITY
Washington, District of Columbia

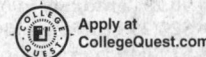 Apply at CollegeQuest.com

■ **Independent**, university, founded 1821
■ **Degrees** associate, bachelor's, master's, doctoral, first professional, post-master's, and postbachelor's certificates
■ **Urban** 36-acre campus
■ **Coed**, 8,168 undergraduate students, 89% full-time, 56% women, 44% men
■ **Very difficult** entrance level, 49% of applicants were admitted
■ **67% graduate** in 6 years or less
■ **$23,375 tuition** and fees
■ **$20,900 average financial aid** package, $18,953 average indebtedness upon graduation, $513 million endowment

Students *Undergraduates:* 7,285 full-time, 883 part-time. Students come from 55 states and territories, 101 other countries. *The most frequently chosen baccalaureate fields are:* business/marketing, psychology, social sciences and history. *Graduate:* 2,073 in professional programs, 9,578 in other graduate degree programs.

From out-of-state	92%	Reside on campus	57%
Age 25 or older	4%	Transferred in	3%
International students	6%	African Americans	7%
Asian Americans/Pacific Islanders	10%	Hispanic Americans	5%
Native Americans	0.4%		

Faculty 739 full-time.
Expenses (1999–2000) *Comprehensive fee:* $31,585 includes full-time tuition ($22,340), mandatory fees ($1035), and room and board ($8210). *College room only:* $5510. Room and board charges vary according to board plan and housing facility. *Part-time tuition:* $722 per credit hour. *Part-time fees:* $34 per credit hour. *Payment plans:* installment, deferred payment. *Waivers:* employees or children of employees.
Library Gelman Library plus 2 others. *Collection:* 1.8 million titles, 14,729 serial subscriptions, 17,246 audiovisual materials.
College life *Housing: Options:* coed, women-only. *Social organizations:* national fraternities, national sororities; 16% of eligible men and 14% of eligible women are members. *Most popular organizations:* Program Board, Student Association, Residence Hall Association, College Democrats, College Republicans.
Campus security 24-hour emergency response devices and patrols, late-night transport-escort service, controlled dormitory access.
After graduation 88 organizations recruited on campus 1997–98. *Career center:* 21 full-time, 1 part-time personnel. Services include job fairs, resume preparation, resume referral, career counseling, careers library, job bank, job interviews. *Graduate education:* 21% of class of 1999 went directly to graduate and professional school: 7% graduate arts and sciences, 6% law, 4% medicine, 2% business. *Major awards:* 1 Marshall, 4 Fulbright Scholars.
Freshmen 14,326 applied, 7,087 admitted, 2,120 enrolled. 36 National Merit Scholars.

SAT verbal scores above 500	95%	SAT math scores above 500	97%
ACT above 18	99%	From top 10% of their h.s. class	47%
From top quarter	84%	From top half	99%
1998 freshmen returning in 1999	92%		

Application *Options:* eApply at www.CollegeQuest.com, Common Application, electronic application, early admission, early decision, deferred entrance. *Application fee:* $60. *Required:* essay or personal statement; high school transcript; 2 letters of recommendation. *Recommended:* interview.
Standardized tests *Admission: Required:* SAT I or ACT. *Recommended:* SAT I, SAT II: Writing Test. *Required for some:* SAT II Subject Tests.
Significant dates *Application deadlines:* 2/1 (freshmen), 6/1 (transfers). *Early decision:* 12/1. *Notification:* 3/15 (freshmen), 12/15 (early decision). *Financial aid deadline priority date:* 2/1.
Freshman Application Contact
Dr. Kathryn M. Napper, Director of Admission, The George Washington University, Office of Undergraduate Admissions, Washington, DC 20052. **Phone:** 202-994-6040. **Toll-free phone:** 800-447-3765. **E-mail:** gwadm@gwis2.circ.gwu.edu
Visit CollegeQuest.com for information on majors offered and athletics. College video available at CollegeQuest.com.

HOWARD UNIVERSITY
Washington, District of Columbia

■ **Independent**, university, founded 1867
■ **Degrees** bachelor's, master's, doctoral, first professional, post-master's, and first professional certificates
■ **Urban** 242-acre campus
■ **Coed**, 6,075 undergraduate students, 85% full-time, 63% women, 37% men
■ **Moderately difficult** entrance level, 56% of applicants were admitted
■ **$9330 tuition** and fees
■ **$296.5 million endowment**

Students *Undergraduates:* 5,145 full-time, 930 part-time. Students come from 50 states and territories. *The most frequently chosen baccalaureate fields* *are:* business/marketing, biological/life sciences, health professions and related sciences. ***Graduate:*** 1,141 in professional programs, 2,363 in other graduate degree programs.

From out-of-state	90%	Reside on campus	57%
Age 25 or older	33%	Transferred in	6%
African Americans	79%	Asian Americans/Pacific Islanders	1%
Hispanic Americans	1%	Native Americans	0.1%

Faculty 1,305 (83% full-time).
Expenses (1999–2000) *Comprehensive fee:* $13,634 includes full-time tuition ($8925), mandatory fees ($405), and room and board ($4304). *College room only:* $2506. Room and board charges vary according to board plan and housing facility. *Part-time tuition:* $372 per credit hour. *Part-time fees:* $232 per term part-time. *Payment plan:* deferred payment. *Waivers:* employees or children of employees.
Library Founders Library plus 8 others. *Operations spending 1999–2000:* $14.5 million. *Collection:* 120,243 audiovisual materials.
College life *Housing:* on-campus residence required through sophomore year. *Option:* coed. *Social organizations:* national fraternities, national sororities, local fraternities; 2% of eligible men and 1% of eligible women are members. *Most popular organizations:* Howard University Student Association, Undergraduate Student Assembly, Campus Pals.
Campus security 24-hour emergency response devices and patrols, student patrols, late-night transport-escort service, controlled dormitory access, security lighting.
After graduation *Career center:* 6 full-time, 2 part-time personnel. Services include job fairs, resume preparation, resume referral, career counseling, careers library, job bank, job interviews. *Graduate education:* 55% of class of 1999 went directly to graduate and professional school.
Freshmen 6,664 applied, 3,701 admitted, 982 enrolled. 41 National Merit Scholars.

Average high school GPA	3.03	SAT verbal scores above 500	N/R
SAT math scores above 500	N/R	ACT above 18	N/R
1998 freshmen returning in 1999	84%		

Application *Options:* electronic application, early admission, early action, deferred entrance. *Application fee:* $45. *Required:* high school transcript. *Required for some:* 2 letters of recommendation.
Standardized tests *Admission:* Required: SAT I or ACT, SAT II: Writing Test.
Significant dates *Application deadlines:* 4/1 (freshmen), 4/1 (transfers). *Early action:* 11/30. *Notification:* 12/25 (early action). **Financial aid deadline priority date:** 2/15.
Freshman Application Contact
Ms. Linda Sanders-Hawkins, Interim Director of Admissions, Howard University, 2400 Sixth Street, NW, Washington, DC 20059-0002. **Phone:** 202-806-2700. **Toll-free phone:** 800-HOWARD-U. **E-mail:** admissions@howard.edu
Visit CollegeQuest.com for information on majors offered and athletics. College video available at CollegeQuest.com.

■ *See page 1806 for a narrative description.*

MOUNT VERNON COLLEGE
District of Columbia—See The George Washington University

POTOMAC COLLEGE
Washington, District of Columbia

- **Proprietary**, 4-year, founded 1991
- **Degree** bachelor's
- **Urban** campus
- **Coed**
- **Noncompetitive** entrance level

Institutional Web site http://www.potomac.edu/
College life *Housing:* college housing not available. *Most popular organization:* Student Government Association.
Campus security 24-hour emergency response devices.

Application *Application fee:* $0. *Required:* high school transcript; interview; 4 years post high school work experience; minimum employment of 20 hours per week.
Admissions Office Contact
Potomac College, 4000 Chesapeake Street, NW, Washington, DC 20016. **Toll-free phone:** 888-686-0876. **Fax:** 202-686-0818. **E-mail:** cdresser@potomac.edu
Visit CollegeQuest.com for information on athletics. Electronic viewbook available at CollegeQuest.com.

SOUTHEASTERN UNIVERSITY
Washington, District of Columbia

- **Independent**, comprehensive, founded 1879
- **Degrees** associate, bachelor's, and master's
- **Urban** 1-acre campus
- **Coed**, 477 undergraduate students, 29% full-time, 66% women, 34% men
- **Noncompetitive** entrance level, 100% of applicants were admitted
- **17.6% graduate** in 6 years or less
- **$7500 tuition** and fees

Students *Undergraduates:* 139 full-time, 338 part-time. Students come from 7 states and territories, 51 other countries. *Graduate:* 503 in graduate degree programs.

From out-of-state	25%	Age 25 or older	55%
Transferred in	1%	International students	18%
African Americans	76%	Asian Americans/Pacific Islanders	4%
Hispanic Americans	1%		

Faculty 82 (12% full-time), 40% with terminal degrees.
Expenses (2000–2001) *Tuition:* full-time $7200; part-time $200 per credit hour. *Required fees:* full-time $300. *Payment plan:* installment. *Waivers:* employees or children of employees.
Library The Learning Resources Center plus 1 other. *Operations spending 1999–2000:* $239,743. *Collection:* 40,000 titles, 110 serial subscriptions.
College life *Housing:* college housing not available. *Social organizations:* national fraternities, national sororities; 2% of eligible men and 2% of eligible women are members. *Most popular organization:* SGA.
Campus security Late-night transport-escort service.
After graduation *Career center:* 1 full-time, 2 part-time personnel. Services include job fairs, resume preparation, interview workshops, resume referral, career/interest testing, career counseling, careers library, job bank, job interviews.
Freshmen 1,099 applied, 1,099 admitted, 95 enrolled.

SAT verbal scores above 500	N/R	SAT math scores above 500	N/R
ACT above 18	N/R	1998 freshmen returning in 1999	55%

Application *Option:* deferred entrance. *Application fee:* $45. *Required:* high school transcript. *Recommended:* essay or personal statement; interview.
Standardized tests *Admission:* Recommended: SAT I or ACT.
Significant dates *Application deadlines:* rolling (freshmen), rolling (transfers). *Financial aid deadline:* continuous.
Freshman Application Contact
Mr. Jack Flinter, Director of Admissions, Southeastern University, 501 I Street, SW, Washington, DC 20024-2788. **Phone:** 202-265-5343 Ext. 211. **Fax:** 202-488-8162. **E-mail:** jackf@admin.seu.edu
Visit CollegeQuest.com for information on majors offered and athletics. Electronic viewbook available at CollegeQuest.com.

■ *See page 2504 for a narrative description.*

STRAYER UNIVERSITY
Washington, District of Columbia

- **Proprietary**, comprehensive, founded 1892
- **Degrees** associate, bachelor's, and master's
- **Urban** campus
- **Coed**
- **Minimally difficult** entrance level

District of Columbia

Strayer University (continued)
- **$7695 tuition** and fees

Expenses (1999–2000) *Tuition:* full-time $7695; part-time $200 per quarter hour. Full-time tuition and fees vary according to course load. Part-time tuition and fees vary according to course load.
Institutional Web site http://www.strayer.edu/
College life *Housing:* college housing not available. *Social organizations:* national sororities; 1% of women are members. *Most popular organizations:* honor society, international club, Association of Information Technology Professionals, business administration club, Human Resource Management club.
Campus security Patrols by trained personnel during operating hours.
Application *Options:* electronic application, early admission, deferred entrance. *Application fee:* $25. *Required:* high school transcript. *Required for some:* 1 letter of recommendation. *Recommended:* essay or personal statement; 1 letter of recommendation; interview.
Standardized tests *Admission: Required:* ACT ASSET tests in English and math. *Recommended:* SAT I.
Admissions Office Contact
Strayer University, 1025 Fifteenth Street, NW, Washington, DC 20005. **Fax:** 202-289-1831. **E-mail:** mw@net.strayer.edu
Visit CollegeQuest.com for information on athletics.

TRINITY COLLEGE
Washington, District of Columbia

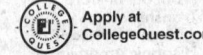 Apply at CollegeQuest.com

- **Independent Roman Catholic**, comprehensive, founded 1897
- **Degrees** bachelor's, master's, and postbachelor's certificates
- **Urban** 26-acre campus
- **Women** only
- **Moderately difficult** entrance level
- **$14,025 tuition** and fees

Trinity College offers women the Foundation for Leadership curriculum, combining liberal arts majors with professional focuses, mentor programs, and internship opportunities. Special programs include the Trinity Center for Women and Public Policy, Executive Women in Government Partnership, and a 5-year academic program combining a liberal arts undergraduate degree with a Master of Arts in Teaching.

Expenses (1999–2000) *Comprehensive fee:* $20,525 includes full-time tuition ($13,875), mandatory fees ($150), and room and board ($6500). *College room only:* $2860. Room and board charges vary according to board plan and housing facility. *Part-time tuition:* $465 per credit hour. *Part-time fees:* $30 per term part-time. Part-time tuition and fees vary according to class time.
Institutional Web site http://www.trinitydc.edu/
College life *Housing:* on-campus residence required through junior year. *Option:* women-only. *Most popular organizations:* Campus Ministry, Athletic Association, international club, Black Student Alliance, Young Democrats/Republicans.
Campus security 24-hour emergency response devices and patrols, late-night transport-escort service, controlled dormitory access.
Application *Options:* eApply at www.CollegeQuest.com, Common Application, electronic application. *Application fee:* $35. *Required:* essay or personal statement; high school transcript; minimum 2.0 GPA; 1 letter of recommendation; interview.
Standardized tests *Admission: Required:* SAT I or ACT. *Recommended:* SAT II Subject Tests.
Admissions Office Contact
Trinity College, 125 Michigan Avenue, NE, Washington, DC 20017-1094. **Fax:** 202-884-9229.

Visit CollegeQuest.com for information on athletics. Electronic viewbook available at CollegeQuest.com.

- *See page 2642 for a narrative description.*

UNIVERSITY OF THE DISTRICT OF COLUMBIA
Washington, District of Columbia

- **District-supported**, comprehensive, founded 1976
- **Degrees** associate, bachelor's, and master's
- **Urban** 28-acre campus
- **Coed**, 4,884 undergraduate students, 32% full-time, 59% women, 41% men
- **Noncompetitive** entrance level, 80% of applicants were admitted
- **$2070 tuition** and fees (in-district); $4710 (out-of-district)
- **$19,000 average indebtedness** upon graduation, $8.7 million endowment

Students *Undergraduates:* 1,584 full-time, 3,300 part-time. Students come from 54 states and territories, 119 other countries. *The most frequently chosen baccalaureate fields are:* business/marketing, computer/information sciences, protective services/public administration. *Graduate:* 237 in graduate degree programs.

From out-of-state	17%	Age 25 or older	56%
Transferred in	5%	International students	5%
African Americans	77%	Asian Americans/Pacific Islanders	2%
Hispanic Americans	4%	Native Americans	0.1%

Faculty 440 (31% full-time).
Expenses (1999–2000) *Tuition, state resident:* full-time $1800; part-time $75 per semester hour. *Tuition, nonresident:* full-time $4440; part-time $185 per semester hour. *Required fees:* full-time $270; $135 per term part-time. Full-time tuition and fees vary according to course load. Part-time tuition and fees vary according to course load. *Payment plans:* installment, deferred payment. *Waivers:* senior citizens and employees or children of employees.
Library Learning Resources Division Library plus 1 other. *Operations spending 1999–2000:* $2 million. *Collection:* 522,123 titles, 543 serial subscriptions, 19,238 audiovisual materials.
College life *Housing:* college housing not available. *Social organizations:* national fraternities, national sororities; 2% of eligible men and 3% of eligible women are members.
Campus security 24-hour patrols.
After graduation *Career center:* 8 full-time personnel. Services include job fairs, resume preparation, resume referral, career counseling, careers library, job bank, job interviews. *Graduate education:* 2% of class of 1999 went directly to graduate and professional school.
Freshmen 3,994 applied, 3,198 admitted, 1,171 enrolled.

SAT verbal scores above 500	N/R	SAT math scores above 500	N/R
ACT above 18	N/R		

Application *Options:* Common Application, deferred entrance. *Preference* given to district residents. *Application fee:* $20. *Required:* high school transcript.
Significant dates *Application deadlines:* 8/1 (freshmen), 8/1 (transfers). *Notification:* continuous until 8/15 (freshmen). *Financial aid deadline priority date:* 3/15.
Freshman Application Contact
Mr. LaHugh Bankston, Registrar and Enrollment Management, University of the District of Columbia, 4200 Connecticut Avenue NW, Building 39—A-Level, Washington, DC 20008. **Phone:** 202-274-6200.
Visit CollegeQuest.com for information on majors offered and athletics.

- *See page 2844 for a narrative description.*

FLORIDA

The Tampa area includes the town of Temple Terrace.

The Miami area includes the towns of Coral Gables, Miami Beach, Miami Shores, and North Miami.

AMERICAN COLLEGE OF PREHOSPITAL MEDICINE
Navarre, Florida

Students *Undergraduates:* Students come from 26 states and territories, 8 other countries. *The most frequently chosen baccalaureate field is:* health professions and related sciences.

Age 25 or older	90%

Faculty 22.

Expenses (2000–2001) *Tuition:* part-time $250 per semester hour. Full-time tuition and fees vary according to degree level. Part-time tuition and fees vary according to degree level. *Payment plans:* guaranteed tuition, installment.

Library American College of Prehospital Medicine Library plus 1 other. *Collection:* 700 titles, 14 serial subscriptions.

College life *Housing:* college housing not available.

Freshmen

SAT verbal scores above 500	N/R	SAT math scores above 500	N/R
ACT above 18	N/R	1998 freshmen returning in 1999	90%

Application *Application fee:* $50. *Required:* high school transcript; emergency medical technician certification or equivalent.

Significant dates *Application deadlines:* rolling (freshmen), rolling (transfers).

Freshman Application Contact
Dr. Richard A. Clinchy, Chairman/CEO, American College of Prehospital Medicine, 7552 Navarre Parkway, Suite 1, Navarre, FL 32566-7312. **Phone:** 504-561-6543. **Toll-free phone:** 800-735-2276. **E-mail:** admit@acpm.edu

Visit CollegeQuest.com for information on majors offered and athletics.

AMERICAN INTERCONTINENTAL UNIVERSITY
Sunrise, Florida

Admissions Office Contact
American InterContinental University, Building B, 1607 North Harrison Parkway, Sunrise, FL 33323. **Fax:** 954-835-1020.

THE ART INSTITUTE OF FORT LAUDERDALE
Fort Lauderdale, Florida

- **Proprietary**, primarily 2-year, founded 1968
- **Degrees** associate and bachelor's
- **Urban** campus with easy access to Miami
- **Coed**, 2,654 undergraduate students
- **Noncompetitive** entrance level
- **20:1 student-to-undergraduate faculty ratio**
- **$11,925 tuition** and fees

Admissions Office Contact
- The Art Institute of Fort Lauderdale, 1799 Southeast 17th Street Causeway, Fort Lauderdale, FL 33316-3000. **Toll-free phone:** 800-275-7603. **Fax:** 954-728-8637.

Visit CollegeQuest.com for information on majors offered and athletics. College video available at CollegeQuest.com.

BARRY UNIVERSITY
Miami Shores, Florida

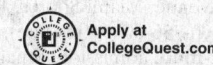 Apply at CollegeQuest.com

- **Independent Roman Catholic**, university, founded 1940
- **Degrees** bachelor's, master's, doctoral, first professional, post-master's, postbachelor's, and first professional certificates
- **Suburban** 122-acre campus with easy access to Miami
- **Coed**, 4,937 undergraduate students, 51% full-time, 66% women, 34% men
- **Moderately difficult** entrance level, 38% of applicants were admitted
- **14:1 student-to-undergraduate faculty ratio**
- **43% graduate** in 6 years or less
- **$15,530 tuition** and fees
- **$14,430 average financial aid** package, $17,469 average indebtedness upon graduation, $18.7 million endowment

Barry University is an independent, coeducational Catholic university that fosters academic distinction in the liberal arts and professional studies. Enrolling 7,909 students, Barry offers more than 60 undergraduate programs and 50 graduate degrees through the Schools of Adult and Continuing Education, Arts and Sciences, Business, Education, Graduate Medical Sciences, Human Performance and Leisure Sciences, Natural and Health Sciences, Nursing, and Social Work.

Students *Undergraduates:* 2,518 full-time, 2,419 part-time. Students come from 46 states and territories, 70 other countries. *The most frequently chosen baccalaureate fields are:* health professions and related sciences, education, liberal arts/general studies. *Graduate:* 252 in professional programs, 2,189 in other graduate degree programs.

From out-of-state	23%	Reside on campus	29%
Age 25 or older	29%	Transferred in	12%
International students	7%	African Americans	17%
Asian Americans/Pacific Islanders	1%	Hispanic Americans	33%
Native Americans	0.2%		

Faculty 620 (43% full-time), 80% with terminal degrees.

Expenses (1999–2000) *Comprehensive fee:* $21,750 includes full-time tuition ($15,530) and room and board ($6220). Full-time tuition and fees vary according to location and program. Room and board charges vary according to board plan. *Part-time tuition:* $455 per credit. Part-time tuition and fees vary according to course load, location, and program. *Payment plans:* tuition prepayment, installment, deferred payment. *Waivers:* employees or children of employees.

Library Monsignor William Barry Memorial Library plus 1 other. *Operations spending 1999–2000:* $1.5 million. *Collection:* 1,788 serial subscriptions, 4,450 audiovisual materials.

College life *Housing:* on-campus residence required in freshman year. *Options:* coed, men-only, women-only, disabled students. *Social organizations:* national fraternities, national sororities; 13% of eligible men and 4% of eligible women are members. *Most popular organizations:* Student Government Association, Campus Activities Board, Scuba Society, Caribbean Students Association, Jamaican Association.

Campus security 24-hour emergency response devices and patrols, late-night transport-escort service.

Florida

Barry University (continued)

After graduation 125 organizations recruited on campus 1997–98. *Career center:* 4 full-time, 1 part-time personnel. Services include job fairs, resume preparation, interview workshops, resume referral, career/interest testing, career counseling, careers library, job bank, job interviews.

Freshmen 5,293 applied, 2,021 admitted, 400 enrolled.

Average high school GPA	3.03	SAT verbal scores above 500	N/R
SAT math scores above 500	N/R	ACT above 18	N/R
1998 freshmen returning in 1999	72%		

Application *Options:* eApply at www.CollegeQuest.com, Common Application, electronic application, early admission, deferred entrance. *Application fee:* $30. *Required:* high school transcript; minimum 2.0 GPA. *Recommended:* essay or personal statement; interview.

Standardized tests *Admission: Required:* SAT I or ACT.

Significant dates *Application deadlines:* rolling (freshmen), rolling (transfers). *Financial aid deadline:* continuous.

Freshman Application Contact
Mr. Dave Fletcher, Director of Admissions, Barry University, , 11300 Northeast Avenue, Miami Shores, FL 33161. **Phone:** 308-699-3146. **Toll-free phone:** 800-756-6000 (in-state); 800-695-2279 (out-of-state). **Fax:** 305-899-2971. **E-mail:** admissions@mail.barry.edu

Visit CollegeQuest.com for information on majors offered and athletics.

■ *See page 1230 for a narrative description.*

BETHUNE-COOKMAN COLLEGE
Daytona Beach, Florida

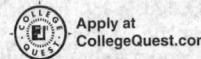 Apply at CollegeQuest.com

- **Independent Methodist**, 4-year, founded 1904
- **Degree** bachelor's
- **Urban** 60-acre campus with easy access to Orlando
- **Coed**, 2,558 undergraduate students, 92% full-time, 56% women, 44% men
- **Minimally difficult** entrance level, 83% of applicants were admitted
- **17:1 student-to-undergraduate faculty ratio**
- **32% graduate** in 6 years or less
- **$8988 tuition** and fees
- **$9855 average financial aid** package, $17,900 average indebtedness upon graduation, $25.4 million endowment

Students *Undergraduates:* 2,357 full-time, 201 part-time. Students come from 35 states and territories, 26 other countries. *The most frequently chosen baccalaureate fields are:* business/marketing, education, protective services/public administration.

From out-of-state	24%	Reside on campus	60%
Age 25 or older	12%	Transferred in	4%
International students	6%	African Americans	91%
Asian Americans/Pacific Islanders	0.3%	Hispanic Americans	1%

Faculty 215 (61% full-time), 37% with terminal degrees.

Expenses (2000–2001, estimated) *Comprehensive fee:* $14,522 includes full-time tuition ($8988) and room and board ($5534). *Part-time tuition:* $375 per credit hour. *Waivers:* employees or children of employees.

Library Carl S. Swisher Library plus 1 other. *Operations spending 1999–2000:* $419,138. *Collection:* 158,528 titles, 770 serial subscriptions, 10,500 audiovisual materials.

College life *Housing:* on-campus residence required in freshman year. *Options:* men-only, women-only. *Social organizations:* national fraternities, national sororities, local fraternities, local sororities; 2% of eligible men and 5% of eligible women are members. *Most popular organizations:* Greek organizations, concert chorale, marching band, inspirational gospel choir, SGA.

Campus security 24-hour emergency response devices and patrols, student patrols, late-night transport-escort service.

After graduation 149 organizations recruited on campus 1997–98. 70% of class of 1998 had job offers within 6 months. *Career center:* 5 full-time personnel. Services include job fairs, resume preparation, interview workshops, resume referral, career/interest testing, career counseling, careers library, job bank, job interviews. *Graduate education:* 26% of class of 1999 went directly to graduate and professional school: 12% business, 11% education, 1% graduate arts and sciences, 1% law, 1% medicine.

Freshmen 2,770 applied, 2,292 admitted, 698 enrolled.

Average high school GPA	2.7	SAT verbal scores above 500	24%
SAT math scores above 500	21%	ACT above 18	26%
From top 10% of their h.s. class	5%	From top quarter	15%
From top half	45%	1998 freshmen returning in 1999	78%

Application *Options:* eApply at www.CollegeQuest.com, early admission, deferred entrance. *Application fee:* $25. *Required:* high school transcript; minimum 2.25 GPA; medical history. *Required for some:* interview.

Standardized tests *Admission: Required:* SAT I or ACT.

Significant dates *Application deadlines:* 7/30 (freshmen), 7/30 (transfers). *Financial aid deadline priority date:* 4/1.

Freshman Application Contact
Mr. William A. T. Byrd, Assistant Vice President for Enrollment Management, Bethune-Cookman College, 640 Dr. Mary McLeod Bethune Boulevard, Daytona Beach, FL 32114-3099. **Phone:** 904-255-1401 Ext. 358. **Toll-free phone:** 800-448-0228. **Fax:** 904-257-5338. **E-mail:** byrdw@cookman.edu

Visit CollegeQuest.com for information on majors offered and athletics. College video and electronic viewbook available at CollegeQuest.com.

■ *See page 1274 for a narrative description.*

CARIBBEAN CENTER FOR ADVANCED STUDIES/MIAMI INSTITUTE OF PSYCHOLOGY
Florida—See Carlos Albizu University

CARLOS ALBIZU UNIVERSITY
Miami, Florida

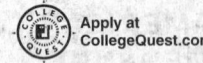 Apply at CollegeQuest.com

- **Independent**, upper-level, founded 1980
- **Degrees** bachelor's, master's, and doctoral
- **Urban** 2-acre campus
- **Coed**, primarily women, 69 undergraduate students, 33% full-time, 83% women, 17% men
- **70% of applicants were admitted**
- **8:1 student-to-undergraduate faculty ratio**
- **$6834 tuition** and fees

Part of Caribbean Center for Advanced Study.

Students *Undergraduates:* 23 full-time, 46 part-time. Students come from 12 other countries. *The most frequently chosen baccalaureate field is:* psychology. *Graduate:* 548 in graduate degree programs.

Age 25 or older	77%	Transferred in	35%
African Americans	7%	Asian Americans/Pacific Islanders	3%
Hispanic Americans	64%		

Faculty 18 (11% full-time), 50% with terminal degrees.

Expenses (1999–2000) *Tuition:* full-time $6300; part-time $210 per credit. *Required fees:* full-time $534; $178 per term part-time. *Payment plan:* installment. *Waivers:* minority students and employees or children of employees.

Library Albizu Library. *Operations spending 1999–2000:* $242,000. *Collection:* 12,688 titles, 195 serial subscriptions, 436 audiovisual materials.

College life *Housing:* college housing not available. *Most popular organizations:* student council, Psi Chi, Students for Cross Cultural Advancement, psychology club.

Campus security 24-hour emergency response devices, late-night transport-escort service.

After graduation *Graduate education:* 23% of class of 1999 went directly to graduate and professional school: 23% graduate arts and sciences.

Application *Options:* eApply at www.CollegeQuest.com, Common Application, deferred entrance. *Application fee:* $25.

Significant dates *Application deadline:* rolling (transfers).

Freshman Application Contact
Mr. Gustavo B. Marin, Recruitment and Outreach Director, Carlos Albizu University, Miami Institute of Psychology, Recruitment and Outreach, 8180

Florida

Northwest 36th Street, Miami, FL 33166. **Phone:** 305-593-1223 Ext. 136. **Toll-free phone:** 800-672-3246. **Fax:** 305-592-7930. **E-mail:** gmarin@mip.ccas.edu
Visit CollegeQuest.com for information on majors offered and athletics.

CLEARWATER CHRISTIAN COLLEGE
Clearwater, Florida

Admissions Office Contact
Clearwater Christian College, 3400 Gulf-to-Bay Boulevard, Clearwater, FL 33759-4595. **Toll-free phone:** 800-348-4463. **Fax:** 727-726-8597. **E-mail:** admissions@clearwater.edu

ECKERD COLLEGE
St. Petersburg, Florida

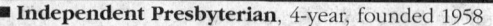

- **Independent Presbyterian**, 4-year, founded 1958
- **Degree** bachelor's
- **Suburban** 267-acre campus with easy access to Tampa
- **Coed**, 1,513 undergraduate students, 99% full-time, 55% women, 45% men
- **Moderately difficult** entrance level, 76% of applicants were admitted
- **14:1 student-to-undergraduate faculty ratio**
- **57.47% graduate** in 6 years or less
- **$18,220 tuition** and fees

Students *Undergraduates:* 1,500 full-time, 13 part-time. Students come from 49 states and territories, 55 other countries. *The most frequently chosen baccalaureate fields are:* biological/life sciences, business/marketing, social sciences and history.

From out-of-state	70%	Reside on campus	71%
Age 25 or older	3%	Transferred in	5%
International students	12%	African Americans	3%
Asian Americans/Pacific Islanders	1%	Hispanic Americans	4%
Native Americans	0.2%		

Faculty 136 (71% full-time), 77% with terminal degrees.
Expenses (1999–2000) *Comprehensive fee:* $23,180 includes full-time tuition ($18,025), mandatory fees ($195), and room and board ($4960). Room and board charges vary according to board plan and housing facility. *Part-time tuition:* $1925 per course. *Payment plan:* installment. *Waivers:* employees or children of employees.
Library William Luther Cobb Library. *Collection:* 150,923 titles, 3,009 serial subscriptions, 1,941 audiovisual materials.
College life *Housing:* on-campus residence required in freshman year. *Options:* coed, men-only, women-only. *Most popular organizations:* Earth Society, Water Search and Rescue Team, Triton Tribune, college choir, Eckerd College Organization of Students.
Campus security 24-hour emergency response devices and patrols, student patrols, late-night transport-escort service, controlled dormitory access.
After graduation 175 organizations recruited on campus 1997–98. 45% of class of 1998 had job offers within 6 months. *Career center:* 3 full-time personnel. Services include job fairs, resume preparation, interview workshops, resume referral, career/interest testing, career counseling, careers library, job bank, job interviews. *Graduate education:* 25% of class of 1999 went directly to graduate and professional school.
Freshmen 1,783 applied, 1,363 admitted, 403 enrolled. 12 National Merit Scholars, 25 class presidents, 25 valedictorians, 115 student government officers.

Average high school GPA	3.24	SAT verbal scores above 500	82%
SAT math scores above 500	84%	ACT above 18	97%
From top 10% of their h.s. class	26%	From top quarter	55%
From top half	82%	1998 freshmen returning in 1999	77%

Application *Options:* eApply at www.CollegeQuest.com, Common Application, electronic application, early admission, deferred entrance. *Application fee:* $25. *Required:* essay or personal statement; high school transcript; 1 letter of recommendation. *Recommended:* minimum 3.0 GPA; interview.
Standardized tests *Admission: Required:* SAT I or ACT. *Recommended:* SAT II Subject Tests, SAT II: Writing Test.

Significant dates *Application deadlines:* rolling (freshmen), rolling (transfers). *Financial aid deadline priority date:* 4/1.
Freshman Application Contact
Dr. Richard R. Hallin, Dean of Admissions, Eckerd College, 4200 54th Avenue South, St. Petersburg, FL 33711. **Phone:** 727-864-8331. **Toll-free phone:** 800-456-9009. **Fax:** 727-866-2304. **E-mail:** admissions@eckerd.edu
Visit CollegeQuest.com for information on majors offered and athletics.

■ *See page 1612 for a narrative description.*

EDUCATION AMERICA– TAMPA TECHNICAL INSTITUTE CAMPUS
Tampa, Florida

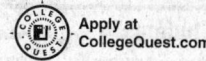

- **Proprietary**, primarily 2-year, founded 1948
- **Degrees** associate and bachelor's
- **Urban** 10-acre campus
- **Coed**, 1,450 undergraduate students
- **Noncompetitive** entrance level

Part of Education America Inc.
Faculty 48 (90% full-time).
Admissions Office Contact
Education America–Tampa Technical Institute Campus, 2410 East Busch Boulevard, Tampa, FL 33612-8410. **Toll-free phone:** 800-992-4850. **E-mail:** rams@ix.netcom.com
Visit CollegeQuest.com for information on majors offered and athletics. College video available at CollegeQuest.com.

EDWARD WATERS COLLEGE
Jacksonville, Florida

- **Independent African Methodist Episcopal**, 4-year, founded 1866
- **Degree** bachelor's
- **Urban** 20-acre campus
- **Coed**
- **Noncompetitive** entrance level
- **$6600 tuition** and fees

Expenses (1999–2000) *Comprehensive fee:* $11,114 includes full-time tuition ($5520), mandatory fees ($1080), and room and board ($4514). *Part-time tuition:* $230 per semester hour. *Part-time fees:* $45 per semester hour.
College life *Housing:* Option: coed.
Campus security 24-hour emergency response devices and patrols, student patrols, late-night transport-escort service, controlled dormitory access.
Application *Option:* Common Application. *Application fee:* $15. *Required:* high school transcript; medical forms.
Standardized tests *Placement: Required:* CAT *Recommended:* SAT I or ACT.
Admissions Office Contact
Edward Waters College, 1658 Kings Road, Jacksonville, FL 32209-6199.
Visit CollegeQuest.com for information on athletics.

EMBRY-RIDDLE AERONAUTICAL UNIVERSITY
Daytona Beach, Florida

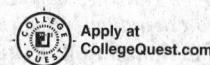

- **Independent**, comprehensive, founded 1926
- **Degrees** associate, bachelor's, and master's
- **Urban** 178-acre campus with easy access to Orlando
- **Coed**, primarily men, 4,581 undergraduate students, 91% full-time, 14% women, 86% men
- **Moderately difficult** entrance level, 78% of applicants were admitted

Florida

Embry-Riddle Aeronautical University (continued)
- **22:1 student-to-undergraduate faculty ratio**
- **49.7% graduate** in 6 years or less
- **$10,700 tuition** and fees
- **$10,679 average financial aid** package, $17,125 average indebtedness upon graduation, $31.7 million endowment

Embry-Riddle teaches science, theory, and business to meet all the demands of employers in the world of aviation and aerospace; the University's impact on the industry through its graduates is significant. Founded just 22 years after the Wright brothers first flew, Embry-Riddle students learn to solve problems in engineering, business, computer science, technology, maintenance, psychology, communication, and flight. Whatever field students choose, they learn from educators and practitioners who are on the leading edge.

Students *Undergraduates:* 4,177 full-time, 404 part-time. Students come from 54 states and territories, 102 other countries. *The most frequently chosen baccalaureate fields are:* engineering/engineering technologies, business/marketing, trade and industry. *Graduate:* 272 in graduate degree programs.

From out-of-state	57%	Reside on campus	41%
Age 25 or older	14%	Transferred in	7%
International students	13%	African Americans	4%
Asian Americans/Pacific Islanders	3%	Hispanic Americans	6%
Native Americans	1%		

Faculty 245 (78% full-time), 59% with terminal degrees.

Expenses (2000–2001) *Comprehensive fee:* $16,140 includes full-time tuition ($10,700) and room and board ($5440). *College room only:* $3100. Full-time tuition and fees vary according to program and student level. Room and board charges vary according to board plan and housing facility. *Part-time tuition:* $605 per credit. Part-time tuition and fees vary according to program and student level. *Payment plans:* installment, deferred payment. *Waivers:* employees or children of employees.

Library Jack R. Hunt Memorial Library. *Operations spending 1999–2000:* $1.9 million. *Collection:* 88,955 titles, 712 serial subscriptions.

College life *Housing:* on-campus residence required through sophomore year. *Options:* coed, men-only, women-only, disabled students. *Social organizations:* national fraternities, national sororities; 52% of eligible men and 64% of eligible women are members. *Most popular organizations:* Society of Automotive Engineers, Caribbean Student Association, Korean Student Association, American Institute of Aeronautics and Astronautics, The Anything Goes Anime Club.

Campus security 24-hour emergency response devices and patrols, student patrols, late-night transport-escort service.

After graduation 185 organizations recruited on campus 1997–98. 94% of class of 1998 had job offers within 6 months. *Career center:* 8 full-time, 6 part-time personnel. Services include job fairs, resume preparation, resume referral, career counseling, careers library, job bank, job interviews. *Graduate education:* 20% of class of 1999 went directly to graduate and professional school.

Freshmen 2,442 applied, 1,902 admitted, 945 enrolled.

Average high school GPA	3.25	SAT verbal scores above 500	70%
SAT math scores above 500	80%	ACT above 18	94%
From top 10% of their h.s. class	16%	From top quarter	45%
From top half	82%	1998 freshmen returning in 1999	78%

Application *Options:* eApply at www.CollegeQuest.com, Common Application, electronic application, early admission, early decision, deferred entrance. *Application fee:* $30. *Required:* high school transcript; minimum 2.0 GPA. *Required for some:* minimum 3.0 GPA; medical examination for flight students. *Recommended:* essay or personal statement; letters of recommendation; interview.

Standardized tests *Admission: Required:* SAT I or ACT.

Significant dates *Application deadlines:* 7/1 (freshmen), 7/1 (transfers). *Early decision:* 12/1. *Notification:* 12/31 (early decision). *Financial aid deadline:* 6/30. *Priority date:* 4/15.

Freshman Application Contact
Ms. Carol Cotman Hogan, Director of Admissions, Embry-Riddle Aeronautical University, 600 South Clyde Morris Boulevard, Daytona Beach, FL 32114-3900. **Phone:** 904-226-6112. **Toll-free phone:** 800-862-2416. **Fax:** 904-226-7070. **E-mail:** admit@db.erau.edu

Visit CollegeQuest.com for information on majors offered and athletics. College video and electronic viewbook available at CollegeQuest.com.

- *See page 1630 for a narrative description.*

EMBRY-RIDDLE AERONAUTICAL UNIVERSITY, EXTENDED CAMPUS
Daytona Beach, Florida

- **Independent**, comprehensive, founded 1970
- **Degrees** associate, bachelor's, and master's (programs offered at 100 military bases worldwide)
- **Coed,** primarily men, 4,549 undergraduate students, 2% full-time, 9% women, 91% men
- **Minimally difficult** entrance level
- **3:1 student-to-undergraduate faculty ratio**
- **$1860 tuition** and fees
- **$17,125 average indebtedness** upon graduation, $31.7 million endowment

Students *Undergraduates:* 77 full-time, 4,472 part-time. *The most frequently chosen baccalaureate fields are:* business/marketing, trade and industry. *Graduate:* 2,471 in graduate degree programs.

International students	2%	African Americans	7%
Asian Americans/Pacific Islanders	3%	Hispanic Americans	7%
Native Americans	1%		

Faculty 2,892 (3% full-time), 22% with terminal degrees.

Expenses (1999–2000) *Tuition:* full-time $1860; part-time $155 per credit. Full-time tuition and fees vary according to location and program. Part-time tuition and fees vary according to location. *Waivers:* employees or children of employees.

Library Jack R. Hunt Memorial Library. *Operations spending 1999–2000:* $1.9 million.

College life *Housing:* college housing not available.

Freshmen 74 enrolled.

SAT verbal scores above 500	N/R	SAT math scores above 500	N/R
ACT above 18	N/R		

Application *Option:* deferred entrance. *Application fee:* $30.

Significant dates *Application deadlines:* rolling (freshmen), rolling (transfers). *Financial aid deadline:* 6/30. *Priority date:* 4/15.

Freshman Application Contact
Mrs. Pam Thomas, Director of Admissions, Records and Registration, Embry-Riddle Aeronautical University, Extended Campus, 600 South Clyde Morris Boulevard, Daytona Beach, FL 32114-3900. **Phone:** 904-226-7610. **Toll-free phone:** 800-862-2416. **Fax:** 904-226-6984. **E-mail:** ecinfo@ec.db.erau.edu

Visit CollegeQuest.com for information on majors offered and athletics.

FLAGLER COLLEGE
St. Augustine, Florida

- **Independent**, 4-year, founded 1968
- **Degree** bachelor's
- **Small-town** 36-acre campus with easy access to Jacksonville
- **Coed**, 1,736 undergraduate students, 98% full-time, 62% women, 38% men
- **Moderately difficult** entrance level, 27% of applicants were admitted
- **19:1 student-to-undergraduate faculty ratio**
- **51.84% graduate** in 6 years or less
- **$6130 tuition** and fees
- **$6743 average financial aid** package, $13,763 average indebtedness upon graduation, $35.2 million endowment

Size, cost, location, and excellent academics are the characteristics most often cited by students in their decision to enroll at Flagler. Interested students are encouraged to visit historic St. Augustine and to learn how Flagler offers high-quality education in a beautiful setting at a reasonable cost. The cost of tuition, room, and board for the 2000–01 year is just $10,230.

Students *Undergraduates:* 1,699 full-time, 37 part-time. Students come from 46 states and territories, 24 other countries. *The most frequently chosen baccalaureate fields are:* business/marketing, communications/communication technologies, education.

From out-of-state	38%	Reside on campus	42%
Age 25 or older	6%	Transferred in	7%
International students	3%	African Americans	1%
Asian Americans/Pacific Islanders	1%	Hispanic Americans	2%
Native Americans	0.1%		

Faculty 152 (38% full-time).

Expenses (1999–2000) *Comprehensive fee:* $9930 includes full-time tuition ($6130) and room and board ($3800). *Part-time tuition:* $250 per credit hour. *Waivers:* employees or children of employees.

Library William L. Proctor Library. *Operations spending 1999–2000:* $428,909. *Collection:* 63,791 titles, 472 serial subscriptions, 2,097 audiovisual materials.

College life *Housing:* on-campus residence required in freshman year. *Options:* men-only, women-only. *Most popular organizations:* Society for Advancement of Management, Student Government Association, women's club, Deaf Awareness Club, sport management club.

Campus security 24-hour emergency response devices and patrols, late-night transport-escort service, controlled dormitory access.

After graduation 80% of class of 1998 had job offers within 6 months. *Career center:* 1 full-time personnel. Services include resume preparation, career/interest testing, career counseling, careers library. *Graduate education:* 20% of class of 1999 went directly to graduate and professional school: 6% education, 4% business, 3% graduate arts and sciences, 2% law, 1% theology.

Freshmen 1,575 applied, 419 admitted, 424 enrolled.

Average high school GPA	2.94	SAT verbal scores above 500	83%
SAT math scores above 500	76%	ACT above 18	98%
From top 10% of their h.s. class	23%	From top quarter	56%
From top half	99%	1998 freshmen returning in 1999	72%

Application *Options:* early admission, early decision, deferred entrance. *Application fee:* $20. *Required:* essay or personal statement; high school transcript; 1 letter of recommendation. *Recommended:* minimum 2.75 GPA; interview; rank in upper 50% of high school class.

Standardized tests *Admission:* Required: SAT I or ACT.

Significant dates *Application deadlines:* 3/1 (freshmen), 3/1 (transfers). *Early decision:* 12/1 (for plan 1), 1/15 (for plan 2). *Notification:* 3/15 (freshmen), 12/15 (early decision plan 1), 2/1 (early decision plan 2). *Financial aid deadline:* continuous.

Freshman Application Contact
Mr. Marc G. Williar, Director of Admissions, Flagler College, PO Box 1027, St. Augustine, FL 32085-1027. **Phone:** 904-829-6481 Ext. 220. **Toll-free phone:** 800-304-4208. **Fax:** 904-826-0094. **E-mail:** admiss@flagler.edu

Visit CollegeQuest.com for information on majors offered and athletics. College video available at CollegeQuest.com.

■ *See page 1670 for a narrative description.*

FLORIDA AGRICULTURAL AND MECHANICAL UNIVERSITY
Tallahassee, Florida

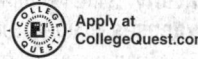
Apply at CollegeQuest.com

- **State-supported**, university, founded 1887
- **Degrees** associate, bachelor's, master's, doctoral, and first professional
- **Urban** 419-acre campus
- **Coed**, 10,328 undergraduate students, 88% full-time, 58% women, 42% men
- **Moderately difficult** entrance level, 70% of applicants were admitted
- **$2187 tuition** and fees (in-state); $8710 (out-of-state)

Part of State University System of Florida.

Students *Undergraduates:* 9,116 full-time, 1,212 part-time. Students come from 46 states and territories, 50 other countries. *The most frequently chosen baccalaureate fields are:* education, engineering/engineering technologies, health professions and related sciences. *Graduate:* 344 in professional programs, 1,047 in other graduate degree programs.

From out-of-state	20%	Age 25 or older	20%
Transferred in	4%	International students	1%
African Americans	95%	Asian Americans/Pacific Islanders	1%
Hispanic Americans	1%	Native Americans	0.05%

Faculty 771 (98% full-time), 90% with terminal degrees.

Expenses (1999–2000) *Tuition, state resident:* full-time $2073; part-time $74 per semester hour. *Tuition, nonresident:* full-time $8596; part-time $307 per semester hour. *Required fees:* full-time $114. Full-time tuition and fees vary according to course load. Part-time tuition and fees vary according to course load. *College room and board:* $3942; room only: $2460. Room and board charges vary according to board plan and housing facility. *Payment plans:* tuition prepayment, deferred payment. *Waivers:* senior citizens and employees or children of employees.

Library Coleman Memorial Library plus 5 others. *Operations spending 1999–2000:* $3.8 million. *Collection:* 529,151 titles, 5,501 serial subscriptions.

College life *Housing:* on-campus residence required in freshman year. *Options:* men-only, women-only. *Social organizations:* national fraternities, national sororities; 16% of eligible men and 19% of eligible women are members. *Most popular organizations:* gospel choir, University Marching Band, Alpha Kappa Alpha, Alpha Phi Alpha, SBI.

Campus security 24-hour emergency response devices and patrols, late-night transport-escort service.

After graduation 534 organizations recruited on campus 1997–98. 68% of class of 1998 had job offers within 6 months. *Career center:* 10 full-time, 2 part-time personnel. Services include job fairs, resume preparation, interview workshops, resume referral, career/interest testing, career counseling, careers library, job bank, job interviews. *Graduate education:* 20% of class of 1999 went directly to graduate and professional school.

Freshmen 5,634 applied, 3,957 admitted, 2,282 enrolled.

Average high school GPA	3.15	SAT verbal scores above 500	N/R
SAT math scores above 500	N/R	ACT above 18	N/R
1998 freshmen returning in 1999	80%		

Application *Options:* eApply at www.CollegeQuest.com, Common Application, electronic application, early admission, deferred entrance. *Preference* given to state residents. *Application fee:* $20. *Required:* high school transcript; minimum 2.0 GPA. *Required for some:* essay or personal statement; letters of recommendation. *Recommended:* minimum 3.0 GPA.

Standardized tests *Admission:* Required: SAT I or ACT.

Significant dates *Application deadlines:* 5/1 (freshmen), 5/1 (transfers). *Notification:* continuous until 8/1 (freshmen). *Financial aid deadline priority date:* 3/1.

Freshman Application Contact
Ms. Barbara R. Cox, Director of Admissions, Florida Agricultural and Mechanical University, Office of Admissions, Tallahassee, FL 32307. **Phone:** 850-599-3796. **Fax:** 850-561-2428. **E-mail:** bcox@ns1.famu.edu

Visit CollegeQuest.com for information on majors offered and athletics. College video and electronic viewbook available at CollegeQuest.com.

■ *See page 1672 for a narrative description.*

FLORIDA ATLANTIC UNIVERSITY
Boca Raton, Florida

- **State-supported**, university, founded 1961
- **Degrees** associate, bachelor's, master's, and doctoral
- **Suburban** 850-acre campus with easy access to Miami
- **Coed**, 14,887 undergraduate students, 54% full-time, 61% women, 39% men
- **Moderately difficult** entrance level, 71% of applicants were admitted
- **15:1 student-to-undergraduate faculty ratio**
- **40% graduate** in 6 years or less
- **$2253 tuition** and fees (in-state); $9242 (out-of-state)
- **$5992 average financial aid** package, $86.3 million endowment

Part of State University System of Florida.

Students *Undergraduates:* 8,061 full-time, 6,826 part-time. Students come from 50 states and territories, 128 other countries. *The most frequently chosen baccalaureate fields are:* business/marketing, education, health professions and related sciences. *Graduate:* 3,656 in graduate degree programs.

From out-of-state	6%	Reside on campus	7%
Age 25 or older	42%	Transferred in	17%
International students	6%	African Americans	14%
Asian Americans/Pacific Islanders	4%	Hispanic Americans	12%
Native Americans	1%		

Faculty 1,188 (55% full-time).

Expenses (1999–2000) *One-time required fee:* $10. *Tuition, state resident:* full-time $2253; part-time $75 per semester hour. *Tuition, nonresident:*

Florida

Florida Atlantic University (continued)
full-time $9242; part-time $308 per semester hour. Full-time tuition and fees vary according to course load. Part-time tuition and fees vary according to course load. *College room and board:* $4774; room only: $2721. Room and board charges vary according to board plan and housing facility. *Payment plans:* installment, deferred payment. *Waivers:* employees or children of employees.

Library S. E. Wimberly Library. *Operations spending 1999–2000:* $5.9 million. *Collection:* 662,269 titles, 4,571 serial subscriptions.

College life *Housing:* on-campus residence required in freshman year. *Option:* coed. *Social organizations:* national fraternities, national sororities; 1% of eligible men and 1% of eligible women are members. *Most popular organizations:* Latin American Student Organization, Alpha Phi Omega, Kombit Kreyol, Program Board, Owl Corral.

Campus security 24-hour emergency response devices and patrols, student patrols, late-night transport-escort service.

After graduation 215 organizations recruited on campus 1997–98. *Career center:* 7 full-time, 2 part-time personnel. Services include job fairs, resume preparation, resume referral, career counseling, careers library, job bank, job interviews.

Freshmen 4,887 applied, 3,470 admitted, 1,547 enrolled.

Average high school GPA	3.3	SAT verbal scores above 500	65%
SAT math scores above 500	65%	ACT above 18	91%
1998 freshmen returning in 1999	67%		

Application *Options:* Common Application, electronic application, early admission, deferred entrance. *Application fee:* $20. *Required:* high school transcript; minimum 2.0 GPA. *Required for some:* 1 letter of recommendation.

Standardized tests *Admission: Required:* SAT I or ACT.

Significant dates *Application deadlines:* rolling (freshmen), rolling (transfers). *Financial aid deadline priority date:* 3/1.

Freshman Application Contact
Mr. Jared Rosenberg, Coordinator, Freshmen Recruitment, Florida Atlantic University, 777 Glades Road, PO Box 3091, Boca Raton, FL 33431-0991. **Phone:** 561-297-2458. **Toll-free phone:** 800-299-4FAU.

Visit CollegeQuest.com for information on majors offered and athletics. College video available at CollegeQuest.com.

■ *See page 1674 for a narrative description.*

FLORIDA BAPTIST THEOLOGICAL COLLEGE
Graceville, Florida

- **Independent Southern Baptist**, 4-year, founded 1943
- **Degrees** associate and bachelor's
- **Small-town** 165-acre campus
- **Coed**, 482 undergraduate students, 85% full-time, 31% women, 69% men
- **Noncompetitive** entrance level, 90% of applicants were admitted
- **15:1** student-to-undergraduate faculty ratio
- **37% graduate** in 6 years or less
- **$3960 tuition** and fees
- **$3000 average financial aid** package, $15,000 average indebtedness upon graduation, $2.4 million endowment

Students *Undergraduates:* 408 full-time, 74 part-time. Students come from 25 states and territories. *The most frequently chosen baccalaureate fields are:* education, philosophy, visual/performing arts.

From out-of-state	32%	Reside on campus	36%
Age 25 or older	41%	Transferred in	18%
African Americans	3%	Asian Americans/Pacific Islanders	1%
Hispanic Americans	1%	Native Americans	1%

Faculty 44 (50% full-time), 39% with terminal degrees.

Expenses (1999–2000) *Comprehensive fee:* $7110 includes full-time tuition ($3760), mandatory fees ($200), and room and board ($3150). Room and board charges vary according to board plan and housing facility. *Part-time tuition:* $120 per semester hour. *Part-time fees:* $100 per term part-time. *Payment plan:* deferred payment. *Waivers:* employees or children of employees.

Library Ida J. MacMillan Library. *Operations spending 1999–2000:* $180,878. *Collection:* 53,851 titles, 1,048 serial subscriptions, 8,777 audiovisual materials.

College life *Housing:* on-campus residence required through senior year. *Options:* men-only, women-only. *Most popular organizations:* Baptist Student Union, Daughters of the King.

Campus security Student patrols, patrols by police officers 11 p.m. to 7 a.m.

After graduation 6 organizations recruited on campus 1997–98. *Career center:* 2 full-time personnel. Services include resume preparation, resume referral, career counseling, job interviews. *Graduate education:* 42% of class of 1999 went directly to graduate and professional school: 35% theology, 7% graduate arts and sciences.

Freshmen 233 applied, 209 admitted, 48 enrolled.

SAT verbal scores above 500	N/R	SAT math scores above 500	N/R
ACT above 18	N/R	1998 freshmen returning in 1999	41%

Application *Options:* Common Application, electronic application, deferred entrance. *Application fee:* $20. *Required:* essay or personal statement; high school transcript; 3 letters of recommendation. *Required for some:* interview.

Standardized tests *Admission: Required for some:* SAT I or ACT.

Significant dates *Application deadlines:* rolling (freshmen), rolling (transfers). *Financial aid deadline priority date:* 4/1.

Freshman Application Contact
Mr. O. Lavan Wilson, Director of Admissions, Florida Baptist Theological College, 5400 College Drive, Graceville, FL 32440-1898. **Phone:** 850-263-3261 Ext. 460. **Toll-free phone:** 800-328-2660 Ext. 460. **Fax:** 850-263-7506. **E-mail:** admissions@fbtc.edu

Visit CollegeQuest.com for information on majors offered and athletics. College video and electronic viewbook available at CollegeQuest.com.

FLORIDA CHRISTIAN COLLEGE
Kissimmee, Florida

- **Independent**, 4-year, founded 1976, affiliated with Christian Churches and Churches of Christ
- **Degrees** associate and bachelor's
- **Small-town** 40-acre campus with easy access to Orlando
- **Coed**, 236 undergraduate students, 75% full-time, 47% women, 53% men
- **Minimally difficult** entrance level
- **11:1** student-to-undergraduate faculty ratio
- **40% graduate** in 6 years or less
- **$5614 tuition** and fees
- **$6935 average financial aid** package, $1.5 million endowment

Students *Undergraduates:* 178 full-time, 58 part-time. Students come from 23 states and territories, 1 other country.

From out-of-state	18%	Reside on campus	65%
Age 25 or older	31%	Transferred in	6%
International students	0.4%	African Americans	3%
Hispanic Americans	6%		

Faculty 34 (24% full-time), 35% with terminal degrees.

Expenses (1999–2000) *One-time required fee:* $40. *Tuition:* full-time $5344; part-time $167 per credit. *Required fees:* full-time $270; $270 per year part-time. *College room only:* $1385. *Payment plan:* installment. *Waivers:* employees or children of employees.

Library *Operations spending 1999–2000:* $117,112. *Collection:* 31,000 titles, 285 serial subscriptions.

College life On-campus residence required in freshman year. *Most popular organizations:* Student Council, camera club, Timothy Club.

After graduation *Career center:* Services include career counseling. *Graduate education:* 30% of class of 1999 went directly to graduate and professional school: 30% theology.

Freshmen 45 enrolled.

SAT verbal scores above 500	N/R	SAT math scores above 500	N/R
ACT above 18	N/R	From top 10% of their h.s. class	16%
From top quarter	42%	From top half	64%
1998 freshmen returning in 1999	58%		

Application *Options:* eApply at www.CollegeQuest.com, early admission, deferred entrance. *Application fee:* $25. *Required:* high school transcript; 3 letters of recommendation.

Standardized tests *Placement: Required:* ACT

Florida

Significant dates *Application deadlines:* 7/15 (freshmen), 7/15 (transfers). *Notification:* continuous until 8/25 (freshmen). *Financial aid deadline:* 8/1. *Priority date:* 5/1.

Freshman Application Contact
Mr. Terry Davis, Admissions Director, Florida Christian College, 1011 Bill Beck Boulevard, Kissimmee, FL 34744-5301. **Phone:** 407-847-8966 Ext. 364. **Fax:** 407-847-3925.

Visit CollegeQuest.com for information on majors offered and athletics.

FLORIDA COLLEGE
Temple Terrace, Florida

- **Independent**, 4-year, founded 1944
- **Degrees** associate and bachelor's
- **Small-town** 95-acre campus with easy access to Tampa
- **Coed**, 530 undergraduate students, 97% full-time, 52% women, 48% men
- **Moderately difficult** entrance level, 74% of applicants were admitted
- **17:1 student-to-undergraduate faculty ratio**
- **$7250 tuition** and fees
- **$11.6 million endowment**

Students *Undergraduates:* 515 full-time, 15 part-time. Students come from 41 states and territories, 7 other countries. *The most frequently chosen baccalaureate field is:* philosophy.

From out-of-state	71%	Reside on campus	90%
Age 25 or older	2%	Transferred in	7%
International students	2%	African Americans	2%
Asian Americans/Pacific Islanders	1%	Hispanic Americans	4%
Native Americans	1%		

Faculty 38 (74% full-time), 24% with terminal degrees.

Expenses (1999–2000) *Comprehensive fee:* $12,790 includes full-time tuition ($7050), mandatory fees ($200), and room and board ($5540). *College room only:* $3200. Room and board charges vary according to housing facility. *Part-time tuition:* $315 per semester hour. *Part-time fees:* $75 per term part-time. *Payment plan:* installment. *Waivers:* employees or children of employees.

Library Chatlos Library. *Operations spending 1999–2000:* $210,747. *Collection:* 44,658 titles, 295 serial subscriptions.

College life *Housing:* on-campus residence required through sophomore year. *Options:* men-only, women-only. *Social organizations:* societies; 67% of eligible men and 84% of eligible women are members. *Most popular organizations:* Drama Workshop, concert band, chorus, SBGA, YWTO.

Campus security Controlled dormitory access, evening patrols by trained security personnel.

After graduation *Career center:* Services include career counseling.

Freshmen 368 applied, 274 admitted, 273 enrolled. 4 National Merit Scholars, 4 valedictorians.

SAT verbal scores above 500	66%	SAT math scores above 500	60%
ACT above 18	84%	1998 freshmen returning in 1999	68%

Application *Option:* electronic application. *Application fee:* $25. *Required:* high school transcript; minimum 2.0 GPA; letters of recommendation. *Required for some:* essay or personal statement.

Standardized tests *Admission: Required:* SAT I or ACT.

Significant dates *Application deadlines:* 8/1 (freshmen), 8/1 (transfers). *Financial aid deadline:* 8/1. *Priority date:* 4/1.

Freshman Application Contact
Mrs. Mari Smith, Assistant Director of Admissions, Florida College, 119 North Glen Arven Avenue, Temple Terrace, FL 33617. **Phone:** 813-988-5131 Ext. 6716. **Toll-free phone:** 800-326-7655. **Fax:** 813-899-6772. **E-mail:** admissions@flcoll.edu

Visit CollegeQuest.com for information on majors offered and athletics. College video and electronic viewbook available at CollegeQuest.com.

FLORIDA GULF COAST UNIVERSITY
Fort Myers, Florida

- **State-supported**, comprehensive, founded 1991
- **Degrees** bachelor's and master's
- **Suburban** 760-acre campus
- **Coed**, 2,087 undergraduate students, 57% full-time, 65% women, 35% men
- **Moderately difficult** entrance level, 61% of applicants were admitted
- **11:1 student-to-undergraduate faculty ratio**
- **$2319 tuition** and fees (in-state); $9308 (out-of-state)
- **$6451 average financial aid** package, $10.6 million endowment

Part of State University System of Florida.

Students *Undergraduates:* 1,187 full-time, 900 part-time. Students come from 18 states and territories, 34 other countries. *The most frequently chosen baccalaureate fields are:* education, health professions and related sciences, protective services/public administration. *Graduate:* 633 in graduate degree programs.

From out-of-state	7%	Reside on campus	8%
Age 25 or older	0.3%	Transferred in	23%
International students	1%	African Americans	4%
Asian Americans/Pacific Islanders	2%	Hispanic Americans	8%
Native Americans	0.3%		

Faculty 196 (98% full-time), 70% with terminal degrees.

Expenses (1999–2000) *One-time required fee:* $10. *Tuition, state resident:* full-time $1990; part-time $66 per credit. *Tuition, nonresident:* full-time $8979; part-time $299 per credit. *Required fees:* full-time $329; $66 per credit. Full-time tuition and fees vary according to course load. Part-time tuition and fees vary according to course load. *College room and board:* $5326; room only: $3208. Room and board charges vary according to board plan. *Waivers:* senior citizens and employees or children of employees.

Library *Operations spending 1999–2000:* $3.8 million. *Collection:* 98,157 titles, 5,625 serial subscriptions, 918 audiovisual materials.

College life *Housing: Option:* coed. *Most popular organizations:* Golden Key National Honor Society, student government, Student Nurses Association, Student Council for Exceptional Children, Physical Therapy Association.

Campus security 24-hour emergency response devices and patrols, late-night transport-escort service.

After graduation 75 organizations recruited on campus 1997–98. *Career center:* 2 part-time personnel. Services include job fairs, resume preparation, interview workshops, resume referral, career/interest testing, career counseling, careers library, job bank, job interviews, portfolio management, skill identification, job search skills, student employment, alumni assistance.

Freshmen 959 applied, 581 admitted, 263 enrolled.

Average high school GPA	3.23	SAT verbal scores above 500	57%
SAT math scores above 500	50%	ACT above 18	87%
From top 10% of their h.s. class	11%	From top quarter	43%
From top half	80%	1998 freshmen returning in 1999	69%

Application *Options:* Common Application, electronic application, early admission, deferred entrance. *Application fee:* $20. *Required:* high school transcript; minimum 2.0 GPA; interview. *Required for some:* essay or personal statement; letters of recommendation.

Standardized tests *Admission: Required:* SAT I or ACT.

Significant dates *Application deadlines:* 8/15 (freshmen), rolling (transfers). *Financial aid deadline priority date:* 5/1.

Freshman Application Contact
Ms. Michele Yovanovich, Director of Admissions, Florida Gulf Coast University, 10501 FGCU Boulevard South, Fort Myers, FL 33965-6565. **Phone:** 941-590-7878. **Toll-free phone:** 800-590-3428. **Fax:** 941-590-7894.

Visit CollegeQuest.com for information on majors offered and athletics. Electronic viewbook available at CollegeQuest.com.

FLORIDA INSTITUTE OF TECHNOLOGY
Melbourne, Florida

Apply at CollegeQuest.com

- **Independent**, university, founded 1958
- **Degrees** associate, bachelor's, master's, doctoral, and postbachelor's certificates
- **Small-town** 130-acre campus with easy access to Orlando
- **Coed**, 1,916 undergraduate students, 93% full-time, 31% women, 69% men
- **Moderately difficult** entrance level, 79% of applicants were admitted
- **12:1 student-to-undergraduate faculty ratio**

Florida

Florida Institute of Technology (continued)
- **49.1% graduate** in 6 years or less
- **$17,300 tuition** and fees
- **$16,462 average financial aid** package, $24,265 average indebtedness upon graduation, $17.5 million endowment

Students *Undergraduates:* 1,787 full-time, 129 part-time. Students come from 49 states and territories, 82 other countries. *The most frequently chosen baccalaureate fields are:* biological/life sciences, engineering/engineering technologies, trade and industry. *Graduate:* 2,245 in graduate degree programs.

From out-of-state	62%	Reside on campus	46%
Age 25 or older	10%	Transferred in	8%
International students	28%	African Americans	5%
Asian Americans/Pacific Islanders	3%	Hispanic Americans	5%
Native Americans	0.3%		

Faculty 191 (84% full-time).
Expenses (1999–2000) *One-time required fee:* $200. *Comprehensive fee:* $22,570 includes full-time tuition ($17,300) and room and board ($5270). *College room only:* $2270. Full-time tuition and fees vary according to program. Room and board charges vary according to board plan. *Part-time tuition:* $525 per credit hour. Part-time tuition and fees vary according to program. *Payment plan:* installment. *Waivers:* senior citizens and employees or children of employees.
Library Evans Library. *Operations spending 1999–2000:* $1.2 million. *Collection:* 3,967 serial subscriptions, 4,097 audiovisual materials.
College life *Housing:* on-campus residence required in freshman year. *Options:* coed, men-only, women-only. *Social organizations:* national fraternities, national sororities, local sororities; 17% of eligible men and 13% of eligible women are members. *Most popular organizations:* Pi Kappa Alpha, Chi Phi, Theta Xi, College Players, Caribbean Student Association.
Campus security 24-hour emergency response devices and patrols, late-night transport-escort service, self-defense education.
After graduation 96 organizations recruited on campus 1997–98. 75% of class of 1998 had job offers within 6 months. *Career center:* 3 full-time personnel. Services include job fairs, resume preparation, interview workshops, resume referral, career counseling, careers library, job bank, job interviews.
Freshmen 1,939 applied, 1,531 admitted, 395 enrolled.

Average high school GPA	3.36	SAT verbal scores above 500	77%
SAT math scores above 500	87%	ACT above 18	95%
From top 10% of their h.s. class	27%	From top quarter	56%
From top half	87%	1998 freshmen returning in 1999	76%

Application *Options:* eApply at www.CollegeQuest.com, Common Application, electronic application, early admission, deferred entrance. *Application fee:* $35. *Required:* high school transcript; minimum 2.5 GPA. *Required for some:* minimum 3.0 GPA. *Recommended:* essay or personal statement; minimum 2.8 GPA; interview.
Standardized tests *Admission: Required:* SAT I or ACT.
Significant dates *Application deadlines:* rolling (freshmen), rolling (transfers). *Financial aid deadline priority date:* 3/15.
Freshman Application Contact
Ms. Judi Marino, Director of Undergraduate Admissions, Florida Institute of Technology, 150 West University Boulevard, Melbourne, FL 32901-6975. **Phone:** 321-674-8030. **Toll-free phone:** 800-348-4636 (in-state); 800-888-4348 (out-of-state). **Fax:** 321-723-9468. **E-mail:** admissions@fit.edu
Visit CollegeQuest.com for information on majors offered and athletics. College video available at CollegeQuest.com.

- *See page 1676 for a narrative description.*

FLORIDA INTERNATIONAL UNIVERSITY
Miami, Florida

- **State-supported**, university, founded 1965
- **Degrees** bachelor's, master's, and doctoral
- **Urban** 573-acre campus
- **Coed**, 22,717 undergraduate students, 58% full-time, 56% women, 44% men
- **Moderately difficult** entrance level, 56% of applicants were admitted
- **14:1 student-to-undergraduate faculty ratio**
- **45.7% graduate** in 6 years or less
- **$2326 tuition** and fees (in-state); $9315 (out-of-state)
- **$18.9 million endowment**

Part of State University System of Florida.
Students *Undergraduates:* 13,110 full-time, 9,607 part-time. Students come from 52 states and territories, 115 other countries. *The most frequently chosen baccalaureate fields are:* business/marketing, education, health professions and related sciences. *Graduate:* 5,584 in graduate degree programs.

From out-of-state	3%	Reside on campus	7%
Age 25 or older	30%	Transferred in	4%
International students	7%	African Americans	15%
Asian Americans/Pacific Islanders	4%	Hispanic Americans	56%
Native Americans	0.1%		

Faculty 1,293 (67% full-time), 66% with terminal degrees.
Expenses (1999–2000) *One-time required fee:* $10. *Tuition, state resident:* full-time $2164; part-time $72 per credit hour. *Tuition, nonresident:* full-time $9153; part-time $305 per credit hour. *Required fees:* full-time $162; $81 per term part-time. Full-time tuition and fees vary according to course load. *College room and board:* $5206; room only: $3176. Room and board charges vary according to board plan and housing facility. *Payment plan:* tuition prepayment. *Waivers:* senior citizens and employees or children of employees.
Library University Park Library plus 2 others. *Operations spending 1999–2000:* $5.2 million. *Collection:* 1.3 million titles, 9,124 serial subscriptions, 112,286 audiovisual materials.
College life *Housing: Option:* coed. *Social organizations:* national fraternities, national sororities; 8% of eligible men and 9% of eligible women are members. *Most popular organizations:* Students for Community Service, Black Student Leadership Council, Hospitality Management Student Club, Hispanic Students Association, Haitian Students Organization.
Campus security 24-hour emergency response devices and patrols, late-night transport-escort service, controlled dormitory access.
After graduation 600 organizations recruited on campus 1997–98. 70% of class of 1998 had job offers within 6 months. *Career center:* 13 full-time, 10 part-time personnel. Services include job fairs, resume preparation, resume referral, career/interest testing, career counseling, careers library, job bank, job interviews.
Freshmen 5,391 applied, 3,006 admitted, 2,551 enrolled. 9 valedictorians.

Average high school GPA	3.47	SAT verbal scores above 500	88%
SAT math scores above 500	86%	ACT above 18	99%
From top 10% of their h.s. class	42%	From top quarter	89%
From top half	99%	1998 freshmen returning in 1999	89%

Application *Options:* Common Application, electronic application, early admission, deferred entrance. *Application fee:* $20. *Required:* high school transcript. *Required for some:* 1 letter of recommendation. *Recommended:* minimum 3.0 GPA.
Standardized tests *Admission: Required:* SAT I or ACT.
Significant dates *Application deadlines:* rolling (freshmen), rolling (transfers). *Notification:* continuous until 8/1 (freshmen). *Financial aid deadline priority date:* 3/1.
Freshman Application Contact
Ms. Carmen Brown, Director of Admissions, Florida International University, University Park, Miami, FL 33199. **Phone:** 305-348-3675. **Fax:** 305-348-3648. **E-mail:** admiss@servms.fiu.edu
Visit CollegeQuest.com for information on majors offered and athletics. Electronic viewbook available at CollegeQuest.com.

- *See page 1678 for a narrative description.*

FLORIDA MEMORIAL COLLEGE
Miami-Dade, Florida

Admissions Office Contact
Florida Memorial College, 15800 NW 42nd Avenue, Miami-Dade, FL 33054. **Toll-free phone:** 800-822-1362.

Florida

FLORIDA METROPOLITAN UNIVERSITY—FORT LAUDERDALE COLLEGE
Fort Lauderdale, Florida

- **Proprietary**, comprehensive, founded 1940
- **Degrees** associate, bachelor's, and master's
- **Suburban** campus with easy access to Miami
- **Coed**
- **Minimally difficult** entrance level
- **$6555 tuition** and fees

Part of Corinthian Colleges, Inc.
Expenses (1999–2000) *Tuition:* full-time $6480; part-time $190 per quarter hour. *Required fees:* full-time $75; $25 per term part-time. Full-time tuition and fees vary according to course load.
College life *Housing:* college housing not available. *Most popular organizations:* American Marketing Association, International Business Club.
Campus security Late-night transport-escort service, building security.
Application *Options:* Common Application, electronic application, deferred entrance. *Application fee:* $25. *Required:* essay or personal statement; high school transcript. *Required for some:* letters of recommendation. *Recommended:* interview.
Standardized tests *Admission: Required:* CPAt. *Recommended:* SAT I or ACT.
Admissions Office Contact
Florida Metropolitan University–Fort Lauderdale College, 1040 Bayview Drive, Fort Lauderdale, FL 33304-2522. **Toll-free phone:** 800-468-0168. **Fax:** 954-568-2008.
Visit CollegeQuest.com for information on athletics.

FLORIDA METROPOLITAN UNIVERSITY—ORLANDO COLLEGE, MELBOURNE
Melbourne, Florida

- **Proprietary**, comprehensive, founded 1953
- **Degrees** associate, bachelor's, and master's
- **Small-town** 5-acre campus with easy access to Orlando
- **Coed**
- **Moderately difficult** entrance level
- **$6555 tuition** and fees

Part of Corinthian Colleges, Inc.
Expenses (1999–2000) *Tuition:* full-time $6480; part-time $190 per quarter hour. *Required fees:* full-time $75; $25 per term part-time. Full-time tuition and fees vary according to course load and program. Part-time tuition and fees vary according to course load.
College life *Housing:* college housing not available.
Campus security 24-hour emergency response devices.
Application *Options:* Common Application, deferred entrance. *Application fee:* $25. *Required:* high school transcript; interview.
Standardized tests *Admission: Required:* CPAt.
Admissions Office Contact
Florida Metropolitan University–Orlando College, Melbourne, 2401 North Harbor City Boulevard, Melbourne, FL 32935-6657. **Fax:** 407-255-2017.
Visit CollegeQuest.com for information on athletics.

FLORIDA METROPOLITAN UNIVERSITY—ORLANDO COLLEGE, NORTH
Orlando, Florida

- **Proprietary**, comprehensive, founded 1953
- **Degrees** associate, bachelor's, and master's
- **Urban** 1-acre campus
- **Coed**
- **Minimally difficult** entrance level
- **$6555 tuition** and fees

Part of Corinthian Colleges, Inc.
Expenses (1999–2000) *Tuition:* full-time $6480; part-time $190 per quarter hour. *Required fees:* full-time $75; $25 per term part-time. Full-time tuition and fees vary according to course load and program.
College life *Housing:* college housing not available.
Campus security Door alarms.
Application *Options:* Common Application, deferred entrance. *Application fee:* $50. *Required:* high school transcript.
Admissions Office Contact
Florida Metropolitan University–Orlando College, North, 5421 Diplomat Circle, Orlando, FL 32810-5674. **Toll-free phone:** 800-628-5870. **Fax:** 407-628-2616.
Visit CollegeQuest.com for information on athletics.

FLORIDA METROPOLITAN UNIVERSITY—ORLANDO COLLEGE, SOUTH
Orlando, Florida

- **Proprietary**, comprehensive
- **Degrees** associate, bachelor's, and master's
- **Coed**
- **Minimally difficult** entrance level
- **$4395 tuition** and fees

Expenses (1999–2000) *Tuition:* full-time $4320; part-time $190 per credit. *Required fees:* full-time $75; $25 per term part-time. Full-time tuition and fees vary according to course load.
College life *Housing:* college housing not available.
Application *Application fee:* $50. *Required:* high school transcript; interview.
Admissions Office Contact
Florida Metropolitan University–Orlando College, South, 2411 Sand Lake Road, Orlando, FL 32809. **Fax:** 407-851-1477.
Visit CollegeQuest.com for information on athletics.

FLORIDA METROPOLITAN UNIVERSITY—TAMPA COLLEGE
Tampa, Florida

- **Proprietary**, comprehensive, founded 1890
- **Degrees** associate, bachelor's, and master's
- **Urban** 4-acre campus
- **Coed**
- **Minimally difficult** entrance level
- **$6879 tuition** and fees

Part of Corinthian Colleges, Inc.
Expenses (1999–2000) *Tuition:* full-time $6804; part-time $199 per quarter hour. *Required fees:* full-time $75; $25 per term part-time. Full-time tuition and fees vary according to course load and program. Part-time tuition and fees vary according to course level and program.
College life *Housing:* college housing not available. *Social organizations:* coed fraternity. *Most popular organizations:* Legal Network, Phi Beta Lambda, PC-MAC Users Group, international club, Art League.
Campus security Evening and Saturday afternoon patrols by trained security personnel.
Application *Options:* Common Application, deferred entrance. *Application fee:* $50. *Required:* high school transcript.
Standardized tests *Admission: Required:* CPAt. *Required for some:* ACT.
Admissions Office Contact
Florida Metropolitan University–Tampa College, 3319 West Hillsborough Avenue, Tampa, FL 33614-5899. **Fax:** 813-871-2483.
Visit CollegeQuest.com for information on athletics.

Peterson's Guide to Four-Year Colleges 2001 www.petersons.com

Florida

FLORIDA METROPOLITAN UNIVERSITY—TAMPA COLLEGE, BRANDON
Tampa, Florida

- **Proprietary**, comprehensive, founded 1890
- **Degrees** associate, bachelor's, and master's
- **Urban** 5-acre campus
- **Coed**, 670 undergraduate students, 83% full-time, 67% women, 33% men
- **Minimally difficult** entrance level, 79% of applicants were admitted
- **14:1 student-to-undergraduate faculty ratio**
- **69% graduate** in 6 years or less
- **$6555 tuition** and fees

Part of Corinthian Colleges, Inc.

Students *Undergraduates:* 556 full-time, 114 part-time. *The most frequently chosen baccalaureate fields are:* business/marketing, computer/information sciences, protective services/public administration. **Graduate:** 47 in graduate degree programs.

Age 25 or older	47%	International students	1%
Africans Americans	31%	Asian Americans/Pacific Islanders	2%
Hispanic Americans	10%	Native Americans	1%

Expenses (1999–2000) *Tuition:* full-time $6480; part-time $190 per quarter hour. *Required fees:* full-time $75; $25 per term part-time. Full-time tuition and fees vary according to course load, degree level, and program. Part-time tuition and fees vary according to course load, degree level, and program. *Payment plan:* installment. *Waivers:* employees or children of employees.

Library Tampa College Library. *Collection:* 1,000 titles, 50 serial subscriptions.

College life *Housing:* college housing not available. *Most popular organizations:* Accounting Club, Medical Assistants Club.

Campus security 24-hour emergency response devices.

After graduation *Career center:* 1 full-time, 2 part-time personnel. Services include job fairs, resume preparation, interview workshops, resume referral, career counseling, careers library, job bank.

Freshmen 165 applied, 130 admitted, 116 enrolled.

| SAT verbal scores above 500 | N/R | SAT math scores above 500 | N/R |
| ACT above 18 | N/R | | |

Application *Options:* Common Application, early admission, deferred entrance. *Application fee:* $50. *Required:* high school transcript; interview; minimum CPAt score of 120.

Standardized tests *Admission: Required:* CPAt.

Significant dates *Application deadlines:* rolling (freshmen), rolling (transfers). *Financial aid deadline:* continuous.

Freshman Application Contact
Ms. Dee Pearson, Director of Admissions, Florida Metropolitan University–Tampa College, Brandon, 3924 Coconut Palm Drive, Tampa, FL 33619. **Phone:** 813-621-0041 Ext. 45. **E-mail:** dpearson@cci.edu

Visit CollegeQuest.com for information on majors offered and athletics.

FLORIDA METROPOLITAN UNIVERSITY—TAMPA COLLEGE, LAKELAND
Lakeland, Florida

- **Proprietary**, comprehensive, founded 1890
- **Degrees** associate, bachelor's, and master's (bachelor's degree in business administration only)
- **Suburban** campus with easy access to Orlando and Tampa–St. Petersburg
- **Coed**
- **Minimally difficult** entrance level
- **$6555 tuition** and fees

Part of Corinthian Colleges, Inc.

Expenses (1999–2000) *Tuition:* full-time $6480; part-time $190 per quarter hour. *Required fees:* full-time $75; $25 per term part-time. Full-time tuition and fees vary according to course load and program. Part-time tuition and fees vary according to course level and program.

Institutional Web site http://www.cci.edu/

College life *Housing:* college housing not available.
Campus security 24-hour patrols.
Application *Options:* Common Application, early admission. *Required:* high school transcript.
Standardized tests *Admission: Required:* CPAt. *Recommended:* SAT I, ACT.

Admissions Office Contact
Florida Metropolitan University–Tampa College, Lakeland, 995 East Memorial Boulevard, Suite 110, Lakeland, FL 33801. **Fax:** 941-688-9881. **E-mail:** dsimmons@cci.edu

Visit CollegeQuest.com for information on athletics.

FLORIDA METROPOLITAN UNIVERSITY—TAMPA COLLEGE, PINELLAS
Clearwater, Florida

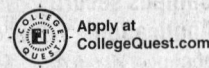
Apply at CollegeQuest.com

- **Proprietary**, comprehensive, founded 1890
- **Degrees** associate, bachelor's, and master's
- **Urban** 3-acre campus with easy access to Tampa–St. Petersburg
- **Coed**
- **Minimally difficult** entrance level
- **$6195 tuition** and fees

Part of Corinthian Colleges, Inc.

Expenses (1999–2000) *One-time required fee:* $150. *Tuition:* full-time $6120; part-time $190 per credit. *Required fees:* full-time $75; $25 per term part-time. Full-time tuition and fees vary according to course load. Part-time tuition and fees vary according to course load.

College life *Housing:* college housing not available. *Most popular organizations:* Human Resource Management Association, American Marketing Association, Criminal Justice Professional Fraternity.

Campus security 24-hour emergency response devices, late-night transport-escort service, evening patrols by security.

Application *Options:* eApply at www.CollegeQuest.com, Common Application, early admission, deferred entrance. *Application fee:* $25. *Required:* high school transcript; interview. *Recommended:* minimum 2.0 GPA.

Standardized tests *Admission: Required:* CPAt. *Recommended:* SAT I or ACT.

Admissions Office Contact
Florida Metropolitan University–Tampa College, Pinellas, 2471 McMullen Booth Road, Suite 200, Clearwater, FL 33759. **Toll-free phone:** 800-353-FMUS. **Fax:** 727-796-3722. **E-mail:** wchilder@cci.edu

Visit CollegeQuest.com for information on athletics.

FLORIDA SOUTHERN COLLEGE
Lakeland, Florida

- **Independent**, comprehensive, founded 1885, affiliated with United Methodist Church
- **Degrees** bachelor's and master's
- **Suburban** 100-acre campus with easy access to Tampa and Orlando
- **Coed**, 1,764 undergraduate students, 95% full-time, 61% women, 39% men
- **Moderately difficult** entrance level, 79% of applicants were admitted
- **16:1 student-to-undergraduate faculty ratio**
- **48.94% graduate** in 6 years or less
- **$12,950 tuition** and fees
- **$12,111 average financial aid** package, $12,678 average indebtedness upon graduation, $72.4 million endowment

Students *Undergraduates:* 1,682 full-time, 82 part-time. Students come from 45 states and territories, 43 other countries. *The most frequently chosen baccalaureate fields are:* business/marketing, education, health professions and related sciences. **Graduate:** 41 in graduate degree programs.

Florida

From out-of-state	22%	Reside on campus	61%
Transferred in	9%	International students	5%
African Americans	5%	Asian Americans/Pacific Islanders	1%
Hispanic Americans	4%	Native Americans	0.4%

Faculty 174 (60% full-time), 53% with terminal degrees.

Expenses (2000–2001) *Comprehensive fee:* $18,500 includes full-time tuition ($12,750), mandatory fees ($200), and room and board ($5550). *College room only:* $2650. Room and board charges vary according to board plan and housing facility. *Part-time tuition:* $370 per semester hour. Part-time tuition and fees vary according to class time. *Payment plan:* installment. *Waivers:* employees or children of employees.

Library E. T. Roux Library plus 1 other. *Operations spending 1999–2000:* $693,857. *Collection:* 125,356 titles, 748 serial subscriptions, 443 audiovisual materials.

College life *Housing:* on-campus residence required through junior year. *Options:* men-only, women-only. *Social organizations:* national fraternities, national sororities; 19% of eligible men and 20% of eligible women are members. *Most popular organizations:* Fellowship of Christian Athletes, Student Government Association, Student Union Board, Shades of Color, International Student Association.

Campus security 24-hour emergency response devices and patrols, student patrols, late-night transport-escort service, controlled dormitory access.

After graduation 44 organizations recruited on campus 1997–98. 74% of class of 1998 had job offers within 6 months. *Career center:* 2 full-time personnel. Services include job fairs, resume preparation, interview workshops, resume referral, career/interest testing, career counseling, careers library, job bank, job interviews. *Graduate education:* 14% of class of 1999 went directly to graduate and professional school: 8% graduate arts and sciences, 3% medicine, 2% law, 1% veterinary medicine.

Freshmen 1,202 applied, 947 admitted, 425 enrolled. 1 National Merit Scholar, 7 valedictorians.

Average high school GPA	3.37	SAT verbal scores above 500	61%
SAT math scores above 500	58%	ACT above 18	84%
From top 10% of their h.s. class	24%	From top quarter	53%
From top half	78%	1998 freshmen returning in 1999	73%

Application *Options:* electronic application, early admission. *Application fee:* $30. *Required:* essay or personal statement; high school transcript; minimum 2.0 GPA; 3 letters of recommendation. *Recommended:* minimum 3.0 GPA; interview.

Standardized tests *Admission: Required:* SAT I or ACT.

Significant dates *Application deadline:* rolling (transfers). *Financial aid deadline:* 8/1. Priority date: 4/1.

Freshman Application Contact
Mr. Robert Palmer, Vice President of Enrollment Management, Florida Southern College, 111 Lake Hollingsworth Drive, Lakeland, FL 33801-5698. **Phone:** 863-680-6212. **Toll-free phone:** 800-274-4131. **Fax:** 863-680-4120. **E-mail:** fscadm@flsouthern.edu

Visit CollegeQuest.com for information on majors offered and athletics. College video available at CollegeQuest.com.

■ *See page 1680 for a narrative description.*

FLORIDA STATE UNIVERSITY
Tallahassee, Florida

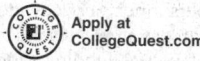
Apply at CollegeQuest.com

- **State-supported**, university, founded 1857
- **Degrees** associate, bachelor's, master's, doctoral, first professional, post-master's, and postbachelor's certificates
- **Suburban** 456-acre campus
- **Coed**, 25,040 undergraduate students, 88% full-time, 55% women, 45% men
- **Very difficult** entrance level, 64% of applicants were admitted
- **64% graduate** in 6 years or less
- **$2196 tuition** and fees (in-state); $9184 (out-of-state)
- **$3127 average financial aid** package, $15,458 average indebtedness upon graduation, $246.7 million endowment

Part of State University System of Florida.

Students *Undergraduates:* 22,151 full-time, 2,889 part-time. Students come from 51 states and territories, 134 other countries. *The most frequently chosen baccalaureate fields are:* business/marketing, education, social sciences and history. *Graduate:* 685 in professional programs, 6,228 in other graduate degree programs.

From out-of-state	20%	Reside on campus	20%
Age 25 or older	11%	Transferred in	9%
International students	1%	African Americans	12%
Asian Americans/Pacific Islanders	3%	Hispanic Americans	8%
Native Americans	0.4%		

Faculty 1,008 full-time.

Expenses (1999–2000) *Tuition, state resident:* full-time $2196; part-time $73 per semester hour. *Tuition, nonresident:* full-time $9184; part-time $306 per semester hour. Full-time tuition and fees vary according to location. Part-time tuition and fees vary according to location. *College room and board:* $4952; room only: $2694. Room and board charges vary according to board plan and housing facility. *Payment plans:* tuition prepayment, installment. *Waivers:* senior citizens and employees or children of employees.

Library Robert Manning Strozier Library plus 6 others. *Operations spending 1999–2000:* $5.8 million. *Collection:* 2.3 million titles, 15,511 serial subscriptions, 43,275 audiovisual materials.

College life *Housing: Options:* coed, women-only, cooperative, disabled students. *Social organizations:* national fraternities, national sororities, local fraternities, local sororities; 7% of eligible men and 8% of eligible women are members. *Most popular organizations:* student government, honors program, sororities/fraternities, Gold Key, Marching Chiefs.

Campus security 24-hour emergency response devices and patrols, late-night transport-escort service, controlled dormitory access.

After graduation 926 organizations recruited on campus 1997–98. *Career center:* 19 full-time personnel. Services include job fairs, resume preparation, interview workshops, resume referral, career/interest testing, career counseling, careers library, job bank, job interviews. *Graduate education:* 35% of class of 1999 went directly to graduate and professional school. *Major awards:* 2 Fulbright Scholars.

Freshmen 21,159 applied, 13,578 admitted, 4,937 enrolled. 97 National Merit Scholars.

Average high school GPA	3.55	SAT verbal scores above 500	87%
SAT math scores above 500	85%	ACT above 18	100%
From top 10% of their h.s. class	47%	From top quarter	86%
From top half	99%	1998 freshmen returning in 1999	85%

Application *Options:* eApply at www.CollegeQuest.com, Common Application, electronic application, early admission. *Application fee:* $20. *Required:* high school transcript. *Required for some:* audition. *Recommended:* essay or personal statement; minimum 3.0 GPA.

Standardized tests *Admission: Required:* SAT I or ACT.

Significant dates *Application deadlines:* 3/3 (freshmen), 7/14 (transfers). *Notification:* continuous until 3/17 (freshmen). *Financial aid deadline priority date:* 2/15.

Freshman Application Contact
Office of Admissions, Florida State University, 2500 University Center, Building A, Tallahassee, FL 32306-2400. **Phone:** 850-644-6200. **Fax:** 850-644-0197. **E-mail:** admissions@admin.fsu.edu

Visit CollegeQuest.com for information on majors offered and athletics. College video and electronic viewbook available at CollegeQuest.com.

■ *See page 1682 for a narrative description.*

HOBE SOUND BIBLE COLLEGE
Hobe Sound, Florida

- **Independent nondenominational**, 4-year, founded 1960
- **Degrees** associate and bachelor's
- **Small-town** 84-acre campus
- **Coed**, 131 undergraduate students, 74% full-time, 53% women, 47% men
- **Noncompetitive** entrance level, 93% of applicants were admitted
- **10:1 student-to-undergraduate faculty ratio**
- **25% graduate** in 6 years or less
- **$4080 tuition** and fees
- **$3520 average financial aid** package, $11,000 average indebtedness upon graduation, $525,932 endowment

Students *Undergraduates:* 97 full-time, 34 part-time. Students come from 17 states and territories, 7 other countries.

Florida

Hobe Sound Bible College (continued)

From out-of-state	50%	Reside on campus	75%
Age 25 or older	3%	Transferred in	5%
International students	15%	African Americans	4%
Hispanic Americans	1%		

Faculty 17 (53% full-time), 6% with terminal degrees.

Expenses (1999–2000) *Comprehensive fee:* $7090 includes full-time tuition ($3940), mandatory fees ($140), and room and board ($3010). Room and board charges vary according to housing facility. *Part-time tuition:* $155 per semester hour. *Payment plan:* installment. *Waivers:* employees or children of employees.

Library College Library. *Collection:* 35,724 titles, 119 serial subscriptions, 2,646 audiovisual materials.

College life *Housing:* on-campus residence required through senior year. *Options:* men-only, women-only.

Campus security Student patrols, late-night transport-escort service, controlled dormitory access.

After graduation *Career center:* Services include career counseling.

Freshmen 41 applied, 38 admitted, 42 enrolled. 1 valedictorian.

Average high school GPA	3.44	SAT verbal scores above 500	80%
SAT math scores above 500	70%	ACT above 18	72%
From top 10% of their h.s. class	10%	From top quarter	30%
From top half	65%	1998 freshmen returning in 1999	67%

Application *Options:* Common Application, early admission. *Preference* given to applicants committed to Wesleyan-Arminian theological position. *Application fee:* $25. *Required:* high school transcript; 3 letters of recommendation; photograph, medical report.

Standardized tests *Placement: Required:* SAT I or ACT

Significant dates *Application deadlines:* rolling (freshmen), rolling (transfers). *Notification:* continuous until 8/30 (freshmen). *Financial aid deadline priority date:* 9/1.

Freshman Application Contact

Mrs. Ann French, Director of Admissions, Hobe Sound Bible College, PO Box 1065, Hobe Sound, FL 33475-1065. **Phone:** 561-546-5534 Ext. 415. **Toll-free phone:** 800-881-5534. **Fax:** 561-545-1422. **E-mail:** hsbcuwin@aol.com

Visit CollegeQuest.com for information on majors offered and athletics.

INTERNATIONAL ACADEMY OF DESIGN

Tampa, Florida

Apply at CollegeQuest.com

- **Proprietary**, 4-year, founded 1984
- **Degrees** associate and bachelor's
- **Urban** 1-acre campus
- **Coed**, 900 undergraduate students, 64% full-time, 67% women, 33% men
- **Noncompetitive** entrance level
- **13:1 student-to-undergraduate faculty ratio**
- **$10,260 tuition** and fees

Part of Career Education Corporation.

Students *Undergraduates:* 579 full-time, 321 part-time. Students come from 18 states and territories, 7 other countries. *The most frequently chosen baccalaureate fields are:* business/marketing, visual/performing arts.

From out-of-state	18%	Age 25 or older	41%
Transferred in	14%	International students	1%
African Americans	11%	Asian Americans/Pacific Islanders	5%
Hispanic Americans	15%	Native Americans	2%

Faculty 84 (10% full-time), 8% with terminal degrees.

Expenses (1999–2000) *Tuition:* full-time $10,260; part-time $285 per credit. *Payment plans:* guaranteed tuition, installment, deferred payment. *Waivers:* employees or children of employees.

Library International Academy Library. *Collection:* 6,321 titles, 236 serial subscriptions, 421 audiovisual materials.

College life *Housing:* college housing not available. *Most popular organizations:* Student Chapter ASID, Dean's Team, Fashion Design International, computer animation club, marketing club.

Campus security 24-hour emergency response devices, late night patrols by trained security personnel.

After graduation 93% of class of 1998 had job offers within 6 months. *Career center:* 1 full-time, 1 part-time personnel. Services include resume preparation, interview workshops, resume referral, career counseling, careers library, job bank, job interviews.

Freshmen 153 enrolled.

SAT verbal scores above 500	N/R	SAT math scores above 500	N/R
ACT above 18	N/R	1998 freshmen returning in 1999	57%

Application *Options:* eApply at www.CollegeQuest.com, Common Application, early admission, deferred entrance. *Application fee:* $100. *Required:* essay or personal statement; high school transcript; interview. *Recommended:* minimum 2.0 GPA.

Significant dates *Application deadlines:* rolling (freshmen), rolling (transfers). *Financial aid deadline:* continuous.

Freshman Application Contact

Mr. Sean Kuhn, Director of Admissions, International Academy of Design, 5225 Memorial Highway, Tampa, FL 33634-7350. **Phone:** 813-881-0007. **Toll-free phone:** 800-ACADEMY. **Fax:** 813-881-0008. **E-mail:** mpage@academy.edu

Visit CollegeQuest.com for information on majors offered and athletics. College video and electronic viewbook available at CollegeQuest.com.

INTERNATIONAL COLLEGE

Naples, Florida

- **Independent**, comprehensive, founded 1990
- **Degrees** associate, bachelor's, and master's
- **Suburban** campus with easy access to Miami
- **Coed**, 782 undergraduate students, 80% full-time, 70% women, 30% men
- **Minimally difficult** entrance level, 59% of applicants were admitted
- **18:1 student-to-undergraduate faculty ratio**
- **$6870 tuition** and fees

Students *Undergraduates:* 623 full-time, 159 part-time. *The most frequently chosen baccalaureate fields are:* (pre)law, business/marketing. *Graduate:* 14 in graduate degree programs.

Age 25 or older	69%	Transferred in	21%
International students	0.3%	African Americans	14%
Asian Americans/Pacific Islanders	2%	Hispanic Americans	10%
Native Americans	1%		

Faculty 68 (43% full-time), 57% with terminal degrees.

Expenses (1999–2000) *Tuition:* full-time $6600; part-time $275 per credit. *Required fees:* full-time $270; $135 per term part-time. *Payment plan:* installment. *Waivers:* employees or children of employees.

Library Information Resource Center plus 1 other. *Operations spending 1999–2000:* $282,590. *Collection:* 18,125 titles, 225 serial subscriptions, 150 audiovisual materials.

College life *Housing:* college housing not available. *Most popular organizations:* AITP, student council, paralegal club, Institute of Managerial Accountants, running club.

Campus security Late-night transport-escort service, building security.

After graduation 40 organizations recruited on campus 1997–98. 92% of class of 1998 had job offers within 6 months. *Career center:* 1 full-time personnel. Services include job fairs, resume preparation, resume referral, career/interest testing, career counseling. *Graduate education:* 5% of class of 1999 went directly to graduate and professional school: 4% business, 1% law.

Freshmen 110 applied, 65 admitted, 65 enrolled.

SAT verbal scores above 500	N/R	SAT math scores above 500	N/R
ACT above 18	N/R		

Application *Options:* Common Application, electronic application, deferred entrance. *Application fee:* $20. *Required:* essay or personal statement; high school transcript; interview.

Standardized tests *Admission: Required:* CPAt. *Recommended:* SAT I.

Significant dates *Application deadlines:* rolling (freshmen), rolling (transfers). *Financial aid deadline:* continuous.

Freshman Application Contact

Ms. Rita Lampus, Director of Admissions, International College, 2654 Tamiami Trail East, Naples, FL 34112. **Phone:** 941-774-4700 Ext. 104. **Toll-free phone:** 800-466-8017. **Fax:** 941-774-4593. **E-mail:** admit@naples.net

Florida

Visit CollegeQuest.com for information on majors offered and athletics.

INTERNATIONAL FINE ARTS COLLEGE
Miami, Florida

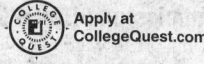

- **Proprietary**, comprehensive, founded 1965
- **Degrees** associate, bachelor's, and master's
- **Urban** 4-acre campus
- **Coed**, 844 undergraduate students, 87% full-time, 48% women, 52% men
- **Moderately difficult** entrance level
- **$11,988 tuition** and fees

Students *Undergraduates:* 731 full-time, 113 part-time. Students come from 45 states and territories, 50 other countries.

Reside on campus	40%	Age 25 or older	22%
International students	22%	African Americans	9%
Asian Americans/Pacific Islanders	2%	Hispanic Americans	40%
Native Americans	0.4%		

Expenses (1999–2000) *Comprehensive fee:* $14,958 includes full-time tuition ($11,463), mandatory fees ($525), and room and board ($2970). Full-time tuition and fees vary according to program. *Payment plans:* tuition prepayment, installment.
Library Daniel Stack Memorial Library plus 2 others. *Collection:* 14,022 titles, 87 serial subscriptions.
College life *Housing:* Option: coed. *Most popular organizations:* Caribbean Students Association, student government, DECA.
Campus security 24-hour emergency response devices, student patrols, late-night transport-escort service, controlled dormitory access, security service.
After graduation 56 organizations recruited on campus 1997–98. 72% of class of 1998 had job offers within 6 months. *Career center:* 1 full-time personnel. Services include resume preparation, resume referral, career counseling, careers library, job bank, job interviews.
Freshmen 338 enrolled.

| SAT verbal scores above 500 | N/R | SAT math scores above 500 | N/R |
| ACT above 18 | N/R | From top half of their h.s. class | 70% |

Application *Options:* eApply at www.CollegeQuest.com, Common Application, deferred entrance. *Application fee:* $50. *Required:* high school transcript; minimum 2.0 GPA; interview; 2 photographs, art portfolio. *Recommended:* essay or personal statement; 2 letters of recommendation.
Standardized tests *Admission: Recommended:* SAT I and SAT II or ACT, SAT II: Writing Test.
Significant dates *Application deadlines:* rolling (freshmen), rolling (transfers).
Freshman Application Contact
Ms. Elsia Suarez, Director of Admissions, International Fine Arts College, 1737 North Bayshore Drive, Miami, FL 33132-1121. **Phone:** 305-373-4684. **Toll-free phone:** 800-225-9023. **Fax:** 305-374-7946.
Visit CollegeQuest.com for information on majors offered and athletics.

ITT TECHNICAL INSTITUTE
Fort Lauderdale, Florida

- **Proprietary**, primarily 2-year, founded 1991
- **Degrees** associate and bachelor's
- **Suburban** campus with easy access to Miami
- **Coed**
- **Minimally difficult** entrance level
- **$9190 tuition** and fees

Part of ITT Educational Services, Inc.
Admissions Office Contact
ITT Technical Institute, 3401 South University Drive, Fort Lauderdale, FL 33328-2021. **Toll-free phone:** 800-488-7797. **Fax:** 954-476-6889.
Visit CollegeQuest.com for information on majors offered and athletics. College video available at CollegeQuest.com.

ITT TECHNICAL INSTITUTE
Jacksonville, Florida

- **Proprietary**, primarily 2-year, founded 1991
- **Degrees** associate and bachelor's
- **Urban** 1-acre campus
- **Coed**
- **Minimally difficult** entrance level
- **$9190 tuition** and fees

Part of ITT Educational Services, Inc.
Admissions Office Contact
ITT Technical Institute, 6600-10 Youngerman Circle, Jacksonville, FL 32244-6630. **Toll-free phone:** 800-318-1264.
Visit CollegeQuest.com for information on majors offered and athletics. College video available at CollegeQuest.com.

ITT TECHNICAL INSTITUTE
Maitland, Florida

- **Proprietary**, primarily 2-year, founded 1989
- **Degrees** associate and bachelor's
- **Suburban** 1-acre campus with easy access to Orlando
- **Coed**
- **Minimally difficult** entrance level
- **$9190 tuition** and fees

Part of ITT Educational Services, Inc.
Admissions Office Contact
ITT Technical Institute, 2600 Lake Lucien Drive, Suite 140, Maitland, FL 32751-7234.
Visit CollegeQuest.com for information on majors offered and athletics. College video available at CollegeQuest.com.

ITT TECHNICAL INSTITUTE
Tampa, Florida

- **Proprietary**, primarily 2-year, founded 1981
- **Degrees** associate and bachelor's
- **Suburban** campus with easy access to St. Petersburg
- **Coed**
- **Minimally difficult** entrance level
- **$9190 tuition** and fees

Part of ITT Educational Services, Inc.
Admissions Office Contact
ITT Technical Institute, 4809 Memorial Highway, Tampa, FL 33634-7151. **Fax:** 813-888-6078.
Visit CollegeQuest.com for information on majors offered and athletics. College video available at CollegeQuest.com.

JACKSONVILLE UNIVERSITY
Jacksonville, Florida

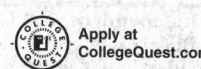

- **Independent**, comprehensive, founded 1934
- **Degrees** bachelor's and master's
- **Suburban** 260-acre campus
- **Coed**, 1,811 undergraduate students, 83% full-time, 52% women, 48% men
- **Moderately difficult** entrance level, 65% of applicants were admitted
- **14:1 student-to-undergraduate faculty ratio**
- **45% graduate** in 6 years or less
- **$14,950 tuition** and fees
- **$13,358 average financial aid** package, $29.5 million endowment

Students *Undergraduates:* 1,504 full-time, 307 part-time. Students come from 45 states and territories, 44 other countries. *The most frequently chosen baccalaureate fields are:* business/marketing, computer/information sciences, health professions and related sciences. *Graduate:* 261 in graduate

Florida

Jacksonville University (continued)
degree programs.

From out-of-state	37%	Reside on campus	50%
Age 25 or older	15%	Transferred in	10%
International students	5%	African Americans	14%
Asian Americans/Pacific Islanders	3%	Hispanic Americans	4%
Native Americans	1%		

Faculty 199 (52% full-time).

Expenses (1999–2000) *Comprehensive fee:* $20,160 includes full-time tuition ($14,390), mandatory fees ($560), and room and board ($5210). *College room only:* $2430. Room and board charges vary according to board plan and housing facility. *Payment plan:* installment. *Waivers:* employees or children of employees.

Library Carl S. Swisher Library. *Operations spending 1999–2000:* $905,759. *Collection:* 306,090 titles, 780 serial subscriptions.

College life *Housing:* on-campus residence required through junior year. *Options:* coed, men-only, women-only. *Social organizations:* national fraternities, national sororities; 18% of eligible men and 18% of eligible women are members. *Most popular organizations:* student government association, sororities, fraternities, Baptist Campus Ministry.

Campus security 24-hour emergency response devices and patrols, student patrols, late-night transport-escort service, controlled dormitory access, code lock doors in residence halls, trained security patrols during evening hours.

After graduation 65 organizations recruited on campus 1997–98. 80% of class of 1998 had job offers within 6 months. *Career center:* 2 full-time personnel. Services include job fairs, resume preparation, interview workshops, resume referral, career/interest testing, career counseling, careers library, job bank, job interviews, on-site corporate visits.

Freshmen 1,600 applied, 1,033 admitted, 315 enrolled.

Average high school GPA	3.06	SAT verbal scores above 500	61%
SAT math scores above 500	60%	ACT above 18	87%
From top 10% of their h.s. class	23%	From top quarter	51%
From top half	75%	1998 freshmen returning in 1999	67%

Application *Options:* eApply at www.CollegeQuest.com, Common Application, electronic application, early admission. *Application fee:* $30. *Required:* essay or personal statement; high school transcript; minimum 2.0 GPA. *Recommended:* letters of recommendation; interview.

Standardized tests *Admission: Required:* SAT I or ACT.

Significant dates *Application deadlines:* rolling (freshmen), rolling (transfers). *Financial aid deadline priority date:* 3/15.

Freshman Application Contact
Ms. Allie Roche-Macom, Associate Director of Admissions, Jacksonville University, 2800 University Boulevard North, Jacksonville, FL 32211-3394. **Phone:** 904-745-7000. **Toll-free phone:** 800-225-2027. **Fax:** 904-745-7012. **E-mail:** admissions@ju.edu

Visit CollegeQuest.com for information on majors offered and athletics. College video and electronic viewbook available at CollegeQuest.com.

■ *See page 1836 for a narrative description.*

JOHNSON & WALES UNIVERSITY
North Miami, Florida

- **Independent**, 4-year, founded 1992
- **Degrees** associate and bachelor's
- **Suburban** 8-acre campus with easy access to Miami
- **Coed**
- **Minimally difficult** entrance level

Institutional Web site http://www.jwu.edu/

College life *Housing:* on-campus residence required in freshman year. *Option:* coed. *Social organizations:* national fraternities, national sororities, local fraternities, local sororities; 25% of eligible men and 25% of eligible women are members. *Most popular organizations:* Vocational Industrial Clubs of America, American Culinary Federation, Collegiate Ambassador Team, New Frontiers, Tasters of the Vine.

Campus security 24-hour emergency response devices and patrols, video camera surveillance throughout campus.

Application *Options:* Common Application, early admission, deferred entrance. *Required:* high school transcript. *Required for some:* essay or personal statement; letters of recommendation; interview. *Recommended:* minimum 2.0 GPA.

Standardized tests *Admission: Required for some:* SAT I or ACT.

Admissions Office Contact
Johnson & Wales University, 1701 Northeast 127th Street, North Miami, FL 33181. **Toll-free phone:** 800-232-2433. **Fax:** 305-892-7030. **E-mail:** admissions@jwu.edu

Visit CollegeQuest.com for information on athletics. College video available at CollegeQuest.com.

JONES COLLEGE
Jacksonville, Florida

- **Independent**, 4-year, founded 1918
- **Degrees** associate and bachelor's
- **Urban** 5-acre campus
- **Coed**, 750 undergraduate students
- **Noncompetitive** entrance level
- **$4530 tuition** and fees

Students *Undergraduates:* Students come from 3 states and territories, 10 other countries. *The most frequently chosen baccalaureate field is:* business/marketing.

| Age 25 or older | 65% |

Faculty 60 (17% full-time).

Expenses (1999–2000) *Tuition:* full-time $4440; part-time $185 per credit hour. *Required fees:* full-time $90; $30 per term part-time.

Library Jerry B. Forrestal Library plus 2 others. *Collection:* 34,000 titles, 161 serial subscriptions.

College life *Housing:* college housing not available. *Social organizations:* national fraternities; 5% of men are members. *Most popular organization:* PBL.

Campus security Late-night transport-escort service.

After graduation 81% of class of 1998 had job offers within 6 months. *Career center:* 2 full-time personnel. Services include job fairs, resume preparation, resume referral, career counseling, careers library, job bank, job interviews.

Freshmen

| SAT verbal scores above 500 | N/R | SAT math scores above 500 | N/R |
| ACT above 18 | N/R | 1998 freshmen returning in 1999 | 68% |

Application *Options:* early admission, deferred entrance. *Application fee:* $0. *Required:* high school transcript; interview.

Standardized tests *Admission: Required:* CPAt.

Significant dates *Application deadlines:* rolling (freshmen), rolling (transfers).

Freshman Application Contact
Mr. Barry Darden, Director of Admissions, Jones College, 5353 Arlington Expressway, Jacksonville, FL 32211-5540. **Phone:** 904-743-1122 Ext. 115. **E-mail:** bdarden@jones.edu

Visit CollegeQuest.com for information on majors offered and athletics.

LYNN UNIVERSITY
Boca Raton, Florida

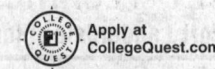
Apply at CollegeQuest.com

- **Independent**, comprehensive, founded 1962
- **Degrees** associate, bachelor's, master's, and doctoral
- **Suburban** 123-acre campus with easy access to Fort Lauderdale
- **Coed**, 1,761 undergraduate students, 77% full-time, 54% women, 46% men
- **Minimally difficult** entrance level, 81% of applicants were admitted
- **19:1 student-to-undergraduate faculty ratio**
- **$19,250 tuition** and fees

The University, ideally located between Palm Beach and Fort Lauderdale, enrolls approximately 2,000 students. The faculty-student ratio of 1:19 provides an academic environment in which the well-being and development of

Florida

the individual are assured. The University currently hosts students from 38 states and 73 nations, creating a community in which each student is provided with a rich multicultural experience and global awareness.

Students *Undergraduates:* Students come from 37 states and territories, 57 other countries.

From out-of-state	61%	Reside on campus	50%
Age 25 or older	24%		

Faculty 168 (36% full-time).

Expenses (2000–2001) *Comprehensive fee:* $26,050 includes full-time tuition ($18,500), mandatory fees ($750), and room and board ($6800). Part-time tuition and fees vary according to class time. *Payment plans:* installment, deferred payment. *Waivers:* employees or children of employees.

Library Eugene M. and Christine E. Lynn Library. *Collection:* 80,341 titles, 840 serial subscriptions.

College life *Housing:* on-campus residence required through sophomore year. *Options:* coed, women-only. *Social organizations:* national fraternities, national sororities; 15% of eligible men and 15% of eligible women are members. *Most popular organizations:* Knights of the Round Table, intramural group, student newspaper, Residence Hall Council, Activities Board.

Campus security 24-hour patrols, late-night transport-escort service, video monitor at residence entrances.

After graduation 125 organizations recruited on campus 1997–98. 86% of class of 1998 had job offers within 6 months. *Career center:* 1 full-time, 1 part-time personnel. Services include job fairs, resume preparation, interview workshops, resume referral, career/interest testing, career counseling, careers library, job bank, job interviews. *Graduate education:* 14% of class of 1999 went directly to graduate and professional school.

Freshmen 1,678 applied, 1,360 admitted.

SAT verbal scores above 500	N/R	SAT math scores above 500	N/R
ACT above 18	N/R	From top half of their h.s. class	80%
1998 freshmen returning in 1999	85%		

Application *Options:* eApply at www.CollegeQuest.com, Common Application, electronic application, early admission, deferred entrance. *Application fee:* $25. *Required:* high school transcript; minimum 2.0 GPA; 2 letters of recommendation. *Recommended:* essay or personal statement; minimum 3.0 GPA; interview.

Standardized tests *Admission: Required:* SAT I or ACT.

Significant dates *Application deadlines:* 8/15 (freshmen), 8/15 (transfers). *Financial aid deadline priority date:* 3/1.

Freshman Application Contact
Mr. James P. Sullivan, Director of Admissions, Lynn University, 3601 North Military Trail, Boca Raton, FL 33431-5598. **Phone:** 561-237-7837. **Toll-free phone:** 800-544-8035. **Fax:** 561-241-3552. **E-mail:** admission@lynn.edu

Visit CollegeQuest.com for information on majors offered and athletics. Electronic viewbook available at CollegeQuest.com.

■ *See page 1966 for a narrative description.*

NEW COLLEGE OF THE UNIVERSITY OF SOUTH FLORIDA
Sarasota, Florida

 Apply at CollegeQuest.com

- **State-supported**, 4-year, founded 1960
- **Degree** bachelor's
- **Suburban** 140-acre campus with easy access to Tampa–St. Petersburg
- **Coed**, 617 undergraduate students, 100% full-time, 63% women, 37% men
- **Very difficult** entrance level, 75% of applicants were admitted
- **11:1 student-to-undergraduate faculty ratio**
- **66% graduate** in 6 years or less
- **$2492 tuition** and fees (in-state); $10,878 (out-of-state)
- **$9962 average financial aid** package, $15,800 average indebtedness upon graduation, $26.5 million endowment

New College offers serious students the opportunity to pursue rigorous academic study in an environment designed to promote depth in thinking, free exchange of ideas, and highly individualized interaction with faculty members. Study is focused in the liberal arts and sciences and is highly accelerated and independent.

Part of State University System of Florida.

Students *Undergraduates:* 617 full-time. *The most frequently chosen baccalaureate field is:* liberal arts/general studies.

From out-of-state	38%	Reside on campus	71%
Age 25 or older	3%	Transferred in	7%
International students	0.3%	African Americans	2%
Asian Americans/Pacific Islanders	5%	Hispanic Americans	7%

Faculty 55 (100% full-time), 98% with terminal degrees.

Expenses (1999–2000) *Tuition, state resident:* full-time $2492. *Tuition, nonresident:* full-time $10,878. Full-time tuition and fees vary according to student level. *College room and board:* $4663. Room and board charges vary according to board plan and housing facility. *Payment plans:* tuition prepayment, installment.

Library Jane Bancroft Cook Library. *Operations spending 1999–2000:* $918,287. *Collection:* 254,889 titles, 1,592 serial subscriptions, 1,168 audiovisual materials.

College life *Housing:* on-campus residence required in freshman year. *Options:* coed, disabled students. *Most popular organizations:* Amnesty International, multicultural club, New College Student Alliance, Gay/Lesbian Student Alliance, The Word (political action group).

Campus security 24-hour emergency response devices and patrols, late-night transport-escort service.

After graduation *Career center:* 2 full-time, 1 part-time personnel. Services include job fairs, resume preparation, interview workshops, career/interest testing, career counseling, careers library, job bank, job interviews. *Graduate education:* 29% of class of 1999 went directly to graduate and professional school: 21% graduate arts and sciences, 4% medicine, 3% law. *Major awards:* 1 Marshall scholar.

Freshmen 298 applied, 223 admitted, 128 enrolled. 12 National Merit Scholars.

Average high school GPA	3.79	SAT verbal scores above 500	98%
SAT math scores above 500	95%	ACT above 18	100%
From top 10% of their h.s. class	53%	From top quarter	84%
From top half	99%	1998 freshmen returning in 1999	88%

Application *Options:* eApply at www.CollegeQuest.com, Common Application, early admission, deferred entrance. *Application fee:* $20. *Required:* essay or personal statement; high school transcript; 2 letters of recommendation; graded writing sample. *Required for some:* interview. *Recommended:* minimum 3.0 GPA; interview.

Standardized tests *Admission: Required:* SAT I or ACT.

Significant dates *Application deadlines:* 5/1 (freshmen), rolling (transfers). *Financial aid deadline priority date:* 3/1.

Freshman Application Contact
Ms. Kathleen Killion, Director of Admissions, New College of the University of South Florida, 5700 North Tamiami Trail, Sarasota, FL 34243-2197. **Phone:** 941-359-4269. **Fax:** 941-359-4435. **E-mail:** ncadmissions@sar.usf.edu

Visit CollegeQuest.com for information on majors offered and athletics.

■ *See page 2146 for a narrative description.*

NEW WORLD SCHOOL OF THE ARTS
Miami, Florida

- **State-supported**, 4-year, founded 1984
- **Degrees** associate and bachelor's
- **Urban** 5-acre campus
- **Coed**, 313 undergraduate students, 100% full-time, 57% women, 43% men
- **Most difficult** entrance level, 39% of applicants were admitted
- **4:1 student-to-undergraduate faculty ratio**
- **$1638 tuition** and fees (in-state); $5722 (out-of-state)
- **$3.2 million endowment**

Students *Undergraduates:* 313 full-time. Students come from 15 states and territories.

Florida

New World School of the Arts (continued)

Age 25 or older	10%	African Americans	16%
Asian Americans/Pacific Islanders	3%	Hispanic Americans	44%

Faculty 96 (21% full-time).

Expenses (1999–2000) *Tuition, state resident:* full-time $1638. *Tuition, nonresident:* full-time $5722. Full-time tuition and fees vary according to course load, degree level, and student level. *Waivers:* employees or children of employees.

College life *Housing:* college housing not available. *Most popular organization:* student government.

Campus security 24-hour patrols.

Freshmen 290 applied, 114 admitted, 122 enrolled.

Average high school GPA	2.8	SAT verbal scores above 500	N/R
SAT math scores above 500	N/R	ACT above 18	N/R
1998 freshmen returning in 1999	80%		

Application *Options:* early admission, deferred entrance. *Application fee:* $20. *Required:* essay or personal statement; high school transcript; 2 letters of recommendation; interview; audition.

Standardized tests *Placement: Recommended:* SAT I or ACT.

Significant dates *Notification:* continuous until 8/1 (freshmen).

Freshman Application Contact
Ms. Pamela Neuman, Recruitment and Admissions Coordinator, New World School of the Arts, 300 NE Second Avenue, Miami, FL 33132. **Phone:** 305-237-7707. **E-mail:** pneuman@mdcc.edu

Visit CollegeQuest.com for information on majors offered and athletics.

NORTHWOOD UNIVERSITY, FLORIDA CAMPUS
West Palm Beach, Florida

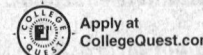

Apply at CollegeQuest.com

- **Independent**, 4-year, founded 1982
- **Degrees** associate and bachelor's
- **Suburban** 90-acre campus with easy access to Miami
- **Coed**, 975 undergraduate students, 77% full-time, 44% women, 56% men
- **Moderately difficult** entrance level, 76% of applicants were admitted
- **38:1 student-to-undergraduate faculty ratio**
- **$11,625 tuition** and fees
- **$13,515 average financial aid** package, $13,378 average indebtedness upon graduation, $42 million system endowment

Students *Undergraduates:* 755 full-time, 220 part-time. Students come from 30 states and territories, 40 other countries. *The most frequently chosen baccalaureate fields are:* business/marketing, computer/information sciences.

From out-of-state	34%	Reside on campus	50%
Age 25 or older	7%	Transferred in	10%
International students	14%	African Americans	11%
Asian Americans/Pacific Islanders	1%	Hispanic Americans	5%

Faculty 25 (48% full-time), 52% with terminal degrees.

Expenses (1999–2000) *Comprehensive fee:* $17,858 includes full-time tuition ($11,325), mandatory fees ($300), and room and board ($6233). Room and board charges vary according to board plan. *Part-time tuition:* $235 per credit hour. Part-time tuition and fees vary according to course load. *Payment plan:* installment. *Waivers:* children of alumni and employees or children of employees.

Library Peter C. Cook Library. *Collection:* 27,000 titles, 285 serial subscriptions.

College life *Housing:* on-campus residence required through sophomore year. *Options:* men-only, women-only.

Campus security 24-hour emergency response devices and patrols, student patrols.

After graduation *Career center:* 1 full-time, 1 part-time personnel. Services include job fairs, resume preparation, resume referral, career counseling, careers library, job bank, job interviews.

Freshmen 572 applied, 436 admitted, 191 enrolled.

Average high school GPA	2.8	SAT verbal scores above 500	N/R
SAT math scores above 500	N/R	ACT above 18	N/R
From top 10% of their h.s. class	3%	From top quarter	20%
From top half	57%	1998 freshmen returning in 1999	55%

Application *Options:* eApply at www.CollegeQuest.com, Common Application, electronic application, early admission, deferred entrance. *Application fee:* $15. *Required:* high school transcript; minimum 2.0 GPA. *Recommended:* essay or personal statement; 1 letter of recommendation; interview.

Standardized tests *Admission: Required:* SAT I or ACT.

Significant dates *Application deadlines:* rolling (freshmen), rolling (transfers). *Financial aid deadline priority date:* 4/1.

Freshman Application Contact
Mr. John M. Letvinchuck, Director of Admissions, Northwood University, Florida Campus, 2600 North Military Trail, West Palm Beach, FL 33409-2911. **Phone:** 561-478-5500. **Toll-free phone:** 800-458-8325. **Fax:** 561-640-3328. **E-mail:** fladmit@northwood.edu

Visit CollegeQuest.com for information on majors offered and athletics. Electronic viewbook available at CollegeQuest.com.

NOVA SOUTHEASTERN UNIVERSITY
Fort Lauderdale, Florida

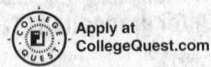

Apply at CollegeQuest.com

- **Independent**, university, founded 1964
- **Degrees** bachelor's, master's, doctoral, first professional, and first professional certificates
- **Suburban** 232-acre campus
- **Coed**, 4,053 undergraduate students, 64% full-time, 71% women, 29% men
- **Moderately difficult** entrance level, 70% of applicants were admitted
- **11:1 student-to-undergraduate faculty ratio**
- **$11,800 tuition** and fees

Nova Southeastern University is located in suburban Fort Lauderdale. Areas of study include majors in business, hospitality, education, computer science, life science (premedical), ocean studies, psychology, legal assisting, legal studies (prelaw), sport and wellness studies, environmental science/studies, accounting, and humanities. All programs can lead to graduate degrees as well as dual-admission programs with NSU's graduate centers.

Students *Undergraduates:* 2,588 full-time, 1,465 part-time. *The most frequently chosen baccalaureate fields are:* business/marketing, education, health professions and related sciences. *Graduate:* 2,927 in professional programs, 10,665 in other graduate degree programs.

From out-of-state	35%	Reside on campus	6%
Age 25 or older	63%	Transferred in	7%
International students	7%	African Americans	19%
Asian Americans/Pacific Islanders	2%	Hispanic Americans	20%
Native Americans	0.5%		

Faculty 1,273 (37% full-time).

Expenses (1999–2000) *Comprehensive fee:* $18,190 includes full-time tuition ($11,600), mandatory fees ($200), and room and board ($6390). Room and board charges vary according to board plan and housing facility. *Part-time tuition:* $387 per credit. *Part-time fees:* $25 per term part-time. *Payment plan:* installment. *Waivers:* employees or children of employees.

Library Einstein Library plus 4 others. *Collection:* 362,611 titles, 8,821 serial subscriptions, 2,591 audiovisual materials.

College life *Housing:* on-campus residence required through sophomore year. *Option:* coed. *Social organizations:* national fraternities, national sororities. *Most popular organizations:* Pre-Med Society, Alpha Phi Omega, Salsa.

Campus security 24-hour emergency response devices and patrols.

After graduation *Career center:* 3 full-time, 3 part-time personnel. Services include job fairs, resume preparation, resume referral, career/interest testing, career counseling, careers library, job bank.

Freshmen 817 applied, 568 admitted, 280 enrolled. 3 class presidents, 6 valedictorians, 49 student government officers.

Florida

Average high school GPA	3.44	SAT verbal scores above 500	69%
SAT math scores above 500	65%	ACT above 18	N/R
From top 10% of their h.s. class	28%	From top quarter	69%
From top half	90%	1998 freshmen returning in 1999	71%

Application *Options:* eApply at www.CollegeQuest.com, Common Application, early admission, deferred entrance. *Application fee:* $25. *Required:* essay or personal statement; high school transcript. *Recommended:* minimum 2.5 GPA; letters of recommendation; interview.
Standardized tests *Admission: Required for some:* SAT I or ACT.
Significant dates *Application deadlines:* 7/1 (freshmen), rolling (transfers). *Notification:* continuous until 8/1 (freshmen). *Financial aid deadline priority date:* 4/1.
Freshman Application Contact
Dr. Jean Lewis, Director of Undergraduate Admissions, Nova Southeastern University, 3301 College Avenue, Fort Lauderdale, FL 33314-7721. **Phone:** 954-262-8000. **Toll-free phone:** 800-541-6682. **Fax:** 954-262-3800. **E-mail:** ncsinfo@polaris.acast.nova.edu
Visit CollegeQuest.com for information on majors offered and athletics.

■ *See page 2204 for a narrative description.*

PALM BEACH ATLANTIC COLLEGE
West Palm Beach, Florida

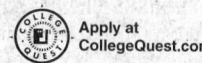

- **Independent nondenominational**, comprehensive, founded 1968
- **Degrees** associate, bachelor's, and master's
- **Urban** 25-acre campus with easy access to Miami
- **Coed**, 1,768 undergraduate students, 93% full-time, 60% women, 40% men
- **18:1 student-to-undergraduate faculty ratio**
- **$11,120 tuition** and fees

At the heart of the Palm Beach Atlantic experience is Workship, a program that combines work and worship and requires full-time students to contribute 45 hours annually to community service. PBA's Workship Program has recorded more than 1 million hours of service since the college was founded in 1968.

Students *Undergraduates:* 1,639 full-time, 129 part-time. Students come from 42 states and territories, 36 other countries. *The most frequently chosen baccalaureate fields are:* business/marketing, education, psychology. *Graduate:* 325 in graduate degree programs.

From out-of-state	24%	Reside on campus	44%
Age 25 or older	26%	Transferred in	33%

Faculty 171 (41% full-time).
Expenses (1999–2000) *Comprehensive fee:* $15,590 includes full-time tuition ($11,040), mandatory fees ($80), and room and board ($4470). *College room only:* $2200. Full-time tuition and fees vary according to class time. Room and board charges vary according to board plan and housing facility. Part-time tuition and fees vary according to class time and course load. *Payment plan:* installment. *Waivers:* senior citizens and employees or children of employees.
Library E. C. Blomeyer Library. *Collection:* 131,124 titles, 2,137 serial subscriptions, 4,806 audiovisual materials.
College life *Housing:* on-campus residence required through sophomore year. *Options:* coed, men-only, women-only.
Campus security 24-hour emergency response devices and patrols, late-night transport-escort service, controlled dormitory access.
Freshmen 1,490 applied, 1,031 admitted, 389 enrolled.

SAT verbal scores above 500	N/R	SAT math scores above 500	N/R
ACT above 18	N/R	1998 freshmen returning in 1999	67%

Application *Options:* eApply at www.CollegeQuest.com, Common Application, electronic application, early admission, deferred entrance. *Application fee:* $25. *Required:* essay or personal statement; high school transcript; minimum 2.0 GPA; 2 letters of recommendation. *Recommended:* minimum 3.0 GPA; interview.
Standardized tests *Admission: Required:* SAT I or ACT.
Significant dates *Application deadlines:* rolling (freshmen), rolling (transfers). *Financial aid deadline:* continuous.
Freshman Application Contact
Mr. Buck James, Dean of Enrollment Services, Palm Beach Atlantic College, 901 South Flagler Dr, PO Box 24708, West Palm Beach, FL 33416-4708. **Phone:** 561-803-2100. **Toll-free phone:** 800-238-3998. **E-mail:** admit@pbac.edu
Visit CollegeQuest.com for information on majors offered and athletics.

■ *See page 2244 for a narrative description.*

RINGLING SCHOOL OF ART AND DESIGN
Sarasota, Florida

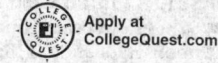

- **Independent**, 4-year, founded 1931
- **Degree** bachelor's
- **Urban** 35-acre campus with easy access to Tampa–St. Petersburg
- **Coed**, 892 undergraduate students, 98% full-time, 43% women, 57% men
- **Moderately difficult** entrance level, 39% of applicants were admitted
- **11:1 student-to-undergraduate faculty ratio**
- **54% graduate** in 6 years or less
- **$15,600 tuition** and fees
- **$10,048 average financial aid** package, $21,966 average indebtedness upon graduation, $3.9 million endowment

Students *Undergraduates:* 871 full-time, 21 part-time. Students come from 47 states and territories, 35 other countries. *The most frequently chosen baccalaureate field is:* visual/performing arts.

From out-of-state	50%	Reside on campus	40%
Age 25 or older	17%	Transferred in	12%
International students	6%	African Americans	2%
Asian Americans/Pacific Islanders	4%	Hispanic Americans	7%
Native Americans	0.4%		

Faculty 116 (38% full-time), 53% with terminal degrees.
Expenses (1999–2000) *One-time required fee:* $250. *Comprehensive fee:* $22,888 includes full-time tuition ($14,500), mandatory fees ($1100), and room and board ($7288). Full-time tuition and fees vary according to course level, course load, program, and student level. Room and board charges vary according to board plan and housing facility. *Part-time tuition:* $700 per credit hour. Part-time tuition and fees vary according to course level, course load, and program. *Payment plan:* installment. *Waivers:* employees or children of employees.
Library Verman Kimbrough Memorial Library. *Operations spending 1999–2000:* $421,007. *Collection:* 32,000 titles, 300 serial subscriptions, 65,600 audiovisual materials.
College life *Housing: Options:* coed, men-only, women-only. *Social organizations:* national fraternities, national sororities; 11% of eligible men and 6% of eligible women are members.
Campus security 24-hour emergency response devices and patrols, late-night transport-escort service, controlled dormitory access.
After graduation 42 organizations recruited on campus 1997–98. 90% of class of 1998 had job offers within 6 months. *Career center:* 2 full-time personnel. Services include resume preparation, interview workshops, career counseling, careers library, job bank, job interviews.
Freshmen 1,078 applied, 416 admitted, 159 enrolled.

SAT verbal scores above 500	N/R	SAT math scores above 500	N/R
ACT above 18	N/R	1998 freshmen returning in 1999	75%

Application *Options:* eApply at www.CollegeQuest.com, electronic application, deferred entrance. *Application fee:* $35. *Required:* essay or personal statement; high school transcript; minimum 2.0 GPA; 2 letters of recommendation; portfolio, resume. *Recommended:* interview.
Standardized tests *Placement: Recommended:* SAT I and SAT II or ACT.
Significant dates *Application deadlines:* rolling (freshmen), rolling (transfers). *Financial aid deadline priority date:* 3/1.
Freshman Application Contact
Mr. James Dean, Dean of Admissions, Ringling School of Art and Design, 2700 North Tamiami Trail, Sarasota, FL 34234-5895. **Phone:** 941-351-5100. **Toll-free phone:** 800-255-7695. **Fax:** 941-359-7517. **E-mail:** admissions@rsad.edu

Florida

Ringling School of Art and Design (continued)
Visit CollegeQuest.com for information on majors offered and athletics.

ROLLINS COLLEGE
Winter Park, Florida

 Apply at CollegeQuest.com

- **Independent**, comprehensive, founded 1885
- **Degrees** bachelor's and master's
- **Suburban** 67-acre campus with easy access to Orlando
- **Coed**, 1,519 undergraduate students, 100% full-time, 60% women, 40% men
- **Very difficult** entrance level, 73% of applicants were admitted
- **12:1** student-to-undergraduate faculty ratio
- **58% graduate** in 6 years or less
- **$21,852 tuition** and fees
- **$23,356 average financial aid** package, $14,600 average indebtedness upon graduation, $135.8 million endowment

As Florida's oldest recognized college, Rollins is noted for its versatile programs with practical applications, international studies programs, internships with a diversity of Central Florida companies, and highly personalized education. Renovation of its lakeside campus, which is minutes from downtown Orlando, include a new campus center, an electronic research and information center, a sports center, a bookstore, and an executive education center that focuses on various aspects of business and health care.

Students *Undergraduates:* 1,519 full-time. Students come from 44 states and territories, 37 other countries. *The most frequently chosen baccalaureate fields are:* psychology, social sciences and history, visual/performing arts. *Graduate:* 737 in graduate degree programs.

From out-of-state	50%	Reside on campus	68%
Age 25 or older	2%	Transferred in	4%
International students	5%	African Americans	2%
Asian Americans/Pacific Islanders	3%	Hispanic Americans	8%
Native Americans	1%		

Faculty 232 (66% full-time), 75% with terminal degrees.

Expenses (1999–2000) *Comprehensive fee:* $28,552 includes full-time tuition ($21,250), mandatory fees ($602), and room and board ($6700). *College room only:* $3850. *Payment plans:* tuition prepayment, installment. *Waivers:* employees or children of employees.

Library Olin Library. *Operations spending 1999–2000:* $1.5 million. *Collection:* 276,144 titles.

College life *Housing: Option:* coed. *Social organizations:* national fraternities, national sororities, local fraternities, local sororities; 27% of eligible men and 27% of eligible women are members. *Most popular organizations:* campus radio station, Greek system, student government, student media, Residential Hall Association.

Campus security 24-hour emergency response devices and patrols, late-night transport-escort service, controlled dormitory access.

After graduation 25 organizations recruited on campus 1997–98. 65% of class of 1998 had job offers within 6 months. *Career center:* 3 full-time personnel. Services include job fairs, resume preparation, interview workshops, resume referral, career/interest testing, career counseling, careers library, job bank, job interviews. *Graduate education:* 29% of class of 1999 went directly to graduate and professional school: 17% graduate arts and sciences, 6% law, 2% business, 2% education, 2% medicine. *Major awards:* 1 Fulbright Scholar.

Freshmen 1,748 applied, 1,275 admitted, 448 enrolled.

SAT verbal scores above 500	85%	SAT math scores above 500	85%
ACT above 18	85%	From top 10% of their h.s. class	37%
From top quarter	64%	From top half	84%
1998 freshmen returning in 1999	82%		

Application *Options:* eApply at www.CollegeQuest.com, Common Application, electronic application, early admission, early decision, deferred entrance. *Application fee:* $40. *Required:* essay or personal statement; high school transcript; 1 letter of recommendation. *Recommended:* interview.

Standardized tests *Admission: Required:* SAT I or ACT. *Recommended:* SAT II Subject Tests.

Significant dates *Application deadlines:* 2/15 (freshmen), 4/15 (transfers). *Early decision:* 11/15 (for plan 1), 1/15 (for plan 2). *Notification:* 4/1 (freshmen), 12/15 (early decision plan 1), 2/1 (early decision plan 2). *Financial aid deadline:* 3/1.

Freshman Application Contact
Mr. David Erdmann, Dean of Admissions and Student Financial Planning, Rollins College, 1000 Holt Avenue, Winter Park, FL 32789-4499. **Phone:** 407-646-2161. **Fax:** 407-646-2600. **E-mail:** admission@rollins.edu

Visit CollegeQuest.com for information on majors offered and athletics. College video and electronic viewbook available at CollegeQuest.com.

- *See page 2354 for a narrative description.*

ST. JOHN VIANNEY COLLEGE SEMINARY
Miami, Florida

- **Independent Roman Catholic**, 4-year, founded 1959
- **Degree** bachelor's
- **Urban** 33-acre campus
- **Coed**, primarily men
- **Moderately difficult** entrance level
- **$7000 tuition** and fees

Expenses (1999–2000) *Comprehensive fee:* $11,000 includes full-time tuition ($6900), mandatory fees ($100), and room and board ($4000). *Part-time tuition:* $150 per credit. *Part-time fees:* $100 per year part-time.

College life *Housing:* on-campus residence required through senior year. *Option:* men-only.

Campus security 24-hour emergency response devices, student patrols.

Application *Preference* given to candidates for the priesthood. *Application fee:* $0. *Required:* high school transcript; minimum 2.0 GPA; 1 letter of recommendation; psychological examination. *Recommended:* interview.

Standardized tests *Admission: Recommended:* SAT I or ACT.

Admissions Office Contact
St. John Vianney College Seminary, 2900 Southwest 87th Avenue, Miami, FL 33165-3244. **E-mail:** academic@sjvcs.edu

Visit CollegeQuest.com for information on athletics.

SAINT LEO UNIVERSITY
Saint Leo, Florida

Apply at CollegeQuest.com

- **Independent Roman Catholic**, comprehensive, founded 1889
- **Degrees** associate, bachelor's, and master's
- **Rural** 170-acre campus with easy access to Tampa and Orlando
- **Coed**, 1,359 undergraduate students, 71% full-time, 57% women, 43% men
- **Moderately difficult** entrance level, 70% of applicants were admitted
- **15:1** student-to-undergraduate faculty ratio
- **31% graduate** in 6 years or less
- **$11,650 tuition** and fees
- **$12,000 average financial aid** package, $12,000 average indebtedness upon graduation, $8.8 million endowment

Students *Undergraduates:* 960 full-time, 399 part-time. Students come from 34 states and territories, 9 other countries. *The most frequently chosen baccalaureate fields are:* business/marketing, protective services/public administration, social sciences and history. *Graduate:* 214 in graduate degree programs.

From out-of-state	13%	Reside on campus	34%
Age 25 or older	46%	Transferred in	13%
International students	3%	African Americans	7%
Asian Americans/Pacific Islanders	1%	Hispanic Americans	8%
Native Americans	1%		

Faculty 49 (92% full-time), 80% with terminal degrees.

Expenses (1999–2000) *Comprehensive fee:* $17,700 includes full-time tuition ($11,450), mandatory fees ($200), and room and board ($6050). *College room only:* $3200. Full-time tuition and fees vary according to class time. Room and board charges vary according to board plan and housing facility. *Part-time tuition:* $300 per credit hour. Part-time tuition and fees vary according to class time. *Payment plan:* installment. *Waivers:* employees or children of employees.

Library Cannon Memorial Library. *Operations spending 1999–2000:* $281,310. *Collection:* 743 serial subscriptions, 5,768 audiovisual materials.

College life *Housing:* on-campus residence required through junior year. *Options:* coed, men-only, women-only, disabled students. *Social organizations:* national fraternities, national sororities, local fraternities, local sororities; 9% of eligible men and 3% of eligible women are members. *Most popular organizations:* Student Government Union, Circle K, Samaritans, American Marketing Association.

Campus security 24-hour emergency response devices and patrols, late-night transport-escort service, controlled dormitory access.

After graduation 25% of class of 1998 had job offers within 6 months. *Career center:* 2 full-time personnel. Services include job fairs, resume preparation, interview workshops, resume referral, career/interest testing, career counseling, careers library. *Graduate education:* 24% of class of 1999 went directly to graduate and professional school.

Freshmen 813 applied, 567 admitted, 202 enrolled.

Average high school GPA	3.01	SAT verbal scores above 500	42%
SAT math scores above 500	44%	ACT above 18	64%
From top 10% of their h.s. class	7%	From top quarter	30%
From top half	57%	1998 freshmen returning in 1999	71%

Application *Options:* eApply at www.CollegeQuest.com, Common Application, electronic application, early admission, deferred entrance. *Application fee:* $35. *Required:* essay or personal statement; high school transcript; minimum 2.0 GPA; 1 letter of recommendation. *Required for some:* interview. *Recommended:* minimum 3.0 GPA; interview.

Standardized tests *Admission: Required:* SAT I or ACT.

Significant dates *Application deadlines:* 8/1 (freshmen), 8/1 (transfers). *Financial aid deadline priority date:* 3/1.

Freshman Application Contact
Dr. Susan Hallenbeck, Director of Undergraduate Admission, Saint Leo University, MC 2008, PO Box 6665, Saint Leo, FL 33574-6665. **Phone:** 352-588-8283. **Toll-free phone:** 800-334-5532. **Fax:** 352-588-8257. **E-mail:** admission@saintleo.edu

Visit CollegeQuest.com for information on majors offered and athletics. College video available at CollegeQuest.com.

■ *See page 2400 for a narrative description.*

ST. THOMAS UNIVERSITY
Miami, Florida

- **Independent Roman Catholic**, comprehensive, founded 1961
- **Degrees** bachelor's, master's, and first professional
- **Suburban** 140-acre campus
- **Coed**, 1,019 undergraduate students, 74% full-time, 55% women, 45% men
- **Moderately difficult** entrance level, 79% of applicants were admitted
- **$13,320 tuition** and fees
- **$12,674 average financial aid** package, $9.1 million endowment

The American Bar Association-accredited Morley School of Law completed a new wing in 1999. A new television production studio and an additional computer lab enrich technical instruction in the communication arts and computer information systems bachelor's degree programs. Study-abroad programs in Spain (El Escorial) and Italy (Assisi) attract students nationally and internationally.

Students *Undergraduates:* 756 full-time, 263 part-time. Students come from 24 states and territories, 59 other countries. *Graduate:* 157 in professional programs, 1,009 in other graduate degree programs.

From out-of-state	4%	Reside on campus	10%
Age 25 or older	37%	Transferred in	15%
International students	16%	African Americans	19%
Asian Americans/Pacific Islanders	1%	Hispanic Americans	50%
Native Americans	0.2%		

Expenses (2000–2001) *Comprehensive fee:* $17,720 includes full-time tuition ($12,720), mandatory fees ($600), and room and board ($4400). Room and board charges vary according to housing facility. *Part-time tuition:* $454 per credit. *Part-time fees:* $45 per term part-time. *Payment plan:* installment. *Waivers:* minority students, children of alumni, and employees or children of employees.

Library St. Thomas University Library plus 1 other. *Operations spending 1999–2000:* $1.6 million. *Collection:* 125,000 titles, 900 serial subscriptions.

College life *Housing: Options:* men-only, women-only. *Most popular organizations:* International Student Organization, Pre-Med Club, Hispanic Heritage Club, Inter-Dorm Council, communicators club.

Campus security 24-hour emergency response devices and patrols, late-night transport-escort service, controlled dormitory access.

After graduation *Career center:* 2 full-time personnel. Services include job fairs, resume preparation, resume referral, career/interest testing, career counseling, careers library, job bank, job interviews.

Freshmen 1,037 applied, 817 admitted, 128 enrolled.

Average high school GPA	2.9	SAT verbal scores above 500	N/R
SAT math scores above 500	N/R	ACT above 18	N/R
From top 10% of their h.s. class	11%	From top quarter	28%
From top half	52%	1998 freshmen returning in 1999	72%

Application *Options:* Common Application, electronic application, early admission, deferred entrance. *Application fee:* $45. *Required:* high school transcript; minimum 2.0 GPA. *Recommended:* essay or personal statement; 1 letter of recommendation; interview.

Standardized tests *Admission: Recommended:* SAT I and SAT II or ACT.

Significant dates *Application deadlines:* rolling (freshmen), rolling (transfers). *Financial aid deadline priority date:* 4/15.

Freshman Application Contact
Mr. Andre Lightbourne, Associate Director of Admissions, St. Thomas University, 16400 Northwest 32nd Avenue, Miami, FL 33054-6459. **Phone:** 305-628-6546. **Toll-free phone:** 800-367-9006 (in-state); 800-367-9010 (out-of-state). **Fax:** 305-628-6591. **E-mail:** signup@stu.edu

Visit CollegeQuest.com for information on majors offered and athletics.

■ *See page 2430 for a narrative description.*

SCHILLER INTERNATIONAL UNIVERSITY
Dunedin, Florida

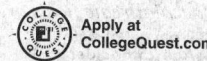

- **Independent**, comprehensive, founded 1991
- **Degrees** associate, bachelor's, and master's
- **Suburban** campus with easy access to Tampa
- **Coed**
- **Noncompetitive** entrance level

Schiller International University is an independent American university with campuses in the US, England, Germany, France, Spain, and Switzerland, among which students can transfer without loss of credit. English is the language of instruction at all campuses. SIU offers undergraduate and graduate students an American education in an international setting.

Part of Schiller International University.

Institutional Web site http://www.schiller.edu/

College life *Housing: Option:* coed. *Most popular organizations:* student government, student newspaper, yearbook staff, Model United Nations.

Campus security Night patrols.

Application *Options:* eApply at www.CollegeQuest.com, Common Application, deferred entrance. *Application fee:* $35. *Required:* essay or personal statement; high school transcript. *Recommended:* minimum 2.0 GPA.

Admissions Office Contact
Schiller International University, 453 Edgewater Drive, Dunedin, FL 34698-7532. **Toll-free phone:** 800-336-4133. **Fax:** 727-734-0359. **E-mail:** study@schiller.edu

Visit CollegeQuest.com for information on athletics. College video available at CollegeQuest.com.

■ *See page 2454 for a narrative description.*

Florida

SOUTH COLLEGE
West Palm Beach, Florida

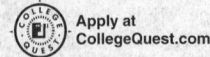

- **Proprietary**, primarily 2-year, founded 1899
- **Degrees** associate and bachelor's
- **Suburban** 1-acre campus with easy access to Miami
- **Coed**, 369 undergraduate students, 59% full-time, 80% women, 20% men
- **Minimally difficult** entrance level
- **8:1** student-to-undergraduate faculty ratio

Faculty 45 (29% full-time), 29% with terminal degrees.
Admissions Office Contact
South College, 1760 North Congress Avenue, West Palm Beach, FL 33409.
Fax: 561-697-9944. **E-mail:** socowpb@icanect.net
Visit CollegeQuest.com for information on majors offered and athletics.

SOUTHEASTERN COLLEGE OF THE ASSEMBLIES OF GOD
Lakeland, Florida

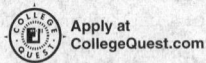

- **Independent**, 4-year, founded 1935, affiliated with Assemblies of God
- **Degree** bachelor's
- **Small-town** 62-acre campus with easy access to Tampa and Orlando
- **Coed**, 1,118 undergraduate students, 91% full-time, 53% women, 47% men
- **Minimally difficult** entrance level, 69% of applicants were admitted
- **18:1** student-to-undergraduate faculty ratio
- **33% graduate** in 6 years or less
- **$6023 tuition** and fees
- **$7456 average financial aid** package, $9775 average indebtedness upon graduation, $1.2 million endowment

Students *Undergraduates:* 1,021 full-time, 97 part-time. Students come from 36 states and territories, 7 other countries. *The most frequently chosen baccalaureate fields are:* education, philosophy, psychology.

From out-of-state	53%	Reside on campus	58%
Age 25 or older	15%	Transferred in	11%
International students	1%	African Americans	4%
Asian Americans/Pacific Islanders	1%	Hispanic Americans	8%
Native Americans	0.4%		

Faculty 81 (58% full-time), 36% with terminal degrees.
Expenses (1999–2000) *Comprehensive fee:* $9531 includes full-time tuition ($5320), mandatory fees ($703), and room and board ($3508). Room and board charges vary according to board plan. *Part-time tuition:* $190 per credit. *Part-time fees:* $352 per term part-time. Part-time tuition and fees vary according to course load and program. *Payment plan:* installment. *Waivers:* employees or children of employees.
Library Steelman Media Center plus 2 others. *Operations spending 1999–2000:* $252,335. *Collection:* 94,167 titles, 600 serial subscriptions.
College life *Housing:* on-campus residence required through senior year. *Options:* men-only, women-only. *Most popular organizations:* Spanish Club, travel music groups, cross-cultural awareness, Castle of the King-Kids, travel drama groups.
Campus security 24-hour emergency response devices and patrols.
After graduation 8 organizations recruited on campus 1997–98. *Career center:* 1 full-time personnel. Services include career/interest testing, career counseling, careers library, job bank, job interviews.
Freshmen 283 applied, 194 admitted, 194 enrolled.

SAT verbal scores above 500	N/R	SAT math scores above 500	N/R
ACT above 18	N/R	1998 freshmen returning in 1999	70%

Application *Options:* eApply at www.CollegeQuest.com, electronic application, early admission, deferred entrance. *Application fee:* $40. *Required:* high school transcript; 2 letters of recommendation. *Required for some:* interview.
Standardized tests *Admission: Required:* SAT I or ACT.
Significant dates *Application deadlines:* 8/1 (freshmen), 8/1 (transfers). *Notification:* continuous until 8/1 (freshmen). **Financial aid deadline** *priority date:* 4/1.

Freshman Application Contact
Ms. Sandy Markharn, Admission Secretary, Southeastern College of the Assemblies of God, 1000 Longfellow Boulevard, Lakeland, FL 33801-6099.
Phone: 863-667-5018. **Toll-free phone:** 800-500-8760. **Fax:** 941-667-5200.
E-mail: admission@secollege.edu
Visit CollegeQuest.com for information on majors offered and athletics. College video available at CollegeQuest.com.

STETSON UNIVERSITY
DeLand, Florida

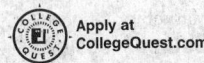

- **Independent**, comprehensive, founded 1883
- **Degrees** bachelor's, master's, first professional, and post-master's certificates
- **Small-town** 162-acre campus with easy access to Orlando
- **Coed**, 2,050 undergraduate students, 96% full-time, 58% women, 42% men
- **Moderately difficult** entrance level, 80% of applicants were admitted
- **10:1** student-to-undergraduate faculty ratio
- **58.5% graduate** in 6 years or less
- **$18,385 tuition** and fees
- **$17,540 average financial aid** package, $17,500 average indebtedness upon graduation, $118.7 million endowment

As Florida's first private university, Stetson University sets a high standard for quality teaching and innovative, superior programs. Stetson maintains a more than century-old commitment to values and social responsibility for its students. Stetson is also committed to making top-quality, private education affordable to a diverse group of qualified students. With a $9.5-million donor-funded construction program, Stetson has added 3 new facilities and renovated a 4th on the historic DeLand campus.

Students *Undergraduates:* 1,965 full-time, 85 part-time. Students come from 42 states and territories, 55 other countries. *The most frequently chosen baccalaureate fields are:* business/marketing, education, social sciences and history. *Graduate:* 673 in professional programs, 318 in other graduate degree programs.

From out-of-state	20%	Reside on campus	73%
Age 25 or older	7%	Transferred in	6%
International students	7%	African Americans	3%
Asian Americans/Pacific Islanders	1%	Hispanic Americans	5%
Native Americans	0.4%		

Faculty 237 (76% full-time).
Expenses (2000–2001, estimated) *Comprehensive fee:* $24,455 includes full-time tuition ($17,475), mandatory fees ($910), and room and board ($6070). *College room only:* $3380. Room and board charges vary according to board plan and housing facility. *Part-time tuition:* $580 per credit hour. Part-time tuition and fees vary according to course load. *Payment plan:* installment. *Waivers:* employees or children of employees.
Library DuPont-Ball Library plus 2 others. *Operations spending 1999–2000:* $1.4 million. *Collection:* 324,000 titles, 1,392 serial subscriptions, 18,178 audiovisual materials.
College life *Housing:* on-campus residence required through junior year. *Options:* coed, men-only, women-only. *Social organizations:* national fraternities, national sororities; 33% of eligible men and 29% of eligible women are members. *Most popular organizations:* Youth Motivators, Habitat for Humanity, Into the Streets, Black Student Association, Best Buddies.
Campus security 24-hour emergency response devices and patrols, late-night transport-escort service.
After graduation 50 organizations recruited on campus 1997–98. *Career center:* 3 full-time personnel. Services include job fairs, resume preparation, interview workshops, resume referral, career/interest testing, career counseling, careers library, job bank, job interviews.
Freshmen 1,913 applied, 1,523 admitted, 550 enrolled. 8 valedictorians.

Average high school GPA	3.54	SAT verbal scores above 500	79%
SAT math scores above 500	77%	ACT above 18	N/R
From top 10% of their h.s. class	30%	From top quarter	65%
From top half	92%	1998 freshmen returning in 1999	81%

Application *Options:* eApply at www.CollegeQuest.com, Common Application, electronic application, early admission, early decision. *Application*

Florida

fee: $35. *Required:* essay or personal statement; high school transcript; letters of recommendation. *Recommended:* interview.
Standardized tests *Admission: Required:* SAT I or ACT. *Recommended:* SAT II Subject Tests.
Significant dates *Application deadlines:* 3/15 (freshmen), rolling (transfers). *Early decision:* 11/1. *Notification:* 11/15 (early decision). **Financial aid deadline priority date:** 4/15.
Freshman Application Contact
Ms. Mary Napier, Dean of Admissions, Stetson University, Unit 8378, DeLand, FL 32720-3781. **Phone:** 904-822-7100. **Toll-free phone:** 800-688-0101. **Fax:** 904-822-8832. **E-mail:** admissions@stetson.edu
Visit CollegeQuest.com for information on majors offered and athletics. College video and electronic viewbook available at CollegeQuest.com.

■ *See page 2574 for a narrative description.*

TALMUDIC COLLEGE OF FLORIDA
Miami Beach, Florida

Admissions Office Contact
Talmudic College of Florida, 4014 Chase Avenue, Miami Beach, FL 33139. **Fax:** 305-534-8444.

TRINITY BAPTIST COLLEGE
Jacksonville, Florida

- **Independent Baptist**, 4-year, founded 1974
- **Degrees** associate and bachelor's
- **Urban** 148-acre campus
- **Coed**, 336 undergraduate students, 84% full-time, 43% women, 57% men
- **Moderately difficult** entrance level, 79% of applicants were admitted
- **11:1 student-to-undergraduate faculty ratio**
- **$3980 tuition** and fees

Students *Undergraduates:* 282 full-time, 54 part-time. Students come from 26 states and territories, 3 other countries. *The most frequently chosen baccalaureate fields are:* education, philosophy.

From out-of-state	35%	Reside on campus	46%
Age 25 or older	26%	Transferred in	7%
International students	1%	African Americans	3%
Asian Americans/Pacific Islanders	2%	Hispanic Americans	0.3%

Faculty 37 (30% full-time), 35% with terminal degrees.
Expenses (1999–2000) *Comprehensive fee:* $6980 includes full-time tuition ($3580), mandatory fees ($400), and room and board ($3000). *College room only:* $1700. Full-time tuition and fees vary according to location. Room and board charges vary according to board plan. *Part-time tuition:* $150 per semester hour. *Part-time fees:* $200 per term part-time. Part-time tuition and fees vary according to course load and location. *Payment plan:* installment. *Waivers:* employees or children of employees.
Library Travis Hudson Library. *Collection:* 33,000 titles, 210 serial subscriptions.
College life *Housing:* on-campus residence required through senior year. *Options:* men-only, women-only. *Social organizations:* societies; 100% of eligible men and 100% of eligible women are members.
Campus security 24-hour emergency response devices, controlled dormitory access, evening security.
After graduation 75% of class of 1998 had job offers within 6 months. *Career center:* Services include career counseling, job bank, job interviews. *Graduate education:* 2% of class of 1999 went directly to graduate and professional school: 2% theology.
Freshmen 121 applied, 95 admitted, 68 enrolled. 5 valedictorians.

Average high school GPA	3.0	SAT verbal scores above 500	N/R
SAT math scores above 500	N/R	ACT above 18	N/R
1998 freshmen returning in 1999	85%		

Application *Option:* Common Application. *Application fee:* $25. *Required:* essay or personal statement; high school transcript; minimum 2.0 GPA; 3 letters of recommendation.
Standardized tests *Admission: Required:* SAT I or ACT.
Significant dates *Application deadlines:* rolling (freshmen), rolling (transfers). *Notification:* continuous until 8/15 (freshmen). **Financial aid deadline:** 6/15. **Priority date:** 5/15.
Freshman Application Contact
Mrs. Shirley F. Hartman, Director of Admissions, Trinity Baptist College, 800 Hammond Boulevard, Jacksonville, FL 32221. **Phone:** 904-596-2450. **Toll-free phone:** 800-786-2206. **Fax:** 904-596-2531. **E-mail:** trinity@tbc.edu
Visit CollegeQuest.com for information on majors offered and athletics. College video available at CollegeQuest.com.

TRINITY COLLEGE OF FLORIDA
New Port Richey, Florida

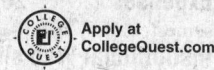
Apply at CollegeQuest.com

- **Independent nondenominational**, 4-year, founded 1932
- **Degrees** associate and bachelor's
- **Small-town** 20-acre campus with easy access to Tampa
- **Coed**, 128 undergraduate students, 77% full-time, 44% women, 56% men
- **Minimally difficult** entrance level
- **12:1 student-to-undergraduate faculty ratio**
- **1% graduate** in 6 years or less
- **$4730 tuition** and fees
- **$1.3 million endowment**

Students *Undergraduates:* 99 full-time, 29 part-time. Students come from 10 states and territories, 9 other countries. *The most frequently chosen baccalaureate field is:* philosophy.

From out-of-state	11%	Reside on campus	30%
Age 25 or older	49%	Transferred in	29%
International students	12%	African Americans	5%
Asian Americans/Pacific Islanders	2%	Hispanic Americans	2%

Faculty 16 (38% full-time), 6% with terminal degrees.
Expenses (1999–2000) *Comprehensive fee:* $7750 includes full-time tuition ($4420), mandatory fees ($310), and room and board ($3020). *Part-time tuition:* $170 per credit hour. *Part-time fees:* $155 per term part-time. Part-time tuition and fees vary according to course load. *Payment plan:* deferred payment. *Waivers:* senior citizens and employees or children of employees.
Library Raymond H. Center, M.D. Library. *Operations spending 1999–2000:* $48,003. *Collection:* 40,000 titles, 245 serial subscriptions.
College life *Housing:* Options: men-only, women-only. *Most popular organizations:* Great Commission Missionary Fellowship, Men's Church League Basketball, music club.
Campus security Controlled dormitory access, on-campus security personnel.
After graduation *Graduate education:* 25% of class of 1999 went directly to graduate and professional school: 25% theology.
Freshmen 23 enrolled. 2 National Merit Scholars.

Average high school GPA	2.85	SAT verbal scores above 500	N/R
SAT math scores above 500	N/R	ACT above 18	N/R
From top 10% of their h.s. class	10%	From top quarter	25%
From top half	52%	1998 freshmen returning in 1999	28%

Application *Options:* eApply at www.CollegeQuest.com, Common Application, early admission, deferred entrance. *Application fee:* $25. *Required:* high school transcript; 3 letters of recommendation. *Required for some:* interview.
Standardized tests *Admission: Required:* SAT I and SAT II or ACT.
Significant dates *Application deadlines:* rolling (freshmen), rolling (transfers). **Financial aid deadline priority date:** 4/14.
Freshman Application Contact
Mr. Paul Heier, Director of Admissions, Trinity College of Florida, 2430 Welbilt Boulevard, New Port Richey, FL 34655. **Phone:** 727-376-6911 Ext. 1120. **Toll-free phone:** 888-776-4999 Ext. 1120. **Fax:** 727-376-0781. **E-mail:** admissions@trinitycollege.edu
Visit CollegeQuest.com for information on majors offered and athletics.

Florida

TRINITY INTERNATIONAL UNIVERSITY, SOUTH FLORIDA CAMPUS
Miami, Florida

- **Independent nondenominational**, comprehensive, founded 1949
- **Degrees** bachelor's and master's
- **Urban** 16-acre campus
- **Coed**
- **Moderately difficult** entrance level
- **$8850 tuition** and fees

Expenses (1999–2000) *Tuition:* full-time $8650; part-time $365 per semester hour. *Required fees:* full-time $200; $50 per term part-time.

Institutional Web site http://www.tiu.edu/

College life *Housing:* college housing not available. *Most popular organizations:* Student Government Association, Youth Workers Support Group, IVMF.

Campus security Student patrols.

Application *Options:* Common Application, early admission, deferred entrance. *Application fee:* $15. *Required:* essay or personal statement; high school transcript; minimum 2.5 GPA; 2 letters of recommendation.

Standardized tests *Admission: Required:* SAT I or ACT.

Admissions Office Contact
Trinity International University, South Florida Campus, 500 Northeast First Avenue, Miami, FL 33132-1996. **Toll-free phone:** 800-288-1138.

Visit CollegeQuest.com for information on athletics.

UNIVERSITY OF CENTRAL FLORIDA
Orlando, Florida

- **State-supported**, university, founded 1963
- **Degrees** associate, bachelor's, master's, and doctoral
- **Suburban** 1,445-acre campus
- **Coed**, 25,749 undergraduate students, 72% full-time, 55% women, 45% men
- **Moderately difficult** entrance level, 62% of applicants were admitted
- **21:1 student-to-undergraduate faculty ratio**
- **51.6% graduate** in 6 years or less
- **$2297 tuition** and fees (in-state); $9286 (out-of-state)
- **$2907 average financial aid** package, $44.5 million endowment

Part of State University System of Florida.

Students *Undergraduates:* 18,459 full-time, 7,290 part-time. Students come from 49 states and territories, 120 other countries. *The most frequently chosen baccalaureate fields are:* business/marketing, education, health professions and related sciences. *Graduate:* 5,188 in graduate degree programs.

From out-of-state	3%	Reside on campus	10%
Age 25 or older	26%	Transferred in	13%
International students	2%	African Americans	8%
Asian Americans/Pacific Islanders	5%	Hispanic Americans	11%
Native Americans	1%		

Faculty 1,705 (51% full-time).

Expenses (1999–2000) *One-time required fee:* $10. *Tuition, state resident:* full-time $2202; part-time $73 per semester hour. *Tuition, nonresident:* full-time $9191; part-time $306 per semester hour. *Required fees:* full-time $95; $47 per term part-time. Full-time tuition and fees vary according to course load. Part-time tuition and fees vary according to course load. *College room and board:* $5215; room only: $3000. Room and board charges vary according to board plan and housing facility. *Payment plans:* tuition prepayment, deferred payment. *Waivers:* senior citizens and employees or children of employees.

Library University Library. *Operations spending 1999–2000:* $8.7 million. *Collection:* 1.2 million titles, 7,086 serial subscriptions, 30,672 audiovisual materials.

College life *Housing: Options:* coed, men-only, women-only. *Social organizations:* national fraternities, national sororities; 13% of eligible men and 11% of eligible women are members. *Most popular organizations:* Campus Activities Board, Student Government Association, Hispanic American Student Association, Volunteer UCF, African-American Student Union.

Campus security 24-hour emergency response devices and patrols, late-night transport-escort service, controlled dormitory access.

After graduation 531 organizations recruited on campus 1997–98. 80% of class of 1998 had job offers within 6 months. *Career center:* 11 full-time, 8 part-time personnel. Services include job fairs, resume preparation, interview workshops, resume referral, career counseling, careers library, job bank, job interviews.

Freshmen 13,703 applied, 8,541 admitted, 4,297 enrolled. 20 National Merit Scholars.

Average high school GPA	3.5	SAT verbal scores above 500	88%
SAT math scores above 500	88%	ACT above 18	100%
1998 freshmen returning in 1999	76%		

Application *Options:* electronic application, early admission. Preference given to state residents. *Application fee:* $20. *Required:* high school transcript; minimum 2.0 GPA. *Required for some:* 1 letter of recommendation. *Recommended:* essay or personal statement.

Standardized tests *Admission: Required:* SAT I or ACT.

Significant dates *Application deadlines:* 5/15 (freshmen), 5/15 (transfers). *Notification:* continuous until 8/15 (freshmen). **Financial aid deadline priority date:** 3/1.

Freshman Application Contact
Dr. Gordon Chavis Jr., Director of Admissions, University of Central Florida, PO Box 160111, Orlando, FL 32816. **Phone:** 407-823-3000. **Fax:** 407-823-3419. **E-mail:** admission@mail.ucf.edu

Visit CollegeQuest.com for information on majors offered and athletics. College video available at CollegeQuest.com.

- *See page 2706 for a narrative description.*

UNIVERSITY OF FLORIDA
Gainesville, Florida

- **State-supported**, university, founded 1853
- **Degrees** associate, bachelor's, master's, doctoral, and first professional
- **Suburban** 2,000-acre campus with easy access to Jacksonville
- **Coed**, 30,883 undergraduate students, 92% full-time, 52% women, 48% men
- **Very difficult** entrance level, 60% of applicants were admitted
- **17:1 student-to-undergraduate faculty ratio**
- **67% graduate** in 6 years or less
- **$2141 tuition** and fees (in-state); $9130 (out-of-state)

Part of State University System of Florida.

Students *Undergraduates:* 28,324 full-time, 2,559 part-time. Students come from 52 states and territories, 114 other countries. *The most frequently chosen baccalaureate fields are:* business/marketing, engineering/engineering technologies, social sciences and history. *Graduate:* 2,927 in professional programs, 8,822 in other graduate degree programs.

From out-of-state	6%	Reside on campus	21%
Age 25 or older	7%	Transferred in	6%
International students	1%	African Americans	7%
Asian Americans/Pacific Islanders	6%	Hispanic Americans	10%
Native Americans	0.4%		

Faculty 1,536 (100% full-time).

Expenses (1999–2000) *Tuition, state resident:* full-time $2141; part-time $71 per semester hour. *Tuition, nonresident:* full-time $9130; part-time $304 per semester hour. *College room and board:* $5040; room only: $2670. Room and board charges vary according to board plan and housing facility. *Payment plan:* tuition prepayment. *Waivers:* senior citizens and employees or children of employees.

Library George A. Smathers Library plus 15 others. *Collection:* 3.4 million titles, 25,213 serial subscriptions, 30,864 audiovisual materials.

College life *Housing: Options:* coed, women-only, cooperative. *Social organizations:* national fraternities, national sororities; 14% of eligible men and 15% of eligible women are members. *Most popular organizations:* Florida Blue Key, student government, Black Student Union, Hispanic Student Association, Reitz Union Program Council.

Campus security 24-hour emergency response devices and patrols, student patrols, late-night transport-escort service, controlled dormitory access, crime and rape prevention programs.

Florida

After graduation 920 organizations recruited on campus 1997–98. *Career center:* 21 full-time, 35 part-time personnel. Services include job fairs, resume preparation, interview workshops, resume referral, career/interest testing, career counseling, careers library, job bank, job interviews, cooperative education employment services. *Graduate education:* 27% of class of 1999 went directly to graduate and professional school. *Major awards:* 1 Rhodes, 5 Fulbright Scholars.

Freshmen 13,967 applied, 8,397 admitted, 5,462 enrolled. 130 National Merit Scholars.

SAT verbal scores above 500	97%	SAT math scores above 500	98%
ACT above 18	100%	From top 10% of their h.s. class	69%
From top quarter	92%	From top half	100%
1998 freshmen returning in 1999	91%		

Application *Options:* Common Application, electronic application, early admission, early decision. *Preference* given to state residents. *Application fee:* $20. *Required:* high school transcript.

Standardized tests *Admission: Required:* SAT I or ACT.

Significant dates *Application deadlines:* 1/29 (freshmen), 1/30 (transfers). *Early decision:* 10/15. *Notification:* 11/15 (early decision). *Financial aid deadline priority date:* 3/15.

Freshman Application Contact
Office of Admissions, University of Florida, PO Box 114000, Gainesville, FL 32611-4000. **Phone:** 352-392-1365.

Visit CollegeQuest.com for information on majors offered and athletics.

UNIVERSITY OF MIAMI
Coral Gables, Florida

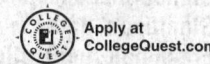 Apply at CollegeQuest.com

- **Independent**, university, founded 1925
- **Degrees** bachelor's, master's, doctoral, first professional, post-master's, and postbachelor's certificates
- **Suburban** 260-acre campus with easy access to Miami
- **Coed**, 8,235 undergraduate students, 94% full-time, 55% women, 45% men
- **Moderately difficult** entrance level, 55% of applicants were admitted
- **13:1 student-to-undergraduate faculty ratio**
- **59.2% graduate** in 6 years or less
- **$21,344 tuition** and fees
- **$19,537 average financial aid** package, $19,108 average indebtedness upon graduation, $428.6 million endowment

Students *Undergraduates:* 7,704 full-time, 531 part-time. Students come from 51 states and territories, 94 other countries. *The most frequently chosen baccalaureate fields are:* business/marketing, health professions and related sciences, visual/performing arts. *Graduate:* 1,807 in professional programs, 3,280 in other graduate degree programs.

From out-of-state	40%	Reside on campus	37%
Age 25 or older	9%	Transferred in	8%
International students	9%	African Americans	11%
Asian Americans/Pacific Islanders	5%	Hispanic Americans	28%
Native Americans	0.3%		

Faculty 1,089 (69% full-time), 75% with terminal degrees.

Expenses (1999–2000) *Comprehensive fee:* $29,126 includes full-time tuition ($20,950), mandatory fees ($394), and room and board ($7782). *College room only:* $4424. Room and board charges vary according to board plan and housing facility. *Payment plans:* tuition prepayment, installment. *Waivers:* employees or children of employees.

Library Otto G. Richter Library plus 2 others. *Operations spending 1999–2000:* $14.3 million. *Collection:* 1.3 million titles, 19,094 serial subscriptions, 102,620 audiovisual materials.

College life *Housing:* on-campus residence required in freshman year. *Options:* coed, disabled students. *Social organizations:* national fraternities, national sororities; 12% of eligible men and 11% of eligible women are members. *Most popular organizations:* student government, international student organizations, sports and recreation clubs, Association of Commuter Students, United Black Students.

Campus security 24-hour emergency response devices and patrols, student patrols, late-night transport-escort service, controlled dormitory access, crime prevention and safety workshops, residential college crime watch.

After graduation 205 organizations recruited on campus 1997–98. 60% of class of 1998 had job offers within 6 months. *Career center:* 10 full-time, 18 part-time personnel. Services include job fairs, resume preparation, interview workshops, resume referral, career/interest testing, career counseling, careers library, job bank, job interviews. *Graduate education:* 36% of class of 1999 went directly to graduate and professional school: 9% graduate arts and sciences, 6% medicine, 5% law, 3% business, 1% education, 1% engineering. *Major awards:* 1 Fulbright Scholar.

Freshmen 12,249 applied, 6,752 admitted, 1,859 enrolled. 61 valedictorians.

Average high school GPA	3.86	SAT verbal scores above 500	84%
SAT math scores above 500	86%	ACT above 18	98%
From top 10% of their h.s. class	46%	From top quarter	76%
From top half	96%	1998 freshmen returning in 1999	83%

Application *Options:* eApply at www.CollegeQuest.com, Common Application, electronic application, early admission, early decision, early action, deferred entrance. *Application fee:* $45. *Required:* essay or personal statement; high school transcript; minimum 2.3 GPA; 1 letter of recommendation. *Recommended:* interview.

Standardized tests *Admission: Required:* SAT I or ACT. *Required for some:* SAT II Subject Tests.

Significant dates *Application deadlines:* 3/1 (freshmen), 3/1 (transfers). *Early decision:* 11/15, 11/15. *Notification:* 4/1 (freshmen), 12/15 (early decision), 1/15 (early action). *Financial aid deadline priority date:* 2/15.

Freshman Application Contact
Mr. Edward M. Gillis, Associate Dean of Enrollments, University of Miami, PO Box 248025, Ashe Building Room 132, 1252 Memorial Drive, Coral Gables, FL 33146-4616. **Phone:** 305-284-4323. **Fax:** 305-284-2507. **E-mail:** admission@miami.edu

Visit CollegeQuest.com for information on majors offered and athletics. College video available at CollegeQuest.com.

UNIVERSITY OF NORTH FLORIDA
Jacksonville, Florida

- **State-supported**, comprehensive, founded 1965
- **Degrees** associate, bachelor's, master's, doctoral, and postbachelor's certificates (doctoral degree in education only)
- **Urban** 1,300-acre campus
- **Coed**, 9,334 undergraduate students, 65% full-time, 58% women, 42% men
- **Very difficult** entrance level, 73% of applicants were admitted
- **18:1 student-to-undergraduate faculty ratio**
- **$1820 tuition** and fees (in-state); $7411 (out-of-state)
- **$2184 average financial aid** package, $11,141 average indebtedness upon graduation, $32.7 million endowment

Part of State University System of Florida.

Students *Undergraduates:* 6,109 full-time, 3,225 part-time. Students come from 46 states and territories, 98 other countries. *The most frequently chosen baccalaureate fields are:* business/marketing, education, health professions and related sciences. *Graduate:* 1,810 in graduate degree programs.

From out-of-state	5%	Reside on campus	16%
Age 25 or older	27%	Transferred in	8%
International students	2%	African Americans	10%
Asian Americans/Pacific Islanders	5%	Hispanic Americans	4%
Native Americans	0.3%		

Faculty 620 (60% full-time).

Expenses (1999–2000) *Tuition, state resident:* full-time $1820; part-time $76 per semester hour. *Tuition, nonresident:* full-time $7411; part-time $309 per semester hour. *College room and board:* $5100; room only: $2790. Room and board charges vary according to board plan and housing facility. *Payment plan:* deferred payment. *Waivers:* senior citizens and employees or children of employees.

Library Thomas G. Carpenter Library. *Operations spending 1999–2000:* $3.7 million. *Collection:* 2,981 serial subscriptions.

College life *Housing: Options:* coed, disabled students. *Social organizations:* national fraternities, national sororities; 5% of eligible men and 3% of eligible women are members. *Most popular organizations:* International Student Association, Filipino Student Association, Student Physical Therapy Association, National Education Association, Student Government Association.

Peterson's Guide to Four-Year Colleges 2001   www.petersons.com

Florida

University of North Florida (continued)

Campus security 24-hour emergency response devices and patrols, student patrols, late-night transport-escort service, controlled dormitory access, electronic parking lot security.

After graduation 140 organizations recruited on campus 1997–98. *Career center:* 6 full-time, 2 part-time personnel. Services include job fairs, resume preparation, interview workshops, resume referral, career/interest testing, career counseling, careers library, job bank, job interviews.

Freshmen 4,895 applied, 3,579 admitted, 1,505 enrolled. 4 National Merit Scholars, 23 class presidents, 8 valedictorians, 212 student government officers.

Average high school GPA	3.4	SAT verbal scores above 500	76%
SAT math scores above 500	76%	ACT above 18	98%
1998 freshmen returning in 1999	78%		

Application *Options:* electronic application, early admission, early action, deferred entrance. *Application fee:* $20. *Required:* high school transcript; minimum 2.0 GPA. *Required for some:* essay or personal statement; letters of recommendation. *Recommended:* minimum 3.0 GPA.

Standardized tests *Admission: Required:* SAT I or ACT.

Significant dates *Application deadlines:* 7/6 (freshmen), 7/16 (transfers). *Early action:* 11/12. *Notification:* 12/1 (early action). *Financial aid deadline priority date:* 4/1.

Freshman Application Contact
Ms. Deborah M. Kaye, Executive Director of Enrollment Services, University of North Florida, 4567 St. Johns Bluff Road South, Jacksonville, FL 32224-2645. **Phone:** 904-620-2624. **Fax:** 904-620-1040. **E-mail:** osprey@unf.edu

Visit CollegeQuest.com for information on majors offered and athletics. College video available at CollegeQuest.com.

UNIVERSITY OF SARASOTA
Sarasota, Florida

Admissions Office Contact
University of Sarasota, 5250 17th Street, Sarasota, FL 34235-8246. **Fax:** 941-379-9464.

UNIVERSITY OF SOUTH FLORIDA
Tampa, Florida

- **State-supported**, university, founded 1956
- **Degrees** associate, bachelor's, master's, doctoral, first professional, and postbachelor's certificates
- **Urban** 1,913-acre campus
- **Coed**, 24,791 undergraduate students, 64% full-time, 58% women, 42% men
- **Moderately difficult** entrance level, 73% of applicants were admitted
- **16:1 student-to-undergraduate faculty ratio**
- **$2256 tuition** and fees (in-state); $9245 (out-of-state)
- **$184.4 million endowment**

Part of State University System of Florida.

Students *Undergraduates:* 15,952 full-time, 8,839 part-time. Students come from 52 states and territories, 101 other countries. *The most frequently chosen baccalaureate fields are:* business/marketing, education, social sciences and history. *Graduate:* 385 in professional programs, 5,817 in other graduate degree programs.

From out-of-state	4%	Reside on campus	11%
Age 25 or older	32%	Transferred in	16%
International students	2%	African Americans	11%
Asian Americans/Pacific Islanders	5%	Hispanic Americans	10%
Native Americans	0.4%		

Faculty 1,624 (92% full-time).

Expenses (1999–2000) *Tuition, state resident:* full-time $2256; part-time $75 per semester hour. *Tuition, nonresident:* full-time $9245; part-time $308 per semester hour. Full-time tuition and fees vary according to course level, course load, and location. Part-time tuition and fees vary according to course level, course load, and location. *College room and board:* $4606; room only: $2406. Room and board charges vary according to board plan, housing facility, and location. *Payment plans:* tuition prepayment, installment. *Waivers:* senior citizens.

Library Tampa Campus Library plus 2 others. *Operations spending 1999–2000:* $11.4 million. *Collection:* 1.4 million titles, 10,155 serial subscriptions, 148,986 audiovisual materials.

College life *Housing: Options:* coed, men-only, women-only, cooperative, disabled students. *Social organizations:* national fraternities, national sororities; 5% of eligible men and 4% of eligible women are members. *Most popular organizations:* student government, Campus Activities Board, USF Ambassadors, student admissions representatives.

Campus security 24-hour emergency response devices and patrols, student patrols, late-night transport-escort service, controlled dormitory access, residence hall lobby personnel 8 p.m. to 6 a.m.

After graduation 260 organizations recruited on campus 1997–98. *Career center:* 9 full-time, 2 part-time personnel. Services include job fairs, resume preparation, interview workshops, resume referral, career counseling, careers library, job bank, job interviews. *Graduate education:* 21% of class of 1999 went directly to graduate and professional school. *Major awards:* 1 Fulbright Scholar.

Freshmen 10,005 applied, 7,267 admitted, 3,588 enrolled. 26 National Merit Scholars, 20 valedictorians.

Average high school GPA	3.5	SAT verbal scores above 500	69%
SAT math scores above 500	71%	ACT above 18	91%

Application *Options:* Common Application, electronic application, early admission. *Application fee:* $20. *Required:* high school transcript; minimum 2.0 GPA. *Required for some:* letters of recommendation.

Standardized tests *Admission: Required:* SAT I or ACT.

Significant dates *Financial aid deadline priority date:* 3/1.

Freshman Application Contact
Ms. Cecelia Leslie, Director of Admissions, University of South Florida, 4202 East Fowler Avenue, SVC 1036, Tampa, FL 33620-9951. **Phone:** 813-974-3350. **Fax:** 813-974-9689. **E-mail:** bullseye@admin.usf.edu

Visit CollegeQuest.com for information on majors offered and athletics.

UNIVERSITY OF SOUTH FLORIDA, NEW COLLEGE
Florida—See New College of the University of South Florida

THE UNIVERSITY OF TAMPA
Tampa, Florida

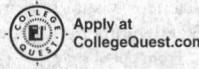
Apply at CollegeQuest.com

- **Independent**, comprehensive, founded 1931
- **Degrees** associate, bachelor's, and master's
- **Urban** 75-acre campus with easy access to Orlando
- **Coed**, 2,750 undergraduate students, 83% full-time, 61% women, 39% men
- **Moderately difficult** entrance level, 80% of applicants were admitted
- **16:1 student-to-undergraduate faculty ratio**
- **53% graduate** in 6 years or less
- **$15,542 tuition** and fees
- **$13,624 average financial aid** package, $17,130 average indebtedness upon graduation, $16.8 million endowment

A diversely populated campus bustles with record enrollments and more than $70 million in recent construction and technology improvements. More than 70 percent of residence halls are less than 4 years old. Tampa Bay was recently named the number one job market in the south and one of the best places to live.

Students *Undergraduates:* 2,284 full-time, 466 part-time. Students come from 50 states and territories, 76 other countries. *The most frequently chosen baccalaureate fields are:* biological/life sciences, business/marketing, communications/communication technologies. *Graduate:* 555 in graduate degree programs.

Florida

From out-of-state	47%	Reside on campus	50%
Age 25 or older	22%	Transferred in	10%
International students	7%	African Americans	7%
Asian Americans/Pacific Islanders	2%	Hispanic Americans	10%
Native Americans	1%		

Faculty 187 (71% full-time).

Expenses (1999–2000) *Comprehensive fee:* $20,717 includes full-time tuition ($14,740), mandatory fees ($802), and room and board ($5175). Room and board charges vary according to housing facility. *Part-time tuition:* $315 per hour. *Part-time fees:* $35 per term part-time. Part-time tuition and fees vary according to class time. *Payment plan:* installment. *Waivers:* employees or children of employees.

Library Merl Kelce Library. *Operations spending 1999–2000:* $1.1 million. *Collection:* 184,219 titles, 854 serial subscriptions, 3,733 audiovisual materials.

College life *Housing:* on-campus residence required through sophomore year. *Options:* coed, women-only. *Social organizations:* national fraternities, national sororities; 17% of eligible men and 12% of eligible women are members. *Most popular organizations:* P.E.A.C.E., student productions, Diplomats, Dance Expressions of the 90's, Christian Student Union.

Campus security 24-hour emergency response devices and patrols, late-night transport-escort service, controlled dormitory access.

After graduation 305 organizations recruited on campus 1997–98. 75% of class of 1998 had job offers within 6 months. *Career center:* 3 full-time personnel. Services include job fairs, resume preparation, interview workshops, resume referral, career/interest testing, career counseling, careers library, job bank, job interviews. *Graduate education:* 14% of class of 1999 went directly to graduate and professional school: 7% business, 4% graduate arts and sciences, 2% medicine, 1% law.

Freshmen 2,812 applied, 2,254 admitted, 614 enrolled.

Average high school GPA	3.13	SAT verbal scores above 500	59%
SAT math scores above 500	59%	ACT above 18	91%
From top 10% of their h.s. class	18%	From top quarter	49%
From top half	80%		

Application *Options:* eApply at www.CollegeQuest.com, Common Application, electronic application, early admission, deferred entrance. *Application fee:* $30. *Required:* essay or personal statement; high school transcript; minimum 2.0 GPA; 1 letter of recommendation. *Recommended:* interview.

Standardized tests *Admission: Required:* SAT I or ACT.

Significant dates *Application deadlines:* rolling (freshmen), rolling (transfers). *Financial aid deadline priority date:* 5/1.

Freshman Application Contact
Ms. Darcy Dwyer, Senior Associate Director of Admissions, The University of Tampa, 401 West Kennedy Boulevard, Tampa, FL 33606-1480. **Phone:** 813-253-6211. **Toll-free phone:** 800-733-4773. **Fax:** 813-254-4955. **E-mail:** admissions@alpha.utampa.edu

Visit CollegeQuest.com for information on majors offered and athletics. College video available at CollegeQuest.com.

■ *See page 2836 for a narrative description.*

UNIVERSITY OF WEST FLORIDA
Pensacola, Florida

- **State-supported**, comprehensive, founded 1963
- **Degrees** bachelor's, master's, and doctoral
- **Suburban** 1,600-acre campus
- **Coed**, 5,898 undergraduate students, 68% full-time, 58% women, 42% men
- **Moderately difficult** entrance level, 83% of applicants were admitted
- **26:1 student-to-undergraduate faculty ratio**
- **39% graduate** in 6 years or less
- **$2294 tuition** and fees (in-state); $9282 (out-of-state)
- **$54.3 million endowment**

The University of West Florida—near historic Pensacola and the world-famous beaches of the Gulf of Mexico—offers an inviting, environmentally friendly setting for study. Small classes, opportunities for individually tailored educational experiences, and scholarships for academic performance help make UWF an extraordinary value in higher education.

Part of State University System of Florida.

Students *Undergraduates:* 4,020 full-time, 1,878 part-time. Students come from 50 states and territories, 75 other countries. *The most frequently chosen baccalaureate fields are:* business/marketing, education, psychology. *Graduate:* 1,677 in graduate degree programs.

Reside on campus	11%	Age 25 or older	34%
Transferred in	17%	International students	2%
African Americans	8%	Asian Americans/Pacific Islanders	5%
Hispanic Americans	3%	Native Americans	1%

Faculty 226 (98% full-time).

Expenses (1999–2000) *Tuition, state resident:* full-time $2294; part-time $76 per semester hour. *Tuition, nonresident:* full-time $9282; part-time $309 per semester hour. *College room and board:* room only: $2310. Room and board charges vary according to housing facility. *Waivers:* senior citizens and employees or children of employees.

Library Pace Library. *Operations spending 1999–2000:* $2.9 million. *Collection:* 594,794 titles, 3,075 serial subscriptions, 160 audiovisual materials.

College life *Housing: Option:* coed. *Social organizations:* national fraternities, national sororities, local sororities; 5% of eligible men and 5% of eligible women are members. *Most popular organizations:* Marketing Association, Student Council for Exceptional Children, Intervarsity Christian Fellowship, Baptist Student Ministry, Golden Key Honor Society.

Campus security 24-hour emergency response devices and patrols, student patrols, late-night transport-escort service, controlled dormitory access.

After graduation 49 organizations recruited on campus 1997–98. *Career center:* 4 full-time personnel. Services include job fairs, resume preparation, interview workshops, resume referral, career counseling, careers library, job bank, job interviews.

Freshmen 1,988 applied, 1,655 admitted, 730 enrolled.

Average high school GPA	3.26	SAT verbal scores above 500	71%
SAT math scores above 500	64%	ACT above 18	95%
1998 freshmen returning in 1999	73%		

Application *Options:* electronic application, early admission, deferred entrance. *Preference* given to applicants with associate degrees from Florida public junior colleges. *Application fee:* $20. *Required:* high school transcript; minimum 2.0 GPA.

Standardized tests *Admission: Required:* SAT I or ACT.

Significant dates *Application deadlines:* 6/30 (freshmen), 6/30 (transfers). *Financial aid deadline:* continuous.

Freshman Application Contact
Ms. Susie Neeley, Director of Admissions, University of West Florida, 11000 University Parkway, Pensacola, FL 32514-5750. **Phone:** 850-474-2230. **Fax:** 850-474-2096. **E-mail:** admissions@uwf.edu

Visit CollegeQuest.com for information on majors offered and athletics.

■ *See page 2858 for a narrative description.*

WARNER SOUTHERN COLLEGE
Lake Wales, Florida

Apply at CollegeQuest.com

- **Independent**, 4-year, founded 1968, affiliated with Church of God
- **Degrees** associate and bachelor's
- **Rural** 320-acre campus with easy access to Tampa and Orlando
- **Coed**, 826 undergraduate students, 90% full-time, 60% women, 40% men
- **Minimally difficult** entrance level, 59% of applicants were admitted
- **14:1 student-to-undergraduate faculty ratio**
- **20.4% graduate** in 6 years or less
- **$8980 tuition** and fees
- **$6.2 million endowment**

Students *Undergraduates:* 745 full-time, 81 part-time. Students come from 23 states and territories, 5 other countries. *The most frequently chosen baccalaureate fields are:* business/marketing, education, philosophy.

From out-of-state	10%	Reside on campus	20%
Age 25 or older	55%	Transferred in	30%
International students	1%	African Americans	12%
Asian Americans/Pacific Islanders	1%	Hispanic Americans	5%
Native Americans	1%		

Faculty 78 (28% full-time), 21% with terminal degrees.

Florida

Warner Southern College *(continued)*

Expenses (1999–2000) *Comprehensive fee:* $13,338 includes full-time tuition ($8340), mandatory fees ($640), and room and board ($4358). *College room only:* $2090. Room and board charges vary according to board plan. *Part-time tuition:* $205 per semester hour. *Part-time fees:* $45 per term part-time. Part-time tuition and fees vary according to course load. *Payment plan:* installment. *Waivers:* senior citizens and employees or children of employees.

Library Learning Resource Center plus 1 other. *Operations spending 1999–2000:* $277,870. *Collection:* 56,419 titles, 224 serial subscriptions, 14,935 audiovisual materials.

College life *Housing:* on-campus residence required through junior year. *Options:* men-only, women-only. *Most popular organizations:* concert choir, Fellowship of Christian Athletes, Young Americans, Student Government Association.

Campus security 24-hour emergency response devices and patrols, late-night transport-escort service, controlled dormitory access.

After graduation *Career center:* 1 part-time personnel. Services include resume preparation, career counseling, careers library. **Graduate education:** 5% of class of 1999 went directly to graduate and professional school.

Freshmen 236 applied, 140 admitted, 78 enrolled.

Average high school GPA	3.32	SAT verbal scores above 500	29%
SAT math scores above 500	30%	ACT above 18	46%
From top 10% of their h.s. class	22%	From top quarter	43%
From top half	84%	1998 freshmen returning in 1999	68%

Application *Options:* eApply at www.CollegeQuest.com, deferred entrance. *Preference* given to Christians. *Application fee:* $20. *Required:* high school transcript; minimum 2.25 GPA; 1 letter of recommendation. *Required for some:* interview. *Recommended:* essay or personal statement.

Standardized tests *Admission: Required:* SAT I or ACT.

Significant dates *Application deadlines:* rolling (freshmen), rolling (transfers). *Financial aid deadline:* continuous.

Freshman Application Contact
Mr. Jason Roe, Director of Admissions, Warner Southern College, 5301 US Highway 27 South, Lake Wales, FL 33853-8725. **Phone:** 863-638-7212 Ext. 7213. **Toll-free phone:** 800-949-7248.

Visit CollegeQuest.com for information on majors offered and athletics. College video available at CollegeQuest.com.

WEBBER COLLEGE
Babson Park, Florida

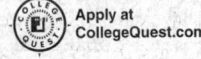 Apply at CollegeQuest.com

- **Independent**, comprehensive, founded 1927
- **Degrees** associate, bachelor's, and master's
- **Small-town** 110-acre campus with easy access to Orlando
- **Coed**, 421 undergraduate students, 83% full-time, 47% women, 53% men
- **Moderately difficult** entrance level, 48% of applicants were admitted
- **19:1 student-to-undergraduate faculty ratio**
- **43% graduate** in 6 years or less
- **$8160 tuition** and fees
- **$8224 average financial aid** package, $11,923 average indebtedness upon graduation, $6.7 million endowment

A 97% placement record: whether a student's goal is to work for one of the business world giants like the Disney Corporation, to return home to manage a family business, or to head out and start a company, Webber prepares students for that challenge.

Students *Undergraduates:* 350 full-time, 71 part-time. Students come from 14 states and territories, 38 other countries. *The most frequently chosen baccalaureate fields are:* business/marketing, parks and recreation. **Graduate:** 37 in graduate degree programs.

From out-of-state	7%	Age 25 or older	32%
Transferred in	11%	International students	33%
African Americans	5%	Hispanic Americans	4%

Faculty 31 (45% full-time), 45% with terminal degrees.

Expenses (1999–2000) *Comprehensive fee:* $11,730 includes full-time tuition ($8160) and room and board ($3570). Room and board charges vary according to board plan. *Part-time tuition:* $155 per credit. Part-time tuition and fees vary according to course load. *Payment plan:* installment. *Waivers:* children of alumni, adult students, senior citizens, and employees or children of employees.

Library Grace and Roger Babson Library plus 1 other. *Operations spending 1999–2000:* $92,138. *Collection:* 27,377 titles, 1,869 serial subscriptions, 551 audiovisual materials.

College life *Housing:* on-campus residence required in freshman year. *Options:* men-only, women-only. *Most popular organizations:* colors and culture club, PBL, student government, travel and hospitality club.

Campus security 24-hour emergency response devices and patrols, late-night transport-escort service, controlled dormitory access.

After graduation 35 organizations recruited on campus 1997–98. 97% of class of 1998 had job offers within 6 months. *Career center:* 1 full-time, 1 part-time personnel. Services include job fairs, resume preparation, resume referral, career counseling, careers library, job bank, job interviews.

Freshmen 249 applied, 119 admitted, 75 enrolled. 5 student government officers.

Average high school GPA	2.85	SAT verbal scores above 500	N/R
SAT math scores above 500	N/R	ACT above 18	N/R
1998 freshmen returning in 1999	60%		

Application *Option:* eApply at www.CollegeQuest.com. *Application fee:* $35. *Required:* essay or personal statement; high school transcript; minimum 2.0 GPA; letters of recommendation. *Recommended:* interview.

Standardized tests *Admission: Required:* SAT I or ACT.

Significant dates *Application deadlines:* rolling (freshmen), rolling (transfers). *Financial aid deadline priority date:* 5/1.

Freshman Application Contact
Mr. Mike Mattison, Director of Admissions, Webber College, PO Box 96, Babson Park, FL 33827-0096. **Phone:** 941-638-2910. **Fax:** 941-638-2823. **E-mail:** warriors@interserv.com

Visit CollegeQuest.com for information on majors offered and athletics. College video available at CollegeQuest.com.

- *See page 2924 for a narrative description.*

GEORGIA

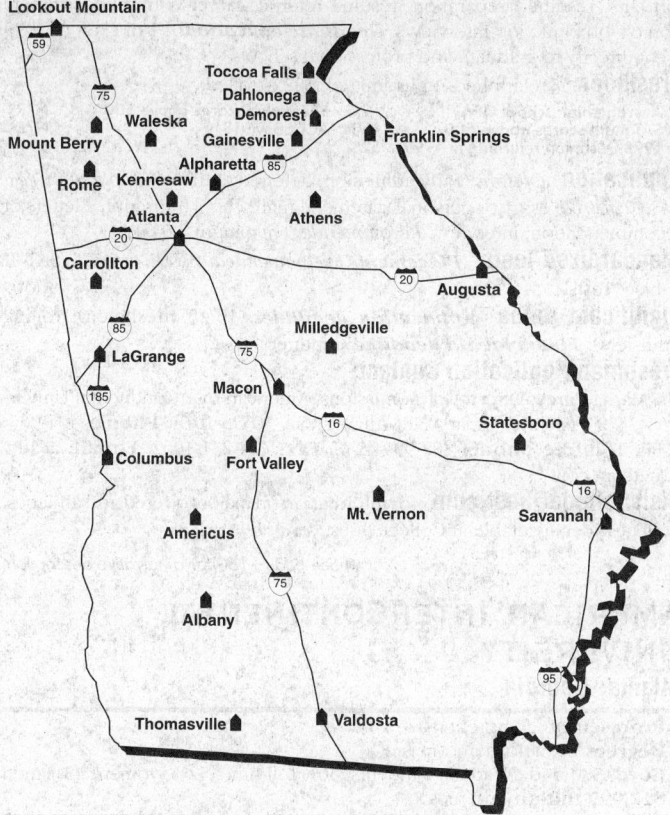

The Atlanta area includes the towns of Decatur, East Point, Lithonia, Marietta, and Morrow.

AGNES SCOTT COLLEGE
Decatur, Georgia

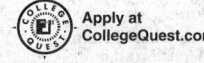 Apply at CollegeQuest.com

- **Independent**, comprehensive, founded 1889, affiliated with Presbyterian Church (U.S.A.)
- **Degrees** bachelor's, master's, and postbachelor's certificates
- **Urban** 100-acre campus with easy access to Atlanta
- **Women** only, 834 undergraduate students, 98% full-time
- **Very difficult** entrance level, 77% of applicants were admitted
- **10:1** student-to-undergraduate faculty ratio
- **50% graduate** in 6 years or less
- **$16,025 tuition** and fees
- **$16,335 average financial aid** package, $14,580 average indebtedness upon graduation, $429.1 million endowment

Students *Undergraduates:* 817 full-time, 17 part-time. Students come from 38 states and territories, 29 other countries. *The most frequently chosen baccalaureate fields are:* biological/life sciences, English, social sciences and history. *Graduate:* 8 in graduate degree programs.

From out-of-state	50%	Reside on campus	90%
Age 25 or older	11%	Transferred in	3%
International students	4%	African Americans	19%
Asian Americans/Pacific Islanders	5%	Hispanic Americans	3%
Native Americans	0.1%		

Faculty 107 (70% full-time).

Expenses (1999–2000) *Comprehensive fee:* $22,685 includes full-time tuition ($15,880), mandatory fees ($145), and room and board ($6660). Room and board charges vary according to board plan and housing facility. *Part-time tuition:* $660 per credit hour. *Part-time fees:* $145 per year part-time. Part-time tuition and fees vary according to course load. *Payment plans:* installment, deferred payment. *Waivers:* employees or children of employees.

Library McCain Library plus 1 other. *Operations spending 1999–2000:* $1.3 million. *Collection:* 204,505 titles, 807 serial subscriptions, 9,406 audiovisual materials.

College life *Housing:* on-campus residence required through senior year. *Option:* women-only. *Most popular organizations:* Student Government Association, Blackfriars, Residence Hall Association, Witkaze, Volunteer Board.

Campus security 24-hour emergency response devices and patrols, late-night transport-escort service, shuttle bus service, security systems in apartments, public safety facility, surveillance equipment.

After graduation 76 organizations recruited on campus 1997–98. 52% of class of 1998 had job offers within 6 months. *Career center:* 2 full-time, 1 part-time personnel. Services include job fairs, resume preparation, interview workshops, resume referral, career/interest testing, career counseling, careers library, job bank, job interviews. *Graduate education:* 21% of class of 1999 went directly to graduate and professional school: 5% graduate arts and sciences, 5% law, 2% engineering, 1% education, 1% medicine.

Freshmen 688 applied, 531 admitted, 241 enrolled. 9 National Merit Scholars.

Average high school GPA	3.67	SAT verbal scores above 500	97%
SAT math scores above 500	87%	ACT above 18	99%
From top 10% of their h.s. class	61%	From top quarter	80%
From top half	93%	1998 freshmen returning in 1999	82%

Application *Options:* eApply at www.CollegeQuest.com, Common Application, electronic application, early admission, early decision, deferred entrance. *Application fee:* $35. *Required:* essay or personal statement; high school transcript; 2 letters of recommendation. *Recommended:* minimum 3.0 GPA; interview.

Standardized tests *Admission: Required:* SAT I or ACT. *Required for some:* SAT II Subject Tests.

Significant dates *Application deadlines:* 3/1 (freshmen), 3/1 (transfers). *Early decision:* 11/15. *Notification:* 3/1 (freshmen), 12/15 (early decision). *Financial aid deadline priority date:* 3/1.

Freshman Application Contact
Ms. Stephanie Balmer, Associate Vice President for Enrollment and Director of Admission, Agnes Scott College, 141 East College Avenue, Decatur, GA 30030-3797. **Phone:** 404-471-6285. **Toll-free phone:** 800-868-8602. **Fax:** 404-471-6414. **E-mail:** admission@agnesscott.edu

Visit CollegeQuest.com for information on majors offered and athletics. College video available at CollegeQuest.com.

■ *See page 1136 for a narrative description.*

ALBANY STATE UNIVERSITY
Albany, Georgia

- **State-supported**, comprehensive, founded 1903
- **Degrees** bachelor's, master's, and post-master's certificates
- **Urban** 144-acre campus
- **Coed**, 2,921 undergraduate students, 83% full-time, 67% women, 33% men
- **Minimally difficult** entrance level
- **20:1** student-to-undergraduate faculty ratio
- **$2700 tuition** and fees (in-state); $8124 (out-of-state)
- **$1 million endowment**

An aggressive $140-million rebuilding project was completed at Albany State University, and the beautiful new campus is nestled along the bank of the Flint River. All-new state-of-the-art facilities include new dormitories, classrooms and laboratories, a dining hall, an athletic complex, and an academic administrative building.

Part of University System of Georgia.

Students *Undergraduates:* 2,416 full-time, 505 part-time. Students come from 10 other countries. *The most frequently chosen baccalaureate fields are:* health professions and related sciences, protective services/public administration, social sciences and history. *Graduate:* 421 in graduate degree programs.

Reside on campus	35%	International students	0.3%
African Americans	80%	Asian Americans/Pacific Islanders	0.03%
Hispanic Americans	0.3%	Native Americans	0.03%

Faculty 137 (100% full-time), 66% with terminal degrees.

Expenses (1999–2000) *Tuition, state resident:* full-time $2254; part-time $76 per credit. *Tuition, nonresident:* full-time $7678; part-time $302 per

Georgia

Albany State University *(continued)*

credit. *Required fees:* full-time $446; $446. Full-time tuition and fees vary according to course load. Part-time tuition and fees vary according to course load. *College room and board:* $3256; room only: $1480. Room and board charges vary according to housing facility. *Waivers:* senior citizens.

Library James Pendergrast Memorial Library. *Operations spending 1999–2000:* $1.1 million. *Collection:* 618 serial subscriptions, 2,531 audiovisual materials.

College life *Housing: Options:* coed, men-only, women-only. *Social organizations:* national fraternities, national sororities; 15% of eligible men and 15% of eligible women are members. *Most popular organizations:* ASC Gospel Choir, Board of Managers, pep band.

Campus security 24-hour emergency response devices and patrols.

After graduation *Career center:* 5 full-time personnel. Services include job fairs, resume preparation, interview workshops, resume referral, career/interest testing, career counseling, careers library, job interviews.

Freshmen 719 enrolled.

| SAT verbal scores above 500 | N/R | SAT math scores above 500 | N/R |
| ACT above 18 | N/R | | |

Application *Options:* early admission, deferred entrance. *Application fee:* $20. *Required:* high school transcript.

Standardized tests *Admission: Required:* SAT I or ACT. *Required for some:* SAT II Subject Tests, SAT II: Writing Test.

Significant dates *Application deadlines:* 7/1 (freshmen), 7/1 (transfers). *Financial aid deadline priority date:* 4/15.

Freshman Application Contact
Mrs. Patricia Price, Assistant Director of Admissions, Albany State University, 504 College Drive, Albany, GA 31705. **Phone:** 912-430-4646. **Toll-free phone:** 800-822-RAMS. **Fax:** 912-430-3936. **E-mail:** kcaldwell@rams.alsnet.peachnet.edu

Visit CollegeQuest.com for information on majors offered and athletics.

■ *See page 1138 for a narrative description.*

THE AMERICAN COLLEGE
Georgia—See American InterContinental University

AMERICAN INTERCONTINENTAL UNIVERSITY
Atlanta, Georgia

- **Proprietary**, 4-year, founded 1977
- **Degrees** associate and bachelor's
- **Urban** campus
- **Coed**, 908 undergraduate students, 54% full-time, 72% women, 28% men
- **Noncompetitive** entrance level, 47% of applicants were admitted
- **12:1 student-to-undergraduate faculty ratio**
- **39% graduate** in 6 years or less
- **$11,430 tuition** and fees

Students *Undergraduates:* 492 full-time, 416 part-time. Students come from 32 states and territories, 47 other countries.

From out-of-state	40%	Reside on campus	14%
Age 25 or older	30%	Transferred in	48%
International students	13%	African Americans	41%
Asian Americans/Pacific Islanders	8%	Hispanic Americans	4%

Faculty 103 (13% full-time), 17% with terminal degrees.

Expenses (1999–2000) *Comprehensive fee:* $15,780 includes full-time tuition ($11,430) and room and board ($4350). Full-time tuition and fees vary according to location. Room and board charges vary according to location. *Part-time tuition:* $1270 per course. Part-time tuition and fees vary according to location. *Waivers:* employees or children of employees.

Library *Operations spending 1999–2000:* $166,660. *Collection:* 19,579 titles, 269 serial subscriptions, 1,133 audiovisual materials.

College life *Most popular organizations:* Student Government Association, Positive Image (Black History), International Student Association, Ministries in Action, Fashion Association.

Campus security 24-hour patrols.

After graduation *Career center:* 5 full-time personnel. Services include job fairs, resume preparation, resume referral, career counseling, careers library, job bank, job interviews. *Graduate education:* 4% of class of 1999 went directly to graduate and professional school.

Freshmen 316 applied, 147 admitted, 122 enrolled.

Average high school GPA	2.5	SAT verbal scores above 500	N/R
SAT math scores above 500	N/R	ACT above 18	N/R
1998 freshmen returning in 1999	52%		

Application *Options:* early admission, deferred entrance. *Application fee:* $35. *Required:* essay or personal statement; high school transcript; 2 letters of recommendation; interview. *Recommended:* minimum 2.0 GPA.

Standardized tests *Placement: Recommended:* SAT I or ACT, SAT II Subject Tests.

Significant dates *Application deadlines:* 10/15 (freshmen), rolling (transfers). *Financial aid deadline:* continuous.

Freshman Application Contact
Ms. Marita Carey, Director of Admissions, American InterContinental University, 3330 Peachtree Road, NE, Atlanta, GA 30326-1016. **Phone:** 404-965-5700. **Toll-free phone:** 888-999-4248. **Fax:** 404-231-1062. **E-mail:** acatl@ix.netcom.com

Visit CollegeQuest.com for information on majors offered and athletics. College video available at CollegeQuest.com.

■ *See page 1160 for a narrative description.*

AMERICAN INTERCONTINENTAL UNIVERSITY
Atlanta, Georgia

- **Proprietary**, comprehensive
- **Degrees** bachelor's and master's
- **Coed**, 380 undergraduate students, 50% full-time, 52% women, 48% men
- **$12,090 tuition** and fees

Students *Undergraduates:* 189 full-time, 191 part-time. Students come from 4 states and territories, 2 other countries. *Graduate:* 625 in graduate degree programs.

From out-of-state	21%	Age 25 or older	92%
Transferred in	30%	International students	0.3%
African Americans	42%	Asian Americans/Pacific Islanders	4%
Hispanic Americans	2%		

Faculty 81 (70% full-time).

Expenses (1999–2000) *Tuition:* full-time 9840; part-time 1760 per term. *Required fees:* full-time 2250; 540 per term part-time. Full-time tuition and fees vary according to class time, degree level, and program. Part-time tuition and fees vary according to class time, degree level, and program. *Payment plan:* installment.

College life *Housing:* college housing not available.

Freshmen 37 enrolled. 1 class president, 3 student government officers.

Average high school GPA	2.7	SAT verbal scores above 500	85%
SAT math scores above 500	65%	ACT above 18	81%
From top 10% of their h.s. class	5%	From top quarter	15%
From top half	60%		

Application *Application fee:* 50. *Required:* essay or personal statement; high school transcript; minimum 2.0 GPA; interview; resume.

Standardized tests *Admission: Recommended:* SAT I or ACT. *Required for some:* ACT ASSET.

Freshman Application Contact
Ms. Marita Carey, Director of Admissions, American InterContinental University, 6600 Peachtree-Dunwoody Road, 500 Embassy Row, Atlanta, GA 30328. **Phone:** 404-965-5700 Ext. 5721. **Toll-free phone:** 800-255-6839. **Fax:** 404-965-6501.

Visit CollegeQuest.com for information on majors offered and athletics.

Georgia

ARMSTRONG ATLANTIC STATE UNIVERSITY
Savannah, Georgia

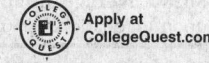 Apply at CollegeQuest.com

- **State-supported**, comprehensive, founded 1935
- **Degrees** associate, bachelor's, and master's
- **Suburban** 250-acre campus
- **Coed**, 4,878 undergraduate students, 59% full-time, 69% women, 31% men
- **Minimally difficult** entrance level, 78% of applicants were admitted
- **18:1 student-to-undergraduate faculty ratio**
- **$2388 tuition** and fees (in-state); $7812 (out-of-state)

Part of University System of Georgia.
Students *Undergraduates:* 2,878 full-time, 2,000 part-time. Students come from 51 states and territories, 50 other countries. *The most frequently chosen baccalaureate fields are:* education, health professions and related sciences, liberal arts/general studies. *Graduate:* 511 in graduate degree programs.

From out-of-state	8%	Reside on campus	3%
Age 25 or older	45%	International students	1%
African Americans	25%	Asian Americans/Pacific Islanders	2%
Hispanic Americans	3%	Native Americans	0.4%

Faculty 241 full-time.
Expenses (1999–2000) *Tuition, state resident:* full-time $2098; part-time $76 per credit hour. *Tuition, nonresident:* full-time $7522; part-time $226 per credit hour. *Required fees:* full-time $290; $145 per term part-time. Part-time tuition and fees vary according to course load. *College room and board:* $4460; room only: $2610. *Waivers:* senior citizens and employees or children of employees.
Library Lane Library. *Operations spending 1999–2000:* $1.4 million. *Collection:* 187,152 titles, 2,684 serial subscriptions, 3,946 audiovisual materials.
College life *Housing: Option:* coed. *Social organizations:* national fraternities, national sororities; 1% of eligible men and 1% of eligible women are members. *Most popular organizations:* Women of Worth, Hispanic Student Society, Ebony Coalition, American Chemical Society, Phi Alpha Theta.
Campus security 24-hour emergency response devices and patrols, student patrols, late-night transport-escort service.
After graduation 90% of class of 1998 had job offers within 6 months. *Career center:* 2 full-time personnel. Services include job fairs, resume preparation, interview workshops, resume referral, career/interest testing, career counseling, careers library, job bank, job interviews.
Freshmen 820 applied, 638 admitted, 750 enrolled.

Average high school GPA	2.87	SAT verbal scores above 500	42%
SAT math scores above 500	34%	ACT above 18	N/R
1998 freshmen returning in 1999	67%		

Application *Options:* eApply at www.CollegeQuest.com, early admission, deferred entrance. *Application fee:* $20. *Required:* high school transcript; proof of immunization.
Standardized tests *Admission: Required:* SAT I or ACT. *Required for some:* SAT II Subject Tests.
Significant dates *Application deadlines:* 7/1 (freshmen), 7/1 (transfers). *Financial aid deadline priority date:* 3/15.
Freshman Application Contact
Ms. Melanie Mirande, Assistant Director of Recruitment, Armstrong Atlantic State University, 11935 Abercorn Street, Savannah, GA 31419-1997. **Phone:** 912-925-5275. **Toll-free phone:** 800-633-2349. **Fax:** 912-921-5462.
Visit CollegeQuest.com for information on majors offered and athletics. Electronic viewbook available at CollegeQuest.com.

THE ART INSTITUTE OF ATLANTA
Atlanta, Georgia

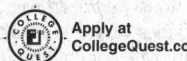 Apply at CollegeQuest.com

- **Proprietary**, primarily 2-year, founded 1949
- **Degrees** associate and bachelor's
- **Urban** 1-acre campus
- **Coed**, 1,909 undergraduate students, 88% full-time, 46% women, 54% men
- **Minimally difficult** entrance level
- **26:1 student-to-undergraduate faculty ratio**
- **$12,624 tuition** and fees

Part of The Art Institutes International.
Faculty 108 (45% full-time), 36% with terminal degrees.
Admissions Office Contact
The Art Institute of Atlanta, 6600 Peachtree Dunwoody Road, 100 Embassy Row, Atlanta, GA 30328. **Toll-free phone:** 800-275-4242. **E-mail:** aiaadm@aii.edu
Visit CollegeQuest.com for information on majors offered and athletics. College video available at CollegeQuest.com.

ATLANTA CHRISTIAN COLLEGE
East Point, Georgia

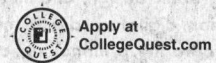 Apply at CollegeQuest.com

- **Independent Christian**, 4-year, founded 1937
- **Degrees** associate and bachelor's
- **Suburban** 52-acre campus with easy access to Atlanta
- **Coed**, 377 undergraduate students, 86% full-time, 49% women, 51% men
- **Minimally difficult** entrance level, 69% of applicants were admitted
- **16:1 student-to-undergraduate faculty ratio**
- **$8398 tuition** and fees

Students *Undergraduates:* Students come from 12 states and territories, 1 other country.

From out-of-state	13%	Reside on campus	47%
Age 25 or older	30%	African Americans	17%
Asian Americans/Pacific Islanders	1%	Hispanic Americans	1%

Faculty 45 (51% full-time), 44% with terminal degrees.
Expenses (1999–2000) *Comprehensive fee:* $12,038 includes full-time tuition ($7900), mandatory fees ($498), and room and board ($3640). Full-time tuition and fees vary according to course load and student level. Room and board charges vary according to board plan. *Part-time tuition:* $359 per semester hour. *Part-time fees:* $249 per term part-time. Part-time tuition and fees vary according to course load and student level. *Payment plan:* installment. *Waivers:* senior citizens and employees or children of employees.
Library Atlanta Christian College Library. *Collection:* 50,000 titles, 187 serial subscriptions.
College life *Housing:* on-campus residence required in freshman year. *Options:* men-only, women-only. *Social organizations:* local fraternities, local sororities; 15% of eligible men and 10% of eligible women are members.
Campus security Controlled dormitory access, 12-hour patrols by security personnel.
After graduation 6 organizations recruited on campus 1997–98. 80% of class of 1998 had job offers within 6 months. *Career center:* Services include career counseling.
Freshmen 341 applied, 235 admitted.

Average high school GPA	2.5	SAT verbal scores above 500	N/R
SAT math scores above 500	N/R	ACT above 18	N/R
From top 10% of their h.s. class	5%	From top quarter	15%
From top half	80%		

Application *Options:* eApply at www.CollegeQuest.com, early admission, deferred entrance. *Preference* given to Christians. *Required:* high school transcript; minimum 2.0 GPA; 2 letters of recommendation; medical history.
Standardized tests *Admission: Required:* SAT I or ACT.
Significant dates *Application deadlines:* rolling (freshmen), rolling (transfers). *Financial aid deadline priority date:* 5/15.
Freshman Application Contact
Mr. Keith Wagner, Director of Admissions, Atlanta Christian College, 2605 Ben Hill Road, East Point, GA 30344-1999. **Phone:** 404-761-8861. **Toll-free phone:** 800-776-1ACC. **E-mail:** admissions@acc.edu
Visit CollegeQuest.com for information on majors offered and athletics. Electronic viewbook available at CollegeQuest.com.

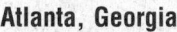

Peterson's Guide to Four-Year Colleges 2001 www.petersons.com

Georgia

ATLANTA COLLEGE OF ART
Atlanta, Georgia

- **Independent**, 4-year, founded 1928
- **Degree** bachelor's
- **Urban** 6-acre campus
- **Coed**, 404 undergraduate students, 93% full-time, 50% women, 50% men
- **Moderately difficult** entrance level, 77% of applicants were admitted
- **11:1 student-to-undergraduate faculty ratio**
- **63% graduate** in 6 years or less
- **$11,587 average financial aid** package, $3.6 million endowment

The Atlanta College of Art is a thriving artistic community that offers the Bachelor of Fine Arts degree in communication design (advertising design, graphic design, and illustration), drawing, electronic arts (computer animation, digital art, digital multimedia, and video), interior design, painting, photography, printmaking, and sculpture.

Students *Undergraduates:* 374 full-time, 30 part-time. Students come from 30 states and territories, 17 other countries. *The most frequently chosen baccalaureate field is:* visual/performing arts.

From out-of-state	50%	Reside on campus	30%
Age 25 or older	16%	Transferred in	16%
International students	8%	African Americans	19%
Asian Americans/Pacific Islanders	6%	Hispanic Americans	2%
Native Americans	1%		

Faculty 81 (30% full-time), 59% with terminal degrees.
Library Atlanta College of Art Library. *Operations spending 1999–2000:* $181,658. *Collection:* 30,000 titles, 200 serial subscriptions, 8,300 audiovisual materials.
College life *Housing:* Option: coed. *Most popular organizations:* Cipher of Peace, outing club, performance art club, student activities club, graphic design club.
Campus security 24-hour patrols, late-night transport-escort service, security cameras.
After graduation 15 organizations recruited on campus 1997–98. *Career center:* 1 part-time personnel. Services include resume preparation, resume referral, career counseling, careers library, job bank, job interviews. *Graduate education:* 35% of class of 1999 went directly to graduate and professional school: 35% graduate arts and sciences.
Freshmen 257 applied, 199 admitted, 65 enrolled.

Average high school GPA	2.73	SAT verbal scores above 500	43%
SAT math scores above 500	41%	ACT above 18	70%
1998 freshmen returning in 1999	66%		

Application *Options:* electronic application, deferred entrance. *Application fee:* $30. *Required:* essay or personal statement; high school transcript; minimum 2.0 GPA; portfolio. *Required for some:* letters of recommendation. *Recommended:* letters of recommendation; interview.
Standardized tests *Admission:* Required: SAT I or ACT.
Significant dates *Application deadlines:* rolling (freshmen), rolling (transfers). *Financial aid deadline priority date:* 3/15.
Freshman Application Contact
Ms. Carol Lee Conchar, Director of Enrollment Management, Atlanta College of Art, 1280 Peachtree Street, NE, Atlanta, GA 30309-3582. **Phone:** 404-733-5101. **Toll-free phone:** 800-832-2104. **Fax:** 404-733-5107. **E-mail:** acainfo@woodruff-arts.org

Visit CollegeQuest.com for information on majors offered and athletics.

- *See page 1202 for a narrative description.*

AUGUSTA STATE UNIVERSITY
Augusta, Georgia

- **State-supported**, comprehensive, founded 1925
- **Degrees** associate, bachelor's, and master's
- **Urban** 72-acre campus
- **Coed**, 4,570 undergraduate students, 63% full-time, 62% women, 38% men
- **Minimally difficult** entrance level, 64% of applicants were admitted
- **17:1 student-to-undergraduate faculty ratio**
- **19.9% graduate** in 6 years or less
- **$2082 tuition** and fees (in-state); $7506 (out-of-state)
- **$6280 average financial aid** package, $12,041 average indebtedness upon graduation, $356,655 endowment

Part of University System of Georgia.
Students *Undergraduates:* 2,896 full-time, 1,674 part-time. Students come from 33 states and territories, 54 other countries. *The most frequently chosen baccalaureate fields are:* business/marketing, education, social sciences and history. *Graduate:* 749 in graduate degree programs.

Age 25 or older	31%	Transferred in	9%
International students	2%	African Americans	25%
Asian Americans/Pacific Islanders	3%	Hispanic Americans	2%
Native Americans	1%		

Faculty 284 (69% full-time), 58% with terminal degrees.
Expenses (1999–2000) *Tuition, state resident:* full-time $1808; part-time $76 per credit. *Tuition, nonresident:* full-time $7232; part-time $302 per credit. *Required fees:* full-time $274; $137 per term part-time. *Waivers:* senior citizens and employees or children of employees.
Library Reese Library. *Operations spending 1999–2000:* $1.4 million. *Collection:* 274,978 titles, 9,884 serial subscriptions.
College life *Housing:* college housing not available. *Social organizations:* national fraternities, national sororities; 5% of eligible men and 5% of eligible women are members. *Most popular organizations:* SGAE, Baptist Student Union, Campus Outreach, College Republicans, Rowing Club.
Campus security 24-hour patrols, late-night transport-escort service.
After graduation 90 organizations recruited on campus 1997–98. *Career center:* 5 full-time personnel. Services include job fairs, resume preparation, resume referral, career counseling, careers library, job bank, job interviews.
Freshmen 1,587 applied, 1,020 admitted, 854 enrolled.

Average high school GPA	2.64	SAT verbal scores above 500	48%
SAT math scores above 500	42%	ACT above 18	N/R
1998 freshmen returning in 1999	49%		

Application *Options:* early admission, deferred entrance. *Application fee:* $20. *Required:* high school transcript; minimum 2.0 GPA.
Standardized tests *Admission:* Required: SAT I or ACT.
Significant dates *Application deadlines:* 7/21 (freshmen), rolling (transfers). *Financial aid deadline priority date:* 4/15.
Freshman Application Contact
Ms. Katherine Sweeney, Director of Admissions and Registrar, Augusta State University, 2500 Walton Way, Augusta, GA 30904-2200. **Phone:** 706-737-1632. **Fax:** 706-737-1774. **E-mail:** admissions@ac.edu
Visit CollegeQuest.com for information on majors offered and athletics.

- *See page 1210 for a narrative description.*

BEACON COLLEGE
Columbus, Georgia

- **Independent religious**, 4-year
- **Degrees** associate and bachelor's
- **Coed**, 57 undergraduate students, 100% full-time, 40% women, 60% men
- **96% of applicants were admitted**
- **5:1 student-to-undergraduate faculty ratio**
- **$2420 tuition** and fees

Students *Undergraduates:* 57 full-time. Students come from 6 states and territories. *The most frequently chosen baccalaureate field is:* philosophy.

From out-of-state	20%	Age 25 or older	53%
African Americans	32%	Hispanic Americans	4%

Faculty 16 (19% full-time), 63% with terminal degrees.
Expenses (1999–2000) *Tuition:* full-time 2400; part-time 110 per semester hour. *Required fees:* full-time 20; 10 per term part-time. Full-time tuition and fees vary according to course load. *Payment plan:* installment. *Waivers:* employees or children of employees.
College life *Housing:* college housing not available. *Most popular organizations:* Student Government Association, practical ministry.
After graduation *Graduate education:* 33% of class of 1999 went directly to graduate and professional school: 33% theology.

Georgia

Freshmen 27 applied, 26 admitted, 25 enrolled.

| SAT verbal scores above 500 | N/R | SAT math scores above 500 | N/R |
| ACT above 18 | N/R | 1998 freshmen returning in 1999 | 59% |

Application *Application fee:* 25. *Required:* high school transcript; minimum 2.0 GPA; 3 letters of recommendation; interview.

Standardized tests *Admission: Recommended:* SAT I or ACT.

Significant dates *Application deadlines:* 9/1 (freshmen), 9/1 (transfers).

Freshman Application Contact
Mrs. Eve Parks, Director of Admissions and Student Records, Beacon College, 1622 13th Avenue, Columbus, GA 31901. **Phone:** 706-323-5364 Ext. 251. **Fax:** 706-323-3236.

Visit CollegeQuest.com for information on majors offered and athletics.

BERRY COLLEGE
Mount Berry, Georgia

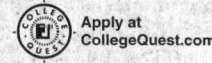

- **Independent interdenominational**, comprehensive, founded 1902
- **Degrees** bachelor's and master's
- **Small-town** 28,000-acre campus with easy access to Atlanta
- **Coed**, 1,890 undergraduate students, 98% full-time, 62% women, 38% men
- **Moderately difficult** entrance level, 68% of applicants were admitted
- **12:1 student-to-undergraduate faculty ratio**
- **$11,550 tuition** and fees
- **$11,100 average financial aid** package, $11,266 average indebtedness upon graduation, $197.2 million endowment

Students *Undergraduates:* 1,860 full-time, 30 part-time. Students come from 30 states and territories, 20 other countries. *Graduate:* 190 in graduate degree programs.

From out-of-state	16%	Reside on campus	69%
Age 25 or older	4%	Transferred in	5%
International students	1%	African Americans	1%
Asian Americans/Pacific Islanders	1%	Hispanic Americans	1%
Native Americans	0.4%		

Expenses (1999–2000) *Comprehensive fee:* $16,822 includes full-time tuition ($11,550) and room and board ($5272). *College room only:* $2892. Room and board charges vary according to board plan. *Part-time tuition:* $385 per semester hour. *Payment plan:* installment. *Waivers:* adult students, senior citizens, and employees or children of employees.

Library Memorial Library plus 1 other. *Operations spending 1999–2000:* $1.5 million. *Collection:* 255,284 titles, 1,418 serial subscriptions.

College life *Housing:* on-campus residence required through sophomore year. *Options:* men-only, women-only. *Most popular organizations:* Student Government Association, Baptist Student Union, Fellowship of Christian Athletes, Block and Bridle, Student Georgia Association of Educators.

Campus security 24-hour emergency response devices and patrols, late-night transport-escort service.

After graduation 103 organizations recruited on campus 1997–98. 99% of class of 1998 had job offers within 6 months. *Career center:* 3 full-time personnel. Services include job fairs, resume preparation, interview workshops, resume referral, career/interest testing, career counseling, careers library, job bank, job interviews. *Graduate education:* 31% of class of 1999 went directly to graduate and professional school.

Freshmen 1,953 applied, 1,320 admitted, 378 enrolled. 5 National Merit Scholars, 12 valedictorians.

Average high school GPA	3.64	SAT verbal scores above 500	92%
SAT math scores above 500	92%	ACT above 18	100%
1998 freshmen returning in 1999	80%		

Application *Options:* eApply at www.CollegeQuest.com, Common Application, electronic application, early admission, deferred entrance. *Application fee:* $25. *Required:* high school transcript.

Standardized tests *Admission: Required:* SAT I or ACT.

Significant dates *Application deadlines:* 7/28 (freshmen), 7/28 (transfers). *Financial aid deadline priority date:* 4/1.

Freshman Application Contact
Mr. George Gaddie, Dean of Admissions, Berry College, PO Box 490159, Mount Berry, GA 30149-0159. **Phone:** 706-236-2215. **Toll-free phone:** 800-237-7942. **Fax:** 706-236-2248. **E-mail:** admissions@berry.edu

Visit CollegeQuest.com for information on majors offered and athletics. College video available at CollegeQuest.com.

BEULAH HEIGHTS BIBLE COLLEGE
Atlanta, Georgia

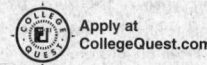

- **Independent Pentecostal**, 4-year, founded 1918
- **Degrees** associate and bachelor's
- **Urban** 10-acre campus
- **Coed**, 591 undergraduate students, 47% full-time, 53% women, 47% men
- **Noncompetitive** entrance level, 90% of applicants were admitted
- **17:1 student-to-undergraduate faculty ratio**
- **37% graduate** in 6 years or less
- **$3200 tuition** and fees
- **$19,750 average indebtedness** upon graduation, $19,881 endowment

Students *Undergraduates:* 279 full-time, 312 part-time. Students come from 19 states and territories, 12 other countries. *The most frequently chosen baccalaureate field is:* philosophy.

From out-of-state	30%	Reside on campus	10%
Age 25 or older	90%	Transferred in	9%
International students	18%	African Americans	75%
Asian Americans/Pacific Islanders	0.3%	Hispanic Americans	0.2%

Faculty 34 (29% full-time), 21% with terminal degrees.

Expenses (1999–2000) *Tuition:* full-time $3120; part-time $130 per semester hour. *Required fees:* full-time $80; $40 per term part-time. Full-time tuition and fees vary according to course load. *College room only:* $1500. *Payment plans:* installment, deferred payment. *Waivers:* employees or children of employees.

Library Barth Memorial Library. *Operations spending 1999–2000:* $85,472. *Collection:* 53,400 titles, 150 serial subscriptions.

College life *Housing: Options:* men-only, women-only.

Campus security 24-hour emergency response devices, student patrols.

After graduation 100% of class of 1998 had job offers within 6 months. *Career center:* Services include career counseling. *Graduate education:* 60% of class of 1999 went directly to graduate and professional school: 60% theology.

Freshmen 175 applied, 158 admitted, 117 enrolled.

Average high school GPA	3.1	SAT verbal scores above 500	N/R
SAT math scores above 500	N/R	ACT above 18	N/R
1998 freshmen returning in 1999	42%		

Application *Options:* eApply at www.CollegeQuest.com, Common Application, early admission. *Application fee:* $20. *Required:* high school transcript; minimum 2.0 GPA; 2 letters of recommendation. *Recommended:* interview.

Standardized tests *Admission: Recommended:* SAT I or ACT, SAT II: Writing Test.

Significant dates *Application deadlines:* rolling (freshmen), rolling (transfers). *Financial aid deadline priority date:* 6/30.

Freshman Application Contact
Ms. Patricia A. Massingil, Registrar, Beulah Heights Bible College, 892 Berne Street, SE, PO Box 18145, Atlanta, GA 30316. **Phone:** 404-627-2681 Ext. 102. **Toll-free phone:** 888-777-BHBC. **Fax:** 404-627-0702. **E-mail:** cjkjr@aol.com

Visit CollegeQuest.com for information on majors offered and athletics.

BRENAU UNIVERSITY
Gainesville, Georgia

- **Independent**, comprehensive, founded 1878
- **Degrees** bachelor's and master's (also offers coed evening and weekend programs with significant enrollment not reflected in profile)
- **Small-town** 57-acre campus with easy access to Atlanta
- **Women** only, 633 undergraduate students, 95% full-time
- **Moderately difficult** entrance level, 73% of applicants were admitted
- **10:1 student-to-undergraduate faculty ratio**
- **$11,730 tuition** and fees

Georgia

Brenau University (continued)

- **$11,907 average financial aid** package, $18,724 average indebtedness upon graduation, $39 million endowment

Students *Undergraduates:* 600 full-time, 33 part-time. Students come from 22 states and territories, 15 other countries. *The most frequently chosen baccalaureate fields are:* education, business/marketing, health professions and related sciences. *Graduate:* 31 in graduate degree programs.

From out-of-state	12%	Reside on campus	54%
Age 25 or older	19%	Transferred in	15%
International students	4%	African Americans	11%
Asian Americans/Pacific Islanders	2%	Hispanic Americans	2%
Native Americans	0.3%		

Faculty 96 (78% full-time), 75% with terminal degrees.

Expenses (1999–2000) *Comprehensive fee:* $18,606 includes full-time tuition ($11,730) and room and board ($6876). Full-time tuition and fees vary according to program. Room and board charges vary according to board plan. *Part-time tuition:* $391 per semester hour. Part-time tuition and fees vary according to program. *Payment plan:* installment. *Waivers:* employees or children of employees.

Library Trustee Library. *Operations spending 1999–2000:* $549,730. *Collection:* 95,894 titles, 617 serial subscriptions, 12,459 audiovisual materials.

College life *Housing:* on-campus residence required through senior year. *Option:* women-only. *Social organizations:* national sororities; 31% of eligible undergrads are members. *Most popular organizations:* student government/Campus Activities Board, Silhouettes (diversity awareness), Recreation Association, Fellowship Association, international club.

Campus security 24-hour emergency response devices and patrols, late-night transport-escort service.

After graduation *Career center:* 1 full-time, 1 part-time personnel. Services include job fairs, resume preparation, interview workshops, career/interest testing, career counseling, careers library, job bank, job interviews.

Freshmen 386 applied, 283 admitted, 131 enrolled.

Average high school GPA	3.4	SAT verbal scores above 500	59%
SAT math scores above 500	54%	ACT above 18	N/R
1998 freshmen returning in 1999	71%		

Application *Options:* eApply at www.CollegeQuest.com, electronic application, early admission, early decision, deferred entrance. *Application fee:* $30. *Required:* high school transcript; minimum 2.5 GPA; 1 letter of recommendation; minimum SAT I score of 900 or ACT score of 19. *Required for some:* interview. *Recommended:* essay or personal statement.

Standardized tests *Admission: Required:* SAT I or ACT.

Significant dates *Application deadlines:* rolling (freshmen), rolling (transfers). *Early decision:* 11/15. *Financial aid deadline priority date:* 5/1.

Freshman Application Contact

Dr. John D. Upchurch, Director of Admissions, Brenau University, One Centennial Circle, Gainesville, GA 30501-3697. **Phone:** 770-534-6100. **Toll-free phone:** 800-252-5119. **Fax:** 770-534-6114. **E-mail:** jupchurch@lib.brenau.edu

Visit CollegeQuest.com for information on majors offered and athletics.

- *See page 1302 for a narrative description.*

BREWTON-PARKER COLLEGE
Mt. Vernon, Georgia

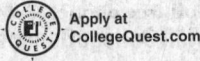
Apply at CollegeQuest.com

- **Independent Southern Baptist**, 4-year, founded 1904
- **Degrees** associate and bachelor's
- **Rural** 280-acre campus
- **Coed**
- **Minimally difficult** entrance level
- **$6340 tuition** and fees

Expenses (1999–2000) *Comprehensive fee:* $9440 includes full-time tuition ($6000), mandatory fees ($340), and room and board ($3100). Full-time tuition and fees vary according to program and reciprocity agreements. Room and board charges vary according to housing facility. *Part-time tuition:* $200 per semester hour. *Part-time fees:* $170 per term part-time. Part-time tuition and fees vary according to program.

Institutional Web site http://www.bpc.edu/

College life *Housing:* on-campus residence required through sophomore year. *Options:* men-only, women-only. *Social organizations:* local fraternities, local sororities; 38% of eligible men and 39% of eligible women are members. *Most popular organizations:* Council of Intramural Activities, Student Activities Council.

Campus security 24-hour emergency response devices and patrols, controlled dormitory access.

Application *Options:* eApply at www.CollegeQuest.com, Common Application, early admission. *Application fee:* $15. *Required:* high school transcript. *Recommended:* minimum 2.0 GPA; interview.

Standardized tests *Placement: Recommended:* SAT I or ACT.

Admissions Office Contact

Brewton-Parker College, Highway 280, Mt. Vernon, GA 30445-0197. **Toll-free phone:** 800-342-1087. **Fax:** 912-583-4498.

Visit CollegeQuest.com for information on athletics. College video available at CollegeQuest.com.

CLARK ATLANTA UNIVERSITY
Atlanta, Georgia

Apply at CollegeQuest.com

- **Independent United Methodist**, university, founded 1865
- **Degrees** bachelor's, master's, and doctoral
- **Urban** 113-acre campus
- **Coed**, 3,878 undergraduate students, 96% full-time, 72% women, 28% men
- **Moderately difficult** entrance level, 67% of applicants were admitted
- **$11,120 tuition** and fees
- **$32.2 million endowment**

Students *Undergraduates:* 3,721 full-time, 157 part-time. Students come from 42 states and territories. *Graduate:* 1,085 in graduate degree programs.

Reside on campus	37%	Age 25 or older	7%
Transferred in	3%	International students	0.1%
African Americans	99%	Asian Americans/Pacific Islanders	0.1%
Hispanic Americans	0.03%		

Faculty 493 (63% full-time).

Expenses (2000–2001) *Comprehensive fee:* $17,094 includes full-time tuition ($10,720), mandatory fees ($400), and room and board ($5974). *College room only:* $3534. Room and board charges vary according to board plan and housing facility. *Payment plan:* deferred payment. *Waivers:* employees or children of employees.

Library Robert W. Woodruff Library. *Collection:* 628,340 titles, 4,506 audiovisual materials.

College life *Housing: Option:* coed. *Social organizations:* national fraternities, national sororities. *Most popular organizations:* student government, honors program, Pre-alumni Council.

Campus security 24-hour emergency response devices and patrols, late-night transport-escort service.

After graduation *Career center:* 1 full-time, 1 part-time personnel. Services include job fairs, resume preparation, resume referral, career counseling, careers library, job bank, job interviews. *Graduate education:* 36% of class of 1999 went directly to graduate and professional school.

Freshmen 6,142 applied, 4,128 admitted, 715 enrolled.

Average high school GPA	3.0	SAT verbal scores above 500	N/R
SAT math scores above 500	N/R	ACT above 18	N/R
1998 freshmen returning in 1999	78%		

Application *Options:* eApply at www.CollegeQuest.com, Common Application, early admission, deferred entrance. *Application fee:* $35. *Required:* essay or personal statement; high school transcript; minimum 2.0 GPA; 2 letters of recommendation. *Recommended:* minimum 2.5 GPA.

Standardized tests *Admission: Required:* SAT I or ACT.

Significant dates *Application deadlines:* 3/1 (freshmen), 3/1 (transfers). *Financial aid deadline priority date:* 3/1.

Freshman Application Contact

Office of Admissions, Clark Atlanta University, 223 James P. Brawley Drive, SW, Atlanta, GA 30314. **Phone:** 404-880-8784 Ext. 6650. **Toll-free phone:** 800-688-3228. **Fax:** 404-880-6174.

Georgia

Visit CollegeQuest.com for information on majors offered and athletics.

■ *See page 1428 for a narrative description.*

CLAYTON COLLEGE & STATE UNIVERSITY
Morrow, Georgia

- **State-supported**, 4-year, founded 1969
- **Degrees** associate and bachelor's
- **Suburban** 163-acre campus with easy access to Atlanta
- **Coed**, 4,398 undergraduate students, 44% full-time, 64% women, 36% men
- **Minimally difficult** entrance level, 75% of applicants were admitted
- **14:1 student-to-undergraduate faculty ratio**
- **11% graduate** in 6 years or less
- **$2702 tuition** and fees (in-state); $8126 (out-of-state)
- **$689,265 endowment**

Part of University System of Georgia.
Students *Undergraduates:* 1,925 full-time, 2,473 part-time. Students come from 18 states and territories, 44 other countries. *The most frequently chosen baccalaureate fields are:* business/marketing, education, health professions and related sciences.

From out-of-state	2%	Age 25 or older	51%
Transferred in	14%	International students	2%
African Americans	35%	Asian Americans/Pacific Islanders	3%
Hispanic Americans	2%	Native Americans	1%

Faculty 378 (29% full-time).
Expenses (1999–2000) *Tuition, state resident:* full-time $1808; part-time $76 per hour. *Tuition, nonresident:* full-time $7232; part-time $302 per hour. *Required fees:* full-time $894; $447 per term part-time. Part-time tuition and fees vary according to program. *Waivers:* senior citizens and employees or children of employees.
Library Clayton College and State University Library plus 1 other. *Operations spending 1999–2000:* $846,563. *Collection:* 86,000 titles, 750 serial subscriptions.
College life *Housing:* college housing not available. *Most popular organizations:* Accounting Club, International Awareness Club, Black Cultural Awareness Association, Student Government Association, Music Club.
Campus security 24-hour emergency response devices and patrols, late-night transport-escort service, lighted pathways.
After graduation 213 organizations recruited on campus 1997–98. 95% of class of 1998 had job offers within 6 months. *Career center:* 6 full-time personnel. Services include job fairs, resume preparation, interview workshops, resume referral, career/interest testing, career counseling, careers library, job bank, job interviews.
Freshmen 2,828 applied, 2,126 admitted, 674 enrolled.

SAT verbal scores above 500	29%	SAT math scores above 500	29%
ACT above 18	52%	1998 freshmen returning in 1999	31%

Application *Options:* Common Application, early admission, deferred entrance. *Application fee:* $20. *Required:* high school transcript; proof of immunization.
Standardized tests *Admission: Required for some:* SAT I or ACT.
Significant dates *Application deadline:* 7/17 (freshmen). *Financial aid deadline priority date:* 4/1.
Freshman Application Contact
Ms. Carol S. Montgomery, Admissions, Clayton College & State University, 5900 North Lee Street, Morrow, GA 30260-0285. **Phone:** 770-961-3500. **Fax:** 770-961-3700. **E-mail:** csc-info@ce.clayton.peachnet.edu
Visit CollegeQuest.com for information on majors offered and athletics. College video and electronic viewbook available at CollegeQuest.com.

COLUMBUS STATE UNIVERSITY
Columbus, Georgia

- **State-supported**, comprehensive, founded 1958
- **Degrees** associate, bachelor's, and master's
- **Suburban** 132-acre campus with easy access to Atlanta
- **Coed**, 4,278 undergraduate students, 61% full-time, 62% women, 38% men
- **Minimally difficult** entrance level, 69% of applicants were admitted
- **$2444 tuition** and fees (in-state); $7868 (out-of-state)

Part of University System of Georgia.
Students *Undergraduates:* Students come from 35 states and territories, 18 other countries. *The most frequently chosen baccalaureate fields are:* business/marketing, education, protective services/public administration. *Graduate:* 633 in graduate degree programs.

From out-of-state	14%	Reside on campus	9%
Age 25 or older	30%	International students	2%
African Americans	26%	Asian Americans/Pacific Islanders	2%
Hispanic Americans	4%	Native Americans	0.5%

Faculty 335 (67% full-time), 53% with terminal degrees.
Expenses (1999–2000) *Tuition, state resident:* full-time $2126; part-time $76 per semester hour. *Tuition, nonresident:* full-time $7550; part-time $502 per semester hour. *Required fees:* full-time $318; $159 per term part-time. Part-time tuition and fees vary according to course load. *College room and board:* $3870. Room and board charges vary according to board plan, gender, and housing facility. *Waivers:* senior citizens and employees or children of employees.
Library Simon Schwob Memorial Library. *Collection:* 250,000 titles, 1,400 serial subscriptions, 2,500 audiovisual materials.
College life *Housing: Options:* coed, men-only. *Social organizations:* national fraternities, national sororities, local sororities; 10% of eligible men and 10% of eligible women are members. *Most popular organizations:* Student Government Association, Student Programming Council, Greek life, Baptist Student Union.
Campus security 24-hour emergency response devices and patrols, late-night transport-escort service.
After graduation 125 organizations recruited on campus 1997–98. *Career center:* 4 full-time, 6 part-time personnel. Services include job fairs, resume preparation, interview workshops, resume referral, career counseling, careers library, job bank, job interviews. *Graduate education:* 17% of class of 1999 went directly to graduate and professional school.
Freshmen 1,708 applied, 1,184 admitted.

Average high school GPA	2.76	SAT verbal scores above 500	46%
SAT math scores above 500	39%	ACT above 18	N/R
1998 freshmen returning in 1999	62%		

Application *Options:* Common Application, early admission, deferred entrance. *Application fee:* $20. *Required:* high school transcript; proof of immunization.
Standardized tests *Admission: Required:* SAT I or ACT. *Required for some:* SAT II Subject Tests.
Significant dates *Application deadlines:* 8/2 (freshmen), 8/2 (transfers). *Financial aid deadline priority date:* 6/1.
Freshman Application Contact
Ms. Susan Webb, Admission Counselor, Columbus State University, 4225 University Avenue, Columbus, GA 31907-5645. **Phone:** 706-568-2035. **Fax:** 706-568-2123.
Visit CollegeQuest.com for information on majors offered and athletics.

COVENANT COLLEGE
Lookout Mountain, Georgia

- **Independent**, comprehensive, founded 1955, affiliated with Presbyterian Church in America
- **Degrees** associate, bachelor's, and master's (master's degree in education only)
- **Suburban** 250-acre campus
- **Coed**, 1,031 undergraduate students, 98% full-time, 58% women, 42% men
- **Moderately difficult** entrance level, 78% of applicants were admitted
- **16:1 student-to-undergraduate faculty ratio**
- **$15,960 tuition** and fees
- **$12,633 average financial aid** package, $17,214 average indebtedness upon graduation, $10.7 million endowment

Students *Undergraduates:* 1,015 full-time, 16 part-time. Students come from 46 states and territories, 18 other countries. *The most frequently chosen*

Georgia

Covenant College (continued)

baccalaureate fields are: business/marketing, education, social sciences and history. *Graduate:* 67 in graduate degree programs.

From out-of-state	78%	Reside on campus	81%
Age 25 or older	3%	Transferred in	3%
International students	3%	African Americans	3%
Asian Americans/Pacific Islanders	1%	Hispanic Americans	2%
Native Americans	1%		

Faculty 67 (75% full-time), 70% with terminal degrees.

Expenses (2000–2001) *Comprehensive fee:* $20,410 includes full-time tuition ($15,600), mandatory fees ($360), and room and board ($4450). Full-time tuition and fees vary according to program. Room and board charges vary according to board plan and housing facility. *Part-time tuition:* $650 per unit. Part-time tuition and fees vary according to program. *Payment plan:* installment. *Waivers:* senior citizens and employees or children of employees.

Library Kresge Memorial Library. *Operations spending 1999–2000:* $244,745. *Collection:* 61,502 titles, 554 serial subscriptions, 11,500 audiovisual materials.

College life *Housing:* on-campus residence required through junior year. *Options:* men-only, women-only. *Most popular organizations:* psychology club, interpretive dance group, drama club, backpacking club.

Campus security Night security guards.

After graduation 100 organizations recruited on campus 1997–98. *Career center:* 2 full-time personnel. Services include job fairs, resume preparation, interview workshops, resume referral, career/interest testing, career counseling, careers library, job bank, job interviews.

Freshmen 654 applied, 507 admitted, 229 enrolled.

Average high school GPA	3.38	SAT verbal scores above 500	85%
SAT math scores above 500	74%	ACT above 18	97%
From top 10% of their h.s. class	26%	From top quarter	56%
From top half	80%	1998 freshmen returning in 1999	79%

Application *Options:* early admission, deferred entrance. *Application fee:* $25. *Required:* essay or personal statement; high school transcript; minimum 2.5 GPA; 2 letters of recommendation; interview.

Standardized tests *Admission: Required:* SAT I or ACT. *Recommended:* SAT I.

Significant dates *Application deadlines:* rolling (freshmen), rolling (transfers). *Financial aid deadline priority date:* 3/1.

Freshman Application Contact
Ms. Leda Goodman, Regional Director, Covenant College, 14049 Scenic Highway, Lookout Mountain, GA 30750. **Phone:** 706-820-1560 Ext. 1644. **Toll-free phone:** 888-451-2683. **E-mail:** admissions@covenant.edu

Visit CollegeQuest.com for information on majors offered and athletics. College video available at CollegeQuest.com.

DALTON STATE COLLEGE
Dalton, Georgia

- **State-supported**, 4-year, founded 1963
- **Degrees** associate and bachelor's
- **Small-town** 141-acre campus
- **Coed**, 3,051 undergraduate students
- **Noncompetitive** entrance level, 60% of applicants were admitted
- **28:1 student-to-undergraduate faculty ratio**
- **$1318 tuition** and fees (in-state); $3744 (out-of-state)
- **$4.6 million endowment**

Part of University System of Georgia.

Students *Undergraduates:* Students come from 5 states and territories, 23 other countries.

From out-of-state	2%	Age 25 or older	37%
African Americans	2%	Asian Americans/Pacific Islanders	1%
Hispanic Americans	2%	Native Americans	0.3%

Faculty 110 (90% full-time).

Expenses (1999–2000) *Tuition, state resident:* full-time $1276; part-time $43 per credit hour. *Tuition, nonresident:* full-time $3702; part-time $123 per credit hour. *Required fees:* full-time $42; $2 per credit hour. *Waivers:* senior citizens.

Library Derrell C. Roberts Library. *Operations spending 1999–2000:* $536,300. *Collection:* 710 serial subscriptions, 6,064 audiovisual materials.

College life *Housing:* college housing not available. *Most popular organizations:* Baptist Student Union, outdoor adventure club, College Bowl, Students in Free Enterprise, environmental club.

Campus security 24-hour emergency response devices and patrols.

After graduation *Career center:* 4 full-time, 2 part-time personnel. Services include job fairs, resume preparation, interview workshops, resume referral, career/interest testing, career counseling, careers library, job bank, job interviews.

Freshmen 1,607 applied, 966 admitted.

Average high school GPA	2.64	SAT verbal scores above 500	N/R
SAT math scores above 500	N/R	ACT above 18	N/R

Application *Options:* Common Application, early admission. *Application fee:* $0. *Required:* high school transcript.

Standardized tests *Admission: Required for some:* SAT I or ACT, SAT II Subject Tests.

Significant dates *Application deadlines:* rolling (freshmen), rolling (transfers). *Financial aid deadline priority date:* 7/1.

Freshman Application Contact
Dr. Angela Harris, Assistant Director of Admissions, Dalton State College, 213 North College Drive, Dalton, GA 30720-3797. **Phone:** 706-272-4476. **Toll-free phone:** 800-829-4436. **Fax:** 706-272-2530. **E-mail:** aharris@em.daltonstate.edu

Visit CollegeQuest.com for information on majors offered and athletics.

DEVRY INSTITUTE OF TECHNOLOGY
Alpharetta, Georgia

- **Proprietary**, 4-year, founded 1997
- **Degrees** associate and bachelor's
- **Suburban** 9-acre campus with easy access to Atlanta
- **Coed**, 1,312 undergraduate students, 71% full-time, 31% women, 69% men
- **Minimally difficult** entrance level, 60% of applicants were admitted
- **27:1 student-to-undergraduate faculty ratio**
- **$7778 tuition** and fees

Part of DeVry, Inc.

Students *Undergraduates:* 937 full-time, 375 part-time. Students come from 27 states and territories, 11 other countries. *The most frequently chosen baccalaureate fields are:* business/marketing, computer/information sciences.

From out-of-state	20%	Age 25 or older	56%
Transferred in	19%	International students	2%
African Americans	32%	Asian Americans/Pacific Islanders	5%
Hispanic Americans	3%	Native Americans	0.2%

Faculty 49 (49% full-time).

Expenses (1999–2000) *Tuition:* full-time $7778; part-time $290 per credit hour. Part-time tuition and fees vary according to class time and course load. *Payment plan:* installment. *Waivers:* employees or children of employees.

Library Learning Resource Center. *Collection:* 4,776 titles, 75 serial subscriptions.

College life *Housing:* college housing not available. *Most popular organizations:* Toastmasters International, Epsilon Delta Pi, International Student Organization, Alpha Sigma Lambda, Institute of electrical and Electronic Engineers.

Campus security 24-hour emergency response devices and patrols, late-night transport-escort service.

Freshmen 953 applied, 569 admitted, 367 enrolled.

SAT verbal scores above 500	N/R	SAT math scores above 500	N/R
ACT above 18	N/R	1998 freshmen returning in 1999	38%

Application *Options:* electronic application, deferred entrance. *Application fee:* $25. *Required:* high school transcript; interview.

Standardized tests *Admission: Required:* CPT. *Recommended:* SAT I or ACT.

Significant dates *Application deadlines:* rolling (freshmen), rolling (transfers). *Financial aid deadline:* continuous.

Freshman Application Contact

Mr. Gerry Purcell, Director of Admissions, DeVry Institute of Technology, 2555 Northwinds Parkway, Alpharetta, GA 30004. **Phone:** 770-664-9520.

Visit CollegeQuest.com for information on majors offered and athletics.

DEVRY INSTITUTE OF TECHNOLOGY
Decatur, Georgia

- **Proprietary**, 4-year, founded 1969
- **Degrees** associate and bachelor's
- **Suburban** 21-acre campus with easy access to Atlanta
- **Coed**, 2,801 undergraduate students, 81% full-time, 40% women, 60% men
- **Minimally difficult** entrance level, 51% of applicants were admitted
- **25:1 student-to-undergraduate faculty ratio**
- **$7778 tuition** and fees

Part of DeVry, Inc.

Students *Undergraduates:* 2,266 full-time, 535 part-time. Students come from 36 states and territories, 23 other countries. *The most frequently chosen baccalaureate fields are:* business/marketing, computer/information sciences, engineering/engineering technologies.

From out-of-state	23%	Age 25 or older	45%
Transferred in	5%	International students	2%
African Americans	76%	Asian Americans/Pacific Islanders	3%
Hispanic Americans	2%	Native Americans	0.2%

Faculty 113 (55% full-time).

Expenses (1999–2000) *Tuition:* full-time $7778; part-time $290 per credit hour. Part-time tuition and fees vary according to class time and course load. *Payment plan:* installment. *Waivers:* employees or children of employees.

Library Learning Resource Center. *Collection:* 16,011 titles, 75 serial subscriptions.

College life *Housing:* college housing not available. *Most popular organizations:* Toastmasters International, Epsilon Delta Pi, Tau Alpha Pi, Institute of Electrical and Electronic Engineers, International Student Organization.

Campus security 24-hour emergency response devices and patrols, late-night transport-escort service.

After graduation 98% of class of 1998 had job offers within 6 months. *Career center:* 7 full-time, 2 part-time personnel. Services include job fairs, resume preparation, career counseling, job bank, job interviews.

Freshmen 2,014 applied, 1,029 admitted, 887 enrolled.

SAT verbal scores above 500	N/R	SAT math scores above 500	N/R
ACT above 18	N/R	1998 freshmen returning in 1999	40%

Application *Options:* electronic application, deferred entrance. *Application fee:* $25. *Required:* high school transcript; interview.

Standardized tests *Admission: Required:* Computerized Placement Test. *Recommended:* SAT I or ACT.

Significant dates *Application deadlines:* rolling (freshmen), rolling (transfers). *Financial aid deadline:* continuous.

Freshman Application Contact

George Ollennu, Director of Admissions, DeVry Institute of Technology, 250 North Arcadia Avenue, Decatur, GA 30030. **Phone:** 404-292-2645 Ext. 430. **Toll-free phone:** 800-221-4771. **Fax:** 404-292-2321 Ext. 2226. **E-mail:** dwalters@admin.atl.devry.edu

Visit CollegeQuest.com for information on majors offered and athletics.

EMMANUEL COLLEGE
Franklin Springs, Georgia

- **Independent**, 4-year, founded 1919, affiliated with Pentecostal Holiness Church
- **Degrees** associate and bachelor's
- **Rural** 90-acre campus with easy access to Atlanta
- **Coed**, 837 undergraduate students, 91% full-time, 54% women, 46% men
- **Minimally difficult** entrance level, 57% of applicants were admitted
- **14:1 student-to-undergraduate faculty ratio**
- **14% graduate** in 6 years or less
- **$7210 tuition** and fees
- **$6456 average financial aid** package, $17,093 average indebtedness upon graduation, $4.1 million endowment

Students *Undergraduates:* 758 full-time, 79 part-time. Students come from 17 states and territories, 12 other countries. *The most frequently chosen baccalaureate fields are:* business/marketing, education, philosophy.

From out-of-state	26%	Reside on campus	51%
Age 25 or older	10%	Transferred in	11%
International students	2%	African Americans	11%
Asian Americans/Pacific Islanders	1%	Hispanic Americans	0.2%
Native Americans	0.1%		

Faculty 68 (74% full-time), 34% with terminal degrees.

Expenses (1999–2000) *Comprehensive fee:* $10,910 includes full-time tuition ($7130), mandatory fees ($80), and room and board ($3700). *College room only:* $1800. Room and board charges vary according to board plan. *Part-time tuition:* $240 per semester hour. *Part-time fees:* $15 per term part-time. *Payment plan:* installment. *Waivers:* adult students, senior citizens, and employees or children of employees.

Library Shaw–Leslie Library. *Operations spending 1999–2000:* $243,123. *Collection:* 44,111 titles, 250 serial subscriptions, 1,110 audiovisual materials.

College life *Housing:* on-campus residence required through sophomore year. *Options:* men-only, women-only.

Campus security 24-hour patrols, controlled dormitory access.

After graduation *Career center:* 3 full-time personnel. Services include career/interest testing, career counseling, careers library.

Freshmen 1,278 applied, 727 admitted, 227 enrolled.

SAT verbal scores above 500	N/R	SAT math scores above 500	N/R
ACT above 18	N/R	1998 freshmen returning in 1999	64%

Application *Options:* eApply at www.CollegeQuest.com, early admission, deferred entrance. *Application fee:* $25. *Required:* high school transcript.

Standardized tests *Admission: Required:* SAT I or ACT.

Significant dates *Application deadlines:* 8/1 (freshmen), 8/1 (transfers). *Notification:* continuous until 8/1 (freshmen). *Financial aid deadline:* 5/15.

Freshman Application Contact

Mr. Tommy Slaton, Director of Admissions, Emmanuel College, PO Box 129, Franklin Springs, GA 30639-0129. **Phone:** 706-245-7226 Ext. 4145. **Toll-free phone:** 800-860-8800. **E-mail:** admissions@emmanuel-college.edu

Visit CollegeQuest.com for information on majors offered and athletics.

EMORY UNIVERSITY
Atlanta, Georgia

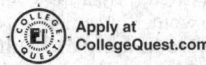

- **Independent Methodist**, university, founded 1836
- **Degrees** bachelor's, master's, doctoral, and first professional (enrollment figures include Emory University, Oxford College; application data for main campus only)
- **Suburban** 631-acre campus
- **Coed**, 6,215 undergraduate students, 97% full-time, 55% women, 45% men
- **Most difficult** entrance level, 43% of applicants were admitted
- **7:1 student-to-undergraduate faculty ratio**
- **84% graduate** in 6 years or less
- **$23,130 tuition** and fees
- **$19,873 average financial aid** package, $16,358 average indebtedness upon graduation, $4.2 billion endowment

For information on Emory University's Oxford campus, please refer to *Peterson's Guide to Colleges in the South*. Oxford provides an intimate living-learning environment for students who want to begin their Emory education in a personalized setting with leadership opportunities. After completing the Oxford program, students automatically continue to Emory in Atlanta for their junior and senior years. See Oxford's Web site at http://www.emory.edu/OXFORD for additional information.

Students *Undergraduates:* 6,055 full-time, 160 part-time. Students come from 49 states and territories, 44 other countries. *The most frequently chosen baccalaureate fields are:* business/marketing, biological/life sciences, psychology. *Graduate:* 1,628 in professional programs, 3,451 in other graduate

Georgia

Emory University *(continued)*
degree programs.

From out-of-state	80%	Reside on campus	63%
Transferred in	2%	International students	2%
African Americans	10%	Asian Americans/Pacific Islanders	15%
Hispanic Americans	3%	Native Americans	0.2%

Faculty 1,848 full-time.

Expenses (1999–2000) *Comprehensive fee:* $30,880 includes full-time tuition ($22,870), mandatory fees ($260), and room and board ($7750). Room and board charges vary according to board plan, housing facility, and student level. *Part-time tuition:* $953 per semester hour. *Part-time fees:* $100 per term part-time. *Payment plans:* tuition prepayment, installment. *Waivers:* employees or children of employees.

Library Robert W. Woodruff Library plus 7 others. *Operations spending 1999–2000:* $22.7 million. *Collection:* 2.3 million titles, 24,687 serial subscriptions.

College life *Housing:* on-campus residence required in freshman year. *Options:* coed, women-only. *Social organizations:* national fraternities, national sororities; 33% of eligible men and 33% of eligible women are members. *Most popular organizations:* Greek life, Volunteer Emory, music/theater, student government.

Campus security 24-hour emergency response devices and patrols, student patrols, late-night transport-escort service.

After graduation 200 organizations recruited on campus 1997–98. *Career center:* 9 full-time, 4 part-time personnel. Services include job fairs, resume preparation, interview workshops, resume referral, career/interest testing, career counseling, careers library, job bank, job interviews. *Graduate education:* 74% of class of 1999 went directly to graduate and professional school: 25% medicine, 22% law, 20% graduate arts and sciences, 6% business, 1% theology. *Major awards:* 1 Rhodes, 7 Fulbright Scholars.

Freshmen 9,850 applied, 4,196 admitted, 1,520 enrolled. 59 National Merit Scholars.

Average high school GPA	3.7	SAT verbal scores above 500	98%
SAT math scores above 500	100%	ACT above 18	100%
From top 10% of their h.s. class	81%	From top quarter	98%
From top half	100%	1998 freshmen returning in 1999	94%

Application *Options:* eApply at www.CollegeQuest.com, Common Application, electronic application, early admission, early decision, deferred entrance. *Application fee:* $40. *Required:* essay or personal statement; high school transcript; 1 letter of recommendation. *Recommended:* minimum 3.0 GPA.

Standardized tests *Admission: Required:* SAT I or ACT. *Recommended:* SAT II Subject Tests.

Significant dates *Application deadlines:* 1/15 (freshmen), 6/1 (transfers). *Early decision:* 11/1 (for plan 1), 1/1 (for plan 2). *Notification:* 4/1 (freshmen), 12/15 (early decision plan 1), 2/1 (early decision plan 2). *Financial aid deadline:* 4/1. *Priority date:* 2/15.

Freshman Application Contact
Mr. Daniel C. Walls, Dean of Admission, Emory University, Boisfeuillet Jones Center–Office of Admissions, Atlanta, GA 30322-1100. **Phone:** 404-727-6036. **Toll-free phone:** 800-727-6036. **E-mail:** admiss@unix.cc.emory.edu

Visit CollegeQuest.com for information on majors offered and athletics. College video available at CollegeQuest.com.

■ *See page 1638 for a narrative description.*

FORT VALLEY STATE UNIVERSITY
Fort Valley, Georgia

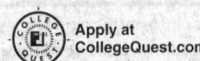
Apply at CollegeQuest.com

- **State-supported**, comprehensive, founded 1895
- **Degrees** associate, bachelor's, master's, doctoral, and first professional
- **Small-town** 1,307-acre campus
- **Coed**, 2,273 undergraduate students, 92% full-time, 55% women, 45% men
- **Moderately difficult** entrance level, 66% of applicants were admitted
- **19:1** student-to-undergraduate faculty ratio
- **$2294 tuition** and fees (in-state); $7718 (out-of-state)
- **$5 million endowment**

Part of University System of Georgia.

Students *Undergraduates:* 2,096 full-time, 177 part-time. Students come from 28 states and territories, 9 other countries. *The most frequently chosen baccalaureate fields are:* business/marketing, biological/life sciences, education. *Graduate:* 324 in graduate degree programs.

Reside on campus	59%

Faculty 148 (95% full-time).

Expenses (1999–2000) *Tuition, state resident:* full-time $1808; part-time $76 per credit. *Tuition, nonresident:* full-time $7232; part-time $302 per credit. *Required fees:* full-time $486; $243 per term part-time. Full-time tuition and fees vary according to course load. Part-time tuition and fees vary according to course load. *College room and board:* $3432; room only: $1700. Room and board charges vary according to board plan. *Waivers:* senior citizens and employees or children of employees.

Library Henry A. Hunt Memorial Library plus 2 others. *Operations spending 1999–2000:* $793,435. *Collection:* 186,365 titles, 1,213 serial subscriptions.

College life *Housing: Options:* coed, men-only, women-only. *Social organizations:* national fraternities, national sororities. *Most popular organizations:* drama group, Christian Student Organization, Habitat for Humanity, debate club.

Campus security 24-hour emergency response devices and patrols, student patrols, late-night transport-escort service.

After graduation 78 organizations recruited on campus 1997–98. *Career center:* 6 full-time, 3 part-time personnel. Services include job fairs, resume preparation, interview workshops, resume referral, career/interest testing, career counseling, careers library, job bank, job interviews. *Graduate education:* 36% of class of 1999 went directly to graduate and professional school.

Freshmen 2,418 applied, 1,602 admitted, 422 enrolled.

Average high school GPA	2.4	SAT verbal scores above 500	N/R
SAT math scores above 500	N/R	ACT above 18	N/R
1998 freshmen returning in 1999	74%		

Application *Options:* eApply at www.CollegeQuest.com, Common Application, electronic application, early admission, deferred entrance. *Application fee:* $20. *Required:* high school transcript.

Standardized tests *Admission: Required:* SAT I or ACT.

Significant dates *Application deadlines:* 8/1 (freshmen), 8/1 (transfers). *Notification:* continuous until 8/10 (freshmen). *Financial aid deadline priority date:* 2/15.

Freshman Application Contact
Mrs. Debra McGhee, Admissions Coordinator, Fort Valley State University, 1005 State University Drive, Fort Valley, GA 31030. **Phone:** 912-825-6307. **Toll-free phone:** 800-248-7343. **E-mail:** admissap@mail.fusu.edu

Visit CollegeQuest.com for information on majors offered and athletics. College video available at CollegeQuest.com.

■ *See page 1686 for a narrative description.*

GEORGIA BAPTIST COLLEGE OF NURSING
Atlanta, Georgia

- **Independent Baptist**, 4-year, founded 1988
- **Degree** bachelor's
- **Urban** 20-acre campus
- **Coed**, primarily women, 336 undergraduate students, 90% full-time, 98% women, 2% men
- **Moderately difficult** entrance level, 33% of applicants were admitted
- **10:1** student-to-undergraduate faculty ratio
- **70% graduate** in 6 years or less
- **$1508 tuition** and fees

Students *Undergraduates:* 303 full-time, 33 part-time. Students come from 5 states and territories. *The most frequently chosen baccalaureate field is:* health professions and related sciences.

From out-of-state	2%	Reside on campus	30%
Age 25 or older	43%	Transferred in	16%
African Americans	20%	Asian Americans/Pacific Islanders	3%
Hispanic Americans	1%		

Faculty 38 (82% full-time), 32% with terminal degrees.
Expenses (1999–2000) *Tuition:* full-time $1024; part-time $318 per semester hour. *Required fees:* full-time $484; $240 per term part-time. Full-time tuition and fees vary according to course level and course load. *College room only:* $1500. *Payment plans:* installment, deferred payment.
Library College of Nursing Library plus 1 other. *Operations spending 1999–2000:* $141,301. *Collection:* 12,836 titles, 182 serial subscriptions, 406 audiovisual materials.
College life *Housing: Option:* coed. *Most popular organizations:* Georgia Baptist Association of Nursing Students, Culturally Diverse Student Organization, Baptist Student Union, Student Government Association, Student Peer Representatives.
Campus security 24-hour emergency response devices and patrols, late-night transport-escort service, controlled dormitory access.
After graduation 100% of class of 1998 had job offers within 6 months. *Career center:* Services include career counseling.
Freshmen 115 applied, 38 admitted, 29 enrolled.

Average high school GPA	3.34	SAT verbal scores above 500	76%
SAT math scores above 500	48%	ACT above 18	N/R
1998 freshmen returning in 1999	69%		

Application *Option:* early admission. *Application fee:* $35. *Required:* essay or personal statement; high school transcript; minimum 2.5 GPA. *Required for some:* letters of recommendation. *Recommendation:* interview.
Standardized tests *Admission: Required:* SAT I or ACT.
Significant dates *Application deadlines:* 5/15 (freshmen), 5/15 (transfers). *Notification:* continuous until 6/1 (freshmen). *Financial aid deadline:* continuous.
Freshman Application Contact
Ms. Kim W. Hays, Associate Director of Admissions, Georgia Baptist College of Nursing, 274 Boulevard, NE, Atlanta, GA 30312. **Phone:** 404-265-4800. **Toll-free phone:** 800-551-8835. **E-mail:** gbcnadm@mindspring.com
Visit CollegeQuest.com for information on majors offered and athletics.

GEORGIA COLLEGE AND STATE UNIVERSITY
Milledgeville, Georgia

- **State-supported**, comprehensive, founded 1889
- **Degrees** bachelor's, master's, and post-master's certificates
- **Small-town** 666-acre campus
- **Coed**, 3,884 undergraduate students, 80% full-time, 62% women, 38% men
- **Moderately difficult** entrance level, 54% of applicants were admitted
- **20:1** student-to-undergraduate faculty ratio
- **30.8% graduate** in 6 years or less
- **$2214 tuition** and fees (in-state); $7638 (out-of-state)
- **$13,206 average indebtedness** upon graduation, $6.3 million endowment

Part of University System of Georgia.
Students *Undergraduates:* 3,094 full-time, 790 part-time. Students come from 26 states and territories, 45 other countries. *The most frequently chosen baccalaureate fields are:* business/marketing, education, health professions and related sciences. *Graduate:* 1,079 in graduate degree programs.

From out-of-state	4%	Reside on campus	26%
Age 25 or older	23%	Transferred in	9%
International students	2%	African Americans	15%
Asian Americans/Pacific Islanders	1%	Hispanic Americans	1%
Native Americans	0.1%		

Faculty 337 (60% full-time).
Expenses (1999–2000) *Tuition, state resident:* full-time $1808; part-time $76 per semester hour. *Tuition, nonresident:* full-time $7232; part-time $302 per semester hour. *Required fees:* full-time $406; $203 per term part-time. Part-time tuition and fees vary according to course load. *College room and board:* $4170; room only: $2210. Room and board charges vary according to board plan and housing facility. *Waivers:* senior citizens.

Library Ina Dillard Russell Library. *Operations spending 1999–2000:* $1.2 million. *Collection:* 183,601 titles, 4,169 audiovisual materials.
College life *Housing: Options:* coed, men-only, women-only. *Social organizations:* national fraternities, national sororities; 9% of eligible men and 8% of eligible women are members. *Most popular organization:* Baptist Student Union.
Campus security 24-hour emergency response devices and patrols, student patrols, late-night transport-escort service, controlled dormitory access.
After graduation 55 organizations recruited on campus 1997–98. *Career center:* 2 full-time personnel. Services include job fairs, resume preparation, resume referral, career counseling, careers library, job bank, job interviews.
Freshmen 2,491 applied, 1,350 admitted, 760 enrolled.

Average high school GPA	3.06	SAT verbal scores above 500	58%
SAT math scores above 500	58%	ACT above 18	85%
1998 freshmen returning in 1999	69%		

Application *Options:* electronic application, early admission. *Application fee:* $25. *Required:* high school transcript; minimum 2.0 GPA; proof of immunization. *Recommended:* interview.
Standardized tests *Admission: Required:* SAT I or ACT.
Significant dates *Application deadlines:* rolling (freshmen), rolling (transfers). *Financial aid deadline priority date:* 3/1.
Freshman Application Contact
Ms. Maryllis Wolfgang, Director of Admissions, Georgia College and State University, CPO Box 023, Milledgeville, GA 31061. **Phone:** 912-445-6285. **Toll-free phone:** 800-342-0471. **Fax:** 912-445-6795. **E-mail:** gcsu@mail.gcsu.edu
Visit CollegeQuest.com for information on majors offered and athletics.

GEORGIA INSTITUTE OF TECHNOLOGY
Atlanta, Georgia

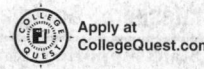

- **State-supported**, university, founded 1885
- **Degrees** bachelor's, master's, and doctoral
- **Urban** 360-acre campus
- **Coed**, 10,171 undergraduate students, 93% full-time, 29% women, 71% men
- **Very difficult** entrance level, 69% of applicants were admitted
- **14:1** student-to-undergraduate faculty ratio
- **69% graduate** in 6 years or less
- **$3108 tuition** and fees (in-state); $10,350 (out-of-state)
- **$5890 average financial aid** package, $358.4 million endowment

Part of University System of Georgia.
Students *Undergraduates:* 9,463 full-time, 708 part-time. Students come from 52 states and territories, 82 other countries. *The most frequently chosen baccalaureate fields are:* business/marketing, computer/information sciences, engineering/engineering technologies. *Graduate:* 3,818 in graduate degree programs.

From out-of-state	33%	Reside on campus	54%
Age 25 or older	5%	Transferred in	4%
International students	4%	African Americans	9%
Asian Americans/Pacific Islanders	13%	Hispanic Americans	3%
Native Americans	0.2%		

Faculty 717 (99% full-time), 93% with terminal degrees.
Expenses (1999–2000) *Tuition, state resident:* full-time $2414; part-time $101 per semester hour. *Tuition, nonresident:* full-time $9656; part-time $403 per semester hour. *Required fees:* full-time $694; $36 per term part-time. Part-time tuition and fees vary according to course load. *College room and board:* $5118; room only: $2800. Room and board charges vary according to board plan and housing facility.
Library Library and Information Center. *Operations spending 1999–2000:* $9.6 million. *Collection:* 83,150 audiovisual materials.
College life *Housing:* on-campus residence required in freshman year. *Option:* coed. *Social organizations:* national fraternities, national sororities; 25% of eligible men and 25% of eligible women are members. *Most popular organizations:* Christian Campus Fellowship, IEEE, Mechanical Engineering Graduate Student Association, Gamma Beta Phi Society.
Campus security 24-hour emergency response devices and patrols, student patrols, late-night transport-escort service, controlled dormitory access.

Georgia

Georgia Institute of Technology (continued)

After graduation 800 organizations recruited on campus 1997–98. 70% of class of 1998 had job offers within 6 months. *Career center:* 8 full-time personnel. Services include job fairs, resume preparation, interview workshops, resume referral, career/interest testing, career counseling, careers library, job bank, job interviews. *Graduate education:* 20% of class of 1999 went directly to graduate and professional school.

Freshmen 7,579 applied, 5,210 admitted, 2,320 enrolled. 91 National Merit Scholars.

Average high school GPA	3.7	SAT verbal scores above 500	96%
SAT math scores above 500	99%	ACT above 18	N/R
From top 10% of their h.s. class	60%	From top quarter	87%
From top half	99%	1998 freshmen returning in 1999	88%

Application *Options:* eApply at www.CollegeQuest.com, electronic application, early admission. *Preference* given to state residents. *Application fee:* $50. *Required:* essay or personal statement; high school transcript.

Standardized tests *Admission: Required:* SAT I or ACT. *Recommended:* SAT I. *Required for some:* SAT II Subject Tests.

Significant dates *Application deadlines:* 1/15 (freshmen), 5/1 (transfers). *Notification:* 3/15 (freshmen). *Financial aid deadline priority date:* 3/1.

Freshman Application Contact
Ms. Deborah Smith, Director of Admissions, Georgia Institute of Technology, 225 North Avenue, NW, Atlanta, GA 30332-0320. **Phone:** 404-894-4154. **Fax:** 404-853-9163. **E-mail:** admissions@success.gatech.edu

Visit CollegeQuest.com for information on majors offered and athletics.

GEORGIA SOUTHERN UNIVERSITY
Statesboro, Georgia

- **State-supported**, comprehensive, founded 1906
- **Degrees** bachelor's, master's, doctoral, and post-master's certificates
- **Small-town** 601-acre campus
- **Coed**, 12,539 undergraduate students, 92% full-time, 53% women, 47% men
- **Moderately difficult** entrance level, 88% of applicants were admitted
- **19:1** student-to-undergraduate faculty ratio
- **35% graduate** in 6 years or less
- **$2432 tuition** and fees (in-state); $7856 (out-of-state)
- **$5306 average financial aid** package, $13,021 average indebtedness upon graduation, $12.6 million endowment

Part of University System of Georgia.

Students *Undergraduates:* 11,529 full-time, 1,010 part-time. Students come from 49 states and territories, 71 other countries. *The most frequently chosen baccalaureate fields are:* business/marketing, education, parks and recreation. *Graduate:* 1,567 in graduate degree programs.

From out-of-state	7%	Reside on campus	22%
Age 25 or older	7%	Transferred in	3%
International students	1%	African Americans	28%
Asian Americans/Pacific Islanders	1%	Hispanic Americans	1%
Native Americans	0.2%		

Faculty 745 (87% full-time), 66% with terminal degrees.

Expenses (1999–2000) *One-time required fee:* $50. *Tuition, state resident:* full-time $1808; part-time $76 per semester hour. *Tuition, nonresident:* full-time $7232; part-time $302 per semester hour. *Required fees:* full-time $624; $312 per term part-time. Part-time tuition and fees vary according to course load. *College room and board:* $4284; room only: $2040. Room and board charges vary according to board plan and housing facility. *Waivers:* senior citizens.

Library Henderson Library. *Operations spending 1999–2000:* $3.5 million. *Collection:* 3,511 serial subscriptions, 29,296 audiovisual materials.

College life *Housing: Options:* coed, men-only, women-only. *Social organizations:* national fraternities, national sororities; 10% of eligible men and 11% of eligible women are members. *Most popular organizations:* Baptist Student Union, Gamma Beta Phi, Black Student Alliance, Golden Key Honor Society, Life Ministries.

Campus security 24-hour emergency response devices and patrols, student patrols, late-night transport-escort service, residence hall security, locked residence hall entrances.

After graduation 95 organizations recruited on campus 1997–98. *Career center:* 8 full-time, 10 part-time personnel. Services include job fairs, resume preparation, interview workshops, resume referral, career/interest testing, career counseling, careers library, job bank, job interviews, online resume.

Freshmen 8,721 applied, 7,640 admitted, 3,291 enrolled.

Average high school GPA	2.93	SAT verbal scores above 500	48%
SAT math scores above 500	44%	ACT above 18	68%
1998 freshmen returning in 1999	70%		

Application *Options:* Common Application, electronic application, early admission, deferred entrance. *Application fee:* $20. *Required:* high school transcript; minimum 2.0 GPA; proof of immunization.

Standardized tests *Admission: Required:* SAT I or ACT.

Significant dates *Application deadlines:* 7/1 (freshmen), rolling (transfers). *Financial aid deadline priority date:* 3/17.

Freshman Application Contact
Dr. Irene Prue, Assistant Director of Admissions, Georgia Southern University, GSU PO Box 8024, Statesboro, GA 30460. **Phone:** 912-681-5977. **Fax:** 912-681-5635. **E-mail:** admissions@gasou.edu

Visit CollegeQuest.com for information on majors offered and athletics. College video and electronic viewbook available at CollegeQuest.com.

GEORGIA SOUTHWESTERN STATE UNIVERSITY
Americus, Georgia

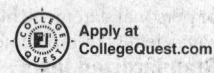

- **State-supported**, comprehensive, founded 1906
- **Degrees** associate, bachelor's, master's, and post-master's certificates
- **Small-town** 255-acre campus
- **Coed**, 2,067 undergraduate students, 70% full-time, 65% women, 35% men
- **Moderately difficult** entrance level, 63% of applicants were admitted
- **12:1** student-to-undergraduate faculty ratio
- **$2312 tuition** and fees (in-state); $7736 (out-of-state)
- **$20,000 average indebtedness** upon graduation, $680,000 endowment

Part of University System of Georgia.

Students *Undergraduates:* 1,442 full-time, 625 part-time. Students come from 23 states and territories, 34 other countries. *The most frequently chosen baccalaureate fields are:* business/marketing, education, social sciences and history. *Graduate:* 502 in graduate degree programs.

From out-of-state	3%	Reside on campus	38%
Age 25 or older	24%	Transferred in	11%
International students	3%	African Americans	29%
Asian Americans/Pacific Islanders	1%	Hispanic Americans	1%
Native Americans	0.3%		

Faculty 171 (71% full-time), 57% with terminal degrees.

Expenses (1999–2000) *Tuition, state resident:* full-time $1808; part-time $76 per semester hour. *Tuition, nonresident:* full-time $7232; part-time $302 per semester hour. *Required fees:* full-time $504; $252 per term part-time. Part-time tuition and fees vary according to course load. *College room and board:* $3484; room only: $1700. Room and board charges vary according to board plan and housing facility. *Waivers:* senior citizens.

Library James Earl Carter Library. *Operations spending 1999–2000:* $715,000. *Collection:* 1,849 audiovisual materials.

College life *Housing:* on-campus residence required through sophomore year. *Options:* coed, men-only, women-only. *Social organizations:* national fraternities, national sororities; 8% of eligible men and 10% of eligible women are members. *Most popular organizations:* Greek organizations, religious clubs and organizations, SABU (Black Student Organization), Biology Club, Gamma Beta Phi.

Campus security 24-hour emergency response devices and patrols, late-night transport-escort service, controlled dormitory access.

After graduation 63 organizations recruited on campus 1997–98. *Career center:* 2 full-time, 1 part-time personnel. Services include job fairs, resume preparation, interview workshops, resume referral, career/interest testing, career counseling, careers library, job bank, job interviews.

Freshmen 1,047 applied, 663 admitted, 284 enrolled. 23 class presidents, 11 valedictorians, 119 student government officers.

Georgia

Average high school GPA	3.16	SAT verbal scores above 500	54%
SAT math scores above 500	53%	ACT above 18	100%
1998 freshmen returning in 1999	71%		

Application *Options:* eApply at www.CollegeQuest.com, Common Application, electronic application, early admission, early decision. *Application fee:* $20. *Required:* high school transcript; minimum 2.0 GPA; proof of immunization. *Recommended:* interview.

Standardized tests *Admission: Required:* SAT I or ACT.

Significant dates *Application deadlines:* rolling (freshmen), rolling (transfers). *Early decision:* 12/15. *Notification:* continuous until 8/1 (freshmen), 1/15 (early decision). *Financial aid deadline priority date:* 4/1.

Freshman Application Contact
Mr. Gary Fallis, Director of Admissions, Georgia Southwestern State University, 800 Wheatley Street, Americus, GA 31709-4693. **Phone:** 912-928-1273. **Toll-free phone:** 800-338-0082. **Fax:** 912-931-2983. **E-mail:** gswapps@canes.gsw.edu

Visit CollegeQuest.com for information on majors offered and athletics. College video and electronic viewbook available at CollegeQuest.com.

■ *See page 1718 for a narrative description.*

GEORGIA STATE UNIVERSITY
Atlanta, Georgia

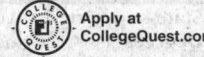
Apply at CollegeQuest.com

- **State-supported**, university, founded 1913
- **Degrees** bachelor's, master's, doctoral, first professional, and post-master's certificates
- **Urban** 24-acre campus
- **Coed**, 15,432 undergraduate students, 61% full-time, 61% women, 39% men
- **Moderately difficult** entrance level, 54% of applicants were admitted
- **15:1** student-to-undergraduate faculty ratio
- **27% graduate** in 6 years or less
- **$2886 tuition** and fees (in-state); $10,128 (out-of-state)
- **$43.7 million endowment**

Part of University System of Georgia.

Students *Undergraduates:* 9,424 full-time, 6,008 part-time. Students come from 49 states and territories, 96 other countries. *The most frequently chosen baccalaureate fields are:* business/marketing, computer/information sciences, social sciences and history. *Graduate:* 605 in professional programs, 6,496 in other graduate degree programs.

From out-of-state	1%	Reside on campus	12%
Age 25 or older	58%	Transferred in	12%
International students	4%	African Americans	33%
Asian Americans/Pacific Islanders	8%	Hispanic Americans	0.1%
Native Americans	0.3%		

Expenses (1999–2000) *Tuition, state resident:* full-time $2414; part-time $101 per credit. *Tuition, nonresident:* full-time $9656; part-time $403 per credit. *Required fees:* full-time $472; $236 per term part-time. Full-time tuition and fees vary according to course load and program. Part-time tuition and fees vary according to course load and program. *College room and board:* room only: $4190. *Waivers:* senior citizens.

Library Pullen Library plus 1 other. *Operations spending 1999–2000:* $8.8 million. *Collection:* 12,053 serial subscriptions, 14,615 audiovisual materials.

College life *Housing: Option:* coed. *Social organizations:* national fraternities, national sororities, local fraternities, local sororities; 4% of eligible men and 3% of eligible women are members. *Most popular organizations:* Spotlight Programs Board, Inter-Fraternity Council, Sports Club Council, Student Government Association, Panhellenic Council.

Campus security 24-hour emergency response devices and patrols, late-night transport-escort service, controlled dormitory access.

After graduation 368 organizations recruited on campus 1997–98. 45% of class of 1998 had job offers within 6 months. *Career center:* 10 full-time, 10 part-time personnel. Services include job fairs, resume preparation, resume referral, career counseling, careers library, job bank, job interviews.

Freshmen 7,042 applied, 3,836 admitted, 1,875 enrolled.

Average high school GPA	3.22	SAT verbal scores above 500	62%
SAT math scores above 500	60%	ACT above 18	89%

Application *Options:* eApply at www.CollegeQuest.com, deferred entrance. *Application fee:* $25. *Required:* high school transcript. *Required for some:* interview. *Recommended:* essay or personal statement; minimum 2.9 GPA.

Standardized tests *Admission: Required:* SAT I or ACT. *Required for some:* SAT II Subject Tests.

Significant dates *Application deadlines:* 5/1 (freshmen), 6/1 (transfers). *Financial aid deadline priority date:* 4/1.

Freshman Application Contact
Mr. Rob Sheinkopf, Dean of Admissions and Acting Dean for Enrollment Services, Georgia State University, PO Box 4009, Atlanta, GA 30302-4009. **Phone:** 404-651-2365. **Toll-free phone:** 404-651-2365.

Visit CollegeQuest.com for information on majors offered and athletics.

■ *See page 1720 for a narrative description.*

HERZING COLLEGE
Atlanta, Georgia

Apply at CollegeQuest.com

- **Proprietary**, primarily 2-year, founded 1949
- **Degrees** associate and bachelor's
- **Urban** campus
- **Coed**, 297 undergraduate students, 88% full-time, 52% women, 48% men
- **Moderately difficult** entrance level
- **8:1** student-to-undergraduate faculty ratio
- **$6720 tuition** and fees

Part of Herzing Institutes, Inc.

Faculty 38 (24% full-time), 100% with terminal degrees.

Admissions Office Contact
Herzing College, 3355 Lenox Road, Suite 100, Atlanta, GA 30326. **Toll-free phone:** 800-573-4533. **Fax:** 404-816-5576. **E-mail:** leec@atl.herzing.edu

Visit CollegeQuest.com for information on majors offered and athletics.

KENNESAW STATE UNIVERSITY
Kennesaw, Georgia

- **State-supported**, comprehensive, founded 1963
- **Degrees** bachelor's and master's
- **Suburban** 185-acre campus with easy access to Atlanta
- **Coed**
- **Moderately difficult** entrance level
- **$2306 tuition** and fees (in-state); $7730 (out-of-state)

Part of University System of Georgia.

Expenses (1999–2000) *Tuition, state resident:* full-time $1808; part-time $76 per credit hour. *Tuition, nonresident:* full-time $7232; part-time $302 per credit hour. *Required fees:* full-time $498; $249 per term part-time.

Institutional Web site http://www.kennesaw.edu/

College life *Housing:* college housing not available. *Social organizations:* national fraternities, national sororities, local sororities.

Campus security 24-hour emergency response devices and patrols, student patrols, late-night transport-escort service.

Application *Options:* early admission, deferred entrance. *Application fee:* $20. *Required:* high school transcript; minimum 2.0 GPA; proof of immunization.

Standardized tests *Admission: Required:* SAT I or ACT.

Admissions Office Contact
Kennesaw State University, 1000 Chastain Road, Kennesaw, GA 30144-5591. **Fax:** 770-423-6541. **E-mail:** ksuadmit@ksumail.kennesaw.edu

Visit CollegeQuest.com for information on athletics. College video available at CollegeQuest.com.

LAGRANGE COLLEGE
LaGrange, Georgia

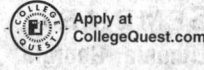
Apply at CollegeQuest.com

- **Independent United Methodist**, comprehensive, founded 1831
- **Degrees** associate, bachelor's, and master's
- **Small-town** 120-acre campus with easy access to Atlanta

Georgia

LaGrange College (continued)
- **Coed**, 951 undergraduate students, 86% full-time, 64% women, 36% men
- **Moderately difficult** entrance level, 86% of applicants were admitted
- **12:1 student-to-undergraduate faculty ratio**
- **43.4% graduate** in 6 years or less
- **$11,001 tuition** and fees
- **$16,831 average financial aid** package, $16,000 average indebtedness upon graduation, $47.9 million endowment

Students *Undergraduates:* 819 full-time, 132 part-time. Students come from 17 states and territories, 13 other countries. *The most frequently chosen baccalaureate fields are:* business/marketing, education, protective services/public administration. *Graduate:* 45 in graduate degree programs.

From out-of-state	10%	Reside on campus	41%
Age 25 or older	20%	Transferred in	7%
International students	4%	African Americans	15%
Asian Americans/Pacific Islanders	1%	Hispanic Americans	1%
Native Americans	0.1%		

Faculty 87 (72% full-time), 66% with terminal degrees.
Expenses (1999–2000) *Comprehensive fee:* $15,657 includes full-time tuition ($10,761), mandatory fees ($240), and room and board ($4656). Full-time tuition and fees vary according to location. *Part-time tuition:* $211 per quarter hour. *Part-time fees:* $80 per term part-time. Part-time tuition and fees vary according to location. *Payment plan:* installment. *Waivers:* employees or children of employees.
Library William and Evelyn Banks Library. *Operations spending 1999–2000:* $349,589. *Collection:* 110,000 titles, 475 serial subscriptions.
College life *Housing:* on-campus residence required through junior year. *Options:* coed, men-only, women-only. *Social organizations:* national fraternities, national sororities; 30% of eligible men and 30% of eligible women are members. *Most popular organizations:* Student Government Association, Greek system, drama/theater groups, Habitat for Humanity, BSU/Wesley Fellowship.
Campus security 24-hour patrols, controlled dormitory access.
After graduation *Career center:* 2 full-time personnel. Services include resume preparation, resume referral, career counseling, careers library, job bank, job interviews.
Freshmen 473 applied, 409 admitted, 186 enrolled.

Average high school GPA	3.01	SAT verbal scores above 500	49%
SAT math scores above 500	53%	ACT above 18	76%
1998 freshmen returning in 1999	69%		

Application *Options:* eApply at www.CollegeQuest.com, Common Application, electronic application, early admission, deferred entrance. *Application fee:* $20. *Required:* essay or personal statement; high school transcript; minimum 2.0 GPA. *Required for some:* 1 letter of recommendation; interview.
Standardized tests *Admission:* Required: SAT I or ACT.
Significant dates *Application deadlines:* 8/15 (freshmen), 8/15 (transfers). *Financial aid deadline priority date:* 5/1.
Freshman Application Contact
Mr. Andy Geeter, Director of Admission, LaGrange College, 601 Broad Street, LaGrange, GA 30240-2999. **Phone:** 706-812-7260. **Toll-free phone:** 800-593-2885. **E-mail:** lgcadmis@lgc.edu
Visit CollegeQuest.com for information on majors offered and athletics.

- *See page 1888 for a narrative description.*

LIFE UNIVERSITY
Marietta, Georgia

Admissions Office Contact
Life University, 1269 Barclay Circle, Marietta, GA 30060-2903.

LUTHER RICE BIBLE COLLEGE AND SEMINARY
Lithonia, Georgia

- **Independent Baptist**, comprehensive, founded 1962
- **Degrees** bachelor's, master's, and doctoral
- **Urban** 5-acre campus with easy access to Atlanta
- **Coed**
- **Noncompetitive** entrance level
- **$2592 tuition** and fees

Expenses (1999–2000) *Tuition:* full-time $2592; part-time $108 per semester hour.
Institutional Web site http://www.lrs.edu/
College life *Housing:* college housing not available.
Campus security 24-hour emergency response devices, late-night transport-escort service.
Application *Options:* Common Application, early admission. *Application fee:* $50. *Required:* high school transcript; letters of recommendation.
Standardized tests *Admission:* Required: Bible examination.
Admissions Office Contact
Luther Rice Bible College and Seminary, 3038 Evans Mill Road, Lithonia, GA 30038-2454. **Toll-free phone:** 800-442-1577. **E-mail:** lrs.@lrs.edu
Visit CollegeQuest.com for information on athletics. College video and electronic viewbook available at CollegeQuest.com.

MACON STATE COLLEGE
Macon, Georgia

- **State-supported**, 4-year, founded 1968
- **Degrees** associate and bachelor's
- **Urban** 167-acre campus
- **Coed**, 3,429 undergraduate students, 36% full-time, 66% women, 34% men
- **Minimally difficult** entrance level
- **17:1 student-to-undergraduate faculty ratio**
- **$1322 tuition** and fees (in-state); $3173 (out-of-state)
- **$3 million endowment**

Part of University System of Georgia.
Students *Undergraduates:* 1,220 full-time, 2,209 part-time. Students come from 11 other countries.

Age 25 or older	49%

Faculty 215 (55% full-time), 49% with terminal degrees.
Expenses (1999–2000) *Tuition, state resident:* full-time $1234; part-time $52 per credit hour. *Tuition, nonresident:* full-time $3085; part-time $207 per credit hour. *Required fees:* full-time $88; $44 per term part-time. Full-time tuition and fees vary according to course level, degree level, and student level. Part-time tuition and fees vary according to course level, course load, degree level, and student level. *Waivers:* senior citizens.
Library Macon State College Library. *Operations spending 1999–2000:* $455,873. *Collection:* 80,000 titles, 513 serial subscriptions.
College life *Housing:* college housing not available. *Most popular organizations:* student government, Macon College Association of Nursing Students.
Campus security 24-hour patrols, late-night transport-escort service.
After graduation 15 organizations recruited on campus 1997–98. *Career center:* 4 full-time personnel. Services include job fairs, resume preparation, interview workshops, career/interest testing, career counseling, careers library, job bank.
Freshmen 607 enrolled.

Average high school GPA	2.78	SAT verbal scores above 500	N/R
SAT math scores above 500	N/R	ACT above 18	N/R

Application *Options:* Common Application, electronic application, early admission. *Application fee:* $10. *Required:* high school transcript.
Standardized tests *Admission:* Required: SAT I or ACT.
Significant dates *Application deadlines:* rolling (freshmen), rolling (transfers). *Financial aid deadline priority date:* 4/1.
Freshman Application Contact
Mr. Terrell Mitchell, Assistant Director of Admissions, Macon State College, 100 College Station Drive, Macon, GA 31206-5144. **Phone:** 912-471-2800. **Toll-free phone:** 800-272-7619. **Fax:** 912-471-2846. **E-mail:** mcinfo@cennet.mc.peachnet.edu
Visit CollegeQuest.com for information on majors offered and athletics. Electronic viewbook available at CollegeQuest.com.

Georgia

MEDICAL COLLEGE OF GEORGIA
Augusta, Georgia

- **State-supported**, upper-level, founded 1828
- **Degrees** bachelor's, master's, doctoral, and first professional
- **Urban** 100-acre campus
- **Coed**, 625 undergraduate students, 95% full-time, 84% women, 16% men
- **Moderately difficult** entrance level, 38% of applicants were admitted
- **$2700 tuition** and fees (in-state); $9942 (out-of-state)

Part of University System of Georgia.

Students *Undergraduates:* 591 full-time, 34 part-time. Students come from 10 states and territories. *The most frequently chosen baccalaureate field is:* health professions and related sciences. *Graduate:* 937 in professional programs, 412 in other graduate degree programs.

From out-of-state	8%	Reside on campus	13%
Age 25 or older	36%	Transferred in	51%
International students	0.2%	African Americans	12%
Asian Americans/Pacific Islanders	4%	Hispanic Americans	1%
Native Americans	0.3%		

Faculty 733 (87% full-time).

Expenses (1999–2000) *Tuition, state resident:* full-time $2414; part-time $101 per semester hour. *Tuition, nonresident:* full-time $9656; part-time $403 per semester hour. *Required fees:* full-time $286; $143 per term part-time. Part-time tuition and fees vary according to course load. *College room and board:* room only: $1302. Room and board charges vary according to housing facility. *Waivers:* senior citizens.

Library Robert B. Greenblatt MD Library. *Collection:* 176,646 titles, 1,401 serial subscriptions, 11,846 audiovisual materials.

College life *Housing: Option:* coed.

Campus security 24-hour emergency response devices and patrols, late-night transport-escort service, controlled dormitory access.

Application *Preference* given to state residents. *Application fee:* $25.

Standardized tests *Admission: Required for some:* SAT I or ACT.

Significant dates *Application deadline:* rolling (transfers). *Financial aid deadline priority date:* 3/31.

Freshman Application Contact
Ms. Elizabeth Griffin, Director of Academic Admissions, Medical College of Georgia, 1120 Fifteenth Street, Augusta, GA 30912. **Phone:** 706-721-2725. **Fax:** 706-721-3461. **E-mail:** underadm@mail.mcg.edu

Visit CollegeQuest.com for information on majors offered and athletics. College video available at CollegeQuest.com.

MERCER UNIVERSITY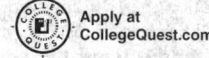
Macon, Georgia

- **Independent Baptist**, comprehensive, founded 1833
- **Degrees** bachelor's, master's, doctoral, first professional, post-master's, and postbachelor's certificates
- **Suburban** 130-acre campus with easy access to Atlanta
- **Coed**, 4,011 undergraduate students, 82% full-time, 65% women, 35% men
- **Moderately difficult** entrance level, 78% of applicants were admitted
- **15:1 student-to-undergraduate faculty ratio**
- **$16,290 tuition** and fees
- **$14,026 average financial aid** package, $12,833 average indebtedness upon graduation, $197.4 million endowment

Students *Undergraduates:* 3,280 full-time, 731 part-time. Students come from 35 states and territories, 62 other countries. *The most frequently chosen baccalaureate fields are:* business/marketing, engineering/engineering technologies, social sciences and history. *Graduate:* 1,238 in professional programs, 1,415 in other graduate degree programs.

From out-of-state	17%	Reside on campus	51%
Age 25 or older	7%	Transferred in	4%
International students	5%	African Americans	23%
Asian Americans/Pacific Islanders	3%	Hispanic Americans	1%
Native Americans	0.5%		

Faculty 504 (56% full-time), 63% with terminal degrees.

Expenses (1999–2000) *Comprehensive fee:* $21,670 includes full-time tuition ($16,290) and room and board ($5380). *College room only:* $2600.

Full-time tuition and fees vary according to course load, location, and program. Room and board charges vary according to board plan and housing facility. *Part-time tuition:* $544 per credit hour. Part-time tuition and fees vary according to course load, location, and program. *Payment plan:* installment. *Waivers:* employees or children of employees.

Library Mercer University Main Library plus 2 others. *Operations spending 1999–2000:* $5.8 million. *Collection:* 418,211 titles, 5,857 serial subscriptions, 57,166 audiovisual materials.

College life *Housing:* on-campus residence required through sophomore year. *Options:* coed, men-only, women-only, disabled students. *Social organizations:* national fraternities, national sororities; 30% of eligible men and 27% of eligible women are members. *Most popular organizations:* Student Union Activities Board, Baptist Student Union, Student Government Association, Reformed University Worship, International Students Organization.

Campus security 24-hour emergency response devices and patrols, student patrols, late-night transport-escort service, controlled dormitory access, patrols by police officers, shuttle bus service.

After graduation 258 organizations recruited on campus 1997–98. 70% of class of 1998 had job offers within 6 months. *Career center:* 5 full-time personnel. Services include job fairs, resume preparation, interview workshops, resume referral, career/interest testing, career counseling, careers library, job bank, job interviews.

Freshmen 3,227 applied, 2,524 admitted, 754 enrolled.

Average high school GPA	3.5	SAT verbal scores above 500	75%
SAT math scores above 500	77%	ACT above 18	93%
From top 10% of their h.s. class	37%	From top quarter	69%
From top half	90%	1998 freshmen returning in 1999	72%

Application *Options:* eApply at www.CollegeQuest.com, Common Application, electronic application, early admission, deferred entrance. *Application fee:* $25. *Required:* high school transcript; counselor's evaluation. *Required for some:* 2 letters of recommendation; interview. *Recommended:* interview.

Standardized tests *Admission: Required:* SAT I or ACT.

Significant dates *Application deadlines:* rolling (freshmen), rolling (transfers). *Financial aid deadline priority date:* 4/1.

Freshman Application Contact
Director of Admission, Mercer University, 1400 Coleman Avenue, Macon, GA 31207-0003. **Phone:** 912-301-2650. **Toll-free phone:** 800-342-0841 (in-state); 800-637-2378 (out-of-state). **Fax:** 912-301-2828. **E-mail:** admissions@mercer.edu

Visit CollegeQuest.com for information on majors offered and athletics. College video available at CollegeQuest.com.

■ *See page 2040 for a narrative description.*

MOREHOUSE COLLEGE
Atlanta, Georgia

- **Independent**, 4-year, founded 1867
- **Degree** bachelor's
- **Urban** 61-acre campus
- **Men** only, 3,012 undergraduate students, 95% full-time
- **Moderately difficult** entrance level, 66% of applicants were admitted
- **15:1 student-to-undergraduate faculty ratio**
- **51% graduate** in 6 years or less
- **$11,738 tuition** and fees
- **$111.5 million endowment**

Students *Undergraduates:* 2,876 full-time, 136 part-time. Students come from 42 states and territories. *The most frequently chosen baccalaureate fields are:* business/marketing, psychology, social sciences and history.

From out-of-state	69%	Reside on campus	50%
Age 25 or older	5%	Transferred in	2%
African Americans	99%	Asian Americans/Pacific Islanders	0.2%
Hispanic Americans	0.2%		

Faculty 234 (79% full-time), 59% with terminal degrees.

Expenses (1999–2000) *Comprehensive fee:* $18,708 includes full-time tuition ($9668), mandatory fees ($2070), and room and board ($6970). *College room only:* $3986. *Part-time tuition:* $422 per semester hour. *Part-time fees:* $975 per term part-time. Part-time tuition and fees vary according to course load. *Payment plan:* installment. *Waivers:* employees or children of employees.

Georgia

Morehouse College (continued)

Library Woodruff Library. *Collection:* 560,000 titles, 1,000 serial subscriptions.

College life *Housing: Option:* men-only. *Social organizations:* national fraternities; 7% of eligible undergrads are members. *Most popular organizations:* The Morehouse Glee Club, political science club, STRIPES.

Campus security 24-hour emergency response devices and patrols, late-night transport-escort service.

After graduation 55 organizations recruited on campus 1997–98. 30% of class of 1998 had job offers within 6 months. *Career center:* 3 full-time personnel. Services include job fairs, resume preparation, resume referral, career counseling, careers library, job bank, job interviews.

Freshmen 2,785 applied, 1,837 admitted, 748 enrolled.

Average high school GPA	3.01	SAT verbal scores above 500	58%
SAT math scores above 500	58%	ACT above 18	81%
From top 10% of their h.s. class	42%	From top quarter	67%
From top half	99%	1998 freshmen returning in 1999	85%

Application *Options:* eApply at www.CollegeQuest.com, Common Application, early admission, early decision, deferred entrance. *Application fee:* $45. *Required:* essay or personal statement; high school transcript; minimum 2.8 GPA; letters of recommendation. *Recommended:* minimum 3.0 GPA; interview.

Standardized tests *Admission: Required:* SAT I or ACT.

Significant dates *Application deadlines:* 2/15 (freshmen), 2/15 (transfers). *Early decision:* 10/15. *Notification:* continuous until 4/1 (freshmen), 12/15 (early decision). *Financial aid deadline priority date:* 4/1.

Freshman Application Contact
Mr. André Pattillo, Director of Admissions, Morehouse College, 830 Westview Drive, SW, Atlanta, GA 30314. **Phone:** 404-215-2632. **Toll-free phone:** 800-851-1254. **Fax:** 404-659-6536. **E-mail:** apattillo@morehouse.edu

Visit CollegeQuest.com for information on majors offered and athletics. College video available at CollegeQuest.com.

MORRIS BROWN COLLEGE
Atlanta, Georgia

- **Independent**, 4-year, founded 1881, affiliated with African Methodist Episcopal Church
- **Degree** bachelor's
- **Urban** 21-acre campus
- **Coed**
- **Minimally difficult** entrance level
- **$9253 tuition** and fees

Expenses (1999–2000) *Comprehensive fee:* $14,265 includes full-time tuition ($7968), mandatory fees ($1285), and room and board ($5012). *Part-time tuition:* $332 per semester hour. *Part-time fees:* $642 per term part-time.

Institutional Web site http://www.morrisbrown.edu/

College life *Housing: Options:* men-only, women-only. *Social organizations:* national fraternities, national sororities.

Campus security 24-hour emergency response devices and patrols.

Application *Options:* Common Application, electronic application, early admission, deferred entrance. *Application fee:* $30. *Required:* high school transcript.

Standardized tests *Placement: Required:* SAT I or ACT

Admissions Office Contact
Morris Brown College, 643 Martin Luther King Jr Drive, NW, Atlanta, GA 30314-4140. **Fax:** 404-220-0267.

Visit CollegeQuest.com for information on athletics.

NORTH GEORGIA COLLEGE & STATE UNIVERSITY
Dahlonega, Georgia

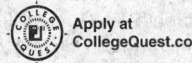

- **State-supported**, comprehensive, founded 1873
- **Degrees** associate, bachelor's, and master's
- **Small-town** 140-acre campus with easy access to Atlanta
- **Coed**, 3,115 undergraduate students, 84% full-time, 64% women, 36% men
- **Moderately difficult** entrance level, 47% of applicants were admitted
- **17:1 student-to-undergraduate faculty ratio**
- **$2210 tuition** and fees (in-state); $7634 (out-of-state)
- **$1.2 million endowment**

Part of University System of Georgia.

Students *Undergraduates:* 2,604 full-time, 511 part-time. Students come from 28 states and territories. *The most frequently chosen baccalaureate fields are:* business/marketing, biological/life sciences, education.

From out-of-state	3%	Reside on campus	34%
Age 25 or older	15%	Transferred in	8%
International students	1%	African Americans	2%
Asian Americans/Pacific Islanders	1%	Hispanic Americans	1%
Native Americans	0.4%		

Faculty 168 (95% full-time), 70% with terminal degrees.

Expenses (1999–2000) *Tuition, state resident:* full-time $1808; part-time $76 per semester hour. *Tuition, nonresident:* full-time $7232; part-time $302 per semester hour. *Required fees:* full-time $402; $201 per term part-time. Part-time tuition and fees vary according to course load. *College room and board:* $3526; room only: $1728. Room and board charges vary according to board plan and housing facility. *Waivers:* senior citizens and employees or children of employees.

Library Stewart Library. *Operations spending 1999–2000:* $75,248. *Collection:* 116,676 titles, 2,464 serial subscriptions, 4,496 audiovisual materials.

College life *Housing:* on-campus residence required through sophomore year. *Options:* men-only, women-only. *Social organizations:* national fraternities, national sororities; 20% of eligible men and 13% of eligible women are members. *Most popular organizations:* Student Government Association, Greek organizations, College Union Board, Resident Student Affairs Board, Baptist Student Union.

Campus security 24-hour emergency response devices and patrols, late-night transport-escort service, controlled dormitory access.

After graduation 126 organizations recruited on campus 1997–98. 60% of class of 1998 had job offers within 6 months. *Career center:* 2 full-time, 1 part-time personnel. Services include job fairs, resume preparation, interview workshops, resume referral, career/interest testing, career counseling, careers library, job bank, job interviews.

Freshmen 2,522 applied, 1,178 admitted, 644 enrolled.

Average high school GPA	3.31	SAT verbal scores above 500	77%
SAT math scores above 500	76%	ACT above 18	N/R
1998 freshmen returning in 1999	83%		

Application *Options:* eApply at www.CollegeQuest.com, electronic application, early admission, deferred entrance. *Application fee:* $25. *Required:* high school transcript; minimum 2.0 GPA; proof of immunization.

Standardized tests *Admission: Required:* SAT I or ACT. *Required for some:* SAT I and SAT II or ACT, SAT II Subject Tests, SAT II: Writing Test.

Significant dates *Application deadlines:* 7/15 (freshmen), 7/1 (transfers). *Notification:* continuous until 8/15 (freshmen). *Financial aid deadline priority date:* 4/15.

Freshman Application Contact
Mr. Bill Smith, Director of Recruitment, North Georgia College & State University, Admissions Center, Dahlonega, GA 30533. **Phone:** 706-864-1800. **Toll-free phone:** 800-498-9581. **Fax:** 706-864-1478. **E-mail:** tdavis@ngcsu.edu

Visit CollegeQuest.com for information on majors offered and athletics. College video and electronic viewbook available at CollegeQuest.com.

■ *See page 2186 for a narrative description.*

OGLETHORPE UNIVERSITY
Atlanta, Georgia

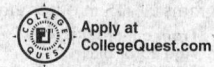

- **Independent**, comprehensive, founded 1835
- **Degrees** bachelor's and master's
- **Suburban** 118-acre campus
- **Coed**, 1,073 undergraduate students, 84% full-time, 66% women, 34% men

Georgia

- **Very difficult** entrance level, 74% of applicants were admitted
- **13:1 student-to-undergraduate faculty ratio**
- **70% graduate** in 6 years or less
- **$17,700 tuition** and fees
- **$16,493 average financial aid** package, $17.5 million endowment

Students *Undergraduates:* 898 full-time, 175 part-time. *The most frequently chosen baccalaureate fields are:* business/marketing, psychology, social sciences and history. *Graduate:* 110 in graduate degree programs.

From out-of-state	45%	Reside on campus	70%
Age 25 or older	4%	Transferred in	10%
International students	2%	African Americans	15%
Asian Americans/Pacific Islanders	4%	Hispanic Americans	3%

Faculty 122 (43% full-time), 89% with terminal degrees.

Expenses (1999–2000) *Comprehensive fee:* $23,000 includes full-time tuition ($17,500), mandatory fees ($200), and room and board ($5300). Room and board charges vary according to board plan and housing facility. *Part-time tuition:* $850 per course. Part-time tuition and fees vary according to class time. *Payment plans:* tuition prepayment, installment. *Waivers:* employees or children of employees.

Library Philip Weltner Library. *Collection:* 131,375 titles, 788 serial subscriptions.

College life *Housing: Options:* coed, men-only, women-only. *Social organizations:* national fraternities, national sororities; 33% of eligible men and 28% of eligible women are members. *Most popular organizations:* fraternities/sororities, Alpha Phi Omega, Oglethorpe Christian Fellowship, International Club, Playmakers.

Campus security 24-hour emergency response devices and patrols, student patrols, late-night transport-escort service, controlled dormitory access.

After graduation 70% of class of 1998 had job offers within 6 months. *Career center:* 2 full-time, 1 part-time personnel. Services include job fairs, resume preparation, interview workshops, resume referral, career/interest testing, career counseling, careers library, job bank, job interviews. *Graduate education:* 34% of class of 1999 went directly to graduate and professional school: 14% business, 11% graduate arts and sciences, 4% medicine, 3% law, 2% education.

Freshmen 744 applied, 553 admitted, 198 enrolled.

Average high school GPA	3.57	SAT verbal scores above 500	89%
SAT math scores above 500	91%	ACT above 18	90%
From top 10% of their h.s. class	38%	From top quarter	65%
From top half	94%	1998 freshmen returning in 1999	81%

Application *Options:* eApply at www.CollegeQuest.com, Common Application, electronic application, early action, deferred entrance. *Application fee:* $30. *Required:* essay or personal statement; high school transcript; 1 letter of recommendation. *Required for some:* interview. *Recommended:* minimum 2.5 GPA; interview.

Standardized tests *Admission: Required:* SAT I or ACT.

Significant dates *Application deadlines:* rolling (freshmen), rolling (transfers). *Early action:* 12/30. *Notification:* continuous until 2/1 (freshmen), 1/15 (early action). *Financial aid deadline:* continuous.

Freshman Application Contact
Mr. Dennis T. Matthews, Associate Dean for Enrollment Management, Oglethorpe University, 4484 Peachtree Road, NE, Atlanta, GA 30319-2797. **Phone:** 404-364-8307. **Toll-free phone:** 800-428-4484. **Fax:** 404-364-8500. **E-mail:** admission@oglethorpe.edu

Visit CollegeQuest.com for information on majors offered and athletics.

■ *See page 2210 for a narrative description.*

PAINE COLLEGE
Augusta, Georgia

- **Independent Methodist**, 4-year, founded 1882
- **Degree** bachelor's
- **Urban** 54-acre campus
- **Coed**, 817 undergraduate students, 89% full-time, 71% women, 29% men
- **Minimally difficult** entrance level, 54% of applicants were admitted
- **12:1 student-to-undergraduate faculty ratio**
- **$7528 tuition** and fees

Students *Undergraduates:* 729 full-time, 88 part-time. Students come from 29 states and territories, 2 other countries. *The most frequently chosen baccalaureate fields are:* business/marketing, education, psychology.

From out-of-state	21%	Reside on campus	58%
Age 25 or older	19%	Transferred in	6%
International students	0.4%	African Americans	99%
Hispanic Americans	0.2%		

Faculty 88 (68% full-time).

Expenses (1999–2000) *Comprehensive fee:* $10,814 includes full-time tuition ($7068), mandatory fees ($460), and room and board ($3286). *College room only:* $1352. Full-time tuition and fees vary according to course load and reciprocity agreements. Room and board charges vary according to housing facility. *Part-time tuition:* $295 per semester hour. *Part-time fees:* $230 per term part-time. Part-time tuition and fees vary according to course load, location, and reciprocity agreements. *Payment plan:* installment. *Waivers:* children of alumni and employees or children of employees.

Library Collins–Callaway Library. *Collection:* 76,120 titles, 4,350 serial subscriptions, 1,407 audiovisual materials.

College life *Housing: Options:* men-only, women-only. *Social organizations:* national fraternities, national sororities, fraternity of Masons; 10% of eligible men and 10% of eligible women are members.

Campus security 24-hour patrols, late-night transport-escort service.

After graduation *Career center:* 1 full-time, 1 part-time personnel. Services include job fairs, resume preparation, interview workshops, resume referral, career/interest testing, career counseling, careers library, job bank, job interviews. *Graduate education:* 10% of class of 1999 went directly to graduate and professional school.

Freshmen 1,323 applied, 709 admitted, 198 enrolled.

Average high school GPA	2.64	SAT verbal scores above 500	47%
SAT math scores above 500	40%	ACT above 18	18%
1998 freshmen returning in 1999	64%		

Application *Options:* early admission, deferred entrance. *Application fee:* $10. *Required:* essay or personal statement; high school transcript; minimum 2.0 GPA; medical history. *Recommended:* 2 letters of recommendation.

Standardized tests *Admission: Required:* SAT I or ACT.

Significant dates *Application deadlines:* 8/1 (freshmen), 8/1 (transfers). *Financial aid deadline:* 5/30. *Priority date:* 4/15.

Freshman Application Contact
Mr. Joseph Tinsley, Director of Admissions, Paine College, 1235 15th Street, Augusta, GA 30901-3182. **Phone:** 706-821-8320. **Toll-free phone:** 800-476-7703. **Fax:** 706-821-8293. **E-mail:** tinsleyj@mail.paine.edu

Visit CollegeQuest.com for information on majors offered and athletics.

■ *See page 2242 for a narrative description.*

PIEDMONT COLLEGE
Demorest, Georgia

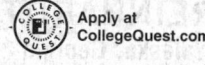
Apply at CollegeQuest.com

- **Independent**, comprehensive, founded 1897, affiliated with Congregational Christian Church
- **Degrees** bachelor's and master's
- **Rural** 115-acre campus with easy access to Atlanta
- **Coed**, 1,042 undergraduate students, 83% full-time, 61% women, 39% men
- **Moderately difficult** entrance level, 69% of applicants were admitted
- **11:1 student-to-undergraduate faculty ratio**
- **25% graduate** in 6 years or less
- **$9500 tuition** and fees
- **$8042 average financial aid** package, $13,048 average indebtedness upon graduation, $44.7 million endowment

Students *Undergraduates:* 868 full-time, 174 part-time. Students come from 15 states and territories. *The most frequently chosen baccalaureate fields are:* business/marketing, education, social sciences and history. *Graduate:* 700 in graduate degree programs.

From out-of-state	3%	Reside on campus	16%
Age 25 or older	31%	Transferred in	13%
International students	0.1%	African Americans	8%
Asian Americans/Pacific Islanders	1%	Hispanic Americans	2%
Native Americans	0.2%		

Faculty 147 (54% full-time).

Expenses (2000–2001) *Comprehensive fee:* $13,900 includes full-time tuition ($9500) and room and board ($4400). *College room only:* $2250.

Georgia

Piedmont College *(continued)*

Full-time tuition and fees vary according to program. Room and board charges vary according to board plan and housing facility. *Part-time tuition:* $396 per credit hour. Part-time tuition and fees vary according to program. *Payment plan:* installment. *Waivers:* employees or children of employees.

Library Piedmont College Library. *Operations spending 1999–2000:* $310,932. *Collection:* 100,000 titles, 488 serial subscriptions, 322 audiovisual materials.

College life *Housing:* on-campus residence required through junior year. *Options:* coed, men-only, women-only, disabled students. *Most popular organizations:* student government, Student Georgia Association of Educators, Students In Free Enterprise, psychology club, Alternatives.

Campus security 24-hour emergency response devices and patrols, late-night transport-escort service.

After graduation 15 organizations recruited on campus 1997–98. 72% of class of 1998 had job offers within 6 months. *Career center:* 1 full-time personnel. Services include job fairs, resume preparation, resume referral, career/interest testing, career counseling, careers library, job bank, job interviews. *Graduate education:* 39% of class of 1999 went directly to graduate and professional school: 18% education, 10% business, 9% graduate arts and sciences, 2% theology.

Freshmen 405 applied, 281 admitted, 236 enrolled.

Average high school GPA	2.95	SAT verbal scores above 500 53%
SAT math scores above 500	43%	ACT above 18 N/R
From top 10% of their h.s. class	6%	From top quarter 15%
From top half	39%	1998 freshmen returning in 1999 73%

Application *Options:* eApply at www.CollegeQuest.com, early admission, deferred entrance. *Application fee:* $20. *Required:* high school transcript; minimum 2.0 GPA. *Required for some:* interview. *Recommended:* essay or personal statement.

Standardized tests *Admission: Required:* SAT I or ACT.

Significant dates *Application deadlines:* rolling (freshmen), rolling (transfers). *Financial aid deadline priority date:* 5/1.

Freshman Application Contact

Ms. Kathy Edwards, Director of Undergraduate Admissions, Piedmont College, PO Box 10, Demorest, GA 30535-0010. **Phone:** 706-776-0103 Ext. 1299. **Toll-free phone:** 800-277-7020. **Fax:** 706-776-6635. **E-mail:** kedwards@piedmont.edu

Visit CollegeQuest.com for information on majors offered and athletics. College video available at CollegeQuest.com.

■ *See page 2268 for a narrative description.*

REINHARDT COLLEGE
Waleska, Georgia

- **Independent**, 4-year, founded 1883, affiliated with United Methodist Church
- **Degrees** associate and bachelor's
- **Rural** 600-acre campus with easy access to Atlanta
- **Coed**, 1,190 undergraduate students, 80% full-time, 63% women, 37% men
- **Moderately difficult** entrance level, 69% of applicants were admitted
- **12:1** student-to-undergraduate faculty ratio
- **24% graduate** in 6 years or less
- **$8800 tuition** and fees
- **$59 million endowment**

Students *Undergraduates:* 948 full-time, 242 part-time. Students come from 8 states and territories, 19 other countries. *The most frequently chosen baccalaureate fields are:* business/marketing, communications/communication technologies, liberal arts/general studies.

From out-of-state	2%	Reside on campus	33%
Age 25 or older	28%	Transferred in	9%
International students	3%	African Americans	4%
Asian Americans/Pacific Islanders	0.3%	Hispanic Americans	1%
Native Americans	0.3%		

Faculty 151 (44% full-time), 58% with terminal degrees.

Expenses (2000–2001) *Comprehensive fee:* $13,550 includes full-time tuition ($8800) and room and board ($4750). *College room only:* $2730. Full-time tuition and fees vary according to course load. Room and board charges vary according to board plan and housing facility. *Part-time tuition:* $275 per credit hour. Part-time tuition and fees vary according to course load and location. *Payment plan:* installment. *Waivers:* children of alumni, senior citizens, and employees or children of employees.

Library Hill Freeman Library. *Operations spending 1999–2000:* $520,000. *Collection:* 32,006 titles, 339 serial subscriptions, 15,330 audiovisual materials.

College life *Housing:* on-campus residence required through sophomore year. *Options:* men-only, women-only. *Most popular organizations:* Student Government Association, Phi Theta Kappa, Phi Beta Lambda, Reach-Out Reinhardt.

Campus security Student patrols, late-night transport-escort service.

After graduation *Career center:* 1 full-time, 1 part-time personnel. Services include job fairs, resume preparation, career counseling, careers library, job bank.

Freshmen 890 applied, 616 admitted, 300 enrolled.

Average high school GPA	2.92	SAT verbal scores above 500	N/R
SAT math scores above 500	N/R	ACT above 18	65%
1998 freshmen returning in 1999	58%		

Application *Options:* eApply at www.CollegeQuest.com, Common Application, electronic application, early admission, early action, deferred entrance. *Application fee:* $15. *Required:* minimum 2.0 GPA. *Required for some:* high school transcript. *Recommended:* essay or personal statement; interview.

Standardized tests *Admission: Required:* SAT I or ACT, ACT COMPASS.

Significant dates *Application deadlines:* rolling (freshmen), rolling (transfers). *Early action:* 1/1. *Notification:* 2/1 (early action). *Financial aid deadline priority date:* 6/1.

Freshman Application Contact

Ms. Jodi Johnson, Director of Admissions, Reinhardt College, 7300 Reinhardt College Circle, Waleska, GA 30183-0128. **Phone:** 770-720-5526. **Fax:** 770-720-5602. **E-mail:** admissions@mail.reinhardt.edu

Visit CollegeQuest.com for information on majors offered and athletics. College video available at CollegeQuest.com.

SAVANNAH COLLEGE OF ART AND DESIGN
Savannah, Georgia

- **Independent**, comprehensive, founded 1978
- **Degrees** bachelor's and master's
- **Urban** campus
- **Coed**, 3,755 undergraduate students, 90% full-time, 43% women, 57% men
- **Moderately difficult** entrance level, 76% of applicants were admitted
- **17:1** student-to-undergraduate faculty ratio
- **57% graduate** in 6 years or less
- **$16,200 tuition** and fees

The College is situated in Savannah's renowned historic district, a creative environment conducive to study, research, and artistic expression. The College exists to prepare talented students for careers. It offers a well-rounded curriculum and emphasizes individual attention. The student body represents all 50 states and more than 80 countries.

Students *Undergraduates:* 3,366 full-time, 389 part-time. Students come from 52 states and territories, 76 other countries. *The most frequently chosen baccalaureate fields are:* architecture, visual/performing arts. *Graduate:* 656 in graduate degree programs.

From out-of-state	82%	Reside on campus	36%
Age 25 or older	8%	Transferred in	9%
International students	8%	African Americans	5%
Asian Americans/Pacific Islanders	2%	Hispanic Americans	3%
Native Americans	0.2%		

Faculty 236 (84% full-time), 88% with terminal degrees.

Expenses (2000–2001) *One-time required fee:* $500. *Comprehensive fee:* $22,950 includes full-time tuition ($16,200) and room and board ($6750). *College room only:* $4200. *Part-time tuition:* $1800 per course. *Payment plan:* installment. *Waivers:* employees or children of employees.

Georgia

Library Savannah College of Art and Design Library plus 1 other. *Operations spending 1999–2000:* $710,906. *Collection:* 46,910 titles, 684 serial subscriptions, 1,285 audiovisual materials.

College life *Housing: Options:* coed, men-only, women-only, disabled students. *Most popular organizations:* United Student Forum, Inter-Club Council, American Institute of Architecture Students, Intercultural Council, American Society of Interior Designers.

Campus security 24-hour emergency response devices and patrols, late-night transport-escort service, video camera surveillance.

After graduation 45 organizations recruited on campus 1997–98. *Career center:* 6 full-time personnel. Services include job fairs, resume preparation, interview workshops, resume referral, career/interest testing, career counseling, careers library, job bank, job interviews, job newsletter. *Graduate education:* 10% of class of 1999 went directly to graduate and professional school: 10% graduate arts and sciences.

Freshmen 3,244 applied, 2,465 admitted, 881 enrolled. 3 National Merit Scholars, 1 class president, 2 valedictorians, 4 student government officers.

SAT verbal scores above 500	70%	SAT math scores above 500	61%
ACT above 18	90%	1998 freshmen returning in 1999	82%

Application *Options:* electronic application, early admission. *Application fee:* $50. *Required:* high school transcript; 3 letters of recommendation. *Recommended:* interview.

Standardized tests *Admission: Required:* SAT I or ACT.

Significant dates *Application deadlines:* rolling (freshmen), rolling (transfers). *Financial aid deadline:* continuous.

Freshman Application Contact
Ms. Pamela Afifi, Vice President of Admissions, Savannah College of Art and Design, 342 Bull Street, PO Box 3146, Savannah, GA 31402-3146. **Phone:** 912-525-5100. **Toll-free phone:** 800-869-7223. **Fax:** 912-238-2436. **E-mail:** admissions@scad.edu

Visit CollegeQuest.com for information on majors offered and athletics. College video and electronic viewbook available at CollegeQuest.com.

■ *See page 2450 for a narrative description.*

SAVANNAH STATE UNIVERSITY
Savannah, Georgia

- **State-supported**, comprehensive, founded 1890
- **Degrees** bachelor's and master's
- **Suburban** 165-acre campus
- **Coed**, 2,042 undergraduate students, 73% full-time, 54% women, 46% men
- **Minimally difficult** entrance level
- **16:1** student-to-undergraduate faculty ratio
- **20% graduate** in 6 years or less
- **$2356 tuition** and fees (in-state); $7780 (out-of-state)
- **$72,919 endowment**

Part of University System of Georgia.

Students *Undergraduates:* 1,494 full-time, 548 part-time. Students come from 28 states and territories, 18 other countries. *Graduate:* 111 in graduate degree programs.

From out-of-state	17%	Reside on campus	45%
Transferred in	4%	International students	2%
African Americans	92%	Asian Americans/Pacific Islanders	0.2%
Hispanic Americans	1%	Native Americans	0.1%

Faculty 143 full-time.

Expenses (1999–2000) *Tuition, state resident:* full-time $1808; part-time $76 per credit. *Tuition, nonresident:* full-time $7232; part-time $302 per credit. *Required fees:* full-time $548; $274 per term part-time. Part-time tuition and fees vary according to course load. *College room and board:* $4084; room only: $2120. Room and board charges vary according to board plan. *Waivers:* senior citizens and employees or children of employees.

Library Asa H. Gordon Library. *Operations spending 1999–2000:* $689,322. *Collection:* 187,916 titles, 812 serial subscriptions.

College life *Housing:* on-campus residence required through junior year. *Options:* men-only, women-only. *Social organizations:* national fraternities, national sororities, local fraternities, local sororities; 35% of eligible men and 38% of eligible women are members. *Most popular organizations:* marching band, gospel choir, concert chair.

Campus security 24-hour patrols.

After graduation *Career center:* 3 full-time personnel. Services include job fairs, resume preparation, interview workshops, resume referral, career/interest testing, career counseling, careers library, job bank, job interviews.

Freshmen 332 enrolled.

Average high school GPA	2.6	SAT verbal scores above 500	N/R
SAT math scores above 500	N/R	ACT above 18	N/R
1998 freshmen returning in 1999	62%		

Application *Options:* Common Application, electronic application, early admission, deferred entrance. *Preference* given to state residents. *Application fee:* $20. *Required:* high school transcript; minimum 2.0 GPA.

Standardized tests *Admission: Required:* SAT I or ACT. *Recommended:* SAT I. *Required for some:* SAT II Subject Tests.

Significant dates *Application deadlines:* 6/1 (freshmen), 6/1 (transfers). *Financial aid deadline priority date:* 5/1.

Freshman Application Contact
Dr. Roy A. Jackson, Director of Admissions, Savannah State University, PO Box 20209, Savannah, GA 31404. **Phone:** 912-356-2181. **Toll-free phone:** 800-788-0478. **Fax:** 912-356-2256.

Visit CollegeQuest.com for information on majors offered and athletics.

■ *See page 2452 for a narrative description.*

SHORTER COLLEGE
Rome, Georgia

- **Independent Baptist**, comprehensive, founded 1873
- **Degrees** bachelor's and master's
- **Small-town** 155-acre campus with easy access to Atlanta
- **Coed**, 1,727 undergraduate students, 97% full-time, 61% women, 39% men
- **Moderately difficult** entrance level, 95% of applicants were admitted
- **15:1** student-to-undergraduate faculty ratio
- **48% graduate** in 6 years or less
- **$9170 tuition** and fees
- **$6993 average financial aid** package, $16,700 average indebtedness upon graduation, $24.5 million endowment

Students *Undergraduates:* 1,678 full-time, 49 part-time. Students come from 14 states and territories, 19 other countries. *The most frequently chosen baccalaureate fields are:* business/marketing, education, visual/performing arts. *Graduate:* 33 in graduate degree programs.

From out-of-state	6%	Reside on campus	68%
Age 25 or older	11%	Transferred in	6%
International students	2%	African Americans	15%
Asian Americans/Pacific Islanders	0.5%	Hispanic Americans	1%
Native Americans	1%		

Faculty 221 (27% full-time), 39% with terminal degrees.

Expenses (1999–2000) *Comprehensive fee:* $13,820 includes full-time tuition ($9050), mandatory fees ($120), and room and board ($4650). *College room only:* $2675. Full-time tuition and fees vary according to location and program. Room and board charges vary according to board plan and housing facility. *Part-time tuition:* $210 per credit hour. *Payment plan:* installment. *Waivers:* senior citizens and employees or children of employees.

Library Livingston Library. *Collection:* 99,486 titles, 599 serial subscriptions, 11,004 audiovisual materials.

College life *Housing:* on-campus residence required through senior year. *Options:* men-only, women-only, disabled students. *Social organizations:* local fraternities, local sororities; 20% of eligible men and 31% of eligible women are members. *Most popular organizations:* Baptist Student Union, Student Government Association.

Campus security 24-hour emergency response devices and patrols.

After graduation 49 organizations recruited on campus 1997–98. *Career center:* 2 full-time personnel. Services include job fairs, resume preparation, career counseling, careers library, job bank, job interviews.

Freshmen 727 applied, 688 admitted, 260 enrolled.

Average high school GPA	3.35	SAT verbal scores above 500	66%
SAT math scores above 500	62%	ACT above 18	84%
1998 freshmen returning in 1999	65%		

Application *Options:* early admission, deferred entrance. *Application fee:* $25. *Required:* essay or personal statement; high school transcript. *Required*

Georgia

Shorter College (continued)
for some: interview; audition for music and theater programs. *Recommended:* minimum 2.0 GPA; 1 letter of recommendation; interview.
Standardized tests *Admission: Required:* SAT I or ACT.
Significant dates *Application deadlines:* rolling (freshmen), rolling (transfers). *Financial aid deadline:* 8/1. *Priority date:* 4/1.
Freshman Application Contact
Ms. Sharon Holcomb, Assistant Director of Admissions, Shorter College, 315 Shorter Avenue, Rome, GA 30165-4298. **Phone:** 706-233-7221. **Toll-free phone:** 800-868-6980. **Fax:** 706-236-1515. **E-mail:** admissions@shorter.edu
Visit CollegeQuest.com for information on majors offered and athletics. College video available at CollegeQuest.com.

■ *See page 2484 for a narrative description.*

SOUTH COLLEGE
Savannah, Georgia

- **Proprietary**, 4-year, founded 1899
- **Degrees** associate and bachelor's
- **Suburban** 6-acre campus
- **Coed,** primarily women
- **Minimally difficult** entrance level

Institutional Web site http://www.southcollege.edu/
College life *Housing:* college housing not available. *Most popular organizations:* Medical Assisting Club, Paralegal Club, Student Advisory Committee.
Campus security Late-night transport-escort service.
Application *Options:* eApply at www.CollegeQuest.com, deferred entrance. *Application fee:* $25. *Required:* interview. *Required for some:* essay or personal statement; 3 letters of recommendation.
Standardized tests *Admission: Required:* SAT I, ACT or CPT.
Admissions Office Contact
South College, 709 Mall Boulevard, Savannah, GA 31406-4881. **Fax:** 912-691-6070. **E-mail:** southcollege@southcollege.edu
Visit CollegeQuest.com for information on athletics.

SOUTHERN POLYTECHNIC STATE UNIVERSITY
Marietta, Georgia

- **State-supported**, comprehensive, founded 1948
- **Degrees** associate, bachelor's, master's, and postbachelor's certificates
- **Suburban** 200-acre campus with easy access to Atlanta
- **Coed**, 2,989 undergraduate students, 59% full-time, 17% women, 83% men
- **Moderately difficult** entrance level, 65% of applicants were admitted
- **19:1** student-to-undergraduate faculty ratio
- **$2134 tuition** and fees (in-state); $7558 (out-of-state)

Part of University System of Georgia.
Students *Undergraduates:* 1,775 full-time, 1,214 part-time. Students come from 40 states and territories. *The most frequently chosen baccalaureate fields are:* computer/information sciences, architecture, engineering/engineering technologies. *Graduate:* 620 in graduate degree programs.

From out-of-state	2%	Reside on campus	12%
Age 25 or older	44%	Transferred in	10%
International students	4%	African Americans	20%
Asian Americans/Pacific Islanders	6%	Hispanic Americans	2%
Native Americans	0.2%		

Faculty 204 (75% full-time).
Expenses (1999–2000) *Tuition, state resident:* full-time $1808; part-time $76 per hour. *Tuition, nonresident:* full-time $7232; part-time $302 per hour. *Required fees:* full-time $326; $163 per term part-time. Part-time tuition and fees vary according to course load. *College room and board:* $4452; room only: $2142. *Waivers:* senior citizens.
Library Lawrence V. Johnson Library. *Collection:* 194,302 titles, 1,415 serial subscriptions, 62 audiovisual materials.

College life *Housing: Option:* coed. *Social organizations:* national fraternities, national sororities, local fraternities; 7% of eligible men and 5% of eligible women are members. *Most popular organizations:* International Student Association, Campus Activities Board, National Society of Black Engineers, Aerial Robotics Team, Intergreek Council.
Campus security 24-hour emergency response devices and patrols, late-night transport-escort service, controlled dormitory access.
After graduation 139 organizations recruited on campus 1997–98. 88% of class of 1998 had job offers within 6 months. *Career center:* 5 full-time personnel. Services include job fairs, resume preparation, resume referral, career counseling, careers library, job bank, job interviews.
Freshmen 867 applied, 560 admitted, 384 enrolled.

Average high school GPA	3.0	SAT verbal scores above 500	56%
SAT math scores above 500	68%	ACT above 18	88%
1998 freshmen returning in 1999	57%		

Application *Options:* early admission, deferred entrance. *Application fee:* $20. *Required:* high school transcript; minimum 2.0 GPA; proof of immunization.
Standardized tests *Admission: Required:* SAT I or ACT. *Required for some:* SAT II Subject Tests.
Significant dates *Application deadlines:* 8/1 (freshmen), 8/1 (transfers). *Financial aid deadline priority date:* 3/15.
Freshman Application Contact
Ms. Virginia A. Head, Director of Admissions, Southern Polytechnic State University, 1100 South Marietta Parkway, Marietta, GA 30060-2896. **Phone:** 770-528-7281. **Toll-free phone:** 800-635-3204. **Fax:** 770-528-7483. **E-mail:** admissions@spsu.edu
Visit CollegeQuest.com for information on majors offered and athletics. College video available at CollegeQuest.com.

■ *See page 2516 for a narrative description.*

SPELMAN COLLEGE
Atlanta, Georgia

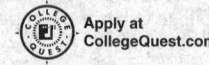

- **Independent**, 4-year, founded 1881
- **Degree** bachelor's
- **Urban** 32-acre campus
- **Women** only, 1,952 undergraduate students, 97% full-time
- **Very difficult** entrance level, 53% of applicants were admitted
- **14:1** student-to-undergraduate faculty ratio
- **$10,985 tuition** and fees
- **$181 million** endowment

Spelman College is a historically black, privately endowed, 4-year liberal arts college for women. Founded in 1881 as the Atlanta Baptist Female Seminary, Spelman today is one of America's top liberal arts colleges, providing academic excellence for women as well as an environment that encourages leadership development and community service experience. Spelman's commitment to excellence is demonstrated by its dedicated, accessible faculty and low student-faculty ratio as well as by the outstanding success of students and alumnae.

Students *Undergraduates:* Students come from 45 states and territories, 21 other countries.

Reside on campus	59%	Age 25 or older	4%

Faculty 147 (100% full-time).
Expenses (1999–2000) *Comprehensive fee:* $17,715 includes full-time tuition ($9260), mandatory fees ($1725), and room and board ($6730). *Part-time tuition:* $380 per hour. *Part-time fees:* $1455 per year part-time. Part-time tuition and fees vary according to course load. *Payment plan:* installment. *Waivers:* employees or children of employees.
Library Robert Woodruff Library. *Collection:* 404,991 titles, 2,693 serial subscriptions.
College life *Housing: Option:* women-only. *Social organizations:* national sororities; 15% of eligible undergrads are members. *Most popular organizations:* Student Government Association, Spotlight (newspaper), Health Career Club.
Campus security 24-hour emergency response devices and patrols, late-night transport-escort service, controlled dormitory access.

After graduation *Career center:* 3 full-time personnel. Services include job fairs, resume preparation, career counseling, careers library, job interviews. *Graduate education:* 38% of class of 1999 went directly to graduate and professional school. *Major awards:* 1 Fulbright Scholar.

Freshmen 3,275 applied, 1,742 admitted. 10 National Merit Scholars, 52 class presidents, 29 student government officers.

Average high school GPA	3.2	SAT verbal scores above 500	78%
SAT math scores above 500	56%	ACT above 18	100%
From top 10% of their h.s. class	47%	From top quarter	83%
From top half	99%	1998 freshmen returning in 1999	90%

Application *Options:* eApply at www.CollegeQuest.com, Common Application, electronic application, early admission, early action. *Application fee:* $35. *Required:* essay or personal statement; high school transcript; minimum 2.0 GPA; 2 letters of recommendation. *Required for some:* interview.

Standardized tests *Admission: Required:* SAT I or ACT.

Significant dates *Application deadlines:* 2/1 (freshmen), 2/1 (transfers). *Early action:* 11/15. *Notification:* 4/1 (freshmen), 12/31 (early action).

Freshman Application Contact Roxie M. Shabazz, Interim Director of Admissions and Orientation Services, Spelman College, 350 Spelman Lane, SW, Atlanta, GA 30314-4399. **Phone:** 404-681-3643 Ext. 2188. **Toll-free phone:** 800-982-2411. **Fax:** 404-215-7788. **E-mail:** admiss@spelman.edu

Visit CollegeQuest.com for information on majors offered and athletics.

■ *See page 2524 for a narrative description.*

STATE UNIVERSITY OF WEST GEORGIA
Carrollton, Georgia

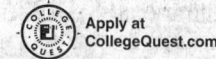 Apply at CollegeQuest.com

- **State-supported**, comprehensive, founded 1933
- **Degrees** associate, bachelor's, and master's
- **Small-town** 400-acre campus with easy access to Atlanta
- **Coed**, 6,644 undergraduate students, 81% full-time, 62% women, 38% men
- **Minimally difficult** entrance level, 68% of applicants were admitted
- **19:1 student-to-undergraduate faculty ratio**
- **28% graduate** in 6 years or less
- **$2212 tuition** and fees (in-state); $7636 (out-of-state)

Part of University System of Georgia.

Students *Undergraduates:* 5,405 full-time, 1,239 part-time. Students come from 28 states and territories, 61 other countries. *The most frequently chosen baccalaureate fields are:* business/marketing, education, psychology.

From out-of-state	3%	Reside on campus	33%
Age 25 or older	14%	Transferred in	7%
International students	1%	African Americans	22%
Asian Americans/Pacific Islanders	1%	Hispanic Americans	1%
Native Americans	0.2%		

Faculty 385 (86% full-time), 74% with terminal degrees.

Expenses (1999–2000) *Tuition, state resident:* full-time $1808; part-time $75 per semester hour. *Tuition, nonresident:* full-time $7232; part-time $301 per semester hour. *Required fees:* full-time $404; $14 per semester hour; $65 per term part-time. Part-time tuition and fees vary according to course load. *College room and board:* $3806; room only: $2026. Room and board charges vary according to board plan and housing facility. *Waivers:* minority students, adult students, and senior citizens.

Library Irvine Sullivan Ingram Library. *Operations spending 1999–2000:* $2.2 million. *Collection:* 332,290 titles, 1,154 serial subscriptions, 25,907 audiovisual materials.

College life *Housing:* on-campus residence required in freshman year. *Options:* coed, men-only, women-only. *Social organizations:* national fraternities, national sororities; 13% of eligible men and 10% of eligible women are members. *Most popular organizations:* Black Student Alliance, Student Activities Council, Baptist Student Union, Campus Outreach, United Voices Gospel Choir.

Campus security 24-hour patrols, late-night transport-escort service, controlled dormitory access.

After graduation 250 organizations recruited on campus 1997–98. 92% of class of 1998 had job offers within 6 months. *Career center:* 5 full-time, 1 part-time personnel. Services include job fairs, resume preparation, interview workshops, resume referral, career counseling, careers library, job bank, job interviews.

Freshmen 4,340 applied, 2,971 admitted, 1,638 enrolled.

Average high school GPA	2.84	SAT verbal scores above 500	31%
SAT math scores above 500	N/R	ACT above 18	62%
1998 freshmen returning in 1999	65%		

Application *Options:* eApply at www.CollegeQuest.com, early admission. *Application fee:* $20. *Required:* high school transcript; proof of immunization. *Required for some:* 2 letters of recommendation; interview.

Standardized tests *Admission: Required:* SAT I or ACT.

Significant dates *Application deadlines:* rolling (freshmen), rolling (transfers). *Financial aid deadline priority date:* 4/15.

Freshman Application Contact Dr. Robert Johnson, Director of Admissions, State University of West Georgia, 1600 Maple Street, Carrollton, GA 30118. **Phone:** 770-836-6416. **Fax:** 770-836-6720. **E-mail:** rjohnson@westga.edu

Visit CollegeQuest.com for information on majors offered and athletics. College video available at CollegeQuest.com.

■ *See page 2568 for a narrative description.*

THOMAS UNIVERSITY
Thomasville, Georgia

- **Independent**, comprehensive, founded 1950
- **Degrees** associate, bachelor's, and master's
- **Small-town** 24-acre campus
- **Coed**, 530 undergraduate students, 73% full-time, 64% women, 36% men
- **Noncompetitive** entrance level, 100% of applicants were admitted
- **10:1 student-to-undergraduate faculty ratio**
- **35% graduate** in 6 years or less
- **$7870 tuition** and fees
- **$4349 average financial aid** package, $2.6 million endowment

Students *Undergraduates:* 386 full-time, 144 part-time. Students come from 6 states and territories, 7 other countries. *The most frequently chosen baccalaureate fields are:* education, health professions and related sciences, protective services/public administration. *Graduate:* 15 in graduate degree programs.

From out-of-state	10%	Age 25 or older	47%
Transferred in	11%	International students	2%
African Americans	28%	Asian Americans/Pacific Islanders	1%
Hispanic Americans	2%	Native Americans	0.2%

Faculty 68 (57% full-time), 37% with terminal degrees.

Expenses (1999–2000) *Tuition:* full-time $7500; part-time $250 per semester hour. *Required fees:* full-time $370; $92 per term part-time. Full-time tuition and fees vary according to course load. Room and board charges vary according to board plan. *Payment plans:* guaranteed tuition, installment, deferred payment. *Waivers:* senior citizens and employees or children of employees.

Library Thomas College Library. *Operations spending 1999–2000:* $228,000. *Collection:* 34,486 titles, 438 serial subscriptions, 35 audiovisual materials.

College life *Housing:* college housing not available. *Most popular organizations:* nursing club, psychology club, Baptist Student Union, equestrian club, outdoor pursuits.

Campus security Late-night transport-escort service, evening security guards.

After graduation 10 organizations recruited on campus 1997–98. *Career center:* 1 full-time personnel. Services include job fairs, resume preparation, interview workshops, resume referral, career counseling, careers library, job bank, job interviews.

Freshmen 141 applied, 141 admitted, 73 enrolled.

| SAT verbal scores above 500 | 26% | SAT math scores above 500 | 29% |
| ACT above 18 | 91% | 1998 freshmen returning in 1999 | 66% |

Application *Options:* Common Application, early admission, deferred entrance. *Application fee:* $25. *Required:* high school transcript; minimum 2.0 GPA.

Standardized tests *Placement: Required:* MAPS *Recommended:* SAT I or ACT.

Georgia

Thomas University (continued)
Significant dates *Application deadlines:* rolling (freshmen), rolling (transfers). *Financial aid deadline:* continuous.
Freshman Application Contact
Ms. Darla Glass, Registrar, Thomas University, 1501 Millpond Road, Thomasville, GA 31792-7499. **Phone:** 912-226-1621 Ext. 122. **Toll-free phone:** 800-538-9784.

Visit CollegeQuest.com for information on majors offered and athletics.

TOCCOA FALLS COLLEGE
Toccoa Falls, Georgia

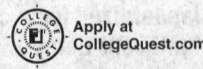 Apply at CollegeQuest.com

- **Independent interdenominational**, comprehensive, founded 1907
- **Degrees** associate, bachelor's, and master's
- **Small-town** 1,100-acre campus
- **Coed**, 924 undergraduate students, 92% full-time, 57% women, 43% men
- **Moderately difficult** entrance level, 64% of applicants were admitted
- **15:1 student-to-undergraduate faculty ratio**
- **$8424 tuition** and fees
- **$1.7 million endowment**

Students *Undergraduates:* 851 full-time, 73 part-time. Students come from 50 states and territories, 25 other countries. *The most frequently chosen baccalaureate fields are:* education, philosophy, psychology. *Graduate:* 37 in graduate degree programs.

From out-of-state	70%
Age 25 or older	11%
African Americans	2%
Hispanic Americans	2%
Reside on campus	65%
International students	4%
Asian Americans/Pacific Islanders	2%

Faculty 67 (75% full-time), 42% with terminal degrees.
Expenses (1999–2000) *One-time required fee:* $20. *Comprehensive fee:* $12,320 includes full-time tuition ($8384), mandatory fees ($40), and room and board ($3896). *Part-time tuition:* $350 per credit hour. *Part-time fees:* $20 per term part-time. *Payment plan:* installment. *Waivers:* children of alumni, senior citizens, and employees or children of employees.
Library Seby Jones Library. *Operations spending 1999–2000:* $265,189. *Collection:* 82,119 titles, 445 serial subscriptions.
College life On-campus residence required through senior year.
Campus security Student patrols.
After graduation *Career center:* 1 part-time personnel. Services include resume preparation, resume referral, career counseling, careers library, job interviews. *Graduate education:* 17% of class of 1999 went directly to graduate and professional school.
Freshmen 1,174 applied, 746 admitted, 314 enrolled. 5 valedictorians.

Average high school GPA	3.13	SAT verbal scores above 500	57%
SAT math scores above 500	47%	ACT above 18	84%
From top 10% of their h.s. class	18%	From top quarter	40%
From top half	69%	1998 freshmen returning in 1999	63%

Application *Options:* eApply at www.CollegeQuest.com, Common Application, electronic application, early admission, deferred entrance. *Application fee:* $20. *Required:* essay or personal statement; high school transcript; 3 letters of recommendation. *Required for some:* interview.
Standardized tests *Admission: Required:* SAT I or ACT.
Significant dates *Application deadlines:* rolling (freshmen), rolling (transfers). *Financial aid deadline priority date:* 3/1.
Freshman Application Contact
Mr. Paul G. Worley, Director of Admissions, Toccoa Falls College, Office of Admissions, Toccoa Falls, GA 30598-1000. **Phone:** 706-886-6831 Ext. 5380. **Toll-free phone:** 800-868-3257. **Fax:** 706-886-6412 Ext. 5380. **E-mail:** admissions@toccoafalls.edu

Visit CollegeQuest.com for information on majors offered and athletics. College video available at CollegeQuest.com.

■ *See page 2626 for a narrative description.*

UNIVERSITY OF GEORGIA
Athens, Georgia

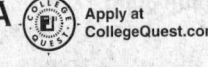 Apply at CollegeQuest.com

- **State-supported**, university, founded 1785
- **Degrees** associate, bachelor's, master's, doctoral, and first professional
- **Suburban** 1,289-acre campus with easy access to Atlanta
- **Coed**, 23,689 undergraduate students, 90% full-time, 54% women, 46% men
- **Moderately difficult** entrance level, 63% of applicants were admitted
- **8:1 student-to-undergraduate faculty ratio**
- **65.7% graduate** in 6 years or less
- **$3024 tuition** and fees (in-state); $10,266 (out-of-state)
- **$5371 average financial aid** package, $13,597 average indebtedness upon graduation, $334.5 million endowment

Part of University System of Georgia.
Students *Undergraduates:* 21,400 full-time, 2,289 part-time. Students come from 53 states and territories, 131 other countries. *The most frequently chosen baccalaureate fields are:* business/marketing, education, social sciences and history. *Graduate:* 1,332 in professional programs, 5,540 in other graduate degree programs.

From out-of-state	18%	Reside on campus	26%
Age 25 or older	6%	Transferred in	8%
International students	1%	African Americans	6%
Asian Americans/Pacific Islanders	3%	Hispanic Americans	1%
Native Americans	0.2%		

Faculty 2,037 (89% full-time).
Expenses (1999–2000) *Tuition, state resident:* full-time $2414; part-time $101 per hour. *Tuition, nonresident:* full-time $9656; part-time $403 per hour. *Required fees:* full-time $610; $310 per term part-time. Full-time tuition and fees vary according to program. Part-time tuition and fees vary according to program. *College room and board:* $4902; room only: $2626. Room and board charges vary according to board plan and housing facility. *Waivers:* senior citizens and employees or children of employees.
Library Ilah Dunlap Little Memorial Library plus 2 others. *Operations spending 1999–2000:* $21.5 million. *Collection:* 3.5 million titles, 45,258 serial subscriptions.
College life *Housing: Options:* coed, men-only, women-only, disabled students. *Social organizations:* national fraternities, national sororities, local fraternities, local sororities; 16% of eligible men and 21% of eligible women are members. *Most popular organizations:* intramurals, recreational sports program, Communiversity, University Union, Red Coat Band.
Campus security 24-hour emergency response devices and patrols, late-night transport-escort service, controlled dormitory access.
After graduation 740 organizations recruited on campus 1997–98. *Career center:* 22 full-time personnel. Services include job fairs, resume preparation, resume referral, career counseling, careers library, job bank, job interviews. *Major awards:* 5 Fulbright Scholars.
Freshmen 13,402 applied, 8,466 admitted, 4,398 enrolled. 1 National Merit Scholar.

Average high school GPA	3.64	SAT verbal scores above 500	94%
SAT math scores above 500	94%	ACT above 18	N/R
1998 freshmen returning in 1999	90%		

Application *Options:* eApply at www.CollegeQuest.com, electronic application, early admission, deferred entrance. *Application fee:* $25. *Required:* high school transcript. *Recommended:* essay or personal statement.
Standardized tests *Admission: Required:* SAT I or ACT.
Significant dates *Application deadlines:* 2/1 (freshmen), 6/15 (transfers). *Notification:* 4/1 (freshmen). *Financial aid deadline priority date:* 3/1.
Freshman Application Contact
Dr. John Albright, Associate Director of Admissions, University of Georgia, Athens, GA 30602. **Phone:** 706-542-3000. **E-mail:** undergrad@admissions.uga.edu

Visit CollegeQuest.com for information on majors offered and athletics. College video available at CollegeQuest.com.

VALDOSTA STATE UNIVERSITY
Valdosta, Georgia

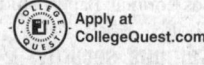 Apply at CollegeQuest.com

- **State-supported**, university, founded 1906
- **Degrees** associate, bachelor's, master's, and doctoral
- **Small-town** 200-acre campus with easy access to Jacksonville

Georgia

- **Coed**, 7,635 undergraduate students, 77% full-time, 60% women, 40% men
- **Moderately difficult** entrance level, 61% of applicants were admitted
- **19:1 student-to-undergraduate faculty ratio**
- **$2290 tuition** and fees (in-state); $7714 (out-of-state)
- **$7557 average financial aid** package, $12,725 average indebtedness upon graduation, $16.6 million endowment

Part of University System of Georgia.

Students *Undergraduates:* 5,850 full-time, 1,785 part-time. Students come from 46 states and territories. *The most frequently chosen baccalaureate fields are:* business/marketing, education, social sciences and history. *Graduate:* 1,117 in graduate degree programs.

From out-of-state	10%	Reside on campus	24%
Age 25 or older	21%	Transferred in	8%
African Americans	22%	Asian Americans/Pacific Islanders	1%
Hispanic Americans	1%	Native Americans	0.2%

Faculty 461 full-time.

Expenses (1999–2000) *Tuition, state resident:* full-time $2290; part-time $76 per semester hour. *Tuition, nonresident:* full-time $7714; part-time $302 per semester hour. Part-time tuition and fees vary according to course load. *College room and board:* $3954; room only: $1844. Room and board charges vary according to board plan. *Waivers:* senior citizens and employees or children of employees.

Library Odom Library. *Collection:* 3,182 serial subscriptions, 18,442 audiovisual materials.

College life *Housing:* on-campus residence required in freshman year. *Options:* coed, men-only, women-only, disabled students. *Social organizations:* national fraternities, national sororities; 5% of eligible men and 11% of eligible women are members. *Most popular organizations:* Blazing Brigade (marching band), SGA (Student Government Association), Greek organizations, intramural athletics, Baptist Student Union.

Campus security 24-hour emergency response devices and patrols, student patrols, late-night transport-escort service, controlled dormitory access, bicycle patrols, security cameras.

After graduation 150 organizations recruited on campus 1997–98. *Career center:* 5 full-time personnel. Services include job fairs, resume preparation, interview workshops, resume referral, career/interest testing, career counseling, careers library, job bank, job interviews. *Graduate education:* 10% of class of 1999 went directly to graduate and professional school.

Freshmen 4,130 applied, 2,516 admitted, 1,259 enrolled.

SAT verbal scores above 500	51%	SAT math scores above 500	43%
ACT above 18	83%	1998 freshmen returning in 1999	68%

Application *Options:* eApply at www.CollegeQuest.com, early admission, deferred entrance. *Application fee:* $20. *Required:* high school transcript; minimum 2.0 GPA; proof of immunization.

Standardized tests *Admission: Required:* SAT I or ACT.

Significant dates *Application deadlines:* 8/1 (freshmen), 8/1 (transfers). *Financial aid deadline priority date:* 4/1.

Freshman Application Contact
Mr. Walter Peacock, Director of Admissions, Valdosta State University, 1500 North Patterson Street, Valdosta, GA 31698. **Phone:** 912-333-5791. **Toll-free phone:** 800-618-1878 Ext. 1. **Fax:** 912-333-5482. **E-mail:** admissions@valdosta.edu

Visit CollegeQuest.com for information on majors offered and athletics.

WESLEYAN COLLEGE
Macon, Georgia

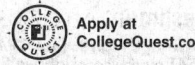

- **Independent United Methodist**, comprehensive, founded 1836
- **Degrees** bachelor's and master's
- **Suburban** 200-acre campus with easy access to Atlanta
- **Women** only, 557 undergraduate students, 80% full-time
- **Moderately difficult** entrance level, 76% of applicants were admitted
- **11:1 student-to-undergraduate faculty ratio**
- **47% graduate** in 6 years or less
- **$16,300 tuition** and fees
- **$12,420 average financial aid** package, $16,250 average indebtedness upon graduation, $47.1 million endowment

Students *Undergraduates:* 443 full-time, 114 part-time. Students come from 26 states and territories, 10 other countries. *The most frequently chosen baccalaureate fields are:* education, business/marketing, psychology. *Graduate:* 22 in graduate degree programs.

From out-of-state	21%	Reside on campus	85%
Age 25 or older	26%	Transferred in	10%
International students	3%	African Americans	30%
Asian Americans/Pacific Islanders	3%	Hispanic Americans	3%
Native Americans	1%		

Faculty 67 (66% full-time), 75% with terminal degrees.

Expenses (1999–2000) *Comprehensive fee:* $22,900 includes full-time tuition ($15,450), mandatory fees ($850), and room and board ($6600). Full-time tuition and fees vary according to class time and course load. Room and board charges vary according to housing facility. *Part-time tuition:* $390 per semester hour. Part-time tuition and fees vary according to class time, course load, and program. *Payment plan:* installment. *Waivers:* children of alumni, senior citizens, and employees or children of employees.

Library Lucy Lester Willet Memorial Library. *Operations spending 1999–2000:* $462,056. *Collection:* 140,579 titles, 650 serial subscriptions, 5,380 audiovisual materials.

College life *Housing:* on-campus residence required through senior year. *Option:* women-only. *Most popular organizations:* Student Recreation Council, Campus Activities Board, Student Government Association, Council on Religious Concerns, Wesleyan Christian Fellowship.

Campus security 24-hour emergency response devices and patrols, late-night transport-escort service, controlled dormitory access.

After graduation 75 organizations recruited on campus 1997–98. 68% of class of 1998 had job offers within 6 months. *Career center:* 1 full-time personnel. Services include job fairs, resume preparation, interview workshops, resume referral, career/interest testing, career counseling, careers library, job bank, job interviews. *Graduate education:* 24% of class of 1999 went directly to graduate and professional school: 14% graduate arts and sciences, 4% business, 3% education, 1% law.

Freshmen 391 applied, 296 admitted, 160 enrolled. 5 National Merit Scholars, 5 valedictorians.

Average high school GPA	3.5	SAT verbal scores above 500	85%
SAT math scores above 500	67%	ACT above 18	98%
From top 10% of their h.s. class	42%	From top quarter	71%
From top half	89%	1998 freshmen returning in 1999	65%

Application *Options:* eApply at www.CollegeQuest.com, Common Application, early admission, early decision, early action, deferred entrance. *Application fee:* $30. *Required:* essay or personal statement; high school transcript; 1 letter of recommendation. *Recommended:* 2 letters of recommendation; interview.

Standardized tests *Admission: Required:* SAT I or ACT.

Significant dates *Application deadlines:* 3/1 (freshmen), rolling (transfers). *Early decision:* 11/1 (for plan 1), 1/15 (for plan 2), 12/15. *Notification:* 4/1 (freshmen), 12/1 (early decision plan 1), 2/1 (early decision plan 2), 1/15 (early action). *Financial aid deadline priority date:* 3/1.

Freshman Application Contact
Mr. Jonathan Stroud, Vice-President for Enrollment and Marketing, Wesleyan College, 4760 Forsyth Road, Macon, GA 31210-4462. **Phone:** 912-757-5206. **Toll-free phone:** 800-447-6610. **Fax:** 912-757-4030. **E-mail:** admissions@wesleyancollege.edu

Visit CollegeQuest.com for information on majors offered and athletics. College video available at CollegeQuest.com.

- *See page 2936 for a narrative description.*

Hawaii

HAWAII

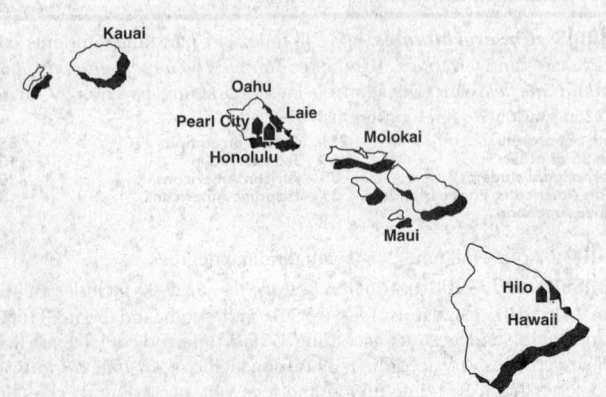

BRIGHAM YOUNG UNIVERSITY—HAWAII CAMPUS
Laie, Hawaii

- **Independent Latter-day Saints**, 4-year, founded 1955
- **Degrees** associate, bachelor's, and postbachelor's certificates
- **Small-town** 60-acre campus with easy access to Honolulu
- **Coed**, 2,276 undergraduate students, 93% full-time, 61% women, 39% men
- **Moderately difficult** entrance level, 37% of applicants were admitted
- **16:1 student-to-undergraduate faculty ratio**
- **$2875 tuition** and fees

Students *Undergraduates:* 2,126 full-time, 150 part-time. Students come from 43 states and territories, 55 other countries. *The most frequently chosen baccalaureate fields are:* business/marketing, computer/information sciences, education.

From out-of-state	42%	Reside on campus	62%
Age 25 or older	26%	Transferred in	8%
International students	37%	African Americans	0.3%
Asian Americans/Pacific Islanders	18%	Hispanic Americans	1%
Native Americans	0.2%		

Faculty 180 (61% full-time).
Expenses (1999–2000) *Comprehensive fee:* $8000 includes full-time tuition ($2875) and room and board ($5125). *College room only:* $2050. Full-time tuition and fees vary according to program. Room and board charges vary according to board plan and housing facility. *Part-time tuition:* $155 per credit. Part-time tuition and fees vary according to program. Tuition for nonchurch members: $4325 full-time, $230 per credit part-time. *Payment plan:* installment. *Waivers:* employees or children of employees.
Library Joseph F. Smith Library. *Collection:* 435,467 titles, 9,180 serial subscriptions, 7,252 audiovisual materials.
College life *Housing:* on-campus residence required in freshman year. *Options:* men-only, women-only. *Most popular organizations:* Tonga club, Samoa club, Hawaiian club, Hong Kong club, Singapore/Malaysia/Indonesia club.
Campus security 24-hour patrols, late-night transport-escort service.
After graduation 65 organizations recruited on campus 1997–98. *Career center:* 1 full-time, 3 part-time personnel. Services include job fairs, resume preparation, interview workshops, resume referral, career/interest testing, career counseling, careers library, job bank, job interviews.
Freshmen 1,110 applied, 407 admitted, 407 enrolled. 1 National Merit Scholar.

Average high school GPA	3.4	SAT verbal scores above 500	N/R
SAT math scores above 500	N/R	ACT above 18	94%

Application *Options:* Common Application, early admission, deferred entrance. *Preference* given to church members. *Application fee:* $25. *Required:* high school transcript; minimum 3.0 GPA; resume of activities. *Required for some:* letters of recommendation. *Recommended:* essay or personal statement.

Standardized tests *Admission: Required:* ACT. *Recommended:* SAT I.
Significant dates *Application deadlines:* 2/15 (freshmen), 3/15 (transfers). *Financial aid deadline:* 4/30.
Freshman Application Contact
Dr. Bruce A. Bowen, Dean for Admissions and Records, Brigham Young University–Hawaii Campus, 55-220 Kulanui Street, Laie, Oahu, HI 96762. **Phone:** 808-293-3738.
Visit CollegeQuest.com for information on majors offered and athletics. College video available at CollegeQuest.com.

CHAMINADE UNIVERSITY OF HONOLULU
Honolulu, Hawaii

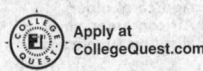

- **Independent Roman Catholic**, comprehensive, founded 1955
- **Degrees** associate, bachelor's, and master's
- **Urban** 62-acre campus
- **Coed**, 1,938 undergraduate students, 58% full-time, 58% women, 42% men
- **Moderately difficult** entrance level, 76% of applicants were admitted
- **16:1 student-to-undergraduate faculty ratio**
- **35.9% graduate** in 6 years or less
- **$11,700 tuition** and fees
- **$9261 average financial aid** package, $21,805 average indebtedness upon graduation, $3.6 million endowment

Students *Undergraduates:* 1,129 full-time, 809 part-time. Students come from 37 states and territories, 5 other countries. *The most frequently chosen baccalaureate fields are:* protective services/public administration, business/marketing, social sciences and history. *Graduate:* 711 in graduate degree programs.

From out-of-state	44%	Reside on campus	13%
Age 25 or older	52%	Transferred in	5%
International students	4%	African Americans	15%
Asian Americans/Pacific Islanders	31%	Hispanic Americans	8%
Native Americans	2%		

Faculty 57 (95% full-time), 60% with terminal degrees.
Expenses (1999–2000) *Comprehensive fee:* $17,370 includes full-time tuition ($11,600), mandatory fees ($100), and room and board ($5670). *College room only:* $3100. Full-time tuition and fees vary according to class time. Room and board charges vary according to board plan and housing facility. *Part-time tuition:* $390 per credit hour. Part-time tuition and fees vary according to class time and course load. *Payment plan:* deferred payment. *Waivers:* employees or children of employees.
Library Sullivan Library. *Operations spending 1999–2000:* $361,138. *Collection:* 139,751 titles, 905 serial subscriptions.
College life *Housing: Options:* coed, women-only. *Most popular organizations:* Chaminade University Student Association, Lumana O Samoa–Chaminade Somoan Club, Chaminade International Student Association, Kaimi Lalakea—Chaminade Hawaiian Club, Residence Hall Association.
Campus security 24-hour emergency response devices and patrols, late-night transport-escort service, controlled dormitory access.
After graduation *Career center:* 1 full-time, 1 part-time personnel. Services include job fairs, resume preparation, interview workshops, resume referral, career/interest testing, career counseling, careers library, job bank, job interviews.
Freshmen 941 applied, 715 admitted, 134 enrolled.

Average high school GPA	3.13	SAT verbal scores above 500	31%
SAT math scores above 500	40%	ACT above 18	84%
From top 10% of their h.s. class	13%	From top quarter	40%
From top half	76%	1998 freshmen returning in 1999	69%

Application *Options:* eApply at www.CollegeQuest.com, Common Application, electronic application, deferred entrance. *Application fee:* $50. *Required:* essay or personal statement; high school transcript. *Required for some:* letters of recommendation; interview.
Standardized tests *Admission: Recommended:* SAT I or ACT.
Significant dates *Application deadlines:* rolling (freshmen), rolling (transfers). *Notification:* 9/8 (freshmen). **Financial aid deadline priority date:** 3/1.

Freshman Application Contact
Office of Admissions, Chaminade University of Honolulu, 3140 Waialae Avenue, Honolulu, HI 96816-1578. **Phone:** 808-735-4735. **Toll-free phone:** 800-735-3733. **Fax:** 808-739-4647. **E-mail:** cuhadmin@lava.net
Visit CollegeQuest.com for information on majors offered and athletics. College video and electronic viewbook available at CollegeQuest.com.

■ *See page 1400 for a narrative description.*

HAWAII PACIFIC UNIVERSITY
Honolulu, Hawaii

- **Independent**, comprehensive, founded 1965
- **Degrees** associate, bachelor's, master's, and postbachelor's certificates
- **Urban** 140-acre campus
- **Coed**, 6,230 undergraduate students, 63% full-time, 52% women, 48% men
- **Moderately difficult** entrance level, 78% of applicants were admitted
- **15:1 student-to-undergraduate faculty ratio**
- **38% graduate** in 6 years or less
- **$8460 tuition** and fees
- **$10,794 average financial aid** package, $15,600 average indebtedness upon graduation, $56.6 million endowment

For the 20th straight year, Hawaii Pacific University has seen an increase in its fall enrollment. Students from all 50 states and more than 100 countries chose HPU to live and learn. Also, HPU will be celebrating its 30th anniversary in September 2000.

Students *Undergraduates:* 3,926 full-time, 2,304 part-time. Students come from 52 states and territories, 101 other countries. *The most frequently chosen baccalaureate fields are:* business/marketing, computer/information sciences, health professions and related sciences. *Graduate:* 1,150 in graduate degree programs.

From out-of-state	35%	Reside on campus	10%
Age 25 or older	28%	Transferred in	17%
International students	27%	African Americans	8%
Asian Americans/Pacific Islanders	26%	Hispanic Americans	5%
Native Americans	1%		

Faculty 705 (32% full-time), 77% with terminal degrees.
Expenses (1999–2000) *Comprehensive fee:* $16,580 includes full-time tuition ($8460) and room and board ($8120). Full-time tuition and fees vary according to program and student level. Room and board charges vary according to housing facility. *Part-time tuition:* $155 per credit. Part-time tuition and fees vary according to course load. *Payment plan:* installment. *Waivers:* employees or children of employees.
Library Meader Library plus 1 other. *Operations spending 1999–2000:* $2.4 million. *Collection:* 160,000 titles, 1,920 serial subscriptions, 5,177 audiovisual materials.
College life *Housing:* Option: coed. *Most popular organizations:* Travel Industry Management Student Organization, International Student Organization, Association of Students of Hawaii Pacific University, President's hosts, Delta Mu Delta.
Campus security 24-hour emergency response devices and patrols, student patrols, late-night transport-escort service.
After graduation 148 organizations recruited on campus 1997–98. 35% of class of 1998 had job offers within 6 months. *Career center:* 10 full-time, 5 part-time personnel. Services include job fairs, resume preparation, interview workshops, resume referral, career/interest testing, career counseling, careers library, job bank, job interviews, pre-employment workshops, career workshops. *Graduate education:* 70% of class of 1999 went directly to graduate and professional school: 40% business, 15% graduate arts and sciences, 5% law.
Freshmen 1,684 applied, 1,306 admitted, 464 enrolled.

Average high school GPA	3.06	SAT verbal scores above 500	50%
SAT math scores above 500	51%	ACT above 18	66%
From top 10% of their h.s. class	10%	From top quarter	30%
From top half	62%		

Application *Options:* eApply at www.CollegeQuest.com, Common Application, electronic application, early admission, deferred entrance. *Application fee:* $50. *Required:* high school transcript; minimum 2.0 GPA. *Required for some:* interview. *Recommended:* essay or personal statement; 2 letters of recommendation.
Standardized tests *Admission: Recommended:* SAT I or ACT.
Significant dates *Application deadlines:* rolling (freshmen), rolling (transfers). *Financial aid deadline priority date:* 3/1.
Freshman Application Contact
Mr. Scott Stensrud, Director of Admissions, Hawaii Pacific University, 1164 Bishop Street, Honolulu, HI 96813-2785. **Phone:** 808-544-0238. **Toll-free phone:** 800-669-4724. **Fax:** 808-544-1136. **E-mail:** admissions@hpu.edu
Visit CollegeQuest.com for information on majors offered and athletics. College video and electronic viewbook available at CollegeQuest.com.

■ *See page 1778 for a narrative description.*

INTERNATIONAL COLLEGE AND GRADUATE SCHOOL
Honolulu, Hawaii

- **Independent interdenominational**, upper-level, founded 1967
- **Degrees** bachelor's, master's, and doctoral
- **Coed**
- **$4100 tuition** and fees

Expenses (1999–2000) *Tuition:* full-time $3840; part-time $160 per semester hour. *Required fees:* full-time $260; $130 per term part-time.
College life *Housing:* college housing not available.
Application *Application fee:* $30.
Admissions Office Contact
International College and Graduate School, 20 Dowsett Avenue, Honolulu, HI 96817. **Fax:** 808-595-4779. **E-mail:** icgs@pixie.com
Visit CollegeQuest.com for information on athletics.

UNIVERSITY OF HAWAII AT HILO
Hilo, Hawaii

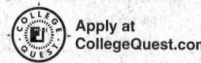

Admissions Office Contact
University of Hawaii at Hilo, 200 West Kawili Street, Hilo, HI 96720-4091. **Toll-free phone:** 800-897-4456. **E-mail:** uhhao@hawaii.edu

UNIVERSITY OF HAWAII AT MANOA
Honolulu, Hawaii

- **State-supported**, university, founded 1907
- **Degrees** bachelor's, master's, doctoral, first professional, and postbachelor's certificates
- **Urban** 300-acre campus
- **Coed**, 11,458 undergraduate students, 83% full-time, 55% women, 45% men
- **Moderately difficult** entrance level, 70% of applicants were admitted
- **11:1 student-to-undergraduate faculty ratio**
- **54.5% graduate** in 6 years or less
- **$3141 tuition** and fees (in-state); $9621 (out-of-state)
- **$5686 average financial aid** package, $12,161 average indebtedness upon graduation, $173.1 million endowment

Part of University of Hawaii System.
Students *Undergraduates:* 9,518 full-time, 1,940 part-time. Students come from 45 states and territories, 82 other countries. *The most frequently chosen baccalaureate fields are:* business/marketing, education, social sciences and history. *Graduate:* 476 in professional programs, 5,197 in other graduate degree programs.

Hawaii–Idaho

University of Hawaii at Manoa *(continued)*

From out-of-state	6%	Reside on campus	21%
Age 25 or older	20%	Transferred in	11%
International students	5%	African Americans	1%
Asian Americans/Pacific Islanders	76%	Hispanic Americans	1%
Native Americans	0.2%		

Faculty 1,136 (92% full-time), 83% with terminal degrees.

Expenses (1999–2000) *Tuition, state resident:* full-time $3024; part-time $126 per credit. *Tuition, nonresident:* full-time $9504; part-time $396 per credit. *Required fees:* full-time $117; $48 per term part-time. Full-time tuition and fees vary according to class time, course load, and program. Part-time tuition and fees vary according to class time, course load, and program. *College room and board:* $5297; room only: $3125. Room and board charges vary according to board plan and housing facility. *Waivers:* minority students, adult students, and employees or children of employees.

Library University of Hawaii at Monoa Library plus 6 others. *Operations spending 1999–2000:* $11 million. *Collection:* 26,895 serial subscriptions.

College life *Housing: Options:* coed, men-only, women-only, disabled students. *Social organizations:* national fraternities, national sororities, local fraternities, local sororities; 2% of eligible men and 1% of eligible women are members. *Most popular organizations:* Associated Students of University of Hawaii, Campus Center Board, Broadcast Communication Authority, Board of Publications, Student Activities and Program Fee Board.

Campus security 24-hour emergency response devices and patrols, late-night transport-escort service, controlled dormitory access.

After graduation 82 organizations recruited on campus 1997–98. *Career center:* 7 full-time personnel. Services include job fairs, resume preparation, interview workshops, resume referral, career counseling, careers library, job bank, job interviews. **Major awards:** 2 Fulbright Scholars.

Freshmen 4,466 applied, 3,113 admitted, 1,529 enrolled.

Average high school GPA	3.36	SAT verbal scores above 500	64%
SAT math scores above 500	83%	ACT above 18	N/R
From top 10% of their h.s. class	31%	From top quarter	63%
From top half	90%	1998 freshmen returning in 1999	82%

Application Preference given to state residents. *Application fee:* $25. *Required:* high school transcript; minimum 2.8 GPA; minimum SAT I score of 510 for verbal and math sections.

Standardized tests *Admission: Required:* SAT I or ACT.

Significant dates *Application deadlines:* 6/1 (freshmen), 6/1 (transfers). *Financial aid deadline priority date:* 3/1.

Freshman Application Contact
Dr. David Robb, Director of Admissions and Records, University of Hawaii at Manoa, 2600 Campus Road, Room 001, Honolulu, HI 96822. **Phone:** 808-956-8975. **Toll-free phone:** 800-823-9771. **E-mail:** ar-info@hawaii.edu

Visit CollegeQuest.com for information on majors offered and athletics.

UNIVERSITY OF HAWAII—WEST OAHU
Pearl City, Hawaii

- **State-supported**, upper-level, founded 1976
- **Degree** bachelor's
- **Small-town** campus with easy access to Honolulu
- **Coed**
- **Moderately difficult** entrance level
- **$1906 tuition** and fees (in-state); $7042 (out-of-state)

Part of University of Hawaii System.

Expenses (1999–2000) *Tuition, state resident:* full-time $1896; part-time $79 per credit. *Tuition, nonresident:* full-time $7032; part-time $293 per credit. *Required fees:* full-time $10; $5 per term part-time.

College life *Housing:* college housing not available.

Campus security 24-hour emergency response devices and patrols, late-night transport-escort service.

Application Preference given to state residents. *Application fee:* $25.

Admissions Office Contact
University of Hawaii–West Oahu, 96-129 Ala Ike, Pearl City, HI 96782-3366. **E-mail:** okazaki@uhwoa.uhwo.hawaii.edu

Visit CollegeQuest.com for information on athletics.

IDAHO

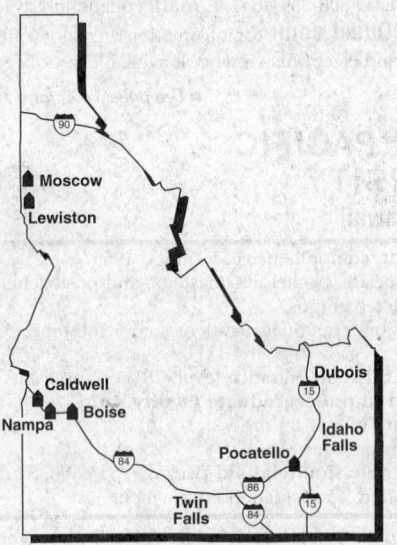

ALBERTSON COLLEGE OF IDAHO
Caldwell, Idaho

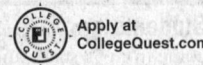
Apply at CollegeQuest.com

- **Independent**, 4-year, founded 1891
- **Degree** bachelor's
- **Small-town** 43-acre campus
- **Coed**, 763 undergraduate students, 96% full-time, 57% women, 43% men
- **Moderately difficult** entrance level, 83% of applicants were admitted
- **12:1 student-to-undergraduate faculty ratio**
- **$16,280 tuition** and fees
- **$11,734 average financial aid** package, $15,460 average indebtedness upon graduation, $63 million endowment

Students *Undergraduates:* 733 full-time, 30 part-time. Students come from 24 states and territories, 7 other countries. *The most frequently chosen baccalaureate fields are:* biological/life sciences, business/marketing, social sciences and history.

Reside on campus	50%	Age 25 or older	3%
Transferred in	6%	International students	2%
African Americans	1%	Asian Americans/Pacific Islanders	4%
Hispanic Americans	4%	Native Americans	1%

Faculty 60, 90% with terminal degrees.

Expenses (1999–2000) *Comprehensive fee:* $20,480 includes full-time tuition ($16,000), mandatory fees ($280), and room and board ($4200). *College room only:* $2000. Room and board charges vary according to board plan and housing facility. *Part-time tuition:* $670 per credit. *Part-time fees:* $69 per term part-time. Part-time tuition and fees vary according to program. *Payment plan:* installment. *Waivers:* children of alumni, adult students, senior citizens, and employees or children of employees.

Library Terteling Library plus 1 other. *Operations spending 1999–2000:* $299,139. *Collection:* 178,719 titles, 75,826 serial subscriptions.

College life *Housing:* on-campus residence required through sophomore year. *Options:* coed, women-only. *Social organizations:* national fraternities, national sororities, local fraternities, local sororities; 15% of eligible men and 15% of eligible women are members. *Most popular organizations:* Scarlet Masque Drama Group, Albertson Latin American Students, Students in Free Enterprise, Theta Theta Theta Sorority, Delta Tau Delta Fraternity.

Campus security 24-hour emergency response devices and patrols, student patrols, late-night transport-escort service, controlled dormitory access.

After graduation 15 organizations recruited on campus 1997–98. 60% of class of 1998 had job offers within 6 months. *Career center:* 1 full-time personnel. Services include job fairs, resume preparation, interview workshops, resume referral, career/interest testing, career counseling, careers

Idaho

library, job bank, job interviews. *Graduate education:* 22% of class of 1999 went directly to graduate and professional school.

Freshmen 887 applied, 734 admitted, 211 enrolled. 10 National Merit Scholars, 26 valedictorians.

Average high school GPA	3.6	SAT verbal scores above 500	77%
SAT math scores above 500	73%	ACT above 18	97%
From top 10% of their h.s. class	33%	From top quarter	59%
From top half	84%	1998 freshmen returning in 1999	73%

Application *Options:* eApply at www.CollegeQuest.com, Common Application, early admission, early action, deferred entrance. *Application fee:* $25. *Required:* essay or personal statement; high school transcript; 1 letter of recommendation. *Recommended:* interview.

Standardized tests *Admission: Required:* SAT I or ACT.

Significant dates *Application deadlines:* 6/1 (freshmen), 8/1 (transfers). *Early action:* 11/15. *Notification:* 12/15 (early action). *Financial aid deadline priority date:* 2/15.

Freshman Application Contact
Mr. Dennis P. Bergvall, Dean of Admissions, Albertson College of Idaho, 2112 Cleveland Boulevard, Caldwell, ID 83605-4494. **Phone:** 208-459-5305. **Toll-free phone:** 800-AC-IDAHO. **Fax:** 208-454-2077. **E-mail:** admission@acofi.edu

Visit CollegeQuest.com for information on majors offered and athletics. College video available at CollegeQuest.com.

■ *See page 1140 for a narrative description.*

BOISE BIBLE COLLEGE
Boise, Idaho

- **Independent nondenominational**, 4-year, founded 1945
- **Degrees** associate and bachelor's
- **Suburban** 17-acre campus
- **Coed**, 104 undergraduate students, 82% full-time, 38% women, 63% men
- **Minimally difficult** entrance level, 98% of applicants were admitted
- **15:1 student-to-undergraduate faculty ratio**
- **20% graduate** in 6 years or less
- **$4630 tuition** and fees
- **$6001 average financial aid** package, $507,870 endowment

Students *Undergraduates:* 85 full-time, 19 part-time. Students come from 9 states and territories. *The most frequently chosen baccalaureate field is:* philosophy.

| Age 25 or older | 24% | Transferred in | 13% |

Faculty 11 (64% full-time).

Expenses (1999–2000) *Comprehensive fee:* $8230 includes full-time tuition ($4560), mandatory fees ($70), and room and board ($3600). Room and board charges vary according to student level. *Part-time tuition:* $190 per semester hour. *Part-time fees:* $2 per semester hour. *Payment plan:* installment. *Waivers:* employees or children of employees.

Library Boise Bible College Library. *Operations spending 1999–2000:* $35,153. *Collection:* 29,431 titles, 115 serial subscriptions.

College life *Housing:* on-campus residence required through sophomore year. *Options:* men-only, women-only. *Most popular organizations:* Concert Choir, Missions, Women's TLC, Spiritual families, drama club.

Campus security Patrols by police officers.

After graduation 6 organizations recruited on campus 1997–98. 100% of class of 1998 had job offers within 6 months. *Career center:* 1 full-time personnel. Services include career counseling.

Freshmen 59 applied, 58 admitted, 26 enrolled.

Average high school GPA	3.19	SAT verbal scores above 500	38%
SAT math scores above 500	38%	ACT above 18	54%
From top 10% of their h.s. class	13%	From top quarter	33%
From top half	67%	1998 freshmen returning in 1999	56%

Application *Option:* deferred entrance. *Application fee:* $25. *Required:* essay or personal statement; high school transcript; minimum 2.0 GPA; 3 letters of recommendation. *Recommended:* interview.

Significant dates *Application deadlines:* rolling (freshmen), rolling (transfers). *Financial aid deadline priority date:* 5/1.

Freshman Application Contact
Mr. Ross Knudsen, Director of Admissions, Boise Bible College, 8695 Marigold Street, Boise, ID 83704. **Phone:** 208-376-7731. **Toll-free phone:** 800-893-7755. **Fax:** 208-376-7743. **E-mail:** boibible@micron.net

Visit CollegeQuest.com for information on majors offered and athletics. College video and electronic viewbook available at CollegeQuest.com.

BOISE STATE UNIVERSITY
Boise, Idaho

- **State-supported**, comprehensive, founded 1932
- **Degrees** associate, bachelor's, master's, and doctoral
- **Urban** 130-acre campus
- **Coed**, 13,129 undergraduate students, 66% full-time, 55% women, 45% men
- **Minimally difficult** entrance level, 82% of applicants were admitted
- **17:1 student-to-undergraduate faculty ratio**
- **21% graduate** in 6 years or less
- **$2283 tuition** and fees (in-state); $8163 (out-of-state)
- **$47.4 million endowment**

Part of Idaho System of Higher Education.

Students *Undergraduates:* 8,659 full-time, 4,470 part-time. Students come from 53 states and territories, 44 other countries. *The most frequently chosen baccalaureate fields are:* business/marketing, education, health professions and related sciences.

From out-of-state	10%	Reside on campus	8%
Age 25 or older	44%	Transferred in	10%
International students	1%	African Americans	1%
Asian Americans/Pacific Islanders	2%	Hispanic Americans	4%
Native Americans	1%		

Faculty 984 (53% full-time), 79% with terminal degrees.

Expenses (1999–2000) *Tuition, state resident:* full-time $0; part-time $115 per credit. *Tuition, nonresident:* full-time $5880; part-time $115 per credit. *Required fees:* full-time $2283. Part-time tuition and fees vary according to course load. *College room and board:* $3558. Room and board charges vary according to board plan and housing facility. *Payment plan:* deferred payment. *Waivers:* senior citizens and employees or children of employees.

Library Albertsons Library. *Operations spending 1999–2000:* $5 million. *Collection:* 505,618 titles, 4,797 serial subscriptions.

College life *Housing: Option:* coed. *Social organizations:* national fraternities, national sororities, local fraternities, local sororities; 1% of eligible men and 1% of eligible women are members. *Most popular organizations:* Latter-Day Saints Student Association, Residence Hall Association, Organization of Student Social Workers, Marching Band Association, Teacher Education Association.

Campus security 24-hour emergency response devices and patrols.

After graduation 40 organizations recruited on campus 1997–98. 85% of class of 1998 had job offers within 6 months. *Career center:* 5 full-time, 1 part-time personnel. Services include job fairs, resume preparation, resume referral, career counseling, careers library, job bank, job interviews. *Graduate education:* 40% of class of 1999 went directly to graduate and professional school: 20% education, 8% business, 5% graduate arts and sciences, 4% engineering.

Freshmen 5,476 applied, 4,496 admitted, 2,083 enrolled.

Average high school GPA	3.1	SAT verbal scores above 500	52%
SAT math scores above 500	49%	ACT above 18	86%
From top 10% of their h.s. class	12%	From top quarter	40%
From top half	75%	1998 freshmen returning in 1999	59%

Application *Option:* electronic application. *Application fee:* $20. *Required for some:* high school transcript; minimum 2.0 GPA.

Standardized tests *Admission: Required for some:* SAT I or ACT.

Significant dates *Application deadlines:* 7/19 (freshmen), 7/19 (transfers). *Financial aid deadline priority date:* 3/30.

Freshman Application Contact
Mr. Mark Wheeler, Dean of Enrollment Services, Boise State University, Enrollment Services, 1910 University Drive, Boise, ID 83725. **Phone:** 208-426-1177. **Toll-free phone:** 800-632-6586 (in-state); 800-824-7017 (out-of-state). **E-mail:** bsuinfo@boisestate.edu

Visit CollegeQuest.com for information on majors offered and athletics.

Idaho

IDAHO STATE UNIVERSITY
Pocatello, Idaho

- **State-supported**, university, founded 1901
- **Degrees** associate, bachelor's, master's, doctoral, first professional, post-master's, and postbachelor's certificates
- **Small-town** 735-acre campus
- **Coed**, 9,585 undergraduate students, 74% full-time, 56% women, 44% men
- **Minimally difficult** entrance level, 75% of applicants were admitted
- **24.1% graduate** in 6 years or less
- **$2398 tuition** and fees (in-state); $8638 (out-of-state)
- **$9030 average financial aid** package, $17,657 average indebtedness upon graduation, $31.9 million endowment

Located in a beautiful mountain valley, ISU is a comprehensive university granting certificates through doctoral degrees in a wide range of programs. It is recognized in the state as a center for health professions and supporting sciences as well as for educator preparation. ISU also emphasizes business, engineering, and the liberal arts and has the largest school in Idaho.

Students *Undergraduates:* 7,135 full-time, 2,450 part-time. Students come from 40 states and territories, 44 other countries. *The most frequently chosen baccalaureate fields are:* business/marketing, education, health professions and related sciences. *Graduate:* 225 in professional programs, 2,038 in other graduate degree programs.

From out-of-state	5%	Reside on campus	6%
Age 25 or older	35%	Transferred in	12%
International students	1%	African Americans	1%
Asian Americans/Pacific Islanders	1%	Hispanic Americans	3%
Native Americans	2%		

Faculty 663 (86% full-time).

Expenses (1999–2000) *Tuition, state resident:* full-time $0. *Tuition, nonresident:* full-time $6240; part-time $90 per credit. *Required fees:* full-time $2398; $119 per credit. Full-time tuition and fees vary according to reciprocity agreements. Part-time tuition and fees vary according to reciprocity agreements. *College room and board:* $3780; room only: $1640. Room and board charges vary according to board plan and housing facility. *Payment plan:* deferred payment. *Waivers:* senior citizens and employees or children of employees.

Library Eli M. Oboler Library. *Operations spending 1999–2000:* $3.9 million. *Collection:* 345,066 titles, 3,336 serial subscriptions, 4,500 audiovisual materials.

College life *Housing: Options:* coed, men-only, women-only, disabled students. *Social organizations:* national fraternities, national sororities, local fraternities, local sororities; 1% of eligible men and 1% of eligible women are members. *Most popular organizations:* International Students Association, Vocational Industrial Clubs of America, Latter Day Saints Student Association, Student American Dental Hygienists Association, Academy of Students of Pharmacy.

Campus security 24-hour emergency response devices and patrols, student patrols, late-night transport-escort service, controlled dormitory access.

After graduation 24 organizations recruited on campus 1997–98. *Career center:* 10 full-time, 6 part-time personnel. Services include job fairs, resume preparation, interview workshops, resume referral, career/interest testing, career counseling, careers library, job bank, job interviews.

Freshmen 3,795 applied, 2,838 admitted, 1,613 enrolled.

Average high school GPA	3.18	SAT verbal scores above 500	N/R
SAT math scores above 500	N/R	ACT above 18	88%
From top quarter of their h.s. class	55%	From top half	90%
1998 freshmen returning in 1999	49%		

Application *Options:* Common Application, early admission, deferred entrance. *Application fee:* $20. *Required:* high school transcript; minimum 2.0 GPA.

Standardized tests *Admission: Required:* SAT I or ACT.

Significant dates *Application deadlines:* 8/1 (freshmen), 8/1 (transfers). *Financial aid deadline:* 6/30. Priority date: 3/15.

Freshman Application Contact
Mr. Guy Hollingsworth, Director of Recruitment, Idaho State University, Campus Box 8270, Pocatello, ID 83209. **Phone:** 208-282-3279. **Fax:** 208-236-4314. **E-mail:** info@isu.edu

Visit CollegeQuest.com for information on majors offered and athletics. College video available at CollegeQuest.com.

■ *See page 1816 for a narrative description.*

ITT TECHNICAL INSTITUTE
Boise, Idaho

- **Proprietary**, primarily 2-year, founded 1906
- **Degrees** associate and bachelor's
- **Urban** 1-acre campus
- **Coed**
- **Minimally difficult** entrance level
- **$9190 tuition** and fees

Part of ITT Educational Services, Inc.

Admissions Office Contact
ITT Technical Institute, 12302 West Explorer Drive, Boise, ID 83713. **Toll-free phone:** 800-666-4888. **Fax:** 208-322-0173.

Visit CollegeQuest.com for information on majors offered and athletics. College video available at CollegeQuest.com.

LEWIS-CLARK STATE COLLEGE
Lewiston, Idaho

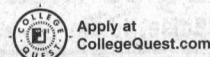
Apply at CollegeQuest.com

- **State-supported**, 4-year, founded 1893
- **Degrees** associate and bachelor's
- **Small-town** 44-acre campus
- **Coed**, 3,151 undergraduate students, 59% full-time, 59% women, 41% men
- **Minimally difficult** entrance level, 82% of applicants were admitted
- **17:1 student-to-undergraduate faculty ratio**
- **$2204 tuition** and fees (in-state); $7476 (out-of-state)
- **$5562 average financial aid** package, $509,158 endowment

Students *Undergraduates:* 1,869 full-time, 1,282 part-time. Students come from 21 states and territories, 21 other countries. *The most frequently chosen baccalaureate fields are:* business/marketing, education, health professions and related sciences.

From out-of-state	16%	Reside on campus	10%
Age 25 or older	40%	Transferred in	9%
International students	4%	African Americans	0.4%
Asian Americans/Pacific Islanders	1%	Hispanic Americans	2%
Native Americans	5%		

Faculty 303 (39% full-time), 86% with terminal degrees.

Expenses (1999–2000) *Tuition, state resident:* full-time $0; part-time $102 per credit. *Tuition, nonresident:* full-time $5272; part-time $102 per credit. *Required fees:* full-time $2204. *College room and board:* $3500. Room and board charges vary according to board plan and housing facility. *Payment plan:* deferred payment. *Waivers:* senior citizens and employees or children of employees.

Library Lewis-Clark State College Library. *Operations spending 1999–2000:* $935,613. *Collection:* 169,481 titles, 1,825 serial subscriptions, 6,797 audiovisual materials.

College life *Housing: Options:* coed, men-only, women-only, cooperative. *Most popular organizations:* Business Students Organization, ambassadors club, international club, Honors Society, Explorers.

Campus security 24-hour emergency response devices and patrols, student patrols, late-night transport-escort service.

After graduation 23 organizations recruited on campus 1997–98. 36% of class of 1998 had job offers within 6 months. *Career center:* 2 full-time, 1 part-time personnel. Services include job fairs, resume preparation, resume referral, career/interest testing, career counseling, careers library, job bank, job interviews. *Graduate education:* 8% of class of 1999 went directly to graduate and professional school.

Idaho

Freshmen 884 applied, 726 admitted, 486 enrolled.

Average high school GPA	2.95	SAT verbal scores above 500	46%
SAT math scores above 500	46%	ACT above 18	69%
From top 10% of their h.s. class	6%	From top quarter	21%
From top half	53%	1998 freshmen returning in 1999	50%

Application *Options:* eApply at www.CollegeQuest.com, Common Application, electronic application, early admission, deferred entrance. *Application fee:* $20. *Required:* high school transcript; minimum 2.0 GPA. *Required for some:* essay or personal statement; interview.

Standardized tests *Admission: Required for some:* SAT I or ACT.

Significant dates *Application deadlines:* rolling (freshmen), rolling (transfers). *Financial aid deadline priority date:* 3/1.

Freshman Application Contact
Ms. Rosanne English, Office Specialist II, Lewis-Clark State College, 500 8th Avenue, Lewiston, ID 83501. **Phone:** 208-799-2210. **Toll-free phone:** 800-933-LCSC Ext. 2210. **Fax:** 208-799-2063. **E-mail:** admoff@lcsc.edu

Visit CollegeQuest.com for information on majors offered and athletics. College video and electronic viewbook available at CollegeQuest.com.

NORTHWEST NAZARENE UNIVERSITY
Nampa, Idaho

- **Independent**, comprehensive, founded 1913, affiliated with Church of the Nazarene
- **Degrees** bachelor's and master's
- **Small-town** 85-acre campus
- **Coed**, 1,085 undergraduate students, 96% full-time, 57% women, 43% men
- **Moderately difficult** entrance level, 71% of applicants were admitted
- **14:1 student-to-undergraduate faculty ratio**
- **$13,500 tuition** and fees
- **$9759 average financial aid** package, $19,545 average indebtedness upon graduation, $11.7 million endowment

NNC has been named a *U.S. News & World Report* "Top Ten Liberal Arts College" for 6 straight years. New programs such as nursing and criminal justice, 3 new buildings in 2 years, and 6 new intercollegiate sports for men and women are just a few signs of change and growth at this forward-moving college.

Students *Undergraduates:* 1,045 full-time, 40 part-time. Students come from 22 states and territories. *The most frequently chosen baccalaureate fields are:* education, business/marketing, philosophy. *Graduate:* 729 in graduate degree programs.

From out-of-state	68%	Reside on campus	68%
Age 25 or older	6%	Transferred in	7%
International students	0.5%	African Americans	1%
Asian Americans/Pacific Islanders	1%	Hispanic Americans	2%
Native Americans	1%		

Faculty 84 (99% full-time).

Expenses (2000–2001) *Comprehensive fee:* $17,520 includes full-time tuition ($12,990), mandatory fees ($510), and room and board ($4020). Room and board charges vary according to board plan and student level. Part-time tuition and fees vary according to course load. *Payment plans:* tuition prepayment, installment. *Waivers:* employees or children of employees.

Library John E. Riley Library. *Operations spending 1999–2000:* $246,797. *Collection:* 100,966 titles, 821 serial subscriptions.

College life *Housing:* on-campus residence required through junior year. *Options:* coed, men-only, women-only. *Most popular organizations:* student government, Are You Serving Him (RUSH), ministry clubs, service clubs, science clubs.

Campus security 24-hour patrols, student patrols, late-night transport-escort service, controlled dormitory access, residence hall check-in system.

After graduation *Career center:* Services include job fairs, resume preparation, interview workshops, resume referral, career/interest testing, career counseling, careers library, job bank, job interviews.

Freshmen 731 applied, 517 admitted, 310 enrolled. 4 National Merit Scholars, 13 valedictorians, 49 student government officers.

Average high school GPA	3.33	SAT verbal scores above 500	N/R
SAT math scores above 500	N/R	ACT above 18	90%
From top 10% of their h.s. class	27%	From top quarter	56%
From top half	73%	1998 freshmen returning in 1999	72%

Application *Options:* electronic application, early admission, deferred entrance. *Application fee:* $20. *Required:* high school transcript; minimum 2.5 GPA; 2 letters of recommendation. *Required for some:* interview.

Standardized tests *Admission: Recommended:* ACT. *Required for some:* ACT.

Significant dates *Application deadlines:* 9/1 (freshmen), 9/1 (transfers). *Financial aid deadline priority date:* 3/1.

Freshman Application Contact
Mr. Jim Butkus, Director of Admissions, Northwest Nazarene University, 623 Holly Street, Nampa, ID 83686. **Phone:** 208-467-8648. **Toll-free phone:** 877-NNU-4YOU. **Fax:** 208-467-8645. **E-mail:** admissions@nnu.edu

Visit CollegeQuest.com for information on majors offered and athletics.

■ *See page 2192 for a narrative description.*

UNIVERSITY OF IDAHO
Moscow, Idaho

- **State-supported**, university, founded 1889
- **Degrees** bachelor's, master's, doctoral, first professional, and post-master's certificates
- **Small-town** 1,450-acre campus
- **Coed**, 7,989 undergraduate students, 92% full-time, 46% women, 54% men
- **Moderately difficult** entrance level, 80% of applicants were admitted
- **17:1 student-to-undergraduate faculty ratio**
- **48.3% graduate** in 6 years or less
- **$2348 tuition** and fees (in-state); $8348 (out-of-state)
- **$4800 average financial aid** package, $18,465 average indebtedness upon graduation, $150.4 million endowment

Students *Undergraduates:* 7,310 full-time, 679 part-time. Students come from 52 states and territories, 40 other countries. *The most frequently chosen baccalaureate fields are:* business/marketing, education, engineering/engineering technologies. *Graduate:* 316 in professional programs, 2,398 in other graduate degree programs.

From out-of-state	20%	Age 25 or older	16%
Transferred in	8%	International students	2%
African Americans	1%	Asian Americans/Pacific Islanders	2%
Hispanic Americans	2%	Native Americans	1%

Expenses (1999–2000) *Tuition, state resident:* full-time $0. *Tuition, nonresident:* full-time $6000; part-time $95 per credit. *Required fees:* full-time $2348; $117 per credit. Full-time tuition and fees vary according to program and reciprocity agreements. Part-time tuition and fees vary according to course load. *College room and board:* $3952. Room and board charges vary according to board plan and housing facility. *Payment plan:* deferred payment. *Waivers:* employees or children of employees.

Library University of Idaho Library plus 1 other. *Operations spending 1999–2000:* $5.7 million. *Collection:* 1.2 million titles, 10,497 serial subscriptions.

College life *Housing: Options:* coed, men-only, women-only, cooperative. *Social organizations:* national fraternities, national sororities; 28% of eligible men and 20% of eligible women are members. *Most popular organizations:* Alpha Phi Omega, Campus Crusade for Christ, Student International Association, OELA, Students of Human Resource Management.

Campus security Late-night transport-escort service, controlled dormitory access.

After graduation 152 organizations recruited on campus 1997–98. 93% of class of 1998 had job offers within 6 months. *Career center:* 5 full-time personnel. Services include job fairs, resume preparation, career counseling, careers library, job interviews. *Major awards:* 4 Fulbright Scholars.

Freshmen 3,687 applied, 2,963 admitted, 1,453 enrolled. 12 National Merit Scholars.

Average high school GPA	3.41	SAT verbal scores above 500	72%
SAT math scores above 500	73%	ACT above 18	93%
From top 10% of their h.s. class	22%	From top quarter	51%
From top half	84%	1998 freshmen returning in 1999	80%

Idaho–Illinois

University of Idaho (continued)

Application *Option:* deferred entrance. *Application fee:* $30. *Required:* high school transcript.

Standardized tests *Admission: Required:* SAT I or ACT.

Significant dates *Application deadlines:* 8/1 (freshmen), rolling (transfers). *Financial aid deadline priority date:* 2/15.

Freshman Application Contact
Mr. Dan Davenport, Director of Admissions, University of Idaho, Admissions Office, Moscow, ID 83844-3133. **Phone:** 208-885-6326. **Toll-free phone:** 888-884-3246. **Fax:** 208-885-5752. **E-mail:** admappl@uidaho.edu

Visit CollegeQuest.com for information on majors offered and athletics.

The Chicago area includes the towns of Aurora, Addison, De Kalb, Deerfield, Elgin, Elmhurst, Evanston, Hoffman Estates, Joliet, Lake Forest, Lisle, Lombard, Mount Prospect, Naperville, North Chicago, Oak Park, Palos Heights, River Forest, Romeoville, Skokie, University Park, and Wheaton.

AMERICAN ACADEMY OF ART
Chicago, Illinois

- **Proprietary**, 4-year, founded 1923
- **Degrees** associate and bachelor's
- **Urban** campus
- **Coed**, 409 undergraduate students, 86% full-time, 34% women, 66% men
- **Moderately difficult** entrance level, 100% of applicants were admitted
- **12:1 student-to-undergraduate faculty ratio**
- **$14,280 tuition** and fees

Students *Undergraduates:* 350 full-time, 59 part-time. Students come from 5 states and territories. *The most frequently chosen baccalaureate field is:* visual/performing arts.

Age 25 or older	34%	Transferred in	9%
International students	0.5%	African Americans	8%
Asian Americans/Pacific Islanders	8%	Hispanic Americans	21%

Faculty 40 (63% full-time), 60% with terminal degrees.

Expenses (1999–2000) *Tuition:* full-time $14,280; part-time $3570 per term. Full-time tuition and fees vary according to course load. Part-time tuition and fees vary according to course load. *Payment plan:* installment. *Waivers:* employees or children of employees.

Library Irving Shapiro Library. *Collection:* 1,730 titles, 62 serial subscriptions, 101 audiovisual materials.

College life *Housing:* college housing not available.

Campus security 24-hour emergency response devices.

After graduation 2 organizations recruited on campus 1997–98. 75% of class of 1998 had job offers within 6 months. *Career center:* 1 full-time personnel. Services include resume preparation, resume referral, career counseling, careers library, job bank, job interviews.

Freshmen 111 applied, 111 admitted, 106 enrolled.

| SAT verbal scores above 500 | N/R | SAT math scores above 500 | N/R |
| ACT above 18 | N/R | 1998 freshmen returning in 1999 | 82% |

Application *Application fee:* $25.

Significant dates *Application deadlines:* rolling (freshmen), rolling (transfers). *Financial aid deadline:* continuous.

Freshman Application Contact
Ms. Ione Fitzgerald, Director of Admissions, American Academy of Art, 332 South Michigan Ave, Suite 300, Chicago, IL 60604-4302. **Phone:** 312-461-0600 Ext. 143.

Visit CollegeQuest.com for information on majors offered and athletics. College video available at CollegeQuest.com.

AUGUSTANA COLLEGE
Rock Island, Illinois

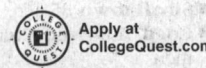 Apply at CollegeQuest.com

- **Independent**, 4-year, founded 1860, affiliated with Evangelical Lutheran Church in America
- **Degree** bachelor's
- **Suburban** 115-acre campus
- **Coed**, 2,184 undergraduate students, 99% full-time, 59% women, 41% men
- **Moderately difficult** entrance level, 80% of applicants were admitted
- **13:1 student-to-undergraduate faculty ratio**
- **$17,187 tuition** and fees
- **$13,518 average financial aid** package, $15,672 average indebtedness upon graduation, $73.8 million endowment

Students *Undergraduates:* 2,167 full-time, 17 part-time. Students come from 26 states and territories. *The most frequently chosen baccalaureate fields are:* biological/life sciences, business/marketing, health professions and related sciences.

From out-of-state	13%	Reside on campus	68%
Age 25 or older	1%	Transferred in	3%
International students	0.4%	African Americans	3%
Asian Americans/Pacific Islanders	2%	Hispanic Americans	3%
Native Americans	0.2%		

Faculty 198 (71% full-time), 63% with terminal degrees.

Expenses (1999–2000) *Comprehensive fee:* $22,224 includes full-time tuition ($16,866), mandatory fees ($321), and room and board ($5037). *College room only:* $2556. Room and board charges vary according to housing facility. *Part-time tuition:* $705 per credit. Part-time tuition and fees vary according to course load. *Payment plans:* tuition prepayment, installment. *Waivers:* employees or children of employees.

Library Augustana College Library plus 3 others. *Operations spending 1999–2000:* $1.5 million. *Collection:* 227,357 titles, 1,870 serial subscriptions, 2,639 audiovisual materials.

College life *Housing:* on-campus residence required through junior year. *Options:* coed, men-only, women-only. *Social organizations:* local fraternities, local sororities; 36% of eligible men and 40% of eligible women are members. *Most popular organizations:* College Union Board of Managers, Student Government Association, Greek Council, Augustana Literacy Council, student radio station.

Campus security 24-hour emergency response devices and patrols, late-night transport-escort service, controlled dormitory access.

After graduation 166 organizations recruited on campus 1997–98. 64% of class of 1998 had job offers within 6 months. *Career center:* 4 full-time, 1

Illinois

part-time personnel. Services include job fairs, resume preparation, interview workshops, resume referral, career/interest testing, career counseling, careers library, job bank, job interviews. *Graduate education:* 33% of class of 1999 went directly to graduate and professional school: 20% graduate arts and sciences, 5% medicine, 3% business, 3% law, 1% dentistry, 1% engineering.

Freshmen 2,293 applied, 1,838 admitted, 565 enrolled.

Average high school GPA	3.5	SAT verbal scores above 500	N/R
SAT math scores above 500	N/R	ACT above 18	100%
From top 10% of their h.s. class	33%	From top quarter	69%
From top half	95%	1998 freshmen returning in 1999	83%

Application *Options:* eApply at www.CollegeQuest.com, Common Application, deferred entrance. *Application fee:* $25. *Required:* high school transcript. *Required for some:* essay or personal statement; 2 letters of recommendation; interview.

Standardized tests *Admission: Required:* SAT I or ACT.

Significant dates *Application deadlines:* rolling (freshmen), rolling (transfers). *Financial aid deadline priority date:* 4/1.

Freshman Application Contact
Mr. Martin Sauer, Director of Admissions, Augustana College, 639 38th Street, Rock Island, IL 61201-2296. **Phone:** 309-794-7341. **Toll-free phone:** 800-798-8100. **Fax:** 309-794-7431. **E-mail:** admissions@augustana.edu

Visit CollegeQuest.com for information on majors offered and athletics. College video available at CollegeQuest.com.

AURORA UNIVERSITY
Aurora, Illinois

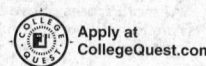
Apply at CollegeQuest.com

- **Independent**, comprehensive, founded 1893
- **Degrees** bachelor's and master's
- **Suburban** 26-acre campus with easy access to Chicago
- **Coed**
- **Moderately difficult** entrance level
- **$12,480 tuition** and fees

Aurora University combines the resources of commuting students with a residence hall population that includes students from 20 states and 5 countries. Curriculum has a strong emphasis on human services supplemented by the John and Judy Dunham School of Business and University College of Arts and Sciences. The YMCA Senior Director Certificate Program is a supplemental major offered in cooperation with the YMCA of the USA.

Expenses (1999–2000) *Comprehensive fee:* $17,142 includes full-time tuition ($12,480) and room and board ($4662). Full-time tuition and fees vary according to course load, location, and program. Room and board charges vary according to board plan and housing facility. *Part-time tuition:* $427 per credit hour. Part-time tuition and fees vary according to location and program.

Institutional Web site http://www.aurora.edu/

College life *Housing: Options:* coed, men-only, women-only. *Social organizations:* national fraternities, national sororities, local fraternities, local sororities; 20% of eligible men and 20% of eligible women are members. *Most popular organizations:* Black Student Association, Aurora University Student Association, Latin American Organization.

Campus security 24-hour patrols, late-night transport-escort service, controlled dormitory access.

Application *Options:* eApply at www.CollegeQuest.com, Common Application, electronic application, early admission, deferred entrance. *Application fee:* $25. *Required:* essay or personal statement; high school transcript. *Required for some:* 2 letters of recommendation; interview. *Recommended:* interview.

Standardized tests *Admission: Required:* ACT. *Recommended:* SAT I.

Admissions Office Contact
Aurora University, 347 South Gladstone Avenue, Aurora, IL 60506-4892. **Toll-free phone:** 800-742-5281. **Fax:** 630-844-5535. **E-mail:** admissions@admin.aurora.edu

Visit CollegeQuest.com for information on athletics. College video available at CollegeQuest.com.

■ *See page 1212 for a narrative description.*

BARAT COLLEGE
Lake Forest, Illinois

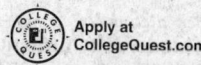
Apply at CollegeQuest.com

- **Independent Roman Catholic**, comprehensive, founded 1858
- **Degrees** bachelor's and master's
- **Suburban** 30-acre campus with easy access to Chicago and Milwaukee
- **Coed**, 725 undergraduate students, 69% full-time, 75% women, 25% men
- **Moderately difficult** entrance level, 94% of applicants were admitted
- **13:1 student-to-undergraduate faculty ratio**
- **38% graduate** in 6 years or less
- **$13,500 tuition** and fees
- **$1.7 million endowment**

Students *Undergraduates:* 503 full-time, 222 part-time. Students come from 24 states and territories. *The most frequently chosen baccalaureate fields are:* social sciences and history, health professions and related sciences, visual/performing arts. *Graduate:* 63 in graduate degree programs.

From out-of-state	20%	Reside on campus	27%
Age 25 or older	41%	International students	0.3%
African Americans	11%	Asian Americans/Pacific Islanders	4%
Hispanic Americans	8%	Native Americans	1%

Faculty 101 (41% full-time), 56% with terminal degrees.

Expenses (1999–2000) *Comprehensive fee:* $18,750 includes full-time tuition ($13,500) and room and board ($5250). Full-time tuition and fees vary according to course load. *Part-time tuition:* $450 per credit hour. Part-time tuition and fees vary according to course load. *Payment plan:* deferred payment. *Waivers:* employees or children of employees.

Library Barat College Library. *Operations spending 1999–2000:* $450,000. *Collection:* 110,000 titles, 400 serial subscriptions.

College life *Housing: Options:* coed, women-only. *Most popular organizations:* Barat Volunteer Coalition, Black Students United, international club, performing arts club.

Campus security 24-hour patrols, late-night transport-escort service, controlled dormitory access.

After graduation *Career center:* 1 full-time personnel. Services include job fairs, resume preparation, resume referral, career counseling, careers library, job bank, job interviews. *Graduate education:* 20% of class of 1999 went directly to graduate and professional school: 12% business, 6% law, 2% medicine.

Freshmen 200 applied, 187 admitted, 127 enrolled.

Average high school GPA	3.0	SAT verbal scores above 500	55%
SAT math scores above 500	65%	ACT above 18	76%
From top 10% of their h.s. class	8%	From top quarter	23%
From top half	42%	1998 freshmen returning in 1999	85%

Application *Options:* eApply at www.CollegeQuest.com, Common Application, electronic application, deferred entrance. *Application fee:* $20. *Required:* essay or personal statement; high school transcript; minimum 2.0 GPA; 2 letters of recommendation. *Required for some:* interview. *Recommended:* interview.

Standardized tests *Admission: Required:* SAT I or ACT.

Significant dates *Application deadlines:* rolling (freshmen), rolling (transfers). *Financial aid deadline priority date:* 4/15.

Freshman Application Contact
Ms. Mary Kay Farrell, Assistant Vice President for Admissions, Barat College, 700 East Westleigh Road, Lake Forest, IL 60045. **Phone:** 847-615-5678. **Fax:** 847-604-6300. **E-mail:** admissions@barat.edu

Visit CollegeQuest.com for information on majors offered and athletics. Electronic viewbook available at CollegeQuest.com.

■ *See page 1226 for a narrative description.*

BENEDICTINE UNIVERSITY
Lisle, Illinois

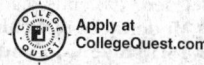
Apply at CollegeQuest.com

- **Independent Roman Catholic**, comprehensive, founded 1887
- **Degrees** associate, bachelor's, master's, and doctoral
- **Suburban** 108-acre campus with easy access to Chicago
- **Coed**, 1,639 undergraduate students, 78% full-time, 58% women, 42% men

Illinois

Benedictine University (continued)
- **Moderately difficult** entrance level, 76% of applicants were admitted
- **14:1 student-to-undergraduate faculty ratio**
- **53% graduate** in 6 years or less
- **$14,060 tuition** and fees
- **$13.1 million endowment**

Students *Undergraduates:* 1,281 full-time, 358 part-time. Students come from 15 states and territories. *The most frequently chosen baccalaureate fields are:* biological/life sciences, business/marketing, health professions and related sciences. *Graduate:* 827 in graduate degree programs.

From out-of-state	4%	Reside on campus	35%
Age 25 or older	22%	Transferred in	14%
African Americans	7%	Asian Americans/Pacific Islanders	14%
Hispanic Americans	8%	Native Americans	0.4%

Faculty 209 (39% full-time), 67% with terminal degrees.
Expenses (1999–2000) *Comprehensive fee:* $19,240 includes full-time tuition ($13,700), mandatory fees ($360), and room and board ($5180). *College room only:* $2180. Full-time tuition and fees vary according to degree level. Room and board charges vary according to board plan and housing facility. *Part-time tuition:* $435 per semester hour. *Part-time fees:* $5 per semester hour. Part-time tuition and fees vary according to class time. *Payment plans:* installment, deferred payment. *Waivers:* children of alumni and employees or children of employees.
Library Lownik Library. *Operations spending 1999–2000:* $262,700. *Collection:* 111,510 titles, 10,140 audiovisual materials.
College life *Housing: Options:* coed, men-only, women-only. *Most popular organizations:* Student Government Association, Campus Ministry, choir/gospel choir.
Campus security 24-hour emergency response devices and patrols, late-night transport-escort service, controlled dormitory access.
After graduation 52 organizations recruited on campus 1997–98. 69% of class of 1998 had job offers within 6 months. *Career center:* 3 full-time, 1 part-time personnel. Services include job fairs, resume preparation, resume referral, career counseling, careers library, job interviews.
Freshmen 892 applied, 674 admitted, 260 enrolled. 10 valedictorians.

Average high school GPA	3.31	SAT verbal scores above 500	N/R
SAT math scores above 500	N/R	ACT above 18	94%
From top 10% of their h.s. class	22%	From top quarter	42%
From top half	76%	1998 freshmen returning in 1999	75%

Application *Options:* eApply at www.CollegeQuest.com, deferred entrance. *Application fee:* $30. *Required:* essay or personal statement; high school transcript; letters of recommendation. *Required for some:* interview. *Recommended:* minimum 2.0 GPA; interview.
Standardized tests *Admission: Required:* SAT I or ACT.
Significant dates *Application deadlines:* rolling (freshmen), rolling (transfers). *Financial aid deadline:* 6/30. Priority date: 4/15.
Freshman Application Contact
Ms. Amy Graham, Undergraduate Admissions Office, Benedictine University, 5700 College Road, Lisle, IL 60532-0900. **Phone:** 630-829-6300. **Toll-free phone:** 800-829-6300. **Fax:** 630-960-1126. **E-mail:** admissions@ben.edu
Visit CollegeQuest.com for information on majors offered and athletics. Electronic viewbook available at CollegeQuest.com.

■ *See page 1252 for a narrative description.*

BLACKBURN COLLEGE
Carlinville, Illinois

- **Independent Presbyterian**, 4-year, founded 1837
- **Degree** bachelor's
- **Small-town** 80-acre campus with easy access to St. Louis
- **Coed**, 498 undergraduate students
- **Moderately difficult** entrance level, 73% of applicants were admitted
- **15:1 student-to-undergraduate faculty ratio**
- **48% graduate** in 6 years or less
- **$8275 tuition** and fees
- **$10.4 million endowment**

Students *Undergraduates:* Students come from 20 states and territories, 7 other countries.

Age 25 or older	6%	International students	3%
African Americans	4%	Asian Americans/Pacific Islanders	1%
Hispanic Americans	1%		

Faculty 46 (67% full-time).
Expenses (2000–2001) *Comprehensive fee:* $11,945 includes full-time tuition ($8190), mandatory fees ($85), and room and board ($3670). Full-time tuition and fees vary according to program. *Part-time tuition:* $334 per semester hour. *Payment plan:* installment. *Waivers:* employees or children of employees.
Library Lumpkin Library. *Operations spending 1999–2000:* $138,634. *Collection:* 82,000 titles, 389 serial subscriptions.
College life *Housing:* on-campus residence required through senior year. *Options:* coed, men-only, women-only. *Most popular organizations:* Cultural Expressions, Residence Hall Association, New Student Orientation Committee, choral groups, student government.
Campus security Student patrols, late-night transport-escort service.
After graduation 100 organizations recruited on campus 1997–98. *Career center:* 2 full-time personnel. Services include job fairs, resume preparation, resume referral, career counseling, careers library, job interviews. **Graduate education:** 18% of class of 1999 went directly to graduate and professional school: 5% law, 4% medicine, 3% business, 3% graduate arts and sciences, 2% engineering. **Major awards:** 1 Fulbright Scholar.
Freshmen 440 applied, 321 admitted. 3 class presidents, 4 valedictorians, 7 student government officers.

Average high school GPA	3.1	SAT verbal scores above 500	N/R
SAT math scores above 500	N/R	ACT above 18	85%
From top 10% of their h.s. class	18%	From top quarter	42%
From top half	82%	1998 freshmen returning in 1999	65%

Application *Options:* early admission, deferred entrance. *Required:* essay or personal statement; high school transcript; minimum 2.0 GPA. *Required for some:* 1 letter of recommendation; interview.
Standardized tests *Admission: Required:* SAT I or ACT.
Significant dates *Application deadlines:* rolling (freshmen), rolling (transfers). *Financial aid deadline priority date:* 4/1.
Freshman Application Contact
Mr. John Malin, Director of Admissions, Blackburn College, 700 College Avenue, Carlinville, IL 62626-1498. **Phone:** 217-854-3231 Ext. 4252. **Toll-free phone:** 800-233-3550. **Fax:** 217-854-3713. **E-mail:** admit@mail.blackburn.edu
Visit CollegeQuest.com for information on majors offered and athletics. College video available at CollegeQuest.com.

■ *See page 1282 for a narrative description.*

BLESSING-RIEMAN COLLEGE OF NURSING
Quincy, Illinois

Apply at CollegeQuest.com

- **Independent**, 4-year, founded 1985
- **Degree** bachelor's
- **Small-town** 1-acre campus
- **Coed**, primarily women, 118 undergraduate students, 88% full-time, 94% women, 6% men
- **Moderately difficult** entrance level, 100% of applicants were admitted
- **8:1 student-to-undergraduate faculty ratio**
- **44% graduate** in 6 years or less
- **$10,400 tuition** and fees
- **$11,000 average indebtedness** upon graduation, $7 million endowment

Students *Undergraduates:* 104 full-time, 14 part-time. Students come from 4 states and territories, 1 other country. *The most frequently chosen baccalaureate field is:* health professions and related sciences.

From out-of-state	37%	Reside on campus	39%
Age 25 or older	28%	Transferred in	17%
International students	1%	African Americans	1%
Asian Americans/Pacific Islanders	1%	Hispanic Americans	2%

Faculty 14 (93% full-time), 14% with terminal degrees.
Expenses (1999–2000) *Comprehensive fee:* $14,970 includes full-time tuition ($10,100), mandatory fees ($300), and room and board ($4570). Full-time tuition and fees vary according to student level. Room and board

Illinois

charges vary according to student level. *Part-time tuition:* $280 per credit. College room and board for freshmen and sophomores is provided by Culver-Stockton College. *Waivers:* employees or children of employees.

Library Blessing-Rieman Library plus 1 other. *Operations spending 1999–2000:* $26,300. *Collection:* 4,275 titles, 112 serial subscriptions.

College life *Housing:* on-campus residence required through sophomore year. *Option:* coed. *Social organizations:* national fraternities, national sororities. *Most popular organization:* Student Nurses Organization.

Campus security 24-hour patrols, late-night transport-escort service.

After graduation 80% of class of 1998 had job offers within 6 months. *Career center:* 1 full-time personnel. Services include career counseling.

Freshmen 21 applied, 21 admitted, 19 enrolled.

Average high school GPA	3.6	SAT verbal scores above 500	N/R
SAT math scores above 500	N/R	ACT above 18	96%
From top 10% of their h.s. class	19%	From top quarter	52%
From top half	100%	1998 freshmen returning in 1999	64%

Application *Options:* eApply at www.CollegeQuest.com, deferred entrance. *Application fee:* $0. *Required:* high school transcript; minimum 3.0 GPA. *Recommended:* essay or personal statement; interview.

Standardized tests *Admission: Required:* SAT I or ACT.

Significant dates *Application deadlines:* rolling (freshmen), rolling (transfers).

Freshman Application Contact
Ms. Linda Cornwell, Director of Support Services/Registrar, Blessing-Rieman College of Nursing, Broadway at 11th, Quincy, IL 62305-7005. **Phone:** 217-228-5520 Ext. 6992. **Toll-free phone:** 800-877-9140. **Fax:** 217-223-6400. **E-mail:** htourney@blessinghospital.com

Visit CollegeQuest.com for information on majors offered and athletics.

BRADLEY UNIVERSITY
Peoria, Illinois

- **Independent**, comprehensive, founded 1897
- **Degrees** bachelor's and master's
- **Urban** 65-acre campus
- **Coed**, 4,946 undergraduate students, 91% full-time, 54% women, 46% men
- **Moderately difficult** entrance level, 81% of applicants were admitted
- **14:1 student-to-undergraduate faculty ratio**
- **65.6% graduate** in 6 years or less
- **$13,960 tuition** and fees
- **$11,112 average financial aid** package, $15,350 average indebtedness upon graduation, $147.4 million endowment

Students *Undergraduates:* 4,483 full-time, 463 part-time. Students come from 43 states and territories, 35 other countries. *The most frequently chosen baccalaureate fields are:* business/marketing, communications/communication technologies, engineering/engineering technologies. *Graduate:* 876 in graduate degree programs.

From out-of-state	19%	Reside on campus	42%
Age 25 or older	10%	Transferred in	7%
International students	2%	African Americans	4%
Asian Americans/Pacific Islanders	2%	Hispanic Americans	2%
Native Americans	0.3%		

Faculty 488 (66% full-time), 55% with terminal degrees.

Expenses (1999–2000) *Comprehensive fee:* $19,260 includes full-time tuition ($13,880), mandatory fees ($80), and room and board ($5300). Room and board charges vary according to board plan. *Part-time tuition:* $377 per credit hour. Part-time tuition and fees vary according to course load. *Payment plans:* installment, deferred payment. *Waivers:* senior citizens and employees or children of employees.

Library Cullom-Davis Library. *Operations spending 1999–2000:* $1.7 million. *Collection:* 508,011 titles, 2,013 serial subscriptions, 11,585 audiovisual materials.

College life *Housing:* on-campus residence required through sophomore year. *Option:* coed. *Social organizations:* national fraternities, national sororities; 41% of eligible men and 28% of eligible women are members. *Most popular organizations:* Alpha Phi Omega, Student Activities Council, Student Action for Environment, investment club, Student Senate.

Campus security 24-hour emergency response devices and patrols, late-night transport-escort service, controlled dormitory access.

After graduation 324 organizations recruited on campus 1997–98. 97% of class of 1998 had job offers within 6 months. *Career center:* 13 full-time personnel. Services include job fairs, resume preparation, resume referral, career counseling, careers library, job bank, job interviews.

Freshmen 4,545 applied, 3,699 admitted, 1,079 enrolled. 17 National Merit Scholars, 50 valedictorians.

SAT verbal scores above 500	88%	SAT math scores above 500	90%
ACT above 18	99%	From top 10% of their h.s. class	31%
From top quarter	59%	From top half	85%
1998 freshmen returning in 1999	84%		

Application *Options:* Common Application, electronic application, early admission, deferred entrance. *Application fee:* $35. *Required:* high school transcript; minimum 2.0 GPA. *Recommended:* essay or personal statement; minimum 3.0 GPA; letters of recommendation; interview.

Standardized tests *Admission: Required:* SAT I or ACT.

Significant dates *Application deadlines:* rolling (freshmen), rolling (transfers). *Financial aid deadline priority date:* 3/1.

Freshman Application Contact
Ms. Nickie Roberson, Director of Admissions, Bradley University, 1501 West Bradley Avenue, Peoria, IL 61625-0002. **Phone:** 309-677-1000. **Toll-free phone:** 800-447-6460. **E-mail:** admissions@bradley.edu

Visit CollegeQuest.com for information on majors offered and athletics. College video available at CollegeQuest.com.

CHICAGO STATE UNIVERSITY
Chicago, Illinois

Apply at CollegeQuest.com

- **State-supported**, comprehensive, founded 1867
- **Degrees** bachelor's and master's
- **Urban** 161-acre campus
- **Coed**, 5,585 undergraduate students, 64% full-time, 73% women, 27% men
- **Moderately difficult** entrance level
- **18:1 student-to-undergraduate faculty ratio**
- **$3151 tuition** and fees (in-state); $7735 (out-of-state)

Students *Undergraduates:* Students come from 12 states and territories, 8 other countries. *Graduate:* 1,995 in graduate degree programs.

Age 25 or older	44%	International students	0.1%
African Americans	91%	Asian Americans/Pacific Islanders	1%
Hispanic Americans	4%	Native Americans	0.1%

Faculty 307 full-time.

Expenses (1999–2000) *Tuition, state resident:* full-time $3151; part-time $96 per credit hour. *Tuition, nonresident:* full-time $7735; part-time $286 per credit hour. *Required fees:* $141 per term part-time. *College room and board:* $5825. *Payment plan:* deferred payment. *Waivers:* senior citizens and employees or children of employees.

Library Paul and Emily Douglas Library. *Operations spending 1999–2000:* $2.2 million. *Collection:* 320,000 titles, 1,539 serial subscriptions.

College life *Housing: Option:* coed. *Social organizations:* national fraternities, national sororities. *Most popular organizations:* Math/Computer Science Club, Geographic Society Club, Gospel Choir, Movie Club.

Campus security 24-hour emergency response devices and patrols, student patrols, controlled dormitory access.

After graduation *Career center:* Services include job fairs, career counseling, careers library, job bank.

Freshmen 5 valedictorians.

SAT verbal scores above 500	N/R	SAT math scores above 500	N/R
ACT above 18	N/R	From top 10% of their h.s. class	12%
From top quarter	34%	From top half	68%

Application *Option:* eApply at www.CollegeQuest.com. *Application fee:* $20. *Required:* high school transcript.

Standardized tests *Admission: Required:* SAT I or ACT.

Significant dates *Application deadlines:* rolling (freshmen), rolling (transfers). *Financial aid deadline priority date:* 3/30.

Illinois

Chicago State University (continued)
Freshman Application Contact
Ms. Addie Epps, Director of Admissions, Chicago State University, 95th Street at King Drive, ADM 200, Chicago, IL 60628. **Phone:** 773-995-2513. **E-mail:** ug-admissions@csu.edu

Visit CollegeQuest.com for information on majors offered and athletics.

CHRISTIAN LIFE COLLEGE
Mount Prospect, Illinois

Admissions Office Contact
Christian Life College, 400 East Gregory Street, Mount Prospect, IL 60056.

COLLEGE OF ST. FRANCIS
Illinois—See University of St. Francis

COLUMBIA COLLEGE CHICAGO
Chicago, Illinois

- **Independent**, comprehensive, founded 1890
- **Degrees** bachelor's and master's
- **Urban** campus
- **Coed**, 8,094 undergraduate students, 78% full-time, 48% women, 52% men
- **Noncompetitive** entrance level, 90% of applicants were admitted
- **13:1** student-to-undergraduate faculty ratio
- **$10,830 tuition** and fees

Students *Undergraduates:* 6,301 full-time, 1,793 part-time. Students come from 36 states and territories, 84 other countries. *Graduate:* 502 in graduate degree programs.

From out-of-state	16%	Reside on campus	4%
Age 25 or older	19%	Transferred in	16%
International students	4%	African Americans	20%
Asian Americans/Pacific Islanders	4%	Hispanic Americans	11%
Native Americans	1%		

Faculty 1,201 (19% full-time), 26% with terminal degrees.
Expenses (1999–2000) *One-time required fee:* $35. *Tuition:* full-time $10,690; part-time $365 per semester hour. *Required fees:* full-time $140; $60 per term part-time. *College room only:* $4988. *Payment plan:* deferred payment. *Waivers:* employees or children of employees.
Library Columbia College Library. *Collection:* 127,494 audiovisual materials.
College life *Housing:* Option: coed. *Most popular organizations:* CUMA (Columbia Urban Music Association), International Student Organization, Acianza Latina, marketing club.
Campus security 24-hour emergency response devices and patrols, late-night transport-escort service, controlled dormitory access.
After graduation 117 organizations recruited on campus 1997–98. *Career center:* 8 full-time, 3 part-time personnel. Services include job fairs, resume preparation, interview workshops, career/interest testing, career counseling, careers library, job bank, job interviews. *Graduate education:* 9% of class of 1999 went directly to graduate and professional school.
Freshmen 2,107 applied, 1,896 admitted, 1,358 enrolled.

Average high school GPA	2.6	SAT verbal scores above 500	N/R
SAT math scores above 500	N/R	ACT above 18	N/R
From top quarter of their h.s. class	35%	From top half	64%

Application *Option:* deferred entrance. *Application fee:* $25. *Required:* essay or personal statement; high school transcript; letters of recommendation. *Required for some:* interview. *Recommended:* interview.
Significant dates *Application deadlines:* 8/15 (freshmen), 8/15 (transfers). *Financial aid deadline priority date:* 1/1.
Freshman Application Contact
Ms. Susan Greenwald, Director of Admissions and Recruitment, Columbia College Chicago, 600 South Michigan Avenue, Chicago, IL 60605-1996. **Phone:** 312-663-1600 Ext. 7133. **E-mail:** admissions@mail.colum.edu

Visit CollegeQuest.com for information on majors offered and athletics. College video available at CollegeQuest.com.

■ *See page 1506 for a narrative description.*

CONCORDIA UNIVERSITY
River Forest, Illinois

- **Independent**, comprehensive, founded 1864, affiliated with Lutheran Church–Missouri Synod
- **Degrees** bachelor's and master's
- **Suburban** 40-acre campus with easy access to Chicago
- **Coed**, 1,260 undergraduate students, 85% full-time, 66% women, 34% men
- **Moderately difficult** entrance level, 72% of applicants were admitted
- **18:1** student-to-undergraduate faculty ratio
- **61% graduate** in 6 years or less
- **$13,860 tuition** and fees
- **$10,000 average financial aid** package, $14,400 average indebtedness upon graduation, $7 million endowment

Part of Concordia University System.
Students *Undergraduates:* 1,077 full-time, 183 part-time. Students come from 34 states and territories, 6 other countries. *Graduate:* 605 in graduate degree programs.

From out-of-state	32%	Reside on campus	65%
Age 25 or older	23%	Transferred in	7%
International students	1%	African Americans	10%
Asian Americans/Pacific Islanders	3%	Hispanic Americans	4%
Native Americans	0.1%		

Faculty 212 (41% full-time), 37% with terminal degrees.
Expenses (2000–2001) *Comprehensive fee:* $19,225 includes full-time tuition ($13,760), mandatory fees ($100), and room and board ($5365). *Part-time tuition:* $430 per semester hour. *Payment plan:* installment. *Waivers:* employees or children of employees.
Library Klinck Memorial Library. *Operations spending 1999–2000:* $507,338. *Collection:* 160,554 titles, 590 serial subscriptions, 5,631 audiovisual materials.
College life *Housing:* on-campus residence required through sophomore year. *Options:* coed, women-only. *Most popular organizations:* Concordia Youth Ministries, Kappelle Choir, wind symphony, student government, intramural sports.
Campus security 24-hour emergency response devices and patrols, student patrols, late-night transport-escort service, emergency call boxes.
After graduation 52 organizations recruited on campus 1997–98. 92% of class of 1998 had job offers within 6 months. *Career center:* 1 full-time, 1 part-time personnel. Services include job fairs, resume preparation, interview workshops, resume referral, career/interest testing, career counseling, careers library, job bank, job interviews. *Graduate education:* 8% of class of 1999 went directly to graduate and professional school: 4% graduate arts and sciences, 3% theology, 1% business.
Freshmen 683 applied, 491 admitted, 248 enrolled. 7 valedictorians.

Average high school GPA	3.1	SAT verbal scores above 500	N/R
SAT math scores above 500	N/R	ACT above 18	83%
From top 10% of their h.s. class	19%	From top quarter	47%
From top half	76%	1998 freshmen returning in 1999	82%

Application *Options:* electronic application, deferred entrance. *Application fee:* $25. *Required:* high school transcript; minimum 2.0 GPA; 1 letter of recommendation; minimum ACT score of 20 or SAT I score of 930. *Required for some:* essay or personal statement; interview.
Standardized tests *Admission:* Required: ACT.
Significant dates *Application deadlines:* rolling (freshmen), rolling (transfers). *Financial aid deadline:* 5/31. *Priority date:* 4/15.
Freshman Application Contact
Mrs. Marsha Hubbuch, Acting Director of Undergraduate Admission, Concordia University, 7400 Augusta Street, River Forest, IL 60305. **Phone:** 708-209-3100. **Toll-free phone:** 800-285-2668. **Fax:** 708-209-3176. **E-mail:** crfadmis@curf.edu

Visit CollegeQuest.com for information on majors offered and athletics.

Illinois

DEPAUL UNIVERSITY
Chicago, Illinois

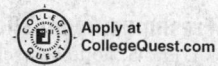 Apply at CollegeQuest.com

- **Independent Roman Catholic**, university, founded 1898
- **Degrees** bachelor's, master's, doctoral, first professional, post-master's, and postbachelor's certificates
- **Urban** 36-acre campus
- **Coed**, 10,914 undergraduate students, 70% full-time, 60% women, 40% men
- **Moderately difficult** entrance level, 78% of applicants were admitted
- **15:1 student-to-undergraduate faculty ratio**
- **56.74% graduate** in 6 years or less
- **$14,700 tuition** and fees

Students *Undergraduates:* 7,611 full-time, 3,303 part-time. Students come from 50 states and territories, 44 other countries. *The most frequently chosen baccalaureate fields are:* business/marketing, liberal arts/general studies, social sciences and history. *Graduate:* 1,170 in professional programs, 6,603 in other graduate degree programs.

From out-of-state	15%	Reside on campus	17%
Age 25 or older	36%	Transferred in	11%
International students	2%	African Americans	12%
Asian Americans/Pacific Islanders	9%	Hispanic Americans	12%
Native Americans	0.3%		

Faculty 1,560 (37% full-time).
Expenses (1999–2000) *Comprehensive fee:* $21,000 includes full-time tuition ($14,670), mandatory fees ($30), and room and board ($6300). *College room only:* $4680. Full-time tuition and fees vary according to program. Room and board charges vary according to board plan and housing facility. *Part-time tuition:* $294 per quarter hour. *Part-time fees:* $10 per term part-time. Part-time tuition and fees vary according to program. *Payment plans:* installment, deferred payment. *Waivers:* employees or children of employees.
Library John T. Richardson Library plus 2 others. *Collection:* 759,569 titles, 16,465 serial subscriptions, 14,000 audiovisual materials.
College life *Housing:* Option: coed. *Social organizations:* national fraternities, national sororities; 3% of eligible men and 3% of eligible women are members. *Most popular organizations:* Student Ambassadors, DePaul Activities Board, DePaul Community Service Association.
Campus security 24-hour emergency response devices and patrols, late-night transport-escort service, controlled dormitory access.
After graduation 1,000 organizations recruited on campus 1997–98. *Career center:* 13 full-time, 25 part-time personnel. Services include job fairs, resume preparation, resume referral, career counseling, careers library, job bank, job interviews.
Freshmen 6,050 applied, 4,737 admitted, 1,750 enrolled. 40 National Merit Scholars.

Average high school GPA	3.3	SAT verbal scores above 500	82%
SAT math scores above 500	75%	ACT above 18	89%
From top 10% of their h.s. class	19%	From top quarter	45%
From top half	75%	1998 freshmen returning in 1999	84%

Application *Options:* eApply at www.CollegeQuest.com, Common Application, electronic application, early admission, early action, deferred entrance. *Application fee:* $25. *Required:* high school transcript; minimum 2.0 GPA; 1 letter of recommendation. *Required for some:* minimum 3.0 GPA; interview; audition. *Recommended:* minimum 3.0 GPA.
Standardized tests *Admission: Required:* SAT I or ACT.
Significant dates *Application deadlines:* rolling (freshmen), rolling (transfers). *Early action:* 12/15. *Notification:* 1/15 (early action). *Financial aid deadline:* 5/1. *Priority date:* 4/1.
Freshman Application Contact
Mr. Ray Kennelley, Dean of Admission, DePaul University, 1 East Jackson Boulevard, Chicago, IL 60604-2287. **Phone:** 312-362-8300. **Toll-free phone:** 800-4DE-PAUL. **Fax:** 312-362-3322. **E-mail:** admitdpu@wppost.depaul.edu
Visit CollegeQuest.com for information on majors offered and athletics.

- *See page 1572 for a narrative description.*

DeVry Institute of Technology
Addison, Illinois

- **Proprietary**, 4-year, founded 1982
- **Degrees** associate and bachelor's
- **Suburban** 14-acre campus with easy access to Chicago
- **Coed**, 4,048 undergraduate students, 62% full-time, 23% women, 77% men
- **Minimally difficult** entrance level, 68% of applicants were admitted
- **22:1 student-to-undergraduate faculty ratio**
- **$7778 tuition** and fees

Part of DeVry, Inc.
Students *Undergraduates:* 2,497 full-time, 1,551 part-time. Students come from 26 states and territories, 29 other countries. *The most frequently chosen baccalaureate fields are:* business/marketing, computer/information sciences, engineering/engineering technologies.

From out-of-state	7%	Age 25 or older	42%
Transferred in	12%	International students	2%
African Americans	9%	Asian Americans/Pacific Islanders	13%
Hispanic Americans	9%	Native Americans	0.4%

Faculty 184 (33% full-time).
Expenses (1999–2000) *Tuition:* full-time $7778; part-time $290 per credit hour. Part-time tuition and fees vary according to class time and course load. *Payment plan:* installment. *Waivers:* employees or children of employees.
Library Learning Resource Center. *Collection:* 12,500 titles, 80 serial subscriptions.
College life *Housing:* college housing not available. *Most popular organizations:* Chi Pi Alpha, computer users group, Black Leadership Association Standing Together, Institute for Electrical and Electronic Engineers, DeVry Telecommunications Management Forum.
Campus security 24-hour emergency response devices, trained security personnel on duty.
After graduation 94% of class of 1998 had job offers within 6 months. *Career center:* 7 full-time, 1 part-time personnel. Services include job fairs, resume preparation, career counseling, job bank, job interviews.
Freshmen 1,553 applied, 1,059 admitted, 835 enrolled.

SAT verbal scores above 500	N/R	SAT math scores above 500	N/R
ACT above 18	N/R	1998 freshmen returning in 1999	52%

Application *Options:* electronic application, deferred entrance. *Application fee:* $25. *Required:* high school transcript; interview.
Standardized tests *Admission: Required:* Computerized Placement Test. *Recommended:* SAT I or ACT.
Significant dates *Application deadlines:* rolling (freshmen), rolling (transfers). *Financial aid deadline:* continuous.
Freshman Application Contact
Sandra Stack, Director of Admissions, DeVry Institute of Technology, 1221 North Swift Road, Addison, IL 60101-6106. **Phone:** 630-953-1300. **Toll-free phone:** 800-346-5420. **Fax:** 630-953-1236.
Visit CollegeQuest.com for information on majors offered and athletics.

DeVry Institute of Technology
Chicago, Illinois

- **Proprietary**, 4-year, founded 1931
- **Degrees** associate and bachelor's
- **Urban** 17-acre campus
- **Coed**, 3,822 undergraduate students, 64% full-time, 33% women, 67% men
- **Minimally difficult** entrance level, 62% of applicants were admitted
- **27:1 student-to-undergraduate faculty ratio**
- **$7778 tuition** and fees

Part of DeVry, Inc.
Students *Undergraduates:* 2,452 full-time, 1,370 part-time. Students come from 20 states and territories, 27 other countries. *The most frequently chosen baccalaureate fields are:* business/marketing, computer/information sciences, engineering/engineering technologies.

Illinois

DeVry Institute of Technology *(continued)*

From out-of-state	2%	Age 25 or older	42%
Transferred in	0.3%	International students	2%
African Americans	32%	Asian Americans/Pacific Islanders	16%
Hispanic Americans	24%	Native Americans	0.4%

Faculty 149 (48% full-time).

Expenses (1999–2000) *Tuition:* full-time $7778; part-time $290 per credit hour. Part-time tuition and fees vary according to class time and course load. *Payment plan:* installment. *Waivers:* employees or children of employees.

Library Learning Resource Center. *Collection:* 11,472 titles, 3,605 serial subscriptions.

College life *Housing:* college housing not available. *Most popular organizations:* Institute of Electrical and Electronic Engineering, Society of Hispanic Professional Engineers, Computer Information Systems, Technicians and Engineering.

Campus security 24-hour emergency response devices, late-night transport-escort service.

After graduation 95% of class of 1998 had job offers within 6 months. *Career center:* 12 full-time, 1 part-time personnel. Services include job fairs, resume preparation, career counseling, job bank, job interviews.

Freshmen 1,651 applied, 1,029 admitted, 1,162 enrolled.

SAT verbal scores above 500	N/R	SAT math scores above 500	N/R
ACT above 18	N/R	1998 freshmen returning in 1999	52%

Application *Options:* electronic application, deferred entrance. *Application fee:* $25. *Required:* high school transcript; interview.

Standardized tests *Admission: Required:* Computerized Placement Test. *Recommended:* SAT I or ACT.

Significant dates *Application deadlines:* rolling (freshmen), rolling (transfers). *Financial aid deadline:* continuous.

Freshman Application Contact Christine Hierl, Director of Admissions, DeVry Institute of Technology, 3300 North Campbell Avenue, Chicago, IL 60618-5994. **Phone:** 773-929-6550. **Toll-free phone:** 800-383-3879.

Visit CollegeQuest.com for information on majors offered and athletics.

DR. WILLIAM M. SCHOLL COLLEGE OF PODIATRIC MEDICINE
Chicago, Illinois

- **Independent**, upper-level, founded 1912
- **Degrees** incidental bachelor's, doctoral, and first professional
- **Urban** campus
- **Coed**
- **Moderately difficult** entrance level
- **7:1 student-to-undergraduate faculty ratio**
- **$20,450 tuition** and fees
- **$11 million endowment**

Students *Undergraduates:* Students come from 35 states and territories, 3 other countries. *Graduate:* 322 in professional programs.

Age 25 or older	64%

Expenses (1999–2000) *Tuition:* full-time $20,450. Full-time tuition and fees vary according to student level. Additional mandatory fees per year: $650 for nonresidents.

Library *Operations spending 1999–2000:* $279,000. *Collection:* 8,000 titles, 285 serial subscriptions.

College life *Housing:* college housing not available. *Social organizations:* coed fraternities; 50% of eligible men and 50% of eligible women are members.

Campus security Motion detectors, night security guard.

After graduation *Career center:* Services include career counseling.

Application *Options:* Common Application, deferred entrance. *Application fee:* $90.

Standardized tests *Admission: Required:* MCAT.

Significant dates *Application deadline:* 4/1 (transfers).

Freshman Application Contact Mr. Eric S. Forte, Associate Dean for Student Affairs, Dr. William M. Scholl College of Podiatric Medicine, 1001 North Dearborn Street, Chicago, IL 60610. **Phone:** 312-280-2940. **Toll-free phone:** 800-843-3059. **Fax:** 312-280-2997. **E-mail:** admiss@scholl.edu

Visit CollegeQuest.com for information on majors offered and athletics. College video available at CollegeQuest.com.

DOMINICAN UNIVERSITY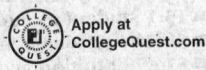
River Forest, Illinois

- **Independent Roman Catholic**, comprehensive, founded 1901
- **Degrees** bachelor's and master's
- **Suburban** 30-acre campus with easy access to Chicago
- **Coed**, 1,048 undergraduate students, 81% full-time, 69% women, 31% men
- **Moderately difficult** entrance level, 78% of applicants were admitted
- **12:1 student-to-undergraduate faculty ratio**
- **57.7% graduate** in 6 years or less
- **$14,820 tuition** and fees
- **$11,539 average financial aid** package, $12,013 average indebtedness upon graduation, $7.9 million endowment

Students *Undergraduates:* 844 full-time, 204 part-time. Students come from 16 states and territories, 17 other countries. *The most frequently chosen baccalaureate fields are:* business/marketing, psychology, social sciences and history. *Graduate:* 1,213 in graduate degree programs.

From out-of-state	5%	Reside on campus	30%
Age 25 or older	24%	Transferred in	14%
International students	3%	African Americans	8%
Asian Americans/Pacific Islanders	2%	Hispanic Americans	12%
Native Americans	0.2%		

Faculty 201 (38% full-time), 31% with terminal degrees.

Expenses (2000–2001) *One-time required fee:* $100. *Comprehensive fee:* $19,850 includes full-time tuition ($14,720), mandatory fees ($100), and room and board ($5030). Room and board charges vary according to board plan and housing facility. *Part-time tuition:* $490 per credit hour. Part-time tuition and fees vary according to program. *Payment plan:* installment. *Waivers:* children of alumni and employees or children of employees.

Library Rebecca Crown Library. *Operations spending 1999–2000:* $315,000. *Collection:* 280,475 titles, 1,388 serial subscriptions.

College life *Housing: Options:* coed, men-only, women-only. *Most popular organizations:* student government, Torch, business club, Resident Student Association, Center Stage.

Campus security 24-hour emergency response devices and patrols, student patrols, late-night transport-escort service, controlled dormitory access, door alarms.

After graduation 95% of class of 1998 had job offers within 6 months. *Career center:* 2 full-time, 1 part-time personnel. Services include job fairs, resume preparation, interview workshops, resume referral, career/interest testing, career counseling, careers library, job interviews. *Graduate education:* 15% of class of 1999 went directly to graduate and professional school.

Freshmen 543 applied, 426 admitted, 201 enrolled. 1 National Merit Scholar, 3 class presidents, 3 valedictorians, 32 student government officers.

Average high school GPA	3.27	SAT verbal scores above 500	N/R
SAT math scores above 500	N/R	ACT above 18	87%
From top 10% of their h.s. class	23%	From top quarter	50%
From top half	79%	1998 freshmen returning in 1999	77%

Application *Option:* eApply at www.CollegeQuest.com. *Application fee:* $20. *Required:* essay or personal statement; high school transcript; minimum 2.5 GPA. *Required for some:* 2 letters of recommendation; interview. *Recommended:* letters of recommendation.

Standardized tests *Admission: Required:* SAT I or ACT.

Significant dates *Application deadlines:* rolling (freshmen), rolling (transfers). *Financial aid deadline priority date:* 6/1.

Freshman Application Contact Ms. Hildegarde Schmidt, Dean of Admissions and Financial Aid, Dominican University, 7900 West Division Street, River Forest, IL 60305-1099. **Phone:** 708-524-6800. **Toll-free phone:** 800-828-8475. **Fax:** 708-366-5360. **E-mail:** domadmis@email.dom.edu

Illinois

Visit CollegeQuest.com for information on majors offered and athletics.

■ *See page 1582 for a narrative description.*

EASTERN ILLINOIS UNIVERSITY
Charleston, Illinois

- **State-supported**, comprehensive, founded 1895
- **Degrees** bachelor's and master's
- **Small-town** 320-acre campus
- **Coed**, 9,707 undergraduate students, 92% full-time, 59% women, 41% men
- **Moderately difficult** entrance level, 72% of applicants were admitted
- **17:1 student-to-undergraduate faculty ratio**
- **$3962 tuition** and fees (in-state); $9782 (out-of-state)
- **$6866 average financial aid** package, $12,211 average indebtedness upon graduation, $19.4 million endowment

Students *Undergraduates:* 8,884 full-time, 823 part-time. Students come from 42 states and territories, 41 other countries. *The most frequently chosen baccalaureate fields are:* business/marketing, education, English. *Graduate:* 1,365 in graduate degree programs.

From out-of-state	2%	Reside on campus	50%
Age 25 or older	10%	Transferred in	11%
International students	1%	African Americans	6%
Asian Americans/Pacific Islanders	1%	Hispanic Americans	2%
Native Americans	0.2%		

Faculty 665 (87% full-time), 66% with terminal degrees.

Expenses (2000–2001) *Tuition, state resident:* full-time $2910; part-time $97 per semester hour. *Tuition, nonresident:* full-time $8730; part-time $291 per semester hour. *Required fees:* full-time $1052; $44 per semester hour. Full-time tuition and fees vary according to course load. Part-time tuition and fees vary according to course load. *College room and board:* $4104. Room and board charges vary according to board plan. *Payment plan:* installment. *Waivers:* employees or children of employees.

Library Booth Library. *Operations spending 1999–2000:* $3.9 million. *Collection:* 477,085 titles, 2,922 serial subscriptions.

College life *Housing:* on-campus residence required in freshman year. *Options:* coed, women-only. *Social organizations:* national fraternities, national sororities; 19% of eligible men and 17% of eligible women are members. *Most popular organizations:* Greek organizations, Black Student Union.

Campus security 24-hour emergency response devices and patrols, student patrols.

After graduation *Career center:* 6 full-time personnel. Services include job fairs, resume preparation, interview workshops, resume referral, career/interest testing, career counseling, careers library, job bank, job interviews. *Graduate education:* 31% of class of 1999 went directly to graduate and professional school.

Freshmen 6,165 applied, 4,411 admitted, 1,495 enrolled.

SAT verbal scores above 500	N/R	SAT math scores above 500	N/R
ACT above 18	95%	From top 10% of their h.s. class	11%
From top quarter	38%	From top half	83%
1998 freshmen returning in 1999	80%		

Application *Application fee:* $25. *Required:* high school transcript; audition for music program. *Required for some:* essay or personal statement; 3 letters of recommendation.

Standardized tests *Admission:* Required: SAT I or ACT.

Significant dates *Application deadlines:* 4/1 (freshmen), rolling (transfers). *Financial aid deadline priority date:* 4/15.

Freshman Application Contact
Mr. Dale W. Wolf, Director of Admissions, Eastern Illinois University, 600 Lincoln Avenue, Charleston, IL 61920-3099. **Phone:** 217-581-2223. **Toll-free phone:** 800-252-5711. **Fax:** 217-581-7060. **E-mail:** admissns@eiu.edu

Visit CollegeQuest.com for information on majors offered and athletics. College video available at CollegeQuest.com.

EAST-WEST UNIVERSITY
Chicago, Illinois

- **Independent**, 4-year, founded 1978
- **Degrees** associate and bachelor's
- **Urban** campus
- **Coed**
- **Minimally difficult** entrance level
- **$8190 tuition** and fees

Expenses (1999–2000) *Tuition:* full-time $7800; part-time $265 per quarter hour. *Required fees:* full-time $390; $125 per term part-time.

College life *Housing:* college housing not available.

Application *Options:* Common Application, electronic application. *Application fee:* $30. *Required:* high school transcript. *Required for some:* 1 letter of recommendation.

Standardized tests *Placement:* Recommended: ACT.

Admissions Office Contact
East-West University, 816 South Michigan Avenue, Chicago, IL 60605-2103. **Fax:** 312-939-0083.

Visit CollegeQuest.com for information on athletics.

ELMHURST COLLEGE
Elmhurst, Illinois

Apply at CollegeQuest.com

- **Independent**, comprehensive, founded 1871, affiliated with United Church of Christ
- **Degrees** bachelor's and master's
- **Suburban** 38-acre campus with easy access to Chicago
- **Coed**, 2,557 undergraduate students, 76% full-time, 64% women, 36% men
- **Moderately difficult** entrance level, 74% of applicants were admitted
- **14:1 student-to-undergraduate faculty ratio**
- **51% graduate** in 6 years or less
- **$13,900 tuition** and fees
- **$13,950 average financial aid** package, $12,850 average indebtedness upon graduation, $66.2 million endowment

Students *Undergraduates:* 1,949 full-time, 608 part-time. Students come from 18 states and territories, 16 other countries. *The most frequently chosen baccalaureate fields are:* business/marketing, education, social sciences and history. *Graduate:* 124 in graduate degree programs.

From out-of-state	8%	Reside on campus	40%
Age 25 or older	39%	Transferred in	11%
International students	1%	African Americans	6%
Asian Americans/Pacific Islanders	3%	Hispanic Americans	6%
Native Americans	0.3%		

Faculty 259 (41% full-time).

Expenses (1999–2000) *Comprehensive fee:* $19,166 includes full-time tuition ($13,900) and room and board ($5266). *College room only:* $2866. Room and board charges vary according to board plan. *Part-time tuition:* $405 per credit hour. *Payment plans:* installment, deferred payment. *Waivers:* senior citizens and employees or children of employees.

Library Buehler Library. *Operations spending 1999–2000:* $911,213. *Collection:* 211,151 titles, 2,000 serial subscriptions, 6,531 audiovisual materials.

College life *Housing: Option:* coed. *Social organizations:* national fraternities, national sororities, local sororities; 3% of eligible men and 3% of eligible women are members. *Most popular organizations:* Programming Board and Student Government, theater and music groups, Black Student Union, residence life groups, Hablamos.

Campus security 24-hour emergency response devices and patrols, late-night transport-escort service, controlled dormitory access.

After graduation 50 organizations recruited on campus 1997–98, 90% of class of 1998 had job offers within 6 months. *Career center:* 3 full-time, 1 part-time personnel. Services include job fairs, resume preparation, interview workshops, resume referral, career/interest testing, career counseling, careers library, job bank, job interviews. *Graduate education:* 22% of class of 1999 went directly to graduate and professional school.

Freshmen 1,014 applied, 753 admitted, 273 enrolled.

Average high school GPA	3.28	SAT verbal scores above 500	N/R
SAT math scores above 500	N/R	ACT above 18	91%
From top 10% of their h.s. class	40%	From top quarter	73%
From top half	93%	1998 freshmen returning in 1999	82%

Application *Options:* eApply at www.CollegeQuest.com, electronic application, early admission, deferred entrance. *Application fee:* $15. *Required:* high school transcript; minimum 2.75 GPA. *Required for some:* essay or

Illinois

Elmhurst College *(continued)*
personal statement; letters of recommendation; interview. *Recommended:* essay or personal statement; minimum 3.0 GPA; interview.
Standardized tests *Admission: Required:* SAT I or ACT.
Significant dates *Application deadlines:* 7/15 (freshmen), 8/1 (transfers). *Financial aid deadline priority date:* 4/15.
Freshman Application Contact
Mr. Stephen Mueller, Director of Freshman Admission, Elmhurst College, 190 Prospect Avenue, Elmhurst, IL 60126-3296. **Phone:** 630-617-3400. **Toll-free phone:** 800-697-1871. **Fax:** 630-617-5501. **E-mail:** admit@elmhurst.edu
Visit CollegeQuest.com for information on majors offered and athletics. Electronic viewbook available at CollegeQuest.com.

■ *See page 1622 for a narrative description.*

EUREKA COLLEGE
Eureka, Illinois

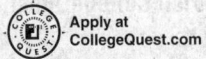 Apply at CollegeQuest.com

- **Independent**, 4-year, founded 1855, affiliated with Christian Church (Disciples of Christ)
- **Degree** bachelor's
- **Small-town** 112-acre campus
- **Coed**
- **Moderately difficult** entrance level
- **$15,450 tuition** and fees

Expenses (1999–2000) *Comprehensive fee:* $20,310 includes full-time tuition ($15,200), mandatory fees ($250), and room and board ($4860). *College room only:* $2320. *Part-time tuition:* $485 per semester hour.
Institutional Web site http://www.eureka.edu/
College life *Housing:* on-campus residence required through senior year. *Option:* coed. *Social organizations:* national fraternities, national sororities, local sororities; 45% of eligible men and 45% of eligible women are members. *Most popular organizations:* College Choral, theater, Campus Activities Board, intercollegiate athletics.
Campus security 24-hour emergency response devices, late night patrols.
Application *Options:* eApply at www.CollegeQuest.com, deferred entrance. *Application fee:* $15. *Required:* high school transcript; minimum 2.0 GPA; 1 letter of recommendation. *Required for some:* essay or personal statement; 3 letters of recommendation. *Recommended:* interview.
Standardized tests *Admission: Required:* SAT I or ACT.
Admissions Office Contact
Eureka College, 300 East College Avenue, Eureka, IL 61530-0128. **Toll-free phone:** 888-4-EUREKA. **Fax:** 309-467-6576. **E-mail:** admissions@eureka.edu
Visit CollegeQuest.com for information on athletics. College video available at CollegeQuest.com.

FINCH UNIVERSITY OF HEALTH SCIENCES/THE CHICAGO MEDICAL SCHOOL
North Chicago, Illinois

- **Independent**, upper-level, founded 1912
- **Degrees** bachelor's, master's, doctoral, and first professional
- **Suburban** 50-acre campus with easy access to Chicago
- **Coed**, 28 undergraduate students, 82% full-time, 100% women
- **Minimally difficult** entrance level
- **$12,903 tuition** and fees

Students *Undergraduates:* 23 full-time, 5 part-time. *The most frequently chosen baccalaureate field is:* health professions and related sciences. **Graduate:** 738 in professional programs, 606 in other graduate degree programs.

Age 25 or older	93%	Transferred in	100%
African Americans	4%	Asian Americans/Pacific Islanders	7%

Expenses (1999–2000) *Tuition:* full-time $12,903; part-time $359 per credit hour. Full-time tuition and fees vary according to program. Part-time tuition and fees vary according to program. *Payment plan:* installment. *Waivers:* employees or children of employees.

Library Boxer University Library. *Collection:* 94,045 titles, 1,063 serial subscriptions, 282 audiovisual materials.
College life *Housing:* college housing not available.
Campus security 24-hour patrols, late-night transport-escort service, outside doors on electric alarm during evening hours.
Application *Option:* Common Application. *Application fee:* $20.
Significant dates *Application deadline:* 8/15 (transfers). *Financial aid deadline:* 1/15.
Freshman Application Contact
Ms. Kristine A. Jones, Director of Admissions and Records, Finch University of Health Sciences/The Chicago Medical School, Undergraduate Admissions, 3333 Green Bay Road, North Chicago, IL 60064. **Phone:** 847-578-3204. **Fax:** 847-578-3284. **E-mail:** admissions@finchcms.edu
Visit CollegeQuest.com for information on majors offered and athletics.

GOVERNORS STATE UNIVERSITY
University Park, Illinois

- **State-supported**, upper-level, founded 1969
- **Degrees** bachelor's and master's
- **Suburban** 750-acre campus with easy access to Chicago
- **Coed**, 3,024 undergraduate students, 32% full-time, 68% women, 32% men
- **Minimally difficult** entrance level, 53% of applicants were admitted
- **$2398 tuition** and fees (in-state); $6814 (out-of-state)

Students *Undergraduates:* Students come from 9 states and territories, 19 other countries. *The most frequently chosen baccalaureate fields are:* business/marketing, computer/information sciences, education. **Graduate:** 2,876 in graduate degree programs.

From out-of-state	3%	Age 25 or older	54%
International students	1%	African Americans	41%
Asian Americans/Pacific Islanders	2%	Hispanic Americans	6%
Native Americans	0.2%		

Faculty 194 (87% full-time), 71% with terminal degrees.
Expenses (1999–2000) *One-time required fee:* $10. *Tuition, state resident:* full-time $2208; part-time $92 per credit hour. *Tuition, nonresident:* full-time $6624; part-time $276 per credit hour. *Required fees:* full-time $190; $95 per term part-time. Full-time tuition and fees vary according to location. Part-time tuition and fees vary according to course load and location. *Payment plans:* installment, deferred payment. *Waivers:* senior citizens and employees or children of employees.
Library University Library. *Collection:* 244,000 titles, 2,300 serial subscriptions.
College life *Housing:* college housing not available. *Most popular organizations:* Future Teachers of America, American College of Health Executives, Circle K, counseling club, African-American Student Association.
Campus security 24-hour patrols, late-night transport-escort service.
After graduation 125 organizations recruited on campus 1997–98. *Career center:* 2 full-time, 2 part-time personnel. Services include job fairs, resume preparation, interview workshops, resume referral, career/interest testing, career counseling, careers library, job bank, job interviews. **Graduate education:** 23% of class of 1999 went directly to graduate and professional school: 6% business, 6% education, 6% graduate arts and sciences, 1% law, 1% medicine, 1% theology.
Application *Option:* deferred entrance. *Application fee:* $0.
Significant dates *Application deadline:* 7/15 (transfers). *Financial aid deadline priority date:* 5/1.
Freshman Application Contact
Dr. Michael Toney, Executive Director of Enrollment Services, Governors State University, One University Parkway, University Park, IL 60466. **Phone:** 708-534-4490. **Fax:** 708-534-1640.
Visit CollegeQuest.com for information on majors offered and athletics.

GREENVILLE COLLEGE
Greenville, Illinois

- **Independent Free Methodist**, comprehensive, founded 1892
- **Degrees** bachelor's and master's

- **Small-town** 12-acre campus with easy access to St. Louis
- **Coed**, 1,030 undergraduate students, 99% full-time, 54% women, 46% men
- **Moderately difficult** entrance level
- **15:1 student-to-undergraduate faculty ratio**
- **44.5% graduate** in 6 years or less
- **$12,586 tuition** and fees
- **$12,608 average financial aid** package, $3.3 million endowment

Students *Undergraduates:* 1,021 full-time, 9 part-time. Students come from 37 states and territories, 14 other countries. *The most frequently chosen baccalaureate fields are:* business/marketing, biological/life sciences, education. *Graduate:* 32 in graduate degree programs.

From out-of-state	31%	Reside on campus	57%
Age 25 or older	19%	Transferred in	7%
International students	1%	African Americans	6%
Asian Americans/Pacific Islanders	1%	Hispanic Americans	2%
Native Americans	1%		

Faculty 99 (57% full-time), 37% with terminal degrees.

Expenses (1999–2000) *Comprehensive fee:* $17,436 includes full-time tuition ($12,576), mandatory fees ($10), and room and board ($4850). *College room only:* $2290. *Part-time tuition:* $370 per credit hour. *Payment plan:* installment. *Waivers:* children of alumni, senior citizens, and employees or children of employees.

Library Ruby E. Dare Library. *Operations spending 1999–2000:* $106,992. *Collection:* 126,210 titles, 490 serial subscriptions, 4,377 audiovisual materials.

College life *Housing:* on-campus residence required through senior year. *Options:* men-only, women-only. *Most popular organizations:* Campus Activity Board, intramurals, Greenville Student Outreach, Habitat for Humanity, Student Senate.

Campus security 24-hour emergency response devices, student patrols, late-night transport-escort service.

After graduation 11 organizations recruited on campus 1997–98. 80% of class of 1998 had job offers within 6 months. *Career center:* 2 full-time personnel. Services include job fairs, resume preparation, interview workshops, career/interest testing, career counseling, careers library, job interviews.

Freshmen 541 applied, 477 admitted, 215 enrolled. 4 National Merit Scholars, 6 valedictorians.

Average high school GPA	3.24	SAT verbal scores above 500	65%
SAT math scores above 500	54%	ACT above 18	83%
From top 10% of their h.s. class	19%	From top quarter	43%
From top half	75%	1998 freshmen returning in 1999	72%

Application *Options:* electronic application, early admission, deferred entrance. *Application fee:* $25. *Required:* essay or personal statement; high school transcript; minimum 2.0 GPA; 2 letters of recommendation; agreement to code of conduct. *Required for some:* interview.

Standardized tests *Admission: Required:* SAT I or ACT.

Significant dates *Application deadlines:* rolling (freshmen), rolling (transfers). *Financial aid deadline:* continuous.

Freshman Application Contact
Mr. Randy Comfort, Dean of Admissions, Greenville College, 315 East College, PO Box 159, Greenville, IL 62246-0159. **Phone:** 618-664-2800 Ext. 4401. **Toll-free phone:** 800-248-2288 (in-state); 800-345-4440 (out-of-state). **Fax:** 618-664-9841. **E-mail:** admissions@greenville.edu

Visit CollegeQuest.com for information on majors offered and athletics. College video available at CollegeQuest.com.

■ *See page 1742 for a narrative description.*

HARRINGTON INSTITUTE OF INTERIOR DESIGN
Chicago, Illinois

- **Proprietary**, 4-year, founded 1931
- **Degrees** associate and bachelor's
- **Urban** campus
- **Coed**, 512 undergraduate students, 49% full-time, 87% women, 13% men
- **Noncompetitive** entrance level, 90% of applicants were admitted
- **12:1 student-to-undergraduate faculty ratio**
- **$11,086 tuition** and fees

Students *Undergraduates:* 250 full-time, 262 part-time. *The most frequently chosen baccalaureate field is:* visual/performing arts.

Age 25 or older	53%	International students	3%
African Americans	6%	Asian Americans/Pacific Islanders	6%
Hispanic Americans	7%		

Faculty 37 (51% full-time).

Expenses (1999–2000) *Tuition:* full-time $11,036; part-time $2586 per term. *Required fees:* full-time $50; $25 per term part-time. *Payment plan:* installment.

Library Harrington Institute Design Library. *Collection:* 22,000 titles, 90 serial subscriptions, 26,000 audiovisual materials.

College life *Housing:* college housing not available. *Most popular organizations:* American Society of Interior Designers, International Interior Design Association.

After graduation 95% of class of 1998 had job offers within 6 months. *Career center:* Services include career counseling.

Freshmen 506 applied, 455 admitted, 37 enrolled.

SAT verbal scores above 500	N/R	SAT math scores above 500	N/R
ACT above 18	N/R		

Application *Option:* deferred entrance. *Application fee:* $50. *Required:* high school transcript; interview.

Significant dates *Application deadline:* rolling (freshmen). *Financial aid deadline priority date:* 5/1.

Freshman Application Contact
Ms. Wendy Stewart, Director of Admissions, Harrington Institute of Interior Design, 410 South Michigan Avenue, Chicago, IL 60605-1496. **Phone:** 312-939-4975. **Toll-free phone:** 877-939-4975. **Fax:** 312-939-8005. **E-mail:** harringtoninstitute@interiordesign.edu

Visit CollegeQuest.com for information on majors offered and athletics. College video available at CollegeQuest.com.

■ *See page 1766 for a narrative description.*

HEBREW THEOLOGICAL COLLEGE
Skokie, Illinois

- **Independent Jewish**, comprehensive, founded 1922
- **Degrees** bachelor's and first professional
- **Suburban** 13-acre campus with easy access to Chicago
- **Men** only, 151 undergraduate students
- **Moderately difficult** entrance level

Coordinate institution with Anne M. Blitstein Teachers Institute of the Hebrew Theological College.

Students *Undergraduates:* Students come from 16 states and territories.

Library Saul Silber Memorial Library plus 2 others. *Collection:* 63,000 titles, 60 serial subscriptions.

College life *Housing: Option:* men-only.

Campus security Controlled dormitory access.

After graduation *Graduate education:* 60% of class of 1999 went directly to graduate and professional school.

Freshmen

SAT verbal scores above 500	N/R	SAT math scores above 500	N/R
ACT above 18	N/R		

Application *Application fee:* $25. *Required:* essay or personal statement; high school transcript; 2 letters of recommendation; interview.

Standardized tests *Admission: Required:* SAT I or ACT.

Significant dates *Application deadline:* rolling (freshmen).

Freshman Application Contact
Office of Admissions, Hebrew Theological College, 7135 North Carpenter Road, Skokie, IL 60077-3263. **Phone:** 847-982-2500.

Visit CollegeQuest.com for information on majors offered and athletics. College video available at CollegeQuest.com.

Illinois

ILLINOIS COLLEGE
Jacksonville, Illinois

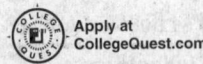
Apply at CollegeQuest.com

- **Independent interdenominational**, 4-year, founded 1829
- **Degree** bachelor's
- **Small-town** 62-acre campus with easy access to St. Louis
- **Coed**, 879 undergraduate students, 99% full-time, 55% women, 45% men
- **Moderately difficult** entrance level, 77% of applicants were admitted
- **14:1 student-to-undergraduate faculty ratio**
- **57.3% graduate** in 6 years or less
- **$10,200 tuition** and fees
- **$10,043 average financial aid** package, $12,801 average indebtedness upon graduation, $103 million endowment

Students *Undergraduates:* 872 full-time, 7 part-time. Students come from 14 states and territories, 5 other countries.

From out-of-state	3%	Reside on campus	75%
Age 25 or older	3%	Transferred in	7%
International students	1%	African Americans	2%
Asian Americans/Pacific Islanders	1%	Hispanic Americans	1%
Native Americans	0.2%		

Faculty 87 (63% full-time).

Expenses (1999–2000) *Comprehensive fee:* $14,700 includes full-time tuition ($10,200) and room and board ($4500). *Part-time tuition:* $425 per credit. *Payment plans:* installment, deferred payment. *Waivers:* employees or children of employees.

Library Schewe Library. *Operations spending 1999–2000:* $535,000. *Collection:* 143,500 titles, 620 serial subscriptions.

College life *Housing:* on-campus residence required through sophomore year. *Options:* coed, men-only, women-only. *Social organizations:* Greek literary societies; 17% of eligible men and 17% of eligible women are members. *Most popular organizations:* Student Activities Board, BACCHUS, Homecoming Committee, BASIC, Action Jacksonville.

Campus security 24-hour emergency response devices and patrols, late-night transport-escort service, controlled dormitory access.

After graduation *Career center:* 2 full-time personnel. Services include job fairs, resume preparation, resume referral, career counseling, careers library, job interviews.

Freshmen 1,050 applied, 811 admitted, 240 enrolled. 1 National Merit Scholar, 12 valedictorians.

Average high school GPA	3.2	SAT verbal scores above 500	55%
SAT math scores above 500	72%	ACT above 18	97%
From top 10% of their h.s. class	21%	From top quarter	45%
From top half	77%	1998 freshmen returning in 1999	93%

Application *Options:* eApply at www.CollegeQuest.com, Common Application, electronic application, early admission. *Application fee:* $10. *Required:* high school transcript; 2 letters of recommendation. *Required for some:* essay or personal statement. *Recommended:* interview.

Standardized tests *Admission:* Required: SAT I or ACT.

Significant dates *Application deadlines:* 8/15 (freshmen), 8/15 (transfers). *Financial aid deadline priority date:* 4/15.

Freshman Application Contact
Gale Vaughn, Director of Enrollment, Illinois College, 1101 West College Avenue, Jacksonville, IL 62650-2299. **Phone:** 217-245-3030. **Toll-free phone:** 888-595-3030. **Fax:** 217-245-3034. **E-mail:** admissions@hilltop.ic.edu

Visit CollegeQuest.com for information on majors offered and athletics.

THE ILLINOIS INSTITUTE OF ART
Chicago, Illinois

- **Proprietary**, 4-year, founded 1916
- **Degrees** associate and bachelor's
- **Urban** campus
- **Coed**
- **Minimally difficult** entrance level
- **$11,904 tuition** and fees

Part of The Art Institutes International.

Expenses (1999–2000) *One-time required fee:* $50. *Tuition:* full-time $11,904; part-time $248 per credit.

Institutional Web site http://www.ilia.aii.edu/

College life *Housing:* college housing not available. *Most popular organizations:* Student Activities Committee, American Society of Interior Designers club, commercial art club, Student Ambassador Program, Fashion Focus.

Campus security 24-hour emergency response devices and patrols.

Application *Options:* Common Application, early admission, deferred entrance. *Application fee:* $50. *Required:* essay or personal statement; high school transcript; interview. *Required for some:* letters of recommendation; portfolio. *Recommended:* minimum 2.0 GPA.

Standardized tests *Placement:* Recommended: SAT I or ACT.

Admissions Office Contact
The Illinois Institute of Art, 350 North Orleans, Chicago, IL 60654. **Toll-free phone:** 800-351-3450 Ext. 132. **Fax:** 312-280-3528. **E-mail:** antonj@aii.edu

Visit CollegeQuest.com for information on athletics. College video available at CollegeQuest.com.

THE ILLINOIS INSTITUTE OF ART AT SCHAUMBURG
Schaumburg, Illinois

- **Proprietary**, 4-year
- **Degrees** associate and bachelor's
- **Coed**, 699 undergraduate students, 81% full-time, 41% women, 59% men
- **99% of applicants were admitted**
- **16:1 student-to-undergraduate faculty ratio**
- **$12,336 tuition** and fees

Part of The Arts Institutes International.

Students *Undergraduates:* 566 full-time, 133 part-time. Students come from 9 states and territories, 2 other countries.

From out-of-state	10%	Age 25 or older	28%
Transferred in	10%	International students	1%
African Americans	3%	Asian Americans/Pacific Islanders	9%
Hispanic Americans	7%		

Faculty 55 (49% full-time), 18% with terminal degrees.

Expenses (2000–2001) *Comprehensive fee:* 17,232 includes full-time tuition (12,336) and room and board (4896). *Payment plans:* guaranteed tuition, tuition prepayment, installment, deferred payment. *Waivers:* employees or children of employees.

College life *Most popular organizations:* animation club, ASID, newspaper, music.

Campus security 24-hour emergency response devices and patrols, student patrols.

Freshmen 304 applied, 303 admitted, 116 enrolled.

Average high school GPA	2.7	SAT verbal scores above 500	N/R
SAT math scores above 500	N/R	ACT above 18	78%
1998 freshmen returning in 1999	8%		

Application *Application fee:* 50. *Required:* essay or personal statement; high school transcript; minimum 2.0 GPA; letters of recommendation. *Required for some:* interview.

Standardized tests *Admission:* Recommended: SAT I and SAT II or ACT.

Freshman Application Contact
John Gescheidle, Director of Admissions, The Illinois Institute of Art at Schaumburg, 1000 Plaza Drive, Schaumburg, IL 60173. **Phone:** 847-619-3450 Ext. 116. **Toll-free phone:** 800-314-3450. **Fax:** 847-619-3064.

Visit CollegeQuest.com for information on majors offered and athletics.

ILLINOIS INSTITUTE OF TECHNOLOGY
Chicago, Illinois

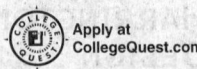
Apply at CollegeQuest.com

- **Independent**, university, founded 1890
- **Degrees** bachelor's, master's, doctoral, first professional, and postbachelor's certificates
- **Urban** 128-acre campus
- **Coed**, 1,539 undergraduate students, 80% full-time, 24% women, 76% men
- **Very difficult** entrance level, 65% of applicants were admitted

- 12:1 student-to-undergraduate faculty ratio
- $17,600 tuition and fees
- $18,080 average financial aid package, $19,138 average indebtedness upon graduation, $175.6 million endowment

IIT is a private, urban, research, PhD-granting university providing small class size, hands-on projects, undergraduate research, co-op learning, combined degree programs, and a distinguished faculty that includes Nobel Laureate Leon Lederman. IIT offers substantial need-based and merit-based scholarship programs. Job placement rates for graduates are over 90%.

Students *Undergraduates:* 1,236 full-time, 303 part-time. Students come from 48 states and territories, 50 other countries. *The most frequently chosen baccalaureate fields are:* architecture, computer/information sciences, engineering/engineering technologies. *Graduate:* 1,142 in professional programs, 3,214 in other graduate degree programs.

From out-of-state	34%	Reside on campus	44%
Age 25 or older	24%	Transferred in	5%
International students	16%	African Americans	8%
Asian Americans/Pacific Islanders	14%	Hispanic Americans	7%
Native Americans	0.3%		

Faculty 500 (56% full-time).

Expenses (1999–2000) *Comprehensive fee:* $22,850 includes full-time tuition ($17,500), mandatory fees ($100), and room and board ($5250). *College room only:* $2350. Room and board charges vary according to board plan. *Part-time tuition:* $550 per semester hour. *Part-time fees:* $2 per semester hour. *Payment plan:* installment. *Waivers:* employees or children of employees.

Library Paul V. Galvin Library plus 5 others. *Operations spending 1999–2000:* $3.1 million. *Collection:* 733,933 titles, 3,500 serial subscriptions, 52,151 audiovisual materials.

College life *Housing:* on-campus residence required in freshman year. *Options:* coed, men-only, women-only. *Social organizations:* national fraternities, local sororities; 15% of eligible men and 10% of eligible women are members. *Most popular organizations:* Union Board, Greek Council, Student Leadership Council, Residence Hall Association, Techmate Commuters.

Campus security 24-hour emergency response devices and patrols, late-night transport-escort service, controlled dormitory access.

After graduation 117 organizations recruited on campus 1997–98. *Career center:* 5 full-time, 1 part-time personnel. Services include job fairs, resume preparation, interview workshops, resume referral, career/interest testing, career counseling, careers library, job bank, job interviews. *Graduate education:* 66% of class of 1999 went directly to graduate and professional school.

Freshmen 2,866 applied, 1,876 admitted, 278 enrolled.

Average high school GPA	3.75	SAT verbal scores above 500	93%
SAT math scores above 500	100%	ACT above 18	100%
From top 10% of their h.s. class	52%	From top quarter	87%
From top half	100%	1998 freshmen returning in 1999	84%

Application *Options:* eApply at www.CollegeQuest.com, Common Application, electronic application, deferred entrance. *Application fee:* $30. *Required:* high school transcript; minimum 3.0 GPA; 1 letter of recommendation. *Required for some:* essay or personal statement; interview.

Standardized tests *Admission: Required:* SAT I or ACT. *Recommended:* SAT II Subject Tests.

Significant dates *Application deadlines:* rolling (freshmen), rolling (transfers). *Financial aid deadline:* continuous.

Freshman Application Contact
Mr. Terry Miller, Associate Dean of Undergraduate Admission, Illinois Institute of Technology, 10 West 33rd Street PH101, Chicago, IL 60616-3793. **Phone:** 312-567-3025. **Toll-free phone:** 800-448-2329. **Fax:** 312-567-6939. **E-mail:** admission@iit.edu
Visit CollegeQuest.com for information on majors offered and athletics. Electronic viewbook available at CollegeQuest.com.

- *See page 1818 for a narrative description.*

ILLINOIS STATE UNIVERSITY
Normal, Illinois

- **State-supported**, university, founded 1857
- **Degrees** bachelor's, master's, doctoral, and post-master's certificates
- **Urban** 850-acre campus
- **Coed**, 17,596 undergraduate students, 92% full-time, 58% women, 42% men
- **Moderately difficult** entrance level, 75% of applicants were admitted
- 19:1 student-to-undergraduate faculty ratio
- 52.6% graduate in 6 years or less
- $4340 tuition and fees (in-state); $10,778 (out-of-state)
- $7120 average financial aid package, $9283 average indebtedness upon graduation, $23.4 million endowment

Students *Undergraduates:* 16,162 full-time, 1,434 part-time. Students come from 36 states and territories, 47 other countries. *The most frequently chosen baccalaureate fields are:* business/marketing, education, social sciences and history. *Graduate:* 2,765 in graduate degree programs.

From out-of-state	2%	Reside on campus	40%
Age 25 or older	9%	Transferred in	10%
International students	1%	African Americans	7%
Asian Americans/Pacific Islanders	2%	Hispanic Americans	2%
Native Americans	0.3%		

Faculty 1,088 (79% full-time), 71% with terminal degrees.

Expenses (1999–2000) *Tuition, state resident:* full-time $3219; part-time $107 per credit. *Tuition, nonresident:* full-time $9657; part-time $322 per credit. *Required fees:* full-time $1121; $39 per credit. Full-time tuition and fees vary according to course load. Part-time tuition and fees vary according to course load. *College room and board:* $4238; room only: $2247. Room and board charges vary according to board plan. *Payment plan:* installment. *Waivers:* minority students, senior citizens, and employees or children of employees.

Library Milner Library. *Operations spending 1999–2000:* $8 million. *Collection:* 1 million titles, 5,724 serial subscriptions, 58,249 audiovisual materials.

College life *Housing:* on-campus residence required through sophomore year. *Options:* coed, women-only, disabled students. *Social organizations:* national fraternities, national sororities; 10% of eligible men and 9% of eligible women are members.

Campus security 24-hour emergency response devices and patrols, late-night transport-escort service, controlled dormitory access.

After graduation 571 organizations recruited on campus 1997–98. *Career center:* 11 full-time, 5 part-time personnel. Services include job fairs, resume preparation, interview workshops, resume referral, career/interest testing, career counseling, careers library, job bank, job interviews.

Freshmen 11,049 applied, 8,251 admitted, 3,080 enrolled. 3 National Merit Scholars, 35 valedictorians.

SAT verbal scores above 500	N/R	SAT math scores above 500	N/R
ACT above 18	97%	From top 10% of their h.s. class	11%
From top quarter	35%	From top half	81%
1998 freshmen returning in 1999	78%		

Application *Option:* early admission. *Required:* high school transcript.

Standardized tests *Admission: Required:* SAT I or ACT. *Recommended:* ACT.

Significant dates *Application deadlines:* 4/1 (freshmen), 6/30 (transfers). *Financial aid deadline priority date:* 3/1.

Freshman Application Contact
Mr. Steve Adams, Director of Admissions, Illinois State University, Campus Box 2200, Normal, IL 61790-2200. **Phone:** 309-438-2181. **Toll-free phone:** 800-366-2478. **Fax:** 309-438-3932. **E-mail:** ugradadm@ilstu.edu
Visit CollegeQuest.com for information on majors offered and athletics. College video available at CollegeQuest.com.

ILLINOIS WESLEYAN UNIVERSITY
Bloomington, Illinois

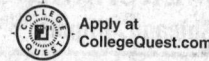
Apply at CollegeQuest.com

- **Independent**, 4-year, founded 1850
- **Degree** bachelor's
- **Suburban** 70-acre campus
- **Coed**, 2,091 undergraduate students, 99% full-time, 56% women, 44% men
- **Very difficult** entrance level, 64% of applicants were admitted
- 13:1 student-to-undergraduate faculty ratio

Illinois

Illinois Wesleyan University (continued)
- **76.5% graduate** in 6 years or less
- **$20,410 tuition** and fees
- **$15,664 average financial aid** package, $16,258 average indebtedness upon graduation, $185.4 million endowment

Students *Undergraduates:* 2,077 full-time, 14 part-time. Students come from 38 states and territories, 25 other countries. *The most frequently chosen baccalaureate fields are:* business/marketing, social sciences and history, visual/performing arts.

From out-of-state	12%	Transferred in	1%
International students	2%	African Americans	3%
Asian Americans/Pacific Islanders	4%	Hispanic Americans	2%
Native Americans	0.05%		

Faculty 179 (84% full-time), 94% with terminal degrees.
Expenses (2000–2001) *Comprehensive fee:* $25,560 includes full-time tuition ($20,284), mandatory fees ($126), and room and board ($5150). *College room only:* $3030. *Payment plan:* installment. *Waivers:* employees or children of employees.
Library Sheean Library. *Operations spending 1999–2000:* $1.5 million. *Collection:* 271,577 titles, 11,577 serial subscriptions, 10,402 audiovisual materials.
College life *Housing:* on-campus residence required through senior year. *Options:* coed, men-only, women-only. *Social organizations:* national fraternities, national sororities; 38% of eligible men and 32% of eligible women are members. *Most popular organizations:* international club, Alpha Phi Omega, Circle K, Student Senate, Habitat for Humanity.
Campus security 24-hour emergency response devices and patrols, student patrols, late-night transport-escort service, student/administration security committee.
After graduation 76 organizations recruited on campus 1997–98. 68% of class of 1998 had job offers within 6 months. *Career center:* 3 full-time, 1 part-time personnel. Services include job fairs, resume preparation, interview workshops, resume referral, career/interest testing, career counseling, careers library, job bank, job interviews. *Graduate education:* 28% of class of 1999 went directly to graduate and professional school: 18% graduate arts and sciences, 4% law, 3% medicine, 2% business, 1% dentistry.
Freshmen 2,565 applied, 1,644 admitted, 553 enrolled. 12 National Merit Scholars.

SAT verbal scores above 500	96%	SAT math scores above 500	98%
ACT above 18	100%	From top 10% of their h.s. class	46%
From top quarter	81%	From top half	100%
1998 freshmen returning in 1999	91%		

Application *Options:* eApply at www.CollegeQuest.com, Common Application, electronic application, early admission, deferred entrance. *Required:* essay or personal statement; high school transcript; minimum 2.0 GPA. *Recommended:* minimum 3.0 GPA; 3 letters of recommendation; interview.
Standardized tests *Admission: Required:* SAT I or ACT.
Significant dates *Application deadlines:* 3/1 (freshmen), rolling (transfers). *Financial aid deadline:* 3/1.
Freshman Application Contact
Mr. James R. Ruoti, Dean of Admissions, Illinois Wesleyan University, PO Box 2900, Bloomington, IL 61702-2900. **Phone:** 309-556-3031. **Toll-free phone:** 800-332-2498. **Fax:** 309-556-3411. **E-mail:** iwuadmit@titan.iwu.edu
Visit CollegeQuest.com for information on majors offered and athletics. College video available at CollegeQuest.com.

INTERNATIONAL ACADEMY OF MERCHANDISING & DESIGN, LTD.
Chicago, Illinois

- **Proprietary**, 4-year, founded 1977
- **Degrees** associate and bachelor's
- **Urban** campus
- **Coed**, 1,383 undergraduate students, 86% full-time, 70% women, 30% men
- **Minimally difficult** entrance level, 49% of applicants were admitted
- **15:1 student-to-undergraduate faculty ratio**
- **$10,692 tuition** and fees

Students *Undergraduates:* 1,193 full-time, 190 part-time. Students come from 9 states and territories.

From out-of-state	7%	Age 25 or older	22%
Transferred in	10%	International students	1%
African Americans	27%	Asian Americans/Pacific Islanders	6%
Hispanic Americans	20%		

Faculty 89 (11% full-time).
Expenses (1999–2000) *Tuition:* full-time $10,692; part-time $799 per course. Full-time tuition and fees vary according to program. Part-time tuition and fees vary according to program. *Payment plans:* installment, deferred payment. *Waivers:* employees or children of employees.
Library International Academy of Merchandising & Design Library. *Operations spending 1999–2000:* $62,327. *Collection:* 3,278 titles, 88 serial subscriptions, 375 audiovisual materials.
College life *Housing:* college housing not available. *Most popular organizations:* ASID, Student Council, Byte-Me Club.
Campus security Building security during hours of operation.
After graduation 31 organizations recruited on campus 1997–98. 100% of class of 1998 had job offers within 6 months. *Career center:* 2 full-time personnel. Services include job fairs, resume preparation, resume referral, career counseling, job bank, job interviews.
Freshmen 998 applied, 493 admitted, 494 enrolled.

Average high school GPA	2.2	SAT verbal scores above 500	N/R
SAT math scores above 500	N/R	ACT above 18	N/R
From top 10% of their h.s. class	5%	From top quarter	15%
From top half	45%	1998 freshmen returning in 1999	71%

Application *Options:* Common Application, early admission, deferred entrance. *Application fee:* $50. *Required:* high school transcript; interview. *Recommended:* essay or personal statement; minimum 2.0 GPA.
Standardized tests *Placement: Recommended:* SAT I and SAT II or ACT, SAT II: Writing Test.
Significant dates *Application deadlines:* rolling (freshmen), rolling (transfers).
Freshman Application Contact
Ms. Robyn Palmersheim, Director of Admissions, International Academy of Merchandising & Design, Ltd., One North State Street, Suite 400, Chicago, IL 60602. **Phone:** 312-541-3900. **Toll-free phone:** 877-ACADEMY. **Fax:** 312-828-9405. **E-mail:** academy@iamd.edu
Visit CollegeQuest.com for information on majors offered and athletics. College video available at CollegeQuest.com.

ITT TECHNICAL INSTITUTE
Hoffman Estates, Illinois

- **Proprietary**, primarily 2-year, founded 1986
- **Degrees** associate and bachelor's
- **Suburban** 1-acre campus with easy access to Chicago
- **Coed**
- **Minimally difficult** entrance level
- **$9190 tuition** and fees

Part of ITT Educational Services, Inc.
Admissions Office Contact
ITT Technical Institute, 375 West Higgins Road, Hoffman Estates, IL 60195-3717.
Visit CollegeQuest.com for information on majors offered and athletics. College video available at CollegeQuest.com.

JUDSON COLLEGE
Elgin, Illinois

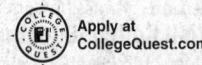
Apply at CollegeQuest.com

- **Independent Baptist**, 4-year, founded 1963
- **Degree** bachelor's
- **Suburban** 80-acre campus with easy access to Chicago
- **Coed**, 1,070 undergraduate students, 77% full-time, 57% women, 43% men
- **Moderately difficult** entrance level, 94% of applicants were admitted
- **$13,890 tuition** and fees

Illinois

Judson College, an evangelical Christian college of the liberal arts, sciences, and professions, emphasizes the integration of faith and learning, theory and practice. Judson is a caring community where faculty and staff members seek to facilitate each student's growth in all areas of life while equipping them for their careers, family life, and service to the community and church.

Students *Undergraduates:* 824 full-time, 246 part-time. Students come from 21 states and territories, 18 other countries.

Reside on campus	65%	Transferred in	7%
International students	3%	African Americans	5%
Asian Americans/Pacific Islanders	1%	Hispanic Americans	6%
Native Americans	0.1%		

Expenses (1999–2000) *Comprehensive fee:* $19,250 includes full-time tuition ($13,340), mandatory fees ($550), and room and board ($5360). *Part-time tuition:* $460 per semester hour. Part-time tuition and fees vary according to course load. *Payment plan:* installment. *Waivers:* senior citizens and employees or children of employees.

Library Benjamin P. Browne Library. *Collection:* 90,000 titles, 430 serial subscriptions.

College life *Housing:* on-campus residence required through junior year. *Options:* men-only, women-only. *Most popular organizations:* Judson Choir, Nowhere Near Broadway, philosophy and religion club, Phi Beta Lambda.

Campus security 24-hour emergency response devices and patrols, controlled dormitory access.

After graduation 79% of class of 1998 had job offers within 6 months. *Career center:* 1 full-time, 1 part-time personnel. Services include job fairs, resume preparation, career counseling, careers library.

Freshmen 576 applied, 539 admitted, 223 enrolled.

SAT verbal scores above 500	69%	SAT math scores above 500	64%
ACT above 18	86%	1998 freshmen returning in 1999	74%

Application *Options:* eApply at www.CollegeQuest.com, early admission, deferred entrance. *Application fee:* $30. *Required:* essay or personal statement; high school transcript; minimum 2.0 GPA. *Required for some:* 1 letter of recommendation; interview.

Standardized tests *Admission: Required:* SAT I or ACT. *Recommended:* ACT.

Significant dates *Application deadlines:* 8/15 (freshmen), rolling (transfers). *Financial aid deadline priority date:* 5/1.

Freshman Application Contact
Director of Admissions, Judson College, 1151 North State Street, Elgin, IL 60123-1498. **Phone:** 847-695-2500 Ext. 2310. **Toll-free phone:** 800-879-5376. **Fax:** 847-695-0216. **E-mail:** admission@judson-il.edu

Visit CollegeQuest.com for information on majors offered and athletics. College video available at CollegeQuest.com.

- *See page 1858 for a narrative description.*

KENDALL COLLEGE
Evanston, Illinois

- **Independent United Methodist**, 4-year, founded 1934
- **Degrees** associate and bachelor's
- **Suburban** 1-acre campus with easy access to Chicago
- **Coed**, 545 undergraduate students
- **Moderately difficult** entrance level, 82% of applicants were admitted
- **11:1 student-to-undergraduate faculty ratio**
- **$11,600 tuition** and fees
- **$5 million endowment**

Students *Undergraduates:* Students come from 18 states and territories, 13 other countries.

Reside on campus	33%	Age 25 or older	45%
International students	3%	African Americans	13%
Asian Americans/Pacific Islanders	4%	Hispanic Americans	8%
Native Americans	0.2%		

Faculty 65 (43% full-time), 43% with terminal degrees.

Expenses (2000–2001, estimated) *Comprehensive fee:* $16,600 includes full-time tuition ($11,500), mandatory fees ($100), and room and board ($5000). Full-time tuition and fees vary according to program. Room and board charges vary according to housing facility. *Part-time tuition:* $348 per credit. *Part-time fees:* $50 per term part-time. Part-time tuition and fees vary according to program. *Payment plan:* installment. *Waivers:* employees or children of employees.

Library Kendall Library plus 1 other. *Collection:* 37,000 titles, 200 serial subscriptions.

College life *Housing:* Option: coed. *Most popular organizations:* debate, mock trial, Students in Free Enterprise, culinary competitions, athletics.

Campus security Student patrols, late night security in dorms.

After graduation *Career center:* 2 full-time personnel. Services include job fairs, resume preparation, resume referral, career counseling, job interviews.

Freshmen 425 applied, 350 admitted.

Average high school GPA	2.5	SAT verbal scores above 500	N/R
SAT math scores above 500	N/R	ACT above 18	93%
From top 10% of their h.s. class	2%	From top quarter	18%
From top half	40%		

Application *Options:* Common Application, deferred entrance. *Application fee:* $30. *Required:* essay or personal statement; high school transcript; minimum ACT score of 18. *Required for some:* letters of recommendation. *Recommended:* minimum 2.0 GPA; interview.

Standardized tests *Admission: Required:* SAT I or ACT.

Significant dates *Application deadlines:* rolling (freshmen), rolling (transfers). *Financial aid deadline priority date:* 3/15.

Admissions Office Contact
Kendall College, 2408 Orrington Avenue, Evanston, IL 60201-2899. **Fax:** 847-866-1320.

Visit CollegeQuest.com for information on majors offered and athletics. College video available at CollegeQuest.com.

KNOX COLLEGE
Galesburg, Illinois

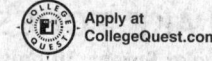
Apply at CollegeQuest.com

- **Independent**, 4-year, founded 1837
- **Degree** bachelor's
- **Small-town** 82-acre campus with easy access to Peoria
- **Coed**, 1,177 undergraduate students, 99% full-time, 55% women, 45% men
- **Very difficult** entrance level, 75% of applicants were admitted
- **12:1 student-to-undergraduate faculty ratio**
- **70% graduate** in 6 years or less
- **$21,174 tuition** and fees
- **$17,686 average financial aid** package, $15,715 average indebtedness upon graduation, $48.9 million endowment

Students *Undergraduates:* 1,168 full-time, 9 part-time. Students come from 47 states and territories, 40 other countries. *The most frequently chosen baccalaureate fields are:* biological/life sciences, social sciences and history, visual/performing arts.

From out-of-state	44%	Reside on campus	92%
Age 25 or older	1%	Transferred in	4%
International students	11%	African Americans	3%
Asian Americans/Pacific Islanders	5%	Hispanic Americans	3%
Native Americans	1%		

Faculty 112 (88% full-time), 88% with terminal degrees.

Expenses (2000–2001) *Comprehensive fee:* $26,610 includes full-time tuition ($20,940), mandatory fees ($234), and room and board ($5436). *College room only:* $2418. Room and board charges vary according to board plan and housing facility. *Payment plans:* tuition prepayment, installment. *Waivers:* employees or children of employees.

Library Seymour Library plus 2 others. *Operations spending 1999-2000:* $930,410. *Collection:* 169,661 titles, 1,500 audiovisual materials.

College life *Housing:* on-campus residence required through senior year. *Options:* coed, men-only, women-only. *Social organizations:* national fraternities, national sororities; 33% of eligible men and 12% of eligible women are members. *Most popular organizations:* international club, Allied Blacks for Liberty and Equality, Sexual Equality Awareness Coalition, Union Board, campus radio station.

Campus security 24-hour emergency response devices and patrols, late-night transport-escort service.

Illinois

Knox College (continued)

After graduation 68 organizations recruited on campus 1997–98. 61% of class of 1998 had job offers within 6 months. *Career center:* 2 full-time personnel. Services include job fairs, resume preparation, interview workshops, resume referral, career/interest testing, career counseling, careers library, job bank, job interviews. *Graduate education:* 35% of class of 1999 went directly to graduate and professional school: 20% graduate arts and sciences, 6% medicine, 5% law, 4% business.

Freshmen 1,357 applied, 1,014 admitted, 300 enrolled. 8 National Merit Scholars, 10 valedictorians.

SAT verbal scores above 500	88%	SAT math scores above 500	89%
ACT above 18	99%	From top 10% of their h.s. class	46%
From top quarter	73%	From top half	94%
1998 freshmen returning in 1999	88%		

Application *Options:* eApply at www.CollegeQuest.com, Common Application, electronic application, early admission, early action, deferred entrance. *Application fee:* $35. *Required:* essay or personal statement; high school transcript; 2 letters of recommendation. *Recommended:* interview.

Standardized tests *Admission: Required:* SAT I or ACT.

Significant dates *Application deadlines:* 2/15 (freshmen), 4/1 (transfers). *Early action:* 12/1. *Notification:* 3/31 (freshmen), 12/31 (early action). *Financial aid deadline priority date:* 3/1.

Freshman Application Contact
Mr. Paul Steenis, Director of Admissions, Knox College, Admission Office, Box K-148, Galesburg, IL 61401. **Phone:** 309-341-7100. **Toll-free phone:** 800-678-KNOX. **Fax:** 309-341-7070. **E-mail:** admission@knox.edu

Visit CollegeQuest.com for information on majors offered and athletics. Electronic viewbook available at CollegeQuest.com.

▪ *See page 1880 for a narrative description.*

LAKE FOREST COLLEGE
Lake Forest, Illinois

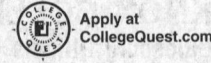 Apply at CollegeQuest.com

- **Independent**, comprehensive, founded 1857
- **Degrees** bachelor's and master's
- **Suburban** 110-acre campus with easy access to Chicago
- **Coed**, 1,214 undergraduate students, 98% full-time, 57% women, 43% men
- **Very difficult** entrance level, 77% of applicants were admitted
- **12:1 student-to-undergraduate faculty ratio**
- **63% graduate** in 6 years or less
- **$21,190 tuition** and fees
- **$17,152 average financial aid** package, $14,604 average indebtedness upon graduation, $61 million endowment

Students *Undergraduates:* 1,195 full-time, 19 part-time. Students come from 44 states and territories, 46 other countries. *The most frequently chosen baccalaureate fields are:* business/marketing, interdisciplinary studies, social sciences and history. *Graduate:* 1 in professional programs, 12 in other graduate degree programs.

From out-of-state	50%	Reside on campus	83%
Age 25 or older	2%	Transferred in	4%
International students	7%	African Americans	6%
Asian Americans/Pacific Islanders	5%	Hispanic Americans	3%
Native Americans	0.3%		

Faculty 132 (61% full-time), 79% with terminal degrees.

Expenses (2000–2001) *Comprehensive fee:* $26,190 includes full-time tuition ($20,900), mandatory fees ($290), and room and board ($5000). *College room only:* $2740. Room and board charges vary according to housing facility. *Part-time tuition:* $2610 per course. *Payment plan:* installment. *Waivers:* employees or children of employees.

Library Donnelley Library plus 1 other. *Operations spending 1999–2000:* $1.1 million. *Collection:* 285,006 titles, 1,111 serial subscriptions, 11,570 audiovisual materials.

College life *Housing:* on-campus residence required in freshman year. *Options:* coed, women-only. *Social organizations:* national fraternities, local fraternities, local sororities; 18% of eligible men and 14% of eligible women are members. *Most popular organizations:* campus newspaper, Garrick Players Drama Group, League for Environmental Awareness and Protection, international student organization, Ambassadors Host Organization.

Campus security 24-hour emergency response devices and patrols, student patrols, late-night transport-escort service.

After graduation 79 organizations recruited on campus 1997–98. 89% of class of 1998 had job offers within 6 months. *Career center:* 2 full-time personnel. Services include job fairs, resume preparation, interview workshops, resume referral, career counseling, careers library, job bank, job interviews. *Graduate education:* 21% of class of 1999 went directly to graduate and professional school: 8% graduate arts and sciences, 5% law, 3% medicine, 2% business, 1% dentistry, 1% veterinary medicine. *Major awards:* 1 Fulbright Scholar.

Freshmen 1,296 applied, 1,004 admitted, 341 enrolled. 1 National Merit Scholar, 17 class presidents, 6 valedictorians, 103 student government officers.

Average high school GPA	3.3	SAT verbal scores above 500	84%
SAT math scores above 500	82%	ACT above 18	100%
From top 10% of their h.s. class	24%	From top quarter	54%
From top half	86%	1998 freshmen returning in 1999	74%

Application *Options:* eApply at www.CollegeQuest.com, Common Application, electronic application, early admission, early decision, early action, deferred entrance. *Application fee:* $35. *Required:* essay or personal statement; high school transcript; 2 letters of recommendation; graded paper. *Recommended:* interview.

Standardized tests *Admission: Required:* SAT I or ACT.

Significant dates *Application deadlines:* 3/1 (freshmen), rolling (transfers). *Early decision:* 1/1, 12/1. *Notification:* 3/23 (freshmen), 1/21 (early decision), 12/20 (early action). *Financial aid deadline priority date:* 3/1.

Freshman Application Contact
Mr. William G. Motzer Jr., Director of Admissions, Lake Forest College, 555 North Sheridan Road, Lake Forest, IL 60045-2399. **Phone:** 847-735-5000. **Toll-free phone:** 800-828-4751. **Fax:** 847-735-6271. **E-mail:** admissions@lfc.edu

Visit CollegeQuest.com for information on majors offered and athletics.

▪ *See page 1892 for a narrative description.*

LAKEVIEW COLLEGE OF NURSING
Danville, Illinois

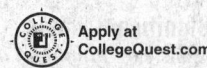 Apply at CollegeQuest.com

- **Independent**, upper-level, founded 1987
- **Degree** bachelor's
- **Small-town** campus
- **Coed,** primarily women, 78 undergraduate students, 27% full-time, 97% women, 3% men
- **Moderately difficult** entrance level
- **5:1 student-to-undergraduate faculty ratio**
- **$7440 tuition** and fees

Students *Undergraduates:* 21 full-time, 57 part-time. Students come from 2 states and territories. *The most frequently chosen baccalaureate field is:* health professions and related sciences.

Age 25 or older	71%	Transferred in	6%
African Americans	6%	Asian Americans/Pacific Islanders	3%
Hispanic Americans	3%		

Faculty 15 (27% full-time), 13% with terminal degrees.

Expenses (1999–2000) *One-time required fee:* $120. *Tuition:* full-time $7440; part-time $240 per credit hour. Full-time tuition and fees vary according to course load. *Payment plans:* installment, deferred payment.

Library Lakeview College of Nursing Library. *Collection:* 1,500 titles, 85 serial subscriptions, 365 audiovisual materials.

College life *Housing:* college housing not available. *Most popular organization:* student nurses association.

Campus security 24-hour emergency response devices.

Application *Options:* eApply at www.CollegeQuest.com, Common Application, deferred entrance. *Application fee:* $50.

Significant dates *Application deadline:* rolling (transfers). *Financial aid deadline priority date:* 4/15.

Admissions Office Contact
Lakeview College of Nursing, 812 North Logan Avenue, Danville, IL 61832. **Fax:** 217-431-4015.

Illinois

Visit CollegeQuest.com for information on majors offered and athletics.

LEWIS UNIVERSITY
Romeoville, Illinois

- **Independent**, comprehensive, founded 1932, affiliated with Roman Catholic Church
- **Degrees** associate, bachelor's, master's, and post-master's certificates
- **Small-town** 600-acre campus with easy access to Chicago
- **Coed**, 3,171 undergraduate students, 64% full-time, 55% women, 45% men
- **Moderately difficult** entrance level, 70% of applicants were admitted
- **15:1 student-to-undergraduate faculty ratio**
- **52% graduate** in 6 years or less
- **$12,810 tuition** and fees
- **$12,039 average financial aid** package, $23.6 million endowment

Lewis University offers bachelor's degrees in 60 majors as well as graduate programs in business administration, counseling psychology, criminal/social justice, education, leadership studies, nursing, and school counseling and guidance. A Christian Brothers university, Lewis is located in Romeoville and is linked by expressway to the Chicago area. Lewis has a widely recognized aviation program and an airport adjacent to campus.

Students *Undergraduates:* 2,022 full-time, 1,149 part-time. Students come from 21 states and territories, 29 other countries. *The most frequently chosen baccalaureate fields are:* business/marketing, health professions and related sciences, protective services/public administration. *Graduate:* 880 in graduate degree programs.

From out-of-state	3%	Reside on campus	28%
Age 25 or older	43%	Transferred in	17%
International students	4%	African Americans	15%
Asian Americans/Pacific Islanders	3%	Hispanic Americans	6%
Native Americans	0.3%		

Faculty 143 full-time.
Expenses (1999–2000) *Comprehensive fee:* $18,540 includes full-time tuition ($12,810) and room and board ($5730). Full-time tuition and fees vary according to course load. Room and board charges vary according to board plan and housing facility. *Part-time tuition:* $427 per credit hour. Part-time tuition and fees vary according to course load. *Payment plan:* installment. *Waivers:* children of alumni and employees or children of employees.
Library Lewis University Library. *Operations spending 1999–2000:* $823,194. *Collection:* 166,134 titles, 732 serial subscriptions.
College life *Housing:* Options: coed, men-only, women-only, disabled students. *Social organizations:* national fraternities, national sororities, local fraternities, local sororities; 7% of eligible men and 4% of eligible women are members. *Most popular organizations:* cultural awareness organizations, Scholars Academy, Black Student Union, Fellowship of Justice.
Campus security 24-hour emergency response devices and patrols, student patrols, late-night transport-escort service, controlled dormitory access.
After graduation 165 organizations recruited on campus 1997–98. 80% of class of 1998 had job offers within 6 months. *Career center:* 12 full-time, 1 part-time personnel. Services include job fairs, resume preparation, interview workshops, resume referral, career/interest testing, career counseling, careers library, job bank, job interviews. *Graduate education:* 10% of class of 1999 went directly to graduate and professional school.
Freshmen 1,217 applied, 857 admitted, 432 enrolled.

SAT verbal scores above 500	N/R	SAT math scores above 500	N/R
ACT above 18	87%	1998 freshmen returning in 1999	78%

Application *Options:* Common Application, deferred entrance. *Application fee:* $30. *Required:* high school transcript; minimum 2.0 GPA. *Required for some:* interview.
Standardized tests *Admission: Required:* ACT.
Significant dates *Application deadlines:* rolling (freshmen), rolling (transfers). *Financial aid deadline priority date:* 5/1.
Freshman Application Contact
Ms. Karen Calloway, Assistant Director of Admissions, Lewis University, Box 297, Romeoville, IL 60446. **Phone:** 815-838-0500 Ext. 5237. **Toll-free phone:** 800-897-9000. **Fax:** 815-838-9456. **E-mail:** admissions@lewisu.edu

---

Visit CollegeQuest.com for information on majors offered and athletics. College video available at CollegeQuest.com.

■ *See page 1922 for a narrative description.*

LINCOLN CHRISTIAN COLLEGE
Lincoln, Illinois

- **Independent**, 4-year, founded 1944, affiliated with Christian Churches and Churches of Christ
- **Degrees** associate and bachelor's
- **Small-town** 227-acre campus
- **Coed**, 576 undergraduate students, 82% full-time, 54% women, 46% men
- **Moderately difficult** entrance level, 82% of applicants were admitted
- **$6708 tuition** and fees

Students *Undergraduates:* 471 full-time, 105 part-time. Students come from 29 states and territories, 7 other countries.

Reside on campus	50%	Age 25 or older	21%
Transferred in	7%		

Expenses (1999–2000) *Comprehensive fee:* $10,608 includes full-time tuition ($5824), mandatory fees ($884), and room and board ($3900). *College room only:* $1790. Room and board charges vary according to board plan. *Part-time tuition:* $182 per semester hour. *Part-time fees:* $12 per hour; $250. Part-time tuition and fees vary according to course load. *Payment plans:* installment, deferred payment. *Waivers:* employees or children of employees.
Library Jessie Eury Library. *Collection:* 90,000 titles, 450 serial subscriptions.
College life *Housing:* on-campus residence required through senior year. *Options:* men-only, women-only.
Campus security 24-hour emergency response devices, student patrols.
After graduation *Career center:* Services include career counseling.
Freshmen 208 applied, 171 admitted, 129 enrolled.

SAT verbal scores above 500	N/R	SAT math scores above 500	N/R
ACT above 18	N/R	From top 10% of their h.s. class	12%
From top quarter	33%	From top half	64%
1998 freshmen returning in 1999	69%		

Application *Option:* deferred entrance. *Preference* given to applicants interested in religious studies. *Application fee:* $20. *Required:* high school transcript; 3 letters of recommendation. *Required for some:* interview.
Standardized tests *Admission: Required:* ACT.
Significant dates *Application deadlines:* rolling (freshmen), rolling (transfers). *Financial aid deadline priority date:* 2/1.
Freshman Application Contact
Ms. Patsy Wilson, Assistant Director of Admissions, Lincoln Christian College, 100 Campus View Drive, Lincoln, IL 62656-2167. **Phone:** 217-732-3168 Ext. 2218. **Toll-free phone:** 888-522-5228. **Fax:** 217-732-5914. **E-mail:** coladmis@lccs.edu
Visit CollegeQuest.com for information on majors offered and athletics. Electronic viewbook available at CollegeQuest.com.

LOYOLA UNIVERSITY CHICAGO
Chicago, Illinois

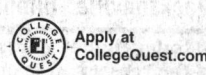
Apply at CollegeQuest.com

- **Independent Roman Catholic (Jesuit)**, university, founded 1870
- **Degrees** bachelor's, master's, doctoral, and first professional (also offers adult part-time program with significant enrollment not reflected in profile)
- **Urban** 105-acre campus
- **Coed**, 6,773 undergraduate students, 78% full-time, 65% women, 35% men
- **Moderately difficult** entrance level, 78% of applicants were admitted
- **11:1 student-to-undergraduate faculty ratio**
- **$18,310 tuition** and fees
- **$17,834 average financial aid** package, $18,300 average indebtedness upon graduation, $307.4 million endowment

Peterson's Guide to Four-Year Colleges 2001 www.petersons.com

Illinois

Loyola University Chicago (continued)

Students *Undergraduates:* 5,310 full-time, 1,463 part-time. Students come from 50 states and territories. *The most frequently chosen baccalaureate fields are:* business/marketing, psychology, social sciences and history. *Graduate:* 1,287 in professional programs, 4,476 in other graduate degree programs.

From out-of-state	28%	Reside on campus	30%
Age 25 or older	6%	Transferred in	6%
International students	1%	African Americans	8%
Asian Americans/Pacific Islanders	13%	Hispanic Americans	9%
Native Americans	0.1%		

Faculty 610 full-time.

Expenses (1999–2000) *Comprehensive fee:* $25,316 includes full-time tuition ($17,750), mandatory fees ($560), and room and board ($7006). *College room only:* $5206. Room and board charges vary according to board plan and housing facility. *Part-time tuition:* $350 per semester hour. *Part-time fees:* $57 per term part-time. Part-time tuition and fees vary according to course load. *Payment plan:* installment. *Waivers:* employees or children of employees.

Library Cudahy Library plus 3 others. *Operations spending 1999–2000:* $10 million. *Collection:* 1.5 million titles, 11,114 serial subscriptions.

College life *Housing:* Option: coed. *Social organizations:* national fraternities, national sororities; 8% of eligible men and 7% of eligible women are members. *Most popular organizations:* Campus Life Union Board, Activities Programming Board, Lake Shore Government Association, Water Tower Government.

Campus security 24-hour emergency response devices and patrols, late-night transport-escort service, controlled dormitory access.

After graduation *Career center:* 11 full-time, 3 part-time personnel. Services include job fairs, resume preparation, resume referral, career counseling, careers library, job interviews.

Freshmen 5,698 applied, 4,467 admitted, 1,067 enrolled. 13 valedictorians.

SAT verbal scores above 500	86%	SAT math scores above 500	82%
ACT above 18	97%	From top 10% of their h.s. class	30%
From top quarter	63%	From top half	92%
1998 freshmen returning in 1999	81%		

Application *Options:* eApply at www.CollegeQuest.com, early admission. *Application fee:* $25. *Required:* essay or personal statement; high school transcript. *Recommended:* interview.

Standardized tests *Admission: Required:* SAT I or ACT.

Significant dates *Application deadlines:* 4/1 (freshmen), 7/9 (transfers). *Notification:* continuous until 8/15 (freshmen). *Financial aid deadline priority date:* 3/1.

Freshman Application Contact Ms. Victoria Valle, Director of Admissions, Loyola University Chicago, 820 North Michigan Avenue, Chicago, IL 60611-2196. **Phone:** 312-915-6500. **Toll-free phone:** 800-262-2373. **E-mail:** admission@luc.edu

Visit CollegeQuest.com for information on majors offered and athletics. College video available at CollegeQuest.com.

■ *See page 1956 for a narrative description.*

MACMURRAY COLLEGE
Jacksonville, Illinois

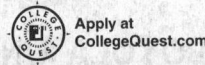

- **Independent United Methodist**, 4-year, founded 1846
- **Degrees** associate and bachelor's
- **Small-town** 60-acre campus
- **Coed**, 686 undergraduate students, 94% full-time, 51% women, 49% men
- **Moderately difficult** entrance level, 76% of applicants were admitted
- **11:1** student-to-undergraduate faculty ratio
- **47% graduate** in 6 years or less
- **$12,375 tuition** and fees
- **$13,376 average financial aid** package, $17,242 average indebtedness upon graduation, $10.7 million endowment

Students *Undergraduates:* 647 full-time, 39 part-time. Students come from 25 states and territories. *The most frequently chosen baccalaureate fields are:* education, protective services/public administration, psychology.

From out-of-state	18%	Reside on campus	66%
Age 25 or older	13%	Transferred in	12%
International students	1%	African Americans	11%
Asian Americans/Pacific Islanders	1%	Hispanic Americans	4%
Native Americans	0.1%		

Faculty 83 (70% full-time).

Expenses (1999–2000) *Comprehensive fee:* $16,805 includes full-time tuition ($12,300), mandatory fees ($75), and room and board ($4430). *College room only:* $1860. *Part-time tuition:* $375 per credit hour. *Payment plan:* installment. *Waivers:* children of alumni, senior citizens, and employees or children of employees.

Library Henry Pfeiffer Library. *Operations spending 1999–2000:* $187,542. *Collection:* 146,000 titles, 103,519 serial subscriptions, 100 audiovisual materials.

College life *Housing:* on-campus residence required through junior year. *Options:* coed, men-only, women-only. *Social organizations:* national fraternities, local sororities; 10% of eligible men and 10% of eligible women are members. *Most popular organizations:* Campus Activity Board, MacMurray Student Association, Sigma Tau Gamma, Alpha Phi Omega, Circle K.

Campus security 24-hour emergency response devices, student patrols, late-night transport-escort service, controlled dormitory access.

After graduation 15 organizations recruited on campus 1997–98. 90% of class of 1998 had job offers within 6 months. *Career center:* 1 full-time, 1 part-time personnel. Services include job fairs, resume preparation, interview workshops, resume referral, career/interest testing, career counseling, careers library, job bank, job interviews.

Freshmen 802 applied, 613 admitted, 186 enrolled. 5 class presidents, 3 valedictorians, 27 student government officers.

Average high school GPA	3.32	SAT verbal scores above 500	N/R
SAT math scores above 500	56%	ACT above 18	68%
From top 10% of their h.s. class	8%	From top quarter	27%
From top half	57%	1998 freshmen returning in 1999	69%

Application *Options:* eApply at www.CollegeQuest.com, Common Application, electronic application, early admission. *Application fee:* $20. *Required:* essay or personal statement; high school transcript; minimum 2.0 GPA. *Required for some:* letters of recommendation; interview.

Standardized tests *Admission: Required:* SAT I or ACT.

Significant dates *Application deadlines:* 7/15 (freshmen), 7/15 (transfers). *Financial aid deadline priority date:* 5/31.

Freshman Application Contact Mrs. Lori A. Hall, Dean of Enrollment, MacMurray College, 447 East College Avenue, Jacksonville, IL 62650. **Phone:** 217-479-7056. **Toll-free phone:** 800-252-7485. **Fax:** 217-245-0405. **E-mail:** admiss@mac.edu

Visit CollegeQuest.com for information on majors offered and athletics. Electronic viewbook available at CollegeQuest.com.

MCKENDREE COLLEGE
Lebanon, Illinois

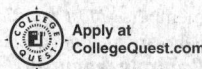

- **Independent**, 4-year, founded 1828, affiliated with United Methodist Church
- **Degree** bachelor's
- **Small-town** 80-acre campus with easy access to St. Louis
- **Coed**, 2,017 undergraduate students, 72% full-time, 63% women, 37% men
- **Moderately difficult** entrance level, 73% of applicants were admitted
- **15:1** student-to-undergraduate faculty ratio
- **56% graduate** in 6 years or less
- **$11,250 tuition** and fees
- **$10,369 average financial aid** package, $11,434 average indebtedness upon graduation, $17.1 million endowment

Students *Undergraduates:* 1,459 full-time, 558 part-time. Students come from 12 states and territories, 13 other countries. *The most frequently chosen baccalaureate fields are:* business/marketing, education, health professions and related sciences.

From out-of-state	30%	Reside on campus	52%
Age 25 or older	40%	Transferred in	8%
International students	2%	African Americans	10%
Asian Americans/Pacific Islanders	1%	Hispanic Americans	1%
Native Americans	0.4%		

Illinois

Faculty 174 (34% full-time), 37% with terminal degrees.
Expenses (1999–2000) *Comprehensive fee:* $15,500 includes full-time tuition ($11,250) and room and board ($4250). Full-time tuition and fees vary according to class time, course load, and location. Room and board charges vary according to board plan and housing facility. *Part-time tuition:* $375 per credit hour. Part-time tuition and fees vary according to class time, course load, and location. *Payment plan:* installment. *Waivers:* employees or children of employees.
Library Holman Library. *Operations spending 1999–2000:* $357,954. *Collection:* 79,963 titles, 501 serial subscriptions, 3,898 audiovisual materials.
College life *Housing:* on-campus residence required through junior year. *Options:* coed, men-only, women-only. *Social organizations:* national fraternities, local fraternities, local sororities; 5% of eligible men and 6% of eligible women are members. *Most popular organizations:* Model United Nations, Campus Christian Fellowship, Residence Hall Association, Student Government Association, Students Against Social Injustice.
Campus security 24-hour emergency response devices and patrols, student patrols, late-night transport-escort service, controlled dormitory access.
After graduation 115 organizations recruited on campus 1997–98. 96% of class of 1998 had job offers within 6 months. *Career center:* 2 full-time personnel. Services include job fairs, resume preparation, interview workshops, resume referral, career/interest testing, career counseling, careers library, job bank, job interviews. *Graduate education:* 12% of class of 1999 went directly to graduate and professional school: 4% business, 4% graduate arts and sciences, 2% law, 1% medicine, 1% theology.
Freshmen 1,049 applied, 766 admitted, 256 enrolled. 1 National Merit Scholar, 16 valedictorians.

Average high school GPA	3.7	SAT verbal scores above 500	N/R
SAT math scores above 500	N/R	ACT above 18	96%
From top 10% of their h.s. class	31%	From top quarter	70%
From top half	88%	1998 freshmen returning in 1999	82%

Application *Options:* eApply at www.CollegeQuest.com, Common Application, deferred entrance. *Application fee:* $0. *Required:* high school transcript; minimum 2.5 GPA; 1 letter of recommendation. *Required for some:* essay or personal statement; interview.
Standardized tests *Admission:* Required: SAT I or ACT.
Significant dates *Application deadlines:* rolling (freshmen), rolling (transfers). *Financial aid deadline priority date:* 5/31.
Freshman Application Contact
Sue Cordon, Dean of Admissions and Financial Aid, McKendree College, 701 College Road, Lebanon, IL 62254. **Phone:** 618-537-4481 Ext. 6831. **Toll-free phone:** 800-232-7228 Ext. 6831. **Fax:** 618-537-6259. **E-mail:** scordon@atlas.mckendree.edu
Visit CollegeQuest.com for information on majors offered and athletics. College video available at CollegeQuest.com.

■ *See page 2030 for a narrative description.*

MENNONITE COLLEGE OF NURSING
Illinois—See Illinois State University

MILLIKIN UNIVERSITY
Decatur, Illinois

- **Independent**, 4-year, founded 1901, affiliated with Presbyterian Church (U.S.A.)
- **Degree** bachelor's
- **Suburban** 70-acre campus
- **Coed**, 2,250 undergraduate students, 97% full-time, 59% women, 41% men
- **Moderately difficult** entrance level, 75% of applicants were admitted
- **13:1 student-to-undergraduate faculty ratio**
- **64% graduate** in 6 years or less
- **$16,008 tuition** and fees
- **$14,497 average financial aid** package, $14,468 average indebtedness upon graduation, $62.8 million endowment

Students *Undergraduates:* 2,172 full-time, 78 part-time. Students come from 36 states and territories, 9 other countries. *The most frequently chosen baccalaureate fields are:* business/marketing, education, visual/performing arts.

From out-of-state	15%	Reside on campus	70%
Age 25 or older	6%	Transferred in	7%
International students	1%	African Americans	7%
Asian Americans/Pacific Islanders	1%	Hispanic Americans	2%
Native Americans	0.2%		

Faculty 227 (63% full-time).
Expenses (1999–2000) *Comprehensive fee:* $21,601 includes full-time tuition ($15,808), mandatory fees ($200), and room and board ($5593). *College room only:* $2938. Full-time tuition and fees vary according to course load. Room and board charges vary according to board plan and housing facility. *Part-time tuition:* $450 per credit. *Payment plan:* installment. *Waivers:* employees or children of employees.
Library Staley Library. *Operations spending 1999–2000:* $611,351. *Collection:* 142,048 titles, 1,008 serial subscriptions, 8,496 audiovisual materials.
College life *Housing:* on-campus residence required through junior year. *Options:* coed, men-only, women-only, disabled students. *Social organizations:* national fraternities, national sororities; 23% of eligible men and 24% of eligible women are members. *Most popular organizations:* University Center Board, Millikin Marketing Association, Student Senate, Alpha Phi Omega, Residence Hall Association.
Campus security 24-hour emergency response devices and patrols, late-night transport-escort service, controlled dormitory access.
After graduation 91 organizations recruited on campus 1997–98. 98% of class of 1998 had job offers within 6 months. *Career center:* 3 full-time, 13 part-time personnel. Services include job fairs, resume preparation, interview workshops, resume referral, career/interest testing, career counseling, careers library, job bank, job interviews. *Graduate education:* 19% of class of 1999 went directly to graduate and professional school: 11% graduate arts and sciences, 2% education, 2% medicine, 1% business, 1% law, 1% veterinary medicine.
Freshmen 2,461 applied, 1,836 admitted, 595 enrolled. 19 valedictorians, 129 student government officers.

SAT verbal scores above 500	75%	SAT math scores above 500	73%
ACT above 18	98%	From top 10% of their h.s. class	22%
From top quarter	51%	From top half	85%
1998 freshmen returning in 1999	77%		

Application *Option:* deferred entrance. *Required:* high school transcript; minimum 2.0 GPA; 2 letters of recommendation. *Required for some:* audition for school of music; portfolio review for art program. *Recommended:* interview.
Standardized tests *Admission:* Required: SAT I or ACT.
Significant dates *Application deadlines:* rolling (freshmen), rolling (transfers). *Financial aid deadline:* 6/1. Priority date: 4/1.
Freshman Application Contact
Mr. Lin Stoner, Dean of Admission, Millikin University, 1184 West Main Street, Decatur, IL 62522-2084. **Phone:** 217-424-6210. **Toll-free phone:** 800-373-7733. **Fax:** 217-425-4669. **E-mail:** admis@mail.millikin.edu
Visit CollegeQuest.com for information on majors offered and athletics.

MONMOUTH COLLEGE
Monmouth, Illinois

Apply at CollegeQuest.com

- **Independent**, 4-year, founded 1853, affiliated with Presbyterian Church
- **Degree** bachelor's
- **Small-town** 40-acre campus with easy access to Peoria
- **Coed**, 1,047 undergraduate students, 99% full-time, 57% women, 43% men
- **Moderately difficult** entrance level, 77% of applicants were admitted
- **14:1 student-to-undergraduate faculty ratio**
- **51.5% graduate** in 6 years or less
- **$15,720 tuition** and fees
- **$52.3 million endowment**

Students *Undergraduates:* 1,037 full-time, 10 part-time. Students come from 20 states and territories, 23 other countries. *The most frequently chosen baccalaureate fields are:* business/marketing, education, social sciences and

Illinois

Monmouth College (continued)
history.

From out-of-state	7%	Reside on campus	90%
Age 25 or older	2%	Transferred in	6%
International students	4%	African Americans	5%
Asian Americans/Pacific Islanders	1%	Hispanic Americans	2%
Native Americans	0.2%		

Faculty 99 (66% full-time), 91% with terminal degrees.
Expenses (1999–2000) *Comprehensive fee:* $20,130 includes full-time tuition ($15,720) and room and board ($4410). *College room only:* $2410. Room and board charges vary according to board plan and housing facility. *Part-time tuition:* $655 per semester hour. *Payment plan:* installment. *Waivers:* employees or children of employees.
Library Hewes Library. *Operations spending 1999–2000:* $687,422. *Collection:* 177,974 titles, 1,709 serial subscriptions, 1,331 audiovisual materials.
College life *Housing:* on-campus residence required through senior year. *Options:* coed, men-only, women-only. *Social organizations:* national fraternities, national sororities; 25% of eligible men and 30% of eligible women are members. *Most popular organizations:* Student Service Organization, Student Association, M-Club, Greek life, Crimson Masque.
Campus security 24-hour emergency response devices, late-night transport-escort service, night security.
After graduation 21 organizations recruited on campus 1997–98. 90% of class of 1998 had job offers within 6 months. *Career center:* 1 full-time, 2 part-time personnel. Services include job fairs, resume preparation, interview workshops, resume referral, career/interest testing, career counseling, careers library, job bank, job interviews. *Graduate education:* 20% of class of 1999 went directly to graduate and professional school.
Freshmen 1,210 applied, 937 admitted, 274 enrolled.

Average high school GPA	3.0	SAT verbal scores above 500	N/R
SAT math scores above 500	N/R	ACT above 18	99%
From top 10% of their h.s. class	14%	From top quarter	52%
From top half	88%	1998 freshmen returning in 1999	78%

Application *Options:* eApply at www.CollegeQuest.com, Common Application, electronic application, deferred entrance. *Application fee:* $0. *Required:* high school transcript. *Required for some:* essay or personal statement. *Recommended:* 2 letters of recommendation; interview.
Standardized tests *Admission: Required:* SAT I or ACT.
Significant dates *Application deadlines:* 5/1 (freshmen), rolling (transfers). *Notification:* continuous until 7/1 (freshmen). *Financial aid deadline priority date:* 4/15.
Freshman Application Contact
Mrs. Marybeth Kemp, Dean of Admission, Monmouth College, 700 East Broadway, Monmouth, IL 61462-1998. **Phone:** 309-457-2131. **Toll-free phone:** 800-747-2687. **Fax:** 309-457-2141. **E-mail:** admit@monm.edu
Visit CollegeQuest.com for information on majors offered and athletics. College video available at CollegeQuest.com.

MOODY BIBLE INSTITUTE
Chicago, Illinois

- **Independent nondenominational**, comprehensive, founded 1886
- **Degrees** bachelor's, master's, and first professional
- **Urban** 25-acre campus
- **Coed**, 1,335 undergraduate students, 96% full-time, 42% women, 58% men
- **Moderately difficult** entrance level, 56% of applicants were admitted
- **18:1 student-to-undergraduate faculty ratio**
- **46% graduate** in 6 years or less
- **$1225 tuition** and fees

Students *Undergraduates:* 1,283 full-time, 52 part-time. Students come from 48 states and territories, 41 other countries. *The most frequently chosen baccalaureate fields are:* communications/communication technologies, foreign language/literature, philosophy. *Graduate:* 62 in professional programs, 61 in other graduate degree programs.

From out-of-state	69%	Reside on campus	90%
Age 25 or older	10%	Transferred in	10%
International students	8%	African Americans	2%
Asian Americans/Pacific Islanders	2%	Hispanic Americans	3%
Native Americans	1%		

Faculty 101 (88% full-time), 70% with terminal degrees.
Expenses (1999–2000) includes mandatory fees ($1225) and room and board ($4770). Room and board charges vary according to housing facility. *Part-time fees:* $630 per term part-time. *Payment plan:* installment. *Waivers:* employees or children of employees.
Library Henry Crowell Learning Center plus 1 other. *Collection:* 135,000 titles, 987 serial subscriptions.
College life *Housing:* on-campus residence required through senior year. *Options:* men-only, women-only. *Social organizations:* 70% of eligible men and 80% of eligible women are members. *Most popular organizations:* Student Missionary Fellowship, Big Brother/Big Sister, music groups, drama group.
Campus security 24-hour emergency response devices and patrols, student patrols, late-night transport-escort service, controlled dormitory access.
After graduation *Career center:* 1 full-time personnel. Services include job fairs, resume preparation, career counseling, careers library, job bank, job interviews.
Freshmen 1,106 applied, 622 admitted, 210 enrolled.

Average high school GPA	3.4	SAT verbal scores above 500	N/R
SAT math scores above 500	N/R	ACT above 18	97%
1998 freshmen returning in 1999	86%		

Application *Options:* early admission, early decision. *Application fee:* $35. *Required:* essay or personal statement; high school transcript; minimum 2.3 GPA; 4 letters of recommendation; Christian testimony. *Required for some:* interview.
Standardized tests *Admission: Required:* SAT I and SAT II or ACT.
Significant dates *Application deadlines:* 3/1 (freshmen), 3/1 (transfers). *Early decision:* 12/1. *Notification:* continuous until 8/1 (freshmen), 1/15 (early decision). *Financial aid deadline:* continuous.
Freshman Application Contact
Mrs. Marthe Campa, Application Coordinator, Moody Bible Institute, 820 North LaSalle Boulevard, Chicago, IL 60610. **Phone:** 312-329-4266. **Toll-free phone:** 800-967-4MBI. **Fax:** 312-329-8987. **E-mail:** admissions@moody.edu
Visit CollegeQuest.com for information on majors offered and athletics. College video available at CollegeQuest.com.

NAES COLLEGE
Chicago, Illinois

- **Independent**, 4-year, founded 1974
- **Degree** bachelor's
- **Coed**, 53 undergraduate students, 87% full-time, 72% women, 28% men
- **Noncompetitive** entrance level, 100% of applicants were admitted
- **$5140 tuition** and fees

Students *Undergraduates:* 46 full-time, 7 part-time.

Age 25 or older	97%	African Americans	2%
Native Americans	89%		

Faculty 43 (9% full-time).
Expenses (1999–2000) *Tuition:* full-time $5000; part-time $208 per credit. *Required fees:* full-time $140; $70 per term part-time. *Payment plan:* tuition prepayment.
Library *Collection:* 6,000 titles, 60 serial subscriptions.
College life *Housing:* college housing not available.
After graduation *Career center:* Services include career counseling.
Freshmen 1 applied, 1 admitted, 1 enrolled.

SAT verbal scores above 500	N/R	SAT math scores above 500	N/R
ACT above 18	N/R		

Application *Required:* high school transcript; interview; employment in an American Indian program.
Significant dates *Application deadlines:* rolling (freshmen), rolling (transfers). *Financial aid deadline priority date:* 6/1.
Freshman Application Contact
Ms. Christine Redcloud, Registrar, NAES College, 2838 West Peterson Avenue, Chicago, IL 60659-3813. **Phone:** 773-761-5000. **Fax:** 773-761-3808.
Visit CollegeQuest.com for information on majors offered and athletics.

Illinois

THE NATIONAL COLLEGE OF CHIROPRACTIC
Lombard, Illinois

- **Independent**, upper-level, founded 1906
- **Degrees** incidental bachelor's, first professional, and first professional certificates
- **Suburban** 32-acre campus with easy access to Chicago
- **Coed**
- **Moderately difficult** entrance level
- **9:1 student-to-undergraduate faculty ratio**
- **$17,203 tuition** and fees

Students *Undergraduates:* Students come from 32 states and territories, 14 other countries. *The most frequently chosen baccalaureate field is:* health professions and related sciences. *Graduate:* 770 in professional programs.

| Reside on campus | 30% | Age 25 or older | 62% |

Expenses (1999–2000) *Tuition:* full-time $16,875. *Required fees:* full-time $328. Full-time tuition and fees vary according to course load. *College room only:* $4281. Room and board charges vary according to housing facility.

Library Learning Resource Center. *Collection:* 25,000 titles, 500 serial subscriptions.

College life *Housing: Options:* coed, men-only, women-only. *Social organizations:* national fraternities; 25% of eligible men and 15% of eligible women are members. *Most popular organizations:* Student American Chiropractic Association, Motion Palpation Club, rugby club, intramurals.

Campus security 24-hour emergency response devices and patrols, late-night transport-escort service.

After graduation *Career center:* Services include resume preparation, career counseling, job bank.

Application *Options:* electronic application, deferred entrance. *Application fee:* $55.

Significant dates *Application deadline:* rolling (transfers). *Financial aid deadline:* continuous.

Freshman Application Contact
Mr. Kurt Schick, Director of Admissions, The National College of Chiropractic, 200 Roosevelt Road, Lombard, IL 60148. **Phone:** 630-889-6572. **Toll-free phone:** 800-826-6285. **E-mail:** admissions@ncc.chiropractic.edu

Visit CollegeQuest.com for information on majors offered and athletics. College video available at CollegeQuest.com.

NATIONAL-LOUIS UNIVERSITY
Evanston, Illinois

- **Independent**, university, founded 1886
- **Degrees** bachelor's, master's, doctoral, post-master's, and postbachelor's certificates
- **12-acre** campus with easy access to Chicago
- **Coed**, 3,545 undergraduate students, 86% full-time, 72% women, 28% men
- **Minimally difficult** entrance level, 99% of applicants were admitted
- **22% graduate** in 6 years or less
- **$13,095 tuition** and fees
- **$13.6 million endowment**

Students *Undergraduates:* 3,064 full-time, 481 part-time. Students come from 19 states and territories. *Graduate:* 3,991 in graduate degree programs.

From out-of-state	1%	Reside on campus	5%
Transferred in	24%	International students	1%
African Americans	26%	Asian Americans/Pacific Islanders	3%
Hispanic Americans	8%	Native Americans	0.3%

Expenses (1999–2000) *Tuition:* full-time $13,095; part-time $291 per quarter hour. Full-time tuition and fees vary according to location and program. Part-time tuition and fees vary according to location and program. Room and board charges vary according to board plan. *Payment plans:* installment, deferred payment. *Waivers:* employees or children of employees.

Library NLU Library plus 5 others. *Operations spending 1999–2000:* $1.7 million. *Collection:* 5,043 audiovisual materials.

College life *Housing: Option:* coed. *Social organizations:* 1% of women are members. *Most popular organizations:* Student Council, Nosotros Unidos, Accounting Club, African-American Club.

Campus security 24-hour emergency response devices and patrols.

After graduation *Career center:* 8 full-time, 6 part-time personnel. Services include job fairs, resume preparation, resume referral, career counseling, careers library, job bank, job interviews.

Freshmen 320 applied, 319 admitted, 209 enrolled.

SAT verbal scores above 500	N/R	SAT math scores above 500	N/R
ACT above 18	47%	From top 10% of their h.s. class	0%
From top quarter	29%	From top half	89%

Application *Option:* deferred entrance. *Application fee:* $25. *Required:* high school transcript; minimum 2.0 GPA. *Required for some:* 2 letters of recommendation. *Recommended:* interview.

Standardized tests *Admission: Required for some:* SAT I or ACT.

Significant dates *Application deadlines:* rolling (freshmen), rolling (transfers). *Financial aid deadline priority date:* 4/15.

Freshman Application Contact
Office of Student Enrollment, National-Louis University, 2840 Sheridan Road, Evanston, IL 60201-1796. **Phone:** 847-465-0575. **Toll-free phone:** 888-NLU-TODAY Ext. 5151 (in-state); 800-443-5522 Ext. 5151 (out-of-state).

Visit CollegeQuest.com for information on majors offered and athletics.

- *See page 2134 for a narrative description.*

NORTH CENTRAL COLLEGE
Naperville, Illinois

 Apply at CollegeQuest.com

- **Independent United Methodist**, comprehensive, founded 1861
- **Degrees** bachelor's and master's
- **Suburban** 56-acre campus with easy access to Chicago
- **Coed**, 1,907 undergraduate students, 88% full-time, 57% women, 43% men
- **Moderately difficult** entrance level, 76% of applicants were admitted
- **13:1 student-to-undergraduate faculty ratio**
- **58.8% graduate** in 6 years or less
- **$15,216 tuition** and fees
- **$13,316 average financial aid** package, $14,061 average indebtedness upon graduation, $52.3 million endowment

Students *Undergraduates:* 1,669 full-time, 238 part-time. Students come from 25 states and territories, 23 other countries. *The most frequently chosen baccalaureate fields are:* business/marketing, communications/communication technologies, education. *Graduate:* 366 in graduate degree programs.

From out-of-state	10%	Reside on campus	41%
Age 25 or older	25%	Transferred in	11%
International students	2%	African Americans	4%
Asian Americans/Pacific Islanders	2%	Hispanic Americans	3%
Native Americans	0.4%		

Faculty 228 (53% full-time), 58% with terminal degrees.

Expenses (1999–2000) *Comprehensive fee:* $20,466 includes full-time tuition ($15,096), mandatory fees ($120), and room and board ($5250). *Part-time tuition:* $441 per credit. Part-time tuition and fees vary according to course load and program. *Payment plan:* installment. *Waivers:* senior citizens and employees or children of employees.

Library Oesterle Library. *Operations spending 1999–2000:* $796,505. *Collection:* 126,057 titles, 659 serial subscriptions, 3,022 audiovisual materials.

College life *Housing: Options:* coed, men-only, women-only. *Most popular organizations:* College Union Activities Board, student radio station, Cards in Action (service group), Black Student Organization, Residence Hall Association.

Campus security Late-night transport-escort service.

After graduation 60 organizations recruited on campus 1997–98. 77% of class of 1998 had job offers within 6 months. *Career center:* 4 full-time personnel. Services include job fairs, resume preparation, resume referral, career counseling, careers library, job bank, job interviews. *Graduate education:* 10% of class of 1999 went directly to graduate and professional school: 6% graduate arts and sciences, 2% business, 1% education, 1% medicine.

Illinois

North Central College (continued)

Freshmen 1,453 applied, 1,111 admitted, 402 enrolled. 3 National Merit Scholars, 13 valedictorians.

Average high school GPA	3.5	SAT verbal scores above 500	85%
SAT math scores above 500	76%	ACT above 18	98%
From top 10% of their h.s. class	25%	From top quarter	57%
From top half	85%	1998 freshmen returning in 1999	80%

Application *Options:* eApply at www.CollegeQuest.com, Common Application, early admission, deferred entrance. *Application fee:* $25. *Required:* high school transcript; minimum 2.0 GPA. *Required for some:* interview. *Recommended:* essay or personal statement; 1 letter of recommendation.

Standardized tests *Admission: Required:* SAT I or ACT. *Recommended:* ACT.

Significant dates *Application deadlines:* rolling (freshmen), rolling (transfers). *Financial aid deadline:* continuous.

Freshman Application Contact Mr. Stephen Potts, Coordinator of Freshman Admission, North Central College, 30 North Brainard Street, PO Box 3063, Naperville, IL 60566-7063. **Phone:** 630-637-5815. **Toll-free phone:** 800-411-1861. **E-mail:** ncadm@noctrl.edu

Visit CollegeQuest.com for information on majors offered and athletics. College video and electronic viewbook available at CollegeQuest.com.

■ *See page 2178 for a narrative description.*

NORTHEASTERN ILLINOIS UNIVERSITY
Chicago, Illinois

- **State-supported**, comprehensive, founded 1961
- **Degrees** bachelor's and master's
- **Urban** 67-acre campus
- **Coed**, 7,911 undergraduate students, 58% full-time, 62% women, 38% men
- **Minimally difficult** entrance level, 71% of applicants were admitted
- **18:1** student-to-undergraduate faculty ratio
- **$2890 tuition** and fees (in-state); $7414 (out-of-state)
- **$999,181 endowment**

Students *Undergraduates:* 4,567 full-time, 3,344 part-time. Students come from 8 states and territories, 41 other countries. *The most frequently chosen baccalaureate fields are:* education, business/marketing, liberal arts/general studies. *Graduate:* 2,732 in graduate degree programs.

From out-of-state	0.4%	Age 25 or older	44%
Transferred in	12%	International students	1%
African Americans	13%	Asian Americans/Pacific Islanders	14%
Hispanic Americans	27%	Native Americans	0.2%

Faculty 462 (68% full-time).

Expenses (1999–2000) *Tuition, state resident:* full-time $2576; part-time $94 per credit hour. *Tuition, nonresident:* full-time $7100; part-time $283 per credit hour. *Required fees:* full-time $314; $13 per credit hour. Full-time tuition and fees vary according to course load. Part-time tuition and fees vary according to course load. *Payment plan:* deferred payment. *Waivers:* senior citizens and employees or children of employees.

Library Ronald Williams Library plus 1 other. *Operations spending 1999-2000:* $3.1 million. *Collection:* 487,510 titles, 3,544 serial subscriptions, 33,443 audiovisual materials.

College life *Housing:* college housing not available. *Social organizations:* national sororities, men's and women's associations; 10% of eligible men and 20% of eligible women are members. *Most popular organizations:* student government, Chimexla, WZRD Radio Club, business and management club, Black Heritage Gospel Choir.

Campus security 24-hour emergency response devices and patrols, late-night transport-escort service.

After graduation 350 organizations recruited on campus 1997–98. 80% of class of 1998 had job offers within 6 months. *Career center:* 7 full-time personnel. Services include job fairs, resume preparation, interview workshops, resume referral, career counseling, careers library, job bank, job interviews.

Freshmen 2,699 applied, 1,915 admitted, 1,012 enrolled.

SAT verbal scores above 500	67%	SAT math scores above 500	33%
ACT above 18	42%	From top 10% of their h.s. class	8%
From top quarter	25%	From top half	57%
1998 freshmen returning in 1999	68%		

Application *Required:* high school transcript.
Standardized tests *Admission: Required:* ACT.
Significant dates *Application deadlines:* 7/1 (freshmen), 7/1 (transfers). *Financial aid deadline:* continuous.

Freshman Application Contact Ms. Kay D. Gulli, Administrative Assistant, Northeastern Illinois University, 500 North St. Louis Avenue, Chicago, IL 60625. **Phone:** 773-583-4050 Ext. 3613. **Fax:** 773-794-6243. **E-mail:** admrec@neiu.edu

Visit CollegeQuest.com for information on majors offered and athletics. College video available at CollegeQuest.com.

NORTHERN ILLINOIS UNIVERSITY
De Kalb, Illinois

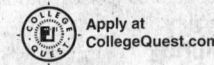
Apply at CollegeQuest.com

- **State-supported**, university, founded 1895
- **Degrees** bachelor's, master's, doctoral, and first professional
- **Small-town** 589-acre campus with easy access to Chicago
- **Coed**, 16,868 undergraduate students, 89% full-time, 54% women, 46% men
- **Moderately difficult** entrance level, 73% of applicants were admitted
- **17:1** student-to-undergraduate faculty ratio
- **50% graduate** in 6 years or less
- **$4099 tuition** and fees (in-state); $7159 (out-of-state)
- **$789,502 endowment**

Students *Undergraduates:* 15,010 full-time, 1,858 part-time. Students come from 50 states and territories, 105 other countries. *The most frequently chosen baccalaureate fields are:* business/marketing, education, English. *Graduate:* 276 in professional programs, 5,674 in other graduate degree programs.

From out-of-state	3%	Reside on campus	36%
Age 25 or older	10%	Transferred in	13%
International students	1%	African Americans	12%
Asian Americans/Pacific Islanders	6%	Hispanic Americans	6%
Native Americans	0.2%		

Faculty 1,230 (82% full-time).

Expenses (1999–2000) *Tuition, state resident:* full-time $3060; part-time $113 per credit hour. *Tuition, nonresident:* full-time $6120; part-time $226 per credit hour. *Required fees:* full-time $1039; $43 per credit hour. Full-time tuition and fees vary according to course load. Part-time tuition and fees vary according to course load. *College room and board:* $4400. Room and board charges vary according to board plan and housing facility. *Payment plan:* installment. *Waivers:* minority students and employees or children of employees.

Library Founders Memorial Library plus 8 others. *Operations spending 1999–2000:* $4 million. *Collection:* 1.6 million titles, 17,000 serial subscriptions, 49,270 audiovisual materials.

College life *Housing:* on-campus residence required in freshman year. *Option:* coed. *Social organizations:* national fraternities, national sororities; 19% of eligible men and 11% of eligible women are members. *Most popular organizations:* American Marketing Association, Delta Sigma Pi, Pi Sigma Epsilon, Black Choir, Student Volunteer Choir.

Campus security 24-hour emergency response devices and patrols, student patrols, late-night transport-escort service, controlled dormitory access.

After graduation 1,100 organizations recruited on campus 1997–98. 77% of class of 1998 had job offers within 6 months. *Career center:* 17 full-time, 3 part-time personnel. Services include job fairs, resume preparation, interview workshops, resume referral, career counseling, careers library, job bank, job interviews. *Graduate education:* 10% of class of 1999 went directly to graduate and professional school. *Major awards:* 1 Fulbright Scholar.

Illinois

Freshmen 13,804 applied, 10,017 admitted, 2,951 enrolled.

SAT verbal scores above 500	N/R	SAT math scores above 500	N/R
ACT above 18	90%	From top 10% of their h.s. class	12%
From top quarter	36%	From top half	78%
1998 freshmen returning in 1999	76%		

Application *Options:* eApply at www.CollegeQuest.com, electronic application. *Required:* high school transcript.

Standardized tests *Admission: Required:* SAT I or ACT.

Significant dates *Application deadlines:* 8/1 (freshmen), 8/1 (transfers). *Financial aid deadline priority date:* 3/1.

Freshman Application Contact Dr. Robert Burk, Director of Admissions, Northern Illinois University, De Kalb, IL 60115-2854. **Phone:** 815-753-0446. **Toll-free phone:** 800-892-3050. **E-mail:** admission-info@niu.edu

Visit CollegeQuest.com for information on majors offered and athletics. College video available at CollegeQuest.com.

NORTH PARK UNIVERSITY
Chicago, Illinois

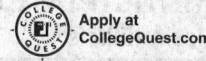
Apply at CollegeQuest.com

- **Independent**, comprehensive, founded 1891, affiliated with Evangelical Covenant Church
- **Degrees** bachelor's, master's, doctoral, and first professional
- **Urban** 30-acre campus
- **Coed**, 1,545 undergraduate students, 77% full-time, 61% women, 39% men
- **Moderately difficult** entrance level, 78% of applicants were admitted
- **16:1 student-to-undergraduate faculty ratio**
- **60% graduate** in 6 years or less
- **$16,180 tuition** and fees
- **$27.3 million endowment**

North Park blends 2 traditions—faith and freedom—and 2 rich environments—the small, residential University and the large, complex city. North Park offers broad exposure to the liberal arts and specific education in a profession. Faculty members are superbly credentialed and devoted to teaching. North Park's city location means unparalleled educational, cultural, recreational, spiritual, and artistic opportunities. Several hundred internships are available in every imaginable vocation. North Park's Urban Outreach Ministries Program has served as a national prototype for urban collegiate service opportunities. An outstanding scholars program includes generous scholarships, special courses, a leadership development program, study abroad, and alumni mentors.

Students *Undergraduates:* 1,194 full-time, 351 part-time. Students come from 36 states and territories, 29 other countries. *The most frequently chosen baccalaureate fields are:* health professions and related sciences, business/marketing, social sciences and history. *Graduate:* 79 in professional programs, 456 in other graduate degree programs.

From out-of-state	32%	Age 25 or older	20%
Transferred in	8%	International students	6%
African Americans	11%	Asian Americans/Pacific Islanders	6%
Hispanic Americans	9%	Native Americans	1%

Faculty 100 (79% full-time), 69% with terminal degrees.

Expenses (1999–2000) *Comprehensive fee:* $21,750 includes full-time tuition ($16,180) and room and board ($5570). *College room only:* $2930. Full-time tuition and fees vary according to program. Room and board charges vary according to board plan, housing facility, and student level. *Part-time tuition:* $550 per semester hour. Part-time tuition and fees vary according to program. *Payment plan:* installment. *Waivers:* adult students and employees or children of employees.

Library Consolidated Library plus 4 others. *Operations spending 1999–2000:* $845,391. *Collection:* 260,685 titles, 1,178 serial subscriptions.

College life *Housing:* on-campus residence required through junior year. *Options:* men-only, women-only. *Most popular organizations:* Student Association, Urban Outreach, College Life, college music.

Campus security 24-hour emergency response devices and patrols, late-night transport-escort service.

After graduation 30 organizations recruited on campus 1997–98. 60% of class of 1998 had job offers within 6 months. *Career center:* 1 full-time, 1 part-time personnel. Services include job fairs, resume preparation, resume referral, career counseling, careers library, job bank, job interviews. **Graduate education:** 20% of class of 1999 went directly to graduate and professional school: 10% graduate arts and sciences, 4% theology, 3% medicine, 2% law, 1% dentistry.

Freshmen 1,049 applied, 813 admitted, 487 enrolled. 5 National Merit Scholars.

SAT verbal scores above 500	83%	SAT math scores above 500	77%
ACT above 18	89%	From top 10% of their h.s. class	20%
From top quarter	45%	From top half	73%
1998 freshmen returning in 1999	70%		

Application *Options:* eApply at www.CollegeQuest.com, early admission. *Application fee:* $20. *Required:* essay or personal statement; high school transcript; minimum 2.0 GPA; 1 letter of recommendation. *Required for some:* interview. *Recommended:* minimum 3.0 GPA.

Standardized tests *Admission: Required:* SAT I or ACT.

Significant dates *Application deadlines:* rolling (freshmen), rolling (transfers). *Financial aid deadline priority date:* 5/1.

Freshman Application Contact Office of Admissions, North Park University, 3225 West Foster Avenue, Chicago, IL 60625-4895. **Phone:** 773-244-5500. **Toll-free phone:** 800-888-NPC8. **Fax:** 773-583-0858. **E-mail:** afao@northpark.edu

Visit CollegeQuest.com for information on majors offered and athletics.

■ *See page 2188 for a narrative description.*

NORTHWESTERN UNIVERSITY
Evanston, Illinois

- **Independent**, university, founded 1851
- **Degrees** bachelor's, master's, doctoral, and first professional
- **Suburban** 250-acre campus with easy access to Chicago
- **Coed**, 7,767 undergraduate students, 99% full-time, 52% women, 48% men
- **Most difficult** entrance level, 32% of applicants were admitted
- **8:1 student-to-undergraduate faculty ratio**
- **90.4% graduate** in 6 years or less
- **$23,562 tuition** and fees
- **$19,985 average financial aid** package, $13,222 average indebtedness upon graduation, $2.4 billion endowment

Students *Undergraduates:* 7,721 full-time, 46 part-time. Students come from 50 states and territories, 80 other countries. *The most frequently chosen baccalaureate fields are:* engineering/engineering technologies, English, social sciences and history. *Graduate:* 1,433 in professional programs, 6,131 in other graduate degree programs.

From out-of-state	73%	Reside on campus	67%
Age 25 or older	1%	Transferred in	1%
International students	3%	African Americans	6%
Asian Americans/Pacific Islanders	17%	Hispanic Americans	4%
Native Americans	0.2%		

Faculty 2,528 (84% full-time), 84% with terminal degrees.

Expenses (1999–2000) *Comprehensive fee:* $30,532 includes full-time tuition ($23,496), mandatory fees ($66), and room and board ($6970). Room and board charges vary according to board plan and housing facility. *Part-time tuition:* $2788 per course. *Payment plan:* installment. *Waivers:* employees or children of employees.

Library Deering Library plus 10 others. *Operations spending 1999–2000:* $19.8 million. *Collection:* 3.9 million titles, 40,124 serial subscriptions.

College life *Housing: Options:* coed, men-only, women-only. *Social organizations:* national fraternities, national sororities; 40% of eligible men and 39% of eligible women are members. *Most popular organizations:* Northwestern Volunteer Network, Daily Northwestern, Activities and Organization Board, dance marathon, Residence Hall Association.

Campus security 24-hour emergency response devices and patrols, late-night transport-escort service, controlled dormitory access.

After graduation 522 organizations recruited on campus 1997–98. *Career center:* 23 full-time personnel. Services include job fairs, resume preparation,

Illinois

Northwestern University (continued)

interview workshops, resume referral, career/interest testing, career counseling, careers library, job bank, job interviews. **Major awards:** 2 Marshall scholars.

Freshmen 15,460 applied, 4,999 admitted, 1,952 enrolled.

SAT verbal scores above 500	98%	SAT math scores above 500	99%
ACT above 18	100%	From top 10% of their h.s. class	83%
From top quarter	96%	From top half	99%
1998 freshmen returning in 1999	95%		

Application *Options:* electronic application, early admission, early decision, deferred entrance. *Application fee:* $55. *Required:* essay or personal statement; high school transcript; 1 letter of recommendation. *Required for some:* audition for music program. *Recommended:* interview.

Standardized tests *Admission: Required:* SAT I or ACT. *Recommended:* SAT II Subject Tests. *Required for some:* SAT II Subject Tests.

Significant dates *Application deadlines:* 1/1 (freshmen), 6/1 (transfers). *Early decision:* 11/1. *Notification:* 4/15 (freshmen), 12/15 (early decision). *Financial aid deadline priority date:* 2/1.

Freshman Application Contact
Ms. Carol Lunkenheimer, Director of Admissions, Northwestern University, 1801 Hinman Avenue, Evanston, IL 60208. **Phone:** 847-491-7271. **E-mail:** ug-admission@nwu.edu

Visit CollegeQuest.com for information on majors offered and athletics. Electronic viewbook available at CollegeQuest.com.

OLIVET NAZARENE UNIVERSITY
Bourbonnais, Illinois

- **Independent**, comprehensive, founded 1907, affiliated with Church of the Nazarene
- **Degrees** bachelor's and master's
- **Small-town** 168-acre campus with easy access to Chicago
- **Coed**, 1,815 undergraduate students, 84% full-time, 59% women, 41% men
- **Moderately difficult** entrance level, 92% of applicants were admitted
- **18:1** student-to-undergraduate faculty ratio
- **48% graduate** in 6 years or less
- **$12,728 tuition** and fees
- **$12,323 average financial aid** package, $15,300 average indebtedness upon graduation, $7.1 million endowment

Students *Undergraduates:* 1,521 full-time, 294 part-time. Students come from 40 states and territories. *The most frequently chosen baccalaureate fields are:* business/marketing, biological/life sciences, health professions and related sciences. *Graduate:* 648 in graduate degree programs.

Reside on campus	72%	Age 25 or older	18%
Transferred in	9%	International students	0.3%
African Americans	9%	Asian Americans/Pacific Islanders	1%
Hispanic Americans	2%	Native Americans	0.3%

Faculty 108 (76% full-time).

Expenses (2000–2001) *Comprehensive fee:* $17,424 includes full-time tuition ($11,928), mandatory fees ($800), and room and board ($4696). Full-time tuition and fees vary according to course load. Room and board charges vary according to board plan. *Part-time tuition:* $480 per hour. *Part-time fees:* $10 per term. Part-time tuition and fees vary according to course load. *Payment plan:* installment. *Waivers:* employees or children of employees.

Library Benner Library. *Operations spending 1999–2000:* $900,000. *Collection:* 140,000 titles, 1,000 serial subscriptions.

College life *Housing:* on-campus residence required through senior year. *Options:* men-only, women-only. *Most popular organizations:* Green Room (drama club), Christian Music Society, Students in Free Enterprise, Student Education Association, Women's Residence Association.

Campus security 24-hour patrols, late-night transport-escort service.

After graduation 15 organizations recruited on campus 1997–98. *Career center:* 2 full-time, 1 part-time personnel. Services include job fairs, resume preparation, interview workshops, resume referral, career/interest testing, career counseling, careers library, job bank, job interviews. **Graduate education:** 10% of class of 1999 went directly to graduate and professional school.

Freshmen 1,026 applied, 948 admitted, 411 enrolled.

Average high school GPA	3.3	SAT verbal scores above 500	N/R
SAT math scores above 500	N/R	ACT above 18	83%
From top 10% of their h.s. class	25%	From top quarter	50%
From top half	75%	1998 freshmen returning in 1999	72%

Application *Options:* electronic application, deferred entrance. *Application fee:* $0. *Required:* high school transcript; minimum 2.0 GPA; 2 letters of recommendation. *Recommended:* interview.

Standardized tests *Admission: Required:* ACT.

Significant dates *Application deadlines:* rolling (freshmen), rolling (transfers). *Financial aid deadline priority date:* 3/1.

Freshman Application Contact
Mr. Brian Parker, Director of Admissions, Olivet Nazarene University, One University Avenue, Bourbonnais, IL 60904-2271. **Phone:** 815-939-5203. **Toll-free phone:** 800-648-1463. **E-mail:** admissions@olivet.edu

Visit CollegeQuest.com for information on majors offered and athletics. Electronic viewbook available at CollegeQuest.com.

■ *See page 2224 for a narrative description.*

PRINCIPIA COLLEGE
Elsah, Illinois

- **Independent Christian Science**, 4-year, founded 1910
- **Degree** bachelor's
- **Rural** 2,600-acre campus with easy access to St. Louis
- **Coed**, 526 undergraduate students, 97% full-time, 54% women, 46% men
- **Moderately difficult** entrance level, 91% of applicants were admitted
- **9:1** student-to-undergraduate faculty ratio
- **74% graduate** in 6 years or less
- **$15,984 tuition** and fees

Students *Undergraduates:* 511 full-time, 15 part-time. Students come from 46 states and territories, 28 other countries. *The most frequently chosen baccalaureate fields are:* business/marketing, social sciences and history, visual/performing arts.

From out-of-state	90%	Reside on campus	100%
Age 25 or older	3%	Transferred in	2%
International students	12%	African Americans	3%
Asian Americans/Pacific Islanders	1%	Hispanic Americans	2%
Native Americans	0.4%		

Faculty 75 (68% full-time), 48% with terminal degrees.

Expenses (2000–2001) *Comprehensive fee:* $21,768 includes full-time tuition ($15,714), mandatory fees ($270), and room and board ($5784). *College room only:* $2808. *Part-time tuition:* $1746 per course. *Payment plan:* installment. *Waivers:* employees or children of employees.

Library Marshall Brooks Library plus 1 other. *Operations spending 1999–2000:* $676,000. *Collection:* 203,000 titles, 900 serial subscriptions, 6,700 audiovisual materials.

College life *Housing:* on-campus residence required through senior year. *Options:* men-only, women-only. *Most popular organizations:* Christian Science Organization, student newspaper, International Students Association, student radio station, Rugby Club.

Campus security 24-hour patrols.

After graduation 30 organizations recruited on campus 1997–98. 21% of class of 1998 had job offers within 6 months. *Career center:* 2 full-time, 1 part-time personnel. Services include job fairs, resume preparation, career counseling, careers library, job bank, job interviews. **Graduate education:** 21% of class of 1999 went directly to graduate and professional school: 16% graduate arts and sciences, 3% law, 2% business.

Freshmen 209 applied, 190 admitted, 127 enrolled. 1 National Merit Scholar, 4 class presidents, 5 valedictorians, 32 student government officers.

Average high school GPA	3.35	SAT verbal scores above 500	85%
SAT math scores above 500	81%	ACT above 18	97%
From top 10% of their h.s. class	21%	From top quarter	24%
From top half	63%	1998 freshmen returning in 1999	84%

Application *Option:* deferred entrance. *Application fee:* $35. *Required:* essay or personal statement; high school transcript; minimum 2.0 GPA; 4 letters of recommendation; Christian Science commitment. *Required for some:* interview. *Recommended:* interview.

Standardized tests *Admission: Required:* SAT I or ACT. *Recommended:* SAT I.

Illinois

Significant dates *Application deadlines:* 3/1 (freshmen), 3/1 (transfers). *Financial aid deadline:* continuous.
Freshman Application Contact
Ms. Martha Green Quirk, Dean of Admissions, Principia College, Office of Admissions and Enrollment, Elsah, IL 62028. **Phone:** 618-374-5180. **Toll-free phone:** 800-277-4648 Ext. 2802. **Fax:** 618-374-4000. **E-mail:** collegeadmissions@prin.edu
Visit CollegeQuest.com for information on majors offered and athletics. College video available at CollegeQuest.com.

QUINCY UNIVERSITY
Quincy, Illinois

- **Independent Roman Catholic**, comprehensive, founded 1860
- **Degrees** associate, bachelor's, and master's
- **Small-town** 75-acre campus
- **Coed**, 1,037 undergraduate students, 95% full-time, 55% women, 45% men
- **Moderately difficult** entrance level, 81% of applicants were admitted
- **13:1 student-to-undergraduate faculty ratio**
- **$14,700 tuition** and fees

Students *Undergraduates:* 985 full-time, 52 part-time. Students come from 35 states and territories, 16 other countries. *The most frequently chosen baccalaureate fields are:* business/marketing, education, social sciences and history. *Graduate:* 135 in graduate degree programs.

From out-of-state	31%	Reside on campus	65%
Age 25 or older	6%	Transferred in	10%
International students	2%	African Americans	6%
Asian Americans/Pacific Islanders	1%	Hispanic Americans	3%
Native Americans	0.4%		

Faculty 111 (56% full-time), 58% with terminal degrees.
Expenses (2000–2001) *Comprehensive fee:* $19,480 includes full-time tuition ($14,300), mandatory fees ($400), and room and board ($4780). Room and board charges vary according to housing facility. *Part-time tuition:* $410 per credit hour. *Payment plans:* guaranteed tuition, installment. *Waivers:* senior citizens and employees or children of employees.
Library Brenner Library. *Operations spending 1999–2000:* $232,680. *Collection:* 236,769 titles, 669 serial subscriptions.
College life *Housing:* on-campus residence required through junior year. *Options:* coed, men-only, women-only. *Social organizations:* national fraternities, national sororities; 11% of eligible men and 4% of eligible women are members. *Most popular organizations:* Student Senate, campus ministry, student programming board, BACCHUS, Students in Free Enterprise.
Campus security 24-hour emergency response devices and patrols, student patrols, late-night transport-escort service, controlled dormitory access.
After graduation 26 organizations recruited on campus 1997–98. 80% of class of 1998 had job offers within 6 months. *Career center:* 1 full-time, 2 part-time personnel. Services include job fairs, resume preparation, interview workshops, resume referral, career/interest testing, career counseling, careers library, job bank, job interviews. *Graduate education:* 18% of class of 1999 went directly to graduate and professional school: 9% graduate arts and sciences, 3% law, 2% business, 2% medicine, 1% dentistry, 1% education.
Freshmen 1,451 applied, 1,170 admitted, 274 enrolled. 1 National Merit Scholar.

Average high school GPA	3.13	SAT verbal scores above 500	55%
SAT math scores above 500	61%	ACT above 18	91%
From top 10% of their h.s. class	15%	From top quarter	34%
From top half	67%	1998 freshmen returning in 1999	73%

Application *Options:* Common Application, electronic application, early admission, deferred entrance. *Application fee:* $25. *Required:* high school transcript. *Recommended:* minimum 2.0 GPA; interview.
Standardized tests *Admission: Required:* SAT I or ACT.
Significant dates *Application deadlines:* rolling (freshmen), rolling (transfers). *Financial aid deadline priority date:* 4/15.
Freshman Application Contact
Mr. Jeff Van Camp, Director of Admissions, Quincy University, 1800 College Avenue, Quincy, IL 62301-2699. **Phone:** 217-222-8020 Ext. 5215. **Toll-free phone:** 800-688-4295. **Fax:** 217-228-5479. **E-mail:** admissions@quincy.edu

Visit CollegeQuest.com for information on majors offered and athletics. College video and electronic viewbook available at CollegeQuest.com.

■ *See page 2302 for a narrative description.*

ROBERT MORRIS COLLEGE
Chicago, Illinois

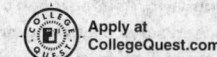

- **Independent**, 4-year, founded 1913
- **Degrees** associate and bachelor's
- **Urban** campus
- **Coed**, 4,028 undergraduate students, 95% full-time, 67% women, 33% men
- **Minimally difficult** entrance level, 68% of applicants were admitted
- **19:1 student-to-undergraduate faculty ratio**
- **64.6% graduate** in 6 years or less
- **$10,950 tuition** and fees
- **$9371 average financial aid** package, $8511 average indebtedness upon graduation, $24.7 million endowment

Students *Undergraduates:* 3,808 full-time, 220 part-time. Students come from 7 states and territories, 10 other countries. *The most frequently chosen baccalaureate field is:* business/marketing.

From out-of-state	1%	Age 25 or older	36%
Transferred in	37%	International students	0.3%
African Americans	41%	Asian Americans/Pacific Islanders	4%
Hispanic Americans	23%	Native Americans	0.4%

Faculty 342 (31% full-time), 18% with terminal degrees.
Expenses (1999–2000) *Tuition:* full-time $10,950; part-time $920 per course. *Payment plan:* installment. *Waivers:* employees or children of employees.
Library Thomas Jefferson Library. *Operations spending 1999–2000:* $526,580. *Collection:* 5,050 audiovisual materials.
College life *Housing:* college housing not available. *Most popular organizations:* Alumni Association, Sigma Beta Delta (honor society), Eagle (newspaper), Accounting Club.
Campus security 24-hour emergency response devices and patrols.
After graduation 125 organizations recruited on campus 1997–98. *Career center:* 22 full-time, 2 part-time personnel. Services include job fairs, resume preparation, interview workshops, resume referral, career counseling, careers library, job bank, job interviews.
Freshmen 3,861 applied, 2,614 admitted, 1,521 enrolled.

Average high school GPA	2.51	SAT verbal scores above 500	N/R
SAT math scores above 500	N/R	ACT above 18	N/R
From top 10% of their h.s. class	8%	From top quarter	23%
From top half	55%	1998 freshmen returning in 1999	62%

Application *Options:* eApply at www.CollegeQuest.com, Common Application, deferred entrance. *Application fee:* $20. *Required:* high school transcript; interview. *Recommended:* minimum 2.0 GPA.
Significant dates *Application deadlines:* rolling (freshmen), rolling (transfers). *Financial aid deadline:* continuous.
Freshman Application Contact
Mr. Vince Norton, Vice President of Enrollment Services, Robert Morris College, 401 South State Street, Chicago, IL 60605. **Phone:** 312-935-6645. **Toll-free phone:** 800-225-1520. **Fax:** 312-836-4599. **E-mail:** enroll@rmcil.edu
Visit CollegeQuest.com for information on majors offered and athletics. College video available at CollegeQuest.com.

■ *See page 2338 for a narrative description.*

ROCKFORD COLLEGE
Rockford, Illinois

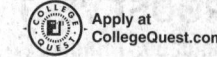

- **Independent**, comprehensive, founded 1847
- **Degrees** bachelor's and master's
- **Suburban** 130-acre campus with easy access to Chicago
- **Coed**, 1,019 undergraduate students, 77% full-time, 69% women, 31% men
- **Moderately difficult** entrance level, 76% of applicants were admitted

Peterson's Guide to Four-Year Colleges 2001   www.petersons.com   251

Illinois

Rockford College (continued)
- 14:1 student-to-undergraduate faculty ratio
- **99% graduate** in 6 years or less
- **$16,800 tuition** and fees
- **$10.3 million endowment**

Rockford College, 1 of 13 colleges in Illinois with a Phi Beta Kappa chapter, is known for its integration of liberal arts and professional programs, community-based service learning programs, and Regent's College in London. Barron's named Rockford a "best buy in higher education." An NCAA Division III football program will begin in fall 2000.

Students *Undergraduates:* Students come from 24 other countries. *The most frequently chosen baccalaureate fields are:* business/marketing, education, health professions and related sciences. *Graduate:* 309 in graduate degree programs.

From out-of-state	39%	Reside on campus	41%
Age 25 or older	39%		

Faculty 125 (64% full-time), 45% with terminal degrees.

Expenses (2000–2001) *Comprehensive fee:* $22,230 includes full-time tuition ($16,800) and room and board ($5430). *College room only:* $3300. Room and board charges vary according to board plan and housing facility. *Payment plans:* installment, deferred payment. *Waivers:* employees or children of employees.

Library Howard Colman Library. *Operations spending 1999–2000:* $479,851. *Collection:* 172,110 titles, 850 serial subscriptions.

College life *Housing:* on-campus residence required through senior year. *Options:* coed, men-only, women-only. *Most popular organizations:* student government, intercultural club, 4Ts (Tomorrow's Teachers Together Today), psychology society, Nursing Student Organization.

Campus security 24-hour emergency response devices and patrols, late-night transport-escort service, controlled dormitory access.

After graduation 68 organizations recruited on campus 1997–98. 93% of class of 1998 had job offers within 6 months. *Career center:* 2 full-time, 4 part-time personnel. Services include job fairs, resume preparation, resume referral, career counseling, careers library, job bank, job interviews. *Graduate education:* 8% of class of 1999 went directly to graduate and professional school: 4% graduate arts and sciences, 2% education, 1% business, 1% medicine.

Freshmen 824 applied, 624 admitted. 4 valedictorians.

Average high school GPA	3.2	SAT verbal scores above 500	27%
SAT math scores above 500	20%	ACT above 18	86%
From top 10% of their h.s. class	27%	From top quarter	68%
From top half	78%	1998 freshmen returning in 1999	67%

Application *Options:* eApply at www.CollegeQuest.com, Common Application, electronic application, early admission, deferred entrance. *Application fee:* $35. *Required:* high school transcript. *Required for some:* essay or personal statement; minimum 2.5 GPA; 2 letters of recommendation. *Recommended:* minimum 2.5 GPA; interview; campus visit.

Standardized tests *Admission: Required:* SAT I or ACT.

Significant dates *Application deadlines:* rolling (freshmen), rolling (transfers). *Financial aid deadline priority date:* 4/15.

Freshman Application Contact
Mr. Paul Hartzog, Associate Director of Admission, Rockford College, Nelson Hall, Rockford, IL 61108-2393. **Phone:** 815-226-4050. **Toll-free phone:** 800-892-2984. **Fax:** 815-226-4119. **E-mail:** admission@rockford.edu

Visit CollegeQuest.com for information on majors offered and athletics. College video available at CollegeQuest.com.

■ *See page 2346 for a narrative description.*

ROOSEVELT UNIVERSITY
Chicago, Illinois

 Apply at CollegeQuest.com

- **Independent**, comprehensive, founded 1945
- **Degrees** bachelor's, master's, and doctoral
- **Urban** campus
- **Coed**
- **Moderately difficult** entrance level
- **$9848 tuition** and fees

Inaugurated in 1998, Roosevelt Scholars is a distinctive honors program open to students who demonstrate outstanding scholarship along with leadership in school/community activities. In addition to enriched academic experiences and scholarship support that averages $5000 annually, students are mentored by Chicago's political, business, and social leaders and participate in internship and research opportunities in their areas of interest.

Expenses (1999–2000) *Comprehensive fee:* $15,698 includes full-time tuition ($9648), mandatory fees ($200), and room and board ($5850). Full-time tuition and fees vary according to course load. Room and board charges vary according to board plan. *Part-time tuition:* $402 per semester hour. *Part-time fees:* $100 per term part-time. Part-time tuition and fees vary according to course load.

Institutional Web site http://www.roosevelt.edu/

College life *Housing: Option:* coed. *Most popular organizations:* International Student Union, RU 10%, Associacion de Latinos Unidos, Black Support Union, Residence Hall Council.

Campus security 24-hour emergency response devices and patrols, controlled dormitory access.

Application *Options:* eApply at www.CollegeQuest.com, Common Application, electronic application, early admission, deferred entrance. *Application fee:* $25. *Required:* essay or personal statement; high school transcript; minimum 2.0 GPA; audition for art and theater programs. *Required for some:* letters of recommendation; interview.

Standardized tests *Admission: Required:* SAT I or ACT.

Admissions Office Contact
Roosevelt University, Office of Admissions, Chicago, IL 60605-1394. **Toll-free phone:** 877-APPLYRU. **E-mail:** applyru@roosevelt.edu

Visit CollegeQuest.com for information on athletics.

■ *See page 2356 for a narrative description.*

RUSH UNIVERSITY
Chicago, Illinois

- **Independent**, upper-level, founded 1969
- **Degrees** bachelor's, master's, doctoral, and first professional
- **Urban** 35-acre campus
- **Coed**, 197 undergraduate students, 93% full-time, 86% women, 14% men
- **Moderately difficult** entrance level
- **$12,270 tuition** and fees
- **$19,230 average indebtedness** upon graduation, $340.2 million endowment

Students *Undergraduates:* 183 full-time, 14 part-time. Students come from 12 states and territories, 2 other countries. *The most frequently chosen baccalaureate field is:* health professions and related sciences. *Graduate:* 485 in professional programs, 617 in other graduate degree programs.

From out-of-state	8%	Reside on campus	27%
Age 25 or older	51%	Transferred in	61%
International students	1%	African Americans	13%
Asian Americans/Pacific Islanders	19%	Hispanic Americans	9%

Expenses (1999–2000) *Tuition:* full-time $12,270; part-time $360 per quarter hour. Full-time tuition and fees vary according to program. Part-time tuition and fees vary according to program. *College room only:* $7284. Room and board charges vary according to housing facility. *Payment plans:* installment, deferred payment. *Waivers:* employees or children of employees.

Library Library of Rush University. *Operations spending 1999–2000:* $1.9 million. *Collection:* 120,042 titles, 1,992 serial subscriptions.

College life *Housing: Option:* coed.

Campus security 24-hour emergency response devices and patrols, late-night transport-escort service, controlled dormitory access.

After graduation *Career center:* Services include career counseling. *Graduate education:* 12% of class of 1999 went directly to graduate and professional school.

Application Preference given to students from affiliate college network. *Application fee:* $40.

Significant dates *Application deadline:* rolling (transfers). *Financial aid deadline:* 4/1. *Priority date:* 3/1.

Illinois

Freshman Application Contact
Ms. Hicela Castruita, Director of College Admission Services, Rush University, 600 S. Paulina—Suite 440, College Admissions Services, Chicago, IL 60612-3878. **Phone:** 312-942-7100. **Fax:** 312-942-2219. **E-mail:** ruadmissions@rushu.rush.edu
Visit CollegeQuest.com for information on majors offered and athletics.

SAINT ANTHONY COLLEGE OF NURSING
Rockford, Illinois

- **Independent Roman Catholic**, upper-level, founded 1915
- **Degree** bachelor's
- **Urban** 17-acre campus with easy access to Chicago
- **Coed,** primarily women, 66 undergraduate students, 91% full-time, 89% women, 11% men
- **Moderately difficult** entrance level, 56% of applicants were admitted
- **5:1 student-to-undergraduate faculty ratio**
- **$11,460 tuition** and fees

Students *Undergraduates:* 60 full-time, 6 part-time. Students come from 3 states and territories. *The most frequently chosen baccalaureate field is:* health professions and related sciences.

From out-of-state	17%	Age 25 or older	50%
Transferred in	24%	African Americans	2%
Asian Americans/Pacific Islanders	2%	Hispanic Americans	7%

Faculty 11 (73% full-time), 18% with terminal degrees.
Expenses (2000–2001) *One-time required fee:* $65. *Tuition:* full-time $11,360; part-time $355 per credit. *Required fees:* full-time $100. Full-time tuition and fees vary according to program. Part-time tuition and fees vary according to program. *Payment plan:* installment.
Library Sister Mary Linus Learning Resource Center plus 1 other. *Operations spending 1999–2000:* $22,716. *Collection:* 1,154 titles, 76 serial subscriptions, 130 audiovisual materials.
College life *Housing:* college housing not available.
Campus security 24-hour emergency response devices and patrols, late-night transport-escort service.
After graduation 4 organizations recruited on campus 1997–98. 90% of class of 1998 had job offers within 6 months. *Career center:* Services include job fairs, resume preparation, career counseling, careers library, job interviews. *Graduate education:* 5% of class of 1999 went directly to graduate and professional school.
Application *Option:* deferred entrance. *Application fee:* $50.
Significant dates *Application deadline:* rolling (transfers). *Financial aid deadline priority date:* 5/1.
Freshman Application Contact
Mr. Steve Crick, Financial Aid Officer, Saint Anthony College of Nursing, 5658 East State Street, Rockford, IL 61108-2468. **Phone:** 815-395-5089. **E-mail:** nancy.sanders@osfhealthcare.org
Visit CollegeQuest.com for information on majors offered and athletics.

ST. AUGUSTINE COLLEGE
Chicago, Illinois

- **Independent**, 4-year, founded 1980
- **Degrees** associate and bachelor's (bilingual Spanish/English degree programs)
- **Urban** 4-acre campus
- **Coed,** 1,202 undergraduate students, 88% full-time, 75% women, 25% men
- **Noncompetitive** entrance level
- **13:1 student-to-undergraduate faculty ratio**
- **$6320 tuition** and fees
- **$685,483 endowment**

Students *Undergraduates:* 1,055 full-time, 147 part-time.

Age 25 or older	59%

Expenses (1999–2000) *Tuition:* full-time $6000; part-time $325 per semester hour. *Required fees:* full-time $320. *Payment plan:* installment. *Waivers:* employees or children of employees.
Library *Collection:* 15,500 titles.
College life *Housing:* college housing not available.
Campus security Late-night transport-escort service.
After graduation *Career center:* 1 full-time personnel. Services include resume preparation, career counseling.
Freshmen 412 enrolled.

SAT verbal scores above 500	N/R	SAT math scores above 500	N/R
ACT above 18	N/R		

Application *Option:* deferred entrance. *Application fee:* $0.
Significant dates *Application deadlines:* rolling (freshmen), rolling (transfers).
Freshman Application Contact
Ms. Guadalupe Moreno, Director of Admissions, St. Augustine College, 1333–1345 West Argyle, Chicago, IL 60640-3501. **Phone:** 773-878-8756 Ext. 232.
Visit CollegeQuest.com for information on majors offered and athletics.

SAINT FRANCIS MEDICAL CENTER COLLEGE OF NURSING
Peoria, Illinois

- **Independent Roman Catholic**, upper-level, founded 1986
- **Degree** bachelor's
- **Urban** campus
- **Coed,** primarily women, 144 undergraduate students, 76% full-time, 93% women, 7% men
- **Moderately difficult** entrance level
- **8:1 student-to-undergraduate faculty ratio**
- **$9200 tuition** and fees

Students *Undergraduates:* Students come from 2 states and territories, 4 other countries. *The most frequently chosen baccalaureate field is:* health professions and related sciences.

From out-of-state	1%	Reside on campus	28%
Age 25 or older	44%	International students	1%
African Americans	5%	Asian Americans/Pacific Islanders	1%
Hispanic Americans	1%	Native Americans	1%

Faculty 17 (100% full-time).
Expenses (1999–2000) *Tuition:* full-time $8880; part-time $370 per semester hour. *Required fees:* full-time $320; $160 per term part-time. Full-time tuition and fees vary according to course load. Part-time tuition and fees vary according to course load. *College room only:* $1680. *Payment plans:* installment, deferred payment. *Waivers:* employees or children of employees.
Library *Collection:* 6,215 titles, 125 serial subscriptions.
College life *Housing:* Option: coed. *Most popular organizations:* student senate, SNAI.
Campus security 24-hour emergency response devices, controlled dormitory access.
Application *Options:* Common Application, deferred entrance. *Application fee:* $25.
Significant dates *Application deadline:* rolling (transfers). *Financial aid deadline priority date:* 3/1.
Freshman Application Contact
Mrs. Janice Farquharson, Director of Admissions and Registrar, Saint Francis Medical Center College of Nursing, 511 Greenleaf Street, Peoria, IL 61603-3783. **Phone:** 309-655-2596. **E-mail:** janice.farquharson@osfhealthcare.org
Visit CollegeQuest.com for information on majors offered and athletics. Electronic viewbook available at CollegeQuest.com.

ST. JOHN'S COLLEGE
Springfield, Illinois

- **Independent Roman Catholic**, upper-level, founded 1886
- **Degree** bachelor's
- **Urban** campus
- **Coed**, 84 undergraduate students, 96% full-time, 99% women, 1% men

Illinois

St. John's College *(continued)*
- **Moderately difficult** entrance level, 70% of applicants were admitted
- **6:1 student-to-undergraduate faculty ratio**
- **$7654 tuition** and fees
- **$310,850 endowment**

Students *Undergraduates:* 81 full-time, 3 part-time. *The most frequently chosen baccalaureate field is:* health professions and related sciences.

Age 25 or older	18%	Transferred in	39%
African Americans	4%		

Faculty 16 (94% full-time), 13% with terminal degrees.

Expenses *(1999–2000)* *One-time required fee:* $67. *Tuition:* full-time $7442. *Required fees:* full-time $212. Full-time tuition and fees vary according to course load and student level. Part-time tuition and fees vary according to course load and student level. *Payment plans:* installment, deferred payment.

Library St. John's Health Science Library. *Collection:* 7,472 titles, 395 serial subscriptions, 887 audiovisual materials.

College life *Housing:* college housing not available. *Most popular organizations:* NSNA, class/student government.

Campus security 24-hour emergency response devices and patrols, late-night transport-escort service.

After graduation 100% of class of 1998 had job offers within 6 months.

Application *Application fee:* $25.

Significant dates *Financial aid deadline priority date:* 5/1.

Freshman Application Contact
Ms. Beth Beasley, Student Development Officer, St. John's College, 421 North Ninth Street, Springfield, IL 62702-5317. **Phone:** 217-525-5628 Ext. 45468.

Visit CollegeQuest.com for information on majors offered and athletics.

SAINT JOSEPH COLLEGE OF NURSING
Illinois—See University of St. Francis

SAINT XAVIER UNIVERSITY
Chicago, Illinois

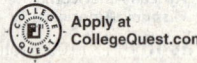
Apply at CollegeQuest.com

- **Independent Roman Catholic**, comprehensive, founded 1847
- **Degrees** bachelor's and master's
- **Urban** 55-acre campus
- **Coed**, 2,401 undergraduate students, 66% full-time, 73% women, 27% men
- **Moderately difficult** entrance level, 76% of applicants were admitted
- **21:1 student-to-undergraduate faculty ratio**
- **$13,760 tuition** and fees
- **$10,865 average financial aid** package, $15,787 average indebtedness upon graduation, $6.1 million endowment

Students *Undergraduates:* 1,594 full-time, 807 part-time. Students come from 13 states and territories, 7 other countries. *The most frequently chosen baccalaureate fields are:* business/marketing, education, health professions and related sciences. *Graduate:* 1,650 in graduate degree programs.

From out-of-state	24%	Reside on campus	12%
Age 25 or older	3%	Transferred in	17%
International students	1%	African Americans	16%
Asian Americans/Pacific Islanders	2%	Hispanic Americans	11%
Native Americans	0.4%		

Faculty 291 (48% full-time), 56% with terminal degrees.

Expenses *(1999–2000)* *Comprehensive fee:* $19,313 includes full-time tuition ($13,650), mandatory fees ($110), and room and board ($5553). *College room only:* $3180. Full-time tuition and fees vary according to course load. Room and board charges vary according to board plan. *Part-time tuition:* $455 per semester hour. *Part-time fees:* $40 per term part-time. Part-time tuition and fees vary according to course load. *Payment plan:* installment. *Waivers:* senior citizens and employees or children of employees.

Library Byrne Memorial Library. *Operations spending 1999–2000:* $738,294. *Collection:* 123,325 titles, 2,199 serial subscriptions, 2,292 audiovisual materials.

College life *Housing:* Option: coed. *Most popular organizations:* Student Activities Board, Black Student Union, UNIDOS (Hispanic Organization), Student Nurses Association, Business Students Association.

Campus security 24-hour emergency response devices and patrols, late-night transport-escort service.

After graduation 96% of class of 1998 had job offers within 6 months. *Career center:* 6 full-time, 1 part-time personnel. Services include job fairs, resume preparation, interview workshops, resume referral, career/interest testing, career counseling, careers library, job bank, job interviews. *Graduate education:* 13% of class of 1999 went directly to graduate and professional school: 3% business, 3% graduate arts and sciences, 2% education, 1% law.

Freshmen 864 applied, 653 admitted, 323 enrolled.

Average high school GPA	2.96	SAT verbal scores above 500	N/R
SAT math scores above 500	N/R	ACT above 18	79%
From top 10% of their h.s. class	23%	From top quarter	45%
From top half	71%	1998 freshmen returning in 1999	76%

Application *Options:* eApply at www.CollegeQuest.com, Common Application, early admission, deferred entrance. *Application fee:* $25. *Required:* high school transcript. *Required for some:* interview. *Recommended:* essay or personal statement; minimum 2.5 GPA; interview.

Standardized tests *Admission:* Required: SAT I or ACT.

Significant dates *Application deadlines:* 8/15 (freshmen), 8/15 (transfers). *Notification:* continuous until 8/30 (freshmen). *Financial aid deadline priority date:* 3/1.

Freshman Application Contact
Ms. Beth Gierach, Director of Enrollment Services, Saint Xavier University, 3700 West 103rd Street, Chicago, IL 60655-3105. **Phone:** 773-298-3063. **Toll-free phone:** 800-462-9288. **Fax:** 773-298-3076 Ext. 3050. **E-mail:** admissions@sxu.edu

Visit CollegeQuest.com for information on majors offered and athletics. College video available at CollegeQuest.com.

- *See page 2432 for a narrative description.*

SCHOOL OF THE ART INSTITUTE OF CHICAGO
Chicago, Illinois

- **Independent**, comprehensive, founded 1866
- **Degrees** bachelor's and master's
- **Urban** 1-acre campus
- **Coed**, 1,819 undergraduate students, 82% full-time, 61% women, 39% men
- **Moderately difficult** entrance level, 73% of applicants were admitted
- **13:1 student-to-undergraduate faculty ratio**
- **40% graduate** in 6 years or less
- **$20,220 tuition** and fees
- **$179.9 million endowment**

Students *Undergraduates:* Students come from 50 states and territories. *Graduate:* 551 in graduate degree programs.

From out-of-state	74%	Reside on campus	24%
International students	9%	African Americans	3%
Asian Americans/Pacific Islanders	8%	Hispanic Americans	5%
Native Americans	1%		

Faculty 456 (23% full-time).

Expenses *(2000–2001, estimated)* *Tuition:* full-time $20,220; part-time $674 per semester hour. *College room only:* $5725. Room and board charges vary according to housing facility. *Payment plan:* installment. *Waivers:* employees or children of employees.

Library Flaxman Memorial Library plus 2 others. *Collection:* 305,886 titles, 2,135 serial subscriptions.

College life *Housing:* Option: coed. *Most popular organizations:* student government, N.I.A. (black student union), L.A.S.O. (Latin Art Student organization), Eye and Ear Clinic (film screening group), Student Union Galleries.

Campus security 24-hour emergency response devices and patrols, late-night transport-escort service, controlled dormitory access.

After graduation *Career center:* 3 full-time personnel. Services include job fairs, resume preparation, interview workshops, career counseling, careers library, job bank, job interviews.

Illinois

Freshmen 1,109 applied, 807 admitted.

SAT verbal scores above 500	N/R	SAT math scores above 500	N/R
ACT above 18	N/R	1998 freshmen returning in 1999	78%

Application *Option:* deferred entrance. *Application fee:* $45. *Required:* essay or personal statement; high school transcript; 1 letter of recommendation; portfolio. *Recommended:* interview.

Standardized tests *Admission: Required:* SAT I or ACT.

Significant dates *Application deadlines:* 8/15 (freshmen), 8/15 (transfers).

Freshman Application Contact
Ms. Kendra Dane, Executive Director of Admissions and Marketing, School of the Art Institute of Chicago, 37 South Wabash, Chicago, IL 60603. **Phone:** 312-899-5219. **Toll-free phone:** 800-232-SAIC. **Fax:** 312-263-0141. **E-mail:** admiss@artic.edu

Visit CollegeQuest.com for information on majors offered and athletics. College video available at CollegeQuest.com.

■ *See page 2456 for a narrative description.*

SHIMER COLLEGE
Waukegan, Illinois

- **Independent**, 4-year, founded 1853
- **Degree** bachelor's
- **Suburban** 3-acre campus with easy access to Chicago and Milwaukee
- **Coed**, 109 undergraduate students, 92% full-time, 61% women, 39% men
- **Moderately difficult** entrance level, 100% of applicants were admitted
- **$14,180 tuition** and fees

Students *Undergraduates:* 100 full-time, 9 part-time. Students come from 22 states and territories, 2 other countries. *The most frequently chosen baccalaureate fields are:* library science, social sciences and history.

From out-of-state	31%	Reside on campus	50%
Age 25 or older	27%	Transferred in	6%
International students	5%	African Americans	5%
Hispanic Americans	2%	Native Americans	2%

Faculty 15 (100% full-time), 100% with terminal degrees.

Expenses (1999–2000) *Tuition:* full-time $14,020; part-time $490 per credit hour. *Required fees:* full-time $160; $80 per term part-time. *College room only:* $1950. Room and board charges vary according to housing facility. *Payment plan:* installment. *Waivers:* minority students, children of alumni, senior citizens, and employees or children of employees.

Library *Collection:* 200,000 titles, 200 serial subscriptions.

College life *Housing: Option:* coed. *Most popular organizations:* student government, drama group.

Campus security 24-hour emergency response devices, late-night transport-escort service.

After graduation *Career center:* 1 part-time personnel. Services include resume preparation, career counseling, careers library, job bank.

Freshmen 33 applied, 33 admitted, 15 enrolled.

Average high school GPA	2.6	SAT verbal scores above 500	100%
SAT math scores above 500	60%	ACT above 18	85%
From top 10% of their h.s. class	0%	From top quarter	25%
From top half	38%	1998 freshmen returning in 1999	66%

Application *Options:* Common Application, electronic application, early admission. *Application fee:* $10. *Required:* essay or personal statement; high school transcript; 1 letter of recommendation; interview.

Standardized tests *Admission: Recommended:* SAT I or ACT. *Required for some:* SAT I or ACT.

Significant dates *Application deadlines:* 7/1 (freshmen), 7/1 (transfers). *Financial aid deadline priority date:* 6/1.

Freshman Application Contact
Mr. David Buchanan, Admissions Counselor, Shimer College, PO Box 500, Waukegan, IL 60079-0500. **Phone:** 847-249-7174. **Toll-free phone:** 800-215-7173. **Fax:** 847-249-7171. **E-mail:** admissions@shimer.edu

Visit CollegeQuest.com for information on majors offered and athletics.

■ *See page 2480 for a narrative description.*

SOUTHERN ILLINOIS UNIVERSITY CARBONDALE
Carbondale, Illinois

- **State-supported**, university, founded 1869
- **Degrees** associate, bachelor's, master's, doctoral, first professional, post-master's, postbachelor's, and first professional certificates
- **Small-town** 1,128-acre campus
- **Coed**, 17,735 undergraduate students, 90% full-time, 43% women, 57% men
- **Moderately difficult** entrance level, 71% of applicants were admitted
- **18:1 student-to-undergraduate faculty ratio**
- **39.1% graduate** in 6 years or less
- **$3936 tuition** and fees (in-state); $6801 (out-of-state)
- **$6217 average financial aid** package, $11,475 average indebtedness upon graduation, $39.5 million endowment

Part of Southern Illinois University.

Students *Undergraduates:* 15,900 full-time, 1,835 part-time. Students come from 51 states and territories. *The most frequently chosen baccalaureate fields are:* education, business/marketing, engineering/engineering technologies. *Graduate:* 674 in professional programs, 3,820 in other graduate degree programs.

From out-of-state	17%	Reside on campus	24%
Age 25 or older	25%	Transferred in	15%
International students	4%	African Americans	14%
Asian Americans/Pacific Islanders	2%	Hispanic Americans	3%
Native Americans	0.4%		

Faculty 1,087 (87% full-time), 72% with terminal degrees.

Expenses (1999–2000) *Tuition, state resident:* full-time $2865; part-time $96 per semester hour. *Tuition, nonresident:* full-time $5730; part-time $191 per semester hour. *Required fees:* full-time $1071; $36 per semester hour. Full-time tuition and fees vary according to course load. Part-time tuition and fees vary according to course load. *College room and board:* $3889. Room and board charges vary according to board plan and housing facility. *Payment plan:* installment. *Waivers:* senior citizens and employees or children of employees.

Library Morris Library plus 1 other. *Operations spending 1999–2000:* $12.7 million. *Collection:* 2.7 million titles, 20,450 serial subscriptions.

College life *Housing:* on-campus residence required in freshman year. *Options:* coed, men-only, women-only, disabled students. *Social organizations:* national fraternities, national sororities, local fraternities; 3% of eligible men and 2% of eligible women are members. *Most popular organizations:* Inter-Greek Council, International Student Council, Student Programming Council, Black Affairs Council.

Campus security 24-hour emergency response devices and patrols, student patrols, late-night transport-escort service, well-lit pathways, night safety vans, student transit system.

After graduation 171 organizations recruited on campus 1997–98. *Career center:* 12 full-time, 1 part-time personnel. Services include job fairs, resume preparation, interview workshops, resume referral, career/interest testing, career counseling, careers library, job bank, job interviews.

Freshmen 11,486 applied, 8,164 admitted, 2,595 enrolled. 5 National Merit Scholars.

SAT verbal scores above 500	N/R	SAT math scores above 500	N/R
ACT above 18	98%	From top 10% of their h.s. class	10%
From top quarter	30%	From top half	65%
1998 freshmen returning in 1999	70%		

Application *Option:* electronic application. *Required:* high school transcript.

Standardized tests *Admission: Required:* SAT I or ACT. *Recommended:* ACT.

Significant dates *Application deadlines:* rolling (freshmen), rolling (transfers). *Financial aid deadline priority date:* 4/1.

Freshman Application Contact
Mr. Walker Allen, Director of Admissions, Southern Illinois University Carbondale, Mail Code 4710, Carbondale, IL 62901-4710. **Phone:** 618-536-4405. **Fax:** 618-453-3250. **E-mail:** admrec@siu.edu

Visit CollegeQuest.com for information on majors offered and athletics. College video and electronic viewbook available at CollegeQuest.com.

■ *See page 2510 for a narrative description.*

Peterson's Guide to Four-Year Colleges 2001   www.petersons.com

Illinois

SOUTHERN ILLINOIS UNIVERSITY EDWARDSVILLE
Edwardsville, Illinois

- **State-supported**, comprehensive, founded 1957
- **Degrees** bachelor's, master's, first professional, and first professional certificates
- **Suburban** 2,660-acre campus with easy access to St. Louis
- **Coed**, 9,313 undergraduate students
- **Moderately difficult** entrance level, 87% of applicants were admitted
- **16:1 student-to-undergraduate faculty ratio**
- **33.7% graduate** in 6 years or less
- **$2827 tuition** and fees (in-state); $5035 (out-of-state)
- **$9553 average financial aid** package, $7 million endowment

Part of Southern Illinois University.

Students *Undergraduates: The most frequently chosen baccalaureate fields are:* business/marketing, education, health professions and related sciences. *Graduate:* 202 in professional programs, 2,362 in other graduate degree programs.

Reside on campus	24%	International students	1%
African Americans	12%	Asian Americans/Pacific Islanders	1%
Hispanic Americans	1%	Native Americans	0.5%

Faculty 726 (68% full-time).

Expenses (2000–2001) *Tuition, state resident:* full-time $2208. *Tuition, nonresident:* full-time $4416. *Required fees:* full-time $619. Full-time tuition and fees vary according to course load. Part-time tuition and fees vary according to course load. *College room and board:* $4290; room only: $2666. Room and board charges vary according to board plan and housing facility. *Payment plan:* installment. *Waivers:* employees or children of employees.

Library Lovejoy Library. *Operations spending 1999–2000:* $4 million. *Collection:* 735,630 titles, 26,950 audiovisual materials.

College life *Housing: Options:* coed, disabled students. *Social organizations:* national fraternities, national sororities; 5% of eligible men and 4% of eligible women are members. *Most popular organizations:* student government, Greek Council, campus newspaper, University Center Board, International Student Council.

Campus security 24-hour emergency response devices and patrols, student patrols, late-night transport-escort service, controlled dormitory access, 24-hour ID check at residence hall entrances.

After graduation 409 organizations recruited on campus 1997–98. *Career center:* 10 full-time, 6 part-time personnel. Services include job fairs, resume preparation, interview workshops, resume referral, career/interest testing, career counseling, careers library, job bank, job interviews. *Graduate education:* 30% of class of 1999 went directly to graduate and professional school.

Freshmen 3,683 applied, 3,197 admitted.

SAT verbal scores above 500	N/R	SAT math scores above 500	N/R
ACT above 18	81%	From top 10% of their h.s. class	13%
From top quarter	40%	From top half	79%
1998 freshmen returning in 1999	71%		

Application *Options:* electronic application, early admission, deferred entrance. *Application fee:* $0. *Required:* high school transcript.

Standardized tests *Admission: Required:* SAT I or ACT.

Significant dates *Application deadlines:* 7/31 (freshmen), 7/31 (transfers). *Notification:* continuous until 8/7 (freshmen). *Financial aid deadline priority date:* 3/1.

Freshman Application Contact
Mr. Boyd Bradshaw, Director of Admissions, Southern Illinois University Edwardsville, Box 1600, Edwardsville, IL 62026-0001. **Phone:** 618-650-3705. **Toll-free phone:** 800-447-SIUE. **Fax:** 618-692-2081. **E-mail:** admis@siue.edu

Visit CollegeQuest.com for information on majors offered and athletics. College video and electronic viewbook available at CollegeQuest.com.

TELSHE YESHIVA—CHICAGO
Chicago, Illinois

Admissions Office Contact
Telshe Yeshiva–Chicago, 3535 West Foster Avenue, Chicago, IL 60625-5598.

TRINITY CHRISTIAN COLLEGE
Palos Heights, Illinois

- **Independent interdenominational**, 4-year, founded 1959
- **Degree** bachelor's
- **Suburban** 53-acre campus with easy access to Chicago
- **Coed**, 679 undergraduate students, 98% full-time, 64% women, 36% men
- **Moderately difficult** entrance level, 99% of applicants were admitted
- **10:1 student-to-undergraduate faculty ratio**
- **53% graduate** in 6 years or less
- **$12,730 tuition** and fees
- **$10,251 average financial aid** package, $3.6 million endowment

Students *Undergraduates:* 665 full-time, 14 part-time. Students come from 29 states and territories, 5 other countries. *The most frequently chosen baccalaureate fields are:* education, business/marketing, health professions and related sciences.

From out-of-state	42%	Reside on campus	66%
Age 25 or older	9%	Transferred in	8%
International students	1%	African Americans	8%
Asian Americans/Pacific Islanders	1%	Hispanic Americans	3%
Native Americans	1%		

Faculty 101 (41% full-time), 36% with terminal degrees.

Expenses (1999–2000) *Comprehensive fee:* $17,740 includes full-time tuition ($12,730) and room and board ($5010). *College room only:* $2580. Room and board charges vary according to board plan. *Part-time tuition:* $425 per credit hour. Part-time tuition and fees vary according to course load. *Payment plan:* installment. *Waivers:* senior citizens and employees or children of employees.

Library Jenny Huizenga Memorial Library. *Operations spending 1999–2000:* $238,124. *Collection:* 55,020 titles, 437 serial subscriptions.

College life *Housing:* on-campus residence required through senior year. *Option:* coed. *Most popular organizations:* Student Association, student ministries, student-run campus newspaper, Pro-Life Task Force, PACE (prison tutoring program).

Campus security Student patrols, late-night transport-escort service.

After graduation 92% of class of 1998 had job offers within 6 months. *Career center:* 1 full-time, 1 part-time personnel. Services include job fairs, resume preparation, interview workshops, resume referral, career/interest testing, career counseling, careers library, job bank, job interviews.

Freshmen 504 applied, 499 admitted, 182 enrolled. 8 valedictorians.

Average high school GPA	3.22	SAT verbal scores above 500	N/R
SAT math scores above 500	N/R	ACT above 18	88%
From top 10% of their h.s. class	14%	From top quarter	34%
From top half	60%	1998 freshmen returning in 1999	76%

Application *Option:* deferred entrance. *Application fee:* $20. *Required:* essay or personal statement; high school transcript; minimum 2.0 GPA; interview. *Required for some:* 1 letter of recommendation.

Standardized tests *Admission: Required:* SAT I or ACT.

Significant dates *Application deadlines:* rolling (freshmen), rolling (transfers). *Financial aid deadline priority date:* 2/15.

Freshman Application Contact
Mr. Peter Hamstra, Dean of Admissions, Trinity Christian College, 6601 West College Drive, Palos Heights, IL 60463-0929. **Phone:** 708-239-4709. **Toll-free phone:** 800-748-0085. **Fax:** 708-239-3995. **E-mail:** admissions@trnty.edu

Visit CollegeQuest.com for information on majors offered and athletics.

- *See page 2638 for a narrative description.*

TRINITY COLLEGE OF NURSING
Moline, Illinois

- **Independent**, 4-year, founded 1994
- **Degrees** associate and bachelor's (general education requirements are taken off campus, usually at Black Hawk College and Western Illinois University)
- **Urban** 1-acre campus
- **Coed**, primarily women
- **Moderately difficult** entrance level

Institutional Web site http://www.trinityqc.com/college_of_nursing/college.htm

College life *Housing: Option:* coed. *Most popular organizations:* Student Nurses Association, student government, BSN Honor Society, Phi Theta Kappa.
Campus security 24-hour emergency response devices, controlled dormitory access.
Application *Option:* Common Application. *Preference* given to students from colleges with whom Trinity College of Nursing has an articulation agreement. *Application fee:* $50. *Required:* high school transcript; minimum 2.5 GPA.
Standardized tests *Admission: Required:* SAT I or ACT.
Admissions Office Contact
Trinity College of Nursing, 555 6th Street, Suite 300, Moline, IL 61265-1216. **Fax:** 309-757-2194. **E-mail:** carterc@trinityqc.com
Visit CollegeQuest.com for information on athletics.

TRINITY INTERNATIONAL UNIVERSITY
Deerfield, Illinois

- **Independent**, university, founded 1897, affiliated with Evangelical Free Church of America
- **Degrees** bachelor's, master's, doctoral, and first professional
- **Suburban** 108-acre campus with easy access to Chicago
- **Coed**
- **Moderately difficult** entrance level
- **$13,630 tuition** and fees

Part of Trinity International University of South Florida.
Expenses (1999–2000) *Comprehensive fee:* $18,580 includes full-time tuition ($13,390), mandatory fees ($240), and room and board ($4950). *College room only:* $2500. Room and board charges vary according to board plan. *Part-time tuition:* $558 per hour. *Part-time fees:* $60 per term part-time.
Institutional Web site http://www.tiu.edu/
College life *Housing:* on-campus residence required through junior year. *Options:* men-only, women-only. *Most popular organizations:* student senate, college union, Trinity Summer Mission, student newspaper, yearbook.
Campus security 24-hour patrols, controlled dormitory access.
Application *Application fee:* $25. *Required:* essay or personal statement; high school transcript; minimum 2.5 GPA; 1 letter of recommendation. *Required for some:* interview. *Recommended:* minimum 3.0 GPA.
Standardized tests *Admission: Required:* SAT I or ACT.
Admissions Office Contact
Trinity International University, 2065 Half Day Road, Deerfield, IL 60015-1284. **Toll-free phone:** 800-822-3225. **Fax:** 847-317-7081. **E-mail:** tcdadm@tiu.edu
Visit CollegeQuest.com for information on athletics.

UNIVERSITY OF CHICAGO
Chicago, Illinois

- **Independent**, university, founded 1891
- **Degrees** bachelor's, master's, doctoral, and first professional
- **Urban** 203-acre campus
- **Coed**, 3,836 undergraduate students, 99% full-time, 49% women, 51% men
- **Most difficult** entrance level, 48% of applicants were admitted
- **4:1 student-to-undergraduate faculty ratio**
- **$24,234 tuition** and fees
- **$1.9 billion endowment**

The Undergraduate College of the University of Chicago is at the heart of one of the world's great intellectual communities and centers of learning, where 71 Nobel laureates have researched, studied, or taught. The College offers 50 concentrations of study and the first established and most extensive general education curriculum.

Students *Undergraduates:* 3,787 full-time, 49 part-time. Students come from 53 states and territories, 34 other countries. *The most frequently chosen baccalaureate fields are:* biological/life sciences, interdisciplinary studies, social sciences and history. *Graduate:* 1,017 in professional programs, 7,142 in other graduate degree programs.

From out-of-state	78%	Reside on campus	66%
Age 25 or older	1%	Transferred in	2%
International students	5%	African Americans	4%
Asian Americans/Pacific Islanders	20%	Hispanic Americans	6%
Native Americans	0.2%		

Faculty 1,789 (87% full-time).
Expenses (1999–2000) *Comprehensive fee:* $32,068 includes full-time tuition ($23,820), mandatory fees ($414), and room and board ($7834). *College room only:* $4378. *Part-time tuition:* $3337 per course. *Part-time fees:* $138 per term part-time. Part-time tuition and fees vary according to course load. *Payment plans:* tuition prepayment, installment. *Waivers:* employees or children of employees.
Library Joseph Regenstein Library plus 8 others. *Operations spending 1999–2000:* $13.2 million. *Collection:* 5.8 million titles, 47,000 serial subscriptions.
College life *Housing:* on-campus residence required in freshman year. *Option:* coed. *Social organizations:* national fraternities, national sororities; 12% of eligible men and 5% of eligible women are members. *Most popular organizations:* Model United Nations, university theater, Documentary Films Club, Major Activities Board, student radio station.
Campus security 24-hour emergency response devices and patrols, late-night transport-escort service, controlled dormitory access.
After graduation *Career center:* 13 full-time, 1 part-time personnel. Services include job fairs, resume preparation, resume referral, career counseling, careers library, job bank, job interviews. *Major awards:* 1 Rhodes, 3 Marshall, 17 Fulbright Scholars.
Freshmen 6,844 applied, 3,252 admitted, 1,005 enrolled. 97 National Merit Scholars, 77 valedictorians.

SAT verbal scores above 500	99%	SAT math scores above 500	99%
ACT above 18	100%	From top 10% of their h.s. class	79%
From top quarter	97%	From top half	100%
1998 freshmen returning in 1999	95%		

Application *Options:* electronic application, early admission, early action, deferred entrance. *Application fee:* $60. *Required:* essay or personal statement; high school transcript; 3 letters of recommendation. *Recommended:* interview.
Standardized tests *Admission: Required:* SAT I or ACT.
Significant dates *Application deadlines:* 1/1 (freshmen), 4/15 (transfers). *Early action:* 11/1. *Notification:* 4/1 (freshmen), 12/15 (early action). *Financial aid deadline priority date:* 2/1.
Freshman Application Contact
Mr. Theodore O'Neill, Dean of Admissions, University of Chicago, 1116 East 59th Street, Chicago, IL 60637-1513. **Phone:** 773-702-8650. **Fax:** 773-702-4199. **E-mail:** college-admissions@uchicago.edu
Visit CollegeQuest.com for information on majors offered and athletics.

■ *See page 2710 for a narrative description.*

UNIVERSITY OF ILLINOIS AT CHICAGO
Chicago, Illinois

- **State-supported**, university, founded 1946
- **Degrees** bachelor's, master's, doctoral, first professional, and first professional certificates
- **Urban** 216-acre campus
- **Coed**, 16,104 undergraduate students, 87% full-time, 54% women, 46% men
- **Moderately difficult** entrance level, 61% of applicants were admitted
- **14:1 student-to-undergraduate faculty ratio**
- **36% graduate** in 6 years or less
- **$4780 tuition** and fees (in-state); $11,244 (out-of-state)
- **$11,200 average financial aid** package, $87.1 million endowment

Part of University of Illinois System.
Students *Undergraduates:* 14,006 full-time, 2,098 part-time. Students come from 42 states and territories, 53 other countries. *The most frequently chosen baccalaureate fields are:* business/marketing, engineering/engineering technologies, psychology. *Graduate:* 2,205 in professional programs, 6,064 in other graduate degree programs.

Illinois

University of Illinois at Chicago (continued)

From out-of-state	2%	Reside on campus	10%
Age 25 or older	15%	Transferred in	11%
International students	2%	African Americans	10%
Asian Americans/Pacific Islanders	23%	Hispanic Americans	17%
Native Americans	0.2%		

Faculty 1,516 (80% full-time).

Expenses (2000–2001) *Tuition, state resident:* full-time $3232; part-time $1077 per term. *Tuition, nonresident:* full-time $9696; part-time $3232 per term. *Required fees:* full-time $1548; $774 per term part-time. Full-time tuition and fees vary according to program. Part-time tuition and fees vary according to course load and program. *College room and board:* $5856. Room and board charges vary according to board plan and housing facility. *Waivers:* senior citizens and employees or children of employees.

Library University Library plus 8 others. *Operations spending 1999–2000:* $14.5 million. *Collection:* 2 million titles, 15,538 serial subscriptions, 25,755 audiovisual materials.

College life *Housing: Option:* coed. *Social organizations:* national fraternities, national sororities, local fraternities, local sororities; 1% of eligible men and 1% of eligible women are members. *Most popular organizations:* Asian American Student Alliance, Health Oriented Latino Association, Muslim Student Association, National Association of Black Accountants, Society of Hispanic Professional Engineers.

Campus security 24-hour emergency response devices and patrols, student patrols, late-night transport-escort service, controlled dormitory access, housing ID stickers, guest escort policy, 24-hour closed circuit videos for exits and entrances, security screen for first floor.

After graduation 829 organizations recruited on campus 1997–98. 92% of class of 1998 had job offers within 6 months. *Career center:* 10 full-time, 21 part-time personnel. Services include job fairs, resume preparation, resume referral, career counseling, careers library, job bank, job interviews.

Freshmen 10,109 applied, 6,127 admitted, 2,616 enrolled.

SAT verbal scores above 500	N/R	SAT math scores above 500	N/R
ACT above 18	93%	From top 10% of their h.s. class	26%
From top quarter	60%	From top half	94%
1998 freshmen returning in 1999	75%		

Application *Option:* early admission. *Application fee:* $40. *Required:* high school transcript. *Required for some:* essay or personal statement; interview.

Standardized tests *Admission: Required:* SAT I or ACT.

Significant dates *Application deadlines:* 2/28 (freshmen), 6/1 (transfers). *Financial aid deadline priority date:* 3/1.

Freshman Application Contact
Ms. Stacey Neil, Associate Director for Undergraduate Admissions, University of Illinois at Chicago, Box 5220, Chicago, IL 60680-5220. **Phone:** 312-996-4350. **E-mail:** uic.admit@uic.edu

Visit CollegeQuest.com for information on majors offered and athletics.

■ *See page 2736 for a narrative description.*

UNIVERSITY OF ILLINOIS AT SPRINGFIELD
Springfield, Illinois

- **State-supported**, upper-level, founded 1969
- **Degrees** bachelor's and master's
- **Suburban** 746-acre campus
- **Coed**, 2,022 undergraduate students, 54% full-time, 62% women, 38% men
- **Minimally difficult** entrance level
- **13:1 student-to-undergraduate faculty ratio**
- **$3042 tuition** and fees (in-state); $8622 (out-of-state)

Students *Undergraduates:* 1,086 full-time, 936 part-time. Students come from 14 states and territories. *The most frequently chosen baccalaureate fields are:* business/marketing, protective services/public administration, psychology. *Graduate:* 1,896 in graduate degree programs.

From out-of-state	2%	Reside on campus	12%
Age 25 or older	43%	Transferred in	24%
International students	1%	African Americans	8%
Asian Americans/Pacific Islanders	1%	Hispanic Americans	1%
Native Americans	0.4%		

Faculty 271 (58% full-time).

Expenses (1999–2000) *Tuition, state resident:* full-time $2790; part-time $93 per semester hour. *Tuition, nonresident:* full-time $8370; part-time $279 per semester hour. *Required fees:* full-time $252; $4 per semester hour; $42 per term part-time. *College room and board:* room only: $2376. Room and board charges vary according to housing facility. *Payment plan:* installment. *Waivers:* employees or children of employees.

Library Brookens Library. *Operations spending 1999–2000:* $2 million. *Collection:* 39,202 audiovisual materials.

College life *Housing: Option:* coed. *Most popular organizations:* International Student Association, Model United Nations, Model Illinois Government, African-American Student Organization.

Campus security 24-hour patrols, late-night transport-escort service.

After graduation *Career center:* 2 full-time, 3 part-time personnel. Services include job fairs, resume preparation, resume referral, career counseling, careers library, job bank, job interviews.

Application *Option:* deferred entrance.

Significant dates *Application deadline:* rolling (transfers). *Financial aid deadline priority date:* 4/15.

Freshman Application Contact
Office of Enrollment Services, University of Illinois at Springfield, PO Box 19243, Springfield, IL 62794-9243. **Phone:** 217-206-6626. **Toll-free phone:** 800-252-8533. **Fax:** 217-206-7188.

Visit CollegeQuest.com for information on majors offered and athletics. College video available at CollegeQuest.com.

UNIVERSITY OF ILLINOIS AT URBANA–CHAMPAIGN
Urbana, Illinois

- **State-supported**, university, founded 1867
- **Degrees** bachelor's, master's, doctoral, and first professional
- **Small-town** 1,470-acre campus
- **Coed**, 27,492 undergraduate students, 98% full-time, 47% women, 53% men
- **Very difficult** entrance level, 71% of applicants were admitted
- **14:1 student-to-undergraduate faculty ratio**
- **77% graduate** in 6 years or less
- **$4752 tuition** and fees (in-state); $12,200 (out-of-state)
- **$7800 average financial aid** package, $10,394 average indebtedness upon graduation, $822.4 million endowment

Part of University of Illinois System.

Students *Undergraduates:* 27,002 full-time, 490 part-time. Students come from 44 states and territories, 122 other countries. *The most frequently chosen baccalaureate fields are:* business/marketing, engineering/engineering technologies, social sciences and history. *Graduate:* 961 in professional programs, 8,974 in other graduate degree programs.

From out-of-state	7%	Reside on campus	30%
Age 25 or older	2%	Transferred in	4%
International students	1%	African Americans	7%
Asian Americans/Pacific Islanders	13%	Hispanic Americans	5%
Native Americans	0.2%		

Faculty 2,529 (85% full-time), 73% with terminal degrees.

Expenses (2000–2001) *Tuition, state resident:* full-time $3724. *Tuition, nonresident:* full-time $11,172. *Required fees:* full-time $1028. Full-time tuition and fees vary according to program and student level. Part-time tuition and fees vary according to course load and student level. *College room and board:* $5424. Room and board charges vary according to board plan and housing facility. *Payment plan:* installment. *Waivers:* senior citizens and employees or children of employees.

Library University Library plus 39 others. *Operations spending 1999–2000:* $26.5 million. *Collection:* 9 million titles, 90,985 serial subscriptions.

College life *Housing:* on-campus residence required in freshman year. *Options:* coed, men-only, women-only, disabled students. *Social organizations:* national fraternities, national sororities, local fraternities, local sororities; 17% of eligible men and 22% of eligible women are members. *Most popular organizations:* Volunteer Illini Project, Alpha Phi Omega, Indian Student Organization, Panhel IFC, Residence Hall Association.

Illinois

Campus security 24-hour emergency response devices and patrols, student patrols, late-night transport-escort service, controlled dormitory access, safety training classes, ID cards with safety numbers.
After graduation 2,247 organizations recruited on campus 1997–98. 86% of class of 1998 had job offers within 6 months. *Career center:* 10 full-time, 18 part-time personnel. Services include job fairs, resume preparation, interview workshops, resume referral, career/interest testing, career counseling, careers library, job bank, job interviews.
Freshmen 17,867 applied, 12,636 admitted, 6,479 enrolled. 53 National Merit Scholars.

SAT verbal scores above 500	89%	SAT math scores above 500	94%
ACT above 18	99%	From top 10% of their h.s. class	50%
From top quarter	86%	From top half	99%
1998 freshmen returning in 1999	92%		

Application *Options:* early admission, deferred entrance. *Application fee:* $40. *Required:* essay or personal statement; high school transcript. *Required for some:* interview; audition, statement of professional interest.
Standardized tests *Admission: Required:* SAT I or ACT.
Significant dates *Application deadlines:* 1/1 (freshmen), 3/15 (transfers). *Financial aid deadline priority date:* 3/15.
Freshman Application Contact
Ms. Tammy Bouseman, Assistant Director of Admissions, University of Illinois at Urbana–Champaign, 901 West Illinois, Urbana, IL 61801. **Phone:** 217-333-0302. **E-mail:** admissions@oar.uiuc.edu
Visit CollegeQuest.com for information on majors offered and athletics. College video and electronic viewbook available at CollegeQuest.com.

UNIVERSITY OF ST. FRANCIS
Joliet, Illinois

- **Independent Roman Catholic**, comprehensive, founded 1920
- **Degrees** bachelor's and master's
- **Suburban** 16-acre campus with easy access to Chicago
- **Coed**, 1,403 undergraduate students, 69% full-time, 61% women, 39% men
- **Moderately difficult** entrance level, 69% of applicants were admitted
- **11:1 student-to-undergraduate faculty ratio**
- **51% graduate** in 6 years or less
- **$13,082 tuition** and fees
- **$11,127 average financial aid** package, $11,506 average indebtedness upon graduation, $9 million endowment

The University of St. Francis announces a new degree in special education. The special education major trains teachers in both learning disabilities and social-emotional disorders, the highest shortage areas nationwide, giving students a wide range of potential career choices.

Students *Undergraduates:* 963 full-time, 440 part-time. Students come from 15 states and territories. *The most frequently chosen baccalaureate fields are:* health professions and related sciences, business/marketing, interdisciplinary studies. *Graduate:* 1,201 in graduate degree programs.

From out-of-state	1%	Reside on campus	24%
Age 25 or older	38%	Transferred in	16%
African Americans	7%	Asian Americans/Pacific Islanders	2%
Hispanic Americans	5%	Native Americans	0.1%

Faculty 139 (50% full-time).
Expenses (1999–2000) *Comprehensive fee:* $18,202 includes full-time tuition ($12,800), mandatory fees ($282), and room and board ($5120). *Part-time tuition:* $370 per credit. *Part-time fees:* $15 per term part-time. Part-time tuition and fees vary according to course load. *Payment plan:* installment. *Waivers:* children of alumni and employees or children of employees.
Library University of St. Francis Library. *Operations spending 1999–2000:* $781,201. *Collection:* 673 serial subscriptions.
College life *Housing: Option:* coed. *Most popular organizations:* Student Business Association, Ethnic Affairs Council, Campus Ministry Poverellos, Student Activity Board, Recreation club.
Campus security 24-hour emergency response devices and patrols, student patrols, late-night transport-escort service, controlled dormitory access.
After graduation 42 organizations recruited on campus 1997–98. 86% of class of 1998 had job offers within 6 months. *Career center:* 2 full-time personnel. Services include job fairs, resume preparation, interview workshops, resume referral, career/interest testing, career counseling, careers library, job bank, job interviews.
Freshmen 799 applied, 553 admitted, 170 enrolled. 4 class presidents, 3 valedictorians.

Average high school GPA	3.29	SAT verbal scores above 500	N/R
SAT math scores above 500	N/R	ACT above 18	96%
From top 10% of their h.s. class	18%	From top quarter	50%
From top half	83%	1998 freshmen returning in 1999	77%

Application *Options:* Common Application, deferred entrance. *Application fee:* $20. *Required:* high school transcript; minimum 2.0 GPA. *Required for some:* essay or personal statement; 1 letter of recommendation; interview.
Standardized tests *Admission: Required:* SAT I or ACT. *Recommended:* ACT.
Significant dates *Application deadlines:* rolling (freshmen), rolling (transfers). *Financial aid deadline:* continuous.
Freshman Application Contact
Mr. Vic Davolt, Director of Admissions, University of St. Francis, 500 North Wilcox Street, Joliet, IL 60435-6188. **Phone:** 815-740-3400. **Toll-free phone:** 800-735-7500. **Fax:** 815-740-4285. **E-mail:** admissions@stfrancis.edu
Visit CollegeQuest.com for information on majors offered and athletics.

■ *See page 2818 for a narrative description.*

VANDERCOOK COLLEGE OF MUSIC
Chicago, Illinois

Apply at CollegeQuest.com

- **Independent**, comprehensive, founded 1909
- **Degrees** bachelor's and master's
- **Urban** 1-acre campus
- **Coed**, 79 undergraduate students
- **Moderately difficult** entrance level, 59% of applicants were admitted
- **9:1 student-to-undergraduate faculty ratio**
- **$12,240 tuition** and fees

Students *Undergraduates:* Students come from 10 states and territories, 3 other countries.

From out-of-state	40%	Reside on campus	15%
Age 25 or older	16%		

Expenses (2000–2001) *Comprehensive fee:* $17,670 includes full-time tuition ($11,870), mandatory fees ($370), and room and board ($5430). Room and board charges vary according to board plan. *Part-time tuition:* $430 per semester hour. Part-time tuition and fees vary according to course load. *Payment plan:* installment. *Waivers:* minority students and employees or children of employees.
Library Harry Ruppel Memorial Library. *Collection:* 5,521 titles, 93 serial subscriptions.
College life *Housing: Option:* coed. *Social organizations:* national fraternities, national sororities, local fraternities, local sororities; 35% of eligible men and 20% of eligible women are members. *Most popular organization:* MENC.
Campus security 24-hour emergency response devices and patrols, late-night transport-escort service, controlled dormitory access.
After graduation 90% of class of 1998 had job offers within 6 months. *Career center:* 1 part-time personnel. Services include resume preparation, resume referral, career counseling, job bank. *Graduate education:* 1% of class of 1999 went directly to graduate and professional school; 1% education.
Freshmen 54 applied, 32 admitted. 2 class presidents, 1 valedictorian, 7 student government officers.

SAT verbal scores above 500	N/R	SAT math scores above 500	N/R
ACT above 18	76%	From top 10% of their h.s. class	28%
From top quarter	39%	From top half	67%
1998 freshmen returning in 1999	90%		

Application *Options:* eApply at www.CollegeQuest.com, deferred entrance. *Application fee:* $35. *Required:* essay or personal statement; high school transcript; 3 letters of recommendation; interview; audition. *Required for some:* minimum 3.0 GPA. *Recommended:* minimum 3.0 GPA.
Standardized tests *Admission: Recommended:* SAT I or ACT.
Significant dates *Application deadlines:* rolling (freshmen), rolling (transfers). *Financial aid deadline:* 7/1. Priority date: 6/1.

Illinois

VanderCook College of Music (continued)
Freshman Application Contact
Mr. George Pierard, Director of Admissions, VanderCook College of Music, 3140 South Federal Street, Chicago, IL 60616-3731. **Phone:** 312-225-6288. **Toll-free phone:** 800-448-2655. **Fax:** 312-225-5211. **E-mail:** gpierard@vandercook.edu
Visit CollegeQuest.com for information on majors offered and athletics.

■ *See page 2878 for a narrative description.*

WESTERN ILLINOIS UNIVERSITY
Macomb, Illinois

- **State-supported**, comprehensive, founded 1899
- **Degrees** bachelor's and master's
- **Small-town** 1,050-acre campus
- **Coed**, 10,423 undergraduate students, 86% full-time, 52% women, 48% men
- **Moderately difficult** entrance level, 66% of applicants were admitted
- **15:1 student-to-undergraduate faculty ratio**
- **45% graduate** in 6 years or less
- **$3610 tuition** and fees (in-state); $6340 (out-of-state)
- **$6526 average financial aid** package, $13,463 average indebtedness upon graduation, $12.7 million endowment

Western Illinois University guarantees a fixed rate of tuition, fees, room, and board for all new undergraduate students, beginning with the fall 1999 entering class. The program establishes and freezes a per-semester-hour cost for students for 4 years as long as they maintain continuous enrollment at Western.

Students *Undergraduates:* 8,940 full-time, 1,483 part-time. Students come from 42 states and territories, 49 other countries. *The most frequently chosen baccalaureate fields are:* education, liberal arts/general studies, protective services/public administration. *Graduate:* 2,500 in graduate degree programs.

From out-of-state	3%	Reside on campus	47%
Age 25 or older	9%	Transferred in	14%
International students	2%	African Americans	7%
Asian Americans/Pacific Islanders	1%	Hispanic Americans	3%
Native Americans	0.2%		

Faculty 665 (91% full-time), 68% with terminal degrees.
Expenses (1999–2000) *Tuition, state resident:* full-time $2730; part-time $91 per credit hour. *Tuition, nonresident:* full-time $5460; part-time $182 per credit hour. *Required fees:* full-time $880; $29 per credit hour. *College room and board:* $4392; room only: $2570. Room and board charges vary according to board plan. *Payment plans:* guaranteed tuition, installment. *Waivers:* senior citizens and employees or children of employees.
Library Western Illinois University Library plus 4 others. *Operations spending 1999–2000:* $3.9 million. *Collection:* 882,087 titles, 3,315 serial subscriptions, 3,046 audiovisual materials.
College life *Housing:* on-campus residence required through sophomore year. *Option:* coed. *Social organizations:* national fraternities, national sororities, local fraternities, local sororities; 12% of eligible men and 10% of eligible women are members. *Most popular organizations:* Student Government Association, Black Student Association, University Union Board, International Friendship Club, Bureau of Cultural Affairs.
Campus security 24-hour emergency response devices and patrols, late-night transport-escort service.
After graduation 405 organizations recruited on campus 1997–98. 90% of class of 1998 had job offers within 6 months. *Career center:* 6 full-time personnel. Services include job fairs, resume preparation, interview workshops, resume referral, career counseling, careers library, job bank, job interviews. *Graduate education:* 25% of class of 1999 went directly to graduate and professional school.
Freshmen 8,529 applied, 5,667 admitted, 1,707 enrolled.

SAT verbal scores above 500	N/R	SAT math scores above 500	N/R
ACT above 18	90%	From top 10% of their h.s. class	6%
From top quarter	27%	From top half	63%
1998 freshmen returning in 1999	74%		

Application *Options:* electronic application, deferred entrance. *Application fee:* $0. *Required:* high school transcript.

Standardized tests *Admission:* Required: SAT I or ACT.
Significant dates *Application deadlines:* 8/1 (freshmen), rolling (transfers). *Notification:* continuous until 8/3 (freshmen). *Financial aid deadline:* continuous.
Freshman Application Contact
Ms. Karen Helmers, Director of Admissions, Western Illinois University, 1 University Circle, 115 Sherman Hall, Macomb, IL 61455-1390. **Phone:** 309-298-3157. **Fax:** 309-298-3111. **E-mail:** karen_helmers@wiu.edu
Visit CollegeQuest.com for information on majors offered and athletics. College video and electronic viewbook available at CollegeQuest.com.

■ *See page 2946 for a narrative description.*

WEST SUBURBAN COLLEGE OF NURSING
Oak Park, Illinois

Admissions Office Contact
West Suburban College of Nursing, 3 Erie Court, Oak Park, IL 60302. **Fax:** 708-763-1531.

WHEATON COLLEGE
Wheaton, Illinois

- **Independent nondenominational**, comprehensive, founded 1860
- **Degrees** bachelor's, master's, doctoral, and postbachelor's certificates
- **Suburban** 80-acre campus with easy access to Chicago
- **Coed**, 2,302 undergraduate students, 99% full-time, 52% women, 48% men
- **Very difficult** entrance level, 53% of applicants were admitted
- **12:1 student-to-undergraduate faculty ratio**
- **83.4% graduate** in 6 years or less
- **$14,930 tuition** and fees
- **$13,109 average financial aid** package, $14,496 average indebtedness upon graduation, $269 million endowment

Students *Undergraduates:* 2,283 full-time, 19 part-time. Students come from 50 states and territories, 13 other countries. *The most frequently chosen baccalaureate fields are:* English, philosophy, social sciences and history. *Graduate:* 394 in graduate degree programs.

From out-of-state	77%	Reside on campus	90%
Age 25 or older	2%	Transferred in	4%
International students	1%	African Americans	2%
Asian Americans/Pacific Islanders	4%	Hispanic Americans	3%
Native Americans	0.4%		

Faculty 271 (63% full-time), 58% with terminal degrees.
Expenses (1999–2000) *Comprehensive fee:* $20,010 includes full-time tuition ($14,930) and room and board ($5080). *College room only:* $2930. Room and board charges vary according to board plan and housing facility. *Part-time tuition:* $625 per hour. *Payment plan:* installment. *Waivers:* employees or children of employees.
Library Buswell Memorial Library plus 1 other. *Operations spending 1999–2000:* $1.6 million. *Collection:* 342,746 titles, 3,264 serial subscriptions, 32,761 audiovisual materials.
College life *Housing:* on-campus residence required through senior year. *Options:* men-only, women-only, cooperative. *Most popular organizations:* Christian Service Council, College Union, music groups, Mu Kappa, student government.
Campus security 24-hour patrols, late-night transport-escort service, controlled dormitory access.
After graduation 179 organizations recruited on campus 1997–98. *Career center:* 3 full-time, 2 part-time personnel. Services include job fairs, resume preparation, interview workshops, resume referral, career/interest testing, career counseling, careers library, job bank, job interviews. *Graduate education:* 25% of class of 1999 went directly to graduate and professional school.
Freshmen 1,964 applied, 1,032 admitted, 583 enrolled. 59 National Merit Scholars.

Illinois–Indiana

Average high school GPA	3.66	SAT verbal scores above 500	98%
SAT math scores above 500	97%	ACT above 18	100%
From top 10% of their h.s. class	61%	From top quarter	86%
From top half	98%	1998 freshmen returning in 1999	92%

Application *Options:* early action, deferred entrance. *Preference* given to Christians. *Application fee:* $35. *Required:* essay or personal statement; high school transcript; 2 letters of recommendation. *Recommended:* interview.
Standardized tests *Admission: Required:* SAT I or ACT. *Recommended:* SAT II: Writing Test.
Significant dates *Application deadlines:* 1/15 (freshmen), 3/1 (transfers). *Early action:* 11/1. *Notification:* 4/1 (freshmen), 1/1 (early action). *Financial aid deadline priority date:* 2/15.
Freshman Application Contact
Mr. Dan Crabtree, Director of Admissions, Wheaton College, 501 East College Avenue, Wheaton, IL 60187-5593. **Phone:** 630-752-5011. **Toll-free phone:** 800-222-2419. **Fax:** 630-752-5285. **E-mail:** admissions@wheaton.edu
Visit CollegeQuest.com for information on majors offered and athletics.

■ *See page 2974 for a narrative description.*

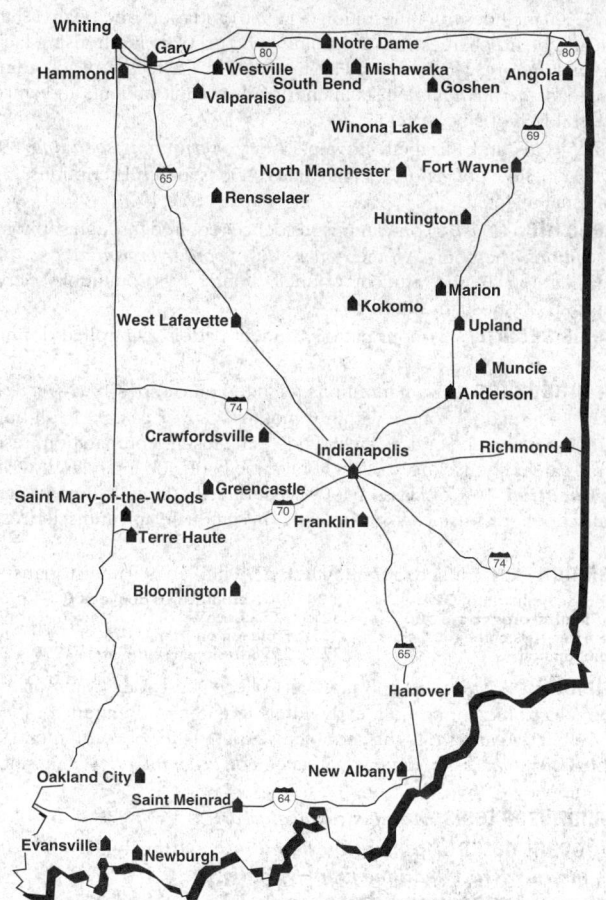

ANDERSON UNIVERSITY
Anderson, Indiana

- **Independent**, comprehensive, founded 1917, affiliated with Church of God
- **Degrees** associate, bachelor's, master's, doctoral, and first professional
- **Suburban** 100-acre campus with easy access to Indianapolis
- **Coed**, 1,978 undergraduate students, 92% full-time, 59% women, 41% men
- **Moderately difficult** entrance level, 80% of applicants were admitted
- **14:1 student-to-undergraduate faculty ratio**
- **49.6% graduate** in 6 years or less

- **$14,680 tuition** and fees
- **$13,530 average financial aid** package, $17,650 average indebtedness upon graduation, $5.1 million endowment

Anderson University is a Christian, liberal arts learning community of 2,300 students. Sixty majors and programs are offered through the College of the Arts, the College of Science and Humanities, and the College of Professional Studies. Each year, hundreds of students express the spirit of the University by volunteering for international service and campus ministries projects.

Students *Undergraduates:* 1,811 full-time, 167 part-time. Students come from 43 states and territories, 12 other countries. *The most frequently chosen baccalaureate fields are:* business/marketing, education, philosophy. *Graduate:* 66 in professional programs, 197 in other graduate degree programs.

From out-of-state	35%	Reside on campus	61%
Age 25 or older	11%	Transferred in	5%
International students	1%	African Americans	4%
Asian Americans/Pacific Islanders	0.5%	Hispanic Americans	1%
Native Americans	0.4%		

Faculty 220 (63% full-time).
Expenses (2000–2001, estimated) *Comprehensive fee:* $19,430 includes full-time tuition ($14,680) and room and board ($4750). *College room only:* $2750. Room and board charges vary according to board plan. *Part-time tuition:* $612 per credit. Part-time tuition and fees vary according to course load. *Payment plan:* installment. *Waivers:* adult students and employees or children of employees.
Library Robert A. Nicholson Library. *Operations spending 1999–2000:* $688,385. *Collection:* 280,575 titles, 928 serial subscriptions, 65 audiovisual materials.
College life *Housing:* on-campus residence required through junior year. *Options:* men-only, women-only. *Most popular organizations:* social clubs, Adult and Continuing Education Students Association, Multicultural Student Union, campus ministries, intramurals.
Campus security 24-hour emergency response devices and patrols, student patrols, late-night transport-escort service, 24-hour crimeline.
After graduation 46 organizations recruited on campus 1997–98. *Career center:* 3 full-time personnel. Services include job fairs, resume preparation, career/interest testing, career counseling, careers library, job interviews. *Graduate education:* 21% of class of 1999 went directly to graduate and professional school.
Freshmen 1,595 applied, 1,278 admitted, 506 enrolled. 24 valedictorians.

Average high school GPA	3.39	SAT verbal scores above 500	62%
SAT math scores above 500	67%	ACT above 18	91%
From top 10% of their h.s. class	29%	From top quarter	53%
From top half	86%	1998 freshmen returning in 1999	76%

Application *Option:* deferred entrance. *Application fee:* $20. *Required:* high school transcript; minimum 2.0 GPA; 2 letters of recommendation; lifestyle statement. *Required for some:* interview. *Recommended:* essay or personal statement.
Standardized tests *Admission: Required:* SAT I or ACT.
Significant dates *Application deadlines:* 8/25 (freshmen), 8/25 (transfers). *Notification:* continuous until 9/1 (freshmen). *Financial aid deadline priority date:* 3/1.
Freshman Application Contact
Mr. Jim King, Director of Admissions, Anderson University, 1100 East Fifth Street, Anderson, IN 46012-3495. **Phone:** 765-641-4080. **Toll-free phone:** 800-421-3014 (in-state); 800-428-6414 (out-of-state). **Fax:** 765-641-3851. **E-mail:** info@anderson.edu
Visit CollegeQuest.com for information on majors offered and athletics.

■ *See page 1170 for a narrative description.*

BALL STATE UNIVERSITY
Muncie, Indiana

- **State-supported**, university, founded 1918
- **Degrees** associate, bachelor's, master's, and doctoral
- **Suburban** 955-acre campus with easy access to Indianapolis
- **Coed**, 15,979 undergraduate students, 91% full-time, 53% women, 47% men
- **Moderately difficult** entrance level, 79% of applicants were admitted

Peterson's Guide to Four-Year Colleges 2001   www.petersons.com   261

Indiana

Ball State University *(continued)*
- 17:1 student-to-undergraduate faculty ratio
- $3686 tuition and fees (in-state); $9846 (out-of-state)

Ball State University is a comprehensive public institution composed of 7 curricular colleges: Applied Sciences and Technology; Architecture and Planning; Business; Communication, Information, and Media; Fine Arts; Sciences and Humanities; and Teachers College. The enrollment of 17,930 includes 15,890 undergraduates. Ball State is located northeast of Indianapolis in Muncie, Indiana.

Students *Undergraduates:* 14,550 full-time, 1,429 part-time. Students come from 52 states and territories. *The most frequently chosen baccalaureate fields are:* business/marketing, communications/communication technologies, education. *Graduate:* 2,524 in graduate degree programs.

From out-of-state	10%	Reside on campus	39%
Age 25 or older	9%	Transferred in	4%
International students	0.01%	African Americans	6%
Asian Americans/Pacific Islanders	1%	Hispanic Americans	1%
Native Americans	0.2%		

Faculty 1,011 (83% full-time).
Expenses (1999–2000) *Tuition, state resident:* full-time $3576; part-time $1125 per term. *Tuition, nonresident:* full-time $9736; part-time $2885 per term. *Required fees:* full-time $110; $55 per term part-time. Part-time tuition and fees vary according to course load. *College room and board:* $4520. Room and board charges vary according to board plan and housing facility. *Payment plan:* installment. *Waivers:* employees or children of employees.
Library Bracken Library plus 3 others. *Operations spending 1999–2000:* $7.9 million. *Collection:* 1 million titles, 3,553 serial subscriptions.
College life *Housing:* on-campus residence required in freshman year. *Option:* coed. *Social organizations:* national fraternities, national sororities; 12% of eligible men and 13% of eligible women are members. *Most popular organizations:* Student Association, Excellence in Leadership, fraternities/sororities, Black Student Association, student voluntary services.
Campus security 24-hour emergency response devices and patrols, late-night transport-escort service, controlled dormitory access.
After graduation 400 organizations recruited on campus 1997–98. *Career center:* 20 full-time personnel. Services include job fairs, resume preparation, interview workshops, resume referral, career counseling, careers library, job bank, job interviews. *Major awards:* 1 Fulbright Scholar.
Freshmen 8,867 applied, 6,972 admitted, 3,649 enrolled. 11 National Merit Scholars, 23 valedictorians.

SAT verbal scores above 500	55%	SAT math scores above 500	55%
ACT above 18	88%	From top 10% of their h.s. class	15%
From top quarter	41%	From top half	79%
1998 freshmen returning in 1999	75%		

Application *Option:* deferred entrance. *Application fee:* $25. *Required:* high school transcript. *Required for some:* essay or personal statement; letters of recommendation; interview.
Standardized tests *Admission: Required:* SAT I or ACT.
Significant dates *Application deadlines:* rolling (freshmen), rolling (transfers). *Financial aid deadline priority date:* 3/1.
Freshman Application Contact
Dr. Lawrence Waters, Dean of Admissions and Financial Aid, Ball State University, Office of Admissions, Muncie, IN 47306-1099. **Phone:** 765-285-8300. **Toll-free phone:** 800-482-4BSU. **Fax:** 765-285-1632. **E-mail:** askus@wp.bsu.edu
Visit CollegeQuest.com for information on majors offered and athletics.

- *See page 1222 for a narrative description.*

BAPTIST BIBLE COLLEGE OF INDIANAPOLIS
Indianapolis, Indiana

Admissions Office Contact
Baptist Bible College of Indianapolis, 601 North Shortridge Road, Indianapolis, IN 46219. **Toll-free phone:** 800-273-2224. **Fax:** 317-352-9145.

BETHEL COLLEGE
Mishawaka, Indiana

- **Independent**, comprehensive, founded 1947, affiliated with Missionary Church
- **Degrees** associate, bachelor's, and master's
- **Suburban** 70-acre campus
- **Coed**, 1,552 undergraduate students, 73% full-time, 66% women, 34% men
- **Moderately difficult** entrance level, 72% of applicants were admitted
- 18:1 student-to-undergraduate faculty ratio
- **$11,950 tuition** and fees
- **$9514 average financial aid** package, $13,517 average indebtedness upon graduation, $3.2 million endowment

Students *Undergraduates:* 1,126 full-time, 426 part-time. Students come from 29 states and territories, 13 other countries. *Graduate:* 88 in graduate degree programs.

From out-of-state	28%	Reside on campus	46%
Age 25 or older	37%	Transferred in	5%
International students	2%	African Americans	9%
Asian Americans/Pacific Islanders	1%	Hispanic Americans	1%
Native Americans	0.2%		

Faculty 128 (54% full-time).
Expenses (1999–2000) *One-time required fee:* $350. *Comprehensive fee:* $15,900 includes full-time tuition ($11,950) and room and board ($3950). Room and board charges vary according to board plan and housing facility. *Part-time tuition:* $240 per hour. Part-time tuition and fees vary according to course load. *Payment plan:* installment. *Waivers:* adult students and employees or children of employees.
Library Otis and Elizabeth Bowen Library. *Operations spending 1999–2000:* $436,359. *Collection:* 90,450 titles, 456 serial subscriptions, 3,389 audiovisual materials.
College life *Housing:* on-campus residence required through sophomore year. *Options:* men-only, women-only. *Most popular organizations:* "Task Force" Mission Teams, Student Council, Center for Community Service, Fellowship of Christian Athletes.
Campus security 24-hour patrols, student patrols, controlled dormitory access.
After graduation 34 organizations recruited on campus 1997–98. 82% of class of 1998 had job offers within 6 months. *Career center:* 1 full-time, 1 part-time personnel. Services include job fairs, resume preparation, resume referral, career counseling, careers library, job bank, job interviews. *Graduate education:* 10% of class of 1999 went directly to graduate and professional school: 4% business, 3% theology, 2% graduate arts and sciences, 1% law.
Freshmen 704 applied, 507 admitted, 277 enrolled. 9 valedictorians.

Average high school GPA	3.34	SAT verbal scores above 500	63%
SAT math scores above 500	52%	ACT above 18	90%
From top 10% of their h.s. class	23%	From top quarter	52%
From top half	77%	1998 freshmen returning in 1999	80%

Application *Options:* eApply at www.CollegeQuest.com, Common Application, electronic application, early admission, deferred entrance. *Application fee:* $25. *Required:* high school transcript; 1 letter of recommendation. *Required for some:* essay or personal statement. *Recommended:* minimum 2.3 GPA; interview.
Standardized tests *Admission: Required:* SAT I or ACT.
Significant dates *Application deadlines:* 8/1 (freshmen), 8/1 (transfers). *Financial aid deadline priority date:* 3/1.
Freshman Application Contact
Ms. Andrea M. Helmuth, Director of Admissions, Bethel College, 1001 West McKinley Avenue, Mishawaka, IN 46545-5591. **Phone:** 219-257-3319. **Toll-free phone:** 800-422-4101. **Fax:** 219-257-3326. **E-mail:** admissions@bethel-in.edu
Visit CollegeQuest.com for information on majors offered and athletics.

BUTLER UNIVERSITY
Indianapolis, Indiana

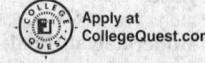

- **Independent**, comprehensive, founded 1855

Indiana

- **Degrees** associate, bachelor's, master's, first professional, and postbachelor's certificates
- **Urban** 290-acre campus
- **Coed**, 3,292 undergraduate students, 97% full-time, 62% women, 38% men
- **Moderately difficult** entrance level, 86% of applicants were admitted
- **14:1 student-to-undergraduate faculty ratio**
- **60% graduate** in 6 years or less
- **$17,360 tuition** and fees
- **$12,212 average financial aid** package, $18,700 average indebtedness upon graduation, $149.9 million endowment

With an undergraduate population of 3,500, Butler University is committed to the interactive learning process encompassing each of the five academic colleges. Students apply practical knowledge gained from the classroom to professional real world experiences. Indianapolis serves as the classroom as students perform internships and co-ops, gaining hands-on experiences tailored to the students' interests and talents.

Students *Undergraduates:* 3,183 full-time, 109 part-time. Students come from 41 states and territories, 38 other countries. *The most frequently chosen baccalaureate fields are:* business/marketing, education, health professions and related sciences. *Graduate:* 118 in professional programs, 735 in other graduate degree programs.

From out-of-state	39%	Reside on campus	62%
Age 25 or older	4%	Transferred in	4%
International students	2%	African Americans	4%
Asian Americans/Pacific Islanders	2%	Hispanic Americans	1%
Native Americans	0.4%		

Faculty 426 (58% full-time), 52% with terminal degrees.
Expenses (1999–2000) *Comprehensive fee:* $23,210 includes full-time tuition ($17,180), mandatory fees ($180), and room and board ($5850). Full-time tuition and fees vary according to program. Room and board charges vary according to board plan and housing facility. *Part-time tuition:* $720 per semester hour. Part-time tuition and fees vary according to program. *Payment plans:* tuition prepayment, installment. *Waivers:* employees or children of employees.
Library Irwin Library System plus 1 other. *Operations spending 1999–2000:* $1.8 million. *Collection:* 2,359 serial subscriptions, 1,664 audiovisual materials.
College life *Housing:* on-campus residence required in freshman year. *Options:* coed, women-only. *Social organizations:* national fraternities, national sororities; 31% of eligible men and 35% of eligible women are members. *Most popular organizations:* Butler University YMCA, Student Government Association, Academic Service Honoraries, Alpha Phi Omega, Mortar Board.
Campus security 24-hour emergency response devices and patrols, late-night transport-escort service, controlled dormitory access.
After graduation 66% of class of 1998 had job offers within 6 months. *Career center:* 7 full-time, 1 part-time personnel. Services include job fairs, resume preparation, resume referral, career counseling, careers library, job bank, job interviews.
Freshmen 3,116 applied, 2,682 admitted, 863 enrolled. 4 National Merit Scholars, 49 valedictorians.

Average high school GPA	3.55	SAT verbal scores above 500	83%
SAT math scores above 500	87%	ACT above 18	100%
From top 10% of their h.s. class	41%	From top quarter	69%
From top half	95%	1998 freshmen returning in 1999	82%

Application *Options:* eApply at www.CollegeQuest.com, Common Application, electronic application, early action, deferred entrance. *Application fee:* $25. *Required:* essay or personal statement; high school transcript. *Required for some:* interview; audition.
Standardized tests *Admission: Required:* SAT I or ACT. *Recommended:* SAT II Subject Tests.
Significant dates *Application deadlines:* 8/15 (freshmen), 8/15 (transfers). *Early action:* 12/1. *Notification:* 1/15 (early action). *Financial aid deadline priority date:* 3/1.
Freshman Application Contact
Mr. William Preble, Director of Admissions, Butler University, 4600 Sunset Avenue, Indianapolis, IN 46208-3485. **Phone:** 317-940-8100 Ext. 8124. **Toll-free phone:** 888-940-8100. **Fax:** 317-940-8150. **E-mail:** admission@butler.edu

Visit CollegeQuest.com for information on majors offered and athletics. College video available at CollegeQuest.com.

- *See page 1328 for a narrative description.*

CALUMET COLLEGE OF SAINT JOSEPH
Whiting, Indiana

Apply at CollegeQuest.com

- **Independent Roman Catholic**, 4-year, founded 1951
- **Degrees** associate and bachelor's
- **Suburban** 25-acre campus with easy access to Chicago
- **Coed**, 1,004 undergraduate students, 35% full-time, 62% women, 38% men
- **Minimally difficult** entrance level
- **$6750 tuition** and fees
- **$1.8 million endowment**

Students *Undergraduates:* 349 full-time, 655 part-time. Students come from 2 states and territories, 4 other countries.

Age 25 or older	74%	International students	0.4%
African Americans	28%	Asian Americans/Pacific Islanders	1%
Hispanic Americans	17%	Native Americans	0.4%

Faculty 81 (26% full-time).
Expenses (1999–2000) *Tuition:* full-time $6750; part-time $225 per credit hour. *Payment plan:* installment. *Waivers:* senior citizens and employees or children of employees.
Library Mary Gorman Specker Memorial Library. *Operations spending 1999–2000:* $200,000. *Collection:* 107,494 titles, 1,578 serial subscriptions.
College life *Housing:* college housing not available. *Most popular organizations:* student government, Los Amigos Hispanic club, criminal justice club, drama club, Black Student Union.
Campus security Late-night transport-escort service, night security.
After graduation 20 organizations recruited on campus 1997–98. *Career center:* 1 full-time personnel. Services include job fairs, resume preparation, interview workshops, resume referral, career/interest testing, career counseling, careers library, job bank, job interviews.
Freshmen 82 enrolled.

SAT verbal scores above 500	N/R	SAT math scores above 500	N/R
ACT above 18	N/R		

Application *Options:* eApply at www.CollegeQuest.com, Common Application, early admission, deferred entrance. *Required:* essay or personal statement; high school transcript; minimum 2.0 GPA. *Recommended:* interview.
Standardized tests *Admission: Required:* ACT COMPASS.
Significant dates *Application deadlines:* rolling (freshmen), rolling (transfers). *Financial aid deadline priority date:* 3/1.
Freshman Application Contact
Mr. Thomas A. Clark, Vice President for Enrollment Management, Calumet College of Saint Joseph, 2400 New York Avenue, Whiting, IN 46394-2195. **Phone:** 219-473-4215. **Toll-free phone:** 877-700-9100. **Fax:** 219-473-4259.
Visit CollegeQuest.com for information on majors offered and athletics. College video available at CollegeQuest.com.

DEPAUW UNIVERSITY
Greencastle, Indiana

Apply at CollegeQuest.com

- **Independent**, 4-year, founded 1837, affiliated with United Methodist Church
- **Degree** bachelor's
- **Small-town** 175-acre campus with easy access to Indianapolis
- **Coed**, 2,173 undergraduate students, 99% full-time, 56% women, 44% men
- **Moderately difficult** entrance level, 67% of applicants were admitted
- **11:1 student-to-undergraduate faculty ratio**
- **77.7% graduate** in 6 years or less
- **$19,730 tuition** and fees

Peterson's Guide to Four-Year Colleges 2001   www.petersons.com   263

Indiana

DePauw University (continued)
- **$17,960 average financial aid** package, $13,218 average indebtedness upon graduation, $430.6 million endowment

DePauw provides its students with a traditional liberal arts education complemented by one of the largest per-capita student internship programs in the nation. Students also gain leadership experience through a wide range of extracurricular opportunities in small, self-governing living units; community service programs; student-run organizations; intercollegiate athletics; numerous productions and ensembles in the performing arts; and other organizations.

Students *Undergraduates:* 2,158 full-time, 15 part-time. Students come from 47 states and territories, 15 other countries. *The most frequently chosen baccalaureate fields are:* communications/communication technologies, English, social sciences and history.

From out-of-state	43%	Reside on campus	94%
Age 25 or older	1%	Transferred in	1%
International students	1%	African Americans	6%
Asian Americans/Pacific Islanders	2%	Hispanic Americans	3%
Native Americans	0.1%		

Faculty 231 (81% full-time), 80% with terminal degrees.

Expenses (1999–2000) *Comprehensive fee:* $25,810 includes full-time tuition ($19,420), mandatory fees ($310), and room and board ($6080). *Part-time tuition:* $607 per semester hour. *Payment plans:* tuition prepayment, installment, deferred payment. *Waivers:* employees or children of employees.

Library Roy O. West Library plus 3 others. *Operations spending 1999–2000:* $2.3 million. *Collection:* 247,587 titles, 1,387 serial subscriptions, 10,259 audiovisual materials.

College life *Housing:* on-campus residence required through senior year. *Option:* coed. *Social organizations:* national fraternities, national sororities, local sororities; 57% of eligible men and 54% of eligible women are members. *Most popular organizations:* fraternities, sororities, DePauw Community Service Program, Union Board, student congress.

Campus security 24-hour emergency response devices and patrols, late-night transport-escort service, controlled dormitory access.

After graduation 52 organizations recruited on campus 1997–98. 82% of class of 1998 had job offers within 6 months. *Career center:* 4 full-time, 4 part-time personnel. Services include job fairs, resume preparation, resume referral, career counseling, careers library, job bank, job interviews. *Graduate education:* 25% of class of 1999 went directly to graduate and professional school: 9% medicine, 7% law, 5% graduate arts and sciences, 3% business, 1% education.

Freshmen 2,687 applied, 1,813 admitted, 581 enrolled. 10 National Merit Scholars, 28 valedictorians.

Average high school GPA	3.66	SAT verbal scores above 500	90%
SAT math scores above 500	93%	ACT above 18	100%
From top 10% of their h.s. class	49%	From top quarter	89%
From top half	100%	1998 freshmen returning in 1999	84%

Application *Options:* eApply at www.CollegeQuest.com, Common Application, electronic application, early admission, early decision, early action, deferred entrance. *Application fee:* $40. *Required:* essay or personal statement; high school transcript; 1 letter of recommendation. *Recommended:* minimum 3.0 GPA; interview.

Standardized tests *Admission: Required:* SAT I or ACT.

Significant dates *Application deadlines:* 2/1 (freshmen), 3/1 (transfers). *Early decision:* 11/1, 12/1. *Notification:* continuous until 4/1 (freshmen), 1/15 (early decision), 2/15 (early action). *Financial aid deadline priority date:* 2/15.

Freshman Application Contact
Mr. Larry West, Director of Admission, DePauw University, 101 East Seminary Street, Greencastle, IN 46135-0037. **Phone:** 765-658-4006. **Toll-free phone:** 800-447-2495. **Fax:** 765-658-4007. **E-mail:** admissions@depauw.edu

Visit CollegeQuest.com for information on majors offered and athletics. College video available at CollegeQuest.com.

- *See page 1574 for a narrative description.*

EARLHAM COLLEGE
Richmond, Indiana

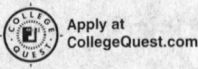
Apply at CollegeQuest.com

- **Independent**, 4-year, founded 1847, affiliated with Society of Friends
- **Degree** bachelor's
- **Small-town** 800-acre campus with easy access to Cincinnati, Indianapolis, and Dayton
- **Coed**, 1,123 undergraduate students, 98% full-time, 57% women, 43% men
- **Moderately difficult** entrance level, 84% of applicants were admitted
- **11:1 student-to-undergraduate faculty ratio**
- **70.4% graduate** in 6 years or less
- **$20,256 tuition** and fees
- **$19,624 average financial aid** package, $10,366 average indebtedness upon graduation, $302.9 million endowment

Students *Undergraduates:* 1,103 full-time, 20 part-time. Students come from 48 states and territories, 22 other countries. *The most frequently chosen baccalaureate fields are:* biological/life sciences, interdisciplinary studies, social sciences and history. *Graduate:* 10 in professional programs, 58 in other graduate degree programs.

From out-of-state	68%	Reside on campus	90%
Age 25 or older	2%	Transferred in	2%
International students	4%	African Americans	8%
Asian Americans/Pacific Islanders	2%	Hispanic Americans	2%
Native Americans	0.4%		

Faculty 90 (83% full-time), 88% with terminal degrees.

Expenses (1999–2000) *Comprehensive fee:* $25,066 includes full-time tuition ($19,684), mandatory fees ($572), and room and board ($4810). *College room only:* $2304. Room and board charges vary according to board plan. *Part-time tuition:* $656 per semester hour. *Payment plans:* tuition prepayment, installment, deferred payment. *Waivers:* employees or children of employees.

Library Lilly Library plus 1 other. *Operations spending 1999–2000:* $457,900. *Collection:* 375,000 titles, 1,188 serial subscriptions.

College life *Housing:* on-campus residence required through senior year. *Options:* coed, men-only, women-only. *Most popular organizations:* Gospel Revelations Chorus, Dance Alloy, club sports, student government, Black Leadership Action Coalition.

Campus security 24-hour emergency response devices and patrols, student patrols, late-night transport-escort service, controlled dormitory access.

After graduation 65 organizations recruited on campus 1997–98. 73% of class of 1998 had job offers within 6 months. *Career center:* 2 full-time personnel. Services include job fairs, resume preparation, interview workshops, resume referral, career/interest testing, career counseling, careers library, job bank, job interviews. *Graduate education:* 23% of class of 1999 went directly to graduate and professional school: 9% graduate arts and sciences, 5% medicine, 3% education, 1% business, 1% engineering, 1% law. *Major awards:* 1 Fulbright Scholar.

Freshmen 1,038 applied, 869 admitted, 296 enrolled. 3 National Merit Scholars, 3 valedictorians.

Average high school GPA	3.3	SAT verbal scores above 500	81%
SAT math scores above 500	78%	ACT above 18	87%
From top 10% of their h.s. class	12%	From top quarter	47%
From top half	77%	1998 freshmen returning in 1999	87%

Application *Options:* eApply at www.CollegeQuest.com, Common Application, electronic application, early admission, early decision, early action, deferred entrance. *Preference* given to Quakers, children of alumni, state residents, minorities. *Application fee:* $30. *Required:* essay or personal statement; high school transcript; minimum 3.0 GPA; 2 letters of recommendation. *Recommended:* interview.

Standardized tests *Admission: Required:* SAT I or ACT. *Recommended:* SAT I.

Significant dates *Application deadlines:* 2/15 (freshmen), 4/1 (transfers). *Early decision:* 12/1, 1/15. *Notification:* 3/15 (freshmen), 12/15 (early decision), 2/1 (early action). *Financial aid deadline priority date:* 3/1.

Freshman Application Contact
Director of Admissions, Earlham College, 801 National Road West, Richmond, IN 47374. **Phone:** 765-983-1200. **Toll-free phone:** 800-327-5426. **Fax:** 765-983-1560. **E-mail:** admission@earlham.edu

Indiana

Visit CollegeQuest.com for information on majors offered and athletics. College video and electronic viewbook available at CollegeQuest.com.

■ *See page 1598 for a narrative description.*

FRANKLIN COLLEGE OF INDIANA
Franklin, Indiana

- **Independent**, 4-year, founded 1834, affiliated with American Baptist Churches in the U.S.A.
- **Degree** bachelor's
- **Small-town** 74-acre campus with easy access to Indianapolis
- **Coed**, 953 undergraduate students, 95% full-time, 50% women, 50% men
- **Moderately difficult** entrance level, 76% of applicants were admitted
- **15:1 student-to-undergraduate faculty ratio**
- **60% graduate** in 6 years or less
- **$13,635 tuition** and fees
- **$13,333 average financial aid** package, $16,050 average indebtedness upon graduation, $83.7 million endowment

A Franklin College education combines traditional liberal arts learning with career-oriented preparation in order to create a solid foundation for lifelong leadership skills and professional success. The College's nationally recognized Leadership and Professional Development Programs are distinguishing features of the Franklin curriculum and serve as proof of their commitment to developing students' broad-based communication, professional, and problem-solving skills. Students are offered a wide variety of diverse opportunities for creative learning and benefit from the small class sizes and personalized relationships with the faculty.

Students *Undergraduates:* 909 full-time, 44 part-time. Students come from 13 states and territories. *The most frequently chosen baccalaureate fields are:* business/marketing, biological/life sciences, education.

From out-of-state	6%	Reside on campus	79%
Age 25 or older	3%	Transferred in	3%
International students	1%	African Americans	1%
Asian Americans/Pacific Islanders	0.1%	Hispanic Americans	1%

Faculty 97 (59% full-time).

Expenses (1999–2000) *One-time required fee:* $135. *Comprehensive fee:* $17,795 includes full-time tuition ($13,500), mandatory fees ($135), and room and board ($4160). *College room only:* $2300. Room and board charges vary according to board plan and housing facility. *Part-time tuition:* $180 per credit. *Part-time fees:* $5 per credit. Part-time tuition and fees vary according to course load. *Payment plan:* installment. *Waivers:* senior citizens and employees or children of employees.

Library Hamilton Library plus 1 other. *Operations spending 1999–2000:* $894,755. *Collection:* 117,232 titles, 843 serial subscriptions, 5,910 audiovisual materials.

College life *Housing:* on-campus residence required through junior year. *Option:* coed. *Social organizations:* national fraternities, national sororities; 55% of eligible men and 48% of eligible women are members. *Most popular organizations:* Intervarsity, FCA, Education Club, Student Congress, Society of Professional Journalist.

Campus security 24-hour emergency response devices and patrols, late-night transport-escort service.

After graduation 5 organizations recruited on campus 1997–98. 76% of class of 1998 had job offers within 6 months. *Career center:* 1 full-time, 1 part-time personnel. Services include job fairs, resume preparation, interview workshops, resume referral, career/interest testing, career counseling, careers library, job bank, job interviews. *Graduate education:* 15% of class of 1999 went directly to graduate and professional school.

Freshmen 850 applied, 645 admitted, 248 enrolled. 8 valedictorians.

SAT verbal scores above 500	57%	SAT math scores above 500	63%
ACT above 18	92%	From top 10% of their h.s. class	21%
From top quarter	54%	From top half	89%
1998 freshmen returning in 1999	78%		

Application *Options:* Common Application, electronic application. *Application fee:* $15. *Required:* essay or personal statement; high school transcript; 1 letter of recommendation. *Recommended:* interview.

Standardized tests *Admission: Required:* SAT I or ACT.

Significant dates *Application deadlines:* rolling (freshmen), rolling (transfers). *Notification:* 8/1 (freshmen). **Financial aid deadline priority date:** 3/1.

Freshman Application Contact Mr. Bruce Stephen Richards, Dean of Admissions and Financial Aid, Franklin College of Indiana, 501 East Monroe Street, Franklin, IN 46131-2598. **Phone:** 317-738-8062. **Toll-free phone:** 800-852-0232. **Fax:** 317-738-8274. **E-mail:** admissions@franklincoll.edu

Visit CollegeQuest.com for information on majors offered and athletics. College video available at CollegeQuest.com.

■ *See page 1694 for a narrative description.*

GOSHEN COLLEGE
Goshen, Indiana

- **Independent Mennonite**, 4-year, founded 1894
- **Degree** bachelor's
- **Small-town** 135-acre campus
- **Coed**, 1,070 undergraduate students, 92% full-time, 57% women, 43% men
- **Moderately difficult** entrance level, 95% of applicants were admitted
- **12:1 student-to-undergraduate faculty ratio**
- **62% graduate** in 6 years or less
- **$13,140 tuition** and fees
- **$12,974 average financial aid** package, $12,552 average indebtedness upon graduation, $84.1 million endowment

Students *Undergraduates:* 981 full-time, 89 part-time. Students come from 38 states and territories, 34 other countries. *The most frequently chosen baccalaureate fields are:* business/marketing, education, health professions and related sciences.

From out-of-state	48%	Reside on campus	64%
Age 25 or older	11%	Transferred in	6%
International students	10%	African Americans	2%
Asian Americans/Pacific Islanders	1%	Hispanic Americans	3%

Faculty 123 (59% full-time).

Expenses (2000–2001, estimated) *Comprehensive fee:* $17,780 includes full-time tuition ($12,870), mandatory fees ($270), and room and board ($4640). *College room only:* $2350. Room and board charges vary according to board plan and student level. Part-time tuition and fees vary according to course load. *Waivers:* employees or children of employees.

Library Harold and Wilma Good Library plus 2 others. *Operations spending 1999–2000:* $573,415. *Collection:* 121,500 titles, 750 serial subscriptions, 1,500 audiovisual materials.

College life *Housing:* on-campus residence required through junior year. *Options:* coed, women-only. *Most popular organizations:* business club, Black Student Union, Nontraditional Student Network, Goshen Student Women's Organization, International Student Club.

Campus security 24-hour emergency response devices and patrols, late-night transport-escort service.

After graduation 40 organizations recruited on campus 1997–98. *Career center:* 1 full-time, 1 part-time personnel. Services include job fairs, resume preparation, resume referral, career/interest testing, career counseling, careers library, job bank, job interviews. *Graduate education:* 40% of class of 1999 went directly to graduate and professional school: 15% graduate arts and sciences, 11% medicine, 5% business, 3% theology, 2% engineering, 2% law, 2% veterinary medicine.

Freshmen 574 applied, 548 admitted, 226 enrolled. 8 National Merit Scholars, 11 valedictorians.

Average high school GPA	3.38	SAT verbal scores above 500	75%
SAT math scores above 500	70%	ACT above 18	N/R
From top 10% of their h.s. class	27%	From top quarter	55%
From top half	81%	1998 freshmen returning in 1999	81%

Application *Options:* Common Application, electronic application, early admission, deferred entrance. *Application fee:* $25. *Required:* high school transcript; minimum 2.0 GPA; 2 letters of recommendation; interview; rank in upper 50% of high school class, minimum SAT score of 920. *Recommended:* essay or personal statement.

Standardized tests *Admission: Required:* SAT I or ACT.

Significant dates *Application deadlines:* rolling (freshmen), rolling (transfers). **Financial aid deadline priority date:** 3/1.

Indiana

Goshen College (continued)
Freshman Application Contact
Ms. Marty Kelley, Director of Admissions, Goshen College, 1700 South Main Street, Goshen, IN 46526-4794. **Phone:** 219-535-7535. **Toll-free phone:** 800-348-7422. **Fax:** 219-535-7060. **E-mail:** admissions@goshen.edu
Visit CollegeQuest.com for information on majors offered and athletics. College video and electronic viewbook available at CollegeQuest.com.

■ *See page 1728 for a narrative description.*

GRACE COLLEGE
Winona Lake, Indiana

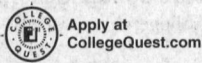
Apply at CollegeQuest.com

- **Independent**, comprehensive, founded 1948, affiliated with Fellowship of Grace Brethren Churches
- **Degrees** associate, bachelor's, and master's
- **Small-town** 160-acre campus
- **Coed**, 923 undergraduate students, 91% full-time, 52% women, 48% men
- **Moderately difficult** entrance level, 87% of applicants were admitted
- **17:1 student-to-undergraduate faculty ratio**
- **$10,500 tuition** and fees
- **$10,490 average financial aid** package, $11,985 average indebtedness upon graduation, $3.5 million endowment

Grace College is a 4-year Christian liberal arts college that applies biblical values in strengthening character, sharpening competence, and preparing for service. Students learn how they can have an effective ministry in any career, from business and education to graphic design and social work. Every year, hundreds of Grace students volunteer in ministries on campus and in the community. Grace seeks to equip students to make a positive impact on their world today and in the future.

Students *Undergraduates:* 844 full-time, 79 part-time. Students come from 35 states and territories, 7 other countries. *The most frequently chosen baccalaureate fields are:* business/marketing, education, psychology. *Graduate:* 122 in graduate degree programs.

From out-of-state	40%	Reside on campus	69%
Age 25 or older	5%	Transferred in	4%
International students	2%	African Americans	3%
Asian Americans/Pacific Islanders	0.4%	Hispanic Americans	1%
Native Americans	0.1%		

Faculty 73 (55% full-time), 48% with terminal degrees.
Expenses (1999–2000) *Comprehensive fee:* $15,100 includes full-time tuition ($10,500) and room and board ($4600). *College room only:* $2200. Room and board charges vary according to board plan and housing facility. *Part-time tuition:* $3750 per term. Part-time tuition and fees vary according to course load. *Payment plan:* installment. *Waivers:* employees or children of employees.
Library Morgan Library. *Operations spending 1999–2000:* $283,498. *Collection:* 140,202 titles, 350 serial subscriptions, 160 audiovisual materials.
College life *Housing:* on-campus residence required through senior year. *Options:* men-only, women-only. *Most popular organizations:* Grace Ministries in Action, Student Activities Board, Funfest, Women's Ministries, Breakout.
Campus security Student patrols, late-night transport-escort service, controlled dormitory access, evening patrols by trained security personnel.
After graduation 35 organizations recruited on campus 1997–98. 70% of class of 1998 had job offers within 6 months. *Career center:* 1 full-time, 1 part-time personnel. Services include job fairs, resume preparation, interview workshops, resume referral, career/interest testing, career counseling, careers library, job bank, job interviews.
Freshmen 501 applied, 435 admitted, 210 enrolled.

Average high school GPA	3.3	
SAT verbal scores above 500		65%
SAT math scores above 500	61%	
ACT above 18		87%
From top 10% of their h.s. class	24%	
From top quarter		46%
From top half	82%	
1998 freshmen returning in 1999		84%

Application *Options:* eApply at www.CollegeQuest.com, electronic application, early admission, deferred entrance. *Application fee:* $20. *Required:* high school transcript; minimum 2.0 GPA; 2 letters of recommendation. *Required for some:* interview.
Standardized tests *Admission: Required:* SAT I or ACT.

Significant dates *Application deadlines:* 8/1 (freshmen), 8/1 (transfers). *Notification:* continuous until 8/15 (freshmen). *Financial aid deadline priority date:* 3/1.
Freshman Application Contact
Mr. Ron Henry, Dean of Admissions, Grace College, 200 Seminary Drive, Winona Lake, IN 46590-1294. **Phone:** 219-372-5100 Ext. 6006. **Toll-free phone:** 800-54-GRACE (in-state); 800-54 GRACE (out-of-state). **Fax:** 219-372-5265. **E-mail:** enroll@grace.edu
Visit CollegeQuest.com for information on majors offered and athletics.

■ *See page 1732 for a narrative description.*

HANOVER COLLEGE
Hanover, Indiana

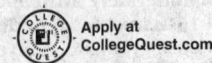
Apply at CollegeQuest.com

- **Independent Presbyterian**, 4-year, founded 1827
- **Degree** bachelor's
- **Rural** 630-acre campus with easy access to Louisville
- **Coed**, 1,111 undergraduate students, 99% full-time, 53% women, 47% men
- **Moderately difficult** entrance level, 82% of applicants were admitted
- **12:1 student-to-undergraduate faculty ratio**
- **62% graduate** in 6 years or less
- **$11,045 tuition** and fees
- **$10,287 average financial aid** package, $11,735 average indebtedness upon graduation, $135.5 million endowment

Hanover College, the oldest private college in Indiana, offers a classic liberal arts education in a value-based environment. Nestled among 650 acres overlooking the Ohio River, Hanover is home to 1,100 students from 38 states and 23 countries who want a varied, individually challenging college experience. Hanover has been consistently ranked by *Money* magazine as one of the best buys among private liberal arts colleges in the nation.

Students *Undergraduates:* 1,104 full-time, 7 part-time. Students come from 38 states and territories, 23 other countries. *The most frequently chosen baccalaureate fields are:* business/marketing, communications/communication technologies, social sciences and history.

From out-of-state	37%	Reside on campus	93%
Age 25 or older	1%	Transferred in	1%
International students	3%	African Americans	1%
Asian Americans/Pacific Islanders	2%	Hispanic Americans	0.4%
Native Americans	0.2%		

Faculty 100 (86% full-time), 79% with terminal degrees.
Expenses (1999–2000) *One-time required fee:* $50. *Comprehensive fee:* $15,700 includes full-time tuition ($10,700), mandatory fees ($345), and room and board ($4655). *College room only:* $2150. Room and board charges vary according to housing facility. *Part-time tuition:* $1190 per unit. *Payment plan:* installment. *Waivers:* senior citizens and employees or children of employees.
Library Duggan Library plus 1 other. *Operations spending 1999–2000:* $880,174. *Collection:* 1,138 serial subscriptions.
College life *Housing:* on-campus residence required through senior year. *Options:* men-only, women-only. *Social organizations:* national fraternities, national sororities; 42% of eligible men and 44% of eligible women are members. *Most popular organizations:* Student Programming Board, Fellowship of Christian Athletes, Student Senate, Link.
Campus security 24-hour emergency response devices and patrols, late-night transport-escort service, controlled dormitory access.
After graduation 36 organizations recruited on campus 1997–98. 87% of class of 1998 had job offers within 6 months. *Career center:* 2 full-time, 2 part-time personnel. Services include job fairs, resume preparation, resume referral, career/interest testing, career counseling, careers library, job interviews. *Graduate education:* 29% of class of 1999 went directly to graduate and professional school: 11% graduate arts and sciences, 6% law, 3% medicine, 2% education, 1% business, 1% veterinary medicine.
Freshmen 1,145 applied, 941 admitted, 342 enrolled.

SAT verbal scores above 500	81%	SAT math scores above 500	86%
ACT above 18	100%	From top 10% of their h.s. class	39%
From top quarter	72%	From top half	95%
1998 freshmen returning in 1999	86%		

Application *Options:* eApply at www.CollegeQuest.com, Common Application, electronic application, early admission, early action, deferred entrance. *Application fee:* $25. *Required:* essay or personal statement; high school transcript; 1 letter of recommendation. *Recommended:* interview.
Standardized tests *Admission: Required:* SAT I or ACT.
Significant dates *Application deadlines:* 3/1 (freshmen), rolling (transfers). *Early action:* 12/1. *Notification:* 12/20 (early action). *Financial aid deadline:* 3/1.
Freshman Application Contact
Mr. Kenneth Moyer Jr., Dean of Admissions, Hanover College, Box 108, Hanover, IN 47243-0108. **Phone:** 812-866-7021. **Toll-free phone:** 800-213-2178. **Fax:** 812-866-7098. **E-mail:** admissions@hanover.edu
Visit CollegeQuest.com for information on majors offered and athletics. College video and electronic viewbook available at CollegeQuest.com.

■ *See page 1762 for a narrative description.*

HUNTINGTON COLLEGE
Huntington, Indiana

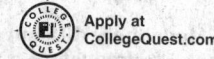

- **Independent**, comprehensive, founded 1897, affiliated with Church of the United Brethren in Christ
- **Degrees** bachelor's, master's, and postbachelor's certificates
- **Small-town** 200-acre campus
- **Coed**, 816 undergraduate students, 96% full-time, 62% women, 38% men
- **Moderately difficult** entrance level, 90% of applicants were admitted
- **61% graduate** in 6 years or less
- **$14,230 tuition** and fees
- **$11,164 average financial aid** package, $18,125 average indebtedness upon graduation, $5.5 million endowment

Huntington College has been honoring Christ in scholarship and service since 1897. Huntington has many distinctions. One of these enables students to freeze their tuition. Others include a beautiful campus with impressive facilities, a chapel program that includes student-led programs, and majors such as theater, youth ministries, graphic design, exercise science, and NCATE-accredited teacher education.

Students *Undergraduates:* 781 full-time, 35 part-time. Students come from 22 states and territories. *The most frequently chosen baccalaureate fields are:* business/marketing, education, philosophy. *Graduate:* 47 in graduate degree programs.

Reside on campus	69%	Transferred in	4%
International students	1%	African Americans	0.2%
Asian Americans/Pacific Islanders	1%	Hispanic Americans	1%

Expenses (2000–2001) *Comprehensive fee:* $19,420 includes full-time tuition ($13,540), mandatory fees ($690), and room and board ($5190). *College room only:* $2350. *Part-time tuition:* $430 per semester hour. Part-time tuition and fees vary according to course load. *Payment plans:* guaranteed tuition, installment. *Waivers:* minority students, children of alumni, adult students, senior citizens, and employees or children of employees.
Library RichLyn Library. *Collection:* 76,954 titles, 553 serial subscriptions.
College life *Housing:* on-campus residence required through junior year. *Options:* men-only, women-only. *Social organizations:* national fraternities, national sororities; 6% of eligible men and 8% of eligible women are members. *Most popular organizations:* Joe Mertz Volunteer Center, Chapel Worship Team, student newspaper, ministry groups, Dormitory Council.
Campus security 24-hour emergency response devices, late-night transport-escort service, night patrols by trained security personnel.
After graduation *Career center:* 1 full-time, 2 part-time personnel. Services include job fairs, resume preparation, resume referral, career counseling, careers library, job bank, job interviews. *Graduate education:* 15% of class of 1999 went directly to graduate and professional school.
Freshmen 630 applied, 565 admitted, 222 enrolled.

Average high school GPA	3.34	SAT verbal scores above 500	69%
SAT math scores above 500	66%	ACT above 18	94%
From top 10% of their h.s. class	23%	From top quarter	53%
From top half	80%		

Application *Options:* eApply at www.CollegeQuest.com, electronic application, deferred entrance. *Application fee:* $15. *Required:* essay or personal statement; high school transcript; minimum 2.3 GPA. *Recommended:* interview.
Standardized tests *Admission: Required:* SAT I or ACT.
Significant dates *Application deadlines:* 8/15 (freshmen), rolling (transfers). *Financial aid deadline priority date:* 3/1.
Freshman Application Contact
Mr. Jeff Berggren, Dean of Enrollment, Huntington College, 2303 College Avenue, Huntington, IN 46750-1299. **Phone:** 219-359-4000 Ext. 4016. **Toll-free phone:** 800-642-6493. **Fax:** 219-356-9448. **E-mail:** admissions@huntington.edu
Visit CollegeQuest.com for information on majors offered and athletics. College video and electronic viewbook available at CollegeQuest.com.

INDIANA INSTITUTE OF TECHNOLOGY
Fort Wayne, Indiana

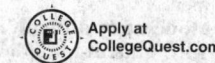

- **Independent**, comprehensive, founded 1930
- **Degrees** associate, bachelor's, and master's
- **Urban** 25-acre campus
- **Coed**, 1,922 undergraduate students, 38% full-time, 53% women, 47% men
- **Moderately difficult** entrance level
- **22:1 student-to-undergraduate faculty ratio**
- **$12,300 tuition** and fees
- **$19 million endowment**

Students *Undergraduates:* 733 full-time, 1,189 part-time. Students come from 31 states and territories, 9 other countries. *The most frequently chosen baccalaureate fields are:* business/marketing, computer/information sciences, engineering/engineering technologies.

From out-of-state	49%	Reside on campus	50%
Age 25 or older	39%	Transferred in	1%
International students	2%	African Americans	6%
Asian Americans/Pacific Islanders	0.2%	Hispanic Americans	1%
Native Americans	0.1%		

Faculty 54 (39% full-time).
Expenses (1999–2000) *Comprehensive fee:* $16,864 includes full-time tuition ($12,300) and room and board ($4564). Full-time tuition and fees vary according to course load. Room and board charges vary according to housing facility and student level. *Part-time tuition:* $2968 per term. Part-time tuition and fees vary according to class time and course load. *Payment plan:* deferred payment. *Waivers:* employees or children of employees.
Library McMillen Library. *Operations spending 1999–2000:* $137,970. *Collection:* 60,000 titles, 175 serial subscriptions.
College life *Housing:* on-campus residence required through sophomore year. *Option:* coed. *Social organizations:* national fraternities, local sororities.
Campus security 24-hour emergency response devices and patrols, controlled dormitory access.
After graduation 90% of class of 1998 had job offers within 6 months. *Career center:* 1 full-time personnel. Services include job fairs, resume preparation, interview workshops, resume referral, career/interest testing, career counseling, careers library, job bank, job interviews. *Graduate education:* 11% of class of 1999 went directly to graduate and professional school: 8% business, 3% engineering.
Freshmen 304 enrolled.

SAT verbal scores above 500	N/R	SAT math scores above 500	N/R
ACT above 18	N/R	From top 10% of their h.s. class	15%
From top quarter	30%	From top half	55%
1998 freshmen returning in 1999	65%		

Application *Options:* eApply at www.CollegeQuest.com, electronic application, early admission, deferred entrance. *Application fee:* $25. *Required:* high school transcript. *Recommended:* minimum 3.0 GPA; interview; 2 references.
Standardized tests *Admission: Required:* SAT I or ACT.
Significant dates *Application deadline:* 9/1 (freshmen). *Financial aid deadline priority date:* 3/1.

Indiana

Indiana Institute of Technology (continued)
Freshman Application Contact
Mrs. Andrea James, Registrar, Indiana Institute of Technology, 1600 East Washington Boulevard, Fort Wayne, IN 46803-1297. **Phone:** 219-422-5561 Ext. 2231. **Toll-free phone:** 800-937-2448 (in-state); 888-666-TECH (out-of-state). **Fax:** 219-422-7696. **E-mail:** filus@indtech.edu
Visit CollegeQuest.com for information on majors offered and athletics. College video and electronic viewbook available at CollegeQuest.com.

INDIANA STATE UNIVERSITY
Terre Haute, Indiana

- **State-supported**, university, founded 1865
- **Degrees** associate, bachelor's, master's, doctoral, and first professional
- **Suburban** 91-acre campus with easy access to Indianapolis
- **Coed**, 9,084 undergraduate students, 87% full-time, 51% women, 49% men
- **Moderately difficult** entrance level, 86% of applicants were admitted
- **15:1 student-to-undergraduate faculty ratio**
- **36.6% graduate** in 6 years or less
- **$3426 tuition** and fees (in-state); $8554 (out-of-state)
- **$5573 average financial aid** package, $4129 average indebtedness upon graduation, $1.2 million endowment

Students *Undergraduates:* 7,927 full-time, 1,157 part-time. Students come from 48 states and territories, 72 other countries. *The most frequently chosen baccalaureate fields are:* business/marketing, education, social sciences and history. *Graduate:* 32 in professional programs, 1,619 in other graduate degree programs.

From out-of-state	7%	Reside on campus	33%
Age 25 or older	19%	Transferred in	8%
International students	3%	African Americans	10%
Asian Americans/Pacific Islanders	1%	Hispanic Americans	1%
Native Americans	0.4%		

Faculty 878 (82% full-time).
Expenses (1999–2000) *Tuition, state resident:* full-time $3426; part-time $123 per credit hour. *Tuition, nonresident:* full-time $8554; part-time $300 per credit hour. Full-time tuition and fees vary according to course load. Part-time tuition and fees vary according to course load. *College room and board:* $4434. Room and board charges vary according to board plan and housing facility. *Payment plans:* installment, deferred payment. *Waivers:* employees or children of employees.
Library Cunningham Memorial Library plus 2 others. *Operations spending 1999–2000:* $4.2 million. *Collection:* 1.2 million titles, 5,128 serial subscriptions, 39,198 audiovisual materials.
College life *Housing:* on-campus residence required through sophomore year. *Options:* coed, men-only, women-only. *Social organizations:* national fraternities, national sororities; 18% of eligible men and 12% of eligible women are members. *Most popular organizations:* Hulman Memorial Union and Junior Union Boards, Student Government Association, Sycamore Ambassadors, Student Alumni Association, Panhellenic, National Panhellenic, and Interfraternity Council.
Campus security 24-hour emergency response devices and patrols, student patrols, late-night transport-escort service, controlled dormitory access.
After graduation 115 organizations recruited on campus 1997–98. *Career center:* 11 full-time personnel. Services include job fairs, resume preparation, interview workshops, resume referral, career/interest testing, career counseling, careers library, job bank, job interviews.
Freshmen 4,900 applied, 4,216 admitted, 2,075 enrolled.

Average high school GPA	2.82	SAT verbal scores above 500	38%
SAT math scores above 500	38%	ACT above 18	68%
From top 10% of their h.s. class	9%	From top quarter	24%
From top half	59%	1998 freshmen returning in 1999	69%

Application *Options:* electronic application, deferred entrance. *Application fee:* $20. *Required:* high school transcript; minimum 2.0 GPA. *Required for some:* letters of recommendation; interview. *Recommended:* essay or personal statement.
Standardized tests *Admission: Required:* SAT I or ACT.
Significant dates *Application deadlines:* 8/15 (freshmen), rolling (transfers). *Financial aid deadline priority date:* 3/1.

Freshman Application Contact
Mr. Ronald Brown, Director of Admissions, Indiana State University, 210 North Seventh Street, Terre Haute, IN 47809-1401. **Phone:** 812-237-2121. **Toll-free phone:** 800-742-0891. **Fax:** 812-237-8023. **E-mail:** admisu@amber.indstate.edu
Visit CollegeQuest.com for information on majors offered and athletics. College video available at CollegeQuest.com.

■ *See page 1822 for a narrative description.*

INDIANA UNIVERSITY BLOOMINGTON
Bloomington, Indiana

- **State-supported**, university, founded 1820
- **Degrees** associate, bachelor's, master's, doctoral, and first professional
- **Small-town** 1,931-acre campus with easy access to Indianapolis
- **Coed**, 27,461 undergraduate students, 95% full-time, 54% women, 46% men
- **Moderately difficult** entrance level, 81% of applicants were admitted
- **66.5% graduate** in 6 years or less
- **$4212 tuition** and fees (in-state); $12,920 (out-of-state)
- **$6335 average financial aid** package, $85.4 million endowment

Part of Indiana University System.
Students *Undergraduates:* 26,139 full-time, 1,322 part-time. Students come from 52 states and territories, 137 other countries. *The most frequently chosen baccalaureate fields are:* business/marketing, education, protective services/public administration. *Graduate:* 904 in professional programs, 6,786 in other graduate degree programs.

From out-of-state	25%	Reside on campus	39%
Age 25 or older	5%	Transferred in	3%
International students	3%	African Americans	4%
Asian Americans/Pacific Islanders	3%	Hispanic Americans	2%
Native Americans	0.3%		

Faculty 1,396 full-time.
Expenses (1999–2000) *Tuition, state resident:* full-time $3752. *Tuition, nonresident:* full-time $12,460. *Required fees:* full-time $460. Part-time tuition and fees vary according to course load. *College room and board:* $5492; room only: $2892. Room and board charges vary according to board plan and housing facility. *Payment plan:* deferred payment. *Waivers:* employees or children of employees.
Library Indiana University Library plus 32 others. *Operations spending 1999–2000:* $22.1 million. *Collection:* 6 million titles, 42,293 serial subscriptions.
College life *Housing: Options:* coed, men-only, women-only. *Social organizations:* national fraternities, national sororities; 7% of eligible men and 7% of eligible women are members. *Most popular organizations:* Union Board, Student Association, Student Foundation, Habitat for Humanity, Student Athletic Board.
Campus security 24-hour emergency response devices and patrols, late-night transport-escort service, safety seminars, lighted pathways, escort service, shuttle bus service, emergency telephones.
After graduation 900 organizations recruited on campus 1997–98. *Career center:* Services include job fairs, resume preparation, resume referral, career counseling, careers library, job bank, job interviews. *Major awards:* 7 Fulbright Scholars.
Freshmen 20,095 applied, 16,238 admitted, 6,583 enrolled. 121 valedictorians.

SAT verbal scores above 500	72%	SAT math scores above 500	74%
ACT above 18	96%	From top 10% of their h.s. class	23%
From top quarter	55%	From top half	93%
1998 freshmen returning in 1999	87%		

Application *Options:* electronic application, deferred entrance. *Preference* given to state residents. *Application fee:* $40. *Required:* high school transcript. *Recommended:* interview.
Standardized tests *Admission: Required:* SAT I or ACT.
Significant dates *Application deadlines:* 2/1 (freshmen), rolling (transfers). *Financial aid deadline priority date:* 3/1.

Freshman Application Contact
Mr. Don Hossler, Vice Chancellor for Enrollment Services, Indiana University Bloomington, 300 North Jordan Avenue, Bloomington, IN 47405-1106. **Phone:** 812-855-0661. **E-mail:** iuadmit@indiana.edu

Visit CollegeQuest.com for information on majors offered and athletics. Electronic viewbook available at CollegeQuest.com.

INDIANA UNIVERSITY EAST
Richmond, Indiana

- **State-supported**, 4-year, founded 1971
- **Degrees** associate and bachelor's
- **Small-town** 194-acre campus with easy access to Indianapolis
- **Coed**, 2,021 undergraduate students, 49% full-time, 70% women, 30% men
- **Moderately difficult** entrance level, 97% of applicants were admitted
- **18.1% graduate** in 6 years or less
- **$3104 tuition** and fees (in-state); $7874 (out-of-state)
- **$6115 average financial aid** package, $506,897 endowment

Part of Indiana University System.

Students *Undergraduates:* 992 full-time, 1,029 part-time. Students come from 10 states and territories, 8 other countries. *The most frequently chosen baccalaureate fields are:* business/marketing, education, health professions and related sciences. *Graduate:* 39 in graduate degree programs.

From out-of-state	5%	Age 25 or older	45%
Transferred in	5%	International students	0.4%
African Americans	4%	Asian Americans/Pacific Islanders	0.4%
Hispanic Americans	1%	Native Americans	0.3%

Faculty 61 full-time.

Expenses (1999–2000) *Tuition, state resident:* full-time $2922; part-time $97 per credit hour. *Tuition, nonresident:* full-time $7692; part-time $256 per credit hour. *Required fees:* full-time $182. Full-time tuition and fees vary according to course load. Part-time tuition and fees vary according to course load. *Payment plan:* deferred payment. *Waivers:* employees or children of employees.

Library Library and Media Services plus 1 other. *Operations spending 1999–2000:* $595,420. *Collection:* 64,052 titles, 460 serial subscriptions.

College life *Housing:* college housing not available. *Most popular organizations:* Student Government Association, Phi Beta Lambda, Multicultural Awareness Association, psychology club, sociology club.

Campus security 24-hour emergency response devices, late-night transport-escort service, safety awareness, lighted pathways, 14-hour foot and vehicle patrol.

After graduation *Career center:* Services include job fairs, resume preparation, career counseling, careers library, job bank, job interviews.

Freshmen 475 applied, 461 admitted, 420 enrolled.

SAT verbal scores above 500	28%	SAT math scores above 500	29%
ACT above 18	59%	From top 10% of their h.s. class	5%
From top quarter	16%	From top half	46%
1998 freshmen returning in 1999	57%		

Application *Options:* early admission, deferred entrance. *Application fee:* $25. *Required:* high school transcript. *Recommended:* minimum 2.0 GPA.

Standardized tests *Admission: Required for some:* SAT I or ACT.

Significant dates *Application deadlines:* rolling (freshmen), rolling (transfers). *Financial aid deadline priority date:* 3/1.

Freshman Application Contact
Ms. Susanna Tanner, Admissions Counselor, Indiana University East, 2325 Chester Boulevard, WZ 116, Richmond, IN 47374-1289. **Phone:** 765-973-8415. **Toll-free phone:** 800-959-3278. **Fax:** 765-973-8288. **E-mail:** eaadmit@indiana.edu

Visit CollegeQuest.com for information on majors offered and athletics.

INDIANA UNIVERSITY KOKOMO
Kokomo, Indiana

- **State-supported**, comprehensive, founded 1945
- **Degrees** associate, bachelor's, and master's
- **Small-town** 51-acre campus with easy access to Indianapolis
- **Coed**, 2,152 undergraduate students, 49% full-time, 72% women, 28% men
- **Minimally difficult** entrance level, 85% of applicants were admitted
- **21.8% graduate** in 6 years or less
- **$3104 tuition** and fees (in-state); $7874 (out-of-state)
- **$4437 average financial aid** package, $425,262 endowment

Part of Indiana University System.

Students *Undergraduates:* 1,061 full-time, 1,091 part-time. Students come from 14 states and territories. *The most frequently chosen baccalaureate fields are:* education, business/marketing, health professions and related sciences. *Graduate:* 308 in graduate degree programs.

Age 25 or older	72%	Transferred in	7%
International students	0.2%	African Americans	3%
Asian Americans/Pacific Islanders	1%	Hispanic Americans	1%
Native Americans	0.4%		

Faculty 67 full-time.

Expenses (1999–2000) *Tuition, state resident:* full-time $2922; part-time $97 per credit hour. *Tuition, nonresident:* full-time $7692; part-time $256 per credit hour. *Required fees:* full-time $182. Full-time tuition and fees vary according to course load. Part-time tuition and fees vary according to course load. *Waivers:* employees or children of employees.

Library Main library plus 1 other. *Operations spending 1999–2000:* $924,997. *Collection:* 127,910 titles, 1,761 serial subscriptions.

College life *Housing:* college housing not available.

Campus security 24-hour patrols, late-night transport-escort service, campus police, lighted pathways.

After graduation *Career center:* Services include job fairs, resume preparation, resume referral, career counseling, careers library, job bank, job interviews.

Freshmen 652 applied, 551 admitted, 434 enrolled.

SAT verbal scores above 500	37%	SAT math scores above 500	35%
ACT above 18	66%	From top 10% of their h.s. class	5%
From top quarter	24%	From top half	58%
1998 freshmen returning in 1999	55%		

Application *Options:* early admission, deferred entrance. *Application fee:* $30. *Required:* high school transcript.

Standardized tests *Admission: Required:* SAT I or ACT.

Significant dates *Application deadlines:* 8/3 (freshmen), 7/15 (transfers). *Financial aid deadline priority date:* 3/1.

Freshman Application Contact
Mr. Darren Bush, Admissions Director, Indiana University Kokomo, PO Box 9003, Kelley Student Center 230A, Kokomo, IN 46904-9003. **Phone:** 765-455-9217. **Toll-free phone:** 888-875-4485. **Fax:** 765-455-9537. **E-mail:** iuadmis@iuk.edu

Visit CollegeQuest.com for information on majors offered and athletics.

INDIANA UNIVERSITY NORTHWEST
Gary, Indiana

- **State-supported**, comprehensive, founded 1959
- **Degrees** associate, bachelor's, and master's
- **Urban** 38-acre campus with easy access to Chicago
- **Coed**, 3,757 undergraduate students, 59% full-time, 71% women, 29% men
- **Minimally difficult** entrance level, 79% of applicants were admitted
- **18.1% graduate** in 6 years or less
- **$3128 tuition** and fees (in-state); $7898 (out-of-state)
- **$5105 average financial aid** package, $808,902 endowment

Part of Indiana University System.

Students *Undergraduates:* 2,232 full-time, 1,525 part-time. Students come from 14 states and territories. *The most frequently chosen baccalaureate fields are:* business/marketing, education, health professions and related sciences. *Graduate:* 578 in graduate degree programs.

Age 25 or older	44%	Transferred in	6%
International students	0.2%	African Americans	25%
Asian Americans/Pacific Islanders	1%	Hispanic Americans	9%
Native Americans	0.2%		

Faculty 138 full-time.

Expenses (1999–2000) *Tuition, state resident:* full-time $2922; part-time $97 per credit hour. *Tuition, nonresident:* full-time $7692; part-time $256 per credit hour. *Required fees:* full-time $206. Full-time tuition and fees vary according to course load. Part-time tuition and fees vary according to course

Indiana

Indiana University Northwest (continued)
load. *Payment plans:* installment, deferred payment. *Waivers:* senior citizens and employees or children of employees.

Library IUN Library. *Operations spending 1999–2000:* $1.2 million. *Collection:* 228,027 titles, 1,882 serial subscriptions.

College life *Housing:* college housing not available. *Social organizations:* national fraternities, national sororities. *Most popular organizations:* Student Government Association, Student Guides Organization, Nursing Association, Dental Association, international affairs club.

Campus security 24-hour emergency response devices and patrols, late-night transport-escort service, lighted pathways.

After graduation *Career center:* Services include job fairs, resume preparation, resume referral, career/interest testing, career counseling, careers library, job bank, job interviews.

Freshmen 1,102 applied, 874 admitted, 680 enrolled. 3 valedictorians.

SAT verbal scores above 500	29%	SAT math scores above 500	24%
ACT above 18	60%	From top 10% of their h.s. class	8%
From top quarter	23%	From top half	55%
1998 freshmen returning in 1999	66%		

Application *Options:* early admission, deferred entrance. *Application fee:* $25. *Required:* high school transcript; minimum 2.0 GPA.

Standardized tests *Admission: Required:* SAT I or ACT.

Significant dates *Application deadline:* 8/1 (freshmen). *Financial aid deadline priority date:* 3/1.

Freshman Application Contact
Mr. William Lee, Director of Admissions, Indiana University Northwest, Hawthorne 100, Gary, IN 46408. **Phone:** 219-980-6991. **Toll-free phone:** 800-437-5409. **Fax:** 219-981-4219. **E-mail:** wlee@iunhaw1.iun.indiana.edu

Visit CollegeQuest.com for information on majors offered and athletics.

INDIANA UNIVERSITY–PURDUE UNIVERSITY FORT WAYNE
Fort Wayne, Indiana

- **State-supported**, comprehensive, founded 1917
- **Degrees** associate, bachelor's, master's, and postbachelor's certificates
- **Urban** 565-acre campus
- **Coed**, 9,445 undergraduate students, 54% full-time, 56% women, 44% men
- **Minimally difficult** entrance level, 96% of applicants were admitted
- **16:1 student-to-undergraduate faculty ratio**
- **15% graduate** in 6 years or less
- **$2827 tuition** and fees (in-state); $6528 (out-of-state)
- **$8088 average indebtedness** upon graduation, $17.5 million endowment

Part of Indiana University System.

Students *Undergraduates:* 5,144 full-time, 4,301 part-time. Students come from 47 states and territories, 68 other countries. *The most frequently chosen baccalaureate fields are:* business/marketing, education, engineering/engineering technologies. *Graduate:* 823 in graduate degree programs.

From out-of-state	7%	Age 25 or older	37%
Transferred in	8%	International students	1%
African Americans	5%	Asian Americans/Pacific Islanders	2%
Hispanic Americans	2%	Native Americans	0.4%

Faculty 636 (51% full-time).

Expenses (1999–2000) *Tuition, state resident:* full-time $2551; part-time $106 per semester hour. *Tuition, nonresident:* full-time $6252; part-time $260 per semester hour. *Required fees:* full-time $276; $12 per semester hour. Full-time tuition and fees vary according to course load. Part-time tuition and fees vary according to course load. *Payment plans:* installment, deferred payment. *Waivers:* senior citizens and employees or children of employees.

Library Helmke Library. *Operations spending 1999–2000:* $1.3 million. *Collection:* 430,619 titles, 2,637 serial subscriptions, 715 audiovisual materials.

College life *Housing:* college housing not available. *Social organizations:* national fraternities, national sororities; 2% of eligible men and 1% of eligible women are members. *Most popular organizations:* Campus Ministry, Hispanos Unidos, Sigma Phi Epsilon, Psi Chi, United Sexualities.

Campus security 24-hour emergency response devices and patrols, late-night transport-escort service.

After graduation 127 organizations recruited on campus 1997–98. *Career center:* 5 full-time, 1 part-time personnel. Services include job fairs, resume preparation, interview workshops, resume referral, career/interest testing, career counseling, careers library, job bank, job interviews. *Graduate education:* 15% of class of 1999 went directly to graduate and professional school.

Freshmen 2,285 applied, 2,186 admitted, 1,604 enrolled.

Average high school GPA	2.8	SAT verbal scores above 500	36%
SAT math scores above 500	38%	ACT above 18	70%
From top 10% of their h.s. class	7%	From top quarter	23%
From top half	53%	1998 freshmen returning in 1999	77%

Application *Options:* early admission, deferred entrance. *Application fee:* $30. *Required:* high school transcript. *Recommended:* rank in upper 50% of high school class.

Standardized tests *Admission: Required:* SAT I or ACT.

Significant dates *Application deadlines:* 8/1 (freshmen), 8/1 (transfers). *Financial aid deadline priority date:* 3/1.

Freshman Application Contact
Ms. Carol Isaacs, Director of Admissions, Indiana University–Purdue University Fort Wayne, Admissions Office, 2101 East Coliseum Boulevard, Fort Wayne, IN 46805-1499. **Phone:** 219-481-6812. **E-mail:** ipfwadms@ipfw.edu

Visit CollegeQuest.com for information on majors offered and athletics. College video and electronic viewbook available at CollegeQuest.com.

INDIANA UNIVERSITY–PURDUE UNIVERSITY INDIANAPOLIS
Indianapolis, Indiana

- **State-supported**, university, founded 1969
- **Degrees** associate, bachelor's, master's, doctoral, and first professional
- **Urban** 511-acre campus
- **Coed**, 20,064 undergraduate students, 57% full-time, 59% women, 41% men
- **Moderately difficult** entrance level, 86% of applicants were admitted
- **17.3% graduate** in 6 years or less
- **$3713 tuition** and fees (in-state); $10,961 (out-of-state)
- **$5754 average financial aid** package, $36.7 million endowment

Part of Indiana University System.

Students *Undergraduates:* 11,491 full-time, 8,573 part-time. Students come from 45 states and territories, 116 other countries. *The most frequently chosen baccalaureate fields are:* business/marketing, education, health professions and related sciences. *Graduate:* 2,379 in professional programs, 4,792 in other graduate degree programs.

From out-of-state	2%	Age 25 or older	39%
Transferred in	7%	International students	1%
African Americans	11%	Asian Americans/Pacific Islanders	2%
Hispanic Americans	2%	Native Americans	0.3%

Faculty 683 full-time.

Expenses (1999–2000) *Tuition, state resident:* full-time $3432; part-time $114 per credit hour. *Tuition, nonresident:* full-time $10,680; part-time $356 per credit hour. *Required fees:* full-time $281. Full-time tuition and fees vary according to course load. Part-time tuition and fees vary according to course load. *College room and board:* $3450; room only: $1850. Room and board charges vary according to board plan and housing facility. *Payment plans:* installment, deferred payment. *Waivers:* employees or children of employees.

Library University Library plus 5 others. *Operations spending 1999–2000:* $6.9 million. *Collection:* 1.3 million titles, 16,865 serial subscriptions.

College life *Housing:* Option: coed. *Social organizations:* national fraternities, national sororities; 1% of eligible men and 1% of eligible women are members. *Most popular organizations:* Undergraduate Student Assembly, Black Student Union, Student Activities Programming Board.

Campus security 24-hour emergency response devices and patrols, late-night transport-escort service, controlled dormitory access, lighted pathways, self-defense education.

Indiana

After graduation *Career center:* Services include job fairs, resume preparation, resume referral, career counseling, careers library, job bank, job interviews.
Freshmen 5,763 applied, 4,956 admitted, 3,455 enrolled.

SAT verbal scores above 500	40%	SAT math scores above 500	39%
ACT above 18	67%	From top 10% of their h.s. class	7%
From top quarter	22%	From top half	52%
1998 freshmen returning in 1999	60%		

Application *Options:* electronic application, early admission, deferred entrance. *Application fee:* $35. *Required:* high school transcript. *Required for some:* interview. *Recommended:* portfolio for art program.
Standardized tests *Admission: Required:* SAT I or ACT. *Recommended:* SAT I.
Significant dates *Application deadlines:* rolling (freshmen), rolling (transfers). *Financial aid deadline priority date:* 3/1.
Freshman Application Contact
Dr. Alan Crist, Executive Director for Enrollment Services, Indiana University–Purdue University Indianapolis, 425 N. University Boulevard, Cavanaugh Hall Room 129, Indianapolis, IN 46202-5143. **Phone:** 317-274-4591. **Fax:** 317-278-1862. **E-mail:** apply@iupui.edu
Visit CollegeQuest.com for information on majors offered and athletics.

INDIANA UNIVERSITY SOUTH BEND
South Bend, Indiana

- **State-supported**, comprehensive, founded 1922
- **Degrees** associate, bachelor's, master's, and postbachelor's certificates
- **Suburban** 73-acre campus with easy access to Chicago
- **Coed**, 5,067 undergraduate students, 55% full-time, 65% women, 35% men
- **Moderately difficult** entrance level, 82% of applicants were admitted
- **24.7% graduate** in 6 years or less
- **$3197 tuition** and fees (in-state); $8481 (out-of-state)
- **$4887 average financial aid** package, $843,146 endowment

Part of Indiana University System.
Students *Undergraduates:* 2,806 full-time, 2,261 part-time. Students come from 30 states and territories, 71 other countries. *The most frequently chosen baccalaureate fields are:* business/marketing, education, liberal arts/general studies. *Graduate:* 1,368 in graduate degree programs.

From out-of-state	3%	Age 25 or older	38%
Transferred in	6%	International students	3%
African Americans	6%	Asian Americans/Pacific Islanders	1%
Hispanic Americans	2%	Native Americans	0.3%

Faculty 202 full-time.
Expenses (1999–2000) *Tuition, state resident:* full-time $2975; part-time $99 per credit hour. *Tuition, nonresident:* full-time $8259; part-time $275 per credit hour. *Required fees:* full-time $222. Full-time tuition and fees vary according to course load. Part-time tuition and fees vary according to course load. *Payment plans:* installment, deferred payment. *Waivers:* employees or children of employees.
Library Franklin D. Schurz Library plus 1 other. *Operations spending 1999–2000:* $1.7 million. *Collection:* 280,427 titles, 2,101 serial subscriptions.
College life *Housing:* college housing not available. *Social organizations:* national fraternities, local sororities.
Campus security 24-hour emergency response devices and patrols, late-night transport-escort service, safety seminars, lighted pathways.
After graduation *Career center:* Services include job fairs, resume preparation, resume referral, career counseling, careers library, job bank, job interviews.
Freshmen 1,467 applied, 1,202 admitted, 870 enrolled.

SAT verbal scores above 500	44%	SAT math scores above 500	40%
ACT above 18	64%	From top 10% of their h.s. class	7%
From top quarter	23%	From top half	59%
1998 freshmen returning in 1999	64%		

Application *Options:* early admission, deferred entrance. *Application fee:* $40. *Required:* high school transcript; minimum 2.0 GPA.
Standardized tests *Admission: Required:* SAT I or ACT.
Significant dates *Application deadlines:* 7/1 (freshmen), 6/1 (transfers). *Financial aid deadline priority date:* 3/1.

Freshman Application Contact
Mr. Peter J. Biegel, Director of Enrollment Management Systems, Indiana University South Bend, Administration Building, Room 169, PO Box 7111, South Bend, IN 46634-7111. **Phone:** 219-237-4839. **Fax:** 219-237-4834. **E-mail:** admissions@iusb.edu
Visit CollegeQuest.com for information on majors offered and athletics. College video available at CollegeQuest.com.

INDIANA UNIVERSITY SOUTHEAST
New Albany, Indiana

- **State-supported**, comprehensive, founded 1941
- **Degrees** associate, bachelor's, and master's
- **Suburban** 177-acre campus with easy access to Louisville
- **Coed**, 4,881 undergraduate students, 57% full-time, 63% women, 37% men
- **Minimally difficult** entrance level, 94% of applicants were admitted
- **21% graduate** in 6 years or less
- **$3092 tuition** and fees (in-state); $7862 (out-of-state)
- **$4449 average financial aid** package, $468,339 endowment

Part of Indiana University System.
Students *Undergraduates:* 2,783 full-time, 2,098 part-time. Students come from 9 states and territories. *The most frequently chosen baccalaureate fields are:* business/marketing, education, health professions and related sciences. *Graduate:* 675 in graduate degree programs.

From out-of-state	3%	Age 25 or older	38%
Transferred in	6%	International students	0.2%
African Americans	3%	Asian Americans/Pacific Islanders	0.5%
Hispanic Americans	1%	Native Americans	0.2%

Faculty 139 full-time.
Expenses (1999–2000) *Tuition, state resident:* full-time $2922; part-time $97 per credit hour. *Tuition, nonresident:* full-time $7692; part-time $256 per credit hour. *Required fees:* full-time $170. Full-time tuition and fees vary according to course load. Part-time tuition and fees vary according to course load. *Waivers:* employees or children of employees.
Library Main library plus 1 other. *Operations spending 1999–2000:* $1.3 million. *Collection:* 192,418 titles, 1,025 serial subscriptions.
College life *Housing:* college housing not available. *Social organizations:* national fraternities, national sororities; 2% of eligible men and 2% of eligible women are members.
Campus security 24-hour emergency response devices and patrols, self-defense education, lighted pathways, police department on campus.
After graduation *Career center:* Services include job fairs, resume preparation, resume referral, career counseling, careers library, job bank, job interviews.
Freshmen 1,323 applied, 1,238 admitted, 956 enrolled.

SAT verbal scores above 500	38%	SAT math scores above 500	33%
ACT above 18	66%	From top 10% of their h.s. class	11%
From top quarter	30%	From top half	60%
1998 freshmen returning in 1999	62%		

Application *Options:* early admission, deferred entrance. *Application fee:* $29. *Required for some:* high school transcript; interview.
Standardized tests *Admission: Required:* SAT I or ACT.
Significant dates *Application deadlines:* 7/15 (freshmen), 7/15 (transfers). *Financial aid deadline priority date:* 3/1.
Freshman Application Contact
Mr. David B. Campbell, Director of Admissions, Indiana University Southeast, University Center Building, Room 100, New Albany, IN 47150. **Phone:** 812-941-2212. **Toll-free phone:** 800-852-8835. **E-mail:** admissions@ius.edu
Visit CollegeQuest.com for information on majors offered and athletics.

INDIANA WESLEYAN UNIVERSITY
Marion, Indiana

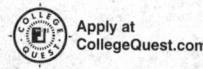

- **Independent Wesleyan**, comprehensive, founded 1920

Peterson's Guide to Four-Year Colleges 2001   www.petersons.com

Indiana

Indiana Wesleyan University (continued)
- **Degrees** associate, bachelor's, and master's (also offers adult program with significant enrollment not reflected in profile)
- **Small-town** 132-acre campus with easy access to Indianapolis
- **Coed,** 4,898 undergraduate students, 90% full-time, 63% women, 37% men
- **Moderately difficult** entrance level, 74% of applicants were admitted
- **17:1 student-to-undergraduate faculty ratio**
- **$11,760 tuition** and fees
- **$14 million endowment**

Independent, religious, comprehensive coed institution founded in 1920. Awards associate, bachelor's, and master's degrees. Setting: 150-acre small-town campus with easy access to Indianapolis and Fort Wayne. Total enrollment is 6,908. Undergraduate faculty—159 (105 full-time, 54 part-time); student-to-undergraduate faculty ratio is 17:1. Graduate and professional fields: business administration (on line), business administration and management, counseling, education, ministry, and nursing: community, health, and primary care.

Students *Undergraduates:* 4,384 full-time, 514 part-time. Students come from 44 states and territories, 15 other countries. *The most frequently chosen baccalaureate fields are:* business/marketing, education, health professions and related sciences. *Graduate:* 2,001 in graduate degree programs.

From out-of-state	47%	Reside on campus	70%
Age 25 or older	9%	Transferred in	2%
International students	1%	African Americans	9%
Asian Americans/Pacific Islanders	0.5%	Hispanic Americans	1%
Native Americans	0.5%		

Faculty 159 (66% full-time), 39% with terminal degrees.
Expenses (1999–2000) *Comprehensive fee:* $16,340 includes full-time tuition ($11,760) and room and board ($4580). *College room only:* $1990. Room and board charges vary according to board plan. *Part-time tuition:* $250 per credit hour. Part-time tuition and fees vary according to course load. *Payment plan:* installment. *Waivers:* employees or children of employees.
Library Goodman Library. *Operations spending 1999–2000:* $1.1 million. *Collection:* 99,340 titles, 5,341 serial subscriptions, 8,984 audiovisual materials.
College life *Housing:* on-campus residence required through junior year. *Options:* men-only, women-only. *Most popular organizations:* student government organization, Student Activities Council, University Players, World Christian Fellowship, International Student Association.
Campus security Late-night transport-escort service, 12-hour evening patrols by trained security personnel.
After graduation 40 organizations recruited on campus 1997–98. *Career center:* 1 full-time, 4 part-time personnel. Services include job fairs, resume preparation, interview workshops, career/interest testing, career counseling, careers library, job bank, job interviews, job newsletter, job search workshop.
Freshmen 1,722 applied, 1,267 admitted, 822 enrolled.

Average high school GPA	3.48	SAT verbal scores above 500	63%
SAT math scores above 500	60%	ACT above 18	93%
1998 freshmen returning in 1999	74%		

Application *Options:* eApply at www.CollegeQuest.com, electronic application, early admission, deferred entrance. *Application fee:* $25. *Required:* essay or personal statement; high school transcript; minimum 2.0 GPA; 1 letter of recommendation. *Required for some:* interview. *Recommended:* interview.
Standardized tests *Admission: Required:* SAT I or ACT.
Significant dates *Application deadlines:* rolling (freshmen), rolling (transfers). *Financial aid deadline priority date:* 3/1.
Freshman Application Contact
Ms. Gaytha Holloway, Director of Admissions, Indiana Wesleyan University, 4201 South Washington Street, Marion, IN 46953-4999. **Phone:** 765-677-2138. **Toll-free phone:** 800-332-6901. **Fax:** 765-677-2333. **E-mail:** admissions@indwes.edu
Visit CollegeQuest.com for information on majors offered and athletics. College video and electronic viewbook available at CollegeQuest.com.

- *See page 1826 for a narrative description.*

INTERNATIONAL BUSINESS COLLEGE
Fort Wayne, Indiana

- **Proprietary**, primarily 2-year, founded 1889
- **Degrees** associate and bachelor's
- **Suburban** 2-acre campus
- **Coed,** primarily women, 738 undergraduate students, 89% full-time, 79% women, 21% men
- **Minimally difficult** entrance level

Part of Bradford Schools, Inc.
Faculty 43 (21% full-time).
Admissions Office Contact
International Business College, 3811 Illinois Road, Fort Wayne, IN 46804-1298. **Toll-free phone:** 800-589-6363. **Fax:** 219-436-1896.
Visit CollegeQuest.com for information on majors offered and athletics.

ITT TECHNICAL INSTITUTE
Fort Wayne, Indiana

- **Proprietary**, primarily 2-year, founded 1967
- **Degrees** associate and bachelor's
- **Coed**
- **Minimally difficult** entrance level
- **$9190 tuition** and fees

Part of ITT Educational Services, Inc.
Admissions Office Contact
ITT Technical Institute, 4919 Coldwater Road, Fort Wayne, IN 46825-5532.
Toll-free phone: 800-866-4488.
Visit CollegeQuest.com for information on majors offered and athletics. College video available at CollegeQuest.com.

ITT TECHNICAL INSTITUTE
Indianapolis, Indiana

- **Proprietary**, primarily 2-year, founded 1966
- **Degrees** associate, bachelor's, and master's
- **Suburban** 10-acre campus
- **Coed**
- **Minimally difficult** entrance level
- **$9190 tuition** and fees

Part of ITT Educational Services, Inc.
Admissions Office Contact
ITT Technical Institute, 9511 Angola Court, Indianapolis, IN 46268-1119.
Toll-free phone: 800-937-4488. **Fax:** 317-875-8641.
Visit CollegeQuest.com for information on majors offered and athletics. College video available at CollegeQuest.com.

ITT TECHNICAL INSTITUTE
Newburgh, Indiana

- **Proprietary**, primarily 2-year, founded 1966
- **Degrees** associate and bachelor's
- **Coed**
- **Minimally difficult** entrance level
- **$9190 tuition** and fees

Part of ITT Educational Services, Inc.
Admissions Office Contact
ITT Technical Institute, 10999 Stahl Road, Newburgh, IN 47630-7430.
Visit CollegeQuest.com for information on majors offered and athletics.

Indiana

LUTHERAN COLLEGE OF HEALTH PROFESSIONS
Indiana—See University of Saint Francis

MANCHESTER COLLEGE
North Manchester, Indiana

 Apply at CollegeQuest.com

- **Independent**, comprehensive, founded 1889, affiliated with Church of the Brethren
- **Degrees** associate, bachelor's, and master's
- **Small-town** 125-acre campus
- **Coed**, 1,039 undergraduate students, 97% full-time, 51% women, 49% men
- **Moderately difficult** entrance level, 82% of applicants were admitted
- **14:1 student-to-undergraduate faculty ratio**
- **51.6% graduate** in 6 years or less
- **$13,930 tuition** and fees
- **$15,220 average financial aid** package, $13,370 average indebtedness upon graduation, $35.1 million endowment

A current student describes Manchester College as a great place for students who hold strong values and seek a better world. Combining the liberal arts and career preparation creates a foundation of critical skills and sound scholarship. Graduates leave with both abilities and convictions and are ready and able to make a difference with their lives.

Students *Undergraduates:* 1,010 full-time, 29 part-time. Students come from 25 states and territories, 23 other countries. *The most frequently chosen baccalaureate fields are:* business/marketing, communications/communication technologies, education. *Graduate:* 16 in graduate degree programs.

From out-of-state	14%	Reside on campus	78%
Age 25 or older	3%	Transferred in	2%
International students	3%	African Americans	3%
Asian Americans/Pacific Islanders	1%	Hispanic Americans	3%
Native Americans	0.5%		

Faculty 80 (85% full-time), 75% with terminal degrees.
Expenses (1999–2000) *Comprehensive fee:* $19,040 includes full-time tuition ($13,930) and room and board ($5110). Room and board charges vary according to board plan and housing facility. *Part-time tuition:* $460 per semester hour. *Payment plans:* installment, deferred payment. *Waivers:* employees or children of employees.
Library Funderburg Library. *Operations spending 1999–2000:* $405,837. *Collection:* 171,000 titles, 740 serial subscriptions, 4,900 audiovisual materials.
College life *Housing:* on-campus residence required through junior year. *Options:* coed, men-only, women-only, disabled students. *Most popular organizations:* volunteer services, Campus Ministry Board, accounting club, Manchester Admissions Recruiting Corps, Student Alumni Council.
Campus security 24-hour emergency response devices and patrols, student patrols, late-night transport-escort service, alarm system, locked residence hall entrances.
After graduation 25 organizations recruited on campus 1997–98. *Career center:* 2 full-time, 1 part-time personnel. Services include job fairs, resume preparation, interview workshops, resume referral, career/interest testing, career counseling, careers library, job bank, job interviews. *Graduate education:* 22% of class of 1999 went directly to graduate and professional school.
Freshmen 1,070 applied, 873 admitted, 329 enrolled.

SAT verbal scores above 500	50%	SAT math scores above 500	53%
ACT above 18	87%	From top 10% of their h.s. class	22%
From top quarter	45%	From top half	82%
1998 freshmen returning in 1999	76%		

Application *Options:* eApply at www.CollegeQuest.com, Common Application, electronic application, deferred entrance. *Application fee:* $20. *Required:* high school transcript; 1 letter of recommendation; rank in upper 50% of high school class. *Required for some:* essay or personal statement; minimum 3.0 GPA; interview. *Recommended:* minimum 2.3 GPA; interview.
Standardized tests *Admission: Required:* SAT I or ACT.
Significant dates *Application deadlines:* rolling (freshmen), rolling (transfers). *Financial aid deadline:* continuous.

Freshman Application Contact
Ms. Jolane Rohr, Director of Admissions, Manchester College, 604 East College Avenue, North Manchester, IN 46962-1225. **Phone:** 219-982-5055. **Toll-free phone:** 800-852-3648. **Fax:** 219-982-5043. **E-mail:** admitinfo@manchester.edu
Visit CollegeQuest.com for information on majors offered and athletics.

■ *See page 1974 for a narrative description.*

MARIAN COLLEGE
Indianapolis, Indiana

- **Independent Roman Catholic**, 4-year, founded 1851
- **Degrees** associate and bachelor's
- **Urban** 114-acre campus
- **Coed**, 1,126 undergraduate students, 77% full-time, 75% women, 25% men
- **Moderately difficult** entrance level, 79% of applicants were admitted
- **13:1 student-to-undergraduate faculty ratio**
- **$14,416 tuition** and fees
- **$12,255 average financial aid** package, $15,674 average indebtedness upon graduation, $5.4 million endowment

Students *Undergraduates:* 867 full-time, 259 part-time. Students come from 15 states and territories, 19 other countries. *The most frequently chosen baccalaureate fields are:* business/marketing, education, health professions and related sciences.

From out-of-state	6%	Reside on campus	33%
Age 25 or older	39%	Transferred in	8%
International students	3%	African Americans	14%
Asian Americans/Pacific Islanders	1%	Hispanic Americans	2%
Native Americans	0.4%		

Faculty 151 (50% full-time).
Expenses (1999–2000) *Comprehensive fee:* $19,292 includes full-time tuition ($14,012), mandatory fees ($404), and room and board ($4876). Room and board charges vary according to board plan and housing facility. *Part-time tuition:* $600 per credit hour. *Part-time fees:* $128 per term part-time. Part-time tuition and fees vary according to class time and course load. *Payment plans:* installment, deferred payment. *Waivers:* children of alumni, senior citizens, and employees or children of employees.
Library Mother Theresa Hackelmeier Memorial Library. *Operations spending 1999–2000:* $274,280. *Collection:* 132,000 titles.
College life *Housing:* on-campus residence required through senior year. *Option:* coed.
Campus security 24-hour patrols, late-night transport-escort service.
After graduation 96% of class of 1998 had job offers within 6 months. *Career center:* 2 full-time personnel. Services include resume preparation, career/interest testing, career counseling, careers library, job interviews.
Freshmen 713 applied, 560 admitted, 265 enrolled. 4 valedictorians.

Average high school GPA	3.0	SAT verbal scores above 500	44%
SAT math scores above 500	42%	ACT above 18	83%
From top 10% of their h.s. class	14%	From top quarter	40%
From top half	73%	1998 freshmen returning in 1999	69%

Application *Options:* early admission, deferred entrance. *Application fee:* $20. *Required:* high school transcript; minimum 2.00 GPA.
Standardized tests *Admission: Required:* SAT I or ACT.
Significant dates *Application deadlines:* 8/15 (freshmen), 8/1 (transfers). *Notification:* continuous until 8/24 (freshmen). *Financial aid deadline priority date:* 3/1.
Freshman Application Contact
Mr. Steve Bushouse, Vice President for Enrollment Management, Marian College, 3200 Cold Spring Road, Indianapolis, IN 46222-1997. **Phone:** 317-955-6300. **Toll-free phone:** 800-772-7264.
Visit CollegeQuest.com for information on majors offered and athletics. College video available at CollegeQuest.com.

■ *See page 1986 for a narrative description.*

Peterson's Guide to Four-Year Colleges 2001 www.petersons.com 273

Indiana

MARTIN UNIVERSITY
Indianapolis, Indiana

- **Independent**, comprehensive, founded 1977
- **Degrees** bachelor's and master's
- **Urban** 5-acre campus
- **Coed**
- **Noncompetitive** entrance level
- **$6720 tuition** and fees

Expenses (1999–2000) *Tuition:* full-time $6600; part-time $275 per credit. *Required fees:* full-time $120; $60 per term part-time.
College life *Housing:* college housing not available.
Campus security Building security, security personnel 7 a.m. to 9:30 p.m.
Application *Options:* early admission, deferred entrance. *Application fee:* $25. *Required:* essay or personal statement; high school transcript; interview; writing sample.
Standardized tests *Placement: Required for some:* Wonderlic aptitude test, Wide Range Achievement Test.
Admissions Office Contact
Martin University, 2171 Avondale Place, PO Box 18567, Indianapolis, IN 46218-3867. **Fax:** 317-543-3257.
Visit CollegeQuest.com for information on athletics.

OAKLAND CITY UNIVERSITY
Oakland City, Indiana

- **Independent General Baptist**, comprehensive, founded 1885
- **Degrees** associate, bachelor's, master's, doctoral, and first professional
- **Rural** 20-acre campus
- **Coed**, 1,258 undergraduate students
- **Minimally difficult** entrance level, 96% of applicants were admitted
- **36:1 student-to-undergraduate faculty ratio**
- **$10,096 tuition** and fees
- **$700,000 endowment**

Students *Undergraduates:* Students come from 15 states and territories. *The most frequently chosen baccalaureate fields are:* business/marketing, education, philosophy.

From out-of-state	23%	Reside on campus	75%
Age 25 or older	40%	International students	0.1%
African Americans	11%	Asian Americans/Pacific Islanders	1%
Hispanic Americans	1%	Native Americans	0.4%

Faculty 44 (84% full-time).
Expenses (1999–2000) *Comprehensive fee:* $13,826 includes full-time tuition ($9900), mandatory fees ($196), and room and board ($3730). *College room only:* $1200. Full-time tuition and fees vary according to location and program. Room and board charges vary according to housing facility. *Part-time tuition:* $330 per credit hour. *Part-time fees:* $63 per term part-time. Part-time tuition and fees vary according to location and program. *Payment plans:* installment, deferred payment. *Waivers:* minority students and employees or children of employees.
Library Founders Memorial Library. *Collection:* 75,000 titles, 350 serial subscriptions.
College life On-campus residence required in freshman year. *Most popular organizations:* Student Government Association, Good News Players, Art Guild.
Campus security 24-hour patrols, student patrols.
After graduation 65% of class of 1998 had job offers within 6 months. *Career center:* 4 full-time personnel. Services include resume preparation, career counseling, careers library.
Freshmen 411 applied, 395 admitted.

Average high school GPA	2.5	SAT verbal scores above 500	N/R
SAT math scores above 500	N/R	ACT above 18	N/R
From top 10% of their h.s. class	6%	From top quarter	26%
From top half	76%	1998 freshmen returning in 1999	91%

Application *Options:* Common Application, early admission, deferred entrance. *Application fee:* $25. *Required:* essay or personal statement; high school transcript; 1 letter of recommendation. *Recommended:* interview.
Standardized tests *Placement: Required:* SAT I or ACT.

Significant dates *Application deadline:* rolling (freshmen). *Financial aid deadline priority date:* 3/1.
Freshman Application Contact
Mr. Jeff Main, Director of Enrollment Management, Oakland City University, 143 North Lucretia Street, Oakland City, IN 47660-1099. **Phone:** 812-749-1222. **Toll-free phone:** 800-737-5125. **Fax:** 812-749-1233.
Visit CollegeQuest.com for information on majors offered and athletics. College video available at CollegeQuest.com.

PURDUE UNIVERSITY
West Lafayette, Indiana

- **State-supported**, university, founded 1869
- **Degrees** associate, bachelor's, master's, doctoral, and first professional
- **Suburban** 1,579-acre campus with easy access to Indianapolis
- **Coed**, 30,300 undergraduate students, 95% full-time, 43% women, 57% men
- **Moderately difficult** entrance level, 84% of applicants were admitted
- **64.8% graduate** in 6 years or less
- **$3724 tuition** and fees (in-state); $12,348 (out-of-state)
- **$6448 average financial aid** package, $15,633 average indebtedness upon graduation, $1.2 billion endowment

Part of Purdue University System.
Students *Undergraduates:* 28,743 full-time, 1,557 part-time. Students come from 53 states and territories, 101 other countries. *The most frequently chosen baccalaureate fields are:* business/marketing, education, engineering/engineering technologies. *Graduate:* 790 in professional programs, 6,137 in other graduate degree programs.

From out-of-state	20%	Reside on campus	36%
Age 25 or older	6%	Transferred in	3%
International students	6%	African Americans	3%
Asian Americans/Pacific Islanders	3%	Hispanic Americans	2%
Native Americans	0.5%		

Faculty 2,287 (88% full-time), 79% with terminal degrees.
Expenses (1999–2000) *Tuition, state resident:* full-time $3724; part-time $134 per semester hour. *Tuition, nonresident:* full-time $12,348; part-time $408 per semester hour. Full-time tuition and fees vary according to course load. Part-time tuition and fees vary according to course load. *College room and board:* $5500. Room and board charges vary according to board plan and housing facility. *Payment plan:* installment. *Waivers:* senior citizens and employees or children of employees.
Library Hicks Undergraduate Library plus 14 others. *Collection:* 2.3 million titles, 19,025 serial subscriptions, 9,195 audiovisual materials.
College life *Housing: Options:* coed, men-only, women-only. *Social organizations:* national fraternities, national sororities; 18% of eligible men and 17% of eligible women are members. *Most popular organizations:* student government, Alpha Phi Omega, Society of Women Engineers, ballroom dancing, Golden Key National Honor Society.
Campus security 24-hour emergency response devices and patrols, student patrols, late-night transport-escort service, controlled dormitory access.
After graduation 802 organizations recruited on campus 1997–98. 90% of class of 1998 had job offers within 6 months. *Career center:* 15 full-time, 2 part-time personnel. Services include job fairs, resume preparation, interview workshops, resume referral, career counseling, careers library, job bank, job interviews. *Major awards:* 1 Fulbright Scholar.
Freshmen 19,625 applied, 16,499 admitted, 6,860 enrolled. 51 National Merit Scholars, 185 valedictorians.

SAT verbal scores above 500	70%	SAT math scores above 500	75%
ACT above 18	96%	From top 10% of their h.s. class	26%
From top quarter	57%	From top half	91%
1998 freshmen returning in 1999	86%		

Application *Option:* early admission. *Preference* given to state residents, children of alumni. *Application fee:* $30. *Required:* high school transcript.
Standardized tests *Admission: Required:* SAT I or ACT.
Significant dates *Application deadlines:* rolling (freshmen), rolling (transfers). *Financial aid deadline priority date:* 3/1.
Freshman Application Contact
Director of Admissions, Purdue University, Schleman Hall, West Lafayette, IN 47907-1080. **Phone:** 765-494-4600. **Fax:** 765-494-0544. **E-mail:** admissions@purdue.edu

Indiana

Visit CollegeQuest.com for information on majors offered and athletics.

PURDUE UNIVERSITY CALUMET
Hammond, Indiana

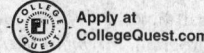
Apply at CollegeQuest.com

- **State-supported**, comprehensive, founded 1951
- **Degrees** associate, bachelor's, master's, and postbachelor's certificates
- **Urban** 167-acre campus with easy access to Chicago
- **Coed**, 7,885 undergraduate students
- **Noncompetitive** entrance level
- **$2577 tuition** and fees (in-state); $6123 (out-of-state)

Part of Purdue University System.

Students

Age 25 or older	47%

Expenses (1999–2000) *Tuition, state resident:* full-time $2341; part-time $98 per credit hour. *Tuition, nonresident:* full-time $5887; part-time $245 per credit hour. *Required fees:* full-time $236; $10 per credit hour. Full-time tuition and fees vary according to course load and program. Part-time tuition and fees vary according to program. *Payment plan:* deferred payment. *Waivers:* senior citizens and employees or children of employees.

Library Purdue Calumet Library. *Collection:* 215,830 titles, 1,736 serial subscriptions.

College life *Housing:* college housing not available. *Social organizations:* national fraternities, national sororities. *Most popular organizations:* Los Latinos, student government, Theater Club, Black Student Union, Song Company.

Campus security 24-hour emergency response devices and patrols, student patrols, late-night transport-escort service.

After graduation 70 organizations recruited on campus 1997–98. 65% of class of 1998 had job offers within 6 months. *Career center:* 3 full-time, 8 part-time personnel. Services include job fairs, resume preparation, resume referral, career counseling, careers library, job interviews.

Freshmen

SAT verbal scores above 500	N/R	SAT math scores above 500	N/R
ACT above 18	N/R	From top 10% of their h.s. class	10%
From top quarter	25%	From top half	60%

Application *Options:* eApply at www.CollegeQuest.com, Common Application, early admission. *Required:* high school transcript.

Standardized tests *Admission: Required for some:* SAT I or ACT.

Significant dates *Application deadlines:* rolling (freshmen), rolling (transfers). *Financial aid deadline priority date:* 3/1.

Freshman Application Contact
Mr. Paul McGuinness, Director of Admissions, Purdue University Calumet, 173rd and Woodmar Avenue, Hammond, IN 46323-2094. **Phone:** 219-989-2289. **Toll-free phone:** 800-447-8738. **Fax:** 219-989-2775. **E-mail:** adms@calumet.purdue.edu

Visit CollegeQuest.com for information on majors offered and athletics. College video available at CollegeQuest.com.

PURDUE UNIVERSITY NORTH CENTRAL
Westville, Indiana

- **State-supported**, comprehensive, founded 1967
- **Degrees** associate, bachelor's, and master's
- **Rural** 264-acre campus with easy access to Chicago
- **Coed**, 3,126 undergraduate students, 55% full-time, 60% women, 40% men
- **Noncompetitive** entrance level, 94% of applicants were admitted
- **6% graduate** in 6 years or less
- **$3211 tuition** and fees (in-state); $7709 (out-of-state)
- **$5000 average financial aid** package, $406,807 endowment

Part of Purdue University System.

Students *Undergraduates:* 1,718 full-time, 1,408 part-time. Students come from 3 states and territories. *The most frequently chosen baccalaureate fields are:* business/marketing, education, liberal arts/general studies. *Graduate:* 47 in graduate degree programs.

Age 25 or older	43%	Transferred in	16%
African Americans	3%	Asian Americans/Pacific Islanders	1%
Hispanic Americans	2%	Native Americans	1%

Faculty 231 (37% full-time), 28% with terminal degrees.

Expenses (1999–2000) *Tuition, state resident:* full-time $2927; part-time $98 per credit hour. *Tuition, nonresident:* full-time $7425; part-time $248 per credit hour. *Required fees:* full-time $284; $9 per credit hour. Full-time tuition and fees vary according to course load. Part-time tuition and fees vary according to course load. *Payment plan:* deferred payment. *Waivers:* senior citizens.

Library Purdue University North Central Library. *Operations spending 1999–2000:* $392,811. *Collection:* 86,557 titles, 417 serial subscriptions, 405 audiovisual materials.

College life *Housing:* college housing not available. *Most popular organizations:* student newspaper, Student Cultural Society, Student Education Association, construction club.

Campus security 24-hour emergency response devices, late-night transport-escort service.

After graduation 250 organizations recruited on campus 1997–98. 67% of class of 1998 had job offers within 6 months. *Career center:* 2 full-time personnel. Services include job fairs, resume preparation, resume referral, career counseling, careers library, job bank, job interviews.

Freshmen 961 applied, 903 admitted, 710 enrolled.

Average high school GPA	2.79	SAT verbal scores above 500	44%
SAT math scores above 500	43%	ACT above 18	88%
From top 10% of their h.s. class	15%	From top quarter	53%
From top half	80%	1998 freshmen returning in 1999	64%

Application *Option:* early admission. *Required:* high school transcript. *Required for some:* essay or personal statement; minimum 2.0 GPA; interview.

Standardized tests *Admission: Recommended:* SAT I, ACT. *Required for some:* SAT I or ACT.

Significant dates *Application deadlines:* 8/6 (freshmen), 8/1 (transfers). *Financial aid deadline priority date:* 3/1.

Freshman Application Contact
Ms. Cathy Buckman, Director of Admissions, Purdue University North Central, 1401 South U.S. Highway 421, Westville, IN 46391. **Phone:** 219-785-5458. **Toll-free phone:** 800-872-1231. **Fax:** 219-785-5538. **E-mail:** cbuckman@purduenc.edu

Visit CollegeQuest.com for information on majors offered and athletics. Electronic viewbook available at CollegeQuest.com.

ROSE-HULMAN INSTITUTE OF TECHNOLOGY
Terre Haute, Indiana

- **Independent**, comprehensive, founded 1874
- **Degrees** bachelor's and master's
- **Rural** 130-acre campus with easy access to Indianapolis
- **Coed**, primarily men, 1,545 undergraduate students, 98% full-time, 17% women, 83% men
- **Very difficult** entrance level, 67% of applicants were admitted
- **14:1** student-to-undergraduate faculty ratio
- **71.3% graduate** in 6 years or less
- **$19,545 tuition** and fees
- **$12,274 average financial aid** package, $22,000 average indebtedness upon graduation, $159 million endowment

Students *Undergraduates:* 1,509 full-time, 36 part-time. Students come from 45 states and territories, 12 other countries. *The most frequently chosen baccalaureate fields are:* computer/information sciences, engineering/engineering technologies, physical sciences. *Graduate:* 133 in graduate degree programs.

From out-of-state	52%	Reside on campus	50%
Age 25 or older	1%	Transferred in	1%
International students	1%	African Americans	1%
Asian Americans/Pacific Islanders	3%	Hispanic Americans	1%
Native Americans	0.2%		

Faculty 133 (89% full-time), 89% with terminal degrees.

Peterson's Guide to Four-Year Colleges 2001 www.petersons.com

Indiana

Rose-Hulman Institute of Technology (continued)

Expenses (1999–2000) *Comprehensive fee:* $25,020 includes full-time tuition ($19,440), mandatory fees ($105), and room and board ($5475). *College room only:* $3000. Full-time tuition and fees vary according to course load and student level. Room and board charges vary according to board plan. *Part-time tuition:* $505 per credit. Part-time tuition and fees vary according to course load. *Payment plans:* tuition prepayment, installment. *Waivers:* employees or children of employees.

Library Logan Library. *Operations spending 1999–2000:* $451,000. *Collection:* 55,000 titles, 170 serial subscriptions.

College life *Housing:* on-campus residence required in freshman year. *Options:* coed, men-only, women-only. *Social organizations:* national fraternities, national sororities; 40% of eligible men and 50% of eligible women are members. *Most popular organizations:* intramurals, fraternities, band, drama club, student government.

Campus security 24-hour emergency response devices and patrols, late-night transport-escort service, controlled dormitory access.

After graduation 280 organizations recruited on campus 1997–98. 99% of class of 1998 had job offers within 6 months. *Career center:* 3 full-time, 4 part-time personnel. Services include job fairs, resume preparation, interview workshops, resume referral, career counseling, careers library, job bank, job interviews. *Major awards:* 1 Fulbright Scholar.

Freshmen 3,295 applied, 2,202 admitted, 395 enrolled. 19 National Merit Scholars, 12 class presidents, 42 valedictorians, 50 student government officers.

SAT verbal scores above 500	99%	SAT math scores above 500	100%
ACT above 18	100%	From top 10% of their h.s. class	51%
From top quarter	100%	From top half	100%
1998 freshmen returning in 1999	96%		

Application *Option:* deferred entrance. *Application fee:* $40. *Required:* high school transcript; minimum 3.5 GPA; 1 letter of recommendation. *Recommended:* essay or personal statement; interview.

Standardized tests *Admission: Required:* SAT I or ACT.

Significant dates *Application deadlines:* 3/1 (freshmen), 7/1 (transfers). *Financial aid deadline priority date:* 3/1.

Freshman Application Contact
Mr. Charles G. Howard, Dean of Admissions/Vice President, Rose-Hulman Institute of Technology, 5500 Wabash Avenue, Terre Haute, IN 47803-3920. **Phone:** 812-877-8213. **Toll-free phone:** 800-552-0725 (in-state); 800-248-7448 (out-of-state). **Fax:** 812-877-8941. **E-mail:** admis.ofc@rose-hulman.edu

Visit CollegeQuest.com for information on majors offered and athletics.

SAINT FRANCIS COLLEGE
Indiana—See University of Saint Francis

SAINT JOSEPH'S COLLEGE
Rensselaer, Indiana

- **Independent Roman Catholic**, comprehensive, founded 1889
- **Degrees** associate, bachelor's, and master's
- **Small-town** 340-acre campus with easy access to Chicago
- **Coed**, 931 undergraduate students, 90% full-time, 53% women, 47% men
- **Moderately difficult** entrance level, 77% of applicants were admitted
- **14:1 student-to-undergraduate faculty ratio**
- **51% graduate** in 6 years or less
- **$14,190 tuition** and fees
- **$12,350 average financial aid** package, $16,730 average indebtedness upon graduation, $8.7 million endowment

Students *Undergraduates:* 834 full-time, 97 part-time. Students come from 26 states and territories, 8 other countries. *The most frequently chosen baccalaureate fields are:* business/marketing, biological/life sciences, education.

From out-of-state	29%	Reside on campus	77%
Age 25 or older	8%	Transferred in	4%
International students	2%	African Americans	5%
Asian Americans/Pacific Islanders	1%	Hispanic Americans	4%
Native Americans	0.2%		

Faculty 82 (65% full-time).

Expenses (1999–2000) *Comprehensive fee:* $19,270 includes full-time tuition ($14,070), mandatory fees ($120), and room and board ($5080). Full-time tuition and fees vary according to reciprocity agreements. *Part-time tuition:* $470 per credit. *Part-time fees:* $2 per credit hour; $60 per term part-time. Part-time tuition and fees vary according to course load and program. *Payment plan:* installment. *Waivers:* minority students, children of alumni, and employees or children of employees.

Library Robinson Memorial Library. *Operations spending 1999–2000:* $357,070. *Collection:* 143,075 titles, 585 serial subscriptions, 21,951 audiovisual materials.

College life *Housing:* on-campus residence required through senior year. *Options:* men-only, women-only, disabled students. *Most popular organizations:* Minority Student Union, Student Senate, Student Union, marching band, Alpha Lambda Delta.

Campus security 24-hour emergency response devices and patrols, student patrols, late-night transport-escort service.

After graduation 41 organizations recruited on campus 1997–98. 95% of class of 1998 had job offers within 6 months. *Career center:* 2 full-time personnel. Services include job fairs, resume preparation, resume referral, career counseling, careers library.

Freshmen 1,297 applied, 1,000 admitted, 301 enrolled.

Average high school GPA	2.99	SAT verbal scores above 500	48%
SAT math scores above 500	57%	ACT above 18	87%
From top 10% of their h.s. class	15%	From top quarter	34%
From top half	63%	1998 freshmen returning in 1999	72%

Application *Options:* Common Application, electronic application, deferred entrance. *Application fee:* $25. *Required:* high school transcript; minimum 2.0 GPA. *Required for some:* interview. *Recommended:* essay or personal statement; letters of recommendation.

Standardized tests *Admission: Required:* SAT I or ACT.

Significant dates *Application deadlines:* rolling (freshmen), rolling (transfers). *Financial aid deadline priority date:* 3/1.

Freshman Application Contact
Mr. Frank P. Bevec, Director of Admissions, Saint Joseph's College, PO Box 815, Rensselaer, IN 47978-0850. **Phone:** 219-866-6170. **Toll-free phone:** 800-447-8781. **Fax:** 219-866-6122. **E-mail:** admissions@saintjoe.edu

Visit CollegeQuest.com for information on majors offered and athletics. College video available at CollegeQuest.com.

■ *See page 2390 for a narrative description.*

SAINT MARY-OF-THE-WOODS COLLEGE
Saint Mary-of-the-Woods, Indiana

Apply at CollegeQuest.com

- **Independent Roman Catholic**, comprehensive, founded 1840
- **Degrees** associate, bachelor's, and master's (also offers external degree program with significant enrollment reflected in profile)
- **Rural** 67-acre campus with easy access to Indianapolis
- **Women** only, 1,199 undergraduate students, 33% full-time
- **Moderately difficult** entrance level, 55% of applicants were admitted
- **12:1 student-to-undergraduate faculty ratio**
- **32% graduate** in 6 years or less
- **$14,660 tuition** and fees
- **$12,000 average financial aid** package, $15,000 average indebtedness upon graduation, $8 million endowment

Students *Undergraduates:* 396 full-time, 803 part-time. Students come from 22 states and territories, 5 other countries. *The most frequently chosen baccalaureate fields are:* business/marketing, education, social sciences and history. *Graduate:* 86 in graduate degree programs.

From out-of-state	30%	Reside on campus	67%
Age 25 or older	50%	Transferred in	11%
International students	1%	African Americans	3%
Asian Americans/Pacific Islanders	0.3%	Hispanic Americans	1%
Native Americans	1%		

Faculty 61 (97% full-time), 64% with terminal degrees.

Expenses (2000–2001) *Comprehensive fee:* $20,070 includes full-time tuition ($14,200), mandatory fees ($460), and room and board ($5410).

Indiana

College room only: $2000. *Part-time tuition:* $570 per credit hour. *Part-time fees:* $230 per term part-time. Part-time tuition and fees vary according to course load and program. *Payment plan:* installment. *Waivers:* minority students, children of alumni, and employees or children of employees.
Library College Library. *Operations spending 1999–2000:* $174,706. *Collection:* 150,437 titles, 479 audiovisual materials.
College life *Housing:* on-campus residence required through senior year. *Option:* women-only. *Most popular organizations:* Student Senate, In-Law, student newspaper, chorale, Green Day.
Campus security 24-hour patrols.
After graduation 94% of class of 1998 had job offers within 6 months. *Career center:* 2 full-time personnel. Services include job fairs, resume preparation, resume referral, career/interest testing, career counseling, careers library, job interviews. *Graduate education:* 25% of class of 1999 went directly to graduate and professional school.
Freshmen 273 applied, 149 admitted, 135 enrolled.

Average high school GPA	3.2	SAT verbal scores above 500	50%
SAT math scores above 500	38%	ACT above 18	94%
From top 10% of their h.s. class	7%	1998 freshmen returning in 1999	68%

Application *Options:* eApply at www.CollegeQuest.com, early admission, early action, deferred entrance. *Application fee:* $30. *Required:* minimum 2.0 GPA; 1 letter of recommendation. *Required for some:* essay or personal statement; high school transcript; interview.
Standardized tests *Admission: Required for some:* SAT I or ACT.
Significant dates *Application deadlines:* 8/15 (freshmen), 8/15 (transfers). *Early action:* 11/15. *Notification:* 12/1 (early action). *Financial aid deadline:* 3/1.
Freshman Application Contact
Ms. Patty R. Young, Director of Admission, Saint Mary-of-the-Woods College, Guerin Hall, Saint Mary-of-the-Woods, IN 47876. **Phone:** 812-535-5106. **Toll-free phone:** 800-926-SMWC. **Fax:** 812-535-5215. **E-mail:** smwcadms@smwc.edu
Visit CollegeQuest.com for information on majors offered and athletics. College video available at CollegeQuest.com.

■ *See page 2406 for a narrative description.*

SAINT MARY'S COLLEGE
Notre Dame, Indiana

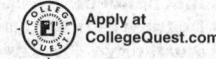
Apply at CollegeQuest.com

- **Independent Roman Catholic**, 4-year, founded 1844
- **Degree** bachelor's
- **Suburban** 275-acre campus
- **Women** only, 1,361 undergraduate students, 99% full-time
- **Moderately difficult** entrance level, 83% of applicants were admitted
- **12:1 student-to-undergraduate faculty ratio**
- **76% graduate** in 6 years or less
- **$16,994 tuition** and fees
- **$14,440 average financial aid** package, $15,894 average indebtedness upon graduation, $81.8 million endowment

Students *Undergraduates:* 1,356 full-time, 5 part-time. Students come from 51 states and territories, 13 other countries. *The most frequently chosen baccalaureate fields are:* business/marketing, education, social sciences and history. *Graduate:* 8 in graduate degree programs.

From out-of-state	75%	Reside on campus	78%
Age 25 or older	1%	Transferred in	3%
International students	1%	African Americans	1%
Asian Americans/Pacific Islanders	1%	Hispanic Americans	5%
Native Americans	0.3%		

Faculty 171 (63% full-time), 61% with terminal degrees.
Expenses (1999–2000) *Comprehensive fee:* $22,956 includes full-time tuition ($16,994) and room and board ($5962). Full-time tuition and fees vary according to location. Room and board charges vary according to housing facility. *Part-time tuition:* $678 per semester hour. *Payment plans:* installment, deferred payment. *Waivers:* adult students, senior citizens, and employees or children of employees.
Library Cushwa-Leighton Library. *Operations spending 1999–2000:* $879,430. *Collection:* 201,253 titles, 758 serial subscriptions.

College life *Housing: Option:* women-only. *Most popular organizations:* Circle K, Toastmasters, volunteers in support of Admissions, student government association, academic clubs.
Campus security 24-hour emergency response devices and patrols, late-night transport-escort service, controlled dormitory access.
After graduation 47 organizations recruited on campus 1997–98. 72% of class of 1998 had job offers within 6 months. *Career center:* 3 full-time, 5 part-time personnel. Services include job fairs, resume preparation, interview workshops, resume referral, career counseling, careers library, job bank, job interviews. *Graduate education:* 15% of class of 1999 went directly to graduate and professional school: 4% graduate arts and sciences, 3% education, 2% business, 1% medicine.
Freshmen 1,041 applied, 869 admitted, 424 enrolled. 6 National Merit Scholars, 15 class presidents, 18 valedictorians, 46 student government officers.

Average high school GPA	3.58	SAT verbal scores above 500	87%
SAT math scores above 500	82%	ACT above 18	99%
From top 10% of their h.s. class	31%	From top quarter	68%
From top half	96%	1998 freshmen returning in 1999	82%

Application *Options:* eApply at www.CollegeQuest.com, electronic application, early admission, early decision, deferred entrance. *Application fee:* $30. *Required:* essay or personal statement; high school transcript; 1 letter of recommendation. *Recommended:* interview.
Standardized tests *Admission: Required:* SAT I and SAT II or ACT.
Significant dates *Application deadlines:* 3/1 (freshmen), rolling (transfers). *Early decision:* 11/15. *Notification:* 12/15 (early decision). *Financial aid deadline priority date:* 3/1.
Freshman Application Contact
Ms. Mary Pat Nolan, Director of Admissions, Saint Mary's College, Notre Dame, IN 46556. **Phone:** 219-284-4587. **Toll-free phone:** 800-551-7621 (in-state); 219-284-4716 (out-of-state). **E-mail:** admission@saintmarys.edu
Visit CollegeQuest.com for information on majors offered and athletics. College video and electronic viewbook available at CollegeQuest.com.

■ *See page 2408 for a narrative description.*

TAYLOR UNIVERSITY
Upland, Indiana

- **Independent interdenominational**, 4-year, founded 1846
- **Degrees** associate and bachelor's
- **Rural** 250-acre campus with easy access to Indianapolis
- **Coed**, 1,869 undergraduate students, 98% full-time, 53% women, 47% men
- **Very difficult** entrance level, 78% of applicants were admitted
- **16:1 student-to-undergraduate faculty ratio**
- **75% graduate** in 6 years or less
- **$15,118 tuition** and fees
- **$11,273 average financial aid** package, $14,655 average indebtedness upon graduation, $37.4 million endowment

Taylor University is anchored by 3 distinctive traditions: Scholarship—students value academic excellence and enjoy personal attention from highly credentialed faculty members; Leadership—Taylor's nationally recognized leadership development program equips students for leadership in career, community, and church; Christian Commitment—every aspect of Taylor life is fully integrated with an active faith in Jesus Christ.

Students *Undergraduates:* 1,840 full-time, 29 part-time. Students come from 48 states and territories, 19 other countries. *The most frequently chosen baccalaureate fields are:* business/marketing, education, psychology.

From out-of-state	73%	Reside on campus	82%
Age 25 or older	2%	Transferred in	2%
International students	2%	African Americans	1%
Asian Americans/Pacific Islanders	1%	Hispanic Americans	2%
Native Americans	1%		

Faculty 144 (78% full-time), 59% with terminal degrees.
Expenses (1999–2000) *Comprehensive fee:* $19,748 includes full-time tuition ($14,900), mandatory fees ($218), and room and board ($4630). *College room only:* $2200. Room and board charges vary according to board

Indiana

Taylor University (continued)
plan and housing facility. Part-time tuition and fees vary according to course load. *Payment plan:* installment. *Waivers:* employees or children of employees.

Library Zondervan Library. *Operations spending 1999–2000:* $673,874. *Collection:* 188,000 titles, 737 serial subscriptions, 6,288 audiovisual materials.

College life *Housing:* on-campus residence required through sophomore year. *Options:* men-only, women-only. *Most popular organizations:* Student Activities Council, Taylor World Outreach, Taylor Student Organization.

Campus security 24-hour patrols, student patrols, late-night transport-escort service.

After graduation 125 organizations recruited on campus 1997–98. 48% of class of 1998 had job offers within 6 months. *Career center:* 1 full-time, 1 part-time personnel. Services include job fairs, resume preparation, resume referral, career/interest testing, career counseling, careers library, job bank, job interviews.

Freshmen 1,624 applied, 1,273 admitted, 475 enrolled. 8 National Merit Scholars, 37 valedictorians.

Average high school GPA	3.6	SAT verbal scores above 500	84%
SAT math scores above 500	86%	ACT above 18	99%
From top 10% of their h.s. class	42%	From top quarter	71%
From top half	92%	1998 freshmen returning in 1999	89%

Application *Options:* electronic application, deferred entrance. *Preference* given to Evangelical Christians. *Application fee:* $20. *Required:* essay or personal statement; high school transcript; 2 letters of recommendation; interview. *Recommended:* minimum 2.8 GPA.

Standardized tests *Admission: Required:* SAT I or ACT.

Significant dates *Application deadlines:* rolling (freshmen), rolling (transfers). *Financial aid deadline:* 3/1.

Freshman Application Contact
Mr. Stephen R. Mortland, Director of Admissions, Taylor University, 236 West Reade Avenue, Upland, IN 46989-1001. **Phone:** 765-998-5134. **Toll-free phone:** 800-882-3456. **Fax:** 765-998-4925. **E-mail:** admissions_u@tayloru.edu

Visit CollegeQuest.com for information on majors offered and athletics.

■ *See page 2592 for a narrative description.*

TAYLOR UNIVERSITY, FORT WAYNE CAMPUS
Fort Wayne, Indiana

- **Independent interdenominational**, 4-year, founded 1992
- **Degrees** associate and bachelor's
- **Suburban** 32-acre campus
- **Coed**, 387 undergraduate students, 82% full-time, 57% women, 43% men
- **Moderately difficult** entrance level, 80% of applicants were admitted
- **12:1** student-to-undergraduate faculty ratio
- **44% graduate** in 6 years or less
- **$12,600 tuition** and fees
- **$12,727 average financial aid** package, $37.4 million endowment

Part of Taylor University.

Students *Undergraduates:* 319 full-time, 68 part-time. Students come from 29 states and territories, 3 other countries. *The most frequently chosen baccalaureate fields are:* education, (pre)law, philosophy.

From out-of-state	28%	Reside on campus	50%
Age 25 or older	27%	Transferred in	6%
International students	1%	African Americans	7%
Asian Americans/Pacific Islanders	0.3%	Hispanic Americans	2%
Native Americans	0.3%		

Faculty 52 (44% full-time), 33% with terminal degrees.

Expenses (1999–2000) *One-time required fee:* $140. *Comprehensive fee:* $16,830 includes full-time tuition ($12,550), mandatory fees ($50), and room and board ($4230). *College room only:* $1800. Room and board charges vary according to board plan. *Part-time tuition:* $170 per hour. *Part-time fees:* $25 per term part-time. Part-time tuition and fees vary according to course load. *Payment plan:* installment. *Waivers:* senior citizens and employees or children of employees.

Library S. A. Lehman Memorial Library. *Operations spending 1999–2000:* $374,697. *Collection:* 72,336 titles, 537 serial subscriptions, 7,834 audiovisual materials.

College life *Housing:* on-campus residence required through junior year. *Options:* men-only, women-only. *Most popular organizations:* Delta Pi Sigma, Married Student Fellowship, Multicultrual Activities Council, World Outreach, Student Activities Council.

Campus security Student patrols, late-night transport-escort service, controlled dormitory access, 12-hour night patrols by trained personnel.

After graduation 50 organizations recruited on campus 1997–98. *Career center:* 2 full-time personnel. Services include job fairs, resume preparation, resume referral, career/interest testing, career counseling, careers library, job bank, job interviews. **Graduate education:** 27% of class of 1999 went directly to graduate and professional school.

Freshmen 585 applied, 468 admitted, 122 enrolled.

Average high school GPA	3.16	SAT verbal scores above 500	51%
SAT math scores above 500	53%	ACT above 18	80%
From top 10% of their h.s. class	13%	From top quarter	38%
From top half	61%	1998 freshmen returning in 1999	59%

Application *Options:* electronic application, deferred entrance. *Application fee:* $20. *Required:* essay or personal statement; high school transcript; minimum 2.0 GPA; 2 letters of recommendation. *Recommended:* minimum 3.0 GPA; interview.

Standardized tests *Admission: Required:* SAT I or ACT.

Significant dates *Application deadlines:* rolling (freshmen), rolling (transfers). *Financial aid deadline priority date:* 3/1.

Freshman Application Contact
Mr. Leo Gonot, Director of Admissions, Taylor University, Fort Wayne Campus, 1025 West Rudisill Boulevard, Fort Wayne, IN 46807-2197. **Phone:** 219-456-2111 Ext. 2274. **Toll-free phone:** 800-233-3922. **Fax:** 219-456-2119. **E-mail:** admissions_f@tayloru.edu

Visit CollegeQuest.com for information on majors offered and athletics.

TRI-STATE UNIVERSITY
Angola, Indiana

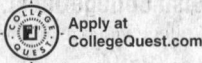
Apply at CollegeQuest.com

- **Independent**, 4-year, founded 1884
- **Degrees** associate and bachelor's
- **Small-town** 400-acre campus
- **Coed**, 1,210 undergraduate students, 91% full-time, 28% women, 72% men
- **Moderately difficult** entrance level, 83% of applicants were admitted
- **17:1** student-to-undergraduate faculty ratio
- **49% graduate** in 6 years or less
- **$13,700 tuition** and fees
- **$11,453 average financial aid** package, $14,000 average indebtedness upon graduation, $16.4 million endowment

In addition to its proven track record in producing work-ready engineers, Tri-State University offers excellent career opportunities for students with an interest in computers. Degree programs in management information systems, computer engineering, and computer science prepare students for highly compensated careers as systems analysts, database managers, or computer engineers.

Students *Undergraduates:* 1,107 full-time, 103 part-time. Students come from 20 states and territories, 22 other countries. *The most frequently chosen baccalaureate fields are:* business/marketing, education, engineering/engineering technologies.

From out-of-state	47%	Reside on campus	48%
Age 25 or older	4%	Transferred in	4%
International students	7%	African Americans	2%
Asian Americans/Pacific Islanders	0.5%	Hispanic Americans	1%
Native Americans	0.4%		

Faculty 86 (65% full-time), 51% with terminal degrees.

Expenses (2000–2001, estimated) *Comprehensive fee:* $18,650 includes full-time tuition ($13,450), mandatory fees ($250), and room and board ($4950). Full-time tuition and fees vary according to class time and program. *Part-time tuition:* $420 per semester hour. *Part-time fees:* $50 per term part-time. Part-time tuition and fees vary according to class time and program. *Payment plan:* installment. *Waivers:* senior citizens and employees or children of employees.

Library Perry Ford Library. *Operations spending 1999–2000:* $174,000. *Collection:* 191,628 titles, 296 serial subscriptions, 5,948 audiovisual materials.

College life *Housing:* on-campus residence required through sophomore year. *Option:* coed. *Social organizations:* national fraternities, local sororities; 25% of eligible men and 15% of eligible women are members. *Most popular organizations:* Circle K, drama club, International Student Association, student newspaper, student radio station.

Campus security 24-hour emergency response devices, late-night transport-escort service.

After graduation 67 organizations recruited on campus 1997–98. 85% of class of 1998 had job offers within 6 months. *Career center:* 2 full-time, 1 part-time personnel. Services include job fairs, resume preparation, interview workshops, resume referral, career counseling, careers library, job interviews. *Graduate education:* 5% of class of 1999 went directly to graduate and professional school: 3% business, 1% engineering, 1% graduate arts and sciences.

Freshmen 1,267 applied, 1,046 admitted, 368 enrolled.

Average high school GPA	3.2	SAT verbal scores above 500	61%
SAT math scores above 500	67%	ACT above 18	94%
From top 10% of their h.s. class	29%	From top quarter	53%
From top half	84%	1998 freshmen returning in 1999	76%

Application *Options:* eApply at www.CollegeQuest.com, Common Application, electronic application. *Application fee:* $20. *Required:* high school transcript; minimum 2.0 GPA. *Recommended:* letters of recommendation; interview.

Standardized tests *Admission: Required:* SAT I or ACT.

Significant dates *Application deadlines:* 6/1 (freshmen), 8/15 (transfers). *Notification:* continuous until 8/15 (freshmen). *Financial aid deadline priority date:* 3/1.

Freshman Application Contact
Mr. Kim Bryan, Director of Admissions, Tri-State University, 1 University Avenue, Angola, IN 46703-1764. **Phone:** 219-665-4139. **Toll-free phone:** 800-347-4TSU. **Fax:** 219-665-4292. **E-mail:** admit@alpha.tristate.edu

Visit CollegeQuest.com for information on majors offered and athletics. College video available at CollegeQuest.com.

■ *See page 2648 for a narrative description.*

UNIVERSITY OF EVANSVILLE
Evansville, Indiana

Apply at CollegeQuest.com

- **Independent**, 4-year, founded 1854, affiliated with United Methodist Church
- **Degrees** associate, bachelor's, and master's
- **Suburban** 75-acre campus
- **Coed**, 2,569 undergraduate students, 94% full-time, 61% women, 39% men
- **Moderately difficult** entrance level, 82% of applicants were admitted
- **13:1 student-to-undergraduate faculty ratio**
- **67% graduate** in 6 years or less
- **$12,606 average financial aid** package, $15,688 average indebtedness upon graduation, $53.8 million endowment

For 7 consecutive years, the University of Evansville has been ranked by *U.S. News & World Report* as one of the top 15 outstanding Midwest regional universities and as one of the best values in the Midwest.

Students *Undergraduates:* 2,416 full-time, 153 part-time. Students come from 45 states and territories, 49 other countries. *The most frequently chosen baccalaureate fields are:* business/marketing, engineering/engineering technologies, health professions and related sciences. *Graduate:* 25 in graduate degree programs.

From out-of-state	40%	Reside on campus	70%
Age 25 or older	5%	Transferred in	4%
International students	6%	African Americans	3%
Asian Americans/Pacific Islanders	1%	Hispanic Americans	1%
Native Americans	0.2%		

Faculty 185 (96% full-time).

Library Bower Suhrheinrich Library plus 1 other. *Operations spending 1999–2000:* $1.2 million. *Collection:* 192,061 titles, 1,352 serial subscriptions, 8,877 audiovisual materials.

College life *Housing:* on-campus residence required in freshman year. *Option:* coed. *Social organizations:* national fraternities, national sororities; 30% of eligible men and 20% of eligible women are members. *Most popular organizations:* Kappa Chi, Admission Ambassadors, Student Activities Board, Phi Eta Sigma, Mortar Board.

Campus security 24-hour emergency response devices and patrols, late-night transport-escort service.

After graduation 95 organizations recruited on campus 1997–98. 60% of class of 1998 had job offers within 6 months. *Career center:* 3 full-time personnel. Services include job fairs, resume preparation, resume referral, career counseling, careers library, job bank, job interviews. *Graduate education:* 16% of class of 1999 went directly to graduate and professional school: 5% business, 4% graduate arts and sciences, 2% medicine, 1% dentistry, 1% engineering, 1% law, 1% theology, 1% veterinary medicine.

Freshmen 2,288 applied, 1,881 admitted, 596 enrolled. 10 National Merit Scholars, 34 valedictorians.

Average high school GPA	3.55	SAT verbal scores above 500	84%
SAT math scores above 500	86%	ACT above 18	100%
From top 10% of their h.s. class	30%	From top quarter	68%
From top half	88%	1998 freshmen returning in 1999	88%

Application *Options:* eApply at www.CollegeQuest.com, Common Application, electronic application, early admission, early action, deferred entrance. *Application fee:* $35. *Required:* high school transcript; minimum 2.0 GPA; 1 letter of recommendation. *Required for some:* essay or personal statement; interview. *Recommended:* minimum 3.0 GPA; interview.

Standardized tests *Admission: Required:* SAT I or ACT.

Significant dates *Application deadlines:* 2/15 (freshmen), 7/1 (transfers). *Early action:* 12/1. *Notification:* 3/1 (freshmen), 12/15 (early action). *Financial aid deadline priority date:* 3/1.

Freshman Application Contact
Mr. Scot Schaeffer, Dean of Admission, University of Evansville, 1800 Lincoln Avenue, Evansville, IN 47722-0002. **Phone:** 812-479-2468. **Toll-free phone:** 800-992-5877 (in-state); 800-423-8633 (out-of-state). **Fax:** 812-474-4076. **E-mail:** admission@evansville.edu

Visit CollegeQuest.com for information on majors offered and athletics. College video and electronic viewbook available at CollegeQuest.com.

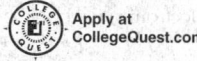

■ *See page 2724 for a narrative description.*

UNIVERSITY OF INDIANAPOLIS
Indianapolis, Indiana

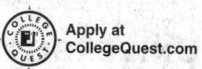
Apply at CollegeQuest.com

- **Independent**, comprehensive, founded 1902, affiliated with United Methodist Church
- **Degrees** associate, bachelor's, master's, and doctoral
- **Suburban** 60-acre campus
- **Coed**, 2,669 undergraduate students, 69% full-time, 65% women, 35% men
- **Moderately difficult** entrance level, 85% of applicants were admitted
- **14:1 student-to-undergraduate faculty ratio**
- **$14,630 tuition** and fees
- **$12,118 average financial aid** package, $16,418 average indebtedness upon graduation, $56.2 million endowment

Students *Undergraduates:* 1,831 full-time, 838 part-time. Students come from 28 states and territories, 55 other countries. *The most frequently chosen baccalaureate fields are:* business/marketing, biological/life sciences, education. *Graduate:* 851 in graduate degree programs.

Indiana

University of Indianapolis (continued)

From out-of-state	12%	Reside on campus	31%
Age 25 or older	28%	Transferred in	4%
International students	5%	African Americans	7%
Asian Americans/Pacific Islanders	0.1%	Hispanic Americans	1%
Native Americans	1%		

Faculty 349 (44% full-time), 49% with terminal degrees.
Expenses (2000–2001) *Comprehensive fee:* $19,855 includes full-time tuition ($14,630) and room and board ($5225). Full-time tuition and fees vary according to course load and program. Room and board charges vary according to board plan. *Part-time tuition:* $610 per credit hour. Part-time tuition and fees vary according to class time and course load. *Payment plans:* installment, deferred payment. *Waivers:* senior citizens and employees or children of employees.
Library Krannert Memorial Library. *Operations spending 1999–2000:* $952,692. *Collection:* 129,799 titles, 1,157 serial subscriptions, 3,592 audiovisual materials.
College life *Housing:* Options: coed, women-only. *Most popular organizations:* Fellowship of Christian Athletes, Intercultural Association, Circle K, Indianapolis Student Government, Residence Hall Association.
Campus security 24-hour emergency response devices and patrols, student patrols, late-night transport-escort service, emergency call boxes.
After graduation 140 organizations recruited on campus 1997–98. *Career center:* 2 full-time, 2 part-time personnel. Services include job fairs, resume preparation, resume referral, career/interest testing, career counseling, careers library, job bank, job interviews. **Graduate education:** 25% of class of 1999 went directly to graduate and professional school: 6% graduate arts and sciences, 5% business, 5% education, 2% law, 1% dentistry, 1% engineering, 1% medicine, 1% theology.
Freshmen 2,407 applied, 2,052 admitted, 606 enrolled. 19 valedictorians.

Average high school GPA	2.94	SAT verbal scores above 500	50%
SAT math scores above 500	53%	ACT above 18	84%
From top 10% of their h.s. class	23%	From top quarter	47%
From top half	77%	1998 freshmen returning in 1999	72%

Application *Options:* eApply at www.CollegeQuest.com, electronic application, deferred entrance. *Application fee:* $20. *Required:* high school transcript; minimum 2.0 GPA. *Required for some:* interview.
Standardized tests *Admission: Required:* SAT I or ACT.
Significant dates *Application deadlines:* rolling (freshmen), rolling (transfers). *Financial aid deadline priority date:* 3/1.
Freshman Application Contact
Mr. Ronald Wilks, Director of Admissions, University of Indianapolis, 1400 East Hanna Avenue, Indianapolis, IN 46227-3697. **Phone:** 317-788-3216. **Toll-free phone:** 800-232-8634 Ext. 3216. **Fax:** 317-788-3300. **E-mail:** admissions@uindy.edu
Visit CollegeQuest.com for information on majors offered and athletics. College video available at CollegeQuest.com.

■ *See page 2738 for a narrative description.*

UNIVERSITY OF NOTRE DAME
Notre Dame, Indiana

- **Independent Roman Catholic**, university, founded 1842
- **Degrees** bachelor's, master's, doctoral, and first professional
- **Suburban** 1,250-acre campus
- **Coed**, 8,005 undergraduate students, 99% full-time, 45% women, 55% men
- **Most difficult** entrance level, 35% of applicants were admitted
- **.94% graduate** in 6 years or less
- **$22,187 tuition** and fees
- **$17,992 average financial aid** package, $19,635 average indebtedness upon graduation, $2 million endowment

Students *Undergraduates:* 7,981 full-time, 24 part-time. Students come from 54 states and territories, 46 other countries. *The most frequently chosen baccalaureate fields are:* business/marketing, engineering/engineering technologies, social sciences and history. *Graduate:* 575 in professional programs, 2,065 in other graduate degree programs.

From out-of-state	90%	Reside on campus	71%
Transferred in	2%	International students	2%
African Americans	3%	Asian Americans/Pacific Islanders	4%
Hispanic Americans	7%	Native Americans	1%

Expenses (1999–2000) *Comprehensive fee:* $27,937 includes full-time tuition ($22,030), mandatory fees ($157), and room and board ($5750). Full-time tuition and fees vary according to program. Room and board charges vary according to housing facility. *Part-time tuition:* $918 per credit. *Part-time fees:* $40 per term part-time. Part-time tuition and fees vary according to course load and program. *Payment plan:* installment. *Waivers:* employees or children of employees.
Library University Libraries of Notre Dame plus 8 others. *Operations spending 1999–2000:* $15 million. *Collection:* 2.6 million titles, 24,106 serial subscriptions, 18,065 audiovisual materials.
College life *Housing:* on-campus residence required in freshman year. *Options:* men-only, women-only. *Most popular organizations:* marching band, Circle K, finance club, Notre Dame/St. Mary's Right to Life.
Campus security 24-hour emergency response devices and patrols, late-night transport-escort service, controlled dormitory access.
After graduation 369 organizations recruited on campus 1997–98. *Career center:* 12 full-time, 3 part-time personnel. Services include job fairs, resume preparation, interview workshops, resume referral, career/interest testing, career counseling, careers library, job bank, job interviews. **Graduate education:** 29% of class of 1999 went directly to graduate and professional school: 8% graduate arts and sciences, 7% law, 6% medicine, 3% education, 2% engineering, 1% business, 1% dentistry, 0.3% veterinary medicine, 0.1% theology.
Freshmen 10,010 applied, 3,500 admitted, 1,967 enrolled. 298 valedictorians.

SAT verbal scores above 500	97%	SAT math scores above 500	99%
ACT above 18	100%	From top 10% of their h.s. class	83%
From top quarter	96%	From top half	99%

Application *Options:* electronic application, early action, deferred entrance. *Application fee:* $40. *Required:* essay or personal statement; high school transcript; 1 letter of recommendation.
Standardized tests *Admission: Required:* SAT I or ACT. *Recommended:* SAT II Subject Tests.
Significant dates *Application deadlines:* 1/7 (freshmen), 4/15 (transfers). *Early action:* 11/1. *Notification:* 4/10 (freshmen), 12/20 (early action). *Financial aid deadline priority date:* 2/15.
Freshman Application Contact
Mr. Daniel J. Saracino, Assistant Provost for Enrollment, University of Notre Dame, 220 Main Building, Notre Dame, IN 46556-5612. **Phone:** 219-631-7505. **Fax:** 219-631-8865. **E-mail:** admissions.admissio.1@nd.edu
Visit CollegeQuest.com for information on majors offered and athletics. Electronic viewbook available at CollegeQuest.com.

■ *See page 2796 for a narrative description.*

UNIVERSITY OF SAINT FRANCIS
Fort Wayne, Indiana

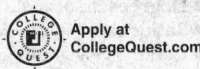
Apply at CollegeQuest.com

- **Independent Roman Catholic**, comprehensive, founded 1890
- **Degrees** associate, bachelor's, master's, and postbachelor's certificates
- **Suburban** 73-acre campus
- **Coed**, 1,387 undergraduate students, 69% full-time, 70% women, 30% men
- **Moderately difficult** entrance level, 43% of applicants were admitted
- **11:1 student-to-undergraduate faculty ratio**
- **$12,495 tuition** and fees
- **$3.3 million endowment**

Students *Undergraduates:* 963 full-time, 424 part-time. Students come from 11 states and territories, 4 other countries. *Graduate:* 90 in graduate degree programs.

From out-of-state	15%	Reside on campus	25%
Age 25 or older	37%	Transferred in	12%
International students	1%	African Americans	6%
Asian Americans/Pacific Islanders	1%	Hispanic Americans	1%
Native Americans	0.4%		

Indiana

Faculty 158 (58% full-time), 30% with terminal degrees.
Expenses (2000–2001) *Comprehensive fee:* $17,295 includes full-time tuition ($12,080), mandatory fees ($415), and room and board ($4800). Full-time tuition and fees vary according to class time. *Part-time tuition:* $380 per semester hour. *Part-time fees:* $8 per semester hour; $70 per term part-time. Part-time tuition and fees vary according to class time and course load. *Payment plan:* installment. *Waivers:* children of alumni, senior citizens, and employees or children of employees.
Library St. Francis College Library. *Operations spending 1999–2000:* $181,000. *Collection:* 85,544 titles, 480 serial subscriptions.
College life *Housing:* on-campus residence required through sophomore year. *Option:* coed. *Most popular organizations:* Student Activities Council, art club, student government organization, honors club, Residence Hall Council.
Campus security 24-hour emergency response devices and patrols, late-night transport-escort service.
After graduation 86% of class of 1998 had job offers within 6 months. *Career center:* 1 full-time personnel. Services include job fairs, resume preparation, interview workshops, career/interest testing, career counseling, careers library. *Graduate education:* 13% of class of 1999 went directly to graduate and professional school.
Freshmen 1,109 applied, 481 admitted, 241 enrolled.

Average high school GPA	2.97	SAT verbal scores above 500	42%
SAT math scores above 500	46%	ACT above 18	78%
From top 10% of their h.s. class	13%	From top quarter	34%
From top half	74%	1998 freshmen returning in 1999	78%

Application *Options:* eApply at www.CollegeQuest.com, Common Application, deferred entrance. *Application fee:* $20. *Required:* essay or personal statement; high school transcript. *Required for some:* minimum 2.0 GPA; letters of recommendation; interview. *Recommended:* minimum 3.0 GPA.
Standardized tests *Admission:* Required: SAT I or ACT.
Significant dates *Application deadlines:* rolling (freshmen), rolling (transfers). *Notification:* continuous until 8/15 (freshmen). *Financial aid deadline priority date:* 3/1.
Freshman Application Contact
Mr. David McMahan, Director of Admissions, University of Saint Francis, 2701 Spring Street, Fort Wayne, IN 46808. **Phone:** 219-434-3279. **Toll-free phone:** 800-729-4732. **E-mail:** admiss@sfc.edu
Visit CollegeQuest.com for information on majors offered and athletics.

UNIVERSITY OF SOUTHERN INDIANA
Evansville, Indiana

- **State-supported**, comprehensive, founded 1965
- **Degrees** associate, bachelor's, master's, and postbachelor's certificates
- **Suburban** 300-acre campus
- **Coed**, 7,783 undergraduate students, 79% full-time, 59% women, 41% men
- **Noncompetitive** entrance level, 97% of applicants were admitted
- **18:1 student-to-undergraduate faculty ratio**
- **24% graduate** in 6 years or less
- **$2920 tuition** and fees (in-state); $7066 (out-of-state)

Part of Indiana Commission for Higher Education.
Students *Undergraduates:* 6,182 full-time, 1,601 part-time. Students come from 26 states and territories, 24 other countries. *The most frequently chosen baccalaureate fields are:* business/marketing, education, health professions and related sciences. *Graduate:* 478 in graduate degree programs.

From out-of-state	9%	Reside on campus	29%
Age 25 or older	24%	Transferred in	8%
International students	0.3%	African Americans	3%
Asian Americans/Pacific Islanders	1%	Hispanic Americans	1%
Native Americans	0.1%		

Faculty 494 (52% full-time).
Expenses (1999–2000) *One-time required fee:* $62. *Tuition, state resident:* full-time $2860; part-time $92 per semester hour. *Tuition, nonresident:* full-time $7006; part-time $226 per semester hour. *Required fees:* full-time $60; $23 per term part-time. Part-time tuition and fees vary according to course load. *College room and board:* room only: $2286. Room and board charges vary according to housing facility. *Payment plan:* installment. *Waivers:* senior citizens and employees or children of employees.

Library David L. Rice Library plus 1 other. *Operations spending 1999–2000:* $1.4 million. *Collection:* 214,709 titles, 1,272 serial subscriptions, 8,224 audiovisual materials.
College life *Housing:* Option: coed. *Social organizations:* national fraternities, national sororities; 5% of eligible men and 4% of eligible women are members. *Most popular organization:* student government.
Campus security 24-hour emergency response devices and patrols, student patrols, late-night transport-escort service.
After graduation 180 organizations recruited on campus 1997–98. 90% of class of 1998 had job offers within 6 months. *Career center:* 5 full-time, 5 part-time personnel. Services include job fairs, resume preparation, interview workshops, resume referral, career counseling, careers library, job bank, job interviews. *Major awards:* 1 Fulbright Scholar.
Freshmen 3,410 applied, 3,301 admitted, 1,809 enrolled.

Average high school GPA	2.88	SAT verbal scores above 500	36%
SAT math scores above 500	39%	ACT above 18	76%
From top 10% of their h.s. class	7%	From top quarter	24%
From top half	56%	1998 freshmen returning in 1999	64%

Application *Option:* deferred entrance. *Application fee:* $25. *Required:* high school transcript. *Required for some:* interview. *Recommended:* essay or personal statement; minimum 2.0 GPA.
Standardized tests *Placement:* Recommended: SAT I or ACT. *Required for some:* SAT I or ACT.
Significant dates *Application deadlines:* 8/15 (freshmen), 8/15 (transfers). *Notification:* continuous until 8/27 (freshmen). *Financial aid deadline priority date:* 3/1.
Freshman Application Contact
Mr. Eric Otto, Director of Admissions, University of Southern Indiana, 8600 University Boulevard, Evansville, IN 47712-3590. **Phone:** 812-464-1765. **Toll-free phone:** 800-467-1965. **Fax:** 812-465-7154. **E-mail:** enroll.ucs@smtp.usi.edu
Visit CollegeQuest.com for information on majors offered and athletics. College video and electronic viewbook available at CollegeQuest.com.

VALPARAISO UNIVERSITY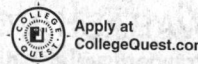
Valparaiso, Indiana

- **Independent**, comprehensive, founded 1859, affiliated with Lutheran Church
- **Degrees** associate, bachelor's, master's, and first professional
- **Small-town** 310-acre campus with easy access to Chicago
- **Coed**, 2,970 undergraduate students, 93% full-time, 53% women, 47% men
- **Moderately difficult** entrance level, 78% of applicants were admitted
- **12:1 student-to-undergraduate faculty ratio**
- **$17,636 tuition** and fees

Students *Undergraduates:* 2,749 full-time, 221 part-time. Students come from 36 states and territories, 50 other countries. *The most frequently chosen baccalaureate fields are:* business/marketing, health professions and related sciences, trade and industry. *Graduate:* 439 in professional programs, 225 in other graduate degree programs.

From out-of-state	65%	Reside on campus	66%
Age 25 or older	2%	Transferred in	2%
International students	3%	African Americans	3%
Asian Americans/Pacific Islanders	2%	Hispanic Americans	2%
Native Americans	1%		

Faculty 355 (63% full-time).
Expenses (2000–2001) *Comprehensive fee:* $22,296 includes full-time tuition ($17,100), mandatory fees ($536), and room and board ($4660). *College room only:* $2970. Full-time tuition and fees vary according to program. Room and board charges vary according to board plan and housing facility. *Part-time tuition:* $380 per credit. *Part-time fees:* $35 per term part-time. Part-time tuition and fees vary according to course load. *Payment plan:* installment. *Waivers:* employees or children of employees.
Library Moellering Library plus 1 other. *Collection:* 353,512 titles, 13,984 serial subscriptions, 10,727 audiovisual materials.
College life *Housing:* on-campus residence required through junior year. *Options:* coed, women-only. *Social organizations:* national fraternities, local sororities; 30% of eligible men and 30% of eligible women are members. *Most*

Indiana

Valparaiso University (continued)
popular organizations: Greek life, Union Board, student government, Student Volunteer Organization, Chapel programs.

Campus security 24-hour emergency response devices and patrols, late-night transport-escort service, controlled dormitory access.

After graduation 63 organizations recruited on campus 1997–98. 71% of class of 1998 had job offers within 6 months. *Career center:* 4 full-time personnel. Services include job fairs, resume preparation, interview workshops, resume referral, career/interest testing, career counseling, careers library, job interviews.

Freshmen 3,494 applied, 2,722 admitted, 734 enrolled. 22 National Merit Scholars, 46 valedictorians, 70 student government officers.

SAT verbal scores above 500	87%	SAT math scores above 500	88%
ACT above 18	100%	From top 10% of their h.s. class	45%
From top quarter	75%	From top half	96%
1998 freshmen returning in 1999	86%		

Application *Options:* eApply at www.CollegeQuest.com, Common Application, electronic application, deferred entrance. *Application fee:* $30. *Required:* high school transcript. *Required for some:* interview. *Recommended:* essay or personal statement; 2 letters of recommendation.

Standardized tests *Admission: Required:* SAT I or ACT.

Significant dates *Application deadlines:* rolling (freshmen), rolling (transfers). *Early action:* 11/1. *Notification:* 12/1 (early action). **Financial aid deadline priority date:** 3/1.

Freshman Application Contact
Ms. Karen Foust, Director of Admissions, Valparaiso University, 651 South College Avenue, Valparaiso, IN 46383-6493. **Phone:** 219-464-5011. **Toll-free phone:** 888-GO-VALPO. **Fax:** 219-464-6898. **E-mail:** undergrad_admissions@valpo.edu

Visit CollegeQuest.com for information on majors offered and athletics.

■ *See page 2874 for a narrative description.*

WABASH COLLEGE
Crawfordsville, Indiana

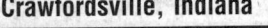 Apply at CollegeQuest.com

- **Independent,** 4-year, founded 1832
- **Degree** bachelor's
- **Small-town** 50-acre campus with easy access to Indianapolis
- **Men** only, 859 undergraduate students, 99% full-time
- **Moderately difficult** entrance level, 75% of applicants were admitted
- **11:1 student-to-undergraduate faculty ratio**
- **69% graduate** in 6 years or less
- **$17,275 tuition** and fees
- **$16,872 average financial aid** package, $13,925 average indebtedness upon graduation, $301 million endowment

Students *Undergraduates:* 853 full-time, 6 part-time. Students come from 35 states and territories, 27 other countries.

From out-of-state	26%	Reside on campus	94%
Age 25 or older	1%	Transferred in	1%
International students	5%	African Americans	5%
Asian Americans/Pacific Islanders	3%	Hispanic Americans	5%

Faculty 80 (99% full-time), 99% with terminal degrees.

Expenses (1999–2000) *Comprehensive fee:* $22,710 includes full-time tuition ($16,975), mandatory fees ($300), and room and board ($5435). *College room only:* $2025. Room and board charges vary according to housing facility. *Part-time tuition:* $2830 per course. Part-time tuition and fees vary according to course load. *Payment plans:* tuition prepayment, installment. *Waivers:* employees or children of employees.

Library Lilly Library. *Operations spending 1999–2000:* $1 million. *Collection:* 409,068 titles, 1,073 serial subscriptions, 8,292 audiovisual materials.

College life *Housing:* on-campus residence required through sophomore year. *Option:* men-only. *Social organizations:* national fraternities, language houses; 70% of eligible undergrads are members. *Most popular organizations:* The Bachelor, Sphinx Club, Alpha Phi Omega, Wabash Christian Fellowship, Malcolm X Institute.

Campus security 24-hour emergency response devices and patrols, late-night transport-escort service.

After graduation 40 organizations recruited on campus 1997–98. 61% of class of 1998 had job offers within 6 months. *Career center:* 3 full-time personnel. Services include job fairs, resume preparation, interview workshops, resume referral, career/interest testing, career counseling, careers library, job bank, job interviews. *Graduate education:* 39% of class of 1999 went directly to graduate and professional school: 10% law, 9% theology, 7% medicine, 5% education, 5% graduate arts and sciences, 3% business.

Freshmen 894 applied, 669 admitted, 292 enrolled. 4 National Merit Scholars, 14 class presidents, 12 valedictorians, 120 student government officers.

Average high school GPA	3.49	SAT verbal scores above 500	81%
SAT math scores above 500	87%	ACT above 18	96%
From top 10% of their h.s. class	36%	From top quarter	68%
From top half	91%	1998 freshmen returning in 1999	81%

Application *Options:* eApply at www.CollegeQuest.com, Common Application, electronic application, early admission, early decision, early action, deferred entrance. *Application fee:* $30. *Required:* essay or personal statement; high school transcript; minimum 2.0 GPA; 1 letter of recommendation. *Recommended:* minimum 3.0 GPA; interview.

Standardized tests *Admission: Required:* SAT I or ACT.

Significant dates *Application deadlines:* 3/1 (freshmen), rolling (transfers). *Early decision:* 11/1, 12/1. *Notification:* continuous until 4/1 (freshmen), 12/1 (early decision), 12/15 (early action). **Financial aid deadline:** 3/1. *Priority date:* 2/15.

Freshman Application Contact
Mr. Steve Klein, Director of Admissions, Wabash College, PO Box 362, Crawfordsville, IN 47933-0352. **Phone:** 765-361-6225. **Toll-free phone:** 800-345-5385. **Fax:** 765-361-6437. **E-mail:** admissions@wabash.edu

Visit CollegeQuest.com for information on majors offered and athletics. College video and electronic viewbook available at CollegeQuest.com.

IOWA

ALLEN COLLEGE
Waterloo, Iowa

- **Independent**, comprehensive, founded 1989
- **Degrees** associate, bachelor's, and master's (only offers nursing courses. General degree requirements must be taken at another institution)
- **Suburban** 20-acre campus
- **Coed**, primarily women, 219 undergraduate students, 74% full-time, 95% women, 5% men
- **Moderately difficult** entrance level, 97% of applicants were admitted
- **11:1 student-to-undergraduate faculty ratio**
- **33.3% graduate** in 6 years or less
- **$8220 tuition** and fees
- **$11,199 average indebtedness** upon graduation, $1.4 million endowment

Students *Undergraduates:* 162 full-time, 57 part-time. Students come from 7 states and territories. *The most frequently chosen baccalaureate field is:* health professions and related sciences. *Graduate:* 18 in graduate degree programs.

From out-of-state	3%	Age 25 or older	32%
African Americans	1%	Asian Americans/Pacific Islanders	1%
Hispanic Americans	0.5%		

Faculty 21 (71% full-time), 10% with terminal degrees.
Expenses (1999–2000) *Tuition:* full-time $8160; part-time $254 per credit hour. *Required fees:* full-time $60; $60 per year part-time. Full-time tuition and fees vary according to course load, location, program, and student level. Part-time tuition and fees vary according to program. *Payment plan:* installment.
Library Barrett Library. *Operations spending 1999–2000:* $21,704. *Collection:* 2,910 titles, 190 serial subscriptions, 370 audiovisual materials.
College life *Housing:* college housing not available. *Most popular organizations:* Allen Student Nurses' Association, Nurses' Christian Fellowship.
Campus security 24-hour patrols.
After graduation 100% of class of 1998 had job offers within 6 months. *Career center:* 3 full-time personnel. Services include resume referral, career counseling.
Freshmen 30 applied, 29 admitted, 23 enrolled.

Average high school GPA	3.15	SAT verbal scores above 500	N/R
SAT math scores above 500	N/R	ACT above 18	100%
From top 10% of their h.s. class	13%	From top quarter	35%
From top half	97%	1998 freshmen returning in 1999	90%

Application *Application fee:* $20. *Required:* essay or personal statement; high school transcript; 1 letter of recommendation. *Required for some:* interview. *Recommended:* minimum 2.3 GPA.
Standardized tests *Admission: Required:* ACT.
Significant dates *Application deadlines:* 8/1 (freshmen), 8/1 (transfers). *Notification:* continuous until 8/20 (freshmen). *Financial aid deadline:* continuous.
Freshman Application Contact
Ms. Lois Hagedorn, Student Services, Allen College, 1825 Logan Avenue, Waterloo, IA 50703. **Phone:** 319-235-3649. **Fax:** 319-235-5280. **E-mail:** studserv@sbtek.net

---

Visit CollegeQuest.com for information on majors offered and athletics.

BRIAR CLIFF COLLEGE
Sioux City, Iowa

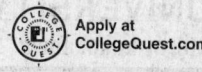 Apply at CollegeQuest.com

- **Independent Roman Catholic**, 4-year, founded 1930
- **Degrees** associate and bachelor's
- **Suburban** 70-acre campus
- **Coed**, 964 undergraduate students, 73% full-time, 65% women, 35% men
- **Moderately difficult** entrance level, 81% of applicants were admitted
- **56.5% graduate** in 6 years or less
- **$13,890 tuition** and fees
- **$13,650 average financial aid** package, $16.5 million endowment

Career success for Briar Cliff students begins in the classroom, where a low student-teacher ratio translates into quality time for each individual. A solid grounding in the liberal arts and a strong emphasis on internship opportunities result in extraordinarily high placement rates: of those BCC responding to a recent survey, 95% had found a job within the field of their choice or had been accepted into graduate school within 6 months of graduation.

Students *Undergraduates:* 706 full-time, 258 part-time. Students come from 23 states and territories, 10 other countries.

From out-of-state	29%	Reside on campus	42%
Age 25 or older	29%	International students	1%
African Americans	2%	Asian Americans/Pacific Islanders	2%
Hispanic Americans	2%	Native Americans	0.4%

Expenses (2000–2001) *Comprehensive fee:* $18,657 includes full-time tuition ($13,560), mandatory fees ($330), and room and board ($4767). *College room only:* $2361. Room and board charges vary according to board plan. *Part-time tuition:* $452 per credit hour. Part-time tuition and fees vary according to class time and course load. *Payment plan:* deferred payment. *Waivers:* adult students, senior citizens, and employees or children of employees.
Library Mueller Library. *Operations spending 1999–2000:* $246,884. *Collection:* 145,138 titles, 2,425 serial subscriptions, 16,387 audiovisual materials.
College life *Housing:* on-campus residence required through junior year. *Option:* coed. *Most popular organizations:* Student Government Association, business and accounting majors and minors club, Residence Hall Association, Commuter Association, Peer Advising Leaders.
Campus security 24-hour emergency response devices and patrols, student patrols, late-night transport-escort service, controlled dormitory access.
After graduation 25 organizations recruited on campus 1997–98. 81% of class of 1998 had job offers within 6 months. *Career center:* 3 full-time personnel. Services include job fairs, resume preparation, resume referral, career counseling, careers library, job bank, job interviews.
Freshmen 602 applied, 490 admitted, 268 enrolled.

Average high school GPA	3.16	SAT verbal scores above 500	23%
SAT math scores above 500	46%	ACT above 18	79%
1998 freshmen returning in 1999	75%		

Application *Options:* eApply at www.CollegeQuest.com, Common Application, early admission, deferred entrance. *Application fee:* $20. *Required:* high school transcript; minimum 2.0 GPA. *Required for some:* 3 letters of recommendation; interview. *Recommended:* essay or personal statement.
Standardized tests *Admission: Required:* SAT I or ACT.
Significant dates *Application deadlines:* rolling (freshmen), rolling (transfers). *Financial aid deadline priority date:* 3/15.
Freshman Application Contact
Ms. Sharisue Wilcoxon, Vice President for Enrollment Management, Briar Cliff College, 3303 Rebecca Street, Sioux City, IA 51104-2100. **Phone:** 712-279-5200 Ext. 1628. **Toll-free phone:** 800-662-3303. **Fax:** 712-279-5410. **E-mail:** admissions@briar-cliff.edu
Visit CollegeQuest.com for information on majors offered and athletics. College video available at CollegeQuest.com.

- *See page 1308 for a narrative description.*

Iowa

BUENA VISTA UNIVERSITY
Storm Lake, Iowa

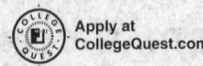

- **Independent**, comprehensive, founded 1891, affiliated with Presbyterian Church (U.S.A.)
- **Degrees** bachelor's and master's
- **Small-town** 60-acre campus
- **Coed**, 1,279 undergraduate students, 97% full-time, 49% women, 51% men
- **Moderately difficult** entrance level, 86% of applicants were admitted
- **16:1** student-to-undergraduate faculty ratio
- **49.1% graduate** in 6 years or less
- **$15,751 tuition** and fees
- **$16,257 average financial aid** package, $15,960 average indebtedness upon graduation, $111.7 million endowment

Students *Undergraduates:* 1,247 full-time, 32 part-time. Students come from 15 states and territories, 6 other countries. *The most frequently chosen baccalaureate fields are:* business/marketing, education, protective services/public administration. *Graduate:* 116 in graduate degree programs.

From out-of-state	14%	Reside on campus	84%
Age 25 or older	2%	Transferred in	5%
International students	2%	African Americans	0.3%
Asian Americans/Pacific Islanders	1%	Hispanic Americans	1%
Native Americans	0.1%		

Faculty 109 (74% full-time), 43% with terminal degrees.

Expenses (1999–2000) *Comprehensive fee:* $20,258 includes full-time tuition ($15,751) and room and board ($4507). *College room only:* $2235. Room and board charges vary according to board plan, housing facility, and location. *Part-time tuition:* $546 per semester hour. Part-time tuition and fees vary according to course load. *Payment plan:* installment. *Waivers:* employees or children of employees.

Library BVU Library. *Operations spending 1999–2000:* $736,690. *Collection:* 124,645 titles, 841 serial subscriptions, 3,077 audiovisual materials.

College life *Housing:* on-campus residence required through senior year. *Option:* coed. *Most popular organizations:* Student Activities Board, student orientation staff, Esprit De Corps, Student Senate, Buena Vista University Marketing Association.

Campus security 24-hour emergency response devices, late-night transport-escort service, controlled dormitory access, night security patrols.

After graduation 50 organizations recruited on campus 1997–98. 95% of class of 1998 had job offers within 6 months. *Career center:* 3 full-time personnel. Services include job fairs, resume preparation, interview workshops, resume referral, career/interest testing, career counseling, careers library, job bank, job interviews. *Graduate education:* 15% of class of 1999 went directly to graduate and professional school: 2% business, 2% graduate arts and sciences, 1% medicine.

Freshmen 1,117 applied, 963 admitted, 325 enrolled. 15 valedictorians.

Average high school GPA	3.3	SAT verbal scores above 500	N/R
SAT math scores above 500	N/R	ACT above 18	91%
From top 10% of their h.s. class	15%	From top quarter	44%
From top half	77%	1998 freshmen returning in 1999	80%

Application *Options:* eApply at www.CollegeQuest.com, Common Application, electronic application, early admission, deferred entrance. *Application fee:* $25. *Required:* high school transcript; letters of recommendation. *Required for some:* essay or personal statement; interview. *Recommended:* minimum 3.0 GPA.

Standardized tests *Admission: Required:* SAT I or ACT.

Significant dates *Application deadlines:* 6/1 (freshmen), 6/1 (transfers). *Financial aid deadline priority date:* 6/1.

Freshman Application Contact
Ms. Louise Cummings-Simmons, Director of Admissions, Buena Vista University, 610 West Fourth Street, Storm Lake, IA 50588. **Phone:** 712-749-2351. **Toll-free phone:** 800-383-9600. **Fax:** 712-749-2037. **E-mail:** admissions@bvu.edu

Visit CollegeQuest.com for information on majors offered and athletics. College video and electronic viewbook available at CollegeQuest.com.

CENTRAL COLLEGE
Pella, Iowa

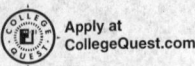

- **Independent**, 4-year, founded 1853, affiliated with Reformed Church in America
- **Degree** bachelor's
- **Small-town** 133-acre campus with easy access to Des Moines
- **Coed**, 1,264 undergraduate students, 99% full-time, 56% women, 44% men
- **Moderately difficult** entrance level, 85% of applicants were admitted
- **13:1** student-to-undergraduate faculty ratio
- **62% graduate** in 6 years or less
- **$14,186 tuition** and fees
- **$13,978 average financial aid** package, $20,665 average indebtedness upon graduation, $44.6 million endowment

Students *Undergraduates:* 1,248 full-time, 16 part-time. Students come from 37 states and territories, 17 other countries. *The most frequently chosen baccalaureate fields are:* business/marketing, communications/communication technologies, English.

From out-of-state	19%	Reside on campus	87%
Age 25 or older	1%	Transferred in	3%
International students	1%	African Americans	0.4%
Asian Americans/Pacific Islanders	1%	Hispanic Americans	1%
Native Americans	0.2%		

Faculty 125 (69% full-time), 89% with terminal degrees.

Expenses (1999–2000) *Comprehensive fee:* $19,130 includes full-time tuition ($14,070), mandatory fees ($116), and room and board ($4944). *College room only:* $2382. Room and board charges vary according to board plan. *Part-time tuition:* $488 per semester hour. *Part-time fees:* $116 per year part-time. Part-time tuition and fees vary according to course load. *Payment plan:* installment. *Waivers:* employees or children of employees.

Library Geisler Library plus 3 others. *Operations spending 1999–2000:* $688,017. *Collection:* 198,000 titles, 924 serial subscriptions.

College life *Housing:* on-campus residence required through senior year. *Option:* coed. *Social organizations:* local fraternities, local sororities; 15% of eligible men and 7% of eligible women are members. *Most popular organizations:* Students Concerned About the Environment, Intervarsity, FCA, Coalition for Multicultural Campus, Student Senate.

Campus security 24-hour emergency response devices, student patrols, late-night transport-escort service, controlled dormitory access.

After graduation 68 organizations recruited on campus 1997–98. 94% of class of 1998 had job offers within 6 months. *Career center:* 2 full-time, 2 part-time personnel. Services include job fairs, resume preparation, resume referral, career counseling, careers library, job bank, job interviews. *Graduate education:* 20% of class of 1999 went directly to graduate and professional school: 10% graduate arts and sciences, 5% medicine, 2% business, 1% law.

Freshmen 1,191 applied, 1,012 admitted, 404 enrolled. 11 valedictorians.

Average high school GPA	3.41	SAT verbal scores above 500	77%
SAT math scores above 500	79%	ACT above 18	97%
From top 10% of their h.s. class	21%	From top quarter	50%
From top half	84%	1998 freshmen returning in 1999	82%

Application *Options:* eApply at www.CollegeQuest.com, Common Application, early admission, deferred entrance. *Application fee:* $25. *Required:* high school transcript. *Required for some:* essay or personal statement; 3 letters of recommendation; interview. *Recommended:* minimum 2.0 GPA; interview.

Standardized tests *Admission: Required:* SAT I or ACT.

Significant dates *Application deadlines:* rolling (freshmen), rolling (transfers). *Notification:* continuous until 8/15 (freshmen). *Financial aid deadline priority date:* 3/1.

Freshman Application Contact
John Olsen, Vice President of Admission and Student Enrollment Services, Central College, 812 University Street, Pella, IA 50219-1999. **Phone:** 515-628-7600. **Toll-free phone:** 800-458-5503. **Fax:** 515-628-5316. **E-mail:** admissions@central.edu

Visit CollegeQuest.com for information on majors offered and athletics. College video and electronic viewbook available at CollegeQuest.com.

- *See page 1392 for a narrative description.*

Iowa

CLARKE COLLEGE
Dubuque, Iowa

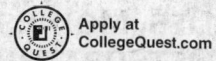 Apply at CollegeQuest.com

- **Independent Roman Catholic**, comprehensive, founded 1843
- **Degrees** associate, bachelor's, and master's
- **Urban** 55-acre campus
- **Coed**, 1,036 undergraduate students, 79% full-time, 67% women, 33% men
- **Moderately difficult** entrance level, 78% of applicants were admitted
- **9:1 student-to-undergraduate faculty ratio**
- **56.8% graduate** in 6 years or less
- **$13,586 tuition** and fees
- **$11,423 average financial aid** package, $16,838 average indebtedness upon graduation, $11.9 million endowment

Students *Undergraduates:* 818 full-time, 218 part-time. Students come from 27 states and territories, 13 other countries. *The most frequently chosen baccalaureate fields are:* business/marketing, computer/information sciences, health professions and related sciences. *Graduate:* 163 in graduate degree programs.

From out-of-state	41%	Reside on campus	70%
Age 25 or older	31%	Transferred in	8%
International students	3%	African Americans	1%
Asian Americans/Pacific Islanders	0.2%	Hispanic Americans	3%
Native Americans	0.2%		

Faculty 149 (58% full-time), 50% with terminal degrees.

Expenses (1999–2000) *Comprehensive fee:* $18,668 includes full-time tuition ($13,196), mandatory fees ($390), and room and board ($5082). *College room only:* $2472. Full-time tuition and fees vary according to class time. Room and board charges vary according to board plan and housing facility. *Part-time tuition:* $315 per credit hour. *Part-time fees:* $5 per credit hour. Part-time tuition and fees vary according to class time. *Payment plans:* installment, deferred payment. *Waivers:* children of alumni, adult students, senior citizens, and employees or children of employees.

Library Nicholas J. Schrupp Library. *Operations spending 1999–2000:* $458,538. *Collection:* 115,562 titles, 936 serial subscriptions, 1,171 audiovisual materials.

College life *Housing:* on-campus residence required through junior year. *Options:* coed, men-only, women-only. *Most popular organizations:* Admissions Student Team, Student Multicultural Organization, Concert Choir, Campus Ministry, student government.

Campus security 24-hour emergency response devices and patrols, late-night transport-escort service, controlled dormitory access.

After graduation 18 organizations recruited on campus 1997–98. 59% of class of 1998 had job offers within 6 months. *Career center:* 3 full-time personnel. Services include job fairs, resume preparation, resume referral, career/interest testing, career counseling, careers library, job bank, job interviews. *Graduate education:* 29% of class of 1999 went directly to graduate and professional school: 2% business, 2% education.

Freshmen 692 applied, 542 admitted, 188 enrolled. 2 valedictorians.

Average high school GPA	3.4	SAT verbal scores above 500	66%
SAT math scores above 500	76%	ACT above 18	99%
From top 10% of their h.s. class	23%	From top quarter	52%
From top half	87%	1998 freshmen returning in 1999	77%

Application *Options:* eApply at www.CollegeQuest.com, Common Application, electronic application, deferred entrance. *Application fee:* $25. *Required:* high school transcript; minimum 2.0 GPA; rank in upper 50% of high school class, minimum ACT score of 21 or SAT score of 1000. *Required for some:* interview.

Standardized tests *Admission: Required:* SAT I or ACT.

Significant dates *Application deadlines:* rolling (freshmen), rolling (transfers). *Notification:* continuous until 7/15 (freshmen). *Financial aid deadline priority date:* 4/15.

Freshman Application Contact
Mr. John D. Foley, Director of Admissions, Clarke College, 1550 Clarke Drive, Dubuque, IA 52001-3198. **Phone:** 319-588-6316. **Toll-free phone:** 800-383-2345. **Fax:** 319-588-6789. **E-mail:** admissions@clarke.edu

Visit CollegeQuest.com for information on majors offered and athletics. Electronic viewbook available at CollegeQuest.com.

COE COLLEGE
Cedar Rapids, Iowa

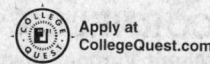 Apply at CollegeQuest.com

- **Independent**, comprehensive, founded 1851, affiliated with Presbyterian Church
- **Degrees** bachelor's and master's
- **Urban** 55-acre campus
- **Coed**, 1,246 undergraduate students, 89% full-time, 54% women, 46% men
- **Moderately difficult** entrance level, 82% of applicants were admitted
- **12:1 student-to-undergraduate faculty ratio**
- **62% graduate** in 6 years or less
- **$17,540 tuition** and fees
- **$18,048 average financial aid** package, $15,310 average indebtedness upon graduation, $58.5 million endowment

Listed among the top 100 liberal arts colleges in America, Coe College is a private, coeducational, church-related college located in Cedar Rapids, Iowa. Coe offers 41 majors, 65 student clubs, and NCAA Division III Iowa Conference competition in 11 men's and 10 women's sports. Ninety-eight percent of Coe graduates are in jobs or graduate school within 6 months of graduation.

Students *Undergraduates:* 1,114 full-time, 132 part-time. Students come from 35 states and territories, 16 other countries. *The most frequently chosen baccalaureate fields are:* business/marketing, social sciences and history, visual/performing arts. *Graduate:* 58 in graduate degree programs.

From out-of-state	43%	Reside on campus	84%
Age 25 or older	7%	Transferred in	4%
International students	4%	African Americans	2%
Asian Americans/Pacific Islanders	1%	Hispanic Americans	1%
Native Americans	0.1%		

Faculty 112 (65% full-time), 67% with terminal degrees.

Expenses (1999–2000) *Comprehensive fee:* $22,560 includes full-time tuition ($17,390), mandatory fees ($150), and room and board ($5020). *College room only:* $2340. Room and board charges vary according to board plan. *Part-time tuition:* $880 per course. *Payment plan:* installment. *Waivers:* children of alumni, adult students, and employees or children of employees.

Library Stewart Memorial Library plus 1 other. *Operations spending 1999–2000:* $845,484. *Collection:* 149,888 titles, 881 serial subscriptions, 8,527 audiovisual materials.

College life *Housing:* on-campus residence required through senior year. *Options:* coed, men-only, women-only. *Social organizations:* national fraternities, national sororities; 24% of eligible men and 15% of eligible women are members. *Most popular organizations:* Student Activities Committee, international club, Student Alumni Association, C-Club, Coe Alliance.

Campus security 24-hour emergency response devices and patrols, late-night transport-escort service, controlled dormitory access.

After graduation 88 organizations recruited on campus 1997–98. 98% of class of 1998 had job offers within 6 months. *Career center:* 3 full-time, 1 part-time personnel. Services include job fairs, resume preparation, interview workshops, career/interest testing, career counseling, careers library, job bank, job interviews.

Freshmen 1,176 applied, 965 admitted, 328 enrolled. 12 valedictorians.

Average high school GPA	3.56	SAT verbal scores above 500	84%
SAT math scores above 500	81%	ACT above 18	98%
From top 10% of their h.s. class	27%	From top quarter	63%
From top half	95%	1998 freshmen returning in 1999	80%

Application *Options:* eApply at www.CollegeQuest.com, electronic application, early admission, early action, deferred entrance. *Required:* essay or personal statement; high school transcript; 1 letter of recommendation. *Recommended:* minimum 3.0 GPA; interview.

Standardized tests *Admission: Required:* SAT I or ACT.

Significant dates *Application deadlines:* 3/1 (freshmen), rolling (transfers). *Early action:* 12/15. *Notification:* 3/15 (freshmen), 1/15 (early action). *Financial aid deadline priority date:* 3/1.

Freshman Application Contact
Mr. Dennis Trotter, Vice President of Admission and Financial Aid, Coe College, 1220 1st Avenue, NE, Cedar Rapids, IA 52402-5070. **Phone:** 319-399-8500. **Toll-free phone:** 877-225-5263. **Fax:** 319-399-8816. **E-mail:** admission@coe.edu

Visit CollegeQuest.com for information on majors offered and athletics.

- *See page 1442 for a narrative description.*

Iowa

CORNELL COLLEGE
Mount Vernon, Iowa

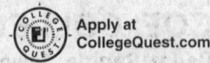 Apply at CollegeQuest.com

- **Independent Methodist**, 4-year, founded 1853
- **Degree** bachelor's
- **Small-town** 129-acre campus
- **Coed**, 946 undergraduate students, 98% full-time, 59% women, 41% men
- **Moderately difficult** entrance level, 72% of applicants were admitted
- **59% graduate** in 6 years or less
- **$18,995 tuition** and fees
- **$17,500 average financial aid** package, $18,025 average indebtedness upon graduation, $64.8 million endowment

Students *Undergraduates:* 929 full-time, 17 part-time. Students come from 40 states and territories, 10 other countries. *The most frequently chosen baccalaureate fields are:* biological/life sciences, psychology, social sciences and history.

From out-of-state	74%	Reside on campus	95%
Age 25 or older	1%	Transferred in	3%
International students	2%	African Americans	2%
Asian Americans/Pacific Islanders	1%	Hispanic Americans	3%
Native Americans	1%		

Faculty 121 (57% full-time), 81% with terminal degrees.

Expenses (1999–2000) *Comprehensive fee:* $24,135 includes full-time tuition ($18,835), mandatory fees ($160), and room and board ($5140). *College room only:* $2350. Full-time tuition and fees vary according to reciprocity agreements. Room and board charges vary according to board plan. *Part-time tuition:* $2355 per unit. Part-time tuition and fees vary according to course load and program. *Payment plan:* installment. *Waivers:* adult students, senior citizens, and employees or children of employees.

Library Cole Library. *Operations spending 1999-2000:* $1.2 million. *Collection:* 865 serial subscriptions, 5,278 audiovisual materials.

College life *Housing:* on-campus residence required through senior year. *Options:* coed, men-only, women-only. *Social organizations:* local fraternities, local sororities; 32% of eligible men and 32% of eligible women are members. *Most popular organizations:* Student Senate, Performing Art and Activity Council, Alpha Phi Omega, chess and games club, Fellowship of Christian Athletes.

Campus security 24-hour emergency response devices and patrols.

After graduation 27 organizations recruited on campus 1997–98. *Career center:* 1 full-time, 3 part-time personnel. Services include job fairs, resume preparation, interview workshops, career/interest testing, career counseling, careers library, job bank, job interviews.

Freshmen 1,102 applied, 791 admitted, 269 enrolled. 1 National Merit Scholar.

Average high school GPA	3.44	SAT verbal scores above 500	87%
SAT math scores above 500	89%	ACT above 18	98%
From top 10% of their h.s. class	31%	From top quarter	65%
From top half	92%	1998 freshmen returning in 1999	80%

Application *Options:* eApply at www.CollegeQuest.com, Common Application, electronic application, early admission, early decision, early action, deferred entrance. *Application fee:* $25. *Required:* essay or personal statement; high school transcript; minimum 2.5 GPA; 1 letter of recommendation. *Recommended:* interview.

Standardized tests *Admission: Required:* SAT I or ACT.

Significant dates *Application deadlines:* 2/1 (freshmen), 2/1 (transfers). *Early decision:* 11/15, 12/15. *Notification:* 3/1 (freshmen), 12/15 (early decision), 1/25 (early action). *Financial aid deadline priority date:* 3/1.

Freshman Application Contact
Ms. Florence W. Hines, Dean of Admission and Financial Assistance, Cornell College, 600 First Street West, Mount Vernon, IA 52314-1098. **Phone:** 319-895-4477. **Toll-free phone:** 800-747-1112. **Fax:** 319-895-4492. **E-mail:** admissions@cornell-iowa.edu

Visit CollegeQuest.com for information on majors offered and athletics. Electronic viewbook available at CollegeQuest.com.

DES MOINES UNIVERSITY OSTEOPATHIC MEDICAL CENTER
Des Moines, Iowa

- **Independent**, upper-level, founded 1898
- **Degrees** bachelor's, master's, and first professional
- **Urban** 20-acre campus
- **Coed**, 62 undergraduate students, 100% full-time, 65% women, 35% men
- **Most difficult** entrance level, 9% of applicants were admitted
- **$12,675 tuition** and fees

Students *Undergraduates:* 62 full-time. Students come from 14 states and territories. *The most frequently chosen baccalaureate field is:* health professions and related sciences. *Graduate:* 1,006 in professional programs, 85 in other graduate degree programs.

From out-of-state	50%	Age 25 or older	50%

Faculty 106 (76% full-time), 98% with terminal degrees.

Expenses (1999–2000) *Tuition:* full-time $12,600. *Required fees:* full-time $75. *Waivers:* employees or children of employees.

Library University Library. *Collection:* 24,000 titles, 285 serial subscriptions.

College life *Housing:* college housing not available.

Campus security Late-night transport-escort service.

After graduation 100% of class of 1998 had job offers within 6 months. *Career center:* Services include career counseling.

Application *Application fee:* $35.

Significant dates *Application deadline:* rolling (transfers). *Financial aid deadline priority date:* 4/1.

Freshman Application Contact
Dr. Dennis Bates, Director of Admissions, Des Moines University Osteopathic Medical Center, Des Moines University, Des Moines, IA 50312. **Phone:** 515-271-1450. **Fax:** 515-271-1578. **E-mail:** pchamberuomhs.edu

Visit CollegeQuest.com for information on majors offered and athletics.

DIVINE WORD COLLEGE
Epworth, Iowa

Admissions Office Contact
Divine Word College, 102 Jacoby Drive SW, Epworth, IA 52045-0380. **Toll-free phone:** 800-553-3321. **Fax:** 319-876-3407.

DORDT COLLEGE
Sioux Center, Iowa

- **Independent Christian Reformed**, comprehensive, founded 1955
- **Degrees** associate, bachelor's, and master's
- **Small-town** 65-acre campus
- **Coed**, 1,430 undergraduate students, 97% full-time, 55% women, 45% men
- **Moderately difficult** entrance level, 95% of applicants were admitted
- **15:1 student-to-undergraduate faculty ratio**
- **65% graduate** in 6 years or less
- **$12,650 tuition** and fees
- **$11,476 average financial aid** package, $14,271 average indebtedness upon graduation, $7 million endowment

Students *Undergraduates:* 1,384 full-time, 46 part-time. Students come from 35 states and territories, 17 other countries. *The most frequently chosen baccalaureate fields are:* business/marketing, education, engineering/engineering technologies.

From out-of-state	54%	Reside on campus	90%
Age 25 or older	5%	Transferred in	3%
International students	12%	African Americans	0.2%
Asian Americans/Pacific Islanders	0.1%	Hispanic Americans	0.2%
Native Americans	0.2%		

Faculty 118 (66% full-time), 49% with terminal degrees.

Expenses (1999–2000) *Comprehensive fee:* $16,250 includes full-time tuition ($12,500), mandatory fees ($150), and room and board ($3600). *College room only:* $1850. Room and board charges vary according to board

Iowa

plan and housing facility. *Part-time tuition:* $525 per credit hour. *Part-time fees:* $75 per term part-time. *Payment plan:* installment. *Waivers:* children of alumni, senior citizens, and employees or children of employees.

Library Dordt College Library plus 1 other. *Operations spending 1999–2000:* $362,778. *Collection:* 185,000 titles, 700 serial subscriptions, 300 audio-visual materials.

College life *Housing:* on-campus residence required through senior year. *Options:* coed, men-only, women-only, disabled students. *Most popular organizations:* PLIA, Future Teachers, Ag Club, soccer club, Community Outreach.

Campus security 24-hour emergency response devices, student patrols, late-night transport-escort service, controlled dormitory access.

After graduation 50 organizations recruited on campus 1997–98. 98% of class of 1998 had job offers within 6 months. *Career center:* 2 full-time personnel. Services include job fairs, resume preparation, resume referral, career/interest testing, career counseling, careers library, job bank, job interviews. *Graduate education:* 11% of class of 1999 went directly to graduate and professional school: 5% graduate arts and sciences, 2% business, 2% engineering, 1% medicine, 1% theology.

Freshmen 831 applied, 789 admitted, 349 enrolled.

Average high school GPA	3.35	SAT verbal scores above 500	73%
SAT math scores above 500	75%	ACT above 18	95%
From top 10% of their h.s. class	22%	From top quarter	44%
From top half	75%	1998 freshmen returning in 1999	89%

Application *Options:* electronic application, deferred entrance. *Application fee:* $25. *Required:* high school transcript; minimum 2.25 GPA; minimum ACT composite score of 19 or combined SAT I score of 920. *Required for some:* interview.

Standardized tests *Admission: Required:* SAT I or ACT.

Significant dates *Application deadlines:* 8/1 (freshmen), 8/1 (transfers). *Notification:* continuous until 9/1 (freshmen). *Financial aid deadline priority date:* 4/1.

Freshman Application Contact
Mr. Quentin Van Essen, Executive Director of Admissions, Dordt College, 498 4th Avenue, NE, Sioux Center, IA 51250-1697. **Phone:** 712-722-6080. **Toll-free phone:** 800-343-6738. **Fax:** 712-722-1967. **E-mail:** admissions@dordt.edu

Visit CollegeQuest.com for information on majors offered and athletics. College video and electronic viewbook available at CollegeQuest.com.

■ *See page 1586 for a narrative description.*

DRAKE UNIVERSITY
Des Moines, Iowa

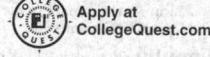
Apply at CollegeQuest.com

- **Independent**, university, founded 1881
- **Degrees** bachelor's, master's, doctoral, and first professional
- **Suburban** 120-acre campus
- **Coed**, 3,099 undergraduate students, 94% full-time, 59% women, 41% men
- **Moderately difficult** entrance level, 90% of applicants were admitted
- **14:1** student-to-undergraduate faculty ratio
- **65% graduate** in 6 years or less
- **$16,580 tuition** and fees
- **$14,149 average financial aid** package, $19,630 average indebtedness upon graduation, $103.5 million endowment

Students *Undergraduates:* 2,910 full-time, 189 part-time. Students come from 46 states and territories, 50 other countries. *The most frequently chosen baccalaureate fields are:* business/marketing, communications/communication technologies, health professions and related sciences. *Graduate:* 380 in professional programs, 1,032 in other graduate degree programs.

From out-of-state	58%	Reside on campus	54%
Age 25 or older	4%	Transferred in	9%
International students	5%	African Americans	3%
Asian Americans/Pacific Islanders	4%	Hispanic Americans	1%
Native Americans	1%		

Faculty 288 (91% full-time).

Expenses (1999–2000) *Comprehensive fee:* $21,450 includes full-time tuition ($16,480), mandatory fees ($100), and room and board ($4870). *College room only:* $2570. Full-time tuition and fees vary according to degree level and student level. Room and board charges vary according to board

plan. *Part-time tuition:* $350 per semester hour. Part-time tuition and fees vary according to class time. *Payment plans:* tuition prepayment, installment. *Waivers:* children of alumni, senior citizens, and employees or children of employees.

Library Cowles Library plus 1 other. *Operations spending 1999–2000:* $2.5 million. *Collection:* 553,569 titles, 2,284 serial subscriptions.

College life *Housing:* on-campus residence required through sophomore year. *Option:* coed. *Social organizations:* national fraternities, national sororities; 32% of eligible men and 30% of eligible women are members. *Most popular organizations:* Student Activities Board, international student organizations, Coalition of Black Students, Habitat for Humanity, Residence Hall Association.

Campus security 24-hour emergency response devices and patrols, late-night transport-escort service, 24-hour desk attendants in residence halls.

After graduation 110 organizations recruited on campus 1997–98. 93% of class of 1998 had job offers within 6 months. *Career center:* 6 full-time, 2 part-time personnel. Services include job fairs, resume preparation, interview workshops, resume referral, career counseling, careers library, job bank, job interviews. *Graduate education:* 21% of class of 1999 went directly to graduate and professional school: 13% graduate arts and sciences, 4% law, 2% business, 2% medicine.

Freshmen 2,388 applied, 2,147 admitted, 676 enrolled. 10 National Merit Scholars.

Average high school GPA	3.55	SAT verbal scores above 500	80%
SAT math scores above 500	83%	ACT above 18	99%
From top 10% of their h.s. class	34%	From top quarter	62%
From top half	90%	1998 freshmen returning in 1999	82%

Application *Options:* eApply at www.CollegeQuest.com, Common Application, electronic application, early admission, deferred entrance. *Application fee:* $25. *Required:* high school transcript; minimum 2.5 GPA; 1 letter of recommendation. *Recommended:* essay or personal statement; interview.

Standardized tests *Admission: Required:* SAT I or ACT. *Required for some:* PCAT for pharmacy transfers.

Significant dates *Application deadlines:* rolling (freshmen), rolling (transfers). *Notification:* continuous until 8/1 (freshmen). *Financial aid deadline priority date:* 3/1.

Freshman Application Contact
Mr. Thomas F. Willoughby, Dean of Admission, Drake University, 2507 University Avenue, Des Moines, IA 50311-4516. **Phone:** 515-271-3181. **Toll-free phone:** 800-44DRAKE. **Fax:** 515-271-2831. **E-mail:** admitinfo@acad.drake.edu

Visit CollegeQuest.com for information on majors offered and athletics. College video available at CollegeQuest.com.

■ *See page 1588 for a narrative description.*

EMMAUS BIBLE COLLEGE
Dubuque, Iowa

- **Independent nondenominational**, 4-year, founded 1941
- **Degrees** associate and bachelor's
- **Small-town** 22-acre campus
- **Coed**, 303 undergraduate students, 91% full-time, 52% women, 48% men
- **Noncompetitive** entrance level, 88% of applicants were admitted
- **15:1** student-to-undergraduate faculty ratio
- **27% graduate** in 6 years or less
- **$5390 tuition** and fees
- **$3425 average financial aid** package, $9400 average indebtedness upon graduation, $464,799 endowment

Students *Undergraduates:* 276 full-time, 27 part-time. Students come from 34 states and territories, 9 other countries. *The most frequently chosen baccalaureate fields are:* education, philosophy.

From out-of-state	55%	Reside on campus	79%
Age 25 or older	13%	Transferred in	15%
International students	6%	African Americans	2%
Asian Americans/Pacific Islanders	3%	Hispanic Americans	3%
Native Americans	1%		

Faculty 24 (63% full-time).

Expenses (1999–2000) *Comprehensive fee:* $8170 includes full-time tuition ($5260), mandatory fees ($130), and room and board ($2780). Full-time tuition and fees vary according to program. *Part-time tuition:* $120 per

Iowa

Emmaus Bible College (continued)
credit. Part-time tuition and fees vary according to course load. *Payment plan:* installment. *Waivers:* employees or children of employees.
Library The Emmaus Bible College Library plus 1 other. *Operations spending 1999–2000:* $108,425. *Collection:* 78,400 titles, 310 serial subscriptions.
College life *Housing:* on-campus residence required through senior year. *Options:* men-only, women-only.
Campus security 24-hour emergency response devices, student patrols, controlled dormitory access.
After graduation *Career center:* Services include career counseling.
Freshmen 94 applied, 83 admitted, 83 enrolled.

Average high school GPA	3.31	SAT verbal scores above 500	69%
SAT math scores above 500	61%	ACT above 18	86%
From top 10% of their h.s. class	10%	From top quarter	44%
From top half	65%	1998 freshmen returning in 1999	83%

Application *Option:* deferred entrance. *Application fee:* $10. *Required:* essay or personal statement; high school transcript; 3 letters of recommendation.
Standardized tests *Placement: Recommended:* SAT I or ACT.
Significant dates *Application deadlines:* 8/1 (freshmen), 8/1 (transfers). *Financial aid deadline priority date:* 7/1.
Freshman Application Contact
Mr. Mark Stevenson, Registrar, Emmaus Bible College, 2570 Asbury Road, Dubuque, IA 52001-3097. **Phone:** 319-588-8000 Ext. 122. **Toll-free phone:** 800-397-2425 Ext. 1. **Fax:** 319-588-1216. **E-mail:** registrar@emmausl.edu
Visit CollegeQuest.com for information on majors offered and athletics.

FAITH BAPTIST BIBLE COLLEGE AND THEOLOGICAL SEMINARY
Ankeny, Iowa

- **Independent**, comprehensive, founded 1921, affiliated with General Association of Regular Baptist Churches
- **Degrees** associate, bachelor's, master's, and first professional
- **Small-town** 52-acre campus
- **Coed**, 360 undergraduate students, 93% full-time, 58% women, 42% men
- **Minimally difficult** entrance level
- **18:1 student-to-undergraduate faculty ratio**
- **57% graduate** in 6 years or less
- **$7886 tuition** and fees
- **$4751 average financial aid** package, $12,979 average indebtedness upon graduation, $3 million endowment

Students *Undergraduates:* 335 full-time, 25 part-time. Students come from 30 states and territories. *The most frequently chosen baccalaureate fields are:* education, philosophy. *Graduate:* 26 in professional programs, 46 in other graduate degree programs.

From out-of-state	54%	Reside on campus	81%
Age 25 or older	6%	Transferred in	7%
African Americans	1%	Asian Americans/Pacific Islanders	1%
Hispanic Americans	1%	Native Americans	1%

Faculty 29 (62% full-time), 55% with terminal degrees.
Expenses (1999–2000) *Comprehensive fee:* $11,236 includes full-time tuition ($7086), mandatory fees ($800), and room and board ($3350). *College room only:* $1250. Full-time tuition and fees vary according to course load. *Part-time tuition:* $268 per semester hour. *Part-time fees:* $195 per term part-time. Part-time tuition and fees vary according to course load. *Payment plan:* installment. *Waivers:* employees or children of employees.
Library Patten Hall plus 1 other. *Operations spending 1999–2000:* $138,398. *Collection:* 61,929 titles, 368 serial subscriptions.
College life *Housing:* on-campus residence required through senior year. *Options:* men-only, women-only. *Most popular organizations:* Student Association, Student Missions Fellowship.
Campus security 24-hour emergency response devices and patrols.
After graduation *Career center:* Services include career counseling. *Graduate education:* 10% of class of 1999 went directly to graduate and professional school; 10% theology.

Freshmen 132 applied, 111 enrolled.

Average high school GPA	3.37	SAT verbal scores above 500	80%
SAT math scores above 500	80%	ACT above 18	82%
From top 10% of their h.s. class	10%	From top quarter	32%
From top half	32%	1998 freshmen returning in 1999	73%

Application *Options:* early admission, deferred entrance. *Application fee:* $25. *Required:* essay or personal statement; high school transcript; 2 letters of recommendation. *Required for some:* interview.
Standardized tests *Admission: Required:* SAT I or ACT.
Significant dates *Application deadlines:* 8/1 (freshmen), 8/1 (transfers). *Financial aid deadline priority date:* 5/1.
Freshman Application Contact
Mr. Tim Nilius, Vice President of Enrollment and Constituent Services, Faith Baptist Bible College and Theological Seminary, 1900 NW 4th Street, Ankeny, IA 50021. **Phone:** 515-964-0601 Ext. 238. **Toll-free phone:** 888-FAITH 4U. **Fax:** 515-964-1638. **E-mail:** admissions@faith.edu
Visit CollegeQuest.com for information on majors offered and athletics.

GRACELAND COLLEGE
Lamoni, Iowa

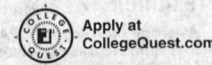
Apply at CollegeQuest.com

- **Independent Reorganized Latter Day Saints**, comprehensive, founded 1895
- **Degrees** bachelor's and master's
- **Small-town** 169-acre campus
- **Coed**, 3,252 undergraduate students, 39% full-time, 78% women, 22% men
- **Moderately difficult** entrance level, 65% of applicants were admitted
- **17:1 student-to-undergraduate faculty ratio**
- **54% graduate** in 6 years or less
- **$11,810 tuition** and fees
- **$13,429 average financial aid** package, $15,649 average indebtedness upon graduation, $20.1 million endowment

Students *Undergraduates:* 1,253 full-time, 1,999 part-time. Students come from 39 states and territories, 30 other countries. *The most frequently chosen baccalaureate fields are:* business/marketing, health professions and related sciences, liberal arts/general studies. *Graduate:* 93 in graduate degree programs.

From out-of-state	57%	Reside on campus	59%
Age 25 or older	12%	Transferred in	43%
International students	3%	African Americans	4%
Asian Americans/Pacific Islanders	2%	Hispanic Americans	2%
Native Americans	1%		

Faculty 91 (87% full-time), 58% with terminal degrees.
Expenses (1999–2000) *One-time required fee:* $100. *Comprehensive fee:* $15,640 includes full-time tuition ($11,700), mandatory fees ($110), and room and board ($3830). *College room only:* $1430. Full-time tuition and fees vary according to course load. Room and board charges vary according to board plan, housing facility, and location. *Part-time tuition:* $365 per semester hour. *Part-time fees:* $55 per term part-time. Part-time tuition and fees vary according to location. *Payment plan:* installment. *Waivers:* senior citizens and employees or children of employees.
Library Frederick Madison Smith Library. *Operations spending 1999–2000:* $348,447. *Collection:* 110,862 titles, 569 serial subscriptions, 2,829 audiovisual materials.
College life *Housing:* on-campus residence required through sophomore year. *Options:* men-only, women-only. *Most popular organizations:* student activities organization, Nontraditional Students, ""Choices Alcohol" Free Night Spot.
Campus security 24-hour emergency response devices and patrols, controlled dormitory access.
After graduation 30 organizations recruited on campus 1997–98. 42% of class of 1998 had job offers within 6 months. *Career center:* 3 full-time, 3 part-time personnel. Services include job fairs, resume preparation, resume referral, career counseling, careers library, job bank, job interviews. *Graduate education:* 17% of class of 1999 went directly to graduate and professional school.

Iowa

Freshmen 1,057 applied, 690 admitted, 307 enrolled.

Average high school GPA	3.27	SAT verbal scores above 500	44%
SAT math scores above 500	55%	ACT above 18	77%
From top 10% of their h.s. class	16%	From top quarter	41%
From top half	77%	1998 freshmen returning in 1999	74%

Application *Options:* eApply at www.CollegeQuest.com, Common Application, electronic application, early admission, deferred entrance. *Application fee:* $30. *Required:* high school transcript; minimum 2.0 GPA. *Required for some:* essay or personal statement; 2 letters of recommendation; interview.

Standardized tests *Admission: Required:* SAT I or ACT.

Significant dates *Application deadlines:* rolling (freshmen), rolling (transfers). *Financial aid deadline:* continuous.

Freshman Application Contact
Ms. Bonita A. Booth, Dean of Admissions, Graceland College, 700 College Avenue, Lamoni, IA 50140. **Phone:** 515-784-5118. **Toll-free phone:** 800-346-9208. **Fax:** 515-784-5480. **E-mail:** admissions@graceland.edu

Visit CollegeQuest.com for information on majors offered and athletics. College video and electronic viewbook available at CollegeQuest.com.

■ *See page 1734 for a narrative description.*

GRAND VIEW COLLEGE
Des Moines, Iowa

- **Independent**, 4-year, founded 1896, affiliated with Evangelical Lutheran Church in America
- **Degrees** associate and bachelor's
- **Urban** 25-acre campus
- **Coed**, 1,366 undergraduate students, 66% full-time, 62% women, 38% men
- **Noncompetitive** entrance level, 82% of applicants were admitted
- **14:1** student-to-undergraduate faculty ratio
- **$12,520 tuition** and fees
- **$11,240 average financial aid** package, $10,762 average indebtedness upon graduation, $7.5 million endowment

Students *Undergraduates:* 908 full-time, 458 part-time. Students come from 15 states and territories, 2 other countries. *The most frequently chosen baccalaureate fields are:* business/marketing, education, health professions and related sciences.

From out-of-state	4%	Reside on campus	20%
Age 25 or older	14%	Transferred in	23%
International students	1%	African Americans	4%
Asian Americans/Pacific Islanders	3%	Hispanic Americans	1%
Native Americans	1%		

Faculty 133 (50% full-time), 36% with terminal degrees.

Expenses (1999–2000) *Comprehensive fee:* $16,352 includes full-time tuition ($12,430), mandatory fees ($90), and room and board ($3832). Room and board charges vary according to board plan, housing facility, and student level. *Part-time tuition:* $380 per credit. Part-time tuition and fees vary according to class time. *Payment plans:* installment, deferred payment. *Waivers:* senior citizens and employees or children of employees.

Library Grand View College Library. *Operations spending 1999–2000:* $296,181. *Collection:* 130,000 titles, 360 serial subscriptions, 6,272 audiovisual materials.

College life *Housing: Options:* coed, men-only, women-only. *Most popular organizations:* Nursing Student Association (NSA), art club, human services club, education club, business club.

Campus security 24-hour emergency response devices, night security patrols.

After graduation 73 organizations recruited on campus 1997–98. 89% of class of 1998 had job offers within 6 months. *Career center:* 2 full-time personnel. Services include job fairs, resume preparation, interview workshops, resume referral, career/interest testing, career counseling, careers library, job bank, job interviews.

Freshmen 601 applied, 490 admitted, 226 enrolled. 1 valedictorian.

Average high school GPA	2.9	SAT verbal scores above 500	N/R
SAT math scores above 500	N/R	ACT above 18	76%
From top 10% of their h.s. class	2%	From top quarter	20%
From top half	37%	1998 freshmen returning in 1999	60%

Application *Options:* Common Application, electronic application, early admission, deferred entrance. *Application fee:* $0. *Required:* high school transcript. *Recommended:* minimum 2.0 GPA.

Standardized tests *Admission: Recommended:* SAT I or ACT.

Significant dates *Application deadlines:* rolling (freshmen), rolling (transfers). *Financial aid deadline priority date:* 3/1.

Freshman Application Contact
Ms. Debbie Barger, Vice President, Enrollment Management, Grand View College, 1200 Grandview Avenue, Des Moines, IA 50316-1599. **Phone:** 515-263-6012. **Toll-free phone:** 800-444-6083. **Fax:** 515-263-2974. **E-mail:** admiss@gvc.edu

Visit CollegeQuest.com for information on majors offered and athletics. Electronic viewbook available at CollegeQuest.com.

■ *See page 1738 for a narrative description.*

GRINNELL COLLEGE
Grinnell, Iowa

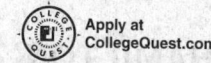
Apply at CollegeQuest.com

- **Independent**, 4-year, founded 1846
- **Degree** bachelor's
- **Small-town** 95-acre campus
- **Coed**, 1,299 undergraduate students, 99% full-time, 55% women, 45% men
- **Very difficult** entrance level, 67% of applicants were admitted
- **83.1% graduate** in 6 years or less
- **$19,460 tuition** and fees
- **$17,122 average financial aid** package, $12,148 average indebtedness upon graduation, $1 billion endowment

The core elements of a Grinnell College education are anchored in one-on-one interactions between students and faculty members committed to teaching. Grinnell has a rigorous academic and diverse extracurricular program. Students develop the intellectual, professional, and social characteristics that support a lifetime of personal achievement and social responsibility.

Students *Undergraduates:* 1,295 full-time, 4 part-time. Students come from 50 states and territories, 47 other countries. *The most frequently chosen baccalaureate fields are:* biological/life sciences, English, social sciences and history.

From out-of-state	86%	Reside on campus	86%
Age 25 or older	0.5%	Transferred in	2%
International students	8%	African Americans	3%
Asian Americans/Pacific Islanders	5%	Hispanic Americans	4%
Native Americans	0.3%		

Faculty 136 (98% full-time), 91% with terminal degrees.

Expenses (1999–2000) *Comprehensive fee:* $25,060 includes full-time tuition ($18,990), mandatory fees ($470), and room and board ($5600). *College room only:* $2610. Room and board charges vary according to board plan. *Payment plans:* tuition prepayment, installment. *Waivers:* employees or children of employees.

Library Burling Library plus 2 others. *Collection:* 267,257 titles, 3,100 serial subscriptions, 17,862 audiovisual materials.

College life *Housing:* on-campus residence required through sophomore year. *Option:* coed. *Most popular organizations:* Environmental Action Group, Chalutzim, Volunteers In Student Admission (VISA), Experimental College, Feminist Action Coalition.

Campus security 24-hour emergency response devices and patrols, student patrols, late-night transport-escort service, controlled dormitory access.

After graduation 52 organizations recruited on campus 1997–98. 55% of class of 1998 had job offers within 6 months. *Career center:* 3 full-time, 4 part-time personnel. Services include resume preparation, interview workshops, resume referral, career/interest testing, career counseling, careers library, job bank, job interviews. *Graduate education:* 33% of class of 1999 went directly to graduate and professional school.

Freshmen 1,757 applied, 1,175 admitted, 325 enrolled. 30 National Merit Scholars, 33 valedictorians, 86 student government officers.

SAT verbal scores above 500	99%	SAT math scores above 500	99%
ACT above 18	100%	From top 10% of their h.s. class	46%
From top half	100%	1998 freshmen returning in 1999	92%

Iowa

Grinnell College (continued)

Application *Options:* eApply at www.CollegeQuest.com, Common Application, early admission, early decision, deferred entrance. *Application fee:* $30. *Required:* essay or personal statement; high school transcript; 2 letters of recommendation. *Recommended:* interview.

Standardized tests *Admission: Required:* SAT I or ACT.

Significant dates *Application deadlines:* 1/20 (freshmen), 5/1 (transfers). *Early decision:* 11/1. *Notification:* 4/1 (freshmen), 12/20 (early decision). *Financial aid deadline:* 2/1.

Freshman Application Contact
Mr. Thomas Crady, Vice President for Student Services, Grinnell College, PO Box 805, Grinnell, IA 50112-0807. **Phone:** 515-269-3600. **Toll-free phone:** 800-247-0113. **Fax:** 515-269-4600. **E-mail:** askgrin@grinnell.edu

Visit CollegeQuest.com for information on majors offered and athletics. College video available at CollegeQuest.com.

■ *See page 1744 for a narrative description.*

HAMILTON TECHNICAL COLLEGE
Davenport, Iowa

- **Proprietary**, 4-year, founded 1969
- **Degrees** associate and bachelor's
- **Urban** campus
- **Coed**, 400 undergraduate students, 100% full-time, 25% women, 75% men
- **Noncompetitive** entrance level
- **$5850 tuition** and fees

Students *Undergraduates: The most frequently chosen baccalaureate field is:* trade and industry.

Faculty 18.

Expenses (1999–2000) *Tuition:* full-time $5850. *Payment plans:* guaranteed tuition, installment.

Library Hamilton Technical College Library. *Collection:* 4,500 titles, 30 serial subscriptions.

College life *Housing:* college housing not available.

Campus security 24-hour emergency response devices.

After graduation *Career center:* 1 full-time personnel. Services include resume preparation, interview workshops, resume referral, career counseling, job interviews.

Freshmen 393 admitted.

SAT verbal scores above 500	N/R	SAT math scores above 500	N/R
ACT above 18	N/R		

Application *Options:* eApply at www.CollegeQuest.com, Common Application, deferred entrance. *Application fee:* $25. *Required:* high school transcript; interview.

Significant dates *Application deadlines:* rolling (freshmen), rolling (transfers). *Financial aid deadline priority date:* 6/30.

Freshman Application Contact
Mr. Robert Hoffmann, Director of Admissions, Hamilton Technical College, 1011 East 53rd Street, Davenport, IA 52807. **Phone:** 319-386-3570. **Fax:** 319-386-6756.

Visit CollegeQuest.com for information on majors offered and athletics.

IOWA STATE UNIVERSITY OF SCIENCE AND TECHNOLOGY
Ames, Iowa

- **State-supported**, university, founded 1858
- **Degrees** bachelor's, master's, doctoral, first professional, and post-master's certificates
- **Suburban** 1,788-acre campus
- **Coed**, 21,503 undergraduate students, 91% full-time, 45% women, 55% men
- **Moderately difficult** entrance level, 88% of applicants were admitted
- **14:1** student-to-undergraduate faculty ratio
- **61.1% graduate** in 6 years or less
- **$3132 tuition** and fees (in-state); $9974 (out-of-state)
- **$6032 average financial aid** package, $16,836 average indebtedness upon graduation, $266.3 million endowment

Students *Undergraduates:* 19,605 full-time, 1,898 part-time. Students come from 53 states and territories, 86 other countries. *The most frequently chosen baccalaureate fields are:* business/marketing, agriculture, engineering/engineering technologies. *Graduate:* 398 in professional programs, 4,209 in other graduate degree programs.

From out-of-state	17%	Reside on campus	35%
Age 25 or older	10%	Transferred in	8%
International students	5%	African Americans	3%
Asian Americans/Pacific Islanders	3%	Hispanic Americans	1%
Native Americans	0.4%		

Faculty 1,667 (86% full-time), 87% with terminal degrees.

Expenses (2000–2001) *Tuition, state resident:* full-time $2906; part-time $122 per semester hour. *Tuition, nonresident:* full-time $9748; part-time $407 per semester hour. *Required fees:* full-time $226. Full-time tuition and fees vary according to class time and program. Part-time tuition and fees vary according to class time, course load, and program. *College room and board:* $4171; room only: $2267. Room and board charges vary according to board plan and housing facility. *Payment plans:* installment, deferred payment.

Library University Library plus 1 other. *Operations spending 1999–2000:* $13.7 million. *Collection:* 2.2 million titles, 22,455 serial subscriptions, 901,338 audiovisual materials.

College life *Housing: Options:* coed, men-only, women-only, disabled students. *Social organizations:* national fraternities, national sororities, local fraternities, local sororities; 16% of eligible men and 16% of eligible women are members. *Most popular organizations:* student government, Student Alumni Association, Greek associations, residence hall associations.

Campus security 24-hour emergency response devices and patrols, student patrols, late-night transport-escort service, controlled dormitory access, crime prevention programs, threat assessment team, motor vehicle help van.

After graduation 1,000 organizations recruited on campus 1997–98. 76% of class of 1998 had job offers within 6 months. *Career center:* 16 full-time, 9 part-time personnel. Services include job fairs, resume preparation, interview workshops, resume referral, career/interest testing, career counseling, careers library, job bank, job interviews.

Freshmen 12,172 applied, 10,717 admitted, 4,085 enrolled. 116 National Merit Scholars, 1 Westinghouse recipient.

Average high school GPA	3.46	SAT verbal scores above 500	81%
SAT math scores above 500	86%	ACT above 18	97%
From top 10% of their h.s. class	25%	From top quarter	56%
From top half	91%	1998 freshmen returning in 1999	84%

Application *Options:* Common Application, electronic application, early admission, deferred entrance. *Application fee:* $20. *Required:* high school transcript; rank in upper 50% of high school class.

Standardized tests *Admission: Required:* SAT I or ACT.

Significant dates *Application deadlines:* 8/21 (freshmen), rolling (transfers). *Financial aid deadline priority date:* 3/1.

Freshman Application Contact
Mr. Phil Caffrey, Associate Director for Freshman Admissions, Iowa State University of Science and Technology, 100 Alumni Hall, Ames, IA 50011-2010. **Phone:** 515-294-5836. **Toll-free phone:** 800-262-3810. **Fax:** 515-294-2592. **E-mail:** admissions@iastate.edu

Visit CollegeQuest.com for information on majors offered and athletics. Electronic viewbook available at CollegeQuest.com.

■ *See page 1832 for a narrative description.*

IOWA WESLEYAN COLLEGE
Mount Pleasant, Iowa

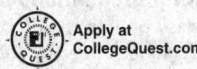

- **Independent United Methodist**, 4-year, founded 1842
- **Degree** bachelor's
- **Small-town** 60-acre campus
- **Coed**, 785 undergraduate students, 63% full-time, 61% women, 39% men
- **Moderately difficult** entrance level, 85% of applicants were admitted
- **12:1** student-to-undergraduate faculty ratio

Iowa

- **34.6% graduate** in 6 years or less
- **$12,700 tuition** and fees
- **$13,478 average financial aid** package, $14,752 average indebtedness upon graduation, $8.8 million endowment

Students *Undergraduates:* 497 full-time, 288 part-time. Students come from 24 states and territories, 11 other countries. *The most frequently chosen baccalaureate fields are:* business/marketing, education, psychology.

From out-of-state	17%	Reside on campus	57%
Age 25 or older	40%	International students	3%
African Americans	5%	Asian Americans/Pacific Islanders	1%
Hispanic Americans	2%	Native Americans	0.1%

Faculty 61 (72% full-time), 30% with terminal degrees.
Expenses (1999–2000) *Comprehensive fee:* $17,070 includes full-time tuition ($12,700) and room and board ($4370). *College room only:* $1850. Room and board charges vary according to board plan and housing facility. *Part-time tuition:* $300 per credit hour. Part-time tuition and fees vary according to class time. *Payment plans:* installment, deferred payment. *Waivers:* employees or children of employees.
Library Chadwick Library plus 1 other. *Operations spending 1999–2000:* $176,463. *Collection:* 109,232 titles, 438 serial subscriptions, 6,614 audiovisual materials.
College life *Housing:* on-campus residence required through junior year. *Options:* men-only, women-only. *Social organizations:* national fraternities, national sororities. *Most popular organizations:* commuter club, Student Senate, international club, behavioral science club, Blue Key.
Campus security 24-hour patrols, late-night transport-escort service, controlled dormitory access.
After graduation 23 organizations recruited on campus 1997–98. 72% of class of 1998 had job offers within 6 months. *Career center:* 1 full-time, 1 part-time personnel. Services include job fairs, resume preparation, resume referral, career/interest testing, career counseling, careers library. *Graduate education:* 2% of class of 1999 went directly to graduate and professional school: 1% business, 1% graduate arts and sciences.
Freshmen 408 applied, 348 admitted, 114 enrolled.

Average high school GPA	2.92	SAT verbal scores above 500	N/R
SAT math scores above 500	N/R	ACT above 18	82%
From top 10% of their h.s. class	8%	From top quarter	16%
From top half	49%	1998 freshmen returning in 1999	55%

Application *Options:* eApply at www.CollegeQuest.com, Common Application, electronic application, early admission, deferred entrance. *Application fee:* $15. *Required:* high school transcript; minimum 2.0 GPA. *Required for some:* essay or personal statement; letters of recommendation. *Recommended:* interview.
Standardized tests *Admission: Required:* SAT I or ACT.
Significant dates *Application deadlines:* 8/15 (freshmen), 8/15 (transfers). *Financial aid deadline priority date:* 4/1.
Freshman Application Contact
Mr. James Lynes, Director of Admissions, Iowa Wesleyan College, 601 North Main Street, Mount Pleasant, IA 52641-1398. **Phone:** 319-385-6230. **Toll-free phone:** 800-582-2383. **Fax:** 319-385-6296. **E-mail:** admitrwl@iwc.edu
Visit CollegeQuest.com for information on majors offered and athletics. College video available at CollegeQuest.com.

LORAS COLLEGE
Dubuque, Iowa

- **Independent Roman Catholic**, comprehensive, founded 1839
- **Degrees** associate, bachelor's, and master's
- **Suburban** 60-acre campus
- **Coed**, 1,551 undergraduate students, 93% full-time, 53% women, 47% men
- **Moderately difficult** entrance level, 81% of applicants were admitted
- **11:1 student-to-undergraduate faculty ratio**
- **$15,350 tuition** and fees
- **$14,108 average financial aid** package, $14,728 average indebtedness upon graduation, $30.4 million endowment

Students *Undergraduates:* 1,439 full-time, 112 part-time. Students come from 24 states and territories, 6 other countries. *The most frequently chosen baccalaureate fields are:* business/marketing, biological/life sciences, education. *Graduate:* 132 in graduate degree programs.

From out-of-state	45%	Reside on campus	71%
Age 25 or older	11%	Transferred in	6%
International students	2%	African Americans	2%
Asian Americans/Pacific Islanders	0.2%	Hispanic Americans	2%
Native Americans	0.1%		

Faculty 166 (70% full-time).
Expenses (2000–2001, estimated) *Comprehensive fee:* $21,154 includes full-time tuition ($15,190), mandatory fees ($160), and room and board ($5804). *College room only:* $2902. Room and board charges vary according to board plan and housing facility. *Part-time tuition:* $344 per credit. *Payment plan:* installment. *Waivers:* children of alumni, senior citizens, and employees or children of employees.
Library Wahlert Memorial Library plus 1 other. *Operations spending 1999–2000:* $757,990. *Collection:* 280,000 titles, 927 serial subscriptions.
College life *Housing:* on-campus residence required through junior year. *Option:* coed. *Social organizations:* national fraternities, national sororities; 10% of eligible men and 20% of eligible women are members. *Most popular organizations:* Student Senate, Campus Ministry, College Activities Board, Residence Hall Councils.
Campus security 24-hour emergency response devices and patrols, late-night transport-escort service, controlled dormitory access.
After graduation 87 organizations recruited on campus 1997–98. *Career center:* 3 full-time personnel. Services include job fairs, resume preparation, interview workshops, career/interest testing, career counseling, careers library, job bank, job interviews. *Graduate education:* 14% of class of 1999 went directly to graduate and professional school: 8% graduate arts and sciences, 3% education, 2% medicine, 1% law, 1% veterinary medicine, 0.3% business, 0.3% engineering, 0.3% theology.
Freshmen 1,278 applied, 1,034 admitted, 376 enrolled. 11 valedictorians.

Average high school GPA	3.21	SAT verbal scores above 500	75%
SAT math scores above 500	85%	ACT above 18	90%
From top 10% of their h.s. class	18%	From top quarter	36%
From top half	67%	1998 freshmen returning in 1999	78%

Application *Options:* eApply at www.CollegeQuest.com, deferred entrance. *Application fee:* $25. *Required:* high school transcript; minimum 2.5 GPA. *Required for some:* interview. *Recommended:* essay or personal statement; 1 letter of recommendation.
Standardized tests *Admission: Required:* SAT I or ACT.
Significant dates *Application deadlines:* rolling (freshmen), rolling (transfers). *Notification:* 7/31 (freshmen). *Financial aid deadline priority date:* 4/15.
Freshman Application Contact
Mr. Tim Hauber, Director of Admissions, Loras College, 1450 Alta Vista, Dubuque, IA 52004-0178. **Phone:** 319-588-7829. **Toll-free phone:** 800-245-6727. **Fax:** 319-588-7964. **E-mail:** adms@loras.edu
Visit CollegeQuest.com for information on majors offered and athletics.

■ *See page 1944 for a narrative description.*

LUTHER COLLEGE
Decorah, Iowa

- **Independent**, 4-year, founded 1861, affiliated with Evangelical Lutheran Church in America
- **Degree** bachelor's
- **Small-town** 800-acre campus
- **Coed**, 2,550 undergraduate students, 97% full-time, 59% women, 41% men
- **Moderately difficult** entrance level, 87% of applicants were admitted
- **13:1 student-to-undergraduate faculty ratio**
- **76% graduate** in 6 years or less
- **$17,290 tuition** and fees
- **$14,316 average financial aid** package, $16,942 average indebtedness upon graduation, $45.7 million endowment

Students *Undergraduates:* 2,478 full-time, 72 part-time. Students come from 35 states and territories, 40 other countries. *The most frequently chosen baccalaureate fields are:* biological/life sciences, business/marketing, visual/performing arts.

Iowa

Luther College (continued)

From out-of-state	62%	Reside on campus	82%
Age 25 or older	3%	Transferred in	3%
International students	5%	African Americans	1%
Asian Americans/Pacific Islanders	1%	Hispanic Americans	1%
Native Americans	0.1%		

Faculty 229 (75% full-time), 66% with terminal degrees.

Expenses (1999–2000) *Comprehensive fee:* $21,100 includes full-time tuition ($17,290) and room and board ($3810). *College room only:* $1980. Full-time tuition and fees vary according to course load. *Part-time tuition:* $618 per semester hour. Part-time tuition and fees vary according to course load. *Payment plan:* installment. *Waivers:* employees or children of employees.

Library Preus Library. *Operations spending 1999–2000:* $1.3 million. *Collection:* 330,160 titles, 1,063 serial subscriptions.

College life *Housing:* on-campus residence required through senior year. *Option:* coed. *Social organizations:* national fraternities, local fraternities, local sororities; 9% of eligible men and 10% of eligible women are members. *Most popular organizations:* National Service Organization, Student Activities Council, intramural clubs and organizations, Inter Greek Council, campus ministry.

Campus security 24-hour emergency response devices and patrols, late-night transport-escort service, controlled dormitory access.

After graduation 102 organizations recruited on campus 1997–98. 63% of class of 1998 had job offers within 6 months. *Career center:* 5 full-time, 2 part-time personnel. Services include job fairs, resume preparation, interview workshops, resume referral, career/interest testing, career counseling, careers library, job bank, job interviews. *Graduate education:* 25% of class of 1999 went directly to graduate and professional school: 11% graduate arts and sciences, 3% medicine, 2% law, 1% business, 1% dentistry, 1% theology.

Freshmen 1,694 applied, 1,475 admitted, 608 enrolled. 11 class presidents, 44 valedictorians, 111 student government officers.

Average high school GPA	3.58	SAT verbal scores above 500	88%
SAT math scores above 500	83%	ACT above 18	99%
From top 10% of their h.s. class	35%	From top quarter	65%
From top half	91%	1998 freshmen returning in 1999	86%

Application *Options:* eApply at www.CollegeQuest.com, Common Application, electronic application, early admission, deferred entrance. *Application fee:* $25. *Required:* essay or personal statement; high school transcript; 1 letter of recommendation. *Recommended:* interview.

Standardized tests *Admission: Required:* SAT I or ACT.

Significant dates *Financial aid deadline priority date:* 3/1.

Freshman Application Contact
Dr. David Sallee, Vice President for Enrollment Management, Luther College, 700 College Drive, Decorah, IA 52101-1045. **Phone:** 319-387-1287. **Toll-free phone:** 800-458-8437. **Fax:** 319-387-2159. **E-mail:** admissions@luther.edu

Visit CollegeQuest.com for information on majors offered and athletics. College video available at CollegeQuest.com.

■ *See page 1960 for a narrative description.*

MAHARISHI UNIVERSITY OF MANAGEMENT
Fairfield, Iowa

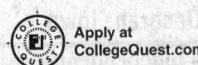
Apply at CollegeQuest.com

- **Independent**, university, founded 1971
- **Degrees** associate, bachelor's, master's, and doctoral
- **Small-town** 262-acre campus
- **Coed**, 206 undergraduate students, 94% full-time, 52% women, 48% men
- **Moderately difficult** entrance level, 78% of applicants were admitted
- **8:1** student-to-undergraduate faculty ratio
- **20% graduate** in 6 years or less
- **$15,630 tuition** and fees
- **$19,495 average financial aid** package, $16,454 average indebtedness upon graduation, $10.6 million endowment

Students *Undergraduates:* 194 full-time, 12 part-time. Students come from 19 states and territories, 19 other countries. *The most frequently chosen baccalaureate fields are:* business/marketing, computer/information sciences, visual/performing arts. *Graduate:* 314 in graduate degree programs.

From out-of-state	38%	Reside on campus	87%
Age 25 or older	26%	Transferred in	11%
International students	31%	African Americans	2%
Asian Americans/Pacific Islanders	1%	Hispanic Americans	3%
Native Americans	0.5%		

Faculty 109 (80% full-time), 59% with terminal degrees.

Expenses (2000–2001) *Comprehensive fee:* $20,830 includes full-time tuition ($15,200), mandatory fees ($430), and room and board ($5200). *College room only:* $2720. Full-time tuition and fees vary according to program. Room and board charges vary according to housing facility. *Part-time tuition:* $3800 per term. Part-time tuition and fees vary according to program. *Payment plan:* installment. *Waivers:* children of alumni, senior citizens, and employees or children of employees.

Library Maharishi University of Management Library. *Operations spending 1999–2000:* $210,000. *Collection:* 150,000 titles, 844 serial subscriptions, 13,276 audiovisual materials.

College life *Housing:* on-campus residence required through senior year. *Options:* men-only, women-only, disabled students. *Most popular organizations:* international student organization, Organization of New Earth, World Congress, Yogic Flying Club.

Campus security 24-hour emergency response devices and patrols, late-night transport-escort service, controlled dormitory access.

After graduation 10 organizations recruited on campus 1997–98. *Career center:* 1 full-time personnel. Services include job fairs, resume preparation, interview workshops, resume referral, career/interest testing, career counseling, careers library, job bank, job interviews.

Freshmen 89 applied, 69 admitted, 68 enrolled. 1 National Merit Scholar, 1 class president, 1 valedictorian, 5 student government officers.

Average high school GPA	3.37	SAT verbal scores above 500	85%
SAT math scores above 500	90%	ACT above 18	92%
1998 freshmen returning in 1999	66%		

Application *Options:* eApply at www.CollegeQuest.com, electronic application, early admission, deferred entrance. *Application fee:* $25. *Required:* essay or personal statement; high school transcript; minimum 2.5 GPA; 2 letters of recommendation; minimum SAT score of 950 or ACT score of 19. *Recommended:* interview.

Standardized tests *Admission: Required:* SAT I or ACT.

Significant dates *Application deadlines:* 8/1 (freshmen), 8/1 (transfers). *Financial aid deadline priority date:* 4/15.

Freshman Application Contact
Mr. Brad Mylett, Director of Admissions, Maharishi University of Management, 1000 North 4th Street, Fairfield, IA 52557. **Phone:** 515-472-1110. **Fax:** 515-472-1189. **E-mail:** admissions@mum.edu

Visit CollegeQuest.com for information on majors offered and athletics. College video available at CollegeQuest.com.

■ *See page 1968 for a narrative description.*

MARYCREST INTERNATIONAL UNIVERSITY
Davenport, Iowa

- **Independent**, comprehensive, founded 1939
- **Degrees** associate, bachelor's, and master's
- **Urban** 30-acre campus
- **Coed**, 345 undergraduate students, 78% full-time, 56% women, 44% men
- **Moderately difficult** entrance level, 77% of applicants were admitted
- **12:1** student-to-undergraduate faculty ratio
- **78% graduate** in 6 years or less
- **$12,760 tuition** and fees
- **$378,053 endowment**

Students *Undergraduates:* 268 full-time, 77 part-time. Students come from 23 states and territories. *The most frequently chosen baccalaureate fields are:* business/marketing, computer/information sciences, health professions and related sciences. *Graduate:* 414 in graduate degree programs.

From out-of-state	27%	Reside on campus	27%
Age 25 or older	43%	Transferred in	24%
International students	10%	African Americans	10%
Asian Americans/Pacific Islanders	1%	Hispanic Americans	5%
Native Americans	0.3%		

Iowa

Faculty 57 (32% full-time), 32% with terminal degrees.
Expenses (1999–2000) *Comprehensive fee:* $17,600 includes full-time tuition ($12,400), mandatory fees ($360), and room and board ($4840). *College room only:* $1900. Room and board charges vary according to housing facility. *Part-time tuition:* $415 per credit hour. *Part-time fees:* $12 per credit hour. Part-time tuition and fees vary according to class time and location. *Payment plans:* installment, deferred payment. *Waivers:* employees or children of employees.
Library Cone Library plus 1 other. *Operations spending 1999–2000:* $96,694. *Collection:* 110,073 titles, 498 serial subscriptions.
College life *Housing: Option:* coed. *Most popular organizations:* coffeehouse, international club, student nurses association, student government association, international business organization.
Campus security 24-hour patrols, late-night transport-escort service.
After graduation 27 organizations recruited on campus 1997–98. 85% of class of 1998 had job offers within 6 months. *Career center:* 1 full-time personnel. Services include job fairs, resume preparation, interview workshops, resume referral, career counseling, careers library, job bank, job interviews. *Graduate education:* 5% of class of 1999 went directly to graduate and professional school: 2% law, 2% medicine, 1% veterinary medicine.
Freshmen 181 applied, 139 admitted, 45 enrolled.

| SAT verbal scores above 500 | N/R | SAT math scores above 500 | N/R |
| ACT above 18 | 91% | 1998 freshmen returning in 1999 | 69% |

Application *Options:* Common Application, electronic application, early admission, deferred entrance. *Application fee:* $25. *Required:* high school transcript; minimum 2.3 GPA. *Required for some:* essay or personal statement; letters of recommendation. *Recommended:* interview.
Standardized tests *Admission: Required:* SAT I or ACT.
Significant dates *Application deadlines:* rolling (freshmen), rolling (transfers). *Notification:* continuous until 8/26 (freshmen). *Financial aid deadline priority date:* 4/1.
Freshman Application Contact
Ms. Meg Farber, Director of Admission, Marycrest International University, 1607 West 12th Street, Davenport, IA 52804. **Phone:** 319-327-9609. **Toll-free phone:** 800-728-9705 Ext. 2225. **Fax:** 319-327-9620. **E-mail:** mfarber@acc.mcrest.edu
Visit CollegeQuest.com for information on majors offered and athletics.

■ *See page 1998 for a narrative description.*

MERCY COLLEGE OF HEALTH SCIENCES
Des Moines, Iowa

Admissions Office Contact
Mercy College of Health Sciences, 928 Sixth Avenue, Des Moines, IA 50309-1239. **Toll-free phone:** 800-637-2994. **Fax:** 515-643-6698.

MORNINGSIDE COLLEGE
Sioux City, Iowa

- **Independent United Methodist**, comprehensive, founded 1894
- **Degrees** bachelor's and master's
- **Suburban** 41-acre campus
- **Coed**, 957 undergraduate students, 92% full-time, 61% women, 39% men
- **Moderately difficult** entrance level, 85% of applicants were admitted
- **11:1** student-to-undergraduate faculty ratio
- **47% graduate** in 6 years or less
- **$13,146 tuition** and fees
- **$13,415 average financial aid** package, $15,028 average indebtedness upon graduation, $31.4 million endowment

Morningside offers a total experience: 45 majors, internships, independent study, and career and graduate school advising services. Within 6 months of graduation, more than 98 percent of students are employed or admitted to graduate school. Merit scholarships for thinkers, doers, and those connected to alumni, the region, or the United Methodist Church are offered. Ninety-six percent of students receive assistance. Resident students have free personal computers and access to e-mail, the Internet, and the online library catalog. There are 33 student organizations, 12 Division II sports, and 35 individual/intramural sports.

Students *Undergraduates:* 882 full-time, 75 part-time. Students come from 20 states and territories, 12 other countries. *The most frequently chosen baccalaureate fields are:* business/marketing, biological/life sciences, education. *Graduate:* 132 in graduate degree programs.

From out-of-state	23%	Reside on campus	62%
Age 25 or older	7%	Transferred in	8%
International students	4%	African Americans	2%
Asian Americans/Pacific Islanders	1%	Hispanic Americans	1%
Native Americans	1%		

Faculty 130 (55% full-time), 45% with terminal degrees.
Expenses (1999–2000) *Comprehensive fee:* $17,782 includes full-time tuition ($12,800), mandatory fees ($346), and room and board ($4636). *College room only:* $2460. Room and board charges vary according to board plan and housing facility. *Part-time tuition:* $420 per semester hour. Part-time tuition and fees vary according to course load. *Payment plan:* installment. *Waivers:* children of alumni, senior citizens, and employees or children of employees.
Library Hickman-Johnson-Furrow Library. *Operations spending 1999–2000:* $197,625. *Collection:* 117,330 titles, 613 serial subscriptions, 3,575 audiovisual materials.
College life *Housing:* on-campus residence required through junior year. *Option:* coed. *Social organizations:* national fraternities, national sororities; 11% of eligible men and 6% of eligible women are members. *Most popular organizations:* Student Government/Activities Council, Student Ambassadors, fraternities and sororities, homecoming committee, new student orientation.
Campus security 24-hour emergency response devices, student patrols, late-night transport-escort service, controlled dormitory access, 18-hour patrols by trained security personnel.
After graduation 40 organizations recruited on campus 1997–98. 99% of class of 1998 had job offers within 6 months. *Career center:* 1 full-time, 2 part-time personnel. Services include job fairs, resume preparation, interview workshops, career/interest testing, career counseling, careers library, job bank, job interviews. *Graduate education:* 9% of class of 1999 went directly to graduate and professional school: 3% graduate arts and sciences, 2% education, 2% law, 1% engineering, 1% medicine. *Major awards:* 1 Fulbright Scholar.
Freshmen 643 applied, 546 admitted, 164 enrolled. 6 valedictorians.

Average high school GPA	3.3	SAT verbal scores above 500	43%
SAT math scores above 500	14%	ACT above 18	93%
From top 10% of their h.s. class	22%	From top quarter	54%
From top half	81%	1998 freshmen returning in 1999	71%

Application *Options:* Common Application, electronic application, early admission, deferred entrance. *Application fee:* $15. *Required:* high school transcript; minimum 2.5 GPA; minimum SAT score of 930 or ACT score of 20 or rank in top 50% of high school class. *Required for some:* essay or personal statement; letters of recommendation; interview.
Standardized tests *Admission: Required:* SAT I or ACT.
Significant dates *Application deadlines:* rolling (freshmen), rolling (transfers). *Financial aid deadline priority date:* 3/1.
Freshman Application Contact
Ms. Terri Curry, Dean of Students/Admissions, Morningside College, 1501 Morningside Avenue, Sioux City, IA 51106-1751. **Phone:** 712-274-5111. **Toll-free phone:** 800-831-0806. **E-mail:** mscadm@alpha.morningside.edu
Visit CollegeQuest.com for information on majors offered and athletics. Electronic viewbook available at CollegeQuest.com.

■ *See page 2100 for a narrative description.*

MOUNT MERCY COLLEGE
Cedar Rapids, Iowa

- **Independent Roman Catholic**, 4-year, founded 1928
- **Degree** bachelor's
- **Suburban** 36-acre campus
- **Coed**, 1,193 undergraduate students, 68% full-time, 68% women, 32% men

Iowa

Mount Mercy College (continued)
- **Moderately difficult** entrance level, 88% of applicants were admitted
- **12:1 student-to-undergraduate faculty ratio**
- **$13,850 tuition** and fees
- **$12,412 average financial aid** package, $16,382 average indebtedness upon graduation, $14.6 million endowment

Students *Undergraduates:* 813 full-time, 380 part-time. Students come from 14 states and territories. *The most frequently chosen baccalaureate fields are:* business/marketing, education, protective services/public administration.

Reside on campus	40%	Age 25 or older	31%
Transferred in	16%	African Americans	1%
Asian Americans/Pacific Islanders	1%	Hispanic Americans	1%
Native Americans	0.1%		

Faculty 125 (51% full-time).

Expenses (2000–2001) *Comprehensive fee:* $18,450 includes full-time tuition ($13,850) and room and board ($4600). *College room only:* $1870. Full-time tuition and fees vary according to course load. Room and board charges vary according to board plan. *Part-time tuition:* $385 per credit hour. Part-time tuition and fees vary according to course load. *Payment plan:* installment. *Waivers:* employees or children of employees.

Library Busse Center. *Operations spending 1999–2000:* $513,520. *Collection:* 107,000 titles, 660 serial subscriptions.

College life *Housing: Option:* coed. *Most popular organizations:* biology club, student teachers club, business club, nursing club, Student Government Association.

Campus security 24-hour emergency response devices and patrols, student patrols, late-night transport-escort service, controlled dormitory access.

After graduation 96% of class of 1998 had job offers within 6 months. *Career center:* 2 full-time personnel. Services include job fairs, resume preparation, resume referral, career counseling, careers library, job bank, job interviews. *Graduate education:* 9% of class of 1999 went directly to graduate and professional school: 6% graduate arts and sciences, 2% business, 1% medicine.

Freshmen 497 applied, 438 admitted, 186 enrolled. 7 valedictorians.

Average high school GPA	3.41	SAT verbal scores above 500	N/R
SAT math scores above 500	N/R	ACT above 18	98%
From top 10% of their h.s. class	19%	From top quarter	56%
From top half	81%	1998 freshmen returning in 1999	86%

Application *Options:* electronic application, early admission, deferred entrance. *Application fee:* $20. *Required:* high school transcript; minimum 2.0 GPA; 1 letter of recommendation. *Required for some:* interview. *Recommended:* essay or personal statement; minimum 3.0 GPA.

Standardized tests *Admission: Required:* SAT I or ACT.

Significant dates *Application deadlines:* 8/15 (freshmen), 8/15 (transfers). *Financial aid deadline priority date:* 3/1.

Freshman Application Contact
Dr. Alex Popovics, Vice President for Enrollment Management, Mount Mercy College, 1330 Elmhurst Drive, NE, Cedar Rapids, IA 52402-4797. **Phone:** 319-368-6460. **Toll-free phone:** 800-248-4504. **Fax:** 319-368-6492. **E-mail:** admission@mmc.mtmercy.edu

Visit CollegeQuest.com for information on majors offered and athletics.

■ *See page 2112 for a narrative description.*

MOUNT ST. CLARE COLLEGE
Clinton, Iowa

- **Independent Roman Catholic**, 4-year, founded 1918
- **Degrees** associate and bachelor's
- **Small-town** 24-acre campus with easy access to Chicago
- **Coed**, 576 undergraduate students, 86% full-time, 55% women, 45% men
- **Minimally difficult** entrance level, 81% of applicants were admitted
- **13:1 student-to-undergraduate faculty ratio**
- **32% graduate** in 6 years or less
- **$12,800 tuition** and fees
- **$10,316 average financial aid** package, $13,219 average indebtedness upon graduation, $1.6 million endowment

Mount St. Clare College holds an annual academic scholarship competition in February. At stake are renewable scholarships that range from $1500 to full tuition in 20 academic areas: accounting, athletic administration, biology, business administration, computer information systems, cytotechnology, education (elementary and secondary), environmental studies, health-care management, journalism, literature, mathematics, music, pre-medical studies, pre-physical therapy, prelaw, psychology, social science, the Spanish language, and visual arts.

Students *Undergraduates:* 496 full-time, 80 part-time. Students come from 13 states and territories, 10 other countries. *The most frequently chosen baccalaureate fields are:* business/marketing, education, liberal arts/general studies. *Graduate:* 79 in graduate degree programs.

From out-of-state	33%	Reside on campus	35%
Age 25 or older	15%	Transferred in	15%
International students	4%	African Americans	7%
Asian Americans/Pacific Islanders	1%	Hispanic Americans	3%

Faculty 71 (38% full-time), 25% with terminal degrees.

Expenses (1999–2000) *One-time required fee:* $20. *Comprehensive fee:* $17,160 includes full-time tuition ($12,580), mandatory fees ($220), and room and board ($4360). *College room only:* $1990. Room and board charges vary according to board plan and housing facility. *Part-time tuition:* $367 per credit hour. *Part-time fees:* $8 per credit hour. Part-time tuition and fees vary according to course load. *Payment plan:* installment. *Waivers:* children of alumni, senior citizens, and employees or children of employees.

Library Mount St. Clare Library. *Operations spending 1999–2000:* $238,779. *Collection:* 78,015 titles, 1,894 serial subscriptions, 1,245 audiovisual materials.

College life *Housing:* on-campus residence required through junior year. *Option:* coed. *Most popular organizations:* student senate, student ambassadors, hall council, Black Student Union, Student Iowa State Education Association.

Campus security 24-hour emergency response devices, student patrols, late-night transport-escort service, controlled dormitory access, self-defense education, lighted pathways.

After graduation 50 organizations recruited on campus 1997–98. 59% of class of 1998 had job offers within 6 months. *Career center:* 1 full-time personnel. Services include job fairs, resume preparation, interview workshops, resume referral, career/interest testing, career counseling, careers library, job bank, job interviews. *Graduate education:* 28% of class of 1999 went directly to graduate and professional school.

Freshmen 355 applied, 286 admitted, 117 enrolled.

Average high school GPA	2.88	SAT verbal scores above 500	50%
SAT math scores above 500	100%	ACT above 18	79%
From top 10% of their h.s. class	5%	From top quarter	16%
From top half	49%	1998 freshmen returning in 1999	59%

Application *Options:* Common Application, early admission. *Application fee:* $20. *Required:* high school transcript. *Required for some:* letters of recommendation; interview. *Recommended:* minimum 2.0 GPA.

Standardized tests *Admission: Required:* SAT I or ACT.

Significant dates *Application deadlines:* 8/15 (freshmen), rolling (transfers). *Financial aid deadline:* 6/1. *Priority date:* 3/1.

Freshman Application Contact
Ms. Waunita M. Sullivan, Director of Enrollment, Mount St. Clare College, 400 North Bluff Boulevard, PO Box 2967, Clinton, IA 52733-2967. **Phone:** 319-242-4023 Ext. 3401. **Toll-free phone:** 800-242-4153 Ext. 3400. **Fax:** 319-242-2003. **E-mail:** admissns@clare.edu

Visit CollegeQuest.com for information on majors offered and athletics. College video available at CollegeQuest.com.

■ *See page 2116 for a narrative description.*

NORTHWESTERN COLLEGE
Orange City, Iowa

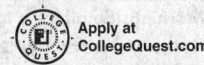

- **Independent**, 4-year, founded 1882, affiliated with Reformed Church in America
- **Degrees** associate and bachelor's

Iowa

- **Rural** 45-acre campus
- **Coed**, 1,219 undergraduate students, 97% full-time, 61% women, 39% men
- **Moderately difficult** entrance level, 92% of applicants were admitted
- **16:1 student-to-undergraduate faculty ratio**
- **54.7% graduate** in 6 years or less
- **$12,270 tuition** and fees
- **$13,471 average financial aid** package, $10,140 average indebtedness upon graduation, $29.3 million endowment

Half of Northwestern's campus has been built or renovated since 1980. The newest buildings say a lot about the College's purpose. New facilities housing nearly all academic departments are important resources for Northwestern's high-quality education. The chapel, student center, cafeteria, and intercollegiate athletic center demonstrate the value of worship and campus life.

Students *Undergraduates:* 1,182 full-time, 37 part-time. Students come from 30 states and territories, 16 other countries. *The most frequently chosen baccalaureate fields are:* business/marketing, biological/life sciences, education.

From out-of-state	36%	Reside on campus	90%
Age 25 or older	3%	Transferred in	5%
International students	3%	African Americans	0.2%
Asian Americans/Pacific Islanders	0.5%	Hispanic Americans	0.4%
Native Americans	0.5%		

Faculty 102 (64% full-time), 43% with terminal degrees.

Expenses (1999–2000) *Comprehensive fee:* $15,770 includes full-time tuition ($12,270) and room and board ($3500). *College room only:* $1500. *Part-time tuition:* $385 per credit hour. Part-time tuition and fees vary according to course load. *Payment plan:* installment. *Waivers:* employees or children of employees.

Library Ramaker Library plus 1 other. *Operations spending 1999–2000:* $399,889. *Collection:* 107,567 titles, 563 serial subscriptions, 5,279 audiovisual materials.

College life *Housing:* on-campus residence required through senior year. *Options:* men-only, women-only, disabled students. *Most popular organizations:* Phi Beta Lambda, Student Ministries Board, Student Iowa State Education Association, Fellowship of Christian Athletes, international club.

Campus security 24-hour emergency response devices, controlled dormitory access.

After graduation 30 organizations recruited on campus 1997–98. 90% of class of 1998 had job offers within 6 months. *Career center:* 1 full-time, 1 part-time personnel. Services include job fairs, resume preparation, interview workshops, resume referral, career/interest testing, career counseling, careers library, job bank, job interviews. *Graduate education:* 9% of class of 1999 went directly to graduate and professional school: 3% theology, 2% graduate arts and sciences, 2% medicine, 1% business, 1% law.

Freshmen 1,080 applied, 998 admitted, 366 enrolled. 2 National Merit Scholars, 32 valedictorians.

Average high school GPA	3.2	SAT verbal scores above 500	78%
SAT math scores above 500	73%	ACT above 18	97%
From top 10% of their h.s. class	28%	From top quarter	57%
From top half	86%	1998 freshmen returning in 1999	75%

Application *Options:* eApply at www.CollegeQuest.com, electronic application, deferred entrance. *Application fee:* $25. *Required:* essay or personal statement; high school transcript; minimum 2.0 GPA; 1 letter of recommendation. *Recommended:* minimum 2.5 GPA; interview.

Standardized tests *Admission: Required:* SAT I or ACT.

Significant dates *Application deadlines:* rolling (freshmen), rolling (transfers). *Notification:* continuous until 8/30 (freshmen). *Financial aid deadline priority date:* 4/1.

Freshman Application Contact
Mr. Ronald K. DeJong, Director of Admissions, Northwestern College, 101 College Lane, Orange City, IA 51041-1996. **Phone:** 712-737-7130. **Toll-free phone:** 800-747-4757. **Fax:** 712-737-7164. **E-mail:** markb@nwciowa.edu
Visit CollegeQuest.com for information on majors offered and athletics. College video available at CollegeQuest.com.

- *See page 2190 for a narrative description.*

PALMER COLLEGE OF CHIROPRACTIC
Davenport, Iowa

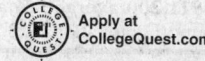
Apply at CollegeQuest.com

- **Independent**, comprehensive, founded 1897
- **Degrees** associate, bachelor's, master's, and first professional
- **Urban** 3-acre campus
- **Coed**, 40 undergraduate students, 70% full-time, 93% women, 8% men
- **Moderately difficult** entrance level, 100% of applicants were admitted
- **$15,705 tuition** and fees
- **$7.8 million endowment**

Part of Palmer Chiropractic University System.

Students *Undergraduates:* 28 full-time, 12 part-time. Students come from 8 states and territories, 1 other country. *The most frequently chosen baccalaureate field is:* interdisciplinary studies. *Graduate:* 1,674 in professional programs, 14 in other graduate degree programs.

From out-of-state	30%	Age 25 or older	37%
Transferred in	15%	International students	3%
Asian Americans/Pacific Islanders	3%	Hispanic Americans	3%

Faculty 67 (79% full-time), 99% with terminal degrees.

Expenses (1999–2000) *One-time required fee:* $150. *Tuition:* full-time $15,645; part-time $200 per credit hour. *Required fees:* full-time $60; $20 per term part-time. Full-time tuition and fees vary according to degree level. Part-time tuition and fees vary according to degree level. *Payment plan:* deferred payment. *Waivers:* employees or children of employees.

Library D. D. Palmer Health Sciences Library. *Operations spending 1999–2000:* $873,360. *Collection:* 49,123 titles, 707 serial subscriptions, 24,020 audiovisual materials.

College life *Housing:* college housing not available. *Social organizations:* local fraternities, local sororities. *Most popular organizations:* Gonstead Club, intramural sports, Campus Guides, Student International Chiropractic Association, Palmer Student Alumni Foundation.

Campus security 24-hour emergency response devices and patrols, late-night transport-escort service.

After graduation *Career center:* 1 full-time personnel. Services include resume preparation, career counseling, careers library, job bank, job interviews.

Freshmen 6 applied, 6 admitted, 6 enrolled.

Average high school GPA	2.8	SAT verbal scores above 500	N/R
SAT math scores above 500	N/R	ACT above 18	N/R
1998 freshmen returning in 1999	94%		

Application *Options:* eApply at www.CollegeQuest.com, Common Application, electronic application, deferred entrance. *Preference* given to students from colleges with whom PCC has an articulation agreement. *Application fee:* $25. *Required:* minimum 2.0 GPA; minimum 2.0 in math, sciences, and English courses.

Significant dates *Application deadline:* rolling (freshmen). *Financial aid deadline:* continuous.

Freshman Application Contact
Dr. David Anderson, Director of Admissions, Palmer College of Chiropractic, 1000 Brady Street, Davenport, IA 52803-5287. **Phone:** 319-884-5656. **Toll-free phone:** 800-722-3648. **Fax:** 319-884-5897. **E-mail:** pcadmit@palmer.edu
Visit CollegeQuest.com for information on majors offered and athletics. College video available at CollegeQuest.com.

ST. AMBROSE UNIVERSITY
Davenport, Iowa

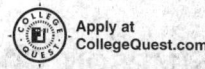
Apply at CollegeQuest.com

- **Independent Roman Catholic**, comprehensive, founded 1882
- **Degrees** bachelor's, master's, doctoral, post-master's, and postbachelor's certificates
- **Urban** 11-acre campus
- **Coed**, 1,924 undergraduate students, 76% full-time, 60% women, 40% men
- **Moderately difficult** entrance level, 85% of applicants were admitted
- **$13,580 tuition** and fees

Peterson's Guide to Four-Year Colleges 2001   www.petersons.com   295

Iowa

St. Ambrose University (continued)
- **$11,200 average financial aid** package, $13,000 average indebtedness upon graduation, $22.1 million endowment

Students *Undergraduates:* 1,455 full-time, 469 part-time. Students come from 19 states and territories, 12 other countries. *Graduate:* 859 in graduate degree programs.

From out-of-state	36%	Reside on campus	45%
Age 25 or older	39%	Transferred in	12%

Faculty 233 (53% full-time).

Expenses (2000–2001) *Comprehensive fee:* $18,730 includes full-time tuition ($13,580) and room and board ($5150). *College room only:* $2270. Full-time tuition and fees vary according to course load and degree level. Room and board charges vary according to board plan and housing facility. *Part-time tuition:* $415 per credit. Part-time tuition and fees vary according to degree level. *Payment plan:* installment. *Waivers:* minority students, children of alumni, adult students, senior citizens, and employees or children of employees.

Library O'Keefe Library plus 1 other. *Operations spending 1999–2000:* $362,192. *Collection:* 115,986 titles, 614 serial subscriptions.

College life *Housing:* on-campus residence required through sophomore year. *Options:* coed, men-only, women-only, disabled students. *Most popular organizations:* Student Government Association, Student Alumni Association, Social Action Group, College Activities Board, Ambrosian's for Peace and Justice.

Campus security 24-hour emergency response devices and patrols, late-night transport-escort service, controlled dormitory access, police officer on campus 10 p.m. to 6 a.m.

After graduation 21 organizations recruited on campus 1997–98. 85% of class of 1998 had job offers within 6 months. *Career center:* 4 full-time personnel. Services include job fairs, resume preparation, interview workshops, resume referral, career/interest testing, career counseling, careers library, job bank, job interviews. *Graduate education:* 18% of class of 1999 went directly to graduate and professional school: 6% business, 6% graduate arts and sciences, 1% education.

Freshmen 1,237 applied, 1,051 admitted, 300 enrolled. 8 National Merit Scholars, 16 valedictorians.

Average high school GPA	3.04	SAT verbal scores above 500	N/R
SAT math scores above 500	N/R	ACT above 18	84%
From top 10% of their h.s. class	13%	From top quarter	33%
From top half	64%	1998 freshmen returning in 1999	70%

Application *Options:* eApply at www.CollegeQuest.com, Common Application, electronic application, deferred entrance. *Application fee:* $25. *Required:* high school transcript; minimum 2.5 GPA; minimum ACT score of 20 or rank in top 50% of high school class. *Required for some:* letters of recommendation; interview. *Recommended:* interview.

Standardized tests *Admission: Required:* SAT I or ACT.

Significant dates *Application deadlines:* rolling (freshmen), rolling (transfers). *Financial aid deadline priority date:* 3/15.

Freshman Application Contact
Ms. Meg Flaherty, Director of Admissions, St. Ambrose University, 518 West Locust, Davenport, IA 52803-2898. **Phone:** 319-333-6300 Ext. 6311. **Toll-free phone:** 800-383-2627. **Fax:** 319-383-8791. **E-mail:** mflahery@saunix.sau.edu

Visit CollegeQuest.com for information on majors offered and athletics. College video available at CollegeQuest.com.

- *See page 2366 for a narrative description.*

SIMPSON COLLEGE
Indianola, Iowa

- **Independent United Methodist**, 4-year, founded 1860
- **Degree** bachelor's
- **Small-town** 68-acre campus
- **Coed**, 1,897 undergraduate students, 69% full-time, 57% women, 43% men
- **Moderately difficult** entrance level, 84% of applicants were admitted
- **17:1** student-to-undergraduate faculty ratio
- **61.7% graduate** in 6 years or less
- **$14,430 tuition** and fees
- **$15,174 average financial aid** package, $16,851 average indebtedness upon graduation, $56.8 million endowment

Simpson is more than a beautiful campus. The College has an outstanding faculty and renowned curricula, including more than 40 majors, minors, and preprofessional programs. A 4-4-1 calendar provides students with many learning opportunities, including internships, career observations, and study programs both abroad and in the United States. Located just 12 miles from Des Moines, Iowa's capital and largest metropolitan area, Simpson's ideal location allows students the opportunity to enjoy both city sophistication and small-town charm.

Students *Undergraduates:* 1,312 full-time, 585 part-time. Students come from 26 states and territories, 10 other countries. *The most frequently chosen baccalaureate fields are:* business/marketing, communications/communication technologies, education.

From out-of-state	11%	Reside on campus	82%
Age 25 or older	26%	Transferred in	4%
International students	1%	African Americans	1%
Asian Americans/Pacific Islanders	1%	Hispanic Americans	1%
Native Americans	1%		

Faculty 110 (73% full-time), 60% with terminal degrees.

Expenses (1999–2000) *Comprehensive fee:* $19,230 includes full-time tuition ($14,300), mandatory fees ($130), and room and board ($4800). *College room only:* $2280. Room and board charges vary according to board plan and housing facility. *Part-time tuition:* $195 per credit. Part-time tuition and fees vary according to class time and course load. *Payment plan:* installment. *Waivers:* employees or children of employees.

Library Dunn Library plus 1 other. *Operations spending 1999–2000:* $591,514. *Collection:* 159,949 titles, 623 serial subscriptions, 1,446 audiovisual materials.

College life *Housing:* on-campus residence required through junior year. *Options:* coed, men-only, women-only. *Social organizations:* national fraternities, national sororities, local fraternities; 23% of eligible men and 31% of eligible women are members. *Most popular organizations:* intramurals, Greek organizations, Religious Life Council, Campus Activities Board, student government.

Campus security 24-hour emergency response devices and patrols, student patrols, late-night transport-escort service, controlled dormitory access.

After graduation 89 organizations recruited on campus 1997–98. 83% of class of 1998 had job offers within 6 months. *Career center:* 3 full-time, 1 part-time personnel. Services include job fairs, resume preparation, interview workshops, resume referral, career/interest testing, career counseling, careers library, job bank, job interviews. *Graduate education:* 16% of class of 1999 went directly to graduate and professional school: 6% graduate arts and sciences, 3% law, 3% medicine, 1% dentistry, 1% education, 1% veterinary medicine.

Freshmen 1,164 applied, 973 admitted, 352 enrolled. 19 valedictorians.

SAT verbal scores above 500	78%	SAT math scores above 500	71%
ACT above 18	100%	From top 10% of their h.s. class	24%
From top quarter	58%	From top half	90%
1998 freshmen returning in 1999	82%		

Application *Options:* early admission, deferred entrance. *Required:* high school transcript; 1 letter of recommendation. *Recommended:* interview; rank in upper 50% of high school class.

Standardized tests *Admission: Required:* SAT I or ACT.

Significant dates *Application deadline:* rolling (transfers). *Financial aid deadline priority date:* 4/1.

Freshman Application Contact
Mr. John Kellogg, Vice President of Enrollment, Simpson College, 701 North C Street, Indianola, IA 50125-1297. **Phone:** 515-961-1624. **Toll-free phone:** 800-362-2454. **Fax:** 515-961-1498. **E-mail:** admiss@simpson.edu

Visit CollegeQuest.com for information on majors offered and athletics. College video available at CollegeQuest.com.

- *See page 2496 for a narrative description.*

Iowa

UNIVERSITY OF DUBUQUE
Dubuque, Iowa

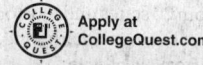
Apply at CollegeQuest.com

- **Independent Presbyterian**, comprehensive, founded 1852
- **Degrees** associate, bachelor's, master's, and first professional
- **Suburban** 56-acre campus
- **Coed**, 680 undergraduate students, 88% full-time, 42% women, 58% men
- **Moderately difficult** entrance level, 91% of applicants were admitted
- **15:1 student-to-undergraduate faculty ratio**
- **$13,530 tuition** and fees
- **$14,582 average financial aid** package, $14,157 average indebtedness upon graduation, $19.4 million endowment

Students *Undergraduates:* 600 full-time, 80 part-time. Students come from 24 states and territories. *The most frequently chosen baccalaureate fields are:* education, social sciences and history, trade and industry. *Graduate:* 104 in professional programs, 172 in other graduate degree programs.

From out-of-state	44%	Reside on campus	45%
Age 25 or older	10%	Transferred in	12%
International students	3%	African Americans	3%
Asian Americans/Pacific Islanders	1%	Hispanic Americans	2%
Native Americans	1%		

Faculty 89 (49% full-time), 53% with terminal degrees.
Expenses (1999–2000) *Comprehensive fee:* $17,810 includes full-time tuition ($13,390), mandatory fees ($140), and room and board ($4280). *College room only:* $2220. Room and board charges vary according to board plan. *Part-time tuition:* $290 per semester hour. *Payment plans:* installment, deferred payment. *Waivers:* children of alumni, senior citizens, and employees or children of employees.
Library Academic Resource Center. *Operations spending 1999–2000:* $440,100. *Collection:* 106,557 titles, 700 serial subscriptions.
College life *Housing:* on-campus residence required through junior year. *Options:* men-only, women-only. *Social organizations:* national fraternities, local fraternities, local sororities; 5% of eligible men and 3% of eligible women are members. *Most popular organizations:* Alpha Phi Omega, Collegiate Singers, Student Activities Board, Student Government Association, Web of Life (environmental science).
Campus security 24-hour patrols, late-night transport-escort service, controlled dormitory access.
After graduation 71 organizations recruited on campus 1997–98. 97% of class of 1998 had job offers within 6 months. *Career center:* 1 full-time personnel. Services include job fairs, resume preparation, resume referral, career/interest testing, career counseling, careers library, job bank, job interviews. *Graduate education:* 67% of class of 1999 went directly to graduate and professional school.
Freshmen 583 applied, 532 admitted, 126 enrolled. 3 valedictorians.

Average high school GPA	3.0	SAT verbal scores above 500	N/R
SAT math scores above 500	N/R	ACT above 18	68%
From top 10% of their h.s. class	10%	From top quarter	30%
From top half	50%	1998 freshmen returning in 1999	58%

Application *Options:* eApply at www.CollegeQuest.com, electronic application. *Application fee:* $25. *Required:* essay or personal statement; high school transcript; minimum 2.0 GPA; 2 letters of recommendation. *Recommended:* interview.
Standardized tests *Admission: Required:* SAT I or ACT.
Significant dates *Application deadlines:* rolling (freshmen), rolling (transfers). *Financial aid deadline priority date:* 4/1.
Freshman Application Contact
Mr. Jesse James, Director of Admissions and Records, University of Dubuque, 2000 University Avenue, Dubuque, IA 52001-5099. **Phone:** 319-589-3214. **Toll-free phone:** 800-722-5583. **Fax:** 319-589-3690. **E-mail:** admssns@dbq.edu
Visit CollegeQuest.com for information on majors offered and athletics.

THE UNIVERSITY OF IOWA
Iowa City, Iowa

- **State-supported**, university, founded 1847
- **Degrees** bachelor's, master's, doctoral, and first professional
- **Small-town** 1,900-acre campus
- **Coed**, 18,770 undergraduate students, 90% full-time, 54% women, 46% men
- **Moderately difficult** entrance level, 83% of applicants were admitted
- **14:1 student-to-undergraduate faculty ratio**
- **63.5% graduate** in 6 years or less
- **$2998 tuition** and fees (in-state); $10,440 (out-of-state)
- **$5981 average financial aid** package, $11,018 average indebtedness upon graduation, $536 million endowment

Students *Undergraduates:* 16,829 full-time, 1,941 part-time. Students come from 51 states and territories, 69 other countries. *The most frequently chosen baccalaureate fields are:* business/marketing, education, social sciences and history. *Graduate:* 2,908 in professional programs, 6,401 in other graduate degree programs.

From out-of-state	28%	Reside on campus	28%
Age 25 or older	10%	Transferred in	7%
International students	1%	African Americans	2%
Asian Americans/Pacific Islanders	3%	Hispanic Americans	2%
Native Americans	0.5%		

Faculty 1,702 (95% full-time), 99% with terminal degrees.
Expenses (1999–2000) *Tuition, state resident:* full-time $2786; part-time $117 per semester hour. *Tuition, nonresident:* full-time $10,228; part-time $427 per semester hour. *Required fees:* full-time $212; $106 per term part-time. Full-time tuition and fees vary according to course load and program. Part-time tuition and fees vary according to course load. *College room and board:* $4370; room only: $2415. Room and board charges vary according to board plan and housing facility. *Payment plan:* installment.
Library Main Library plus 12 others. *Operations spending 1999–2000:* $18.7 million. *Collection:* 3.9 million titles, 47,401 serial subscriptions.
College life *Housing:* Option: coed. *Social organizations:* national fraternities, national sororities; 11% of eligible men and 12% of eligible women are members. *Most popular organizations:* Association of Students of Engineering, Association of Residence Halls, Newman Center, Friendship Association of Chinese Scholars, May Co.
Campus security 24-hour emergency response devices and patrols, late-night transport-escort service, controlled dormitory access.
After graduation 320 organizations recruited on campus 1997-98. *Career center:* Services include job fairs, resume preparation, interview workshops, resume referral, career/interest testing, career counseling, careers library, job bank, job interviews, online resume. *Major awards:* 6 Fulbright Scholars.
Freshmen 11,358 applied, 9,437 admitted, 3,859 enrolled. 30 National Merit Scholars, 146 valedictorians.

Average high school GPA	3.45	SAT verbal scores above 500	80%
SAT math scores above 500	86%	ACT above 18	99%
From top 10% of their h.s. class	21%	From top quarter	50%
From top half	89%	1998 freshmen returning in 1999	82%

Application *Options:* electronic application, early admission, deferred entrance. *Application fee:* $30. *Required:* high school transcript.
Standardized tests *Admission: Required:* SAT I or ACT.
Significant dates *Application deadlines:* 5/15 (freshmen), 5/15 (transfers). *Financial aid deadline priority date:* 1/1.
Freshman Application Contact
Mr. Michael Barron, Director of Admissions, The University of Iowa, 107 Calvin Hall, Iowa City, IA 52242. **Phone:** 319-335-3847. **Toll-free phone:** 800-553-4692. **Fax:** 319-335-1535. **E-mail:** admissions@uiowa.edu
Visit CollegeQuest.com for information on majors offered and athletics. Electronic viewbook available at CollegeQuest.com.

UNIVERSITY OF NORTHERN IOWA
Cedar Falls, Iowa

- **State-supported**, comprehensive, founded 1876
- **Degrees** bachelor's, master's, and doctoral
- **Small-town** 940-acre campus
- **Coed**, 12,100 undergraduate students, 89% full-time, 57% women, 43% men
- **Moderately difficult** entrance level, 82% of applicants were admitted
- **16:1 student-to-undergraduate faculty ratio**
- **62.2% graduate** in 6 years or less
- **$3130 tuition** and fees (in-state); $8094 (out-of-state)

Peterson's Guide to Four-Year Colleges 2001   www.petersons.com

Iowa

University of Northern Iowa (continued)
- **$4771 average financial aid** package, $16,983 average indebtedness upon graduation, $42.4 million endowment

Part of Iowa State Board of Regents.

Students *Undergraduates:* 10,716 full-time, 1,384 part-time. Students come from 45 states and territories, 67 other countries. *The most frequently chosen baccalaureate fields are:* business/marketing, education, social sciences and history. *Graduate:* 1,711 in graduate degree programs.

From out-of-state	4%	Reside on campus	60%
Age 25 or older	9%	Transferred in	9%
International students	1%	African Americans	2%
Asian Americans/Pacific Islanders	1%	Hispanic Americans	1%
Native Americans	0.2%		

Faculty 880 (76% full-time), 60% with terminal degrees.

Expenses (2000–2001) *Tuition, state resident:* full-time $2906; part-time $122 per semester hour. *Tuition, nonresident:* full-time $7870; part-time $328 per semester hour. *Required fees:* full-time $224; $15 per term part-time. Part-time tuition and fees vary according to course load. *College room and board:* $4200; room only: $1927. Room and board charges vary according to board plan and housing facility. *Payment plan:* installment.

Library Rod Library plus 1 other. *Operations spending 1999–2000:* $5.3 million. *Collection:* 977,485 titles, 19,037 audiovisual materials.

College life *Housing: Options:* coed, men-only, women-only. *Social organizations:* national fraternities, national sororities; 5% of eligible men and 4% of eligible women are members. *Most popular organizations:* American Marketing Association, Public Relations Student Society, Iowa State Education Association, Greek system, United Students of Iowa.

Campus security 24-hour emergency response devices and patrols, student patrols, late-night transport-escort service.

After graduation 2,116 organizations recruited on campus 1997–98. 86% of class of 1998 had job offers within 6 months. *Career center:* 16 full-time, 2 part-time personnel. Services include job fairs, resume preparation, interview workshops, resume referral, career counseling, careers library, job bank, job interviews. *Graduate education:* 13% of class of 1999 went directly to graduate and professional school: 9% graduate arts and sciences, 1% business, 1% education, 1% law, 1% medicine.

Freshmen 4,700 applied, 3,851 admitted, 2,176 enrolled. 102 valedictorians.

SAT verbal scores above 500	N/R	SAT math scores above 500	N/R
ACT above 18	95%	From top 10% of their h.s. class	18%
From top quarter	50%	From top half	91%
1998 freshmen returning in 1999	81%		

Application *Option:* electronic application. *Application fee:* $20. *Required:* high school transcript. *Required for some:* interview.

Standardized tests *Admission: Required:* SAT I or ACT. *Recommended:* ACT.

Significant dates *Application deadlines:* 8/15 (freshmen), 8/15 (transfers). *Financial aid deadline:* continuous.

Freshman Application Contact
Mr. Clark Elmer, Director of Enrollment Management and Admissions, University of Northern Iowa, 120 Gilchrist Hall, Cedar Falls, IA 50614-0018. **Phone:** 319-273-2281. **Toll-free phone:** 800-772-2037. **Fax:** 319-273-2885. **E-mail:** admissions@uni.edu

Visit CollegeQuest.com for information on majors offered and athletics. College video available at CollegeQuest.com.

UPPER IOWA UNIVERSITY
Fayette, Iowa

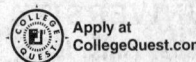

- **Independent**, comprehensive, founded 1857
- **Degrees** associate, bachelor's, and master's (also offers continuing education program with significant enrollment not reflected in profile)
- **Rural** 80-acre campus
- **Coed**, 671 undergraduate students, 97% full-time, 38% women, 62% men
- **Moderately difficult** entrance level, 74% of applicants were admitted
- **16:1** student-to-undergraduate faculty ratio
- **$10,752 tuition** and fees

Students *Undergraduates:* 652 full-time, 19 part-time. Students come from 20 states and territories. *The most frequently chosen baccalaureate fields are:* business/marketing, education, psychology.

From out-of-state	40%	Reside on campus	70%
Transferred in	28%		

Faculty 52 (62% full-time), 27% with terminal degrees.

Expenses (1999–2000) *Comprehensive fee:* $14,908 includes full-time tuition ($10,752) and room and board ($4156). Full-time tuition and fees vary according to location. *Part-time tuition:* $360 per semester hour. Part-time tuition and fees vary according to location. *Payment plan:* installment. *Waivers:* employees or children of employees.

Library Henderson Wilder Library. *Collection:* 98,007 titles, 284 serial subscriptions, 3,818 audiovisual materials.

College life *Housing:* on-campus residence required through sophomore year. *Options:* coed, men-only, women-only. *Social organizations:* local fraternities, local sororities; 30% of eligible men and 30% of eligible women are members. *Most popular organizations:* Outdoor Pursuits, Sigma Delta Phi, Alpha Nu Omega, psychology club, Campus Events Council.

Campus security Late-night transport-escort service, controlled dormitory access.

After graduation 4 organizations recruited on campus 1997–98. 85% of class of 1998 had job offers within 6 months. *Career center:* 1 full-time, 1 part-time personnel. Services include job fairs, resume preparation, interview workshops, resume referral, career/interest testing, career counseling, careers library, job bank, job interviews.

Freshmen 529 applied, 391 admitted, 140 enrolled. 2 class presidents, 4 valedictorians, 25 student government officers.

Average high school GPA	2.86	SAT verbal scores above 500	N/R
SAT math scores above 500	N/R	ACT above 18	73%
From top 10% of their h.s. class	5%	From top quarter	20%
From top half	70%	1998 freshmen returning in 1999	61%

Application *Options:* eApply at www.CollegeQuest.com, Common Application, early admission, deferred entrance. *Application fee:* $15. *Required:* high school transcript; minimum 2.0 GPA. *Required for some:* essay or personal statement; letters of recommendation; interview.

Standardized tests *Admission: Required:* SAT I or ACT.

Significant dates *Application deadlines:* rolling (freshmen), rolling (transfers). *Financial aid deadline priority date:* 6/1.

Freshman Application Contact
Mr. Kent McElvania, Director of Admissions, Upper Iowa University, Box 1859, Fayette, IA 52142-1857. **Phone:** 319-425-5281 Ext. 5279. **Toll-free phone:** 800-553-4150. **Fax:** 319-425-5277. **E-mail:** admission@uiu.edu

Visit CollegeQuest.com for information on majors offered and athletics.

WALDORF COLLEGE
Forest City, Iowa

- **Independent Lutheran**, primarily 2-year, founded 1903
- **Degrees** associate and bachelor's
- **Small-town** 29-acre campus
- **Coed**, 291 undergraduate students, 80% full-time, 45% women, 55% men
- **Moderately difficult** entrance level
- **12:1** student-to-undergraduate faculty ratio
- **$13,522 tuition** and fees

Faculty 53 (68% full-time), 30% with terminal degrees.

Admissions Office Contact
Waldorf College, 106 South 6th Street, Forest City, IA 50436. **Toll-free phone:** 800-292-1903. **Fax:** 515-582-8194. **E-mail:** admissions@waldorf.edu

Visit CollegeQuest.com for information on majors offered and athletics. College video available at CollegeQuest.com.

WARTBURG COLLEGE
Waverly, Iowa

- **Independent Lutheran**, 4-year, founded 1852
- **Degree** bachelor's
- **Small-town** 118-acre campus

Iowa

- **Coed**, 1,499 undergraduate students, 98% full-time, 57% women, 43% men
- **Moderately difficult** entrance level, 87% of applicants were admitted
- **14:1 student-to-undergraduate faculty ratio**
- **62% graduate** in 6 years or less
- **$15,765 tuition** and fees
- **$14,306 average financial aid** package, $14,826 average indebtedness upon graduation, $33.1 million endowment

Wartburg's integrated approach to education combines the liberal arts with an emphasis on leadership education and global and multicultural studies. Cultural immersion programs offer academic credit and give students the opportunity to live and work in Australia, Brazil, China, England, France, Germany, Ghana, Guyana, Indonesia, Jamaica, Mexico, Palestine, Spain, Tanzania, and Turkey.

Students *Undergraduates:* 1,476 full-time, 23 part-time. Students come from 26 states and territories, 25 other countries. *The most frequently chosen baccalaureate fields are:* business/marketing, biological/life sciences, education.

From out-of-state	22%	Reside on campus	76%
Age 25 or older	3%	Transferred in	4%
International students	4%	African Americans	4%
Asian Americans/Pacific Islanders	1%	Hispanic Americans	1%
Native Americans	0.3%		

Faculty 142 (66% full-time), 52% with terminal degrees.

Expenses (2000–2001) *Comprehensive fee:* $20,165 includes full-time tuition ($15,510), mandatory fees ($255), and room and board ($4400). *College room only:* $2100. Room and board charges vary according to board plan and housing facility. Part-time tuition and fees vary according to class time and course load. *Payment plan:* installment. *Waivers:* senior citizens and employees or children of employees.

Library Engelbrecht Library. *Operations spending 1999–2000:* $523,824. *Collection:* 104,140 titles, 732 serial subscriptions, 2,260 audiovisual materials.

College life *Housing:* on-campus residence required through senior year. *Options:* coed, men-only, women-only, disabled students. *Most popular organizations:* Entertainment To Knight, Wartburg choir, Student Senate, campus ministry, Wartburg band.

Campus security 24-hour emergency response devices and patrols, late-night transport-escort service, controlled dormitory access.

After graduation 15 organizations recruited on campus 1997–98. 74% of class of 1998 had job offers within 6 months. *Career center:* 2 full-time personnel. Services include job fairs, resume preparation, interview workshops, resume referral, career/interest testing, career counseling, careers library, job bank, job interviews.

Freshmen 1,385 applied, 1,201 admitted, 411 enrolled. 4 National Merit Scholars.

Average high school GPA	3.5	SAT verbal scores above 500	77%
SAT math scores above 500	79%	ACT above 18	86%
From top 10% of their h.s. class	35%	From top quarter	59%
From top half	86%	1998 freshmen returning in 1999	77%

Application *Options:* eApply at www.CollegeQuest.com, Common Application, deferred entrance. *Application fee:* $20. *Required:* high school transcript; minimum 2.0 GPA; letters of recommendation. *Required for some:* interview. *Recommended:* interview.

Significant dates *Application deadlines:* 6/1 (freshmen), 12/1 (transfers). *Financial aid deadline priority date:* 3/1.

Freshman Application Contact
Doug Bowman, Director of Admissions, Wartburg College, 222 Ninth Street, NW, PO Box 1003, Waverly, IA 50677-1003. **Phone:** 319-352-8264. **Toll-free phone:** 800-772-2085. **Fax:** 319-352-8279. **E-mail:** admissions@wartburg.edu

Visit CollegeQuest.com for information on majors offered and athletics. College video and electronic viewbook available at CollegeQuest.com.

■ *See page 2912 for a narrative description.*

WILLIAM PENN UNIVERSITY
Oskaloosa, Iowa

- **Independent**, 4-year, founded 1873, affiliated with Society of Friends
- **Degree** bachelor's
- **Rural** 40-acre campus with easy access to Des Moines
- **Coed**, 1,252 undergraduate students, 96% full-time, 53% women, 47% men
- **Moderately difficult** entrance level, 78% of applicants were admitted
- **14:1 student-to-undergraduate faculty ratio**
- **$12,770 tuition** and fees
- **$9305 average financial aid** package, $3.9 million endowment

Students *Undergraduates:* 1,208 full-time, 44 part-time. Students come from 41 states and territories, 2 other countries. *The most frequently chosen baccalaureate fields are:* business/marketing, education, engineering/engineering technologies.

From out-of-state	36%	Reside on campus	40%
Age 25 or older	24%	Transferred in	10%
International students	1%	African Americans	8%
Asian Americans/Pacific Islanders	1%	Hispanic Americans	2%
Native Americans	0.4%		

Faculty 59 (61% full-time), 24% with terminal degrees.

Expenses (2000–2001) *Comprehensive fee:* $16,910 includes full-time tuition ($12,400), mandatory fees ($370), and room and board ($4140). *Part-time tuition:* $200 per credit hour. *Part-time fees:* $12 per credit hour. Part-time tuition and fees vary according to course load. *Payment plan:* installment. *Waivers:* senior citizens and employees or children of employees.

Library Wilcox Library. *Collection:* 72,907 titles, 354 serial subscriptions, 738 audiovisual materials.

College life *Housing:* on-campus residence required through junior year. *Options:* coed, women-only. *Social organizations:* national fraternities, local fraternities, local sororities; 10% of eligible men and 10% of eligible women are members. *Most popular organizations:* Fellowship of Christian Athletes, Lettermen's Club, Literacy Tutoring Project, student government.

Campus security 24-hour emergency response devices and patrols, controlled dormitory access.

After graduation 40 organizations recruited on campus 1997–98. *Career center:* 2 part-time personnel. Services include job fairs, resume preparation, interview workshops, career/interest testing, career counseling, careers library, job bank, job interviews.

Freshmen 579 applied, 453 admitted, 440 enrolled.

SAT verbal scores above 500	N/R	SAT math scores above 500	N/R
ACT above 18	82%	From top quarter of their h.s. class	18%
From top half	48%	1998 freshmen returning in 1999	55%

Application *Options:* electronic application, early admission, deferred entrance. *Application fee:* $20. *Required:* high school transcript; minimum 2.0 GPA. *Required for some:* essay or personal statement; letters of recommendation; interview.

Standardized tests *Admission:* Required: SAT I and SAT II or ACT.

Significant dates *Financial aid deadline priority date:* 4/15.

Freshman Application Contact
Mrs. Mary Boyd, Director of Admissions, William Penn University, 201 Trueblood Avenue, Oskaloosa, IA 52577. **Phone:** 515-673-1012 Ext. 2015. **Toll-free phone:** 800-779-7366. **Fax:** 515-673-1396. **E-mail:** admissions@wmpenn.edu

Visit CollegeQuest.com for information on majors offered and athletics. Electronic viewbook available at CollegeQuest.com.

■ *See page 3002 for a narrative description.*

Kansas

KANSAS

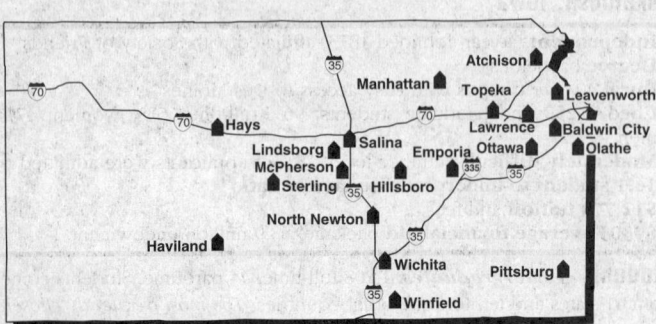

BAKER UNIVERSITY
Baldwin City, Kansas

- **Independent United Methodist**, comprehensive, founded 1858
- **Degrees** associate, bachelor's, and master's
- **Small-town** 26-acre campus with easy access to Kansas City
- **Coed**, 1,741 undergraduate students, 47% full-time, 60% women, 40% men
- **Moderately difficult** entrance level, 82% of applicants were admitted
- **12:1 student-to-undergraduate faculty ratio**
- **$11,750 tuition** and fees
- **$29.6 million endowment**

Students *Undergraduates:* 814 full-time, 927 part-time. Students come from 18 states and territories, 9 other countries. *The most frequently chosen baccalaureate fields are:* business/marketing, education, health professions and related sciences. *Graduate:* 918 in graduate degree programs.

From out-of-state	33%	Reside on campus	90%
Age 25 or older	49%	Transferred in	3%
International students	1%	African Americans	6%
Asian Americans/Pacific Islanders	1%	Hispanic Americans	3%
Native Americans	1%		

Faculty 62 full-time.
Expenses (1999–2000) *One-time required fee:* $80. *Comprehensive fee:* $16,450 includes full-time tuition ($11,750) and room and board ($4700). Full-time tuition and fees vary according to location and program. Room and board charges vary according to board plan and housing facility. *Part-time tuition:* $455 per credit hour. Part-time tuition and fees vary according to course load. *Payment plan:* installment. *Waivers:* senior citizens and employees or children of employees.
Library Collins Library. *Operations spending 1999–2000:* $430,138. *Collection:* 75,000 titles, 342 serial subscriptions, 1,300 audiovisual materials.
College life *Housing:* on-campus residence required through senior year. *Options:* coed, men-only, women-only, disabled students. *Social organizations:* national fraternities, national sororities, local fraternities; 50% of eligible men and 50% of eligible women are members. *Most popular organizations:* Delta Sigma Pi, Earth We Are, Mungano, Fellowship of Christian Athletes.
Campus security 24-hour emergency response devices and patrols, student patrols.
After graduation 63 organizations recruited on campus 1997–98. 68% of class of 1998 had job offers within 6 months. *Career center:* 2 full-time, 1 part-time personnel. Services include job fairs, resume preparation, interview workshops, resume referral, career/interest testing, career counseling, careers library, job bank, job interviews. *Graduate education:* 27% of class of 1999 went directly to graduate and professional school.
Freshmen 594 applied, 486 admitted, 229 enrolled.

Average high school GPA	3.49	SAT verbal scores above 500	66%
SAT math scores above 500	80%	ACT above 18	96%
From top 10% of their h.s. class	39%	From top quarter	65%
From top half	74%	1998 freshmen returning in 1999	86%

Application *Options:* electronic application, deferred entrance. *Application fee:* $20. *Required:* high school transcript; minimum 3.0 GPA; 1 letter of recommendation. *Required for some:* essay or personal statement; interview.
Standardized tests *Admission: Required:* SAT I or ACT.
Significant dates *Application deadlines:* rolling (freshmen), rolling (transfers). *Financial aid deadline priority date:* 3/1.

Freshman Application Contact
Ms. Paige Illum, Director of Admission, Baker University, PO Box 65, Baldwin City, KS 66006-0065. **Phone:** 785-594-6451 Ext. 458. **Toll-free phone:** 800-873-4282. **Fax:** 785-594-6721. **E-mail:** admission@george.bakeru.edu
Visit CollegeQuest.com for information on majors offered and athletics. Electronic viewbook available at CollegeQuest.com.

■ *See page 1220 for a narrative description.*

BARCLAY COLLEGE
Haviland, Kansas

- **Independent**, 4-year, founded 1917, affiliated with Society of Friends
- **Degrees** associate and bachelor's
- **Rural** 13-acre campus
- **Coed**, 169 undergraduate students, 93% full-time, 50% women, 50% men
- **Minimally difficult** entrance level, 29% of applicants were admitted
- **11:1 student-to-undergraduate faculty ratio**
- **$6250 tuition** and fees
- **$7500 average financial aid** package, $10,000 average indebtedness upon graduation, $263,836 endowment

Barclay College is a coed, 4-year, accredited Christian College located in Haviland, Kansas, and was founded in 1917 by the Evangelical Friends. Barclay offers bachelor's degrees in bible/theology, business administration, church music, Christian school elementary education, English, pastoral ministries, psychology/family counseling, and youth ministries and 2 associate degrees. Tuition, room and board, and fees total $10,495.

Students *Undergraduates:* 157 full-time, 12 part-time. Students come from 15 states and territories, 2 other countries. *The most frequently chosen baccalaureate fields are:* business/marketing, philosophy, psychology.

From out-of-state	33%	Age 25 or older	47%
Transferred in	10%	International students	1%
African Americans	4%	Asian Americans/Pacific Islanders	2%
Hispanic Americans	4%	Native Americans	1%

Faculty 35 (23% full-time), 17% with terminal degrees.
Expenses (1999–2000) *Comprehensive fee:* $9350 includes full-time tuition ($5650), mandatory fees ($600), and room and board ($3100). *College room only:* $950. Room and board charges vary according to board plan. *Part-time tuition:* $230 per credit hour. *Part-time fees:* $35 per credit hour. Part-time tuition and fees vary according to course load. *Payment plan:* installment. *Waivers:* employees or children of employees.
Library Worden Memorial Library. *Operations spending 1999–2000:* $48,040. *Collection:* 55,480 titles, 194 serial subscriptions.
College life *Housing:* on-campus residence required through senior year. *Options:* men-only, women-only. *Most popular organizations:* pep club, drama club, missions club.
Campus security Student patrols.
After graduation 3 organizations recruited on campus 1997–98. 80% of class of 1998 had job offers within 6 months. *Career center:* 1 full-time, 1 part-time personnel. Services include resume preparation, career counseling, careers library, job bank. *Graduate education:* 8% of class of 1999 went directly to graduate and professional school: 4% business, 4% theology.
Freshmen 78 applied, 23 admitted, 23 enrolled.

Average high school GPA	3.13	SAT verbal scores above 500	N/R
SAT math scores above 500	N/R	ACT above 18	94%
From top 10% of their h.s. class	33%	From top quarter	66%
From top half	66%		

Application *Options:* early admission, deferred entrance. *Application fee:* $25. *Required:* essay or personal statement; high school transcript; 3 letters of recommendation.
Standardized tests *Admission: Required:* SAT I or ACT.
Significant dates *Application deadlines:* 9/1 (freshmen), 9/1 (transfers). *Financial aid deadline priority date:* 3/15.
Freshman Application Contact
Mr. Ryan Haase, Director of Admissions, Barclay College, 607 North Kingman, Haviland, KS 67059. **Phone:** 316-862-5252 Ext. 41. **Toll-free phone:** 800-862-0226. **Fax:** 316-862-5403. **E-mail:** barclaycollege@havilandteko.com
Visit CollegeQuest.com for information on majors offered and athletics.

Kansas

BENEDICTINE COLLEGE
Atchison, Kansas

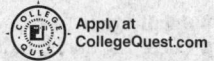

- **Independent Roman Catholic**, comprehensive, founded 1859
- **Degrees** associate, bachelor's, and master's
- **Small-town** 225-acre campus with easy access to Kansas City
- **Coed**, 1,084 undergraduate students, 73% full-time, 45% women, 55% men
- **Moderately difficult** entrance level, 97% of applicants were admitted
- **15:1 student-to-undergraduate faculty ratio**
- **42% graduate** in 6 years or less
- **$12,316 tuition** and fees
- **$12,960 average financial aid** package, $15,539 average indebtedness upon graduation, $4.6 million endowment

Benedictine College, America's Discovery College, is a 4-year Catholic, residential, liberal arts Benedictine college that provides an outstanding education for students of all backgrounds and faiths. Benedictine is distinguished by its distinctive student-centered academic program that offers students exceptional opportunities for research and personal growth.

Students *Undergraduates:* 795 full-time, 289 part-time. Students come from 34 states and territories, 15 other countries. *The most frequently chosen baccalaureate fields are:* education, biological/life sciences, social sciences and history. *Graduate:* 44 in graduate degree programs.

From out-of-state	53%	Reside on campus	75%
Age 25 or older	6%	Transferred in	6%
International students	3%	African Americans	4%
Asian Americans/Pacific Islanders	1%	Hispanic Americans	6%
Native Americans	0.5%		

Faculty 76 (67% full-time), 55% with terminal degrees.

Expenses (1999–2000) *Comprehensive fee:* $17,116 includes full-time tuition ($12,116), mandatory fees ($200), and room and board ($4800). *College room only:* $2140. Full-time tuition and fees vary according to course load and degree level. Room and board charges vary according to board plan and housing facility. *Part-time tuition:* $230 per credit hour. *Part-time fees:* $100 per term part-time. Part-time tuition and fees vary according to course load and degree level. *Payment plan:* installment. *Waivers:* senior citizens and employees or children of employees.

Library Benedictine College Library. *Operations spending 1999–2000:* $108,389. *Collection:* 328,143 titles, 30,999 serial subscriptions, 2,048 audiovisual materials.

College life *Housing:* on-campus residence required through sophomore year. *Options:* men-only, women-only. *Most popular organizations:* student government, Students in Free Enterprise, Knights of Columbus, Concert Chorale/Chamber Singers, Campus Activities Board.

Campus security 24-hour emergency response devices and patrols, late-night transport-escort service.

After graduation 24 organizations recruited on campus 1997–98. 99% of class of 1998 had job offers within 6 months. *Career center:* 1 full-time, 1 part-time personnel. Services include job fairs, resume preparation, resume referral, career counseling, careers library, job bank, job interviews.

Freshmen 644 applied, 622 admitted, 246 enrolled. 5 class presidents, 15 valedictorians.

Average high school GPA	3.14	SAT verbal scores above 500	51%
SAT math scores above 500	54%	ACT above 18	94%
From top 10% of their h.s. class	13%	From top quarter	31%
From top half	59%	1998 freshmen returning in 1999	75%

Application *Options:* eApply at www.CollegeQuest.com, Common Application, electronic application, deferred entrance. *Application fee:* $25. *Required:* high school transcript; minimum 2.0 GPA; letters of recommendation. *Required for some:* interview.

Standardized tests *Admission: Required:* SAT I or ACT.

Significant dates *Financial aid deadline:* continuous.

Freshman Application Contact
Ms. Kelly Vowels, Dean of Enrollment Management, Benedictine College, 1020 N. 2nd Street, Atchison, KS 66002. **Phone:** 913-367-5340 Ext. 2476. **Toll-free phone:** 800-467-5340. **Fax:** 913-367-3673. **E-mail:** bcadmiss@benedictine.edu

Visit CollegeQuest.com for information on majors offered and athletics. College video and electronic viewbook available at CollegeQuest.com.

■ *See page 1250 for a narrative description.*

BETHANY COLLEGE
Lindsborg, Kansas

- **Independent Lutheran**, 4-year, founded 1881
- **Degree** bachelor's
- **Small-town** 80-acre campus
- **Coed**, 587 undergraduate students, 93% full-time, 45% women, 55% men
- **Moderately difficult** entrance level, 73% of applicants were admitted
- **12:1 student-to-undergraduate faculty ratio**
- **43% graduate** in 6 years or less
- **$12,304 tuition** and fees
- **$7438 average financial aid** package, $15,296 average indebtedness upon graduation, $14.3 million endowment

Students *Undergraduates:* 546 full-time, 41 part-time. Students come from 20 states and territories, 9 other countries. *The most frequently chosen baccalaureate fields are:* business/marketing, education, protective services/public administration.

From out-of-state	35%	Reside on campus	84%
Age 25 or older	31%	Transferred in	9%
International students	1%	African Americans	5%
Asian Americans/Pacific Islanders	1%	Hispanic Americans	4%
Native Americans	2%		

Faculty 65 (55% full-time), 51% with terminal degrees.

Expenses (2000–2001, estimated) *Comprehensive fee:* $16,084 includes full-time tuition ($12,154), mandatory fees ($150), and room and board ($3780). *College room only:* $1660. Full-time tuition and fees vary according to location. Room and board charges vary according to board plan and housing facility. *Part-time tuition:* $195 per credit hour. Part-time tuition and fees vary according to course load. *Payment plan:* installment. *Waivers:* employees or children of employees.

Library Wallerstedt Library plus 1 other. *Operations spending 1999–2000:* $154,561. *Collection:* 609 serial subscriptions, 3,518 audiovisual materials.

College life *Housing:* on-campus residence required through senior year. *Options:* coed, women-only. *Social organizations:* local fraternities, local sororities; 15% of eligible men and 17% of eligible women are members. *Most popular organizations:* business club, Bethany Student Education Association, Multicultural Student Association.

Campus security 24-hour emergency response devices, student patrols, late-night transport-escort service, controlled dormitory access, night patrols by security personnel.

After graduation 25 organizations recruited on campus 1997–98. 88% of class of 1998 had job offers within 6 months. *Career center:* 2 full-time, 6 part-time personnel. Services include job fairs, resume preparation, resume referral, career/interest testing, career counseling, careers library, job bank, job interviews, career seminars. *Graduate education:* 22% of class of 1999 went directly to graduate and professional school: 10% graduate arts and sciences, 4% business, 3% medicine, 2% education, 1% engineering, 1% veterinary medicine.

Freshmen 673 applied, 493 admitted, 176 enrolled.

Average high school GPA	3.31	SAT verbal scores above 500	N/R
SAT math scores above 500	N/R	ACT above 18	82%
1998 freshmen returning in 1999	66%		

Application *Option:* deferred entrance. *Application fee:* $20. *Required:* high school transcript; minimum 2.5 GPA. *Required for some:* essay or personal statement; letters of recommendation; interview.

Standardized tests *Admission: Required:* SAT I or ACT. *Recommended:* ACT.

Significant dates *Application deadlines:* 7/1 (freshmen), rolling (transfers). *Financial aid deadline priority date:* 3/15.

Freshman Application Contact
Daniel McKinney, Dean of Admissions and Financial Aid, Bethany College, 421 North First Street, Lindsborg, KS 67456-1897. **Phone:** 785-227-3311 Ext. 8108. **Toll-free phone:** 800-826-2281. **Fax:** 785-227-2860. **E-mail:** admissions@bethany.bethanylb.edu

Visit CollegeQuest.com for information on majors offered and athletics. College video available at CollegeQuest.com.

Kansas

BETHEL COLLEGE
North Newton, Kansas

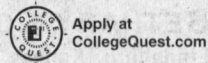 Apply at CollegeQuest.com

- **Independent**, 4-year, founded 1887, affiliated with General Conference Mennonite Church
- **Degree** bachelor's
- **Small-town** 60-acre campus with easy access to Wichita
- **Coed**, 462 undergraduate students, 92% full-time, 52% women, 48% men
- **Moderately difficult** entrance level, 84% of applicants were admitted
- **10:1 student-to-undergraduate faculty ratio**
- **51.3% graduate** in 6 years or less
- **$11,800 tuition** and fees
- **$12,777 average financial aid** package, $13,610 average indebtedness upon graduation, $15.9 million endowment

Students *Undergraduates:* 427 full-time, 35 part-time. Students come from 24 states and territories, 13 other countries. *The most frequently chosen baccalaureate fields are:* business/marketing, health professions and related sciences, visual/performing arts.

From out-of-state	31%	Reside on campus	66%
Age 25 or older	15%	Transferred in	7%

Faculty 65 (60% full-time), 63% with terminal degrees.

Expenses (2000–2001) *Comprehensive fee:* $16,500 includes full-time tuition ($11,700), mandatory fees ($100), and room and board ($4700). *College room only:* $2200. Full-time tuition and fees vary according to course load. Room and board charges vary according to board plan and housing facility. *Part-time tuition:* $430 per credit hour. Part-time tuition and fees vary according to course load. *Payment plan:* installment. *Waivers:* senior citizens and employees or children of employees.

Library Mantz Library plus 1 other. *Operations spending 1999–2000:* $261,000. *Collection:* 128,039 titles, 625 serial subscriptions, 154,354 audiovisual materials.

College life *Housing:* on-campus residence required through senior year. *Options:* coed, men-only, women-only. *Most popular organizations:* Bethel College Service Corps, The Collegian (newspaper), Student Alumni Association, Student Senate, Student Activities Board.

Campus security 24-hour emergency response devices, student patrols, community police patrols.

After graduation 35 organizations recruited on campus 1997–98. 67% of class of 1998 had job offers within 6 months. *Career center:* 1 full-time personnel. Services include job fairs, resume preparation, interview workshops, resume referral, career/interest testing, career counseling, careers library, job bank, job interviews. *Graduate education:* 11% of class of 1999 went directly to graduate and professional school.

Freshmen 303 applied, 255 admitted, 120 enrolled. 8 valedictorians.

Average high school GPA	3.38	SAT verbal scores above 500	N/R
SAT math scores above 500	N/R	ACT above 18	96%
From top 10% of their h.s. class	17%	From top quarter	36%
From top half	68%	1998 freshmen returning in 1999	67%

Application *Options:* eApply at www.CollegeQuest.com, deferred entrance. *Application fee:* $20. *Required:* high school transcript; minimum 2.5 GPA. *Required for some:* essay or personal statement; 2 letters of recommendation. *Recommended:* interview.

Standardized tests *Admission: Required:* SAT I or ACT.

Significant dates *Application deadlines:* 8/15 (freshmen), 8/15 (transfers). *Financial aid deadline priority date:* 3/1.

Freshman Application Contact Dr. Shirley King, Dean of Enrollment Services, Bethel College, 300 East 27th Street, North Newton, KS 67117. **Phone:** 316-283-2500 Ext. 230. **Toll-free phone:** 800-522-1887. **Fax:** 316-284-5286. **E-mail:** admissions@bethelks.edu

Visit CollegeQuest.com for information on majors offered and athletics.

- *See page 1268 for a narrative description.*

CENTRAL CHRISTIAN COLLEGE OF KANSAS
McPherson, Kansas

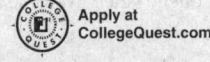 Apply at CollegeQuest.com

- **Independent Free Methodist**, primarily 2-year, founded 1884
- **Degrees** associate and bachelor's
- **Small-town** 16-acre campus
- **Coed**, 226 undergraduate students, 100% full-time, 49% women, 51% men
- **Minimally difficult** entrance level
- **14:1 student-to-undergraduate faculty ratio**
- **$10,600 tuition** and fees

Faculty 27 (63% full-time), 11% with terminal degrees.

Admissions Office Contact Central Christian College of Kansas, PO Box 1403, McPherson, KS 67460. **Toll-free phone:** 800-835-0078. **Fax:** 316-241-6032. **E-mail:** admissions@centralchristian.edu

Visit CollegeQuest.com for information on majors offered and athletics. College video available at CollegeQuest.com.

EMPORIA STATE UNIVERSITY
Emporia, Kansas

- **State-supported**, comprehensive, founded 1863
- **Degrees** bachelor's, master's, and doctoral
- **Small-town** 207-acre campus with easy access to Wichita
- **Coed**, 4,028 undergraduate students, 90% full-time, 60% women, 40% men
- **Noncompetitive** entrance level, 100% of applicants were admitted
- **19:1 student-to-undergraduate faculty ratio**
- **41% graduate** in 6 years or less
- **$2086 tuition** and fees (in-state); $6552 (out-of-state)
- **$4929 average financial aid** package, $12,827 average indebtedness upon graduation, $33.5 million endowment

Part of Kansas Board of Regents.

Students *Undergraduates:* 3,615 full-time, 413 part-time. Students come from 46 states and territories, 56 other countries. *The most frequently chosen baccalaureate fields are:* business/marketing, education, social sciences and history. *Graduate:* 1,448 in graduate degree programs.

From out-of-state	8%	Reside on campus	18%
Age 25 or older	16%	Transferred in	11%
International students	2%	African Americans	3%
Asian Americans/Pacific Islanders	1%	Hispanic Americans	3%
Native Americans	0.5%		

Faculty 322 (74% full-time), 59% with terminal degrees.

Expenses (1999–2000) *Tuition, state resident:* full-time $1574; part-time $52 per credit hour. *Tuition, nonresident:* full-time $6040; part-time $201 per credit hour. *Required fees:* full-time $512; $29 per credit hour. *College room and board:* $3656; room only: $1780. Room and board charges vary according to board plan and housing facility. *Payment plans:* installment, deferred payment. *Waivers:* senior citizens and employees or children of employees.

Library William Allen White Library. *Operations spending 1999–2000:* $1.8 million. *Collection:* 629,699 titles, 1,405 serial subscriptions, 2,891 audiovisual materials.

College life *Housing:* on-campus residence required in freshman year. *Options:* coed, disabled students. *Social organizations:* national fraternities, national sororities; 15% of eligible men and 9% of eligible women are members. *Most popular organizations:* Associated Student Government, Union Activities Council, Panhellenic Association, Residence Hall Association, Interfraternity Council.

Campus security 24-hour emergency response devices and patrols, late-night transport-escort service, controlled dormitory access, 24-hour residence hall monitoring, safety and self-awareness programs.

After graduation 205 organizations recruited on campus 1997–98. 84% of class of 1998 had job offers within 6 months. *Career center:* 8 full-time, 1 part-time personnel. Services include job fairs, resume preparation, interview workshops, resume referral, career counseling, careers library, job bank, job interviews.

Freshmen 1,434 applied, 1,434 admitted, 809 enrolled.

SAT verbal scores above 500	N/R	SAT math scores above 500	N/R
ACT above 18	84%	1998 freshmen returning in 1999	69%

Application *Options:* early admission, deferred entrance. *Application fee:* $20. *Required:* high school transcript.

Standardized tests *Placement: Recommended:* ACT.

Significant dates *Application deadlines:* rolling (freshmen), rolling (transfers). *Financial aid deadline priority date:* 3/15.

Freshman Application Contact
Ms. Melissa Jones, Director of Admissions, Emporia State University, 1200 Commercial Street, Emporia, KS 66801-5087. **Phone:** 316-341-5465. **Toll-free phone:** 800-896-7544. **E-mail:** ugadmiss@esumail.emporia.edu
Visit CollegeQuest.com for information on majors offered and athletics. College video available at CollegeQuest.com.

FORT HAYS STATE UNIVERSITY
Hays, Kansas

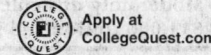
Apply at CollegeQuest.com

- **State-supported**, comprehensive, founded 1902
- **Degrees** associate, bachelor's, and master's
- **Small-town** 200-acre campus
- **Coed**, 4,414 undergraduate students, 85% full-time, 54% women, 46% men
- **Noncompetitive** entrance level, 100% of applicants were admitted
- **40.4% graduate** in 6 years or less
- **$2063 tuition** and fees (in-state); $6531 (out-of-state)
- **$30.5 million endowment**

Part of Kansas Board of Regents.
Students *Undergraduates:* Students come from 36 states and territories. *The most frequently chosen baccalaureate fields are:* business/marketing, education, health professions and related sciences.

| Reside on campus | 23% |

Faculty 273 (94% full-time), 70% with terminal degrees.
Expenses (1999–2000) *Tuition, state resident:* full-time $2063; part-time $69 per credit hour. *Tuition, nonresident:* full-time $6531; part-time $218 per credit hour. Full-time tuition and fees vary according to course load, location, and reciprocity agreements. Part-time tuition and fees vary according to course load and location. *College room and board:* $3770; room only: $1915. Room and board charges vary according to board plan, housing facility, and student level. *Payment plan:* installment. *Waivers:* senior citizens.
Library Forsyth Library. *Operations spending 1999–2000:* $2 million. *Collection:* 195,000 titles, 3,400 serial subscriptions.
College life *Housing:* on-campus residence required in freshman year. *Options:* coed, men-only, women-only. *Social organizations:* national fraternities, national sororities; 2% of eligible men and 2% of eligible women are members. *Most popular organizations:* Student Government Association, Union Activities Board, Residence Hall Association, International Student Union, Block and Bridle.
Campus security 24-hour emergency response devices and patrols, late-night transport-escort service, controlled dormitory access.
After graduation 190 organizations recruited on campus 1997–98. 90% of class of 1998 had job offers within 6 months. *Career center:* 5 full-time, 8 part-time personnel. Services include job fairs, resume preparation, interview workshops, resume referral, career/interest testing, career counseling, careers library, job bank, job interviews.
Freshmen 1,413 applied, 1,413 admitted.

SAT verbal scores above 500	N/R	SAT math scores above 500	N/R
ACT above 18	83%	From top quarter of their h.s. class	48%
From top half	83%	1998 freshmen returning in 1999	66%

Application *Options:* eApply at www.CollegeQuest.com, Common Application, electronic application. *Application fee:* $20. *Required:* high school transcript.
Significant dates *Application deadlines:* rolling (freshmen), rolling (transfers). *Financial aid deadline priority date:* 3/15.
Freshman Application Contact
Mr. Joey Linn, Director of Admissions, Fort Hays State University, 600 Park Street, Hays, KS 67601-4099. **Phone:** 785-628-5666. **Toll-free phone:** 800-432-0248. **Fax:** 785-628-4014. **E-mail:** tigers@fhsu.edu
Visit CollegeQuest.com for information on majors offered and athletics. College video and electronic viewbook available at CollegeQuest.com.

FRIENDS UNIVERSITY
Wichita, Kansas

- **Independent**, comprehensive, founded 1898
- **Degrees** associate, bachelor's, and master's
- **Urban** 45-acre campus
- **Coed**, 2,614 undergraduate students
- **Moderately difficult** entrance level, 93% of applicants were admitted
- **$11,010 tuition** and fees

Students *Undergraduates:* Students come from 30 states and territories, 25 other countries.

| From out-of-state | 10% | Reside on campus | 18% |
| Age 25 or older | 0.3% | | |

Faculty 212 (34% full-time).
Expenses (1999–2000) *Comprehensive fee:* $14,430 includes full-time tuition ($10,920), mandatory fees ($90), and room and board ($3420). Full-time tuition and fees vary according to course load. Room and board charges vary according to student level. *Part-time tuition:* $364 per semester hour. *Part-time fees:* $3 per semester hour. Part-time tuition and fees vary according to course load. *Payment plan:* installment. *Waivers:* senior citizens and employees or children of employees.
Library Edmund Stanley Library plus 3 others. *Collection:* 105,989 titles, 857 serial subscriptions.
College life *Housing:* *Options:* men-only, women-only. *Social organizations:* local fraternities, local sororities. *Most popular organizations:* Singing Quakers, Phi Beta Lambda, Student Association.
Campus security 24-hour patrols, late-night transport-escort service.
After graduation *Career center:* 1 full-time personnel. Services include job fairs, resume preparation, career/interest testing, career counseling, careers library, job bank, job interviews. *Graduate education:* 33% of class of 1999 went directly to graduate and professional school.
Freshmen 668 applied, 620 admitted.

Average high school GPA	3.4	SAT verbal scores above 500	N/R
SAT math scores above 500	N/R	ACT above 18	N/R
1998 freshmen returning in 1999	63%		

Application *Option:* early admission. *Application fee:* $15. *Required:* high school transcript. *Required for some:* essay or personal statement; 1 letter of recommendation. *Recommended:* interview.
Standardized tests *Admission:* Required: SAT I or ACT.
Significant dates *Application deadlines:* rolling (freshmen), rolling (transfers). *Financial aid deadline priority date:* 4/1.
Freshman Application Contact
Mr. Tony Meyers, Director of Admissions, Friends University, 2100 West University Street, Wichita, KS 67213. **Phone:** 316-295-5100. **Toll-free phone:** 800-577-2233. **Fax:** 316-262-5027. **E-mail:** tonym@friends.edu
Visit CollegeQuest.com for information on majors offered and athletics.

HASKELL INDIAN NATIONS UNIVERSITY
Lawrence, Kansas

- **Federally supported**, primarily 2-year, founded 1884
- **Degrees** associate and bachelor's
- **Suburban** 320-acre campus
- **Coed**, 898 undergraduate students
- **Minimally difficult** entrance level

Faculty 68 (93% full-time).
Admissions Office Contact
Haskell Indian Nations University, 155 Indian Avenue, #5031, Lawrence, KS 66046-4800. **Fax:** 785-749-8429.
Visit CollegeQuest.com for information on majors offered and athletics. College video available at CollegeQuest.com.

Kansas

KANSAS NEWMAN COLLEGE
Kansas—See Newman University

KANSAS STATE UNIVERSITY
Manhattan, Kansas

- **State-supported**, university, founded 1863
- **Degrees** associate, bachelor's, master's, doctoral, and first professional
- **Suburban** 668-acre campus with easy access to Kansas City
- **Coed**, 17,809 undergraduate students, 86% full-time, 47% women, 53% men
- **Noncompetitive** entrance level, 65% of applicants were admitted
- **15:1 student-to-undergraduate faculty ratio**
- **45% graduate** in 6 years or less
- **$2592 tuition** and fees (in-state); $9195 (out-of-state)

Students *Undergraduates:* 15,348 full-time, 2,461 part-time. Students come from 50 states and territories, 101 other countries. *The most frequently chosen baccalaureate fields are:* agriculture, business/marketing, education. *Graduate:* 396 in professional programs, 3,244 in other graduate degree programs.

From out-of-state	8%	Reside on campus	29%
Age 25 or older	11%	Transferred in	9%
International students	1%	African Americans	3%
Asian Americans/Pacific Islanders	1%	Hispanic Americans	2%
Native Americans	1%		

Expenses (1999–2000) *Tuition, state resident:* full-time $2090; part-time $70 per semester hour. *Tuition, nonresident:* full-time $8693; part-time $290 per semester hour. *Required fees:* full-time $502; $17 per semester hour; $47 per term part-time. Full-time tuition and fees vary according to degree level and location. Part-time tuition and fees vary according to degree level and location. *College room and board:* $3950. *Payment plans:* installment, deferred payment.

Library Hale Library plus 3 others. *Collection:* 935,312 titles, 12,104 serial subscriptions, 35,894 audiovisual materials.

College life *Housing: Options:* coed, men-only, women-only, cooperative. *Social organizations:* national fraternities, national sororities; 20% of eligible men and 20% of eligible women are members. *Most popular organizations:* athletic department groups, marching band, Union Governing Board, theater productions, debate team.

Campus security 24-hour emergency response devices and patrols, late-night transport-escort service, controlled dormitory access.

After graduation 470 organizations recruited on campus 1997–98. 62% of class of 1998 had job offers within 6 months. *Career center:* 14 full-time, 16 part-time personnel. Services include job fairs, resume preparation, interview workshops, resume referral, career/interest testing, career counseling, careers library, job bank, job interviews. *Graduate education:* 41% of class of 1999 went directly to graduate and professional school. *Major awards:* 1 Fulbright Scholar.

Freshmen 10,457 applied, 6,751 admitted, 3,504 enrolled. 27 National Merit Scholars, 253 valedictorians.

Average high school GPA	3.39	SAT verbal scores above 500	N/R
SAT math scores above 500	N/R	ACT above 18	90%
From top quarter of their h.s. class	60%	From top half	89%
1998 freshmen returning in 1999	78%		

Application *Options:* Common Application, electronic application. *Application fee:* $20. *Required:* minimum 2.0 GPA. *Required for some:* high school transcript.

Standardized tests *Admission: Required for some:* SAT I or ACT.

Significant dates *Application deadlines:* rolling (freshmen), rolling (transfers). *Financial aid deadline priority date:* 3/1.

Freshman Application Contact
Mr. Larry Moeder, Interim Director of Admissions, Kansas State University, Anderson Hall, Room 1, Manhattan, KS 66506. **Phone:** 785-532-6250. **Toll-free phone:** 800-432-8270. **Fax:** 785-532-6393. **E-mail:** kstate@ksu.edu

Visit CollegeQuest.com for information on majors offered and athletics. College video available at CollegeQuest.com.

■ *See page 1862 for a narrative description.*

KANSAS WESLEYAN UNIVERSITY
Salina, Kansas

- **Independent United Methodist**, comprehensive, founded 1886
- **Degrees** associate, bachelor's, and master's
- **Urban** 28-acre campus
- **Coed**
- **Moderately difficult** entrance level
- **$11,000 tuition** and fees

Expenses (1999–2000) *Comprehensive fee:* $15,000 includes full-time tuition ($11,000) and room and board ($4000). *Part-time tuition:* $160 per credit. Part-time tuition and fees vary according to course load.

Institutional Web site http://www.kwu.edu/

College life *Housing:* on-campus residence required through sophomore year. *Options:* men-only, women-only. *Social organizations:* local fraternities, local sororities, societies; 1% of eligible men and 1% of eligible women are members. *Most popular organizations:* Fellowship of Christian Athletes, student government, Wesleyan Chorale, Multicultural Student Association, business club.

Campus security 24-hour emergency response devices, student patrols, late-night transport-escort service, controlled dormitory access, evening patrols by security.

Application *Options:* eApply at www.CollegeQuest.com, Common Application, electronic application, deferred entrance. *Application fee:* $15. *Required:* high school transcript; minimum 2.5 GPA; minimum ACT composite score of 18. *Required for some:* essay or personal statement; 2 letters of recommendation; interview.

Standardized tests *Admission: Required:* SAT I or ACT. *Recommended:* SAT I, ACT.

Admissions Office Contact
Kansas Wesleyan University, 100 East Claflin, Salina, KS 67401-6196. **Toll-free phone:** 800-874-1154 Ext. 1285. **Fax:** 785-827-0927. **E-mail:** admissions@diamond.kwu.edu

Visit CollegeQuest.com for information on athletics. Electronic viewbook available at CollegeQuest.com.

MANHATTAN CHRISTIAN COLLEGE
Manhattan, Kansas

- **Independent**, 4-year, founded 1927, affiliated with Christian Churches and Churches of Christ
- **Degrees** associate and bachelor's
- **Small-town** 10-acre campus
- **Coed**, 373 undergraduate students, 84% full-time, 56% women, 44% men
- **Minimally difficult** entrance level, 94% of applicants were admitted
- **21:1 student-to-undergraduate faculty ratio**
- **20.7% graduate** in 6 years or less
- **$6870 tuition** and fees
- **$5278 average financial aid** package, $939,895 endowment

Students *Undergraduates:* 312 full-time, 61 part-time. Students come from 17 states and territories. *The most frequently chosen baccalaureate fields are:* business/marketing, philosophy.

From out-of-state	24%	Reside on campus	65%
Age 25 or older	14%	Transferred in	9%
African Americans	3%	Asian Americans/Pacific Islanders	1%
Hispanic Americans	1%	Native Americans	1%

Faculty 27 (41% full-time), 15% with terminal degrees.

Expenses (2000–2001) *One-time required fee:* $30. *Comprehensive fee:* $10,480 includes full-time tuition ($6870) and room and board ($3610). Room and board charges vary according to board plan. *Part-time tuition:* $160 per hour. Part-time tuition and fees vary according to course load. *Payment plan:* installment. *Waivers:* senior citizens and employees or children of employees.

Library Manhattan Christian College Library. *Operations spending 1999–2000:* $65,147. *Collection:* 2,500 titles, 45 serial subscriptions.

Kansas

College life *Housing:* on-campus residence required through sophomore year. *Options:* men-only, women-only. *Most popular organizations:* Student Council, Unspoken Message (drama and dance team), praise bands, drama team, prison ministry.
Campus security Controlled dormitory access.
After graduation *Career center:* Services include career counseling. *Graduate education:* 1% of class of 1999 went directly to graduate and professional school: 1% theology.
Freshmen 125 applied, 118 admitted, 108 enrolled. 3 class presidents, 2 valedictorians, 32 student government officers.

Average high school GPA	3.34	SAT verbal scores above 500	N/R
SAT math scores above 500	N/R	ACT above 18	94%
1998 freshmen returning in 1999	63%		

Application *Option:* eApply at www.CollegeQuest.com. *Application fee:* $25. *Required:* high school transcript; minimum 2.0 GPA; 3 letters of recommendation. *Required for some:* interview. *Recommended:* essay or personal statement.
Standardized tests *Admission: Required:* SAT I or ACT.
Significant dates *Application deadlines:* rolling (freshmen), rolling (transfers). *Financial aid deadline priority date:* 4/1.
Freshman Application Contact
Mr. John W. Poulson, Vice President of Admissions, Manhattan Christian College, 1415 Anderson, Manhattan, KS 66502-4081. **Phone:** 785-539-3571 Ext. 30. **Toll-free phone:** 877-246-4622. **Fax:** 785-539-0832.
Visit CollegeQuest.com for information on majors offered and athletics.

MCPHERSON COLLEGE
McPherson, Kansas

- **Independent**, 4-year, founded 1887, affiliated with Church of the Brethren
- **Degrees** associate and bachelor's
- **Small-town** 26-acre campus
- **Coed**, 467 undergraduate students, 93% full-time, 44% women, 56% men
- **Moderately difficult** entrance level, 72% of applicants were admitted
- **12:1 student-to-undergraduate faculty ratio**
- **45% graduate** in 6 years or less
- **$11,700 tuition** and fees
- **$12,152 average financial aid** package, $19,075 average indebtedness upon graduation, $25.7 million endowment

Students *Undergraduates:* 434 full-time, 33 part-time. Students come from 38 states and territories, 5 other countries. *The most frequently chosen baccalaureate fields are:* business/marketing, biological/life sciences, education.

From out-of-state	54%	Reside on campus	70%
Age 25 or older	12%	Transferred in	10%
International students	2%	African Americans	6%
Asian Americans/Pacific Islanders	3%	Hispanic Americans	6%
Native Americans	1%		

Faculty 51 (78% full-time), 61% with terminal degrees.
Expenses (2000–2001) *Comprehensive fee:* $16,600 includes full-time tuition ($11,500), mandatory fees ($200), and room and board ($4900). Room and board charges vary according to board plan and housing facility. Part-time tuition and fees vary according to course load. *Waivers:* senior citizens and employees or children of employees.
Library Miller Library. *Operations spending 1999–2000:* $197,546. *Collection:* 4,045 audiovisual materials.
College life *Housing:* on-campus residence required through senior year. *Options:* coed, men-only, disabled students. *Most popular organizations:* Today's Educators, Spectator (newspaper), drama productions, athletics, choir.
Campus security Student patrols, controlled dormitory access.
After graduation *Career center:* 2 part-time personnel. Services include job fairs, resume preparation, career counseling, careers library, job interviews.

Freshmen 786 applied, 563 admitted, 129 enrolled.

Average high school GPA	3.7	SAT verbal scores above 500	N/R
SAT math scores above 500	N/R	ACT above 18	N/R
From top 10% of their h.s. class	22%	From top quarter	47%
From top half	71%	1998 freshmen returning in 1999	60%

Application *Option:* deferred entrance. *Application fee:* $25. *Required:* high school transcript; minimum 2.0 GPA.
Standardized tests *Admission: Required:* SAT I or ACT.
Significant dates *Application deadlines:* rolling (freshmen), rolling (transfers). *Financial aid deadline priority date:* 3/1.
Freshman Application Contact
Mr. Fred Schmidt, Director of Admission and Financial Aid, McPherson College, , 1600 East Euclid, PO Box 1402, McPherson, KS 67460-1402. **Phone:** 316-241-0731 Ext. 1270. **Toll-free phone:** 800-365-7402 Ext. 1270. **Fax:** 316-241-8443 Ext. 1270. **E-mail:** admiss@mcpherson.edu
Visit CollegeQuest.com for information on majors offered and athletics.

MIDAMERICA NAZARENE UNIVERSITY
Olathe, Kansas

- **Independent**, comprehensive, founded 1966, affiliated with Church of the Nazarene
- **Degrees** associate, bachelor's, and master's
- **Suburban** 112-acre campus with easy access to Kansas City
- **Coed**, 1,173 undergraduate students, 92% full-time, 54% women, 46% men
- **Minimally difficult** entrance level, 53% of applicants were admitted
- **16:1 student-to-undergraduate faculty ratio**
- **43.19% graduate** in 6 years or less
- **$10,474 tuition** and fees
- **$13.3 million endowment**

MidAmerica is a comprehensive, Christian liberal arts university committed to transforming students for a life of service to God, their country, and their world. The University offers 5 degree options and 39 majors in such areas as business, education, nursing, psychology, and criminal justice. The University is located just 20 miles from Kansas City.

Students *Undergraduates:* 1,078 full-time, 95 part-time. Students come from 31 states and territories, 8 other countries. *The most frequently chosen baccalaureate fields are:* communications/communication technologies, engineering/engineering technologies, home economics/vocational home economics. *Graduate:* 386 in graduate degree programs.

From out-of-state	43%	Reside on campus	62%
Age 25 or older	11%	Transferred in	7%
International students	1%	African Americans	4%
Asian Americans/Pacific Islanders	1%	Hispanic Americans	1%
Native Americans	1%		

Faculty 123 (56% full-time), 35% with terminal degrees.
Expenses (1999–2000) *Comprehensive fee:* $15,534 includes full-time tuition ($9580), mandatory fees ($894), and room and board ($5060). Full-time tuition and fees vary according to course load. Room and board charges vary according to board plan and housing facility. *Part-time tuition:* $320 per semester hour. *Part-time fees:* $319 per term part-time. Part-time tuition and fees vary according to course load. *Payment plan:* installment. *Waivers:* senior citizens and employees or children of employees.
Library Mabee Library. *Operations spending 1999–2000:* $356,298. *Collection:* 80,560 titles, 1,025 serial subscriptions.
College life *Housing:* on-campus residence required through senior year. *Options:* men-only, women-only. *Most popular organizations:* Associated Student Government, Circle K, ministry groups, College Republicans, gospel station.
Campus security 24-hour emergency response devices and patrols, student patrols, late-night transport-escort service, controlled dormitory access.
After graduation 40 organizations recruited on campus 1997–98. *Career center:* 2 full-time, 1 part-time personnel. Services include job fairs, resume preparation, interview workshops, career/interest testing, career counseling, careers library, job bank, job interviews.
Freshmen 449 applied, 239 admitted, 222 enrolled. 1 National Merit Scholar.

Kansas

MidAmerica Nazarene University (continued)

Average high school GPA	3.28	SAT verbal scores above 500	79%
SAT math scores above 500	65%	ACT above 18	67%
From top 10% of their h.s. class	17%	From top quarter	40%
From top half	68%	1998 freshmen returning in 1999	69%

Application *Options:* early admission, deferred entrance. *Application fee:* $15. *Required:* high school transcript; minimum 2.0 GPA; 2 letters of recommendation.
Standardized tests *Admission: Required:* SAT I or ACT.
Significant dates *Application deadlines:* 8/1 (freshmen), 8/1 (transfers). *Financial aid deadline priority date:* 3/1.
Freshman Application Contact Dr. Daniel Martin, Executive Director of Enrollment Development, MidAmerica Nazarene University, 2030 East College Way, Olathe, KS 66062-1899. **Phone:** 913-791-3380 Ext. 481. **Toll-free phone:** 800-800-8887. **Fax:** 913-791-3481. **E-mail:** admissions@mnu.edu
Visit CollegeQuest.com for information on majors offered and athletics. College video available at CollegeQuest.com.

NEWMAN UNIVERSITY
Wichita, Kansas

- **Independent Roman Catholic**, comprehensive, founded 1933
- **Degrees** associate, bachelor's, and master's
- **Urban** 53-acre campus
- **Coed**, 1,195 undergraduate students, 74% full-time, 67% women, 33% men
- **Minimally difficult** entrance level, 84% of applicants were admitted
- **11:1 student-to-undergraduate faculty ratio**
- **47% graduate** in 6 years or less
- **$10,268 tuition** and fees
- **$8872 average financial aid** package, $18.3 million endowment

Students *Undergraduates:* 888 full-time, 307 part-time. Students come from 25 states and territories, 26 other countries. *The most frequently chosen baccalaureate fields are:* education, business/marketing, home economics/vocational home economics. *Graduate:* 414 in graduate degree programs.

From out-of-state	12%	Reside on campus	13%
Age 25 or older	46%	Transferred in	19%
International students	2%	African Americans	6%
Asian Americans/Pacific Islanders	2%	Hispanic Americans	4%
Native Americans	1%		

Faculty 81 full-time.
Expenses (2000–2001) *Comprehensive fee:* $14,218 includes full-time tuition ($10,148), mandatory fees ($120), and room and board ($3950). *College room only:* $1850. Full-time tuition and fees vary according to class time. Room and board charges vary according to housing facility. *Part-time tuition:* $337 per semester hour. *Part-time fees:* $5 per semester hour. Part-time tuition and fees vary according to class time. *Payment plans:* installment, deferred payment. *Waivers:* minority students, children of alumni, and employees or children of employees.
Library Ryan Library. *Operations spending 1999–2000:* $228,391. *Collection:* 88,000 titles, 450 serial subscriptions.
College life *Housing:* on-campus residence required through sophomore year. *Options:* coed, women-only. *Most popular organizations:* Student Activities Board, chorale, international club, Chemistry/Pre-Med Club, Kansas Newman Occupational Therapy Student Association.
Campus security 24-hour patrols, late-night transport-escort service.
After graduation *Career center:* 1 full-time, 1 part-time personnel. Services include job fairs, career counseling, job bank.
Freshmen 340 applied, 286 admitted, 159 enrolled. 5 valedictorians.

Average high school GPA	3.35	SAT verbal scores above 500	75%
SAT math scores above 500	75%	ACT above 18	86%
From top 10% of their h.s. class	18%	From top quarter	43%
From top half	78%	1998 freshmen returning in 1999	66%

Application *Options:* early admission, deferred entrance. *Application fee:* $15. *Required:* high school transcript; minimum 2.0 GPA. *Recommended:* interview.
Standardized tests *Admission: Required:* SAT I or ACT.
Significant dates *Application deadlines:* rolling (freshmen), rolling (transfers). *Financial aid deadline priority date:* 3/1.

Freshman Application Contact Mr. Thomas C. Green, Dean of Enrollment Services, Newman University, 3100 McCormick Avenue, Wichita, KS 67213-2097. **Phone:** 316-942-4291 Ext. 241. **Toll-free phone:** 877-NEWMANU. **Fax:** 316-942-4483. **E-mail:** admissions@newmanu.edu
Visit CollegeQuest.com for information on majors offered and athletics. College video available at CollegeQuest.com.

OTTAWA UNIVERSITY
Ottawa, Kansas

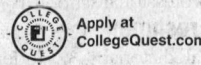

- **Independent American Baptist**, comprehensive, founded 1865
- **Degrees** bachelor's and master's (also offers adult, international and on-line education programs with significant enrollment not reflected in profile)
- **Small-town** 60-acre campus with easy access to Kansas City
- **Coed**, 459 undergraduate students, 97% full-time, 42% women, 58% men
- **Moderately difficult** entrance level, 70% of applicants were admitted
- **19:1 student-to-undergraduate faculty ratio**
- **35% graduate** in 6 years or less
- **$10,250 tuition** and fees
- **$5974 average financial aid** package, $14,000 average indebtedness upon graduation, $12.7 million endowment

Students *Undergraduates:* 443 full-time, 16 part-time. Students come from 23 states and territories, 6 other countries. *The most frequently chosen baccalaureate fields are:* education, communications/communication technologies, social sciences and history.

From out-of-state	44%	Reside on campus	52%
Age 25 or older	6%	International students	5%
African Americans	11%	Asian Americans/Pacific Islanders	0.4%
Hispanic Americans	4%	Native Americans	2%

Faculty 33 (58% full-time), 42% with terminal degrees.
Expenses (1999–2000) *Comprehensive fee:* $14,470 includes full-time tuition ($10,040), mandatory fees ($210), and room and board ($4220). *College room only:* $2000. Full-time tuition and fees vary according to course load. Room and board charges vary according to board plan and housing facility. *Part-time tuition:* $335 per credit hour. *Part-time fees:* $55 per term part-time. Part-time tuition and fees vary according to course load. *Payment plans:* installment, deferred payment. *Waivers:* senior citizens and employees or children of employees.
Library Myers Library. *Operations spending 1999–2000:* $146,329. *Collection:* 80,000 titles, 164 serial subscriptions.
College life *Housing:* on-campus residence required through junior year. *Options:* men-only, women-only. *Social organizations:* university social clubs; 20% of eligible men and 25% of eligible women are members. *Most popular organizations:* Christian Faith In Action, Student Activities Force, education club, Whole Earth club, Fellowship of Christian Athletes.
Campus security 24-hour emergency response devices and patrols, locked residence hall entrances.
After graduation 105 organizations recruited on campus 1997–98. 57% of class of 1998 had job offers within 6 months. *Career center:* 2 full-time, 1 part-time personnel. Services include job fairs, resume preparation, interview workshops, resume referral, career/interest testing, career counseling, careers library, job interviews. *Graduate education:* 20% of class of 1999 went directly to graduate and professional school.
Freshmen 754 applied, 528 admitted, 136 enrolled. 3 valedictorians.

Average high school GPA	3.17	SAT verbal scores above 500	N/R
SAT math scores above 500	N/R	ACT above 18	83%
From top 10% of their h.s. class	8%	From top quarter	28%
From top half	71%	1998 freshmen returning in 1999	54%

Application *Options:* eApply at www.CollegeQuest.com, electronic application. *Application fee:* $15. *Required:* high school transcript; minimum 2.5 GPA. *Required for some:* essay or personal statement. *Recommended:* 2 letters of recommendation; interview.
Standardized tests *Admission: Required:* SAT I or ACT.
Significant dates *Application deadlines:* rolling (freshmen), rolling (transfers). *Financial aid deadline priority date:* 3/15.

Kansas

Freshman Application Contact
Mr. Tim Albers, Director of Admissions, Ottawa University, 1001 South Cedar, Ottawa, KS 66067-3399. **Phone:** 785-242-5200 Ext. 5558. **Toll-free phone:** 800-755-5200. **Fax:** 785-242-7429. **E-mail:** wwwadmiss@ottawa.edu
Visit CollegeQuest.com for information on majors offered and athletics. College video available at CollegeQuest.com.

PITTSBURG STATE UNIVERSITY
Pittsburg, Kansas

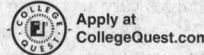

- **State-supported**, comprehensive, founded 1903
- **Degrees** associate, bachelor's, and master's
- **Small-town** 233-acre campus
- **Coed**, 5,211 undergraduate students, 90% full-time, 47% women, 53% men
- **Noncompetitive** entrance level
- **23:1 student-to-undergraduate faculty ratio**
- **$2142 tuition** and fees (in-state); $6608 (out-of-state)
- **$5553 average financial aid** package, $10,433 average indebtedness upon graduation, $27 million endowment

Part of Kansas Board of Regents.
Students *Undergraduates:* Students come from 49 states and territories, 51 other countries. *Graduate:* 1,078 in graduate degree programs.

From out-of-state	13%	Reside on campus	20%
Age 25 or older	19%	International students	3%
African Americans	3%	Asian Americans/Pacific Islanders	1%
Hispanic Americans	1%	Native Americans	2%

Faculty 372 (77% full-time), 76% with terminal degrees.
Expenses (1999–2000) *Tuition, state resident:* full-time $2142; part-time $78 per semester hour. *Tuition, nonresident:* full-time $6608; part-time $227 per semester hour. *College room and board:* $3715. Room and board charges vary according to board plan. *Payment plan:* installment. *Waivers:* employees or children of employees.
Library Leonard H. Axe Library plus 2 others. *Collection:* 290,798 titles, 1,368 serial subscriptions.
College life *Housing:* on-campus residence required in freshman year. *Option:* coed. *Social organizations:* national fraternities, national sororities; 10% of eligible men and 6% of eligible women are members. *Most popular organizations:* Student Government Association, student yearbook, student newspaper.
Campus security 24-hour emergency response devices and patrols, student patrols, controlled dormitory access.
After graduation 145 organizations recruited on campus 1997–98. *Career center:* 3 full-time, 3 part-time personnel. Services include job fairs, resume preparation, resume referral, career/interest testing, career counseling, careers library, job bank, job interviews.
Freshmen

SAT verbal scores above 500	N/R	SAT math scores above 500	N/R
ACT above 18	79%	From top quarter of their h.s. class	32%
From top half	63%	1998 freshmen returning in 1999	87%

Application *Options:* eApply at www.CollegeQuest.com, Common Application, electronic application, early admission, deferred entrance. *Application fee:* $20. *Required:* high school transcript. *Required for some:* minimum 2.0 GPA.
Standardized tests *Admission: Required:* ACT.
Significant dates *Application deadlines:* rolling (freshmen), rolling (transfers). *Financial aid deadline priority date:* 3/1.
Freshman Application Contact
Ms. Ange Peterson, Director of Admissions and Retention, Pittsburg State University, 1701 South Broadway, Pittsburg, KS 66762-5880. **Phone:** 316-235-4252. **Toll-free phone:** 800-854-7488 Ext. 2. **Fax:** 316-235-4080. **E-mail:** psuadmit@pittstate.edu
Visit CollegeQuest.com for information on majors offered and athletics. College video available at CollegeQuest.com.

SAINT MARY COLLEGE
Leavenworth, Kansas

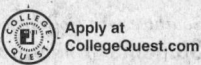

- **Independent Roman Catholic**, comprehensive, founded 1923
- **Degrees** associate, bachelor's, and master's
- **Small-town** 240-acre campus with easy access to Kansas City
- **Coed**, 486 undergraduate students, 72% full-time, 62% women, 38% men
- **Moderately difficult** entrance level, 90% of applicants were admitted
- **11:1 student-to-undergraduate faculty ratio**
- **41% graduate** in 6 years or less
- **$11,390 tuition** and fees
- **$9.3 million endowment**

Students *Undergraduates:* 352 full-time, 134 part-time. *The most frequently chosen baccalaureate fields are:* education, psychology, social sciences and history. *Graduate:* 184 in graduate degree programs.

Age 25 or older	11%	Transferred in	10%
International students	1%	African Americans	14%
Asian Americans/Pacific Islanders	2%	Hispanic Americans	5%
Native Americans	1%		

Faculty 39 (92% full-time), 59% with terminal degrees.
Expenses (2000–2001) *Comprehensive fee:* $15,990 includes full-time tuition ($11,390) and room and board ($4600). *College room only:* $2140. Full-time tuition and fees vary according to class time. Room and board charges vary according to housing facility. *Part-time tuition:* $375 per credit hour. Part-time tuition and fees vary according to class time. *Payment plan:* installment. *Waivers:* minority students, adult students, and employees or children of employees.
Library De Paul Library. *Operations spending 1999–2000:* $177,750. *Collection:* 114,175 titles, 363 serial subscriptions, 1,742 audiovisual materials.
College life *Housing:* on-campus residence required through senior year. *Option:* coed. *Most popular organizations:* student government association, BACCHUS, Theatrical Union, Campus Ministry, Amnesty International.
Campus security Late-night transport-escort service, controlled dormitory access.
After graduation 88% of class of 1998 had job offers within 6 months. *Career center:* 1 full-time, 3 part-time personnel. Services include job fairs, resume preparation, interview workshops, resume referral, career/interest testing, career counseling, careers library, job bank, job interviews.
Freshmen 324 applied, 290 admitted, 121 enrolled.

Average high school GPA	3.45	SAT verbal scores above 500	N/R
SAT math scores above 500	N/R	ACT above 18	N/R
From top 10% of their h.s. class	15%	From top quarter	35%
From top half	85%		

Application *Options:* eApply at www.CollegeQuest.com, Common Application, electronic application, early admission, deferred entrance. *Application fee:* $25. *Required:* high school transcript; minimum 2.2 GPA; 1 letter of recommendation. *Recommended:* interview.
Standardized tests *Admission: Required:* SAT I or ACT.
Significant dates *Application deadlines:* rolling (freshmen), rolling (transfers). *Financial aid deadline priority date:* 4/1.
Freshman Application Contact
Mr. John Wilbur, Enrollment Services, Saint Mary College, 4100 South Fourth Street, Leavenworth, KS 66048. **Phone:** 913-682-5151 Ext. 6118. **Toll-free phone:** 800-758-6140. **E-mail:** admiss@hub.smcks.edu
Visit CollegeQuest.com for information on majors offered and athletics. College video and electronic viewbook available at CollegeQuest.com.

SOUTHWESTERN COLLEGE
Winfield, Kansas

- **Independent United Methodist**, comprehensive, founded 1885
- **Degrees** bachelor's and master's
- **Small-town** 70-acre campus with easy access to Wichita
- **Coed**, 890 undergraduate students, 66% full-time, 55% women, 45% men
- **Moderately difficult** entrance level, 95% of applicants were admitted
- **13:1 student-to-undergraduate faculty ratio**
- **51% graduate** in 6 years or less
- **$10,560 tuition** and fees
- **$11,123 average financial aid** package, $13,803 average indebtedness upon graduation, $22 million endowment

Peterson's Guide to Four-Year Colleges 2001 www.petersons.com

Kansas

Southwestern College (continued)

Students *Undergraduates:* 590 full-time, 300 part-time. Students come from 26 states and territories, 14 other countries. *The most frequently chosen baccalaureate fields are:* business/marketing, biological/life sciences, health professions and related sciences. *Graduate:* 26 in graduate degree programs.

From out-of-state	18%	Reside on campus	63%
Age 25 or older	37%	Transferred in	7%
International students	4%	African Americans	4%
Asian Americans/Pacific Islanders	1%	Hispanic Americans	3%
Native Americans	2%		

Faculty 90 (53% full-time), 51% with terminal degrees.

Expenses (1999–2000) *Comprehensive fee:* $14,830 includes full-time tuition ($10,560) and room and board ($4270). *College room only:* $1750. Full-time tuition and fees vary according to degree level and location. Room and board charges vary according to board plan, housing facility, and location. *Part-time tuition:* $440 per semester hour. Part-time tuition and fees vary according to degree level and location. *Payment plan:* installment. *Waivers:* senior citizens and employees or children of employees.

Library Memorial Library plus 1 other. *Operations spending 1999–2000:* $248,501. *Collection:* 75,000 titles, 300 serial subscriptions.

College life *Housing:* on-campus residence required in freshman year. *Options:* coed, men-only, women-only. *Social organizations:* national fraternities, local fraternities, local sororities; 15% of eligible men and 12% of eligible women are members. *Most popular organizations:* Student Activities Association, student government, Fellowship of Christian Athletes, Campus Council on Ministries, international club.

Campus security 24-hour emergency response devices, late-night transport-escort service.

After graduation 15 organizations recruited on campus 1997–98. *Career center:* 1 full-time, 1 part-time personnel. Services include resume preparation, interview workshops, career/interest testing, career counseling, careers library, job bank, job interviews.

Freshmen 273 applied, 258 admitted, 136 enrolled.

SAT verbal scores above 500	10%	SAT math scores above 500	48%
ACT above 18	88%	From top quarter of their h.s. class	50%
From top half	77%	1998 freshmen returning in 1999	67%

Application *Option:* deferred entrance. *Application fee:* $20. *Required:* essay or personal statement; high school transcript; minimum 2.0 GPA. *Required for some:* interview.

Standardized tests *Admission: Required:* SAT I or ACT.

Significant dates *Application deadlines:* 8/1 (freshmen), 8/1 (transfers). *Financial aid deadline:* 8/1. *Priority date:* 7/1.

Freshman Application Contact
Ms. Brenda D. Hicks, Director of Admission, Southwestern College, 100 College Street, Winfield, KS 67156-2499. **Phone:** 316-221-8236. **Toll-free phone:** 800-846-1543 Ext. 236. **Fax:** 316-221-8344 Ext. 236. **E-mail:** scadmit@sckans.edu

Visit CollegeQuest.com for information on majors offered and athletics.

STERLING COLLEGE
Sterling, Kansas

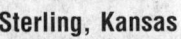
Apply at CollegeQuest.com

- **Independent Presbyterian**, 4-year, founded 1887
- **Degree** bachelor's
- **Small-town** 46-acre campus
- **Coed**, 410 undergraduate students, 97% full-time, 53% women, 47% men
- **Minimally difficult** entrance level, 73% of applicants were admitted
- **12:1 student-to-undergraduate faculty ratio**
- **45% graduate** in 6 years or less
- **$11,030 tuition** and fees
- **$9000 average financial aid** package, $12,287 average indebtedness upon graduation, $6.1 million endowment

Students *Undergraduates:* 398 full-time, 12 part-time. Students come from 25 states and territories, 1 other country. *The most frequently chosen baccalaureate fields are:* biological/life sciences, business/marketing, education.

From out-of-state	41%	Reside on campus	77%
Age 25 or older	2%	Transferred in	7%
International students	0.2%	African Americans	4%
Asian Americans/Pacific Islanders	0.2%	Hispanic Americans	4%
Native Americans	1%		

Faculty 47 (70% full-time), 34% with terminal degrees.

Expenses (1999–2000) *One-time required fee:* $100. *Comprehensive fee:* $15,616 includes full-time tuition ($11,030) and room and board ($4586). Full-time tuition and fees vary according to course load. Room and board charges vary according to board plan and housing facility. *Part-time tuition:* $236 per credit. Part-time tuition and fees vary according to course load. *Payment plan:* installment. *Waivers:* senior citizens and employees or children of employees.

Library Mabee Library. *Operations spending 1999–2000:* $222,031. *Collection:* 85,484 titles, 482 serial subscriptions, 1,871 audiovisual materials.

College life *Housing:* on-campus residence required through senior year. *Options:* men-only, women-only. *Most popular organizations:* Fellowship of Christian Athletes, Student Activities Council, My Brother's Keeper, Community Outreach, Youth Ministries.

Campus security Late night security patrol.

After graduation *Career center:* 2 full-time personnel. Services include job fairs, resume preparation, interview workshops, resume referral, career/interest testing, career counseling, careers library, job bank, job interviews.

Freshmen 434 applied, 315 admitted, 115 enrolled. 9 valedictorians.

Average high school GPA	3.52	SAT verbal scores above 500	77%
SAT math scores above 500	77%	ACT above 18	94%
From top 10% of their h.s. class	18%	From top quarter	45%
From top half	75%	1998 freshmen returning in 1999	50%

Application *Options:* eApply at www.CollegeQuest.com, electronic application, deferred entrance. *Application fee:* $10. *Required:* high school transcript; minimum 2.2 GPA. *Required for some:* letters of recommendation. *Recommended:* essay or personal statement.

Standardized tests *Admission: Required:* SAT I or ACT.

Significant dates *Application deadlines:* rolling (freshmen), rolling (transfers). *Financial aid deadline priority date:* 3/15.

Freshman Application Contact
Susan Sankey, Director of Admissions, Sterling College, PO Box 98, Sterling, KS 67579-0098. **Phone:** 316-278-4364 Ext. 364. **Toll-free phone:** 800-346-1017. **Fax:** 316-278-3690. **E-mail:** admissions@sterling.edu

Visit CollegeQuest.com for information on majors offered and athletics. College video available at CollegeQuest.com.

TABOR COLLEGE
Hillsboro, Kansas

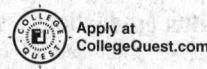
Apply at CollegeQuest.com

- **Independent Mennonite Brethren**, comprehensive, founded 1908
- **Degrees** associate and bachelor's
- **Small-town** 26-acre campus with easy access to Wichita
- **Coed**, 538 undergraduate students, 72% full-time, 49% women, 51% men
- **Moderately difficult** entrance level, 63% of applicants were admitted
- **14:1 student-to-undergraduate faculty ratio**
- **59% graduate** in 6 years or less
- **$12,410 tuition** and fees
- **$11,260 average financial aid** package, $16,452 average indebtedness upon graduation, $2.3 million endowment

Students *Undergraduates:* 389 full-time, 149 part-time. Students come from 22 states and territories. *The most frequently chosen baccalaureate fields are:* business/marketing, education, philosophy.

From out-of-state	37%	Reside on campus	79%
Age 25 or older	20%	International students	1%
African Americans	3%	Asian Americans/Pacific Islanders	1%
Hispanic Americans	2%	Native Americans	1%

Faculty 37 (92% full-time), 43% with terminal degrees.

Expenses (2000–2001) *Comprehensive fee:* $16,890 includes full-time tuition ($12,090), mandatory fees ($320), and room and board ($4480). *College room only:* $1700. Room and board charges vary according to board plan, housing facility, and location. Part-time tuition and fees vary according to course load. *Payment plan:* installment. *Waivers:* children of alumni, adult students, senior citizens, and employees or children of employees.

Library Tabor College Library plus 2 others. *Operations spending 1999–2000:* $97,391. *Collection:* 76,730 titles, 298 serial subscriptions, 945 audiovisual materials.

College life *Housing:* on-campus residence required through senior year. *Options:* men-only, women-only. *Most popular organizations:* Student Activities Board, Stuco, Campus Ministries Council, Fellowship of Christian Athletes.

Campus security Student patrols, controlled dormitory access.

After graduation 40 organizations recruited on campus 1997–98. *Career center:* 1 full-time, 1 part-time personnel. Services include job fairs, resume preparation, resume referral, career counseling, careers library, job bank, job interviews. *Graduate education:* 20% of class of 1999 went directly to graduate and professional school.

Freshmen 363 applied, 227 admitted, 138 enrolled.

Average high school GPA	3.34	SAT verbal scores above 500	N/R
SAT math scores above 500	N/R	ACT above 18	69%
From top 10% of their h.s. class	18%	From top quarter	41%
From top half	73%	1998 freshmen returning in 1999	63%

Application *Options:* eApply at www.CollegeQuest.com, Common Application, electronic application, deferred entrance. *Application fee:* $10. *Required:* essay or personal statement; high school transcript; minimum 2.0 GPA; 2 letters of recommendation. *Recommended:* minimum 3.0 GPA; interview.

Standardized tests *Admission: Required:* SAT I or ACT. *Recommended:* SAT II Subject Tests, SAT II: Writing Test.

Significant dates *Application deadlines:* 8/1 (freshmen), 8/1 (transfers). *Financial aid deadline:* 8/15. *Priority date:* 3/1.

Freshman Application Contact
Mr. Glenn Lygrisse, Vice President for Enrollment Management, Tabor College, 400 South Jefferson, Hillsboro, KS 67063. **Phone:** 316-947-3121 Ext. 1723. **Toll-free phone:** 800-822-6799. **Fax:** 316-947-2607. **E-mail:** admissions@tcnet.tabor.edu

Visit CollegeQuest.com for information on majors offered and athletics. Electronic viewbook available at CollegeQuest.com.

UNIVERSITY OF KANSAS
Lawrence, Kansas

- **State-supported**, university, founded 1866
- **Degrees** bachelor's, master's, doctoral, first professional, post-master's, and first professional certificates (University of Kansas is a single institution with academic programs and facilities at two primary locations: Lawrence and Kansas City. Undergraduate, graduate, and professional education are the principal missions of the Lawrence campus, with medicine and related professional education the focus of the Kansas City campus)
- **Suburban** 1,000-acre campus with easy access to Kansas City
- **Coed**, 19,271 undergraduate students, 90% full-time, 53% women, 47% men
- **Moderately difficult** entrance level, 69% of applicants were admitted
- **14:1** student-to-undergraduate faculty ratio
- **54.4% graduate** in 6 years or less
- **$2518 tuition** and fees (in-state); $9121 (out-of-state)
- **$5686 average financial aid** package, $979 million endowment

Students *Undergraduates:* 17,332 full-time, 1,939 part-time. Students come from 52 states and territories, 110 other countries. *The most frequently chosen baccalaureate fields are:* business/marketing, health professions and related sciences, social sciences and history. *Graduate:* 1,235 in professional programs, 7,126 in other graduate degree programs.

From out-of-state	24%	Reside on campus	24%
Age 25 or older	9%	Transferred in	7%
International students	3%	African Americans	3%
Asian Americans/Pacific Islanders	3%	Hispanic Americans	2%
Native Americans	1%		

Faculty 2,020 (75% full-time).

Expenses (1999–2000) *Tuition, state resident:* full-time $2090; part-time $70 per credit hour. *Tuition, nonresident:* full-time $8693; part-time $290 per credit hour. *Required fees:* full-time $428; $31 per credit hour. Full-time tuition and fees vary according to course load and program. Part-time tuition and fees vary according to course load and program. *College room and board:* $3941. Room and board charges vary according to board plan and housing facility. *Payment plan:* installment. *Waivers:* senior citizens and employees or children of employees.

Library Watson Library plus 11 others. *Collection:* 4.3 million titles, 33,515 serial subscriptions, 45,332 audiovisual materials.

College life *Housing: Options:* coed, women-only, cooperative. *Social organizations:* national fraternities, national sororities; 19% of eligible men and 21% of eligible women are members.

Campus security 24-hour emergency response devices and patrols, late-night transport-escort service, controlled dormitory access.

After graduation 400 organizations recruited on campus 1997–98. *Career center:* 7 full-time, 8 part-time personnel. Services include job fairs, resume preparation, interview workshops, resume referral, career counseling, careers library, job bank, job interviews. *Graduate education:* 32% of class of 1999 went directly to graduate and professional school. *Major awards:* 1 Marshall scholar.

Freshmen 8,409 applied, 5,762 admitted, 3,878 enrolled. 101 National Merit Scholars.

Average high school GPA	3.4	SAT verbal scores above 500	N/R
SAT math scores above 500	N/R	ACT above 18	95%
From top 10% of their h.s. class	26%	From top quarter	56%
From top half	87%		

Application *Option:* deferred entrance. *Preference* given to state residents. *Application fee:* $20. *Required:* high school transcript; minimum 2.0 GPA. *Required for some:* minimum 2.5 GPA.

Standardized tests *Admission: Required:* SAT I or ACT.

Significant dates *Application deadlines:* 4/1 (freshmen), rolling (transfers). *Financial aid deadline priority date:* 3/1.

Freshman Application Contact
Mr. Alan Cerveny, Director of Admissions and Scholarships, University of Kansas, KU Visitor Center, 1502 Iowa Street, Lawrence, KS 66045-1910. **Phone:** 785-864-3911. **Toll-free phone:** 888-686-7323. **Fax:** 785-864-5006. **E-mail:** adm@ukans.edu

Visit CollegeQuest.com for information on majors offered and athletics. College video available at CollegeQuest.com.

WASHBURN UNIVERSITY OF TOPEKA
Topeka, Kansas

- **City-supported**, comprehensive, founded 1865
- **Degrees** associate, bachelor's, master's, and first professional
- **Urban** 160-acre campus with easy access to Kansas City
- **Coed**
- **Noncompetitive** entrance level
- **$2934 tuition** and fees (in-state); $6546 (out-of-state)

Expenses (1999–2000) *Tuition, state resident:* full-time $2884; part-time $103 per credit hour. *Tuition, nonresident:* full-time $6496; part-time $232 per credit hour. *Required fees:* full-time $50; $25 per term part-time. Part-time tuition and fees vary according to course load. *College room and board:* $3320. Room and board charges vary according to board plan and housing facility.

Institutional Web site http://www.washburn.edu/

College life *Housing: Option:* coed. *Social organizations:* national fraternities, national sororities, local fraternities; 5% of eligible men and 5% of eligible women are members. *Most popular organizations:* Washburn Student Association, Campus Activities Board, Student Alumni Association, Learning in the Community, Washburn Education Association.

Campus security 24-hour emergency response devices and patrols, late-night transport-escort service.

Application *Options:* electronic application, early admission. *Required:* high school transcript.

Standardized tests *Admission: Required:* ACT.

Admissions Office Contact
Washburn University of Topeka, 1700 SW College Avenue, Topeka, KS 66621. **Toll-free phone:** 800-332-0291. **Fax:** 785-231-1089. **E-mail:** zzhansen@acc.washburn.edu

Visit CollegeQuest.com for information on athletics. College video and electronic viewbook available at CollegeQuest.com.

Kansas–Kentucky

WICHITA STATE UNIVERSITY
Wichita, Kansas

- **State-supported**, university, founded 1895
- **Degrees** associate, bachelor's, master's, doctoral, and post-master's certificates
- **Urban** 335-acre campus
- **Coed**, 10,142 undergraduate students, 60% full-time, 56% women, 44% men
- **Noncompetitive** entrance level, 76% of applicants were admitted
- **19:1 student-to-undergraduate faculty ratio**
- **23% graduate** in 6 years or less
- **$2573 tuition** and fees (in-state); $9026 (out-of-state)
- **$4966 average financial aid** package, $122 million endowment

Part of Kansas Board of Regents.

Students *Undergraduates:* 6,096 full-time, 4,046 part-time. Students come from 48 states and territories, 100 other countries. *The most frequently chosen baccalaureate fields are:* business/marketing, education, health professions and related sciences. *Graduate:* 3,186 in graduate degree programs.

From out-of-state	11%	Reside on campus	6%
Age 25 or older	35%	Transferred in	36%
International students	5%	African Americans	7%
Asian Americans/Pacific Islanders	7%	Hispanic Americans	4%
Native Americans	1%		

Faculty 501 (92% full-time), 76% with terminal degrees.

Expenses (1999–2000) *Tuition, state resident:* full-time $1976; part-time $66 per credit hour. *Tuition, nonresident:* full-time $8429; part-time $281 per credit hour. *Required fees:* full-time $597; $19 per credit hour; $17 per term part-time. Full-time tuition and fees vary according to course load. *College room and board:* $4070. Room and board charges vary according to board plan and housing facility. *Payment plan:* deferred payment. *Waivers:* senior citizens.

Library Ablah Library plus 2 others. *Operations spending 1999–2000:* $4.3 million. *Collection:* 1.1 million titles, 12,055 serial subscriptions, 2,572 audio-visual materials.

College life *Housing:* on-campus residence required in freshman year. *Option:* coed. *Social organizations:* national fraternities, national sororities; 12% of eligible men and 7% of eligible women are members. *Most popular organizations:* Association of Malaysian Students, Organization of Pakistani Students, psychology club, nursing students, Institute of Aeronautics.

Campus security 24-hour emergency response devices and patrols, student patrols, late-night transport-escort service, controlled dormitory access, bicycle patrols by campus security.

After graduation 75 organizations recruited on campus 1997–98. 68% of class of 1998 had job offers within 6 months. *Career center:* 7 full-time, 1 part-time personnel. Services include job fairs, resume preparation, resume referral, career counseling, careers library, job bank, job interviews.

Freshmen 3,142 applied, 2,375 admitted, 1,316 enrolled.

Average high school GPA	3.0	SAT verbal scores above 500	N/R
SAT math scores above 500	N/R	ACT above 18	80%
From top 10% of their h.s. class	14%	From top quarter	34%
From top half	62%	1998 freshmen returning in 1999	67%

Application *Options:* Common Application, deferred entrance. *Application fee:* $20. *Required:* high school transcript. *Required for some:* minimum 2.0 GPA.

Standardized tests *Admission: Required for some:* ACT.

Significant dates *Application deadlines:* rolling (freshmen), rolling (transfers). *Financial aid deadline priority date:* 3/15.

Freshman Application Contact
Ms. Christine Schneikart-Luebbe, Director of Admissions, Wichita State University, 1845 North Fairmount, Wichita, KS 67260. **Phone:** 316-978-3085. **Toll-free phone:** 800-362-2594. **Fax:** 316-978-3795. **E-mail:** wsuadmis@twsuvm.uc.twsu.edu

Visit CollegeQuest.com for information on majors offered and athletics. College video available at CollegeQuest.com.

KENTUCKY

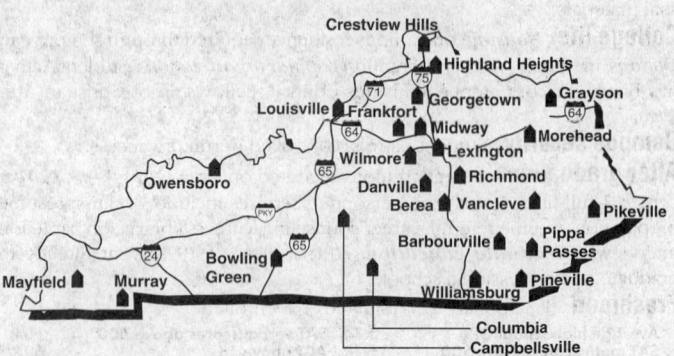

ALICE LLOYD COLLEGE
Pippa Passes, Kentucky

Apply at CollegeQuest.com

- **Independent**, 4-year, founded 1923
- **Degree** bachelor's
- **Rural** 175-acre campus
- **Coed**, 509 undergraduate students, 100% full-time, 60% women, 40% men
- **Moderately difficult** entrance level, 66% of applicants were admitted
- **$360 tuition** and fees
- **$3371 average indebtedness** upon graduation, $14.5 million endowment

Students *Undergraduates:* 509 full-time. Students come from 7 states and territories, 3 other countries. *The most frequently chosen baccalaureate fields are:* biological/life sciences, business/marketing, education.

From out-of-state	30%	Age 25 or older	10%
Transferred in	3%	International students	1%
African Americans	0.2%	Asian Americans/Pacific Islanders	1%
Hispanic Americans	0.4%	Native Americans	0.2%

Faculty 40 (65% full-time), 55% with terminal degrees.

Expenses (1999–2000) includes mandatory fees ($360) and room and board ($2680). *College room only:* $1200. Full-time tuition and fees vary according to reciprocity agreements. *Part-time tuition:* $95 per credit hour. Full-time tuition: $0 for residents of 100 counties in Kentucky, Ohio, Tennessee, Virginia and West Virginia. Tuition for students who are not residents of participating counties: $4000. *Payment plan:* installment. *Waivers:* employees or children of employees.

Library McGaw Library and Learning Center. *Collection:* 80,000 titles, 400 serial subscriptions.

College life On-campus residence required through senior year. *Most popular organizations:* choral group, Phi Beta Lambda, All Scholastic Society, Math/Science Club, Allied Health Sciences Club.

Campus security 24-hour patrols, late-night transport-escort service.

After graduation 10 organizations recruited on campus 1997–98. 85% of class of 1998 had job offers within 6 months. *Career center:* 1 full-time personnel. Services include job fairs, resume preparation, resume referral, career counseling, careers library, job bank, job interviews. *Graduate education:* 30% of class of 1999 went directly to graduate and professional school.

Freshmen 767 applied, 509 admitted, 170 enrolled.

Average high school GPA	3.38	SAT verbal scores above 500	N/R
SAT math scores above 500	N/R	ACT above 18	96%
From top 10% of their h.s. class	11%	From top quarter	32%
From top half	57%	1998 freshmen returning in 1999	58%

Application *Options:* eApply at www.CollegeQuest.com, deferred entrance. *Application fee:* $0. *Required:* high school transcript. *Required for some:* essay or personal statement; 1 letter of recommendation; interview.

Standardized tests *Admission: Required:* SAT I or ACT.

Significant dates *Application deadlines:* 8/1 (freshmen), rolling (transfers). *Notification:* continuous until 8/1 (freshmen). *Financial aid deadline priority date:* 3/15.

Freshman Application Contact
John Mills, Director of Admissions, Alice Lloyd College, 100 Purpose Road, Pippa Passes, KY 41844. **Phone:** 606-368-2101 Ext. 6134. **Fax:** 606-368-2125.

Kentucky

Visit CollegeQuest.com for information on majors offered and athletics.

ASBURY COLLEGE
Wilmore, Kentucky

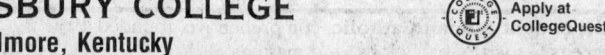

- **Independent nondenominational**, 4-year, founded 1890
- **Degree** bachelor's
- **Small-town** 400-acre campus with easy access to Lexington
- **Coed**, 1,287 undergraduate students, 98% full-time, 58% women, 42% men
- **Moderately difficult** entrance level, 87% of applicants were admitted
- **13:1 student-to-undergraduate faculty ratio**
- **51.12% graduate** in 6 years or less
- **$13,784 tuition** and fees
- **$10,010 average financial aid** package, $17,222 average indebtedness upon graduation, $28.2 million endowment

Students *Undergraduates:* 1,260 full-time, 27 part-time. Students come from 43 states and territories, 20 other countries. *The most frequently chosen baccalaureate fields are:* education, English, philosophy.

From out-of-state	73%	Reside on campus	84%
Age 25 or older	5%	Transferred in	5%
International students	2%	African Americans	1%
Asian Americans/Pacific Islanders	1%	Hispanic Americans	1%
Native Americans	0.5%		

Faculty 147 (59% full-time), 50% with terminal degrees.

Expenses (2000–2001) *Comprehensive fee:* $17,350 includes full-time tuition ($13,644), mandatory fees ($140), and room and board ($3566). *College room only:* $1838. Full-time tuition and fees vary according to course load. Room and board charges vary according to board plan, gender, and housing facility. *Part-time tuition:* $560 per semester hour. Part-time tuition and fees vary according to course load. *Payment plans:* installment, deferred payment. *Waivers:* senior citizens and employees or children of employees.

Library Morrison Kenyon Library. *Operations spending 1999–2000:* $377,978. *Collection:* 123,351 titles, 575 serial subscriptions.

College life *Housing:* on-campus residence required through senior year. *Options:* men-only, women-only, disabled students. *Most popular organizations:* Fellowship of Christian Athletes, Impact (community service), Christian Service Association, ministry teams, Student-Faculty Council.

Campus security 24-hour emergency response devices, late-night transport-escort service, controlled dormitory access, late night security personnel.

After graduation 20 organizations recruited on campus 1997–98. *Career center:* 1 full-time personnel. Services include job fairs, resume preparation, interview workshops, resume referral, career/interest testing, career counseling, careers library, job bank, job interviews.

Freshmen 838 applied, 729 admitted, 328 enrolled. 9 National Merit Scholars, 18 valedictorians.

Average high school GPA	3.51	SAT verbal scores above 500	88%
SAT math scores above 500	76%	ACT above 18	100%
From top 10% of their h.s. class	34%	From top quarter	58%
From top half	86%	1998 freshmen returning in 1999	84%

Application *Options:* eApply at www.CollegeQuest.com, early admission, deferred entrance. *Application fee:* $25. *Required:* essay or personal statement; high school transcript; minimum 2.5 GPA; 3 letters of recommendation. *Required for some:* interview.

Standardized tests *Admission:* Required: SAT I or ACT. *Required for some:* ACT.

Significant dates *Application deadlines:* rolling (freshmen), rolling (transfers). *Financial aid deadline priority date:* 3/1.

Freshman Application Contact Mr. Stan F. Wiggam, Dean of Admissions, Asbury College, 1 Macklem Drive, Wilmore, KY 40390. **Phone:** 606-858-3511 Ext. 2142. **Toll-free phone:** 800-888-1818. **Fax:** 606-858-3921. **E-mail:** admissions@asbury.edu

Visit CollegeQuest.com for information on majors offered and athletics. College video and electronic viewbook available at CollegeQuest.com.

■ *See page 1196 for a narrative description.*

BELLARMINE COLLEGE
Louisville, Kentucky

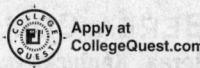

- **Independent Roman Catholic**, comprehensive, founded 1950
- **Degrees** bachelor's and master's
- **Suburban** 120-acre campus
- **Coed**, 1,702 undergraduate students, 77% full-time, 64% women, 36% men
- **Moderately difficult** entrance level, 95% of applicants were admitted
- **14:1 student-to-undergraduate faculty ratio**
- **53% graduate** in 6 years or less
- **$12,650 tuition** and fees
- **$14,200 average indebtedness** upon graduation, $17.2 million endowment

Students *Undergraduates:* 1,306 full-time, 396 part-time. Students come from 19 states and territories, 12 other countries. *The most frequently chosen baccalaureate fields are:* business/marketing, health professions and related sciences, social sciences and history. **Graduate:** 507 in graduate degree programs.

From out-of-state	31%	Reside on campus	37%
Age 25 or older	23%	Transferred in	11%
International students	1%	African Americans	3%
Asian Americans/Pacific Islanders	1%	Hispanic Americans	1%
Native Americans	0.2%		

Faculty 244 (41% full-time), 45% with terminal degrees.

Expenses (1999–2000) *Comprehensive fee:* $16,590 includes full-time tuition ($12,480), mandatory fees ($170), and room and board ($3940). *College room only:* $2440. Room and board charges vary according to housing facility. *Part-time tuition:* $330 per credit. Part-time tuition and fees vary according to course load. *Payment plans:* installment, deferred payment. *Waivers:* senior citizens and employees or children of employees.

Library W.L. Lyons Brown Library. *Operations spending 1999–2000:* $605,888. *Collection:* 97,737 titles, 401 serial subscriptions, 3,853 audiovisual materials.

College life *Housing:* on-campus residence required through sophomore year. *Options:* coed, men-only, women-only, disabled students. *Social organizations:* national fraternities, national sororities; 3% of eligible men and 3% of eligible women are members. *Most popular organizations:* student government, Delta Sigma Pi, Fellowship of Christian Athletes, Campus Ministry, Residence Hall Council.

Campus security 24-hour emergency response devices and patrols, late-night transport-escort service, 24-hour locked residence hall entrances, security cameras.

After graduation 42 organizations recruited on campus 1997–98, 75% of class of 1998 had job offers within 6 months. *Career center:* 2 full-time personnel. Services include job fairs, resume preparation, interview workshops, resume referral, career/interest testing, career counseling, careers library, job bank, job interviews.

Freshmen 887 applied, 843 admitted, 329 enrolled. 6 National Merit Scholars, 1 class president, 16 valedictorians, 52 student government officers.

Average high school GPA	3.4	SAT verbal scores above 500	77%
SAT math scores above 500	83%	ACT above 18	97%
From top 10% of their h.s. class	28%	From top quarter	55%
From top half	79%	1998 freshmen returning in 1999	83%

Application *Options:* eApply at www.CollegeQuest.com, Common Application, electronic application, early admission, early action, deferred entrance. *Application fee:* $25. *Required:* essay or personal statement; high school transcript; minimum 2.5 GPA; letters of recommendation. *Recommended:* interview.

Standardized tests *Admission:* Required: SAT I or ACT.

Significant dates *Application deadlines:* 8/15 (freshmen), 8/15 (transfers). *Early action:* 10/15. *Notification:* 12/1 (early action). *Financial aid deadline priority date:* 3/1.

Freshman Application Contact Mr. Timothy A. Sturgeon, Dean of Admission, Bellarmine College, 2001 Newburg Road, Louisville, KY 40205-0671. **Phone:** 502-452-8131. **Toll-free phone:** 800-274-4723 Ext. 8131. **Fax:** 502-452-8002. **E-mail:** admissions@bellarmine.edu

Visit CollegeQuest.com fr information on majors offered and athletics.

Peterson's Guide to Four-Year Colleges 2001   www.petersons.com

Kentucky

BEREA COLLEGE
Berea, Kentucky

- **Independent**, 4-year, founded 1855
- **Degree** bachelor's
- **Small-town** 140-acre campus
- **Coed**, 1,496 undergraduate students, 99% full-time, 57% women, 43% men
- **Moderately difficult** entrance level, 34% of applicants were admitted
- **11:1 student-to-undergraduate faculty ratio**
- **51.9% graduate** in 6 years or less
- **$199 tuition** and fees
- **$19,042 average financial aid** package, $630 million endowment

Berea College is a small, residential, nonsectarian Christian college recognized for its distinctive academic and work programs and for its special interest in Appalachia. Financial need is an absolute prerequisite for admission. Every accepted student is awarded a full tuition scholarship currently worth $16,600 per year. All students participate in a work program on campus for 10–15 hours per week.

Students *Undergraduates:* 1,491 full-time, 5 part-time. Students come from 42 states and territories. *The most frequently chosen baccalaureate fields are:* business/marketing, home economics/vocational home economics, social sciences and history.

From out-of-state	52%	Reside on campus	82%
Age 25 or older	5%	Transferred in	4%
African Americans	12%	Asian Americans/Pacific Islanders	2%
Hispanic Americans	1%	Native Americans	0.3%

Faculty 146 (84% full-time), 76% with terminal degrees.
Expenses (1999–2000) includes mandatory fees ($199) and room and board ($3686). Financial aid is provided to all students for tuition costs. *Payment plan:* deferred payment.
Library Hutchins Library plus 2 others. *Operations spending 1999–2000:* $968,509. *Collection:* 322,626 titles, 1,662 serial subscriptions, 4,178 audiovisual materials.
College life *Housing:* on-campus residence required through senior year. *Options:* men-only, women-only. *Most popular organizations:* Campus Activities Board, Cosmopolitan Club, Students for Appalachia, flag football and basketball intramurals, Baptist Student Union.
Campus security 24-hour emergency response devices and patrols, late-night transport-escort service, controlled dormitory access, crime prevention programs.
After graduation 75 organizations recruited on campus 1997–98. *Career center:* 1 full-time, 1 part-time personnel. Services include job fairs, resume preparation, resume referral, career counseling, careers library, job bank, job interviews.
Freshmen 1,751 applied, 595 admitted, 423 enrolled.

Average high school GPA	3.47	SAT verbal scores above 500	63%
SAT math scores above 500	59%	ACT above 18	97%
From top 10% of their h.s. class	58%	From top quarter	67%
From top half	92%	1998 freshmen returning in 1999	79%

Application *Option:* early admission. *Preference* given to Appalachian residents with high ability and limited economic resources. *Application fee:* $0. *Required:* essay or personal statement; high school transcript; financial aid application. *Required for some:* interview. *Recommended:* 2 letters of recommendation.
Standardized tests *Admission: Required:* SAT I or ACT.
Significant dates *Application deadlines:* 4/15 (freshmen), 4/15 (transfers). *Notification:* 4/20 (freshmen). *Financial aid deadline priority date:* 2/1.
Freshman Application Contact
Mr. Joseph Bagnoli, Director of Admissions, Berea College, CPO 2220, Berea, KY 40404. **Phone:** 606-986-9341 Ext. 5083. **Toll-free phone:** 800-326-5948. **E-mail:** admissions@berea.edu
Visit CollegeQuest.com for information on majors offered and athletics. College video available at CollegeQuest.com.

■ *See page 1258 for a narrative description.*

BRESCIA UNIVERSITY
Owensboro, Kentucky

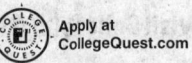
Apply at CollegeQuest.com

- **Independent Roman Catholic**, comprehensive, founded 1950
- **Degrees** associate, bachelor's, and master's
- **Urban** 6-acre campus
- **Coed**, 583 undergraduate students, 83% full-time, 65% women, 35% men
- **Moderately difficult** entrance level, 81% of applicants were admitted
- **14:1 student-to-undergraduate faculty ratio**
- **42% graduate** in 6 years or less
- **$9545 tuition** and fees
- **$8720 average financial aid** package, $8.6 million endowment

Brescia University is a Catholic, career-oriented, coed, liberal arts institution that offers 8 associate, 31 bachelor's, and 9 preprofessional degree programs as well as a Master of Science in Management. Brescia offers the only accredited ministry formation undergraduate program in the nation. Eighty-five percent of Brescia students receive some form of financial aid, including scholarships. World Wide Web: http://www.brescia.edu.

Students *Undergraduates:* 485 full-time, 98 part-time. Students come from 13 states and territories, 13 other countries. *The most frequently chosen baccalaureate fields are:* business/marketing, health professions and related sciences, protective services/public administration. **Graduate:** 37 in graduate degree programs.

From out-of-state	19%	Reside on campus	28%
Age 25 or older	36%	Transferred in	14%
International students	5%	African Americans	3%
Asian Americans/Pacific Islanders	0.3%	Hispanic Americans	1%
Native Americans	1%		

Faculty 70 (57% full-time), 46% with terminal degrees.
Expenses (2000–2001) *Comprehensive fee:* $13,785 includes full-time tuition ($9390), mandatory fees ($155), and room and board ($4240). Room and board charges vary according to board plan and housing facility. *Part-time tuition:* $315 per credit hour. *Part-time fees:* $40 per term part-time. Part-time tuition and fees vary according to course load. *Payment plan:* deferred payment. *Waivers:* children of alumni, senior citizens, and employees or children of employees.
Library Brescia University Library. *Operations spending 1999–2000:* $167,291. *Collection:* 6,717 audiovisual materials.
College life *Housing:* on-campus residence required in freshman year. *Options:* men-only, women-only. *Most popular organizations:* Student Government Association, Brescia Students National Education Association, National Student Speech-Language-Hearing Association, Brescia Student Social Work Association, International Student Organization.
Campus security Late-night transport-escort service, controlled dormitory access.
After graduation 1 organization recruited on campus 1997–98. 95% of class of 1998 had job offers within 6 months. *Career center:* 1 part-time personnel. Services include job fairs, resume preparation, interview workshops, resume referral, career/interest testing, career counseling, careers library, job bank, job interviews.
Freshmen 285 applied, 232 admitted, 92 enrolled. 4 valedictorians.

Average high school GPA	3.24	SAT verbal scores above 500	N/R
SAT math scores above 500	N/R	ACT above 18	85%
From top 10% of their h.s. class	19%	From top quarter	40%
From top half	77%	1998 freshmen returning in 1999	70%

Application *Options:* eApply at www.CollegeQuest.com, Common Application, electronic application, early admission, deferred entrance. *Application fee:* $25. *Required:* high school transcript; minimum 2.5 GPA; minimum ACT score of 18, rank in upper 50% of high school class. *Required for some:* essay or personal statement; 1 letter of recommendation; interview.
Standardized tests *Admission: Required:* SAT I or ACT.
Significant dates *Application deadlines:* rolling (freshmen), rolling (transfers). *Financial aid deadline priority date:* 3/1.
Freshman Application Contact
Mr. Rick Eber, Director of Admissions, Brescia University, 717 Frederica Street, Owensboro, KY 42301-3023. **Phone:** 270-686-4241 Ext. 241. **Toll-free phone:** 877-BRESCIA. **Fax:** 270-686-4266. **E-mail:** admissions@brescia.edu
Visit CollegeQuest.com for information on majors offered and athletics. College video available at CollegeQuest.com.

■ *See page 1304 for a narrative description.*

Kentucky

CAMPBELLSVILLE UNIVERSITY
Campbellsville, Kentucky

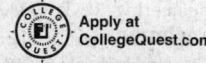 Apply at CollegeQuest.com

- **Independent**, comprehensive, founded 1906, affiliated with Kentucky Baptist Convention
- **Degrees** associate, bachelor's, master's, and postbachelor's certificates
- **Small-town** 70-acre campus
- **Coed**, 1,299 undergraduate students, 91% full-time, 59% women, 41% men
- **Moderately difficult** entrance level, 72% of applicants were admitted
- **16:1 student-to-undergraduate faculty ratio**
- **$8240 tuition** and fees

Students *Undergraduates:* 1,177 full-time, 122 part-time. Students come from 28 states and territories, 17 other countries. *Graduate:* 60 in graduate degree programs.

From out-of-state	10%	Reside on campus	52%
Age 25 or older	14%	Transferred in	11%
International students	5%	African Americans	5%
Asian Americans/Pacific Islanders	0.1%	Hispanic Americans	1%
Native Americans	0.3%		

Faculty 147 (50% full-time), 68% with terminal degrees.

Expenses (1999–2000) *Comprehensive fee:* $12,230 includes full-time tuition ($8000), mandatory fees ($240), and room and board ($3990). *College room only:* $1730. Room and board charges vary according to board plan and housing facility. *Part-time tuition:* $336 per credit. *Part-time fees:* $30 per term part-time. *Payment plans:* installment, deferred payment. *Waivers:* minority students, senior citizens, and employees or children of employees.

Library Montgomery Library. *Collection:* 108,000 titles, 500 serial subscriptions.

College life *Housing:* on-campus residence required through sophomore year. *Options:* men-only, women-only. *Most popular organizations:* Student Government Association, Baptist Student Union, Phi Beta Lambda, African-American Leadership League, Fellowship of Christian Athletics.

Campus security 24-hour emergency response devices and patrols, student patrols, late-night transport-escort service, controlled dormitory access.

After graduation 60 organizations recruited on campus 1997–98. *Career center:* 1 full-time, 1 part-time personnel. Services include job fairs, resume preparation, resume referral, career counseling, careers library, job bank, job interviews. *Graduate education:* 48% of class of 1999 went directly to graduate and professional school.

Freshmen 786 applied, 563 admitted, 308 enrolled. 11 class presidents, 7 valedictorians, 80 student government officers.

Average high school GPA	3.67	SAT verbal scores above 500	36%
SAT math scores above 500	N/R	ACT above 18	71%
From top 10% of their h.s. class	17%	From top quarter	43%
From top half	78%	1998 freshmen returning in 1999	78%

Application *Options:* eApply at www.CollegeQuest.com, Common Application, electronic application, deferred entrance. *Application fee:* $20. *Required:* high school transcript; minimum 2.0 GPA. *Recommended:* essay or personal statement; minimum 3.0 GPA; letters of recommendation; interview.

Standardized tests *Admission: Required:* SAT I or ACT.

Significant dates *Application deadlines:* rolling (freshmen), rolling (transfers). *Financial aid deadline priority date:* 3/1.

Freshman Application Contact
Mr. R. Trent Argo, Director of Admissions, Campbellsville University, 1 University Drive, Campbellsville, KY 42718-2799. **Phone:** 270-789-5552. **Toll-free phone:** 800-264-6014. **Fax:** 270-789-5071. **E-mail:** admissions@campbellsvil.edu

Visit CollegeQuest.com for information on majors offered and athletics. College video available at CollegeQuest.com.

CENTRE COLLEGE
Danville, Kentucky

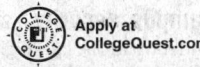 Apply at CollegeQuest.com

- **Independent**, 4-year, founded 1819, affiliated with Presbyterian Church (U.S.A.)
- **Degree** bachelor's
- **Small-town** 100-acre campus
- **Coed**, 1,015 undergraduate students, 99% full-time, 51% women, 49% men
- **Very difficult** entrance level, 86% of applicants were admitted
- **10:1 student-to-undergraduate faculty ratio**
- **73% graduate** in 6 years or less
- **$21,350 comprehensive fee**
- **$15,120 average financial aid** package, $13,000 average indebtedness upon graduation, $154.7 million endowment

Students *Undergraduates:* 1,013 full-time, 2 part-time. Students come from 39 states and territories, 7 other countries. *The most frequently chosen baccalaureate fields are:* English, biological/life sciences, social sciences and history.

From out-of-state	35%	Reside on campus	95%
Age 25 or older	1%	Transferred in	2%
International students	1%	African Americans	3%
Asian Americans/Pacific Islanders	1%	Hispanic Americans	0.5%
Native Americans	0.1%		

Faculty 100 (91% full-time), 87% with terminal degrees.

Expenses (1999–2000) *Comprehensive fee:* $21,350. Room and board charges vary according to board plan. *Part-time tuition:* $495 per semester hour. Part-time tuition and fees vary according to course load. *Payment plan:* installment. *Waivers:* children of alumni and employees or children of employees.

Library Doherty Library plus 1 other. *Operations spending 1999–2000:* $740,479. *Collection:* 265,000 titles, 850 serial subscriptions.

College life *Housing:* on-campus residence required through sophomore year. *Options:* coed, men-only, women-only. *Social organizations:* national fraternities, national sororities; 60% of eligible men and 65% of eligible women are members. *Most popular organizations:* CARE (Centre Action Reaches Everyone), Centre Christian Fellowship, College Democrats and Republicans, Student Congress, outdoors club.

Campus security 24-hour emergency response devices and patrols, late-night transport-escort service, controlled dormitory access.

After graduation 25 organizations recruited on campus 1997–98. 70% of class of 1998 had job offers within 6 months. *Career center:* 3 full-time personnel. Services include job fairs, resume preparation, interview workshops, resume referral, career counseling, careers library, job bank, job interviews. *Graduate education:* 40% of class of 1999 went directly to graduate and professional school: 21% graduate arts and sciences, 9% law, 5% medicine, 2% business, 1% dentistry, 1% engineering, 1% theology. *Major awards:* 1 Rhodes, 1 Fulbright Scholar.

Freshmen 1,142 applied, 977 admitted, 250 enrolled. 6 National Merit Scholars, 22 valedictorians, 108 student government officers.

Average high school GPA	3.68	SAT verbal scores above 500	98%
SAT math scores above 500	95%	ACT above 18	100%
From top 10% of their h.s. class	50%	From top quarter	84%
From top half	97%	1998 freshmen returning in 1999	87%

Application *Options:* eApply at www.CollegeQuest.com, Common Application, early admission, early decision, early action, deferred entrance. *Application fee:* $30. *Required:* essay or personal statement; high school transcript; 1 letter of recommendation. *Recommended:* interview.

Standardized tests *Admission: Required:* SAT I or ACT. *Recommended:* SAT II: Writing Test.

Significant dates *Application deadlines:* 2/1 (freshmen), 6/1 (transfers). *Early decision:* 11/15, 12/1. *Notification:* 3/1 (freshmen), 12/15 (early decision), 1/1 (early action). *Financial aid deadline:* 3/1.

Freshman Application Contact
Mr. J. Carey Thompson, Dean of Admission and Financial Aid, Centre College, 600 West Walnut Street, Danville, KY 40422-1394. **Phone:** 606-238-5350. **Toll-free phone:** 800-423-6236. **Fax:** 606-238-5456. **E-mail:** admission@centre.edu

Visit CollegeQuest.com for information on majors offered and athletics. College video available at CollegeQuest.com.

CLEAR CREEK BAPTIST BIBLE COLLEGE
Pineville, Kentucky

- **Independent Southern Baptist**, 4-year, founded 1926
- **Degrees** associate and bachelor's

Kentucky

Clear Creek Baptist Bible College (continued)
- **Rural** 700-acre campus
- **Coed,** primarily men
- **Noncompetitive** entrance level
- **$3170 tuition** and fees

Expenses (1999–2000) *Comprehensive fee:* $5910 includes full-time tuition ($2820), mandatory fees ($350), and room and board ($2740). Room and board charges vary according to housing facility. *Part-time tuition:* $160 per semester hour. *Part-time fees:* $110 per term part-time.
Institutional Web site http://www.ccbbc.edu/
College life *Housing: Option:* coed.
Campus security 24-hour emergency response devices, student patrols.
Application *Options:* Common Application, deferred entrance. *Application fee:* $40. *Required:* essay or personal statement; 4 letters of recommendation; age 21 or over. *Recommended:* high school transcript; interview.
Admissions Office Contact
Clear Creek Baptist Bible College, 300 Clear Creek Road, Pineville, KY 40977-9754. **E-mail:** ccbbc@tcnet.net
Visit CollegeQuest.com for information on athletics. College video available at CollegeQuest.com.

CUMBERLAND COLLEGE
Williamsburg, Kentucky

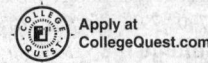

- **Independent Kentucky Baptist,** comprehensive, founded 1889
- **Degrees** bachelor's and master's
- **Rural** 30-acre campus with easy access to Knoxville
- **Coed,** 1,393 undergraduate students, 98% full-time, 53% women, 47% men
- **Moderately difficult** entrance level, 69% of applicants were admitted
- **17:1 student-to-undergraduate faculty ratio**
- **$9920 tuition** and fees
- **$10,631 average financial aid** package, $14,469 average indebtedness upon graduation, $39.9 million endowment

Cumberland College is a 4-year, private, liberal arts college situated in the foothills of the Kentucky mountains. Founded in 1889, the College strives to provide a high-quality education at a reasonable cost while maintaining a strong commitment to the Christian values established by its founders.

Students *Undergraduates:* 1,361 full-time, 32 part-time. Students come from 36 states and territories, 14 other countries. *The most frequently chosen baccalaureate fields are:* business/marketing, education, psychology. **Graduate:** 122 in graduate degree programs.

From out-of-state	35%	Reside on campus	53%
Age 25 or older	7%	Transferred in	6%
International students	2%	African Americans	4%
Asian Americans/Pacific Islanders	0.3%	Hispanic Americans	1%

Faculty 101 (96% full-time), 64% with terminal degrees.
Expenses (2000–2001) *Comprehensive fee:* $14,196 includes full-time tuition ($9698), mandatory fees ($222), and room and board ($4276). *Part-time fees:* $46 per term part-time. Part-time tuition and fees vary according to course load. *Payment plan:* installment. *Waivers:* employees or children of employees.
Library Norma Perkins Hagan Memorial Library. *Operations spending 1999–2000:* $562,833. *Collection:* 159,068 titles, 2,020 serial subscriptions, 6,756 audiovisual materials.
College life *Housing:* on-campus residence required through junior year. *Options:* men-only, women-only. *Most popular organizations:* Baptist Student Union, Student Government Association, Campus Activity Board, Mountain Outreach, Fellowship of Christian Athletes.
Campus security 24-hour emergency response devices and patrols, student patrols, late-night transport-escort service.
After graduation 60 organizations recruited on campus 1997–98. 90% of class of 1998 had job offers within 6 months. *Career center:* 2 full-time, 1 part-time personnel. Services include job fairs, resume preparation, interview workshops, resume referral, career/interest testing, career counseling, careers library, job interviews. **Graduate education:** 29% of class of 1999 went directly to graduate and professional school: 15% education, 3% graduate arts and sciences, 3% medicine, 2% business, 2% theology, 1% dentistry, 1% engineering, 1% law, 1% veterinary medicine.

Freshmen 961 applied, 666 admitted, 403 enrolled. 16 valedictorians.

Average high school GPA	3.24	SAT verbal scores above 500	49%
SAT math scores above 500	57%	ACT above 18	99%
From top 10% of their h.s. class	19%	From top quarter	42%
From top half	72%	1998 freshmen returning in 1999	63%

Application *Options:* eApply at www.CollegeQuest.com, deferred entrance. *Application fee:* $25. *Required:* essay or personal statement; high school transcript; minimum 2.0 GPA; 2 letters of recommendation. *Recommended:* interview.
Standardized tests *Admission: Required:* SAT I or ACT.
Significant dates *Application deadlines:* rolling (freshmen), rolling (transfers). *Financial aid deadline priority date:* 3/1.
Freshman Application Contact
Mrs. Erica Harris, Coordinator of Admissions, Cumberland College, 6178 College Station Drive, Williamsburg, KY 40769. **Phone:** 606-539-4241. **Toll-free phone:** 800-343-1609. **Fax:** 606-539-4303. **E-mail:** admiss@cc.cumber.edu
Visit CollegeQuest.com for information on majors offered and athletics. College video available at CollegeQuest.com.

- *See page 1546 for a narrative description.*

EASTERN KENTUCKY UNIVERSITY
Richmond, Kentucky

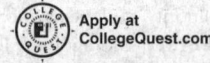

- **State-supported,** comprehensive, founded 1906
- **Degrees** associate, bachelor's, and master's
- **Small-town** 500-acre campus with easy access to Lexington
- **Coed,** 12,141 undergraduate students, 84% full-time, 60% women, 40% men
- **Noncompetitive** entrance level, 52% of applicants were admitted
- **17:1 student-to-undergraduate faculty ratio**
- **27% graduate** in 6 years or less
- **$2390 tuition** and fees (in-state); $6430 (out-of-state)

Part of Kentucky Council on Post Secondary Education.
Students *Undergraduates:* 10,147 full-time, 1,994 part-time. Students come from 49 states and territories. *The most frequently chosen baccalaureate fields are:* education, health professions and related sciences, protective services/public administration. **Graduate:** 1,919 in graduate degree programs.

From out-of-state	7%	Reside on campus	33%
Age 25 or older	27%	Transferred in	8%
International students	1%	African Americans	4%
Asian Americans/Pacific Islanders	0.5%	Hispanic Americans	0.4%
Native Americans	0.2%		

Faculty 680.
Expenses (1999–2000) *Tuition, state resident:* full-time $2390; part-time $100 per semester hour. *Tuition, nonresident:* full-time $6430; part-time $261 per semester hour. Part-time tuition and fees vary according to course load. *College room and board:* $3676; room only: $1356. Room and board charges vary according to board plan and housing facility. *Payment plan:* deferred payment. *Waivers:* employees or children of employees.
Library John Grant Crabbe Library plus 2 others. *Collection:* 865,009 titles, 3,907 serial subscriptions.
College life *Housing:* on-campus residence required through senior year. *Options:* coed, men-only, women-only. *Social organizations:* national fraternities, national sororities; 13% of eligible men and 15% of eligible women are members. *Most popular organizations:* fraternities, sororities, honor society, regular society.
Campus security 24-hour emergency response devices and patrols, student patrols, late-night transport-escort service.
After graduation *Career center:* 5 full-time, 5 part-time personnel. Services include job fairs, resume preparation, resume referral, career counseling, careers library, job bank, job interviews. **Graduate education:** 24% of class of 1999 went directly to graduate and professional school.

Kentucky

Freshmen 9,794 applied, 5,100 admitted, 2,157 enrolled.

| SAT verbal scores above 500 | N/R | SAT math scores above 500 | N/R |
| ACT above 18 | 66% | | |

Application *Options:* eApply at www.CollegeQuest.com, Common Application, deferred entrance. *Required:* high school transcript.
Standardized tests *Admission: Required:* ACT.
Significant dates *Application deadlines:* rolling (freshmen), rolling (transfers). *Financial aid deadline priority date:* 4/1.
Freshman Application Contact
Mr. James L. Grigsby, Director of Admissions, Eastern Kentucky University, 521 Lancaster Avenue, Richmond, KY 40475-3102. **Phone:** 606-622-2106. **Toll-free phone:** 800-262-7493.
Visit CollegeQuest.com for information on majors offered and athletics.

GEORGETOWN COLLEGE
Georgetown, Kentucky

Apply at CollegeQuest.com

- **Independent**, comprehensive, founded 1829, affiliated with Baptist Church
- **Degrees** bachelor's and master's
- **Suburban** 110-acre campus with easy access to Cincinnati
- **Coed**, 1,320 undergraduate students, 98% full-time, 58% women, 42% men
- **Moderately difficult** entrance level, 89% of applicants were admitted
- **13:1 student-to-undergraduate faculty ratio**
- **$12,390 tuition** and fees
- **$11,821 average financial aid** package, $14,393 average indebtedness upon graduation, $35.7 million endowment

Students *Undergraduates:* 1,298 full-time, 22 part-time. Students come from 26 states and territories, 5 other countries. *The most frequently chosen baccalaureate fields are:* biological/life sciences, business/marketing, psychology. *Graduate:* 334 in graduate degree programs.

From out-of-state	16%	Reside on campus	90%
Age 25 or older	2%	Transferred in	3%
International students	1%	African Americans	3%
Asian Americans/Pacific Islanders	0.1%	Hispanic Americans	0.2%
Native Americans	0.1%		

Faculty 139 (63% full-time), 71% with terminal degrees.
Expenses (2000–2001) *Comprehensive fee:* $16,990 includes full-time tuition ($12,150), mandatory fees ($240), and room and board ($4600). *College room only:* $2220. Room and board charges vary according to board plan, housing facility, and location. *Part-time tuition:* $470 per semester hour. *Part-time fees:* $15 per term. Part-time tuition and fees vary according to course load. *Payment plan:* deferred payment. *Waivers:* employees or children of employees.
Library Anna Ashcraft Ensor Learning Resource Center plus 1 other. *Operations spending 1999–2000:* $625,883. *Collection:* 139,940 titles, 1,105 serial subscriptions, 2,327 audiovisual materials.
College life *Housing:* on-campus residence required through senior year. *Options:* men-only, women-only. *Social organizations:* national fraternities, national sororities, local fraternities; 33% of eligible men and 35% of eligible women are members. *Most popular organizations:* Campus Ministries, Association of Georgetown Students, Harper-Gatlon Leadership Center, President's Ambassadors, Phi Beta Lambda.
Campus security 24-hour patrols, late-night transport-escort service.
After graduation 40 organizations recruited on campus 1997–98. *Career center:* 1 full-time personnel. Services include job fairs, resume preparation, interview workshops, resume referral, career/interest testing, career counseling, careers library, job bank, job interviews. *Major awards:* 1 Fulbright Scholar.
Freshmen 810 applied, 721 admitted, 340 enrolled. 33 valedictorians.

Average high school GPA	3.53	SAT verbal scores above 500	75%
SAT math scores above 500	69%	ACT above 18	99%
From top 10% of their h.s. class	38%	From top quarter	66%
From top half	92%	1998 freshmen returning in 1999	78%

Application *Options:* eApply at www.CollegeQuest.com, electronic application, early decision. *Application fee:* $25. *Required:* essay or personal statement; high school transcript; minimum 2.5 GPA. *Required for some:* letters of recommendation; interview.

Standardized tests *Admission: Required:* SAT I or ACT. *Recommended:* ACT.
Significant dates *Application deadlines:* 7/1 (freshmen), rolling (transfers). *Early decision:* 9/15. *Notification:* 10/15 (early decision). *Financial aid deadline priority date:* 2/15.
Freshman Application Contact
Ms. Dana Hall, Interim Director of Admissions, Georgetown College, 400 East College Street, Georgetown, KY 40324-1696. **Phone:** 502-863-8009. **Toll-free phone:** 800-788-9985. **Fax:** 502-868-8891. **E-mail:** admissions@georgetowncollege.edu
Visit CollegeQuest.com for information on majors offered and athletics.

■ *See page 1712 for a narrative description.*

KENTUCKY CHRISTIAN COLLEGE
Grayson, Kentucky

- **Independent**, 4-year, founded 1919, affiliated with Christian Churches and Churches of Christ
- **Degrees** associate and bachelor's
- **Rural** 124-acre campus
- **Coed**, 564 undergraduate students, 96% full-time, 54% women, 46% men
- **Moderately difficult** entrance level, 88% of applicants were admitted
- **16:1 student-to-undergraduate faculty ratio**
- **41.3% graduate** in 6 years or less
- **$6880 tuition** and fees
- **$8404 average financial aid** package, $17,119 average indebtedness upon graduation, $4.2 million endowment

Students *Undergraduates:* 540 full-time, 24 part-time. Students come from 27 states and territories, 8 other countries. *The most frequently chosen baccalaureate fields are:* education, business/marketing, philosophy.

From out-of-state	72%	Reside on campus	90%
Age 25 or older	6%	Transferred in	6%
International students	2%	African Americans	1%
Asian Americans/Pacific Islanders	0.2%	Hispanic Americans	1%
Native Americans	1%		

Faculty 49 (59% full-time), 57% with terminal degrees.
Expenses (1999–2000) *Comprehensive fee:* $10,794 includes full-time tuition ($6880) and room and board ($3914). Room and board charges vary according to board plan. *Part-time tuition:* $215 per credit hour. *Payment plans:* tuition prepayment, installment. *Waivers:* minority students and employees or children of employees.
Library Young Library. *Operations spending 1999–2000:* $179,282. *Collection:* 447 serial subscriptions, 326 audiovisual materials.
College life *Housing:* on-campus residence required through senior year. *Options:* men-only, women-only. *Most popular organizations:* Rotaract, SIFE, Matheteuo, Pi Chi Delta, Laos Alpha.
Campus security 24-hour emergency response devices, late-night transport-escort service, late night security patrols.
After graduation *Career center:* Services include career counseling.
Freshmen 272 applied, 240 admitted, 157 enrolled. 4 valedictorians.

Average high school GPA	3.04	SAT verbal scores above 500	51%
SAT math scores above 500	44%	ACT above 18	68%
From top 10% of their h.s. class	13%	From top quarter	31%
From top half	58%	1998 freshmen returning in 1999	49%

Application *Option:* Common Application. *Application fee:* $25. *Required:* essay or personal statement; high school transcript; 3 letters of recommendation. *Required for some:* interview. *Recommended:* minimum 2.0 GPA.
Standardized tests *Admission: Required:* SAT I or ACT.
Significant dates *Application deadlines:* rolling (freshmen), rolling (transfers). *Financial aid deadline priority date:* 4/1.
Freshman Application Contact
Mrs. Sandra Deakins, Director of Admissions, Kentucky Christian College, 100 Academic Parkway, Grayson, KY 41143-2205. **Phone:** 606-474-3266. **Toll-free phone:** 800-522-3181. **Fax:** 606-474-3155. **E-mail:** knights@email.kcc.edu
Visit CollegeQuest.com for information on majors offered and athletics.

Kentucky

KENTUCKY MOUNTAIN BIBLE COLLEGE
Vancleve, Kentucky

- **Independent interdenominational**, 4-year, founded 1931
- **Degrees** associate and bachelor's
- **Rural** 35-acre campus
- **Coed**, 72 undergraduate students, 88% full-time, 44% women, 56% men
- **Minimally difficult** entrance level
- **5:1 student-to-undergraduate faculty ratio**
- **20% graduate** in 6 years or less
- **$4170 tuition** and fees
- **$144,301 endowment**

Students *Undergraduates:* 63 full-time, 9 part-time. Students come from 11 states and territories, 4 other countries. *The most frequently chosen baccalaureate field is:* philosophy.

From out-of-state	72%	Reside on campus	93%
Age 25 or older	30%	Transferred in	13%
International students	6%	Asian Americans/Pacific Islanders	1%
Hispanic Americans	3%	Native Americans	1%

Faculty 15 (53% full-time).
Expenses (2000–2001) *Comprehensive fee:* $6970 includes full-time tuition ($3750), mandatory fees ($420), and room and board ($2800). *College room only:* $750. Full-time tuition and fees vary according to course load. Room and board charges vary according to housing facility. *Part-time tuition:* $125 per credit. *Part-time fees:* $88 per term part-time. Part-time tuition and fees vary according to course load. *Payment plan:* installment. *Waivers:* employees or children of employees.
Library Gibson Library. *Operations spending 1999–2000:* $18,000. *Collection:* 22,500 titles, 200 serial subscriptions.
College life *Housing:* on-campus residence required through senior year. *Options:* men-only, women-only. *Most popular organizations:* drama team, choral groups, student council, band, Student Involvement (missionary group).
Campus security Student patrols.
After graduation *Graduate education:* 9% of class of 1999 went directly to graduate and professional school: 9% theology.
Freshmen 15 enrolled.

SAT verbal scores above 500	N/R	SAT math scores above 500	N/R
ACT above 18	N/R		

Application *Option:* deferred entrance. *Preference* given to Christians. *Application fee:* $25. *Required:* essay or personal statement; high school transcript; minimum 2.0 GPA. *Recommended:* interview.
Standardized tests *Admission:* Required: SAT I or ACT.
Significant dates *Application deadlines:* rolling (freshmen), rolling (transfers). *Financial aid deadline:* 8/31. *Priority date:* 3/31.
Freshman Application Contact
Mr. James Nelson, Director of Recruiting, Kentucky Mountain Bible College, PO Box 10, Vancleve, KY 41385-0010. **Phone:** 606-666-5000 Ext. 130. **Toll-free phone:** 800-879-KMBC. **Fax:** 606-666-7744. **E-mail:** jnelson@kmbc.edu
Visit CollegeQuest.com for information on majors offered and athletics. College video available at CollegeQuest.com.

KENTUCKY STATE UNIVERSITY
Frankfort, Kentucky

- **State-related**, comprehensive, founded 1886
- **Degrees** associate, bachelor's, and master's (Louisville)
- **Small-town** 485-acre campus with easy access to Louisville
- **Coed**, 2,062 undergraduate students, 81% full-time, 57% women, 43% men
- **Minimally difficult** entrance level, 45% of applicants were admitted
- **17% graduate** in 6 years or less
- **$2300 tuition** and fees (in-state); $6340 (out-of-state)

Students *Undergraduates:* 1,673 full-time, 389 part-time. Students come from 29 states and territories, 26 other countries. *The most frequently chosen baccalaureate fields are:* education, business/marketing, protective services/public administration. *Graduate:* 116 in graduate degree programs.

From out-of-state	32%	Reside on campus	36%
Age 25 or older	27%	Transferred in	4%
International students	1%	African Americans	64%
Asian Americans/Pacific Islanders	1%	Hispanic Americans	1%
Native Americans	0.1%		

Faculty 130 (97% full-time).
Expenses (1999–2000) *Tuition, state resident:* full-time $2020; part-time $91 per credit hour. *Tuition, nonresident:* full-time $6060; part-time $260 per credit hour. *Required fees:* full-time $280; $20 per term part-time. *College room and board:* $3446; room only: $1576. *Payment plans:* installment, deferred payment. *Waivers:* senior citizens and employees or children of employees.
Library Blazer Library. *Operations spending 1999–2000:* $709,584. *Collection:* 1,181 serial subscriptions, 1,832 audiovisual materials.
College life *Housing:* Options: men-only, women-only. *Social organizations:* national fraternities, national sororities, local fraternities, local sororities; 6% of eligible men and 4% of eligible women are members. *Most popular organizations:* Baptist Student Union, student government.
Campus security 24-hour patrols, controlled dormitory access.
After graduation 26 organizations recruited on campus 1997–98. 50% of class of 1998 had job offers within 6 months. *Career center:* 4 full-time personnel. Services include job fairs, resume preparation, resume referral, career counseling, careers library, job bank, job interviews.
Freshmen 1,134 applied, 511 admitted, 373 enrolled.

Average high school GPA	2.7	SAT verbal scores above 500	N/R
SAT math scores above 500	N/R	ACT above 18	N/R
1998 freshmen returning in 1999	74%		

Application *Option:* early admission. *Application fee:* $15. *Required:* high school transcript. *Required for some:* essay or personal statement; minimum 3.0 GPA; 2 letters of recommendation; interview. *Recommended:* minimum 2.0 GPA.
Standardized tests *Admission:* Required: SAT I or ACT. *Recommended:* ACT.
Significant dates *Application deadlines:* rolling (freshmen), rolling (transfers). *Financial aid deadline:* 5/31. *Priority date:* 4/15.
Freshman Application Contact
Mr. Jimmy Arrington, Director of Records, Registration, and Admission, Kentucky State University, East Main Street, Dept. PG-92, Frankfort, KY 40601. **Phone:** 502-227-6340. **Toll-free phone:** 800-633-9415 (in-state); 800-325-1716 (out-of-state). **E-mail:** jarrington@gwmail.kysu.edu
Visit CollegeQuest.com for information on majors offered and athletics. College video available at CollegeQuest.com.

■ *See page 1872 for a narrative description.*

KENTUCKY WESLEYAN COLLEGE
Owensboro, Kentucky

Apply at CollegeQuest.com

- **Independent Methodist**, 4-year, founded 1858
- **Degree** bachelor's
- **Suburban** 52-acre campus
- **Coed**, 728 undergraduate students, 94% full-time, 57% women, 43% men
- **Moderately difficult** entrance level, 84% of applicants were admitted
- **15:1 student-to-undergraduate faculty ratio**
- **36% graduate** in 6 years or less
- **$10,020 tuition** and fees
- **$12,250 average financial aid** package, $12,000 average indebtedness upon graduation, $10.5 million endowment

Students *Undergraduates:* 687 full-time, 41 part-time. Students come from 8 states and territories, 6 other countries. *The most frequently chosen baccalaureate fields are:* business/marketing, education, health professions and related sciences.

Reside on campus	49%	International students	1%
African Americans	5%		

Faculty 71 (62% full-time).
Expenses (1999–2000) *Comprehensive fee:* $14,790 includes full-time tuition ($10,020) and room and board ($4770). *College room only:* $2190. Full-time tuition and fees vary according to course load. *Part-time tuition:*

$310 per semester hour. *Part-time fees:* $50 per term part-time. Part-time tuition and fees vary according to course load. *Payment plans:* installment, deferred payment. *Waivers:* children of alumni, senior citizens, and employees or children of employees.
Library Library Learning Center. *Operations spending 1999–2000:* $250,184. *Collection:* 74,066 titles, 462 serial subscriptions.
College life *Housing:* on-campus residence required through junior year. *Options:* coed, men-only, women-only. *Social organizations:* national fraternities, national sororities; 14% of eligible men and 33% of eligible women are members. *Most popular organizations:* student government association, student activities programming board, Leadership KWC, pre-professional society, Wesley club.
Campus security Late-night transport-escort service, 12-hour patrols by trained security personnel.
After graduation 16 organizations recruited on campus 1997–98. 97% of class of 1998 had job offers within 6 months. *Career center:* 2 full-time personnel. Services include job fairs, resume preparation, career/interest testing, career counseling, careers library, job bank, job interviews. *Graduate education:* 30% of class of 1999 went directly to graduate and professional school: 15% graduate arts and sciences, 4% business, 4% medicine, 3% law.
Freshmen 618 applied, 518 admitted, 194 enrolled. 1 National Merit Scholar, 10 valedictorians.

Average high school GPA	3.36	SAT verbal scores above 500	54%
SAT math scores above 500	52%	ACT above 18	94%
1998 freshmen returning in 1999	74%		

Application *Options:* eApply at www.CollegeQuest.com, Common Application, electronic application, early admission, deferred entrance. *Application fee:* $20. *Required:* essay or personal statement; high school transcript. *Required for some:* letters of recommendation. *Recommended:* letters of recommendation.
Standardized tests *Admission: Required:* SAT I or ACT.
Significant dates *Application deadlines:* 8/21 (freshmen), 8/21 (transfers). *Financial aid deadline priority date:* 3/1.
Freshman Application Contact
Mr. Pat Fawcett, Dean of Admission, Kentucky Wesleyan College, 3000 Frederica Street, PO Box 1039, Owensboro, KY 42302-1039. **Phone:** 270-926-3111 Ext. 5145. **Toll-free phone:** 800-999-0592 (in-state); 270-999-0592 (out-of-state). **Fax:** 270-926-3196. **E-mail:** admission@kwc.edu
Visit CollegeQuest.com for information on majors offered and athletics.

■ *See page 1874 for a narrative description.*

LINDSEY WILSON COLLEGE
Columbia, Kentucky

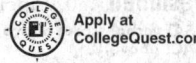
Apply at CollegeQuest.com

- **Independent United Methodist**, comprehensive, founded 1903
- **Degrees** associate, bachelor's, and master's
- **Rural** 40-acre campus
- **Coed**, 1,366 undergraduate students, 90% full-time, 63% women, 37% men
- **Minimally difficult** entrance level, 83% of applicants were admitted
- **20:1 student-to-undergraduate faculty ratio**
- **$9768 tuition** and fees
- **$28 million endowment**

Students *Undergraduates:* Students come from 18 states and territories, 22 other countries. *Graduate:* 49 in graduate degree programs.

From out-of-state	8%	Reside on campus	44%
Age 25 or older	29%	International students	4%
African Americans	7%	Asian Americans/Pacific Islanders	1%
Hispanic Americans	1%	Native Americans	0.3%

Faculty 98 (58% full-time).
Expenses (2000–2001) *Comprehensive fee:* $14,448 includes full-time tuition ($9648), mandatory fees ($120), and room and board ($4680). *College room only:* $1780. *Part-time tuition:* $402 per semester hour. *Payment plan:* installment. *Waivers:* employees or children of employees.
Library Katie Murrell Library. *Operations spending 1999–2000:* $355,000. *Collection:* 80,000 titles, 1,500 serial subscriptions.

College life *Housing:* on-campus residence required through senior year. *Options:* men-only, women-only, disabled students.
Campus security 24-hour emergency response devices and patrols.
After graduation 40 organizations recruited on campus 1997–98. 30% of class of 1998 had job offers within 6 months. *Career center:* 1 full-time, 1 part-time personnel. Services include job fairs, resume preparation, interview workshops, resume referral, career/interest testing, career counseling, careers library, job bank, job interviews.
Freshmen 1,355 applied, 1,119 admitted. 5 class presidents, 7 valedictorians, 5 student government officers.

Average high school GPA	2.9	SAT verbal scores above 500	N/R
SAT math scores above 500	N/R	ACT above 18	80%
From top 10% of their h.s. class	14%	From top quarter	42%
From top half	65%	1998 freshmen returning in 1999	52%

Application *Options:* eApply at www.CollegeQuest.com, early admission, deferred entrance. *Required:* high school transcript. *Required for some:* 3 letters of recommendation. *Recommended:* interview.
Standardized tests *Admission: Required:* ACT.
Significant dates *Application deadlines:* rolling (freshmen), rolling (transfers). *Financial aid deadline priority date:* 4/1.
Freshman Application Contact
Mr. Claude Bacon, Director of Admissions, Lindsey Wilson College, 210 Lindsey Wilson Street, Columbia, KY 42728-1298. **Phone:** 270-384-8100 Ext. 8008. **Toll-free phone:** 800-264-0138. **Fax:** 502-384-8200. **E-mail:** baconc@lindsey.edu
Visit CollegeQuest.com for information on majors offered and athletics.

MID-CONTINENT COLLEGE
Mayfield, Kentucky

- **Independent Southern Baptist**, 4-year, founded 1949
- **Degree** bachelor's
- **Small-town** 60-acre campus
- **Coed**, 211 undergraduate students, 77% full-time, 41% women, 59% men
- **Noncompetitive** entrance level, 100% of applicants were admitted
- **8:1 student-to-undergraduate faculty ratio**
- **$2960 tuition** and fees
- **$4565 average financial aid** package, $9960 average indebtedness upon graduation, $2.1 million endowment

Students *Undergraduates:* 163 full-time, 48 part-time. Students come from 10 states and territories, 5 other countries. *The most frequently chosen baccalaureate field is:* philosophy.

From out-of-state	24%	Reside on campus	17%
Age 25 or older	57%	Transferred in	29%
International students	2%	African Americans	5%
Asian Americans/Pacific Islanders	1%		

Faculty 42 (33% full-time), 36% with terminal degrees.
Expenses (1999–2000) *Comprehensive fee:* $5948 includes full-time tuition ($2640), mandatory fees ($320), and room and board ($2988). *College room only:* $1412. Full-time tuition and fees vary according to course load and program. Room and board charges vary according to board plan. *Part-time tuition:* $110 per semester hour. *Part-time fees:* $12 per semester hour; $45 per term part-time. Part-time tuition and fees vary according to course load and program. *Waivers:* employees or children of employees.
Library Anne P. Markham Library. *Operations spending 1999–2000:* $56,020. *Collection:* 29,731 titles, 147 serial subscriptions, 290 audiovisual materials.
College life *Housing: Options:* men-only, women-only. *Most popular organizations:* Baptist Student Union, student government.
Campus security Student patrols.
After graduation *Career center:* Services include resume referral, career counseling, job interviews. *Graduate education:* 21% of class of 1999 went directly to graduate and professional school.
Freshmen 50 applied, 50 admitted, 43 enrolled.

SAT verbal scores above 500	N/R	SAT math scores above 500	N/R
ACT above 18	63%	1998 freshmen returning in 1999	58%

Application *Options:* Common Application, early admission. *Application fee:* $10. *Required:* high school transcript; 2 letters of recommendation; interview. *Recommended:* minimum 2.0 GPA.

Kentucky

Mid-Continent College (continued)

Standardized tests *Admission: Required:* ACT.

Significant dates *Application deadlines:* rolling (freshmen), rolling (transfers). *Financial aid deadline priority date:* 4/1.

Freshman Application Contact
Mr. Jerry Muniz, Dean of Enrollment and Retention Management, Mid-Continent College, 99 Powell Road East, Mayfield, KY 42066. **Phone:** 270-247-8521 Ext. 19. **Toll-free phone:** 800-232-4662. **Fax:** 270-247-3115. **E-mail:** mcc@midcontinent.edu

Visit CollegeQuest.com for information on majors offered and athletics.

MIDWAY COLLEGE
Midway, Kentucky

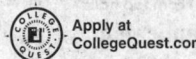
Apply at CollegeQuest.com

- **Independent**, 4-year, founded 1847, affiliated with Christian Church (Disciples of Christ)
- **Degrees** associate and bachelor's
- **Small-town** 105-acre campus with easy access to Louisville and Lexington
- **Women** only, 803 undergraduate students, 62% full-time
- **Minimally difficult** entrance level, 43% of applicants were admitted
- **10:1 student-to-undergraduate faculty ratio**
- **26.3% graduate** in 6 years or less
- **$9122 tuition** and fees
- **$9287 average financial aid** package, $15,946 average indebtedness upon graduation, $17.2 million endowment

Students *Undergraduates:* 495 full-time, 308 part-time. Students come from 30 states and territories. *The most frequently chosen baccalaureate fields are:* business/marketing, education, health professions and related sciences.

From out-of-state	11%	Reside on campus	25%
Age 25 or older	52%	Transferred in	10%
International students	0.5%	African Americans	4%
Hispanic Americans	0.1%	Native Americans	0.2%

Faculty 120 (35% full-time), 31% with terminal degrees.

Expenses (1999–2000) *Comprehensive fee:* $13,972 includes full-time tuition ($9062), mandatory fees ($60), and room and board ($4850). *College room only:* $2275. Full-time tuition and fees vary according to program. Room and board charges vary according to board plan. *Part-time tuition:* $302 per semester hour. *Part-time fees:* $2 per semester hour. Part-time tuition and fees vary according to class time and course load. *Payment plan:* installment. *Waivers:* senior citizens and employees or children of employees.

Library Little Memorial Library. *Operations spending 1999–2000:* $246,551.

College life *Housing:* on-campus residence required through sophomore year. *Option:* women-only. *Most popular organizations:* student government, Midway Chorale, Midway Association of Nursing Students, Council on Religious Activities, Midway Horse Women's Association.

Campus security 24-hour emergency response devices and patrols, late-night transport-escort service, controlled dormitory access.

After graduation *Career center:* 1 full-time personnel. Services include resume preparation, interview workshops, career/interest testing, career counseling, careers library.

Freshmen 648 applied, 277 admitted, 128 enrolled. 2 valedictorians, 12 student government officers.

Average high school GPA	3.01	SAT verbal scores above 500	53%
SAT math scores above 500	37%	ACT above 18	82%
From top 10% of their h.s. class	9%	From top quarter	32%
From top half	57%	1998 freshmen returning in 1999	69%

Application *Options:* eApply at www.CollegeQuest.com, early admission, deferred entrance. *Application fee:* $15. *Required:* high school transcript. *Required for some:* essay or personal statement; letters of recommendation; interview.

Standardized tests *Admission: Required:* SAT I or ACT.

Significant dates *Application deadlines:* rolling (freshmen), rolling (transfers). *Financial aid deadline priority date:* 3/15.

Freshman Application Contact
Mr. K. Bryan, Director of Admissions, Midway College, 512 East Stephens Street, Midway, KY 40347-1120. **Phone:** 606-846-5346. **Toll-free phone:** 800-755-0031. **Fax:** 606-846-5823. **E-mail:** admissions@midway.edu

Visit CollegeQuest.com for information on majors offered and athletics. College video and electronic viewbook available at CollegeQuest.com.

■ *See page 2056 for a narrative description.*

MOREHEAD STATE UNIVERSITY
Morehead, Kentucky

- **State-supported**, comprehensive, founded 1922
- **Degrees** associate, bachelor's, master's, and post-master's certificates
- **Small-town** 809-acre campus
- **Coed**, 6,397 undergraduate students, 87% full-time, 59% women, 41% men
- **Minimally difficult** entrance level, 80% of applicants were admitted
- **18:1 student-to-undergraduate faculty ratio**
- **$2440 tuition** and fees (in-state); $6480 (out-of-state)
- **$5252 average financial aid** package, $13,230 average indebtedness upon graduation, $1.3 million endowment

Students *Undergraduates:* 5,584 full-time, 813 part-time. Students come from 40 states and territories, 33 other countries. *The most frequently chosen baccalaureate fields are:* business/marketing, education, social sciences and history. *Graduate:* 1,522 in graduate degree programs.

From out-of-state	12%	Reside on campus	36%
Age 25 or older	18%	Transferred in	6%
International students	1%	African Americans	4%
Asian Americans/Pacific Islanders	0.2%	Hispanic Americans	0.4%
Native Americans	0.4%		

Faculty 440 (73% full-time), 46% with terminal degrees.

Expenses (1999–2000) *Tuition, state resident:* full-time $2440; part-time $102 per credit hour. *Tuition, nonresident:* full-time $6480; part-time $270 per credit hour. *College room and board:* $3300. Room and board charges vary according to board plan and housing facility. *Payment plans:* installment, deferred payment. *Waivers:* senior citizens and employees or children of employees.

Library Camden Carroll Library. *Operations spending 1999–2000:* $2.2 million. *Collection:* 21,033 audiovisual materials.

College life *Housing:* on-campus residence required through sophomore year. *Options:* coed, men-only, women-only, disabled students. *Social organizations:* national fraternities, national sororities; 20% of eligible men and 20% of eligible women are members.

Campus security 24-hour emergency response devices and patrols, late-night transport-escort service.

After graduation 150 organizations recruited on campus 1997–98. *Career center:* 2 full-time personnel. Services include job fairs, resume preparation, resume referral, career counseling, careers library, job bank, job interviews.

Freshmen 4,079 applied, 3,243 admitted, 1,372 enrolled.

SAT verbal scores above 500	N/R	SAT math scores above 500	N/R
ACT above 18	N/R		

Application *Options:* electronic application, early admission, deferred entrance. *Required:* high school transcript. *Required for some:* letters of recommendation.

Standardized tests *Admission: Required:* SAT I or ACT. *Recommended:* ACT.

Significant dates *Application deadlines:* rolling (freshmen), rolling (transfers). *Financial aid deadline priority date:* 3/15.

Freshman Application Contact
Mr. Tim Rhodes, Director of Admissions and Financial Aid, Morehead State University, Howell McDowell 301, Morehead, KY 40351. **Phone:** 606-783-2000. **Toll-free phone:** 800-585-6781. **Fax:** 606-783-5038. **E-mail:** admissions@morehead-st.edu

Visit CollegeQuest.com for information on majors offered and athletics. College video available at CollegeQuest.com.

■ *See page 2096 for a narrative description.*

MURRAY STATE UNIVERSITY
Murray, Kentucky

- **State-supported**, comprehensive, founded 1922
- **Degrees** associate, bachelor's, and master's

Kentucky

- **Small-town** 238-acre campus
- **Coed**, 7,065 undergraduate students, 88% full-time, 56% women, 44% men
- **Moderately difficult** entrance level, 78% of applicants were admitted
- **17:1 student-to-undergraduate faculty ratio**
- **45.3% graduate** in 6 years or less
- **$2606 tuition and fees** (out-of-state)
- **$4570 average financial aid** package, $14,375 average indebtedness upon graduation, $15.7 million endowment

Part of Kentucky Council on Post Secondary Education.

Students *Undergraduates:* 6,229 full-time, 836 part-time. Students come from 48 states and territories, 62 other countries. *The most frequently chosen baccalaureate fields are:* business/marketing, education, health professions and related sciences. *Graduate:* 1,615 in graduate degree programs.

From out-of-state	28%	Reside on campus	40%
Age 25 or older	22%	International students	3%
African Americans	6%	Asian Americans/Pacific Islanders	1%
Hispanic Americans	1%	Native Americans	0.3%

Faculty 397 (93% full-time), 90% with terminal degrees.

Expenses (2000–2001) *Tuition, state resident:* part-time $111 per credit hour. *Tuition, nonresident:* full-time $2256; part-time $292 per credit hour. *Required fees:* full-time $350; $90 per term part-time. Full-time tuition and fees vary according to reciprocity agreements. Part-time tuition and fees vary according to course load and reciprocity agreements. *College room and board:* $3570; room only: $1750. *Payment plans:* installment, deferred payment. *Waivers:* children of alumni, senior citizens, and employees or children of employees.

Library Harry Lee Waterfield Library plus 1 other. *Operations spending 1999–2000:* $2.6 million. *Collection:* 470,000 titles, 3,000 serial subscriptions.

College life *Housing:* on-campus residence required through sophomore year. *Option:* coed. *Social organizations:* national fraternities, national sororities, local fraternities, local sororities; 25% of eligible men and 25% of eligible women are members. *Most popular organizations:* student government, Student Alumni, Phi Mu Alpha.

Campus security 24-hour emergency response devices and patrols, student patrols, late-night transport-escort service, controlled dormitory access.

After graduation 400 organizations recruited on campus 1997–98. *Career center:* 5 full-time, 2 part-time personnel. Services include job fairs, resume preparation, interview workshops, resume referral, career/interest testing, career counseling, careers library, job bank, job interviews.

Freshmen 2,728 applied, 2,115 admitted, 1,206 enrolled. 24 National Merit Scholars, 61 valedictorians.

SAT verbal scores above 500	N/R	SAT math scores above 500	N/R
ACT above 18	100%	From top 10% of their h.s. class	35%
From top quarter	69%	From top half	100%
1998 freshmen returning in 1999	79%		

Application *Options:* electronic application, early admission, deferred entrance. *Application fee:* $20. *Required:* high school transcript; rank in top 50% of graduating class. *Required for some:* letters of recommendation. *Recommended:* interview.

Standardized tests *Admission: Required:* ACT.

Significant dates *Application deadlines:* rolling (freshmen), 8/1 (out-of-state freshmen), rolling (transfers). *Financial aid deadline priority date:* 4/1.

Freshman Application Contact
Mrs. Stacy Bell, Admission Clerk, Murray State University, PO Box 9, Murray, KY 42071-0009. **Phone:** 270-762-3035. **Toll-free phone:** 800-272-4678. **Fax:** 270-762-3050. **E-mail:** phil.bryan@murraystate.edu

Visit CollegeQuest.com for information on majors offered and athletics. College video available at CollegeQuest.com.

NORTHERN KENTUCKY UNIVERSITY
Highland Heights, Kentucky

- **State-supported**, comprehensive, founded 1968
- **Degrees** associate, bachelor's, master's, first professional, and post-master's certificates
- **Suburban** 300-acre campus with easy access to Cincinnati
- **Coed**, 10,644 undergraduate students, 70% full-time, 59% women, 41% men
- **Noncompetitive** entrance level, 97% of applicants were admitted
- **16:1 student-to-undergraduate faculty ratio**
- **30% graduate** in 6 years or less
- **$2442 tuition** and fees (in-state); $6482 (out-of-state)

Students *Undergraduates:* 7,435 full-time, 3,209 part-time. Students come from 42 states and territories, 73 other countries. *The most frequently chosen baccalaureate fields are:* business/marketing, education, social sciences and history. *Graduate:* 358 in professional programs, 821 in other graduate degree programs.

From out-of-state	23%	Reside on campus	23%
Age 25 or older	28%	Transferred in	5%
International students	1%	African Americans	3%
Asian Americans/Pacific Islanders	1%	Hispanic Americans	1%
Native Americans	0.2%		

Faculty 780 (54% full-time).

Expenses (1999–2000) *Tuition, state resident:* full-time $2100; part-time $89 per semester hour. *Tuition, nonresident:* full-time $6140; part-time $257 per semester hour. *Required fees:* full-time $342; $14 per semester hour. Full-time tuition and fees vary according to course load. Part-time tuition and fees vary according to course load. *College room and board:* $3654; room only: $3326. Room and board charges vary according to board plan and housing facility. *Payment plan:* installment. *Waivers:* senior citizens and employees or children of employees.

Library Steely Library plus 2 others. *Operations spending 1999–2000:* $3.1 million.

College life *Housing: Options:* coed, men-only, women-only, disabled students. *Social organizations:* national fraternities, national sororities, women's association; 4% of eligible men and 4% of eligible women are members. *Most popular organizations:* Greek organizations, campus ministries, academic organizations, student government, activities program board.

Campus security 24-hour emergency response devices and patrols, late-night transport-escort service, controlled dormitory access.

After graduation 60 organizations recruited on campus 1997–98. 85% of class of 1998 had job offers within 6 months. *Career center:* 5 full-time, 3 part-time personnel. Services include job fairs, resume preparation, resume referral, career counseling, careers library, job bank, job interviews.

Freshmen 3,086 applied, 2,978 admitted, 1,873 enrolled.

SAT verbal scores above 500	N/R	SAT math scores above 500	N/R
ACT above 18	73%	1998 freshmen returning in 1999	70%

Application *Options:* early admission, deferred entrance. *Application fee:* $25. *Required:* high school transcript.

Standardized tests *Admission: Required:* SAT I or ACT.

Significant dates *Application deadlines:* 8/23 (freshmen), 8/1 (transfers). *Financial aid deadline priority date:* 3/1.

Freshman Application Contact
Mrs. Debbie Poweleit, Associate Director of Admissions, Northern Kentucky University, Administrative Center 400, Highland Heights, KY 41099-7010. **Phone:** 606-572-5220 Ext. 5154. **Toll-free phone:** 800-637-9948. **E-mail:** admitnku@nku.edu

Visit CollegeQuest.com for information on majors offered and athletics.

- *See page 2184 for a narrative description.*

PIKEVILLE COLLEGE
Pikeville, Kentucky

- **Independent**, comprehensive, founded 1889, affiliated with Presbyterian Church (U.S.A.)
- **Degrees** associate, bachelor's, and first professional
- **Small-town** 25-acre campus
- **Coed**, 769 undergraduate students, 94% full-time, 67% women, 33% men
- **Noncompetitive** entrance level, 100% of applicants were admitted
- **15:1 student-to-undergraduate faculty ratio**
- **18% graduate** in 6 years or less
- **$7800 tuition** and fees
- **$8500 average financial aid** package, $12,000 average indebtedness upon graduation, $13.6 million endowment

Students *Undergraduates:* 722 full-time, 47 part-time. Students come from 9 states and territories, 2 other countries. *The most frequently chosen*

Kentucky

Pikeville College (continued)
baccalaureate fields are: business/marketing, education, psychology. ***Graduate:*** 180 in professional programs.

From out-of-state	11%	Reside on campus	39%
Age 25 or older	17%	Transferred in	15%
African Americans	1%	Asian Americans/Pacific Islanders	0.3%
Hispanic Americans	0.3%	Native Americans	0.1%

Faculty 60 (82% full-time), 43% with terminal degrees.
Expenses (2000–2001) *Comprehensive fee:* $11,140 includes full-time tuition ($7800) and room and board ($3340). *Part-time tuition:* $310 per semester hour. *Payment plan:* installment. *Waivers:* senior citizens and employees or children of employees.
Library Allara Library. *Operations spending 1999–2000:* $234,381. *Collection:* 61,000 titles, 320 serial subscriptions.
College life *Housing:* Options: coed, men-only, women-only. *Most popular organizations:* Pre-Professional, Phi Beta Lambda, Rotaract, Psychology Round Table, nursing club.
Campus security Controlled dormitory access, 12-hour weekday patrols, 24-hour weekend patrols by trained security personnel.
After graduation 25 organizations recruited on campus 1997–98. 65% of class of 1998 had job offers within 6 months. *Career center:* 2 part-time personnel. Services include job fairs, resume preparation, interview workshops, resume referral, career counseling, careers library, job bank, job interviews. ***Graduate education:*** 3% of class of 1999 went directly to graduate and professional school: 2% medicine, 1% law.
Freshmen 890 applied, 890 admitted, 207 enrolled. 6 valedictorians, 4 student government officers.

Average high school GPA	3.2	SAT verbal scores above 500	N/R
SAT math scores above 500	N/R	ACT above 18	71%
From top 10% of their h.s. class	6%	From top quarter	75%
From top half	90%	1998 freshmen returning in 1999	60%

Application *Option:* electronic application. *Application fee:* $0. *Required:* high school transcript. *Recommended:* interview.
Standardized tests *Admission: Required:* SAT I or ACT.
Significant dates *Application deadlines:* 8/20 (freshmen), 8/20 (transfers). *Notification:* continuous until 8/20 (freshmen). **Financial aid deadline priority date:** 3/15.
Freshman Application Contact
Ms. Melinda Lynch, Director of Admissions, Pikeville College, Sycamore Street, Pikeville, KY 41501. **Phone:** 606-432-9322. **Fax:** 606-432-9328.
Visit CollegeQuest.com for information on majors offered and athletics. College video and electronic viewbook available at CollegeQuest.com.

SOUTHERN BAPTIST THEOLOGICAL SEMINARY
Louisville, Kentucky

Admissions Office Contact
Southern Baptist Theological Seminary, 2825 Lexington Road, Louisville, KY 40280-0004.

SPALDING UNIVERSITY
Louisville, Kentucky

- **Independent**, comprehensive, founded 1814, affiliated with Roman Catholic Church
- **Degrees** associate, bachelor's, master's, and doctoral
- **Urban** 5-acre campus
- **Coed**, 1,001 undergraduate students, 74% full-time, 79% women, 21% men
- **Moderately difficult** entrance level, 83% of applicants were admitted
- **$10,996 tuition** and fees
- **$10,500 average financial aid** package, $11,620 average indebtedness upon graduation, $4.6 million endowment

Students *Undergraduates:* 742 full-time, 259 part-time. Students come from 10 states and territories, 16 other countries. ***Graduate:*** 491 in graduate degree programs.

From out-of-state	14%	Reside on campus	13%
Age 25 or older	43%	Transferred in	9%
International students	5%	African Americans	15%
Asian Americans/Pacific Islanders	1%	Hispanic Americans	1%
Native Americans	0.1%		

Faculty 149 (56% full-time).
Expenses (1999–2000) *Comprehensive fee:* $13,806 includes full-time tuition ($10,900), mandatory fees ($96), and room and board ($2810). *College room only:* $1500. Room and board charges vary according to board plan. *Part-time tuition:* $335 per semester hour. *Part-time fees:* $4 per semester hour. Part-time tuition and fees vary according to program. *Payment plan:* installment. *Waivers:* children of alumni, senior citizens, and employees or children of employees.
Library Spalding Library. *Operations spending 1999–2000:* $498,528. *Collection:* 217,838 titles, 604 serial subscriptions, 2,875 audiovisual materials.
College life *Housing:* Option: coed. *Most popular organizations:* student government, Model United Nations/International Club, Nursing Society, National Education Association, Student Occupational Therapy Association.
Campus security 24-hour emergency response devices and patrols, late-night transport-escort service.
After graduation 20 organizations recruited on campus 1997–98. 62% of class of 1998 had job offers within 6 months. *Career center:* 1 full-time personnel. Services include job fairs, resume preparation, interview workshops, resume referral, career/interest testing, career counseling, careers library, job bank, internet job search support. ***Graduate education:*** 5% of class of 1999 went directly to graduate and professional school.
Freshmen 369 applied, 307 admitted, 116 enrolled. 6 valedictorians.

Average high school GPA	3.22	SAT verbal scores above 500	50%
SAT math scores above 500	40%	ACT above 18	74%
From top 10% of their h.s. class	21%	From top quarter	50%
From top half	80%	1998 freshmen returning in 1999	74%

Application *Options:* Common Application, electronic application, early admission, deferred entrance. *Application fee:* $20. *Required:* high school transcript; minimum 2.0 GPA. *Recommended:* minimum 3.0 GPA; interview.
Standardized tests *Admission: Required:* SAT I or ACT.
Significant dates *Application deadlines:* 8/15 (freshmen), 8/15 (transfers). **Financial aid deadline priority date:** 3/1.
Freshman Application Contact
Ms. Gayle Milam, Associate Director of Admissions, Spalding University, 851 South Fourth Street, Louisville, KY 40203-2188. **Phone:** 502-585-7111 Ext. 2229. **Toll-free phone:** 800-896-8941 Ext. 111. **Fax:** 502-585-7158. **E-mail:** admissions@spalding.edu
Visit CollegeQuest.com for information on majors offered and athletics.

SULLIVAN COLLEGE
Louisville, Kentucky

- **Proprietary**, comprehensive, founded 1864
- **Degrees** associate, bachelor's, and master's (master's degree in business administration only)
- **Suburban** 10-acre campus
- **Coed**
- **Minimally difficult** entrance level
- **$9600 tuition** and fees

Expenses (1999–2000) *One-time required fee:* $325. *Tuition:* full-time $9600; part-time $160 per credit. *Required fees:* $12 per course. Full-time tuition and fees vary according to program. Part-time tuition and fees vary according to program. *College room only:* $2790.
Institutional Web site http://www.sullivan.edu/
College life *Housing:* Option: coed. *Social organizations:* local sororities; 10% of women are members. *Most popular organizations:* student government, Travel Club, Sullivan Student Paralegal Association, American Marketing Association, Society of Hosteurs.
Campus security 24-hour patrols.
Application *Application fee:* $80. *Required:* high school transcript; interview.
Standardized tests *Admission: Required:* ACT or CPAt. *Recommended:* ACT.

Admissions Office Contact

Sullivan College, 3101 Bardstown Road, Louisville, KY 40205. **Toll-free phone:** 800-844-1354. **Fax:** 502-456-0040. **E-mail:** tfd@corp.sullivan.edu

Visit CollegeQuest.com for information on athletics. College video available at CollegeQuest.com.

■ *See page 2580 for a narrative description.*

THOMAS MORE COLLEGE
Crestview Hills, Kentucky

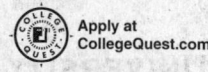

- **Independent Roman Catholic**, comprehensive, founded 1921
- **Degrees** associate, bachelor's, and master's
- **Suburban** 100-acre campus with easy access to Cincinnati
- **Coed**, 1,325 undergraduate students, 59% full-time, 57% women, 43% men
- **Moderately difficult** entrance level, 88% of applicants were admitted
- **10:1 student-to-undergraduate faculty ratio**
- **$12,580 tuition** and fees
- **$10,865 average financial aid** package, $18,931 average indebtedness upon graduation, $6.3 million endowment

Thomas More College is dedicated to the individual learning experience, offering majors and preprofessional programs. The College provides an outstanding liberal arts education that is carefully combined with practical professional training through cooperative education. The Thomas More experience is an education for all seasons of life.

Students *Undergraduates:* 784 full-time, 541 part-time. Students come from 10 states and territories, 12 other countries. *The most frequently chosen baccalaureate fields are:* biological/life sciences, business/marketing, liberal arts/general studies. *Graduate:* 156 in graduate degree programs.

From out-of-state	39%	Reside on campus	18%
Age 25 or older	36%	Transferred in	3%

Faculty 127 (55% full-time).

Expenses (1999–2000) *Comprehensive fee:* $16,336 includes full-time tuition ($12,300), mandatory fees ($280), and room and board ($3756). *College room only:* $2156. Room and board charges vary according to board plan and housing facility. *Part-time tuition:* $314 per credit hour. *Part-time fees:* $10 per credit hour; $10 per term part-time. Part-time tuition and fees vary according to course load and program. *Payment plans:* installment, deferred payment. *Waivers:* children of alumni and employees or children of employees.

Library Thomas More Library. *Operations spending 1999–2000:* $302,752. *Collection:* 131,694 titles, 571 serial subscriptions, 1,756 audiovisual materials.

College life *Housing:* Options: men-only, women-only. *Most popular organizations:* ACT More Program Board, Student Government Association, orientation team, Athletic Student Trainers Association, outdoors club.

Campus security 24-hour patrols, late-night transport-escort service, controlled dormitory access.

After graduation 97 organizations recruited on campus 1997–98. *Career center:* 2 full-time, 1 part-time personnel. Services include job fairs, resume preparation, interview workshops, resume referral, career/interest testing, career counseling, careers library, job bank, job interviews. *Graduate education:* 20% of class of 1999 went directly to graduate and professional school.

Freshmen 787 applied, 694 admitted, 287 enrolled. 2 National Merit Scholars, 3 valedictorians.

Average high school GPA	3.11	SAT verbal scores above 500	N/R
SAT math scores above 500	N/R	ACT above 18	93%
From top 10% of their h.s. class	20%	From top quarter	21%
From top half	71%	1998 freshmen returning in 1999	72%

Application *Options:* eApply at www.CollegeQuest.com, Common Application, deferred entrance. *Application fee:* $25. *Required:* high school transcript; minimum 2.0 GPA. *Required for some:* essay or personal statement; letters of recommendation. *Recommended:* interview.

Standardized tests *Admission:* Required: SAT I or ACT.

Significant dates *Application deadlines:* 8/15 (freshmen), 8/15 (transfers). *Financial aid deadline priority date:* 3/1.

Freshman Application Contact

Mr. Robert A. McDermott, Director of Admissions, Thomas More College, 333 Thomas More Parkway, Crestview Hills, KY 41017. **Phone:** 606-344-3332. **Toll-free phone:** 800-825-4557. **Fax:** 606-344-3638. **E-mail:** robert.mcdermott@thomasmore.edu

Visit CollegeQuest.com for information on majors offered and athletics. College video available at CollegeQuest.com.

■ *See page 2620 for a narrative description.*

TRANSYLVANIA UNIVERSITY
Lexington, Kentucky

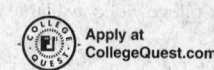

- **Independent**, 4-year, founded 1780, affiliated with Christian Church (Disciples of Christ)
- **Degree** bachelor's
- **Urban** 35-acre campus with easy access to Cincinnati and Louisville
- **Coed**, 1,065 undergraduate students, 99% full-time, 59% women, 41% men
- **Very difficult** entrance level, 89% of applicants were admitted
- **13:1 student-to-undergraduate faculty ratio**
- **67.45% graduate** in 6 years or less
- **$14,600 tuition** and fees
- **$13,021 average financial aid** package, $14,650 average indebtedness upon graduation, $124.5 million endowment

Students *Undergraduates:* 1,060 full-time, 5 part-time. Students come from 28 states and territories, 3 other countries. *The most frequently chosen baccalaureate fields are:* biological/life sciences, business/marketing, social sciences and history.

From out-of-state	18%	Reside on campus	80%
Age 25 or older	1%	Transferred in	2%
International students	1%	African Americans	2%
Asian Americans/Pacific Islanders	3%	Hispanic Americans	0.5%
Native Americans	0.4%		

Faculty 102 (69% full-time), 74% with terminal degrees.

Expenses (1999–2000) *Comprehensive fee:* $19,950 includes full-time tuition ($14,050), mandatory fees ($550), and room and board ($5350). *College room only:* $2996. Room and board charges vary according to board plan and housing facility. *Part-time tuition:* $1561 per course. *Part-time fees:* $61 per course. *Payment plans:* tuition prepayment, installment, deferred payment. *Waivers:* employees or children of employees.

Library Transylvania Library. *Operations spending 1999–2000:* $462,330. *Collection:* 94,926 titles, 1,464 audiovisual materials.

College life *Housing:* on-campus residence required through junior year. *Options:* coed, men-only, women-only. *Social organizations:* national fraternities, national sororities; 60% of eligible men and 60% of eligible women are members. *Most popular organizations:* Student Alumni Association, Student Government Association, Student Activities Board, Crimson Crew, Alternative Spring Break.

Campus security 24-hour emergency response devices and patrols, late-night transport-escort service.

After graduation 66 organizations recruited on campus 1997–98. 45% of class of 1998 had job offers within 6 months. *Career center:* 3 full-time personnel. Services include job fairs, resume preparation, interview workshops, resume referral, career/interest testing, career counseling, careers library, job bank, job interviews. *Graduate education:* 44% of class of 1999 went directly to graduate and professional school: 22% graduate arts and sciences, 11% medicine, 6% law, 2% education, 1% business, 1% dentistry, 1% theology.

Freshmen 1,011 applied, 902 admitted, 308 enrolled. 16 National Merit Scholars, 31 valedictorians.

Average high school GPA	3.49	SAT verbal scores above 500	85%
SAT math scores above 500	83%	ACT above 18	100%
From top 10% of their h.s. class	54%	From top quarter	76%
From top half	97%	1998 freshmen returning in 1999	81%

Application *Options:* eApply at www.CollegeQuest.com, Common Application, electronic application, early admission, deferred entrance. *Application fee:* $30. *Required:* essay or personal statement; high school transcript; minimum 2.75 GPA; 2 letters of recommendation. *Required for some:* interview. *Recommended:* interview.

Kentucky

Transylvania University (continued)

Standardized tests *Admission:* Required: SAT I or ACT.
Significant dates *Application deadlines:* 2/1 (freshmen), rolling (transfers). *Notification:* 3/1 (freshmen). *Financial aid deadline priority date:* 3/1.
Freshman Application Contact
Ms. Sarah Coen, Director of Admissions, Transylvania University, 300 North Broadway, Lexington, KY 40508-1797. **Phone:** 606-233-8242. **Toll-free phone:** 800-872-6798. **Fax:** 606-233-8797. **E-mail:** admissions@transy.edu
Visit CollegeQuest.com for information on majors offered and athletics. College video available at CollegeQuest.com.

■ *See page 2632 for a narrative description.*

UNION COLLEGE
Barbourville, Kentucky

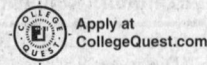
Apply at CollegeQuest.com

■ **Independent United Methodist**, comprehensive, founded 1879
■ **Degrees** bachelor's and master's
■ **Small-town** 110-acre campus
■ **Coed**, 541 undergraduate students, 92% full-time, 48% women, 52% men
■ **Moderately difficult** entrance level, 39% of applicants were admitted
■ **12:1 student-to-undergraduate faculty ratio**
■ **30% graduate** in 6 years or less
■ **$11,320 tuition** and fees

Union College has embarked on the most ambitious facilities project in its history. Phase One of the project includes construction of a new student apartment building, the conversion of Stevenson Hall into a state-of-the-art academic center, improvements to the athletic fields, and renovations to Speed Hall, the current administration building.

Students *Undergraduates:* 496 full-time, 45 part-time. Students come from 28 states and territories, 4 other countries. *Graduate:* 294 in graduate degree programs.

From out-of-state	50%	Age 25 or older	30%

Faculty 53 (94% full-time), 64% with terminal degrees.
Expenses (2000–2001) *Tuition:* full-time $11,070; part-time $225 per hour. *Required fees:* full-time $250. Room and board charges vary according to board plan and housing facility. *Payment plan:* installment. *Waivers:* minority students, children of alumni, senior citizens, and employees or children of employees.
Library Townsend-Weeks Memorial Library. *Collection:* 96,671 titles, 736 serial subscriptions.
College life *Housing:* on-campus residence required through sophomore year. *Options:* coed, men-only, women-only. *Most popular organizations:* Fellowship of Christian Athletes, Baptist Student Union, Thespian Society, Newman Club, Dawg Pound.
Campus security 24-hour emergency response devices and patrols, late-night transport-escort service, controlled dormitory access.
After graduation 2 organizations recruited on campus 1997–98. *Career center:* 1 full-time, 1 part-time personnel. Services include job fairs, resume preparation, career counseling, careers library.
Freshmen 631 applied, 245 admitted, 93 enrolled.

Average high school GPA	3.16	SAT verbal scores above 500	37%
SAT math scores above 500	50%	ACT above 18	73%
From top 10% of their h.s. class	10%	From top quarter	33%
From top half	66%	1998 freshmen returning in 1999	63%

Application *Options:* eApply at www.CollegeQuest.com, Common Application, electronic application, early admission, deferred entrance. *Application fee:* $20. *Required:* high school transcript; minimum 2.0 GPA. *Required for some:* essay or personal statement; letters of recommendation. *Recommended:* interview.
Standardized tests *Admission:* Required: SAT I or ACT.
Significant dates *Application deadlines:* 8/1 (freshmen), 8/31 (transfers). *Financial aid deadline priority date:* 3/15.

Freshman Application Contact
Ms. Joretta Nelson, Vice President for Enrollment and Recruitment, Union College, 310 College Street, Barbourville, KY 40906-1499. **Phone:** 606-546-1220. **Toll-free phone:** 800-489-8646. **Fax:** 606-546-1667. **E-mail:** enroll@unionky.edu
Visit CollegeQuest.com for information on majors offered and athletics. College video and electronic viewbook available at CollegeQuest.com.

■ *See page 2658 for a narrative description.*

UNIVERSITY OF KENTUCKY
Lexington, Kentucky

■ **State-supported**, university, founded 1865
■ **Degrees** bachelor's, master's, doctoral, and first professional
■ **Urban** 685-acre campus with easy access to Cincinnati and Louisville
■ **Coed**, 16,481 undergraduate students, 90% full-time, 52% women, 48% men
■ **Moderately difficult** entrance level, 73% of applicants were admitted
■ **51% graduate** in 6 years or less
■ **$3296 tuition** and fees (in-state); $9216 (out-of-state)
■ **$335.1 million endowment**

Students *Undergraduates:* 14,824 full-time, 1,657 part-time. Students come from 50 states and territories, 84 other countries. *The most frequently chosen baccalaureate fields are:* business/marketing, engineering/engineering technologies, health professions and related sciences. *Graduate:* 1,397 in professional programs, 4,822 in other graduate degree programs.

From out-of-state	14%	Reside on campus	35%
Age 25 or older	11%	Transferred in	9%
International students	2%	African Americans	6%
Asian Americans/Pacific Islanders	2%	Hispanic Americans	1%
Native Americans	0.2%		

Faculty 1,239 full-time.
Expenses (1999–2000) *Tuition, state resident:* full-time $2960; part-time $124 per semester hour. *Tuition, nonresident:* full-time $8880; part-time $370 per semester hour. *Required fees:* full-time $336; $7 per semester hour. Full-time tuition and fees vary according to reciprocity agreements. Part-time tuition and fees vary according to course load and reciprocity agreements. *College room and board:* $3722. Room and board charges vary according to board plan and housing facility. *Waivers:* senior citizens and employees or children of employees.
Library William T. Young Library plus 12 others. *Operations spending 1999–2000:* $19.9 million. *Collection:* 2.7 million titles, 28,535 serial subscriptions, 72,508 audiovisual materials.
College life *Housing: Options:* coed, men-only, women-only. *Social organizations:* national fraternities, national sororities; 8% of eligible men and 10% of eligible women are members.
Campus security 24-hour emergency response devices and patrols, late-night transport-escort service, controlled dormitory access.
After graduation *Career center:* 11 full-time, 1 part-time personnel. Services include job fairs, resume preparation, interview workshops, resume referral, career counseling, careers library, job bank, job interviews. *Major awards:* 1 Marshall scholar.
Freshmen 8,320 applied, 6,096 admitted, 2,681 enrolled. 67 National Merit Scholars, 106 valedictorians.

Average high school GPA	3.51	SAT verbal scores above 500	N/R
SAT math scores above 500	N/R	ACT above 18	99%
From top 10% of their h.s. class	24%	From top quarter	52%
From top half	77%	1998 freshmen returning in 1999	80%

Application *Option:* early admission. *Preference* given to state residents for certain programs. *Application fee:* $20. *Required:* high school transcript; minimum 2.0 GPA.
Standardized tests *Admission:* Required: SAT I or ACT.
Significant dates *Application deadlines:* 2/15 (freshmen), 6/1 (transfers). *Financial aid deadline priority date:* 2/15.
Freshman Application Contact
Mr. Randy Mills, Senior Associate Director of Admissions, University of Kentucky, 100 W.D. Funkhouser Building, Lexington, KY 40506-0054. **Phone:** 606-257-2000. **Toll-free phone:** 800-432-0967. **E-mail:** admissio@pop.uky.edu

Kentucky

Visit CollegeQuest.com for information on majors offered and athletics.

UNIVERSITY OF LOUISVILLE
Louisville, Kentucky

- **State-supported**, university, founded 1798
- **Degrees** associate, bachelor's, master's, doctoral, first professional, post-master's, and postbachelor's certificates
- **Urban** 169-acre campus
- **Coed**, 13,116 undergraduate students, 72% full-time, 54% women, 46% men
- **Moderately difficult** entrance level, 75% of applicants were admitted
- **31.9% graduate** in 6 years or less
- **$3246 tuition** and fees (in-state); $9166 (out-of-state)
- **$6488 average financial aid** package, $350.8 million endowment

Students *Undergraduates:* 9,498 full-time, 3,618 part-time. Students come from 47 states and territories, 69 other countries. *The most frequently chosen baccalaureate fields are:* business/marketing, engineering/engineering technologies, social sciences and history. *Graduate:* 1,257 in professional programs, 3,941 in other graduate degree programs.

From out-of-state	14%	Reside on campus	7%
Age 25 or older	31%	Transferred in	11%
International students	1%	African Americans	13%
Asian Americans/Pacific Islanders	3%	Hispanic Americans	1%
Native Americans	0.3%		

Faculty 1,857 (67% full-time).

Expenses (1999–2000) *Tuition, state resident:* full-time $2960; part-time $123 per hour. *Tuition, nonresident:* full-time $8880; part-time $370 per hour. *Required fees:* full-time $286; $10 per hour; $15 per term part-time. Part-time tuition and fees vary according to course load. *College room and board:* $3400. Room and board charges vary according to board plan and housing facility. *Payment plan:* installment. *Waivers:* senior citizens and employees or children of employees.

Library William F. Ekstrom Library plus 5 others. *Operations spending 1999–2000:* $11.5 million. *Collection:* 969,925 titles, 13,333 serial subscriptions.

College life *Housing: Options:* coed, disabled students. *Social organizations:* national fraternities, national sororities; 15% of eligible men and 10% of eligible women are members. *Most popular organizations:* spirit club, Alpha Phi Omega, Student Organization for Alumni Relations, Golden Key.

Campus security 24-hour emergency response devices and patrols, late-night transport-escort service, controlled dormitory access.

After graduation 300 organizations recruited on campus 1997–98. *Career center:* 12 full-time, 1 part-time personnel. Services include job fairs, resume preparation, resume referral, career counseling, careers library, job bank, job interviews.

Freshmen 4,087 applied, 3,078 admitted, 2,447 enrolled. 15 National Merit Scholars.

Average high school GPA	3.15	SAT verbal scores above 500	N/R
SAT math scores above 500	N/R	ACT above 18	82%
From top 10% of their h.s. class	15%	From top quarter	37%
From top half	64%	1998 freshmen returning in 1999	69%

Application *Options:* electronic application, early admission, deferred entrance. *Application fee:* $25. *Required:* high school transcript; minimum 2.25 GPA.

Standardized tests *Admission: Required:* SAT I or ACT.

Significant dates *Application deadlines:* rolling (freshmen), rolling (transfers). *Financial aid deadline priority date:* 3/15.

Freshman Application Contact
Ms. Jenny Sawyer, Executive Director for Admissions, University of Louisville, 2211 South Brook, Louisville, KY 40292. **Phone:** 502-852-6531. **Toll-free phone:** 502-852-6531 (in-state); 800-334-8635 (out-of-state). **Fax:** 502-852-4776 Ext. 6531. **E-mail:** admitme@gwise.louisville.edu

Visit CollegeQuest.com for information on majors offered and athletics. College video available at CollegeQuest.com.

WESTERN KENTUCKY UNIVERSITY
Bowling Green, Kentucky

- **State-supported**, comprehensive, founded 1906
- **Degrees** associate, bachelor's, and master's
- **Suburban** 223-acre campus with easy access to Nashville
- **Coed**, 12,507 undergraduate students, 83% full-time, 58% women, 42% men
- **Moderately difficult** entrance level, 85% of applicants were admitted
- **18:1 student-to-undergraduate faculty ratio**
- **39% graduate** in 6 years or less
- **$2390 tuition** and fees (in-state); $6430 (out-of-state)
- **$5795 average financial aid** package, $31.8 million endowment

Students *Undergraduates:* 10,403 full-time, 2,104 part-time. Students come from 49 states and territories, 48 other countries. *The most frequently chosen baccalaureate fields are:* business/marketing, communications/communication technologies, education. *Graduate:* 2,202 in graduate degree programs.

From out-of-state	13%	Reside on campus	33%
Age 25 or older	22%	Transferred in	6%
International students	0.5%	African Americans	8%
Asian Americans/Pacific Islanders	1%	Hispanic Americans	1%
Native Americans	0.3%		

Faculty 885 (59% full-time).

Expenses (1999–2000) *Tuition, state resident:* full-time $2020; part-time $97 per semester hour. *Tuition, nonresident:* full-time $6060; part-time $265 per semester hour. *Required fees:* full-time $370; $18 per semester hour. Full-time tuition and fees vary according to reciprocity agreements. Part-time tuition and fees vary according to reciprocity agreements. *College room and board:* $3460; room only: $1660. Room and board charges vary according to board plan and housing facility. *Payment plans:* installment, deferred payment. *Waivers:* children of alumni, senior citizens, and employees or children of employees.

Library Helm-Cravens Library plus 3 others. *Operations spending 1999–2000:* $4.8 million. *Collection:* 664,272 titles, 4,900 serial subscriptions, 22,485 audiovisual materials.

College life *Housing:* on-campus residence required through sophomore year. *Options:* coed, men-only, women-only, disabled students. *Social organizations:* national fraternities, national sororities, local sororities; 12% of eligible men and 8% of eligible women are members. *Most popular organizations:* Student Government Association, University Center Board Council, Campus Crusade for Christ, campus ministries, Residence Hall Association.

Campus security 24-hour emergency response devices and patrols, student patrols, late-night transport-escort service, controlled dormitory access.

After graduation 502 organizations recruited on campus 1997–98. 87% of class of 1998 had job offers within 6 months. *Career center:* 9 full-time, 5 part-time personnel. Services include job fairs, resume preparation, interview workshops, resume referral, career/interest testing, career counseling, careers library, job bank, job interviews.

Freshmen 4,773 applied, 4,069 admitted, 2,552 enrolled. 7 National Merit Scholars, 57 valedictorians.

Average high school GPA	3.08	SAT verbal scores above 500	62%
SAT math scores above 500	56%	ACT above 18	78%
From top 10% of their h.s. class	17%	From top quarter	40%
From top half	70%	1998 freshmen returning in 1999	71%

Application *Application fee:* $25. *Required:* high school transcript; minimum 2.5 GPA.

Standardized tests *Admission: Required:* SAT I or ACT.

Significant dates *Application deadlines:* 8/1 (freshmen); 6/1 (out-of-state freshmen), 8/1 (transfers). *Notification:* continuous until continuous (out-of-state freshmen). *Financial aid deadline priority date:* 3/1.

Freshman Application Contact
Ms. Sharon Dyrsen, Director of Admissions and Academic Services, Western Kentucky University, Potter Hall 117, 1 Big Red Way, Bowling Green, KY 42101-3576. **Phone:** 270-745-4241. **Toll-free phone:** 800-495-8463. **Fax:** 270-745-6133. **E-mail:** admission@wku.edu

Visit CollegeQuest.com for information on majors offered and athletics. College video and electronic viewbook available at CollegeQuest.com.

Peterson's Guide to Four-Year Colleges 2001 www.petersons.com

Louisiana

LOUISIANA

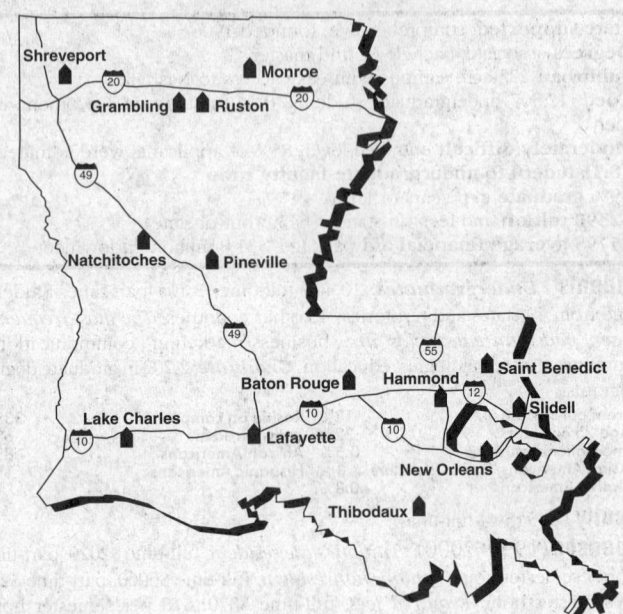

CENTENARY COLLEGE OF LOUISIANA
Shreveport, Louisiana

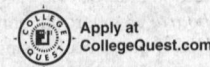 Apply at CollegeQuest.com

- **Independent United Methodist**, comprehensive, founded 1825
- **Degrees** bachelor's and master's
- **Suburban** 65-acre campus
- **Coed**, 868 undergraduate students, 98% full-time, 59% women, 41% men
- **Moderately difficult** entrance level, 83% of applicants were admitted
- **12:1 student-to-undergraduate faculty ratio**
- **50% graduate** in 6 years or less
- **$14,600 tuition** and fees
- **$10,512 average financial aid** package, $16,500 average indebtedness upon graduation, $111.9 million endowment

Students *Undergraduates:* 853 full-time, 15 part-time. Students come from 32 states and territories, 7 other countries. *The most frequently chosen baccalaureate fields are:* business/marketing, biological/life sciences, social sciences and history. *Graduate:* 142 in graduate degree programs.

From out-of-state	38%	Reside on campus	62%
Age 25 or older	3%	Transferred in	4%
International students	2%	African Americans	6%
Asian Americans/Pacific Islanders	1%	Hispanic Americans	3%
Native Americans	1%		

Faculty 122 (57% full-time), 64% with terminal degrees.

Expenses (2000–2001, estimated) *Comprehensive fee:* $19,100 includes full-time tuition ($14,200), mandatory fees ($400), and room and board ($4500). *College room only:* $2000. Full-time tuition and fees vary according to course load and student level. *Part-time tuition:* $473 per semester hour. *Part-time fees:* $30 per term part-time. *Payment plans:* guaranteed tuition, installment, deferred payment. *Waivers:* employees or children of employees.

Library Magale Library plus 1 other. *Collection:* 181,000 titles, 1,190 serial subscriptions, 10,235 audiovisual materials.

College life *Housing:* on-campus residence required through senior year. *Options:* coed, men-only, women-only. *Social organizations:* national fraternities, national sororities; 27% of eligible men and 27% of eligible women are members. *Most popular organizations:* intramural sports, Student Activities Board, crew, Church Career/Campus Ministries, student media.

Campus security 24-hour emergency response devices and patrols, late-night transport-escort service, controlled dormitory access.

After graduation 40 organizations recruited on campus 1997–98. 51% of class of 1998 had job offers within 6 months. *Career center:* 1 full-time personnel. Services include job fairs, resume preparation, resume referral, career/interest testing, career counseling, careers library, job bank, job interviews.

Freshmen 727 applied, 605 admitted, 269 enrolled.

SAT verbal scores above 500	72%	SAT math scores above 500	75%
ACT above 18	95%	From top 10% of their h.s. class	35%
From top quarter	62%	From top half	86%
1998 freshmen returning in 1999	75%		

Application *Options:* eApply at www.CollegeQuest.com, Common Application, early admission, early decision, deferred entrance. *Application fee:* $30. *Required:* essay or personal statement; high school transcript; minimum 2.0 GPA; 1 letter of recommendation. *Recommended:* interview; class rank.

Standardized tests *Admission: Required:* SAT I or ACT. *Required for some:* SAT II Subject Tests.

Significant dates *Application deadlines:* 3/1 (freshmen), 8/1 (transfers). *Early decision:* 1/1. *Notification:* 3/15 (freshmen), 1/15 (early decision). *Financial aid deadline priority date:* 2/15.

Freshman Application Contact
Mr. J. Timothy Martin, Dean of Enrollment Management, Centenary College of Louisiana, 2911 Centenary Blvd, PO Box 41188, Shreveport, LA 71134-1188. **Phone:** 318-869-5131. **Toll-free phone:** 800-234-4448. **Fax:** 318-869-5005. **E-mail:** jtmartin@centenary.edu

Visit CollegeQuest.com for information on majors offered and athletics. College video available at CollegeQuest.com.

DILLARD UNIVERSITY
New Orleans, Louisiana

- **Independent interdenominational**, 4-year, founded 1869
- **Degree** bachelor's
- **Urban** 46-acre campus
- **Coed**
- **Moderately difficult** entrance level
- **$8900 tuition** and fees

Expenses (1999–2000) *Comprehensive fee:* $13,800 includes full-time tuition ($8900) and room and board ($4900). Full-time tuition and fees vary according to program. *Part-time tuition:* $155 per credit hour. Part-time tuition and fees vary according to class time and program.

College life *Social organizations:* national fraternities, national sororities; 18% of eligible men and 21% of eligible women are members.

Campus security 24-hour patrols.

Application *Options:* Common Application, electronic application, early admission. *Application fee:* $10. *Required:* essay or personal statement; high school transcript; minimum 2.0 GPA; 2 letters of recommendation. *Recommended:* interview.

Standardized tests *Admission: Required:* SAT I or ACT. *Recommended:* SAT II Subject Tests.

Admissions Office Contact
Dillard University, 2601 Gentilly Boulevard, New Orleans, LA 70122-3097. **Fax:** 504-286-4895.

Visit CollegeQuest.com for information on athletics.

GRAMBLING STATE UNIVERSITY
Grambling, Louisiana

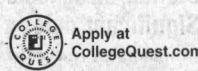 Apply at CollegeQuest.com

- **State-supported**, comprehensive, founded 1901
- **Degrees** associate, bachelor's, master's, and doctoral
- **Small-town** 340-acre campus
- **Coed**
- **Noncompetitive** entrance level
- **$2301 tuition** and fees (in-state); $7651 (out-of-state)

Expenses (1999–2000) *Tuition, state resident:* full-time $2301; part-time $708 per term. *Tuition, nonresident:* full-time $7651; part-time $2,046 per term. Part-time tuition and fees vary according to course load. *College room and board:* $2636.

College life *Social organizations:* national fraternities, national sororities, local fraternities, local sororities.
Campus security 24-hour patrols, student patrols, controlled dormitory access.
Application *Options:* eApply at www.CollegeQuest.com, Common Application, early admission, early decision, deferred entrance. *Application fee:* $10. *Required:* high school transcript.
Standardized tests *Placement: Required:* SAT I or ACT
Admissions Office Contact
Grambling State University, PO Box 607, Grambling, LA 71245. **Fax:** 318-274-6172. **E-mail:** bingamann@medgar.gram.edu
Visit CollegeQuest.com for information on athletics.

GRANTHAM COLLEGE OF ENGINEERING
Slidell, Louisiana

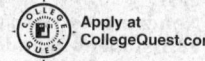

- **Proprietary**, 4-year, founded 1951
- **Degrees** associate and bachelor's (offers only external degree programs)
- **Small-town** campus
- **Coed,** primarily men, 1,200 undergraduate students
- **Noncompetitive** entrance level
- **$5250 tuition** and fees

Students *Undergraduates:* Students come from 52 states and territories, 25 other countries.

Age 25 or older	96%

Faculty 13 (77% full-time).
Expenses (1999–2000) *Tuition:* full-time $5250. *Payment plans:* guaranteed tuition, tuition prepayment, deferred payment.
College life *Housing:* college housing not available.
Freshmen

SAT verbal scores above 500	N/R	SAT math scores above 500	N/R
ACT above 18	N/R		

Application *Option:* eApply at www.CollegeQuest.com.
Significant dates *Application deadlines:* rolling (freshmen), rolling (transfers).
Freshman Application Contact
Mrs. Maria Adcock, Director of Student Services, Grantham College of Engineering, PO Box 5700, Slidell, LA 70460-6815. **Phone:** 504-649-4191. **Toll-free phone:** 800-955-2527. **Fax:** 504-649-4183. **E-mail:** gce@grantham.edu
Visit CollegeQuest.com for information on majors offered and athletics.

LOUISIANA COLLEGE
Pineville, Louisiana

- **Independent Southern Baptist**, 4-year, founded 1906
- **Degrees** associate and bachelor's
- **Small-town** 81-acre campus
- **Coed,** 950 undergraduate students, 94% full-time, 59% women, 41% men
- **Moderately difficult** entrance level, 82% of applicants were admitted
- **16:1 student-to-undergraduate faculty ratio**
- **$7413 tuition** and fees
- **$26.4 million endowment**

Students *Undergraduates:* 893 full-time, 57 part-time. Students come from 18 states and territories. *The most frequently chosen baccalaureate fields are:* business/marketing, education, health professions and related sciences.

From out-of-state	7%	Reside on campus	42%
Age 25 or older	14%	Transferred in	6%
International students	1%	African Americans	8%
Asian Americans/Pacific Islanders	1%	Hispanic Americans	2%
Native Americans	1%		

Faculty 63 (100% full-time).
Expenses (1999–2000) *Comprehensive fee:* $10,573 includes full-time tuition ($6912), mandatory fees ($501), and room and board ($3160). *College room only:* $1400. Full-time tuition and fees vary according to program. Room and board charges vary according to board plan and housing facility. *Part-time tuition:* $216 per credit hour. Part-time tuition and fees vary according to course load and program. *Waivers:* senior citizens and employees or children of employees.
Library Richard W. Morton Memorial Library. *Operations spending 1999–2000:* $510,929. *Collection:* 131,000 titles, 600 serial subscriptions.
College life On-campus residence required through senior year. *Social organizations:* local fraternities, local sororities; 10% of eligible men and 20% of eligible women are members. *Most popular organizations:* Baptist Student Union, Delta Xi Omega, Student Government Association, Union Board, Lambda Chi Beta.
Campus security 24-hour patrols, student patrols, late-night transport-escort service, controlled dormitory access.
After graduation 65 organizations recruited on campus 1997–98. *Career center:* 1 full-time personnel. Services include job fairs, resume preparation, resume referral, career counseling, careers library, job bank, job interviews. *Graduate education:* 48% of class of 1999 went directly to graduate and professional school: 12% medicine, 11% graduate arts and sciences, 10% law, 7% theology, 5% business, 1% dentistry, 1% veterinary medicine.
Freshmen 530 applied, 437 admitted, 269 enrolled. 5 class presidents, 53 student government officers.

Average high school GPA	3.3	SAT verbal scores above 500	N/R
SAT math scores above 500	N/R	ACT above 18	95%
From top 10% of their h.s. class	34%	From top quarter	62%
From top half	86%	1998 freshmen returning in 1999	65%

Application *Option:* early admission. *Application fee:* $25. *Required:* high school transcript; letters of recommendation. *Required for some:* minimum 2.0 GPA; 3 letters of recommendation; class rank. *Recommended:* interview.
Standardized tests *Admission: Required:* SAT I or ACT.
Significant dates *Application deadlines:* 8/1 (freshmen), 8/1 (transfers). *Financial aid deadline priority date:* 3/31.
Freshman Application Contact
Mr. Byron McGee, Director of Admissions, Louisiana College, Box 560, Pineville, LA 71359-0001. **Phone:** 318-487-7259 Ext. 7301. **Toll-free phone:** 800-487-1906. **Fax:** 318-487-7550. **E-mail:** admissions@andria.lacollege.edu
Visit CollegeQuest.com for information on majors offered and athletics. College video available at CollegeQuest.com.

LOUISIANA STATE UNIVERSITY AND AGRICULTURAL AND MECHANICAL COLLEGE
Baton Rouge, Louisiana

- **State-supported**, university, founded 1860
- **Degrees** bachelor's, master's, doctoral, first professional, and post-master's certificates
- **Urban** 2,000-acre campus with easy access to New Orleans
- **Coed,** 24,771 undergraduate students, 92% full-time, 53% women, 47% men
- **Moderately difficult** entrance level, 82% of applicants were admitted
- **21:1 student-to-undergraduate faculty ratio**
- **$2881 tuition** and fees (in-state); $7081 (out-of-state)
- **$5876 average financial aid** package, $17,093 average indebtedness upon graduation, $165.1 million endowment

Part of Louisiana State University System.
Students *Undergraduates:* 22,827 full-time, 1,944 part-time. Students come from 51 states and territories, 107 other countries. *The most frequently chosen baccalaureate fields are:* business/marketing, education, engineering/engineering technologies. *Graduate:* 326 in professional programs, 4,729 in other graduate degree programs.

From out-of-state	9%	Reside on campus	23%
Age 25 or older	12%	Transferred in	4%
International students	3%	African Americans	9%
Asian Americans/Pacific Islanders	4%	Hispanic Americans	2%
Native Americans	0.4%		

Faculty 1,397 (93% full-time), 77% with terminal degrees.
Expenses (1999–2000) *Tuition, state resident:* full-time $2301; part-time $495 per term. *Tuition, nonresident:* full-time $6501; part-time $1385 per

Louisiana

Louisiana State University and Agricultural and Mechanical College (continued)

term. *Required fees:* full-time $580. *College room and board:* $4220; room only: $2300. Room and board charges vary according to board plan and housing facility. *Payment plan:* deferred payment. *Waivers:* children of alumni, senior citizens, and employees or children of employees.

Library Troy H. Middleton Library plus 7 others. *Operations spending 1999–2000:* $12.9 million. *Collection:* 17,975 serial subscriptions, 2,043 audiovisual materials.

College life *Housing:* Options: men-only, women-only, disabled students. *Social organizations:* national fraternities, national sororities; 10% of eligible men and 15% of eligible women are members. *Most popular organizations:* intramural athletics, student political organizations, Greek organizations, student professional organizations, religious organizations.

Campus security 24-hour emergency response devices and patrols, late-night transport-escort service, controlled dormitory access, self-defense education, crime prevention programs.

After graduation 1,300 organizations recruited on campus 1997–98. *Career center:* 15 full-time, 25 part-time personnel. Services include job fairs, resume preparation, interview workshops, resume referral, career/interest testing, career counseling, careers library, job bank, job interviews.

Freshmen 9,661 applied, 7,936 admitted, 5,187 enrolled. 38 National Merit Scholars, 148 valedictorians.

Average high school GPA	3.19	SAT verbal scores above 500	N/R
SAT math scores above 500	N/R	ACT above 18	97%
From top 10% of their h.s. class	25%	From top quarter	53%
From top half	84%	1998 freshmen returning in 1999	83%

Application *Option:* early admission. *Application fee:* $25. *Required:* high school transcript; minimum 2.3 GPA. *Required for some:* 1 letter of recommendation; minimum ACT score of 17 or SAT I score of 830.

Standardized tests *Admission:* Required: SAT I or ACT. *Required for some:* SAT I and SAT II or ACT.

Significant dates *Application deadlines:* 5/1 (freshmen), 5/1 (transfers). *Financial aid deadline priority date:* 4/1.

Freshman Application Contact
Interim Director of Admissions, Louisiana State University and Agricultural and Mechanical College, 110 Thomas Boyd Hall, Baton Rouge, LA 70803-3103. **Phone:** 225-388-1175. **Fax:** 225-388-4433. **E-mail:** lsuadmit@lsu.edu
Visit CollegeQuest.com for information on majors offered and athletics. College video available at CollegeQuest.com.

■ *See page 1948 for a narrative description.*

LOUISIANA STATE UNIVERSITY HEALTH SCIENCES CENTER
New Orleans, Louisiana

■ **$20.4 million endowment**

Part of Louisiana State University System.
Students *Undergraduates:* Students come from 14 states and territories. *The most frequently chosen baccalaureate field is:* health professions and related sciences.

From out-of-state	2%	Age 25 or older	24%
African Americans	9%	Asian Americans/Pacific Islanders	6%
Hispanic Americans	3%	Native Americans	0.1%

Expenses (1999–2000) *Payment plan:* deferred payment. *Waivers:* children of alumni, senior citizens, and employees or children of employees.
Library John P. Ische Library plus 2 others. *Operations spending 1999–2000:* $3.7 million. *Collection:* 389,486 titles, 3,500 serial subscriptions, 9,454 audiovisual materials.
College life *Housing:* Option: coed.
Campus security 24-hour patrols, late-night transport-escort service, controlled dormitory access.
Freshmen

| SAT verbal scores above 500 | N/R | SAT math scores above 500 | N/R |
| ACT above 18 | N/R | | |

Application *Application fee:* $50.
Standardized tests *Admission:* Required for some: SAT I or ACT.

Significant dates *Application deadline:* 3/1 (transfers).
Freshman Application Contact
Mr. Edmund A. Vidacovich, Registrar, Louisiana State University Health Sciences Center, 433 Bolivar Street, New Orleans, LA 70112-2223. **Phone:** 504-568-4829.
Visit CollegeQuest.com for information on majors offered and athletics.

LOUISIANA STATE UNIVERSITY IN SHREVEPORT
Shreveport, Louisiana

■ **State-supported**, comprehensive, founded 1965
■ **Degrees** bachelor's and master's
■ **Urban** 200-acre campus
■ **Coed**, 3,480 undergraduate students, 65% full-time, 61% women, 39% men
■ **Noncompetitive** entrance level, 99% of applicants were admitted
■ **18:1 student-to-undergraduate faculty ratio**
■ **18.4% graduate** in 6 years or less
■ **$2200 tuition** and fees (in-state); $6360 (out-of-state)
■ **$3.5 million endowment**

Part of Louisiana State University System.
Students *Undergraduates:* 2,267 full-time, 1,213 part-time. Students come from 28 states and territories, 8 other countries. *The most frequently chosen baccalaureate fields are:* business/marketing, education, liberal arts/general studies. *Graduate:* 686 in graduate degree programs.

From out-of-state	2%	Reside on campus	5%
Age 25 or older	37%	Transferred in	14%
International students	0.2%	African Americans	19%
Asian Americans/Pacific Islanders	2%	Hispanic Americans	2%
Native Americans	1%		

Faculty 220 (60% full-time), 55% with terminal degrees.
Expenses (1999–2000) *Tuition, state resident:* full-time $1950; part-time $225 per course. *Tuition, nonresident:* full-time $6110; part-time $715 per course. *Required fees:* full-time $250; $5 per credit hour; $65 per term part-time. Full-time tuition and fees vary according to course load. Part-time tuition and fees vary according to course load and location. *College room and board:* room only: $4032. Room and board charges vary according to housing facility. *Payment plan:* deferred payment. *Waivers:* senior citizens and employees or children of employees.
Library Noel Memorial Library. *Operations spending 1999–2000:* $1.3 million. *Collection:* 279,821 titles, 1,190 serial subscriptions, 1,914 audiovisual materials.
College life *Housing:* Options: coed, men-only, women-only. *Social organizations:* national fraternities, national sororities; 5% of eligible men and 5% of eligible women are members. *Most popular organizations:* American Humanics, The Louisiana Association of Educators, Catholic Student Union, Biology/Health Club, psychology club.
Campus security 24-hour patrols, student patrols, controlled dormitory access.
After graduation 75 organizations recruited on campus 1997–98. *Career center:* 2 full-time personnel. Services include job fairs, resume preparation, interview workshops, resume referral, career/interest testing, career counseling, careers library, job bank, job interviews.
Freshmen 785 applied, 780 admitted, 501 enrolled. 3 National Merit Scholars.

Average high school GPA	3.03	SAT verbal scores above 500	N/R
SAT math scores above 500	N/R	ACT above 18	N/R
1998 freshmen returning in 1999	61%		

Application *Options:* early admission, deferred entrance. *Application fee:* $10. *Required:* high school transcript; minimum 2.0 GPA. *Required for some:* minimum ACT score of 17 for nonresidents.
Standardized tests *Admission:* Required: SAT I or ACT.
Significant dates *Application deadlines:* 8/5 (freshmen), 8/5 (transfers). *Financial aid deadline priority date:* 6/1.

Louisiana

Freshman Application Contact
Ms. Julie Wilkins, Assistant Director of Admissions and Records, Louisiana State University in Shreveport, One University Place, Shreveport, LA 71115-2399. **Phone:** 318-797-5057. **Toll-free phone:** 800-229-5957. **Fax:** 318-797-5286. **E-mail:** admissions@pilot.lsus.edu
Visit CollegeQuest.com for information on majors offered and athletics.

LOUISIANA TECH UNIVERSITY
Ruston, Louisiana

- **State-supported**, university, founded 1894
- **Degrees** associate, bachelor's, master's, and doctoral
- **Small-town** 247-acre campus
- **Coed**, 8,735 undergraduate students
- **Moderately difficult** entrance level, 91% of applicants were admitted
- **27:1 student-to-undergraduate faculty ratio**
- **$2549 tuition** and fees (in-state); $6929 (out-of-state)

Louisiana Tech University is known for high graduation rates, entrance exam scores, and overall academic quality. Quarter terms provide flexible scheduling. Family atmosphere enhances creativity and opportunity for participation in the many student organizations.

Students *Undergraduates:* Students come from 44 states and territories, 61 other countries.

From out-of-state	13%	Reside on campus	30%
Age 25 or older	22%	International students	1%
African Americans	14%	Asian Americans/Pacific Islanders	1%
Hispanic Americans	1%	Native Americans	0.5%

Faculty 446 (83% full-time).
Expenses (1999–2000) *Tuition, state resident:* full-time $2379; part-time $546 per term. *Tuition, nonresident:* full-time $6759; part-time $1366 per term. *Required fees:* full-time $170; $5 per credit hour. Full-time tuition and fees vary according to program. Part-time tuition and fees vary according to course load and program. *College room and board:* $3120. Room and board charges vary according to board plan and housing facility. *Waivers:* children of alumni, senior citizens, and employees or children of employees.
Library Prescott Memorial Library. *Collection:* 2,469 serial subscriptions, 14,532 audiovisual materials.
College life *Housing:* on-campus residence required through sophomore year. *Options:* men-only, women-only, disabled students. *Social organizations:* national fraternities, national sororities; 10% of eligible men and 12% of eligible women are members. *Most popular organizations:* Student Government Association, Association of Women's Studies, Union Board.
Campus security 24-hour emergency response devices and patrols, student patrols, late-night transport-escort service, controlled dormitory access.
After graduation 921 organizations recruited on campus 1997–98. *Career center:* 5 full-time personnel. Services include job fairs, resume preparation, interview workshops, resume referral, career/interest testing, career counseling, careers library, job bank, job interviews. *Graduate education:* 32% of class of 1999 went directly to graduate and professional school.
Freshmen 3,096 applied, 2,803 admitted. 3 National Merit Scholars, 73 valedictorians.

Average high school GPA	3.2	SAT verbal scores above 500	N/R
SAT math scores above 500	N/R	ACT above 18	87%
From top 10% of their h.s. class	39%	From top quarter	68%
From top half	85%	1998 freshmen returning in 1999	78%

Application *Options:* Common Application, early admission, deferred entrance. *Application fee:* $20. *Required:* high school transcript; minimum 2.0 GPA.
Standardized tests *Admission: Required:* SAT I or ACT.
Significant dates *Application deadlines:* rolling (freshmen), rolling (transfers). *Financial aid deadline priority date:* 4/15.
Freshman Application Contact
Mrs. Jan B. Albritton, Director of Admissions, Louisiana Tech University, PO Box 3168, Ruston, LA 71272. **Phone:** 318-257-3036. **Toll-free phone:** 800-LATECH1. **E-mail:** usjba@latech.edu
Visit CollegeQuest.com for information on majors offered and athletics. College video available at CollegeQuest.com.

■ *See page 1950 for a narrative description.*

LOYOLA UNIVERSITY NEW ORLEANS
New Orleans, Louisiana

- **Independent Roman Catholic (Jesuit)**, comprehensive, founded 1912
- **Degrees** bachelor's, master's, and first professional
- **Urban** 26-acre campus
- **Coed**, 3,384 undergraduate students, 82% full-time, 63% women, 37% men
- **Moderately difficult** entrance level, 83% of applicants were admitted
- **12:1 student-to-undergraduate faculty ratio**
- **53.3% graduate** in 6 years or less
- **$15,481 tuition** and fees
- **$13,122 average financial aid** package, $15,887 average indebtedness upon graduation, $293.7 million endowment

As Loyola builds for the future, physical evidence around campus points to a university on the move. The new 150,000-square-foot library has more than 630 simultaneous computer links as well as a media center, a visual arts center, and the Lindy Boggs National Center for Community Literacy. A new 7-story, 327-bed residence hall was completed in summer 1999.

Students *Undergraduates:* 2,790 full-time, 594 part-time. Students come from 50 states and territories, 56 other countries. *The most frequently chosen baccalaureate fields are:* business/marketing, communications/communication technologies, social sciences and history. *Graduate:* 645 in professional programs, 885 in other graduate degree programs.

From out-of-state	46%	Reside on campus	33%
Age 25 or older	8%	Transferred in	5%
International students	3%	African Americans	12%
Asian Americans/Pacific Islanders	4%	Hispanic Americans	9%
Native Americans	1%		

Faculty 384 (64% full-time), 67% with terminal degrees.
Expenses (2000–2001) *Comprehensive fee:* $21,597 includes full-time tuition ($14,989), mandatory fees ($492), and room and board ($6116). *College room only:* $3638. Room and board charges vary according to board plan and housing facility. *Part-time tuition:* $530 per credit hour. *Payment plan:* installment. *Waivers:* senior citizens and employees or children of employees.
Library University Library plus 1 other. *Operations spending 1999–2000:* $3.9 million. *Collection:* 384,142 titles, 4,897 serial subscriptions, 13,500 audiovisual materials.
College life *Housing:* on-campus residence required in freshman year. *Options:* coed, women-only, disabled students. *Social organizations:* national fraternities, national sororities; 17% of eligible men and 17% of eligible women are members. *Most popular organizations:* University Programming Board, Community Action Program, Black Student Union, Student Government Association.
Campus security 24-hour emergency response devices and patrols, late-night transport-escort service, controlled dormitory access, self-defense education, bicycle patrols, closed circuit TV monitors, door alarms, shuttle service, crime prevention programs.
After graduation 275 organizations recruited on campus 1997–98. 62% of class of 1998 had job offers within 6 months. *Career center:* 5 full-time, 2 part-time personnel. Services include job fairs, resume preparation, interview workshops, resume referral, career counseling, careers library, job interviews. *Graduate education:* 16% of class of 1999 went directly to graduate and professional school: 11% graduate arts and sciences, 3% law, 2% medicine, 1% business.
Freshmen 2,190 applied, 1,817 admitted, 814 enrolled. 1 National Merit Scholar, 9 valedictorians.

Average high school GPA	3.57	SAT verbal scores above 500	88%
SAT math scores above 500	83%	ACT above 18	100%
From top 10% of their h.s. class	26%	From top quarter	58%
From top half	88%		

Application *Options:* Common Application, electronic application, deferred entrance. *Application fee:* $20. *Required:* essay or personal statement; high school transcript; 1 letter of recommendation. *Required for some:* interview. *Recommended:* interview.
Standardized tests *Admission: Required:* SAT I or ACT. *Required for some:* PAA.
Significant dates *Application deadlines:* rolling (freshmen), rolling (transfers). *Financial aid deadline priority date:* 5/1.

Peterson's Guide to Four-Year Colleges 2001   www.petersons.com

Louisiana

Loyola University New Orleans (continued)
Freshman Application Contact
Ms. Debbie Stieffel, Director of Admission and Enrollment Management, Loyola University New Orleans, 6363 Saint Charles Avenue, Box 18, New Orleans, LA 70118-6195. **Phone:** 504-865-3240. **Toll-free phone:** 800-4-LOYOLA. **Fax:** 504-865-3383. **E-mail:** admit@loyno.edu
Visit CollegeQuest.com for information on majors offered and athletics.

■ *See page 1958 for a narrative description.*

MCNEESE STATE UNIVERSITY
Lake Charles, Louisiana

- **State-supported**, comprehensive, founded 1939
- **Degrees** associate, bachelor's, and master's
- **Suburban** 580-acre campus
- **Coed**, 6,865 undergraduate students, 81% full-time, 57% women, 43% men
- **Noncompetitive** entrance level
- **25:1 student-to-undergraduate faculty ratio**
- **25.5% graduate** in 6 years or less
- **$2113 tuition** and fees (in-state); $7983 (out-of-state)
- **$3693 average financial aid** package, $19.5 million endowment

Students *Undergraduates:* 5,544 full-time, 1,321 part-time. Students come from 41 states and territories, 30 other countries. *The most frequently chosen baccalaureate fields are:* business/marketing, education, social sciences and history. *Graduate:* 1,014 in graduate degree programs.

Reside on campus	12%	Age 25 or older	24%
Transferred in	4%	International students	1%
African Americans	16%	Asian Americans/Pacific Islanders	1%
Hispanic Americans	1%	Native Americans	1%

Faculty 330 (85% full-time), 57% with terminal degrees.
Expenses (1999–2000) *Tuition, state resident:* full-time $1650; part-time $412 per course. *Tuition, nonresident:* full-time $7520; part-time $1,710 per course. *Required fees:* full-time $463; $176 per term part-time. Full-time tuition and fees vary according to course load. Part-time tuition and fees vary according to course load. *College room and board:* $2328; room only: $1110. Room and board charges vary according to board plan and housing facility. *Payment plan:* installment. *Waivers:* senior citizens and employees or children of employees.
Library Frazer Memorial Library plus 1 other. *Operations spending 1999–2000:* $1.2 million. *Collection:* 250,482 titles, 1,641 serial subscriptions.
College life *Housing:* on-campus residence required in freshman year. *Options:* coed, men-only, women-only. *Social organizations:* national fraternities, national sororities; 7% of eligible men and 6% of eligible women are members. *Most popular organizations:* Student Government Association, International Students Association, Resident Student Association.
Campus security 24-hour emergency response devices and patrols, late-night transport-escort service, controlled dormitory access.
After graduation 108 organizations recruited on campus 1997–98. 81% of class of 1998 had job offers within 6 months. *Career center:* 2 full-time personnel. Services include job fairs, resume preparation, resume referral, career counseling, careers library, job bank, job interviews.
Freshmen 1,332 admitted, 1,332 enrolled.

SAT verbal scores above 500	N/R	SAT math scores above 500	N/R
ACT above 18	63%		

Application *Option:* early admission. *Application fee:* $10. *Required:* high school transcript. *Required for some:* minimum 2.0 GPA.
Standardized tests *Admission: Required:* ACT.
Significant dates *Application deadlines:* 7/15 (freshmen), 7/15 (transfers). *Notification:* continuous until 8/12 (freshmen). **Financial aid deadline priority date:** 5/1.
Freshman Application Contact
Ms. Stephanie Tarver, Admissions Counselor, McNeese State University, PO Box 92495, Lake Charles, LA 70609-2495. **Phone:** 318-475-5148. **Toll-free phone:** 800-622-3352.
Visit CollegeQuest.com for information on majors offered and athletics. College video and electronic viewbook available at CollegeQuest.com.

NEW ORLEANS BAPTIST THEOLOGICAL SEMINARY
New Orleans, Louisiana

- **Independent Southern Baptist**, comprehensive, founded 1917
- **Degrees** associate, bachelor's, master's, doctoral, and first professional
- **Suburban** 81-acre campus
- **Coed**
- **Minimally difficult** entrance level
- **$2400 tuition** and fees

Expenses (1999–2000) *Tuition:* full-time $2400; part-time $95 per credit.
Institutional Web site http://www.nobts.edu/
College life *Social organizations:* state clubs.
Campus security 24-hour emergency response devices and patrols.
Application *Option:* deferred entrance. *Application fee:* $25. *Recommended:* minimum 2.0 GPA.
Admissions Office Contact
New Orleans Baptist Theological Seminary, 3939 Gentilly Boulevard, New Orleans, LA 70126-4858. **Toll-free phone:** 800-662-8701.
Visit CollegeQuest.com for information on athletics. College video available at CollegeQuest.com.

NICHOLLS STATE UNIVERSITY
Thibodaux, Louisiana

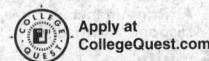 Apply at CollegeQuest.com

- **State-supported**, comprehensive, founded 1948
- **Degrees** associate, bachelor's, master's, and post-master's certificates
- **Small-town** 210-acre campus with easy access to New Orleans
- **Coed**, 6,490 undergraduate students, 83% full-time, 63% women, 37% men
- **Noncompetitive** entrance level, 93% of applicants were admitted
- **23:1 student-to-undergraduate faculty ratio**
- **22.3% graduate** in 6 years or less
- **$2589 tuition** and fees (in-state); $6861 (out-of-state)
- **$4.9 million endowment**

Part of Louisiana State University System.
Students *Undergraduates:* 5,372 full-time, 1,118 part-time. Students come from 32 states and territories, 33 other countries. *The most frequently chosen baccalaureate fields are:* education, business/marketing, liberal arts/general studies. *Graduate:* 752 in graduate degree programs.

From out-of-state	2%	Reside on campus	14%
Age 25 or older	23%	Transferred in	4%
International students	1%	African Americans	15%
Asian Americans/Pacific Islanders	1%	Hispanic Americans	1%
Native Americans	2%		

Faculty 270 (97% full-time), 52% with terminal degrees.
Expenses (1999–2000) *Tuition, state resident:* full-time $2117; part-time $504 per term. *Tuition, nonresident:* full-time $6389; part-time $1,440 per term. *Required fees:* full-time $472; $64 per term part-time. Part-time tuition and fees vary according to course load. *College room and board:* $2850. *Waivers:* senior citizens and employees or children of employees.
Library Allen J. Ellender Memorial Library. *Operations spending 1999–2000:* $1.7 million. *Collection:* 532,948 titles, 1,341 serial subscriptions, 3,374 audiovisual materials.
College life *Housing: Options:* coed, men-only, women-only, disabled students. *Social organizations:* national fraternities, national sororities; 5% of eligible men and 5% of eligible women are members. *Most popular organizations:* Student Government Association, Student Programming Association, Residence Hall Association, Food Advisory Association, Intrafraternity Council.
Campus security 24-hour emergency response devices and patrols, student patrols, late-night transport-escort service.
After graduation 368 organizations recruited on campus 1997–98. *Career center:* 2 full-time personnel. Services include job fairs, resume preparation, interview workshops, resume referral, career/interest testing, career counseling, careers library, job bank, job interviews.

Louisiana

Freshmen 2,420 applied, 2,251 admitted, 1,469 enrolled.
Average high school GPA	2.5	SAT verbal scores above 500	N/R
SAT math scores above 500	N/R	ACT above 18	65%
1998 freshmen returning in 1999	60%		

Application *Options:* eApply at www.CollegeQuest.com, electronic application, early admission, deferred entrance. *Application fee:* $10. *Required:* high school transcript.

Standardized tests *Placement: Required:* ACT

Significant dates *Application deadlines:* rolling (freshmen), rolling (transfers). *Notification:* continuous until 8/24 (freshmen).

Freshman Application Contact
Mrs. Becky L. Durocher, Director of Admissions, Nicholls State University, PO Box 2004-NSU, Thibodaux, LA 70310. **Phone:** 504-448-4507. **Toll-free phone:** 877-NICHOLLS (in-state); 877-NICHOLS (out-of-state). **Fax:** 504-448-4929. **E-mail:** nicholls@server.nich.edu

Visit CollegeQuest.com for information on majors offered and athletics. Electronic viewbook available at CollegeQuest.com.

NORTHEAST LOUISIANA UNIVERSITY
Louisiana—See University of Louisiana at Monroe

NORTHWESTERN STATE UNIVERSITY OF LOUISIANA
Natchitoches, Louisiana

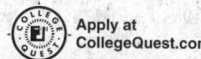
Apply at CollegeQuest.com

- **State-supported**, comprehensive, founded 1884
- **Degrees** associate, bachelor's, master's, and doctoral
- **Small-town** 1,000-acre campus
- **Coed**, 8,040 undergraduate students, 78% full-time, 65% women, 35% men
- **Noncompetitive** entrance level, 98% of applicants were admitted
- **24:1 student-to-undergraduate faculty ratio**
- **25.9% graduate** in 6 years or less
- **$2327 tuition** and fees (in-state); $7553 (out-of-state)

Northwestern is a friendly, vibrant, student-oriented institution that is, in the words of one alumnus, "large enough to serve you but small enough to know you." The University places its highest premium on excellence in teaching. NSU is committed to making a positive difference in the lives of its students.

Students *Undergraduates:* 6,273 full-time, 1,767 part-time. Students come from 43 states and territories, 25 other countries. *The most frequently chosen baccalaureate fields are:* education, health professions and related sciences, liberal arts/general studies. *Graduate:* 965 in graduate degree programs.

From out-of-state	6%	Reside on campus	35%
Age 25 or older	29%	International students	1%
African Americans	25%	Asian Americans/Pacific Islanders	1%
Hispanic Americans	2%	Native Americans	2%

Faculty 310 (78% full-time), 60% with terminal degrees.

Expenses (1999–2000) *Tuition, state resident:* full-time $2030. *Tuition, nonresident:* full-time $7256. *Required fees:* full-time $297. Part-time tuition and fees vary according to course load. *College room and board:* $2596; room only: $1300. Room and board charges vary according to board plan and housing facility. *Payment plan:* installment. *Waivers:* children of alumni and employees or children of employees.

Library Eugene P. Watson Memorial Library. *Operations spending 1999–2000:* $1.7 million. *Collection:* 320,545 titles, 1,682 serial subscriptions, 5,845 audiovisual materials.

College life *Housing:* on-campus residence required through junior year. *Options:* men-only, women-only. *Social organizations:* national fraternities, national sororities; 19% of eligible men and 29% of eligible women are members.

Campus security 24-hour emergency response devices and patrols, late-night transport-escort service, controlled dormitory access.

After graduation 139 organizations recruited on campus 1997–98. *Career center:* 3 full-time, 3 part-time personnel. Services include job fairs, resume preparation, resume referral, career counseling, careers library, job bank, job interviews.

Freshmen 2,814 applied, 2,768 admitted, 1,813 enrolled.
SAT verbal scores above 500	N/R	SAT math scores above 500	N/R
ACT above 18	67%	1998 freshmen returning in 1999	65%

Application *Options:* eApply at www.CollegeQuest.com, early admission. *Application fee:* $15. *Required:* high school transcript.

Standardized tests *Placement: Required:* ACT

Significant dates *Application deadlines:* rolling (freshmen), rolling (transfers). *Financial aid deadline priority date:* 5/3.

Freshman Application Contact
Ms. Jana Lucky, Director of Recruiting and Admissions, Northwestern State University of Louisiana, Roy Hall, Room 101, Natchitoches, LA 71497. **Phone:** 318-357-4503. **Toll-free phone:** 800-426-3754 (in-state); 800-327-1903 (out-of-state). **E-mail:** admissions@alpha.nsula.edu

Visit CollegeQuest.com for information on majors offered and athletics. College video available at CollegeQuest.com.

■ *See page 1946 for a narrative description.*

OUR LADY OF HOLY CROSS COLLEGE
New Orleans, Louisiana

- **Independent Roman Catholic**, comprehensive, founded 1916
- **Degrees** associate, bachelor's, master's, and postbachelor's certificates
- **Suburban** 40-acre campus
- **Coed**, 1,086 undergraduate students, 60% full-time, 76% women, 24% men
- **Minimally difficult** entrance level, 44% of applicants were admitted
- **21:1 student-to-undergraduate faculty ratio**
- **$5950 tuition** and fees
- **$18,500 average indebtedness** upon graduation, $4.6 million endowment

Our Lady of Holy Cross College, a Catholic, coeducational liberal arts college, was founded in 1916. With a low student-faculty ratio, Our Lady of Holy Cross College provides high-quality education at reasonable tuition rates. Associate, baccalaureate, and master's programs are offered, and financial aid is available.

Students *Undergraduates:* 654 full-time, 432 part-time. Students come from 5 states and territories. *The most frequently chosen baccalaureate fields are:* education, business/marketing, health professions and related sciences. *Graduate:* 157 in graduate degree programs.

From out-of-state	0.4%	Age 25 or older	35%
Transferred in	13%	African Americans	11%
Asian Americans/Pacific Islanders	2%	Hispanic Americans	5%
Native Americans	1%		

Faculty 93 (31% full-time), 54% with terminal degrees.

Expenses (1999–2000) *Tuition:* full-time $5700; part-time $190 per semester hour. *Required fees:* full-time $250; $125 per term part-time. *Payment plan:* installment. *Waivers:* employees or children of employees.

Library Blaine Kern Library. *Operations spending 1999–2000:* $278,909. *Collection:* 85,404 titles, 970 serial subscriptions, 14,513 audiovisual materials.

College life *Housing:* college housing not available. *Most popular organizations:* Innovators, student government, Association of Student Nurses, Delta Sigma Pi, Louisiana Association of Educators/Student Programs.

Campus security 24-hour patrols.

After graduation 12 organizations recruited on campus 1997–98. *Career center:* 1 full-time personnel. Services include job fairs, resume preparation, resume referral, career/interest testing, career counseling, careers library, job bank, job interviews. *Graduate education:* 20% of class of 1999 went directly to graduate and professional school: 10% business, 10% education.

Freshmen 200 applied, 88 admitted, 146 enrolled.
SAT verbal scores above 500	N/R	SAT math scores above 500	N/R
ACT above 18	70%	1998 freshmen returning in 1999	64%

Peterson's Guide to Four-Year Colleges 2001   www.petersons.com   329

Louisiana

Our Lady of Holy Cross College (continued)

Application *Options:* Common Application, electronic application, early admission, deferred entrance. *Application fee:* $15. *Required:* high school transcript. *Recommended:* minimum 2.0 GPA.

Standardized tests *Placement: Recommended:* SAT I or ACT.

Significant dates *Application deadlines:* rolling (freshmen), rolling (transfers). *Financial aid deadline priority date:* 4/15.

Freshman Application Contact

Ms. Kristine Hatfield Kopecky, Director of Student Affairs and Admissions, Our Lady of Holy Cross College, 4123 Woodland Drive, New Orleans, LA 70131-7399. **Phone:** 504-394-7744 Ext. 185. **Toll-free phone:** 800-259-7744 Ext. 175. **Fax:** 504-391-2421.

Visit CollegeQuest.com for information on majors offered and athletics. College video available at CollegeQuest.com.

OUR LADY OF THE LAKE COLLEGE
Baton Rouge, Louisiana

- **Independent Roman Catholic**, primarily 2-year, founded 1990
- **Degrees** associate and bachelor's
- **Suburban** 5-acre campus with easy access to New Orleans
- **Coed**, 916 undergraduate students
- **Noncompetitive** entrance level
- **24:1 student-to-undergraduate faculty ratio**
- **$4360 tuition** and fees

Faculty 72 (56% full-time), 85% with terminal degrees.

Admissions Office Contact

Our Lady of the Lake College, 5345 Brittany Drive, Baton Rouge, LA 70808. **Fax:** 225-768-1726. **E-mail:** admission@ololcollege.edu

Visit CollegeQuest.com for information on majors offered and athletics.

SAINT JOSEPH SEMINARY COLLEGE
Saint Benedict, Louisiana

Admissions Office Contact

Saint Joseph Seminary College, Saint Benedict, LA 70457.

SOUTHEASTERN LOUISIANA UNIVERSITY
Hammond, Louisiana

- **State-supported**, comprehensive, founded 1925
- **Degrees** associate, bachelor's, and master's
- **Small-town** 375-acre campus with easy access to New Orleans
- **Coed**, 13,205 undergraduate students, 86% full-time, 61% women, 39% men
- **Noncompetitive** entrance level, 88% of applicants were admitted
- **27:1 student-to-undergraduate faculty ratio**
- **19% graduate** in 6 years or less
- **$2217 tuition** and fees (in-state); $7545 (out-of-state)
- **$5249 average financial aid** package, $12.6 million endowment

Part of University of Louisiana System.

Students *Undergraduates:* 11,292 full-time, 1,913 part-time. Students come from 40 states and territories, 39 other countries. *The most frequently chosen baccalaureate fields are:* business/marketing, education, health professions and related sciences. *Graduate:* 1,699 in graduate degree programs.

From out-of-state	2%	Reside on campus	12%
Age 25 or older	24%	Transferred in	5%
International students	0.5%	African Americans	13%
Asian Americans/Pacific Islanders	0.4%	Hispanic Americans	2%
Native Americans	1%		

Faculty 472 (95% full-time), 62% with terminal degrees.

Expenses (1999–2000) *Tuition, state resident:* full-time $2030. *Tuition, nonresident:* full-time $7358. *Required fees:* full-time $187. Part-time tuition and fees vary according to course load. *College room and board:* $2770. Room and board charges vary according to board plan and housing facility. *Payment plans:* installment, deferred payment. *Waivers:* senior citizens and employees or children of employees.

Library Sims Memorial Library. *Operations spending 1999–2000:* $2.7 million. *Collection:* 584,987 titles, 2,315 serial subscriptions.

College life *Housing:* on-campus residence required through sophomore year. *Options:* coed, men-only, women-only. *Social organizations:* national fraternities, national sororities, local fraternities, local sororities; 8% of eligible men and 4% of eligible women are members. *Most popular organizations:* Gamma Beta Phi, Phi Kappa Phi, South Eastern Oaks Residential Community Organization, Sigma Sigma Sigma, Phi Mu.

Campus security 24-hour emergency response devices and patrols, late-night transport-escort service, controlled dormitory access.

After graduation 93 organizations recruited on campus 1997–98. *Career center:* 4 full-time, 3 part-time personnel. Services include job fairs, resume preparation, interview workshops, resume referral, career/interest testing, career counseling, careers library, job bank, job interviews.

Freshmen 3,237 applied, 2,851 admitted, 2,448 enrolled.

SAT verbal scores above 500	N/R	SAT math scores above 500	N/R
ACT above 18	65%	1998 freshmen returning in 1999	63%

Application *Options:* early admission, deferred entrance. *Application fee:* $10. *Required:* high school transcript; proof of immunization.

Standardized tests *Placement: Required:* SAT I or ACT.

Significant dates *Application deadlines:* 7/15 (freshmen), rolling (transfers). *Financial aid deadline priority date:* 5/1.

Freshman Application Contact

Ms. Pat Duplessis, University Admissions Analyst, Southeastern Louisiana University, SLU 10752, Hammond, LA 70402. **Phone:** 504-549-2066. **Toll-free phone:** 800-222-7358. **Fax:** 504-549-5095. **E-mail:** ssoutullo@selu.edu

Visit CollegeQuest.com for information on majors offered and athletics. College video available at CollegeQuest.com.

SOUTHERN UNIVERSITY AND AGRICULTURAL AND MECHANICAL COLLEGE
Baton Rouge, Louisiana

- **State-supported**, comprehensive, founded 1880
- **Degrees** associate, bachelor's, master's, doctoral, and first professional
- **Suburban** 964-acre campus
- **Coed**
- **Noncompetitive** entrance level
- **$2286 tuition** and fees (in-state); $8078 (out-of-state)

Part of Southern University System.

Expenses (1999–2000) *Tuition, state resident:* full-time $2286; part-time $646 per term. *Tuition, nonresident:* full-time $8078; part-time $3542 per term. Part-time tuition and fees vary according to course load and location. *College room and board:* $3339. Room and board charges vary according to board plan and housing facility.

Institutional Web site http://www.subr.edu/

College life *Housing: Options:* men-only, women-only. *Social organizations:* national fraternities, national sororities, local fraternities, local sororities; 8% of eligible men and 4% of eligible women are members.

Campus security 24-hour emergency response devices and patrols.

Application *Options:* Common Application, early admission. *Application fee:* $5. *Required:* high school transcript.

Standardized tests *Placement: Required:* SAT I or ACT

Admissions Office Contact

Southern University and Agricultural and Mechanical College, PO Box 9901, Baton Rouge, LA 70813.

Visit CollegeQuest.com for information on athletics.

SOUTHERN UNIVERSITY AT NEW ORLEANS
New Orleans, Louisiana

Admissions Office Contact

Southern University at New Orleans, 6400 Press Drive, New Orleans, LA 70126-1009.

Louisiana

TULANE UNIVERSITY
New Orleans, Louisiana

 Apply at CollegeQuest.com

- **Independent**, university, founded 1834
- **Degrees** associate, bachelor's, master's, doctoral, and first professional
- **Urban** 110-acre campus
- **Coed**, 7,163 undergraduate students, 79% full-time, 53% women, 47% men
- **Very difficult** entrance level, 78% of applicants were admitted
- **9:1 student-to-undergraduate faculty ratio**
- **72% graduate** in 6 years or less
- **$24,214 tuition** and fees
- **$22,948 average financial aid** package, $20,040 average indebtedness upon graduation, $550 million endowment

Students *Undergraduates:* 5,633 full-time, 1,530 part-time. Students come from 52 states and territories, 64 other countries. *The most frequently chosen baccalaureate fields are:* business/marketing, engineering/engineering technologies, social sciences and history. *Graduate:* 1,576 in professional programs, 2,699 in other graduate degree programs.

From out-of-state	66%	Reside on campus	41%
Age 25 or older	15%	Transferred in	2%
International students	4%	African Americans	5%
Asian Americans/Pacific Islanders	7%	Hispanic Americans	4%
Native Americans	0.4%		

Faculty 1,059 (59% full-time), 74% with terminal degrees.

Expenses (1999–2000) *Comprehensive fee:* $31,256 includes full-time tuition ($22,590), mandatory fees ($1624), and room and board ($7042). *College room only:* $3892. Room and board charges vary according to board plan and housing facility. *Part-time tuition:* $941 per credit hour. *Part-time fees:* $195 per credit hour; $60 per term part-time. *Payment plan:* installment. *Waivers:* employees or children of employees.

Library Howard Tilton Memorial Library plus 8 others. *Operations spending 1999–2000:* $10.9 million. *Collection:* 2.1 million titles, 14,986 serial subscriptions, 83,774 audiovisual materials.

College life *Housing:* on-campus residence required in freshman year. *Options:* coed, women-only. *Social organizations:* national fraternities, national sororities; 16% of eligible men and 19% of eligible women are members. *Most popular organizations:* Community Action Council of Tulane University Students, Tulane University Campus Programming, African-American Congress of Tulane, club sports, Tsunami.

Campus security 24-hour emergency response devices and patrols, student patrols, late-night transport-escort service, controlled dormitory access, on and off-campus shuttle service, crime prevention programs.

After graduation 557 organizations recruited on campus 1997–98. *Career center:* 7 full-time personnel. Services include job fairs, resume preparation, resume referral, career counseling, careers library, job bank, job interviews. *Major awards:* 1 Marshall scholar.

Freshmen 8,388 applied, 6,547 admitted, 2,445 enrolled.

SAT verbal scores above 500	95%	SAT math scores above 500	97%
ACT above 18	N/R	From top 10% of their h.s. class	52%
From top half	97%	1998 freshmen returning in 1999	86%

Application *Options:* eApply at www.CollegeQuest.com, Common Application, electronic application, early admission, early decision, early action, deferred entrance. *Application fee:* $45. *Required:* essay or personal statement; high school transcript; 1 letter of recommendation.

Standardized tests *Admission: Required:* SAT I or ACT. *Recommended:* SAT II Subject Tests. *Required for some:* SAT II Subject Tests.

Significant dates *Application deadlines:* 1/15 (freshmen), 6/1 (transfers). *Early decision:* 11/1. *Notification:* continuous until 4/1 (freshmen), 12/15 (early decision). *Financial aid deadline:* 2/1. *Priority date:* 1/15.

Freshman Application Contact
Mr. Richard Whiteside, Vice President of Enrollment Management and Institutional Research, Tulane University, 6823 St Charles Avenue, New Orleans, LA 70118-5669. **Phone:** 504-865-5731. **Toll-free phone:** 800-873-9283. **Fax:** 504-862-8715. **E-mail:** undergrad.admission@tulane.edu

Visit CollegeQuest.com for information on majors offered and athletics. College video and electronic viewbook available at CollegeQuest.com.

■ *See page 2652 for a narrative description.*

UNIVERSITY OF LOUISIANA AT LAFAYETTE
Lafayette, Louisiana

- **State-supported**, university, founded 1898
- **Degrees** associate, bachelor's, master's, doctoral, and post-master's certificates
- **Urban** 1,375-acre campus
- **Coed**, 14,418 undergraduate students, 83% full-time, 56% women, 44% men
- **Minimally difficult** entrance level, 83% of applicants were admitted
- **24:1 student-to-undergraduate faculty ratio**
- **25.1% graduate** in 6 years or less
- **$2013 tuition** and fees (in-state); $7245 (out-of-state)
- **$5400 average financial aid** package, $53 million endowment

Part of University of Louisiana System.

Students *Undergraduates:* 11,997 full-time, 2,421 part-time. Students come from 48 states and territories, 101 other countries. *The most frequently chosen baccalaureate fields are:* business/marketing, education, liberal arts/general studies. *Graduate:* 1,451 in graduate degree programs.

From out-of-state	4%	Reside on campus	13%
Age 25 or older	24%	Transferred in	4%
International students	2%	African Americans	19%
Asian Americans/Pacific Islanders	1%	Hispanic Americans	2%
Native Americans	1%		

Faculty 666 (82% full-time), 63% with terminal degrees.

Expenses (1999–2000) *One-time required fee:* $7.50. *Tuition, state resident:* full-time $2013; part-time $525 per term. *Tuition, nonresident:* full-time $7245; part-time $1833 per term. Part-time tuition and fees vary according to course load. *College room and board:* $2656. Room and board charges vary according to board plan. *Payment plan:* deferred payment. *Waivers:* senior citizens and employees or children of employees.

Library Edith Garland Dupre Library. *Operations spending 1999–2000:* $2.9 million. *Collection:* 419,447 titles, 5,174 serial subscriptions, 5,755 audiovisual materials.

College life *Housing:* on-campus residence required in freshman year. *Options:* men-only, women-only. *Social organizations:* national fraternities, national sororities; 3% of eligible men and 3% of eligible women are members.

Campus security 24-hour emergency response devices and patrols, late-night transport-escort service.

After graduation 116 organizations recruited on campus 1997–98. *Career center:* 1 full-time personnel. Services include job fairs, resume preparation, resume referral, career counseling, careers library, job bank, job interviews.

Freshmen 4,335 applied, 3,610 admitted, 2,529 enrolled.

SAT verbal scores above 500	N/R	SAT math scores above 500	N/R
ACT above 18	79%	From top quarter of their h.s. class	37%
From top half	72%	1998 freshmen returning in 1999	64%

Application *Options:* early admission, deferred entrance. *Application fee:* $20. *Required:* high school transcript.

Standardized tests *Admission: Required:* SAT I or ACT.

Significant dates *Application deadlines:* rolling (freshmen), rolling (transfers). *Financial aid deadline priority date:* 3/1.

Freshman Application Contact
Mr. Leroy Broussard Jr., Director of Admissions, University of Louisiana at Lafayette, PO Drawer 41210, Lafayette, LA 70504. **Phone:** 337-482-6473. **Toll-free phone:** 800-752-6553. **E-mail:** admissions@louisiana.edu

Visit CollegeQuest.com for information on majors offered and athletics. College video available at CollegeQuest.com.

■ *See page 2744 for a narrative description.*

UNIVERSITY OF LOUISIANA AT MONROE
Monroe, Louisiana

- **State-supported**, comprehensive, founded 1931
- **Degrees** associate, bachelor's, master's, and doctoral
- **Urban** 238-acre campus
- **Coed**, 8,542 undergraduate students, 85% full-time, 61% women, 39% men

Louisiana

University of Louisiana at Monroe (continued)
- **Noncompetitive** entrance level, 95% of applicants were admitted
- **25% graduate** in 6 years or less
- **$2052 tuition** and fees (in-state); $8432 (out-of-state)

Students *Undergraduates:* 7,223 full-time, 1,319 part-time. Students come from 39 states and territories, 44 other countries. *Graduate:* 170 in professional programs, 1,108 in other graduate degree programs.

From out-of-state	5%	Reside on campus	22%
Age 25 or older	28%	Transferred in	7%
International students	1%	African Americans	27%
Asian Americans/Pacific Islanders	3%	Hispanic Americans	1%
Native Americans	0.4%		

Faculty 516 (89% full-time), 51% with terminal degrees.

Expenses (1999–2000) *Tuition, state resident:* full-time $1644; part-time $414 per term. *Tuition, nonresident:* full-time $8024; part-time $1488 per term. *Required fees:* full-time $408; $153 per term part-time. Part-time tuition and fees vary according to course load. *College room and board:* $3660; room only: $2560. Room and board charges vary according to board plan and housing facility. *Waivers:* children of alumni, senior citizens, and employees or children of employees.

Library Sandel Library. *Operations spending 1999–2000:* $637,814. *Collection:* 355,748 titles, 2,912 serial subscriptions, 331 audiovisual materials.

College life *Housing:* on-campus residence required through senior year. *Options:* coed, men-only, women-only. *Social organizations:* national fraternities, national sororities; 5% of eligible men and 4% of eligible women are members. *Most popular organizations:* Panhellenic Council, Intrafraternity Council, Union Board, Student Government Association.

Campus security 24-hour emergency response devices and patrols, student patrols, late-night transport-escort service.

After graduation 382 organizations recruited on campus 1997–98. *Career center:* 6 full-time personnel. Services include job fairs, resume preparation, career counseling, careers library, job bank, job interviews.

Freshmen 2,432 applied, 2,309 admitted, 1,529 enrolled.

SAT verbal scores above 500	N/R	SAT math scores above 500	N/R
ACT above 18	63%	From top quarter of their h.s. class	41%
From top half	74%	1998 freshmen returning in 1999	64%

Application *Application fee:* $15. *Required for some:* high school transcript.

Standardized tests *Placement: Required:* ACT

Significant dates *Application deadlines:* rolling (freshmen), rolling (transfers). *Financial aid deadline priority date:* 4/1.

Freshman Application Contact
Ms. Carlette Browder, Associate Director of Admissions, University of Louisiana at Monroe, Monroe, LA 71209-1115. **Phone:** 318-342-5252. **Toll-free phone:** 800-372-5127. **Fax:** 318-342-1049. **E-mail:** rebrowder@ulm.edu

Visit CollegeQuest.com for information on majors offered and athletics.

UNIVERSITY OF NEW ORLEANS
New Orleans, Louisiana

Apply at CollegeQuest.com

- **State-supported**, university, founded 1958
- **Degrees** bachelor's, master's, and doctoral
- **Urban** 345-acre campus
- **Coed**, 11,872 undergraduate students, 71% full-time, 57% women, 43% men
- **Moderately difficult** entrance level, 83% of applicants were admitted
- **19:1 student-to-undergraduate faculty ratio**
- **18% graduate** in 6 years or less
- **$2532 tuition** and fees (in-state); $8058 (out-of-state)
- **$10 million endowment**

Part of Louisiana State University System.

Students *Undergraduates:* 8,461 full-time, 3,411 part-time. Students come from 46 states and territories, 91 other countries. *The most frequently chosen baccalaureate fields are:* business/marketing, education, liberal arts/general studies. *Graduate:* 3,996 in graduate degree programs.

From out-of-state	4%	Reside on campus	5%
Age 25 or older	27%	Transferred in	10%
International students	3%	African Americans	21%
Asian Americans/Pacific Islanders	5%	Hispanic Americans	6%
Native Americans	0.5%		

Faculty 776 (68% full-time), 61% with terminal degrees.

Expenses (1999–2000) *Tuition, state resident:* full-time $2362; part-time $735 per term. *Tuition, nonresident:* full-time $7888; part-time $2119 per term. *Required fees:* full-time $170; $5 per semester hour; $10 per term part-time. Part-time tuition and fees vary according to course load. *College room and board:* $3175; room only: $1575. Room and board charges vary according to board plan and housing facility. *Payment plan:* deferred payment. *Waivers:* senior citizens and employees or children of employees.

Library Earl K. Long Library. *Operations spending 1999–2000:* $3.8 million. *Collection:* 577,525 titles, 3,690 serial subscriptions, 117,086 audiovisual materials.

College life *Housing:* Option: coed. *Social organizations:* national fraternities, national sororities, local fraternities; 2% of eligible men and 2% of eligible women are members. *Most popular organizations:* Student Government Association, Student Government Activities Council, Circle K International, International Student Organization, Progressive Black Student Union.

Campus security 24-hour emergency response devices and patrols, late-night transport-escort service, controlled dormitory access.

After graduation 400 organizations recruited on campus 1997–98. 80% of class of 1998 had job offers within 6 months. *Career center:* 4 full-time, 1 part-time personnel. Services include job fairs, resume preparation, resume referral, career counseling, careers library, job bank, job interviews.

Freshmen 3,612 applied, 2,991 admitted, 1,872 enrolled. 1 National Merit Scholar.

SAT verbal scores above 500	65%	SAT math scores above 500	57%
ACT above 18	77%	1998 freshmen returning in 1999	68%

Application *Options:* eApply at www.CollegeQuest.com, Common Application, electronic application, early admission, deferred entrance. *Application fee:* $20. *Required:* high school transcript. *Required for some:* essay or personal statement; minimum 2.0 GPA; 3 letters of recommendation; interview; 2.0 high school GPA on high school core program.

Standardized tests *Admission: Required:* SAT I or ACT.

Significant dates *Application deadlines:* rolling (freshmen), rolling (transfers).

Freshman Application Contact
Ms. Roslyn S. Sheley, Director of Admissions, University of New Orleans, Lake Front, New Orleans, LA 70145. **Phone:** 504-280-6595. **Toll-free phone:** 888-514-4275. **Fax:** 504-280-5522. **E-mail:** admission@uno.edu

Visit CollegeQuest.com for information on majors offered and athletics. College video and electronic viewbook available at CollegeQuest.com.

- *See page 2792 for a narrative description.*

UNIVERSITY OF SOUTHWESTERN LOUISIANA
Louisiana—See University of Louisiana at Lafayette

XAVIER UNIVERSITY OF LOUISIANA
New Orleans, Louisiana

- **Independent Roman Catholic**, comprehensive, founded 1925
- **Degrees** bachelor's, master's, and first professional
- **Urban** 23-acre campus
- **Coed**, 3,201 undergraduate students, 98% full-time, 72% women, 28% men
- **Moderately difficult** entrance level, 85% of applicants were admitted
- **16:1 student-to-undergraduate faculty ratio**
- **$9700 tuition** and fees
- **$27.5 million endowment**

Students *Undergraduates:* 3,131 full-time, 70 part-time. Students come from 41 states and territories, 27 other countries. *The most frequently chosen*

Louisiana–Maine

baccalaureate fields are: biological/life sciences, physical sciences, psychology. *Graduate:* 232 in professional programs, 310 in other graduate degree programs.

From out-of-state	55%	Reside on campus	60%
Age 25 or older	3%	Transferred in	4%
International students	2%	African Americans	94%
Asian Americans/Pacific Islanders	2%	Hispanic Americans	0.3%
Native Americans	0.03%		

Faculty 250 (86% full-time), 82% with terminal degrees.

Expenses (1999–2000) *Comprehensive fee:* $14,800 includes full-time tuition ($8900), mandatory fees ($800), and room and board ($5100). Full-time tuition and fees vary according to program. Room and board charges vary according to housing facility. *Part-time tuition:* $375 per semester hour. *Part-time fees:* $75 per term part-time. Part-time tuition and fees vary according to course load and program. *Payment plan:* installment. *Waivers:* senior citizens and employees or children of employees.

Library Xavier Library plus 1 other. *Collection:* 100,431 titles, 1,863 serial subscriptions, 4,778 audiovisual materials.

College life *Housing:* Options: coed, men-only, women-only. *Social organizations:* national fraternities, national sororities; 2% of eligible men and 6% of eligible women are members. *Most popular organizations:* Mobilization at Xavier, AWARE, NAACP, California club, Beta Beta Beta.

Campus security 24-hour emergency response devices and patrols, student patrols, bicycle patrols.

After graduation 70 organizations recruited on campus 1997–98. *Career center:* 4 full-time personnel. Services include job fairs, resume preparation, resume referral, career/interest testing, career counseling, careers library, job bank, job interviews.

Freshmen 3,401 applied, 2,898 admitted, 898 enrolled.

Average high school GPA	3.0	SAT verbal scores above 500	51%
SAT math scores above 500	43%	ACT above 18	81%
From top 10% of their h.s. class	29%	From top quarter	54%
From top half	80%		

Application *Options:* Common Application, early admission, early action. *Application fee:* $25. *Required:* high school transcript; minimum 2.0 GPA; 1 letter of recommendation. *Required for some:* interview.

Standardized tests *Admission: Required:* SAT I or ACT.

Significant dates *Application deadlines:* 3/1 (freshmen), 6/1 (transfers). *Early action:* 1/15. *Notification:* 4/15 (freshmen), 2/1 (early action). *Financial aid deadline:* continuous.

Freshman Application Contact
Mr. Winston Brown, Dean of Admissions, Xavier University of Louisiana, 7325 Palmetto Street, New Orleans, LA 70125. **Phone:** 504-483-7388. **E-mail:** apply@xula.edu

Visit CollegeQuest.com for information on majors offered and athletics. College video available at CollegeQuest.com.

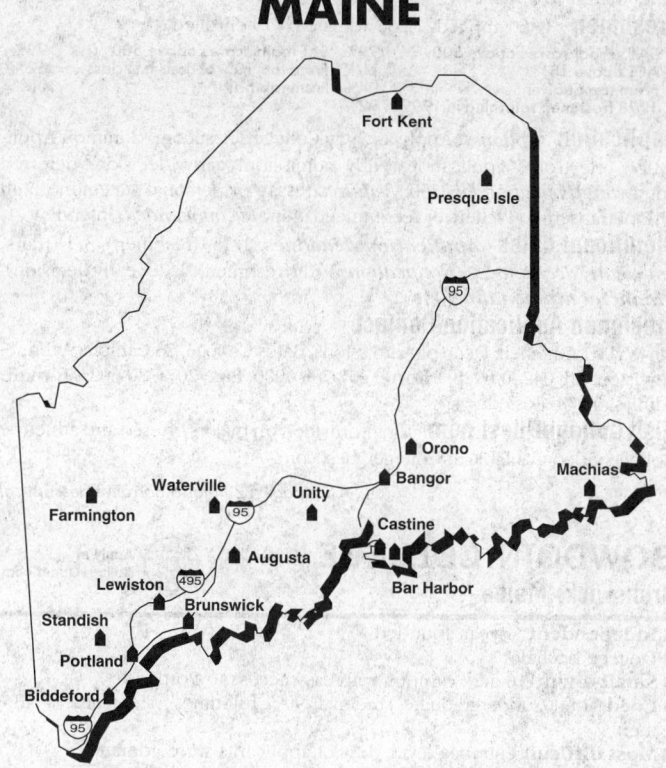

MAINE

BATES COLLEGE
Lewiston, Maine

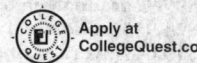
Apply at CollegeQuest.com

- **Independent**, 4-year, founded 1855
- **Degree** bachelor's
- **Suburban** 109-acre campus
- **Coed**, 1,706 undergraduate students, 100% full-time, 51% women, 49% men
- **Most difficult** entrance level, 33% of applicants were admitted
- **10:1 student-to-undergraduate faculty ratio**
- **83.5% graduate** in 6 years or less
- **$31,400 comprehensive fee**
- **$20,487 average financial aid** package, $15,129 average indebtedness upon graduation, $162.4 million endowment

Students *Undergraduates:* 1,706 full-time. Students come from 48 states and territories, 46 other countries. *The most frequently chosen baccalaureate fields are:* biological/life sciences, psychology, social sciences and history.

From out-of-state	89%	Reside on campus	90%
Age 25 or older	1%	Transferred in	0.1%
International students	4%	African Americans	2%
Asian Americans/Pacific Islanders	4%	Hispanic Americans	1%
Native Americans	0.1%		

Faculty 181 (91% full-time).

Expenses (1999–2000) *Comprehensive fee:* $31,400. *Payment plan:* installment. *Waivers:* employees or children of employees.

Library Ladd Library. *Collection:* 547,220 titles, 1,715 serial subscriptions, 48,233 audiovisual materials.

College life *Housing:* on-campus residence required in freshman year. *Options:* coed, men-only, women-only. *Most popular organizations:* Representative Assembly, International Club, Outing Club, student radio station, The Student (newspaper).

Campus security 24-hour emergency response devices and patrols, student patrols, late-night transport-escort service, controlled dormitory access.

After graduation 75 organizations recruited on campus 1997–98. *Career center:* 6 full-time personnel. Services include job fairs, resume preparation, interview workshops, resume referral, career/interest testing, career counseling, careers library, job bank, job interviews. *Graduate education:* 17% of class of 1999 went directly to graduate and professional school.

Maine

Bates College (continued)

Freshmen 3,860 applied, 1,266 admitted, 479 enrolled.

SAT verbal scores above 500	99%	SAT math scores above 500	99%
ACT above 18	N/R	From top 10% of their h.s. class	62%
From top quarter		From top half	100%
1998 freshmen returning in 1999	92%		

Application *Options:* eApply at www.CollegeQuest.com, Common Application, electronic application, early admission, early decision, deferred entrance. *Application fee:* $50. *Required:* essay or personal statement; high school transcript; 3 letters of recommendation. *Recommended:* interview.

Significant dates *Application deadlines:* 1/15 (freshmen), 3/1 (transfers). *Early decision:* 1/1. *Notification:* 3/31 (freshmen), 1/20 (early decision). *Financial aid deadline:* 1/15.

Freshman Application Contact

Mr. Wylie L. Mitchell, Dean of Admissions, Bates College, 23 Campus Avenue, Lewiston, ME 04240-6028. **Phone:** 207-786-6000. **Fax:** 207-786-6025. **E-mail:** admissions@bates.edu

Visit CollegeQuest.com for information on majors offered and athletics. College video available at CollegeQuest.com.

■ *See page 1234 for a narrative description.*

BOWDOIN COLLEGE
Brunswick, Maine

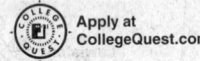
Apply at CollegeQuest.com

- **Independent**, 4-year, founded 1794
- **Degree** bachelor's
- **Small-town** 110-acre campus with easy access to Portland
- **Coed**, 1,600 undergraduate students, 99% full-time, 52% women, 48% men
- **Most difficult** entrance level, 32% of applicants were admitted
- **10:1 student-to-undergraduate faculty ratio**
- **89.5% graduate** in 6 years or less
- **$24,955 tuition** and fees
- **$19,647 average financial aid** package, $16,077 average indebtedness upon graduation, $406.9 million endowment

Students *Undergraduates:* 1,598 full-time, 2 part-time. Students come from 50 states and territories, 32 other countries. *The most frequently chosen baccalaureate fields are:* biological/life sciences, foreign language/literature, social sciences and history.

From out-of-state	85%	Reside on campus	85%
Age 25 or older	0.3%	Transferred in	1%
International students	2%	African Americans	2%
Asian Americans/Pacific Islanders	7%	Hispanic Americans	3%
Native Americans	0.4%		

Faculty 152 (74% full-time), 95% with terminal degrees.

Expenses (1999–2000) *Comprehensive fee:* $31,475 includes full-time tuition ($24,435), mandatory fees ($520), and room and board ($6520). *College room only:* $2890. Room and board charges vary according to housing facility. *Payment plan:* installment. *Waivers:* employees or children of employees.

Library Hawthorne-Longfellow Library plus 5 others. *Operations spending 1999–2000:* $3.6 million. *Collection:* 888,377 titles, 2,272 serial subscriptions, 16,684 audiovisual materials.

College life *Housing:* on-campus residence required through sophomore year. *Option:* coed. *Most popular organizations:* outing club, men's and women's rugby, volunteer programs, ballroom dance club, Campus Activities Board.

Campus security 24-hour emergency response devices and patrols, student patrols, late-night transport-escort service, controlled dormitory access, self-defense education, whistle program.

After graduation 50 organizations recruited on campus 1997–98. 70% of class of 1998 had job offers within 6 months. *Career center:* 6 full-time personnel. Services include job fairs, resume preparation, interview workshops, resume referral, career/interest testing, career counseling, careers library, job bank, job interviews. *Graduate education:* 20% of class of 1999 went directly to graduate and professional school: 8% graduate arts and sciences, 4% law, 4% medicine, 1% business, 1% education, 1% engineering, 1% veterinary medicine. *Major awards:* 6 Fulbright Scholars.

Freshmen 3,942 applied, 1,263 admitted, 464 enrolled. 18 National Merit Scholars, 42 valedictorians.

SAT verbal scores above 500	99%	SAT math scores above 500	100%
ACT above 18	N/R	From top 10% of their h.s. class	77%
From top quarter	95%	From top half	100%
1998 freshmen returning in 1999	94%		

Application *Options:* eApply at www.CollegeQuest.com, Common Application, early admission, early decision, deferred entrance. *Application fee:* $55. *Required:* essay or personal statement; high school transcript; 3 letters of recommendation. *Recommended:* interview.

Standardized tests *Placement:* Required: SAT I

Significant dates *Application deadlines:* 1/1 (freshmen), 3/1 (transfers). *Early decision:* 11/15. *Notification:* 4/15 (freshmen), 12/15 (early decision). *Financial aid deadline priority date:* 2/15.

Freshman Application Contact

Dr. Richard E. Steele, Dean of Admissions, Bowdoin College, 5000 College Station, Brunswick, ME 04011-8441. **Phone:** 207-725-3100. **Fax:** 207-725-3003. **E-mail:** admissions-lit@polar.bowdoin.edu

Visit CollegeQuest.com for information on majors offered and athletics. College video available at CollegeQuest.com.

■ *See page 1294 for a narrative description.*

COLBY COLLEGE
Waterville, Maine

Apply at CollegeQuest.com

- **Independent**, 4-year, founded 1813
- **Degree** bachelor's
- **Small-town** 714-acre campus
- **Coed**, 1,764 undergraduate students, 100% full-time, 52% women, 48% men
- **Most difficult** entrance level, 33% of applicants were admitted
- **11:1 student-to-undergraduate faculty ratio**
- **89% graduate** in 6 years or less
- **$31,580 comprehensive fee**
- **$20,100 average financial aid** package, $16,300 average indebtedness upon graduation, $290.4 million endowment

Colby, located in central Maine on one of America's most beautiful campuses, is among the nation's oldest and most respected colleges. Colby has a tradition of innovation, having pioneered the January Program of independent study (1962), African-American studies (program founded 1969), and universal e-mail accounts for students (1983). Among colleges, Colby is a national leader in study-abroad programs (two thirds of Colby students participate), interdisciplinary study options, and extracurricular programs.

Students *Undergraduates:* 1,764 full-time. Students come from 46 states and territories, 52 other countries. *The most frequently chosen baccalaureate fields are:* biological/life sciences, English, social sciences and history.

From out-of-state	89%	Reside on campus	98%
Age 25 or older	4%	Transferred in	1%
International students	4%	African Americans	3%
Asian Americans/Pacific Islanders	5%	Hispanic Americans	2%
Native Americans	0.2%		

Faculty 164 (90% full-time).

Expenses (1999–2000) *Comprehensive fee:* $31,580. *Payment plan:* installment. *Waivers:* adult students, senior citizens, and employees or children of employees.

Library Miller Library plus 2 others. *Operations spending 1999–2000:* $3.6 million. *Collection:* 591,845 titles, 2,390 serial subscriptions, 18,375 audiovisual materials.

College life *Housing:* on-campus residence required through senior year. *Options:* coed, cooperative. *Most popular organizations:* mountaineering club, outing club, student government, volunteer center.

Campus security 24-hour emergency response devices and patrols, late-night transport-escort service, controlled dormitory access, campus lighting, student emergency response team.

After graduation 55 organizations recruited on campus 1997–98. 80% of class of 1998 had job offers within 6 months. *Career center:* 4 full-time personnel. Services include job fairs, resume preparation, interview workshops, resume referral, career/interest testing, career counseling, careers library, job bank, job interviews.

Maine

Freshmen 4,363 applied, 1,425 admitted, 489 enrolled. 9 valedictorians.

SAT verbal scores above 500	99%	SAT math scores above 500	97%
ACT above 18	99%	From top 10% of their h.s. class	52%
From top quarter	86%	From top half	98%
1998 freshmen returning in 1999	91%		

Application *Options:* eApply at www.CollegeQuest.com, Common Application, electronic application, early decision, deferred entrance. *Application fee:* $50. *Required:* essay or personal statement; high school transcript; 2 letters of recommendation. *Recommended:* interview.

Standardized tests *Admission: Required:* SAT I or ACT.

Significant dates *Application deadlines:* 1/15 (freshmen), 3/1 (transfers). *Early decision:* 11/15 (for plan 1), 1/1 (for plan 2). *Notification:* 4/1 (freshmen), 12/15 (early decision plan 1), 2/1 (early decision plan 2). *Financial aid deadline:* 2/1.

Freshman Application Contact Mr. Parker J. Beverage, Dean of Admissions and Financial Aid, Colby College, Office of Admissions and Financial Aid, 4800 Mayflower Hill, Waterville, ME 04901-8848. **Phone:** 207-872-3168. **Toll-free phone:** 800-723-3032. **Fax:** 207-872-3474. **E-mail:** admissions@colby.edu

Visit CollegeQuest.com for information on majors offered and athletics. Electronic viewbook available at CollegeQuest.com.

■ *See page 1448 for a narrative description.*

Average high school GPA	3.74	SAT verbal scores above 500	100%
SAT math scores above 500	90%	ACT above 18	100%
From top 10% of their h.s. class	28%	From top quarter	78%
From top half	98%	1998 freshmen returning in 1999	93%

Application *Options:* eApply at www.CollegeQuest.com, electronic application, early admission, early decision, deferred entrance. *Application fee:* $45. *Required:* essay or personal statement; high school transcript; 3 letters of recommendation. *Required for some:* interview. *Recommended:* minimum 3.0 GPA; interview.

Standardized tests *Admission: Recommended:* SAT I and SAT II or ACT.

Significant dates *Application deadlines:* 3/1 (freshmen), 5/1 (transfers). *Early decision:* 12/1 (for plan 1), 1/10 (for plan 2). *Notification:* 4/1 (freshmen), 12/15 (early decision plan 1), 1/25 (early decision plan 2). *Financial aid deadline priority date:* 2/15.

Freshman Application Contact Mr. David Mahoney, Director of Admission and Financial Aid, College of the Atlantic, 105 Eden Street, Bar Harbor, ME 04609-1198. **Phone:** 207-288-5015 Ext. 233. **Toll-free phone:** 800-528-0025. **Fax:** 207-288-4126. **E-mail:** inquiry@ecology.coa.edu

Visit CollegeQuest.com for information on majors offered and athletics. Electronic viewbook available at CollegeQuest.com.

■ *See page 1488 for a narrative description.*

COLLEGE OF THE ATLANTIC
Bar Harbor, Maine

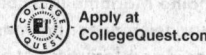

- **Independent**, comprehensive, founded 1969
- **Degrees** bachelor's and master's
- **Small-town** 25-acre campus
- **Coed**, 273 undergraduate students, 96% full-time, 67% women, 33% men
- **Very difficult** entrance level, 73% of applicants were admitted
- **4:1** student-to-undergraduate faculty ratio
- **68% graduate** in 6 years or less
- **$19,485 tuition** and fees
- **$15,771 average financial aid** package, $13,887 average indebtedness upon graduation, $7 million endowment

Students *Undergraduates:* 262 full-time, 11 part-time. Students come from 38 states and territories, 9 other countries. *The most frequently chosen baccalaureate field is:* liberal arts/general studies. *Graduate:* 5 in graduate degree programs.

From out-of-state	79%	Reside on campus	40%
Transferred in	6%	African Americans	0.4%
Asian Americans/Pacific Islanders	1%	Hispanic Americans	1%
Native Americans	0.4%		

Faculty 30 (63% full-time).

Expenses (1999–2000) *Comprehensive fee:* $24,705 includes full-time tuition ($19,248), mandatory fees ($237), and room and board ($5220). *College room only:* $3180. Room and board charges vary according to board plan. *Part-time tuition:* $2566 per term. *Part-time fees:* $79 per term part-time. *Payment plan:* installment. *Waivers:* adult students and employees or children of employees.

Library Thorndike Library plus 1 other. *Operations spending 1999-2000:* $245,000. *Collection:* 33,032 titles.

College life *Housing: Option:* coed. *Most popular organizations:* outing club, environmental awareness club, students for a free Tibet, All-Campus Meeting, choral group.

Campus security 24-hour emergency response devices and patrols, late-night transport-escort service.

After graduation 75% of class of 1998 had job offers within 6 months. *Career center:* 1 full-time, 1 part-time personnel. Services include resume preparation, resume referral, career counseling, careers library, job bank, job interviews. *Graduate education:* 7% of class of 1999 went directly to graduate and professional school: 2% education, 2% graduate arts and sciences, 2% law, 1% veterinary medicine.

Freshmen 234 applied, 171 admitted, 73 enrolled. 8 National Merit Scholars, 4 class presidents, 1 valedictorian, 11 student government officers.

HUSSON COLLEGE
Bangor, Maine

- **Independent**, comprehensive, founded 1898
- **Degrees** associate, bachelor's, master's, post-master's, and postbachelor's certificates
- **Suburban** 170-acre campus
- **Coed**, 1,394 undergraduate students, 61% full-time, 65% women, 35% men
- **Moderately difficult** entrance level, 93% of applicants were admitted
- **19:1** student-to-undergraduate faculty ratio
- **54% graduate** in 6 years or less
- **$9310 tuition** and fees
- **$9410 average financial aid** package, $17,125 average indebtedness upon graduation, $2.1 million endowment

Students *Undergraduates:* 844 full-time, 550 part-time. Students come from 27 states and territories, 6 other countries. *The most frequently chosen baccalaureate fields are:* business/marketing, computer/information sciences, health professions and related sciences. *Graduate:* 342 in graduate degree programs.

From out-of-state	25%	Reside on campus	41%
Age 25 or older	22%	Transferred in	7%

Faculty 98 (54% full-time), 30% with terminal degrees.

Expenses (1999–2000) *Comprehensive fee:* $14,300 includes full-time tuition ($9210), mandatory fees ($100), and room and board ($4990). Full-time tuition and fees vary according to class time. *Part-time tuition:* $307 per semester hour. Part-time tuition and fees vary according to class time and course load. *Payment plans:* tuition prepayment, installment. *Waivers:* senior citizens and employees or children of employees.

Library Husson College Library plus 1 other. *Operations spending 1999-2000:* $136,952. *Collection:* 34,536 titles, 450 serial subscriptions, 50 audiovisual materials.

College life *Housing:* on-campus residence required through senior year. *Option:* coed. *Social organizations:* national fraternities, local fraternities, local sororities; 3% of eligible men and 6% of eligible women are members. *Most popular organizations:* student government, Organization of Student Nurses, Organization of Physical Therapy Students, Accounting Society, Phi Beta Lambda.

Campus security 24-hour emergency response devices and patrols.

After graduation 30 organizations recruited on campus 1997–98. 94% of class of 1998 had job offers within 6 months. *Career center:* 2 full-time personnel. Services include job fairs, resume preparation, interview workshops, resume referral, career/interest testing, career counseling, careers library, job bank, job interviews. *Graduate education:* 2% of class of 1999 went directly to graduate and professional school: 2% business.

Maine

Husson College (continued)

Freshmen 708 applied, 657 admitted, 183 enrolled. 6 class presidents, 1 valedictorian, 6 student government officers.

Average high school GPA	3.1	SAT verbal scores above 500	44%
SAT math scores above 500	37%	ACT above 18	100%
From top 10% of their h.s. class	7%	From top quarter	34%
From top half	63%	1998 freshmen returning in 1999	65%

Application *Options:* eApply at www.CollegeQuest.com, electronic application, early admission, early action, deferred entrance. *Application fee:* $25. *Required:* essay or personal statement; high school transcript; 1 letter of recommendation. *Recommended:* interview.
Standardized tests *Admission: Required:* SAT I or ACT.
Significant dates *Application deadlines:* 9/1 (freshmen), 9/1 (transfers). *Early action:* 12/15. *Notification:* 1/2 (early action). *Financial aid deadline priority date:* 4/1.
Freshman Application Contact
Mrs. Jane Goodwin, Director of Admissions, Husson College, One College Circle, Bangor, ME 04401-2999. **Phone:** 207-941-7100. **Toll-free phone:** 800-4-HUSSON. **Fax:** 207-941-7935. **E-mail:** admit@husson.edu
Visit CollegeQuest.com for information on majors offered and athletics. College video available at CollegeQuest.com.

■ *See page 1814 for a narrative description.*

MAINE COLLEGE OF ART
Portland, Maine

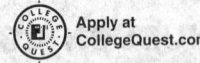

- **Independent**, comprehensive, founded 1882
- **Degrees** bachelor's and master's
- **Urban** campus with easy access to Boston
- **Coed**, 380 undergraduate students, 84% full-time, 58% women, 42% men
- **Moderately difficult** entrance level, 91% of applicants were admitted
- **10:1** student-to-undergraduate faculty ratio
- **35.42% graduate** in 6 years or less
- **$16,718 tuition** and fees
- **$13,135 average financial aid** package, $2.2 million endowment

Students *Undergraduates:* 321 full-time, 59 part-time. Students come from 23 states and territories. *The most frequently chosen baccalaureate field is:* visual/performing arts. *Graduate:* 26 in graduate degree programs.

Reside on campus	20%	Age 25 or older	23%
Transferred in	14%	African Americans	1%
Asian Americans/Pacific Islanders	3%	Native Americans	1%

Faculty 52 (58% full-time), 100% with terminal degrees.
Expenses (1999–2000) *One-time required fee:* $22. *Comprehensive fee:* $23,107 includes full-time tuition ($16,530), mandatory fees ($188), and room and board ($6389). *College room only:* $3965. Room and board charges vary according to housing facility. *Part-time tuition:* $689 per credit hour. *Payment plans:* installment, deferred payment.
Library Maine College of Art Library. *Operations spending 1999–2000:* $105,000. *Collection:* 19,700 titles, 98 serial subscriptions, 150 audiovisual materials.
College life *Housing:* Option: coed. *Most popular organizations:* Student Representative Association, Outdoor Group, The Canvas—student newspaper, Ski and Snowboard Club, Movie Club.
Campus security 24-hour emergency response devices and patrols, controlled dormitory access.
After graduation *Career center:* 2 full-time personnel. Services include resume preparation, career counseling, careers library.
Freshmen 301 applied, 273 admitted, 86 enrolled.

Average high school GPA	2.9	SAT verbal scores above 500	66%
SAT math scores above 500	44%	ACT above 18	80%
From top 10% of their h.s. class	21%	From top quarter	25%
From top half	45%	1998 freshmen returning in 1999	52%

Application *Options:* eApply at www.CollegeQuest.com, Common Application, electronic application, early admission, deferred entrance. *Application fee:* $40. *Required:* essay or personal statement; high school transcript; minimum 2.0 GPA; 2 letters of recommendation; portfolio. *Recommended:* interview.
Standardized tests *Admission: Required:* SAT I or ACT. *Recommended:* SAT II Subject Tests.
Significant dates *Application deadlines:* rolling (freshmen), rolling (transfers). *Notification:* continuous until 8/31 (freshmen). *Financial aid deadline priority date:* 3/1.
Freshman Application Contact
Ms. Meg Widmer, Admissions Coordinator, Maine College of Art, 97 Spring Street, Portland, ME 04101-3987. **Phone:** 207-775-3052 Ext. 225. **Toll-free phone:** 800-639-4808. **Fax:** 207-772-5069. **E-mail:** admissions@meca.edu
Visit CollegeQuest.com for information on majors offered and athletics. College video available at CollegeQuest.com.

■ *See page 1970 for a narrative description.*

MAINE MARITIME ACADEMY
Castine, Maine

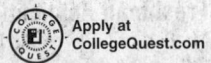

- **State-supported**, comprehensive, founded 1941
- **Degrees** associate, bachelor's, master's, and postbachelor's certificates
- **Small-town** 35-acre campus
- **Coed**, 680 undergraduate students, 98% full-time, 14% women, 86% men
- **Moderately difficult** entrance level, 80% of applicants were admitted
- **12:1** student-to-undergraduate faculty ratio
- **$5092 tuition** and fees (in-state); $8900 (out-of-state)
- **$8431 average financial aid** package, $13,358 average indebtedness upon graduation, $7 million endowment

Maine Maritime is a college awarding associate and bachelor's degrees in marine engineering, marine transportation, ocean studies, international business, and logistics. A 500-foot training ship, a fleet of 90 vessels, annual cruises, high-tech simulation, 4 USCG licenses. Telephone: 800-464-6565 (toll-free, in-state); 800-227-8465 (toll-free, out-of-state). Web site: http://www.mainemaritime.edu.

Students *Undergraduates:* 668 full-time, 12 part-time. Students come from 37 states and territories, 6 other countries. *The most frequently chosen baccalaureate fields are:* engineering/engineering technologies, biological/life sciences, trade and industry. *Graduate:* 16 in graduate degree programs.

From out-of-state	47%	Reside on campus	80%
Age 25 or older	15%	Transferred in	0.1%

Faculty 53 (100% full-time).
Expenses (1999–2000) *Tuition, state resident:* full-time $4462; part-time $153 per credit hour. *Tuition, nonresident:* full-time $8270; part-time $274 per credit hour. *Required fees:* full-time $630; $315 per term part-time. Full-time tuition and fees vary according to course load, reciprocity agreements, and student level. Part-time tuition and fees vary according to program. *College room and board:* $5022. Room and board charges vary according to board plan. *Payment plan:* installment. *Waivers:* employees or children of employees.
Library Nutting Memorial Library. *Collection:* 82,216 titles, 462 serial subscriptions, 3,192 audiovisual materials.
College life *Housing:* on-campus residence required through junior year. *Option:* coed. *Social organizations:* coed fraternity; 6% of eligible men and 25% of eligible women are members. *Most popular organizations:* Alpha Phi Omega, yacht club, outing club, Social Council, drill team.
Campus security 24-hour patrols, student patrols.
After graduation 40 organizations recruited on campus 1997–98. 100% of class of 1998 had job offers within 6 months. *Career center:* 2 full-time personnel. Services include resume preparation, interview workshops, resume referral, career counseling, careers library, job bank, job interviews. *Graduate education:* 2% of class of 1999 went directly to graduate and professional school.
Freshmen 473 applied, 380 admitted, 152 enrolled.

Average high school GPA	2.8	SAT verbal scores above 500	N/R
SAT math scores above 500	N/R	ACT above 18	N/R
From top 10% of their h.s. class	25%	From top quarter	42%
From top half	74%	1998 freshmen returning in 1999	75%

Application *Options:* eApply at www.CollegeQuest.com, electronic application, early decision, deferred entrance. *Application fee:* $15. *Required:* high school transcript; 1 letter of recommendation; physical examination. *Recommended:* interview.

Maine

Standardized tests *Admission: Required:* SAT I or ACT.
Significant dates *Application deadlines:* 7/1 (freshmen), 7/1 (transfers). *Early decision:* 12/20. *Notification:* 1/1 (early decision). *Financial aid deadline priority date:* 4/15.
Freshman Application Contact
Mr. Jeffrey C. Wright, Director of Admissions, Maine Maritime Academy, 67 Pleasant Street, Castine, ME 04420. **Phone:** 207-326-2215. **Toll-free phone:** 800-464-6565 (in-state); 800-227-8465 (out-of-state). **Fax:** 207-326-2515. **E-mail:** admissions@bell.mma.edu
Visit CollegeQuest.com for information on majors offered and athletics. College video and electronic viewbook available at CollegeQuest.com.

SAINT JOSEPH'S COLLEGE
Standish, Maine

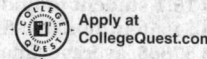 Apply at CollegeQuest.com

- **Independent**, comprehensive, founded 1912, affiliated with Roman Catholic Church
- **Degrees** associate, bachelor's, and master's (profile does not include enrollment in distance learning master's program)
- **Small-town** 330-acre campus
- **Coed**, 820 undergraduate students, 95% full-time, 66% women, 34% men
- **Moderately difficult** entrance level, 91% of applicants were admitted
- **$13,735 tuition** and fees
- **$12,276 average financial aid** package, $16,122 average indebtedness upon graduation, $3.7 million endowment

Sponsored by the Sisters of Mercy, Saint Joseph's College is the only Catholic college in Maine. For more than 85 years, the College has offered a liberal arts education to men and women of all ages and faiths. The intellectual, spiritual, and social growth of its students within a values-centered environment is integral to a Saint Joseph's College education.

Students *Undergraduates:* 782 full-time, 38 part-time. Students come from 17 states and territories, 3 other countries. *The most frequently chosen baccalaureate fields are:* education, business/marketing, health professions and related sciences.

From out-of-state	49%	Age 25 or older	65%
Transferred in	4%	International students	0.1%
African Americans	1%	Asian Americans/Pacific Islanders	1%
Hispanic Americans	0.4%	Native Americans	0.1%

Faculty 98 (51% full-time).
Expenses (1999–2000) *Comprehensive fee:* $19,685 includes full-time tuition ($13,240), mandatory fees ($495), and room and board ($5950). *Part-time tuition:* $235 per credit hour. *Part-time fees:* $100 per term part-time. Part-time tuition and fees vary according to course load. *Payment plan:* installment. *Waivers:* senior citizens and employees or children of employees.
Library Wellehan Library. *Collection:* 77,446 titles, 474 serial subscriptions.
College life *Housing: Option:* coed. *Most popular organizations:* church ministry, Theater Guild, Student Government Association, outing club, Inter-Hall Council.
Campus security 24-hour emergency response devices and patrols, late-night transport-escort service, controlled dormitory access.
After graduation 40 organizations recruited on campus 1997–98. 81% of class of 1998 had job offers within 6 months. *Career center:* 2 full-time personnel. Services include job fairs, resume preparation, resume referral, career counseling, careers library, job bank, job interviews. *Graduate education:* 17% of class of 1999 went directly to graduate and professional school.
Freshmen 892 applied, 812 admitted, 281 enrolled.

Average high school GPA	3.0	SAT verbal scores above 500	53%
SAT math scores above 500	48%	ACT above 18	N/R
From top 10% of their h.s. class	13%	From top quarter	40%
From top half	76%	1998 freshmen returning in 1999	72%

Application *Options:* eApply at www.CollegeQuest.com, Common Application, electronic application, early admission, deferred entrance. *Application fee:* $0. *Required:* essay or personal statement; high school transcript; minimum 2.0 GPA. *Recommended:* letters of recommendation; interview.

Standardized tests *Admission: Required:* SAT I or ACT.
Significant dates *Application deadlines:* rolling (freshmen), rolling (transfers). *Financial aid deadline priority date:* 3/1.
Freshman Application Contact
Mr. William Dunfey, Dean of Enrollment Management, Saint Joseph's College, 278 Whites Bridge Road, Standish, ME 04084-5263. **Phone:** 207-893-7746 Ext. 7741. **Toll-free phone:** 800-338-7057. **Fax:** 207-893-7862. **E-mail:** admissions@sjcme.edu
Visit CollegeQuest.com for information on majors offered and athletics.

■ *See page 2392 for a narrative description.*

THOMAS COLLEGE
Waterville, Maine

Apply at CollegeQuest.com

- **Independent**, comprehensive, founded 1894
- **Degrees** associate, bachelor's, and master's
- **Small-town** 70-acre campus
- **Coed**, 696 undergraduate students, 69% full-time, 56% women, 44% men
- **Minimally difficult** entrance level, 96% of applicants were admitted
- **54% graduate** in 6 years or less
- **$12,290 tuition** and fees
- **$15,018 average financial aid** package, $19,125 average indebtedness upon graduation, $891,991 endowment

Students *Undergraduates:* 481 full-time, 215 part-time. Students come from 5 states and territories, 3 other countries. *The most frequently chosen baccalaureate fields are:* business/marketing, computer/information sciences, parks and recreation. *Graduate:* 185 in graduate degree programs.

From out-of-state	10%	Reside on campus	60%
Age 25 or older	34%	Transferred in	4%
International students	1%	African Americans	0.3%
Asian Americans/Pacific Islanders	1%	Hispanic Americans	0.3%
Native Americans	0.3%		

Faculty 84 (26% full-time), 43% with terminal degrees.
Expenses (1999–2000) *One-time required fee:* $75. *Comprehensive fee:* $17,840 includes full-time tuition ($12,000), mandatory fees ($290), and room and board ($5550). Room and board charges vary according to housing facility. *Part-time tuition:* $1500 per course. *Part-time fees:* $145 per term part-time. Part-time tuition and fees vary according to class time and course load. *Payment plan:* installment. *Waivers:* employees or children of employees.
Library Marriner Library. *Operations spending 1999–2000:* $111,118. *Collection:* 28,000 titles, 80 serial subscriptions, 250 audiovisual materials.
College life *Housing:* on-campus residence required through senior year. *Option:* coed. *Social organizations:* national fraternities, national sororities, local fraternities, local sororities; 3% of eligible men and 5% of eligible women are members. *Most popular organizations:* Phi Beta Lambda, students club, GLOBE, Campus Activity Board, peer advisors.
Campus security 24-hour emergency response devices and patrols, student patrols.
After graduation 40 organizations recruited on campus 1997–98. 97% of class of 1998 had job offers within 6 months. *Career center:* 2 full-time, 1 part-time personnel. Services include job fairs, resume preparation, interview workshops, resume referral, career counseling, careers library, job bank, job interviews. *Graduate education:* 6% of class of 1999 went directly to graduate and professional school: 6% business.
Freshmen 341 applied, 329 admitted, 164 enrolled. 1 valedictorian.

Average high school GPA	2.81	SAT verbal scores above 500	28%
SAT math scores above 500	39%	ACT above 18	N/R
From top 10% of their h.s. class	10%	From top quarter	22%
From top half	57%	1998 freshmen returning in 1999	71%

Application *Options:* eApply at www.CollegeQuest.com, electronic application, early action, deferred entrance. *Application fee:* $25. *Required:* essay or personal statement; high school transcript; 1 letter of recommendation. *Recommended:* minimum 2.0 GPA; interview; rank in upper 50% of high school class.
Standardized tests *Admission: Recommended:* SAT I. *Required for some:* SAT I or ACT.
Significant dates *Application deadlines:* rolling (freshmen), rolling (transfers). *Early action:* 12/1. *Notification:* 12/15 (early action). *Financial aid deadline priority date:* 2/15.

Maine

Thomas College (continued)
Freshman Application Contact
Mr. Robert Callahan, Director of Admissions, Thomas College, 180 West River Road, Waterville, ME 04901. **Phone:** 207-859-1101. **Toll-free phone:** 800-339-7001. **Fax:** 207-859-1114. **E-mail:** admiss@host2.thomas.edu
Visit CollegeQuest.com for information on majors offered and athletics. Electronic viewbook available at CollegeQuest.com.

UNITY COLLEGE
Unity, Maine

- **Independent**, 4-year, founded 1965
- **Degrees** associate and bachelor's
- **Rural** 205-acre campus
- **Coed**, 512 undergraduate students, 96% full-time, 31% women, 69% men
- **Moderately difficult** entrance level, 92% of applicants were admitted
- **16:1 student-to-undergraduate faculty ratio**
- **30% graduate** in 6 years or less
- **$12,780 tuition** and fees
- **$9022 average financial aid** package, $2.1 million endowment

Unity College's Learning Resource Center provides academic support services for students who need academic improvement. The center offers courses, advising, tutoring, study skills workshops, and counseling. The staff consists of 6 full-time faculty members, including a learning disabilities specialist. The 4-week Summer Institute prepares entering students for the academic challenges of college.

Students *Undergraduates:* 492 full-time, 20 part-time. Students come from 21 states and territories, 2 other countries. *The most frequently chosen baccalaureate fields are:* natural resources/environmental science, liberal arts/general studies, parks and recreation.

From out-of-state	62%	Reside on campus	72%
Age 25 or older	8%	Transferred in	5%
International students	1%	African Americans	1%
Asian Americans/Pacific Islanders	0.2%	Hispanic Americans	0.2%

Faculty 72 (49% full-time), 29% with terminal degrees.
Expenses (2000–2001) *One-time required fee:* $150. *Comprehensive fee:* $18,080 includes full-time tuition ($12,330), mandatory fees ($450), and room and board ($5300). *Part-time tuition:* $415 per credit hour. Part-time tuition and fees vary according to course load. *Payment plan:* installment. *Waivers:* employees or children of employees.
Library Dorothy Webb Quimby Library. *Operations spending 1999–2000:* $273,740. *Collection:* 46,000 titles, 650 serial subscriptions.
College life *Housing:* on-campus residence required through sophomore year. *Option:* coed.
Campus security 24-hour patrols.
After graduation 65 organizations recruited on campus 1997–98. 91% of class of 1998 had job offers within 6 months. *Career center:* 2 full-time, 2 part-time personnel. Services include job fairs, resume preparation, interview workshops, resume referral, career counseling, job bank, job interviews. *Graduate education:* 12% of class of 1999 went directly to graduate and professional school.
Freshmen 500 applied, 458 admitted, 146 enrolled.

SAT verbal scores above 500	18%	SAT math scores above 500	13%
ACT above 18	N/R	From top 10% of their h.s. class	4%
From top quarter	10%	From top half	41%
1998 freshmen returning in 1999	66%		

Application *Options:* eApply at www.CollegeQuest.com, Common Application, electronic application, early admission, early action, deferred entrance. *Application fee:* $25. *Required:* essay or personal statement; high school transcript; 2 letters of recommendation. *Required for some:* interview. *Recommended:* minimum 2.0 GPA; interview.
Standardized tests *Placement: Recommended:* SAT I or ACT.
Significant dates *Application deadlines:* rolling (freshmen), rolling (transfers). *Early action:* 1/15. *Notification:* 2/1 (early action). *Financial aid deadline priority date:* 3/1.
Freshman Application Contact
Dr. John M. B. Craig, Vice President and Dean for Admissions, Unity College, PO Box 532, Unity, ME 04988-0532. **Phone:** 207-948-3131 Ext. 222. **Fax:** 207-948-6277.

Visit CollegeQuest.com for information on majors offered and athletics. College video and electronic viewbook available at CollegeQuest.com.

■ *See page 2672 for a narrative description.*

UNIVERSITY OF MAINE
Orono, Maine

- **State-supported**, university, founded 1865
- **Degrees** bachelor's, master's, doctoral, post-master's, and postbachelor's certificates
- **Small-town** 3,298-acre campus
- **Coed**, 6,936 undergraduate students, 90% full-time, 48% women, 52% men
- **Moderately difficult** entrance level, 85% of applicants were admitted
- **15:1 student-to-undergraduate faculty ratio**
- **$4656 tuition** and fees (in-state); $11,946 (out-of-state)
- **$7888 average financial aid** package, $15,000 average indebtedness upon graduation, $134.2 million endowment

Part of University of Maine System.
Students *Undergraduates:* 6,246 full-time, 690 part-time. Students come from 37 states and territories, 49 other countries. *The most frequently chosen baccalaureate fields are:* education, business/marketing, engineering/engineering technologies. *Graduate:* 2,063 in graduate degree programs.

From out-of-state	15%	Reside on campus	44%
Age 25 or older	14%	Transferred in	7%
International students	2%	African Americans	1%
Asian Americans/Pacific Islanders	1%	Hispanic Americans	1%
Native Americans	2%		

Faculty 644 (75% full-time), 74% with terminal degrees.
Expenses (1999–2000) *One-time required fee:* $15. *Tuition, state resident:* full-time $3960; part-time $132 per credit hour. *Tuition, nonresident:* full-time $11,250; part-time $375 per credit hour. *Required fees:* full-time $696; $135 per term part-time. Full-time tuition and fees vary according to course load and reciprocity agreements. Part-time tuition and fees vary according to course load and reciprocity agreements. *College room and board:* $5256. Room and board charges vary according to board plan and housing facility. *Payment plan:* installment. *Waivers:* employees or children of employees.
Library Fogler Library. *Operations spending 1999–2000:* $5.6 million. *Collection:* 1.2 million titles, 5,400 serial subscriptions, 23,979 audiovisual materials.
College life *Housing:* on-campus residence required in freshman year. *Options:* coed, women-only, disabled students. *Social organizations:* national fraternities, national sororities; 14% of eligible men and 6% of eligible women are members. *Most popular organizations:* Volunteers in Community Efforts, Alternative Spring Break, student government, Alpha Phi Omega, Gamma Sigma Sigma.
Campus security 24-hour emergency response devices and patrols, late-night transport-escort service, controlled dormitory access.
After graduation *Career center:* 6 full-time personnel. Services include job fairs, resume preparation, resume referral, career counseling, careers library, job bank, job interviews.
Freshmen 4,568 applied, 3,877 admitted, 1,573 enrolled. 24 valedictorians, 277 student government officers.

Average high school GPA	3.1	SAT verbal scores above 500	69%
SAT math scores above 500	68%	ACT above 18	N/R
From top 10% of their h.s. class	18%	From top quarter	45%
From top half	81%	1998 freshmen returning in 1999	80%

Application *Options:* eApply at www.CollegeQuest.com, electronic application, early admission, deferred entrance. *Application fee:* $25. *Required:* essay or personal statement; high school transcript; 1 letter of recommendation.
Standardized tests *Admission: Required:* SAT I or ACT.
Significant dates *Application deadlines:* rolling (freshmen), rolling (transfers). *Financial aid deadline priority date:* 3/1.
Freshman Application Contact
Mr. Jonathan H. Henry, Director, University of Maine, 5713 Chadbourne Hall, Orono, ME 04469-5713. **Phone:** 207-581-1561. **Toll-free phone:** 877-486-2364. **Fax:** 207-581-1213. **E-mail:** um-admit@maine.edu

Maine

Visit CollegeQuest.com for information on majors offered and athletics. College video available at CollegeQuest.com.

■ *See page 2746 for a narrative description.*

THE UNIVERSITY OF MAINE AT AUGUSTA
Augusta, Maine

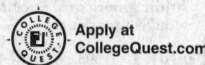 Apply at CollegeQuest.com

- **State-supported**, 4-year, founded 1965
- **Degrees** associate and bachelor's (also offers some graduate courses and continuing education program with significant enrollment not reflected in profile)
- **Small-town** 165-acre campus
- **Coed**, 3,997 undergraduate students, 38% full-time, 76% women, 24% men
- **Noncompetitive** entrance level, 67% of applicants were admitted
- **20:1 student-to-undergraduate faculty ratio**
- **$3366 tuition** and fees (in-state); $7866 (out-of-state)

Part of University of Maine System.
Students *Undergraduates:* 1,514 full-time, 2,483 part-time. Students come from 12 states and territories, 2 other countries. *The most frequently chosen baccalaureate fields are:* business/marketing, liberal arts/general studies, protective services/public administration.

From out-of-state	1%	Age 25 or older	60%
Transferred in	13%	International students	0.03%
African Americans	1%	Asian Americans/Pacific Islanders	0.5%
Hispanic Americans	1%	Native Americans	3%

Faculty 266 (38% full-time), 32% with terminal degrees.
Expenses (1999–2000) *Tuition, state resident:* full-time $3090; part-time $103 per credit. *Tuition, nonresident:* full-time $7590; part-time $252 per credit. *Required fees:* full-time $276; $12 per credit. Full-time tuition and fees vary according to reciprocity agreements. Part-time tuition and fees vary according to reciprocity agreements. *Payment plan:* installment. *Waivers:* senior citizens and employees or children of employees.
Library Learning Resources Center. *Collection:* 44,000 titles, 560 serial subscriptions.
College life *Housing:* college housing not available. *Most popular organizations:* Phi Theta Kappa, student government.
Campus security 24-hour emergency response devices.
After graduation *Career center:* 2 full-time personnel. Services include job fairs, resume preparation, career counseling, careers library.
Freshmen 2,233 applied, 1,501 admitted, 654 enrolled.

SAT verbal scores above 500	N/R	SAT math scores above 500	N/R
ACT above 18	N/R		

Application *Options:* eApply at www.CollegeQuest.com, Common Application, electronic application, early admission, early action, deferred entrance. *Required:* high school transcript.
Standardized tests *Placement: Recommended:* SAT I. *Required for some:* SAT I.
Significant dates *Application deadlines:* rolling (freshmen), rolling (transfers). *Early action:* 11/1. *Notification:* 12/1 (early action).
Freshman Application Contact
Mr. William Clark Ketcham, Director of Enrollment Services, The University of Maine at Augusta, 46 University Drive, Augusta, ME 04330-9410. **Phone:** 207-621-3185. **Toll-free phone:** 800-696-6000 Ext. 3185. **Fax:** 207-621-3116. **E-mail:** umaar@maine.maine.edu
Visit CollegeQuest.com for information on majors offered and athletics. College video available at CollegeQuest.com.

UNIVERSITY OF MAINE AT FARMINGTON
Farmington, Maine

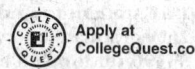 Apply at CollegeQuest.com

- **State-supported**, 4-year, founded 1863
- **Degree** bachelor's
- **Small-town** 50-acre campus
- **Coed**, 2,262 undergraduate students, 90% full-time, 69% women, 31% men
- **Moderately difficult** entrance level, 65% of applicants were admitted
- **18:1 student-to-undergraduate faculty ratio**
- **52.3% graduate** in 6 years or less
- **$3776 tuition** and fees (in-state); $8666 (out-of-state)
- **$5.4 million endowment**

Part of University of Maine System.
Students *Undergraduates:* 2,025 full-time, 237 part-time. Students come from 32 states and territories, 14 other countries. *The most frequently chosen baccalaureate fields are:* education, interdisciplinary studies, psychology.

From out-of-state	15%	Reside on campus	43%
Age 25 or older	10%	Transferred in	5%
International students	1%	African Americans	0.2%
Asian Americans/Pacific Islanders	1%	Hispanic Americans	0.2%
Native Americans	1%		

Faculty 179 (64% full-time), 53% with terminal degrees.
Expenses (1999–2000) *One-time required fee:* $15. *Tuition, state resident:* full-time $3390; part-time $113 per credit hour. *Tuition, nonresident:* full-time $8280; part-time $276 per credit hour. *Required fees:* full-time $386; $5 per credit hour; $59 per term part-time. Full-time tuition and fees vary according to course load and reciprocity agreements. Part-time tuition and fees vary according to course load and reciprocity agreements. *College room and board:* $4614; room only: $2384. Room and board charges vary according to board plan and housing facility. *Payment plan:* installment. *Waivers:* minority students, senior citizens, and employees or children of employees.
Library Mantor Library. *Collection:* 91,519 titles, 1,581 serial subscriptions, 8,369 audiovisual materials.
College life *Housing: Options:* coed, women-only. *Most popular organizations:* Program Board, Intramural Board, Campus Residence Council, campus radio station, Commuter Council.
Campus security 24-hour emergency response devices and patrols, late-night transport-escort service, controlled dormitory access, safety whistles.
After graduation 25 organizations recruited on campus 1997–98. 80% of class of 1998 had job offers within 6 months. *Career center:* 5 full-time personnel. Services include job fairs, resume preparation, interview workshops, resume referral, career counseling, careers library, job bank, job interviews. *Graduate education:* 18% of class of 1999 went directly to graduate and professional school: 11% graduate arts and sciences, 3% business, 2% education, 1% law, 1% medicine.
Freshmen 1,510 applied, 980 admitted, 480 enrolled. 20 class presidents, 3 valedictorians, 110 student government officers.

SAT verbal scores above 500	65%	SAT math scores above 500	55%
ACT above 18	N/R	From top 10% of their h.s. class	10%
From top quarter	45%	From top half	85%
1998 freshmen returning in 1999	69%		

Application *Options:* eApply at www.CollegeQuest.com, electronic application, early admission, early action, deferred entrance. *Application fee:* $25. *Required:* essay or personal statement; high school transcript; minimum 2.0 GPA; 1 letter of recommendation. *Recommended:* interview.
Standardized tests *Placement: Recommended:* SAT I.
Significant dates *Application deadlines:* 4/15 (freshmen), 5/1 (transfers). *Early action:* 12/15. *Notification:* 1/8 (early action). *Financial aid deadline priority date:* 3/1.
Freshman Application Contact
Mr. James G. Collins, Associate Director of Admissions, University of Maine at Farmington, 102 Main Street, Farmington, ME 04938-1994. **Phone:** 207-778-7050. **Fax:** 207-778-8182. **E-mail:** umfadmit@maine.maine.edu
Visit CollegeQuest.com for information on majors offered and athletics.

UNIVERSITY OF MAINE AT FORT KENT
Fort Kent, Maine

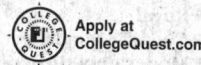 Apply at CollegeQuest.com

- **State-supported**, 4-year, founded 1878
- **Degrees** associate and bachelor's
- **Rural** 52-acre campus
- **Coed**, 926 undergraduate students, 66% full-time, 64% women, 36% men
- **Moderately difficult** entrance level, 93% of applicants were admitted

Maine

University of Maine at Fort Kent (continued)

- 18:1 student-to-undergraduate faculty ratio
- $3375 tuition and fees (in-state); $7845 (out-of-state)

Part of University of Maine System.

Students *Undergraduates:* 607 full-time, 319 part-time. Students come from 10 states and territories, 2 other countries. *The most frequently chosen baccalaureate fields are:* business/marketing, education, psychology.

From out-of-state	31%	Age 25 or older	7%
Transferred in	16%	International students	26%
African Americans	1%	Asian Americans/Pacific Islanders	0.2%
Native Americans	1%		

Faculty 33 (100% full-time), 70% with terminal degrees.

Expenses (1999–2000) *One-time required fee:* $15. *Tuition, state resident:* full-time $3120; part-time $104 per credit hour. *Tuition, nonresident:* full-time $7590; part-time $253 per credit hour. *Required fees:* full-time $255; $8 per credit hour. Full-time tuition and fees vary according to course load and reciprocity agreements. Part-time tuition and fees vary according to course load and reciprocity agreements. *College room and board:* $4000; room only: $2020. Room and board charges vary according to board plan. *Payment plan:* installment. *Waivers:* senior citizens and employees or children of employees.

Library Waneta Blake Library plus 1 other. *Operations spending 1999–2000:* $205,168. *Collection:* 60,000 titles, 378 serial subscriptions, 750 audiovisual materials.

College life *Housing: Option:* coed. *Social organizations:* national fraternities, national sororities, local fraternities, local sororities; 5% of eligible men and 5% of eligible women are members. *Most popular organizations:* Performing Arts, Future Teachers Organization.

Campus security Controlled dormitory access, 8-hour night patrols by security personnel.

After graduation 50 organizations recruited on campus 1997–98. *Career center:* 2 part-time personnel. Services include job fairs, resume preparation, resume referral, career counseling, careers library, job bank, job interviews.

Freshmen 260 applied, 243 admitted, 130 enrolled.

Average high school GPA	2.49	SAT verbal scores above 500	26%
SAT math scores above 500	25%	ACT above 18	N/R
From top 10% of their h.s. class	6%	From top quarter	14%
From top half	48%	1998 freshmen returning in 1999	78%

Application *Options:* eApply at www.CollegeQuest.com, Common Application, electronic application, early admission, deferred entrance. *Application fee:* $25. *Required:* essay or personal statement; high school transcript. *Recommended:* interview.

Standardized tests *Placement: Recommended:* SAT I, SAT II Subject Tests.

Significant dates *Application deadlines:* rolling (freshmen), rolling (transfers). *Financial aid deadline priority date:* 3/15.

Freshman Application Contact
Mr. Jerald R. Nadeau, Director of Admissions, University of Maine at Fort Kent, 25 Pleasant Street, Fort Kent, ME 04743-1292. **Phone:** 207-834-7600. **Toll-free phone:** 888-TRY-UMFK. **Fax:** 207-834-7609. **E-mail:** umfkadm@maine.maine.edu

Visit CollegeQuest.com for information on majors offered and athletics.

- *See page 2748 for a narrative description.*

UNIVERSITY OF MAINE AT MACHIAS
Machias, Maine

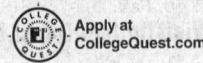
Apply at CollegeQuest.com

- **State-supported**, 4-year, founded 1909
- **Degrees** associate and bachelor's
- **Rural** 42-acre campus
- **Coed**, 731 undergraduate students, 68% full-time, 65% women, 35% men
- **Moderately difficult** entrance level, 84% of applicants were admitted
- 13:1 student-to-undergraduate faculty ratio
- 40.6% graduate in 6 years or less
- $3445 tuition and fees (in-state); $7975 (out-of-state)
- $864,822 endowment

Part of University of Maine System.

Students *Undergraduates:* 497 full-time, 234 part-time. Students come from 20 states and territories, 12 other countries. *The most frequently chosen baccalaureate fields are:* education, business/marketing, natural resources/environmental science.

From out-of-state	16%	Reside on campus	33%
Age 25 or older	33%	Transferred in	7%
International students	3%	African Americans	1%
Asian Americans/Pacific Islanders	0.3%	Hispanic Americans	1%
Native Americans	4%		

Faculty 63 (63% full-time), 52% with terminal degrees.

Expenses (1999–2000) *One-time required fee:* $15. *Tuition, state resident:* full-time $3090; part-time $103 per credit. *Tuition, nonresident:* full-time $7620; part-time $254 per credit. *Required fees:* full-time $355; $11 per credit; $20 per term part-time. Full-time tuition and fees vary according to course load and reciprocity agreements. Part-time tuition and fees vary according to course load and reciprocity agreements. *College room and board:* $4330; room only: $2140. *Payment plans:* installment, deferred payment. *Waivers:* senior citizens and employees or children of employees.

Library Merrill Library plus 1 other. *Operations spending 1999–2000:* $238,727. *Collection:* 80,745 titles, 476 serial subscriptions, 557 audiovisual materials.

College life *Housing: Option:* coed. *Social organizations:* national fraternities, national sororities, local fraternities, local sororities; 17% of eligible men and 12% of eligible women are members.

Campus security 24-hour emergency response devices, late-night transport-escort service, controlled dormitory access, night security guard.

After graduation 7 organizations recruited on campus 1997–98. *Career center:* 1 part-time personnel. Services include job fairs, resume preparation, resume referral, career counseling, careers library, job interviews. *Graduate education:* 10% of class of 1999 went directly to graduate and professional school: 8% graduate arts and sciences, 2% business.

Freshmen 397 applied, 332 admitted, 144 enrolled.

SAT verbal scores above 500	59%	SAT math scores above 500	57%
ACT above 18	96%	From top 10% of their h.s. class	17%
From top quarter	46%	From top half	89%
1998 freshmen returning in 1999	76%		

Application *Options:* eApply at www.CollegeQuest.com, Common Application, electronic application, early admission, early action, deferred entrance. *Application fee:* $25. *Required:* essay or personal statement; high school transcript; 1 letter of recommendation. *Required for some:* minimum 2.0 GPA. *Recommended:* 2 letters of recommendation; interview.

Standardized tests *Admission: Required for some:* SAT I or ACT.

Significant dates *Application deadlines:* rolling (freshmen), rolling (transfers). *Early action:* 12/15. *Financial aid deadline priority date:* 3/1.

Freshman Application Contact
Mr. David Baldwin, Director of Admissions, University of Maine at Machias, 9 O'Brien Avenue, Machias, ME 04654-1321. **Phone:** 207-255-1318. **Toll-free phone:** 888-GOTOUMM. **Fax:** 207-255-1363. **E-mail:** admissions@acad.umm.maine.edu

Visit CollegeQuest.com for information on majors offered and athletics. College video available at CollegeQuest.com.

- *See page 2750 for a narrative description.*

UNIVERSITY OF MAINE AT PRESQUE ISLE
Presque Isle, Maine

- **State-supported**, 4-year, founded 1903
- **Degrees** associate and bachelor's
- **Small-town** 150-acre campus
- **Coed**, 1,204 undergraduate students, 81% full-time, 61% women, 39% men
- **Minimally difficult** entrance level, 89% of applicants were admitted
- 14:1 student-to-undergraduate faculty ratio
- 26% graduate in 6 years or less
- $3390 tuition and fees (in-state); $7860 (out-of-state)

Part of University of Maine System.

Students *Undergraduates:* 975 full-time, 229 part-time. Students come from 19 states and territories, 9 other countries. *The most frequently chosen*

Maine

baccalaureate fields are: education, interdisciplinary studies, liberal arts/general studies.

From out-of-state	3%	Reside on campus	26%
Age 25 or older	29%	Transferred in	14%
International students	15%	African Americans	0.3%
Asian Americans/Pacific Islanders	1%	Hispanic Americans	1%
Native Americans	2%		

Faculty 113 (52% full-time), 40% with terminal degrees.

Expenses (1999–2000) *One-time required fee:* $15. *Tuition, state resident:* full-time $3090; part-time $103 per credit hour. *Tuition, nonresident:* full-time $7560; part-time $252 per credit hour. *Required fees:* full-time $300; $8 per credit hour; $20 per term part-time. Full-time tuition and fees vary according to course load and reciprocity agreements. Part-time tuition and fees vary according to course load and reciprocity agreements. *College room and board:* $4048; room only: $2060. Room and board charges vary according to board plan. *Payment plans:* installment, deferred payment. *Waivers:* minority students, children of alumni, adult students, senior citizens, and employees or children of employees.

Library *Collection:* 232,975 titles, 450 serial subscriptions, 2,275 audiovisual materials.

College life *Housing:* Option: coed. *Social organizations:* national fraternities, national sororities; 2% of eligible men and 1% of eligible women are members. *Most popular organizations:* parks and recreation club, UMPI hockey, international student club, Student Senate, physical education majors club.

Campus security Student patrols, late-night transport-escort service, crime prevention programs, lighted pathways.

After graduation 12 organizations recruited on campus 1997–98. 70% of class of 1998 had job offers within 6 months. *Career center:* 1 part-time personnel. Services include resume preparation, interview workshops, resume referral, career/interest testing, career counseling, careers library, job bank, job interviews. *Graduate education:* 7% of class of 1999 went directly to graduate and professional school: 7% education, 2% graduate arts and sciences.

Freshmen 857 applied, 766 admitted, 223 enrolled. 1 class president.

SAT verbal scores above 500	34%	SAT math scores above 500	33%
ACT above 18	N/R	From top 10% of their h.s. class	8%
From top quarter	25%	From top half	63%
1998 freshmen returning in 1999	62%		

Application *Options:* Common Application, electronic application, early admission, deferred entrance. *Application fee:* $25. *Required:* essay or personal statement; high school transcript; minimum 2.0 GPA; 1 letter of recommendation. *Recommended:* interview.

Standardized tests *Admission: Required:* SAT I or ACT. *Recommended:* SAT II Subject Tests.

Significant dates *Application deadlines:* rolling (freshmen), rolling (transfers). *Financial aid deadline priority date:* 4/1.

Freshman Application Contact
Mr. Michael Sullivan, Admissions Representative, University of Maine at Presque Isle, 181 Main Street, Presque Isle, ME 04769. **Phone:** 207-768-9534. **Fax:** 207-768-9608. **E-mail:** infoumpi@polaris.umpi.maine.edu

Visit CollegeQuest.com for information on majors offered and athletics. College video and electronic viewbook available at CollegeQuest.com.

UNIVERSITY OF NEW ENGLAND
Biddeford, Maine

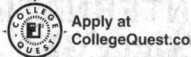

- **Independent**, comprehensive, founded 1831
- **Degrees** associate, bachelor's, master's, and first professional
- **Small-town** 410-acre campus
- **Coed**, 1,473 undergraduate students, 85% full-time, 81% women, 19% men
- **Moderately difficult** entrance level, 90% of applicants were admitted
- **$15,500 tuition** and fees
- **$21.8 million endowment**

Students *Undergraduates:* 1,257 full-time, 216 part-time. Students come from 30 states and territories. *The most frequently chosen baccalaureate fields are:* biological/life sciences, business/marketing, health professions and related sciences. *Graduate:* 457 in professional programs, 793 in other graduate degree programs.

From out-of-state	47%	Reside on campus	35%
Age 25 or older	19%	Transferred in	7%
International students	17%	African Americans	1%
Asian Americans/Pacific Islanders	1%	Hispanic Americans	1%
Native Americans	0.2%		

Faculty 240 (56% full-time).

Expenses (1999–2000) *Comprehensive fee:* $21,700 includes full-time tuition ($14,990), mandatory fees ($510), and room and board ($6200). Room and board charges vary according to housing facility. *Part-time tuition:* $500 per credit. *Part-time fees:* $230 per year part-time. Part-time tuition and fees vary according to course load. *Payment plans:* installment, deferred payment. *Waivers:* employees or children of employees.

Library Ketchum Library plus 1 other. *Operations spending 1999–2000:* $1.1 million. *Collection:* 1,294 serial subscriptions, 14,555 audiovisual materials.

College life *Housing:* on-campus residence required through sophomore year. *Options:* coed, women-only. *Most popular organizations:* Student Senate, Earth's Eco, Campus Programming Board, Rotoract, outing club.

Campus security 24-hour patrols, late-night transport-escort service.

After graduation *Career center:* 1 full-time personnel. Services include job fairs, resume preparation, resume referral, career counseling, careers library, job bank, job interviews.

Freshmen 1,237 applied, 1,110 admitted, 310 enrolled.

Average high school GPA	3.2	SAT verbal scores above 500	58%
SAT math scores above 500	55%	ACT above 18	N/R
From top 10% of their h.s. class	18%	From top quarter	42%
From top half	85%		

Application *Options:* eApply at www.CollegeQuest.com, early decision, deferred entrance. *Application fee:* $40. *Required:* essay or personal statement; high school transcript; 2 letters of recommendation. *Required for some:* interview. *Recommended:* interview.

Standardized tests *Admission: Required:* SAT I or ACT.

Significant dates *Application deadlines:* rolling (freshmen), rolling (transfers). *Early decision:* 11/15. *Notification:* 12/15 (early decision). **Financial aid deadline:** 5/1. *Priority date:* 3/1.

Freshman Application Contact
Ms. Patricia Cribby, Dean of Admissions, University of New England, Hills Beach Road, Biddeford, ME 04005-9526. **Phone:** 207-283-0171 Ext. 2240. **Toll-free phone:** 800-477-4UNE. **E-mail:** dvallee@mailbox.une.edu

Visit CollegeQuest.com for information on majors offered and athletics.

■ *See page 2788 for a narrative description.*

UNIVERSITY OF SOUTHERN MAINE
Portland, Maine

- **State-supported**, comprehensive, founded 1878
- **Degrees** associate, bachelor's, master's, doctoral, first professional, and post-master's certificates
- **Suburban** 144-acre campus
- **Coed**, 6,524 undergraduate students, 60% full-time, 61% women, 39% men
- **Moderately difficult** entrance level, 69% of applicants were admitted
- **13:1 student-to-undergraduate faculty ratio**
- **27% graduate** in 6 years or less
- **$4192 tuition** and fees (in-state); $10,672 (out-of-state)
- **$7446 average financial aid** package, $12.5 million endowment

Combining a small-school atmosphere with the choices of a larger university, USM is just 2 hours from Boston, with access to the ocean, lakes, and ski resorts. Features include dedicated faculty members, small class sizes, a diverse student body, internships and cooperative education, a new field house and ice arena, and a dual residential campus (urban and suburban). USM provides students with real value: a high-quality education at an affordable cost.

Part of University of Maine System.

Students *Undergraduates:* 3,938 full-time, 2,586 part-time. Students come from 32 states and territories. *The most frequently chosen baccalaureate fields are:* health professions and related sciences, business/marketing,

Maine–Maryland

University of Southern Maine (continued)
social sciences and history. **Graduate:** 266 in professional programs, 1,676 in other graduate degree programs.

From out-of-state	6%	Reside on campus	18%
Age 25 or older	40%	Transferred in	13%
International students	0.03%	African Americans	1%
Asian Americans/Pacific Islanders	1%	Hispanic Americans	1%
Native Americans	1%		

Faculty 665 (54% full-time), 43% with terminal degrees.
Expenses (1999–2000) *One-time required fee:* $15. *Tuition, state resident:* full-time $3630; part-time $121 per credit hour. *Tuition, nonresident:* full-time $10,110; part-time $337 per credit hour. *Required fees:* full-time $562; $13 per credit hour; $70 per term part-time. Full-time tuition and fees vary according to course load, degree level, location, and reciprocity agreements. Part-time tuition and fees vary according to course load, degree level, location, and reciprocity agreements. *College room and board:* $4926; room only: $2548. Room and board charges vary according to housing facility. *Payment plan:* installment. *Waivers:* minority students, senior citizens, and employees or children of employees.
Library University of Southern Maine Library plus 4 others. *Operations spending 1999–2000:* $3.2 million. *Collection:* 379,554 titles, 3,626 serial subscriptions, 1,344 audiovisual materials.
College life *Housing:* Option: coed. *Social organizations:* national fraternities, national sororities, local fraternities, local sororities; 2% of eligible men and 2% of eligible women are members. *Most popular organizations:* outing and ski clubs, fraternities and sororities, Gorham Events Board, Commuter Student Group, Circle K.
Campus security 24-hour emergency response devices and patrols, student patrols, late-night transport-escort service, controlled dormitory access, security lighting, preventative programs within residence halls.
After graduation 45 organizations recruited on campus 1997–98. *Career center:* 9 full-time personnel. Services include job fairs, resume preparation, interview workshops, career/interest testing, career counseling, careers library, job bank, job interviews.
Freshmen 2,758 applied, 1,908 admitted, 953 enrolled. 1 valedictorian.

SAT verbal scores above 500	64%	SAT math scores above 500	62%
ACT above 18	N/R	From top 10% of their h.s. class	10%
From top quarter	35%	From top half	80%
1998 freshmen returning in 1999	70%		

Application *Options:* eApply at www.CollegeQuest.com, electronic application, early admission. *Application fee:* $25. *Required:* essay or personal statement; high school transcript; minimum 2.5 GPA. *Required for some:* audition. *Recommended:* 1 letter of recommendation; interview.
Standardized tests *Admission: Required:* SAT I or ACT.
Significant dates *Application deadlines:* 2/1 (freshmen), 2/1 (transfers). *Financial aid deadline priority date:* 2/15.
Freshman Application Contact
Mr. David M. Pirani, Director of Admission, University of Southern Maine, 37 College Avenue, Gorham, ME 04038. **Phone:** 207-780-5670. **Toll-free phone:** 800-800-4USM Ext. 5670. **Fax:** 207-780-5640. **E-mail:** usmadm@maine.maine.edu
Visit CollegeQuest.com for information on majors offered and athletics.

■ *See page 2834 for a narrative description.*

WESTBROOK COLLEGE
Maine—See University of New England

MARYLAND

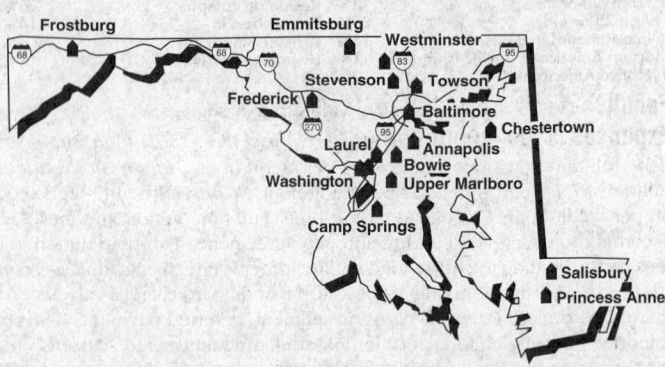

The Washington area includes the towns of Capital Heights College Park, Lanham, St. Mary's City, Silver Spring, and Takoma Park.

BALTIMORE HEBREW UNIVERSITY
Baltimore, Maryland

Apply at CollegeQuest.com

- **Independent**, comprehensive, founded 1919
- **Degrees** associate, bachelor's, master's, and doctoral
- **Urban** 2-acre campus
- **Coed**
- **Moderately difficult** entrance level
- **$5630 tuition** and fees

Expenses (1999–2000) *Tuition:* full-time $5600; part-time $700 per course. *Required fees:* full-time $30; $15 per term part-time. Full-time tuition and fees vary according to course load. Part-time tuition and fees vary according to course load.
Institutional Web site http://www.bhu.edu/
College life *Housing:* college housing not available. *Social organizations:* Hebrew Ulpan social club. *Most popular organizations:* Israeli dance, Chug Ivri Club for advanced Hebrew speakers, Yiddish Club.
Campus security 24-hour patrols, guards on duty during class hours, patrols by security, well-lit parking lots.
Application *Options:* eApply at www.CollegeQuest.com, Common Application, early admission, deferred entrance. *Application fee:* $20. *Required:* high school transcript; interview. *Required for some:* 3 letters of recommendation.
Admissions Office Contact
Baltimore Hebrew University, 5800 Park Heights Avenue, Baltimore, MD 21215-3996. **Toll-free phone:** 888-248-7420. **Fax:** 410-578-6940. **E-mail:** bhu@bhu.edu
Visit CollegeQuest.com for information on athletics.

BALTIMORE INTERNATIONAL COLLEGE
Baltimore, Maryland

Apply at CollegeQuest.com

- **Independent**, 4-year, founded 1972
- **Degrees** associate and bachelor's
- **Urban** 6-acre campus with easy access to Washington, DC
- **Coed**, 470 undergraduate students, 94% full-time, 43% women, 57% men
- **Minimally difficult** entrance level, 47% of applicants were admitted
- **21:1** student-to-undergraduate faculty ratio
- **$15,830 tuition** and fees
- **$579,082 endowment**

Students *Undergraduates:* 440 full-time, 30 part-time. Students come from 30 states and territories, 5 other countries.

Maryland

Reside on campus	24%	Age 25 or older	38%
Transferred in	4%	African Americans	40%
Asian Americans/Pacific Islanders	2%	Hispanic Americans	4%
Native Americans	1%		

Faculty 28 (61% full-time), 32% with terminal degrees.
Expenses (1999–2000) *Comprehensive fee:* $21,014 includes full-time tuition ($15,670), mandatory fees ($160), and room and board ($5184). Full-time tuition and fees vary according to class time, degree level, and program. Room and board charges vary according to housing facility. *Payment plans:* tuition prepayment, installment. *Waivers:* employees or children of employees.
Library George A. Piendak Library. *Operations spending 1999–2000:* $160,795. *Collection:* 12,000 titles, 200 serial subscriptions, 770 audiovisual materials.
College life *Housing:* on-campus residence required in freshman year. *Option:* coed. *Social organizations:* local fraternities; 2% of men are members. *Most popular organizations:* American Culinary Federation, Beta Iota Kappa.
Campus security Late-night transport-escort service, controlled dormitory access.
After graduation 105 organizations recruited on campus 1997–98. 98% of class of 1998 had job offers within 6 months. *Career center:* 1 full-time, 1 part-time personnel. Services include job fairs, resume preparation, interview workshops, resume referral, career counseling, careers library, job bank, job interviews.
Freshmen 736 applied, 345 admitted, 92 enrolled.

Average high school GPA	2.5	SAT verbal scores above 500	N/R
SAT math scores above 500	N/R	ACT above 18	N/R
From top 10% of their h.s. class	15%	From top quarter	20%
From top half	30%		

Application *Options:* eApply at www.CollegeQuest.com, Common Application, electronic application, deferred entrance. *Application fee:* $35. *Required:* high school transcript. *Recommended:* interview.
Standardized tests *Admission: Required for some:* SAT I or ACT.
Significant dates *Application deadlines:* rolling (freshmen), rolling (transfers). *Notification:* continuous until 8/15 (freshmen). **Financial aid deadline:** continuous.
Freshman Application Contact
Mr. Michael Smith, Director of Admissions, Baltimore International College, Commerce Exchange, 17 Commerce Street, Baltimore, MD 21202-3230. **Phone:** 410-752-4710 Ext. 125. **Toll-free phone:** 800-624-9926 Ext. 120. **Fax:** 410-752-3730. **E-mail:** admissions@bic.edu
Visit CollegeQuest.com for information on majors offered and athletics. Electronic viewbook available at CollegeQuest.com.

■ *See page 1224 for a narrative description.*

BOWIE STATE UNIVERSITY
Bowie, Maryland

■ **State-supported**, comprehensive, founded 1865
■ **Degrees** bachelor's and master's
■ **Small-town** 312-acre campus with easy access to Baltimore and Washington, DC
■ **Coed**, 3,114 undergraduate students, 71% full-time, 61% women, 39% men
■ **Minimally difficult** entrance level, 43% of applicants were admitted
■ **$3664 tuition** and fees (in-state); $8981 (out-of-state)
■ **$5957 average financial aid** package, $2.7 million endowment

Part of University System of Maryland.
Students *Undergraduates:* 2,214 full-time, 900 part-time. Students come from 40 states and territories. *The most frequently chosen baccalaureate fields are:* business/marketing, psychology, social sciences and history. *Graduate:* 1,656 in graduate degree programs.

From out-of-state	6%	Reside on campus	24%
Age 25 or older	33%	Transferred in	14%
International students	1%	African Americans	86%
Asian Americans/Pacific Islanders	2%	Hispanic Americans	1%
Native Americans	0.4%		

Faculty 341 (46% full-time), 56% with terminal degrees.

Expenses (1999–2000) *Tuition, state resident:* full-time $2828; part-time $124 per credit. *Tuition, nonresident:* full-time $8145; part-time $341 per credit. *Required fees:* full-time $836; $122 per term part-time. Part-time tuition and fees vary according to course load. *College room and board:* $4012; room only: $2072. Room and board charges vary according to board plan and housing facility. *Payment plan:* deferred payment. *Waivers:* senior citizens and employees or children of employees.
Library Thurgood Marshall Library. *Operations spending 1999–2000:* $971,900. *Collection:* 211,844 titles, 1,364 serial subscriptions.
College life *Housing: Options:* coed, men-only, women-only. *Social organizations:* national fraternities, national sororities; 2% of eligible men and 2% of eligible women are members.
Campus security 24-hour emergency response devices and patrols, late-night transport-escort service, controlled dormitory access.
After graduation 108 organizations recruited on campus 1997–98. *Career center:* Services include job fairs, resume preparation, resume referral, career counseling, careers library, job interviews.
Freshmen 1,603 applied, 694 admitted, 361 enrolled.

Average high school GPA	2.83	SAT verbal scores above 500	29%
SAT math scores above 500	22%	ACT above 18	N/R
1998 freshmen returning in 1999	72%		

Application *Option:* electronic application. *Preference* given to state residents. *Application fee:* $40. *Required:* high school transcript; minimum 2.2 GPA. *Required for some:* letters of recommendation. *Recommended:* letters of recommendation.
Standardized tests *Admission: Required:* SAT I or ACT.
Significant dates *Application deadlines:* 4/1 (freshmen), 4/1 (transfers). **Financial aid deadline priority date:** 4/1.
Freshman Application Contact
Ms. Hope Ransom, Coordinator of Undergraduate Enrollment, Bowie State University, 14000 Jericho Park Road, Bowie, MD 20715-9465. **Phone:** 301-464-6563. **Fax:** 301-464-7521. **E-mail:** dkiah@bowiestate.edu
Visit CollegeQuest.com for information on majors offered and athletics. College video available at CollegeQuest.com.

■ *See page 1296 for a narrative description.*

CAPITOL COLLEGE
Laurel, Maryland

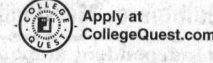
Apply at CollegeQuest.com

■ **Independent**, comprehensive, founded 1964
■ **Degrees** associate, bachelor's, master's, and postbachelor's certificates
■ **Suburban** 52-acre campus with easy access to Baltimore and Washington, DC
■ **Coed**, 572 undergraduate students, 59% full-time, 20% women, 80% men
■ **Minimally difficult** entrance level, 84% of applicants were admitted
■ **13:1 student-to-undergraduate faculty ratio**
■ **$12,308 tuition** and fees
■ **$7600 average financial aid** package, $12,000 average indebtedness upon graduation, $1.5 million endowment

In addition to comprehensive degree programs in engineering, technology, and management, Capitol guarantees its qualified BS graduates placement in high-technology careers at nationally competitive salaries within 90 days of commencement. Capitol also offers certifications in A+ and MCSE and has recently upgraded its MS programs to include electronic commerce management.

Students *Undergraduates:* 335 full-time, 237 part-time. Students come from 16 states and territories, 21 other countries. *The most frequently chosen baccalaureate field is:* engineering/engineering technologies. *Graduate:* 111 in graduate degree programs.

From out-of-state	28%	Reside on campus	34%
Age 25 or older	40%	Transferred in	7%
International students	7%	African Americans	38%
Asian Americans/Pacific Islanders	5%	Hispanic Americans	5%
Native Americans	0.4%		

Faculty 49 (39% full-time), 18% with terminal degrees.
Expenses (1999–2000) *Tuition:* full-time $11,808; part-time $447 per semester hour. *Required fees:* full-time $500; $10 per semester hour; $7 per

Maryland

Capitol College *(continued)*
term part-time. Part-time tuition and fees vary according to course load. *College room only:* $3240. *Payment plans:* guaranteed tuition, installment, deferred payment. *Waivers:* employees or children of employees.
Library Puente Library. *Operations spending 1999–2000:* $119,953. *Collection:* 11,000 titles, 130 serial subscriptions.
College life *Housing:* Option: coed. *Most popular organizations:* IEEE, NSDE, SWE.
Campus security Night security patrols.
After graduation 100% of class of 1998 had job offers within 6 months. *Career center:* 1 full-time, 1 part-time personnel. Services include job fairs, resume preparation, resume referral, career counseling, careers library, job bank, job interviews. *Graduate education:* 5% of class of 1999 went directly to graduate and professional school: 3% business, 3% engineering.
Freshmen 172 applied, 145 admitted, 76 enrolled.

Average high school GPA	3.02	SAT verbal scores above 500	33%
SAT math scores above 500	32%	ACT above 18	N/R
1998 freshmen returning in 1999	59%		

Application *Options:* eApply at www.CollegeQuest.com, early admission, deferred entrance. *Application fee:* $25. *Required:* high school transcript. *Required for some:* essay or personal statement; 2 letters of recommendation; interview. *Recommended:* minimum 2.2 GPA; interview.
Standardized tests *Admission: Required:* SAT I or ACT.
Significant dates *Application deadlines:* rolling (freshmen), rolling (transfers). *Financial aid deadline priority date:* 2/1.
Freshman Application Contact
Mr. Anthony G. Miller, Director of Admissions, Capitol College, 11301 Springfield Road, Laurel, MD 20708-9759. **Phone:** 301-953-3200. **Toll-free phone:** 800-950-1992. **E-mail:** admissions@capitol-college.edu
Visit CollegeQuest.com for information on majors offered and athletics. College video available at CollegeQuest.com.

■ *See page 1356 for a narrative description.*

COLLEGE OF NOTRE DAME OF MARYLAND
Baltimore, Maryland

- **Independent Roman Catholic**, comprehensive, founded 1873
- **Degrees** bachelor's, master's, and postbachelor's certificates
- **Suburban** 58-acre campus
- **Women** only, 2,037 undergraduate students, 33% full-time
- **Moderately difficult** entrance level, 74% of applicants were admitted
- **15:1** student-to-undergraduate faculty ratio
- **63% graduate** in 6 years or less
- **$15,875 tuition** and fees

The vision of the College of Notre Dame of Maryland as it charts its 2nd century is to become a learning community of excellence for the 21st-century woman. Excellence in learning means a liberal education that liberates minds, hearts, and spirits to think critically, communicate effectively, and develop holistically. Essential components of a Notre Dame education are the integration of a global perspective and the development of leadership skills.

Students *Undergraduates:* Students come from 23 states and territories. *The most frequently chosen baccalaureate fields are:* business/marketing, education, health professions and related sciences. *Graduate:* 1,102 in graduate degree programs.

From out-of-state	6%	Reside on campus	57%
International students	3%	African Americans	19%
Asian Americans/Pacific Islanders	2%	Hispanic Americans	2%
Native Americans	0.2%		

Faculty 91 (89% full-time), 68% with terminal degrees.
Expenses (2000–2001) *Comprehensive fee:* $22,675 includes full-time tuition ($15,600), mandatory fees ($275), and room and board ($6800). *Part-time tuition:* $255 per credit. *Part-time fees:* $30 per term part-time. *Payment plan:* installment. *Waivers:* employees or children of employees.
Library Loyola/Notre Dame Library. *Collection:* 360,000 titles, 2,100 serial subscriptions.

College life *Housing:* on-campus residence required through sophomore year. *Option:* women-only. *Most popular organizations:* Black Student Association, Kymry, Commuter Association, Community Service Organization, campus ministry.
Campus security 24-hour emergency response devices and patrols, late-night transport-escort service, controlled dormitory access, emergency call boxes.
After graduation *Career center:* 2 full-time, 1 part-time personnel. Services include job fairs, resume preparation, interview workshops, resume referral, career/interest testing, career counseling, careers library, job bank, job interviews.
Freshmen 377 applied, 278 admitted.

Average high school GPA	3.33	SAT verbal scores above 500	65%
SAT math scores above 500	49%	ACT above 18	N/R
From top 10% of their h.s. class	33%	From top quarter	59%
From top half	90%	1998 freshmen returning in 1999	82%

Application *Options:* Common Application, electronic application, early admission, early action, deferred entrance. *Application fee:* $25. *Required:* essay or personal statement; high school transcript; minimum 2.0 GPA; 2 letters of recommendation. *Recommended:* minimum 3.0 GPA; interview.
Standardized tests *Admission: Required:* SAT I or ACT.
Significant dates *Application deadlines:* rolling (freshmen), rolling (transfers). *Early action:* 12/3. *Notification:* continuous until 6/30 (freshmen), 1/1 (early action). *Financial aid deadline priority date:* 2/15.
Freshman Application Contact
Mrs. Karen Stakem Hornig, Vice President for Enrollment Management, College of Notre Dame of Maryland, 4701 North Charles Street, Baltimore, MD 21210. **Phone:** 410-532-5330. **Toll-free phone:** 800-435-0200 (in-state); 800-435-0300 (out-of-state). **Fax:** 410-532-6287. **E-mail:** admiss@ndm.edu
Visit CollegeQuest.com for information on majors offered and athletics. College video and electronic viewbook available at CollegeQuest.com.

■ *See page 1468 for a narrative description.*

COLUMBIA UNION COLLEGE
Takoma Park, Maryland

- **Independent Seventh-day Adventist**, 4-year, founded 1904
- **Degrees** associate and bachelor's
- **Suburban** 19-acre campus with easy access to Washington, DC
- **Coed**, 964 undergraduate students, 41% full-time, 39% women, 61% men
- **Minimally difficult** entrance level, 70% of applicants were admitted
- **13:1** student-to-undergraduate faculty ratio
- **42% graduate** in 6 years or less
- **$12,660 tuition** and fees
- **$3.1 million endowment**

Students *Undergraduates:* Students come from 38 states and territories, 39 other countries. *The most frequently chosen baccalaureate fields are:* business/marketing, health professions and related sciences, psychology.

From out-of-state	60%	Reside on campus	56%
International students	5%	African Americans	43%
Asian Americans/Pacific Islanders	7%	Hispanic Americans	8%
Native Americans	0.1%		

Faculty 44 (89% full-time), 52% with terminal degrees.
Expenses (1999–2000) *Comprehensive fee:* $17,060 includes full-time tuition ($12,200), mandatory fees ($460), and room and board ($4400). *Part-time tuition:* $510 per semester hour. *Part-time fees:* $230 per term part-time. *Payment plans:* installment, deferred payment. *Waivers:* adult students, senior citizens, and employees or children of employees.
Library Theofield G. Weis Library. *Operations spending 1999–2000:* $378,211. *Collection:* 126,909 titles, 431 serial subscriptions.
College life *Housing:* on-campus residence required through senior year. *Options:* men-only, women-only. *Most popular organization:* Student Association.
Campus security 24-hour emergency response devices, student patrols, late-night transport-escort service.

Maryland

Freshmen 624 applied, 437 admitted. 1 valedictorian.

Average high school GPA	3.14	SAT verbal scores above 500	48%
SAT math scores above 500	44%	ACT above 18	78%
1998 freshmen returning in 1999	62%		

Application *Option:* deferred entrance. *Application fee:* $25. *Required:* high school transcript; 2 letters of recommendation. *Required for some:* essay or personal statement; interview.

Standardized tests *Admission: Required:* SAT I or ACT.

Significant dates *Application deadlines:* 8/15 (freshmen), rolling (transfers). *Financial aid deadline:* 5/1. *Priority date:* 3/1.

Freshman Application Contact
Ms. Cindy Carreno, Director of Admissions, Columbia Union College, 7600 Flower Avenue, Takoma Park, MD 20912-7796. **Phone:** 301-891-4080. **Toll-free phone:** 800-492-1715 (in-state); 800-835-4212 (out-of-state). **Fax:** 301-891-4230.

Visit CollegeQuest.com for information on majors offered and athletics. College video available at CollegeQuest.com.

■ *See page 1512 for a narrative description.*

COPPIN STATE COLLEGE
Baltimore, Maryland

Apply at CollegeQuest.com

- **State-supported**, comprehensive, founded 1900
- **Degrees** bachelor's and master's
- **Urban** 33-acre campus
- **Coed**, 3,217 undergraduate students
- **Moderately difficult** entrance level, 47% of applicants were admitted
- **$3973 tuition** and fees (in-state); $8865 (out-of-state)

Part of University System of Maryland.

Students *Undergraduates:* Students come from 20 states and territories, 19 other countries.

Reside on campus	10%	Age 25 or older	50%
International students	2%	African Americans	96%
Asian Americans/Pacific Islanders	0.2%	Hispanic Americans	0.4%
Native Americans	0.2%		

Faculty 202 (54% full-time).

Expenses (1999–2000) *Tuition, state resident:* full-time $3272; part-time $110 per credit hour. *Tuition, nonresident:* full-time $8164; part-time $262 per credit hour. *Required fees:* full-time $701; $18 per credit hour; $66 per term part-time. Part-time tuition and fees vary according to course load. *College room and board:* $5274; room only: $3380. Room and board charges vary according to housing facility. *Payment plan:* deferred payment. *Waivers:* employees or children of employees.

Library Parlett L. Moore Library. *Collection:* 134,983 titles, 665 serial subscriptions.

College life *Housing: Option:* coed. *Social organizations:* national fraternities, national sororities, local fraternities, local sororities; 5% of eligible men and 4% of eligible women are members. *Most popular organizations:* International Students Association, class government, Nursing Students' Association, Coppin Models Fashion Club, Student Honors Association.

Campus security 24-hour emergency response devices and patrols, late-night transport-escort service, controlled dormitory access.

After graduation 67 organizations recruited on campus 1997–98. *Career center:* 3 full-time personnel. Services include job fairs, resume preparation, interview workshops, resume referral, career/interest testing, career counseling, careers library, job bank, job interviews. *Graduate education:* 17% of class of 1999 went directly to graduate and professional school.

Freshmen 2,270 applied, 1,078 admitted.

Average high school GPA	2.96	SAT verbal scores above 500	N/R
SAT math scores above 500	N/R	ACT above 18	N/R
From top 10% of their h.s. class	10%	From top quarter	20%
From top half	60%		

Application *Options:* eApply at www.CollegeQuest.com, Common Application, electronic application, early admission, deferred entrance. *Application fee:* $25. *Required:* high school transcript. *Required for some:* 2 letters of recommendation. *Recommended:* minimum 2.5 GPA; interview.

Standardized tests *Admission: Required:* SAT I or ACT.

Significant dates *Application deadlines:* 7/15 (freshmen), 7/15 (transfers). *Financial aid deadline:* continuous.

Freshman Application Contact
Ms. Michelle Gross, Director of Admissions, Coppin State College, 2500 West North Avenue, Baltimore, MD 21216. **Phone:** 410-383-5990. **Toll-free phone:** 800-635-3674. **Fax:** 410-523-7238. **E-mail:** mgross@coppin.edu

Visit CollegeQuest.com for information on majors offered and athletics. College video and electronic viewbook available at CollegeQuest.com.

FROSTBURG STATE UNIVERSITY
Frostburg, Maryland

- **State-supported**, comprehensive, founded 1898
- **Degrees** bachelor's and master's
- **Small-town** 260-acre campus with easy access to Baltimore and Washington, DC
- **Coed**, 4,240 undergraduate students, 93% full-time, 54% women, 46% men
- **Moderately difficult** entrance level, 77% of applicants were admitted
- **17:1** student-to-undergraduate faculty ratio
- **53.87%** graduate in 6 years or less
- **$4132 tuition** and fees (in-state); $9282 (out-of-state)
- **$4583 average financial aid** package, $13,103 average indebtedness upon graduation, $4.8 million endowment

Part of University System of Maryland.

Students *Undergraduates:* 3,952 full-time, 288 part-time. Students come from 34 states and territories. *The most frequently chosen baccalaureate fields are:* business/marketing, education, social sciences and history. *Graduate:* 885 in graduate degree programs.

From out-of-state	11%	Reside on campus	39%
Age 25 or older	9%	Transferred in	8%
International students	0.4%	African Americans	11%
Asian Americans/Pacific Islanders	2%	Hispanic Americans	2%
Native Americans	0.4%		

Faculty 323 (74% full-time), 83% with terminal degrees.

Expenses (2000–2001) *Tuition, state resident:* full-time $3342; part-time $138 per credit hour. *Tuition, nonresident:* full-time $8492; part-time $244 per credit hour. *Required fees:* full-time $790; $33 per credit hour; $9 per term part-time. Full-time tuition and fees vary according to course load and program. Part-time tuition and fees vary according to course load and program. *College room and board:* $5214; room only: $2650. Room and board charges vary according to board plan and housing facility. *Payment plans:* installment, deferred payment. *Waivers:* senior citizens and employees or children of employees.

Library Lewis J. Ort Library plus 1 other. *Operations spending 1999–2000:* $538,420. *Collection:* 256,977 titles, 1,963 serial subscriptions, 7,096 audiovisual materials.

College life *Housing: Options:* coed, men-only, women-only. *Social organizations:* national fraternities, national sororities; 10% of eligible men and 10% of eligible women are members. *Most popular organizations:* Student Government Association, Black Student Association, Campus Activities Board, Residence Hall Association.

Campus security 24-hour emergency response devices and patrols, student patrols, late-night transport-escort service, controlled dormitory access, bicycle patrols.

After graduation 200 organizations recruited on campus 1997–98. 91% of class of 1998 had job offers within 6 months. *Career center:* 2 full-time personnel. Services include job fairs, resume preparation, interview workshops, resume referral, career/interest testing, career counseling, careers library, job bank, job interviews. *Graduate education:* 20% of class of 1999 went directly to graduate and professional school.

Freshmen 3,180 applied, 2,457 admitted, 937 enrolled.

Average high school GPA	2.74	SAT verbal scores above 500	44%
SAT math scores above 500	45%	ACT above 18	N/R
1998 freshmen returning in 1999	73%		

Application *Options:* electronic application, early admission. *Application fee:* $30. *Required:* high school transcript; minimum 2.0 GPA. *Required for some:* essay or personal statement. *Recommended:* letters of recommendation; interview.

Standardized tests *Admission: Required:* SAT I or ACT.

Significant dates *Application deadlines:* rolling (freshmen), rolling (transfers). *Financial aid deadline:* 3/1. *Priority date:* 2/15.

Maryland

Frostburg State University (continued)
Freshman Application Contact
Mr. Bernard Wynder, Director of Admissions, Frostburg State University, 101 Braddock Road, Frostburg, MD 21532-1099. **Phone:** 301-687-4201. **Fax:** 301-687-7074. **E-mail:** fsuadmissions@frostburg.edu
Visit CollegeQuest.com for information on majors offered and athletics. College video available at CollegeQuest.com.

■ *See page 1700 for a narrative description.*

GOUCHER COLLEGE
Baltimore, Maryland

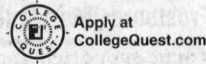 Apply at CollegeQuest.com

- **Independent**, comprehensive, founded 1885
- **Degrees** bachelor's and master's
- **Suburban** 287-acre campus
- **Coed**, 1,119 undergraduate students, 96% full-time, 73% women, 27% men
- **Moderately difficult** entrance level, 85% of applicants were admitted
- **11:1 student-to-undergraduate faculty ratio**
- **70% graduate** in 6 years or less
- **$20,485 tuition** and fees
- **$15,700 average financial aid** package, $6928 average indebtedness upon graduation, $151.9 million endowment

Students *Undergraduates:* 1,076 full-time, 43 part-time. Students come from 43 states and territories, 21 other countries. *The most frequently chosen baccalaureate fields are:* biological/life sciences, English, visual/performing arts. *Graduate:* 569 in graduate degree programs.

From out-of-state	59%	Reside on campus	71%
Age 25 or older	4%	Transferred in	3%
International students	2%	African Americans	8%
Asian Americans/Pacific Islanders	3%	Hispanic Americans	3%
Native Americans	0.2%		

Faculty 144 (54% full-time), 76% with terminal degrees.
Expenses (1999–2000) *Comprehensive fee:* $27,865 includes full-time tuition ($20,200), mandatory fees ($285), and room and board ($7380). *College room only:* $4910. Room and board charges vary according to board plan. *Part-time tuition:* $710 per semester hour. *Payment plan:* installment. *Waivers:* adult students and employees or children of employees.
Library Julia Rogers Library. *Operations spending 1999–2000:* $1.3 million. *Collection:* 295,593 titles, 1,138 serial subscriptions, 8,532 audiovisual materials.
College life *Housing:* on-campus residence required through sophomore year. *Options:* coed, women-only. *Most popular organizations:* CAUSE (Community Auxiliary for Service), Umoja: The African Alliance, Quindecim (newspaper), BGlad, Hillel.
Campus security 24-hour emergency response devices and patrols, late-night transport-escort service.
After graduation 17 organizations recruited on campus 1997–98. 84% of class of 1998 had job offers within 6 months. *Career center:* 3 full-time, 2 part-time personnel. Services include job fairs, resume preparation, career counseling, careers library, job bank, job interviews. *Graduate education:* 25% of class of 1999 went directly to graduate and professional school: 15% graduate arts and sciences, 4% medicine, 3% business, 2% law, 1% dentistry.
Freshmen 2,078 applied, 1,760 admitted, 303 enrolled. 6 valedictorians.

Average high school GPA	3.11	SAT verbal scores above 500	85%
SAT math scores above 500	84%	ACT above 18	99%
From top 10% of their h.s. class	27%	From top quarter	60%
From top half	90%	1998 freshmen returning in 1999	82%

Application *Options:* eApply at www.CollegeQuest.com, Common Application, electronic application, early admission, early decision, early action, deferred entrance. *Application fee:* $40. *Required:* essay or personal statement; high school transcript; minimum 2.0 GPA; 3 letters of recommendation. *Recommended:* minimum 3.0 GPA; interview.
Standardized tests *Admission: Required:* SAT I or ACT. *Recommended:* SAT II Subject Tests, SAT II: Writing Test.
Significant dates *Application deadlines:* 2/1 (freshmen), 4/1 (transfers). *Early decision:* 11/15, 12/1. *Notification:* 4/1 (freshmen), 1/15 (early decision), 1/15 (early action). *Financial aid deadline priority date:* 2/15.

Freshman Application Contact
Mr. Carlton E. Surbeck III, Director of Admissions, Goucher College, 1021 Dulaney Valley Road, Baltimore, MD 21204-2794. **Phone:** 410-337-6100. **Toll-free phone:** 800-GOUCHER. **Fax:** 410-337-6123. **E-mail:** admission@goucher.edu
Visit CollegeQuest.com for information on majors offered and athletics. College video available at CollegeQuest.com.

■ *See page 1730 for a narrative description.*

GRIGGS UNIVERSITY
Silver Spring, Maryland

- **Independent Seventh-day Adventist**, 4-year, founded 1990
- **Degrees** associate and bachelor's (offers only external degree programs)
- **Suburban** campus
- **Coed,** primarily men, 397 undergraduate students
- **Minimally difficult** entrance level
- **$5160 tuition** and fees

Students *Undergraduates: The most frequently chosen baccalaureate fields are:* business/marketing, philosophy.
Faculty 40, 43% with terminal degrees.
Expenses (1999–2000) *Tuition:* full-time $5100; part-time $170 per semester hour. *Required fees:* full-time $60; $60 per year part-time. Full-time tuition and fees vary according to course load. *Payment plan:* installment. *Waivers:* senior citizens.
College life *Housing:* college housing not available.
Freshmen

SAT verbal scores above 500	N/R	SAT math scores above 500	N/R
ACT above 18	N/R		

Application *Options:* Common Application, early admission, deferred entrance. *Application fee:* $50. *Required:* essay or personal statement; high school transcript; minimum 2.0 GPA.
Significant dates *Application deadlines:* rolling (freshmen), rolling (transfers).
Freshman Application Contact
Ms. Eva Michel, Enrollment Officer, Griggs University, PO Box 4437, Silver Spring, MD 20914-4437. **Phone:** 301-680-6593. **Toll-free phone:** 800-782-4769. **Fax:** 301-680-6577. **E-mail:** 74617.74@compuserve.com
Visit CollegeQuest.com for information on majors offered and athletics.

HOOD COLLEGE
Frederick, Maryland

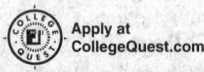 Apply at CollegeQuest.com

- **Independent**, comprehensive, founded 1893, affiliated with United Church of Christ
- **Degrees** bachelor's and master's (also offers adult program with significant enrollment not reflected in profile)
- **Suburban** 50-acre campus with easy access to Baltimore and Washington, DC
- **Women** only, 810 undergraduate students, 75% full-time
- **Moderately difficult** entrance level, 77% of applicants were admitted
- **10:1 student-to-undergraduate faculty ratio**
- **65% graduate** in 6 years or less
- **$17,600 tuition** and fees
- **$18,873 average financial aid** package, $12,255 average indebtedness upon graduation, $83 million endowment

Students *Undergraduates:* 610 full-time, 200 part-time. Students come from 28 states and territories, 31 other countries. *The most frequently chosen baccalaureate fields are:* psychology, biological/life sciences, social sciences and history. *Graduate:* 882 in graduate degree programs.

From out-of-state	23%	Reside on campus	51%
Age 25 or older	28%	Transferred in	10%
International students	5%	African Americans	12%
Asian Americans/Pacific Islanders	2%	Hispanic Americans	3%
Native Americans	1%		

Faculty 91 (80% full-time).

Maryland

Expenses (1999–2000) *Comprehensive fee:* $24,500 includes full-time tuition ($17,275), mandatory fees ($325), and room and board ($6900). *College room only:* $3600. Room and board charges vary according to board plan. *Part-time tuition:* $500 per credit. *Part-time fees:* $100 per term part-time. Part-time tuition and fees vary according to course load. *Payment plans:* tuition prepayment, installment, deferred payment. *Waivers:* senior citizens and employees or children of employees.

Library Beneficial-Hodson Library and Information Technology Center. *Operations spending 1999–2000:* $600,000. *Collection:* 178,727 titles, 1,216 serial subscriptions.

College life *Housing:* on-campus residence required through sophomore year. *Options:* women-only, disabled students. *Social organizations:* 70% of eligible undergrads are members. *Most popular organizations:* Education Club, Black Student Union, Campus Activities Board.

Campus security 24-hour emergency response devices and patrols, late-night transport-escort service, controlled dormitory access, residence hall security.

After graduation 262 organizations recruited on campus 1997–98. 80% of class of 1998 had job offers within 6 months. *Career center:* 3 full-time, 2 part-time personnel. Services include job fairs, resume preparation, interview workshops, resume referral, career/interest testing, career counseling, careers library, job bank, job interviews. *Graduate education:* 36% of class of 1999 went directly to graduate and professional school: 20% graduate arts and sciences, 12% business, 2% law, 2% medicine.

Freshmen 533 applied, 413 admitted, 169 enrolled. 22 National Merit Scholars, 8 valedictorians, 13 student government officers.

Average high school GPA	3.46	SAT verbal scores above 500	84%
SAT math scores above 500	72%	ACT above 18	N/R
From top 10% of their h.s. class	40%	From top quarter	71%
From top half	95%	1998 freshmen returning in 1999	84%

Application *Options:* eApply at www.CollegeQuest.com, Common Application, electronic application, early admission, early action, deferred entrance. *Application fee:* $35. *Required:* essay or personal statement; high school transcript; 2 letters of recommendation. *Recommended:* minimum 3.0 GPA; interview.

Standardized tests *Admission: Required:* SAT I or ACT. *Recommended:* SAT II Subject Tests, SAT II: Writing Test.

Significant dates *Application deadlines:* 2/15 (freshmen), 3/1 (transfers). *Early action:* 11/15. *Notification:* 3/15 (freshmen), 12/15 (early action). *Financial aid deadline:* 2/15.

Freshman Application Contact
Ms. Mauree Donahue, Director of Admissions, Hood College, 401 Rosemont Avenue, Frederick, MD 21701-8575. **Phone:** 301-696-3400. **Toll-free phone:** 800-922-1599. **E-mail:** admissions@hood.edu

Visit CollegeQuest.com for information on majors offered and athletics. Electronic viewbook available at CollegeQuest.com.

▪ *See page 1800 for a narrative description.*

JOHNS HOPKINS UNIVERSITY
Baltimore, Maryland

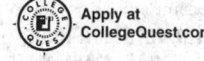
Apply at CollegeQuest.com

- **Independent**, university, founded 1876
- **Degrees** bachelor's, master's, and doctoral
- **Urban** 140-acre campus with easy access to Washington, DC
- **Coed**, 3,910 undergraduate students, 99% full-time, 41% women, 59% men
- **Most difficult** entrance level
- **10:1 student-to-undergraduate faculty ratio**
- **89% graduate** in 6 years or less
- **$23,660 tuition** and fees
- **$22,436 average financial aid** package, $16,100 average indebtedness upon graduation, $1.5 billion endowment

The name Johns Hopkins often brings to mind the term premed. However, literary scholars, anthropologists, engineers, filmmakers, mathematicians, musicians, and business leaders, as well as doctors, come from this diverse academic community. The common thread is a love of learning and the thrill of discovering new ideas.

Students *Undergraduates:* 3,900 full-time, 10 part-time. Students come from 55 states and territories, 47 other countries. *Graduate:* 1,369 in graduate degree programs.

From out-of-state	86%	Reside on campus	68%
Transferred in	1%	International students	8%
African Americans	6%	Asian Americans/Pacific Islanders	19%
Hispanic Americans	2%	Native Americans	0.1%

Faculty 913 (41% full-time), 99% with terminal degrees.

Expenses (1999–2000) *One-time required fee:* $500. *Comprehensive fee:* $31,530 includes full-time tuition ($23,660) and room and board ($7870). *College room only:* $4500. Room and board charges vary according to board plan and housing facility. *Part-time tuition:* $790 per credit. *Payment plans:* tuition prepayment, installment. *Waivers:* employees or children of employees.

Library Milton S. Eisenhower Library plus 6 others. *Operations spending 1999–2000:* $12.7 million. *Collection:* 6.8 million titles, 19,827 serial subscriptions, 298,353 audiovisual materials.

College life *Housing:* on-campus residence required through sophomore year. *Options:* coed, men-only, women-only. *Social organizations:* national fraternities, national sororities; 35% of eligible men and 40% of eligible women are members. *Most popular organizations:* Barnstormers, Hopkins Symphony, student government, student newspaper, volunteer services.

Campus security 24-hour emergency response devices and patrols, student patrols, late-night transport-escort service, controlled dormitory access.

After graduation 125 organizations recruited on campus 1997–98. 34% of class of 1998 had job offers within 6 months. *Career center:* 5 full-time, 1 part-time personnel. Services include job fairs, resume preparation, interview workshops, resume referral, career/interest testing, career counseling, careers library, job bank, job interviews. *Graduate education:* 70% of class of 1999 went directly to graduate and professional school: 22% medicine, 13% engineering, 13% graduate arts and sciences, 12% business, 10% law.

Freshmen 9,496 applied, 3,160 admitted, 1,018 enrolled. 48 National Merit Scholars, 117 valedictorians.

Average high school GPA	3.9	SAT verbal scores above 500	96%
SAT math scores above 500	99%	ACT above 18	100%
From top 10% of their h.s. class	73%	From top quarter	95%
From top half	99%	1998 freshmen returning in 1999	97%

Application *Options:* eApply at www.CollegeQuest.com, Common Application, electronic application, early admission, early decision, deferred entrance. *Application fee:* $55. *Required:* essay or personal statement; high school transcript; 1 letter of recommendation. *Recommended:* interview.

Standardized tests *Admission: Required:* SAT I and SAT II or ACT, SAT II: Writing Test. *Required for some:* SAT II Subject Tests.

Significant dates *Application deadlines:* 1/1 (freshmen), 3/15 (transfers). *Early decision:* 11/15. *Notification:* 4/1 (freshmen), 12/15 (early decision). *Financial aid deadline:* 2/15. *Priority date:* 2/1.

Freshman Application Contact
Mr. Paul White, Director of Undergraduate Admissions, Johns Hopkins University, 140 Garland Hall, 3400 North Charles Street, Baltimore, MD 21218-2699. **Phone:** 410-516-8171. **Fax:** 410-516-6025. **E-mail:** gotojhu@jhu.edu

Visit CollegeQuest.com for information on majors offered and athletics. College video and electronic viewbook available at CollegeQuest.com.

▪ *See pages 1848 and 1850 for narrative descriptions.*

LOYOLA COLLEGE IN MARYLAND
Baltimore, Maryland

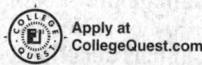
Apply at CollegeQuest.com

- **Independent Roman Catholic (Jesuit)**, comprehensive, founded 1852
- **Degrees** bachelor's, master's, doctoral, post-master's, and postbachelor's certificates
- **Urban** 89-acre campus with easy access to Washington, DC
- **Coed**, 3,357 undergraduate students, 98% full-time, 55% women, 45% men
- **Moderately difficult** entrance level, 66% of applicants were admitted
- **14:1 student-to-undergraduate faculty ratio**
- **$18,830 tuition** and fees

Maryland

Loyola College in Maryland (continued)

Students *Undergraduates:* 3,299 full-time, 58 part-time. *Graduate:* 2,886 in graduate degree programs.

International students	1%	African Americans	5%
Asian Americans/Pacific Islanders	2%	Hispanic Americans	2%
Native Americans	0.1%		

Expenses (2000–2001) *Comprehensive fee:* $26,430 includes full-time tuition ($18,310), mandatory fees ($520), and room and board ($7600). Full-time tuition and fees vary according to student level. Room and board charges vary according to board plan and housing facility. *Part-time tuition:* $365 per credit. *Part-time fees:* $25 per term part-time. *Payment plan:* guaranteed tuition. *Waivers:* employees or children of employees.

Library Loyola/Notre Dame Library. *Collection:* 347,158 titles, 2,081 serial subscriptions, 26,514 audiovisual materials.

College life *Housing:* on-campus residence required in freshman year. *Option:* coed.

Campus security 24-hour emergency response devices and patrols, late-night transport-escort service, controlled dormitory access.

After graduation 265 organizations recruited on campus 1997–98. 70% of class of 1998 had job offers within 6 months. *Career center:* 4 full-time, 4 part-time personnel. Services include job fairs, resume preparation, interview workshops, resume referral, career/interest testing, career counseling, careers library, job bank, job interviews.

Freshmen 6,129 applied, 4,037 admitted, 940 enrolled.

Average high school GPA	3.4	SAT verbal scores above 500	95%
SAT math scores above 500	95%	ACT above 18	N/R
From top 10% of their h.s. class	29%	From top quarter	68%
From top half	97%		

Application *Options:* eApply at www.CollegeQuest.com, Common Application, early admission, deferred entrance. *Application fee:* $30. *Required:* essay or personal statement; high school transcript. *Recommended:* interview.

Standardized tests *Admission: Required:* SAT I.

Significant dates *Application deadline:* 1/15 (freshmen). *Notification:* 4/15 (freshmen). *Financial aid deadline:* 2/1.

Freshman Application Contact

Mr. William Bossemeyer, Dean of Admissions, Loyola College in Maryland, 4501 North Charles Street, Baltimore, MD 21210-2699. **Phone:** 410-617-2000 Ext. 2252. **Toll-free phone:** 800-221-9107 Ext. 2252. **Fax:** 410-323-2768.

Visit CollegeQuest.com for information on majors offered and athletics. College video available at CollegeQuest.com.

■ *See page 1952 for a narrative description.*

MAPLE SPRINGS BAPTIST BIBLE COLLEGE AND SEMINARY
Capitol Heights, Maryland

- **Independent Baptist**, comprehensive, founded 1986
- **Degrees** associate, bachelor's, master's, and doctoral
- **Suburban** 1-acre campus with easy access to Washington, DC
- **Minimally difficult** entrance level
- **$2340 tuition** and fees

Expenses (1999–2000) *Tuition:* full-time $2280; part-time $95 per credit. *Required fees:* full-time $60; $30 per term part-time.

College life *Housing:* college housing not available. *Most popular organizations:* Student Government Association, newsletter.

Campus security 24-hour emergency response devices, part-time security personnel.

Application *Option:* deferred entrance. *Application fee:* $25. *Required:* essay or personal statement; high school transcript; 3 letters of recommendation; interview.

Standardized tests *Placement: Required:* Bible examination.

Admissions Office Contact

Maple Springs Baptist Bible College and Seminary, 4130 Belt Road, Capitol Heights, MD 20743. **Fax:** 301-735-6507.

Visit CollegeQuest.com for information on athletics.

MARYLAND INSTITUTE, COLLEGE OF ART
Baltimore, Maryland

- **Independent**, comprehensive, founded 1826
- **Degrees** bachelor's, master's, and postbachelor's certificates
- **Urban** 12-acre campus with easy access to Washington, DC
- **Coed**, 1,115 undergraduate students, 98% full-time, 57% women, 43% men
- **Very difficult** entrance level, 52% of applicants were admitted
- **10:1 student-to-undergraduate faculty ratio**
- **$18,710 tuition** and fees
- **$28.4 million endowment**

Students *Undergraduates:* 1,094 full-time, 21 part-time. Students come from 47 states and territories, 54 other countries. *The most frequently chosen baccalaureate field is:* visual/performing arts. *Graduate:* 139 in graduate degree programs.

From out-of-state	75%	Reside on campus	88%
Age 25 or older	5%	Transferred in	7%
International students	6%	African Americans	4%
Asian Americans/Pacific Islanders	6%	Hispanic Americans	4%
Native Americans	0.3%		

Faculty 195 (46% full-time), 39% with terminal degrees.

Expenses (1999–2000) *Tuition:* full-time $18,460; part-time $770 per credit. *Required fees:* full-time $250; $125 per term part-time. *College room only:* $4400. Room and board charges vary according to board plan and housing facility. *Payment plan:* installment. *Waivers:* employees or children of employees.

Library Decker Library. *Operations spending 1999–2000:* $729,441. *Collection:* 50,000 titles, 305 serial subscriptions, 2,400 audiovisual materials.

College life *Housing: Options:* coed, disabled students. *Most popular organizations:* Animation Club, Black Student Union, Outdoors Club, Amnesty International, Koinonia (Christian Fellowship).

Campus security 24-hour emergency response devices and patrols, student patrols, late-night transport-escort service, controlled dormitory access, self-defense education, lighted pathways, building security, safety awareness programs.

After graduation 30 organizations recruited on campus 1997–98. *Career center:* 3 full-time personnel. Services include job fairs, resume preparation, interview workshops, resume referral, career/interest testing, career counseling, careers library, job bank, job interviews. *Graduate education:* 20% of class of 1999 went directly to graduate and professional school: 14% graduate arts and sciences, 6% education. *Major awards:* 1 Fulbright Scholar.

Freshmen 1,496 applied, 776 admitted, 305 enrolled.

Average high school GPA	3.3	SAT verbal scores above 500	85%
SAT math scores above 500	70%	ACT above 18	N/R
From top 10% of their h.s. class	15%	From top quarter	50%
From top half	78%	1998 freshmen returning in 1999	82%

Application *Options:* electronic application, early admission, early decision, deferred entrance. *Application fee:* $45. *Required:* essay or personal statement; high school transcript; art portfolio. *Recommended:* 2 letters of recommendation; interview.

Standardized tests *Admission: Required for some:* SAT I or ACT.

Significant dates *Application deadlines:* 1/15 (freshmen), 3/15 (transfers). *Early decision:* 11/15. *Notification:* 3/15 (freshmen), 12/15 (early decision). *Financial aid deadline priority date:* 3/1.

Freshman Application Contact

Ms. Danielle Salisbury, Director of Undergraduate Admission, Maryland Institute, College of Art, 1300 Mount Royal Avenue, Baltimore, MD 21217-4191. **Phone:** 410-225-2222. **Fax:** 410-225-2337. **E-mail:** admissions@mica.edu

Visit CollegeQuest.com for information on majors offered and athletics.

■ *See page 2002 for a narrative description.*

MORGAN STATE UNIVERSITY
Baltimore, Maryland

- **State-supported**, university, founded 1867
- **Degrees** bachelor's, master's, and doctoral

Maryland

- **Urban** 140-acre campus with easy access to Washington, DC
- **Coed**, 5,805 undergraduate students, 86% full-time, 58% women, 42% men
- **Moderately difficult** entrance level, 55% of applicants were admitted
- **18:1** student-to-undergraduate faculty ratio
- **$3874 tuition** and fees (in-state); $9458 (out-of-state)

Students *Undergraduates:* Students come from 47 states and territories, 30 other countries.

| Reside on campus | 30% | Age 25 or older | 27% |

Expenses (1999–2000) *Tuition, state resident:* full-time $2906; part-time $131 per semester hour. *Tuition, nonresident:* full-time $8490; part-time $295 per semester hour. *Required fees:* full-time $968; $175 per term part-time. *College room and board:* $5718; room only: $3150. Room and board charges vary according to board plan and housing facility. *Payment plans:* installment, deferred payment. *Waivers:* senior citizens and employees or children of employees.

Library Morris Soper Library. *Collection:* 333,101 titles, 2,526 serial subscriptions.

College life *Housing: Option:* coed. *Social organizations:* national fraternities, national sororities; 10% of eligible men and 10% of eligible women are members. *Most popular organizations:* Student Government Association, choir, band.

Campus security 24-hour emergency response devices and patrols, late-night transport-escort service, controlled dormitory access.

After graduation 200 organizations recruited on campus 1997–98. *Career center:* 4 full-time personnel. Services include job fairs, resume preparation, resume referral, career counseling, careers library, job bank, job interviews. *Major awards:* 1 Fulbright Scholar.

Freshmen 5,840 applied, 3,235 admitted.

Average high school GPA	3.1	SAT verbal scores above 500	N/R
SAT math scores above 500	N/R	ACT above 18	N/R
From top half of their h.s. class	40%	1998 freshmen returning in 1999	76%

Application *Options:* eApply at www.CollegeQuest.com, Common Application, electronic application, early admission, deferred entrance. *Preference* given to state residents. *Application fee:* $25. *Required:* high school transcript; minimum 2.0 GPA. *Required for some:* 2 letters of recommendation; interview. *Recommended:* essay or personal statement.

Standardized tests *Admission: Required:* SAT I or ACT.

Significant dates *Application deadlines:* rolling (freshmen), rolling (transfers). *Financial aid deadline priority date:* 4/1.

Freshman Application Contact
Ms. Delores Norris, Acting Director of Admission and Recruitment, Morgan State University, 1700 East Cold Spring Lane, Baltimore, MD 21251. **Phone:** 443-885-3000. **Toll-free phone:** 800-332-6674.

Visit CollegeQuest.com for information on majors offered and athletics.

■ *See page 2098 for a narrative description.*

MOUNT SAINT MARY'S COLLEGE AND SEMINARY
Emmitsburg, Maryland

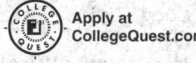
Apply at CollegeQuest.com

- **Independent Roman Catholic**, comprehensive, founded 1808
- **Degrees** bachelor's, master's, and first professional
- **Rural** 1,400-acre campus with easy access to Baltimore and Washington, DC
- **Coed**, 1,268 undergraduate students, 99% full-time, 57% women, 43% men
- **Moderately difficult** entrance level, 81% of applicants were admitted
- **13:1** student-to-undergraduate faculty ratio
- **64% graduate** in 6 years or less
- **$16,720 tuition** and fees
- **$12,856 average financial aid** package, $15,463 average indebtedness upon graduation, $29.6 million endowment

The Mount has expanded the concentrations in the business administration major to include sports management as well as finance, international business, management, and marketing. The sports management concentration includes courses in sport history, marketing, economics, and a required internship in the field. More than one third of Mount students enhance their majors with internships and study abroad programs. The Mount is proud to award academic scholarships ranging from $5000 to more than $17,000 per year for qualified students.

Students *Undergraduates:* 1,255 full-time, 13 part-time. Students come from 29 states and territories, 17 other countries. *The most frequently chosen baccalaureate fields are:* business/marketing, education, social sciences and history. *Graduate:* 139 in professional programs, 237 in other graduate degree programs.

From out-of-state	49%	Reside on campus	84%
Age 25 or older	7%	Transferred in	2%
International students	2%	African Americans	6%
Asian Americans/Pacific Islanders	2%	Hispanic Americans	3%
Native Americans	0.2%		

Faculty 123 (70% full-time).

Expenses (1999–2000) *Comprehensive fee:* $23,370 includes full-time tuition ($16,520), mandatory fees ($200), and room and board ($6650). *College room only:* $3325. Room and board charges vary according to board plan. *Part-time tuition:* $550 per credit. *Part-time fees:* $5 per credit. Part-time tuition and fees vary according to course load. *Payment plans:* tuition prepayment, installment. *Waivers:* employees or children of employees.

Library Phillips Library. *Operations spending 1999–2000:* $786,002. *Collection:* 201,755 titles, 966 serial subscriptions, 9,440 audiovisual materials.

College life *Housing:* on-campus residence required in freshman year. *Option:* coed. *Most popular organizations:* campus ministry, rugby team club, ice hockey club, Circle K, International Affairs Organization.

Campus security 24-hour emergency response devices and patrols, late-night transport-escort service, controlled dormitory access.

After graduation 57 organizations recruited on campus 1997–98. *Career center:* 4 full-time personnel. Services include job fairs, resume preparation, interview workshops, resume referral, career/interest testing, career counseling, careers library, job bank, job interviews.

Freshmen 1,466 applied, 1,187 admitted, 369 enrolled.

Average high school GPA	3.0	SAT verbal scores above 500	69%
SAT math scores above 500	63%	ACT above 18	N/R
From top 10% of their h.s. class	15%	From top quarter	36%
From top half	76%	1998 freshmen returning in 1999	80%

Application *Options:* eApply at www.CollegeQuest.com, early admission, early action, deferred entrance. *Application fee:* $25. *Required:* high school transcript; minimum 2.0 GPA; 1 letter of recommendation. *Recommended:* essay or personal statement; minimum 3.0 GPA; interview.

Standardized tests *Admission: Required:* SAT I or ACT.

Significant dates *Application deadlines:* 3/1 (freshmen), 6/1 (transfers). *Early action:* 12/1. *Notification:* 4/1 (freshmen), 12/15 (early action). *Financial aid deadline:* 3/15. *Priority date:* 2/15.

Freshman Application Contact
Mr. Stephen Neitz, Executive Director of Admissions and Financial Aid, Mount Saint Mary's College and Seminary, 16300 Old Emmitsburg Road, Emmitsburg, MD 21727-7799. **Phone:** 301-447-5214. **Toll-free phone:** 800-448-4347. **E-mail:** admissions@msmary.edu

Visit CollegeQuest.com for information on majors offered and athletics. College video available at CollegeQuest.com.

■ *See page 2122 for a narrative description.*

NER ISRAEL RABBINICAL COLLEGE
Baltimore, Maryland

Admissions Office Contact
Ner Israel Rabbinical College, Mount Wilson Lane, Baltimore, MD 21208.

PEABODY CONSERVATORY OF MUSIC OF THE JOHNS HOPKINS UNIVERSITY
Baltimore, Maryland

- **Independent**, comprehensive, founded 1857
- **Degrees** bachelor's, master's, and doctoral
- **Urban** campus with easy access to Washington, DC
- **Coed**, 348 undergraduate students, 96% full-time, 52% women, 48% men

Maryland

Peabody Conservatory of Music of The Johns Hopkins University *(continued)*
- **Very difficult** entrance level, 54% of applicants were admitted
- **70% graduate** in 6 years or less
- **$21,975 tuition** and fees
- **$16,145 average financial aid** package, $25 million endowment

Students *Undergraduates:* 333 full-time, 15 part-time. Students come from 39 states and territories, 8 other countries. *The most frequently chosen baccalaureate fields are:* education, visual/performing arts. *Graduate:* 302 in graduate degree programs.

Age 25 or older	6%	Transferred in	6%
International students	16%	African Americans	2%
Asian Americans/Pacific Islanders	7%	Hispanic Americans	4%

Faculty 150.

Expenses (1999–2000) *One-time required fee:* $500. *Comprehensive fee:* $30,035 includes full-time tuition ($21,700), mandatory fees ($275), and room and board ($8060). Room and board charges vary according to board plan and housing facility. *Part-time tuition:* $620 per semester hour. Part-time tuition and fees vary according to course load. *Waivers:* employees or children of employees.

Library Arthur Friedheim Library. *Collection:* 80,430 titles, 245 serial subscriptions, 21,840 audiovisual materials.

College life *Housing:* on-campus residence required through sophomore year. *Options:* coed, women-only. *Most popular organizations:* Student Council, Residence Hall Council.

Campus security 24-hour emergency response devices, late-night transport-escort service, controlled dormitory access.

After graduation 20% of class of 1998 had job offers within 6 months. *Career center:* 1 full-time personnel. Services include resume preparation, resume referral, career counseling, careers library, job bank, job interviews.

Freshmen 583 applied, 317 admitted, 86 enrolled.

SAT verbal scores above 500	81%	SAT math scores above 500	90%
ACT above 18	N/R	1998 freshmen returning in 1999	90%

Application *Application fee:* $50. *Required:* high school transcript; 3 letters of recommendation; interview; audition. *Required for some:* essay or personal statement.

Standardized tests *Admission: Required for some:* SAT I or ACT.

Significant dates *Application deadlines:* 12/15 (freshmen), 12/15 (transfers). *Notification:* 4/1 (freshmen). *Financial aid deadline priority date:* 2/1.

Freshman Application Contact
Mr. David Lane, Director of Admissions, Peabody Conservatory of Music of The Johns Hopkins University, 1 East Mount Vernon Place, Baltimore, MD 21202-2397. **Phone:** 410-659-8110. **Toll-free phone:** 800-368-2521.

Visit CollegeQuest.com for information on majors offered and athletics.

ST. JOHN'S COLLEGE
Annapolis, Maryland

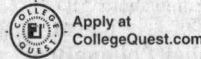 Apply at CollegeQuest.com

- **Independent**, comprehensive, founded 1784
- **Degrees** bachelor's and master's
- **Small-town** 36-acre campus with easy access to Baltimore and Washington, DC
- **Coed**, 452 undergraduate students, 99% full-time, 45% women, 55% men
- **Moderately difficult** entrance level, 78% of applicants were admitted
- **8:1 student-to-undergraduate faculty ratio**
- **69% graduate** in 6 years or less
- **$23,490 tuition** and fees
- **$20,763 average financial aid** package, $17,125 average indebtedness upon graduation, $54 million endowment

Students *Undergraduates:* 451 full-time, 1 part-time. Students come from 44 states and territories, 13 other countries. *The most frequently chosen baccalaureate field is:* liberal arts/general studies. *Graduate:* 64 in graduate degree programs.

From out-of-state	82%	Reside on campus	75%
Age 25 or older	4%	Transferred in	2%
International students	4%	African Americans	1%
Asian Americans/Pacific Islanders	2%	Hispanic Americans	2%

Faculty 70 (91% full-time), 67% with terminal degrees.

Expenses (1999–2000) *Comprehensive fee:* $29,850 includes full-time tuition ($23,290), mandatory fees ($200), and room and board ($6360). *College room only:* $3150. Room and board charges vary according to board plan. *Payment plans:* tuition prepayment, installment. *Waivers:* employees or children of employees.

Library Greenfield Library plus 1 other. *Operations spending 1999–2000:* $387,230. *Collection:* 102,133 titles, 114 serial subscriptions, 920 audiovisual materials.

College life *Housing:* on-campus residence required in freshman year. *Option:* coed. *Most popular organizations:* King William Players, Polity, Political Forum, Student Committee on Instruction, rowing club.

Campus security 24-hour emergency response devices and patrols, late-night transport-escort service, controlled dormitory access.

After graduation 7 organizations recruited on campus 1997–98. 50% of class of 1998 had job offers within 6 months. *Career center:* 1 full-time, 1 part-time personnel. Services include job fairs, resume preparation, resume referral, career/interest testing, career counseling, careers library, job bank, job interviews, web site job listing on college homepage. *Major awards:* 2 Fulbright Scholars.

Freshmen 446 applied, 349 admitted, 133 enrolled. 6 National Merit Scholars.

SAT verbal scores above 500	99%	SAT math scores above 500	95%
ACT above 18	N/R	From top 10% of their h.s. class	36%
From top quarter	61%	From top half	91%
1998 freshmen returning in 1999	81%		

Application *Options:* eApply at www.CollegeQuest.com, early admission, deferred entrance. *Application fee:* $0. *Required:* essay or personal statement; high school transcript; 2 letters of recommendation. *Recommended:* interview.

Standardized tests *Admission: Recommended:* SAT I or ACT. *Required for some:* SAT I or ACT.

Significant dates *Application deadlines:* rolling (freshmen), rolling (transfers). *Financial aid deadline priority date:* 2/15.

Freshman Application Contact
Mr. John Christensen, Director of Admissions, St. John's College, PO Box 2800, 60 College Avenue, Annapolis, MD 21404. **Phone:** 410-626-2522. **Toll-free phone:** 800-727-9238. **E-mail:** admissions@sjca.edu

Visit CollegeQuest.com for information on majors offered and athletics.

- *See page 2384 for a narrative description.*

ST. MARY'S COLLEGE OF MARYLAND
St. Mary's City, Maryland

 Apply at CollegeQuest.com

- **State-supported**, 4-year, founded 1840
- **Degree** bachelor's
- **Rural** 275-acre campus
- **Coed**, 1,458 undergraduate students, 96% full-time, 58% women, 42% men
- **Moderately difficult** entrance level, 65% of applicants were admitted
- **12:1 student-to-undergraduate faculty ratio**
- **71.8% graduate** in 6 years or less
- **$7360 tuition** and fees (in-state); $12,200 (out-of-state)
- **$5455 average financial aid** package, $14,399 average indebtedness upon graduation, $22.4 million endowment

St. Mary's College, designated a Public Honors College specializing in liberal arts and sciences, occupies a waterfront location in historic St. Mary's City. The renovation of the campus center is scheduled for completion in fall 1999. The renovation and addition to the athletic and recreation complex begins in summer 1999, with completion of the recreation complex during spring 2001. An innovative student-designed major and the St. Mary's Project were recently added.

Part of Maryland State Colleges and Universities System.

Students *Undergraduates:* 1,394 full-time, 64 part-time. Students come from 36 states and territories. *The most frequently chosen baccalaureate fields are:* psychology, biological/life sciences, social sciences and history.

From out-of-state	16%	Reside on campus	69%
Age 25 or older	6%	Transferred in	6%
International students	1%	African Americans	10%
Asian Americans/Pacific Islanders	4%	Hispanic Americans	2%
Native Americans	0.4%		

Faculty 172 (68% full-time), 79% with terminal degrees.

Expenses (2000–2001) *Tuition, state resident:* full-time $6285; part-time $110 per credit. *Tuition, nonresident:* full-time $11,125; part-time $110 per credit. *Required fees:* full-time $1075; $250 per term part-time. Part-time tuition and fees vary according to course load. *College room and board:* $6325; room only: $3425. Room and board charges vary according to board plan and housing facility. *Waivers:* senior citizens and employees or children of employees.

Library Baltimore Hall. *Operations spending 1999–2000:* $1.6 million. *Collection:* 110,642 titles, 15,211 audiovisual materials.

College life *Housing: Options:* coed, men-only, women-only. *Most popular organizations:* Black Student Union, economics club, women's rugby, crew, For Goodness Sake (community service).

Campus security 24-hour emergency response devices and patrols, student patrols, late-night transport-escort service, controlled dormitory access.

After graduation 9 organizations recruited on campus 1997–98. *Career center:* 3 full-time personnel. Services include job fairs, resume preparation, interview workshops, resume referral, career/interest testing, career counseling, careers library, job bank, job interviews. *Graduate education:* 37% of class of 1999 went directly to graduate and professional school: 28% graduate arts and sciences, 4% law, 3% business, 2% medicine.

Freshmen 1,285 applied, 837 admitted, 276 enrolled. 11 National Merit Scholars, 13 valedictorians.

Average high school GPA	3.4	SAT verbal scores above 500	96%
SAT math scores above 500	94%	ACT above 18	N/R
From top 10% of their h.s. class	50%	From top quarter	78%
From top half	97%	1998 freshmen returning in 1999	85%

Application *Options:* eApply at www.CollegeQuest.com, early admission, early decision. *Application fee:* $25. *Required:* essay or personal statement; high school transcript; minimum 2.0 GPA. *Recommended:* 3 letters of recommendation; interview.

Standardized tests *Admission: Required:* SAT I or ACT.

Significant dates *Application deadlines:* 1/15 (freshmen), 3/15 (transfers). *Early decision:* 12/1 (for plan 1), 1/15 (for plan 2). *Notification:* 4/1 (freshmen), 1/1 (early decision plan 1), 2/15 (early decision plan 2). ***Financial aid deadline:*** 3/1.

Freshman Application Contact
Mr. Richard J. Edgar, Director of Admissions, St. Mary's College of Maryland, 18952 East Fisher Road, St. Mary's City, MD 20686-3001. **Phone:** 301-862-0292. **Toll-free phone:** 800-492-7181. **Fax:** 301-862-0906. **E-mail:** admissions@honors.smcm.edu

Visit CollegeQuest.com for information on majors offered and athletics. College video and electronic viewbook available at CollegeQuest.com.

■ *See page 2414 for a narrative description.*

SALISBURY STATE UNIVERSITY
Salisbury, Maryland

- **State-supported**, comprehensive, founded 1925
- **Degrees** bachelor's and master's
- **Small-town** 140-acre campus
- **Coed**, 5,039 undergraduate students, 92% full-time, 57% women, 43% men
- **Moderately difficult** entrance level, 57% of applicants were admitted
- **17:1 student-to-undergraduate faculty ratio**
- **63% graduate** in 6 years or less
- **$4156 tuition** and fees (in-state); $8550 (out-of-state)
- **$5120 average financial aid** package, $14,000 average indebtedness upon graduation, $12.7 million endowment

Salisbury State University is a rarity among public institutions in Maryland—all 4 of its schools are endowed. These multimillion-dollar gifts have expanded scholarships and other opportunities for students. With an emphasis on active learning, including undergraduate research, internships, community service, and travel abroad, SSU is earning a national reputation for educating undergraduates. Publications such as *U.S. News & World Report*, *Kiplinger's*, and *Princeton Review* rank SSU among the nation's best schools.

Part of University System of Maryland.

Students *Undergraduates:* 4,639 full-time, 400 part-time. Students come from 34 states and territories. *The most frequently chosen baccalaureate fields are:* business/marketing, biological/life sciences, education. **Graduate:** 524 in graduate degree programs.

From out-of-state	20%	Reside on campus	37%
Age 25 or older	13%	Transferred in	11%
International students	0.5%	African Americans	6%
Asian Americans/Pacific Islanders	1%	Hispanic Americans	1%
Native Americans	0.3%		

Faculty 394 (66% full-time).

Expenses (1999–2000) *Tuition, state resident:* full-time $2972; part-time $125 per semester hour. *Tuition, nonresident:* full-time $7366; part-time $308 per semester hour. *Required fees:* full-time $1184; $4 per semester hour. *College room and board:* $5590; room only: $2900. Room and board charges vary according to board plan and housing facility. *Payment plan:* installment. *Waivers:* senior citizens and employees or children of employees.

Library Blackwell Library plus 1 other. *Operations spending 1999–2000:* $1.7 million. *Collection:* 243,698 titles, 1,661 serial subscriptions.

College life *Housing: Options:* coed, men-only, women-only. *Social organizations:* national fraternities, national sororities; 75% of eligible men and 75% of eligible women are members. *Most popular organizations:* Student Government Association, campus radio station, Programming Board, Greek Council, Union of African-American Students.

Campus security 24-hour emergency response devices and patrols, student patrols, late-night transport-escort service, controlled dormitory access.

After graduation 300 organizations recruited on campus 1997–98. *Career center:* 4 full-time, 1 part-time personnel. Services include job fairs, resume preparation, interview workshops, resume referral, career/interest testing, career counseling, careers library, job bank, job interviews.

Freshmen 4,501 applied, 2,572 admitted, 871 enrolled. 10 valedictorians.

Average high school GPA	3.4	SAT verbal scores above 500	86%
SAT math scores above 500	88%	ACT above 18	100%
From top 10% of their h.s. class	20%	From top quarter	57%
From top half	89%	1998 freshmen returning in 1999	81%

Application *Options:* Common Application, electronic application, early admission, early decision. *Application fee:* $30. *Required:* high school transcript; minimum 2.0 GPA. *Required for some:* letters of recommendation. *Recommended:* essay or personal statement.

Standardized tests *Admission: Required:* SAT I or ACT.

Significant dates *Application deadlines:* 1/15 (freshmen), rolling (transfers). *Early decision:* 12/15. *Notification:* 3/15 (freshmen), 1/15 (early decision). ***Financial aid deadline priority date:*** 2/15.

Freshman Application Contact
Mrs. Jane H. Dané, Dean of Admissions, Salisbury State University, Admissions House, 1101 Camden Avenue, Salisbury, MD 21801. **Phone:** 410-543-6161. **Toll-free phone:** 888-543-0148. **Fax:** 410-548-2587. **E-mail:** admissions@ssu.edu

Visit CollegeQuest.com for information on majors offered and athletics. Electronic viewbook available at CollegeQuest.com.

■ *See page 2438 for a narrative description.*

SOJOURNER-DOUGLASS COLLEGE
Baltimore, Maryland

Admissions Office Contact
Sojourner-Douglass College, 500 North Caroline Street, Baltimore, MD 21205-1814. **Fax:** 410-675-1810.

TOWSON UNIVERSITY
Towson, Maryland

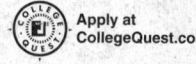
Apply at CollegeQuest.com

- **State-supported**, comprehensive, founded 1866

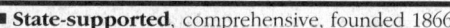

Maryland

Towson University (continued)
- **Degrees** bachelor's, master's, post-master's, and postbachelor's certificates
- **Suburban** 321-acre campus with easy access to Baltimore and Washington, DC
- **Coed**, 13,027 undergraduate students, 87% full-time, 59% women, 41% men
- **Moderately difficult** entrance level, 69% of applicants were admitted
- **16:1 student-to-undergraduate faculty ratio**
- **57.5% graduate** in 6 years or less
- **$4710 tuition** and fees (in-state); $11,140 (out-of-state)
- **$7851 average financial aid** package, $10.7 million endowment

Part of University System of Maryland.

Students *Undergraduates:* 11,281 full-time, 1,746 part-time. Students come from 48 states and territories, 87 other countries. *The most frequently chosen baccalaureate fields are:* business/marketing, communications/communication technologies, education. *Graduate:* 2,666 in graduate degree programs.

From out-of-state	18%	Reside on campus	25%
Age 25 or older	14%	Transferred in	14%
International students	3%	African Americans	10%
Asian Americans/Pacific Islanders	3%	Hispanic Americans	1%
Native Americans	0.2%		

Faculty 1,140 (46% full-time), 42% with terminal degrees.
Expenses (1999–2000) *Tuition, state resident:* full-time $3466; part-time $150 per credit hour. *Tuition, nonresident:* full-time $9896; part-time $362 per credit hour. *Required fees:* full-time $1244; $43 per credit hour. *College room and board:* $5800; room only: $3350. Room and board charges vary according to board plan and housing facility. *Payment plan:* installment. *Waivers:* senior citizens and employees or children of employees.
Library Cook Library. *Operations spending 1999–2000:* $2.9 million. *Collection:* 363,430 titles, 2,227 serial subscriptions.
College life *Housing: Options:* coed, disabled students. *Social organizations:* national fraternities, national sororities; 10% of eligible men and 7% of eligible women are members. *Most popular organizations:* Black Student Union, Student Government Association, Habitat for Humanity, Circle K, University Residence Government.
Campus security 24-hour emergency response devices and patrols, late-night transport-escort service, controlled dormitory access.
After graduation 90 organizations recruited on campus 1997–98. *Career center:* 10 full-time, 4 part-time personnel. Services include job fairs, resume preparation, interview workshops, resume referral, career counseling, careers library, job bank, job interviews. *Graduate education:* 26% of class of 1999 went directly to graduate and professional school.
Freshmen 7,799 applied, 5,390 admitted, 2,079 enrolled.

Average high school GPA	3.2	SAT verbal scores above 500	72%
SAT math scores above 500	73%	ACT above 18	74%
From top 10% of their h.s. class	16%	From top quarter	45%
From top half	82%	1998 freshmen returning in 1999	83%

Application *Options:* eApply at www.CollegeQuest.com, electronic application, early admission, deferred entrance. *Application fee:* $30. *Required:* high school transcript. *Required for some:* interview. *Recommended:* essay or personal statement; minimum 2.75 GPA; letters of recommendation; interview.
Standardized tests *Admission: Required:* SAT I or ACT.
Significant dates *Application deadlines:* 5/1 (freshmen), rolling (transfers). *Notification:* 10/1 (freshmen). *Financial aid deadline priority date:* 2/15.
Freshman Application Contact
Ms. Louise Shulack, Acting Director of Admissions, Towson University, 8000 York Road, Towson, MD 21252. **Phone:** 410-830-3333. **Toll-free phone:** 888-4TOWSON. **Fax:** 410-830-3030. **E-mail:** admissions@towson.edu
Visit CollegeQuest.com for information on majors offered and athletics. College video available at CollegeQuest.com.

- *See page 2630 for a narrative description.*

UNITED STATES NAVAL ACADEMY
Annapolis, Maryland

- **Federally supported**, 4-year, founded 1845
- **Degree** bachelor's
- **Small-town** 329-acre campus with easy access to Baltimore and Washington, DC
- **Coed**, primarily men, 4,123 undergraduate students, 100% full-time, 15% women, 85% men
- **Very difficult** entrance level, 15% of applicants were admitted
- **9:1 student-to-undergraduate faculty ratio**
- **76.48% graduate** in 6 years or less
- **$0 comprehensive fee**

Students *Undergraduates:* 4,123 full-time. Students come from 54 states and territories, 20 other countries. *The most frequently chosen baccalaureate fields are:* engineering/engineering technologies, physical sciences, social sciences and history.

From out-of-state	96%	Reside on campus	100%
Age 25 or older	1%	International students	1%
African Americans	6%	Asian Americans/Pacific Islanders	4%
Hispanic Americans	7%	Native Americans	1%

Faculty 553 (100% full-time), 46% with terminal degrees.
Expenses (1999–2000) Tuition, room and board, and medical and dental care are provided by the U.S. government. Each midshipman receives a salary from which to pay for uniforms, supplies, and personal expenses. Entering freshmen are required to deposit $2250 to defray the initial cost of uniforms and equipment.
Library Nimitz Library plus 1 other. *Collection:* 800,000 titles, 1,892 serial subscriptions.
College life *Housing:* on-campus residence required through senior year. *Option:* coed. *Most popular organizations:* Mountaineering Club, Semper Fi, Black Studies Club, Midshipmen Action Club, Martial Arts Club.
Campus security 24-hour emergency response devices and patrols, student patrols, front gate security.
After graduation 100% of class of 1998 had job offers within 6 months. *Career center:* Services include career counseling. *Graduate education:* 2% of class of 1999 went directly to graduate and professional school; 1% medicine. *Major awards:* 1 Marshall scholar.
Freshmen 10,145 applied, 1,511 admitted, 1,144 enrolled. 1 Westinghouse recipient, 148 class presidents, 123 student government officers.

SAT verbal scores above 500	100%	SAT math scores above 500	100%
ACT above 18	N/R	From top 10% of their h.s. class	61%
From top quarter	84%	From top half	97%
1998 freshmen returning in 1999	94%		

Application *Application fee:* $0. *Required:* essay or personal statement; high school transcript; minimum 2.0 GPA; 2 letters of recommendation; interview; authorized nomination.
Standardized tests *Admission: Required:* SAT I or ACT.
Significant dates *Application deadline:* 2/28 (freshmen). *Notification:* 4/15 (freshmen).
Freshman Application Contact
Col. David A. Vetter, Dean of Admissions, United States Naval Academy, 117 Decatur Road, Annapolis, MD 21402-5000. **Phone:** 410-293-4361. **Fax:** 410-293-4348.
Visit CollegeQuest.com for information on majors offered and athletics. College video available at CollegeQuest.com.

UNIVERSITY OF BALTIMORE
Baltimore, Maryland

- **State-supported**, upper-level, founded 1925
- **Degrees** bachelor's, master's, doctoral, and first professional
- **Urban** 49-acre campus
- **Coed**, 1,802 undergraduate students, 45% full-time, 61% women, 39% men
- **Noncompetitive** entrance level, 81% of applicants were admitted
- **16:1 student-to-undergraduate faculty ratio**
- **$4122 tuition** and fees (in-state); $11,464 (out-of-state)
- **$18.1 million endowment**

Maryland

Part of University System of Maryland.

Students *Undergraduates:* 813 full-time, 989 part-time. Students come from 7 states and territories, 50 other countries. *The most frequently chosen baccalaureate fields are:* business/marketing, interdisciplinary studies, protective services/public administration. *Graduate:* 953 in professional programs, 1,724 in other graduate degree programs.

From out-of-state	0.3%	Age 25 or older	73%
Transferred in	25%	International students	3%
African Americans	27%	Asian Americans/Pacific Islanders	3%
Hispanic Americans	1%	Native Americans	1%

Faculty 325 (46% full-time), 75% with terminal degrees.

Expenses (1999–2000) *Tuition, state resident:* full-time $3542; part-time $163 per credit. *Tuition, nonresident:* full-time $10,884; part-time $454 per credit. *Required fees:* full-time $580; $20 per credit; $60 per term part-time. Full-time tuition and fees vary according to course level. *Payment plan:* deferred payment. *Waivers:* senior citizens and employees or children of employees.

Library Langsdale Library plus 1 other. *Operations spending 1999–2000:* $2 million. *Collection:* 730 serial subscriptions, 3,314 audiovisual materials.

College life *Housing:* college housing not available. *Most popular organizations:* Project Hunger, Student Events Board, student government association.

Campus security 24-hour emergency response devices and patrols, late-night transport-escort service.

After graduation 116 organizations recruited on campus 1997–98. 88% of class of 1998 had job offers within 6 months. *Career center:* 6 full-time, 3 part-time personnel. Services include job fairs, resume preparation, resume referral, career counseling, careers library, job bank, job interviews.

Application *Option:* electronic application. *Application fee:* $20.

Significant dates *Application deadline:* rolling (transfers). *Financial aid deadline priority date:* 4/1.

Freshman Application Contact
Ms. Julia Pitman, Associate Director of Admissions, University of Baltimore, 1420 North Charles St., Baltimore, MD 21201. **Phone:** 410-837-4777. **Toll-free phone:** 877-APPLYUB. **Fax:** 410-837-4793. **E-mail:** admissions@ubmail.ubalt.edu

Visit CollegeQuest.com for information on majors offered and athletics.

■ *See page 2696 for a narrative description.*

UNIVERSITY OF MARYLAND, BALTIMORE COUNTY
Baltimore, Maryland

- **State-supported**, university, founded 1963
- **Degrees** bachelor's, master's, and doctoral
- **Suburban** 500-acre campus
- **Coed**, 8,592 undergraduate students, 81% full-time, 50% women, 50% men
- **Moderately difficult** entrance level, 69% of applicants were admitted
- **17:1 student-to-undergraduate faculty ratio**
- **$5160 tuition** and fees (in-state); $9632 (out-of-state)

Some of the most exciting students and best teaching talents anywhere are coming together at a young university located in the suburbs of Baltimore that has approximately 9,000 undergraduates. UMBC's leadership in technology, friendly campus climate, business and industry partnerships, and ability to place students in leading graduate programs and promising careers are just a few of the reasons why students who could attend any college are choosing UMBC.

Part of University System of Maryland.

Students *Undergraduates:* 6,955 full-time, 1,637 part-time. Students come from 42 states and territories, 70 other countries. *The most frequently chosen baccalaureate fields are:* computer/information sciences, psychology, social sciences and history. *Graduate:* 1,411 in graduate degree programs.

From out-of-state	7%	Reside on campus	27%
Age 25 or older	21%	Transferred in	12%
International students	4%	African Americans	16%
Asian Americans/Pacific Islanders	17%	Hispanic Americans	2%
Native Americans	1%		

Faculty 736 (56% full-time).

Expenses (1999–2000) *Tuition, state resident:* full-time $4046; part-time $170 per credit hour. *Tuition, nonresident:* full-time $8518; part-time $353 per credit hour. *Required fees:* full-time $1114; $57 per credit hour. Part-time tuition and fees vary according to course load. *College room and board:* $5694; room only: $3414. Room and board charges vary according to board plan and housing facility. *Payment plan:* installment. *Waivers:* senior citizens and employees or children of employees.

Library Albin O. Kuhn Library and Gallery. *Operations spending 1999–2000:* $2.7 million. *Collection:* 983,052 titles, 4,142 serial subscriptions, 1.5 million audiovisual materials.

College life *Housing: Option:* coed. *Social organizations:* national fraternities, national sororities; 2% of eligible men and 2% of eligible women are members. *Most popular organizations:* student government association, student events board, Retriever Weekly, resident student association, Black Student Union.

Campus security 24-hour emergency response devices, late-night transport-escort service.

After graduation 843 organizations recruited on campus 1997–98. 87% of class of 1998 had job offers within 6 months. *Career center:* 6 full-time, 1 part-time personnel. Services include job fairs, resume preparation, interview workshops, resume referral, career counseling, careers library, job bank, job interviews. *Graduate education:* 36% of class of 1999 went directly to graduate and professional school: 25% graduate arts and sciences, 2% business, 2% law, 2% medicine.

Freshmen 5,128 applied, 3,542 admitted, 1,398 enrolled. 3 National Merit Scholars.

Average high school GPA	3.35	SAT verbal scores above 500	85%
SAT math scores above 500	90%	ACT above 18	91%
From top 10% of their h.s. class	30%	From top quarter	59%
From top half	85%	1998 freshmen returning in 1999	83%

Application *Options:* early admission, deferred entrance. *Application fee:* $45. *Required:* essay or personal statement; high school transcript; minimum 2.0 GPA.

Standardized tests *Admission: Required:* SAT I or ACT. *Recommended:* SAT I.

Significant dates *Application deadlines:* 3/15 (freshmen), rolling (transfers). *Financial aid deadline priority date:* 3/1.

Freshman Application Contact
Ms. Janice Doyle, Enrollment Services, University of Maryland, Baltimore County, 1000 Hilltop Circle, Baltimore, MD 21250-5398. **Phone:** 410-455-4835. **Toll-free phone:** 800-UMBC-4U2 (in-state); 800-862-2402 (out-of-state). **Fax:** 410-455-1094. **E-mail:** admissions@umbc.edu

Visit CollegeQuest.com for information on majors offered and athletics. College video available at CollegeQuest.com.

■ *See page 2754 for a narrative description.*

UNIVERSITY OF MARYLAND, COLLEGE PARK
College Park, Maryland

- **State-supported**, university, founded 1856
- **Degrees** bachelor's, master's, doctoral, and post-master's certificates
- **Suburban** 3,650-acre campus with easy access to Baltimore and Washington, DC
- **Coed**, 24,028 undergraduate students, 90% full-time, 49% women, 51% men
- **Moderately difficult** entrance level, 54% of applicants were admitted
- **14:1 student-to-undergraduate faculty ratio**
- **63.98% graduate** in 6 years or less
- **$4939 tuition** and fees (in-state); $11,827 (out-of-state)
- **$7019 average financial aid** package, $14,076 average indebtedness upon graduation, $273.8 million endowment

Part of University System of Maryland.

Maryland

University of Maryland, College Park *(continued)*

Students *Undergraduates:* 21,707 full-time, 2,321 part-time. Students come from 54 states and territories, 150 other countries. *The most frequently chosen baccalaureate fields are:* business/marketing, biological/life sciences, social sciences and history. *Graduate:* 8,147 in graduate degree programs.

From out-of-state	27%	Reside on campus	36%
Age 25 or older	12%	Transferred in	9%
International students	3%	African Americans	14%
Asian Americans/Pacific Islanders	14%	Hispanic Americans	5%
Native Americans	0.3%		

Faculty 1,918 (72% full-time), 80% with terminal degrees.

Expenses (1999–2000) *Tuition, state resident:* full-time $4050; part-time $170 per semester hour. *Tuition, nonresident:* full-time $10,938; part-time $456 per semester hour. *Required fees:* full-time $889; $198 per term part-time. *College room and board:* $6306; room only: $3686. Room and board charges vary according to board plan. *Payment plans:* installment, deferred payment. *Waivers:* senior citizens and employees or children of employees.

Library McKeldin Library plus 6 others. *Operations spending 1999–2000:* $16.6 million. *Collection:* 2.7 million titles, 27,137 serial subscriptions, 175,602 audiovisual materials.

College life *Housing: Options:* coed, men-only, women-only, disabled students. *Social organizations:* national fraternities, national sororities; 9% of eligible men and 10% of eligible women are members. *Most popular organizations:* Student Government Association, Residence Hall Association, Black Student Union, Interfraternity Council, Stamp Union Program Council.

Campus security 24-hour emergency response devices and patrols, student patrols, late-night transport-escort service, controlled dormitory access, campus police, video camera surveillance.

After graduation 525 organizations recruited on campus 1997–98. 86% of class of 1998 had job offers within 6 months. *Career center:* 22 full-time, 12 part-time personnel. Services include job fairs, resume preparation, interview workshops, resume referral, career/interest testing, career counseling, careers library, job bank, job interviews. *Graduate education:* 33% of class of 1999 went directly to graduate and professional school: 15% graduate arts and sciences, 9% law, 4% medicine, 2% business, 1% dentistry. *Major awards:* 2 Fulbright Scholars.

Freshmen 18,731 applied, 10,169 admitted, 3,916 enrolled. 52 National Merit Scholars.

Average high school GPA	3.61	SAT verbal scores above 500	92%
SAT math scores above 500	93%	ACT above 18	N/R
From top 10% of their h.s. class	45%	From top quarter	83%
From top half	98%	1998 freshmen returning in 1999	90%

Application *Options:* electronic application, early admission, early action. *Preference* given to state residents. *Application fee:* $45. *Required:* essay or personal statement; high school transcript; 1 letter of recommendation. *Recommended:* 2 letters of recommendation; resume of activities.

Standardized tests *Admission: Required:* SAT I or ACT.

Significant dates *Application deadlines:* 2/15 (freshmen), 7/1 (transfers). *Early action:* 12/1. *Notification:* continuous until 4/1 (freshmen), 2/1 (early action). *Financial aid deadline priority date:* 2/15.

Freshman Application Contact

Dr. Linda Clement, Assistant Vice President and Director of Undergraduate Admissions, University of Maryland, College Park, Mitchell Building, College Park, MD 20742-5235. **Phone:** 301-314-8385. **Toll-free phone:** 800-422-5867. **Fax:** 301-314-9693. **E-mail:** um-admit@uga.umd.edu

Visit CollegeQuest.com for information on majors offered and athletics. College video and electronic viewbook available at CollegeQuest.com.

■ *See page 2756 for a narrative description.*

UNIVERSITY OF MARYLAND EASTERN SHORE
Princess Anne, Maryland

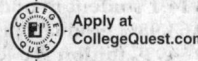

- **State-supported**, university, founded 1886
- **Degrees** bachelor's, master's, and doctoral
- **Rural** 700-acre campus
- **Coed**
- **Moderately difficult** entrance level
- **$3833 tuition** and fees (in-state); $8443 (out-of-state)

Part of University System of Maryland.

Expenses (1999–2000) *Tuition, state resident:* full-time $2680; part-time $124 per credit. *Tuition, nonresident:* full-time $7290; part-time $245 per credit. *Required fees:* full-time $1153; $25 per term part-time. *College room and board:* $4730. Room and board charges vary according to board plan and housing facility.

Institutional Web site http://www.umes.umd.edu/

College life *Housing: Options:* coed, men-only, women-only. *Social organizations:* national fraternities, national sororities, local fraternities, local sororities; 25% of eligible men and 30% of eligible women are members.

Campus security 24-hour emergency response devices and patrols, student patrols, late-night transport-escort service, controlled dormitory access.

Application *Options:* eApply at www.CollegeQuest.com, Common Application, electronic application, early admission, deferred entrance. *Preference* given to state residents. *Application fee:* $25. *Required:* essay or personal statement; high school transcript; minimum 2.5 GPA. *Recommended:* interview.

Standardized tests *Admission: Required:* SAT I or ACT.

Admissions Office Contact

University of Maryland Eastern Shore, Princess Anne, MD 21853-1299. **Fax:** 410-651-7922.

Visit CollegeQuest.com for information on athletics. College video and electronic viewbook available at CollegeQuest.com.

■ *See page 2758 for a narrative description.*

UNIVERSITY OF MARYLAND UNIVERSITY COLLEGE
College Park, Maryland

- **State-supported**, comprehensive, founded 1947
- **Degrees** associate, bachelor's, master's, doctoral, post-master's, and postbachelor's certificates (offers primarily part-time evening and weekend degree programs at more than 30 off-campus locations in Maryland and the Washington, DC area, and more than 180 military communities in Europe and Asia with military enrollment not reflected in this profile; associate of arts program available to military students only)
- **Suburban** campus with easy access to Washington, DC
- **Coed**, 11,507 undergraduate students, 12% full-time, 57% women, 43% men
- **Noncompetitive** entrance level, 100% of applicants were admitted
- **$4416 tuition** and fees (in-state); $5664 (out-of-state)

Part of University System of Maryland.

Students *Undergraduates:* 1,401 full-time, 10,106 part-time. Students come from 54 states and territories, 90 other countries. *The most frequently chosen baccalaureate field is:* interdisciplinary studies. *Graduate:* 4,070 in graduate degree programs.

From out-of-state	21%	Age 25 or older	85%
Transferred in	10%	International students	2%
African Americans	30%	Asian Americans/Pacific Islanders	7%
Hispanic Americans	4%	Native Americans	0.5%

Faculty 720 (% full-time), 100% with terminal degrees.

Expenses (1999–2000) *Tuition, state resident:* full-time $4416; part-time $184 per semester hour. *Tuition, nonresident:* full-time $5664; part-time $236 per semester hour. *Waivers:* senior citizens and employees or children of employees.

Library Information and Library Services plus 1 other. *Collection:* 4,623 titles, 65 serial subscriptions.

College life *Housing:* college housing not available.

Campus security 24-hour emergency response devices and patrols, late-night transport-escort service.

After graduation *Career center:* 1 full-time personnel. Services include interview workshops, resume referral, career counseling, careers library, job bank.

Maryland

Freshmen 1,090 applied, 1,090 admitted, 516 enrolled.

| SAT verbal scores above 500 | N/R | SAT math scores above 500 | N/R |
| ACT above 18 | N/R | | |

Application *Options:* electronic application, deferred entrance. *Application fee:* $30. *Required:* high school transcript.

Significant dates *Application deadlines:* rolling (freshmen), rolling (transfers). *Financial aid deadline priority date:* 6/1.

Freshman Application Contact Ms. Anne Rahill, Technical Director, Admissions, University of Maryland University College, University Boulevard at Adelphi Road, College Park, MD 20742-1600. **Phone:** 301-985-7000. **Toll-free phone:** 800-888-UMUC. **Fax:** 301-985-7678. **E-mail:** umucinfo@nova.umuc.ed

Visit CollegeQuest.com for information on majors offered and athletics.

■ *See pages 2760 for a narrative description.*

VILLA JULIE COLLEGE
Stevenson, Maryland

 Apply at CollegeQuest.com

- **Independent**, comprehensive, founded 1952
- **Degrees** associate, bachelor's, and master's
- **Suburban** 60-acre campus with easy access to Baltimore
- **Coed**, 1,985 undergraduate students, 75% full-time, 72% women, 28% men
- **Moderately difficult** entrance level, 75% of applicants were admitted
- **13:1** student-to-undergraduate faculty ratio
- **48% graduate** in 6 years or less
- **$10,980 tuition** and fees

Students *Undergraduates:* 1,487 full-time, 498 part-time. Students come from 11 states and territories, 3 other countries. *Graduate:* 67 in graduate degree programs.

From out-of-state	2%	Reside on campus	10%
Age 25 or older	30%	Transferred in	7%
International students	0.1%	African Americans	9%
Asian Americans/Pacific Islanders	2%	Hispanic Americans	1%
Native Americans	0.05%		

Faculty 196 (38% full-time), 46% with terminal degrees.

Expenses (1999–2000) *Tuition:* full-time $10,250; part-time $305 per credit. *Required fees:* full-time $730; $30 per term part-time. *College room only:* $3650. *Waivers:* employees or children of employees.

Library Villa Julie College Library. *Collection:* 86,000 titles, 605 serial subscriptions, 2,500 audiovisual materials.

College life *Housing: Option:* coed. *Social organizations:* national sororities. *Most popular organizations:* Student Government Association, Wilderness Club, Black Student Union, National Student Nurses Association, pre-medical club.

Campus security 24-hour emergency response devices, late-night transport-escort service, controlled dormitory access, patrols by trained security personnel during campus hours.

After graduation 60 organizations recruited on campus 1997–98. 99% of class of 1998 had job offers within 6 months. *Career center:* 3 full-time, 2 part-time personnel. Services include job fairs, resume preparation, interview workshops, resume referral, career/interest testing, career counseling, careers library, job bank, job interviews. *Graduate education:* 8% of class of 1999 went directly to graduate and professional school: 5% graduate arts and sciences, 2% law, 1% business.

Freshmen 965 applied, 720 admitted, 430 enrolled.

Average high school GPA	3.3	SAT verbal scores above 500	N/R
SAT math scores above 500	66%	ACT above 18	N/R
1998 freshmen returning in 1999	80%		

Application *Options:* eApply at www.CollegeQuest.com, electronic application, early admission, deferred entrance. *Application fee:* $25. *Required:* essay or personal statement; high school transcript; 2 letters of recommendation; interview. *Recommended:* minimum 3.0 GPA.

Standardized tests *Admission: Required:* SAT I or ACT.

Significant dates *Application deadlines:* 7/15 (freshmen), 7/15 (transfers). *Financial aid deadline priority date:* 3/1.

Freshman Application Contact Mr. Mark Hergan, Director of Admissions, Villa Julie College, 125 Greenspring Valley Road, Stevenson, MD 21153. **Phone:** 410-486-7001. **Toll-free phone:** 877-468-6852 (in-state); 877-468-3852 (out-of-state). **E-mail:** admissions@vjc.edu

Visit CollegeQuest.com for information on majors offered and athletics.

■ *See page 2886 for a narrative description.*

WASHINGTON BIBLE COLLEGE
Lanham, Maryland

- **Independent nondenominational**, 4-year, founded 1938
- **Degrees** associate and bachelor's
- **Suburban** 63-acre campus with easy access to Washington, DC
- **Coed**, 313 undergraduate students, 46% full-time, 41% women, 59% men
- **Moderately difficult** entrance level, 53% of applicants were admitted
- **13:1** student-to-undergraduate faculty ratio
- **60% graduate** in 6 years or less
- **$6460 tuition** and fees

Since 1938, Washington Bible College has been preparing students for God-centered lives and careers through programs that include biblical, general, and professional studies. Located on a 63-acre campus in suburban Maryland, WBC fosters an environment that enables students to grow spiritually, socially, and intellectually.

Students *Undergraduates:* 143 full-time, 170 part-time. Students come from 14 states and territories, 9 other countries. *The most frequently chosen baccalaureate field is:* philosophy.

From out-of-state	24%	Reside on campus	28%
Age 25 or older	63%	Transferred in	16%
International students	4%	African Americans	47%
Asian Americans/Pacific Islanders	7%	Hispanic Americans	1%
Native Americans	0.3%		

Faculty 26 (42% full-time), 19% with terminal degrees.

Expenses (1999–2000) *Comprehensive fee:* $10,710 includes full-time tuition ($6240), mandatory fees ($220), and room and board ($4250). *College room only:* $1770. Room and board charges vary according to board plan. *Part-time tuition:* $260 per credit hour. Part-time tuition and fees vary according to course load and location. *Payment plans:* installment, deferred payment. *Waivers:* employees or children of employees.

Library Oyer Memorial Library plus 1 other. *Collection:* 78,000 titles, 525 serial subscriptions, 3,824 audiovisual materials.

College life *Housing:* on-campus residence required through senior year. *Options:* men-only, women-only. *Most popular organizations:* Student Missions Fellowship, School Choir and Ensemble, Korean Student Fellowship.

Campus security 24-hour patrols, student patrols, late-night transport-escort service, secured campus entrances, trained guards on duty.

After graduation *Career center:* Services include career counseling.

Freshmen 182 applied, 97 admitted, 34 enrolled.

Average high school GPA	2.83	SAT verbal scores above 500	N/R
SAT math scores above 500	N/R	ACT above 18	N/R
From top 10% of their h.s. class	13%	From top quarter	31%
From top half	56%	1998 freshmen returning in 1999	70%

Application *Options:* early admission, deferred entrance. *Application fee:* $15. *Required:* essay or personal statement; high school transcript; 2 letters of recommendation; Christian testimony. *Required for some:* interview.

Standardized tests *Admission: Required:* SAT I or ACT.

Significant dates *Application deadlines:* rolling (freshmen), rolling (transfers). *Notification:* continuous until 8/15 (freshmen). *Financial aid deadline priority date:* 6/1.

Freshman Application Contact Mrs. Shea Kaurin, Director of Admissions, Washington Bible College, 6511 Princess Garden Parkway, Lanham, MD 20706. **Phone:** 301-552-1400 Ext. 213. **Toll-free phone:** 800-787-0256 Ext. 212. **Fax:** 301-552-2775. **E-mail:** admissions@bible.edu

Visit CollegeQuest.com for information on majors offered and athletics.

Maryland

WASHINGTON COLLEGE
Chestertown, Maryland

 Apply at CollegeQuest.com

- **Independent**, comprehensive, founded 1782
- **Degrees** bachelor's and master's
- **Small-town** 120-acre campus with easy access to Baltimore and Washington, DC
- **Coed**, 1,037 undergraduate students, 99% full-time, 59% women, 41% men
- **Moderately difficult** entrance level, 85% of applicants were admitted
- **12:1 student-to-undergraduate faculty ratio**
- **64% graduate** in 6 years or less
- **$20,200 tuition** and fees
- **$17,977 average financial aid** package, $17,278 average indebtedness upon graduation, $88.9 million endowment

Washington College has initiated a $40,000 scholarship program expressly for National Honor Society and Cum Laude Society members. Washington College NHS/CLS Scholarships are $10,000 annual awards renewable through the completion of 8 semesters. To be eligible for scholarship consideration, a student must apply for freshman aid no later than February 15 of the senior year. For more information, students should contact the Admissions Office or visit the WC Web Site at http://www.washcoll.edu.

Students *Undergraduates:* 1,026 full-time, 11 part-time. Students come from 40 states and territories, 42 other countries. *The most frequently chosen baccalaureate fields are:* business/marketing, foreign language/literature, social sciences and history. *Graduate:* 77 in graduate degree programs.

From out-of-state	50%	Reside on campus	80%
Age 25 or older	2%	Transferred in	3%
International students	9%	African Americans	4%
Asian Americans/Pacific Islanders	2%	Hispanic Americans	2%
Native Americans	0.4%		

Faculty 103 (75% full-time), 79% with terminal degrees.

Expenses (1999–2000) *Comprehensive fee:* $25,940 includes full-time tuition ($19,750), mandatory fees ($450), and room and board ($5740). *College room only:* $2600. Full-time tuition and fees vary according to program. Room and board charges vary according to board plan and housing facility. *Part-time tuition:* $3291 per course. *Part-time fees:* $75 per course. Part-time tuition and fees vary according to course load and program. *Payment plan:* installment. *Waivers:* adult students and employees or children of employees.

Library Clifton M. Miller Library. *Operations spending 1999–2000:* $718,000. *Collection:* 217,000 titles, 823 serial subscriptions.

College life *Housing:* on-campus residence required through sophomore year. *Option:* coed. *Social organizations:* national fraternities, national sororities; 25% of eligible men and 25% of eligible women are members. *Most popular organizations:* Writers Union, Student Government Association, Hands Out, Omicron Delta Kappa, Dale Adams Society.

Campus security 24-hour emergency response devices and patrols, student patrols, late-night transport-escort service.

After graduation *Career center:* 2 full-time personnel. Services include job fairs, resume preparation, resume referral, career counseling, careers library, job bank, job interviews. *Graduate education:* 35% of class of 1999 went directly to graduate and professional school.

Freshmen 1,479 applied, 1,264 admitted, 282 enrolled.

Average high school GPA	3.2	SAT verbal scores above 500	78%
SAT math scores above 500	74%	ACT above 18	N/R
From top 10% of their h.s. class	30%	From top quarter	70%
From top half	91%	1998 freshmen returning in 1999	78%

Application *Options:* eApply at www.CollegeQuest.com, Common Application, electronic application, early admission, early decision, deferred entrance. *Application fee:* $40. *Required:* essay or personal statement; high school transcript; 2 letters of recommendation. *Required for some:* interview. *Recommended:* interview.

Standardized tests *Admission: Required:* SAT I or ACT.

Significant dates *Application deadlines:* 2/15 (freshmen), rolling (transfers). *Early decision:* 12/1. *Notification:* continuous until 4/1 (freshmen), 12/15 (early decision). **Financial aid deadline priority date:** 2/15.

Freshman Application Contact
Mr. Kevin Coveney, Vice President for Admissions, Washington College, 300 Washington Avenue, Chestertown, MD 21620-1197. **Phone:** 410-778-7700. **Toll-free phone:** 800-422-1782. **Fax:** 410-778-7287. **E-mail:** admissions_office@washcoll.edu.
Visit CollegeQuest.com for information on majors offered and athletics. College video and electronic viewbook available at CollegeQuest.com.

- *See page 2918 for a narrative description.*

WESTERN MARYLAND COLLEGE
Westminster, Maryland

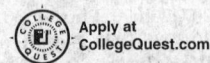 Apply at CollegeQuest.com

- **Independent**, comprehensive, founded 1867
- **Degrees** bachelor's and master's
- **Small-town** 160-acre campus with easy access to Baltimore and Washington, DC
- **Coed**, 1,593 undergraduate students, 98% full-time, 54% women, 46% men
- **Moderately difficult** entrance level, 81% of applicants were admitted
- **13:1 student-to-undergraduate faculty ratio**
- **58.1% graduate** in 6 years or less
- **$19,600 tuition** and fees
- **$17,067 average financial aid** package, $15,799 average indebtedness upon graduation, $48.7 million endowment

Students *Undergraduates:* 1,562 full-time, 31 part-time. Students come from 31 states and territories, 24 other countries. *The most frequently chosen baccalaureate fields are:* business/marketing, psychology, social sciences and history. *Graduate:* 1,692 in graduate degree programs.

From out-of-state	33%	Reside on campus	72%
Age 25 or older	4%	Transferred in	4%
International students	5%	African Americans	5%
Asian Americans/Pacific Islanders	2%	Hispanic Americans	2%
Native Americans	0.1%		

Faculty 162 (52% full-time), 62% with terminal degrees.

Expenses (2000–2001) *One-time required fee:* $300. *Comprehensive fee:* $24,950 includes full-time tuition ($19,600) and room and board ($5350). *College room only:* $2540. Room and board charges vary according to board plan and housing facility. *Part-time tuition:* $613 per semester hour. *Payment plans:* tuition prepayment, installment. *Waivers:* employees or children of employees.

Library Hoover Library. *Operations spending 1999–2000:* $996,427. *Collection:* 198,000 titles, 1,090 serial subscriptions, 5,000 audiovisual materials.

College life *Housing:* on-campus residence required through junior year. *Options:* coed, men-only, women-only. *Social organizations:* national fraternities, national sororities, local fraternities, local sororities; 15% of eligible men and 17% of eligible women are members. *Most popular organizations:* Christian Fellowship, Beta Beta Beta, Cap Bank, SERVE, Black Student Union.

Campus security 24-hour emergency response devices and patrols, student patrols, late-night transport-escort service, controlled dormitory access.

After graduation 118 organizations recruited on campus 1997–98. 75% of class of 1998 had job offers within 6 months. *Career center:* 1 full-time, 1 part-time personnel. Services include job fairs, resume preparation, interview workshops, resume referral, career/interest testing, career counseling, careers library, job bank, job interviews, internship search assistance.

Freshmen 1,717 applied, 1,390 admitted, 412 enrolled. 3 National Merit Scholars, 21 class presidents, 34 valedictorians.

Average high school GPA	3.37	SAT verbal scores above 500	82%
SAT math scores above 500	74%	ACT above 18	N/R
From top 10% of their h.s. class	50%	From top quarter	70%
From top half	93%	1998 freshmen returning in 1999	83%

Application *Options:* eApply at www.CollegeQuest.com, Common Application, electronic application, early admission, early action, deferred entrance. *Application fee:* $40. *Required:* essay or personal statement; high school transcript; minimum 2.5 GPA. *Required for some:* interview. *Recommended:* letters of recommendation; interview.

Standardized tests *Admission: Required:* SAT I or ACT. *Recommended:* SAT II Subject Tests.

Maryland–Massachusetts

Significant dates *Application deadlines:* 3/15 (freshmen), 7/1 (transfers). *Early action:* 12/1. *Notification:* 4/1 (freshmen), 12/15 (early action). *Financial aid deadline priority date:* 3/1.

Freshman Application Contact
Ms. M. Martha O'Connell, Dean of Admissions, Western Maryland College, 2 College Hill, Westminster, MD 21157-4390. **Phone:** 410-857-2230. **Toll-free phone:** 800-638-5005. **Fax:** 410-857-2729. **E-mail:** admissio@ns1.wmc.car.md.us

Visit CollegeQuest.com for information on majors offered and athletics.

■ *See page 2948 for a narrative description.*

MASSACHUSETTS

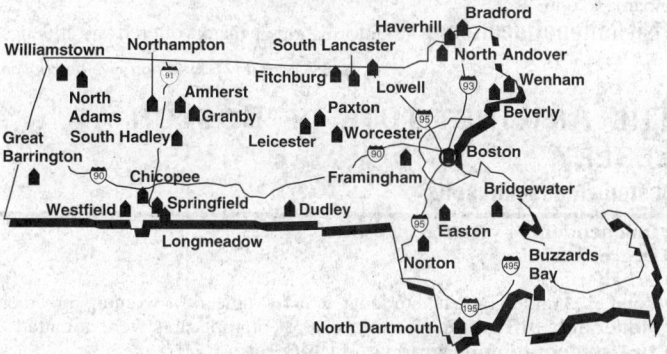

The Boston area includes the towns of Babson Park, Brighton, Brookline, Chestnut Hill, Cambridge, Medford, Milton, Newton, Newton Centre, Quincy, Salem, Waltham, Wellesley, and Weston.

AMERICAN INTERNATIONAL COLLEGE
Springfield, Massachusetts

- **Independent**, comprehensive, founded 1885
- **Degrees** associate, bachelor's, master's, doctoral, and post-master's certificates
- **Urban** 58-acre campus
- **Coed**, 1,236 undergraduate students, 87% full-time, 53% women, 47% men
- **Moderately difficult** entrance level, 81% of applicants were admitted
- **15:1** student-to-undergraduate faculty ratio
- **45% graduate** in 6 years or less
- **$12,900 tuition** and fees
- **$12,600 average financial aid** package, $17,000 average indebtedness upon graduation, $13.4 million endowment

Students *Undergraduates:* 1,074 full-time, 162 part-time. Students come from 26 states and territories, 52 other countries. *The most frequently chosen baccalaureate fields are:* business/marketing, health professions and related sciences, protective services/public administration. *Graduate:* 501 in graduate degree programs.

From out-of-state	41%	Reside on campus	58%
Age 25 or older	25%	Transferred in	15%
International students	5%	African Americans	19%
Asian Americans/Pacific Islanders	2%	Hispanic Americans	7%
Native Americans	0.2%		

Faculty 122 (61% full-time), 57% with terminal degrees.

Expenses (1999–2000) *Comprehensive fee:* $19,548 includes full-time tuition ($12,900) and room and board ($6648). *Part-time tuition:* $315 per credit. *Part-time fees:* $25 per term part-time. *Payment plans:* tuition prepayment, installment, deferred payment. *Waivers:* senior citizens and employees or children of employees.

Library James J. Shea Jr. Library. *Operations spending 1999–2000:* $481,286. *Collection:* 118,000 titles, 390 serial subscriptions.

College life *Housing:* on-campus residence required through sophomore year. *Options:* coed, men-only, women-only. *Social organizations:* national fraternities, national sororities, local fraternities, local sororities; 20% of eligible men and 21% of eligible women are members. *Most popular organizations:* student activities committee, Golden Key Society, PRIDE (Persons Ready in Defense of Ebony), student government.

Campus security 24-hour emergency response devices and patrols, student patrols, late-night transport-escort service, controlled dormitory access.

After graduation 45 organizations recruited on campus 1997–98. 85% of class of 1998 had job offers within 6 months. *Career center:* 3 full-time personnel. Services include job fairs, resume preparation, resume referral, career/interest testing, career counseling, careers library, job bank, job interviews. *Graduate education:* 25% of class of 1999 went directly to graduate and professional school: 8% business, 8% education, 4% law, 3% graduate arts and sciences, 1% dentistry, 1% medicine.

Freshmen 1,145 applied, 932 admitted, 253 enrolled. 16 class presidents, 2 valedictorians, 114 student government officers.

Average high school GPA	2.75	SAT verbal scores above 500	45%
SAT math scores above 500	54%	ACT above 18	N/R
From top 10% of their h.s. class	8%	From top quarter	37%
From top half	75%	1998 freshmen returning in 1999	62%

Application *Options:* Common Application, early admission, early decision, deferred entrance. *Application fee:* $20. *Required:* high school transcript; 1 letter of recommendation. *Required for some:* interview. *Recommended:* interview.

Standardized tests *Admission: Required:* SAT I or ACT.

Significant dates *Application deadlines:* rolling (freshmen), rolling (transfers). *Early decision:* 11/15. *Notification:* 12/15 (early decision). *Financial aid deadline priority date:* 4/1.

Freshman Application Contact
Mr. Peter Miller, Dean of Admissions, American International College, 1000 State Street, Springfield, MA 01109-3189. **Phone:** 413-747-6201. **Toll-free phone:** 800-242-3142. **Fax:** 413-737-2803. **E-mail:** inquiry@www.aic.edu

Visit CollegeQuest.com for information on majors offered and athletics. College video available at CollegeQuest.com.

■ *See page 1162 for a narrative description.*

AMHERST COLLEGE
Amherst, Massachusetts

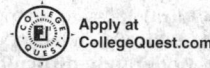
Apply at CollegeQuest.com

- **Independent**, 4-year, founded 1821
- **Degree** bachelor's
- **Small-town** 964-acre campus
- **Coed**, 1,664 undergraduate students, 100% full-time, 48% women, 52% men
- **Most difficult** entrance level, 19% of applicants were admitted
- **9:1** student-to-undergraduate faculty ratio
- **97% graduate** in 6 years or less
- **$25,259 tuition** and fees
- **$22,705 average financial aid** package, $12,340 average indebtedness upon graduation, $634.5 million endowment

Students *Undergraduates:* 1,664 full-time. Students come from 52 states and territories, 29 other countries. *The most frequently chosen baccalaureate fields are:* English, foreign language/literature, social sciences and history.

From out-of-state	86%	Reside on campus	98%
Transferred in	0.3%	International students	4%
African Americans	6%	Asian Americans/Pacific Islanders	12%
Hispanic Americans	7%	Native Americans	0.3%

Faculty 200 (90% full-time), 93% with terminal degrees.

Expenses (1999–2000) *Comprehensive fee:* $31,819 includes full-time tuition ($24,800), mandatory fees ($459), and room and board ($6560). *College room only:* $3280. *Payment plans:* installment, deferred payment.

Library Robert Frost Library plus 5 others. *Operations spending 1999–2000:* $3.8 million. *Collection:* 866,452 titles, 5,053 serial subscriptions, 53,126 audiovisual materials.

College life *Housing:* on-campus residence required in freshman year. *Options:* coed, cooperative. *Most popular organizations:* choral groups, WAMH (campus radio station), OUTREACH (Community Service), literary magazines, The Amherst Student (school newspaper).

Campus security 24-hour emergency response devices and patrols, student patrols, late-night transport-escort service, controlled dormitory access.

Massachusetts

Amherst College *(continued)*

After graduation 65 organizations recruited on campus 1997–98. 63% of class of 1998 had job offers within 6 months. *Career center:* 6 full-time, 1 part-time personnel. Services include job fairs, resume preparation, interview workshops, resume referral, career/interest testing, career counseling, careers library, job bank, job interviews. *Graduate education:* 30% of class of 1999 went directly to graduate and professional school. *Major awards:* 1 Rhodes scholar.

Freshmen 5,198 applied, 999 admitted, 422 enrolled. 84 National Merit Scholars, 49 valedictorians.

SAT verbal scores above 500	99%
ACT above 18	100%
From top quarter	98%
1998 freshmen returning in 1999	97%
SAT math scores above 500	99%
From top 10% of their h.s. class	87%
From top half	100%

Application *Options:* eApply at www.CollegeQuest.com, Common Application, early decision, deferred entrance. *Application fee:* $55. *Required:* essay or personal statement; high school transcript; 3 letters of recommendation.

Standardized tests *Admission: Required:* SAT I or ACT, 3 SAT II Subject Tests. *Recommended:* SAT II: Writing Test.

Significant dates *Application deadlines:* 12/31 (freshmen), 2/1 (transfers). *Early decision:* 11/15. *Notification:* 4/15 (freshmen), 12/15 (early decision). *Financial aid deadline priority date:* 2/1.

Freshman Application Contact
Mr. Thomas Parker, Dean of Admission and Financial Aid, Amherst College, PO Box 5000, Amherst, MA 01002. **Phone:** 413-542-2328. **Fax:** 413-542-2040. **E-mail:** admissions@amherst.edu

Visit CollegeQuest.com for information on majors offered and athletics.

ANNA MARIA COLLEGE
Paxton, Massachusetts

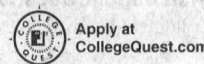 Apply at CollegeQuest.com

- **Independent Roman Catholic**, comprehensive, founded 1946
- **Degrees** associate, bachelor's, master's, and post-master's certificates
- **Rural** 180-acre campus with easy access to Boston
- **Coed**, 694 undergraduate students, 71% full-time, 64% women, 36% men
- **Moderately difficult** entrance level, 85% of applicants were admitted
- **13:1** student-to-undergraduate faculty ratio
- **74% graduate** in 6 years or less
- **$12,950 tuition** and fees
- **$11,354 average financial aid** package, $1.7 million endowment

Students *Undergraduates:* 495 full-time, 199 part-time. Students come from 13 states and territories, 8 other countries. *The most frequently chosen baccalaureate fields are:* business/marketing, education, protective services/public administration. *Graduate:* 574 in graduate degree programs.

From out-of-state	22%	Reside on campus	66%
Age 25 or older	29%	Transferred in	6%
International students	2%	African Americans	1%
Asian Americans/Pacific Islanders	2%	Hispanic Americans	3%
Native Americans	0.1%		

Faculty 196 (18% full-time), 39% with terminal degrees.

Expenses (1999–2000) *Comprehensive fee:* $18,900 includes full-time tuition ($12,200), mandatory fees ($750), and room and board ($5950). Full-time tuition and fees vary according to program. *Part-time tuition:* $590 per course. *Payment plans:* guaranteed tuition, installment. *Waivers:* children of alumni, senior citizens, and employees or children of employees.

Library Mondor-Eagen Library. *Operations spending 1999–2000:* $192,157. *Collection:* 110,586 titles, 288 serial subscriptions.

College life *Housing: Option:* coed. *Most popular organizations:* Student Government Association, drama club, ski club, chorus, criminal justice club.

Campus security 24-hour emergency response devices and patrols, late-night transport-escort service, controlled dormitory access.

After graduation *Career center:* 1 full-time, 1 part-time personnel. Services include resume preparation, interview workshops, career/interest testing, career counseling, careers library, job bank.

Freshmen 502 applied, 427 admitted, 134 enrolled.

Average high school GPA	2.7	SAT verbal scores above 500	45%
SAT math scores above 500	38%	ACT above 18	N/R
From top 10% of their h.s. class	2%	From top quarter	13%
From top half	42%	1998 freshmen returning in 1999	80%

Application *Options:* eApply at www.CollegeQuest.com, early admission, deferred entrance. *Application fee:* $30. *Required:* essay or personal statement; high school transcript; 2 letters of recommendation. *Required for some:* audition for music programs, portfolio for art programs. *Recommended:* minimum 2 GPA; interview.

Standardized tests *Admission: Required:* SAT I or ACT.

Significant dates *Application deadlines:* rolling (freshmen), rolling (transfers). *Financial aid deadline priority date:* 3/15.

Freshman Application Contact
Ms. Laurie Peltier, Director of Admissions, Anna Maria College, Box O, Sunset Lane, Paxton, MA 01612. **Phone:** 508-849-3360. **E-mail:** admissions@annamaria.edu

Visit CollegeQuest.com for information on majors offered and athletics.

■ *See page 1176 for a narrative description.*

THE ART INSTITUTE OF BOSTON AT LESLEY
Boston, Massachusetts

- **Independent**, 4-year, founded 1912
- **Degree** bachelor's
- **Urban** campus
- **Coed**, 472 undergraduate students, 92% full-time, 50% women, 50% men
- **Moderately difficult** entrance level, 35% of applicants were admitted
- **10:1** student-to-undergraduate faculty ratio
- **$13,970 tuition** and fees
- **$28.5 million endowment**

Students *Undergraduates:* 434 full-time, 38 part-time. Students come from 28 states and territories, 27 other countries. *The most frequently chosen baccalaureate field is:* visual/performing arts.

From out-of-state	36%	Reside on campus	15%
Age 25 or older	57%	Transferred in	19%
International students	15%	African Americans	1%
Asian Americans/Pacific Islanders	1%	Hispanic Americans	3%

Faculty 102 (22% full-time), 65% with terminal degrees.

Expenses (1999–2000) *Comprehensive fee:* $21,920 includes full-time tuition ($13,250), mandatory fees ($720), and room and board ($7950). Full-time tuition and fees vary according to program. Room and board charges vary according to housing facility. *Part-time tuition:* $520 per credit. *Part-time fees:* $230 per term part-time. Part-time tuition and fees vary according to program. *Payment plan:* installment. *Waivers:* adult students, senior citizens, and employees or children of employees.

Library The Art Institute of Boston Library plus 1 other. *Operations spending 1999–2000:* $98,518. *Collection:* 9,015 titles, 77 serial subscriptions, 365 audiovisual materials.

College life *Housing: Option:* coed. *Most popular organizations:* Peer Advisors, International Student Association, Student Gallery Committee, Literary Journal.

Campus security 24-hour emergency response devices, student patrols, controlled dormitory access.

After graduation *Career center:* Services include careers library, job bank.

Freshmen 675 applied, 235 admitted, 112 enrolled.

Average high school GPA	2.77	SAT verbal scores above 500	53%
SAT math scores above 500	44%	ACT above 18	N/R
1998 freshmen returning in 1999	62%		

Application *Options:* Common Application, deferred entrance. *Application fee:* $30. *Required:* essay or personal statement; high school transcript; portfolio. *Recommended:* minimum 2.0 GPA; letters of recommendation; interview.

Standardized tests *Admission: Required:* SAT I or ACT.

Significant dates *Application deadlines:* rolling (freshmen), rolling (transfers). *Financial aid deadline priority date:* 3/14.

Massachusetts

Freshman Application Contact
Mr. Brad White, Director of Admissions, The Art Institute of Boston at Lesley, 700 Beacon Street, Boston, MA 02215-2598. **Phone:** 617-262-1223 Ext. 304. **Toll-free phone:** 800-773-0494. **Fax:** 617-437-1226. **E-mail:** admissions@aiboston.edu

Visit CollegeQuest.com for information on majors offered and athletics.

■ *See page 1190 for a narrative description.*

ASSUMPTION COLLEGE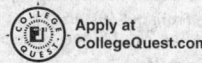
Worcester, Massachusetts

- **Independent Roman Catholic**, comprehensive, founded 1904
- **Degrees** associate, bachelor's, master's, and post-master's certificates
- **Urban** 145-acre campus with easy access to Boston
- **Coed**, 2,352 undergraduate students, 81% full-time, 65% women, 35% men
- **Moderately difficult** entrance level, 74% of applicants were admitted
- **14:1 student-to-undergraduate faculty ratio**
- **63% graduate** in 6 years or less
- **$17,490 tuition** and fees
- **$13,065 average financial aid** package, $16,400 average indebtedness upon graduation, $33.3 million endowment

Students *Undergraduates:* 1,903 full-time, 449 part-time. Students come from 20 states and territories, 9 other countries. *The most frequently chosen baccalaureate fields are:* business/marketing, health professions and related sciences, social sciences and history. *Graduate:* 342 in graduate degree programs.

From out-of-state	29%	Reside on campus	87%
Age 25 or older	1%	Transferred in	1%
International students	1%	African Americans	1%
Asian Americans/Pacific Islanders	1%	Hispanic Americans	1%
Native Americans	0.04%		

Faculty 242 (46% full-time), 69% with terminal degrees.
Expenses (1999–2000) *Comprehensive fee:* $24,250 includes full-time tuition ($17,320), mandatory fees ($170), and room and board ($6760). *College room only:* $4140. Full-time tuition and fees vary according to course load and reciprocity agreements. Room and board charges vary according to board plan and housing facility. *Part-time tuition:* $577 per credit. *Part-time fees:* $170 per year part-time. Part-time tuition and fees vary according to course load and student level. *Payment plan:* installment. *Waivers:* minority students and employees or children of employees.
Library Emmanuel D'alzon Library. *Operations spending 1999–2000:* $862,857. *Collection:* 176,587 titles, 1,135 serial subscriptions, 1,155 audiovisual materials.
College life *Housing: Options:* coed, women-only. *Most popular organizations:* Volunteer Center, Campus Activities Board, student government, Campus Ministry, college chorale.
Campus security 24-hour emergency response devices and patrols, student patrols, late-night transport-escort service, front gate security, well-lit pathways.
After graduation 105 organizations recruited on campus 1997–98. 86% of class of 1998 had job offers within 6 months. *Career center:* 2 full-time personnel. Services include job fairs, resume preparation, interview workshops, career/interest testing, career counseling, careers library, job bank, job interviews, time management workshops.
Freshmen 2,639 applied, 1,948 admitted, 492 enrolled.

SAT verbal scores above 500	74%	SAT math scores above 500	67%
ACT above 18	94%	From top 10% of their h.s. class	13%
From top quarter	42%	From top half	80%
1998 freshmen returning in 1999	85%		

Application *Options:* eApply at www.CollegeQuest.com, Common Application, electronic application, early admission, early decision, deferred entrance. *Application fee:* $40. *Required:* high school transcript; 1 letter of recommendation. *Recommended:* essay or personal statement; interview.
Standardized tests *Admission: Required:* SAT I or ACT.
Significant dates *Application deadlines:* 3/1 (freshmen), 5/1 (transfers). *Early decision:* 11/1. *Notification:* continuous until 5/1 (freshmen), 12/15 (early decision). *Financial aid deadline:* 3/1. Priority date: 2/1.

Freshman Application Contact
Ms. Mary Bresnahan, Dean of Admission, Assumption College, 500 Salisbury Street, PO Box 15005, Worcester, MA 01615-0005. **Phone:** 508-767-7362. **Toll-free phone:** 888-882-7786. **Fax:** 508-799-4412. **E-mail:** admiss@assumption.edu

Visit CollegeQuest.com for information on majors offered and athletics. College video available at CollegeQuest.com.

■ *See page 1200 for a narrative description.*

ATLANTIC UNION COLLEGE
South Lancaster, Massachusetts

- **Independent Seventh-day Adventist**, comprehensive, founded 1882
- **Degrees** associate, bachelor's, and master's
- **Small-town** 314-acre campus with easy access to Boston
- **Coed**, 661 undergraduate students, 70% full-time, 58% women, 42% men
- **Moderately difficult** entrance level, 42% of applicants were admitted
- **$12,634 tuition** and fees
- **$12,050 average financial aid** package, $13,319 average indebtedness upon graduation, $1.7 million endowment

Students *Undergraduates:* 460 full-time, 201 part-time. Students come from 20 states and territories, 21 other countries. *Graduate:* 81 in graduate degree programs.

From out-of-state	85%	Reside on campus	68%
Age 25 or older	88%	International students	6%
African Americans	32%	Asian Americans/Pacific Islanders	1%
Hispanic Americans	16%	Native Americans	0.5%

Faculty 42 (90% full-time), 55% with terminal degrees.
Expenses (1999–2000) *Comprehensive fee:* $16,654 includes full-time tuition ($11,904), mandatory fees ($730), and room and board ($4020). *College room only:* $2160. Full-time tuition and fees vary according to class time and program. Room and board charges vary according to board plan and housing facility. *Part-time tuition:* $496 per hour. *Payment plan:* installment. *Waivers:* senior citizens and employees or children of employees.
Library G. Eric Jones Library. *Operations spending 1999–2000:* $448,696. *Collection:* 126,475 titles, 828 serial subscriptions.
College life *Housing:* on-campus residence required through senior year. *Options:* coed, men-only, women-only. *Most popular organizations:* Student Association, Black Christian Union, choir, CHISPA (Hispanic group).
Campus security 24-hour patrols, late-night transport-escort service.
After graduation *Career center:* 1 full-time, 1 part-time personnel. Services include job fairs, resume preparation, career counseling, job bank, job interviews. *Graduate education:* 10% of class of 1999 went directly to graduate and professional school.
Freshmen 485 applied, 202 admitted, 122 enrolled.

SAT verbal scores above 500	N/R	SAT math scores above 500	N/R
ACT above 18	N/R	1998 freshmen returning in 1999	75%

Application *Option:* Common Application. *Application fee:* $25. *Required:* high school transcript; minimum 2.0 GPA; 2 letters of recommendation. *Required for some:* essay or personal statement; interview. *Recommended:* essay or personal statement.
Standardized tests *Placement: Required:* ACT. *Recommended:* SAT I.
Significant dates *Application deadlines:* 8/1 (freshmen), 8/1 (transfers). *Financial aid deadline priority date:* 4/1.

Freshman Application Contact
Mrs. Rosita Lashley, Associate Director for Admissions, Atlantic Union College, PO Box 1000, South Lancaster, MA 01561. **Phone:** 978-368-2239. **Toll-free phone:** 800-282-2030. **Fax:** 978-368-2015. **E-mail:** enroll@math.atlanticuc.edu

Visit CollegeQuest.com for information on majors offered and athletics.

BABSON COLLEGE
Wellesley, Massachusetts

- **Independent**, comprehensive, founded 1919
- **Degrees** bachelor's and master's
- **Suburban** 450-acre campus with easy access to Boston

Peterson's Guide to Four-Year Colleges 2001 • www.petersons.com

Massachusetts

Babson College (continued)
- **Coed**, 1,701 undergraduate students, 100% full-time, 36% women, 64% men
- **Very difficult** entrance level, 45% of applicants were admitted
- **11:1 student-to-undergraduate faculty ratio**
- **$21,952 tuition** and fees
- **$16,903 average financial aid** package, $20,000 average indebtedness upon graduation, $149.6 million endowment

Students *Undergraduates:* 1,701 full-time. Students come from 40 states and territories, 70 other countries. *The most frequently chosen baccalaureate field is:* business/marketing. *Graduate:* 1,730 in graduate degree programs.

From out-of-state	38%	Reside on campus	85%
Age 25 or older	1%	Transferred in	3%
International students	19%	African Americans	2%
Asian Americans/Pacific Islanders	6%	Hispanic Americans	4%
Native Americans	0.3%		

Faculty 192 (83% full-time), 91% with terminal degrees.

Expenses (2000–2001, estimated) *Comprehensive fee:* $30,698 includes full-time tuition ($21,952) and room and board ($8746). *College room only:* $5640. Full-time tuition and fees vary according to course load. Room and board charges vary according to board plan and housing facility. *Payment plan:* installment. *Waivers:* employees or children of employees.

Library Horn Library plus 1 other. *Operations spending 1999–2000:* $1.9 million. *Collection:* 90,543 titles, 1,510 serial subscriptions, 3,883 audiovisual materials.

College life *Housing:* on-campus residence required in freshman year. *Options:* coed, men-only, disabled students. *Social organizations:* national fraternities, national sororities; 10% of eligible men and 10% of eligible women are members. *Most popular organizations:* student government, Babson Free Press, admission assistant program, Babson Dance Ensemble, Campus Activities Board.

Campus security 24-hour emergency response devices and patrols, late-night transport-escort service.

After graduation 479 organizations recruited on campus 1997–98. 95% of class of 1998 had job offers within 6 months. *Career center:* 7 full-time personnel. Services include job fairs, resume preparation, interview workshops, resume referral, career/interest testing, career counseling, careers library, job bank, job interviews. *Graduate education:* 2% of class of 1999 went directly to graduate and professional school: 2% law.

Freshmen 2,582 applied, 1,170 admitted, 414 enrolled. 18 class presidents, 100 student government officers.

SAT verbal scores above 500	92%	SAT math scores above 500	79%
ACT above 18	N/R	From top 10% of their h.s. class	29%
From top quarter	71%	From top half	92%
1998 freshmen returning in 1999	90%		

Application *Options:* eApply at www.CollegeQuest.com, Common Application, electronic application, early decision, early action, deferred entrance. *Application fee:* $50. *Required:* essay or personal statement; high school transcript; 2 letters of recommendation. *Recommended:* interview.

Standardized tests *Admission: Required:* SAT I or ACT.

Significant dates *Application deadlines:* 2/1 (freshmen), 4/1 (transfers). *Early decision:* 12/1 (for plan 1), 1/1 (for plan 2), 12/1. *Notification:* 4/1 (freshmen), 1/1 (early decision plan 1), 2/1 (early decision plan 2), 1/1 (early action). *Financial aid deadline:* 2/15.

Freshman Application Contact
Ms. Amy Reuben, Acting Dean of Undergraduate Admission, Babson College, Office of Undergraduate Admissions, Mustard Hall, Babson Park, MA 02457-0310. **Phone:** 781-239-5522. **Toll-free phone:** 800-488-3696. **Fax:** 781-239-5614. **E-mail:** ugradadmission@babson.edu

Visit CollegeQuest.com for information on majors offered and athletics. College video available at CollegeQuest.com.

■ *See page 1218 for a narrative description.*

BAY PATH COLLEGE
Longmeadow, Massachusetts

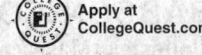
Apply at CollegeQuest.com

- **Independent**, 4-year, founded 1897
- **Degrees** associate and bachelor's
- **Suburban** 44-acre campus with easy access to Boston
- **Women** only, 656 undergraduate students, 66% full-time
- **Moderately difficult** entrance level
- **10:1 student-to-undergraduate faculty ratio**
- **$13,010 tuition** and fees
- **$12,700 average financial aid** package, $21.1 million endowment

Students *Undergraduates:* Students come from 12 states and territories, 9 other countries. *The most frequently chosen baccalaureate fields are:* business/marketing, (pre)law, psychology.

From out-of-state	44%	Reside on campus	40%
Age 25 or older	37%		

Faculty 68 (41% full-time), 46% with terminal degrees.

Expenses (1999–2000) *One-time required fee:* $250. *Comprehensive fee:* $19,874 includes full-time tuition ($13,010) and room and board ($6864). Full-time tuition and fees vary according to course load. Room and board charges vary according to board plan. *Part-time tuition:* $350 per credit. Part-time tuition and fees vary according to course load. *Payment plans:* tuition prepayment, installment, deferred payment. *Waivers:* employees or children of employees.

Library Frank and Marion Hatch Library. *Operations spending 1999–2000:* $223,362. *Collection:* 40,317 titles, 315 serial subscriptions, 1,134 audiovisual materials.

College life *Housing: Option:* women-only. *Most popular organizations:* student government, Theater Workshop, Golden Z Service Club, Phi Beta Lambda, Ambassador Club.

Campus security 24-hour emergency response devices and patrols, late-night transport-escort service, controlled dormitory access.

After graduation 26 organizations recruited on campus 1997–98. 68% of class of 1998 had job offers within 6 months. *Career center:* 1 full-time, 1 part-time personnel. Services include job fairs, resume preparation, interview workshops, resume referral, career counseling, careers library, job bank, job interviews. *Graduate education:* 17% of class of 1999 went directly to graduate and professional school.

Freshmen

Average high school GPA	2.8	SAT verbal scores above 500	N/R
SAT math scores above 500	N/R	ACT above 18	N/R
1998 freshmen returning in 1999	79%		

Application *Options:* eApply at www.CollegeQuest.com, Common Application, electronic application, early admission, early action, deferred entrance. *Application fee:* $25. *Required:* high school transcript; 2 letters of recommendation. *Required for some:* essay or personal statement; minimum 2.3 GPA; interview. *Recommended:* minimum 2.0 GPA; interview.

Standardized tests *Admission: Required:* SAT I or ACT.

Significant dates *Application deadlines:* rolling (freshmen), rolling (transfers). *Early action:* 12/1. *Notification:* 12/15 (early action). *Financial aid deadline priority date:* 3/15.

Freshman Application Contact
Mr. William F. Campanella, Dean of Enrollment Services, Bay Path College, 588 Longmeadow Street, Longmeadow, MA 01106-2292. **Phone:** 413-565-1000 Ext. 335. **Toll-free phone:** 800-782-7284. **Fax:** 413-567-0501. **E-mail:** admiss@baypath.edu

Visit CollegeQuest.com for information on majors offered and athletics. Electronic viewbook available at CollegeQuest.com.

■ *See page 1238 for a narrative description.*

BECKER COLLEGE
Worcester, Massachusetts

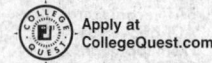
Apply at CollegeQuest.com

- **Independent**, 4-year, founded 1784
- **Degrees** associate and bachelor's (also includes Leicester, MA small town campus)
- **Urban** campus with easy access to Boston
- **Coed**, 1,010 undergraduate students, 83% full-time, 75% women, 25% men
- **Minimally difficult** entrance level, 81% of applicants were admitted
- **15:1 student-to-undergraduate faculty ratio**
- **$11,710 tuition** and fees
- **$6756 average financial aid** package, $16,410 average indebtedness upon graduation, $11 million endowment

Massachusetts

Becker College's small classes and supportive academic atmosphere offer students the individual attention and recognition they deserve. The 2 campuses allow students the unique opportunity to choose the environment that best suits their personal tastes: an urban neighborhood setting or a small New England town.

Students *Undergraduates:* 834 full-time, 176 part-time. Students come from 18 states and territories. *The most frequently chosen baccalaureate fields are:* business/marketing, (pre)law, psychology.

From out-of-state	28%	Reside on campus	60%
Age 25 or older	9%	Transferred in	8%
African Americans	5%	Asian Americans/Pacific Islanders	3%
Hispanic Americans	4%	Native Americans	0.4%

Faculty 101 (43% full-time), 17% with terminal degrees.

Expenses (1999–2000) *Comprehensive fee:* $17,540 includes full-time tuition ($11,490), mandatory fees ($220), and room and board ($5830). Full-time tuition and fees vary according to class time, course load, and program. *Part-time tuition:* $383 per credit. Part-time tuition and fees vary according to class time, course load, and program. *Payment plan:* installment. *Waivers:* senior citizens and employees or children of employees.

Library Ruska Library plus 1 other. *Operations spending 1999–2000:* $301,066. *Collection:* 65,000 titles, 400 serial subscriptions, 2,900 audiovisual materials.

College life *Housing:* on-campus residence required in freshman year. *Options:* coed, men-only, women-only. *Most popular organizations:* student government, Student Activities Committee, travel club, ski club, drama club.

Campus security 24-hour emergency response devices and patrols, late-night transport-escort service, controlled dormitory access.

After graduation 55% of class of 1998 had job offers within 6 months. *Career center:* 1 full-time personnel. Services include job fairs, resume preparation, interview workshops, career/interest testing, career counseling, careers library, job bank, job interviews. *Graduate education:* 13% of class of 1999 went directly to graduate and professional school.

Freshmen 1,556 applied, 1,262 admitted, 420 enrolled.

Average high school GPA	2.5	SAT verbal scores above 500	N/R
SAT math scores above 500	N/R	ACT above 18	N/R
1998 freshmen returning in 1999	87%		

Application *Options:* eApply at www.CollegeQuest.com, Common Application, deferred entrance. *Application fee:* $25. *Required:* high school transcript; minimum 2.0 GPA. *Required for some:* interview. *Recommended:* essay or personal statement; letters of recommendation.

Standardized tests *Admission: Required:* SAT I or ACT.

Significant dates *Application deadlines:* rolling (freshmen), rolling (transfers). *Financial aid deadline priority date:* 4/1.

Freshman Application Contact
Ms. Shannon Sutton, Admissions Receptionist, Becker College, 61 Sever Street, Worcester, MA 01609. **Phone:** 508-791-9241 Ext. 245. **Toll-free phone:** 877-5BECKER Ext. 245. **Fax:** 508-831-7505. **E-mail:** admissions@beckercollege.edu

Visit CollegeQuest.com for information on majors offered and athletics.

■ *See page 1242 for a narrative description.*

BENTLEY COLLEGE
Waltham, Massachusetts

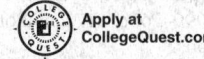 Apply at CollegeQuest.com

- **Independent**, comprehensive, founded 1917
- **Degrees** associate, bachelor's, and master's
- **Suburban** 143-acre campus with easy access to Boston
- **Coed**, 4,114 undergraduate students, 84% full-time, 42% women, 58% men
- **Moderately difficult** entrance level, 57% of applicants were admitted
- **16:1 student-to-undergraduate faculty ratio**
- **74% graduate** in 6 years or less
- **$18,910 tuition** and fees
- **$16,899 average financial aid** package, $17,438 average indebtedness upon graduation, $136.9 million endowment

Students *Undergraduates:* 3,446 full-time, 668 part-time. Students come from 38 states and territories, 64 other countries. *The most frequently chosen baccalaureate fields are:* business/marketing, computer/information sciences, interdisciplinary studies. *Graduate:* 1,500 in graduate degree programs.

From out-of-state	40%	Reside on campus	74%
Age 25 or older	14%	Transferred in	3%
International students	8%	African Americans	3%
Asian Americans/Pacific Islanders	7%	Hispanic Americans	2%
Native Americans	0.1%		

Faculty 224 (100% full-time), 82% with terminal degrees.

Expenses (2000–2001) *Comprehensive fee:* $27,510 includes full-time tuition ($18,795), mandatory fees ($115), and room and board ($8600). *College room only:* $4740. Room and board charges vary according to board plan and housing facility. Part-time tuition and fees vary according to class time. *Payment plan:* installment. *Waivers:* employees or children of employees.

Library Soloman R. Baker Library. *Operations spending 1999–2000:* $1.4 million. *Collection:* 208,956 titles, 9,319 serial subscriptions.

College life *Social organizations:* national fraternities, national sororities, local fraternities. *Most popular organizations:* Student Government Association, Campus Activities Board, Hall Council Advisory Board, Greek Council, WBTY.

Campus security 24-hour emergency response devices and patrols, late-night transport-escort service, controlled dormitory access, security cameras.

After graduation 286 organizations recruited on campus 1997–98. 94% of class of 1998 had job offers within 6 months. *Career center:* 9 full-time, 1 part-time personnel. Services include job fairs, resume preparation, resume referral, career counseling, careers library, job bank, job interviews.

Freshmen 4,600 applied, 2,622 admitted, 916 enrolled.

SAT verbal scores above 500	72%	SAT math scores above 500	86%
ACT above 18	86%	From top 10% of their h.s. class	20%
From top quarter	54%	From top half	90%
1998 freshmen returning in 1999	91%		

Application *Options:* eApply at www.CollegeQuest.com, Common Application, electronic application, early admission, early decision, early action, deferred entrance. *Application fee:* $35. *Required:* essay or personal statement; high school transcript; 2 letters of recommendation. *Recommended:* interview.

Standardized tests *Admission: Required:* SAT I or ACT.

Significant dates *Application deadlines:* 2/15 (freshmen), 5/15 (transfers). *Early decision:* 12/1, 12/1. *Notification:* 4/1 (freshmen), 12/29 (early decision), 1/26 (early action). *Financial aid deadline:* 2/1.

Freshman Application Contact
Ms. M.J. Knoll, Director of Admission, Bentley College, 175 Forest Street, Waltham, MA 02452-4705. **Phone:** 781-891-2244. **Toll-free phone:** 800-523-2354. **Fax:** 781-891-3414. **E-mail:** ugadmission@bentley.edu

Visit CollegeQuest.com for information on majors offered and athletics. College video available at CollegeQuest.com.

■ *See page 1256 for a narrative description.*

BERKLEE COLLEGE OF MUSIC
Boston, Massachusetts

- **Independent**, 4-year, founded 1945
- **Degree** bachelor's
- **Urban** campus
- **Coed**, 3,012 undergraduate students, 90% full-time, 23% women, 77% men
- **Moderately difficult** entrance level, 76% of applicants were admitted
- **12:1 student-to-undergraduate faculty ratio**
- **$16,627 tuition** and fees
- **$123.4 million endowment**

Students *Undergraduates:* 2,706 full-time, 306 part-time. Students come from 45 states and territories, 44 other countries. *The most frequently chosen baccalaureate field is:* visual/performing arts.

From out-of-state	79%	Reside on campus	25%
Age 25 or older	14%	Transferred in	9%
International students	35%	African Americans	4%
Asian Americans/Pacific Islanders	2%	Hispanic Americans	3%
Native Americans	0.2%		

Peterson's Guide to Four-Year Colleges 2001   www.petersons.com

Massachusetts

Berklee College of Music (continued)
Faculty 391 (40% full-time).
Expenses (2000–2001) *One-time required fee:* $250. *Comprehensive fee:* $25,517 includes full-time tuition ($16,590), mandatory fees ($37), and room and board ($8890). *Payment plan:* installment. *Waivers:* employees or children of employees.
Library The Stan Getz Media Center and Library. *Operations spending 1999–2000:* $644,500. *Collection:* 35,000 titles, 77 serial subscriptions.
College life *Housing: Option:* coed. *Most popular organizations:* Musical Theater at Berklee Club, Yoga Society, Black Student Union, Christian Fellowship.
Campus security 24-hour patrols.
After graduation 4 organizations recruited on campus 1997–98. *Career center:* 2 full-time, 2 part-time personnel. Services include job fairs, resume preparation, interview workshops, resume referral, career/interest testing, career counseling, careers library, job bank, job interviews, career advisory network.
Freshmen 1,498 applied, 1,138 admitted, 509 enrolled.

SAT verbal scores above 500	N/R	SAT math scores above 500	N/R
ACT above 18	N/R		

Application *Option:* deferred entrance. *Application fee:* $65. *Required:* essay or personal statement; high school transcript; 2 letters of recommendation; 2 years of formal musical experience or study. *Required for some:* interview. *Recommended:* interview.
Standardized tests *Admission: Required for some:* SAT I or ACT.
Significant dates *Application deadlines:* rolling (freshmen), rolling (transfers). *Financial aid deadline priority date:* 4/24.
Freshman Application Contact
Ms. Marsha Ginn, Director of Admissions, Berklee College of Music, 1140 Boyleston Street, Boston, MA 02215-3693. **Phone:** 617-266-1400 Ext. 2367. **Toll-free phone:** 800-421-0084. **Fax:** 617-747-2047. **E-mail:** admissions@berklee.edu
Visit CollegeQuest.com for information on majors offered and athletics. College video and electronic viewbook available at CollegeQuest.com.

■ *See page 1262 for a narrative description.*

BOSTON ARCHITECTURAL CENTER
Boston, Massachusetts

- **Independent**, comprehensive, founded 1889
- **Degrees** bachelor's, master's, and first professional
- **Urban** campus
- **Coed**, 495 undergraduate students, 86% full-time, 26% women, 74% men
- **Noncompetitive** entrance level, 94% of applicants were admitted
- **6.77% graduate** in 6 years or less
- **$6330 tuition** and fees
- **$6 million endowment**

Students *Undergraduates:* 425 full-time, 70 part-time. Students come from 43 states and territories, 1 other country. *The most frequently chosen baccalaureate field is:* architecture. *Graduate:* 180 in graduate degree programs.

From out-of-state	47%	Age 25 or older	67%
Transferred in	16%	African Americans	3%
Asian Americans/Pacific Islanders	5%	Hispanic Americans	5%
Native Americans	1%		

Faculty 275, 80% with terminal degrees.
Expenses (1999–2000) *Tuition:* full-time $6245; part-time $508 per credit. *Required fees:* full-time $85. Part-time tuition and fees vary according to program. *Payment plan:* deferred payment.
Library Shaw and Stone Library plus 1 other. *Operations spending 1999–2000:* $280,926. *Collection:* 25,000 titles, 140 serial subscriptions.
College life *Housing:* college housing not available.
Campus security 24-hour emergency response devices and patrols, electronically operated building access.
After graduation *Career center:* 2 full-time, 1 part-time personnel. Services include resume preparation, career counseling, job bank.

Freshmen 368 applied, 347 admitted, 111 enrolled.

SAT verbal scores above 500	N/R	SAT math scores above 500	N/R
ACT above 18	N/R	1998 freshmen returning in 1999	53%

Application *Application fee:* $50. *Required:* high school transcript.
Significant dates *Application deadlines:* rolling (freshmen), rolling (transfers). *Financial aid deadline priority date:* 6/1.
Freshman Application Contact
Ms. Valerie Nyce, Director of Admission, Boston Architectural Center, 320 Newbury Street, Boston, MA 02115-2795. **Phone:** 617-585-0123. **Toll-free phone:** 877-585-0100. **Fax:** 617-585-0111. **E-mail:** admissions@the-bac.edu
Visit CollegeQuest.com for information on majors offered and athletics.

■ *See page 1288 for a narrative description.*

BOSTON COLLEGE
Chestnut Hill, Massachusetts

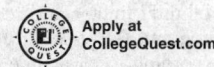
Apply at CollegeQuest.com

- **Independent Roman Catholic (Jesuit)**, university, founded 1863
- **Degrees** bachelor's, master's, doctoral, first professional, and post-master's certificates (also offers continuing education program with significant enrollment not reflected in profile)
- **Suburban** 240-acre campus with easy access to Boston
- **Coed**, 9,190 undergraduate students, 100% full-time, 53% women, 47% men
- **Very difficult** entrance level, 35% of applicants were admitted
- **14:1 student-to-undergraduate faculty ratio**
- **85% graduate** in 6 years or less
- **$22,256 tuition** and fees
- **$19,036 average financial aid** package, $16,417 average indebtedness upon graduation, $910.9 million endowment

Boston College's international stature is strengthened by the more than 450-year tradition of Jesuit education. Students are challenged to fulfill their potential as scholars through honors programs, research with faculty members, independent study, study abroad, and service learning. Students are also challenged to fulfill their potential as caring, thoughtful individuals and future leaders in society with artistic, cultural, service, social, religious, and athletic opportunities that abound on campus and throughout Boston.

Students *Undergraduates:* 9,190 full-time. Students come from 53 states and territories, 63 other countries. *The most frequently chosen baccalaureate fields are:* business/marketing, education, social sciences and history. *Graduate:* 829 in professional programs, 3,834 in other graduate degree programs.

From out-of-state	73%	Reside on campus	73%
Transferred in	2%	International students	2%
African Americans	4%	Asian Americans/Pacific Islanders	8%
Hispanic Americans	5%	Native Americans	0.4%

Faculty 1,146 (55% full-time).
Expenses (1999–2000) *Comprehensive fee:* $30,506 includes full-time tuition ($21,700), mandatory fees ($556), and room and board ($8250). *College room only:* $4620. Room and board charges vary according to housing facility. *Payment plans:* tuition prepayment, installment. *Waivers:* employees or children of employees.
Library Thomas P. O'Neill Library plus 6 others. *Operations spending 1999–2000:* $17.2 million. *Collection:* 1.6 million titles, 18,300 serial subscriptions.
College life *Housing: Options:* coed, women-only. *Most popular organizations:* ski club, The Bostonians, Boston College Bop.
Campus security 24-hour emergency response devices and patrols, late-night transport-escort service, controlled dormitory access.
After graduation *Career center:* 10 full-time, 5 part-time personnel. Services include job fairs, resume preparation, interview workshops, resume referral, career/interest testing, career counseling, careers library, job bank, job interviews. *Graduate education:* 16% of class of 1999 went directly to graduate and professional school: 5% law, 4% business, 4% graduate arts and sciences, 2% medicine. *Major awards:* 14 Fulbright Scholars.
Freshmen 19,746 applied, 6,976 admitted, 2,284 enrolled. 7 National Merit Scholars, 138 student government officers.

Massachusetts

SAT verbal scores above 500	95%	SAT math scores above 500	96%
ACT above 18	N/R	From top 10% of their h.s. class	62%
From top quarter	91%	From top half	99%
1998 freshmen returning in 1999	94%		

Application *Options:* eApply at www.CollegeQuest.com, Common Application, electronic application, early admission, early action, deferred entrance. *Application fee:* $55. *Required:* essay or personal statement; high school transcript; 2 letters of recommendation.

Standardized tests *Admission: Required:* SAT I and SAT II or ACT, SAT II: Writing Test.

Significant dates *Application deadlines:* 1/15 (freshmen), 4/15 (transfers). *Early action:* 11/1. *Notification:* 4/15 (freshmen), 12/24 (early action). *Financial aid deadline priority date:* 2/1.

Freshman Application Contact
Mr. John L. Mahoney Jr., Director of Undergraduate Admission, Boston College, 140 Commonwealth Avenue, Devlin Hall 208, Chestnut Hill, MA 02167-3809. **Phone:** 617-552-3100. **Toll-free phone:** 800-360-2522. **Fax:** 617-552-0798. **E-mail:** ugadmis@bc.edu

Visit CollegeQuest.com for information on majors offered and athletics. College video and electronic viewbook available at CollegeQuest.com.

■ *See page 1290 for a narrative description.*

BOSTON CONSERVATORY
Boston, Massachusetts

- **Independent**, comprehensive, founded 1867
- **Degrees** bachelor's and master's
- **Urban** campus
- **Coed**
- **Moderately difficult** entrance level
- **$18,135 tuition** and fees

Expenses (1999–2000) *Comprehensive fee:* $26,335 includes full-time tuition ($17,300), mandatory fees ($835), and room and board ($8200). Full-time tuition and fees vary according to course load, degree level, and program. *Part-time tuition:* $710 per credit. Part-time tuition and fees vary according to course load, degree level, and program.

Institutional Web site http://www.bostonconservatory.edu/

College life *Housing:* on-campus residence required in freshman year. *Options:* coed, women-only. *Social organizations:* national fraternities, national sororities; 25% of eligible men and 15% of eligible women are members. *Most popular organizations:* Student Government Association, Korean Student Association, Chinese Student Association, Sigma Alpha Iota.

Campus security 24-hour emergency response devices and patrols, controlled dormitory access.

Application *Options:* early admission, deferred entrance. *Application fee:* $60. *Required:* essay or personal statement; high school transcript; minimum 2.7 GPA; 4 letters of recommendation; audition. *Required for some:* interview.

Standardized tests *Admission: Required:* SAT I or ACT.

Admissions Office Contact
Boston Conservatory, 8 The Fenway, Boston, MA 02215. **Fax:** 617-536-3176.

Visit CollegeQuest.com for information on athletics.

BOSTON UNIVERSITY
Boston, Massachusetts

- **Independent**, university, founded 1839
- **Degrees** bachelor's, master's, doctoral, first professional, and post-master's certificates
- **Urban** 132-acre campus
- **Coed**, 15,469 undergraduate students, 97% full-time, 60% women, 40% men
- **Very difficult** entrance level, 55% of applicants were admitted
- **13:1 student-to-undergraduate faculty ratio**
- **67.9% graduate** in 6 years or less
- **$24,100 tuition** and fees
- **$21,654 average financial aid** package, $18,702 average indebtedness upon graduation, $640 million endowment

The spirit of Boston University is in the possibilities: the excitement of living and learning in one of the world's greatest cities and America's largest college town. With students from more than 100 countries, Boston University has one of the most culturally diverse student bodies. The 10 undergraduate schools and colleges offer more than 130 programs of study in areas as diverse as biochemistry, theater, physical therapy, elementary education, biomedical engineering, management, broadcast journalism, and graphic design. Students further enhance their degree programs through internships, field work, research, and study abroad.

Students *Undergraduates:* 15,034 full-time, 435 part-time. Students come from 54 states and territories, 105 other countries. *The most frequently chosen baccalaureate fields are:* communications/communication technologies, business/marketing, social sciences and history. *Graduate:* 1,951 in professional programs, 8,518 in other graduate degree programs.

From out-of-state	77%	Reside on campus	64%
Age 25 or older	4%	Transferred in	1%
International students	8%	African Americans	3%
Asian Americans/Pacific Islanders	12%	Hispanic Americans	6%
Native Americans	0.4%		

Faculty 3,277 (71% full-time).

Expenses (1999–2000) *Comprehensive fee:* $32,230 includes full-time tuition ($23,770), mandatory fees ($330), and room and board ($8130). *College room only:* $5020. Room and board charges vary according to board plan and housing facility. *Part-time tuition:* $743 per credit. *Part-time fees:* $40 per term part-time. *Payment plans:* tuition prepayment, installment. *Waivers:* senior citizens and employees or children of employees.

Library Mugar Memorial Library plus 18 others. *Operations spending 1999–2000:* $11.7 million. *Collection:* 2.1 million titles, 28,535 serial subscriptions, 145,863 audiovisual materials.

College life *Housing:* on-campus residence required in freshman year. *Options:* coed, women-only, cooperative. *Social organizations:* national fraternities, national sororities; 3% of eligible men and 4% of eligible women are members. *Most popular organizations:* performing and acappella groups, cultural organizations, service organizations, student government, residence hall associations.

Campus security 24-hour emergency response devices and patrols, late-night transport-escort service, controlled dormitory access, security personnel at residence hall entrances, self-defense education, well-lit sidewalks.

After graduation 400 organizations recruited on campus 1997–98. *Career center:* 10 full-time personnel. Services include job fairs, resume preparation, interview workshops, resume referral, career/interest testing, career counseling, careers library, job bank, job interviews. *Graduate education:* 25% of class of 1999 went directly to graduate and professional school. *Major awards:* 2 Fulbright Scholars.

Freshmen 28,090 applied, 15,561 admitted, 4,225 enrolled. 49 National Merit Scholars, 139 valedictorians.

Average high school GPA	3.49	SAT verbal scores above 500	99%
SAT math scores above 500	100%	ACT above 18	99%
From top 10% of their h.s. class	55%	From top quarter	90%
From top half	99%	1998 freshmen returning in 1999	85%

Application *Options:* eApply at www.CollegeQuest.com, Common Application, electronic application, early admission, early decision, deferred entrance. *Application fee:* $60. *Required:* essay or personal statement; high school transcript; 2 letters of recommendation. *Required for some:* interview; audition, portfolio. *Recommended:* minimum 3.0 GPA.

Standardized tests *Admission: Required:* SAT I or ACT. *Required for some:* SAT II Subject Tests, SAT II: Writing Test.

Significant dates *Application deadlines:* 1/1 (freshmen), 4/1 (transfers). *Early decision:* 11/1. *Notification:* continuous until 4/15 (freshmen), 12/15 (early decision). *Financial aid deadline priority date:* 2/15.

Freshman Application Contact
Ms. Kelly A. Walter, Director of Undergraduate Admissions, Boston University, 121 Bay State Road, Boston, MA 02215. **Phone:** 617-353-2300. **Fax:** 617-353-9695. **E-mail:** admissions@bu.edu

Visit CollegeQuest.com for information on majors offered and athletics. College video and electronic viewbook available at CollegeQuest.com.

■ *See page 1292 for a narrative description.*

Massachusetts

BRANDEIS UNIVERSITY
Waltham, Massachusetts

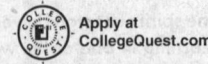 Apply at CollegeQuest.com

- **Independent**, university, founded 1948
- **Degrees** bachelor's, master's, doctoral, and postbachelor's certificates
- **Suburban** 235-acre campus with easy access to Boston
- **Coed**, 3,040 undergraduate students, 99% full-time, 56% women, 44% men
- **Most difficult** entrance level, 52% of applicants were admitted
- **9:1 student-to-undergraduate faculty ratio**
- **79% graduate** in 6 years or less
- **$25,174 tuition** and fees
- **$19,589 average financial aid** package, $355 million endowment

A recent major study ranked Brandeis 9th among all United States private research universities, based on the faculty's contribution to the generation of new knowledge. To assist students of exceptional scholarly achievement and promise to study with this teaching faculty, Brandeis offers a significant number of academic merit-based scholarships of up to 75% of tuition.

Students *Undergraduates:* 3,032 full-time, 8 part-time. Students come from 45 states and territories, 50 other countries. *The most frequently chosen baccalaureate fields are:* biological/life sciences, psychology, social sciences and history. *Graduate:* 1,415 in graduate degree programs.

From out-of-state	60%	Reside on campus	85%
Age 25 or older	1%	Transferred in	2%
International students	5%	African Americans	2%
Asian Americans/Pacific Islanders	10%	Hispanic Americans	2%
Native Americans	0.3%		

Faculty 461 (69% full-time), 93% with terminal degrees.
Expenses (1999–2000) *Comprehensive fee:* $32,214 includes full-time tuition ($24,421), mandatory fees ($753), and room and board ($7040). Room and board charges vary according to board plan and housing facility. *Payment plans:* tuition prepayment, installment. *Waivers:* employees or children of employees.
Library Goldfarb Library plus 2 others. *Operations spending 1999–2000:* $7.5 million. *Collection:* 1.1 million titles, 6,000 serial subscriptions, 29,453 audiovisual materials.
College life *Housing: Options:* coed, disabled students. *Most popular organizations:* Waltham Group, Student Programming Board, performing groups, religious groups, student publications.
Campus security 24-hour emergency response devices and patrols, late-night transport-escort service, controlled dormitory access.
After graduation 200 organizations recruited on campus 1997–98. *Career center:* 7 full-time, 1 part-time personnel. Services include job fairs, resume preparation, interview workshops, resume referral, career/interest testing, career counseling, careers library, job bank, job interviews. *Major awards:* 1 Fulbright Scholar.
Freshmen 5,792 applied, 2,989 admitted, 794 enrolled. 23 National Merit Scholars.

Average high school GPA	3.5	SAT verbal scores above 500	99%
SAT math scores above 500	98%	ACT above 18	N/R
From top 10% of their h.s. class	63%	From top quarter	95%
From top half	100%	1998 freshmen returning in 1999	92%

Application *Options:* eApply at www.CollegeQuest.com, Common Application, electronic application, early decision, deferred entrance. *Application fee:* $50. *Required:* essay or personal statement; high school transcript; 2 letters of recommendation. *Recommended:* minimum 3.0 GPA; interview.
Standardized tests *Admission: Required:* SAT I and SAT II or ACT.
Significant dates *Application deadlines:* 1/31 (freshmen), 4/1 (transfers). *Early decision:* 1/1. *Notification:* 4/15 (freshmen), 2/1 (early decision). *Financial aid deadline priority date:* 1/31.
Freshman Application Contact
Mr. Michael Kalafatas, Director of Admissions, Brandeis University, 415 South Street, Waltham, MA 02254-9110. **Phone:** 781-736-3500. **Toll-free phone:** 800-622-0622. **Fax:** 781-736-3536. **E-mail:** sendinfo@brandeis.edu
Visit CollegeQuest.com for information on majors offered and athletics.

■ *See page 1300 for a narrative description.*

BRIDGEWATER STATE COLLEGE
Bridgewater, Massachusetts

- **State-supported**, comprehensive, founded 1840
- **Degrees** bachelor's, master's, post-master's, and postbachelor's certificates
- **Suburban** 235-acre campus with easy access to Boston
- **Coed**, 6,477 undergraduate students, 81% full-time, 62% women, 38% men
- **Moderately difficult** entrance level, 75% of applicants were admitted
- **49% graduate** in 6 years or less
- **$2123 tuition** and fees (in-state); $8141 (out-of-state)

Part of Massachusetts Public Higher Education System.

Students *Undergraduates:* 5,274 full-time, 1,203 part-time. Students come from 23 states and territories. *The most frequently chosen baccalaureate fields are:* business/marketing, education, social sciences and history. *Graduate:* 1,800 in graduate degree programs.

From out-of-state	9%	Age 25 or older	20%
Transferred in	10%	International students	2%
African Americans	4%	Asian Americans/Pacific Islanders	1%
Hispanic Americans	1%	Native Americans	0.3%

Faculty 255 (100% full-time).
Expenses (1999–2000) *Tuition, state resident:* full-time $1032; part-time $43 per semester hour. *Tuition, nonresident:* full-time $7050; part-time $294 per semester hour. *Required fees:* full-time $1091; $66 per semester hour; $12 per term part-time. *College room and board:* $4704; room only: $2684. Room and board charges vary according to board plan and housing facility. *Payment plan:* installment. *Waivers:* employees or children of employees.
Library Clement Maxwell Library. *Operations spending 1999–2000:* $1.9 million. *Collection:* 250,000 titles, 1,500 serial subscriptions, 250 audiovisual materials.
College life *Housing: Options:* coed, women-only, disabled students. *Social organizations:* national fraternities, national sororities, coed fraternities; 9% of eligible men and 6% of eligible women are members. *Most popular organizations:* Greek life, Children's Developmental Clinic, Student Government Association, Afro-American/Latino Club, Program Committee.
Campus security 24-hour emergency response devices and patrols, late-night transport-escort service, controlled dormitory access.
After graduation 70 organizations recruited on campus 1997–98. 85% of class of 1998 had job offers within 6 months. *Career center:* 3 full-time, 1 part-time personnel. Services include job fairs, resume preparation, interview workshops, resume referral, career/interest testing, career counseling, careers library, job bank, job interviews. *Graduate education:* 15% of class of 1999 went directly to graduate and professional school: 9% education, 5% graduate arts and sciences, 1% law.
Freshmen 4,909 applied, 3,668 admitted, 1,096 enrolled.

Average high school GPA	2.81	SAT verbal scores above 500	53%
SAT math scores above 500	47%	ACT above 18	N/R
From top 10% of their h.s. class	4%	From top quarter	22%
From top half	66%	1998 freshmen returning in 1999	75%

Application *Options:* Common Application, electronic application, early admission, early action, deferred entrance. *Application fee:* $40 for nonresidents. *Required:* essay or personal statement; high school transcript; minimum 2.7 GPA. *Recommended:* letters of recommendation.
Standardized tests *Admission: Required:* SAT I or ACT.
Significant dates *Application deadlines:* 3/1 (freshmen), 4/1 (transfers). *Early action:* 11/15. *Notification:* continuous until 4/15 (freshmen), 12/15 (early action). *Financial aid deadline priority date:* 3/1.
Freshman Application Contact
Mr. Steve King, Director of Admissions, Bridgewater State College, Admission Office, Bridgewater, MA 02325-0001. **Phone:** 508-531-1237. **Fax:** 508-531-1746. **E-mail:** admission@bridgew.edu
Visit CollegeQuest.com for information on majors offered and athletics. Electronic viewbook available at CollegeQuest.com.

■ *See page 1314 for a narrative description.*

Massachusetts

CAMBRIDGE COLLEGE
Cambridge, Massachusetts

- **Independent**, comprehensive, founded 1971
- **Degrees** bachelor's and master's
- **Urban** campus with easy access to Boston
- **Coed**, 285 undergraduate students
- **Minimally difficult** entrance level, 100% of applicants were admitted
- **$7620 tuition** and fees

Cambridge College's innovative Bachelor of Arts program is designed for working adults. It offers an empowering learning model, emphasizes peer support and assessment, and encourages personal and professional development. Students may choose a concentration in educational psychology, family and community systems: human services, or organizational psychology and management.

Students *Undergraduates:* The most frequently chosen baccalaureate field is: psychology.

| From out-of-state | 2% | Age 25 or older | 95% |

Faculty 50.

Expenses (1999–2000) *Tuition:* full-time $7500; part-time $250 per credit hour. *Required fees:* full-time $120; $60 per term part-time.

Library Operations spending 1999–2000: $45,000.

College life *Housing:* college housing not available.

Freshmen 100 applied, 100 admitted.

| SAT verbal scores above 500 | N/R | SAT math scores above 500 | N/R |
| ACT above 18 | N/R |

Application *Option:* deferred entrance. *Application fee:* $30. *Required:* essay or personal statement; high school transcript; interview.

Standardized tests *Placement: Required:* ACCUPLACER

Significant dates *Application deadlines:* rolling (freshmen), rolling (transfers). *Financial aid deadline:* continuous.

Freshman Application Contact
Ms. Joy King, Associate Director of Enrollment Services, Cambridge College, 1000 Massachusetts Avenue, Cambridge, MA 02138-5304. **Phone:** 617-868-1000. **Toll-free phone:** 800-877-4723. **Fax:** 617-349-3545. **E-mail:** enroll@idea.cambridge.edu

Visit CollegeQuest.com for information on majors offered and athletics.

■ *See page 1348 for a narrative description.*

CLARK UNIVERSITY
Worcester, Massachusetts

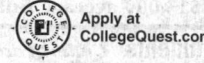
Apply at CollegeQuest.com

- **Independent**, university, founded 1887
- **Degrees** bachelor's, master's, doctoral, post-master's, and postbachelor's certificates
- **Urban** 50-acre campus with easy access to Boston
- **Coed**, 2,013 undergraduate students, 96% full-time, 60% women, 40% men
- **Moderately difficult** entrance level, 73% of applicants were admitted
- **12:1 student-to-undergraduate faculty ratio**
- **65% graduate** in 6 years or less
- **$22,620 tuition** and fees
- **$18,138 average financial aid** package, $17,224 average indebtedness upon graduation, $124.2 million endowment

Students *Undergraduates:* 1,925 full-time, 88 part-time. Students come from 40 states and territories, 63 other countries. *The most frequently chosen baccalaureate fields are:* psychology, biological/life sciences, social sciences and history. *Graduate:* 821 in graduate degree programs.

From out-of-state	59%	Reside on campus	71%
Age 25 or older	2%	Transferred in	2%
International students	11%	African Americans	3%
Asian Americans/Pacific Islanders	4%	Hispanic Americans	3%
Native Americans	0.2%		

Faculty 237 (63% full-time), 63% with terminal degrees.

Expenses (1999–2000) *Comprehensive fee:* $26,970 includes full-time tuition ($22,400), mandatory fees ($220), and room and board ($4350). *College room only:* $2650. Room and board charges vary according to board plan and housing facility. *Part-time tuition:* $2800 per course. *Payment plans:* tuition prepayment, installment. *Waivers:* employees or children of employees.

Library Robert Hutchings Goddard Library plus 4 others. *Operations spending 1999–2000:* $1.9 million. *Collection:* 3,593 serial subscriptions, 1,158 audiovisual materials.

College life *Housing:* on-campus residence required through sophomore year. *Options:* coed, women-only, disabled students. *Most popular organizations:* Main South Big Brothers/Big Sisters, COUNT, Student Activities Board, Speakers Forum, Clark University Players Society.

Campus security 24-hour emergency response devices and patrols, student patrols, late-night transport-escort service, controlled dormitory access.

After graduation 64 organizations recruited on campus 1997–98. 65% of class of 1998 had job offers within 6 months. *Career center:* 3 full-time, 2 part-time personnel. Services include job fairs, resume preparation, interview workshops, resume referral, career counseling, careers library, job bank, job interviews. *Graduate education:* 29% of class of 1999 went directly to graduate and professional school.

Freshmen 3,231 applied, 2,372 admitted, 481 enrolled.

Average high school GPA	3.27	SAT verbal scores above 500	82%
SAT math scores above 500	82%	ACT above 18	100%
From top 10% of their h.s. class	30%	From top quarter	68%
From top half	90%	1998 freshmen returning in 1999	87%

Application *Options:* eApply at www.CollegeQuest.com, Common Application, early admission, early decision, deferred entrance. *Application fee:* $40. *Required:* essay or personal statement; high school transcript. *Recommended:* minimum 3.0 GPA; 2 letters of recommendation; interview.

Standardized tests *Admission: Required:* SAT I or ACT, SAT II: Writing Test. *Recommended:* SAT II Subject Tests.

Significant dates *Application deadlines:* 2/1 (freshmen), 4/15 (transfers). *Early decision:* 11/15. *Notification:* 4/1 (freshmen), 12/15 (early decision). *Financial aid deadline priority date:* 2/1.

Freshman Application Contact
Mr. Harold M. Wingood, Dean of Admissions, Clark University, 950 Main Street, Worcester, MA 01610-1477. **Phone:** 508-793-7431. **Toll-free phone:** 800-GO-CLARK. **Fax:** 508-793-8821. **E-mail:** admissions@admissions.clark.edu

Visit CollegeQuest.com for information on majors offered and athletics. College video available at CollegeQuest.com.

COLLEGE OF OUR LADY OF THE ELMS
Chicopee, Massachusetts

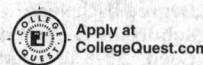
Apply at CollegeQuest.com

- **Independent Roman Catholic**, comprehensive, founded 1928
- **Degrees** bachelor's and master's
- **Suburban** 32-acre campus
- **Coed**, primarily women, 724 undergraduate students, 69% full-time, 90% women, 10% men
- **Moderately difficult** entrance level, 88% of applicants were admitted
- **12:1 student-to-undergraduate faculty ratio**
- **77% graduate** in 6 years or less
- **$14,720 tuition** and fees
- **$11,892 average financial aid** package, $11,868 average indebtedness upon graduation, $3.8 million endowment

Students *Undergraduates:* 502 full-time, 222 part-time. Students come from 10 states and territories, 3 other countries. *The most frequently chosen baccalaureate fields are:* health professions and related sciences, business/marketing, social sciences and history. *Graduate:* 176 in graduate degree programs.

From out-of-state	9%	Reside on campus	39%
Age 25 or older	52%	Transferred in	34%
International students	1%	African Americans	6%
Asian Americans/Pacific Islanders	2%	Hispanic Americans	6%
Native Americans	0.3%		

Faculty 71 (62% full-time), 58% with terminal degrees.

Expenses (2000–2001) *Comprehensive fee:* $20,286 includes full-time tuition ($14,144), mandatory fees ($576), and room and board ($5566). Room and board charges vary according to board plan. *Part-time tuition:* $310 per credit. *Waivers:* senior citizens and employees or children of employees.

Massachusetts

College of Our Lady of the Elms (continued)

Library Alumnae Library. *Operations spending 1999–2000:* $403,247. *Collection:* 113,382 titles, 688 serial subscriptions, 2,551 audiovisual materials.

College life *Housing: Options:* coed, women-only. *Most popular organizations:* Student Government Association, Zonta, Elmscript, Umoja, social work club.

Campus security 24-hour emergency response devices and patrols, late-night transport-escort service, controlled dormitory access.

After graduation 5% of class of 1998 had job offers within 6 months. *Career center:* 1 full-time personnel. Services include job fairs, resume preparation, interview workshops, resume referral, career/interest testing, career counseling, careers library, job bank, job interviews. *Graduate education:* 5% of class of 1999 went directly to graduate and professional school: 2% education, 1% business, 1% graduate arts and sciences, 1% law.

Freshmen 372 applied, 328 admitted, 334 enrolled.

Average high school GPA	3.22	SAT verbal scores above 500	41%
SAT math scores above 500	34%	ACT above 18	N/R
From top 10% of their h.s. class	17%	From top quarter	44%
From top half	73%	1998 freshmen returning in 1999	83%

Application *Options:* eApply at www.CollegeQuest.com, Common Application, early admission, deferred entrance. *Application fee:* $30. *Required:* essay or personal statement; high school transcript; minimum 2.0 GPA; 2 letters of recommendation. *Recommended:* interview.

Standardized tests *Admission: Required:* SAT I or ACT. *Recommended:* SAT II Subject Tests.

Significant dates *Application deadlines:* rolling (freshmen), rolling (transfers). *Financial aid deadline priority date:* 3/1.

Admissions Office Contact
College of Our Lady of the Elms, 291 Springfield Street, Chicopee, MA 01013-2839. **Toll-free phone:** 800-255-ELMS. **Fax:** 413-594-2781. **E-mail:** admissions@elms.edu

Visit CollegeQuest.com for information on majors offered and athletics.

■ *See page 1470 for a narrative description.*

COLLEGE OF THE HOLY CROSS
Worcester, Massachusetts

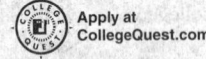
Apply at CollegeQuest.com

- **Independent Roman Catholic (Jesuit)**, 4-year, founded 1843
- **Degree** bachelor's
- **Suburban** 174-acre campus with easy access to Boston
- **Coed**, 2,778 undergraduate students, 100% full-time, 52% women, 48% men
- **Very difficult** entrance level, 44% of applicants were admitted
- **13:1** student-to-undergraduate faculty ratio
- **93% graduate** in 6 years or less
- **$23,815 tuition** and fees
- **$17,236 average financial aid** package, $16,430 average indebtedness upon graduation, $352 million endowment

Students *Undergraduates:* 2,778 full-time. Students come from 49 states and territories. *The most frequently chosen baccalaureate fields are:* English, psychology, social sciences and history.

From out-of-state	67%	Reside on campus	80%
Transferred in	1%	International students	1%
African Americans	3%	Asian Americans/Pacific Islanders	3%
Hispanic Americans	5%	Native Americans	0.1%

Faculty 267 (83% full-time), 84% with terminal degrees.

Expenses (2000–2001) *Comprehensive fee:* $31,355 includes full-time tuition ($23,400), mandatory fees ($415), and room and board ($7540). *College room only:* $3770. Room and board charges vary according to board plan and housing facility. *Payment plans:* tuition prepayment, installment. *Waivers:* employees or children of employees.

Library Dinand Library plus 2 others. *Operations spending 1999–2000:* $2.3 million. *Collection:* 548,492 titles, 1,689 serial subscriptions, 22,050 audiovisual materials.

College life *Housing: Option:* coed. *Most popular organizations:* SPUD (community service organization), choral and music groups, Campus Activities Board, Student Government Association, Purple Key Society.

Campus security 24-hour emergency response devices and patrols, late-night transport-escort service, controlled dormitory access.

After graduation 77 organizations recruited on campus 1997–98. *Career center:* 5 full-time, 1 part-time personnel. Services include job fairs, resume preparation, interview workshops, resume referral, career/interest testing, career counseling, careers library, job interviews, individual career counseling, alumni career advisors, job posting. *Graduate education:* 15% of class of 1999 went directly to graduate and professional school: 6% graduate arts and sciences, 4% law, 1% business, 1% dentistry, 1% education, 1% medicine. *Major awards:* 6 Fulbright Scholars.

Freshmen 4,834 applied, 2,114 admitted, 722 enrolled.

SAT verbal scores above 500	97%	SAT math scores above 500	98%
ACT above 18	N/R	From top 10% of their h.s. class	54%
From top half	99%	1998 freshmen returning in 1999	94%

Application *Options:* eApply at www.CollegeQuest.com, Common Application, electronic application, early admission, early decision, deferred entrance. *Application fee:* $50. *Required:* essay or personal statement; high school transcript; 2 letters of recommendation. *Recommended:* interview.

Standardized tests *Admission: Required:* SAT I and SAT II or ACT, SAT II: Writing Test.

Significant dates *Application deadlines:* 1/15 (freshmen), 5/1 (transfers). *Early decision:* 12/15. *Notification:* 4/1 (freshmen), 2/16 (early decision). *Financial aid deadline priority date:* 2/1.

Freshman Application Contact
Ms. Ann Bowe McDermott, Director of Admissions, College of the Holy Cross, , 1 College Street, Worcester, MA 01610. **Phone:** 508-793-2443. **Toll-free phone:** 800-442-2421. **Fax:** 508-793-3888. **E-mail:** admissions@holycross.edu

Visit CollegeQuest.com for information on majors offered and athletics. College video available at CollegeQuest.com.

CURRY COLLEGE
Milton, Massachusetts

- **Independent**, comprehensive, founded 1879
- **Degrees** bachelor's and master's
- **Suburban** 131-acre campus with easy access to Boston
- **Coed**, 1,894 undergraduate students, 63% full-time, 53% women, 47% men
- **Moderately difficult** entrance level, 77% of applicants were admitted
- **12:1** student-to-undergraduate faculty ratio
- **53% graduate** in 6 years or less
- **$17,300 tuition** and fees
- **$13,000 average financial aid** package, $2.5 million endowment

Students *Undergraduates:* 1,195 full-time, 699 part-time. Students come from 31 states and territories, 12 other countries. *The most frequently chosen baccalaureate fields are:* health professions and related sciences, business/marketing, protective services/public administration. *Graduate:* 119 in graduate degree programs.

From out-of-state	21%	Reside on campus	65%
Age 25 or older	43%	Transferred in	4%
International students	1%	African Americans	4%
Asian Americans/Pacific Islanders	1%	Hispanic Americans	2%
Native Americans	0.2%		

Faculty 330 (24% full-time).

Expenses (1999–2000) *Comprehensive fee:* $24,010 includes full-time tuition ($16,500), mandatory fees ($800), and room and board ($6710). *College room only:* $3600. Room and board charges vary according to board plan. *Part-time tuition:* $550 per credit hour. *Payment plan:* installment. *Waivers:* children of alumni, senior citizens, and employees or children of employees.

Library Levin Library plus 1 other. *Operations spending 1999–2000:* $542,934. *Collection:* 90,000 titles, 625 serial subscriptions.

College life *Housing: Options:* coed, men-only, women-only. *Most popular organizations:* student radio station, student government, Community Service Organization, student newspaper, drama club.

Campus security 24-hour emergency response devices and patrols, late-night transport-escort service, controlled dormitory access.

After graduation 35 organizations recruited on campus 1997–98. 85% of class of 1998 had job offers within 6 months. *Career center:* 1 full-time, 1

Massachusetts

part-time personnel. Services include job fairs, resume preparation, resume referral, career counseling, careers library, job bank. *Graduate education:* 17% of class of 1999 went directly to graduate and professional school: 10% graduate arts and sciences, 4% education, 2% business, 1% law.

Freshmen 1,416 applied, 1,085 admitted, 373 enrolled.

Average high school GPA	2.3	SAT verbal scores above 500	29%
SAT math scores above 500	16%	ACT above 18	N/R
From top 10% of their h.s. class	3%	From top quarter	22%
From top half	52%	1998 freshmen returning in 1999	65%

Application *Options:* electronic application, early admission, early decision, deferred entrance. *Application fee:* $40. *Required:* essay or personal statement; high school transcript; minimum 2.0 GPA; 1 letter of recommendation. *Required for some:* interview. *Recommended:* interview.

Standardized tests *Admission: Required for some:* SAT I or ACT, Wechsler Adult Intelligence Scale-Revised.

Significant dates *Application deadlines:* 4/1 (freshmen), 7/1 (transfers). *Early decision:* 12/1. *Notification:* continuous until 5/1 (freshmen), 12/15 (early decision). *Financial aid deadline priority date:* 3/1.

Freshman Application Contact
Mr. Michael Poll, Dean of Admissions and Financial Aid, Curry College, 1071 Blue Hill Avenue, Milton, MA 02186. **Phone:** 617-333-2210. **Toll-free phone:** 800-669-0686. **Fax:** 617-333-6860. **E-mail:** curryadm@curry.edu.8080

Visit CollegeQuest.com for information on majors offered and athletics. Electronic viewbook available at CollegeQuest.com.

■ *See page 1548 for a narrative description.*

EASTERN NAZARENE COLLEGE
Quincy, Massachusetts

- **Independent**, comprehensive, founded 1918, affiliated with Church of the Nazarene
- **Degrees** associate, bachelor's, and master's
- **Suburban** 15-acre campus with easy access to Boston
- **Coed**, 1,338 undergraduate students, 99% full-time, 58% women, 42% men
- **Moderately difficult** entrance level, 65% of applicants were admitted
- **10:1 student-to-undergraduate faculty ratio**
- **48% graduate** in 6 years or less
- **$14,060 tuition** and fees
- **$9471 average financial aid** package, $7.6 million endowment

Students *Undergraduates:* 1,322 full-time, 16 part-time. Students come from 32 states and territories. *The most frequently chosen baccalaureate fields are:* business/marketing, biological/life sciences, education. *Graduate:* 217 in graduate degree programs.

From out-of-state	28%	Reside on campus	82%
Age 25 or older	50%	Transferred in	2%
International students	2%	African Americans	9%
Asian Americans/Pacific Islanders	2%	Hispanic Americans	3%
Native Americans	1%		

Faculty 82 (71% full-time), 54% with terminal degrees.

Expenses (2000–2001, estimated) *Comprehensive fee:* $18,610 includes full-time tuition ($13,235), mandatory fees ($825), and room and board ($4550). Room and board charges vary according to board plan. *Part-time tuition:* $446 per credit. *Part-time fees:* $15 per term part-time. Part-time tuition and fees vary according to course load. *Payment plan:* installment. *Waivers:* employees or children of employees.

Library Nease Library. *Operations spending 1999–2000:* $543,000. *Collection:* 94,111 titles, 3,062 serial subscriptions, 2,566 audiovisual materials.

College life *Housing:* on-campus residence required through senior year. *Options:* men-only, women-only, disabled students. *Most popular organizations:* AMS Associated Men Students, AWS Associated Women Students, gospel choir, ACTS Actors Christians Teachers Singers, Kid's Club.

Campus security 24-hour emergency response devices and patrols, late-night transport-escort service, controlled dormitory access.

After graduation *Career center:* 1 full-time, 1 part-time personnel. Services include resume preparation, career/interest testing, career counseling, careers library.

Freshmen 546 applied, 354 admitted, 179 enrolled. 4 valedictorians.

Average high school GPA	2.91	SAT verbal scores above 500	62%
SAT math scores above 500	56%	ACT above 18	86%
From top 10% of their h.s. class	13%	From top quarter	39%
From top half	66%	1998 freshmen returning in 1999	75%

Application *Options:* early admission, deferred entrance. *Application fee:* $25. *Required:* high school transcript; 2 letters of recommendation. *Recommended:* essay or personal statement; interview.

Standardized tests *Admission: Required:* SAT I or ACT.

Significant dates *Application deadlines:* rolling (freshmen), rolling (transfers). *Financial aid deadline priority date:* 3/1.

Freshman Application Contact
Mr. James F. Heyward II, Director of Admissions, Eastern Nazarene College, 23 East Elm Avenue, Quincy, MA 02170. **Phone:** 617-745-3868. **Toll-free phone:** 800-88-ENC88. **Fax:** 617-745-3907. **E-mail:** admissions@enc.edu

Visit CollegeQuest.com for information on majors offered and athletics.

■ *See page 1606 for a narrative description.*

ELMS COLLEGE
Massachusetts—See College of Our Lady of the Elms

EMERSON COLLEGE
Boston, Massachusetts

Apply at CollegeQuest.com

- **Independent**, comprehensive, founded 1880
- **Degrees** bachelor's, master's, doctoral, and first professional certificates
- **Urban** campus
- **Coed**, 3,135 undergraduate students, 85% full-time, 58% women, 42% men
- **Moderately difficult** entrance level, 65% of applicants were admitted
- **16:1 student-to-undergraduate faculty ratio**
- **$19,316 tuition** and fees
- **$12,600 average financial aid** package, $17,125 average indebtedness upon graduation, $23.2 million endowment

Emerson College, founded in 1880, is the nation's only 4-year independent college exclusively devoted to the study of communication and the performing arts. A privately supported, coeducational college, Emerson provides a curriculum that integrates the liberal arts with specialized academic study. More than 1,500 internships provide students with professional experience. Students can visit the College's Web site at http://www.emerson.edu/admiss/

Students *Undergraduates:* 2,660 full-time, 475 part-time. Students come from 48 states and territories, 66 other countries. *Graduate:* 852 in graduate degree programs.

From out-of-state	71%	Reside on campus	51%
Age 25 or older	6%	Transferred in	7%
International students	7%	African Americans	2%
Asian Americans/Pacific Islanders	2%	Hispanic Americans	2%
Native Americans	0.4%		

Faculty 309 (36% full-time), 25% with terminal degrees.

Expenses (1999–2000) *Comprehensive fee:* $28,050 includes full-time tuition ($18,816), mandatory fees ($500), and room and board ($8734). *College room only:* $5200. Full-time tuition and fees vary according to course load and program. Room and board charges vary according to board plan. *Part-time tuition:* $588 per credit. *Part-time fees:* $196 per term part-time. Part-time tuition and fees vary according to course load and program. *Payment plans:* tuition prepayment, deferred payment. *Waivers:* employees or children of employees.

Library Emerson Library plus 1 other. *Operations spending 1999–2000:* $2.2 million. *Collection:* 195,000 titles, 1,043 serial subscriptions.

College life *Housing:* on-campus residence required in freshman year. *Option:* coed. *Social organizations:* national fraternities, national sororities, local fraternities, local sororities; 4% of eligible men and 6% of eligible women are members. *Most popular organizations:* Emerson Independent Video, student radio station, Musical Theatre Society, Berkeley Beacon, international student association.

Massachusetts

Emerson College (continued)

Campus security 24-hour emergency response devices and patrols, late-night transport-escort service, controlled dormitory access.

After graduation *Career center:* 5 full-time, 1 part-time personnel. Services include job fairs, resume preparation, interview workshops, resume referral, career/interest testing, career counseling, careers library, job bank, job interviews. *Graduate education:* 10% of class of 1999 went directly to graduate and professional school.

Freshmen 2,747 applied, 1,791 admitted, 652 enrolled. 5 valedictorians.

Average high school GPA	3.17	SAT verbal scores above 500	95%
SAT math scores above 500	85%	ACT above 18	70%
From top 10% of their h.s. class	18%	From top quarter	53%
From top half	87%	1998 freshmen returning in 1999	82%

Application *Options:* eApply at www.CollegeQuest.com, Common Application, electronic application, early admission, early action, deferred entrance. *Application fee:* $45. *Required:* essay or personal statement; high school transcript; 2 letters of recommendation. *Required for some:* interview; audition for acting, dance, and musical theatre majors.

Standardized tests *Admission: Required:* SAT I or ACT.

Significant dates *Application deadlines:* 2/1 (freshmen), 3/1 (transfers). *Early action:* 11/15. *Notification:* 3/15 (freshmen), 12/15 (early action). *Financial aid deadline priority date:* 3/1.

Freshman Application Contact
Ms. Sara Ramirez, Director of Admission, Emerson College, 100 Beacon Street, Boston, MA 02116-1596. **Phone:** 617-824-8600. **Fax:** 617-824-8609. **E-mail:** admission@emerson.edu

Visit CollegeQuest.com for information on majors offered and athletics. Electronic viewbook available at CollegeQuest.com.

■ *See page 1632 for a narrative description.*

EMMANUEL COLLEGE
Boston, Massachusetts

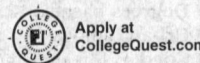 Apply at CollegeQuest.com

- **Independent Roman Catholic**, comprehensive, founded 1919
- **Degrees** bachelor's and master's
- **Urban** 16-acre campus
- **Women** only, 1,303 undergraduate students, 55% full-time
- **Moderately difficult** entrance level, 78% of applicants were admitted
- **15:1 student-to-undergraduate faculty ratio**
- **45% graduate** in 6 years or less
- **$16,612 tuition** and fees
- **$19,350 average financial aid** package, $19,349 average indebtedness upon graduation, $3.3 million endowment

Students *Undergraduates:* 718 full-time, 585 part-time. Students come from 23 states and territories, 36 other countries. *The most frequently chosen baccalaureate fields are:* business/marketing, health professions and related sciences, interdisciplinary studies. *Graduate:* 177 in graduate degree programs.

From out-of-state	12%	Reside on campus	65%
Age 25 or older	63%	Transferred in	2%
International students	6%	African Americans	10%
Asian Americans/Pacific Islanders	3%	Hispanic Americans	4%
Native Americans	0.2%		

Faculty 65 (69% full-time), 66% with terminal degrees.

Expenses (2000–2001) *Comprehensive fee:* $24,002 includes full-time tuition ($16,112), mandatory fees ($500), and room and board ($7390). Part-time tuition and fees vary according to program. *Payment plans:* installment, deferred payment. *Waivers:* employees or children of employees.

Library Cardinal Cushing Library. *Operations spending 1999–2000:* $406,890. *Collection:* 95,000 titles, 876 serial subscriptions, 459 audiovisual materials.

College life *Housing:* Option: women-only. *Social organizations:* 45% of eligible undergrads are members. *Most popular organizations:* Student Government Association, peace and justice club, Theatre Guild, Student Activity Committee, political science club.

Campus security 24-hour emergency response devices and patrols, late-night transport-escort service, controlled dormitory access, 24-hour security personnel on duty at front desk in residence halls.

After graduation *Career center:* 1 full-time personnel. Services include job fairs, resume preparation, career counseling, careers library, job bank.

Freshmen 510 applied, 398 admitted, 144 enrolled.

Average high school GPA	3.28	SAT verbal scores above 500	62%
SAT math scores above 500	45%	ACT above 18	70%
From top 10% of their h.s. class	10%	From top quarter	49%
From top half	77%	1998 freshmen returning in 1999	77%

Application *Options:* eApply at www.CollegeQuest.com, Common Application, electronic application, early admission, early decision, deferred entrance. *Application fee:* $40. *Required:* essay or personal statement; high school transcript; minimum 2.0 GPA; 2 letters of recommendation. *Required for some:* interview.

Standardized tests *Admission: Required:* SAT I or ACT.

Significant dates *Application deadlines:* rolling (freshmen), rolling (transfers). *Early decision:* 11/1. *Notification:* 12/1 (early decision). *Financial aid deadline priority date:* 4/15.

Freshman Application Contact
Ms. Meg Miller, Director of Admissions, Emmanuel College, 400 The Fenway, Boston, MA 02115. **Phone:** 617-735-9715. **Fax:** 617-735-9801. **E-mail:** enroll@emmanuel.edu

Visit CollegeQuest.com for information on majors offered and athletics. College video available at CollegeQuest.com.

■ *See page 1634 for a narrative description.*

ENDICOTT COLLEGE
Beverly, Massachusetts

- **Independent**, comprehensive, founded 1939
- **Degrees** associate, bachelor's, and master's
- **Suburban** 200-acre campus with easy access to Boston
- **Coed**, 1,395 undergraduate students, 90% full-time, 68% women, 32% men
- **Moderately difficult** entrance level, 75% of applicants were admitted
- **13:1 student-to-undergraduate faculty ratio**
- **$14,556 tuition** and fees
- **$11,170 average financial aid** package, $16,060 average indebtedness upon graduation, $6.7 million endowment

Students *Undergraduates:* 1,250 full-time, 145 part-time. Students come from 24 states and territories, 32 other countries. *The most frequently chosen baccalaureate fields are:* business/marketing, personal/miscellaneous services, psychology. *Graduate:* 117 in graduate degree programs.

From out-of-state	44%	Reside on campus	81%
Age 25 or older	14%	Transferred in	6%
International students	7%	African Americans	1%
Asian Americans/Pacific Islanders	1%	Hispanic Americans	2%
Native Americans	1%		

Faculty 170 (40% full-time), 31% with terminal degrees.

Expenses (1999–2000) *Comprehensive fee:* $21,966 includes full-time tuition ($14,000), mandatory fees ($556), and room and board ($7410). *College room only:* $5200. Room and board charges vary according to board plan and housing facility. *Part-time tuition:* $429 per credit. *Part-time fees:* $141 per term part-time. Part-time tuition and fees vary according to program. *Payment plan:* installment. *Waivers:* senior citizens and employees or children of employees.

Library Endicott College Library. *Operations spending 1999–2000:* $300,757. *Collection:* 47,500 titles, 1,750 serial subscriptions, 430 audiovisual materials.

College life *Housing:* on-campus residence required through senior year. *Options:* coed, women-only. *Most popular organizations:* student activities committee, student government, yearbook, Admissions Ambassadors, Adventure Base Council.

Campus security 24-hour emergency response devices and patrols, late-night transport-escort service, controlled dormitory access.

After graduation 170 organizations recruited on campus 1997–98. 97% of class of 1998 had job offers within 6 months. *Career center:* 1 full-time personnel. Services include job fairs, resume preparation, interview workshops, resume referral, career/interest testing, career counseling, careers library, job bank, job interviews, job bulletin, mentoring program. *Graduate education:* 8% of class of 1999 went directly to graduate and professional school: 1% business.

Massachusetts

Freshmen 1,594 applied, 1,203 admitted, 407 enrolled.

SAT verbal scores above 500	50%	SAT math scores above 500	43%
ACT above 18	N/R	From top 10% of their h.s. class	4%
From top quarter	22%	From top half	63%
1998 freshmen returning in 1999	75%		

Application *Options:* Common Application, electronic application, deferred entrance. *Application fee:* $25. *Required:* essay or personal statement; high school transcript; minimum 2.0 GPA; letters of recommendation. *Required for some:* interview. *Recommended:* interview.

Standardized tests *Admission: Required:* SAT I or ACT.

Significant dates *Application deadlines:* rolling (freshmen), rolling (transfers). *Financial aid deadline priority date:* 3/15.

Freshman Application Contact
Mr. Thomas J. Redman, Vice President of Admissions and Financial Aid, Endicott College, 376 Hale Street, Beverly, MA 01915. **Phone:** 978-921-1000. **Toll-free phone:** 800-325-1114. **Fax:** 978-927-0084. **E-mail:** admissio@endicott.edu

Visit CollegeQuest.com for information on majors offered and athletics. College video available at CollegeQuest.com.

■ *See page 1640 for a narrative description.*

FISHER COLLEGE
Boston, Massachusetts

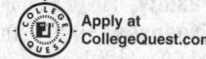 Apply at CollegeQuest.com

- **Independent**, primarily 2-year, founded 1903
- **Degrees** associate and bachelor's
- **Urban** 3-acre campus
- **Coed**, 2,638 undergraduate students
- **Minimally difficult** entrance level
- **$13,900 tuition** and fees

Faculty 36 (39% full-time).

Admissions Office Contact
Fisher College, 118 Beacon Street, Boston, MA 02116-1500. **Toll-free phone:** 800-821-3050 (in-state); 800-446-1226 (out-of-state). **Fax:** 617-236-8858. **E-mail:** admissions@fisher.edu

Visit CollegeQuest.com for information on majors offered and athletics. College video available at CollegeQuest.com.

■ *See page 1662 for a narrative description.*

FITCHBURG STATE COLLEGE
Fitchburg, Massachusetts

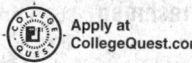 Apply at CollegeQuest.com

- **State-supported**, comprehensive, founded 1894
- **Degrees** bachelor's, master's, and post-master's certificates
- **Small-town** 45-acre campus with easy access to Boston
- **Coed**, 2,857 undergraduate students, 77% full-time, 58% women, 42% men
- **Moderately difficult** entrance level, 71% of applicants were admitted
- **14:1 student-to-undergraduate faculty ratio**
- **43.9% graduate** in 6 years or less
- **$3018 tuition** and fees (in-state); $8978 (out-of-state)
- **$6.8 million endowment**

Part of Massachusetts Public Higher Education System.

Students *Undergraduates:* 2,208 full-time, 649 part-time. Students come from 12 states and territories, 8 other countries. *The most frequently chosen baccalaureate fields are:* business/marketing, education, health professions and related sciences. *Graduate:* 2,205 in graduate degree programs.

From out-of-state	6%	Reside on campus	35%
Age 25 or older	30%	Transferred in	7%
International students	1%	African Americans	5%
Asian Americans/Pacific Islanders	1%	Hispanic Americans	3%
Native Americans	0.1%		

Faculty 304 (67% full-time).

Expenses (1999–2000) *Tuition, state resident:* full-time $1090; part-time $45 per semester hour. *Tuition, nonresident:* full-time $7050; part-time $294 per semester hour. *Required fees:* full-time $1928; $80 per semester hour.

Full-time tuition and fees vary according to class time, course load, and reciprocity agreements. Part-time tuition and fees vary according to class time, course load, and reciprocity agreements. *College room and board:* $4540. Room and board charges vary according to board plan and housing facility. *Payment plan:* installment. *Waivers:* senior citizens and employees or children of employees.

Library Hammond Library. *Operations spending 1999–2000:* $1.2 million. *Collection:* 222,581 titles, 1,874 serial subscriptions, 460,560 audiovisual materials.

College life *Housing: Option:* coed. *Social organizations:* national fraternities, national sororities, local fraternities, local sororities; 10% of eligible men and 15% of eligible women are members. *Most popular organizations:* Student Government Association, Rescue Squad, student radio station, student newspaper, Black Student Union.

Campus security 24-hour emergency response devices and patrols, late-night transport-escort service, controlled dormitory access.

After graduation 30 organizations recruited on campus 1997–98. 84% of class of 1998 had job offers within 6 months. *Career center:* 3 full-time personnel. Services include job fairs, resume preparation, interview workshops, resume referral, career/interest testing, career counseling, careers library, job bank, job interviews. *Graduate education:* 7% of class of 1999 went directly to graduate and professional school: 3% business, 2% education, 2% graduate arts and sciences.

Freshmen 1,493 applied, 1,058 admitted, 401 enrolled.

Average high school GPA	2.8	SAT verbal scores above 500	43%
SAT math scores above 500	42%	ACT above 18	N/R
1998 freshmen returning in 1999	71%		

Application *Options:* eApply at www.CollegeQuest.com, Common Application, early admission, deferred entrance. *Application fee:* $10. *Required:* essay or personal statement; high school transcript; minimum 2.9 GPA. *Recommended:* letters of recommendation; interview.

Standardized tests *Admission: Required:* SAT I or ACT.

Significant dates *Application deadlines:* 4/1 (freshmen), 4/1 (transfers). *Financial aid deadline priority date:* 3/1.

Freshman Application Contact
Mr. James Dupont, Director of Admissions, Fitchburg State College, 160 Pearl Street, Fitchburg, MA 01420-2697. **Phone:** 978-665-3144. **Toll-free phone:** 800-705-9692. **Fax:** 978-665-4540. **E-mail:** admissions@fsc.edu

Visit CollegeQuest.com for information on majors offered and athletics. College video available at CollegeQuest.com.

■ *See page 1666 for a narrative description.*

FRAMINGHAM STATE COLLEGE
Framingham, Massachusetts

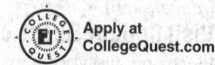 Apply at CollegeQuest.com

- **State-supported**, comprehensive, founded 1839
- **Degrees** bachelor's, master's, and postbachelor's certificates
- **Suburban** 73-acre campus with easy access to Boston
- **Coed**, 3,599 undergraduate students, 83% full-time, 67% women, 33% men
- **Moderately difficult** entrance level, 60% of applicants were admitted
- **15:1 student-to-undergraduate faculty ratio**
- **45% graduate** in 6 years or less
- **$2830 tuition** and fees (in-state); $8850 (out-of-state)
- **$5025 average financial aid** package, $12,339 average indebtedness upon graduation, $4.7 million endowment

Framingham State College announces the September 2000 opening of its new Athletic and Recreation Center. The center will house a 2-court gymnasium, a fitness/cardiovascular area, multipurpose studios, and training-room and locker-room facilities.

Part of Massachusetts Public Higher Education System.

Students *Undergraduates:* 2,983 full-time, 616 part-time. Students come from 18 states and territories, 19 other countries. *The most frequently chosen baccalaureate fields are:* business/marketing, psychology, social sciences and history. *Graduate:* 1,401 in graduate degree programs.

Massachusetts

Framingham State College (continued)

From out-of-state	8%	Reside on campus	40%
Age 25 or older	19%	International students	3%
African Americans	5%	Asian Americans/Pacific Islanders	2%
Hispanic Americans	3%	Native Americans	0.4%

Faculty 314 (52% full-time), 73% with terminal degrees.

Expenses (2000–2001, estimated) *One-time required fee:* $86. *Tuition, state resident:* full-time $1030; part-time $182 per course. *Tuition, nonresident:* full-time $7050; part-time $1175 per course. *Required fees:* full-time $1800; $86 per credit hour. Full-time tuition and fees vary according to class time and student level. Part-time tuition and fees vary according to class time, course load, and student level. *College room and board:* $4154. Room and board charges vary according to board plan. *Payment plan:* installment. *Waivers:* senior citizens and employees or children of employees.

Library Whittemore Library. *Operations spending 1999–2000:* $1.4 million. *Collection:* 191,969 titles, 1,598 serial subscriptions, 2,217 audiovisual materials.

College life *Housing: Options:* coed, women-only. *Most popular organizations:* Student Union Activities Board, Student Government Association, Gatepost (student newspaper), Hilltop Players, literary magazine.

Campus security 24-hour emergency response devices and patrols, student patrols, late-night transport-escort service, controlled dormitory access.

After graduation 22 organizations recruited on campus 1997–98. 80% of class of 1998 had job offers within 6 months. *Career center:* 4 full-time personnel. Services include job fairs, resume preparation, interview workshops, resume referral, career counseling, careers library, job bank, job interviews. *Graduate education:* 15% of class of 1999 went directly to graduate and professional school.

Freshmen 3,196 applied, 1,928 admitted, 625 enrolled.

Average high school GPA	2.87	SAT verbal scores above 500	54%
SAT math scores above 500	49%	ACT above 18	N/R
From top 10% of their h.s. class	6%	From top quarter	27%
From top half	75%	1998 freshmen returning in 1999	68%

Application *Options:* eApply at www.CollegeQuest.com, electronic application, early admission, early action, deferred entrance. *Preference* given to state residents. *Application fee:* $10. *Required:* high school transcript. *Required for some:* essay or personal statement; interview. *Recommended:* essay or personal statement; minimum 2.9 GPA; letters of recommendation.

Standardized tests *Admission: Required:* SAT I or ACT.

Significant dates *Application deadlines:* 3/15 (freshmen), 3/15 (transfers). *Early action:* 11/15. *Notification:* 12/15 (early action). *Financial aid deadline priority date:* 3/1.

Freshman Application Contact
Dr. Philip M. Dooher, Dean of Admissions and Enrollment Services, Framingham State College, 100 State Street, PO Box 9101, Framingham, MA 01701-9101. **Phone:** 508-626-4500. **Fax:** 508-626-4017. **E-mail:** admiss@frc.mass.edu

Visit CollegeQuest.com for information on majors offered and athletics. Electronic viewbook available at CollegeQuest.com.

■ *See page 1688 for a narrative description.*

FRANKLIN INSTITUTE OF BOSTON
Boston, Massachusetts

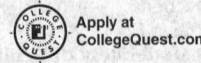
Apply at CollegeQuest.com

- **Independent**, primarily 2-year, founded 1908
- **Degrees** associate and bachelor's
- **Urban** 3-acre campus
- **Coed**, primarily men, 342 undergraduate students, 97% full-time, 11% women, 89% men
- **Minimally difficult** entrance level
- **10:1 student-to-undergraduate faculty ratio**
- **$10,120 tuition** and fees

Faculty 35 (86% full-time).

Admissions Office Contact
Franklin Institute of Boston, 41 Berkeley Street, Boston, MA 02116-6296. **Fax:** 617-482-3706. **E-mail:** fibadm@franklin-fib.edu

Visit CollegeQuest.com for information on majors offered and athletics. Electronic viewbook available at CollegeQuest.com.

GORDON COLLEGE
Wenham, Massachusetts

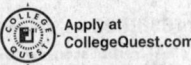
Apply at CollegeQuest.com

- **Independent nondenominational**, comprehensive, founded 1889
- **Degrees** bachelor's and master's
- **Small-town** 500-acre campus with easy access to Boston
- **Coed**, 1,487 undergraduate students, 97% full-time, 65% women, 35% men
- **Moderately difficult** entrance level, 76% of applicants were admitted
- **18:1 student-to-undergraduate faculty ratio**
- **65% graduate** in 6 years or less
- **$16,420 tuition** and fees
- **$13,675 average financial aid** package, $10,429 average indebtedness upon graduation, $21.1 million endowment

Students *Undergraduates:* 1,439 full-time, 48 part-time. Students come from 40 states and territories, 18 other countries. *The most frequently chosen baccalaureate fields are:* English, philosophy, social sciences and history. *Graduate:* 61 in graduate degree programs.

From out-of-state	70%	Reside on campus	84%
Age 25 or older	3%	Transferred in	3%
International students	2%	African Americans	1%
Asian Americans/Pacific Islanders	2%	Hispanic Americans	1%
Native Americans	0.2%		

Faculty 116 (72% full-time).

Expenses (1999–2000) *Comprehensive fee:* $21,470 includes full-time tuition ($15,740), mandatory fees ($680), and room and board ($5050). *College room only:* $3400. Room and board charges vary according to board plan and housing facility. *Part-time tuition:* $4320 per term. *Part-time fees:* $170 per term part-time. Part-time tuition and fees vary according to course load. *Payment plans:* tuition prepayment, installment. *Waivers:* employees or children of employees.

Library Jenks Learning Resource Center. *Operations spending 1999–2000:* $534,131. *Collection:* 169,521 titles, 5,751 serial subscriptions, 7,079 audiovisual materials.

College life *Housing: Options:* coed, men-only, women-only, disabled students. *Most popular organizations:* Student Government Association, student ministries, diverse music ensembles.

Campus security 24-hour emergency response devices and patrols, late-night transport-escort service.

After graduation 48 organizations recruited on campus 1997–98. *Career center:* 3 full-time personnel. Services include job fairs, resume preparation, interview workshops, resume referral, career/interest testing, career counseling, careers library, job bank, job interviews. *Graduate education:* 19% of class of 1999 went directly to graduate and professional school.

Freshmen 963 applied, 734 admitted, 385 enrolled. 5 National Merit Scholars.

Average high school GPA	3.46	SAT verbal scores above 500	91%
SAT math scores above 500	88%	ACT above 18	100%
From top 10% of their h.s. class	36%	From top quarter	67%
From top half	92%	1998 freshmen returning in 1999	87%

Application *Options:* eApply at www.CollegeQuest.com, electronic application, early admission, early decision, deferred entrance. *Application fee:* $40. *Required:* essay or personal statement; high school transcript; 2 letters of recommendation; interview; pastoral recommendation, statement of Christian faith. *Recommended:* minimum 2.5 GPA.

Standardized tests *Admission: Required:* SAT I or ACT.

Significant dates *Application deadlines:* rolling (freshmen), rolling (transfers). *Early decision:* 12/1. *Notification:* 1/15 (early decision). *Financial aid deadline priority date:* 3/1.

Freshman Application Contact
Mr. Silvio E. Vazquez, Dean of Admissions, Gordon College, 255 Grapevine Road, Wenham, MA 01984-1899. **Phone:** 978-927-2300 Ext. 4218. **Toll-free phone:** 800-343-1379. **Fax:** 978-524-3704. **E-mail:** admissions@hope.gordon.edu

Visit CollegeQuest.com for information on majors offered and athletics. College video available at CollegeQuest.com.

■ *See page 1726 for a narrative description.*

Massachusetts

HAMPSHIRE COLLEGE
Amherst, Massachusetts

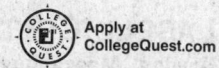 Apply at CollegeQuest.com

- **Independent**, 4-year, founded 1965
- **Degree** bachelor's
- **Rural** 800-acre campus
- **Coed**, 1,162 undergraduate students, 100% full-time, 56% women, 44% men
- **Moderately difficult** entrance level, 61% of applicants were admitted
- **12:1 student-to-undergraduate faculty ratio**
- **55.8% graduate** in 6 years or less
- **$25,400 tuition** and fees
- **$21,500 average financial aid** package, $16,000 average indebtedness upon graduation, $22.1 million endowment

Hampshire College's bold, innovative approach to the liberal arts creates an academic atmosphere that energizes students to work hard and grow tremendously, both personally and intellectually. Students have the freedom to design an individualized course of study in a graduate school–like environment, culminating in original final projects such as science or social science research, academic study, or a body of work in writing, performing, visual, or media arts. Students work closely with faculty mentors, often integrating different disciplines. Independent thinking is expected. Hampshire students and faculty agree: if what a student loves is incorporated into his or her education, the student will love his or her education.

Students *Undergraduates:* 1,162 full-time. Students come from 50 states and territories, 31 other countries.

From out-of-state	83%	Reside on campus	94%
Age 25 or older	2%	Transferred in	4%
International students	5%	African Americans	4%
Asian Americans/Pacific Islanders	4%	Hispanic Americans	3%
Native Americans	0.2%		

Faculty 94 (90% full-time).
Expenses (1999–2000) *One-time required fee:* $90. *Comprehensive fee:* $32,022 includes full-time tuition ($24,984), mandatory fees ($416), and room and board ($6622). *College room only:* $4209. Room and board charges vary according to board plan. *Waivers:* employees or children of employees.
Library Harold F. Johnson Library. *Operations spending 1999–2000:* $1.2 million. *Collection:* 120,918 titles, 760 serial subscriptions, 35,657 audiovisual materials.
College life *Housing:* on-campus residence required through senior year. *Options:* coed, disabled students. *Most popular organizations:* SOURCE groups, Human Rights, Student Action, Sports Co-Op, Women's Center organizations.
Campus security 24-hour emergency response devices and patrols, student patrols, late-night transport-escort service.
After graduation *Career center:* 2 full-time, 1 part-time personnel. Services include job fairs, resume preparation, interview workshops, career/interest testing, career counseling, careers library, job bank, job interviews. *Major awards:* 1 Fulbright Scholar.
Freshmen 1,774 applied, 1,079 admitted, 295 enrolled.

Average high school GPA	3.29	SAT verbal scores above 500	97%
SAT math scores above 500	93%	ACT above 18	90%
From top 10% of their h.s. class	22%	From top quarter	58%
From top half	90%	1998 freshmen returning in 1999	77%

Application *Options:* eApply at www.CollegeQuest.com, Common Application, early admission, early decision, early action, deferred entrance. *Application fee:* $50. *Required:* essay or personal statement; high school transcript; 2 letters of recommendation. *Recommended:* interview.
Significant dates *Application deadlines:* 2/1 (freshmen), 3/15 (transfers). *Early decision:* 11/15, 1/1. *Notification:* 4/1 (freshmen), 12/15 (early decision), 2/1 (early action). *Financial aid deadline priority date:* 2/1.
Freshman Application Contact
Ms. Audrey Smith, Director of Admissions, Hampshire College, 839 West Street, Amherst, MA 01002. **Phone:** 413-559-5471. **Fax:** 413-582-5631. **E-mail:** admissions@hampshire.edu
Visit CollegeQuest.com for information on majors offered and athletics. College video available at CollegeQuest.com.

■ *See page 1758 for a narrative description.*

HARVARD UNIVERSITY
Cambridge, Massachusetts

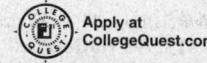 Apply at CollegeQuest.com

- **Independent**, university, founded 1636
- **Degrees** bachelor's, master's, doctoral, and first professional
- **Urban** 380-acre campus with easy access to Boston
- **Coed**, 6,684 undergraduate students, 99% full-time, 46% women, 54% men
- **Most difficult** entrance level, 11% of applicants were admitted
- **8:1 student-to-undergraduate faculty ratio**
- **97% graduate** in 6 years or less
- **$24,407 tuition** and fees
- **$22,010 average financial aid** package, $14,744 average indebtedness upon graduation, $14.5 billion endowment

Students *Undergraduates:* Students come from 53 states and territories, 93 other countries.

Reside on campus	96%	Age 25 or older	1%
International students	7%	African Americans	8%
Asian Americans/Pacific Islanders	17%	Hispanic Americans	8%
Native Americans	1%		

Faculty 2,336 (73% full-time), 72% with terminal degrees.
Expenses (1999–2000) *Comprehensive fee:* $32,164 includes full-time tuition ($22,054), mandatory fees ($2353), and room and board ($7757). *College room only:* $4072. *Payment plans:* tuition prepayment, installment.
Library Widener Library plus 90 others. *Operations spending 1999–2000:* $91 million. *Collection:* 13.4 million titles, 97,568 serial subscriptions.
College life *Housing:* on-campus residence required in freshman year. *Option:* coed. *Social organizations:* "House" system; 99% of eligible men and 99% of eligible women are members. *Most popular organizations:* Phillips Brooks House, Asian-American Association, International Relations Council, Harvard Crimson (newspaper), Harvard/Radcliffe Chorus.
Campus security 24-hour emergency response devices and patrols, late-night transport-escort service, controlled dormitory access, required and optional safety courses.
After graduation *Career center:* 15 full-time, 14 part-time personnel. Services include job fairs, resume preparation, interview workshops, career counseling, careers library, job bank, job interviews. *Major awards:* 2 Rhodes, 7 Marshall scholars.
Freshmen 18,161 applied, 2,068 admitted. 370 National Merit Scholars, 5 Westinghouse recipients.

SAT verbal scores above 500	N/R	SAT math scores above 500	N/R
ACT above 18	N/R	From top 10% of their h.s. class	95%
From top quarter	99%	From top half	100%
1998 freshmen returning in 1999	97%		

Application *Options:* eApply at www.CollegeQuest.com, Common Application, early action, deferred entrance. *Application fee:* $60. *Required:* essay or personal statement; high school transcript; 2 letters of recommendation; interview.
Standardized tests *Admission: Required:* SAT I or ACT, SAT II Subject Tests.
Significant dates *Application deadlines:* 1/1 (freshmen), 2/1 (transfers). *Early action:* 11/1. *Notification:* 4/1 (freshmen), 12/15 (early action). *Financial aid deadline priority date:* 2/1.
Freshman Application Contact
Office of Admissions and Financial Aid, Harvard University, Byerly Hall, 8 Garden Street, Cambridge, MA 02138. **Phone:** 617-495-1551. **E-mail:** college@harvard.edu
Visit CollegeQuest.com for information on majors offered and athletics. College video available at CollegeQuest.com.

■ *See page 1772 for a narrative description.*

HEBREW COLLEGE
Brookline, Massachusetts

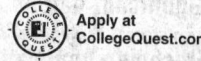 Apply at CollegeQuest.com

- **Independent Jewish**, comprehensive, founded 1921
- **Degrees** bachelor's and master's
- **Suburban** 3-acre campus with easy access to Boston
- **Coed**
- **Noncompetitive** entrance level

Peterson's Guide to Four-Year Colleges 2001   www.petersons.com

Massachusetts

Hebrew College (continued)
- **$13,590 tuition** and fees

Expenses (1999–2000) *Tuition:* full-time $13,500; part-time $450 per credit. *Required fees:* full-time $90; $45 per term part-time.
Institutional Web site http://www.hebrewcollege.edu/
College life *Housing:* college housing not available.
Application *Options:* eApply at www.CollegeQuest.com, Common Application, early decision, deferred entrance. *Application fee:* $25. *Required:* essay or personal statement; high school transcript; minimum 2.0 GPA; 2 letters of recommendation. *Recommended:* interview.
Standardized tests *Placement: Required:* SAT I
Admissions Office Contact
Hebrew College, 43 Hawes Street, Brookline, MA 02446-5495. **Toll-free phone:** 800-866-4814. **Fax:** 617-734-9769. **E-mail:** nfrankel@lynx.neu.edu
Visit CollegeQuest.com for information on athletics.

HELLENIC COLLEGE
Brookline, Massachusetts

- **Independent Greek Orthodox**, 4-year, founded 1937
- **Degree** bachelor's
- **Suburban** 52-acre campus with easy access to Boston
- **Coed**, 51 undergraduate students, 100% full-time, 29% women, 71% men
- **Minimally difficult** entrance level, 74% of applicants were admitted
- **6:1 student-to-undergraduate faculty ratio**
- **$8615 tuition** and fees
- **$8000 average financial aid** package, $15,000 average indebtedness upon graduation, $16.2 million endowment

Students *Undergraduates:* 51 full-time. Students come from 29 states and territories, 6 other countries. *The most frequently chosen baccalaureate fields are:* education, foreign language/literature, philosophy.

From out-of-state	87%	Reside on campus	90%
Age 25 or older	10%	Transferred in	10%
International students	25%		

Faculty 29 (28% full-time).
Expenses (1999–2000) *One-time required fee:* $50. *Comprehensive fee:* $15,215 includes full-time tuition ($8400), mandatory fees ($215), and room and board ($6600). Room and board charges vary according to housing facility. *Part-time tuition:* $350 per credit. *Part-time fees:* $50 per term part-time. *Waivers:* minority students, children of alumni, and employees or children of employees.
Library Archbishop Iakoros Library. *Operations spending 1999–2000:* $312,390. *Collection:* 109,000 titles, 770 serial subscriptions, 1,340 audiovisual materials.
College life *Housing:* on-campus residence required through senior year. *Option:* coed.
Campus security Controlled dormitory access.
After graduation *Career center:* Services include interview workshops, career counseling, careers library.
Freshmen 19 applied, 14 admitted, 5 enrolled.

Average high school GPA	2.53	SAT verbal scores above 500	N/R
SAT math scores above 500	N/R	ACT above 18	N/R
1998 freshmen returning in 1999	100%		

Application *Options:* Common Application, deferred entrance. *Application fee:* $35. *Required:* essay or personal statement; high school transcript; minimum 2.0 GPA; letters of recommendation; interview; health certificate.
Standardized tests *Admission: Required:* SAT I or ACT. *Required for some:* SAT II: Writing Test.
Significant dates *Application deadlines:* rolling (freshmen), rolling (transfers). *Financial aid deadline priority date:* 5/1.
Freshman Application Contact
Rev. Deacon Gerasimos Michaleas, Director of Admissions and Records, Hellenic College, 50 Goddard Avenue, Brookline, MA 02445-7496. **Phone:** 617-731-3500 Ext. 1260. **Fax:** 617-232-7819. **E-mail:** admissions@hchc.edu
Visit CollegeQuest.com for information on majors offered and athletics. College video available at CollegeQuest.com.

LASELL COLLEGE
Newton, Massachusetts

- **Independent**, 4-year, founded 1851
- **Degrees** associate and bachelor's
- **Suburban** 50-acre campus with easy access to Boston
- **Coed**, 706 undergraduate students, 97% full-time, 80% women, 20% men
- **Moderately difficult** entrance level, 82% of applicants were admitted
- **10:1 student-to-undergraduate faculty ratio**
- **$14,900 tuition** and fees
- **$15,967 average financial aid** package, $17,209 average indebtedness upon graduation, $12.1 million endowment

The Lasell Plan of Education is distinguished by a philosophy called connected learning. In connected learning, students practice classroom theory in practical settings. In addition to off-campus internship sites, students gain practical experience in on-campus labs, which include 2 renowned child-study centers, a state-of-the-art business technology center, travel agency, bed and breakfast, fashion design and merchandising center, allied health labs, CADD lab, and an art center.

Students *Undergraduates:* 687 full-time, 19 part-time. Students come from 20 states and territories, 8 other countries. *The most frequently chosen baccalaureate fields are:* business/marketing, education, protective services/public administration.

From out-of-state	36%	Reside on campus	70%
Age 25 or older	15%	Transferred in	6%
International students	1%	African Americans	12%
Asian Americans/Pacific Islanders	4%	Hispanic Americans	6%

Faculty 131 (31% full-time), 37% with terminal degrees.
Expenses (1999–2000) *One-time required fee:* $400. *Comprehensive fee:* $22,400 includes full-time tuition ($14,300), mandatory fees ($600), and room and board ($7500). Full-time tuition and fees vary according to program. *Part-time tuition:* $475 per semester hour. *Part-time fees:* $150 per term part-time. Part-time tuition and fees vary according to course load and program. One-time mandatory fee for part-time students: $200. *Payment plan:* installment. *Waivers:* children of alumni and employees or children of employees.
Library Brennan Library plus 1 other. *Operations spending 1999–2000:* $251,333. *Collection:* 51,219 titles, 521 serial subscriptions, 2,145 audiovisual materials.
College life *Housing: Option:* women-only. *Most popular organizations:* Center for Public Service, student government, Umoja-Nia, yearbook, fashion board.
Campus security 24-hour emergency response devices and patrols, late-night transport-escort service, controlled dormitory access.
After graduation 40 organizations recruited on campus 1997–98. 85% of class of 1998 had job offers within 6 months. *Career center:* 1 full-time, 1 part-time personnel. Services include job fairs, resume preparation, interview workshops, resume referral, career/interest testing, career counseling, careers library, job bank, job interviews. *Graduate education:* 8% of class of 1999 went directly to graduate and professional school: 5% education, 1% business, 1% graduate arts and sciences, 1% law.
Freshmen 1,314 applied, 1,081 admitted, 276 enrolled. 3 class presidents, 70 student government officers.

Average high school GPA	2.4	SAT verbal scores above 500	46%
SAT math scores above 500	41%	ACT above 18	N/R
From top 10% of their h.s. class	6%	From top quarter	32%
From top half	62%	1998 freshmen returning in 1999	82%

Application *Options:* Common Application, electronic application, deferred entrance. *Application fee:* $25. *Required:* high school transcript; minimum 2.0 GPA; 1 letter of recommendation. *Recommended:* essay or personal statement; interview.
Standardized tests *Admission: Required:* SAT I or ACT.
Significant dates *Application deadlines:* rolling (freshmen), rolling (transfers). *Financial aid deadline priority date:* 4/1.
Freshman Application Contact
Mr. David Eddy, Director of Admission, Lasell College, 1844 Commonwealth Avenue, Newton, MA 02466-2709. **Phone:** 617-243-2225. **Toll-free phone:** 888-LASELL-4. **Fax:** 617-796-4343.
Visit CollegeQuest.com for information on majors offered and athletics.

- *See page 1902 for a narrative description.*

Massachusetts

LESLEY COLLEGE
Cambridge, Massachusetts

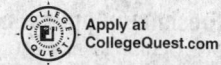 Apply at CollegeQuest.com

- **Independent**, comprehensive, founded 1909
- **Degrees** associate, bachelor's, master's, doctoral, and post-master's certificates
- **Urban** 5-acre campus with easy access to Boston
- **Women** only, 571 undergraduate students
- **Moderately difficult** entrance level, 82% of applicants were admitted
- **15:1** student-to-undergraduate faculty ratio
- **$15,600 tuition** and fees
- **$11,200 average financial aid** package, $13,378 average indebtedness upon graduation, $28.5 million endowment

Located in Cambridge, Massachusetts, Lesley College offers women academic programs in art therapy, counseling, education, human services, management, and the liberal arts. An education at Lesley combines theoretical and practical approaches to learning, blending a strong liberal arts foundation with solid professional preparation. Field exposure begins freshman year and complements classroom instruction throughout the undergraduate program.

Students *Undergraduates:* Students come from 32 states and territories, 10 other countries. *The most frequently chosen baccalaureate fields are:* health professions and related sciences, education, liberal arts/general studies.

From out-of-state	32%	Reside on campus	59%
International students	5%	African Americans	6%
Asian Americans/Pacific Islanders	5%	Hispanic Americans	8%
Native Americans	0.2%		

Faculty 37 (100% full-time), 70% with terminal degrees.
Expenses (1999–2000) *Comprehensive fee:* $22,800 includes full-time tuition ($15,450), mandatory fees ($150), and room and board ($7200). Full-time tuition and fees vary according to course load. *Part-time tuition:* $454 per credit. *Payment plan:* installment. *Waivers:* employees or children of employees.
Library Eleanor DeWolfe Ludcke Library. *Operations spending 1999–2000:* $1.2 million. *Collection:* 100,992 titles, 91,873 serial subscriptions, 1,308 audiovisual materials.
College life *Housing: Option:* women-only. *Most popular organizations:* Student Senate, Gay/Straight/Bisexual Alliance, Education Council, LINC (Learning in Neighborhood Communities), spirit club.
Campus security 24-hour emergency response devices and patrols, late-night transport-escort service.
After graduation 77 organizations recruited on campus 1997–98. 83% of class of 1998 had job offers within 6 months. *Career center:* 5 full-time personnel. Services include job fairs, resume preparation, interview workshops, career/interest testing, career counseling, careers library, job bank, job interviews. *Graduate education:* 13% of class of 1999 went directly to graduate and professional school.
Freshmen 333 applied, 272 admitted.

Average high school GPA	2.8	SAT verbal scores above 500	53%
SAT math scores above 500	39%	ACT above 18	N/R
From top 10% of their h.s. class	13%	From top quarter	34%
From top half	71%	1998 freshmen returning in 1999	80%

Application *Options:* eApply at www.CollegeQuest.com, electronic application, early decision, deferred entrance. *Application fee:* $35. *Required:* essay or personal statement; high school transcript; 3 letters of recommendation. *Recommended:* interview.
Standardized tests *Admission: Required:* SAT I or ACT.
Significant dates *Application deadlines:* 3/17 (freshmen), 5/1 (transfers). *Early decision:* 12/1. *Notification:* 12/15 (early decision). *Financial aid deadline priority date:* 2/1.
Freshman Application Contact
Ms. Jane A. Raley, Director of Women's College Admissions, Lesley College, 29 Everett Street, Cambridge, MA 02138-2790. **Phone:** 617-349-8800. **Toll-free phone:** 800-999-1959 Ext. 8800. **Fax:** 617-349-8150. **E-mail:** ugadm@mail.lesley.edu

Visit CollegeQuest.com for information on majors offered and athletics.

- *See page 1918 for a narrative description.*

MASSACHUSETTS COLLEGE OF ART
Boston, Massachusetts

- **State-supported**, comprehensive, founded 1873
- **Degrees** bachelor's, master's, and postbachelor's certificates
- **Urban** 5-acre campus
- **Coed**, 1,511 undergraduate students, 82% full-time, 61% women, 39% men
- **Very difficult** entrance level, 47% of applicants were admitted
- **13:1** student-to-undergraduate faculty ratio
- **53% graduate** in 6 years or less
- **$3808 tuition** and fees (in-state); $10,668 (out-of-state)
- **$8440 average financial aid** package, $16,760 average indebtedness upon graduation, $1.4 million endowment

Part of Massachusetts Public Higher Education System.

Students *Undergraduates:* 1,244 full-time, 267 part-time. Students come from 34 states and territories, 36 other countries. *The most frequently chosen baccalaureate fields are:* education, architecture, visual/performing arts. *Graduate:* 105 in graduate degree programs.

From out-of-state	22%	Reside on campus	14%
Age 25 or older	22%	Transferred in	10%
International students	5%	African Americans	3%
Asian Americans/Pacific Islanders	3%	Hispanic Americans	3%
Native Americans	0.2%		

Faculty 193 (37% full-time).
Expenses (1999–2000) *Tuition, state resident:* full-time $1140; part-time $142 per course. *Tuition, nonresident:* full-time $8000; part-time $1000 per course. *Required fees:* full-time $2668; $935 per term part-time. Full-time tuition and fees vary according to reciprocity agreements. Part-time tuition and fees vary according to class time, course load, and reciprocity agreements. *College room and board:* $7164. Room and board charges vary according to housing facility. *Payment plan:* installment. *Waivers:* senior citizens and employees or children of employees.
Library Morton R. Godine Library. *Operations spending 1999–2000:* $877,611. *Collection:* 757 serial subscriptions, 125,000 audiovisual materials.
College life *Housing: Option:* coed. *Most popular organizations:* international students, Design Research Unit, Spectrum, film society, Event Works.
Campus security 24-hour emergency response devices and patrols, late-night transport-escort service, security lighting, self-defense workshops.
After graduation 8 organizations recruited on campus 1997–98. *Career center:* 3 full-time, 1 part-time personnel. Services include resume preparation, resume referral, career counseling, careers library, job bank, job interviews. *Graduate education:* 5% of class of 1999 went directly to graduate and professional school.
Freshmen 1,049 applied, 497 admitted, 250 enrolled.

Average high school GPA	3.14	SAT verbal scores above 500	80%
SAT math scores above 500	74%	ACT above 18	N/R
From top 10% of their h.s. class	16%	From top quarter	56%
From top half	88%	1998 freshmen returning in 1999	86%

Application *Options:* early admission, early decision, deferred entrance. *Preference* given to state residents. *Application fee:* $65 for nonresidents. *Required:* essay or personal statement; high school transcript; minimum 2.9 GPA; portfolio. *Recommended:* letters of recommendation.
Standardized tests *Admission: Required:* SAT I or ACT.
Significant dates *Application deadlines:* 3/1 (freshmen), 4/1 (transfers). *Early decision:* 12/1. *Notification:* continuous until 4/20 (freshmen). *Financial aid deadline priority date:* 3/15.
Freshman Application Contact
Ms. Kay Ransdell, Dean of Admissions, Massachusetts College of Art, 621 Huntington Avenue, Boston, MA 02115-5882. **Phone:** 617-232-1555 Ext. 235. **Fax:** 617-739-9744. **E-mail:** admissions@massart.edu

Visit CollegeQuest.com for information on majors offered and athletics. College video available at CollegeQuest.com.

Massachusetts

MASSACHUSETTS COLLEGE OF LIBERAL ARTS
North Adams, Massachusetts

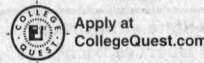 Apply at CollegeQuest.com

- **State-supported**, comprehensive, founded 1894
- **Degrees** bachelor's, master's, and postbachelor's certificates
- **Small-town** 80-acre campus
- **Coed**, 1,246 undergraduate students, 85% full-time, 61% women, 39% men
- **Moderately difficult** entrance level, 70% of applicants were admitted
- **13:1 student-to-undergraduate faculty ratio**
- **33.5% graduate** in 6 years or less
- **$3357 tuition** and fees (in-state); $9317 (out-of-state)
- **$6217 average financial aid** package, $15,524 average indebtedness upon graduation, $3.5 million endowment

North Adams State College changed its name to Massachusetts College of Liberal Arts to officially recognize the institution's liberal arts character. With this new designation, Massachusetts College joins the 2 other specialized institutions in the public sector (Massachusetts College of Art and Massachusetts Maritime Academy) in providing a distinctive educational experience.

Part of Massachusetts Public Higher Education System.

Students *Undergraduates:* 1,058 full-time, 188 part-time. Students come from 20 states and territories. *The most frequently chosen baccalaureate fields are:* business/marketing, English, social sciences and history. *Graduate:* 128 in graduate degree programs.

From out-of-state	16%	Reside on campus	50%
Age 25 or older	23%	Transferred in	9%
African Americans	5%	Asian Americans/Pacific Islanders	1%
Hispanic Americans	2%	Native Americans	1%

Faculty 134 (63% full-time), 47% with terminal degrees.

Expenses (2000–2001) *Tuition, area resident:* part-time $370 per credit. *Tuition, state resident:* full-time $1090. *Tuition, nonresident:* full-time $7050. *Required fees:* full-time $2267. Full-time tuition and fees vary according to reciprocity agreements. Part-time tuition and fees vary according to reciprocity agreements. *College room and board:* $4290; room only: $2748. Room and board charges vary according to board plan and housing facility. *Payment plan:* installment. *Waivers:* senior citizens and employees or children of employees.

Library Freel Library. *Operations spending 1999–2000:* $701,667. *Collection:* 541 serial subscriptions, 4,567 audiovisual materials.

College life *Housing:* on-campus residence required through junior year. *Options:* coed, disabled students. *Social organizations:* national fraternities, national sororities, local fraternities, local sororities; 5% of eligible men and 10% of eligible women are members. *Most popular organizations:* Student Activities Council, weightlifting club, Non-Traditional Student Organization, outing club, lacrosse club.

Campus security 24-hour emergency response devices and patrols, late-night transport-escort service, controlled dormitory access.

After graduation 15 organizations recruited on campus 1997–98. 79% of class of 1998 had job offers within 6 months. *Career center:* 4 full-time personnel. Services include job fairs, resume preparation, interview workshops, resume referral, career/interest testing, career counseling, careers library, job bank, job interviews. *Graduate education:* 7% of class of 1999 went directly to graduate and professional school.

Freshmen 1,019 applied, 718 admitted, 225 enrolled.

Average high school GPA	2.94	SAT verbal scores above 500	61%
SAT math scores above 500	54%	ACT above 18	N/R
1998 freshmen returning in 1999	72%		

Application *Options:* eApply at www.CollegeQuest.com, Common Application, electronic application, early action, deferred entrance. *Application fee:* $10. *Required:* essay or personal statement; high school transcript; minimum 2.7 GPA. *Required for some:* interview. *Recommended:* letters of recommendation; interview.

Standardized tests *Admission: Required:* SAT I or ACT.

Significant dates *Application deadlines:* rolling (freshmen), rolling (transfers). *Early action:* 12/1. *Notification:* 12/15 (early action). **Financial aid deadline priority date:** 4/1.

Freshman Application Contact
Ms. Denise Richardello, Dean of Enrollment Management, Massachusetts College of Liberal Arts, 375 Church Street, North Adams, MA 01247-4100. **Phone:** 413-662-5410 Ext. 5416. **Toll-free phone:** 800-292-6632. **Fax:** 413-662-5179. **E-mail:** admissions@mcla.mass.edu
Visit CollegeQuest.com for information on majors offered and athletics. College video available at CollegeQuest.com.

■ *See page 2020 for a narrative description.*

MASSACHUSETTS COLLEGE OF PHARMACY AND HEALTH SCIENCES
Boston, Massachusetts

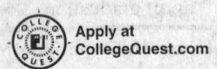 Apply at CollegeQuest.com

- **Independent**, university, founded 1823
- **Degrees** bachelor's, master's, doctoral, first professional, and first professional certificates (bachelor of science in nursing program for registered nurses only)
- **Urban** 2-acre campus
- **Coed**, 920 undergraduate students, 88% full-time, 63% women, 37% men
- **Moderately difficult** entrance level
- **14:1 student-to-undergraduate faculty ratio**
- **$17,320 tuition** and fees
- **$14,774 average financial aid** package, $23,372 average indebtedness upon graduation, $22.5 million endowment

An 8-story, 280,000-square-foot facility was completed in 1996. Connected to the White Building by an atrium, the Fennell-Iorio Wing houses a residence hall, dining commons, sophisticated research facilities, laboratories, offices, and classrooms. MCPHS offers the following programs: PharmD, 6 years; MS in physician assistant studies (6 years); BS in chemistry, health psychology, health communications, premed and health studies, pharmaceutical sciences, radiological sciences; and a completion program for RN to BSN and MSN.

Students *Undergraduates:* 808 full-time, 112 part-time. Students come from 30 states and territories, 8 other countries. *The most frequently chosen baccalaureate field is:* health professions and related sciences. *Graduate:* 974 in professional programs, 89 in other graduate degree programs.

From out-of-state	30%	Reside on campus	15%
Transferred in	29%		

Faculty 99 (90% full-time).

Expenses (1999–2000) *Comprehensive fee:* $25,220 includes full-time tuition ($16,900), mandatory fees ($420), and room and board ($7900). Full-time tuition and fees vary according to course level and program. *Part-time tuition:* $487 per semester hour. *Part-time fees:* $210 per term part-time. Part-time tuition and fees vary according to course level and program. *Payment plan:* installment. *Waivers:* employees or children of employees.

Library Shepard Library. *Collection:* 60,000 titles, 790 serial subscriptions, 750 audiovisual materials.

College life *Housing: Option:* coed. *Social organizations:* national fraternities, national sororities, local fraternities, local sororities; 35% of eligible men and 30% of eligible women are members. *Most popular organizations:* student government, Vietnamese Student Organization, Academy of Students of Pharmacy, Physician Assistant Student Society, Lambda Kappa Sigma.

Campus security 24-hour emergency response devices and patrols, controlled dormitory access, electronically operated academic area entrances.

After graduation 45 organizations recruited on campus 1997–98. *Career center:* Services include resume preparation, interview workshops, career counseling, job interviews.

Freshmen 10 enrolled.

Average high school GPA	3.17	SAT verbal scores above 500	57%
SAT math scores above 500	74%	ACT above 18	N/R
From top 10% of their h.s. class	28%	From top quarter	58%
From top half	90%	1998 freshmen returning in 1999	3%

Application *Options:* eApply at www.CollegeQuest.com, Common Application, early admission, early decision, deferred entrance. *Application fee:* $60. *Required:* essay or personal statement; high school transcript; 2 letters of recommendation. *Required for some:* 3 letters of recommendation; interview. *Recommended:* interview.

Massachusetts

Standardized tests *Admission: Required:* SAT I or ACT.
Significant dates *Application deadlines:* 3/1 (freshmen), 3/1 (transfers). *Early decision:* 11/1. *Notification:* continuous until 8/1 (freshmen), 12/1 (early decision). *Financial aid deadline priority date:* 3/15.
Freshman Application Contact
Ms. Kathleen Houghton, Director of Admission, Massachusetts College of Pharmacy and Health Sciences, 179 Longwood Avenue, Boston, MA 02115-5896. **Phone:** 617-732-2850 Ext. 2791. **Toll-free phone:** 800-225-5506. **Fax:** 617-732-2801. **E-mail:** admissions@mcp.edu
Visit CollegeQuest.com for information on majors offered and athletics. Electronic viewbook available at CollegeQuest.com.

■ *See page 2022 for a narrative description.*

MASSACHUSETTS INSTITUTE OF TECHNOLOGY
Cambridge, Massachusetts

- **Independent**, university, founded 1861
- **Degrees** bachelor's, master's, and doctoral
- **Urban** 154-acre campus with easy access to Boston
- **Coed**, 4,292 undergraduate students, 99% full-time, 41% women, 59% men
- **Most difficult** entrance level, 19% of applicants were admitted
- **92% graduate** in 6 years or less
- **$25,000 tuition** and fees
- **$23,445 average financial aid** package, $4.3 billion endowment

Students *Undergraduates:* 4,240 full-time, 52 part-time. Students come from 53 states and territories, 81 other countries. *The most frequently chosen baccalaureate fields are:* computer/information sciences, biological/life sciences, engineering/engineering technologies. *Graduate:* 183 in professional programs, 5,489 in other graduate degree programs.

From out-of-state	90%	Reside on campus	95%
Age 25 or older	1%	Transferred in	1%
International students	8%	African Americans	6%
Asian Americans/Pacific Islanders	28%	Hispanic Americans	11%
Native Americans	2%		

Faculty 1,571 (76% full-time).
Expenses (1999–2000) *Comprehensive fee:* $31,900 includes full-time tuition ($25,000) and room and board ($6900). Room and board charges vary according to board plan and housing facility. *Payment plan:* deferred payment. *Waivers:* employees or children of employees.
Library Main library plus 11 others. *Collection:* 2.5 million titles, 18,359 serial subscriptions, 572,094 audiovisual materials.
College life *Housing:* on-campus residence required in freshman year. *Options:* coed, women-only. *Social organizations:* national fraternities, national sororities, local fraternities; 50% of eligible men and 25% of eligible women are members. *Most popular organizations:* Interfraternity Council, Undergraduate Association, Sangam (Indian Students Association), Hillel, Chinese students club.
Campus security 24-hour emergency response devices and patrols, student patrols, late-night transport-escort service, controlled dormitory access.
After graduation 700 organizations recruited on campus 1997–98. 41% of class of 1998 had job offers within 6 months. *Career center:* 11 full-time, 3 part-time personnel. Services include job fairs, resume preparation, resume referral, career counseling, careers library, job bank, job interviews.
Freshmen 9,136 applied, 1,742 admitted, 1,048 enrolled. 133 National Merit Scholars, 55 class presidents, 218 valedictorians, 132 student government officers.

SAT verbal scores above 500	99%	SAT math scores above 500	100%
ACT above 18	100%	From top 10% of their h.s. class	95%
From top quarter	100%	From top half	100%
1998 freshmen returning in 1999	98%		

Application *Options:* electronic application, early action, deferred entrance. *Application fee:* $55. *Required:* essay or personal statement; high school transcript; 2 letters of recommendation; interview.
Standardized tests *Admission: Required:* SAT I or ACT, SAT II Subject Tests.

Significant dates *Application deadlines:* 1/1 (freshmen), 3/15 (transfers). *Early action:* 11/1. *Notification:* 4/1 (freshmen), 12/15 (early action). *Financial aid deadline priority date:* 1/11.
Freshman Application Contact
Ms. Marilee Jones, Dean of Admissions, Massachusetts Institute of Technology, 77 Massachusetts Avenue, Cambridge, MA 02139-4307. **Phone:** 617-253-4791. **Fax:** 617-258-8304. **E-mail:** mitfrosh@mit.edu
Visit CollegeQuest.com for information on majors offered and athletics. College video available at CollegeQuest.com.

■ *See page 2024 for a narrative description.*

MASSACHUSETTS MARITIME ACADEMY
Buzzards Bay, Massachusetts

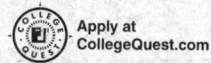
Apply at CollegeQuest.com

- **State-supported**, 4-year, founded 1891
- **Degree** bachelor's
- **Small-town** 55-acre campus with easy access to Boston
- **Coed**, 778 undergraduate students, 97% full-time, 14% women, 86% men
- **Moderately difficult** entrance level, 81% of applicants were admitted
- **12:1** student-to-undergraduate faculty ratio
- **64% graduate** in 6 years or less
- **$2873 tuition** and fees (in-state); $10,953 (out-of-state)
- **$6706 average financial aid** package, $4.1 million endowment

Engineering, international business, transportation and environmental science are all majors at Massachusetts Maritime Academy. The semester at sea takes students on an international odyssey to more than a dozen countries. Paid cooperatives and internships provide the opportunity to learn and earn, while a regimented lifestyle prepares students to lead in industry or the US armed services. Web site: www.mma.mass.edu.

Part of Massachusetts Public Higher Education System.
Students *Undergraduates:* 757 full-time, 21 part-time. Students come from 26 states and territories, 5 other countries. *The most frequently chosen baccalaureate fields are:* engineering/engineering technologies, natural resources/environmental science.

From out-of-state	25%	Age 25 or older	7%
Transferred in	5%		

Faculty 70 (84% full-time), 61% with terminal degrees.
Expenses (2000–2001) *One-time required fee:* $1450. *Tuition, state resident:* full-time $1090. *Tuition, nonresident:* full-time $9170. *Required fees:* full-time $1783. Full-time tuition and fees vary according to reciprocity agreements. *College room and board:* $4560; room only: $2260. *Waivers:* employees or children of employees.
Library Hurley Library. *Operations spending 1999–2000:* $286,500. *Collection:* 42,000 titles, 505 serial subscriptions.
College life *Housing:* on-campus residence required through senior year. *Option:* coed. *Most popular organizations:* club hockey, water sports, sailing/cruising, rugby club, scuba club.
Campus security 24-hour emergency response devices and patrols, late-night transport-escort service.
After graduation *Career center:* 3 full-time personnel. Services include resume preparation, resume referral, career counseling, careers library, job bank, job interviews. *Graduate education:* 1% of class of 1999 went directly to graduate and professional school: 1% engineering.
Freshmen 515 applied, 416 admitted, 181 enrolled.

Average high school GPA	2.8	SAT verbal scores above 500	N/R
SAT math scores above 500	N/R	ACT above 18	N/R
From top 10% of their h.s. class	4%	From top quarter	30%
From top half	60%	1998 freshmen returning in 1999	79%

Application *Options:* eApply at www.CollegeQuest.com, early decision, deferred entrance. *Application fee:* $40 for nonresidents. *Required:* essay or personal statement; high school transcript; 2 letters of recommendation; interview; physical examination.
Standardized tests *Admission: Required:* SAT I. *Recommended:* SAT II Subject Tests.

Massachusetts

Massachusetts Maritime Academy (continued)
Significant dates *Application deadlines:* rolling (freshmen), rolling (transfers). *Early decision:* 11/1. *Notification:* 12/15 (early decision). *Financial aid deadline priority date:* 3/15.
Freshman Application Contact
Roy Fulgueras, Director of Admissions, Massachusetts Maritime Academy, 101 Academy Drive, Buzzards Bay, MA 02532-1803. **Phone:** 508-830-5031. **Toll-free phone:** 800-544-3411. **Fax:** 508-830-5077. **E-mail:** admissions@mma.mass.edu
Visit CollegeQuest.com for information on majors offered and athletics. College video available at CollegeQuest.com.

■ *See page 2026 for a narrative description.*

MERRIMACK COLLEGE
North Andover, Massachusetts

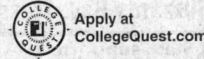 Apply at CollegeQuest.com

- **Independent Roman Catholic**, comprehensive, founded 1947
- **Degrees** associate, bachelor's, and master's
- **Suburban** 220-acre campus with easy access to Boston
- **Coed**, 2,677 undergraduate students, 79% full-time, 50% women, 50% men
- **Moderately difficult** entrance level, 72% of applicants were admitted
- **15:1 student-to-undergraduate faculty ratio**
- **55.8% graduate** in 6 years or less
- **$15,710 tuition** and fees
- **$13,800 average financial aid** package, $22.4 million endowment

Merrimack College recently completed a number of ventures that further enhance the quality of life at the College. Two new majors—communication studies and digital media/graphic design—add to the extensive offerings in the Liberal Arts, Business, Science, and Engineering Schools. With renovations in technology to all classrooms and residence halls, a 1999 opening of the Rogers Center for the Performing Arts, and completion of the Campus Center in January 2001, Merrimack is experiencing a growth to match the enthusiasm of students, alumni, and community alike to become active members in the College.

Students *Undergraduates:* 2,124 full-time, 553 part-time. Students come from 25 states and territories, 20 other countries. *The most frequently chosen baccalaureate fields are:* business/marketing, psychology, social sciences and history.

From out-of-state	21%	Reside on campus	60%
Age 25 or older	3%	Transferred in	4%
International students	2%	African Americans	1%
Asian Americans/Pacific Islanders	1%	Hispanic Americans	2%
Native Americans	0.2%		

Faculty 198 (65% full-time), 93% with terminal degrees.
Expenses (1999–2000) *Comprehensive fee:* $23,210 includes full-time tuition ($15,710) and room and board ($7500). *College room only:* $4200. Room and board charges vary according to board plan and housing facility. *Part-time tuition:* $580 per credit. Part-time tuition and fees vary according to class time. *Payment plans:* installment, deferred payment. *Waivers:* senior citizens and employees or children of employees.
Library McQuade Library. *Operations spending 1999–2000:* $688,292. *Collection:* 120,369 titles, 967 serial subscriptions, 1,300 audiovisual materials.
College life *Housing: Option:* coed. *Social organizations:* national fraternities, national sororities, local fraternities, local sororities; 13% of eligible men and 12% of eligible women are members. *Most popular organizations:* Merrimaction Community Outreach, MORE Retreat Program, Merrimack Marketing Association, Orientation Committee Coordinators, Developing Leaders Program.
Campus security 24-hour emergency response devices and patrols, student patrols, late-night transport-escort service, controlled dormitory access.
After graduation 330 organizations recruited on campus 1997–98. 88% of class of 1998 had job offers within 6 months. *Career center:* 7 full-time personnel. Services include job fairs, resume preparation, interview workshops, resume referral, career/interest testing, career counseling, careers library, job bank, job interviews, alumni resource nights. *Graduate education:* 10% of class of 1999 went directly to graduate and professional school.

Freshmen 2,750 applied, 1,977 admitted, 787 enrolled. 1 National Merit Scholar, 19 class presidents, 6 valedictorians, 182 student government officers.

Average high school GPA	3.1	SAT verbal scores above 500	94%
SAT math scores above 500	88%	ACT above 18	99%
From top 10% of their h.s. class	17%	From top quarter	35%
From top half	82%	1998 freshmen returning in 1999	76%

Application *Options:* eApply at www.CollegeQuest.com, Common Application, electronic application, early admission, early decision, deferred entrance. *Application fee:* $40. *Required:* essay or personal statement; high school transcript. *Required for some:* interview. *Recommended:* minimum 2.5 GPA; 1 letter of recommendation; interview.
Standardized tests *Admission: Required:* SAT I or ACT.
Significant dates *Application deadlines:* 2/15 (freshmen), 6/1 (transfers). *Early decision:* 11/30. *Notification:* continuous until 4/15 (freshmen), 12/15 (early decision). *Financial aid deadline:* 2/15.
Freshman Application Contact
Ms. MaryLou Retelle, Dean of Admissions and Financial Aid, Merrimack College, Austin Hall, A22, North Andover, MA 01845. **Phone:** 978-837-5100 Ext. 5120. **Fax:** 978-837-5222. **E-mail:** admissions@merrimack.edu
Visit CollegeQuest.com for information on majors offered and athletics.

■ *See page 2048 for a narrative description.*

MONTSERRAT COLLEGE OF ART
Beverly, Massachusetts

- **Independent**, 4-year, founded 1970
- **Degrees** bachelor's and postbachelor's certificates
- **Suburban** 10-acre campus with easy access to Boston
- **Coed**, 383 undergraduate students, 91% full-time, 54% women, 46% men
- **Moderately difficult** entrance level, 28% of applicants were admitted
- **16:1 student-to-undergraduate faculty ratio**
- **31% graduate** in 6 years or less
- **$12,950 tuition** and fees
- **$8536 average financial aid** package, $11,000 average indebtedness upon graduation, $250,000 endowment

Students *Undergraduates:* 347 full-time, 36 part-time. Students come from 9 other countries. *The most frequently chosen baccalaureate field is:* visual/performing arts.

From out-of-state	48%	Reside on campus	62%
Age 25 or older	13%	Transferred in	3%
International students	3%	African Americans	1%
Asian Americans/Pacific Islanders	2%	Hispanic Americans	1%
Native Americans	1%		

Faculty 63 (30% full-time), 56% with terminal degrees.
Expenses (1999–2000) *Tuition:* full-time $12,550; part-time $418 per credit. *Required fees:* full-time $400; $48 per course. Full-time tuition and fees vary according to course load. Part-time tuition and fees vary according to course load. *College room only:* $3650. Room and board charges vary according to housing facility. *Payment plan:* installment. *Waivers:* employees or children of employees.
Library Paul Scott Library plus 1 other. *Operations spending 1999–2000:* $80,564. *Collection:* 12,000 titles, 73 serial subscriptions, 35,000 audiovisual materials.
College life *Housing: Option:* coed. *Most popular organizations:* student council, Coffee House Committee, peer advisors, Fashion Show Committee, coed intramural sports.
Campus security Late-night transport-escort service, 24-hour residence hall monitoring.
After graduation 20% of class of 1998 had job offers within 6 months. *Career center:* 1 part-time personnel. Services include job fairs, resume preparation, career counseling, careers library, job bank. *Graduate education:* 26% of class of 1999 went directly to graduate and professional school: 26% graduate arts and sciences.
Freshmen 385 applied, 106 admitted, 106 enrolled.

Average high school GPA	2.61	SAT verbal scores above 500	64%
SAT math scores above 500	35%	ACT above 18	N/R
1998 freshmen returning in 1999	81%		

Application *Options:* early action, deferred entrance. *Application fee:* $40. *Required:* essay or personal statement; high school transcript; minimum 2.0 GPA; 2 letters of recommendation; portfolio. *Recommended:* minimum 3.0 GPA; interview.
Standardized tests *Admission: Required:* SAT I or ACT.
Significant dates *Application deadlines:* 7/15 (freshmen), rolling (transfers). *Early action:* 12/15. *Notification:* continuous until 8/1 (freshmen), 12/20 (early action). *Financial aid deadline priority date:* 3/1.
Freshman Application Contact
Mr. Stephen M. Negron, Director of Recruitment, Montserrat College of Art, 41 Essex Street, Beverly, MA 01945. **Phone:** 978-921-4242 Ext. 1153. **Toll-free phone:** 800-836-0487. **Fax:** 978-922-4268. **E-mail:** admiss@montserrat.edu
Visit CollegeQuest.com for information on majors offered and athletics.

■ *See page 2090 for a narrative description.*

MOUNT HOLYOKE COLLEGE
South Hadley, Massachusetts

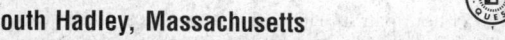

- **Independent**, 4-year, founded 1837
- **Degree** bachelor's
- **Small-town** 800-acre campus
- **Women** only, 1,915 undergraduate students, 98% full-time
- **Very difficult** entrance level, 60% of applicants were admitted
- **10:1** student-to-undergraduate faculty ratio
- **79% graduate** in 6 years or less
- **$24,354 tuition** and fees
- **$20,966 average financial aid** package, $15,000 average indebtedness upon graduation, $363.8 million endowment

Students *Undergraduates:* 1,879 full-time, 36 part-time. Students come from 50 states and territories, 76 other countries. *The most frequently chosen baccalaureate fields are:* biological/life sciences, English, social sciences and history. *Graduate:* 3 in graduate degree programs.

From out-of-state	66%	Reside on campus	96%
Age 25 or older	8%	Transferred in	3%
International students	12%	African Americans	5%
Asian Americans/Pacific Islanders	9%	Hispanic Americans	5%
Native Americans	1%		

Faculty 231 (78% full-time), 88% with terminal degrees.
Expenses (1999–2000) *Comprehensive fee:* $31,464 includes full-time tuition ($24,200), mandatory fees ($154), and room and board ($7110). *College room only:* $3480. *Part-time tuition:* $755 per credit hour. *Part-time fees:* $154 per year part-time. *Payment plans:* tuition prepayment, installment. *Waivers:* employees or children of employees.
Library Williston Memorial Library plus 1 other. *Operations spending 1999–2000:* $3.4 million. *Collection:* 2,696 serial subscriptions, 1,801 audio-visual materials.
College life *Housing:* on-campus residence required through senior year. *Option:* women-only. *Most popular organizations:* Student Government Association, Mount Holyoke College News, student radio station, The Network, community service.
Campus security 24-hour emergency response devices and patrols, student patrols, late-night transport-escort service, controlled dormitory access.
After graduation 60 organizations recruited on campus 1997–98. *Career center:* 11 full-time personnel. Services include job fairs, resume preparation, interview workshops, resume referral, career/interest testing, career counseling, careers library, job bank, job interviews, on-site corporate visits. *Graduate education:* 25% of class of 1999 went directly to graduate and professional school. *Major awards:* 1 Marshall, 1 Fulbright Scholar.
Freshmen 2,435 applied, 1,458 admitted, 554 enrolled. 20 National Merit Scholars, 21 valedictorians.

Average high school GPA	3.65	SAT verbal scores above 500	95%
SAT math scores above 500	94%	ACT above 18	100%
From top 10% of their h.s. class	48%	From top half	97%
1998 freshmen returning in 1999	94%		

Application *Options:* eApply at www.CollegeQuest.com, Common Application, early admission, early decision, deferred entrance. *Application fee:* $55. *Required:* essay or personal statement; high school transcript; 2 letters of recommendation. *Recommended:* interview.
Standardized tests *Admission: Required:* SAT I or ACT.
Significant dates *Application deadlines:* 1/15 (freshmen), 5/31 (transfers). *Early decision:* 12/1 (for plan 1), 1/1 (for plan 2). *Notification:* 4/1 (freshmen), 1/1 (early decision plan 1), 2/1 (early decision plan 2). *Financial aid deadline:* 2/15.
Freshman Application Contact
Diane Anci, Director of Admission, Mount Holyoke College, 50 College Street, South Hadley, MA 01075. **Phone:** 413-538-2023. **Fax:** 413-538-2409. **E-mail:** admissions@mtholyoke.edu
Visit CollegeQuest.com for information on majors offered and athletics. Electronic viewbook available at CollegeQuest.com.

■ *See page 2104 for a narrative description.*

MOUNT IDA COLLEGE
Newton Centre, Massachusetts

- **Independent**, 4-year, founded 1899
- **Degrees** associate and bachelor's
- **Suburban** 85-acre campus with easy access to Boston
- **Coed**, 1,471 undergraduate students, 88% full-time, 59% women, 41% men
- **Moderately difficult** entrance level
- **$15,830 tuition** and fees
- **$9.4 million endowment**

Students *Undergraduates:* 1,290 full-time, 181 part-time. Students come from 29 states and territories, 42 other countries.

Reside on campus	38%	Age 25 or older	8%
International students	10%	African Americans	18%
Asian Americans/Pacific Islanders	5%	Hispanic Americans	6%
Native Americans	1%		

Faculty 176 (40% full-time).
Expenses (2000–2001) *Comprehensive fee:* $24,780 includes full-time tuition ($15,300), mandatory fees ($530), and room and board ($8950). *Part-time tuition:* $1050 per course. Part-time tuition and fees vary according to course load. *Payment plan:* installment. *Waivers:* employees or children of employees.
Library Wadsworth Learning Resource Center plus 1 other. *Collection:* 100,695 titles, 533 serial subscriptions.
College life *Housing:* Option: coed. *Social organizations:* national fraternities, national sororities; 4% of men are members. *Most popular organizations:* Leadership Students, student government, Phi Theta Kappa, Residence Council, Alpha Chi.
Campus security 24-hour emergency response devices and patrols, student patrols, late-night transport-escort service, controlled residence hall entrances, secured campus entrance.
After graduation 80 organizations recruited on campus 1997–98. *Career center:* 1 full-time, 6 part-time personnel. Services include job fairs, resume preparation, career counseling, careers library, job bank.
Freshmen 650 applied, 542 enrolled.

Average high school GPA	2.5	SAT verbal scores above 500	24%
SAT math scores above 500	16%	ACT above 18	N/R
1998 freshmen returning in 1999	94%		

Application *Options:* eApply at www.CollegeQuest.com, Common Application, electronic application, early action, deferred entrance. *Application fee:* $25. *Required:* essay or personal statement; high school transcript; 2 letters of recommendation. *Recommended:* minimum 2.0 GPA; interview.
Standardized tests *Admission: Required:* SAT I or ACT. *Placement: Required:* SAT I or ACT
Significant dates *Application deadline:* rolling (transfers). *Early action:* 10/30. *Financial aid deadline priority date:* 6/1.
Freshman Application Contact
Ms. Nancy Lemelman, Director of Admissions, Mount Ida College, 777 Dedham Street, Newton Centre, MA 02459. **Phone:** 617-928-4500. **Fax:** 617-928-4507. **E-mail:** admissions@mountida.edu
Visit CollegeQuest.com for information on majors offered and athletics. College video and electronic viewbook available at CollegeQuest.com.

■ *See page 2106 for a narrative description.*

Massachusetts

NEWBURY COLLEGE
Brookline, Massachusetts

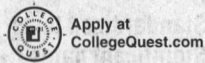 Apply at CollegeQuest.com

- **Independent**, primarily 2-year, founded 1962
- **Degrees** associate and bachelor's
- **Suburban** 10-acre campus with easy access to Boston
- **Coed**, 2,376 undergraduate students, 33% full-time, 66% women, 34% men
- **Minimally difficult** entrance level
- **17:1 student-to-undergraduate faculty ratio**
- **$13,680 tuition** and fees

Just minutes from Boston, Newbury College features an ideal collegiate setting in a safe, elite neighborhood with easy access to public transportation. Skilled and experienced faculty members, small classes, personalized attention, and hands-on training opportunities make Newbury graduates among the most employable. Students may pursue bachelor's and associate degrees.

Faculty 101 (47% full-time), 53% with terminal degrees.
Admissions Office Contact
Newbury College, Admission Office, 129 Fisher Avenue, Brookline, MA 02445-5796. **Toll-free phone:** 800-NEWBURY. **Fax:** 617-731-9618. **E-mail:** info@newbury.edu
Visit CollegeQuest.com for information on majors offered and athletics. Electronic viewbook available at CollegeQuest.com.

- See page 2142 for a narrative description.

NEW ENGLAND COLLEGE OF FINANCE
Boston, Massachusetts

- **Independent**, primarily 2-year, founded 1909
- **Degrees** associate and bachelor's (offers primarily part-time evening degree programs; bachelor's degree offered jointly with Bentley College, Assumption College, Providence College, University of Hartford, and University System College for Lifelong Learning)
- **Urban** campus
- **Coed**, 955 undergraduate students, 82% women, 18% men
- **Noncompetitive** entrance level

Faculty 171.
Admissions Office Contact
New England College of Finance, 1 Lincoln Plaza, Boston, MA 02111-2645. **Toll-free phone:** 888-696-NECF. **Fax:** 617-951-2533.
Visit CollegeQuest.com for information on majors offered and athletics.

NEW ENGLAND COLLEGE OF OPTOMETRY
Boston, Massachusetts

Admissions Office Contact
New England College of Optometry, 424 Beacon Street, Boston, MA 02115-1100. **Toll-free phone:** 800-824-5526.

NEW ENGLAND CONSERVATORY OF MUSIC
Boston, Massachusetts

- **Independent**, comprehensive, founded 1867
- **Degrees** bachelor's, master's, and doctoral
- **Urban** campus
- **Coed**, 398 undergraduate students, 90% full-time, 50% women, 50% men
- **Very difficult** entrance level, 49% of applicants were admitted
- **$19,800 tuition** and fees
- **$14,957 average financial aid** package, $19,000 average indebtedness upon graduation, $46.4 million endowment

Students *Undergraduates:* 357 full-time, 41 part-time. Students come from 37 states and territories, 21 other countries. *The most frequently chosen baccalaureate field is:* visual/performing arts. **Graduate:** 370 in graduate degree programs.

From out-of-state	81%	Reside on campus	40%
Age 25 or older	6%	Transferred in	8%
International students	22%	African Americans	5%
Asian Americans/Pacific Islanders	7%	Hispanic Americans	5%
Native Americans	1%		

Faculty 77 full-time.
Expenses (1999–2000) *Comprehensive fee:* $28,400 includes full-time tuition ($19,650), mandatory fees ($150), and room and board ($8600). Full-time tuition and fees vary according to program. Room and board charges vary according to housing facility. *Part-time tuition:* $635 per credit hour. *Part-time fees:* $150 per year part-time. Part-time tuition and fees vary according to program. Tuition for studio instruction: $4915 per term.
Library Spaulding Library plus 1 other. *Operations spending 1999–2000:* $413,480. *Collection:* 71,000 titles, 260 serial subscriptions.
College life *Housing:* on-campus residence required in freshman year. *Option:* coed. *Social organizations:* local fraternities. *Most popular organizations:* NEC Student Association, Chinese Student Association, Christian Fellowship, vegetarian club, soccer club.
Campus security 24-hour patrols, late-night transport-escort service.
After graduation 58 organizations recruited on campus 1997–98. *Career center:* 2 full-time personnel. Services include job fairs, resume preparation, interview workshops, career counseling, careers library, job bank, job bulletin, career workshops.
Freshmen 1,502 applied, 734 admitted, 84 enrolled.

Average high school GPA	3.05	SAT verbal scores above 500	N/R
SAT math scores above 500	N/R	ACT above 18	N/R

Application *Option:* deferred entrance. *Application fee:* $75. *Required:* essay or personal statement; high school transcript; 2 letters of recommendation; audition.
Standardized tests *Admission:* Required: SAT I or ACT.
Significant dates *Notification:* 4/1 (freshmen). **Financial aid deadline priority date:** 2/2.
Freshman Application Contact
Ms. Allison T. Ball, Dean of Enrollment Services, New England Conservatory of Music, 290 Huntington Avenue, Boston, MA 02115-5000. **Phone:** 617-585-1101. **Fax:** 617-585-1115.
Visit CollegeQuest.com for information on majors offered and athletics.

NEW ENGLAND INSTITUTE OF APPLIED ARTS AND SCIENCES
Massachusetts—See Mount Ida College

THE NEW ENGLAND SCHOOL OF ART AND DESIGN AT SUFFOLK UNIVERSITY
Massachusetts—See Suffolk University

NICHOLS COLLEGE
Dudley, Massachusetts

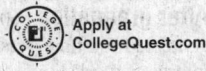 Apply at CollegeQuest.com

- **Independent**, comprehensive, founded 1815
- **Degrees** associate, bachelor's, and master's
- **Rural** 210-acre campus with easy access to Boston
- **Coed**, 1,088 undergraduate students, 61% full-time, 51% women, 49% men
- **Moderately difficult** entrance level, 92% of applicants were admitted
- **22:1 student-to-undergraduate faculty ratio**
- **$14,550 tuition** and fees

Students *Undergraduates:* 661 full-time, 427 part-time. Students come from 23 states and territories, 5 other countries. *The most frequently chosen baccalaureate fields are:* business/marketing, English, psychology. **Graduate:** 256 in graduate degree programs.

Massachusetts

From out-of-state	40%	Reside on campus	80%
Age 25 or older	5%	Transferred in	3%
International students	1%	African Americans	3%
Asian Americans/Pacific Islanders	1%	Hispanic Americans	1%
Native Americans	0.5%		

Faculty 30 (63% full-time).

Expenses (1999–2000) *Comprehensive fee:* $21,090 includes full-time tuition ($14,200), mandatory fees ($350), and room and board ($6540). *College room only:* $3220. Full-time tuition and fees vary according to course load. Room and board charges vary according to housing facility. *Part-time tuition:* $474 per credit. Part-time tuition and fees vary according to class time, course load, and location. *Payment plan:* installment. *Waivers:* employees or children of employees.

Library Conant Library plus 1 other. *Collection:* 60,000 titles, 450 serial subscriptions.

College life *Housing:* on-campus residence required through senior year. *Options:* coed, men-only, women-only. *Most popular organizations:* rugby club, accounting club, racquetball club, student publications.

Campus security 24-hour patrols, late-night transport-escort service.

After graduation 60 organizations recruited on campus 1997–98. 94% of class of 1998 had job offers within 6 months. *Career center:* 1 full-time, 1 part-time personnel. Services include job fairs, resume preparation, interview workshops, resume referral, career/interest testing, career counseling, careers library, job bank, job interviews. *Graduate education:* 2% of class of 1999 went directly to graduate and professional school.

Freshmen 734 applied, 672 admitted, 225 enrolled.

Average high school GPA	2.31	SAT verbal scores above 500	26%
SAT math scores above 500	33%	ACT above 18	N/R
From top 10% of their h.s. class	2%	From top quarter	21%
From top half	42%	1998 freshmen returning in 1999	76%

Application *Options:* eApply at www.CollegeQuest.com, electronic application, early admission, deferred entrance. *Application fee:* $25. *Required:* essay or personal statement; high school transcript; 1 letter of recommendation. *Required for some:* interview.

Standardized tests *Admission: Required:* SAT I or ACT.

Significant dates *Application deadlines:* rolling (freshmen), rolling (transfers). *Financial aid deadline priority date:* 3/1.

Freshman Application Contact
Susan Montville, Admissions Assistant, Nichols College, P.O. Box 5000, Office of Admissions, Dudley, MA 01571. **Phone:** 508-213-1560. **Toll-free phone:** 800-470-3379. **Fax:** 508-213-9885. **E-mail:** admissions@nichols.edu

Visit CollegeQuest.com for information on majors offered and athletics.

■ *See page 2170 for a narrative description.*

NORTH ADAMS STATE COLLEGE
Massachusetts—See Massachusetts College of Liberal Arts

NORTHEASTERN UNIVERSITY
Boston, Massachusetts

- **Independent**, university, founded 1898
- **Degrees** associate, bachelor's, master's, doctoral, first professional, and post-master's certificates
- **Urban** 60-acre campus
- **Coed**, 12,183 undergraduate students, 100% full-time, 49% women, 51% men
- **Moderately difficult** entrance level, 62% of applicants were admitted
- **14:1 student-to-undergraduate faculty ratio**
- **45% graduate** in 6 years or less
- **$18,867 tuition** and fees
- **$11,653 average financial aid** package, $405.8 million endowment

Northeastern University is the internationally recognized leader in cooperative education and offers more than 80 programs of study in 6 colleges. Students alternate between academic quarters and co-op employment opportunities in Boston, throughout the United States, or overseas. Individually assigned advisers provide academic and co-op counseling. All this in Boston, a center of education, culture, business, history, and sports.

Students *Undergraduates:* 12,183 full-time. Students come from 50 states and territories, 120 other countries. *The most frequently chosen baccalaureate fields are:* business/marketing, engineering/engineering technologies, health professions and related sciences. *Graduate:* 579 in professional programs, 3,749 in other graduate degree programs.

From out-of-state	55%	Reside on campus	65%
Age 25 or older	5%	Transferred in	6%
International students	7%	African Americans	6%
Asian Americans/Pacific Islanders	7%	Hispanic Americans	3%
Native Americans	0.2%		

Faculty 1,041 (72% full-time).

Expenses (1999–2000) *Comprehensive fee:* $27,477 includes full-time tuition ($18,675), mandatory fees ($192), and room and board ($8610). *College room only:* $4485. Full-time tuition and fees vary according to class time and student level. Room and board charges vary according to board plan and housing facility. Part-time tuition and fees vary according to class time and program. *Payment plans:* installment, deferred payment. *Waivers:* senior citizens and employees or children of employees.

Library Snell Library plus 6 others. *Collection:* 870,475 titles, 8,417 serial subscriptions, 18,282 audiovisual materials.

College life *Housing:* on-campus residence required in freshman year. *Options:* coed, women-only. *Social organizations:* national fraternities, national sororities, local fraternities; 1% of eligible men and 1% of eligible women are members. *Most popular organizations:* student government, Northeastern hiking and outdoor club, International Student Forum, Council for University Programs, Resident Student Association.

Campus security 24-hour emergency response devices and patrols, late-night transport-escort service.

After graduation 200 organizations recruited on campus 1997–98. 91% of class of 1998 had job offers within 6 months. *Career center:* 13 full-time, 3 part-time personnel. Services include job fairs, resume preparation, interview workshops, resume referral, career/interest testing, career counseling, careers library, job bank, job interviews. *Graduate education:* 13% of class of 1999 went directly to graduate and professional school.

Freshmen 16,418 applied, 10,174 admitted, 2,395 enrolled.

Average high school GPA	3.1	SAT verbal scores above 500	80%
SAT math scores above 500	85%	ACT above 18	97%
From top 10% of their h.s. class	18%	From top quarter	51%
From top half	86%	1998 freshmen returning in 1999	80%

Application *Options:* electronic application, early admission, deferred entrance. *Application fee:* $45. *Required:* essay or personal statement; high school transcript. *Required for some:* interview. *Recommended:* minimum 2.0 GPA; 2 letters of recommendation.

Standardized tests *Admission: Required:* SAT I or ACT.

Significant dates *Application deadlines:* rolling (freshmen), rolling (transfers). *Financial aid deadline priority date:* 2/15.

Freshman Application Contact
Mr. Alan Kines, Dean of Admissions, Northeastern University, 150 Richards Hall, Boston, MA 02115-5096. **Phone:** 617-373-2200. **Fax:** 617-373-8780. **E-mail:** admissions@neu.edu

Visit CollegeQuest.com for information on majors offered and athletics. College video and electronic viewbook available at CollegeQuest.com.

■ *See page 2180 for a narrative description.*

PINE MANOR COLLEGE
Chestnut Hill, Massachusetts

- **Independent**, 4-year, founded 1911
- **Degrees** associate, bachelor's, and master's
- **Suburban** 65-acre campus with easy access to Boston
- **Women** only, 323 undergraduate students, 97% full-time
- **Moderately difficult** entrance level, 81% of applicants were admitted
- **17:1 student-to-undergraduate faculty ratio**
- **43% graduate** in 6 years or less
- **$11,440 tuition** and fees
- **$14,492 average financial aid** package, $15,229 average indebtedness upon graduation, $22 million endowment

Students *Undergraduates:* 313 full-time, 10 part-time. Students come from 27 states and territories, 22 other countries. *The most frequently chosen*

Massachusetts

Pine Manor College *(continued)*
baccalaureate fields are: business/marketing, psychology, visual/performing arts.

From out-of-state	38%	Reside on campus	73%
Age 25 or older	10%	Transferred in	5%

Expenses (1999–2000) *Comprehensive fee:* $18,600 includes full-time tuition ($11,440) and room and board ($7160). *College room only:* $3580. Room and board charges vary according to housing facility. *Part-time tuition:* $210 per credit. *Payment plans:* tuition prepayment, installment. *Waivers:* children of alumni, adult students, and employees or children of employees.

Library Annenberg Library. *Operations spending 1999–2000:* $257,066. *Collection:* 64,647 titles, 1,645 serial subscriptions, 4,085 audiovisual materials.

College life *Housing:* on-campus residence required in freshman year. *Option:* women-only. *Most popular organizations:* Student Government Association, ALANA, business club, Pine Manor Post, Campus Activities Board.

Campus security 24-hour emergency response devices and patrols, student patrols, late-night transport-escort service, controlled dormitory access.

After graduation 49% of class of 1998 had job offers within 6 months. *Career center:* 1 full-time, 1 part-time personnel. Services include job fairs, resume preparation, interview workshops, resume referral, career/interest testing, career counseling, careers library, job bank.

Freshmen 331 applied, 268 admitted, 98 enrolled. 1 class president, 1 valedictorian, 1 student government officer.

Average high school GPA	2.51	SAT verbal scores above 500	33%
SAT math scores above 500	25%	ACT above 18	40%
From top 10% of their h.s. class	12%	From top quarter	32%
From top half	56%	1998 freshmen returning in 1999	72%

Application *Options:* Common Application, electronic application, early admission, deferred entrance. *Preference* given to students from colleges with whom PMC has an articulation agreement. *Application fee:* $25. *Required:* essay or personal statement; high school transcript; 1 letter of recommendation. *Recommended:* minimum 2.0 GPA; interview.

Standardized tests *Admission: Required:* SAT I or ACT.

Significant dates *Application deadlines:* rolling (freshmen), rolling (transfers). *Financial aid deadline priority date:* 3/1.

Freshman Application Contact
Dean of Admissions, Pine Manor College, 400 Heath Street, Chestnut Hill, MA 02167-2332. **Phone:** 617-731-7104. **Toll-free phone:** 800-762-1357. **Fax:** 617-731-7199. **E-mail:** admission@pmc.edu

Visit CollegeQuest.com for information on majors offered and athletics. College video available at CollegeQuest.com.

■ *See page 2270 for a narrative description.*

REGIS COLLEGE
Weston, Massachusetts

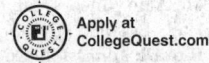 Apply at CollegeQuest.com

- **Independent Roman Catholic**, comprehensive, founded 1927
- **Degrees** associate, bachelor's, and master's
- **Small-town** 168-acre campus with easy access to Boston
- **Women** only, 889 undergraduate students, 77% full-time
- **Moderately difficult** entrance level, 94% of applicants were admitted
- **10:1 student-to-undergraduate faculty ratio**
- **73% graduate** in 6 years or less
- **$16,860 tuition** and fees
- **$12,479 average financial aid** package, $18,443 average indebtedness upon graduation, $35.2 million endowment

Students *Undergraduates:* 684 full-time, 205 part-time. Students come from 23 states and territories, 7 other countries. *The most frequently chosen baccalaureate fields are:* health professions and related sciences, communications/communication technologies, social sciences and history. *Graduate:* 242 in graduate degree programs.

From out-of-state	22%	Reside on campus	56%
Age 25 or older	13%	Transferred in	4%
International students	3%	African Americans	4%
Asian Americans/Pacific Islanders	4%	Hispanic Americans	4%
Native Americans	0.1%		

Faculty 135 (50% full-time), 61% with terminal degrees.

Expenses (1999–2000) *Comprehensive fee:* $24,730 includes full-time tuition ($16,860) and room and board ($7870). *Part-time tuition:* $1950 per course. Part-time tuition and fees vary according to class time and course load. *Payment plans:* tuition prepayment, installment, deferred payment. *Waivers:* employees or children of employees.

Library Regis College Library. *Operations spending 1999–2000:* $1 million. *Collection:* 107,359 titles, 1,179 serial subscriptions, 4,897 audiovisual materials.

College life *Housing: Option:* women-only. *Most popular organizations:* Tower Society-Admission Ambassadors, student government, glee club, orientation committee, AHANA Club.

Campus security 24-hour emergency response devices and patrols, late-night transport-escort service, controlled dormitory access.

After graduation 37 organizations recruited on campus 1997–98. 77% of class of 1998 had job offers within 6 months. *Career center:* 3 full-time personnel. Services include job fairs, resume preparation, resume referral, career/interest testing, career counseling, careers library, job bank, job interviews, internship advising. *Graduate education:* 12% of class of 1999 went directly to graduate and professional school: 7% graduate arts and sciences, 2% education, 1% business, 1% law, 1% medicine.

Freshmen 562 applied, 526 admitted, 175 enrolled.

Average high school GPA	3.1	SAT verbal scores above 500	56%
SAT math scores above 500	45%	ACT above 18	N/R
From top 10% of their h.s. class	12%	From top quarter	40%
From top half	70%	1998 freshmen returning in 1999	73%

Application *Options:* eApply at www.CollegeQuest.com, Common Application, electronic application, deferred entrance. *Application fee:* $30. *Required:* essay or personal statement; high school transcript; minimum 2.5 GPA; 2 letters of recommendation. *Required for some:* interview. *Recommended:* minimum 3.0 GPA; interview; rank in upper 50% of high school class.

Standardized tests *Admission: Required:* SAT I or ACT. *Recommended:* SAT II Subject Tests.

Significant dates *Application deadlines:* rolling (freshmen), rolling (transfers). *Financial aid deadline priority date:* 3/1.

Freshman Application Contact
Ms. Donna L. Gibbons, Director of Admission, Regis College, 235 Wellesley Street, Weston, MA 02493. **Phone:** 781-768-7065. **Toll-free phone:** 800-456-1820. **Fax:** 781-768-8339. **E-mail:** admission@regiscollege.edu/

Visit CollegeQuest.com for information on majors offered and athletics. College video available at CollegeQuest.com.

■ *See page 2318 for a narrative description.*

SAINT JOHN'S SEMINARY COLLEGE OF LIBERAL ARTS
Brighton, Massachusetts

- **Independent Roman Catholic**, 4-year, founded 1884
- **Degrees** associate and bachelor's
- **Urban** 70-acre campus with easy access to Boston
- **Men** only, 31 undergraduate students, 100% full-time
- **Minimally difficult** entrance level, 93% of applicants were admitted
- **$5800 tuition** and fees
- **$9.2 million endowment**

Students *Undergraduates:* 31 full-time. Students come from 8 states and territories. *The most frequently chosen baccalaureate field is:* philosophy.

From out-of-state	38%	Reside on campus	100%
Age 25 or older	50%	Transferred in	29%

Faculty 14 (57% full-time), 79% with terminal degrees.

Expenses (1999–2000) *Comprehensive fee:* $8800 includes full-time tuition ($5800) and room and board ($3000). *Part-time tuition:* $200 per credit hour. *Payment plan:* installment.

Library Saint John's Library. *Operations spending 1999–2000:* $168,187. *Collection:* 150,000 titles, 345 serial subscriptions.

College life *Housing:* on-campus residence required through senior year. *Option:* men-only. *Social organizations:* national fraternities; 60% of eligible undergrads are members.

Massachusetts

Campus security 24-hour patrols.
After graduation *Career center:* Services include career counseling. *Graduate education:* 90% of class of 1999 went directly to graduate and professional school; 90% theology.
Freshmen 15 applied, 14 admitted, 7 enrolled. 2 class presidents, 1 student government officer.

SAT verbal scores above 500	N/R	SAT math scores above 500	N/R
ACT above 18	N/R	From top 10% of their h.s. class	0%
From top quarter	20%	From top half	40%
1998 freshmen returning in 1999	89%		

Application *Application fee:* $0. *Required:* essay or personal statement; high school transcript; 4 letters of recommendation; interview. *Required for some:* bishop's sponsorship.
Standardized tests *Admission: Required:* SAT I.
Significant dates *Application deadlines:* 8/1 (freshmen), 8/1 (transfers). *Financial aid deadline priority date:* 5/1.
Freshman Application Contact
Rev. Robert W. Flagg, Dean of the College, Saint John's Seminary College of Liberal Arts, 127 Lake Street, Brighton, MA 02135. **Phone:** 617-746-5460.
Visit CollegeQuest.com for information on majors offered and athletics.

SALEM STATE COLLEGE
Salem, Massachusetts

- **State-supported**, comprehensive, founded 1854
- **Degrees** bachelor's and master's
- **Small-town** 62-acre campus with easy access to Boston
- **Coed**, 5,952 undergraduate students, 72% full-time, 62% women, 38% men
- **Minimally difficult** entrance level, 55% of applicants were admitted
- **14:1** student-to-undergraduate faculty ratio
- **36.92%** graduate in 6 years or less
- **$2958 tuition** and fees (in-state); $8978 (out-of-state)
- **$5942 average financial aid** package, $5.2 million endowment

Part of Massachusetts Public Higher Education System.
Students *Undergraduates:* 4,257 full-time, 1,695 part-time. Students come from 18 states and territories, 12 other countries. *The most frequently chosen baccalaureate fields are:* business/marketing, education, health professions and related sciences. *Graduate:* 1,243 in graduate degree programs.

From out-of-state	16%	Reside on campus	22%
Age 25 or older	18%	Transferred in	12%
International students	3%	African Americans	4%
Asian Americans/Pacific Islanders	2%	Hispanic Americans	4%
Native Americans	1%		

Faculty 421 (76% full-time), 77% with terminal degrees.
Expenses (1999–2000) *Tuition, state resident:* full-time $1030; part-time $43 per hour. *Tuition, nonresident:* full-time $7050; part-time $294 per hour. *Required fees:* full-time $1928; $80 per hour. Full-time tuition and fees vary according to class time. Part-time tuition and fees vary according to class time. *College room and board:* $4044; room only: $2500. Room and board charges vary according to board plan and housing facility. *Payment plans:* installment, deferred payment. *Waivers:* minority students, senior citizens, and employees or children of employees.
Library Salem State College Library. *Operations spending 1999–2000:* $1.9 million. *Collection:* 236,337 titles, 1,360 serial subscriptions.
College life *Housing: Option:* coed. *Most popular organizations:* Student Government Association, Program Council, Hispanic American Student Association, GLBT Alliance, WMWM Radio.
Campus security 24-hour emergency response devices and patrols, late-night transport-escort service.
After graduation *Career center:* 3 full-time, 1 part-time personnel. Services include job fairs, resume preparation, resume referral, career counseling, careers library, job bank, job interviews. *Graduate education:* 9% of class of 1999 went directly to graduate and professional school.
Freshmen 4,013 applied, 2,197 admitted, 671 enrolled.

Average high school GPA	2.79	SAT verbal scores above 500	36%
SAT math scores above 500	30%	ACT above 18	N/R
From top 10% of their h.s. class	8%	From top quarter	10%
From top half	40%	1998 freshmen returning in 1999	67%

Application *Option:* early admission. *Preference* given to state residents. *Application fee:* $10. *Required:* high school transcript; minimum 2.9 GPA; letters of recommendation. *Required for some:* interview. *Recommended:* essay or personal statement.
Standardized tests *Admission: Required:* SAT I or ACT.
Significant dates *Application deadlines:* rolling (freshmen), rolling (transfers). *Financial aid deadline priority date:* 4/1.
Freshman Application Contact
Mr. Nate Bryant, Director of Admissions, Salem State College, 352 Lafayette Street, Salem, MA 01970-5353. **Phone:** 978-542-6200. **Fax:** 978-542-6126.
Visit CollegeQuest.com for information on majors offered and athletics. College video available at CollegeQuest.com.

SCHOOL OF THE MUSEUM OF FINE ARTS
Boston, Massachusetts

- **Independent**, comprehensive, founded 1876
- **Degrees** bachelor's, master's, and postbachelor's certificates
- **Urban** 14-acre campus
- **Coed**, 1,095 undergraduate students
- **Moderately difficult** entrance level
- **$18,580 tuition** and fees
- **$8778 average financial aid** package, $9.6 million endowment

Students *Undergraduates:* Students come from 33 states and territories, 30 other countries. *Graduate:* 92 in graduate degree programs.

From out-of-state	40%	Age 25 or older	26%
International students	8%	African Americans	1%
Asian Americans/Pacific Islanders	4%	Hispanic Americans	2%
Native Americans	0.2%		

Expenses (2000–2001) *Tuition:* full-time $17,880. *Required fees:* full-time $700. Full-time tuition and fees vary according to program. Part-time tuition and fees vary according to program. *Payment plan:* installment. *Waivers:* employees or children of employees.
Library William Morris Hunt Memorial Library plus 1 other. *Operations spending 1999–2000:* $148,507. *Collection:* 657 serial subscriptions, 220 audiovisual materials.
College life *Housing:* college housing not available. *Most popular organization:* Gay/Lesbian/Bisexual Alliance.
Campus security 24-hour emergency response devices and patrols, late-night transport-escort service.
After graduation *Career center:* 2 part-time personnel. Services include resume preparation, career counseling, careers library, job bank.
Freshmen

SAT verbal scores above 500	N/R	SAT math scores above 500	N/R
ACT above 18	N/R		

Application *Option:* deferred entrance. *Application fee:* $35. *Required:* essay or personal statement; high school transcript; portfolio. *Required for some:* interview.
Standardized tests *Placement: Recommended:* SAT I, ACT, SAT II Subject Tests.
Significant dates *Application deadlines:* rolling (freshmen), rolling (transfers). *Financial aid deadline priority date:* 3/15.
Freshman Application Contact
Mr. John A. Williamson, Director of Enrollment and Student Services, School of the Museum of Fine Arts, 230 The Fenway, Boston, MA 02115. **Phone:** 617-369-3626. **Toll-free phone:** 800-643-6078. **Fax:** 617-369-3679. **E-mail:** admissions@smfa.edu
Visit CollegeQuest.com for information on majors offered and athletics. Electronic viewbook available at CollegeQuest.com.

■ *See page 2458 for a narrative description.*

SIMMONS COLLEGE
Boston, Massachusetts

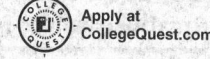

- **Independent**, comprehensive, founded 1899

Massachusetts

Simmons College (continued)
- **Degrees** bachelor's, master's, doctoral, post-master's, and postbachelor's certificates
- **Urban** 12-acre campus
- **Women** only, 1,235 undergraduate students, 88% full-time
- **Moderately difficult** entrance level, 72% of applicants were admitted
- **10:1 student-to-undergraduate faculty ratio**
- **69% graduate** in 6 years or less
- **$20,134 tuition** and fees
- **$19,059 average financial aid** package, $19,650 average indebtedness upon graduation, $150.2 million endowment

Students *Undergraduates:* 1,090 full-time, 145 part-time. Students come from 37 states and territories, 29 other countries. *The most frequently chosen baccalaureate fields are:* health professions and related sciences, biological/life sciences, social sciences and history. *Graduate:* 2,060 in graduate degree programs.

From out-of-state	40%	Reside on campus	70%
Age 25 or older	17%	Transferred in	4%
International students	4%	African Americans	6%
Asian Americans/Pacific Islanders	6%	Hispanic Americans	3%
Native Americans	0.1%		

Faculty 399 (53% full-time).
Expenses (1999–2000) *Comprehensive fee:* $28,180 includes full-time tuition ($19,520), mandatory fees ($614), and room and board ($8046). Full-time tuition and fees vary according to course load. *Part-time tuition:* $610 per semester hour. Part-time tuition and fees vary according to course load. *Payment plan:* installment. *Waivers:* adult students, senior citizens, and employees or children of employees.
Library Beatley Library plus 5 others. *Operations spending 1999–2000:* $1.6 million. *Collection:* 270,402 titles, 1,757 serial subscriptions, 1,923 audio-visual materials.
College life *Housing:* Options: women-only, disabled students. *Social organizations:* 30% of eligible undergrads are members. *Most popular organizations:* Student Government Association, Quadside Committee, Activities Programming Board, Black Student Organization, Simmons News.
Campus security 24-hour emergency response devices and patrols, late-night transport-escort service, controlled dormitory access.
After graduation 25 organizations recruited on campus 1997–98. 75% of class of 1998 had job offers within 6 months. *Career center:* 4 full-time personnel. Services include job fairs, resume preparation, interview workshops, career/interest testing, career counseling, careers library, job bank, job interviews. *Graduate education:* 10% of class of 1999 went directly to graduate and professional school: 4% education, 4% graduate arts and sciences, 2% business, 1% law.
Freshmen 1,184 applied, 849 admitted, 271 enrolled.

SAT verbal scores above 500	79%	SAT math scores above 500	72%
ACT above 18	N/R	From top 10% of their h.s. class	23%
From top quarter	55%	From top half	90%
1998 freshmen returning in 1999	83%		

Application *Options:* eApply at www.CollegeQuest.com, Common Application, early admission, early action, deferred entrance. *Application fee:* $35. *Required:* essay or personal statement; high school transcript; 2 letters of recommendation. *Recommended:* minimum 3.0 GPA; interview.
Standardized tests *Admission: Required:* SAT I or ACT.
Significant dates *Application deadlines:* 2/1 (freshmen), 4/1 (transfers). *Early action:* 12/1. *Notification:* 4/15 (freshmen), 1/20 (early action). *Financial aid deadline priority date:* 2/1.
Freshman Application Contact
Ms. Patricia A. Tencza, Director of Undergraduate Admissions, Simmons College, 300 The Fenway, Boston, MA 02115. **Phone:** 617-521-2051. **Toll-free phone:** 800-345-8468. **Fax:** 617-521-3199. **E-mail:** ugadm@simmons.edu
Visit CollegeQuest.com for information on majors offered and athletics. College video available at CollegeQuest.com.

■ *See page 2492 for a narrative description.*

SIMON'S ROCK COLLEGE OF BARD
Great Barrington, Massachusetts

- **Independent**, 4-year, founded 1964
- **Degrees** associate and bachelor's
- **Rural** 275-acre campus with easy access to Albany and Springfield
- **Coed**, 366 undergraduate students, 100% full-time, 57% women, 43% men
- **Very difficult** entrance level
- **8:1 student-to-undergraduate faculty ratio**
- **$23,300 tuition** and fees
- **$15,908 average financial aid** package, $6.3 million endowment

Students *Undergraduates:* 366 full-time. Students come from 39 states and territories, 4 other countries. *The most frequently chosen baccalaureate fields are:* social sciences and history, physical sciences, visual/performing arts.

From out-of-state	81%	Reside on campus	94%
Transferred in	1%	International students	1%
African Americans	3%	Asian Americans/Pacific Islanders	4%
Hispanic Americans	2%	Native Americans	1%

Faculty 63 (56% full-time), 86% with terminal degrees.
Expenses (1999–2000) *Comprehensive fee:* $29,710 includes full-time tuition ($20,800), mandatory fees ($2500), and room and board ($6410). *College room only:* $3130. Full-time tuition and fees vary according to course load. Room and board charges vary according to board plan and housing facility. *Part-time tuition:* $795 per credit hour. *Part-time fees:* $150 per term part-time. Part-time tuition and fees vary according to course load. *Payment plan:* installment. *Waivers:* employees or children of employees.
Library Alumni Library. *Operations spending 1999–2000:* $348,000. *Collection:* 70,000 titles, 350 serial subscriptions, 3,350 audiovisual materials.
College life *Housing:* on-campus residence required through sophomore year. *Option:* coed. *Most popular organizations:* women's center, math and sciences club, multicultural student organization, Community Health Institute, Community Service Program.
Campus security 24-hour emergency response devices, late-night transport-escort service, controlled dormitory access, 24-hour weekend patrols by trained security personnel.
After graduation 56% of class of 1998 had job offers within 6 months. *Career center:* 1 full-time personnel. Services include job fairs, resume preparation, resume referral, career counseling, careers library, job bank, job interviews.
Freshmen 246 applied, 208 admitted, 143 enrolled.

SAT verbal scores above 500	92%	SAT math scores above 500	92%
ACT above 18	100%	1998 freshmen returning in 1999	76%

Application *Options:* electronic application, early admission, deferred entrance. *Application fee:* $40. *Required:* essay or personal statement; high school transcript; minimum 2.0 GPA; 2 letters of recommendation; interview; parent application. *Recommended:* minimum 3.0 GPA.
Standardized tests *Admission: Required:* SAT I, PSAT. *Recommended:* ACT.
Significant dates *Application deadlines:* 6/15 (freshmen), 7/15 (transfers). *Financial aid deadline priority date:* 6/30.
Freshman Application Contact
Ms. Mary King Austin, Director of Admissions, Simon's Rock College of Bard, 84 Alford Road, Great Barrington, MA 01230-9702. **Phone:** 413-528-7317. **Toll-free phone:** 800-235-7186. **Fax:** 413-528-7334. **E-mail:** admit@simons-rock.edu
Visit CollegeQuest.com for information on majors offered and athletics. College video and electronic viewbook available at CollegeQuest.com.

■ *See page 2494 for a narrative description.*

SMITH COLLEGE
Northampton, Massachusetts

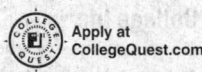

- **Independent**, comprehensive, founded 1871
- **Degrees** bachelor's, master's, doctoral, post-master's, and postbachelor's certificates
- **Urban** 125-acre campus with easy access to Hartford
- **Women** only, 2,665 undergraduate students, 98% full-time
- **Very difficult** entrance level, 56% of applicants were admitted
- **10:1 student-to-undergraduate faculty ratio**
- **83% graduate** in 6 years or less
- **$22,622 tuition** and fees
- **$21,548 average financial aid** package, $15,142 average indebtedness upon graduation, $884.8 million endowment

Massachusetts

Students *Undergraduates:* 2,604 full-time, 61 part-time. Students come from 53 states and territories, 48 other countries. *The most frequently chosen baccalaureate fields are:* social sciences and history, biological/life sciences, visual/performing arts. *Graduate:* 503 in graduate degree programs.

From out-of-state	78%	Reside on campus	92%
Age 25 or older	8%	Transferred in	3%
International students	6%	African Americans	4%
Asian Americans/Pacific Islanders	9%	Hispanic Americans	4%
Native Americans	1%		

Faculty 272 (94% full-time), 97% with terminal degrees.

Expenses (1999–2000) *Comprehensive fee:* $30,442 includes full-time tuition ($22,440), mandatory fees ($182), and room and board ($7820). *College room only:* $3520. Room and board charges vary according to housing facility. *Part-time tuition:* $705 per credit. *Payment plans:* tuition prepayment, installment. *Waivers:* employees or children of employees.

Library Neilson Library plus 3 others. *Operations spending 1999–2000:* $5.5 million. *Collection:* 1.2 million titles, 4,957 serial subscriptions, 59,481 audiovisual materials.

College life *Housing:* on-campus residence required through senior year. *Options:* women-only, cooperative. *Most popular organizations:* Recreation Council, debate team, glee club and choirs, Athletic Association, Black Student Alliance.

Campus security 24-hour emergency response devices and patrols, late-night transport-escort service, self-defense workshops, emergency telephones, programs in crime and sexual assault prevention.

After graduation 550 organizations recruited on campus 1997–98. *Career center:* 10 full-time, 2 part-time personnel. Services include job fairs, resume preparation, interview workshops, resume referral, career/interest testing, career counseling, careers library, job bank, job interviews. *Graduate education:* 15% of class of 1999 went directly to graduate and professional school: 7% graduate arts and sciences, 3% law, 1% business, 1% education, 1% medicine, 0.4% engineering, 0.4% theology.

Freshmen 2,998 applied, 1,681 admitted, 667 enrolled.

Average high school GPA	3.74	SAT verbal scores above 500	98%
SAT math scores above 500	96%	ACT above 18	100%
From top 10% of their h.s. class	52%	From top quarter	89%
From top half	98%	1998 freshmen returning in 1999	89%

Application *Options:* eApply at www.CollegeQuest.com, Common Application, electronic application, early admission, early decision, deferred entrance. *Application fee:* $50. *Required:* essay or personal statement; high school transcript; 2 letters of recommendation. *Recommended:* interview.

Standardized tests *Admission: Required:* SAT I or ACT. *Recommended:* SAT II Subject Tests, SAT II: Writing Test.

Significant dates *Application deadlines:* 1/15 (freshmen), 6/1 (transfers). *Early decision:* 11/15 (for plan 1), 1/1 (for plan 2). *Notification:* 4/11 (freshmen), 12/15 (early decision plan 1), 2/1 (early decision plan 2). *Financial aid deadline:* 2/1.

Freshman Application Contact
Ms. Nanci Tessier, Director of Admissions, Smith College, 7 College Lane, Northampton, MA 01063. **Phone:** 413-585-2500. **Fax:** 413-585-2123. **E-mail:** admission@smith.edu

Visit CollegeQuest.com for information on majors offered and athletics. College video available at CollegeQuest.com.

■ *See page 2502 for a narrative description.*

SPRINGFIELD COLLEGE
Springfield, Massachusetts

- **Independent**, comprehensive, founded 1885
- **Degrees** bachelor's, master's, and doctoral
- **Suburban** 167-acre campus
- **Coed**
- **Moderately difficult** entrance level
- **$16,898 tuition** and fees

Springfield College was founded in 1885 as a pioneer in teaching and scholarship related to physical education, wellness, and the training of YMCA executives. Its humanics philosophy calls for educating the whole person—spirit, mind, and body—for leadership in service to humanity. Today, the College continues to educate leaders for the physical education, allied health, and human service professions.

Expenses (1999–2000) *Comprehensive fee:* $22,754 includes full-time tuition ($16,698), mandatory fees ($200), and room and board ($5856). *College room only:* $3106. Room and board charges vary according to board plan and housing facility. *Part-time tuition:* $506 per credit hour. *Part-time fees:* $100 per term part-time.

Institutional Web site http://www.spfldcol.edu/

College life *Housing:* on-campus residence required through junior year. *Options:* coed, men-only, women-only.

Application *Options:* Common Application, electronic application, early admission, early decision, deferred entrance. *Preference* given to children of alumni. *Application fee:* $30. *Required:* essay or personal statement; high school transcript; 2 letters of recommendation; interview. *Required for some:* portfolio.

Standardized tests *Admission: Required:* SAT I.

Admissions Office Contact
Springfield College, 263 Alden Street, Springfield, MA 01109-3797. **Toll-free phone:** 800-343-1257. **Fax:** 413-748-3764. **E-mail:** admissions@spfldcol.edu

Visit CollegeQuest.com for information on athletics.

■ *See page 2528 for a narrative description.*

STONEHILL COLLEGE
Easton, Massachusetts

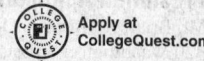
Apply at CollegeQuest.com

- **Independent Roman Catholic**, comprehensive, founded 1948
- **Degrees** bachelor's and master's
- **Suburban** 375-acre campus with easy access to Boston
- **Coed**, 2,360 undergraduate students, 88% full-time, 59% women, 41% men
- **Moderately difficult** entrance level, 53% of applicants were admitted
- **12:1 student-to-undergraduate faculty ratio**
- **77% graduate** in 6 years or less
- **$16,336 tuition** and fees
- **$12,129 average financial aid** package, $10,115 average indebtedness upon graduation, $87.5 million endowment

Located 20 miles south of Boston, Stonehill combines a community atmosphere and a beautiful 375-acre campus with easy access to America's premier college town. Exciting special programs, such as full-time international internships, study abroad, domestic internships, and Stonehill Undergraduate Research Experience (SURE), complement the College's rigorous education in the liberal arts, sciences, and business. More than 70% of graduating students take advantage of these enriching programs.

Students *Undergraduates:* 2,080 full-time, 280 part-time. Students come from 26 states and territories, 17 other countries. *The most frequently chosen baccalaureate fields are:* business/marketing, education, social sciences and history. *Graduate:* 16 in graduate degree programs.

From out-of-state	39%	Reside on campus	83%
Age 25 or older	1%	Transferred in	2%
International students	1%	African Americans	2%
Asian Americans/Pacific Islanders	2%	Hispanic Americans	2%
Native Americans	0.2%		

Faculty 254 (48% full-time).

Expenses (1999–2000) *Comprehensive fee:* $24,188 includes full-time tuition ($15,736), mandatory fees ($600), and room and board ($7852). Full-time tuition and fees vary according to class time and course load. Room and board charges vary according to board plan. *Part-time tuition:* $1574 per course. *Part-time fees:* $60 per course. Part-time tuition and fees vary according to class time. *Payment plans:* tuition prepayment, installment. *Waivers:* minority students, senior citizens, and employees or children of employees.

Library Bartley MacPhaidin, C.S.C. Library plus 1 other. *Operations spending 1999–2000:* $1.2 million. *Collection:* 180,000 titles, 1,134 serial subscriptions, 2,900 audiovisual materials.

College life *Housing: Options:* coed, women-only, disabled students. *Most popular organizations:* Into the Streets, student radio station, student government, Ski Club, sports clubs.

Massachusetts

Stonehill College (continued)

Campus security 24-hour emergency response devices and patrols, late-night transport-escort service.

After graduation 117 organizations recruited on campus 1997–98. 87% of class of 1998 had job offers within 6 months. *Career center:* 4 full-time, 1 part-time personnel. Services include job fairs, resume preparation, interview workshops, resume referral, career/interest testing, career counseling, careers library, job bank, job interviews. *Graduate education:* 17% of class of 1999 went directly to graduate and professional school.

Freshmen 4,432 applied, 2,366 admitted, 589 enrolled. 4 National Merit Scholars, 3 valedictorians, 38 student government officers.

Average high school GPA	3.4	SAT verbal scores above 500	89%
SAT math scores above 500	88%	ACT above 18	N/R
From top 10% of their h.s. class	31%	From top quarter	77%
From top half	98%	1998 freshmen returning in 1999	88%

Application *Options:* eApply at www.CollegeQuest.com, Common Application, early admission, early decision, deferred entrance. *Application fee:* $50. *Required:* essay or personal statement; high school transcript; 1 letter of recommendation. *Required for some:* interview. *Recommended:* campus visit.

Standardized tests *Admission: Required:* SAT I or ACT.

Significant dates *Application deadlines:* 2/1 (freshmen), 4/1 (transfers). *Early decision:* 11/1. *Notification:* 4/1 (freshmen), 12/31 (early decision). *Financial aid deadline priority date:* 2/1.

Freshman Application Contact
Mr. Brian P. Murphy, Dean of Admissions and Enrollment, Stonehill College, 320 Washington Street, Easton, MA 02357-5610. **Phone:** 508-565-1373. **Fax:** 508-565-1500. **E-mail:** admissions@stonehill.edu

Visit CollegeQuest.com for information on majors offered and athletics.

■ *See page 2578 for a narrative description.*

SUFFOLK UNIVERSITY
Boston, Massachusetts

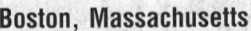

■ **Independent**, comprehensive, founded 1906
■ **Degrees** associate, bachelor's, master's, doctoral, first professional, post-master's, and postbachelor's certificates (doctoral degree in law)
■ **Urban** 2-acre campus
■ **Coed**, 3,160 undergraduate students, 84% full-time, 57% women, 43% men
■ **Moderately difficult** entrance level, 77% of applicants were admitted
■ **12:1 student-to-undergraduate faculty ratio**
■ **52% graduate** in 6 years or less
■ **$14,660 tuition** and fees
■ **$11,402 average financial aid** package, $20,384 average indebtedness upon graduation, $50.6 million endowment

Students *Undergraduates:* 2,651 full-time, 509 part-time. Students come from 29 states and territories, 96 other countries. *The most frequently chosen baccalaureate fields are:* business/marketing, communications/communication technologies, social sciences and history. *Graduate:* 1,708 in professional programs, 1,444 in other graduate degree programs.

From out-of-state	17%	Reside on campus	18%
Age 25 or older	15%	Transferred in	8%
International students	18%	African Americans	4%
Asian Americans/Pacific Islanders	6%	Hispanic Americans	4%
Native Americans	0.3%		

Faculty 678 (40% full-time), 67% with terminal degrees.

Expenses (1999–2000) *Comprehensive fee:* $23,870 includes full-time tuition ($14,580), mandatory fees ($80), and room and board ($9210). Room and board charges vary according to housing facility. *Part-time tuition:* $386 per semester hour. *Part-time fees:* $10 per term part-time. *Payment plans:* installment, deferred payment. *Waivers:* senior citizens and employees or children of employees.

Library Mildred Sawyer Library plus 3 others. *Operations spending 1999–2000:* $3.4 million. *Collection:* 288,620 titles, 5,238 serial subscriptions, 236 audiovisual materials.

College life *Housing: Option:* coed. *Social organizations:* national fraternities; 1% of eligible men and 1% of eligible women are members. *Most popular organizations:* Student Government Association, Program Council, Black Student Union, Evening Student Association, International Student Association.

Campus security 24-hour emergency response devices, late-night transport-escort service, controlled dormitory access.

After graduation 88 organizations recruited on campus 1997–98. *Career center:* 7 full-time personnel. Services include job fairs, resume preparation, interview workshops, resume referral, career/interest testing, career counseling, careers library, job bank, job interviews. *Graduate education:* 22% of class of 1999 went directly to graduate and professional school: 7% graduate arts and sciences, 5% education, 5% law, 2% business, 1% engineering, 1% theology.

Freshmen 2,897 applied, 2,234 admitted, 678 enrolled.

Average high school GPA	2.7	SAT verbal scores above 500	51%
SAT math scores above 500	41%	ACT above 18	N/R
From top 10% of their h.s. class	9%	From top half	66%
1998 freshmen returning in 1999	77%		

Application *Options:* eApply at www.CollegeQuest.com, Common Application, early admission, early action, deferred entrance. *Application fee:* $40. *Required:* essay or personal statement; high school transcript; 2 letters of recommendation. *Required for some:* interview. *Recommended:* minimum 2.5 GPA.

Standardized tests *Admission: Required:* SAT I or ACT.

Significant dates *Application deadlines:* rolling (freshmen), rolling (transfers). *Early action:* 11/15. *Notification:* 12/1 (early action). *Financial aid deadline priority date:* 3/1.

Freshman Application Contact
Mr. Walter Caffey, Director of Undergraduate Admission, Suffolk University, 8 Ashburton Place, Boston, MA 02108-2770. **Phone:** 617-573-8460. **Toll-free phone:** 800-6-SUFFOLK. **Fax:** 617-742-4291. **E-mail:** admission@admin.suffolk.edu

Visit CollegeQuest.com for information on majors offered and athletics. College video available at CollegeQuest.com.

TUFTS UNIVERSITY
Medford, Massachusetts

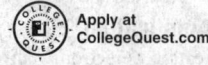

■ **Independent**, university, founded 1852
■ **Degrees** bachelor's, master's, doctoral, first professional, and post-master's certificates
■ **Suburban** 150-acre campus with easy access to Boston
■ **Coed**, 4,950 undergraduate students, 99% full-time, 53% women, 47% men
■ **Most difficult** entrance level, 32% of applicants were admitted
■ **10:1 student-to-undergraduate faculty ratio**
■ **86% graduate** in 6 years or less
■ **$24,751 tuition** and fees
■ **$19,785 average financial aid** package, $14,834 average indebtedness upon graduation, $483.7 million endowment

Students *Undergraduates:* 4,926 full-time, 24 part-time. Students come from 52 states and territories, 69 other countries. *The most frequently chosen baccalaureate fields are:* engineering/engineering technologies, biological/life sciences, social sciences and history. *Graduate:* 1,636 in professional programs, 2,656 in other graduate degree programs.

From out-of-state	75%	Reside on campus	80%
Transferred in	0.4%	International students	8%
African Americans	6%	Asian Americans/Pacific Islanders	13%
Hispanic Americans	6%	Native Americans	0.2%

Faculty 1,059 (61% full-time).

Expenses (1999–2000) *Comprehensive fee:* $32,126 includes full-time tuition ($24,126), mandatory fees ($625), and room and board ($7375). *College room only:* $3775. Room and board charges vary according to board plan. *Payment plans:* tuition prepayment, installment. *Waivers:* employees or children of employees.

Library Tisch Library plus 1 other. *Collection:* 957,500 titles, 5,282 serial subscriptions, 28,000 audiovisual materials.

College life *Housing:* on-campus residence required through sophomore year. *Options:* coed, women-only, cooperative. *Social organizations:* national fraternities, national sororities; 15% of eligible men and 4% of eligible women

Massachusetts

are members. *Most popular organizations:* Leonard Carmichael Society, Tufts Mountain Club, Environmental Consciousness Outreach.

Campus security 24-hour emergency response devices and patrols, late-night transport-escort service, controlled dormitory access, security lighting, call boxes to campus police.

After graduation 214 organizations recruited on campus 1997–98. *Career center:* 8 full-time, 1 part-time personnel. Services include job fairs, resume preparation, interview workshops, resume referral, career counseling, careers library, job bank, job interviews. *Graduate education:* 30% of class of 1999 went directly to graduate and professional school: 11% law, 9% medicine, 8% business, 1% dentistry, 1% veterinary medicine. *Major awards:* 10 Fulbright Scholars.

Freshmen 13,471 applied, 4,313 admitted, 1,351 enrolled. 35 National Merit Scholars.

SAT verbal scores above 500	98%	SAT math scores above 500	98%
ACT above 18	100%	From top 10% of their h.s. class	70%
From top quarter	95%	From top half	99%
1998 freshmen returning in 1999	99%		

Application *Options:* eApply at www.CollegeQuest.com, Common Application, electronic application, early admission, early decision, deferred entrance. *Application fee:* $55. *Required:* essay or personal statement; high school transcript; 1 letter of recommendation. *Recommended:* interview.

Standardized tests *Admission: Required:* SAT I and SAT II or ACT, SAT II: Writing Test.

Significant dates *Application deadlines:* 1/1 (freshmen), 3/1 (transfers). *Early decision:* 11/15 (for plan 1), 1/1 (for plan 2). *Notification:* 4/1 (freshmen), 12/15 (early decision plan 1), 2/1 (early decision plan 2). *Financial aid deadline:* 2/15. *Priority date:* 2/1.

Freshman Application Contact
Mr. David D. Cuttino, Dean of Undergraduate Admissions, Tufts University, Bendetson Hall, Tufts University, Medford, MA 02155. **Phone:** 617-627-3170. **Fax:** 617-627-3860. **E-mail:** uadmiss_inquiry@infonet.tufts.edu

Visit CollegeQuest.com for information on majors offered and athletics. Electronic viewbook available at CollegeQuest.com.

UNIVERSITY OF MASSACHUSETTS AMHERST
Amherst, Massachusetts

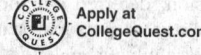
Apply at CollegeQuest.com

- **State-supported**, university, founded 1863
- **Degrees** associate, bachelor's, master's, doctoral, and post-master's certificates
- **Small-town** 1,463-acre campus with easy access to Hartford
- **Coed**, 18,619 undergraduate students, 95% full-time, 50% women, 50% men
- **Moderately difficult** entrance level, 69% of applicants were admitted
- **18:1 student-to-undergraduate faculty ratio**
- **57.1% graduate** in 6 years or less
- **$5212 tuition** and fees (in-state); $13,254 (out-of-state)
- **$8069 average financial aid** package, $16,255 average indebtedness upon graduation, $49 million endowment

The Commonwealth College Honors Program combines an innovative curriculum, rigorous standards, and a residential academic experience. The College encourages creativity, initiative, responsibility, collaboration, and independent thought. Profile of first-year honors students: SAT, 1329; median GPA, 3.9; top 8% of their high school class.

Part of University of Massachusetts.

Students *Undergraduates:* 17,643 full-time, 976 part-time. Students come from 50 states and territories, 60 other countries. *The most frequently chosen baccalaureate fields are:* business/marketing, communications/communication technologies, social sciences and history. *Graduate:* 5,659 in graduate degree programs.

From out-of-state	24%	Reside on campus	58%
Age 25 or older	6%	Transferred in	6%
International students	2%	African Americans	5%
Asian Americans/Pacific Islanders	6%	Hispanic Americans	4%
Native Americans	0.4%		

Faculty 1,291 (90% full-time), 90% with terminal degrees.

Expenses (1999–2000) *One-time required fee:* $153. *Tuition, state resident:* full-time $1714; part-time $72 per credit. *Tuition, nonresident:* full-time $9756; part-time $406 per credit. *Required fees:* full-time $3498; $494 per term part-time. Full-time tuition and fees vary according to reciprocity agreements. Part-time tuition and fees vary according to course load and reciprocity agreements. *College room and board:* $4790; room only: $2638. Room and board charges vary according to board plan. *Payment plan:* installment. *Waivers:* senior citizens and employees or children of employees.

Library W. E. B. Du Bois Library plus 3 others. *Operations spending 1999–2000:* $11.5 million. *Collection:* 2.9 million titles, 15,835 serial subscriptions.

College life *Housing:* on-campus residence required through sophomore year. *Options:* coed, men-only, women-only, disabled students. *Social organizations:* national fraternities, national sororities, local fraternities, local sororities; 5% of eligible men and 4% of eligible women are members. *Most popular organizations:* Minutemen Marching Band, Theater Guild, Ski Club, Outing Club, student newspaper.

Campus security 24-hour emergency response devices and patrols, student patrols, late-night transport-escort service, controlled dormitory access, residence halls locked nights and weekends.

After graduation 568 organizations recruited on campus 1997–98. 97% of class of 1998 had job offers within 6 months. *Career center:* 27 full-time, 2 part-time personnel. Services include job fairs, resume preparation, interview workshops, resume referral, career/interest testing, career counseling, careers library, job bank, job interviews, shadowing programs, computerized alumni network. *Graduate education:* 13% of class of 1999 went directly to graduate and professional school. *Major awards:* 3 Fulbright Scholars.

Freshmen 19,914 applied, 13,727 admitted, 4,196 enrolled. 40 valedictorians.

Average high school GPA	3.26	SAT verbal scores above 500	82%
SAT math scores above 500	83%	ACT above 18	N/R
From top 10% of their h.s. class	19%	From top quarter	50%
From top half	93%	1998 freshmen returning in 1999	81%

Application *Options:* eApply at www.CollegeQuest.com, Common Application, early admission, deferred entrance. *Application fee:* $40 for nonresidents. *Required:* essay or personal statement; high school transcript; minimum 2.0 GPA. *Recommended:* letters of recommendation.

Standardized tests *Admission: Required:* SAT I or ACT.

Significant dates *Application deadlines:* 2/1 (freshmen), 5/1 (transfers). *Financial aid deadline priority date:* 3/1.

Freshman Application Contact
Mr. Joseph Marshall, Assistant Dean for Enrollment Services, University of Massachusetts Amherst, Amherst, MA 01003. **Phone:** 413-545-0222. **Fax:** 413-545-4312. **E-mail:** mail@admissions.umass.edu

Visit CollegeQuest.com for information on majors offered and athletics. College video available at CollegeQuest.com.

■ *See page 2762 for a narrative description.*

UNIVERSITY OF MASSACHUSETTS BOSTON
Boston, Massachusetts

- **State-supported**, university, founded 1964
- **Degrees** bachelor's, master's, doctoral, and post-master's certificates
- **Urban** 177-acre campus
- **Coed**, 8,575 undergraduate students, 66% full-time, 57% women, 43% men
- **Moderately difficult** entrance level, 62% of applicants were admitted
- **25% graduate** in 6 years or less
- **$4307 tuition** and fees (in-state); $12,351 (out-of-state)
- **$9.7 million endowment**

The University of Massachusetts Boston is a public urban university, located on a peninsula in Boston Harbor, just 3 miles south of the city and adjacent to the John F. Kennedy Library and Museum. Established in 1964, the University enrolls more than 13,000 students in both undergraduate and graduate programs.

Massachusetts

University of Massachusetts Boston (continued)
Part of University of Massachusetts.

Students *Undergraduates:* 5,680 full-time, 2,895 part-time. Students come from 30 states and territories, 74 other countries. *The most frequently chosen baccalaureate fields are:* business/marketing, psychology, social sciences and history. *Graduate:* 3,199 in graduate degree programs.

From out-of-state	5%	Age 25 or older	47%
Transferred in	19%	International students	6%
African Americans	14%	Asian Americans/Pacific Islanders	11%
Hispanic Americans	6%	Native Americans	0.4%

Faculty 861 (53% full-time).

Expenses (1999–2000) *One-time required fee:* $150. *Tuition, state resident:* full-time $1714; part-time $72 per credit. *Tuition, nonresident:* full-time $9758; part-time $406 per credit. *Required fees:* full-time $2593; $482 per term part-time. Part-time tuition and fees vary according to course load. Additional part-time mandatory fees per term: $15 for nonresidents. *Payment plan:* installment. *Waivers:* senior citizens and employees or children of employees.

Library Joseph P. Healey Library. *Operations spending 1999–2000:* $3.1 million. *Collection:* 580,810 titles, 435,612 serial subscriptions, 1,826 audiovisual materials.

College life *Housing:* college housing not available. *Most popular organizations:* women's center, black student center, Asian student center, veterans student center, disabilities student center.

Campus security 24-hour emergency response devices and patrols, late-night transport-escort service, crime prevention program, bicycle patrols.

After graduation 70 organizations recruited on campus 1997–98. *Career center:* 7 full-time, 2 part-time personnel. Services include job fairs, resume preparation, interview workshops, resume referral, career counseling, careers library, job bank, job interviews.

Freshmen 2,724 applied, 1,694 admitted, 789 enrolled.

Average high school GPA	2.84	SAT verbal scores above 500	61%
SAT math scores above 500	58%	ACT above 18	N/R
1998 freshmen returning in 1999	67%		

Application *Options:* Common Application, electronic application, deferred entrance. *Application fee:* $25. *Required:* high school transcript; minimum 2.75 GPA. *Required for some:* essay or personal statement; letters of recommendation; interview. *Recommended:* essay or personal statement.

Standardized tests *Admission: Required:* SAT I or ACT. *Placement: Required:* SAT I or ACT

Significant dates *Application deadlines:* 3/1 (freshmen), 3/1 (transfers). *Financial aid deadline priority date:* 3/1.

Freshman Application Contact
Office of Admissions Information Service, University of Massachusetts Boston, 100 Morrissey Boulevard, Boston, MA 02125-3393. **Phone:** 617-287-6000. **E-mail:** bos.admiss@umassp.edu

Visit CollegeQuest.com for information on majors offered and athletics. Electronic viewbook available at CollegeQuest.com.

■ *See page 2764 for a narrative description.*

UNIVERSITY OF MASSACHUSETTS DARTMOUTH
North Dartmouth, Massachusetts

- **State-supported**, comprehensive, founded 1895
- **Degrees** bachelor's, master's, doctoral, post-master's, and postbachelor's certificates
- **Suburban** 710-acre campus with easy access to Boston and Providence
- **Coed**, 5,464 undergraduate students, 86% full-time, 53% women, 47% men
- **Moderately difficult** entrance level, 65% of applicants were admitted
- **15:1** student-to-undergraduate faculty ratio
- **49% graduate** in 6 years or less
- **$4129 tuition** and fees (in-state); $11,783 (out-of-state)
- **$6912 average financial aid** package, $13,446 average indebtedness upon graduation, $6 million endowment

The University of Massachusetts Dartmouth enrolls more than 5,500 students on its 710-acre campus in southeastern Massachusetts. Five colleges offer 42 undergraduate and 17 graduate degrees. Publicly supported, the University provides affordable options in professional and preprofessional programs as well as in a variety of cocurricular activities, organizations, and teams.

Part of University of Massachusetts.

Students *Undergraduates:* 4,724 full-time, 740 part-time. Students come from 25 states and territories, 30 other countries. *The most frequently chosen baccalaureate fields are:* business/marketing, psychology, social sciences and history. *Graduate:* 801 in graduate degree programs.

From out-of-state	7%	Reside on campus	42%
Age 25 or older	16%	Transferred in	8%
International students	2%	African Americans	6%
Asian Americans/Pacific Islanders	3%	Hispanic Americans	2%
Native Americans	1%		

Faculty 453 (75% full-time).

Expenses (1999–2000) *Tuition, state resident:* full-time $1417; part-time $59 per credit hour. *Tuition, nonresident:* full-time $9071; part-time $327 per credit hour. *Required fees:* full-time $2712; $113 per credit hour. Part-time tuition and fees vary according to course load and program. *College room and board:* $4992; room only: $2827. Room and board charges vary according to board plan and housing facility. *Payment plan:* installment. *Waivers:* senior citizens and employees or children of employees.

Library University of Massachusetts Dartmouth Library. *Operations spending 1999–2000:* $3.2 million. *Collection:* 14,303 audiovisual materials.

College life *Housing: Options:* coed, disabled students. *Social organizations:* national fraternities, national sororities. *Most popular organizations:* Student Activities Board, Outing Club, Phi Sigma Sigma, Portuguese Language Club, United Brothers and Sisters.

Campus security 24-hour emergency response devices and patrols, student patrols, late-night transport-escort service, controlled dormitory access.

After graduation 400 organizations recruited on campus 1997–98. 90% of class of 1998 had job offers within 6 months. *Career center:* 7 full-time personnel. Services include job fairs, resume preparation, resume referral, career counseling, careers library, job bank, job interviews. *Major awards:* 1 Fulbright Scholar.

Freshmen 4,831 applied, 3,127 admitted, 1,142 enrolled. 4 valedictorians.

Average high school GPA	2.92	SAT verbal scores above 500	63%
SAT math scores above 500	66%	ACT above 18	100%
From top 10% of their h.s. class	11%	From top quarter	37%
From top half	78%	1998 freshmen returning in 1999	80%

Application *Options:* Common Application, early admission, early decision, deferred entrance. *Application fee:* $40 for nonresidents. *Required:* essay or personal statement; high school transcript; minimum 3.0 GPA. *Recommended:* letters of recommendation.

Standardized tests *Admission: Required:* SAT I or ACT. *Recommended:* SAT I.

Significant dates *Application deadlines:* rolling (freshmen), rolling (transfers). *Early decision:* 11/15. *Notification:* 12/15 (early decision). *Financial aid deadline priority date:* 3/1.

Freshman Application Contact
Mr. Steven Briggs, Director of Admissions, University of Massachusetts Dartmouth, 285 Old Westport Road, North Dartmouth, MA 02747-2300. **Phone:** 508-999-8606. **Fax:** 508-999-8755. **E-mail:** admissions@umassd.edu

Visit CollegeQuest.com for information on majors offered and athletics. College video available at CollegeQuest.com.

■ *See page 2766 for a narrative description.*

UNIVERSITY OF MASSACHUSETTS LOWELL
Lowell, Massachusetts

- **State-supported**, university, founded 1894
- **Degrees** associate, bachelor's, master's, and doctoral
- **Urban** 100-acre campus with easy access to Boston
- **Coed**, 5,851 undergraduate students, 88% full-time, 41% women, 59% men
- **Moderately difficult** entrance level, 71% of applicants were admitted
- **43% graduate** in 6 years or less
- **$4255 tuition** and fees (in-state); $10,892 (out-of-state)
- **$6702 average financial aid** package, $15,735 average indebtedness upon graduation, $6.6 million endowment

Massachusetts

Part of University of Massachusetts.
Students *Undergraduates:* 5,139 full-time, 712 part-time. Students come from 38 states and territories, 51 other countries. *The most frequently chosen baccalaureate fields are:* business/marketing, engineering/engineering technologies, health professions and related sciences. *Graduate:* 2,684 in graduate degree programs.

From out-of-state	13%	Reside on campus	32%
Age 25 or older	30%	Transferred in	11%
International students	3%	African Americans	3%
Asian Americans/Pacific Islanders	7%	Hispanic Americans	4%
Native Americans	0.2%		

Faculty 561 (73% full-time).
Expenses (1999–2000) *Tuition, state resident:* full-time $1454; part-time $61 per credit. *Tuition, nonresident:* full-time $8091; part-time $328 per credit. *Required fees:* full-time $2801; $129 per credit. *College room and board:* $4726; room only: $2800. Room and board charges vary according to board plan and housing facility. *Payment plan:* installment. *Waivers:* senior citizens and employees or children of employees.
Library O'Leary Library plus 2 others. *Collection:* 446,309 titles, 5,590 serial subscriptions, 6,000 audiovisual materials.
College life *Housing: Options:* coed, men-only, women-only.
Campus security 24-hour emergency response devices and patrols, late-night transport-escort service, controlled dormitory access.
After graduation 567 organizations recruited on campus 1997–98. *Career center:* 4 full-time personnel. Services include job fairs, resume preparation, interview workshops, resume referral, career/interest testing, career counseling, careers library, job bank, job interviews.
Freshmen 3,135 applied, 2,225 admitted, 950 enrolled.

Average high school GPA	3.0	SAT verbal scores above 500	59%
SAT math scores above 500	N/R	ACT above 18	N/R
1998 freshmen returning in 1999	76%		

Application *Options:* electronic application, deferred entrance. *Application fee:* $35 for nonresidents. *Required:* essay or personal statement; high school transcript; minimum 3.00 GPA. *Required for some:* interview. *Recommended:* 1 letter of recommendation.
Standardized tests *Admission: Required:* SAT I or ACT.
Significant dates *Application deadlines:* rolling (freshmen), rolling (transfers). *Financial aid deadline priority date:* 3/1.
Freshman Application Contact
Ms. Rayanne Lapierre, Assistant Director of Admissions, University of Massachusetts Lowell, 883 Broadway Street, Room 110, Lowell, MA 01854-5104. **Phone:** 978-934-3944. **Toll-free phone:** 800-410-4607. **Fax:** 978-934-3000. **E-mail:** admissions@uml.edu
Visit CollegeQuest.com for information on majors offered and athletics. College video and electronic viewbook available at CollegeQuest.com.

■ *See page 2768 for a narrative description.*

WELLESLEY COLLEGE
Wellesley, Massachusetts

Apply at CollegeQuest.com

- **Independent**, 4-year, founded 1870
- **Degree** bachelor's (double bachelor's degree with Massachusetts Institute of Technology)
- **Suburban** 500-acre campus with easy access to Boston
- **Women** only, 2,290 undergraduate students, 98% full-time
- **Most difficult** entrance level, 46% of applicants were admitted
- **10:1** student-to-undergraduate faculty ratio
- **88% graduate** in 6 years or less
- **$23,320 tuition** and fees
- **$18,704 average financial aid** package, $17,664 average indebtedness upon graduation, $887.5 million endowment

Students *Undergraduates:* 2,235 full-time, 55 part-time. Students come from 53 states and territories, 77 other countries. *The most frequently chosen baccalaureate fields are:* psychology, English, social sciences and history.

From out-of-state	77%	Reside on campus	93%
Age 25 or older	4%	Transferred in	1%
International students	6%	African Americans	7%
Asian Americans/Pacific Islanders	23%	Hispanic Americans	6%
Native Americans	1%		

Faculty 333 (67% full-time), 88% with terminal degrees.

Expenses (1999–2000) *Comprehensive fee:* $30,554 includes full-time tuition ($22,894), mandatory fees ($426), and room and board ($7234). *College room only:* $3664. Room and board charges vary according to board plan. *Part-time tuition:* $2916 per course. *Payment plans:* tuition prepayment, installment. *Waivers:* employees or children of employees.
Library Margaret Clapp Library plus 3 others. *Operations spending 1999–2000:* $4.8 million. *Collection:* 689,627 titles, 4,756 serial subscriptions, 20,532 audiovisual materials.
College life *Housing: Options:* women-only, cooperative, disabled students. *Most popular organizations:* student government, radio station, cultural clubs, rugby club, theater groups.
Campus security 24-hour emergency response devices and patrols, late-night transport-escort service, controlled dormitory access.
After graduation 124 organizations recruited on campus 1997–98. 71% of class of 1998 had job offers within 6 months. *Career center:* Services include job fairs, resume preparation, interview workshops, resume referral, career counseling, careers library, job bank, job interviews. *Graduate education:* 28% of class of 1999 went directly to graduate and professional school. *Major awards:* 1 Marshall, 3 Fulbright Scholars.
Freshmen 2,862 applied, 1,311 admitted, 596 enrolled.

SAT verbal scores above 500	96%	SAT math scores above 500	99%
ACT above 18	N/R	From top 10% of their h.s. class	70%
From top quarter	97%	From top half	100%
1998 freshmen returning in 1999	95%		

Application *Options:* eApply at www.CollegeQuest.com, Common Application, early admission, early decision, deferred entrance. *Application fee:* $50. *Required:* essay or personal statement; high school transcript; 3 letters of recommendation. *Required for some:* interview. *Recommended:* interview.
Standardized tests *Admission: Required:* SAT I and SAT II or ACT.
Significant dates *Application deadlines:* 1/15 (freshmen), 2/10 (transfers). *Early decision:* 11/1. *Notification:* 4/1 (freshmen), 12/15 (early decision). *Financial aid deadline priority date:* 1/15.
Freshman Application Contact
Ms. Janet Lavin Rapelye, Dean of Admission, Wellesley College, 106 Central Street, Wellesley, MA 02481-8203. **Phone:** 781-283-2270. **Fax:** 781-283-3678. **E-mail:** admission@wellesley.edu
Visit CollegeQuest.com for information on majors offered and athletics. College video and electronic viewbook available at CollegeQuest.com.

■ *See page 2930 for a narrative description.*

WENTWORTH INSTITUTE OF TECHNOLOGY
Boston, Massachusetts

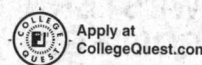

Apply at CollegeQuest.com

- **Independent**, 4-year, founded 1904
- **Degrees** associate and bachelor's
- **Urban** 35-acre campus
- **Coed**, primarily men, 3,168 undergraduate students, 78% full-time, 16% women, 84% men
- **Moderately difficult** entrance level, 65% of applicants were admitted
- **$12,450 tuition** and fees
- **$7681 average financial aid** package, $19,500 average indebtedness upon graduation, $76.9 million endowment

Founded in 1904, Wentworth Institute of Technology offers bachelor's degrees in architecture, computer science, design, engineering, engineering technology, and management of technology. Wentworth provides an education that balances classroom theory with laboratory/studio practice and work experience through its strong co-op program. More than 3,000 students attend this private coeducational institution, located on a 35-acre campus on Huntington Avenue, across from Boston's Museum of Fine Arts.

Students *Undergraduates:* 2,459 full-time, 709 part-time. *The most frequently chosen baccalaureate fields are:* architecture, computer/information sciences, engineering/engineering technologies.

Reside on campus	50%	Age 25 or older	4%
Transferred in	6%	International students	8%
African Americans	6%	Asian Americans/Pacific Islanders	6%
Hispanic Americans	4%	Native Americans	1%

Massachusetts

Wentworth Institute of Technology (continued)

Faculty 239 (48% full-time).

Expenses (1999–2000) *Comprehensive fee:* $18,950 includes full-time tuition ($12,450) and room and board ($6500). Room and board charges vary according to board plan and housing facility. *Part-time tuition:* $330 per credit. Part-time tuition and fees vary according to class time. *Payment plan:* installment. *Waivers:* employees or children of employees.

Library Wentworth Alumni Library. *Operations spending 1999–2000:* $659,000. *Collection:* 77,000 titles, 500 serial subscriptions.

College life *Housing: Option:* coed. *Most popular organizations:* intramural sports, Wentworth Events Board, Asian Students Association, ski and adventure club.

Campus security 24-hour emergency response devices and patrols, student patrols, late-night transport-escort service, controlled dormitory access.

After graduation 160 organizations recruited on campus 1997–98. 98% of class of 1998 had job offers within 6 months. *Career center:* 8 full-time personnel. Services include job fairs, resume preparation, interview workshops, resume referral, career/interest testing, career counseling, careers library, job bank, job interviews. *Graduate education:* 5% of class of 1999 went directly to graduate and professional school: 3% engineering, 2% business.

Freshmen 3,100 applied, 2,014 admitted, 972 enrolled.

| SAT verbal scores above 500 | 51% | SAT math scores above 500 | 58% |
| ACT above 18 | N/R | 1998 freshmen returning in 1999 | 75% |

Application *Options:* eApply at www.CollegeQuest.com, Common Application, electronic application, deferred entrance. *Application fee:* $30. *Required:* high school transcript. *Recommended:* essay or personal statement; minimum 2.0 GPA; letters of recommendation; interview.

Standardized tests *Admission: Required:* SAT I or ACT.

Significant dates *Application deadlines:* rolling (freshmen), rolling (transfers). *Financial aid deadline priority date:* 3/1.

Freshman Application Contact
Ms. Keiko S. Broomhead, Associate Director of Admissions, Wentworth Institute of Technology, 550 Huntington Avenue, Boston, MA 02115-5998. **Phone:** 617-989-4009. **Toll-free phone:** 800-556-0610. **Fax:** 617-989-4010. **E-mail:** admissions@wit.edu

Visit CollegeQuest.com for information on majors offered and athletics. Electronic viewbook available at CollegeQuest.com.

■ *See page 2934 for a narrative description.*

WESTERN NEW ENGLAND COLLEGE
Springfield, Massachusetts

Apply at CollegeQuest.com

- **Independent**, comprehensive, founded 1919
- **Degrees** associate, bachelor's, master's, and first professional
- **Suburban** 185-acre campus
- **Coed**, 3,288 undergraduate students, 59% full-time, 34% women, 66% men
- **Moderately difficult** entrance level, 77% of applicants were admitted
- **47% graduate** in 6 years or less
- **$15,504 tuition** and fees
- **$9909 average financial aid** package, $23,000 average indebtedness upon graduation, $34 million endowment

Students *Undergraduates:* 1,943 full-time, 1,345 part-time. Students come from 25 states and territories, 15 other countries. *The most frequently chosen baccalaureate fields are:* business/marketing, engineering/engineering technologies, protective services/public administration. *Graduate:* 567 in professional programs, 1,183 in other graduate degree programs.

From out-of-state	52%	Reside on campus	72%
Age 25 or older	40%	Transferred in	3%
International students	1%	African Americans	3%
Asian Americans/Pacific Islanders	2%	Hispanic Americans	3%
Native Americans	0.2%		

Faculty 253 (45% full-time).

Expenses (2000–2001) *Comprehensive fee:* $22,554 includes full-time tuition ($14,354), mandatory fees ($1150), and room and board ($7050). Room and board charges vary according to board plan and housing facility. *Part-time tuition:* $356 per semester hour. *Part-time fees:* $9 per semester hour; $20 per term part-time. *Payment plans:* tuition prepayment, installment, deferred payment. *Waivers:* senior citizens and employees or children of employees.

Library D'Amour Library plus 1 other. *Operations spending 1999–2000:* $922,298. *Collection:* 307,011 titles.

College life *Housing: Options:* coed, men-only, women-only. *Most popular organizations:* Student Senate, Residence Hall Association, Campus Activities Board, student radio station, Management Association.

Campus security 24-hour emergency response devices and patrols, student patrols, late-night transport-escort service, controlled dormitory access, security cameras.

After graduation 29 organizations recruited on campus 1997–98. *Career center:* 7 full-time, 4 part-time personnel. Services include job fairs, resume preparation, interview workshops, resume referral, career/interest testing, career counseling, careers library, job bank, job interviews. *Graduate education:* 10% of class of 1999 went directly to graduate and professional school.

Freshmen 3,223 applied, 2,489 admitted, 612 enrolled. 2 valedictorians.

Average high school GPA	2.92	SAT verbal scores above 500	55%
SAT math scores above 500	58%	ACT above 18	N/R
From top 10% of their h.s. class	9%	From top quarter	31%
From top half	69%	1998 freshmen returning in 1999	75%

Application *Options:* eApply at www.CollegeQuest.com, Common Application, electronic application. *Application fee:* $30. *Required:* high school transcript; minimum 2.2 GPA; 1 letter of recommendation. *Recommended:* essay or personal statement; interview.

Standardized tests *Admission: Required:* SAT I or ACT.

Significant dates *Application deadlines:* rolling (freshmen), rolling (transfers). *Financial aid deadline:* continuous.

Freshman Application Contact
Dr. Charles R. Pollock, Dean of Enrollment Management, Western New England College, , 1215 Wilbraham Road, Springfield, MA 01119. **Phone:** 413-782-1321. **Toll-free phone:** 800-325-1122 Ext. 1321. **Fax:** 413-782-1777. **E-mail:** ugradmis@wnec.edu

Visit CollegeQuest.com for information on majors offered and athletics. College video available at CollegeQuest.com.

■ *See page 2954 for a narrative description.*

WESTFIELD STATE COLLEGE
Westfield, Massachusetts

- **State-supported**, comprehensive, founded 1838
- **Degrees** bachelor's, master's, post-master's, and postbachelor's certificates
- **Small-town** 227-acre campus
- **Coed**, 3,935 undergraduate students, 87% full-time, 54% women, 46% men
- **Moderately difficult** entrance level, 65% of applicants were admitted
- **18:1 student-to-undergraduate faculty ratio**
- **$2974 tuition** and fees (in-state); $8934 (out-of-state)

Part of Massachusetts Public Higher Education System.

Students *Undergraduates:* 3,406 full-time, 529 part-time. Students come from 14 states and territories, 1 other country. *The most frequently chosen baccalaureate fields are:* education, business/marketing, protective services/public administration. *Graduate:* 703 in graduate degree programs.

From out-of-state	7%	Reside on campus	59%
Age 25 or older	6%	Transferred in	6%
International students	0.2%	African Americans	3%
Asian Americans/Pacific Islanders	1%	Hispanic Americans	2%
Native Americans	0.1%		

Faculty 297 (57% full-time).

Expenses (1999–2000) *Tuition, state resident:* full-time $1090; part-time $135 per credit hour. *Tuition, nonresident:* full-time $7050. *Required fees:* full-time $1884. Full-time tuition and fees vary according to reciprocity agreements and student level. *College room and board:* $4174; room only: $2440. Room and board charges vary according to board plan and housing facility. *Payment plan:* installment. *Waivers:* senior citizens and employees or children of employees.

Library Ely Library. *Collection:* 176,589 titles, 1,028 serial subscriptions.
College life *Housing: Options:* coed, disabled students.
Campus security 24-hour emergency response devices and patrols, student patrols, late-night transport-escort service.
After graduation *Career center:* 1 full-time, 1 part-time personnel. Services include job fairs, resume preparation, career counseling, careers library, job bank. *Graduate education:* 10% of class of 1999 went directly to graduate and professional school: 5% graduate arts and sciences, 4% business, 1% law.
Freshmen 3,440 applied, 2,227 admitted, 899 enrolled.

Average high school GPA	2.9	SAT verbal scores above 500	54%
SAT math scores above 500	57%	ACT above 18	N/R
1998 freshmen returning in 1999	74%		

Application *Option:* electronic application. *Application fee:* $10. *Required:* high school transcript; minimum 2.0 GPA. *Recommended:* letters of recommendation.
Standardized tests *Admission: Required:* SAT I. *Required for some:* SAT II Subject Tests.
Significant dates *Application deadlines:* 3/1 (freshmen), 4/1 (transfers). *Notification:* 4/15 (freshmen). *Financial aid deadline priority date:* 3/1.
Freshman Application Contact
Ms. Michelle Mattie, Director of Admission and Financial Aid, Westfield State College, Western Avenue, Westfield, MA 01086. **Phone:** 413-572-5218. **Toll-free phone:** 800-322-8401. **E-mail:** admission@wsc.mass.edu
Visit CollegeQuest.com for information on majors offered and athletics.

WHEATON COLLEGE
Norton, Massachusetts

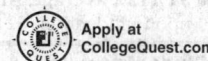 Apply at CollegeQuest.com

- **Independent**, 4-year, founded 1834
- **Degree** bachelor's
- **Small-town** 385-acre campus with easy access to Boston
- **Coed**, 1,485 undergraduate students, 99% full-time, 66% women, 34% men
- **Moderately difficult** entrance level, 71% of applicants were admitted
- **13:1 student-to-undergraduate faculty ratio**
- **68% graduate** in 6 years or less
- **$23,150 tuition** and fees
- **$18,068 average financial aid** package, $16,193 average indebtedness upon graduation, $126.3 million endowment

Students *Undergraduates:* 1,478 full-time, 7 part-time. Students come from 40 states and territories, 29 other countries. *The most frequently chosen baccalaureate fields are:* psychology, social sciences and history, visual/performing arts.

From out-of-state	58%	Reside on campus	98%
Age 25 or older	1%	Transferred in	1%
International students	2%	African Americans	4%
Asian Americans/Pacific Islanders	3%	Hispanic Americans	4%
Native Americans	0.5%		

Faculty 140 (69% full-time), 84% with terminal degrees.
Expenses (1999–2000) *Comprehensive fee:* $29,880 includes full-time tuition ($22,950), mandatory fees ($200), and room and board ($6730). *College room only:* $3550. *Part-time tuition:* $2869 per course. *Payment plans:* tuition prepayment, installment, deferred payment. *Waivers:* employees or children of employees.
Library Madeleine Clark Wallace Library plus 1 other. *Operations spending 1999–2000:* $2.4 million. *Collection:* 361,860 titles, 2,252 serial subscriptions, 10,967 audiovisual materials.
College life *Housing:* on-campus residence required through senior year. *Options:* coed, men-only, women-only. *Most popular organizations:* Student Government Association, Community Service Network, Amnesty International, a cappella singing groups, Programming Council.
Campus security 24-hour emergency response devices and patrols, student patrols, late-night transport-escort service, controlled dormitory access.
After graduation 25 organizations recruited on campus 1997–98. 60% of class of 1998 had job offers within 6 months. *Career center:* 6 full-time, 3 part-time personnel. Services include job fairs, resume preparation, interview workshops, resume referral, career/interest testing, career counseling, careers library, job bank, job interviews, internship assistance. *Major awards:* 1 Fulbright Scholar.
Freshmen 2,463 applied, 1,759 admitted, 427 enrolled. 125 student government officers.

Average high school GPA	3.05	SAT verbal scores above 500	95%
SAT math scores above 500	96%	ACT above 18	N/R
From top 10% of their h.s. class	25%	From top quarter	59%
From top half	90%	1998 freshmen returning in 1999	85%

Application *Options:* eApply at www.CollegeQuest.com, Common Application, electronic application, early admission, early decision, early action, deferred entrance. *Application fee:* $50. *Required:* essay or personal statement; high school transcript; 2 letters of recommendation. *Recommended:* interview.
Significant dates *Application deadlines:* 2/1 (freshmen), 4/1 (transfers). *Early decision:* 11/15, 12/15. *Notification:* 4/1 (freshmen), 12/15 (early decision), 2/1 (early action). *Financial aid deadline:* 2/1.
Freshman Application Contact
Ms. Lynne M. Stack, Director of Admission, Wheaton College, East Main Street, Norton, MA 02766. **Phone:** 508-286-8251. **Toll-free phone:** 800-394-6003. **Fax:** 508-285-8271. **E-mail:** admission@wheatonma.edu
Visit CollegeQuest.com for information on majors offered and athletics. College video available at CollegeQuest.com.

■ *See page 2976 for a narrative description.*

WHEELOCK COLLEGE
Boston, Massachusetts

 Apply at CollegeQuest.com

- **Independent**, comprehensive, founded 1888
- **Degrees** bachelor's and master's
- **Urban** 5-acre campus
- **Coed**, primarily women, 604 undergraduate students, 99% full-time, 96% women, 4% men
- **Moderately difficult** entrance level, 86% of applicants were admitted
- **11:1 student-to-undergraduate faculty ratio**
- **$17,410 tuition** and fees
- **$11,900 average financial aid** package, $20,000 average indebtedness upon graduation, $37.6 million endowment

Students *Undergraduates:* 597 full-time, 7 part-time. Students come from 20 states and territories, 6 other countries. *The most frequently chosen baccalaureate fields are:* education, health professions and related sciences, protective services/public administration. *Graduate:* 728 in graduate degree programs.

From out-of-state	45%	Reside on campus	69%
Age 25 or older	8%	Transferred in	9%
International students	1%	African Americans	5%
Asian Americans/Pacific Islanders	3%	Hispanic Americans	4%
Native Americans	0.5%		

Faculty 213 (32% full-time), 40% with terminal degrees.
Expenses (2000–2001) *Comprehensive fee:* $24,355 includes full-time tuition ($17,410) and room and board ($6945). *Part-time tuition:* $544 per credit. *Payment plan:* installment. *Waivers:* employees or children of employees.
Library Wheelock College Library plus 1 other. *Operations spending 1999–2000:* $534,000. *Collection:* 94,000 titles, 541 serial subscriptions.
College life *Housing:* on-campus residence required in freshman year. *Options:* coed, women-only, cooperative. *Most popular organizations:* Student Government Association, theatre club, AHANA Club, residence hall councils, class councils.
Campus security 24-hour patrols, late-night transport-escort service, controlled dormitory access, self-defense education.
After graduation 63 organizations recruited on campus 1997–98. 68% of class of 1998 had job offers within 6 months. *Career center:* 2 full-time, 1 part-time personnel. Services include job fairs, resume preparation, interview workshops, career counseling, careers library, job bank. *Graduate education:* 12% of class of 1999 went directly to graduate and professional school.

Massachusetts

Wheelock College (continued)

Freshmen 415 applied, 355 admitted, 127 enrolled. 1 valedictorian.

Average high school GPA	2.9	SAT verbal scores above 500	49%
SAT math scores above 500	36%	ACT above 18	N/R
From top 10% of their h.s. class	9%	From top quarter	21%
From top half	56%	1998 freshmen returning in 1999	82%

Application *Options:* eApply at www.CollegeQuest.com, electronic application, early decision, deferred entrance. *Application fee:* $30. *Required:* essay or personal statement; high school transcript; 2 letters of recommendation. *Recommended:* interview.

Standardized tests *Admission: Required:* SAT I or ACT.

Significant dates *Application deadlines:* 3/1 (freshmen), 4/15 (transfers). *Early decision:* 12/1. *Notification:* continuous until 4/15 (freshmen), 1/1 (early decision). *Financial aid deadline priority date:* 3/1.

Freshman Application Contact
Ms. Lynne E. Dailey, Dean of Admissions, Wheelock College, 200 the Riverway, Boston, MA 02215. **Phone:** 617-734-5200 Ext. 204. **Toll-free phone:** 800-734-5212. **Fax:** 617-566-7369. **E-mail:** undergrad@wheelock.edu

Visit CollegeQuest.com for information on majors offered and athletics. College video available at CollegeQuest.com.

■ *See page 2980 for a narrative description.*

WILLIAMS COLLEGE
Williamstown, Massachusetts

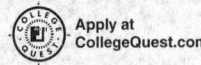 Apply at CollegeQuest.com

■ **Independent**, comprehensive, founded 1793
■ **Degrees** bachelor's and master's
■ **Small-town** 450-acre campus with easy access to Albany
■ **Coed**, 2,052 undergraduate students, 100% full-time, 49% women, 51% men
■ **Most difficult** entrance level, 23% of applicants were admitted
■ **93% graduate** in 6 years or less
■ **$24,790 tuition** and fees
■ **$21,955 average financial aid** package, $14,328 average indebtedness upon graduation, $980.2 million endowment

Students *Undergraduates:* 2,052 full-time. Students come from 51 states and territories, 32 other countries. *The most frequently chosen baccalaureate fields are:* biological/life sciences, English, social sciences and history. *Graduate:* 49 in graduate degree programs.

From out-of-state	85%	Reside on campus	96%
Age 25 or older	2%	Transferred in	0.4%
International students	6%	African Americans	7%
Asian Americans/Pacific Islanders	9%	Hispanic Americans	6%
Native Americans	0.4%		

Faculty 301 (80% full-time).

Expenses (1999–2000) *Comprehensive fee:* $31,520 includes full-time tuition ($24,619), mandatory fees ($171), and room and board ($6730). *College room only:* $3340. Room and board charges vary according to board plan. *Payment plan:* installment. *Waivers:* employees or children of employees.

Library Sawyer Library plus 9 others. *Operations spending 1999–2000:* $3.6 million. *Collection:* 420,144 titles, 2,853 serial subscriptions, 31,659 audiovisual materials.

College life *Housing:* on-campus residence required through senior year. *Option:* coed.

Campus security 24-hour emergency response devices and patrols, student patrols, late-night transport-escort service, controlled dormitory access.

After graduation 100 organizations recruited on campus 1997–98. 65% of class of 1998 had job offers within 6 months. *Career center:* 5 full-time, 2 part-time personnel. Services include job fairs, resume preparation, interview workshops, resume referral, career counseling, careers library, job bank, job interviews. *Graduate education:* 19% of class of 1999 went directly to graduate and professional school.

Freshmen 5,007 applied, 1,157 admitted, 544 enrolled. 1 Westinghouse recipient.

SAT verbal scores above 500	99%	SAT math scores above 500	99%
ACT above 18	N/R	From top 10% of their h.s. class	84%
From top quarter	97%	From top half	99%
1998 freshmen returning in 1999	98%		

Application *Options:* eApply at www.CollegeQuest.com, Common Application, electronic application, early admission, early decision, deferred entrance. *Application fee:* $50. *Required:* essay or personal statement; high school transcript; 2 letters of recommendation.

Standardized tests *Admission: Required:* SAT I and SAT II or ACT.

Significant dates *Application deadlines:* 1/1 (freshmen), 3/1 (transfers). *Early decision:* 11/15. *Notification:* 4/8 (freshmen), 12/15 (early decision). *Financial aid deadline:* 2/1.

Freshman Application Contact
Mr. Thomas H. Parker, Director of Admission, Williams College, 988 Main Street, Williamstown, MA 01267. **Phone:** 413-597-2211. **E-mail:** admission@williams.edu

Visit CollegeQuest.com for information on majors offered and athletics. College video available at CollegeQuest.com.

WORCESTER POLYTECHNIC INSTITUTE
Worcester, Massachusetts

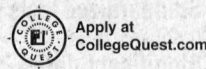 Apply at CollegeQuest.com

■ **Independent**, university, founded 1865
■ **Degrees** bachelor's, master's, and doctoral
■ **Suburban** 80-acre campus with easy access to Boston
■ **Coed**, 2,737 undergraduate students, 98% full-time, 22% women, 78% men
■ **Very difficult** entrance level, 79% of applicants were admitted
■ **13:1 student-to-undergraduate faculty ratio**
■ **78% graduate** in 6 years or less
■ **$22,108 tuition** and fees
■ **$17,122 average financial aid** package, $18,596 average indebtedness upon graduation, $213.3 million endowment

Students *Undergraduates:* 2,675 full-time, 62 part-time. Students come from 51 states and territories, 40 other countries. *The most frequently chosen baccalaureate fields are:* biological/life sciences, computer/information sciences, engineering/engineering technologies. *Graduate:* 1,091 in graduate degree programs.

Reside on campus	50%	Age 25 or older	2%
Transferred in	2%	International students	5%
African Americans	2%	Asian Americans/Pacific Islanders	7%
Hispanic Americans	3%	Native Americans	0.3%

Expenses (1999–2000) *One-time required fee:* $180. *Comprehensive fee:* $29,020 includes full-time tuition ($21,770), mandatory fees ($338), and room and board ($6912). *College room only:* $3600. Room and board charges vary according to board plan and housing facility. *Part-time tuition:* $1,814 per course. *Waivers:* employees or children of employees.

Library Gordon Library. *Operations spending 1999–2000:* $1.7 million. *Collection:* 170,000 titles, 1,400 serial subscriptions.

College life *Housing: Options:* coed, men-only. *Social organizations:* national fraternities, national sororities; 35% of eligible men and 40% of eligible women are members. *Most popular organizations:* student government, Masque (Drama Group), music groups, intramural sports, ethnic clubs.

Campus security 24-hour emergency response devices and patrols, student patrols, late-night transport-escort service.

After graduation 150 organizations recruited on campus 1997–98. *Career center:* 3 full-time, 3 part-time personnel. Services include job fairs, resume preparation, interview workshops, resume referral, career/interest testing, career counseling, careers library, job bank, job interviews.

Freshmen 3,231 applied, 2,556 admitted, 664 enrolled. 30 National Merit Scholars.

SAT verbal scores above 500	93%	SAT math scores above 500	100%
ACT above 18	N/R	From top 10% of their h.s. class	43%
From top quarter	82%	From top half	98%
1998 freshmen returning in 1999	91%		

Application *Options:* eApply at www.CollegeQuest.com, Common Application, electronic application, early admission, early decision, deferred entrance. *Application fee:* $60. *Required:* high school transcript; 1 letter of recommendation. *Recommended:* essay or personal statement.

Standardized tests *Admission: Required:* SAT I and SAT II or ACT.

Massachusetts–Michigan

Significant dates *Application deadlines:* 2/1 (freshmen), 4/15 (transfers). *Early decision:* 11/15. *Notification:* 4/1 (freshmen), 12/15 (early decision). *Financial aid deadline priority date:* 3/1.

Freshman Application Contact
Ms. Monica Inzer, Director of Admissions, Worcester Polytechnic Institute, 100 Institute Road, Worcester, MA 01609. **Phone:** 508-831-5286. **Fax:** 508-831-5875. **E-mail:** admissions@wpi.edu

Visit CollegeQuest.com for information on majors offered and athletics. College video available at CollegeQuest.com.

WORCESTER STATE COLLEGE
Worcester, Massachusetts

- **State-supported**, comprehensive, founded 1874
- **Degrees** bachelor's and master's
- **Urban** 53-acre campus with easy access to Boston
- **Coed**, 3,493 undergraduate students, 73% full-time, 63% women, 37% men
- **Moderately difficult** entrance level, 52% of applicants were admitted
- **20:1 student-to-undergraduate faculty ratio**
- **32.7% graduate** in 6 years or less
- **$2458 tuition** and fees (in-state); $8418 (out-of-state)
- **$3.4 million endowment**

Part of Massachusetts Public Higher Education System.

Students *Undergraduates:* 2,561 full-time, 932 part-time. Students come from 20 states and territories, 84 other countries. *The most frequently chosen baccalaureate fields are:* business/marketing, health professions and related sciences, psychology. *Graduate:* 747 in graduate degree programs.

From out-of-state	4%	Reside on campus	16%
Age 25 or older	34%	Transferred in	11%
International students	2%	African Americans	4%
Asian Americans/Pacific Islanders	3%	Hispanic Americans	3%
Native Americans	1%		

Faculty 258 (65% full-time).

Expenses (1999–2000) *Tuition, state resident:* full-time $1090; part-time $45 per credit. *Tuition, nonresident:* full-time $7050; part-time $294 per credit. *Required fees:* full-time $1368; $57 per credit. Full-time tuition and fees vary according to reciprocity agreements. Part-time tuition and fees vary according to reciprocity agreements. *College room and board:* $4369; room only: $2985. Room and board charges vary according to board plan and housing facility. *Payment plan:* deferred payment. *Waivers:* senior citizens and employees or children of employees.

Library Learning Resources Center. *Collection:* 1,137 serial subscriptions, 11,963 audiovisual materials.

College life *Housing: Options:* men-only, women-only, disabled students. *Most popular organizations:* Third World Alliance, ski club, Program Council, pep club.

Campus security 24-hour emergency response devices and patrols, late-night transport-escort service, controlled dormitory access, well-lit campus, limited access to campus at night.

After graduation *Career center:* 1 full-time, 1 part-time personnel. Services include job fairs, resume preparation, career counseling, careers library, job bank, job interviews.

Freshmen 2,451 applied, 1,275 admitted, 461 enrolled.

Average high school GPA	2.88	SAT verbal scores above 500	N/R
SAT math scores above 500	N/R	ACT above 18	N/R
1998 freshmen returning in 1999	75%		

Application *Options:* electronic application, early admission, deferred entrance. *Application fee:* $40 for nonresidents. *Required:* high school transcript; minimum 2.9 GPA.

Standardized tests *Admission: Required for some:* SAT I or ACT.

Significant dates *Application deadlines:* 8/1 (freshmen), 8/1 (transfers). *Financial aid deadline priority date:* 3/1.

Freshman Application Contact
Mr. Michael Backes, Dean of Enrollment Management, Worcester State College, 486 Chandler Street, Worcester, MA 01602-2597. **Phone:** 508-929-8040. **Fax:** 508-929-8131. **E-mail:** admissions@worcester.edu

Visit CollegeQuest.com for information on majors offered and athletics. College video and electronic viewbook available at CollegeQuest.com.

■ *See page 3018 for a narrative description.*

MICHIGAN

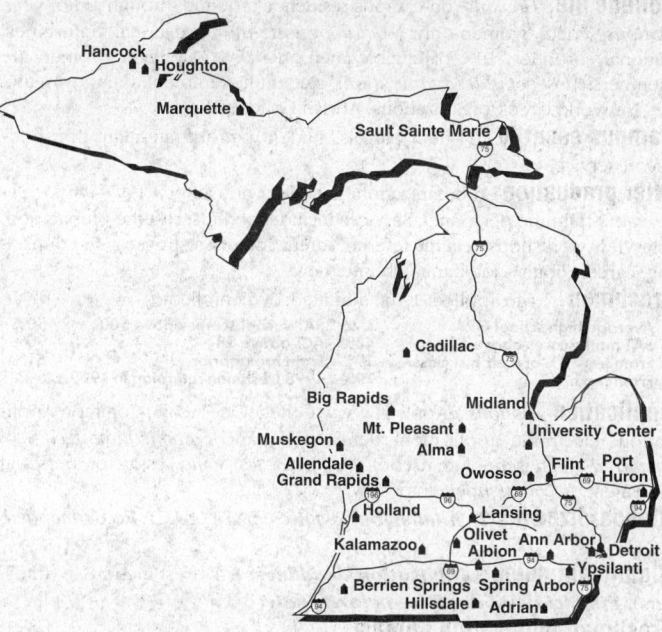

The Detroit area includes the towns of Auburn Hills, Clinton Township, Dearborn, Farmington Hills, Livonia, Oak Park, Orchard Lake, Rochester, Rochester Hills, Southfield, Troy, and Warren.

The Lansing area includes the town of East Lansing.

ADRIAN COLLEGE
Adrian, Michigan

 Apply at CollegeQuest.com

- **Independent**, 4-year, founded 1859, affiliated with United Methodist Church
- **Degrees** associate and bachelor's
- **Small-town** 100-acre campus with easy access to Detroit and Toledo
- **Coed**, 1,029 undergraduate students, 96% full-time, 52% women, 48% men
- **Moderately difficult** entrance level, 80% of applicants were admitted
- **13:1 student-to-undergraduate faculty ratio**
- **53% graduate** in 6 years or less
- **$13,750 tuition** and fees
- **$12,920 average financial aid** package, $15,187 average indebtedness upon graduation, $41.9 million endowment

Adrian College offers more than 30 majors that are complemented by a liberal arts core. Academic and cocurricular opportunities develop students' fullest potential. Students have free Internet and e-mail access, internships, and study-abroad options, and there is a 90% placement record for graduates. *U.S. News & World Report* identified the Adrian faculty as outstanding in their commitment to undergraduate students.

Students *Undergraduates:* 985 full-time, 44 part-time. Students come from 18 states and territories, 8 other countries. *The most frequently chosen baccalaureate fields are:* business/marketing, parks and recreation, social sciences and history.

From out-of-state	19%	Reside on campus	75%
Age 25 or older	1%	Transferred in	4%
International students	1%	African Americans	6%
Asian Americans/Pacific Islanders	1%	Hispanic Americans	2%
Native Americans	0.3%		

Faculty 115 (56% full-time), 57% with terminal degrees.

Michigan

Adrian College (continued)

Expenses (1999–2000) *Comprehensive fee:* $18,530 includes full-time tuition ($13,650), mandatory fees ($100), and room and board ($4780). *College room only:* $2030. Room and board charges vary according to board plan. *Payment plan:* installment. *Waivers:* employees or children of employees.

Library Shipman Library. *Operations spending 1999–2000:* $405,000. *Collection:* 82,687 titles, 783 serial subscriptions, 1,048 audiovisual materials.

College life *Housing:* on-campus residence required through junior year. *Options:* coed, women-only. *Social organizations:* national fraternities, national sororities; 19% of eligible men and 25% of eligible women are members. *Most popular organizations:* student government, Campus Activities Network, Greek organizations, Adrian College Theatre.

Campus security 24-hour patrols, student patrols, late-night transport-escort service.

After graduation 6 organizations recruited on campus 1997–98. *Career center:* 2 full-time personnel. Services include job fairs, resume preparation, interview workshops, resume referral, career/interest testing, career counseling, careers library, job bank, job interviews.

Freshmen 1,446 applied, 1,160 admitted, 296 enrolled.

Average high school GPA	3.26	SAT verbal scores above 500	50%
SAT math scores above 500	43%	ACT above 18	90%
From top 10% of their h.s. class	19%	From top quarter	51%
From top half	79%	1998 freshmen returning in 1999	69%

Application *Options:* eApply at www.CollegeQuest.com, Common Application, electronic application, deferred entrance. *Application fee:* $20. *Required:* high school transcript. *Required for some:* essay or personal statement. *Recommended:* interview.

Standardized tests *Admission: Required:* SAT I or ACT. *Recommended:* ACT.

Significant dates *Application deadlines:* 8/1 (freshmen), 8/1 (transfers). *Financial aid deadline priority date:* 3/15.

Freshman Application Contact
Ms. Janel Sutkus, Director of Admissions, Adrian College, 110 South Madison Street, Adrian, MI 49221-2575. **Phone:** 517-265-5161 Ext. 4326. **Toll-free phone:** 800-877-2246. **Fax:** 517-265-3331. **E-mail:** admissions@adrian.edu

Visit CollegeQuest.com for information on majors offered and athletics.

■ *See page 1134 for a narrative description.*

ALBION COLLEGE
Albion, Michigan

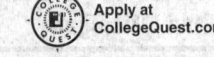 Apply at CollegeQuest.com

- **Independent Methodist**, 4-year, founded 1835
- **Degree** bachelor's
- **Small-town** 225-acre campus with easy access to Detroit
- **Coed**, 1,425 undergraduate students, 99% full-time, 54% women, 46% men
- **Moderately difficult** entrance level, 84% of applicants were admitted
- **14:1 student-to-undergraduate faculty ratio**
- **77% graduate** in 6 years or less
- **$18,160 tuition** and fees
- **$16,429 average financial aid** package, $18,085 average indebtedness upon graduation, $165.8 million endowment

Preparation for success in graduate and professional school is a hallmark of an Albion College liberal arts education. Special academic institutes in law and public policy, economics and business, and environmental studies combine with the Honors Institute, Fritz Shurmur Education Institute, and Pre-med/Allied Health Institute to offer special opportunities for success and distinction.

Students *Undergraduates:* 1,411 full-time, 14 part-time. Students come from 33 states and territories. *The most frequently chosen baccalaureate fields are:* biological/life sciences, business/marketing, social sciences and history.

From out-of-state	16%	Reside on campus	99%
Age 25 or older	2%	Transferred in	2%
International students	0.4%	African Americans	3%
Asian Americans/Pacific Islanders	2%	Hispanic Americans	1%
Native Americans	0.5%		

Faculty 117 (94% full-time).

Expenses (1999–2000) *One-time required fee:* $100. *Comprehensive fee:* $23,380 includes full-time tuition ($17,984), mandatory fees ($176), and room and board ($5220). *College room only:* $2554. *Part-time tuition:* $3072 per unit. *Payment plan:* deferred payment. *Waivers:* employees or children of employees.

Library Stockwell Mudd Libraries. *Operations spending 1999–2000:* $1.3 million. *Collection:* 400,000 titles, 900 serial subscriptions.

College life *Housing:* on-campus residence required through senior year. *Options:* coed, women-only. *Social organizations:* national fraternities, national sororities; 45% of eligible men and 44% of eligible women are members. *Most popular organizations:* fraternities/sororities, Alpha Phi Omega, Union Board, Inter Varsity Christian Fellowship, Student Senate.

Campus security 24-hour emergency response devices and patrols, student patrols, late-night transport-escort service, controlled dormitory access.

After graduation 36 organizations recruited on campus 1997–98. 69% of class of 1998 had job offers within 6 months. *Career center:* 2 full-time, 1 part-time personnel. Services include job fairs, resume preparation, interview workshops, resume referral, career counseling, careers library, job bank, job interviews.

Freshmen 1,413 applied, 1,183 admitted, 409 enrolled. 6 National Merit Scholars, 17 class presidents, 21 valedictorians, 119 student government officers.

Average high school GPA	3.6	SAT verbal scores above 500	84%
SAT math scores above 500	88%	ACT above 18	100%
From top 10% of their h.s. class	37%	From top quarter	64%
From top half	95%	1998 freshmen returning in 1999	84%

Application *Options:* eApply at www.CollegeQuest.com, Common Application, electronic application, early admission, early decision, early action, deferred entrance. *Application fee:* $20. *Required:* high school transcript; 1 letter of recommendation. *Required for some:* interview. *Recommended:* essay or personal statement; minimum 3.0 GPA.

Standardized tests *Admission: Required:* SAT I or ACT.

Significant dates *Application deadlines:* 5/1 (freshmen), rolling (transfers). *Early decision:* 11/15, 12/10. *Notification:* 12/10 (early decision), 12/20 (early action). *Financial aid deadline priority date:* 2/15.

Freshman Application Contact
Ms. Sharon P. Crawford, Director of Admission, Albion College, 611 East Porter Street, Albion, MI 48224. **Phone:** 517-629-0600. **Toll-free phone:** 800-858-6770. **Fax:** 517-629-0569. **E-mail:** admissions@albion.edu

Visit CollegeQuest.com for information on majors offered and athletics. College video available at CollegeQuest.com.

■ *See page 1144 for a narrative description.*

ALMA COLLEGE
Alma, Michigan

 Apply at CollegeQuest.com

- **Independent Presbyterian**, 4-year, founded 1886
- **Degree** bachelor's
- **Small-town** 100-acre campus
- **Coed**, 1,350 undergraduate students, 99% full-time, 57% women, 43% men
- **Moderately difficult** entrance level, 83% of applicants were admitted
- **15:1 student-to-undergraduate faculty ratio**
- **$15,142 tuition** and fees
- **$13,635 average financial aid** package, $115.2 million endowment

Students *Undergraduates:* 1,330 full-time, 20 part-time. Students come from 19 states and territories, 12 other countries. *The most frequently chosen baccalaureate fields are:* biological/life sciences, business/marketing, health professions and related sciences.

From out-of-state	5%	Reside on campus	82%
Age 25 or older	1%	Transferred in	3%
International students	0.4%	African Americans	2%
Asian Americans/Pacific Islanders	0.4%	Hispanic Americans	2%
Native Americans	1%		

Faculty 129 (70% full-time), 63% with terminal degrees.

Expenses (1999–2000) *Comprehensive fee:* $20,602 includes full-time tuition ($14,998), mandatory fees ($144), and room and board ($5460). *College room only:* $2704. Room and board charges vary according to board plan and housing facility. *Part-time tuition:* $576 per credit. Part-time tuition and fees vary according to course load. *Payment plans:* installment, deferred payment. *Waivers:* employees or children of employees.

Michigan

Library Kerhl Building-Monteith Library. *Operations spending 1999–2000:* $1 million. *Collection:* 223,446 titles, 1,178 serial subscriptions.

College life *Housing:* on-campus residence required through senior year. *Options:* coed, women-only. *Social organizations:* national fraternities, national sororities, local fraternities, local sororities; 23% of eligible men and 23% of eligible women are members. *Most popular organizations:* Alma Ambassadors, Almanian (student newspaper), MEGA-Mentoring Program, student government, SOS (Students Offering Service).

Campus security 24-hour emergency response devices and patrols.

After graduation 25 organizations recruited on campus 1997–98. 69% of class of 1998 had job offers within 6 months. *Career center:* 3 full-time, 1 part-time personnel. Services include job fairs, resume preparation, interview workshops, resume referral, career/interest testing, career counseling, careers library, job bank, job interviews. *Graduate education:* 30% of class of 1999 went directly to graduate and professional school: 12% graduate arts and sciences, 3% engineering, 3% law, 3% medicine, 2% education, 1% dentistry.

Freshmen 1,366 applied, 1,133 admitted, 335 enrolled. 24 valedictorians, 109 student government officers.

Average high school GPA	3.6	SAT verbal scores above 500	N/R
SAT math scores above 500	N/R	ACT above 18	99%
From top 10% of their h.s. class	37%	From top quarter	77%
From top half	95%	1998 freshmen returning in 1999	89%

Application *Options:* eApply at www.CollegeQuest.com, early admission, early decision, deferred entrance. *Application fee:* $20. *Required:* high school transcript; minimum 2.0 GPA; 2 letters of recommendation. *Required for some:* interview. *Recommended:* essay or personal statement.

Standardized tests *Admission: Required:* SAT I or ACT. *Recommended:* ACT.

Significant dates *Application deadlines:* rolling (freshmen), rolling (transfers). *Early decision:* 11/1. *Notification:* 12/15 (early decision). *Financial aid deadline priority date:* 2/15.

Freshman Application Contact Acting Director of Admissions, Alma College, Admissions Office, Alma, MI 48801-1599. **Phone:** 517-463-7139. **Toll-free phone:** 800-321-ALMA. **Fax:** 517-463-7057. **E-mail:** admissions@alma.edu

Visit CollegeQuest.com for information on majors offered and athletics. College video and electronic viewbook available at CollegeQuest.com.

■ *See page 1154 for a narrative description.*

ANDREWS UNIVERSITY
Berrien Springs, Michigan

- **Independent Seventh-day Adventist**, university, founded 1874
- **Degrees** associate, bachelor's, master's, doctoral, and first professional
- **Small-town** 1,650-acre campus
- **Coed**, 1,793 undergraduate students, 84% full-time, 57% women, 43% men
- **Moderately difficult** entrance level, 60% of applicants were admitted
- **10:1** student-to-undergraduate faculty ratio
- **$12,339 tuition** and fees
- **$13,593 average financial aid** package, $21.9 million endowment

Students *Undergraduates:* 1,508 full-time, 285 part-time. Students come from 44 states and territories, 55 other countries. *The most frequently chosen baccalaureate fields are:* biological/life sciences, education, health professions and related sciences. *Graduate:* 300 in professional programs, 843 in other graduate degree programs.

From out-of-state	45%	Reside on campus	51%
Age 25 or older	21%	Transferred in	13%
International students	14%	African Americans	21%
Asian Americans/Pacific Islanders	8%	Hispanic Americans	7%
Native Americans	0.2%		

Faculty 259 (92% full-time), 63% with terminal degrees.

Expenses (1999–2000) *Comprehensive fee:* $16,104 includes full-time tuition ($12,030), mandatory fees ($309), and room and board ($3765). *College room only:* $2235. *Part-time tuition:* $305 per quarter hour. *Payment plan:* installment. *Waivers:* senior citizens and employees or children of employees.

Library James White Library plus 2 others. *Operations spending 1999–2000:* $2.1 million. *Collection:* 666,377 titles, 2,952 serial subscriptions, 120,041 audiovisual materials.

College life *Housing:* on-campus residence required through senior year. *Options:* men-only, women-only.

Campus security 24-hour emergency response devices and patrols, controlled dormitory access.

After graduation 62 organizations recruited on campus 1997–98. *Career center:* 2 full-time, 4 part-time personnel. Services include job fairs, resume preparation, interview workshops, resume referral, career counseling, careers library, job bank, job interviews.

Freshmen 971 applied, 578 admitted, 324 enrolled.

Average high school GPA	3.14	SAT verbal scores above 500	60%
SAT math scores above 500	55%	ACT above 18	80%
From top 10% of their h.s. class	13%	From top quarter	29%
From top half	65%	1998 freshmen returning in 1999	71%

Application *Options:* early admission, deferred entrance. *Application fee:* $30. *Required:* high school transcript; 2 letters of recommendation. *Recommended:* minimum 2.0 GPA.

Standardized tests *Admission: Required:* SAT I or ACT. *Recommended:* ACT.

Significant dates *Application deadlines:* rolling (freshmen), rolling (transfers). *Financial aid deadline:* continuous.

Freshman Application Contact Ms. Charlotte Coy, Admissions Supervisor, Andrews University, Berrien Springs, MI 49104. **Phone:** 616-471-7771. **Toll-free phone:** 800-253-2874. **Fax:** 616-471-3228. **E-mail:** enroll@andrews.edu

Visit CollegeQuest.com for information on majors offered and athletics. College video available at CollegeQuest.com.

■ *See page 1172 for a narrative description.*

AQUINAS COLLEGE
Grand Rapids, Michigan

- **Independent Roman Catholic**, comprehensive, founded 1886
- **Degrees** associate, bachelor's, and master's
- **Suburban** 107-acre campus with easy access to Detroit
- **Coed**, 1,922 undergraduate students, 74% full-time, 66% women, 34% men
- **Moderately difficult** entrance level, 84% of applicants were admitted
- **13:1** student-to-undergraduate faculty ratio
- **46.4%** graduate in 6 years or less
- **$14,034 tuition** and fees
- **$12,958 average financial aid** package, $12,348 average indebtedness upon graduation, $23.2 million endowment

Students *Undergraduates:* 1,423 full-time, 499 part-time. Students come from 25 states and territories. *The most frequently chosen baccalaureate fields are:* business/marketing, education, social sciences and history. *Graduate:* 564 in graduate degree programs.

From out-of-state	5%	Reside on campus	51%
Age 25 or older	3%	Transferred in	4%
International students	0.1%	African Americans	5%
Asian Americans/Pacific Islanders	1%	Hispanic Americans	2%
Native Americans	1%		

Faculty 260 (41% full-time), 34% with terminal degrees.

Expenses (2000–2001) *Comprehensive fee:* $18,918 includes full-time tuition ($14,034) and room and board ($4884). *College room only:* $2256. Full-time tuition and fees vary according to course load. Room and board charges vary according to board plan and housing facility. *Part-time tuition:* $280 per credit hour. Part-time tuition and fees vary according to course load. *Payment plans:* installment, deferred payment. *Waivers:* children of alumni and employees or children of employees.

Library Woodhouse Library. *Operations spending 1999–2000:* $851,022. *Collection:* 118,913 titles, 843 serial subscriptions, 6,170 audiovisual materials.

College life *Housing:* on-campus residence required through sophomore year. *Option:* coed. *Most popular organizations:* Community Senate Programming Board, JAMMIN (multicultural group), BACCHUS (alcohol awareness group).

Campus security 24-hour emergency response devices and patrols, student patrols, late-night transport-escort service, controlled dormitory access.

Michigan

Aquinas College (continued)

After graduation 25 organizations recruited on campus 1997–98. 80% of class of 1998 had job offers within 6 months. *Career center:* 5 full-time, 2 part-time personnel. Services include job fairs, resume preparation, resume referral, career counseling, careers library, job interviews. **Graduate education:** 4% of class of 1999 went directly to graduate and professional school: 1% education, 1% engineering, 1% law, 1% medicine.

Freshmen 1,114 applied, 939 admitted, 354 enrolled. 10 valedictorians.

Average high school GPA	3.3	SAT verbal scores above 500	N/R
SAT math scores above 500	N/R	ACT above 18	92%
From top 10% of their h.s. class	20%	From top quarter	48%
From top half	81%	1998 freshmen returning in 1999	74%

Application *Options:* electronic application, early admission, deferred entrance. *Application fee:* $25. *Required:* high school transcript; minimum 2.5 GPA. *Required for some:* essay or personal statement; interview.

Standardized tests *Admission: Required:* ACT. *Recommended:* SAT I.

Significant dates *Application deadlines:* rolling (freshmen), rolling (transfers). *Financial aid deadline priority date:* 2/15.

Freshman Application Contact
Ms. Mary Kwiatkowski, Staff Assistant/Applications Secretary, Aquinas College, 1607 Robinson Road, SE, Grand Rapids, MI 49506-1799. **Phone:** 616-732-4460 Ext. 5150. **Toll-free phone:** 800-678-9593. **Fax:** 616-459-2563. **E-mail:** admissions@aquinas.edu

Visit CollegeQuest.com for information on majors offered and athletics. College video and electronic viewbook available at CollegeQuest.com.

■ *See page 1180 for a narrative description.*

BAKER COLLEGE OF AUBURN HILLS
Auburn Hills, Michigan

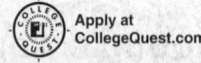
Apply at CollegeQuest.com

- **Independent**, 4-year, founded 1990
- **Degrees** associate, bachelor's, and postbachelor's certificates
- **Urban** 7-acre campus with easy access to Detroit
- **Coed**, 1,456 undergraduate students, 51% full-time, 70% women, 30% men
- **Noncompetitive** entrance level, 100% of applicants were admitted
- **30:1 student-to-undergraduate faculty ratio**
- **$7200 tuition** and fees

Part of Baker College System.

Students *Undergraduates:* 747 full-time, 709 part-time.

Age 25 or older	41%	Transferred in	21%

Faculty 83 (10% full-time), 11% with terminal degrees.

Expenses (1999–2000) *Tuition:* full-time $7200; part-time $145 per quarter hour. *Payment plan:* installment. *Waivers:* employees or children of employees.

Library Baker College of Auburn Hills Library. *Collection:* 5,400 titles, 95 serial subscriptions.

College life *Housing:* college housing not available. *Most popular organizations:* Baker Business Club, Interior Design Society, Students Action in Engineering, Marketing Club.

Campus security 24-hour emergency response devices.

After graduation 12 organizations recruited on campus 1997–98. 98% of class of 1998 had job offers within 6 months. *Career center:* 1 full-time personnel. Services include job fairs, resume preparation, resume referral, career counseling, careers library, job bank, job interviews.

Freshmen 851 applied, 851 admitted, 482 enrolled.

SAT verbal scores above 500	N/R	SAT math scores above 500	N/R
ACT above 18	N/R		

Application *Options:* eApply at www.CollegeQuest.com, early admission, deferred entrance. *Application fee:* $20. *Required:* high school transcript.

Significant dates *Application deadlines:* rolling (freshmen), rolling (transfers).

Freshman Application Contact
Ms. Jan Bohlen, Director of Admissions, Baker College of Auburn Hills, 1500 University Drive, Auburn Hills, MI 48326-1586. **Phone:** 248-340-0600. **Toll-free phone:** 888-429-0410. **E-mail:** bohlen_j@auburnhills.baker.edu

Visit CollegeQuest.com for information on majors offered and athletics. College video available at CollegeQuest.com.

BAKER COLLEGE OF CADILLAC
Cadillac, Michigan

- **Independent**, 4-year, founded 1986
- **Degrees** associate and bachelor's
- **Small-town** 40-acre campus
- **Coed**
- **Noncompetitive** entrance level
- **$6743 tuition** and fees

Part of Baker College System.

Expenses (1999–2000) *Tuition:* full-time $6743; part-time $145 per quarter hour. Full-time tuition and fees vary according to program. Part-time tuition and fees vary according to program.

Institutional Web site http://www.baker.edu/

College life *Housing:* college housing not available.

Campus security 24-hour emergency response devices.

Application *Options:* early admission, deferred entrance. *Application fee:* $20. *Required:* high school transcript. *Recommended:* interview.

Standardized tests *Placement: Required:* ACT ASSET

Admissions Office Contact
Baker College of Cadillac, 9600 East 13th Street, Cadillac, MI 49601. **Fax:** 231-775-8505. **E-mail:** runstr_e@cadillac.baker.edu

Visit CollegeQuest.com for information on athletics. College video available at CollegeQuest.com.

BAKER COLLEGE OF FLINT
Flint, Michigan

- **Independent**, 4-year, founded 1911
- **Degrees** associate and bachelor's
- **Urban** 30-acre campus with easy access to Detroit
- **Coed**, 3,816 undergraduate students, 50% full-time, 67% women, 33% men
- **Noncompetitive** entrance level, 100% of applicants were admitted
- **32:1 student-to-undergraduate faculty ratio**
- **$5260 tuition** and fees

Part of Baker College System.

Students *Undergraduates:* 1,919 full-time, 1,897 part-time. Students come from 5 states and territories. *The most frequently chosen baccalaureate fields are:* business/marketing, health professions and related sciences, visual/performing arts.

From out-of-state	1%	Reside on campus	2%
Transferred in	17%	African Americans	14%
Asian Americans/Pacific Islanders	4%	Hispanic Americans	2%
Native Americans	1%		

Faculty 183 (19% full-time), 12% with terminal degrees.

Expenses (1999–2000) *Tuition:* full-time $5240; part-time $145 per quarter hour. *Required fees:* full-time $20. Full-time tuition and fees vary according to program. Part-time tuition and fees vary according to program. *College room only:* $1950. *Payment plan:* installment. *Waivers:* employees or children of employees.

Library Marianne Jewell Library. *Collection:* 168,700 titles.

College life *Housing: Option:* coed. *Most popular organizations:* travel club, occupational therapy club, interior design society, medical assistants student organization, physical therapist assistant club.

Campus security 24-hour patrols, late-night transport-escort service, controlled dormitory access, video monitoring of high traffic areas.

After graduation 100 organizations recruited on campus 1997–98. 98% of class of 1998 had job offers within 6 months. *Career center:* 6 full-time personnel. Services include job fairs, resume preparation, resume referral, career counseling, careers library, job bank, job interviews.

Michigan

Freshmen 1,861 applied, 1,861 admitted, 961 enrolled.
SAT verbal scores above 500 N/R   SAT math scores above 500 N/R
ACT above 18 N/R

Application *Options:* early admission, deferred entrance. *Application fee:* $20. *Required:* high school transcript.

Significant dates *Application deadlines:* 9/20 (freshmen), 9/20 (transfers).

Freshman Application Contact
Mr. Mark Heaton, Vice President for Admissions, Baker College of Flint, 1050 West Bristol Road, Flint, MI 48507-5508. **Phone:** 810-766-4015. **Toll-free phone:** 800-964-4299. **Fax:** 810-766-4049. **E-mail:** heaton_m@fafl.baker.edu

Visit CollegeQuest.com for information on majors offered and athletics. College video available at CollegeQuest.com.

BAKER COLLEGE OF JACKSON
Jackson, Michigan

- **Independent**, 4-year, founded 1994
- **Degrees** associate and bachelor's
- **Urban** 42-acre campus with easy access to Lansing
- **Coed**, 999 undergraduate students, 49% full-time, 73% women, 27% men
- **Noncompetitive** entrance level, 100% of applicants were admitted
- **$7200 tuition** and fees

Part of Baker College System.

Students *Undergraduates:* 486 full-time, 513 part-time. *The most frequently chosen baccalaureate field is:* business/marketing.
Age 25 or older 56%   Transferred in 21%

Faculty 73 (8% full-time), 8% with terminal degrees.

Expenses (2000-2001) *Tuition:* full-time $7200; part-time $150 per credit. Full-time tuition and fees vary according to program. Part-time tuition and fees vary according to program. *Waivers:* employees or children of employees.

Library Baker College of Jackson Library. *Collection:* 7,000 titles, 150 serial subscriptions.

College life *Housing:* college housing not available.

Campus security 24-hour emergency response devices.

After graduation 100% of class of 1998 had job offers within 6 months. *Career center:* 1 full-time personnel. Services include job fairs, resume preparation, resume referral, career counseling, careers library, job bank, job interviews.

Freshmen 375 applied, 375 admitted, 375 enrolled.
SAT verbal scores above 500 N/R   SAT math scores above 500 N/R
ACT above 18 N/R

Application *Options:* early admission, deferred entrance. *Application fee:* $20. *Required:* high school transcript.

Significant dates *Application deadlines:* 9/19 (freshmen), rolling (transfers).

Freshman Application Contact
Mr. Steve Kim, Director of Admissions, Baker College of Jackson, 2800 Springport Road, Jackson, MI 49202. **Phone:** 517-788-7800. **E-mail:** kim_s@jackson.baker.edu

Visit CollegeQuest.com for information on majors offered and athletics. College video available at CollegeQuest.com.

BAKER COLLEGE OF MOUNT CLEMENS
Clinton Township, Michigan

- **Independent**, 4-year, founded 1990
- **Degrees** associate and bachelor's
- **Urban** campus with easy access to Detroit
- **Coed**
- **Noncompetitive** entrance level
- **$6525 tuition** and fees

Part of Baker College System.

Expenses (1999-2000) *Tuition:* full-time $6525; part-time $145 per quarter hour. Full-time tuition and fees vary according to program. Part-time tuition and fees vary according to program.

Institutional Web site http://www.baker.edu/

College life *Housing:* college housing not available.

Campus security Evening security guard.

Application *Options:* early admission, deferred entrance. *Application fee:* $20. *Required:* high school transcript.

Standardized tests *Placement:* Required: ACT ASSET

Admissions Office Contact
Baker College of Mount Clemens, 34950 Little Mack Avenue, Clinton Township, MI 48035-4701. **Fax:** 810-791-6611. **E-mail:** looser_a@mtclemens.baker.edu

Visit CollegeQuest.com for information on athletics. College video available at CollegeQuest.com.

BAKER COLLEGE OF MUSKEGON
Muskegon, Michigan

- **Independent**, 4-year, founded 1888
- **Degrees** associate and bachelor's
- **Suburban** 40-acre campus with easy access to Grand Rapids
- **Coed**, 2,249 undergraduate students, 56% full-time, 71% women, 29% men
- **Noncompetitive** entrance level, 73% of applicants were admitted
- **32:1 student-to-undergraduate faculty ratio**
- **$7200 tuition** and fees

Part of Baker College System.

Students *Undergraduates:* 1,261 full-time, 988 part-time. Students come from 4 states and territories. *The most frequently chosen baccalaureate fields are:* business/marketing, engineering/engineering technologies, health professions and related sciences.

From out-of-state	1%	Reside on campus	11%
Age 25 or older	43%	Transferred in	17%
African Americans	12%	Asian Americans/Pacific Islanders	1%
Hispanic Americans	3%	Native Americans	1%

Faculty 138 (10% full-time), 4% with terminal degrees.

Expenses (2000-2001) *Tuition:* full-time $7200; part-time $150 per quarter hour. Full-time tuition and fees vary according to program. Part-time tuition and fees vary according to program. *College room only:* $2100. Room and board charges vary according to housing facility. *Payment plans:* installment, deferred payment. *Waivers:* employees or children of employees.

Library Marianne Jewell Library. *Operations spending 1999-2000:* $241,725. *Collection:* 32,000 titles, 140 serial subscriptions.

College life *Housing:* on-campus residence required in freshman year. *Options:* coed, disabled students. *Most popular organizations:* accounting club, rehab club, travel club, culinary club.

Campus security 24-hour patrols, late-night transport-escort service, controlled dormitory access, 24-hour security camera surveillance.

After graduation 35 organizations recruited on campus 1997-98. 99% of class of 1998 had job offers within 6 months. *Career center:* 3 full-time, 2 part-time personnel. Services include job fairs, resume preparation, resume referral, career/interest testing, career counseling, careers library, job bank, job interviews. *Graduate education:* 1% of class of 1999 went directly to graduate and professional school: 1% business.

Freshmen 1,000 applied, 726 admitted, 726 enrolled.
SAT verbal scores above 500 N/R   SAT math scores above 500 N/R
ACT above 18 N/R

Application *Options:* early admission, deferred entrance. *Application fee:* $20. *Required:* high school transcript.

Significant dates *Application deadlines:* 9/19 (freshmen), rolling (transfers).

Freshman Application Contact
Ms. Kathy Jacobson, Director of Admissions, Baker College of Muskegon, 1903 Marquette Avenue, Muskegon, MI 49442-3497. **Phone:** 231-777-5207. **Toll-free phone:** 800-937-0337. **Fax:** 231-777-5265. **E-mail:** jacobs_k@muskegon.baker.edu

Michigan

Baker College of Muskegon (continued)
Visit CollegeQuest.com for information on majors offered and athletics. College video available at CollegeQuest.com.

BAKER COLLEGE OF OWOSSO
Owosso, Michigan

- **Independent**, 4-year, founded 1984
- **Degrees** associate and bachelor's
- **Small-town** 32-acre campus
- **Coed**, 1,711 undergraduate students, 70% full-time, 70% women, 30% men
- **Noncompetitive** entrance level, 100% of applicants were admitted
- **23:1 student-to-undergraduate faculty ratio**
- **$6960 tuition** and fees

Part of Baker College System.
Students *Undergraduates:* 1,193 full-time, 518 part-time. Students come from 3 states and territories. *The most frequently chosen baccalaureate fields are:* business/marketing, computer/information sciences, health professions and related sciences.

From out-of-state	0.4%	Reside on campus	15%
Age 25 or older	41%	Transferred in	16%
African Americans	1%	Asian Americans/Pacific Islanders	0.3%
Hispanic Americans	2%	Native Americans	1%

Faculty 114 (4% full-time), 60% with terminal degrees.
Expenses (1999–2000) *Tuition:* full-time $6960; part-time $145 per quarter hour. Full-time tuition and fees vary according to program. Part-time tuition and fees vary according to program. *College room only:* $1800. *Waivers:* employees or children of employees.
Library Baker College of Owosso Library. *Operations spending 1999–2000:* $214,072. *Collection:* 34,000 titles, 165 serial subscriptions.
College life *Housing:* Option: coed. *Most popular organizations:* accounting club, travel club, management club, Baker Health Information Management Club, RAD Club.
Campus security 24-hour emergency response devices and patrols, late-night transport-escort service.
After graduation 14 organizations recruited on campus 1997–98. 94% of class of 1998 had job offers within 6 months. *Career center:* 2 full-time, 2 part-time personnel. Services include job fairs, resume preparation, resume referral, career counseling, careers library, job bank, job interviews.
Freshmen 785 applied, 785 admitted, 581 enrolled.

SAT verbal scores above 500	N/R	SAT math scores above 500	N/R
ACT above 18	N/R		

Application *Options:* Common Application, early admission, deferred entrance. *Application fee:* $20. *Required:* high school transcript.
Significant dates *Application deadlines:* rolling (freshmen), rolling (transfers).
Freshman Application Contact
Ms. Michelle Murray, Director, Baker College of Owosso, 1020 South Washington Street, Owosso, MI 48867-4400. **Phone:** 517-729-3353. **Toll-free phone:** 800-879-3797. **Fax:** 517-729-3411. **E-mail:** murray_m@owosso.baker.edu
Visit CollegeQuest.com for information on majors offered and athletics. College video available at CollegeQuest.com.

BAKER COLLEGE OF PORT HURON
Port Huron, Michigan

- **Independent**, 4-year, founded 1990
- **Degrees** associate and bachelor's
- **Urban** 10-acre campus with easy access to Detroit
- **Coed**, 976 undergraduate students, 58% full-time, 79% women, 21% men
- **Noncompetitive** entrance level, 84% of applicants were admitted
- **13:1 student-to-undergraduate faculty ratio**
- **$7200 tuition** and fees

Part of Baker College System.
Students *Undergraduates:* 562 full-time, 414 part-time.

From out-of-state	10%	Age 25 or older	51%
African Americans	2%	Asian Americans/Pacific Islanders	1%
Hispanic Americans	2%	Native Americans	0.3%

Faculty 85 (12% full-time), 6% with terminal degrees.
Expenses (1999–2000) *Tuition:* full-time $7200; part-time $150 per quarter hour. Full-time tuition and fees vary according to program. Part-time tuition and fees vary according to program. *Waivers:* employees or children of employees.
Library Baker College of Port Huron Library.
College life *Housing:* college housing not available. *Most popular organizations:* travel club, Student Association Dental Hygienists of America.
Campus security 24-hour emergency response devices, late-night transport-escort service.
After graduation 50 organizations recruited on campus 1997–98. 100% of class of 1998 had job offers within 6 months. *Career center:* 1 full-time personnel. Services include job fairs, resume preparation, interview workshops, resume referral, career counseling, careers library, job bank, job interviews.
Freshmen 498 applied, 416 admitted, 294 enrolled.

SAT verbal scores above 500	N/R	SAT math scores above 500	N/R
ACT above 18	N/R		

Application *Options:* early admission, deferred entrance. *Application fee:* $20. *Required:* high school transcript; interview.
Significant dates *Application deadlines:* 9/19 (freshmen), rolling (transfers).
Freshman Application Contact
Mr. Daniel Kenny, Director of Admissions, Baker College of Port Huron, 3403 Lapeer Road, Port Huron, MI 48060-2597. **Phone:** 810-985-7000. **Fax:** 810-985-7066. **E-mail:** kenny_d@porthuron.baker.edu
Visit CollegeQuest.com for information on majors offered and athletics. College video available at CollegeQuest.com.

CALVIN COLLEGE
Grand Rapids, Michigan

Apply at CollegeQuest.com

- **Independent**, comprehensive, founded 1876, affiliated with Christian Reformed Church
- **Degrees** bachelor's, master's, and postbachelor's certificates
- **Suburban** 370-acre campus
- **Coed**, 4,117 undergraduate students, 98% full-time, 56% women, 44% men
- **Moderately difficult** entrance level, 99% of applicants were admitted
- **16:1 student-to-undergraduate faculty ratio**
- **68.4% graduate** in 6 years or less
- **$14,040 tuition** and fees
- **$10,350 average financial aid** package, $16,000 average indebtedness upon graduation, $50.7 million endowment

Academic excellence, Christian commitment, reasonable cost, more than 4,200 students, 80 academic options. Calvin College is recognized by *U.S. News & World Report's America's Best Colleges*, *The National Review College Guide*, the *Templeton Guide: Colleges that Encourage Character Development*, the *Fiske Guide to Colleges*, and *Barron's Best Buys in College Education*.

Students *Undergraduates:* 4,018 full-time, 99 part-time. Students come from 44 states and territories, 31 other countries. *The most frequently chosen baccalaureate fields are:* business/marketing, education, social sciences and history. *Graduate:* 46 in graduate degree programs.

From out-of-state	43%	Reside on campus	58%
Transferred in	3%	International students	7%
African Americans	1%	Asian Americans/Pacific Islanders	2%
Hispanic Americans	1%	Native Americans	0.2%

Faculty 329 (83% full-time), 68% with terminal degrees.
Expenses (2000–2001) *Comprehensive fee:* $18,930 includes full-time tuition ($14,040) and room and board ($4890). *College room only:* $2100. Room and board charges vary according to board plan. *Part-time tuition:* $340 per credit hour. Part-time tuition and fees vary according to course load. *Payment plans:* tuition prepayment, installment. *Waivers:* employees or children of employees.

Michigan

Library Hekman Library. *Operations spending 1999–2000:* $1.6 million. *Collection:* 2,721 serial subscriptions, 20,405 audiovisual materials.
College life *Housing:* on-campus residence required through sophomore year. *Options:* men-only, women-only. *Most popular organizations:* Association for Supervision and Curriculum Development, Environmental Stewardship Coalition, China Club, Young Life, Dance Guild.
Campus security 24-hour emergency response devices and patrols, student patrols, late-night transport-escort service, controlled dormitory access, crime prevention programs, crime alert bulletins.
After graduation 154 organizations recruited on campus 1997–98. 72% of class of 1998 had job offers within 6 months. *Career center:* 6 full-time, 3 part-time personnel. Services include job fairs, resume preparation, interview workshops, resume referral, career/interest testing, career counseling, careers library, job bank, job interviews.
Freshmen 1,971 applied, 1,945 admitted, 1,061 enrolled. 20 National Merit Scholars, 41 valedictorians.

Average high school GPA	3.49	SAT verbal scores above 500	83%
SAT math scores above 500	86%	ACT above 18	98%
From top 10% of their h.s. class	26%	From top quarter	52%
From top half	80%	1998 freshmen returning in 1999	85%

Application *Options:* eApply at www.CollegeQuest.com, Common Application, deferred entrance. *Application fee:* $35. *Required:* essay or personal statement; high school transcript; minimum 2.5 GPA; 1 letter of recommendation.
Standardized tests *Admission: Required:* SAT I or ACT. *Recommended:* ACT.
Significant dates *Application deadlines:* 8/15 (freshmen), rolling (transfers). *Financial aid deadline priority date:* 2/15.
Freshman Application Contact
Mr. Dale D. Kuiper, Director of Admissions, Calvin College, 3201 Burton Street, SE, Grand Rapids, MI 49546-4388. **Phone:** 616-957-6106. **Toll-free phone:** 800-668-0122. **E-mail:** admissions@calvin.edu
Visit CollegeQuest.com for information on majors offered and athletics.

■ *See page 1346 for a narrative description.*

CENTER FOR CREATIVE STUDIES—COLLEGE OF ART AND DESIGN
Detroit, Michigan

- **Independent**, 4-year, founded 1926
- **Degree** bachelor's
- **Urban** 11-acre campus
- **Coed**, 1,025 undergraduate students, 87% full-time, 41% women, 59% men
- **Moderately difficult** entrance level, 70% of applicants were admitted
- **9:1 student-to-undergraduate faculty ratio**
- **$16,526 tuition** and fees
- **$11.2 million endowment**

Students *Undergraduates:* 892 full-time, 133 part-time. Students come from 28 states and territories, 8 other countries. *The most frequently chosen baccalaureate field is:* visual/performing arts.

From out-of-state	15%	Reside on campus	20%
Age 25 or older	28%	Transferred in	12%
International students	4%	African Americans	9%
Asian Americans/Pacific Islanders	5%	Hispanic Americans	3%
Native Americans	1%		

Faculty 206 (22% full-time).
Expenses (2000–2001) *Tuition:* full-time $15,630; part-time $521 per credit hour. *Required fees:* full-time $896; $329 per term part-time. Part-time tuition and fees vary according to course load. *College room only:* $3200. Room and board charges vary according to housing facility. *Payment plans:* installment, deferred payment. *Waivers:* employees or children of employees.
Library Center for Creative Studies Library. *Operations spending 1999–2000:* $113,864. *Collection:* 24,000 titles, 75 serial subscriptions.
College life *Housing: Option:* coed.
Campus security 24-hour patrols.

After graduation 70 organizations recruited on campus 1997–98. *Career center:* 1 full-time personnel. Services include job fairs, resume preparation, interview workshops, resume referral, career counseling, careers library, job bank, job interviews.
Freshmen 393 applied, 275 admitted, 166 enrolled.

Average high school GPA	3.02	SAT verbal scores above 500	64%
SAT math scores above 500	66%	ACT above 18	94%
1998 freshmen returning in 1999	72%		

Application *Option:* deferred entrance. *Application fee:* $35. *Required:* essay or personal statement; high school transcript; portfolio. *Required for some:* letters of recommendation; interview. *Recommended:* minimum 2.5 GPA.
Standardized tests *Admission: Required:* SAT I or ACT.
Significant dates *Application deadlines:* rolling (freshmen), rolling (transfers). *Financial aid deadline priority date:* 2/21.
Freshman Application Contact
Office of Admissions, Center for Creative Studies—College of Art and Design, 201 East Kirby, Detroit, MI 48202-4034. **Phone:** 313-664-7425. **Toll-free phone:** 800-952-ARTS. **Fax:** 313-872-2739. **E-mail:** admissions@ccscad.edu
Visit CollegeQuest.com for information on majors offered and athletics. Electronic viewbook available at CollegeQuest.com.

■ *See page 1390 for a narrative description.*

CENTRAL MICHIGAN UNIVERSITY
Mount Pleasant, Michigan

Apply at CollegeQuest.com

- **State-supported**, university, founded 1892
- **Degrees** bachelor's, master's, doctoral, post-master's, and postbachelor's certificates
- **Small-town** 854-acre campus
- **Coed**, 17,602 undergraduate students, 85% full-time, 59% women, 41% men
- **Moderately difficult** entrance level, 83% of applicants were admitted
- **22:1 student-to-undergraduate faculty ratio**
- **50% graduate** in 6 years or less
- **$3630 tuition** and fees (in-state); $8655 (out-of-state)
- **$7121 average financial aid** package, $16,757 average indebtedness upon graduation, $36.1 million endowment

Students *Undergraduates:* 14,970 full-time, 2,632 part-time. Students come from 44 states and territories, 48 other countries. *The most frequently chosen baccalaureate fields are:* business/marketing, education, health professions and related sciences. *Graduate:* 8,455 in graduate degree programs.

From out-of-state	2%	Reside on campus	35%
Age 25 or older	8%	Transferred in	6%
International students	1%	African Americans	5%
Asian Americans/Pacific Islanders	1%	Hispanic Americans	1%
Native Americans	1%		

Faculty 941 (68% full-time), 82% with terminal degrees.
Expenses (1999–2000) *Tuition, state resident:* full-time $3150; part-time $105 per credit. *Tuition, nonresident:* full-time $8175; part-time $272 per credit. *Required fees:* full-time $480; $90 per term part-time. *College room and board:* $4620; room only: $2310. Room and board charges vary according to board plan and housing facility. *Waivers:* senior citizens and employees or children of employees.
Library Park Library plus 1 other. *Operations spending 1999–2000:* $5.6 million. *Collection:* 923,243 titles, 4,309 serial subscriptions, 23,336 audiovisual materials.
College life *Housing:* on-campus residence required through sophomore year. *Options:* coed, men-only, women-only, disabled students. *Social organizations:* national fraternities, national sororities; 12% of eligible men and 10% of eligible women are members. *Most popular organizations:* Residence Hall Assembly, Student Government Association, Big Brothers/Big Sisters, Organization for Black Unity, Program Board.
Campus security 24-hour patrols, late-night transport-escort service.
After graduation 504 organizations recruited on campus 1997–98. 95% of class of 1998 had job offers within 6 months. *Career center:* 14 full-time personnel. Services include job fairs, resume preparation, interview workshops, resume referral, career/interest testing, career counseling, careers

Michigan

Central Michigan University (continued)

library, job interviews. **Graduate education:** 12% of class of 1999 went directly to graduate and professional school.

Freshmen 10,019 applied, 8,287 admitted, 3,449 enrolled.

Average high school GPA	3.31	SAT verbal scores above 500	N/R
SAT math scores above 500	N/R	ACT above 18	86%
1998 freshmen returning in 1999	77%		

Application *Options:* eApply at www.CollegeQuest.com, electronic application, early admission, deferred entrance. *Application fee:* $25. *Required:* high school transcript. *Required for some:* essay or personal statement; letters of recommendation; interview. *Recommended:* minimum 3.0 GPA.

Standardized tests *Admission: Required:* ACT.

Significant dates *Application deadlines:* rolling (freshmen), rolling (transfers). *Financial aid deadline priority date:* 2/21.

Freshman Application Contact
Mrs. Betty J. Wagner, Director of Admissions, Central Michigan University, Office of Admissions, 105 Warriner Hall, Mt. Pleasant, MI 48859. **Phone:** 517-774-3076. **Fax:** 517-774-3537. **E-mail:** cmuadmit@cmich.edu

Visit CollegeQuest.com for information on majors offered and athletics. Electronic viewbook available at CollegeQuest.com.

CLEARY COLLEGE
Howell, Michigan

- **Independent**, 4-year, founded 1883
- **Degrees** associate and bachelor's
- **Small-town** 27-acre campus with easy access to Detroit and Lansing
- **Coed**, 642 undergraduate students, 67% full-time, 66% women, 34% men
- **Noncompetitive** entrance level
- **$7605 tuition** and fees

Students *Undergraduates:* Students come from 2 states and territories, 1 other country.

From out-of-state	1%	Age 25 or older	70%

Faculty 101 (11% full-time), 12% with terminal degrees.

Expenses (1999–2000) *Tuition:* full-time $7605; part-time $169 per credit hour. *Payment plans:* installment, deferred payment. *Waivers:* senior citizens and employees or children of employees.

Library Richards Library plus 1 other. *Collection:* 1,100 titles, 47 serial subscriptions.

College life *Housing:* college housing not available.

Campus security 24-hour emergency response devices.

After graduation *Career center:* 1 full-time personnel. Services include job fairs, resume preparation, resume referral, career counseling, job bank. **Graduate education:** 35% of class of 1999 went directly to graduate and professional school.

Freshmen

SAT verbal scores above 500	N/R	SAT math scores above 500	N/R
ACT above 18	N/R		

Application *Options:* Common Application, electronic application, early admission, deferred entrance. *Application fee:* $25. *Required:* high school transcript; minimum 2.5 GPA. *Required for some:* essay or personal statement; 2 letters of recommendation. *Recommended:* interview.

Standardized tests *Placement: Required:* SAT I or ACT.

Significant dates *Application deadlines:* rolling (freshmen), rolling (transfers). *Financial aid deadline priority date:* 3/1.

Freshman Application Contact
Ms. Mary Krowleski, Admissions Representative, Cleary College, 3750 Cleary College Drive, Howell, MI 48843. **Phone:** 517-548-3670 Ext. 2215. **Toll-free phone:** 800-589-1979 Ext. 2249. **Fax:** 517-548-2170.

Visit CollegeQuest.com for information on majors offered and athletics.

■ *See page 1434 for a narrative description.*

CONCORDIA COLLEGE
Ann Arbor, Michigan

- **Independent**, 4-year, founded 1963, affiliated with Lutheran Church–Missouri Synod
- **Degrees** associate and bachelor's
- **Suburban** 234-acre campus with easy access to Detroit
- **Coed**, 558 undergraduate students, 81% full-time, 61% women, 39% men
- **Moderately difficult** entrance level, 74% of applicants were admitted
- **$13,800 tuition** and fees
- **$12,072 average financial aid** package, $20,026 average indebtedness upon graduation, $6.2 million endowment

Part of Concordia University System.

Students *Undergraduates:* 453 full-time, 105 part-time. Students come from 20 states and territories, 4 other countries. *The most frequently chosen baccalaureate fields are:* business/marketing, education, health professions and related sciences.

From out-of-state	30%	Reside on campus	60%
Age 25 or older	35%	Transferred in	6%
International students	1%	African Americans	7%
Asian Americans/Pacific Islanders	0.4%	Hispanic Americans	1%
Native Americans	0.2%		

Faculty 51 (88% full-time).

Expenses (2000–2001) *One-time required fee:* $100. *Comprehensive fee:* $19,600 includes full-time tuition ($13,400), mandatory fees ($400), and room and board ($5800). Full-time tuition and fees vary according to class time and program. Room and board charges vary according to board plan and housing facility. *Part-time tuition:* $450 per credit hour. Part-time tuition and fees vary according to class time, course load, and program. *Waivers:* employees or children of employees.

Library Zimmerman Library. *Operations spending 1999–2000:* $349,269. *Collection:* 120,000 titles, 1,400 serial subscriptions, 8,112 audiovisual materials.

College life *Housing:* on-campus residence required through sophomore year. *Options:* men-only, women-only. *Most popular organizations:* Student Activities Committee, drama club, Student Senate, Spiritual Life Committee, Off-Campus Ministries.

Campus security Student patrols, late-night transport-escort service.

After graduation *Career center:* 1 full-time, 1 part-time personnel. Services include job fairs, resume preparation, resume referral, career/interest testing, career counseling, careers library, job bank.

Freshmen 287 applied, 212 admitted, 90 enrolled.

Average high school GPA	3.22	SAT verbal scores above 500	N/R
SAT math scores above 500	N/R	ACT above 18	N/R
1998 freshmen returning in 1999	77%		

Application *Option:* deferred entrance. *Application fee:* $25. *Required:* high school transcript; minimum 2.5 GPA; 1 letter of recommendation. *Required for some:* essay or personal statement; interview.

Standardized tests *Admission: Required:* SAT I or ACT.

Significant dates *Application deadlines:* rolling (freshmen), rolling (transfers). *Financial aid deadline priority date:* 5/1.

Freshman Application Contact
Ms. Kathleen Rowe, Director of Admissions, Concordia College, 4090 Geddes Road, Ann Arbor, MI 48105. **Phone:** 734-995-7322 Ext. 7311. **Toll-free phone:** 800-253-0680. **Fax:** 734-995-4610. **E-mail:** admissions@ccaa.edu

Visit CollegeQuest.com for information on majors offered and athletics. College video available at CollegeQuest.com.

CORNERSTONE UNIVERSITY
Grand Rapids, Michigan

- **Independent Baptist**, 4-year, founded 1941
- **Degrees** associate and bachelor's
- **Suburban** 132-acre campus
- **Coed**, 1,495 undergraduate students, 92% full-time, 60% women, 40% men
- **Moderately difficult** entrance level, 91% of applicants were admitted
- **35.4% graduate** in 6 years or less
- **$10,344 tuition** and fees
- **$4.6 million endowment**

Students *Undergraduates:* 1,382 full-time, 113 part-time. Students come from 29 states and territories, 4 other countries. *The most frequently chosen baccalaureate fields are:* business/marketing, education, English.

Michigan

From out-of-state	18%	Age 25 or older	5%
Transferred in	6%	International students	1%
African Americans	3%	Asian Americans/Pacific Islanders	1%
Hispanic Americans	2%	Native Americans	0.3%

Faculty 110 (51% full-time).

Expenses (1999–2000) *Comprehensive fee:* $15,056 includes full-time tuition ($9664), mandatory fees ($680), and room and board ($4712). *College room only:* $2160. *Part-time tuition:* $347 per credit hour. Part-time tuition and fees vary according to course load. *Payment plan:* installment. *Waivers:* employees or children of employees.

Library Miller Library. *Operations spending 1999–2000:* $433,000. *Collection:* 90,444 titles, 4,700 audiovisual materials.

College life *Housing:* on-campus residence required through junior year. *Options:* men-only, women-only, disabled students. *Most popular organizations:* student government, Student Education Association, Breakpoint, Student Activities Council.

Campus security 24-hour emergency response devices and patrols, student patrols, late-night transport-escort service.

After graduation 35 organizations recruited on campus 1997–98. 95% of class of 1998 had job offers within 6 months. *Career center:* 3 full-time personnel. Services include job fairs, resume preparation, resume referral, career counseling, careers library, job bank, job interviews. *Graduate education:* 14% of class of 1999 went directly to graduate and professional school.

Freshmen 725 applied, 657 admitted, 366 enrolled. 7 valedictorians.

Average high school GPA	3.42	SAT verbal scores above 500	N/R
SAT math scores above 500	N/R	ACT above 18	96%
From top 10% of their h.s. class	15%	From top quarter	39%
From top half	73%	1998 freshmen returning in 1999	67%

Application *Option:* deferred entrance. *Application fee:* $25. *Required:* essay or personal statement; high school transcript; minimum 2.25 GPA; 1 letter of recommendation. *Recommended:* interview.

Standardized tests *Admission: Required:* SAT I or ACT.

Significant dates *Application deadlines:* rolling (freshmen), rolling (transfers). *Financial aid deadline priority date:* 3/21.

Freshman Application Contact
Mr. Brent Rudin, Director of Enrollment Management, Cornerstone University, 1001 East Beltline Avenue, NE, Grand Rapids, MI 49325-5597. **Phone:** 616-222-1426. **Toll-free phone:** 800-968-4722. **Fax:** 616-949-0875. **E-mail:** admissions@cornerstone.edu

Visit CollegeQuest.com for information on majors offered and athletics. College video and electronic viewbook available at CollegeQuest.com.

DAVENPORT COLLEGE OF BUSINESS
Grand Rapids, Michigan

- **Independent**, comprehensive, founded 1866
- **Degrees** associate, bachelor's, and master's
- **Urban** 5-acre campus
- **Coed**, 1,985 undergraduate students, 38% full-time, 69% women, 31% men
- **Noncompetitive** entrance level
- **$9116 tuition** and fees

Part of Davenport Educational System.

Students *Undergraduates:* 762 full-time, 1,223 part-time. *The most frequently chosen baccalaureate fields are:* (pre)law, business/marketing, computer/information sciences. *Graduate:* 64 in graduate degree programs.

Reside on campus	10%	Age 25 or older	59%
Transferred in	17%	International students	1%
African Americans	8%	Asian Americans/Pacific Islanders	2%
Hispanic Americans	5%	Native Americans	1%

Faculty 144 (26% full-time).

Expenses (1999–2000) *Tuition:* full-time $9016; part-time $196 per credit hour. *Required fees:* full-time $100; $25 per term part-time. Full-time tuition and fees vary according to course load. *College room only:* $3200.

Library Sneden Library plus 1 other. *Collection:* 35,584 titles, 1,027 serial subscriptions.

Campus security 24-hour emergency response devices and patrols, late-night transport-escort service, controlled dormitory access.

After graduation *Career center:* 2 full-time, 2 part-time personnel. Services include job fairs, resume preparation, resume referral, career counseling, careers library, job bank, job interviews. *Graduate education:* 10% of class of 1999 went directly to graduate and professional school.

Freshmen 333 enrolled.

| SAT verbal scores above 500 | N/R | SAT math scores above 500 | N/R |
| ACT above 18 | N/R | 1998 freshmen returning in 1999 | 40% |

Application *Options:* Common Application, early admission, deferred entrance. *Application fee:* $25. *Required:* high school transcript. *Recommended:* essay or personal statement; interview.

Standardized tests *Placement: Recommended:* ACT.

Significant dates *Application deadlines:* rolling (freshmen), 9/15 (out-of-state freshmen), rolling (transfers). *Notification:* continuous until continuous (out-of-state freshmen). *Financial aid deadline priority date:* 3/15.

Freshman Application Contact
Ms. Colleen Wolfe, Dean of Enrollment Management and Student Services, Davenport College of Business, 415 East Fulton, Grand Rapids, MI 49503. **Phone:** 616-732-1200. **Toll-free phone:** 800-632-9569.

Visit CollegeQuest.com for information on majors offered and athletics. College video available at CollegeQuest.com.

DAVENPORT COLLEGE OF BUSINESS, KALAMAZOO CAMPUS
Kalamazoo, Michigan

- **Independent**, 4-year, founded 1866
- **Degrees** associate, bachelor's, and postbachelor's certificates
- **Suburban** 5-acre campus
- **Coed**, 1,231 undergraduate students, 30% full-time, 77% women, 23% men
- **Noncompetitive** entrance level
- **13:1 student-to-undergraduate faculty ratio**
- **$8895 tuition** and fees

Part of Davenport Educational System.

Students *Undergraduates:* 369 full-time, 862 part-time. Students come from 2 states and territories, 6 other countries. *The most frequently chosen baccalaureate fields are:* (pre)law, business/marketing, computer/information sciences.

From out-of-state	1%	Age 25 or older	71%
International students	0.2%	African Americans	17%
Asian Americans/Pacific Islanders	1%	Hispanic Americans	2%
Native Americans	0.5%		

Faculty 110 (22% full-time), 13% with terminal degrees.

Expenses (1999–2000) *Tuition:* full-time $8820; part-time $196 per credit hour. *Required fees:* full-time $75; $25 per term part-time. Part-time tuition and fees vary according to program. *Payment plans:* installment, deferred payment. *Waivers:* employees or children of employees.

Library T. F. Reed Library. *Collection:* 10,257 titles, 949 audiovisual materials.

College life *Housing:* college housing not available. *Most popular organizations:* management/marketing club, Institute of Management Accountants, Paralegal Association, Data Processing Management Association.

Campus security Late-night transport-escort service.

After graduation *Career center:* 2 full-time personnel. Services include job fairs, resume preparation, resume referral, career counseling, job bank, job interviews.

Freshmen 244 enrolled.

| SAT verbal scores above 500 | N/R | SAT math scores above 500 | N/R |
| ACT above 18 | N/R | | |

Application *Options:* Common Application, electronic application, early admission, deferred entrance. *Application fee:* $25. *Required:* essay or personal statement; high school transcript.

Significant dates *Application deadlines:* rolling (freshmen), rolling (transfers). *Financial aid deadline priority date:* 2/21.

Michigan

Davenport College of Business, Kalamazoo Campus (continued)
Freshman Application Contact
Ms. Deb Burley, Admissions Director, Davenport College of Business, Kalamazoo Campus, 4123 West Main Street, Kalamazoo, MI 49006-2791. **Phone:** 616-382-2835 Ext. 3309. **Toll-free phone:** 800-632-8928 Ext. 3308.
Visit CollegeQuest.com for information on majors offered and athletics.

DAVENPORT COLLEGE OF BUSINESS, LANSING CAMPUS
Lansing, Michigan

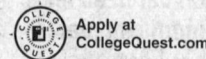

- **Independent**, 4-year, founded 1979
- **Degrees** associate and bachelor's
- **Suburban** 2-acre campus with easy access to Detroit
- **Coed**, 1,215 undergraduate students, 39% full-time, 73% women, 27% men
- **Noncompetitive** entrance level
- **$8111 tuition** and fees

Part of Davenport Educational System.
Students *Undergraduates:* 475 full-time, 740 part-time.

Age 25 or older	45%	Transferred in	27%
International students	0.2%	African Americans	13%
Asian Americans/Pacific Islanders	2%	Hispanic Americans	6%
Native Americans	0.5%		

Faculty 105 (15% full-time).
Expenses (1999–2000) *Tuition:* full-time $8036; part-time $196 per credit hour. *Required fees:* full-time $75; $25 per term part-time. *Payment plan:* installment. *Waivers:* senior citizens.
Library *Collection:* 10,680 titles, 850 serial subscriptions.
College life *Housing:* college housing not available. *Most popular organizations:* Student Accounting Society, Management Marketing Association, Student Leadership Council, Data Processing Management Association, Professional Secretaries International.
Campus security 24-hour emergency response devices, late-night transport-escort service.
After graduation 90% of class of 1998 had job offers within 6 months. *Career center:* 1 full-time personnel. Services include job fairs, resume preparation, resume referral, career/interest testing, career counseling, job bank, job interviews. *Graduate education:* 3% of class of 1999 went directly to graduate and professional school: 3% business.
Freshmen 397 enrolled.

SAT verbal scores above 500	N/R	SAT math scores above 500	N/R
ACT above 18	N/R	1998 freshmen returning in 1999	43%

Application *Options:* eApply at www.CollegeQuest.com, Common Application, electronic application, early admission, deferred entrance. *Application fee:* $25. *Required:* high school transcript. *Recommended:* interview.
Standardized tests *Placement: Required for some:* ACT.
Significant dates *Application deadlines:* 9/15 (freshmen), 9/15 (transfers). *Notification:* continuous until 9/15 (freshmen). *Financial aid deadline priority date:* 3/15.
Freshman Application Contact
Mr. Tom Woods, Enrollment Coordinator, Davenport College of Business, Lansing Campus, 220 East Kalamazoo, Lansing, MI 48933-2197. **Phone:** 517-484-2600 Ext. 288. **Toll-free phone:** 800-331-3306. **Fax:** 517-484-9719. **E-mail:** laadmissions@davenport.edu
Visit CollegeQuest.com for information on majors offered and athletics.

DETROIT COLLEGE OF BUSINESS
Dearborn, Michigan

- **Independent**, comprehensive, founded 1962
- **Degrees** associate, bachelor's, and master's
- **Suburban** 17-acre campus with easy access to Detroit
- **Coed**, 2,959 undergraduate students, 52% full-time, 76% women, 24% men
- **Noncompetitive** entrance level, 57% of applicants were admitted
- **23:1 student-to-undergraduate faculty ratio**
- **$6768 tuition** and fees

Part of Davenport Educational Systems.
Students *Undergraduates:* 1,538 full-time, 1,421 part-time. *The most frequently chosen baccalaureate fields are:* business/marketing, health professions and related sciences. *Graduate:* 195 in graduate degree programs.

From out-of-state	1%	Age 25 or older	71%
International students	0.3%	African Americans	58%
Asian Americans/Pacific Islanders	1%	Hispanic Americans	2%
Native Americans	0.3%		

Faculty 242 (11% full-time).
Expenses (1999–2000) *Tuition:* full-time $6768; part-time $188 per quarter hour. Full-time tuition and fees vary according to course load and location. Part-time tuition and fees vary according to course load and location. *Payment plans:* installment, deferred payment. *Waivers:* children of alumni and employees or children of employees.
Library Dearborn Campus Library. *Collection:* 31,035 titles, 218 serial subscriptions, 218 audiovisual materials.
College life *Housing:* college housing not available. *Most popular organizations:* Health Occupations Students of America (HOSA), student newspaper, student council, Allman Rafiki Society (ARS), President's Council.
Campus security Late-night transport-escort service.
After graduation 42 organizations recruited on campus 1997–98. *Career center:* 4 full-time, 4 part-time personnel. Services include job fairs, resume preparation, resume referral, career counseling, careers library, job bank, job interviews.
Freshmen 1,375 applied, 790 admitted, 339 enrolled.

SAT verbal scores above 500	N/R	SAT math scores above 500	N/R
ACT above 18	N/R	1998 freshmen returning in 1999	42%

Application *Options:* early admission, deferred entrance. *Application fee:* $20. *Required:* high school transcript. *Recommended:* interview.
Significant dates *Application deadlines:* rolling (freshmen), rolling (transfers). *Financial aid deadline priority date:* 3/21.
Freshman Application Contact
Ms. Jennifer Miller, Director of Admissions, Detroit College of Business, 4801 Oakman Boulevard, Dearborn, MI 48126-3799. **Phone:** 313-581-4400. **Fax:** 313-581-1985. **E-mail:** dbgjmiller@dcb.edu
Visit CollegeQuest.com for information on majors offered and athletics.

DETROIT COLLEGE OF BUSINESS—FLINT
Flint, Michigan

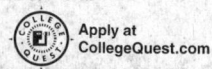

- **Independent**, 4-year, founded 1974
- **Degrees** associate and bachelor's
- **Suburban** 1-acre campus with easy access to Detroit
- **Coed**, 901 undergraduate students, 63% full-time, 79% women, 21% men
- **Noncompetitive** entrance level, 100% of applicants were admitted
- **18:1 student-to-undergraduate faculty ratio**
- **$5004 tuition** and fees

Part of Davenport Educational System.
Students *Undergraduates:* 565 full-time, 336 part-time. *The most frequently chosen baccalaureate fields are:* business/marketing, health professions and related sciences. *Graduate:* 12 in graduate degree programs.

Age 25 or older	68%	African Americans	39%
Asian Americans/Pacific Islanders	0.1%	Hispanic Americans	1%
Native Americans	1%		

Faculty 145 (2% full-time).
Expenses (1999–2000) *Tuition:* full-time $5004; part-time $139 per quarter hour. Full-time tuition and fees vary according to location. Part-time tuition and fees vary according to location. *Payment plans:* installment, deferred payment. *Waivers:* children of alumni and employees or children of employees.
Library Flint Campus Library. *Collection:* 9,101 titles, 103 serial subscriptions, 115 audiovisual materials.

Michigan

College life *Housing:* college housing not available. *Most popular organizations:* Student Government Council, student newspaper, Alumni Association, Student Personnel Association.
Campus security Late-night transport-escort service.
After graduation 20 organizations recruited on campus 1997–98. *Career center:* 1 full-time, 1 part-time personnel. Services include job fairs, resume preparation, resume referral, career counseling, careers library, job bank, job interviews.
Freshmen 194 applied, 194 admitted, 144 enrolled.

SAT verbal scores above 500	N/R	SAT math scores above 500	N/R
ACT above 18	N/R	1998 freshmen returning in 1999	40%

Application *Options:* eApply at www.CollegeQuest.com, early admission, deferred entrance. *Application fee:* $20. *Required:* high school transcript. *Recommended:* interview.
Significant dates *Application deadlines:* rolling (freshmen), rolling (transfers). *Financial aid deadline priority date:* 3/21.
Freshman Application Contact
Ms. Wilma Collins, Director of Admissions, Detroit College of Business–Flint, 3488 North Jennings Road, Flint, MI 48504. **Phone:** 810-789-2200. **Toll-free phone:** 800-727-1443. **Fax:** 810-789-2266. **E-mail:** flwcollins@dbc.edu
Visit CollegeQuest.com for information on majors offered and athletics.

DETROIT COLLEGE OF BUSINESS, WARREN CAMPUS
Warren, Michigan

- **Independent**, comprehensive, founded 1962
- **Degrees** associate, bachelor's, and master's
- **Suburban** 9-acre campus with easy access to Detroit
- **Coed**, 1,985 undergraduate students, 45% full-time, 75% women, 25% men
- **Noncompetitive** entrance level, 67% of applicants were admitted
- **$6768 tuition** and fees

Part of Davenport Educational System, Inc.
Students *Undergraduates:* 902 full-time, 1,083 part-time. Students come from 2 other countries. *The most frequently chosen baccalaureate fields are:* business/marketing, health professions and related sciences. *Graduate:* 69 in graduate degree programs.

Age 25 or older	69%	International students	0.1%
African Americans	39%	Asian Americans/Pacific Islanders	2%
Hispanic Americans	1%	Native Americans	0.3%

Faculty 155 (8% full-time).
Expenses (2000–2001, estimated) *Tuition:* full-time $6768. Full-time tuition and fees vary according to course load. Part-time tuition and fees vary according to course load. *Payment plans:* installment, deferred payment. *Waivers:* children of alumni and employees or children of employees.
Library Detroit College of Business-Warren Library. *Collection:* 8,000 titles, 185 serial subscriptions, 195 audiovisual materials.
College life *Housing:* college housing not available. *Most popular organizations:* Business Olympics, marketing club, management club, campus newspaper, accounting club.
Campus security Late-night transport-escort service.
After graduation *Career center:* 1 full-time, 3 part-time personnel. Services include job fairs, resume preparation, resume referral, career counseling, careers library, job bank, job interviews.
Freshmen 699 applied, 468 admitted, 237 enrolled.

SAT verbal scores above 500	N/R	SAT math scores above 500	N/R
ACT above 18	N/R	1998 freshmen returning in 1999	42%

Application *Options:* early admission, deferred entrance. *Application fee:* $20. *Required:* high school transcript.
Significant dates *Application deadlines:* rolling (freshmen), rolling (transfers). *Financial aid deadline priority date:* 3/21.
Freshman Application Contact
Ms. Gerri Pauvall, Director of Admissions, Detroit College of Business, Warren Campus, 27500 Dequindre Road, Warren, MI 48092-5209. **Phone:** 810-558-8700. **Fax:** 810-558-7868. **E-mail:** wagpauval@dcb.edu

Visit CollegeQuest.com for information on majors offered and athletics.

EASTERN MICHIGAN UNIVERSITY
Ypsilanti, Michigan

- **State-supported**, comprehensive, founded 1849
- **Degrees** bachelor's, master's, doctoral, and post-master's certificates
- **Suburban** 460-acre campus with easy access to Detroit
- **Coed**, 17,859 undergraduate students, 69% full-time, 60% women, 40% men
- **Moderately difficult** entrance level, 80% of applicants were admitted
- **19:1 student-to-undergraduate faculty ratio**
- **35% graduate** in 6 years or less
- **$3754 tuition** and fees (in-state); $8822 (out-of-state)
- **$8300 average financial aid** package, $11,719 average indebtedness upon graduation, $32.2 million endowment

Students *Undergraduates:* 12,234 full-time, 5,625 part-time. Students come from 44 states and territories, 60 other countries. *The most frequently chosen baccalaureate fields are:* business/marketing, education, social sciences and history. *Graduate:* 4,913 in graduate degree programs.

From out-of-state	11%	Reside on campus	20%
Age 25 or older	27%	Transferred in	9%
International students	2%	African Americans	15%
Asian Americans/Pacific Islanders	2%	Hispanic Americans	2%
Native Americans	1%		

Faculty 1,167 (59% full-time).
Expenses (1999–2000) *Tuition, state resident:* full-time $3147; part-time $102 per credit hour. *Tuition, nonresident:* full-time $8215; part-time $265 per credit hour. *Required fees:* full-time $607; $17 per credit hour; $40 per term part-time. Full-time tuition and fees vary according to course level and reciprocity agreements. Part-time tuition and fees vary according to course level and reciprocity agreements. *College room and board:* $4842. Room and board charges vary according to board plan, housing facility, and location. *Payment plan:* installment. *Waivers:* employees or children of employees.
Library Bruce T. Halle Library. *Operations spending 1999–2000:* $5.4 million. *Collection:* 890,525 titles, 5,263 serial subscriptions, 6,407 audiovisual materials.
College life *Housing:* on-campus residence required through sophomore year. *Options:* coed, women-only, disabled students. *Social organizations:* national fraternities, national sororities, local fraternities, local sororities.
Campus security 24-hour emergency response devices and patrols, student patrols, late-night transport-escort service, controlled dormitory access, bicycle patrols, local police in dormitories.
After graduation 640 organizations recruited on campus 1997–98. *Career center:* 18 full-time, 2 part-time personnel. Services include job fairs, resume preparation, interview workshops, resume referral, career/interest testing, career counseling, careers library, job bank, job interviews. *Graduate education:* 20% of class of 1999 went directly to graduate and professional school.
Freshmen 8,688 applied, 6,938 admitted, 2,902 enrolled.

Average high school GPA	2.99	SAT verbal scores above 500	50%
SAT math scores above 500	47%	ACT above 18	79%
1998 freshmen returning in 1999	73%		

Application *Application fee:* $25. *Required:* high school transcript; minimum 2.0 GPA. *Required for some:* 1 letter of recommendation; interview.
Standardized tests *Admission:* Required: SAT I or ACT.
Significant dates *Application deadlines:* 8/1 (freshmen), 8/3 (transfers). *Financial aid deadline priority date:* 3/15.
Freshman Application Contact
Ms. Judy Benfield-Tatum, Director of Admissions, Eastern Michigan University, Ypsilanti, MI 48197. **Phone:** 734-487-3060. **Toll-free phone:** 800-GO TO EMU. **Fax:** 734-487-1484.
Visit CollegeQuest.com for information on majors offered and athletics.

Michigan

FERRIS STATE UNIVERSITY
Big Rapids, Michigan

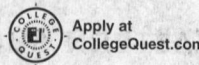

- **State-supported**, comprehensive, founded 1884
- **Degrees** associate, bachelor's, master's, and first professional
- **Small-town** 600-acre campus with easy access to Grand Rapids
- **Coed**, 8,882 undergraduate students, 81% full-time, 44% women, 56% men
- **Minimally difficult** entrance level, 86% of applicants were admitted
- **16:1 student-to-undergraduate faculty ratio**
- **$4195 tuition** and fees (in-state); $8803 (out-of-state)
- **$7574 average financial aid** package, $13,000 average indebtedness upon graduation, $15.4 million endowment

Students *Undergraduates:* 7,188 full-time, 1,694 part-time. Students come from 41 states and territories, 57 other countries. *The most frequently chosen baccalaureate fields are:* business/marketing, engineering/engineering technologies, health professions and related sciences. *Graduate:* 163 in professional programs, 314 in other graduate degree programs.

From out-of-state	6%	Reside on campus	47%
Age 25 or older	26%	Transferred in	11%
International students	3%	African Americans	11%
Asian Americans/Pacific Islanders	2%	Hispanic Americans	1%
Native Americans	1%		

Faculty 612 (72% full-time).
Expenses (1999–2000) *Tuition, state resident:* full-time $4118; part-time $172 per credit hour. *Tuition, nonresident:* full-time $8726; part-time $366 per credit hour. *Required fees:* full-time $77; $38 per term part-time. Full-time tuition and fees vary according to reciprocity agreements. Part-time tuition and fees vary according to course load and reciprocity agreements. *College room and board:* $5110. Room and board charges vary according to board plan and housing facility. *Payment plans:* installment, deferred payment. *Waivers:* employees or children of employees.
Library Timme Library plus 1 other. *Operations spending 1999–2000:* $2.8 million. *Collection:* 416,352 titles, 3,995 serial subscriptions.
College life *Housing:* on-campus residence required through sophomore year. *Options:* coed, men-only, women-only. *Social organizations:* national fraternities, national sororities, local fraternities, local sororities; 4% of eligible men and 2% of eligible women are members. *Most popular organizations:* Associated Student Government, intramural sports club, University Theatre, Music Club, Forensics Club.
Campus security 24-hour emergency response devices, student patrols, late-night transport-escort service.
After graduation 175 organizations recruited on campus 1997–98. *Career center:* 5 full-time, 1 part-time personnel. Services include job fairs, resume preparation, interview workshops, resume referral, career/interest testing, career counseling, careers library, job bank, job interviews.
Freshmen 5,815 applied, 5,006 admitted, 2,142 enrolled.

Average high school GPA	2.85	SAT verbal scores above 500	N/R
SAT math scores above 500	N/R	ACT above 18	N/R
1998 freshmen returning in 1999	64%		

Application *Options:* eApply at www.CollegeQuest.com, electronic application, deferred entrance. *Application fee:* $20. *Required:* high school transcript; minimum 2.0 GPA. *Required for some:* interview. *Recommended:* interview.
Standardized tests *Admission: Required:* ACT.
Significant dates *Application deadlines:* rolling (freshmen), rolling (transfers). *Financial aid deadline priority date:* 3/15.
Freshman Application Contact
Mr. Don Mullens, Assistant Vice President/Dean of Enrollment Services, Ferris State University, PRK 110, Big Rapids, MI 49307-2742. **Phone:** 231-591-2100. **Toll-free phone:** 800-433-7747. **Fax:** 231-591-2978. **E-mail:** admissions@ferris.edu
Visit CollegeQuest.com for information on majors offered and athletics. College video available at CollegeQuest.com.

- *See page 1656 for a narrative description.*

FINLANDIA UNIVERSITY
Hancock, Michigan

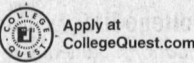

- **Independent**, 4-year, founded 1896, affiliated with Evangelical Lutheran Church in America
- **Degrees** associate and bachelor's
- **Small-town** 25-acre campus
- **Coed**, 363 undergraduate students, 84% full-time, 71% women, 29% men
- **Minimally difficult** entrance level, 83% of applicants were admitted
- **11:1 student-to-undergraduate faculty ratio**
- **$12,260 tuition** and fees
- **$4.1 million endowment**

Students *Undergraduates:* 305 full-time, 58 part-time. Students come from 8 states and territories, 4 other countries. *The most frequently chosen baccalaureate field is:* business/marketing.

From out-of-state	6%	Reside on campus	28%
Age 25 or older	34%	Transferred in	17%
International students	5%	African Americans	6%
Native Americans	2%		

Faculty 40 (78% full-time), 100% with terminal degrees.
Expenses (2000–2001) *Comprehensive fee:* $16,600 includes full-time tuition ($11,700), mandatory fees ($560), and room and board ($4340). *College room only:* $2340. *Part-time tuition:* $390 per credit. *Part-time fees:* $560 per year. Part-time tuition and fees vary according to course load. *Payment plan:* installment. *Waivers:* employees or children of employees.
Library Suomi College Library. *Operations spending 1999–2000:* $134,000. *Collection:* 61,631 titles, 313 serial subscriptions, 15,694 audiovisual materials.
College life *Housing:* on-campus residence required through junior year. *Option:* coed. *Most popular organizations:* student senate, community service club, Suomi business group, Campus Enrichment, hall government.
Campus security 24-hour patrols, late-night transport-escort service.
After graduation 50% of class of 1998 had job offers within 6 months. *Career center:* 1 full-time personnel. Services include resume preparation, career counseling, careers library.
Freshmen 170 applied, 141 admitted, 107 enrolled.

Average high school GPA	2.72	SAT verbal scores above 500	N/R
SAT math scores above 500	N/R	ACT above 18	N/R
From top 10% of their h.s. class	5%	From top quarter	6%
From top half	14%	1998 freshmen returning in 1999	54%

Application *Options:* eApply at www.CollegeQuest.com, Common Application, early admission. *Application fee:* $20. *Required:* high school transcript; minimum 2.00 GPA. *Required for some:* essay or personal statement; letters of recommendation; interview.
Standardized tests *Admission: Recommended:* SAT I or ACT.
Significant dates *Application deadlines:* 8/15 (freshmen), 8/15 (transfers). *Financial aid deadline:* 5/1. Priority date: 2/15.
Freshman Application Contact
Mr. Ben Larson, Director of Admissions, Finlandia University, 601 Quincy Street, Hancock, MI 49930. **Phone:** 906-487-7311 Ext. 311. **Toll-free phone:** 800-682-7604. **Fax:** 906-487-7300. **E-mail:** admissions@suomi.edu
Visit CollegeQuest.com for information on majors offered and athletics. College video available at CollegeQuest.com.

- *See page 1660 for a narrative description.*

GMI ENGINEERING & MANAGEMENT INSTITUTE
Michigan—See Kettering University

GRACE BIBLE COLLEGE
Grand Rapids, Michigan

- **Independent**, 4-year, founded 1945, affiliated with Grace Gospel Fellowship
- **Degrees** associate and bachelor's
- **Suburban** 16-acre campus

Michigan

- **Coed**, 143 undergraduate students, 92% full-time, 52% women, 48% men
- **Minimally difficult** entrance level, 54% of applicants were admitted
- **11:1 student-to-undergraduate faculty ratio**
- **31% graduate** in 6 years or less
- **$7100 tuition** and fees
- **$6928 average financial aid** package, $15,632 average indebtedness upon graduation, $1.8 million endowment

Students *Undergraduates:* 132 full-time, 11 part-time. Students come from 17 states and territories, 4 other countries. *The most frequently chosen baccalaureate fields are:* business/marketing, education, visual/performing arts.

From out-of-state	33%	Reside on campus	64%
Age 25 or older	19%	Transferred in	8%
International students	3%	African Americans	1%
Asian Americans/Pacific Islanders	1%	Hispanic Americans	1%
Native Americans	1%		

Faculty 23 (35% full-time), 100% with terminal degrees.

Expenses (1999–2000) *Comprehensive fee:* $11,250 includes full-time tuition ($6800), mandatory fees ($300), and room and board ($4150). *College room only:* $1800. Room and board charges vary according to housing facility. *Part-time tuition:* $285 per semester hour. Part-time tuition and fees vary according to course load. *Payment plan:* installment. *Waivers:* senior citizens and employees or children of employees.

Library Bultema Memorial Library. *Operations spending 1999–2000:* $92,800. *Collection:* 38,884 titles, 134 serial subscriptions, 272 audiovisual materials.

College life *Housing:* on-campus residence required through sophomore year. *Options:* men-only, women-only. *Most popular organizations:* Ambassador Fellowship, Student Activities Committee, student council, Ambassador Staff.

Campus security Student patrols, controlled dormitory access.

After graduation *Career center:* 1 part-time personnel. Services include career counseling, careers library.

Freshmen 130 applied, 70 admitted, 42 enrolled.

Average high school GPA	3.26	SAT verbal scores above 500	N/R
SAT math scores above 500	N/R	ACT above 18	71%
From top 10% of their h.s. class	7%	From top quarter	24%
From top half	50%	1998 freshmen returning in 1999	60%

Application *Options:* early admission, deferred entrance. *Application fee:* $0. *Required:* high school transcript; 2 letters of recommendation. *Required for some:* interview. *Recommended:* minimum 2.5 GPA.

Standardized tests *Admission: Required:* ACT.

Significant dates *Application deadline:* 7/15 (freshmen). *Notification:* continuous until 8/1 (freshmen). *Financial aid deadline priority date:* 2/15.

Freshman Application Contact
Mr. Kevin Gilliam, Director of Enrollment, Grace Bible College, 1011 Aldon Street SW, PO Box 910, Grand Rapids, MI 49509-0910. **Phone:** 616-538-2330. **Toll-free phone:** 800-968-1887. **Fax:** 616-538-0599. **E-mail:** gbc@gbcol.edu

Visit CollegeQuest.com for information on majors offered and athletics. College video available at CollegeQuest.com.

GRAND VALLEY STATE UNIVERSITY
Allendale, Michigan

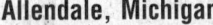
Apply at CollegeQuest.com

- **State-supported**, comprehensive, founded 1960
- **Degrees** bachelor's, master's, and post-master's certificates
- **Small-town** 900-acre campus with easy access to Grand Rapids
- **Coed**, 13,820 undergraduate students, 83% full-time, 60% women, 40% men
- **Moderately difficult** entrance level, 76% of applicants were admitted
- **21:1 student-to-undergraduate faculty ratio**
- **48.3% graduate** in 6 years or less
- **$4108 tuition** and fees (in-state); $8890 (out-of-state)
- **$5518 average financial aid** package, $11,600 average indebtedness upon graduation, $35.9 million endowment

Students *Undergraduates:* 11,407 full-time, 2,413 part-time. Students come from 42 states and territories, 24 other countries. *The most frequently chosen baccalaureate fields are:* business/marketing, health professions and related sciences, protective services/public administration. **Graduate:** 3,223 in graduate degree programs.

From out-of-state	3%	Reside on campus	23%
Age 25 or older	16%	Transferred in	9%
International students	0.4%	African Americans	5%
Asian Americans/Pacific Islanders	1%	Hispanic Americans	2%
Native Americans	1%		

Faculty 965 (62% full-time).

Expenses (1999–2000) *Tuition, state resident:* full-time $4048; part-time $179 per semester hour. *Tuition, nonresident:* full-time $8830; part-time $378 per semester hour. *Required fees:* full-time $60. Full-time tuition and fees vary according to student level. Part-time tuition and fees vary according to student level. *College room and board:* $4910. Room and board charges vary according to board plan and housing facility. *Payment plans:* installment, deferred payment. *Waivers:* employees or children of employees.

Library James H. Zumberge Library. *Operations spending 1999–2000:* $3.3 million. *Collection:* 501,376 titles, 2,835 serial subscriptions.

College life *Housing: Option:* coed. *Social organizations:* national fraternities, national sororities, local fraternities, local sororities; 3% of eligible men and 2% of eligible women are members. *Most popular organizations:* Black Student Union, Residence Hall Association, Crew Club, student senate, Student Organization Network.

Campus security 24-hour emergency response devices and patrols, student patrols, late-night transport-escort service.

After graduation 127 organizations recruited on campus 1997–98. 73% of class of 1998 had job offers within 6 months. *Career center:* 7 full-time, 2 part-time personnel. Services include job fairs, resume preparation, interview workshops, resume referral, career/interest testing, career counseling, careers library, job bank, job interviews.

Freshmen 8,403 applied, 6,422 admitted, 2,572 enrolled.

Average high school GPA	3.3	SAT verbal scores above 500	N/R
SAT math scores above 500	N/R	ACT above 18	97%
From top 10% of their h.s. class	15%	From top quarter	43%
From top half	82%	1998 freshmen returning in 1999	75%

Application *Options:* eApply at www.CollegeQuest.com, electronic application. *Application fee:* $20. *Required:* high school transcript. *Required for some:* essay or personal statement; interview.

Standardized tests *Admission: Required:* SAT I or ACT.

Significant dates *Application deadlines:* 7/26 (freshmen), 7/26 (transfers). *Notification:* continuous until 8/25 (freshmen). *Financial aid deadline priority date:* 2/15.

Freshman Application Contact
Mr. William Eilola, Director of Admissions, Grand Valley State University, 1 Campus Drive, Allendale, MI 49401-9403. **Phone:** 616-895-2025. **Toll-free phone:** 800-748-0246. **Fax:** 616-895-2000. **E-mail:** go2gvsu@gvsu.edu

Visit CollegeQuest.com for information on majors offered and athletics. College video available at CollegeQuest.com.

GREAT LAKES CHRISTIAN COLLEGE
Lansing, Michigan

- **Independent**, 4-year, founded 1949, affiliated with Christian Churches and Churches of Christ
- **Degrees** associate and bachelor's
- **Suburban** 50-acre campus
- **Coed**
- **Moderately difficult** entrance level
- **$6424 tuition** and fees

Expenses (1999–2000) *Comprehensive fee:* $10,424 includes full-time tuition ($6000), mandatory fees ($424), and room and board ($4000). Full-time tuition and fees vary according to course load. Room and board charges vary according to board plan and housing facility. *Part-time tuition:* $198 per credit hour. *Part-time fees:* $227 per term part-time.

Institutional Web site http://www.glcc.edu/

College life *Housing:* on-campus residence required through senior year. *Options:* men-only, women-only.

Campus security Evening security patrols.

Michigan

Great Lakes Christian College (continued)
Application *Options:* early admission, deferred entrance. *Application fee:* $30. *Required:* essay or personal statement; high school transcript; minimum 2.25 GPA; 3 letters of recommendation.
Standardized tests *Admission: Required:* SAT I and SAT II or ACT.
Admissions Office Contact
Great Lakes Christian College, 6211 West Willow Highway, Lansing, MI 48917-1299. **Toll-free phone:** 800-YES-GLCC. **Fax:** 517-321-5902.
Visit CollegeQuest.com for information on athletics.

HILLSDALE COLLEGE
Hillsdale, Michigan

- **Independent**, 4-year, founded 1844
- **Degree** bachelor's
- **Small-town** 200-acre campus
- **Coed**, 1,167 undergraduate students, 98% full-time, 52% women, 48% men
- **Very difficult** entrance level, 84% of applicants were admitted
- **11:1 student-to-undergraduate faculty ratio**
- **70.2% graduate** in 6 years or less
- **$13,460 tuition** and fees
- **$13,524 average financial aid** package, $13,385 average indebtedness upon graduation, $180 million endowment

Students *Undergraduates:* 1,138 full-time, 29 part-time. Students come from 47 states and territories, 10 other countries. *The most frequently chosen baccalaureate fields are:* business/marketing, biological/life sciences, social sciences and history.

From out-of-state	49%	Reside on campus	85%
Age 25 or older	1%	Transferred in	3%

Faculty 127 (76% full-time), 83% with terminal degrees.
Expenses (1999–2000) *Comprehensive fee:* $19,090 includes full-time tuition ($13,220), mandatory fees ($240), and room and board ($5630). *College room only:* $2630. Room and board charges vary according to board plan. *Part-time tuition:* $520 per semester hour. Part-time tuition and fees vary according to course load. *Payment plan:* installment. *Waivers:* employees or children of employees.
Library Mossey Learning Center plus 3 others. *Operations spending 1999–2000:* $1.1 million. *Collection:* 180,000 titles, 19,200 serial subscriptions, 6,500 audiovisual materials.
College life *Housing:* on-campus residence required through sophomore year. *Options:* men-only, women-only. *Social organizations:* national fraternities, national sororities; 35% of eligible men and 45% of eligible women are members. *Most popular organizations:* Greek system, Intervarsity Christian Fellowship, H-Club, Student Federation, Prelaw Society.
Campus security 24-hour emergency response devices and patrols, late-night transport-escort service, controlled dormitory access.
After graduation 44 organizations recruited on campus 1997–98. 97% of class of 1998 had job offers within 6 months. *Career center:* 3 full-time, 2 part-time personnel. Services include job fairs, resume preparation, interview workshops, resume referral, career/interest testing, career counseling, careers library, job bank, job interviews. *Major awards:* 1 Fulbright Scholar.
Freshmen 1,008 applied, 849 admitted, 323 enrolled. 11 National Merit Scholars, 20 valedictorians.

Average high school GPA	3.55	SAT verbal scores above 500	93%
SAT math scores above 500	91%	ACT above 18	100%
From top 10% of their h.s. class	40%	From top quarter	73%
From top half	99%	1998 freshmen returning in 1999	90%

Application *Options:* eApply at www.CollegeQuest.com, Common Application, electronic application, early admission, deferred entrance. *Application fee:* $15. *Required:* essay or personal statement; high school transcript; minimum 3.1 GPA; 1 letter of recommendation. *Required for some:* interview. *Recommended:* interview.
Standardized tests *Admission: Required:* SAT I or ACT. *Recommended:* SAT II Subject Tests, SAT II: Writing Test.
Significant dates *Application deadlines:* rolling (freshmen), rolling (transfers). *Notification:* continuous until 7/15 (freshmen). *Financial aid deadline priority date:* 3/15.

Freshman Application Contact
Mr. Jeffrey S. Lantis, Director of Admissions, Hillsdale College, 33 East College Street, Hillsdale, MI 49242-1298. **Phone:** 517-437-7341 Ext. 2327. **Fax:** 517-437-0190. **E-mail:** admissions@ac.hillsdale.edu
Visit CollegeQuest.com for information on majors offered and athletics. College video available at CollegeQuest.com.

■ *See page 1790 for a narrative description.*

HOPE COLLEGE
Holland, Michigan

- **Independent**, 4-year, founded 1866, affiliated with Reformed Church in America
- **Degree** bachelor's
- **Small-town** 45-acre campus with easy access to Grand Rapids
- **Coed**, 2,812 undergraduate students, 98% full-time, 60% women, 40% men
- **Moderately difficult** entrance level, 89% of applicants were admitted
- **14:1 student-to-undergraduate faculty ratio**
- **68.85% graduate** in 6 years or less
- **$16,024 tuition** and fees
- **$14,227 average financial aid** package, $16,259 average indebtedness upon graduation, $106 million endowment

Students *Undergraduates:* 2,747 full-time, 65 part-time. Students come from 36 states and territories, 27 other countries. *The most frequently chosen baccalaureate fields are:* biological/life sciences, business/marketing, English.

From out-of-state	23%	Reside on campus	76%
Age 25 or older	3%	Transferred in	2%
International students	1%	African Americans	1%
Asian Americans/Pacific Islanders	2%	Hispanic Americans	1%
Native Americans	0.2%		

Faculty 292 (70% full-time), 57% with terminal degrees.
Expenses (1999–2000) *Comprehensive fee:* $21,054 includes full-time tuition ($15,934), mandatory fees ($90), and room and board ($5030). *College room only:* $2294. Room and board charges vary according to board plan and housing facility. Part-time tuition and fees vary according to course load. *Payment plan:* installment. *Waivers:* employees or children of employees.
Library Van Wylen Library plus 1 other. *Operations spending 1999–2000:* $1.8 million. *Collection:* 318,386 titles, 1,945 serial subscriptions.
College life *Housing:* on-campus residence required through junior year. *Option:* coed. *Social organizations:* local fraternities, local sororities; 9% of eligible men and 10% of eligible women are members. *Most popular organizations:* Fellowship of Christian Athletes, Social Activities Committee, Greek organizations.
Campus security 24-hour emergency response devices and patrols, late-night transport-escort service, controlled dormitory access.
After graduation 54 organizations recruited on campus 1997–98. *Career center:* 2 full-time, 2 part-time personnel. Services include job fairs, resume preparation, interview workshops, resume referral, career/interest testing, career counseling, careers library, job bank, job interviews. *Graduate education:* 27% of class of 1999 went directly to graduate and professional school: 17% graduate arts and sciences, 2% engineering, 2% law, 2% medicine, 2% theology, 1% dentistry.
Freshmen 2,089 applied, 1,863 admitted, 755 enrolled. 15 National Merit Scholars, 18 valedictorians.

Average high school GPA	3.64	SAT verbal scores above 500	84%
SAT math scores above 500	89%	ACT above 18	N/R
From top 10% of their h.s. class	37%	From top quarter	61%
From top half	94%	1998 freshmen returning in 1999	87%

Application *Options:* eApply at www.CollegeQuest.com, Common Application, electronic application, early admission, deferred entrance. *Application fee:* $25. *Required:* essay or personal statement; high school transcript. *Required for some:* 1 letter of recommendation. *Recommended:* interview.
Standardized tests *Admission: Required:* SAT I or ACT.
Significant dates *Application deadlines:* rolling (freshmen), rolling (transfers). *Financial aid deadline priority date:* 2/15.
Freshman Application Contact
Office of Admissions, Hope College, 69 East 10th Street, PO Box 9000, Holland, MI 49422-9000. **Phone:** 616-395-7850. **Toll-free phone:** 800-968-7850. **Fax:** 616-395-7130. **E-mail:** admissions@hope.edu

Michigan

Visit CollegeQuest.com for information on majors offered and athletics. College video available at CollegeQuest.com.

■ *See page 1802 for a narrative description.*

KALAMAZOO COLLEGE
Kalamazoo, Michigan

- **Independent**, 4-year, founded 1833, affiliated with American Baptist Churches in the U.S.A.
- **Degree** bachelor's
- **Suburban** 60-acre campus
- **Coed**, 1,367 undergraduate students, 100% full-time, 56% women, 44% men
- **Very difficult** entrance level, 77% of applicants were admitted
- **14:1 student-to-undergraduate faculty ratio**
- **$19,188 tuition** and fees
- **$15,408 average financial aid** package, $17,100 average indebtedness upon graduation, $104 million endowment

Students *Undergraduates:* 1,367 full-time. Students come from 42 states and territories, 14 other countries. *The most frequently chosen baccalaureate fields are:* biological/life sciences, business/marketing, social sciences and history.

From out-of-state	30%	Reside on campus	74%
Age 25 or older	1%	Transferred in	1%
International students	2%	African Americans	3%
Asian Americans/Pacific Islanders	4%	Hispanic Americans	1%
Native Americans	0.1%		

Faculty 107 (84% full-time), 80% with terminal degrees.

Expenses (1999–2000) *One-time required fee:* $70. *Comprehensive fee:* $24,975 includes full-time tuition ($19,188) and room and board ($5787). *College room only:* $2865. Room and board charges vary according to board plan and housing facility. Part-time tuition and fees vary according to course load. *Payment plans:* installment, deferred payment. *Waivers:* employees or children of employees.

Library Upjohn Library plus 1 other. *Operations spending 1999–2000:* $840,550. *Collection:* 305,874 titles, 1,311 serial subscriptions, 15,102 audiovisual materials.

College life *Housing:* on-campus residence required in freshman year. *Option:* coed. *Most popular organizations:* Student Activities Committee, Student Commission, Index (college newspaper), Intervarsity Christian Fellowship, Project Brave volunteer organization.

Campus security 24-hour emergency response devices and patrols, late-night transport-escort service, controlled dormitory access.

After graduation 23 organizations recruited on campus 1997–98. *Career center:* 3 full-time, 2 part-time personnel. Services include job fairs, resume preparation, resume referral, career counseling, careers library, job bank, job interviews. *Graduate education:* 37% of class of 1999 went directly to graduate and professional school: 6% medicine, 4% graduate arts and sciences, 2% law, 1% business.

Freshmen 1,410 applied, 1,087 admitted, 370 enrolled. 10 National Merit Scholars, 20 valedictorians.

Average high school GPA	3.69	SAT verbal scores above 500	93%
SAT math scores above 500	93%	ACT above 18	100%
From top 10% of their h.s. class	47%	From top quarter	80%
From top half	99%	1998 freshmen returning in 1999	89%

Application *Options:* eApply at www.CollegeQuest.com, Common Application, electronic application, early decision, early action, deferred entrance. *Application fee:* $35. *Required:* essay or personal statement; high school transcript; 2 letters of recommendation. *Recommended:* minimum 3.0 GPA; interview.

Standardized tests *Admission: Required:* SAT I or ACT.

Significant dates *Application deadlines:* 2/1 (freshmen), 2/1 (transfers). *Early decision:* 11/15, 12/1. *Notification:* 4/1 (freshmen), 12/1 (early decision), 12/15 (early action). *Financial aid deadline priority date:* 2/15.

Freshman Application Contact
Mrs. Munselle Pientka, Records Manager, Kalamazoo College, Mandelle Hall, 1200 Academy Street, Kalamazoo, MI 49006-3295. **Phone:** 616-337-7166. **Toll-free phone:** 800-253-3602. **Fax:** 616-337-7251. **E-mail:** admission@kzoo.edu

---

Visit CollegeQuest.com for information on majors offered and athletics. College video available at CollegeQuest.com.

KENDALL COLLEGE OF ART AND DESIGN
Grand Rapids, Michigan

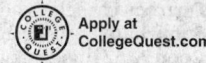

- **Independent**, 4-year, founded 1928
- **Degree** bachelor's
- **Urban** campus
- **Coed**, 637 undergraduate students, 75% full-time, 53% women, 47% men
- **Minimally difficult** entrance level
- **12:1 student-to-undergraduate faculty ratio**
- **28% graduate** in 6 years or less
- **$10,860 tuition** and fees
- **$7885 average financial aid** package, $18,861 average indebtedness upon graduation, $2.5 million endowment

Kendall was founded as a living memorial to one of America's most renowned and innovative furniture designers. David Wolcott Kendall was considered truly avant-garde in arts education. The College today continues to push the envelope, offering leading-edge professional programs that blur the distinction between making art and making a living.

Students *Undergraduates:* 476 full-time, 161 part-time. Students come from 17 states and territories, 9 other countries. *The most frequently chosen baccalaureate fields are:* trade and industry, visual/performing arts.

From out-of-state	8%	Age 25 or older	27%
Transferred in	15%	International students	1%
African Americans	5%	Asian Americans/Pacific Islanders	2%
Hispanic Americans	2%	Native Americans	0.5%

Faculty 74 (43% full-time).

Expenses (1999–2000) *Tuition:* full-time $10,500; part-time $350 per credit. *Required fees:* full-time $360; $130 per term part-time. Full-time tuition and fees vary according to course load. Part-time tuition and fees vary according to course load. *Payment plans:* tuition prepayment, installment, deferred payment. *Waivers:* employees or children of employees.

Library Van Steenburg Library. *Operations spending 1999–2000:* $102,590. *Collection:* 21,324 titles, 111 serial subscriptions, 311 audiovisual materials.

College life *Housing:* college housing not available. *Most popular organizations:* student government association, graphics club, American Society of Interior Designers, Industrial Designers Society of America.

Campus security 24-hour emergency response devices, late-night transport-escort service.

After graduation *Career center:* 1 full-time personnel. Services include resume preparation, interview workshops, career counseling, careers library, job bank, job interviews.

Freshmen 121 admitted, 122 enrolled.

Average high school GPA	2.8	SAT verbal scores above 500	50%
SAT math scores above 500	35%	ACT above 18	N/R
From top 10% of their h.s. class	3%	From top quarter	16%
From top half	54%	1998 freshmen returning in 1999	70%

Application *Options:* eApply at www.CollegeQuest.com, Common Application, early admission, early decision, deferred entrance. *Application fee:* $35. *Required:* essay or personal statement; high school transcript; minimum 2.0 GPA; portfolio. *Recommended:* interview.

Standardized tests *Admission: Required:* SAT I and SAT II or ACT.

Significant dates *Application deadlines:* rolling (freshmen), rolling (transfers). *Financial aid deadline priority date:* 2/15.

Freshman Application Contact
Ms. Amy Packard, Director of Admissions, Kendall College of Art and Design, 111 Division Avenue North, Grand Rapids, MI 49503-3194. **Phone:** 616-451-2787 Ext. 109. **Toll-free phone:** 800-676-2787.

Visit CollegeQuest.com for information on majors offered and athletics.

■ *See page 1868 for a narrative description.*

Michigan

KETTERING UNIVERSITY
Flint, Michigan

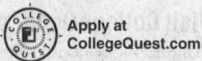

- **Independent**, comprehensive, founded 1919
- **Degrees** bachelor's and master's
- **Suburban** 45-acre campus with easy access to Detroit
- **Coed**, 2,524 undergraduate students, 100% full-time, 20% women, 80% men
- **Very difficult** entrance level, 75% of applicants were admitted
- **9:1 student-to-undergraduate faculty ratio**
- **$14,775 tuition** and fees
- **$5465 average financial aid** package, $30,000 average indebtedness upon graduation, $34.4 million endowment

Kettering University (formerly GMI Engineering & Management Institute) will jump-start your career in engineering, math, applied sciences, or business. With our renowned professional co-op program, students alternate 12-week class terms with 12-week paid work experience terms with one of more than 750 corporate employers. Ninety-nine of seniors receive job offers or are accepted by graduate schools before they receive their diplomas. Kettering University provides education for the real world.

Students *Undergraduates:* 2,524 full-time. Students come from 48 states and territories, 18 other countries. *The most frequently chosen baccalaureate fields are:* business/marketing, engineering/engineering technologies, mathematics. *Graduate:* 613 in graduate degree programs.

From out-of-state	40%	Reside on campus	43%
Age 25 or older	3%	Transferred in	2%
International students	5%	African Americans	7%
Asian Americans/Pacific Islanders	4%	Hispanic Americans	2%
Native Americans	0.2%		

Faculty 157 (89% full-time), 78% with terminal degrees.
Expenses (1999–2000) *Comprehensive fee:* $18,795 includes full-time tuition ($14,640), mandatory fees ($135), and room and board ($4020). *College room only:* $2540. Room and board charges vary according to student level. *Payment plan:* installment. *Waivers:* employees or children of employees.
Library Kettering University Library plus 1 other. *Operations spending 1999–2000:* $819,904. *Collection:* 94,738 titles, 540 serial subscriptions, 276 audiovisual materials.
College life *Housing:* on-campus residence required in freshman year. *Option:* coed. *Social organizations:* national fraternities, national sororities; 50% of eligible men and 50% of eligible women are members. *Most popular organizations:* student government, Society of Automotive Engineers, National Society of Black Engineers, outdoors club, Christians in Action.
Campus security 24-hour emergency response devices and patrols, late-night transport-escort service, controlled dormitory access.
After graduation 550 organizations recruited on campus 1997–98. 98% of class of 1998 had job offers within 6 months. *Career center:* 16 full-time personnel. Services include resume preparation, interview workshops, resume referral, career/interest testing, career counseling, job bank, job interviews, cooperative education employment services. *Graduate education:* 33% of class of 1999 went directly to graduate and professional school: 17% business, 10% engineering, 4% graduate arts and sciences, 2% law.
Freshmen 1,616 applied, 1,217 admitted, 525 enrolled. 18 valedictorians.

Average high school GPA	3.5	SAT verbal scores above 500	82%
SAT math scores above 500	100%	ACT above 18	99%
From top 10% of their h.s. class	33%	From top quarter	70%
From top half	96%	1998 freshmen returning in 1999	85%

Application *Options:* eApply at www.CollegeQuest.com, electronic application, deferred entrance. *Application fee:* $25. *Required:* essay or personal statement; high school transcript; minimum 3.0 GPA. *Recommended:* interview.
Standardized tests *Admission: Required:* SAT I or ACT. *Recommended:* SAT II Subject Tests.
Significant dates *Application deadlines:* rolling (freshmen), rolling (transfers). *Financial aid deadline priority date:* 2/14.
Freshman Application Contact
Mr. Rawlan Lillard II, Director of Admissions, Kettering University, 1700 West Third Avenue, Flint, MI 48504-4898. **Phone:** 810-762-7865. **Toll-free phone:** 800-955-4464 Ext. 7865 (in-state); 800-955-4464 (out-of-state). **Fax:** 810-762-9837. **E-mail:** admissions@kettering.edu

Visit CollegeQuest.com for information on majors offered and athletics. College video and electronic viewbook available at CollegeQuest.com.

- *See page 1876 for a narrative description.*

LAKE SUPERIOR STATE UNIVERSITY
Sault Sainte Marie, Michigan

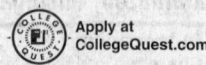

- **State-supported**, comprehensive, founded 1946
- **Degrees** associate, bachelor's, and master's
- **Small-town** 121-acre campus
- **Coed**, 2,909 undergraduate students, 84% full-time, 53% women, 47% men
- **Moderately difficult** entrance level, 75% of applicants were admitted
- **21:1 student-to-undergraduate faculty ratio**
- **37% graduate** in 6 years or less
- **$4034 tuition** and fees (in-state); $7738 (out-of-state)
- **$3382 average financial aid** package, $5.3 million endowment

Students *Undergraduates:* 2,442 full-time, 467 part-time. Students come from 20 states and territories, 12 other countries. *The most frequently chosen baccalaureate fields are:* business/marketing, engineering/engineering technologies, protective services/public administration. *Graduate:* 80 in graduate degree programs.

From out-of-state	3%	Reside on campus	29%
Age 25 or older	22%	Transferred in	8%
International students	15%	African Americans	0.3%
Asian Americans/Pacific Islanders	1%	Hispanic Americans	1%
Native Americans	7%		

Faculty 115 (100% full-time), 48% with terminal degrees.
Expenses (1999–2000) *Tuition, state resident:* full-time $3838; part-time $160 per semester hour. *Tuition, nonresident:* full-time $7542; part-time $314 per semester hour. *Required fees:* full-time $196; $98 per term part-time. Full-time tuition and fees vary according to reciprocity agreements. Part-time tuition and fees vary according to reciprocity agreements. *College room and board:* $4930; room only: $4273. Room and board charges vary according to board plan. *Waivers:* minority students, children of alumni, senior citizens, and employees or children of employees.
Library Kenneth Shouldice Library. *Operations spending 1999–2000:* $887,578. *Collection:* 112,920 titles, 714 serial subscriptions.
College life *Housing:* on-campus residence required through sophomore year. *Options:* coed, men-only, women-only. *Social organizations:* national fraternities, national sororities, local fraternities, local sororities.
Campus security 24-hour patrols, student patrols, late-night transport-escort service.
After graduation 188 organizations recruited on campus 1997–98. 80% of class of 1998 had job offers within 6 months. *Career center:* 2 full-time personnel. Services include job fairs, resume preparation, resume referral, career counseling, careers library, job interviews. *Graduate education:* 10% of class of 1999 went directly to graduate and professional school.
Freshmen 2,302 applied, 1,719 admitted, 520 enrolled.

Average high school GPA	2.99	SAT verbal scores above 500	N/R
SAT math scores above 500	N/R	ACT above 18	79%
From top 10% of their h.s. class	12%	From top quarter	31%
From top half	59%	1998 freshmen returning in 1999	65%

Application *Options:* eApply at www.CollegeQuest.com, deferred entrance. *Application fee:* $25. *Required:* high school transcript. *Required for some:* minimum 2.0 GPA.
Standardized tests *Admission: Required:* ACT.
Significant dates *Application deadlines:* 8/15 (freshmen), rolling (transfers). *Financial aid deadline:* continuous.
Freshman Application Contact
Mr. Kevin Pollock, Director of Admissions, Lake Superior State University, 650 W Easterday Avenue, Sault Sainte Marie, MI 49783-1626. **Phone:** 906-635-2670. **Toll-free phone:** 888-800-LSSU Ext. 2231. **Fax:** 906-635-6669. **E-mail:** admissions@gw.lssu.edu
Visit CollegeQuest.com for information on majors offered and athletics. College video and electronic viewbook available at CollegeQuest.com.

- *See page 1896 for a narrative description.*

Michigan

LAWRENCE TECHNOLOGICAL UNIVERSITY
Southfield, Michigan

- **Independent**, comprehensive, founded 1932
- **Degrees** associate, bachelor's, and master's
- **Suburban** 110-acre campus with easy access to Detroit
- **Coed**, 2,942 undergraduate students
- **Moderately difficult** entrance level, 82% of applicants were admitted
- **12:1** student-to-undergraduate faculty ratio
- **$10,340 tuition** and fees
- **$15,400 average indebtedness** upon graduation, $14 million endowment

Students *Undergraduates:* Students come from 39 states and territories, 34 other countries.

From out-of-state	8%	Reside on campus	9%

Expenses (1999–2000) *Tuition:* full-time $10,140; part-time $330 per credit hour. *Required fees:* full-time $200; $100 per term part-time. Full-time tuition and fees vary according to program and student level. Part-time tuition and fees vary according to program and student level. *College room only:* $2385. Room and board charges vary according to housing facility. *Payment plan:* installment. *Waivers:* employees or children of employees.

Library Lawrence Technological University Library plus 1 other. *Operations spending 1999–2000:* $600,000. *Collection:* 107,000 titles, 665 serial subscriptions.

College life *Housing: Option:* coed. *Social organizations:* national fraternities, national sororities, local sororities; 10% of eligible men and 10% of eligible women are members. *Most popular organizations:* Society of Automotive Engineers, Institute of Electric and Electronic Engineers, Michigan Society of Professional Engineers, American Institute of Architecture Students, American Society of Civil Engineers.

Campus security 24-hour patrols, late-night transport-escort service, controlled dormitory access.

After graduation 100 organizations recruited on campus 1997–98. 90% of class of 1998 had job offers within 6 months. *Career center:* 5 full-time, 2 part-time personnel. Services include job fairs, resume preparation, interview workshops, resume referral, career counseling, job bank, job interviews. *Graduate education:* 15% of class of 1999 went directly to graduate and professional school: 7% business, 7% engineering, 2% graduate arts and sciences, 0.15% law.

Freshmen 2,061 applied, 1,693 admitted.

Average high school GPA	3.2	SAT verbal scores above 500	N/R
SAT math scores above 500	N/R	ACT above 18	99%
From top 10% of their h.s. class	30%	1998 freshmen returning in 1999	75%

Application *Options:* electronic application, early admission, deferred entrance. *Application fee:* $30. *Required:* high school transcript; minimum 2.0 GPA. *Required for some:* essay or personal statement; letters of recommendation; interview. *Recommended:* essay or personal statement.

Standardized tests *Admission: Required:* SAT I or ACT.

Significant dates *Application deadlines:* 4/15 (freshmen), 8/15 (transfers). *Notification:* continuous until 8/26 (freshmen). *Financial aid deadline priority date:* 8/1.

Freshman Application Contact
Mrs. Lisa Kujawa, Director of Admissions, Lawrence Technological University, 2100 West 10 Mile Road, Southfield, MI 48075. **Phone:** 248-204-3180. **Toll-free phone:** 800-225-5588. **Fax:** 248-204-3727. **E-mail:** admissions@ltu.edu

Visit CollegeQuest.com for information on majors offered and athletics. College video available at CollegeQuest.com.

- *See page 1904 for a narrative description.*

MADONNA UNIVERSITY
Livonia, Michigan

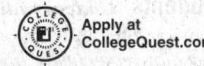 Apply at CollegeQuest.com

- **Independent Roman Catholic**, comprehensive, founded 1947
- **Degrees** associate, bachelor's, and master's
- **Suburban** 49-acre campus with easy access to Detroit
- **Coed**, 2,852 undergraduate students, 48% full-time, 77% women, 23% men
- **Moderately difficult** entrance level, 59% of applicants were admitted
- **17:1** student-to-undergraduate faculty ratio
- **45% graduate** in 6 years or less
- **$6610 tuition** and fees
- **$32 million endowment**

Students *Undergraduates:* 1,370 full-time, 1,482 part-time. Students come from 10 states and territories, 38 other countries. *The most frequently chosen baccalaureate fields are:* health professions and related sciences, business/marketing, protective services/public administration. **Graduate:** 723 in graduate degree programs.

From out-of-state	1%	Reside on campus	3%
Age 25 or older	56%	Transferred in	65%
International students	2%	African Americans	11%
Asian Americans/Pacific Islanders	1%	Hispanic Americans	2%
Native Americans	0.4%		

Faculty 274 (47% full-time), 44% with terminal degrees.

Expenses (1999–2000) *Comprehensive fee:* $11,286 includes full-time tuition ($6510), mandatory fees ($100), and room and board ($4676). *College room only:* $2526. Full-time tuition and fees vary according to course load and program. Room and board charges vary according to board plan. *Part-time tuition:* $217 per semester hour. *Part-time fees:* $50 per term part-time. Part-time tuition and fees vary according to course load and program. *Payment plan:* deferred payment. *Waivers:* employees or children of employees.

Library Madonna University Library. *Operations spending 1999–2000:* $1.3 million. *Collection:* 199,144 titles, 1,679 serial subscriptions.

College life *Housing: Option:* coed. *Social organizations:* national sororities; 2% of eligible men and 2% of eligible women are members.

Campus security 24-hour emergency response devices and patrols, late-night transport-escort service.

After graduation *Career center:* 3 full-time, 1 part-time personnel. Services include job fairs, resume preparation, interview workshops, resume referral, career/interest testing, career counseling, careers library, job bank, job interviews. *Graduate education:* 40% of class of 1999 went directly to graduate and professional school.

Freshmen 1,446 applied, 860 admitted, 246 enrolled.

Average high school GPA	3.26	SAT verbal scores above 500	N/R
SAT math scores above 500	N/R	ACT above 18	97%
From top 10% of their h.s. class	28%	From top quarter	41%
From top half	91%	1998 freshmen returning in 1999	74%

Application *Options:* eApply at www.CollegeQuest.com, early admission, deferred entrance. *Application fee:* $0. *Required:* high school transcript; minimum 2.75 GPA. *Required for some:* 2 letters of recommendation.

Standardized tests *Admission: Required:* ACT.

Significant dates *Application deadlines:* rolling (freshmen), rolling (transfers). *Financial aid deadline priority date:* 3/1.

Freshman Application Contact
Mr. Frank J. Hribar, Director of Enrollment Management, Madonna University, 36600 Schoolcraft Road, Livonia, MI 48150-1173. **Phone:** 734-432-5317. **Toll-free phone:** 800-852-4951. **Fax:** 734-432-5393. **E-mail:** muinfo@smtp.munet.edu

Visit CollegeQuest.com for information on majors offered and athletics. College video available at CollegeQuest.com.

MARYGROVE COLLEGE
Detroit, Michigan

 Apply at CollegeQuest.com

- **Independent Roman Catholic**, comprehensive, founded 1905
- **Degrees** associate, bachelor's, master's, and postbachelor's certificates
- **Urban** 50-acre campus
- **Coed,** primarily women, 853 undergraduate students, 40% full-time, 82% women, 18% men
- **Moderately difficult** entrance level, 58% of applicants were admitted
- **15:1** student-to-undergraduate faculty ratio
- **$10,375 tuition** and fees
- **$8.7 million endowment**

Students *Undergraduates:* 340 full-time, 513 part-time. Students come from 4 other countries. *The most frequently chosen baccalaureate fields are:*

Michigan

Marygrove College (continued)
business/marketing, education, protective services/public administration.

From out-of-state	2%	Reside on campus	4%
Age 25 or older	80%	Transferred in	13%

Faculty 63 (83% full-time).

Expenses (2000–2001) *Comprehensive fee:* $15,575 includes full-time tuition ($10,140), mandatory fees ($235), and room and board ($5200). *Part-time tuition:* $366 per credit. *Part-time fees:* $5 per credit; $50 per term part-time. *Payment plan:* installment. *Waivers:* senior citizens and employees or children of employees.

Library *Operations spending 1999–2000:* $400,000. *Collection:* 160,230 titles, 550 serial subscriptions.

College life *Housing:* Option: coed. *Most popular organizations:* Association of Black Social Workers, Council of Student Organization, political science club, United Brotherhood, Marygrove Business Association.

Campus security 24-hour emergency response devices and patrols, late-night transport-escort service.

After graduation *Career center:* 2 full-time, 2 part-time personnel. Services include job fairs, resume preparation, resume referral, career counseling, careers library, job bank. *Graduate education:* 35% of class of 1999 went directly to graduate and professional school: 25% graduate arts and sciences, 10% business.

Freshmen 617 applied, 358 admitted, 90 enrolled.

Average high school GPA	2.7	SAT verbal scores above 500	N/R
SAT math scores above 500	N/R	ACT above 18	N/R
1998 freshmen returning in 1999	79%		

Application *Options:* eApply at www.CollegeQuest.com, early admission, deferred entrance. *Application fee:* $25. *Required:* high school transcript; minimum 2.7 GPA. *Required for some:* letters of recommendation; interview.

Standardized tests *Admission:* Required: ACT.

Significant dates *Application deadlines:* 8/15 (freshmen), 8/15 (transfers). *Notification:* continuous until 9/1 (freshmen).

Freshman Application Contact
Ms. Carla R. Mathews, Director of Undergraduate Admissions, Marygrove College, 8425 West McNichols Road, Detroit, MI 48221-2599. **Phone:** 313-927-1240. **Fax:** 313-927-1345. **E-mail:** info@marygrove.edu

Visit CollegeQuest.com for information on majors offered and athletics. College video available at CollegeQuest.com.

■ *See page 2000 for a narrative description.*

MICHIGAN CHRISTIAN COLLEGE
Michigan—See Rochester College

MICHIGAN STATE UNIVERSITY
East Lansing, Michigan

- **State-supported**, university, founded 1855
- **Degrees** bachelor's, master's, doctoral, and first professional
- **Suburban** campus with easy access to Detroit
- **Coed**, 33,687 undergraduate students, 87% full-time, 53% women, 47% men
- **Moderately difficult** entrance level, 71% of applicants were admitted
- **18:1 student-to-undergraduate faculty ratio**
- **66% graduate** in 6 years or less
- **$5590 tuition** and fees (in-state); $12,992 (out-of-state)

Students *Undergraduates:* 29,324 full-time, 4,363 part-time. Students come from 54 states and territories, 85 other countries. *The most frequently chosen baccalaureate fields are:* business/marketing, engineering/engineering technologies, social sciences and history. *Graduate:* 1,340 in professional programs, 7,732 in other graduate degree programs.

From out-of-state	6%	Reside on campus	44%
Age 25 or older	9%	Transferred in	5%
International students	2%	African Americans	9%
Asian Americans/Pacific Islanders	4%	Hispanic Americans	2%
Native Americans	1%		

Faculty 2,518 (92% full-time), 92% with terminal degrees.

Expenses (1999–2000) *Tuition, state resident:* full-time $5004; part-time $147 per semester hour. *Tuition, nonresident:* full-time $12,406; part-time $394 per semester hour. *Required fees:* full-time $586; $241 per term part-time. Full-time tuition and fees vary according to program and student level. Part-time tuition and fees vary according to course load, program, and student level. *College room and board:* $4298; room only: $1860. Room and board charges vary according to board plan and housing facility. *Payment plans:* guaranteed tuition, deferred payment. *Waivers:* employees or children of employees.

Library Main Library plus 15 others. *Collection:* 4.2 million titles, 267,344 audiovisual materials.

College life *Housing:* on-campus residence required in freshman year. *Options:* coed, women-only, disabled students. *Social organizations:* national fraternities, national sororities; 8% of eligible men and 8% of eligible women are members.

Campus security 24-hour emergency response devices and patrols, late-night transport-escort service, self-defense workshops.

After graduation 620 organizations recruited on campus 1997–98. 80% of class of 1998 had job offers within 6 months. *Career center:* 28 full-time personnel. Services include job fairs, resume preparation, resume referral, career counseling, careers library, job interviews. *Graduate education:* 20% of class of 1999 went directly to graduate and professional school. *Major awards:* 3 Fulbright Scholars.

Freshmen 22,623 applied, 16,084 admitted, 6,716 enrolled. 150 National Merit Scholars, 100 valedictorians.

Average high school GPA	3.44	SAT verbal scores above 500	72%
SAT math scores above 500	75%	ACT above 18	95%
From top 10% of their h.s. class	23%	From top quarter	56%
From top half	91%	1998 freshmen returning in 1999	87%

Application *Options:* eApply at www.CollegeQuest.com, electronic application, deferred entrance. *Application fee:* $30. *Required:* high school transcript.

Standardized tests *Admission:* Required: SAT I or ACT.

Significant dates *Application deadlines:* 7/30 (freshmen), 7/30 (transfers). *Financial aid deadline:* 6/30. *Priority date:* 2/21.

Freshman Application Contact
Dr. Gordon Stanley, Assistant to the Provost for Enrollment and Director of Admissions, Michigan State University, East Lansing, MI 48824-1020. **Phone:** 517-355-8332. **E-mail:** admis@msu.edu

Visit CollegeQuest.com for information on majors offered and athletics. College video and electronic viewbook available at CollegeQuest.com.

■ *See page 1838 for a narrative description.*

MICHIGAN TECHNOLOGICAL UNIVERSITY
Houghton, Michigan

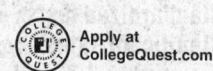

- **State-supported**, university, founded 1885
- **Degrees** associate, bachelor's, master's, and doctoral
- **Small-town** 240-acre campus
- **Coed**, 5,474 undergraduate students, 94% full-time, 26% women, 74% men
- **Moderately difficult** entrance level, 94% of applicants were admitted
- **16:1 student-to-undergraduate faculty ratio**
- **62.9% graduate** in 6 years or less
- **$4491 tuition** and fees (in-state); $10,704 (out-of-state)
- **$6397 average financial aid** package, $6397 average indebtedness upon graduation, $26.3 million endowment

Students *Undergraduates:* 5,142 full-time, 332 part-time. Students come from 43 states and territories, 63 other countries. *The most frequently chosen baccalaureate fields are:* business/marketing, computer/information sciences, engineering/engineering technologies. *Graduate:* 660 in graduate degree programs.

Michigan

From out-of-state	19%	Reside on campus	43%
Age 25 or older	9%	Transferred in	5%
International students	5%	African Americans	2%
Asian Americans/Pacific Islanders	1%	Hispanic Americans	1%
Native Americans	1%		

Faculty 395 (93% full-time), 85% with terminal degrees.
Expenses (1999–2000) *Tuition, state resident:* full-time $4365; part-time $122 per credit hour. *Tuition, nonresident:* full-time $10,578; part-time $294 per credit hour. *Required fees:* full-time $126; $42 per term part-time. Full-time tuition and fees vary according to student level. Part-time tuition and fees vary according to course load and student level. *College room and board:* $4726. Room and board charges vary according to board plan and housing facility. *Payment plan:* installment. *Waivers:* children of alumni, senior citizens, and employees or children of employees.
Library J. R. Van Pelt Library. *Operations spending 1999–2000:* $3.1 million. *Collection:* 5,149 serial subscriptions, 3,209 audiovisual materials.
College life *Housing:* on-campus residence required in freshman year. *Options:* coed, men-only, women-only. *Social organizations:* national fraternities, national sororities, local fraternities, local sororities; 85% of eligible men and 15% of eligible women are members. *Most popular organizations:* Inter-fraternity Council, Film Board, undergraduate student government, Inter-Residence Hall Council, Blue Key National Honor Fraternity.
Campus security 24-hour emergency response devices and patrols, late-night transport-escort service.
After graduation 183 organizations recruited on campus 1997–98. 91% of class of 1998 had job offers within 6 months. *Career center:* 7 full-time, 1 part-time personnel. Services include job fairs, resume preparation, resume referral, career counseling, careers library, job bank, job interviews. *Graduate education:* 20% of class of 1999 went directly to graduate and professional school.
Freshmen 2,689 applied, 2,541 admitted, 1,155 enrolled. 7 National Merit Scholars, 63 valedictorians.

Average high school GPA	3.51	SAT verbal scores above 500	83%
SAT math scores above 500	93%	ACT above 18	97%
From top 10% of their h.s. class	34%	From top quarter	64%
From top half	90%	1998 freshmen returning in 1999	82%

Application *Options:* eApply at www.CollegeQuest.com, Common Application, electronic application, deferred entrance. *Application fee:* $30. *Required:* high school transcript. *Recommended:* interview.
Standardized tests *Admission: Recommended:* SAT I or ACT.
Significant dates *Application deadlines:* rolling (freshmen), rolling (transfers). *Financial aid deadline priority date:* 2/21.
Freshman Application Contact
Ms. Nancy Rehling, Director of Undergraduate Admissions, Michigan Technological University, 1400 Townsend Drive, Houghton, MI 49931-1295. **Phone:** 906-487-2335. **Fax:** 906-487-3343. **E-mail:** mtu4u@mtu.edu
Visit CollegeQuest.com for information on majors offered and athletics. College video and electronic viewbook available at CollegeQuest.com.

NORTHERN MICHIGAN UNIVERSITY
Marquette, Michigan

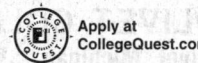
Apply at CollegeQuest.com

- **State-supported**, comprehensive, founded 1899
- **Degrees** associate, bachelor's, and master's
- **Small-town** 300-acre campus
- **Coed**, 7,254 undergraduate students, 85% full-time, 54% women, 46% men
- **Minimally difficult** entrance level, 86% of applicants were admitted
- **20:1 student-to-undergraduate faculty ratio**
- **$3146 tuition** and fees (in-state); $5582 (out-of-state)
- **$14.5 million endowment**

Part of Michigan Department of Education.
Students *Undergraduates:* Students come from 46 states and territories, 36 other countries. *Graduate:* 838 in graduate degree programs.

| From out-of-state | 14% | Reside on campus | 30% |
| Age 25 or older | 16% | | |

Faculty 338 (87% full-time), 80% with terminal degrees.
Expenses (1999–2000) *Tuition, state resident:* full-time $2772; part-time $116 per credit hour. *Tuition, nonresident:* full-time $5208; part-time $217 per credit hour. *Required fees:* full-time $374; $115 per term part-time. Part-time tuition and fees vary according to course load. *College room and board:* $4640; room only: $2242. Room and board charges vary according to housing facility. *Payment plan:* installment. *Waivers:* children of alumni, senior citizens, and employees or children of employees.
Library Lydia Olson Library plus 1 other. *Operations spending 1999–2000:* $2.2 million. *Collection:* 514,168 titles.
College life *Housing:* on-campus residence required through sophomore year. *Options:* coed, disabled students. *Social organizations:* national fraternities, national sororities; 2% of eligible men and 2% of eligible women are members. *Most popular organizations:* Associated Students of Northern Michigan University, Platform Personalities, campus cinema, Northern Arts and Entertainment, Student Leader Fellowship Program.
Campus security 24-hour emergency response devices and patrols, student patrols, late-night transport-escort service.
After graduation 74% of class of 1998 had job offers within 6 months. *Career center:* 6 full-time, 1 part-time personnel. Services include job fairs, resume preparation, interview workshops, resume referral, career/interest testing, career counseling, careers library, job bank, job interviews.
Freshmen 3,619 applied, 3,098 admitted. 19 National Merit Scholars, 10 valedictorians.

Average high school GPA	2.85	SAT verbal scores above 500	N/R
SAT math scores above 500	N/R	ACT above 18	90%
1998 freshmen returning in 1999	69%		

Application *Options:* eApply at www.CollegeQuest.com, Common Application, electronic application, deferred entrance. *Application fee:* $25. *Required:* high school transcript. *Required for some:* minimum 2.25 GPA.
Standardized tests *Admission: Required:* SAT I or ACT.
Significant dates *Application deadlines:* rolling (freshmen), rolling (transfers). *Notification:* 6/1 (freshmen). *Financial aid deadline priority date:* 2/21.
Freshman Application Contact
Ms. Gerri Daniels, Northern Michigan University, 304 Cohodas, Marquette, MI 49855-5301. **Phone:** 906-227-2650. **Toll-free phone:** 800-682-9797 Ext. 1 (in-state); 800-682-9797 (out-of-state). **Fax:** 906-227-1747. **E-mail:** admiss@nmu.edu
Visit CollegeQuest.com for information on majors offered and athletics. College video available at CollegeQuest.com.

NORTHWOOD UNIVERSITY
Midland, Michigan

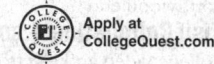
Apply at CollegeQuest.com

- **Independent**, comprehensive, founded 1959
- **Degrees** associate, bachelor's, and master's
- **Small-town** 434-acre campus
- **Coed**, 3,190 undergraduate students, 60% full-time, 47% women, 53% men
- **Moderately difficult** entrance level, 93% of applicants were admitted
- **26:1 student-to-undergraduate faculty ratio**
- **$11,625 tuition** and fees
- **$42 million system endowment**

Exciting programs: a major in international business; an honors program for the most capable students; automotive aftermarket management and hotel, restaurant, and resort management majors at the BBA and associate degree levels; new health-care management curriculum. Through the EXCEL Program, students participate in valuable, documentable activities and receive a Student Development Transcript in addition to an academic transcript. Potential employers of Northwood graduates see the experiences, attitudes, and leadership abilities gained by these students.

Students *Undergraduates:* 1,925 full-time, 1,265 part-time. Students come from 23 states and territories, 32 other countries. *The most frequently chosen baccalaureate fields are:* business/marketing, computer/information sciences. *Graduate:* 183 in graduate degree programs.

Peterson's Guide to Four-Year Colleges 2001 www.petersons.com

Michigan

Northwood University (continued)

From out-of-state	19%	Reside on campus	53%
Age 25 or older	3%	Transferred in	7%
International students	6%	African Americans	7%
Asian Americans/Pacific Islanders	0.3%	Hispanic Americans	1%
Native Americans	0.2%		

Faculty 103 (44% full-time).

Expenses (1999–2000) *Comprehensive fee:* $16,833 includes full-time tuition ($11,325), mandatory fees ($300), and room and board ($5208). Room and board charges vary according to board plan. *Part-time tuition:* $235 per credit hour. Part-time tuition and fees vary according to course load. *Payment plan:* installment. *Waivers:* children of alumni and employees or children of employees.

Library Strosacker Library. *Operations spending 1999–2000:* $371,526. *Collection:* 45,913 titles, 410 serial subscriptions.

College life *Housing:* on-campus residence required in freshman year. *Options:* men-only, women-only. *Social organizations:* national fraternities, national sororities, local fraternities, local sororities. *Most popular organizations:* fraternities/sororities, student senate, intramural sports.

Campus security 24-hour emergency response devices and patrols.

After graduation 81 organizations recruited on campus 1997–98. 97% of class of 1998 had job offers within 6 months. *Career center:* 2 full-time personnel. Services include job fairs, resume preparation, interview workshops, resume referral, career/interest testing, career counseling, careers library, job bank, job interviews. *Graduate education:* 4% of class of 1999 went directly to graduate and professional school.

Freshmen 1,186 applied, 1,099 admitted, 463 enrolled. 12 valedictorians.

Average high school GPA	2.9	SAT verbal scores above 500	25%
SAT math scores above 500	38%	ACT above 18	90%
From top 10% of their h.s. class	8%	From top quarter	28%
From top half	60%	1998 freshmen returning in 1999	76%

Application *Options:* eApply at www.CollegeQuest.com, Common Application, electronic application, early admission, deferred entrance. *Application fee:* $15. *Required:* high school transcript. *Recommended:* essay or personal statement; minimum 2.0 GPA; 1 letter of recommendation; interview.

Standardized tests *Admission: Required:* SAT I or ACT.

Significant dates *Application deadlines:* rolling (freshmen), rolling (transfers). *Financial aid deadline:* continuous.

Freshman Application Contact Dr. David D. Long, University Dean of Enrollment Management, Northwood University, 4000 Whiting Drive, Midland, MI 48640. **Phone:** 517-837-4273. **Toll-free phone:** 800-457-7878. **Fax:** 517-837-4104. **E-mail:** admissions@northwood.edu

Visit CollegeQuest.com for information on majors offered and athletics. College video and electronic viewbook available at CollegeQuest.com.

■ *See page 2194 for a narrative description.*

OAKLAND UNIVERSITY
Rochester, Michigan

- **State-supported**, university, founded 1957
- **Degrees** bachelor's, master's, doctoral, post-master's, and postbachelor's certificates
- **Suburban** 1,444-acre campus with easy access to Detroit
- **Coed**, 11,037 undergraduate students, 68% full-time, 65% women, 35% men
- **Moderately difficult** entrance level, 75% of applicants were admitted
- **18:1 student-to-undergraduate faculty ratio**
- **41% graduate** in 6 years or less
- **$4292 tuition** and fees (in-state); $11,686 (out-of-state)
- **$5750 average financial aid** package, $25.7 million endowment

Students *Undergraduates:* 7,516 full-time, 3,521 part-time. Students come from 34 states and territories, 56 other countries. *The most frequently chosen baccalaureate fields are:* business/marketing, education, health professions and related sciences. *Graduate:* 3,040 in graduate degree programs.

From out-of-state	2%	Reside on campus	11%
Age 25 or older	28%	Transferred in	11%
International students	2%	African Americans	7%
Asian Americans/Pacific Islanders	3%	Hispanic Americans	1%
Native Americans	0.5%		

Expenses (1999–2000) *Tuition, state resident:* full-time $3864; part-time $119 per credit hour. *Tuition, nonresident:* full-time $11,258; part-time $350 per credit hour. *Required fees:* full-time $428; $214 per term part-time. Full-time tuition and fees vary according to program and student level. Part-time tuition and fees vary according to program and student level. *College room and board:* $4715. Room and board charges vary according to housing facility. *Payment plans:* installment, deferred payment. *Waivers:* employees or children of employees.

Library Kresge Library plus 1 other. *Operations spending 1999–2000:* $3.3 million. *Collection:* 640,000 titles, 2,104 serial subscriptions.

College life *Housing:* on-campus residence required in freshman year. *Options:* coed, disabled students. *Social organizations:* national fraternities, national sororities, local fraternities, local sororities; 1% of eligible men and 2% of eligible women are members. *Most popular organizations:* Golden Key National Honor Society, Association of Black Students, Order of Leibowitz, Greek Council, Lutheran Students Fellowship.

Campus security 24-hour emergency response devices and patrols, student patrols, late-night transport-escort service.

After graduation 124 organizations recruited on campus 1997–98. 79% of class of 1998 had job offers within 6 months. *Career center:* 12 full-time, 1 part-time personnel. Services include job fairs, resume preparation, interview workshops, resume referral, career counseling, careers library, job bank, job interviews. *Graduate education:* 16% of class of 1999 went directly to graduate and professional school.

Freshmen 4,966 applied, 3,722 admitted, 1,813 enrolled.

Average high school GPA	3.1	SAT verbal scores above 500	N/R
SAT math scores above 500	N/R	ACT above 18	88%
1998 freshmen returning in 1999	75%		

Application *Options:* Common Application, electronic application, early action, deferred entrance. *Application fee:* $25. *Required:* high school transcript; minimum 2.5 GPA. *Required for some:* minimum 3.0 GPA; letters of recommendation; interview.

Standardized tests *Admission: Required:* ACT.

Significant dates *Application deadlines:* 8/28 (freshmen), 8/28 (transfers). *Financial aid deadline priority date:* 4/1.

Freshman Application Contact Mr. Robert E. Johnson, Associate Vice President for Enrollment Management, Oakland University, 101 North Foundation Hall, Rochester, MI 48309-4401. **Phone:** 248-370-3360. **Toll-free phone:** 800-OAK-UNIV. **Fax:** 248-370-4462. **E-mail:** ouinfo@oakland.edu

Visit CollegeQuest.com for information on majors offered and athletics. College video available at CollegeQuest.com.

■ *See page 2206 for a narrative description.*

OLIVET COLLEGE
Olivet, Michigan

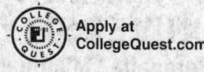
Apply at CollegeQuest.com

- **Independent**, comprehensive, founded 1844, affiliated with Congregational Christian Church
- **Degrees** bachelor's and master's
- **Small-town** 92-acre campus
- **Coed**
- **Moderately difficult** entrance level
- **$13,158 tuition** and fees

Expenses (1999–2000) *Comprehensive fee:* $17,410 includes full-time tuition ($12,948), mandatory fees ($210), and room and board ($4252). *College room only:* $2264. Room and board charges vary according to board plan and housing facility. *Part-time tuition:* $460 per semester hour. *Part-time fees:* $105 per term part-time. Part-time tuition and fees vary according to course load.

Institutional Web site http://www.olivetnet.edu/

College life *Housing:* on-campus residence required through junior year. *Options:* coed, men-only, women-only. *Social organizations:* local fraternities, local sororities; 15% of eligible men and 15% of eligible women are

Michigan

members. *Most popular organizations:* Campus Activities Board, Black Student Union, international club, non-traditional student organization, Omicron Delta Kappa.

Campus security 24-hour emergency response devices and patrols, late-night transport-escort service.

Application *Options:* eApply at www.CollegeQuest.com, Common Application, electronic application, deferred entrance. *Application fee:* $25. *Required:* high school transcript. *Required for some:* essay or personal statement; letters of recommendation. *Recommended:* minimum 2.6 GPA; interview.

Standardized tests *Admission: Recommended:* SAT I or ACT.

Admissions Office Contact
Olivet College, 320 South Main Street, Olivet, MI 49076-9701. **Toll-free phone:** 800-456-7189. **Fax:** 616-749-3821. **E-mail:** admissions@olivetnet.edu

Visit CollegeQuest.com for information on athletics.

REFORMED BIBLE COLLEGE
Grand Rapids, Michigan

- **Independent religious**, 4-year, founded 1939
- **Degrees** associate and bachelor's
- **Suburban** 27-acre campus
- **Coed**, 301 undergraduate students
- **Moderately difficult** entrance level
- **10:1 student-to-undergraduate faculty ratio**
- **$7371 tuition** and fees

Reformed Bible College is dedicated to improving the spiritual lives of students and preparing them for careers in Christian service. The College is an interdenominational college with students of various ages from around the world. Each semester, students are involved in practical field education as well as their class work. Reformed Bible College offers associate and bachelor's degrees. The College was established in 1939 and is located on a 27-acre suburban campus.

Students *Undergraduates:* Students come from 18 states and territories. *The most frequently chosen baccalaureate field is:* philosophy.

Reside on campus	40%	Age 25 or older	36%
International students	1%	African Americans	4%
Asian Americans/Pacific Islanders	1%	Hispanic Americans	1%
Native Americans	1%		

Faculty 23 (52% full-time), 35% with terminal degrees.

Expenses (1999–2000) *Comprehensive fee:* $11,471 includes full-time tuition ($7150), mandatory fees ($221), and room and board ($4100). *Part-time tuition:* $298 per credit. *Part-time fees:* $34 per term part-time. Part-time tuition and fees vary according to course load. *Payment plan:* deferred payment. *Waivers:* employees or children of employees.

Library Zondervan Library. *Operations spending 1999–2000:* $123,000. *Collection:* 53,000 titles, 210 serial subscriptions.

College life On-campus residence required through sophomore year. *Most popular organizations:* Bible study and prayer groups, Student Council, yearbook, Student Activities, Wellspring drama club.

Campus security Student patrols, controlled dormitory access.

After graduation 105 organizations recruited on campus 1997–98. *Career center:* 1 full-time, 1 part-time personnel. Services include job fairs, resume preparation, career counseling, careers library.

Freshmen

Average high school GPA	2.81	SAT verbal scores above 500	N/R
SAT math scores above 500	N/R	ACT above 18	N/R
From top 10% of their h.s. class	20%	From top quarter	28%
From top half	57%	1998 freshmen returning in 1999	92%

Application *Options:* eApply at www.CollegeQuest.com, Common Application, deferred entrance. *Application fee:* $25. *Required:* essay or personal statement; high school transcript; minimum 2.5 GPA; 2 letters of recommendation; interview.

Standardized tests *Admission: Required:* SAT I or ACT.

Significant dates *Application deadlines:* rolling (freshmen), rolling (transfers). *Financial aid deadline priority date:* 2/15.

Freshman Application Contact
Ms. Sarah Couwenhoven Behm, Associate Director of Admissions, Reformed Bible College, 333 East Beltline North East, Grand Rapids, MI 49525. **Phone:** 616-222-3000 Ext. 631. **Fax:** 616-222-3045. **E-mail:** admissions@reformed.edu

Visit CollegeQuest.com for information on majors offered and athletics.

ROCHESTER COLLEGE
Rochester Hills, Michigan

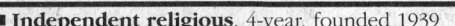

- **Independent**, 4-year, founded 1959, affiliated with Church of Christ
- **Degrees** associate and bachelor's
- **Suburban** 83-acre campus with easy access to Detroit
- **Coed**, 550 undergraduate students, 72% full-time, 48% women, 52% men
- **Minimally difficult** entrance level
- **$8304 tuition** and fees

Students *Undergraduates:* 397 full-time, 153 part-time. Students come from 25 states and territories, 11 other countries. *The most frequently chosen baccalaureate fields are:* business/marketing, English, psychology.

From out-of-state	17%	Reside on campus	63%
Age 25 or older	10%	Transferred in	10%
International students	5%	African Americans	11%
Asian Americans/Pacific Islanders	1%	Hispanic Americans	1%
Native Americans	0.2%		

Faculty 66 (42% full-time), 39% with terminal degrees.

Expenses (1999–2000) *Comprehensive fee:* $12,720 includes full-time tuition ($7808), mandatory fees ($496), and room and board ($4416). *Part-time tuition:* $244 per credit hour. *Part-time fees:* $108 per term part-time. Part-time tuition and fees vary according to course load. *Payment plan:* installment. *Waivers:* children of alumni, senior citizens, and employees or children of employees.

Library Muirhead Library. *Collection:* 41,234 titles, 285 serial subscriptions, 459 audiovisual materials.

College life *Housing:* on-campus residence required through junior year. *Options:* men-only, women-only. *Social organizations:* social clubs.

Campus security 24-hour emergency response devices, evening security guards.

After graduation 85% of class of 1998 had job offers within 6 months. *Career center:* 1 part-time personnel. Services include job fairs, resume preparation, career/interest testing, career counseling, careers library, job bank. *Graduate education:* 11% of class of 1999 went directly to graduate and professional school.

Freshmen 108 enrolled.

SAT verbal scores above 500	N/R	SAT math scores above 500	N/R
ACT above 18	N/R		

Application *Options:* eApply at www.CollegeQuest.com, early admission, deferred entrance. *Application fee:* $25. *Required:* high school transcript. *Required for some:* interview. *Recommended:* essay or personal statement; minimum 2.25 GPA.

Standardized tests *Admission: Required:* SAT I and SAT II or ACT.

Significant dates *Application deadlines:* rolling (freshmen), rolling (transfers). *Financial aid deadline priority date:* 3/1.

Freshman Application Contact
Mr. Larry Norman, Vice President for Enrollment Management, Rochester College, 800 West Avon Road, Rochester Hills, MI 48307-2764. **Phone:** 248-218-2032. **Toll-free phone:** 800-521-6010. **Fax:** 248-218-2005. **E-mail:** admissions@rc.edu

Visit CollegeQuest.com for information on majors offered and athletics.

SACRED HEART MAJOR SEMINARY
Detroit, Michigan

- **Independent Roman Catholic**, comprehensive, founded 1919
- **Degrees** associate, bachelor's, master's, and first professional
- **Urban** 24-acre campus
- **Coed**, 30 undergraduate students, 100% full-time, 99.9% women, 100% men
- **Moderately difficult** entrance level, 100% of applicants were admitted

Michigan

Sacred Heart Major Seminary (continued)
- 8:1 student-to-undergraduate faculty ratio
- $6114 tuition and fees
- $2.3 million endowment

Students *Undergraduates:* 30 full-time. Students come from 3 states and territories, 2 other countries. *The most frequently chosen baccalaureate field is:* philosophy. *Graduate:* 48 in professional programs, 52 in other graduate degree programs.

From out-of-state	6%	Age 25 or older	40%
Transferred in	27%	Asian Americans/Pacific Islanders	10%
Hispanic Americans	10%	Native Americans	7%

Faculty 32 (47% full-time), 78% with terminal degrees.
Expenses (1999–2000) *Comprehensive fee:* $10,504 includes full-time tuition ($6074), mandatory fees ($40), and room and board ($4390). Full-time tuition and fees vary according to course load. *Part-time tuition:* $192 per credit. *Part-time fees:* $20 per term part-time. Part-time tuition and fees vary according to course load. *Payment plans:* installment, deferred payment. *Waivers:* employees or children of employees.
Library Szoka Library. *Operations spending 1999–2000:* $268,145. *Collection:* 120,000 titles, 495 serial subscriptions.
Campus security 24-hour emergency response devices, late-night transport-escort service.
After graduation *Graduate education:* 100% of class of 1999 went directly to graduate and professional school: 100% theology.
Freshmen 8 applied, 8 admitted, 8 enrolled.

SAT verbal scores above 500	N/R	SAT math scores above 500	N/R
ACT above 18	N/R	From top half of their h.s. class	100%
1998 freshmen returning in 1999	100%		

Application *Option:* deferred entrance. *Preference* given to candidates for the priesthood. *Application fee:* $30. *Required:* essay or personal statement; high school transcript; minimum 2.0 GPA; 1 letter of recommendation; interview.
Significant dates *Application deadlines:* 7/31 (freshmen), 7/31 (transfers). *Notification:* continuous until 8/15 (freshmen). *Financial aid deadline priority date:* 4/1.
Freshman Application Contact
Rev. Earl Boyea, Dean of Studies, Sacred Heart Major Seminary, 2701 Chicago Boulevard, Detroit, MI 48206. **Phone:** 313-883-8556.
Visit CollegeQuest.com for information on majors offered and athletics.

SAGINAW VALLEY STATE UNIVERSITY
University Center, Michigan

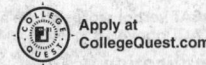
Apply at CollegeQuest.com

- **State-supported**, comprehensive, founded 1963
- **Degrees** bachelor's, master's, and post-master's certificates
- **Rural** 782-acre campus
- **Coed**, 6,107 undergraduate students, 68% full-time, 59% women, 41% men
- **Moderately difficult** entrance level, 97% of applicants were admitted
- 19:1 student-to-undergraduate faculty ratio
- 30% graduate in 6 years or less
- $3512 tuition and fees (in-state); $7051 (out-of-state)
- $16.8 million endowment

Students *Undergraduates:* 4,183 full-time, 1,924 part-time. Students come from 17 states and territories, 48 other countries. *The most frequently chosen baccalaureate fields are:* business/marketing, education, protective services/public administration. *Graduate:* 1,512 in graduate degree programs.

From out-of-state	1%	Reside on campus	14%
Age 25 or older	29%	Transferred in	10%
International students	2%	African Americans	7%
Asian Americans/Pacific Islanders	1%	Hispanic Americans	3%
Native Americans	1%		

Faculty 497 (43% full-time), 35% with terminal degrees.
Expenses (1999–2000) *Tuition, state resident:* full-time $3243; part-time $108 per credit hour. *Tuition, nonresident:* full-time $6782; part-time $226 per credit hour. *Required fees:* full-time $269; $9 per credit hour. Full-time tuition and fees vary according to course load, location, and program. Part-time tuition and fees vary according to course load, location, and program. *College room and board:* $4800. Room and board charges vary according to board plan and housing facility. *Payment plan:* installment. *Waivers:* employees or children of employees.
Library Zahnow Library. *Operations spending 1999–2000:* $1.5 million. *Collection:* 3,119 serial subscriptions, 19,231 audiovisual materials.
College life *Housing: Options:* coed, disabled students. *Social organizations:* national fraternities, national sororities; 5% of eligible men and 5% of eligible women are members. *Most popular organizations:* Alpha Sigma Alpha, biology club, Alpha Psi Omega, Phi Beta Sigma, Resident Hall Association.
Campus security 24-hour emergency response devices, late-night transport-escort service, controlled dormitory access, rape prevention program.
After graduation 12 organizations recruited on campus 1997–98. *Career center:* 1 full-time personnel. Services include job fairs, resume preparation, interview workshops, resume referral, career/interest testing, career counseling, careers library, job bank, job interviews.
Freshmen 2,373 applied, 2,307 admitted, 1,083 enrolled. 11 valedictorians.

Average high school GPA	3.11	SAT verbal scores above 500	N/R
SAT math scores above 500	N/R	ACT above 18	78%
1998 freshmen returning in 1999	52%		

Application *Options:* eApply at www.CollegeQuest.com, deferred entrance. *Application fee:* $25. *Required:* high school transcript. *Recommended:* minimum 2.5 GPA.
Standardized tests *Admission: Required:* SAT I or ACT.
Significant dates *Application deadlines:* rolling (freshmen), rolling (transfers). *Financial aid deadline priority date:* 2/14.
Freshman Application Contact
Mr. James P. Dwyer, Director of Admissions, Saginaw Valley State University, 7400 Bay Road, University Center, MI 48710. **Phone:** 517-790-4200. **Toll-free phone:** 800-968-9500. **Fax:** 517-790-0180. **E-mail:** admissions@svsu.edu
Visit CollegeQuest.com for information on majors offered and athletics.

SAINT MARY'S COLLEGE
Orchard Lake, Michigan

- **Independent Roman Catholic**, 4-year, founded 1885
- **Degree** bachelor's
- **Suburban** 120-acre campus with easy access to Detroit
- **Coed**, 381 undergraduate students, 50% full-time, 40% women, 60% men
- **Moderately difficult** entrance level, 61% of applicants were admitted
- 14:1 student-to-undergraduate faculty ratio
- $7524 tuition and fees

Students *Undergraduates:* 191 full-time, 190 part-time. Students come from 5 states and territories, 11 other countries. *The most frequently chosen baccalaureate fields are:* biological/life sciences, communications/communication technologies, psychology.

From out-of-state	2%	Reside on campus	18%
Age 25 or older	32%	Transferred in	14%
International students	29%	African Americans	8%
Asian Americans/Pacific Islanders	1%	Hispanic Americans	1%
Native Americans	1%		

Faculty 46 (24% full-time), 59% with terminal degrees.
Expenses (1999–2000) *Comprehensive fee:* $12,024 includes full-time tuition ($7380), mandatory fees ($144), and room and board ($4500). *College room only:* $1900. Full-time tuition and fees vary according to course load. Room and board charges vary according to board plan and housing facility. *Part-time tuition:* $246 per credit hour. Part-time tuition and fees vary according to course load. *Payment plan:* installment. *Waivers:* employees or children of employees.
Library Alumni Memorial Library. *Operations spending 1999–2000:* $158,450. *Collection:* 68,000 titles, 450 serial subscriptions.
College life *Housing: Options:* men-only, women-only. *Most popular organizations:* drama club, campus ministry, student government, Galicja (dance ensemble).
Campus security 24-hour emergency response devices, security patrols until 2 a.m.

412   www.petersons.com   *Peterson's Guide to Four-Year Colleges 2001*

Michigan

After graduation *Career center:* 1 full-time, 1 part-time personnel. Services include resume preparation, interview workshops, resume referral, career/interest testing, career counseling, careers library, job bank, job interviews.
Freshmen 228 applied, 138 admitted, 176 enrolled. 1 valedictorian, 2 student government officers.

Average high school GPA	2.71	SAT verbal scores above 500	N/R
SAT math scores above 500	N/R	ACT above 18	60%
From top 10% of their h.s. class	5%	From top quarter	70%
From top half	94%		

Application *Option:* early admission. *Application fee:* $25. *Required:* essay or personal statement; high school transcript. *Required for some:* interview. *Recommended:* 2 letters of recommendation.
Standardized tests *Admission: Required:* SAT I or ACT. *Recommended:* SAT II Subject Tests.
Significant dates *Application deadlines:* rolling (freshmen), rolling (transfers). *Financial aid deadline:* 4/30. *Priority date:* 2/21.
Freshman Application Contact
Mr. James Bass, Director of Admissions, Saint Mary's College, 3535 Indian Trail, Orchard Lake, MI 48324-1623. **Phone:** 248-683-0523. **Toll-free phone:** 877-252 Ext. 3131. **E-mail:** jbass@stmarys.ols.edu
Visit CollegeQuest.com for information on majors offered and athletics. College video available at CollegeQuest.com.

■ *See page 2410 for a narrative description.*

SIENA HEIGHTS UNIVERSITY
Adrian, Michigan

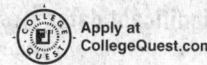 Apply at CollegeQuest.com

- **Independent Roman Catholic**, comprehensive, founded 1919
- **Degrees** associate, bachelor's, and master's
- **Small-town** 140-acre campus with easy access to Detroit
- **Coed**, 1,662 undergraduate students, 47% full-time, 64% women, 36% men
- **Moderately difficult** entrance level, 79% of applicants were admitted
- **41% graduate** in 6 years or less
- **$12,400 tuition** and fees

Siena Heights University students integrate liberal arts and career preparation. Rooted in the heritage and mission of the University, the curriculum reflects a strong commitment to interdisciplinary learning and emphasizes the mixture of theoretical and experiential knowledge. Through internships and special programs, students apply career skills prior to graduation.

Students *Undergraduates:* 785 full-time, 877 part-time. Students come from 8 states and territories. *The most frequently chosen baccalaureate fields are:* business/marketing, education, health professions and related sciences. *Graduate:* 235 in graduate degree programs.

Reside on campus	33%	Age 25 or older	51%
Transferred in	4%	International students	0.2%
African Americans	8%	Asian Americans/Pacific Islanders	1%
Hispanic Americans	2%	Native Americans	0.3%

Faculty 72 full-time.
Expenses (2000–2001) *Comprehensive fee:* $16,902 includes full-time tuition ($12,100), mandatory fees ($300), and room and board ($4502). Room and board charges vary according to board plan and housing facility. *Part-time tuition:* $307 per credit. *Part-time fees:* $75 per term part-time. Part-time tuition and fees vary according to course load. *Payment plans:* installment, deferred payment. *Waivers:* children of alumni, senior citizens, and employees or children of employees.
Library *Collection:* 120,407 titles, 451 serial subscriptions.
College life *Housing:* on-campus residence required through sophomore year. *Option:* coed. *Social organizations:* national fraternities, national sororities, local fraternities, local sororities; 5% of eligible men and 5% of eligible women are members. *Most popular organizations:* Student Programming Association, Residence Hall Counsel, Student Senate, Siena Heights African American Knowledge Association, Greek Council.
Campus security 24-hour patrols, student patrols, late-night transport-escort service.

After graduation 55 organizations recruited on campus 1997–98. 98% of class of 1998 had job offers within 6 months. *Career center:* 2 full-time personnel. Services include job fairs, resume preparation, interview workshops, resume referral, career/interest testing, career counseling, careers library, job bank, job interviews. *Graduate education:* 9% of class of 1999 went directly to graduate and professional school.
Freshmen 620 applied, 487 admitted, 218 enrolled. 6 valedictorians.

Average high school GPA	3.1	SAT verbal scores above 500	N/R
SAT math scores above 500	N/R	ACT above 18	88%
From top 10% of their h.s. class	22%	From top quarter	31%
From top half	71%	1998 freshmen returning in 1999	70%

Application *Options:* eApply at www.CollegeQuest.com, Common Application, electronic application, deferred entrance. *Application fee:* $25. *Required:* high school transcript. *Required for some:* essay or personal statement; letters of recommendation; interview. *Recommended:* minimum 2.3 GPA; interview.
Standardized tests *Admission: Required:* SAT I or ACT.
Significant dates *Application deadlines:* rolling (freshmen), rolling (transfers). *Financial aid deadline priority date:* 3/15.
Freshman Application Contact
Mr. Kevin Kucera, Dean of Admissions and Enrollment Services, Siena Heights University, 1247 East Siena Heights Drive, Adrian, MI 49221-1796. **Phone:** 517-264-7180. **Toll-free phone:** 800-521-0009. **Fax:** 517-264-7745. **E-mail:** admissions@sienahts.edu
Visit CollegeQuest.com for information on majors offered and athletics. College video available at CollegeQuest.com.

■ *See page 2488 for a narrative description.*

SPRING ARBOR COLLEGE
Spring Arbor, Michigan

- **Independent Free Methodist**, comprehensive, founded 1873
- **Degrees** associate, bachelor's, and master's
- **Small-town** 70-acre campus
- **Coed**, 2,139 undergraduate students, 83% full-time, 67% women, 33% men
- **Moderately difficult** entrance level, 88% of applicants were admitted
- **16:1 student-to-undergraduate faculty ratio**
- **47% graduate** in 6 years or less
- **$11,706 tuition** and fees

Students *Undergraduates:* 1,774 full-time, 365 part-time. Students come from 8 other countries. *The most frequently chosen baccalaureate fields are:* business/marketing, education, social sciences and history. *Graduate:* 295 in graduate degree programs.

From out-of-state	11%	Reside on campus	52%
Age 25 or older	24%	Transferred in	4%
International students	1%	African Americans	14%
Asian Americans/Pacific Islanders	1%	Hispanic Americans	1%
Native Americans	0.3%		

Faculty 76 (71% full-time).
Expenses (1999–2000) *Comprehensive fee:* $16,166 includes full-time tuition ($11,600), mandatory fees ($106), and room and board ($4460). *Part-time tuition:* $215 per credit. *Part-time fees:* $25 per term part-time. Part-time tuition and fees vary according to course load. *Payment plans:* installment, deferred payment. *Waivers:* senior citizens and employees or children of employees.
Library Hugh A. White Library. *Collection:* 84,225 titles, 5,120 audiovisual materials.
College life *Housing:* on-campus residence required through senior year. *Options:* men-only, women-only, disabled students. *Most popular organizations:* Action Jackson, Cougarettes, Multicultural Organization.
Campus security Late-night transport-escort service.
After graduation *Career center:* 2 full-time, 4 part-time personnel. Services include job fairs, resume preparation, career counseling, careers library, job bank, job interviews. *Graduate education:* 12% of class of 1999 went directly to graduate and professional school.

Michigan

Spring Arbor College (continued)

Freshmen 597 applied, 527 admitted, 185 enrolled.

Average high school GPA	3.3	SAT verbal scores above 500	N/R
SAT math scores above 500	N/R	ACT above 18	84%
From top 10% of their h.s. class	19%	From top quarter	45%
From top half	77%	1998 freshmen returning in 1999	80%

Application *Options:* early admission, deferred entrance. *Application fee:* $15. *Required:* high school transcript. *Required for some:* letters of recommendation. *Recommended:* essay or personal statement; interview; guidance counselor's evaluation form.

Standardized tests *Admission: Required:* SAT I or ACT.

Significant dates *Application deadlines:* rolling (freshmen), rolling (transfers). *Financial aid deadline priority date:* 2/15.

Freshman Application Contact
Mr. Jim Weidman, Director of Admissions, Spring Arbor College, 106 East Main Street, Spring Arbor, MI 49283-9799. **Phone:** 517-750-1200 Ext. 1475. **Toll-free phone:** 800-968-0011. **Fax:** 517-750-1604. **E-mail:** shellya@admin.arbor.edu

Visit CollegeQuest.com for information on majors offered and athletics. College video available at CollegeQuest.com.

■ *See page 2526 for a narrative description.*

SUOMI COLLEGE
Michigan—See Finlandia University

UNIVERSITY OF DETROIT MERCY
Detroit, Michigan

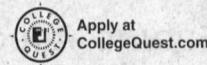
Apply at CollegeQuest.com

- **Independent Roman Catholic (Jesuit)**, university, founded 1877
- **Degrees** associate, bachelor's, master's, doctoral, first professional, post-master's, and postbachelor's certificates
- **Urban** 70-acre campus
- **Coed**, 3,514 undergraduate students, 60% full-time, 64% women, 36% men
- **Moderately difficult** entrance level, 77% of applicants were admitted
- **16:1 student-to-undergraduate faculty ratio**
- **48.3% graduate** in 6 years or less
- **$14,332 tuition** and fees

The University of Detroit Mercy, a Catholic university in the Jesuit and Mercy traditions, provides excellent student-centered undergraduate and graduate education in an urban context. Detroit is surrounded by thousands of exciting sports, music and entertainment venues, museums and art galleries, and restaurants and pubs. UDM's urban location allows faculty members and students to partner with leaders in the health-care, business, and automotive industries. With one of the oldest cooperative education programs in the nation, UDM students can earn professional experience (and a professional paycheck) during the undergraduate experience. UDM professors are not only accessible but also proactive in getting to know their students. UDM's comfortably safe campus in an urban setting is the perfect place for students who value a real-world experience with all the benefits of an attentive faculty. Generous academic scholarships and financial aid packages are available.

Students *Undergraduates:* 2,101 full-time, 1,413 part-time. Students come from 27 states and territories, 21 other countries. *The most frequently chosen baccalaureate fields are:* business/marketing, engineering/engineering technologies, health professions and related sciences. *Graduate:* 663 in professional programs, 1,617 in other graduate degree programs.

From out-of-state	4%	Reside on campus	21%
Age 25 or older	47%	Transferred in	11%
International students	2%	African Americans	36%
Asian Americans/Pacific Islanders	2%	Hispanic Americans	3%
Native Americans	1%		

Faculty 407 (73% full-time).

Expenses (1999–2000) *One-time required fee:* $694. *Comprehensive fee:* $19,802 includes full-time tuition ($14,100), mandatory fees ($232), and room and board ($5470). *College room only:* $3300. Full-time tuition and fees vary according to program. Room and board charges vary according to board plan and housing facility. *Part-time tuition:* $350 per credit hour. *Part-time fees:* $83 per term part time. Part-time tuition and fees vary according to program. *Payment plans:* installment, deferred payment. *Waivers:* children of alumni, senior citizens, and employees or children of employees.

Library McNichols Campus Library plus 3 others. *Collection:* 9,340 serial subscriptions, 32,053 audiovisual materials.

College life *Housing: Option:* coed. *Social organizations:* national fraternities, national sororities, local fraternities, local sororities; 22% of eligible men and 13% of eligible women are members.

Campus security 24-hour emergency response devices and patrols, student patrols, late-night transport-escort service.

After graduation 225 organizations recruited on campus 1997–98. *Career center:* 11 full-time personnel. Services include job fairs, resume preparation, interview workshops, resume referral, career/interest testing, career counseling, careers library, job bank, job interviews. *Graduate education:* 20% of class of 1999 went directly to graduate and professional school: 6% business, 4% engineering, 3% dentistry, 3% graduate arts and sciences, 2% law, 2% medicine.

Freshmen 1,414 applied, 1,089 admitted, 448 enrolled.

Average high school GPA	3.25	SAT verbal scores above 500	N/R
SAT math scores above 500	N/R	ACT above 18	86%
From top 10% of their h.s. class	30%	From top quarter	56%
From top half	82%	1998 freshmen returning in 1999	78%

Application *Options:* eApply at www.CollegeQuest.com, early admission, deferred entrance. *Application fee:* $25. *Required:* high school transcript. *Required for some:* 1 letter of recommendation; interview.

Standardized tests *Admission: Required:* SAT I or ACT.

Significant dates *Application deadlines:* 7/1 (freshmen), 8/15 (transfers). *Notification:* continuous until 9/2 (freshmen). *Financial aid deadline priority date:* 4/1.

Freshman Application Contact
Ms. Colleen Ezzeddine, Admissions Counselor, University of Detroit Mercy, PO Box 19900, Detroit, MI 48219-0900. **Phone:** 313-993-1245. **Toll-free phone:** 800-635-5020. **Fax:** 313-993-3326. **E-mail:** admissions@udmercy.edu

Visit CollegeQuest.com for information on majors offered and athletics.

■ *See page 2722 for a narrative description.*

UNIVERSITY OF MICHIGAN
Ann Arbor, Michigan

- **State-supported**, university, founded 1817
- **Degrees** bachelor's, master's, doctoral, first professional, and post-master's certificates
- **Suburban** 2,861-acre campus with easy access to Detroit
- **Coed**, 24,493 undergraduate students, 94% full-time, 50% women, 50% men
- **Very difficult** entrance level, 59% of applicants were admitted
- **11:1 student-to-undergraduate faculty ratio**
- **83% graduate** in 6 years or less
- **$6333 tuition** and fees (in-state); $19,761 (out-of-state)
- **$10,405 average financial aid** package, $14,534 average indebtedness upon graduation, $2.3 billion endowment

Students *Undergraduates:* 23,063 full-time, 1,430 part-time. Students come from 53 states and territories, 90 other countries. *The most frequently chosen baccalaureate fields are:* engineering/engineering technologies, psychology, social sciences and history. *Graduate:* 2,290 in professional programs, 11,063 in other graduate degree programs.

From out-of-state	28%	Reside on campus	39%
Age 25 or older	3%	Transferred in	3%
International students	4%	African Americans	8%
Asian Americans/Pacific Islanders	12%	Hispanic Americans	4%
Native Americans	1%		

Faculty 3,710 (81% full-time), 76% with terminal degrees.

Expenses (1999–2000) *Tuition, state resident:* full-time $6148; part-time $232 per credit hour. *Tuition, nonresident:* full-time $19,576; part-time $792 per credit hour. *Required fees:* full-time $185. Full-time tuition and fees vary according to program and student level. Part-time tuition and fees vary according to course load, program, and student level. *College room and*

Michigan

board: $5614. Room and board charges vary according to board plan and housing facility. *Payment plan:* installment. *Waivers:* senior citizens and employees or children of employees.

Library University Library plus 20 others. *Operations spending 1999–2000:* $39.1 million. *Collection:* 7.1 million titles, 69,280 serial subscriptions, 52,827 audiovisual materials.

College life *Housing:* Options: coed, women-only, cooperative, disabled students. *Social organizations:* national fraternities, national sororities, local fraternities, local sororities; 18% of eligible men and 18% of eligible women are members. *Most popular organizations:* University Activities Center, Hillel, Project Serve, Residence Hall Association, Black Student Union.

Campus security 24-hour emergency response devices and patrols, student patrols, late-night transport-escort service, controlled dormitory access, bicycle patrols.

After graduation 950 organizations recruited on campus 1997–98. *Career center:* 20 full-time, 1 part-time personnel. Services include job fairs, resume preparation, interview workshops, resume referral, career/interest testing, career counseling, careers library, job bank, job interviews. *Graduate education:* 34% of class of 1999 went directly to graduate and professional school: 11% graduate arts and sciences, 5% law, 5% medicine, 4% engineering, 2% education, 1% business, 1% dentistry, 1% theology, 1% veterinary medicine. *Major awards:* 17 Fulbright Scholars.

Freshmen 21,324 applied, 12,590 admitted, 5,559 enrolled. 37 National Merit Scholars.

Average high school GPA	3.6	SAT verbal scores above 500	93%
SAT math scores above 500	95%	ACT above 18	99%
From top 10% of their h.s. class	63%	From top quarter	90%
From top half	99%	1998 freshmen returning in 1999	95%

Application *Options:* electronic application, deferred entrance. *Preference* given to state residents. *Application fee:* $40. *Required:* essay or personal statement; high school transcript. *Required for some:* letters of recommendation; interview.

Standardized tests *Admission: Required:* SAT I or ACT. *Required for some:* SAT II Subject Tests, SAT II: Writing Test.

Significant dates *Application deadlines:* 2/1 (freshmen), 3/1 (transfers). *Notification:* continuous until 4/1 (freshmen). *Financial aid deadline:* 9/30. *Priority date:* 2/15.

Freshman Application Contact
Mr. Ted Spencer, Director of Undergraduate Admissions, University of Michigan, Ann Arbor, MI 48109-1316. **Phone:** 734-764-7433. **Fax:** 734-936-0740. **E-mail:** ugadmiss@umich.edu

Visit CollegeQuest.com for information on majors offered and athletics. College video and electronic viewbook available at CollegeQuest.com.

UNIVERSITY OF MICHIGAN—DEARBORN
Dearborn, Michigan

- **State-supported**, comprehensive, founded 1959
- **Degrees** bachelor's and master's
- **Suburban** 210-acre campus with easy access to Detroit
- **Coed**, 5,953 undergraduate students, 61% full-time, 53% women, 47% men
- **Moderately difficult** entrance level, 72% of applicants were admitted
- **$4361 tuition** and fees (in-state); $11,849 (out-of-state)

Part of University of Michigan System.

Students *Undergraduates:* 3,616 full-time, 2,337 part-time. Students come from 25 states and territories, 22 other countries. *The most frequently chosen baccalaureate fields are:* business/marketing, engineering/engineering technologies, psychology. *Graduate:* 1,553 in graduate degree programs.

From out-of-state	1%	Age 25 or older	31%
Transferred in	11%	International students	1%
African Americans	7%	Asian Americans/Pacific Islanders	6%
Hispanic Americans	2%	Native Americans	0.5%

Faculty 438 (55% full-time), 67% with terminal degrees.

Expenses (1999–2000) *Tuition, state resident:* full-time $4077; part-time $161 per credit. *Tuition, nonresident:* full-time $11,565; part-time $460 per credit. *Required fees:* full-time $284; $10 per credit; $62 per term part-time. Full-time tuition and fees vary according to course level, course load, program, and student level. Part-time tuition and fees vary according to

course level, course load, program, and student level. *Payment plan:* installment. *Waivers:* senior citizens and employees or children of employees.

Library Mardigian Library. *Operations spending 1999–2000:* $92,001. *Collection:* 299,792 titles, 1,169 serial subscriptions.

College life *Housing:* college housing not available. *Social organizations:* national fraternities, national sororities; 6% of eligible men and 5% of eligible women are members. *Most popular organizations:* Dearborn Campus Engineers, student radio station, Association for African-American Students.

Campus security 24-hour emergency response devices and patrols, late-night transport-escort service.

After graduation 66 organizations recruited on campus 1997–98. 24% of class of 1998 had job offers within 6 months. *Career center:* 6 full-time personnel. Services include job fairs, resume preparation, resume referral, career counseling, careers library, job interviews. *Graduate education:* 23% of class of 1999 went directly to graduate and professional school.

Freshmen 2,187 applied, 1,577 admitted, 767 enrolled.

SAT verbal scores above 500	N/R	SAT math scores above 500	N/R
ACT above 18	N/R		

Application *Application fee:* $30. *Required:* high school transcript; minimum 3.0 GPA. *Required for some:* interview.

Standardized tests *Admission: Required:* SAT I or ACT.

Significant dates *Application deadlines:* rolling (freshmen), rolling (transfers). *Notification:* continuous until 9/15 (freshmen). *Financial aid deadline priority date:* 4/1.

Freshman Application Contact
Mr. David Placey, Director of Admissions, University of Michigan–Dearborn, 4901 Evergreen Road, Dearborn, MI 48128-1491. **Phone:** 313-593-5100. **E-mail:** umdgoblu@umd.umich.edu

Visit CollegeQuest.com for information on majors offered and athletics. College video available at CollegeQuest.com.

UNIVERSITY OF MICHIGAN—FLINT
Flint, Michigan

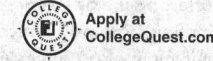
Apply at CollegeQuest.com

- **State-supported**, comprehensive, founded 1956
- **Degrees** bachelor's, master's, and postbachelor's certificates
- **Urban** 72-acre campus with easy access to Detroit
- **Coed**, 5,994 undergraduate students, 56% full-time, 65% women, 35% men
- **Moderately difficult** entrance level, 87% of applicants were admitted
- **34% graduate** in 6 years or less
- **$3800 tuition** and fees (in-state); $10,990 (out-of-state)

Part of University of Michigan System.

Students *Undergraduates:* Students come from 18 states and territories. *Graduate:* 530 in graduate degree programs.

From out-of-state	1%	Age 25 or older	40%
International students	0.1%	African Americans	11%
Asian Americans/Pacific Islanders	2%	Hispanic Americans	2%
Native Americans	1%		

Expenses (1999–2000) *Tuition, state resident:* full-time $3546; part-time $152 per credit. *Tuition, nonresident:* full-time $10,736; part-time $450 per credit. *Required fees:* full-time $254; $116 per term part-time. Full-time tuition and fees vary according to program and student level. Part-time tuition and fees vary according to program and student level. *Payment plan:* deferred payment. *Waivers:* minority students and senior citizens.

Library *Collection:* 184,120 titles, 1,202 serial subscriptions, 27,759 audiovisual materials.

College life *Housing:* college housing not available. *Social organizations:* national fraternities, national sororities; 1% of eligible men and 1% of eligible women are members.

Campus security 24-hour emergency response devices and patrols, student patrols, late-night transport-escort service.

After graduation *Career center:* 2 full-time, 2 part-time personnel. Services include job fairs, resume preparation, resume referral, career counseling, careers library, job bank, job interviews. *Graduate education:* 18% of class of 1999 went directly to graduate and professional school.

Michigan

University of Michigan–Flint (continued)

Freshmen 1,142 applied, 999 admitted.

Average high school GPA	3.23	SAT verbal scores above 500	N/R
SAT math scores above 500	N/R	ACT above 18	83%
From top 10% of their h.s. class	16%	From top quarter	43%
From top half	81%	1998 freshmen returning in 1999	74%

Application *Options:* eApply at www.CollegeQuest.com, deferred entrance. *Application fee:* $30. *Required:* high school transcript. *Recommended:* essay or personal statement.

Standardized tests *Admission: Required:* SAT I or ACT.

Significant dates *Application deadlines:* 9/2 (freshmen), 8/21 (transfers). *Financial aid deadline priority date:* 2/21.

Freshman Application Contact Dr. Virginia R. Allen, Vice Chancellor for Student Services and Enrollment, University of Michigan–Flint, 303 Kearsley Street, Flint, MI 48502-1950. **Phone:** 810-762-3434. **Toll-free phone:** 800-942-5636. **E-mail:** admissions@list.flint.umich.edu

Visit CollegeQuest.com for information on majors offered and athletics.

WALSH COLLEGE OF ACCOUNTANCY AND BUSINESS ADMINISTRATION
Troy, Michigan

- **Independent**, upper-level, founded 1922
- **Degrees** bachelor's and master's
- **Suburban** 29-acre campus with easy access to Detroit
- **Coed**, 1,176 undergraduate students, 16% full-time, 61% women, 39% men
- **Noncompetitive** entrance level
- **21:1 student-to-undergraduate faculty ratio**
- **$5275 tuition** and fees
- **$12,700 average indebtedness** upon graduation, $1.4 million endowment

Walsh College in Troy, Michigan, specializes in a business curriculum that offers bachelor's degree completion programs in accounting, computer information systems, finance, general business, management, and marketing. A minimum of 60 semester credit hours are needed to transfer. Graduate programs include the MBA and Master of Science degrees in finance, information management and communication, management, professional accountancy, and taxation. Extension sites include the Novi Campus and University Centers in Port Huron and Clinton Township.

Students *Undergraduates:* 190 full-time, 986 part-time. Students come from 24 other countries. *Graduate:* 1,750 in graduate degree programs.

Age 25 or older	75%	Transferred in	20%
International students	4%	African Americans	4%
Asian Americans/Pacific Islanders	2%	Hispanic Americans	1%
Native Americans	0.2%		

Faculty 141 (10% full-time), 23% with terminal degrees.

Expenses (1999–2000) *Tuition:* full-time $5125; part-time $205 per credit hour. *Required fees:* full-time $150; $75 per term part-time. Full-time tuition and fees vary according to course load. Part-time tuition and fees vary according to course load. *Payment plan:* deferred payment. *Waivers:* employees or children of employees.

Library Vollbrecht Library. *Operations spending 1999–2000:* $661,135. *Collection:* 26,000 titles, 495 serial subscriptions, 137 audiovisual materials.

College life *Housing:* college housing not available. *Most popular organizations:* student government, American Marketing Association, economics/finance club, accounting club, National Association of Black Accountants.

Campus security 24-hour emergency response devices.

After graduation 132 organizations recruited on campus 1997–98. 99% of class of 1998 had job offers within 6 months. *Career center:* 3 full-time, 2 part-time personnel. Services include job fairs, resume preparation, interview workshops, resume referral, career/interest testing, career counseling, careers library, job bank, job interviews.

Application *Options:* Common Application, deferred entrance. *Application fee:* $25.

Significant dates *Application deadline:* rolling (transfers). *Financial aid deadline:* continuous.

Freshman Application Contact Ms. Diane Zalapi, Director of Admissions, Walsh College of Accountancy and Business Administration, 3838 Livernois, PO Box 7006, Troy, MI 48007-7006. **Phone:** 248-689-8282 Ext. 294. **Fax:** 248-524-2520. **E-mail:** admissions@walshcol.edu

Visit CollegeQuest.com for information on majors offered and athletics.

WAYNE STATE UNIVERSITY
Detroit, Michigan

- **State-supported**, university, founded 1868
- **Degrees** bachelor's, master's, doctoral, first professional, post-master's, and postbachelor's certificates
- **Urban** 203-acre campus
- **Coed**, 16,542 undergraduate students, 53% full-time, 60% women, 40% men
- **Moderately difficult** entrance level, 82% of applicants were admitted
- **$3809 tuition** and fees (in-state); $8249 (out-of-state)
- **$4804 average financial aid** package, $14,834 average indebtedness upon graduation, $118.2 million endowment

Students *Undergraduates:* 8,749 full-time, 7,793 part-time. Students come from 30 states and territories, 64 other countries. *The most frequently chosen baccalaureate fields are:* education, engineering/engineering technologies, health professions and related sciences. *Graduate:* 2,803 in professional programs, 9,829 in other graduate degree programs.

From out-of-state	1%	Age 25 or older	41%
Transferred in	10%	International students	3%
African Americans	30%	Asian Americans/Pacific Islanders	5%
Hispanic Americans	2%	Native Americans	0.4%

Faculty 2,762 (64% full-time).

Expenses (1999–2000) *Tuition, state resident:* full-time $3420; part-time $114 per semester hour. *Tuition, nonresident:* full-time $7860; part-time $262 per semester hour. *Required fees:* full-time $389; $10 per semester hour; $71 per term part-time. Full-time tuition and fees vary according to course level and student level. Part-time tuition and fees vary according to course level and student level. *College room and board:* room only: $4152. Room and board charges vary according to housing facility. *Payment plan:* installment. *Waivers:* senior citizens and employees or children of employees.

Library David Adamany Undergraduate Library plus 6 others. *Operations spending 1999–2000:* $15.3 million. *Collection:* 24,200 serial subscriptions, 38,070 audiovisual materials.

College life *Housing: Option:* coed. *Social organizations:* national fraternities, national sororities, local fraternities; 1% of eligible men and 1% of eligible women are members. *Most popular organizations:* Indian Student Association, Golden Key Honor Society, Campus Crusade for Christ, Friendship Association of Chinese Students, Project Volunteer/Students of Service.

Campus security 24-hour emergency response devices and patrols, late-night transport-escort service.

After graduation 161 organizations recruited on campus 1997–98. *Career center:* 22 full-time, 4 part-time personnel. Services include job fairs, resume preparation, interview workshops, resume referral, career/interest testing, career counseling, careers library, job bank, job interviews.

Freshmen 5,230 applied, 4,297 admitted, 2,014 enrolled.

SAT verbal scores above 500	N/R	SAT math scores above 500	N/R
ACT above 18	70%		

Application *Application fee:* $20. *Required:* high school transcript; minimum 2.0 GPA. *Required for some:* letters of recommendation; interview; portfolio.

Standardized tests *Admission: Required:* SAT I or ACT.

Significant dates *Application deadlines:* 8/1 (freshmen), 8/1 (transfers). *Notification:* continuous until 9/1 (freshmen). *Financial aid deadline priority date:* 3/1.

Freshman Application Contact Mr. Michael Wood, Interim Director of University Admissions, Wayne State University, 3E HNJ, Detroit, MI 48202. **Phone:** 313-577-3581. **Fax:** 313-577-7536. **E-mail:** admissions@wayne.edu

Visit CollegeQuest.com for information on majors offered and athletics.

Michigan

WESTERN MICHIGAN UNIVERSITY
Kalamazoo, Michigan

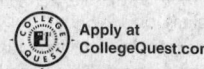 Apply at CollegeQuest.com

- **State-supported**, university, founded 1903
- **Degrees** bachelor's, master's, doctoral, and post-master's certificates
- **Urban** 504-acre campus
- **Coed**, 21,548 undergraduate students, 83% full-time, 54% women, 46% men
- **Moderately difficult** entrance level, 85% of applicants were admitted
- **16:1 student-to-undergraduate faculty ratio**
- **$3944 tuition** and fees (in-state); $8990 (out-of-state)
- **$4078 average financial aid** package, $16,000 average indebtedness upon graduation, $92.6 million endowment

Students *Undergraduates:* 17,828 full-time, 3,720 part-time. Students come from 52 states and territories, 99 other countries. *The most frequently chosen baccalaureate fields are:* business/marketing, education, social sciences and history. *Graduate:* 5,915 in graduate degree programs.

From out-of-state	6%	Reside on campus	30%
Age 25 or older	15%	Transferred in	9%
International students	4%	African Americans	6%
Asian Americans/Pacific Islanders	1%	Hispanic Americans	2%
Native Americans	1%		

Faculty 1,334 (65% full-time).
Expenses (1999–2000) *Tuition, state resident:* full-time $3342; part-time $111 per credit hour. *Tuition, nonresident:* full-time $8388; part-time $280 per credit hour. *Required fees:* full-time $602; $132 per term part-time. Full-time tuition and fees vary according to course load and student level. Part-time tuition and fees vary according to course load and student level. *College room and board:* $4831. Room and board charges vary according to board plan. *Payment plan:* installment. *Waivers:* senior citizens and employees or children of employees.
Library Waldo Library plus 4 others. *Operations spending 1999–2000:* $9.7 million. *Collection:* 886,145 titles, 6,734 serial subscriptions, 109,069 audiovisual materials.
College life *Housing:* Options: coed, men-only, women-only, disabled students. *Social organizations:* national fraternities, national sororities, local fraternities, local sororities. *Most popular organizations:* Intrafraternity Council, National Panhellenic Conference, Golden Key, Inter-Varsity Christian Fellowship, Malaysian Student Organization.
Campus security 24-hour emergency response devices and patrols, student patrols, late-night transport-escort service, controlled dormitory access.
After graduation 293 organizations recruited on campus 1997–98. *Career center:* 12 full-time, 1 part-time personnel. Services include job fairs, resume preparation, interview workshops, resume referral, career/interest testing, career counseling, careers library, job bank, job interviews.
Freshmen 12,929 applied, 11,000 admitted, 4,344 enrolled.

Average high school GPA	3.22	SAT verbal scores above 500	N/R
SAT math scores above 500	N/R	ACT above 18	92%
From top 10% of their h.s. class	14%	From top quarter	35%
From top half	69%	1998 freshmen returning in 1999	80%

Application *Options:* eApply at www.CollegeQuest.com, electronic application, early admission. *Application fee:* $25. *Required:* high school transcript. *Required for some:* interview.
Standardized tests *Placement: Required:* ACT
Significant dates *Application deadlines:* rolling (freshmen), rolling (transfers). *Financial aid deadline priority date:* 1/31.
Freshman Application Contact
Mr. John Fraire, Dean, Office of Admissions and Orientation, Western Michigan University, Office of Admissions and Orientation, Kalamazoo, MI 49008. **Phone:** 616-387-2000. **Toll-free phone:** 800-400-4968. **Fax:** 616-387-2096. **E-mail:** ask-wmu@wmich.edu
Visit CollegeQuest.com for information on majors offered and athletics. Electronic viewbook available at CollegeQuest.com.

- *See page 2950 for a narrative description.*

WILLIAM TYNDALE COLLEGE
Farmington Hills, Michigan

- **Independent religious**, 4-year, founded 1945
- **Degrees** associate and bachelor's
- **Suburban** 28-acre campus with easy access to Detroit
- **Coed**, 637 undergraduate students, 64% full-time, 53% women, 47% men
- **Minimally difficult** entrance level, 86% of applicants were admitted
- **12:1 student-to-undergraduate faculty ratio**
- **24% graduate** in 6 years or less
- **$7050 tuition** and fees
- **$4782 average financial aid** package, $9500 average indebtedness upon graduation, $270,141 endowment

Students *Undergraduates:* 409 full-time, 228 part-time. Students come from 6 states and territories, 10 other countries. *The most frequently chosen baccalaureate fields are:* business/marketing, philosophy, psychology.

From out-of-state	1%	Reside on campus	8%
Age 25 or older	62%	Transferred in	14%
International students	3%	African Americans	35%
Asian Americans/Pacific Islanders	1%	Native Americans	0.3%

Faculty 92 (16% full-time).
Expenses (2000–2001) *Comprehensive fee:* $9850 includes full-time tuition ($7050) and room and board ($2800). Room and board charges vary according to housing facility. *Part-time tuition:* $235 per credit. *Payment plan:* deferred payment. *Waivers:* senior citizens and employees or children of employees.
Library William Tyndale College Library. *Operations spending 1999–2000:* $171,217. *Collection:* 63,500 titles, 230 serial subscriptions, 3,300 audiovisual materials.
College life *Housing:* Option: coed. *Most popular organizations:* choir, drama club, Student Executive Board.
After graduation *Career center:* Services include resume preparation, interview workshops, resume referral, career counseling.
Freshmen 140 applied, 120 admitted, 90 enrolled.

Average high school GPA	3.14	SAT verbal scores above 500	N/R
SAT math scores above 500	N/R	ACT above 18	89%
From top 10% of their h.s. class	2%	From top quarter	11%
From top half	40%	1998 freshmen returning in 1999	70%

Application *Options:* early admission, deferred entrance. *Application fee:* $25. *Required:* high school transcript; minimum 2.25 GPA. *Required for some:* essay or personal statement; letters of recommendation; interview. *Recommended:* minimum 3.0 GPA.
Standardized tests *Admission: Required:* SAT I or ACT.
Significant dates *Application deadlines:* rolling (freshmen), rolling (transfers). *Notification:* continuous until 9/1 (freshmen). *Financial aid deadline:* 6/30. *Priority date:* 2/21.
Freshman Application Contact
Ms. Dianne Larimer, Counselor, William Tyndale College, 37500 West Twelve Mile Road, Farmington Hills, MI 48331. **Phone:** 248-553-7200. **Toll-free phone:** 800-483-0707. **Fax:** 248-553-5963.
Visit CollegeQuest.com for information on majors offered and athletics.

YESHIVA GEDDOLAH OF GREATER DETROIT RABBINICAL COLLEGE
Oak Park, Michigan

Admissions Office Contact
Yeshiva Geddolah of Greater Detroit Rabbinical College, 24600 Greenfield, Oak Park, MI 48237-1544.

Minnesota

MINNESOTA

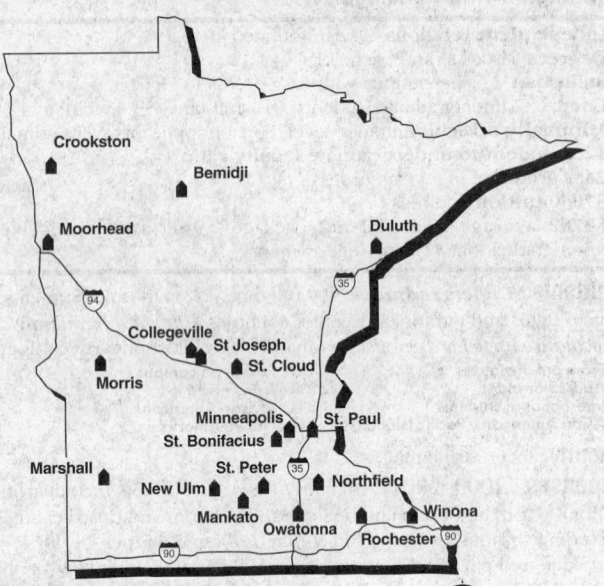

AUGSBURG COLLEGE
Minneapolis, Minnesota

Apply at CollegeQuest.com

- **Independent Lutheran**, comprehensive, founded 1869
- **Degrees** bachelor's, master's, and postbachelor's certificates
- **Urban** 23-acre campus
- **Coed**, 2,455 undergraduate students, 83% full-time, 59% women, 41% men
- **Moderately difficult** entrance level, 77% of applicants were admitted
- **14:1 student-to-undergraduate faculty ratio**
- **49.6% graduate** in 6 years or less
- **$15,250 tuition** and fees
- **$9428 average financial aid** package, $20,846 average indebtedness upon graduation, $20.3 million endowment

Augsburg College, an urban liberal arts college, draws upon the cultural and corporate resources of Minneapolis to complement the campus and classroom learning experience. A college of diversity, it serves people of all colors and nationalities and of many religions. Affiliated with the Evangelical Lutheran Church of America, Augsburg is a college of intellectual challenge, academic excellence, and career preparation.

Students *Undergraduates:* 2,041 full-time, 414 part-time. Students come from 36 states and territories, 45 other countries. *The most frequently chosen baccalaureate fields are:* business/marketing, education, psychology. ***Graduate:*** 178 in graduate degree programs.

From out-of-state	13%	Reside on campus	53%
Age 25 or older	12%	Transferred in	14%
International students	2%	African Americans	6%
Asian Americans/Pacific Islanders	4%	Hispanic Americans	1%
Native Americans	1%		

Faculty 282 (48% full-time), 67% with terminal degrees.
Expenses (1999–2000) *Comprehensive fee:* $20,490 includes full-time tuition ($15,084), mandatory fees ($166), and room and board ($5240). *College room only:* $2676. Room and board charges vary according to board plan and housing facility. *Part-time tuition:* $1630 per course. *Part-time fees:* $42 per term part-time. Part-time tuition and fees vary according to course load. *Payment plans:* installment, deferred payment. *Waivers:* children of alumni, senior citizens, and employees or children of employees.
Library James G. Lindell Library plus 2 others. *Operations spending 1999–2000:* $787,586. *Collection:* 136,250 titles, 991 serial subscriptions, 6,150 audiovisual materials.
College life *Housing: Options:* coed, men-only, women-only, disabled students. *Most popular organizations:* Student Activities Council, student government, newspaper/yearbook, Campus Ministry, intramurals.
Campus security 24-hour emergency response devices and patrols, late-night transport-escort service, controlled dormitory access.

After graduation 60 organizations recruited on campus 1997–98. 88% of class of 1998 had job offers within 6 months. *Career center:* 3 full-time personnel. Services include job fairs, resume preparation, interview workshops, resume referral, career/interest testing, career counseling, careers library, job bank. ***Graduate education:*** 12% of class of 1999 went directly to graduate and professional school.
Freshmen 829 applied, 636 admitted, 323 enrolled.

Average high school GPA	3.25	SAT verbal scores above 500	73%
SAT math scores above 500	87%	ACT above 18	90%
From top 10% of their h.s. class	18%	From top quarter	40%
From top half	75%	1998 freshmen returning in 1999	75%

Application *Options:* eApply at www.CollegeQuest.com, deferred entrance. *Application fee:* $25. *Required:* essay or personal statement; high school transcript; minimum 2.5 GPA. *Required for some:* 2 letters of recommendation. *Recommended:* interview.
Standardized tests *Admission: Required:* SAT I or ACT.
Significant dates *Application deadlines:* 8/15 (freshmen), 8/10 (transfers). *Financial aid deadline:* 4/15.
Freshman Application Contact
Ms. Sally Daniels, Director of Undergraduate Day Admissions, Augsburg College, 2211 Riverside Avenue, Minneapolis, MN 55454-1351. **Phone:** 612-330-1001. **Toll-free phone:** 800-788-5678. **Fax:** 612-330-1649. **E-mail:** admissions@augsburg.edu
Visit CollegeQuest.com for information on majors offered and athletics. College video available at CollegeQuest.com.

BEMIDJI STATE UNIVERSITY
Bemidji, Minnesota

- **State-supported**, comprehensive, founded 1919
- **Degrees** associate, bachelor's, and master's
- **Small-town** 89-acre campus
- **Coed**, 3,814 undergraduate students, 83% full-time, 54% women, 46% men
- **Moderately difficult** entrance level, 75% of applicants were admitted
- **20:1 student-to-undergraduate faculty ratio**
- **37% graduate** in 6 years or less
- **$3579 tuition** and fees (in-state); $6549 (out-of-state)
- **$5128 average financial aid** package, $12,670 average indebtedness upon graduation, $4.4 million endowment

Part of Minnesota State Colleges and Universities System.
Students *Undergraduates:* 3,165 full-time, 649 part-time. Students come from 38 states and territories, 35 other countries. *The most frequently chosen baccalaureate fields are:* business/marketing, education, protective services/public administration. ***Graduate:*** 246 in graduate degree programs.

From out-of-state	11%	Reside on campus	26%
Age 25 or older	27%	Transferred in	12%
International students	6%	African Americans	1%
Asian Americans/Pacific Islanders	2%	Hispanic Americans	1%
Native Americans	4%		

Faculty 221 (75% full-time), 56% with terminal degrees.
Expenses (1999–2000) *Tuition, state resident:* full-time $2970; part-time $100 per semester hour. *Tuition, nonresident:* full-time $5940; part-time $196 per semester hour. *Required fees:* full-time $609; $43 per semester hour. Full-time tuition and fees vary according to reciprocity agreements. Part-time tuition and fees vary according to course load and reciprocity agreements. *College room and board:* $3778; room only: $2048. Room and board charges vary according to board plan and housing facility. *Payment plan:* installment. *Waivers:* senior citizens and employees or children of employees.
Library A. C. Clark Library. *Operations spending 1999–2000:* $919,419. *Collection:* 4,462 audiovisual materials.
College life *Housing: Option:* coed. *Social organizations:* national fraternities, national sororities, local fraternities; 2% of eligible men and 1% of eligible women are members.
Campus security 24-hour emergency response devices and patrols, late-night transport-escort service, controlled dormitory access.
After graduation 12 organizations recruited on campus 1997–98. *Career center:* 3 full-time personnel. Services include job fairs, resume preparation, interview workshops, resume referral, career/interest testing, career counseling, careers library, job bank, job interviews.

Minnesota

Freshmen 1,260 applied, 940 admitted, 616 enrolled.

Average high school GPA	3.33	SAT verbal scores above 500	N/R
SAT math scores above 500	N/R	ACT above 18	89%
From top 10% of their h.s. class	10%	From top quarter	50%
From top half	90%	1998 freshmen returning in 1999	72%

Application *Options:* Common Application, electronic application, deferred entrance. *Application fee:* $20. *Required:* high school transcript. *Required for some:* essay or personal statement; letters of recommendation; interview.

Standardized tests *Admission: Required:* ACT.

Significant dates *Application deadlines:* rolling (freshmen), rolling (transfers). *Financial aid deadline priority date:* 5/15.

Freshman Application Contact
Mr. Paul Muller, Director of Admissions, Bemidji State University, Deputy-102, Bemidji, MN 56601. **Phone:** 218-755-2040. **Toll-free phone:** 800-475-2001 (in-state); 800-652-9747 (out-of-state). **Fax:** 218-755-2074. **E-mail:** admissions@vax1.bemidji.msus.edu

Visit CollegeQuest.com for information on majors offered and athletics. College video and electronic viewbook available at CollegeQuest.com.

BETHANY LUTHERAN COLLEGE
Mankato, Minnesota

- **Independent Lutheran**, primarily 2-year, founded 1927
- **Degrees** associate and bachelor's
- **Small-town** 50-acre campus with easy access to Minneapolis–St. Paul
- **Coed**, 406 undergraduate students, 96% full-time, 52% women, 48% men
- **Moderately difficult** entrance level
- **10:1 student-to-undergraduate faculty ratio**
- **$10,366 tuition** and fees

Faculty 60 (50% full-time), 13% with terminal degrees.

Admissions Office Contact
Bethany Lutheran College, 700 Luther Drive, Mankato, MN 56001-6163. **Toll-free phone:** 800-944-3066. **Fax:** 507-344-7376. **E-mail:** admiss@blc.edu

Visit CollegeQuest.com for information on majors offered and athletics.

BETHEL COLLEGE
St. Paul, Minnesota

- **Independent**, comprehensive, founded 1871, affiliated with Baptist General Conference
- **Degrees** associate, bachelor's, and master's
- **Suburban** 231-acre campus
- **Coed**, 2,708 undergraduate students, 93% full-time, 63% women, 37% men
- **Moderately difficult** entrance level, 81% of applicants were admitted
- **16:1 student-to-undergraduate faculty ratio**
- **75% graduate** in 6 years or less
- **$15,335 tuition** and fees
- **$12,726 average financial aid** package, $16,903 average indebtedness upon graduation, $15.7 million endowment

Bethel College provides academic excellence in a dynamic Christian environment. *U.S. News and World Report* has recognized Bethel as one of the top ten liberal arts colleges in the Midwest. What makes Bethel outstanding are its excellent students, expert faculty, and dedicated staff. Bethel is committed to providing a high-quality liberal arts education to prepare tomorrow's leaders to make a difference in their community, the church, and the world.

Students *Undergraduates:* 2,515 full-time, 193 part-time. Students come from 38 states and territories. *The most frequently chosen baccalaureate fields are:* business/marketing, health professions and related sciences, interdisciplinary studies. *Graduate:* 262 in graduate degree programs.

From out-of-state	28%	Reside on campus	70%
Transferred in	5%	African Americans	2%
Asian Americans/Pacific Islanders	3%	Hispanic Americans	1%
Native Americans	0.3%		

Faculty 261 (51% full-time), 37% with terminal degrees.

Expenses (1999–2000) *Comprehensive fee:* $20,745 includes full-time tuition ($15,300), mandatory fees ($35), and room and board ($5410). *College room only:* $3140. Room and board charges vary according to board plan. *Part-time tuition:* $580 per credit hour. Part-time tuition and fees vary according to course load. *Payment plan:* installment. *Waivers:* senior citizens and employees or children of employees.

Library Learning Resource Center. *Operations spending 1999–2000:* $776,407. *Collection:* 150,203 titles, 3,449 serial subscriptions, 6,270 audiovisual materials.

College life *Housing:* on-campus residence required through sophomore year. *Options:* coed, disabled students. *Most popular organizations:* United Cultures of Bethel, Student Senate, Bethel Student Association, Habitat for Humanity, Tri Beta.

Campus security 24-hour emergency response devices and patrols, student patrols, late-night transport-escort service, controlled dormitory access.

After graduation *Career center:* 3 full-time, 1 part-time personnel. Services include job fairs, resume preparation, interview workshops, resume referral, career/interest testing, career counseling, careers library, job bank, job interviews.

Freshmen 1,526 applied, 1,241 admitted, 519 enrolled.

SAT verbal scores above 500	81%	SAT math scores above 500	79%
ACT above 18	91%	From top 10% of their h.s. class	30%
From top quarter	59%	From top half	87%
1998 freshmen returning in 1999	83%		

Application *Option:* deferred entrance. *Application fee:* $25. *Required:* essay or personal statement; high school transcript; 2 letters of recommendation. *Required for some:* interview. *Recommended:* interview.

Standardized tests *Admission: Required:* SAT I, ACT or PSAT.

Significant dates *Application deadlines:* 6/1 (freshmen), 8/1 (transfers). *Financial aid deadline priority date:* 4/15.

Freshman Application Contact
Mr. John C. Lassen, Director of Admissions, Bethel College, 3900 Bethel Drive, St. Paul, MN 55112. **Phone:** 651-638-6436. **Toll-free phone:** 800-255-8706 Ext. 6242. **E-mail:** bcoll-admit@bethel.edu

Visit CollegeQuest.com for information on majors offered and athletics. Electronic viewbook available at CollegeQuest.com.

- *See page 1270 for a narrative description.*

CARLETON COLLEGE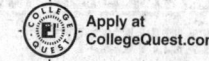
Northfield, Minnesota

- **Independent**, 4-year, founded 1866
- **Degree** bachelor's
- **Small-town** 955-acre campus with easy access to Minneapolis–St. Paul
- **Coed**, 1,882 undergraduate students, 100% full-time, 53% women, 47% men
- **Very difficult** entrance level, 46% of applicants were admitted
- **10:1 student-to-undergraduate faculty ratio**
- **88.3% graduate** in 6 years or less
- **$23,469 tuition** and fees
- **$18,824 average financial aid** package, $14,720 average indebtedness upon graduation, $551 million endowment

Students *Undergraduates:* 1,882 full-time. Students come from 50 states and territories, 15 other countries. *The most frequently chosen baccalaureate fields are:* physical sciences, biological/life sciences, social sciences and history.

From out-of-state	78%	Reside on campus	89%
Transferred in	1%	International students	2%
African Americans	3%	Asian Americans/Pacific Islanders	9%
Hispanic Americans	3%	Native Americans	0.4%

Faculty 207 (86% full-time), 93% with terminal degrees.

Expenses (1999–2000) *Comprehensive fee:* $28,230 includes full-time tuition ($23,325), mandatory fees ($144), and room and board ($4761). *College room only:* $2067. Room and board charges vary according to board plan. *Payment plans:* tuition prepayment, installment.

Library Carleton Library plus 1 other. *Operations spending 1999–2000:* $3.5 million. *Collection:* 514,029 titles, 1,505 serial subscriptions.

College life *Housing:* on-campus residence required in freshman year. *Options:* coed, disabled students. *Most popular organizations:* CANOE (Carleton Association of Nature and Outdoor Enthusiasts), Farm Club, Amnesty International, WHIMS (Women in Math and Science), Ebony II.

Minnesota

Carleton College (continued)

Campus security 24-hour emergency response devices and patrols, student patrols, late-night transport-escort service, controlled dormitory access.

After graduation 60 organizations recruited on campus 1997–98. 63% of class of 1998 had job offers within 6 months. *Career center:* 3 full-time, 5 part-time personnel. Services include job fairs, resume preparation, interview workshops, resume referral, career counseling, careers library, job interviews. *Graduate education:* 17% of class of 1999 went directly to graduate and professional school: 12% graduate arts and sciences, 2% medicine, 1% business, 1% education, 1% engineering, 1% law. *Major awards:* 4 Fulbright Scholars.

Freshmen 3,457 applied, 1,606 admitted, 510 enrolled. 85 National Merit Scholars, 45 valedictorians.

SAT verbal scores above 500	99%	SAT math scores above 500	100%
ACT above 18	100%	From top 10% of their h.s. class	61%
From top quarter	89%	From top half	99%
1998 freshmen returning in 1999	95%		

Application *Options:* eApply at www.CollegeQuest.com, Common Application, electronic application, early admission, early decision, deferred entrance. *Application fee:* $30. *Required:* essay or personal statement; high school transcript; 2 letters of recommendation. *Recommended:* interview.

Standardized tests *Admission: Required:* SAT I or ACT. *Recommended:* SAT II Subject Tests, SAT II: Writing Test.

Significant dates *Application deadlines:* 1/15 (freshmen), 3/31 (transfers). *Early decision:* 11/15 (for plan 1), 1/15 (for plan 2). *Notification:* 4/15 (freshmen), 12/15 (early decision plan 1), 2/15 (early decision plan 2). *Financial aid deadline:* 2/1. *Priority date:* 1/15.

Freshman Application Contact
Mr. Paul Thiboutot, Dean of Admissions, Carleton College, One North College Street, Northfield, MN 55057. **Phone:** 507-646-4190. **Toll-free phone:** 800-995-2275. **Fax:** 507-646-4526. **E-mail:** admissions@acs.carleton.edu

Visit CollegeQuest.com for information on majors offered and athletics. College video available at CollegeQuest.com.

■ *See page 1360 for a narrative description.*

COLLEGE OF SAINT BENEDICT
Saint Joseph, Minnesota

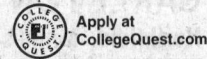 Apply at CollegeQuest.com

- **Independent Roman Catholic**, 4-year, founded 1887
- **Degree** bachelor's
- **Small-town** 315-acre campus with easy access to Minneapolis–St. Paul
- **Women** only, 2,000 undergraduate students, 98% full-time
- **Moderately difficult** entrance level, 88% of applicants were admitted
- **13:1 student-to-undergraduate faculty ratio**
- **74% graduate** in 6 years or less
- **$16,441 tuition** and fees
- **$14,488 average financial aid** package, $17,445 average indebtedness upon graduation, $16.9 million endowment

The College of Saint Benedict, through its coordinate relationship with Saint John's University for men, offers the best features of both a coeducational and a women's college. While all classes, facilities, and social and cultural functions are shared, each campus maintains its own residence halls, student development programming, student governments, and athletics. See full description of the College of Saint Benedict and Saint John's University.

Coordinate institution with Saint John's University (MN).

Students *Undergraduates:* 1,952 full-time, 48 part-time. Students come from 30 states and territories, 17 other countries. *The most frequently chosen baccalaureate fields are:* business/marketing, health professions and related sciences, social sciences and history.

From out-of-state	13%	Reside on campus	74%
Age 25 or older	4%	Transferred in	3%
International students	3%	African Americans	1%
Asian Americans/Pacific Islanders	2%	Hispanic Americans	1%
Native Americans	0.3%		

Faculty 150 (84% full-time), 65% with terminal degrees.

Expenses (1999–2000) *Comprehensive fee:* $21,481 includes full-time tuition ($16,195), mandatory fees ($246), and room and board ($5040). *College room only:* $2700. Room and board charges vary according to board plan and housing facility. *Part-time tuition:* $675 per credit. *Part-time fees:* $123 per term part-time. *Payment plans:* tuition prepayment, installment, deferred payment.

Library Clemens Library plus 2 others. *Operations spending 1999–2000:* $1.1 million. *Collection:* 726,844 titles, 8,564 serial subscriptions, 18,824 audiovisual materials.

College life *Housing:* on-campus residence required through sophomore year. *Option:* women-only. *Most popular organizations:* Volunteers in Service to Others, student newspaper, Joint Events Council, Collegiate Management Association, Cultural Affairs Board.

Campus security 24-hour emergency response devices and patrols, student patrols, late-night transport-escort service, controlled dormitory access, well-lit pathways.

After graduation 85 organizations recruited on campus 1997–98. 84% of class of 1998 had job offers within 6 months. *Career center:* 3 full-time, 2 part-time personnel. Services include job fairs, resume preparation, interview workshops, resume referral, career/interest testing, career counseling, careers library, job bank, job interviews. *Graduate education:* 14% of class of 1999 went directly to graduate and professional school: 8% graduate arts and sciences, 3% medicine, 2% law, 1% business.

Freshmen 1,159 applied, 1,024 admitted, 515 enrolled.

Average high school GPA	3.7	SAT verbal scores above 500	87%
SAT math scores above 500	82%	ACT above 18	100%
From top 10% of their h.s. class	36%	From top quarter	71%
From top half	95%	1998 freshmen returning in 1999	89%

Application *Options:* eApply at www.CollegeQuest.com, Common Application, electronic application, early admission, deferred entrance. *Application fee:* $25. *Required:* essay or personal statement; high school transcript. *Required for some:* letters of recommendation. *Recommended:* minimum 2.8 GPA; interview.

Standardized tests *Admission: Required:* SAT I or ACT.

Significant dates *Application deadlines:* rolling (freshmen), rolling (transfers). *Financial aid deadline priority date:* 4/1.

Freshman Application Contact
Ms. Mary Milbert, Dean of Admissions, College of Saint Benedict, 37 South College Avenue, Saint Joseph, MN 56374-2091. **Phone:** 320-363-5308. **Toll-free phone:** 800-544-1489. **Fax:** 320-363-5010. **E-mail:** admissions@csbsju.edu

Visit CollegeQuest.com for information on majors offered and athletics. College video and electronic viewbook available at CollegeQuest.com.

■ *See page 1472 for a narrative description.*

COLLEGE OF ST. CATHERINE
St. Paul, Minnesota

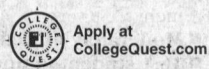 Apply at CollegeQuest.com

- **Independent Roman Catholic**, comprehensive, founded 1905
- **Degrees** bachelor's, master's, and postbachelor's certificates
- **Urban** 110-acre campus with easy access to Minneapolis
- **Women** only, 2,430 undergraduate students, 82% full-time
- **Moderately difficult** entrance level, 87% of applicants were admitted
- **12:1 student-to-undergraduate faculty ratio**
- **52.5% graduate** in 6 years or less
- **$15,578 tuition** and fees
- **$16,277 average financial aid** package, $17,341 average indebtedness upon graduation, $36.7 million endowment

Students *Undergraduates:* 2,004 full-time, 426 part-time. Students come from 29 states and territories, 30 other countries. *The most frequently chosen baccalaureate fields are:* education, business/marketing, health professions and related sciences. *Graduate:* 898 in graduate degree programs.

From out-of-state	13%	Reside on campus	38%
Age 25 or older	42%	Transferred in	21%
International students	4%	African Americans	3%
Asian Americans/Pacific Islanders	3%	Hispanic Americans	2%
Native Americans	0.4%		

Faculty 286 (48% full-time), 83% with terminal degrees.

Expenses (1999–2000) *Comprehensive fee:* $20,128 includes full-time tuition ($15,456), mandatory fees ($122), and room and board ($4550).

Minnesota

College room only: $2570. Full-time tuition and fees vary according to class time. Room and board charges vary according to board plan and housing facility. *Part-time tuition:* $483 per credit. *Part-time fees:* $61 per term part-time. Part-time tuition and fees vary according to class time. *Payment plan:* installment. *Waivers:* senior citizens and employees or children of employees.

Library St. Catherine Library plus 1 other. *Operations spending 1999-2000:* $2.3 million. *Collection:* 10,706 audiovisual materials.

College life *Housing: Option:* women-only. *Most popular organizations:* student government, Residence Hall Association, Women Helping Women, Student Nursing Association, social work club.

Campus security 24-hour emergency response devices and patrols, student patrols, late-night transport-escort service, controlled dormitory access.

After graduation 75% of class of 1998 had job offers within 6 months. *Career center:* 4 full-time, 3 part-time personnel. Services include job fairs, resume preparation, interview workshops, resume referral, career/interest testing, career counseling, careers library, job bank, job interviews. *Graduate education:* 19% of class of 1999 went directly to graduate and professional school: 6% graduate arts and sciences, 3% medicine, 3% theology, 2% business, 2% education, 1% law.

Freshmen 674 applied, 587 admitted, 282 enrolled. 2 National Merit Scholars, 6 valedictorians.

Average high school GPA	3.37	SAT verbal scores above 500	74%
SAT math scores above 500	68%	ACT above 18	86%
From top 10% of their h.s. class	19%	From top quarter	49%
From top half	79%	1998 freshmen returning in 1999	79%

Application *Options:* eApply at www.CollegeQuest.com, Common Application, deferred entrance. *Application fee:* $20. *Required:* high school transcript; 1 letter of recommendation. *Required for some:* essay or personal statement; interview. *Recommended:* interview.

Standardized tests *Admission: Required:* SAT I or ACT.

Significant dates *Application deadlines:* 8/15 (freshmen), rolling (transfers). *Financial aid deadline priority date:* 4/1.

Freshman Application Contact
Ms. Cory Piper-Hauswirth, Associate Director of Admission and Financial Aid, College of St. Catherine, 2004 Randolph Avenue, St. Paul, MN 55105-1789. **Phone:** 651-690-6047. **Toll-free phone:** 800-945-4599. **Fax:** 651-690-6042. **E-mail:** admissions@stkate.edu

Visit CollegeQuest.com for information on majors offered and athletics. College video available at CollegeQuest.com.

■ *See page 1474 for a narrative description.*

COLLEGE OF ST. CATHERINE—MINNEAPOLIS
Minneapolis, Minnesota

- **Independent Roman Catholic**, primarily 2-year, founded 1964
- **Degrees** associate and bachelor's
- **Urban** 1-acre campus
- **Coed,** primarily women, 905 undergraduate students, 28% full-time, 92% women, 8% men
- **Minimally difficult** entrance level
- **6:1 student-to-undergraduate faculty ratio**
- **$10,500 tuition** and fees

Faculty 129 (39% full-time).

Admissions Office Contact
College of St. Catherine–Minneapolis, 601 25th Avenue South, Minneapolis, MN 55454-1494. **Fax:** 651-690-8107. **E-mail:** pajohnson@stkate.edu

Visit CollegeQuest.com for information on majors offered and athletics.

THE COLLEGE OF ST. SCHOLASTICA
Duluth, Minnesota

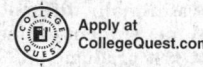
Apply at CollegeQuest.com

- **Independent**, comprehensive, founded 1912, affiliated with Roman Catholic Church
- **Degrees** bachelor's and master's
- **Suburban** 160-acre campus
- **Coed**, 1,429 undergraduate students, 90% full-time, 74% women, 26% men
- **Moderately difficult** entrance level, 37% of applicants were admitted
- **13:1 student-to-undergraduate faculty ratio**
- **47% graduate** in 6 years or less
- **$15,510 tuition** and fees
- **$11,602 average financial aid** package, $20,224 average indebtedness upon graduation, $15.2 million endowment

Students *Undergraduates:* 1,287 full-time, 142 part-time. Students come from 23 states and territories, 9 other countries. *The most frequently chosen baccalaureate fields are:* biological/life sciences, health professions and related sciences, parks and recreation. *Graduate:* 650 in graduate degree programs.

From out-of-state	13%	Reside on campus	34%
Age 25 or older	18%	Transferred in	13%
International students	1%	African Americans	1%
Asian Americans/Pacific Islanders	1%	Hispanic Americans	1%
Native Americans	1%		

Faculty 171 (64% full-time), 32% with terminal degrees.

Expenses (1999–2000) *Comprehensive fee:* $20,270 includes full-time tuition ($15,420), mandatory fees ($90), and room and board ($4760). Room and board charges vary according to board plan and housing facility. *Part-time tuition:* $482 per credit. *Part-time fees:* $45 per term part-time. Part-time tuition and fees vary according to course load. *Payment plan:* installment. *Waivers:* senior citizens and employees or children of employees.

Library College of St. Scholastica Library plus 1 other. *Operations spending 1999–2000:* $180,029. *Collection:* 118,703 titles, 759 serial subscriptions.

College life *Housing: Option:* coed. *Most popular organizations:* Campus Activity Board (CAB), Intervarsity, SOTA, SHIMA, social work club.

Campus security 24-hour emergency response devices and patrols, late-night transport-escort service, controlled dormitory access, student door monitor at night.

After graduation 4 organizations recruited on campus 1997–98. 62% of class of 1998 had job offers within 6 months. *Career center:* 1 full-time personnel. Services include job fairs, resume preparation, interview workshops, resume referral, career/interest testing, career counseling, careers library, job bank, job interviews. *Graduate education:* 38% of class of 1999 went directly to graduate and professional school: 35% graduate arts and sciences, 2% medicine.

Freshmen 826 applied, 308 admitted, 300 enrolled. 14 valedictorians.

Average high school GPA	3.52	SAT verbal scores above 500	80%
SAT math scores above 500	75%	ACT above 18	94%
From top 10% of their h.s. class	33%	From top quarter	62%
From top half	84%	1998 freshmen returning in 1999	83%

Application *Options:* eApply at www.CollegeQuest.com, Common Application, electronic application, early admission, deferred entrance. *Application fee:* $25. *Required:* high school transcript. *Required for some:* minimum 2.0 GPA; interview. *Recommended:* essay or personal statement; letters of recommendation; interview.

Standardized tests *Admission: Required:* SAT I or ACT. *Recommended:* PSAT.

Significant dates *Application deadlines:* rolling (freshmen), rolling (transfers). *Financial aid deadline priority date:* 3/15.

Freshman Application Contact
Mr. Brian Dalton, Vice President for Enrollment Management, The College of St. Scholastica, 1200 Kenwood Avenue, Duluth, MN 55811-4199. **Phone:** 218-723-6053. **Toll-free phone:** 800-447-5444. **Fax:** 218-723-6290. **E-mail:** admissions@css.edu

Visit CollegeQuest.com for information on majors offered and athletics.

■ *See page 1482 for a narrative description.*

COLLEGE OF VISUAL ARTS
St. Paul, Minnesota

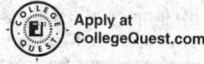
Apply at CollegeQuest.com

- **Independent**, 4-year, founded 1924
- **Degree** bachelor's

Minnesota

College of Visual Arts (continued)
- **Urban** 2-acre campus with easy access to Minneapolis
- **Coed**, 264 undergraduate students, 93% full-time, 56% women, 44% men
- **Minimally difficult** entrance level, 65% of applicants were admitted
- 10:1 student-to-undergraduate faculty ratio
- $11,020 tuition and fees
- $600,000 endowment

Students *Undergraduates:* 246 full-time, 18 part-time. Students come from 8 states and territories, 3 other countries. *The most frequently chosen baccalaureate field is:* visual/performing arts.

From out-of-state	20%	Age 25 or older	17%
Transferred in	15%	International students	3%
African Americans	2%	Asian Americans/Pacific Islanders	4%
Hispanic Americans	4%	Native Americans	1%

Faculty 61 (18% full-time).
Expenses (1999–2000) *Tuition:* full-time $10,910; part-time $455 per credit. *Required fees:* full-time $110. Part-time tuition and fees vary according to course load. *Waivers:* children of alumni and employees or children of employees.
Library College of Visual Arts Library. *Collection:* 6,000 titles, 35 serial subscriptions, 15,000 audiovisual materials.
College life *Housing:* college housing not available. *Most popular organization:* AIGA Student Chapter.
Campus security 24-hour patrols, late-night transport-escort service.
After graduation 60% of class of 1998 had job offers within 6 months. *Career center:* 1 part-time personnel. Services include resume preparation, interview workshops, resume referral, career/interest testing, career counseling, careers library, job interviews, speaker series.
Freshmen 135 applied, 88 admitted, 50 enrolled. 2 valedictorians.

Average high school GPA	2.9	SAT verbal scores above 500	N/R
SAT math scores above 500	N/R	ACT above 18	N/R
1998 freshmen returning in 1999	76%		

Application *Options:* eApply at www.CollegeQuest.com, Common Application, electronic application, deferred entrance. *Application fee:* $25. *Required:* essay or personal statement; high school transcript; minimum 2.0 GPA; portfolio. *Recommended:* minimum 3.0 GPA; letters of recommendation; interview.
Standardized tests *Admission: Required for some:* SAT I or ACT.
Significant dates *Application deadlines:* rolling (freshmen), rolling (transfers). *Financial aid deadline:* continuous.
Freshman Application Contact
Ms. Lynn E. Tanaka, Director of Admissions, College of Visual Arts, 344 Summit Avenue, St. Paul, MN 55102-2124. **Phone:** 651-224-3416. **Toll-free phone:** 800-224-1536. **Fax:** 651-224-8854. **E-mail:** info@cva.edu
Visit CollegeQuest.com for information on majors offered and athletics.

CONCORDIA COLLEGE
Moorhead, Minnesota

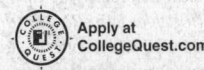
Apply at CollegeQuest.com

- **Independent**, 4-year, founded 1891, affiliated with Evangelical Lutheran Church in America
- **Degree** bachelor's
- **Suburban** 120-acre campus
- **Coed**, 2,883 undergraduate students, 98% full-time, 63% women, 37% men
- **Moderately difficult** entrance level, 88% of applicants were admitted
- 14:1 student-to-undergraduate faculty ratio
- 70% **graduate** in 6 years or less
- $14,020 **tuition** and fees
- **$11,209 average financial aid** package, $18,135 average indebtedness upon graduation, $70.5 million endowment

Ranked by *U.S. News & World Report* as a national liberal arts college, Concordia is distinctive as one of the largest in that group, offering more than 80 majors. The College is also noted for the friendliness of the student body and for both the safety and opportunities of a small city environment.

Students *Undergraduates:* 2,812 full-time, 71 part-time. Students come from 37 states and territories, 34 other countries. *The most frequently chosen baccalaureate fields are:* business/marketing, biological/life sciences, education.

From out-of-state	39%	Reside on campus	58%
Age 25 or older	8%	Transferred in	2%
International students	4%	African Americans	0.4%
Asian Americans/Pacific Islanders	2%	Hispanic Americans	1%
Native Americans	0.3%		

Faculty 237 (77% full-time), 59% with terminal degrees.
Expenses (2000–2001) *Comprehensive fee:* $17,920 includes full-time tuition ($13,904), mandatory fees ($116), and room and board ($3900). *College room only:* $1700. Room and board charges vary according to board plan and housing facility. *Part-time tuition:* $2185 per course. *Part-time fees:* $116 per year part-time. Part-time tuition and fees vary according to course load. *Payment plan:* installment. *Waivers:* employees or children of employees.
Library Carl B. Ylvisaker Library. *Operations spending 1999–2000:* $1.1 million. *Collection:* 300,000 titles, 1,440 serial subscriptions.
College life *Housing:* on-campus residence required through sophomore year. *Options:* coed, men-only, women-only. *Social organizations:* local fraternities, local sororities, local coed fraternity; 4% of eligible men and 4% of eligible women are members. *Most popular organizations:* Sources of Service, Habitat for Humanity, Student Minnesota Education Association, language clubs, health professions interest club.
Campus security 24-hour emergency response devices and patrols, student patrols, late-night transport-escort service, well-lit campus; 24-hour locked wing doors.
After graduation 60 organizations recruited on campus 1997–98. 75% of class of 1998 had job offers within 6 months. *Career center:* 6 full-time, 2 part-time personnel. Services include job fairs, resume preparation, interview workshops, resume referral, career/interest testing, career counseling, careers library, job bank, job interviews. *Graduate education:* 18% of class of 1999 went directly to graduate and professional school: 6% graduate arts and sciences, 3% medicine, 2% business, 2% law, 1% dentistry, 1% education, 1% engineering, 1% theology, 1% veterinary medicine.
Freshmen 2,112 applied, 1,854 admitted, 797 enrolled. 5 National Merit Scholars.

SAT verbal scores above 500	84%	SAT math scores above 500	81%
ACT above 18	96%	From top 10% of their h.s. class	29%
From top quarter	57%	From top half	87%
1998 freshmen returning in 1999	79%		

Application *Options:* eApply at www.CollegeQuest.com, Common Application, electronic application, early admission, deferred entrance. *Application fee:* $20. *Required:* high school transcript; 2 letters of recommendation. *Recommended:* interview.
Standardized tests *Admission: Required:* SAT I or ACT.
Significant dates *Application deadlines:* rolling (freshmen), rolling (transfers). *Financial aid deadline:* continuous.
Freshman Application Contact
Mr. Scott E. Ellingson, Interim Director of Admissions, Concordia College, 901 8th Street South, Moorhead, MN 56562. **Phone:** 218-299-3004. **Toll-free phone:** 800-699-9897. **Fax:** 218-299-3947. **E-mail:** admissions@cord.edu
Visit CollegeQuest.com for information on majors offered and athletics. Electronic viewbook available at CollegeQuest.com.

CONCORDIA UNIVERSITY AT ST. PAUL
St. Paul, Minnesota

Apply at CollegeQuest.com

- **Independent**, comprehensive, founded 1893, affiliated with Lutheran Church–Missouri Synod
- **Degrees** associate, bachelor's, and master's
- **Urban** 37-acre campus
- **Coed**, 1,038 undergraduate students, 86% full-time, 56% women, 44% men
- **Minimally difficult** entrance level, 67% of applicants were admitted
- 14:1 student-to-undergraduate faculty ratio
- 35% **graduate** in 6 years or less
- $14,752 **tuition** and fees

Part of Concordia University System.

Students *Undergraduates:* 892 full-time, 146 part-time. Students come from 45 states and territories, 4 other countries. *The most frequently chosen baccalaureate fields are:* business/marketing, education, philosophy. *Graduate:* 207 in graduate degree programs.

From out-of-state	25%	Reside on campus	48%
Age 25 or older	37%	Transferred in	12%
International students	1%	African Americans	7%
Asian Americans/Pacific Islanders	9%	Hispanic Americans	2%
Native Americans	0.1%		

Faculty 239 (33% full-time), 33% with terminal degrees.

Expenses (2000–2001) *Comprehensive fee:* $19,912 includes full-time tuition ($14,752) and room and board ($5160). *Part-time tuition:* $614 per semester hour. Part-time tuition and fees vary according to course load. *Payment plan:* installment. *Waivers:* senior citizens and employees or children of employees.

Library Buenger Memorial Library plus 1 other. *Operations spending 1999–2000:* $436,972. *Collection:* 125,000 titles, 1,400 serial subscriptions, 6,000 audiovisual materials.

College life *Housing:* on-campus residence required in freshman year. *Options:* coed, men-only, women-only, disabled students. *Most popular organizations:* church vocations, Minority Students, ministry, community based outreach.

Campus security 24-hour emergency response devices and patrols, student patrols, late-night transport-escort service.

After graduation 50 organizations recruited on campus 1997–98. *Career center:* 1 part-time personnel. Services include job fairs, resume preparation, interview workshops, resume referral, career/interest testing, career counseling, careers library, job bank, job interviews.

Freshmen 736 applied, 496 admitted, 308 enrolled.

Average high school GPA	3.21	SAT verbal scores above 500	70%
SAT math scores above 500	62%	ACT above 18	86%
From top 10% of their h.s. class	19%	From top quarter	43%
From top half	72%	1998 freshmen returning in 1999	62%

Application *Options:* eApply at www.CollegeQuest.com, Common Application, electronic application, early admission, deferred entrance. *Application fee:* $20. *Required:* high school transcript; 2 letters of recommendation. *Required for some:* essay or personal statement. *Recommended:* minimum 2.0 GPA; interview.

Standardized tests *Admission: Required:* ACT.

Significant dates *Application deadlines:* 8/15 (freshmen), 8/15 (transfers). *Financial aid deadline:* continuous.

Freshman Application Contact
Mr. Tim Utter, Director of Admissions, Concordia University at St. Paul, 275 Syndicate North, St. Paul, MN 55104-5494. **Phone:** 651-641-8230. **Toll-free phone:** 800-333-4705. **Fax:** 651-659-0207. **E-mail:** admiss@luther.csp.edu

Visit CollegeQuest.com for information on majors offered and athletics. Electronic viewbook available at CollegeQuest.com.

CROWN COLLEGE
St. Bonifacius, Minnesota

- **Independent**, comprehensive, founded 1916, affiliated with The Christian and Missionary Alliance
- **Degrees** associate, bachelor's, and master's
- **Suburban** 193-acre campus with easy access to Minneapolis–St. Paul
- **Coed**, 474 undergraduate students, 95% full-time, 55% women, 45% men
- **Minimally difficult** entrance level, 93% of applicants were admitted
- **14:1 student-to-undergraduate faculty ratio**
- **51% graduate** in 6 years or less
- **$10,570 tuition** and fees
- **$11,780 average financial aid** package, $17,067 average indebtedness upon graduation, $1.8 million endowment

Students *Undergraduates:* 451 full-time, 23 part-time. Students come from 22 states and territories. *The most frequently chosen baccalaureate fields are:* education, business/marketing, philosophy. *Graduate:* 6 in graduate degree programs.

From out-of-state	22%	Reside on campus	78%
Age 25 or older	7%	Transferred in	8%
African Americans	1%	Asian Americans/Pacific Islanders	4%
Hispanic Americans	1%		

Faculty 52 (52% full-time), 31% with terminal degrees.

Expenses (2000–2001) *Comprehensive fee:* $14,990 includes full-time tuition ($9840), mandatory fees ($730), and room and board ($4420). *College room only:* $2056. *Part-time tuition:* $328 per credit hour. *Part-time fees:* $192 per term part-time. Part-time tuition and fees vary according to course load. *Payment plan:* installment. *Waivers:* employees or children of employees.

Library Peter Watne Memorial Library plus 1 other. *Operations spending 1999–2000:* $160,696. *Collection:* 190,000 titles, 1,311 audiovisual materials.

College life *Housing:* on-campus residence required through senior year. *Options:* men-only, women-only. *Most popular organizations:* Missions Support Teams, Hmong Student Fellowship, Married Student Fellowship, Senate/Student Services Board, newspaper/yearbook staff.

Campus security 24-hour emergency response devices, late-night transport-escort service, controlled dormitory access.

After graduation 50 organizations recruited on campus 1997–98. *Career center:* 1 full-time personnel. Services include resume preparation, interview workshops, career/interest testing, career counseling, careers library, job bank, job interviews. *Graduate education:* 11% of class of 1999 went directly to graduate and professional school: 8% theology, 2% business, 1% education.

Freshmen 254 applied, 237 admitted, 135 enrolled.

SAT verbal scores above 500	N/R	SAT math scores above 500	N/R
ACT above 18	82%	From top 10% of their h.s. class	15%
From top quarter	34%	From top half	60%
1998 freshmen returning in 1999	73%		

Application *Options:* early admission, deferred entrance. *Application fee:* $35. *Required:* essay or personal statement; high school transcript; minimum 2.0 GPA; 2 letters of recommendation. *Required for some:* interview.

Standardized tests *Admission: Required:* SAT I or ACT.

Significant dates *Application deadlines:* rolling (freshmen), rolling (transfers). *Financial aid deadline priority date:* 8/1.

Freshman Application Contact
Ms. Kimberely LaQuay, Application Coordinator, Crown College, 6425 County Road 30, St. Bonifacius, MN 55375-9002. **Phone:** 612-446-4143. **Toll-free phone:** 800-68-CROWN. **Fax:** 612-446-4149. **E-mail:** info@crown.edu

Visit CollegeQuest.com for information on majors offered and athletics. College video and electronic viewbook available at CollegeQuest.com.

■ *See page 1540 for a narrative description.*

GUSTAVUS ADOLPHUS COLLEGE
St. Peter, Minnesota

Apply at CollegeQuest.com

- **Independent**, 4-year, founded 1862, affiliated with Evangelical Lutheran Church in America
- **Degree** bachelor's
- **Small-town** 330-acre campus with easy access to Minneapolis–St. Paul
- **Coed**, 2,500 undergraduate students, 99% full-time, 56% women, 44% men
- **Very difficult** entrance level, 79% of applicants were admitted
- **13:1 student-to-undergraduate faculty ratio**
- **75.1% graduate** in 6 years or less
- **$17,430 tuition** and fees
- **$13,459 average financial aid** package, $16,952 average indebtedness upon graduation, $74.8 million endowment

Additions to the 340-acre campus include an international education center and residence hall, a 9-lane outdoor track with access to an indoor track facility, an international soccer field, Campus Center housing, the Market Place and Courtyard Café, a diversity center, a student activities and ticket office, a bookstore, a health center, and student organization offices.

Students *Undergraduates:* 2,481 full-time, 19 part-time. Students come from 42 states and territories, 17 other countries. *The most frequently chosen baccalaureate fields are:* business/marketing, biological/life sciences, social

Minnesota

Gustavus Adolphus College (continued)
sciences and history.

From out-of-state	23%	Reside on campus	85%
Transferred in	1%	International students	1%
African Americans	1%	Asian Americans/Pacific Islanders	3%
Hispanic Americans	1%	Native Americans	0.2%

Faculty 233 (73% full-time), 67% with terminal degrees.

Expenses (1999–2000) *Comprehensive fee:* $21,750 includes full-time tuition ($17,200), mandatory fees ($230), and room and board ($4320). *College room only:* $2050. Full-time tuition and fees vary according to student level. Room and board charges vary according to board plan, housing facility, and student level. *Part-time tuition:* $1875 per course. *Part-time fees:* $165 per year part-time. *Payment plans:* tuition prepayment, installment. *Waivers:* senior citizens and employees or children of employees.

Library Folke Bernadotte Memorial Library plus 4 others. *Operations spending 1999–2000:* $1.5 million. *Collection:* 254,086 titles, 1,752 serial subscriptions, 13,245 audiovisual materials.

College life *Housing:* on-campus residence required through senior year. *Option:* coed. *Social organizations:* local fraternities, local sororities; 20% of eligible men and 25% of eligible women are members. *Most popular organizations:* Campus Activity Board, Gustavus Choir, Greens.

Campus security 24-hour emergency response devices and patrols, late-night transport-escort service, controlled dormitory access.

After graduation 92% of class of 1998 had job offers within 6 months. *Career center:* 3 full-time personnel. Services include job fairs, resume preparation, resume referral, career counseling, careers library, job bank, job interviews. *Graduate education:* 36% of class of 1999 went directly to graduate and professional school: 13% graduate arts and sciences, 7% business, 5% law, 3% engineering, 3% medicine, 2% theology, 1% dentistry, 1% education, 1% veterinary medicine.

Freshmen 1,993 applied, 1,565 admitted, 654 enrolled. 8 National Merit Scholars, 50 valedictorians.

Average high school GPA	3.61	SAT verbal scores above 500	93%
SAT math scores above 500	94%	ACT above 18	99%
From top 10% of their h.s. class	35%	From top quarter	69%
From top half	94%	1998 freshmen returning in 1999	91%

Application *Options:* eApply at www.CollegeQuest.com, Common Application, electronic application, early admission, early decision, early action, deferred entrance. *Application fee:* $25. *Required:* essay or personal statement; high school transcript; 2 letters of recommendation. *Recommended:* interview.

Standardized tests *Admission: Required:* SAT I or ACT.

Significant dates *Application deadlines:* 4/1 (freshmen), 4/1 (transfers). *Early decision:* 11/15, 12/31. *Notification:* continuous until 5/1 (freshmen), 12/1 (early decision), 1/15 (early action). *Financial aid deadline priority date:* 2/15.

Freshman Application Contact
Mr. Mark H. Anderson, Dean of Admission, Gustavus Adolphus College, 800 West College Avenue, St. Peter, MN 56082-1498. **Phone:** 507-933-7676. **Toll-free phone:** 800-GUSTAVU(S). **E-mail:** admission@gac.edu

Visit CollegeQuest.com for information on majors offered and athletics. College video available at CollegeQuest.com.

■ *See page 1750 for a narrative description.*

HAMLINE UNIVERSITY
St. Paul, Minnesota

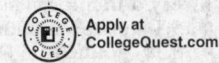
Apply at CollegeQuest.com

- **Independent**, comprehensive, founded 1854, affiliated with United Methodist Church
- **Degrees** bachelor's, master's, doctoral, and first professional
- **Urban** 50-acre campus
- **Coed**, 1,601 undergraduate students, 97% full-time, 65% women, 35% men
- **Moderately difficult** entrance level, 83% of applicants were admitted
- **14:1** student-to-undergraduate faculty ratio
- **60% graduate** in 6 years or less
- **$15,798 tuition** and fees
- **$15,205 average financial aid** package, $18,887 average indebtedness upon graduation, $42.4 million endowment

Students *Undergraduates:* 1,548 full-time, 53 part-time. Students come from 27 states and territories, 34 other countries. *The most frequently chosen baccalaureate fields are:* business/marketing, psychology, social sciences and history. *Graduate:* 488 in professional programs, 790 in other graduate degree programs.

From out-of-state	21%	Reside on campus	47%
Age 25 or older	8%	Transferred in	8%
International students	3%	African Americans	3%
Asian Americans/Pacific Islanders	3%	Hispanic Americans	1%
Native Americans	0.5%		

Faculty 301 (51% full-time), 60% with terminal degrees.

Expenses (1999–2000) *Comprehensive fee:* $21,089 includes full-time tuition ($15,574), mandatory fees ($224), and room and board ($5291). *College room only:* $2728. Room and board charges vary according to board plan. *Part-time tuition:* $1947 per course. *Part-time fees:* $112 per term part-time. Part-time tuition and fees vary according to course load. *Payment plan:* installment. *Waivers:* employees or children of employees.

Library Bush Library plus 1 other. *Operations spending 1999–2000:* $1.8 million. *Collection:* 445,902 titles, 3,803 serial subscriptions, 2,040 audiovisual materials.

College life *Housing: Option:* coed. *Social organizations:* local sororities, international dining club; 5% of women are members. *Most popular organizations:* student congress, Acting in the Community Together, Minnesota Public Interest Research Group, residential hall councils, Affordable Arts.

Campus security 24-hour emergency response devices and patrols, student patrols, late-night transport-escort service, controlled dormitory access.

After graduation 71% of class of 1998 had job offers within 6 months. *Career center:* 5 full-time, 3 part-time personnel. Services include job fairs, resume preparation, interview workshops, resume referral, career counseling, careers library, job bank, job interviews. *Graduate education:* 26% of class of 1999 went directly to graduate and professional school: 14% graduate arts and sciences, 5% law, 4% education, 2% business, 1% medicine. *Major awards:* 1 Fulbright Scholar.

Freshmen 1,230 applied, 1,023 admitted, 421 enrolled. 6 National Merit Scholars, 16 valedictorians.

Average high school GPA	3.41	SAT verbal scores above 500	90%
SAT math scores above 500	87%	ACT above 18	96%
From top 10% of their h.s. class	29%	From top quarter	60%
From top half	90%	1998 freshmen returning in 1999	83%

Application *Options:* eApply at www.CollegeQuest.com, electronic application, early admission, early action, deferred entrance. *Required:* essay or personal statement; high school transcript; 2 letters of recommendation. *Recommended:* interview.

Standardized tests *Admission: Required:* SAT I or ACT.

Significant dates *Application deadlines:* rolling (freshmen), rolling (transfers). *Early action:* 12/1. *Notification:* 12/15 (early action). *Financial aid deadline priority date:* 5/1.

Freshman Application Contact
Mr. Steven Bjork, Director of Undergraduate Admission, Hamline University, 1536 Hewitt Avenue C1930, St. Paul, MN 55104-1284. **Phone:** 651-523-2207. **Toll-free phone:** 800-753-9753. **Fax:** 651-523-2458. **E-mail:** cla-admis@gw.hamline.edu

Visit CollegeQuest.com for information on majors offered and athletics. Electronic viewbook available at CollegeQuest.com.

MACALESTER COLLEGE
St. Paul, Minnesota

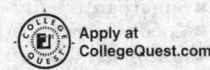
Apply at CollegeQuest.com

- **Independent Presbyterian**, 4-year, founded 1874
- **Degree** bachelor's
- **Urban** 53-acre campus
- **Coed**, 1,794 undergraduate students, 98% full-time, 58% women, 42% men
- **Very difficult** entrance level, 53% of applicants were admitted
- **11:1** student-to-undergraduate faculty ratio
- **78% graduate** in 6 years or less
- **$20,688 tuition** and fees
- **$16,006 average financial aid** package, $14,350 average indebtedness upon graduation, $517.2 million endowment

Minnesota

Students *Undergraduates:* 1,765 full-time, 29 part-time. Students come from 50 states and territories, 81 other countries. *The most frequently chosen baccalaureate fields are:* biological/life sciences, psychology, social sciences and history.

From out-of-state	62%	Reside on campus	70%
Age 25 or older	0.4%	Transferred in	2%
International students	11%	African Americans	4%
Asian Americans/Pacific Islanders	5%	Hispanic Americans	3%
Native Americans	0.4%		

Faculty 201 (73% full-time), 83% with terminal degrees.
Expenses (1999–2000) *Comprehensive fee:* $26,448 includes full-time tuition ($20,560), mandatory fees ($128), and room and board ($5760). *College room only:* $2990. *Part-time tuition:* $645 per semester hour. *Payment plan:* installment. *Waivers:* employees or children of employees.
Library DeWitt Wallace Library. *Operations spending 1999–2000:* $2.1 million. *Collection:* 390,025 titles, 1,703 serial subscriptions, 7,018 audiovisual materials.
College life *Housing:* on-campus residence required through sophomore year. *Options:* coed, cooperative. *Most popular organizations:* Community Service Organization, student publications, multicultural organization, MPIRG, outing club.
Campus security 24-hour emergency response devices and patrols, late-night transport-escort service, controlled dormitory access.
After graduation 100 organizations recruited on campus 1997–98. 65% of class of 1998 had job offers within 6 months. *Career center:* 3 full-time, 2 part-time personnel. Services include job fairs, resume preparation, interview workshops, resume referral, career/interest testing, career counseling, careers library, job bank, job interviews. *Graduate education:* 18% of class of 1999 went directly to graduate and professional school: 12% graduate arts and sciences, 3% law, 3% medicine. *Major awards:* 1 Marshall, 3 Fulbright Scholars.
Freshmen 3,161 applied, 1,681 admitted, 460 enrolled. 39 National Merit Scholars, 29 valedictorians.

SAT verbal scores above 500	99%	SAT math scores above 500	98%
ACT above 18	100%	From top 10% of their h.s. class	59%
From top quarter	94%	From top half	100%
1998 freshmen returning in 1999	90%		

Application *Options:* eApply at www.CollegeQuest.com, Common Application, electronic application, early admission, early decision, deferred entrance. *Application fee:* $40. *Required:* essay or personal statement; high school transcript; 3 letters of recommendation. *Recommended:* interview.
Standardized tests *Admission: Required:* SAT I or ACT. *Recommended:* SAT II Subject Tests.
Significant dates *Application deadlines:* 1/15 (freshmen), 3/15 (transfers). *Early decision:* 11/15 (for plan 1), 1/15 (for plan 2). *Notification:* 3/30 (freshmen), 12/15 (early decision plan 1), 2/7 (early decision plan 2). *Financial aid deadline priority date:* 2/8.
Freshman Application Contact
Mr. Lorne T. Robinson, Dean of Admissions and Financial Aid, Macalester College, 1600 Grand Avenue, St. Paul, MN 55105-1899. **Phone:** 651-696-6357. **Toll-free phone:** 800-231-7974. **Fax:** 651-696-6500. **E-mail:** admissions@macalester.edu
Visit CollegeQuest.com for information on majors offered and athletics.

MANKATO STATE UNIVERSITY
Minnesota—See Minnesota State University, Mankato

MARTIN LUTHER COLLEGE
New Ulm, Minnesota

- **Independent**, 4-year, founded 1995, affiliated with Wisconsin Evangelical Lutheran Synod
- **Degree** bachelor's
- **Small-town** 50-acre campus
- **Coed**, 909 undergraduate students, 99% full-time, 50% women, 50% men
- **Moderately difficult** entrance level, 94% of applicants were admitted
- **9:1 student-to-undergraduate faculty ratio**
- **66% graduate** in 6 years or less

- **$5145 tuition** and fees

Students *Undergraduates:* 902 full-time, 7 part-time. Students come from 35 states and territories, 9 other countries. *The most frequently chosen baccalaureate fields are:* education, interdisciplinary studies, philosophy.

From out-of-state	77%	Reside on campus	86%
Age 25 or older	3%	Transferred in	4%
International students	1%	African Americans	0.3%
Asian Americans/Pacific Islanders	1%	Hispanic Americans	0.3%
Native Americans	0.1%		

Faculty 78 (81% full-time), 41% with terminal degrees.
Expenses (2000–2001) *Comprehensive fee:* $7485 includes full-time tuition ($4610), mandatory fees ($535), and room and board ($2340). *College room only:* $600. *Part-time tuition:* $125 per semester hour. *Part-time fees:* $65 per term part-time. *Payment plan:* installment.
Library Martin Luther College Library. *Operations spending 1999–2000:* $188,649. *Collection:* 160,753 titles, 385 serial subscriptions, 5,469 audiovisual materials.
College life *Housing:* on-campus residence required through junior year. *Options:* men-only, women-only. *Most popular organizations:* drama club, Color Guard, Pom Poms.
Campus security 24-hour emergency response devices, student patrols, controlled dormitory access.
Freshmen 326 applied, 305 admitted, 242 enrolled. 7 valedictorians.

Average high school GPA	3.43	SAT verbal scores above 500	N/R
SAT math scores above 500	N/R	ACT above 18	N/R
From top 10% of their h.s. class	19%	From top quarter	45%
From top half	75%	1998 freshmen returning in 1999	87%

Application *Option:* deferred entrance. *Application fee:* $25. *Required:* high school transcript; minimum 2.0 GPA; letters of recommendation.
Standardized tests *Admission: Required:* ACT.
Significant dates *Application deadlines:* 5/1 (freshmen), 5/1 (transfers). *Notification:* continuous until 5/1 (freshmen). *Financial aid deadline:* 5/1.
Freshman Application Contact
Prof. Ronald B. Brutlag, Associate Director of Admissions, Martin Luther College, 1995 Luther Court, New Ulm, MN 56073-3965. **Phone:** 507-354-8221 Ext. 280. **Fax:** 507-354-8225. **E-mail:** brutlaro@mlc-wels.edu
Visit CollegeQuest.com for information on majors offered and athletics. College video available at CollegeQuest.com.

MAYO SCHOOL OF HEALTH-RELATED SCIENCES
Rochester, Minnesota

- **Independent**, upper-level, founded 1973
- **Degrees** associate, bachelor's, master's, and postbachelor's certificates
- **Urban** campus
- **Coed**
- **Moderately difficult** entrance level

Institutional Web site http://www.mayo.edu/hrs/hrs.htm
College life *Housing:* college housing not available.
Campus security 24-hour emergency response devices, late-night transport-escort service.
Application *Option:* Common Application.
Standardized tests *Admission: Required:* SAT I and SAT II or ACT.
Admissions Office Contact
Mayo School of Health-Related Sciences, 200 First Street, SW, Rochester, MN 55905. **Toll-free phone:** 800-626-9041. **Fax:** 507-284-0999. **E-mail:** kray@mayo.edu
Visit CollegeQuest.com for information on athletics. Electronic viewbook available at CollegeQuest.com.

METROPOLITAN STATE UNIVERSITY
St. Paul, Minnesota

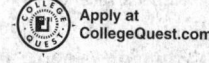

- **State-supported**, comprehensive, founded 1971

Minnesota

Metropolitan State University (continued)
- **Degrees** bachelor's and master's (offers primarily part-time evening degree programs)
- **Urban** campus
- **Coed**, 4,653 undergraduate students
- **Moderately difficult** entrance level
- **$2269 tuition** and fees (in-state); $4831 (out-of-state)

Part of Minnesota State Colleges and Universities System.

Students *Undergraduates:* Students come from 5 states and territories, 13 other countries.

Age 25 or older	86%

Faculty 497 (5% full-time).

Expenses (1999–2000) *Tuition, state resident:* full-time $2117; part-time $8820 per credit. *Tuition, nonresident:* full-time $4679; part-time $195 per credit. *Required fees:* full-time $152; $6 per credit. Full-time tuition and fees vary according to course load. *Waivers:* senior citizens and employees or children of employees.

College life *Housing:* college housing not available.

Campus security Late-night transport-escort service.

After graduation *Career center:* 2 full-time personnel. Services include job fairs, resume preparation, career counseling. *Graduate education:* 23% of class of 1999 went directly to graduate and professional school.

Freshmen

SAT verbal scores above 500	N/R	SAT math scores above 500		N/R
ACT above 18	N/R	1998 freshmen returning in 1999		68%

Application *Options:* eApply at www.CollegeQuest.com, deferred entrance. *Application fee:* $20. *Required:* high school transcript; minimum 2.0 GPA.

Standardized tests *Admission: Required for some:* ACT.

Significant dates *Application deadlines:* rolling (freshmen), rolling (transfers). *Financial aid deadline priority date:* 6/1.

Freshman Application Contact
Ms. Cindy Olson, Registrar, Metropolitan State University, 700 East 7th Street, St. Paul, MN 55106-5000. **Phone:** 651-772-7776. **Fax:** 651-772-7632.

Visit CollegeQuest.com for information on majors offered and athletics.

MINNEAPOLIS COLLEGE OF ART AND DESIGN
Minneapolis, Minnesota

- **Independent**, comprehensive, founded 1886
- **Degrees** bachelor's, master's, and postbachelor's certificates
- **Urban** 7-acre campus
- **Coed**, 558 undergraduate students, 89% full-time, 42% women, 58% men
- **Moderately difficult** entrance level, 73% of applicants were admitted
- **11:1 student-to-undergraduate faculty ratio**
- **62% graduate** in 6 years or less
- **$18,190 tuition** and fees
- **$12,081 average financial aid** package, $22,250 average indebtedness upon graduation, $35.1 million endowment

Located in a culturally supportive city, the Minneapolis College of Art and Design offers a rigorous BFA curriculum that teaches students to think conceptually and creatively and to explore various techniques and technology. In addition, MCAD also offers a BS in visualization, which offers course work in visual persuasion and information techniques. MCAD's facilities are extensive and include individual studio spaces, state-of-the-art computer and media areas, and student galleries.

Students *Undergraduates:* 494 full-time, 64 part-time. Students come from 36 states and territories. *The most frequently chosen baccalaureate field is:* visual/performing arts. *Graduate:* 25 in graduate degree programs.

From out-of-state	36%	Reside on campus	33%
Age 25 or older	15%	Transferred in	13%
African Americans	2%	Asian Americans/Pacific Islanders	6%
Hispanic Americans	1%	Native Americans	0.2%

Faculty 108 (48% full-time), 14% with terminal degrees.

Expenses (1999–2000) *Tuition:* full-time $17,910; part-time $597 per credit. *Required fees:* full-time $280; $40 per term part-time. *College room only:* $2900. Room and board charges vary according to housing facility. *Payment plan:* installment. *Waivers:* children of alumni and employees or children of employees.

Library Minneapolis College of Art and Design Library. *Operations spending 1999–2000:* $264,400. *Collection:* 47,166 titles, 196 serial subscriptions, 139,245 audiovisual materials.

College life *Housing: Option:* coed.

Campus security 24-hour emergency response devices and patrols, late-night transport-escort service.

After graduation 6 organizations recruited on campus 1997–98. 90% of class of 1998 had job offers within 6 months. *Career center:* 2 full-time personnel. Services include resume preparation, interview workshops, career counseling, careers library, job bank, job interviews. *Graduate education:* 10% of class of 1999 went directly to graduate and professional school: 10% graduate arts and sciences.

Freshmen 317 applied, 230 admitted, 87 enrolled.

Average high school GPA	3.02	SAT verbal scores above 500	75%
SAT math scores above 500	50%	ACT above 18	83%
From top 10% of their h.s. class	5%	From top quarter	36%
From top half	79%	1998 freshmen returning in 1999	77%

Application *Options:* Common Application, deferred entrance. *Application fee:* $35. *Required:* essay or personal statement; high school transcript; 1 letter of recommendation. *Required for some:* portfolio. *Recommended:* interview.

Standardized tests *Admission: Required:* SAT I or ACT.

Significant dates *Application deadlines:* rolling (freshmen), rolling (transfers). *Financial aid deadline:* continuous.

Freshman Application Contact
Ms. Susan Neppl, Director of Enrollment and Student Financial Services, Minneapolis College of Art and Design, 2501 Stevens Avenue South, Minneapolis, MN 55404-4347. **Phone:** 612-874-3762. **Toll-free phone:** 800-874-6223. **Fax:** 612-874-3704. **E-mail:** admissions@mn.mcad.edu

Visit CollegeQuest.com for information on majors offered and athletics.

- *See page 2066 for a narrative description.*

MINNESOTA BIBLE COLLEGE
Rochester, Minnesota

- **Independent**, 4-year, founded 1913, affiliated with Christian Churches and Churches of Christ
- **Degrees** associate and bachelor's
- **Urban** 40-acre campus with easy access to Minneapolis–St. Paul
- **Coed**, 114 undergraduate students, 88% full-time, 43% women, 57% men
- **Noncompetitive** entrance level, 90% of applicants were admitted
- **8:1 student-to-undergraduate faculty ratio**
- **63% graduate** in 6 years or less
- **$6056 tuition** and fees
- **$18,558 average indebtedness** upon graduation, $672,000 endowment

Students *Undergraduates:* 100 full-time, 14 part-time. Students come from 9 states and territories, 5 other countries. *The most frequently chosen baccalaureate field is:* philosophy.

From out-of-state	43%	Reside on campus	78%
Age 25 or older	28%	Transferred in	14%
International students	5%	African Americans	4%
Asian Americans/Pacific Islanders	4%	Hispanic Americans	3%

Faculty 21 (43% full-time), 38% with terminal degrees.

Expenses (1999–2000) *Tuition:* full-time $5746; part-time $169 per semester hour. *Required fees:* full-time $310. *College room only:* $1800. Room and board charges vary according to housing facility. *Payment plan:* installment. *Waivers:* senior citizens and employees or children of employees.

Library G. H. Cachiaras Memorial Library. *Operations spending 1999–2000:* $75,888. *Collection:* 31,116 titles, 175 serial subscriptions, 1,242 audiovisual materials.

College life *Housing:* on-campus residence required through senior year. *Options:* men-only, women-only. *Most popular organizations:* Christian Outdoors, Musical Outreach, Ambassadors Mission Group.

Campus security Student patrols, late-night transport-escort service.

After graduation 10 organizations recruited on campus 1997–98. 29% of class of 1998 had job offers within 6 months. *Career center:* 1 full-time, 6

part-time personnel. Services include resume preparation, career counseling, careers library, job bank. *Graduate education:* 8% of class of 1999 went directly to graduate and professional school: 8% theology.

Freshmen 21 applied, 19 admitted, 16 enrolled.

Average high school GPA	3.05	SAT verbal scores above 500	N/R
SAT math scores above 500	N/R	ACT above 18	67%
From top quarter of their h.s. class	20%	From top half	40%
1998 freshmen returning in 1999	54%		

Application *Option:* deferred entrance. *Application fee:* $30. *Required:* essay or personal statement; high school transcript; 3 letters of recommendation. *Required for some:* interview.

Standardized tests *Admission: Required:* SAT I or ACT.

Significant dates *Application deadlines:* 8/15 (freshmen), 8/15 (transfers). *Notification:* continuous until 9/1 (freshmen). *Financial aid deadline priority date:* 6/1.

Freshman Application Contact
Mr. Alan D. Wager, Director of Admissions, Minnesota Bible College, 920 Mayowood Road, SW, Rochester, MN 55902-2382. **Phone:** 507-288-4563 Ext. 246. **Toll-free phone:** 800-456-7651. **Fax:** 507-288-9046. **E-mail:** admissions@mnbc.edu

Visit CollegeQuest.com for information on majors offered and athletics. College video available at CollegeQuest.com.

MINNESOTA STATE UNIVERSITY, MANKATO
Mankato, Minnesota

- **State-supported**, comprehensive, founded 1868
- **Degrees** associate, bachelor's, master's, and post-master's certificates
- **Small-town** 303-acre campus with easy access to Minneapolis–St. Paul
- **Coed**, 10,087 undergraduate students, 87% full-time, 53% women, 47% men
- **Moderately difficult** entrance level, 91% of applicants were admitted
- **20:1 student-to-undergraduate faculty ratio**
- **42.4% graduate** in 6 years or less
- **$3492 tuition** and fees (in-state); $6292 (out-of-state)
- **$1.5 million endowment**

Part of Minnesota State Colleges and Universities System.

Students *Undergraduates:* 8,809 full-time, 1,278 part-time. Students come from 39 states and territories, 70 other countries. *The most frequently chosen baccalaureate fields are:* business/marketing, education, protective services/public administration. *Graduate:* 1,643 in graduate degree programs.

From out-of-state	14%	Reside on campus	25%
Age 25 or older	14%	Transferred in	9%
International students	2%	African Americans	1%
Asian Americans/Pacific Islanders	2%	Hispanic Americans	1%
Native Americans	0.2%		

Faculty 584 (90% full-time), 64% with terminal degrees.

Expenses (1999–2000) *Tuition, state resident:* full-time $2996; part-time $104 per credit. *Tuition, nonresident:* full-time $5796; part-time $220 per credit. *Required fees:* full-time $496; $21 per credit. Full-time tuition and fees vary according to course load and reciprocity agreements. Part-time tuition and fees vary according to course load and reciprocity agreements. *College room and board:* $5348; room only: $2004. Room and board charges vary according to board plan. *Payment plan:* installment. *Waivers:* senior citizens and employees or children of employees.

Library Memorial Library. *Operations spending 1999–2000:* $3.5 million. *Collection:* 1 million titles, 3,200 serial subscriptions.

College life *Housing: Option:* coed. *Social organizations:* national fraternities, national sororities; 4% of eligible men and 4% of eligible women are members.

Campus security 24-hour emergency response devices and patrols, student patrols, late-night transport-escort service, Night Owl security program in residence halls, closed circuit cameras in parking lots.

After graduation 400 organizations recruited on campus 1997–98. *Career center:* 6 full-time, 3 part-time personnel. Services include job fairs, resume preparation, interview workshops, resume referral, career/interest testing, career counseling, careers library, job bank, job interviews.

Freshmen 4,511 applied, 4,094 admitted, 2,038 enrolled.

SAT verbal scores above 500	N/R	SAT math scores above 500	N/R
ACT above 18	89%	From top 10% of their h.s. class	9%
From top quarter	30%	From top half	71%
1998 freshmen returning in 1999	77%		

Application *Options:* electronic application, early admission, deferred entrance. *Application fee:* $20. *Required:* high school transcript. *Required for some:* essay or personal statement; 3 letters of recommendation.

Standardized tests *Admission: Required:* ACT.

Significant dates *Application deadlines:* rolling (freshmen), rolling (transfers).

Freshman Application Contact
Mr. Walt Wolff, Director of Admissions, Minnesota State University, Mankato, 209 Wigley Administration Center, Mankato, MN 56001. **Phone:** 507-389-6670. **Toll-free phone:** 800-722-0544. **E-mail:** admissions@mankato.msus.edu

Visit CollegeQuest.com for information on majors offered and athletics.

MINNESOTA STATE UNIVERSITY MOORHEAD
Moorhead, Minnesota

- **State-supported**, comprehensive, founded 1885
- **Degrees** associate, bachelor's, master's, and post-master's certificates
- **Urban** 118-acre campus
- **Coed**, 6,129 undergraduate students, 86% full-time, 62% women, 38% men
- **Moderately difficult** entrance level, 91% of applicants were admitted
- **38.5% graduate** in 6 years or less
- **$3179 tuition** and fees (in-state); $6568 (out-of-state)

Part of Minnesota State Colleges and Universities System.

Students *Undergraduates:* 5,244 full-time, 885 part-time. Students come from 39 states and territories, 25 other countries. *The most frequently chosen baccalaureate fields are:* business/marketing, education, protective services/public administration. *Graduate:* 330 in graduate degree programs.

From out-of-state	39%	Reside on campus	27%
Age 25 or older	19%	Transferred in	11%
International students	1%	African Americans	1%
Asian Americans/Pacific Islanders	1%	Hispanic Americans	1%
Native Americans	1%		

Faculty 272 (96% full-time), 65% with terminal degrees.

Expenses (1999–2000) *Tuition, state resident:* full-time $2729; part-time $85 per credit. *Tuition, nonresident:* full-time $6118; part-time $191 per credit. *Required fees:* full-time $450; $19 per credit. Full-time tuition and fees vary according to reciprocity agreements. Part-time tuition and fees vary according to reciprocity agreements. *College room and board:* $3264; room only: $1978. Room and board charges vary according to board plan. *Payment plan:* deferred payment. *Waivers:* senior citizens and employees or children of employees.

Library Livingston Lord Library. *Operations spending 1999–2000:* $1.4 million. *Collection:* 367,334 titles, 1,539 serial subscriptions.

College life *Housing: Options:* coed, men-only, women-only. *Social organizations:* national fraternities, national sororities, local fraternities; 3% of eligible men and 2% of eligible women are members. *Most popular organizations:* residence hall associations, campus activities board, Pi Sigma Epsilon, Campus Crusade for Christ, transfer club.

Campus security 24-hour emergency response devices and patrols, student patrols, late-night transport-escort service, controlled dormitory access.

After graduation 160 organizations recruited on campus 1997–98. *Career center:* 4 full-time, 12 part-time personnel. Services include job fairs, resume preparation, resume referral, career counseling, careers library, job bank, job interviews. *Graduate education:* 7% of class of 1999 went directly to graduate and professional school.

Freshmen 1,993 applied, 1,818 admitted, 1,158 enrolled.

SAT verbal scores above 500	N/R	SAT math scores above 500	N/R
ACT above 18	88%	From top 10% of their h.s. class	11%
From top quarter	39%	From top half	84%
1998 freshmen returning in 1999	69%		

Application *Options:* early admission, deferred entrance. *Application fee:* $20. *Required:* high school transcript.

Minnesota

Minnesota State University Moorhead (continued)
Standardized tests *Admission: Required:* SAT I or ACT, PSAT.
Significant dates *Application deadlines:* 8/7 (freshmen), 8/7 (transfers). *Financial aid deadline priority date:* 3/1.
Freshman Application Contact
Ms. Jean Butler, Director of Admissions, Minnesota State University Moorhead, Owens Hall, Moorhead, MN 56563-0002. **Phone:** 218-236-2548. **Toll-free phone:** 800-593-7246. **Fax:** 218-236-2168.
Visit CollegeQuest.com for information on majors offered and athletics. College video available at CollegeQuest.com.

MOORHEAD STATE UNIVERSITY
Minnesota—See Minnesota State University Moorhead

NATIONAL AMERICAN UNIVERSITY—ST. PAUL CAMPUS
St. Paul, Minnesota

- **Proprietary**, 4-year, founded 1974
- **Degrees** associate and bachelor's
- **Urban** 1-acre campus
- **Coed**, 412 undergraduate students, 53% full-time, 49% women, 51% men
- **Noncompetitive** entrance level, 100% of applicants were admitted
- **10:1 student-to-undergraduate faculty ratio**
- **$10,080 tuition** and fees

Part of National American University.
Students *Undergraduates:* 220 full-time, 192 part-time. Students come from 5 states and territories. *The most frequently chosen baccalaureate fields are:* business/marketing, computer/information sciences.

Age 25 or older	50%	International students	5%
African Americans	18%	Asian Americans/Pacific Islanders	16%
Hispanic Americans	3%	Native Americans	0.4%

Faculty 32 (16% full-time), 22% with terminal degrees.
Expenses (1999–2000) *Tuition:* full-time $10,080; part-time $210 per credit. Full-time tuition and fees vary according to program. Part-time tuition and fees vary according to program. *Payment plan:* installment. *Waivers:* employees or children of employees.
Library National College Library plus 1 other. *Operations spending 1999–2000:* $75,000. *Collection:* 1,500 titles, 25 serial subscriptions.
College life *Housing:* college housing not available. *Most popular organizations:* Southeast Asian Student Organization, Phi Beta Lambda/Lambda Beta Omicron, Student Government Association, International Student Organization.
Campus security Late-night transport-escort service.
After graduation 5 organizations recruited on campus 1997–98. 94% of class of 1998 had job offers within 6 months. *Career center:* 2 full-time, 1 part-time personnel. Services include job fairs, resume preparation, resume referral, career/interest testing, career counseling, careers library, job bank, job interviews.
Freshmen 259 applied, 259 admitted, 45 enrolled.

SAT verbal scores above 500	N/R	SAT math scores above 500	N/R
ACT above 18	N/R	1998 freshmen returning in 1999	52%

Application *Options:* Common Application, deferred entrance. *Application fee:* $25. *Required:* high school transcript. *Required for some:* essay or personal statement. *Recommended:* minimum 2.0 GPA; interview.
Significant dates *Application deadlines:* rolling (freshmen), rolling (transfers). *Financial aid deadline:* continuous.
Freshman Application Contact
Mrs. Cindy Olson, Director of Admissions, National American University–St. Paul Campus, 1380 Energy Lane, Suite 13, St. Paul, MN 55108-9952. **Phone:** 651-644-1265. **Fax:** 651-644-0690. **E-mail:** natcoll@iaxs.net
Visit CollegeQuest.com for information on majors offered and athletics.

NORTH CENTRAL UNIVERSITY
Minneapolis, Minnesota

- **Independent**, 4-year, founded 1930, affiliated with Assemblies of God
- **Degrees** associate and bachelor's
- **Urban** 9-acre campus
- **Coed**, 1,172 undergraduate students, 89% full-time, 57% women, 43% men
- **Noncompetitive** entrance level, 77% of applicants were admitted
- **18:1 student-to-undergraduate faculty ratio**
- **62.5% graduate** in 6 years or less
- **$8020 tuition** and fees
- **$969,948 endowment**

Students *Undergraduates:* 1,043 full-time, 129 part-time. Students come from 40 states and territories, 11 other countries. *The most frequently chosen baccalaureate fields are:* education, communications/communication technologies, philosophy.

From out-of-state	50%	Reside on campus	65%
Age 25 or older	16%	Transferred in	11%
International students	3%	African Americans	5%
Asian Americans/Pacific Islanders	1%	Hispanic Americans	3%
Native Americans	1%		

Faculty 88 (57% full-time), 26% with terminal degrees.
Expenses (1999–2000) *Comprehensive fee:* $11,920 includes full-time tuition ($7350), mandatory fees ($670), and room and board ($3900). *College room only:* $1710. Room and board charges vary according to board plan and housing facility. *Part-time tuition:* $245 per credit. *Part-time fees:* $35 per credit. Part-time tuition and fees vary according to course load. *Payment plan:* installment. *Waivers:* senior citizens and employees or children of employees.
Library T. J. Jones Information Resource Center. *Operations spending 1999–2000:* $282,286. *Collection:* 70,041 titles, 384 serial subscriptions.
College life *Housing:* on-campus residence required through senior year. *Options:* men-only, women-only. *Most popular organizations:* athletics, Mu Kappa, musical organizations, student government, student ministries.
Campus security 24-hour emergency response devices and patrols, late-night transport-escort service, controlled dormitory access.
After graduation 15 organizations recruited on campus 1997–98. *Career center:* Services include job fairs, resume preparation, resume referral, career counseling, job interviews.
Freshmen 551 applied, 427 admitted, 270 enrolled.

SAT verbal scores above 500	N/R	SAT math scores above 500	N/R
ACT above 18	N/R	From top 10% of their h.s. class	8%
From top quarter	26%	From top half	70%
1998 freshmen returning in 1999	68%		

Application *Options:* Common Application, deferred entrance. *Application fee:* $25. *Required:* essay or personal statement; high school transcript; minimum 2.2 GPA; letters of recommendation; Christian testimony.
Standardized tests *Admission: Required:* SAT I or ACT.
Significant dates *Application deadlines:* 6/1 (freshmen), 6/1 (transfers). *Notification:* 7/1 (freshmen). *Financial aid deadline priority date:* 4/30.
Freshman Application Contact
Ms. Mary Jo Meier, Admissions Secretary, North Central University, 910 Elliot Avenue, Minneapolis, MN 55404. **Phone:** 612-343-4401. **Toll-free phone:** 800-289-6222. **Fax:** 612-343-4778. **E-mail:** admissions@northcentral.edu
Visit CollegeQuest.com for information on majors offered and athletics. College video available at CollegeQuest.com.

NORTHWESTERN COLLEGE
St. Paul, Minnesota

- **Independent nondenominational**, 4-year, founded 1902
- **Degrees** associate and bachelor's
- **Suburban** 100-acre campus
- **Coed**, 1,623 undergraduate students, 95% full-time, 61% women, 39% men
- **Moderately difficult** entrance level, 71% of applicants were admitted
- **14:1 student-to-undergraduate faculty ratio**
- **52% graduate** in 6 years or less

Minnesota

- **$14,982 tuition** and fees
- **$16,000 average indebtedness** upon graduation, $4 million endowment

NWC is a nondenominational Christian college where students earn an equivalent of a double major in an academic area and the Bible. More than 1,400 students enjoy a Christian community atmosphere, music, athletics, drama, and missions opportunities. Daily chapel services, 41 academic majors, and the Minneapolis–St. Paul location are benefits of NWC.

Students *Undergraduates:* 1,538 full-time, 85 part-time. Students come from 35 states and territories, 22 other countries. *The most frequently chosen baccalaureate fields are:* business/marketing, education, psychology.

From out-of-state	36%	Reside on campus	62%
Age 25 or older	15%	Transferred in	5%
International students	1%	African Americans	2%
Asian Americans/Pacific Islanders	2%	Hispanic Americans	1%
Native Americans	0.1%		

Faculty 127 (51% full-time), 50% with terminal degrees.

Expenses (2000–2001) *Comprehensive fee:* $19,430 includes full-time tuition ($14,982) and room and board ($4448). *College room only:* $2566. Full-time tuition and fees vary according to course load and program. Room and board charges vary according to board plan. *Part-time tuition:* $625 per credit. Part-time tuition and fees vary according to program. *Payment plan:* installment. *Waivers:* senior citizens and employees or children of employees.

Library Berntsen Resource Center. *Operations spending 1999–2000:* $561,109. *Collection:* 74,857 titles, 1,695 serial subscriptions.

College life *Housing:* on-campus residence required through sophomore year. *Options:* men-only, women-only, disabled students. *Most popular organizations:* NWSA (student government association), Edge (religious group), Transfer Connection, Guardian Angels, Mu Kappa.

Campus security 24-hour patrols, late-night transport-escort service, controlled dormitory access.

After graduation 147 organizations recruited on campus 1997–98. 77% of class of 1998 had job offers within 6 months. *Career center:* 2 full-time personnel. Services include job fairs, resume preparation, interview workshops, resume referral, career/interest testing, career counseling, careers library, job bank, job interviews. *Graduate education:* 6% of class of 1999 went directly to graduate and professional school: 2% graduate arts and sciences, 1% education, 1% law, 1% medicine, 1% theology.

Freshmen 1,181 applied, 841 admitted, 404 enrolled. 19 valedictorians.

Average high school GPA	3.47	SAT verbal scores above 500	85%
SAT math scores above 500	80%	ACT above 18	94%
From top 10% of their h.s. class	25%	From top quarter	54%
From top half	89%	1998 freshmen returning in 1999	77%

Application *Options:* electronic application, early admission, deferred entrance. *Application fee:* $20. *Required:* essay or personal statement; high school transcript; minimum 2.0 GPA; 2 letters of recommendation; lifestyle agreement, statement of Christian faith. *Required for some:* interview. *Recommended:* minimum 3.0 GPA; interview.

Standardized tests *Admission: Required:* SAT I or ACT.

Significant dates *Application deadlines:* 8/15 (freshmen), 8/15 (transfers). *Notification:* continuous until 8/24 (freshmen). *Financial aid deadline priority date:* 3/1.

Freshman Application Contact
Mr. Kenneth K. Faffler, Director of Recruitment, Northwestern College, 3003 Snelling Avenue North, St. Paul, MN 55113-1598. **Phone:** 651-631-5209. **Toll-free phone:** 800-827-6827. **Fax:** 651-631-5680.
Visit CollegeQuest.com for information on majors offered and athletics. College video available at CollegeQuest.com.

NORTHWESTERN HEALTH SCIENCES UNIVERSITY
Bloomington, Minnesota

Admissions Office Contact
Northwestern Health Sciences University, 2501 West 84th Street, Bloomington, MN 55431-1599. **Toll-free phone:** 800-888-4777.

OAK HILLS CHRISTIAN COLLEGE
Bemidji, Minnesota

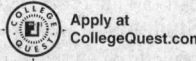
Apply at CollegeQuest.com

- **Independent interdenominational**, 4-year, founded 1946
- **Degrees** associate and bachelor's
- **Rural** 180-acre campus
- **Coed**, 150 undergraduate students, 87% full-time, 50% women, 50% men
- **Minimally difficult** entrance level, 55% of applicants were admitted
- **11:1 student-to-undergraduate faculty ratio**
- **10.34% graduate** in 6 years or less
- **$8590 tuition** and fees
- **$193,184 endowment**

Students *Undergraduates:* 131 full-time, 19 part-time. Students come from 13 states and territories. *The most frequently chosen baccalaureate field is:* philosophy.

Reside on campus	80%	Age 25 or older	12%
Transferred in	10%	Native Americans	1%

Faculty 16 (50% full-time).

Expenses (1999–2000) *Comprehensive fee:* $11,690 includes full-time tuition ($7970), mandatory fees ($620), and room and board ($3100). *College room only:* $1480. Full-time tuition and fees vary according to course load. Room and board charges vary according to housing facility. *Part-time tuition:* $250 per semester hour. *Part-time fees:* $310 per term part-time. Part-time tuition and fees vary according to course load. *Payment plan:* installment. *Waivers:* employees or children of employees.

Library Cummings Library. *Operations spending 1999–2000:* $82,767. *Collection:* 22,000 titles, 150 serial subscriptions.

College life *Housing:* on-campus residence required through sophomore year. *Options:* men-only, women-only. *Most popular organizations:* student council, Students Older Than Average.

Campus security 24-hour emergency response devices, evening patrols by trained security personnel.

After graduation 10 organizations recruited on campus 1997–98. *Career center:* 1 part-time personnel. Services include resume preparation, career/interest testing, career counseling, careers library.

Freshmen 67 applied, 37 admitted, 33 enrolled.

Average high school GPA	3.1	SAT verbal scores above 500	N/R
SAT math scores above 500	N/R	ACT above 18	80%
From top 10% of their h.s. class	8%	From top quarter	60%
From top half	92%	1998 freshmen returning in 1999	48%

Application *Options:* eApply at www.CollegeQuest.com, deferred entrance. *Application fee:* $20. *Required:* essay or personal statement; high school transcript; 2 letters of recommendation. *Required for some:* minimum 2.0 GPA.

Standardized tests *Admission: Required for some:* ACT.

Significant dates *Application deadlines:* rolling (freshmen), rolling (transfers). *Financial aid deadline:* continuous.

Freshman Application Contact
Mr. Dan Hovestol, Admissions Director, Oak Hills Christian College, 1600 Oak Hills Road, SW, Bemidji, MN 56601-8832. **Phone:** 218-751-8670 Ext. 220. **Toll-free phone:** 888-751-8670 Ext. 285. **Fax:** 218-751-8825. **E-mail:** admissions@oakhill.edu
Visit CollegeQuest.com for information on majors offered and athletics.

ST. CLOUD STATE UNIVERSITY
St. Cloud, Minnesota

- **State-supported**, comprehensive, founded 1869
- **Degrees** associate, bachelor's, master's, and doctoral
- **Suburban** 108-acre campus with easy access to Minneapolis–St. Paul
- **Coed**, 13,372 undergraduate students, 78% full-time, 54% women, 46% men
- **Moderately difficult** entrance level, 82% of applicants were admitted
- **18:1 student-to-undergraduate faculty ratio**
- **40.8% graduate** in 6 years or less
- **$2881 tuition** and fees (in-state); $5304 (out-of-state)
- **$13.2 million endowment**

Minnesota

St. Cloud State University *(continued)*
Part of Minnesota State Colleges and Universities System.

Students *Undergraduates:* 10,475 full-time, 2,897 part-time. Students come from 49 states and territories, 32 other countries. *The most frequently chosen baccalaureate fields are:* business/marketing, education, social sciences and history. *Graduate:* 1,179 in graduate degree programs.

From out-of-state	12%	Reside on campus	20%
Age 25 or older	8%	Transferred in	10%
International students	4%	African Americans	1%
Asian Americans/Pacific Islanders	1%	Hispanic Americans	1%
Native Americans	1%		

Faculty 728 (89% full-time), 62% with terminal degrees.

Expenses (1999–2000) *Tuition, state resident:* full-time $2475; part-time $86 per credit hour. *Tuition, nonresident:* full-time $4898; part-time $187 per credit hour. *Required fees:* full-time $406; $17 per credit hour. Full-time tuition and fees vary according to course load, location, and reciprocity agreements. Part-time tuition and fees vary according to course load, location, and reciprocity agreements. *College room and board:* $3422. Room and board charges vary according to board plan and housing facility. *Payment plan:* deferred payment. *Waivers:* senior citizens and employees or children of employees.

Library Centennial Hall Library. *Operations spending 1999–2000:* $5.1 million. *Collection:* 597,137 titles, 2,859 serial subscriptions, 31,970 audiovisual materials.

College life *Housing:* Options: coed, disabled students. *Social organizations:* national fraternities, national sororities, local sororities; 5% of eligible men and 5% of eligible women are members. *Most popular organizations:* Residence Hall Association, aero club, Phi Kappa Phi, University program committees, accounting club.

Campus security 24-hour emergency response devices and patrols, late-night transport-escort service.

After graduation 240 organizations recruited on campus 1997–98. 63% of class of 1998 had job offers within 6 months. *Career center:* 6 full-time, 2 part-time personnel. Services include job fairs, resume preparation, resume referral, career counseling, careers library, job bank, job interviews. *Graduate education:* 10% of class of 1999 went directly to graduate and professional school.

Freshmen 5,171 applied, 4,220 admitted, 2,404 enrolled. 3 National Merit Scholars.

SAT verbal scores above 500	N/R	SAT math scores above 500	N/R
ACT above 18	88%	From top 10% of their h.s. class	10%
From top quarter	33%	From top half	75%
1998 freshmen returning in 1999	73%		

Application *Options:* electronic application, early admission, deferred entrance. *Application fee:* $20. *Required:* high school transcript. *Required for some:* letters of recommendation.

Standardized tests *Admission: Required:* ACT.

Significant dates *Application deadlines:* 7/15 (freshmen), 7/15 (transfers). *Financial aid deadline priority date:* 5/1.

Freshman Application Contact
Ms. Annette Day, Director of Admissions, St. Cloud State University, 720 4th Avenue South, St. Cloud, MN 56301-4498. **Phone:** 320-255-2244. **Toll-free phone:** 877-654-7278. **E-mail:** scsu4u@stcloudstate.edu

Visit CollegeQuest.com for information on majors offered and athletics. Electronic viewbook available at CollegeQuest.com.

SAINT JOHN'S UNIVERSITY
Collegeville, Minnesota

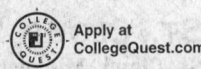

- **Independent Roman Catholic**, comprehensive, founded 1857
- **Degrees** bachelor's, master's, and first professional
- **Rural** 2,400-acre campus with easy access to Minneapolis–St. Paul
- **Men** only, 1,803 undergraduate students, 97% full-time
- **Moderately difficult** entrance level, 85% of applicants were admitted
- **13:1** student-to-undergraduate faculty ratio
- **68% graduate** in 6 years or less
- **$16,441 tuition** and fees
- **$13,677 average financial aid** package, $16,487 average indebtedness upon graduation, $98 million endowment

Saint John's University, through its coordinate relationship with the College of Saint Benedict for women, offers the best features of both a coeducational and a men's college. While all classes, facilities, and social and cultural functions are shared, each campus maintains its own residence halls, student governments, and athletics. See full description of the College of Saint Benedict and Saint John's University.

Coordinate institution with College of Saint Benedict.

Students *Undergraduates:* 1,754 full-time, 49 part-time. Students come from 29 states and territories, 24 other countries. *The most frequently chosen baccalaureate fields are:* business/marketing, biological/life sciences, social sciences and history. *Graduate:* 3 in professional programs, 126 in other graduate degree programs.

From out-of-state	15%	Reside on campus	78%
Age 25 or older	2%	Transferred in	2%
International students	2%	African Americans	0.3%
Asian Americans/Pacific Islanders	1%	Hispanic Americans	1%
Native Americans	0.3%		

Faculty 177 (88% full-time), 77% with terminal degrees.

Expenses (1999–2000) *Comprehensive fee:* $21,371 includes full-time tuition ($16,195), mandatory fees ($246), and room and board ($4930). *College room only:* $2364. Room and board charges vary according to board plan and housing facility. *Part-time tuition:* $675 per credit. *Payment plans:* tuition prepayment, installment, deferred payment.

Library Alcuin Library plus 2 others. *Operations spending 1999–2000:* $1.1 million. *Collection:* 726,844 titles, 8,564 serial subscriptions, 18,824 audiovisual materials.

College life *Housing:* on-campus residence required through sophomore year. *Option:* men-only. *Most popular organizations:* Volunteers in Service to Others, Joint Events Council, Cultural Affairs Board, Collegiate Management Association, student newspapers.

Campus security 24-hour emergency response devices and patrols, late-night transport-escort service, well-lit pathways, 911 center on campus, closed circuit TV monitors.

After graduation 85 organizations recruited on campus 1997–98. 79% of class of 1998 had job offers within 6 months. *Career center:* 4 full-time, 1 part-time personnel. Services include job fairs, resume preparation, interview workshops, resume referral, career/interest testing, career counseling, careers library, job bank, job interviews. *Graduate education:* 19% of class of 1999 went directly to graduate and professional school: 7% graduate arts and sciences, 5% law, 4% business, 3% medicine.

Freshmen 1,119 applied, 950 admitted, 475 enrolled.

Average high school GPA	3.5	SAT verbal scores above 500	83%
SAT math scores above 500	89%	ACT above 18	100%
From top 10% of their h.s. class	21%	From top quarter	58%
From top half	90%	1998 freshmen returning in 1999	92%

Application *Options:* eApply at www.CollegeQuest.com, Common Application, electronic application, early admission, deferred entrance. *Application fee:* $25. *Required:* essay or personal statement; high school transcript. *Required for some:* 3 letters of recommendation. *Recommended:* minimum 2.8 GPA; interview.

Standardized tests *Admission: Required:* SAT I or ACT.

Significant dates *Application deadlines:* rolling (freshmen), rolling (transfers). *Financial aid deadline priority date:* 3/1.

Freshman Application Contact
Ms. Mary Milbert, Dean of Admissions, Saint John's University, PO Box 7155, Collegeville, MN 56321-7155. **Phone:** 320-363-2196. **Toll-free phone:** 800-24JOHNS. **Fax:** 320-363-3206. **E-mail:** admissions@csbsju.edu

Visit CollegeQuest.com for information on majors offered and athletics. College video and electronic viewbook available at CollegeQuest.com.

SAINT MARY'S UNIVERSITY OF MINNESOTA
Winona, Minnesota

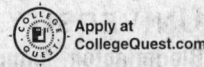

- **Independent Roman Catholic**, comprehensive, founded 1912
- **Degrees** bachelor's, master's, doctoral, and post-master's certificates
- **Small-town** 350-acre campus

Minnesota

- **Coed**, 1,716 undergraduate students, 76% full-time, 49% women, 51% men
- **Moderately difficult** entrance level, 93% of applicants were admitted
- **14:1 student-to-undergraduate faculty ratio**
- **52% graduate** in 6 years or less
- **$13,645 tuition** and fees
- **$11,485 average financial aid** package, $14.8 million endowment

Students *Undergraduates:* 1,302 full-time, 414 part-time. Students come from 22 states and territories, 19 other countries. *The most frequently chosen baccalaureate fields are:* business/marketing, education, protective services/public administration. *Graduate:* 4,557 in graduate degree programs.

From out-of-state	44%	Reside on campus	85%
Age 25 or older	3%	Transferred in	2%
International students	2%	African Americans	1%
Asian Americans/Pacific Islanders	2%	Hispanic Americans	1%
Native Americans	0.2%		

Faculty 101 full-time.

Expenses (1999–2000) *Comprehensive fee:* $18,065 includes full-time tuition ($13,300), mandatory fees ($345), and room and board ($4420). Full-time tuition and fees vary according to course load and reciprocity agreements. *Part-time tuition:* $444 per credit. *Payment plan:* installment. *Waivers:* employees or children of employees.

Library Fitzgerald Library. *Operations spending 1999–2000:* $622,368. *Collection:* 145,667 titles, 711 serial subscriptions, 1,526 audiovisual materials.

College life *Housing:* on-campus residence required through sophomore year. *Options:* coed, men-only, women-only. *Social organizations:* national fraternities, national sororities; 4% of eligible men and 4% of eligible women are members. *Most popular organizations:* Student Activity Committee, Good Times Committee (chapter of BACCHUS), Volunteers in Service to Others, Serving Others United in Love (Soul), concert choir/chamber singers.

Campus security 24-hour emergency response devices and patrols, late-night transport-escort service, controlled dormitory access.

After graduation 120 organizations recruited on campus 1997–98. 62% of class of 1998 had job offers within 6 months. *Career center:* 1 full-time, 1 part-time personnel. Services include job fairs, resume preparation, interview workshops, resume referral, career/interest testing, career counseling, careers library, job bank, job interviews. *Graduate education:* 20% of class of 1999 went directly to graduate and professional school: 11% graduate arts and sciences, 4% theology, 2% business, 2% medicine, 1% law.

Freshmen 955 applied, 891 admitted, 418 enrolled.

Average high school GPA	2.9	SAT verbal scores above 500	N/R
SAT math scores above 500	N/R	ACT above 18	90%
From top 10% of their h.s. class	15%	From top quarter	33%
From top half	64%	1998 freshmen returning in 1999	75%

Application *Options:* eApply at www.CollegeQuest.com, electronic application, early admission, deferred entrance. *Application fee:* $25. *Required:* essay or personal statement; high school transcript; minimum 2.2 GPA. *Required for some:* interview. *Recommended:* 2 letters of recommendation.

Standardized tests *Admission: Required:* SAT I or ACT.

Significant dates *Application deadlines:* rolling (freshmen), rolling (transfers). *Financial aid deadline priority date:* 3/15.

Freshman Application Contact
Mr. Anthony M. Piscitiello, Vice President for Admission, Saint Mary's University of Minnesota, 700 Terrace Heights, Winona, MN 55987-1399. **Phone:** 507-457-1700. **Toll-free phone:** 800-635-5987. **Fax:** 507-457-1722. **E-mail:** admissions@smumn.edu

Visit CollegeQuest.com for information on majors offered and athletics. College video and electronic viewbook available at CollegeQuest.com.

■ *See page 2418 for a narrative description.*

ST. OLAF COLLEGE
Northfield, Minnesota

Apply at CollegeQuest.com

- **Independent Lutheran**, 4-year, founded 1874
- **Degree** bachelor's
- **Small-town** 350-acre campus with easy access to Minneapolis–St. Paul
- **Coed**, 2,879 undergraduate students, 99% full-time, 57% women, 43% men
- **Very difficult** entrance level, 76% of applicants were admitted
- **12:1 student-to-undergraduate faculty ratio**
- **78% graduate** in 6 years or less
- **$19,400 tuition** and fees
- **$14,654 average financial aid** package, $15,991 average indebtedness upon graduation, $134.3 million endowment

Students *Undergraduates:* 2,868 full-time, 11 part-time. Students come from 46 states and territories, 27 other countries. *The most frequently chosen baccalaureate fields are:* social sciences and history, English, visual/performing arts.

From out-of-state	47%	Reside on campus	96%
Age 25 or older	1%	Transferred in	2%
International students	2%	African Americans	1%
Asian Americans/Pacific Islanders	3%	Hispanic Americans	1%
Native Americans	0.2%		

Faculty 366 (59% full-time).

Expenses (2000–2001) *Comprehensive fee:* $23,900 includes full-time tuition ($19,400) and room and board ($4500). *College room only:* $2100. Room and board charges vary according to board plan. *Part-time tuition:* $2280 per course. *Payment plans:* tuition prepayment, installment. *Waivers:* employees or children of employees.

Library Rolvaag Memorial Library plus 3 others. *Operations spending 1999–2000:* $1.4 million. *Collection:* 488,299 titles, 1,703 serial subscriptions.

College life *Housing:* on-campus residence required through senior year. *Option:* coed. *Most popular organizations:* Student Congregation, Student Government Association, Fellowship of Christian Athletes, Alpha Phi Omega, Habitat for Humanity.

Campus security 24-hour emergency response devices and patrols, late-night transport-escort service, controlled dormitory access.

After graduation 33 organizations recruited on campus 1997–98. 70% of class of 1998 had job offers within 6 months. *Career center:* 4 full-time, 2 part-time personnel. Services include job fairs, resume preparation, interview workshops, resume referral, career/interest testing, career counseling, careers library, job bank, job interviews. *Graduate education:* 23% of class of 1999 went directly to graduate and professional school: 10% graduate arts and sciences, 2% education, 2% law, 2% medicine, 1% business, 1% dentistry, 1% theology, 0.3% engineering, 0.3% veterinary medicine. *Major awards:* 1 Rhodes, 4 Fulbright Scholars.

Freshmen 2,359 applied, 1,803 admitted, 766 enrolled. 32 National Merit Scholars, 41 class presidents, 62 valedictorians, 171 student government officers.

Average high school GPA	3.67	SAT verbal scores above 500	95%
SAT math scores above 500	96%	ACT above 18	99%
From top 10% of their h.s. class	48%	From top quarter	76%
From top half	96%	1998 freshmen returning in 1999	92%

Application *Options:* eApply at www.CollegeQuest.com, Common Application, electronic application, early admission, early decision, early action, deferred entrance. *Application fee:* $35. *Required:* essay or personal statement; high school transcript; minimum 3.0 GPA; 2 letters of recommendation. *Recommended:* interview.

Standardized tests *Admission: Required:* SAT I or ACT.

Significant dates *Application deadlines:* rolling (freshmen), rolling (transfers). *Early decision:* 11/15, 12/15. *Notification:* continuous until 6/15 (freshmen), 12/10 (early decision), 1/15 (early action). *Financial aid deadline priority date:* 3/1.

Freshman Application Contact
Ms. Sara Kyle, Interim Director of Admissions, St. Olaf College, 1520 St. Olaf Avenue, Northfield, MN 55057-1098. **Phone:** 507-646-3025. **Toll-free phone:** 800-800-3025. **Fax:** 507-646-3832. **E-mail:** admiss@stolaf.edu

Visit CollegeQuest.com for information on majors offered and athletics. College video and electronic viewbook available at CollegeQuest.com.

SOUTHWEST STATE UNIVERSITY
Marshall, Minnesota

- **State-supported**, comprehensive, founded 1963
- **Degrees** associate, bachelor's, and master's
- **Small-town** 216-acre campus
- **Coed**, 3,999 undergraduate students, 53% full-time, 58% women, 42% men

Minnesota

Southwest State University (continued)
- **Moderately difficult** entrance level, 51% of applicants were admitted
- **18:1 student-to-undergraduate faculty ratio**
- **29% graduate** in 6 years or less
- **$3428 tuition** and fees (in-state); $6924 (out-of-state)
- **$6255 average financial aid** package, $3.1 million endowment

Part of Minnesota State Colleges and Universities System.
Students *Undergraduates:* 2,130 full-time, 1,869 part-time. Students come from 24 states and territories, 30 other countries. *The most frequently chosen baccalaureate fields are:* business/marketing, education, social sciences and history. *Graduate:* 522 in graduate degree programs.

From out-of-state	19%	Reside on campus	53%
Age 25 or older	7%	Transferred in	6%
International students	1%	African Americans	1%
Asian Americans/Pacific Islanders	1%	Hispanic Americans	0.4%
Native Americans	0.4%		

Faculty 156 (80% full-time).
Expenses (2000–2001, estimated) *Tuition, state resident:* full-time $2790; part-time $93 per credit hour. *Tuition, nonresident:* full-time $6286; part-time $206 per credit hour. *Required fees:* full-time $638; $21 per credit hour. Full-time tuition and fees vary according to course load, location, and reciprocity agreements. Part-time tuition and fees vary according to course load, location, and reciprocity agreements. *College room and board:* $3588; room only: $2580. Room and board charges vary according to board plan and housing facility. *Payment plans:* installment, deferred payment. *Waivers:* senior citizens and employees or children of employees.
Library Southwest State University. *Operations spending 1999–2000:* $856,659. *Collection:* 188,861 titles, 748 serial subscriptions, 9,819 audiovisual materials.
College life *Housing:* Options: coed, men-only, women-only.
Campus security 24-hour emergency response devices and patrols, student patrols, late-night transport-escort service.
After graduation 35 organizations recruited on campus 1997–98. 66% of class of 1998 had job offers within 6 months. *Career center:* 1 full-time, 1 part-time personnel. Services include job fairs, resume preparation, interview workshops, resume referral, career/interest testing, career counseling, careers library, job bank, job interviews. *Graduate education:* 4% of class of 1999 went directly to graduate and professional school.
Freshmen 1,204 applied, 609 admitted, 528 enrolled.

SAT verbal scores above 500	N/R	SAT math scores above 500	N/R
ACT above 18	90%	From top 10% of their h.s. class	8%
From top quarter	26%	From top half	67%
1998 freshmen returning in 1999	87%		

Application *Options:* Common Application, electronic application, early admission, deferred entrance. *Application fee:* $20. *Required:* essay or personal statement; high school transcript.
Standardized tests *Admission: Required:* SAT I or ACT.
Significant dates *Application deadlines:* rolling (freshmen), rolling (transfers). *Financial aid deadline priority date:* 4/1.
Freshman Application Contact
Mr. Richard Shearer, Director of Enrollment Services, Southwest State University, 1501 State Street, Marshall, MN 56258-1598. **Phone:** 507-537-6286. **Toll-free phone:** 800-642-0684. **Fax:** 507-537-7154. **E-mail:** shearerr@southwest.msus.edu

Visit CollegeQuest.com for information on majors offered and athletics. College video available at CollegeQuest.com.

UNIVERSITY OF MINNESOTA, CROOKSTON
Crookston, Minnesota

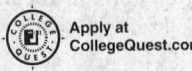 Apply at CollegeQuest.com

- **State-supported**, 4-year, founded 1966
- **Degrees** associate and bachelor's
- **Rural** 95-acre campus
- **Coed**, 1,002 undergraduate students, 90% full-time, 42% women, 58% men
- **Noncompetitive** entrance level, 95% of applicants were admitted
- **17:1 student-to-undergraduate faculty ratio**
- **$5020 tuition** and fees (in-state); $5020 (out-of-state)
- **$4.3 million endowment**

Part of University of Minnesota System.
Students *Undergraduates:* 899 full-time, 103 part-time. Students come from 21 states and territories, 18 other countries.

Age 25 or older	3%	Transferred in	10%
International students	3%	African Americans	3%
Asian Americans/Pacific Islanders	1%	Hispanic Americans	1%
Native Americans	1%		

Expenses (2000–2001) *Tuition, state resident:* full-time $3780; part-time $126 per credit. *Tuition, nonresident:* full-time $3780; part-time $126 per credit. *Required fees:* full-time $1240; $480 per term part-time. Full-time tuition and fees vary according to reciprocity agreements. Part-time tuition and fees vary according to course load. *College room and board:* $4046; room only: $1861. Room and board charges vary according to board plan and housing facility. *Payment plans:* guaranteed tuition, installment. *Waivers:* senior citizens.
Library *Operations spending 1999–2000:* $518,767. *Collection:* 30,000 titles, 700 serial subscriptions.
College life *Housing:* Option: coed.
Campus security Student patrols, controlled dormitory access.
After graduation 25 organizations recruited on campus 1997–98. 75% of class of 1998 had job offers within 6 months. *Career center:* 2 full-time personnel. Services include job fairs, resume preparation, interview workshops, resume referral, career/interest testing, career counseling, careers library, job bank, job interviews.
Freshmen 465 applied, 440 admitted, 303 enrolled. 5 valedictorians.

SAT verbal scores above 500	N/R	SAT math scores above 500	N/R
ACT above 18	N/R	From top 10% of their h.s. class	4%
From top quarter	20%	From top half	52%
1998 freshmen returning in 1999	62%		

Application *Options:* eApply at www.CollegeQuest.com, Common Application, electronic application, deferred entrance. *Required:* high school transcript.
Standardized tests *Admission: Required:* ACT.
Significant dates *Application deadlines:* rolling (freshmen), rolling (transfers). *Financial aid deadline priority date:* 3/31.
Freshman Application Contact
Mr. Russ Kreager, Director of Admissions and Enrollment Manager, University of Minnesota, Crookston, 2900 University Avenue, Crookston, MN 56716-5001. **Phone:** 218-281-8568. **Toll-free phone:** 800-232-6466. **Fax:** 218-281-8050. **E-mail:** info@mail.crk.umn.edu

Visit CollegeQuest.com for information on majors offered and athletics. Electronic viewbook available at CollegeQuest.com.

■ *See page 2772 for a narrative description.*

UNIVERSITY OF MINNESOTA, DULUTH
Duluth, Minnesota

- **State-supported**, comprehensive, founded 1947
- **Degrees** bachelor's, master's, and first professional
- **Suburban** 250-acre campus
- **Coed**, 7,473 undergraduate students, 91% full-time, 50% women, 50% men
- **Moderately difficult** entrance level, 83% of applicants were admitted
- **20:1 student-to-undergraduate faculty ratio**
- **42% graduate** in 6 years or less
- **$4903 tuition** and fees (in-state); $12,673 (out-of-state)
- **$6494 average financial aid** package, $11,500 average indebtedness upon graduation, $39.5 million endowment

Part of University of Minnesota System.
Students *Undergraduates:* 6,828 full-time, 645 part-time. Students come from 25 states and territories, 34 other countries. *The most frequently chosen baccalaureate fields are:* business/marketing, education, social sciences and history. *Graduate:* 106 in professional programs, 439 in other graduate degree programs.

Reside on campus	38%	Age 25 or older	11%
Transferred in	6%	International students	2%
African Americans	1%	Asian Americans/Pacific Islanders	2%
Hispanic Americans	1%	Native Americans	1%

Minnesota

Faculty 446 (74% full-time), 64% with terminal degrees.
Expenses (1999–2000) *Tuition, state resident:* full-time $4230; part-time $141 per credit. *Tuition, nonresident:* full-time $12,000; part-time $400 per credit. *Required fees:* full-time $673; $302 per term part-time. Full-time tuition and fees vary according to course level, course load, reciprocity agreements, and student level. Part-time tuition and fees vary according to course level, course load, reciprocity agreements, and student level. *College room and board:* $4132. Room and board charges vary according to board plan and housing facility. Additional part-time mandatory fees per term: $124 for nonresidents. *Payment plan:* installment. *Waivers:* senior citizens and employees or children of employees.
Library University of Minnesota, Duluth Library plus 1 other. *Operations spending 1999–2000:* $2.9 million. *Collection:* 614,367 titles, 2,181 serial subscriptions, 15,580 audiovisual materials.
College life *Housing: Options:* coed, men-only, women-only. *Social organizations:* national fraternities, national sororities, local fraternities, local sororities; 1% of eligible men and 1% of eligible women are members. *Most popular organizations:* recreational sports, departmental clubs, outdoor recreation clubs.
Campus security 24-hour emergency response devices and patrols, late-night transport-escort service.
After graduation 188 organizations recruited on campus 1997–98. 75% of class of 1998 had job offers within 6 months. *Career center:* 5 full-time personnel. Services include job fairs, resume preparation, interview workshops, resume referral, career/interest testing, career counseling, careers library, job bank, job interviews. *Graduate education:* 23% of class of 1999 went directly to graduate and professional school.
Freshmen 5,388 applied, 4,475 admitted, 1,922 enrolled. 33 valedictorians.

Average high school GPA	3.2	SAT verbal scores above 500	N/R
SAT math scores above 500	N/R	ACT above 18	97%
From top 10% of their h.s. class	16%	From top quarter	46%
From top half	86%	1998 freshmen returning in 1999	78%

Application *Application fee:* $25. *Required:* high school transcript.
Standardized tests *Admission: Required:* SAT I or ACT.
Significant dates *Application deadlines:* 2/1 (freshmen), 8/1 (transfers). *Financial aid deadline priority date:* 3/1.
Freshman Application Contact
Ms. Beth Esselstrom, Director of Admissions, University of Minnesota, Duluth, , 184 Darland Administration Building, 10 University Drive, Duluth, MN 55812. **Phone:** 218-726-7171. **Toll-free phone:** 800-232-1339. **Fax:** 218-726-6394. **E-mail:** umdadmis@d.umn.edu
Visit CollegeQuest.com for information on majors offered and athletics. Electronic viewbook available at CollegeQuest.com.

UNIVERSITY OF MINNESOTA, MORRIS
Morris, Minnesota

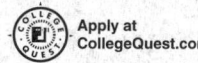
Apply at CollegeQuest.com

- **State-supported**, 4-year, founded 1959
- **Degree** bachelor's
- **Small-town** 130-acre campus
- **Coed**, 1,789 undergraduate students, 96% full-time, 58% women, 42% men
- **Moderately difficult** entrance level, 97% of applicants were admitted
- **15:1 student-to-undergraduate faculty ratio**
- **63% graduate** in 6 years or less
- **$5312 tuition** and fees (in-state); $10,014 (out-of-state)

Part of University of Minnesota System.
Students *Undergraduates:* 1,722 full-time, 67 part-time. Students come from 31 states and territories. *The most frequently chosen baccalaureate fields are:* biological/life sciences, business/marketing, social sciences and history.

From out-of-state	17%	Reside on campus	48%
Age 25 or older	5%	Transferred in	6%
International students	0.3%	African Americans	5%
Asian Americans/Pacific Islanders	3%	Hispanic Americans	1%
Native Americans	7%		

Faculty 122 (100% full-time).
Expenses (1999–2000) *Tuition, state resident:* full-time $4778; part-time $159 per credit. *Tuition, nonresident:* full-time $9480; part-time $318 per credit. *Required fees:* full-time $534; $267 per term part-time. Part-time tuition and fees vary according to course load. *College room and board:* $3910; room only: $2080. Room and board charges vary according to board plan and housing facility. *Payment plans:* installment, deferred payment. *Waivers:* minority students.
Library Rodney A. Briggs Library. *Operations spending 1999–2000:* $831,991. *Collection:* 1,100 serial subscriptions, 4,522 audiovisual materials.
College life *Housing: Option:* coed. *Social organizations:* local fraternities; 1% of men are members. *Most popular organizations:* student radio station, Intervarsity Christian Fellowship, jazz ensemble/concert choir, Big Friend, Little Friend, student newspaper.
Campus security 24-hour emergency response devices and patrols, late-night transport-escort service, controlled dormitory access.
After graduation 70 organizations recruited on campus 1997–98. 80% of class of 1998 had job offers within 6 months. *Career center:* 1 full-time, 12 part-time personnel. Services include job fairs, resume preparation, interview workshops, resume referral, career/interest testing, career counseling, careers library, job bank, job interviews. *Graduate education:* 27% of class of 1999 went directly to graduate and professional school: 16% graduate arts and sciences, 3% business, 3% law, 3% medicine, 1% dentistry, 1% veterinary medicine.
Freshmen 994 applied, 961 admitted, 457 enrolled.

SAT verbal scores above 500	70%	SAT math scores above 500	83%
ACT above 18	94%	From top 10% of their h.s. class	45%
From top quarter	76%	From top half	98%
1998 freshmen returning in 1999	78%		

Application *Options:* eApply at www.CollegeQuest.com, electronic application, early admission, early action, deferred entrance. *Application fee:* $25. *Required:* essay or personal statement; high school transcript. *Required for some:* interview. *Recommended:* minimum 3.0 GPA.
Standardized tests *Admission: Required:* SAT I or ACT.
Significant dates *Application deadlines:* 3/15 (freshmen), 5/1 (transfers). *Early action:* 12/1. *Notification:* 4/1 (freshmen), 12/20 (early action). *Financial aid deadline priority date:* 4/1.
Freshman Application Contact
Mr. Scott K. Hagg, Acting Director of Admissions, University of Minnesota, Morris, 600 East 4th Street, Morris, MN 56267-2199. **Phone:** 320-539-6036. **Toll-free phone:** 800-992-8863. **Fax:** 320-589-6399. **E-mail:** admissions@caa.mrs.umn.edu
Visit CollegeQuest.com for information on majors offered and athletics. College video available at CollegeQuest.com.

UNIVERSITY OF MINNESOTA, TWIN CITIES CAMPUS
Minneapolis, Minnesota

- **State-supported**, university, founded 1851
- **Degrees** bachelor's, master's, doctoral, first professional, post-master's, and postbachelor's certificates
- **Urban** 2,000-acre campus
- **Coed**, 26,968 undergraduate students, 77% full-time, 52% women, 48% men
- **Moderately difficult** entrance level, 73% of applicants were admitted
- **$4649 tuition** and fees (in-state); $12,789 (out-of-state)

Part of University of Minnesota System.
Students *Undergraduates:* 20,757 full-time, 6,211 part-time. Students come from 55 states and territories, 85 other countries. *The most frequently chosen baccalaureate fields are:* engineering/engineering technologies, business/marketing, social sciences and history. *Graduate:* 2,583 in professional programs, 10,436 in other graduate degree programs.

From out-of-state	28%	Reside on campus	19%
Age 25 or older	15%	Transferred in	8%
International students	2%	African Americans	4%
Asian Americans/Pacific Islanders	8%	Hispanic Americans	2%
Native Americans	1%		

Faculty 2,862 (89% full-time), 92% with terminal degrees.
Expenses (1999–2000) *Tuition, state resident:* full-time $4172; part-time $154 per credit. *Tuition, nonresident:* full-time $12,312; part-time $456 per credit. *Required fees:* full-time $477; $238 per term part-time. Full-time tuition

Minnesota

University of Minnesota, Twin Cities Campus (continued)
and fees vary according to program, reciprocity agreements, and student level. Part-time tuition and fees vary according to course load, program, reciprocity agreements, and student level. *College room and board:* $4494. Room and board charges vary according to board plan, housing facility, and location. *Payment plans:* guaranteed tuition, installment. *Waivers:* senior citizens and employees or children of employees.

Library Wilson Library plus 17 others. *Collection:* 5.5 million titles, 48,105 serial subscriptions.

College life *Housing: Options:* coed, cooperative, disabled students. *Social organizations:* national fraternities, national sororities, local sororities; 3% of eligible men and 3% of eligible women are members. *Most popular organizations:* sports clubs, student government, sororities/fraternities, religious organizations, departmental/professional organizations.

Campus security 24-hour emergency response devices and patrols, student patrols, late-night transport-escort service, controlled dormitory access, safety/security orientation, security lighting.

After graduation *Career center:* Services include job fairs, resume preparation, resume referral, career counseling, careers library, job bank, job interviews. *Major awards:* 1 Marshall, 7 Fulbright Scholars.

Freshmen 15,319 applied, 11,216 admitted, 5,141 enrolled. 223 valedictorians.

SAT verbal scores above 500	85%
ACT above 18	95%
From top quarter	60%
1998 freshmen returning in 1999	82%
SAT math scores above 500	90%
From top 10% of their h.s. class	29%
From top half	90%

Application *Options:* electronic application, early admission, deferred entrance. *Application fee:* $25. *Required:* high school transcript. *Recommended:* minimum 2.0 GPA.

Standardized tests *Admission: Required:* SAT I or ACT.

Significant dates *Application deadlines:* rolling (freshmen), 3/1 (transfers). *Financial aid deadline priority date:* 2/15.

Freshman Application Contact
Ms. Patricia Jones Whyte, Associate Director of Admissions, University of Minnesota, Twin Cities Campus, 240 Williamson, Minneapolis, MN 55455-0213. **Phone:** 612-625-2008. **Toll-free phone:** 800-752-1000. **Fax:** 612-626-1693. **E-mail:** admissions@tc.umn.edu

Visit CollegeQuest.com for information on majors offered and athletics. College video and electronic viewbook available at CollegeQuest.com.

UNIVERSITY OF ST. THOMAS
St. Paul, Minnesota

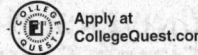
Apply at CollegeQuest.com

- **Independent Roman Catholic**, university, founded 1885
- **Degrees** bachelor's, master's, doctoral, first professional, post-master's, and postbachelor's certificates
- **Urban** 78-acre campus with easy access to Minneapolis
- **Coed**, 5,195 undergraduate students, 89% full-time, 54% women, 46% men
- **Moderately difficult** entrance level, 85% of applicants were admitted
- **14:1 student-to-undergraduate faculty ratio**
- **66% graduate** in 6 years or less
- **$16,340 tuition** and fees
- **$13,310 average financial aid** package, $16,245 average indebtedness upon graduation, $230.7 million endowment

St. Thomas, a coeducational, Catholic liberal arts university with more than 10,000 undergraduate and graduate students—the largest independent university in Minnesota—is located in a quiet neighborhood only 10 minutes from the downtown areas of both St. Paul and Minneapolis. St. Thomas offers nearly 80 majors, including business administration, computer science, journalism, biology, engineering, and preprofessional programs. St. Thomas emphasizes values-centered, career-oriented education.

Students *Undergraduates:* 4,599 full-time, 596 part-time. Students come from 46 states and territories, 34 other countries. *The most frequently chosen baccalaureate fields are:* business/marketing, communications/communication technologies, social sciences and history. *Graduate:* 80 in professional programs, 5,450 in other graduate degree programs.

From out-of-state	18%	Reside on campus	42%
Age 25 or older	12%	Transferred in	6%
International students	1%	African Americans	2%
Asian Americans/Pacific Islanders	4%	Hispanic Americans	2%
Native Americans	1%		

Faculty 789 (45% full-time), 55% with terminal degrees.

Expenses (1999–2000) *Comprehensive fee:* $21,520 includes full-time tuition ($16,128), mandatory fees ($212), and room and board ($5180). *College room only:* $3058. Full-time tuition and fees vary according to course load. Room and board charges vary according to board plan and housing facility. *Part-time tuition:* $504 per credit. *Part-time fees:* $78 per term part-time. Part-time tuition and fees vary according to course load. *Payment plans:* installment, deferred payment. *Waivers:* senior citizens and employees or children of employees.

Library O'Shaughnessy-Frey Library plus 2 others. *Operations spending 1999–2000:* $4.8 million. *Collection:* 262,603 titles, 2,537 serial subscriptions.

College life *Housing: Options:* men-only, women-only, disabled students. *Social organizations:* national fraternities, national sororities, local fraternities, local sororities.

Campus security 24-hour emergency response devices and patrols, late-night transport-escort service, controlled dormitory access.

After graduation 80 organizations recruited on campus 1997–98. *Career center:* 10 full-time, 2 part-time personnel. Services include job fairs, resume preparation, interview workshops, career/interest testing, career counseling, careers library, job bank, job interviews.

Freshmen 2,853 applied, 2,437 admitted, 1,055 enrolled. 2 National Merit Scholars.

Average high school GPA	3.55	SAT verbal scores above 500	86%
SAT math scores above 500	87%	ACT above 18	99%
From top 10% of their h.s. class	30%	From top quarter	62%
From top half	91%	1998 freshmen returning in 1999	86%

Application *Options:* eApply at www.CollegeQuest.com, Common Application, electronic application, deferred entrance. *Application fee:* $30. *Required:* essay or personal statement; high school transcript. *Recommended:* letters of recommendation; interview.

Standardized tests *Admission: Required:* SAT I or ACT. *Recommended:* ACT.

Significant dates *Application deadlines:* rolling (freshmen), 8/1 (transfers). *Financial aid deadline priority date:* 4/1.

Freshman Application Contact
Ms. Marla Friederichs, Associate Vice President of Enrollment Management, University of St. Thomas, Mail #32F-1, 2115 Summit Avenue, St. Paul, MN 55105-1096. **Phone:** 651-962-6150. **Toll-free phone:** 800-328-6819 Ext. 26150. **Fax:** 651-962-6160. **E-mail:** admissions@stthomas.edu

Visit CollegeQuest.com for information on majors offered and athletics. Electronic viewbook available at CollegeQuest.com.

- *See page 2820 for a narrative description.*

WINONA STATE UNIVERSITY
Winona, Minnesota

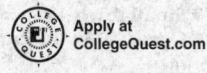
Apply at CollegeQuest.com

- **State-supported**, comprehensive, founded 1858
- **Degrees** associate, bachelor's, master's, and post-master's certificates
- **Small-town** 40-acre campus
- **Coed**, 6,049 undergraduate students, 89% full-time, 62% women, 38% men
- **Moderately difficult** entrance level, 65% of applicants were admitted
- **19:1 student-to-undergraduate faculty ratio**
- **38% graduate** in 6 years or less
- **$3300 tuition** and fees (in-state); $6700 (out-of-state)
- **$4875 average financial aid** package, $2.8 million endowment

Part of Minnesota State Colleges and Universities System.

Students *Undergraduates:* 5,389 full-time, 660 part-time. Students come from 40 states and territories, 53 other countries. *The most frequently chosen baccalaureate fields are:* business/marketing, education, health professions and related sciences. *Graduate:* 654 in graduate degree programs.

434   www.petersons.com   *Peterson's Guide to Four-Year Colleges 2001*

Minnesota–Mississippi

From out-of-state	30%	Reside on campus	35%
Age 25 or older	8%	Transferred in	8%
International students	5%	African Americans	1%
Asian Americans/Pacific Islanders	1%	Hispanic Americans	1%
Native Americans	0.2%		

Faculty 357 (88% full-time), 62% with terminal degrees.

Expenses (2000–2001) *Tuition, state resident:* full-time $2800; part-time $93 per semester hour. *Tuition, nonresident:* full-time $6200; part-time $206 per semester hour. *Required fees:* full-time $500; $19 per semester hour. Full-time tuition and fees vary according to course load and reciprocity agreements. Part-time tuition and fees vary according to course load and reciprocity agreements. *College room and board:* $3500. Room and board charges vary according to board plan, housing facility, and location. *Waivers:* senior citizens and employees or children of employees.

Library Maxwell Library. *Operations spending 1999–2000:* $1.9 million. *Collection:* 243,500 titles, 1,950 serial subscriptions.

College life *Housing: Options:* coed, men-only, women-only. *Social organizations:* national fraternities, national sororities, local fraternities, local sororities; 3% of eligible men and 3% of eligible women are members. *Most popular organizations:* University Program Activities Committee, student senate, Inter-residence Hall Council.

Campus security 24-hour emergency response devices and patrols, student patrols, late-night transport-escort service, controlled dormitory access, security cameras.

After graduation 240 organizations recruited on campus 1997–98. 80% of class of 1998 had job offers within 6 months. *Career center:* 2 full-time, 1 part-time personnel. Services include job fairs, resume preparation, interview workshops, resume referral, career counseling, careers library, job bank, job interviews. *Graduate education:* 25% of class of 1999 went directly to graduate and professional school: 10% graduate arts and sciences, 6% business, 4% engineering, 1% dentistry, 1% law, 1% medicine, 1% theology, 1% veterinary medicine.

Freshmen 3,400 applied, 2,200 admitted, 1,479 enrolled. 2 National Merit Scholars, 60 class presidents, 30 valedictorians, 400 student government officers.

Average high school GPA	3.3	SAT verbal scores above 500	N/R
SAT math scores above 500	N/R	ACT above 18	99%
From top 10% of their h.s. class	20%	From top quarter	50%
From top half	96%	1998 freshmen returning in 1999	75%

Application *Options:* eApply at www.CollegeQuest.com, Common Application, electronic application, early admission, early action, deferred entrance. *Application fee:* $20. *Required:* high school transcript; class rank. *Required for some:* essay or personal statement; letters of recommendation; interview.

Standardized tests *Admission: Required:* SAT I or ACT.

Significant dates *Application deadlines:* rolling (freshmen), rolling (transfers). *Financial aid deadline:* continuous.

Freshman Application Contact
Dr. Jim Mootz, Director of Enrollment Services, Winona State University, PO Box 5838, Winona, MN 55987. **Phone:** 507-457-5100 Ext. 5105. **Toll-free phone:** 800-DIAL WSU. **Fax:** 507-457-5620. **E-mail:** admissions@vax2.winona.msus.edu

Visit CollegeQuest.com for information on majors offered and athletics. College video and electronic viewbook available at CollegeQuest.com.

MISSISSIPPI

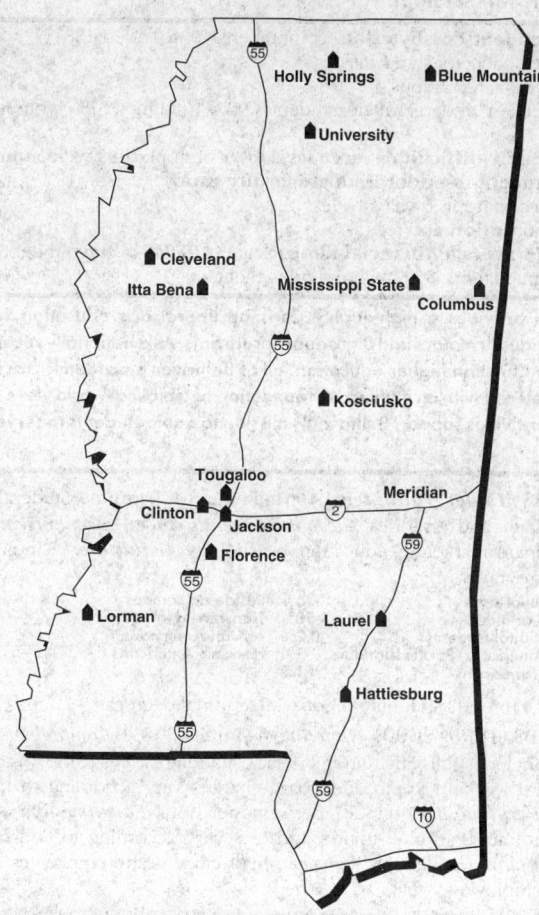

ALCORN STATE UNIVERSITY
Alcorn State, Mississippi

- **State-supported**, comprehensive, founded 1871
- **Degrees** associate, bachelor's, master's, and post-master's certificates
- **Rural** 1,756-acre campus
- **Coed**
- **Minimally difficult** entrance level
- **$2685 tuition** and fees (in-state); $5546 (out-of-state)

Part of Mississippi Institutions of Higher Learning.

Expenses (1999–2000) *Tuition, state resident:* full-time $2685; part-time $104 per semester hour. *Tuition, nonresident:* full-time $5546; part-time $223 per semester hour. *College room and board:* $2627.

Institutional Web site http://www.alcorn.edu/

College life *Housing: Options:* men-only, women-only. *Social organizations:* national fraternities, national sororities; 8% of eligible men and 10% of eligible women are members. *Most popular organizations:* Pan-Hellenic Council, Intramural sports, marching band, Gospel Choir, interfaith choir.

Campus security 24-hour patrols.

Application *Options:* Common Application, early admission, deferred entrance. *Preference* given to state residents. *Application fee:* $0. *Required:* high school transcript; minimum 2.0 GPA.

Standardized tests *Admission: Required:* SAT I or ACT.

Admissions Office Contact
Alcorn State University, 1000 ASU Drive, Alcorn State, MS 39096-7500. **Toll-free phone:** 800-222-6790. **E-mail:** ebarnes@loman.alcorn.edu

Visit CollegeQuest.com for information on athletics. College video available at CollegeQuest.com.

Mississippi

BELHAVEN COLLEGE
Jackson, Mississippi

- **Independent Presbyterian**, comprehensive, founded 1883
- **Degrees** bachelor's and master's
- **Urban** 42-acre campus
- **Coed**, 1,294 undergraduate students, 90% full-time, 62% women, 38% men
- **Moderately difficult** entrance level, 64% of applicants were admitted
- **16:1 student-to-undergraduate faculty ratio**
- **34% graduate** in 6 years or less
- **$10,340 tuition** and fees
- **$10,875 average financial aid** package, $10,255 average indebtedness upon graduation, $6.3 million endowment

Belhaven provides a high-quality Christian liberal arts education with 25 undergraduate majors and 3 graduate programs. As a nationally recognized leader in Christian higher education, all of Belhaven's academic classes are Christ centered with an intellectual foundation of a biblical world view, and all campus activities support Belhaven's mission to equip students to serve Christ Jesus.

Students *Undergraduates:* 1,166 full-time, 128 part-time. Students come from 30 states and territories. *The most frequently chosen baccalaureate fields are:* business/marketing, education, psychology. *Graduate:* 98 in graduate degree programs.

From out-of-state	26%	Reside on campus	32%
Age 25 or older	50%	Transferred in	12%
International students	0.2%	African Americans	30%
Asian Americans/Pacific Islanders	2%	Hispanic Americans	1%
Native Americans	1%		

Faculty 163 (31% full-time), 33% with terminal degrees.
Expenses (1999–2000) *One-time required fee:* $30. *Comprehensive fee:* $14,190 includes full-time tuition ($9960), mandatory fees ($380), and room and board ($3850). Room and board charges vary according to housing facility. *Part-time tuition:* $267 per semester hour. *Part-time fees:* $50 per term part-time. Part-time tuition and fees vary according to course load. *Payment plan:* installment. *Waivers:* senior citizens and employees or children of employees.
Library Hood Library. *Operations spending 1999–2000:* $223,941. *Collection:* 84,662 titles, 498 serial subscriptions, 10,897 audiovisual materials.
College life *Housing:* on-campus residence required through sophomore year. *Options:* men-only, women-only. *Social organizations:* local sororities; 1% of women are members. *Most popular organizations:* Student Government Association, Reformed University Fellowship, Kappa Delta Epsilon, Black Student Association, math/computer science club.
Campus security 24-hour emergency response devices and patrols, late-night transport-escort service, controlled dormitory access.
After graduation 28 organizations recruited on campus 1997–98. 72% of class of 1998 had job offers within 6 months. *Career center:* 1 part-time personnel. Services include job fairs, resume preparation, resume referral, career/interest testing, career counseling, careers library, job bank, job interviews.
Freshmen 518 applied, 333 admitted, 147 enrolled. 1 National Merit Scholar, 4 valedictorians.

Average high school GPA	3.23	SAT verbal scores above 500	93%
SAT math scores above 500	85%	ACT above 18	100%
From top 10% of their h.s. class	16%	From top half	74%
1998 freshmen returning in 1999	56%		

Application *Options:* early admission, deferred entrance. *Application fee:* $25. *Required:* high school transcript; minimum 2.0 GPA; 1 letter of recommendation; 1 academic reference. *Required for some:* essay or personal statement; interview.
Standardized tests *Admission: Required:* SAT I or ACT.
Significant dates *Application deadlines:* rolling (freshmen), rolling (transfers). *Financial aid deadline priority date:* 4/1.
Freshman Application Contact
Dr. Stephen Livesay, Vice President for Advancement, Belhaven College, 150 Peachtree Street, Jackson, MS 39202. **Phone:** 601-968-5940. **Toll-free phone:** 800-960-5940. **Fax:** 601-968-9998. **E-mail:** admissions@belhaven.edu
Visit CollegeQuest.com for information on majors offered and athletics.

BLUE MOUNTAIN COLLEGE
Blue Mountain, Mississippi

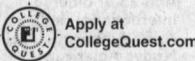
Apply at CollegeQuest.com

- **Independent Southern Baptist**, 4-year, founded 1873
- **Degree** bachelor's
- **Rural** 44-acre campus with easy access to Memphis
- **Coed**, primarily women, 435 undergraduate students, 79% full-time, 82% women, 18% men
- **Noncompetitive** entrance level, 69% of applicants were admitted
- **15:1 student-to-undergraduate faculty ratio**
- **35% graduate** in 6 years or less
- **$5340 tuition** and fees

Students *Undergraduates:* 342 full-time, 93 part-time. Students come from 10 states and territories. *The most frequently chosen baccalaureate fields are:* education, philosophy, social sciences and history.

From out-of-state	12%	Reside on campus	23%
Age 25 or older	24%	Transferred in	19%
African Americans	12%	Asian Americans/Pacific Islanders	0.5%
Native Americans	1%		

Faculty 32 (81% full-time), 38% with terminal degrees.
Expenses (1999–2000) *Comprehensive fee:* $8106 includes full-time tuition ($4980), mandatory fees ($360), and room and board ($2766). *College room only:* $966. Full-time tuition and fees vary according to course load. Room and board charges vary according to board plan and housing facility. *Part-time tuition:* $166 per semester hour. *Part-time fees:* $65 per term part-time. Part-time tuition and fees vary according to course load. *Payment plan:* installment. *Waivers:* employees or children of employees.
Library Guyton Library. *Collection:* 58,372 titles, 197 serial subscriptions, 4,210 audiovisual materials.
College life *Housing:* on-campus residence required through senior year. *Option:* women-only. *Social organizations:* societies for women; 50% of women are members. *Most popular organizations:* Baptist Student Union, student government association, athletic association, commuter club, Mississippi Association of Educators/Student Program.
Campus security 24-hour patrols.
After graduation 3 organizations recruited on campus 1997–98. 75% of class of 1998 had job offers within 6 months. *Career center:* 1 part-time personnel. Services include resume preparation, interview workshops, career counseling, job interviews. *Graduate education:* 7% of class of 1999 went directly to graduate and professional school: 5% theology, 2% education.
Freshmen 99 applied, 68 admitted, 50 enrolled.

Average high school GPA	3.0	SAT verbal scores above 500	N/R
SAT math scores above 500	N/R	ACT above 18	55%
From top half of their h.s. class	52%	1998 freshmen returning in 1999	65%

Application *Options:* eApply at www.CollegeQuest.com, early admission. *Application fee:* $10. *Required:* high school transcript. *Required for some:* 2 letters of recommendation; interview. *Recommended:* minimum 2.0 GPA.
Standardized tests *Admission: Required:* SAT I or ACT.
Significant dates *Application deadlines:* rolling (freshmen), rolling (transfers). *Financial aid deadline priority date:* 5/1.
Freshman Application Contact
Ms. Charlotte Lewis, Director of Admissions, Blue Mountain College, PO Box 160, Blue Mountain, MS 38610-0160. **Phone:** 662-685-4161 Ext. 176. **Toll-free phone:** 800-235-0136. **Fax:** 662-685-4776. **E-mail:** clewis@bmc.edu
Visit CollegeQuest.com for information on majors offered and athletics.

DELTA STATE UNIVERSITY
Cleveland, Mississippi

- **State-supported**, comprehensive, founded 1924
- **Degrees** bachelor's, master's, and doctoral
- **Small-town** 332-acre campus
- **Coed**, 3,469 undergraduate students, 82% full-time, 60% women, 40% men
- **Minimally difficult** entrance level, 84% of applicants were admitted
- **14:1 student-to-undergraduate faculty ratio**
- **45% graduate** in 6 years or less
- **$2596 tuition** and fees (in-state); $5546 (out-of-state)

- **$12,900 average indebtedness** upon graduation, $7.8 million endowment

Part of Mississippi Institutions of Higher Learning.

Students *Undergraduates:* 2,854 full-time, 615 part-time. Students come from 23 states and territories. *The most frequently chosen baccalaureate fields are:* business/marketing, education, social sciences and history. *Graduate:* 558 in graduate degree programs.

From out-of-state	6%	Reside on campus	38%
Age 25 or older	23%	Transferred in	18%
African Americans	28%	Asian Americans/Pacific Islanders	1%
Hispanic Americans	0.3%	Native Americans	0.3%

Expenses (1999–2000) *Tuition, state resident:* full-time $2596; part-time $91 per semester hour. *Tuition, nonresident:* full-time $5546; part-time $214 per semester hour. *College room and board:* $2730. *Payment plan:* installment. *Waivers:* children of alumni, senior citizens, and employees or children of employees.

Library W. B. Roberts Library plus 1 other. *Operations spending 1999–2000:* $1.4 million. *Collection:* 203,045 titles, 1,337 serial subscriptions, 15,523 audiovisual materials.

College life *Housing: Options:* men-only, women-only. *Social organizations:* national fraternities, national sororities; 17% of eligible men and 13% of eligible women are members. *Most popular organizations:* Student Government Association, Delta Volunteers, Student Alumni Association, Baptist Student Union, Reform University Fellowship.

Campus security 24-hour emergency response devices and patrols, late-night transport-escort service, controlled dormitory access.

After graduation 204 organizations recruited on campus 1997–98. 67% of class of 1998 had job offers within 6 months. *Career center:* 2 full-time personnel. Services include job fairs, resume preparation, interview workshops, resume referral, career counseling, careers library, job interviews.

Freshmen 578 applied, 488 admitted, 465 enrolled.

Average high school GPA	3.03	SAT verbal scores above 500	N/R
SAT math scores above 500	N/R	ACT above 18	74%
From top quarter of their h.s. class	46%	From top half	74%
1998 freshmen returning in 1999	76%		

Application *Options:* electronic application, early admission, deferred entrance. *Application fee:* $0. *Required:* high school transcript.

Standardized tests *Admission: Required:* SAT I or ACT.

Significant dates *Application deadlines:* rolling (freshmen), rolling (transfers). *Financial aid deadline priority date:* 5/1.

Freshman Application Contact
Ms. Debbie Heslep, Coordinator of Admissions, Delta State University, Kethley 107, Cleveland, MS 38733-0001. **Phone:** 662-846-4018. **Toll-free phone:** 800-468-6378. **Fax:** 662-846-4016. **E-mail:** jdcooper@dsu.deltast.edu
Visit CollegeQuest.com for information on majors offered and athletics. College video available at CollegeQuest.com.

JACKSON STATE UNIVERSITY
Jackson, Mississippi

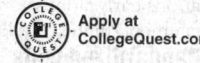
Apply at CollegeQuest.com

- **State-supported**, university, founded 1877
- **Degrees** bachelor's, master's, and doctoral
- **Urban** 128-acre campus
- **Coed**
- **Minimally difficult** entrance level
- **$2688 tuition** and fees (in-state); $5546 (out-of-state)

Part of Mississippi Institutions of Higher Learning.

Expenses (1999–2000) *Tuition, state resident:* full-time $2688; part-time $112 per credit hour. *Tuition, nonresident:* full-time $5546; part-time $231 per credit hour. *College room and board:* $3366; room only: $2036. Room and board charges vary according to board plan and housing facility.

Institutional Web site http://www.jsums.edu/

College life *Social organizations:* national fraternities, national sororities; 4% of eligible men and 4% of eligible women are members.

Campus security 24-hour emergency response devices and patrols, late-night transport-escort service, controlled dormitory access.

Application *Options:* eApply at www.CollegeQuest.com, Common Application, electronic application, early admission, deferred entrance. *Application fee:* $0. *Required:* high school transcript; minimum 3.0 GPA. *Required for some:* 3 letters of recommendation.

Standardized tests *Admission: Required:* ACT. *Required for some:* SAT I.

Admissions Office Contact
Jackson State University, PO Box 17330, 1400 John R. Lynch Street, Jackson, MS 39217. **Toll-free phone:** 800-682-5390 (in-state); 800-848-6817 (out-of-state). **E-mail:** schatman@ccaix.jsums.edu
Visit CollegeQuest.com for information on athletics.

MAGNOLIA BIBLE COLLEGE
Kosciusko, Mississippi

- **Independent**, 4-year, founded 1976, affiliated with Church of Christ
- **Degree** bachelor's
- **Small-town** 5-acre campus
- **Coed**, primarily men, 29 undergraduate students, 66% full-time, 21% women, 79% men
- **Noncompetitive** entrance level, 84% of applicants were admitted
- **6:1** student-to-undergraduate faculty ratio
- **25% graduate** in 6 years or less
- **$4540 tuition** and fees
- **$4072 average financial aid** package, $5258 average indebtedness upon graduation, $591,090 endowment

Students *Undergraduates:* 19 full-time, 10 part-time. Students come from 5 states and territories, 4 other countries. *The most frequently chosen baccalaureate field is:* philosophy.

| From out-of-state | 10% | Reside on campus | 63% |
| Age 25 or older | 63% | Transferred in | 14% |

Faculty 10 (40% full-time), 20% with terminal degrees.

Expenses (1999–2000) *Comprehensive fee:* $6284 includes full-time tuition ($4500), mandatory fees ($40), and room and board ($1744). *College room only:* $1000. Room and board charges vary according to housing facility. *Part-time tuition:* $150 per semester hour. *Part-time fees:* $20 per term part-time. *Payment plan:* deferred payment. *Waivers:* employees or children of employees.

Library John and Phillip Gaunt Library. *Operations spending 1999–2000:* $60,335. *Collection:* 36,650 titles, 278 serial subscriptions, 1,403 audiovisual materials.

College life On-campus residence required through sophomore year.

After graduation *Career center:* 1 part-time personnel. Services include resume preparation, interview workshops, career/interest testing, career counseling, job bank.

Freshmen 19 applied, 16 admitted, 1 enrolled.

Average high school GPA	2.66	SAT verbal scores above 500	N/R
SAT math scores above 500	N/R	ACT above 18	N/R
1998 freshmen returning in 1999	100%		

Application *Preference* given to Christians. *Application fee:* $0. *Required:* essay or personal statement; high school transcript; 3 letters of recommendation.

Standardized tests *Placement: Recommended:* SAT I or ACT.

Significant dates *Application deadlines:* 8/31 (freshmen), 8/31 (transfers). *Financial aid deadline priority date:* 8/1.

Freshman Application Contact
Mr. Allen Coker, Admissions Officer, Magnolia Bible College, PO Box 1109, Kosciusko, MS 39090-1109. **Phone:** 601-289-2896 Ext. 106. **Toll-free phone:** 800-748-8655. **E-mail:** mbcgary@kopower.com
Visit CollegeQuest.com for information on majors offered and athletics. College video available at CollegeQuest.com.

MILLSAPS COLLEGE
Jackson, Mississippi

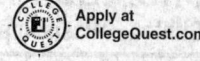
Apply at CollegeQuest.com

- **Independent United Methodist**, comprehensive, founded 1890
- **Degrees** bachelor's and master's

Mississippi

Millsaps College (continued)
- **Urban** 100-acre campus
- **Coed**, 1,191 undergraduate students, 94% full-time, 55% women, 45% men
- **Moderately difficult** entrance level, 87% of applicants were admitted
- **14:1 student-to-undergraduate faculty ratio**
- **76% graduate** in 6 years or less
- **$15,029 tuition** and fees
- **$15,692 average financial aid** package, $18,743 average indebtedness upon graduation, $93.1 million endowment

Students *Undergraduates:* 1,117 full-time, 74 part-time. Students come from 26 states and territories, 6 other countries. *The most frequently chosen baccalaureate fields are:* business/marketing, English, social sciences and history. *Graduate:* 123 in graduate degree programs.

From out-of-state	43%	Reside on campus	78%
Age 25 or older	1%	Transferred in	4%
International students	1%	African Americans	9%
Asian Americans/Pacific Islanders	3%	Hispanic Americans	1%
Native Americans	0.4%		

Faculty 97 (92% full-time), 92% with terminal degrees.

Expenses (1999–2000) *Comprehensive fee:* $21,135 includes full-time tuition ($14,190), mandatory fees ($839), and room and board ($6106). *College room only:* $3684. Room and board charges vary according to housing facility. Part-time tuition and fees vary according to course load. *Payment plan:* installment. *Waivers:* employees or children of employees.

Library Millsaps Wilson Library. *Operations spending 1999–2000:* $909,367. *Collection:* 117,705 titles, 656 serial subscriptions.

College life *Housing:* on-campus residence required through sophomore year. *Options:* coed, men-only, women-only. *Social organizations:* national fraternities, national sororities; 59% of eligible men and 56% of eligible women are members. *Most popular organizations:* fraternities/sororities, Campus Ministry Team, National Leadership Organization, Habitat for Humanity, Student Body Association.

Campus security 24-hour emergency response devices and patrols, student patrols, late-night transport-escort service, controlled dormitory access, self-defense education, lighted pathways.

After graduation 60 organizations recruited on campus 1997–98. 44% of class of 1998 had job offers within 6 months. *Career center:* 3 full-time, 1 part-time personnel. Services include job fairs, resume preparation, interview workshops, resume referral, career/interest testing, career counseling, careers library, job bank, job interviews. *Graduate education:* 35% of class of 1999 went directly to graduate and professional school.

Freshmen 912 applied, 792 admitted, 284 enrolled. 7 National Merit Scholars, 19 class presidents, 19 valedictorians, 89 student government officers.

Average high school GPA	3.26	SAT verbal scores above 500	90%
SAT math scores above 500	85%	ACT above 18	100%
From top 10% of their h.s. class	44%	From top quarter	71%
From top half	90%	1998 freshmen returning in 1999	85%

Application *Options:* eApply at www.CollegeQuest.com, Common Application, electronic application, early action, deferred entrance. *Application fee:* $25. *Required:* essay or personal statement; high school transcript; minimum 2.75 GPA. *Recommended:* letters of recommendation; interview.

Standardized tests *Admission: Required:* SAT I or ACT.

Significant dates *Application deadlines:* 7/1 (freshmen), rolling (transfers). *Early action:* 12/1. *Notification:* 12/20 (early action). *Financial aid deadline:* continuous.

Freshman Application Contact
Mr. John Gaines, Director of Admissions, Millsaps College, 1701 North State Street, Jackson, MS 39210-0001. **Phone:** 601-974-1050. **Toll-free phone:** 800-352-1050. **Fax:** 601-974-1059. **E-mail:** admissions@millsaps.edu

Visit CollegeQuest.com for information on majors offered and athletics. College video and electronic viewbook available at CollegeQuest.com.

MISSISSIPPI COLLEGE
Clinton, Mississippi

Apply at CollegeQuest.com

- **Independent Southern Baptist**, comprehensive, founded 1826
- **Degrees** bachelor's, master's, first professional, and post-master's certificates
- **Suburban** 320-acre campus
- **Coed**, 2,506 undergraduate students, 86% full-time, 57% women, 43% men
- **Moderately difficult** entrance level, 93% of applicants were admitted
- **15:1 student-to-undergraduate faculty ratio**
- **$9614 tuition** and fees
- **$12,369 average financial aid** package, $22,588 average indebtedness upon graduation, $39.9 million endowment

Founded in 1826 and located in Clinton, Mississippi College is the state's oldest institution of higher learning and the second-oldest Baptist university in the nation. With an undergraduate enrollment of more than 2,300, Mississippi College is also the largest private university in the state. At Mississippi College, 170 years of tradition blends with state-of-the-art technology to provide a 4-year liberal arts education of unrivaled quality.

Students *Undergraduates:* 2,145 full-time, 361 part-time. Students come from 29 states and territories, 7 other countries. *The most frequently chosen baccalaureate fields are:* business/marketing, education, health professions and related sciences. *Graduate:* 371 in professional programs, 667 in other graduate degree programs.

From out-of-state	15%	Reside on campus	69%
Age 25 or older	16%	Transferred in	11%
International students	0.4%	African Americans	12%
Asian Americans/Pacific Islanders	1%	Hispanic Americans	0.4%
Native Americans	0.2%		

Faculty 285 (55% full-time), 51% with terminal degrees.

Expenses (2000–2001) *Comprehensive fee:* $13,790 includes full-time tuition ($9090), mandatory fees ($524), and room and board ($4176). *College room only:* $1980. Full-time tuition and fees vary according to course load. Room and board charges vary according to board plan and housing facility. *Part-time tuition:* $303 per credit hour. *Part-time fees:* $75 per term part-time. Part-time tuition and fees vary according to course load. *Payment plans:* installment, deferred payment. *Waivers:* employees or children of employees.

Library Leland Speed Library plus 1 other. *Operations spending 1999–2000:* $1.9 million. *Collection:* 317,804 titles.

College life *Housing:* on-campus residence required through senior year. *Options:* men-only, women-only, disabled students. *Most popular organizations:* Baptist Student Union, Nenamoosha Social Tribe, Circle K, Nurses' Fellowship.

Campus security 24-hour emergency response devices and patrols, late-night transport-escort service, controlled dormitory access.

After graduation 65 organizations recruited on campus 1997–98. *Career center:* 1 full-time personnel. Services include job fairs, resume preparation, career counseling, careers library, job interviews.

Freshmen 805 applied, 749 admitted, 405 enrolled. 23 National Merit Scholars.

SAT verbal scores above 500	N/R	SAT math scores above 500	N/R
ACT above 18	N/R	1998 freshmen returning in 1999	85%

Application *Options:* eApply at www.CollegeQuest.com, Common Application, early admission. *Application fee:* $25. *Required:* essay or personal statement; high school transcript.

Standardized tests *Admission: Required:* SAT I or ACT.

Significant dates *Application deadlines:* rolling (freshmen), rolling (transfers). *Financial aid deadline priority date:* 3/1.

Freshman Application Contact
Dr. Jim Turcotte, Dean of Enrollment Services, Mississippi College, PO Box 4026, Clinton, MS 39058. **Phone:** 601-925-3240. **Toll-free phone:** 800-738-1236. **Fax:** 601-925-3804. **E-mail:** admissions@mc.edu

Visit CollegeQuest.com for information on majors offered and athletics. Electronic viewbook available at CollegeQuest.com.

MISSISSIPPI STATE UNIVERSITY
Mississippi State, Mississippi

- **State-supported**, university, founded 1878
- **Degrees** bachelor's, master's, doctoral, first professional, and post-master's certificates
- **Small-town** 4,200-acre campus

Mississippi

- **Coed**, 12,879 undergraduate students, 86% full-time, 45% women, 55% men
- **Moderately difficult** entrance level, 70% of applicants were admitted
- **15:1 student-to-undergraduate faculty ratio**
- **49.5% graduate** in 6 years or less
- **$3,330 tuition** and fees (in-state); $6,432 (out-of-state)
- **$5440 average financial aid** package, $17,712 average indebtedness upon graduation, $160.4 million endowment

Students *Undergraduates:* 11,125 full-time, 1,754 part-time. Students come from 52 states and territories, 52 other countries. *The most frequently chosen baccalaureate fields are:* business/marketing, education, engineering/engineering technologies. *Graduate:* 193 in professional programs, 3,004 in other graduate degree programs.

From out-of-state	22%	Reside on campus	30%
Age 25 or older	15%	Transferred in	11%
International students	2%	African Americans	18%
Asian Americans/Pacific Islanders	1%	Hispanic Americans	1%
Native Americans	1%		

Faculty 1,020 (87% full-time), 74% with terminal degrees.

Expenses (1999–2000) *Tuition, state resident:* full-time $3017; part-time $126 per credit hour. *Tuition, nonresident:* full-time $6119; part-time $255 per credit hour. *Required fees:* full-time $312. Full-time tuition and fees vary according to location. Part-time tuition and fees vary according to course load and location. *College room and board:* $3690; room only: $1800. Room and board charges vary according to board plan and housing facility. *Waivers:* children of alumni, senior citizens, and employees or children of employees.

Library Mitchell Memorial Library plus 2 others. *Operations spending 1999–2000:* $5.8 million. *Collection:* 10,118 serial subscriptions, 44,263 audiovisual materials.

College life *Housing: Options:* coed, men-only, women-only, disabled students. *Social organizations:* national fraternities, national sororities; 17% of eligible men and 18% of eligible women are members. *Most popular organizations:* student association, Black Student Alliance, Residence Hall Association, Fashion Board, Campus Activities Board.

Campus security 24-hour emergency response devices, late-night transport-escort service, controlled dormitory access, bicycle patrols, crime prevention program, RAD program, general law enforcement services.

After graduation 377 organizations recruited on campus 1997–98. 60% of class of 1998 had job offers within 6 months. *Career center:* 10 full-time personnel. Services include job fairs, resume preparation, interview workshops, resume referral, career/interest testing, career counseling, careers library, job bank, job interviews.

Freshmen 5,949 applied, 4,175 admitted, 2,024 enrolled. 40 National Merit Scholars.

Average high school GPA	3.23	SAT verbal scores above 500	N/R
SAT math scores above 500	N/R	ACT above 18	93%
From top 10% of their h.s. class	26%	From top quarter	54%
From top half	81%	1998 freshmen returning in 1999	78%

Application *Options:* electronic application, early admission, deferred entrance. *Application fee:* $25 for nonresidents. *Required:* high school transcript; minimum 2.0 GPA. *Required for some:* letters of recommendation; interview.

Standardized tests *Admission: Required:* SAT I or ACT. *Required for some:* ACCUPLACER.

Significant dates *Application deadlines:* 8/1 (freshmen), 8/1 (transfers). *Financial aid deadline priority date:* 4/1.

Freshman Application Contact
Mr. Jerry Inmon, Director of Admissions, Mississippi State University, PO Box 6305, Mississippi State, MS 39762. **Phone:** 601-325-2224. **Fax:** 662-325-3299. **E-mail:** admit@admissions.msstate.edu

Visit CollegeQuest.com for information on majors offered and athletics.

MISSISSIPPI UNIVERSITY FOR WOMEN
Columbus, Mississippi

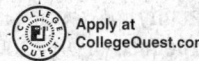 Apply at CollegeQuest.com

- **State-supported**, comprehensive, founded 1884
- **Degrees** associate, bachelor's, and master's
- **Small-town** 110-acre campus
- **Coed**, 3,180 undergraduate students, 60% full-time, 81% women, 19% men
- **Moderately difficult** entrance level, 79% of applicants were admitted
- **$2556 tuition** and fees (in-state); $5546 (out-of-state)
- **$16.2 million endowment**

Part of Mississippi Institutions of Higher Learning.

Students *Undergraduates:* 1,910 full-time, 1,270 part-time. Students come from 26 states and territories, 36 other countries. *Graduate:* 134 in graduate degree programs.

From out-of-state	11%	Reside on campus	21%
Age 25 or older	42%	Transferred in	17%
International students	2%	African Americans	28%
Asian Americans/Pacific Islanders	0.3%	Hispanic Americans	1%
Native Americans	0.2%		

Faculty 206 (63% full-time).

Expenses (1999–2000) *Tuition, state resident:* full-time $2556; part-time $106 per semester hour. *Tuition, nonresident:* full-time $5546; part-time $231 per semester hour. *College room and board:* $2590; room only: $1260. Room and board charges vary according to board plan. *Payment plans:* installment, deferred payment. *Waivers:* minority students, children of alumni, adult students, and employees or children of employees.

Library John Clayton Fant Memorial Library. *Operations spending 1999–2000:* $708,933. *Collection:* 426,543 titles, 1,629 serial subscriptions, 164 audiovisual materials.

College life *Housing: Options:* men-only, women-only. *Social organizations:* national fraternities, national sororities, local fraternities, local sororities; 10% of eligible men and 20% of eligible women are members. *Most popular organizations:* Student Government Association, Union Advisory Cabinet, Black Student Council, W Angels, Student Alumni Ambassadors.

Campus security 24-hour patrols, student patrols, late-night transport-escort service.

After graduation 56 organizations recruited on campus 1997–98. *Career center:* 2 full-time personnel. Services include job fairs, resume preparation, interview workshops, resume referral, career/interest testing, career counseling, careers library, job bank, job interviews.

Freshmen 758 applied, 599 admitted, 332 enrolled. 10 class presidents, 23 valedictorians, 26 student government officers.

Average high school GPA	3.2	SAT verbal scores above 500	N/R
SAT math scores above 500	N/R	ACT above 18	90%
From top quarter of their h.s. class	59%	From top half	88%
1998 freshmen returning in 1999	71%		

Application *Options:* eApply at www.CollegeQuest.com, Common Application, electronic application, early admission. *Application fee:* $25 for nonresidents. *Required:* high school transcript. *Required for some:* minimum 2.0 GPA; letters of recommendation; rank in upper 50% of high school class.

Standardized tests *Admission: Recommended:* SAT I or ACT. *Required for some:* SAT I or ACT.

Significant dates *Application deadlines:* 9/6 (freshmen), 9/6 (transfers). *Financial aid deadline priority date:* 4/15.

Freshman Application Contact
Ms. Melanie Freeman, Director of Admissions, Mississippi University for Women, PO Box 1613, Columbus, MS 39701-9998. **Phone:** 601-329-7106. **Toll-free phone:** 877-GO 2 THE W. **Fax:** 662-329-7297. **E-mail:** admissions@muw.edu

Visit CollegeQuest.com for information on majors offered and athletics.

MISSISSIPPI VALLEY STATE UNIVERSITY
Itta Bena, Mississippi

- **State-supported**, comprehensive, founded 1946
- **Degrees** bachelor's and master's
- **Small-town** 450-acre campus
- **Coed**, 2,212 undergraduate students, 86% full-time, 62% women, 38% men
- **Minimally difficult** entrance level, 21% of applicants were admitted
- **19:1 student-to-undergraduate faculty ratio**
- **25% graduate** in 6 years or less
- **$2346 tuition** and fees (in-state); $5091 (out-of-state)

Peterson's Guide to Four-Year Colleges 2001   www.petersons.com   439

Mississippi

Mississippi Valley State University (continued)
■ $989,369 endowment

Part of Mississippi Institutions of Higher Learning.
Students *Undergraduates:* 1,913 full-time, 299 part-time. Students come from 27 states and territories. *The most frequently chosen baccalaureate fields are:* business/marketing, education, protective services/public administration. *Graduate:* 297 in graduate degree programs.

From out-of-state	7%	Reside on campus	53%
Age 25 or older	27%	Transferred in	7%
African Americans	97%	Asian Americans/Pacific Islanders	0.3%
Hispanic Americans	0.05%		

Faculty 129 (89% full-time), 55% with terminal degrees.
Expenses (1999–2000) *Tuition, state resident:* full-time $2126; part-time $110 per semester hour. *Tuition, nonresident:* full-time $4871; part-time $121 per semester hour. *Required fees:* full-time $220. Full-time tuition and fees vary according to course load. Part-time tuition and fees vary according to course load. *College room and board:* $2844. *Payment plan:* installment. *Waivers:* children of alumni and employees or children of employees.
Library James H. White Library plus 1 other. *Operations spending 1999–2000:* $648,931. *Collection:* 145,979 titles, 573 serial subscriptions.
College life *Housing:* on-campus residence required through senior year. *Options:* men-only, women-only. *Social organizations:* national fraternities, national sororities, local fraternities, local sororities; 20% of eligible men and 25% of eligible women are members. *Most popular organizations:* Student Government Association, Baptist Student Union, Black Student Fellowship, Panhellenic Council, National Education Association.
Campus security 24-hour emergency response devices and patrols, controlled dormitory access.
After graduation 45 organizations recruited on campus 1997–98. 40% of class of 1998 had job offers within 6 months. *Career center:* 2 full-time personnel. Services include job fairs, resume preparation, resume referral, career counseling, careers library, job bank, job interviews. *Graduate education:* 40% of class of 1999 went directly to graduate and professional school.
Freshmen 2,766 applied, 587 admitted, 560 enrolled.

Average high school GPA	2.0	SAT verbal scores above 500	N/R
SAT math scores above 500	N/R	ACT above 18	42%
From top 10% of their h.s. class	3%	From top quarter	5%
From top half	15%	1998 freshmen returning in 1999	78%

Application *Option:* deferred entrance. *Required:* high school transcript. *Recommended:* letters of recommendation; interview.
Standardized tests *Admission: Required:* SAT I or ACT. *Recommended:* ACT.
Significant dates *Application deadlines:* rolling (freshmen), rolling (transfers). *Financial aid deadline priority date:* 4/1.
Freshman Application Contact
Mrs. Maxine B. Rush, Director of Admissions and Recruitment, Mississippi Valley State University, 14000 Highway 82 West, Itta Bena, MS 38941-1400. **Phone:** 662-254-3344. **Toll-free phone:** 800-844-6885. **Fax:** 662-254-7900.
Visit CollegeQuest.com for information on majors offered and athletics. College video available at CollegeQuest.com.

RUST COLLEGE
Holly Springs, Mississippi

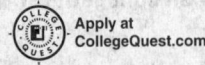

■ **Independent United Methodist**, 4-year, founded 1866
■ **Degrees** associate and bachelor's
■ **Rural** 126-acre campus with easy access to Memphis
■ **Coed**, 733 undergraduate students, 88% full-time, 56% women, 44% men
■ **Moderately difficult** entrance level, 47% of applicants were admitted
■ **16:1** student-to-undergraduate faculty ratio
■ **46.18% graduate** in 6 years or less
■ **$5200 tuition** and fees

Students *Undergraduates:* 645 full-time, 88 part-time. Students come from 23 states and territories, 6 other countries. *The most frequently chosen baccalaureate fields are:* business/marketing, computer/information sciences, social sciences and history.

From out-of-state	35%	Reside on campus	29%
Age 25 or older	26%	International students	5%
African Americans	95%		

Faculty 48 (92% full-time), 52% with terminal degrees.
Expenses (1999–2000) *Comprehensive fee:* $7600 includes full-time tuition ($5200) and room and board ($2400). *Part-time tuition:* $225 per credit hour. *Payment plan:* installment. *Waivers:* employees or children of employees.
Library Leontyne Price Library. *Collection:* 112,000 titles, 339 serial subscriptions.
College life *Housing: Options:* men-only, women-only. *Social organizations:* national fraternities, national sororities.
Campus security 24-hour emergency response devices and patrols, late-night transport-escort service.
After graduation *Career center:* 2 full-time personnel. Services include job fairs, resume preparation, resume referral, career counseling, careers library, job interviews.
Freshmen 1,795 applied, 849 admitted, 208 enrolled.

SAT verbal scores above 500	N/R	SAT math scores above 500	N/R
ACT above 18	N/R		

Application *Options:* eApply at www.CollegeQuest.com, Common Application, deferred entrance. *Application fee:* $10. *Required:* high school transcript; letters of recommendation. *Required for some:* essay or personal statement.
Standardized tests *Admission: Required:* ACT.
Significant dates *Application deadlines:* rolling (freshmen), rolling (transfers). *Financial aid deadline priority date:* 4/1.
Freshman Application Contact
Mr. Johnny McDonald, Director of Enrollment Services, Rust College, 150 Rust Avenue, Holly Springs, MS 38635-2328. **Phone:** 601-252-8000 Ext. 4065. **Toll-free phone:** 888-886-8492 Ext. 4065. **Fax:** 662-252-6107. **E-mail:** admissions@rustcollege.edu
Visit CollegeQuest.com for information on majors offered and athletics. College video available at CollegeQuest.com.

SOUTHEASTERN BAPTIST COLLEGE
Laurel, Mississippi

Admissions Office Contact
Southeastern Baptist College, 4229 Highway 15 North, Laurel, MS 39440-1096.

TOUGALOO COLLEGE
Tougaloo, Mississippi

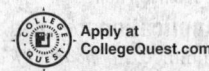

■ **Independent**, 4-year, founded 1869, affiliated with United Church of Christ
■ **Degrees** associate and bachelor's
■ **Suburban** 500-acre campus
■ **Coed**, 965 undergraduate students, 95% full-time, 72% women, 28% men
■ **Minimally difficult** entrance level, 99% of applicants were admitted
■ **18:1** student-to-undergraduate faculty ratio
■ **35.7% graduate** in 6 years or less
■ **$7110 tuition** and fees

Students *Undergraduates:* 913 full-time, 52 part-time. Students come from 24 states and territories. *The most frequently chosen baccalaureate fields are:* psychology, business/marketing, social sciences and history.

From out-of-state	14%	Age 25 or older	10%
Transferred in	5%	African Americans	100%

Faculty 90 (67% full-time).
Expenses (1999–2000) *Comprehensive fee:* $10,170 includes full-time tuition ($6400), mandatory fees ($710), and room and board ($3060). *College room only:* $1760. *Part-time tuition:* $240 per hour. *Part-time fees:* $710 per year part-time. *Payment plans:* installment, deferred payment. *Waivers:* adult students, senior citizens, and employees or children of employees.

Library L. Zenobiz Coleman Library. *Collection:* 137,000 titles, 432 serial subscriptions.
College life *Housing: Options:* men-only, women-only. *Social organizations:* national fraternities, national sororities; 30% of eligible men and 35% of eligible women are members. *Most popular organizations:* Concert Choir, Student Government Association, Gospel Choir, NAACP, Pre-Alumni.
Campus security 24-hour emergency response devices and patrols.
After graduation *Career center:* 1 full-time personnel. Services include job fairs, resume preparation, resume referral, career counseling, careers library, job bank, job interviews.
Freshmen 646 applied, 639 admitted, 251 enrolled.

Average high school GPA	3.15	SAT verbal scores above 500	N/R
SAT math scores above 500	N/R	ACT above 18	N/R
From top 10% of their h.s. class	24%	From top quarter	40%
From top half	60%	1998 freshmen returning in 1999	68%

Application *Options:* eApply at www.CollegeQuest.com, Common Application, early admission. *Application fee:* $5. *Required:* high school transcript; minimum 2.0 GPA.
Standardized tests *Admission: Required:* SAT I or ACT.
Significant dates *Application deadlines:* rolling (freshmen), rolling (transfers). *Financial aid deadline priority date:* 4/15.
Freshman Application Contact
Ms. Felicia Smith, Data Entry Specialist, Tougaloo College, Student Enrollment Management Center, 500 West County Line Road, Tougaloo, MS 39174. **Phone:** 601-977-7768. **Toll-free phone:** 888-42GALOO. **Fax:** 601-977-7739. **E-mail:** carolyn.evans@tougaloo.edu
Visit CollegeQuest.com for information on majors offered and athletics. College video available at CollegeQuest.com.

UNIVERSITY OF MISSISSIPPI
Oxford, Mississippi

- **State-supported**, university, founded 1844
- **Degrees** bachelor's, master's, doctoral, and first professional
- **Small-town** 2,500-acre campus with easy access to Memphis
- **Coed**, 9,062 undergraduate students, 92% full-time, 52% women, 48% men
- **Moderately difficult** entrance level, 76% of applicants were admitted
- **17:1** student-to-undergraduate faculty ratio
- **48% graduate** in 6 years or less
- **$3053 tuition** and fees (in-state); $6155 (out-of-state)
- **$6523 average financial aid** package, $14,795 average indebtedness upon graduation, $17.1 million endowment

Part of Mississippi Institutions of Higher Learning.
Students *Undergraduates:* 8,356 full-time, 706 part-time. Students come from 47 states and territories, 46 other countries. *The most frequently chosen baccalaureate fields are:* business/marketing, education, health professions and related sciences. *Graduate:* 596 in professional programs, 1,819 in other graduate degree programs.

From out-of-state	35%	Reside on campus	33%
Age 25 or older	10%	Transferred in	9%
International students	2%	African Americans	11%
Asian Americans/Pacific Islanders	1%	Hispanic Americans	1%
Native Americans	0.3%		

Faculty 584 (85% full-time), 55% with terminal degrees.
Expenses (1999–2000) *Tuition, state resident:* full-time $3053; part-time $127 per semester hour. *Tuition, nonresident:* full-time $6155; part-time $256 per semester hour. Part-time tuition and fees vary according to course load. *College room and board:* $3414. Room and board charges vary according to board plan and housing facility. *Payment plans:* tuition prepayment, deferred payment. *Waivers:* children of alumni, senior citizens, and employees or children of employees.
Library J. D. Williams Library plus 3 others. *Operations spending 1999–2000:* $7.1 million. *Collection:* 951,259 titles, 8,495 serial subscriptions, 143,717 audiovisual materials.
College life On-campus residence required in freshman year. *Social organizations:* national fraternities, national sororities; 28% of eligible men and 35% of eligible women are members. *Most popular organizations:* Associated Student Body, School Spirit, sport clubs, Black Student Union, Student Programming Board.

Campus security 24-hour emergency response devices and patrols, late-night transport-escort service, controlled dormitory access, crime prevention programs.
After graduation 245 organizations recruited on campus 1997–98. *Career center:* 7 full-time, 7 part-time personnel. Services include job fairs, resume preparation, interview workshops, resume referral, career counseling, careers library, job bank, job interviews.
Freshmen 4,196 applied, 3,180 admitted, 1,826 enrolled. 27 National Merit Scholars.

SAT verbal scores above 500	N/R	SAT math scores above 500	N/R
ACT above 18	94%	From top 10% of their h.s. class	38%
From top quarter	54%	From top half	86%
1998 freshmen returning in 1999	75%		

Application *Options:* electronic application, early admission. *Application fee:* $25 for nonresidents. *Required:* high school transcript; minimum 2.0 GPA.
Standardized tests *Admission: Required for some:* SAT I or ACT.
Significant dates *Application deadlines:* 7/24 (freshmen), 7/24 (transfers). *Notification:* continuous until 8/16 (freshmen). *Financial aid deadline priority date:* 3/15.
Freshman Application Contact
Mr. Beckett Howorth, Director of Admissions, University of Mississippi, Office of Admissions, 145 Martindale Student Services Center, University, MS 38677. **Phone:** 662-915-7226. **Toll-free phone:** 662-915-7226 (in-state); 662-915-5869 (out-of-state). **Fax:** 662-232-5869. **E-mail:** admissions@olemiss.edu
Visit CollegeQuest.com for information on majors offered and athletics. College video available at CollegeQuest.com.

UNIVERSITY OF MISSISSIPPI MEDICAL CENTER
Jackson, Mississippi

- **State-supported**, upper-level, founded 1955
- **Degrees** bachelor's, master's, doctoral, and first professional
- **Urban** 164-acre campus
- **Coed**, 532 undergraduate students, 100% full-time, 83% women, 17% men
- **Moderately difficult** entrance level, 31% of applicants were admitted
- **$3168 tuition** and fees (in-state); $8819 (out-of-state)
- **$9500 average indebtedness** upon graduation, $29.1 million endowment

Part of University of Mississippi.
Students *Undergraduates:* 532 full-time. Students come from 3 states and territories. *The most frequently chosen baccalaureate field is:* health professions and related sciences. *Graduate:* 497 in professional programs, 731 in other graduate degree programs.

From out-of-state	3%	Age 25 or older	28%
Transferred in	56%	African Americans	14%
Asian Americans/Pacific Islanders	1%	Hispanic Americans	1%
Native Americans	0.4%		

Faculty 662 (80% full-time), 100% with terminal degrees.
Expenses (1999–2000) *Tuition, state resident:* full-time $3168. *Tuition, nonresident:* full-time $8819. *College room and board:* room only: $1530. Room and board charges vary according to housing facility. *Payment plans:* installment, deferred payment. *Waivers:* employees or children of employees.
Library Rowland Medical Library. *Operations spending 1999–2000:* $2.8 million. *Collection:* 244,460 titles, 2,371 serial subscriptions, 17,084 audiovisual materials.
College life *Housing: Option:* women-only.
Campus security 24-hour emergency response devices and patrols, late-night transport-escort service, controlled dormitory access.
After graduation 100% of class of 1998 had job offers within 6 months. *Career center:* Services include career counseling.
Application *Preference* given to state residents. *Application fee:* $10.
Standardized tests *Admission: Required for some:* ACT.
Significant dates *Application deadline:* 2/15 (transfers). *Notification:* continuous until 5/1 (transfers). *Financial aid deadline priority date:* 4/1.

Mississippi

University of Mississippi Medical Center (continued)
Freshman Application Contact
Dr. Billy M. Bishop, Director of Student Services and Records, University of Mississippi Medical Center, 2500 North State Street, Jackson, MS 39216-4505. **Phone:** 601-984-1080. **Fax:** 601-984-1080.
Visit CollegeQuest.com for information on majors offered and athletics.

UNIVERSITY OF SOUTHERN MISSISSIPPI
Hattiesburg, Mississippi

- **State-supported**, university, founded 1910
- **Degrees** bachelor's, master's, and doctoral
- **Suburban** 1,090-acre campus with easy access to New Orleans
- **Coed**, 11,987 undergraduate students, 84% full-time, 60% women, 40% men
- **Moderately difficult** entrance level, 63% of applicants were admitted
- **40% graduate** in 6 years or less
- **$2870 tuition** and fees (in-state); $5972 (out-of-state)

Students *Undergraduates:* 10,114 full-time, 1,873 part-time. Students come from 49 states and territories, 62 other countries. *The most frequently chosen baccalaureate fields are:* business/marketing, education, health professions and related sciences. *Graduate:* 2,375 in graduate degree programs.

From out-of-state	12%	Reside on campus	33%
Age 25 or older	20%	Transferred in	13%
International students	2%	African Americans	21%
Asian Americans/Pacific Islanders	1%	Hispanic Americans	1%
Native Americans	0.3%		

Faculty 747 (88% full-time), 53% with terminal degrees.
Expenses (1999–2000) *Tuition, state resident:* full-time $2870; part-time $105 per credit. *Tuition, nonresident:* full-time $5972; part-time $234 per credit. Part-time tuition and fees vary according to course load. *College room and board:* $3345; room only: $1785. Room and board charges vary according to board plan and housing facility. *Payment plans:* tuition prepayment, installment. *Waivers:* children of alumni, senior citizens, and employees or children of employees.
Library Cook Memorial Library plus 3 others. *Operations spending 1999–2000:* $5.4 million. *Collection:* 745,653 titles, 19,013 audiovisual materials.
College life *Housing: Options:* men-only, women-only, disabled students. *Social organizations:* national fraternities, national sororities; 16% of eligible men and 15% of eligible women are members. *Most popular organizations:* University Activities Council, residence halls associations, Greek life, Student Government Association.
Campus security 24-hour emergency response devices and patrols, late-night transport-escort service, controlled dormitory access.
After graduation 259 organizations recruited on campus 1997–98. 73% of class of 1998 had job offers within 6 months. *Career center:* 11 full-time, 2 part-time personnel. Services include job fairs, resume preparation, interview workshops, resume referral, career/interest testing, career counseling, careers library, job bank, job interviews.
Freshmen 4,533 applied, 2,877 admitted, 1,307 enrolled. 6 National Merit Scholars.

Average high school GPA	3.24	SAT verbal scores above 500	N/R
SAT math scores above 500	N/R	ACT above 18	76%
From top 10% of their h.s. class	35%	From top quarter	49%
From top half	80%	1998 freshmen returning in 1999	70%

Application *Options:* electronic application, early admission, deferred entrance. *Application fee:* $0. *Required:* high school transcript; minimum 2.0 GPA. *Required for some:* interview.
Standardized tests *Admission: Required:* SAT I or ACT.
Significant dates *Application deadlines:* rolling (freshmen), rolling (transfers). *Financial aid deadline priority date:* 3/15.

Freshman Application Contact
Dr. Homer Wesley, Dean of Admissions, University of Southern Mississippi, Box 5166, Hattiesburg, MS 39406-5166. **Phone:** 601-266-5000. **E-mail:** admissions@usm.edu
Visit CollegeQuest.com for information on majors offered and athletics. College video and electronic viewbook available at CollegeQuest.com.

WESLEY COLLEGE
Florence, Mississippi

- **Independent Congregational Methodist**, 4-year, founded 1944
- **Degree** bachelor's
- **Small-town** 40-acre campus with easy access to Jackson
- **Coed**, 101 undergraduate students, 70% full-time, 41% women, 59% men
- **Noncompetitive** entrance level
- **$2800 tuition** and fees
- **$353,038 endowment**

Students *Undergraduates:* 71 full-time, 30 part-time. Students come from 10 states and territories, 3 other countries. *The most frequently chosen baccalaureate field is:* philosophy.

From out-of-state	35%	Reside on campus	69%
Age 25 or older	40%	Transferred in	10%
International students	3%	African Americans	26%
Asian Americans/Pacific Islanders	1%		

Expenses (1999–2000) *Comprehensive fee:* $5250 includes full-time tuition ($2500), mandatory fees ($300), and room and board ($2450). Full-time tuition and fees vary according to course load. Room and board charges vary according to housing facility. *Part-time tuition:* $105 per semester hour. *Part-time fees:* $75 per term part-time. Part-time tuition and fees vary according to course load. *Payment plan:* installment. *Waivers:* senior citizens and employees or children of employees.
Library *Operations spending 1999–2000:* $28,515. *Collection:* 25,000 titles, 96 serial subscriptions, 51 audiovisual materials.
College life *Housing: Options:* men-only, women-only. *Most popular organizations:* Missionary Prayer Band, Ministerial Union.
Campus security 24-hour emergency response devices.
Freshmen 29 enrolled.

SAT verbal scores above 500	100%	SAT math scores above 500	0%
ACT above 18	77%	1998 freshmen returning in 1999	14%

Application *Application fee:* $20. *Required:* essay or personal statement; high school transcript; 3 letters of recommendation. *Recommended:* interview.
Standardized tests *Admission: Required:* SAT I or ACT.
Significant dates *Application deadlines:* rolling (freshmen), rolling (transfers). *Financial aid deadline priority date:* 8/20.
Freshman Application Contact
Rev. Chris Lohrstorfer, Director of Admissions, Wesley College, PO Box 1070, Florence, MS 39073-1070. **Phone:** 601-845-2265 Ext. 21. **Toll-free phone:** 800-748-9972. **Fax:** 601-845-2266. **E-mail:** wcadmit@aol.com
Visit CollegeQuest.com for information on majors offered and athletics.

WILLIAM CAREY COLLEGE
Hattiesburg, Mississippi

Admissions Office Contact
William Carey College, 498 Tuscan Avenue, Hattiesburg, MS 39401-5499. **Toll-free phone:** 800-962-5991. **Fax:** 601-582-6454. **E-mail:** admiss@mail.wmcarey.edu

Missouri

MISSOURI

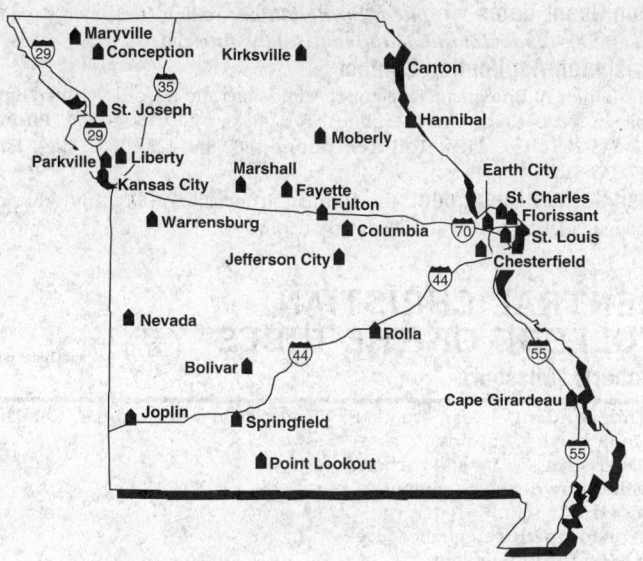

AVILA COLLEGE
Kansas City, Missouri

 Apply at CollegeQuest.com

- **Independent Roman Catholic**, comprehensive, founded 1916
- **Degrees** bachelor's and master's
- **Suburban** 50-acre campus
- **Coed**, 955 undergraduate students, 66% full-time, 73% women, 27% men
- **Minimally difficult** entrance level, 92% of applicants were admitted
- **11:1** student-to-undergraduate faculty ratio
- **32% graduate** in 6 years or less
- **$11,960 tuition** and fees
- **$17,125 average indebtedness** upon graduation, $4.4 million endowment

Students *Undergraduates:* 634 full-time, 321 part-time. Students come from 20 states and territories, 23 other countries. *The most frequently chosen baccalaureate fields are:* business/marketing, education, health professions and related sciences. *Graduate:* 191 in graduate degree programs.

From out-of-state	29%	Reside on campus	14%
Age 25 or older	45%	Transferred in	14%
International students	3%	African Americans	14%
Asian Americans/Pacific Islanders	1%	Hispanic Americans	3%
Native Americans	1%		

Faculty 167 (34% full-time), 46% with terminal degrees.
Expenses (1999–2000) *Comprehensive fee:* $16,760 includes full-time tuition ($11,800), mandatory fees ($160), and room and board ($4800). Room and board charges vary according to housing facility. *Part-time tuition:* $260 per credit hour. *Part-time fees:* $3 per credit hour. *Payment plans:* guaranteed tuition, installment, deferred payment. *Waivers:* children of alumni, senior citizens, and employees or children of employees.
Library Hooley Bundshu Library plus 1 other. *Operations spending 1999–2000:* $269,684. *Collection:* 70,935 titles, 551 serial subscriptions, 3,094 audiovisual materials.
College life *Housing:* on-campus residence required through sophomore year. *Options:* coed, men-only, women-only. *Most popular organizations:* Student Union Board, Avila Student Nurses Association, Residence Hall Association, Student Senate, Avila Education Association.
Campus security Student patrols, controlled dormitory access, 8-hour patrols by trained security personnel.
After graduation 89% of class of 1998 had job offers within 6 months. *Career center:* 1 full-time personnel. Services include job fairs, resume preparation, resume referral, career counseling, careers library, job bank, job interviews. *Graduate education:* 10% of class of 1999 went directly to graduate and professional school.

Freshmen 389 applied, 358 admitted, 115 enrolled.

Average high school GPA	3.22	SAT verbal scores above 500	N/R
SAT math scores above 500	N/R	ACT above 18	86%
From top 10% of their h.s. class	12%	From top quarter	39%
From top half	79%	1998 freshmen returning in 1999	68%

Application *Options:* eApply at www.CollegeQuest.com, Common Application, early admission. *Application fee:* $0. *Required:* high school transcript; minimum 2.5 GPA. *Required for some:* essay or personal statement; letters of recommendation. *Recommended:* interview.
Standardized tests *Admission:* Required: SAT I or ACT.
Significant dates *Application deadlines:* rolling (freshmen), rolling (transfers). *Financial aid deadline:* continuous.
Freshman Application Contact
Mr. Todd H. Moore, Director of Admissions, Avila College, 11901 Wornall Road, Kansas City, MO 64145-1698. **Phone:** 816-942-8400 Ext. 3500. **Toll-free phone:** 800-GO-AVILA. **Fax:** 816-942-3362. **E-mail:** admissions@mail.avila.edu
Visit CollegeQuest.com for information on majors offered and athletics.

BAPTIST BIBLE COLLEGE
Springfield, Missouri

- **Independent Baptist**, comprehensive, founded 1950
- **Degrees** associate, bachelor's, and master's
- **38-acre** campus
- **Coed**
- **Noncompetitive** entrance level
- **$2888 tuition** and fees

Expenses (1999–2000) *Comprehensive fee:* $6500 includes full-time tuition ($2478), mandatory fees ($410), and room and board ($3612). Full-time tuition and fees vary according to program. *Part-time tuition:* $105 per hour.
Institutional Web site http://www.bbcnet.edu/bbgst.html
College life on-campus residence required through senior year.
Application *Options:* early admission, deferred entrance. *Preference* given to members of supporting churches. *Required:* high school transcript; 1 letter of recommendation.
Standardized tests *Placement:* Required: ACT
Admissions Office Contact
Baptist Bible College, 628 East Kearney, Springfield, MO 65803-3498. **Fax:** 417-831-8029.
Visit CollegeQuest.com for information on athletics. College video available at CollegeQuest.com.

CALVARY BIBLE COLLEGE AND THEOLOGICAL SEMINARY
Kansas City, Missouri

- **Independent interdenominational**, comprehensive, founded 1932
- **Degrees** associate, bachelor's, master's, and doctoral
- **Suburban** 55-acre campus
- **Coed**, 229 undergraduate students
- **Minimally difficult** entrance level
- **10:1** student-to-undergraduate faculty ratio
- **$5170 tuition** and fees

Students *Undergraduates:* Students come from 25 states and territories, 5 other countries.

Age 25 or older	50%	International students	1%
African Americans	6%	Asian Americans/Pacific Islanders	7%
Hispanic Americans	2%		

Faculty 17 (65% full-time), 35% with terminal degrees.
Expenses (2000–2001) *Comprehensive fee:* $8320 includes full-time tuition ($4760), mandatory fees ($410), and room and board ($3150). *College room only:* $1300. *Part-time tuition:* $170 per semester hour. *Part-time fees:* $16 per semester hour. *Payment plans:* installment, deferred payment. *Waivers:* children of alumni, senior citizens, and employees or children of employees.

Missouri

Calvary Bible College and Theological Seminary *(continued)*

Library Hilda Kroeker Library. *Collection:* 59,000 titles, 307 serial subscriptions.

College life *Housing:* on-campus residence required through senior year. *Options:* men-only, women-only.

Campus security Night patrols by trained security personnel.

After graduation *Career center:* Services include job fairs, career counseling.

Freshmen

| SAT verbal scores above 500 | N/R | SAT math scores above 500 | N/R |
| ACT above 18 | N/R | From top half of their h.s. class | 35% |

Application *Options:* early admission, deferred entrance. *Application fee:* $25. *Required:* essay or personal statement; high school transcript; 2 letters of recommendation; statement of faith. *Recommended:* interview.

Standardized tests *Admission: Required:* SAT I or ACT.

Significant dates *Application deadlines:* rolling (freshmen), rolling (transfers). *Financial aid deadline:* 3/31.

Freshman Application Contact
Mr. Mike Piburn, Director of Admissions, Calvary Bible College and Theological Seminary, 15800 Calvary Road, Kansas City, MO 64147-1341. **Phone:** 816-322-0110 Ext. 1326. **Toll-free phone:** 800-326-3960. **E-mail:** admissions@calvary.edu

Visit CollegeQuest.com for information on majors offered and athletics.

CENTRAL BIBLE COLLEGE
Springfield, Missouri

- **Independent**, 4-year, founded 1922, affiliated with Assemblies of God
- **Degrees** associate and bachelor's
- **Suburban** 108-acre campus
- **Coed**, 949 undergraduate students, 91% full-time, 41% women, 59% men
- **Moderately difficult** entrance level, 94% of applicants were admitted
- **20:1 student-to-undergraduate faculty ratio**
- **$6260 tuition** and fees

Students *Undergraduates:* 866 full-time, 83 part-time. Students come from 47 states and territories, 3 other countries. *The most frequently chosen baccalaureate field is:* philosophy.

From out-of-state	78%	Reside on campus	65%
Age 25 or older	15%	Transferred in	10%
International students	0.4%	African Americans	1%
Asian Americans/Pacific Islanders	2%	Hispanic Americans	3%
Native Americans	0.4%		

Faculty 60 (70% full-time), 25% with terminal degrees.

Expenses (2000–2001) *Comprehensive fee:* $9660 includes full-time tuition ($5760), mandatory fees ($500), and room and board ($3400). Full-time tuition and fees vary according to course load. Room and board charges vary according to housing facility. *Part-time tuition:* $230 per semester hour. *Part-time fees:* $180 per term part-time. Part-time tuition and fees vary according to course load. *Payment plan:* installment. *Waivers:* senior citizens and employees or children of employees.

Library Meyer Pearlman Library. *Operations spending 1999–2000:* $186,610. *Collection:* 107,924 titles, 544 serial subscriptions.

College life *Housing:* on-campus residence required through senior year. *Options:* men-only, women-only.

Campus security 24-hour emergency response devices and patrols, student patrols.

After graduation *Career center:* 2 full-time, 2 part-time personnel. Services include resume preparation, resume referral, career counseling, job bank, job interviews.

Freshmen 239 applied, 224 admitted, 172 enrolled.

Average high school GPA	3.13	SAT verbal scores above 500	71%
SAT math scores above 500	52%	ACT above 18	68%
From top 10% of their h.s. class	12%	From top quarter	13%
From top half	43%	1998 freshmen returning in 1999	74%

Application *Options:* early admission, deferred entrance. *Preference* given to Christians. *Application fee:* $75. *Required:* essay or personal statement; high school transcript; 3 letters of recommendation. *Required for some:* interview. *Recommended:* minimum 2.0 GPA.

Standardized tests *Admission: Required:* SAT I or ACT. *Recommended:* ACT.

Significant dates *Application deadlines:* rolling (freshmen), rolling (transfers). *Financial aid deadline priority date:* 5/1.

Freshman Application Contact
Mrs. Eunice A. Bruegman, Director of Admissions and Records, Central Bible College, 3000 North Grant Avenue, Springfield, MO 65803-1096. **Phone:** 417-833-2551 Ext. 1184. **Toll-free phone:** 800-831-4222 Ext. 1184. **Fax:** 417-833-5141.

Visit CollegeQuest.com for information on majors offered and athletics. College video available at CollegeQuest.com.

CENTRAL CHRISTIAN COLLEGE OF THE BIBLE
Moberly, Missouri

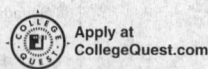 Apply at CollegeQuest.com

- **Independent**, 4-year, founded 1957, affiliated with Christian Churches and Churches of Christ
- **Degrees** associate and bachelor's
- **Small-town** 40-acre campus
- **Coed**
- **Noncompetitive** entrance level
- **$4500 tuition** and fees

Expenses (1999–2000) *Comprehensive fee:* $7100 includes full-time tuition ($4000), mandatory fees ($500), and room and board ($2600). Room and board charges vary according to board plan. *Part-time tuition:* $125 per credit. *Part-time fees:* $40 per term part-time. Part-time tuition and fees vary according to course load.

Institutional Web site http://www.cccb.edu/

College life *Housing:* on-campus residence required through senior year. *Options:* men-only, women-only. *Most popular organization:* Harvesters.

Application *Options:* eApply at www.CollegeQuest.com, early admission, deferred entrance. *Preference* given to Christians. *Application fee:* $25. *Required:* high school transcript; 3 letters of recommendation.

Standardized tests *Admission: Required:* SAT I or ACT.

Admissions Office Contact
Central Christian College of the Bible, 911 Urbandale Drive East, Moberly, MO 65270-1997. **Toll-free phone:** 888-263-3900. **Fax:** 660-263-3936. **E-mail:** iwant2be@cccb.edu

Visit CollegeQuest.com for information on athletics.

CENTRAL METHODIST COLLEGE
Fayette, Missouri

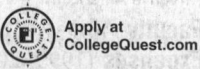 Apply at CollegeQuest.com

- **Independent Methodist**, comprehensive, founded 1854
- **Degrees** associate, bachelor's, and master's
- **Small-town** 52-acre campus
- **Coed**, 1,209 undergraduate students, 90% full-time, 60% women, 40% men
- **Moderately difficult** entrance level, 87% of applicants were admitted
- **15:1 student-to-undergraduate faculty ratio**
- **$11,760 tuition** and fees
- **$11,207 average financial aid** package, $16,252 average indebtedness upon graduation, $15.1 million endowment

Students at CMC are offered superior programs in prelaw, criminal justice, premedicine, nursing, teacher education, computer science, athletic training, business, Christian service, communications, music, theater, and the arts. Located near Columbia and within easy driving distance of Kansas City and St. Louis, CMC has blended a values-based liberal arts tradition with professional preparation to help students develop into "leaders of character."

Students *Undergraduates:* 1,092 full-time, 117 part-time. Students come from 22 states and territories. *The most frequently chosen baccalaureate fields are:* business/marketing, education, health professions and related sciences. *Graduate:* 45 in graduate degree programs.

Missouri

From out-of-state	9%	Reside on campus	68%
Age 25 or older	3%	Transferred in	6%
International students	1%	African Americans	9%
Asian Americans/Pacific Islanders	0.1%	Hispanic Americans	1%
Native Americans	1%		

Faculty 94 (57% full-time), 38% with terminal degrees.

Expenses (2000–2001) *Comprehensive fee:* $16,090 includes full-time tuition ($11,390), mandatory fees ($370), and room and board ($4330). *College room only:* $1980. *Part-time tuition:* $470 per credit hour.

Library Smiley Library plus 1 other. *Operations spending 1999–2000:* $233,675. *Collection:* 98,640 titles, 1,700 serial subscriptions, 3,382 audiovisual materials.

College life *Housing:* on-campus residence required through senior year. *Options:* coed, men-only, women-only. *Social organizations:* local fraternities, local sororities; 60% of eligible men and 60% of eligible women are members. *Most popular organizations:* Student Government Association, Wesley Foundation, Alpha Phi Omega, Christian Students United in Christ, Big Brothers/Big Sisters program.

Campus security 24-hour emergency response devices, late-night transport-escort service, controlled dormitory access.

After graduation 20 organizations recruited on campus 1997–98. 60% of class of 1998 had job offers within 6 months. *Career center:* 1 part-time personnel. Services include job fairs, resume preparation, interview workshops, resume referral, career counseling, careers library, job bank, job interviews. *Graduate education:* 25% of class of 1999 went directly to graduate and professional school.

Freshmen 909 applied, 788 admitted, 236 enrolled. 1 National Merit Scholar, 8 class presidents, 12 valedictorians.

SAT verbal scores above 500	N/R	SAT math scores above 500	N/R
ACT above 18	80%	From top 10% of their h.s. class	9%
From top quarter	31%	From top half	67%
1998 freshmen returning in 1999	60%		

Application *Options:* eApply at www.CollegeQuest.com, Common Application, electronic application, early admission, deferred entrance. *Application fee:* $20. *Required:* high school transcript; minimum 2.0 GPA. *Required for some:* 2 letters of recommendation; interview.

Standardized tests *Admission: Required:* SAT I or ACT. *Recommended:* ACT.

Significant dates *Application deadlines:* 8/15 (freshmen), rolling (transfers). *Financial aid deadline:* continuous.

Freshman Application Contact

Mr. David Heringer, Vice President for Enrollment Management and Student Development, Central Methodist College, 411 Central Methodist Square, Fayette, MO 65248-1198. **Phone:** 660-248-6247. **Toll-free phone:** 888-262-1854. **Fax:** 660-248-2287. **E-mail:** dheringe@cmc.edu

Visit CollegeQuest.com for information on majors offered and athletics.

CENTRAL MISSOURI STATE UNIVERSITY
Warrensburg, Missouri

- **State-supported**, comprehensive, founded 1871
- **Degrees** associate, bachelor's, master's, and post-master's certificates
- **Small-town** 1,240-acre campus with easy access to Kansas City
- **Coed**, 8,522 undergraduate students, 82% full-time, 53% women, 47% men
- **Moderately difficult** entrance level, 90% of applicants were admitted
- **17:1 student-to-undergraduate faculty ratio**
- **38% graduate** in 6 years or less
- **$2970 tuition** and fees (in-state); $5940 (out-of-state)
- **$7975 average financial aid** package, $1.6 million endowment

Central Missouri State University offers outstanding career-oriented programs in more than 150 areas of study within the arts and sciences, applied sciences and technology, business and economics, and education and human services. A friendly environment, an excellent faculty, and state-of-the-art facilities make the 1,240-acre campus an exciting place to learn and live.

Students *Undergraduates:* 7,019 full-time, 1,503 part-time. Students come from 46 states and territories, 62 other countries. *The most frequently chosen baccalaureate fields are:* business/marketing, education, protective services/public administration. *Graduate:* 1,820 in graduate degree programs.

From out-of-state	7%	Reside on campus	34%
Age 25 or older	18%	Transferred in	11%
International students	3%	African Americans	5%
Asian Americans/Pacific Islanders	1%	Hispanic Americans	1%
Native Americans	1%		

Faculty 520 (86% full-time), 74% with terminal degrees.

Expenses (1999–2000) *Tuition, state resident:* full-time $2970; part-time $99 per credit hour. *Tuition, nonresident:* full-time $5940; part-time $198 per credit hour. *College room and board:* $4104; room only: $2600. Room and board charges vary according to board plan and housing facility. *Payment plans:* installment, deferred payment. *Waivers:* children of alumni, senior citizens, and employees or children of employees.

Library Ward Edwards Library. *Operations spending 1999–2000:* $3.4 million. *Collection:* 556,190 titles, 3,557 serial subscriptions.

College life *Housing:* on-campus residence required in freshman year. *Options:* coed, men-only, women-only, disabled students. *Social organizations:* national fraternities, national sororities; 15% of eligible men and 12% of eligible women are members. *Most popular organizations:* Student Government Association, University Program Council, Association of Black Collegiates, University Student Housing Council, International Student Organization.

Campus security 24-hour emergency response devices and patrols, student patrols, late-night transport-escort service, controlled dormitory access.

After graduation 600 organizations recruited on campus 1997–98. 94% of class of 1998 had job offers within 6 months. *Career center:* 8 full-time personnel. Services include job fairs, resume preparation, interview workshops, resume referral, career/interest testing, career counseling, careers library, job bank, job interviews. *Graduate education:* 14% of class of 1999 went directly to graduate and professional school.

Freshmen 2,857 applied, 2,578 admitted, 1,412 enrolled.

SAT verbal scores above 500	N/R	SAT math scores above 500	N/R
ACT above 18	90%	From top 10% of their h.s. class	11%
From top quarter	37%	From top half	70%
1998 freshmen returning in 1999	73%		

Application *Options:* Common Application, electronic application, deferred entrance. *Application fee:* $25. *Required:* high school transcript; rank in upper two-thirds of high school class. *Required for some:* letters of recommendation.

Standardized tests *Admission: Required:* SAT I or ACT.

Significant dates *Application deadlines:* rolling (freshmen), rolling (transfers). *Financial aid deadline priority date:* 3/1.

Freshman Application Contact

Mr. Charles Petentler, Associate Director of Admissions, Central Missouri State University, Administration Building Room 104, Warrensburg, MO 64093. **Phone:** 660-543-4290. **Toll-free phone:** 800-956-0177. **Fax:** 660-543-8517. **E-mail:** admit@cmsuvmb.cmsu.edu

Visit CollegeQuest.com for information on majors offered and athletics. College video and electronic viewbook available at CollegeQuest.com.

■ *See page 1396 for a narrative description.*

CLEVELAND CHIROPRACTIC COLLEGE OF KANSAS CITY
Kansas City, Missouri

Admissions Office Contact

Cleveland Chiropractic College of Kansas City, 6401 Rockhill Road, Kansas City, MO 64131-1181. **Fax:** 816-361-0272.

COLLEGE OF THE OZARKS
Point Lookout, Missouri

- **Independent Presbyterian**, 4-year, founded 1906
- **Degree** bachelor's
- **Small-town** 1,000-acre campus
- **Coed**, 1,429 undergraduate students, 88% full-time, 53% women, 47% men
- **Moderately difficult** entrance level, 18% of applicants were admitted

Missouri

College of the Ozarks (continued)
- **14:1 student-to-undergraduate faculty ratio**
- **$150 tuition** and fees
- **$271 million endowment**

Students *Undergraduates:* 1,261 full-time, 168 part-time. Students come from 34 states and territories, 27 other countries. *The most frequently chosen baccalaureate fields are:* business/marketing, agriculture, education.

From out-of-state	34%	Reside on campus	68%
Age 25 or older	6%	Transferred in	5%
International students	3%	African Americans	0.4%
Asian Americans/Pacific Islanders	0.5%	Hispanic Americans	1%
Native Americans	1%		

Faculty 122 (73% full-time).

Expenses (2000–2001, estimated) includes mandatory fees ($150) and room and board ($2500). *Part-time tuition:* $125 per credit hour. *Part-time fees:* $75 per term part-time. Full-time students work 15 hours per week plus two 40-hour work weeks per year to defray the cost of tuition.

Library Lyons Memorial Library plus 1 other. *Operations spending 1999–2000:* $500,310. *Collection:* 114,549 titles, 4,895 audiovisual materials.

College life *Housing:* on-campus residence required through senior year. *Options:* men-only, women-only. *Most popular organizations:* aviation club, Student Senate, Baptist Student Union, Aggie club, Business Undergraduate Society.

Campus security 24-hour emergency response devices and patrols, controlled dormitory access, front gate closed 1 a.m. to 6 a.m., gate security 5:30 p.m. to 1 a.m.

After graduation 192 organizations recruited on campus 1997–98. 97% of class of 1998 had job offers within 6 months. *Career center:* 1 full-time, 6 part-time personnel. Services include job fairs, resume preparation, resume referral, career counseling, careers library, job bank, job interviews. *Graduate education:* 12% of class of 1999 went directly to graduate and professional school: 7% graduate arts and sciences, 2% business, 2% education, 2% medicine, 1% law.

Freshmen 2,752 applied, 495 admitted, 270 enrolled.

Average high school GPA	2.89	SAT verbal scores above 500	N/R
SAT math scores above 500	N/R	ACT above 18	N/R
From top 10% of their h.s. class	24%	From top quarter	48%
From top half	82%	1998 freshmen returning in 1999	74%

Application *Option:* early admission. *Preference* given to needy students. *Application fee:* $0. *Required:* high school transcript; 2 letters of recommendation; interview; medical history, financial statement. *Recommended:* essay or personal statement; minimum 2.0 GPA.

Standardized tests *Admission: Required:* SAT I or ACT.

Significant dates *Application deadlines:* 8/15 (freshmen), 1/18 (transfers). *Financial aid deadline priority date:* 3/15.

Freshman Application Contact
Mrs. Janet Miller, Admissions Secretary, College of the Ozarks, Point Lookout, MO 65726. **Phone:** 417-334-6411 Ext. 4217. **Toll-free phone:** 800-222-0525. **Fax:** 417-335-2618. **E-mail:** admiss4@cofo.edu

Visit CollegeQuest.com for information on majors offered and athletics. College video available at CollegeQuest.com.

COLUMBIA COLLEGE
Columbia, Missouri

- **Independent**, comprehensive, founded 1851, affiliated with Christian Church (Disciples of Christ)
- **Degrees** associate, bachelor's, and master's
- **Small-town** 29-acre campus
- **Coed**, 7,275 undergraduate students, 59% full-time, 58% women, 42% men
- **Moderately difficult** entrance level, 85% of applicants were admitted
- **11:1 student-to-undergraduate faculty ratio**
- **34% graduate** in 6 years or less
- **$9808 tuition** and fees
- **$6193 average financial aid** package, $13,576 average indebtedness upon graduation, $5.5 million endowment

Students *Undergraduates:* 4,274 full-time, 3,001 part-time. Students come from 29 states and territories, 46 other countries. *The most frequently chosen baccalaureate fields are:* business/marketing, liberal arts/general studies, protective services/public administration. *Graduate:* 137 in graduate degree programs.

From out-of-state	10%	Reside on campus	33%
Age 25 or older	42%	Transferred in	13%
International students	2%	African Americans	15%
Asian Americans/Pacific Islanders	2%	Hispanic Americans	5%
Native Americans	1%		

Expenses (1999–2000) *Comprehensive fee:* $14,207 includes full-time tuition ($9808) and room and board ($4399). *College room only:* $2767. Full-time tuition and fees vary according to class time and course load. Room and board charges vary according to board plan. *Part-time tuition:* $175 per credit hour. Part-time tuition and fees vary according to class time. *Payment plan:* deferred payment. *Waivers:* children of alumni, senior citizens, and employees or children of employees.

Library Stafford Library. *Operations spending 1999–2000:* $407,337. *Collection:* 52,959 titles, 718 serial subscriptions.

College life *Housing:* on-campus residence required through sophomore year. *Options:* coed, women-only. *Most popular organizations:* Students in Free Enterprise, Campus Community Government, Student Leaders Advocating Teaching Excellence, Spanish club, Criminal Justice Association.

Campus security 24-hour emergency response devices and patrols, late-night transport-escort service, controlled dormitory access.

After graduation 85 organizations recruited on campus 1997–98. *Career center:* 2 full-time personnel. Services include job fairs, resume preparation, career/interest testing, career counseling, careers library, job bank, job interviews.

Freshmen 2,582 applied, 2,202 admitted, 1,269 enrolled. 6 valedictorians.

Average high school GPA	3.1	SAT verbal scores above 500	N/R
SAT math scores above 500	N/R	ACT above 18	87%
From top 10% of their h.s. class	8%	From top quarter	28%
From top half	63%	1998 freshmen returning in 1999	66%

Application *Options:* Common Application, early admission, deferred entrance. *Application fee:* $25. *Required:* high school transcript; minimum 2.0 GPA. *Required for some:* essay or personal statement; letters of recommendation; interview. *Recommended:* rank in upper 50% of high school class.

Standardized tests *Admission: Recommended:* SAT I and SAT II or ACT.

Significant dates *Application deadlines:* rolling (freshmen), rolling (transfers). *Financial aid deadline priority date:* 3/1.

Freshman Application Contact
Ms. Regina Morin, Director of Admissions, Columbia College, 1001 Rogers Street, Columbia, MO 65216. **Phone:** 573-875-7352. **Toll-free phone:** 800-231-2391 Ext. 7366. **Fax:** 573-875-7506. **E-mail:** admissions@email.ccis.edu

Visit CollegeQuest.com for information on majors offered and athletics.

■ *See page 1502 for a narrative description.*

CONCEPTION SEMINARY COLLEGE
Conception, Missouri

- **Independent Roman Catholic**, 4-year, founded 1886
- **Degree** bachelor's
- **Rural** 30-acre campus
- **Men** only, 92 undergraduate students, 89% full-time
- **Noncompetitive** entrance level, 100% of applicants were admitted
- **23:1 student-to-undergraduate faculty ratio**
- **$8650 tuition** and fees

Students *Undergraduates:* 82 full-time, 10 part-time. Students come from 13 states and territories, 3 other countries. *The most frequently chosen baccalaureate fields are:* liberal arts/general studies, philosophy.

From out-of-state	67%	Reside on campus	100%
Age 25 or older	63%	Transferred in	18%
International students	4%	Asian Americans/Pacific Islanders	13%
Hispanic Americans	2%		

Faculty 28 (61% full-time), 61% with terminal degrees.

Expenses (2000–2001) *Comprehensive fee:* $13,718 includes full-time tuition ($8650) and room and board ($5068). *College room only:* $2078. Room and board charges vary according to board plan.

Library *Collection:* 130,000 titles, 230,000 serial subscriptions, 3,500 audiovisual materials.

Missouri

College life *Housing:* on-campus residence required through senior year. *Option:* men-only. *Most popular organizations:* Vocation Committee, drama club, Apostolics, Fine Arts Committee, Social Concerns Committee.

After graduation *Career center:* Services include career counseling.

Freshmen 11 applied, 11 admitted, 9 enrolled. 2 class presidents, 5 student government officers.

Average high school GPA	2.7	SAT verbal scores above 500	N/R
SAT math scores above 500	N/R	ACT above 18	N/R
From top 10% of their h.s. class	15%	1998 freshmen returning in 1999	43%

Application *Options:* early admission, deferred entrance. *Preference* given to Catholic seminarians. *Application fee:* $0. *Required:* essay or personal statement; high school transcript; 2 letters of recommendation; church certificate, medical history. *Recommended:* minimum 2.0 GPA.

Standardized tests *Admission: Required:* SAT I or ACT.

Significant dates *Application deadlines:* 7/31 (freshmen), 7/31 (transfers). *Notification:* continuous until 8/15 (freshmen). *Financial aid deadline:* continuous.

Freshman Application Contact
Mr. Keith Jiron, Director of Recruitment and Admissions, Conception Seminary College, PO Box 502, Highway 136 & VV, Conception, MO 64433-0502. **Phone:** 660-944-2886. **Fax:** 660-944-2829. **E-mail:** vocations@conception.edu

Visit CollegeQuest.com for information on majors offered and athletics. College video available at CollegeQuest.com.

CULVER-STOCKTON COLLEGE
Canton, Missouri

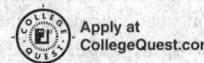 Apply at CollegeQuest.com

- **Independent**, 4-year, founded 1853, affiliated with Christian Church (Disciples of Christ)
- **Degree** bachelor's
- **Rural** 143-acre campus
- **Coed**, 870 undergraduate students, 92% full-time, 58% women, 42% men
- **Moderately difficult** entrance level, 92% of applicants were admitted
- **15:1** student-to-undergraduate faculty ratio
- **45% graduate** in 6 years or less
- **$10,650 tuition** and fees
- **$8318 average financial aid** package, $8204 average indebtedness upon graduation, $22.6 million endowment

Students *Undergraduates:* 797 full-time, 73 part-time. Students come from 26 states and territories, 6 other countries. *The most frequently chosen baccalaureate fields are:* business/marketing, education, health professions and related sciences.

From out-of-state	44%	Reside on campus	74%
Age 25 or older	10%	Transferred in	6%
International students	2%	African Americans	2%
Asian Americans/Pacific Islanders	0.1%	Hispanic Americans	1%
Native Americans	0.2%		

Faculty 71 (76% full-time), 56% with terminal degrees.

Expenses (2000-2001) *Comprehensive fee:* $15,400 includes full-time tuition ($10,650) and room and board ($4750). *Payment plan:* installment. *Waivers:* children of alumni, adult students, senior citizens, and employees or children of employees.

Library Johann Memorial Library. *Operations spending 1999-2000:* $327,598. *Collection:* 147,418 titles, 3,164 audiovisual materials.

College life *Housing:* on-campus residence required through senior year. *Options:* coed, men-only, women-only. *Social organizations:* national fraternities, national sororities; 41% of eligible men and 37% of eligible women are members. *Most popular organizations:* C-S Teachers Organization, varsity club, Christian Fellowship group, student parliament, student nurses organization.

Campus security 24-hour emergency response devices, late-night transport-escort service.

After graduation 24 organizations recruited on campus 1997-98. 97% of class of 1998 had job offers within 6 months. *Career center:* 2 full-time personnel. Services include job fairs, resume preparation, interview workshops, resume referral, career/interest testing, career counseling, careers library, job bank, job interviews.

Freshmen 396 applied, 363 admitted, 175 enrolled. 1 National Merit Scholar, 10 valedictorians.

Average high school GPA	3.26	SAT verbal scores above 500	N/R
SAT math scores above 500	N/R	ACT above 18	91%
From top 10% of their h.s. class	11%	From top quarter	39%
From top half	72%	1998 freshmen returning in 1999	76%

Application *Options:* eApply at www.CollegeQuest.com, Common Application, electronic application, early decision, early action, deferred entrance. *Application fee:* $25. *Required:* essay or personal statement; high school transcript; minimum 2.0 GPA; 1 letter of recommendation. *Required for some:* interview. *Recommended:* interview.

Standardized tests *Admission: Required:* SAT I or ACT.

Significant dates *Application deadlines:* 2/1 (freshmen), 6/1 (transfers). *Early decision:* 11/15, 1/1. *Notification:* 4/1 (freshmen), 12/15 (early decision), 2/1 (early action). *Financial aid deadline:* 6/15. Priority date: 3/15.

Freshman Application Contact
Mr. Ian Symmonds, Dean of Enrollment Services, Culver-Stockton College, One College Hill, Canton, MO 63435-1299. **Phone:** 217-231-6466. **Toll-free phone:** 800-537-1883. **Fax:** 217-231-6611. **E-mail:** enrollment@culver.edu

Visit CollegeQuest.com for information on majors offered and athletics.

■ *See page 1544 for a narrative description.*

DEACONESS COLLEGE OF NURSING
St. Louis, Missouri

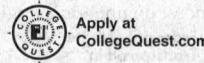 Apply at CollegeQuest.com

- **Proprietary**, 4-year, founded 1889
- **Degrees** associate and bachelor's
- **Urban** 15-acre campus
- **Coed**, 245 undergraduate students, 72% full-time, 96% women, 4% men
- **Moderately difficult** entrance level, 40% of applicants were admitted
- **12:1** student-to-undergraduate faculty ratio
- **$8575 tuition** and fees
- **$6796 average financial aid** package, $516,640 endowment

Students *Undergraduates:* 177 full-time, 68 part-time. Students come from 7 states and territories. *The most frequently chosen baccalaureate field is:* health professions and related sciences.

Reside on campus	21%	Age 25 or older	23%
Transferred in	4%	International students	0.4%
African Americans	24%	Asian Americans/Pacific Islanders	1%
Hispanic Americans	1%		

Faculty 19.

Expenses (1999-2000) *Comprehensive fee:* $12,565 includes full-time tuition ($8500), mandatory fees ($75), and room and board ($3990). Room and board charges vary according to board plan and housing facility. *Part-time tuition:* $330 per credit. *Part-time fees:* $75 per term part-time. *Payment plans:* installment, deferred payment.

Library Drusch Professional Library. *Collection:* 8,700 titles, 233 serial subscriptions.

College life *Most popular organizations:* Deaconess Ambassadors, National Student Nurses Association, Student Government Association.

Campus security 24-hour patrols, late-night transport-escort service, controlled dormitory access.

After graduation 4 organizations recruited on campus 1997-98. 100% of class of 1998 had job offers within 6 months. *Career center:* 1 full-time personnel. Services include career counseling, careers library, job bank, job interviews.

Freshmen 121 applied, 48 admitted, 39 enrolled.

Average high school GPA	3.0	SAT verbal scores above 500	N/R
SAT math scores above 500	N/R	ACT above 18	97%
From top 10% of their h.s. class	10%	From top quarter	45%
From top half	86%		

Application *Options:* eApply at www.CollegeQuest.com, deferred entrance. *Application fee:* $30. *Required:* essay or personal statement; high school transcript. *Required for some:* letters of recommendation; interview. *Recommended:* minimum 2.5 GPA.

Standardized tests *Admission: Required:* SAT I or ACT.

Missouri

Deaconess College of Nursing (continued)

Significant dates *Application deadlines:* rolling (freshmen), rolling (transfers). *Financial aid deadline priority date:* 4/1.

Freshman Application Contact
Ms. Peggy Hudson, Admissions Coordinator, Deaconess College of Nursing, 6150 Oakland Avenue, St. Louis, MO 63139-3215. **Phone:** 314-768-3044. **Toll-free phone:** 800-942-4310. **Fax:** 314-768-5673.

Visit CollegeQuest.com for information on majors offered and athletics.

DEVRY INSTITUTE OF TECHNOLOGY
Kansas City, Missouri

- **Proprietary**, 4-year, founded 1931
- **Degrees** associate and bachelor's
- **Urban** 12-acre campus
- **Coed**, 2,547 undergraduate students, 70% full-time, 24% women, 76% men
- **Minimally difficult** entrance level, 69% of applicants were admitted
- **22:1 student-to-undergraduate faculty ratio**
- **$7778 tuition** and fees

Part of DeVry, Inc.

Students *Undergraduates:* 1,786 full-time, 761 part-time. Students come from 38 states and territories, 4 other countries. *The most frequently chosen baccalaureate fields are:* business/marketing, computer/information sciences, engineering/engineering technologies.

From out-of-state	45%	Age 25 or older	49%
Transferred in	16%	International students	1%
African Americans	12%	Asian Americans/Pacific Islanders	2%
Hispanic Americans	2%	Native Americans	1%

Faculty 114 (60% full-time).

Expenses (1999–2000) *Tuition:* full-time $7778; part-time $290 per credit hour. Part-time tuition and fees vary according to class time and course load. *Payment plan:* installment. *Waivers:* employees or children of employees.

Library James E. Lovan Library. *Collection:* 9,915 titles, 43 serial subscriptions.

College life *Housing:* college housing not available. *Most popular organizations:* Phi Beta Lambda, American Production and Inventory Control Society, Volleyball Club, Tau Alpha Pi, Institute for Electrical and Electronic Engineers.

Campus security 24-hour emergency response devices, student patrols.

After graduation 97% of class of 1998 had job offers within 6 months. *Career center:* 7 full-time, 1 part-time personnel. Services include job fairs, resume preparation, career counseling, job bank, job interviews.

Freshmen 947 applied, 651 admitted, 499 enrolled.

SAT verbal scores above 500	N/R	SAT math scores above 500	N/R
ACT above 18	N/R	1998 freshmen returning in 1999	50%

Application *Options:* electronic application, deferred entrance. *Application fee:* $25. *Required:* high school transcript; interview.

Standardized tests *Admission: Required:* Computerized Placement Test. *Recommended:* SAT I or ACT. *Placement: Recommended:* SAT I or ACT.

Significant dates *Application deadlines:* rolling (freshmen), rolling (transfers). *Financial aid deadline:* continuous.

Freshman Application Contact
Mike Wimer, Director of Admissions, DeVry Institute of Technology, 11224 Holmes Road, Kansas City, MO 64131. **Phone:** 816-941-2810. **Toll-free phone:** 800-821-3766. **Fax:** 816-941-0896.

Visit CollegeQuest.com for information on majors offered and athletics.

DRURY UNIVERSITY
Springfield, Missouri

Apply at CollegeQuest.com

- **Independent**, comprehensive, founded 1873
- **Degrees** bachelor's and master's (also offers evening program with significant enrollment not reflected in profile)
- **Urban** 60-acre campus
- **Coed**, 1,427 undergraduate students, 98% full-time, 53% women, 47% men
- **Moderately difficult** entrance level, 91% of applicants were admitted
- **12:1 student-to-undergraduate faculty ratio**
- **61% graduate** in 6 years or less
- **$10,695 tuition** and fees
- **$7983 average financial aid** package, $12,800 average indebtedness upon graduation, $88.1 million endowment

Students *Undergraduates:* 1,403 full-time, 24 part-time. *Graduate:* 329 in graduate degree programs.

From out-of-state	20%	Reside on campus	50%
Transferred in	5%		

Faculty 162 (73% full-time), 65% with terminal degrees.

Expenses (1999–2000) *One-time required fee:* $75. *Comprehensive fee:* $14,825 includes full-time tuition ($10,450), mandatory fees ($245), and room and board ($4130). Room and board charges vary according to board plan and housing facility. *Part-time tuition:* $346 per semester hour. *Payment plans:* tuition prepayment, installment, deferred payment. *Waivers:* adult students, senior citizens, and employees or children of employees.

Library F. W. Olin Library plus 1 other. *Operations spending 1999–2000:* $1.1 million. *Collection:* 164,457 titles, 1,101 serial subscriptions, 2,101 audio-visual materials.

College life *Housing:* on-campus residence required in freshman year. *Options:* coed, men-only, women-only. *Social organizations:* national fraternities, national sororities; 35% of eligible men and 35% of eligible women are members. *Most popular organizations:* Student Union Board, Community Service Coalition, choral groups and bands, International Student Organization, academic department clubs.

Campus security 24-hour emergency response devices and patrols, student patrols, late-night transport-escort service, controlled dormitory access.

After graduation 69% of class of 1998 had job offers within 6 months. *Career center:* 2 full-time, 4 part-time personnel. Services include job fairs, resume preparation, interview workshops, resume referral, career counseling, careers library, job bank, job interviews. *Graduate education:* 26% of class of 1999 went directly to graduate and professional school.

Freshmen 994 applied, 902 admitted, 364 enrolled. 7 National Merit Scholars.

Average high school GPA	3.54	SAT verbal scores above 500	N/R
SAT math scores above 500	N/R	ACT above 18	100%
From top 10% of their h.s. class	27%	From top quarter	57%
From top half	87%	1998 freshmen returning in 1999	80%

Application *Options:* eApply at www.CollegeQuest.com, Common Application, electronic application, deferred entrance. *Application fee:* $20. *Required:* essay or personal statement; high school transcript; 1 letter of recommendation. *Recommended:* interview.

Standardized tests *Admission: Required:* SAT I or ACT.

Significant dates *Application deadlines:* rolling (freshmen), rolling (transfers). *Financial aid deadline priority date:* 3/15.

Freshman Application Contact
Mr. Michael Thomas, Director of Admissions, Drury University, 900 North Benton, Springfield, MO 65802. **Phone:** 417-873-7205. **Toll-free phone:** 800-922-2274. **Fax:** 417-873-7529. **E-mail:** druryad@drury.edu

Visit CollegeQuest.com for information on majors offered and athletics. College video available at CollegeQuest.com.

EVANGEL UNIVERSITY
Springfield, Missouri

- **Independent**, comprehensive, founded 1955, affiliated with Assemblies of God
- **Degrees** associate, bachelor's, and master's
- **Urban** 80-acre campus
- **Coed**, 1,525 undergraduate students, 94% full-time, 58% women, 42% men
- **Moderately difficult** entrance level, 98% of applicants were admitted
- **18:1 student-to-undergraduate faculty ratio**
- **58% graduate** in 6 years or less
- **$9720 tuition** and fees

Missouri

Evangel, a 4-year arts and sciences college of the Assemblies of God, offers baccalaureate and master's degrees and is accredited by NCACS, NCATE, NASM, and CSWE. The mission of Evangel is to develop students academically, spiritually, emotionally, and culturally in a Christian atmosphere and to serve God and their fellow man in their chosen careers.

Students *Undergraduates:* 1,431 full-time, 94 part-time. Students come from 49 states and territories. *The most frequently chosen baccalaureate fields are:* business/marketing, education, psychology. *Graduate:* 39 in graduate degree programs.

From out-of-state	58%	Reside on campus	82%
Age 25 or older	3%	Transferred in	8%
International students	0.3%	African Americans	5%
Asian Americans/Pacific Islanders	0.4%	Hispanic Americans	0.5%
Native Americans	0.3%		

Expenses (2000–2001) *One-time required fee:* $20. *Comprehensive fee:* $13,490 includes full-time tuition ($9250), mandatory fees ($470), and room and board ($3770). Full-time tuition and fees vary according to course load. Room and board charges vary according to board plan. *Part-time tuition:* $360 per credit hour. *Payment plan:* installment. *Waivers:* employees or children of employees.

Library Claude Kendrick Library. *Collection:* 96,487 titles, 748 serial subscriptions.

College life *Housing:* on-campus residence required through senior year. *Option:* coed.

Campus security 24-hour emergency response devices and patrols, student patrols, late-night transport-escort service, controlled dormitory access.

After graduation *Career center:* 2 full-time personnel. Services include resume preparation, interview workshops, resume referral, career/interest testing, career counseling, careers library, job bank, job interviews.

Freshmen 641 applied, 626 admitted, 318 enrolled. 7 valedictorians.

Average high school GPA	3.1	SAT verbal scores above 500	N/R
SAT math scores above 500	N/R	ACT above 18	94%
From top 10% of their h.s. class	19%	From top quarter	45%
From top half	77%	1998 freshmen returning in 1999	76%

Application *Option:* deferred entrance. *Application fee:* $25. *Required:* high school transcript. *Recommended:* minimum 2.0 GPA.

Standardized tests *Admission: Required:* SAT I or ACT.

Significant dates *Application deadlines:* 8/15 (freshmen), 8/15 (transfers). *Financial aid deadline priority date:* 4/1.

Freshman Application Contact
Mr. David I. Schoolfield, Director of Enrollment Management, Evangel University, 1111 North Glenstone, Springfield, MO 65802-2191. **Phone:** 417-865-2811 Ext. 7202. **Toll-free phone:** 800-382-6435. **Fax:** 417-865-9599. **E-mail:** admissions@mail4.evangel.edu

Visit CollegeQuest.com for information on majors offered and athletics. College video available at CollegeQuest.com.

FONTBONNE COLLEGE
St. Louis, Missouri

- **Independent Roman Catholic**, comprehensive, founded 1917
- **Degrees** bachelor's and master's
- **Suburban** 13-acre campus
- **Coed**, 1,262 undergraduate students, 86% full-time, 72% women, 28% men
- **Moderately difficult** entrance level, 87% of applicants were admitted
- **$11,343 tuition** and fees
- **$8500 average financial aid** package, $7 million endowment

Students *Undergraduates:* 1,089 full-time, 173 part-time. Students come from 16 states and territories, 18 other countries. *The most frequently chosen baccalaureate fields are:* business/marketing, education, visual/performing arts. *Graduate:* 714 in graduate degree programs.

Reside on campus	35%	Age 25 or older	37%
Transferred in	10%	International students	2%
African Americans	15%	Asian Americans/Pacific Islanders	1%
Hispanic Americans	1%	Native Americans	0.4%

Faculty 180 (27% full-time).

Expenses (1999–2000) *Comprehensive fee:* $16,193 includes full-time tuition ($11,183), mandatory fees ($160), and room and board ($4850). Full-time tuition and fees vary according to class time, program, and reciprocity agreements. Room and board charges vary according to board plan and housing facility. *Part-time tuition:* $346 per hour. *Part-time fees:* $7 per hour. Part-time tuition and fees vary according to class time, course load, program, and reciprocity agreements. *Payment plans:* installment, deferred payment. *Waivers:* senior citizens and employees or children of employees.

Library Fontbonne Library. *Operations spending 1999–2000:* $324,080. *Collection:* 95,000 titles, 485 serial subscriptions.

College life *Housing: Option:* coed. *Social organizations:* local fraternities. *Most popular organizations:* Student Government Association, Residents Hall Council.

Campus security 24-hour patrols, late-night transport-escort service, controlled dormitory access.

After graduation 96% of class of 1998 had job offers within 6 months. *Career center:* 1 full-time, 1 part-time personnel. Services include job fairs, resume preparation, resume referral, career counseling, careers library, job bank, job interviews. *Graduate education:* 25% of class of 1999 went directly to graduate and professional school.

Freshmen 395 applied, 345 admitted, 146 enrolled. 10 class presidents, 2 valedictorians, 42 student government officers.

Average high school GPA	3.1	SAT verbal scores above 500	N/R
SAT math scores above 500	N/R	ACT above 18	88%
From top 10% of their h.s. class	15%	From top quarter	46%
From top half	85%	1998 freshmen returning in 1999	71%

Application *Options:* Common Application, electronic application, early admission, deferred entrance. *Application fee:* $20. *Required:* essay or personal statement; high school transcript; minimum 2.5 GPA. *Recommended:* 2 letters of recommendation; interview.

Standardized tests *Admission: Required:* SAT I or ACT.

Significant dates *Application deadlines:* 8/1 (freshmen), rolling (transfers). *Financial aid deadline:* 7/1. *Priority date:* 4/1.

Freshman Application Contact
Ms. Peggy Musen, Associate Dean for Enrollment Management, Fontbonne College, 6800 Wydown Boulevard, St. Louis, MO 63105-3098. **Phone:** 314-889-1400. **Fax:** 314-719-8021. **E-mail:** pmusen@fontbonne.edu

Visit CollegeQuest.com for information on majors offered and athletics. College video available at CollegeQuest.com.

GLOBAL UNIVERSITY OF THE ASSEMBLIES OF GOD
Springfield, Missouri

- **Independent**, comprehensive, founded 1948, affiliated with Assemblies of God
- **Degrees** associate, bachelor's, and master's (offers only external degree programs)
- **Coed**, 7,510 undergraduate students, 2% full-time, 27% women, 73% men
- **Noncompetitive** entrance level
- **$1800 tuition** and fees
- **$210,000 endowment**

Global University offers AA, BA, and MA degrees in Bible and related areas by distance education. Adult continuing education courses are also offered. Many courses are offered in Spanish. The school is accredited by the accrediting commission of the Distance Education and Training Council. Degree-level courses are approved by DANTES for veteran's benefits. Telephone: 800-443-1083 (toll-free).

Students *Undergraduates:* Students come from 50 states and territories, 136 other countries. *The most frequently chosen baccalaureate field is:* philosophy. *Graduate:* 171 in graduate degree programs.

From out-of-state	93%	Age 25 or older	92%

Faculty 450 (10% full-time), 40% with terminal degrees.

Expenses (1999–2000) *Tuition:* full-time $1800; part-time $75 per credit hour. Full-time tuition and fees vary according to location and reciprocity agreements. Part-time tuition and fees vary according to course load, location, and reciprocity agreements. *Payment plan:* installment. *Waivers:* employees or children of employees.

Missouri

Global University of the Assemblies of God (continued)
Library *Operations spending 1999–2000:* $152,000.
College life *Housing:* college housing not available.
Campus security 24-hour emergency response devices.
Freshmen
| SAT verbal scores above 500 | N/R | SAT math scores above 500 | N/R |
| ACT above 18 | N/R | | |

Application *Application fee:* $35. *Required:* high school transcript. *Required for some:* 1 letter of recommendation. *Recommended:* essay or personal statement.
Significant dates *Application deadlines:* rolling (freshmen), rolling (transfers).
Freshman Application Contact
Lattice Campbell, Dean of Student Affairs, Global University of the Assemblies of God, 1211 South Glenstone Avenue, Springfield, MO 65804. **Phone:** 800-443-1083. **Toll-free phone:** 800-443-1083. **Fax:** 417-862-5318.
Visit CollegeQuest.com for information on majors offered and athletics. College video and electronic viewbook available at CollegeQuest.com.

HANNIBAL-LAGRANGE COLLEGE
Hannibal, Missouri

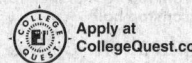
Apply at CollegeQuest.com

- **Independent Southern Baptist**, 4-year, founded 1858
- **Degrees** associate and bachelor's
- **Small-town** 110-acre campus
- **Coed**, 1,132 undergraduate students, 59% full-time, 66% women, 34% men
- **Moderately difficult** entrance level, 41% of applicants were admitted
- **18:1 student-to-undergraduate faculty ratio**
- **41% graduate** in 6 years or less
- **$8440 tuition** and fees
- **$14,563 average indebtedness** upon graduation, $4.8 million endowment

Students *Undergraduates:* 663 full-time, 469 part-time. Students come from 21 states and territories, 4 other countries.
From out-of-state	14%	Reside on campus	35%
Age 25 or older	28%	Transferred in	8%
International students	1%	African Americans	1%
Asian Americans/Pacific Islanders	0.2%	Hispanic Americans	1%
Native Americans	0.3%		

Faculty 108 (44% full-time), 19% with terminal degrees.
Expenses (1999–2000) *Comprehensive fee:* $11,666 includes full-time tuition ($8160), mandatory fees ($280), and room and board ($3226). Full-time tuition and fees vary according to program. Room and board charges vary according to board plan and housing facility. *Part-time tuition:* $272 per credit hour. *Part-time fees:* $55 per term part-time. Part-time tuition and fees vary according to course load and program. *Payment plan:* deferred payment. *Waivers:* senior citizens and employees or children of employees.
Library L. A. Foster Library. *Operations spending 1999–2000:* $300,051. *Collection:* 68,906 titles, 521 serial subscriptions, 5,772 audiovisual materials.
College life *Housing:* on-campus residence required through senior year. *Options:* men-only, women-only. *Most popular organizations:* Phi Beta Lambda, Baptist Student Union, Alpha Chi Honor Society, Phi Beta Delta.
Campus security 24-hour emergency response devices, late-night transport-escort service, controlled dormitory access.
After graduation 27 organizations recruited on campus 1997–98. *Career center:* 2 full-time personnel. Services include job fairs, resume preparation, resume referral, career/interest testing, career counseling, careers library, job bank, job interviews.
Freshmen 311 applied, 128 admitted, 128 enrolled.
SAT verbal scores above 500	N/R	SAT math scores above 500	N/R
ACT above 18	100%	From top 10% of their h.s. class	12%
From top quarter	45%	From top half	92%
1998 freshmen returning in 1999	76%		

Application *Options:* eApply at www.CollegeQuest.com, early admission, deferred entrance. *Application fee:* $25. *Required:* high school transcript; 2 letters of recommendation.

Standardized tests *Admission: Required:* SAT I or ACT.
Significant dates *Application deadlines:* 8/26 (freshmen), rolling (transfers). *Financial aid deadline:* continuous.
Freshman Application Contact
Mr. Raymond Carty, Dean of Enrollment Management, Hannibal-LaGrange College, 2800 Palmyra Road, Hannibal, MO 63401-1999. **Phone:** 573-221-3113. **Toll-free phone:** 800-HLG-1119. **Fax:** 573-221-6594. **E-mail:** admissio@hlg.edu
Visit CollegeQuest.com for information on majors offered and athletics. Electronic viewbook available at CollegeQuest.com.

HARRIS-STOWE STATE COLLEGE
St. Louis, Missouri

- **State-supported**, 4-year, founded 1857
- **Degree** bachelor's
- **Urban** 22-acre campus
- **Coed**, 1,422 undergraduate students, 51% full-time, 70% women, 30% men
- **Moderately difficult** entrance level, 66% of applicants were admitted
- **18:1 student-to-undergraduate faculty ratio**
- **18% graduate** in 6 years or less
- **$2064 tuition** and fees (in-state); $4056 (out-of-state)

Part of Missouri Coordinating Board for Higher Education.
Students *Undergraduates:* 721 full-time, 701 part-time. Students come from 5 states and territories, 21 other countries.
From out-of-state	8%	Transferred in	21%
International students	2%	African Americans	76%
Asian Americans/Pacific Islanders	0.2%	Hispanic Americans	1%
Native Americans	0.1%		

Expenses (1999–2000) *One-time required fee:* $15. *Tuition, state resident:* full-time $2064; part-time $86 per credit hour. *Tuition, nonresident:* full-time $4056; part-time $169 per credit hour. Full-time tuition and fees vary according to course load. *Payment plan:* installment. *Waivers:* employees or children of employees.
Library Southwestern Bell Library and Technology Center. *Operations spending 1999–2000:* $354,589. *Collection:* 60,000 titles, 340 serial subscriptions.
College life *Housing:* college housing not available. *Social organizations:* national fraternities, national sororities; 1% of eligible men and 1% of eligible women are members. *Most popular organizations:* drama club, concert chorale, Student Government Association.
Campus security 24-hour emergency response devices, late-night transport-escort service, 16-hour patrols by trained security personnel Monday through Friday, 24-hour weekend and holiday patrols.
After graduation *Career center:* 2 full-time personnel. Services include job fairs, resume preparation, interview workshops, resume referral, career/interest testing, career counseling, careers library, job bank, job interviews.
Freshmen 319 applied, 210 admitted, 181 enrolled. 21 valedictorians.
Average high school GPA	2.9	SAT verbal scores above 500	26%
SAT math scores above 500	31%	ACT above 18	56%
From top 10% of their h.s. class	10%	From top quarter	38%
From top half	60%	1998 freshmen returning in 1999	60%

Application *Options:* early admission, deferred entrance. *Required:* high school transcript; minimum 2.0 GPA.
Standardized tests *Admission: Required:* SAT I or ACT.
Significant dates *Application deadlines:* rolling (freshmen), rolling (transfers). *Financial aid deadline priority date:* 4/1.
Freshman Application Contact
Ms. Valerie A. Beeson, Director of Admissions and Academic Advisement, Harris-Stowe State College, 3026 Laclede Avenue, St. Louis, MO 63103. **Phone:** 314-340-3300. **Fax:** 314-340-3322. **E-mail:** curriderd@mail1.hssc.edu
Visit CollegeQuest.com for information on majors offered and athletics. College video available at CollegeQuest.com.

Missouri

ITT TECHNICAL INSTITUTE
Earth City, Missouri

- **Proprietary**, primarily 2-year, founded 1936
- **Degrees** associate and bachelor's
- **Suburban** 2-acre campus with easy access to St. Louis
- **Coed**
- **Minimally difficult** entrance level
- **$9190 tuition** and fees

Part of ITT Educational Services, Inc.

Admissions Office Contact
ITT Technical Institute, 13505 Lakefront Drive, Earth City, MO 63045-1412. **Toll-free phone:** 800-235-5488. **Fax:** 314-298-0559.
Visit CollegeQuest.com for information on majors offered and athletics. College video available at CollegeQuest.com.

JEWISH HOSPITAL COLLEGE OF NURSING AND ALLIED HEALTH
St. Louis, Missouri

- **Independent**, comprehensive, founded 1902
- **Degrees** associate, bachelor's, master's, post-master's, and postbachelor's certificates
- **Urban** campus
- **Coed,** primarily women, 388 undergraduate students, 41% full-time, 89% women, 11% men
- **Moderately difficult** entrance level, 100% of applicants were admitted
- **$10,034 tuition** and fees
- **$8000 average financial aid** package, $10,000 average indebtedness upon graduation, $4.1 million endowment

Students *Undergraduates:* 159 full-time, 229 part-time. Students come from 6 states and territories. *Graduate:* 91 in graduate degree programs.

Reside on campus	8%	Age 25 or older	60%
International students	0.3%	African Americans	15%
Asian Americans/Pacific Islanders	2%	Hispanic Americans	1%
Native Americans	0.3%		

Faculty 43 (77% full-time), 40% with terminal degrees.
Expenses (1999–2000) *Tuition:* full-time $9834; part-time $298 per credit hour. *Required fees:* full-time $200; $35 per term part-time. Full-time tuition and fees vary according to program. Part-time tuition and fees vary according to course load and program. *College room only:* $2210. Room and board charges vary according to housing facility. *Payment plans:* installment, deferred payment.
Library George and Juanita Way Library plus 4 others. *Operations spending 1999–2000:* $156,000. *Collection:* 2,801 titles, 187 serial subscriptions.
College life *Housing: Option:* coed. *Most popular organization:* Student Council.
Campus security 24-hour patrols, late-night transport-escort service, controlled dormitory access.
After graduation 45% of class of 1998 had job offers within 6 months. *Career center:* Services include resume preparation, career counseling, job bank. *Graduate education:* 10% of class of 1999 went directly to graduate and professional school.
Freshmen 9 applied, 9 admitted, 9 enrolled. 3 student government officers.

Average high school GPA	3.1	SAT verbal scores above 500	N/R
SAT math scores above 500	N/R	ACT above 18	100%
From top 10% of their h.s. class	33%	From top quarter	100%
From top half	100%		

Application *Application fee:* $25. *Required:* essay or personal statement; high school transcript; minimum 2.5 GPA; 2 letters of recommendation. *Required for some:* interview.
Standardized tests *Admission: Required:* SAT I or ACT. *Required for some:* SCAT, Nelson Denny Reading Test.
Significant dates *Application deadlines:* rolling (freshmen), rolling (transfers). *Financial aid deadline priority date:* 4/1.
Freshman Application Contact
Ms. Constance J. Stohlman, Director of Enrollment and Management, Jewish Hospital College of Nursing and Allied Health, 306 South Kingshighway, St. Louis, MO 63110-1091. **Phone:** 314-454-7057. **Toll-free phone:** 800-832-9009. **Fax:** 314-454-5239. **E-mail:** jxi4885@bjcmail.carenet.org
Visit CollegeQuest.com for information on majors offered and athletics. College video available at CollegeQuest.com.

KANSAS CITY ART INSTITUTE
Kansas City, Missouri

- **Independent**, 4-year, founded 1885
- **Degree** bachelor's
- **Urban** 12-acre campus
- **Coed,** 550 undergraduate students, 99% full-time, 52% women, 48% men
- **Moderately difficult** entrance level, 83% of applicants were admitted
- **14:1 student-to-undergraduate faculty ratio**
- **65% graduate** in 6 years or less
- **$19,010 tuition** and fees
- **$13,241 average financial aid** package, $17,125 average indebtedness upon graduation, $19.6 million endowment

Students *Undergraduates:* 545 full-time, 5 part-time. Students come from 43 states and territories. *The most frequently chosen baccalaureate field is:* visual/performing arts.

From out-of-state	77%	Reside on campus	25%
Age 25 or older	10%	Transferred in	9%
International students	0.4%	African Americans	1%
Asian Americans/Pacific Islanders	1%	Hispanic Americans	5%
Native Americans	1%		

Faculty 85 (48% full-time), 78% with terminal degrees.
Expenses (2000–2001) *Comprehensive fee:* $24,510 includes full-time tuition ($18,218), mandatory fees ($792), and room and board ($5500). Room and board charges vary according to board plan and housing facility. *Part-time tuition:* $700 per credit hour. *Waivers:* employees or children of employees.
Library Charles T. and Marion M. Thompson Library. *Operations spending 1999–2000:* $177,288. *Collection:* 29,129 titles, 129 serial subscriptions.
College life *Housing:* on-campus residence required in freshman year. *Option:* coed. *Most popular organizations:* Student Union, Student Gallery Committee, Ethnic Student Association.
Campus security 24-hour emergency response devices and patrols, late-night transport-escort service, controlled dormitory access.
After graduation 15 organizations recruited on campus 1997–98. 50% of class of 1998 had job offers within 6 months. *Career center:* 1 full-time, 1 part-time personnel. Services include job fairs, resume preparation, interview workshops, career counseling, careers library, job bank, job interviews. *Graduate education:* 35% of class of 1999 went directly to graduate and professional school: 35% graduate arts and sciences.
Freshmen 430 applied, 357 admitted, 128 enrolled. 1 National Merit Scholar.

Average high school GPA	3.23	SAT verbal scores above 500	82%
SAT math scores above 500	68%	ACT above 18	94%
From top 10% of their h.s. class	12%	From top quarter	24%
From top half	70%	1998 freshmen returning in 1999	79%

Application *Option:* deferred entrance. *Application fee:* $25. *Required:* essay or personal statement; high school transcript; minimum 2.5 GPA; 2 letters of recommendation; portfolio, statement of purpose. *Recommended:* interview.
Standardized tests *Admission: Required:* SAT I or ACT.
Significant dates *Application deadlines:* rolling (freshmen), rolling (transfers). *Notification:* continuous until 8/1 (freshmen). *Financial aid deadline priority date:* 2/15.
Freshman Application Contact
Mr. Gerald Valet, Admissions Office Supervisor, Kansas City Art Institute, 4415 Warwick Boulevard, Kansas City, MO 64111-1874. **Phone:** 816-474-5224. **Toll-free phone:** 800-522-5224. **Fax:** 816-531-6296. **E-mail:** admiss@kcai.edu
Visit CollegeQuest.com for information on majors offered and athletics.

Missouri

LESTER L. COX COLLEGE OF NURSING AND HEALTH SCIENCES
Springfield, Missouri

- **Independent**, 4-year
- **Degrees** associate and bachelor's
- **Coed**, primarily women, 250 undergraduate students, 56% full-time, 91% women, 9% men
- **56% of applicants were admitted**
- **$6430 tuition** and fees

Students *Undergraduates:* Students come from 4 states and territories. *The most frequently chosen baccalaureate field is:* health professions and related sciences.

From out-of-state	1%	Reside on campus	15%
Age 25 or older	48%	African Americans	1%
Asian Americans/Pacific Islanders	1%	Hispanic Americans	2%
Native Americans	0.4%		

Faculty 35 (40% full-time), 26% with terminal degrees.
Expenses (1999–2000) *Tuition:* full-time 5880; part-time 252 per credit hour. *Required fees:* full-time 550. Full-time tuition and fees vary according to course load and program. Part-time tuition and fees vary according to course load and program. *College room only:* 1650. *Payment plan:* deferred payment.
College life *Housing: Option:* coed. *Most popular organizations:* Student Nurses Association, National Student Nurses Association, Student Council, Residence Hall Council, Christian Fellowship.
Campus security 24-hour patrols, late-night transport-escort service.
Freshmen 50 applied, 28 admitted.

Average high school GPA	3.48	SAT verbal scores above 500	N/R
SAT math scores above 500	N/R	ACT above 18	100%
1998 freshmen returning in 1999	80%		

Application *Option:* early decision. *Application fee:* 30. *Required:* high school transcript.
Standardized tests *Admission: Required:* ACT.
Significant dates *Application deadline:* 2/1 (freshmen). *Early decision:* 11/1. *Notification:* 3/1 (freshmen), 12/1 (early decision).
Freshman Application Contact
Ms. Virginia Mace, Admissions Counselor, Lester L. Cox College of Nursing and Health Sciences, 1423 North Jefferson, Springfield, MO 65802. **Phone:** 417-269-3069. **E-mail:** vsmace@coxnet.org
Visit CollegeQuest.com for information on majors offered and athletics.

LINCOLN UNIVERSITY
Jefferson City, Missouri

- **State-supported**, comprehensive, founded 1866
- **Degrees** associate, bachelor's, and master's
- **Small-town** 152-acre campus
- **Coed**, 3,088 undergraduate students, 66% full-time, 59% women, 41% men
- **Noncompetitive** entrance level, 99% of applicants were admitted
- **14:1 student-to-undergraduate faculty ratio**
- **$2368 tuition** and fees (in-state); **$4576** (out-of-state)
- **$8625 average financial aid** package, $17,125 average indebtedness upon graduation, $132,399 endowment

Part of Missouri Coordinating Board for Higher Education.
Students *Undergraduates:* Students come from 56 states and territories, 29 other countries. *Graduate:* 259 in graduate degree programs.

From out-of-state	22%	Reside on campus	73%
Age 25 or older	5%	International students	5%
African Americans	35%	Asian Americans/Pacific Islanders	1%
Hispanic Americans	1%	Native Americans	1%

Faculty 231 (55% full-time), 31% with terminal degrees.
Expenses (1999–2000) *One-time required fee:* $142. *Tuition, state resident:* full-time $2208; part-time $92 per credit hour. *Tuition, nonresident:* full-time $4416; part-time $184 per credit hour. *Required fees:* full-time $160; $5 per credit hour; $20 per term part-time. *College room and board:* $3790; room only:* $1850. *Payment plan:* deferred payment. *Waivers:* senior citizens and employees or children of employees.

Library Inman Page Library. *Operations spending 1999–2000:* $711,077. *Collection:* 151,595 titles, 761 serial subscriptions.
College life *Housing:* on-campus residence required through sophomore year. *Options:* men-only, women-only. *Social organizations:* national fraternities, national sororities, local fraternities, local sororities; 4% of women are members.
Campus security 24-hour emergency response devices and patrols, student patrols, late-night transport-escort service, controlled dormitory access.
After graduation *Career center:* 2 full-time personnel. Services include job fairs, resume preparation, resume referral, career counseling, careers library, job bank, job interviews.
Freshmen 1,296 applied, 1,290 admitted.

SAT verbal scores above 500	N/R	SAT math scores above 500	N/R
ACT above 18	40%	From top 10% of their h.s. class	5%
From top quarter	23%	From top half	44%
1998 freshmen returning in 1999	73%		

Application *Options:* Common Application, early admission, deferred entrance. *Application fee:* $17. *Required:* high school transcript; 1 letter of recommendation.
Standardized tests *Admission: Required:* SAT I or ACT.
Significant dates *Application deadlines:* 7/15 (freshmen), 6/15 (transfers). *Financial aid deadline priority date:* 3/31.
Freshman Application Contact
Executive Director of Enrollment Management, Lincoln University, 820 Chestnut, Jefferson City, MO 65102. **Phone:** 573-681-5599. **Toll-free phone:** 800-521-5052. **Fax:** 573-681-6074.
Visit CollegeQuest.com for information on majors offered and athletics. College video available at CollegeQuest.com.

LINDENWOOD UNIVERSITY
St. Charles, Missouri

Apply at CollegeQuest.com

- **Independent Presbyterian**, comprehensive, founded 1827
- **Degrees** bachelor's, master's, and post-master's certificates
- **Suburban** 358-acre campus with easy access to St. Louis
- **Coed**, 3,566 undergraduate students, 95% full-time, 58% women, 42% men
- **Moderately difficult** entrance level, 44% of applicants were admitted
- **17:1 student-to-undergraduate faculty ratio**
- **$10,550 tuition** and fees
- **$15 million endowment**

Students *Undergraduates:* 3,402 full-time, 164 part-time. Students come from 45 states and territories, 50 other countries. *The most frequently chosen baccalaureate fields are:* business/marketing, communications/communication technologies, education. *Graduate:* 1,907 in graduate degree programs.

From out-of-state	12%	Reside on campus	48%
Age 25 or older	35%	Transferred in	19%
International students	5%	African Americans	8%
Asian Americans/Pacific Islanders	1%	Hispanic Americans	1%
Native Americans	1%		

Faculty 136 (55% full-time).
Expenses (1999–2000) *Comprehensive fee:* $16,000 includes full-time tuition ($10,400), mandatory fees ($150), and room and board ($5450). *College room only:* $2800. *Part-time tuition:* $295 per credit hour. Part-time tuition and fees vary according to course load. *Payment plans:* installment, deferred payment. *Waivers:* senior citizens and employees or children of employees.
Library Butler Library. *Operations spending 1999–2000:* $549,187. *Collection:* 222,071 titles, 519 serial subscriptions.
College life *Housing: Options:* men-only, women-only. *Social organizations:* national fraternities, national sororities, local fraternities, local sororities; 13% of eligible men and 11% of eligible women are members. *Most popular organizations:* Lindenwood Student Government, American Humanics, Circle K, international club, Honors Club.
Campus security 24-hour emergency response devices and patrols, late-night transport-escort service, controlled dormitory access.
After graduation 150 organizations recruited on campus 1997–98. *Career center:* 1 full-time, 1 part-time personnel. Services include job fairs, resume

preparation, interview workshops, resume referral, career/interest testing, career counseling, careers library, job bank, job interviews.

Freshmen 1,635 applied, 717 admitted, 583 enrolled. 1 National Merit Scholar, 5 class presidents, 3 valedictorians, 20 student government officers.

Average high school GPA	3.07	SAT verbal scores above 500	N/R
SAT math scores above 500	N/R	ACT above 18	80%
From top 10% of their h.s. class	10%	From top quarter	38%
From top half	66%	1998 freshmen returning in 1999	81%

Application *Options:* eApply at www.CollegeQuest.com, early admission, deferred entrance. *Application fee:* $25. *Required:* high school transcript; minimum 2.0 GPA. *Required for some:* essay or personal statement; letters of recommendation; interview.

Standardized tests *Admission: Required:* SAT I or ACT.

Significant dates *Application deadlines:* rolling (freshmen), rolling (transfers). *Financial aid deadline priority date:* 3/15.

Freshman Application Contact
Dr. David R. Williams, Dean of Admissions and Financial Aid, Lindenwood University, 209 South Kingshighway, St. Charles, MO 63301-1695. **Phone:** 636-949-4902. **Fax:** 636-949-4910.

Visit CollegeQuest.com for information on majors offered and athletics. College video available at CollegeQuest.com.

■ *See page 1930 for a narrative description.*

LOGAN UNIVERSITY OF CHIROPRACTIC
Chesterfield, Missouri

- **Independent**, upper-level, founded 1935
- **Degrees** incidental bachelor's and first professional
- **Suburban** 100-acre campus with easy access to St. Louis
- **Coed**, 74 undergraduate students, 61% full-time, 30% women, 70% men
- **Moderately difficult** entrance level
- **$9360 tuition** and fees

Students *Undergraduates:* 45 full-time, 29 part-time. *The most frequently chosen baccalaureate field is:* biological/life sciences. *Graduate:* 880 in professional programs.

Faculty 83 (49% full-time), 99% with terminal degrees.

Expenses (1999–2000) *Tuition:* full-time $9190; part-time $95 per credit hour. *Required fees:* full-time $170; $35 per term part-time. *Payment plan:* installment. *Waivers:* employees or children of employees.

Library Learning Resource Center plus 1 other. *Operations spending 1999–2000:* $107,615. *Collection:* 12,000 titles, 300 serial subscriptions.

College life *Housing:* college housing not available. *Social organizations:* national fraternities, national sororities; 5% of eligible men and 2% of eligible women are members.

Campus security 24-hour patrols.

After graduation *Career center:* 1 full-time personnel. Services include resume referral, career counseling, job bank, job interviews.

Application *Option:* deferred entrance. *Application fee:* $35.

Significant dates *Application deadline:* rolling (transfers). *Financial aid deadline:* continuous.

Freshman Application Contact
Mr. Patrick Browne, Dean of Admissions, Logan University of Chiropractic, 1851 Schoettler Road, Box 1065, Chesterfield, MO 63006-1065. **Phone:** 636-227-2100 Ext. 156. **Toll-free phone:** 800-782-3344. **Fax:** 636-227-9338. **E-mail:** loganadm@logan.edu

Visit CollegeQuest.com for information on majors offered and athletics. College video available at CollegeQuest.com.

MARYVILLE UNIVERSITY OF SAINT LOUIS
St. Louis, Missouri

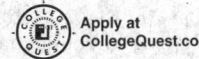
Apply at CollegeQuest.com

- **Independent**, comprehensive, founded 1872
- **Degrees** bachelor's and master's
- **Suburban** 130-acre campus

- **Coed**, 2,506 undergraduate students, 54% full-time, 71% women, 29% men
- **Moderately difficult** entrance level, 80% of applicants were admitted
- **13:1 student-to-undergraduate faculty ratio**
- **63% graduate** in 6 years or less
- **$12,280 tuition** and fees
- **$10,279 average financial aid** package, $11,751 average indebtedness upon graduation, $41.9 million endowment

Outstanding programs in actuarial science, interior design, music therapy, physical therapy, and teacher education prepare students for rewarding careers. Business majors enhance their studies with cooperative education experiences at corporate headquarters at the Maryville Centre. Maryville provides an extensive program of academic scholarships for students with outstanding high school records.

Students *Undergraduates:* 1,350 full-time, 1,156 part-time. Students come from 15 states and territories, 38 other countries. *The most frequently chosen baccalaureate fields are:* business/marketing, health professions and related sciences, psychology. *Graduate:* 530 in graduate degree programs.

From out-of-state	8%	Reside on campus	22%
Age 25 or older	51%	Transferred in	15%
International students	5%	African Americans	5%
Asian Americans/Pacific Islanders	2%	Hispanic Americans	1%
Native Americans	0.4%		

Faculty 279 (33% full-time), 40% with terminal degrees.

Expenses (1999–2000) *Comprehensive fee:* $17,680 includes full-time tuition ($12,160), mandatory fees ($120), and room and board ($5400). *Part-time tuition:* $347 per credit hour. *Part-time fees:* $30 per term part-time. Part-time tuition and fees vary according to class time. *Payment plans:* installment, deferred payment. *Waivers:* senior citizens and employees or children of employees.

Library Maryville University Library. *Operations spending 1999–2000:* $846,330. *Collection:* 125,950 titles, 1,558 serial subscriptions, 9,596 audiovisual materials.

College life *Housing: Option:* coed. *Most popular organizations:* Ambassadors, Physical Therapy Club, Student Nurses Association, Occupational Therapy Club, drama club.

Campus security 24-hour emergency response devices and patrols, late-night transport-escort service, controlled dormitory access, video security system in residence halls, self-defense and education programs.

After graduation 70 organizations recruited on campus 1997–98. *Career center:* 5 full-time personnel. Services include job fairs, resume preparation, interview workshops, resume referral, career/interest testing, career counseling, careers library, job bank, job interviews, portfolio development.

Freshmen 653 applied, 522 admitted, 221 enrolled. 3 valedictorians.

Average high school GPA	3.39	SAT verbal scores above 500	66%
SAT math scores above 500	57%	ACT above 18	91%
From top 10% of their h.s. class	27%	From top quarter	57%
From top half	84%	1998 freshmen returning in 1999	73%

Application *Options:* eApply at www.CollegeQuest.com, Common Application, electronic application, early admission, deferred entrance. *Application fee:* $20. *Required:* high school transcript; minimum 2.5 GPA. *Required for some:* essay or personal statement; letters of recommendation; interview; audition, portfolio.

Standardized tests *Admission: Required:* SAT I or ACT.

Significant dates *Application deadlines:* 8/15 (freshmen), rolling (transfers). *Financial aid deadline priority date:* 4/1.

Freshman Application Contact
Dr. Martha Wade, Vice President of Admissions and Enrollment Management, Maryville University of Saint Louis, 13550 Conway Road, St. Louis, MO 63141-7299. **Phone:** 314-529-9350. **Toll-free phone:** 800-627-9855. **Fax:** 314-529-9927. **E-mail:** admissions@maryville.edu

Visit CollegeQuest.com for information on majors offered and athletics. College video available at CollegeQuest.com.

■ *See page 2014 for a narrative description.*

Missouri

MESSENGER COLLEGE
Joplin, Missouri

- **Independent Pentecostal**, 4-year, founded 1987
- **Degrees** associate and bachelor's
- **Small-town** 16-acre campus with easy access to Springfield
- **Coed**, 98 undergraduate students, 89% full-time, 48% women, 52% men
- **Moderately difficult** entrance level, 86% of applicants were admitted
- **$3430 tuition** and fees
- **$248,626 endowment**

Students *Undergraduates:* 87 full-time, 11 part-time. Students come from 25 states and territories. *The most frequently chosen baccalaureate fields are:* philosophy, visual/performing arts.

From out-of-state	81%	Age 25 or older	23%
Transferred in	9%	African Americans	3%
Hispanic Americans	4%	Native Americans	1%

Faculty 10 (40% full-time), 30% with terminal degrees.

Expenses (1999–2000) *Comprehensive fee:* $6370 includes full-time tuition ($3150), mandatory fees ($280), and room and board ($2940). *Part-time tuition:* $105 per credit. *Part-time fees:* $7 per credit. *Payment plan:* installment. *Waivers:* employees or children of employees.

Library McDole-McDonald Library. *Operations spending 1999–2000:* $25,000. *Collection:* 26,653 titles, 139 serial subscriptions.

College life *Housing:* on-campus residence required through sophomore year. *Options:* men-only, women-only.

Campus security 24-hour emergency response devices.

Freshmen 35 applied, 30 admitted, 31 enrolled.

Average high school GPA	2.5	SAT verbal scores above 500	N/R
SAT math scores above 500	N/R	ACT above 18	N/R
1998 freshmen returning in 1999	47%		

Application *Application fee:* $10. *Required:* essay or personal statement; high school transcript; minimum 2.0 GPA; 2 letters of recommendation. *Required for some:* interview.

Standardized tests *Admission: Required:* SAT I or ACT.

Significant dates *Application deadlines:* 9/1 (freshmen), 9/1 (transfers). *Financial aid deadline:* continuous.

Freshman Application Contact
Mrs. Gwendolyn Minor, Vice President of Academic Affairs, Messenger College, PO Box 4050, Joplin, MO 64803. **Phone:** 417-624-7070, **Fax:** 417-624-5070.

Visit CollegeQuest.com for information on majors offered and athletics.

MISSOURI BAPTIST COLLEGE
St. Louis, Missouri

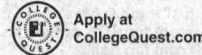
Apply at CollegeQuest.com

- **Independent Southern Baptist**, 4-year, founded 1964
- **Degrees** associate and bachelor's (also offers some graduate courses)
- **Suburban** 65-acre campus
- **Coed**, 2,963 undergraduate students
- **Moderately difficult** entrance level, 72% of applicants were admitted
- **14:1 student-to-undergraduate faculty ratio**
- **41% graduate** in 6 years or less
- **$9408 tuition** and fees
- **$4925 average financial aid** package, $2.6 million endowment

Students *Undergraduates:* Students come from 22 states and territories, 22 other countries. *The most frequently chosen baccalaureate fields are:* business/marketing, education, psychology.

From out-of-state	10%	Reside on campus	18%
Age 25 or older	33%	International students	4%
African Americans	7%	Asian Americans/Pacific Islanders	1%
Hispanic Americans	2%	Native Americans	0.1%

Faculty 127 (28% full-time), 24% with terminal degrees.

Expenses (1999–2000) *Comprehensive fee:* $13,888 includes full-time tuition ($9090), mandatory fees ($318), and room and board ($4480). Full-time tuition and fees vary according to course load, location, and program. *Part-time tuition:* $320 per credit hour. *Part-time fees:* $4 per credit hour; $15 per term part-time. Part-time tuition and fees vary according to course load and location. *Payment plan:* installment. *Waivers:* children of alumni, senior citizens, and employees or children of employees.

Library Jung-Kellogg Library. *Operations spending 1999–2000:* $207,078. *Collection:* 170,282 titles, 430 serial subscriptions, 4,066 audiovisual materials.

College life *Housing: Options:* men-only, women-only. *Social organizations:* university social clubs. *Most popular organizations:* Baptist Student Union, Student Government Association, Missouri State Teacher's Association, Fellowship of Christian Athletes, Ministerial Alliance.

Campus security 24-hour patrols, late-night transport-escort service, controlled dormitory access, self-defense classes.

After graduation 43 organizations recruited on campus 1997–98. *Career center:* 1 full-time, 1 part-time personnel. Services include job fairs, resume preparation, interview workshops, resume referral, career/interest testing, career counseling, careers library, job bank.

Freshmen 333 applied, 241 admitted. 1 National Merit Scholar, 7 valedictorians.

Average high school GPA	3.16	SAT verbal scores above 500	N/R
SAT math scores above 500	N/R	ACT above 18	91%
From top 10% of their h.s. class	17%	From top quarter	39%
From top half	72%	1998 freshmen returning in 1999	69%

Application *Options:* eApply at www.CollegeQuest.com, Common Application, electronic application. *Application fee:* $25. *Required:* high school transcript; minimum 2.0 GPA; letters of recommendation; interview.

Standardized tests *Admission: Required:* SAT I or ACT.

Significant dates *Application deadlines:* rolling (freshmen), rolling (transfers). *Financial aid deadline:* 11/15.

Freshman Application Contact
Mr. Robert Cornwell, Associate Director of Admissions, Missouri Baptist College, 1 College Park Drive, St. Louis, MO 63141-8698. **Phone:** 314-392-2293. **Toll-free phone:** 877-434-1115 Ext. 2290. **Fax:** 314-434-7596. **E-mail:** admissions@mobap.edu

Visit CollegeQuest.com for information on majors offered and athletics. College video and electronic viewbook available at CollegeQuest.com.

MISSOURI SOUTHERN STATE COLLEGE
Joplin, Missouri

- **State-supported**, 4-year, founded 1937
- **Degrees** associate and bachelor's
- **Small-town** 350-acre campus
- **Coed**, 5,495 undergraduate students, 68% full-time, 56% women, 44% men
- **Moderately difficult** entrance level, 87% of applicants were admitted
- **18:1 student-to-undergraduate faculty ratio**
- **27% graduate** in 6 years or less
- **$2496 tuition** and fees (in-state); $4866 (out-of-state)
- **$3354 average financial aid** package, $11,571 average indebtedness upon graduation, $1,743 endowment

Part of Missouri Coordinating Board for Higher Education.

Students *Undergraduates:* 3,732 full-time, 1,763 part-time. Students come from 37 states and territories, 30 other countries. *The most frequently chosen baccalaureate fields are:* business/marketing, education, protective services/public administration.

From out-of-state	11%	Reside on campus	11%
Age 25 or older	30%	Transferred in	7%
International students	1%	African Americans	3%
Asian Americans/Pacific Islanders	1%	Hispanic Americans	1%
Native Americans	3%		

Faculty 309 (66% full-time), 49% with terminal degrees.

Expenses (2000–2001) *One-time required fee:* $15. *Tuition, state resident:* full-time $2370; part-time $79 per credit. *Tuition, nonresident:* full-time $4740; part-time $158 per credit. *Required fees:* full-time $126; $43 per term part-time. Full-time tuition and fees vary according to course load. *College room and board:* $3610; room only: $2410. Room and board charges vary according to housing facility. *Payment plan:* deferred payment. *Waivers:* senior citizens and employees or children of employees.

Library Spiva Library plus 1 other. *Operations spending 1999–2000:* $1 million. *Collection:* 425,116 titles, 1,235 serial subscriptions, 13,724 audiovisual materials.

Missouri

College life *Housing:* on-campus residence required through sophomore year. *Options:* men-only, women-only, disabled students. *Social organizations:* national fraternities, national sororities, local fraternities; 1% of eligible men and 1% of eligible women are members. *Most popular organizations:* Koinonia, Campus Activities Board, Residence Hall Association, Baptist Student Union, Student Senate.

Campus security 24-hour emergency response devices and patrols, late-night transport-escort service, controlled dormitory access.

After graduation 47 organizations recruited on campus 1997–98. 36% of class of 1998 had job offers within 6 months. *Career center:* 3 full-time, 2 part-time personnel. Services include job fairs, resume preparation, resume referral, career counseling, careers library, job bank, job interviews.

Freshmen 1,829 applied, 1,600 admitted, 950 enrolled. 18 valedictorians.

SAT verbal scores above 500	N/R	SAT math scores above 500	N/R
ACT above 18	87%	From top 10% of their h.s. class	13%
From top quarter	38%	From top half	70%
1998 freshmen returning in 1999	67%		

Application *Options:* Common Application, electronic application, deferred entrance. *Application fee:* $15. *Required:* high school transcript.

Standardized tests *Admission: Required:* SAT I or ACT. *Required for some:* Michigan Test of English Language Proficiency.

Significant dates *Application deadlines:* 8/17 (freshmen), 8/17 (transfers). *Financial aid deadline priority date:* 2/15.

Freshman Application Contact
Mr. Derek Skaggs, Director of Enrollment Services, Missouri Southern State College, 3950 East Newman Road, Joplin, MO 64801-1595. **Phone:** 417-625-9537. **Toll-free phone:** 800-606-MSSC. **Fax:** 417-659-4429. **E-mail:** admissions@mail.mssc.edu

Visit CollegeQuest.com for information on majors offered and athletics. College video available at CollegeQuest.com.

■ *See page 2068 for a narrative description.*

MISSOURI TECH
St. Louis, Missouri

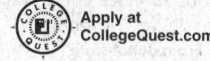
Apply at CollegeQuest.com

- **Proprietary**, 4-year, founded 1932
- **Degrees** associate and bachelor's
- **Suburban** campus
- **Coed**
- **Moderately difficult** entrance level
- **$8850 tuition** and fees

Expenses (1999–2000) *Tuition:* full-time $8850; part-time $295 per credit hour. Full-time tuition and fees vary according to course load. Part-time tuition and fees vary according to course load. *College room only:* $3600.

Institutional Web site http://www.motech.edu/

College life *Housing: Options:* men-only, women-only.

Campus security 24-hour emergency response devices.

Application *Options:* eApply at www.CollegeQuest.com, Common Application. *Required for some:* interview; minimum ACT score of 20.

Standardized tests *Admission: Recommended:* ACT.

Admissions Office Contact
Missouri Tech, 1167 Corporate Lake Drive, St. Louis, MO 63132-1716. **Toll-free phone:** 800-230-3600. **Fax:** 314-569-1167. **E-mail:** rhonaker@motech.edu

Visit CollegeQuest.com for information on athletics. College video and electronic viewbook available at CollegeQuest.com.

MISSOURI VALLEY COLLEGE
Marshall, Missouri

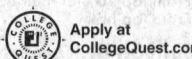
Apply at CollegeQuest.com

- **Independent**, 4-year, founded 1889, affiliated with Presbyterian Church
- **Degrees** associate and bachelor's
- **Small-town** 140-acre campus with easy access to Kansas City
- **Coed**, 1,328 undergraduate students, 98% full-time, 40% women, 60% men
- **Moderately difficult** entrance level, 84% of applicants were admitted

- **$11,900 tuition** and fees
- **$15,300 average indebtedness** upon graduation, $1.9 million endowment

Students *Undergraduates:* 1,307 full-time, 21 part-time. Students come from 37 states and territories, 15 other countries.

From out-of-state	40%	Reside on campus	80%
Age 25 or older	2%	Transferred in	8%
International students	3%	African Americans	16%
Asian Americans/Pacific Islanders	3%	Hispanic Americans	4%
Native Americans	1%		

Faculty 61 full-time.

Expenses (2000–2001) *Comprehensive fee:* $16,900 includes full-time tuition ($11,500), mandatory fees ($400), and room and board ($5000). *Payment plan:* installment. *Waivers:* children of alumni, senior citizens, and employees or children of employees.

Library Murrell Memorial Library plus 1 other. *Operations spending 1999–2000:* $261,000. *Collection:* 55,206 titles, 1,192 serial subscriptions, 1,191 audiovisual materials.

College life *Housing: Options:* coed, men-only, women-only. *Social organizations:* national fraternities, national sororities, local fraternities; 30% of eligible men and 25% of eligible women are members. *Most popular organizations:* V Club, fraternities, sororities, Rodeo Club, Musical Theatre.

Campus security 24-hour emergency response devices, student patrols, controlled dormitory access.

After graduation 37 organizations recruited on campus 1997–98. *Career center:* 1 part-time personnel. Services include job fairs, resume preparation, interview workshops, career/interest testing, career counseling, careers library, job interviews. *Graduate education:* 20% of class of 1999 went directly to graduate and professional school.

Freshmen 1,672 applied, 1,410 admitted, 474 enrolled. 11 class presidents, 6 valedictorians, 64 student government officers.

Average high school GPA	2.7	SAT verbal scores above 500	22%
SAT math scores above 500	24%	ACT above 18	66%
From top 10% of their h.s. class	9%	From top quarter	39%
From top half	69%	1998 freshmen returning in 1999	50%

Application *Options:* eApply at www.CollegeQuest.com, Common Application, electronic application, early admission, deferred entrance. *Application fee:* $10. *Required:* high school transcript. *Recommended:* interview.

Standardized tests *Admission: Required:* ACT, SAT I and SAT II or ACT. *Recommended:* SAT II: Writing Test.

Significant dates *Application deadlines:* rolling (freshmen), rolling (transfers). *Financial aid deadline:* 9/15. *Priority date:* 3/20.

Freshman Application Contact
Ms. Debbie Bultman, Admissions, Missouri Valley College, 500 East College, Marshall, MO 65340-3197. **Phone:** 660-831-4114. **Fax:** 660-831-4039. **E-mail:** mo-valley@juno.com

Visit CollegeQuest.com for information on majors offered and athletics. Electronic viewbook available at CollegeQuest.com.

■ *See page 2070 for a narrative description.*

MISSOURI WESTERN STATE COLLEGE
St. Joseph, Missouri

- **State-supported**, 4-year, founded 1915
- **Degrees** associate and bachelor's
- **Suburban** 744-acre campus with easy access to Kansas City
- **Coed**, 4,878 undergraduate students, 79% full-time, 61% women, 39% men
- **Noncompetitive** entrance level, 100% of applicants were admitted
- **19:1 student-to-undergraduate faculty ratio**
- **27% graduate** in 6 years or less
- **$2774 tuition** and fees (in-state); $4982 (out-of-state)

Missouri Western State College affords quality instruction in a wide range of programs, reasonable costs, scholarships, and a well-rounded college experience. A friendly, personal atmosphere pervades classroom and campus. The College serves a 4-state area and attracts students nationwide. Its small student-faculty ratio allows hands-on emphasis in all academic areas.

Peterson's Guide to Four-Year Colleges 2001   www.petersons.com

Missouri

Missouri Western State College (continued)

Students *Undergraduates:* 3,872 full-time, 1,006 part-time. Students come from 31 states and territories, 3 other countries. *The most frequently chosen baccalaureate fields are:* business/marketing, education, protective services/public administration.

From out-of-state	9%	Reside on campus	20%
Age 25 or older	23%	Transferred in	6%
International students	0.2%	African Americans	9%
Asian Americans/Pacific Islanders	1%	Hispanic Americans	1%
Native Americans	1%		

Faculty 311 (61% full-time), 47% with terminal degrees.

Expenses (1999–2000) *One-time required fee:* $15. *Tuition, state resident:* full-time $2622; part-time $96 per hour. *Tuition, nonresident:* full-time $4830; part-time $171 per hour. *Required fees:* full-time $152; $5 per hour; $10 per term part-time. *College room and board:* $3600. Room and board charges vary according to board plan and housing facility. *Payment plans:* installment, deferred payment. *Waivers:* senior citizens and employees or children of employees.

Library Warren E. Hearnes Library. *Collection:* 145,311 titles, 1,068 serial subscriptions, 12,825 audiovisual materials.

College life *Housing:* Option: coed. *Social organizations:* national fraternities, national sororities; 6% of eligible men and 3% of eligible women are members.

Campus security 24-hour emergency response devices and patrols, student patrols, late-night transport-escort service, controlled dormitory access.

After graduation *Career center:* 2 full-time personnel. Services include job fairs, resume preparation, interview workshops, career/interest testing, career counseling, careers library, job interviews.

Freshmen 2,039 applied, 2,039 admitted, 1,060 enrolled.

SAT verbal scores above 500	N/R	SAT math scores above 500	N/R
ACT above 18	63%	From top 10% of their h.s. class	10%
From top quarter	28%	From top half	59%
1998 freshmen returning in 1999	61%		

Application *Option:* early admission. *Application fee:* $15. *Required:* high school transcript.

Standardized tests *Placement: Required:* ACT

Significant dates *Application deadlines:* 7/30 (freshmen), 7/30 (transfers). *Notification:* continuous until 8/10 (freshmen). *Financial aid deadline priority date:* 3/1.

Freshman Application Contact
Mr. Howard McCauley, Director of Admissions, Missouri Western State College, 4525 Downs Drive, St. Joseph, MO 64507-2294. **Phone:** 816-271-4267. **Toll-free phone:** 800-662-7041 Ext. 60. **Fax:** 816-271-5833. **E-mail:** admissn@giffon.mwsc.edu

Visit CollegeQuest.com for information on majors offered and athletics.

NATIONAL AMERICAN UNIVERSITY
Kansas City, Missouri

- **Proprietary**, 4-year, founded 1941
- **Degrees** associate and bachelor's
- **Urban** 1-acre campus
- **Coed**, 350 undergraduate students
- **Noncompetitive** entrance level, 95% of applicants were admitted
- **$8880 tuition** and fees

Part of National College.

Students *Undergraduates:* Students come from 2 states and territories, 5 other countries.

Age 25 or older	97%

Faculty 30.

Expenses (1999–2000) *Tuition:* full-time $8880; part-time $185 per credit. *Payment plan:* installment.

Library Learning Resource Center plus 1 other. *Collection:* 1,500 titles, 60 serial subscriptions.

College life *Housing:* college housing not available. *Most popular organizations:* Phi Beta Lambda, Student Senate.

Campus security 24-hour patrols.

After graduation *Career center:* 1 full-time personnel. Services include resume preparation, career counseling, careers library, job interviews. *Graduate education:* 40% of class of 1999 went directly to graduate and professional school: 40% business.

Freshmen 61 applied, 58 admitted.

SAT verbal scores above 500	N/R	SAT math scores above 500	N/R
ACT above 18	N/R	1998 freshmen returning in 1999	81%

Application *Options:* early admission, deferred entrance. *Application fee:* $25. *Required:* high school transcript; interview.

Significant dates *Application deadline:* rolling (freshmen). *Notification:* continuous until 9/12 (freshmen). *Financial aid deadline:* continuous.

Freshman Application Contact
Ms. Tanya Carr, Director of Admissions, National American University, 4200 Blue Ridge Boulevard, Kansas City, MO 64133-1612. **Phone:** 816-353-4554. **Fax:** 816-353-1176.

Visit CollegeQuest.com for information on majors offered and athletics.

NORTHWEST MISSOURI STATE UNIVERSITY
Maryville, Missouri

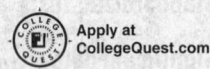
Apply at CollegeQuest.com

- **State-supported**, comprehensive, founded 1905
- **Degrees** bachelor's and master's
- **Small-town** 240-acre campus with easy access to Kansas City
- **Coed**, 5,096 undergraduate students, 94% full-time, 56% women, 44% men
- **Moderately difficult** entrance level, 87% of applicants were admitted
- **22:1** student-to-undergraduate faculty ratio
- **$3330 tuition** and fees (in-state); $5588 (out-of-state)

Part of Missouri Coordinating Board for Higher Education.

Students *Undergraduates:* 4,804 full-time, 292 part-time. Students come from 52 states and territories, 28 other countries. *Graduate:* 1,149 in graduate degree programs.

From out-of-state	35%	Reside on campus	49%
Age 25 or older	4%	International students	2%
African Americans	3%	Asian Americans/Pacific Islanders	0.3%
Hispanic Americans	1%	Native Americans	0.3%

Faculty 242 (98% full-time), 69% with terminal degrees.

Expenses (2000–2001) *Tuition, state resident:* full-time $3210; part-time $107 per credit hour. *Tuition, nonresident:* full-time $5468; part-time $182 per credit hour. *Required fees:* full-time $120; $4 per credit hour. *College room and board:* $4150. Room and board charges vary according to housing facility. *Payment plan:* installment. *Waivers:* senior citizens and employees or children of employees.

Library B. D. Owens Library plus 1 other. *Operations spending 1999–2000:* $1.6 million. *Collection:* 305,982 titles, 1,469 serial subscriptions.

College life *Housing:* on-campus residence required in freshman year. *Option:* coed. *Social organizations:* national fraternities, national sororities; 20% of eligible men and 20% of eligible women are members. *Most popular organizations:* Greek system, student government.

Campus security 24-hour patrols, student patrols, late-night transport-escort service.

After graduation 120 organizations recruited on campus 1997–98. 90% of class of 1998 had job offers within 6 months. *Career center:* 5 full-time, 2 part-time personnel. Services include job fairs, resume preparation, resume referral, career counseling, careers library, job bank, job interviews.

Freshmen 2,752 applied, 2,389 admitted, 1,214 enrolled.

Average high school GPA	3.2	SAT verbal scores above 500	N/R
SAT math scores above 500	N/R	ACT above 18	N/R
From top 10% of their h.s. class	10%	From top quarter	36%
From top half	73%	1998 freshmen returning in 1999	72%

Application *Options:* eApply at www.CollegeQuest.com, early admission, deferred entrance. *Preference* given to state residents. *Application fee:* $15. *Required:* high school transcript; minimum 2.0 GPA. *Required for some:* interview.

Standardized tests *Admission: Required:* SAT I or ACT.

Missouri

Significant dates *Application deadlines:* rolling (freshmen), rolling (transfers). *Notification:* continuous until 7/31 (freshmen). *Financial aid deadline priority date:* 3/1.
Freshman Application Contact
Ms. Beverly Schenkel, Associate Director of Admission, Northwest Missouri State University, 800 University Drive, Maryville, MO 64468-6001. **Phone:** 660-562-1149. **Toll-free phone:** 800-633-1175. **Fax:** 660-562-1121. **E-mail:** admissions@acad.nwmissouri.edu
Visit CollegeQuest.com for information on majors offered and athletics. College video available at CollegeQuest.com.

OZARK CHRISTIAN COLLEGE
Joplin, Missouri

- **Independent Christian**, 4-year, founded 1942
- **Degrees** associate and bachelor's
- **Suburban** 110-acre campus
- **Coed**, 697 undergraduate students, 84% full-time, 48% women, 52% men
- **Noncompetitive** entrance level, 100% of applicants were admitted
- **20:1 student-to-undergraduate faculty ratio**
- **24% graduate** in 6 years or less
- **$5325 tuition** and fees

Students *Undergraduates:* Students come from 31 states and territories, 3 other countries. *The most frequently chosen baccalaureate field is:* philosophy.

From out-of-state	70%	Reside on campus	63%
Age 25 or older	25%	International students	0.4%
African Americans	1%	Asian Americans/Pacific Islanders	0.1%
Hispanic Americans	1%	Native Americans	1%

Faculty 44 (59% full-time), 18% with terminal degrees.
Expenses (2000–2001) *Comprehensive fee:* $8805 includes full-time tuition ($4640), mandatory fees ($685), and room and board ($3480). *College room only:* $1590. Room and board charges vary according to board plan. *Part-time tuition:* $145 per credit. *Payment plans:* installment, deferred payment. *Waivers:* senior citizens and employees or children of employees.
Library Seth Wilson Library. *Collection:* 50,000 titles, 382 serial subscriptions, 18,000 audiovisual materials.
College life *Housing:* on-campus residence required through senior year. *Options:* men-only, women-only. *Most popular organizations:* Family Outreach Group, God's Spokesman, International Club, Lord's Reapers.
Campus security 24-hour emergency response devices, 12-hour patrols by trained security personnel.
After graduation *Career center:* Services include resume preparation.
Freshmen 297 applied, 297 admitted.

SAT verbal scores above 500	N/R	SAT math scores above 500	N/R
ACT above 18	N/R	1998 freshmen returning in 1999	68%

Application *Option:* deferred entrance. *Application fee:* $30. *Required:* essay or personal statement; high school transcript; 4 letters of recommendation. *Required for some:* interview.
Standardized tests *Admission: Required:* SAT I or ACT.
Significant dates *Application deadlines:* 8/15 (freshmen), rolling (transfers). *Financial aid deadline:* 4/1.
Freshman Application Contact
Mr. Jim Marcum, Director of Admissions, Ozark Christian College, 1111 North Main Street, Joplin, MO 64801-4804. **Phone:** 417-624-2518 Ext. 2021. **Toll-free phone:** 800-299-4622. **Fax:** 417-624-0090. **E-mail:** occadmin@occ.edu
Visit CollegeQuest.com for information on majors offered and athletics. College video available at CollegeQuest.com.

PARK UNIVERSITY
Parkville, Missouri

 Apply at CollegeQuest.com

- **Independent**, comprehensive, founded 1875, affiliated with Reorganized Church of Jesus Christ of Latter Day Saints
- **Degrees** associate, bachelor's, and master's
- **Suburban** 800-acre campus with easy access to Kansas City
- **Coed**, 1,066 undergraduate students, 73% full-time, 61% women, 39% men
- **Moderately difficult** entrance level, 87% of applicants were admitted
- **14:1 student-to-undergraduate faculty ratio**
- **31% graduate** in 6 years or less
- **$4770 tuition** and fees
- **$6377 average financial aid** package, $10,250 average indebtedness upon graduation, $22.9 million endowment

Students *Undergraduates:* 779 full-time, 287 part-time. Students come from 23 states and territories, 26 other countries. *The most frequently chosen baccalaureate fields are:* business/marketing, education, social sciences and history. *Graduate:* 102 in graduate degree programs.

From out-of-state	20%	Reside on campus	12%
Age 25 or older	33%	Transferred in	23%
International students	8%	African Americans	14%
Asian Americans/Pacific Islanders	2%	Hispanic Americans	5%
Native Americans	1%		

Faculty 98 (51% full-time).
Expenses (1999–2000) *Comprehensive fee:* $9560 includes full-time tuition ($4770) and room and board ($4790). Room and board charges vary according to housing facility. *Part-time tuition:* $159 per credit hour. *Payment plan:* installment. *Waivers:* senior citizens and employees or children of employees.
Library McAfee Memorial Library. *Operations spending 1999–2000:* $446,643. *Collection:* 134,748 titles, 775 serial subscriptions.
College life *Housing:* on-campus residence required through junior year. *Option:* coed. *Most popular organizations:* World Student Union, Student Senate, radio club, Latin American Student Organization, marketing club.
Campus security 24-hour patrols, student patrols.
After graduation 44 organizations recruited on campus 1997–98. 73% of class of 1998 had job offers within 6 months. *Career center:* 1 full-time personnel. Services include job fairs, resume preparation, resume referral, career/interest testing, career counseling, careers library, job bank, job interviews. *Graduate education:* 7% of class of 1999 went directly to graduate and professional school: 6% graduate arts and sciences, 1% business.
Freshmen 264 applied, 230 admitted, 145 enrolled. 2 class presidents, 1 valedictorian, 20 student government officers.

Average high school GPA	2.99	SAT verbal scores above 500	N/R
SAT math scores above 500	N/R	ACT above 18	N/R
From top 10% of their h.s. class	6%	From top quarter	30%
From top half	58%	1998 freshmen returning in 1999	75%

Application *Options:* eApply at www.CollegeQuest.com, electronic application, early admission, deferred entrance. *Application fee:* $25. *Required:* high school transcript; minimum 2.0 GPA. *Required for some:* 2 letters of recommendation; interview. *Recommended:* essay or personal statement.
Standardized tests *Admission: Required:* SAT I or ACT.
Significant dates *Application deadlines:* 8/1 (freshmen), 8/1 (transfers). *Financial aid deadline priority date:* 4/1.
Freshman Application Contact
Dr. Ron Carruth, Director of Student Recruiting and Marketing, Park University, 8700 NW River Park Drive, Campus Box 1, Parkville, MO 64152. **Phone:** 816-741-2000 Ext. 6215. **Toll-free phone:** 800-745-7275. **Fax:** 816-741-4462. **E-mail:** admissions@mail.park.edu
Visit CollegeQuest.com for information on majors offered and athletics. College video available at CollegeQuest.com.

RESEARCH COLLEGE OF NURSING
Kansas City, Missouri

- **Independent**, comprehensive, founded 1980
- **Degrees** bachelor's and master's (jointly with Rockhurst College)
- **Urban** 66-acre campus
- **Coed**
- **Moderately difficult** entrance level
- **$12,840 tuition** and fees

Expenses (1999–2000) *One-time required fee:* $40. *Comprehensive fee:* $18,070 includes full-time tuition ($12,500), mandatory fees ($340), and room and board ($5230). Full-time tuition and fees vary according to program.

Missouri

Research College of Nursing *(continued)*
Room and board charges vary according to board plan. *Part-time tuition:* $420 per credit hour. *Part-time fees:* $170 per term part-time. Part-time tuition and fees vary according to class time and program.
College life on-campus residence required in freshman year. *Social organizations:* national fraternities, national sororities, local sororities.
Campus security 24-hour emergency response devices and patrols, late-night transport-escort service, controlled dormitory access.
Application *Option:* deferred entrance. *Application fee:* $20. *Required:* high school transcript; 1 letter of recommendation. *Recommended:* interview.
Standardized tests *Admission: Required:* SAT I or ACT.
Admissions Office Contact
Research College of Nursing, 2316 East Meyer Boulevard, Kansas City, MO 64132. **Toll-free phone:** 800-842-6776. **Fax:** 816-501-4588. **E-mail:** mendenhall@vax2.rockhurst.edu
Visit CollegeQuest.com for information on athletics. College video available at CollegeQuest.com.

ROCKHURST UNIVERSITY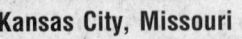
Kansas City, Missouri

- **Independent Roman Catholic (Jesuit)**, comprehensive, founded 1910
- **Degrees** bachelor's, master's, and postbachelor's certificates
- **Urban** 35-acre campus
- **Coed**, 2,050 undergraduate students, 62% full-time, 57% women, 43% men
- **Moderately difficult** entrance level, 90% of applicants were admitted
- **9:1 student-to-undergraduate faculty ratio**
- **65% graduate** in 6 years or less
- **$13,845 tuition** and fees
- **$12,785 average financial aid** package, $15,106 average indebtedness upon graduation, $41 million endowment

With its proximity to the new Stowers Institute, one of the world's largest molecular and genetic research facilities, Rockhurst University has elevated its opportunities for molecular biology to a full program. Students have the opportunity to be involved in investigative techniques used in modern molecular and cell studies.

Students *Undergraduates:* 1,274 full-time, 776 part-time. Students come from 25 states and territories, 9 other countries. *The most frequently chosen baccalaureate fields are:* business/marketing, health professions and related sciences, psychology. *Graduate:* 858 in graduate degree programs.

From out-of-state	31%	Reside on campus	52%
Age 25 or older	14%	Transferred in	7%
International students	1%	African Americans	7%
Asian Americans/Pacific Islanders	3%	Hispanic Americans	4%
Native Americans	1%		

Faculty 196 (59% full-time), 58% with terminal degrees.
Expenses (2000–2001, estimated) *One-time required fee:* $40. *Comprehensive fee:* $18,865 includes full-time tuition ($13,500), mandatory fees ($345), and room and board ($5020). *College room only:* $2375. Full-time tuition and fees vary according to course load. Room and board charges vary according to board plan, gender, and housing facility. *Part-time tuition:* $453 per semester hour. *Part-time fees:* $15 per term part-time. Part-time tuition and fees vary according to class time, course load, and program. *Payment plans:* installment, deferred payment. *Waivers:* children of alumni, senior citizens, and employees or children of employees.
Library Greenlease Library. *Operations spending 1999–2000:* $549,926. *Collection:* 53,720 titles, 100 serial subscriptions, 2,730 audiovisual materials.
College life *Housing:* on-campus residence required through sophomore year. *Options:* coed, men-only, women-only. *Social organizations:* national fraternities, national sororities; 50% of eligible men and 50% of eligible women are members. *Most popular organizations:* Student Activities Board, Rockhurst Organization of Collegiate Women, Black Student Union, Student Organization of Latinos, Rockhurst College Players.
Campus security 24-hour emergency response devices and patrols, student patrols, late-night transport-escort service, controlled dormitory access, closed circuit TV monitors.
After graduation 55 organizations recruited on campus 1997–98. 63% of class of 1998 had job offers within 6 months. *Career center:* 5 full-time personnel. Services include job fairs, resume preparation, interview workshops, resume referral, career/interest testing, career counseling, careers library, job bank, job interviews. **Graduate education:** 27% of class of 1999 went directly to graduate and professional school: 20% graduate arts and sciences, 3% business, 2% law, 2% medicine.
Freshmen 1,186 applied, 1,063 admitted, 309 enrolled, 5 valedictorians.

Average high school GPA	3.1	SAT verbal scores above 500	81%
SAT math scores above 500	74%	ACT above 18	95%
From top 10% of their h.s. class	22%	From top quarter	45%
From top half	75%	1998 freshmen returning in 1999	83%

Application *Options:* eApply at www.CollegeQuest.com, Common Application, early admission, early action, deferred entrance. *Application fee:* $20. *Required:* high school transcript; minimum 2.0 GPA; 1 letter of recommendation. *Required for some:* essay or personal statement; interview.
Standardized tests *Admission: Required:* SAT I or ACT.
Significant dates *Application deadlines:* 6/30 (freshmen), rolling (transfers). *Early action:* 5/1. *Notification:* 7/1 (early action). *Financial aid deadline priority date:* 2/15.
Freshman Application Contact
Mr. Mark Kopenski, Vice President of Enrollment Management Services, Rockhurst University, 1100 Rockhurst Road, Kansas City, MO 64110-2561. **Phone:** 816-501-4100. **Toll-free phone:** 800-842-6776. **Fax:** 816-501-4241. **E-mail:** admission@rockhurst.edu
Visit CollegeQuest.com for information on majors offered and athletics. College video and electronic viewbook available at CollegeQuest.com.

■ *See page 2348 for a narrative description.*

ST. LOUIS CHRISTIAN COLLEGE
Florissant, Missouri

- **Independent Christian**, 4-year, founded 1956
- **Degrees** associate and bachelor's
- **Suburban** 20-acre campus with easy access to St. Louis
- **Coed**, 203 undergraduate students, 64% full-time, 43% women, 57% men
- **Minimally difficult** entrance level, 37% of applicants were admitted
- **10:1 student-to-undergraduate faculty ratio**
- **14% graduate** in 6 years or less
- **$4950 tuition** and fees
- **$5797 average financial aid** package, $577,910 endowment

Students *Undergraduates:* 130 full-time, 73 part-time. Students come from 8 states and territories, 6 other countries. *The most frequently chosen baccalaureate fields are:* education, philosophy, social sciences and history.

From out-of-state	48%	Reside on campus	48%
Age 25 or older	50%	Transferred in	12%
International students	3%	African Americans	21%
Asian Americans/Pacific Islanders	1%	Hispanic Americans	1%
Native Americans	0.5%		

Faculty 30 (30% full-time), 23% with terminal degrees.
Expenses (1999–2000) *Comprehensive fee:* $8070 includes full-time tuition ($4950) and room and board ($3120). *College room only:* $1560. Room and board charges vary according to board plan and housing facility. *Part-time tuition:* $165 per credit hour. *Payment plan:* installment. *Waivers:* employees or children of employees.
Library St. Louis Christian College Library. *Operations spending 1999–2000:* $70,631. *Collection:* 39,728 titles, 144 serial subscriptions.
College life *Housing:* on-campus residence required through senior year. *Options:* men-only, women-only. *Most popular organizations:* World Christians Unlimited, drama club, pep band.
Campus security 24-hour emergency response devices and patrols, controlled dormitory access, night security.
After graduation 64% of class of 1998 had job offers within 6 months. *Career center:* Services include resume preparation, career counseling. **Graduate education:** 10% of class of 1999 went directly to graduate and professional school: 10% theology.
Freshmen 120 applied, 44 admitted, 38 enrolled.

SAT verbal scores above 500	N/R	SAT math scores above 500	N/R
ACT above 18	72%	From top 10% of their h.s. class	15%
From top quarter	33%	From top half	52%
1998 freshmen returning in 1999	53%		

Missouri

Application *Options:* early admission, deferred entrance. *Application fee:* $20. *Required:* essay or personal statement; high school transcript; 2 letters of recommendation. *Required for some:* interview. *Recommended:* minimum 2.0 GPA.
Standardized tests *Admission: Required:* ACT.
Significant dates *Application deadlines:* 8/20 (freshmen), 8/20 (transfers). *Financial aid deadline priority date:* 5/1.
Freshman Application Contact Mr. Richard Fordyce, Registrar, St. Louis Christian College, 1360 Grandview Drive, Florissant, MO 63033-6499. **Phone:** 314-837-6777 Ext. 1500. **Fax:** 314-837-8291. **E-mail:** questions@slcc4ministry.edu
Visit CollegeQuest.com for information on majors offered and athletics.

ST. LOUIS COLLEGE OF PHARMACY
St. Louis, Missouri

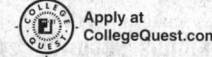 Apply at CollegeQuest.com

- **Independent**, comprehensive, founded 1864
- **Degrees** bachelor's, master's, and first professional
- **Urban** 5-acre campus
- **Coed**, 815 undergraduate students, 99% full-time, 66% women, 34% men
- **Moderately difficult** entrance level, 62% of applicants were admitted
- **$13,370 tuition** and fees
- **$8469 average financial aid** package, $45,108 average indebtedness upon graduation, $45.6 million endowment

Students *Undergraduates:* 805 full-time, 10 part-time. Students come from 15 states and territories. *Graduate:* 49 in professional programs, 11 in other graduate degree programs.

Reside on campus	26%	Age 25 or older	15%
Transferred in	9%	African Americans	5%
Asian Americans/Pacific Islanders	11%	Hispanic Americans	2%

Faculty 108 (58% full-time), 64% with terminal degrees.
Expenses (2000–2001, estimated) *Comprehensive fee:* $18,745 includes full-time tuition ($13,250), mandatory fees ($120), and room and board ($5375). *Payment plan:* deferred payment. *Waivers:* employees or children of employees.
Library O. J. Cloughly Alumni Library. *Operations spending 1999–2000:* $378,306. *Collection:* 27,391 titles, 308 serial subscriptions, 1,067 audiovisual materials.
College life *Housing:* on-campus residence required in freshman year. *Option:* coed. *Social organizations:* national fraternities, national sororities; 70% of eligible men and 65% of eligible women are members. *Most popular organizations:* Gateway Academy of Student Pharmacists, Student Council, International Student Council, Student Ambassadors, Student Alumni Association.
Campus security 24-hour emergency response devices and patrols, late-night transport-escort service, controlled dormitory access.
After graduation *Graduate education:* 6% of class of 1999 went directly to graduate and professional school: 2% business, 2% graduate arts and sciences, 1% law, 1% medicine.
Freshmen 268 applied, 166 admitted, 132 enrolled. 10 valedictorians.

Average high school GPA	3.64	SAT verbal scores above 500	N/R
SAT math scores above 500	N/R	ACT above 18	100%
1998 freshmen returning in 1999	89%		

Application *Options:* eApply at www.CollegeQuest.com, electronic application. *Application fee:* $35. *Required:* essay or personal statement; high school transcript; minimum 2.5 GPA; letters of recommendation. *Recommended:* minimum 3.0 GPA.
Standardized tests *Admission: Required:* SAT I or ACT.
Significant dates *Application deadlines:* rolling (freshmen), 2/1 (transfers). *Notification:* continuous until 8/1 (freshmen). *Financial aid deadline:* 11/15. *Priority date:* 4/1.
Freshman Application Contact Ms. Penny Bryant, Director of Admissions, St. Louis College of Pharmacy, 4588 Parkview Place, St. Louis, MO 63110-1088. **Phone:** 314-367-8700 Ext. 1067. **Toll-free phone:** 800-278-5267. **Fax:** 314-367-2784. **E-mail:** pbryant@stlcop.edu

Visit CollegeQuest.com for information on majors offered and athletics. College video available at CollegeQuest.com.

■ *See page 2402 for a narrative description.*

SAINT LOUIS UNIVERSITY
St. Louis, Missouri

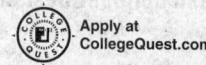 Apply at CollegeQuest.com

- **Independent Roman Catholic (Jesuit)**, university, founded 1818
- **Degrees** associate, bachelor's, master's, doctoral, first professional, post-master's, and postbachelor's certificates
- **Urban** 279-acre campus
- **Coed**, 6,308 undergraduate students, 89% full-time, 55% women, 45% men
- **Moderately difficult** entrance level, 69% of applicants were admitted
- **14:1 student-to-undergraduate faculty ratio**
- **64.1% graduate** in 6 years or less
- **$17,268 tuition** and fees
- **$19,058 average indebtedness** upon graduation, $900 million endowment

Students *Undergraduates:* 5,628 full-time, 680 part-time. Students come from 50 states and territories, 83 other countries. *The most frequently chosen baccalaureate fields are:* business/marketing, health professions and related sciences, psychology. *Graduate:* 1,387 in professional programs, 2,793 in other graduate degree programs.

From out-of-state	38%	Reside on campus	46%
Age 25 or older	16%	Transferred in	8%
International students	6%	African Americans	9%
Asian Americans/Pacific Islanders	5%	Hispanic Americans	2%
Native Americans	0.3%		

Faculty 1,612 (71% full-time).
Expenses (1999–2000) *Comprehensive fee:* $23,168 includes full-time tuition ($17,230), mandatory fees ($38), and room and board ($5900). *College room only:* $3000. Room and board charges vary according to board plan and housing facility. *Part-time tuition:* $605 per credit hour. Part-time tuition and fees vary according to class time and program. *Payment plan:* installment. *Waivers:* employees or children of employees.
Library Pius XII Memorial Library plus 3 others. *Operations spending 1999–2000:* $8.8 million. *Collection:* 1.2 million titles, 13,941 serial subscriptions, 196,770 audiovisual materials.
College life *Housing: Options:* coed, women-only, disabled students. *Social organizations:* national fraternities, national sororities; 17% of eligible men and 13% of eligible women are members. *Most popular organizations:* volunteer groups, Greek organizations, student government bodies, residence hall councils, sports clubs.
Campus security 24-hour emergency response devices and patrols, student patrols, late-night transport-escort service, controlled dormitory access, crime prevention program, bicycle patrols.
After graduation 142 organizations recruited on campus 1997–98. 75% of class of 1998 had job offers within 6 months. *Career center:* 9 full-time, 7 part-time personnel. Services include job fairs, resume preparation, interview workshops, resume referral, career/interest testing, career counseling, careers library, job bank, job interviews. *Graduate education:* 25% of class of 1999 went directly to graduate and professional school. *Major awards:* 2 Fulbright Scholars.
Freshmen 4,990 applied, 3,440 admitted, 1,274 enrolled. 23 National Merit Scholars.

Average high school GPA	3.46	SAT verbal scores above 500	N/R
SAT math scores above 500	N/R	ACT above 18	98%
From top 10% of their h.s. class	36%	From top quarter	65%
From top half	88%	1998 freshmen returning in 1999	87%

Application *Options:* eApply at www.CollegeQuest.com, Common Application, electronic application, early admission, deferred entrance. *Application fee:* $25. *Required:* essay or personal statement; high school transcript; secondary school report form. *Recommended:* 2 letters of recommendation; interview.
Standardized tests *Admission: Required:* ACT.
Significant dates *Application deadlines:* rolling (freshmen), rolling (transfers). *Financial aid deadline priority date:* 3/1.

Missouri

Saint Louis University *(continued)*

Freshman Application Contact
Ms. Patsy Brooks, Credential Evaluator for Undergraduate Admissions, Saint Louis University, 221 North Grand Boulevard, St. Louis, MO 63103-2097. **Phone:** 314-977-2500. **Toll-free phone:** 800-758-3678. **Fax:** 314-977-7136. **E-mail:** admitme@slu.edu
Visit CollegeQuest.com for information on majors offered and athletics. College video available at CollegeQuest.com.

SAINT LUKE'S COLLEGE
Kansas City, Missouri

- **Independent Episcopal**, upper-level, founded 1903
- **Degree** bachelor's
- **Urban** 3-acre campus
- **Coed**, 112 undergraduate students, 75% full-time, 92% women, 8% men
- **Very difficult** entrance level, 40% of applicants were admitted
- **7:1 student-to-undergraduate faculty ratio**
- **$8600 tuition** and fees
- **$21,000 average indebtedness** upon graduation, $1.8 million endowment

Students *Undergraduates:* 84 full-time, 28 part-time. *The most frequently chosen baccalaureate field is:* health professions and related sciences.

Reside on campus	4%	Age 25 or older	80%
Transferred in	46%	International students	1%
African Americans	4%	Asian Americans/Pacific Islanders	4%
Hispanic Americans	5%	Native Americans	1%

Faculty 18 (89% full-time), 6% with terminal degrees.
Expenses (1999–2000) *Comprehensive fee:* $11,600 includes full-time tuition ($8250), mandatory fees ($350), and room and board ($3000). Full-time tuition and fees vary according to course load. *Part-time tuition:* $275 per credit hour. Part-time tuition and fees vary according to course load.
College life *Housing: Option:* coed. *Most popular organization:* Saint Luke's Student Nurse Association.
Campus security 24-hour emergency response devices and patrols, late-night transport-escort service, controlled dormitory access.
Application *Option:* Common Application. *Application fee:* $20.
Significant dates *Application deadline:* 12/21 (transfers). *Notification:* continuous until 2/15 (transfers).
Freshman Application Contact
Ms. Marsha Thomas, Director, Admissions and Records, Saint Luke's College, 4426 Wornall Road, Kansas City, MO 64111. **Phone:** 816-932-2073. **E-mail:** mjthomas@saint-lukes.org
Visit CollegeQuest.com for information on majors offered and athletics.

SOUTHEAST MISSOURI STATE UNIVERSITY
Cape Girardeau, Missouri

 Apply at CollegeQuest.com

- **State-supported**, comprehensive, founded 1873
- **Degrees** associate, bachelor's, and master's
- **Small-town** 693-acre campus with easy access to St. Louis
- **Coed**, 7,474 undergraduate students, 77% full-time, 60% women, 40% men
- **Moderately difficult** entrance level, 88% of applicants were admitted
- **16:1 student-to-undergraduate faculty ratio**
- **39% graduate** in 6 years or less
- **$3225 tuition** and fees (in-state); $5805 (out-of-state)
- **$3940 average financial aid** package, $14,090 average indebtedness upon graduation, $24.7 million endowment

Part of Missouri Coordinating Board for Higher Education.
Students *Undergraduates:* Students come from 37 states and territories, 39 other countries. *The most frequently chosen baccalaureate fields are:* business/marketing, education, protective services/public administration. *Graduate:* 1,389 in graduate degree programs.

From out-of-state	11%	Reside on campus	25%
Age 25 or older	19%	International students	2%
African Americans	5%	Asian Americans/Pacific Islanders	1%
Hispanic Americans	1%	Native Americans	1%

Faculty 535 (73% full-time).
Expenses (1999–2000) *Tuition, state resident:* full-time $2979; part-time $99 per credit hour. *Tuition, nonresident:* full-time $5559; part-time $185 per credit hour. *Required fees:* full-time $246; $8 per credit hour. *College room and board:* $4401. Room and board charges vary according to board plan, housing facility, and location. *Payment plans:* installment, deferred payment. *Waivers:* senior citizens and employees or children of employees.
Library Kent Library. *Operations spending 1999–2000:* $2.8 million. *Collection:* 408,875 titles, 2,469 serial subscriptions.
College life *Housing:* on-campus residence required through sophomore year. *Option:* coed. *Social organizations:* national fraternities, national sororities; 14% of eligible men and 13% of eligible women are members. *Most popular organizations:* student government, Greek life, Residence Hall Association, marketing club.
Campus security 24-hour emergency response devices and patrols, late-night transport-escort service, controlled dormitory access.
After graduation *Career center:* 5 full-time, 4 part-time personnel. Services include job fairs, resume preparation, resume referral, career counseling, careers library, job bank, job interviews.
Freshmen 2,907 applied, 2,572 admitted.

Average high school GPA	3.07	SAT verbal scores above 500	N/R
SAT math scores above 500	N/R	ACT above 18	89%
From top 10% of their h.s. class	17%	From top quarter	45%
From top half	66%	1998 freshmen returning in 1999	70%

Application *Options:* eApply at www.CollegeQuest.com, Common Application, early admission. *Application fee:* $20. *Required:* high school transcript; minimum 2.0 GPA.
Standardized tests *Admission: Required:* ACT.
Significant dates *Application deadlines:* 7/15 (freshmen), 8/15 (transfers). *Financial aid deadline priority date:* 3/1.
Freshman Application Contact
Mr. Jay Goff, Director of Admissions, Southeast Missouri State University, One University Plaza, Cape Girardeau, MO 63701-4799. **Phone:** 573-651-2590.
Visit CollegeQuest.com for information on majors offered and athletics. College video available at CollegeQuest.com.

SOUTHWEST BAPTIST UNIVERSITY
Bolivar, Missouri

- **Independent Southern Baptist**, comprehensive, founded 1878
- **Degrees** associate, bachelor's, and master's
- **Small-town** 152-acre campus
- **Coed**, 2,755 undergraduate students, 70% full-time, 65% women, 35% men
- **Moderately difficult** entrance level, 86% of applicants were admitted
- **19:1 student-to-undergraduate faculty ratio**
- **$9290 tuition** and fees
- **$7885 average financial aid** package, $12,756 average indebtedness upon graduation, $8.8 million endowment

SBU is a Christ-centered, caring academic community preparing students to be servant leaders in a global society. SBU is a fully accredited university located in a thriving small-town environment just minutes from a metropolitan area. Academic programs include both liberal arts and professional degrees. Graduate degrees in administration, education, and physical therapy are offered. Popular majors include biology, business, education, music, and religious studies.

Students *Undergraduates:* 1,933 full-time, 822 part-time. Students come from 39 states and territories, 8 other countries. *The most frequently chosen baccalaureate fields are:* business/marketing, education, health professions and related sciences. *Graduate:* 833 in graduate degree programs.

Missouri

From out-of-state	18%	Reside on campus	35%
Age 25 or older	27%	Transferred in	6%
International students	1%	African Americans	2%
Asian Americans/Pacific Islanders	1%	Hispanic Americans	1%
Native Americans	1%		

Faculty 242 (43% full-time), 23% with terminal degrees.

Expenses (1999–2000) *Comprehensive fee:* $12,120 includes full-time tuition ($8940), mandatory fees ($350), and room and board ($2830). *College room only:* $1400. Full-time tuition and fees vary according to location. Room and board charges vary according to board plan and housing facility. *Part-time tuition:* $372 per credit hour. *Part-time fees:* $9 per credit hour. Part-time tuition and fees vary according to location. *Payment plan:* installment. *Waivers:* employees or children of employees.

Library Harriett K. Hutchens Library. *Operations spending 1999–2000:* $1 million. *Collection:* 108,128 titles, 2,518 serial subscriptions, 9,370 audiovisual materials.

College life *Housing:* on-campus residence required through senior year. *Options:* men-only, women-only. *Most popular organizations:* small group ministries, Christian Service Organization, Student Government Association, Student Missouri State Teachers Association, revival teams.

Campus security 24-hour emergency response devices and patrols.

After graduation 630 organizations recruited on campus 1997–98. 80% of class of 1998 had job offers within 6 months. *Career center:* 2 full-time, 1 part-time personnel. Services include job fairs, resume preparation, interview workshops, resume referral, career/interest testing, career counseling, careers library, job bank, job interviews.

Freshmen 883 applied, 759 admitted, 528 enrolled.

Average high school GPA	3.24	SAT verbal scores above 500	65%
SAT math scores above 500	39%	ACT above 18	88%
From top 10% of their h.s. class	23%	From top quarter	47%
From top half	75%	1998 freshmen returning in 1999	70%

Application *Options:* electronic application, early action. *Application fee:* $25. *Required:* high school transcript. *Recommended:* interview.

Standardized tests *Admission: Required:* SAT I or ACT.

Significant dates *Application deadlines:* rolling (freshmen), rolling (transfers). *Early action:* 12/31. *Financial aid deadline priority date:* 3/15.

Freshman Application Contact
Mr. Rob Harris, Director of Admissions, Southwest Baptist University, 1600 University Avenue, Bolivar, MO 65613-2597. **Phone:** 417-328-1809. **Toll-free phone:** 800-526-5859. **Fax:** 417-328-1514. **E-mail:** rharris@sbuniv.edu

Visit CollegeQuest.com for information on majors offered and athletics. College video and electronic viewbook available at CollegeQuest.com.

SOUTHWEST MISSOURI STATE UNIVERSITY
Springfield, Missouri

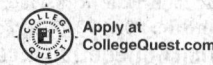

- **State-supported**, comprehensive, founded 1905
- **Degrees** bachelor's, master's, and postbachelor's certificates
- **Suburban** 225-acre campus
- **Coed**, 13,699 undergraduate students, 86% full-time, 54% women, 46% men
- **Moderately difficult** entrance level, 80% of applicants were admitted
- **18:1** student-to-undergraduate faculty ratio
- **$3564 tuition** and fees (in-state); $6744 (out-of-state)
- **$7000 average financial aid** package, $13,455 average indebtedness upon graduation, $28.1 million endowment

SMSU is the 2nd-largest university in Missouri, and undergraduate education is its highest priority. High-quality instruction, excellent classroom facilities and residence halls, generous scholarship programs, and many opportunities for student employment and recreation in a mild, 4-season climate attract students. Through its public affairs mission, the University is committed to preparing students for success in their chosen careers as well as in their lifelong careers as citizens and leaders.

Students *Undergraduates:* 11,756 full-time, 1,943 part-time. Students come from 46 states and territories, 74 other countries. *The most frequently chosen baccalaureate fields are:* business/marketing, communications/communication technologies, education. *Graduate:* 2,873 in graduate degree programs.

From out-of-state	8%	Reside on campus	28%
Age 25 or older	16%	Transferred in	7%
International students	2%	African Americans	2%
Asian Americans/Pacific Islanders	1%	Hispanic Americans	1%
Native Americans	1%		

Faculty 927 (76% full-time), 67% with terminal degrees.

Expenses (2000–2001) *Tuition, state resident:* full-time $3180; part-time $106 per credit hour. *Tuition, nonresident:* full-time $6360; part-time $212 per credit hour. *Required fees:* full-time $384. Full-time tuition and fees vary according to course load. Part-time tuition and fees vary according to course load. *College room and board:* $3846. Room and board charges vary according to board plan and housing facility. *Payment plan:* deferred payment. *Waivers:* senior citizens and employees or children of employees.

Library Meyer Library plus 3 others. *Operations spending 1999–2000:* $5.1 million. *Collection:* 711,122 titles, 5,038 serial subscriptions, 31,129 audiovisual materials.

College life *Housing:* on-campus residence required through sophomore year. *Options:* coed, disabled students. *Social organizations:* national fraternities, national sororities; 12% of eligible men and 11% of eligible women are members. *Most popular organizations:* Pride Marching Band, Student Government Association, Residence Hall Association.

Campus security 24-hour emergency response devices and patrols, late-night transport-escort service, controlled dormitory access, on-campus police substation.

After graduation 350 organizations recruited on campus 1997–98. *Career center:* 6 full-time, 2 part-time personnel. Services include job fairs, resume preparation, interview workshops, resume referral, career/interest testing, career counseling, careers library, job bank, job interviews.

Freshmen 6,714 applied, 5,373 admitted, 2,673 enrolled. 8 National Merit Scholars, 77 valedictorians.

SAT verbal scores above 500	N/R	SAT math scores above 500	N/R
ACT above 18	97%	From top 10% of their h.s. class	21%
From top quarter	47%	From top half	82%
1998 freshmen returning in 1999	73%		

Application *Options:* eApply at www.CollegeQuest.com, Common Application, electronic application. *Application fee:* $25. *Required:* high school transcript. *Required for some:* essay or personal statement; interview.

Standardized tests *Admission: Required:* SAT I or ACT. *Recommended:* ACT.

Significant dates *Application deadlines:* 8/1 (freshmen), 8/1 (transfers). *Financial aid deadline priority date:* 3/31.

Freshman Application Contact
Ms. Jill Duncan, Associate Director of Admissions, Southwest Missouri State University, 901 South National, Springfield, MO 65804. **Phone:** 417-836-5517. **Toll-free phone:** 800-492-7900. **Fax:** 417-836-6334. **E-mail:** smsuinfo@mail.smsu.edu

Visit CollegeQuest.com for information on majors offered and athletics. College video available at CollegeQuest.com.

■ *See page 2520 for a narrative description.*

STEPHENS COLLEGE
Columbia, Missouri

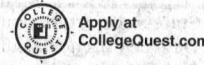

- **Independent**, comprehensive, founded 1833
- **Degrees** associate, bachelor's, and master's
- **Urban** 202-acre campus
- **Women** only, 734 undergraduate students, 62% full-time
- **Moderately difficult** entrance level, 84% of applicants were admitted
- **10:1** student-to-undergraduate faculty ratio
- **44% graduate** in 6 years or less
- **$15,770 tuition** and fees
- **$18.9 million endowment**

Students *Undergraduates:* 455 full-time, 279 part-time. Students come from 42 states and territories, 3 other countries. *The most frequently chosen baccalaureate fields are:* education, communications/communication technologies, visual/performing arts. *Graduate:* 54 in graduate degree programs.

Missouri

Stephens College (continued)
From out-of-state 71% Reside on campus 88%
Age 25 or older 9% Transferred in 4%

Faculty 45 full-time, 80% with terminal degrees.
Expenses (2000–2001) *Comprehensive fee:* $21,640 includes full-time tuition ($15,770) and room and board ($5870). Room and board charges vary according to board plan. *Payment plan:* installment. *Waivers:* employees or children of employees.
Library Hugh Stephens Library. *Operations spending 1999–2000:* $279,575. *Collection:* 123,535 titles, 395 serial subscriptions, 4,705 audiovisual materials.
College life *Housing:* on-campus residence required through senior year. *Option:* women-only. *Social organizations:* national sororities; 20% of eligible undergrads are members. *Most popular organizations:* Student Government Association, Martin Luther King Jr. Student Union, Stephens Ambassadors Association, Stephens Christian Fellowship, Young Women's Political Caucus.
Campus security 24-hour emergency response devices and patrols, student patrols, late-night transport-escort service, controlled dormitory access.
After graduation 113 organizations recruited on campus 1997–98. *Career center:* 1 full-time, 1 part-time personnel. Services include job fairs, resume preparation, interview workshops, career/interest testing, career counseling, careers library, job bank. *Graduate education:* 34% of class of 1999 went directly to graduate and professional school.
Freshmen 286 applied, 240 admitted, 134 enrolled.

Average high school GPA	3.31	SAT verbal scores above 500	82%
SAT math scores above 500	64%	ACT above 18	100%
From top 10% of their h.s. class	14%	From top quarter	40%
From top half	82%	1998 freshmen returning in 1999	64%

Application *Options:* eApply at www.CollegeQuest.com, Common Application, early admission, early decision, deferred entrance. *Application fee:* $25. *Required:* essay or personal statement; high school transcript; minimum 2.5 GPA; 1 letter of recommendation. *Required for some:* interview. *Recommended:* interview.
Standardized tests *Admission: Required:* SAT I or ACT.
Significant dates *Application deadlines:* 7/31 (freshmen), 7/31 (transfers). *Early decision:* 12/15. *Notification:* continuous until 8/15 (freshmen), 1/20 (early decision). *Financial aid deadline priority date:* 3/15.
Freshman Application Contact
Ms. Margaret Herron, Associate Dean of Enrollment Services, Stephens College, Box 2121, Columbia, MO 65215-0002. **Phone:** 573-876-7207. **Toll-free phone:** 800-876-7207. **Fax:** 573-876-7237. **E-mail:** apply@sc.stephens.edu
Visit CollegeQuest.com for information on majors offered and athletics.

■ *See page 2570 for a narrative description.*

TRUMAN STATE UNIVERSITY
Kirksville, Missouri

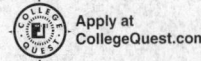
Apply at CollegeQuest.com

- **State-supported**, comprehensive, founded 1867
- **Degrees** bachelor's and master's
- **Small-town** 140-acre campus
- **Coed**, 5,847 undergraduate students, 98% full-time, 58% women, 42% men
- **Moderately difficult** entrance level, 81% of applicants were admitted
- **16:1 student-to-undergraduate faculty ratio**
- **63.7% graduate** in 6 years or less
- **$3562 tuition** and fees (in-state); $6362 (out-of-state)
- **$5200 average financial aid** package, $15,357 average indebtedness upon graduation, $12.5 million endowment

Students *Undergraduates:* 5,727 full-time, 120 part-time. Students come from 43 states and territories, 51 other countries. *The most frequently chosen baccalaureate fields are:* biological/life sciences, business/marketing, English. *Graduate:* 273 in graduate degree programs.

From out-of-state 28% Reside on campus 45%
Age 25 or older 2% Transferred in 2%
International students 3% African Americans 3%
Asian Americans/Pacific Islanders 2% Hispanic Americans 2%
Native Americans 0.2%

Faculty 396 (92% full-time).
Expenses (1999–2000) *Tuition, state resident:* full-time $3544. *Tuition, nonresident:* full-time $6344. *Required fees:* full-time $18. Part-time tuition and fees vary according to course load. *College room and board:* $4400. Room and board charges vary according to board plan and housing facility. *Payment plan:* installment. *Waivers:* senior citizens and employees or children of employees.
Library Pickler Memorial Library plus 1 other. *Operations spending 1999–2000:* $3.2 million. *Collection:* 398,749 titles, 3,541 serial subscriptions, 32,225 audiovisual materials.
College life *Housing:* on-campus residence required in freshman year. *Options:* coed, women-only. *Social organizations:* national fraternities, national sororities, local sororities; 30% of eligible men and 21% of eligible women are members. *Most popular organizations:* Campus Christian Fellowship, Alpha Phi Omega, student ambassadors, Phi Sigma Pi, Alpha Gamma Sigma.
Campus security 24-hour emergency response devices and patrols, student patrols, late-night transport-escort service, patrols by commissioned officers.
After graduation 220 organizations recruited on campus 1997–98. 58% of class of 1998 had job offers within 6 months. *Career center:* 4 full-time, 22 part-time personnel. Services include job fairs, resume preparation, resume referral, career counseling, careers library, job bank, job interviews.
Freshmen 5,159 applied, 4,166 admitted, 1,457 enrolled. 18 National Merit Scholars, 115 class presidents, 137 valedictorians, 210 student government officers.

Average high school GPA	3.72	SAT verbal scores above 500	93%
SAT math scores above 500	93%	ACT above 18	100%
From top 10% of their h.s. class	45%	From top quarter	81%
From top half	99%	1998 freshmen returning in 1999	84%

Application *Options:* eApply at www.CollegeQuest.com, electronic application, early admission, early action, deferred entrance. *Preference* given to state residents. *Application fee:* $0. *Required:* essay or personal statement; high school transcript. *Recommended:* minimum 3.0 GPA; interview.
Standardized tests *Admission: Required:* SAT I or ACT. *Recommended:* ACT.
Significant dates *Application deadlines:* 3/1 (freshmen), 4/1 (transfers). *Early action:* 11/15. *Notification:* 12/20 (early action). *Financial aid deadline priority date:* 4/1.
Freshman Application Contact
Mr. Brad Chambers, Co-Director of Admissions, Truman State University, 205 McClain Hall, Kirksville, MO 63501-4221. **Phone:** 660-785-4114. **Toll-free phone:** 800-892-7792. **Fax:** 660-785-7456. **E-mail:** admissions@truman.edu
Visit CollegeQuest.com for information on majors offered and athletics. Electronic viewbook available at CollegeQuest.com.

UNIVERSITY OF MISSOURI—COLUMBIA
Columbia, Missouri

- **State-supported**, university, founded 1839
- **Degrees** bachelor's, master's, doctoral, and first professional
- **Small-town** 1,348-acre campus
- **Coed**, 17,517 undergraduate students, 94% full-time, 53% women, 47% men
- **Moderately difficult** entrance level, 90% of applicants were admitted
- **16:1 student-to-undergraduate faculty ratio**
- **60.3% graduate** in 6 years or less
- **$4581 tuition** and fees (in-state); $12,495 (out-of-state)
- **$6159 average financial aid** package, $16,161 average indebtedness upon graduation, $331.3 million endowment

Part of University of Missouri System.
Students *Undergraduates:* 16,522 full-time, 995 part-time. Students come from 50 states and territories, 90 other countries. *The most frequently chosen baccalaureate fields are:* business/marketing, communications/communication

technologies, education. *Graduate:* 1,148 in professional programs, 3,971 in other graduate degree programs.

From out-of-state	12%	Reside on campus	47%
Age 25 or older	19%	Transferred in	6%
International students	2%	African Americans	6%
Asian Americans/Pacific Islanders	2%	Hispanic Americans	1%
Native Americans	0.5%		

Faculty 1,741 (96% full-time), 86% with terminal degrees.

Expenses (1999–2000) *Tuition, state resident:* full-time $3978; part-time $133 per credit hour. *Tuition, nonresident:* full-time $11,892; part-time $396 per credit hour. *Required fees:* full-time $603; $18 per credit hour. *College room and board:* $4545. Room and board charges vary according to board plan and housing facility. *Payment plan:* installment. *Waivers:* employees or children of employees.

Library Ellis Library plus 11 others. *Operations spending 1999–2000:* $12.9 million. *Collection:* 2.9 million titles, 23,522 serial subscriptions, 16,472 audiovisual materials.

College life *Housing:* on-campus residence required in freshman year. *Options:* coed, men-only, women-only, disabled students. *Social organizations:* national fraternities, national sororities; 23% of eligible men and 25% of eligible women are members. *Most popular organizations:* Missouri Students Association, Residence Hall Association, Honors International Organization.

Campus security 24-hour emergency response devices and patrols, late-night transport-escort service, controlled dormitory access.

After graduation 665 organizations recruited on campus 1997–98. *Career center:* 5 full-time personnel. Services include resume preparation, career counseling, careers library, job bank, job interviews.

Freshmen 9,091 applied, 8,143 admitted, 3,932 enrolled. 33 National Merit Scholars, 133 valedictorians.

SAT verbal scores above 500	N/R	SAT math scores above 500	N/R
ACT above 18	100%	From top 10% of their h.s. class	31%
From top quarter	62%	From top half	90%
1998 freshmen returning in 1999	84%		

Application *Option:* deferred entrance. *Application fee:* $25. *Required:* high school transcript.

Standardized tests *Admission:* Required: ACT.

Significant dates *Application deadlines:* rolling (freshmen), rolling (transfers). *Financial aid deadline priority date:* 3/1.

Freshman Application Contact
Ms. Georgeanne Porter, Director of Undergraduate Admissions, University of Missouri–Columbia, 225 Jesse Hall, Columbia, MO 65211. **Phone:** 573-882-7786. **Toll-free phone:** 800-225-6075. **Fax:** 573-882-7887. **E-mail:** mu4u@missouri.edu

Visit CollegeQuest.com for information on majors offered and athletics. College video available at CollegeQuest.com.

UNIVERSITY OF MISSOURI–KANSAS CITY
Kansas City, Missouri

- **State-supported**, university, founded 1929
- **Degrees** bachelor's, master's, doctoral, first professional, and first professional certificates
- **Urban** 191-acre campus
- **Coed**, 5,400 undergraduate students, 72% full-time, 58% women, 42% men
- **Moderately difficult** entrance level, 68% of applicants were admitted
- **8:1 student-to-undergraduate faculty ratio**
- **$3852 tuition** and fees (in-state); $10,387 (out-of-state)
- **$11,920 average financial aid** package, $22,127 average indebtedness upon graduation, $193.7 million endowment

Part of University of Missouri System.

Students *Undergraduates:* 3,879 full-time, 1,521 part-time. Students come from 43 states and territories, 66 other countries. *The most frequently chosen baccalaureate fields are:* biological/life sciences, business/marketing, liberal arts/general studies. *Graduate:* 1,362 in professional programs, 3,366 in other graduate degree programs.

From out-of-state	20%	Reside on campus	5%
Age 25 or older	30%	International students	4%
African Americans	12%	Asian Americans/Pacific Islanders	7%
Hispanic Americans	4%	Native Americans	1%

Faculty 895 (64% full-time).

Expenses (2000–2001) *Tuition, state resident:* full-time $3822; part-time $137 per credit hour. *Tuition, nonresident:* full-time $10,357; part-time $409 per credit hour. *Required fees:* full-time $30; $22 per credit hour; $30 per term part-time. Full-time tuition and fees vary according to student level. Part-time tuition and fees vary according to student level. Room and board charges vary according to board plan and housing facility. *Waivers:* employees or children of employees.

Library Miller-Nichols Library plus 3 others. *Operations spending 1999–2000:* $7 million. *Collection:* 1.4 million titles, 12,472 serial subscriptions, 363,933 audiovisual materials.

College life *Housing:* Option: coed. *Social organizations:* national fraternities, national sororities, local sororities; 18% of eligible men and 18% of eligible women are members. *Most popular organizations:* African-American Student Association, International Student Council, Greek system, Alpha Phi Omega, Activities and Programs Council.

Campus security 24-hour emergency response devices and patrols, late-night transport-escort service, controlled dormitory access.

After graduation 390 organizations recruited on campus 1997–98. 85% of class of 1998 had job offers within 6 months. *Career center:* 7 full-time, 15 part-time personnel. Services include job fairs, resume preparation, resume referral, career counseling, careers library, job bank, job interviews.

Freshmen 2,583 applied, 1,767 admitted, 688 enrolled.

SAT verbal scores above 500	N/R	SAT math scores above 500	N/R
ACT above 18	98%	From top 10% of their h.s. class	37%
From top quarter	63%	From top half	89%
1998 freshmen returning in 1999	73%		

Application *Options:* early admission, deferred entrance. *Application fee:* $25. *Required:* high school transcript.

Standardized tests *Admission:* Required: ACT.

Significant dates *Application deadlines:* rolling (freshmen), rolling (transfers). *Financial aid deadline priority date:* 3/15.

Freshman Application Contact
Mr. Melvin C. Tyler, Director of Admissions, University of Missouri–Kansas City, 5100 Rockhill Road, Kansas City, MO 64110-2499. **Phone:** 816-235-1111. **Fax:** 816-235-1717. **E-mail:** admit@umkc.edu

Visit CollegeQuest.com for information on majors offered and athletics.

■ *See page 2774 for a narrative description.*

UNIVERSITY OF MISSOURI–ROLLA
Rolla, Missouri

- **State-supported**, university, founded 1870
- **Degrees** bachelor's, master's, and doctoral
- **Small-town** 284-acre campus
- **Coed**, 3,811 undergraduate students, 89% full-time, 23% women, 77% men
- **Very difficult** entrance level, 89% of applicants were admitted
- **55% graduate** in 6 years or less
- **$4665 tuition** and fees (in-state); $12,579 (out-of-state)
- **$8067 average financial aid** package, $15,000 average indebtedness upon graduation, $49.1 million endowment

University of Missouri–Rolla educates students in engineering, science, and the liberal arts. This internationally known research institution offers a 13:1 student-faculty ratio, small class sizes, and an active student body. With high-quality instruction, a dedicated faculty, and top laboratories, the University of Missouri–Rolla educates tomorrow's leaders.

Part of University of Missouri System.

Students *Undergraduates:* 3,409 full-time, 402 part-time. Students come from 46 states and territories, 35 other countries. *The most frequently chosen baccalaureate fields are:* computer/information sciences, engineering/engineering technologies, physical sciences. *Graduate:* 833 in graduate degree programs.

Missouri

University of Missouri–Rolla (continued)

From out-of-state	25%	Reside on campus	56%
Age 25 or older	9%	Transferred in	6%
International students	4%	African Americans	4%
Asian Americans/Pacific Islanders	3%	Hispanic Americans	1%
Native Americans	1%		

Faculty 399 (84% full-time), 84% with terminal degrees.
Expenses (1999–2000) *Tuition, state resident:* full-time $3978; part-time $133 per credit hour. *Tuition, nonresident:* full-time $11,892; part-time $396 per credit hour. *Required fees:* full-time $687; $24 per credit hour; $60 per term part-time. Full-time tuition and fees vary according to course load and program. Part-time tuition and fees vary according to course load and program. *College room and board:* $4557; room only: $2670. Room and board charges vary according to board plan and housing facility. *Payment plan:* installment. *Waivers:* minority students, children of alumni, and employees or children of employees.
Library Curtis Laws Wilson Library. *Operations spending 1999–2000:* $2.2 million. *Collection:* 195,089 titles, 5,880 serial subscriptions, 79,691 audiovisual materials.
College life *Housing:* on-campus residence required through sophomore year. *Options:* coed, men-only, women-only. *Social organizations:* national fraternities, national sororities, local sororities; 28% of eligible men and 22% of eligible women are members. *Most popular organizations:* student government, service organizations, academic organizations.
Campus security 24-hour emergency response devices and patrols, student patrols, late-night transport-escort service, controlled dormitory access, crime prevention programs.
After graduation 542 organizations recruited on campus 1997–98. 79% of class of 1998 had job offers within 6 months. *Career center:* 7 full-time, 1 part-time personnel. Services include job fairs, resume preparation, resume referral, career counseling, careers library, job bank, job interviews. *Graduate education:* 16% of class of 1999 went directly to graduate and professional school.
Freshmen 1,699 applied, 1,508 admitted, 688 enrolled.

Average high school GPA	3.5	SAT verbal scores above 500	92%
SAT math scores above 500	99%	ACT above 18	100%
From top 10% of their h.s. class	48%	From top quarter	77%
From top half	96%	1998 freshmen returning in 1999	84%

Application *Options:* Common Application, electronic application, early admission, deferred entrance. *Application fee:* $25. *Required:* high school transcript.
Standardized tests *Admission: Required:* SAT I or ACT.
Significant dates *Application deadlines:* 6/1 (freshmen), rolling (transfers). *Financial aid deadline priority date:* 3/1.
Freshman Application Contact
Ms. Martina Hahn, Director of Admission and Student Financial Assistance, University of Missouri–Rolla, 102 Parker Hall, Rolla, MO 65409. **Phone:** 573-341-4164. **Toll-free phone:** 800-522-0938. **E-mail:** umrolla@umr.edu
Visit CollegeQuest.com for information on majors offered and athletics. College video and electronic viewbook available at CollegeQuest.com.

■ *See page 2776 for a narrative description.*

UNIVERSITY OF MISSOURI–ST. LOUIS
St. Louis, Missouri

■ **State-supported**, university, founded 1963
■ **Degrees** bachelor's, master's, doctoral, and first professional
■ **Suburban** 250-acre campus
■ **Coed**, 9,118 undergraduate students, 57% full-time, 58% women, 42% men
■ **Moderately difficult** entrance level, 78% of applicants were admitted
■ **14:1 student-to-undergraduate faculty ratio**
■ **29% graduate** in 6 years or less
■ **$4798 tuition** and fees (in-state); $12,712 (out-of-state)
■ **$31.2 million endowment**

Part of University of Missouri System.
Students *Undergraduates:* 5,218 full-time, 3,900 part-time. Students come from 46 states and territories, 50 other countries. *The most frequently chosen baccalaureate fields are:* business/marketing, education, social sciences and history. *Graduate:* 173 in professional programs, 2,435 in other graduate degree programs.

From out-of-state	4%	Reside on campus	7%
Age 25 or older	36%	Transferred in	20%
International students	2%	African Americans	14%
Asian Americans/Pacific Islanders	3%	Hispanic Americans	1%
Native Americans	0.3%		

Faculty 966 (52% full-time), 51% with terminal degrees.
Expenses (1999–2000) *Tuition, state resident:* full-time $3978; part-time $133 per credit hour. *Tuition, nonresident:* full-time $11,892; part-time $396 per credit hour. *Required fees:* full-time $820; $32 per credit hour. Part-time tuition and fees vary according to course load. *College room and board:* $4500; room only: $2900. Room and board charges vary according to board plan and housing facility. *Payment plan:* installment. *Waivers:* employees or children of employees.
Library Thomas Jefferson Library plus 3 others. *Operations spending 1999–2000:* $4.2 million. *Collection:* 1 million titles, 3,922 serial subscriptions, 3,602 audiovisual materials.
College life *Housing: Options:* coed, women-only. *Social organizations:* national fraternities, national sororities, local sororities; 1% of eligible men and 1% of eligible women are members. *Most popular organizations:* Student Government Association, Associated Black Collegians, Pierre laclede Honors College Student Association, Residence Hall Council, International Student Association.
Campus security 24-hour emergency response devices and patrols, late-night transport-escort service, controlled dormitory access.
After graduation 268 organizations recruited on campus 1997–98. 95% of class of 1998 had job offers within 6 months. *Career center:* 9 full-time, 4 part-time personnel. Services include job fairs, resume preparation, interview workshops, resume referral, career/interest testing, career counseling, careers library, job bank, job interviews, online resume, listing service.
Freshmen 1,826 applied, 1,428 admitted, 655 enrolled.

SAT verbal scores above 500	N/R	SAT math scores above 500	N/R
ACT above 18	97%	From top 10% of their h.s. class	18%
From top quarter	43%	From top half	78%
1998 freshmen returning in 1999	58%		

Application *Options:* electronic application, early admission. *Application fee:* $25. *Required:* high school transcript.
Standardized tests *Admission: Required:* SAT I or ACT.
Significant dates *Application deadlines:* rolling (freshmen), rolling (transfers). *Financial aid deadline priority date:* 4/1.
Freshman Application Contact
Mr. Curtis C. Coonrod, Director of Admissions, University of Missouri–St. Louis, Woods Hall, St. Louis, MO 63121-4499. **Phone:** 314-516-5460. **Fax:** 314-516-5310. **E-mail:** curt_coonrod@umsl.edu
Visit CollegeQuest.com for information on majors offered and athletics. Electronic viewbook available at CollegeQuest.com.

■ *See page 2778 for a narrative description.*

WASHINGTON UNIVERSITY IN ST. LOUIS
St. Louis, Missouri

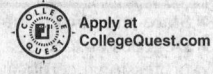
Apply at CollegeQuest.com

■ **Independent**, university, founded 1853
■ **Degrees** bachelor's, master's, doctoral, first professional, and postbachelor's certificates
■ **Suburban** 169-acre campus
■ **Coed**, 5,993 undergraduate students, 95% full-time, 50% women, 50% men
■ **Very difficult** entrance level, 34% of applicants were admitted
■ **7:1 student-to-undergraduate faculty ratio**
■ **86% graduate** in 6 years or less
■ **$24,745 tuition** and fees
■ **$20,682 average financial aid** package, $3.9 billion endowment

Students *Undergraduates:* 5,664 full-time, 329 part-time. Students come from 52 states and territories, 86 other countries. *The most frequently chosen baccalaureate fields are:* engineering/engineering technologies, business/marketing, social sciences and history. *Graduate:* 1,057 in professional

Missouri

programs, 4,522 in other graduate degree programs.

From out-of-state	87%	Reside on campus	77%
Age 25 or older	1%	Transferred in	3%
International students	5%	African Americans	7%
Asian Americans/Pacific Islanders	11%	Hispanic Americans	2%
Native Americans	0.2%		

Faculty 1,197 (62% full-time).

Expenses (2000–2001) *Comprehensive fee:* $32,469 includes full-time tuition ($24,500), mandatory fees ($245), and room and board ($7724). *College room only:* $4602. Room and board charges vary according to board plan and housing facility. Part-time tuition and fees vary according to class time. *Payment plans:* tuition prepayment, installment. *Waivers:* employees or children of employees.

Library John M. Olin Library plus 13 others. *Operations spending 1999-2000:* $19.3 million. *Collection:* 1.4 million titles, 20,278 serial subscriptions, 41,929 audiovisual materials.

College life *Housing:* on-campus residence required in freshman year. *Options:* coed, men-only, women-only. *Social organizations:* national fraternities, national sororities; 22% of eligible men and 21% of eligible women are members. *Most popular organizations:* Campus Y, multicultural organizations, Student Publications Media, student government, performing arts groups.

Campus security 24-hour emergency response devices and patrols, student patrols, late-night transport-escort service, controlled dormitory access.

After graduation 280 organizations recruited on campus 1997–98. 65% of class of 1998 had job offers within 6 months. *Career center:* 18 full-time, 6 part-time personnel. Services include job fairs, resume preparation, interview workshops, resume referral, career/interest testing, career counseling, careers library, job bank, job interviews.

Freshmen 17,109 applied, 5,806 admitted, 1,384 enrolled. 157 National Merit Scholars, 23 class presidents, 138 valedictorians, 195 student government officers.

SAT verbal scores above 500	98%	SAT math scores above 500	100%
ACT above 18	100%	From top 10% of their h.s. class	79%
From top quarter	97%	From top half	100%
1998 freshmen returning in 1999	96%		

Application *Options:* eApply at www.CollegeQuest.com, Common Application, electronic application, early admission, early decision, deferred entrance. *Application fee:* $55. *Required:* essay or personal statement; high school transcript; 2 letters of recommendation. *Recommended:* minimum 3.0 GPA; portfolio for art and architecture programs.

Standardized tests *Admission: Required:* SAT I or ACT.

Significant dates *Application deadlines:* 1/15 (freshmen), 4/15 (transfers). *Early decision:* 11/15 (for plan 1), 1/1 (for plan 2). *Notification:* 4/1 (freshmen), 12/15 (early decision plan 1), 1/15 (early decision plan 2). *Financial aid deadline:* 2/15.

Freshman Application Contact
Ms. Nanette Tarbouni, Director of Admissions, Washington University in St. Louis, Campus Box 1089, 1 Brookings Drive, St. Louis, MO 63130-4899. **Phone:** 314-935-6000. **Toll-free phone:** 800-638-0700. **Fax:** 314-935-4290. **E-mail:** admissions@wustl.edu

Visit CollegeQuest.com for information on majors offered and athletics. College video available at CollegeQuest.com.

■ *See page 2920 for a narrative description.*

WEBSTER UNIVERSITY
St. Louis, Missouri

- **Independent**, comprehensive, founded 1915
- **Degrees** bachelor's, master's, and doctoral
- **Suburban** 47-acre campus
- **Coed**, 3,341 undergraduate students, 64% full-time, 63% women, 37% men
- **Moderately difficult** entrance level, 62% of applicants were admitted
- **15:1** student-to-undergraduate faculty ratio
- **$12,450 tuition** and fees
- **$12,709 average financial aid** package, $31.8 million endowment

Students *Undergraduates:* 2,126 full-time, 1,215 part-time. Students come from 45 states and territories, 34 other countries. *The most frequently chosen baccalaureate fields are:* business/marketing, communications/communication technologies, health professions and related sciences. *Graduate:* 9,337 in graduate degree programs.

From out-of-state	17%	Reside on campus	25%
Age 25 or older	41%	Transferred in	13%
International students	2%	African Americans	10%
Asian Americans/Pacific Islanders	1%	Hispanic Americans	2%
Native Americans	0.4%		

Faculty 1,280 (11% full-time), 97% with terminal degrees.

Expenses (1999–2000) *Comprehensive fee:* $17,890 includes full-time tuition ($12,150), mandatory fees ($300), and room and board ($5440). Full-time tuition and fees vary according to program. Room and board charges vary according to board plan and housing facility. *Part-time tuition:* $368 per credit hour. Part-time tuition and fees vary according to location. *Payment plan:* installment. *Waivers:* employees or children of employees.

Library Eden-Webster Library. *Operations spending 1999–2000:* $2.1 million. *Collection:* 156,523 titles, 3,880 serial subscriptions, 7,389 audiovisual materials.

College life *Housing:* on-campus residence required in freshman year. *Option:* coed. *Most popular organizations:* Student Government Association, Student Activities Council, Thai Students Association, International Student Association, Women in Media.

Campus security 24-hour emergency response devices and patrols, student patrols, late-night transport-escort service.

After graduation 56 organizations recruited on campus 1997–98. 89% of class of 1998 had job offers within 6 months. *Career center:* 4 full-time personnel. Services include job fairs, resume preparation, interview workshops, resume referral, career/interest testing, career counseling, careers library, job bank, job interviews.

Freshmen 990 applied, 616 admitted, 404 enrolled. 2 National Merit Scholars, 20 class presidents, 8 valedictorians, 58 student government officers.

Average high school GPA	3.4	SAT verbal scores above 500	84%
SAT math scores above 500	73%	ACT above 18	N/R
From top 10% of their h.s. class	30%	From top quarter	58%
From top half	85%	1998 freshmen returning in 1999	81%

Application *Options:* eApply at www.CollegeQuest.com, Common Application, electronic application, early admission, deferred entrance. *Application fee:* $25. *Required:* essay or personal statement; high school transcript; minimum 2.5 GPA; 1 letter of recommendation. *Required for some:* audition. *Recommended:* minimum 3.0 GPA; interview.

Standardized tests *Admission: Required:* SAT I or ACT.

Significant dates *Application deadlines:* 3/1 (freshmen), 8/1 (transfers). *Financial aid deadline priority date:* 4/1.

Freshman Application Contact
Mr. Andrew Laue, Associate Director of Undergraduate Admission, Webster University, 470 East Lockwood Avenue, St. Louis, MO 63119-3194. **Phone:** 314-961-2660 Ext. 7012. **Toll-free phone:** 800-75-ENROL. **Fax:** 314-968-7115. **E-mail:** admit@webster.edu

Visit CollegeQuest.com for information on majors offered and athletics. College video available at CollegeQuest.com.

■ *See page 2928 for a narrative description.*

WESTMINSTER COLLEGE
Fulton, Missouri

- **Independent**, 4-year, founded 1851, affiliated with Presbyterian Church
- **Degree** bachelor's
- **Small-town** 65-acre campus
- **Coed**, 686 undergraduate students, 99% full-time, 42% women, 58% men
- **Moderately difficult** entrance level, 81% of applicants were admitted
- **12:1** student-to-undergraduate faculty ratio
- **48% graduate** in 6 years or less
- **$14,070 tuition** and fees
- **$12,400 average financial aid** package, $12,600 average indebtedness upon graduation, $40.4 million endowment

Students *Undergraduates:* 679 full-time, 7 part-time. Students come from 19 states and territories, 14 other countries. *The most frequently chosen baccalaureate fields are:* business/marketing, psychology, social sciences

Missouri

Westminster College (continued)
and history.

From out-of-state	33%	Reside on campus	80%
Age 25 or older	1%	Transferred in	5%
International students	3%	African Americans	2%
Asian Americans/Pacific Islanders	1%	Hispanic Americans	2%
Native Americans	1%		

Faculty 79 (62% full-time), 61% with terminal degrees.

Expenses (1999–2000) *Comprehensive fee:* $18,950 includes full-time tuition ($13,490), mandatory fees ($580), and room and board ($4880). *College room only:* $2460. Full-time tuition and fees vary according to course load. Room and board charges vary according to housing facility and student level. *Part-time tuition:* $562 per credit hour. *Part-time fees:* $120 per term part-time. Part-time tuition and fees vary according to course load. *Payment plan:* installment. *Waivers:* employees or children of employees.

Library Reeves Memorial Library plus 1 other. *Operations spending 1999–2000:* $200,757. *Collection:* 87,715 titles, 489 serial subscriptions.

College life *Housing:* on-campus residence required through junior year. *Options:* coed, women-only. *Social organizations:* national fraternities, national sororities; 72% of eligible men and 68% of eligible women are members. *Most popular organizations:* Student Government Association, Environmentally Concerned Students, International Student Club.

Campus security 24-hour emergency response devices and patrols, late-night transport-escort service, controlled dormitory access, self-defense education, well-lit campus.

After graduation 45 organizations recruited on campus 1997–98. 75% of class of 1998 had job offers within 6 months. *Career center:* 3 full-time personnel. Services include job fairs, resume preparation, resume referral, career/interest testing, career counseling, careers library, job interviews.

Freshmen 822 applied, 666 admitted, 201 enrolled.

Average high school GPA	3.31	SAT verbal scores above 500	82%
SAT math scores above 500	84%	ACT above 18	98%
From top 10% of their h.s. class	22%	From top quarter	49%
From top half	90%	1998 freshmen returning in 1999	67%

Application *Options:* eApply at www.CollegeQuest.com, Common Application, electronic application, early admission, deferred entrance. *Application fee:* $25. *Required:* essay or personal statement; high school transcript; 1 letter of recommendation. *Required for some:* interview.

Standardized tests *Admission: Required:* SAT I or ACT.

Significant dates *Application deadlines:* rolling (freshmen), rolling (transfers). *Financial aid deadline priority date:* 2/28.

Freshman Application Contact
Dr. Patrick Kirby, Dean of Enrollment Services, Westminster College, 501 Westminster Avenue, Fulton, MO 65251-1299. **Phone:** 573-592-5251. **Toll-free phone:** 800-475-3361. **Fax:** 573-592-5227. **E-mail:** admissions@jaynet.wcmo.edu

Visit CollegeQuest.com for information on majors offered and athletics. College video and electronic viewbook available at CollegeQuest.com.

■ *See page 2962 for a narrative description.*

WILLIAM JEWELL COLLEGE
Liberty, Missouri

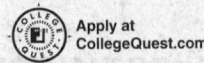
Apply at CollegeQuest.com

- **Independent Baptist**, 4-year, founded 1849
- **Degree** bachelor's (also offers evening program with significant enrollment not reflected in profile)
- **Small-town** 149-acre campus with easy access to Kansas City
- **Coed**, 1,116 undergraduate students, 97% full-time, 58% women, 42% men
- **Moderately difficult** entrance level, 86% of applicants were admitted
- **10:1** student-to-undergraduate faculty ratio
- **57% graduate** in 6 years or less
- **$13,020 tuition** and fees
- **$17,908 average indebtedness** upon graduation, $80.3 million endowment

The Oxbridge Honors Program, a program of tutorials and examinations through which a small number of academically outstanding students may pursue their areas of concentration, is available at William Jewell College. As its name implies, it is an American adaptation of the educational method of the great English universities, Oxford and Cambridge.

Students *Undergraduates:* 1,088 full-time, 28 part-time. Students come from 32 states and territories, 12 other countries. *The most frequently chosen baccalaureate fields are:* business/marketing, education, psychology.

From out-of-state	23%	Reside on campus	70%
Age 25 or older	3%	Transferred in	6%
International students	2%	African Americans	3%
Asian Americans/Pacific Islanders	1%	Hispanic Americans	2%
Native Americans	0.4%		

Faculty 141 (60% full-time), 54% with terminal degrees.

Expenses (1999–2000) *Comprehensive fee:* $17,030 includes full-time tuition ($13,020) and room and board ($4010). Full-time tuition and fees vary according to class time and course load. Room and board charges vary according to board plan and housing facility. *Part-time tuition:* $525 per semester hour. Part-time tuition and fees vary according to class time. *Payment plans:* tuition prepayment, installment. *Waivers:* senior citizens and employees or children of employees.

Library Charles F. Curry Library plus 1 other. *Operations spending 1999–2000:* $919,013. *Collection:* 248,310 titles, 899 serial subscriptions, 26,334 audiovisual materials.

College life *Housing:* on-campus residence required through junior year. *Options:* coed, men-only, women-only. *Social organizations:* national fraternities, national sororities; 43% of eligible men and 34% of eligible women are members. *Most popular organizations:* Christian Student Ministries, college union activities, Fellowship of Christian Athletes, Alpha Omega, Earth Rocks.

Campus security 24-hour emergency response devices and patrols, late-night transport-escort service, controlled dormitory access.

After graduation 119 organizations recruited on campus 1997–98. 80% of class of 1998 had job offers within 6 months. *Career center:* 2 full-time, 1 part-time personnel. Services include job fairs, resume preparation, interview workshops, resume referral, career counseling, careers library, job bank, job interviews, career courses. *Graduate education:* 19% of class of 1999 went directly to graduate and professional school: 10% graduate arts and sciences, 4% medicine, 3% business, 3% law.

Freshmen 739 applied, 634 admitted, 285 enrolled. 24 valedictorians.

Average high school GPA	3.59	SAT verbal scores above 500	76%
SAT math scores above 500	66%	ACT above 18	98%
From top 10% of their h.s. class	31%	From top quarter	65%
From top half	91%	1998 freshmen returning in 1999	77%

Application *Options:* eApply at www.CollegeQuest.com, Common Application, electronic application, early admission, early action, deferred entrance. *Application fee:* $25. *Required:* high school transcript; minimum 2.0 GPA. *Recommended:* essay or personal statement; minimum 2.5 GPA; 2 letters of recommendation; interview.

Standardized tests *Admission: Required:* SAT I or ACT. *Recommended:* ACT.

Significant dates *Application deadlines:* 3/15 (freshmen), rolling (transfers). *Early action:* 11/15. *Notification:* 12/1 (early action). *Financial aid deadline priority date:* 3/1.

Freshman Application Contact
Mr. Chad Jolly, Dean of Enrollment Development, William Jewell College, 500 College Hill, Liberty, MO 64068-1843. **Phone:** 816-781-7700. **Toll-free phone:** 800-753-7009. **Fax:** 816-415-5027. **E-mail:** admission@william.jewell.edu

Visit CollegeQuest.com for information on majors offered and athletics.

■ *See page 2998 for a narrative description.*

WILLIAM WOODS UNIVERSITY
Fulton, Missouri

- **Independent**, comprehensive, founded 1870, affiliated with Christian Church (Disciples of Christ)
- **Degrees** associate, bachelor's, and master's
- **Small-town** 170-acre campus with easy access to St. Louis
- **Coed**, 790 undergraduate students, 90% full-time, 75% women, 25% men
- **Moderately difficult** entrance level, 82% of applicants were admitted
- **54% graduate** in 6 years or less
- **$13,050 tuition** and fees

- $11.4 million endowment

Students *Undergraduates:* 714 full-time, 76 part-time. Students come from 35 states and territories. *Graduate:* 412 in graduate degree programs.

Reside on campus	80%	Age 25 or older	40%
Transferred in	6%	African Americans	3%
Asian Americans/Pacific Islanders	7%	Hispanic Americans	2%
Native Americans	1%		

Expenses (1999–2000) *Comprehensive fee:* $18,450 includes full-time tuition ($12,900), mandatory fees ($150), and room and board ($5400). *College room only:* $2640. Full-time tuition and fees vary according to program. *Part-time tuition:* $225 per credit hour. *Part-time fees:* $15 per term part-time. *Payment plan:* installment. *Waivers:* employees or children of employees.

Library Dulany Library. *Operations spending 1999–2000:* $366,677. *Collection:* 93,917 titles, 26,773 audiovisual materials.

College life *Housing:* on-campus residence required through senior year. *Options:* coed, men-only, women-only. *Social organizations:* national sororities; 40% of women are members. *Most popular organizations:* Campus Government Association, Panhellenic Council, Paddock club, Little Brother/Little Sister, Leader Scholars.

Campus security 24-hour patrols, late-night transport-escort service, controlled dormitory access.

After graduation 60 organizations recruited on campus 1997–98. 85% of class of 1998 had job offers within 6 months. *Career center:* 1 full-time personnel. Services include job fairs, resume preparation, interview workshops, resume referral, career/interest testing, career counseling, careers library, job bank, job interviews. *Graduate education:* 15% of class of 1999 went directly to graduate and professional school.

Freshmen 499 applied, 410 admitted, 130 enrolled. 16 class presidents, 2 valedictorians, 100 student government officers.

Average high school GPA	3.2	SAT verbal scores above 500	52%
SAT math scores above 500	40%	ACT above 18	89%
From top 10% of their h.s. class	12%	From top quarter	35%
From top half	75%	1998 freshmen returning in 1999	70%

Application *Options:* electronic application, early admission, deferred entrance. *Application fee:* $25. *Required:* high school transcript; 2 letters of recommendation. *Required for some:* essay or personal statement. *Recommended:* interview.

Standardized tests *Admission: Required:* SAT I or ACT.

Significant dates *Application deadlines:* rolling (freshmen), rolling (transfers). *Financial aid deadline:* 9/1. *Priority date:* 3/1.

Freshman Application Contact
Ms. Mary Hawk, Dean of Admission, William Woods University, 200 West 12th Street, Fulton, MO 65251. **Phone:** 573-592-4221 Ext. 4220. **Toll-free phone:** 800-995-3159 Ext. 4221. **Fax:** 573-592-1146. **E-mail:** mhawk@iris.wmwoods.edu

Visit CollegeQuest.com for information on majors offered and athletics.

- *See page 3004 for a narrative description.*

MONTANA

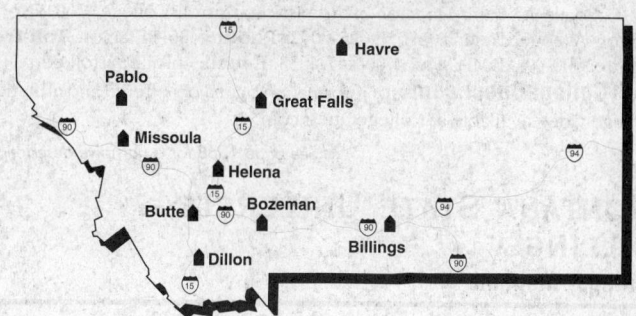

CARROLL COLLEGE
Helena, Montana

- **Independent Roman Catholic**, 4-year, founded 1909
- **Degrees** associate and bachelor's
- **Small-town** 64-acre campus
- **Coed**, 1,063 undergraduate students, 94% full-time, 58% women, 42% men
- **Moderately difficult** entrance level, 91% of applicants were admitted
- **12:1** student-to-undergraduate faculty ratio
- **43% graduate** in 6 years or less
- **$11,778 tuition** and fees
- **$11,670 average financial aid** package, $20 million endowment

Students *Undergraduates:* 1,002 full-time, 61 part-time. Students come from 28 states and territories, 10 other countries.

From out-of-state	29%	Reside on campus	44%
Age 25 or older	17%	Transferred in	8%
International students	3%	Asian Americans/Pacific Islanders	1%
Hispanic Americans	2%	Native Americans	1%

Faculty 128 (60% full-time).

Expenses (1999–2000) *Comprehensive fee:* $16,494 includes full-time tuition ($11,778) and room and board ($4716). Room and board charges vary according to board plan, housing facility, and student level. *Part-time tuition:* $393 per semester hour. *Payment plan:* installment. *Waivers:* senior citizens and employees or children of employees.

Library Corette Library plus 1 other. *Operations spending 1999–2000:* $355,521. *Collection:* 86,889 titles, 607 serial subscriptions, 3,053 audiovisual materials.

College life *Housing:* on-campus residence required through sophomore year. *Options:* coed, men-only, women-only. *Most popular organizations:* student government, drama club, Into the Streets, radio club, soccer club.

Campus security Late-night transport-escort service.

After graduation 95 organizations recruited on campus 1997–98. 66% of class of 1998 had job offers within 6 months. *Career center:* 1 full-time, 1 part-time personnel. Services include job fairs, resume preparation, interview workshops, resume referral, career/interest testing, career counseling, careers library, job bank, job interviews. *Graduate education:* 28% of class of 1999 went directly to graduate and professional school: 9% graduate arts and sciences, 4% business, 4% law, 4% medicine, 3% engineering, 2% education, 1% dentistry, 1% veterinary medicine.

Freshmen 608 applied, 554 admitted, 245 enrolled. 17 valedictorians.

Average high school GPA	3.39	SAT verbal scores above 500	76%
SAT math scores above 500	64%	ACT above 18	96%
From top 10% of their h.s. class	26%	From top quarter	52%
From top half	80%	1998 freshmen returning in 1999	80%

Application *Options:* eApply at www.CollegeQuest.com, electronic application, early admission, deferred entrance. *Application fee:* $25. *Required:* essay or personal statement; high school transcript; minimum 2.0 GPA; 1 letter of recommendation. *Required for some:* interview. *Recommended:* minimum 3.0 GPA; interview.

Standardized tests *Admission: Required:* SAT I or ACT. *Required for some:* SAT II Subject Tests, SAT II: Writing Test.

Significant dates *Application deadlines:* 6/1 (freshmen), 6/1 (transfers). *Notification:* continuous until 8/20 (freshmen). *Financial aid deadline priority date:* 3/1.

Montana

Carroll College (continued)
Freshman Application Contact
Ms. Candace A. Cain, Director of Admission, Carroll College, 1601 North Benton Avenue, Helena, MT 59625-0002. **Phone:** 406-447-4384. **Toll-free phone:** 800-99-ADMIT. **Fax:** 406-447-4533. **E-mail:** enroll@carroll.edu
Visit CollegeQuest.com for information on majors offered and athletics. College video available at CollegeQuest.com.

■ *See page 1368 for a narrative description.*

MONTANA STATE UNIVERSITY–BILLINGS
Billings, Montana

- **State-supported**, comprehensive, founded 1927
- **Degrees** associate, bachelor's, and master's
- **Urban** 92-acre campus
- **Coed**, 3,799 undergraduate students, 79% full-time, 63% women, 37% men
- **Moderately difficult** entrance level
- **19:1 student-to-undergraduate faculty ratio**
- **33% graduate** in 6 years or less
- **$2922 tuition** and fees (in-state); $7885 (out-of-state)
- **$4877 average financial aid** package, $13,555 average indebtedness upon graduation; $7 million endowment

Part of Montana University System.

Students *Undergraduates:* 2,987 full-time, 812 part-time. Students come from 32 states and territories, 13 other countries. *The most frequently chosen baccalaureate fields are:* business/marketing, education, liberal arts/general studies. *Graduate:* 406 in graduate degree programs.

From out-of-state	7%	Reside on campus	14%
Age 25 or older	35%	Transferred in	10%
International students	1%	African Americans	0.3%
Asian Americans/Pacific Islanders	1%	Hispanic Americans	2%
Native Americans	6%		

Faculty 272 (58% full-time).
Expenses (1999–2000) *One-time required fee:* $5. *Tuition, state resident:* full-time $2922; part-time $696 per term. *Tuition, nonresident:* full-time $7885; part-time $1,841 per term. Full-time tuition and fees vary according to course load and reciprocity agreements. Part-time tuition and fees vary according to course load and reciprocity agreements. *College room and board:* $4200. Room and board charges vary according to board plan and housing facility. *Payment plan:* installment. *Waivers:* senior citizens and employees or children of employees.
Library Montana State University-Billings Library. *Operations spending 1999–2000:* $178,157. *Collection:* 418,000 titles, 865 serial subscriptions.
College life *Housing:* on-campus residence required in freshman year. *Options:* coed, men-only, women-only. *Social organizations:* local fraternities, local sororities; 5% of eligible men and 10% of eligible women are members. *Most popular organizations:* Art Student League, band club, Inter-varsity Christian Fellowship, Residence Hall Association, Student Council for Exceptional Children.
Campus security 24-hour patrols, late-night transport-escort service, controlled dormitory access.
After graduation 33 organizations recruited on campus 1997–98. 85% of class of 1998 had job offers within 6 months. *Career center:* 3 full-time, 2 part-time personnel. Services include job fairs, resume preparation, resume referral, career counseling, careers library, job bank, job interviews. *Graduate education:* 7% of class of 1999 went directly to graduate and professional school: 4% graduate arts and sciences, 2% education, 1% business.
Freshmen 774 admitted, 777 enrolled.

Average high school GPA	2.95	SAT verbal scores above 500	N/R
SAT math scores above 500	N/R	ACT above 18	80%
From top 10% of their h.s. class	8%	From top quarter	22%
From top half	54%	1998 freshmen returning in 1999	70%

Application *Options:* Common Application, early admission, deferred entrance. *Application fee:* $30. *Required:* high school transcript; minimum 2.5 GPA.
Standardized tests *Admission: Required:* SAT I or ACT.
Significant dates *Application deadlines:* 7/1 (freshmen), rolling (transfers). *Financial aid deadline priority date:* 3/1.

Freshman Application Contact
Ms. Karen Everett, Director, Admissions and Records, Montana State University–Billings, 1500 North 30th Street, Billings, MT 59101-9984. **Phone:** 406-657-2158. **Toll-free phone:** 800-565-6782. **Fax:** 406-657-2302. **E-mail:** keverett@msubillings.edu
Visit CollegeQuest.com for information on majors offered and athletics. Electronic viewbook available at CollegeQuest.com.

■ *See page 2080 for a narrative description.*

MONTANA STATE UNIVERSITY–BOZEMAN
Bozeman, Montana

- **State-supported**, university, founded 1893
- **Degrees** bachelor's, master's, and doctoral
- **Small-town** 1,170-acre campus
- **Coed**, 10,331 undergraduate students, 88% full-time, 45% women, 55% men
- **Moderately difficult** entrance level, 87% of applicants were admitted
- **20:1 student-to-undergraduate faculty ratio**
- **42% graduate** in 6 years or less
- **$2965 tuition** and fees (in-state); $8715 (out-of-state)
- **$6141 average financial aid** package, $17,000 average indebtedness upon graduation, $24.5 million endowment

Part of Montana University System.

Students *Undergraduates:* 9,077 full-time, 1,254 part-time. Students come from 50 states and territories, 56 other countries. *The most frequently chosen baccalaureate fields are:* business/marketing, education, engineering/engineering technologies. *Graduate:* 1,200 in graduate degree programs.

From out-of-state	26%	Reside on campus	26%
Age 25 or older	16%	Transferred in	8%
International students	2%	African Americans	0.4%
Asian Americans/Pacific Islanders	1%	Hispanic Americans	1%
Native Americans	2%		

Faculty 685 (76% full-time), 67% with terminal degrees.
Expenses (1999–2000) *Tuition, state resident:* full-time $2965; part-time $91 per credit. *Tuition, nonresident:* full-time $8715; part-time $327 per credit. Full-time tuition and fees vary according to course load and reciprocity agreements. Part-time tuition and fees vary according to course load and reciprocity agreements. *College room and board:* $4650. Room and board charges vary according to board plan and housing facility. *Payment plans:* installment, deferred payment. *Waivers:* minority students, senior citizens, and employees or children of employees.
Library Renne Library plus 1 other. *Operations spending 1999–2000:* $3.5 million. *Collection:* 574,634 titles, 3,790 serial subscriptions, 2,925 audiovisual materials.
College life *Housing:* on-campus residence required in freshman year. *Options:* coed, men-only, women-only, cooperative. *Social organizations:* national fraternities, national sororities; 5% of eligible men and 5% of eligible women are members. *Most popular organizations:* Spurs, Intervarsity Christian Fellowship, Campus Crusade for Christ, Fangs, Mortar Board.
Campus security 24-hour emergency response devices and patrols, student patrols, late-night transport-escort service, 24-hour residence hall monitoring.
After graduation 157 organizations recruited on campus 1997–98. *Career center:* 5 full-time personnel. Services include job fairs, resume preparation, interview workshops, resume referral, career/interest testing, career counseling, careers library, job bank, job interviews. *Major awards:* 1 Rhodes scholar.
Freshmen 3,758 applied, 3,286 admitted, 2,015 enrolled. 93 valedictorians.

Average high school GPA	3.29	SAT verbal scores above 500	71%
SAT math scores above 500	76%	ACT above 18	92%
From top 10% of their h.s. class	20%	From top quarter	43%
From top half	76%	1998 freshmen returning in 1999	70%

Application *Options:* electronic application, early admission, deferred entrance. *Application fee:* $30. *Required:* high school transcript; minimum 2.5 GPA.
Standardized tests *Admission: Required:* SAT I or ACT.
Significant dates *Application deadlines:* rolling (freshmen), rolling (transfers). *Financial aid deadline priority date:* 3/1.

Freshman Application Contact
Ms. Ronda Russell, Director of New Student Services, Montana State University–Bozeman, PO Box 172190, Bozeman, MT 59717-2190. **Phone:** 406-994-2452. **Toll-free phone:** 888-MSU-CATS. **E-mail:** admissions@montana.edu
Visit CollegeQuest.com for information on majors offered and athletics. College video and electronic viewbook available at CollegeQuest.com.

■ *See page 2082 for a narrative description.*

MONTANA STATE UNIVERSITY– NORTHERN
Havre, Montana

- **State-supported**, comprehensive, founded 1929
- **Degrees** associate, bachelor's, and master's
- **Small-town** 105-acre campus
- **Coed**, 1,487 undergraduate students, 74% full-time, 53% women, 47% men
- **Moderately difficult** entrance level
- **$2691 tuition** and fees (in-state); $7857 (out-of-state)
- **$100,858 endowment**

Part of Montana University System.
Students *Undergraduates:* 1,101 full-time, 386 part-time. Students come from 24 states and territories, 5 other countries. *Graduate:* 217 in graduate degree programs.

Age 25 or older	47%

Faculty 118 (60% full-time).
Expenses (1999–2000) *Tuition, state resident:* full-time $2691; part-time $101 per credit. *Tuition, nonresident:* full-time $7857; part-time $286 per credit. Full-time tuition and fees vary according to course load, location, and reciprocity agreements. Part-time tuition and fees vary according to course load, location, and reciprocity agreements. *College room and board:* $3800. *Payment plan:* deferred payment. *Waivers:* minority students, senior citizens, and employees or children of employees.
Library VandeBogart Libraries. *Operations spending 1999–2000:* $298,488. *Collection:* 128,000 titles, 1,729 serial subscriptions.
College life *Housing:* on-campus residence required in freshman year. *Option:* coed. *Most popular organizations:* Vocational and Industrial Clubs of America, Student Nurses Association of America, Student Education Association.
After graduation 20 organizations recruited on campus 1997–98. 75% of class of 1998 had job offers within 6 months. *Career center:* 4 full-time personnel. Services include job fairs, resume preparation, resume referral, career counseling, careers library, job bank, job interviews.
Freshmen 290 enrolled.

SAT verbal scores above 500	N/R	SAT math scores above 500	N/R
ACT above 18	N/R	1998 freshmen returning in 1999	65%

Application *Options:* early admission, deferred entrance. *Application fee:* $30. *Required:* high school transcript. *Required for some:* minimum 2.0 GPA.
Standardized tests *Placement: Required:* ACT
Significant dates *Application deadlines:* rolling (freshmen), rolling (transfers). *Financial aid deadline priority date:* 3/1.
Freshman Application Contact
Ms. Rosalie Spinler, Director of Admissions, Montana State University–Northern, PO Box 7751, Havre, MT 59501-7751. **Phone:** 406-265-3704. **Toll-free phone:** 800-662-6132. **Fax:** 406-265-3777. **E-mail:** msunadmit@nmc1.nmclites.edu
Visit CollegeQuest.com for information on majors offered and athletics. Electronic viewbook available at CollegeQuest.com.

MONTANA TECH OF THE UNIVERSITY OF MONTANA
Butte, Montana

- **State-supported**, comprehensive, founded 1895
- **Degrees** associate, bachelor's, and master's
- **Small-town** 56-acre campus
- **Coed**, 1,798 undergraduate students, 84% full-time, 44% women, 56% men
- **Moderately difficult** entrance level, 95% of applicants were admitted
- **16:1 student-to-undergraduate faculty ratio**
- **$2865 tuition** and fees (in-state); $8162 (out-of-state)
- **$6000 average financial aid** package, $11,500 average indebtedness upon graduation, $9.7 million endowment

Part of Montana University System.
Students *Undergraduates:* 1,513 full-time, 285 part-time. Students come from 34 states and territories, 17 other countries. *The most frequently chosen baccalaureate fields are:* business/marketing, engineering/engineering technologies, health professions and related sciences. *Graduate:* 95 in graduate degree programs.

From out-of-state	13%	Reside on campus	15%
Age 25 or older	24%	Transferred in	6%

Faculty 143 (77% full-time), 65% with terminal degrees.
Expenses (1999–2000) *Tuition, state resident:* full-time $2865; part-time $711 per term. *Tuition, nonresident:* full-time $8162; part-time $2,035 per term. Full-time tuition and fees vary according to course level, course load, degree level, reciprocity agreements, and student level. Part-time tuition and fees vary according to course level, course load, degree level, reciprocity agreements, and student level. *College room and board:* $4090. Room and board charges vary according to housing facility. *Payment plan:* deferred payment. *Waivers:* minority students, senior citizens, and employees or children of employees.
Library Montana Tech Library plus 1 other. *Operations spending 1999–2000:* $480,000. *Collection:* 140,205 titles, 1,707 serial subscriptions, 12 audiovisual materials.
College life *Housing:* on-campus residence required in freshman year. *Option:* coed. *Social organizations:* International Club. *Most popular organizations:* environmental engineering club, SH/IH Club, Petroleum Club SPE, Marcus Daly Mining, chemistry club.
Campus security 24-hour patrols, controlled dormitory access.
After graduation 82 organizations recruited on campus 1997–98. 96% of class of 1998 had job offers within 6 months. *Career center:* 2 full-time, 1 part-time personnel. Services include resume preparation, resume referral, career counseling, careers library, job interviews. *Graduate education:* 10% of class of 1999 went directly to graduate and professional school.
Freshmen 577 applied, 546 admitted, 378 enrolled. 22 valedictorians.

Average high school GPA	3.49	SAT verbal scores above 500	69%
SAT math scores above 500	72%	ACT above 18	84%
From top 10% of their h.s. class	22%	From top quarter	48%
From top half	77%	1998 freshmen returning in 1999	71%

Application *Options:* electronic application, early admission. *Application fee:* $30. *Required:* high school transcript; minimum 2.5 GPA; proof of immunization.
Standardized tests *Admission: Required:* SAT I or ACT.
Significant dates *Application deadlines:* rolling (freshmen), rolling (transfers). *Financial aid deadline priority date:* 3/1.
Freshman Application Contact
Tony Campeau, Associate Director of Admissions, Montana Tech of The University of Montana, 1300 West Park Street, Butte, MT 59701-8997. **Phone:** 406-496-4178. **Toll-free phone:** 800-445-TECH Ext. 1. **Fax:** 406-496-4710. **E-mail:** admissions@mtech.edu
Visit CollegeQuest.com for information on majors offered and athletics. College video and electronic viewbook available at CollegeQuest.com.

■ *See page 2084 for a narrative description.*

ROCKY MOUNTAIN COLLEGE
Billings, Montana

 Apply at CollegeQuest.com

- **Independent interdenominational**, 4-year, founded 1878
- **Degrees** associate and bachelor's
- **Urban** 60-acre campus
- **Coed**, 787 undergraduate students, 89% full-time, 53% women, 47% men
- **Moderately difficult** entrance level, 99% of applicants were admitted

Montana

Rocky Mountain College (continued)
- **14:1 student-to-undergraduate faculty ratio**
- **$12,243 tuition** and fees

Rocky Mountain College nurtures its students while challenging them to reach their full potential. The individual attention Rocky students receive inspires them to excel in many areas. At Rocky, students enjoy internships, cooperative education, and many social and outdoor recreation opportunities. After graduation, Rocky students succeed in business, industry, and graduate and professional schools.

Students *Undergraduates:* 701 full-time, 86 part-time. Students come from 35 states and territories, 10 other countries. *The most frequently chosen baccalaureate fields are:* business/marketing, education, parks and recreation.

From out-of-state	28%	Reside on campus	37%
Age 25 or older	29%	Transferred in	12%
International students	2%	African Americans	0.4%
Asian Americans/Pacific Islanders	1%	Hispanic Americans	1%
Native Americans	7%		

Faculty 80 (53% full-time).

Expenses (2000–2001, estimated) *Comprehensive fee:* $16,390 includes full-time tuition ($12,088), mandatory fees ($155), and room and board ($4147). *College room only:* $1625. Full-time tuition and fees vary according to course load, program, and reciprocity agreements. Room and board charges vary according to board plan and housing facility. *Part-time tuition:* $504 per semester hour. *Part-time fees:* $35 per term part-time. Part-time tuition and fees vary according to course load and program. *Payment plan:* installment. *Waivers:* employees or children of employees.

Library Paul Adams Library. *Operations spending 1999–2000:* $174,806. *Collection:* 86,449 titles.

College life *Housing:* on-campus residence required through sophomore year. *Option:* coed. *Most popular organizations:* Ambassador, equestrian club, Aviation club, Indian club, Sojourners.

Campus security 24-hour emergency response devices, student patrols, controlled dormitory access.

After graduation 75 organizations recruited on campus 1997–98. 95% of class of 1998 had job offers within 6 months. *Career center:* 1 full-time personnel. Services include job fairs, resume preparation, interview workshops, resume referral, career/interest testing, career counseling, careers library, job bank, job interviews. *Graduate education:* 13% of class of 1999 went directly to graduate and professional school: 9% graduate arts and sciences, 2% medicine, 1% law, 1% veterinary medicine.

Freshmen 378 applied, 373 admitted, 147 enrolled.

Average high school GPA	3.26	SAT verbal scores above 500	59%
SAT math scores above 500	54%	ACT above 18	91%
From top 10% of their h.s. class	12%	From top quarter	41%
From top half	70%	1998 freshmen returning in 1999	72%

Application *Options:* eApply at www.CollegeQuest.com, Common Application, electronic application, early admission, deferred entrance. *Application fee:* $25. *Required:* high school transcript; minimum 2.5 GPA. *Required for some:* essay or personal statement; interview. *Recommended:* 2 letters of recommendation.

Standardized tests *Admission: Required:* SAT I or ACT. *Recommended:* ACT.

Significant dates *Application deadlines:* rolling (freshmen), rolling (transfers). *Financial aid deadline priority date:* 4/1.

Freshman Application Contact
Mr. Craig Gould, Director of Admissions, Rocky Mountain College, 1511 Poly Drive, Billings, MT 59102-1796. **Phone:** 406-657-1026. **Toll-free phone:** 800-877-6259. **Fax:** 406-259-9751. **E-mail:** admissions@rocky.edu

Visit CollegeQuest.com for information on majors offered and athletics.

- *See page 2350 for a narrative description.*

SALISH KOOTENAI COLLEGE
Pablo, Montana

- **Independent**, primarily 2-year, founded 1977
- **Degrees** associate and bachelor's
- **Rural** 4-acre campus
- **Coed**, 641 undergraduate students, 73% full-time, 68% women, 32% men
- **Noncompetitive** entrance level

Faculty 55 (36% full-time).

Admissions Office Contact
Salish Kootenai College, PO Box 117, Pablo, MT 59855-0117. **Fax:** 406-675-4801. **E-mail:** jackie_moran@skc.edu

Visit CollegeQuest.com for information on majors offered and athletics.

UNIVERSITY OF GREAT FALLS
Great Falls, Montana

- **Independent Roman Catholic**, comprehensive, founded 1932
- **Degrees** associate, bachelor's, and master's
- **Urban** 40-acre campus
- **Coed**, 825 undergraduate students, 67% full-time, 72% women, 28% men
- **Noncompetitive** entrance level, 100% of applicants were admitted
- **15:1 student-to-undergraduate faculty ratio**
- **16% graduate** in 6 years or less
- **$8420 tuition** and fees
- **$9165 average financial aid** package, $20,750 average indebtedness upon graduation, $6.5 million endowment

Students *Undergraduates:* 550 full-time, 275 part-time. Students come from 8 states and territories. *The most frequently chosen baccalaureate fields are:* computer/information sciences, health professions and related sciences, protective services/public administration. *Graduate:* 111 in graduate degree programs.

From out-of-state	4%	Reside on campus	8%
Age 25 or older	71%	Transferred in	32%

Faculty 109 (40% full-time).

Expenses (1999–2000) *One-time required fee:* $8. *Tuition:* full-time $8160; part-time $255 per credit. *Required fees:* full-time $260; $5 per credit; $70 per term part-time. Full-time tuition and fees vary according to course load. Part-time tuition and fees vary according to course load. *College room only:* $1500. Room and board charges vary according to board plan. *Payment plan:* deferred payment. *Waivers:* senior citizens and employees or children of employees.

Library University of Great Falls Library. *Operations spending 1999–2000:* $376,355. *Collection:* 72,829 titles, 549 serial subscriptions, 5,070 audiovisual materials.

College life *Housing: Option:* coed. *Most popular organizations:* Student Montana Education Association, Student Senate, Lumen Press (school newspaper), Law and Justice Club, computer science club.

Campus security 24-hour emergency response devices.

After graduation 4 organizations recruited on campus 1997–98. *Career center:* 2 full-time personnel. Services include job fairs, resume preparation, interview workshops, career/interest testing, career counseling, careers library. *Graduate education:* 12% of class of 1999 went directly to graduate and professional school.

Freshmen 144 applied, 144 admitted, 119 enrolled.

SAT verbal scores above 500	N/R	SAT math scores above 500	N/R
ACT above 18	N/R	1998 freshmen returning in 1999	45%

Application *Options:* early admission, deferred entrance. *Application fee:* $25. *Required:* high school transcript. *Recommended:* interview.

Standardized tests *Placement: Recommended:* SAT I or ACT.

Significant dates *Application deadlines:* rolling (freshmen), rolling (transfers). *Financial aid deadline priority date:* 4/1.

Freshman Application Contact
Mr. Robert Hensley, Vice President for Enrollment Management, University of Great Falls, 1301 Twentieth Street South, Great Falls, MT 59405. **Phone:** 406-791-5200. **Toll-free phone:** 800-856-9544. **Fax:** 406-791-5209. **E-mail:** adminrec@ugf.edu

Visit CollegeQuest.com for information on majors offered and athletics.

- *See page 2728 for a narrative description.*

Montana

THE UNIVERSITY OF MONTANA—MISSOULA
Missoula, Montana

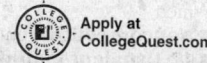

- **State-supported**, university, founded 1893
- **Degrees** associate, bachelor's, master's, doctoral, and first professional
- **Urban** 220-acre campus
- **Coed**, 10,307 undergraduate students, 87% full-time, 53% women, 47% men
- **Moderately difficult** entrance level, 88% of applicants were admitted
- **19:1 student-to-undergraduate faculty ratio**
- **39.4% graduate** in 6 years or less
- **$2967 tuition** and fees (in-state); $8077 (out-of-state)
- **$7807 average financial aid** package, $16,000 average indebtedness upon graduation, $68.5 million endowment

Part of Montana University System.

Students *Undergraduates:* 8,991 full-time, 1,316 part-time. Students come from 52 states and territories, 60 other countries. *Graduate:* 241 in professional programs, 1,510 in other graduate degree programs.

From out-of-state	30%	Reside on campus	23%
Age 25 or older	17%	Transferred in	29%
International students	2%	African Americans	0.4%
Asian Americans/Pacific Islanders	1%	Hispanic Americans	1%
Native Americans	3%		

Faculty 672 (64% full-time), 69% with terminal degrees.

Expenses (1999–2000) *Tuition, state resident:* full-time $2048. *Tuition, nonresident:* full-time $7158. *Required fees:* full-time $919. Full-time tuition and fees vary according to program and student level. Part-time tuition and fees vary according to course load and program. *College room and board:* $4496; room only: $2054. Room and board charges vary according to board plan and housing facility. *Payment plan:* installment. *Waivers:* minority students and senior citizens.

Library Maureen and Mike Mansfield Library plus 2 others. *Operations spending 1999–2000:* $5.3 million. *Collection:* 6,248 serial subscriptions, 118,190 audiovisual materials.

College life *Housing:* on-campus residence required in freshman year. *Options:* coed, men-only, women-only, disabled students. *Social organizations:* national fraternities, national sororities; 10% of eligible men and 7% of eligible women are members. *Most popular organizations:* Forestry Club, Honors Student Association, Campus Outdoor Program, International Organization, Kyio Indian Club.

Campus security 24-hour emergency response devices and patrols, student patrols, late-night transport-escort service, controlled dormitory access.

After graduation 49 organizations recruited on campus 1997–98. *Career center:* 5 full-time, 1 part-time personnel. Services include job fairs, resume preparation, interview workshops, resume referral, career/interest testing, career counseling, careers library, job interviews. *Graduate education:* 28% of class of 1999 went directly to graduate and professional school. *Major awards:* 3 Fulbright Scholars.

Freshmen 4,506 applied, 3,978 admitted, 2,060 enrolled. 14 National Merit Scholars, 66 valedictorians.

Average high school GPA	3.21	SAT verbal scores above 500	70%
SAT math scores above 500	100%	ACT above 18	88%
From top 10% of their h.s. class	16%	From top quarter	37%
From top half	70%	1998 freshmen returning in 1999	71%

Application *Options:* eApply at www.CollegeQuest.com, Common Application, electronic application, early admission, deferred entrance. *Application fee:* $30. *Required:* high school transcript; minimum 2.5 GPA.

Standardized tests *Admission: Required:* SAT I or ACT. *Required for some:* ACT ASSET or ACT COMPASS.

Significant dates *Application deadlines:* 7/1 (freshmen), rolling (transfers). *Financial aid deadline priority date:* 3/1.

Freshman Application Contact
Office of New Student Services, The University of Montana–Missoula, Missoula, MT 59812-0002. **Phone:** 406-243-6266. **Toll-free phone:** 800-462-8636. **Fax:** 406-243-5711. **E-mail:** admiss@selway.umt.edu

Visit CollegeQuest.com for information on majors offered and athletics. College video and electronic viewbook available at CollegeQuest.com.

WESTERN MONTANA COLLEGE OF THE UNIVERSITY OF MONTANA
Dillon, Montana

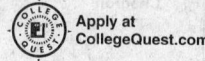

- **State-supported**, 4-year, founded 1893
- **Degrees** associate and bachelor's
- **Small-town** 36-acre campus
- **Coed**, 975 undergraduate students, 86% full-time, 52% women, 48% men
- **Moderately difficult** entrance level, 99% of applicants were admitted
- **17:1 student-to-undergraduate faculty ratio**
- **30% graduate** in 6 years or less
- **$2545 tuition** and fees (in-state); $7427 (out-of-state)
- **$5728 average financial aid** package, $13,867 average indebtedness upon graduation, $5 million endowment

Part of Montana University System.

Students *Undergraduates:* 841 full-time, 134 part-time. Students come from 21 states and territories, 4 other countries. *The most frequently chosen baccalaureate fields are:* business/marketing, biological/life sciences, education.

From out-of-state	14%	Reside on campus	27%
Age 25 or older	30%	Transferred in	13%
International students	1%	African Americans	1%
Asian Americans/Pacific Islanders	1%	Hispanic Americans	1%
Native Americans	2%		

Faculty 75 (67% full-time).

Expenses (1999–2000) *Tuition, state resident:* full-time $1880; part-time $78 per credit. *Tuition, nonresident:* full-time $6762; part-time $282 per credit. *Required fees:* full-time $665; $7 per credit; $84 per term part-time. Full-time tuition and fees vary according to course level, course load, and reciprocity agreements. Part-time tuition and fees vary according to course level, course load, and reciprocity agreements. *College room and board:* $3810. Room and board charges vary according to board plan and housing facility. *Payment plan:* deferred payment. *Waivers:* minority students, senior citizens, and employees or children of employees.

Library Lucy Carson Memorial Library. *Operations spending 1999–2000:* $277,487. *Collection:* 63,000 titles, 550 serial subscriptions, 10,000 audiovisual materials.

College life *Housing:* on-campus residence required in freshman year. *Options:* coed, men-only, women-only, disabled students. *Most popular organizations:* soccer, IGNU-Poetry Club, admissions volunteers, Rodeo Club, Chi Alpha-Christian Fellowship.

Campus security 24-hour emergency response devices and patrols, late-night transport-escort service.

After graduation 70% of class of 1998 had job offers within 6 months. *Career center:* 1 full-time personnel. Services include job fairs, resume preparation, resume referral, career/interest testing, career counseling, careers library, job interviews.

Freshmen 352 applied, 348 admitted, 226 enrolled. 4 valedictorians.

Average high school GPA	3.0	SAT verbal scores above 500	43%
SAT math scores above 500	37%	ACT above 18	66%
From top 10% of their h.s. class	6%	From top quarter	18%
From top half	55%	1998 freshmen returning in 1999	60%

Application *Options:* eApply at www.CollegeQuest.com, Common Application, early admission, deferred entrance. *Application fee:* $30. *Required:* high school transcript; minimum 2.5 GPA.

Standardized tests *Admission: Required:* SAT I or ACT.

Significant dates *Application deadlines:* 7/1 (freshmen), 7/1 (transfers). *Financial aid deadline priority date:* 3/1.

Freshman Application Contact
Ms. Kay Leum, Director of Admissions and New Student Services, Western Montana College of The University of Montana, 710 South Atlantic, Dillon, MT 59725. **Phone:** 406-683-7331. **Toll-free phone:** 800-WMC-MONT. **Fax:** 406-683-7493. **E-mail:** admissions@wmc.edu

Visit CollegeQuest.com for information on majors offered and athletics.

■ *See page 2952 for a narrative description.*

Nebraska

NEBRASKA

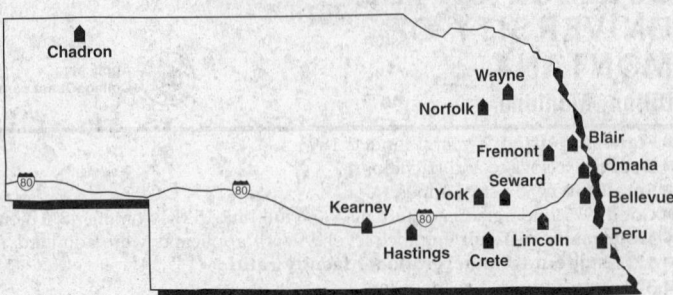

BELLEVUE UNIVERSITY
Bellevue, Nebraska

- **Independent**, comprehensive, founded 1965
- **Degrees** bachelor's and master's
- **Suburban** 19-acre campus with easy access to Omaha
- **Coed**, 2,486 undergraduate students
- **Noncompetitive** entrance level
- **23:1 student-to-undergraduate faculty ratio**
- **$4030 tuition** and fees
- **$18 million endowment**

Students *Undergraduates:* Students come from 6 states and territories, 40 other countries. *The most frequently chosen baccalaureate fields are:* business/marketing, computer/information sciences, psychology.

From out-of-state	15%	Age 25 or older	80%
International students	11%	African Americans	8%
Asian Americans/Pacific Islanders	1%	Hispanic Americans	2%
Native Americans	1%		

Faculty 131 (43% full-time).
Expenses (2000–2001) *Tuition:* full-time $3960; part-time $132 per credit hour. *Required fees:* full-time $70; $35 per term part-time. Full-time tuition and fees vary according to program. *Payment plans:* installment, deferred payment. *Waivers:* employees or children of employees.
Library Freeman/Lozier Library. *Operations spending 1999–2000:* $361,107. *Collection:* 130,000 titles, 2,787 serial subscriptions, 2,865 audiovisual materials.
College life *Housing:* college housing not available.
Campus security 24-hour emergency response devices.
After graduation *Career center:* 1 full-time personnel. Services include job fairs, resume preparation, resume referral, career counseling, careers library, job bank, job interviews. *Graduate education:* 15% of class of 1999 went directly to graduate and professional school.

Freshmen

SAT verbal scores above 500	N/R	SAT math scores above 500	N/R
ACT above 18	N/R	From top 10% of their h.s. class	8%
From top quarter	37%	From top half	57%

Application *Option:* deferred entrance. *Application fee:* $25. *Required:* high school transcript; interview. *Required for some:* 3 letters of recommendation.
Standardized tests *Placement: Required for some:* SAT I or ACT.
Significant dates *Application deadlines:* rolling (freshmen), rolling (transfers). *Financial aid deadline:* continuous.
Freshman Application Contact
Ms. Sharon Thonen, Director of Admissions, Bellevue University, 1000 Galvin Road South, Bellevue, NE 68005-3098. **Phone:** 402-293-3711. **Toll-free phone:** 800-756-7920. **Fax:** 402-293-2020. **E-mail:** set@scholars.bellevue.edu
Visit CollegeQuest.com for information on majors offered and athletics.

CHADRON STATE COLLEGE
Chadron, Nebraska

- **State-supported**, comprehensive, founded 1911
- **Degrees** bachelor's and master's
- **Small-town** 281-acre campus

- **Coed**, 2,269 undergraduate students, 82% full-time, 58% women, 42% men
- **Noncompetitive** entrance level, 100% of applicants were admitted
- **17:1 student-to-undergraduate faculty ratio**
- **33.16% graduate** in 6 years or less
- **$2263 tuition** and fees (in-state); $4138 (out-of-state)
- **$11,000 average indebtedness** upon graduation, $5.5 million endowment

Part of Nebraska State College System.
Students *Undergraduates:* 1,870 full-time, 399 part-time. Students come from 31 states and territories, 7 other countries. *The most frequently chosen baccalaureate fields are:* business/marketing, education, protective services/public administration. *Graduate:* 285 in graduate degree programs.

From out-of-state	30%	Reside on campus	38%
Age 25 or older	14%	Transferred in	10%
International students	1%	African Americans	1%
Asian Americans/Pacific Islanders	0.4%	Hispanic Americans	2%
Native Americans	1%		

Faculty 152 (68% full-time), 45% with terminal degrees.
Expenses (1999–2000) *Tuition, state resident:* full-time $1875; part-time $62 per semester hour. *Tuition, nonresident:* full-time $3750; part-time $125 per semester hour. *Required fees:* full-time $388; $11 per semester hour; $15 per term part-time. Full-time tuition and fees vary according to course load. Part-time tuition and fees vary according to course load. *College room and board:* $3300; room only: $1566. Room and board charges vary according to board plan and housing facility. *Payment plan:* installment. *Waivers:* senior citizens and employees or children of employees.
Library Reta King Library. *Operations spending 1999–2000:* $675,287. *Collection:* 129,660 titles, 5,596 audiovisual materials.
College life *Housing:* on-campus residence required in freshman year. *Options:* coed, men-only, women-only.
Campus security 24-hour emergency response devices and patrols, student patrols, late-night transport-escort service.
After graduation 30 organizations recruited on campus 1997–98. 95% of class of 1998 had job offers within 6 months. *Career center:* 3 full-time personnel. Services include job fairs, resume preparation, resume referral, career counseling, careers library, job interviews.
Freshmen 986 applied, 986 admitted, 449 enrolled.

Average high school GPA	3.17	SAT verbal scores above 500	29%
SAT math scores above 500	43%	ACT above 18	80%
From top 10% of their h.s. class	11%	From top quarter	30%
From top half	60%	1998 freshmen returning in 1999	82%

Application *Option:* early admission. *Application fee:* $15. *Required:* high school transcript; health forms.
Standardized tests *Admission: Required:* SAT I or ACT.
Significant dates *Application deadlines:* rolling (freshmen), rolling (transfers). *Financial aid deadline priority date:* 6/1.
Freshman Application Contact
Ms. Terie Dawson, Director of Enrollment Management, Chadron State College, 1000 Main Street, Chadron, NE 69337-2690. **Phone:** 308-432-6263. **Toll-free phone:** 800-CHADRON. **Fax:** 308-432-6229. **E-mail:** inquire@csc1.csc.edu
Visit CollegeQuest.com for information on majors offered and athletics. College video and electronic viewbook available at CollegeQuest.com.

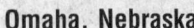 *See page 1398 for a narrative description.*

CLARKSON COLLEGE
Omaha, Nebraska

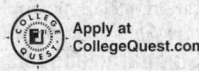 Apply at CollegeQuest.com

- **Independent**, comprehensive, founded 1888, affiliated with Episcopal Church
- **Degrees** associate, bachelor's, master's, and post-master's certificates
- **Urban** 3-acre campus
- **Coed**, 274 undergraduate students, 48% full-time, 89% women, 11% men
- **Moderately difficult** entrance level, 62% of applicants were admitted
- **12:1 student-to-undergraduate faculty ratio**
- **$7176 tuition** and fees
- **$2.2 million endowment**

472   www.petersons.com   *Peterson's Guide to Four-Year Colleges 2001*

Nebraska

Clarkson College focuses on student success, with a nationally recognized faculty, a beautiful campus, and high-tech facilities. The College offers full- and part-time undergraduate degrees in nursing, radiologic technology, medical imaging, business, physical therapist assistant studies, and occupational therapy assistant studies; graduate degrees in nursing; and a postgraduate certificate in family nurse practitioner studies through on-campus and distance education courses.

Students *Undergraduates:* 132 full-time, 142 part-time. Students come from 35 states and territories, 1 other country. *The most frequently chosen baccalaureate fields are:* business/marketing, health professions and related sciences. *Graduate:* 132 in graduate degree programs.

From out-of-state	33%	Reside on campus	10%
Age 25 or older	40%	Transferred in	20%
International students	0.4%	African Americans	2%
Asian Americans/Pacific Islanders	1%	Hispanic Americans	4%

Faculty 41 (100% full-time), 39% with terminal degrees.

Expenses (1999–2000) *Tuition:* full-time $6768; part-time $282 per credit. *Required fees:* full-time $408; $17 per credit. *College room only:* $2800. Room and board charges vary according to housing facility and location. *Payment plans:* installment, deferred payment. *Waivers:* minority students and employees or children of employees.

Library Clarkson College Library. *Operations spending 1999–2000:* $258,319. *Collection:* 8,200 titles, 282 serial subscriptions, 302 audiovisual materials.

College life *Housing: Option:* coed. *Most popular organizations:* Clarkson Student Nurses Association, Clarkson Radiology Student Association, Student Government Association, Student Ambassadors, Clarkson Fellows Program.

Campus security 24-hour emergency response devices and patrols, late-night transport-escort service, controlled dormitory access.

After graduation 50 organizations recruited on campus 1997–98. 98% of class of 1998 had job offers within 6 months. *Career center:* 1 full-time, 1 part-time personnel. Services include job fairs, resume preparation, interview workshops, resume referral, career/interest testing, career counseling, careers library, job bank, job interviews. *Graduate education:* 10% of class of 1999 went directly to graduate and professional school: 10% graduate arts and sciences.

Freshmen 92 applied, 57 admitted, 29 enrolled.

Average high school GPA	3.29	SAT verbal scores above 500	N/R
SAT math scores above 500	N/R	ACT above 18	95%
From top 10% of their h.s. class	15%	From top quarter	30%
From top half	70%	1998 freshmen returning in 1999	80%

Application *Options:* eApply at www.CollegeQuest.com, electronic application, deferred entrance. *Application fee:* $15. *Required:* essay or personal statement; high school transcript; minimum 2.5 GPA. *Required for some:* 2 letters of recommendation. *Recommended:* minimum 3.0 GPA.

Standardized tests *Admission: Required for some:* SAT I or ACT.

Significant dates *Application deadlines:* rolling (freshmen), rolling (transfers). *Financial aid deadline priority date:* 4/1.

Freshman Application Contact
Mr. Tony Damewood, Director of Enrollment Services, Clarkson College, 101 South 42nd Street, Omaha, NE 68131-2739. **Phone:** 402-552-6109. **Toll-free phone:** 800-647-5500. **Fax:** 402-552-6057. **E-mail:** admiss@clrkcol.crhsnet.edu

Visit CollegeQuest.com for information on majors offered and athletics. College video and electronic viewbook available at CollegeQuest.com.

■ *See page 1430 for a narrative description.*

COLLEGE OF SAINT MARY
Omaha, Nebraska

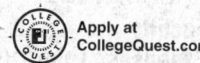
Apply at CollegeQuest.com

- **Independent Roman Catholic**, 4-year, founded 1923
- **Degrees** associate and bachelor's
- **Suburban** 25-acre campus
- **Women** only, 827 undergraduate students, 67% full-time
- **Moderately difficult** entrance level, 88% of applicants were admitted
- **10:1 student-to-undergraduate faculty ratio**
- **47% graduate** in 6 years or less
- **$12,836 tuition** and fees

- **$6.7 million endowment**

Students *Undergraduates:* 553 full-time, 274 part-time. Students come from 20 states and territories, 2 other countries. *The most frequently chosen baccalaureate fields are:* business/marketing, education, health professions and related sciences.

From out-of-state	16%	Reside on campus	15%
Age 25 or older	48%	Transferred in	9%
International students	1%	African Americans	3%
Asian Americans/Pacific Islanders	1%	Hispanic Americans	4%

Faculty 55 (69% full-time), 24% with terminal degrees.

Expenses (1999–2000) *One-time required fee:* $25. *Comprehensive fee:* $17,434 includes full-time tuition ($12,428), mandatory fees ($408), and room and board ($4598). Room and board charges vary according to board plan and housing facility. *Part-time tuition:* $414 per credit hour. *Part-time fees:* $18 per credit hour. Part-time tuition and fees vary according to class time. *Payment plans:* installment, deferred payment. *Waivers:* senior citizens and employees or children of employees.

Library College of Saint Mary Library. *Operations spending 1999–2000:* $257,406. *Collection:* 53,867 titles, 1,616 serial subscriptions, 2,029 audiovisual materials.

College life *Housing:* on-campus residence required through sophomore year. *Option:* women-only. *Most popular organizations:* student senate, Campus Faith Council, Student Nurses Association, Student Occupational Therapy Club, Student Ambassadors.

Campus security 24-hour emergency response devices and patrols, late-night transport-escort service, controlled dormitory access, external cameras at residence hall entrances.

After graduation 68 organizations recruited on campus 1997–98. *Career center:* 1 full-time personnel. Services include job fairs, resume preparation, interview workshops, career/interest testing, career counseling, careers library, job bank, job interviews. *Graduate education:* 10% of class of 1999 went directly to graduate and professional school: 2% education, 2% graduate arts and sciences, 1% business, 1% law, 1% medicine, 1% veterinary medicine.

Freshmen 447 applied, 394 admitted, 118 enrolled.

Average high school GPA	2.57	SAT verbal scores above 500	N/R
SAT math scores above 500	N/R	ACT above 18	85%
From top 10% of their h.s. class	18%	From top quarter	39%
From top half	74%	1998 freshmen returning in 1999	67%

Application *Options:* eApply at www.CollegeQuest.com, Common Application, electronic application. *Application fee:* $20. *Required:* high school transcript; minimum 2.0 GPA. *Required for some:* minimum 3.0 GPA; 2 letters of recommendation; interview.

Standardized tests *Admission: Required:* SAT I or ACT.

Significant dates *Application deadlines:* rolling (freshmen), rolling (transfers). *Notification:* continuous until 8/24 (freshmen). *Financial aid deadline priority date:* 4/1.

Freshman Application Contact
Ms. Sue Kropf, Director of Enrollment Services, College of Saint Mary, 1901 South 72nd Street, Omaha, NE 68124-2377. **Phone:** 402-399-2425. **Toll-free phone:** 800-926-5534. **Fax:** 402-399-2412. **E-mail:** enroll@csm.edu

Visit CollegeQuest.com for information on majors offered and athletics. Electronic viewbook available at CollegeQuest.com.

CONCORDIA UNIVERSITY
Seward, Nebraska

- **Independent**, comprehensive, founded 1894, affiliated with Lutheran Church–Missouri Synod
- **Degrees** bachelor's and master's
- **Small-town** 120-acre campus with easy access to Omaha
- **Coed**, 1,094 undergraduate students, 99% full-time, 54% women, 46% men
- **Moderately difficult** entrance level, 89% of applicants were admitted
- **$11,876 tuition** and fees
- **$13,165 average financial aid** package, $12.9 million endowment

Part of Concordia University System.

Students *Undergraduates:* 1,078 full-time, 16 part-time. Students come from 36 states and territories, 12 other countries. *Graduate:* 67 in graduate

Peterson's Guide to Four-Year Colleges 2001   www.petersons.com

Nebraska

Concordia University (continued)
degree programs.

From out-of-state	62%	Reside on campus	77%
Age 25 or older	4%	Transferred in	4%
International students	0.5%	African Americans	1%
Asian Americans/Pacific Islanders	2%	Hispanic Americans	2%
Native Americans	0.1%		

Faculty 124 (52% full-time), 42% with terminal degrees.

Expenses (1999–2000) *Comprehensive fee:* $15,814 includes full-time tuition ($11,876) and room and board ($3938). Room and board charges vary according to board plan. *Part-time tuition:* $361 per credit. Part-time tuition and fees vary according to course load. *Payment plans:* installment, deferred payment. *Waivers:* employees or children of employees.

Library Link Library. *Operations spending 1999–2000:* $347,766. *Collection:* 171,688 titles, 575 serial subscriptions, 12,068 audiovisual materials.

College life *Housing:* on-campus residence required through senior year. *Options:* men-only, women-only, disabled students. *Most popular organizations:* Student Activities Council, musical groups, Men's and Women's C-Club, Student Senate, Concordia Youth Ministry.

Campus security 24-hour emergency response devices and patrols, controlled dormitory access.

After graduation *Career center:* 2 full-time personnel. Services include job fairs, resume preparation, resume referral, career/interest testing, career counseling, job bank.

Freshmen 825 applied, 737 admitted, 262 enrolled.

SAT verbal scores above 500	N/R	SAT math scores above 500	N/R
ACT above 18	N/R	1998 freshmen returning in 1999	80%

Application *Options:* electronic application, deferred entrance. *Application fee:* $15. *Required:* high school transcript. *Required for some:* letters of recommendation. *Recommended:* minimum 2.0 GPA; interview.

Standardized tests *Admission: Required:* SAT I or ACT.

Significant dates *Application deadlines:* 8/1 (freshmen), 8/1 (transfers). *Financial aid deadline priority date:* 3/1.

Freshman Application Contact
Mr. Don Vos, Director of Admissions, Concordia University, 800 North Columbia Avenue, Seward, NE 68434-1599. **Phone:** 402-643-7233. **Toll-free phone:** 800-535-5494. **Fax:** 402-643-4073. **E-mail:** admiss@seward.ccsn.edu

Visit CollegeQuest.com for information on majors offered and athletics. Electronic viewbook available at CollegeQuest.com.

CREIGHTON UNIVERSITY
Omaha, Nebraska

- **Independent Roman Catholic (Jesuit)**, university, founded 1878
- **Degrees** associate, bachelor's, master's, doctoral, and first professional
- **Urban** 90-acre campus
- **Coed**, 3,554 undergraduate students, 96% full-time, 58% women, 42% men
- **Moderately difficult** entrance level, 91% of applicants were admitted
- **14:1 student-to-undergraduate faculty ratio**
- **72% graduate** in 6 years or less
- **$14,132 tuition** and fees
- **$13,169 average financial aid** package, $19,441 average indebtedness upon graduation, $205 million endowment

Students *Undergraduates:* 3,425 full-time, 129 part-time. Students come from 48 states and territories, 58 other countries. *The most frequently chosen baccalaureate fields are:* business/marketing, biological/life sciences, health professions and related sciences. *Graduate:* 1,873 in professional programs, 476 in other graduate degree programs.

From out-of-state	54%	Age 25 or older	13%
Transferred in	3%	International students	4%
African Americans	3%	Asian Americans/Pacific Islanders	12%
Hispanic Americans	3%	Native Americans	1%

Faculty 1,438.

Expenses (1999–2000) *Comprehensive fee:* $19,578 includes full-time tuition ($13,566), mandatory fees ($566), and room and board ($5446). *College room only:* $3222. Room and board charges vary according to board plan and housing facility. *Part-time tuition:* $424 per credit. *Part-time fees:* $30 per term part-time. Part-time tuition and fees vary according to course load. *Payment plan:* installment. *Waivers:* adult students and employees or children of employees.

Library Reinert Alumni Memorial Library plus 2 others. *Operations spending 1999–2000:* $4.8 million. *Collection:* 5,923 audiovisual materials.

College life *Housing:* on-campus residence required through sophomore year. *Options:* coed, women-only, disabled students. *Social organizations:* national fraternities, national sororities; 29% of eligible men and 30% of eligible women are members. *Most popular organizations:* Alpha Phi Omega, Student Education Association of Nebraska, Alpha Kappa Psi, Occupational Therapy Association, Knights of Columbus.

Campus security 24-hour emergency response devices and patrols, student patrols, late-night transport-escort service, controlled dormitory access.

After graduation 101 organizations recruited on campus 1997–98. *Career center:* 3 full-time, 2 part-time personnel. Services include job fairs, resume preparation, interview workshops, resume referral, career/interest testing, career counseling, careers library, job bank, job interviews, CAP planning guide.

Freshmen 3,112 applied, 2,830 admitted, 834 enrolled.

Average high school GPA	3.67	SAT verbal scores above 500	84%
SAT math scores above 500	83%	ACT above 18	99%
From top 10% of their h.s. class	41%	From top quarter	72%
From top half	94%	1998 freshmen returning in 1999	85%

Application *Options:* electronic application, deferred entrance. *Application fee:* $30. *Required:* high school transcript; minimum 2.75 GPA; 1 letter of recommendation. *Recommended:* essay or personal statement.

Standardized tests *Admission: Required:* SAT I or ACT.

Significant dates *Application deadlines:* 8/1 (freshmen), rolling (transfers). *Financial aid deadline priority date:* 5/15.

Freshman Application Contact
Mr. Dennis J. O'Driscoll, Director of Admissions, Creighton University, 2500 California Plaza, Omaha, NE 68178-0001. **Phone:** 402-280-2703. **Toll-free phone:** 800-282-5835. **Fax:** 402-280-2685. **E-mail:** admissions@creighton.edu

Visit CollegeQuest.com for information on majors offered and athletics. College video available at CollegeQuest.com.

■ *See page 1538 for a narrative description.*

DANA COLLEGE
Blair, Nebraska

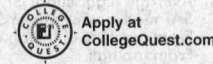

- **Independent**, 4-year, founded 1884, affiliated with Evangelical Lutheran Church in America
- **Degree** bachelor's
- **Small-town** 150-acre campus with easy access to Omaha
- **Coed**, 527 undergraduate students, 98% full-time, 51% women, 49% men
- **Moderately difficult** entrance level, 84% of applicants were admitted
- **12:1 student-to-undergraduate faculty ratio**
- **$12,700 tuition** and fees
- **$12,080 average financial aid** package, $14,735 average indebtedness upon graduation, $7.5 million endowment

Students *Undergraduates:* 517 full-time, 10 part-time. Students come from 25 states and territories. *The most frequently chosen baccalaureate fields are:* business/marketing, education, protective services/public administration.

From out-of-state	45%	Reside on campus	68%
Age 25 or older	30%	Transferred in	7%
International students	2%	African Americans	4%
Asian Americans/Pacific Islanders	5%	Hispanic Americans	2%
Native Americans	1%		

Faculty 78 (54% full-time), 41% with terminal degrees.

Expenses (1999–2000) *Comprehensive fee:* $16,774 includes full-time tuition ($12,150), mandatory fees ($550), and room and board ($4074). *College room only:* $1600. Room and board charges vary according to board plan and housing facility. *Part-time tuition:* $390 per semester hour. *Part-time fees:* $30 per term part-time. Part-time tuition and fees vary according to course load. *Waivers:* employees or children of employees.

Library C. A. Dana-Life Library plus 1 other. *Operations spending 1999–2000:* $220,395. *Collection:* 191,000 titles, 1,488 serial subscriptions, 3,757 audiovisual materials.

Nebraska

College life *Housing:* on-campus residence required through junior year. *Options:* coed, women-only. *Most popular organizations:* Residence Hall Association, Social Awareness Organization, Fellowship of Christian Athletes, Campus Ministry, HOPE (Helping Our People Expand).
Campus security 24-hour emergency response devices and patrols, late-night transport-escort service, controlled dormitory access.
After graduation 92% of class of 1998 had job offers within 6 months. *Career center:* 1 full-time, 1 part-time personnel. Services include job fairs, resume preparation, interview workshops, resume referral, career/interest testing, career counseling, careers library, job bank, job interviews.
Freshmen 453 applied, 382 admitted, 148 enrolled. 1 National Merit Scholar, 3 valedictorians.

Average high school GPA	3.1	SAT verbal scores above 500	26%
SAT math scores above 500	31%	ACT above 18	80%
From top 10% of their h.s. class	13%	From top quarter	29%
From top half	64%	1998 freshmen returning in 1999	68%

Application *Options:* eApply at www.CollegeQuest.com, Common Application, electronic application, deferred entrance. *Application fee:* $20. *Required:* essay or personal statement; high school transcript; minimum 2.0 GPA; class rank. *Required for some:* 1 letter of recommendation; interview.
Standardized tests *Admission: Required:* SAT I or ACT.
Significant dates *Financial aid deadline priority date:* 4/1.
Freshman Application Contact
Ms. Judy Mathiesen, Office Manager, Dana College, 2848 College Drive, Blair, NE 68008-1099. **Phone:** 402-426-7337. **Toll-free phone:** 800-444-3262. **Fax:** 402-426-7386. **E-mail:** admissions@dana.edu
Visit CollegeQuest.com for information on majors offered and athletics. Electronic viewbook available at CollegeQuest.com.

DOANE COLLEGE
Crete, Nebraska

- **Independent**, comprehensive, founded 1872, affiliated with United Church of Christ
- **Degrees** bachelor's and master's (nontraditional undergraduate programs and graduate programs offered at Lincoln campus)
- **Small-town** 300-acre campus with easy access to Omaha
- **Coed**, 1,579 undergraduate students, 71% full-time, 53% women, 47% men
- **Moderately difficult** entrance level, 89% of applicants were admitted
- **15:1 student-to-undergraduate faculty ratio**
- **66% graduate** in 6 years or less
- **$12,280 tuition** and fees
- **$11,161 average financial aid** package, $15,716 average indebtedness upon graduation, $56.6 million endowment

Students *Undergraduates:* 1,125 full-time, 454 part-time. Students come from 23 states and territories. *The most frequently chosen baccalaureate fields are:* business/marketing, education, social sciences and history. *Graduate:* 555 in graduate degree programs.

From out-of-state	18%	Reside on campus	74%
Age 25 or older	35%	Transferred in	2%
International students	1%	African Americans	2%
Asian Americans/Pacific Islanders	1%	Hispanic Americans	2%
Native Americans	0.1%		

Faculty 109 (58% full-time), 45% with terminal degrees.
Expenses (1999–2000) *Comprehensive fee:* $16,010 includes full-time tuition ($12,010), mandatory fees ($270), and room and board ($3730). Full-time tuition and fees vary according to location. Room and board charges vary according to board plan and location. *Part-time tuition:* $400 per credit. *Part-time fees:* $135 per term part-time. Part-time tuition and fees vary according to course load and location. *Payment plan:* installment. *Waivers:* senior citizens and employees or children of employees.
Library Perkins Library. *Operations spending 1999–2000:* $449,280. *Collection:* 179,394 titles, 3,143 serial subscriptions, 2,043 audiovisual materials.
College life *Housing:* on-campus residence required through senior year. *Option:* coed. *Social organizations:* local fraternities, local sororities; 40% of eligible men and 40% of eligible women are members. *Most popular organizations:* Greek society, Student Activities Council, Hansen Leadership Program, band/choir, Doane Ambassadors.

Campus security Student patrols, evening patrols by trained security personnel.
After graduation 78% of class of 1998 had job offers within 6 months. *Career center:* 2 full-time personnel. Services include job fairs, resume preparation, interview workshops, resume referral, career/interest testing, career counseling, careers library, job interviews.
Freshmen 922 applied, 818 admitted, 279 enrolled. 1 National Merit Scholar, 18 valedictorians.

Average high school GPA	3.4	SAT verbal scores above 500	N/R
SAT math scores above 500	N/R	ACT above 18	93%
From top 10% of their h.s. class	21%	From top quarter	48%
From top half	81%	1998 freshmen returning in 1999	78%

Application *Options:* early admission, deferred entrance. *Application fee:* $15. *Required:* high school transcript; 2 letters of recommendation. *Required for some:* interview. *Recommended:* minimum 2.0 GPA.
Standardized tests *Admission: Required:* SAT I or ACT.
Significant dates *Application deadlines:* 8/15 (freshmen), 8/15 (transfers). *Financial aid deadline priority date:* 3/1.
Freshman Application Contact
Mr. Dan Kunzman, Dean of Admissions, Doane College, 1014 Boswell Avenue, Crete, NE 68333-2430. **Phone:** 402-826-8222. **Toll-free phone:** 800-333-6263. **Fax:** 402-826-8600. **E-mail:** admissions@doane.edu
Visit CollegeQuest.com for information on majors offered and athletics. College video available at CollegeQuest.com.

GRACE UNIVERSITY
Omaha, Nebraska

- **Independent interdenominational**, comprehensive, founded 1943
- **Degrees** associate, bachelor's, and master's
- **Urban** 15-acre campus
- **Coed**
- **Moderately difficult** entrance level
- **$7964 tuition** and fees

Expenses (1999–2000) *Comprehensive fee:* $11,364 includes full-time tuition ($7440), mandatory fees ($524), and room and board ($3400). Room and board charges vary according to board plan and housing facility. *Part-time tuition:* $248 per credit hour. *Part-time fees:* $122 per term part-time. Part-time tuition and fees vary according to course load.
Institutional Web site http://www.graceu.edu/
College life *Housing:* on-campus residence required through senior year. *Options:* men-only, women-only.
Campus security Late-night transport-escort service, controlled dormitory access.
Application *Options:* electronic application, early admission, deferred entrance. *Application fee:* $25. *Required:* essay or personal statement; high school transcript; minimum 2.0 GPA; 3 letters of recommendation. *Required for some:* interview.
Standardized tests *Admission: Required:* SAT I or ACT. *Recommended:* ACT.
Admissions Office Contact
Grace University, 1311 South Ninth Street, Omaha, NE 68108. **Toll-free phone:** 800-383-1422. **Fax:** 402-341-9587. **E-mail:** admissions@graceu.edu
Visit CollegeQuest.com for information on athletics. College video available at CollegeQuest.com.

HASTINGS COLLEGE
Hastings, Nebraska

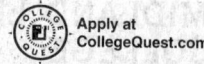

- **Independent Presbyterian**, comprehensive, founded 1882
- **Degrees** bachelor's and master's
- **Small-town** 88-acre campus
- **Coed**, 1,082 undergraduate students, 98% full-time, 52% women, 48% men
- **Moderately difficult** entrance level, 86% of applicants were admitted
- **13:1 student-to-undergraduate faculty ratio**
- **57.5% graduate** in 6 years or less

Nebraska

Hastings College (continued)
- $12,916 tuition and fees
- $10,292 average financial aid package, $15,778 average indebtedness upon graduation, $57.9 million endowment

Students *Undergraduates:* 1,057 full-time, 25 part-time. Students come from 28 states and territories, 6 other countries. *The most frequently chosen baccalaureate fields are:* business/marketing, education, psychology. *Graduate:* 30 in graduate degree programs.

From out-of-state	22%	Reside on campus	55%
Transferred in	3%	International students	1%
African Americans	1%	Asian Americans/Pacific Islanders	0.3%
Hispanic Americans	2%	Native Americans	0.4%

Faculty 114 (61% full-time), 50% with terminal degrees.

Expenses (2000–2001) *Comprehensive fee:* $16,982 includes full-time tuition ($12,396), mandatory fees ($520), and room and board ($4066). *College room only:* $1714. Full-time tuition and fees vary according to degree level and program. Room and board charges vary according to board plan. Part-time tuition and fees vary according to course load, degree level, and program. *Payment plans:* installment, deferred payment. *Waivers:* adult students and employees or children of employees.

Library Perkins Library. *Operations spending 1999–2000:* $418,213. *Collection:* 123,512 titles, 583 serial subscriptions.

College life *Housing:* on-campus residence required through sophomore year. *Options:* coed, men-only, women-only. *Social organizations:* local fraternities, local sororities; 20% of eligible men and 32% of eligible women are members. *Most popular organizations:* Student Association, Public Relations Council, Fellowship of Christian Athletes, Phi Mu Alpha Sinfonia, Hastings College Singers.

Campus security 24-hour emergency response devices, student patrols, late-night transport-escort service, controlled dormitory access.

After graduation 18 organizations recruited on campus 1997–98. 72% of class of 1998 had job offers within 6 months. *Career center:* 2 full-time personnel. Services include job fairs, resume preparation, interview workshops, resume referral, career/interest testing, career counseling, careers library, job bank, job interviews, internship assistance. *Graduate education:* 17% of class of 1999 went directly to graduate and professional school: 10% graduate arts and sciences, 1% education, 1% law, 1% medicine.

Freshmen 1,098 applied, 946 admitted, 288 enrolled. 1 National Merit Scholar, 31 class presidents, 22 valedictorians, 81 student government officers.

SAT verbal scores above 500	64%	SAT math scores above 500	69%
ACT above 18	98%	From top 10% of their h.s. class	24%
From top quarter	51%	From top half	81%
1998 freshmen returning in 1999	75%		

Application *Options:* eApply at www.CollegeQuest.com, Common Application, electronic application. *Application fee:* $20. *Required:* high school transcript; minimum 2.0 GPA; counselor's recommendation. *Required for some:* essay or personal statement; 2 letters of recommendation; interview.

Standardized tests *Admission: Required:* SAT I or ACT.

Significant dates *Application deadlines:* 8/1 (freshmen), rolling (transfers). *Financial aid deadline:* 9/1. *Priority date:* 5/1.

Freshman Application Contact
Mr. Michael Karloff, Director of Admissions, Hastings College, 800 North Turner Avenue, Hastings, NE 68901-7696. **Phone:** 402-461-7316. **Toll-free phone:** 800-532-7642. **Fax:** 402-463-3002. **E-mail:** admissions@hastings.edu
Visit CollegeQuest.com for information on majors offered and athletics. College video and electronic viewbook available at CollegeQuest.com.

MIDLAND LUTHERAN COLLEGE
Fremont, Nebraska

Apply at CollegeQuest.com

- **Independent Lutheran**, 4-year, founded 1883
- **Degrees** associate and bachelor's
- **Small-town** 27-acre campus with easy access to Omaha
- **Coed**, 984 undergraduate students, 93% full-time, 60% women, 40% men
- **Moderately difficult** entrance level, 92% of applicants were admitted
- **15:1** student-to-undergraduate faculty ratio
- **$13,320** tuition and fees
- **$12,381** average financial aid package, $18,491 average indebtedness upon graduation, $23 million endowment

Midland's Anderson Complex, dedicated in 1985, houses modern facilities for business, education, humanities, journalism, and nursing. Classrooms, laboratories, and faculty offices make this building a campus landmark. Computer facilities are available for student use throughout the campus. A 15:1 student-faculty ratio promotes personal attention for individual students.

Students *Undergraduates:* 917 full-time, 67 part-time. Students come from 24 states and territories, 3 other countries. *The most frequently chosen baccalaureate fields are:* business/marketing, biological/life sciences, education.

From out-of-state	24%	Reside on campus	52%
Age 25 or older	15%	Transferred in	5%
International students	1%	African Americans	5%
Asian Americans/Pacific Islanders	0.3%	Hispanic Americans	1%
Native Americans	0.1%		

Faculty 90 (67% full-time), 41% with terminal degrees.

Expenses (1999–2000) *Comprehensive fee:* $16,930 includes full-time tuition ($13,320) and room and board ($3610). *College room only:* $1530. Full-time tuition and fees vary according to course load. Room and board charges vary according to board plan. *Part-time tuition:* $330 per credit hour. Part-time tuition and fees vary according to course load. *Payment plan:* installment. *Waivers:* senior citizens and employees or children of employees.

Library Luther Library. *Collection:* 110,000 titles, 900 serial subscriptions.

College life *Housing:* on-campus residence required through sophomore year. *Options:* coed, men-only, women-only. *Social organizations:* local fraternities, local sororities; 40% of eligible men and 40% of eligible women are members. *Most popular organizations:* Student Nurses Association, Student Education Association, Phi Beta Lambda, Society for Collegiate Journalists, Circle K.

Campus security 24-hour emergency response devices, student patrols, late-night transport-escort service, controlled dormitory access.

After graduation 24 organizations recruited on campus 1997–98. 94% of class of 1998 had job offers within 6 months. *Career center:* 2 full-time personnel. Services include job fairs, resume preparation, resume referral, career counseling, careers library, job interviews. *Graduate education:* 12% of class of 1999 went directly to graduate and professional school.

Freshmen 747 applied, 690 admitted, 272 enrolled. 11 valedictorians.

Average high school GPA	3.09	SAT verbal scores above 500	N/R
SAT math scores above 500	N/R	ACT above 18	88%
From top 10% of their h.s. class	21%	From top quarter	50%
From top half	83%	1998 freshmen returning in 1999	76%

Application *Options:* eApply at www.CollegeQuest.com, electronic application, early admission. *Application fee:* $30. *Required:* high school transcript.

Standardized tests *Admission: Required:* SAT I or ACT.

Significant dates *Application deadlines:* rolling (freshmen), rolling (transfers). *Notification:* continuous until 9/1 (freshmen). *Financial aid deadline:* continuous.

Freshman Application Contact
Mr. Roland R. Kahnk, Vice President for Enrollment Services, Midland Lutheran College, Admissions Office, Fremont, NE 68025-4200. **Phone:** 402-721-5487 Ext. 6500. **Toll-free phone:** 800-642-8382 Ext. 6500. **Fax:** 402-721-0250. **E-mail:** rkahnk@admin.mlc.edu
Visit CollegeQuest.com for information on majors offered and athletics. College video and electronic viewbook available at CollegeQuest.com.

- *See page 2054 for a narrative description.*

NEBRASKA CHRISTIAN COLLEGE
Norfolk, Nebraska

Apply at CollegeQuest.com

- **Independent**, 4-year, founded 1944, affiliated with Christian Churches and Churches of Christ
- **Degrees** associate and bachelor's
- **Small-town** 85-acre campus

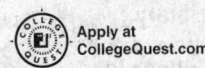

Nebraska

- **Coed**, 130 undergraduate students, 85% full-time, 43% women, 57% men
- **Minimally difficult** entrance level, 100% of applicants were admitted
- **$4930 tuition** and fees
- **$200,000 endowment**

Students *Undergraduates:* Students come from 16 states and territories, 2 other countries. *The most frequently chosen baccalaureate fields are:* liberal arts/general studies, philosophy.

Reside on campus	85%	Age 25 or older	12%
International students	2%	African Americans	1%
Asian Americans/Pacific Islanders	1%	Hispanic Americans	1%

Faculty 13.

Expenses (1999–2000) *Comprehensive fee:* $7890 includes full-time tuition ($4500), mandatory fees ($430), and room and board ($2960). *College room only:* $1350. *Part-time tuition:* $150 per credit hour. *Part-time fees:* $108 per term part-time. Part-time tuition and fees vary according to course load. *Waivers:* employees or children of employees.

Library Swedberg Library. *Collection:* 250,000 titles, 149 serial subscriptions.

College life On-campus residence required through senior year.

After graduation 69% of class of 1998 had job offers within 6 months. *Career center:* Services include career counseling. *Graduate education:* 8% of class of 1999 went directly to graduate and professional school: 8% theology.

Freshmen 89 applied, 89 admitted.

SAT verbal scores above 500	N/R	SAT math scores above 500	N/R
ACT above 18	N/R	From top 10% of their h.s. class	13%
From top quarter	32%	From top half	56%
1998 freshmen returning in 1999	66%		

Application *Option:* eApply at www.CollegeQuest.com. *Required:* high school transcript; 2 letters of recommendation. *Required for some:* interview.

Standardized tests *Admission: Required:* ACT.

Significant dates *Application deadlines:* rolling (freshmen), rolling (transfers). *Notification:* continuous until 9/1 (freshmen). *Financial aid deadline:* continuous.

Freshman Application Contact
Mr. Jerry Hopkins, Director of Admissions, Nebraska Christian College, 1800 Syracuse Avenue, Norfolk, NE 68701-2458. **Phone:** 402-379-5000.

Visit CollegeQuest.com for information on majors offered and athletics.

NEBRASKA METHODIST COLLEGE OF NURSING AND ALLIED HEALTH
Omaha, Nebraska

- **Independent**, comprehensive, founded 1891, affiliated with United Methodist Church
- **Degrees** associate, bachelor's, and master's
- **Urban** 5-acre campus
- **Coed**, primarily women, 387 undergraduate students, 57% full-time, 93% women, 7% men
- **Moderately difficult** entrance level, 93% of applicants were admitted
- **10:1 student-to-undergraduate faculty ratio**
- **$8700 tuition** and fees
- **$8325 average financial aid** package, $35 million endowment

Students *Undergraduates:* 219 full-time, 168 part-time. Students come from 8 states and territories. *The most frequently chosen baccalaureate field is:* health professions and related sciences. *Graduate:* 24 in graduate degree programs.

Reside on campus	20%	Age 25 or older	45%
Transferred in	21%	African Americans	5%
Asian Americans/Pacific Islanders	1%	Hispanic Americans	3%
Native Americans	0.3%		

Faculty 40 (70% full-time).

Expenses (1999–2000) *Tuition:* full-time $8160; part-time $272 per credit hour. *Required fees:* full-time $540; $18 per credit hour. *College room only:* $1480. Room and board charges vary according to housing facility and location. *Payment plan:* installment.

Library John Moritz Library plus 1 other. *Operations spending 1999–2000:* $350,002. *Collection:* 15,176 titles, 374 serial subscriptions.

College life *Housing: Option:* coed. *Most popular organizations:* Student Senate, Student Nurses Association, Methodist Allied Health Student Association, Student Ambassadors, Orientation Team.

Campus security 24-hour emergency response devices, late-night transport-escort service, controlled dormitory access.

After graduation 4 organizations recruited on campus 1997–98. 75% of class of 1998 had job offers within 6 months. *Career center:* 1 full-time personnel. Services include job fairs, resume preparation, resume referral, career counseling, job bank. *Graduate education:* 3% of class of 1999 went directly to graduate and professional school: 2% medicine, 1% graduate arts and sciences.

Freshmen 40 applied, 37 admitted, 39 enrolled.

Average high school GPA	3.34	SAT verbal scores above 500	N/R
SAT math scores above 500	N/R	ACT above 18	79%
From top 10% of their h.s. class	12%	From top quarter	38%
From top half	38%	1998 freshmen returning in 1999	75%

Application *Option:* deferred entrance. *Application fee:* $25. *Required:* essay or personal statement; high school transcript; minimum 2.0 GPA; 3 letters of recommendation; interview.

Standardized tests *Admission: Required:* SAT I or ACT.

Significant dates *Application deadlines:* 4/1 (freshmen), 4/1 (transfers). *Notification:* 4/15 (freshmen). *Financial aid deadline priority date:* 5/1.

Freshman Application Contact
Ms. Deann Sterner, Director of Admissions, Nebraska Methodist College of Nursing and Allied Health, 8501 West Dodge Road, Omaha, NE 68114-3426. **Phone:** 402-354-4922. **Toll-free phone:** 800-335-5510. **Fax:** 402-354-4819. **E-mail:** dsterne@nmns.org

Visit CollegeQuest.com for information on majors offered and athletics. College video available at CollegeQuest.com.

NEBRASKA WESLEYAN UNIVERSITY
Lincoln, Nebraska

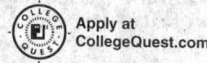
Apply at CollegeQuest.com

- **Independent United Methodist**, 4-year, founded 1887
- **Degree** bachelor's
- **Suburban** 50-acre campus with easy access to Omaha
- **Coed**, 1,607 undergraduate students, 91% full-time, 57% women, 43% men
- **Moderately difficult** entrance level, 94% of applicants were admitted
- **14:1 student-to-undergraduate faculty ratio**
- **62.5% graduate** in 6 years or less
- **$12,826 tuition** and fees
- **$9748 average financial aid** package, $35.3 million endowment

Students *Undergraduates:* 1,461 full-time, 146 part-time. Students come from 24 states and territories. *The most frequently chosen baccalaureate fields are:* biological/life sciences, business/marketing, psychology.

From out-of-state	6%	Reside on campus	38%
Age 25 or older	7%	Transferred in	3%
International students	0.4%	African Americans	1%
Asian Americans/Pacific Islanders	1%	Hispanic Americans	1%
Native Americans	0.2%		

Faculty 159 (58% full-time), 47% with terminal degrees.

Expenses (1999–2000) *One-time required fee:* $80. *Comprehensive fee:* $16,800 includes full-time tuition ($12,584), mandatory fees ($242), and room and board ($3974). Room and board charges vary according to board plan. *Part-time tuition:* $475 per hour. Part-time tuition and fees vary according to class time and course load. *Payment plan:* installment. *Waivers:* adult students, senior citizens, and employees or children of employees.

Library Cochrane Woods Library. *Operations spending 1999–2000:* $627,976. *Collection:* 132,758 titles, 741 serial subscriptions, 7,670 audiovisual materials.

College life *Housing:* on-campus residence required through sophomore year. *Options:* coed, men-only, women-only. *Social organizations:* national fraternities, national sororities, local fraternities, local sororities; 42% of eligible men and 34% of eligible women are members. *Most popular organizations:* Student Affairs Senate, Union programs, Ambassadors, FCA.

Nebraska

Nebraska Wesleyan University *(continued)*

Campus security 24-hour patrols, late-night transport-escort service, controlled dormitory access.

After graduation 77 organizations recruited on campus 1997–98. *Career center:* 3 full-time, 1 part-time personnel. Services include job fairs, resume preparation, interview workshops, career/interest testing, career counseling, careers library, job interviews.

Freshmen 1,105 applied, 1,041 admitted, 359 enrolled. 22 valedictorians.

SAT verbal scores above 500	N/R	SAT math scores above 500	N/R
ACT above 18	99%	From top 10% of their h.s. class	26%
From top quarter	55%	From top half	89%
1998 freshmen returning in 1999	79%		

Application *Options:* eApply at www.CollegeQuest.com, Common Application, electronic application, early decision, deferred entrance. *Application fee:* $20. *Required:* high school transcript; minimum 2.0 GPA. *Required for some:* essay or personal statement; resume of activities. *Recommended:* letters of recommendation; interview.

Standardized tests *Admission: Required:* SAT I or ACT.

Significant dates *Application deadlines:* 1/5 (freshmen), rolling (transfers). *Early decision:* 11/15. *Notification:* 12/15 (early decision). ***Financial aid deadline:*** 3/1.

Freshman Application Contact
Mr. Kendal E. Sieg, Director of Admissions, Nebraska Wesleyan University, 5000 Saint Paul Avenue, Lincoln, NE 68504-2796. **Phone:** 402-465-2218. **Toll-free phone:** 800-541-3818. **Fax:** 402-465-2179. **E-mail:** adm@nebrwesleyan.edu

Visit CollegeQuest.com for information on majors offered and athletics. College video available at CollegeQuest.com.

PERU STATE COLLEGE
Peru, Nebraska

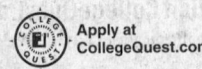
Apply at CollegeQuest.com

- **State-supported**, comprehensive, founded 1867
- **Degrees** bachelor's and master's
- **Rural** 103-acre campus
- **Coed**, 1,454 undergraduate students, 60% full-time, 55% women, 45% men
- **Noncompetitive** entrance level, 63% of applicants were admitted
- **14:1** student-to-undergraduate faculty ratio
- **$2271 tuition** and fees (in-state); $4146 (out-of-state)

Part of Nebraska State College System.

Students *Undergraduates:* 876 full-time, 578 part-time. Students come from 31 states and territories, 1 other country. *The most frequently chosen baccalaureate fields are:* biological/life sciences, education, interdisciplinary studies. *Graduate:* 210 in graduate degree programs.

From out-of-state	14%	Age 25 or older	8%
Transferred in	7%	International students	1%
African Americans	2%	Asian Americans/Pacific Islanders	1%
Hispanic Americans	1%	Native Americans	1%

Faculty 170 (26% full-time).

Expenses (1999–2000) *Tuition, state resident:* full-time $1875; part-time $62 per semester hour. *Tuition, nonresident:* full-time $3750; part-time $125 per semester hour. *Required fees:* full-time $396; $8 per semester hour; $55 per term part-time. Full-time tuition and fees vary according to course load. Part-time tuition and fees vary according to course load. *College room and board:* $3304; room only: $1586. Room and board charges vary according to board plan and housing facility. *Waivers:* employees or children of employees.

Library Peru State College Library. *Collection:* 177,373 titles, 232 serial subscriptions.

College life *Housing:* on-campus residence required through sophomore year. *Option:* coed. *Most popular organizations:* Peru Chorus, Campus Activities Board, marching band, student government, Peru Players.

Campus security 24-hour patrols.

After graduation 55 organizations recruited on campus 1997–98. 86% of class of 1998 had job offers within 6 months. *Career center:* 3 full-time, 2 part-time personnel. Services include job fairs, resume preparation, resume referral, career counseling, careers library, job bank, job interviews. ***Graduate education:*** 13% of class of 1999 went directly to graduate and professional school: 7% business, 4% graduate arts and sciences, 1% law, 1% medicine.

Freshmen 460 applied, 291 admitted, 193 enrolled.

Average high school GPA	2.89	SAT verbal scores above 500	N/R
SAT math scores above 500	N/R	ACT above 18	69%
From top 10% of their h.s. class	10%	From top quarter	14%
From top half	43%	1998 freshmen returning in 1999	53%

Application *Options:* eApply at www.CollegeQuest.com, Common Application, early admission, deferred entrance. *Application fee:* $10. *Required:* high school transcript. *Required for some:* minimum 2.0 GPA; letters of recommendation.

Standardized tests *Placement: Required:* SAT I or ACT.

Significant dates *Application deadlines:* rolling (freshmen), rolling (transfers). *Financial aid deadline priority date:* 3/1.

Freshman Application Contact
Mr. Robert Lopez, Director of Enrollment Management, Peru State College, Administration Building, Peru, NE 68421. **Phone:** 402-872-3815 Ext. 2221. **Toll-free phone:** 800-742-4412. **E-mail:** rlopez@oakmail.peru.edu

Visit CollegeQuest.com for information on majors offered and athletics.

■ *See page 2262 for a narrative description.*

UNION COLLEGE
Lincoln, Nebraska

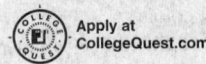
Apply at CollegeQuest.com

- **Independent Seventh-day Adventist**, 4-year, founded 1891
- **Degrees** associate and bachelor's
- **Suburban** 26-acre campus with easy access to Omaha
- **Coed**, 776 undergraduate students, 87% full-time, 55% women, 45% men
- **Minimally difficult** entrance level, 58% of applicants were admitted
- **14:1** student-to-undergraduate faculty ratio
- **$10,696 tuition** and fees
- **$8245 average financial aid** package, $10,736 average indebtedness upon graduation, $6.9 million endowment

Students *Undergraduates:* 677 full-time, 99 part-time. Students come from 41 states and territories, 29 other countries. *The most frequently chosen baccalaureate fields are:* business/marketing, education, health professions and related sciences.

From out-of-state	77%	Reside on campus	69%
Age 25 or older	8%	Transferred in	10%
International students	12%	African Americans	3%
Asian Americans/Pacific Islanders	2%	Hispanic Americans	5%
Native Americans	2%		

Faculty 85 (64% full-time), 24% with terminal degrees.

Expenses (1999–2000) *Comprehensive fee:* $13,726 includes full-time tuition ($10,590), mandatory fees ($106), and room and board ($3030). *College room only:* $2080. Full-time tuition and fees vary according to course load. *Part-time tuition:* $442 per semester hour. *Payment plans:* tuition prepayment, installment. *Waivers:* senior citizens and employees or children of employees.

Library Ella Johnson Crandall Library. *Operations spending 1999–2000:* $334,953. *Collection:* 150,032 titles, 4,048 audiovisual materials.

College life *Housing:* on-campus residence required through senior year. *Options:* men-only, women-only.

Campus security 24-hour emergency response devices, student patrols, late-night transport-escort service.

After graduation 110 organizations recruited on campus 1997–98. 89% of class of 1998 had job offers within 6 months. *Career center:* 2 full-time, 1 part-time personnel. Services include job fairs, resume preparation, interview workshops, resume referral, career/interest testing, career counseling, careers library, job bank, job interviews.

Freshmen 464 applied, 271 admitted, 184 enrolled. 3 National Merit Scholars, 7 class presidents, 9 valedictorians, 42 student government officers.

Average high school GPA	3.17	SAT verbal scores above 500	N/R
SAT math scores above 500	N/R	ACT above 18	89%
1998 freshmen returning in 1999	93%		

Application *Options:* eApply at www.CollegeQuest.com, Common Application, electronic application, early admission, deferred entrance. *Application fee:* $0. *Required:* high school transcript; minimum 2.5 GPA; 3 letters of recommendation. *Required for some:* interview. *Recommended:* essay or personal statement; interview.
Standardized tests *Admission: Required:* ACT.
Significant dates *Application deadlines:* rolling (freshmen), rolling (transfers). *Financial aid deadline priority date:* 5/1.
Freshman Application Contact
Huda McClelland, Director of Admissions, Union College, 3800 South 48th Street, Lincoln, NE 68516. **Phone:** 402-486-2504. **Toll-free phone:** 800-228-4600. **Fax:** 402-486-2895. **E-mail:** ucenrol@ucollege.edu
Visit CollegeQuest.com for information on majors offered and athletics.

■ *See page 2660 for a narrative description.*

UNIVERSITY OF NEBRASKA AT KEARNEY
Kearney, Nebraska

- **State-supported**, comprehensive, founded 1903
- **Degrees** bachelor's, master's, and post-master's certificates
- **Small-town** 235-acre campus
- **Coed**, 5,805 undergraduate students, 87% full-time, 56% women, 44% men
- **Moderately difficult** entrance level, 95% of applicants were admitted
- **43% graduate** in 6 years or less
- **$2728 tuition** and fees (in-state); $4581 (out-of-state)

Part of University of Nebraska System.
Students *Undergraduates:* 5,047 full-time, 758 part-time. Students come from 39 states and territories, 45 other countries. *The most frequently chosen baccalaureate fields are:* business/marketing, education, protective services/public administration. *Graduate:* 975 in graduate degree programs.

From out-of-state	6%	Reside on campus	33%
Age 25 or older	12%	Transferred in	6%
International students	3%	African Americans	1%
Asian Americans/Pacific Islanders	0.5%	Hispanic Americans	2%
Native Americans	0.3%		

Faculty 412 (78% full-time).
Expenses (1999–2000) *One-time required fee:* $30. *Tuition, state resident:* full-time $2122; part-time $71 per semester hour. *Tuition, nonresident:* full-time $3975; part-time $132 per semester hour. *Required fees:* full-time $606; $11 per semester hour; $5 per term part-time. Full-time tuition and fees vary according to course load. Part-time tuition and fees vary according to course load. *College room and board:* $3430; room only: $1720. Room and board charges vary according to board plan and housing facility. *Payment plan:* installment. *Waivers:* employees or children of employees.
Library Calvin T. Ryan Library. *Operations spending 1999–2000:* $2 million. *Collection:* 286,555 titles, 1,637 serial subscriptions.
College life *Housing:* on-campus residence required in freshman year. *Options:* coed, men-only, women-only. *Social organizations:* national fraternities, national sororities; 9% of eligible men and 9% of eligible women are members. *Most popular organizations:* Student Activities Council, Intramurals Council, Residence Hall Association, International Student Association, Panhellenic/Interfraternity Council.
Campus security 24-hour emergency response devices and patrols, late-night transport-escort service.
After graduation 54 organizations recruited on campus 1997–98. 50% of class of 1998 had job offers within 6 months. *Career center:* 4 full-time, 1 part-time personnel. Services include job fairs, resume preparation, interview workshops, resume referral, career/interest testing, career counseling, careers library, job bank, job interviews.
Freshmen 2,503 applied, 2,382 admitted, 1,224 enrolled.

Average high school GPA	3.37	SAT verbal scores above 500	N/R
SAT math scores above 500	N/R	ACT above 18	89%
From top 10% of their h.s. class	10%	From top quarter	49%
From top half	89%	1998 freshmen returning in 1999	77%

Application *Option:* Common Application. *Application fee:* $25. *Required:* high school transcript. *Required for some:* essay or personal statement; 3 letters of recommendation.
Standardized tests *Admission: Required:* SAT I or ACT. *Recommended:* ACT.
Significant dates *Application deadlines:* 8/1 (freshmen), 8/1 (transfers). *Financial aid deadline:* continuous.
Freshman Application Contact
Mr. John Kundel, Director of Admissions and Financial Aid, University of Nebraska at Kearney, 905 West 25th Street, Kearney, NE 68849-0001. **Phone:** 308-865-8526. **Toll-free phone:** 800-445-3434. **Fax:** 308-865-8987. **E-mail:** admissionsug@unk.edu
Visit CollegeQuest.com for information on majors offered and athletics. Electronic viewbook available at CollegeQuest.com.

UNIVERSITY OF NEBRASKA AT OMAHA
Omaha, Nebraska

- **State-supported**, university, founded 1908
- **Degrees** associate, bachelor's, master's, and doctoral
- **Urban** 88-acre campus
- **Coed**, 10,342 undergraduate students, 69% full-time, 53% women, 47% men
- **Minimally difficult** entrance level, 90% of applicants were admitted
- **19:1 student-to-undergraduate faculty ratio**
- **25.16% graduate** in 6 years or less
- **$2823 tuition** and fees (in-state); $6888 (out-of-state)
- **$14,200 average indebtedness** upon graduation, $7.3 million endowment

Part of University of Nebraska System.
Students *Undergraduates:* 7,120 full-time, 3,222 part-time. Students come from 42 states and territories, 84 other countries. *The most frequently chosen baccalaureate fields are:* business/marketing, education, protective services/public administration. *Graduate:* 2,605 in graduate degree programs.

From out-of-state	8%	Age 25 or older	26%
Transferred in	10%	International students	3%
African Americans	6%	Asian Americans/Pacific Islanders	2%
Hispanic Americans	3%	Native Americans	1%

Faculty 853 (50% full-time), 45% with terminal degrees.
Expenses (1999–2000) *Tuition, state resident:* full-time $2393; part-time $80 per semester hour. *Tuition, nonresident:* full-time $6458; part-time $215 per semester hour. *Required fees:* full-time $430; $12 per semester hour; $60 per term part-time. Full-time tuition and fees vary according to course load and program. Part-time tuition and fees vary according to program. *College room and board:* $5290; room only: $2151. *Payment plan:* deferred payment.
Library University Library. *Operations spending 1999–2000:* $4.5 million. *Collection:* 817,238 titles, 9,741 serial subscriptions.
College life *Social organizations:* national fraternities, national sororities; 1% of eligible men and 1% of eligible women are members. *Most popular organizations:* Student Programming Organization, fraternities/sororities.
Campus security 24-hour emergency response devices, late-night transport-escort service.
After graduation 145 organizations recruited on campus 1997–98. 86% of class of 1998 had job offers within 6 months. *Career center:* 7 full-time, 12 part-time personnel. Services include job fairs, resume preparation, resume referral, career counseling, careers library, job bank, job interviews.
Freshmen 3,448 applied, 3,103 admitted, 1,620 enrolled.

Average high school GPA	3.19	SAT verbal scores above 500	N/R
SAT math scores above 500	N/R	ACT above 18	88%
From top 10% of their h.s. class	10%	From top quarter	30%
From top half	66%	1998 freshmen returning in 1999	66%

Application *Option:* deferred entrance. *Application fee:* $25. *Required:* high school transcript; rank in upper 50% of high school class.
Standardized tests *Admission: Required:* SAT I or ACT.
Significant dates *Application deadlines:* rolling (freshmen), rolling (transfers). *Financial aid deadline priority date:* 3/1.
Freshman Application Contact
Ms. Jolene Adams, Associate Director of Admissions, University of Nebraska at Omaha, 6001 Dodge Street, Omaha, NE 68182. **Phone:** 402-554-2416. **Toll-free phone:** 800-858-8648. **Fax:** 402-554-3472.

Nebraska

University of Nebraska at Omaha (continued)
Visit CollegeQuest.com for information on majors offered and athletics. College video available at CollegeQuest.com.

UNIVERSITY OF NEBRASKA—LINCOLN
Lincoln, Nebraska

- **State-supported**, university, founded 1869
- **Degrees** associate, bachelor's, master's, doctoral, first professional, and post-master's certificates
- **Urban** 623-acre campus with easy access to Omaha
- **Coed**, 17,804 undergraduate students, 88% full-time, 47% women, 53% men
- **Moderately difficult** entrance level, 92% of applicants were admitted
- **18:1 student-to-undergraduate faculty ratio**
- **46.4% graduate** in 6 years or less
- **$3338 tuition** and fees (in-state); $7845 (out-of-state)

Part of University of Nebraska System.
Students *Undergraduates:* Students come from 48 states and territories, 109 other countries. *The most frequently chosen baccalaureate fields are:* business/marketing, education, engineering/engineering technologies. *Graduate:* 384 in professional programs, 3,954 in other graduate degree programs.

Reside on campus	24%	Age 25 or older	10%
International students	3%	African Americans	2%
Asian Americans/Pacific Islanders	2%	Hispanic Americans	2%
Native Americans	0.4%		

Faculty 1,099 (97% full-time), 96% with terminal degrees.
Expenses (1999–2000) *Tuition, state resident:* full-time $2618; part-time $87 per credit hour. *Tuition, nonresident:* full-time $7125; part-time $238 per credit hour. *Required fees:* full-time $720; $5 per credit hour; $119 per term part-time. Full-time tuition and fees vary according to course load. Part-time tuition and fees vary according to course load. *College room and board:* $4070; room only: $1880. Room and board charges vary according to board plan and housing facility. *Waivers:* employees or children of employees.
Library Love Memorial Library plus 10 others. *Collection:* 23,244 serial subscriptions, 47,794 audiovisual materials.
College life *Housing:* on-campus residence required in freshman year. *Options:* coed, men-only, women-only, cooperative. *Social organizations:* national fraternities, national sororities, local fraternities, local sororities; 18% of eligible men and 16% of eligible women are members. *Most popular organizations:* Student Alumni Association, University Ambassadors, University Program Council, Golden Key.
Campus security 24-hour emergency response devices and patrols, student patrols, late-night transport-escort service, controlled dormitory access.
After graduation 300 organizations recruited on campus 1997–98. *Career center:* 9 full-time, 4 part-time personnel. Services include job fairs, resume preparation, interview workshops, resume referral, career/interest testing, career counseling, careers library, job bank, job interviews. *Major awards:* 1 Fulbright Scholar.
Freshmen 6,977 applied, 6,453 admitted. 30 National Merit Scholars.

SAT verbal scores above 500	76%	SAT math scores above 500	80%
ACT above 18	97%	From top 10% of their h.s. class	25%
From top quarter	53%	From top half	85%
1998 freshmen returning in 1999	79%		

Application *Application fee:* $25. *Required:* high school transcript. *Required for some:* rank in upper 50% of high school class.
Standardized tests *Admission:* Required: SAT I or ACT.
Significant dates *Application deadlines:* 6/30 (freshmen), 6/30 (transfers). *Financial aid deadline:* continuous.
Freshman Application Contact
Dr. Larry Routh, Director of Admissions, Interim, University of Nebraska–Lincoln, 1410 Q Street, Lincoln, NE 68588-0417. **Phone:** 402-472-2030. **Toll-free phone:** 800-742-8800. **Fax:** 402-472-0670. **E-mail:** nuhusker@unl.edu
Visit CollegeQuest.com for information on majors offered and athletics. College video and electronic viewbook available at CollegeQuest.com.

■ *See page 2782 for a narrative description.*

UNIVERSITY OF NEBRASKA MEDICAL CENTER
Omaha, Nebraska

- **State-supported**, upper-level, founded 1869
- **Degrees** bachelor's, master's, doctoral, first professional, post-master's, postbachelor's, and first professional certificates
- **Urban** 51-acre campus
- **Coed**, 752 undergraduate students, 92% full-time, 86% women, 14% men
- **Moderately difficult** entrance level
- **$2838 tuition** and fees (in-state); $7345 (out-of-state)
- **$24,100 average indebtedness** upon graduation, $9.4 million endowment

Part of University of Nebraska System.
Students *Undergraduates:* 694 full-time, 58 part-time. Students come from 3 other countries. *The most frequently chosen baccalaureate field is:* health professions and related sciences. *Graduate:* 925 in professional programs, 901 in other graduate degree programs.

From out-of-state	9%	Age 25 or older	41%
Transferred in	33%	International students	0.4%
African Americans	1%	Asian Americans/Pacific Islanders	2%
Hispanic Americans	2%	Native Americans	1%

Faculty 786 (80% full-time).
Expenses (1999–2000) *Tuition, state resident:* full-time $2618; part-time $87 per hour. *Tuition, nonresident:* full-time $7125; part-time $238 per hour. *Required fees:* full-time $220; $110 per term part-time. Full-time tuition and fees vary according to location and program. Part-time tuition and fees vary according to course load, location, and program.
Library McGoogan Medical Library. *Operations spending 1999–2000:* $3 million. *Collection:* 243,256 titles, 2,133 serial subscriptions, 4,179 audiovisual materials.
College life *Housing:* college housing not available. *Social organizations:* national fraternities, national sororities; 10% of eligible men and 10% of eligible women are members. *Most popular organizations:* student government, Toastmasters, Student Alliance for Global Health, Christian Medical Society, Student Research Group.
Campus security 24-hour emergency response devices and patrols, late-night transport-escort service.
Application *Preference* given to state residents. *Application fee:* $25.
Significant dates *Application deadline:* rolling (transfers). *Financial aid deadline priority date:* 2/1.
Freshman Application Contact
Ms. Jo Wagner, Assistant Director of Academic Records, University of Nebraska Medical Center, 984230 Nebraska Medical Center, Omaha, NE 68198-4230. **Phone:** 402-559-6468. **Toll-free phone:** 800-626-8431. **Fax:** 402-559-6796.
Visit CollegeQuest.com for information on majors offered and athletics.

WAYNE STATE COLLEGE
Wayne, Nebraska

Apply at CollegeQuest.com

- **State-supported**, comprehensive, founded 1910
- **Degrees** bachelor's, master's, and post-master's certificates
- **Small-town** 128-acre campus
- **Coed**, 3,036 undergraduate students, 91% full-time, 56% women, 44% men
- **Noncompetitive** entrance level, 100% of applicants were admitted
- **19:1 student-to-undergraduate faculty ratio**
- **$2271 tuition** and fees (in-state); $4146 (out-of-state)

Part of Nebraska State College System.
Students *Undergraduates:* 2,772 full-time, 264 part-time. Students come from 25 states and territories, 10 other countries. *The most frequently chosen baccalaureate fields are:* business/marketing, education, parks and recreation. *Graduate:* 565 in graduate degree programs.

From out-of-state	18%	Reside on campus	44%
Age 25 or older	10%	Transferred in	7%
International students	1%	African Americans	3%
Asian Americans/Pacific Islanders	1%	Hispanic Americans	1%
Native Americans	1%		

Faculty 199 (70% full-time), 56% with terminal degrees.

Nebraska

Expenses (1999–2000) *Tuition, state resident:* full-time $1875; part-time $62 per semester hour. *Tuition, nonresident:* full-time $3750; part-time $125 per semester hour. *Required fees:* full-time $396; $16 per semester hour. *College room and board:* $3300; room only: $1520. Room and board charges vary according to board plan and housing facility. *Payment plan:* installment. *Waivers:* employees or children of employees.

Library U. S. Conn Library plus 1 other. *Operations spending 1999–2000:* $756,766. *Collection:* 145,070 titles, 2,690 serial subscriptions, 4,524 audiovisual materials.

College life *Housing:* on-campus residence required in freshman year. *Option:* coed. *Social organizations:* national fraternities, national sororities.

Campus security 24-hour patrols, student patrols, late-night transport-escort service, controlled dormitory access.

After graduation 36 organizations recruited on campus 1997–98. *Career center:* 5 full-time personnel. Services include job fairs, resume preparation, career counseling, careers library, job bank, job interviews.

Freshmen 1,360 applied, 1,360 admitted, 668 enrolled.

Average high school GPA	3.0	SAT verbal scores above 500	N/R
SAT math scores above 500	N/R	ACT above 18	76%
From top 10% of their h.s. class	10%	From top quarter	26%
From top half	53%	1998 freshmen returning in 1999	62%

Application *Options:* eApply at www.CollegeQuest.com, Common Application, deferred entrance. *Application fee:* $10. *Required:* high school transcript. *Required for some:* minimum 2.0 GPA. *Recommended:* minimum 3.0 GPA; interview.

Standardized tests *Placement: Recommended:* SAT I or ACT.

Significant dates *Application deadlines:* rolling (freshmen), rolling (transfers). *Financial aid deadline:* continuous.

Freshman Application Contact
Mr. Brian Taylor, Director of Admissions, Wayne State College, 1111 Main Street, Wayne, NE 68787. **Phone:** 402-375-7234. **Toll-free phone:** 800-228-9972. **Fax:** 402-375-7204. **E-mail:** wscadmit@wscgate.wsc.edu

Visit CollegeQuest.com for information on majors offered and athletics. College video and electronic viewbook available at CollegeQuest.com.

YORK COLLEGE
York, Nebraska

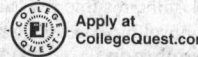
Apply at CollegeQuest.com

- **Independent**, 4-year, founded 1890, affiliated with Church of Christ
- **Degrees** associate and bachelor's
- **Small-town** 44-acre campus
- **Coed**, 485 undergraduate students
- **Moderately difficult** entrance level, 59% of applicants were admitted
- **$8000 tuition** and fees
- **$7681 average financial aid** package, $1.8 million endowment

York College, founded in 1890, is a private, liberal arts college offering 4 bachelor's degrees in 29 fields to a student body of more than 500. York is one of the most affordable Christian colleges in America and is accredited by NCACS. It offers NAIA sports and is located in one of the top 20 Best Small Towns in America.

Students *Undergraduates:* Students come from 32 states and territories, 16 other countries.

From out-of-state	80%	Reside on campus	62%
Age 25 or older	12%		

Faculty 54 (67% full-time).

Expenses (1999–2000) *Comprehensive fee:* $11,300 includes full-time tuition ($7200), mandatory fees ($800), and room and board ($3300). *College room only:* $1400. Full-time tuition and fees vary according to course load. Room and board charges vary according to board plan and housing facility. *Part-time tuition:* $225 per credit hour. *Part-time fees:* $50 per term part-time. Part-time tuition and fees vary according to course load. *Payment plan:* installment. *Waivers:* employees or children of employees.

Library Levitt Library. *Collection:* 38,835 titles, 223 serial subscriptions.

College life On-campus residence required through junior year. *Social organizations:* local fraternities, local sororities; 75% of eligible men and 75% of eligible women are members. *Most popular organizations:* concert choir, Student Association, Promethians, social organizations, Marksmen.

Campus security 24-hour patrols, student patrols, controlled dormitory access.

After graduation 30 organizations recruited on campus 1997–98. 100% of class of 1998 had job offers within 6 months. *Career center:* 2 part-time personnel. Services include job fairs, resume preparation, career/interest testing, career counseling, careers library, job bank, job interviews. *Graduate education:* 8% of class of 1999 went directly to graduate and professional school: 3% education, 2% business, 1% law, 1% medicine, 1% theology.

Freshmen 346 applied, 204 admitted. 3 class presidents, 2 valedictorians, 15 student government officers.

Average high school GPA	3.28	SAT verbal scores above 500	N/R
SAT math scores above 500	N/R	ACT above 18	N/R
From top 10% of their h.s. class	10%	From top quarter	33%
From top half	63%	1998 freshmen returning in 1999	82%

Application *Options:* eApply at www.CollegeQuest.com, Common Application, electronic application, early admission, deferred entrance. *Application fee:* $20. *Required:* high school transcript; 2 letters of recommendation. *Required for some:* minimum 2.0 GPA. *Recommended:* minimum 2.0 GPA.

Standardized tests *Admission: Required:* SAT I or ACT.

Significant dates *Application deadlines:* rolling (freshmen), rolling (transfers). *Financial aid deadline priority date:* 4/1.

Freshman Application Contact
Dr. James White, Vice President of Enrollment, York College, 1125 East 8th Street, York, NE 68467-2699. **Phone:** 402-363-5668. **Toll-free phone:** 800-950-9675. **Fax:** 402-363-5623. **E-mail:** enroll@york.edu

Visit CollegeQuest.com for information on majors offered and athletics.

Nevada

NEVADA

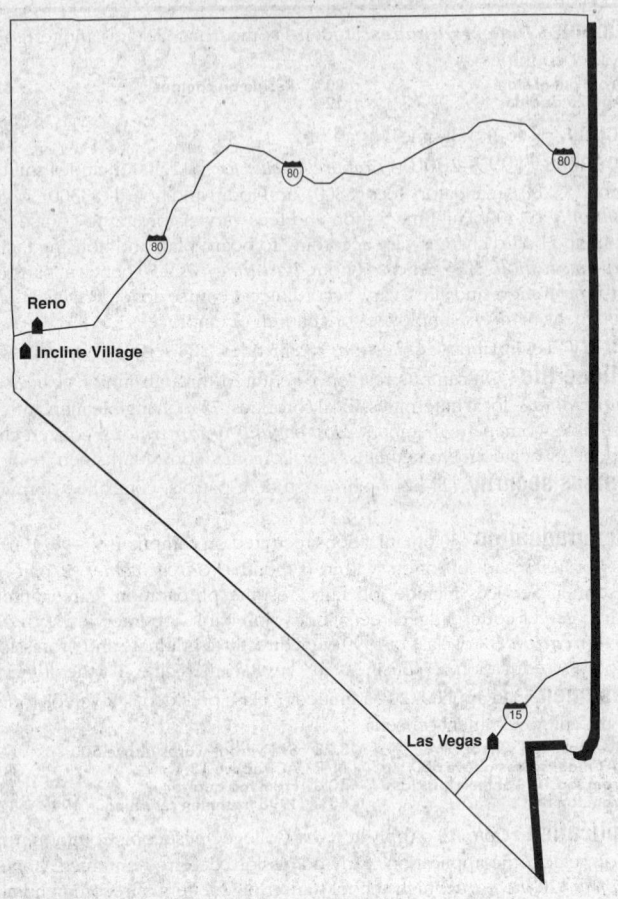

MORRISON UNIVERSITY
Reno, Nevada

- **Proprietary**, comprehensive, founded 1902
- **Degrees** associate, bachelor's, and master's
- **Urban** 2-acre campus
- **Coed**
- **Noncompetitive** entrance level
- **$5580 tuition** and fees

Expenses (1999–2000) *One-time required fee:* $75. *Tuition:* full-time $5580; part-time $155 per credit. Full-time tuition and fees vary according to degree level.

Institutional Web site http://www.morrison.edu/

College life *Housing:* college housing not available. *Social organizations:* national fraternities, national sororities; 25% of eligible men and 35% of eligible women are members. *Most popular organization:* Phi Beta Lambda.

Campus security 24-hour emergency response devices, late-night transport-escort service, evening patrols by security.

Application *Options:* early admission, deferred entrance. *Application fee:* $25. *Required:* high school transcript; interview. *Required for some:* essay or personal statement. *Recommended:* CPAt of 160 for paralegal program.

Admissions Office Contact
Morrison University, 140 Washington Street, Reno, NV 89503-5600. **Toll-free phone:** 800-369-6144. **Fax:** 775-323-8495.

Visit CollegeQuest.com for information on athletics.

SIERRA NEVADA COLLEGE
Incline Village, Nevada

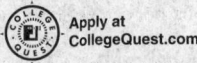 Apply at CollegeQuest.com

- **Independent**, comprehensive, founded 1969
- **Degrees** bachelor's and postbachelor's certificates
- **Small-town** 20-acre campus with easy access to Reno
- **Coed**, 347 undergraduate students, 84% full-time, 51% women, 49% men
- **Moderately difficult** entrance level, 55% of applicants were admitted
- **12:1 student-to-undergraduate faculty ratio**
- **5% graduate** in 6 years or less
- **$11,600 tuition** and fees
- **$12,250 average indebtedness** upon graduation, $2.8 million endowment

Students *Undergraduates:* 290 full-time, 57 part-time. Students come from 30 states and territories, 7 other countries.

From out-of-state	84%	Reside on campus	30%
Age 25 or older	29%	Transferred in	16%
International students	3%	African Americans	1%
Hispanic Americans	1%	Native Americans	0.3%

Faculty 40 (25% full-time).

Expenses (1999–2000) *One-time required fee:* $630. *Comprehensive fee:* $17,200 includes full-time tuition ($11,400), mandatory fees ($200), and room and board ($5600). *College room only:* $2600. Full-time tuition and fees vary according to course load, location, and program. Room and board charges vary according to housing facility. *Part-time tuition:* $380 per semester hour. *Part-time fees:* $100 per term part-time. Part-time tuition and fees vary according to course load, location, and program. *Payment plan:* deferred payment. *Waivers:* employees or children of employees.

Library MacLean Library. *Operations spending 1999–2000:* $32,790. *Collection:* 18,500 titles, 175 serial subscriptions.

College life *Housing: Options:* coed, men-only, women-only. *Most popular organizations:* Hotel Students of America, ski club (NASIS), enviroaction club, snowboard club, Rotaract.

Campus security 24-hour emergency response devices and patrols.

After graduation *Career center:* 1 full-time personnel. Services include job fairs, resume preparation, resume referral, career/interest testing, career counseling, careers library, job bank.

Freshmen 210 applied, 115 admitted, 125 enrolled.

Average high school GPA	2.8	SAT verbal scores above 500	N/R
SAT math scores above 500	N/R	ACT above 18	N/R
From top 10% of their h.s. class	12%	From top quarter	35%
From top half	58%	1998 freshmen returning in 1999	47%

Application *Options:* eApply at www.CollegeQuest.com, Common Application, electronic application, deferred entrance. *Application fee:* $35. *Required:* essay or personal statement; high school transcript; minimum 2.0 GPA; 2 letters of recommendation. *Recommended:* interview.

Standardized tests *Placement: Required:* SAT I or ACT

Significant dates *Application deadlines:* rolling (freshmen), rolling (transfers). *Financial aid deadline:* continuous.

Freshman Application Contact
Dr. Marcia Hoch, Dean of Student Services, Sierra Nevada College, 999 Tahoe Boulevard, PO Box 4269, Incline Village, NV 89480-4269. **Phone:** 775-831-1314 Ext. 1639. **Toll-free phone:** 800-332-8666 Ext. 1632. **Fax:** 775-831-1347. **E-mail:** admissions@sierranevada.edu

Visit CollegeQuest.com for information on majors offered and athletics. College video and electronic viewbook available at CollegeQuest.com.

- *See page 2490 for a narrative description.*

UNIVERSITY OF NEVADA, LAS VEGAS
Las Vegas, Nevada

- **State-supported**, university, founded 1957
- **Degrees** bachelor's, master's, doctoral, first professional, post-master's, and postbachelor's certificates
- **Urban** 335-acre campus
- **Coed**, 14,779 undergraduate students, 63% full-time, 55% women, 45% men

Nevada

- **Moderately difficult** entrance level, 78% of applicants were admitted
- **19:1 student-to-undergraduate faculty ratio**
- **28.7% graduate** in 6 years or less
- **$2386 tuition** and fees (in-state); $9366 (out-of-state)
- **$9360 average financial aid** package, $11,470 average indebtedness upon graduation, $44.7 million endowment

UNLV, America's youngest major university, offers excellent undergraduate and graduate degree programs, reasonable tuition, modern learning facilities, and extracurricular activities and organizations. UNLV's fields of study, considered among the best available anywhere, include business, hotel administration, education, law, liberal arts, fine arts, engineering, health sciences, physical therapy, natural sciences, and communication studies.

Part of University and Community College System of Nevada.

Students *Undergraduates:* 9,286 full-time, 5,493 part-time. Students come from 53 states and territories, 67 other countries. *The most frequently chosen baccalaureate fields are:* business/marketing, education, social sciences and history. *Graduate:* 273 in professional programs, 4,007 in other graduate degree programs.

From out-of-state	19%	Reside on campus	8%
Transferred in	15%	International students	5%
African Americans	7%	Asian Americans/Pacific Islanders	12%
Hispanic Americans	8%	Native Americans	1%

Faculty 1,064 (64% full-time).

Expenses (1999–2000) *Tuition, state resident:* full-time $2340; part-time $72 per credit hour. *Tuition, nonresident:* full-time $9320; part-time $150 per credit hour. *Required fees:* full-time $46; $23 per term part-time. Full-time tuition and fees vary according to course load and reciprocity agreements. Part-time tuition and fees vary according to course load and reciprocity agreements. *College room and board:* $5694; room only: $3522. Room and board charges vary according to board plan. *Payment plan:* deferred payment. *Waivers:* children of alumni, senior citizens, and employees or children of employees.

Library James R. Dickinson Library. *Operations spending 1999–2000:* $8.6 million. *Collection:* 810,000 titles, 7,600 serial subscriptions.

College life *Housing:* on-campus residence required in freshman year. *Options:* coed, women-only, disabled students. *Social organizations:* national fraternities, national sororities; 6% of eligible men and 4% of eligible women are members. *Most popular organizations:* Inter-Varsity Christian Fellowship, Rebel Ski Club, Student Organization of Latinos, Latter Day Saints, Hawaii club.

Campus security 24-hour emergency response devices and patrols, late-night transport-escort service, controlled dormitory access.

After graduation 450 organizations recruited on campus 1997–98. *Career center:* 7 full-time, 8 part-time personnel. Services include job fairs, resume preparation, career counseling, careers library, job bank, job interviews. *Graduate education:* 9% of class of 1999 went directly to graduate and professional school.

Freshmen 3,967 applied, 3,113 admitted, 1,794 enrolled.

Average high school GPA	3.2	SAT verbal scores above 500	51%
SAT math scores above 500	56%	ACT above 18	86%
From top 10% of their h.s. class	18%	From top quarter	46%
From top half	81%	1998 freshmen returning in 1999	74%

Application *Options:* early action, deferred entrance. *Application fee:* $40. *Required:* high school transcript; minimum 2.5 GPA. *Required for some:* 2 letters of recommendation.

Standardized tests *Admission: Recommended:* SAT I or ACT. *Required for some:* SAT I or ACT.

Significant dates *Application deadlines:* 7/15 (freshmen), 8/15 (transfers). *Early action:* 2/1. *Notification:* 2/1 (early action). **Financial aid deadline priority date:** 2/1.

Freshman Application Contact
Susan Horning, Assistant Director of Admissions, University of Nevada, Las Vegas, 4505 Maryland Parkway, Box 451021, Las Vegas, NV 89154-1021. **Phone:** 702-895-3443. **Toll-free phone:** 800-334-UNLV. **Fax:** 702-895-1118. **E-mail:** undrgradadmision@ccmail.nevada.edu

Visit CollegeQuest.com for information on majors offered and athletics. College video available at CollegeQuest.com.

- *See page 2784 for a narrative description.*

UNIVERSITY OF NEVADA, RENO
Reno, Nevada

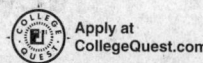
Apply at CollegeQuest.com

- **State-supported**, university, founded 1874
- **Degrees** bachelor's, master's, doctoral, first professional, post-master's, and postbachelor's certificates
- **Urban** 200-acre campus
- **Coed**, 8,818 undergraduate students, 75% full-time, 55% women, 45% men
- **Moderately difficult** entrance level, 91% of applicants were admitted
- **19:1 student-to-undergraduate faculty ratio**
- **42.2% graduate** in 6 years or less
- **$2259 tuition** and fees (in-state); $8606 (out-of-state)
- **$9500 average financial aid** package, $81.1 million endowment

Part of University and Community College System of Nevada.

Students *Undergraduates:* 6,636 full-time, 2,182 part-time. Students come from 51 states and territories, 63 other countries. *The most frequently chosen baccalaureate fields are:* business/marketing, education, social sciences and history. *Graduate:* 207 in professional programs, 2,923 in other graduate degree programs.

From out-of-state	16%	Reside on campus	13%
Age 25 or older	24%	Transferred in	10%
International students	4%	African Americans	2%
Asian Americans/Pacific Islanders	6%	Hispanic Americans	5%
Native Americans	2%		

Faculty 670 (88% full-time), 88% with terminal degrees.

Expenses (1999–2000) *Tuition, state resident:* full-time $2145; part-time $72 per credit. *Tuition, nonresident:* full-time $8492; part-time $150 per credit. *Required fees:* full-time $114; $57 per term part-time. Full-time tuition and fees vary according to course load. Part-time tuition and fees vary according to course load. *College room and board:* $5295; room only: $2860. Room and board charges vary according to board plan and housing facility. *Payment plan:* deferred payment. *Waivers:* children of alumni, senior citizens, and employees or children of employees.

Library Getchell Library plus 5 others. *Operations spending 1999–2000:* $7.8 million. *Collection:* 455,372 titles, 5,567 serial subscriptions, 395,862 audiovisual materials.

College life *Housing: Options:* coed, men-only, women-only, disabled students. *Social organizations:* national fraternities, national sororities; 9% of eligible men and 6% of eligible women are members. *Most popular organizations:* Asian-American Student Association, Ambassadors, Non-Traditional Student Union, The Alliance, Orvis Nursing Student Association.

Campus security 24-hour emergency response devices and patrols, late-night transport-escort service, controlled dormitory access.

After graduation 250 organizations recruited on campus 1997–98. *Career center:* 9 full-time, 2 part-time personnel. Services include job fairs, resume preparation, interview workshops, resume referral, career/interest testing, career counseling, careers library, job bank, job interviews.

Freshmen 2,903 applied, 2,642 admitted, 1,548 enrolled.

Average high school GPA	3.33	SAT verbal scores above 500	61%
SAT math scores above 500	66%	ACT above 18	91%
1998 freshmen returning in 1999	76%		

Application *Options:* eApply at www.CollegeQuest.com, deferred entrance. *Application fee:* $40. *Required:* high school transcript; minimum 2.5 GPA.

Standardized tests *Placement: Required:* SAT I or ACT

Significant dates *Application deadlines:* 3/1 (freshmen), rolling (transfers). **Financial aid deadline priority date:** 2/1.

Freshman Application Contact
Dr. Melissa N. Choroszy, Associate Dean of Records and Enrollment Services, University of Nevada, Reno, Mail Stop 120, Reno, NV 89557. **Phone:** 702-784-6865. **Toll-free phone:** 800-622-4867. **E-mail:** unrug@unr.edu

Visit CollegeQuest.com for information on majors offered and athletics.

- *See page 2786 for a narrative description.*

Peterson's Guide to Four-Year Colleges 2001 www.petersons.com

New Hampshire

NEW HAMPSHIRE

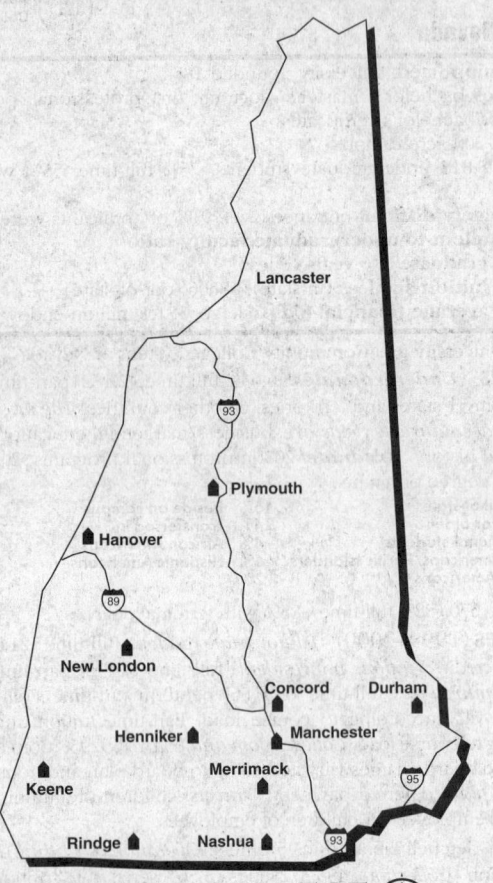

COLBY-SAWYER COLLEGE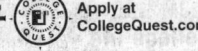
New London, New Hampshire

- **Independent**, 4-year, founded 1837
- **Degrees** associate and bachelor's
- **Small-town** 190-acre campus
- **Coed**, 788 undergraduate students, 97% full-time, 65% women, 35% men
- **Moderately difficult** entrance level, 84% of applicants were admitted
- **13:1 student-to-undergraduate faculty ratio**
- **59% graduate** in 6 years or less
- **$19,110 tuition** and fees
- **$13.5 million endowment**

Students *Undergraduates:* 763 full-time, 25 part-time. Students come from 27 states and territories, 8 other countries. *The most frequently chosen baccalaureate fields are:* parks and recreation, business/marketing, psychology.

From out-of-state	66%	Reside on campus	88%
Age 25 or older	4%	Transferred in	4%
International students	3%	African Americans	0.4%
Asian Americans/Pacific Islanders	1%	Hispanic Americans	1%
Native Americans	0.4%		

Faculty 87 (51% full-time), 56% with terminal degrees.

Expenses (2000–2001) *Comprehensive fee:* $26,350 includes full-time tuition ($18,960), mandatory fees ($150), and room and board ($7240). *College room only:* $3980. *Part-time tuition:* $630 per credit hour. *Part-time fees:* $75 per term part-time. Part-time tuition and fees vary according to course load. *Payment plan:* installment. *Waivers:* employees or children of employees.

Library Susan Colgate Cleveland Library Learning Center. *Operations spending 1999–2000:* $358,009. *Collection:* 67,090 titles, 1,023 serial subscriptions, 1,785 audiovisual materials.

College life *Housing:* on-campus residence required in freshman year. *Options:* coed, women-only, disabled students. *Most popular organizations:* campus activities, Student Government Association, campus radio station, Alpha Chi Honor Society, outing club.

Campus security 24-hour emergency response devices and patrols, late-night transport-escort service, controlled dormitory access, awareness seminars.

After graduation 8 organizations recruited on campus 1997–98. *Career center:* 2 full-time, 1 part-time personnel. Services include job fairs, resume preparation, interview workshops, career/interest testing, career counseling, careers library, job bank, job interviews.

Freshmen 1,188 applied, 1,002 admitted, 236 enrolled.

Average high school GPA	2.79	SAT verbal scores above 500	55%
SAT math scores above 500	50%	ACT above 18	86%
1998 freshmen returning in 1999	80%		

Application *Options:* eApply at www.CollegeQuest.com, Common Application, early admission, early action, deferred entrance. *Application fee:* $40. *Required:* essay or personal statement; high school transcript; minimum 2.0 GPA; 2 letters of recommendation. *Recommended:* interview.

Standardized tests *Admission: Required:* SAT I or ACT.

Significant dates *Application deadlines:* rolling (freshmen), rolling (transfers). *Early action:* 12/1. *Notification:* 1/1 (early action). *Financial aid deadline priority date:* 3/1.

Freshman Application Contact Ms. Wendy Beckemeyer, Vice President for Enrollment Management and Dean of Admissions, Colby-Sawyer College, 100 Main Street, New London, NH 03257-4648. **Phone:** 603-526-3700. **Toll-free phone:** 800-272-1015. **Fax:** 603-526-3452. **E-mail:** csadmiss@colby-sawyer.edu

Visit CollegeQuest.com for information on majors offered and athletics.

■ *See page 1450 for a narrative description.*

COLLEGE FOR LIFELONG LEARNING OF THE UNIVERSITY SYSTEM OF NEW HAMPSHIRE
New Hampshire—See University System College for Lifelong Learning

DANIEL WEBSTER COLLEGE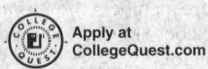
Nashua, New Hampshire

- **Independent**, 4-year, founded 1965
- **Degrees** associate and bachelor's
- **Suburban** 50-acre campus with easy access to Boston
- **Coed**, 918 undergraduate students, 82% full-time, 32% women, 68% men
- **Moderately difficult** entrance level, 83% of applicants were admitted
- **13:1 student-to-undergraduate faculty ratio**
- **$15,650 tuition** and fees
- **$13,000 average financial aid** package, $20,875 average indebtedness upon graduation, $700,000 endowment

Students *Undergraduates:* 753 full-time, 165 part-time. Students come from 24 states and territories, 8 other countries. *The most frequently chosen baccalaureate fields are:* business/marketing, computer/information sciences, trade and industry.

Reside on campus	70%	Age 25 or older	6%
International students	1%	African Americans	4%
Asian Americans/Pacific Islanders	1%	Hispanic Americans	2%
Native Americans	0.4%		

Faculty 53 (49% full-time), 30% with terminal degrees.

Expenses (1999–2000) *Comprehensive fee:* $21,652 includes full-time tuition ($15,330), mandatory fees ($320), and room and board ($6002). *College room only:* $3116. Full-time tuition and fees vary according to class time and course load. Room and board charges vary according to board plan and housing facility. *Part-time tuition:* $638 per credit. *Part-time fees:* $200 per term part-time. Part-time tuition and fees vary according to class time. *Payment plan:* installment. *Waivers:* senior citizens and employees or children of employees.

Library Ann Bridge Baddour Library and Learning Center. *Operations spending 1999–2000:* $287,668. *Collection:* 35,000 titles, 300 serial subscriptions, 730 audiovisual materials.

New Hampshire

College life *Housing:* on-campus residence required through sophomore year. *Options:* coed, men-only, women-only, disabled students. *Most popular organizations:* Alpha Eta Rho Society, Flight Team, ice hockey club, student government, The Talon (newspaper).

Campus security 24-hour emergency response devices and patrols, student patrols, late-night transport-escort service, controlled dormitory access.

After graduation 51 organizations recruited on campus 1997–98. 92% of class of 1998 had job offers within 6 months. *Career center:* 1 full-time personnel. Services include job fairs, resume preparation, interview workshops, career/interest testing, career counseling, careers library, job bank, job interviews. *Graduate education:* 4% of class of 1999 went directly to graduate and professional school.

Freshmen 757 applied, 627 admitted, 179 enrolled. 1 valedictorian.

Average high school GPA	2.96	SAT verbal scores above 500	65%
SAT math scores above 500	66%	ACT above 18	N/R
From top 10% of their h.s. class	10%	From top quarter	27%
From top half	64%	1998 freshmen returning in 1999	55%

Application *Options:* eApply at www.CollegeQuest.com, Common Application, electronic application, early admission, deferred entrance. *Application fee:* $35. *Required:* high school transcript. *Recommended:* 1 letter of recommendation; interview.

Standardized tests *Admission: Required:* SAT I and SAT II or ACT.

Significant dates *Application deadlines:* rolling (freshmen), rolling (transfers). *Financial aid deadline priority date:* 3/1.

Freshman Application Contact Mr. Paul D. LaBarre, Director of Enrollment Services, Daniel Webster College, 20 University Drive, Nashua, NH 03063. **Phone:** 603-577-6603. **Toll-free phone:** 800-325-6876. **Fax:** 603-577-6001. **E-mail:** admissions@dwc.edu

Visit CollegeQuest.com for information on majors offered and athletics.

■ *See page 1556 for a narrative description.*

DARTMOUTH COLLEGE
Hanover, New Hampshire

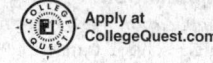 Apply at CollegeQuest.com

- **Independent**, university, founded 1769
- **Degrees** bachelor's, master's, doctoral, and first professional
- **Rural** 265-acre campus
- **Coed**, 3,998 undergraduate students, 99% full-time, 48% women, 52% men
- **Most difficult** entrance level, 21% of applicants were admitted
- **9:1 student-to-undergraduate faculty ratio**
- **93.9% graduate** in 6 years or less
- **$24,884 tuition** and fees
- **$23,331 average financial aid** package, $14,818 average indebtedness upon graduation, $1.7 billion endowment

Students *Undergraduates:* 3,992 full-time, 6 part-time. Students come from 52 states and territories, 47 other countries. *The most frequently chosen baccalaureate fields are:* biological/life sciences, English, social sciences and history. *Graduate:* 272 in professional programs, 1,015 in other graduate degree programs.

From out-of-state	97%	Reside on campus	85%
Age 25 or older	27%	Transferred in	1%
International students	4%	African Americans	5%
Asian Americans/Pacific Islanders	10%	Hispanic Americans	5%
Native Americans	2%		

Faculty 658 (67% full-time), 89% with terminal degrees.

Expenses (1999–2000) *One-time required fee:* $90. *Comprehensive fee:* $31,274 includes full-time tuition ($24,624), mandatory fees ($260), and room and board ($6390). *College room only:* $4230. Room and board charges vary according to board plan and housing facility. *Payment plans:* tuition prepayment, installment.

Library Baker Library plus 8 others. *Collection:* 2.3 million titles, 20,043 serial subscriptions, 74,547 audiovisual materials.

College life *Housing:* on-campus residence required in freshman year. *Options:* coed, cooperative. *Social organizations:* national fraternities, national sororities, local fraternities, local sororities, coed fraternities; 41% of eligible men and 28% of eligible women are members. *Most popular organizations:* Dartmouth Outing Club, Programming Board, Student Assembly, class councils, African-American society.

Campus security 24-hour emergency response devices and patrols, student patrols, late-night transport-escort service.

After graduation 215 organizations recruited on campus 1997–98. *Career center:* 10 full-time, 1 part-time personnel. Services include job fairs, resume preparation, resume referral, career counseling, careers library, job bank, job interviews. *Graduate education:* 20% of class of 1999 went directly to graduate and professional school. *Major awards:* 5 Fulbright Scholars.

Freshmen 10,259 applied, 2,131 admitted, 1,054 enrolled. 53 National Merit Scholars, 196 valedictorians.

SAT verbal scores above 500	100%	SAT math scores above 500	100%
ACT above 18	N/R	From top 10% of their h.s. class	87%
From top quarter	98%	From top half	100%
1998 freshmen returning in 1999	98%		

Application *Options:* eApply at www.CollegeQuest.com, Common Application, electronic application, early admission, early decision, deferred entrance. *Application fee:* $60. *Required:* essay or personal statement; high school transcript; 2 letters of recommendation. *Recommended:* interview.

Standardized tests *Admission: Required:* SAT I and SAT II or ACT.

Significant dates *Application deadlines:* 1/1 (freshmen), 3/1 (transfers). *Early decision:* 11/1. *Notification:* 4/10 (freshmen), 12/15 (early decision). *Financial aid deadline:* 2/1.

Freshman Application Contact Mr. Karl M. Furstenberg, Dean of Admissions and Financial Aid, Dartmouth College, 6016 McNutt Hall, Hanover, NH 03755. **Phone:** 603-646-2875. **Fax:** 603-646-1216. **E-mail:** admissions.office@dartmouth.edu

Visit CollegeQuest.com for information on majors offered and athletics.

■ *See page 1558 for a narrative description.*

FRANKLIN PIERCE COLLEGE
Rindge, New Hampshire

 Apply at CollegeQuest.com

- **Independent**, comprehensive, founded 1962
- **Degrees** associate, bachelor's, and master's (profile does not reflect significant enrollment at 6 continuing education sites; master's degree is only offered at these sites)
- **Rural** 1,000-acre campus
- **Coed**, 1,350 undergraduate students, 99% full-time, 48% women, 52% men
- **Moderately difficult** entrance level, 77% of applicants were admitted
- **14:1 student-to-undergraduate faculty ratio**
- **43% graduate** in 6 years or less
- **$17,990 tuition** and fees
- **$14,769 average financial aid** package, $18,000 average indebtedness upon graduation, $5.6 million endowment

Students *Undergraduates:* 1,331 full-time, 19 part-time. Students come from 32 states and territories, 23 other countries. *The most frequently chosen baccalaureate fields are:* business/marketing, communications/communication technologies, social sciences and history.

From out-of-state	75%	Reside on campus	93%
Age 25 or older	2%	Transferred in	3%
International students	2%	African Americans	3%
Asian Americans/Pacific Islanders	1%	Hispanic Americans	3%
Native Americans	0.2%		

Faculty 156 (46% full-time), 60% with terminal degrees.

Expenses (1999–2000) *Comprehensive fee:* $24,040 includes full-time tuition ($17,250), mandatory fees ($740), and room and board ($6050). *College room only:* $3300. *Part-time tuition:* $575 per credit. *Payment plan:* installment. *Waivers:* senior citizens and employees or children of employees.

Library Franklin Pierce College Library. *Collection:* 100,916 titles, 3,091 audiovisual materials.

College life *Housing:* on-campus residence required through senior year. *Options:* coed, disabled students. *Most popular organizations:* outing club, WFPR-Radio, Student Senate, law club, business club.

Campus security 24-hour emergency response devices and patrols, student patrols, late-night transport-escort service, controlled dormitory access.

After graduation 47 organizations recruited on campus 1997–98. *Career center:* 1 full-time, 1 part-time personnel. Services include job fairs, resume

New Hampshire

Franklin Pierce College (continued)

preparation, interview workshops, resume referral, career/interest testing, career counseling, careers library, job bank, job interviews. **Graduate education:** 19% of class of 1999 went directly to graduate and professional school: 12% graduate arts and sciences, 5% business, 2% law, 1% education.

Freshmen 3,622 applied, 2,772 admitted, 436 enrolled.

Average high school GPA	2.78	SAT verbal scores above 500	46%
SAT math scores above 500	45%	ACT above 18	64%
1998 freshmen returning in 1999	63%		

Application *Options:* eApply at www.CollegeQuest.com, Common Application, electronic application, early admission, deferred entrance. *Application fee:* $0. *Required:* essay or personal statement; high school transcript; 1 letter of recommendation. *Recommended:* minimum 2.0 GPA; interview.

Standardized tests *Admission: Required:* SAT I or ACT.

Significant dates *Application deadlines:* rolling (freshmen), rolling (transfers). *Notification:* continuous until 9/1 (freshmen). **Financial aid deadline:** continuous.

Freshman Application Contact
Ms. Lucy C. Shonk, Director of Admissions, Franklin Pierce College, Box 60, College Road, Rindge, NH 03461. **Phone:** 603-899-4050. **Toll-free phone:** 800-437-0048. **Fax:** 603-899-4372. **E-mail:** admissions@rindge.fpc.edu

Visit CollegeQuest.com for information on majors offered and athletics. College video and electronic viewbook available at CollegeQuest.com.

HESSER COLLEGE
Manchester, New Hampshire

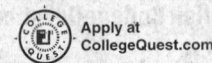 Apply at CollegeQuest.com

- **Proprietary**, primarily 2-year, founded 1900
- **Degrees** associate and bachelor's
- **Urban** 1-acre campus with easy access to Boston
- **Coed**, 3,181 undergraduate students, 54% full-time, 69% women, 31% men
- **Moderately difficult** entrance level
- **18:1** student-to-undergraduate faculty ratio
- **$8640 tuition** and fees

Faculty 250 (20% full-time).

Admissions Office Contact
Hesser College, 3 Sundial Avenue, Manchester, NH 03103. **Toll-free phone:** 800-526-9231. **E-mail:** admissions@hesser.edu

Visit CollegeQuest.com for information on majors offered and athletics. College video available at CollegeQuest.com.

■ *See page 1784 for a narrative description.*

KEENE STATE COLLEGE
Keene, New Hampshire

- **State-supported**, comprehensive, founded 1909
- **Degrees** associate, bachelor's, master's, post-master's, and postbachelor's certificates
- **Small-town** 160-acre campus
- **Coed**, 3,820 undergraduate students, 93% full-time, 58% women, 42% men
- **Moderately difficult** entrance level, 81% of applicants were admitted
- **19:1** student-to-undergraduate faculty ratio
- **48% graduate** in 6 years or less
- **$5046 tuition** and fees (in-state); $10,356 (out-of-state)
- **$6923 average financial aid** package, $16,439 average indebtedness upon graduation, $7.8 million endowment

Keene State College, a public institution grounded in the liberal arts, offers programs in 35 academic areas. The campus, with 21st-century technology housed in traditional ivy-covered brick buildings, is located in the Monadnock Region of southwestern New Hampshire. KSC has an enrollment of 4,700 full- and part-time students.

Part of University System of New Hampshire.

Students *Undergraduates:* 3,558 full-time, 262 part-time. Students come from 30 states and territories. *The most frequently chosen baccalaureate fields are:* education, psychology, visual/performing arts. *Graduate:* 219 in graduate degree programs.

From out-of-state	42%	Reside on campus	51%
Age 25 or older	10%	Transferred in	5%
International students	0.3%	African Americans	0.3%
Asian Americans/Pacific Islanders	1%	Hispanic Americans	1%
Native Americans	0.2%		

Faculty 326 (45% full-time).

Expenses (1999–2000) *Tuition, state resident:* full-time $3830; part-time $164 per credit. *Tuition, nonresident:* full-time $9140; part-time $460 per credit. *Required fees:* full-time $1216; $48 per credit; $10 per term part-time. Part-time tuition and fees vary according to course load. *College room and board:* $4938; room only: $3358. Room and board charges vary according to board plan and housing facility. *Payment plan:* installment. *Waivers:* employees or children of employees.

Library Mason Library. *Operations spending 1999–2000:* $1.5 million. *Collection:* 165,105 titles, 880 audiovisual materials.

College life *Housing: Options:* coed, women-only, disabled students. *Social organizations:* national fraternities, national sororities, local fraternities, local sororities, coed organization; 11% of eligible men and 8% of eligible women are members. *Most popular organizations:* Social Activities Council, Concerned Students Coalition, Pride, Habitat for Humanity, sports club.

Campus security 24-hour emergency response devices and patrols, late-night transport-escort service, controlled dormitory access.

After graduation 136 organizations recruited on campus 1997–98. *Career center:* 4 full-time personnel. Services include job fairs, resume preparation, interview workshops, resume referral, career/interest testing, career counseling, careers library, job bank, job interviews.

Freshmen 3,116 applied, 2,526 admitted, 1,019 enrolled.

SAT verbal scores above 500	49%	SAT math scores above 500	45%
ACT above 18	79%	From top 10% of their h.s. class	4%
From top quarter	19%	From top half	56%
1998 freshmen returning in 1999	77%		

Application *Option:* deferred entrance. *Preference* given to state residents. *Application fee:* $35 for nonresidents. *Required:* essay or personal statement; high school transcript; 1 letter of recommendation. *Required for some:* interview. *Recommended:* interview.

Standardized tests *Admission: Required:* SAT I or ACT.

Significant dates *Application deadlines:* 4/1 (freshmen), 5/1 (transfers). *Financial aid deadline priority date:* 3/1.

Freshman Application Contact
Mrs. Kathryn G. Dodge, Director of Admissions, Keene State College, 229 Main Street, Keene, NH 03435. **Phone:** 603-358-2276. **Toll-free phone:** 800-572-1909. **Fax:** 603-358-2767. **E-mail:** admissions@keene.edu

Visit CollegeQuest.com for information on majors offered and athletics. College video available at CollegeQuest.com.

■ *See page 1866 for a narrative description.*

MAGDALEN COLLEGE
Warner, New Hampshire

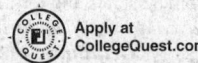 Apply at CollegeQuest.com

- **Independent Roman Catholic**, 4-year, founded 1973
- **Degree** bachelor's
- **Coed**, 74 undergraduate students, 100% full-time, 51% women, 49% men
- **65%** of applicants were admitted
- **9:1** student-to-undergraduate faculty ratio
- **28% graduate** in 6 years or less
- **$6950 tuition** and fees
- **$1.4 million endowment**

Students *Undergraduates:* 74 full-time. Students come from 19 states and territories. *The most frequently chosen baccalaureate field is:* liberal arts/general studies.

| From out-of-state | 74% | Reside on campus | 100% |
| Age 25 or older | 3% | | |

Faculty 8 (100% full-time), 100% with terminal degrees.

Expenses (2000–2001) *Comprehensive fee:* 11,950 includes full-time tuition (6950) and room and board (5000). *Part-time tuition:* 200 per credit. *Payment plan:* installment. *Waivers:* employees or children of employees.

Library *Operations spending 1999–2000:* $17,663.

College life *Housing:* on-campus residence required through senior year. *Options:* men-only, women-only. *Most popular organizations:* Performance Choir, Polophony Choir, Drama Club, intramural sports, Leisure Activities Programs.
Campus security 24-hour emergency response devices, student patrols.
Freshmen 49 applied, 32 admitted, 32 enrolled.

Average high school GPA	3.4	SAT verbal scores above 500	72%
SAT math scores above 500	63%	ACT above 18	90%
1998 freshmen returning in 1999	81%		

Application *Options:* eApply at www.CollegeQuest.com, early decision. *Application fee:* 35. *Required:* essay or personal statement; high school transcript; 2 letters of recommendation; interview; medical examination form.
Standardized tests *Admission: Required:* SAT I or ACT.
Significant dates *Application deadline:* 5/1 (freshmen). *Early decision:* 1/1.
Freshman Application Contact
Mr. Paul V. Sullivan, Director of Admissions, Magdalen College, 511 Kearsarge Mountain Road, Warner, NH 03278. **Phone:** 603-456-2656 Ext. 11. **Fax:** 603-456-2660. **E-mail:** admissions@magdalen.edu
Visit CollegeQuest.com for information on majors offered and athletics.

NEW ENGLAND COLLEGE
Henniker, New Hampshire

- **Independent**, comprehensive, founded 1946
- **Degrees** bachelor's and master's
- **Small-town** 225-acre campus with easy access to Boston
- **Coed**, 707 undergraduate students, 89% full-time, 52% women, 48% men
- **Moderately difficult** entrance level, 91% of applicants were admitted
- **11:1 student-to-undergraduate faculty ratio**
- **42% graduate** in 6 years or less
- **$18,097 tuition** and fees
- **$16,651 average financial aid** package, $14,750 average indebtedness upon graduation, $5.7 million endowment

Students *Undergraduates:* 630 full-time, 77 part-time. Students come from 27 states and territories, 25 other countries. *The most frequently chosen baccalaureate fields are:* business/marketing, psychology, social sciences and history. *Graduate:* 50 in graduate degree programs.

From out-of-state	76%	Age 25 or older	11%
Transferred in	3%	International students	5%
African Americans	3%	Asian Americans/Pacific Islanders	0.4%
Hispanic Americans	0.1%		

Faculty 85 (60% full-time), 48% with terminal degrees.
Expenses (1999–2000) *Comprehensive fee:* $24,311 includes full-time tuition ($17,674), mandatory fees ($423), and room and board ($6214). Room and board charges vary according to board plan. *Part-time tuition:* $737 per credit. *Part-time fees:* $110 per term part-time. Part-time tuition and fees vary according to course load. *Payment plan:* installment. *Waivers:* employees or children of employees.
Library Danforth Library. *Operations spending 1999–2000:* $362,000. *Collection:* 107,200 titles, 650 serial subscriptions, 2,050 audiovisual materials.
College life *Housing:* on-campus residence required through sophomore year. *Option:* coed. *Social organizations:* national fraternities, local fraternities, local sororities; 18% of eligible men and 14% of eligible women are members. *Most popular organizations:* student senate, Campus Activities Board, ServCorps, International Diplomacy Council, Carriage Theater.
Campus security 24-hour emergency response devices and patrols, student patrols, late-night transport-escort service.
After graduation *Career center:* 1 full-time, 1 part-time personnel. Services include job fairs, resume preparation, career counseling, careers library, job bank, job interviews. *Graduate education:* 8% of class of 1999 went directly to graduate and professional school: 3% graduate arts and sciences, 2% business, 2% education, 1% law.
Freshmen 737 applied, 673 admitted, 213 enrolled. 3 class presidents, 2 valedictorians, 30 student government officers.

Average high school GPA	2.76	SAT verbal scores above 500	N/R
SAT math scores above 500	N/R	ACT above 18	N/R
From top 10% of their h.s. class	21%	From top quarter	27%
From top half	43%	1998 freshmen returning in 1999	66%

Application *Options:* Common Application, electronic application, early action, deferred entrance. *Application fee:* $30. *Required:* essay or personal statement; high school transcript; 1 letter of recommendation. *Required for some:* interview. *Recommended:* interview.
Significant dates *Application deadlines:* rolling (freshmen), rolling (transfers). *Early action:* 12/4. *Notification:* 12/17 (early action). *Financial aid deadline priority date:* 3/1.
Freshman Application Contact
Mr. Donald N. Parker, Dean of Admission, New England College, 26 Bridge Street, Henniker, NH 03242. **Phone:** 603-428-2223. **Toll-free phone:** 800-521-7642. **E-mail:** admis@nec1.nec.edu
Visit CollegeQuest.com for information on majors offered and athletics.

■ *See page 2148 for a narrative description.*

NEW HAMPSHIRE COLLEGE
Manchester, New Hampshire

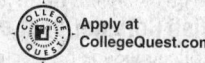
Apply at CollegeQuest.com

- **Independent**, comprehensive, founded 1932
- **Degrees** associate, bachelor's, master's, and doctoral
- **Suburban** 280-acre campus with easy access to Boston
- **Coed**, 4,058 undergraduate students, 32% full-time, 52% women, 48% men
- **Moderately difficult** entrance level, 80% of applicants were admitted
- **18:1 student-to-undergraduate faculty ratio**
- **$15,848 tuition** and fees
- **$7.6 million endowment**

New Hampshire College (NHC) is where the world comes to mind. It is a college that is enhanced by growth and response to the changing times; a private institution that offers a wide variety of majors under the Divisions of Business, Liberal Arts, and Hospitality; and a college that also awards master's and doctoral degrees through the Graduate School of Business. NHC is a place where learning never ends.

Students *Undergraduates:* 1,316 full-time, 2,742 part-time. Students come from 31 states and territories, 38 other countries. *Graduate:* 1,522 in graduate degree programs.

From out-of-state	70%	Reside on campus	80%
Age 25 or older	1%	Transferred in	3%
International students	4%	African Americans	2%
Asian Americans/Pacific Islanders	1%	Hispanic Americans	2%
Native Americans	0.1%		

Faculty 252 (39% full-time), 52% with terminal degrees.
Expenses (2000–2001) *Comprehensive fee:* $22,638 includes full-time tuition ($15,598), mandatory fees ($250), and room and board ($6790). *College room only:* $4750. Full-time tuition and fees vary according to class time. Room and board charges vary according to board plan and housing facility. *Part-time tuition:* $650 per credit. Part-time tuition and fees vary according to class time. *Payment plans:* installment, deferred payment. *Waivers:* senior citizens and employees or children of employees.
Library Harry A. B. and Gertrude C. Shapiro Library. *Operations spending 1999–2000:* $932,653. *Collection:* 1,943 audiovisual materials.
College life *Housing:* on-campus residence required in freshman year. *Options:* coed, men-only, women-only, disabled students. *Social organizations:* national fraternities, national sororities, local fraternities, local sororities; 15% of eligible men and 15% of eligible women are members. *Most popular organizations:* Student Government Association, Intergreek Council, Student Programming Board, Association Cultural Exchange, commuter club.
Campus security 24-hour emergency response devices and patrols, student patrols, late-night transport-escort service, controlled dormitory access.
After graduation 160 organizations recruited on campus 1997–98. 95% of class of 1998 had job offers within 6 months. *Career center:* 3 full-time, 2 part-time personnel. Services include job fairs, resume preparation, interview workshops, resume referral, career counseling, careers library, job bank, job interviews.

New Hampshire

New Hampshire College (continued)

Freshmen 1,650 applied, 1,328 admitted, 933 enrolled.

Average high school GPA	2.8	SAT verbal scores above 500	45%
SAT math scores above 500	45%	ACT above 18	N/R
From top 10% of their h.s. class	5%	From top quarter	26%
From top half	54%	1998 freshmen returning in 1999	75%

Application *Options:* eApply at www.CollegeQuest.com, Common Application, electronic application, early action, deferred entrance. *Application fee:* $0. *Required:* essay or personal statement; high school transcript; minimum 2.0 GPA; 1 letter of recommendation from guidance counselor. *Recommended:* interview.

Standardized tests *Admission: Required:* SAT I or ACT.

Significant dates *Application deadlines:* rolling (freshmen), rolling (transfers). *Early action:* 11/15. *Notification:* 12/15 (early action). *Financial aid deadline priority date:* 3/15.

Freshman Application Contact
Mr. Brad Poznanski, Director of Admission and Enrollment Planning, New Hampshire College, 2500 North River Road, Manchester, NH 03106-1045. **Phone:** 603-645-9611 Ext. 9633. **Toll-free phone:** 800-NHC-4YOU. **Fax:** 603-645-9693. **E-mail:** admission@nhc.edu

Visit CollegeQuest.com for information on majors offered and athletics. College video and electronic viewbook available at CollegeQuest.com.

■ *See page 2150 for a narrative description.*

NOTRE DAME COLLEGE
Manchester, New Hampshire

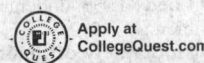 Apply at CollegeQuest.com

- **Independent Roman Catholic**, comprehensive, founded 1950
- **Degrees** associate, bachelor's, and master's
- **Suburban** 8-acre campus with easy access to Boston
- **Coed**, 685 undergraduate students, 70% full-time, 76% women, 24% men
- **Moderately difficult** entrance level, 88% of applicants were admitted
- **13:1 student-to-undergraduate faculty ratio**
- **45% graduate** in 6 years or less
- **$14,378 tuition** and fees
- **$1.8 million endowment**

Students *Undergraduates:* 482 full-time, 203 part-time. Students come from 19 states and territories, 3 other countries. *The most frequently chosen baccalaureate fields are:* biological/life sciences, education, interdisciplinary studies. *Graduate:* 531 in graduate degree programs.

From out-of-state	22%	Reside on campus	25%
Age 25 or older	34%	Transferred in	10%
International students	0.4%	African Americans	2%
Asian Americans/Pacific Islanders	1%	Hispanic Americans	1%
Native Americans	0.3%		

Faculty 58 (79% full-time), 52% with terminal degrees.

Expenses (1999–2000) *Comprehensive fee:* $20,091 includes full-time tuition ($14,098), mandatory fees ($280), and room and board ($5713). *College room only:* $2715. Full-time tuition and fees vary according to course load and program. Room and board charges vary according to housing facility. *Part-time tuition:* $220 per credit. Part-time tuition and fees vary according to class time and course load. *Payment plan:* installment. *Waivers:* children of alumni and employees or children of employees.

Library Harvey Library. *Operations spending 1999–2000:* $262,985. *Collection:* 55,000 titles, 6,800 audiovisual materials.

College life *Housing: Options:* coed, men-only, women-only. *Most popular organizations:* Student Senate, Student Activities Union, Outing Club, Campus Ministry Council, Habitat for Humanity.

Campus security 24-hour emergency response devices and patrols, late-night transport-escort service, educational and informational programs, campus alert notices.

After graduation 30 organizations recruited on campus 1997–98. *Career center:* 1 full-time, 1 part-time personnel. Services include job fairs, resume preparation, resume referral, career counseling, careers library, job bank, job interviews. *Graduate education:* 24% of class of 1999 went directly to graduate and professional school: 18% medicine, 2% graduate arts and sciences, 1% business, 1% education, 1% law.

Freshmen 542 applied, 477 admitted, 136 enrolled.

Average high school GPA	2.76	SAT verbal scores above 500	35%
SAT math scores above 500	29%	ACT above 18	N/R
1998 freshmen returning in 1999	69%		

Application *Options:* eApply at www.CollegeQuest.com, Common Application, deferred entrance. *Application fee:* $25. *Required:* essay or personal statement; high school transcript; portfolio for art program. *Recommended:* letters of recommendation; interview.

Standardized tests *Admission: Required:* SAT I or ACT.

Significant dates *Application deadlines:* rolling (freshmen), rolling (transfers). *Financial aid deadline priority date:* 3/15.

Freshman Application Contact
Ms. Tracy Fontaine, Dean of Graduate and Undergraduate Enrollment, Notre Dame College, 2321 Elm Street, Manchester, NH 03104. **Phone:** 603-669-4298 Ext. 163. **Toll-free phone:** 800-754-0405. **Fax:** 603-644-8316. **E-mail:** admissions@notredame.edu

Visit CollegeQuest.com for information on majors offered and athletics. College video available at CollegeQuest.com.

■ *See page 2198 for a narrative description.*

PLYMOUTH STATE COLLEGE
Plymouth, New Hampshire

- **State-supported**, comprehensive, founded 1871
- **Degrees** associate, bachelor's, master's, post-master's, and postbachelor's certificates
- **Small-town** 170-acre campus
- **Coed**, 3,251 undergraduate students, 96% full-time, 48% women, 52% men
- **Moderately difficult** entrance level, 77% of applicants were admitted
- **15:1 student-to-undergraduate faculty ratio**
- **52.14% graduate** in 6 years or less
- **$5032 tuition** and fees (in-state); $10,342 (out-of-state)
- **$7226 average financial aid** package, $16,343 average indebtedness upon graduation, $2.9 million endowment

Part of University System of New Hampshire.

Students *Undergraduates:* 3,125 full-time, 126 part-time. Students come from 26 states and territories, 11 other countries. *The most frequently chosen baccalaureate fields are:* business/marketing, education, social sciences and history. *Graduate:* 480 in graduate degree programs.

Reside on campus	55%	Age 25 or older	9%
Transferred in	6%	International students	1%
African Americans	1%	Asian Americans/Pacific Islanders	1%
Hispanic Americans	1%	Native Americans	0.5%

Faculty 321 (50% full-time).

Expenses (1999–2000) *Tuition, state resident:* full-time $3830; part-time $164 per credit hour. *Tuition, nonresident:* full-time $9140; part-time $457 per credit hour. *Required fees:* full-time $1202; $56 per credit hour. Full-time tuition and fees vary according to reciprocity agreements. Part-time tuition and fees vary according to course load. *College room and board:* $5030; room only: $3354. Room and board charges vary according to board plan and housing facility. *Payment plan:* installment. *Waivers:* senior citizens and employees or children of employees.

Library Lamson Library. *Operations spending 1999–2000:* $1.4 million. *Collection:* 243,717 titles, 1,065 serial subscriptions, 20,541 audiovisual materials.

College life *Housing: Options:* coed, men-only, women-only, disabled students. *Social organizations:* national fraternities, national sororities, local fraternities, local sororities; 5% of eligible men and 6% of eligible women are members. *Most popular organizations:* Programming Activities in College Environment, Student Senate, Student Leadership Institute, Residence Housing Association, OSSIPEE—student wellness organization.

Campus security 24-hour emergency response devices and patrols, student patrols, late-night transport-escort service, controlled dormitory access, shuttle bus service, crime prevention programs, self-defense education.

After graduation 80 organizations recruited on campus 1997–98. 85% of class of 1998 had job offers within 6 months. *Career center:* 3 full-time, 10 part-time personnel. Services include job fairs, resume preparation, interview workshops, career/interest testing, career counseling, careers library, job

bank, job interviews. **Graduate education:** 15% of class of 1999 went directly to graduate and professional school.
Freshmen 2,843 applied, 2,181 admitted, 783 enrolled. 140 student government officers.

Average high school GPA	2.8	SAT verbal scores above 500	42%
SAT math scores above 500	41%	ACT above 18	46%
From top 10% of their h.s. class	4%	From top quarter	18%
From top half	53%	1998 freshmen returning in 1999	71%

Application *Options:* electronic application, early admission, deferred entrance. *Application fee:* $30. *Required:* essay or personal statement; high school transcript; 2 letters of recommendation. *Required for some:* interview. *Recommended:* minimum 2.0 GPA.
Standardized tests *Admission: Required:* SAT I or ACT.
Significant dates *Application deadlines:* 4/1 (freshmen), 4/1 (transfers). *Notification:* continuous until 7/1 (freshmen). **Financial aid deadline priority date:** 3/1.
Freshman Application Contact
Mr. Eugene Fahey, Senior Associate Director of Admission, Plymouth State College, 17 High Street, MSC #52, Plymouth, NH 03264-1595. **Phone:** 800-842-6900. **Toll-free phone:** 800-842-6900. **Fax:** 603-535-2714. **E-mail:** pscadmit@mail.plymouth.edu
Visit CollegeQuest.com for information on majors offered and athletics.

■ *See page 2276 for a narrative description.*

RIVIER COLLEGE
Nashua, New Hampshire

- **Independent Roman Catholic**, comprehensive, founded 1933
- **Degrees** associate, bachelor's, master's, post-master's, and postbachelor's certificates
- **Suburban** 64-acre campus with easy access to Boston
- **Coed**, 1,330 undergraduate students, 53% full-time, 82% women, 18% men
- **Moderately difficult** entrance level, 78% of applicants were admitted
- **13:1 student-to-undergraduate faculty ratio**
- **$14,260 tuition** and fees
- **$11,730 average financial aid** package, $16,555 average indebtedness upon graduation, $13.9 million endowment

Rivier's School of Undergraduate Studies enrolls approximately 800 day students and 750 evening students. Students pursue Rivier's commitment to social justice through service-learning experiences in the community, combining academic achievement in the liberal arts and professional studies with hands-on preparation for the future. Special opportunities, such as the honors program, offer added challenges and enrichment.

Students *Undergraduates:* 704 full-time, 626 part-time. Students come from 10 states and territories, 6 other countries. *The most frequently chosen baccalaureate fields are:* education, health professions and related sciences, psychology. *Graduate:* 1,046 in graduate degree programs.

From out-of-state	32%	Reside on campus	40%
Age 25 or older	47%	Transferred in	9%
International students	1%	African Americans	1%
Asian Americans/Pacific Islanders	1%	Hispanic Americans	2%
Native Americans	0.2%		

Faculty 209 (38% full-time).
Expenses (1999–2000) *Comprehensive fee:* $19,950 includes full-time tuition ($13,950), mandatory fees ($310), and room and board ($5690). *Part-time tuition:* $465 per credit hour. *Part-time fees:* $2 per credit hour; $25 per term part-time. Part-time tuition and fees vary according to class time. *Payment plans:* installment, deferred payment. *Waivers:* senior citizens and employees or children of employees.
Library Regina Library plus 1 other. *Operations spending 1999–2000:* $474,719. *Collection:* 105,000 titles, 1,802 serial subscriptions, 29,094 audio-visual materials.
College life *Housing: Option:* coed. *Most popular organizations:* Student Government Association, Residence Hall Council, Paralegal Society, Student Admissions Committee, Behavioral Sciences Association.
Campus security 24-hour emergency response devices and patrols, late-night transport-escort service, controlled dormitory access.

After graduation 72% of class of 1998 had job offers within 6 months. *Career center:* 1 full-time, 1 part-time personnel. Services include job fairs, resume preparation, interview workshops, career/interest testing, career counseling, careers library, job bank. **Graduate education:** 21% of class of 1999 went directly to graduate and professional school: 7% business, 7% education, 6% graduate arts and sciences, 1% law, 1% medicine.
Freshmen 658 applied, 514 admitted, 194 enrolled.

Average high school GPA	3.0	SAT verbal scores above 500	38%
SAT math scores above 500	32%	ACT above 18	N/R
From top 10% of their h.s. class	9%	From top quarter	24%
From top half	70%	1998 freshmen returning in 1999	78%

Application *Options:* Common Application, early action, deferred entrance. *Application fee:* $25. *Required:* essay or personal statement; high school transcript; 1 letter of recommendation. *Required for some:* interview; portfolio for art program. *Recommended:* minimum 2.3 GPA; interview.
Standardized tests *Admission: Required:* SAT I or ACT. *Required for some:* nursing examination.
Significant dates *Application deadlines:* rolling (freshmen), rolling (transfers). *Early action:* 11/15. *Notification:* 12/1 (early action). **Financial aid deadline priority date:** 2/1.
Freshman Application Contact
Ms. Lynn A. Petrillo, Director of Undergraduate Admissions, Rivier College, Office of Undergraduate Admissions, 420 Main Street, Nashua, NH 03060. **Phone:** 603-897-8502. **Toll-free phone:** 800-44RIVIER. **Fax:** 603-891-1799. **E-mail:** rivadmit@rivier.edu
Visit CollegeQuest.com for information on majors offered and athletics.

■ *See page 2336 for a narrative description.*

SAINT ANSELM COLLEGE
Manchester, New Hampshire

Apply at CollegeQuest.com

- **Independent Roman Catholic**, 4-year, founded 1889
- **Degree** bachelor's
- **Suburban** 450-acre campus with easy access to Boston
- **Coed**, 1,937 undergraduate students, 98% full-time, 56% women, 44% men
- **Moderately difficult** entrance level, 72% of applicants were admitted
- **15:1 student-to-undergraduate faculty ratio**
- **71% graduate** in 6 years or less
- **$17,640 tuition** and fees
- **$16,448 average indebtedness** upon graduation, $45.7 million endowment

Students *Undergraduates:* 1,899 full-time, 38 part-time. Students come from 29 states and territories, 9 other countries. *The most frequently chosen baccalaureate fields are:* business/marketing, health professions and related sciences, social sciences and history.

From out-of-state	77%	Reside on campus	80%
Transferred in	2%	International students	0.5%
African Americans	0.2%	Asian Americans/Pacific Islanders	1%
Hispanic Americans	1%	Native Americans	0.1%

Faculty 170 (66% full-time), 84% with terminal degrees.
Expenses (1999–2000) *Comprehensive fee:* $24,160 includes full-time tuition ($17,300), mandatory fees ($340), and room and board ($6520). Room and board charges vary according to housing facility. *Part-time tuition:* $1730 per course. *Payment plans:* installment, deferred payment. *Waivers:* senior citizens and employees or children of employees.
Library Geisel Library. *Operations spending 1999–2000:* $1.1 million. *Collection:* 205,136 titles, 1,745 serial subscriptions.
College life *Housing:* on-campus residence required in freshman year. *Options:* men-only, women-only, disabled students. *Most popular organizations:* Center for Volunteers, Anselmian Abbey Players, Knights of Columbus, My College, International Relations Club.
Campus security 24-hour emergency response devices and patrols, late-night transport-escort service, controlled dormitory access.
After graduation 165 organizations recruited on campus 1997–98. *Career center:* 2 full-time personnel. Services include job fairs, resume preparation, interview workshops, resume referral, career counseling, careers library, job bank, job interviews. **Graduate education:** 22% of class of 1999 went

New Hampshire

Saint Anselm College (continued)

directly to graduate and professional school: 8% business, 5% graduate arts and sciences, 4% law, 2% dentistry, 2% education, 1% medicine.

Freshmen 2,547 applied, 1,842 admitted, 536 enrolled. 23 class presidents, 7 valedictorians, 79 student government officers.

Average high school GPA	3.01	SAT verbal scores above 500	81%
SAT math scores above 500	79%	ACT above 18	N/R
From top 10% of their h.s. class	18%	From top quarter	53%
From top half	90%	1998 freshmen returning in 1999	82%

Application *Options:* eApply at www.CollegeQuest.com, Common Application, electronic application, early admission, early decision, deferred entrance. *Application fee:* $35. *Required:* essay or personal statement; high school transcript; minimum 2.0 GPA; 2 letters of recommendation. *Recommended:* interview.

Standardized tests *Admission: Required:* SAT I or ACT.

Significant dates *Application deadlines:* rolling (freshmen), rolling (transfers). *Early decision:* 12/1. *Notification:* 12/15 (early decision). *Financial aid deadline:* 4/15. *Priority date:* 3/1.

Freshman Application Contact
Mr. Donald E. Healy, Director of Admissions, Saint Anselm College, 100 Saint Anselm Drive, Manchester, NH 03102-1310. **Phone:** 603-641-7500 Ext. 7171. **Toll-free phone:** 888-4ANSELM. **Fax:** 603-641-7550. **E-mail:** admissions@anselm.edu

Visit CollegeQuest.com for information on majors offered and athletics. Electronic viewbook available at CollegeQuest.com.

■ *See page 2370 for a narrative description.*

THOMAS MORE COLLEGE OF LIBERAL ARTS
Merrimack, New Hampshire

- **Independent**, 4-year, founded 1978, affiliated with Roman Catholic Church
- **Degree** bachelor's
- **Small-town** 14-acre campus with easy access to Boston
- **Coed**, 72 undergraduate students, 99% full-time, 53% women, 47% men
- **Moderately difficult** entrance level, 100% of applicants were admitted
- **13:1 student-to-undergraduate faculty ratio**
- **$9600 tuition** and fees

Students *Undergraduates:* 71 full-time, 1 part-time. Students come from 28 states and territories, 2 other countries. *The most frequently chosen baccalaureate fields are:* foreign language/literature, philosophy, social sciences and history.

From out-of-state	94%	Reside on campus	98%
Age 25 or older	5%	Transferred in	13%
International students	6%	Asian Americans/Pacific Islanders	1%
Hispanic Americans	7%		

Expenses (1999–2000) *Comprehensive fee:* $17,000 includes full-time tuition ($9600) and room and board ($7400). *Payment plans:* installment, deferred payment. *Waivers:* employees or children of employees.

Library Warren Memorial Library. *Operations spending 1999–2000:* $26,319. *Collection:* 30,000 titles.

College life *Housing:* on-campus residence required through senior year. *Options:* men-only, women-only.

Campus security Student patrols, late-night transport-escort service.

After graduation 50% of class of 1998 had job offers within 6 months. *Career center:* Services include career counseling. *Graduate education:* 67% of class of 1999 went directly to graduate and professional school: 56% graduate arts and sciences.

Freshmen 36 applied, 36 admitted, 17 enrolled.

Average high school GPA	3.1	SAT verbal scores above 500	87%
SAT math scores above 500	74%	ACT above 18	100%
1998 freshmen returning in 1999	75%		

Application *Options:* early admission, deferred entrance. *Application fee:* $25. *Required:* essay or personal statement; high school transcript; 2 letters of recommendation. *Required for some:* interview.

Standardized tests *Admission: Required:* SAT I or ACT.

Significant dates *Application deadlines:* rolling (freshmen), rolling (transfers). *Financial aid deadline priority date:* 5/1.

Freshman Application Contact
Dr. Kristen S. Kelly, Director of Admissions, Thomas More College of Liberal Arts, 6 Manchester Street, Merrimack, NH 03054-4818. **Phone:** 603-880-8308. **Fax:** 603-880-9280. **E-mail:** thomaemorae@earthlink.com

Visit CollegeQuest.com for information on majors offered and athletics.

■ *See page 2622 for a narrative description.*

UNIVERSITY OF NEW HAMPSHIRE
Durham, New Hampshire

- **State-supported**, university, founded 1866
- **Degrees** associate, bachelor's, master's, doctoral, and post-master's certificates
- **Small-town** 200-acre campus with easy access to Boston
- **Coed**, 10,215 undergraduate students, 95% full-time, 59% women, 41% men
- **Moderately difficult** entrance level, 81% of applicants were admitted
- **14:1 student-to-undergraduate faculty ratio**
- **72.9% graduate** in 6 years or less
- **$6939 tuition** and fees (in-state); $15,829 (out-of-state)
- **$10,405 average financial aid** package, $19,712 average indebtedness upon graduation, $148.7 million endowment

Part of University System of New Hampshire.

Students *Undergraduates:* 9,750 full-time, 465 part-time. Students come from 40 states and territories, 34 other countries. *The most frequently chosen baccalaureate fields are:* business/marketing, health professions and related sciences, social sciences and history. *Graduate:* 2,714 in graduate degree programs.

From out-of-state	40%	Reside on campus	50%
Age 25 or older	6%	Transferred in	5%
International students	1%	African Americans	1%
Asian Americans/Pacific Islanders	1%	Hispanic Americans	1%
Native Americans	0.2%		

Faculty 707 (83% full-time).

Expenses (1999–2000) *Tuition, state resident:* full-time $5450; part-time $227 per credit. *Tuition, nonresident:* full-time $14,340; part-time $598 per credit. *Required fees:* full-time $1489; $15 per term part-time. Full-time tuition and fees vary according to program. Part-time tuition and fees vary according to course load. *College room and board:* $4798; room only: $2820. Room and board charges vary according to board plan and housing facility. *Waivers:* minority students, senior citizens, and employees or children of employees.

Library Dimond Library plus 4 others. *Operations spending 1999–2000:* $6.8 million. *Collection:* 801,013 titles, 9,136 serial subscriptions, 19,959 audiovisual materials.

College life *Housing: Option:* coed. *Social organizations:* national fraternities, national sororities; 5% of eligible men and 5% of eligible women are members. *Most popular organizations:* Outing Club, student government, Diversity Support Coalition, Campus Activities Board, Memorial Union Student Organization (MUSO).

Campus security 24-hour emergency response devices and patrols, student patrols, late-night transport-escort service, controlled dormitory access.

After graduation 260 organizations recruited on campus 1997–98. *Career center:* 5 full-time, 4 part-time personnel. Services include job fairs, resume preparation, interview workshops, resume referral, career/interest testing, career counseling, careers library, job bank, job interviews. *Major awards:* 2 Fulbright Scholars.

Freshmen 8,833 applied, 7,183 admitted, 2,556 enrolled.

SAT verbal scores above 500	76%	SAT math scores above 500	79%
ACT above 18	N/R	From top 10% of their h.s. class	21%
From top quarter	57%	From top half	94%
1998 freshmen returning in 1999	84%		

Application *Options:* Common Application, electronic application, early action, deferred entrance. *Preference* given to state residents. *Application fee:* $50 for nonresidents. *Required:* essay or personal statement; high school transcript; 1 letter of recommendation. *Recommended:* minimum 3.0 GPA; interview.

Standardized tests *Admission: Required:* SAT I or ACT. *Recommended:* SAT II Subject Tests.

New Hampshire

Significant dates *Application deadlines:* 2/1 (freshmen), 3/1 (transfers). *Early action:* 12/1. *Notification:* 4/15 (freshmen), 1/15 (early action). *Financial aid deadline:* 3/1.
Freshman Application Contact
Mr. James Washington Jr., Director of Admissions, University of New Hampshire, Grant House, 4 Garrison Avenue, Durham, NH 03824. **Phone:** 603-862-1360. **E-mail:** admissions@unh.edu
Visit CollegeQuest.com for information on majors offered and athletics. Electronic viewbook available at CollegeQuest.com.

UNIVERSITY OF NEW HAMPSHIRE AT MANCHESTER
Manchester, New Hampshire

- **State-supported**, 4-year, founded 1967
- **Degrees** associate and bachelor's
- **Urban** 800-acre campus with easy access to Boston
- **Coed**, 704 undergraduate students, 56% full-time, 64% women, 36% men
- **Moderately difficult** entrance level, 73% of applicants were admitted
- **13:1 student-to-undergraduate faculty ratio**
- **$4684 tuition** and fees (in-state); $12,244 (out-of-state)
- **$18,851 endowment**

Part of University System of New Hampshire.
Students *Undergraduates:* 394 full-time, 310 part-time. Students come from 4 states and territories. *The most frequently chosen baccalaureate fields are:* foreign language/literature, communications/communication technologies, psychology. *Graduate:* 70 in graduate degree programs.

Transferred in	17%	International students	1%
African Americans	2%	Asian Americans/Pacific Islanders	1%
Hispanic Americans	1%	Native Americans	0.3%

Faculty 108 (21% full-time), 43% with terminal degrees.
Expenses (1999–2000) *Tuition, state resident:* full-time $4630; part-time $172 per credit. *Tuition, nonresident:* full-time $12,190; part-time $190 per credit. *Required fees:* full-time $54; $17 per term part-time. Part-time tuition and fees vary according to program. *Payment plan:* installment. *Waivers:* senior citizens and employees or children of employees.
Library Norma K. Oudens Memorial Library. *Operations spending 1999–2000:* $282,343. *Collection:* 25,000 titles, 550 serial subscriptions, 1,256 audiovisual materials.
College life *Housing:* college housing not available. *Most popular organization:* Student Council.
Campus security Late-night transport-escort service.
After graduation *Career center:* 3 full-time personnel. Services include resume preparation, career/interest testing, career counseling, careers library.
Freshmen 221 applied, 161 admitted, 107 enrolled.

SAT verbal scores above 500	66%	SAT math scores above 500	51%
ACT above 18	N/R	From top 10% of their h.s. class	3%
From top quarter	15%	From top half	52%

Application *Option:* deferred entrance. *Application fee:* $50 for nonresidents. *Required:* essay or personal statement; high school transcript; 1 letter of recommendation. *Recommended:* interview.
Standardized tests *Admission: Recommended:* ACT. *Required for some:* SAT I.
Significant dates *Application deadlines:* 6/15 (freshmen), 6/15 (transfers). *Financial aid deadline priority date:* 5/1.
Freshman Application Contact
Ms. Susan Miller, Admissions Secretary, University of New Hampshire at Manchester, 220 Hackett Hill Road, Manchester, NH 03102-8597. **Phone:** 603-629-4150. **Fax:** 603-623-2745. **E-mail:** unhm@unh.edu
Visit CollegeQuest.com for information on majors offered and athletics. College video available at CollegeQuest.com.

UNIVERSITY SYSTEM COLLEGE FOR LIFELONG LEARNING
Concord, New Hampshire

- **State and locally supported**, 4-year, founded 1972
- **Degrees** associate, bachelor's, and postbachelor's certificates (offers primarily part-time degree programs; courses offered at 50 locations in New Hampshire)
- **Rural** campus
- **Coed**
- **Noncompetitive** entrance level
- **10:1 student-to-undergraduate faculty ratio**
- **$3920 tuition** and fees (in-state); $4376 (out-of-state)

Part of University System of New Hampshire.
Students *Undergraduates: The most frequently chosen baccalaureate fields are:* business/marketing, liberal arts/general studies, social sciences and history.
Faculty 498, 22% with terminal degrees.
Expenses (1999–2000) *Tuition, state resident:* full-time $3840; part-time $160 per semester hour. *Tuition, nonresident:* full-time $4296; part-time $179 per semester hour. *Required fees:* full-time $80; $20 per term part-time. Full-time tuition and fees vary according to course load. Part-time tuition and fees vary according to course load. *Payment plan:* installment. *Waivers:* employees or children of employees.
Library *Operations spending 1999–2000:* $80,000.
College life *Housing:* college housing not available. *Most popular organization:* Alumni Learner Association.
After graduation *Career center:* 1 part-time personnel. Services include job fairs, resume preparation, interview workshops, resume referral, career/interest testing, career counseling, careers library.
Freshmen

SAT verbal scores above 500	N/R	SAT math scores above 500	N/R
ACT above 18	N/R		

Application *Application fee:* $35.
Significant dates *Application deadlines:* rolling (freshmen), rolling (transfers).
Freshman Application Contact
Ms. Teresa McDonnell, Associate Dean of Learner Services, University System College for Lifelong Learning, 125 North State Street, Concord, NH 03301. **Phone:** 603-228-3000 Ext. 308. **Toll-free phone:** 800-582-7248 Ext. 313. **Fax:** 603-229-0964. **E-mail:** n_dumont@unhf.unh.edu
Visit CollegeQuest.com for information on majors offered and athletics.

WHITE PINES COLLEGE
Chester, New Hampshire

Apply at CollegeQuest.com

- **Independent**, 4-year, founded 1965
- **Degrees** associate and bachelor's
- **Rural** 83-acre campus with easy access to Boston
- **Coed**, 100 undergraduate students, 76% full-time, 65% women, 35% men
- **Minimally difficult** entrance level, 80% of applicants were admitted
- **7:1 student-to-undergraduate faculty ratio**
- **$10,100 tuition** and fees

Students *Undergraduates:* 76 full-time, 24 part-time. Students come from 10 states and territories.

Age 25 or older	9%	African Americans	1%
Asian Americans/Pacific Islanders	3%	Hispanic Americans	3%

Expenses (2000–2001) *Comprehensive fee:* $15,600 includes full-time tuition ($10,100) and room and board ($5500). *Part-time tuition:* $340 per credit. *Payment plan:* installment. *Waivers:* employees or children of employees.
Library Wadleigh Library. *Collection:* 20,000 titles, 100 serial subscriptions.
College life *Housing:* on-campus residence required in freshman year. *Option:* coed.
After graduation *Career center:* Services include career counseling.
Freshmen 179 applied, 144 admitted, 70 enrolled. 5 student government officers.

SAT verbal scores above 500	N/R	SAT math scores above 500	N/R
ACT above 18	N/R	From top 10% of their h.s. class	10%
From top quarter	29%	From top half	52%

Peterson's Guide to Four-Year Colleges 2001   www.petersons.com

New Hampshire–New Jersey

White Pines College (continued)

Application *Options:* eApply at www.CollegeQuest.com, deferred entrance. *Application fee:* $25. *Required:* essay or personal statement; high school transcript; 3 letters of recommendation. *Recommended:* minimum 2.0 GPA; interview.

Standardized tests *Admission: Recommended:* SAT I and SAT II or ACT.

Significant dates *Application deadlines:* rolling (freshmen), rolling (transfers). *Financial aid deadline priority date:* 3/1.

Freshman Application Contact Ms. Sue Dugas, Director of Admissions and Enrollment, White Pines College, 40 Chester Street, Chester, NH 03036. **Phone:** 603-887-7400. **Toll-free phone:** 800-974-6372.

Visit CollegeQuest.com for information on majors offered and athletics.

■ *See page 2982 for a narrative description.*

NEW JERSEY

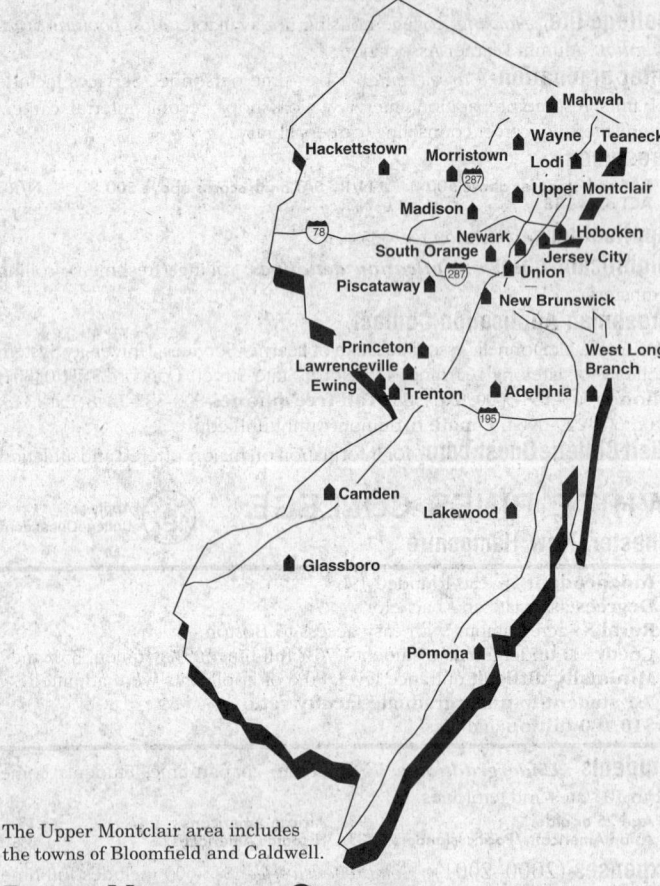

The Upper Montclair area includes the towns of Bloomfield and Caldwell.

BETH MEDRASH GOVOHA
Lakewood, New Jersey

Admissions Office Contact
Beth Medrash Govoha, 617 Sixth Street, Lakewood, NJ 08701-2797.

BLOOMFIELD COLLEGE
Bloomfield, New Jersey

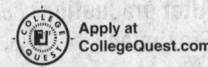 Apply at CollegeQuest.com

- **Independent**, 4-year, founded 1868, affiliated with Presbyterian Church (U.S.A.)
- **Degree** bachelor's
- **Suburban** 12-acre campus with easy access to New York City
- **Coed**, 1,756 undergraduate students, 72% full-time, 70% women, 30% men

- **Minimally difficult** entrance level, 28% of applicants were admitted
- **14:1 student-to-undergraduate faculty ratio**
- **26% graduate** in 6 years or less
- **$10,450 tuition** and fees
- **$9841 average financial aid** package, $12,967 average indebtedness upon graduation, $6 million endowment

Diversity is the hallmark of Bloomfield College, attracting resident students from a wide geographic range and commuter students from the New Jersey/New York metropolitan area. They come from a rich mixture of backgrounds and experiences. Reflecting the contemporary world, they learn together, share interests, build friendships to last a lifetime, and graduate fully prepared for careers and continued education.

Students *Undergraduates:* 1,272 full-time, 484 part-time. Students come from 10 states and territories, 55 other countries. *The most frequently chosen baccalaureate fields are:* business/marketing, biological/life sciences, social sciences and history.

From out-of-state	2%	Reside on campus	13%
Age 25 or older	41%	Transferred in	9%
International students	2%	African Americans	48%
Asian Americans/Pacific Islanders	3%	Hispanic Americans	16%
Native Americans	0.2%		

Faculty 199 (32% full-time).

Expenses (1999–2000) *Comprehensive fee:* $15,600 includes full-time tuition ($10,300), mandatory fees ($150), and room and board ($5150). Full-time tuition and fees vary according to course load and program. Room and board charges vary according to board plan. *Part-time tuition:* $1040 per course. *Part-time fees:* $25 per term part-time. Part-time tuition and fees vary according to course load and program. *Payment plans:* installment, deferred payment. *Waivers:* senior citizens and employees or children of employees.

Library Talbott Hall Library plus 1 other. *Operations spending 1999–2000:* $544,505. *Collection:* 64,700 titles, 4,818 serial subscriptions.

College life *Housing:* Option: coed. *Social organizations:* national fraternities, national sororities, local fraternities, local sororities, coed social clubs; 2% of eligible men and 2% of eligible women are members. *Most popular organizations:* Nursing Student Association, Black Students for Progress, Haitian Student Association, Association of Latin American Students, Caribbean Students Association.

Campus security 24-hour emergency response devices and patrols, escort service.

After graduation 45 organizations recruited on campus 1997–98. 80% of class of 1998 had job offers within 6 months. *Career center:* 2 full-time, 1 part-time personnel. Services include resume preparation, interview workshops, resume referral, career/interest testing, career counseling, careers library, job bank, job interviews. *Graduate education:* 7% of class of 1999 went directly to graduate and professional school.

Freshmen 1,390 applied, 392 admitted, 249 enrolled.

Average high school GPA	2.4	SAT verbal scores above 500	7%
SAT math scores above 500	10%	ACT above 18	N/R
From top 10% of their h.s. class	5%	From top quarter	20%
From top half	49%	1998 freshmen returning in 1999	68%

Application *Options:* eApply at www.CollegeQuest.com, Common Application, early admission, early action, deferred entrance. *Application fee:* $25. *Required:* high school transcript; minimum 2.3 GPA; 2 letters of recommendation. *Recommended:* essay or personal statement; interview.

Standardized tests *Admission: Required:* SAT I or ACT.

Significant dates *Application deadlines:* 8/1 (freshmen), rolling (transfers). *Early action:* 1/7. *Notification:* 1/21 (early action). *Financial aid deadline priority date:* 6/1.

Freshman Application Contact Office of Admission, Bloomfield College, 467 Franklin Street, Bloomfield, NJ 07003-9981. **Phone:** 973-748-9000 Ext. 230. **Toll-free phone:** 800-848-4555. **Fax:** 973-748-0916. **E-mail:** admission@bloomfield.edu

Visit CollegeQuest.com for information on majors offered and athletics.

■ *See page 1284 for a narrative description.*

New Jersey

CALDWELL COLLEGE
Caldwell, New Jersey

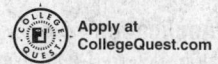

- **Independent Roman Catholic**, comprehensive, founded 1939
- **Degrees** bachelor's, master's, and post-master's certificates
- **Suburban** 100-acre campus with easy access to New York City
- **Coed**, 1,756 undergraduate students, 52% full-time, 69% women, 31% men
- **Moderately difficult** entrance level, 75% of applicants were admitted
- **13:1** student-to-undergraduate faculty ratio
- **$12,400 tuition** and fees
- **$7925 average financial aid** package, $11,350 average indebtedness upon graduation, $3.9 million endowment

Plans are underway during 2000–01 to open a 47,300-square-foot Student Activities and Recreation Building to meet the social needs of a growing student population. Despite its growth, the College still maintains its liberal arts character by providing students will close, personal attention while enhancing technological facilities on campus.

Students *Undergraduates:* 909 full-time, 847 part-time. Students come from 3 states and territories, 18 other countries. *The most frequently chosen baccalaureate fields are:* business/marketing, education, psychology. **Graduate:** 250 in graduate degree programs.

From out-of-state	13%	Reside on campus	36%
Age 25 or older	2%	Transferred in	2%
International students	4%	African Americans	12%
Asian Americans/Pacific Islanders	3%	Hispanic Americans	7%

Faculty 137 (53% full-time), 34% with terminal degrees.

Expenses (1999–2000) *Comprehensive fee:* $18,300 includes full-time tuition ($12,400) and room and board ($5900). Full-time tuition and fees vary according to program. *Part-time tuition:* $319 per credit. Part-time tuition and fees vary according to course load and program. *Payment plans:* installment, deferred payment. *Waivers:* senior citizens and employees or children of employees.

Library Jennings Library. *Operations spending 1999–2000:* $701,169. *Collection:* 121,184 titles, 710 serial subscriptions, 2,596 audiovisual materials.

College life *Housing: Option:* coed. *Most popular organizations:* Student Government Association, International Students Organization, Caldwell College Education Association, Circle K, Black Student Cooperative Unit.

Campus security 24-hour patrols, late-night transport-escort service, controlled dormitory access, dusk-to-dawn patrols by trained security personnel.

After graduation 30 organizations recruited on campus 1997–98. *Career center:* 2 full-time, 3 part-time personnel. Services include job fairs, resume preparation, interview workshops, career/interest testing, career counseling, careers library, job interviews.

Freshmen 1,027 applied, 766 admitted, 271 enrolled.

Average high school GPA	2.81	SAT verbal scores above 500	26%
SAT math scores above 500	27%	ACT above 18	N/R
From top 10% of their h.s. class	4%	From top quarter	13%
From top half	38%		

Application *Options:* eApply at www.CollegeQuest.com, Common Application, early admission, early action, deferred entrance. *Application fee:* $40. *Required:* essay or personal statement; high school transcript; minimum 2.0 GPA; 2 letters of recommendation. *Required for some:* interview. *Recommended:* essay or personal statement.

Standardized tests *Admission: Required:* SAT I or ACT.

Significant dates *Application deadline:* rolling (transfers). *Early action:* 1/1. *Notification:* 1/15 (early action). *Financial aid deadline priority date:* 4/15.

Freshman Application Contact
Mr. Raymond Sheenan, Executive Director of Admissions, Caldwell College, 9 Ryerson Avenue, Caldwell, NJ 07006. **Phone:** 973-618-3220. **Toll-free phone:** 888-864-9516. **E-mail:** admissions@caldwell.edu

Visit CollegeQuest.com for information on majors offered and athletics. College video available at CollegeQuest.com.

- *See page 1332 for a narrative description.*

CAMDEN COLLEGE OF ARTS AND SCIENCES
New Jersey—See Rutgers, The State University of New Jersey, Camden College of Arts and Sciences

CENTENARY COLLEGE
Hackettstown, New Jersey

- **Independent**, comprehensive, founded 1867, affiliated with United Methodist Church
- **Degrees** associate, bachelor's, master's, and postbachelor's certificates
- **Suburban** 42-acre campus with easy access to New York City
- **Coed**, 734 undergraduate students, 78% full-time, 72% women, 28% men
- **Moderately difficult** entrance level, 83% of applicants were admitted
- **14:1** student-to-undergraduate faculty ratio
- **45% graduate** in 6 years or less
- **$14,340 tuition** and fees
- **$12,873 average financial aid** package, $1.9 million endowment

New majors are computer information systems, sociology, and theater arts. New programs are criminal justice, sports management, and student-run television station. New services include waived fees for online applications/financial estimates, a renewable scholarship program, computers and printers in each dorm room, voice mail, Internet access, e-mail, cable television, and a library catalog system.

Students *Undergraduates:* 572 full-time, 162 part-time. Students come from 21 states and territories, 16 other countries. *The most frequently chosen baccalaureate fields are:* business/marketing, liberal arts/general studies, psychology. **Graduate:** 83 in graduate degree programs.

From out-of-state	15%	Reside on campus	55%
Age 25 or older	53%	Transferred in	25%
International students	8%	African Americans	4%
Asian Americans/Pacific Islanders	1%	Hispanic Americans	3%
Native Americans	1%		

Faculty 137 (31% full-time).

Expenses (1999–2000) *Comprehensive fee:* $20,490 includes full-time tuition ($13,800), mandatory fees ($540), and room and board ($6150). Full-time tuition and fees vary according to program. *Part-time tuition:* $268 per credit. *Part-time fees:* $20 per term part-time. Part-time tuition and fees vary according to course load and program. *Payment plan:* installment. *Waivers:* senior citizens and employees or children of employees.

Library Taylor Memorial Library. *Operations spending 1999–2000:* $236,584. *Collection:* 67,272 titles, 485 serial subscriptions.

College life *Housing: Options:* coed, women-only. *Social organizations:* local fraternities, local sororities; 10% of eligible men and 30% of eligible women are members. *Most popular organizations:* Essence, equestrian teams, Quill, student government, Kappa Delta Epsilon.

Campus security Late-night transport-escort service, controlled dormitory access, patrols by trained security personnel 4 p.m. to 8 a.m.

After graduation 35 organizations recruited on campus 1997–98. 70% of class of 1998 had job offers within 6 months. *Career center:* 2 full-time, 1 part-time personnel. Services include job fairs, resume preparation, interview workshops, resume referral, career/interest testing, career counseling, careers library, job bank. **Graduate education:** 19% of class of 1999 went directly to graduate and professional school: 5% education, 4% graduate arts and sciences, 1% business, 1% law, 1% medicine, 1% veterinary medicine.

Freshmen 375 applied, 310 admitted, 142 enrolled. 2 valedictorians.

Average high school GPA	2.55	SAT verbal scores above 500	30%
SAT math scores above 500	24%	ACT above 18	60%
From top 10% of their h.s. class	6%	From top quarter	18%
From top half	56%	1998 freshmen returning in 1999	54%

Application *Options:* eApply at www.CollegeQuest.com, Common Application, electronic application, deferred entrance. *Application fee:* $25. *Required:* essay or personal statement; high school transcript. *Required for some:* interview; portfolio. *Recommended:* minimum 2.0 GPA; letters of recommendation; interview.

Standardized tests *Admission: Required:* SAT I or ACT.

Significant dates *Application deadlines:* rolling (freshmen), rolling (transfers). *Financial aid deadline priority date:* 4/15.

New Jersey

Centenary College (continued)
Freshman Application Contact
Mr. Dennis Kelly, Vice President for Enrollment Management, Centenary College, 400 Jefferson Street, Hackettstown, NJ 07840-2100. **Phone:** 908-852-1400 Ext. 2217. **Toll-free phone:** 800-236-8679. **Fax:** 908-852-3454. **E-mail:** admissions@centenarycollege.edu
Visit CollegeQuest.com for information on majors offered and athletics. College video available at CollegeQuest.com.

■ *See page 1388 for a narrative description.*

THE COLLEGE OF NEW JERSEY
Ewing, New Jersey

- **State-supported**, comprehensive, founded 1855
- **Degrees** bachelor's and master's
- **Suburban** 255-acre campus with easy access to Philadelphia
- **Coed**, 5,930 undergraduate students, 93% full-time, 60% women, 40% men
- **Very difficult** entrance level, 55% of applicants were admitted
- **12:1 student-to-undergraduate faculty ratio**
- **80% graduate** in 6 years or less
- **$5685 tuition** and fees (in-state); $9002 (out-of-state)
- **$6000 average financial aid** package, $13,000 average indebtedness upon graduation, $4.1 million endowment

The College of New Jersey (TCNJ) is a mid-sized, comprehensive public college that concentrates primarily on the undergraduate experience. Known for the quality of its academic offerings, TCNJ serves a highly selective, diverse, and achievement-oriented student body. Set on 289 acres in the suburban township of Ewing, New Jersey, The College of New Jersey is recognized as one of the finest institution of its type in the nation.

Students *Undergraduates:* 5,539 full-time, 391 part-time. Students come from 20 states and territories, 13 other countries. *The most frequently chosen baccalaureate fields are:* business/marketing, education, English. *Graduate:* 817 in graduate degree programs.

From out-of-state	4%	Reside on campus	60%
Age 25 or older	7%	Transferred in	4%
International students	0.2%	African Americans	6%
Asian Americans/Pacific Islanders	5%	Hispanic Americans	5%
Native Americans	0.2%		

Faculty 635 (52% full-time), 46% with terminal degrees.
Expenses (1999–2000) *Tuition, state resident:* full-time $4445; part-time $151 per semester hour. *Tuition, nonresident:* full-time $7762; part-time $265 per semester hour. *Required fees:* full-time $1240; $41 per semester hour; $2 per term part-time. *College room and board:* $6330. Room and board charges vary according to board plan. *Payment plans:* installment, deferred payment. *Waivers:* senior citizens and employees or children of employees.
Library Roscoe L. West Library. *Collection:* 520,000 titles, 4,700 serial subscriptions, 2,500 audiovisual materials.
College life *Housing:* Option: coed. *Social organizations:* national fraternities, national sororities, local fraternities, local sororities; 20% of eligible men and 20% of eligible women are members. *Most popular organizations:* Student Government Association, College Union Board, Inter-Greek Council, The Signal, intramurals.
Campus security 24-hour emergency response devices and patrols, student patrols, late-night transport-escort service, controlled dormitory access.
After graduation 265 organizations recruited on campus 1997–98. 65% of class of 1998 had job offers within 6 months. *Career center:* 7 full-time, 1 part-time personnel. Services include job fairs, resume preparation, resume referral, career counseling, careers library, job bank, job interviews. *Graduate education:* 25% of class of 1999 went directly to graduate and professional school: 8% education, 7% graduate arts and sciences, 6% business, 3% law, 1% engineering, 1% medicine.
Freshmen 5,755 applied, 3,163 admitted, 1,209 enrolled. 31 valedictorians.

Average high school GPA	3.25	SAT verbal scores above 500	94%
SAT math scores above 500	96%	ACT above 18	N/R
From top 10% of their h.s. class	57%	From top quarter	92%
From top half	98%	1998 freshmen returning in 1999	93%

Application *Options:* electronic application, early admission, early decision, deferred entrance. *Application fee:* $50. *Required:* essay or personal statement; high school transcript; minimum 2.0 GPA. *Required for some:* interview.
Standardized tests *Admission: Required:* SAT I, SAT II: Writing Test.
Significant dates *Application deadlines:* 2/15 (freshmen), 2/15 (transfers). *Early decision:* 11/15. *Notification:* 4/1 (freshmen), 12/15 (early decision). *Financial aid deadline:* 6/1. *Priority date:* 3/1.
Freshman Application Contact
Ms. Lisa Angeloni, Director of Admissions, The College of New Jersey, The College of New Jersey, Admission Office, PO Box 7718, Ewing, NJ 08628. **Phone:** 609-771-2131. **Toll-free phone:** 800-624-0967. **E-mail:** admiss@vm.tcnj.edu
Visit CollegeQuest.com for information on majors offered and athletics. Electronic viewbook available at CollegeQuest.com.

■ *See page 1462 for a narrative description.*

COLLEGE OF SAINT ELIZABETH
Morristown, New Jersey

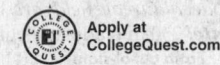
Apply at CollegeQuest.com

- **Independent Roman Catholic**, comprehensive, founded 1899
- **Degrees** bachelor's, master's, and postbachelor's certificates
- **Suburban** 188-acre campus with easy access to New York City
- **Women** only, 1,090 undergraduate students, 54% full-time
- **Moderately difficult** entrance level, 83% of applicants were admitted
- **11:1 student-to-undergraduate faculty ratio**
- **64% graduate** in 6 years or less
- **$14,030 tuition** and fees
- **$16,470 average financial aid** package, $14,261 average indebtedness upon graduation, $18.5 million endowment

The College of Saint Elizabeth is a private women's college in the Catholic liberal arts tradition, located in suburban Morristown, New Jersey. Students learn in an environment focused on women in which high-quality teaching is a primary goal, along with the development of leadership in the spirit of service and social responsibility.

Students *Undergraduates:* 589 full-time, 501 part-time. Students come from 9 states and territories, 21 other countries. *The most frequently chosen baccalaureate fields are:* business/marketing, education, psychology. *Graduate:* 459 in graduate degree programs.

From out-of-state	3%	Reside on campus	72%
Age 25 or older	1%	Transferred in	6%

Faculty 181 (29% full-time), 50% with terminal degrees.
Expenses (1999–2000) *Comprehensive fee:* $20,470 includes full-time tuition ($13,500), mandatory fees ($530), and room and board ($6440). *Part-time tuition:* $410 per semester hour. *Part-time fees:* $55 per course; $15 per term part-time. *Payment plan:* installment. *Waivers:* senior citizens and employees or children of employees.
Library Mahoney Library. *Operations spending 1999–2000:* $1.2 million. *Collection:* 140,202 titles, 848 serial subscriptions, 525 audiovisual materials.
College life *Housing:* Option: women-only. *Most popular organizations:* Elizabethan Education Club, Students Take Action Committee, International/Intercultural Club, student activities committee, campus ministry.
Campus security 24-hour emergency response devices and patrols, late-night transport-escort service, controlled dormitory access, self-defense education.
After graduation 46% of class of 1998 had job offers within 6 months. *Career center:* 1 full-time, 1 part-time personnel. Services include resume preparation, interview workshops, resume referral, career/interest testing, career counseling, careers library, job bank, job interviews. *Graduate education:* 18% of class of 1999 went directly to graduate and professional school.

New Jersey

Freshmen 412 applied, 343 admitted, 135 enrolled. 1 valedictorian.

Average high school GPA	3.12	SAT verbal scores above 500	58%
SAT math scores above 500	45%	ACT above 18	N/R
From top 10% of their h.s. class	15%	From top quarter	36%
From top half	71%	1998 freshmen returning in 1999	81%

Application *Options:* eApply at www.CollegeQuest.com, early admission, deferred entrance. *Application fee:* $35. *Required:* essay or personal statement; high school transcript; 2 letters of recommendation. *Recommended:* interview.

Standardized tests *Admission: Required:* SAT I or ACT.

Significant dates *Application deadlines:* 8/15 (freshmen), rolling (transfers). *Notification:* 11/15 (freshmen). *Financial aid deadline priority date:* 3/1.

Freshman Application Contact
Ms. Donna Yamanis, Dean of Admissions and Financial Aid, College of Saint Elizabeth, 2 Convent Road, Morristown, NJ 07960. **Phone:** 973-290-4700. **Toll-free phone:** 800-210-7900. **Fax:** 973-290-4710. **E-mail:** apply@liza.st-elizabeth.edu

Visit CollegeQuest.com for information on majors offered and athletics.

■ *See page 1476 for a narrative description.*

COOK COLLEGE
New Jersey—See Rutgers, The State University of New Jersey, Cook College

DEVRY INSTITUTE
North Brunswick, New Jersey

- **Proprietary**, 4-year, founded 1969
- **Degrees** associate and bachelor's
- **Urban** 10-acre campus with easy access to New York City
- **Coed**, 3,608 undergraduate students, 62% full-time, 22% women, 78% men
- **Minimally difficult** entrance level, 56% of applicants were admitted
- **22:1 student-to-undergraduate faculty ratio**
- **$7778 tuition** and fees

Part of DeVry, Inc.

Students *Undergraduates:* 2,230 full-time, 1,378 part-time. Students come from 20 states and territories, 13 other countries.

From out-of-state	15%	Age 25 or older	46%
Transferred in	0.03%	International students	1%
African Americans	22%	Asian Americans/Pacific Islanders	6%
Hispanic Americans	15%	Native Americans	0.2%

Faculty 162 (61% full-time).

Expenses (1999–2000) *Tuition:* full-time $7778; part-time $290 per credit hour. Part-time tuition and fees vary according to class time and course load. *Payment plan:* deferred payment. *Waivers:* employees or children of employees.

Library Learning Resource Center. *Collection:* 19,152 titles, 208 serial subscriptions.

College life *Housing:* college housing not available. *Most popular organizations:* Phi Theta Kappa, Data Processing Management Association, Telecommunications Management Association, Institute of Electrical and Electronics Engineering.

Campus security 24-hour emergency response devices and patrols, late-night transport-escort service.

After graduation 90% of class of 1998 had job offers within 6 months. *Career center:* 11 full-time personnel. Services include job fairs, resume preparation, resume referral, career counseling, careers library.

Freshmen 2,268 applied, 1,268 admitted, 1,400 enrolled.

| SAT verbal scores above 500 | N/R | SAT math scores above 500 | N/R |
| ACT above 18 | N/R | 1998 freshmen returning in 1999 | 51% |

Application *Options:* eApply at www.CollegeQuest.com, electronic application, deferred entrance. *Application fee:* $25. *Required:* high school transcript; interview.

Standardized tests *Admission: Required:* CPT. *Recommended:* SAT I or ACT.

Significant dates *Application deadlines:* rolling (freshmen), rolling (transfers). *Financial aid deadline:* continuous.

Freshman Application Contact
Ms. Danielle DiNapoli, Director of Admission, DeVry Institute, 630 US Highway One, North Brunswick, NJ 08902-3362. **Phone:** 732-435-4850. **Toll-free phone:** 800-333-3879.

Visit CollegeQuest.com for information on majors offered and athletics.

DOUGLASS COLLEGE
New Jersey—See Rutgers, The State University of New Jersey, Douglass College

DREW UNIVERSITY
Madison, New Jersey

- **Independent**, university, founded 1867, affiliated with United Methodist Church
- **Degrees** bachelor's, master's, doctoral, first professional, and postbachelor's certificates
- **Suburban** 186-acre campus with easy access to New York City
- **Coed**, 1,421 undergraduate students, 98% full-time, 58% women, 42% men
- **Very difficult** entrance level, 75% of applicants were admitted
- **11:1 student-to-undergraduate faculty ratio**
- **77.4% graduate** in 6 years or less
- **$23,008 tuition** and fees
- **$20,137 average financial aid** package, $12,880 average indebtedness upon graduation, $163.5 million endowment

Drew is educating students to help shape the world of tomorrow. With its roots in the best traditions of the liberal arts, Drew blends inspired teaching on a technologically integrated campus with numerous opportunities for academic internships in nearby corporate headquarters and research centers. Drew's innovative international seminars program and semesters in New York on Wall Street and in the UN, for example, provide students with an understanding of the issues that affect a global society.

Students *Undergraduates:* 1,394 full-time, 27 part-time. Students come from 42 states and territories, 11 other countries. *The most frequently chosen baccalaureate fields are:* psychology, English, social sciences and history. *Graduate:* 185 in professional programs, 711 in other graduate degree programs.

From out-of-state	43%	Reside on campus	91%
Age 25 or older	3%	Transferred in	2%
International students	1%	African Americans	4%
Asian Americans/Pacific Islanders	6%	Hispanic Americans	5%
Native Americans	0.4%		

Faculty 155 (75% full-time), 70% with terminal degrees.

Expenses (1999–2000) *Comprehensive fee:* $29,572 includes full-time tuition ($22,462), mandatory fees ($546), and room and board ($6564). Room and board charges vary according to board plan and housing facility. *Part-time tuition:* $936 per credit. *Part-time fees:* $23 per credit. *Payment plans:* tuition prepayment, installment. *Waivers:* senior citizens and employees or children of employees.

Library Drew University Library. *Collection:* 462,498 titles, 2,257 serial subscriptions.

College life *Housing:* on-campus residence required in freshman year. *Options:* coed, women-only, cooperative, disabled students. *Most popular organizations:* Drew University Drama Society, Student Government Association.

Campus security 24-hour emergency response devices and patrols, late-night transport-escort service, controlled dormitory access.

After graduation *Career center:* 4 full-time, 1 part-time personnel. Services include resume preparation, resume referral, career counseling, careers

New Jersey

Drew University (continued)
library, job bank, job interviews. **Graduate education:** 27% of class of 1999 went directly to graduate and professional school: 19% graduate arts and sciences, 5% medicine, 3% law.

Freshmen 2,400 applied, 1,799 admitted, 407 enrolled. 15 National Merit Scholars.

SAT verbal scores above 500	91%	SAT math scores above 500	91%
ACT above 18	N/R	From top 10% of their h.s. class	44%
From top quarter	70%	From top half	92%
1998 freshmen returning in 1999	87%		

Application *Options:* eApply at www.CollegeQuest.com, Common Application, early decision, deferred entrance. *Application fee:* $40. *Required:* essay or personal statement; high school transcript; 2 letters of recommendation. *Recommended:* interview.

Standardized tests *Admission: Required:* SAT I or ACT. *Recommended:* SAT I.

Significant dates *Application deadlines:* 2/15 (freshmen), 8/1 (transfers). *Early decision:* 12/1 (for plan 1), 1/15 (for plan 2). *Notification:* 3/15 (freshmen), 12/24 (early decision plan 1), 2/15 (early decision plan 2). *Financial aid deadline:* 3/1.

Freshman Application Contact
Mr. Roberto Noya, Dean of Admissions for the College of Liberal Arts, Drew University, 36 Madison Avenue, Madison, NJ 07940-1493. **Phone:** 973-408-3739. **Fax:** 973-408-3939. **E-mail:** cadm@drew.edu

Visit CollegeQuest.com for information on majors offered and athletics. College video available at CollegeQuest.com.

■ *See page 1590 for a narrative description.*

FAIRLEIGH DICKINSON UNIVERSITY, FLORHAM-MADISON CAMPUS
Madison, New Jersey

- **Independent**, comprehensive, founded 1942
- **Degrees** associate, bachelor's, master's, post-master's, and postbachelor's certificates
- **Suburban** 178-acre campus with easy access to New York City
- **Coed**, 2,433 undergraduate students
- **Moderately difficult** entrance level, 73% of applicants were admitted
- **15:1** student-to-undergraduate faculty ratio
- **48% graduate** in 6 years or less
- **$15,593 tuition** and fees
- **$15,303 average financial aid** package, $15,968 average indebtedness upon graduation, $19.3 million endowment

Students *Undergraduates: The most frequently chosen baccalaureate fields are:* business/marketing, liberal arts/general studies, psychology.

Reside on campus	56%	Age 25 or older	34%
International students	3%	African Americans	5%
Asian Americans/Pacific Islanders	2%	Hispanic Americans	6%
Native Americans	0.2%		

Faculty 335 (30% full-time).

Expenses (1999–2000) *Comprehensive fee:* $22,193 includes full-time tuition ($14,732), mandatory fees ($861), and room and board ($6600). *College room only:* $3900. Room and board charges vary according to board plan and housing facility. *Part-time tuition:* $478 per credit. *Part-time fees:* $212 per term part-time. Part-time tuition and fees vary according to course load and program. *Payment plans:* installment, deferred payment. *Waivers:* senior citizens and employees or children of employees.

Library Friendship Library plus 1 other. *Operations spending 1999–2000:* $1.9 million. *Collection:* 860 serial subscriptions, 330 audiovisual materials.

College life *Housing: Option:* coed. *Social organizations:* national fraternities, national sororities; 10% of eligible men and 12% of eligible women are members. *Most popular organizations:* student government, Student Activities Programming Board, Greek Council, Association of Black Collegians, "Metro" Newspaper.

Campus security 24-hour emergency response devices and patrols, late-night transport-escort service, trained law enforcement personnel on staff.

After graduation 50 organizations recruited on campus 1997–98. *Career center:* 3 full-time, 1 part-time personnel. Services include job fairs, resume preparation, resume referral, career/interest testing, career counseling, careers library, job bank, job interviews.

Freshmen 2,166 applied, 1,592 admitted.

SAT verbal scores above 500	54%	SAT math scores above 500	56%
ACT above 18	N/R	From top 10% of their h.s. class	10%
From top quarter	24%	From top half	61%
1998 freshmen returning in 1999	76%		

Application *Options:* Common Application, early admission, early decision, deferred entrance. *Application fee:* $35. *Required:* essay or personal statement; high school transcript. *Recommended:* 1 letter of recommendation; interview.

Standardized tests *Admission: Required:* SAT I or ACT.

Significant dates *Application deadlines:* rolling (freshmen), rolling (transfers). *Early decision:* 12/1. *Notification:* 12/15 (early decision). *Financial aid deadline priority date:* 3/15.

Freshman Application Contact
Admissions Office, Fairleigh Dickinson University, Florham-Madison Campus, 1000 River Road, Teaneck, NJ 07666-1914. **Phone:** 973-443-8900. **Toll-free phone:** 800-338-8803.

Visit CollegeQuest.com for information on majors offered and athletics.

FAIRLEIGH DICKINSON UNIVERSITY, TEANECK–HACKENSACK CAMPUS
Teaneck, New Jersey

- **Independent**, comprehensive, founded 1942
- **Degrees** associate, bachelor's, master's, doctoral, post-master's, postbachelor's, and first professional certificates
- **Suburban** 125-acre campus with easy access to New York City
- **Coed**, 2,482 undergraduate students, 76% full-time, 56% women, 44% men
- **Moderately difficult** entrance level, 81% of applicants were admitted
- **14:1** student-to-undergraduate faculty ratio
- **$15,330 tuition** and fees
- **$15,776 average financial aid** package, $18,493 average indebtedness upon graduation, $27.6 million endowment

Fairleigh Dickinson University offers two uniquely different campuses in northern New Jersey, an international learning experience (including the option to attend FDU's own campus in England), and outstanding career development opportunities that take advantage of the University's proximity to New York City and New Jersey's corporate corridor.

Students *Undergraduates:* 1,876 full-time, 606 part-time. Students come from 25 states and territories, 49 other countries. *The most frequently chosen baccalaureate fields are:* business/marketing, communications/communication technologies, health professions and related sciences. **Graduate:** 1,774 in graduate degree programs.

From out-of-state	15%	Reside on campus	28%
Age 25 or older	21%	Transferred in	12%
International students	10%	African Americans	22%
Asian Americans/Pacific Islanders	6%	Hispanic Americans	13%
Native Americans	0.4%		

Faculty 493 (32% full-time), 27% with terminal degrees.

Expenses (1999–2000) *Comprehensive fee:* $21,866 includes full-time tuition ($14,732), mandatory fees ($598), and room and board ($6536). *College room only:* $3908. Full-time tuition and fees vary according to degree level and program. Room and board charges vary according to board plan and housing facility. *Part-time tuition:* $478 per credit. *Part-time fees:* $106 per term part-time. Part-time tuition and fees vary according to program. *Payment plans:* installment, deferred payment. *Waivers:* senior citizens and employees or children of employees.

Library Weiner Library plus 2 others. *Operations spending 1999–2000:* $1.9 million. *Collection:* 280,608 titles, 1,284 serial subscriptions.

College life *Housing: Options:* coed, men-only, women-only. *Social organizations:* national fraternities, national sororities; 4% of eligible men and 3% of eligible women are members. *Most popular organizations:* student government, Student Activities Programming Planning Board, Greek Council, Multicultural Council, Media Organization.

New Jersey

Campus security 24-hour emergency response devices and patrols, late-night transport-escort service, controlled dormitory access, trained law enforcement personnel on staff.
After graduation 200 organizations recruited on campus 1997–98. *Career center:* 6 full-time personnel. Services include job fairs, resume preparation, resume referral, career/interest testing, career counseling, careers library, job bank, job interviews.
Freshmen 2,581 applied, 2,098 admitted, 581 enrolled.

SAT verbal scores above 500	40%	SAT math scores above 500	45%
ACT above 18	N/R	From top 10% of their h.s. class	15%
From top quarter	32%	From top half	72%
1998 freshmen returning in 1999	66%		

Application *Options:* Common Application, early admission, early decision, deferred entrance. *Application fee:* $40. *Required:* essay or personal statement; high school transcript. *Recommended:* 1 letter of recommendation; interview.
Standardized tests *Admission: Required:* SAT I or ACT.
Significant dates *Application deadlines:* rolling (freshmen), rolling (transfers). *Early decision:* 12/1. *Notification:* 12/15 (early decision). **Financial aid deadline priority date:** 3/15.
Freshman Application Contact
Dean of Admissions, Fairleigh Dickinson University, Teaneck–Hackensack Campus, Office of University Admissions, 1000 River Road, Teaneck, NJ 07666. **Phone:** 201-692-2000. **Toll-free phone:** 800-338-8803. **E-mail:** info@admit.fdu.edu
Visit CollegeQuest.com for information on majors offered and athletics.

■ *See page 1648 for a narrative description.*

FELICIAN COLLEGE
Lodi, New Jersey

- **Independent Roman Catholic**, comprehensive, founded 1942
- **Degrees** associate, bachelor's, master's, post-master's, and postbachelor's certificates
- **Suburban** 37-acre campus with easy access to New York City
- **Coed**, 1,082 undergraduate students, 70% full-time, 79% women, 21% men
- **Moderately difficult** entrance level, 74% of applicants were admitted
- **10:1 student-to-undergraduate faculty ratio**
- **$11,060 tuition** and fees
- **$10,500 average financial aid** package, $18,000 average indebtedness upon graduation, $3 million endowment

Students *Undergraduates:* 754 full-time, 328 part-time. Students come from 12 states and territories, 17 other countries. *The most frequently chosen baccalaureate fields are:* education, English, health professions and related sciences. *Graduate:* 53 in graduate degree programs.

From out-of-state	3%	Reside on campus	18%
Age 25 or older	46%	Transferred in	14%

Faculty 144 (39% full-time), 47% with terminal degrees.
Expenses (1999–2000) *Comprehensive fee:* $16,730 includes full-time tuition ($10,560), mandatory fees ($500), and room and board ($5670). *College room only:* $2835. Full-time tuition and fees vary according to course load. *Part-time tuition:* $352 per semester hour. *Part-time fees:* $100 per term part-time. Part-time tuition and fees vary according to course load. *Payment plans:* installment, deferred payment. *Waivers:* senior citizens and employees or children of employees.
Library Felician College Library. *Operations spending 1999–2000:* $422,840. *Collection:* 115,331 titles, 795 serial subscriptions, 14,845 audiovisual materials.
College life *Housing: Options:* men-only, women-only. *Social organizations:* local fraternities, local sororities; 15% of eligible men and 20% of eligible women are members. *Most popular organizations:* Student Nurses Association, Zeta Alpha Zeta teaching sorority, Campus Activity Board, Students In Free Enterprise, Student Government Association.
Campus security 24-hour patrols, student patrols, late-night transport-escort service.
After graduation 26 organizations recruited on campus 1997–98. *Career center:* 1 full-time personnel. Services include job fairs, resume preparation,

interview workshops, resume referral, career/interest testing, career counseling, careers library, job bank. **Graduate education:** 12% of class of 1999 went directly to graduate and professional school: 3% graduate arts and sciences, 2% business, 2% education, 1% dentistry, 1% law, 1% medicine, 1% theology.
Freshmen 788 applied, 584 admitted, 241 enrolled.

Average high school GPA	3.0	SAT verbal scores above 500	21%
SAT math scores above 500	18%	ACT above 18	N/R
From top 10% of their h.s. class	6%	From top quarter	42%
From top half	79%	1998 freshmen returning in 1999	64%

Application *Option:* deferred entrance. *Application fee:* $25. *Required:* high school transcript; minimum 2.0 GPA. *Required for some:* essay or personal statement; interview.
Standardized tests *Admission: Required:* SAT I.
Significant dates *Application deadlines:* rolling (freshmen), rolling (transfers). **Financial aid deadline priority date:** 3/15.
Freshman Application Contact
Ms. Cynthia Sievewright, Director of Admission, Felician College, 262 South Main Street, Lodi, NJ 07644. **Phone:** 201-559-6131. **Fax:** 973-778-4111. **E-mail:** admissions@inet.felician.edu
Visit CollegeQuest.com for information on majors offered and athletics. College video available at CollegeQuest.com.

■ *See page 1654 for a narrative description.*

GEORGIAN COURT COLLEGE
Lakewood, New Jersey

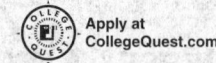

- **Independent Roman Catholic**, comprehensive, founded 1908
- **Degrees** bachelor's and master's
- **Suburban** 150-acre campus with easy access to New York City and Philadelphia
- **Women** only, 1,353 undergraduate students, 76% full-time
- **Moderately difficult** entrance level, 91% of applicants were admitted
- **11:1 student-to-undergraduate faculty ratio**
- **$12,334 tuition** and fees

Georgian Court College is a comprehensive college offering 20 majors in the liberal arts and sciences and 3 professional studies majors. The Department of Art offers a BFA degree, with majors in general fine arts and graphic design/illustration. The Department of Business Administration, Accounting and Economics was recently accredited by the Association of Collegiate Business Schools and Programs. The Department of Social Work received accreditation by the Council on Social Work Education.

Students *Undergraduates:* 1,028 full-time, 325 part-time. Students come from 5 states and territories, 3 other countries. *The most frequently chosen baccalaureate fields are:* business/marketing, education, psychology. *Graduate:* 838 in graduate degree programs.

From out-of-state	1%	Reside on campus	26%
Age 25 or older	35%	Transferred in	16%
International students	0.3%	African Americans	7%
Asian Americans/Pacific Islanders	1%	Hispanic Americans	4%
Native Americans	0.4%		

Faculty 215 (42% full-time), 30% with terminal degrees.
Expenses (1999–2000) *Comprehensive fee:* $16,334 includes full-time tuition ($12,134), mandatory fees ($200), and room and board ($4000). Room and board charges vary according to board plan and housing facility. *Part-time tuition:* $337 per credit. *Part-time fees:* $48 per term part-time. *Payment plans:* installment, deferred payment. *Waivers:* senior citizens and employees or children of employees.
Library Georgian Court College Library. *Collection:* 121,724 titles, 1,076 serial subscriptions.
College life *Most popular organizations:* student government, Sigma Phi Sigma (National Mercy Honor Society).
Campus security 24-hour emergency response devices and patrols, late-night transport-escort service.
After graduation 57 organizations recruited on campus 1997–98. 85% of class of 1998 had job offers within 6 months. *Career center:* 2 full-time

New Jersey

Georgian Court College (continued)

personnel. Services include job fairs, resume preparation, career counseling, careers library, job interviews. **Graduate education:** 16% of class of 1999 went directly to graduate and professional school: 5% business, 0.3% law, 0.3% medicine.

Freshmen 296 applied, 270 admitted, 142 enrolled.

SAT verbal scores above 500	46%	SAT math scores above 500	35%
ACT above 18	N/R	From top 10% of their h.s. class	11%
From top quarter	47%	From top half	84%
1998 freshmen returning in 1999	84%		

Application *Options:* eApply at www.CollegeQuest.com, Common Application, early admission, early action. *Application fee:* $30. *Required:* essay or personal statement; high school transcript; minimum 2.0 GPA. *Recommended:* letters of recommendation; interview.

Standardized tests *Admission: Required:* SAT I or ACT.

Significant dates *Application deadlines:* 8/1 (freshmen), 8/1 (transfers). *Early action:* 11/15. *Notification:* 12/30 (early action). **Financial aid deadline:** continuous.

Freshman Application Contact
Ms. Marjorie Cooke, Interim Director of Admissions, Georgian Court College, Office of Admissions, 900 Lakewood Avenue, Lakewood, NJ 08701-2697. **Phone:** 732-364-2200 Ext. 760. **Toll-free phone:** 800-458-8422. **Fax:** 732-364-4442. **E-mail:** admissions-ugrad@georgian.edu

Visit CollegeQuest.com for information on majors offered and athletics. College video available at CollegeQuest.com.

■ *See page 1716 for a narrative description.*

JERSEY CITY STATE COLLEGE
New Jersey—See New Jersey City University

KEAN UNIVERSITY
Union, New Jersey

- **State-supported**, comprehensive, founded 1855
- **Degrees** bachelor's, master's, post-master's, and postbachelor's certificates
- **Urban** 151-acre campus with easy access to New York City
- **Coed**, 8,702 undergraduate students, 71% full-time, 64% women, 36% men
- **Moderately difficult** entrance level, 57% of applicants were admitted
- **20:1 student-to-undergraduate faculty ratio**
- **36.8% graduate** in 6 years or less
- **$4384 tuition** and fees (in-state); $6081 (out-of-state)

Kean University offers its diverse student body personal attention and a wide variety of academic disciplines. The Center for New Students helps entering students adjust to the college experience. Nationally known for its innovative educational initiatives, Kean continues to prepare its students for success in the 21st century.

Part of New Jersey State College System.

Students *Undergraduates:* 6,176 full-time, 2,526 part-time. Students come from 13 states and territories, 89 other countries. *The most frequently chosen baccalaureate fields are:* business/marketing, education, protective services/public administration. *Graduate:* 1,971 in graduate degree programs.

From out-of-state	1%	Reside on campus	12%
Age 25 or older	39%	Transferred in	11%
International students	3%	African Americans	19%
Asian Americans/Pacific Islanders	7%	Hispanic Americans	19%
Native Americans	0.2%		

Faculty 366 (96% full-time), 86% with terminal degrees.

Expenses (1999–2000) *Tuition, state resident:* full-time $3373; part-time $113 per hour. *Tuition, nonresident:* full-time $5070; part-time $170 per hour. *Required fees:* full-time $1011; $31 per hour. *College room and board:* room only: $4330. Room and board charges vary according to board plan and housing facility. *Payment plans:* installment, deferred payment. *Waivers:* senior citizens and employees or children of employees.

Library Nancy Thompson Library plus 1 other. *Operations spending 1999–2000:* $2.1 million. *Collection:* 285,550 titles.

College life *Housing: Option:* coed. *Social organizations:* national fraternities, national sororities, local fraternities, local sororities, eating clubs. *Most popular organizations:* student organization, Greek Cooperative Council.

Campus security 24-hour emergency response devices, student patrols, late-night transport-escort service, controlled dormitory access, 24-hour patrols by campus police.

After graduation *Career center:* 4 full-time, 2 part-time personnel. Services include job fairs, resume preparation, resume referral, career counseling, careers library, job bank, job interviews.

Freshmen 4,206 applied, 2,408 admitted, 1,036 enrolled.

SAT verbal scores above 500	33%	SAT math scores above 500	37%
ACT above 18	N/R	From top 10% of their h.s. class	7%
From top quarter	32%	From top half	62%
1998 freshmen returning in 1999	79%		

Application *Options:* electronic application, early admission. *Application fee:* $35. *Required:* essay or personal statement; high school transcript; minimum 2.0 GPA. *Required for some:* interview.

Standardized tests *Admission: Required:* SAT I or ACT.

Significant dates *Application deadlines:* 5/31 (freshmen), 7/15 (transfers). *Notification:* continuous until 8/1 (freshmen). **Financial aid deadline priority date:** 3/15.

Freshman Application Contact
Mr. Audley Bridges, Director of Admissions, Kean University, 1000 Morris Avenue, Union, NJ 07083. **Phone:** 908-527-2195. **Fax:** 908-355-5143. **E-mail:** admitme@turbo.kean.edu

Visit CollegeQuest.com for information on majors offered and athletics. College video available at CollegeQuest.com.

■ *See page 1864 for a narrative description.*

LIVINGSTON COLLEGE
New Jersey—See Rutgers, The State University of New Jersey, Livingston College

MASON GROSS SCHOOL OF THE ARTS
New Jersey—See Rutgers, The State University of New Jersey, Mason Gross School of the Arts

MONMOUTH UNIVERSITY
West Long Branch, New Jersey

- **Independent**, comprehensive, founded 1933
- **Degrees** associate, bachelor's, master's, and post-master's certificates
- **Suburban** 147-acre campus with easy access to New York City and Philadelphia
- **Coed**, 3,931 undergraduate students, 87% full-time, 58% women, 42% men
- **Moderately difficult** entrance level, 87% of applicants were admitted
- **15:1 student-to-undergraduate faculty ratio**
- **$15,686 tuition** and fees
- **$11,181 average financial aid** package, $18,750 average indebtedness upon graduation, $19.9 million endowment

Students *Undergraduates:* 3,437 full-time, 494 part-time. Students come from 23 states and territories. *The most frequently chosen baccalaureate fields are:* business/marketing, communications/communication technologies, education. *Graduate:* 1,421 in graduate degree programs.

From out-of-state	6%	Reside on campus	40%
Age 25 or older	15%	Transferred in	10%
International students	1%	African Americans	6%
Asian Americans/Pacific Islanders	2%	Hispanic Americans	4%
Native Americans	0.2%		

Faculty 459 (43% full-time), 44% with terminal degrees.

Expenses (1999–2000) *Comprehensive fee:* $22,162 includes full-time tuition ($15,138), mandatory fees ($548), and room and board ($6476).

College room only: $3376. Room and board charges vary according to board plan and housing facility. *Part-time tuition:* $438 per credit. *Part-time fees:* $137 per term part-time. *Payment plan:* installment. *Waivers:* senior citizens and employees or children of employees.

Library Murry and Leonie Guggenheim Memorial Library. *Operations spending 1999–2000:* $1.1 million. *Collection:* 252,497 titles, 1,250 serial subscriptions.

College life *Housing:* Option: coed. *Social organizations:* national fraternities, national sororities; 8% of eligible men and 9% of eligible women are members. *Most popular organizations:* student-run radio station, Student Government Association, student newspaper, Student Activities Board, Shadows Yearbook.

Campus security 24-hour emergency response devices and patrols, late-night transport-escort service, controlled dormitory access.

After graduation 90 organizations recruited on campus 1997–98. 70% of class of 1998 had job offers within 6 months. *Career center:* 3 full-time, 2 part-time personnel. Services include job fairs, resume preparation, resume referral, career/interest testing, career counseling, careers library, job bank, job interviews.

Freshmen 4,549 applied, 3,935 admitted, 836 enrolled.

Average high school GPA	2.7	SAT verbal scores above 500	52%
SAT math scores above 500	57%	ACT above 18	73%
From top 10% of their h.s. class	9%	From top quarter	26%
From top half	61%	1998 freshmen returning in 1999	70%

Application *Options:* eApply at www.CollegeQuest.com, early admission, deferred entrance. *Application fee:* $35. *Required:* high school transcript. *Required for some:* minimum 2.0 GPA. *Recommended:* essay or personal statement; interview.

Standardized tests *Admission: Recommended:* SAT I or ACT.

Significant dates *Application deadlines:* rolling (freshmen), rolling (transfers). *Financial aid deadline:* continuous.

Freshman Application Contact
Ms. Christine Benol, Associate Director of Undergraduate Admission, Monmouth University, 400 Cedar Avenue, West Long Branch, NJ 07764-1898. **Phone:** 732-571-3456. **Toll-free phone:** 800-543-9671. **Fax:** 732-263-5166. **E-mail:** cbenol@mondec.monmouth.edu

Visit CollegeQuest.com for information on majors offered and athletics.

■ *See page 2076 for a narrative description.*

MONTCLAIR STATE UNIVERSITY
Upper Montclair, New Jersey

- **State-supported**, comprehensive, founded 1908
- **Degrees** bachelor's, master's, and doctoral
- **Suburban** 200-acre campus with easy access to New York City
- **Coed**
- **Moderately difficult** entrance level
- **$4320 tuition** and fees (in-state); $6235 (out-of-state)

Expenses (1999–2000) *Tuition, state resident:* full-time $3365; part-time $105 per credit. *Tuition, nonresident:* full-time $5280; part-time $165 per credit. *Required fees:* full-time $955; $30 per credit. *College room and board:* $6212; room only: $4160. Room and board charges vary according to board plan and housing facility.

Institutional Web site http://www.montclair.edu/

College life *Housing:* Option: coed. *Social organizations:* national fraternities, national sororities, local fraternities, local sororities.

Campus security 24-hour emergency response devices and patrols, late-night transport-escort service, controlled dormitory access, video surveillance, student escorts.

Application *Option:* deferred entrance. *Preference* given to state residents. *Application fee:* $40. *Required:* high school transcript. *Required for some:* interview.

Standardized tests *Admission: Required:* SAT I or ACT.

Admissions Office Contact
Montclair State University, Valley Road and Normal Avenue, Upper Montclair, NJ 07043-1624. **Toll-free phone:** 800-331-9205. **Fax:** 973-893-5455. **E-mail:** msuadm@saturn.montclair.edu

Visit CollegeQuest.com for information on athletics. College video and electronic viewbook available at CollegeQuest.com.

■ *See page 2086 for a narrative description.*

NEWARK COLLEGE OF ARTS AND SCIENCES
New Jersey—See Rutgers, The State University of New Jersey, Newark College of Arts and Sciences

NEW JERSEY CITY UNIVERSITY
Jersey City, New Jersey

- **State-supported**, comprehensive, founded 1927
- **Degrees** bachelor's and master's
- **Urban** 46-acre campus with easy access to New York City
- **Coed**, 5,564 undergraduate students, 67% full-time, 60% women, 40% men
- **Moderately difficult** entrance level, 67% of applicants were admitted
- **16:1 student-to-undergraduate faculty ratio**
- **$4358 tuition** and fees (in-state); $7546 (out-of-state)
- **$1.8 million endowment**

New Jersey's only 4-year urban public university offers 25 undergraduate degree programs in the liberal arts, professional studies, and education. Cooperative education internships are available in all majors. The University is a center of cultural diversity and intellectual opportunity. The 47-acre campus is ideal for quiet study, although it is located just minutes from New York City.

Students *Undergraduates:* 3,725 full-time, 1,839 part-time. Students come from 10 states and territories, 47 other countries. *The most frequently chosen baccalaureate fields are:* business/marketing, health professions and related sciences, social sciences and history.

From out-of-state	4%	Reside on campus	4%
Age 25 or older	49%	Transferred in	9%

Faculty 490 (49% full-time).

Expenses (1999–2000) *Tuition, state resident:* full-time $3330; part-time $111 per credit. *Tuition, nonresident:* full-time $6518; part-time $217 per credit. *Required fees:* full-time $1028; $34 per credit. Part-time tuition and fees vary according to course load. *College room and board:* $5400. *Payment plan:* deferred payment. *Waivers:* senior citizens and employees or children of employees.

Library Forrest A. Irwin Library. *Operations spending 1999–2000:* $1.8 million. *Collection:* 245,000 titles, 1,260 serial subscriptions, 2,286 audiovisual materials.

College life *Housing:* Option: coed. *Social organizations:* national fraternities, local fraternities, local sororities, "forority"; 1% of eligible men and 1% of eligible women are members. *Most popular organizations:* International Student Association, Black Freedom Society, Latin Power Association.

Campus security 24-hour emergency response devices and patrols, late-night transport-escort service.

After graduation 125 organizations recruited on campus 1997–98. *Career center:* 25 full-time personnel. Services include job fairs, resume preparation, resume referral, career counseling, careers library, job bank, job interviews.

Freshmen 2,919 applied, 1,959 admitted, 857 enrolled.

SAT verbal scores above 500	50%	SAT math scores above 500	36%
ACT above 18	N/R	From top 10% of their h.s. class	5%
From top quarter	23%	From top half	60%

Application *Options:* electronic application, deferred entrance. *Application fee:* $35. *Required:* essay or personal statement; high school transcript; minimum 2.0 GPA. *Required for some:* interview. *Recommended:* 1 letter of recommendation.

Standardized tests *Admission: Required:* SAT I.

Significant dates *Application deadlines:* 4/1 (freshmen), 4/1 (transfers). *Financial aid deadline priority date:* 4/15.

New Jersey

New Jersey City University (continued)
Freshman Application Contact
Ms. Drusilla Blackman, Director of Admissions, New Jersey City University, 2039 Kennedy Boulevard, Jersey City, NJ 07305-1597. **Phone:** 201-200-3234. **Toll-free phone:** 800-441-NJCU. **Fax:** 201-200-2044. **E-mail:** admissions@njcu.edu

Visit CollegeQuest.com for information on majors offered and athletics. College video and electronic viewbook available at CollegeQuest.com.

■ *See page 2152 for a narrative description.*

NEW JERSEY INSTITUTE OF TECHNOLOGY
Newark, New Jersey

- **State-supported**, university, founded 1881
- **Degrees** bachelor's, master's, and doctoral
- **Urban** 45-acre campus with easy access to New York City
- **Coed**, 4,668 undergraduate students, 77% full-time, 20% women, 80% men
- **Moderately difficult** entrance level, 60% of applicants were admitted
- **14:1 student-to-undergraduate faculty ratio**
- **40% graduate** in 6 years or less
- **$6480 tuition** and fees (in-state); $10,824 (out-of-state)
- **$8817 average financial aid** package, $36.8 million endowment

The Albert Dorman Honors College is one of the nation's leading technologically oriented honors programs. Admission is highly selective; successful applicants generally rank in the top 10% of their high schools, with SAT I scores above 1250. Honors College scholars receive at least a one-half-tuition scholarship award. Exceptionally well prepared students may be eligible for additional scholarships and partial room grants. All degree programs are available through the Albert Dorman Honors College.

Students *Undergraduates:* 3,597 full-time, 1,071 part-time. Students come from 33 states and territories, 42 other countries. *The most frequently chosen baccalaureate fields are:* computer/information sciences, architecture, engineering/engineering technologies. *Graduate:* 2,991 in graduate degree programs.

From out-of-state	10%	Reside on campus	33%
Age 25 or older	35%	Transferred in	9%
International students	6%	African Americans	12%
Asian Americans/Pacific Islanders	21%	Hispanic Americans	13%
Native Americans	0.2%		

Faculty 399 full-time.
Expenses (1999–2000) *Tuition, state resident:* full-time $5508; part-time $206 per credit. *Tuition, nonresident:* full-time $9852; part-time $424 per credit. *Required fees:* full-time $972; $41 per credit. Full-time tuition and fees vary according to degree level. Part-time tuition and fees vary according to degree level. *College room and board:* $7050. Room and board charges vary according to board plan and housing facility. *Payment plans:* installment, deferred payment. *Waivers:* employees or children of employees.
Library Van Houten Library plus 1 other. *Operations spending 1999–2000:* $1.6 million. *Collection:* 140,575 titles, 997 serial subscriptions.
College life *Housing: Option:* coed. *Social organizations:* national fraternities, national sororities, local fraternities, local sororities; 12% of eligible men and 9% of eligible women are members. *Most popular organizations:* fraternities/sororities, Student Senate, Student Activities Council, Microcomputers Users Group, Chess Club.
Campus security 24-hour emergency response devices and patrols, late-night transport-escort service, controlled dormitory access, bicycle patrols, sexual assault response team.
After graduation 100 organizations recruited on campus 1997–98. 70% of class of 1998 had job offers within 6 months. *Career center:* 17 full-time, 1 part-time personnel. Services include job fairs, resume preparation, resume referral, career counseling, careers library, job bank, job interviews. *Graduate education:* 22% of class of 1999 went directly to graduate and professional school.

Freshmen 2,369 applied, 1,415 admitted, 681 enrolled.

SAT verbal scores above 500	68%	SAT math scores above 500	94%
ACT above 18	N/R	From top 10% of their h.s. class	14%
From top quarter	36%	From top half	57%
1998 freshmen returning in 1999	82%		

Application *Options:* electronic application, early admission, early action, deferred entrance. *Preference* given to state residents. *Application fee:* $35. *Required:* high school transcript. *Required for some:* essay or personal statement; interview. *Recommended:* 1 letter of recommendation.
Standardized tests *Admission: Required:* SAT I or ACT. *Required for some:* SAT II Subject Tests.
Significant dates *Application deadlines:* 4/1 (freshmen), 6/1 (transfers). *Early action:* 12/1. *Notification:* 12/31 (early action). *Financial aid deadline priority date:* 4/15.
Freshman Application Contact
Ms. Kathy Kelly, Director of Admissions, New Jersey Institute of Technology, University Heights, Newark, NJ 07102-1982. **Phone:** 973-596-3300. **Toll-free phone:** 800-925-NJIT. **Fax:** 973-802-1854. **E-mail:** admissions@njit.edu
Visit CollegeQuest.com for information on majors offered and athletics. Electronic viewbook available at CollegeQuest.com.

■ *See page 2154 for a narrative description.*

PRINCETON UNIVERSITY
Princeton, New Jersey

- **Independent**, university, founded 1746
- **Degrees** bachelor's, master's, and doctoral
- **Suburban** 600-acre campus with easy access to New York City and Philadelphia
- **Coed**, 4,556 undergraduate students, 100% full-time, 47% women, 53% men
- **Most difficult** entrance level, 11% of applicants were admitted
- **96% graduate** in 6 years or less
- **$24,630 tuition** and fees
- **$21,800 average financial aid** package, $15,500 average indebtedness upon graduation, $6.5 billion endowment

Students *Undergraduates:* 4,556 full-time. Students come from 53 states and territories, 55 other countries. *The most frequently chosen baccalaureate fields are:* engineering/engineering technologies, biological/life sciences, social sciences and history. *Graduate:* 1,768 in graduate degree programs.

From out-of-state	85%	Reside on campus	97%
International students	5%	African Americans	7%
Asian Americans/Pacific Islanders	12%	Hispanic Americans	6%
Native Americans	1%		

Faculty 902 (80% full-time), 83% with terminal degrees.
Expenses (1999–2000) *Comprehensive fee:* $31,599 includes full-time tuition ($24,630) and room and board ($6969). *College room only:* $3262. *Payment plans:* installment, deferred payment. *Waivers:* employees or children of employees.
Library Harvey S. Firestone Memorial Library plus 22 others. *Operations spending 1999–2000:* $30.3 million. *Collection:* 5.1 million titles, 34,348 serial subscriptions, 398,347 audiovisual materials.
College life *Housing:* on-campus residence required through sophomore year. *Options:* coed, men-only, women-only, disabled students. *Social organizations:* eating clubs; 70% of eligible men and 70% of eligible women are members. *Most popular organizations:* Student Volunteer Council, Undergraduate Student Government, Princeton University Band, American Whig-Cliosophic Society, Princeton University Players Club.
Campus security 24-hour emergency response devices and patrols, student patrols, late-night transport-escort service, controlled dormitory access.
After graduation 300 organizations recruited on campus 1997–98. 47% of class of 1998 had job offers within 6 months. *Career center:* 6 full-time, 2 part-time personnel. Services include job fairs, resume preparation, interview workshops, resume referral, career/interest testing, career counseling, careers library, job bank, job interviews. *Graduate education:* 24% of class of 1999 went directly to graduate and professional school: 8% graduate arts and sciences, 5% law, 5% medicine, 3% engineering, 0.2% education, 0.2% theology. *Major awards:* 1 Marshall, 18 Fulbright Scholars.
Freshmen 14,875 applied, 1,694 admitted, 1,148 enrolled. 1 Westinghouse recipient.

New Jersey

Average high school GPA	3.82	SAT verbal scores above 500	99%
SAT math scores above 500	100%	ACT above 18	N/R
From top 10% of their h.s. class	92%	From top half	100%
1998 freshmen returning in 1999	99%		

Application *Options:* early admission, early decision, deferred entrance. *Application fee:* $60. *Required:* essay or personal statement; high school transcript; 3 letters of recommendation. *Recommended:* interview.

Standardized tests *Admission: Required:* SAT I, SAT II Subject Tests.

Significant dates *Application deadline:* 1/1 (freshmen). *Early decision:* 11/1. *Notification:* 4/3 (freshmen), 12/15 (early decision). *Financial aid deadline priority date:* 2/1.

Freshman Application Contact
Mr. Fred A. Hargadon, Dean of Admission, Princeton University, PO Box 430, Princeton, NJ 08544. **Phone:** 609-258-3062.

Visit CollegeQuest.com for information on majors offered and athletics. Electronic viewbook available at CollegeQuest.com.

■ *See page 2292 for a narrative description.*

RABBINICAL COLLEGE OF AMERICA
Morristown, New Jersey

Admissions Office Contact
Rabbinical College of America, Box 1996, Morristown, NJ 07962. **Fax:** 973-267-5208.

RAMAPO COLLEGE OF NEW JERSEY
Mahwah, New Jersey

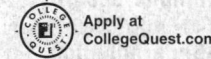

- **State-supported**, comprehensive, founded 1969
- **Degrees** bachelor's and master's
- **Suburban** 315-acre campus with easy access to New York City
- **Coed**, 4,131 undergraduate students, 73% full-time, 58% women, 42% men
- **Moderately difficult** entrance level, 47% of applicants were admitted
- **16:1** student-to-undergraduate faculty ratio
- **41.1% graduate** in 6 years or less
- **$5110 tuition** and fees (in-state); $7976 (out-of-state)
- **$5594 average financial aid** package, $11,498 average indebtedness upon graduation, $1 million endowment

As "the College of Choice for a Global Education," Ramapo College provides students with the opportunity to encounter the world beyond the campus through study-abroad and cooperative education programs and teleconferences. Undergraduate experiences through these programs have taken students to faraway countries; to internationally recognized institutions such as Regents College in London, Czech Technical Institute in Prague, Shanghai Teacher's University in Shanghai, and Volgograd Pedagogical Institute in Russia; and to corporate offices in the US and abroad.

Part of New Jersey State College System.

Students *Undergraduates:* 2,996 full-time, 1,135 part-time. Students come from 22 states and territories, 57 other countries. *The most frequently chosen baccalaureate fields are:* business/marketing, communications/communication technologies, psychology. *Graduate:* 213 in graduate degree programs.

From out-of-state	9%	Reside on campus	31%
Age 25 or older	30%	Transferred in	14%
International students	4%	African Americans	8%
Asian Americans/Pacific Islanders	4%	Hispanic Americans	7%
Native Americans	0.3%		

Faculty 285 (50% full-time), 48% with terminal degrees.

Expenses (1999–2000) *Tuition, state resident:* full-time $3822; part-time $119 per credit. *Tuition, nonresident:* full-time $6688; part-time $209 per credit. *Required fees:* full-time $1288; $36 per credit; $65 per term part-time. Full-time tuition and fees vary according to reciprocity agreements. Part-time tuition and fees vary according to course load and reciprocity agreements. *College room and board:* $6790; room only: $4550. Room and board charges vary according to board plan and housing facility. *Payment plan:* installment. *Waivers:* senior citizens and employees or children of employees.

Library George T. Potter Library plus 1 other. *Operations spending 1999–2000:* $1.9 million. *Collection:* 158,615 titles, 719 serial subscriptions, 1,726 audiovisual materials.

College life *Housing: Options:* coed, disabled students. *Social organizations:* national fraternities, national sororities, coed fraternity; 8% of eligible men and 7% of eligible women are members. *Most popular organizations:* Organization of African Unity, Student Activities Program Board, Ramapo News, International Student Organization, Student Activities Program Board.

Campus security 24-hour emergency response devices and patrols, late-night transport-escort service, controlled dormitory access, surveillance cameras, patrols by trained security personnel.

After graduation 143 organizations recruited on campus 1997–98. *Career center:* 9 full-time, 5 part-time personnel. Services include job fairs, resume preparation, interview workshops, resume referral, career/interest testing, career counseling, careers library, job bank, job interviews.

Freshmen 2,705 applied, 1,276 admitted, 536 enrolled.

Average high school GPA	3.1	SAT verbal scores above 500	60%
SAT math scores above 500	63%	ACT above 18	N/R
From top 10% of their h.s. class	16%	From top quarter	40%
From top half	84%	1998 freshmen returning in 1999	83%

Application *Options:* eApply at www.CollegeQuest.com, early admission, deferred entrance. *Application fee:* $45. *Required:* essay or personal statement; high school transcript; 1 letter of recommendation. *Recommended:* minimum 3.0 GPA; interview.

Standardized tests *Admission: Required:* SAT I. *Required for some:* ACT.

Significant dates *Application deadlines:* 3/15 (freshmen), 5/1 (transfers). *Notification:* continuous until 5/15 (freshmen). *Financial aid deadline priority date:* 3/1.

Freshman Application Contact
Ms. Nancy Jaeger, Director of Admissions, Ramapo College of New Jersey, 505 Ramapo Valley Road, Mahwah, NJ 07430-1680. **Phone:** 201-684-7300 Ext. 7601. **Toll-free phone:** 800-9RAMAPO. **Fax:** 201-684-7508. **E-mail:** adm@ramapo.edu

Visit CollegeQuest.com for information on majors offered and athletics. College video available at CollegeQuest.com.

■ *See page 2308 for a narrative description.*

THE RICHARD STOCKTON COLLEGE OF NEW JERSEY
Pomona, New Jersey

- **State-supported**, comprehensive, founded 1969
- **Degrees** bachelor's and master's
- **Suburban** 1,600-acre campus with easy access to Philadelphia
- **Coed**, 5,607 undergraduate students, 86% full-time, 56% women, 44% men
- **Very difficult** entrance level, 48% of applicants were admitted
- **20:1** student-to-undergraduate faculty ratio
- **60% graduate** in 6 years or less
- **$4400 tuition** and fees (in-state); $6432 (out-of-state)
- **$7980 average financial aid** package, $13,135 average indebtedness upon graduation, $2.4 million endowment

State-supported, 4-year coed college founded in 1969. Located 12 miles from Atlantic City, Stockton is primarily an undergraduate arts and sciences college within the New Jersey system. Special educational experiences are encouraged, including study abroad, internships, field studies, and independent study. Admission is selective.

Part of New Jersey State College System.

Students *Undergraduates:* 4,805 full-time, 802 part-time. Students come from 23 states and territories, 27 other countries. *The most frequently chosen baccalaureate fields are:* biological/life sciences, business/marketing, social sciences and history. *Graduate:* 323 in graduate degree programs.

New Jersey

The Richard Stockton College of New Jersey (continued)

From out-of-state	2%	Reside on campus	42%
Age 25 or older	21%	Transferred in	16%
International students	1%	African Americans	8%
Asian Americans/Pacific Islanders	4%	Hispanic Americans	5%
Native Americans	0.4%		

Faculty 344 (58% full-time), 81% with terminal degrees.

Expenses (1999–2000) *Tuition, state resident:* full-time $3280; part-time $102 per credit hour. *Tuition, nonresident:* full-time $5312; part-time $166 per credit hour. *Required fees:* full-time $1120; $35 per credit hour. Full-time tuition and fees vary according to course load. *College room and board:* $5381; room only: $3485. Room and board charges vary according to board plan and housing facility. *Payment plan:* installment. *Waivers:* senior citizens.

Library The Richard Stockton College of New Jersey Library. *Operations spending 1999–2000:* $2.9 million. *Collection:* 287,769 titles, 7,682 audiovisual materials.

College life *Housing: Option:* coed. *Social organizations:* national fraternities, national sororities; 5% of eligible men and 5% of eligible women are members. *Most popular organizations:* Stockton Action Volunteers for the Environment, Board of Activities, Stockton Television, Unified Black Student Society, Stockton Residents Association.

Campus security 24-hour emergency response devices and patrols, late-night transport-escort service, on-campus police force.

After graduation 148 organizations recruited on campus 1997–98. 83% of class of 1998 had job offers within 6 months. *Career center:* 3 full-time personnel. Services include job fairs, resume preparation, interview workshops, resume referral, career/interest testing, career counseling, careers library, job bank, job interviews.

Freshmen 3,138 applied, 1,493 admitted, 732 enrolled. 24 class presidents, 3 valedictorians, 238 student government officers.

Average high school GPA	3.2	SAT verbal scores above 500	72%
SAT math scores above 500	77%	ACT above 18	N/R
From top 10% of their h.s. class	18%	From top quarter	59%
From top half	92%	1998 freshmen returning in 1999	84%

Application *Options:* eApply at www.CollegeQuest.com, electronic application, early action. *Application fee:* $35. *Required:* essay or personal statement; high school transcript; minimum 2.0 GPA. *Recommended:* minimum 3.0 GPA; letters of recommendation.

Standardized tests *Admission: Required:* SAT I or ACT.

Significant dates *Application deadlines:* 5/1 (freshmen), 6/1 (transfers). *Early action:* 2/1. *Notification:* continuous until 5/15 (freshmen). *Financial aid deadline priority date:* 3/1.

Freshman Application Contact
Mr. Salvatore Catalfamo, Dean of Enrollment Management, The Richard Stockton College of New Jersey, PO Box 195, Jimmie Leeds Road, Pomona, NJ 08240-0195. **Phone:** 609-652-4261. **Fax:** 609-748-5541. **E-mail:** admissions@pollux.stockton.edu

Visit CollegeQuest.com for information on majors offered and athletics.

■ *See page 2328 for a narrative description.*

RIDER UNIVERSITY
Lawrenceville, New Jersey

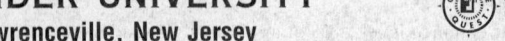

- **Independent**, comprehensive, founded 1865
- **Degrees** associate, bachelor's, master's, post-master's, and postbachelor's certificates
- **Suburban** 340-acre campus with easy access to New York City and Philadelphia
- **Coed**, 3,873 undergraduate students, 83% full-time, 58% women, 42% men
- **Moderately difficult** entrance level, 80% of applicants were admitted
- **13:1 student-to-undergraduate faculty ratio**
- **55.4% graduate** in 6 years or less
- **$16,820 tuition** and fees
- **$14,650 average financial aid** package, $12,500 average indebtedness upon graduation, $49.7 million endowment

Rider University offers majors in business, education, liberal arts, science, and music. Rider's formula for career success includes a combination of small classes, personal advising, experiential learning, and use of modern facilities.

Students enjoy activities ranging from social organizations to Division I athletics. More than 75 percent of the 2,900 full-time undergraduates receive financial assistance.

Students *Undergraduates:* 3,231 full-time, 642 part-time. Students come from 43 states and territories, 24 other countries. *The most frequently chosen baccalaureate fields are:* business/marketing, education, English. *Graduate:* 1,125 in graduate degree programs.

From out-of-state	26%	Reside on campus	66%
Age 25 or older	6%	Transferred in	5%
International students	2%	African Americans	7%
Asian Americans/Pacific Islanders	3%	Hispanic Americans	4%
Native Americans	0.5%		

Faculty 435 (51% full-time).

Expenses (1999–2000) *Comprehensive fee:* $23,590 includes full-time tuition ($16,520), mandatory fees ($300), and room and board ($6770). *College room only:* $4260. Full-time tuition and fees vary according to course load. Room and board charges vary according to housing facility. *Part-time tuition:* $550 per semester hour. *Part-time fees:* $10 per course. Part-time tuition and fees vary according to course load. *Payment plan:* installment. *Waivers:* employees or children of employees.

Library Franklin F. Moore Library. *Operations spending 1999–2000:* $2 million. *Collection:* 376,495 titles, 2,715 serial subscriptions, 23,095 audiovisual materials.

College life *Housing: Options:* coed, men-only, women-only, disabled students. *Social organizations:* national fraternities, national sororities; 12% of eligible men and 12% of eligible women are members. *Most popular organizations:* Student Government Association, Student Entertainment Council, Association of Commuter Students, Greek organizations, Latin American Student Organization.

Campus security 24-hour emergency response devices and patrols, student patrols, late-night transport-escort service, controlled dormitory access.

After graduation 151 organizations recruited on campus 1997–98. 81% of class of 1998 had job offers within 6 months. *Career center:* 5 full-time, 1 part-time personnel. Services include job fairs, resume preparation, resume referral, career counseling, careers library, job interviews.

Freshmen 4,037 applied, 3,223 admitted, 829 enrolled. 3 class presidents.

Average high school GPA	3.02	SAT verbal scores above 500	58%
SAT math scores above 500	59%	ACT above 18	N/R
From top 10% of their h.s. class	9%	From top quarter	29%
From top half	68%	1998 freshmen returning in 1999	78%

Application *Options:* eApply at www.CollegeQuest.com, early admission, early action, deferred entrance. *Application fee:* $35. *Required:* essay or personal statement; high school transcript. *Required for some:* interview. *Recommended:* minimum 2.0 GPA; 2 letters of recommendation; interview.

Standardized tests *Admission: Required:* SAT I or ACT.

Significant dates *Application deadlines:* rolling (freshmen), rolling (transfers). *Early action:* 11/15. *Notification:* 12/15 (early action). *Financial aid deadline priority date:* 3/1.

Freshman Application Contact
Mrs. Susan C. Christian, Director, Office of Admissions, Rider University, 2083 Lawrenceville Road, Lawrenceville, NJ 08648-3099. **Phone:** 609-895-5768. **Toll-free phone:** 800-257-9026. **Fax:** 609-895-6645. **E-mail:** admissions@rider.edu

Visit CollegeQuest.com for information on majors offered and athletics. College video available at CollegeQuest.com.

■ *See page 2332 for a narrative description.*

ROWAN UNIVERSITY
Glassboro, New Jersey

- **State-supported**, comprehensive, founded 1923
- **Degrees** bachelor's, master's, and doctoral
- **Small-town** 200-acre campus with easy access to Philadelphia
- **Coed**, 7,672 undergraduate students, 85% full-time, 56% women, 44% men
- **Moderately difficult** entrance level, 54% of applicants were admitted
- **16:1 student-to-undergraduate faculty ratio**
- **52.8% graduate** in 6 years or less
- **$4921 tuition** and fees (in-state); $8671 (out-of-state)

New Jersey

- **$5235 average financial aid** package, $86.9 million endowment

Rowan University is a selective public university offering undergraduate majors plus graduate degrees and certificates. Included are nationally recognized programs in business, engineering, fine and performing arts, liberal arts and sciences, communications, and teacher education. The 200-acre campus hosts 6,200 full-time undergraduates in Glassboro, a southern New Jersey town.

Part of New Jersey State College System.

Students *Undergraduates:* 6,541 full-time, 1,131 part-time. Students come from 17 states and territories, 23 other countries. *The most frequently chosen baccalaureate fields are:* business/marketing, communications/communication technologies, education. *Graduate:* 1,245 in graduate degree programs.

From out-of-state	4%	Reside on campus	30%
Age 25 or older	26%	Transferred in	10%
African Americans	9%	Asian Americans/Pacific Islanders	4%
Hispanic Americans	5%	Native Americans	0.4%

Faculty 695 (53% full-time).

Expenses (1999–2000) *Tuition, state resident:* full-time $3750; part-time $114 per credit. *Tuition, nonresident:* full-time $7500; part-time $228 per credit. *Required fees:* full-time $1171; $37 per credit. *College room and board:* $5766; room only: $3660. Room and board charges vary according to board plan and housing facility. *Payment plan:* deferred payment. *Waivers:* employees or children of employees.

Library Main library plus 2 others. *Operations spending 1999–2000:* $3 million.

College life *Housing:* on-campus residence required in freshman year. *Options:* coed, women-only, disabled students. *Social organizations:* national fraternities, national sororities, local fraternities, local sororities. *Most popular organizations:* Greek organizations, Student Government Association, Student Activities Board.

Campus security 24-hour emergency response devices and patrols, late-night transport-escort service, controlled dormitory access.

After graduation 65 organizations recruited on campus 1997–98. *Career center:* 8 full-time, 4 part-time personnel. Services include job fairs, resume preparation, interview workshops, resume referral, career/interest testing, career counseling, careers library, job bank, job interviews. *Graduate education:* 10% of class of 1999 went directly to graduate and professional school.

Freshmen 5,311 applied, 2,851 admitted, 1,129 enrolled.

SAT verbal scores above 500	74%	SAT math scores above 500	78%
ACT above 18	N/R	From top 10% of their h.s. class	16%
From top quarter	50%	From top half	88%
1998 freshmen returning in 1999	87%		

Application *Option:* deferred entrance. *Application fee:* $50. *Required:* essay or personal statement; high school transcript; minimum 2.0 GPA; 1 letter of recommendation. *Required for some:* interview. *Recommended:* minimum 3.0 GPA.

Standardized tests *Admission: Required:* SAT I or ACT. *Recommended:* SAT I.

Significant dates *Application deadlines:* 3/15 (freshmen), 3/15 (transfers). *Notification:* 4/15 (freshmen). *Financial aid deadline:* 3/15.

Freshman Application Contact
Mr. Marvin G. Sills, Director of Admissions, Rowan University, 201 Mullica Hill Road, Glassboro, NJ 08028-1701. **Phone:** 856-256-4200. **Toll-free phone:** 800-447-1165. **E-mail:** admissions@rowan.edu

Visit CollegeQuest.com for information on majors offered and athletics.

■ *See page 2360 for a narrative description.*

RUTGERS, THE STATE UNIVERSITY OF NEW JERSEY, CAMDEN COLLEGE OF ARTS AND SCIENCES
Camden, New Jersey

- **State-supported**, 4-year, founded 1927
- **Degree** bachelor's
- **Urban** 25-acre campus with easy access to Philadelphia
- **Coed**, 2,811 undergraduate students, 81% full-time, 58% women, 42% men
- **Moderately difficult** entrance level, 62% of applicants were admitted
- **11:1 student-to-undergraduate faculty ratio**
- **50% graduate** in 6 years or less
- **$5874 tuition** and fees (in-state); $10,804 (out-of-state)
- **$7720 average financial aid** package, $15,709 average indebtedness upon graduation, $342 million system endowment

Part of Rutgers, The State University of New Jersey.

Students *Undergraduates:* 2,269 full-time, 542 part-time. Students come from 19 states and territories, 9 other countries. *The most frequently chosen baccalaureate fields are:* psychology, health professions and related sciences, social sciences and history.

From out-of-state	4%	Transferred in	13%
International students	1%	African Americans	14%
Asian Americans/Pacific Islanders	8%	Hispanic Americans	6%
Native Americans	0.5%		

Faculty 357 (60% full-time), 98% with terminal degrees.

Expenses (1999–2000) *Tuition, state resident:* full-time $4762. *Tuition, nonresident:* full-time $9692. *Required fees:* full-time $1112. Full-time tuition and fees vary according to location. Part-time tuition and fees vary according to course load. *College room and board:* $5548; room only: $3348. Room and board charges vary according to board plan and housing facility. *Payment plan:* deferred payment. *Waivers:* employees or children of employees.

Library Paul Robeson Library plus 2 others. *System-wide operations spending 1999–2000:* $29.4 million. *Collection:* 6.4 million titles, 28,934 serial subscriptions, 119,880 audiovisual materials.

College life *Housing: Options:* coed, disabled students. *Social organizations:* national fraternities, national sororities; 10% of eligible men and 6% of eligible women are members. *Most popular organizations:* Black Student Union, Political Science Society, Asian Pacific Students Association, English Students Organization, Latin Students Organization.

Campus security 24-hour emergency response devices and patrols, student patrols, late-night transport-escort service, controlled dormitory access.

After graduation 90 organizations recruited on campus 1997–98. 75% of class of 1998 had job offers within 6 months. *Career center:* 5 full-time, 2 part-time personnel. Services include job fairs, resume preparation, interview workshops, resume referral, career/interest testing, career counseling, careers library, job bank, job interviews.

Freshmen 4,332 applied, 2,668 admitted, 299 enrolled. 2 valedictorians.

SAT verbal scores above 500	65%	SAT math scores above 500	64%
ACT above 18	N/R	From top 10% of their h.s. class	20%
From top quarter	62%	From top half	94%
1998 freshmen returning in 1999	86%		

Application *Options:* electronic application, early admission, deferred entrance. *Preference* given to state residents. *Application fee:* $50. *Required:* high school transcript.

Standardized tests *Admission: Required:* SAT I or ACT. *Required for some:* SAT II Subject Tests.

Significant dates *Application deadlines:* 12/15 (freshmen), 3/1 (transfers). *Notification:* continuous until 2/27 (freshmen). *Financial aid deadline priority date:* 3/15.

Freshman Application Contact
Ms. Diane Wms. Harris, Associate Director of University Undergraduate Admissions, Rutgers, The State University of New Jersey, Camden College of Arts and Sciences, 65 Davidson Road, Room 202, Piscataway, NJ 08854-8097. **Phone:** 732-732-4636. **Fax:** 732-445-0237. **E-mail:** admissions@asb-ugadm.rutgers.edu

Visit CollegeQuest.com for information on majors offered and athletics. Electronic viewbook available at CollegeQuest.com.

RUTGERS, THE STATE UNIVERSITY OF NEW JERSEY, COLLEGE OF NURSING
Newark, New Jersey

- **State-supported**, comprehensive, founded 1956
- **Degrees** bachelor's, master's, and doctoral (master's and doctoral degrees offered jointly with Rutgers Graduate School–Newark)
- **Urban** 34-acre campus with easy access to New York City

New Jersey

Rutgers, The State University of New Jersey, College of Nursing (continued)
- **Coed**, 443 undergraduate students, 75% full-time, 92% women, 8% men
- **Moderately difficult** entrance level, 26% of applicants were admitted
- **11:1 student-to-undergraduate faculty ratio**
- **64% graduate** in 6 years or less
- **$5792 tuition** and fees (in-state); $10,722 (out-of-state)
- **$8444 average financial aid** package, $17,701 average indebtedness upon graduation, $342 million system endowment

Part of Rutgers, The State University of New Jersey.

Students *Undergraduates:* 332 full-time, 111 part-time. Students come from 7 states and territories. *The most frequently chosen baccalaureate field is:* health professions and related sciences.

From out-of-state	4%	Transferred in	17%
International students	1%	African Americans	18%
Asian Americans/Pacific Islanders	16%	Hispanic Americans	12%

Faculty 61 (59% full-time), 97% with terminal degrees.

Expenses (1999–2000) *Tuition, state resident:* full-time $4762. *Tuition, nonresident:* full-time $9692. *Required fees:* full-time $1030. Part-time tuition and fees vary according to course load and location. *College room and board:* $6110; room only: $3348. Room and board charges vary according to board plan and housing facility. *Payment plan:* deferred payment. *Waivers:* employees or children of employees.

Library John Cotton Dana Library plus 4 others. *System-wide operations spending 1999–2000:* $29.4 million. *Collection:* 6.4 million titles, 28,934 serial subscriptions, 119,880 audiovisual materials.

College life *Housing: Options:* coed, disabled students. *Social organizations:* national fraternities, national sororities, local fraternities, local sororities. *Most popular organizations:* College of Nursing Senate, Rutgers Nursing Students Association, Rutgers Ethnic Nursing Students Association.

Campus security 24-hour emergency response devices and patrols, student patrols, late-night transport-escort service, controlled dormitory access, 24-hour security in residence halls.

After graduation 395 organizations recruited on campus 1997–98. *Career center:* 3 full-time, 2 part-time personnel. Services include job fairs, resume preparation, interview workshops, resume referral, career/interest testing, career counseling, careers library, job bank, job interviews, career guidance software.

Freshmen 711 applied, 182 admitted, 46 enrolled. 1 valedictorian.

SAT verbal scores above 500	72%	SAT math scores above 500	85%
ACT above 18	N/R	From top 10% of their h.s. class	20%
From top quarter	67%	From top half	96%
1998 freshmen returning in 1999	94%		

Application *Options:* electronic application, early admission, deferred entrance. *Preference* given to state residents. *Application fee:* $50. *Required:* high school transcript. *Required for some:* letters of recommendation.

Standardized tests *Admission: Required:* SAT I or ACT. *Required for some:* SAT II Subject Tests.

Significant dates *Application deadlines:* 12/15 (freshmen), 3/1 (transfers). *Notification:* continuous until 2/27 (freshmen). **Financial aid deadline priority date:** 3/15.

Freshman Application Contact
Ms. Diane Wms. Harris, Associate Director of University Undergraduate Admissions, Rutgers, The State University of New Jersey, College of Nursing, 65 Davidson Road, Piscataway, NJ 08854-8097. **Phone:** 732-932-4636. **Fax:** 732-445-0237. **E-mail:** admissions@asb-ugadm.rutgers.edu

Visit CollegeQuest.com for information on majors offered and athletics. Electronic viewbook available at CollegeQuest.com.

RUTGERS, THE STATE UNIVERSITY OF NEW JERSEY, COLLEGE OF PHARMACY
Piscataway, New Jersey

- **State-supported**, comprehensive, founded 1927
- **Degrees** incidental bachelor's, doctoral, and first professional (6-year doctor of pharmacy [PharmD] degree program is offered to students applying directly from high school)
- **Small-town** 2,695-acre campus with easy access to New York City and Philadelphia
- **Coed**, 825 undergraduate students, 99% full-time, 64% women, 36% men
- **Most difficult** entrance level, 45% of applicants were admitted
- **11:1 student-to-undergraduate faculty ratio**
- **76% graduate** in 6 years or less
- **$6576 tuition** and fees (in-state); $12,044 (out-of-state)
- **$8611 average financial aid** package, $16,760 average indebtedness upon graduation, $342 million system endowment

Part of Rutgers, The State University of New Jersey.

Students *Undergraduates:* 813 full-time, 12 part-time. Students come from 18 states and territories, 9 other countries. *The most frequently chosen baccalaureate field is:* health professions and related sciences. **Graduate:** 191 in professional programs.

From out-of-state	15%	Reside on campus	62%
Age 25 or older	6%	Transferred in	2%
International students	2%	African Americans	6%
Asian Americans/Pacific Islanders	48%	Hispanic Americans	7%

Faculty 85 (74% full-time), 98% with terminal degrees.

Expenses (1999–2000) *Tuition, state resident:* full-time $5286; part-time $174 per credit hour. *Tuition, nonresident:* full-time $10,754; part-time $358 per credit hour. *Required fees:* full-time $1290. Full-time tuition and fees vary according to location. *College room and board:* $6098; room only: $3348. Room and board charges vary according to board plan, housing facility, and location. *Payment plan:* deferred payment. *Waivers:* employees or children of employees.

Library Archibald S. Alexander Library plus 14 others. *System-wide operations spending 1999–2000:* $29.4 million. *Collection:* 6.4 million titles, 28,934 serial subscriptions, 119,880 audiovisual materials.

College life *Housing: Options:* coed, men-only, women-only, disabled students. *Social organizations:* national fraternities, national sororities; 8% of eligible men and 5% of eligible women are members. *Most popular organizations:* Pharmacy Governing Council, Academy of Students of Pharmacy, Lambda Kappa Sigma, Rho Chi Pharmacy Honor Society, Alpha Zeta Omega.

Campus security 24-hour emergency response devices and patrols, student patrols, late-night transport-escort service, controlled dormitory access.

After graduation 500 organizations recruited on campus 1997–98. 80% of class of 1998 had job offers within 6 months. *Career center:* 25 full-time, 5 part-time personnel. Services include job fairs, resume preparation, interview workshops, resume referral, career/interest testing, career counseling, careers library, job bank, job interviews.

Freshmen 1,401 applied, 630 admitted, 164 enrolled. 14 valedictorians.

SAT verbal scores above 500	98%	SAT math scores above 500	100%
ACT above 18	N/R	From top 10% of their h.s. class	68%
From top quarter	96%	From top half	100%
1998 freshmen returning in 1999	92%		

Application *Options:* electronic application, early admission, deferred entrance. *Preference* given to state residents. *Application fee:* $50. *Required:* high school transcript.

Standardized tests *Admission: Required:* SAT I or ACT. *Required for some:* SAT II Subject Tests.

Significant dates *Application deadlines:* 12/15 (freshmen), 3/1 (transfers). *Notification:* continuous until 2/27 (freshmen). **Financial aid deadline priority date:** 3/15.

Freshman Application Contact
Ms. Diane Wms. Harris, Associate Director of University Undergraduate Admissions, Rutgers, The State University of New Jersey, College of Pharmacy, 65 Davidson Road, Room 202, Piscataway, NJ 08854-8097. **Phone:** 732-932-4636. **Fax:** 732-445-0237. **E-mail:** admissions@asb-ugadm.rutgers.edu

Visit CollegeQuest.com for information on majors offered and athletics. Electronic viewbook available at CollegeQuest.com.

RUTGERS, THE STATE UNIVERSITY OF NEW JERSEY, COOK COLLEGE
New Brunswick, New Jersey

- **State-supported**, 4-year, founded 1921
- **Degree** bachelor's
- **Small-town** 2,695-acre campus with easy access to New York City and Philadelphia
- **Coed**, 3,178 undergraduate students, 93% full-time, 50% women, 50% men

New Jersey

- **Very difficult** entrance level, 64% of applicants were admitted
- **11:1 student-to-undergraduate faculty ratio**
- **73% graduate** in 6 years or less
- **$6544 tuition** and fees (in-state); $12,012 (out-of-state)
- **$8198 average financial aid** package, $16,078 average indebtedness upon graduation, $342 million system endowment

Part of Rutgers, The State University of New Jersey.

Students *Undergraduates:* 2,961 full-time, 217 part-time. Students come from 27 states and territories, 23 other countries. *The most frequently chosen baccalaureate fields are:* biological/life sciences, agriculture, natural resources/environmental science.

From out-of-state	9%	Reside on campus	56%
Age 25 or older	9%	Transferred in	7%
International students	2%	African Americans	6%
Asian Americans/Pacific Islanders	13%	Hispanic Americans	6%
Native Americans	0.3%		

Faculty 290 (88% full-time), 98% with terminal degrees.

Expenses (1999–2000) *Tuition, state resident:* full-time $5286. *Tuition, nonresident:* full-time $10,754. *Required fees:* full-time $1258. Full-time tuition and fees vary according to location. *College room and board:* $6098; room only: $3348. Room and board charges vary according to board plan and housing facility. *Payment plan:* deferred payment. *Waivers:* employees or children of employees.

Library Archibald S. Alexander Library plus 14 others. *System-wide operations spending 1999–2000:* $29.4 million. *Collection:* 6.4 million titles, 28,934 serial subscriptions, 119,880 audiovisual materials.

College life *Housing: Options:* coed, men-only, cooperative, disabled students. *Social organizations:* national fraternities, national sororities; 5% of eligible men and 4% of eligible women are members. *Most popular organizations:* student advisers, Recreation Advisory Council, Cook Leadership, environmental science club, Alpha Zeta.

Campus security 24-hour emergency response devices and patrols, student patrols, late-night transport-escort service, controlled dormitory access.

After graduation 500 organizations recruited on campus 1997–98. 80% of class of 1998 had job offers within 6 months. *Career center:* 25 full-time, 5 part-time personnel. Services include job fairs, resume preparation, interview workshops, resume referral, career/interest testing, career counseling, careers library, job bank, job interviews.

Freshmen 6,673 applied, 4,267 admitted, 464 enrolled. 5 National Merit Scholars, 6 valedictorians.

SAT verbal scores above 500	81%	SAT math scores above 500	86%
ACT above 18	N/R	From top 10% of their h.s. class	28%
From top quarter	69%	From top half	98%
1998 freshmen returning in 1999	91%		

Application *Options:* electronic application, early admission, deferred entrance. *Preference* given to state residents. *Application fee:* $50. *Required:* high school transcript.

Standardized tests *Admission: Required:* SAT I or ACT. *Required for some:* SAT II Subject Tests.

Significant dates *Application deadlines:* 12/15 (freshmen), 3/1 (transfers). *Notification:* continuous until 2/27 (freshmen). **Financial aid deadline priority date:** 3/15.

Freshman Application Contact
Ms. Diane Wms. Harris, Associate Director of University Undergraduate Admissions, Rutgers, The State University of New Jersey, Cook College, 65 Davidson Road, Room 202, Piscataway, NJ 08854-8097. **Phone:** 732-932-4636. **Fax:** 732-445-0237. **E-mail:** admissions@asb-ugadm.rutgers.edu

Visit CollegeQuest.com for information on majors offered and athletics. Electronic viewbook available at CollegeQuest.com.

RUTGERS, THE STATE UNIVERSITY OF NEW JERSEY, DOUGLASS COLLEGE
New Brunswick, New Jersey

- **State-supported**, 4-year, founded 1918
- **Degree** bachelor's
- **Small-town** 2,695-acre campus with easy access to New York City and Philadelphia
- **Women** only, 3,094 undergraduate students, 95% full-time

---

- **Moderately difficult** entrance level, 68% of applicants were admitted
- **15:1 student-to-undergraduate faculty ratio**
- **77% graduate** in 6 years or less
- **$6017 tuition** and fees (in-state); $10,947 (out-of-state)
- **$8541 average financial aid** package, $16,496 average indebtedness upon graduation, $342 million system endowment

Part of Rutgers, The State University of New Jersey.

Students *Undergraduates:* 2,951 full-time, 143 part-time. Students come from 29 states and territories, 25 other countries. *The most frequently chosen baccalaureate fields are:* psychology, communications/communication technologies, social sciences and history.

From out-of-state	6%	Reside on campus	54%
Age 25 or older	7%	Transferred in	9%
International students	2%	African Americans	12%
Asian Americans/Pacific Islanders	14%	Hispanic Americans	8%
Native Americans	0.2%		

Faculty 1,562 (67% full-time), 98% with terminal degrees.

Expenses (1999–2000) *Tuition, state resident:* full-time $4762. *Tuition, nonresident:* full-time $9692. *Required fees:* full-time $1255. Full-time tuition and fees vary according to location. Part-time tuition and fees vary according to course load and location. *College room and board:* $6098; room only: $3348. Room and board charges vary according to board plan and housing facility. *Payment plan:* deferred payment. *Waivers:* employees or children of employees.

Library Archibald S. Alexander Library plus 14 others. *System-wide operations spending 1999–2000:* $29.4 million. *Collection:* 6.4 million titles, 28,934 serial subscriptions, 119,880 audiovisual materials.

College life *Housing:* on-campus residence required in freshman year. *Options:* women-only, disabled students. *Social organizations:* national sororities; 5% of eligible undergrads are members. *Most popular organizations:* Douglass College Governing Association, Douglass College Activities Board, Voorhees Choir, Recreation Association, Douglass Asian Women's Association.

Campus security 24-hour emergency response devices and patrols, student patrols, late-night transport-escort service, controlled dormitory access.

After graduation 500 organizations recruited on campus 1997–98. 80% of class of 1998 had job offers within 6 months. *Career center:* 25 full-time, 5 part-time personnel. Services include job fairs, resume preparation, interview workshops, resume referral, career/interest testing, career counseling, careers library, job bank, job interviews.

Freshmen 6,453 applied, 4,419 admitted, 519 enrolled. 3 valedictorians.

SAT verbal scores above 500	75%	SAT math scores above 500	74%
ACT above 18	N/R	From top 10% of their h.s. class	19%
From top quarter	53%	From top half	98%
1998 freshmen returning in 1999	88%		

Application *Options:* electronic application, early admission, deferred entrance. *Preference* given to state residents. *Application fee:* $50. *Required:* high school transcript.

Standardized tests *Admission: Required:* SAT I or ACT. *Required for some:* SAT II Subject Tests.

Significant dates *Application deadlines:* 12/15 (freshmen), 3/1 (transfers). *Notification:* continuous until 2/27 (freshmen). **Financial aid deadline priority date:** 3/15.

Freshman Application Contact
Ms. Diane Wms. Harris, Associate Director of University Undergraduate Admissions, Rutgers, The State University of New Jersey, Douglass College, 65 Davidson Road, Room 202, Piscataway, NJ 08854-8097. **Phone:** 732-932-4636. **Fax:** 732-445-0237. **E-mail:** admissions@asb-ugadm.rutgers.edu

Visit CollegeQuest.com for information on majors offered and athletics. Electronic viewbook available at CollegeQuest.com.

RUTGERS, THE STATE UNIVERSITY OF NEW JERSEY, LIVINGSTON COLLEGE
Piscataway, New Jersey

- **State-supported**, 4-year, founded 1969
- **Degree** bachelor's
- **Small-town** 2,695-acre campus with easy access to New York City and Philadelphia

New Jersey

Rutgers, The State University of New Jersey, Livingston College (continued)
- **Coed**, 3,529 undergraduate students, 95% full-time, 39% women, 61% men
- **Moderately difficult** entrance level, 60% of applicants were admitted
- **15:1 student-to-undergraduate faculty ratio**
- **65.4% graduate** in 6 years or less
- **$6038 tuition** and fees (in-state); $10,968 (out-of-state)
- **$8392 average financial aid** package, $15,942 average indebtedness upon graduation, $342 million system endowment

Part of Rutgers, The State University of New Jersey.

Students *Undergraduates:* 3,353 full-time, 176 part-time. Students come from 31 states and territories, 84 other countries. *The most frequently chosen baccalaureate fields are:* protective services/public administration, psychology, social sciences and history.

From out-of-state	8%	Transferred in	6%
International students	2%	African Americans	10%
Asian Americans/Pacific Islanders	18%	Hispanic Americans	8%
Native Americans	0.1%		

Faculty 1,562 (67% full-time), 98% with terminal degrees.

Expenses (1999–2000) *Tuition, state resident:* full-time $4762. *Tuition, nonresident:* full-time $9692. *Required fees:* full-time $1276. Full-time tuition and fees vary according to location. Part-time tuition and fees vary according to course load. *College room and board:* $6098; room only: $3348. Room and board charges vary according to board plan and housing facility. *Payment plan:* deferred payment. *Waivers:* employees or children of employees.

Library Archibald S. Alexander Library plus 14 others. *System-wide operations spending 1999–2000:* $29.4 million. *Collection:* 6.4 million titles, 28,934 serial subscriptions, 119,880 audiovisual materials.

College life *Housing: Options:* coed, disabled students. *Social organizations:* national fraternities, national sororities; 8% of eligible men and 5% of eligible women are members. *Most popular organizations:* Livingston College Governing Association, Livingston's Own Concert Organization, program board, LUEP (Latinos Unidos en Poder), BUST (Blacks United to Save Themselves).

Campus security 24-hour emergency response devices and patrols, student patrols, late-night transport-escort service, controlled dormitory access.

After graduation 500 organizations recruited on campus 1997–98. 80% of class of 1998 had job offers within 6 months. *Career center:* 25 full-time, 5 part-time personnel. Services include job fairs, resume preparation, interview workshops, resume referral, career/interest testing, career counseling, careers library, job bank, job interviews.

Freshmen 14,995 applied, 8,927 admitted, 712 enrolled. 6 National Merit Scholars, 1 valedictorian.

SAT verbal scores above 500	75%	SAT math scores above 500	82%
ACT above 18	N/R	From top 10% of their h.s. class	9%
From top quarter	42%	From top half	95%
1998 freshmen returning in 1999	86%		

Application *Options:* electronic application, early admission, deferred entrance. *Preference* given to state residents. *Application fee:* $50. *Required:* high school transcript.

Standardized tests *Admission: Required:* SAT I or ACT. *Required for some:* SAT II Subject Tests.

Significant dates *Application deadlines:* 12/15 (freshmen), 3/1 (transfers). *Notification:* continuous until 2/27 (freshmen). *Financial aid deadline priority date:* 3/15.

Freshman Application Contact
Ms. Diane Wms. Harris, Associate Director of University Undergraduate Admissions, Rutgers, The State University of New Jersey, Livingston College, 65 Davidson Road, Room 202, Piscataway, NJ 08854-8097. **Phone:** 732-932-4636. **Fax:** 732-445-0237. **E-mail:** admissions@asb-ugadm.rutgers.edu

Visit CollegeQuest.com for information on majors offered and athletics. Electronic viewbook available at CollegeQuest.com.

RUTGERS, THE STATE UNIVERSITY OF NEW JERSEY, MASON GROSS SCHOOL OF THE ARTS
New Brunswick, New Jersey

- **State-supported**, comprehensive, founded 1976
- **Degrees** bachelor's, master's, and doctoral (also offers artist diploma)
- **Small-town** 2,695-acre campus with easy access to New York City and Philadelphia
- **Coed**, 617 undergraduate students, 98% full-time, 57% women, 43% men
- **Very difficult** entrance level, 22% of applicants were admitted
- **6:1 student-to-undergraduate faculty ratio**
- **53% graduate** in 6 years or less
- **$6052 tuition** and fees (in-state); $10,982 (out-of-state)
- **$7817 average financial aid** package, $18,141 average indebtedness upon graduation, $342 million system endowment

Part of Rutgers, The State University of New Jersey.

Students *Undergraduates:* 604 full-time, 13 part-time. Students come from 27 states and territories, 6 other countries. *The most frequently chosen baccalaureate field is:* visual/performing arts. *Graduate:* 234 in graduate degree programs.

From out-of-state	18%	Reside on campus	47%
Age 25 or older	4%	Transferred in	7%
International students	1%	African Americans	5%
Asian Americans/Pacific Islanders	6%	Hispanic Americans	4%
Native Americans	1%		

Faculty 148 (53% full-time), 98% with terminal degrees.

Expenses (1999–2000) *Tuition, state resident:* full-time $4762; part-time $154 per credit hour. *Tuition, nonresident:* full-time $9692; part-time $314 per credit hour. *Required fees:* full-time $1290. Full-time tuition and fees vary according to location. *College room and board:* $6098; room only: $3348. Room and board charges vary according to board plan, housing facility, and location. *Payment plan:* deferred payment. *Waivers:* employees or children of employees.

Library Archibald S. Alexander Library plus 14 others. *System-wide operations spending 1999–2000:* $29.4 million. *Collection:* 6.4 million titles, 28,934 serial subscriptions, 119,880 audiovisual materials.

College life *Housing: Options:* coed, men-only, women-only, disabled students. *Social organizations:* national fraternities, national sororities; 8% of eligible men and 5% of eligible women are members. *Most popular organization:* Mason Gross Student Government Association.

Campus security 24-hour emergency response devices and patrols, student patrols, late-night transport-escort service, controlled dormitory access.

After graduation 500 organizations recruited on campus 1997–98. 80% of class of 1998 had job offers within 6 months. *Career center:* 25 full-time, 5 part-time personnel. Services include job fairs, resume preparation, interview workshops, resume referral, career/interest testing, career counseling, careers library, job bank, job interviews.

Freshmen 1,603 applied, 356 admitted, 112 enrolled. 2 valedictorians.

SAT verbal scores above 500	80%	SAT math scores above 500	74%
ACT above 18	N/R	From top 10% of their h.s. class	17%
From top quarter	45%	From top half	79%
1998 freshmen returning in 1999	90%		

Application *Options:* electronic application, early admission, deferred entrance. *Preference* given to state residents. *Application fee:* $50. *Required:* high school transcript; audition, portfolio, or interview.

Standardized tests *Admission: Required:* SAT I or ACT. *Required for some:* SAT II Subject Tests.

Significant dates *Application deadlines:* 12/15 (freshmen), 3/1 (transfers). *Notification:* continuous until 2/27 (freshmen). *Financial aid deadline priority date:* 3/15.

Freshman Application Contact
Ms. Diane Wms. Harris, Associate Director of University Undergraduate Admissions, Rutgers, The State University of New Jersey, Mason Gross School of the Arts, 65 Davidson Road, Room 202, Piscataway, NJ 08854-8097. **Phone:** 732-932-4636. **Fax:** 732-445-0237. **E-mail:** admissions@asb-ugadm.rutgers.edu

Visit CollegeQuest.com for information on majors offered and athletics. Electronic viewbook available at CollegeQuest.com.

New Jersey

RUTGERS, THE STATE UNIVERSITY OF NEW JERSEY, NEWARK COLLEGE OF ARTS AND SCIENCES
Newark, New Jersey

- **State-supported**, 4-year, founded 1946
- **Degree** bachelor's
- **Urban** 34-acre campus with easy access to New York City
- **Coed**, 3,650 undergraduate students, 85% full-time, 56% women, 44% men
- **Moderately difficult** entrance level, 57% of applicants were admitted
- **9:1 student-to-undergraduate faculty ratio**
- **52% graduate** in 6 years or less
- **$5814 tuition** and fees (in-state); $10,744 (out-of-state)
- **$7876 average financial aid** package, $14,313 average indebtedness upon graduation, $342 million system endowment

Part of Rutgers, The State University of New Jersey.

Students *Undergraduates:* 3,089 full-time, 561 part-time. Students come from 19 states and territories. *The most frequently chosen baccalaureate fields are:* biological/life sciences, business/marketing, protective services/public administration.

From out-of-state	4%	Transferred in	9%
International students	4%	African Americans	16%
Asian Americans/Pacific Islanders	20%	Hispanic Americans	19%
Native Americans	0.2%		

Faculty 573 (68% full-time), 98% with terminal degrees.

Expenses (1999–2000) *Tuition, state resident:* full-time $4762. *Tuition, nonresident:* full-time $9692. *Required fees:* full-time $1052. Full-time tuition and fees vary according to location. Part-time tuition and fees vary according to course load. *College room and board:* $6110; room only: $3348. Room and board charges vary according to board plan and housing facility. *Payment plan:* deferred payment. *Waivers:* employees or children of employees.

Library John Cotton Dana Library plus 4 others. *System-wide operations spending 1999–2000:* $29.4 million. *Collection:* 6.4 million titles, 28,934 serial subscriptions, 119,880 audiovisual materials.

College life *Housing: Options:* coed, disabled students. *Social organizations:* national fraternities, national sororities, local fraternities, local sororities. *Most popular organizations:* Interfraternity/Sorority Council, Filipino Students Organization, Hellenic Students Organization, Latino Students Organization.

Campus security 24-hour emergency response devices and patrols, student patrols, late-night transport-escort service, controlled dormitory access, 24-hour security in residence halls.

After graduation 395 organizations recruited on campus 1997–98. *Career center:* 3 full-time, 2 part-time personnel. Services include job fairs, resume preparation, interview workshops, resume referral, career/interest testing, career counseling, careers library, job bank, job interviews, career guidance software.

Freshmen 6,620 applied, 3,749 admitted, 598 enrolled. 4 valedictorians.

SAT verbal scores above 500	52%	SAT math scores above 500	66%
ACT above 18	N/R	From top 10% of their h.s. class	24%
From top quarter	52%	From top half	94%
1998 freshmen returning in 1999	86%		

Application *Options:* electronic application, early admission, deferred entrance. *Preference* given to state residents. *Application fee:* $50. *Required:* high school transcript.

Standardized tests *Admission: Required:* SAT I or ACT. *Required for some:* SAT II Subject Tests.

Significant dates *Application deadlines:* 12/15 (freshmen), 3/1 (transfers). *Notification:* continuous until 2/27 (freshmen). **Financial aid deadline priority date:** 3/15.

Freshman Application Contact
Ms. Diane Wms. Harris, Associate Director of University Undergraduate Admissions, Rutgers, The State University of New Jersey, Newark College of Arts and Sciences, 65 Davidson Road, Piscataway, NJ 08854-8097. **Phone:** 732-932-4636. **Fax:** 732-445-0237. **E-mail:** admissions@asb-ugadm.rutgers.edu

Visit CollegeQuest.com for information on majors offered and athletics. Electronic viewbook available at CollegeQuest.com.

RUTGERS, THE STATE UNIVERSITY OF NEW JERSEY, RUTGERS COLLEGE
New Brunswick, New Jersey

- **State-supported**, 4-year, founded 1766
- **Degree** bachelor's
- **Small-town** 2,695-acre campus with easy access to New York City and Philadelphia
- **Coed**, 10,894 undergraduate students, 97% full-time, 51% women, 49% men
- **Very difficult** entrance level, 48% of applicants were admitted
- **15:1 student-to-undergraduate faculty ratio**
- **77% graduate** in 6 years or less
- **$6052 tuition** and fees (in-state); $10,982 (out-of-state)
- **$8586 average financial aid** package, $15,560 average indebtedness upon graduation, $342 million system endowment

Part of Rutgers, The State University of New Jersey.

Students *Undergraduates:* 10,602 full-time, 292 part-time. Students come from 43 states and territories, 69 other countries. *The most frequently chosen baccalaureate fields are:* psychology, biological/life sciences, social sciences and history.

From out-of-state	10%	Reside on campus	54%
Age 25 or older	3%	Transferred in	4%
International students	3%	African Americans	7%
Asian Americans/Pacific Islanders	20%	Hispanic Americans	9%
Native Americans	0.1%		

Faculty 1,562 (67% full-time), 98% with terminal degrees.

Expenses (1999–2000) *Tuition, state resident:* full-time $4762. *Tuition, nonresident:* full-time $9692. *Required fees:* full-time $1290. Full-time tuition and fees vary according to location. *College room and board:* $6098; room only: $3348. Room and board charges vary according to board plan and housing facility. *Payment plan:* installment. *Waivers:* employees or children of employees.

Library Archibald S. Alexander Library plus 14 others. *System-wide operations spending 1999–2000:* $29.4 million. *Collection:* 6.4 million titles, 28,934 serial subscriptions, 119,880 audiovisual materials.

College life *Housing: Options:* coed, disabled students. *Social organizations:* national fraternities, national sororities; 8% of eligible men and 5% of eligible women are members. *Most popular organizations:* Rutgers College Governing Association, Golden Key, BIGLARU (Bisexual, Gay, Lesbian Alliance of Rutgers University), Children's AIDS Network.

Campus security 24-hour emergency response devices and patrols, student patrols, late-night transport-escort service, controlled dormitory access.

After graduation 500 organizations recruited on campus 1997–98. 80% of class of 1998 had job offers within 6 months. *Career center:* 25 full-time, 5 part-time personnel. Services include job fairs, resume preparation, interview workshops, resume referral, career/interest testing, career counseling, careers library, job bank, job interviews. **Major awards:** 10 Fulbright Scholars.

Freshmen 20,441 applied, 9,896 admitted, 1,765 enrolled. 24 valedictorians.

SAT verbal scores above 500	87%	SAT math scores above 500	91%
ACT above 18	N/R	From top 10% of their h.s. class	43%
From top quarter	82%	From top half	99%
1998 freshmen returning in 1999	90%		

Application *Options:* electronic application, early admission, deferred entrance. *Preference* given to state residents. *Application fee:* $50. *Required:* high school transcript.

Standardized tests *Admission: Required:* SAT I or ACT. *Required for some:* SAT II Subject Tests.

Significant dates *Application deadlines:* 12/15 (freshmen), 3/1 (transfers). *Notification:* continuous until 2/27 (freshmen). **Financial aid deadline priority date:** 3/15.

Freshman Application Contact
Ms. Diane Wms. Harris, Associate Director of University Undergraduate Admissions, Rutgers, The State University of New Jersey, Rutgers College, 65 Davidson Road, Piscataway, NJ 08854-8097. **Phone:** 732-932-4636. **Fax:** 732-445-0237. **E-mail:** admissions@asb-ugadm.rutgers.edu

Visit CollegeQuest.com for information on majors offered and athletics. Electronic viewbook available at CollegeQuest.com.

New Jersey

RUTGERS, THE STATE UNIVERSITY OF NEW JERSEY, SCHOOL OF ENGINEERING
Piscataway, New Jersey

- **State-supported**, 4-year, founded 1864
- **Degree** bachelor's (master of science, master of philosophy, and doctor of philosophy degrees are offered through the Graduate School, New Brunswick)
- **Small-town** 2,695-acre campus with easy access to New York City and Philadelphia
- **Coed**, 2,181 undergraduate students, 96% full-time, 22% women, 78% men
- **Very difficult** entrance level, 68% of applicants were admitted
- **15:1 student-to-undergraduate faculty ratio**
- **68% graduate** in 6 years or less
- **$6576 tuition** and fees (in-state); $12,044 (out-of-state)
- **$8988 average financial aid** package, $16,386 average indebtedness upon graduation, $342 million system endowment

Part of Rutgers, The State University of New Jersey.
Students *Undergraduates:* 2,104 full-time, 77 part-time. Students come from 19 states and territories, 39 other countries. *The most frequently chosen baccalaureate field is:* engineering/engineering technologies.

From out-of-state	9%	Reside on campus	56%
Age 25 or older	5%	Transferred in	3%
International students	6%	African Americans	7%
Asian Americans/Pacific Islanders	27%	Hispanic Americans	6%
Native Americans	0.05%		

Faculty 149 (93% full-time).
Expenses (1999–2000) *Tuition, state resident:* full-time $5286; part-time $174 per credit hour. *Tuition, nonresident:* full-time $10,754; part-time $358 per credit hour. *Required fees:* full-time $1290. Full-time tuition and fees vary according to location. *College room and board:* $6098; room only: $3348. Room and board charges vary according to board plan and housing facility. *Payment plan:* deferred payment. *Waivers:* employees or children of employees.
Library Archibald S. Alexander Library plus 14 others. *System-wide operations spending 1999–2000:* $29.4 million. *Collection:* 6.4 million titles, 28,934 serial subscriptions, 119,880 audiovisual materials.
College life *Housing: Options:* coed, men-only, women-only, cooperative, disabled students. *Social organizations:* national fraternities, national sororities; 8% of eligible men and 5% of eligible women are members. *Most popular organizations:* Institute of Industrial Engineers, Tau Beta Pi, Engineering Governing Council, Society of Women Engineers, Minority Engineering Educational Task.
Campus security 24-hour emergency response devices and patrols, student patrols, late-night transport-escort service, controlled dormitory access.
After graduation 500 organizations recruited on campus 1997–98. 80% of class of 1998 had job offers within 6 months. *Career center:* 25 full-time, 5 part-time personnel. Services include job fairs, resume preparation, interview workshops, resume referral, career/interest testing, career counseling, careers library, job bank, job interviews.
Freshmen 3,806 applied, 2,593 admitted, 394 enrolled. 7 valedictorians.

SAT verbal scores above 500	85%	SAT math scores above 500	97%
ACT above 18	N/R	From top 10% of their h.s. class	35%
From top quarter	73%	From top half	98%
1998 freshmen returning in 1999	88%		

Application *Options:* electronic application, early admission, deferred entrance. *Preference* given to state residents. *Application fee:* $50. *Required:* high school transcript.
Standardized tests *Admission: Required:* SAT I or ACT. *Required for some:* SAT II Subject Tests.
Significant dates *Application deadlines:* 12/15 (freshmen), 3/1 (transfers). *Notification:* continuous until 2/27 (freshmen). *Financial aid deadline priority date:* 3/15.
Freshman Application Contact
Ms. Diane Wms. Harris, Associate Director of University Undergraduate Admissions, Rutgers, The State University of New Jersey, School of Engineering, 65 Davidson Road, Room 202, Piscataway, NJ 08854-8097. **Phone:** 732-932-4636. **Fax:** 732-445-0237. **E-mail:** admissions@asb-ugadm.rutgers.edu

Visit CollegeQuest.com for information on majors offered and athletics. Electronic viewbook available at CollegeQuest.com.

RUTGERS, THE STATE UNIVERSITY OF NEW JERSEY, UNIVERSITY COLLEGE—CAMDEN
Camden, New Jersey

- **$6692 average financial aid** package, $15,780 average indebtedness upon graduation, $342 million system endowment

Part of Rutgers, The State University of New Jersey.
Students *Undergraduates:* 301 full-time, 303 part-time. Students come from 5 states and territories. *The most frequently chosen baccalaureate fields are:* psychology, computer/information sciences, social sciences and history.

From out-of-state	2%	International students	0.2%
African Americans	18%	Asian Americans/Pacific Islanders	6%
Hispanic Americans	3%	Native Americans	1%

Faculty 357 (60% full-time), 98% with terminal degrees.
Expenses (1999–2000) *Tuition, state resident:* part-time $154 per credit hour. *Tuition, nonresident:* part-time $314 per credit hour. *Required fees:* $170 per term part-time. Part-time tuition and fees vary according to course load. *Payment plan:* installment. *Waivers:* employees or children of employees.
Library Paul Robeson Library plus 2 others. *System-wide operations spending 1999–2000:* $29.4 million. *Collection:* 6.4 million titles, 28,934 serial subscriptions, 119,880 audiovisual materials.
College life *Housing: Option:* coed. *Social organizations:* national fraternities, national sororities. *Most popular organizations:* Student Council, Return Students.
Campus security 24-hour emergency response devices and patrols, late-night transport-escort service.
After graduation 90 organizations recruited on campus 1997–98. 75% of class of 1998 had job offers within 6 months. *Career center:* 5 full-time, 2 part-time personnel. Services include job fairs, resume preparation, interview workshops, resume referral, career/interest testing, career counseling, careers library, job bank, job interviews.
Freshmen 217 applied, 26 admitted, 4 enrolled.

SAT verbal scores above 500	N/R	SAT math scores above 500	N/R
ACT above 18	N/R		

Application *Options:* electronic application, early admission, deferred entrance. *Application fee:* $50. *Required:* high school transcript.
Standardized tests *Admission: Required:* SAT I or ACT. *Required for some:* SAT II Subject Tests.
Significant dates *Application deadlines:* 12/15 (freshmen), 3/1 (transfers). *Notification:* continuous until 2/27 (freshmen). *Financial aid deadline priority date:* 3/15.
Freshman Application Contact
Ms. Diane Wms. Harris, Associate Director of University Undergraduate Admissions, Rutgers, The State University of New Jersey, University College–Camden, 65 Davidson Road, Piscataway, NJ 08854-8097. **Phone:** 732-932-4636. **Fax:** 732-445-0237. **E-mail:** admissions@asb.ugadm-rutgers.edu
Visit CollegeQuest.com for information on majors offered and athletics. Electronic viewbook available at CollegeQuest.com.

RUTGERS, THE STATE UNIVERSITY OF NEW JERSEY, UNIVERSITY COLLEGE—NEWARK
Newark, New Jersey

- **$7470 average financial aid** package, $17,030 average indebtedness upon graduation, $342 million system endowment

Part of Rutgers, The State University of New Jersey.
Students *Undergraduates:* 622 full-time, 733 part-time. Students come from 9 states and territories. *The most frequently chosen baccalaureate fields*

New Jersey

are: business/marketing, protective services/public administration, social sciences and history.

From out-of-state	5%	International students	2%
African Americans	35%	Asian Americans/Pacific Islanders	9%
Hispanic Americans	19%	Native Americans	0.1%

Faculty 573 (68% full-time), 98% with terminal degrees.
Expenses (1999–2000) *Tuition, state resident:* part-time $154 per credit hour. *Tuition, nonresident:* part-time $314 per credit hour. *Required fees:* $128 per term part-time. Part-time tuition and fees vary according to course load. *Payment plan:* deferred payment. *Waivers:* employees or children of employees.
Library John Cotton Dana Library plus 4 others. *System-wide operations spending 1999–2000:* $29.4 million. *Collection:* 6.4 million titles, 28,934 serial subscriptions, 119,880 audiovisual materials.
College life *Housing: Option:* coed. *Social organizations:* national fraternities, national sororities, local fraternities, local sororities. *Most popular organizations:* University College Student Government, Untitled Magazine, UC Newsletter.
Campus security 24-hour emergency response devices and patrols, student patrols, late-night transport-escort service.
After graduation 339 organizations recruited on campus 1997–98. *Career center:* Services include job fairs, resume preparation, interview workshops, resume referral, career/interest testing, career counseling, careers library, job bank, job interviews.
Freshmen 357 applied, 160 admitted, 70 enrolled.

| SAT verbal scores above 500 | N/R | SAT math scores above 500 | N/R |
| ACT above 18 | N/R | | |

Application *Options:* electronic application, early admission, deferred entrance. *Application fee:* $50. *Required:* high school transcript.
Significant dates *Application deadlines:* 12/15 (freshmen), 3/1 (transfers). *Notification:* continuous until 2/28 (freshmen). *Financial aid deadline priority date:* 3/15.
Freshman Application Contact
Ms. Diane Wms. Harris, Associate Director of University Undergraduate Admissions, Rutgers, The State University of New Jersey, University College–Newark, 65 Davidson Road, Piscataway, NJ 08854-8097. **Phone:** 732-932-4636. **Fax:** 732-445-0237. **E-mail:** admissions@asb-ugadm.rutgers.edu
Visit CollegeQuest.com for information on majors offered and athletics. Electronic viewbook available at CollegeQuest.com.

RUTGERS, THE STATE UNIVERSITY OF NEW JERSEY, UNIVERSITY COLLEGE– NEW BRUNSWICK
New Brunswick, New Jersey

- **$7559 average financial aid** package, $16,737 average indebtedness upon graduation, $342 million system endowment

Part of Rutgers, The State University of New Jersey.
Students *Undergraduates:* 1,324 full-time, 1,596 part-time. Students come from 19 states and territories. *The most frequently chosen baccalaureate fields are:* psychology, business/marketing, social sciences and history.

From out-of-state	4%	International students	2%
African Americans	9%	Asian Americans/Pacific Islanders	10%
Hispanic Americans	6%	Native Americans	0.5%

Faculty 1,562 (67% full-time), 98% with terminal degrees.
Expenses (1999–2000) *Tuition, state resident:* part-time $154 per credit hour. *Tuition, nonresident:* part-time $314 per credit hour. Part-time tuition and fees vary according to course load. *Payment plan:* installment. *Waivers:* employees or children of employees.
Library Archibald S. Alexander Library plus 14 others. *System-wide operations spending 1999–2000:* $29.4 million. *Collection:* 6.4 million titles, 28,934 serial subscriptions, 119,880 audiovisual materials.
College life *Housing: Option:* coed. *Most popular organizations:* University College Governing Association, student newspaper.
Campus security 24-hour emergency response devices and patrols, student patrols, late-night transport-escort service.

After graduation 500 organizations recruited on campus 1997–98. 80% of class of 1998 had job offers within 6 months. *Career center:* Services include job fairs, resume preparation, interview workshops, resume referral, career/interest testing, career counseling, careers library, job bank, job interviews.
Freshmen 352 applied, 154 admitted, 54 enrolled.

| SAT verbal scores above 500 | N/R | SAT math scores above 500 | N/R |
| ACT above 18 | N/R | | |

Application *Options:* electronic application, deferred entrance. *Application fee:* $50. *Required:* high school transcript.
Standardized tests *Admission: Required for some:* CAT.
Significant dates *Application deadlines:* 12/15 (freshmen), 3/1 (transfers). *Notification:* continuous until 2/27 (freshmen). *Financial aid deadline priority date:* 3/15.
Freshman Application Contact
Mr. Raul Barriera, Director of Admissions, Rutgers, The State University of New Jersey, University College–New Brunswick, 14 College Avenue, Miller Hall, New Brunswick, NJ 08903. **Phone:** 732-932-7276. **Fax:** 732-932-8767. **E-mail:** ucnb@rci.rutgers.edu
Visit CollegeQuest.com for information on majors offered and athletics. Electronic viewbook available at CollegeQuest.com.

SAINT PETER'S COLLEGE
Jersey City, New Jersey

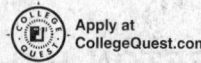
Apply at CollegeQuest.com

- **Independent Roman Catholic (Jesuit)**, comprehensive, founded 1872
- **Degrees** associate, bachelor's, and master's
- **Urban** 15-acre campus with easy access to New York City
- **Coed**, 2,604 undergraduate students, 83% full-time, 55% women, 45% men
- **Moderately difficult** entrance level, 84% of applicants were admitted
- **20:1 student-to-undergraduate faculty ratio**
- **45% graduate** in 6 years or less
- **$15,606 tuition** and fees
- **$20 million endowment**

Saint Peter's College has one of the lowest tuition rates of all Jesuit colleges in the East as well as an average financial aid package of $14,410 for commuter students and $15,340 for students living on campus. A student-faculty ratio of 14:1 upholds its commitment to personal care. SPC's location, just minutes from Manhattan, allows students to benefit from a myriad of opportunities, especially through the nationally ranked Cooperative Education Program.

Students *Undergraduates:* 2,172 full-time, 432 part-time. Students come from 28 states and territories, 9 other countries. *The most frequently chosen baccalaureate fields are:* business/marketing, education, health professions and related sciences. *Graduate:* 518 in graduate degree programs.

From out-of-state	13%	Reside on campus	27%
Age 25 or older	19%	Transferred in	3%
International students	1%	African Americans	16%
Asian Americans/Pacific Islanders	8%	Hispanic Americans	27%
Native Americans	0.3%		

Faculty 289 (40% full-time), 46% with terminal degrees.
Expenses (2000–2001) *Comprehensive fee:* $22,052 includes full-time tuition ($15,240), mandatory fees ($366), and room and board ($6446). *College room only:* $3990. Full-time tuition and fees vary according to course load and location. Room and board charges vary according to board plan and housing facility. *Part-time tuition:* $508 per credit. Part-time tuition and fees vary according to class time and course load. *Payment plans:* installment, deferred payment. *Waivers:* employees or children of employees.
Library Theresa and Edward O'Toole Library plus 1 other. *Operations spending 1999–2000:* $1.2 million. *Collection:* 178,587 titles, 1,741 serial subscriptions, 330 audiovisual materials.
College life *Housing: Options:* coed, women-only. *Most popular organizations:* Caribbean Culture Club, Black Action Committee, Asian American Student Union, Argus Eyes Dramatic Society, Voices of Praise Gospel Choir.
Campus security 24-hour emergency response devices and patrols, late-night transport-escort service, controlled dormitory access, ID checks at residence halls and library.
After graduation 140 organizations recruited on campus 1997–98. 77% of class of 1998 had job offers within 6 months. *Career center:* 3 full-time

New Jersey

Saint Peter's College (continued)

personnel. Services include job fairs, resume preparation, interview workshops, resume referral, career/interest testing, career counseling, careers library, job bank, job interviews.

Freshmen 2,016 applied, 1,689 admitted, 601 enrolled. 5 valedictorians.

Average high school GPA	2.9	SAT verbal scores above 500	29%
SAT math scores above 500	29%	ACT above 18	N/R
From top 10% of their h.s. class	15%	From top quarter	43%
From top half	64%	1998 freshmen returning in 1999	66%

Application *Options:* eApply at www.CollegeQuest.com, Common Application, early admission, deferred entrance. *Application fee:* $30. *Required:* essay or personal statement; high school transcript; minimum 2.0 GPA; 2 letters of recommendation. *Required for some:* interview. *Recommended:* interview.

Standardized tests *Admission: Required:* SAT I or ACT.

Significant dates *Application deadlines:* rolling (freshmen), 6/1 (transfers). *Financial aid deadline priority date:* 3/15.

Freshman Application Contact
Stephanie Decker, Director of Recruitment, Saint Peter's College, 2627 Kennedy Blvd., Jersey City, NJ 07306. **Phone:** 201-915-9213. **Toll-free phone:** 888-SPC-9933. **Fax:** 201-432-5860. **E-mail:** admissions@spcvxa.spc.edu

Visit CollegeQuest.com for information on majors offered and athletics.

■ *See page 2426 for a narrative description.*

SETON HALL UNIVERSITY
South Orange, New Jersey

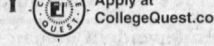
Apply at CollegeQuest.com

- ■ **Independent Roman Catholic**, university, founded 1856
- ■ **Degrees** bachelor's, master's, doctoral, first professional, and postmaster's certificates
- ■ **Suburban** 58-acre campus with easy access to New York City
- ■ **Coed**, 4,801 undergraduate students, 90% full-time, 55% women, 45% men
- ■ **Moderately difficult** entrance level, 76% of applicants were admitted
- ■ **14:1 student-to-undergraduate faculty ratio**
- ■ **60% graduate** in 6 years or less
- ■ **$17,360 tuition** and fees
- ■ **$11,608 average financial aid** package, $15,824 average indebtedness upon graduation, $129.4 million endowment

Distinctive among colleges and universities is Seton Hall's Mobile Computing Program offered to freshmen. The hallmark of the computing program transforms the classroom by incorporating information technology into the curriculum. The University realizes the impact of technology on the future and has created a multifaceted educational program using IBM ThinkPads. All freshmen receive these laptops and use them for research, writing, and communicating around the world. Seton Hall's mobile computing program helps students acquire essential computing skills and gain access to networked learning sources. By working closely with faculty members, students are prepared to work in the 21st century.

Students *Undergraduates:* 4,322 full-time, 479 part-time. Students come from 45 states and territories, 43 other countries. *The most frequently chosen baccalaureate fields are:* business/marketing, communications/communication technologies, protective services/public administration. *Graduate:* 1,220 in professional programs, 3,411 in other graduate degree programs.

From out-of-state	18%	Reside on campus	40%
Age 25 or older	9%	Transferred in	5%
International students	2%	African Americans	12%
Asian Americans/Pacific Islanders	6%	Hispanic Americans	9%
Native Americans	0.1%		

Faculty 802 (47% full-time).

Expenses (1999–2000) *Comprehensive fee:* $24,856 includes full-time tuition ($15,480), mandatory fees ($1880), and room and board ($7496). *College room only:* $5290. Full-time tuition and fees vary according to course load and student level. Room and board charges vary according to board plan and housing facility. *Part-time tuition:* $516 per credit. *Part-time fees:* $185 per term part-time. Part-time tuition and fees vary according to course load and student level. *Payment plans:* installment, deferred payment. *Waivers:* senior citizens and employees or children of employees.

Library Walsh Library plus 1 other. *Operations spending 1999–2000:* $8.8 million. *Collection:* 385,000 titles, 2,271 serial subscriptions, 3,558 audiovisual materials.

College life *Housing: Option:* coed. *Social organizations:* national fraternities, national sororities, local fraternities, local sororities; 15% of eligible men and 12% of eligible women are members. *Most popular organizations:* Martin Luther King Jr. Scholars Association, Adelante/Caribe, Black Student Union, National Council of Negro Women.

Campus security 24-hour emergency response devices and patrols, late-night transport-escort service, controlled dormitory access.

After graduation 200 organizations recruited on campus 1997–98. 50% of class of 1998 had job offers within 6 months. *Career center:* 11 full-time, 4 part-time personnel. Services include job fairs, resume preparation, interview workshops, resume referral, career/interest testing, career counseling, careers library, job bank, job interviews. *Graduate education:* 20% of class of 1999 went directly to graduate and professional school: 7% graduate arts and sciences, 7% law, 3% medicine, 2% business, 1% education.

Freshmen 4,941 applied, 3,767 admitted, 1,083 enrolled.

SAT verbal scores above 500	69%	SAT math scores above 500	68%
ACT above 18	93%	From top 10% of their h.s. class	15%
From top quarter	37%	From top half	67%
1998 freshmen returning in 1999	80%		

Application *Options:* eApply at www.CollegeQuest.com, Common Application, electronic application, deferred entrance. *Application fee:* $45. *Required:* high school transcript. *Required for some:* minimum 3.0 GPA; interview. *Recommended:* essay or personal statement; minimum 3.0 GPA; letters of recommendation; interview.

Standardized tests *Admission: Required:* SAT I or ACT.

Significant dates *Application deadlines:* 3/1 (freshmen), 6/1 (transfers). *Financial aid deadline:* continuous.

Freshman Application Contact
Ms. Alyssa McCloud, Acting Director of Admissions, Seton Hall University, Enrollment Services, Bayley Hall, South Orange, NJ 07079-2697. **Phone:** 973-275-2576. **Toll-free phone:** 800-THE HALL. **Fax:** 973-761-9452. **E-mail:** thehall@shu.edu

Visit CollegeQuest.com for information on majors offered and athletics. College video available at CollegeQuest.com.

■ *See page 2470 for a narrative description.*

STEVENS INSTITUTE OF TECHNOLOGY
Hoboken, New Jersey

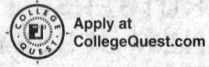
Apply at CollegeQuest.com

- ■ **Independent**, university, founded 1870
- ■ **Degrees** bachelor's, master's, doctoral, and postbachelor's certificates
- ■ **Urban** 55-acre campus with easy access to New York City
- ■ **Coed**, 1,560 undergraduate students, 99% full-time, 23% women, 78% men
- ■ **Very difficult** entrance level, 59% of applicants were admitted
- ■ **9:1 student-to-undergraduate faculty ratio**
- ■ **$21,140 tuition** and fees
- ■ **$19,815 average financial aid** package, $12,900 average indebtedness upon graduation, $180.5 million endowment

Stevens ranks in the top 5% of the nation's technological universities. The rigorous curricula in business, engineering, the sciences, computer science, and humanities fosters critical analysis and creativity, as well as hands-on research and development with faculty members. It also enables Stevens graduates to meet their goals and succeed in an increasingly technological environment.

Students *Undergraduates:* 1,540 full-time, 20 part-time. Students come from 34 states and territories, 50 other countries. *The most frequently chosen baccalaureate fields are:* computer/information sciences, biological/life sciences, engineering/engineering technologies. *Graduate:* 1,903 in graduate degree programs.

New Jersey

From out-of-state	30%	Reside on campus	80%
Age 25 or older	4%	Transferred in	4%
International students	8%	African Americans	5%
Asian Americans/Pacific Islanders	22%	Hispanic Americans	12%
Native Americans	0.3%		

Faculty 212 (48% full-time), 100% with terminal degrees.

Expenses (1999–2000) *Comprehensive fee:* $28,420 includes full-time tuition ($20,890), mandatory fees ($250), and room and board ($7280). Room and board charges vary according to board plan and housing facility. *Payment plan:* installment. *Waivers:* employees or children of employees.

Library S. C. Williams Library. *Operations spending 1999–2000:* $1.9 million. *Collection:* 57,671 titles, 145 serial subscriptions.

College life *Housing: Options:* coed, men-only, women-only. *Social organizations:* national fraternities, national sororities, local sororities; 30% of eligible men and 33% of eligible women are members. *Most popular organizations:* drama society, Student Council including Ethnic Student Council, foreign student clubs, Interdormitory Council, student newspaper.

Campus security 24-hour emergency response devices and patrols, late-night transport-escort service, controlled dormitory access.

After graduation 350 organizations recruited on campus 1997–98. 90% of class of 1998 had job offers within 6 months. *Career center:* 4 full-time, 1 part-time personnel. Services include job fairs, resume preparation, interview workshops, resume referral, career/interest testing, career counseling, careers library, job bank, job interviews. *Graduate education:* 21% of class of 1999 went directly to graduate and professional school.

Freshmen 1,894 applied, 1,123 admitted, 372 enrolled.

Average high school GPA	3.7	SAT verbal scores above 500	87%
SAT math scores above 500	98%	ACT above 18	N/R
From top 10% of their h.s. class	53%	From top quarter	84%
From top half	99%	1998 freshmen returning in 1999	87%

Application *Options:* eApply at www.CollegeQuest.com, Common Application, electronic application, early admission, early decision, deferred entrance. *Application fee:* $45. *Required:* high school transcript; interview. *Recommended:* essay or personal statement; letters of recommendation.

Standardized tests *Admission: Required:* SAT I or ACT. *Recommended:* SAT II Subject Tests, SAT II: Writing Test. *Required for some:* SAT I and SAT II or ACT, SAT II Subject Tests, SAT II: Writing Test.

Significant dates *Application deadlines:* 3/1 (freshmen), 7/1 (transfers). *Early decision:* 11/15. *Notification:* continuous until 5/1 (freshmen), 12/15 (early decision). *Financial aid deadline priority date:* 2/15.

Freshman Application Contact Mr. Daniel Gallagher, Director of Undergraduate Admissions, Stevens Institute of Technology, Castle Point on Hudson, Hoboken, NJ 07030. **Phone:** 201-216-5197. **Toll-free phone:** 800-458-5323. **Fax:** 201-216-8348. **E-mail:** admissions@stevens-tech.edu

Visit CollegeQuest.com for information on majors offered and athletics. Electronic viewbook available at CollegeQuest.com.

■ *See page 2576 for a narrative description.*

TALMUDICAL ACADEMY OF NEW JERSEY
Adelphia, New Jersey

Admissions Office Contact Talmudical Academy of New Jersey, Route 524, Adelphia, NJ 07710.

THOMAS EDISON STATE COLLEGE
Trenton, New Jersey

■ **$407,361 endowment**

Students *Undergraduates:* Students come from 52 states and territories, 86 other countries. *The most frequently chosen baccalaureate fields are:* business/marketing, physical sciences, social sciences and history. *Graduate:* 124 in graduate degree programs.

From out-of-state	32%	Age 25 or older	97%
International students	5%	African Americans	9%
Asian Americans/Pacific Islanders	2%	Hispanic Americans	4%
Native Americans	1%		

Faculty 516.

Expenses (2000–2001) Tuition and fees vary depending on type of credit attempted. Fees are charged for transfer credit, Guided Study program, Portfolio/Practicum assessment, and the college's own examination program. *Payment plan:* installment. *Waivers:* senior citizens and employees or children of employees.

College life *Housing:* college housing not available.

Campus security Guard from 7 a.m. to 11 p.m., local police patrol.

Freshmen

SAT verbal scores above 500	N/R	SAT math scores above 500	N/R
ACT above 18	N/R		

Application *Option:* electronic application. *Application fee:* $75. *Required:* age 21 or over and a high school graduate.

Significant dates *Application deadline:* rolling (transfers).

Freshman Application Contact Mr. Gordon Holly, Director of Admissions Services, Thomas Edison State College, 101 West State Street, Trenton, NJ 08608-1176. **Phone:** 609-984-1150. **Toll-free phone:** 888-442-8372. **Fax:** 609-292-9000. **E-mail:** admissions@call.tesc.edu

Visit CollegeQuest.com for information on majors offered and athletics.

■ *See page 2616 for a narrative description.*

UNIVERSITY OF MEDICINE AND DENTISTRY OF NEW JERSEY
Newark, New Jersey

Admissions Office Contact University of Medicine and Dentistry of New Jersey, 65 Bergen Street, Newark, NJ 07107-3001.

WESTMINSTER CHOIR COLLEGE OF RIDER UNIVERSITY
Princeton, New Jersey

■ **Independent**, comprehensive, founded 1926
■ **Degrees** bachelor's and master's
■ **Small-town** 23-acre campus with easy access to New York City and Philadelphia
■ **Coed**, 275 undergraduate students
■ **Moderately difficult** entrance level, 74% of applicants were admitted
■ **$16,760 tuition** and fees

Students *Undergraduates:* Students come from 38 states and territories, 12 other countries. *The most frequently chosen baccalaureate field is:* visual/performing arts.

From out-of-state	70%	Reside on campus	58%

Expenses (1999–2000) *Comprehensive fee:* $23,840 includes full-time tuition ($16,520), mandatory fees ($240), and room and board ($7080). *College room only:* $3220. *Part-time tuition:* $550 per credit. *Part-time fees:* $120 per term part-time. *Payment plan:* installment. *Waivers:* employees or children of employees.

Library Talbott Library-Learning Center. *Collection:* 55,000 titles, 160 serial subscriptions.

College life *Housing:* on-campus residence required through junior year. *Option:* coed. *Most popular organizations:* Westminster Choir, Westminster Singers, Black and Hispanic Alliance, Westminster Handbell Choir, Student Activities Committee.

Campus security 24-hour emergency response devices, late-night transport-escort service, security guards from 4 p.m. to 7 a.m.

After graduation *Career center:* 2 full-time personnel. Services include resume preparation, career counseling, job bank, job interviews.

Freshmen 161 applied, 119 admitted. 1 class president, 10 student government officers.

Average high school GPA	3.0	SAT verbal scores above 500	75%
SAT math scores above 500	58%	ACT above 18	N/R
1998 freshmen returning in 1999	84%		

New Jersey–New Mexico

Westminster Choir College of Rider University *(continued)*

Application *Options:* early admission, early decision, deferred entrance. *Application fee:* $40. *Required:* essay or personal statement; high school transcript; 2 letters of recommendation; audition, music examination. *Recommended:* minimum 2.5 GPA; interview.

Standardized tests *Admission: Required:* SAT I or ACT.

Significant dates *Application deadlines:* rolling (freshmen), rolling (transfers). *Early decision:* 11/1. *Notification:* 12/15 (early decision). *Financial aid deadline priority date:* 3/1.

Freshman Application Contact
Ms. Monica Thomas Tritto, Assistant Director of Admissions, Westminster Choir College of Rider University, 101 Walnut Lane, Princeton, NJ 08540-3899. **Phone:** 609-921-7144 Ext. 103. **Toll-free phone:** 800-96-CHOIR. **Fax:** 609-921-2538. **E-mail:** wccadmission@rider.edu

Visit CollegeQuest.com for information on majors offered and athletics.

■ *See page 2960 for a narrative description.*

WILLIAM PATERSON UNIVERSITY OF NEW JERSEY
Wayne, New Jersey

- **State-supported**, comprehensive, founded 1855
- **Degrees** bachelor's and master's
- **Suburban** 300-acre campus with easy access to New York City
- **Coed**, 7,940 undergraduate students, 76% full-time, 58% women, 42% men
- **Moderately difficult** entrance level, 50% of applicants were admitted
- **41.5% graduate** in 6 years or less
- **$4690 tuition** and fees (in-state); $7360 (out-of-state)
- **$6675 average financial aid** package, $11,728 average indebtedness upon graduation, $3.1 million endowment

Committed to student success, William Paterson University seeks ambitious students who are up to its challenge. Small classes and a distinguished faculty; 29 majors; preprofessional programs in dentistry, engineering, medicine, law, and communication disorders; and seven distinctive honors programs provide a rewarding educational experience that far exceeds its cost.

Part of New Jersey State College System.

Students *Undergraduates:* 6,066 full-time, 1,874 part-time. Students come from 13 states and territories, 20 other countries. *Graduate:* 1,313 in graduate degree programs.

Reside on campus	30%	Age 25 or older	26%
Transferred in	11%		

Faculty 335 (93% full-time).

Expenses (1999–2000) *Tuition, state resident:* full-time $4690; part-time $106 per credit. *Tuition, nonresident:* full-time $7360; part-time $238 per credit. *Required fees:* $44 per credit. *College room and board:* $5650; room only: $3700. Room and board charges vary according to board plan and housing facility. *Payment plan:* installment.

Library Sarah Byrd Askew Library. *Operations spending 1999–2000:* $3.3 million. *Collection:* 320,000 titles, 1,400 serial subscriptions.

College life *Housing: Option:* coed. *Social organizations:* national fraternities, national sororities, local fraternities, local sororities. *Most popular organizations:* Greek Senate, Caribbean Student Association, Organization of Latin American Students (OLAS), Sisters of Awareness, Student Activities Committee.

Campus security 24-hour emergency response devices and patrols, controlled dormitory access.

After graduation *Career center:* 7 full-time personnel. Services include job fairs, resume preparation, resume referral, career counseling, careers library, job bank, job interviews. *Graduate education:* 7% of class of 1999 went directly to graduate and professional school.

Freshmen 5,240 applied, 2,606 admitted, 1,261 enrolled.

SAT verbal scores above 500	N/R	SAT math scores above 500	N/R
ACT above 18	N/R	From top quarter of their h.s. class	36%
From top half	72%	1998 freshmen returning in 1999	81%

Application *Options:* Common Application, electronic application, early admission, deferred entrance. *Application fee:* $35. *Required:* essay or personal statement; high school transcript. *Required for some:* letters of recommendation; interview. *Recommended:* minimum 2.5 GPA.

Standardized tests *Admission: Required:* SAT I or ACT.

Significant dates *Application deadlines:* 5/1 (freshmen), 6/1 (transfers). *Notification:* continuous until 8/1 (freshmen). *Financial aid deadline priority date:* 4/1.

Freshman Application Contact
Mr. Leo DeBartolo, Director of Admissions, William Paterson University of New Jersey, 300 Pompton Road, Wayne, NJ 07470. **Phone:** 973-720-2906. **Fax:** 973-720-2910. **E-mail:** christensen_@wpc.wilpaterson.edu

Visit CollegeQuest.com for information on majors offered and athletics. College video available at CollegeQuest.com.

■ *See page 3000 for a narrative description.*

NEW MEXICO

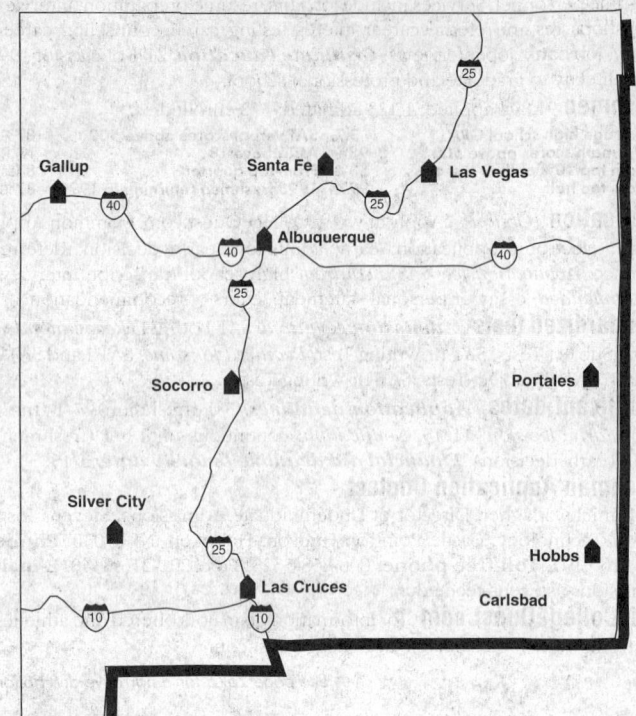

COLLEGE OF SANTA FE
Santa Fe, New Mexico

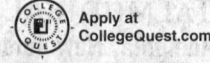
Apply at CollegeQuest.com

- **Independent**, comprehensive, founded 1947
- **Degrees** associate, bachelor's, and master's
- **Suburban** 100-acre campus with easy access to Albuquerque
- **Coed**, 1,180 undergraduate students, 54% full-time, 61% women, 39% men
- **Moderately difficult** entrance level, 84% of applicants were admitted
- **13:1 student-to-undergraduate faculty ratio**
- **33% graduate** in 6 years or less
- **$16,110 tuition** and fees
- **$12,000 average financial aid** package, $4.9 million endowment

Students *Undergraduates:* 641 full-time, 539 part-time. Students come from 44 states and territories, 6 other countries. *The most frequently chosen baccalaureate fields are:* business/marketing, education, visual/performing arts. *Graduate:* 221 in graduate degree programs.

From out-of-state	60%	Reside on campus	53%
Age 25 or older	19%	Transferred in	5%

Faculty 280 (26% full-time), 35% with terminal degrees.

Expenses (2000–2001) *One-time required fee:* $10. *Comprehensive fee:* $21,182 includes full-time tuition ($15,750), mandatory fees ($360), and room and board ($5072). *College room only:* $2424. Full-time tuition and fees vary according to program. Room and board charges vary according to board plan and housing facility. *Part-time tuition:* $524 per semester hour. *Part-time fees:* $5 per semester hour. Part-time tuition and fees vary according to program. *Payment plan:* installment. *Waivers:* senior citizens and employees or children of employees.
Library Fogelson Library Center. *Operations spending 1999–2000:* $381,763. *Collection:* 240,956 titles, 500 serial subscriptions, 11,935 audiovisual materials.
College life *Housing:* on-campus residence required in freshman year. *Options:* coed, men-only, women-only. *Most popular organizations:* Model UN Group, Renaissance club, Moving Image Student Council, social science club, Student Management Association.
Campus security 24-hour patrols, late-night transport-escort service.
After graduation 60% of class of 1998 had job offers within 6 months. *Career center:* 1 full-time personnel. Services include job fairs, resume preparation, interview workshops, resume referral, career/interest testing, career counseling, careers library, job bank, job interviews. *Graduate education:* 21% of class of 1999 went directly to graduate and professional school.
Freshmen 491 applied, 411 admitted, 486 enrolled.

Average high school GPA	3.08	SAT verbal scores above 500	83%
SAT math scores above 500	68%	ACT above 18	95%
From top 10% of their h.s. class	11%	From top quarter	37%
From top half	67%	1998 freshmen returning in 1999	68%

Application *Options:* eApply at www.CollegeQuest.com, Common Application, electronic application, early admission, early decision, deferred entrance. *Application fee:* $25. *Required:* essay or personal statement; high school transcript; 2 letters of recommendation; interview; portfolio or audition for visual and performing arts programs. *Recommended:* minimum 3.0 GPA.
Standardized tests *Admission: Required:* SAT I or ACT.
Significant dates *Application deadlines:* rolling (freshmen), rolling (transfers). *Early decision:* 11/15. *Notification:* 12/15 (early decision). *Financial aid deadline priority date:* 3/1.
Freshman Application Contact
Mr. Dale H. Reinhart, Director of Admissions and Enrollment Management, College of Santa Fe, Admissions Office, 1600 St. Michael's Drive, Santa Fe, NM 87505-7634. **Phone:** 505-473-6133. **Toll-free phone:** 800-456-2673. **Fax:** 505-473-6127 Ext. 6133. **E-mail:** admissions@csf.edu
Visit CollegeQuest.com for information on majors offered and athletics. College video available at CollegeQuest.com.

■ *See page 1484 for a narrative description.*

COLLEGE OF THE SOUTHWEST
Hobbs, New Mexico

- **Independent**, comprehensive, founded 1962
- **Degrees** bachelor's and master's
- **Small-town** 162-acre campus
- **Coed**, 515 undergraduate students, 66% full-time, 73% women, 27% men
- **Moderately difficult** entrance level, 71% of applicants were admitted
- **11:1** student-to-undergraduate faculty ratio
- **$4640 tuition** and fees
- **$6415 average financial aid** package, $11,687 average indebtedness upon graduation, $497,253 endowment

Students *Undergraduates:* 338 full-time, 177 part-time. Students come from 10 states and territories, 2 other countries. *The most frequently chosen baccalaureate fields are:* education, English, psychology. *Graduate:* 120 in graduate degree programs.

From out-of-state	87%	Reside on campus	12%
Age 25 or older	62%	Transferred in	18%
International students	1%	African Americans	3%
Asian Americans/Pacific Islanders	0.4%	Hispanic Americans	20%
Native Americans	1%		

Faculty 73 (27% full-time), 12% with terminal degrees.
Expenses (1999–2000) *Comprehensive fee:* $8140 includes full-time tuition ($4500), mandatory fees ($140), and room and board ($3500). *College room only:* $1575. Room and board charges vary according to housing facility. *Part-time tuition:* $150 per semester hour. *Part-time fees:* $70 per term part-time. *Payment plan:* deferred payment. *Waivers:* employees or children of employees.
Library Scarborough Memorial Library plus 1 other. *Operations spending 1999–2000:* $134,503. *Collection:* 59,500 titles, 300 serial subscriptions, 454 audiovisual materials.
College life *Housing:* on-campus residence required through sophomore year. *Option:* coed. *Most popular organizations:* student government, Students in Free Enterprise, Southwest Association of Teachers, Fellowship of Christian Athletes.
Campus security Student patrols, night security.
After graduation *Career center:* 1 full-time personnel. Services include job fairs, resume preparation, careers library, job bank, job interviews.
Freshmen 45 applied, 32 admitted, 33 enrolled.

Average high school GPA	3.26	SAT verbal scores above 500	N/R
SAT math scores above 500	N/R	ACT above 18	N/R
From top 10% of their h.s. class	3%	From top quarter	41%
From top half	76%	1998 freshmen returning in 1999	51%

Application *Options:* early admission, deferred entrance. *Application fee:* $25. *Required:* high school transcript; 2 letters of recommendation; medical history.
Standardized tests *Admission: Required:* SAT I or ACT.
Significant dates *Application deadlines:* rolling (freshmen), rolling (transfers). *Financial aid deadline priority date:* 4/1.
Freshman Application Contact
Mr. Buster Jamieson, Director of Student Services, College of the Southwest, 6610 Lovington Highway, Hobbs, NM 88240-9129. **Phone:** 505-392-6561. **Toll-free phone:** 800-530-4400 Ext. 347.
Visit CollegeQuest.com for information on majors offered and athletics.

■ *See page 1490 for a narrative description.*

EASTERN NEW MEXICO UNIVERSITY
Portales, New Mexico

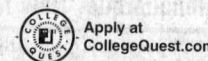
Apply at CollegeQuest.com

- **State-supported**, comprehensive, founded 1934
- **Degrees** associate, bachelor's, and master's
- **Rural** 240-acre campus
- **Coed**, 2,980 undergraduate students, 83% full-time, 59% women, 41% men
- **Minimally difficult** entrance level, 60% of applicants were admitted
- **17:1** student-to-undergraduate faculty ratio
- **26% graduate** in 6 years or less
- **$1830 tuition** and fees (in-state); $6714 (out-of-state)
- **$5861 average financial aid** package, $16,511 average indebtedness upon graduation, $5.9 million endowment

Part of Eastern New Mexico University System.
Students *Undergraduates:* 2,480 full-time, 500 part-time. Students come from 48 states and territories, 8 other countries. *The most frequently chosen baccalaureate fields are:* education, business/marketing, social sciences and history. *Graduate:* 550 in graduate degree programs.

From out-of-state	18%	Reside on campus	23%
Age 25 or older	29%	Transferred in	11%
International students	1%	African Americans	3%
Asian Americans/Pacific Islanders	1%	Hispanic Americans	26%
Native Americans	3%		

Faculty 252 (54% full-time), 49% with terminal degrees.
Expenses (1999–2000) *Tuition, state resident:* full-time $1272; part-time $53 per credit hour. *Tuition, nonresident:* full-time $6156; part-time $256 per credit hour. *Required fees:* full-time $558; $23 per credit hour. *College room and board:* $3690; room only: $1890. Room and board charges vary according to board plan. *Payment plan:* installment. *Waivers:* employees or children of employees.
Library Golden Library. *Operations spending 1999–2000:* $1.2 million. *Collection:* 496,992 titles, 1,703 serial subscriptions, 7,550 audiovisual materials.

New Mexico

Eastern New Mexico University (continued)

College life *Housing: Options:* coed, women-only. *Social organizations:* national fraternities, national sororities. *Most popular organizations:* Student Government Association, Student Activities Board, Residence Hall Association, IFC, Panhellenic Council.

Campus security 24-hour emergency response devices and patrols, late-night transport-escort service, controlled dormitory access.

After graduation 104 organizations recruited on campus 1997–98. *Career center:* 2 full-time, 8 part-time personnel. Services include job fairs, resume preparation, resume referral, career counseling, careers library, job bank, job interviews.

Freshmen 1,648 applied, 985 admitted, 493 enrolled.

Average high school GPA	3.08	SAT verbal scores above 500	42%
SAT math scores above 500	44%	ACT above 18	66%
1998 freshmen returning in 1999	62%		

Application *Options:* eApply at www.CollegeQuest.com, Common Application, electronic application, early admission, deferred entrance. *Application fee:* $0. *Required:* high school transcript; minimum 2.0 GPA.

Standardized tests *Admission: Required:* SAT I or ACT.

Significant dates *Application deadlines:* rolling (freshmen), rolling (transfers). *Financial aid deadline priority date:* 3/1.

Freshman Application Contact
Dr. Karyl C. Lyne, Assistant Vice President for Student Affairs, Eastern New Mexico University, Station #7 ENMU, Portales, NM 88130. **Phone:** 505-562-2178. **Toll-free phone:** 800-367-3668. **Fax:** 505-562-2118. **E-mail:** karyl.lyne@enmu.edu

Visit CollegeQuest.com for information on majors offered and athletics. College video and electronic viewbook available at CollegeQuest.com.

■ *See page 1608 for a narrative description.*

ITT TECHNICAL INSTITUTE
Albuquerque, New Mexico

- **Proprietary**, primarily 2-year, founded 1989
- **Degrees** associate and bachelor's
- **Minimally difficult** entrance level
- **$9190 tuition** and fees

Part of ITT Educational Services, Inc.

Admissions Office Contact
ITT Technical Institute, 5100 Masthead, NE, Albuquerque, NM 87109-4366. **Toll-free phone:** 800-636-1114. **Fax:** 505-828-1849.

Visit CollegeQuest.com for information on majors offered and athletics. College video available at CollegeQuest.com.

METROPOLITAN COLLEGE OF COURT REPORTING
Albuquerque, New Mexico

Admissions Office Contact
Metropolitan College of Court Reporting, 1717 Louisiana Boulevard NE, Suite 207, Albuquerque, NM 87110-7027. **Fax:** 505-254-3738.

NATIONAL AMERICAN UNIVERSITY
Albuquerque, New Mexico

Apply at CollegeQuest.com

- **Proprietary**, 4-year, founded 1941
- **Degrees** associate and bachelor's
- **Suburban** campus
- **Coed**
- **Noncompetitive** entrance level

Part of National College.

College life *Housing:* college housing not available.

Campus security 24-hour patrols, late-night transport-escort service.

Application *Option:* eApply at www.CollegeQuest.com. *Required:* high school transcript.

Admissions Office Contact
National American University, 1202 Pennsylvania Avenue, NE, Albuquerque, NM 87110. **Toll-free phone:** 800-843-8892. **Fax:** 505-265-7542.

Visit CollegeQuest.com for information on athletics.

NAZARENE INDIAN BIBLE COLLEGE
Albuquerque, New Mexico

- **Independent**, 4-year, founded 1976, affiliated with Church of the Nazarene
- **Degrees** associate and bachelor's
- **Suburban** campus
- **Coed**, 37 undergraduate students, 84% full-time, 46% women, 54% men
- **Moderately difficult** entrance level, 80% of applicants were admitted
- **$4020 tuition** and fees

Students *Undergraduates:* 31 full-time, 6 part-time.

Transferred in	19%	Hispanic Americans	8%
Native Americans	68%		

Faculty 12 (42% full-time).

Expenses (1999–2000) *Comprehensive fee:* $5595 includes full-time tuition ($3960), mandatory fees ($60), and room and board ($1575). *Waivers:* employees or children of employees.

Library Nazarene Indian Bible College Library. *Collection:* 25,348 titles, 45 serial subscriptions, 180 audiovisual materials.

College life *Housing: Options:* men-only, women-only.

Freshmen 25 applied, 20 admitted, 8 enrolled.

SAT verbal scores above 500	N/R	SAT math scores above 500	N/R
ACT above 18	N/R	1998 freshmen returning in 1999	60%

Application *Option:* Common Application. *Required:* essay or personal statement; high school transcript. *Recommended:* letters of recommendation.

Significant dates *Application deadlines:* rolling (freshmen), rolling (transfers). *Financial aid deadline:* continuous.

Freshman Application Contact
Ms. Yolanda Vielle, Registrar, Nazarene Indian Bible College, 2315 Markham Road, SW, Albuquerque, NM 87105. **Phone:** 505-877-0240 Ext. 107. **Toll-free phone:** 888-877-NIBC.

Visit CollegeQuest.com for information on majors offered and athletics.

NEW MEXICO HIGHLANDS UNIVERSITY
Las Vegas, New Mexico

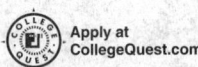
Apply at CollegeQuest.com

- **State-supported**, comprehensive, founded 1893
- **Degrees** associate, bachelor's, and master's
- **Small-town** 120-acre campus
- **Coed**, 1,945 undergraduate students, 79% full-time, 58% women, 42% men
- **Minimally difficult** entrance level, 84% of applicants were admitted
- **21% graduate** in 6 years or less
- **$1866 tuition** and fees (in-state); $7578 (out-of-state)

Students *Undergraduates:* Students come from 40 states and territories, 10 other countries. *The most frequently chosen baccalaureate fields are:* business/marketing, education, protective services/public administration.

From out-of-state	11%	Age 25 or older	26%
International students	1%	African Americans	3%
Asian Americans/Pacific Islanders	2%	Hispanic Americans	63%
Native Americans	8%		

Faculty 169 (64% full-time).

Expenses (1999–2000) *One-time required fee:* $5. *Tuition, state resident:* full-time $1866; part-time $78 per semester hour. *Tuition, nonresident:* full-time $7578; part-time $316 per semester hour. Full-time tuition and fees vary according to degree level. Part-time tuition and fees vary according to course load and degree level. *College room and board:* $2730. Room and board charges vary according to board plan and housing facility. *Payment plan:* deferred payment. *Waivers:* senior citizens and employees or children of employees.

Library Donnelly Library. *Collection:* 561,500 titles, 47,100 serial subscriptions.

College life *Housing: Options:* coed, women-only.

Campus security 24-hour emergency response devices and patrols, late-night transport-escort service, controlled dormitory access.

After graduation 100 organizations recruited on campus 1997–98. *Career center:* 5 full-time personnel. Services include job fairs, resume preparation, career counseling, careers library, job interviews.

Freshmen 1,141 applied, 956 admitted.

Average high school GPA	2.95	SAT verbal scores above 500	N/R
SAT math scores above 500	N/R	ACT above 18	60%
From top 10% of their h.s. class	14%	From top quarter	33%
From top half	65%	1998 freshmen returning in 1999	56%

Application *Options:* eApply at www.CollegeQuest.com, Common Application, electronic application, early admission, deferred entrance. *Application fee:* $15. *Required:* high school transcript; minimum 2.0 GPA. *Required for some:* 2 letters of recommendation; interview.

Standardized tests *Placement: Required:* ACT

Significant dates *Application deadlines:* rolling (freshmen), rolling (transfers). *Financial aid deadline priority date:* 3/1.

Freshman Application Contact
Ms. Lou Ann Romero, Director of Student Recruitment, New Mexico Highlands University, , Box 9000, Las Vegas, NM 87701. **Phone:** 505-454-3256. **Toll-free phone:** 800-338-6648. **Fax:** 505-454-3311. **E-mail:** admission@venus.nmnu.edu

Visit CollegeQuest.com for information on majors offered and athletics. College video available at CollegeQuest.com.

NEW MEXICO INSTITUTE OF MINING AND TECHNOLOGY
Socorro, New Mexico

- **State-supported**, university, founded 1889
- **Degrees** associate, bachelor's, master's, and doctoral
- **Small-town** 320-acre campus with easy access to Albuquerque
- **Coed**, 1,047 undergraduate students, 95% full-time, 32% women, 68% men
- **Moderately difficult** entrance level, 70% of applicants were admitted
- **11:1 student-to-undergraduate faculty ratio**
- **37% graduate** in 6 years or less
- **$2328 tuition** and fees (in-state); $7328 (out-of-state)
- **$7979 average financial aid** package, $14,500 average indebtedness upon graduation, $16.9 million endowment

Students *Undergraduates:* 990 full-time, 57 part-time. Students come from 52 states and territories, 14 other countries. *The most frequently chosen baccalaureate fields are:* engineering/engineering technologies, biological/life sciences, physical sciences. *Graduate:* 295 in graduate degree programs.

From out-of-state	36%	Reside on campus	49%
Age 25 or older	32%	Transferred in	5%
International students	2%	African Americans	1%
Asian Americans/Pacific Islanders	3%	Hispanic Americans	18%
Native Americans	4%		

Faculty 99 (100% full-time), 100% with terminal degrees.

Expenses (1999–2000) *One-time required fee:* $16. *Tuition, state resident:* full-time $1600; part-time $67 per credit hour. *Tuition, nonresident:* full-time $6600; part-time $275 per credit hour. *Required fees:* full-time $728; $22 per credit hour; $27 per term part-time. Part-time tuition and fees vary according to course load. *College room and board:* $3584. Room and board charges vary according to board plan and housing facility. *Payment plan:* deferred payment. *Waivers:* senior citizens and employees or children of employees.

Library New Mexico Tech Library plus 1 other. *Operations spending 1999–2000:* $875,373. *Collection:* 89,725 titles, 766 serial subscriptions, 2,065 audiovisual materials.

College life *Housing: Options:* coed, men-only, women-only. *Most popular organizations:* Search and Rescue, Society for Creative Anachronism, Amateur Astronomers, ski club.

Campus security 24-hour emergency response devices and patrols, late-night transport-escort service.

After graduation 22 organizations recruited on campus 1997–98. *Career center:* 1 full-time, 1 part-time personnel. Services include job fairs, resume preparation, interview workshops, resume referral, career/interest testing, career counseling, careers library, job bank, job interviews. *Graduate education:* 26% of class of 1999 went directly to graduate and professional school: 14% graduate arts and sciences, 9% engineering, 2% education, 1% law.

Freshmen 1,168 applied, 817 admitted, 249 enrolled.

Average high school GPA	3.5	SAT verbal scores above 500	N/R
SAT math scores above 500	N/R	ACT above 18	100%
From top 10% of their h.s. class	31%	From top quarter	65%
From top half	90%	1998 freshmen returning in 1999	67%

Application *Options:* eApply at www.CollegeQuest.com, electronic application, deferred entrance. *Application fee:* $15. *Required:* high school transcript; minimum 2.0 GPA. *Required for some:* 2 letters of recommendation. *Recommended:* interview.

Standardized tests *Admission: Required:* SAT I or ACT. *Recommended:* SAT II Subject Tests.

Significant dates *Application deadlines:* 8/1 (freshmen), 8/1 (transfers). *Financial aid deadline priority date:* 3/1.

Freshman Application Contact
Ms. Melissa Jaramillo-Fleming, Director of Admissions, New Mexico Institute of Mining and Technology, 801 Leroy Place, Socorro, NM 87801. **Phone:** 505-835-5424. **Toll-free phone:** 800-428-TECH. **Fax:** 505-835-5989. **E-mail:** admission@admin.nmt.edu

Visit CollegeQuest.com for information on majors offered and athletics. Electronic viewbook available at CollegeQuest.com.

■ *See page 2156 for a narrative description.*

NEW MEXICO STATE UNIVERSITY
Las Cruces, New Mexico

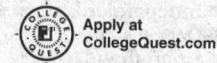

- **State-supported**, university, founded 1888
- **Degrees** associate, bachelor's, master's, doctoral, and post-master's certificates
- **Suburban** 900-acre campus with easy access to El Paso
- **Coed**, 11,783 undergraduate students, 83% full-time, 53% women, 47% men
- **Moderately difficult** entrance level, 68% of applicants were admitted
- **41.49% graduate** in 6 years or less
- **$2502 tuition** and fees (in-state); $8166 (out-of-state)
- **$43.7 million endowment**

Part of New Mexico State University System.

Students *Undergraduates:* 9,729 full-time, 2,054 part-time. Students come from 51 states and territories, 49 other countries. *The most frequently chosen baccalaureate fields are:* business/marketing, education, engineering/engineering technologies. *Graduate:* 2,618 in graduate degree programs.

From out-of-state	20%	Reside on campus	25%
Age 25 or older	19%	Transferred in	6%
International students	1%	African Americans	3%
Asian Americans/Pacific Islanders	2%	Hispanic Americans	41%
Native Americans	3%		

Faculty 630 (96% full-time), 83% with terminal degrees.

Expenses (1999–2000) *Tuition, state resident:* full-time $2502; part-time $104 per credit. *Tuition, nonresident:* full-time $8166; part-time $340 per credit. *Required fees:* $16 per term part-time. *College room and board:* $3726; room only: $1976. Room and board charges vary according to board plan and housing facility. *Payment plans:* installment, deferred payment. *Waivers:* senior citizens and employees or children of employees.

Library New Library plus 1 other. *Operations spending 1999–2000:* $6.4 million. *Collection:* 11,784 serial subscriptions, 320 audiovisual materials.

New Mexico

New Mexico State University (continued)

College life Housing: Options: coed, men-only, women-only, disabled students. Social organizations: national fraternities, national sororities; 8% of eligible men and 5% of eligible women are members.
Campus security 24-hour emergency response devices and patrols, late-night transport-escort service, controlled dormitory access.
After graduation 345 organizations recruited on campus 1997–98. Career center: 13 full-time, 1 part-time personnel. Services include job fairs, resume preparation, resume referral, career counseling, careers library, job bank, job interviews.
Freshmen 6,624 applied, 4,483 admitted, 2,266 enrolled. 1 class president, 1 valedictorian.

Average high school GPA	3.3	SAT verbal scores above 500	N/R
SAT math scores above 500	N/R	ACT above 18	80%
From top 10% of their h.s. class	20%	From top quarter	48%
From top half	79%	1998 freshmen returning in 1999	72%

Application Options: eApply at www.CollegeQuest.com, electronic application, early admission, deferred entrance. Application fee: $15. Required: high school transcript; minimum 2.0 GPA.
Standardized tests Admission: Required: SAT I or ACT.
Significant dates Application deadlines: 8/14 (freshmen), 8/14 (transfers). Financial aid deadline: continuous.
Freshman Application Contact
Ms. Angela Mora-Riley, Director of Admissions, New Mexico State University, Box 30001, MSC, Las Cruces, NM 88003-8001. **Phone:** 505-646-3121. **Toll-free phone:** 800-662-6678. **Fax:** 505-646-6330. **E-mail:** admssions@nmsu.edu
Visit CollegeQuest.com for information on majors offered and athletics. College video and electronic viewbook available at CollegeQuest.com.

■ See page 2158 for a narrative description.

ST. JOHN'S COLLEGE
Santa Fe, New Mexico

Apply at CollegeQuest.com

- **Independent**, comprehensive, founded 1964
- **Degrees** bachelor's and master's
- **Small-town** 250-acre campus
- **Coed**, 431 undergraduate students, 99% full-time, 43% women, 57% men
- **Moderately difficult** entrance level, 84% of applicants were admitted
- **8:1 student-to-undergraduate faculty ratio**
- **56% graduate** in 6 years or less
- **$22,200 tuition** and fees
- **$20,220 average financial aid** package, $17,125 average indebtedness upon graduation, $20.3 million endowment

Students Undergraduates: 425 full-time, 6 part-time. Students come from 48 states and territories, 1 other country. The most frequently chosen baccalaureate field is: liberal arts/general studies. Graduate: 26 in professional programs, 99 in other graduate degree programs.

From out-of-state	89%	Reside on campus	71%
Age 25 or older	6%	Transferred in	9%
International students	0.2%	African Americans	0.2%
Asian Americans/Pacific Islanders	2%	Hispanic Americans	7%
Native Americans	2%		

Faculty 59 (92% full-time), 76% with terminal degrees.
Expenses (1999–2000) Comprehensive fee: $28,586 includes full-time tuition ($22,000), mandatory fees ($200), and room and board ($6386). Room and board charges vary according to board plan. Payment plans: tuition prepayment, installment. Waivers: employees or children of employees.
Library Meem Library. Operations spending 1999–2000: $213,990. Collection: 40,103 titles, 135 serial subscriptions.
College life Housing: on-campus residence required through junior year. Options: coed, men-only, disabled students. Most popular organizations: student government, film society, Search and Rescue Team, student newspaper, theatre group.
Campus security 24-hour emergency response devices and patrols, student patrols, late-night transport-escort service.
After graduation 20 organizations recruited on campus 1997–98. Career center: 1 full-time, 1 part-time personnel. Services include job fairs, resume preparation, resume referral, career counseling, careers library, job bank, job interviews. **Graduate education:** 75% of class of 1999 went directly to graduate and professional school: 37% graduate arts and sciences, 10% law, 7% business, 7% theology, 6% medicine, 5% education, 3% engineering.
Freshmen 355 applied, 297 admitted, 109 enrolled. 1 National Merit Scholar, 4 class presidents, 4 valedictorians.

SAT verbal scores above 500	100%	SAT math scores above 500	93%
ACT above 18	100%	From top 10% of their h.s. class	29%
From top quarter	72%	From top half	90%
1998 freshmen returning in 1999	73%		

Application Options: eApply at www.CollegeQuest.com, Common Application, early admission, deferred entrance. Application fee: $0. Required: essay or personal statement; high school transcript; 3 letters of recommendation. Required for some: interview. Recommended: interview.
Standardized tests Admission: Required for some: SAT I or ACT.
Significant dates Application deadlines: rolling (freshmen), rolling (transfers). Financial aid deadline: 2/15. Priority date: 12/1.
Freshman Application Contact
Mr. Larry Clendenin, Director of Admissions, St. John's College, 1160 Camino Cruz Blanca, Santa Fe, NM 87501. **Phone:** 505-984-6060. **Toll-free phone:** 800-331-5232. **E-mail:** admissions@mail.sjcsf.edu
Visit CollegeQuest.com for information on majors offered and athletics.

UNIVERSITY OF NEW MEXICO
Albuquerque, New Mexico

- **State-supported**, university, founded 1889
- **Degrees** associate, bachelor's, master's, doctoral, first professional, and post-master's certificates
- **Urban** 625-acre campus
- **Coed**, 15,510 undergraduate students, 77% full-time, 58% women, 42% men
- **Moderately difficult** entrance level, 91% of applicants were admitted
- **37% graduate** in 6 years or less
- **$2430 tuition** and fees (in-state); $9170 (out-of-state)
- **$8074 average financial aid** package, $15,896 average indebtedness upon graduation, $319 million endowment

Students Undergraduates: 11,912 full-time, 3,598 part-time. Students come from 50 states and territories, 20 other countries. The most frequently chosen baccalaureate fields are: education, business/marketing, health professions and related sciences. Graduate: 927 in professional programs, 6,630 in other graduate degree programs.

From out-of-state	17%	Reside on campus	13%
Age 25 or older	31%	Transferred in	7%
International students	1%	African Americans	3%
Asian Americans/Pacific Islanders	3%	Hispanic Americans	31%
Native Americans	6%		

Faculty 2,164 (72% full-time).
Expenses (1999–2000) Tuition, state resident: full-time $2430; part-time $101 per credit hour. Tuition, nonresident: full-time $9170; part-time $101 per credit hour. Part-time tuition and fees vary according to course load. College room and board: $4800. Room and board charges vary according to board plan and housing facility. Payment plan: installment. Waivers: senior citizens and employees or children of employees.
Library Zimmerman Library plus 7 others. Operations spending 1999–2000: $17.7 million. Collection: 17,963 serial subscriptions, 1.6 million audio-visual materials.
College life Housing: Options: coed, women-only. Social organizations: national fraternities, national sororities; 7% of eligible men and 3% of eligible women are members. Most popular organizations: Golden Key National Honor Society, Associated Students of UNM, Graduate and Professional Students Association.
Campus security 24-hour emergency response devices and patrols, student patrols, late-night transport-escort service, controlled dormitory access.
After graduation 210 organizations recruited on campus 1997–98. Career center: 14 full-time, 13 part-time personnel. Services include job fairs, resume preparation, resume referral, career counseling, careers library, job bank, job interviews. **Major awards:** 1 Marshall, 1 Fulbright Scholar.

New Mexico

Freshmen 4,179 applied, 3,818 admitted, 2,649 enrolled.

Average high school GPA	3.25	SAT verbal scores above 500	72%
SAT math scores above 500	69%	ACT above 18	87%
From top 10% of their h.s. class	20%	From top quarter	47%
From top half	80%	1998 freshmen returning in 1999	73%

Application *Options:* electronic application, early admission, deferred entrance. *Application fee:* $15. *Required:* high school transcript; minimum 2.25 GPA. *Recommended:* essay or personal statement.

Standardized tests *Admission: Required:* SAT I or ACT. *Required for some:* SAT II Subject Tests, SAT II: Writing Test.

Significant dates *Application deadlines:* 6/15 (freshmen), 6/15 (transfers). *Financial aid deadline priority date:* 3/1.

Freshman Application Contact
Ms. Robin Ryan, Associate Director of Admissions, University of New Mexico, Albuquerque, NM 87131-2046. **Phone:** 505-277-2446. **Toll-free phone:** 800-CALLUNM. **Fax:** 505-277-6686. **E-mail:** apply@unm.edu

Visit CollegeQuest.com for information on majors offered and athletics. College video and electronic viewbook available at CollegeQuest.com.

UNIVERSITY OF NEW MEXICO—GALLUP
Gallup, New Mexico

- **State-supported**, primarily 2-year, founded 1968
- **Degrees** associate and bachelor's
- **Small-town** 80-acre campus
- **Coed**, 2,612 undergraduate students
- **Noncompetitive** entrance level

Part of New Mexico Commission on Higher Education.

Faculty 159 (47% full-time).

Admissions Office Contact
University of New Mexico–Gallup, 200 College Road, Gallup, NM 87301-5603. **Fax:** 505-863-7532. **E-mail:** pmorris@gallup.unm.edu

Visit CollegeQuest.com for information on majors offered and athletics.

WESTERN NEW MEXICO UNIVERSITY
Silver City, New Mexico

- **State-supported**, comprehensive, founded 1893
- **Degrees** associate, bachelor's, and master's
- **Rural** 83-acre campus
- **Coed**
- **Noncompetitive** entrance level
- **$1768 tuition** and fees (in-state); $6456 (out-of-state)

Expenses (1999–2000) *Tuition, state resident:* full-time $1768; part-time $57 per hour. *Tuition, nonresident:* full-time $6456; part-time $57 per hour. Full-time tuition and fees vary according to program. Part-time tuition and fees vary according to course load and program. *College room and board:* $2938; room only: $1122.

Institutional Web site http://www.wnmu.edu/

College life *Housing:* on-campus residence required in freshman year. *Option:* coed.

Campus security 24-hour emergency response devices and patrols, student patrols, late-night transport-escort service.

Application *Options:* Common Application, early admission, deferred entrance. *Application fee:* $10. *Required:* high school transcript.

Standardized tests *Placement: Required:* ACT COMPASS

Admissions Office Contact
Western New Mexico University, College Avenue, Silver City, NM 88062-0680. **Toll-free phone:** 800-872-WNMU. **Fax:** 505-538-6155.

Visit CollegeQuest.com for information on athletics. College video available at CollegeQuest.com.

New York

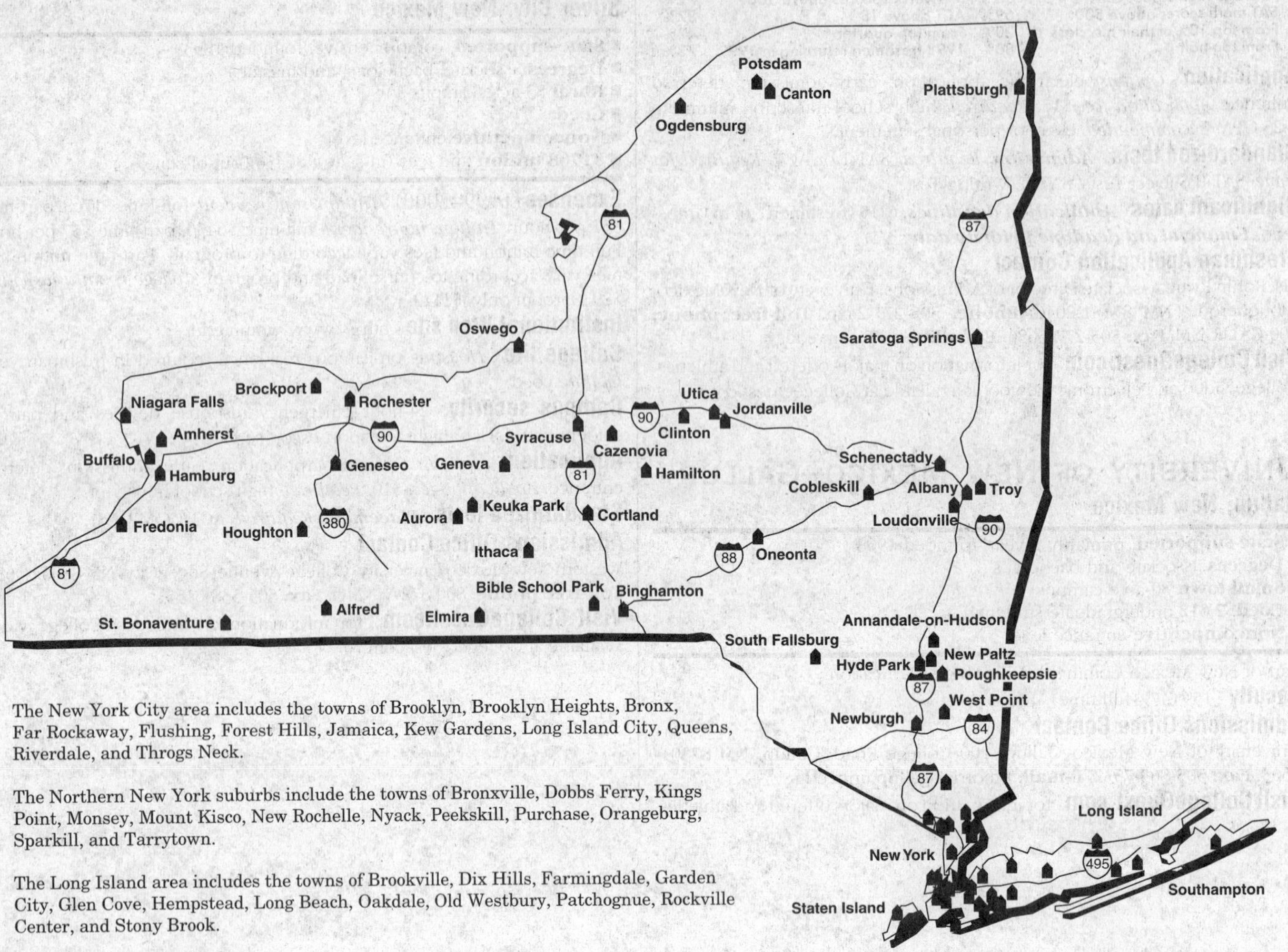

NEW YORK

[Map of New York State showing college locations in cities including Potsdam, Canton, Ogdensburg, Plattsburgh, Oswego, Saratoga Springs, Niagara Falls, Brockport, Rochester, Utica, Jordanville, Amherst, Buffalo, Geneseo, Syracuse, Clinton, Schenectady, Hamburg, Geneva, Cazenovia, Hamilton, Cobleskill, Albany, Troy, Fredonia, Aurora, Keuka Park, Cortland, Loudonville, Houghton, Ithaca, Oneonta, St. Bonaventure, Alfred, Bible School Park, Binghamton, Annandale-on-Hudson, Elmira, South Fallsburg, New Paltz, Hyde Park, Poughkeepsie, West Point, Newburgh, Long Island, New York, Staten Island, Southampton]

The New York City area includes the towns of Brooklyn, Brooklyn Heights, Bronx, Far Rockaway, Flushing, Forest Hills, Jamaica, Kew Gardens, Long Island City, Queens, Riverdale, and Throgs Neck.

The Northern New York suburbs include the towns of Bronxville, Dobbs Ferry, Kings Point, Monsey, Mount Kisco, New Rochelle, Nyack, Peekskill, Purchase, Orangeburg, Sparkill, and Tarrytown.

The Long Island area includes the towns of Brookville, Dix Hills, Farmingdale, Garden City, Glen Cove, Hempstead, Long Beach, Oakdale, Old Westbury, Patchognue, Rockville Center, and Stony Brook.

ADELPHI UNIVERSITY
Garden City, New York

 Apply at CollegeQuest.com

- **Independent**, university, founded 1896
- **Degrees** associate, bachelor's, master's, doctoral, post-master's, and postbachelor's certificates
- **Suburban** 75-acre campus with easy access to New York City
- **Coed**, 2,865 undergraduate students, 73% full-time, 69% women, 31% men
- **Moderately difficult** entrance level, 68% of applicants were admitted
- **13:1** student-to-undergraduate faculty ratio
- **45.9% graduate** in 6 years or less
- **$14,920 tuition** and fees

Adelphi is a private, coeducational university offering degrees in the liberal arts and the professions at the bachelor's, master's, and doctoral levels. Undergraduate student–faculty ratio is 13:1. Entrance difficulty level is competitive and is highly competitive for the Honors College. Merit and talent scholarships as well as need-based aid are available.

Students *Undergraduates:* 2,100 full-time, 765 part-time. Students come from 53 other countries. *The most frequently chosen baccalaureate fields are:* business/marketing, health professions and related sciences, trade and industry. *Graduate:* 3,000 in graduate degree programs.

From out-of-state	10%	Reside on campus	21%
Age 25 or older	37%	Transferred in	14%
International students	4%	African Americans	12%
Asian Americans/Pacific Islanders	3%	Hispanic Americans	6%
Native Americans	0.1%		

Faculty 584 (34% full-time), 27% with terminal degrees.

Expenses (1999–2000) *Comprehensive fee:* $22,100 includes full-time tuition ($14,750), mandatory fees ($170), and room and board ($7180). Full-time tuition and fees vary according to program. Room and board charges vary according to board plan and housing facility. *Part-time tuition:* $450 per credit. Part-time tuition and fees vary according to program. *Payment plans:* tuition prepayment, installment, deferred payment. *Waivers:* employees or children of employees.

Library Swirbul Library plus 2 others. *Collection:* 627,875 titles.

College life *Housing: Options:* coed, disabled students. *Social organizations:* national fraternities, national sororities, local fraternities, local sororities; 7% of eligible men and 5% of eligible women are members. *Most popular organizations:* Student Activities Board, Student Government Association, Circle K, Model United Nations.

Campus security 24-hour emergency response devices and patrols, late-night transport-escort service, controlled dormitory access.

After graduation *Career center:* 5 full-time personnel. Services include job fairs, resume preparation, career counseling, careers library, job bank, job interviews.

Freshmen 3,142 applied, 2,127 admitted, 554 enrolled.

Average high school GPA	3.3	SAT verbal scores above 500	61%
SAT math scores above 500	62%	ACT above 18	N/R
1998 freshmen returning in 1999	74%		

Application *Options:* eApply at www.CollegeQuest.com, Common Application, early admission, early action, deferred entrance. *Application fee:* $35. *Required:* essay or personal statement; high school transcript. *Recommended:* minimum 3.0 GPA; 1 letter of recommendation; interview.

Standardized tests *Admission: Required:* SAT I or ACT.

518 www.petersons.com *Peterson's Guide to Four-Year Colleges 2001*

New York

Significant dates *Application deadlines:* rolling (freshmen), rolling (transfers). *Early action:* 12/1. *Notification:* 12/31 (early action). *Financial aid deadline priority date:* 2/15.

Freshman Application Contact
Mr. Joseph Posillico, Acting Director of Admissions/Director of Student Financial Services, Adelphi University, South Avenue, Garden City, NY 11530. **Phone:** 516-877-3052. **Toll-free phone:** 800-ADELPHI. **Fax:** 516-877-3039. **E-mail:** admissions@adelphi.edu
Visit CollegeQuest.com for information on majors offered and athletics. College video available at CollegeQuest.com.

■ *See page 1132 for a narrative description.*

ALBANY COLLEGE OF PHARMACY OF UNION UNIVERSITY
Albany, New York

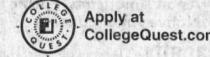
Apply at CollegeQuest.com

- **Independent**, comprehensive, founded 1881
- **Degrees** bachelor's and first professional
- **Urban** 1-acre campus
- **Coed**
- **Moderately difficult** entrance level
- **$12,173 tuition** and fees

Part of Union University (Albany Law School, Albany Medical College, Union College, NY).
Expenses (1999–2000) *Comprehensive fee:* $17,273 includes full-time tuition ($11,950), mandatory fees ($223), and room and board ($5100). *College room only:* $3500. Room and board charges vary according to student level. *Part-time tuition:* $398 per semester hour. *Part-time fees:* $223 per year part-time. Part-time tuition and fees vary according to course load.
Institutional Web site http://panther.acp.edu/
College life *Housing:* on-campus residence required in freshman year. *Option:* coed. *Social organizations:* national fraternities, national sororities; 30% of eligible men and 30% of eligible women are members.
Campus security 24-hour emergency response devices, controlled dormitory access.
Application *Options:* eApply at www.CollegeQuest.com, early admission. *Application fee:* $50. *Required:* essay or personal statement; high school transcript; 2 letters of recommendation. *Recommended:* minimum 2.0 GPA; interview.
Standardized tests *Admission: Required:* SAT I or ACT.
Admissions Office Contact
Albany College of Pharmacy of Union University, 106 New Scotland Avenue, Albany, NY 12208-3425. **Fax:** 518-445-7202. **E-mail:** admissions@panther.acp.edu
Visit CollegeQuest.com for information on athletics.

ALBERT A. LIST COLLEGE OF JEWISH STUDIES
New York—See Jewish Theological Seminary of America

ALFRED UNIVERSITY
Alfred, New York

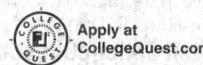
Apply at CollegeQuest.com

- **Independent**, university, founded 1836
- **Degrees** bachelor's, master's, and doctoral
- **Rural** 232-acre campus with easy access to Rochester
- **Coed**, 2,058 undergraduate students, 98% full-time, 50% women, 50% men
- **Moderately difficult** entrance level, 81% of applicants were admitted
- **12:1** student-to-undergraduate faculty ratio
- **68.9% graduate** in 6 years or less
- **$9448 tuition** and fees (in-state); $12,808 (out-of-state)

■ **$22,350 average financial aid** package, $17,500 average indebtedness upon graduation, $55.7 million endowment

Alfred University continues its plan that holds tuition costs steady for incoming freshmen at the 1996 rate. The University also continues to expand and improve its programs and facilities. Nine buildings have been renovated or constructed to enhance the academic, cultural, and social lives of students. Included are a new campus center, a performing arts building, and a renovated castle that houses the Career Development Center.

Students *Undergraduates:* 2,025 full-time, 33 part-time. Students come from 37 states and territories, 11 other countries. *The most frequently chosen baccalaureate fields are:* business/marketing, engineering/engineering technologies, psychology. *Graduate:* 324 in graduate degree programs.

From out-of-state	32%	Reside on campus	65%
Age 25 or older	10%	Transferred in	5%
International students	1%	African Americans	3%
Asian Americans/Pacific Islanders	2%	Hispanic Americans	4%
Native Americans	0.4%		

Faculty 212 (81% full-time), 81% with terminal degrees.
Expenses (1999–2000) *One-time required fee:* $300. *Comprehensive fee:* $26,248 includes full-time tuition ($18,498), mandatory fees ($576), and room and board ($7174). *College room only:* $3740. Full-time tuition and fees vary according to program and student level. Room and board charges vary according to board plan and housing facility. *Part-time tuition:* $494 per credit. *Part-time fees:* $29 per term part-time. *Payment plans:* tuition prepayment, installment, deferred payment. *Waivers:* employees or children of employees.
Library Herrick Memorial Library plus 1 other. *Operations spending 1999–2000:* $1.5 million. *Collection:* 330,522 titles, 1,722 serial subscriptions, 158,620 audiovisual materials.
College life *Housing:* on-campus residence required through sophomore year. *Option:* coed. *Social organizations:* national fraternities, national sororities, local fraternities, local sororities; 20% of eligible men and 11% of eligible women are members. *Most popular organizations:* Student Activities Board, Spectrum, WALF, Student Senate, Fiat Lux.
Campus security 24-hour emergency response devices, student patrols, late-night transport-escort service.
After graduation 79 organizations recruited on campus 1997–98. 71% of class of 1998 had job offers within 6 months. *Career center:* 6 full-time personnel. Services include job fairs, resume preparation, resume referral, career/interest testing, career counseling, careers library, job bank, job interviews. *Graduate education:* 22% of class of 1999 went directly to graduate and professional school.
Freshmen 1,954 applied, 1,592 admitted, 543 enrolled. 15 National Merit Scholars, 15 student government officers.

SAT verbal scores above 500	76%	SAT math scores above 500	77%
ACT above 18	N/R	From top 10% of their h.s. class	23%
From top quarter	51%	From top half	83%
1998 freshmen returning in 1999	85%		

Application *Options:* eApply at www.CollegeQuest.com, Common Application, electronic application, early admission, early decision, deferred entrance. *Application fee:* $40. *Required:* essay or personal statement; high school transcript; 1 letter of recommendation. *Required for some:* interview; portfolio. *Recommended:* interview.
Standardized tests *Admission: Required:* SAT I or ACT. *Recommended:* SAT II: Writing Test.
Significant dates *Application deadlines:* 2/1 (freshmen), 8/1 (transfers). *Early decision:* 12/1. *Notification:* 3/15 (freshmen), 12/15 (early decision). *Financial aid deadline:* continuous.
Freshman Application Contact
Katherine M. McCarthy, Director of Admissions, Alfred University, Alumni Hall, Alfred, NY 14802-1205. **Phone:** 607-871-2115. **Toll-free phone:** 800-541-9229. **Fax:** 607-871-2198. **E-mail:** admwww@alfred.edu
Visit CollegeQuest.com for information on majors offered and athletics. College video available at CollegeQuest.com.

■ *See page 1150 for a narrative description.*

Peterson's Guide to Four-Year Colleges 2001   www.petersons.com

New York

ARNOLD & MARIE SCHWARTZ COLLEGE OF PHARMACY AND HEALTH SCIENCES
New York—See Long Island University, Brooklyn Campus

AUDREY COHEN COLLEGE
New York, New York

- **Independent**, comprehensive, founded 1964
- **Degrees** associate, bachelor's, and master's
- **Urban** campus
- **Coed**, 1,093 undergraduate students, 100% full-time, 80% women, 20% men
- **Moderately difficult** entrance level, 74% of applicants were admitted
- **25:1 student-to-undergraduate faculty ratio**
- **$14,480 tuition** and fees

Three times each year, Audrey Cohen College students create or enhance career opportunities in business management and human services through the only college curriculum designed to link learning to practice. Students earn credit for applying theoretical concepts mastered in the liberal arts, business, and professional studies to practical experience gained in professional work or internship settings. Students can complete a bachelor's degree in 2 years and 8 months or associate degree in 1 year and 4 months.

Students *Undergraduates:* 1,093 full-time. Students come from 5 states and territories. *Graduate:* 129 in graduate degree programs.

From out-of-state	2%	Age 25 or older	65%
African Americans	64%	Asian Americans/Pacific Islanders	1%
Hispanic Americans	18%	Native Americans	1%

Expenses (1999–2000) *Tuition:* full-time $14,160; part-time $295 per credit. *Required fees:* full-time $320. Full-time tuition and fees vary according to program. *Payment plans:* guaranteed tuition, installment. *Waivers:* employees or children of employees.
Library Main Library. *Collection:* 26,800 titles, 3,414 serial subscriptions.
College life *Housing:* college housing not available. *Most popular organizations:* student government, student newsletter, honor societies, networking club, yearbook committee.
Campus security 24-hour patrols.
After graduation 50 organizations recruited on campus 1997–98. 92% of class of 1998 had job offers within 6 months. *Career center:* 1 full-time, 2 part-time personnel. Services include job fairs, resume preparation, resume referral, career counseling, careers library, job bank, job interviews.
Freshmen 352 applied, 261 admitted, 173 enrolled.

SAT verbal scores above 500	N/R	SAT math scores above 500	N/R
ACT above 18	N/R	From top 10% of their h.s. class	4%
From top quarter	20%	From top half	60%
1998 freshmen returning in 1999	72%		

Application *Options:* early admission, deferred entrance. *Application fee:* $20. *Required:* essay or personal statement; high school transcript; 2 letters of recommendation; interview. *Recommended:* minimum 3.0 GPA.
Standardized tests *Admission: Required:* TABE. *Recommended:* SAT I.
Significant dates *Application deadlines:* 8/15 (freshmen), 8/15 (transfers). *Notification:* continuous until 8/31 (freshmen). *Financial aid deadline:* continuous.
Freshman Application Contact
Ms. Jennifer Gass, Admissions Counselor, Audrey Cohen College, 75 Varick Street, 12th Floor, New York, NY 10013. **Phone:** 212-343-1234 Ext. 2704. **Toll-free phone:** 800-33-THINK Ext. 5001. **Fax:** 212-343-8470.
Visit CollegeQuest.com for information on majors offered and athletics. College video available at CollegeQuest.com.

■ *See page 1206 for a narrative description.*

BARD COLLEGE
Annandale-on-Hudson, New York

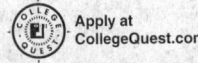 Apply at CollegeQuest.com

- **Independent**, comprehensive, founded 1860
- **Degrees** bachelor's, master's, and doctoral
- **Rural** 600-acre campus
- **Coed**, 1,233 undergraduate students, 92% full-time, 58% women, 42% men
- **Very difficult** entrance level, 47% of applicants were admitted
- **9:1 student-to-undergraduate faculty ratio**
- **65% graduate** in 6 years or less
- **$24,000 tuition** and fees
- **$19,325 average financial aid** package, $15,400 average indebtedness upon graduation, $99 million endowment

Students *Undergraduates:* 1,135 full-time, 98 part-time. Students come from 50 states and territories, 47 other countries. *The most frequently chosen baccalaureate fields are:* social sciences and history, foreign language/literature, visual/performing arts. *Graduate:* 194 in graduate degree programs.

From out-of-state	72%	Reside on campus	82%
Age 25 or older	1%	Transferred in	3%
International students	6%	African Americans	2%
Asian Americans/Pacific Islanders	3%	Hispanic Americans	4%
Native Americans	0.3%		

Faculty 167 (63% full-time).
Expenses (1999–2000) *Comprehensive fee:* $31,220 includes full-time tuition ($23,480), mandatory fees ($520), and room and board ($7220). *College room only:* $3620. Room and board charges vary according to board plan. *Part-time tuition:* $734 per credit. *Part-time fees:* $160 per term part-time. Part-time tuition and fees vary according to course load. *Payment plan:* installment. *Waivers:* employees or children of employees.
Library Stevenson Library plus 3 others. *Operations spending 1999–2000:* $955,789. *Collection:* 260,000 titles, 1,075 serial subscriptions, 5,600 audiovisual materials.
College life *Housing:* on-campus residence required in freshman year. *Option:* coed. *Most popular organizations:* student government, Social Action Workshop, Model United Nations, student newspaper, International Student Organization.
Campus security 24-hour emergency response devices and patrols, student patrols, late-night transport-escort service, controlled dormitory access.
After graduation 198 organizations recruited on campus 1997–98. *Career center:* 1 full-time, 1 part-time personnel. Services include job fairs, resume preparation, resume referral, career counseling, careers library, job bank, job interviews. *Graduate education:* 55% of class of 1999 went directly to graduate and professional school: 43% graduate arts and sciences, 5% law, 3% business, 3% medicine, 1% engineering. *Major awards:* 1 Fulbright Scholar.
Freshmen 2,508 applied, 1,177 admitted, 335 enrolled. 1 National Merit Scholar, 12 class presidents, 13 valedictorians, 76 student government officers.

Average high school GPA	3.5	SAT verbal scores above 500	96%
SAT math scores above 500	96%	ACT above 18	100%
From top 10% of their h.s. class	60%	From top quarter	91%
From top half	99%	1998 freshmen returning in 1999	83%

Application *Options:* eApply at www.CollegeQuest.com, Common Application, early admission, early action, deferred entrance. *Application fee:* $40. *Required:* essay or personal statement; high school transcript; 3 letters of recommendation. *Required for some:* interview. *Recommended:* minimum 3.0 GPA; interview.
Standardized tests *Admission: Recommended:* SAT I or ACT.
Significant dates *Application deadlines:* 1/15 (freshmen), 1/31 (transfers). *Early action:* 11/1. *Notification:* 4/1 (freshmen), 1/1 (early action). *Financial aid deadline:* 3/15. *Priority date:* 2/15.
Freshman Application Contact
Ms. Mary Inga Backlund, Director of Admissions, Bard College, Annandale-on-Hudson, NY 12504. **Phone:** 914-758-7472. **E-mail:** admission@bard.edu
Visit CollegeQuest.com for information on majors offered and athletics. Electronic viewbook available at CollegeQuest.com.

BARNARD COLLEGE
New York, New York

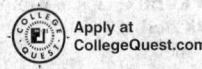 Apply at CollegeQuest.com

- **Independent**, 4-year, founded 1889
- **Degree** bachelor's
- **Urban** 4-acre campus

New York

- **Women** only, 2,294 undergraduate students, 98% full-time
- **Most difficult** entrance level, 37% of applicants were admitted
- **11:1** student-to-undergraduate faculty ratio
- **82% graduate** in 6 years or less
- **$22,316 tuition** and fees
- **$21,706 average financial aid** package, $13,430 average indebtedness upon graduation, $152.2 million endowment

Part of Columbia University.

Students *Undergraduates:* 2,244 full-time, 50 part-time. Students come from 49 states and territories, 25 other countries. *The most frequently chosen baccalaureate fields are:* English, psychology, social sciences and history.

From out-of-state	63%	Reside on campus	88%
Age 25 or older	1%	Transferred in	3%
International students	3%	African Americans	4%
Asian Americans/Pacific Islanders	23%	Hispanic Americans	6%
Native Americans	0.3%		

Faculty 268 (66% full-time).

Expenses (1999–2000) *Comprehensive fee:* $31,400 includes full-time tuition ($21,410), mandatory fees ($906), and room and board ($9084). *College room only:* $5632. Room and board charges vary according to board plan and housing facility. *Part-time tuition:* $714 per credit. *Payment plans:* tuition prepayment, installment, deferred payment. *Waivers:* employees or children of employees.

Library Wollman Library. *Operations spending 1999–2000:* $1.5 million. *Collection:* 198,020 titles, 900 serial subscriptions, 12,425 audiovisual materials.

College life *Housing: Options:* coed, women-only, disabled students. *Most popular organizations:* Community Impact, Student Government Association, Student Activities Council, WBAR Radio, Asian-American Alliance.

Campus security 24-hour emergency response devices and patrols, late-night transport-escort service, 4 permanent security posts.

After graduation 106 organizations recruited on campus 1997–98. 67% of class of 1998 had job offers within 6 months. *Career center:* 8 full-time, 3 part-time personnel. Services include job fairs, resume preparation, interview workshops, resume referral, career/interest testing, career counseling, careers library, job bank, job interviews. *Graduate education:* 22% of class of 1999 went directly to graduate and professional school: 6% graduate arts and sciences, 5% medicine, 4% law. *Major awards:* 1 Fulbright Scholar.

Freshmen 3,883 applied, 1,443 admitted, 558 enrolled. 2 National Merit Scholars.

Average high school GPA	3.81	SAT verbal scores above 500	99%
SAT math scores above 500	99%	ACT above 18	100%
From top 10% of their h.s. class	74%	From top quarter	96%
From top half	100%	1998 freshmen returning in 1999	95%

Application *Options:* eApply at www.CollegeQuest.com, Common Application, early admission, early decision, deferred entrance. *Application fee:* $45. *Required:* essay or personal statement; high school transcript; 3 letters of recommendation. *Recommended:* interview.

Standardized tests *Admission: Required:* SAT I and SAT II or ACT, SAT II: Writing Test.

Significant dates *Application deadlines:* 1/15 (freshmen), 5/1 (transfers). *Early decision:* 11/15. *Notification:* 4/1 (freshmen), 12/15 (early decision). *Financial aid deadline:* 2/1.

Freshman Application Contact
Ms. Doris Davis, Dean of Admissions, Barnard College, 3009 Broadway, New York, NY 10027. **Phone:** 212-854-2014. **Fax:** 212-854-6220. **E-mail:** admissions@barnard.edu

Visit CollegeQuest.com for information on majors offered and athletics.

- *See page 1228 for a narrative description.*

BERKELEY COLLEGE
New York, New York

- **Proprietary**, primarily 2-year, founded 1936
- **Degrees** associate and bachelor's
- **Urban** campus
- **Coed**, 1,687 undergraduate students, 89% full-time, 74% women, 26% men
- **Minimally difficult** entrance level
- **23:1** student-to-undergraduate faculty ratio
- **$12,945 tuition** and fees

Faculty 134 (27% full-time).

Admissions Office Contact
Berkeley College, 3 East 43rd Street, New York, NY 10017. **Toll-free phone:** 800-446-5400. **Fax:** 212-697-3371. **E-mail:** ny@berkeleycollege.edu

Visit CollegeQuest.com for information on majors offered and athletics. College video available at CollegeQuest.com.

- *See page 1260 for a narrative description.*

BERKELEY COLLEGE
White Plains, New York

- **Proprietary**, primarily 2-year, founded 1945
- **Degrees** associate and bachelor's
- **Suburban** 10-acre campus with easy access to New York City
- **Coed**, 654 undergraduate students, 84% full-time, 74% women, 26% men
- **Minimally difficult** entrance level
- **21:1** student-to-undergraduate faculty ratio
- **$12,945 tuition** and fees

Faculty 53 (28% full-time).

Admissions Office Contact
Berkeley College, 40 West Red Oak Lane, White Plains, NY 10604. **Toll-free phone:** 800-446-5400. **Fax:** 914-694-5832. **E-mail:** wpcampus@berkeleycollege.edu

Visit CollegeQuest.com for information on majors offered and athletics.

BERNARD M. BARUCH COLLEGE OF THE CITY UNIVERSITY OF NEW YORK
New York, New York

- **State and locally supported**, comprehensive, founded 1919
- **Degrees** bachelor's, master's, doctoral, and post-master's certificates
- **Urban** campus
- **Coed**, 12,325 undergraduate students, 67% full-time, 57% women, 43% men
- **Moderately difficult** entrance level, 22% of applicants were admitted
- **$3340 tuition** and fees (in-state); $6940 (out-of-state)

Part of City University of New York System.

Students *Undergraduates:* 8,217 full-time, 4,108 part-time. Students come from 144 other countries. *The most frequently chosen baccalaureate fields are:* business/marketing, psychology, social sciences and history. *Graduate:* 2,656 in graduate degree programs.

From out-of-state	1%	Age 25 or older	37%
International students	8%	African Americans	21%
Asian Americans/Pacific Islanders	23%	Hispanic Americans	20%
Native Americans	0.1%		

Faculty 1,063 (39% full-time), 60% with terminal degrees.

Expenses (1999–2000) *Tuition, state resident:* full-time $3200; part-time $138 per credit. *Tuition, nonresident:* full-time $6800; part-time $228 per credit. *Required fees:* full-time $140; $38 per term. Full-time tuition and fees vary according to class time. Part-time tuition and fees vary according to class time. *Payment plans:* installment, deferred payment. *Waivers:* senior citizens and employees or children of employees.

Library The William and Anita Newman Library plus 1 other. *Collection:* 4,263 serial subscriptions, 770 audiovisual materials.

College life *Housing:* college housing not available. *Social organizations:* local fraternities, local sororities. *Most popular organizations:* Accounting Society, Asian Student Association, Caribbean Student Association, Golden Key National Honor Society, Helpline.

Campus security 24-hour emergency response devices and patrols, late-night transport-escort service, controlled access by ID card.

After graduation 300 organizations recruited on campus 1997–98. *Career center:* 3 full-time, 2 part-time personnel. Services include job fairs, resume preparation, resume referral, career counseling, careers library, job bank, job interviews.

New York

Bernard M. Baruch College of the City University of New York (continued)
Freshmen 12,222 applied, 2,683 admitted, 1,165 enrolled.

SAT verbal scores above 500	55%	SAT math scores above 500	72%
ACT above 18	N/R	From top 10% of their h.s. class	25%
From top quarter	59%	From top half	87%
1998 freshmen returning in 1999	83%		

Application *Option:* deferred entrance. *Application fee:* $40. *Required:* high school transcript; minimum 3.0 GPA.
Standardized tests *Admission: Required:* SAT I.
Significant dates *Application deadlines:* 5/1 (freshmen), 6/1 (transfers). *Notification:* continuous until 7/30 (freshmen). **Financial aid deadline:** 4/30. *Priority date:* 3/15.
Freshman Application Contact
Mr. James F. Murphy, Director of Undergraduate Admissions and Financial Aid, Bernard M. Baruch College of the City University of New York, Box H-0720, New York, NY 10010-5585. **Phone:** 212-802-2300. **E-mail:** admissions@baruch.cuny.edu
Visit CollegeQuest.com for information on majors offered and athletics. College video available at CollegeQuest.com.

■ *See page 1264 for a narrative description.*

BETH HAMEDRASH SHAAREI YOSHER INSTITUTE
Brooklyn, New York

Admissions Office Contact
Beth HaMedrash Shaarei Yosher Institute, 4102-10 Sixteenth Avenue, Brooklyn, NY 11204.

BETH HATALMUD RABBINICAL COLLEGE
Brooklyn, New York

Admissions Office Contact
Beth Hatalmud Rabbinical College, 2127 Eighty-second Street, Brooklyn, NY 11214.

BORICUA COLLEGE
New York, New York

Admissions Office Contact
Boricua College, 3755 Broadway, New York, NY 10032-1560.

BRIARCLIFFE COLLEGE
Bethpage, New York

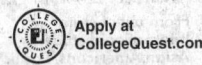 Apply at CollegeQuest.com

■ **Proprietary**, 4-year, founded 1966
■ **Degrees** associate and bachelor's
■ **Suburban** 18-acre campus with easy access to New York City
■ **Coed**, 1,457 undergraduate students, 70% full-time, 55% women, 45% men
■ **Minimally difficult** entrance level, 55% of applicants were admitted
■ **13:1** student-to-undergraduate faculty ratio
■ **$9070 tuition** and fees

Students *Undergraduates:* 1,019 full-time, 438 part-time. Students come from 3 states and territories, 1 other country.

From out-of-state	0.2%	Age 25 or older	47%
Transferred in	9%	International students	0.4%
African Americans	10%	Asian Americans/Pacific Islanders	1%
Hispanic Americans	12%	Native Americans	0.3%

Faculty 118 (31% full-time).
Expenses (1999–2000) *Tuition:* full-time $8700; part-time $290 per credit. *Required fees:* full-time $370; $18 per credit. *Payment plans:* installment, deferred payment. *Waivers:* senior citizens and employees or children of employees.
Library Briarcliffe Library. *Collection:* 11,834 titles, 191 serial subscriptions.

College life *Housing:* college housing not available. *Most popular organizations:* Student Government Association, Telecommunication Club, Graphic Design Club, Law Club.
Campus security Late-night transport-escort service.
After graduation 95 organizations recruited on campus 1997–98. 72% of class of 1998 had job offers within 6 months. *Career center:* 4 full-time, 1 part-time personnel. Services include job fairs, resume preparation, resume referral, career counseling, careers library, job bank, job interviews.
Freshmen 626 applied, 345 admitted, 525 enrolled.

Average high school GPA	2.5	SAT verbal scores above 500	N/R
SAT math scores above 500	N/R	ACT above 18	N/R
From top 10% of their h.s. class	10%	From top quarter	40%
From top half	70%		

Application *Options:* eApply at www.CollegeQuest.com, deferred entrance. *Application fee:* $25. *Required:* high school transcript; interview.
Standardized tests *Admission: Recommended:* SAT I and SAT II or ACT.
Significant dates *Application deadlines:* rolling (freshmen), rolling (transfers). **Financial aid deadline:** continuous.
Freshman Application Contact
Ms. Theresa Donohue, Dean of Marketing and Admissions, Briarcliffe College, 1055 Stewart Avenue, Bethpage, NY 11714. **Phone:** 516-470-6008 Ext. 233. **Fax:** 516-470-6020. **E-mail:** info@bcl.edu
Visit CollegeQuest.com for information on majors offered and athletics.

■ *See page 1310 for a narrative description.*

BROOKLYN COLLEGE OF THE CITY UNIVERSITY OF NEW YORK
Brooklyn, New York

■ **State and locally supported**, comprehensive, founded 1930
■ **Degrees** bachelor's, master's, and post-master's certificates
■ **Urban** 26-acre campus
■ **Coed**, 9,868 undergraduate students, 68% full-time, 61% women, 39% men
■ **Moderately difficult** entrance level
■ **20:1** student-to-undergraduate faculty ratio
■ **$3393 tuition** and fees (in-state); $6993 (out-of-state)
■ **$27 million endowment**

Part of City University of New York System.
Students *Undergraduates:* 6,714 full-time, 3,154 part-time. Students come from 20 states and territories, 50 other countries. *The most frequently chosen baccalaureate fields are:* business/marketing, education, psychology. *Graduate:* 4,874 in graduate degree programs.

Age 25 or older	29%	Transferred in	11%
International students	3%	African Americans	29%
Asian Americans/Pacific Islanders	8%	Hispanic Americans	11%
Native Americans	0.1%		

Faculty 1,046 (45% full-time).
Expenses (1999–2000) *Tuition, state resident:* full-time $3200; part-time $135 per credit. *Tuition, nonresident:* full-time $6800; part-time $285 per credit. *Required fees:* full-time $193; $97 per term part-time. Full-time tuition and fees vary according to class time and course load. Part-time tuition and fees vary according to class time and course load. *Payment plan:* installment. *Waivers:* senior citizens and employees or children of employees.
Library Brooklyn College Library plus 1 other. *Operations spending 1999–2000:* $3.2 million. *Collection:* 1.2 million titles, 4,803 serial subscriptions.
College life *Housing:* college housing not available. *Social organizations:* national fraternities, national sororities, local fraternities, local sororities; 5% of eligible men and 5% of eligible women are members. *Most popular organizations:* Academic Club Association, Kingsman, and Excelsior Newspaper, NY Public Interest Group (NYPIRG), Student government CIAS, SGS, and GSO, Student Forensics.
Campus security 24-hour emergency response devices and patrols, late-night transport-escort service.
After graduation 150 organizations recruited on campus 1997–98. 40% of class of 1998 had job offers within 6 months. *Career center:* 4 full-time, 1 part-time personnel. Services include job fairs, resume preparation, resume referral, career counseling, careers library, job bank, job interviews.

New York

Freshmen 1,057 admitted, 1,057 enrolled.

| SAT verbal scores above 500 | N/R | SAT math scores above 500 | N/R |
| ACT above 18 | N/R | | |

Application *Options:* Common Application, early admission, deferred entrance. *Application fee:* $40. *Required:* high school transcript; minimum 2.8 GPA. *Required for some:* essay or personal statement; letters of recommendation; interview. *Recommended:* minimum 3.0 GPA.
Standardized tests *Placement: Required:* SAT I, ACT
Significant dates *Application deadlines:* 12/1 (freshmen), 3/1 (transfers). *Financial aid deadline:* continuous.
Freshman Application Contact
Ms. Celia Adams, Admissions Counselor/Recruiter, Brooklyn College of the City University of New York, 1203 Plaza, Brooklyn, NY 11210-2889. **Phone:** 718-951-5001. **E-mail:** admissions@brooklyn.cuny.edu
Visit CollegeQuest.com for information on majors offered and athletics.

■ *See page 1318 for a narrative description.*

CANISIUS COLLEGE
Buffalo, New York

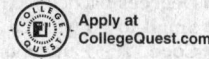 Apply at CollegeQuest.com

■ **Independent Roman Catholic (Jesuit)**, comprehensive, founded 1870
■ **Degrees** associate, bachelor's, and master's
■ **Urban** 26-acre campus
■ **Coed**, 3,329 undergraduate students, 86% full-time, 51% women, 49% men
■ **Moderately difficult** entrance level, 81% of applicants were admitted
■ **54% graduate** in 6 years or less
■ **$15,548 tuition** and fees
■ **$16,910 average financial aid** package, $60.8 million endowment

Students *Undergraduates:* Students come from 35 states and territories, 31 other countries. *The most frequently chosen baccalaureate fields are:* business/marketing, education, liberal arts/general studies. *Graduate:* 1,410 in graduate degree programs.

From out-of-state	6%	Reside on campus	32%
Age 25 or older	15%	International students	3%
African Americans	6%	Asian Americans/Pacific Islanders	2%
Hispanic Americans	3%	Native Americans	0.3%

Faculty 411 (46% full-time).
Expenses (1999–2000) *Comprehensive fee:* $21,888 includes full-time tuition ($15,160), mandatory fees ($388), and room and board ($6340). *College room only:* $3360. Room and board charges vary according to board plan, housing facility, and student level. *Part-time tuition:* $433 per credit hour. *Payment plans:* installment, deferred payment. *Waivers:* employees or children of employees.
Library Andrew L. Bouwhuis Library plus 1 other. *Operations spending 1999–2000:* $1.1 million. *Collection:* 308,508 titles, 1,818 serial subscriptions, 6,460 audiovisual materials.
College life *Housing: Option:* coed. *Social organizations:* national fraternities, national sororities; 4% of eligible men and 4% of eligible women are members. *Most popular organizations:* Campus Programming Board, Undergraduate Student Association, Afro-American Society, Residence Hall Association, commuter club.
Campus security 24-hour emergency response devices and patrols, late-night transport-escort service, controlled dormitory access, crime prevention programs, closed-circuit television monitors.
After graduation 37 organizations recruited on campus 1997–98. *Career center:* 2 full-time, 2 part-time personnel. Services include job fairs, resume preparation, interview workshops, resume referral, career/interest testing, career counseling, careers library, job bank, job interviews. *Graduate education:* 10% of class of 1999 went directly to graduate and professional school. *Major awards:* 1 Fulbright Scholar.
Freshmen 3,473 applied, 2,816 admitted. 1 National Merit Scholar, 13 valedictorians.

Average high school GPA	3.43	SAT verbal scores above 500	74%
SAT math scores above 500	76%	ACT above 18	96%
From top 10% of their h.s. class	22%	From top quarter	57%
From top half	86%	1998 freshmen returning in 1999	85%

Application *Options:* eApply at www.CollegeQuest.com, Common Application, electronic application, early admission, deferred entrance. *Application fee:* $25. *Required:* high school transcript. *Required for some:* interview. *Recommended:* letters of recommendation; interview.
Standardized tests *Admission: Required:* SAT I or ACT.
Significant dates *Application deadlines:* rolling (freshmen), rolling (transfers). *Financial aid deadline priority date:* 2/1.
Freshman Application Contact
Miss Penelope H. Lips, Director of Admissions, Canisius College, 2001 Main Street, Buffalo, NY 14208-1098. **Phone:** 716-888-2200. **Toll-free phone:** 800-843-1517. **Fax:** 716-888-2377. **E-mail:** inquiry@canisius.edu
Visit CollegeQuest.com for information on majors offered and athletics. College video and electronic viewbook available at CollegeQuest.com.

■ *See page 1352 for a narrative description.*

CAZENOVIA COLLEGE
Cazenovia, New York

■ **Independent**, 4-year, founded 1824
■ **Degrees** associate and bachelor's
■ **Small-town** 40-acre campus with easy access to Syracuse
■ **Coed**, 741 undergraduate students, 97% full-time, 68% women, 32% men
■ **Minimally difficult** entrance level, 89% of applicants were admitted
■ **13:1 student-to-undergraduate faculty ratio**
■ **$12,140 tuition** and fees
■ **$40.8 million endowment**

In 1999, Cazenovia College introduced new baccalaureate programs in early childhood education and program administration, social science, and English and a specialization in accounting.

Students *Undergraduates:* 722 full-time, 19 part-time. Students come from 1 other country. *The most frequently chosen baccalaureate fields are:* business/marketing, home economics/vocational home economics, visual/performing arts.

From out-of-state	10%	Reside on campus	71%
Age 25 or older	8%	Transferred in	8%
International students	0.3%	African Americans	8%
Asian Americans/Pacific Islanders	1%	Hispanic Americans	2%
Native Americans	1%		

Faculty 79 (53% full-time), 78% with terminal degrees.
Expenses (1999–2000) *Comprehensive fee:* $18,068 includes full-time tuition ($11,640), mandatory fees ($500), and room and board ($5928). *College room only:* $3178. Room and board charges vary according to board plan. *Part-time tuition:* $297 per credit. Part-time tuition and fees vary according to class time and course load. *Payment plan:* installment. *Waivers:* employees or children of employees.
Library Witheral Library. *Operations spending 1999–2000:* $401,870. *Collection:* 61,694 titles, 526 serial subscriptions.
College life *Housing:* on-campus residence required through sophomore year. *Option:* coed. *Most popular organizations:* Activities Board, Multicultural Student Group, performing arts, student radio station, yearbook.
Campus security 24-hour emergency response devices and patrols, late-night transport-escort service, controlled dormitory access.
After graduation 25 organizations recruited on campus 1997–98. 15% of class of 1998 had job offers within 6 months. *Career center:* 1 full-time personnel. Services include job fairs, resume preparation, resume referral, career counseling, careers library, job bank, job interviews. *Graduate education:* 31% of class of 1999 went directly to graduate and professional school.
Freshmen 851 applied, 761 admitted, 292 enrolled.

Average high school GPA	2.73	SAT verbal scores above 500	31%
SAT math scores above 500	27%	ACT above 18	79%
From top 10% of their h.s. class	3%	From top quarter	13%
From top half	50%	1998 freshmen returning in 1999	62%

Application *Options:* Common Application, early admission, deferred entrance. *Application fee:* $25. *Required:* high school transcript.
Standardized tests *Admission: Recommended:* SAT I and SAT II or ACT.
Significant dates *Application deadlines:* rolling (freshmen), rolling (transfers). *Financial aid deadline priority date:* 3/15.

New York

Cazenovia College (continued)
Freshman Application Contact
Mr. Tim Williams, Dean of Admission, Financial Aid, and Retention, Cazenovia College, Cazenovia, NY 13035-1084. **Phone:** 315-655-7208. **Toll-free phone:** 800-654-3210. **Fax:** 315-655-2190.
Visit CollegeQuest.com for information on majors offered and athletics. College video available at CollegeQuest.com.

■ *See page 1384 for a narrative description.*

CENTRAL YESHIVA TOMCHEI TMIMIM-LUBAVITCH
Brooklyn, New York

Admissions Office Contact
Central Yeshiva Tomchei Tmimim-Lubavitch, 841-853 Ocean Parkway, Brooklyn, NY 11230.

CITY COLLEGE OF THE CITY UNIVERSITY OF NEW YORK
New York, New York

- **State and locally supported**, university, founded 1847
- **Degrees** bachelor's, master's, and doctoral
- **Urban** 35-acre campus
- **Coed**, 8,041 undergraduate students, 66% full-time, 52% women, 48% men
- **Moderately difficult** entrance level, 59% of applicants were admitted
- **$3309 tuition** and fees (in-state); $6909 (out-of-state)

For more than 150 years, the City College of New York (CUNY) has provided an excellent higher education to generations of New Yorkers. City College offers degree programs in architecture, the arts, biomedical education, computer science, education, engineering, humanities, sciences, and social sciences. Conveniently located in New York City, students can take advantage of an environment that is diverse, politically and socially active, and artistically and intellectually stimulating. For more information, students should visit the Web site (http://www.ccny.cuny.edu).

Part of City University of New York System.
Students *Undergraduates:* 5,344 full-time, 2,697 part-time. Students come from 52 states and territories, 80 other countries. *Graduate:* 2,644 in graduate degree programs.

Age 25 or older	39%	International students	11%
African Americans	37%	Asian Americans/Pacific Islanders	11%
Hispanic Americans	31%	Native Americans	0.2%

Faculty 968 (48% full-time).
Expenses (1999–2000) *Tuition, state resident:* full-time $3200; part-time $135 per credit. *Tuition, nonresident:* full-time $6800; part-time $285 per credit. *Required fees:* full-time $109; $27 per term part-time. Full-time tuition and fees vary according to class time and program. Part-time tuition and fees vary according to class time and program. *Payment plan:* deferred payment. *Waivers:* senior citizens.
Library Morris Raphael Cohen Library. *Operations spending 1999–2000:* $3.9 million. *Collection:* 1.2 million titles, 2,700 serial subscriptions.
College life *Housing:* college housing not available. *Social organizations:* national fraternities.
Campus security 24-hour patrols.
After graduation 50 organizations recruited on campus 1997–98. *Career center:* 2 full-time, 7 part-time personnel. Services include job fairs, resume preparation, career counseling, careers library, job bank, job interviews.
Freshmen 3,252 applied, 1,919 admitted, 828 enrolled.

SAT verbal scores above 500	N/R	SAT math scores above 500	N/R
ACT above 18	N/R	From top 10% of their h.s. class	8%
From top half	81%	1998 freshmen returning in 1999	80%

Application *Options:* early admission, deferred entrance. *Application fee:* $40. *Required:* high school transcript.
Standardized tests *Placement: Required for some:* SAT I or ACT.

Significant dates *Application deadlines:* rolling (freshmen), rolling (transfers). *Notification:* continuous until 8/15 (freshmen). **Financial aid deadline priority date:** 5/1.
Freshman Application Contact
Mr. William Di Brienza, Acting Director of Admissions, City College of the City University of New York, Convent Avenue at 138th Street, New York, NY 10031-9198. **Phone:** 212-650-6977. **Fax:** 212-650-6417. **E-mail:** adocc@cunyvm.cuny.edu
Visit CollegeQuest.com for information on majors offered and athletics. College video available at CollegeQuest.com.

■ *See page 1420 for a narrative description.*

CLARKSON UNIVERSITY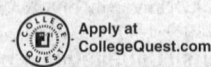
Potsdam, New York

- **Independent**, university, founded 1896
- **Degrees** bachelor's, master's, and doctoral
- **Small-town** 640-acre campus
- **Coed**, 2,533 undergraduate students, 99% full-time, 26% women, 74% men
- **Very difficult** entrance level, 83% of applicants were admitted
- **16:1 student-to-undergraduate faculty ratio**
- **$20,225 tuition** and fees
- **$14,647 average financial aid** package, $18,110 average indebtedness upon graduation, $105.8 million endowment

Students *Undergraduates:* 2,514 full-time, 19 part-time. Students come from 36 states and territories, 28 other countries. *The most frequently chosen baccalaureate fields are:* business/marketing, engineering/engineering technologies, interdisciplinary studies. *Graduate:* 321 in graduate degree programs.

From out-of-state	28%	Reside on campus	70%
Age 25 or older	2%	Transferred in	6%
International students	3%	African Americans	3%
Asian Americans/Pacific Islanders	2%	Hispanic Americans	2%
Native Americans	1%		

Faculty 181 (85% full-time), 82% with terminal degrees.
Expenses (1999–2000) *Comprehensive fee:* $27,709 includes full-time tuition ($19,825), mandatory fees ($400), and room and board ($7484). *College room only:* $3900. Full-time tuition and fees vary according to course load. Room and board charges vary according to housing facility. *Part-time tuition:* $661 per credit hour. *Part-time fees:* $105 per term part-time. Part-time tuition and fees vary according to course load. *Payment plan:* installment. *Waivers:* employees or children of employees.
Library Andrew S. Schuler Educational Resources Center. *Operations spending 1999–2000:* $1.3 million. *Collection:* 237,251 titles, 1,705 serial subscriptions, 1,524 audiovisual materials.
College life *Housing:* on-campus residence required through senior year. *Options:* coed, men-only, women-only. *Social organizations:* national fraternities, national sororities, local fraternities; 15% of eligible men and 17% of eligible women are members. *Most popular organizations:* Outing Club, Auto Club, Ski Club, Pep Band, Men's Rugby.
Campus security 24-hour emergency response devices and patrols, late-night transport-escort service, controlled dormitory access.
After graduation 167 organizations recruited on campus 1997–98. 97% of class of 1998 had job offers within 6 months. *Career center:* 5 full-time personnel. Services include job fairs, resume preparation, interview workshops, resume referral, career counseling, careers library, job bank, job interviews. *Graduate education:* 16% of class of 1999 went directly to graduate and professional school: 6% engineering, 6% graduate arts and sciences, 3% business, 1% law, 0.2% medicine.
Freshmen 2,568 applied, 2,119 admitted, 707 enrolled. 6 National Merit Scholars, 22 valedictorians.

Average high school GPA	3.31	SAT verbal scores above 500	87%
SAT math scores above 500	95%	ACT above 18	N/R
From top 10% of their h.s. class	39%	From top quarter	76%
From top half	95%	1998 freshmen returning in 1999	85%

Application *Options:* eApply at www.CollegeQuest.com, Common Application, early admission, early decision, deferred entrance. *Application fee:* $30. *Required:* high school transcript; 1 letter of recommendation. *Recommended:* interview.

New York

Standardized tests *Admission: Required:* SAT I or ACT. *Recommended:* SAT II Subject Tests.
Significant dates *Application deadlines:* 3/15 (freshmen), rolling (transfers). *Early decision:* 12/1 (for plan 1), 1/15 (for plan 2). *Notification:* 12/15 (early decision plan 1), 2/1 (early decision plan 2). *Financial aid deadline priority date:* 3/1.
Freshman Application Contact
Mr. Brian T. Grant, Director of Enrollment Operations, Clarkson University, Holcroft House, Potsdam, NY 13699. **Phone:** 315-268-6479. **Toll-free phone:** 800-527-6577. **Fax:** 315-268-7647. **E-mail:** admission@clarkson.edu
Visit CollegeQuest.com for information on majors offered and athletics. College video available at CollegeQuest.com.

■ *See page 1432 for a narrative description.*

COLGATE UNIVERSITY
Hamilton, New York

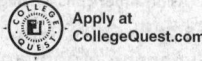

- **Independent**, comprehensive, founded 1819
- **Degrees** bachelor's and master's
- **Rural** 515-acre campus
- **Coed**, 2,868 undergraduate students, 98% full-time, 52% women, 48% men
- **Very difficult** entrance level, 42% of applicants were admitted
- **10:1 student-to-undergraduate faculty ratio**
- **89% graduate** in 6 years or less
- **$24,750 tuition** and fees
- **$21,543 average financial aid** package, $12,777 average indebtedness upon graduation, $380.3 million endowment

Students *Undergraduates:* 2,806 full-time, 62 part-time. Students come from 44 states and territories, 29 other countries. *The most frequently chosen baccalaureate fields are:* biological/life sciences, English, social sciences and history. *Graduate:* 8 in graduate degree programs.

From out-of-state	68%	Reside on campus	91%
Transferred in	1%	International students	2%
African Americans	5%	Asian Americans/Pacific Islanders	6%
Hispanic Americans	4%	Native Americans	1%

Faculty 279 (82% full-time), 92% with terminal degrees.
Expenses (1999–2000) *Comprehensive fee:* $31,080 includes full-time tuition ($24,575), mandatory fees ($175), and room and board ($6330). *College room only:* $3055. Full-time tuition and fees vary according to course load. Room and board charges vary according to board plan and housing facility. *Part-time tuition:* $3071 per course. Part-time tuition and fees vary according to course load. *Payment plans:* tuition prepayment, installment, deferred payment. *Waivers:* employees or children of employees.
Library Everett Needham Case Library plus 1 other. *Operations spending 1999–2000:* $3.7 million. *Collection:* 600,000 titles, 2,250 serial subscriptions, 5,752 audiovisual materials.
College life *Housing:* on-campus residence required through sophomore year. *Option:* coed. *Social organizations:* national fraternities, national sororities, local fraternities; 33% of eligible men and 31% of eligible women are members. *Most popular organizations:* Volunteer Colgate, student government, cultural/ethnic interest groups, student publications, performance groups.
Campus security 24-hour emergency response devices and patrols, student patrols, late-night transport-escort service, controlled dormitory access.
After graduation 109 organizations recruited on campus 1997–98. 79% of class of 1998 had job offers within 6 months. *Career center:* 7 full-time personnel. Services include job fairs, resume preparation, interview workshops, resume referral, career counseling, careers library, job bank, job interviews. *Graduate education:* 14% of class of 1999 went directly to graduate and professional school: 5% graduate arts and sciences, 4% law, 4% medicine, 1% business.
Freshmen 5,590 applied, 2,345 admitted, 750 enrolled. 31 valedictorians.

Average high school GPA	3.39	SAT verbal scores above 500	98%
SAT math scores above 500	97%	ACT above 18	89%
From top 10% of their h.s. class	66%	From top quarter	84%
From top half	98%	1998 freshmen returning in 1999	98%

Application *Options:* eApply at www.CollegeQuest.com, Common Application, electronic application, early admission, early decision, deferred entrance. *Application fee:* $50. *Required:* essay or personal statement; high school transcript; 3 letters of recommendation.
Standardized tests *Admission: Required:* SAT I with 3 SAT II Subject Tests (including SAT II: Writing Test) or ACT.
Significant dates *Application deadlines:* 1/15 (freshmen), 3/15 (transfers). *Early decision:* 11/15 (for plan 1), 1/15 (for plan 2). *Notification:* 4/1 (freshmen), 12/15 (early decision plan 1), 2/15 (early decision plan 2). *Financial aid deadline:* 2/1.
Freshman Application Contact
Ms. Mary F. Hill, Dean of Admission, Colgate University, 13 Oak Drive, Hamilton, NY 13346-1386. **Phone:** 315-228-7401. **Fax:** 315-228-7798. **E-mail:** admission@mail.colgate.edu
Visit CollegeQuest.com for information on majors offered and athletics.

COLLEGE OF AERONAUTICS
Flushing, New York

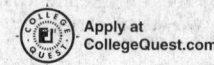

- **Independent**, 4-year, founded 1932
- **Degrees** associate and bachelor's
- **Urban** 6-acre campus
- **Coed**, primarily men, 1,264 undergraduate students, 74% full-time, 7% women, 93% men
- **Minimally difficult** entrance level, 45% of applicants were admitted
- **11:1 student-to-undergraduate faculty ratio**
- **51% graduate** in 6 years or less
- **$8500 tuition** and fees
- **$8148 average financial aid** package, $18,000 average indebtedness upon graduation, $39.5 million endowment

Students *Undergraduates:* 932 full-time, 332 part-time. Students come from 10 states and territories, 15 other countries.

From out-of-state	6%	Age 25 or older	35%
Transferred in	6%	International students	5%
African Americans	23%	Asian Americans/Pacific Islanders	14%
Hispanic Americans	36%	Native Americans	0.1%

Faculty 60 (87% full-time).
Expenses (1999–2000) *Tuition:* full-time $8250; part-time $275 per credit. *Required fees:* full-time $250; $125 per term part-time. Full-time tuition and fees vary according to program. *Payment plan:* installment.
Library George A. Vaughn Memorial Library. *Operations spending 1999–2000:* $166,000. *Collection:* 62,000 titles, 400 serial subscriptions.
College life *Most popular organizations:* Hispanic Society of Aeronautical Engineers, student government, Women in Aviation International, Society of Automotive Engineers, American Association of Airport Executives.
Campus security 24-hour emergency response devices and patrols.
After graduation 94% of class of 1998 had job offers within 6 months. *Career center:* 2 full-time personnel. Services include job fairs, resume preparation, resume referral, career counseling, job interviews. *Graduate education:* 20% of class of 1999 went directly to graduate and professional school.
Freshmen 772 applied, 351 admitted, 320 enrolled. 2 National Merit Scholars, 3 class presidents, 8 student government officers.

Average high school GPA	2.8	SAT verbal scores above 500	N/R
SAT math scores above 500	N/R	ACT above 18	N/R
From top 10% of their h.s. class	5%	From top quarter	15%
From top half	57%	1998 freshmen returning in 1999	67%

Application *Options:* eApply at www.CollegeQuest.com, deferred entrance. *Application fee:* $25. *Required:* high school transcript; minimum 2.0 GPA. *Required for some:* interview. *Recommended:* interview.
Standardized tests *Admission: Required for some:* SAT I.
Significant dates *Application deadlines:* rolling (freshmen), rolling (transfers). *Financial aid deadline:* continuous.
Freshman Application Contact
Mr. Vincent J. Montera, Director of Admissions, College of Aeronautics, 8601 23rd Avenue, Flushing, NY 11369-1037. **Phone:** 718-429-6600 Ext. 188. **Toll-free phone:** 800-776-2376. **Fax:** 718-429-0256. **E-mail:** pro@aero.edu
Visit CollegeQuest.com for information on majors offered and athletics. College video and electronic viewbook available at CollegeQuest.com.

■ *See page 1454 for a narrative description.*

New York

COLLEGE OF INSURANCE
New York, New York

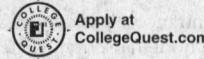 Apply at CollegeQuest.com

- **Independent**, comprehensive, founded 1962
- **Degrees** associate, bachelor's, and master's
- **Urban** 2-acre campus
- **Coed**, 182 undergraduate students, 56% full-time, 53% women, 47% men
- **Very difficult** entrance level, 71% of applicants were admitted
- **11:1 student-to-undergraduate faculty ratio**
- **50% graduate** in 6 years or less
- **$14,612 tuition** and fees
- **$17,397 average financial aid** package, $16,435 average indebtedness upon graduation, $7.4 million endowment

Students *Undergraduates:* 102 full-time, 80 part-time. Students come from 20 other countries. *The most frequently chosen baccalaureate field is:* business/marketing. *Graduate:* 87 in graduate degree programs.

From out-of-state	18%	Reside on campus	50%
Age 25 or older	24%		

Faculty 35 (29% full-time), 29% with terminal degrees.

Expenses (1999–2000) *Comprehensive fee:* $22,512 includes full-time tuition ($14,252), mandatory fees ($360), and room and board ($7900). Full-time tuition and fees vary according to program. Room and board charges vary according to board plan. *Part-time tuition:* $495 per credit. *Part-time fees:* $15 per credit. Part-time tuition and fees vary according to course load, degree level, and program. *Payment plan:* installment. *Waivers:* employees or children of employees.

Library The Kathryn and Shelby Cullom Davis Library plus 1 other. *Operations spending 1999–2000:* $365,770. *Collection:* 418 serial subscriptions, 175 audiovisual materials.

College life *Housing: Option:* coed. *Social organizations:* national fraternities. *Most popular organizations:* Gamma Iota Sigma, Commuter Forum, Golf Club.

Campus security 24-hour emergency response devices and patrols.

After graduation 30 organizations recruited on campus 1997–98. 95% of class of 1998 had job offers within 6 months. *Career center:* 1 full-time personnel. Services include job fairs, resume preparation, resume referral, career counseling, careers library, job bank, job interviews.

Freshmen 56 applied, 40 admitted, 13 enrolled.

SAT verbal scores above 500	88%	SAT math scores above 500	93%
ACT above 18	N/R	From top 10% of their h.s. class	35%
From top quarter	70%	From top half	85%
1998 freshmen returning in 1999	72%		

Application *Options:* eApply at www.CollegeQuest.com, Common Application, electronic application, early decision, deferred entrance. *Application fee:* $30. *Required:* essay or personal statement; high school transcript; minimum 2.5 GPA; interview. *Recommended:* letters of recommendation.

Standardized tests *Admission: Required:* SAT I or ACT.

Significant dates *Application deadlines:* 5/1 (freshmen), 8/1 (transfers). *Early decision:* 12/1. *Notification:* 1/1 (early decision). *Financial aid deadline:* continuous.

Freshman Application Contact
Ms. Theresa C. Marro, Director of Admissions, College of Insurance, 101 Murray Street, New York, NY 10007. **Phone:** 212-815-9232. **Toll-free phone:** 800-356-5146. **E-mail:** admissions@tci.edu

Visit CollegeQuest.com for information on majors offered and athletics. College video available at CollegeQuest.com.

■ *See page 1456 for a narrative description.*

COLLEGE OF MOUNT SAINT VINCENT
Riverdale, New York

Apply at CollegeQuest.com

- **Independent**, comprehensive, founded 1911
- **Degrees** associate, bachelor's, master's, and post-master's certificates
- **Suburban** 70-acre campus with easy access to New York City
- **Coed**, 1,202 undergraduate students, 81% full-time, 78% women, 22% men
- **Moderately difficult** entrance level, 73% of applicants were admitted
- **12:1 student-to-undergraduate faculty ratio**
- **$15,070 tuition** and fees
- **$12,000 average financial aid** package, $3.6 million endowment

The College has 27 majors and 10 programs of study, including business, education, health sciences, and liberal arts. The CMSV internship program offers more than 500 opportunities annually within corporations in the New York metropolitan area. Internships are available in every major. World Wide Web: http://www.cmsv.edu.

Students *Undergraduates:* 970 full-time, 232 part-time. Students come from 14 states and territories, 8 other countries. *The most frequently chosen baccalaureate fields are:* education, health professions and related sciences, social sciences and history. *Graduate:* 225 in graduate degree programs.

From out-of-state	5%	Reside on campus	48%
Age 25 or older	22%	Transferred in	4%
International students	1%	African Americans	19%
Asian Americans/Pacific Islanders	9%	Hispanic Americans	29%

Faculty 149 (48% full-time), 50% with terminal degrees.

Expenses (1999–2000) *Comprehensive fee:* $22,090 includes full-time tuition ($14,910), mandatory fees ($160), and room and board ($7020). *Part-time tuition:* $435 per credit. *Part-time fees:* $25 per term part-time. *Payment plan:* installment. *Waivers:* senior citizens and employees or children of employees.

Library Elizabeth Seton Library. *Operations spending 1999–2000:* $434,483. *Collection:* 169,529 titles, 616 serial subscriptions, 6,642 audiovisual materials.

College life *Housing: Options:* coed, women-only. *Most popular organizations:* Latino Club, Players, Dance Club, Student Nurse Association, Black Student Union.

Campus security 24-hour emergency response devices and patrols, late-night transport-escort service, controlled dormitory access, emergency call boxes.

After graduation 130 organizations recruited on campus 1997–98. 83% of class of 1998 had job offers within 6 months. *Career center:* 2 full-time personnel. Services include job fairs, resume preparation, interview workshops, resume referral, career counseling, careers library, job bank, job interviews. *Graduate education:* 15% of class of 1999 went directly to graduate and professional school.

Freshmen 1,173 applied, 851 admitted, 248 enrolled.

SAT verbal scores above 500	40%	SAT math scores above 500	32%
ACT above 18	N/R	From top 10% of their h.s. class	16%
From top quarter	31%	From top half	50%
1998 freshmen returning in 1999	82%		

Application *Options:* eApply at www.CollegeQuest.com, Common Application, electronic application, early admission, early decision, deferred entrance. *Application fee:* $25. *Required:* high school transcript; minimum 2.0 GPA; 1 letter of recommendation. *Required for some:* interview. *Recommended:* essay or personal statement; 2 letters of recommendation; interview.

Standardized tests *Admission: Required:* SAT I or ACT.

Significant dates *Application deadlines:* rolling (freshmen), rolling (transfers). *Early decision:* 11/15. *Notification:* 12/15 (early decision). *Financial aid deadline priority date:* 3/1.

Freshman Application Contact
Mrs. Lenore M. Mott, Dean of Admissions and Financial Aid, College of Mount Saint Vincent, 6301 Riverdale Avenue, Riverdale, NY 10471-1093. **Phone:** 718-405-3268. **Toll-free phone:** 800-665-CMSV. **Fax:** 718-549-7945. **E-mail:** admissns@cmsv.edu

Visit CollegeQuest.com for information on majors offered and athletics. College video available at CollegeQuest.com.

■ *See page 1460 for a narrative description.*

THE COLLEGE OF NEW ROCHELLE
New Rochelle, New York

 Apply at CollegeQuest.com

- **Independent**, comprehensive, founded 1904
- **Degrees** bachelor's and master's
- **Suburban** 20-acre campus with easy access to New York City

New York

- **Coed**, primarily women, 5,511 undergraduate students, 85% full-time, 87% women, 13% men
- **Moderately difficult** entrance level, 74% of applicants were admitted
- **10:1 student-to-undergraduate faculty ratio**
- **$11,700 tuition** and fees
- **$11,878 average financial aid** package, $16.6 million endowment

Students *Undergraduates:* 4,704 full-time, 807 part-time. Students come from 13 states and territories. *The most frequently chosen baccalaureate fields are:* health professions and related sciences, education, liberal arts/general studies. *Graduate:* 1,709 in graduate degree programs.

From out-of-state	17%	Reside on campus	58%
Age 25 or older	13%	Transferred in	1%
African Americans	37%	Asian Americans/Pacific Islanders	1%
Hispanic Americans	10%	Native Americans	0.2%

Faculty 157 (41% full-time).

Expenses (1999–2000) *Comprehensive fee:* $17,700 includes full-time tuition ($11,600), mandatory fees ($100), and room and board ($6000). Full-time tuition and fees vary according to course load and program. Room and board charges vary according to housing facility. *Part-time tuition:* $390 per credit. Part-time tuition and fees vary according to course load. *Payment plans:* tuition prepayment, installment. *Waivers:* senior citizens and employees or children of employees.

Library Gill Library. *Operations spending 1999–2000:* $1.4 million. *Collection:* 189,800 titles, 1,441 serial subscriptions, 6,881 audiovisual materials.

College life *Housing: Option:* women-only. *Most popular organizations:* drama club, Science and Math Society, Business Board, Latin-American Women's Society, karate club.

Campus security 24-hour emergency response devices and patrols, late-night transport-escort service, controlled dormitory access, 24-hour monitored security cameras at residence hall entrances.

After graduation 27 organizations recruited on campus 1997–98. *Career center:* 5 full-time, 1 part-time personnel. Services include job fairs, resume preparation, resume referral, career/interest testing, career counseling, careers library, job bank, job interviews. **Graduate education:** 37% of class of 1999 went directly to graduate and professional school.

Freshmen 663 applied, 491 admitted, 1,013 enrolled.

Average high school GPA	2.9	SAT verbal scores above 500	51%
SAT math scores above 500	32%	ACT above 18	100%
From top 10% of their h.s. class	21%	From top quarter	36%
From top half	73%	1998 freshmen returning in 1999	78%

Application *Options:* eApply at www.CollegeQuest.com, Common Application, early admission, deferred entrance. *Application fee:* $20. *Required:* high school transcript. *Recommended:* essay or personal statement; 2 letters of recommendation; interview.

Standardized tests *Admission: Required:* SAT I or ACT.

Significant dates *Application deadlines:* rolling (freshmen), rolling (transfers). *Financial aid deadline:* continuous.

Freshman Application Contact
Mrs. Kelly Getman-Crowley, Director of Admission, The College of New Rochelle, 29 Castle Place, New Rochelle, NY 10805-2339. **Phone:** 914-654-5452. **Toll-free phone:** 800-933-5923. **Fax:** 914-654-5554.

Visit CollegeQuest.com for information on majors offered and athletics. College video available at CollegeQuest.com.

- *See page 1464 for a narrative description.*

THE COLLEGE OF SAINT ROSE
Albany, New York

Apply at CollegeQuest.com

- **Independent**, comprehensive, founded 1920
- **Degrees** bachelor's and master's
- **Urban** 22-acre campus
- **Coed**, 2,729 undergraduate students, 76% full-time, 73% women, 27% men
- **Moderately difficult** entrance level, 75% of applicants were admitted
- **15:1 student-to-undergraduate faculty ratio**
- **65% graduate** in 6 years or less
- **$12,654 tuition** and fees

- **$10,225 average financial aid** package, $16,379 average indebtedness upon graduation, $14 million endowment

Students *Undergraduates:* 2,085 full-time, 644 part-time. *The most frequently chosen baccalaureate fields are:* business/marketing, education, health professions and related sciences. *Graduate:* 1,438 in graduate degree programs.

From out-of-state	3%	Reside on campus	30%
Age 25 or older	34%	Transferred in	12%
International students	0.4%	African Americans	3%
Asian Americans/Pacific Islanders	1%	Hispanic Americans	2%
Native Americans	0.3%		

Faculty 326 (43% full-time), 32% with terminal degrees.

Expenses (1999–2000) *Comprehensive fee:* $19,012 includes full-time tuition ($12,434), mandatory fees ($220), and room and board ($6358). *College room only:* $2970. Full-time tuition and fees vary according to course load and program. Room and board charges vary according to board plan. *Part-time tuition:* $414 per credit. *Part-time fees:* $2 per credit; $15 per term part-time. Part-time tuition and fees vary according to class time. *Waivers:* employees or children of employees.

Library Neil Hellman Library plus 1 other. *Operations spending 1999–2000:* $767,142. *Collection:* 133,175 titles, 1,042 serial subscriptions.

College life *Housing: Options:* coed, men-only, women-only. *Most popular organizations:* Student Association, Student Events Board, Circle K, Student Education Association, Student Speech, Hearing and Language Association.

Campus security 24-hour emergency response devices and patrols, student patrols, late-night transport-escort service, controlled dormitory access.

After graduation 121 organizations recruited on campus 1997–98. *Career center:* 3 full-time, 1 part-time personnel. Services include job fairs, resume preparation, interview workshops, resume referral, career/interest testing, career counseling, careers library, job bank, job interviews. **Graduate education:** 42% of class of 1999 went directly to graduate and professional school.

Freshmen 1,371 applied, 1,035 admitted, 406 enrolled.

SAT verbal scores above 500	69%	SAT math scores above 500	65%
ACT above 18	N/R	From top 10% of their h.s. class	12%
From top quarter	43%	From top half	82%
1998 freshmen returning in 1999	87%		

Application *Options:* eApply at www.CollegeQuest.com, Common Application, electronic application, early admission, deferred entrance. *Application fee:* $30. *Required:* essay or personal statement; high school transcript; 1 letter of recommendation. *Required for some:* interview. *Recommended:* minimum 3.0 GPA; interview.

Standardized tests *Admission: Required:* SAT I or ACT.

Significant dates *Application deadlines:* 2/1 (freshmen), 7/1 (transfers). *Financial aid deadline:* 3/1.

Freshman Application Contact
Ms. Mary Elizabeth Amico, Associate Dean of Admissions and Enrollment Services, The College of Saint Rose, 432 Western Avenue, Albany, NY 12203-1419. **Phone:** 518-454-5150. **Toll-free phone:** 800-637-8556. **Fax:** 518-451-2013. **E-mail:** admit@mail.strose.edu

Visit CollegeQuest.com for information on majors offered and athletics. College video available at CollegeQuest.com.

- *See page 1480 for a narrative description.*

COLLEGE OF STATEN ISLAND OF THE CITY UNIVERSITY OF NEW YORK
Staten Island, New York

- **State and locally supported**, comprehensive, founded 1955
- **Degrees** associate, bachelor's, master's, and post-master's certificates
- **Urban** 204-acre campus with easy access to New York City
- **Coed**, 9,858 undergraduate students, 65% full-time, 58% women, 42% men
- **Noncompetitive** entrance level
- **$3316 tuition** and fees (in-state); $6916 (out-of-state)
- **$2.7 million endowment**

New York

College of Staten Island of the City University of New York (continued)
The College of Staten Island/CUNY, a senior college, offers 11,000 students a state-of-the-art, picturesque 204-acre campus and a comprehensive range of bachelor's degrees and selected associate and master's degree programs in liberal arts and sciences, engineering science and physics, and such professional areas as business, education, nursing, and social work. For more information, students should visit the Web site (http://www.csi.cuny.edu).

Part of City University of New York System.

Students *Undergraduates:* 6,439 full-time, 3,419 part-time. Students come from 3 states and territories, 98 other countries. *Graduate:* 1,240 in graduate degree programs.

Transferred in	6%	International students	2%
African Americans	12%	Asian Americans/Pacific Islanders	9%
Hispanic Americans	9%	Native Americans	0.2%

Faculty 780 (39% full-time).

Expenses (1999–2000) *Tuition, state resident:* full-time $3200; part-time $135 per semester hour. *Tuition, nonresident:* full-time $6800; part-time $285 per semester hour. *Required fees:* full-time $116; $32 per term part-time. *Payment plan:* deferred payment. *Waivers:* senior citizens and employees or children of employees.

Library College of Staten Island Library. *Operations spending 1999–2000:* $2 million. *Collection:* 203,368 titles, 11,074 serial subscriptions, 14,350 audiovisual materials.

College life *Housing:* college housing not available. *Most popular organizations:* High Society Club, Spanish, Hispanic Club, Chinese Student Association, Fashion Club, Apostolic Christian Life Center.

Campus security 24-hour emergency response devices and patrols, late-night transport-escort service, emergency call boxes, bicycle patrols.

After graduation 110 organizations recruited on campus 1997–98. *Career center:* 4 full-time, 2 part-time personnel. Services include job fairs, resume preparation, interview workshops, resume referral, career counseling, careers library, job bank, job interviews.

Freshmen 1,851 enrolled.

SAT verbal scores above 500	N/R	SAT math scores above 500	N/R
ACT above 18	N/R	1998 freshmen returning in 1999	83%

Application *Application fee:* $40. *Required:* high school transcript.

Significant dates *Application deadlines:* rolling (freshmen), rolling (transfers). *Financial aid deadline:* continuous.

Freshman Application Contact
Mr. Earl Teasley, Director of Admissions and Recruitment, College of Staten Island of the City University of New York, 2800 Victory Boulevard, Staten Island, NY 10314-6600. **Phone:** 718-982-2011. **Fax:** 718-982-2500.

Visit CollegeQuest.com for information on majors offered and athletics.

■ *See page 1486 for a narrative description.*

COLUMBIA COLLEGE
New York, New York

- **Independent**, 4-year, founded 1754
- **Degree** bachelor's
- **Urban** 35-acre campus
- **Coed**, 3,913 undergraduate students, 100% full-time, 51% women, 49% men
- **Most difficult** entrance level, 14% of applicants were admitted
- **7:1 student-to-undergraduate faculty ratio**
- **$24,974 tuition** and fees
- **$21,365 average financial aid** package, $3.4 billion system endowment

Part of Columbia University.

Students *Undergraduates:* 3,913 full-time. Students come from 49 states and territories, 39 other countries.

Reside on campus	90%	Transferred in	2%

Faculty 632 full-time.

Expenses (1999–2000) *One-time required fee:* $45. *Comprehensive fee:* $32,706 includes full-time tuition ($24,150), mandatory fees ($824), and room and board ($7732). *Payment plans:* tuition prepayment, installment. *Waivers:* employees or children of employees.

Library Butler Library plus 20 others. *Collection:* 6.8 million titles, 66,000 serial subscriptions.

College life *Housing:* on-campus residence required in freshman year. *Options:* coed, men-only, women-only. *Social organizations:* national fraternities, national sororities, coed fraternities; 19% of eligible men and 25% of eligible women are members.

Campus security 24-hour emergency response devices and patrols, late-night transport-escort service, 24-hour ID check at door.

After graduation *Career center:* 17 full-time personnel. Services include job fairs, resume preparation, resume referral, career counseling, careers library, job bank, job interviews. *Graduate education:* 80% of class of 1999 went directly to graduate and professional school. *Major awards:* 1 Rhodes, 2 Marshall, 12 Fulbright Scholars.

Freshmen 13,013 applied, 1,767 admitted, 964 enrolled. 1 Westinghouse recipient.

SAT verbal scores above 500	N/R	SAT math scores above 500	N/R
ACT above 18	N/R	1998 freshmen returning in 1999	96%

Application *Options:* early admission, early decision, deferred entrance. *Application fee:* $50. *Required:* essay or personal statement; high school transcript; 3 letters of recommendation. *Recommended:* interview.

Standardized tests *Admission: Required:* SAT I or ACT, SAT II Subject Tests, SAT II: Writing Test.

Significant dates *Application deadlines:* 1/1 (freshmen), 4/1 (transfers). *Early decision:* 11/1. *Notification:* 3/31 (freshmen), 12/15 (early decision). *Financial aid deadline:* 2/10.

Freshman Application Contact
Mr. Eric Furda, Director of Undergraduate Admissions, Columbia College, 1130 Amsterdam Avenue MC 2807, New York, NY 10027. **Phone:** 212-854-2522. **Fax:** 212-854-1209. **E-mail:** ugrad-admiss@columbia.edu

Visit CollegeQuest.com for information on majors offered and athletics. Electronic viewbook available at CollegeQuest.com.

■ *See page 1514 for a narrative description.*

COLUMBIA UNIVERSITY, BARNARD COLLEGE
New York—See Barnard College

COLUMBIA UNIVERSITY, COLUMBIA COLLEGE
New York—See Columbia College

COLUMBIA UNIVERSITY, SCHOOL OF GENERAL STUDIES
New York, New York

- **Independent**, 4-year, founded 1754
- **Degree** bachelor's
- **Urban** 36-acre campus
- **Coed**, 1,145 undergraduate students, 48% full-time, 55% women, 45% men
- **Most difficult** entrance level, 46% of applicants were admitted
- **7:1 student-to-undergraduate faculty ratio**
- **$23,740 tuition** and fees
- **$12.1 million endowment**

Part of Columbia University.

Students *Undergraduates:* Students come from 36 states and territories. *The most frequently chosen baccalaureate field is:* liberal arts/general studies.

From out-of-state	42%	Age 25 or older	75%
African Americans	9%	Asian Americans/Pacific Islanders	10%
Hispanic Americans	8%	Native Americans	0.3%

Faculty 632 (100% full-time), 100% with terminal degrees.

New York

Expenses (1999–2000) *One-time required fee:* $30. *Comprehensive fee:* $32,740 includes full-time tuition ($23,040), mandatory fees ($700), and room and board ($9000). Full-time tuition and fees vary according to course load. Room and board charges vary according to housing facility. *Part-time tuition:* $768 per credit. Part-time tuition and fees vary according to course load. *Payment plans:* tuition prepayment, deferred payment. *Waivers:* employees or children of employees.
Library Butler Library plus 21 others. *Collection:* 5.6 million titles, 59,400 serial subscriptions.
College life *Housing: Option:* coed. *Social organizations:* national fraternities, national sororities. *Most popular organizations:* Columbia Dramatists, writers club, General Studies Student Council, The Observer.
Campus security 24-hour emergency response devices and patrols, late-night transport-escort service.
After graduation *Career center:* Services include resume preparation, career counseling, careers library, job bank, job interviews.
Freshmen 783 applied, 360 admitted.

| SAT verbal scores above 500 | N/R | SAT math scores above 500 | N/R |
| ACT above 18 | N/R | 1998 freshmen returning in 1999 | 90% |

Application *Options:* electronic application, deferred entrance. *Application fee:* $50. *Required:* essay or personal statement; high school transcript. *Required for some:* interview.
Standardized tests *Admission: Required for some:* SAT I or ACT.
Significant dates *Application deadlines:* 7/1 (freshmen), 7/1 (transfers). *Financial aid deadline priority date:* 7/1.
Freshman Application Contact
Mr. Carlos A. Porro, Director of Admissions, Columbia University, School of General Studies, Mail Code 4101, Lewisohn Hall, 2970 Broadway, New York, NY 10027-9829. **Phone:** 212-854-2772. **Toll-free phone:** 800-895-1169. **E-mail:** gsdegree@columbia.edu
Visit CollegeQuest.com for information on majors offered and athletics. Electronic viewbook available at CollegeQuest.com.

■ *See page 1516 for a narrative description.*

COLUMBIA UNIVERSITY, THE FU FOUNDATION SCHOOL OF ENGINEERING AND APPLIED SCIENCE
New York, New York

- **Independent**, university, founded 1864
- **Degrees** bachelor's, master's, and doctoral
- **Urban** campus
- **Coed**, 1,248 undergraduate students, 100% full-time, 27% women, 73% men
- **Most difficult** entrance level, 29% of applicants were admitted
- **5:1** student-to-undergraduate faculty ratio
- **$24,974 tuition** and fees
- **$22,438 average financial aid** package, $16,449 average indebtedness upon graduation, $3.4 billion system endowment

Part of Columbia University.
Students *Undergraduates:* 1,248 full-time. Students come from 44 states and territories, 31 other countries.

| Reside on campus | 90% | Transferred in | 1% |

Faculty 108 full-time.
Expenses (1999–2000) *One-time required fee:* $45. *Comprehensive fee:* $32,706 includes full-time tuition ($24,150), mandatory fees ($824), and room and board ($7732). *Payment plans:* tuition prepayment, installment, deferred payment. *Waivers:* minority students and employees or children of employees.
Library Butler Library plus 20 others. *Collection:* 6.8 million titles, 66,000 serial subscriptions.
College life *Housing:* on-campus residence required in freshman year. *Options:* coed, men-only, women-only. *Social organizations:* national fraternities, national sororities, coed fraternities; 19% of eligible men and 25% of eligible women are members.
Campus security 24-hour emergency response devices and patrols, late-night transport-escort service, 24-hour ID check at door.

After graduation *Career center:* 17 full-time personnel. Services include job fairs, resume preparation, resume referral, career counseling, careers library, job bank, job interviews.
Freshmen 2,293 applied, 661 admitted, 316 enrolled.

| SAT verbal scores above 500 | N/R | SAT math scores above 500 | N/R |
| ACT above 18 | N/R | 1998 freshmen returning in 1999 | 89% |

Application *Options:* early admission, early decision, deferred entrance. *Application fee:* $50. *Required:* essay or personal statement; high school transcript; 3 letters of recommendation. *Recommended:* minimum 3.0 GPA; interview.
Standardized tests *Admission: Required:* SAT I or ACT, SAT II Subject Tests, SAT II: Writing Test.
Significant dates *Application deadlines:* 1/1 (freshmen), 4/1 (transfers). *Early decision:* 11/1. *Notification:* 3/31 (freshmen), 12/15 (early decision). *Financial aid deadline:* 2/10.
Freshman Application Contact
Mr. Eric Furda, Director of Undergraduate Admissions, Columbia University, The Fu Foundation School of Engineering and Applied Science, 1130 Amsterdam Avenue MC 2807, New York, NY 10027. **Phone:** 212-854-2522. **Fax:** 212-854-1209. **E-mail:** ugrad-admiss@columbia.edu
Visit CollegeQuest.com for information on majors offered and athletics. Electronic viewbook available at CollegeQuest.com.

CONCORDIA COLLEGE
Bronxville, New York

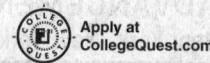
Apply at CollegeQuest.com

- **Independent Lutheran**, 4-year, founded 1881
- **Degrees** associate and bachelor's
- **Suburban** 33-acre campus with easy access to New York City
- **Coed**, 539 undergraduate students, 95% full-time, 59% women, 41% men
- **Moderately difficult** entrance level, 70% of applicants were admitted
- **10:1** student-to-undergraduate faculty ratio
- **41.5% graduate** in 6 years or less
- **$14,350 tuition** and fees
- **$6.4 million endowment**

Part of Concordia University System.
Students *Undergraduates:* 511 full-time, 28 part-time. Students come from 18 states and territories. *The most frequently chosen baccalaureate fields are:* business/marketing, biological/life sciences, education.

From out-of-state	30%	Reside on campus	68%
Age 25 or older	18%	Transferred in	6%
International students	1%	African Americans	16%
Asian Americans/Pacific Islanders	5%	Hispanic Americans	12%

Faculty 57 (60% full-time), 81% with terminal degrees.
Expenses (2000–2001) *Comprehensive fee:* $20,550 includes full-time tuition ($14,350) and room and board ($6200). *College room only:* $3100. Room and board charges vary according to board plan. *Part-time tuition:* $388 per credit hour. Part-time tuition and fees vary according to course load. *Payment plan:* installment. *Waivers:* senior citizens and employees or children of employees.
Library Scheele Memorial Library. *Operations spending 1999–2000:* $276,825. *Collection:* 71,500 titles, 467 serial subscriptions, 7,660 audiovisual materials.
College life *Housing: Options:* men-only, women-only. *Social organizations:* national fraternities, national sororities; 5% of eligible men and 5% of eligible women are members. *Most popular organizations:* Campus Christian Ministries, drama club, Student Government Association, International and Afro/Latin American Club, yearbook and newspaper.
Campus security 24-hour emergency response devices and patrols, late-night transport-escort service, controlled dormitory access.
After graduation 72% of class of 1998 had job offers within 6 months. *Career center:* 2 full-time personnel. Services include resume preparation, resume referral, career/interest testing, career counseling, careers library, job bank, job interviews. *Graduate education:* 25% of class of 1999 went directly to graduate and professional school: 20% education, 3% business, 2% theology.
Freshmen 510 applied, 357 admitted, 118 enrolled. 8 class presidents, 3 valedictorians, 24 student government officers.

Peterson's Guide to Four-Year Colleges 2001 www.petersons.com

New York

Concordia College (continued)

Average high school GPA	3.01	SAT verbal scores above 500	41%
SAT math scores above 500	34%	ACT above 18	N/R
From top 10% of their h.s. class	20%	From top quarter	40%
From top half	40%	1998 freshmen returning in 1999	71%

Application *Options:* eApply at www.CollegeQuest.com, electronic application, early admission, deferred entrance. *Application fee:* $30. *Required:* high school transcript; 1 letter of recommendation. *Required for some:* interview. *Recommended:* essay or personal statement; minimum 2.5 GPA.

Standardized tests *Admission: Required:* SAT I or ACT.

Significant dates *Application deadlines:* 3/15 (freshmen), 7/15 (transfers). *Notification:* continuous until 2/1 (freshmen). *Financial aid deadline priority date:* 3/15.

Freshman Application Contact
Ms. Becky Hendricks, Dean of Enrollment Management, Concordia College, 171 White Plains Road, Bronxville, NY 10708. **Phone:** 914-337-9300. **Toll-free phone:** 800-YES-COLLEGE. **Fax:** 914-395-4500. **E-mail:** admission@concordia-ny.edu

Visit CollegeQuest.com for information on majors offered and athletics.

■ *See page 1522 for a narrative description.*

COOPER UNION FOR THE ADVANCEMENT OF SCIENCE AND ART
New York, New York

■ **$183.4 million endowment**

Cooper Union awards full tuition scholarships to every registered student. The value of the scholarship is approximately $100,000 for 4 years. Cooper Union has been cited by *U.S. News & World Report* as the number one engineering school of its kind and as one of the most selective colleges in the country.

Students *Undergraduates:* 841 full-time, 4 part-time. Students come from 33 states and territories. *The most frequently chosen baccalaureate fields are:* engineering/engineering technologies, architecture, visual/performing arts. *Graduate:* 37 in graduate degree programs.

From out-of-state	37%	Reside on campus	19%
Age 25 or older	2%	Transferred in	5%
International students	10%	African Americans	5%
Asian Americans/Pacific Islanders	25%	Hispanic Americans	8%
Native Americans	0.4%		

Faculty 244 (22% full-time), 38% with terminal degrees.

Expenses (2000–2001) All students are awarded full-tuition scholarships. Living expenses subsidized by college-administered financial aid.

Library Cooper Union Library. *Operations spending 1999–2000:* $683,432. *Collection:* 97,000 titles, 370 serial subscriptions.

College life *Housing: Option:* coed. *Social organizations:* national fraternities, national sororities; 20% of eligible men and 10% of eligible women are members. *Most popular organizations:* Campus Crusade for Christ, Chinese Students Association, Kesher, Cooper Union Athletic Association, Muslim Students Organization.

Campus security 24-hour emergency response devices and patrols, security guards.

After graduation 80 organizations recruited on campus 1997–98. 98% of class of 1998 had job offers within 6 months. *Career center:* 2 full-time, 1 part-time personnel. Services include job fairs, resume preparation, interview workshops, resume referral, career counseling, careers library, job bank, job interviews. *Graduate education:* 43% of class of 1999 went directly to graduate and professional school: 15% engineering, 14% graduate arts and sciences, 6% law, 5% medicine, 3% business, 1% dentistry, 1% veterinary medicine. *Major awards:* 2 Fulbright Scholars.

Freshmen 2,216 applied, 290 admitted, 186 enrolled.

Average high school GPA	3.4	SAT verbal scores above 500	N/R
SAT math scores above 500	N/R	ACT above 18	N/R
From top 10% of their h.s. class	80%	1998 freshmen returning in 1999	92%

Application *Options:* early admission, early decision, deferred entrance. *Application fee:* $35. *Required:* high school transcript; minimum 2.0 GPA. *Required for some:* essay or personal statement; 3 letters of recommendation; portfolio, home examination. *Recommended:* minimum 3.0 GPA.

Standardized tests *Admission: Required:* SAT I or ACT. *Required for some:* SAT II Subject Tests.

Significant dates *Financial aid deadline:* 5/1. *Priority date:* 4/15.

Freshman Application Contact
Mr. Richard Bory, Dean of Admissions and Records and Registrar, Cooper Union for the Advancement of Science and Art, 30 Cooper Square, New York, NY 10003-7120. **Phone:** 212-353-4120. **Fax:** 212-353-4343. **E-mail:** admission@cooper.edu

Visit CollegeQuest.com for information on majors offered and athletics.

■ *See page 1534 for a narrative description.*

CORNELL UNIVERSITY
Ithaca, New York

■ **Independent**, university, founded 1865
■ **Degrees** bachelor's, master's, doctoral, and first professional
■ **Small-town** 745-acre campus with easy access to Syracuse
■ **Coed**, 13,639 undergraduate students, 100% full-time, 48% women, 52% men
■ **Most difficult** entrance level, 33% of applicants were admitted
■ **11:1 student-to-undergraduate faculty ratio**
■ **91% graduate** in 6 years or less
■ **$10,418 tuition** and fees (in-state); $19,988 (out-of-state)
■ **$18,700 average financial aid** package, $16,900 average indebtedness upon graduation, $2.4 billion endowment

Students *Undergraduates:* 13,639 full-time. Students come from 56 states and territories, 81 other countries. *The most frequently chosen baccalaureate fields are:* agriculture, business/marketing, engineering/engineering technologies. *Graduate:* 843 in professional programs, 4,509 in other graduate degree programs.

From out-of-state	55%	Reside on campus	56%
Age 25 or older	2%	Transferred in	4%
International students	7%	African Americans	4%
Asian Americans/Pacific Islanders	16%	Hispanic Americans	6%
Native Americans	1%		

Faculty 1,722 (92% full-time), 89% with terminal degrees.

Expenses (1999–2000) *Comprehensive fee:* $31,675 includes full-time tuition ($23,760), mandatory fees ($88), and room and board ($7827). *College room only:* $4687. Room and board charges vary according to board plan and housing facility. *Payment plans:* tuition prepayment, installment. *Waivers:* employees or children of employees.

Library Olin Library plus 17 others. *Operations spending 1999–2000:* $17.6 million. *Collection:* 6.3 million titles, 61,941 serial subscriptions, 140,443 audiovisual materials.

College life *Housing: Options:* coed, men-only, women-only, cooperative, disabled students. *Social organizations:* national fraternities, national sororities, local fraternities; 22% of eligible men and 19% of eligible women are members. *Most popular organizations:* Student Assembly, residence hall association, Cornell Catholic Community, Cornell Hillel, Concert Commission.

Campus security 24-hour emergency response devices and patrols, late-night transport-escort service, controlled dormitory access, escort service.

After graduation 500 organizations recruited on campus 1997–98. 66% of class of 1998 had job offers within 6 months. *Career center:* 37 full-time personnel. Services include job fairs, resume preparation, resume referral, career counseling, careers library, job bank, job interviews. *Graduate education:* 32% of class of 1999 went directly to graduate and professional school. *Major awards:* 1 Marshall, 9 Fulbright Scholars.

Freshmen 19,949 applied, 6,561 admitted, 3,136 enrolled. 47 National Merit Scholars, 1 Westinghouse recipient.

SAT verbal scores above 500	98%	SAT math scores above 500	99%
ACT above 18	N/R	From top 10% of their h.s. class	80%
From top quarter	94%	From top half	100%
1998 freshmen returning in 1999	93%		

Application *Options:* electronic application, early admission, early decision, deferred entrance. *Preference* given to state residents for state-supported programs. *Application fee:* $65. *Required:* essay or personal statement; high school transcript; 1 letter of recommendation. *Required for some:* interview.

New York

Standardized tests *Admission: Required:* SAT I or ACT. *Required for some:* SAT II Subject Tests, SAT II: Writing Test.

Significant dates *Application deadlines:* 1/1 (freshmen), 3/15 (transfers). *Early decision:* 11/10. *Notification:* 4/3 (freshmen), 12/15 (early decision). *Financial aid deadline:* 2/14.

Freshman Application Contact
Ms. Doris Davis, Associate Provost of Admissions and Financial Aid, Cornell University, 410 Thurston Avenue, Ithaca, NY 14850. **Phone:** 607-255-3316. **Fax:** 607-255-0659. **E-mail:** admissions@cornell.edu

Visit CollegeQuest.com for information on majors offered and athletics. College video available at CollegeQuest.com.

■ *See page 1536 for a narrative description.*

THE CULINARY INSTITUTE OF AMERICA
Hyde Park, New York

- **Independent**, 4-year, founded 1946
- **Degrees** associate and bachelor's
- **Small-town** 150-acre campus
- **Coed**, 2,120 undergraduate students, 100% full-time, 27% women, 73% men
- **Moderately difficult** entrance level, 60% of applicants were admitted
- **18:1 student-to-undergraduate faculty ratio**
- **$15,605 tuition** and fees
- **$8325 average financial aid** package, $18,500 average indebtedness upon graduation, $19.5 million endowment

Students *Undergraduates:* 2,120 full-time. Students come from 43 states and territories, 25 other countries.

From out-of-state	74%	Age 25 or older	40%
International students	3%	African Americans	2%
Asian Americans/Pacific Islanders	3%	Hispanic Americans	5%
Native Americans	0.4%		

Faculty 119.

Expenses (2000–2001) *Comprehensive fee:* $20,985 includes full-time tuition ($15,400), mandatory fees ($205), and room and board ($5380). Full-time tuition and fees vary according to course level, degree level, program, and student level. Room and board charges vary according to housing facility. *Payment plan:* installment. *Waivers:* minority students and employees or children of employees.

Library Conrad N. Hilton Library. *Collection:* 52,626 titles, 296 serial subscriptions, 404 audiovisual materials.

College life *Housing: Option:* coed. *Most popular organizations:* Gourmet Society, Women Chefs and Restaurateurs, International Club, Black Culinary Society, The Service Club.

Campus security 24-hour emergency response devices and patrols, late-night transport-escort service, controlled dormitory access.

After graduation 200 organizations recruited on campus 1997–98. 95% of class of 1998 had job offers within 6 months. *Career center:* 8 full-time personnel. Services include job fairs, resume preparation, interview workshops, resume referral, career counseling, careers library, job bank, job interviews.

Freshmen 1,174 applied, 703 admitted, 503 enrolled.

Average high school GPA	2.5	SAT verbal scores above 500	N/R
SAT math scores above 500	N/R	ACT above 18	N/R
From top 10% of their h.s. class	7%	From top quarter	18%
From top half	43%		

Application *Option:* deferred entrance. *Preference* given to candidates with prior food service experience. *Application fee:* $30. *Required:* essay or personal statement; high school transcript; 2 letters of recommendation. *Required for some:* interview.

Significant dates *Application deadlines:* rolling (freshmen), rolling (transfers). *Early decision:* 12/15. *Notification:* 1/15 (early decision). *Financial aid deadline:* continuous.

Freshman Application Contact
Mr. Dennis Craig, Director of Admissions, The Culinary Institute of America, 433 Albany Post Road, Hyde Park, NY 12538-1499. **Phone:** 914-451-1534. **Toll-free phone:** 800-CULINARY. **Fax:** 914-452-8629. **E-mail:** admissions@culinary.edu

Visit CollegeQuest.com for information on majors offered and athletics. College video and electronic viewbook available at CollegeQuest.com.

■ *See page 1542 for a narrative description.*

C.W. POST CAMPUS OF LONG ISLAND UNIVERSITY
New York—See Long Island University, C.W. Post Campus

DAEMEN COLLEGE
Amherst, New York

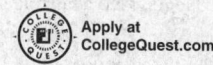
Apply at CollegeQuest.com

- **Independent**, comprehensive, founded 1947
- **Degrees** bachelor's, master's, post-master's, and postbachelor's certificates
- **Suburban** 35-acre campus with easy access to Buffalo
- **Coed**, 1,568 undergraduate students, 81% full-time, 75% women, 25% men
- **Moderately difficult** entrance level, 73% of applicants were admitted
- **14:1 student-to-undergraduate faculty ratio**
- **29% graduate** in 6 years or less
- **$12,220 tuition** and fees
- **$8440 average financial aid** package, $19,500 average indebtedness upon graduation, $1.8 million endowment

Students *Undergraduates:* 1,264 full-time, 304 part-time. Students come from 22 states and territories, 8 other countries. *The most frequently chosen baccalaureate fields are:* education, business/marketing, health professions and related sciences. *Graduate:* 110 in graduate degree programs.

From out-of-state	9%	Reside on campus	27%
Age 25 or older	29%	Transferred in	13%
International students	2%	African Americans	10%
Asian Americans/Pacific Islanders	3%	Hispanic Americans	1%
Native Americans	1%		

Faculty 175 (41% full-time), 54% with terminal degrees.

Expenses (1999–2000) *Comprehensive fee:* $18,320 includes full-time tuition ($11,800), mandatory fees ($420), and room and board ($6100). Room and board charges vary according to board plan. *Part-time tuition:* $390 per credit. *Part-time fees:* $3 per credit; $68 per term part-time. Part-time tuition and fees vary according to course load. *Payment plans:* installment, deferred payment. *Waivers:* children of alumni, senior citizens, and employees or children of employees.

Library Marian Library plus 1 other. *Operations spending 1999–2000:* $611,232. *Collection:* 123,835 titles, 983 serial subscriptions, 16,457 audiovisual materials.

College life *Housing: Options:* men-only, women-only. *Social organizations:* local fraternities, local sororities; 5% of eligible men and 3% of eligible women are members. *Most popular organizations:* Multicultural Association, Greek organizations, Student Association, ski club, resident council.

Campus security 24-hour emergency response devices and patrols, late-night transport-escort service, 24-hour security cameras.

After graduation 80 organizations recruited on campus 1997–98. 79% of class of 1998 had job offers within 6 months. *Career center:* 2 full-time personnel. Services include job fairs, resume preparation, interview workshops, resume referral, career/interest testing, career counseling, careers library, job bank, job interviews. *Graduate education:* 9% of class of 1999 went directly to graduate and professional school: 5% medicine, 3% education, 1% business.

Freshmen 1,847 applied, 1,348 admitted, 295 enrolled.

Average high school GPA	3.4	SAT verbal scores above 500	47%
SAT math scores above 500	49%	ACT above 18	72%
From top 10% of their h.s. class	13%	From top quarter	33%
From top half	69%	1998 freshmen returning in 1999	57%

Application *Options:* eApply at www.CollegeQuest.com, Common Application, early admission, early action, deferred entrance. *Application fee:* $25. *Required:* high school transcript; minimum 2.0 GPA. *Required for some:* essay or personal statement; 3 letters of recommendation; interview; portfolio for art program, supplemental application for physician's assistant program. *Recommended:* interview.

New York

Daemen College (continued)
Standardized tests *Admission: Required:* SAT I or ACT.
Significant dates *Application deadlines:* rolling (freshmen), rolling (transfers). *Early action:* 8/30. *Notification:* 9/1 (early action). *Financial aid deadline priority date:* 2/15.
Freshman Application Contact
Ms. Maria P. Dillard, Dean of Admissions and Enrollment Management, Daemen College, 4380 Main Street, Amherst, NY 14226-3592. **Phone:** 716-839-8225. **Toll-free phone:** 800-462-7652. **Fax:** 716-839-8516. **E-mail:** admissions@daemen.edu
Visit CollegeQuest.com for information on majors offered and athletics. College video available at CollegeQuest.com.

■ *See page 1550 for a narrative description.*

DARKEI NOAM RABBINICAL COLLEGE
Brooklyn, New York

Admissions Office Contact
Darkei Noam Rabbinical College, 2822 Avenue J, Brooklyn, NY 11210.

DEVRY INSTITUTE OF TECHNOLOGY
Long Island City, New York

- **Proprietary**, 4-year, founded 1998
- **Degrees** associate and bachelor's
- **Urban** campus
- **Coed**, 1,245 undergraduate students, 68% full-time, 21% women, 79% men
- **Minimally difficult** entrance level, 47% of applicants were admitted
- **21:1** student-to-undergraduate faculty ratio
- **$8776 tuition** and fees

Part of DeVry Inc.
Students *Undergraduates:* 849 full-time, 396 part-time. Students come from 18 states and territories, 14 other countries.

From out-of-state	5%	Age 25 or older	40%
International students	4%	African Americans	28%
Asian Americans/Pacific Islanders	4%	Hispanic Americans	22%
Native Americans	1%		

Faculty 60 (32% full-time).
Expenses (1999–2000) *Tuition:* full-time $8776; part-time $325 per credit hour. Part-time tuition and fees vary according to class time and course load. *Payment plan:* installment. *Waivers:* employees or children of employees.
College life *Housing:* college housing not available. *Most popular organizations:* Health Newsletter Club, CIS Club, Association of Information Technology, Year Book Club, Institute of Electrical and Electronics Engineers.
Campus security 24-hour emergency response devices and patrols, late-night transport-escort service.
Freshmen 1,401 applied, 661 admitted, 785 enrolled.

| SAT verbal scores above 500 | N/R | SAT math scores above 500 | N/R |
| ACT above 18 | N/R | 1998 freshmen returning in 1999 | 47% |

Application *Options:* electronic application, deferred entrance. *Application fee:* $25. *Required:* high school transcript; interview.
Standardized tests *Admission: Required:* CPT. *Recommended:* SAT I or ACT.
Significant dates *Application deadlines:* rolling (freshmen), rolling (transfers). *Financial aid deadline:* continuous.
Freshman Application Contact
Mr. Christopher Wargo, Director of Admissions, DeVry Institute of Technology, 30-20 Thomson Avenue, Long Island City, NY 11101. **Phone:** 718-361-0004. **Toll-free phone:** 888-713-3879.
Visit CollegeQuest.com for information on majors offered and athletics.

DOMINICAN COLLEGE OF BLAUVELT
Orangeburg, New York

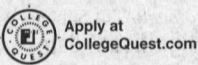
Apply at CollegeQuest.com

- **Independent**, comprehensive, founded 1952
- **Degrees** associate, bachelor's, and master's
- **Suburban** 14-acre campus with easy access to New York City
- **Coed**, 1,645 undergraduate students, 46% full-time, 75% women, 25% men
- **Moderately difficult** entrance level, 73% of applicants were admitted
- **12:1** student-to-undergraduate faculty ratio
- **41.7% graduate** in 6 years or less
- **$12,370 tuition** and fees

Students *Undergraduates:* 759 full-time, 886 part-time. Students come from 19 states and territories. *The most frequently chosen baccalaureate fields are:* business/marketing, health professions and related sciences, social sciences and history. *Graduate:* 43 in graduate degree programs.

From out-of-state	24%	Age 25 or older	66%
African Americans	12%	Asian Americans/Pacific Islanders	5%
Hispanic Americans	10%		

Faculty 159 (36% full-time), 26% with terminal degrees.
Expenses (1999–2000) *Comprehensive fee:* $19,370 includes full-time tuition ($12,000), mandatory fees ($370), and room and board ($7000). Room and board charges vary according to board plan. *Part-time tuition:* $400 per credit. *Part-time fees:* $10 per credit. *Payment plans:* guaranteed tuition, installment. *Waivers:* senior citizens and employees or children of employees.
Library Pius X Hall plus 1 other. *Operations spending 1999–2000:* $477,000. *Collection:* 103,350 titles, 650 serial subscriptions.
College life *Housing:* Option: coed. *Most popular organizations:* student government association, Student Ambassadors, Aquin Players, school newspaper, Teachers of Tomorrow.
Campus security 24-hour emergency response devices and patrols, student patrols, late-night transport-escort service, controlled dormitory access.
After graduation *Career center:* 1 full-time, 1 part-time personnel. Services include job fairs, resume preparation, resume referral, career counseling, careers library, job bank, job interviews. *Graduate education:* 35% of class of 1999 went directly to graduate and professional school.
Freshmen 565 applied, 411 admitted, 135 enrolled.

SAT verbal scores above 500	32%	SAT math scores above 500	32%
ACT above 18	N/R	From top 10% of their h.s. class	14%
From top quarter	29%	From top half	55%
1998 freshmen returning in 1999	77%		

Application *Options:* eApply at www.CollegeQuest.com, Common Application, early admission, deferred entrance. *Application fee:* $35. *Required:* high school transcript; minimum 2.0 GPA. *Required for some:* interview. *Recommended:* 2 letters of recommendation.
Standardized tests *Admission: Required:* SAT I or ACT.
Significant dates *Application deadlines:* rolling (freshmen), rolling (transfers). *Financial aid deadline priority date:* 2/15.
Freshman Application Contact
Ms. Joyce Elbe, Director of Admissions, Dominican College of Blauvelt, 470 Western Highway, Orangeburg, NY 10962-1210. **Phone:** 914-359-7800 Ext. 271. **Fax:** 914-359-2313. **E-mail:** admissions@dc.edu
Visit CollegeQuest.com for information on majors offered and athletics. College video available at CollegeQuest.com.

■ *See page 1580 for a narrative description.*

DOWLING COLLEGE
Oakdale, New York

- **Independent**, comprehensive, founded 1955
- **Degrees** bachelor's, master's, doctoral, and post-master's certificates
- **Suburban** 156-acre campus with easy access to New York City
- **Coed**, 2,922 undergraduate students, 62% full-time, 59% women, 41% men
- **Moderately difficult** entrance level, 89% of applicants were admitted
- **36% graduate** in 6 years or less

New York

- $14,070 tuition and fees

Students *Undergraduates:* 1,815 full-time, 1,107 part-time. Students come from 27 states and territories. *Graduate:* 2,852 in graduate degree programs.

From out-of-state	6%	Reside on campus	13%
Age 25 or older	54%	Transferred in	12%
International students	0.2%	African Americans	7%
Asian Americans/Pacific Islanders	3%	Hispanic Americans	8%
Native Americans	0.2%		

Faculty 430 (27% full-time), 37% with terminal degrees.

Expenses (1999–2000) *Tuition:* full-time $13,350; part-time $445 per credit hour. *Required fees:* full-time $720; $240 per term part-time. Full-time tuition and fees vary according to course load and degree level. Part-time tuition and fees vary according to course load and degree level. *College room only:* $4800. Room and board charges vary according to housing facility and location. *Payment plans:* guaranteed tuition, installment, deferred payment. *Waivers:* minority students, children of alumni, adult students, senior citizens, and employees or children of employees.

Library Dowling College Library. *Collection:* 118,830 titles, 3,131 serial subscriptions.

College life *Housing:* Option: coed. *Most popular organizations:* Student Government Association, Residence Hall Council, Pan African-American Caribbean Club, aeronautics club, Lion's Voice: The Student Newspaper.

Campus security 24-hour emergency response devices and patrols, late-night transport-escort service.

After graduation 115 organizations recruited on campus 1997–98. *Career center:* 3 full-time, 1 part-time personnel. Services include job fairs, resume preparation, resume referral, career counseling, job bank, job interviews.

Freshmen 1,606 applied, 1,431 admitted, 339 enrolled.

Average high school GPA	2.8	SAT verbal scores above 500	32%
SAT math scores above 500	66%	ACT above 18	N/R
1998 freshmen returning in 1999	65%		

Application *Options:* Common Application, electronic application, deferred entrance. *Application fee:* $25. *Required:* high school transcript. *Recommended:* interview.

Standardized tests *Admission: Recommended:* SAT I or ACT.

Significant dates *Application deadlines:* rolling (freshmen), rolling (transfers). *Financial aid deadline:* continuous.

Freshman Application Contact
Mr. Stephen Dougherty, Special Assistant for Student Recruitment, Dowling College, 150 Idle Hour Boulevard, Oakdale, NY 11769. **Phone:** 631-244-3497. **Toll-free phone:** 800-DOWLING. **Fax:** 631-563-3827. **E-mail:** macdonar@dowling.edu

Visit CollegeQuest.com for information on majors offered and athletics. College video available at CollegeQuest.com.

D'YOUVILLE COLLEGE
Buffalo, New York

- **Independent**, comprehensive, founded 1908
- **Degrees** bachelor's, master's, post-master's, and postbachelor's certificates
- **Urban** 7-acre campus
- **Coed**, 1,062 undergraduate students, 81% full-time, 74% women, 26% men
- **Moderately difficult** entrance level, 72% of applicants were admitted
- **12:1 student-to-undergraduate faculty ratio**
- **47% graduate** in 6 years or less
- **$11,250 tuition** and fees

The College offers a bachelor's degree in physician assistant studies. A 5-year combined bachelor's/master's degree is offered in physical therapy, occupational therapy, international business, nursing, and dietetics. These programs are direct entry, with no requirement to reapply for upper-division status. All dual-degree students pay undergraduate full-time tuition all 5 years.

Students *Undergraduates:* 858 full-time, 204 part-time. Students come from 25 states and territories, 4 other countries. *The most frequently chosen baccalaureate fields are:* health professions and related sciences, business/marketing, home economics/vocational home economics. *Graduate:* 1,059 in graduate degree programs.

From out-of-state	20%	Reside on campus	20%
Age 25 or older	35%	Transferred in	16%
International students	12%	African Americans	10%
Asian Americans/Pacific Islanders	3%	Hispanic Americans	4%
Native Americans	1%		

Faculty 175 (54% full-time).

Expenses (1999–2000) *Comprehensive fee:* $16,630 includes full-time tuition ($10,900), mandatory fees ($350), and room and board ($5380). *Part-time tuition:* $300 per credit. *Part-time fees:* $2 per credit; $115 per term part-time. Part-time tuition and fees vary according to course load. *Payment plans:* guaranteed tuition, installment, deferred payment. *Waivers:* minority students, children of alumni, adult students, and employees or children of employees.

Library D'Youville College Library. *Operations spending 1999–2000:* $366,123. *Collection:* 73,169 titles, 3,379 serial subscriptions, 3,379 audiovisual materials.

College life *Housing:* on-campus residence required through sophomore year. *Option:* coed. *Most popular organizations:* Student Association, Occupational Therapy Student Association, Physical Therapy Student Association, Student Nurses Association, Black Student Union.

Campus security 24-hour emergency response devices and patrols, late-night transport-escort service.

After graduation 15 organizations recruited on campus 1997–98. 90% of class of 1998 had job offers within 6 months. *Career center:* 2 full-time personnel. Services include job fairs, resume preparation, interview workshops, career/interest testing, career counseling, careers library, job bank, job interviews. *Graduate education:* 11% of class of 1999 went directly to graduate and professional school.

Freshmen 715 applied, 515 admitted, 125 enrolled. 2 valedictorians.

Average high school GPA	3.0	SAT verbal scores above 500	8%
SAT math scores above 500	63%	ACT above 18	64%
1998 freshmen returning in 1999	40%		

Application *Option:* deferred entrance. *Application fee:* $25. *Required:* high school transcript; minimum 2.0 GPA. *Required for some:* essay or personal statement; letters of recommendation; interview. *Recommended:* minimum 3.0 GPA.

Standardized tests *Admission: Required:* SAT I or ACT.

Significant dates *Application deadlines:* rolling (freshmen), rolling (transfers). *Financial aid deadline priority date:* 3/1.

Freshman Application Contact
Mr. Ron Dannecker, Director of Admissions and Financial Aid, D'Youville College, 320 Porter Avenue, Buffalo, NY 14201-1084. **Phone:** 716-881-7600. **Toll-free phone:** 800-777-3921. **Fax:** 716-881-7790. **E-mail:** admiss@dyc.edu

Visit CollegeQuest.com for information on majors offered and athletics. College video available at CollegeQuest.com.

- *See page 1596 for a narrative description.*

EASTMAN SCHOOL OF MUSIC
New York—See University of Rochester

ELMIRA COLLEGE
Elmira, New York

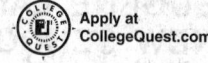
Apply at CollegeQuest.com

- **Independent**, comprehensive, founded 1855
- **Degrees** bachelor's and master's
- **Small-town** 42-acre campus
- **Coed**, 1,640 undergraduate students, 73% full-time, 69% women, 31% men
- **Moderately difficult** entrance level, 72% of applicants were admitted
- **12:1 student-to-undergraduate faculty ratio**
- **55% graduate** in 6 years or less
- **$22,540 tuition** and fees
- **$18,957 average financial aid** package, $29.7 million endowment

Students *Undergraduates:* 1,191 full-time, 449 part-time. Students come from 30 states and territories, 15 other countries. *The most frequently chosen*

New York

Elmira College (continued)
baccalaureate fields are: education, business/marketing, psychology. *Graduate:* 418 in graduate degree programs.

From out-of-state	42%	Reside on campus	95%
Age 25 or older	4%	Transferred in	4%
International students	3%	African Americans	1%
Asian Americans/Pacific Islanders	0.4%	Hispanic Americans	1%
Native Americans	0.2%		

Faculty 107 (73% full-time), 100% with terminal degrees.

Expenses (2000–2001, estimated) *Comprehensive fee:* $29,820 includes full-time tuition ($21,960), mandatory fees ($580), and room and board ($7280). *College room only:* $4450. *Part-time tuition:* $240 per credit hour. *Payment plans:* tuition prepayment, installment. *Waivers:* employees or children of employees.

Library Gannet-Tripp Library. *Operations spending 1999–2000:* $475,000. *Collection:* 389,036 titles, 855 serial subscriptions, 6,261 audiovisual materials.

College life *Housing:* on-campus residence required through senior year. *Options:* coed, women-only. *Most popular organizations:* student radio station, Student Activities Board, psychology club, ski club, Pal Program.

Campus security 24-hour patrols, late-night transport-escort service, 24-hour locked residence hall entrances.

After graduation 58 organizations recruited on campus 1997–98. 50% of class of 1998 had job offers within 6 months. *Career center:* 2 full-time, 8 part-time personnel. Services include job fairs, resume preparation, interview workshops, resume referral, career/interest testing, career counseling, careers library, job interviews. *Graduate education:* 41% of class of 1999 went directly to graduate and professional school: 18% graduate arts and sciences, 11% business, 7% education, 3% law, 1% dentistry, 1% medicine.

Freshmen 1,520 applied, 1,093 admitted, 366 enrolled. 1 National Merit Scholar, 27 class presidents, 32 valedictorians, 163 student government officers.

Average high school GPA	3.5	SAT verbal scores above 500	68%
SAT math scores above 500	68%	ACT above 18	91%
From top 10% of their h.s. class	31%	From top quarter	54%
From top half	78%	1998 freshmen returning in 1999	80%

Application *Options:* eApply at www.CollegeQuest.com, Common Application, early admission, early decision, deferred entrance. *Application fee:* $40. *Required:* essay or personal statement; high school transcript; minimum 2.0 GPA; 2 letters of recommendation. *Required for some:* interview. *Recommended:* interview.

Standardized tests *Admission: Required:* SAT I or ACT.

Significant dates *Application deadlines:* 4/15 (freshmen), 8/1 (transfers). *Early decision:* 1/15. *Notification:* continuous until 5/1 (freshmen), 2/1 (early decision). *Financial aid deadline priority date:* 2/1.

Freshman Application Contact
Mr. William S. Neal, Dean of Admissions, Elmira College, Office of Admissions, Elmira, NY 14901. **Phone:** 607-735-1724. **Toll-free phone:** 800-935-6472. **Fax:** 607-735-1718. **E-mail:** admissions@elmira.edu

Visit CollegeQuest.com for information on majors offered and athletics. College video available at CollegeQuest.com.

■ *See page 1624 for a narrative description.*

EUGENE LANG COLLEGE, NEW SCHOOL UNIVERSITY
New York, New York

Apply at CollegeQuest.com

■ **Independent**, 4-year, founded 1978
■ **Degree** bachelor's
■ **Urban** 5-acre campus
■ **Coed**, 480 undergraduate students, 94% full-time, 67% women, 33% men
■ **Moderately difficult** entrance level, 54% of applicants were admitted
■ **10:1** student-to-undergraduate faculty ratio
■ **40% graduate** in 6 years or less
■ **$19,915 tuition** and fees
■ **$14,861 average financial aid** package, $17,125 average indebtedness upon graduation, $86.9 million system endowment

Eugene Lang offers undergraduates a seminar style of learning that emphasizes interdisciplinary liberal arts courses in discussion-based classes of no more than 15 students. The internship program encourages students to extend their learning beyond the classroom. The Greenwich location means that all the cultural treasures of New York City—museums, theater, dance, and music—are at a student's doorstep.

Part of New School University.

Students *Undergraduates:* 452 full-time, 28 part-time. Students come from 41 states and territories, 20 other countries. *The most frequently chosen baccalaureate field is:* liberal arts/general studies.

From out-of-state	59%	Reside on campus	30%
Age 25 or older	5%	Transferred in	13%
International students	5%	African Americans	7%
Asian Americans/Pacific Islanders	5%	Hispanic Americans	11%
Native Americans	1%		

Faculty 76 (18% full-time).

Expenses (1999–2000) *Comprehensive fee:* $28,920 includes full-time tuition ($19,620), mandatory fees ($295), and room and board ($9005). *College room only:* $6485. Room and board charges vary according to board plan and housing facility. *Part-time tuition:* $720 per credit. *Part-time fees:* $58 per term part-time. Part-time tuition and fees vary according to course load. *Payment plan:* installment. *Waivers:* employees or children of employees.

Library Fogelman Library plus 2 others. *System-wide operations spending 1999–2000:* $1.8 million. *Collection:* 191,789 titles, 896 serial subscriptions, 137,878 audiovisual materials.

College life *Housing: Option:* coed. *Most popular organizations:* Student Union, Theater Club, student newspaper, literary journal, ethnic organizations.

Campus security 24-hour emergency response devices, controlled dormitory access, 24-hour desk attendants in residence halls.

After graduation 82% of class of 1998 had job offers within 6 months. *Career center:* 3 full-time, 3 part-time personnel. Services include resume preparation, interview workshops, resume referral, career counseling, careers library, job bank.

Freshmen 718 applied, 390 admitted, 110 enrolled. 3 class presidents, 2 valedictorians, 20 student government officers.

Average high school GPA	3.0	SAT verbal scores above 500	94%
SAT math scores above 500	83%	ACT above 18	N/R
From top 10% of their h.s. class	24%	From top quarter	27%
From top half	33%	1998 freshmen returning in 1999	73%

Application *Options:* eApply at www.CollegeQuest.com, Common Application, early admission, early decision, deferred entrance. *Application fee:* $30. *Required:* essay or personal statement; high school transcript; minimum 2.0 GPA; 2 letters of recommendation; interview. *Recommended:* minimum 3.0 GPA.

Standardized tests *Admission: Required:* SAT I or ACT or 4 SAT II Subject Tests.

Significant dates *Application deadlines:* 2/1 (freshmen), 5/15 (transfers). *Early decision:* 11/15. *Notification:* 4/1 (freshmen), 12/15 (early decision). *Financial aid deadline priority date:* 3/1.

Freshman Application Contact
Ms. Jennifer Fondiller, Director of Admissions, Eugene Lang College, New School University, 65 West 11th Street, New York, NY 10011-8601. **Phone:** 212-229-5665. **Fax:** 212-229-5355. **E-mail:** lang@newschool.edu

Visit CollegeQuest.com for information on majors offered and athletics.

■ *See page 1644 for a narrative description.*

FASHION INSTITUTE OF TECHNOLOGY
New York, New York

■ **State and locally supported**, comprehensive, founded 1944
■ **Degrees** associate, bachelor's, and master's
■ **Urban** 5-acre campus
■ **Coed**, 7,003 undergraduate students, 81% full-time, 83% women, 17% men
■ **Moderately difficult** entrance level
■ **13:1** student-to-undergraduate faculty ratio

New York

■ **$3195 tuition** and fees (in-state); $7475 (out-of-state)

Part of State University of New York System.

Students *Undergraduates:* 5,685 full-time, 1,318 part-time. Students come from 51 states and territories, 70 other countries. *The most frequently chosen baccalaureate fields are:* business/marketing, engineering/engineering technologies, visual/performing arts. *Graduate:* 103 in graduate degree programs.

From out-of-state	17%	Age 25 or older	30%
Transferred in	14%	International students	11%
African Americans	8%	Asian Americans/Pacific Islanders	12%
Hispanic Americans	10%	Native Americans	0.1%

Faculty 863 (20% full-time).

Expenses (1999–2000) *Tuition, state resident:* full-time $2985; part-time $125 per credit. *Tuition, nonresident:* full-time $7265; part-time $310 per credit. *Required fees:* full-time $210; $5 per term part-time. Full-time tuition and fees vary according to degree level and program. Part-time tuition and fees vary according to degree level and program. *College room and board:* $7339. Room and board charges vary according to board plan and housing facility. *Payment plan:* installment. *Waivers:* employees or children of employees.

Library Gladys Marcus Library. *Collection:* 154,015 titles, 3,871 audiovisual materials.

College life *Housing: Options:* coed, women-only. *Most popular organizations:* American Marketing Association, Distributive Education Clubs of America, Merchandising Society, literary magazine.

Campus security 24-hour emergency response devices and patrols.

After graduation 95 organizations recruited on campus 1997–98. 86% of class of 1998 had job offers within 6 months. *Career center:* 12 full-time, 4 part-time personnel. Services include job fairs, resume preparation, interview workshops, career counseling, careers library, job bank.

Freshmen 3,961 applied, 1,103 enrolled.

Average high school GPA	3.3	SAT verbal scores above 500	N/R
SAT math scores above 500	N/R	ACT above 18	N/R
From top 10% of their h.s. class	8%	From top quarter	25%
From top half	70%	1998 freshmen returning in 1999	78%

Application *Options:* electronic application, deferred entrance. *Application fee:* $30. *Required:* essay or personal statement; high school transcript; portfolio for art and design programs.

Standardized tests *Placement: Recommended:* SAT I or ACT.

Significant dates *Application deadlines:* 1/15 (freshmen), 1/15 (transfers). *Financial aid deadline priority date:* 3/1.

Freshman Application Contact
Mr. Jim Pidgeon, Director of Admissions, Fashion Institute of Technology, Seventh Avenue at 27th Street, New York, NY 10001-5992. **Phone:** 212-217-7675. **Toll-free phone:** 800-GOTOFIT. **Fax:** 212-217-7481. **E-mail:** fitinfo@sfitva.cc.fitsuny.edu

Visit CollegeQuest.com for information on majors offered and athletics.

■ *See page 1652 for a narrative description.*

FIVE TOWNS COLLEGE
Dix Hills, New York

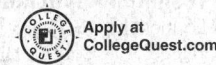 Apply at CollegeQuest.com

- **Independent**, comprehensive, founded 1972
- **Degrees** associate, bachelor's, and master's
- **Suburban** 40-acre campus with easy access to New York City
- **Coed**, 803 undergraduate students, 94% full-time, 27% women, 73% men
- **Minimally difficult** entrance level, 96% of applicants were admitted
- **13:1 student-to-undergraduate faculty ratio**
- **$9620 tuition** and fees

Five Towns College offers 2-year, 4-year, and master's degree programs. Students may select from more than 30 different majors, including audio recording technology, music business, jazz/commercial music, music teacher education, and film/video. New programs include broadcasting, telecommunications, dramatic arts, and literature. The College is accredited by the Middle States Association and the New York State Board of Regents.

Students *Undergraduates:* 752 full-time, 51 part-time. Students come from 12 states and territories, 10 other countries. *The most frequently chosen baccalaureate fields are:* education, visual/performing arts. *Graduate:* 45 in graduate degree programs.

Reside on campus	12%	International students	2%
African Americans	22%	Asian Americans/Pacific Islanders	2%
Hispanic Americans	12%		

Faculty 55 (27% full-time), 27% with terminal degrees.

Expenses (2000–2001) *Tuition:* full-time $9300; part-time $390 per credit. *Required fees:* full-time $320; $70 per term. Room and board charges vary according to board plan. *Payment plans:* installment, deferred payment. *Waivers:* senior citizens and employees or children of employees.

Library Five Towns College Library. *Collection:* 32,000 titles, 450 serial subscriptions.

College life *Housing: Option:* coed. *Most popular organizations:* concert choir, live audio club, dance club, musical theatre, yearbook.

Campus security 24-hour patrols, late-night transport-escort service.

After graduation 15 organizations recruited on campus 1997–98. 85% of class of 1998 had job offers within 6 months. *Career center:* 1 full-time, 1 part-time personnel. Services include job fairs, resume preparation, interview workshops, resume referral, career/interest testing, career counseling, careers library, job bank, job interviews. *Graduate education:* 12% of class of 1999 went directly to graduate and professional school.

Freshmen 375 applied, 359 admitted, 271 enrolled.

Average high school GPA	2.7	SAT verbal scores above 500	40%
SAT math scores above 500	31%	ACT above 18	N/R
From top 10% of their h.s. class	5%	From top quarter	22%
From top half	56%	1998 freshmen returning in 1999	76%

Application *Options:* eApply at www.CollegeQuest.com, early admission, deferred entrance. *Application fee:* $25. *Required:* essay or personal statement; high school transcript; minimum 2.0 GPA. *Required for some:* interview.

Standardized tests *Admission: Required:* SAT I and SAT II or ACT.

Significant dates *Application deadlines:* rolling (freshmen), rolling (transfers). *Financial aid deadline priority date:* 4/30.

Freshman Application Contact
Mr. Jerry Cohen, Enrollment Services, Five Towns College, 305 North Service Road, Dix Hills, NY 11746-6055. **Phone:** 631-424-7000 Ext. 110. **Fax:** 516-424-7008.

Visit CollegeQuest.com for information on majors offered and athletics.

■ *See page 1668 for a narrative description.*

FORDHAM UNIVERSITY
New York, New York

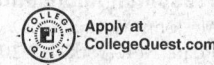 Apply at CollegeQuest.com

- **Independent Roman Catholic (Jesuit)**, university, founded 1841
- **Degrees** bachelor's, master's, doctoral, and first professional (branch locations: an 85-acre campus at Rose Hill and an 8-acre campus at Lincoln Center)
- **Urban** 85-acre campus
- **Coed**, 6,407 undergraduate students, 88% full-time, 59% women, 41% men
- **Very difficult** entrance level, 62% of applicants were admitted
- **10:1 student-to-undergraduate faculty ratio**
- **68.6% graduate** in 6 years or less
- **$19,660 tuition** and fees
- **$16,351 average financial aid** package, $15,379 average indebtedness upon graduation, $163.6 million endowment

Fordham, an independent institution offering an education based on the Jesuit tradition, has 2 major campuses in New York City. The Rose Hill campus is set on 85 acres and is the largest green campus in New York City. The Lincoln Center campus, with a new 20-story residence hall, is located in the heart of midtown Manhattan.

Students *Undergraduates:* 5,669 full-time, 738 part-time. Students come from 48 states and territories, 38 other countries. *The most frequently chosen baccalaureate fields are:* business/marketing, communications/communication technologies, social sciences and history. *Graduate:* 1,442 in professional programs, 5,531 in other graduate degree programs.

New York

Fordham University (continued)

From out-of-state	34%	Reside on campus	60%
International students	1%	African Americans	5%
Asian Americans/Pacific Islanders	4%	Hispanic Americans	12%
Native Americans	0.2%		

Faculty 1,125 (53% full-time).

Expenses (1999–2000) *Comprehensive fee:* $26,140 includes full-time tuition ($19,200), mandatory fees ($460), and room and board ($6480). *College room only:* $3580. Room and board charges vary according to housing facility. *Part-time tuition:* $640 per credit. *Part-time fees:* $230 per term part-time. Part-time tuition and fees vary according to class time and location. *Payment plans:* tuition prepayment, installment. *Waivers:* employees or children of employees.

Library Walsh Library plus 4 others. *Operations spending 1999–2000:* $8.2 million. *Collection:* 1.9 million titles, 12,022 serial subscriptions.

College life *Housing: Option:* coed. *Most popular organizations:* United Student Government, Commuting Student Association, Residence Hall Association, Ambassador Program.

Campus security 24-hour emergency response devices and patrols, student patrols, late-night transport-escort service, controlled dormitory access.

After graduation 500 organizations recruited on campus 1997–98. 90% of class of 1998 had job offers within 6 months. *Career center:* 8 full-time, 2 part-time personnel. Services include job fairs, resume preparation, resume referral, career/interest testing, career counseling, careers library, job bank, job interviews. *Graduate education:* 25% of class of 1999 went directly to graduate and professional school: 7% graduate arts and sciences, 6% law, 5% business, 5% education, 2% medicine. *Major awards:* 1 Marshall scholar.

Freshmen 8,600 applied, 5,352 admitted, 1,584 enrolled. 20 valedictorians.

Average high school GPA	3.51	SAT verbal scores above 500	89%
SAT math scores above 500	85%	ACT above 18	98%
From top 10% of their h.s. class	29%	From top quarter	60%
From top half	92%	1998 freshmen returning in 1999	88%

Application *Options:* eApply at www.CollegeQuest.com, Common Application, early admission, early decision, deferred entrance. *Preference* given to children of alumni. *Application fee:* $50. *Required:* essay or personal statement; high school transcript; 1 letter of recommendation. *Required for some:* interview. *Recommended:* minimum 3.0 GPA; interview.

Standardized tests *Admission: Required:* SAT I or ACT. *Recommended:* SAT II Subject Tests.

Significant dates *Application deadlines:* 2/1 (freshmen), 7/1 (transfers). *Early decision:* 11/1. *Notification:* 4/1 (freshmen), 12/15 (early decision). *Financial aid deadline priority date:* 2/1.

Freshman Application Contact
Mr. John W. Buckley, Dean of Admission, Fordham University, East Fordham Road, New York, NY 10458. **Phone:** 718-817-4000. **Toll-free phone:** 800-FORDHAM. **Fax:** 718-367-9404. **E-mail:** ad_buckley@lars.fordham.edu

Visit CollegeQuest.com for information on majors offered and athletics. College video available at CollegeQuest.com.

■ *See page 1684 for a narrative description.*

FRIENDS WORLD COLLEGE
New York—See Long Island University, Southampton College, Friends World Program

HAMILTON COLLEGE
Clinton, New York

- **Independent**, 4-year, founded 1812
- **Degree** bachelor's
- **Rural** 1,200-acre campus
- **Coed**, 1,712 undergraduate students, 99% full-time, 49% women, 51% men
- **Very difficult** entrance level, 42% of applicants were admitted
- **9:1 student-to-undergraduate faculty ratio**
- **85.9% graduate** in 6 years or less
- **$25,050 tuition** and fees

■ $19,490 average financial aid package, $16,776 average indebtedness upon graduation, $401.6 million endowment

Students *Undergraduates:* 1,709 full-time, 3 part-time. Students come from 41 states and territories, 33 other countries. *The most frequently chosen baccalaureate fields are:* English, social sciences and history, visual/performing arts.

From out-of-state	57%	Reside on campus	96%
Age 25 or older	1%	Transferred in	1%
International students	3%	African Americans	3%
Asian Americans/Pacific Islanders	4%	Hispanic Americans	4%
Native Americans	0.2%		

Faculty 189 (88% full-time), 89% with terminal degrees.

Expenses (1999–2000) *Comprehensive fee:* $31,250 includes full-time tuition ($25,000), mandatory fees ($50), and room and board ($6200). Room and board charges vary according to board plan. *Part-time tuition:* $2400 per unit. *Payment plans:* installment, deferred payment. *Waivers:* adult students and employees or children of employees.

Library Burke Library plus 3 others. *Operations spending 1999–2000:* $2.8 million. *Collection:* 890,591 titles, 3,585 serial subscriptions, 52,051 audiovisual materials.

College life *Housing:* on-campus residence required through senior year. *Option:* coed. *Social organizations:* national fraternities, local sororities, private society; 29% of eligible men and 12% of eligible women are members. *Most popular organizations:* community service group, outing club, student newspaper.

Campus security 24-hour emergency response devices and patrols, late-night transport-escort service, controlled dormitory access, student safety program.

After graduation 32 organizations recruited on campus 1997–98. 90% of class of 1998 had job offers within 6 months. *Career center:* 4 full-time, 4 part-time personnel. Services include job fairs, resume preparation, interview workshops, resume referral, career/interest testing, career counseling, careers library, job bank, job interviews. *Graduate education:* 15% of class of 1999 went directly to graduate and professional school.

Freshmen 3,909 applied, 1,660 admitted, 500 enrolled. 10 National Merit Scholars, 7 valedictorians.

SAT verbal scores above 500	97%	SAT math scores above 500	94%
ACT above 18	N/R	From top 10% of their h.s. class	48%
From top quarter	79%	From top half	98%
1998 freshmen returning in 1999	92%		

Application *Options:* eApply at www.CollegeQuest.com, Common Application, electronic application, early admission, early decision, deferred entrance. *Application fee:* $50. *Required:* essay or personal statement; high school transcript; 1 letter of recommendation; sample of expository prose. *Recommended:* interview.

Standardized tests *Admission: Required:* SAT I or ACT.

Significant dates *Application deadlines:* 1/15 (freshmen), 3/15 (transfers). *Early decision:* 11/15 (for plan 1), 1/10 (for plan 2). *Notification:* 4/1 (freshmen), 12/15 (early decision plan 1), 2/10 (early decision plan 2). *Financial aid deadline:* 2/1.

Freshman Application Contact
Mr. Richard M. Fuller, Dean of Admission and Financial Aid, Hamilton College, 198 College Hill Road, Clinton, NY 13323-1296. **Phone:** 315-859-4421. **Toll-free phone:** 800-843-2655. **Fax:** 315-859-4124. **E-mail:** admission@hamilton.edu

Visit CollegeQuest.com for information on majors offered and athletics. College video available at CollegeQuest.com.

■ *See page 1754 for a narrative description.*

HARTWICK COLLEGE
Oneonta, New York

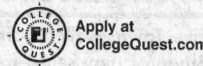

- **Independent**, 4-year, founded 1797
- **Degree** bachelor's
- **Small-town** 425-acre campus with easy access to Albany
- **Coed**, 1,395 undergraduate students, 75% full-time, 52% women, 48% men
- **Moderately difficult** entrance level, 79% of applicants were admitted
- **11:1 student-to-undergraduate faculty ratio**

New York

- 64% **graduate** in 6 years or less
- **$23,800 tuition** and fees
- **$82.2 million endowment**

Students *Undergraduates:* 1,052 full-time, 343 part-time. Students come from 32 states and territories. *The most frequently chosen baccalaureate fields are:* psychology, business/marketing, social sciences and history.

From out-of-state	37%	Reside on campus	84%
Age 25 or older	12%	Transferred in	2%
International students	2%	African Americans	4%
Asian Americans/Pacific Islanders	1%	Hispanic Americans	3%
Native Americans	0.3%		

Faculty 147 (73% full-time).

Expenses (1999–2000) *Comprehensive fee:* $30,140 includes full-time tuition ($23,475), mandatory fees ($325), and room and board ($6340). *College room only:* $3175. Room and board charges vary according to board plan and housing facility. *Part-time tuition:* $2638 per course. *Payment plan:* installment. *Waivers:* employees or children of employees.

Library Stevens-German Library. *Operations spending 1999–2000:* $538,710. *Collection:* 284,280 titles, 1,815 serial subscriptions, 6,000 audiovisual materials.

College life *Housing:* on-campus residence required through junior year. *Options:* coed, men-only, women-only. *Social organizations:* national fraternities, national sororities, local fraternities, local sororities; 15% of eligible men and 17% of eligible women are members. *Most popular organizations:* Student Union, student radio station, Student Senate, Hilltops, Cardboard Alley Players.

Campus security 24-hour emergency response devices and patrols, late-night transport-escort service.

After graduation 71% of class of 1998 had job offers within 6 months. *Career center:* 4 full-time, 1 part-time personnel. Services include job fairs, resume preparation, interview workshops, resume referral, career/interest testing, career counseling, careers library, job bank, job interviews. *Major awards:* 1 Fulbright Scholar.

Freshmen 2,174 applied, 1,723 admitted, 396 enrolled. 21 class presidents, 5 valedictorians.

Average high school GPA	3.0	SAT verbal scores above 500	76%
SAT math scores above 500	77%	ACT above 18	97%
From top 10% of their h.s. class	17%	From top quarter	46%
From top half	79%	1998 freshmen returning in 1999	77%

Application *Options:* eApply at www.CollegeQuest.com, Common Application, electronic application, early admission, early decision, deferred entrance. *Application fee:* $35. *Required:* essay or personal statement; high school transcript; 2 letters of recommendation; audition for music program. *Recommended:* minimum 3.0 GPA; interview.

Standardized tests *Admission: Recommended:* SAT I or ACT.

Significant dates *Application deadlines:* 2/15 (freshmen), 8/1 (transfers). *Early decision:* 1/15. *Notification:* 3/15 (freshmen). *Financial aid deadline:* 2/1.

Freshman Application Contact
Ms. Susan Dileno, Dean of Admissions, Hartwick College, PO Box 4022, Oneonta, NY 13820-4022. **Phone:** 607-431-4150. **Toll-free phone:** 888-HARTWICK. **Fax:** 607-431-4138. **E-mail:** admissions@hartwick.edu

Visit CollegeQuest.com for information on majors offered and athletics. Electronic viewbook available at CollegeQuest.com.

- *See page 1770 for a narrative description.*

HILBERT COLLEGE
Hamburg, New York

- **Independent**, 4-year, founded 1957
- **Degrees** associate and bachelor's
- **Small-town** 40-acre campus with easy access to Buffalo
- **Coed**, 808 undergraduate students, 68% full-time, 67% women, 33% men
- **Minimally difficult** entrance level, 86% of applicants were admitted
- **16:1 student-to-undergraduate faculty ratio**
- **31.3% graduate** in 6 years or less
- **$10,800 tuition** and fees
- **$6738 average financial aid** package, $2.1 million endowment

Hilbert College has added two new baccalaureate programs—economic crime investigation and liberal studies. The economic crime investigation program is 1 of 2 such programs in the country and offers students career education in the fields of computer investigation and forensic accounting. The liberal studies program offers avenues into the fields of law, government, and city planning.

Students *Undergraduates:* 551 full-time, 257 part-time. Students come from 3 states and territories, 1 other country. *The most frequently chosen baccalaureate fields are:* business/marketing, health professions and related sciences, protective services/public administration.

From out-of-state	0.4%	Reside on campus	10%
Age 25 or older	40%	Transferred in	15%
International students	0.1%	African Americans	5%
Hispanic Americans	1%	Native Americans	1%

Faculty 79 (44% full-time), 34% with terminal degrees.

Expenses (1999–2000) *Comprehensive fee:* $15,340 includes full-time tuition ($10,250), mandatory fees ($550), and room and board ($4540). *College room only:* $1790. Room and board charges vary according to board plan and housing facility. *Part-time tuition:* $267 per credit. *Part-time fees:* $12 per credit; $5 per term part-time. *Payment plans:* installment, deferred payment. *Waivers:* senior citizens and employees or children of employees.

Library McGrath Library. *Operations spending 1999–2000:* $371,824. *Collection:* 34,005 titles, 2,352 serial subscriptions, 465 audiovisual materials.

College life *Housing: Option:* coed. *Most popular organizations:* Student Government Association, Phi Beta Lambda, wellness club, Human Services Club, criminal justice association.

Campus security 24-hour emergency response devices and patrols, student patrols, late-night transport-escort service, controlled dormitory access.

After graduation 45 organizations recruited on campus 1997–98. 68% of class of 1998 had job offers within 6 months. *Career center:* 1 full-time, 1 part-time personnel. Services include job fairs, resume preparation, resume referral, career/interest testing, career counseling, careers library, job bank, job interviews. *Graduate education:* 25% of class of 1999 went directly to graduate and professional school: 12% business, 3% law, 2% education, 2% graduate arts and sciences.

Freshmen 250 applied, 216 admitted, 114 enrolled. 1 valedictorian, 2 student government officers.

Average high school GPA	2.2	SAT verbal scores above 500	30%
SAT math scores above 500	28%	ACT above 18	75%
From top 10% of their h.s. class	5%	From top quarter	19%
From top half	51%	1998 freshmen returning in 1999	72%

Application *Options:* Common Application, early admission, deferred entrance. *Application fee:* $20. *Required:* high school transcript. *Required for some:* interview. *Recommended:* letters of recommendation; interview.

Standardized tests *Admission: Recommended:* SAT I or ACT.

Significant dates *Application deadlines:* 9/1 (freshmen), 8/1 (transfers). *Financial aid deadline:* 5/1. *Priority date:* 3/1.

Freshman Application Contact
Ms. Michele Sojda, Admissions Counselor, Hilbert College, 5200 South Park Avenue, Hamburg, NY 14075-1597. **Phone:** 716-649-7900 Ext. 211. **Fax:** 716-649-0702.

Visit CollegeQuest.com for information on majors offered and athletics. College video available at CollegeQuest.com.

- *See page 1788 for a narrative description.*

HOBART AND WILLIAM SMITH COLLEGES
Geneva, New York

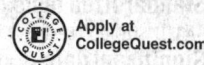
Apply at CollegeQuest.com

- **Independent**, 4-year, founded 1822
- **Degree** bachelor's
- **Small-town** 200-acre campus with easy access to Rochester and Syracuse
- **Coed**, 1,823 undergraduate students, 100% full-time, 52% women, 48% men
- **Moderately difficult** entrance level, 75% of applicants were admitted
- **13:1 student-to-undergraduate faculty ratio**
- **83.3% graduate** in 6 years or less
- **$24,342 tuition** and fees

Peterson's Guide to Four-Year Colleges 2001   www.petersons.com

New York

Hobart and William Smith Colleges (continued)

- **$21,368 average financial aid** package, $15,338 average indebtedness upon graduation, $106.2 million endowment

Hobart and William Smith Colleges are joined in a distinctive coordinate system that reflects the institutions' commitment to equity and the intentional creation of community. The Colleges are dedicated to providing a liberal arts education that is not merely informative but also transformative, one that generates not only knowledge but also ideals. Key to this emphasis on the intersection of difference in order to create a more humane community is the commitment to an interdisciplinary curriculum and international education, with nearly 2/3 of the students participating in one of the college-sponsored programs in nearly 30 different locales.

Students *Undergraduates:* 1,823 full-time. Students come from 40 states and territories, 19 other countries. *The most frequently chosen baccalaureate fields are:* English, psychology, social sciences and history.

From out-of-state	50%	Reside on campus	95%
Transferred in	2%	International students	1%
African Americans	6%	Asian Americans/Pacific Islanders	2%
Hispanic Americans	4%	Native Americans	0.2%

Faculty 168 (80% full-time), 93% with terminal degrees.

Expenses (1999–2000) *Comprehensive fee:* $31,224 includes full-time tuition ($23,865), mandatory fees ($477), and room and board ($6882). *College room only:* $3507. Room and board charges vary according to board plan and housing facility. *Part-time tuition:* $2652 per course. Part-time tuition and fees vary according to course load. *Payment plans:* tuition prepayment, installment, deferred payment. *Waivers:* employees or children of employees.

Library Warren Hunting Smith Library plus 1 other. *Operations spending 1999–2000:* $1.6 million. *Collection:* 340,185 titles, 1,562 serial subscriptions, 6,101 audiovisual materials.

College life *Housing:* on-campus residence required through senior year. *Options:* coed, men-only, women-only, cooperative. *Social organizations:* national fraternities; 19% of men are members. *Most popular organizations:* Student Life and Leadership, student government, African-American Student Coalition, service network, sports clubs.

Campus security 24-hour emergency response devices and patrols, late-night transport-escort service, controlled dormitory access.

After graduation 48 organizations recruited on campus 1997–98. 70% of class of 1998 had job offers within 6 months. *Career center:* 3 full-time, 4 part-time personnel. Services include job fairs, resume preparation, interview workshops, resume referral, career/interest testing, career counseling, careers library, job bank, job interviews. *Graduate education:* 30% of class of 1999 went directly to graduate and professional school: 14% graduate arts and sciences, 5% medicine, 4% law, 2% business, 2% education, 2% theology, 1% veterinary medicine.

Freshmen 2,634 applied, 1,970 admitted, 503 enrolled. 8 National Merit Scholars, 9 class presidents, 5 valedictorians, 30 student government officers.

Average high school GPA	3.25	SAT verbal scores above 500	88%
SAT math scores above 500	88%	ACT above 18	N/R
From top 10% of their h.s. class	25%	From top quarter	60%
From top half	90%	1998 freshmen returning in 1999	88%

Application *Options:* eApply at www.CollegeQuest.com, Common Application, electronic application, early admission, early decision, deferred entrance. *Application fee:* $45. *Required:* essay or personal statement; high school transcript; 2 letters of recommendation. *Recommended:* interview.

Standardized tests *Admission: Required:* SAT I or ACT. *Recommended:* SAT II Subject Tests.

Significant dates *Application deadlines:* 2/1 (freshmen), rolling (transfers). *Early decision:* 11/15 (for plan 1), 1/1 (for plan 2). *Notification:* 4/1 (freshmen), 12/15 (early decision plan 1), 2/1 (early decision plan 2). *Financial aid deadline:* 3/15. *Priority date:* 2/15.

Freshman Application Contact
Ms. Mara O'Laughlin, Director of Admissions, Hobart and William Smith Colleges, Geneva, NY 14456-3397. **Phone:** 315-781-3472. **Toll-free phone:** 800-245-0100. **Fax:** 315-781-5471. **E-mail:** hoadm@hws.edu

Visit CollegeQuest.com for information on majors offered and athletics. College video available at CollegeQuest.com.

- *See page 1794 for a narrative description.*

HOFSTRA UNIVERSITY
Hempstead, New York

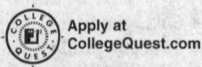
Apply at CollegeQuest.com

- **Independent**, university, founded 1935
- **Degrees** associate, bachelor's, master's, doctoral, first professional, and postbachelor's certificates
- **Suburban** 240-acre campus with easy access to New York City
- **Coed**, 9,173 undergraduate students, 87% full-time, 54% women, 46% men
- **Moderately difficult** entrance level, 82% of applicants were admitted
- **13:1 student-to-undergraduate faculty ratio**
- **62.3% graduate** in 6 years or less
- **$14,512 tuition** and fees
- **$7839 average financial aid** package, $105.7 million endowment

Founded in 1935, Hofstra University has grown to be recognized both nationally and internationally for its resources, academic offerings, accreditations, conferences, and cultural events. Hofstra's undergraduate education places great emphasis on the role of the student in the life of the University. Hofstra also offers graduate programs in business, education, liberal arts, and law. Students have easy access to the theater and cultural life of New York City, yet have a learning environment on Long Island on a 240-acre campus that is also an accredited arboretum and museum.

Students *Undergraduates:* 7,947 full-time, 1,226 part-time. Students come from 44 states and territories. *The most frequently chosen baccalaureate fields are:* business/marketing, communications/communication technologies, psychology. *Graduate:* 834 in professional programs, 3,007 in other graduate degree programs.

From out-of-state	11%	Reside on campus	43%
Age 25 or older	11%	Transferred in	10%
International students	0.02%	African Americans	8%
Asian Americans/Pacific Islanders	5%	Hispanic Americans	6%
Native Americans	0.2%		

Faculty 1,176 (42% full-time), 56% with terminal degrees.

Expenses (1999–2000) *Comprehensive fee:* $21,572 includes full-time tuition ($13,750), mandatory fees ($762), and room and board ($7060). *College room only:* $4670. Room and board charges vary according to board plan and housing facility. *Part-time tuition:* $452 per semester hour. *Part-time fees:* $112 per term part-time. Part-time tuition and fees vary according to course load. *Payment plans:* installment, deferred payment. *Waivers:* senior citizens and employees or children of employees.

Library Axinn Library plus 1 other. *Operations spending 1999–2000:* $5.1 million. *Collection:* 1.4 million titles, 7,017 serial subscriptions.

College life *Housing: Options:* coed, women-only, disabled students. *Social organizations:* national fraternities, national sororities, local fraternities, local sororities; 10% of eligible men and 10% of eligible women are members. *Most popular organizations:* Student Government Association, Organization of Commuter Students, Interfraternity/Sorority Council, Entertainment Unlimited, Resident Students Association.

Campus security 24-hour emergency response devices and patrols, student patrols, late-night transport-escort service, controlled dormitory access, security booths at each residence hall.

After graduation 190 organizations recruited on campus 1997–98. *Career center:* 7 full-time, 11 part-time personnel. Services include job fairs, resume preparation, interview workshops, resume referral, career/interest testing, career counseling, careers library, job bank, job interviews.

Freshmen 8,997 applied, 7,363 admitted, 1,906 enrolled. 17 valedictorians.

Average high school GPA	3.0	SAT verbal scores above 500	79%
SAT math scores above 500	77%	ACT above 18	97%
From top 10% of their h.s. class	12%	From top quarter	49%
From top half	92%	1998 freshmen returning in 1999	78%

Application *Options:* eApply at www.CollegeQuest.com, Common Application, electronic application, early admission, early decision, deferred entrance. *Application fee:* $40. *Required:* high school transcript; 1 letter of recommendation. *Required for some:* essay or personal statement; interview.

Standardized tests *Admission: Required:* SAT I or ACT. *Recommended:* SAT II Subject Tests.

Significant dates *Application deadlines:* rolling (freshmen), rolling (transfers). *Early decision:* 12/1. *Notification:* 12/30 (early decision). *Financial aid deadline priority date:* 2/15.

Freshman Application Contact
Ms. Mary Beth Carey, Executive Dean of Enrollment Management, Hofstra University, 100 Hofstra University, Hempstead, NY 11549. **Phone:** 516-463-6700. **Toll-free phone:** 800-HOFSTRA. **Fax:** 516-560-7660. **E-mail:** hofstra@hofstra.edu

Visit CollegeQuest.com for information on majors offered and athletics. College video available at CollegeQuest.com.

■ *See page 1796 for a narrative description.*

HOLY TRINITY ORTHODOX SEMINARY
Jordanville, New York

- **Independent Russian Orthodox**, 5-year, founded 1948
- **Degree** bachelor's
- **Rural** 900-acre campus
- **Men** only, 42 undergraduate students, 100% full-time
- **Noncompetitive** entrance level, 43% of applicants were admitted
- **$2000 tuition** and fees

Students *Undergraduates:* 42 full-time. Students come from 5 states and territories, 5 other countries.

| From out-of-state | 30% | Reside on campus | 95% |
| Age 25 or older | 30% | | |

Faculty 19.
Expenses (2000–2001) *Comprehensive fee:* $4000 includes full-time tuition ($2000) and room and board ($2000).
Library Holy Trinity Orthodox Seminary Library plus 1 other. *Collection:* 30,000 titles, 200 serial subscriptions.
College life *Housing:* on-campus residence required through senior year. *Option:* men-only. *Most popular organization:* Student Union.
Campus security 24-hour emergency response devices.
After graduation *Graduate education:* 5% of class of 1999 went directly to graduate and professional school: 5% graduate arts and sciences.
Freshmen 28 applied, 12 admitted, 12 enrolled.

| SAT verbal scores above 500 | N/R | SAT math scores above 500 | N/R |
| ACT above 18 | N/R | 1998 freshmen returning in 1999 | 100% |

Application *Application fee:* $0. *Required:* essay or personal statement; high school transcript; letters of recommendation; special examination, proficiency in Russian, Eastern Orthodox baptism. *Recommended:* minimum 3.0 GPA.
Significant dates *Application deadlines:* 5/1 (freshmen), 5/1 (transfers).
Freshman Application Contact
Fr. Vladimir von Tsurikov, Secretary, Holy Trinity Orthodox Seminary, PO Box 36, Jordanville, NY 13361. **Phone:** 315-858-0945. **Fax:** 315-858-0945. **E-mail:** seminary@telenet.net

Visit CollegeQuest.com for information on majors offered and athletics.

HOUGHTON COLLEGE
Houghton, New York

- **Independent Wesleyan**, 4-year, founded 1883
- **Degrees** associate and bachelor's
- **Rural** 1,300-acre campus with easy access to Buffalo and Rochester
- **Coed**, 1,378 undergraduate students, 96% full-time, 63% women, 37% men
- **Moderately difficult** entrance level, 89% of applicants were admitted
- **14:1 student-to-undergraduate faculty ratio**
- **63.85% graduate** in 6 years or less
- **$15,140 tuition** and fees
- **$12,340 average financial aid** package, $16,850 average indebtedness upon graduation, $15.2 million endowment

Houghton College is a selective Christian liberal arts college of more than 1,200 undergraduates. Located on 1,300 acres in western New York, the College attracts talented students from around the world. Small classes in a traditional liberal arts curriculum of 49 majors and programs characterize Houghton's academic life. More than 90 percent of students receive financial aid.

Students *Undergraduates:* 1,316 full-time, 62 part-time. Students come from 37 states and territories, 27 other countries. *The most frequently chosen baccalaureate fields are:* business/marketing, education, social sciences and history.

From out-of-state	36%	Reside on campus	78%
Age 25 or older	8%	Transferred in	7%
International students	5%	African Americans	3%
Asian Americans/Pacific Islanders	1%	Hispanic Americans	1%
Native Americans	1%		

Faculty 99 (79% full-time), 74% with terminal degrees.
Expenses (2000–2001, estimated) *Comprehensive fee:* $20,540 includes full-time tuition ($15,140) and room and board ($5400). *College room only:* $2700. Full-time tuition and fees vary according to course load and program. Room and board charges vary according to board plan and housing facility. *Part-time tuition:* $630 per hour. Part-time tuition and fees vary according to course load. *Payment plan:* installment. *Waivers:* senior citizens and employees or children of employees.
Library Willard J. Houghton Library. *Operations spending 1999–2000:* $683,000. *Collection:* 217,618 titles, 3,027 serial subscriptions, 4,927 audiovisual materials.
College life *Housing:* on-campus residence required through sophomore year. *Options:* men-only, women-only. *Most popular organizations:* student government, World Mission Fellowship, Allegany County Outreach, Youth for Christ, climbing club.
Campus security 24-hour patrols, late-night transport-escort service, controlled dormitory access, phone connection to security patrols.
After graduation 26 organizations recruited on campus 1997–98. 69% of class of 1998 had job offers within 6 months. *Career center:* 2 full-time personnel. Services include job fairs, resume preparation, interview workshops, resume referral, career/interest testing, career counseling, careers library, job bank, job interviews. *Graduate education:* 25% of class of 1999 went directly to graduate and professional school.
Freshmen 1,030 applied, 913 admitted, 294 enrolled. 8 class presidents, 16 valedictorians, 72 student government officers.

Average high school GPA	3.19	SAT verbal scores above 500	86%
SAT math scores above 500	85%	ACT above 18	99%
From top 10% of their h.s. class	35%	From top quarter	61%
From top half	87%	1998 freshmen returning in 1999	82%

Application *Options:* early admission, early action, deferred entrance. Preference given to Evangelical Christians and members of the Wesleyan Church. *Application fee:* $25. *Required:* essay or personal statement; high school transcript; 1 letter of recommendation; pastoral recommendation. *Recommended:* minimum 2.5 GPA; interview.
Standardized tests *Admission: Required:* SAT I or ACT.
Significant dates *Application deadlines:* rolling (freshmen), 8/1 (transfers). *Early action:* 11/15. *Notification:* 1/1 (early action). *Financial aid deadline priority date:* 3/1.
Freshman Application Contact
Mr. Timothy Fuller, Vice President for Enrollment, Houghton College, PO Box 128, Houghton, NY 14744. **Phone:** 716-567-9353. **Toll-free phone:** 800-777-2556. **Fax:** 716-567-9522. **E-mail:** admission@houghton.edu

Visit CollegeQuest.com for information on majors offered and athletics.

■ *See page 1804 for a narrative description.*

HUNTER COLLEGE OF THE CITY UNIVERSITY OF NEW YORK
New York, New York

- **State and locally supported**, comprehensive, founded 1870
- **Degrees** bachelor's and master's
- **Urban** campus
- **Coed**, 14,426 undergraduate students, 67% full-time, 71% women, 29% men
- **Moderately difficult** entrance level, 42% of applicants were admitted
- **$3333 tuition** and fees (in-state); $6933 (out-of-state)

Part of City University of New York System.

New York

Hunter College of the City University of New York (continued)

Students *Undergraduates:* 9,696 full-time, 4,730 part-time. Students come from 29 states and territories. *Graduate:* 4,433 in graduate degree programs.

From out-of-state	3%	Reside on campus	1%
Age 25 or older	40%	Transferred in	12%
International students	6%	African Americans	20%
Asian Americans/Pacific Islanders	14%	Hispanic Americans	23%
Native Americans	0.2%		

Faculty 1,249 (47% full-time).

Expenses (1999–2000) *Tuition, state resident:* full-time $3200; part-time $135 per credit. *Tuition, nonresident:* full-time $6800; part-time $285 per credit. *Required fees:* full-time $133; $49 per term part-time. Room and board charges vary according to housing facility. *Payment plan:* deferred payment. *Waivers:* senior citizens.

Library Hunter College Library. *Collection:* 521,955 titles, 2,419 serial subscriptions, 12,515 audiovisual materials.

College life *Housing:* Option: coed. *Most popular organizations:* Caribbean Student Union, Asian Students in Action, National Golden Key Honor Society.

Campus security 24-hour emergency response devices and patrols.

After graduation 65 organizations recruited on campus 1997–98. *Career center:* 4 full-time, 3 part-time personnel. Services include job fairs, resume preparation, interview workshops, resume referral, career/interest testing, career counseling, careers library, job bank, job interviews.

Freshmen 6,986 applied, 2,914 admitted, 1,920 enrolled.

Average high school GPA	2.74	SAT verbal scores above 500	42%
SAT math scores above 500	43%	ACT above 18	N/R
From top 10% of their h.s. class	14%	From top quarter	44%
From top half	81%	1998 freshmen returning in 1999	79%

Application *Option:* early admission. *Application fee:* $40. *Required:* high school transcript.

Standardized tests *Admission: Required:* SAT I or ACT.

Significant dates *Application deadlines:* 1/15 (freshmen), 3/1 (transfers). *Financial aid deadline:* 5/15.

Freshman Application Contact
Office of Admissions, Hunter College of the City University of New York, 695 Park Avenue, New York, NY 10021-5085. **Phone:** 212-772-4490.

Visit CollegeQuest.com for information on majors offered and athletics.

■ *See page 1808 for a narrative description.*

IONA COLLEGE
New Rochelle, New York

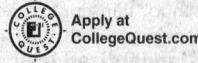
Apply at CollegeQuest.com

- **Independent**, comprehensive, founded 1940, affiliated with Roman Catholic Church
- **Degrees** associate, bachelor's, and master's
- **Suburban** 35-acre campus with easy access to New York City
- **Coed**, 3,447 undergraduate students, 84% full-time, 51% women, 49% men
- **Moderately difficult** entrance level, 77% of applicants were admitted
- **17:1 student-to-undergraduate faculty ratio**
- **54% graduate** in 6 years or less
- **$15,070 tuition** and fees
- **$14,955 average financial aid** package, $16,086 average indebtedness upon graduation, $17.8 million endowment

Founded in 1940, Iona College is dedicated to personal teaching in the tradition of American Catholic higher education and the Christian Brothers. The College endeavors to develop informed, critical, and responsible individuals who are equipped to participate actively in culture and society. At Iona College, students are the first priority.

Students *Undergraduates:* 2,893 full-time, 554 part-time. Students come from 26 states and territories, 36 other countries. *The most frequently chosen baccalaureate fields are:* business/marketing, communications/communication technologies, protective services/public administration. *Graduate:* 1,070 in graduate degree programs.

From out-of-state	13%	Reside on campus	15%
Age 25 or older	18%	Transferred in	4%
International students	0.03%	African Americans	11%
Asian Americans/Pacific Islanders	1%	Hispanic Americans	12%
Native Americans	0.1%		

Faculty 348 (49% full-time).

Expenses (1999–2000) *One-time required fee:* $25. *Comprehensive fee:* $23,500 includes full-time tuition ($14,700), mandatory fees ($370), and room and board ($8430). Full-time tuition and fees vary according to class time. *Part-time tuition:* $490 per credit. *Part-time fees:* $185 per term part-time. Part-time tuition and fees vary according to class time and course load. *Payment plans:* installment, deferred payment. *Waivers:* senior citizens and employees or children of employees.

Library Ryan Library. *Operations spending 1999–2000:* $1.5 million. *Collection:* 2,611 audiovisual materials.

College life *Housing:* Option: coed. *Social organizations:* national fraternities, national sororities, local fraternities, local sororities; 5% of eligible men and 5% of eligible women are members. *Most popular organizations:* Council of Multicultural Leaders, student government, The Ionian, LASO, WICR.

Campus security 24-hour patrols, controlled dormitory access.

After graduation *Career center:* 4 full-time personnel. Services include job fairs, resume preparation, resume referral, career counseling, careers library, job bank, job interviews.

Freshmen 2,986 applied, 2,304 admitted, 844 enrolled.

Average high school GPA	2.8	SAT verbal scores above 500	52%
SAT math scores above 500	52%	ACT above 18	N/R
From top 10% of their h.s. class	11%	From top quarter	30%
From top half	69%	1998 freshmen returning in 1999	79%

Application *Options:* eApply at www.CollegeQuest.com, Common Application, early action, deferred entrance. *Application fee:* $25. *Required:* high school transcript. *Recommended:* essay or personal statement; minimum 2.5 GPA; letters of recommendation; interview.

Standardized tests *Admission: Required:* SAT I or ACT. *Recommended:* SAT II Subject Tests, SAT II: Writing Test.

Significant dates *Application deadlines:* 3/15 (freshmen), 8/1 (transfers). *Early action:* 12/1. *Notification:* 12/20 (early action). *Financial aid deadline:* continuous.

Freshman Application Contact
Mr. Tom Delahunt, Director of Undergraduate Admissions, Iona College, 715 North Avenue, New Rochelle, NY 10801-1890. **Phone:** 914-633-2502. **Fax:** 914-633-2096.

Visit CollegeQuest.com for information on majors offered and athletics. College video available at CollegeQuest.com.

■ *See page 1830 for a narrative description.*

ITHACA COLLEGE
Ithaca, New York

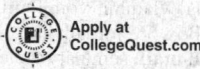
Apply at CollegeQuest.com

- **Independent**, comprehensive, founded 1892
- **Degrees** bachelor's and master's
- **Small-town** 757-acre campus with easy access to Syracuse
- **Coed**, 5,588 undergraduate students, 99% full-time, 56% women, 44% men
- **Moderately difficult** entrance level, 73% of applicants were admitted
- **11:1 student-to-undergraduate faculty ratio**
- **69% graduate** in 6 years or less
- **$18,410 tuition** and fees
- **$16,634 average financial aid** package, $16,673 average indebtedness upon graduation, $121.3 million endowment

Students *Undergraduates:* 5,525 full-time, 63 part-time. Students come from 47 states and territories, 78 other countries. *The most frequently chosen baccalaureate fields are:* communications/communication technologies, health professions and related sciences, visual/performing arts. *Graduate:* 258 in graduate degree programs.

From out-of-state	50%	Reside on campus	70%
Age 25 or older	2%	Transferred in	3%
International students	2%	African Americans	2%
Asian Americans/Pacific Islanders	2%	Hispanic Americans	3%
Native Americans	0.3%		

Faculty 514 (76% full-time), 83% with terminal degrees.

Expenses (1999–2000) *Comprehensive fee:* $26,366 includes full-time tuition ($18,410) and room and board ($7956). *College room only:* $3980. Room and board charges vary according to housing facility. *Part-time tuition:* $575 per credit. *Part-time fees:* $15 per term part-time. *Payment plan:* installment. *Waivers:* employees or children of employees.

Library Ithaca College Library. *Operations spending 1999–2000:* $2.6 million. *Collection:* 356,229 titles, 2,541 serial subscriptions, 31,019 audiovisual materials.

College life *Housing:* on-campus residence required through senior year. *Options:* coed, women-only, disabled students. *Most popular organizations:* student government, Student Activities Board, African-Latino Society, Residence Hall Association, Community Service Network.

Campus security 24-hour emergency response devices, student patrols, late-night transport-escort service, patrols by trained security personnel 11 p.m. to 7 a.m.

After graduation 300 organizations recruited on campus 1997–98. *Career center:* 6 full-time personnel. Services include job fairs, resume preparation, interview workshops, resume referral, career/interest testing, career counseling, careers library, job bank, job interviews. *Graduate education:* 33% of class of 1999 went directly to graduate and professional school. 26% graduate arts and sciences, 4% education, 1% business, 1% law. *Major awards:* 1 Fulbright Scholar.

Freshmen 8,301 applied, 6,100 admitted, 1,589 enrolled. 6 National Merit Scholars, 26 valedictorians.

SAT verbal scores above 500	87%	SAT math scores above 500	86%
ACT above 18	N/R	From top 10% of their h.s. class	30%
From top quarter	61%	From top half	88%
1998 freshmen returning in 1999	87%		

Application *Options:* eApply at www.CollegeQuest.com, Common Application, electronic application, early admission, early decision, deferred entrance. *Application fee:* $45. *Required:* essay or personal statement; high school transcript; 1 letter of recommendation. *Required for some:* audition for music and theater programs. *Recommended:* minimum 3.0 GPA; interview.

Standardized tests *Admission: Required:* SAT I or ACT.

Significant dates *Application deadlines:* 3/1 (freshmen), 7/15 (transfers). *Early decision:* 11/1. *Notification:* continuous until 4/15 (freshmen), 12/15 (early decision). *Financial aid deadline priority date:* 2/1.

Freshman Application Contact
Ms. Paula J. Mitchell, Director of Admission, Ithaca College, 100 Job Hall, Ithaca, NY 14850-7020. **Phone:** 607-274-3124. **Toll-free phone:** 800-429-4274. **Fax:** 607-274-1900. **E-mail:** admission@ithaca.edu

Visit CollegeQuest.com for information on majors offered and athletics. College video and electronic viewbook available at CollegeQuest.com.

■ *See page 1834 for a narrative description.*

JEWISH THEOLOGICAL SEMINARY OF AMERICA
New York, New York

- **Independent Jewish**, university, founded 1886
- **Degrees** bachelor's, master's, and doctoral (double bachelor's degree with Barnard College, Columbia University)
- **Urban** 1-acre campus
- **Coed**, 172 undergraduate students, 100% full-time, 56% women, 44% men
- **Very difficult** entrance level, 63% of applicants were admitted
- **$8720 tuition** and fees

Two undergraduate degrees can be earned in dual-degree programs: one in Jewish studies from List College, the Seminary's undergraduate school, the other in any liberal arts major at Columbia University or Barnard College. Majors at List include Bible, Jewish history, Jewish music, literature or philosophy, Midrash, and Talmud. Honors Program and study in Israel available. Coed residential campus. Access to vast cultural activities of New York City.

Students *Undergraduates:* 172 full-time. Students come from 22 states and territories, 3 other countries. *The most frequently chosen baccalaureate field is:* philosophy. *Graduate:* 399 in graduate degree programs.

From out-of-state	67%	Reside on campus	77%
Age 25 or older	1%	Transferred in	4%

Expenses (1999–2000) *Tuition:* full-time $8320; part-time $445 per credit. *Required fees:* full-time $400; $200 per term part-time. Full-time tuition and fees vary according to program. Part-time tuition and fees vary according to program. *College room only:* $5000. Room and board charges vary according to housing facility. *Payment plan:* installment. *Waivers:* senior citizens and employees or children of employees.

Library *Collection:* 271,000 titles, 720 serial subscriptions.

College life *Housing: Option:* coed.

Campus security 24-hour emergency response devices and patrols, late-night transport-escort service, controlled dormitory access.

After graduation *Career center:* 1 part-time personnel. Services include resume preparation, career counseling, careers library. *Graduate education:* 60% of class of 1999 went directly to graduate and professional school.

Freshmen 138 applied, 87 admitted, 48 enrolled.

Average high school GPA	3.75	SAT verbal scores above 500	98%
SAT math scores above 500	96%	ACT above 18	100%
From top 10% of their h.s. class	39%	From top quarter	78%
From top half	100%	1998 freshmen returning in 1999	86%

Application *Options:* early admission, early decision, deferred entrance. *Application fee:* $60. *Required:* essay or personal statement; high school transcript; 2 letters of recommendation. *Recommended:* minimum 3.0 GPA; interview.

Standardized tests *Admission: Required:* SAT I and SAT II or ACT, SAT II: Writing Test.

Significant dates *Application deadlines:* 2/15 (freshmen), 5/1 (transfers). *Early decision:* 11/15 (for plan 1), 1/15 (for plan 2). *Notification:* continuous until 4/15 (freshmen), 12/15 (early decision plan 1), 2/15 (early decision plan 2). *Financial aid deadline:* 3/1.

Freshman Application Contact
Reena Gold, Assistant Director of Admissions, Jewish Theological Seminary of America, Room 614 Schiff, 3080 Broadway, New York, NY 10027-4649. **Phone:** 212-678-8832. **Fax:** 212-678-8947. **E-mail:** regold@jtsa.edu

Visit CollegeQuest.com for information on majors offered and athletics.

■ *See page 1840 for a narrative description.*

JOHN JAY COLLEGE OF CRIMINAL JUSTICE OF THE CITY UNIVERSITY OF NEW YORK
New York, New York

- **State and locally supported**, comprehensive, founded 1964
- **Degrees** associate, bachelor's, and master's
- **Urban** campus
- **Coed**, 9,213 undergraduate students, 75% full-time, 58% women, 42% men
- **Moderately difficult** entrance level, 73% of applicants were admitted
- **20:1 student-to-undergraduate faculty ratio**
- **26% graduate** in 6 years or less
- **$3312 tuition** and fees (in-state); $6912 (out-of-state)
- **$4800 average financial aid** package, $10,000 average indebtedness upon graduation, $221,000 endowment

Part of City University of New York System.

Students *Undergraduates:* 6,905 full-time, 2,308 part-time. Students come from 10 states and territories, 12 other countries. *The most frequently chosen baccalaureate fields are:* protective services/public administration, psychology, social sciences and history. *Graduate:* 1,141 in graduate degree programs.

Age 25 or older	35%	International students	1%
African Americans	31%	Asian Americans/Pacific Islanders	5%
Hispanic Americans	37%	Native Americans	0.2%

Faculty 628 (44% full-time), 61% with terminal degrees.

Expenses (2000–2001) *Tuition, state resident:* full-time $3200; part-time $135 per credit. *Tuition, nonresident:* full-time $6800; part-time $285 per credit. *Required fees:* full-time $112; $46 per term part-time. Full-time tuition and fees vary according to course level and course load. Part-time tuition and fees vary according to course level.

New York

John Jay College of Criminal Justice of the City University of New York *(continued)*

Library Lloyd George Sealy Library. *Operations spending 1999–2000:* $1.5 million. *Collection:* 310,000 titles, 1,325 serial subscriptions.

College life *Housing:* college housing not available. *Most popular organizations:* Organization of Black Students, Latino Diversity Club, Lex Review, Women's Awareness Club, Forensic Psychology Society.

Campus security 24-hour emergency response devices and patrols.

After graduation *Career center:* 2 full-time, 2 part-time personnel. Services include job fairs, resume preparation, resume referral, career counseling, careers library, job bank. *Graduate education:* 13% of class of 1999 went directly to graduate and professional school.

Freshmen 3,144 applied, 2,299 admitted, 1,407 enrolled.

SAT verbal scores above 500	N/R	SAT math scores above 500	N/R
ACT above 18	N/R	From top quarter of their h.s. class	20%
From top half	66%	1998 freshmen returning in 1999	72%

Application *Options:* early admission, deferred entrance. *Application fee:* $40. *Required:* high school transcript.

Significant dates *Application deadlines:* rolling (freshmen), rolling (transfers). *Financial aid deadline priority date:* 6/1.

Freshman Application Contact Mr. Richard Saulnier, Acting Dean for Admissions and Registration, John Jay College of Criminal Justice of the City University of New York, 899 Tenth Avenue, New York, NY 10019-1093. **Phone:** 212-237-8878.

Visit CollegeQuest.com for information on majors offered and athletics.

■ *See page 1846 for a narrative description.*

THE JUILLIARD SCHOOL
New York, New York

- **Independent**, comprehensive, founded 1905
- **Degrees** bachelor's, master's, and doctoral
- **Urban** campus
- **Coed**, 473 undergraduate students, 99% full-time, 51% women, 49% men
- **Most difficult** entrance level, 8% of applicants were admitted
- **75% graduate** in 6 years or less
- **$16,600 tuition** and fees
- **$15,188 average financial aid** package, $17,298 average indebtedness upon graduation, $436 million endowment

Students *Undergraduates:* 468 full-time, 5 part-time. Students come from 39 states and territories, 26 other countries. *The most frequently chosen baccalaureate field is:* visual/performing arts. *Graduate:* 296 in graduate degree programs.

From out-of-state	83%	Reside on campus	48%
Age 25 or older	5%	Transferred in	6%
International students	22%	African Americans	12%
Asian Americans/Pacific Islanders	12%	Hispanic Americans	4%
Native Americans	0.2%		

Expenses (1999–2000) *Comprehensive fee:* $23,450 includes full-time tuition ($16,000), mandatory fees ($600), and room and board ($6850). Room and board charges vary according to housing facility. *Payment plan:* installment. *Waivers:* employees or children of employees.

Library Lila Acheson Wallace Library. *Operations spending 1999–2000:* $566,000. *Collection:* 65,000 titles, 200 serial subscriptions.

College life *Housing:* on-campus residence required in freshman year. *Option:* coed. *Most popular organizations:* Christian Fellowship, Korean Crusade for Christ, Mu Phi Epsilon (music honor society), Greens, Gay Student Organization.

Campus security 24-hour emergency response devices and patrols, controlled dormitory access, electronically operated main building entrances.

After graduation *Career center:* 3 full-time personnel. Services include resume preparation, resume referral, career counseling, careers library, job interviews.

Freshmen 1,755 applied, 132 admitted, 94 enrolled.

SAT verbal scores above 500	N/R	SAT math scores above 500	N/R
ACT above 18	N/R	1998 freshmen returning in 1999	95%

Application *Option:* early admission. *Application fee:* $100. *Required:* high school transcript; audition. *Required for some:* essay or personal statement.

Significant dates *Application deadlines:* 12/1 (freshmen), 12/1 (transfers). *Notification:* 4/1 (freshmen). *Financial aid deadline priority date:* 3/1.

Freshman Application Contact Ms. Mary K. Gray, Director of Admissions, The Juilliard School, 60 Lincoln Center Plaza, New York, NY 10023-6588. **Phone:** 212-799-5000 Ext. 223. **Fax:** 212-724-0263. **E-mail:** webmaster@juilliard.edu

Visit CollegeQuest.com for information on majors offered and athletics.

KEHILATH YAKOV RABBINICAL SEMINARY
Brooklyn, New York

Admissions Office Contact Kehilath Yakov Rabbinical Seminary, 206 Wilson Street, Brooklyn, NY 11211-7207. **Fax:** 718-387-8586.

KEUKA COLLEGE
Keuka Park, New York

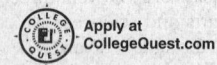

- **Independent**, 4-year, founded 1890, affiliated with American Baptist Churches in the U.S.A.
- **Degree** bachelor's
- **Rural** 173-acre campus with easy access to Rochester
- **Coed**, 893 undergraduate students, 97% full-time, 75% women, 25% men
- **Moderately difficult** entrance level, 94% of applicants were admitted
- **13:1 student-to-undergraduate faculty ratio**
- **48.1% graduate** in 6 years or less
- **$13,085 tuition** and fees

Students *Undergraduates:* 870 full-time, 23 part-time. Students come from 15 states and territories. *The most frequently chosen baccalaureate fields are:* education, business/marketing, health professions and related sciences.

From out-of-state	8%	Reside on campus	75%
Age 25 or older	12%	Transferred in	10%
African Americans	3%	Asian Americans/Pacific Islanders	1%
Hispanic Americans	1%	Native Americans	0.3%

Faculty 76 (63% full-time), 42% with terminal degrees.

Expenses (1999–2000) *Comprehensive fee:* $19,455 includes full-time tuition ($12,730), mandatory fees ($355), and room and board ($6370). Full-time tuition and fees vary according to program. Room and board charges vary according to board plan and housing facility. *Part-time tuition:* $425 per credit hour. Part-time tuition and fees vary according to program. *Payment plan:* installment. *Waivers:* employees or children of employees.

Library Lightner Library. *Operations spending 1999–2000:* $344,681. *Collection:* 70,285 titles, 3,170 audiovisual materials.

College life *Housing:* on-campus residence required through senior year. *Options:* coed, women-only, cooperative. *Most popular organizations:* Student Senate, Campus Activities Board, OTTERS (occupational therapy club), education club, BAKU.

Campus security 24-hour emergency response devices and patrols, late-night transport-escort service.

After graduation *Career center:* 2 full-time personnel. Services include job fairs, resume preparation, interview workshops, career/interest testing, career counseling, careers library, job bank. *Graduate education:* 16% of class of 1999 went directly to graduate and professional school: 3% law, 2% business, 1% medicine.

Freshmen 831 applied, 778 admitted, 270 enrolled. 3 valedictorians.

Average high school GPA	3.0	SAT verbal scores above 500	44%
SAT math scores above 500	50%	ACT above 18	83%
From top 10% of their h.s. class	10%	From top quarter	33%
From top half	70%	1998 freshmen returning in 1999	68%

Application *Options:* eApply at www.CollegeQuest.com, Common Application, electronic application, early admission, early decision, deferred entrance. *Application fee:* $30. *Required:* essay or personal statement; high school transcript; letters of recommendation. *Required for some:* interview. *Recommended:* minimum 2.75 GPA; interview.

Standardized tests *Admission: Required:* SAT I or ACT.

Significant dates *Application deadlines:* rolling (freshmen), rolling (transfers). *Early decision:* 12/15. *Notification:* 1/15 (early decision). *Financial aid deadline priority date:* 3/15.

Freshman Application Contact
Mr. Joel Wincowski, Dean of Admissions and Financial Aid, Keuka College, Office of Admissions, Keuka Park, NY 14478-0098. **Phone:** 315-536-4411 Ext. 5254. **Toll-free phone:** 800-33-KEUKA. **Fax:** 315-536-5386. **E-mail:** admissions@mail.keuka.edu

Visit CollegeQuest.com for information on majors offered and athletics. College video available at CollegeQuest.com.

KOL YAAKOV TORAH CENTER
Monsey, New York

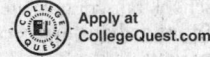

- **Independent Jewish**, comprehensive, founded 1980
- **Degrees** bachelor's and master's
- **Small-town** 3-acre campus with easy access to New York City
- **Men** only
- **Minimally difficult** entrance level, 50% of applicants were admitted

Students *Undergraduates:* Students come from 15 states and territories.
Age 25 or older   7%

Faculty 12 (17% full-time).
Library *Collection:* 2,000 titles.
Campus security 24-hour emergency response devices.
After graduation *Career center:* Services include career counseling.
Freshmen 10 applied, 5 admitted.

| SAT verbal scores above 500 | N/R | SAT math scores above 500 | N/R |
| ACT above 18 | N/R | | |

Application *Options:* eApply at www.CollegeQuest.com, early admission. *Required:* high school transcript; interview. *Recommended:* letters of recommendation.

Significant dates *Application deadlines:* rolling (freshmen), rolling (transfers).

Freshman Application Contact
Mr. Aaron Parry, Assistant Director of Admissions, Kol Yaakov Torah Center, 29 West Maple Avenue, Monsey, NY 10952-2954. **Phone:** 914-425-3871. **E-mail:** horizonss@aol.com

Visit CollegeQuest.com for information on majors offered and athletics.

LABORATORY INSTITUTE OF MERCHANDISING
New York, New York

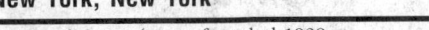

- **Proprietary**, 4-year, founded 1939
- **Degrees** associate and bachelor's
- **Urban** campus
- **Coed**, primarily women, 267 undergraduate students, 96% full-time, 97% women, 3% men
- **Moderately difficult** entrance level, 76% of applicants were admitted
- **8:1 student-to-undergraduate faculty ratio**
- **$12,950 tuition** and fees

A private, Middle States–accredited 4-year college offering bachelor's and associate degrees in fashion merchandising, marketing, and visual merchandising. Distinctive educational opportunity through a combination of academics and industry work-study/co-ops. Prepares students for careers in fashion marketing, buying, product development, retail management, production, cosmetics, magazines, and more. Experience broadened by weekly field trips and guest lectures. Campus setting is in the finest area of New York City near business, fashion, and cultural centers. Summer sessions available for high school and college students.

Students *Undergraduates:* 256 full-time, 11 part-time. Students come from 9 states and territories, 6 other countries. *The most frequently chosen baccalaureate field is:* business/marketing.

From out-of-state	54%	Age 25 or older	1%
Transferred in	9%	International students	3%
African Americans	19%	Asian Americans/Pacific Islanders	6%
Hispanic Americans	13%	Native Americans	1%

Faculty 38 (24% full-time), 16% with terminal degrees.
Expenses (2000–2001) *Tuition:* full-time $12,800; part-time $390 per credit. *Required fees:* full-time $150; $75 per term part-time. *Payment plan:* installment.
Library *Collection:* 10,702 titles, 80 serial subscriptions, 390 audiovisual materials.
College life *Housing:* college housing not available. *Most popular organizations:* student government, LIMlight club (yearbook), Fashion club, Latin Cultures club, Marketing club/SIFE.
After graduation 97% of class of 1998 had job offers within 6 months. *Career center:* 1 full-time personnel. Services include job fairs, resume preparation, interview workshops, resume referral, career counseling, careers library, job bank, job interviews.
Freshmen 249 applied, 189 admitted, 79 enrolled.

SAT verbal scores above 500	26%	SAT math scores above 500	12%
ACT above 18	0%	From top 10% of their h.s. class	1%
From top quarter	18%	From top half	46%

Application *Options:* eApply at www.CollegeQuest.com, deferred entrance. *Application fee:* $35. *Required:* essay or personal statement; high school transcript; interview. *Recommended:* minimum 2.5 GPA; letters of recommendation.
Standardized tests *Admission: Required:* SAT I or ACT.
Significant dates *Application deadlines:* rolling (freshmen), rolling (transfers). *Financial aid deadline:* continuous.
Freshman Application Contact
Mr. Drew Ippolito, Director of Admissions, Laboratory Institute of Merchandising, 12 East 53rd Street, New York, NY 10022-5268. **Phone:** 212-752-1530. **Toll-free phone:** 800-677-1323. **Fax:** 212-832-6708. **E-mail:** admissions@limcollege.edu

Visit CollegeQuest.com for information on majors offered and athletics. College video and electronic viewbook available at CollegeQuest.com.

■ *See page 1884 for a narrative description.*

LEHMAN COLLEGE OF THE CITY UNIVERSITY OF NEW YORK
Bronx, New York

- **State and locally supported**, comprehensive, founded 1931
- **Degrees** bachelor's and master's
- **Urban** 37-acre campus
- **Coed**, 7,228 undergraduate students
- **Moderately difficult** entrance level
- **$3320 tuition** and fees (in-state); $6920 (out-of-state)

Part of City University of New York System.

Students *Undergraduates:* Students come from 91 other countries.
Age 25 or older   54%

Faculty 694 (41% full-time).
Expenses (2000–2001) *Tuition, state resident:* full-time $3200; part-time $135 per credit. *Tuition, nonresident:* full-time $6800; part-time $285 per credit. *Required fees:* full-time $120; $40 per term part-time. Full-time tuition and fees vary according to course load and program. Part-time tuition and fees vary according to course load and program. *Payment plan:* installment. *Waivers:* senior citizens.
Library Lehman College Library plus 1 other. *Collection:* 541,944 titles, 1,350 serial subscriptions.
College life *Housing:* college housing not available. *Social organizations:* national sororities. *Most popular organizations:* Club Mac, Central and South American Club, Dominican Student Association, Health Services Association, academic society.
Campus security 24-hour emergency response devices and patrols, student patrols.

New York

Lehman College of the City University of New York (continued)
After graduation 45 organizations recruited on campus 1997–98. *Career center:* 2 full-time, 1 part-time personnel. Services include job fairs, resume preparation, resume referral, career counseling, careers library, job bank, job interviews.
Freshmen

SAT verbal scores above 500	N/R	SAT math scores above 500	N/R
ACT above 18	N/R	1998 freshmen returning in 1999	69%

Application *Option:* deferred entrance. *Application fee:* $40. *Required:* high school transcript; minimum 3.0 GPA. *Required for some:* letters of recommendation; interview.
Standardized tests *Admission: Recommended:* SAT I, ACT.
Significant dates *Application deadlines:* rolling (freshmen), rolling (transfers). *Financial aid deadline:* continuous.
Freshman Application Contact
Ms. Gloria Ortiz, Assistant Director of Undergraduate Admissions, Lehman College of the City University of New York, 250 Bedford Park Boulevard West, Bronx, NY 10468. **Phone:** 718-960-8096. **Toll-free phone:** 877-Lehman1. **Fax:** 718-960-8712. **E-mail:** cawic@cunyum.cunx.edu
Visit CollegeQuest.com for information on majors offered and athletics. College video available at CollegeQuest.com.

■ *See page 1912 for a narrative description.*

LE MOYNE COLLEGE
Syracuse, New York

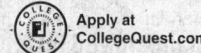
Apply at CollegeQuest.com

- **Independent Roman Catholic (Jesuit)**, comprehensive, founded 1946
- **Degrees** bachelor's, master's, and postbachelor's certificates
- **Suburban** 151-acre campus
- **Coed**, 2,131 undergraduate students, 92% full-time, 59% women, 41% men
- **Moderately difficult** entrance level, 80% of applicants were admitted
- **14:1 student-to-undergraduate faculty ratio**
- **73% graduate** in 6 years or less
- **$14,980 tuition** and fees
- **$12,578 average financial aid** package, $16,000 average indebtedness upon graduation, $28.7 million endowment

Le Moyne is a comprehensive liberal arts college, nationally recognized for quality and value, founded in the Jesuit tradition of academic excellence. That powerful tradition, present in the College's strong academic programs, caring faculty members, and reassuring Jesuit presence, emphasizes developing students' abilities to think clearly and communicate well and prepares them for life.

Students *Undergraduates:* 1,971 full-time, 160 part-time. Students come from 24 states and territories, 7 other countries. *The most frequently chosen baccalaureate fields are:* business/marketing, psychology, social sciences and history. *Graduate:* 729 in graduate degree programs.

From out-of-state	6%	Reside on campus	64%
Age 25 or older	18%	Transferred in	6%
International students	0.1%	African Americans	4%
Asian Americans/Pacific Islanders	1%	Hispanic Americans	3%
Native Americans	1%		

Faculty 239 (53% full-time), 64% with terminal degrees.
Expenses (1999–2000) *Comprehensive fee:* $21,300 includes full-time tuition ($14,580), mandatory fees ($400), and room and board ($6320). *College room only:* $3860. Room and board charges vary according to board plan and housing facility. *Part-time tuition:* $329 per credit hour. Part-time tuition and fees vary according to class time. *Payment plans:* installment, deferred payment. *Waivers:* employees or children of employees.
Library Noreen Reale Falcone Library. *Operations spending 1999–2000:* $1.3 million. *Collection:* 231,283 titles, 1,710 serial subscriptions, 9,539 audio-visual materials.
College life *Housing:* on-campus residence required through senior year. *Options:* coed, men-only, women-only. *Most popular organizations:* Le Moyne Student Programming Board, Outing Club, theater group, Le Moyne Student Dancers, El Progresso (Latino organization).
Campus security 24-hour emergency response devices and patrols, late-night transport-escort service, controlled dormitory access, campus watch, self-defense education, lighted pathways, closed circuit TV monitors.

After graduation 70 organizations recruited on campus 1997–98. 65% of class of 1998 had job offers within 6 months. *Career center:* 3 full-time, 1 part-time personnel. Services include job fairs, resume preparation, interview workshops, resume referral, career/interest testing, career counseling, careers library, job bank, job interviews, career advisory network.
Freshmen 2,275 applied, 1,831 admitted, 473 enrolled. 3 National Merit Scholars, 2 valedictorians.

Average high school GPA	2.71	SAT verbal scores above 500	67%
SAT math scores above 500	69%	ACT above 18	96%
From top 10% of their h.s. class	15%	From top quarter	43%
From top half	85%	1998 freshmen returning in 1999	84%

Application *Options:* eApply at www.CollegeQuest.com, Common Application, electronic application, early admission, early decision, deferred entrance. *Application fee:* $35. *Required:* essay or personal statement; high school transcript; 2 letters of recommendation. *Recommended:* interview.
Standardized tests *Admission: Required:* SAT I or ACT.
Significant dates *Application deadlines:* 3/1 (freshmen), 6/1 (transfers). *Early decision:* 12/1. *Notification:* continuous until 5/1 (freshmen), 12/15 (early decision). *Financial aid deadline priority date:* 2/1.
Freshman Application Contact
Director of Admission, Le Moyne College, 1419 Salt Spring Road, Syracuse, NY 13214-1399. **Phone:** 315-445-4300. **Toll-free phone:** 800-333-4733. **Fax:** 315-445-4711. **E-mail:** admsoffc@maple.lemoyne.edu
Visit CollegeQuest.com for information on majors offered and athletics. College video available at CollegeQuest.com.

■ *See page 1914 for a narrative description.*

LIST COLLEGE OF JEWISH STUDIES
New York—See Jewish Theological Seminary of America

LONG ISLAND UNIVERSITY, BRENTWOOD CAMPUS
Brentwood, New York

- **Independent**, upper-level, founded 1959
- **Degrees** bachelor's and master's
- **Coed**, 98 undergraduate students, 33% full-time, 62% women, 38% men
- **100% of applicants were admitted**
- **$15,960 tuition** and fees

Part of Long Island University.
Students *Undergraduates:* 32 full-time, 66 part-time. *The most frequently chosen baccalaureate fields are:* business/marketing, protective services/public administration. *Graduate:* 626 in graduate degree programs.

From out-of-state	1%	Age 25 or older	95%
Transferred in	99.9%	African Americans	7%
Asian Americans/Pacific Islanders	1%	Hispanic Americans	12%
Native Americans	1%		

Faculty 110 (18% full-time), 86% with terminal degrees.
Expenses (1999–2000) *Tuition:* full-time 15,340. *Required fees:* full-time 620; 145 per term part-time.
Campus security Evening security guard.
Significant dates *Application deadline:* 9/14 (transfers).
Admissions Office Contact
Long Island University, Brentwood Campus, 100 Second Avenue, Brentwood, NY 11717.
Visit CollegeQuest.com for information on majors offered and athletics.

LONG ISLAND UNIVERSITY, BROOKLYN CAMPUS
Brooklyn, New York

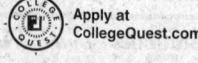
Apply at CollegeQuest.com

- **Independent**, comprehensive, founded 1926

New York

- **Degrees** associate, bachelor's, master's, doctoral, first professional, and postbachelor's certificates
- **Urban** 10-acre campus
- **Coed**, 5,929 undergraduate students, 82% full-time, 71% women, 29% men
- **Minimally difficult** entrance level, 84% of applicants were admitted
- **$15,450 tuition** and fees
- **$13,709 average financial aid** package, $19,380 average indebtedness upon graduation, $31.6 million system endowment

Part of Long Island University.

Students *Undergraduates:* 4,891 full-time, 1,038 part-time. Students come from 35 states and territories. *Graduate:* 14 in professional programs, 2,037 in other graduate degree programs.

From out-of-state	10%	Reside on campus	5%
Age 25 or older	33%	Transferred in	10%
International students	1%	African Americans	47%
Asian Americans/Pacific Islanders	11%	Hispanic Americans	16%
Native Americans	0.3%		

Faculty 923 (27% full-time).

Expenses (1999–2000) *Comprehensive fee:* $20,550 includes full-time tuition ($14,750), mandatory fees ($700), and room and board ($5100). *College room only:* $4300. Room and board charges vary according to board plan. *Part-time tuition:* $487 per credit. Part-time tuition and fees vary according to course load. *Waivers:* senior citizens and employees or children of employees.

Library Selena Library. *Operations spending 1999–2000:* $3.1 million. *Collection:* 149,455 titles, 1,667 serial subscriptions, 23,794 audiovisual materials.

College life *Housing: Option:* coed. *Social organizations:* national fraternities, local fraternities, local sororities; 30% of eligible men and 30% of eligible women are members. *Most popular organizations:* Caribbean Students Movement, Asian Students Association, African Students United, Speech and Hearing Society, Hillel.

Campus security 24-hour emergency response devices and patrols.

After graduation 63 organizations recruited on campus 1997–98. 70% of class of 1998 had job offers within 6 months. *Career center:* 14 full-time, 6 part-time personnel. Services include job fairs, resume preparation, interview workshops, resume referral, career/interest testing, career counseling, careers library, job bank, job interviews.

Freshmen 3,277 applied, 2,739 admitted, 1,124 enrolled.

Average high school GPA	3.0	SAT verbal scores above 500	N/R
SAT math scores above 500	N/R	ACT above 18	N/R
From top 10% of their h.s. class	11%	From top quarter	32%
From top half	34%		

Application *Options:* eApply at www.CollegeQuest.com, Common Application, electronic application, early action, deferred entrance. *Application fee:* $30. *Required:* high school transcript; minimum 2.0 GPA. *Required for some:* 2 letters of recommendation; interview. *Recommended:* essay or personal statement.

Standardized tests *Admission: Required for some:* SAT I or ACT.

Significant dates *Application deadlines:* rolling (freshmen), rolling (transfers). *Early action:* 12/15. *Notification:* 1/2 (early action). *Financial aid deadline:* continuous.

Freshman Application Contact
Mr. Alan B. Chaves, Dean of Admissions, Long Island University, Brooklyn Campus, One University Plaza, Brooklyn, NY 11201-8423. **Phone:** 718-488-1011. **Toll-free phone:** 800-LIU-PLAN. **E-mail:** admissions@brooklyn.liu.edu

Visit CollegeQuest.com for information on majors offered and athletics. College video available at CollegeQuest.com.

- *See page 1936 for a narrative description.*

LONG ISLAND UNIVERSITY, C.W. POST CAMPUS
Brookville, New York

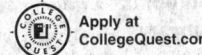

- **Independent**, comprehensive, founded 1954
- **Degrees** associate, bachelor's, master's, and doctoral
- **Suburban** 308-acre campus with easy access to New York City
- **Coed**, 5,748 undergraduate students, 63% full-time, 57% women, 43% men
- **Moderately difficult** entrance level, 85% of applicants were admitted
- **14:1 student-to-undergraduate faculty ratio**
- **99% graduate** in 6 years or less
- **$31.6 million system endowment**

Part of Long Island University.

Students *Undergraduates:* 3,641 full-time, 2,107 part-time. Students come from 34 states and territories, 40 other countries. *The most frequently chosen baccalaureate fields are:* computer/information sciences, education, visual/performing arts. *Graduate:* 3,533 in graduate degree programs.

From out-of-state	6%	Reside on campus	37%
Age 25 or older	23%	Transferred in	13%
International students	2%	African Americans	7%
Asian Americans/Pacific Islanders	2%	Hispanic Americans	7%
Native Americans	1%		

Faculty 657 (47% full-time).

Library B. Davis Schwartz Memorial Library. *Operations spending 1999–2000:* $4 million. *Collection:* 859,212 titles, 11,446 serial subscriptions, 34,530 audiovisual materials.

College life *Housing: Option:* coed. *Social organizations:* national fraternities, national sororities, local fraternities, local sororities; 1% of eligible men and 1% of eligible women are members. *Most popular organizations:* Student Government Association, Campus Activities Board, C.W. Post Earth Club.

Campus security 24-hour emergency response devices and patrols, student patrols, late-night transport-escort service, controlled dormitory access, closed campus after hours.

After graduation 500 organizations recruited on campus 1997–98. 94% of class of 1998 had job offers within 6 months. *Career center:* 12 full-time, 3 part-time personnel. Services include job fairs, resume preparation, interview workshops, resume referral, career/interest testing, career counseling, careers library, job bank, job interviews. *Graduate education:* 26% of class of 1999 went directly to graduate and professional school: 12% graduate arts and sciences, 7% education, 4% business, 3% medicine, 2% engineering.

Freshmen 3,315 applied, 2,813 admitted, 725 enrolled. 12 National Merit Scholars, 9 class presidents, 4 valedictorians, 63 student government officers.

Average high school GPA	3.55	SAT verbal scores above 500	64%
SAT math scores above 500	58%	ACT above 18	N/R
From top 10% of their h.s. class	10%	From top quarter	26%
From top half	61%	1998 freshmen returning in 1999	87%

Application *Options:* eApply at www.CollegeQuest.com, Common Application, electronic application, deferred entrance. *Application fee:* $30. *Required:* high school transcript; minimum 2.5 GPA. *Recommended:* essay or personal statement; minimum 3.0 GPA; 2 letters of recommendation; interview.

Standardized tests *Admission: Required:* SAT I or ACT.

Significant dates *Application deadlines:* rolling (freshmen), rolling (transfers). *Financial aid deadline:* 5/15. *Priority date:* 3/15.

Freshman Application Contact
Mr. Jeffrey Lang, Associate Director of Admissions, Long Island University, C.W. Post Campus, 720 Northern Boulevard, Brookville, NY 11548-1300. **Phone:** 516-299-2900. **Toll-free phone:** 800-LIU-PLAN. **E-mail:** enroll@cwpost.liu.edu

Visit CollegeQuest.com for information on majors offered and athletics.

- *See page 1938 for a narrative description.*

LONG ISLAND UNIVERSITY, SOUTHAMPTON COLLEGE
Southampton, New York

- **Independent**, comprehensive, founded 1963
- **Degrees** bachelor's and master's
- **Rural** 110-acre campus
- **Coed**, 1,433 undergraduate students, 93% full-time, 67% women, 33% men
- **Moderately difficult** entrance level, 67% of applicants were admitted
- **11:1 student-to-undergraduate faculty ratio**

New York

Long Island University, Southampton College *(continued)*
- **$16,120 tuition** and fees
- **$12,874 average financial aid** package, $15,235 average indebtedness upon graduation, $35.9 million endowment

Part of Long Island University.

Students *Undergraduates:* 1,332 full-time, 101 part-time. Students come from 46 states and territories, 15 other countries. *The most frequently chosen baccalaureate fields are:* biological/life sciences, business/marketing, liberal arts/general studies. *Graduate:* 230 in graduate degree programs.

From out-of-state	30%	Reside on campus	54%
Transferred in	9%	International students	2%
African Americans	4%	Asian Americans/Pacific Islanders	2%
Hispanic Americans	5%	Native Americans	1%

Faculty 255 (31% full-time).

Expenses (1999–2000) *Comprehensive fee:* $23,910 includes full-time tuition ($15,340), mandatory fees ($780), and room and board ($7790). *College room only:* $4200. Full-time tuition and fees vary according to location. Room and board charges vary according to board plan and housing facility. *Part-time tuition:* $478 per credit hour. *Part-time fees:* $185 per term part-time. Part-time tuition and fees vary according to course load and location. *Payment plans:* installment, deferred payment. *Waivers:* children of alumni, senior citizens, and employees or children of employees.

Library Southampton Campus Library plus 1 other. *Operations spending 1999–2000:* $981,359. *Collection:* 145,332 titles, 660 serial subscriptions, 886 audiovisual materials.

College life *Housing:* on-campus residence required in freshman year. *Options:* coed, women-only. *Most popular organizations:* student government association, marine science club, Submersibles, PEACE environmental club, women's issues collective.

Campus security 24-hour emergency response devices and patrols, student patrols, late-night transport-escort service, controlled dormitory access, bicycle patrol.

After graduation 24 organizations recruited on campus 1997–98. 61% of class of 1998 had job offers within 6 months. *Career center:* 7 full-time personnel. Services include job fairs, resume preparation, interview workshops, resume referral, career/interest testing, career counseling, careers library, job bank, job interviews. *Graduate education:* 22% of class of 1999 went directly to graduate and professional school. *Major awards:* 1 Fulbright Scholar.

Freshmen 1,530 applied, 1,022 admitted, 335 enrolled.

SAT verbal scores above 500	76%	SAT math scores above 500	68%
ACT above 18	95%	From top 10% of their h.s. class	19%
From top quarter	49%	From top half	84%
1998 freshmen returning in 1999	40%		

Application *Options:* eApply at www.CollegeQuest.com, Common Application, electronic application, early admission, early decision, deferred entrance. *Application fee:* $30. *Required:* high school transcript. *Recommended:* essay or personal statement; minimum 2.5 GPA; 2 letters of recommendation; interview.

Standardized tests *Admission: Required:* SAT I or ACT.

Significant dates *Application deadlines:* rolling (freshmen), rolling (transfers). *Early decision:* 12/1. *Notification:* 12/20 (early decision). *Financial aid deadline:* continuous.

Freshman Application Contact
Mr. Michael Brophy, Associate Provost, Long Island University, Southampton College, 239 Montauk Highway, Southampton, NY 11968-9822. **Phone:** 631-287-8200. **Toll-free phone:** 800-LIU PLAN Ext. 2. **Fax:** 631-283-4081. **E-mail:** admissions@southampton.liu.edu

Visit CollegeQuest.com for information on majors offered and athletics. College video and electronic viewbook available at CollegeQuest.com.

- *See page 1942 for a narrative description.*

LONG ISLAND UNIVERSITY, SOUTHAMPTON COLLEGE, FRIENDS WORLD PROGRAM
Southampton, New York

- **Independent**, 4-year, founded 1965
- **Degree** bachelor's
- **Rural** 110-acre campus
- **Coed**, 219 undergraduate students, 99% full-time, 72% women, 28% men
- **Noncompetitive** entrance level, 82% of applicants were admitted
- **$16,120 tuition** and fees

Friends World is committed to global education for social change. With dedicated faculty members at all 8 of the international centers, FW offers a truly unique college experience. In 1991, the academic programs of Friends World College were affiliated with Long Island University and became Friends World Program. See Long Island University, Friends World Program, in the In-Depth Descriptions section of this guide.

Part of Long Island University.

Students *Undergraduates:* 216 full-time, 3 part-time. Students come from 39 states and territories, 5 other countries. *The most frequently chosen baccalaureate field is:* interdisciplinary studies.

From out-of-state	74%	Age 25 or older	7%
Transferred in	18%		

Faculty 41 (39% full-time), 41% with terminal degrees.

Expenses (1999–2000) *Comprehensive fee:* $23,850 includes full-time tuition ($15,340), mandatory fees ($780), and room and board ($7730). Full-time tuition and fees vary according to location. Room and board charges vary according to board plan, housing facility, and location. *Part-time tuition:* $478 per credit. Part-time tuition and fees vary according to course load. *Payment plan:* installment. *Waivers:* senior citizens and employees or children of employees.

Library *Operations spending 1999–2000:* $22,000.

College life *Housing:* on-campus residence required in freshman year. *Option:* coed. *Most popular organizations:* Activist Club, P.E.A.C.E., LaFuenza Latina, Caribbean Student Association, women's issues collective.

After graduation 60% of class of 1998 had job offers within 6 months. *Career center:* Services include job fairs, resume preparation, resume referral, career counseling, careers library, job bank, job interviews. *Graduate education:* 10% of class of 1999 went directly to graduate and professional school: 10% graduate arts and sciences.

Freshmen 190 applied, 155 admitted, 54 enrolled.

Average high school GPA	3.4	SAT verbal scores above 500	N/R
SAT math scores above 500	N/R	ACT above 18	N/R
1998 freshmen returning in 1999	78%		

Application *Options:* electronic application, early admission, deferred entrance. *Application fee:* $30. *Required:* essay or personal statement; high school transcript; interview. *Recommended:* minimum 3.0 GPA; 2 letters of recommendation.

Significant dates *Application deadlines:* rolling (freshmen), rolling (transfers).

Freshman Application Contact
Ms. Joyce Tuttle, Associate Director of Enrollment, Long Island University, Southampton College, Friends World Program, 239 Montauk Highway, Southampton, NY 11968. **Phone:** 631-257-8474. **Toll-free phone:** 800-LIU PLAN. **Fax:** 631-287-8463. **E-mail:** fw@southampton.liu.edu

Visit CollegeQuest.com for information on majors offered and athletics. College video and electronic viewbook available at CollegeQuest.com.

- *See page 1940 for a narrative description.*

MACHZIKEI HADATH RABBINICAL COLLEGE
Brooklyn, New York

- **Independent Jewish**, comprehensive, founded 1956
- **Degrees** bachelor's and master's
- **Men** only
- **Moderately difficult** entrance level

Students *Undergraduates:* Students come from 4 states and territories.
Library Abraham Koppel Library plus 1 other. *Collection:* 20,000 titles.
Freshmen

SAT verbal scores above 500	N/R	SAT math scores above 500	N/R
ACT above 18	N/R		

New York

Application *Required:* interview.
Significant dates *Application deadline:* rolling (freshmen).
Freshman Application Contact
Rabbi Abraham M. Lezerowitz, Director of Admissions, Machzikei Hadath Rabbinical College, 5407 Sixteenth Avenue, Brooklyn, NY 11204-1805. **Phone:** 718-854-8777.

Visit CollegeQuest.com for information on majors offered and athletics.

MANHATTAN COLLEGE
Riverdale, New York

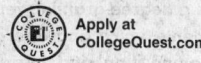 Apply at CollegeQuest.com

- **Independent**, comprehensive, founded 1853, affiliated with Roman Catholic Church
- **Degrees** bachelor's and master's
- **Urban** 31-acre campus with easy access to New York City
- **Coed**, 2,703 undergraduate students, 92% full-time, 46% women, 54% men
- **Moderately difficult** entrance level, 73% of applicants were admitted
- **14:1 student-to-undergraduate faculty ratio**
- **64.8% graduate** in 6 years or less
- **$15,810 tuition** and fees
- **$12,198 average financial aid** package, $21.5 million endowment

Radiation therapy is commonly used in hospitals to help cancer patients and ease pain in others. The program at Manhattan College includes 24 credits of clinical internship courses, equal to about 275 days in a Radiation Therapy Department in 1 of 8 hospitals, such as New York University Hospital, St. Vincent's Hospital, and Westchester Medical Center.

Students *Undergraduates:* 2,495 full-time, 208 part-time. Students come from 35 states and territories, 35 other countries. *The most frequently chosen baccalaureate fields are:* business/marketing, education, engineering/engineering technologies. *Graduate:* 384 in graduate degree programs.

From out-of-state	18%	Reside on campus	60%
Age 25 or older	7%	Transferred in	5%
International students	2%	African Americans	7%
Asian Americans/Pacific Islanders	6%	Hispanic Americans	17%
Native Americans	0.1%		

Faculty 244 (67% full-time), 92% with terminal degrees.
Expenses (1999-2000) *One-time required fee:* $200. *Comprehensive fee:* $23,260 includes full-time tuition ($15,500), mandatory fees ($310), and room and board ($7450). Full-time tuition and fees vary according to program. Room and board charges vary according to board plan. *Part-time tuition:* $425 per credit hour. *Part-time fees:* $100 per term part-time. *Payment plan:* installment. *Waivers:* employees or children of employees.
Library Cardinal Hayes Library plus 1 other. *Operations spending 1999-2000:* $1.3 million. *Collection:* 193,100 titles, 1,527 serial subscriptions, 3,680 audiovisual materials.
College life *Housing: Option:* coed. *Social organizations:* national fraternities, national sororities, local fraternities; 7% of eligible men and 5% of eligible women are members. *Most popular organizations:* Minority Student Union, student government, student radio station, Manhattan College Singers, Resident/Commuter Student Association.
Campus security 24-hour patrols, student patrols, late-night transport-escort service, controlled dormitory access.
After graduation 202 organizations recruited on campus 1997-98. 73% of class of 1998 had job offers within 6 months. *Career center:* 5 full-time, 1 part-time personnel. Services include job fairs, resume preparation, interview workshops, resume referral, career/interest testing, career counseling, careers library, job bank, job interviews.
Freshmen 3,767 applied, 2,749 admitted, 647 enrolled.

Average high school GPA	3.0	SAT verbal scores above 500	69%
SAT math scores above 500	68%	ACT above 18	N/R
1998 freshmen returning in 1999	85%		

Application *Options:* eApply at www.CollegeQuest.com, Common Application, early admission, early decision, deferred entrance. *Application fee:* $35. *Required:* essay or personal statement; high school transcript; 1 letter of recommendation. *Required for some:* interview. *Recommended:* interview.
Standardized tests *Admission: Required:* SAT I or ACT.
Significant dates *Application deadlines:* 3/1 (freshmen), 7/1 (transfers). *Early decision:* 11/15. *Notification:* continuous until 8/15 (freshmen), 12/1 (early decision). *Financial aid deadline priority date:* 3/1.
Freshman Application Contact
Mr. William J. Bisset Jr., Dean of Admissions and Financial Aid, Manhattan College, 4513 Manhattan College Parkway, Riverdale, NY 10471. **Phone:** 718-862-7200. **Toll-free phone:** 800-622-9235. **Fax:** 718-862-8019. **E-mail:** admit@manhattan.edu

Visit CollegeQuest.com for information on majors offered and athletics. College video available at CollegeQuest.com.

■ *See page 1976 for a narrative description.*

MANHATTAN SCHOOL OF MUSIC
New York, New York

- **Independent**, comprehensive, founded 1917
- **Degrees** bachelor's, master's, doctoral, post-master's, and postbachelor's certificates
- **Urban** 1-acre campus
- **Coed**, 391 undergraduate students, 98% full-time, 46% women, 54% men
- **Very difficult** entrance level, 33% of applicants were admitted
- **8:1 student-to-undergraduate faculty ratio**
- **55% graduate** in 6 years or less
- **$19,580 tuition** and fees
- **$15,915 average financial aid** package, $17,125 average indebtedness upon graduation, $12 million endowment

Students *Undergraduates:* 383 full-time, 8 part-time. Students come from 40 states and territories, 40 other countries. *The most frequently chosen baccalaureate field is:* visual/performing arts. *Graduate:* 427 in graduate degree programs.

From out-of-state	78%	Reside on campus	28%
Age 25 or older	10%	Transferred in	10%
International students	28%	African Americans	4%
Asian Americans/Pacific Islanders	9%	Hispanic Americans	5%
Native Americans	0.3%		

Faculty 275 (18% full-time).
Expenses (1999-2000) *Tuition:* full-time $19,000. *Required fees:* full-time $580. *College room only:* $5250. *Payment plan:* installment. *Waivers:* employees or children of employees.
Library Francis Hall Ballard Library. *Operations spending 1999-2000:* $480,000. *Collection:* 39,684 titles, 134 serial subscriptions, 25,074 audiovisual materials.
College life *Housing:* on-campus residence required through sophomore year. *Option:* coed. *Most popular organizations:* Pan-African Student Union, Composers Now, Chinese Student Association, Korean Student Association, Gay/Lesbian/Bisexual Students Association.
Campus security 24-hour patrols.
After graduation *Career center:* 2 full-time, 1 part-time personnel. Services include resume preparation, resume referral, career counseling, careers library, job bank. *Graduate education:* 60% of class of 1999 went directly to graduate and professional school: 60% graduate arts and sciences. *Major awards:* 1 Fulbright Scholar.
Freshmen 665 applied, 219 admitted, 84 enrolled.

SAT verbal scores above 500	N/R	SAT math scores above 500	N/R
ACT above 18	N/R	1998 freshmen returning in 1999	82%

Application *Application fee:* $90. *Required:* essay or personal statement; high school transcript; minimum 2.0 GPA; audition. *Recommended:* minimum 3.0 GPA; 1 letter of recommendation; interview.
Standardized tests *Admission: Recommended:* SAT I or ACT.
Significant dates *Application deadlines:* 12/15 (freshmen), 12/15 (transfers). *Notification:* 4/1 (freshmen). *Financial aid deadline priority date:* 3/15.
Freshman Application Contact
Ms. Lee Cioppa, Director of Admission, Manhattan School of Music, 120 Claremont Avenue, New York, NY 10040. **Phone:** 212-749-2802 Ext. 2. **Fax:** 212-749-5471. **E-mail:** admission@msmnyc.edu

Visit CollegeQuest.com for information on majors offered and athletics.

■ *See page 1978 for a narrative description.*

Peterson's Guide to Four-Year Colleges 2001   www.petersons.com   547

New York

MANHATTANVILLE COLLEGE
Purchase, New York

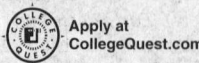 Apply at CollegeQuest.com

- **Independent**, comprehensive, founded 1841
- **Degrees** bachelor's and master's
- **Suburban** 100-acre campus with easy access to New York City
- **Coed**, 1,509 undergraduate students
- **Moderately difficult** entrance level, 66% of applicants were admitted
- **10:1 student-to-undergraduate faculty ratio**
- **$19,620 tuition** and fees

Manhattanville College, founded in 1841, is a private, coeducational, 4-year, comprehensive liberal arts institution. Located in scenic Westchester County, NY, approximately 30 minutes northeast of New York City. The College offers more than 30 academic areas of concentration. An active social life involves nearly 50 student organizations, 18 Division III varsity teams, intramurals, and sports clubs to choose from.

Students *Undergraduates:* Students come from 31 states and territories, 41 other countries.

From out-of-state	38%	Reside on campus	70%
Age 25 or older	5%	International students	6%
African Americans	6%	Asian Americans/Pacific Islanders	3%
Hispanic Americans	13%	Native Americans	0.2%

Faculty 198 (34% full-time), 76% with terminal degrees.
Expenses (2000–2001) *Comprehensive fee:* $27,620 includes full-time tuition ($18,860), mandatory fees ($760), and room and board ($8000). Part-time tuition and fees vary according to program. *Payment plans:* installment, deferred payment. *Waivers:* senior citizens and employees or children of employees.
Library Manhattanville College Library plus 1 other. *Operations spending 1999–2000:* $655,000. *Collection:* 182,789 titles, 912 serial subscriptions, 3,096 audiovisual materials.
College life *Housing:* Options: coed, women-only, disabled students. *Most popular organizations:* student government, International Student Organization, Touchstone (newspaper), WMVL (radio station), philosophy club.
Campus security 24-hour emergency response devices and patrols, late-night transport-escort service, controlled dormitory access.
After graduation 85% of class of 1998 had job offers within 6 months. *Career center:* 4 full-time, 1 part-time personnel. Services include job fairs, resume preparation, interview workshops, resume referral, career/interest testing, career counseling, careers library, job bank, job interviews.
Freshmen 1,803 applied, 1,186 admitted. 3 valedictorians.

Average high school GPA	3.0	SAT verbal scores above 500	66%
SAT math scores above 500	67%	ACT above 18	83%
1998 freshmen returning in 1999	82%		

Application *Options:* eApply at www.CollegeQuest.com, Common Application, early admission, early decision. *Application fee:* $40. *Required:* high school transcript; minimum 2.0 GPA; 2 letters of recommendation. *Recommended:* essay or personal statement; minimum 3.0 GPA; interview.
Standardized tests *Admission: Required:* SAT I. *Required for some:* SAT II Subject Tests.
Significant dates *Application deadlines:* 3/1 (freshmen), rolling (transfers). *Early decision:* 12/1. *Notification:* 12/31 (early decision). *Financial aid deadline priority date:* 4/15.
Freshman Application Contact
Mr. Jose Flores, Director of Admissions, Manhattanville College, 2900 Purchase Street, Purchase, NY 10577-2132. **Phone:** 914-323-5124. **Toll-free phone:** 800-328-4553. **Fax:** 914-694-1732.
Visit CollegeQuest.com for information on majors offered and athletics.

■ *See page 1980 for a narrative description.*

MANNES COLLEGE OF MUSIC, NEW SCHOOL UNIVERSITY
New York, New York

- **Independent**, comprehensive, founded 1916
- **Degrees** bachelor's, master's, and post-master's certificates
- **Urban** campus
- **Coed**, 160 undergraduate students, 100% full-time, 56% women, 44% men
- **Very difficult** entrance level, 31% of applicants were admitted
- **8:1 student-to-undergraduate faculty ratio**
- **$18,000 tuition** and fees
- **$9528 average financial aid** package, $18,380 average indebtedness upon graduation, $86.9 million system endowment

The Mannes College of Music, a division of the New School for Social Research, is a degree-granting music conservatory with majors in all orchestral instruments, voice and opera, piano, guitar, historical performance, conducting, composition, and theory. Dormitory housing and scholarships are available. Distinguished by small enrollment, a world-class faculty, and internationally acclaimed curriculum.

Part of New School University.
Students *Undergraduates:* 160 full-time. Students come from 24 states and territories, 42 other countries. *The most frequently chosen baccalaureate field is:* visual/performing arts. *Graduate:* 163 in graduate degree programs.

From out-of-state	61%	Reside on campus	10%
Age 25 or older	23%	Transferred in	20%

Faculty 210 (12% full-time).
Expenses (1999–2000) *Tuition:* full-time $18,000. *College room only:* $6875. *Payment plan:* installment. *Waivers:* employees or children of employees.
Library Harry Scherman Library plus 2 others. *System-wide operations spending 1999–2000:* $1.8 million. *Collection:* 191,789 titles, 896 serial subscriptions, 137,878 audiovisual materials.
College life *Housing: Option:* coed.
Campus security 24-hour emergency response devices, controlled dormitory access.
After graduation *Career center:* 1 full-time personnel. Services include resume preparation, resume referral, career counseling, careers library, job bank, job interviews. *Graduate education:* 45% of class of 1999 went directly to graduate and professional school: 45% graduate arts and sciences.
Freshmen 257 applied, 80 admitted, 28 enrolled.

SAT verbal scores above 500	N/R	SAT math scores above 500	N/R
ACT above 18	N/R	1998 freshmen returning in 1999	75%

Application *Option:* deferred entrance. *Application fee:* $100. *Required:* high school transcript; 1 letter of recommendation; audition. *Recommended:* interview.
Significant dates *Application deadlines:* 12/15 (freshmen), rolling (transfers). *Financial aid deadline priority date:* 3/1.
Freshman Application Contact
Ms. Emily E. Taxson, Associate Director of Admissions, Mannes College of Music, New School University, 150 West 85th Street, New York, NY 10024-4402. **Phone:** 212-580-0210 Ext. 246. **Toll-free phone:** 800-292-3040. **Fax:** 212-580-1738. **E-mail:** mannasadmissions@newschool.edu
Visit CollegeQuest.com for information on majors offered and athletics.

■ *See page 1982 for a narrative description.*

MARIST COLLEGE
Poughkeepsie, New York

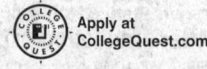 Apply at CollegeQuest.com

- **Independent**, comprehensive, founded 1929
- **Degrees** bachelor's and master's
- **Small-town** 135-acre campus with easy access to Albany and New York City
- **Coed**, 4,314 undergraduate students, 87% full-time, 57% women, 43% men
- **Moderately difficult** entrance level, 56% of applicants were admitted
- **14:1 student-to-undergraduate faculty ratio**
- **66.8% graduate** in 6 years or less
- **$14,754 tuition** and fees
- **$11.8 million endowment**

Marist is a small college with a national reputation for excellence in education. The College's focus on technology in the educational experience provides students with today's most advanced learning tools. The fully networked

New York

campus includes a voice and data telecommunications system that extends to all areas of the College—and the world—through the Internet and the World Wide Web. Students enjoy a curriculum that provides for dual majors, a major and minor option, extensive internship opportunities, and exceptional international study options. The Honors Program and special academic advising services, open to all majors, allow students to enjoy a challenging and fulfilling educational experience.

Students *Undergraduates:* 3,764 full-time, 550 part-time. Students come from 31 states and territories, 18 other countries. *The most frequently chosen baccalaureate fields are:* business/marketing, communications/communication technologies, protective services/public administration. *Graduate:* 582 in graduate degree programs.

From out-of-state	35%	Reside on campus	70%
Age 25 or older	13%	Transferred in	3%
International students	1%	African Americans	3%
Asian Americans/Pacific Islanders	1%	Hispanic Americans	4%
Native Americans	0.1%		

Faculty 496 (33% full-time).

Expenses (1999–2000) *One-time required fee:* $25. *Comprehensive fee:* $22,172 includes full-time tuition ($14,374), mandatory fees ($380), and room and board ($7418). *College room only:* $4624. Room and board charges vary according to board plan and housing facility. *Part-time tuition:* $335 per credit. *Part-time fees:* $60 per term part-time. *Payment plan:* installment. *Waivers:* employees or children of employees.

Library Marist College Library. *Operations spending 1999–2000:* $1.5 million. *Collection:* 170,000 titles, 1,825 serial subscriptions.

College life *Housing: Option:* coed. *Social organizations:* national fraternities, local fraternities, local sororities; 9% of eligible men and 11% of eligible women are members. *Most popular organizations:* outback club, student newspaper, student government, theater club, community service and campus ministry.

Campus security 24-hour emergency response devices and patrols, student patrols, late-night transport-escort service, controlled dormitory access, night residence hall monitors.

After graduation 175 organizations recruited on campus 1997–98. 72% of class of 1998 had job offers within 6 months. *Career center:* 6 full-time, 1 part-time personnel. Services include job fairs, resume preparation, interview workshops, resume referral, career/interest testing, career counseling, careers library, job bank, job interviews. *Graduate education:* 19% of class of 1999 went directly to graduate and professional school: 11% graduate arts and sciences, 1% business, 1% law, 1% medicine.

Freshmen 6,179 applied, 3,449 admitted, 1,124 enrolled. 3 National Merit Scholars, 21 class presidents, 7 valedictorians, 152 student government officers.

Average high school GPA	3.2	SAT verbal scores above 500	82%
SAT math scores above 500	82%	ACT above 18	N/R
From top 10% of their h.s. class	21%	From top quarter	47%
From top half	90%	1998 freshmen returning in 1999	88%

Application *Options:* eApply at www.CollegeQuest.com, Common Application, electronic application, early admission, early action, deferred entrance. *Application fee:* $35. *Required:* high school transcript; 1 letter of recommendation. *Recommended:* essay or personal statement.

Standardized tests *Admission: Required:* SAT I or ACT.

Significant dates *Application deadlines:* 3/1 (freshmen), rolling (transfers). *Early action:* 12/1. *Notification:* 1/1 (early action). *Financial aid deadline priority date:* 2/15.

Freshman Application Contact
Mr. Jay Murray, Associate Director of Admissions, Marist College, 290 North Road, Poughkeepsie, NY 12601-1387. **Phone:** 914-575-3226 Ext. 2441. **Toll-free phone:** 800-436-5483. **E-mail:** admissions@marist.edu

Visit CollegeQuest.com for information on majors offered and athletics.

■ *See page 1990 for a narrative description.*

MARYMOUNT COLLEGE
Tarrytown, New York

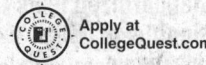

- **Independent**, 4-year, founded 1907
- **Degrees** associate and bachelor's
- **Suburban** 25-acre campus with easy access to New York City
- **Women** only, 847 undergraduate students, 80% full-time
- **Moderately difficult** entrance level, 85% of applicants were admitted
- **9:1 student-to-undergraduate faculty ratio**
- **48.5% graduate** in 6 years or less
- **$15,130 tuition** and fees
- **$5.9 million endowment**

Marymount College, a pioneer in women's education for more than 90 years, is an independent liberal arts college in the Catholic tradition. Through career development, internships, study-abroad programs, and more than 30 majors, Marymount equips and empowers women to achieve their full potential in a rapidly changing world. Conveniently located just 25 miles north of New York City, students enjoy rich cultural, intellectual, and professional offerings while living in a safe, suburban atmosphere.

Students *Undergraduates:* 674 full-time, 173 part-time. Students come from 29 states and territories, 14 other countries. *The most frequently chosen baccalaureate fields are:* business/marketing, computer/information sciences, psychology.

From out-of-state	23%	Reside on campus	65%
Age 25 or older	38%	Transferred in	11%
International students	8%	African Americans	13%
Asian Americans/Pacific Islanders	6%	Hispanic Americans	16%
Native Americans	0.2%		

Faculty 148 (40% full-time), 64% with terminal degrees.

Expenses (2000–2001) *Comprehensive fee:* $22,930 includes full-time tuition ($14,700), mandatory fees ($430), and room and board ($7800). *Part-time tuition:* $475 per semester hour. *Part-time fees:* $108 per term part-time. Part-time tuition and fees vary according to class time and course load. *Payment plans:* installment, deferred payment. *Waivers:* employees or children of employees.

Library Gloria Gaines Memorial Library plus 1 other. *Operations spending 1999–2000:* $108,295. *Collection:* 428 serial subscriptions, 275 audiovisual materials.

College life *Housing: Option:* women-only. *Most popular organizations:* Campus Activities Board, Student Government Association, Latin Unity, Black Student Union, international club.

Campus security 24-hour emergency response devices and patrols, late-night transport-escort service, controlled dormitory access.

After graduation 54 organizations recruited on campus 1997–98. 77% of class of 1998 had job offers within 6 months. *Career center:* 2 full-time, 1 part-time personnel. Services include job fairs, resume preparation, interview workshops, resume referral, career/interest testing, career counseling, careers library, job bank, job interviews.

Freshmen 508 applied, 431 admitted, 166 enrolled. 1 class president, 5 student government officers.

Average high school GPA	2.8	SAT verbal scores above 500	37%
SAT math scores above 500	22%	ACT above 18	N/R
From top 10% of their h.s. class	14%	From top quarter	32%
From top half	70%	1998 freshmen returning in 1999	69%

Application *Options:* eApply at www.CollegeQuest.com, Common Application, early admission, early action, deferred entrance. *Application fee:* $30. *Required:* high school transcript; minimum 2.0 GPA. *Recommended:* essay or personal statement; minimum 3.0 GPA; 1 letter of recommendation; interview.

Standardized tests *Admission: Required:* SAT I.

Significant dates *Application deadlines:* 8/15 (freshmen), rolling (transfers). *Early action:* 9/30. *Notification:* 10/15 (early action). *Financial aid deadline:* 5/1. *Priority date:* 2/15.

Freshman Application Contact
Ms. Daniela Esposito, Director of Admissions, Marymount College, 100 Marymount Avenue, Tarrytown, NY 10591-3796. **Phone:** 914-332-8295. **Toll-free phone:** 800-724-4312. **Fax:** 914-332-4956. **E-mail:** admiss@mmc.marymt.edu

Visit CollegeQuest.com for information on majors offered and athletics. College video available at CollegeQuest.com.

■ *See page 2006 for a narrative description.*

New York

MARYMOUNT MANHATTAN COLLEGE
New York, New York

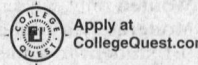
Apply at CollegeQuest.com

- **Independent**, 4-year, founded 1936
- **Degree** bachelor's
- **Urban** 1-acre campus
- **Coed**, 2,274 undergraduate students, 70% full-time, 81% women, 19% men
- **Moderately difficult** entrance level, 67% of applicants were admitted
- **18:1 student-to-undergraduate faculty ratio**
- **35% graduate** in 6 years or less
- **$13,605 tuition** and fees
- **$12,504 average financial aid** package, $8.3 million endowment

Marymount offers a bachelor's degree program in international business communications with École Française des Attachés de Presse (EFAP), Europe's largest communications school. EFAP-MMC integrates Marymount's liberal arts curriculum with EFAP's knowledge of cross-cultural public relations. Marymount Manhattan offers a combined BS/MBA degree with St. John's University; after 5 years of study at MMC, students not only have an undergraduate degree in business management or accounting but also a Master of Business Administration degree.

Students *Undergraduates:* 1,601 full-time, 673 part-time. Students come from 42 states and territories, 60 other countries. *The most frequently chosen baccalaureate fields are:* business/marketing, communications/communication technologies, visual/performing arts.

From out-of-state	35%	Reside on campus	15%
Age 25 or older	40%	Transferred in	6%
International students	6%	African Americans	22%
Asian Americans/Pacific Islanders	4%	Hispanic Americans	17%
Native Americans	0.4%		

Faculty 342 (22% full-time), 42% with terminal degrees.
Expenses (1999–2000) *Tuition:* full-time $13,050; part-time $365 per credit. *Required fees:* full-time $555; $210 per term part-time. *College room only:* $6750. Room and board charges vary according to housing facility. *Payment plan:* installment. *Waivers:* senior citizens and employees or children of employees.
Library Shanahan Library. *Operations spending 1999–2000:* $430,000. *Collection:* 100,535 titles, 600 serial subscriptions, 13,285 audiovisual materials.
College life *Housing: Option:* coed. *Most popular organizations:* education club, African-American Heritage Club, Asian-American Heritage Club, Latino Heritage Club, business club.
Campus security 24-hour emergency response devices and patrols, student patrols, 24-hour security in residence halls.
After graduation 15 organizations recruited on campus 1997–98. 65% of class of 1998 had job offers within 6 months. *Career center:* 1 full-time personnel. Services include job fairs, resume preparation, career counseling, careers library, job bank. *Graduate education:* 30% of class of 1999 went directly to graduate and professional school: 11% business, 7% graduate arts and sciences, 6% law, 5% medicine, 1% education.
Freshmen 1,703 applied, 1,148 admitted, 528 enrolled.

Average high school GPA	3.4	SAT verbal scores above 500	67%
SAT math scores above 500	45%	ACT above 18	N/R
From top 10% of their h.s. class	25%	From top quarter	75%
From top half	89%	1998 freshmen returning in 1999	77%

Application *Options:* eApply at www.CollegeQuest.com, electronic application, early admission, early decision, deferred entrance. *Application fee:* $50. *Required:* high school transcript; 2 letters of recommendation; audition for dance and theater programs. *Required for some:* interview. *Recommended:* essay or personal statement.
Standardized tests *Admission: Required:* SAT I or ACT.
Significant dates *Application deadlines:* rolling (freshmen), rolling (transfers). *Early decision:* 11/1. *Notification:* 12/1 (early decision). *Financial aid deadline priority date:* 2/15.
Freshman Application Contact
Mr. Thomas Friebel, Associate Vice President for Enrollment Services, Marymount Manhattan College, 221 East 71st Street, New York, NY 10021. **Phone:** 212-517-0430. **Toll-free phone:** 800-MARYMOUNT. **E-mail:** admissions@mmm.edu

---

Visit CollegeQuest.com for information on majors offered and athletics.
■ *See page 2008 for a narrative description.*

MEDAILLE COLLEGE
Buffalo, New York

- **Independent**, comprehensive, founded 1875
- **Degrees** associate, bachelor's, and master's
- **Urban** 13-acre campus
- **Coed**, 1,215 undergraduate students, 79% full-time, 72% women, 28% men
- **Moderately difficult** entrance level, 39% of applicants were admitted
- **17:1 student-to-undergraduate faculty ratio**
- **29.35% graduate** in 6 years or less
- **$11,450 tuition** and fees
- **$622,087 endowment**

Medaille is a small private college that offers 16 distinctive academic programs, each designed to help students realize their potential in their personal and professional lives. Degree programs allow students ample opportunity to customize course work through required internships, starting as early as the sophomore year. A Medaille education provides students with skills that are both fulfilling and highly valued by employers.

Students *Undergraduates:* 963 full-time, 252 part-time. Students come from 4 states and territories, 2 other countries. *The most frequently chosen baccalaureate fields are:* business/marketing, education, liberal arts/general studies. *Graduate:* 113 in graduate degree programs.

From out-of-state	1%	Reside on campus	8%
Age 25 or older	53%	Transferred in	16%
International students	5%	African Americans	14%
Asian Americans/Pacific Islanders	0.2%	Hispanic Americans	1%
Native Americans	0.2%		

Faculty 104 (41% full-time), 56% with terminal degrees.
Expenses (1999–2000) *Comprehensive fee:* $16,750 includes full-time tuition ($11,190), mandatory fees ($260), and room and board ($5300). Full-time tuition and fees vary according to location. Room and board charges vary according to board plan and housing facility. *Part-time tuition:* $373 per credit hour. *Part-time fees:* $78 per term part-time. Part-time tuition and fees vary according to course load. *Payment plan:* installment. *Waivers:* adult students, senior citizens, and employees or children of employees.
Library Medaille College Library. *Operations spending 1999–2000:* $248,000. *Collection:* 53,215 titles, 240 serial subscriptions, 1,372 audiovisual materials.
College life *Housing: Options:* coed, men-only, women-only, disabled students. *Most popular organizations:* student government, radio station, ASRA (Admissions Club), Student Activities Board, Teach.
Campus security 24-hour emergency response devices, late-night transport-escort service.
After graduation 85% of class of 1998 had job offers within 6 months. *Career center:* 1 full-time personnel. Services include job fairs, resume preparation, interview workshops, resume referral, career/interest testing, career counseling, careers library, job bank, job interviews. *Graduate education:* 24% of class of 1999 went directly to graduate and professional school: 12% education, 10% graduate arts and sciences, 1% business, 1% law.
Freshmen 385 applied, 149 admitted, 179 enrolled. 1 class president, 1 valedictorian.

SAT verbal scores above 500	26%	SAT math scores above 500	26%
ACT above 18	N/R	From top 10% of their h.s. class	3%
From top quarter	38%	From top half	72%
1998 freshmen returning in 1999	67%		

Application *Options:* Common Application, electronic application, early admission, deferred entrance. *Application fee:* $25. *Required:* high school transcript; interview. *Recommended:* essay or personal statement; minimum 2.0 GPA; 1 letter of recommendation; 2.5 high school GPA for veterinary technology and elementary teacher education majors.
Standardized tests *Admission: Required:* SAT I or ACT.
Significant dates *Application deadlines:* 8/1 (freshmen), rolling (transfers). *Financial aid deadline priority date:* 3/15.

Freshman Application Contact
Mrs. Jacqueline S. Matheny, Director of Enrollment Management, Medaille College, Medaille College, Office of Admissions, Buffalo, NY 14214. **Phone:** 716-884-3281 Ext. 203. **Toll-free phone:** 800-292-1582. **Fax:** 716-884-0291.
Visit CollegeQuest.com for information on majors offered and athletics.

MEDGAR EVERS COLLEGE OF THE CITY UNIVERSITY OF NEW YORK
Brooklyn, New York

- **State and locally supported**, 4-year, founded 1969
- **Degrees** associate and bachelor's
- **Urban** 1-acre campus
- **Coed**, 5,009 undergraduate students, 54% full-time, 78% women, 22% men
- **Noncompetitive** entrance level
- **18:1** student-to-undergraduate faculty ratio
- **$3282 tuition** and fees (in-state); $6882 (out-of-state)

Part of City University of New York System.
Students *Undergraduates:* 2,702 full-time, 2,307 part-time. Students come from 3 states and territories, 50 other countries. *The most frequently chosen baccalaureate fields are:* business/marketing, education, health professions and related sciences.

From out-of-state	1%	Age 25 or older	70%
Transferred in	6%	International students	2%
African Americans	71%	Asian Americans/Pacific Islanders	1%
Hispanic Americans	5%	Native Americans	0.3%

Faculty 133 (72% full-time), 78% with terminal degrees.
Expenses (1999–2000) *Tuition, state resident:* full-time $3200; part-time $135 per credit. *Tuition, nonresident:* full-time $6800; part-time $285 per credit. *Required fees:* full-time $82; $41 per term part-time.
Library Charles Innis Memorial Library. *Collection:* 74,826 titles, 585 serial subscriptions.
College life *Housing:* college housing not available. *Most popular organizations:* Caribbean American Student Association, African Heritage, Phi Beta Sigma, Black Social Worker, Latino Club.
After graduation *Career center:* 3 full-time personnel. Services include job fairs, resume preparation, interview workshops, career counseling, job bank.
Freshmen 717 admitted, 717 enrolled.

SAT verbal scores above 500	N/R	SAT math scores above 500	N/R
ACT above 18	N/R		

Application *Options:* Common Application, deferred entrance. *Preference* given to city residents. *Application fee:* $40. *Required:* high school transcript.
Standardized tests *Placement: Recommended:* SAT I.
Significant dates *Application deadlines:* rolling (freshmen), rolling (transfers). *Financial aid deadline priority date:* 6/1.
Freshman Application Contact
Ms. Shannon Clarke, Acting Director of Admissions, Medgar Evers College of the City University of New York, 1650 Bedford Avenue, Brooklyn, NY 11225-2298. **Phone:** 718-270-6025.
Visit CollegeQuest.com for information on majors offered and athletics.

MERCY COLLEGE
Dobbs Ferry, New York

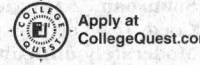
Apply at CollegeQuest.com

- **Independent**, comprehensive, founded 1951
- **Degrees** associate, bachelor's, and master's
- **Suburban** 60-acre campus with easy access to New York City
- **Coed**, 5,223 undergraduate students, 65% full-time, 62% women, 38% men
- **Noncompetitive** entrance level
- **$7950 tuition** and fees

Students *Undergraduates:* 3,397 full-time, 1,826 part-time. Students come from 6 states and territories, 49 other countries. *Graduate:* 1,922 in graduate degree programs.

New York

Age 25 or older	58%

Faculty 665 (25% full-time).
Expenses (1999–2000) *Comprehensive fee:* $15,450 includes full-time tuition ($7950) and room and board ($7500). Full-time tuition and fees vary according to course load and degree level. Room and board charges vary according to board plan and housing facility. *Part-time tuition:* $335 per credit. *Payment plans:* installment, deferred payment. *Waivers:* children of alumni, senior citizens, and employees or children of employees.
Library Mercy College Library. *Collection:* 322,610 titles, 1,765 serial subscriptions.
College life *Housing: Option:* coed.
Campus security 24-hour patrols.
After graduation *Career center:* Services include job fairs, resume preparation, interview workshops, career counseling, careers library, job bank.
Freshmen 2,708 applied, 1,146 enrolled.

SAT verbal scores above 500	N/R	SAT math scores above 500	N/R
ACT above 18	N/R	From top 10% of their h.s. class	1%
From top quarter	5%	From top half	45%

Application *Options:* eApply at www.CollegeQuest.com, electronic application, early admission, deferred entrance. *Application fee:* $35. *Required:* high school transcript; 1 letter of recommendation. *Recommended:* interview.
Standardized tests *Placement: Recommended:* SAT I or ACT.
Significant dates *Application deadlines:* rolling (freshmen), rolling (transfers). *Financial aid deadline priority date:* 2/1.
Freshman Application Contact
Ms. Kathy O'Brien, Assistant Dean for Admissions, Mercy College, 555 Broadway, Dobbs Ferry, NY 10522-1189. **Phone:** 914-674-7535. **Toll-free phone:** 800-MERCY-NY. **Fax:** 914-674-7382. **E-mail:** admission@merlin.mercynet.edu
Visit CollegeQuest.com for information on majors offered and athletics. Electronic viewbook available at CollegeQuest.com.

■ *See page 2042 for a narrative description.*

MESIVTA OF EASTERN PARKWAY RABBINICAL SEMINARY
Brooklyn, New York

Admissions Office Contact
Mesivta of Eastern Parkway Rabbinical Seminary, 510 Dahill Road, Brooklyn, NY 11218-5559.

MESIVTA TIFERETH JERUSALEM OF AMERICA
New York, New York

Admissions Office Contact
Mesivta Tifereth Jerusalem of America, 141 East Broadway, New York, NY 10002-6301.

MESIVTA TORAH VODAATH RABBINICAL SEMINARY
Brooklyn, New York

- **Independent Jewish**, comprehensive, founded 1918
- **Degrees** bachelor's and master's
- **Men** only
- **Moderately difficult** entrance level
- **$3300 tuition** and fees

Expenses (1999–2000) *Comprehensive fee:* 6800 includes full-time tuition (3300) and room and board (3500).
Library *Collection:* 40,000 titles, 12 serial subscriptions.

New York

Mesivta Torah Vodaath Rabbinical Seminary (continued)

Freshmen

| SAT verbal scores above 500 | N/R | SAT math scores above 500 | N/R |
| ACT above 18 | N/R | | |

Application *Options:* early admission, deferred entrance. *Preference* given to Orthodox Jews. *Required:* high school transcript; 2 letters of recommendation.

Significant dates *Application deadlines:* rolling (freshmen), rolling (transfers).

Freshman Application Contact
Rabbi Issac Braun, Admisistrator, Mesivta Torah Vodaath Rabbinical Seminary, 425 East Ninth Street, Brooklyn, NY 11218-5209. **Phone:** 718-941-8000. **Fax:** 718-941-8032.

Visit CollegeQuest.com for information on majors offered and athletics.

MIRRER YESHIVA
Brooklyn, New York

Admissions Office Contact
Mirrer Yeshiva, 1795 Ocean Parkway, Brooklyn, NY 11223-2010.

MOLLOY COLLEGE
Rockville Centre, New York

- **Independent**, comprehensive, founded 1955
- **Degrees** associate, bachelor's, master's, and post-master's certificates
- **Suburban** 25-acre campus with easy access to New York City
- **Coed**, 1,857 undergraduate students, 68% full-time, 80% women, 20% men
- **Moderately difficult** entrance level, 90% of applicants were admitted
- **9:1 student-to-undergraduate faculty ratio**
- **65% graduate** in 6 years or less
- **$12,470 tuition** and fees

Students *Undergraduates:* 1,266 full-time, 591 part-time. Students come from 4 states and territories, 9 other countries. *The most frequently chosen baccalaureate fields are:* health professions and related sciences, business/marketing, psychology. *Graduate:* 427 in graduate degree programs.

Age 25 or older	38%	Transferred in	20%
International students	0.5%	African Americans	13%
Asian Americans/Pacific Islanders	2%	Hispanic Americans	6%
Native Americans	0.2%		

Faculty 298 (46% full-time), 34% with terminal degrees.

Expenses (1999–2000) *Tuition:* full-time $11,900; part-time $395 per credit. *Required fees:* full-time $570; $215 per term part-time. Part-time tuition and fees vary according to course load. *Payment plan:* installment. *Waivers:* minority students, children of alumni, senior citizens, and employees or children of employees.

Library James Edward Tobin Library. *Collection:* 133,035 titles, 2,950 serial subscriptions.

College life *Housing:* college housing not available. *Most popular organizations:* Nursing Student Association, African-American Caribbean Organization, Gaelic Society, Education Club, International Society.

Campus security 24-hour emergency response devices and patrols, late-night transport-escort service.

After graduation 50 organizations recruited on campus 1997–98. *Career center:* 3 full-time personnel. Services include job fairs, resume preparation, career/interest testing, career counseling, careers library, job bank.

Freshmen 598 applied, 539 admitted, 225 enrolled.

SAT verbal scores above 500	50%	SAT math scores above 500	51%
ACT above 18	N/R	From top 10% of their h.s. class	13%
From top quarter	54%	From top half	78%
1998 freshmen returning in 1999	80%		

Application *Options:* Common Application, early admission, early decision, deferred entrance. *Application fee:* $25. *Required:* essay or personal statement; high school transcript. *Required for some:* 1 letter of recommendation. *Recommended:* interview.

Standardized tests *Admission: Required:* SAT I or ACT.

Significant dates *Application deadlines:* rolling (freshmen), rolling (transfers). *Early decision:* 11/1. *Notification:* 12/1 (early decision). *Financial aid deadline priority date:* 4/15.

Freshman Application Contact
Mrs. Linda Finley Albanese, Director of Admissions, Molloy College, 1000 Hempstead Avenue, PO Box 5002, Rockville Centre, NY 11571-5002. **Phone:** 516-678-5000 Ext. 6240. **Toll-free phone:** 888-4MOLLOY. **E-mail:** mlane@mooloy.edu

Visit CollegeQuest.com for information on majors offered and athletics. College video available at CollegeQuest.com.

■ *See page 2074 for a narrative description.*

MONROE COLLEGE
Bronx, New York

- **Proprietary**, primarily 2-year, founded 1933
- **Degrees** associate and bachelor's
- **Urban** campus
- **Coed**, 3,336 undergraduate students, 78% full-time, 72% women, 28% men
- **Moderately difficult** entrance level
- **$7160 tuition** and fees

Faculty 115 (53% full-time).

Admissions Office Contact
Monroe College, Monroe College Way, Bronx, NY 10468-5407. **Toll-free phone:** 800-55MONROE.

Visit CollegeQuest.com for information on majors offered and athletics. College video available at CollegeQuest.com.

■ *See page 2078 for a narrative description.*

MONROE COLLEGE
New Rochelle, New York

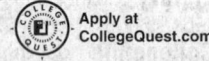

- **Proprietary**, primarily 2-year, founded 1983
- **Degrees** associate and bachelor's
- **Urban** campus with easy access to New York City
- **Coed**, 843 undergraduate students, 78% full-time, 67% women, 33% men
- **Moderately difficult** entrance level

Faculty 38 (55% full-time).

Admissions Office Contact
Monroe College, 434 Main Street, New Rochelle, NY 10801. **Toll-free phone:** 800-55-monroe.

Visit CollegeQuest.com for information on majors offered and athletics. College video available at CollegeQuest.com.

MOUNT SAINT MARY COLLEGE
Newburgh, New York

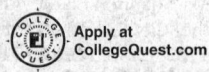

- **Independent**, comprehensive, founded 1960
- **Degrees** bachelor's and master's
- **Suburban** 72-acre campus with easy access to New York City
- **Coed**, 1,598 undergraduate students
- **Moderately difficult** entrance level
- **16:1 student-to-undergraduate faculty ratio**
- **$11,470 tuition** and fees
- **$8200 average financial aid** package, $14,500 average indebtedness upon graduation, $3.2 million endowment

Students *Undergraduates:* Students come from 16 states and territories, 6 other countries.

From out-of-state	7%	Reside on campus	70%
Age 25 or older	30%	International students	0.2%
African Americans	8%	Asian Americans/Pacific Islanders	2%
Hispanic Americans	8%	Native Americans	0.3%

Faculty 199 (31% full-time).

Expenses (1999–2000) *One-time required fee:* $15. *Comprehensive fee:* $17,170 includes full-time tuition ($11,100), mandatory fees ($370), and room and board ($5700). Room and board charges vary according to board plan and student level. *Part-time tuition:* $370 per credit hour. *Part-time fees:* $15 per term part-time. *Payment plan:* installment. *Waivers:* employees or children of employees.
Library Curtin Memorial Library plus 1 other. *Operations spending 1999–2000:* $495,000. *Collection:* 119,146 titles, 1,117 serial subscriptions.
College life *Housing: Options:* men-only, women-only. *Most popular organizations:* Student Government Association, Different Stages, Peer Educators, Black and Latin student unions, CARE.
Campus security 24-hour emergency response devices and patrols, student patrols, late-night transport-escort service, controlled dormitory access, monitored surveillance cameras in all residence halls.
After graduation 32 organizations recruited on campus 1997–98. 82% of class of 1998 had job offers within 6 months. *Career center:* 1 full-time, 1 part-time personnel. Services include job fairs, resume preparation, interview workshops, resume referral, career/interest testing, career counseling, careers library, job bank, job interviews.
Freshmen 1,420 applied, 1,169 admitted. 27 class presidents, 1 valedictorian, 63 student government officers.

Average high school GPA	3.1	SAT verbal scores above 500	60%
SAT math scores above 500	58%	ACT above 18	N/R
From top 10% of their h.s. class	17%	From top quarter	63%
From top half	81%	1998 freshmen returning in 1999	78%

Application *Options:* eApply at www.CollegeQuest.com, deferred entrance. *Application fee:* $25. *Required:* high school transcript. *Required for some:* essay or personal statement; 3 letters of recommendation; interview. *Recommended:* 3 letters of recommendation; interview.
Standardized tests *Admission: Required:* SAT I or ACT.
Significant dates *Application deadlines:* rolling (freshmen), rolling (transfers). *Financial aid deadline priority date:* 3/15.
Freshman Application Contact
Mr. J. Randall Ognibene, Director of Admissions, Mount Saint Mary College, 330 Powell Avenue, Newburgh, NY 12550-3494. **Phone:** 914-569-3248. **Toll-free phone:** 888-937-6762. **Fax:** 914-562-6762. **E-mail:** admissions@msmc.edu
Visit CollegeQuest.com for information on majors offered and athletics. College video available at CollegeQuest.com.

■ *See page 2118 for a narrative description.*

NAZARETH COLLEGE OF ROCHESTER
Rochester, New York

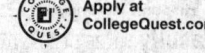
Apply at CollegeQuest.com

- **Independent**, comprehensive, founded 1924
- **Degrees** bachelor's and master's
- **Suburban** 75-acre campus
- **Coed**, 1,693 undergraduate students, 89% full-time, 75% women, 25% men
- **Moderately difficult** entrance level, 81% of applicants were admitted
- **13:1 student-to-undergraduate faculty ratio**
- **70.68% graduate** in 6 years or less
- **$14,046 tuition** and fees
- **$13,245 average financial aid** package, $18,095 average indebtedness upon graduation, $40.2 million endowment

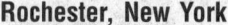

Students *Undergraduates:* 1,515 full-time, 178 part-time. Students come from 20 states and territories. *Graduate:* 1,081 in graduate degree programs.

From out-of-state	4%	Age 25 or older	14%
Transferred in	8%	International students	0.1%
African Americans	3%	Asian Americans/Pacific Islanders	1%
Hispanic Americans	2%	Native Americans	1%

Faculty 187 (65% full-time).
Expenses (1999–2000) *Comprehensive fee:* $20,422 includes full-time tuition ($13,620), mandatory fees ($426), and room and board ($6376). *College room only:* $3660. Full-time tuition and fees vary according to course load. Room and board charges vary according to board plan and housing facility. *Part-time tuition:* $378 per credit hour. *Part-time fees:* $20 per term part-time. *Payment plan:* installment. *Waivers:* employees or children of employees.
Library Lorette Wilmot Library. *Operations spending 1999–2000:* $1.5 million. *Collection:* 278,216 titles, 2,006 serial subscriptions, 18,554 audiovisual materials.
College life *Housing: Options:* coed, women-only, disabled students. *Most popular organizations:* student activities council, French club, theater club, Campus Ministry Council, Coffeehouse, Arts, Lecture, Entertainment Board (CALEB).
Campus security 24-hour emergency response devices and patrols, student patrols, late-night transport-escort service, controlled dormitory access, alarm system, security beeper.
After graduation 69% of class of 1998 had job offers within 6 months. *Career center:* 3 full-time personnel. Services include job fairs, resume preparation, resume referral, career counseling, careers library, job bank, job interviews. *Graduate education:* 37% of class of 1999 went directly to graduate and professional school.
Freshmen 1,248 applied, 1,017 admitted, 332 enrolled.

Average high school GPA	3.4	SAT verbal scores above 500	83%
SAT math scores above 500	82%	ACT above 18	97%
From top 10% of their h.s. class	33%	From top quarter	69%
From top half	93%	1998 freshmen returning in 1999	85%

Application *Options:* eApply at www.CollegeQuest.com, Common Application, electronic application, early admission, early decision, deferred entrance. *Application fee:* $40. *Required:* essay or personal statement; high school transcript; 1 letter of recommendation. *Recommended:* interview.
Standardized tests *Admission: Required:* SAT I or ACT.
Significant dates *Application deadlines:* 3/1 (freshmen), 3/15 (transfers). *Early decision:* 11/15. *Notification:* 12/15 (early decision). *Financial aid deadline priority date:* 2/15.
Freshman Application Contact
Mr. Thomas K. DaRin, Dean of Admissions, Nazareth College of Rochester, 4245 East Avenue, Rochester, NY 14618-3790. **Phone:** 716-389-2860. **Toll-free phone:** 800-462-3944. **Fax:** 716-389-2826. **E-mail:** admissions@naz.edu
Visit CollegeQuest.com for information on majors offered and athletics.

■ *See page 2136 for a narrative description.*

NEW SCHOOL BACHELOR OF ARTS, NEW SCHOOL UNIVERSITY
New York, New York

- **Independent**, upper-level, founded 1919
- **Degrees** bachelor's, master's, and doctoral
- **Urban** campus
- **Coed**, 430 undergraduate students, 38% full-time, 72% women, 28% men
- **Moderately difficult** entrance level
- **$13,068 tuition** and fees
- **$9743 average financial aid** package, $14,500 average indebtedness upon graduation, $86.9 million endowment

The New School offers an individualized undergraduate program in the liberal arts designed for adults. Students select their curriculum from nearly 800 courses offered each semester. Special features include the DIAL program, which offers courses at a distance via computer conferencing; accelerated BA/MA programs, which enable undergraduates to begin graduate study; and credit for prior experiential learning through testing and portfolio assessment.

Part of New School University.
Students *Undergraduates:* 163 full-time, 267 part-time. Students come from 16 states and territories, 20 other countries. *The most frequently chosen baccalaureate fields are:* liberal arts/general studies, visual/performing arts. *Graduate:* 503 in graduate degree programs.

From out-of-state	22%	Age 25 or older	77%
Transferred in	29%	International students	7%
African Americans	11%	Asian Americans/Pacific Islanders	3%
Hispanic Americans	9%	Native Americans	1%

Expenses (1999–2000) *Tuition:* full-time $12,672; part-time $528 per credit. *Required fees:* full-time $396; $198 per term part-time. *College room*

New York

New School Bachelor of Arts, New School University (continued)
only: $6310. Room and board charges vary according to housing facility. *Payment plan:* installment. *Waivers:* employees or children of employees.

Library Raymond Fogelman Library plus 2 others. *Operations spending 1999–2000:* $1.8 million. *Collection:* 191,789 titles, 896 serial subscriptions, 137,878 audiovisual materials.

College life *Housing: Option:* coed. *Most popular organizations:* university committees, B.A. program committees, student advisory committees, publications.

Campus security 24-hour emergency response devices, controlled dormitory access, trained security personnel in central buildings.

After graduation *Graduate education:* 30% of class of 1999 went directly to graduate and professional school: 25% graduate arts and sciences, 5% education.

Application *Option:* deferred entrance. *Application fee:* $30.

Significant dates *Application deadline:* 8/1 (transfers). *Financial aid deadline priority date:* 3/1.

Freshman Application Contact
Ms. Gerianne Brusati, Director of Educational Advising and Admissions, New School Bachelor of Arts, New School University, 66 West 12th Street, New York, NY 10011-8603. **Phone:** 212-229-5630. **E-mail:** admissions@dialnsa.edu

Visit CollegeQuest.com for information on majors offered and athletics.

■ *See page 2160 for a narrative description.*

NEW SCHOOL UNIVERSITY, EUGENE LANG COLLEGE
New York—See Eugene Lang College, New School University

NEW SCHOOL UNIVERSITY, MANNES COLLEGE OF MUSIC
New York—See Mannes College of Music, New School University

NEW SCHOOL UNIVERSITY, PARSONS SCHOOL OF DESIGN
New York—See Parsons School of Design, New School University

NEW YORK CITY TECHNICAL COLLEGE OF THE CITY UNIVERSITY OF NEW YORK
Brooklyn, New York

- **State and locally supported**, primarily 2-year, founded 1946
- **Degrees** associate and bachelor's
- **Urban** campus
- **Coed**, 11,180 undergraduate students, 70% full-time, 48% women, 52% men
- **Noncompetitive** entrance level

Part of City University of New York System.

Faculty 893 (30% full-time).

Admissions Office Contact
New York City Technical College of the City University of New York, 300 Jay Street, Brooklyn, NY 11201-2983. **Fax:** 718-260-5198. **E-mail:** jlento@nyctc.cuny.edu

Visit CollegeQuest.com for information on majors offered and athletics.

THE NEW YORK COLLEGE FOR WHOLISTIC HEALTH EDUCATION & RESEARCH
Syosset, New York

- **Independent**, primarily 2-year, founded 1981
- **Degrees** associate, incidental bachelor's, and master's
- **Suburban** campus with easy access to New York City
- **Coed**, 800 undergraduate students
- **Moderately difficult** entrance level

The New York College provides the highest standard of medical education and training for practitioners of holistic medicine. Combined bachelor's/master's degree programs in acupuncture and oriental medicine lead to national certification and licensing. The New York College also offers a 68-credit massage therapy program that leads to an associate degree in occupational studies.

Admissions Office Contact
The New York College for Wholistic Health Education & Research, 6801 Jericho Turnpike, Suite 300, Syosset, NY 11791-4413. **Toll-free phone:** 800-922-7337. **Fax:** 516-364-0989.

Visit CollegeQuest.com for information on majors offered and athletics.

NEW YORK INSTITUTE OF TECHNOLOGY
Old Westbury, New York

- **Independent**, comprehensive, founded 1955
- **Degrees** associate, bachelor's, master's, first professional, and postbachelor's certificates
- **Suburban** 1,050-acre campus with easy access to New York City
- **Coed**, 5,399 undergraduate students, 74% full-time, 39% women, 61% men
- **Moderately difficult** entrance level, 82% of applicants were admitted
- **16:1 student-to-undergraduate faculty ratio**
- **$11,990 tuition** and fees

Students *Undergraduates:* 3,987 full-time, 1,412 part-time. Students come from 29 states and territories, 85 other countries. *The most frequently chosen baccalaureate fields are:* architecture, business/marketing, engineering/engineering technologies. *Graduate:* 1,027 in professional programs, 2,515 in other graduate degree programs.

From out-of-state	11%	Reside on campus	5%
Age 25 or older	38%	International students	8%
African Americans	17%	Asian Americans/Pacific Islanders	11%
Hispanic Americans	10%	Native Americans	0.2%

Faculty 1,254 (20% full-time).

Expenses (1999–2000) *Comprehensive fee:* $18,500 includes full-time tuition ($11,990) and room and board ($6510). *College room only:* $3480. Full-time tuition and fees vary according to program. Room and board charges vary according to board plan and housing facility. *Part-time tuition:* $370 per credit. *Part-time fees:* $90 per term part-time. Part-time tuition and fees vary according to course load and program. *Payment plan:* installment. *Waivers:* senior citizens and employees or children of employees.

Library George and Gertrude Wisser Memorial Library plus 4 others. *Collection:* 201,028 titles, 3,196 serial subscriptions, 40,582 audiovisual materials.

College life *Housing: Option:* coed. *Social organizations:* national fraternities, national sororities, local fraternities, local sororities; 2% of eligible men and 1% of eligible women are members. *Most popular organizations:* Physical Therapy Society, Occupational Therapy Association, ASHRAM, Bio-Medical Society, National Society of Black Engineers.

Campus security 24-hour emergency response devices and patrols, late-night transport-escort service, controlled dormitory access.

After graduation 112 organizations recruited on campus 1997–98. *Career center:* 2 full-time, 2 part-time personnel. Services include job fairs, resume preparation, interview workshops, resume referral, career/interest testing, career counseling, careers library, job bank, job interviews. *Graduate education:* 48% of class of 1999 went directly to graduate and professional school: 14% business, 10% education, 10% graduate arts and sciences, 7% engineering, 3% law, 2% medicine, 2% theology.

New York

Freshmen 2,781 applied, 2,280 admitted, 785 enrolled.
Average high school GPA 3.0 SAT verbal scores above 500 67%
SAT math scores above 500 78% ACT above 18 100%
1998 freshmen returning in 1999 67%

Application *Options:* Common Application, electronic application, deferred entrance. *Application fee:* $50. *Required:* essay or personal statement; high school transcript. *Required for some:* letters of recommendation; interview.

Standardized tests *Admission: Required:* SAT I or ACT.

Significant dates *Application deadlines:* rolling (freshmen), rolling (transfers). *Financial aid deadline priority date:* 2/15.

Freshman Application Contact
Mr. James Newell, Director of Financial Aid, New York Institute of Technology, PO Box 8000, Old Westbury, NY 11568. **Phone:** 516-686-7680. **Toll-free phone:** 800-345-NYIT. **Fax:** 516-686-7613. **E-mail:** admissions@nyit.edu

Visit CollegeQuest.com for information on majors offered and athletics. College video available at CollegeQuest.com.

■ *See page 2162 for a narrative description.*

NEW YORK SCHOOL OF INTERIOR DESIGN
New York, New York

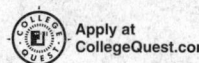
Apply at CollegeQuest.com

■ **Independent**, comprehensive, founded 1916
■ **Degrees** associate, bachelor's, and master's
■ **Urban** campus
■ **Coed**, 554 undergraduate students, 20% full-time, 84% women, 16% men
■ **Moderately difficult** entrance level
■ **7:1 student-to-undergraduate faculty ratio**
■ **$16,070 tuition** and fees

The New York School of Interior Design is an NASAD-accredited private college devoted to interior design education. The Bachelor of Fine Arts degree is FIDER-accredited. Located on Manhattan's Upper East Side, the School is surrounded by many famous museums and buildings of great architectural interest.

Students *Undergraduates:* 111 full-time, 443 part-time. Students come from 17 states and territories, 24 other countries. *The most frequently chosen baccalaureate field is:* visual/performing arts. *Graduate:* 12 in graduate degree programs.

From out-of-state 15% Age 25 or older 64%
Transferred in 2%

Expenses (2000–2001) *Tuition:* full-time $16,000; part-time $500 per credit. *Required fees:* full-time $70; $35 per term part-time. Full-time tuition and fees vary according to course load. Part-time tuition and fees vary according to course load. *Payment plans:* installment, deferred payment. *Waivers:* employees or children of employees.

Library NYSID Library. *Collection:* 5,500 titles, 90 serial subscriptions, 100 audiovisual materials.

College life *Housing:* college housing not available. *Most popular organization:* ASID.

Campus security Security during school hours.

After graduation *Career center:* 1 part-time personnel. Services include resume preparation, resume referral, career counseling, job bank, job interviews.

Freshmen 199 enrolled.
SAT verbal scores above 500 N/R SAT math scores above 500 N/R
ACT above 18 N/R

Application *Options:* eApply at www.CollegeQuest.com, Common Application, deferred entrance. *Application fee:* $50. *Required:* essay or personal statement; high school transcript; minimum 2.5 GPA; 2 letters of recommendation; portfolio. *Required for some:* interview. *Recommended:* interview.

Standardized tests *Admission: Required:* SAT I or ACT.

Significant dates *Application deadlines:* rolling (freshmen), rolling (transfers). *Financial aid deadline priority date:* 5/1.

Freshman Application Contact
Ms. Lydia Paiste, Admissions Associate, New York School of Interior Design, 170 East 70th Street, New York, NY 10021-5110. **Phone:** 212-472-1500 Ext. 204. **Toll-free phone:** 800-336-9743. **Fax:** 212-472-1867. **E-mail:** admissions@nysid.edu

Visit CollegeQuest.com for information on majors offered and athletics.

■ *See page 2164 for a narrative description.*

NEW YORK STATE COLLEGE OF CERAMICS
New York—See Alfred University

NEW YORK UNIVERSITY
New York, New York

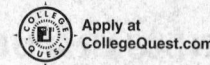
Apply at CollegeQuest.com

■ **Independent**, university, founded 1831
■ **Degrees** associate, bachelor's, master's, doctoral, first professional, and post-master's certificates
■ **Urban** 28-acre campus
■ **Coed**, 17,776 undergraduate students, 89% full-time, 59% women, 41% men
■ **Most difficult** entrance level, 32% of applicants were admitted
■ **13:1 student-to-undergraduate faculty ratio**
■ **72% graduate** in 6 years or less
■ **$23,456 tuition** and fees
■ **$15,999 average financial aid** package, $17,985 average indebtedness upon graduation, $1 billion endowment

Students *Undergraduates:* 15,734 full-time, 2,042 part-time. Students come from 52 states and territories, 120 other countries. *The most frequently chosen baccalaureate fields are:* business/marketing, social sciences and history, visual/performing arts. *Graduate:* 3,286 in professional programs, 15,642 in other graduate degree programs.

From out-of-state 47% Reside on campus 48%
Transferred in 5% International students 5%
African Americans 7% Asian Americans/Pacific Islanders 16%
Hispanic Americans 8% Native Americans 0.1%

Faculty 3,507 (42% full-time).

Expenses (1999–2000) *Comprehensive fee:* $32,316 includes full-time tuition ($23,456) and room and board ($8860). Full-time tuition and fees vary according to program. Room and board charges vary according to board plan and housing facility. *Part-time tuition:* $644 per credit. Part-time tuition and fees vary according to program. *Payment plans:* tuition prepayment, installment, deferred payment. *Waivers:* employees or children of employees.

Library Elmer H. Bobst Library plus 7 others. *Operations spending 1999–2000:* $38.7 million. *Collection:* 4.1 million titles, 29,244 serial subscriptions.

College life *Housing: Options:* coed, disabled students. *Social organizations:* national fraternities, national sororities, local sororities; 7% of eligible men and 6% of eligible women are members.

Campus security 24-hour emergency response devices and patrols, student patrols, late-night transport-escort service, controlled dormitory access, 24-hour security in residence halls.

After graduation 400 organizations recruited on campus 1997–98. *Career center:* 18 full-time, 30 part-time personnel. Services include job fairs, resume preparation, interview workshops, resume referral, career/interest testing, career counseling, careers library, job bank, job interviews.

Freshmen 28,794 applied, 9,140 admitted, 3,642 enrolled. 126 National Merit Scholars.
Average high school GPA 3.53 SAT verbal scores above 500 99%
SAT math scores above 500 99% ACT above 18 N/R
From top 10% of their h.s. class 61% From top quarter 92%
From top half 100% 1998 freshmen returning in 1999 88%

Application *Options:* eApply at www.CollegeQuest.com, Common Application, electronic application, early admission, early decision, deferred entrance. *Application fee:* $50. *Required:* essay or personal statement; high school transcript; minimum 3.0 GPA; 2 letters of recommendation. *Required for some:* interview; audition, portfolio.

New York

New York University (continued)

Standardized tests *Admission: Required:* SAT I or ACT. *Recommended:* SAT II Subject Tests, SAT II: Writing Test. *Required for some:* SAT II Subject Tests.

Significant dates *Application deadlines:* 1/15 (freshmen), 4/1 (transfers). *Early decision:* 11/15. *Notification:* 4/1 (freshmen), 1/15 (early decision). *Financial aid deadline priority date:* 2/15.

Freshman Application Contact
Mr. Richard Avitabile, Assistant Vice President for Enrollment Services, New York University, 22 Washington Square North, New York, NY 10011. **Phone:** 212-998-4500. **Fax:** 212-995-4902.

Visit CollegeQuest.com for information on majors offered and athletics. College video available at CollegeQuest.com.

■ *See page 2166 for a narrative description.*

NIAGARA UNIVERSITY
Niagara Falls, New York

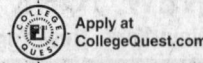
Apply at CollegeQuest.com

- **Independent**, comprehensive, founded 1856, affiliated with Roman Catholic Church
- **Degrees** associate, bachelor's, master's, and post-master's certificates
- **Suburban** 160-acre campus with easy access to Buffalo and Toronto
- **Coed**, 2,331 undergraduate students, 92% full-time, 62% women, 38% men
- **Moderately difficult** entrance level, 84% of applicants were admitted
- **15:1** student-to-undergraduate faculty ratio
- **50% graduate** in 6 years or less
- **$13,940 tuition** and fees
- **$14,720 average financial aid** package, $12,743 average indebtedness upon graduation, $38.8 million endowment

Niagara University offers an extensive merit scholarship and grant program. Students, regardless of need, may be eligible to receive an academic award ranging from $3500 up to full tuition. These merit-based grants, awards, and scholarships are renewable. To be considered, students must meet certain academic criteria and other NU guidelines.

Students *Undergraduates:* 2,153 full-time, 178 part-time. Students come from 19 states and territories, 16 other countries. *The most frequently chosen baccalaureate fields are:* business/marketing, education, social sciences and history. *Graduate:* 583 in graduate degree programs.

From out-of-state	7%	Reside on campus	59%
Age 25 or older	11%	Transferred in	6%
International students	4%	African Americans	4%
Asian Americans/Pacific Islanders	1%	Hispanic Americans	2%
Native Americans	1%		

Faculty 258 (47% full-time).

Expenses (1999–2000) *One-time required fee:* $100. *Comprehensive fee:* $20,270 includes full-time tuition ($13,400), mandatory fees ($540), and room and board ($6330). Room and board charges vary according to board plan. *Part-time tuition:* $406 per credit hour. *Part-time fees:* $10 per term part-time. Part-time tuition and fees vary according to program. *Payment plans:* installment, deferred payment. *Waivers:* employees or children of employees.

Library Our Lady of Angels Library. *Operations spending 1999–2000:* $893,393. *Collection:* 309,014 titles, 1,429 serial subscriptions.

College life *Housing:* on-campus residence required through sophomore year. *Options:* coed, women-only. *Social organizations:* national fraternities. *Most popular organizations:* Niagara University Community Action Program, student government, Programming Board.

Campus security 24-hour emergency response devices and patrols, late-night transport-escort service, controlled dormitory access, 24-hour escort service.

After graduation 139 organizations recruited on campus 1997–98. *Career center:* 6 full-time personnel. Services include job fairs, resume preparation, interview workshops, resume referral, career/interest testing, career counseling, careers library, job bank, job interviews.

Freshmen 2,061 applied, 1,731 admitted, 580 enrolled.

Average high school GPA	3.0	SAT verbal scores above 500	63%
SAT math scores above 500	61%	ACT above 18	91%
From top 10% of their h.s. class	13%	From top quarter	42%
From top half	75%	1998 freshmen returning in 1999	76%

Application *Options:* eApply at www.CollegeQuest.com, electronic application, early admission, deferred entrance. *Application fee:* $30. *Required:* high school transcript. *Recommended:* minimum 3.0 GPA; 3 letters of recommendation; interview.

Standardized tests *Admission: Required:* SAT I or ACT.

Significant dates *Application deadlines:* 8/1 (freshmen), 8/15 (transfers). *Financial aid deadline priority date:* 2/15.

Freshman Application Contact
Ms. Christine M. McDermott, Associate Director of Admissions, Niagara University, Niagara University, NY 14109. **Phone:** 716-286-8700 Ext. 8715. **Toll-free phone:** 800-462-2111. **Fax:** 716-286-8355. **E-mail:** admissions@niagara.edu

Visit CollegeQuest.com for information on majors offered and athletics. College video available at CollegeQuest.com.

■ *See page 2168 for a narrative description.*

NYACK COLLEGE
Nyack, New York

- **Independent**, 4-year, founded 1882, affiliated with The Christian and Missionary Alliance
- **Degrees** associate, bachelor's, master's, first professional, and postbachelor's certificates
- **Suburban** 102-acre campus with easy access to New York City
- **Coed**, 1,415 undergraduate students, 93% full-time, 56% women, 44% men
- **Moderately difficult** entrance level
- **$12,740 tuition** and fees
- **$13,073 average financial aid** package, $17,000 average indebtedness upon graduation, $3.4 million endowment

Students *Undergraduates:* 1,314 full-time, 101 part-time. Students come from 41 states and territories, 38 other countries. *The most frequently chosen baccalaureate fields are:* business/marketing, education, philosophy. *Graduate:* 191 in professional programs, 199 in other graduate degree programs.

From out-of-state	43%	Reside on campus	59%
Age 25 or older	85%	Transferred in	18%
International students	6%	African Americans	25%
Asian Americans/Pacific Islanders	7%	Hispanic Americans	14%
Native Americans	0.2%		

Expenses (2000–2001) *Comprehensive fee:* $18,540 includes full-time tuition ($11,990), mandatory fees ($750), and room and board ($5800). Full-time tuition and fees vary according to location and program. Room and board charges vary according to housing facility. *Part-time tuition:* $500 per credit hour. *Part-time fees:* $170 per term. Part-time tuition and fees vary according to course load, location, and program. *Payment plan:* installment. *Waivers:* employees or children of employees.

Library Nyack College Library plus 1 other. *Collection:* 81,029 titles, 874 serial subscriptions, 3,723 audiovisual materials.

College life *Housing: Options:* men-only, women-only. *Most popular organizations:* Gospel Teams, Drama Club, Student Government Association.

Campus security 24-hour emergency response devices and patrols, student patrols, late-night transport-escort service.

After graduation *Career center:* 1 full-time, 1 part-time personnel. Services include job fairs, resume preparation, interview workshops, career/interest testing, career counseling, careers library, job bank, job interviews.

Freshmen 330 enrolled.

Average high school GPA	2.87	SAT verbal scores above 500	45%
SAT math scores above 500	39%	ACT above 18	77%
From top 10% of their h.s. class	10%	From top quarter	28%
From top half	60%	1998 freshmen returning in 1999	64%

Application *Options:* early admission, deferred entrance. *Application fee:* $15. *Required:* essay or personal statement; high school transcript; minimum 2.0 GPA; 3 letters of recommendation. *Required for some:* interview.

Standardized tests *Admission: Required:* SAT I or ACT.
Significant dates *Application deadline:* 9/1 (freshmen). *Financial aid deadline priority date:* 3/1.
Freshman Application Contact
Miguel A. Sanchez, Director of Admissions, Nyack College, 1 South Boulevard, Nyack, NY 10960-3698. **Phone:** 914-358-1710 Ext. 350. **Toll-free phone:** 800-33-NYACK. **Fax:** 914-358-3047. **E-mail:** enroll@nyack.edu
Visit CollegeQuest.com for information on majors offered and athletics. College video available at CollegeQuest.com.

OHR HAMEIR THEOLOGICAL SEMINARY
Peekskill, New York

Admissions Office Contact
Ohr Hameir Theological Seminary, Furnace Woods Road, Peekskill, NY 10566.

OHR SOMAYACH/JOSEPH TANENBAUM EDUCATIONAL CENTER
Monsey, New York

Admissions Office Contact
Ohr Somayach/Joseph Tanenbaum Educational Center, PO Box 334, Monsey, NY 10952-0334.

PACE UNIVERSITY, NEW YORK CITY CAMPUS
New York, New York

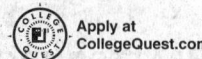
Apply at CollegeQuest.com

- **Independent**, university, founded 1906
- **Degrees** associate, bachelor's, master's, doctoral, post-master's, and postbachelor's certificates
- **Coed**, 5,791 undergraduate students, 72% full-time, 61% women, 39% men
- **Moderately difficult** entrance level, 70% of applicants were admitted
- **50% graduate** in 6 years or less
- **$15,490 tuition** and fees
- **$78.1 million endowment**

Pace offers a variety of scholarships and grants that range from $1000 to $10,000 per year. Candidates are encouraged to apply early. Pace's outstanding co-op education program also helps qualified students finance and enhance their education through paid career-related work experiences in the public and private sectors.

Students *Undergraduates:* 4,154 full-time, 1,637 part-time. Students come from 42 states and territories, 58 other countries. *The most frequently chosen baccalaureate fields are:* business/marketing, computer/information sciences, health professions and related sciences. *Graduate:* 2,102 in graduate degree programs.

From out-of-state	14%	Reside on campus	23%
Age 25 or older	22%	International students	8%
African Americans	14%	Asian Americans/Pacific Islanders	15%
Hispanic Americans	13%	Native Americans	0.1%

Faculty 554 (38% full-time), 54% with terminal degrees.
Expenses (1999–2000) *Comprehensive fee:* $22,040 includes full-time tuition ($15,130), mandatory fees ($360), and room and board ($6550). *College room only:* $4750. Room and board charges vary according to board plan and housing facility. *Part-time tuition:* $475 per credit. *Part-time fees:* $84 per term part-time. Part-time tuition and fees vary according to course load. *Payment plan:* installment. *Waivers:* senior citizens and employees or children of employees.
Library Henry Birnbaum Library plus 3 others. *Operations spending 1999–2000:* $5.5 million. *Collection:* 547,658 titles, 7,826 serial subscriptions, 482 audiovisual materials.
College life *Housing:* Option: coed. *Social organizations:* national fraternities, national sororities, local fraternities, local sororities; 5% of eligible men and 3% of eligible women are members. *Most popular organizations:* student government, Pace Press Newspaper, United Chinese Students Association, Alianza Latina, Black Student Organization.
Campus security 24-hour emergency response devices and patrols, late-night transport-escort service, controlled dormitory access.
After graduation 325 organizations recruited on campus 1997–98. 83% of class of 1998 had job offers within 6 months. *Career center:* 35 full-time, 1 part-time personnel. Services include job fairs, resume preparation, interview workshops, resume referral, career/interest testing, career counseling, careers library, job bank, job interviews.
Freshmen 4,457 applied, 3,136 admitted, 1,137 enrolled.

Average high school GPA	3.0	SAT verbal scores above 500	54%
SAT math scores above 500	63%	ACT above 18	100%
From top 10% of their h.s. class	20%	From top quarter	54%
From top half	86%	1998 freshmen returning in 1999	73%

Application *Options:* eApply at www.CollegeQuest.com, Common Application, electronic application, early action, deferred entrance. *Application fee:* $35. *Required:* high school transcript. *Recommended:* essay or personal statement; minimum 3.0 GPA; letters of recommendation; interview.
Standardized tests *Admission: Required:* SAT I or ACT.
Significant dates *Application deadlines:* rolling (freshmen), rolling (transfers). *Early action:* 11/1. *Notification:* 12/15 (early action). *Financial aid deadline priority date:* 2/15.
Freshman Application Contact
Mr. Richard Alvarez, Director of Admission, Pace University, New York City Campus, One Pace Plaza, New York, NY 10038. **Phone:** 212-346-1225. **Toll-free phone:** 800-874-7223. **Fax:** 212-346-1040. **E-mail:** infoctr@pace.edu
Visit CollegeQuest.com for information on majors offered and athletics. Electronic viewbook available at CollegeQuest.com.

■ *See page 2234 for a narrative description.*

PACE UNIVERSITY, PLEASANTVILLE/BRIARCLIFF CAMPUS
Pleasantville, New York

- **Independent**, comprehensive
- **Degrees** associate, bachelor's, master's, doctoral, post-master's, and postbachelor's certificates
- **Coed**, 3,389 undergraduate students, 70% full-time, 59% women, 41% men
- **75% of applicants were admitted**
- **57% graduate** in 6 years or less
- **$15,490 tuition** and fees
- **$78.1 million endowment**

Students *Undergraduates:* 2,383 full-time, 1,006 part-time. Students come from 42 states and territories, 58 other countries. *The most frequently chosen baccalaureate fields are:* business/marketing, computer/information sciences, health professions and related sciences. *Graduate:* 138 in graduate degree programs.

From out-of-state	14%	Reside on campus	23%
Age 25 or older	22%	International students	4%
African Americans	9%	Asian Americans/Pacific Islanders	4%
Hispanic Americans	7%	Native Americans	0.3%

Faculty 371 (43% full-time).
Expenses (1999–2000) *Comprehensive fee:* 22,040 includes full-time tuition (15,130), mandatory fees (360), and room and board (6550). *College room only:* 4750. Room and board charges vary according to board plan and housing facility. *Part-time tuition:* 475 per credit. *Part-time fees:* 84 per term part-time. Part-time tuition and fees vary according to course load. *Payment plan:* installment. *Waivers:* senior citizens and employees or children of employees.
Library *Operations spending 1999–2000:* $5.5 million.
College life *Housing:* Option: coed. *Social organizations:* national fraternities, national sororities, local fraternities, local sororities; 5% of eligible men and 3% of eligible women are members. *Most popular organizations:* student government, Pace Press Newspaper, United Chinese Students Association, Alianza Latina, Black Student Organization.
Campus security 24-hour emergency response devices and patrols, late-night transport-escort service, controlled dormitory access.

New York

Pace University, Pleasantville/Briarcliff Campus (continued)

Freshmen 2,611 applied, 1,964 admitted, 854 enrolled.

Average high school GPA	3.0	SAT verbal scores above 500	54%
SAT math scores above 500	63%	ACT above 18	100%
From top 10% of their h.s. class	20%	From top quarter	54%
From top half	86%	1998 freshmen returning in 1999	73%

Application *Option:* early action. *Application fee:* 35. *Required:* high school transcript. *Recommended:* essay or personal statement; minimum 3.0 GPA; letters of recommendation; interview.

Standardized tests *Admission: Required:* SAT I or ACT.

Significant dates *Application deadlines:* rolling (freshmen), rolling (transfers). *Early action:* 11/1. *Notification:* 12/15 (early action).

Freshman Application Contact
Mr. Richard Alvarez, Director of Admission, Pace University, Pleasantville/Briarcliff Campus, 861 Bedford Road, Pleasantville, NY 10570. **Phone:** 212-346-1225. **Toll-free phone:** 800-874-7223. **Fax:** 914-773-3851.

Visit CollegeQuest.com for information on majors offered and athletics.

PARSONS SCHOOL OF DESIGN, NEW SCHOOL UNIVERSITY
New York, New York

- **Independent**, comprehensive, founded 1896
- **Degrees** associate, bachelor's, and master's
- **Urban** 2-acre campus
- **Coed**, 2,322 undergraduate students, 91% full-time, 72% women, 28% men
- **Very difficult** entrance level, 44% of applicants were admitted
- **12:1 student-to-undergraduate faculty ratio**
- **55% graduate** in 6 years or less
- **$21,790 tuition** and fees
- **$13,782 average financial aid** package, $27,125 average indebtedness upon graduation, $86.9 million system endowment

Part of New School University.

Students *Undergraduates:* 2,118 full-time, 204 part-time. Students come from 47 states and territories, 65 other countries. *The most frequently chosen baccalaureate fields are:* communications/communication technologies, business/marketing, visual/performing arts. *Graduate:* 319 in graduate degree programs.

From out-of-state	48%	Reside on campus	66%
Age 25 or older	25%	Transferred in	13%
International students	30%	African Americans	4%
Asian Americans/Pacific Islanders	17%	Hispanic Americans	8%
Native Americans	0.4%		

Faculty 709 (4% full-time), 1% with terminal degrees.

Expenses (2000–2001) *Tuition:* full-time $21,550; part-time $734 per credit. *Required fees:* full-time $240. Part-time tuition and fees vary according to program. Room and board charges vary according to board plan. *Payment plan:* installment. *Waivers:* employees or children of employees.

Library Adam L. and Sophie Gimbel Library plus 2 others. *System-wide operations spending 1999–2000:* $1.8 million. *Collection:* 191,789 titles, 896 serial subscriptions, 137,878 audiovisual materials.

College life *Housing: Option:* coed. *Most popular organizations:* gallery committees, Latino/Latina Student Group, Chinese Student Association, American Institute of Architectural Students.

Campus security 24-hour emergency response devices, controlled dormitory access.

After graduation 100 organizations recruited on campus 1997–98. *Career center:* 2 full-time personnel. Services include job fairs, resume preparation, resume referral, career counseling, job bank, job interviews. *Graduate education:* 5% of class of 1999 went directly to graduate and professional school; 5% graduate arts and sciences.

Freshmen 1,617 applied, 706 admitted, 371 enrolled.

Average high school GPA	2.9	SAT verbal scores above 500	64%
SAT math scores above 500	65%	ACT above 18	N/R
1998 freshmen returning in 1999	80%		

Application *Option:* early admission. *Application fee:* $40. *Required:* high school transcript; minimum 2.0 GPA; portfolio, home examination. *Required for some:* essay or personal statement; interview. *Recommended:* minimum 3.0 GPA.

Standardized tests *Admission: Required:* SAT I or ACT.

Significant dates *Application deadlines:* 7/1 (freshmen), 7/1 (transfers). *Financial aid deadline priority date:* 3/1.

Freshman Application Contact
Ms. Nadine M. Bourgeois, Assistant Dean and Director of Admissions, Parsons School of Design, New School University, 66 Fifth Avenue, New York, NY 10011-8878. **Phone:** 212-229-8910. **Toll-free phone:** 800-252-0852. **Fax:** 212-229-8975. **E-mail:** parsadm@newschool.edu

Visit CollegeQuest.com for information on majors offered and athletics. Electronic viewbook available at CollegeQuest.com.

PAUL SMITH'S COLLEGE OF ARTS AND SCIENCES
Paul Smiths, New York

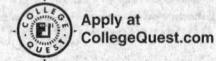
Apply at CollegeQuest.com

- **Independent**, primarily 2-year, founded 1937
- **Degrees** associate and bachelor's
- **Rural** 14,200-acre campus
- **Coed**, 806 undergraduate students
- **Minimally difficult** entrance level

Faculty 97 (90% full-time).

Admissions Office Contact
Paul Smith's College of Arts and Sciences, Paul Smiths, NY 12970-0265. **Toll-free phone:** 800-421-2605. **Fax:** 518-327-6060.

Visit CollegeQuest.com for information on majors offered and athletics. College video available at CollegeQuest.com.

■ *See page 2246 for a narrative description.*

PLATTSBURGH STATE UNIVERSITY OF NEW YORK
Plattsburgh, New York

- **State-supported**, comprehensive, founded 1889
- **Degrees** bachelor's, master's, and post-master's certificates
- **Small-town** 265-acre campus with easy access to Montreal
- **Coed**, 5,176 undergraduate students, 95% full-time, 57% women, 43% men
- **Moderately difficult** entrance level, 69% of applicants were admitted
- **17:1 student-to-undergraduate faculty ratio**
- **57.6% graduate** in 6 years or less
- **$3957 tuition** and fees (in-state); $8857 (out-of-state)
- **$6701 average financial aid** package, $15,474 average indebtedness upon graduation, $8.7 million endowment

Plattsburg combines the best of all worlds by offering a high-quality college experience in a region of exceptional beauty and recreational opportunities. The University excels at preparing graduates for successful careers as professionals through a combination of liberal arts and science study, professional programs, internships, and study-abroad options.

Part of State University of New York System.

Students *Undergraduates:* 4,897 full-time, 279 part-time. Students come from 20 states and territories, 19 other countries. *The most frequently chosen baccalaureate fields are:* business/marketing, communications/communication technologies, education. *Graduate:* 689 in graduate degree programs.

From out-of-state	2%	Reside on campus	44%
Age 25 or older	10%	Transferred in	13%
International students	2%	African Americans	3%
Asian Americans/Pacific Islanders	1%	Hispanic Americans	3%
Native Americans	1%		

Faculty 400 (70% full-time), 63% with terminal degrees.

Expenses (1999–2000) *Tuition, state resident:* full-time $3400; part-time $137 per credit hour. *Tuition, nonresident:* full-time $8300; part-time $346 per credit hour. *Required fees:* full-time $557; $19 per credit hour. Part-time tuition and fees vary according to course load. *College room and board:* $4850; room only: $2800. Room and board charges vary according to board plan. *Payment plans:* installment, deferred payment. *Waivers:* senior citizens and employees or children of employees.

New York

Library Feinberg Library. *Operations spending 1999–2000:* $2.4 million. *Collection:* 471,818 titles, 1,412 serial subscriptions, 23,123 audiovisual materials.

College life *Housing:* on-campus residence required through sophomore year. *Options:* coed, disabled students. *Social organizations:* national fraternities, national sororities, local fraternities, local sororities; 6% of eligible men and 5% of eligible women are members. *Most popular organizations:* Student Association, honor societies, student media organizations, service/leadership organizations, intramural and recreational sports.

Campus security 24-hour emergency response devices and patrols, late-night transport-escort service, controlled dormitory access, enhanced 911 system.

After graduation 120 organizations recruited on campus 1997–98. 79% of class of 1998 had job offers within 6 months. *Career center:* 4 full-time, 1 part-time personnel. Services include job fairs, resume preparation, interview workshops, resume referral, career/interest testing, career counseling, careers library, job bank, job interviews. *Graduate education:* 32% of class of 1999 went directly to graduate and professional school.

Freshmen 4,559 applied, 3,135 admitted, 887 enrolled.

Average high school GPA	3.5	SAT verbal scores above 500	72%
SAT math scores above 500	66%	ACT above 18	N/R
From top 10% of their h.s. class	7%	From top quarter	28%
From top half	77%	1998 freshmen returning in 1999	79%

Application *Options:* electronic application, early admission, early decision, deferred entrance. *Application fee:* $30. *Required:* high school transcript; minimum 2.5 GPA. *Recommended:* essay or personal statement; minimum 3.4 GPA; letters of recommendation; interview.

Standardized tests *Admission: Required:* SAT I or ACT.

Significant dates *Application deadlines:* rolling (freshmen), rolling (transfers). *Early decision:* 11/1. *Notification:* 12/15 (early decision). *Financial aid deadline priority date:* 3/1.

Freshman Application Contact
Mr. Richard Higgins, Director of Admissions, Plattsburgh State University of New York, 101 Broad Street, Plattsburgh, NY 12901-2681. **Phone:** 518-564-2040. **Toll-free phone:** 800-388-6473. **Fax:** 518-564-2045. **E-mail:** admissions@splava.cc.plattsburgh.edu

Visit CollegeQuest.com for information on majors offered and athletics. College video and electronic viewbook available at CollegeQuest.com.

■ *See page 2274 for a narrative description.*

POLYTECHNIC UNIVERSITY, BROOKLYN CAMPUS
Brooklyn, New York

Apply at CollegeQuest.com

- **Independent**, university, founded 1854
- **Degrees** bachelor's, master's, and doctoral (most information given is for both Brooklyn and Farmingdale campuses)
- **Urban** 3-acre campus
- **Coed**, 1,785 undergraduate students, 92% full-time, 18% women, 82% men
- **Very difficult** entrance level, 70% of applicants were admitted
- **12:1 student-to-undergraduate faculty ratio**
- **52% graduate** in 6 years or less
- **$20,810 tuition** and fees
- **$17,554 average financial aid** package, $19,341 average indebtedness upon graduation, $171 million system endowment

Polytechnic University is one of the nation's leading technological universities. Founded in 1854 and today a private, coeducational institution, Polytechnic is the New York metro area's preeminent educational resource in science and technology. The University awards bachelor's, master's, and PhD degrees. With 3 campuses—at MetroTech in downtown Brooklyn; in Farmingdale, Long Island; and the Westchester Graduate Center—Polytechnic is ideally situated to serve the needs of the metro area's growing high-tech economy.

Students *Undergraduates:* 1,647 full-time, 138 part-time. Students come from 6 states and territories, 19 other countries. *The most frequently chosen baccalaureate fields are:* computer/information sciences, engineering/engineering technologies, physical sciences. *Graduate:* 1,613 in graduate degree programs.

From out-of-state	3%	Age 25 or older	6%
Transferred in	7%	International students	3%
African Americans	11%	Asian Americans/Pacific Islanders	37%
Hispanic Americans	6%	Native Americans	0.4%

Faculty 312 (52% full-time).

Expenses (1999–2000) *Comprehensive fee:* $26,280 includes full-time tuition ($20,210), mandatory fees ($600), and room and board ($5470). Full-time tuition and fees vary according to course load. Room and board charges vary according to board plan. *Part-time tuition:* $640 per credit. *Part-time fees:* $200 per term part-time. Part-time tuition and fees vary according to course load. College room and board is available through Long Island University. *Payment plans:* tuition prepayment, deferred payment. *Waivers:* minority students and employees or children of employees.

Library Bern Dibner Library. *Operations spending 1999–2000:* $1.2 million. *Collection:* 148,000 titles, 613 serial subscriptions, 235 audiovisual materials.

College life *Housing:* college housing not available. *Social organizations:* national fraternities, local fraternities, coed fraternity; 6% of eligible men and 3% of eligible women are members. *Most popular organizations:* National Society of Black Engineers, Society of Hispanic Professional Engineers, Association for Computing Machinery, Alpha Phi Omega Service Fraternity, Chinese Student Society.

Campus security 24-hour patrols.

After graduation *Career center:* 6 full-time personnel. Services include job fairs, resume preparation, interview workshops, resume referral, career counseling, careers library, job bank, job interviews. *Graduate education:* 8% of class of 1999 went directly to graduate and professional school.

Freshmen 1,389 applied, 979 admitted, 468 enrolled.

Average high school GPA	3.3	SAT verbal scores above 500	76%
SAT math scores above 500	99%	ACT above 18	N/R
1998 freshmen returning in 1999	79%		

Application *Options:* eApply at www.CollegeQuest.com, Common Application, electronic application, deferred entrance. *Application fee:* $40. *Required:* essay or personal statement; high school transcript; 2 letters of recommendation. *Recommended:* interview.

Standardized tests *Admission: Required:* SAT I or ACT. *Recommended:* SAT II Subject Tests, SAT II: Writing Test.

Significant dates *Application deadlines:* rolling (freshmen), rolling (transfers). *Financial aid deadline:* continuous.

Freshman Application Contact
Mr. John S. Kerge, Dean of Admissions, Polytechnic University, Brooklyn Campus, Six Metrotech Center, Brooklyn, NY 11201-2990. **Phone:** 718-260-3100. **Toll-free phone:** 800-POLYTECH. **Fax:** 718-260-3136. **E-mail:** admitme@poly.edu

Visit CollegeQuest.com for information on majors offered and athletics.

■ *See page 2280 for a narrative description.*

POLYTECHNIC UNIVERSITY, FARMINGDALE CAMPUS
Farmingdale, New York

- **Independent**, university, founded 1854
- **Degrees** bachelor's, master's, and doctoral (most information given is for both Brooklyn and Farmingdale campuses)
- **Suburban** 25-acre campus with easy access to New York City
- **Coed**, 1,785 undergraduate students, 92% full-time, 18% women, 82% men
- **Very difficult** entrance level, 70% of applicants were admitted
- **12:1 student-to-undergraduate faculty ratio**
- **52% graduate** in 6 years or less
- **$20,810 tuition** and fees
- **$171 million system endowment**

Students *Undergraduates:* 1,647 full-time, 138 part-time. Students come from 6 states and territories, 19 other countries. *The most frequently chosen baccalaureate fields are:* computer/information sciences, engineering/

Peterson's Guide to Four-Year Colleges 2001 www.petersons.com

New York

Polytechnic University, Farmingdale Campus (continued)
engineering technologies, physical sciences. **Graduate:** 1,613 in graduate degree programs.

From out-of-state	3%	Reside on campus	35%
Age 25 or older	6%	Transferred in	7%
International students	3%	African Americans	11%
Asian Americans/Pacific Islanders	37%	Hispanic Americans	6%
Native Americans	0.4%		

Faculty 312 (52% full-time).

Expenses (1999–2000) *Comprehensive fee:* $26,280 includes full-time tuition ($20,210), mandatory fees ($600), and room and board ($5470). Full-time tuition and fees vary according to course load. Room and board charges vary according to housing facility and location. *Part-time tuition:* $640 per credit. *Part-time fees:* $200 per term part-time. Part-time tuition and fees vary according to course load. *Payment plans:* tuition prepayment, deferred payment. *Waivers:* minority students and employees or children of employees.

Library Long Island Center Library. *Operations spending 1999–2000:* $1.2 million. *Collection:* 48,100 titles, 110 serial subscriptions, 50 audiovisual materials.

College life *Housing:* Option: coed. *Social organizations:* national fraternities, local fraternities, local sororities, coed fraternity; 15% of eligible men and 15% of eligible women are members. *Most popular organizations:* Tau Delta Phi, Omega Phi Alpha, Society of Women Engineers, Residence Hall Association, Student Government Organization.

Campus security Controlled dormitory access, patrols by trained security personnel.

After graduation *Career center:* 2 full-time, 1 part-time personnel. Services include job fairs, resume preparation, interview workshops, resume referral, career counseling, careers library, job bank, job interviews. **Graduate education:** 8% of class of 1999 went directly to graduate and professional school.

Freshmen 1,389 applied, 979 admitted, 468 enrolled.

Average high school GPA	3.3	SAT verbal scores above 500	76%
SAT math scores above 500	99%	ACT above 18	N/R
1998 freshmen returning in 1999	79%		

Application *Options:* Common Application, electronic application, deferred entrance. *Application fee:* $40. *Required:* essay or personal statement; high school transcript; 2 letters of recommendation. *Recommended:* interview.

Standardized tests *Admission: Required:* SAT I or ACT. *Recommended:* SAT II Subject Tests, SAT II: Writing Test.

Significant dates *Application deadlines:* rolling (freshmen), rolling (transfers). *Financial aid deadline:* continuous.

Freshman Application Contact
Mr. John Steven Kerge, Dean of Admissions, Long Island Center, Polytechnic University, Farmingdale Campus, Route 110, Farmingdale, NY 11735-3995. **Phone:** 516-755-4200. **Toll-free phone:** 800-POLYTECH. **Fax:** 516-755-4404. **E-mail:** admitme@poly.edu

Visit CollegeQuest.com for information on majors offered and athletics.

PRACTICAL BIBLE COLLEGE
Bible School Park, New York

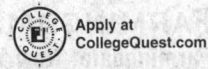
Apply at CollegeQuest.com

- **Independent nondenominational**, 4-year, founded 1900
- **Degrees** associate and bachelor's
- **Suburban** 22-acre campus with easy access to Syracuse
- **Coed**, 209 undergraduate students, 87% full-time, 43% women, 57% men
- **Minimally difficult** entrance level, 86% of applicants were admitted
- **18:1 student-to-undergraduate faculty ratio**
- **$6370 tuition** and fees
- **$4630 average financial aid** package, $4804 average indebtedness upon graduation, $1.9 million endowment

Students *Undergraduates:* 181 full-time, 28 part-time. Students come from 10 states and territories, 3 other countries. *The most frequently chosen baccalaureate field is:* philosophy.

From out-of-state	21%	Reside on campus	61%
Age 25 or older	29%	Transferred in	10%
International students	2%	African Americans	1%
Asian Americans/Pacific Islanders	2%	Hispanic Americans	1%

Faculty 23 (26% full-time), 43% with terminal degrees.

Expenses (1999–2000) *Comprehensive fee:* $10,170 includes full-time tuition ($5800), mandatory fees ($570), and room and board ($3800). Room and board charges vary according to housing facility. *Part-time tuition:* $245 per credit. *Part-time fees:* $215 per term part-time. Part-time tuition and fees vary according to class time and course load. *Payment plan:* installment. *Waivers:* children of alumni and employees or children of employees.

Library Alice E. Chatlos Library. *Operations spending 1999–2000:* $116,609. *Collection:* 57,000 titles, 644 serial subscriptions, 7,957 audiovisual materials.

College life *Housing:* on-campus residence required through senior year. *Options:* men-only, women-only. *Most popular organizations:* Student Missionary Fellowship, Student Wives Fellowship, Student Life Committee, Married Couples Fellowship.

Campus security 24-hour emergency response devices and patrols, student patrols, late-night transport-escort service.

After graduation *Career center:* 1 full-time personnel. Services include resume referral, career counseling.

Freshmen 64 applied, 55 admitted, 48 enrolled.

Average high school GPA	3.21	SAT verbal scores above 500	N/R
SAT math scores above 500	N/R	ACT above 18	62%
From top 10% of their h.s. class	11%	From top quarter	18%
From top half	41%	1998 freshmen returning in 1999	82%

Application *Options:* eApply at www.CollegeQuest.com, Common Application, deferred entrance. *Application fee:* $25. *Required:* high school transcript; 2 letters of recommendation; references. *Required for some:* essay or personal statement. *Recommended:* minimum 2.0 GPA; interview.

Standardized tests *Admission: Required:* SAT I or ACT. *Recommended:* ACT.

Significant dates *Application deadlines:* rolling (freshmen), rolling (transfers). *Financial aid deadline priority date:* 7/15.

Freshman Application Contact
Mrs. Suzanne VanWormer, Associate Director of Admissions, Practical Bible College, PO Box 601, Bible School Park, NY 13737-0601. **Phone:** 607-729-1581 Ext. 406. **Toll-free phone:** 800-331-4137 Ext. 406. **Fax:** 607-729-2962. **E-mail:** pbc@lakenet.org

Visit CollegeQuest.com for information on majors offered and athletics. College video available at CollegeQuest.com.

PRATT INSTITUTE
Brooklyn, New York

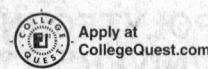
Apply at CollegeQuest.com

- **Independent**, comprehensive, founded 1887
- **Degrees** associate, bachelor's, and master's
- **Urban** 25-acre campus
- **Coed**, 2,752 undergraduate students, 91% full-time, 49% women, 51% men
- **Moderately difficult** entrance level, 50% of applicants were admitted
- **12:1 student-to-undergraduate faculty ratio**
- **$20,084 tuition** and fees
- **$12,590 average financial aid** package, $20.8 million endowment

Pratt Institute, one of the premier art, design, writing, and architecture schools nationwide, is located in the historic Clinton Hill section of Brooklyn, just 25 minutes from downtown Manhattan. The majority of Pratt's freshmen live on the Institute's 25-acre tree-lined campus. Pratt offers 4-year bachelor's, 2-year associate, and combined bachelor's and master's degrees.

Students *Undergraduates:* 2,510 full-time, 242 part-time. Students come from 41 states and territories, 38 other countries. **Graduate:** 1,396 in graduate degree programs.

Reside on campus	55%	Age 25 or older	27%
Transferred in	11%	International students	16%
African Americans	8%	Asian Americans/Pacific Islanders	10%
Hispanic Americans	7%	Native Americans	0.1%

Faculty 653 (15% full-time).

Expenses (2000–2001) *Comprehensive fee:* $27,884 includes full-time tuition ($19,524), mandatory fees ($560), and room and board ($7800).

College room only: $4700. *Part-time tuition:* $620 per credit. *Part-time fees:* $167 per term part-time. *Payment plans:* installment, deferred payment. *Waivers:* employees or children of employees.

Library Pratt Institute Library. *Operations spending 1999–2000:* $1.2 million. *Collection:* 172,000 titles, 540 serial subscriptions, 2,851 audiovisual materials.

College life *Housing: Option:* coed. *Social organizations:* national fraternities, local fraternities, local sororities; 5% of eligible men and 3% of eligible women are members. *Most popular organizations:* Travel and Recreation, student newspaper, athletic clubs, Performing Arts Committee.

Campus security 24-hour emergency response devices and patrols, late-night transport-escort service.

After graduation 23 organizations recruited on campus 1997–98. 95% of class of 1998 had job offers within 6 months. *Career center:* 5 full-time personnel. Services include resume preparation, resume referral, career counseling, careers library, job bank, job interviews.

Freshmen 3,387 applied, 1,702 admitted, 644 enrolled.

Average high school GPA	3.2	SAT verbal scores above 500	65%
SAT math scores above 500	56%	ACT above 18	N/R
From top 10% of their h.s. class	20%	From top quarter	42%
From top half	83%	1998 freshmen returning in 1999	90%

Application *Options:* eApply at www.CollegeQuest.com, Common Application, electronic application, early decision, deferred entrance. *Application fee:* $35. *Required:* essay or personal statement; high school transcript; 1 letter of recommendation. *Required for some:* interview; portfolio. *Recommended:* minimum 3.0 GPA.

Standardized tests *Admission: Required:* SAT I or ACT.

Significant dates *Application deadlines:* 2/1 (freshmen), rolling (transfers). *Early decision:* 11/1. *Notification:* 12/1 (early decision). *Financial aid deadline priority date:* 2/1.

Freshman Application Contact
Ms. Judith Aaron, Vice President for Enrollment, Pratt Institute, DeKalb Hall, 200 Willoughby Avenue, Brooklyn, NY 11205-3899. **Phone:** 718-636-3669. **Toll-free phone:** 800-331-0834. **Fax:** 718-636-3670. **E-mail:** info@pratt.edu

Visit CollegeQuest.com for information on majors offered and athletics.

■ *See page 2286 for a narrative description.*

PURCHASE COLLEGE, STATE UNIVERSITY OF NEW YORK
Purchase, New York

- **State-supported**, comprehensive, founded 1967
- **Degrees** bachelor's and master's
- **Small-town** 500-acre campus with easy access to New York City
- **Coed**, 2,991 undergraduate students, 92% full-time, 56% women, 44% men
- **Moderately difficult** entrance level, 35% of applicants were admitted
- **22:1** student-to-undergraduate faculty ratio
- **37% graduate** in 6 years or less
- **$3949 tuition** and fees (in-state); $8849 (out-of-state)
- **$8510 average financial aid** package, $26 million endowment

Purchase College combines excellent liberal arts and sciences programs with professional conservatory programs in the visual and performing arts. Purchase offers undergraduate degree programs in music, film, acting, stage design/technology (including costume design), dance, art and design, humanities, social sciences, and natural sciences. New programs in new media arts management and journalism are developing. Purchase is a small college community that offers students the opportunity to enter into apprentice relationships with artists, performers, scholars, and scientists who are making significant contributions to their fields. Purchase is committed to fostering educational creativity in a climate of artistic and intellectual freedom.

Part of State University of New York System.

Students *Undergraduates:* 2,748 full-time, 243 part-time. Students come from 44 states and territories, 29 other countries. *The most frequently chosen baccalaureate fields are:* liberal arts/general studies, English, visual/performing arts. *Graduate:* 119 in graduate degree programs.

From out-of-state	17%	Reside on campus	54%
Age 25 or older	16%	Transferred in	14%
International students	4%	African Americans	9%
Asian Americans/Pacific Islanders	3%	Hispanic Americans	10%
Native Americans	0.3%		

Faculty 365 (32% full-time).

Expenses (1999–2000) *Tuition, state resident:* full-time $3400; part-time $137 per credit. *Tuition, nonresident:* full-time $8300; part-time $346 per credit. *Required fees:* full-time $549; $18 per credit. *College room and board:* $5942; room only: $3572. Room and board charges vary according to board plan and housing facility. *Payment plan:* installment. *Waivers:* senior citizens and employees or children of employees.

Library Purchase College Library. *Operations spending 1999–2000:* $1.2 million. *Collection:* 171,998 titles, 1,131 serial subscriptions, 13,449 audiovisual materials.

College life *Housing: Option:* coed. *Most popular organizations:* Student Union, WPUR radio station, Latinos Unidos, Gay/Lesbian/Bi-Sexual/Transgender Union, Organization of African People in America.

Campus security 24-hour emergency response devices and patrols, late-night transport-escort service, controlled dormitory access, 24-hour patrols by police officers.

After graduation 49% of class of 1998 had job offers within 6 months. *Career center:* 2 full-time personnel. Services include resume preparation, interview workshops, career/interest testing, career counseling, careers library, job bank, job interviews.

Freshmen 5,384 applied, 1,892 admitted, 646 enrolled.

SAT verbal scores above 500	67%	SAT math scores above 500	54%
ACT above 18	91%	1998 freshmen returning in 1999	71%

Application *Options:* early admission, deferred entrance. *Application fee:* $30. *Required:* high school transcript; minimum 3.0 GPA. *Required for some:* essay or personal statement; 1 letter of recommendation; interview; audition; portfolio.

Standardized tests *Admission: Required:* SAT I.

Significant dates *Application deadlines:* 7/1 (freshmen), rolling (transfers). *Financial aid deadline priority date:* 3/15.

Freshman Application Contact
Ms. Betsy Immergut, Director of Admissions, Purchase College, State University of New York, 735 Anderson Hill Road, Purchase, NY 10577-1400. **Phone:** 914-251-6300. **E-mail:** admissn@brick.purchase.edu

Visit CollegeQuest.com for information on majors offered and athletics.

■ *See page 2296 for a narrative description.*

QUEENS COLLEGE OF THE CITY UNIVERSITY OF NEW YORK
Flushing, New York

- **State and locally supported**, comprehensive, founded 1937
- **Degrees** bachelor's and master's
- **Urban** 76-acre campus
- **Coed**, 11,041 undergraduate students, 65% full-time, 63% women, 37% men
- **Very difficult** entrance level, 58% of applicants were admitted
- **19:1** student-to-undergraduate faculty ratio
- **40.71% graduate** in 6 years or less
- **$3403 tuition** and fees (in-state); $7003 (out-of-state)

College years are a time to discover and dream, a time to broaden horizons. Queens College gives students sophisticated technology, distinguished professors teaching innovative programs, and a stimulating environment. Students come from around the globe and around the corner and help fellow students travel the world without leaving New York. Discover Queens College and get more than a piece of paper—get an education.

Part of City University of New York System.

Students *Undergraduates:* 7,170 full-time, 3,871 part-time. Students come from 10 states and territories, 130 other countries. *The most frequently chosen baccalaureate fields are:* business/marketing, education, social sciences and history. *Graduate:* 4,120 in graduate degree programs.

New York

Queens College of the City University of New York (continued)

From out-of-state	0.1%	Age 25 or older	39%
Transferred in	11%	International students	4%
African Americans	10%	Asian Americans/Pacific Islanders	16%
Hispanic Americans	16%	Native Americans	0.1%

Faculty 899 (60% full-time).

Expenses (2000–2001) *Tuition, state resident:* full-time $3200; part-time $135 per credit. *Tuition, nonresident:* full-time $6800; part-time $285 per credit. *Required fees:* full-time $203; $71 per term part-time. Full-time tuition and fees vary according to program. Part-time tuition and fees vary according to program. *Payment plan:* installment. *Waivers:* senior citizens and employees or children of employees.

Library Benjamin S. Rosenthal Library plus 1 other. *Collection:* 3,439 serial subscriptions, 94,631 audiovisual materials.

College life *Housing:* college housing not available. *Social organizations:* national fraternities, national sororities, social clubs; 35% of eligible men and 30% of eligible women are members.

Campus security 24-hour emergency response devices and patrols.

After graduation 100 organizations recruited on campus 1997–98. *Career center:* 3 full-time personnel. Services include job fairs, resume preparation, resume referral, career/interest testing, career counseling, careers library, job bank, job interviews. *Graduate education:* 25% of class of 1999 went directly to graduate and professional school: 3% medicine, 1% business, 1% law.

Freshmen 4,632 applied, 2,686 admitted, 1,037 enrolled.

Average high school GPA	3.4	SAT verbal scores above 500	70%
SAT math scores above 500	76%	ACT above 18	N/R
From top 10% of their h.s. class	24%	From top quarter	61%
From top half	95%	1998 freshmen returning in 1999	82%

Application *Options:* electronic application, early admission, deferred entrance. *Application fee:* $40. *Required:* high school transcript; minimum 3.0 GPA. *Required for some:* essay or personal statement; 2 letters of recommendation; interview.

Standardized tests *Admission: Required:* SAT I or ACT. *Recommended:* SAT II Subject Tests. *Required for some:* SAT II Subject Tests.

Significant dates *Application deadlines:* 1/1 (freshmen), 3/1 (transfers). *Notification:* continuous until 6/1 (freshmen). **Financial aid deadline priority date:** 5/1.

Freshman Application Contact
Undergraduate Admissions Office, Queens College of the City University of New York, Undergraduate Admissions, Kiely Hall 217, 65-30 Kissena Boulevard, Flushing, NY 11367. **Phone:** 718-997-5600. **Fax:** 718-997-5617. **E-mail:** admissions@qc.edu

Visit CollegeQuest.com for information on majors offered and athletics. College video available at CollegeQuest.com.

■ *See page 2298 for a narrative description.*

RABBINICAL ACADEMY MESIVTA RABBI CHAIM BERLIN
Brooklyn, New York

Admissions Office Contact
Rabbinical Academy Mesivta Rabbi Chaim Berlin, 1605 Coney Island Avenue, Brooklyn, NY 11230-4715.

RABBINICAL COLLEGE BETH SHRAGA
Monsey, New York

Admissions Office Contact
Rabbinical College Beth Shraga, 28 Saddle River Road, Monsey, NY 10952-3035.

RABBINICAL COLLEGE BOBOVER YESHIVA B'NEI ZION
Brooklyn, New York

Admissions Office Contact
Rabbinical College Bobover Yeshiva B'nei Zion, 1577 Forty-eighth Street, Brooklyn, NY 11219.

RABBINICAL COLLEGE CH'SAN SOFER
Brooklyn, New York

Admissions Office Contact
Rabbinical College Ch'san Sofer, 1876 Fiftieth Street, Brooklyn, NY 11204.

RABBINICAL COLLEGE OF LONG ISLAND
Long Beach, New York

Admissions Office Contact
Rabbinical College of Long Island, 201 Magnolia Boulevard, Long Beach, NY 11561-3305.

RABBINICAL SEMINARY ADAS YEREIM
Brooklyn, New York

Admissions Office Contact
Rabbinical Seminary Adas Yereim, 185 Wilson Street, Brooklyn, NY 11211-7206.

RABBINICAL SEMINARY M'KOR CHAIM
Brooklyn, New York

Admissions Office Contact
Rabbinical Seminary M'kor Chaim, 1571 Fifty-fifth Street, Brooklyn, NY 11219.

RABBINICAL SEMINARY OF AMERICA
Forest Hills, New York

- **Independent Jewish**, comprehensive, founded 1933
- **Degrees** bachelor's, master's, and first professional
- **Urban** campus with easy access to New York City
- **Men** only
- **Very difficult** entrance level

Students *Undergraduates:* Students come from 18 states and territories, 2 other countries.

| Reside on campus | 90% | Age 25 or older | 2% |

Library Rabbinical Seminary of America Otzar HaSeforim Library plus 3 others. *Collection:* 30,000 titles, 50 serial subscriptions.

After graduation *Career center:* Services include resume referral, career counseling, job interviews. *Graduate education:* 100% of class of 1999 went directly to graduate and professional school: 67% theology, 33% graduate arts and sciences.

Freshmen

| SAT verbal scores above 500 | N/R | SAT math scores above 500 | N/R |
| ACT above 18 | N/R | | |

Application *Option:* early admission. *Application fee:* $0. *Required:* high school transcript; interview.

Significant dates *Application deadline:* 12/1 (freshmen).

Freshman Application Contact
Rabbi Abraham Semmel, Director of Admissions, Rabbinical Seminary of America, 92-15 Sixty-ninth Avenue, Forest Hills, NY 11375. **Phone:** 718-268-4700.

Visit CollegeQuest.com for information on majors offered and athletics.

REGENTS COLLEGE
Albany, New York

Regents College offers the independent learner significant flexibility in completing accredited associate, bachelor's, and master's degrees. Regents College has no residency requirement, allows students to transfer credit from a wide variety of sources, and is ideal for the student who has difficulty meeting

New York

matriculation requirements at traditional campuses. World Wide Web: http://www.regents.edu.

Students *Undergraduates:* Students come from 50 states and territories, 58 other countries. *Graduate:* 43 in graduate degree programs.

From out-of-state	83%	Age 25 or older	97%
International students	1%	African Americans	12%
Asian Americans/Pacific Islanders	5%	Hispanic Americans	4%
Native Americans	1%		

Expenses (1999–2000) *Tuition:* part-time $800 per year. *Required fees:* $350 per year part-time. Full-time tuition and fees vary according to degree level. Part-time tuition and fees vary according to degree level. *Payment plans:* tuition prepayment, installment, deferred payment. *Waivers:* employees or children of employees.

College life *Housing:* college housing not available.

After graduation *Career center:* Services include resume preparation, career/interest testing, career counseling, careers library.

Freshmen 9,113 applied, 9,113 admitted.

SAT verbal scores above 500	N/R	SAT math scores above 500	N/R
ACT above 18	N/R		

Application *Application fee:* $0.

Significant dates *Application deadlines:* rolling (freshmen), rolling (transfers). *Financial aid deadline priority date:* 7/1.

Freshman Application Contact Ms. Chari Leader, Dean of Enrollment Management, Regents College, 7 Columbia Circle, Albany, NY 12203-5159. **Phone:** 518-464-8500. **Toll-free phone:** 888-647-2388. **Fax:** 518-464-8777. **E-mail:** rcinfo@regents.edu

Visit CollegeQuest.com for information on majors offered and athletics.

■ *See page 2316 for a narrative description.*

RENSSELAER POLYTECHNIC INSTITUTE
Troy, New York

Apply at CollegeQuest.com

- **Independent**, university, founded 1824
- **Degrees** bachelor's, master's, and doctoral
- **Suburban** 260-acre campus with easy access to Albany
- **Coed**, 4,867 undergraduate students, 99% full-time, 24% women, 76% men
- **Very difficult** entrance level, 78% of applicants were admitted
- **18:1 student-to-undergraduate faculty ratio**
- **73% graduate** in 6 years or less
- **$22,955 tuition** and fees
- **$17,537 average financial aid** package, $22,300 average indebtedness upon graduation, $516.2 million endowment

Hands-on programs emphasize the practical and responsible application of technology and prepare students for meaningful careers in a global society. Tomorrow's leaders are educated in the fields of architecture, engineering, humanities and social sciences, information technology, management, and science. The 4,800 undergraduate students come from all 50 states and 78 countries.

Students *Undergraduates:* 4,850 full-time, 17 part-time. Students come from 53 states and territories, 78 other countries. *The most frequently chosen baccalaureate fields are:* business/marketing, architecture, engineering/engineering technologies. *Graduate:* 2,724 in graduate degree programs.

From out-of-state	49%	Reside on campus	57%
Age 25 or older	3%	Transferred in	3%
International students	4%	African Americans	4%
Asian Americans/Pacific Islanders	11%	Hispanic Americans	4%
Native Americans	0.4%		

Faculty 360 (95% full-time), 96% with terminal degrees.

Expenses (1999–2000) *Comprehensive fee:* $30,647 includes full-time tuition ($22,300), mandatory fees ($655), and room and board ($7692). *College room only:* $4250. Room and board charges vary according to board plan, housing facility, and student level. *Part-time tuition:* $665 per credit hour. *Part-time fees:* $328 per term part-time. Part-time tuition and fees vary according to location. *Payment plan:* installment. *Waivers:* employees or children of employees.

Library Folsom Library plus 1 other. *Collection:* 309,171 titles, 10,210 serial subscriptions.

College life *Housing:* on-campus residence required in freshman year. *Options:* coed, men-only, disabled students. *Social organizations:* national fraternities, national sororities, local fraternities, local sororities; 30% of eligible men and 20% of eligible women are members. *Most popular organizations:* Ski Club, musical organizations, weightlifting, ballroom dance, campus radio station.

Campus security 24-hour emergency response devices and patrols, late-night transport-escort service, controlled dormitory access, campus foot patrols at night.

After graduation 377 organizations recruited on campus 1997–98. 77% of class of 1998 had job offers within 6 months. *Career center:* 5 full-time, 6 part-time personnel. Services include job fairs, resume preparation, interview workshops, resume referral, career/interest testing, career counseling, careers library, job bank, job interviews. *Graduate education:* 21% of class of 1999 went directly to graduate and professional school.

Freshmen 5,264 applied, 4,126 admitted, 1,323 enrolled. 26 National Merit Scholars, 101 valedictorians.

SAT verbal scores above 500	94%	SAT math scores above 500	100%
ACT above 18	100%	From top 10% of their h.s. class	54%
From top quarter	86%	From top half	98%
1998 freshmen returning in 1999	90%		

Application *Options:* eApply at www.CollegeQuest.com, Common Application, electronic application, early admission, early decision, deferred entrance. *Application fee:* $50. *Required:* essay or personal statement; high school transcript; 1 letter of recommendation. *Required for some:* portfolio for architecture program.

Standardized tests *Admission:* Required: SAT I or ACT. *Required for some:* SAT II Subject Tests.

Significant dates *Application deadlines:* 1/1 (freshmen), 7/1 (transfers). *Early decision:* 11/15. *Notification:* 3/15 (freshmen), 12/18 (early decision). *Financial aid deadline priority date:* 2/15.

Freshman Application Contact Ms. Teresa Duffy, Dean of Admissions, Rensselaer Polytechnic Institute, 110 8th Street, Troy, NY 12180-3590. **Phone:** 518-276-6216. **Toll-free phone:** 800-448-6562. **Fax:** 518-276-4072. **E-mail:** admissions@rpi.edu

Visit CollegeQuest.com for information on majors offered and athletics. College video and electronic viewbook available at CollegeQuest.com.

■ *See page 2322 for a narrative description.*

ROBERTS WESLEYAN COLLEGE
Rochester, New York

- **Independent**, comprehensive, founded 1866, affiliated with Free Methodist Church of North America
- **Degrees** associate, bachelor's, and master's
- **Suburban** 75-acre campus
- **Coed**, 1,128 undergraduate students, 93% full-time, 66% women, 34% men
- **Moderately difficult** entrance level, 94% of applicants were admitted
- **14:1 student-to-undergraduate faculty ratio**
- **$13,614 tuition** and fees
- **$12,503 average financial aid** package, $17,436 average indebtedness upon graduation, $8.7 million endowment

Roberts Wesleyan College President William C. Crothers is among only 50 American college and university presidents recognized by the John Templeton Foundation for outstanding leadership in student character development. Dr. Crothers is profiled in the recently released *Templeton Guide: Colleges That Encourage Character Development*. Roberts Wesleyan College is also profiled for its character development programs.

Students *Undergraduates:* 1,051 full-time, 77 part-time. Students come from 11 other countries. *The most frequently chosen baccalaureate fields are:* business/marketing, education, health professions and related sciences. *Graduate:* 256 in graduate degree programs.

New York

Roberts Wesleyan College (continued)

From out-of-state 11% Reside on campus 66%
Age 25 or older 63% Transferred in 5%
International students 5% African Americans 4%
Asian Americans/Pacific Islanders 1% Hispanic Americans 2%
Native Americans 0.4%

Faculty 128 (59% full-time), 47% with terminal degrees.

Expenses (1999–2000) *One-time required fee:* $100. *Comprehensive fee:* $18,228 includes full-time tuition ($13,100), mandatory fees ($514), and room and board ($4614). *College room only:* $3174. Room and board charges vary according to board plan. *Part-time tuition:* $270 per hour. Part-time tuition and fees vary according to course load. *Payment plan:* installment. *Waivers:* employees or children of employees.

Library Ora A. Sprague Library. *Operations spending 1999–2000:* $396,000. *Collection:* 106,970 titles, 792 serial subscriptions, 3,412 audiovisual materials.

College life *Housing:* on-campus residence required through senior year. *Options:* men-only, women-only. *Most popular organizations:* Habitat for Humanity, Foot of the Cross, Radiant Light, nursing club, drama club.

Campus security 24-hour emergency response devices and patrols, late-night transport-escort service, controlled dormitory access, 24-hour Resident Life staff on-call.

After graduation 90 organizations recruited on campus 1997–98. 80% of class of 1998 had job offers within 6 months. *Career center:* 1 full-time personnel. Services include job fairs, resume preparation, interview workshops, career/interest testing, career counseling, careers library, job bank, job interviews. *Graduate education:* 19% of class of 1999 went directly to graduate and professional school: 6% business, 6% education, 4% theology, 1% law, 1% medicine.

Freshmen 522 applied, 489 admitted, 272 enrolled. 7 valedictorians.

Average high school GPA 3.1 SAT verbal scores above 500 68%
SAT math scores above 500 60% ACT above 18 89%
From top 10% of their h.s. class 22% From top quarter 49%
From top half 85% 1998 freshmen returning in 1999 78%

Application *Options:* early admission, deferred entrance. *Application fee:* $35. *Required:* essay or personal statement; high school transcript; 2 letters of recommendation. *Recommended:* minimum 2.5 GPA; interview.

Standardized tests *Admission: Required:* SAT I and SAT II or ACT.

Significant dates *Application deadlines:* 2/1 (freshmen), rolling (transfers). *Financial aid deadline priority date:* 3/15.

Freshman Application Contact
Ms. Linda Kurtz, Director of Admissions, Roberts Wesleyan College, 2301 Westside Drive, Rochester, NY 14624-1997. **Phone:** 716-594-6400. **Toll-free phone:** 800-777-4RWC. **Fax:** 716-594-6371.

Visit CollegeQuest.com for information on majors offered and athletics. College video available at CollegeQuest.com.

■ *See page 2342 for a narrative description.*

ROCHESTER INSTITUTE OF TECHNOLOGY
Rochester, New York

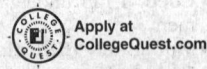
Apply at CollegeQuest.com

- **Independent**, comprehensive, founded 1829
- **Degrees** associate, bachelor's, master's, doctoral, and postbachelor's certificates
- **Suburban** 1,300-acre campus with easy access to Buffalo
- **Coed**, 9,902 undergraduate students, 85% full-time, 34% women, 66% men
- **Moderately difficult** entrance level, 77% of applicants were admitted
- **13:1 student-to-undergraduate faculty ratio**
- **60% graduate** in 6 years or less
- **$17,637 tuition** and fees
- **$14,700 average financial aid** package, $467.2 million endowment

Students *Undergraduates:* 8,446 full-time, 1,456 part-time. Students come from 50 states and territories, 85 other countries. *The most frequently chosen baccalaureate fields are:* engineering/engineering technologies, business/marketing, visual/performing arts. *Graduate:* 2,029 in graduate degree programs.

From out-of-state 40% Reside on campus 60%
Age 25 or older 24% Transferred in 9%
International students 5% African Americans 5%
Asian Americans/Pacific Islanders 5% Hispanic Americans 3%
Native Americans 0.4%

Faculty 1,091 (55% full-time), 44% with terminal degrees.

Expenses (1999–2000) *Comprehensive fee:* $24,489 includes full-time tuition ($17,328), mandatory fees ($309), and room and board ($6852). *College room only:* $3774. Full-time tuition and fees vary according to course load and program. Room and board charges vary according to board plan and housing facility. *Part-time tuition:* $414 per credit hour. *Part-time fees:* $22 per term part-time. Part-time tuition and fees vary according to class time, course level, course load, and program. *Payment plans:* tuition prepayment, installment, deferred payment. *Waivers:* employees or children of employees.

Library Wallace Memorial Library. *Operations spending 1999–2000:* $3.8 million. *Collection:* 350,000 titles, 4,305 serial subscriptions, 8,215 audiovisual materials.

College life *Housing:* on-campus residence required in freshman year. *Options:* coed, men-only, women-only, disabled students. *Social organizations:* national fraternities, national sororities, local fraternities, local sororities; 8% of eligible men and 8% of eligible women are members. *Most popular organizations:* fraternities/sororities, campus radio station, Campus Weekly Magazine, student government, Off-Campus Student Association.

Campus security 24-hour emergency response devices and patrols, student patrols, late-night transport-escort service.

After graduation 600 organizations recruited on campus 1997–98. 92% of class of 1998 had job offers within 6 months. *Career center:* 20 full-time, 6 part-time personnel. Services include job fairs, resume preparation, interview workshops, resume referral, career/interest testing, career counseling, careers library, job bank, job interviews, electronic resume submission on internet. *Graduate education:* 10% of class of 1999 went directly to graduate and professional school.

Freshmen 7,497 applied, 5,744 admitted, 2,186 enrolled. 16 National Merit Scholars, 40 valedictorians.

Average high school GPA 3.7 SAT verbal scores above 500 85%
SAT math scores above 500 92% ACT above 18 99%
From top 10% of their h.s. class 25% From top quarter 58%
From top half 89% 1998 freshmen returning in 1999 84%

Application *Options:* eApply at www.CollegeQuest.com, Common Application, electronic application, early admission, early decision, deferred entrance. *Application fee:* $40. *Required:* essay or personal statement; high school transcript. *Required for some:* portfolio for art program. *Recommended:* minimum 3.0 GPA; 1 letter of recommendation; interview.

Standardized tests *Admission: Required:* SAT I or ACT.

Significant dates *Application deadlines:* 7/1 (freshmen), rolling (transfers). *Early decision:* 12/15. *Notification:* 1/15 (early decision). *Financial aid deadline priority date:* 3/15.

Freshman Application Contact
Mr. Daniel Shelley, Director of Admissions, Rochester Institute of Technology, 60 Lomb Memorial Drive, Rochester, NY 14623-5604. **Phone:** 716-475-6631. **Fax:** 716-475-7424. **E-mail:** admissons@rit.edu

Visit CollegeQuest.com for information on majors offered and athletics. College video and electronic viewbook available at CollegeQuest.com.

■ *See page 2344 for a narrative description.*

RUSSELL SAGE COLLEGE
Troy, New York

Apply at CollegeQuest.com

- **Independent**, 4-year, founded 1916
- **Degree** bachelor's
- **Urban** 8-acre campus
- **Women** only, 827 undergraduate students, 94% full-time
- **Moderately difficult** entrance level, 93% of applicants were admitted
- **11:1 student-to-undergraduate faculty ratio**
- **68% graduate** in 6 years or less
- **$15,300 tuition** and fees
- **$12,583 average financial aid** package, $11,350 average indebtedness upon graduation, $31.2 million system endowment

New York

Russell Sage College, located in the Capital Region of New York State, is a small college for women where individuals count and are consistently challenged. The College offers liberal arts and professional degree programs in fields such as the health sciences, humanities, natural sciences and mathematics, and social and professional sciences. To schedule a campus visit, students should call 518-244-2217 or 888-VERY-SAGE (toll-free). E-mail: rscadmin@sage.edu; Web site: http://www.sage.edu.

Part of The Sage Colleges.

Students *Undergraduates:* 779 full-time, 48 part-time. Students come from 18 states and territories, 1 other country. *The most frequently chosen baccalaureate fields are:* education, health professions and related sciences, visual/performing arts.

From out-of-state	15%	Reside on campus	52%
Age 25 or older	19%	Transferred in	11%
African Americans	5%	Asian Americans/Pacific Islanders	3%
Hispanic Americans	3%	Native Americans	0.4%

Faculty 108 (65% full-time), 41% with terminal degrees.

Expenses (1999–2000) *Comprehensive fee:* $21,650 includes full-time tuition ($14,920), mandatory fees ($380), and room and board ($6350). *College room only:* $3250. Room and board charges vary according to board plan and housing facility. *Part-time tuition:* $500 per credit hour. Part-time tuition and fees vary according to program. *Waivers:* senior citizens and employees or children of employees.

Library Troy and Albany Campus Libraries plus 2 others. *System-wide operations spending 1999–2000:* $1.5 million. *Collection:* 204,667 titles, 1,372 serial subscriptions, 12,680 audiovisual materials.

College life *Housing:* on-campus residence required through senior year. *Option:* women-only. *Most popular organizations:* student government, Sage Recreation Association, physical therapy club, crew club, Black-Latin Student Alliance.

Campus security 24-hour emergency response devices and patrols, late-night transport-escort service, controlled dormitory access.

After graduation 33 organizations recruited on campus 1997–98. 70% of class of 1998 had job offers within 6 months. *Career center:* 7 full-time, 3 part-time personnel. Services include job fairs, resume preparation, resume referral, career/interest testing, career counseling, careers library, job bank, job interviews. *Graduate education:* 42% of class of 1999 went directly to graduate and professional school: 34% graduate arts and sciences, 3% education, 2% law, 1% business.

Freshmen 377 applied, 349 admitted, 109 enrolled.

SAT verbal scores above 500	70%	SAT math scores above 500	60%
ACT above 18	100%	From top 10% of their h.s. class	18%
From top quarter	53%	From top half	85%
1998 freshmen returning in 1999	80%		

Application *Options:* eApply at www.CollegeQuest.com, Common Application, electronic application, early admission, early decision, deferred entrance. *Application fee:* $30. *Required:* essay or personal statement; high school transcript; minimum 2.0 GPA; 2 letters of recommendation. *Recommended:* interview.

Standardized tests *Admission: Required:* SAT I or ACT.

Significant dates *Application deadlines:* 8/1 (freshmen), rolling (transfers). *Early decision:* 12/1. *Notification:* 12/15 (early decision). *Financial aid deadline priority date:* 3/1.

Freshman Application Contact
Ms. Joanna Boyd, Associate Director of Admissions, Russell Sage College, 45 Ferry Street, Troy, NY 12180-4115. **Phone:** 518-244-2217. **Toll-free phone:** 888-VERY-SAGE (in-state); 888-VERY SAGE (out-of-state). **Fax:** 518-244-6880. **E-mail:** rscadm@sage.edu

Visit CollegeQuest.com for information on majors offered and athletics.

■ *See page 2362 for a narrative description.*

ST. BONAVENTURE UNIVERSITY
St. Bonaventure, New York

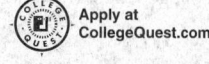
Apply at CollegeQuest.com

■ **Independent**, comprehensive, founded 1858, affiliated with Roman Catholic Church

■ **Degrees** bachelor's, master's, post-master's, and postbachelor's certificates
■ **Small-town** 600-acre campus
■ **Coed**, 2,116 undergraduate students, 99% full-time, 52% women, 48% men
■ **Moderately difficult** entrance level, 91% of applicants were admitted
■ **17:1 student-to-undergraduate faculty ratio**
■ **64.17% graduate** in 6 years or less
■ **$14,430 tuition** and fees
■ **$12,811 average financial aid** package, $16,402 average indebtedness upon graduation, $14.5 million endowment

Offering more than 30 majors and Division I athletics, St. Bonaventure University attracts exceptional students from 36 states and 10 countries. Adding to the Bonaventure experience are a broadcast journalism laboratory, an expanded fiber-optic computer network, an endowed visiting professorship, a modern language laboratory, a regional arts center, and a dynamic intramural program. *U.S. News & World Report* repeatedly ranks St. Bonaventure in its "top tier" of regional universities.

Students *Undergraduates:* 2,090 full-time, 26 part-time. Students come from 36 states and territories, 9 other countries. *The most frequently chosen baccalaureate fields are:* business/marketing, education, social sciences and history. *Graduate:* 622 in graduate degree programs.

From out-of-state	21%	Reside on campus	77%
Age 25 or older	2%	Transferred in	3%
International students	1%	African Americans	1%
Asian Americans/Pacific Islanders	1%	Hispanic Americans	1%
Native Americans	0.3%		

Faculty 221 (67% full-time), 81% with terminal degrees.

Expenses (1999–2000) *Comprehensive fee:* $20,230 includes full-time tuition ($13,880), mandatory fees ($550), and room and board ($5800). *Part-time tuition:* $440 per credit hour. *Payment plans:* installment, deferred payment. *Waivers:* senior citizens and employees or children of employees.

Library Friedsam Library. *Operations spending 1999–2000:* $906,811. *Collection:* 224,160 titles.

College life *Housing:* on-campus residence required through junior year. *Options:* coed, men-only, women-only, disabled students. *Most popular organizations:* student government, Student Programming Board, campus media, Bonaventure Business Association, Student Ambassadors.

Campus security 24-hour emergency response devices and patrols, student patrols, late-night transport-escort service.

After graduation 20 organizations recruited on campus 1997–98. *Career center:* 3 full-time personnel. Services include job fairs, resume preparation, interview workshops, resume referral, career/interest testing, career counseling, careers library, job bank, job interviews.

Freshmen 1,546 applied, 1,407 admitted, 520 enrolled.

Average high school GPA	3.1	SAT verbal scores above 500	67%
SAT math scores above 500	71%	ACT above 18	69%
From top 10% of their h.s. class	12%	From top quarter	40%
From top half	73%	1998 freshmen returning in 1999	84%

Application *Options:* eApply at www.CollegeQuest.com, Common Application, early admission, deferred entrance. *Application fee:* $30. *Required:* high school transcript; 1 letter of recommendation. *Required for some:* essay or personal statement. *Recommended:* essay or personal statement; minimum 3.0 GPA; 3 letters of recommendation; interview.

Standardized tests *Admission: Required:* SAT I or ACT.

Significant dates *Application deadlines:* 4/1 (freshmen), 8/15 (transfers). *Financial aid deadline:* continuous.

Freshman Application Contact
Mr. Alexander P. Nazemetz, Director of Admissions, St. Bonaventure University, PO Box D, St. Bonaventure, NY 14778-2284. **Phone:** 716-375-2400. **Toll-free phone:** 800-462-5050. **Fax:** 716-375-2005. **E-mail:** admissions@sbu.edu

Visit CollegeQuest.com for information on majors offered and athletics.

■ *See page 2372 for a narrative description.*

New York

ST. FRANCIS COLLEGE
Brooklyn Heights, New York

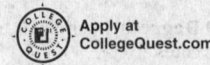 Apply at CollegeQuest.com

- **Independent Roman Catholic**, 4-year, founded 1884
- **Degrees** associate and bachelor's
- **Urban** 1-acre campus with easy access to New York City
- **Coed**, 2,305 undergraduate students, 81% full-time, 60% women, 40% men
- **Moderately difficult** entrance level, 76% of applicants were admitted
- **27:1 student-to-undergraduate faculty ratio**
- **47% graduate** in 6 years or less
- **$8410 tuition** and fees
- **$7990 average financial aid** package, $39.1 million endowment

St. Francis College offers an exceptional value in private college education in the New York area with low tuition and an emphasis on the values of the Franciscan tradition. Small, urban, friendly, and caring, St. Francis provides students with a college experience that translates into development of the whole person as well as academic achievement. Bachelor's and associate degrees in arts and science are offered in a wide array of disciplines. Proximity to Manhattan extends the classroom to offer students diverse cultural and career opportunities.

Students *Undergraduates:* Students come from 23 states and territories, 84 other countries.

From out-of-state	1%	Age 25 or older	24%
International students	10%	African Americans	21%
Asian Americans/Pacific Islanders	2%	Hispanic Americans	14%

Faculty 201 (33% full-time).
Expenses (1999–2000) *One-time required fee:* $25. *Tuition:* full-time $8250; part-time $285 per credit. *Required fees:* full-time $160; $20 per term part-time. Full-time tuition and fees vary according to course load. Part-time tuition and fees vary according to course load. *Payment plan:* installment. *Waivers:* employees or children of employees.
Library McGarry Library. *Operations spending 1999–2000:* $564,717. *Collection:* 139,725 titles, 571 serial subscriptions, 2,000 audiovisual materials.
College life *Housing:* college housing not available. *Social organizations:* national fraternities, local fraternities, local sororities; 5% of eligible men and 5% of eligible women are members. *Most popular organizations:* Troupers Drama Club, psychology club, Latin American Society, Caribbean Student Association, Black Student Association.
Campus security ID checks, crime awareness workshops.
After graduation 38 organizations recruited on campus 1997–98. 20% of class of 1998 had job offers within 6 months. *Career center:* 3 full-time personnel. Services include resume preparation, interview workshops, resume referral, career counseling, careers library, job bank, job interviews. *Graduate education:* 29% of class of 1999 went directly to graduate and professional school: 20% business, 6% graduate arts and sciences, 2% law, 1% medicine.
Freshmen 1,486 applied, 1,131 admitted. 3 class presidents, 4 valedictorians, 14 student government officers.

SAT verbal scores above 500	32%	SAT math scores above 500	33%
ACT above 18	N/R	1998 freshmen returning in 1999	82%

Application *Options:* eApply at www.CollegeQuest.com, electronic application, deferred entrance. *Application fee:* $20. *Required:* essay or personal statement; high school transcript; 1 letter of recommendation. *Required for some:* interview. *Recommended:* interview.
Standardized tests *Admission: Required:* SAT I or ACT.
Significant dates *Application deadlines:* rolling (freshmen), rolling (transfers). *Financial aid deadline priority date:* 2/15.
Freshman Application Contact
Br. George Larkin OSF, Dean of Admissions, St. Francis College, 180 Remsen Street, Brooklyn Heights, NY 11201-4398. **Phone:** 718-489-5200. **Fax:** 718-522-1274.
Visit CollegeQuest.com for information on majors offered and athletics.

■ *See page 2376 for a narrative description.*

ST. JOHN FISHER COLLEGE
Rochester, New York

- **Independent**, comprehensive, founded 1948, affiliated with Roman Catholic Church
- **Degrees** bachelor's and master's
- **Suburban** 136-acre campus
- **Coed**, 2,123 undergraduate students
- **Moderately difficult** entrance level, 80% of applicants were admitted
- **16:1 student-to-undergraduate faculty ratio**
- **62% graduate** in 6 years or less
- **$14,140 tuition** and fees
- **$10,794 average financial aid** package, $18,400 average indebtedness upon graduation, $22.5 million endowment

St. John Fisher College is in the midst of a $12-million building project designed to enhance both the academic and athletic facilities of the College. Classrooms and laboratories have been outfitted with state-of-the-market educational technology. An academic gateway, complete with a cyberspace café and learning resource center, is being built in summer 2000. This comes at a time when the College is experiencing record enrollment and the curriculum is expanding to meet the changing needs of the marketplace.

Students *Undergraduates:* Students come from 15 states and territories.

From out-of-state	3%

Faculty 228 (44% full-time).
Expenses (1999–2000) *One-time required fee:* $200. *Comprehensive fee:* $20,190 includes full-time tuition ($13,990), mandatory fees ($150), and room and board ($6050). Full-time tuition and fees vary according to course load. Room and board charges vary according to board plan. *Part-time tuition:* $395 per credit hour. Part-time tuition and fees vary according to course load. *Payment plans:* installment, deferred payment. *Waivers:* senior citizens and children of employees.
Library Charles V. Lavery Library plus 1 other. *Operations spending 1999–2000:* $795,633. *Collection:* 195,000 titles, 1,330 serial subscriptions, 27,666 audiovisual materials.
College life *Housing:* Options: coed, women-only, disabled students. *Most popular organizations:* student government, Student Activities Board, Commuter Council, Resident Student Network.
Campus security 24-hour emergency response devices and patrols, late-night transport-escort service.
After graduation 73 organizations recruited on campus 1997–98. *Career center:* 1 full-time personnel. Services include job fairs, resume preparation, resume referral, career counseling, careers library, job bank, job interviews. *Graduate education:* 12% of class of 1999 went directly to graduate and professional school.
Freshmen 1,482 applied, 1,180 admitted.

Average high school GPA	3.1	SAT verbal scores above 500	61%
SAT math scores above 500	61%	ACT above 18	91%
From top 10% of their h.s. class	16%	From top quarter	45%
From top half	78%	1998 freshmen returning in 1999	83%

Application *Options:* Common Application, electronic application, early admission, early decision, deferred entrance. *Application fee:* $25. *Required:* high school transcript; 1 letter of recommendation. *Recommended:* essay or personal statement; interview.
Standardized tests *Admission: Required:* SAT I or ACT.
Significant dates *Application deadlines:* rolling (freshmen), rolling (transfers). *Early decision:* 12/1. *Notification:* continuous until 9/1 (freshmen), 12/20 (early decision). *Financial aid deadline priority date:* 2/15.
Freshman Application Contact
Mr. Gerard J. Rooney, Vice President of Enrollment Management, St. John Fisher College, 3690 East Avenue, Rochester, NY 14618-3597. **Phone:** 716-385-8064. **Toll-free phone:** 800-444-4640. **Fax:** 716-385-8386. **E-mail:** admissions@sjfc.edu
Visit CollegeQuest.com for information on majors offered and athletics. College video available at CollegeQuest.com.

■ *See page 2382 for a narrative description.*

New York

ST. JOHN'S UNIVERSITY
Jamaica, New York

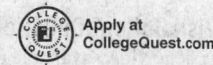
Apply at CollegeQuest.com

- **Independent**, university, founded 1870, affiliated with Roman Catholic Church
- **Degrees** associate, bachelor's, master's, doctoral, first professional, and post-master's certificates
- **Urban** 95-acre campus with easy access to New York City
- **Coed**, 11,973 undergraduate students, 91% full-time, 56% women, 44% men
- **Moderately difficult** entrance level, 83% of applicants were admitted
- **19:1 student-to-undergraduate faculty ratio**
- **66% graduate** in 6 years or less
- **$14,420 tuition** and fees
- **$10,517 average financial aid** package, $14,393 average indebtedness upon graduation, $107.9 million endowment

Founded in 1870, St. John's University prepares students for personal and professional success. St. John's combines a rigorous academic program, a close-knit campus environment, and nationally renowned athletic teams with the vast business and cultural opportunities of New York City. With magnificent new residence halls and the latest academic technologies, a St. John's education is the right step toward a bright future.

Students *Undergraduates:* 10,924 full-time, 1,049 part-time. Students come from 34 states and territories, 126 other countries. *The most frequently chosen baccalaureate fields are:* business/marketing, education, health professions and related sciences. *Graduate:* 1,027 in professional programs, 3,416 in other graduate degree programs.

From out-of-state	5%	Reside on campus	5%
Age 25 or older	10%	Transferred in	5%
International students	3%	African Americans	12%
Asian Americans/Pacific Islanders	13%	Hispanic Americans	15%
Native Americans	0.2%		

Faculty 1,087 (50% full-time).
Expenses (1999–2000) *Comprehensive fee:* $22,970 includes full-time tuition ($13,990), mandatory fees ($430), and room and board ($8550). Full-time tuition and fees vary according to class time, course level, course load, program, and student level. Room and board charges vary according to housing facility. *Part-time tuition:* $466 per credit. *Part-time fees:* $70 per term part-time. Part-time tuition and fees vary according to class time, course level, course load, program, and student level. *Payment plans:* guaranteed tuition, installment, deferred payment. *Waivers:* senior citizens and employees or children of employees.
Library St. John's University Library plus 2 others. *Operations spending 1999–2000:* $9.4 million. *Collection:* 14,275 serial subscriptions, 21,402 audiovisual materials.
College life *Housing: Option:* coed. *Social organizations:* national fraternities, national sororities, local fraternities, local sororities; 9% of eligible men and 8% of eligible women are members. *Most popular organizations:* Student Government, Incorporated, Student Programming Board, Community and University Services in Education, Haraya, American Pharmaceutical Association.
Campus security 24-hour emergency response devices and patrols, student patrols, late-night transport-escort service, controlled dormitory access.
After graduation 65% of class of 1998 had job offers within 6 months. *Career center:* 10 full-time, 2 part-time personnel. Services include job fairs, resume preparation, interview workshops, resume referral, career/interest testing, career counseling, careers library, job bank, job interviews. *Graduate education:* 18% of class of 1999 went directly to graduate and professional school: 5% graduate arts and sciences, 3% business, 3% education, 3% law, 1% medicine.
Freshmen 8,283 applied, 6,836 admitted, 2,696 enrolled.

Average high school GPA	3.4	SAT verbal scores above 500	48%
SAT math scores above 500	52%	ACT above 18	N/R
From top 10% of their h.s. class	16%	From top quarter	37%
From top half	70%	1998 freshmen returning in 1999	85%

Application *Options:* eApply at www.CollegeQuest.com, Common Application, electronic application, deferred entrance. *Application fee:* $30. *Required:* essay or personal statement; high school transcript; letters of recommendation.
Standardized tests *Admission: Required:* SAT I or ACT.

Significant dates *Application deadlines:* rolling (freshmen), rolling (transfers). *Financial aid deadline priority date:* 2/1.
Freshman Application Contact
Mr. Glenn Sklarin, Associate Vice President and Dean, Office of Enrollment Management, St. John's University, 8000 Utopia Parkway, Jamaica, NY 11439. **Phone:** 718-990-1984. **Toll-free phone:** 800-232-4SJU. **E-mail:** admissions@stjohns.edu
Visit CollegeQuest.com for information on majors offered and athletics.

- *See page 2386 for a narrative description.*

ST. JOSEPH'S COLLEGE, NEW YORK
Brooklyn, New York

- **Independent**, 4-year, founded 1916
- **Degree** bachelor's
- **Urban** campus
- **Coed**, 1,194 undergraduate students, 50% full-time, 78% women, 22% men
- **Moderately difficult** entrance level, 52% of applicants were admitted
- **13:1 student-to-undergraduate faculty ratio**
- **64% graduate** in 6 years or less
- **$8922 tuition** and fees
- **$7000 average financial aid** package, $14,000 average indebtedness upon graduation, $23.4 million endowment

For more than 80 years, St. Joseph's has provided a high-quality liberal arts education to a diverse group of students. Students can take advantage of small classes and individualized academic and career counseling. Preprofessional programs in law and medicine and career-oriented majors (education and accounting) afford students the opportunity to prepare for a successful career while obtaining a traditional liberal arts education.

Students *Undergraduates:* 592 full-time, 602 part-time. *The most frequently chosen baccalaureate fields are:* education, business/marketing, health professions and related sciences. *Graduate:* 27 in graduate degree programs.

From out-of-state	1%	Age 25 or older	66%
Transferred in	17%	African Americans	40%
Asian Americans/Pacific Islanders	5%	Hispanic Americans	8%

Faculty 143 (32% full-time).
Expenses (1999–2000) *Tuition:* full-time $8600; part-time $276 per credit. *Required fees:* full-time $322; $11 per credit; $5 per term part-time. Part-time tuition and fees vary according to course load. *Payment plans:* installment, deferred payment. *Waivers:* employees or children of employees.
Library McEntegart Hall Library. *Operations spending 1999–2000:* $1.1 million. *Collection:* 100,000 titles, 432 serial subscriptions, 4,482 audiovisual materials.
College life *Housing:* college housing not available. *Social organizations:* local fraternities, local sororities; 10% of eligible men and 6% of eligible women are members. *Most popular organizations:* admissions club, science club, dramatics, child study club, dance team.
Campus security Late-night transport-escort service.
After graduation 32 organizations recruited on campus 1997–98. 60% of class of 1998 had job offers within 6 months. *Career center:* 1 full-time personnel. Services include job fairs, resume preparation, career/interest testing, career counseling, careers library, job interviews. *Graduate education:* 40% of class of 1999 went directly to graduate and professional school.
Freshmen 542 applied, 281 admitted, 91 enrolled.

Average high school GPA	3.0	SAT verbal scores above 500	59%
SAT math scores above 500	44%	ACT above 18	N/R
From top 10% of their h.s. class	16%	From top quarter	49%
From top half	67%	1998 freshmen returning in 1999	87%

Application *Options:* early admission, deferred entrance. *Application fee:* $25. *Required:* high school transcript; minimum 3.0 GPA. *Required for some:* interview. *Recommended:* essay or personal statement; 2 letters of recommendation.
Standardized tests *Admission: Required:* SAT I.

New York

St. Joseph's College, New York (continued)

Significant dates *Application deadlines:* 8/15 (freshmen), 8/15 (transfers). *Notification:* continuous until 8/30 (freshmen). *Financial aid deadline priority date:* 2/25.

Freshman Application Contact
Ms. Mary Elizabeth Rohan, Director of Admissions, St. Joseph's College, New York, 245 Clinton Avenue, Brooklyn, NY 11205-3688. **Phone:** 718-636-6868. **Fax:** 718-636-7242. **E-mail:** mrohan@sjeny.edu

Visit CollegeQuest.com for information on majors offered and athletics. College video available at CollegeQuest.com.

■ *See page 2394 for a narrative description.*

ST. JOSEPH'S COLLEGE, SUFFOLK CAMPUS
Patchogue, New York

- **Independent**, comprehensive, founded 1916
- **Degrees** bachelor's and master's (master's degree in education only)
- **Small-town** 28-acre campus with easy access to New York City
- **Coed**, 2,859 undergraduate students, 69% full-time, 78% women, 22% men
- **Moderately difficult** entrance level, 78% of applicants were admitted
- **16:1 student-to-undergraduate faculty ratio**
- **$9182 tuition** and fees

Students *Undergraduates:* 1,964 full-time, 895 part-time. Students come from 2 states and territories. *The most frequently chosen baccalaureate fields are:* business/marketing, education, health professions and related sciences. *Graduate:* 80 in graduate degree programs.

Age 25 or older	36%	Transferred in	14%
African Americans	3%	Asian Americans/Pacific Islanders	1%
Hispanic Americans	5%	Native Americans	0.2%

Faculty 280 (29% full-time), 15% with terminal degrees.

Expenses (1999–2000) *Tuition:* full-time $8850; part-time $286 per credit. *Required fees:* full-time $332; $96 per term part-time. Part-time tuition and fees vary according to course load. *Payment plan:* installment. *Waivers:* senior citizens and employees or children of employees.

Library Callahan Library. *Collection:* 65,530 titles, 514 serial subscriptions, 727 audiovisual materials.

College life *Housing:* college housing not available. *Social organizations:* national fraternities, national sororities; 2% of eligible men and 4% of eligible women are members. *Most popular organizations:* Circle K, business/accounting club, STARS (Students Taking an Active Role in Society).

Campus security 24-hour patrols, late-night transport-escort service.

After graduation 50 organizations recruited on campus 1997–98. 75% of class of 1998 had job offers within 6 months. *Career center:* 1 full-time, 1 part-time personnel. Services include job fairs, resume preparation, interview workshops, resume referral, career/interest testing, career counseling, careers library, job bank. *Graduate education:* 32% of class of 1999 went directly to graduate and professional school: 23% education, 5% graduate arts and sciences, 2% business, 1% law, 1% medicine.

Freshmen 634 applied, 493 admitted, 246 enrolled. 10 student government officers.

Average high school GPA	3.5	SAT verbal scores above 500	58%
SAT math scores above 500	64%	ACT above 18	100%
From top 10% of their h.s. class	14%	From top quarter	49%
From top half	94%	1998 freshmen returning in 1999	90%

Application *Options:* early admission, deferred entrance. *Application fee:* $25. *Required:* high school transcript; minimum 2.0 GPA. *Required for some:* 2 letters of recommendation. *Recommended:* essay or personal statement; interview.

Standardized tests *Admission: Required:* SAT I or ACT.

Significant dates *Application deadlines:* rolling (freshmen), rolling (transfers). *Financial aid deadline priority date:* 2/25.

Freshman Application Contact
Mrs. Marion E. Salgado, Director of Admissions, St. Joseph's College, Suffolk Campus, 155 West Roe Boulevard, Patchogue, NY 11772. **Phone:** 631-447-3219. **Fax:** 631-447-1734.

Visit CollegeQuest.com for information on majors offered and athletics. College video available at CollegeQuest.com.

ST. LAWRENCE UNIVERSITY
Canton, New York

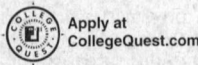
Apply at CollegeQuest.com

- **Independent**, comprehensive, founded 1856
- **Degrees** bachelor's, master's, and post-master's certificates
- **Small-town** 1,000-acre campus with easy access to Ottawa
- **Coed**, 1,851 undergraduate students, 99% full-time, 51% women, 49% men
- **Very difficult** entrance level, 74% of applicants were admitted
- **11:1 student-to-undergraduate faculty ratio**
- **$23,165 tuition** and fees
- **$22,736 average financial aid** package, $226.8 million endowment

Students *Undergraduates:* 1,840 full-time, 11 part-time. Students come from 38 states and territories, 18 other countries. *The most frequently chosen baccalaureate fields are:* biological/life sciences, psychology, social sciences and history. *Graduate:* 103 in graduate degree programs.

Reside on campus	95%	Age 25 or older	1%
Transferred in	1%	International students	3%
African Americans	2%	Asian Americans/Pacific Islanders	1%
Hispanic Americans	2%	Native Americans	0.5%

Faculty 182 (86% full-time).

Expenses (1999–2000) *Comprehensive fee:* $30,370 includes full-time tuition ($22,905), mandatory fees ($260), and room and board ($7205). *College room only:* $3875. Full-time tuition and fees vary according to student level. Room and board charges vary according to board plan. *Payment plans:* installment, deferred payment. *Waivers:* employees or children of employees.

Library Owen D. Young Library plus 1 other. *Operations spending 1999–2000:* $2.5 million. *Collection:* 484,460 titles, 1,972 serial subscriptions.

College life *Housing:* on-campus residence required through senior year. *Option:* coed. *Social organizations:* national fraternities, national sororities, local sororities; 19% of eligible men and 28% of eligible women are members. *Most popular organizations:* outing club, student newspaper, student government, Environmental Action, Habitat for Humanity.

Campus security 24-hour emergency response devices and patrols, student patrols, late-night transport-escort service, controlled dormitory access.

After graduation 73% of class of 1998 had job offers within 6 months. *Career center:* 4 full-time, 1 part-time personnel. Services include job fairs, resume preparation, interview workshops, resume referral, career/interest testing, career counseling, careers library, job bank, job interviews. *Graduate education:* 23% of class of 1999 went directly to graduate and professional school.

Freshmen 2,235 applied, 1,647 admitted, 575 enrolled. 16 valedictorians.

Average high school GPA	3.28	SAT verbal scores above 500	83%
SAT math scores above 500	82%	ACT above 18	96%
From top 10% of their h.s. class	30%	From top quarter	61%
From top half	88%	1998 freshmen returning in 1999	83%

Application *Options:* eApply at www.CollegeQuest.com, Common Application, electronic application, early decision, deferred entrance. *Application fee:* $50. *Required:* essay or personal statement; high school transcript; 2 letters of recommendation. *Recommended:* minimum 2.0 GPA; interview.

Standardized tests *Admission: Required:* SAT I or ACT. *Recommended:* SAT II Subject Tests.

Significant dates *Application deadlines:* 2/15 (freshmen), 4/1 (transfers). *Early decision:* 11/15 (for plan 1), 11/15 (for plan 2). *Notification:* 3/31 (freshmen), 12/15 (early decision plan 1), 12/15 (early decision plan 2). *Financial aid deadline priority date:* 2/15.

Freshman Application Contact
Ms. Terry Cowdrey, Dean of Admissions and Financial Aid, St. Lawrence University, Canton, NY 13617-1455. **Phone:** 315-229-5261. **Toll-free phone:** 800-285-1856. **Fax:** 315-229-5502. **E-mail:** admissions@stlawu.edu

Visit CollegeQuest.com for information on majors offered and athletics. Electronic viewbook available at CollegeQuest.com.

■ *See page 2398 for a narrative description.*

New York

ST. THOMAS AQUINAS COLLEGE
Sparkill, New York

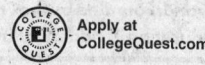 Apply at CollegeQuest.com

- **Independent**, comprehensive, founded 1952
- **Degrees** bachelor's, master's, and post-master's certificates
- **Suburban** 46-acre campus with easy access to New York City
- **Coed**
- **Moderately difficult** entrance level
- **$12,120 tuition** and fees

Expenses (1999–2000) *Comprehensive fee:* $19,270 includes full-time tuition ($11,800), mandatory fees ($320), and room and board ($7150). *College room only:* $4040. Room and board charges vary according to board plan and housing facility. *Part-time tuition:* $390 per credit. *Part-time fees:* $75 per term part-time.

Institutional Web site http://www.stac.edu/

Campus security 24-hour emergency response devices and patrols, late-night transport-escort service, controlled dormitory access.

Application *Options:* eApply at www.CollegeQuest.com, Common Application, electronic application, early admission, early decision, early action, deferred entrance. *Application fee:* $25. *Required:* high school transcript; minimum 2.0 GPA. *Required for some:* 3 letters of recommendation. *Recommended:* essay or personal statement; interview.

Standardized tests *Admission: Required:* SAT I or ACT.

Admissions Office Contact
St. Thomas Aquinas College, 125 Route 340, Sparkill, NY 10976. **Toll-free phone:** 800-999-STAC. **E-mail:** joestacenroll@rockland.net

Visit CollegeQuest.com for information on athletics. College video available at CollegeQuest.com.

■ *See page 2428 for a narrative description.*

SARAH LAWRENCE COLLEGE
Bronxville, New York

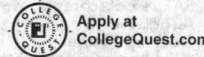 Apply at CollegeQuest.com

- **Independent**, comprehensive, founded 1926
- **Degrees** bachelor's and master's
- **Suburban** 40-acre campus with easy access to New York City
- **Coed**, 1,057 undergraduate students, 96% full-time, 74% women, 26% men
- **Very difficult** entrance level, 43% of applicants were admitted
- **6:1 student-to-undergraduate faculty ratio**
- **65% graduate** in 6 years or less
- **$25,406 tuition** and fees
- **$17,957 average financial aid** package, $16,362 average indebtedness upon graduation, $42.8 million endowment

At the heart of the Sarah Lawrence learning experience is the seminar and conference system. Every course has 2 parts: a seminar limited to 15 students and an individual meeting held every 2 weeks between student and teacher, during which they create a project that extends the seminar material and connects it to the student's academic goals and aspirations. Through dialogue, reading, and research, students work with their teachers to create an individualized education.

Students *Undergraduates:* 1,020 full-time, 37 part-time. Students come from 51 states and territories, 27 other countries. *The most frequently chosen baccalaureate field is:* liberal arts/general studies. *Graduate:* 317 in graduate degree programs.

From out-of-state	79%	Reside on campus	90%
Age 25 or older	1%	Transferred in	3%
International students	2%	African Americans	6%
Asian Americans/Pacific Islanders	5%	Hispanic Americans	5%
Native Americans	0.4%		

Faculty 218 (82% full-time).

Expenses (1999–2000) *Comprehensive fee:* $34,054 includes full-time tuition ($24,810), mandatory fees ($596), and room and board ($8648). *College room only:* $5638. Full-time tuition and fees vary according to course load. Room and board charges vary according to board plan. *Part-time tuition:* $827 per credit. *Part-time fees:* $149 per term part-time. Part-time tuition and fees vary according to course load. *Payment plan:* installment. *Waivers:* employees or children of employees.

Library Esther Rauschenbush Library plus 2 others. *Operations spending 1999–2000:* $2.1 million. *Collection:* 292,839 titles, 1,068 serial subscriptions, 17,881 audiovisual materials.

College life *Housing:* on-campus residence required in freshman year. *Options:* coed, men-only, women-only, cooperative. *Most popular organizations:* Student Senate, Chavarah, UNIDAD, Res Moranda, Amnesty International.

Campus security 24-hour emergency response devices and patrols, student patrols, late-night transport-escort service, controlled dormitory access.

After graduation 58 organizations recruited on campus 1997–98. 65% of class of 1998 had job offers within 6 months. *Career center:* 3 full-time personnel. Services include job fairs, resume preparation, resume referral, career counseling, careers library, job bank, job interviews. *Graduate education:* 30% of class of 1999 went directly to graduate and professional school: 10% graduate arts and sciences, 10% law, 5% education, 1% medicine, 1% theology. *Major awards:* 1 Fulbright Scholar.

Freshmen 2,070 applied, 895 admitted, 277 enrolled. 5 National Merit Scholars, 4 valedictorians.

Average high school GPA	3.3	SAT verbal scores above 500	96%
SAT math scores above 500	85%	ACT above 18	98%
From top 10% of their h.s. class	38%	From top quarter	77%
From top half	94%	1998 freshmen returning in 1999	92%

Application *Options:* eApply at www.CollegeQuest.com, Common Application, early admission, early decision, deferred entrance. *Application fee:* $50. *Required:* essay or personal statement; high school transcript; 3 letters of recommendation. *Recommended:* minimum 3.0 GPA; interview.

Standardized tests *Admission: Required:* SAT I or ACT or any 3 SAT II Subject Tests.

Significant dates *Application deadlines:* 2/1 (freshmen), 3/1 (transfers). *Early decision:* 11/15 (for plan 1), 1/1 (for plan 2). *Notification:* 4/1 (freshmen), 12/15 (early decision plan 1), 2/15 (early decision plan 2). *Financial aid deadline:* 2/1.

Freshman Application Contact
Ms. Thyra L. Briggs, Dean of Admissions, Sarah Lawrence College, 1 Mead Way, Bronxville, NY 10708-5999. **Phone:** 914-395-2510. **Toll-free phone:** 800-888-2858. **Fax:** 914-395-2668. **E-mail:** slcadmit@slc.edu

Visit CollegeQuest.com for information on majors offered and athletics. Electronic viewbook available at CollegeQuest.com.

■ *See page 2448 for a narrative description.*

SCHOOL OF VISUAL ARTS
New York, New York

- **Proprietary**, comprehensive, founded 1947
- **Degrees** bachelor's and master's
- **Urban** 1-acre campus
- **Coed**, 2,946 undergraduate students, 89% full-time, 47% women, 53% men
- **Moderately difficult** entrance level, 64% of applicants were admitted
- **4:1 student-to-undergraduate faculty ratio**
- **45.28% graduate** in 6 years or less
- **$15,320 tuition** and fees

SVA's mission to educate artists and the students' objective to become artists are the same. The School achieves its mission, in part, through a faculty of 800 working professionals who bring their individuality and insight into the challenging and exhilarating process of becoming an artist or designer. They encourage students to create work of excellence while in college and, once they are professionals, to create work that will influence and help shape the vision of art in the next millennium.

Students *Undergraduates:* 2,625 full-time, 321 part-time. Students come from 44 states and territories, 21 other countries. *The most frequently chosen baccalaureate field is:* visual/performing arts. *Graduate:* 313 in graduate degree programs.

New York

School of Visual Arts (continued)

From out-of-state	38%	Reside on campus	24%
Age 25 or older	16%	Transferred in	17%
International students	23%	African Americans	3%
Asian Americans/Pacific Islanders	6%	Hispanic Americans	8%
Native Americans	0.5%		

Faculty 852 (12% full-time), 24% with terminal degrees.
Expenses (1999–2000) *Tuition:* full-time $15,000; part-time $630 per credit. *Required fees:* full-time $320. Full-time tuition and fees vary according to program. *College room only:* $6400. Room and board charges vary according to gender and housing facility. *Payment plan:* installment. *Waivers:* employees or children of employees.
Library School of Visual Arts Library. *Operations spending 1999–2000:* $556,000. *Collection:* 70,680 titles, 306 serial subscriptions, 1,600 audiovisual materials.
College life *Housing: Options:* coed, women-only. *Most popular organizations:* Visual Arts Student Association, Film Club, Korean Christian, Asian Association, Bible Study.
Campus security 24-hour patrols.
After graduation 50 organizations recruited on campus 1997–98. *Career center:* 4 full-time personnel. Services include resume preparation, resume referral, career counseling, job bank, job interviews. *Graduate education:* 4% of class of 1999 went directly to graduate and professional school: 4% graduate arts and sciences.
Freshmen 1,647 applied, 1,056 admitted, 513 enrolled.

Average high school GPA	3.0	SAT verbal scores above 500	64%
SAT math scores above 500	55%	ACT above 18	82%
1998 freshmen returning in 1999	88%		

Application *Options:* early decision, deferred entrance. *Application fee:* $45. *Required:* essay or personal statement; high school transcript; minimum 2.3 GPA; portfolio. *Required for some:* 1 letter of recommendation. *Recommended:* interview.
Standardized tests *Admission: Required:* SAT I or ACT.
Significant dates *Application deadlines:* rolling (freshmen), rolling (transfers). *Early decision:* 12/1. *Notification:* 1/16 (early decision). *Financial aid deadline:* 5/1. *Priority date:* 2/1.
Freshman Application Contact
Mr. Richard M. Longo, Director of Admissions, School of Visual Arts, 209 East 23rd Street, New York, NY 10010-3994. **Phone:** 212-592-2100. **Toll-free phone:** 800-436-4204. **Fax:** 212-592-2116. **E-mail:** admissions@adm.schoolofvisualarts.edu
Visit CollegeQuest.com for information on majors offered and athletics.

■ *See page 2460 for a narrative description.*

SH'OR YOSHUV RABBINICAL COLLEGE
Far Rockaway, New York

Admissions Office Contact
Sh'or Yoshuv Rabbinical College, 1284 Central Avenue, Far Rockaway, NY 11691-4002.

SIENA COLLEGE
Loudonville, New York

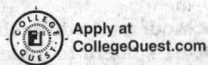

- **Independent Roman Catholic**, comprehensive, founded 1937
- **Degrees** bachelor's and master's
- **Suburban** 155-acre campus
- **Coed**, 2,812 undergraduate students, 92% full-time, 53% women, 47% men
- **Moderately difficult** entrance level, 73% of applicants were admitted
- **14:1 student-to-undergraduate faculty ratio**
- **75.81% graduate** in 6 years or less
- **$14,130 tuition** and fees
- **$10,440 average financial aid** package, $14,000 average indebtedness upon graduation, $41.8 million endowment

Located in Loudonville, New York, Siena is a community of about 2,700 men and women that offers degrees in arts, business, and science. Student-focused professors are the heart of a supportive learning environment that prepares students for careers, for active roles in their communities, and for the real world. Founded by the Franciscans, Siena provides a personal, values-oriented education 1 student at a time.

Students *Undergraduates:* 2,590 full-time, 222 part-time. Students come from 28 states and territories, 6 other countries. *The most frequently chosen baccalaureate fields are:* business/marketing, English, social sciences and history. *Graduate:* 22 in graduate degree programs.

From out-of-state	16%	Reside on campus	76%
Age 25 or older	9%	Transferred in	6%
International students	0.3%	African Americans	2%
Asian Americans/Pacific Islanders	3%	Hispanic Americans	3%
Native Americans	0.2%		

Faculty 252 (61% full-time), 76% with terminal degrees.
Expenses (1999–2000) *Comprehensive fee:* $20,345 includes full-time tuition ($13,660), mandatory fees ($470), and room and board ($6215). *College room only:* $3795. Room and board charges vary according to board plan and housing facility. *Part-time tuition:* $250 per credit hour. *Part-time fees:* $25 per term part-time. *Payment plan:* installment. *Waivers:* senior citizens and employees or children of employees.
Library Jerome Dawson Memorial Library. *Operations spending 1999–2000:* $1.1 million. *Collection:* 206,559 titles, 1,606 serial subscriptions, 4,679 audiovisual materials.
College life *Housing:* on-campus residence required in freshman year. *Option:* coed. *Most popular organizations:* Student Senate, Student Events Board, Big Brothers/Big Sisters, Gaelic Society, outing club.
Campus security 24-hour emergency response devices and patrols, late-night transport-escort service, controlled dormitory access, call boxes in parking lots and on roadways.
After graduation 180 organizations recruited on campus 1997–98. 74% of class of 1998 had job offers within 6 months. *Career center:* 5 full-time, 1 part-time personnel. Services include job fairs, resume preparation, interview workshops, resume referral, career/interest testing, career counseling, careers library, job bank, job interviews.
Freshmen 3,121 applied, 2,272 admitted, 680 enrolled.

SAT verbal scores above 500	77%	SAT math scores above 500	80%
ACT above 18	96%	From top 10% of their h.s. class	20%
From top quarter	56%	From top half	88%
1998 freshmen returning in 1999	89%		

Application *Options:* eApply at www.CollegeQuest.com, electronic application, early admission, early decision, early action, deferred entrance. *Application fee:* $40. *Required:* essay or personal statement; high school transcript; 1 letter of recommendation. *Required for some:* interview.
Standardized tests *Admission: Required:* SAT I or ACT.
Significant dates *Application deadlines:* 3/1 (freshmen), 9/1 (transfers). *Early decision:* 12/1, 12/1. *Notification:* 3/15 (freshmen), 12/15 (early decision), 12/30 (early action). *Financial aid deadline priority date:* 2/1.
Freshman Application Contact
Mr. Edward Jones, Director of Admissions, Siena College, 515 Loudon Road, Loudonville, NY 12211-1462. **Phone:** 518-783-2423. **Toll-free phone:** 800-45SIENA. **Fax:** 518-783-4293. **E-mail:** admit@siena.edu
Visit CollegeQuest.com for information on majors offered and athletics. Electronic viewbook available at CollegeQuest.com.

■ *See page 2486 for a narrative description.*

SKIDMORE COLLEGE
Saratoga Springs, New York

- **Independent**, comprehensive, founded 1903
- **Degrees** bachelor's and master's
- **Small-town** 800-acre campus with easy access to Albany
- **Coed**, 2,501 undergraduate students, 90% full-time, 60% women, 40% men
- **Very difficult** entrance level, 49% of applicants were admitted
- **11:1 student-to-undergraduate faculty ratio**
- **$24,259 tuition** and fees
- **$18,355 average financial aid** package, $14,400 average indebtedness upon graduation, $129.5 million endowment

Students *Undergraduates:* 2,262 full-time, 239 part-time. Students come from 43 states and territories, 25 other countries. *The most frequently chosen*

baccalaureate fields are: business/marketing, social sciences and history, visual/performing arts. *Graduate:* 52 in graduate degree programs.

From out-of-state	73%	Reside on campus	76%
Transferred in	0.4%	International students	1%
African Americans	2%	Asian Americans/Pacific Islanders	3%
Hispanic Americans	5%	Native Americans	0.3%

Faculty 199 (95% full-time), 82% with terminal degrees.

Expenses (1999–2000) *Comprehensive fee:* $31,200 includes full-time tuition ($24,000), mandatory fees ($259), and room and board ($6950). *College room only:* $3900. Room and board charges vary according to board plan and housing facility. *Part-time tuition:* $800 per semester hour. *Part-time fees:* $25 per year part-time. *Payment plans:* tuition prepayment, installment. *Waivers:* employees or children of employees.

Library Scribner Library. *Operations spending 1999–2000:* $2.2 million. *Collection:* 673,877 titles, 1,843 serial subscriptions, 112,591 audiovisual materials.

College life *Housing:* on-campus residence required through sophomore year. *Options:* coed, women-only. *Most popular organizations:* Student Government Association, student radio station, Student Volunteer Bureau, outing club, Skidmore News.

Campus security 24-hour emergency response devices and patrols, late-night transport-escort service, controlled dormitory access, well-lit campus.

After graduation 206 organizations recruited on campus 1997–98. 76% of class of 1998 had job offers within 6 months. *Career center:* 4 full-time, 2 part-time personnel. Services include job fairs, resume preparation, interview workshops, resume referral, career/interest testing, career counseling, careers library, job bank, job interviews. *Graduate education:* 15% of class of 1999 went directly to graduate and professional school: 7% graduate arts and sciences, 3% law, 1% business, 1% education, 1% medicine.

Freshmen 5,414 applied, 2,647 admitted, 648 enrolled.

SAT verbal scores above 500	95%	SAT math scores above 500	95%
ACT above 18	100%	From top 10% of their h.s. class	27%
From top quarter	61%	From top half	91%
1998 freshmen returning in 1999	91%		

Application *Options:* eApply at www.CollegeQuest.com, Common Application, early admission, early decision, deferred entrance. *Application fee:* $50. *Required:* essay or personal statement; high school transcript; 2 letters of recommendation. *Recommended:* interview.

Standardized tests *Admission: Required:* SAT I or ACT. *Recommended:* SAT II Subject Tests, SAT II: Writing Test.

Significant dates *Application deadlines:* 1/15 (freshmen), 4/1 (transfers). *Early decision:* 12/1 (for plan 1), 1/15 (for plan 2). *Notification:* 4/1 (freshmen), 1/1 (early decision plan 1), 2/15 (early decision plan 2). *Financial aid deadline:* 2/1.

Freshman Application Contact
Ms. Mary Lou W. Bates, Director of Admissions, Skidmore College, 815 North Broadway, Saratoga Springs, NY 12866-1632. **Phone:** 518-580-5570. **Toll-free phone:** 800-867-6007. **Fax:** 518-581-7462. **E-mail:** admissions@skidmore.edu

Visit CollegeQuest.com for information on majors offered and athletics. College video available at CollegeQuest.com.

■ *See page 2498 for a narrative description.*

SOUTHAMPTON COLLEGE OF LONG ISLAND UNIVERSITY

New York—See Long Island University, Southampton College

STATE UNIVERSITY OF NEW YORK AT ALBANY
Albany, New York

- **State-supported**, university, founded 1844
- **Degrees** bachelor's, master's, doctoral, and post-master's certificates
- **Suburban** 560-acre campus

- **Coed**, 11,002 undergraduate students, 95% full-time, 49% women, 51% men
- **Moderately difficult** entrance level, 61% of applicants were admitted
- **18:1 student-to-undergraduate faculty ratio**
- **66.37% graduate** in 6 years or less
- **$4338 tuition** and fees (in-state); $9238 (out-of-state)
- **$6962 average financial aid** package, $12.9 million endowment

Part of State University of New York System.

Students *Undergraduates:* 10,410 full-time, 592 part-time. Students come from 38 states and territories, 36 other countries. *The most frequently chosen baccalaureate fields are:* mathematics, health professions and related sciences, protective services/public administration. *Graduate:* 5,164 in graduate degree programs.

From out-of-state	33%	Reside on campus	54%
Age 25 or older	10%	Transferred in	11%
International students	1%	African Americans	9%
Asian Americans/Pacific Islanders	8%	Hispanic Americans	6%
Native Americans	0.3%		

Faculty 877 (67% full-time).

Expenses (1999–2000) *Tuition, state resident:* full-time $3400; part-time $138 per credit hour. *Tuition, nonresident:* full-time $8300; part-time $347 per credit hour. *Required fees:* full-time $938; $27 per credit hour. Part-time tuition and fees vary according to course load. *College room and board:* $5828; room only: $3740. Room and board charges vary according to board plan and housing facility. *Payment plan:* installment. *Waivers:* senior citizens.

Library University Library plus 1 other. *Operations spending 1999–2000:* $8.3 million. *Collection:* 1.1 million titles, 16,103 serial subscriptions.

College life *Housing:* on-campus residence required through sophomore year. *Options:* coed, men-only, women-only. *Social organizations:* national fraternities, national sororities, local fraternities, local sororities; 15% of eligible men and 15% of eligible women are members. *Most popular organizations:* intramural athletics, cultural organizations, political organizations.

Campus security 24-hour emergency response devices and patrols, late-night transport-escort service, controlled dormitory access.

After graduation 120 organizations recruited on campus 1997–98. *Career center:* Services include job fairs, resume preparation, resume referral, career counseling, careers library, job bank, job interviews. *Graduate education:* 45% of class of 1999 went directly to graduate and professional school: 21% graduate arts and sciences, 9% law, 6% business, 5% medicine, 2% dentistry, 2% education. *Major awards:* 1 Fulbright Scholar.

Freshmen 15,312 applied, 9,410 admitted, 2,282 enrolled. 3 valedictorians.

SAT verbal scores above 500	78%	SAT math scores above 500	83%
ACT above 18	N/R	From top 10% of their h.s. class	12%
From top quarter	45%	From top half	89%
1998 freshmen returning in 1999	83%		

Application *Options:* electronic application, early admission, early action, deferred entrance. *Application fee:* $30. *Required:* high school transcript. *Required for some:* portfolio, audition. *Recommended:* essay or personal statement.

Standardized tests *Admission: Required:* SAT I or ACT.

Significant dates *Application deadlines:* 3/1 (freshmen), 4/1 (transfers). *Early action:* 12/1. *Notification:* 1/1 (early action). *Financial aid deadline priority date:* 3/15.

Freshman Application Contact
Mr. Harry Wood, Director of Undergraduate Admissions, State University of New York at Albany, 1400 Washington Avenue, Albany, NY 12222-0001. **Phone:** 518-442-5435. **E-mail:** ugadmit@safnet.albany.edu

Visit CollegeQuest.com for information on majors offered and athletics.

■ *See page 2532 for a narrative description.*

STATE UNIVERSITY OF NEW YORK AT BINGHAMTON
Binghamton, New York

- **State-supported**, university, founded 1946
- **Degrees** bachelor's, master's, doctoral, and post-master's certificates
- **Suburban** 606-acre campus
- **Coed**, 9,710 undergraduate students, 98% full-time, 53% women, 47% men

New York

State University of New York at Binghamton (continued)
- **Very difficult** entrance level, 42% of applicants were admitted
- **18:1 student-to-undergraduate faculty ratio**
- **82% graduate** in 6 years or less
- **$4416 tuition** and fees (in-state); $9316 (out-of-state)
- **$9573 average financial aid** package, $11,856 average indebtedness upon graduation, $32.2 million endowment

Part of State University of New York System.

Students *Undergraduates:* 9,468 full-time, 242 part-time. Students come from 33 states and territories, 43 other countries. *The most frequently chosen baccalaureate fields are:* business/marketing, psychology, social sciences and history. *Graduate:* 2,692 in graduate degree programs.

From out-of-state	4%	Reside on campus	55%
Age 25 or older	6%	Transferred in	7%
International students	2%	African Americans	5%
Asian Americans/Pacific Islanders	17%	Hispanic Americans	6%
Native Americans	0.2%		

Faculty 803 (64% full-time).

Expenses (1999–2000) *Tuition, state resident:* full-time $3400; part-time $137 per credit. *Tuition, nonresident:* full-time $8300; part-time $346 per credit. *Required fees:* full-time $1016; $38 per credit; $37 per term part-time. *College room and board:* $5516; room only: $3430. Room and board charges vary according to board plan and housing facility. *Payment plan:* installment. *Waivers:* employees or children of employees.

Library Glenn G. Bartle Library plus 1 other. *Operations spending 1999–2000:* $10.8 million. *Collection:* 1.6 million titles, 7,265 serial subscriptions.

College life *Housing:* on-campus residence required in freshman year. *Options:* coed, disabled students. *Social organizations:* national fraternities, national sororities, local fraternities, local sororities; 18% of eligible men and 14% of eligible women are members. *Most popular organizations:* student radio station, student association, student newspaper, cultural organizations, peer counseling/mentoring/volunteering program.

Campus security 24-hour emergency response devices and patrols, student patrols, late-night transport-escort service, controlled dormitory access, safety awareness programs, well-lit campus, self-defense education, secured campus entrance 12 a.m. to 5 a.m., emergency telephones.

After graduation 200 organizations recruited on campus 1997–98. *Career center:* 7 full-time, 3 part-time personnel. Services include job fairs, resume preparation, interview workshops, resume referral, career counseling, careers library, job bank, job interviews, career software, online catalog to career library. *Graduate education:* 38% of class of 1999 went directly to graduate and professional school: 15% graduate arts and sciences, 6% law, 4% medicine, 3% education, 2% business, 2% engineering, 1% dentistry. **Major awards:** 2 Fulbright Scholars.

Freshmen 16,386 applied, 6,902 admitted, 2,050 enrolled. 18 valedictorians.

Average high school GPA	3.6	SAT verbal scores above 500	88%
SAT math scores above 500	95%	ACT above 18	N/R
From top 10% of their h.s. class	50%	From top quarter	96%
From top half	100%	1998 freshmen returning in 1999	91%

Application *Options:* electronic application, early admission, early action, deferred entrance. *Application fee:* $30. *Required:* essay or personal statement; high school transcript. *Required for some:* 1 letter of recommendation; portfolio, audition.

Standardized tests *Admission: Required:* SAT I or ACT.

Significant dates *Application deadlines:* rolling (freshmen), rolling (transfers). *Early action:* 11/15. **Financial aid deadline priority date:** 3/1.

Freshman Application Contact Mr. Geoffrey D. Gould, Director of Admissions, State University of New York at Binghamton, PO Box 6001, Binghamton, NY 13902-6001. **Phone:** 607-777-2171. **E-mail:** admit@binghamton.edu

Visit CollegeQuest.com for information on majors offered and athletics. College video and electronic viewbook available at CollegeQuest.com.

- *See page 2534 for a narrative description.*

STATE UNIVERSITY OF NEW YORK AT BUFFALO
Buffalo, New York

- **State-supported**, university, founded 1846
- **Degrees** bachelor's, master's, doctoral, first professional, and post-master's certificates
- **Suburban** 1,350-acre campus
- **Coed**, 15,572 undergraduate students, 90% full-time, 47% women, 53% men
- **Moderately difficult** entrance level, 74% of applicants were admitted
- **13:1 student-to-undergraduate faculty ratio**
- **60% graduate** in 6 years or less
- **$4655 tuition** and fees (in-state); $9555 (out-of-state)
- **$5940 average financial aid** package, $15,250 average indebtedness upon graduation, $457.6 million endowment

UB is committed to enhancing students' life quality by offering new on-campus apartment housing options, NCAA Division I men's and women's athletics, and recreational, intramural, and club sports. UB attracts highly qualified students with its honors program—the largest in the SUNY system—and an expanded merit scholarship program. UB offers a growing number of combined bachelor's and master's programs. The University is committed to providing educational technology and assistance, exposing students to computer-enhanced classwork and training them for the 21st century.

Part of State University of New York System.

Students *Undergraduates:* 14,041 full-time, 1,531 part-time. Students come from 36 states and territories, 66 other countries. *The most frequently chosen baccalaureate fields are:* business/marketing, health professions and related sciences, social sciences and history. *Graduate:* 1,664 in professional programs, 6,334 in other graduate degree programs.

From out-of-state	2%	Reside on campus	21%
Age 25 or older	17%	Transferred in	10%
International students	3%	African Americans	9%
Asian Americans/Pacific Islanders	11%	Hispanic Americans	4%
Native Americans	1%		

Faculty 1,869 (65% full-time), 98% with terminal degrees.

Expenses (1999–2000) *Tuition, state resident:* full-time $3400; part-time $137 per credit hour. *Tuition, nonresident:* full-time $8300; part-time $346 per credit hour. *Required fees:* full-time $1255; $52 per credit hour. *College room and board:* $5904; room only: $3424. Room and board charges vary according to board plan and housing facility. *Payment plan:* installment.

Library Lockwood Library plus 7 others. *Operations spending 1999–2000:* $16.8 million. *Collection:* 3.1 million titles, 21,262 serial subscriptions, 157,312 audiovisual materials.

College life *Housing: Option:* coed. *Social organizations:* national fraternities, national sororities, local fraternities, local sororities; 1% of eligible men and 1% of eligible women are members. *Most popular organizations:* Schussmeisters Ski Club, student association, Black Student Union.

Campus security 24-hour emergency response devices and patrols, student patrols, late-night transport-escort service, controlled dormitory access, self-defense and awareness programs.

After graduation *Career center:* 15 full-time, 4 part-time personnel. Services include job fairs, resume preparation, interview workshops, resume referral, career/interest testing, career counseling, careers library, job bank, job interviews. **Major awards:** 4 Fulbright Scholars.

Freshmen 14,836 applied, 11,031 admitted, 3,223 enrolled.

Average high school GPA	3.1	SAT verbal scores above 500	72%
SAT math scores above 500	80%	ACT above 18	93%
From top 10% of their h.s. class	18%	From top quarter	50%
From top half	88%	1998 freshmen returning in 1999	84%

Application *Options:* Common Application, electronic application, early admission, early decision. *Application fee:* $30. *Required:* high school transcript. *Required for some:* letters of recommendation; portfolio, audition.

Standardized tests *Admission: Required:* SAT I or ACT.

Significant dates *Application deadlines:* rolling (freshmen), rolling (transfers). *Early decision:* 11/1. *Notification:* 12/15 (early decision). **Financial aid deadline priority date:** 3/1.

Freshman Application Contact
Ms. Regina Toomey, Director of Admissions, State University of New York at Buffalo, Capen Hall, Room 17, North Campus, Buffalo, NY 14260-1660. **Phone:** 716-645-6900. **Fax:** 716-645-6411. **E-mail:** ubadmissions@admissions.buffalo.edu

Visit CollegeQuest.com for information on majors offered and athletics. Electronic viewbook available at CollegeQuest.com.

■ See pages 2536 and 2538 for narrative descriptions.

STATE UNIVERSITY OF NEW YORK AT FARMINGDALE
Farmingdale, New York

- **State-supported**, 4-year, founded 1912
- **Degrees** associate and bachelor's (one bachelor's degree program is upper level)
- **Small-town** 380-acre campus with easy access to New York City
- **Coed**, 4,114 undergraduate students, 69% full-time, 42% women, 58% men
- **Moderately difficult** entrance level, 51% of applicants were admitted
- **17:1 student-to-undergraduate faculty ratio**
- **$4075 tuition** and fees (in-state); $8975 (out-of-state)
- **$444,187 endowment**

SUNY Farmingdale, a specialized 4-year college of technology, offers 12 bachelor's degrees, 20 associate degrees, 15 certificate programs, and workshops in engineering technologies, business, health, human services, and liberal arts and sciences. Credit and credit-free classes are available during the day and evening and on the weekends.

Part of State University of New York System.
Students *Undergraduates:* 2,858 full-time, 1,256 part-time. Students come from 8 states and territories. *The most frequently chosen baccalaureate fields are:* business/marketing, engineering/engineering technologies.

From out-of-state	1%	Reside on campus	12%
Age 25 or older	28%	Transferred in	10%
African Americans	15%	Asian Americans/Pacific Islanders	4%
Hispanic Americans	9%	Native Americans	0.2%

Faculty 295 (58% full-time).
Expenses (1999–2000) *Tuition, state resident:* full-time $3400; part-time $137 per credit. *Tuition, nonresident:* full-time $8300; part-time $346 per credit. *Required fees:* full-time $675; $19 per credit. Full-time tuition and fees vary according to degree level. Part-time tuition and fees vary according to course load and degree level. *College room and board:* $6114; room only: $3390. Room and board charges vary according to board plan and housing facility. *Payment plans:* installment, deferred payment. *Waivers:* senior citizens.
Library Greenley Hall. *Operations spending 1999–2000:* $943,063. *Collection:* 132,049 titles, 1,185 serial subscriptions, 18,021 audiovisual materials.
College life *Housing:* Option: coed. *Most popular organizations:* liberal arts club, Campus Activities Board, student government association, student radio station, Rambler Newspaper.
Campus security 24-hour emergency response devices and patrols.
After graduation 150 organizations recruited on campus 1997–98. *Career center:* 2 full-time, 1 part-time personnel. Services include job fairs, resume preparation, interview workshops, career/interest testing, career counseling, careers library, job bank, job interviews. *Graduate education:* 2% of class of 1999 went directly to graduate and professional school.
Freshmen 3,165 applied, 1,623 admitted, 1,058 enrolled.

Average high school GPA	2.9	SAT verbal scores above 500	25%
SAT math scores above 500	34%	ACT above 18	N/R
From top 10% of their h.s. class	3%	From top quarter	14%
From top half	52%		

Application *Options:* electronic application, early admission. *Application fee:* $30. *Required:* high school transcript; minimum 2.0 GPA. *Required for some:* portfolio.
Standardized tests *Admission: Required:* SAT I or ACT.
Significant dates *Application deadlines:* rolling (freshmen), rolling (transfers). *Financial aid deadline priority date:* 4/1.

Freshman Application Contact
Mr. George Kraus, Associate Director, State University of New York at Farmingdale, Memorial Hall, Farmingdale, NY 11735. **Phone:** 516-420-2457. **Toll-free phone:** 877-4-FARMINGDALE. **Fax:** 516-420-2633. **E-mail:** admissions@farmingdale.edu

Visit CollegeQuest.com for information on majors offered and athletics. Electronic viewbook available at CollegeQuest.com.

■ See page 2540 for a narrative description.

STATE UNIVERSITY OF NEW YORK AT NEW PALTZ
New Paltz, New York

- **State-supported**, comprehensive, founded 1828
- **Degrees** bachelor's, master's, doctoral, and post-master's certificates
- **Small-town** 216-acre campus
- **Coed**, 5,706 undergraduate students, 88% full-time, 64% women, 36% men
- **Moderately difficult** entrance level, 46% of applicants were admitted
- **19:1 student-to-undergraduate faculty ratio**
- **50.3% graduate** in 6 years or less
- **$3985 tuition** and fees (in-state); $8885 (out-of-state)
- **$7500 average financial aid** package, $5.6 million endowment

Part of State University of New York System.
Students *Undergraduates:* 5,026 full-time, 680 part-time. Students come from 25 states and territories, 30 other countries. *The most frequently chosen baccalaureate fields are:* communications/communication technologies, education, social sciences and history. *Graduate:* 1,663 in graduate degree programs.

From out-of-state	4%	Reside on campus	52%
Age 25 or older	10%	Transferred in	14%
International students	0.1%	African Americans	7%
Asian Americans/Pacific Islanders	4%	Hispanic Americans	10%
Native Americans	0.3%		

Faculty 564 (49% full-time).
Expenses (2000–2001, estimated) *Tuition, state resident:* full-time $3400; part-time $137 per credit. *Tuition, nonresident:* full-time $8300; part-time $346 per credit. *Required fees:* full-time $585; $19 per credit; $60 per term part-time. *College room and board:* $5368; room only: $3200. Room and board charges vary according to board plan. *Payment plan:* installment.
Library Sojourner Truth Library. *Operations spending 1999–2000:* $2.3 million. *Collection:* 1,500 serial subscriptions, 310 audiovisual materials.
College life *Housing:* on-campus residence required in freshman year. *Options:* coed, disabled students. *Social organizations:* national fraternities, national sororities, local fraternities, local sororities; 1% of eligible men and 3% of eligible women are members. *Most popular organizations:* outing club, Greek letter organizations, intramurals, Residence Hall Student Association, Student Art Alliance.
Campus security 24-hour emergency response devices and patrols, late-night transport-escort service, controlled dormitory access, safety seminars.
After graduation 399 organizations recruited on campus 1997–98. *Career center:* 2 full-time personnel. Services include job fairs, resume preparation, interview workshops, resume referral, career counseling, careers library, job bank, job interviews. *Graduate education:* 38% of class of 1999 went directly to graduate and professional school.
Freshmen 9,115 applied, 4,154 admitted, 977 enrolled. 3 valedictorians.

Average high school GPA	3.25	SAT verbal scores above 500	84%
SAT math scores above 500	82%	ACT above 18	N/R
From top 10% of their h.s. class	18%	From top quarter	46%
From top half	92%	1998 freshmen returning in 1999	79%

Application *Options:* electronic application, early decision, deferred entrance. *Application fee:* $30. *Required:* high school transcript; portfolio for art program, audition for music and theater programs. *Required for some:* essay or personal statement; letters of recommendation; interview. *Recommended:* minimum 3.0 GPA.
Standardized tests *Admission: Required:* SAT I or ACT.
Significant dates *Application deadlines:* 4/15 (freshmen), 5/1 (transfers). *Early decision:* 11/15. *Notification:* 12/15 (early decision). *Financial aid deadline priority date:* 3/1.

New York

State University of New York at New Paltz (continued)
Freshman Application Contact
Ms. Mary Claire Bauer, Dean of Admission, State University of New York at New Paltz, 75 South Manheim Boulevard, Suite 1, New Paltz, NY 12561-2499. **Phone:** 914-257-3200. **Toll-free phone:** 888-639-7589. **Fax:** 914-257-3209. **E-mail:** admiss@npvm.newpaltz.edu
Visit CollegeQuest.com for information on majors offered and athletics.

STATE UNIVERSITY OF NEW YORK AT OSWEGO
Oswego, New York

- **State-supported**, comprehensive, founded 1861
- **Degrees** bachelor's, master's, and post-master's certificates
- **Small-town** 696-acre campus with easy access to Syracuse
- **Coed**, 6,550 undergraduate students, 92% full-time, 54% women, 46% men
- **Moderately difficult** entrance level, 59% of applicants were admitted
- **20:1 student-to-undergraduate faculty ratio**
- **62.4% graduate** in 6 years or less
- **$3975 tuition** and fees (in-state); $8875 (out-of-state)
- **$7049 average financial aid** package, $14,649 average indebtedness upon graduation, $3.6 million endowment

Part of State University of New York System.
Students *Undergraduates:* 6,031 full-time, 519 part-time. Students come from 28 states and territories, 26 other countries. *The most frequently chosen baccalaureate fields are:* business/marketing, communications/communication technologies, education. *Graduate:* 1,095 in graduate degree programs.

From out-of-state	1%	Reside on campus	53%
Age 25 or older	15%	Transferred in	12%
International students	0.3%	African Americans	4%
Asian Americans/Pacific Islanders	2%	Hispanic Americans	3%
Native Americans	1%		

Faculty 360 (85% full-time), 76% with terminal degrees.
Expenses (1999–2000) *Tuition, state resident:* full-time $3400; part-time $137 per credit hour. *Tuition, nonresident:* full-time $8300; part-time $346 per credit hour. *Required fees:* full-time $575; $18 per credit hour. Part-time tuition and fees vary according to class time and location. *College room and board:* $6160; room only: $3540. Room and board charges vary according to board plan and housing facility. *Payment plans:* installment, deferred payment.
Library Penfield Library plus 1 other. *Operations spending 1999–2000:* $2.6 million. *Collection:* 455,145 titles, 1,501 serial subscriptions, 42,000 audiovisual materials.
College life *Housing:* on-campus residence required through sophomore year. *Options:* coed, disabled students. *Social organizations:* national fraternities, national sororities, local fraternities, local sororities; 12% of eligible men and 12% of eligible women are members. *Most popular organizations:* club sports, student radio/television stations, outing/recreation club, student government, ski club.
Campus security 24-hour emergency response devices and patrols, student patrols, controlled dormitory access.
After graduation 120 organizations recruited on campus 1997–98. 73% of class of 1998 had job offers within 6 months. *Career center:* 4 full-time, 1 part-time personnel. Services include job fairs, resume preparation, interview workshops, resume referral, career/interest testing, career counseling, careers library, job bank, job interviews.
Freshmen 7,274 applied, 4,310 admitted, 1,258 enrolled.

Average high school GPA	3.1	SAT verbal scores above 500	76%
SAT math scores above 500	77%	ACT above 18	97%
From top 10% of their h.s. class	10%	From top quarter	43%
From top half	86%	1998 freshmen returning in 1999	80%

Application *Options:* electronic application, early admission, early decision, deferred entrance. *Application fee:* $30. *Required:* high school transcript. *Required for some:* letters of recommendation. *Recommended:* essay or personal statement; interview.
Standardized tests *Admission: Required:* SAT I or ACT.
Significant dates *Application deadlines:* rolling (freshmen), rolling (transfers). *Early decision:* 11/15. *Notification:* 1/15 (freshmen), 12/15 (early decision). *Financial aid deadline priority date:* 4/1.

Freshman Application Contact
Mr. Robert Stewart, Senior Associate Director, State University of New York at Oswego, 7060 State Route 104, Oswego, NY 13126. **Phone:** 315-341-2250. **Fax:** 315-341-3260. **E-mail:** admiss@oswego.edu
Visit CollegeQuest.com for information on majors offered and athletics. College video and electronic viewbook available at CollegeQuest.com.

■ *See page 2542 for a narrative description.*

STATE UNIVERSITY OF NEW YORK AT STONY BROOK
Stony Brook, New York

- **State-supported**, university, founded 1957
- **Degrees** bachelor's, master's, doctoral, first professional, and post-master's certificates
- **Small-town** 1,100-acre campus with easy access to New York City
- **Coed**, 12,480 undergraduate students, 91% full-time, 50% women, 50% men
- **Very difficult** entrance level, 58% of applicants were admitted
- **18:1 student-to-undergraduate faculty ratio**
- **$4141 tuition** and fees (in-state); $9041 (out-of-state)
- **$7157 average financial aid** package, $19.4 million endowment

Since its founding in 1956, SUNY at Stony Brook has grown tremendously and is now recognized as one of the nation's leading centers of learning and scholarship. A recent study published by Johns Hopkins University Press ranked Stony Brook 2nd in the nation among all public research universities. Stony Brook is at the forefront of integrating research and education at the undergraduate level and prides itself on the quality of its academic programs and outstanding faculty.

Part of State University of New York System.
Students *Undergraduates:* 11,346 full-time, 1,134 part-time. Students come from 37 states and territories, 47 other countries. *The most frequently chosen baccalaureate fields are:* psychology, biological/life sciences, social sciences and history. *Graduate:* 561 in professional programs, 5,887 in other graduate degree programs.

From out-of-state	2%	Age 25 or older	11%
Transferred in	10%	International students	3%
African Americans	9%	Asian Americans/Pacific Islanders	22%
Hispanic Americans	7%	Native Americans	0.2%

Faculty 1,737 (74% full-time).
Expenses (1999–2000) *Tuition, state resident:* full-time $3400; part-time $137 per credit. *Tuition, nonresident:* full-time $8300; part-time $346 per credit. *Required fees:* full-time $741; $35 per credit. *College room and board:* $6421; room only: $4021. Room and board charges vary according to board plan and housing facility. *Payment plans:* installment, deferred payment. *Waivers:* minority students.
Library Frank Melville, Jr. Building Library plus 7 others. *Collection:* 1.9 million titles, 14,024 serial subscriptions.
College life *Housing: Option:* coed. *Social organizations:* national fraternities, national sororities, local fraternities, local sororities; 1% of eligible men and 3% of eligible women are members. *Most popular organizations:* Lambda Upsilon Lambda Fraternity, Sigma Iota Alpha Sorority, Omega Phi Beta Sorority, Sigma Lambda Gamma Sorority, Delta Sigma Phi Fraternity.
Campus security 24-hour emergency response devices and patrols, late-night transport-escort service.
After graduation 147 organizations recruited on campus 1997–98. *Career center:* Services include job fairs, resume preparation, resume referral, career counseling, careers library, job bank. *Graduate education:* 47% of class of 1999 went directly to graduate and professional school. *Major awards:* 2 Fulbright Scholars.
Freshmen 14,892 applied, 8,649 admitted, 2,269 enrolled.

Average high school GPA	3.1	SAT verbal scores above 500	66%
SAT math scores above 500	80%	ACT above 18	N/R
From top 10% of their h.s. class	24%	From top quarter	63%
From top half	98%	1998 freshmen returning in 1999	81%

Application *Options:* Common Application, early admission, early decision, deferred entrance. *Application fee:* $30. *Required:* high school transcript; minimum 3.0 GPA. *Recommended:* 2 letters of recommendation; interview.

Standardized tests *Admission: Required:* SAT I or ACT.
Significant dates *Application deadlines:* rolling (freshmen), rolling (transfers). *Early decision:* 11/1. *Notification:* 12/15 (early decision). *Financial aid deadline priority date:* 3/1.

Freshman Application Contact
Ms. Gigi Lamens, Director of Admissions, State University of New York at Stony Brook, Nicolls Road, Stony Brook, NY 11794. **Phone:** 631-632-6868. **Toll-free phone:** 800-USB-SUNY. **E-mail:** admiss@mail.upsa.sunysb.edu
Visit CollegeQuest.com for information on majors offered and athletics. College video available at CollegeQuest.com.

■ *See page 2544 for a narrative description.*

STATE UNIVERSITY OF NEW YORK COLLEGE AT BROCKPORT
Brockport, New York

- **State-supported**, comprehensive, founded 1867
- **Degrees** bachelor's, master's, and postbachelor's certificates
- **Small-town** 435-acre campus with easy access to Rochester
- **Coed**, 6,457 undergraduate students, 85% full-time, 57% women, 43% men
- **Moderately difficult** entrance level, 55% of applicants were admitted
- **19:1 student-to-undergraduate faculty ratio**
- **47.7% graduate** in 6 years or less
- **$4014 tuition** and fees (in-state); $8914 (out-of-state)
- **$7017 average financial aid** package, $15,514 average indebtedness upon graduation, $2.3 million endowment

Part of State University of New York System.

Students *Undergraduates:* 5,479 full-time, 978 part-time. Students come from 33 states and territories, 12 other countries. *The most frequently chosen baccalaureate fields are:* health professions and related sciences, business/marketing, protective services/public administration. *Graduate:* 1,806 in graduate degree programs.

From out-of-state	2%	Reside on campus	33%
Age 25 or older	24%	Transferred in	14%
International students	0.4%	African Americans	7%
Asian Americans/Pacific Islanders	1%	Hispanic Americans	2%
Native Americans	0.3%		

Faculty 560 (50% full-time), 63% with terminal degrees.
Expenses (1999–2000) *Comprehensive fee:* $9424 includes mandatory fees ($614) and room and board ($5410). *College room only:* $3340. Full-time tuition and fees vary according to course load. Room and board charges vary according to board plan and housing facility. *Part-time fees:* $26 per credit hour. Part-time tuition and fees vary according to course load. *Payment plans:* installment, deferred payment. *Waivers:* senior citizens and employees or children of employees.
Library Drake Memorial Library. *Operations spending 1999–2000:* $2.7 million. *Collection:* 550,000 titles, 2,000 serial subscriptions, 5,500 audiovisual materials.
College life *Housing:* on-campus residence required in freshman year. *Options:* coed, disabled students. *Social organizations:* national fraternities, national sororities; 5% of eligible men and 5% of eligible women are members. *Most popular organizations:* fine arts clubs, criminal justice club, communication club, student radio station, sports clubs.
Campus security 24-hour emergency response devices and patrols, student patrols, late-night transport-escort service, controlled dormitory access.
After graduation 300 organizations recruited on campus 1997–98. *Career center:* 9 full-time personnel. Services include job fairs, resume preparation, resume referral, career counseling, careers library, job bank, job interviews. *Graduate education:* 16% of class of 1999 went directly to graduate and professional school: 10% education, 2% business.
Freshmen 6,306 applied, 3,459 admitted, 987 enrolled. 7 valedictorians.

Average high school GPA	2.9	SAT verbal scores above 500	56%
SAT math scores above 500	62%	ACT above 18	93%
From top 10% of their h.s. class	8%	From top quarter	31%
From top half	76%	1998 freshmen returning in 1999	71%

Application *Options:* electronic application, deferred entrance. *Application fee:* $30. *Required:* high school transcript. *Required for some:* essay or personal statement; letters of recommendation; interview; supplemental information form. *Recommended:* minimum 2.5 GPA; letters of recommendation; supplemental information form.
Standardized tests *Admission: Required:* SAT I or ACT.
Significant dates *Application deadlines:* rolling (freshmen), rolling (transfers). *Financial aid deadline priority date:* 3/15.
Freshman Application Contact
Bernie Valento, Assistant Director of Admission, State University of New York College at Brockport, 350 New Campus Drive, Brockport, NY 14420-2997. **Phone:** 716-395-5059 Ext. 5059. **Toll-free phone:** 800-382-8447. **Fax:** 716-395-5452. **E-mail:** admit@po.brockport.edu
Visit CollegeQuest.com for information on majors offered and athletics. College video available at CollegeQuest.com.

■ *See page 2546 for a narrative description.*

STATE UNIVERSITY OF NEW YORK COLLEGE AT BUFFALO
Buffalo, New York

- **State-supported**, comprehensive, founded 1867
- **Degrees** bachelor's and master's
- **Urban** 115-acre campus
- **Coed**, 9,252 undergraduate students, 80% full-time, 57% women, 43% men
- **Moderately difficult** entrance level, 63% of applicants were admitted
- **19:1 student-to-undergraduate faculty ratio**
- **$3909 tuition** and fees (in-state); $8809 (out-of-state)
- **$8.4 million endowment**

The largest SUNY college, Buffalo State offers 76 majors and 49 minors to undergraduates seeking an outstanding, affordable education. Experienced professors emphasize teaching, mentoring, and helping students achieve success. Buffalo State tailors small classes, studios, labs, and internships to meet students' career interests.

Part of State University of New York System.
Students *Undergraduates:* Students come from 18 states and territories, 20 other countries. *The most frequently chosen baccalaureate fields are:* business/marketing, education, social sciences and history. *Graduate:* 1,910 in graduate degree programs.

From out-of-state	1%	Reside on campus	15%
Age 25 or older	24%	International students	1%
African Americans	11%	Asian Americans/Pacific Islanders	1%
Hispanic Americans	3%	Native Americans	1%

Faculty 670 (58% full-time).
Expenses (1999–2000) *Tuition, state resident:* full-time $3400; part-time $137 per semester hour. *Tuition, nonresident:* full-time $8300; part-time $346 per semester hour. *Required fees:* full-time $509; $21 per semester hour. *College room and board:* $5170; room only: $3190. Room and board charges vary according to board plan, housing facility, and student level. *Payment plan:* installment. *Waivers:* employees or children of employees.
Library E. H. Butler Library. *Operations spending 1999–2000:* $2.8 million. *Collection:* 470,176 titles, 3,100 serial subscriptions, 20,840 audiovisual materials.
College life *Housing:* on-campus residence required through sophomore year. *Option:* coed. *Social organizations:* national fraternities, national sororities, local fraternities, local sororities; 1% of eligible men and 1% of eligible women are members. *Most popular organizations:* United Student Government, African-American Student Organization, Caribbean Student Organization, The Record, WBNY Radio.
Campus security 24-hour emergency response devices and patrols, student patrols, late-night transport-escort service, controlled dormitory access.
After graduation *Career center:* 4 full-time, 1 part-time personnel. Services include job fairs, resume preparation, interview workshops, resume referral, career/interest testing, career counseling, careers library, job bank, job interviews. *Graduate education:* 30% of class of 1999 went directly to graduate and professional school: 15% graduate arts and sciences, 4% education, 0.3% business, 0.3% law.

New York

State University of New York College at Buffalo (continued)

Freshmen 6,062 applied, 3,813 admitted.

Average high school GPA	3.0	SAT verbal scores above 500	46%
SAT math scores above 500	49%	ACT above 18	N/R
From top 10% of their h.s. class	9%	From top quarter	25%
From top half	49%	1998 freshmen returning in 1999	73%

Application *Options:* early admission, early decision, deferred entrance. *Application fee:* $30. *Required:* high school transcript; minimum 3.0 GPA. *Required for some:* essay or personal statement; letters of recommendation; interview.

Standardized tests *Admission: Required:* SAT I. *Recommended:* ACT.

Significant dates *Application deadlines:* rolling (freshmen), rolling (transfers). *Early decision:* 11/15. *Notification:* 12/15 (early decision). *Financial aid deadline priority date:* 3/15.

Freshman Application Contact
Ms. Lesa Loritts, Director of Admissions, State University of New York College at Buffalo, 1300 Elmwood Avenue, Buffalo, NY 14222-1095. **Phone:** 716-878-5519. **Fax:** 716-878-6100. **E-mail:** admissio@buffalostate.edu

Visit CollegeQuest.com for information on majors offered and athletics.

■ *See page 2548 for a narrative description.*

STATE UNIVERSITY OF NEW YORK COLLEGE AT CORTLAND
Cortland, New York

- **State-supported**, comprehensive, founded 1868
- **Degrees** bachelor's, master's, post-master's, and postbachelor's certificates
- **Small-town** 191-acre campus with easy access to Syracuse
- **Coed**, 5,132 undergraduate students, 97% full-time, 57% women, 43% men
- **Moderately difficult** entrance level, 64% of applicants were admitted
- **16:1** student-to-undergraduate faculty ratio
- **$4104 tuition** and fees (in-state); $9004 (out-of-state)
- **$8400 average financial aid** package, $18,279 average indebtedness upon graduation, $5.7 million endowment

Part of State University of New York System.

Students *Undergraduates:* 4,954 full-time, 178 part-time. Students come from 20 states and territories. *The most frequently chosen baccalaureate fields are:* education, health professions and related sciences, social sciences and history. *Graduate:* 1,287 in graduate degree programs.

From out-of-state	2%	Reside on campus	55%
Age 25 or older	9%	Transferred in	12%
International students	0.2%	African Americans	2%
Asian Americans/Pacific Islanders	1%	Hispanic Americans	2%
Native Americans	1%		

Faculty 507 (52% full-time).

Expenses (1999–2000) *Tuition, state resident:* full-time $3400; part-time $137 per credit. *Tuition, nonresident:* full-time $8300; part-time $346 per credit. *Required fees:* full-time $704; $28 per credit. Part-time tuition and fees vary according to course load. *College room and board:* $5530; room only: $3250. Room and board charges vary according to board plan. *Payment plan:* installment. *Waivers:* employees or children of employees.

Library Memorial Library. *Operations spending 1999–2000:* $1.7 million. *Collection:* 396,222 titles, 2,744 serial subscriptions, 4,557 audiovisual materials.

College life *Housing:* on-campus residence required through sophomore year. *Option:* coed. *Social organizations:* national fraternities, national sororities, local sororities; 4% of eligible men and 9% of eligible women are members.

Campus security 24-hour emergency response devices and patrols, late-night transport-escort service.

After graduation 230 organizations recruited on campus 1997–98. *Career center:* 6 full-time, 1 part-time personnel. Services include job fairs, resume preparation, interview workshops, resume referral, career/interest testing, career counseling, careers library, job bank, job interviews.

Freshmen 7,359 applied, 4,716 admitted, 1,022 enrolled.

Average high school GPA	3.44	SAT verbal scores above 500	52%
SAT math scores above 500	60%	ACT above 18	95%
From top 10% of their h.s. class	5%	From top quarter	33%
From top half	84%	1998 freshmen returning in 1999	77%

Application *Options:* electronic application, early admission, early decision, deferred entrance. *Application fee:* $30. *Required:* essay or personal statement; high school transcript; minimum 2.3 GPA; 1 letter of recommendation. *Recommended:* minimum 3.0 GPA; 3 letters of recommendation; interview.

Standardized tests *Admission: Required:* SAT I or ACT.

Significant dates *Application deadline:* 3/15 (transfers). *Early decision:* 11/15. *Notification:* 12/15 (early decision). *Financial aid deadline:* 4/1.

Freshman Application Contact
Mr. Gradon Avery, Director of Admission, State University of New York College at Cortland, PO Box 2000, Cortland, NY 13045. **Phone:** 607-753-4711. **Fax:** 607-753-5999. **E-mail:** admssn_info@snycorva.cortland.edu

Visit CollegeQuest.com for information on majors offered and athletics. College video and electronic viewbook available at CollegeQuest.com.

STATE UNIVERSITY OF NEW YORK COLLEGE AT FREDONIA
Fredonia, New York

- **State-supported**, comprehensive, founded 1826
- **Degrees** bachelor's and master's
- **Small-town** 266-acre campus with easy access to Buffalo
- **Coed**, 4,676 undergraduate students, 95% full-time, 59% women, 41% men
- **Moderately difficult** entrance level, 62% of applicants were admitted
- **20:1** student-to-undergraduate faculty ratio
- **66% graduate** in 6 years or less
- **$4125 tuition** and fees (in-state); $9025 (out-of-state)
- **$6046 average financial aid** package, $12,691 average indebtedness upon graduation, $8.6 million endowment

Part of State University of New York System.

Students *Undergraduates:* 4,455 full-time, 221 part-time. Students come from 27 states and territories, 9 other countries. *The most frequently chosen baccalaureate fields are:* business/marketing, education, visual/performing arts. *Graduate:* 293 in graduate degree programs.

From out-of-state	2%	Reside on campus	53%
Age 25 or older	7%	Transferred in	9%
International students	0.4%	African Americans	2%
Asian Americans/Pacific Islanders	1%	Hispanic Americans	1%
Native Americans	.		

Faculty 380 (59% full-time), 54% with terminal degrees.

Expenses (1999–2000) *Tuition, state resident:* full-time 3400; part-time 137 per credit hour. *Tuition, nonresident:* full-time 8300; part-time 346 per credit hour. *Required fees:* full-time 725; 310 per credit hour. *College room and board:* 5200; room only: 3150. Room and board charges vary according to board plan and housing facility. *Payment plan:* installment.

Library Reed Library. *Operations spending 1999–2000:* $1.5 million. *Collection:* 397,162 titles, 1,960 serial subscriptions, 20,619 audiovisual materials.

College life *Housing:* on-campus residence required through sophomore year. *Options:* coed, men-only, women-only. *Social organizations:* national fraternities, national sororities; 5% of eligible men and 3% of eligible women are members. *Most popular organizations:* Student Association, Undergraduate Alumni Council, communication club, Greek organizations, ethnic organizations.

Campus security 24-hour emergency response devices and patrols, late-night transport-escort service, controlled dormitory access.

After graduation 50 organizations recruited on campus 1997–98. 71% of class of 1998 had job offers within 6 months. *Career center:* 2 full-time, 1 part-time personnel. Services include job fairs, resume preparation, interview workshops, resume referral, career/interest testing, career counseling, careers library, job bank, job interviews. *Graduate education:* 26% of class of 1999 went directly to graduate and professional school.

New York

Freshmen 5,148 applied, 3,213 admitted, 1,073 enrolled. 6 valedictorians.

Average high school GPA	3.32	SAT verbal scores above 500	82%
SAT math scores above 500	82%	ACT above 18	100%
From top 10% of their h.s. class	14%	From top quarter	46%
From top half	90%	1998 freshmen returning in 1999	81%

Application *Options:* electronic application, early admission, early decision, deferred entrance. *Application fee:* $30. *Required:* high school transcript; minimum 2.5 GPA. *Required for some:* essay or personal statement; interview; audition for music and theater programs, portfolio for art programs, essay for media arts program. *Recommended:* letters of recommendation.

Standardized tests *Admission: Required:* SAT I or ACT.

Significant dates *Application deadlines:* rolling (freshmen), rolling (transfers). *Early decision:* 11/1. *Notification:* 12/15 (early decision). **Financial aid deadline priority date:** 2/15.

Freshman Application Contact
Mr. J. Denis Bolton, Director of Admissions, State University of New York College at Fredonia, Fredonia, NY 14063. **Phone:** 716-673-3251. **Toll-free phone:** 800-252-1212. **Fax:** 716-673-3249. **E-mail:** admissionsinq@fredonia.edu

Visit CollegeQuest.com for information on majors offered and athletics. College video and electronic viewbook available at CollegeQuest.com.

■ *See page 2550 for a narrative description.*

STATE UNIVERSITY OF NEW YORK COLLEGE AT GENESEO
Geneseo, New York

- **State-supported**, comprehensive, founded 1871
- **Degrees** bachelor's and master's
- **Small-town** 220-acre campus with easy access to Rochester
- **Coed**, 5,322 undergraduate students, 98% full-time, 66% women, 34% men
- **Very difficult** entrance level, 52% of applicants were admitted
- **19:1** student-to-undergraduate faculty ratio
- **77% graduate** in 6 years or less
- **$4221 tuition** and fees (in-state); $9121 (out-of-state)
- **$6730 average financial aid** package, $12,500 average indebtedness upon graduation, $6.2 million endowment

Part of State University of New York System.

Students *Undergraduates:* 5,213 full-time, 109 part-time. Students come from 18 states and territories, 9 other countries. *The most frequently chosen baccalaureate fields are:* education, business/marketing, social sciences and history. *Graduate:* 282 in graduate degree programs.

From out-of-state	2%	Reside on campus	57%
Age 25 or older	4%	Transferred in	6%
International students	0.2%	African Americans	2%
Asian Americans/Pacific Islanders	4%	Hispanic Americans	3%
Native Americans	0.3%		

Faculty 350 (73% full-time), 68% with terminal degrees.

Expenses (1999–2000) *Tuition, state resident:* full-time $3400; part-time $137 per credit. *Tuition, nonresident:* full-time $8300; part-time $346 per credit. *Required fees:* full-time $821; $34 per credit. *College room and board:* $4940. Room and board charges vary according to board plan and housing facility. *Payment plans:* installment, deferred payment.

Library Milne Library plus 1 other. *Operations spending 1999–2000:* $2 million. *Collection:* 493,299 titles, 3,117 serial subscriptions.

College life *Housing:* on-campus residence required in freshman year. *Option:* coed. *Social organizations:* national fraternities, national sororities, local fraternities, local sororities; 10% of eligible men and 10% of eligible women are members.

Campus security 24-hour emergency response devices and patrols, student patrols, late-night transport-escort service, controlled dormitory access.

After graduation 40 organizations recruited on campus 1997–98. 54% of class of 1998 had job offers within 6 months. *Career center:* 5 full-time, 1 part-time personnel. Services include job fairs, resume preparation, interview workshops, resume referral, career/interest testing, career counseling, careers library, job bank, job interviews. *Major awards:* 2 Fulbright Scholars.

Freshmen 7,974 applied, 4,148 admitted, 1,169 enrolled.

Average high school GPA	3.62	SAT verbal scores above 500	95%
SAT math scores above 500	97%	ACT above 18	100%
From top 10% of their h.s. class	44%	From top quarter	92%
From top half	100%	1998 freshmen returning in 1999	92%

Application *Options:* electronic application, early admission, early decision, deferred entrance. *Application fee:* $30. *Required:* essay or personal statement; high school transcript. *Recommended:* letters of recommendation; interview.

Standardized tests *Admission: Required:* SAT I or ACT.

Significant dates *Application deadlines:* 2/15 (freshmen), rolling (transfers). *Early decision:* 11/15. *Notification:* continuous until 3/15 (freshmen), 12/15 (early decision). **Financial aid deadline priority date:** 2/15.

Freshman Application Contact
Mr. Scott Hooker, Director of Admissions, State University of New York College at Geneseo, 1 College Circle, Geneseo, NY 14454-1401. **Phone:** 716-245-5571. **Fax:** 716-245-5005. **E-mail:** admissions@geneseo.edu

Visit CollegeQuest.com for information on majors offered and athletics. College video and electronic viewbook available at CollegeQuest.com.

■ *See page 2552 for a narrative description.*

STATE UNIVERSITY OF NEW YORK COLLEGE AT OLD WESTBURY
Old Westbury, New York

- **State-supported**, 4-year, founded 1965
- **Degree** bachelor's
- **Suburban** 605-acre campus with easy access to New York City
- **Coed**, 3,245 undergraduate students, 78% full-time, 57% women, 43% men
- **Minimally difficult** entrance level, 87% of applicants were admitted
- **17:1** student-to-undergraduate faculty ratio
- **31.4% graduate** in 6 years or less
- **$3946 tuition** and fees (in-state); $8846 (out-of-state)

SUNY Old Westbury has exchange programs with colleges and universities in the Far East, South Africa, and Europe. SUNY tuition, room and board costs, and fees are paid to the College at Old Westbury. Travel is the only additional expense. Exchange faculty members from China and Korea are regularly on campus.

Part of State University of New York System.

Students *Undergraduates:* Students come from 7 states and territories, 20 other countries. *The most frequently chosen baccalaureate fields are:* business/marketing, education, psychology.

From out-of-state	1%	Reside on campus	23%
Age 25 or older	36%	International students	1%
African Americans	29%	Asian Americans/Pacific Islanders	8%
Hispanic Americans	15%	Native Americans	0.4%

Faculty 228 (52% full-time).

Expenses (1999–2000) *One-time required fee:* $100. *Tuition, state resident:* full-time $3400; part-time $138 per credit. *Tuition, nonresident:* full-time $8300; part-time $346 per credit. *Required fees:* full-time $546; $67 per term part-time. Part-time tuition and fees vary according to course load. *College room and board:* $5345; room only: $3547. Room and board charges vary according to board plan and housing facility. *Payment plan:* installment. *Waivers:* senior citizens.

Library SUNY College at Old Westbury Library. *Collection:* 216,289 titles, 850 serial subscriptions.

College life *Housing: Option:* coed. *Social organizations:* national fraternities, national sororities, local fraternities, local sororities; 5% of eligible men and 5% of eligible women are members. *Most popular organizations:* Alianza Latina, Caribbean Student Association, Asian Club, Finance/Accounting Society.

Campus security 24-hour emergency response devices and patrols, student patrols, late-night transport-escort service, controlled dormitory access.

After graduation 75 organizations recruited on campus 1997–98. *Career center:* 1 full-time personnel. Services include job fairs, resume preparation, interview workshops, resume referral, career/interest testing, career counseling, careers library, job bank, job interviews.

New York

State University of New York College at Old Westbury (continued)

Freshmen 2,193 applied, 1,914 admitted.

SAT verbal scores above 500	N/R	SAT math scores above 500	N/R
ACT above 18	N/R	From top 10% of their h.s. class	5%
From top quarter	20%	From top half	59%
1998 freshmen returning in 1999	56%		

Application *Options:* electronic application, early admission, early decision, deferred entrance. *Application fee:* $30. *Required:* high school transcript. *Required for some:* essay or personal statement; 2 letters of recommendation; interview.

Standardized tests *Admission: Required:* SAT I or ACT.

Significant dates *Application deadlines:* rolling (freshmen), rolling (transfers). *Early decision:* 11/1. *Notification:* 12/15 (early decision). *Financial aid deadline priority date:* 5/15.

Freshman Application Contact
Ms. Mary Marquez Bell, Director, State University of New York College at Old Westbury, PO Box 307, Old Westbury, NY 11568. **Phone:** 516-876-3073. **Fax:** 516-876-3307.

Visit CollegeQuest.com for information on majors offered and athletics. College video available at CollegeQuest.com.

■ *See page 2554 for a narrative description.*

STATE UNIVERSITY OF NEW YORK COLLEGE AT ONEONTA
Oneonta, New York

- **State-supported**, comprehensive, founded 1889
- **Degrees** bachelor's, master's, and postbachelor's certificates
- **Small-town** 250-acre campus
- **Coed**, 5,042 undergraduate students, 97% full-time, 59% women, 41% men
- **Moderately difficult** entrance level, 65% of applicants were admitted
- **21:1 student-to-undergraduate faculty ratio**
- **55% graduate** in 6 years or less
- **$4123 tuition** and fees (in-state); $9023 (out-of-state)
- **$7997 average financial aid** package, $15,100 average indebtedness upon graduation, $12.8 million endowment

The College at Oneonta is a comprehensive college with studies that include the arts and sciences, elementary and secondary education, business, accounting, computer science, music industry, and prelaw as well as premedicine. An exceptional library, outstanding campuswide computing facilities, and a distinctive student center for volunteering enhance students' intellectual and personal development in a safe, scenic, and convenient campus environment.

Part of State University of New York System.

Students *Undergraduates:* 4,889 full-time, 153 part-time. Students come from 14 states and territories, 20 other countries. *The most frequently chosen baccalaureate fields are:* business/marketing, education, home economics/vocational home economics. *Graduate:* 260 in graduate degree programs.

From out-of-state	2%	Reside on campus	58%
Age 25 or older	11%	Transferred in	13%
International students	1%	African Americans	3%
Asian Americans/Pacific Islanders	2%	Hispanic Americans	4%
Native Americans	0.2%		

Faculty 351 (56% full-time), 46% with terminal degrees.

Expenses (2000–2001, estimated) *Tuition, state resident:* full-time $3400; part-time $137 per semester hour. *Tuition, nonresident:* full-time $8300; part-time $346 per semester hour. *Required fees:* full-time $723; $27 per semester hour. Part-time tuition and fees vary according to course load. *College room and board:* $5456; room only: $3006. Room and board charges vary according to board plan and housing facility. *Payment plan:* installment. *Waivers:* employees or children of employees.

Library Milne Library. *Collection:* 546,123 titles, 16,024 audiovisual materials.

College life *Housing:* on-campus residence required through sophomore year. *Option:* coed. *Social organizations:* national sororities, local sororities; 7% of women are members. *Most popular organizations:* Center for Social Responsibility and Community, Mask and Hammer, Terpsichorean, student government, WONY Radio Station.

Campus security 24-hour emergency response devices and patrols, late-night transport-escort service, controlled dormitory access.

After graduation 41 organizations recruited on campus 1997–98. 75% of class of 1998 had job offers within 6 months. *Career center:* 2 full-time personnel. Services include job fairs, resume preparation, career counseling, careers library, job bank, job interviews. *Graduate education:* 37% of class of 1999 went directly to graduate and professional school. *Major awards:* 1 Fulbright Scholar.

Freshmen 8,379 applied, 5,462 admitted, 1,152 enrolled.

Average high school GPA	2.85	SAT verbal scores above 500	61%
SAT math scores above 500	62%	ACT above 18	95%
From top 10% of their h.s. class	5%	From top quarter	25%
From top half	70%	1998 freshmen returning in 1999	66%

Application *Options:* electronic application, early admission, early decision, deferred entrance. *Application fee:* $30. *Required:* essay or personal statement; high school transcript. *Recommended:* minimum 3.0 GPA; 3 letters of recommendation.

Standardized tests *Admission: Required:* SAT I or ACT.

Significant dates *Application deadlines:* rolling (freshmen), rolling (transfers). *Early decision:* 11/1 (for plan 1), 12/15 (for plan 2). *Notification:* 11/15 (early decision plan 1), 12/30 (early decision plan 2). *Financial aid deadline priority date:* 3/15.

Freshman Application Contact
Ms. Karen A. Brown, Director of Admissions, State University of New York College at Oneonta, Alumni Hall 116, Oneonta, NY 13820-4015. **Phone:** 607-436-2524 Ext. 3002. **Toll-free phone:** 800-SUNY-123. **Fax:** 607-436-3074. **E-mail:** admissions@oneonta.edu

Visit CollegeQuest.com for information on majors offered and athletics. College video and electronic viewbook available at CollegeQuest.com.

■ *See page 2556 for a narrative description.*

STATE UNIVERSITY OF NEW YORK COLLEGE AT PLATTSBURGH
New York—See Plattsburgh State University of New York

STATE UNIVERSITY OF NEW YORK COLLEGE AT POTSDAM
Potsdam, New York

- **State-supported**, comprehensive, founded 1816
- **Degrees** bachelor's and master's
- **Small-town** 240-acre campus
- **Coed**, 3,515 undergraduate students, 96% full-time, 59% women, 41% men
- **Moderately difficult** entrance level, 81% of applicants were admitted
- **19:1 student-to-undergraduate faculty ratio**
- **$3935 tuition** and fees (in-state); $8835 (out-of-state)
- **$9198 average financial aid** package, $15,303 average indebtedness upon graduation, $10.1 million endowment

Potsdam, the oldest liberal arts college of SUNY, has strong programs in the arts and sciences, teacher education, and the Crane School of Music. With more than 270 faculty members, the student-faculty ratio is 16:1. Within the Crane School of Music, the ratio is 11:1. Potsdam is within an easy drive of Interstates 81 and 87, Lake Placid, Ottawa, Syracuse, and Montreal. Potsdam offers more than 40 majors, including new programs in archeological studies, business economics, community health, computer and information science, and the business of music.

Part of State University of New York System.

Students *Undergraduates:* 3,385 full-time, 130 part-time. Students come from 25 states and territories, 9 other countries. *The most frequently chosen baccalaureate fields are:* psychology, education, social sciences and history. *Graduate:* 540 in graduate degree programs.

New York

From out-of-state	3%	Reside on campus	50%
Age 25 or older	13%	Transferred in	10%
International students	1%	African Americans	3%
Asian Americans/Pacific Islanders	1%	Hispanic Americans	2%
Native Americans	2%		

Faculty 293 (74% full-time), 63% with terminal degrees.
Expenses (1999–2000) *Tuition, state resident:* full-time $3400; part-time $137 per credit hour. *Tuition, nonresident:* full-time $8300; part-time $346 per credit hour. *Required fees:* full-time $535; $28 per credit hour. *College room and board:* $5750; room only: $3300. Room and board charges vary according to board plan and housing facility. *Payment plan:* installment.
Library F. W. Crumb Memorial Library plus 1 other. *Collection:* 401,579 titles, 1,265 serial subscriptions, 15,267 audiovisual materials.
College life *Housing:* on-campus residence required through junior year. *Options:* coed, men-only, women-only. *Social organizations:* national fraternities, national sororities, local fraternities, local sororities; 10% of eligible men and 10% of eligible women are members. *Most popular organizations:* College Union Board, Students for Environmental Awareness, Crane Student Association.
Campus security 24-hour emergency response devices and patrols, late-night transport-escort service, controlled dormitory access.
After graduation 35 organizations recruited on campus 1997–98. 57% of class of 1998 had job offers within 6 months. *Career center:* 4 full-time personnel. Services include job fairs, resume preparation, interview workshops, resume referral, career/interest testing, career counseling, careers library, job bank, job interviews. *Graduate education:* 25% of class of 1999 went directly to graduate and professional school.
Freshmen 3,108 applied, 2,525 admitted, 750 enrolled.

SAT verbal scores above 500	59%	SAT math scores above 500	56%
ACT above 18	89%	From top 10% of their h.s. class	11%
From top quarter	31%	From top half	64%
1998 freshmen returning in 1999	74%		

Application *Options:* electronic application, early admission, early decision, deferred entrance. *Application fee:* $30. *Required:* high school transcript; minimum 3.0 GPA. *Required for some:* essay or personal statement; audition for music program. *Recommended:* interview.
Standardized tests *Admission: Required:* SAT I or ACT.
Significant dates *Application deadlines:* rolling (freshmen), rolling (transfers). *Early decision:* 11/15. *Notification:* 10/15 (freshmen), 12/15 (early decision). *Financial aid deadline:* continuous.
Freshman Application Contact
Director of Admissions, State University of New York College at Potsdam, 44 Pierrepont Avenue, Potsdam, NY 13676. **Phone:** 315-267-2180. **Fax:** 315-267-2163. **E-mail:** admissions@potsdam.edu
Visit CollegeQuest.com for information on majors offered and athletics. College video and electronic viewbook available at CollegeQuest.com.

■ *See page 2558 for a narrative description.*

STATE UNIVERSITY OF NEW YORK COLLEGE AT PURCHASE
New York—See Purchase College, State University of New York

STATE UNIVERSITY OF NEW YORK COLLEGE OF AGRICULTURE AND TECHNOLOGY AT COBLESKILL
Cobleskill, New York

■ **State-supported**, primarily 2-year, founded 1916
■ **Degrees** associate and bachelor's
■ **Rural** 750-acre campus
■ **Coed**, 2,320 undergraduate students, 93% full-time, 45% women, 55% men
■ **Moderately difficult** entrance level

Part of State University of New York System.
Faculty 145 (86% full-time).
Admissions Office Contact
State University of New York College of Agriculture and Technology at Cobleskill, Cobleskill, NY 12043. **Toll-free phone:** 800-295-8988. **Fax:** 518-255-5333. **E-mail:** admissions@snycob.cobleskill.edu
Visit CollegeQuest.com for information on majors offered and athletics. College video available at CollegeQuest.com.

■ *See page 2560 for a narrative description.*

STATE UNIVERSITY OF NEW YORK COLLEGE OF AGRICULTURE AND TECHNOLOGY AT MORRISVILLE
Morrisville, New York

■ **State-supported**, primarily 2-year, founded 1908
■ **Degrees** associate and bachelor's
■ **Rural** 740-acre campus with easy access to Syracuse
■ **Coed**, 2,767 undergraduate students, 83% full-time, 51% women, 49% men
■ **Minimally difficult** entrance level

Part of State University of New York System.
Faculty 171 (74% full-time).
Admissions Office Contact
State University of New York College of Agriculture and Technology at Morrisville, PO Box 901, Morrisville, NY 13408-0901. **Toll-free phone:** 800-258-0111. **Fax:** 315-684-6116.
Visit CollegeQuest.com for information on majors offered and athletics. College video available at CollegeQuest.com.

STATE UNIVERSITY OF NEW YORK COLLEGE OF ENVIRONMENTAL SCIENCE AND FORESTRY
Syracuse, New York

■ **State-supported**, university, founded 1911
■ **Degrees** bachelor's, master's, and doctoral
■ **Urban** 12-acre campus
■ **Coed**, 1,156 undergraduate students, 97% full-time, 37% women, 63% men
■ **Very difficult** entrance level, 50% of applicants were admitted
■ **$3762 tuition** and fees (in-state); $8662 (out-of-state)
■ **$8456 average financial aid** package, $15,000 average indebtedness upon graduation, $7.5 million endowment

Part of State University of New York System.
Students *Undergraduates:* 1,116 full-time, 40 part-time. Students come from 18 states and territories, 7 other countries. *Graduate:* 558 in graduate degree programs.

From out-of-state	7%	Reside on campus	33%
Age 25 or older	15%	Transferred in	26%
International students	1%	African Americans	3%
Asian Americans/Pacific Islanders	1%	Hispanic Americans	2%
Native Americans	0.3%		

Faculty 136 (84% full-time).
Expenses (1999–2000) *Tuition, state resident:* full-time $3400; part-time $137 per credit hour. *Tuition, nonresident:* full-time $8300; part-time $346 per credit hour. *Required fees:* full-time $362; $12 per credit hour. Full-time tuition and fees vary according to location. Part-time tuition and fees vary according to course load and location. *College room and board:* $8310; room only: $4170. Room and board charges vary according to board plan, housing facility, and location. College room and board are provided by Syracuse University. *Payment plans:* installment, deferred payment.
Library F. Franklin Moon Library plus 1 other. *Operations spending 1999–2000:* $1 million. *Collection:* 122,377 titles, 732 audiovisual materials.
College life *Housing:* on-campus residence required in freshman year. *Option:* coed. *Social organizations:* national fraternities, national sororities;

New York

State University of New York College of Environmental Science and Forestry (continued)

10% of eligible men and 10% of eligible women are members. *Most popular organizations:* Wildlife Society, forestry club, Environmental Education Organization.

Campus security 24-hour emergency response devices and patrols, late-night transport-escort service.

After graduation 25 organizations recruited on campus 1997–98. 73% of class of 1998 had job offers within 6 months. *Career center:* 1 full-time personnel. Services include job fairs, resume preparation, interview workshops, resume referral, career/interest testing, career counseling, careers library, job bank, job interviews. *Graduate education:* 21% of class of 1999 went directly to graduate and professional school: 13% graduate arts and sciences, 2% education, 2% engineering, 2% law, 1% business, 1% medicine.

Freshmen 587 applied, 295 admitted, 142 enrolled. 3 class presidents, 4 valedictorians, 21 student government officers.

Average high school GPA	3.64	SAT verbal scores above 500	86%
SAT math scores above 500	89%	ACT above 18	100%
From top 10% of their h.s. class	31%	From top quarter	67%
From top half	98%	1998 freshmen returning in 1999	91%

Application *Options:* electronic application, early admission, early decision, deferred entrance. *Application fee:* $30. *Required:* essay or personal statement; high school transcript; minimum 3.3 GPA; inventory of courses-in-progress form. *Recommended:* 3 letters of recommendation; interview.

Standardized tests *Admission: Required:* SAT I or ACT.

Significant dates *Application deadlines:* rolling (freshmen), rolling (transfers). *Early decision:* 11/15. *Notification:* 12/15 (early decision). *Financial aid deadline priority date:* 3/1.

Freshman Application Contact
Ms. Susan Sanford, Director of Admissions, State University of New York College of Environmental Science and Forestry, 1 Forestry Drive, Syracuse, NY 13210-2779. **Phone:** 315-470-6600. **Toll-free phone:** 800-777-7373. **Fax:** 315-470-6933. **E-mail:** esfinfo@esf.edu

Visit CollegeQuest.com for information on majors offered and athletics. College video available at CollegeQuest.com.

■ *See page 2562 for a narrative description.*

STATE UNIVERSITY OF NEW YORK COLLEGE OF TECHNOLOGY AT ALFRED
Alfred, New York

- **State-supported**, primarily 2-year, founded 1908
- **Degrees** associate and bachelor's
- **Rural** 175-acre campus
- **Coed**, 1,264 undergraduate students, 100% full-time, 28% women, 72% men
- **Moderately difficult** entrance level
- **2:1 student-to-undergraduate faculty ratio**
- **$3830 tuition** and fees (in-state); $5630 (out-of-state)

Part of State University of New York System.
Faculty 247 (85% full-time).

Admissions Office Contact
State University of New York College of Technology at Alfred, Huntington Administration Building, Alfred, NY 14802. **Toll-free phone:** 800-4-ALFRED. **Fax:** 607-587-4299. **E-mail:** admissions@alfredtech.edu

Visit CollegeQuest.com for information on majors offered and athletics. College video and electronic viewbook available at CollegeQuest.com.

STATE UNIVERSITY OF NEW YORK COLLEGE OF TECHNOLOGY AT CANTON
Canton, New York

- **State-supported**, 4-year, founded 1906
- **Degrees** associate and bachelor's
- **Small-town** 555-acre campus
- **Coed**, 1,833 undergraduate students, 100% full-time, 46% women, 54% men

- **Minimally difficult** entrance level, 79% of applicants were admitted
- **17:1 student-to-undergraduate faculty ratio**
- **$3.2 million endowment**

Part of State University of New York System.

Students *Undergraduates:* 1,833 full-time. Students come from 16 states and territories, 5 other countries.

From out-of-state	2%	Reside on campus	55%
Age 25 or older	28%	Transferred in	7%

Library Southworth Library. *Operations spending 1999–2000:* $292,924. *Collection:* 69,388 titles, 382 serial subscriptions, 1,782 audiovisual materials.

College life *Housing:* on-campus residence required through sophomore year. *Options:* coed, men-only, women-only. *Social organizations:* local fraternities, local sororities; 2% of eligible men and 1% of eligible women are members. *Most popular organizations:* karate club, Mortuary Science club, gospel choir, WATC-Radio, Afro-Latin Society.

Campus security 24-hour emergency response devices and patrols, late-night transport-escort service, controlled dormitory access.

After graduation 40 organizations recruited on campus 1997–98. *Career center:* 2 full-time personnel. Services include resume preparation, interview workshops, resume referral, career/interest testing, career counseling, careers library, job bank, job interviews.

Freshmen 2,559 applied, 2,034 admitted, 1,371 enrolled.

SAT verbal scores above 500	N/R	SAT math scores above 500	N/R
ACT above 18	N/R	From top 10% of their h.s. class	3%
From top quarter	12%	From top half	40%

Application *Options:* electronic application, early admission, deferred entrance. *Application fee:* $30. *Required:* high school transcript. *Required for some:* interview. *Recommended:* minimum 2.0 GPA.

Significant dates *Application deadlines:* rolling (freshmen), rolling (transfers). *Financial aid deadline priority date:* 3/15.

Freshman Application Contact
Mr. David M. Gerlach, Interim Dean of Enrollment Management, State University of New York College of Technology at Canton, Cornell Drive, Canton, NY 13617. **Phone:** 315-386-7123. **Toll-free phone:** 800-388-7123. **Fax:** 315-386-7930. **E-mail:** williama@scanva.canton.edu

Visit CollegeQuest.com for information on majors offered and athletics. College video available at CollegeQuest.com.

STATE UNIVERSITY OF NEW YORK COLLEGE OF TECHNOLOGY AT DELHI
Delhi, New York

- **State-supported**, primarily 2-year, founded 1913
- **Degrees** associate and bachelor's
- **Small-town** 1,100-acre campus
- **Coed**, 1,899 undergraduate students, 97% full-time, 43% women, 57% men
- **Moderately difficult** entrance level

Part of State University of New York System.
Faculty 141 (70% full-time).

Admissions Office Contact
State University of New York College of Technology at Delhi, Main Street, Delhi, NY 13753. **Fax:** 607-746-4104.

Visit CollegeQuest.com for information on majors offered and athletics. College video available at CollegeQuest.com.

STATE UNIVERSITY OF NEW YORK EMPIRE STATE COLLEGE
Saratoga Springs, New York

- **State-supported**, comprehensive, founded 1971
- **Degrees** associate, bachelor's, and master's (branch locations at 7 regional centers with 38 auxiliary units)
- **Small-town** campus
- **Coed**
- **Minimally difficult** entrance level

New York

- **$3555 tuition** and fees (in-state); $8455 (out-of-state)

SUNY Empire State College is an international leader in adult higher education. Students design their own individualized associate, bachelor's, and master's degree programs based on their academic and professional goals. Students benefit from flexible, guided independent study, credit earned for learning gained in work and life, and low SUNY tuition. Empire State College, accredited by the Middle States Association of Colleges and Schools, has more than 40 locations throughout New York State as well as distance learning options.

Part of State University of New York System.

Expenses (1999–2000) *One-time required fee:* $300. *Tuition, state resident:* full-time $3400; part-time $904 per term. *Tuition, nonresident:* full-time $8300; part-time $2216 per term. *Required fees:* full-time $155; $71 per term part-time. Part-time tuition and fees vary according to course load.

Institutional Web site http://www.esc.edu/

College life *Housing:* college housing not available.

Application *Option:* early admission. *Application fee:* $0. *Required:* essay or personal statement. *Required for some:* interview.

Admissions Office Contact
State University of New York Empire State College, 2 Union Avenue, Saratoga Springs, NY 12866-4397. **Toll-free phone:** 800-847-3000. **Fax:** 518-587-2100 Ext. 326.

Visit CollegeQuest.com for information on athletics.

STATE UNIVERSITY OF NEW YORK HEALTH SCIENCE CENTER AT BROOKLYN
Brooklyn, New York

Admissions Office Contact
State University of New York Health Science Center at Brooklyn, 450 Clarkson Avenue, Brooklyn, NY 11203-2098. **Fax:** 718-270-7592.

STATE UNIVERSITY OF NEW YORK INSTITUTE OF TECHNOLOGY AT UTICA/ROME
Utica, New York

- **State-supported**, upper-level, founded 1966
- **Degrees** bachelor's and master's
- **Suburban** 800-acre campus
- **Coed**, 1,987 undergraduate students, 63% full-time, 49% women, 51% men
- **Moderately difficult** entrance level
- **19:1 student-to-undergraduate faculty ratio**
- **$3975 tuition** and fees (in-state); $8875 (out-of-state)
- **$1.1 million endowment**

As an upper-division college, SUNY Utica/Rome is designed to meet the special needs of 2-year college transfer and graduate students. Residence halls feature town house-style suites. Distinctive programs include computer science, telecommunications, professional and technical communications, health information management, health services management, and engineering technologies. A variety of transfer scholarships are available to reward academic excellence.

Part of State University of New York System.

Students *Undergraduates:* 1,247 full-time, 740 part-time. Students come from 8 states and territories, 9 other countries. *The most frequently chosen baccalaureate fields are:* business/marketing, engineering/engineering technologies, health professions and related sciences. *Graduate:* 387 in graduate degree programs.

From out-of-state	2%	Reside on campus	22%
Age 25 or older	65%	Transferred in	32%
International students	2%	African Americans	5%
Asian Americans/Pacific Islanders	2%	Hispanic Americans	2%
Native Americans	0.3%		

Faculty 164 (50% full-time), 37% with terminal degrees.

Expenses (1999–2000) *Tuition, state resident:* full-time $3400; part-time $137 per semester hour. *Tuition, nonresident:* full-time $8300; part-time $346 per semester hour. *Required fees:* full-time $575; $22 per semester hour. Part-time tuition and fees vary according to course load. *College room and board:* $6100; room only: $3900. Room and board charges vary according to board plan and housing facility. *Payment plan:* installment.

Library Kunsela Library plus 1 other. *Operations spending 1999–2000:* $747,700. *Collection:* 189,657 titles, 974 serial subscriptions, 3,822 audiovisual materials.

College life *Housing: Option:* coed. *Most popular organizations:* telecommunications club, Ski and Snowboard Club, Phi Beta Lambda, Black Student Union, American Society of Manufacturing Engineers.

Campus security 24-hour emergency response devices and patrols, late-night transport-escort service, controlled dormitory access, closed circuit TV monitors.

After graduation 63 organizations recruited on campus 1997–98. 85% of class of 1998 had job offers within 6 months. *Career center:* 3 full-time personnel. Services include job fairs, resume preparation, interview workshops, resume referral, career/interest testing, career counseling, careers library, job bank, job interviews. *Graduate education:* 2% of class of 1999 went directly to graduate and professional school.

Application *Options:* electronic application, deferred entrance. *Application fee:* $30.

Significant dates *Application deadline:* rolling (transfers). *Financial aid deadline:* continuous.

Freshman Application Contact
Ms. Marybeth Lyons, Director of Admissions, State University of New York Institute of Technology at Utica/Rome, PO Box 3050, Utica, NY 13504-3050. **Phone:** 315-792-7500. **Toll-free phone:** 800-SUNYTEC. **Fax:** 315-792-7837. **E-mail:** admissions@sunyit.edu

Visit CollegeQuest.com for information on majors offered and athletics. College video available at CollegeQuest.com.

- *See page 2564 for a narrative description.*

STATE UNIVERSITY OF NEW YORK MARITIME COLLEGE
Throggs Neck, New York

- **State-supported**, comprehensive, founded 1874
- **Degrees** associate, bachelor's, and master's
- **Suburban** 56-acre campus
- **Coed**, 666 undergraduate students, 100% full-time, 14% women, 86% men
- **Moderately difficult** entrance level, 31% of applicants were admitted
- **100% graduate** in 6 years or less
- **$4195 tuition** and fees (in-state); $9095 (out-of-state)
- **$10,000 average financial aid** package, $12,000 average indebtedness upon graduation, $1 million endowment

Maritime College's primary mission is the preparation of men and women for the full spectrum of professional careers in the maritime industry, including the US Merchant Marine. Its graduates receive a well-rounded education that enables them to pursue career options in industry or government service or at sea as civilian officers of merchant ships, research ships, and other US vessels. All students participate in 3 summer sea terms aboard the training ship *Empire State VI* in preparation for the US Merchant Marine Officer's license as 3rd mate or 3rd assistant engineer. In addition, commissioning options exist for those seeking careers as officers in the US Navy, Marine Corps, Coast Guard, or Air Force or in the National Oceanographic and Atmospheric Administration (NOAA). Maritime College is the only college that hosts a Naval ROTC program in the greater New York metropolitan area.

Part of State University of New York System.

New York

State University of New York Maritime College (continued)

Students *Undergraduates:* 666 full-time. Students come from 23 states and territories, 15 other countries. *Graduate:* 163 in graduate degree programs.

From out-of-state	24%	Reside on campus	96%
Age 25 or older	8%	Transferred in	8%
International students	5%	African Americans	7%
Asian Americans/Pacific Islanders	4%	Hispanic Americans	7%
Native Americans	0.2%		

Expenses (1999–2000) *One-time required fee:* $1900. *Tuition, state resident:* full-time $3400; part-time $157 per credit. *Tuition, nonresident:* full-time $8300; part-time $546 per credit. *Required fees:* full-time $795; $11 per credit. Full-time tuition and fees vary according to reciprocity agreements. Part-time tuition and fees vary according to reciprocity agreements. *College room and board:* $5600; room only: $3400. Room and board charges vary according to board plan. Tuition and fees for mandatory summer sea term: $1600. *Payment plan:* installment.

Library Stephen Luce Library. *Operations spending 1999–2000:* $425,100. *Collection:* 69,593 titles, 2,043 serial subscriptions, 6,280 audiovisual materials.

College life *Housing:* on-campus residence required through senior year. *Option:* coed. *Social organizations:* local fraternities; 4% of men are members. *Most popular organizations:* Sailing Club, Eagle Scout Fraternity, Ski Club, Culture Club.

Campus security 24-hour emergency response devices and patrols, student patrols, late-night transport-escort service.

After graduation 30 organizations recruited on campus 1997–98. 100% of class of 1998 had job offers within 6 months. *Career center:* 3 full-time personnel. Services include job fairs, resume preparation, resume referral, career counseling, careers library, job bank, job interviews. *Graduate education:* 4% of class of 1999 went directly to graduate and professional school: 2% business, 2% engineering.

Freshmen 663 applied, 207 admitted, 156 enrolled.

Average high school GPA	2.9	SAT verbal scores above 500	56%
SAT math scores above 500	64%	ACT above 18	N/R
From top 10% of their h.s. class	3%	From top quarter	16%
From top half	48%	1998 freshmen returning in 1999	84%

Application *Options:* electronic application, early admission, early decision, early action, deferred entrance. *Application fee:* $30. *Required:* high school transcript; minimum 2.5 GPA; 1 letter of recommendation; medical history. *Recommended:* essay or personal statement; interview.

Standardized tests *Admission: Required:* SAT I or ACT. *Recommended:* SAT II Subject Tests.

Significant dates *Application deadlines:* rolling (freshmen), rolling (transfers). *Early decision:* 11/15, 12/1. *Notification:* 12/15 (early decision), 1/15 (early action). *Financial aid deadline priority date:* 2/15.

Freshman Application Contact
Ms. Deidre Whitman, Vice President of Enrollment and Campus Life, State University of New York Maritime College, 6 Pennyfield Avenue, Fort Schuyler, Throggs Neck, NY 10465-4198. **Phone:** 718-409-7220 Ext. 7222. **Toll-free phone:** 800-654-1874 (in-state); 800-642-1874 (out-of-state). **Fax:** 718-409-7392. **E-mail:** admissions@sunymaritime.edu

Visit CollegeQuest.com for information on majors offered and athletics. College video available at CollegeQuest.com.

■ *See page 2566 for a narrative description.*

STATE UNIVERSITY OF NEW YORK UPSTATE MEDICAL UNIVERSITY
Syracuse, New York

- **State-supported**, upper-level, founded 1950
- **Degrees** bachelor's, master's, doctoral, and first professional
- **Urban** 25-acre campus
- **Coed**, 300 undergraduate students, 60% full-time, 72% women, 28% men
- **Moderately difficult** entrance level, 32% of applicants were admitted
- **$3810 tuition** and fees (in-state); $8710 (out-of-state)

Part of State University of New York System.

Students *Undergraduates:* 180 full-time, 120 part-time. Students come from 5 states and territories. *The most frequently chosen baccalaureate field is:* health professions and related sciences. *Graduate:* 631 in professional programs, 222 in other graduate degree programs.

African Americans	5%	Asian Americans/Pacific Islanders	4%
Hispanic Americans	3%	Native Americans	1%

Expenses (1999–2000) *Tuition, state resident:* full-time $3400; part-time $137 per credit. *Tuition, nonresident:* full-time $8300; part-time $346 per credit. *Required fees:* full-time $410; $9 per credit; $32 per term part-time. Full-time tuition and fees vary according to degree level. Part-time tuition and fees vary according to course load and degree level. *College room and board:* $6515; room only: $4175. Room and board charges vary according to housing facility. *Payment plan:* installment.

Library Weiskotten Library. *Collection:* 132,500 titles, 1,800 serial subscriptions, 29,515 audiovisual materials.

College life *Housing: Option:* coed. *Most popular organizations:* Undergraduate Student Council, Diversity in Allied Health.

Campus security Late-night transport-escort service.

After graduation 100% of class of 1998 had job offers within 6 months. *Career center:* Services include job fairs, resume preparation, career counseling, careers library, job bank.

Application *Options:* early admission, early action, deferred entrance. *Preference* given to state residents. *Application fee:* $30.

Significant dates *Application deadline:* rolling (transfers). *Financial aid deadline:* 4/1. *Priority date:* 3/1.

Freshman Application Contact
Ms. Jennifer Welch, Assistant Director of Admissions, State University of New York Upstate Medical University, 155 Elizabeth Blackwell Street, Syracuse, NY 13210. **Phone:** 315-464-4570. **Fax:** 315-464-8823.

Visit CollegeQuest.com for information on majors offered and athletics.

STERN COLLEGE FOR WOMEN
New York—See Yeshiva University

SYRACUSE UNIVERSITY
Syracuse, New York

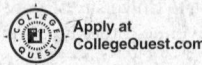 Apply at CollegeQuest.com

- **Independent**, university, founded 1870
- **Degrees** bachelor's, master's, doctoral, first professional, and post-master's certificates
- **Urban** 200-acre campus
- **Coed**, 10,685 undergraduate students, 98% full-time, 54% women, 46% men
- **Very difficult** entrance level, 59% of applicants were admitted
- **12:1 student-to-undergraduate faculty ratio**
- **71.2% graduate** in 6 years or less
- **$19,784 tuition** and fees
- **$15,700 average financial aid** package, $18,600 average indebtedness upon graduation, $657.7 million endowment

Students *Undergraduates:* 10,482 full-time, 203 part-time. Students come from 53 states and territories, 62 other countries. *The most frequently chosen baccalaureate fields are:* business/marketing, communications/communication technologies, social sciences and history. *Graduate:* 764 in professional programs, 3,219 in other graduate degree programs.

From out-of-state	53%	Reside on campus	72%
Age 25 or older	3%	Transferred in	3%
International students	4%	African Americans	7%
Asian Americans/Pacific Islanders	4%	Hispanic Americans	4%
Native Americans	0.3%		

Faculty 1,386 (59% full-time), 51% with terminal degrees.

Expenses (1999–2000) *One-time required fee:* $50. *Comprehensive fee:* $28,184 includes full-time tuition ($19,360), mandatory fees ($424), and room and board ($8400). *College room only:* $4430. Room and board charges vary according to board plan and housing facility. *Part-time tuition:* $844 per credit hour. *Part-time fees:* $62 per year part-time. Part-time tuition and fees vary according to course load, location, and program. *Payment plans:* tuition prepayment, installment. *Waivers:* employees or children of employees.

Library E. S. Bird Library plus 6 others. *Operations spending 1999–2000:* $12.7 million. *Collection:* 2.7 million titles, 16,700 serial subscriptions.

New York

College life *Housing:* on-campus residence required through sophomore year. *Option:* coed. *Social organizations:* national fraternities, national sororities, local fraternities; 20% of eligible men and 30% of eligible women are members. *Most popular organizations:* Panhellenic Association, Student Government Association, university union, interfraternity council, Student African-American Society.

Campus security 24-hour emergency response devices and patrols, late-night transport-escort service, controlled dormitory access, crime prevention programs.

After graduation 230 organizations recruited on campus 1997–98. 80% of class of 1998 had job offers within 6 months. *Career center:* 10 full-time, 6 part-time personnel. Services include job fairs, resume preparation, interview workshops, resume referral, career counseling, careers library, job bank, job interviews, salary negotiation workshops. *Graduate education:* 20% of class of 1999 went directly to graduate and professional school: 6% business, 4% law, 4% medicine, 3% education, 2% engineering, 1% graduate arts and sciences.

Freshmen 12,663 applied, 7,459 admitted, 2,752 enrolled. 39 valedictorians.

Average high school GPA	3.46	SAT verbal scores above 500	90%
SAT math scores above 500	94%	ACT above 18	N/R
From top 10% of their h.s. class	38%	From top quarter	75%
From top half	97%		

Application *Options:* eApply at www.CollegeQuest.com, Common Application, early admission, early decision, deferred entrance. *Application fee:* $40. *Required:* essay or personal statement; high school transcript; 2 letters of recommendation. *Required for some:* audition for drama and music programs, portfolio for art and architecture programs. *Recommended:* interview.

Standardized tests *Admission: Required:* SAT I or ACT.

Significant dates *Application deadlines:* 1/15 (freshmen), 1/15 (transfers). *Early decision:* 11/15. *Notification:* 3/15 (freshmen), 12/31 (early decision). *Financial aid deadline priority date:* 2/15.

Freshman Application Contact
Office of Admissions, Syracuse University, 201 Tolley Administration Building, Syracuse, NY 13244-1100. **Phone:** 315-443-3611. **E-mail:** orange@syr.edu

Visit CollegeQuest.com for information on majors offered and athletics. College video and electronic viewbook available at CollegeQuest.com.

■ *See page 2588 for a narrative description.*

SYRACUSE UNIVERSITY, UTICA COLLEGE
New York—See Utica College of Syracuse University

TALMUDICAL INSTITUTE OF UPSTATE NEW YORK
Rochester, New York

- **Independent Jewish**, 5-year, founded 1974
- **Degree** bachelor's (also offers some graduate courses)
- **Urban** 1-acre campus
- **Men** only
- **Noncompetitive** entrance level

College life *Housing: Option:* men-only.
Campus security Student patrols.
Application *Options:* Common Application, early admission. *Application fee:* $0. *Required:* high school transcript. *Required for some:* interview.

Admissions Office Contact
Talmudical Institute of Upstate New York, 769 Park Avenue, Rochester, NY 14607-3046. **Fax:** 716-442-0417.

Visit CollegeQuest.com for information on athletics.

TALMUDICAL SEMINARY OHOLEI TORAH
Brooklyn, New York

Admissions Office Contact
Talmudical Seminary Oholei Torah, 667 Eastern Parkway, Brooklyn, NY 11213-3310.

TORAH TEMIMAH TALMUDICAL SEMINARY
Brooklyn, New York

Admissions Office Contact
Torah Temimah Talmudical Seminary, 555 Ocean Parkway, Brooklyn, NY 11218-5913.

TOURO COLLEGE
New York, New York

- **Independent**, comprehensive, founded 1971
- **Degrees** associate, bachelor's, master's, doctoral, and first professional
- **Urban** campus
- **Coed**, 6,661 undergraduate students, 91% full-time, 68% women, 32% men
- **Moderately difficult** entrance level
- **12:1 student-to-undergraduate faculty ratio**
- **$9250 tuition** and fees

Students *Undergraduates:* Students come from 17 states and territories. *Graduate:* 959 in professional programs, 582 in other graduate degree programs.

Age 25 or older	51%	International students	0.04%
African Americans	10%	Asian Americans/Pacific Islanders	5%
Hispanic Americans	9%	Native Americans	0.1%

Faculty 937 (29% full-time).

Expenses (1999–2000) *Tuition:* full-time $9250; part-time $390 per credit. Full-time tuition and fees vary according to program. Part-time tuition and fees vary according to program. Room and board charges vary according to gender. *Waivers:* employees or children of employees.

Library *Collection:* 534,280 titles, 4,715 serial subscriptions.

Campus security 24-hour emergency response devices and patrols.

After graduation *Career center:* 5 full-time, 1 part-time personnel. Services include job fairs, resume preparation, resume referral, career counseling, job interviews.

Freshmen

SAT verbal scores above 500	N/R	SAT math scores above 500	N/R
ACT above 18	N/R		

Application *Options:* early admission, deferred entrance. *Application fee:* $35. *Required:* high school transcript. *Required for some:* 2 letters of recommendation; interview. *Recommended:* essay or personal statement; 1 letter of recommendation.

Standardized tests *Admission: Recommended:* SAT I or ACT.

Significant dates *Application deadlines:* rolling (freshmen), rolling (transfers). *Financial aid deadline priority date:* 5/15.

Freshman Application Contact
Ms. Amy Harrison, Director of Admissions, Touro College, 27-33 West 23rd Street, New York, NY 10010. **Phone:** 212-463-0400. **Fax:** 212-779-2344.

Visit CollegeQuest.com for information on majors offered and athletics. College video available at CollegeQuest.com.

■ *See page 2628 for a narrative description.*

UNION COLLEGE
Schenectady, New York

Apply at CollegeQuest.com

- **Independent**, comprehensive, founded 1795
- **Degrees** bachelor's and master's
- **Suburban** 100-acre campus

New York

Union College (continued)
- **Coed**, 2,112 undergraduate students, 99% full-time, 48% women, 52% men
- **Very difficult** entrance level, 46% of applicants were admitted
- **11:1 student-to-undergraduate faculty ratio**
- **83% graduate** in 6 years or less
- **$24,099 tuition** and fees
- **$21,084 average financial aid** package, $17,650 average indebtedness upon graduation, $271.6 million endowment

Major additions to the Union College campus as of fall 1998 were the F. W. Olin Center, a $9-million high-technology classroom and laboratory building funded by the F. W. Olin Foundation of New York City, and the $17.6-million renovated and expanded College library.

Students *Undergraduates:* 2,084 full-time, 28 part-time. Students come from 37 states and territories, 22 other countries. *The most frequently chosen baccalaureate fields are:* biological/life sciences, psychology, social sciences and history. *Graduate:* 282 in graduate degree programs.

From out-of-state	49%	Reside on campus	78%
Age 25 or older	2%	Transferred in	2%
International students	3%	African Americans	4%
Asian Americans/Pacific Islanders	5%	Hispanic Americans	4%
Native Americans	0.2%		

Faculty 213 (89% full-time), 85% with terminal degrees.

Expenses (1999–2000) *Comprehensive fee:* $30,573 includes full-time tuition ($23,892), mandatory fees ($207), and room and board ($6474). *College room only:* $3492. Room and board charges vary according to board plan. *Part-time tuition:* $2655 per course. *Payment plan:* installment. *Waivers:* senior citizens and employees or children of employees.

Library Schaffer Library. *Operations spending 1999–2000:* $2.4 million. *Collection:* 275,064 titles, 2,766 serial subscriptions, 6,002 audiovisual materials.

College life *Housing:* on-campus residence required through senior year. *Options:* coed, men-only, women-only, cooperative. *Social organizations:* national fraternities, national sororities, local fraternities, local sororities, theme houses; 31% of eligible men and 26% of eligible women are members. *Most popular organizations:* Big Brothers/Big Sisters, We Care About U Schenectady, student radio station, student newspaper, African and Latino Alliance of Students.

Campus security 24-hour emergency response devices and patrols, student patrols, late-night transport-escort service, controlled dormitory access, awareness programs, bicycle patrol, shuttle service.

After graduation 54 organizations recruited on campus 1997–98. *Career center:* 3 full-time, 2 part-time personnel. Services include job fairs, resume preparation, interview workshops, resume referral, career/interest testing, career counseling, careers library, job bank, job interviews. **Graduate education:** 30% of class of 1999 went directly to graduate and professional school: 9% graduate arts and sciences, 7% medicine, 5% education, 5% law, 3% business, 1% engineering.

Freshmen 3,761 applied, 1,745 admitted, 535 enrolled. 125 student government officers.

Average high school GPA	3.45	SAT verbal scores above 500	95%
SAT math scores above 500	98%	ACT above 18	N/R
From top 10% of their h.s. class	50%	From top quarter	77%
From top half	98%	1998 freshmen returning in 1999	94%

Application *Options:* eApply at www.CollegeQuest.com, Common Application, electronic application, early admission, early decision, deferred entrance. *Application fee:* $50. *Required:* essay or personal statement; high school transcript; 2 letters of recommendation. *Recommended:* interview.

Standardized tests *Admission: Required:* SAT I or ACT or 3 SAT II Subject Tests (including SAT II: Writing Test).

Significant dates *Application deadlines:* 2/1 (freshmen), 6/1 (transfers). *Early decision:* 11/15 (for plan 1), 1/15 (for plan 2). *Notification:* 4/1 (freshmen), 12/15 (early decision plan 1), 2/1 (early decision plan 2). *Financial aid deadline priority date:* 2/1.

Freshman Application Contact
Mr. Daniel Lundquist, Vice President for Admissions and Financial Aid, Union College, Schenectady, NY 12308-2311. **Phone:** 518-388-6112. **Toll-free phone:** 888-843-6688. **Fax:** 518-388-6986. **E-mail:** admissions@union.edu

Visit CollegeQuest.com for information on majors offered and athletics. College video and electronic viewbook available at CollegeQuest.com.

- *See page 2662 for a narrative description.*

UNITED STATES MERCHANT MARINE ACADEMY
Kings Point, New York

- **Federally supported**, 4-year, founded 1943
- **Degree** bachelor's
- **Suburban** 80-acre campus with easy access to New York City
- **Coed**, 921 undergraduate students, 100% full-time, 10% women, 90% men
- **Very difficult** entrance level, 40% of applicants were admitted
- **$0 comprehensive fee**

Students *Undergraduates:* Students come from 53 states and territories, 3 other countries. *The most frequently chosen baccalaureate fields are:* engineering/engineering technologies, military science/technologies.

Faculty 90 (89% full-time).

Expenses (1999–2000) Tuition, room and board, and medical and dental care provided by the U.S. government. Each midshipman receives a monthly salary while assigned aboard ship for training. Entering freshmen are required to deposit $4852 to defray the initial cost of computer equipment and activities fees.

Library Schuyler Otis Bland Memorial Library. *Collection:* 232,576 titles, 985 serial subscriptions.

College life *Housing:* on-campus residence required through senior year. *Option:* coed.

Campus security 24-hour patrols.

After graduation 34 organizations recruited on campus 1997–98. 96% of class of 1998 had job offers within 6 months. *Career center:* 2 full-time personnel. Services include resume preparation, resume referral, career counseling, careers library, job bank, job interviews. **Graduate education:** 2% of class of 1999 went directly to graduate and professional school: 1% business, 1% engineering.

Freshmen 910 applied, 365 admitted.

Average high school GPA	3.5	SAT verbal scores above 500	100%
SAT math scores above 500	100%	ACT above 18	N/R
From top 10% of their h.s. class	34%	From top quarter	97%
From top half	100%	1998 freshmen returning in 1999	87%

Application *Application fee:* $0. *Required:* essay or personal statement; high school transcript; 3 letters of recommendation. *Recommended:* interview.

Standardized tests *Admission: Required:* SAT I or ACT. *Required for some:* SAT II Subject Tests.

Significant dates *Application deadlines:* 3/1 (freshmen), 3/1 (transfers). *Notification:* continuous until 4/1 (freshmen).

Freshman Application Contact
Capt. James M. Skinner, Director of Admissions, United States Merchant Marine Academy, Kings Point, NY 11024-1699. **Phone:** 516-773-5391. **Toll-free phone:** 800-732-6267. **Fax:** 516-773-5390. **E-mail:** admissions@usmma.edu

Visit CollegeQuest.com for information on majors offered and athletics. College video available at CollegeQuest.com.

- *See page 2668 for a narrative description.*

UNITED STATES MILITARY ACADEMY
West Point, New York

- **Federally supported**, 4-year, founded 1802
- **Degree** bachelor's
- **Small-town** 16,080-acre campus with easy access to New York City
- **Coed**, primarily men, 4,154 undergraduate students, 100% full-time, 15% women, 85% men
- **Most difficult** entrance level, 13% of applicants were admitted
- **7:1 student-to-undergraduate faculty ratio**
- **82.4% graduate** in 6 years or less

New York

- $0 comprehensive fee

Become a leader who can make a difference for the nation in the 21st century. West Point offers this opportunity, challenging outstanding young men and women in academics, leadership, and physical development. The West Point experience builds a foundation for career success as an Army officer; it is tough but rewarding. Graduates earn a Bachelor of Science degree and a commission as a second lieutenant in the U.S. Army.

Students *Undergraduates:* 4,154 full-time. Students come from 53 states and territories, 18 other countries. *The most frequently chosen baccalaureate fields are:* engineering/engineering technologies, physical sciences, social sciences and history.

From out-of-state	92%	Reside on campus	100%
International students	1%	African Americans	8%
Asian Americans/Pacific Islanders	5%	Hispanic Americans	6%
Native Americans	1%		

Faculty 575 (100% full-time), 39% with terminal degrees.

Expenses (1999–2000) Tuition, room and board, and medical and dental care are provided by the U.S. government. Each cadet receives a salary from which to pay for personal computer, uniforms, activities, books, services, and personal expenses. Entering freshmen are required to deposit $2400 to defray the initial cost of uniforms, books, supplies, equipment and fees.

Library United States Military Academy Library plus 1 other. *Collection:* 457,340 titles, 2,220 serial subscriptions, 8,000 audiovisual materials.

College life *Housing:* on-campus residence required through senior year. *Option:* coed. *Most popular organizations:* rugby club, chapel choirs, Big Brothers/Big Sisters, Orienteering Team, Spirit Support Group.

Campus security 24-hour emergency response devices and patrols, student patrols, late-night transport-escort service.

After graduation *Graduate education:* 2% of class of 1999 went directly to graduate and professional school: 2% medicine. *Major awards:* 3 Rhodes scholars.

Freshmen 11,490 applied, 1,484 admitted, 1,100 enrolled. 227 National Merit Scholars, 208 class presidents, 82 valedictorians, 404 student government officers.

SAT verbal scores above 500	95%	SAT math scores above 500	79%
ACT above 18	100%	From top 10% of their h.s. class	50%
From top quarter	81%	From top half	97%
1998 freshmen returning in 1999	92%		

Application *Option:* early action. *Application fee:* $0. *Required:* essay or personal statement; high school transcript; 4 letters of recommendation; medical examination, authorized nomination. *Recommended:* interview.

Standardized tests *Admission: Required:* SAT I or ACT.

Significant dates *Application deadlines:* 3/21 (freshmen), 3/21 (transfers). *Early action:* 10/25. *Notification:* continuous until 6/1 (freshmen), 1/5 (early action).

Freshman Application Contact
Col. Michael C. Jones, Director of Admissions, United States Military Academy, United States Military Academy, West Point, NY 10996. **Phone:** 914-938-4041. **Fax:** 914-938-3021. **E-mail:** 8dad@sunams.usma.army.mil

Visit CollegeQuest.com for information on majors offered and athletics. College video and electronic viewbook available at CollegeQuest.com.

■ *See page 2670 for a narrative description.*

UNITED TALMUDICAL SEMINARY
Brooklyn, New York

Admissions Office Contact
United Talmudical Seminary, 82 Lee Avenue, Brooklyn, NY 11211-7900.

UNIVERSITY AT ALBANY, STATE UNIVERSITY OF NEW YORK
New York—See State University of New York at Albany

UNIVERSITY OF ROCHESTER
Rochester, New York

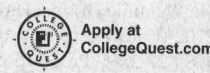
Apply at CollegeQuest.com

- **Independent**, university, founded 1850
- **Degrees** bachelor's, master's, doctoral, and first professional
- **Suburban** 534-acre campus
- **Coed**, 4,445 undergraduate students, 97% full-time, 48% women, 52% men
- **Very difficult** entrance level, 66% of applicants were admitted
- **12:1 student-to-undergraduate faculty ratio**
- **76% graduate** in 6 years or less
- **$22,864 tuition** and fees
- **$21,103 average financial aid** package, $1.1 billion endowment

Rochester is a leading private university with a rich diversity of programs and personal attention that allows close contact with faculty members. Distinctive opportunities include the nationally recognized Take Five program for a tuition-free 5th year, the management certificate, and, for selected students, simultaneous admission to the undergraduate and medical schools.

Students *Undergraduates:* 4,300 full-time, 145 part-time. Students come from 52 states and territories, 45 other countries. *The most frequently chosen baccalaureate fields are:* biological/life sciences, psychology, visual/performing arts. *Graduate:* 763 in professional programs, 2,405 in other graduate degree programs.

Reside on campus	85%	Transferred in	3%
International students	5%	African Americans	5%
Asian Americans/Pacific Islanders	12%	Hispanic Americans	4%
Native Americans	0.2%		

Faculty 1,371 (90% full-time).

Expenses (1999–2000) *Comprehensive fee:* $30,376 includes full-time tuition ($22,300), mandatory fees ($564), and room and board ($7512). *College room only:* $4560. Room and board charges vary according to board plan. *Part-time tuition:* $697 per credit hour. *Payment plans:* tuition prepayment, installment. *Waivers:* children of alumni and employees or children of employees.

Library Rush Rhees Library plus 5 others. *Collection:* 3 million titles, 11,254 serial subscriptions, 78,600 audiovisual materials.

College life *Housing:* on-campus residence required through sophomore year. *Options:* coed, men-only, women-only. *Social organizations:* national fraternities, national sororities; 20% of eligible men and 15% of eligible women are members. *Most popular organizations:* campus newspaper, student radio station, Cinema Group, Debate Union, Campus Board Program.

Campus security 24-hour emergency response devices and patrols, late-night transport-escort service, controlled dormitory access.

After graduation 127 organizations recruited on campus 1997–98. 57% of class of 1998 had job offers within 6 months. *Career center:* 10 full-time personnel. Services include job fairs, resume preparation, resume referral, career/interest testing, career counseling, careers library, job bank, job interviews. *Graduate education:* 50% of class of 1999 went directly to graduate and professional school: 20% graduate arts and sciences, 10% law, 9% medicine, 5% education, 3% engineering, 2% business, 2% dentistry, 1% theology.

Freshmen 8,656 applied, 5,714 admitted, 1,212 enrolled. 25 National Merit Scholars, 53 valedictorians.

Average high school GPA	3.61	SAT verbal scores above 500	95%
SAT math scores above 500	98%	ACT above 18	100%
From top 10% of their h.s. class	57%	From top quarter	86%
From top half	99%	1998 freshmen returning in 1999	93%

Application *Options:* eApply at www.CollegeQuest.com, Common Application, electronic application, early admission, early decision, deferred entrance. *Application fee:* $50. *Required:* essay or personal statement; high school transcript; 1 letter of recommendation. *Required for some:* audition, portfolio. *Recommended:* 2 letters of recommendation.

New York

University of Rochester (continued)
Standardized tests *Admission: Required:* SAT I or ACT. *Recommended:* SAT II Subject Tests.
Significant dates *Application deadlines:* 1/15 (freshmen), rolling (transfers). *Early decision:* 11/1. *Notification:* 4/15 (freshmen), 12/15 (early decision). *Financial aid deadline priority date:* 2/1.
Freshman Application Contact
Mr. W. Jamie Hobba, Director of Admissions, University of Rochester, PO Box 270251, Rochester, NY 14627-0001. **Phone:** 716-275-3221. **Toll-free phone:** 888-822-2256. **Fax:** 716-273-1118. **E-mail:** admit@admissions.cc.rochester.edu
Visit CollegeQuest.com for information on majors offered and athletics. College video available at CollegeQuest.com.

■ *See page 2816 for a narrative description.*

UNIVERSITY OF THE STATE OF NEW YORK, REGENTS COLLEGE
New York—See Regents College

UTICA COLLEGE OF SYRACUSE UNIVERSITY
Utica, New York

- **Independent**, comprehensive, founded 1946
- **Degrees** bachelor's and master's
- **Suburban** 138-acre campus
- **Coed**, 1,835 undergraduate students, 88% full-time, 63% women, 37% men
- **Moderately difficult** entrance level, 84% of applicants were admitted
- **13:1 student-to-undergraduate faculty ratio**
- **47.1% graduate** in 6 years or less
- **$16,410 tuition** and fees
- **$10.2 million endowment**

Utica College offers a warm, friendly atmosphere with small classes and a dedicated faculty. Students choose from 33 majors in both the liberal arts and professional career programs. Extensive cooperative education and internship opportunities provide students with valuable experience in the workplace. Upon graduation, Utica College students receive the internationally recognized Syracuse University degree.

Part of Syracuse University.
Students *Undergraduates:* 1,609 full-time, 226 part-time. Students come from 21 states and territories, 18 other countries. *The most frequently chosen baccalaureate fields are:* business/marketing, health professions and related sciences, psychology. *Graduate:* 42 in graduate degree programs.

From out-of-state	9%	Reside on campus	41%
Age 25 or older	30%	Transferred in	11%
International students	2%	African Americans	8%
Asian Americans/Pacific Islanders	2%	Hispanic Americans	4%
Native Americans	0.5%		

Faculty 203 (49% full-time), 46% with terminal degrees.
Expenses (1999–2000) *Comprehensive fee:* $22,760 includes full-time tuition ($16,150), mandatory fees ($260), and room and board ($6350). *College room only:* $3200. Room and board charges vary according to board plan and housing facility. *Part-time tuition:* $545 per credit hour. *Payment plan:* deferred payment. *Waivers:* senior citizens and employees or children of employees.
Library Gannett Memorial Library. *Operations spending 1999–2000:* $726,326. *Collection:* 176,849 titles, 1,268 serial subscriptions, 62 audiovisual materials.
College life *Housing:* on-campus residence required through sophomore year. *Option:* coed. *Social organizations:* national fraternities, national sororities, local fraternities, local sororities; 3% of eligible men and 3% of eligible women are members. *Most popular organizations:* Occupational Therapy Society, Students of African Descent Alliance, Radio Station Circle, Student Nurses, Young Scholars Liberty Partnership Program.

Campus security 24-hour emergency response devices and patrols, late-night transport-escort service, controlled dormitory access.
After graduation 115 organizations recruited on campus 1997–98. 91% of class of 1998 had job offers within 6 months. *Career center:* 4 full-time personnel. Services include job fairs, resume preparation, interview workshops, resume referral, career/interest testing, career counseling, careers library, job bank, job interviews. *Graduate education:* 10% of class of 1999 went directly to graduate and professional school: 8% graduate arts and sciences, 1% law, 1% medicine.
Freshmen 1,467 applied, 1,233 admitted, 366 enrolled. 2 valedictorians, 29 student government officers.

Average high school GPA	3.2	SAT verbal scores above 500	61%
SAT math scores above 500	60%	ACT above 18	N/R
From top 10% of their h.s. class	9%	From top quarter	71%
From top half	80%	1998 freshmen returning in 1999	80%

Application *Options:* eApply at www.CollegeQuest.com, Common Application. *Application fee:* $35. *Required:* essay or personal statement; high school transcript; minimum 2.0 GPA. *Required for some:* minimum 3.0 GPA. *Recommended:* letters of recommendation; interview.
Standardized tests *Admission: Recommended:* SAT I or ACT. *Required for some:* SAT I or ACT.
Significant dates *Application deadlines:* rolling (freshmen), rolling (transfers). *Financial aid deadline priority date:* 2/15.
Freshman Application Contact
Ms. Leslie North, Vice President for Enrollment Management, Utica College of Syracuse University, 160 Burrstone Road, Utica, NY 13502. **Phone:** 315-792-3006. **Toll-free phone:** 800-782-8884. **Fax:** 315-792-3003. **E-mail:** admiss@utica.ucsu.edu
Visit CollegeQuest.com for information on majors offered and athletics.

■ *See page 2872 for a narrative description.*

VASSAR COLLEGE
Poughkeepsie, New York

- **Independent**, comprehensive, founded 1861
- **Degrees** bachelor's and master's
- **Suburban** 1,000-acre campus with easy access to New York City
- **Coed**, 2,298 undergraduate students, 99% full-time, 61% women, 39% men
- **Very difficult** entrance level, 43% of applicants were admitted
- **10:1 student-to-undergraduate faculty ratio**
- **86.8% graduate** in 6 years or less
- **$24,030 tuition** and fees
- **$20,820 average financial aid** package, $15,772 average indebtedness upon graduation, $578.4 million endowment

Students *Undergraduates:* 2,275 full-time, 23 part-time. Students come from 51 states and territories, 46 other countries. *The most frequently chosen baccalaureate fields are:* English, social sciences and history, visual/performing arts.

From out-of-state	60%	Reside on campus	98%
Age 25 or older	1%	Transferred in	1%
International students	5%	African Americans	5%
Asian Americans/Pacific Islanders	9%	Hispanic Americans	5%
Native Americans	0.4%		

Faculty 289 (85% full-time), 81% with terminal degrees.
Expenses (1999–2000) *Comprehensive fee:* $30,800 includes full-time tuition ($23,700), mandatory fees ($330), and room and board ($6770). *College room only:* $3600. Room and board charges vary according to board plan. *Part-time tuition:* $2790 per unit. Part-time tuition and fees vary according to program. *Payment plan:* installment. *Waivers:* employees or children of employees.
Library Frederick Ferris Thompson Memorial Library. *Operations spending 1999–2000:* $4 million. *Collection:* 780,651 titles, 4,799 serial subscriptions, 16,672 audiovisual materials.
College life *Housing:* on-campus residence required in freshman year. *Options:* coed, women-only. *Most popular organizations:* Vassar Student Association, Black Students Union, VICE (Programming Social Events), Student Activists' Union, Poder Latino.
Campus security 24-hour emergency response devices and patrols, student patrols, late-night transport-escort service, controlled dormitory access.

New York

After graduation 66% of class of 1998 had job offers within 6 months. *Career center:* 5 full-time, 1 part-time personnel. Services include job fairs, resume preparation, resume referral, career counseling, careers library, job bank, job interviews. **Graduate education:** 20% of class of 1999 went directly to graduate and professional school: 13% graduate arts and sciences, 5% law, 2% medicine. **Major awards:** 3 Fulbright Scholars.

Freshmen 4,777 applied, 2,039 admitted, 635 enrolled. 36 class presidents, 26 valedictorians, 100 student government officers.

SAT verbal scores above 500	99%	SAT math scores above 500	99%
ACT above 18	N/R	From top 10% of their h.s. class	63%
From top quarter	90%	From top half	99%
1998 freshmen returning in 1999	92%		

Application *Options:* eApply at www.CollegeQuest.com, Common Application, early admission, early decision, deferred entrance. *Application fee:* $60. *Required:* essay or personal statement; high school transcript; 2 letters of recommendation. *Recommended:* interview.

Standardized tests *Admission: Required:* SAT I and SAT II or ACT.

Significant dates *Application deadlines:* 1/1 (freshmen), 4/15 (transfers). *Early decision:* 11/15 (for plan 1), 1/1 (for plan 2). *Notification:* 4/1 (freshmen), 12/15 (early decision plan 1), 2/1 (early decision plan 2). *Financial aid deadline:* 1/10.

Freshman Application Contact
Dr. David M. Borus, Dean of Admission and Financial Aid, Vassar College, 124 Raymond Avenue, Poughkeepsie, NY 12604. **Phone:** 914-437-7300. **Toll-free phone:** 800-827-7270. **Fax:** 914-437-7063. **E-mail:** admissions@vassar.edu

Visit CollegeQuest.com for information on majors offered and athletics.

See page 2882 for a narrative description.

WADHAMS HALL SEMINARY-COLLEGE
Ogdensburg, New York

- **Independent Roman Catholic**, 4-year, founded 1924
- **Degrees** bachelor's and postbachelor's certificates
- **Rural** 208-acre campus with easy access to Ottawa
- **Coed**, primarily men, 21 undergraduate students, 100% full-time, 100% men
- **Moderately difficult** entrance level, 100% of applicants were admitted
- **3:1 student-to-undergraduate faculty ratio**
- **100% graduate** in 6 years or less
- **$5525 tuition** and fees
- **$10,500 average financial aid** package, $6800 average indebtedness upon graduation, $3.1 million endowment

Students *Undergraduates:* 21 full-time. Students come from 2 states and territories, 1 other country. *The most frequently chosen baccalaureate field is:* philosophy.

From out-of-state	14%	Reside on campus	100%
Age 25 or older	36%	Transferred in	24%
International students	14%		

Faculty 12 (58% full-time), 50% with terminal degrees.

Expenses (1999–2000) *Comprehensive fee:* $10,300 includes full-time tuition ($5100), mandatory fees ($425), and room and board ($4775). *College room only:* $2275. *Part-time tuition:* $170 per credit hour. *Payment plans:* installment, deferred payment.

Library Reverend Richard S. Sturtz Library. *Operations spending 1999–2000:* $63,387. *Collection:* 99,771 titles, 305 serial subscriptions, 4,772 audio-visual materials.

College life *Housing:* on-campus residence required through senior year. *Option:* men-only. *Most popular organization:* Community Service Program.

Campus security 24-hour emergency response devices.

After graduation *Career center:* Services include career counseling. **Graduate education:** 75% of class of 1999 went directly to graduate and professional school: 75% theology.

Freshmen 3 applied, 3 admitted, 4 enrolled.

Average high school GPA	3.5	SAT verbal scores above 500	100%
SAT math scores above 500	100%	ACT above 18	N/R
1998 freshmen returning in 1999	80%		

Application *Option:* Common Application. *Application fee:* $15. *Required:* essay or personal statement; high school transcript; 3 letters of recommendation; interview.

Standardized tests *Admission: Required:* SAT I or ACT, MAPS. *Recommended:* SAT II Subject Tests.

Significant dates *Application deadlines:* 8/15 (freshmen), 8/15 (transfers). *Financial aid deadline priority date:* 7/1.

Freshman Application Contact
Rev. Timothy G. Canaan, Director of Admissions, Wadhams Hall Seminary-College, 6866 State Highway 37, Ogdensburg, NY 13669. **Phone:** 315-393-4231 Ext. 224. **Fax:** 315-393-4249.

Visit CollegeQuest.com for information on majors offered and athletics.

WAGNER COLLEGE
Staten Island, New York

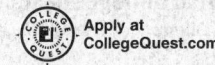
Apply at CollegeQuest.com

- **Independent**, comprehensive, founded 1883
- **Degrees** bachelor's and master's
- **Urban** 105-acre campus with easy access to New York City
- **Coed**, 1,616 undergraduate students, 95% full-time, 60% women, 40% men
- **Moderately difficult** entrance level, 70% of applicants were admitted
- **14:1 student-to-undergraduate faculty ratio**
- **71.3% graduate** in 6 years or less
- **$18,000 tuition** and fees
- **$12,103 average financial aid** package, $7 million endowment

Rated "top tier" by *U.S. News & World Report*, Wagner's curriculum has been recognized for its excellence and innovation while still rooted in the classical liberal arts tradition. The integration of internships and field experiences into the curriculum secures Wagner's place as New York City's only residential liberal arts college.

Students *Undergraduates:* 1,539 full-time, 77 part-time. Students come from 38 states and territories, 13 other countries. *The most frequently chosen baccalaureate fields are:* biological/life sciences, business/marketing, education. *Graduate:* 384 in graduate degree programs.

From out-of-state	31%	Reside on campus	65%
Age 25 or older	9%	Transferred in	3%
International students	2%	African Americans	5%
Asian Americans/Pacific Islanders	3%	Hispanic Americans	5%
Native Americans	0.3%		

Faculty 177 (47% full-time), 61% with terminal degrees.

Expenses (1999–2000) *Comprehensive fee:* $24,500 includes full-time tuition ($18,000) and room and board ($6500). *Part-time tuition:* $600 per credit. Part-time tuition and fees vary according to course load. *Payment plan:* installment. *Waivers:* senior citizens and employees or children of employees.

Library August Horrmann Library. *Operations spending 1999–2000:* $743,210. *Collection:* 310,000 titles, 1,000 serial subscriptions.

College life *Housing: Option:* coed. *Social organizations:* national fraternities, national sororities, local fraternities, local sororities; 20% of eligible men and 15% of eligible women are members. *Most popular organizations:* Student Government Association, Student Activities Board, Wagner College Theatre, Wagner College Choir, student newspaper.

Campus security 24-hour emergency response devices and patrols, late-night transport-escort service, controlled dormitory access.

After graduation 68% of class of 1998 had job offers within 6 months. *Career center:* 3 full-time, 1 part-time personnel. Services include job fairs, resume preparation, interview workshops, resume referral, career/interest testing, career counseling, careers library, job bank, job interviews. **Graduate education:** 29% of class of 1999 went directly to graduate and professional school.

Freshmen 2,156 applied, 1,518 admitted, 478 enrolled. 14 class presidents, 6 valedictorians.

Average high school GPA	2.9	SAT verbal scores above 500	74%
SAT math scores above 500	73%	ACT above 18	99%
From top 10% of their h.s. class	16%	From top quarter	46%
From top half	84%	1998 freshmen returning in 1999	82%

Application *Options:* eApply at www.CollegeQuest.com, Common Application, electronic application, early admission, early decision, deferred

New York

Wagner College (continued)
entrance. *Application fee:* $45. *Required:* essay or personal statement; high school transcript; minimum 2.7 GPA; 2 letters of recommendation. *Recommended:* minimum 3.0 GPA; interview.

Standardized tests *Admission: Required:* SAT I or ACT. *Recommended:* SAT II Subject Tests.

Significant dates *Application deadlines:* 2/15 (freshmen), rolling (transfers). *Early decision:* 12/1. *Notification:* 3/1 (freshmen), 1/1 (early decision). *Financial aid deadline priority date:* 2/15.

Freshman Application Contact
Mr. Angelo Araimo, Dean of Admissions, Wagner College, One Campus Road, Staten Island, NY 10301. **Phone:** 718-390-3411. **Toll-free phone:** 800-221-1010. **Fax:** 718-390-3105. **E-mail:** admissions@wagner.edu

Visit CollegeQuest.com for information on majors offered and athletics. College video available at CollegeQuest.com.

■ *See page 2904 for a narrative description.*

WEBB INSTITUTE
Glen Cove, New York

- **Independent**, 4-year, founded 1889
- **Degree** bachelor's
- **Suburban** 26-acre campus with easy access to New York City
- **Coed**, 81 undergraduate students, 100% full-time, 17% women, 83% men
- **Most difficult** entrance level, 46% of applicants were admitted
- **7:1 student-to-undergraduate faculty ratio**
- **78% graduate** in 6 years or less
- **$0 tuition** and fees
- **$5250 average financial aid** package, $16,600 average indebtedness upon graduation, $70.7 million endowment

Private engineering college, with all undergraduate students on full-tuition scholarship. BS degree in naval architecture and marine engineering. Cooperative work term in each year; 100% employment. Competitive selection of students based on academic record, standardized test scores, and motivation for program. Fully accredited.

Students *Undergraduates:* 81 full-time. Students come from 28 states and territories. *The most frequently chosen baccalaureate field is:* engineering/engineering technologies.

| From out-of-state | 77% | Reside on campus | 99% |
| Asian Americans/Pacific Islanders | 1% | | |

Faculty 15 (53% full-time), 60% with terminal degrees.

Expenses (2000–2001) includes room and board ($6250). *College room only:* $2800.

Library Livingston Library. *Operations spending 1999–2000:* $146,796. *Collection:* 39,318 titles, 255 serial subscriptions, 1,829 audiovisual materials.

College life *Housing:* on-campus residence required through senior year. *Options:* coed, men-only, women-only. *Most popular organizations:* Webb Student Organization, Society of Naval Architects and Marine Engineers.

Campus security 24-hour emergency response devices and patrols, controlled dormitory access.

After graduation 11 organizations recruited on campus 1997–98. *Career center:* 1 part-time personnel. Services include resume preparation, resume referral, career counseling, job bank, job interviews. *Graduate education:* 38% of class of 1999 went directly to graduate and professional school: 38% engineering.

Freshmen 70 applied, 32 admitted, 22 enrolled. 1 National Merit Scholar, 2 valedictorians, 5 student government officers.

Average high school GPA	3.9	SAT verbal scores above 500	99%
SAT math scores above 500	100%	ACT above 18	N/R
From top 10% of their h.s. class	75%	From top quarter	100%
From top half	100%	1998 freshmen returning in 1999	96%

Application *Option:* early decision. *Application fee:* $25. *Required:* high school transcript; minimum 3.5 GPA; 2 letters of recommendation; interview; proof of U.S. citizenship.

Standardized tests *Admission: Required:* SAT I, SAT II: Writing Test, SAT II Subject Tests in math and either physics or chemistry.

Significant dates *Application deadlines:* 2/15 (freshmen), 2/15 (transfers). *Early decision:* 10/15. *Notification:* continuous until 4/15 (freshmen), 12/10 (early decision). *Financial aid deadline priority date:* 7/1.

Freshman Application Contact
Mr. William G. Murray, Executive Director of Student Administrative Services, Webb Institute, Crescent Beach Road, Glen Cove, NY 11542-1398. **Phone:** 516-671-2213. **Fax:** 516-674-9838. **E-mail:** admissions@webb-institute.edu

Visit CollegeQuest.com for information on majors offered and athletics. College video available at CollegeQuest.com.

■ *See page 2926 for a narrative description.*

WELLS COLLEGE
Aurora, New York

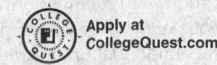
Apply at CollegeQuest.com

- **Independent**, 4-year, founded 1868
- **Degree** bachelor's
- **Rural** 365-acre campus with easy access to Syracuse
- **Women** only, 385 undergraduate students, 98% full-time
- **Moderately difficult** entrance level, 90% of applicants were admitted
- **8:1 student-to-undergraduate faculty ratio**
- **60% graduate** in 6 years or less
- **$12,300 tuition** and fees
- **$13,807 average financial aid** package, $17,125 average indebtedness upon graduation, $52.5 million endowment

Wells College believes that the 21st century will be a time of unprecedented opportunity for women. Women who are prepared for leadership roles will have a distinct advantage. Wells College has an integrative liberal arts curriculum designed to prepare women for the leadership roles they will assume in all areas of life in the next century. Wells women are being prepared to become the leaders in a variety of fields: business, government, the arts, sciences, medicine, and education. The liberal arts curriculum, combined with a wide array of internships, outstanding study-abroad opportunities, leadership programs, and a wealth of cocurricular activities, helps Wells women realize their potential and career goals.

Students *Undergraduates:* 376 full-time, 9 part-time. Students come from 24 states and territories, 9 other countries. *The most frequently chosen baccalaureate fields are:* biological/life sciences, social sciences and history, visual/performing arts.

From out-of-state	35%	Age 25 or older	7%
Transferred in	8%	International students	3%
African Americans	4%	Asian Americans/Pacific Islanders	6%
Hispanic Americans	2%	Native Americans	1%

Faculty 55 (76% full-time), 85% with terminal degrees.

Expenses (1999–2000) *Comprehensive fee:* $18,400 includes full-time tuition ($11,850), mandatory fees ($450), and room and board ($6100). *Part-time tuition:* $250 per semester hour. *Payment plan:* installment. *Waivers:* senior citizens and employees or children of employees.

Library Louis Jefferson Long Library. *Operations spending 1999–2000:* $364,284. *Collection:* 248,130 titles, 412 serial subscriptions, 782 audiovisual materials.

College life *Housing:* on-campus residence required through senior year. *Option:* women-only. *Most popular organizations:* creative and performing arts groups, POWER, Amnesty International, Athletic Association, choral groups.

Campus security 24-hour emergency response devices and patrols, late-night transport-escort service, controlled dormitory access.

After graduation 39% of class of 1998 had job offers within 6 months. *Career center:* 2 full-time personnel. Services include job fairs, resume preparation, interview workshops, resume referral, career/interest testing, career counseling, careers library, job bank. *Graduate education:* 15% of class of 1999 went directly to graduate and professional school: 11% graduate arts and sciences, 2% education, 2% medicine, 1% veterinary medicine.

Freshmen 410 applied, 368 admitted, 135 enrolled. 3 valedictorians.

Average high school GPA	3.5	SAT verbal scores above 500	83%
SAT math scores above 500	72%	ACT above 18	96%
From top 10% of their h.s. class	33%	From top quarter	72%
From top half	94%	1998 freshmen returning in 1999	80%

New York

Application *Options:* eApply at www.CollegeQuest.com, Common Application, early admission, early decision, early action, deferred entrance. *Application fee:* $40. *Required:* essay or personal statement; high school transcript; 2 letters of recommendation. *Recommended:* interview.
Standardized tests *Admission: Required:* SAT I or ACT.
Significant dates *Application deadlines:* 3/1 (freshmen), rolling (transfers). *Early decision:* 12/15, 12/15. *Notification:* 4/1 (freshmen), 1/15 (early decision), 2/1 (early action). *Financial aid deadline priority date:* 2/15.
Freshman Application Contact
Ms. Susan Raith Sloan, Director of Admissions, Wells College, MacMillan Hall, Aurora, NY 13026. **Phone:** 315-364-3264. **Toll-free phone:** 800-952-9355. **Fax:** 315-364-3362. **E-mail:** admissions@wells.edu
Visit CollegeQuest.com for information on majors offered and athletics.

■ *See page 2932 for a narrative description.*

WILLIAM SMITH COLLEGE
New York—See Hobart and William Smith Colleges

YESHIVA COLLEGE
New York—See Yeshiva University

YESHIVA DERECH CHAIM
Brooklyn, New York

Admissions Office Contact
Yeshiva Derech Chaim, 4907 18th Avenue, Brooklyn, NY 11218.

YESHIVA KARLIN STOLIN RABBINICAL INSTITUTE
Brooklyn, New York

- **Independent Jewish**, comprehensive, founded 1948
- **Degrees** bachelor's and master's
- **Urban** campus
- **Men** only, 38 undergraduate students, 100% full-time
- **Very difficult** entrance level
- **$5200 tuition** and fees

Students *Undergraduates:* 38 full-time. Students come from 3 other countries. *Graduate:* 15 in graduate degree programs.
   Transferred in   8%
Faculty 7 (57% full-time).
Expenses (1999–2000) *Comprehensive fee:* $8400 includes full-time tuition ($5200) and room and board ($3200). *College room only:* $1800. *Payment plan:* installment.
Library *Operations spending 1999–2000:* $15,000. *Collection:* 6,000 titles.
Campus security 24-hour emergency response devices.
Freshmen 14 enrolled.

SAT verbal scores above 500	N/R
ACT above 18	N/R
From top quarter	75%
1998 freshmen returning in 1999	70%
SAT math scores above 500	N/R
From top 10% of their h.s. class	33%
From top half	100%

Application *Preference* given to students from Mesivta Karlin Stolin. *Required:* high school transcript; interview.
Significant dates *Application deadlines:* rolling (freshmen), rolling (transfers). *Financial aid deadline priority date:* 11/1.
Freshman Application Contact
Mr. Arych L. Wolpin, Director of Admissions, Yeshiva Karlin Stolin Rabbinical Institute, 1818 Fifty-fourth Street, Brooklyn, NY 11204. **Phone:** 718-232-7800. **Fax:** 718-331-4833.
Visit CollegeQuest.com for information on majors offered and athletics.

YESHIVA OF NITRA RABBINICAL COLLEGE
Mount Kisco, New York

Admissions Office Contact
Yeshiva of Nitra Rabbinical College, Pines Bridge Road, Mount Kisco, NY 10549.

YESHIVA SHAAR HATORAH TALMUDIC RESEARCH INSTITUTE
Kew Gardens, New York

Admissions Office Contact
Yeshiva Shaar Hatorah Talmudic Research Institute, 83-96 117th Street, Kew Gardens, NY 11418-1469.

YESHIVATH VIZNITZ
Monsey, New York

Admissions Office Contact
Yeshivath Viznitz, Phyllis Terrace, PO Box 446, Monsey, NY 10952.

YESHIVATH ZICHRON MOSHE
South Fallsburg, New York

Admissions Office Contact
Yeshivath Zichron Moshe, Laurel Park Road, South Fallsburg, NY 12779.

YESHIVAT MIKDASH MELECH
Brooklyn, New York

Admissions Office Contact
Yeshivat Mikdash Melech, 1326 Ocean Parkway, Brooklyn, NY 11230-5601.

YESHIVA UNIVERSITY
New York, New York

- **Independent**, university, founded 1886
- **Degrees** bachelor's, master's, doctoral, and first professional (Yeshiva College and Stern College for Women are coordinate undergraduate colleges of arts and sciences for men and women, respectively. Sy Syms School of Business offers programs at both campuses)
- **Urban** campus
- **Coed**, 2,529 undergraduate students, 98% full-time, 44% women, 56% men
- **Moderately difficult** entrance level
- **$15,960 tuition** and fees
- **$493 million endowment**

Students *Undergraduates:* 2,467 full-time, 62 part-time. Students come from 31 states and territories, 30 other countries. *Graduate:* 1,617 in professional programs, 1,335 in other graduate degree programs.
   Age 25 or older   1%
Expenses (1999–2000) *Comprehensive fee:* $21,230 includes full-time tuition ($15,650), mandatory fees ($310), and room and board ($5270). *College room only:* $3770. *Part-time tuition:* $560 per credit. *Part-time fees:* $25 per term part-time. *Payment plan:* installment. *Waivers:* employees or children of employees.
Library Mendel Gottesman Library plus 6 others. *Collection:* 995,312 titles, 9,760 serial subscriptions.
College life *Most popular organizations:* dramatics societies, student newspapers, social action groups.
Campus security 24-hour emergency response devices and patrols, late-night transport-escort service.

New York–North Carolina

Yeshiva University (continued)

After graduation 50 organizations recruited on campus 1997–98. *Career center:* 4 full-time personnel. Services include job fairs, resume preparation, resume referral, career counseling, careers library, job bank, job interviews.

Freshmen 671 enrolled.

Average high school GPA	3.4	SAT verbal scores above 500	N/R
SAT math scores above 500	N/R	ACT above 18	N/R
1998 freshmen returning in 1999	83%		

Application *Options:* early admission, deferred entrance. *Application fee:* $40. *Required:* high school transcript; 2 letters of recommendation; interview. *Recommended:* essay or personal statement.

Standardized tests *Admission: Required:* SAT I or ACT. *Recommended:* SAT II Subject Tests.

Significant dates *Application deadlines:* 2/15 (freshmen), 2/15 (transfers). *Financial aid deadline:* continuous.

Freshman Application Contact
Mr. Michael Kranzler, Director of Undergraduate Admissions, Yeshiva University, 500 West 185th Street, New York, NY 10033-3201. **Phone:** 212-960-5400 Ext. 277. **Fax:** 212-960-0086. **E-mail:** yuadmit@ymail.yu.edu

Visit CollegeQuest.com for information on majors offered and athletics. College video available at CollegeQuest.com.

YORK COLLEGE OF THE CITY UNIVERSITY OF NEW YORK
Jamaica, New York

- **State and locally supported**, 4-year, founded 1967
- **Degree** bachelor's
- **Urban** 50-acre campus with easy access to New York City
- **Coed**, 4,979 undergraduate students, 59% full-time, 71% women, 29% men
- **Noncompetitive** entrance level, 52% of applicants were admitted
- **18:1 student-to-undergraduate faculty ratio**
- **$3292 tuition** and fees (in-state); $6892 (out-of-state)

Part of City University of New York System.

Students *Undergraduates:* 2,918 full-time, 2,061 part-time. Students come from 100 other countries. *The most frequently chosen baccalaureate fields are:* business/marketing, education, psychology.

From out-of-state	4%	Age 25 or older	58%
Transferred in	10%	International students	3%
African Americans	50%	Asian Americans/Pacific Islanders	7%
Hispanic Americans	14%	Native Americans	0.4%

Faculty 385 (43% full-time), 47% with terminal degrees.

Expenses (1999–2000) *Tuition, state resident:* full-time $3200; part-time $135 per credit. *Tuition, nonresident:* full-time $6800; part-time $285 per credit. *Required fees:* full-time $92; $26 per term part-time.

Library *Collection:* 174,915 titles, 1,094 serial subscriptions.

College life *Housing:* college housing not available. *Most popular organizations:* Haitian Students Association, Caribbean Students Association, Haitian Cultural Association, Latin Caucus.

Campus security 24-hour emergency response devices and patrols, late-night transport-escort service.

After graduation *Career center:* 3 full-time, 2 part-time personnel. Services include job fairs, resume preparation, resume referral, career counseling, job bank, job interviews.

Freshmen 734 applied, 381 admitted, 461 enrolled.

Average high school GPA	2.42	SAT verbal scores above 500	15%
SAT math scores above 500	18%	ACT above 18	N/R

Application *Options:* Common Application, early admission, deferred entrance. *Application fee:* $40. *Required:* high school transcript; minimum 2.0 GPA. *Required for some:* minimum 2.5 GPA. *Recommended:* minimum 3.0 GPA.

Standardized tests *Admission: Recommended:* SAT I and SAT II or ACT. *Required for some:* SAT I and SAT II or ACT.

Significant dates *Application deadlines:* rolling (freshmen), rolling (transfers). *Financial aid deadline:* 5/1.

Freshman Application Contact
Ms. Sally Nelson, Director of Admissions, York College of the City University of New York, 94-20 Guy R. Brewer Boulevard, Jamaica, NY 11451. **Phone:** 718-262-2165.

Visit CollegeQuest.com for information on majors offered and athletics. College video available at CollegeQuest.com.

■ *See page 3024 for a narrative description.*

NORTH CAROLINA

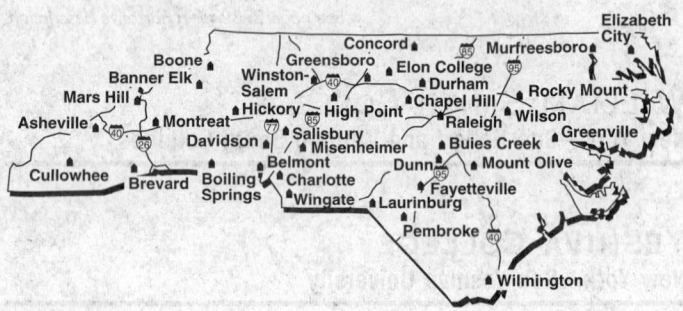

APPALACHIAN STATE UNIVERSITY
Boone, North Carolina

- **State-supported**, comprehensive, founded 1899
- **Degrees** bachelor's, master's, doctoral, and post-master's certificates
- **Small-town** 255-acre campus
- **Coed**, 10,994 undergraduate students, 95% full-time, 51% women, 49% men
- **Moderately difficult** entrance level, 66% of applicants were admitted
- **17:1 student-to-undergraduate faculty ratio**
- **$2088 tuition** and fees (in-state); $9358 (out-of-state)

Part of University of North Carolina System.

Students *Undergraduates:* 10,391 full-time, 603 part-time. Students come from 38 states and territories. *The most frequently chosen baccalaureate fields are:* business/marketing, education, social sciences and history. *Graduate:* 1,209 in graduate degree programs.

Reside on campus	48%	Age 25 or older	9%
Transferred in	7%	International students	0.3%
African Americans	3%	Asian Americans/Pacific Islanders	1%
Hispanic Americans	1%	Native Americans	0.3%

Faculty 829 (71% full-time), 61% with terminal degrees.

Expenses (2000–2001, estimated) *Tuition, state resident:* full-time $962. *Tuition, nonresident:* full-time $8232. *Required fees:* full-time $1126. Part-time tuition and fees vary according to course load. *College room and board:* $3560; room only: $2110. Room and board charges vary according to board plan and housing facility. *Payment plan:* installment. *Waivers:* senior citizens.

Library Carol Grotnes Belk Library plus 1 other. *Operations spending 1999–2000:* $6.1 million. *Collection:* 564,252 titles, 29,347 audiovisual materials.

College life *Housing:* on-campus residence required in freshman year. *Option:* coed. *Social organizations:* national fraternities, national sororities; 27% of eligible men and 34% of eligible women are members. *Most popular organizations:* Baptist Student Union, Inter-University Christian Fellowship, Campus Crusade for Christ, Circle K, Criminal Justice Association.

Campus security 24-hour emergency response devices and patrols, late-night transport-escort service, controlled dormitory access.

After graduation 200 organizations recruited on campus 1997–98. 85% of class of 1998 had job offers within 6 months. *Career center:* 10 full-time personnel. Services include job fairs, resume preparation, resume referral, career counseling, careers library, job bank, job interviews. *Graduate education:* 15% of class of 1999 went directly to graduate and professional school.

North Carolina

Freshmen 8,049 applied, 5,318 admitted, 2,209 enrolled.

Average high school GPA	3.55	SAT verbal scores above 500	70%
SAT math scores above 500	69%	ACT above 18	N/R
From top 10% of their h.s. class	15%	From top quarter	49%
From top half	86%		

Application *Options:* Common Application, early admission, deferred entrance. *Application fee:* $35. *Required:* high school transcript.

Standardized tests *Admission: Required:* SAT I or ACT.

Significant dates *Financial aid deadline priority date:* 3/15.

Freshman Application Contact
Mr. Joe Watts, Associate Vice Chancellor, Appalachian State University, John Thomas Hall, Boone, NC 28608. **Phone:** 828-262-2120. **Fax:** 828-262-3296. **E-mail:** admissions@appstate.edu

Visit CollegeQuest.com for information on majors offered and athletics. College video available at CollegeQuest.com.

BARBER-SCOTIA COLLEGE
Concord, North Carolina

- **Independent**, 4-year, founded 1867, affiliated with Presbyterian Church (U.S.A.)
- **Degree** bachelor's
- **Small-town** 23-acre campus with easy access to Charlotte
- **Coed**, 480 undergraduate students, 98% full-time, 44% women, 56% men
- **Minimally difficult** entrance level, 51% of applicants were admitted
- **18:1 student-to-undergraduate faculty ratio**
- **$7866 tuition** and fees
- **$8741 average financial aid** package, $12,125 average indebtedness upon graduation, $4.3 million endowment

Students *Undergraduates:* 472 full-time, 8 part-time. Students come from 23 states and territories. *The most frequently chosen baccalaureate fields are:* business/marketing, parks and recreation, social sciences and history.

From out-of-state	39%	Reside on campus	90%
Age 25 or older	9%	Transferred in	6%
African Americans	99%	Hispanic Americans	0.2%

Faculty 33 (67% full-time), 48% with terminal degrees.

Expenses (1999–2000) *Comprehensive fee:* $11,366 includes full-time tuition ($7400), mandatory fees ($466), and room and board ($3500). *College room only:* $1800. Full-time tuition and fees vary according to course load. *Part-time tuition:* $310 per semester hour. *Part-time fees:* $44 per year part-time. Part-time tuition and fees vary according to course load. *Payment plan:* installment. *Waivers:* employees or children of employees.

Library Sage Memorial Library. *Operations spending 1999–2000:* $210,925. *Collection:* 24,270 titles, 193 serial subscriptions.

College life On-campus residence required through senior year. *Social organizations:* national fraternities, national sororities; 10% of eligible men and 12% of eligible women are members. *Most popular organizations:* SGA (Student Government Association), Student Christian Association, Pre-Alumni Council, Scotia Express, yearbook.

Campus security 24-hour emergency response devices and patrols.

After graduation *Career center:* 1 full-time, 1 part-time personnel. Services include job fairs, resume preparation, resume referral, career counseling, careers library, job bank, job interviews. *Graduate education:* 7% of class of 1999 went directly to graduate and professional school: 5% graduate arts and sciences, 2% theology.

Freshmen 838 applied, 431 admitted, 143 enrolled.

Average high school GPA	2.12	SAT verbal scores above 500	N/R
SAT math scores above 500	N/R	ACT above 18	N/R
From top 10% of their h.s. class	3%	From top quarter	10%
From top half	17%	1998 freshmen returning in 1999	69%

Application *Options:* Common Application, electronic application, early admission. *Application fee:* $15. *Required:* high school transcript; letters of recommendation. *Recommended:* essay or personal statement; interview.

Standardized tests *Admission: Required:* SAT I or ACT.

Significant dates *Application deadlines:* rolling (freshmen), rolling (transfers). *Financial aid deadline priority date:* 8/1.

Freshman Application Contact
Dr. Alexander Erwin, Academic Dean, Barber-Scotia College, 145 Cabarrus Avenue, West, Concord, NC 28025-5187. **Phone:** 704-789-2948. **Toll-free phone:** 800-610-0778. **Fax:** 704-784-3817.

Visit CollegeQuest.com for information on majors offered and athletics.

BARTON COLLEGE
Wilson, North Carolina

- **Independent**, 4-year, founded 1902, affiliated with Christian Church (Disciples of Christ)
- **Degree** bachelor's
- **Small-town** 62-acre campus
- **Coed**, 1,233 undergraduate students, 78% full-time, 68% women, 32% men
- **Minimally difficult** entrance level, 90% of applicants were admitted
- **$10,834 tuition** and fees
- **$9282 average financial aid** package, $11,500 average indebtedness upon graduation, $19 million endowment

Students *Undergraduates:* 958 full-time, 275 part-time. Students come from 26 states and territories, 22 other countries. *The most frequently chosen baccalaureate fields are:* business/marketing, education, health professions and related sciences.

From out-of-state	26%	Reside on campus	40%
Age 25 or older	25%	Transferred in	12%
International students	2%	African Americans	15%
Asian Americans/Pacific Islanders	1%	Hispanic Americans	1%
Native Americans	0.5%		

Faculty 92 (28% full-time).

Expenses (1999–2000) *Comprehensive fee:* $14,726 includes full-time tuition ($10,030), mandatory fees ($804), and room and board ($3892). *College room only:* $1784. Full-time tuition and fees vary according to course load. Room and board charges vary according to board plan and housing facility. *Part-time tuition:* $206 per semester hour. Part-time tuition and fees vary according to course load and program. *Payment plan:* installment. *Waivers:* adult students and employees or children of employees.

Library Willis N. Hackney Library. *Operations spending 1999–2000:* $328,000. *Collection:* 179,758 titles, 725 serial subscriptions, 4,656 audiovisual materials.

College life *Housing:* on-campus residence required through sophomore year. *Options:* coed, women-only. *Social organizations:* national fraternities, national sororities; 6% of eligible men and 9% of eligible women are members. *Most popular organizations:* Barton College Association of Nurses, Black Student Awareness, Stage and Script, Campus Activities Board.

Campus security 24-hour emergency response devices and patrols, student patrols, late-night transport-escort service, controlled dormitory access.

After graduation 85 organizations recruited on campus 1997–98. 90% of class of 1998 had job offers within 6 months. *Career center:* 2 full-time personnel. Services include job fairs, resume preparation, resume referral, career counseling, careers library, job interviews. *Graduate education:* 6% of class of 1999 went directly to graduate and professional school.

Freshmen 870 applied, 781 admitted, 285 enrolled.

Average high school GPA	2.6	SAT verbal scores above 500	26%
SAT math scores above 500	29%	ACT above 18	N/R
From top 10% of their h.s. class	12%	From top quarter	29%
From top half	70%	1998 freshmen returning in 1999	75%

Application *Options:* electronic application, early admission, deferred entrance. *Application fee:* $25. *Required:* high school transcript. *Recommended:* essay or personal statement; minimum 2.5 GPA; 2 letters of recommendation; interview.

Standardized tests *Admission: Required:* SAT I or ACT.

Significant dates *Application deadlines:* rolling (freshmen), rolling (transfers). *Financial aid deadline priority date:* 4/15.

Freshman Application Contact
Ms. Amy Denton, Director of In-State Admissions, Barton College, 400 North Atlantic Christian College Drive, Wilson, NC 27893-7000. **Phone:** 252-399-6314. **Toll-free phone:** 800-345-4973. **Fax:** 252-237-4957. **E-mail:** enroll@barton.edu

Visit CollegeQuest.com for information on majors offered and athletics.

- *See page 1232 for a narrative description.*

North Carolina

BELMONT ABBEY COLLEGE
Belmont, North Carolina

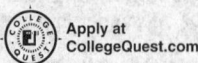
Apply at CollegeQuest.com

- **Independent Roman Catholic**, 4-year, founded 1876
- **Degree** bachelor's
- **Small-town** 650-acre campus with easy access to Charlotte
- **Coed**, 926 undergraduate students, 85% full-time, 54% women, 46% men
- **Moderately difficult** entrance level, 98% of applicants were admitted
- **17:1 student-to-undergraduate faculty ratio**
- **39.5% graduate** in 6 years or less
- **$12,712 tuition** and fees
- **$14,000 average financial aid** package, $4000 average indebtedness upon graduation, $16 million endowment

Students *Undergraduates:* 789 full-time, 137 part-time. Students come from 35 states and territories, 12 other countries. *The most frequently chosen baccalaureate fields are:* business/marketing, computer/information sciences, education.

From out-of-state	55%	Reside on campus	80%
Age 25 or older	40%	Transferred in	11%
International students	2%	African Americans	8%
Asian Americans/Pacific Islanders	1%	Hispanic Americans	1%
Native Americans	1%		

Faculty 75 (53% full-time).

Expenses (2000–2001) *Comprehensive fee:* $19,240 includes full-time tuition ($12,116), mandatory fees ($596), and room and board ($6528). *College room only:* $3676. Full-time tuition and fees vary according to class time, course load, and student level. Room and board charges vary according to board plan and housing facility. *Part-time tuition:* $379 per credit hour. *Part-time fees:* $38 per credit hour. Part-time tuition and fees vary according to class time and course load. *Payment plan:* installment. *Waivers:* senior citizens and employees or children of employees.

Library Abbot Vincent Taylor Library plus 1 other. *Operations spending 1999–2000:* $414,939. *Collection:* 110,050 titles, 609 serial subscriptions.

College life *Housing:* on-campus residence required through senior year. *Options:* coed, disabled students. *Social organizations:* national fraternities, national sororities, local fraternities, local sororities; 35% of eligible men and 40% of eligible women are members. *Most popular organizations:* Greek system, College Union, WABY (student radio station), Abbey Players.

Campus security 24-hour emergency response devices and patrols, late-night transport-escort service.

After graduation *Career center:* 1 part-time personnel. Services include job fairs, resume preparation, interview workshops, resume referral, career counseling, careers library, job bank, job interviews.

Freshmen 571 applied, 557 admitted, 199 enrolled.

Average high school GPA	2.9	SAT verbal scores above 500	49%
SAT math scores above 500	48%	ACT above 18	N/R
1998 freshmen returning in 1999	48%		

Application *Options:* eApply at www.CollegeQuest.com, Common Application. *Application fee:* $25. *Required:* high school transcript. *Required for some:* essay or personal statement; 2 letters of recommendation. *Recommended:* minimum 2.0 GPA; interview.

Standardized tests *Admission: Required:* SAT I or ACT. *Recommended:* SAT II Subject Tests.

Significant dates *Application deadlines:* 8/1 (freshmen), 8/15 (transfers). *Financial aid deadline priority date:* 4/1.

Freshman Application Contact
Mr. Denis Stokes, Vice President of Enrollment Management, Belmont Abbey College, 100 Belmont-Mt. Holly Road, Belmont, NC 28012-1802. **Phone:** 704-825-6665. **Toll-free phone:** 888-BAC-0110. **Fax:** 704-825-6670. **E-mail:** admissions@crusader.bac.edu

Visit CollegeQuest.com for information on majors offered and athletics.

- *See page 1244 for a narrative description.*

BENNETT COLLEGE
Greensboro, North Carolina

- **Independent United Methodist**, 4-year, founded 1873
- **Degree** bachelor's
- **Urban** 55-acre campus
- **Women** only, 637 undergraduate students, 99% full-time
- **Moderately difficult** entrance level, 84% of applicants were admitted
- **10:1 student-to-undergraduate faculty ratio**
- **37% graduate** in 6 years or less
- **$8460 tuition** and fees

Students *Undergraduates:* 633 full-time, 4 part-time. Students come from 34 states and territories, 6 other countries. *The most frequently chosen baccalaureate fields are:* biological/life sciences, business/marketing, psychology.

From out-of-state	74%	Reside on campus	81%
Age 25 or older	4%	Transferred in	2%
International students	3%	African Americans	97%

Faculty 67 (87% full-time), 66% with terminal degrees.

Expenses (1999–2000) *Comprehensive fee:* $12,162 includes full-time tuition ($6720), mandatory fees ($1740), and room and board ($3702). *College room only:* $1784. *Part-time tuition:* $292 per semester hour. *Payment plan:* deferred payment. *Waivers:* employees or children of employees.

Library Holgate Library. *Collection:* 105,000 titles, 310 serial subscriptions.

College life On-campus residence required through sophomore year. *Social organizations:* national sororities; 20% of eligible undergrads are members. *Most popular organizations:* Christian Fellowship, Pre-Alumnae Council, Belles of Harmony, Campus Girl Scouts, National Council of Negro Women.

Campus security 24-hour patrols, late-night transport-escort service.

After graduation 60 organizations recruited on campus 1997–98. 70% of class of 1998 had job offers within 6 months. *Career center:* 2 full-time personnel. Services include job fairs, resume preparation, resume referral, career counseling, careers library, job bank, job interviews.

Freshmen 420 applied, 352 admitted, 238 enrolled.

Average high school GPA	3.21	SAT verbal scores above 500	N/R
SAT math scores above 500	N/R	ACT above 18	N/R
1998 freshmen returning in 1999	63%		

Application *Option:* deferred entrance. *Application fee:* $20. *Required:* essay or personal statement; high school transcript; minimum 2.0 GPA; letters of recommendation. *Required for some:* interview.

Standardized tests *Admission: Required:* SAT I or ACT.

Significant dates *Application deadlines:* rolling (freshmen), rolling (transfers). *Financial aid deadline priority date:* 3/1.

Freshman Application Contact
Ms. Linda K. Torrence, Director of Admissions, Bennett College, 900 East Washington Street, Greensboro, NC 27401-3239. **Phone:** 336-370-8624.

Visit CollegeQuest.com for information on majors offered and athletics.

BREVARD COLLEGE
Brevard, North Carolina

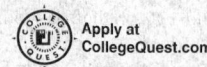
Apply at CollegeQuest.com

- **Independent United Methodist**, 4-year, founded 1853
- **Degrees** associate and bachelor's
- **Small-town** 120-acre campus
- **Coed**, 661 undergraduate students, 96% full-time, 46% women, 54% men
- **Minimally difficult** entrance level, 88% of applicants were admitted
- **10:1 student-to-undergraduate faculty ratio**
- **$12,310 tuition** and fees
- **$10,231 average financial aid** package, $8618 average indebtedness upon graduation, $23.3 million endowment

Students *Undergraduates:* 633 full-time, 28 part-time. Students come from 36 states and territories, 20 other countries. *The most frequently chosen baccalaureate fields are:* parks and recreation, English, visual/performing arts.

From out-of-state	51%	Reside on campus	65%
Age 25 or older	8%	Transferred in	11%
International students	6%	African Americans	7%
Asian Americans/Pacific Islanders	0.1%	Hispanic Americans	1%

Faculty 97 (63% full-time), 34% with terminal degrees.

Expenses (1999–2000) *Comprehensive fee:* $17,130 includes full-time tuition ($11,480), mandatory fees ($830), and room and board ($4820). Room and board charges vary according to housing facility. *Part-time tuition:* $330

North Carolina

per semester hour. Part-time tuition and fees vary according to course load. *Payment plan:* installment. *Waivers:* employees or children of employees.
Library Jones Library plus 1 other. *Operations spending 1999-2000:* $264,320. *Collection:* 42,224 titles, 270 serial subscriptions, 5,555 audiovisual materials.
College life *Housing:* on-campus residence required through sophomore year. *Options:* coed, men-only, women-only. *Most popular organizations:* fine arts organizations, Phi Theta Kappa, Fellowship of Christian Athletes, Student Ambassadors, Service Learning.
Campus security 24-hour emergency response devices and patrols.
After graduation *Career center:* 1 part-time personnel. Services include job fairs, resume preparation, interview workshops, career/interest testing, career counseling, careers library, job bank, job interviews. *Graduate education:* 7% of class of 1999 went directly to graduate and professional school; 7% graduate arts and sciences. *Major awards:* 1 Fulbright Scholar.
Freshmen 596 applied, 526 admitted, 204 enrolled.

Average high school GPA	2.51	SAT verbal scores above 500	47%
SAT math scores above 500	45%	ACT above 18	N/R
1998 freshmen returning in 1999	56%		

Application *Options:* eApply at www.CollegeQuest.com, Common Application, electronic application, early admission, deferred entrance. *Application fee:* $20. *Required:* essay or personal statement; high school transcript; minimum 2.0 GPA. *Required for some:* 3 letters of recommendation; interview.
Standardized tests *Admission: Required:* SAT I or ACT.
Significant dates *Application deadlines:* rolling (freshmen), rolling (transfers). *Financial aid deadline priority date:* 4/15.
Freshman Application Contact
Mr. Theodore J. Wiard, Director of Admissions, Brevard College, 400 North Broad Street, Brevard, NC 28712-3306. **Phone:** 828-884-8300. **Toll-free phone:** 800-527-9090. **Fax:** 828-884-3790. **E-mail:** admissions@brevard.edu
Visit CollegeQuest.com for information on majors offered and athletics. College video and electronic viewbook available at CollegeQuest.com.

■ *See page 1306 for a narrative description.*

CAMPBELL UNIVERSITY
Buies Creek, North Carolina

- **Independent Baptist**, university, founded 1887
- **Degrees** associate, bachelor's, master's, doctoral, and first professional
- **Rural** 850-acre campus with easy access to Raleigh
- **Coed**, 2,201 undergraduate students, 96% full-time, 56% women, 44% men
- **Moderately difficult** entrance level, 70% of applicants were admitted
- **18:1 student-to-undergraduate faculty ratio**
- **$10,997 tuition** and fees

Campbell's ROTC program is currently rated as the best in America. The Norman Adrian Wiggins School of Law has received the Gumpert Award for excellence in the teaching of trial advocacy. The BBA in golf management, offered by the School of Business, is PGA-certified and has gained national attention. Graduate programs include the MS in clinical research, the PharmD in the School of Pharmacy, the MEd and MA in the School of Education, the MBA in the School of Business, and the MDiv and MA in the School of Divinity. Education has a nearly 97 percent passage rate on licensure exams.

Students *Undergraduates:* 2,107 full-time, 94 part-time. Students come from 50 states and territories, 46 other countries. *The most frequently chosen baccalaureate fields are:* business/marketing, psychology, social sciences and history. *Graduate:* 797 in professional programs, 267 in other graduate degree programs.

From out-of-state	30%	Reside on campus	74%
Age 25 or older	10%	Transferred in	9%
International students	3%	African Americans	10%
Hispanic Americans	3%	Native Americans	0.2%

Faculty 439 (41% full-time), 56% with terminal degrees.
Expenses (1999-2000) *Comprehensive fee:* $14,947 includes full-time tuition ($10,807), mandatory fees ($190), and room and board ($3950). Room and board charges vary according to board plan and housing facility.

Part-time tuition: $180 per semester hour. *Payment plan:* installment. *Waivers:* employees or children of employees.
Library Carrie Rich Memorial Library plus 2 others. *Collection:* 189,763 titles, 1,298 audiovisual materials.
College life *Housing:* on-campus residence required in freshman year. *Options:* men-only, women-only. *Most popular organizations:* Student Government Association, Baptist Student Union, Young Catholic Adults, Presidential Scholars Club, pre-pharmacy club.
Campus security 24-hour emergency response devices and patrols, late-night transport-escort service, controlled dormitory access.
After graduation 20 organizations recruited on campus 1997-98. 80% of class of 1998 had job offers within 6 months. *Career center:* 2 full-time personnel. Services include job fairs, resume preparation, resume referral, career counseling, careers library, job interviews. *Graduate education:* 25% of class of 1999 went directly to graduate and professional school; 8% business, 6% graduate arts and sciences, 4% law, 3% education, 3% theology, 1% medicine.
Freshmen 1,902 applied, 1,337 admitted, 544 enrolled. 6 National Merit Scholars, 19 class presidents, 24 valedictorians, 75 student government officers.

Average high school GPA	2.8	SAT verbal scores above 500	51%
SAT math scores above 500	56%	ACT above 18	N/R
From top 10% of their h.s. class	16%	From top quarter	32%
From top half	61%	1998 freshmen returning in 1999	71%

Application *Options:* Common Application, electronic application, early admission, deferred entrance. *Application fee:* $15. *Required:* high school transcript; minimum 2.0 GPA. *Required for some:* 3 letters of recommendation. *Recommended:* interview.
Standardized tests *Admission: Required:* SAT I or ACT.
Significant dates *Application deadlines:* rolling (freshmen), rolling (transfers). *Financial aid deadline priority date:* 3/15.
Freshman Application Contact
Mrs. Charlotte Bohn, Director of Admissions, Campbell University, PO Box 546, Buies Creek, NC 27506. **Phone:** 910-893-1300. **Toll-free phone:** 800-334-4111. **Fax:** 910-893-1288. **E-mail:** satterfiel@mailcenter.campbell.edu
Visit CollegeQuest.com for information on majors offered and athletics. College video available at CollegeQuest.com.

■ *See page 1350 for a narrative description.*

CATAWBA COLLEGE
Salisbury, North Carolina

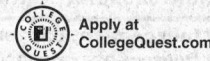
Apply at CollegeQuest.com

- **Independent**, comprehensive, founded 1851, affiliated with United Church of Christ
- **Degrees** bachelor's and master's
- **Small-town** 210-acre campus with easy access to Charlotte
- **Coed**, 1,195 undergraduate students, 97% full-time, 50% women, 50% men
- **Moderately difficult** entrance level, 78% of applicants were admitted
- **15:1 student-to-undergraduate faculty ratio**
- **47% graduate** in 6 years or less
- **$12,600 tuition** and fees
- **$27.2 million endowment**

Students *Undergraduates:* 1,164 full-time, 31 part-time. Students come from 32 states and territories, 9 other countries. *The most frequently chosen baccalaureate fields are:* business/marketing, education, social sciences and history. *Graduate:* 22 in graduate degree programs.

From out-of-state	41%	Reside on campus	55%
Age 25 or older	18%	Transferred in	10%
International students	2%	African Americans	14%
Asian Americans/Pacific Islanders	1%	Hispanic Americans	1%
Native Americans	0.4%		

Faculty 114 (60% full-time), 48% with terminal degrees.
Expenses (1999-2000) *One-time required fee:* $275. *Comprehensive fee:* $17,440 includes full-time tuition ($12,600) and room and board ($4840). *Part-time tuition:* $390 per semester hour. *Part-time fees:* $30 per term part-time. *Payment plan:* installment. *Waivers:* employees or children of employees.

North Carolina

Catawba College (continued)

Library Corriher-Linn-Black Memorial Library plus 1 other. *Operations spending 1999–2000:* $496,767. *Collection:* 144,788 titles, 3,661 serial subscriptions, 24,281 audiovisual materials.

College life *Housing:* on-campus residence required through sophomore year. *Options:* coed, men-only, women-only. *Most popular organizations:* United In Service, Catawba Guides, Blue Masque (drama), L'il Chiefs, Wigwam Productions.

Campus security 24-hour emergency response devices and patrols, late-night transport-escort service, controlled dormitory access.

After graduation 18 organizations recruited on campus 1997–98. *Career center:* 2 full-time, 1 part-time personnel. Services include job fairs, resume preparation, career counseling, careers library, job interviews. *Graduate education:* 10% of class of 1999 went directly to graduate and professional school: 5% graduate arts and sciences, 3% business, 1% law, 1% medicine.

Freshmen 1,179 applied, 920 admitted, 276 enrolled.

Average high school GPA	2.85	SAT verbal scores above 500	46%
SAT math scores above 500	49%	ACT above 18	N/R
From top 10% of their h.s. class	7%	From top quarter	24%
From top half	57%	1998 freshmen returning in 1999	57%

Application *Options:* eApply at www.CollegeQuest.com, Common Application, electronic application, early admission, deferred entrance. *Application fee:* $25. *Required:* high school transcript; minimum 2.0 GPA. *Recommended:* essay or personal statement; letters of recommendation; interview.

Standardized tests *Admission: Required:* SAT I or ACT.

Significant dates *Application deadlines:* rolling (freshmen), rolling (transfers). *Financial aid deadline priority date:* 3/1.

Freshman Application Contact
Mr. Brian Best, Chief Enrollment Officer, Catawba College, 2300 West Innes Street, Salisbury, NC 28144-2488. **Phone:** 704-637-4111. **Toll-free phone:** 800-CATAWBA. **E-mail:** bdbest@catawba.edu

Visit CollegeQuest.com for information on majors offered and athletics. College video available at CollegeQuest.com.

■ *See page 1380 for a narrative description.*

CHOWAN COLLEGE
Murfreesboro, North Carolina

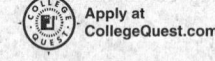 Apply at CollegeQuest.com

- **Independent Baptist**, 4-year, founded 1848
- **Degrees** associate and bachelor's
- **Rural** 300-acre campus with easy access to Norfolk
- **Coed**, 726 undergraduate students, 96% full-time, 43% women, 57% men
- **Minimally difficult** entrance level, 90% of applicants were admitted
- **12:1 student-to-undergraduate faculty ratio**
- **$11,520 tuition** and fees
- **$12,203 average financial aid** package, $17,056 average indebtedness upon graduation, $15.4 million endowment

Set among woodlands and lakes, the relaxed family-like campus counterbalances the technologically advanced approach to a liberal arts education at Chowan. Setting the standard for ethics-enriched learning, Chowan offers 30 bachelor's degrees with varying emphases. An extensive academic grant and scholarship program helps make a private education affordable for many students. Students are encouraged to call 800-488-4101 (toll-free) for more information.

Students *Undergraduates:* 696 full-time, 30 part-time. Students come from 23 states and territories, 6 other countries. *The most frequently chosen baccalaureate fields are:* business/marketing; computer/information sciences, education.

From out-of-state	58%	Reside on campus	84%
Age 25 or older	12%	Transferred in	6%
International students	2%	African Americans	25%
Asian Americans/Pacific Islanders	1%	Hispanic Americans	2%
Native Americans	1%		

Faculty 70 (76% full-time), 47% with terminal degrees.

Expenses (1999–2000) *Comprehensive fee:* $16,120 includes full-time tuition ($11,470), mandatory fees ($50), and room and board ($4600). *College room only:* $2130. Room and board charges vary according to board plan. *Part-time tuition:* $260 per hour. Part-time tuition and fees vary according to course load and program. *Payment plans:* installment, deferred payment. *Waivers:* senior citizens and employees or children of employees.

Library Whitaker Library plus 1 other. *Operations spending 1999–2000:* $645,900. *Collection:* 96,994 titles, 925 serial subscriptions, 3,991 audiovisual materials.

College life *Housing:* on-campus residence required through sophomore year. *Options:* coed, men-only, women-only. *Social organizations:* national fraternities, local sororities; 12% of eligible men and 13% of eligible women are members. *Most popular organizations:* Christian Student Union, Student Government Association, Habitat for Humanity, Phi Kappa Tau, SNCAE (Students of North Carolina Association of Educators).

Campus security 24-hour emergency response devices and patrols, late-night transport-escort service, controlled dormitory access.

After graduation 25 organizations recruited on campus 1997–98. 86% of class of 1998 had job offers within 6 months. *Career center:* 2 full-time personnel. Services include job fairs, resume preparation, interview workshops, resume referral, career/interest testing, career counseling, careers library, job bank, job interviews. *Graduate education:* 5% of class of 1999 went directly to graduate and professional school: 2% business, 1% education.

Freshmen 1,297 applied, 1,166 admitted, 254 enrolled.

Average high school GPA	2.73	SAT verbal scores above 500	31%
SAT math scores above 500	23%	ACT above 18	34%
From top 10% of their h.s. class	5%	From top quarter	19%
From top half	55%	1998 freshmen returning in 1999	49%

Application *Options:* eApply at www.CollegeQuest.com, electronic application, early admission, deferred entrance. *Application fee:* $20. *Required:* high school transcript. *Required for some:* essay or personal statement; interview. *Recommended:* minimum 2.0 GPA; 2 letters of recommendation.

Standardized tests *Admission: Required:* SAT I or ACT.

Significant dates *Application deadlines:* rolling (freshmen), rolling (transfers). *Financial aid deadline priority date:* 5/1.

Freshman Application Contact
Mrs. Stephanie Harrell, Director of Admissions, Chowan College, 200 Jones Drive, Murfreesboro, NC 27855. **Phone:** 252-398-6314. **Toll-free phone:** 800-488-4101. **Fax:** 252-398-1190. **E-mail:** admissions@chowan.edu

Visit CollegeQuest.com for information on majors offered and athletics. Electronic viewbook available at CollegeQuest.com.

■ *See page 1414 for a narrative description.*

DAVIDSON COLLEGE
Davidson, North Carolina

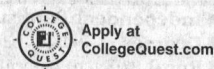 Apply at CollegeQuest.com

- **Independent Presbyterian**, 4-year, founded 1837
- **Degree** bachelor's
- **Small-town** 464-acre campus with easy access to Charlotte
- **Coed**, 1,649 undergraduate students, 100% full-time, 50% women, 50% men
- **Very difficult** entrance level, 38% of applicants were admitted
- **11:1 student-to-undergraduate faculty ratio**
- **92% graduate** in 6 years or less
- **$22,228 tuition** and fees
- **$13,889 average financial aid** package, $14,011 average indebtedness upon graduation, $274.7 million endowment

Students *Undergraduates:* 1,649 full-time. Students come from 46 states and territories, 37 other countries. *The most frequently chosen baccalaureate fields are:* biological/life sciences, English, social sciences and history.

From out-of-state	81%	Reside on campus	89%
Age 25 or older	0.3%	Transferred in	1%
International students	3%	African Americans	5%
Asian Americans/Pacific Islanders	2%	Hispanic Americans	2%
Native Americans	0.3%		

Faculty 167 (91% full-time), 98% with terminal degrees.

Expenses (1999–2000) *Comprehensive fee:* $28,568 includes full-time tuition ($22,014), mandatory fees ($214), and room and board ($6340). *College room only:* $3352. Room and board charges vary according to board plan and housing facility. *Payment plan:* installment. *Waivers:* employees or children of employees.

Library E. H. Little Library plus 1 other. *Collection:* 395,794 titles, 2,829 serial subscriptions, 2,468 audiovisual materials.

North Carolina

College life *Housing:* on-campus residence required through senior year. *Options:* coed, men-only, women-only. *Social organizations:* national fraternities, women's eating houses; 55% of eligible men and 65% of eligible women are members. *Most popular organizations:* Intervarsity Christian Fellowship, Dean Rusk Program Student Advisory Council, music organizations, Community Service Council, Student Government Association.

Campus security 24-hour emergency response devices and patrols, late-night transport-escort service, controlled dormitory access.

After graduation 90 organizations recruited on campus 1997–98. 68% of class of 1998 had job offers within 6 months. *Career center:* 6 full-time personnel. Services include job fairs, resume preparation, interview workshops, resume referral, career/interest testing, career counseling, careers library, job bank, job interviews. *Major awards:* 1 Rhodes, 2 Fulbright Scholars.

Freshmen 2,824 applied, 1,080 admitted, 455 enrolled.

SAT verbal scores above 500	98%	SAT math scores above 500	99%
ACT above 18	N/R	From top 10% of their h.s. class	74%
From top quarter	95%	From top half	100%
1998 freshmen returning in 1999	97%		

Application *Options:* eApply at www.CollegeQuest.com, Common Application, early admission, early decision, deferred entrance. *Application fee:* $50. *Required:* essay or personal statement; high school transcript; 4 letters of recommendation. *Recommended:* interview.

Standardized tests *Admission: Required:* SAT I or ACT. *Recommended:* SAT II Subject Tests, SAT II: Writing Test.

Significant dates *Application deadlines:* 1/2 (freshmen), rolling (transfers). *Early decision:* 11/10 (for plan 1), 1/2 (for plan 2). *Notification:* 4/1 (freshmen), 12/15 (early decision plan 1), 2/1 (early decision plan 2). *Financial aid deadline priority date:* 2/15.

Freshman Application Contact
Dr. Nancy J. Cable, Dean of Admission and Financial Aid, Davidson College, PO Box 1719, Davidson, NC 28036-1719. **Phone:** 704-892-2230. **Toll-free phone:** 800-768-0380. **Fax:** 704-892-2016. **E-mail:** admission@davidson.edu

Visit CollegeQuest.com for information on majors offered and athletics. College video available at CollegeQuest.com.

■ *See page 1562 for a narrative description.*

DUKE UNIVERSITY
Durham, North Carolina

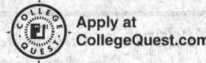

- **Independent**, university, founded 1838, affiliated with United Methodist Church
- **Degrees** bachelor's, master's, doctoral, and first professional
- **Suburban** 8,500-acre campus
- **Coed**, 6,232 undergraduate students, 99% full-time, 48% women, 52% men
- **Most difficult** entrance level, 28% of applicants were admitted
- **8:1 student-to-undergraduate faculty ratio**
- **92% graduate** in 6 years or less
- **$24,751 tuition** and fees
- **$19,056 average financial aid** package, $16,098 average indebtedness upon graduation, $1.8 billion endowment

Students *Undergraduates:* 6,207 full-time, 25 part-time. Students come from 52 states and territories, 77 other countries. *The most frequently chosen baccalaureate fields are:* biological/life sciences, engineering/engineering technologies, social sciences and history. *Graduate:* 1,556 in professional programs, 3,887 in other graduate degree programs.

From out-of-state	88%	Reside on campus	82%
Age 25 or older	1%	Transferred in	0.2%
International students	4%	African Americans	9%
Asian Americans/Pacific Islanders	13%	Hispanic Americans	4%
Native Americans	0.4%		

Faculty 2,168 (100% full-time), 95% with terminal degrees.

Expenses (1999–2000) *Comprehensive fee:* $31,839 includes full-time tuition ($24,040), mandatory fees ($711), and room and board ($7088). *College room only:* $3788. Full-time tuition and fees vary according to program and student level. Room and board charges vary according to board plan and housing facility. *Part-time tuition:* $3005 per course. *Part-time fees:* $215 per term part-time. Part-time tuition and fees vary according to program and student level. *Payment plans:* tuition prepayment, installment, deferred payment. *Waivers:* employees or children of employees.

Library Perkins Library plus 11 others. *Operations spending 1999–2000:* $24.6 million. *Collection:* 4.6 million titles, 33,003 serial subscriptions.

College life *Housing:* on-campus residence required in freshman year. *Options:* coed, men-only, women-only. *Social organizations:* national fraternities, national sororities; 29% of eligible men and 42% of eligible women are members.

Campus security 24-hour emergency response devices and patrols, late-night transport-escort service, controlled dormitory access.

After graduation 210 organizations recruited on campus 1997–98. 45% of class of 1998 had job offers within 6 months. *Career center:* 15 full-time, 9 part-time personnel. Services include job fairs, resume preparation, interview workshops, resume referral, career counseling, careers library, job bank, job interviews. *Graduate education:* 25% of class of 1999 went directly to graduate and professional school: 9% medicine, 8% law, 7% graduate arts and sciences, 2% engineering, 1% business. *Major awards:* 1 Rhodes, 12 Fulbright Scholars.

Freshmen 13,407 applied, 3,777 admitted, 1,630 enrolled. 2 Westinghouse recipients, 216 valedictorians.

SAT verbal scores above 500	98%	SAT math scores above 500	99%
ACT above 18	100%	From top 10% of their h.s. class	88%
From top quarter	97%	From top half	100%
1998 freshmen returning in 1999	97%		

Application *Options:* eApply at www.CollegeQuest.com, Common Application, early admission, early decision, deferred entrance. *Preference* given to children of alumni, minorities, state residents. *Application fee:* $60. *Required:* essay or personal statement; high school transcript; 3 letters of recommendation. *Recommended:* minimum 3.0 GPA; interview; audition tape for applicants with outstanding dance, dramatic, or musical talent; slides of artwork.

Standardized tests *Admission: Required:* SAT I or ACT. *Required for some:* SAT II Subject Tests, SAT II: Writing Test.

Significant dates *Application deadlines:* 1/2 (freshmen), 4/1 (transfers). *Early decision:* 11/1. *Notification:* 4/15 (freshmen), 12/15 (early decision). *Financial aid deadline:* 2/1.

Freshman Application Contact
Mr. Christoph Guttentag, Director of Admissions, Duke University, Durham, NC 27708-0586. **Phone:** 919-684-3214. **Fax:** 919-681-8941. **E-mail:** askduke@admiss.duke.edu

Visit CollegeQuest.com for information on majors offered and athletics.

■ *See page 1594 for a narrative description.*

EAST CAROLINA UNIVERSITY
Greenville, North Carolina

- **State-supported**, university, founded 1907
- **Degrees** bachelor's, master's, doctoral, first professional, and post-master's certificates
- **Urban** 465-acre campus
- **Coed**, 15,177 undergraduate students, 91% full-time, 58% women, 42% men
- **Moderately difficult** entrance level, 80% of applicants were admitted
- **16:1 student-to-undergraduate faculty ratio**
- **49% graduate** in 6 years or less
- **$1998 tuition** and fees (in-state); $9564 (out-of-state)
- **$14,105 average indebtedness** upon graduation, $10.1 million endowment

Part of University of North Carolina System.

Students *Undergraduates:* 13,808 full-time, 1,369 part-time. Students come from 46 states and territories, 34 other countries. *The most frequently chosen baccalaureate fields are:* business/marketing, education, health professions and related sciences. *Graduate:* 300 in professional programs, 3,265 in other graduate degree programs.

From out-of-state	15%	Reside on campus	31%
Age 25 or older	14%	Transferred in	7%
International students	1%	African Americans	13%
Asian Americans/Pacific Islanders	2%	Hispanic Americans	1%
Native Americans	1%		

Faculty 1,081 (82% full-time), 61% with terminal degrees.

North Carolina

East Carolina University (continued)

Expenses (1999–2000) *Tuition, state resident:* full-time $992. *Tuition, nonresident:* full-time $8558. *Required fees:* full-time $1006. Part-time tuition and fees vary according to course load. *College room and board:* $4070; room only: $2050. Room and board charges vary according to board plan and housing facility. *Payment plans:* installment, deferred payment. *Waivers:* senior citizens and employees or children of employees.

Library Joyner Library plus 1 other. *Operations spending 1999–2000:* $7.7 million. *Collection:* 1.2 million titles, 7,788 serial subscriptions.

College life *Housing: Option:* coed. *Social organizations:* national fraternities, national sororities; 10% of eligible men and 6% of eligible women are members. *Most popular organizations:* Student Government Association, Pan Hellenic Association, Student Union, Interfraternity Council, Residence Hall Association.

Campus security 24-hour emergency response devices and patrols, student patrols, late-night transport-escort service, Operation ID.

After graduation 400 organizations recruited on campus 1997–98. 74% of class of 1998 had job offers within 6 months. *Career center:* 7 full-time personnel. Services include job fairs, resume preparation, interview workshops, resume referral, career/interest testing, career counseling, careers library, job bank, job interviews.

Freshmen 10,076 applied, 8,062 admitted, 3,270 enrolled.

Average high school GPA	3.18	SAT verbal scores above 500	55%
SAT math scores above 500	54%	ACT above 18	74%
From top 10% of their h.s. class	11%	From top quarter	38%
From top half	81%	1998 freshmen returning in 1999	79%

Application *Options:* electronic application, early admission. *Preference* given to state residents. *Application fee:* $40. *Required:* high school transcript; minimum 2.0 GPA.

Standardized tests *Admission: Required:* SAT I or ACT.

Significant dates *Application deadlines:* 3/15 (freshmen), 4/15 (transfers). *Financial aid deadline priority date:* 4/15.

Freshman Application Contact
Dr. Thomas Powell Jr., Director of Admissions, East Carolina University, East Fifth Street, Greenville, NC 27858-4353. **Phone:** 252-328-6640. **Fax:** 252-328-6495.

Visit CollegeQuest.com for information on majors offered and athletics. College video available at CollegeQuest.com.

ELIZABETH CITY STATE UNIVERSITY
Elizabeth City, North Carolina

- **State-supported**, 4-year, founded 1891
- **Degree** bachelor's
- **Small-town** 125-acre campus with easy access to Norfolk
- **Coed**, 1,968 undergraduate students
- **Moderately difficult** entrance level, 27% of applicants were admitted
- **$1851 tuition** and fees (in-state); $8411 (out-of-state)

Part of University of North Carolina System.

Students *Undergraduates:* Students come from 23 states and territories, 8 other countries.

| From out-of-state | 12% | Reside on campus | 54% |
| Age 25 or older | 25% | African Americans | 75% |

Faculty 139 (81% full-time).

Expenses (1999–2000) *Tuition, state resident:* full-time $806; part-time $202 per term. *Tuition, nonresident:* full-time $7366; part-time $1806 per term. *Required fees:* full-time $1045; $201 per term part-time. Part-time tuition and fees vary according to course load. *College room and board:* $3898. *Waivers:* senior citizens.

Library G. R. Little Library. *Collection:* 147,479 titles, 1,665 serial subscriptions.

College life *Housing: Options:* men-only, women-only. *Social organizations:* national fraternities, national sororities, local fraternities; 10% of eligible men and 10% of eligible women are members.

Campus security 24-hour emergency response devices and patrols.

After graduation *Career center:* 2 full-time personnel. Services include job fairs, resume preparation, career/interest testing, career counseling, careers library, job bank, job interviews.

Freshmen 1,965 applied, 524 admitted.

Average high school GPA	2.69	SAT verbal scores above 500	N/R
SAT math scores above 500	N/R	ACT above 18	N/R
From top 10% of their h.s. class	7%	From top quarter	30%
From top half	70%	1998 freshmen returning in 1999	75%

Application *Options:* electronic application, deferred entrance. *Preference* given to state residents. *Application fee:* $30. *Required:* high school transcript; minimum 2.0 GPA.

Standardized tests *Admission: Required:* SAT I or ACT.

Significant dates *Application deadlines:* rolling (freshmen), rolling (transfers). *Financial aid deadline priority date:* 3/15.

Freshman Application Contact
Ms. Bridgett N. Golman, Director of Admissions, Elizabeth City State University, Campus Box 901, Elizabeth City, NC 27909-7806. **Phone:** 252-335-3305. **Toll-free phone:** 800-347-3278. **Fax:** 252-335-3731. **E-mail:** admissions@mail.ecsu.edu

Visit CollegeQuest.com for information on majors offered and athletics. College video available at CollegeQuest.com.

■ *See page 1618 for a narrative description.*

ELON COLLEGE
Elon College, North Carolina

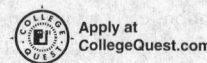
Apply at CollegeQuest.com

- **Independent**, comprehensive, founded 1889, affiliated with United Church of Christ
- **Degrees** bachelor's and master's
- **Suburban** 500-acre campus with easy access to Raleigh
- **Coed**, 3,642 undergraduate students, 98% full-time, 60% women, 40% men
- **Moderately difficult** entrance level, 59% of applicants were admitted
- **16:1 student-to-undergraduate faculty ratio**
- **$12,896 tuition** and fees
- **$9365 average financial aid** package, $17,408 average indebtedness upon graduation, $49.4 million endowment

The largest of North Carolina's primarily undergraduate private colleges, Elon offers students the varied opportunities of a university as well as small classes and individual attention. Elon offers 46 majors as well as exceptional programs in study abroad, undergraduate research, career preparation, service learning, and leadership.

Students *Undergraduates:* 3,562 full-time, 80 part-time. Students come from 44 states and territories, 35 other countries. *The most frequently chosen baccalaureate fields are:* business/marketing, communications/communication technologies, education. *Graduate:* 260 in graduate degree programs.

From out-of-state	75%	Reside on campus	63%
Age 25 or older	2%	Transferred in	2%
International students	2%	African Americans	7%
Asian Americans/Pacific Islanders	1%	Hispanic Americans	1%
Native Americans	0.1%		

Faculty 259 (74% full-time), 71% with terminal degrees.

Expenses (1999–2000) *Comprehensive fee:* $17,447 includes full-time tuition ($12,671), mandatory fees ($225), and room and board ($4551). Room and board charges vary according to board plan and housing facility. *Part-time tuition:* $257 per semester hour. Part-time tuition and fees vary according to course load. *Payment plan:* installment. *Waivers:* employees or children of employees.

Library Iris Holt McEwen Library. *Operations spending 1999–2000:* $1.4 million. *Collection:* 212,262 titles, 8,164 audiovisual materials.

College life *Housing:* on-campus residence required through sophomore year. *Options:* coed, men-only, women-only. *Social organizations:* national fraternities, national sororities; 22% of eligible men and 37% of eligible women are members. *Most popular organizations:* Elon Volunteers, Student Media, Greek Affairs, intramural athletics, Religious Life.

Campus security 24-hour emergency response devices and patrols, student patrols, late-night transport-escort service, controlled dormitory access, residence hall entrances locked at dusk with combination locks.

After graduation 150 organizations recruited on campus 1997–98. 90% of class of 1998 had job offers within 6 months. *Career center:* 6 full-time

personnel. Services include job fairs, resume preparation, interview workshops, resume referral, career/interest testing, career counseling, careers library, job bank, job interviews.

Freshmen 5,322 applied, 3,166 admitted, 1,000 enrolled. 11 valedictorians.

Average high school GPA	3.4	SAT verbal scores above 500	81%
SAT math scores above 500	83%	ACT above 18	N/R
From top 10% of their h.s. class	18%	From top quarter	51%
From top half	87%	1998 freshmen returning in 1999	85%

Application *Options:* eApply at www.CollegeQuest.com, Common Application, early admission, early decision, deferred entrance. *Application fee:* $25. *Required:* high school transcript; minimum 2.5 GPA; 1 letter of recommendation.

Standardized tests *Admission: Required:* SAT I or ACT.

Significant dates *Application deadlines:* rolling (freshmen), rolling (transfers). *Early decision:* 11/15. ***Financial aid deadline priority date:*** 2/15.

Freshman Application Contact
Ms. Susan C. Klopman, Assistant Dean of Admissions, Elon College, 2700 Campus Box, Elon College, NC 27244. **Phone:** 336-538-2772. **Toll-free phone:** 800-334-8448. **Fax:** 336-538-3986. **E-mail:** admissions@elon.edu

Visit CollegeQuest.com for information on majors offered and athletics. College video available at CollegeQuest.com.

■ *See page 1626 for a narrative description.*

FAYETTEVILLE STATE UNIVERSITY
Fayetteville, North Carolina

Admissions Office Contact
Fayetteville State University, 1200 Murchison Road, Fayetteville, NC 28301-4298. **Toll-free phone:** 800-672-6667 (in-state); 800-222-2594 (out-of-state). **Fax:** 910-486-6024.

GARDNER-WEBB UNIVERSITY
Boiling Springs, North Carolina

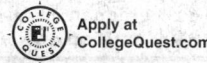 Apply at CollegeQuest.com

- **Independent Baptist**, comprehensive, founded 1905
- **Degrees** associate, bachelor's, and master's
- **Small-town** 200-acre campus with easy access to Charlotte
- **Coed**, 2,337 undergraduate students, 83% full-time, 64% women, 36% men
- **Moderately difficult** entrance level, 80% of applicants were admitted
- **16:1 student-to-undergraduate faculty ratio**
- **30% graduate** in 6 years or less
- **$11,660 tuition** and fees
- **$9576 average financial aid** package, $25.5 million endowment

Students *Undergraduates:* 1,937 full-time, 400 part-time. Students come from 36 states and territories. *The most frequently chosen baccalaureate fields are:* business/marketing, education, social sciences and history. *Graduate:* 134 in professional programs, 497 in other graduate degree programs.

From out-of-state	26%	Reside on campus	42%
Age 25 or older	34%	Transferred in	18%
International students	0.3%	African Americans	13%
Asian Americans/Pacific Islanders	2%	Hispanic Americans	1%
Native Americans	0.2%		

Faculty 158 (77% full-time), 63% with terminal degrees.

Expenses (1999–2000) *Comprehensive fee:* $16,420 includes full-time tuition ($11,660) and room and board ($4760). *College room only:* $2320. Room and board charges vary according to board plan and housing facility. *Part-time tuition:* $240 per credit hour. Part-time tuition and fees vary according to course load.

Library Dover Memorial Library. *Operations spending 1999–2000:* $584,618. *Collection:* 200,333 titles, 885 serial subscriptions, 8,587 audiovisual materials.

College life *Housing:* on-campus residence required through senior year. *Options:* men-only, women-only. *Most popular organizations:* Student Volunteer Corps, GAP (God and People), Fellowship of Christian Athletes, gospel choir, outdoor explorers club.

Campus security 24-hour patrols.

After graduation 20 organizations recruited on campus 1997–98. 75% of class of 1998 had job offers within 6 months. *Career center:* 1 full-time, 1 part-time personnel. Services include job fairs, resume preparation, resume referral, career counseling, careers library, job bank, job interviews. ***Graduate education:*** 25% of class of 1999 went directly to graduate and professional school: 9% theology, 8% business, 5% education, 2% law, 1% medicine.

Freshmen 1,849 applied, 1,481 admitted, 407 enrolled. 5 class presidents, 5 valedictorians, 75 student government officers.

Average high school GPA	3.4	SAT verbal scores above 500	53%
SAT math scores above 500	51%	ACT above 18	N/R
From top 10% of their h.s. class	30%	From top quarter	51%
From top half	70%	1998 freshmen returning in 1999	80%

Application *Options:* eApply at www.CollegeQuest.com, Common Application, electronic application, early admission, deferred entrance. *Application fee:* $25. *Required:* essay or personal statement; high school transcript; minimum 2.2 GPA. *Required for some:* letters of recommendation.

Standardized tests *Admission: Required:* SAT I or ACT.

Significant dates *Application deadlines:* rolling (freshmen), rolling (transfers). ***Financial aid deadline:*** continuous.

Freshman Application Contact
Mr. Ray McKay Hardee, Dean of Admissions and Enrollment Management, Gardner-Webb University, PO Box 817, Boiling Springs, NC 28017. **Phone:** 704-434-4491. **Toll-free phone:** 800-253-6472. **Fax:** 704-434-4488. **E-mail:** admissions@gardner-webb.edu

Visit CollegeQuest.com for information on majors offered and athletics. College video available at CollegeQuest.com.

■ *See page 1704 for a narrative description.*

GREENSBORO COLLEGE
Greensboro, North Carolina

 Apply at CollegeQuest.com

- **Independent United Methodist**, 4-year, founded 1838
- **Degree** bachelor's
- **Urban** 40-acre campus
- **Coed**, 991 undergraduate students, 83% full-time, 53% women, 47% men
- **Moderately difficult** entrance level, 72% of applicants were admitted
- **13:1 student-to-undergraduate faculty ratio**
- **38% graduate** in 6 years or less
- **$11,700 tuition** and fees
- **$6942 average financial aid** package, $12,229 average indebtedness upon graduation, $32 million endowment

Students *Undergraduates:* 820 full-time, 171 part-time. Students come from 30 states and territories. *The most frequently chosen baccalaureate fields are:* business/marketing, biological/life sciences, education.

From out-of-state	40%	Reside on campus	52%
Age 25 or older	22%	Transferred in	11%
International students	1%	African Americans	16%
Asian Americans/Pacific Islanders	1%	Hispanic Americans	2%
Native Americans	0.4%		

Faculty 105 (49% full-time), 56% with terminal degrees.

Expenses (1999–2000) *Comprehensive fee:* $16,600 includes full-time tuition ($11,500), mandatory fees ($200), and room and board ($4900). Full-time tuition and fees vary according to course load. Room and board charges vary according to housing facility. *Part-time tuition:* $275 per semester hour. Part-time tuition and fees vary according to course load. *Payment plan:* installment. *Waivers:* employees or children of employees.

Library James Addison Jones Library. *Operations spending 1999–2000:* $344,904. *Collection:* 2,032 audiovisual materials.

College life *Housing:* on-campus residence required through sophomore year. *Options:* coed, men-only. *Most popular organizations:* Student Christian Fellowship, Campus Activities Board, student government, Peer Awareness With Students, Celebrating Diversity.

Campus security 24-hour patrols, late-night transport-escort service, controlled dormitory access.

After graduation 77% of class of 1998 had job offers within 6 months. *Career center:* 1 full-time, 2 part-time personnel. Services include job fairs, resume preparation, interview workshops, resume referral, career/interest

North Carolina

Greensboro College (continued)

testing, career counseling, careers library, job bank, job interviews. **Graduate education:** 9% of class of 1999 went directly to graduate and professional school: 3% graduate arts and sciences, 2% business, 2% medicine, 1% education, 1% law, 1% theology.

Freshmen 799 applied, 578 admitted, 229 enrolled. 2 valedictorians, 54 student government officers.

Average high school GPA	2.99	SAT verbal scores above 500	42%
SAT math scores above 500	45%	ACT above 18	72%
From top 10% of their h.s. class	12%	From top quarter	30%
From top half	62%	1998 freshmen returning in 1999	63%

Application *Options:* eApply at www.CollegeQuest.com, Common Application, electronic application, early admission, early action, deferred entrance. *Application fee:* $35. *Required:* essay or personal statement; high school transcript. *Required for some:* 2 letters of recommendation; interview. *Recommended:* interview.

Standardized tests *Admission: Required:* SAT I or ACT.

Significant dates *Application deadlines:* rolling (freshmen), rolling (transfers). *Early action:* 12/15. *Notification:* 1/15 (early action). *Financial aid deadline priority date:* 3/15.

Freshman Application Contact
Mr. Randy Doss, Vice President of Admissions, Greensboro College, 815 West Market Street, Greensboro, NC 27401-1875. **Phone:** 336-272-7102 Ext. 211. **Toll-free phone:** 800-346-8226. **Fax:** 336-271-6634. **E-mail:** admissions@gborocollege.edu

Visit CollegeQuest.com for information on majors offered and athletics. College video available at CollegeQuest.com.

■ *See page 1740 for a narrative description.*

GUILFORD COLLEGE
Greensboro, North Carolina

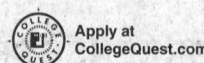
Apply at CollegeQuest.com

- **Independent**, 4-year, founded 1837, affiliated with Society of Friends
- **Degree** bachelor's
- **Suburban** 340-acre campus
- **Coed**, 1,245 undergraduate students, 90% full-time, 54% women, 46% men
- **Moderately difficult** entrance level, 76% of applicants were admitted
- **13:1 student-to-undergraduate faculty ratio**
- **$16,970 tuition** and fees
- **$14,420 average financial aid** package, $14,260 average indebtedness upon graduation, $63.4 million endowment

Students *Undergraduates:* 1,120 full-time, 125 part-time. Students come from 42 states and territories, 30 other countries. *The most frequently chosen baccalaureate fields are:* business/marketing, psychology, social sciences and history.

From out-of-state	75%	Reside on campus	78%
Age 25 or older	1%	Transferred in	2%
International students	3%	African Americans	7%
Asian Americans/Pacific Islanders	1%	Hispanic Americans	3%
Native Americans	1%		

Faculty 123 (72% full-time), 89% with terminal degrees.

Expenses (2000–2001) *Comprehensive fee:* $22,580 includes full-time tuition ($16,400), mandatory fees ($570), and room and board ($5610). *College room only:* $2960. Room and board charges vary according to board plan and housing facility. *Part-time tuition:* $497 per credit. *Part-time fees:* $15 per term part-time. Part-time tuition and fees vary according to course load. *Payment plan:* installment. *Waivers:* employees or children of employees.

Library Hege Library. *Operations spending 1999–2000:* $842,037. *Collection:* 250,000 titles, 1,059 serial subscriptions, 8,826 audiovisual materials.

College life *Housing:* on-campus residence required through junior year. *Options:* coed, men-only, women-only, cooperative. *Most popular organizations:* student government, student radio station, student newspaper, Project Community, Ultimate Frisbee.

Campus security 24-hour emergency response devices and patrols, student patrols, late-night transport-escort service, controlled dormitory access.

After graduation 115 organizations recruited on campus 1997–98. 50% of class of 1998 had job offers within 6 months. *Career center:* 3 full-time, 1 part-time personnel. Services include job fairs, resume preparation, resume referral, career/interest testing, career counseling, careers library, job bank, job interviews.

Freshmen 1,227 applied, 938 admitted, 223 enrolled. 8 National Merit Scholars, 4 class presidents, 10 valedictorians, 47 student government officers.

Average high school GPA	3.27	SAT verbal scores above 500	89%
SAT math scores above 500	85%	ACT above 18	99%
From top 10% of their h.s. class	16%	From top quarter	26%
From top half	51%	1998 freshmen returning in 1999	78%

Application *Options:* eApply at www.CollegeQuest.com, Common Application, electronic application, early admission, early decision, early action, deferred entrance. *Application fee:* $25. *Required:* essay or personal statement; high school transcript; minimum 2.0 GPA; 2 letters of recommendation. *Recommended:* minimum 3.0 GPA; interview.

Standardized tests *Admission: Required:* SAT I or ACT.

Significant dates *Application deadlines:* 2/15 (freshmen), 4/1 (transfers). *Early decision:* 11/15, 1/15. *Notification:* 4/1 (freshmen), 12/15 (early decision), 2/15 (early action). *Financial aid deadline priority date:* 3/1.

Freshman Application Contact
Mr. Randy Doss, Dean of Enrollment, Guilford College, 5800 West Friendly Avenue, Greensboro, NC 27410-4173. **Phone:** 336-316-2100. **Toll-free phone:** 800-992-7759. **Fax:** 336-316-2954. **E-mail:** admission@guilford.edu

Visit CollegeQuest.com for information on majors offered and athletics.

■ *See page 1748 for a narrative description.*

HERITAGE BIBLE COLLEGE
Dunn, North Carolina

- **Independent Pentecostal Free Will Baptist**, 4-year, founded 1971
- **Degrees** associate and bachelor's
- **Small-town** 82-acre campus with easy access to Raleigh-Durham
- **Coed**, 86 undergraduate students, 67% full-time, 26% women, 74% men
- **Minimally difficult** entrance level, 100% of applicants were admitted
- **20:1 student-to-undergraduate faculty ratio**
- **44% graduate** in 6 years or less
- **$4000 tuition** and fees

Students *Undergraduates:* 58 full-time, 28 part-time. Students come from 3 states and territories, 2 other countries.

From out-of-state	4%	Reside on campus	2%
Age 25 or older	65%	Transferred in	19%
International students	2%	African Americans	16%
Asian Americans/Pacific Islanders	2%	Hispanic Americans	5%
Native Americans	1%		

Faculty 13 (31% full-time), 15% with terminal degrees.

Expenses (1999–2000) *Comprehensive fee:* $6236 includes full-time tuition ($3600), mandatory fees ($400), and room and board ($2236). *College room only:* $1320. Full-time tuition and fees vary according to course load. Room and board charges vary according to board plan and housing facility. *Part-time tuition:* $120 per credit hour. *Part-time fees:* $100 per term part-time. Part-time tuition and fees vary according to course load. *Payment plans:* installment, deferred payment.

Library Alphin Learning Center. *Operations spending 1999–2000:* $60,464. *Collection:* 14,187 titles, 72 serial subscriptions.

College life *Housing: Option:* coed.

After graduation *Graduate education:* 2% of class of 1999 went directly to graduate and professional school: 2% theology.

Freshmen 31 applied, 31 admitted, 31 enrolled.

SAT verbal scores above 500	N/R	SAT math scores above 500	N/R
ACT above 18	N/R	1998 freshmen returning in 1999	63%

Application *Option:* Common Application. *Application fee:* $20. *Required:* essay or personal statement; high school transcript; letters of recommendation.

Standardized tests *Placement: Required:* ACT ASSET

Significant dates *Application deadlines:* rolling (freshmen), rolling (transfers). *Financial aid deadline priority date:* 5/20.

Freshman Application Contact
Mr. Elvin Butts, Director of Admissions and Registrar, Heritage Bible College, PO Box 1628, Dunn, NC 28335. **Phone:** 910-892-4268. **Fax:** 910-892-1809.

North Carolina

Visit CollegeQuest.com for information on majors offered and athletics.

HIGH POINT UNIVERSITY
High Point, North Carolina

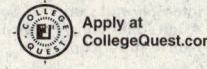
Apply at CollegeQuest.com

- **Independent United Methodist**, comprehensive, founded 1924
- **Degrees** bachelor's and master's
- **Suburban** 77-acre campus with easy access to Charlotte
- **Coed**, 2,489 undergraduate students, 94% full-time, 56% women, 44% men
- **Moderately difficult** entrance level, 90% of applicants were admitted
- **16:1** student-to-undergraduate faculty ratio
- **48% graduate** in 6 years or less
- **$12,440 tuition** and fees
- **$42.1 million endowment**

Students *Undergraduates:* 2,334 full-time, 155 part-time. Students come from 38 states and territories. *The most frequently chosen baccalaureate fields are:* business/marketing, computer/information sciences, education. *Graduate:* 173 in graduate degree programs.

From out-of-state	50%	Reside on campus	60%
Age 25 or older	20%	Transferred in	5%
International students	1%	African Americans	15%
Asian Americans/Pacific Islanders	1%	Hispanic Americans	1%
Native Americans	0.2%		

Faculty 210 (57% full-time), 49% with terminal degrees.

Expenses (2000–2001) *Comprehensive fee:* $18,210 includes full-time tuition ($11,260), mandatory fees ($1180), and room and board ($5770). *College room only:* $2480. Full-time tuition and fees vary according to class time. Room and board charges vary according to board plan. *Part-time tuition:* $193 per semester hour. *Waivers:* employees or children of employees.

Library Herman and Louise Smith Library. *Operations spending 1999–2000:* $696,967. *Collection:* 102,040 titles, 6,130 serial subscriptions, 8,000 audiovisual materials.

College life *Housing:* Options: coed, men-only, women-only, disabled students. *Social organizations:* national fraternities, national sororities, local fraternities, local sororities; 33% of eligible men and 33% of eligible women are members. *Most popular organizations:* student government, Habitat for Humanity, international club, Student Activities Board, honors club.

Campus security 24-hour emergency response devices and patrols, student patrols, late-night transport-escort service, controlled dormitory access.

After graduation 97 organizations recruited on campus 1997–98. 96% of class of 1998 had job offers within 6 months. *Career center:* 1 full-time, 2 part-time personnel. Services include job fairs, resume preparation, interview workshops, resume referral, career counseling, careers library, job bank, job interviews. *Graduate education:* 16% of class of 1999 went directly to graduate and professional school: 6% graduate arts and sciences, 4% education, 1% business, 1% dentistry, 1% law, 1% medicine, 1% theology, 1% veterinary medicine.

Freshmen 1,536 applied, 1,387 admitted, 507 enrolled. 8 class presidents, 10 valedictorians, 153 student government officers.

Average high school GPA	2.6	SAT verbal scores above 500	56%
SAT math scores above 500	52%	ACT above 18	N/R
From top 10% of their h.s. class	15%	From top quarter	38%
From top half	71%	1998 freshmen returning in 1999	76%

Application *Options:* eApply at www.CollegeQuest.com, Common Application, electronic application, deferred entrance. *Application fee:* $25. *Required:* high school transcript; minimum 2.0 GPA; 2 letters of recommendation. *Recommended:* essay or personal statement; minimum 3.0 GPA; interview.

Standardized tests *Admission: Required:* SAT I or ACT. *Recommended:* SAT II Subject Tests, SAT II: Writing Test.

Significant dates *Application deadlines:* 8/31 (freshmen), 8/31 (transfers). *Financial aid deadline priority date:* 3/1.

Freshman Application Contact
Mr. James L. Schlimmer, Dean of Admissions, High Point University, University Station, Montlieu Avenue, High Point, NC 27262-3598. **Phone:** 336-841-9216. **Toll-free phone:** 800-345-6993. **Fax:** 336-841-5123. **E-mail:** admiss@highpoint.edu

Visit CollegeQuest.com for information on majors offered and athletics. Electronic viewbook available at CollegeQuest.com.

■ *See page 1786 for a narrative description.*

JOHNSON C. SMITH UNIVERSITY
Charlotte, North Carolina

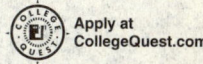
Apply at CollegeQuest.com

- **Independent**, 4-year, founded 1867
- **Degree** bachelor's
- **Urban** 105-acre campus
- **Coed**, 1,591 undergraduate students, 97% full-time, 60% women, 40% men
- **Minimally difficult** entrance level, 35% of applicants were admitted
- **16:1** student-to-undergraduate faculty ratio
- **36% graduate** in 6 years or less
- **$9974 tuition** and fees
- **$6200 average financial aid** package, $22,000 average indebtedness upon graduation, $29 million endowment

Johnson C. Smith University is committed to maintaining its rich liberal arts heritage while concurrently developing new programs that are responsive to the needs of society, including infusing technology into the curriculum through the IBM ThinkPad Initiative and developing programs that focus on banking and finance, computer science, and computer engineering.

Students *Undergraduates:* 1,546 full-time, 45 part-time. Students come from 35 states and territories.

From out-of-state	75%	Reside on campus	80%
Age 25 or older	6%	Transferred in	3%
African Americans	99%	Hispanic Americans	0.3%

Faculty 119 (75% full-time), 70% with terminal degrees.

Expenses (1999–2000) *Comprehensive fee:* $13,849 includes full-time tuition ($8857), mandatory fees ($1117), and room and board ($3875). *College room only:* $2202. Room and board charges vary according to board plan, housing facility, and location. *Part-time tuition:* $192 per semester hour. *Part-time fees:* $61 per term part-time. Part-time tuition and fees vary according to course load. *Payment plan:* installment. *Waivers:* employees or children of employees.

Library James B. Duke Library plus 1 other. *Operations spending 1999–2000:* $692,945. *Collection:* 112,477 titles, 800 serial subscriptions, 1,993 audiovisual materials.

College life *Housing:* on-campus residence required in freshman year. *Options:* coed, men-only, women-only. *Social organizations:* national fraternities, national sororities, local fraternities; 10% of eligible men and 8% of eligible women are members. *Most popular organizations:* Union Program Board, Royal Golden Bull Pep Squad, health and physical education club, Delta Sigma Theta, Alpha Kappa Alpha.

Campus security 24-hour emergency response devices and patrols, late-night transport-escort service, controlled dormitory access.

After graduation 107 organizations recruited on campus 1997–98. *Career center:* 3 full-time personnel. Services include job fairs, resume preparation, resume referral, career/interest testing, career counseling, careers library, job bank, job interviews. *Graduate education:* 17% of class of 1999 went directly to graduate and professional school: 6% graduate arts and sciences, 3% business, 3% medicine, 2% education, 2% law, 1% dentistry.

Freshmen 2,951 applied, 1,026 admitted, 595 enrolled. 10 class presidents, 4 valedictorians, 50 student government officers.

Average high school GPA	2.56	SAT verbal scores above 500	11%
SAT math scores above 500	1%	ACT above 18	N/R
From top 10% of their h.s. class	17%	From top quarter	33%
From top half	45%	1998 freshmen returning in 1999	70%

Application *Options:* eApply at www.CollegeQuest.com, Common Application, electronic application, early admission, deferred entrance. *Application fee:* $25. *Required:* high school transcript. *Required for some:* letters of recommendation. *Recommended:* essay or personal statement; interview.

Standardized tests *Admission: Required:* SAT I and SAT II or ACT.

Significant dates *Application deadlines:* 8/1 (freshmen), 8/1 (transfers). *Financial aid deadline priority date:* 4/1.

North Carolina

Johnson C. Smith University *(continued)*
Freshman Application Contact
Ms. Bridgett N. Golman, Director of Admissions, Johnson C. Smith University, 100 Beatties Ford Road, Charlotte, NC 28216. **Phone:** 704-378-1010. **Toll-free phone:** 800-782-7303.
Visit CollegeQuest.com for information on majors offered and athletics. Electronic viewbook available at CollegeQuest.com.

■ *See page 1854 for a narrative description.*

JOHN WESLEY COLLEGE
High Point, North Carolina

- **Independent interdenominational**, 4-year, founded 1932
- **Degrees** associate and bachelor's
- **Urban** 24-acre campus
- **Coed**, 154 undergraduate students, 71% full-time, 47% women, 53% men
- **Minimally difficult** entrance level, 56% of applicants were admitted
- **12:1** student-to-undergraduate faculty ratio
- **$5556 tuition** and fees
- **$661,176 endowment**

Students *Undergraduates:* 109 full-time, 45 part-time. Students come from 3 states and territories, 1 other country. *The most frequently chosen baccalaureate fields are:* business/marketing, education, philosophy.

From out-of-state	5%	Reside on campus	24%
Age 25 or older	75%	Transferred in	58%
International students	1%	African Americans	14%
Asian Americans/Pacific Islanders	1%	Hispanic Americans	1%

Faculty 7 (71% full-time), 100% with terminal degrees.
Expenses (1999–2000) *Tuition:* full-time $5336; part-time $220 per semester hour. *Required fees:* full-time $220; $110 per term part-time. Part-time tuition and fees vary according to course load. *College room only:* $1750. Room and board charges vary according to housing facility. *Payment plan:* installment. *Waivers:* employees or children of employees.
Library Temple Library. *Collection:* 40,796 titles, 146 serial subscriptions, 2,886 audiovisual materials.
College life On-campus residence required through senior year.
Freshmen 18 applied, 10 admitted, 10 enrolled.

Average high school GPA	2.5	SAT verbal scores above 500	N/R
SAT math scores above 500	N/R	ACT above 18	N/R
From top 10% of their h.s. class	40%	1998 freshmen returning in 1999	80%

Application *Options:* early admission, deferred entrance. *Application fee:* $30. *Required:* high school transcript; 2 letters of recommendation; interview. *Recommended:* minimum 2.0 GPA.
Standardized tests *Placement: Recommended:* SAT I and SAT II or ACT, SAT II: Writing Test.
Significant dates *Application deadlines:* 8/1 (freshmen), 8/1 (transfers). *Notification:* continuous until 8/10 (freshmen). **Financial aid deadline priority date:** 8/1.
Freshman Application Contact
Mr. Greg Workman, Admissions Officer, John Wesley College, 2314 North Centennial Street, High Point, NC 27265-3197. **Phone:** 336-889-2262 Ext. 127. **E-mail:** gworkman@johnwesley.edu
Visit CollegeQuest.com for information on majors offered and athletics.

LEES-MCRAE COLLEGE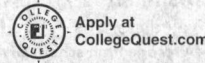
Banner Elk, North Carolina

Apply at CollegeQuest.com

- **Independent**, 4-year, founded 1900, affiliated with Presbyterian Church (U.S.A.)
- **Degree** bachelor's
- **Rural** 400-acre campus
- **Coed**, 643 undergraduate students, 97% full-time, 51% women, 49% men
- **Minimally difficult** entrance level, 86% of applicants were admitted
- **15:1** student-to-undergraduate faculty ratio
- **$11,200 tuition** and fees
- **$11 million endowment**

Students *Undergraduates:* 625 full-time, 18 part-time. Students come from 21 states and territories, 12 other countries.

From out-of-state	45%	Reside on campus	70%
Age 25 or older	7%	Transferred in	6%
International students	5%	African Americans	4%
Asian Americans/Pacific Islanders	0.5%	Hispanic Americans	1%
Native Americans	1%		

Faculty 57 (68% full-time).
Expenses (2000–2001) *Comprehensive fee:* $15,300 includes full-time tuition ($11,200) and room and board ($4100). *College room only:* $1890. *Part-time tuition:* $340 per credit hour. *Payment plan:* installment. *Waivers:* employees or children of employees.
Library James H. Carson Library. *Operations spending 1999-2000:* $173,903. *Collection:* 88,756 titles, 429 serial subscriptions.
College life On-campus residence required through sophomore year. *Most popular organizations:* Student Government Association, Students Against a Vanishing Environment, Student Activity Board, Order of the Tower, Student Ambassadors.
Campus security 24-hour emergency response devices, 16-hour patrols by trained security personnel.
After graduation *Career center:* 1 full-time, 1 part-time personnel. Services include job fairs, resume preparation, career counseling, job interviews. *Graduate education:* 27% of class of 1999 went directly to graduate and professional school: 22% business, 5% education.
Freshmen 438 applied, 378 admitted, 183 enrolled.

Average high school GPA	2.8	SAT verbal scores above 500	42%
SAT math scores above 500	39%	ACT above 18	N/R
From top 10% of their h.s. class	6%	From top quarter	21%
From top half	54%	1998 freshmen returning in 1999	83%

Application *Options:* eApply at www.CollegeQuest.com, electronic application, early admission, deferred entrance. *Application fee:* $15. *Required:* high school transcript; minimum 2.0 GPA. *Required for some:* letters of recommendation; interview. *Recommended:* essay or personal statement.
Standardized tests *Admission: Required:* SAT I or ACT.
Significant dates *Application deadlines:* 8/1 (freshmen), 8/1 (transfers). *Notification:* continuous until 8/15 (freshmen). **Financial aid deadline priority date:** 3/15.
Freshman Application Contact
J. Alan Coheley, Dean of Admissions and Financial Aid, Lees-McRae College, PO Box 128, Banner Elk, NC 28604-0128. **Phone:** 828-898-8702. **Toll-free phone:** 800-280-4562. **Fax:** 828-898-8814. **E-mail:** admissions@lmc.edu
Visit CollegeQuest.com for information on majors offered and athletics. College video available at CollegeQuest.com.

LENOIR-RHYNE COLLEGE
Hickory, North Carolina

Apply at CollegeQuest.com

- **Independent Lutheran**, comprehensive, founded 1891
- **Degrees** bachelor's and master's
- **Small-town** 100-acre campus with easy access to Charlotte
- **Coed**, 1,353 undergraduate students
- **Moderately difficult** entrance level, 86% of applicants were admitted
- **12:1** student-to-undergraduate faculty ratio
- **$13,356 tuition** and fees
- **$40.6 million endowment**

Lenoir-Rhyne College is proud to provide an outstanding program for hearing-impaired students. Each year, more than 20 hearing-impaired students are totally integrated into the academic and social life of the campus. Notetakers and interpreters, as well as tutors and counseling services, are provided for all students.

Students *Undergraduates:* Students come from 29 states and territories.

From out-of-state	29%	Reside on campus	60%
Age 25 or older	22%	International students	0.2%
African Americans	7%	Asian Americans/Pacific Islanders	1%
Hispanic Americans	1%	Native Americans	0.1%

Faculty 159 (67% full-time), 73% with terminal degrees.
Expenses (2000–2001) *Comprehensive fee:* $18,276 includes full-time tuition ($12,870), mandatory fees ($486), and room and board ($4920). Room

North Carolina

and board charges vary according to board plan. Part-time tuition and fees vary according to class time. *Payment plans:* installment, deferred payment. *Waivers:* employees or children of employees.

Library Carl Rudisill Library plus 3 others. *Operations spending 1999–2000:* $561,436. *Collection:* 139,726 titles, 2,335 serial subscriptions, 36,728 audiovisual materials.

College life *Housing:* on-campus residence required through junior year. *Options:* coed, men-only, women-only, disabled students. *Social organizations:* national fraternities, national sororities; 23% of eligible men and 27% of eligible women are members. *Most popular organizations:* Student Government Association, religious clubs, outdoors and service club, Playmakers, Bear Trackers (Student Recruitment Organization).

Campus security 24-hour emergency response devices and patrols, late-night transport-escort service, controlled dormitory access.

After graduation 150 organizations recruited on campus 1997–98. *Career center:* 2 full-time personnel. Services include job fairs, resume preparation, interview workshops, resume referral, career/interest testing, career counseling, careers library, job bank, job interviews.

Freshmen 1,037 applied, 889 admitted. 5 valedictorians.

Average high school GPA	3.43	SAT verbal scores above 500	58%
SAT math scores above 500	60%	ACT above 18	84%
From top 10% of their h.s. class	20%	From top quarter	54%
From top half	82%		

Application *Options:* eApply at www.CollegeQuest.com, Common Application, electronic application, early admission, deferred entrance. *Application fee:* $25. *Required:* high school transcript; minimum 2.5 GPA. *Recommended:* interview.

Standardized tests *Admission: Required:* SAT I or ACT.

Significant dates *Application deadlines:* rolling (freshmen), rolling (transfers). *Financial aid deadline priority date:* 3/1.

Freshman Application Contact
Mrs. Rachel Nichols, Director of Admissions, Lenoir-Rhyne College, PO Box 7227, Hickory, NC 28603. **Phone:** 828-328-7300 Ext. 300. **Toll-free phone:** 800-277-5721. **Fax:** 828-328-7338. **E-mail:** admission@lrc.edu

Visit CollegeQuest.com for information on majors offered and athletics. College video available at CollegeQuest.com.

■ *See page 1916 for a narrative description.*

LIVINGSTONE COLLEGE
Salisbury, North Carolina

- **Independent**, 4-year, founded 1879, affiliated with African Methodist Episcopal Zion Church
- **Degree** bachelor's
- **Small-town** 272-acre campus
- **Coed**
- **Minimally difficult** entrance level
- **$8400 tuition** and fees

Expenses (1999–2000) *Comprehensive fee:* $12,520 includes full-time tuition ($7200), mandatory fees ($1200), and room and board ($4120). *College room only:* $1500. *Part-time tuition:* $300 per credit hour. *Part-time fees:* $50 per credit hour.

Institutional Web site http://www.catawba.edu/html/businf/livingst/html/

College life *Social organizations:* national fraternities, national sororities, local fraternities, local sororities; 10% of eligible men and 10% of eligible women are members.

Campus security 24-hour patrols.

Application *Option:* deferred entrance. *Application fee:* $15. *Required:* high school transcript; 2 letters of recommendation.

Standardized tests *Admission: Required:* SAT I or ACT.

Admissions Office Contact
Livingstone College, 701 West Monroe Street, Salisbury, NC 28144-5298. **Toll-free phone:** 800-835-3435. **Fax:** 704-797-1217.

Visit CollegeQuest.com for information on athletics.

MARS HILL COLLEGE
Mars Hill, North Carolina

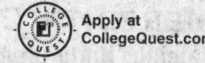

- **Independent Baptist**, 4-year, founded 1856
- **Degree** bachelor's
- **Small-town** 194-acre campus
- **Coed**, 1,177 undergraduate students, 91% full-time, 56% women, 44% men
- **Moderately difficult** entrance level, 90% of applicants were admitted
- **13:1** student-to-undergraduate faculty ratio
- **$11,600 tuition** and fees
- **$22.7 million endowment**

Students *Undergraduates:* 1,068 full-time, 109 part-time. Students come from 25 states and territories, 16 other countries. *The most frequently chosen baccalaureate fields are:* business/marketing, education, social sciences and history.

From out-of-state	34%	Reside on campus	65%
Age 25 or older	18%	Transferred in	6%
International students	2%	African Americans	10%
Asian Americans/Pacific Islanders	0.2%	Hispanic Americans	1%
Native Americans	1%		

Faculty 143 (52% full-time), 44% with terminal degrees.

Expenses (1999–2000) *Comprehensive fee:* $15,900 includes full-time tuition ($10,800), mandatory fees ($800), and room and board ($4300). *College room only:* $2200. Full-time tuition and fees vary according to course load. Room and board charges vary according to board plan and housing facility. *Part-time tuition:* $345 per credit. Part-time tuition and fees vary according to course load. *Payment plan:* installment. *Waivers:* employees or children of employees.

Library Renfro Library plus 1 other. *Operations spending 1999–2000:* $326,575. *Collection:* 98,150 titles, 650 serial subscriptions.

College life On-campus residence required through sophomore year. *Social organizations:* national fraternities, national sororities, local fraternities, local sororities; 40% of eligible men and 40% of eligible women are members. *Most popular organizations:* Student Government Association, Fellowship of Christian Athletes, Christian Student Movement, Student Union Board, Inter-Greek Council.

Campus security 24-hour emergency response devices and patrols, late-night transport-escort service, controlled dormitory access.

After graduation 57% of class of 1998 had job offers within 6 months. *Career center:* 1 full-time personnel. Services include job fairs, resume preparation, interview workshops, resume referral, career/interest testing, career counseling, careers library, job bank, job interviews. *Graduate education:* 22% of class of 1999 went directly to graduate and professional school: 7% theology, 5% business, 4% law, 3% graduate arts and sciences, 2% medicine, 1% dentistry, 1% veterinary medicine.

Freshmen 963 applied, 862 admitted, 347 enrolled.

Average high school GPA	3.01	SAT verbal scores above 500	57%
SAT math scores above 500	56%	ACT above 18	100%
From top 10% of their h.s. class	10%	From top quarter	23%
From top half	58%	1998 freshmen returning in 1999	80%

Application *Options:* eApply at www.CollegeQuest.com, early admission, deferred entrance. *Application fee:* $25. *Required:* high school transcript; minimum 2.0 GPA. *Required for some:* interview. *Recommended:* minimum 3.0 GPA.

Standardized tests *Admission: Required:* SAT I or ACT.

Significant dates *Application deadlines:* rolling (freshmen), rolling (transfers). *Financial aid deadline priority date:* 4/15.

Freshman Application Contact
Ms. Cathy Beard, Director of Admissions, Mars Hill College, PO Box 370, Mars Hill, NC 28754. **Phone:** 828-689-1201. **Toll-free phone:** 800-543-1514. **Fax:** 828-689-1474. **E-mail:** admissions@mhc.edu

Visit CollegeQuest.com for information on majors offered and athletics. College video available at CollegeQuest.com.

■ *See page 1996 for a narrative description.*

Peterson's Guide to Four-Year Colleges 2001 www.petersons.com 601

North Carolina

MEREDITH COLLEGE
Raleigh, North Carolina

- **Independent**, comprehensive, founded 1891, affiliated with Baptist Church
- **Degrees** bachelor's, master's, and postbachelor's certificates
- **Urban** 225-acre campus
- **Women** only, 2,166 undergraduate students, 83% full-time
- **Moderately difficult** entrance level, 85% of applicants were admitted
- **13:1** student-to-undergraduate faculty ratio
- **68.8% graduate** in 6 years or less
- **$9840 tuition** and fees
- **$8649 average financial aid** package, $52.9 million endowment

Students *Undergraduates:* 1,787 full-time, 379 part-time. Students come from 33 states and territories, 24 other countries. *The most frequently chosen baccalaureate fields are:* business/marketing, home economics/vocational home economics, visual/performing arts. *Graduate:* 186 in graduate degree programs.

From out-of-state	12%	Reside on campus	51%
Age 25 or older	21%	Transferred in	4%
International students	1%	African Americans	6%
Asian Americans/Pacific Islanders	2%	Hispanic Americans	1%
Native Americans	0.1%		

Faculty 268 (42% full-time), 47% with terminal degrees.

Expenses (2000–2001) *Comprehensive fee:* $14,100 includes full-time tuition ($9840) and room and board ($4260). *Part-time tuition:* $295 per semester hour. *Payment plan:* installment. *Waivers:* employees or children of employees.

Library Carlyle Campbell Library plus 1 other. *Operations spending 1999–2000:* $904,373. *Collection:* 113,179 titles, 4,952 serial subscriptions, 11,751 audiovisual materials.

College life *Housing:* on-campus residence required through sophomore year. *Option:* women-only. *Most popular organizations:* Student Government Association, Entertainment Association, Recreation Association, Christian Association, choral groups.

Campus security 24-hour emergency response devices and patrols, controlled dormitory access.

After graduation 70 organizations recruited on campus 1997–98. 86% of class of 1998 had job offers within 6 months. *Career center:* 5 full-time personnel. Services include job fairs, resume preparation, interview workshops, resume referral, career/interest testing, career counseling, careers library, job bank, job interviews. *Graduate education:* 12% of class of 1999 went directly to graduate and professional school: 5% graduate arts and sciences, 2% education, 1% medicine.

Freshmen 1,088 applied, 927 admitted, 460 enrolled. 10 valedictorians.

Average high school GPA	3.09	SAT verbal scores above 500	60%
SAT math scores above 500	60%	ACT above 18	65%
From top 10% of their h.s. class	24%	From top quarter	60%
From top half	92%	1998 freshmen returning in 1999	86%

Application *Options:* Common Application, electronic application, early admission, early decision, deferred entrance. *Application fee:* $35. *Required:* high school transcript; minimum 2.0 GPA; 2 letters of recommendation. *Required for some:* essay or personal statement; interview.

Standardized tests *Admission: Required:* SAT I or ACT. *Required for some:* SAT I and SAT II or ACT.

Significant dates *Application deadlines:* 2/15 (freshmen), 2/15 (transfers). *Early decision:* 10/15. *Notification:* 11/1 (early decision). *Financial aid deadline priority date:* 2/15.

Freshman Application Contact
Ms. Carol R. Kercheval, Director of Admissions, Meredith College, 3800 Hillsborough Street, Raleigh, NC 27607-5298. **Phone:** 919-760-8581. **Toll-free phone:** 800-MEREDITH. **Fax:** 919-829-2348. **E-mail:** admissions@meredith.edu

Visit CollegeQuest.com for information on majors offered and athletics. College video available at CollegeQuest.com.

■ *See page 2046 for a narrative description.*

METHODIST COLLEGE
Fayetteville, North Carolina

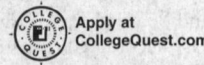 Apply at CollegeQuest.com

- **Independent United Methodist**, 4-year, founded 1956
- **Degrees** associate and bachelor's
- **Suburban** 600-acre campus with easy access to Raleigh-Durham
- **Coed**, 1,940 undergraduate students, 82% full-time, 46% women, 54% men
- **Moderately difficult** entrance level, 93% of applicants were admitted
- **17:1** student-to-undergraduate faculty ratio
- **35% graduate** in 6 years or less
- **$12,704 tuition** and fees
- **$10,800 average financial aid** package, $17,944 average indebtedness upon graduation, $8.2 million endowment

Students *Undergraduates:* 1,600 full-time, 340 part-time. Students come from 46 states and territories. *The most frequently chosen baccalaureate fields are:* business/marketing, health professions and related sciences, social sciences and history.

From out-of-state	49%	Reside on campus	50%
Age 25 or older	2%	Transferred in	3%
International students	1%	African Americans	21%
Asian Americans/Pacific Islanders	1%	Hispanic Americans	4%
Native Americans	1%		

Expenses (1999–2000) *Comprehensive fee:* $17,534 includes full-time tuition ($12,600), mandatory fees ($104), and room and board ($4830). *College room only:* $2330. Full-time tuition and fees vary according to program. Room and board charges vary according to board plan and housing facility. *Part-time tuition:* $420 per semester hour. Part-time tuition and fees vary according to program. *Payment plans:* installment, deferred payment. *Waivers:* senior citizens and employees or children of employees.

Library Davis Memorial Library plus 1 other. *Operations spending 1999–2000:* $733,773. *Collection:* 93,773 titles, 620 serial subscriptions.

College life *Housing: Options:* coed, men-only, women-only. *Most popular organizations:* Student Activities Council, Student Government Association, Student Education Association, Fellowship of Christian Athletes.

Campus security 24-hour emergency response devices and patrols, late-night transport-escort service, controlled dormitory access, campus police station.

After graduation 200 organizations recruited on campus 1997–98. 58% of class of 1998 had job offers within 6 months. *Career center:* 1 full-time personnel. Services include job fairs, resume preparation, interview workshops, career/interest testing, career counseling, careers library, job bank, job interviews.

Freshmen 1,148 applied, 1,070 admitted, 775 enrolled.

Average high school GPA	3.11	SAT verbal scores above 500	34%
SAT math scores above 500	42%	ACT above 18	N/R
From top 10% of their h.s. class	10%	From top quarter	28%
From top half	68%	1998 freshmen returning in 1999	52%

Application *Options:* eApply at www.CollegeQuest.com, early admission, deferred entrance. *Application fee:* $25. *Required:* high school transcript; minimum 2.0 GPA. *Required for some:* essay or personal statement; 2 letters of recommendation. *Recommended:* 2 letters of recommendation; interview.

Standardized tests *Admission: Required:* SAT I or ACT.

Significant dates *Application deadlines:* rolling (freshmen), rolling (transfers). *Notification:* continuous until 8/15 (freshmen). *Financial aid deadline priority date:* 5/1.

Freshman Application Contact
Mr. Rick Lowe, Vice President of Enrollment Services, Methodist College, Admissions Office, 5400 Ramsey Street, Fayetteville, NC 28311. **Phone:** 910-630-7027. **Toll-free phone:** 800-488-7110 Ext. 7027. **Fax:** 910-630-2123. **E-mail:** admissions@methodist.edu

Visit CollegeQuest.com for information on majors offered and athletics. College video available at CollegeQuest.com.

MONTREAT COLLEGE
Montreat, North Carolina

- **Independent Presbyterian**, comprehensive, founded 1916
- **Degrees** associate, bachelor's, and master's
- **Small-town** 100-acre campus

602   www.petersons.com   Peterson's Guide to Four-Year Colleges 2001

North Carolina

- **Coed**, 992 undergraduate students, 98% full-time, 57% women, 43% men
- **Moderately difficult** entrance level, 80% of applicants were admitted
- **$10,862 tuition** and fees
- **$9446 average financial aid** package, $16,274 average indebtedness upon graduation, $12 million endowment

Students *Undergraduates:* Students come from 30 states and territories, 9 other countries. *Graduate:* 62 in graduate degree programs.

Age 25 or older	64%	International students	1%
African Americans	15%	Asian Americans/Pacific Islanders	0.4%
Hispanic Americans	1%	Native Americans	1%

Faculty 57 (58% full-time).

Expenses (1999–2000) *Comprehensive fee:* $15,274 includes full-time tuition ($10,862) and room and board ($4412). *Part-time tuition:* $240 per semester hour. *Payment plan:* installment. *Waivers:* senior citizens and employees or children of employees.

Library L. Nelson Bell Library. *Operations spending 1999–2000:* $307,200. *Collection:* 67,378 titles, 426 serial subscriptions.

College life On-campus residence required through sophomore year. *Most popular organizations:* student government, Student Christian Association, Intervarsity Missions Fellowship, paint ball club, business club.

Campus security 24-hour emergency response devices and patrols, controlled dormitory access.

After graduation 17 organizations recruited on campus 1997–98. 70% of class of 1998 had job offers within 6 months. *Career center:* 1 full-time personnel. Services include resume preparation, career counseling, careers library. *Graduate education:* 17% of class of 1999 went directly to graduate and professional school.

Freshmen 382 applied, 306 admitted.

Average high school GPA	3.13	SAT verbal scores above 500	54%
SAT math scores above 500	49%	ACT above 18	N/R
From top 10% of their h.s. class	10%	From top quarter	32%
From top half	69%	1998 freshmen returning in 1999	81%

Application *Options:* early admission, deferred entrance. *Application fee:* $15. *Required:* essay or personal statement; high school transcript; 1 letter of recommendation. *Required for some:* interview.

Standardized tests *Admission: Required:* SAT I or ACT.

Significant dates *Application deadlines:* 8/20 (freshmen), 8/20 (transfers). *Financial aid deadline priority date:* 5/15.

Freshman Application Contact
Ms. Anita Darby, Director of Admissions, Montreat College, PO Box 1267, Montreat, NC 28757-1267. **Phone:** 828-669-8012 Ext. 3784. **Toll-free phone:** 800-622-6968. **Fax:** 828-669-0120. **E-mail:** admissions@montreat.edu

Visit CollegeQuest.com for information on majors offered and athletics. College video available at CollegeQuest.com.

■ *See page 2088 for a narrative description.*

MOUNT OLIVE COLLEGE

 Apply at CollegeQuest.com

Mount Olive, North Carolina

- **Independent Free Will Baptist**, 4-year, founded 1951
- **Degrees** associate and bachelor's
- **Small-town** 123-acre campus with easy access to Raleigh
- **Coed**, 1,752 undergraduate students, 85% full-time, 53% women, 47% men
- **Minimally difficult** entrance level, 91% of applicants were admitted
- **17:1 student-to-undergraduate faculty ratio**
- **$9210 tuition** and fees
- **$6627 average financial aid** package, $7453 average indebtedness upon graduation, $9.8 million endowment

Students *Undergraduates:* 1,491 full-time, 261 part-time. Students come from 17 states and territories. *The most frequently chosen baccalaureate fields are:* business/marketing, parks and recreation, protective services/public administration.

From out-of-state	29%	Reside on campus	22%
Age 25 or older	48%	Transferred in	4%
African Americans	21%	Asian Americans/Pacific Islanders	0.3%
Hispanic Americans	1%	Native Americans	0.2%

Faculty 115 (35% full-time), 24% with terminal degrees.

Expenses (2000–2001) *Comprehensive fee:* $13,210 includes full-time tuition ($9100), mandatory fees ($110), and room and board ($4000). *College room only:* $1850. Full-time tuition and fees vary according to location. Room and board charges vary according to board plan and housing facility. *Part-time tuition:* $210 per semester hour. Part-time tuition and fees vary according to course load and location. *Payment plan:* installment. *Waivers:* senior citizens and employees or children of employees.

Library Moye Library. *Operations spending 1999–2000:* $197,232. *Collection:* 65,000 titles, 559 serial subscriptions, 1,958 audiovisual materials.

College life *Housing: Options:* men-only, women-only. *Most popular organizations:* Student Government Association, Phi Beta Lambda, commuters organization, Christian Student Fellowship, English Society.

Campus security Overnight security patrols; weekend patrols.

After graduation 75 organizations recruited on campus 1997–98. 82% of class of 1998 had job offers within 6 months. *Career center:* 2 full-time personnel. Services include job fairs, resume preparation, resume referral, career counseling, careers library, job bank, job interviews. *Graduate education:* 15% of class of 1999 went directly to graduate and professional school.

Freshmen 385 applied, 349 admitted, 149 enrolled.

Average high school GPA	2.98	SAT verbal scores above 500	33%
SAT math scores above 500	33%	ACT above 18	48%
From top 10% of their h.s. class	8%	From top quarter	31%
From top half	68%	1998 freshmen returning in 1999	90%

Application *Options:* eApply at www.CollegeQuest.com, Common Application, early admission, deferred entrance. *Application fee:* $20. *Required:* high school transcript; minimum 2.0 GPA. *Recommended:* 2 letters of recommendation; interview.

Standardized tests *Admission: Required:* SAT I or ACT. *Recommended:* SAT I.

Significant dates *Application deadlines:* rolling (freshmen), rolling (transfers). *Financial aid deadline priority date:* 3/1.

Freshman Application Contact
Mr. Tim Woodard, Director of Admissions, Mount Olive College, 634 Henderson Street, Mount Olive, NC 28365. **Phone:** 919-658-2502 Ext. 3009. **Toll-free phone:** 800-653-0854. **Fax:** 919-658-8934.

Visit CollegeQuest.com for information on majors offered and athletics.

■ *See page 2114 for a narrative description.*

NORTH CAROLINA AGRICULTURAL AND TECHNICAL STATE UNIVERSITY

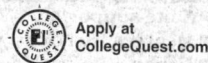 Apply at CollegeQuest.com

Greensboro, North Carolina

- **State-supported**, university, founded 1891
- **Degrees** bachelor's, master's, and doctoral
- **Urban** 191-acre campus
- **Coed**, 6,484 undergraduate students, 90% full-time, 52% women, 48% men
- **Moderately difficult** entrance level, 72% of applicants were admitted
- **43.5% graduate** in 6 years or less
- **$1889 tuition** and fees (in-state); $9159 (out-of-state)
- **$8643 average financial aid** package, $10.4 million endowment

Part of University of North Carolina System.

Students *Undergraduates:* 5,851 full-time, 633 part-time. Students come from 42 states and territories. *Graduate:* 919 in graduate degree programs.

From out-of-state	18%	Reside on campus	42%
Age 25 or older	20%	Transferred in	5%
International students	1%	African Americans	93%
Asian Americans/Pacific Islanders	1%	Hispanic Americans	0.4%
Native Americans	0.3%		

Faculty 470 (95% full-time).

Expenses (1999–2000) *Tuition, state resident:* full-time $962; part-time $241 per term. *Tuition, nonresident:* full-time $8232; part-time $2058 per term. *Required fees:* full-time $927; $304 per term part-time. Part-time tuition

North Carolina

North Carolina Agricultural and Technical State University *(continued)*
and fees vary according to course load. *College room and board:* $4010. Room and board charges vary according to board plan. *Payment plan:* deferred payment.

Library F. D. Bluford Library plus 1 other. *Operations spending 1999–2000:* $4.4 million. *Collection:* 449,766 titles, 4,004 serial subscriptions.

College life *Housing: Options:* men-only, women-only. *Social organizations:* national fraternities, national sororities, local fraternities, local sororities; 1% of eligible men and 1% of eligible women are members. *Most popular organization:* student government.

Campus security 24-hour emergency response devices and patrols, late-night transport-escort service, controlled dormitory access.

After graduation 995 organizations recruited on campus 1997–98. 85% of class of 1998 had job offers within 6 months. *Career center:* 7 full-time personnel. Services include job fairs, resume preparation, resume referral, career counseling, careers library, job bank, job interviews.

Freshmen 4,392 applied, 3,156 admitted, 1,538 enrolled. 7 National Merit Scholars.

Average high school GPA	2.75	SAT verbal scores above 500	21%
SAT math scores above 500	21%	ACT above 18	N/R
From top 10% of their h.s. class	6%	From top quarter	20%
From top half	20%	1998 freshmen returning in 1999	75%

Application *Options:* eApply at www.CollegeQuest.com, early admission, early action, deferred entrance. *Application fee:* $35. *Required:* high school transcript; minimum 2.0 GPA.

Standardized tests *Admission: Required:* SAT I or ACT.

Significant dates *Application deadlines:* 6/1 (freshmen), 6/1 (transfers). *Early action:* 11/1. *Notification:* 12/15 (early action). *Financial aid deadline priority date:* 3/15.

Freshman Application Contact
Mr. John Smith, Director of Admissions, North Carolina Agricultural and Technical State University, 1601 East Market Street, Webb Hall, Greensboro, NC 27411. **Phone:** 336-334-7946. **Toll-free phone:** 800-443-8964. **Fax:** 336-334-7082.

Visit CollegeQuest.com for information on majors offered and athletics. College video available at CollegeQuest.com.

■ *See page 2172 for a narrative description.*

NORTH CAROLINA CENTRAL UNIVERSITY
Durham, North Carolina

- **State-supported**, comprehensive, founded 1910
- **Degrees** bachelor's, master's, and first professional
- **Urban** 103-acre campus
- **Coed**, 3,906 undergraduate students, 81% full-time, 63% women, 37% men
- **Minimally difficult** entrance level, 71% of applicants were admitted
- **11:1 student-to-undergraduate faculty ratio**
- **$1887 tuition** and fees (in-state); $9157 (out-of-state)

A historically black constituent institution of the UNC System, NCCU is located in Durham, near Research Triangle, NC. Raleigh, Durham, and Chapel Hill are a hotbed of academic institutions. Both major private grant and federal funding support opportunities for undergraduate involvement in meaningful research activity under the guidance of a faculty mentor.

Part of University of North Carolina System.

Students *Undergraduates:* 3,148 full-time, 758 part-time. Students come from 34 states and territories, 14 other countries. *The most frequently chosen baccalaureate fields are:* education, health professions and related sciences, liberal arts/general studies. *Graduate:* 367 in professional programs, 1,192 in other graduate degree programs.

From out-of-state	17%	Age 25 or older	33%
Transferred in	7%	International students	2%
African Americans	90%	Asian Americans/Pacific Islanders	0.3%
Hispanic Americans	1%	Native Americans	0.2%

Faculty 410 (69% full-time), 62% with terminal degrees.

Expenses (1999–2000) *Tuition, state resident:* full-time $962. *Tuition, nonresident:* full-time $8232. *Required fees:* full-time $925. Part-time tuition and fees vary according to course load. *College room and board:* $3904; room only: $2250. *Waivers:* employees or children of employees.

Library Shepherd Library plus 1 other. *Collection:* 621,164 titles, 6,162 serial subscriptions, 6,058 audiovisual materials.

College life *Housing: Option:* coed. *Social organizations:* national fraternities, national sororities, local fraternities, local sororities.

Campus security 24-hour emergency response devices and patrols, controlled dormitory access.

After graduation *Career center:* 3 full-time, 1 part-time personnel. Services include job fairs, resume preparation, resume referral, career counseling, job bank, job interviews.

Freshmen 1,808 applied, 1,289 admitted, 653 enrolled.

Average high school GPA	2.6	SAT verbal scores above 500	21%
SAT math scores above 500	19%	ACT above 18	32%
From top 10% of their h.s. class	10%	From top quarter	26%
From top half	51%		

Application *Preference* given to qualified state residents. *Application fee:* $30. *Required:* high school transcript.

Standardized tests *Admission: Required:* SAT I or ACT.

Significant dates *Application deadlines:* 7/1 (freshmen), 7/1 (transfers). *Financial aid deadline priority date:* 4/1.

Freshman Application Contact
Dr. Roger G. Bryant, Interim Director of Admissions, North Carolina Central University, 1801 Fayetteville Street, Durham, NC 27707-3129. **Phone:** 919-560-6298. **E-mail:** ebridges@wpo.nccu.edu

Visit CollegeQuest.com for information on majors offered and athletics.

■ *See page 2174 for a narrative description.*

NORTH CAROLINA SCHOOL OF THE ARTS
Winston-Salem, North Carolina

- **State-supported**, comprehensive, founded 1963
- **Degrees** bachelor's and master's
- **Urban** 57-acre campus
- **Coed**, 700 undergraduate students, 99% full-time, 39% women, 61% men
- **Very difficult** entrance level, 46% of applicants were admitted
- **8:1 student-to-undergraduate faculty ratio**
- **37% graduate** in 6 years or less
- **$2517 tuition** and fees (in-state); $11,145 (out-of-state)
- **$6476 average financial aid** package, $16,300 average indebtedness upon graduation, $15 million endowment

Part of University of North Carolina System.

Students *Undergraduates:* 696 full-time, 4 part-time. Students come from 40 states and territories, 16 other countries. *The most frequently chosen baccalaureate field is:* visual/performing arts. *Graduate:* 67 in graduate degree programs.

From out-of-state	52%	Reside on campus	55%
Age 25 or older	10%	Transferred in	9%
International students	3%	African Americans	8%
Asian Americans/Pacific Islanders	2%	Hispanic Americans	2%
Native Americans	0.4%		

Faculty 132 (92% full-time).

Expenses (1999–2000) *Tuition, state resident:* full-time $1497. *Tuition, nonresident:* full-time $10,125. *Required fees:* full-time $1020. Full-time tuition and fees vary according to program. Part-time tuition and fees vary according to course load. *College room and board:* $4462; room only: $2315. Room and board charges vary according to board plan and housing facility.

Library Semans Library plus 1 other. *Operations spending 1999–2000:* $779,670. *Collection:* 69,510 audiovisual materials.

College life *Housing:* on-campus residence required through sophomore year. *Option:* coed. *Most popular organizations:* Pride (gay/lesbian organization), Appreciation of Black Artists.

Campus security 24-hour emergency response devices and patrols, controlled dormitory access.

After graduation *Career center:* 1 full-time personnel. Services include career counseling, careers library.

North Carolina

Freshmen 638 applied, 295 admitted, 176 enrolled.

Average high school GPA	3.27	SAT verbal scores above 500	80%
SAT math scores above 500	69%	ACT above 18	90%
From top 10% of their h.s. class	16%	From top quarter	35%
From top half	72%	1998 freshmen returning in 1999	62%

Application *Application fee:* $35. *Required:* high school transcript; 2 letters of recommendation; audition. *Required for some:* essay or personal statement; interview.

Standardized tests *Admission: Required:* SAT I or ACT.

Significant dates *Application deadlines:* rolling (freshmen), rolling (transfers). *Financial aid deadline priority date:* 3/1.

Freshman Application Contact
Mrs. Kelye Suzanne Bush, Director of Admissions, North Carolina School of the Arts, 1533 South Main Street, PO Box 12189, Winston-Salem, NC 27127-2188. **Phone:** 336-770-3290. **Fax:** 336-770-3370. **E-mail:** admissions@ncarts.edu

Visit CollegeQuest.com for information on majors offered and athletics.

NORTH CAROLINA STATE UNIVERSITY
Raleigh, North Carolina

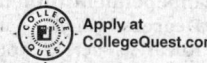

- **State-supported**, university, founded 1887
- **Degrees** associate, bachelor's, master's, doctoral, first professional, and first professional certificates
- **Suburban** 1,623-acre campus
- **Coed**, 19,337 undergraduate students, 90% full-time, 40% women, 60% men
- **Very difficult** entrance level, 62% of applicants were admitted
- **13:1 student-to-undergraduate faculty ratio**
- **63% graduate** in 6 years or less
- **$2514 tuition** and fees (in-state); $12,566 (out-of-state)
- **$5661 average financial aid** package, $14,801 average indebtedness upon graduation, $275.5 million endowment

Part of University of North Carolina System.

Students *Undergraduates:* 17,463 full-time, 1,874 part-time. Students come from 51 states and territories, 65 other countries. *The most frequently chosen baccalaureate fields are:* business/marketing, agriculture, engineering/engineering technologies. *Graduate:* 289 in professional programs, 6,038 in other graduate degree programs.

From out-of-state	8%	Reside on campus	35%
Age 25 or older	10%	Transferred in	6%
International students	1%	African Americans	10%
Asian Americans/Pacific Islanders	5%	Hispanic Americans	2%
Native Americans	1%		

Expenses (1999–2000) *Tuition, state resident:* full-time $1528; part-time $667 per term. *Tuition, nonresident:* full-time $11,580; part-time $2959 per term. *Required fees:* full-time $986. Full-time tuition and fees vary according to program. Part-time tuition and fees vary according to course load and program. *College room and board:* $4560; room only: $2370. Room and board charges vary according to board plan and housing facility. *Waivers:* senior citizens.

Library D. H. Hill Library plus 4 others. *Operations spending 1999–2000:* $17.3 million. *Collection:* 35,194 serial subscriptions, 138,608 audiovisual materials.

College life *Housing: Options:* coed, men-only, women-only, disabled students. *Social organizations:* national fraternities, national sororities. *Most popular organizations:* student government, student media, student musical groups, intramural sports.

Campus security 24-hour emergency response devices and patrols, student patrols, late-night transport-escort service, controlled dormitory access.

After graduation 498 organizations recruited on campus 1997–98. *Career center:* 10 full-time, 1 part-time personnel. Services include job fairs, resume preparation, interview workshops, resume referral, career/interest testing, career counseling, careers library, job bank, job interviews. *Graduate education:* 20% of class of 1999 went directly to graduate and professional school. *Major awards:* 2 Fulbright Scholars.

Freshmen 12,227 applied, 7,555 admitted, 3,666 enrolled. 41 National Merit Scholars, 75 valedictorians.

Average high school GPA	3.86	SAT verbal scores above 500	87%
SAT math scores above 500	92%	ACT above 18	97%
From top 10% of their h.s. class	36%	From top quarter	78%
From top half	98%	1998 freshmen returning in 1999	88%

Application *Options:* eApply at www.CollegeQuest.com, electronic application, early action, deferred entrance. *Preference* given to state residents. *Application fee:* $55. *Required:* high school transcript. *Required for some:* 1 letter of recommendation; interview. *Recommended:* essay or personal statement; minimum 3.0 GPA.

Standardized tests *Admission: Required:* SAT I or ACT.

Significant dates *Application deadlines:* 12/1 (freshmen), rolling (transfers). *Early action:* 11/15. *Notification:* 12/30 (early action). *Financial aid deadline priority date:* 3/1.

Freshman Application Contact
Dr. George R. Dixon, Vice Provost and Director of Admissions, North Carolina State University, Box 7103, 112 Peele Hall, Raleigh, NC 27695. **Phone:** 919-515-2434. **Fax:** 919-515-5039. **E-mail:** undergrad_admissions@ncsu.edu

Visit CollegeQuest.com for information on majors offered and athletics. College video and electronic viewbook available at CollegeQuest.com.

NORTH CAROLINA WESLEYAN COLLEGE
Rocky Mount, North Carolina

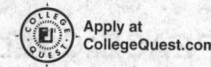

- **Independent**, 4-year, founded 1956, affiliated with United Methodist Church
- **Degree** bachelor's (also offers adult part-time degree program with significant enrollment not reflected in profile)
- **Suburban** 200-acre campus
- **Coed**, 2,024 undergraduate students, 56% full-time, 57% women, 43% men
- **Moderately difficult** entrance level, 91% of applicants were admitted
- **15:1 student-to-undergraduate faculty ratio**
- **95% graduate** in 6 years or less
- **$8556 tuition** and fees
- **$4.1 million endowment**

North Carolina Wesleyan, a private liberal arts college affiliated with the Methodist Church, educates men and women for productive and fulfilling lives, rewarding careers, and service to their community. The curriculum, both in traditional and preprofessional fields, emphasizes critical thinking, reading and writing, listening and speaking, and making informed decisions. The College focuses on personal attention and student self-development.

Students *Undergraduates:* 1,134 full-time, 890 part-time. Students come from 22 states and territories, 6 other countries.

From out-of-state	32%	Transferred in	4%
International students	0.3%	African Americans	30%
Asian Americans/Pacific Islanders	0.4%	Hispanic Americans	2%
Native Americans	0.4%		

Expenses (1999–2000) *Comprehensive fee:* $14,528 includes full-time tuition ($7724), mandatory fees ($832), and room and board ($5972). *College room only:* $3088. Room and board charges vary according to board plan and housing facility. *Part-time tuition:* $167 per credit. *Part-time fees:* $4 per credit; $69 per term part-time. Part-time tuition and fees vary according to course load. *Payment plan:* installment. *Waivers:* senior citizens and employees or children of employees.

Library Elizabeth Braswell Pearsall Library. *Collection:* 75,000 titles, 565 serial subscriptions.

College life *Housing:* on-campus residence required through sophomore year. *Options:* coed, men-only, women-only. *Social organizations:* national fraternities, national sororities; 14% of eligible men and 13% of eligible women are members. *Most popular organizations:* Club Dramatica, Student Government Association, Gospel Choir, Wesleyan Singers, pep band.

Campus security 24-hour emergency response devices and patrols, student patrols, late-night transport-escort service, controlled dormitory access.

After graduation 60 organizations recruited on campus 1997–98. 65% of class of 1998 had job offers within 6 months. *Career center:* 2 full-time personnel. Services include job fairs, resume preparation, resume referral, career counseling, careers library, job bank, job interviews. *Graduate*

North Carolina

North Carolina Wesleyan College (continued)
education: 16% of class of 1999 went directly to graduate and professional school: 7% business, 6% education, 2% medicine, 1% law.

Freshmen 663 applied, 606 admitted, 216 enrolled.

Average high school GPA	2.7	SAT verbal scores above 500	27%
SAT math scores above 500	32%	ACT above 18	N/R
1998 freshmen returning in 1999	67%		

Application *Options:* eApply at www.CollegeQuest.com, Common Application, electronic application, early admission, deferred entrance. *Application fee:* $25. *Required:* high school transcript. *Required for some:* essay or personal statement; interview. *Recommended:* minimum 2.0 GPA; 2 letters of recommendation; interview.

Standardized tests *Admission: Required:* SAT I or ACT.

Significant dates *Application deadlines:* rolling (freshmen), rolling (transfers). *Financial aid deadline priority date:* 4/15.

Freshman Application Contact
Cecelia Summers, Associate Director of Admissions, North Carolina Wesleyan College, 4300 N Wesleyan Blvd., Attn: Office of Admission, Rocky Mount, NC 27804. **Phone:** 800-488-6292 Ext. 5202. **Toll-free phone:** 800-488-6292. **Fax:** 252-985-5325. **E-mail:** adm@ncwc.edu

Visit CollegeQuest.com for information on majors offered and athletics.

■ *See page 2176 for a narrative description.*

PEACE COLLEGE
Raleigh, North Carolina

 Apply at CollegeQuest.com

- **Independent**, 4-year, founded 1857, affiliated with Presbyterian Church (U.S.A.)
- **Degrees** associate and bachelor's
- **Urban** 16-acre campus
- **Women** only, 550 undergraduate students, 100% full-time
- **Moderately difficult** entrance level, 86% of applicants were admitted
- **13:1 student-to-undergraduate faculty ratio**
- **$9927 tuition** and fees
- **$8320 average financial aid** package, $43.3 million endowment

Students *Undergraduates:* 550 full-time. Students come from 14 states and territories, 2 other countries. *The most frequently chosen baccalaureate fields are:* business/marketing, communications/communication technologies, liberal arts/general studies.

From out-of-state	13%	Reside on campus	82%
Age 25 or older	4%	Transferred in	2%
International students	0.4%	African Americans	6%
Asian Americans/Pacific Islanders	1%	Hispanic Americans	1%
Native Americans	0.4%		

Faculty 68 (54% full-time), 54% with terminal degrees.

Expenses (2000–2001) *Comprehensive fee:* $14,927 includes full-time tuition ($9727), mandatory fees ($200), and room and board ($5000). *Part-time tuition:* $300 per semester hour. *Payment plan:* installment. *Waivers:* employees or children of employees.

Library Lucy Cooper Finch Library. *Operations spending 1999–2000:* $221,500. *Collection:* 51,118 titles, 3,900 serial subscriptions, 1,200 audiovisual materials.

College life *Housing:* on-campus residence required through sophomore year. *Option:* women-only. *Most popular organizations:* Student Government Association, Peace Student Christian Association, Recreation Association, Human Resources Society, psychology club.

Campus security 24-hour emergency response devices and patrols, late-night transport-escort service, controlled dormitory access.

After graduation *Career center:* 1 full-time personnel. Services include job fairs, resume preparation, interview workshops, resume referral, career/interest testing, career counseling, careers library, job bank, job interviews. *Graduate education:* 6% of class of 1999 went directly to graduate and professional school: 2% graduate arts and sciences, 2% law, 2% medicine.

Freshmen 348 applied, 301 admitted, 171 enrolled. 4 valedictorians.

Average high school GPA	2.83	SAT verbal scores above 500	N/R
SAT math scores above 500	N/R	ACT above 18	N/R
1998 freshmen returning in 1999	69%		

Application *Options:* eApply at www.CollegeQuest.com, early admission, deferred entrance. *Application fee:* $25. *Required:* essay or personal statement; high school transcript; minimum 2.0 GPA; 2 letters of recommendation. *Recommended:* interview.

Standardized tests *Admission: Required:* SAT I or ACT.

Significant dates *Application deadlines:* rolling (freshmen), rolling (transfers). *Financial aid deadline priority date:* 4/1.

Freshman Application Contact
Dr. E. Carole Tyler, Dean of Admissions and Financial Aid, Peace College, Admissions and Financial Aid, Raleigh, NC 27604. **Phone:** 919-508-2214. **Toll-free phone:** 800-PEACE-47. **Fax:** 919-508-2328. **E-mail:** chill@peace.edu

Visit CollegeQuest.com for information on majors offered and athletics. College video available at CollegeQuest.com.

■ *See page 2248 for a narrative description.*

PFEIFFER UNIVERSITY
Misenheimer, North Carolina

- **Independent United Methodist**, comprehensive, founded 1885
- **Degrees** bachelor's and master's
- **Rural** 300-acre campus with easy access to Charlotte
- **Coed**, 926 undergraduate students, 87% full-time, 57% women, 43% men
- **Moderately difficult** entrance level, 80% of applicants were admitted
- **15:1 student-to-undergraduate faculty ratio**
- **42.2% graduate** in 6 years or less
- **$10,844 tuition** and fees
- **$7369 average financial aid** package, $11 million endowment

Students *Undergraduates:* 802 full-time, 124 part-time. Students come from 27 states and territories, 21 other countries. *The most frequently chosen baccalaureate fields are:* business/marketing, health professions and related sciences, protective services/public administration. *Graduate:* 643 in graduate degree programs.

From out-of-state	22%	Reside on campus	65%
Age 25 or older	41%	Transferred in	8%
International students	3%	African Americans	18%
Asian Americans/Pacific Islanders	1%	Hispanic Americans	2%
Native Americans	0.3%		

Faculty 124, 73% with terminal degrees.

Expenses (1999–2000) *Comprehensive fee:* $15,211 includes full-time tuition ($10,844) and room and board ($4367). *College room only:* $2270. Full-time tuition and fees vary according to course load. Room and board charges vary according to board plan and housing facility. *Part-time tuition:* $249 per semester hour. *Payment plans:* installment, deferred payment. *Waivers:* employees or children of employees.

Library Gustavus A. Pfeiffer Library. *Operations spending 1999–2000:* $324,861. *Collection:* 116,200 titles, 415 serial subscriptions, 2,349 audiovisual materials.

College life *Housing:* on-campus residence required through senior year. *Options:* coed, men-only, women-only. *Most popular organizations:* Student Government Association, Religious Life Council, Commuter Student Association, Programming Activities Council, Residence Hall Association.

Campus security 24-hour emergency response devices and patrols, late-night transport-escort service, controlled dormitory access.

After graduation 12 organizations recruited on campus 1997–98. *Career center:* 1 full-time, 1 part-time personnel. Services include job fairs, resume preparation, interview workshops, career/interest testing, career counseling, careers library, job bank, job interviews. *Graduate education:* 28% of class of 1999 went directly to graduate and professional school: 17% graduate arts and sciences, 5% business, 2% law, 2% theology, 1% engineering, 1% medicine.

Freshmen 709 applied, 568 admitted, 159 enrolled.

Average high school GPA	2.85	SAT verbal scores above 500	42%
SAT math scores above 500	43%	ACT above 18	72%
From top 10% of their h.s. class	6%	From top quarter	28%
From top half	63%	1998 freshmen returning in 1999	68%

Application *Options:* Common Application, early admission, deferred entrance. *Application fee:* $25. *Required:* high school transcript. *Required for some:* 2 letters of recommendation. *Recommended:* minimum 2.0 GPA; interview.

Standardized tests *Admission: Required:* SAT I or ACT.
Significant dates *Application deadlines:* rolling (freshmen), rolling (transfers). *Financial aid deadline priority date:* 3/15.
Freshman Application Contact
Mr. Steve Cumming, Director of Admissions, Pfeiffer University, PO Box 960, Highway 52 North, Misenheimer, NC 28109. **Phone:** 704-463-1360 Ext. 2079. **Toll-free phone:** 800-338-2060. **Fax:** 704-463-1363. **E-mail:** admiss@pfeiffer.edu
Visit CollegeQuest.com for information on majors offered and athletics. College video and electronic viewbook available at CollegeQuest.com.

■ *See page 2264 for a narrative description.*

PIEDMONT BAPTIST COLLEGE
Winston-Salem, North Carolina

- **Independent Baptist**, comprehensive, founded 1947
- **Degrees** associate, bachelor's, and master's
- **Urban** 12-acre campus
- **Coed**, 275 undergraduate students, 77% full-time, 47% women, 53% men
- **Noncompetitive** entrance level, 100% of applicants were admitted
- **$5750 tuition** and fees

Students *Undergraduates:* 211 full-time, 64 part-time. Students come from 25 states and territories. *Graduate:* 20 in graduate degree programs.

From out-of-state	42%	Reside on campus	32%
Age 25 or older	42%	Transferred in	10%
African Americans	3%	Asian Americans/Pacific Islanders	10%
Hispanic Americans	1%	Native Americans	0.3%

Faculty 38 (50% full-time).
Expenses (1999-2000) *Comprehensive fee:* $9150 includes full-time tuition ($5270), mandatory fees ($480), and room and board ($3400). Full-time tuition and fees vary according to course load. *Part-time tuition:* $215 per credit hour. *Part-time fees:* $140 per term part-time. Part-time tuition and fees vary according to course load. *Payment plan:* installment. *Waivers:* children of alumni, adult students, and employees or children of employees.
Library George Manuel Memorial Library. *Collection:* 46,485 titles, 204 serial subscriptions.
College life *Housing:* on-campus residence required through senior year. *Options:* men-only, women-only. *Most popular organizations:* Piedmont Missions Fellowship, Piedmont Preachers Fellowship, Piedmont Educators' Fellowship, Piedmont Music Fellowship, Student Government Association.
Campus security Student patrols, late-night transport-escort service, controlled dormitory access, security guards on duty during evening hours.
After graduation 25 organizations recruited on campus 1997-98. 90% of class of 1998 had job offers within 6 months. *Career center:* Services include career counseling. *Graduate education:* 11% of class of 1999 went directly to graduate and professional school: 8% theology, 3% graduate arts and sciences.
Freshmen 78 applied, 78 admitted, 50 enrolled. 3 valedictorians, 6 student government officers.

SAT verbal scores above 500	34%	SAT math scores above 500	18%
ACT above 18	13%	From top 10% of their h.s. class	13%
From top quarter	33%	From top half	69%
1998 freshmen returning in 1999	68%		

Application *Options:* early admission, early action, deferred entrance. *Application fee:* $30. *Required:* essay or personal statement; high school transcript; 3 letters of recommendation; medical history, proof of immunization. *Recommended:* minimum 2.0 GPA; interview.
Standardized tests *Placement: Required:* SAT I or ACT. *Recommended:* SAT II Subject Tests.
Significant dates *Application deadlines:* rolling (freshmen), rolling (transfers). *Early action:* 11/1. *Notification:* 11/30 (early action). *Financial aid deadline priority date:* 6/1.
Freshman Application Contact
Mrs. Carole Beverly, Director of Admissions, Piedmont Baptist College, 716 Franklin Street, Winston-Salem, NC 27101-5197. **Phone:** 336-725-8344. **Toll-free phone:** 800-937-5097. **Fax:** 336-725-5522. **E-mail:** admissions@pbc.edu
Visit CollegeQuest.com for information on majors offered and athletics. College video available at CollegeQuest.com.

QUEENS COLLEGE
Charlotte, North Carolina

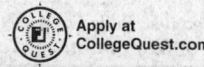

- **Independent Presbyterian**, comprehensive, founded 1857
- **Degrees** bachelor's, master's, and postbachelor's certificates
- **Suburban** 25-acre campus
- **Coed**, 1,048 undergraduate students, 62% full-time, 80% women, 20% men
- **Moderately difficult** entrance level, 73% of applicants were admitted
- **11:1 student-to-undergraduate faculty ratio**
- **52.1% graduate** in 6 years or less
- **$10,680 tuition** and fees
- **$11,440 average financial aid** package, $15,300 average indebtedness upon graduation, $37.8 million endowment

Students *Undergraduates:* 649 full-time, 399 part-time. Students come from 33 states and territories, 24 other countries. *Graduate:* 448 in graduate degree programs.

From out-of-state	33%	Reside on campus	75%
Transferred in	6%	International students	5%
African Americans	15%	Asian Americans/Pacific Islanders	1%
Hispanic Americans	2%	Native Americans	1%

Faculty 125 (49% full-time), 50% with terminal degrees.
Expenses (2000-2001) *Comprehensive fee:* $16,570 includes full-time tuition ($10,680) and room and board ($5890). *Part-time tuition:* $225 per credit hour. *Part-time fees:* $15 per term part-time. *Payment plan:* installment. *Waivers:* employees or children of employees.
Library Everett Library plus 1 other. *Operations spending 1999-2000:* $406,627. *Collection:* 98,878 titles, 632 serial subscriptions, 845 audiovisual materials.
College life *Housing:* on-campus residence required in freshman year. *Options:* coed, men-only, women-only. *Social organizations:* national fraternities, national sororities; 20% of eligible men and 35% of eligible women are members. *Most popular organizations:* Senate, College Union Board, Admissions Ambassadors, Baptist Student Union, International Club.
Campus security 24-hour emergency response devices and patrols, late-night transport-escort service, controlled dormitory access.
After graduation 75% of class of 1998 had job offers within 6 months. *Career center:* 4 full-time personnel. Services include job fairs, resume preparation, interview workshops, resume referral, career/interest testing, career counseling, careers library, job bank, job interviews.
Freshmen 577 applied, 424 admitted, 123 enrolled. 2 class presidents, 2 valedictorians, 14 student government officers.

Average high school GPA	3.1	SAT verbal scores above 500	62%
SAT math scores above 500	51%	ACT above 18	81%
From top 10% of their h.s. class	13%	From top quarter	42%
From top half	77%	1998 freshmen returning in 1999	73%

Application *Options:* eApply at www.CollegeQuest.com, Common Application, early admission, deferred entrance. *Application fee:* $25. *Required:* essay or personal statement; high school transcript; minimum 2.0 GPA; 2 letters of recommendation. *Recommended:* interview.
Standardized tests *Admission: Required:* SAT I or ACT.
Significant dates *Application deadlines:* rolling (freshmen), rolling (transfers). *Financial aid deadline priority date:* 3/1.
Freshman Application Contact
Ms. Eileen T. Dills, Dean of Admissions and Financial Aid, Queens College, 1900 Selwyn Avenue, Charlotte, NC 28274-0002. **Phone:** 704-337-2212. **Toll-free phone:** 800-849-0202. **Fax:** 704-337-2403. **E-mail:** cas@queens.edu
Visit CollegeQuest.com for information on majors offered and athletics. College video available at CollegeQuest.com.

ROANOKE BIBLE COLLEGE
Elizabeth City, North Carolina

- **Independent Christian**, 4-year, founded 1948
- **Degrees** associate and bachelor's
- **Small-town** 19-acre campus with easy access to Norfolk
- **Coed**
- **Minimally difficult** entrance level

North Carolina

Roanoke Bible College (continued)
- **$5610 tuition** and fees

Expenses (1999–2000) *Comprehensive fee:* $9070 includes full-time tuition ($4960), mandatory fees ($650), and room and board ($3460). Room and board charges vary according to housing facility. *Part-time tuition:* $155 per semester hour. *Part-time fees:* $35 per semester hour. Part-time tuition and fees vary according to course load.
Institutional Web site http://www.roanokebible.edu/
College life *Housing:* on-campus residence required through senior year. *Options:* men-only, women-only. *Most popular organizations:* Student Advisory Council, counseling club, drama club, choral group.
Campus security 24-hour emergency response devices, controlled dormitory access.
Application *Options:* eApply at www.CollegeQuest.com, electronic application, early admission, deferred entrance. *Application fee:* $25. *Required:* essay or personal statement; high school transcript; reference from church. *Required for some:* interview.
Standardized tests *Placement: Required:* SAT I or ACT
Admissions Office Contact
Roanoke Bible College, 715 North Poindexter Street, Elizabeth City, NC 27909-4054. **Toll-free phone:** 800-RBC-8980. **Fax:** 252-334-2071. **E-mail:** admissions@roanokebible.edu
Visit CollegeQuest.com for information on athletics.

ST. ANDREWS PRESBYTERIAN COLLEGE
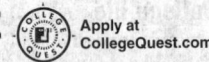
Laurinburg, North Carolina

- **Independent Presbyterian**, 4-year, founded 1958
- **Degree** bachelor's
- **Small-town** 600-acre campus
- **Coed**, 584 undergraduate students, 91% full-time, 58% women, 42% men
- **Moderately difficult** entrance level, 81% of applicants were admitted
- **10:1** student-to-undergraduate faculty ratio
- **37% graduate** in 6 years or less
- **$13,735 tuition** and fees
- **$12,388 average financial aid** package, $10 million endowment

Students *Undergraduates:* 533 full-time, 51 part-time. Students come from 42 states and territories, 15 other countries. *The most frequently chosen baccalaureate fields are:* business/marketing, education, psychology.

From out-of-state	56%	Reside on campus	83%
Age 25 or older	19%	Transferred in	7%
International students	5%	African Americans	13%
Asian Americans/Pacific Islanders	2%	Hispanic Americans	1%
Native Americans	0.5%		

Faculty 76 (45% full-time), 36% with terminal degrees.
Expenses (1999–2000) *Comprehensive fee:* $19,035 includes full-time tuition ($13,515), mandatory fees ($220), and room and board ($5300). *College room only:* $2115. *Part-time tuition:* $410 per credit. *Payment plan:* installment. *Waivers:* adult students and employees or children of employees.
Library DeTamble Library. *Operations spending 1999–2000:* $301,395. *Collection:* 108,734 titles, 436 serial subscriptions, 4,405 audiovisual materials.
College life *Housing:* on-campus residence required through senior year. *Options:* coed, men-only, women-only. *Most popular organizations:* business club, Breaking the Mirror (women's group), Writer's Forum, Student Activities Union, Eco-Action.
Campus security 24-hour emergency response devices and patrols, late-night transport-escort service.
After graduation 4 organizations recruited on campus 1997–98. 75% of class of 1998 had job offers within 6 months. *Career center:* 1 full-time, 1 part-time personnel. Services include job fairs, resume preparation, interview workshops, resume referral, career/interest testing, career counseling, careers library, job bank, job interviews. **Graduate education:** 16% of class of 1999 went directly to graduate and professional school.

Freshmen 842 applied, 681 admitted, 152 enrolled.

Average high school GPA	2.88	SAT verbal scores above 500	56%
SAT math scores above 500	33%	ACT above 18	N/R
1998 freshmen returning in 1999	40%		

Application *Options:* eApply at www.CollegeQuest.com, Common Application, electronic application, early admission, early decision, deferred entrance. *Application fee:* $25. *Required:* high school transcript; 1 letter of recommendation. *Required for some:* essay or personal statement; interview. *Recommended:* minimum 2.0 GPA.
Standardized tests *Admission: Required:* SAT I or ACT.
Significant dates *Application deadlines:* rolling (freshmen), rolling (transfers). *Early decision:* 12/1. *Notification:* 1/1 (early decision). *Financial aid deadline:* continuous.
Freshman Application Contact
Ms. Marcia Nance, Dean for Student Affairs and Enrollment, St. Andrews Presbyterian College, 1700 Dogwood Mile, Laurinburg, NC 28352-5598. **Phone:** 910-277-5555. **Toll-free phone:** 800-763-0198. **Fax:** 910-277-5087. **E-mail:** admission@sapc.edu
Visit CollegeQuest.com for information on majors offered and athletics. College video and electronic viewbook available at CollegeQuest.com.

- *See page 2368 for a narrative description.*

SAINT AUGUSTINE'S COLLEGE
Raleigh, North Carolina

- **Independent Episcopal**, 4-year, founded 1867
- **Degree** bachelor's
- **Urban** 110-acre campus
- **Coed**, 1,464 undergraduate students, 93% full-time, 58% women, 42% men
- **Minimally difficult** entrance level, 45% of applicants were admitted
- **16:1** student-to-undergraduate faculty ratio
- **30% graduate** in 6 years or less
- **$7182 tuition** and fees
- **$8762 average financial aid** package, $18,000 average indebtedness upon graduation, $21 million endowment

Students *Undergraduates:* 1,357 full-time, 107 part-time. Students come from 50 states and territories, 20 other countries. *The most frequently chosen baccalaureate fields are:* business/marketing, psychology, social sciences and history.

From out-of-state	41%	Reside on campus	62%
Age 25 or older	17%	Transferred in	3%
International students	9%	African Americans	90%
Hispanic Americans	0.2%		

Faculty 111 (78% full-time), 51% with terminal degrees.
Expenses (1999–2000) *One-time required fee:* $275. *Comprehensive fee:* $11,690 includes full-time tuition ($5132), mandatory fees ($2050), and room and board ($4508). Full-time tuition and fees vary according to program. Room and board charges vary according to housing facility and location. *Part-time tuition:* $210 per semester hour. *Part-time fees:* $210 per term part-time. Part-time tuition and fees vary according to program. *Payment plan:* installment. *Waivers:* employees or children of employees.
Library Prezell R. Robinson Library. *Collection:* 500 serial subscriptions, 300 audiovisual materials.
College life *Housing: Options:* men-only, women-only. *Social organizations:* national fraternities, national sororities, local fraternities, local sororities; 6% of eligible men and 12% of eligible women are members. *Most popular organizations:* chorale group, jazz band, International Student Organization, Pershing Rifles.
Campus security 24-hour emergency response devices and patrols.
After graduation 25 organizations recruited on campus 1997–98. 40% of class of 1998 had job offers within 6 months. *Career center:* 5 full-time personnel. Services include job fairs, resume preparation, interview workshops, resume referral, career/interest testing, career counseling, careers library, job bank, job interviews.

North Carolina

Freshmen 2,187 applied, 994 admitted, 338 enrolled.

Average high school GPA	2.34	SAT verbal scores above 500	11%
SAT math scores above 500	11%	ACT above 18	78%
From top 10% of their h.s. class	4%	From top quarter	10%
From top half	31%	1998 freshmen returning in 1999	62%

Application *Options:* eApply at www.CollegeQuest.com, electronic application, deferred entrance. *Application fee:* $25. *Required:* essay or personal statement; high school transcript; 3 letters of recommendation; medical history. *Recommended:* minimum 2.0 GPA.

Standardized tests *Admission: Required:* SAT I or ACT.

Significant dates *Application deadlines:* 7/1 (freshmen), rolling (transfers). *Financial aid deadline priority date:* 4/15.

Freshman Application Contact
Ms. Sha-Ron Jones, Dean for Enrollment Management, Saint Augustine's College, 1315 Oakwood Avenue, Raleigh, NC 27610-2298. **Phone:** 919-516-4011. **Toll-free phone:** 800-948-1126. **Fax:** 919-516-4415. **E-mail:** admissions@es.st-aug.edu

Visit CollegeQuest.com for information on majors offered and athletics.

SALEM COLLEGE
Winston-Salem, North Carolina

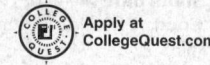
Apply at CollegeQuest.com

- **Independent Moravian**, comprehensive, founded 1772
- **Degrees** bachelor's and master's (only students 23 or over are eligible to enroll part-time; men may attend evening program only)
- **Urban** 57-acre campus
- **Women** only, 918 undergraduate students
- **Moderately difficult** entrance level, 89% of applicants were admitted
- **13:1 student-to-undergraduate faculty ratio**
- **54% graduate** in 6 years or less
- **$13,415 tuition** and fees
- **$49.2 million endowment**

Salem College's honors scholarship program recognizes superior academic achievement as well as leadership and service. Scholarships range from $7000 to $13,000 and are renewable annually. They are awarded on a competitive basis to entering freshmen.

Students *Undergraduates:* Students come from 25 states and territories, 16 other countries. *The most frequently chosen baccalaureate fields are:* business/marketing, social sciences and history, visual/performing arts.

From out-of-state	48%	Age 25 or older	36%
International students	3%	African Americans	17%
Asian Americans/Pacific Islanders	1%	Hispanic Americans	2%
Native Americans	1%		

Faculty 86 (60% full-time), 70% with terminal degrees.

Expenses (1999–2000) *Comprehensive fee:* $21,335 includes full-time tuition ($13,200), mandatory fees ($215), and room and board ($7920). *Part-time tuition:* $720 per course. *Payment plan:* installment. *Waivers:* employees or children of employees.

Library Gramley Library plus 2 others. *Operations spending 1999–2000:* $543,126. *Collection:* 121,783 titles, 11,784 audiovisual materials.

College life On-campus residence required through senior year. *Most popular organizations:* Campus Activities Council, Onua, Big 3+3, Fremdendienerin, Ambassadors.

Campus security 24-hour emergency response devices and patrols, late-night transport-escort service, controlled dormitory access.

After graduation 77% of class of 1998 had job offers within 6 months. *Career center:* 1 full-time, 1 part-time personnel. Services include job fairs, resume preparation, resume referral, career counseling, careers library, job interviews. *Graduate education:* 20% of class of 1999 went directly to graduate and professional school: 13% graduate arts and sciences, 3% education, 1% business, 1% law, 1% medicine.

Freshmen 380 applied, 339 admitted.

Average high school GPA	3.5	SAT verbal scores above 500	74%
SAT math scores above 500	56%	ACT above 18	84%
From top 10% of their h.s. class	32%	From top quarter	62%
From top half	89%	1998 freshmen returning in 1999	78%

Application *Options:* eApply at www.CollegeQuest.com, Common Application, electronic application, early admission, early action, deferred entrance. *Application fee:* $25. *Required:* essay or personal statement; high school transcript; 2 letters of recommendation. *Recommended:* interview.

Standardized tests *Admission: Required:* SAT I or ACT.

Significant dates *Application deadlines:* rolling (freshmen), rolling (transfers). *Early action:* 12/1. *Notification:* 1/1 (early action). *Financial aid deadline priority date:* 3/15.

Freshman Application Contact
Ms. Katherine Knapp-Watts, Dean of Admissions and Financial Aid, Salem College, PO Box 10548, Winston-Salem, NC 27108-0548. **Phone:** 336-721-2621. **Toll-free phone:** 800-327-2536. **Fax:** 336-724-7102. **E-mail:** admissions@salem.edu

Visit CollegeQuest.com for information on majors offered and athletics. College video available at CollegeQuest.com.

■ *See page 2434 for a narrative description.*

SHAW UNIVERSITY
Raleigh, North Carolina

- **Independent Baptist**, comprehensive, founded 1865
- **Degrees** associate, bachelor's, and first professional
- **Urban** 18-acre campus
- **Coed**, 2,529 undergraduate students, 85% full-time, 63% women, 37% men
- **Minimally difficult** entrance level, 68% of applicants were admitted
- **16:1 student-to-undergraduate faculty ratio**
- **25% graduate** in 6 years or less
- **$6854 tuition** and fees

Students *Undergraduates:* 2,161 full-time, 368 part-time. Students come from 35 states and territories. *The most frequently chosen baccalaureate fields are:* business/marketing, protective services/public administration, social sciences and history. *Graduate:* 141 in professional programs.

From out-of-state	25%	Reside on campus	41%
Age 25 or older	49%	Transferred in	12%
African Americans	85%	Asian Americans/Pacific Islanders	0.1%
Hispanic Americans	0.4%	Native Americans	0.3%

Faculty 295 (29% full-time), 43% with terminal degrees.

Expenses (1999–2000) *Comprehensive fee:* $11,196 includes full-time tuition ($6272), mandatory fees ($582), and room and board ($4342). Full-time tuition and fees vary according to degree level. *Part-time tuition:* $261 per credit hour. *Part-time fees:* $134 per term part-time. Part-time tuition and fees vary according to degree level. *Payment plans:* installment, deferred payment. *Waivers:* employees or children of employees.

Library James E. Cheek Learning Resources Center plus 2 others. *Collection:* 136,851 titles, 4,982 serial subscriptions, 435 audiovisual materials.

College life *Housing:* on-campus residence required in freshman year. *Options:* men-only, women-only. *Social organizations:* national fraternities, national sororities, social fellowships; 4% of eligible men and 5% of eligible women are members. *Most popular organizations:* Student Government Association, choir, university band, Shaw Players, academic clubs.

Campus security 24-hour emergency response devices and patrols, late-night transport-escort service, 24-hour electronic surveillance cameras.

After graduation 130 organizations recruited on campus 1997–98. *Career center:* 3 full-time personnel. Services include job fairs, resume preparation, interview workshops, resume referral, career/interest testing, career counseling, careers library, job bank, job interviews.

Freshmen 1,791 applied, 1,215 admitted, 464 enrolled.

Average high school GPA	2.32	SAT verbal scores above 500	N/R
SAT math scores above 500	N/R	ACT above 18	N/R
From top 10% of their h.s. class	4%	From top quarter	10%
From top half	30%	1998 freshmen returning in 1999	42%

Application *Options:* Common Application, electronic application, early admission, deferred entrance. *Application fee:* $25. *Required:* essay or personal statement; high school transcript; minimum 2.0 GPA.

Standardized tests *Admission: Required:* SAT I or ACT.

Significant dates *Application deadlines:* 7/30 (freshmen), 7/30 (transfers). *Notification:* continuous until 8/25 (freshmen). *Financial aid deadline priority date:* 4/1.

North Carolina

Shaw University (continued)
Freshman Application Contact
Mr. Keith Smith, Director of Admissions and Recruitment, Shaw University, 118 East South Street, Raleigh, NC 27601-2399. **Phone:** 919-546-8275. **Toll-free phone:** 800-214-6683. **Fax:** 919-546-8271. **E-mail:** ksmith@shawu.edu
Visit CollegeQuest.com for information on majors offered and athletics. College video available at CollegeQuest.com.

THE UNIVERSITY OF NORTH CAROLINA AT ASHEVILLE
Asheville, North Carolina

Apply at CollegeQuest.com

- **State-supported**, comprehensive, founded 1927
- **Degrees** bachelor's and master's
- **Suburban** 265-acre campus
- **Coed**, 2,767 undergraduate students, 84% full-time, 58% women, 42% men
- **Moderately difficult** entrance level, 61% of applicants were admitted
- **13:1 student-to-undergraduate faculty ratio**
- **52.1% graduate** in 6 years or less
- **$1960 tuition** and fees (in-state); $8580 (out-of-state)
- **$6014 average financial aid** package, $13,118 average indebtedness upon graduation, $15.9 million endowment

Part of University of North Carolina System.
Students *Undergraduates:* 2,323 full-time, 444 part-time. Students come from 43 states and territories, 23 other countries. *The most frequently chosen baccalaureate fields are:* business/marketing, psychology, social sciences and history. *Graduate:* 39 in graduate degree programs.

From out-of-state	10%	Reside on campus	35%
Age 25 or older	21%	Transferred in	12%
International students	1%	African Americans	3%
Asian Americans/Pacific Islanders	1%	Hispanic Americans	1%
Native Americans	0.4%		

Faculty 282 (55% full-time), 60% with terminal degrees.
Expenses (1999–2000) *Tuition, state resident:* full-time $806; part-time $302 per term. *Tuition, nonresident:* full-time $7426; part-time $2785 per term. *Required fees:* full-time $1154; $432 per term part-time. Part-time tuition and fees vary according to course load. *College room and board:* $4179; room only: $2039. Room and board charges vary according to board plan and housing facility. *Payment plan:* installment. *Waivers:* senior citizens and employees or children of employees.
Library D. Hidden Ramsey Library. *Operations spending 1999–2000:* $1.8 million. *Collection:* 589,777 titles, 2,251 serial subscriptions.
College life *Housing:* on-campus residence required in freshman year. *Options:* coed, men-only, women-only, disabled students. *Social organizations:* national fraternities, national sororities; 10% of eligible men and 6% of eligible women are members. *Most popular organizations:* Student Government Association, Underdog Productions, Residence Hall Association, African-American Association, International Student Association.
Campus security 24-hour patrols, late-night transport-escort service, controlled dormitory access.
After graduation 149 organizations recruited on campus 1997–98. 75% of class of 1998 had job offers within 6 months. *Career center:* 2 full-time, 1 part-time personnel. Services include job fairs, resume preparation, resume referral, career counseling, careers library, job bank, job interviews. *Graduate education:* 20% of class of 1999 went directly to graduate and professional school.
Freshmen 1,866 applied, 1,137 admitted, 460 enrolled. 2 valedictorians.

Average high school GPA	3.69	SAT verbal scores above 500	86%
SAT math scores above 500	83%	ACT above 18	98%
From top 10% of their h.s. class	22%	From top quarter	63%
From top half	99%	1998 freshmen returning in 1999	78%

Application *Options:* eApply at www.CollegeQuest.com, Common Application, early action, deferred entrance. *Application fee:* $45. *Required:* high school transcript. *Required for some:* interview. *Recommended:* essay or personal statement; minimum 3.0 GPA.
Standardized tests *Admission: Required:* SAT I or ACT.

Significant dates *Application deadlines:* 3/15 (freshmen), 6/1 (transfers). *Early action:* 10/15. *Notification:* 12/5 (early action). **Financial aid deadline priority date:** 3/1.
Freshman Application Contact
Mr. John W. White, Director of Admissions, The University of North Carolina at Asheville, Lipinsky Hall, CPO 2210, Asheville, NC 28804-8510. **Phone:** 828-251-6481. **Toll-free phone:** 800-531-9842. **Fax:** 828-251-6385. **E-mail:** admissions@unca.edu
Visit CollegeQuest.com for information on majors offered and athletics. College video and electronic viewbook available at CollegeQuest.com.

THE UNIVERSITY OF NORTH CAROLINA AT CHAPEL HILL
Chapel Hill, North Carolina

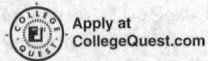
Apply at CollegeQuest.com

- **State-supported**, university, founded 1789
- **Degrees** bachelor's, master's, doctoral, first professional, and post-master's certificates
- **Suburban** 789-acre campus with easy access to Raleigh-Durham
- **Coed**, 14,969 undergraduate students, 97% full-time, 61% women, 39% men
- **Very difficult** entrance level, 39% of applicants were admitted
- **82% graduate** in 6 years or less
- **$2365 tuition** and fees (in-state); $11,531 (out-of-state)
- **$6772 average financial aid** package, $12,800 average indebtedness upon graduation, $586.5 million endowment

Part of University of North Carolina System.
Students *Undergraduates:* 14,589 full-time, 380 part-time. Students come from 52 states and territories, 99 other countries. *The most frequently chosen baccalaureate fields are:* communications/communication technologies, biological/life sciences, social sciences and history. *Graduate:* 1,899 in professional programs, 7,020 in other graduate degree programs.

From out-of-state	18%	Reside on campus	40%
Age 25 or older	5%	Transferred in	5%
International students	1%	African Americans	11%
Asian Americans/Pacific Islanders	5%	Hispanic Americans	1%
Native Americans	1%		

Faculty 2,861 (91% full-time), 85% with terminal degrees.
Expenses (1999–2000) *Tuition, state resident:* full-time $1528. *Tuition, nonresident:* full-time $10,694. *Required fees:* full-time $837. Full-time tuition and fees vary according to program and student level. Part-time tuition and fees vary according to course load and program. *College room and board:* $5280; room only: $2460. Room and board charges vary according to board plan, housing facility, and location. *Payment plan:* deferred payment. *Waivers:* senior citizens and employees or children of employees.
Library Davis Library plus 14 others. *Operations spending 1999–2000:* $26 million. *Collection:* 4.9 million titles, 44,023 serial subscriptions, 176,445 audiovisual materials.
College life *Housing: Options:* coed, men-only, women-only, disabled students. *Social organizations:* national fraternities, national sororities, local sororities; 19% of eligible men and 19% of eligible women are members. *Most popular organizations:* Campus Y, Black Student Movement, Carolina Athletic Association, Residence Hall Association, Campus Crusade for Christ.
Campus security 24-hour emergency response devices and patrols, student patrols, late-night transport-escort service, controlled dormitory access, crime prevention programs.
After graduation 512 organizations recruited on campus 1997–98. 72% of class of 1998 had job offers within 6 months. *Career center:* 14 full-time, 8 part-time personnel. Services include job fairs, resume preparation, interview workshops, resume referral, career/interest testing, career counseling, careers library, job bank, job interviews. *Major awards:* 13 Fulbright Scholars.
Freshmen 16,022 applied, 6,177 admitted, 3,396 enrolled.

Average high school GPA	4.0	SAT verbal scores above 500	93%
SAT math scores above 500	94%	ACT above 18	N/R
From top 10% of their h.s. class	68%	From top quarter	92%
From top half	98%	1998 freshmen returning in 1999	94%

North Carolina

Application *Options:* eApply at www.CollegeQuest.com, electronic application, early decision, early action, deferred entrance. *Preference* given to state residents. *Application fee:* $55. *Required:* essay or personal statement; high school transcript.

Standardized tests *Admission: Required:* SAT I or ACT.

Significant dates *Application deadlines:* 1/15 (freshmen), 3/1 (transfers). *Early decision:* 10/15, 11/15. *Notification:* 3/31 (freshmen), 12/7 (early decision), 1/30 (early action). *Financial aid deadline priority date:* 3/1.

Freshman Application Contact
Mr. Jerome A. Lucido, Associate Vice Chancellor/Director of Undergraduate Admissions, The University of North Carolina at Chapel Hill, Office of Undergraduate Admissions, Jackson Hall 153A, Campus Box 2200, Chapel Hill, NC 27599-2200. **Phone:** 919-966-3621. **E-mail:** uadm@email.unc.edu

Visit CollegeQuest.com for information on majors offered and athletics. Electronic viewbook available at CollegeQuest.com.

THE UNIVERSITY OF NORTH CAROLINA AT CHARLOTTE
Charlotte, North Carolina

- **State-supported**, university, founded 1946
- **Degrees** bachelor's, master's, doctoral, and post-master's certificates
- **Suburban** 1,000-acre campus
- **Coed**, 13,237 undergraduate students, 79% full-time, 53% women, 47% men
- **Moderately difficult** entrance level, 70% of applicants were admitted
- **16:1 student-to-undergraduate faculty ratio**
- **50.92% graduate** in 6 years or less
- **$1920 tuition** and fees (in-state); $9190 (out-of-state)
- **$6629 average financial aid** package, $7848 average indebtedness upon graduation, $78.8 million endowment

Part of University of North Carolina System.

Students *Undergraduates:* 10,448 full-time, 2,789 part-time. Students come from 50 states and territories, 77 other countries. *The most frequently chosen baccalaureate fields are:* business/marketing, engineering/engineering technologies, social sciences and history. **Graduate:** 2,755 in graduate degree programs.

From out-of-state	10%	Reside on campus	22%
Age 25 or older	24%	International students	2%
African Americans	18%	Asian Americans/Pacific Islanders	5%
Hispanic Americans	2%	Native Americans	0.5%

Faculty 991 (68% full-time), 70% with terminal degrees.

Expenses (1999–2000) *Tuition, state resident:* full-time $962; part-time $240 per term. *Tuition, nonresident:* full-time $8232; part-time $2058 per term. *Required fees:* full-time $958; $252 per term part-time. Full-time tuition and fees vary according to course load. Part-time tuition and fees vary according to course load. *College room and board:* $3816; room only: $1996. Room and board charges vary according to board plan and housing facility. *Waivers:* senior citizens.

Library J. Murrey Atkins Library. *Operations spending 1999–2000:* $8.1 million. *Collection:* 822,297 titles, 39,966 audiovisual materials.

College life *Housing: Options:* coed, women-only, disabled students. *Social organizations:* national fraternities, national sororities; 9% of eligible men and 7% of eligible women are members. *Most popular organizations:* University Program Board, Student Government Association, Resident Student Association, Black Student Union, Greek Council.

Campus security 24-hour emergency response devices and patrols, late-night transport-escort service, controlled dormitory access.

After graduation 244 organizations recruited on campus 1997–98. 89% of class of 1998 had job offers within 6 months. *Career center:* 12 full-time, 5 part-time personnel. Services include job fairs, resume preparation, interview workshops, resume referral, career counseling, careers library, job bank, job interviews, cooperative education employment services.

Freshmen 6,941 applied, 4,853 admitted, 2,122 enrolled.

Average high school GPA	3.43	SAT verbal scores above 500	58%
SAT math scores above 500	62%	ACT above 18	85%
From top 10% of their h.s. class	13%	From top quarter	46%
From top half	88%	1998 freshmen returning in 1999	79%

Application *Options:* Common Application, electronic application, early admission, deferred entrance. *Preference* given to state residents. *Application fee:* $35. *Required:* high school transcript; minimum 2.0 GPA; 1 letter of recommendation; medical history. *Required for some:* interview.

Standardized tests *Admission: Required:* SAT I or ACT.

Significant dates *Application deadlines:* 7/1 (freshmen), 7/1 (transfers). *Financial aid deadline priority date:* 4/1.

Freshman Application Contact
Mr. Craig Fulton, Director of Admissions, The University of North Carolina at Charlotte, 9201 University City Boulevard, Charlotte, NC 28223-0001. **Phone:** 704-547-2213. **Fax:** 704-510-6483. **E-mail:** unccadm@email.uncc.edu

Visit CollegeQuest.com for information on majors offered and athletics. College video available at CollegeQuest.com.

THE UNIVERSITY OF NORTH CAROLINA AT GREENSBORO
Greensboro, North Carolina

- **State-supported**, university, founded 1891
- **Degrees** bachelor's, master's, and doctoral
- **Urban** 200-acre campus
- **Coed**, 9,963 undergraduate students, 84% full-time, 67% women, 33% men
- **Moderately difficult** entrance level, 77% of applicants were admitted
- **19:1 student-to-undergraduate faculty ratio**
- **$2136 tuition** and fees (in-state); $10,590 (out-of-state)
- **$5000 average financial aid** package, $10,026 average indebtedness upon graduation, $94.4 million endowment

Part of University of North Carolina System.

Students *Undergraduates:* 8,335 full-time, 1,628 part-time. Students come from 41 states and territories, 55 other countries. *The most frequently chosen baccalaureate fields are:* business/marketing, health professions and related sciences, home economics/vocational home economics. **Graduate:** 2,712 in graduate degree programs.

From out-of-state	9%	Age 25 or older	22%
Transferred in	11%	International students	1%
African Americans	18%	Asian Americans/Pacific Islanders	3%
Hispanic Americans	1%	Native Americans	0.4%

Faculty 644 (95% full-time), 88% with terminal degrees.

Expenses (1999–2000) *Tuition, state resident:* full-time $1086; part-time $136 per credit. *Tuition, nonresident:* full-time $9540; part-time $1193 per credit. *Required fees:* full-time $1050; $43 per credit. Part-time tuition and fees vary according to course load. *College room and board:* $4064; room only: $2164. Room and board charges vary according to board plan and housing facility. *Waivers:* senior citizens and employees or children of employees.

Library Jackson Library plus 1 other. *Operations spending 1999–2000:* $6.6 million. *Collection:* 914,914 titles, 5,317 serial subscriptions.

College life *Housing: Options:* coed, men-only, women-only. *Social organizations:* national fraternities, national sororities; 6% of eligible men and 4% of eligible women are members. *Most popular organizations:* Campus Activities Board, Neo-Black Society, religious organizations, International Students Association.

Campus security 24-hour emergency response devices and patrols, late-night transport-escort service, controlled dormitory access.

After graduation 81 organizations recruited on campus 1997–98. *Career center:* 9 full-time, 2 part-time personnel. Services include job fairs, resume preparation, resume referral, career counseling, careers library, job bank, job interviews. *Graduate education:* 13% of class of 1999 went directly to graduate and professional school. *Major awards:* 1 Fulbright Scholar.

Freshmen 6,650 applied, 5,103 admitted, 1,939 enrolled.

Average high school GPA	3.43	SAT verbal scores above 500	60%
SAT math scores above 500	57%	ACT above 18	N/R
From top 10% of their h.s. class	13%	From top quarter	43%
From top half	86%	1998 freshmen returning in 1999	74%

Application *Option:* early admission. *Application fee:* $35. *Required:* high school transcript; minimum 2.0 GPA.

Standardized tests *Admission: Required:* SAT I or ACT. *Recommended:* SAT II Subject Tests.

North Carolina

The University of North Carolina at Greensboro (continued)
Significant dates *Application deadlines:* 8/1 (freshmen), 8/1 (transfers). *Financial aid deadline priority date:* 3/1.
Freshman Application Contact
Mr. Peter Lindsey, Director of Admissions, The University of North Carolina at Greensboro, 1000 Spring Garden Street, Greensboro, NC 27412-5001. **Phone:** 336-334-5243. **Fax:** 336-334-4180. **E-mail:** undergrad_admissions@uncg.edu
Visit CollegeQuest.com for information on majors offered and athletics. College video available at CollegeQuest.com.

THE UNIVERSITY OF NORTH CAROLINA AT PEMBROKE
Pembroke, North Carolina

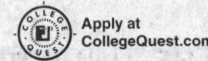
Apply at CollegeQuest.com

- **State-supported**, comprehensive, founded 1887
- **Degrees** bachelor's and master's
- **Rural** 126-acre campus
- **Coed**, 2,581 undergraduate students, 83% full-time, 60% women, 40% men
- **Moderately difficult** entrance level, 87% of applicants were admitted
- **18:1 student-to-undergraduate faculty ratio**
- **33.8% graduate** in 6 years or less
- **$1706 tuition** and fees (in-state); $8976 (out-of-state)
- **$4630 average financial aid** package, $4.6 million endowment

Part of University of North Carolina System.
Students *Undergraduates:* 2,134 full-time, 447 part-time. Students come from 18 states and territories, 12 other countries. *The most frequently chosen baccalaureate fields are:* education, business/marketing, protective services/public administration. *Graduate:* 273 in graduate degree programs.

From out-of-state	3%	Reside on campus	22%
Age 25 or older	37%	Transferred in	13%
International students	1%	African Americans	18%
Asian Americans/Pacific Islanders	2%	Hispanic Americans	2%
Native Americans	24%		

Faculty 210 (70% full-time), 60% with terminal degrees.
Expenses (1999–2000) *Tuition, state resident:* full-time $962; part-time $241 per term. *Tuition, nonresident:* full-time $8232; part-time $2058 per term. *Required fees:* full-time $744; $158 per term part-time. Part-time tuition and fees vary according to course load. *College room and board:* $3358; room only: $1758. Room and board charges vary according to board plan and housing facility. *Payment plan:* installment. *Waivers:* senior citizens.
Library Sampson-Livermore Library. *Operations spending 1999–2000:* $1.8 million. *Collection:* 200,969 titles, 1,341 serial subscriptions.
College life *Housing: Options:* men-only, women-only. *Social organizations:* national fraternities, national sororities, local fraternities, local sororities; 5% of eligible men and 8% of eligible women are members. *Most popular organizations:* Phi Kappa Tau, Zeta Tau Alpha, Tau Kappa Epsilon, Sigma Sigma Sigma, Pi Lambda Upsilon.
Campus security 24-hour emergency response devices and patrols, late-night transport-escort service, controlled dormitory access.
After graduation 137 organizations recruited on campus 1997–98. *Career center:* 2 full-time personnel. Services include job fairs, resume preparation, interview workshops, resume referral, career/interest testing, career counseling, careers library, job interviews. *Graduate education:* 15% of class of 1999 went directly to graduate and professional school.
Freshmen 962 applied, 840 admitted, 481 enrolled.

Average high school GPA	3.0	SAT verbal scores above 500	34%
SAT math scores above 500	29%	ACT above 18	48%
From top 10% of their h.s. class	10%	From top quarter	31%
From top half	62%	1998 freshmen returning in 1999	67%

Application *Options:* eApply at www.CollegeQuest.com, Common Application, early admission, deferred entrance. *Application fee:* $25. *Required:* high school transcript. *Required for some:* letters of recommendation, interview. *Recommended:* essay or personal statement; minimum 2.0 GPA.
Standardized tests *Admission: Required:* SAT I or ACT.
Significant dates *Application deadlines:* rolling (freshmen), rolling (transfers). *Financial aid deadline priority date:* 3/15.

Freshman Application Contact
Ms. Jacqueline Clark, Director of Admissions, The University of North Carolina at Pembroke, One University Drive, PO Box 1510, Pembroke, NC 28372-1510. **Phone:** 910-521-6262. **Toll-free phone:** 800-822-2185.
Visit CollegeQuest.com for information on majors offered and athletics. College video available at CollegeQuest.com.

■ *See page 2794 for a narrative description.*

THE UNIVERSITY OF NORTH CAROLINA AT WILMINGTON
Wilmington, North Carolina

- **State-supported**, comprehensive, founded 1947
- **Degrees** bachelor's and master's
- **Urban** 650-acre campus
- **Coed**, 8,728 undergraduate students, 90% full-time, 59% women, 41% men
- **Moderately difficult** entrance level, 58% of applicants were admitted
- **18:1 student-to-undergraduate faculty ratio**
- **52.4% graduate** in 6 years or less
- **$2068 tuition** and fees (in-state); $9338 (out-of-state)
- **$7282 average financial aid** package, $12,559 average indebtedness upon graduation, $20.6 million endowment

Part of University of North Carolina System.
Students *Undergraduates:* 7,849 full-time, 879 part-time. Students come from 49 states and territories, 40 other countries. *The most frequently chosen baccalaureate fields are:* business/marketing, biological/life sciences, English. *Graduate:* 690 in graduate degree programs.

From out-of-state	13%	Reside on campus	23%
Age 25 or older	16%	Transferred in	10%
International students	1%	African Americans	5%
Asian Americans/Pacific Islanders	1%	Hispanic Americans	1%
Native Americans	1%		

Faculty 579 (71% full-time), 61% with terminal degrees.
Expenses (1999–2000) *Tuition, state resident:* full-time $962. *Tuition, nonresident:* full-time $8232. *Required fees:* full-time $1106. Part-time tuition and fees vary according to course load and program. *College room and board:* $4656. Room and board charges vary according to board plan and housing facility. *Payment plan:* installment. *Waivers:* senior citizens and employees or children of employees.
Library William M. Randall Library. *Operations spending 1999–2000:* $4.1 million. *Collection:* 1,408 serial subscriptions, 40,366 audiovisual materials.
College life *Housing: Options:* coed, women-only. *Social organizations:* national fraternities, national sororities, local sororities; 13% of eligible men and 14% of eligible women are members. *Most popular organizations:* student government association, Association of Campus Entertainment, Residence Hall Association, Greek governing bodies, sailing club.
Campus security 24-hour emergency response devices and patrols, late-night transport-escort service, controlled dormitory access, escort service.
After graduation 154 organizations recruited on campus 1997–98. *Career center:* 9 full-time personnel. Services include job fairs, resume preparation, interview workshops, resume referral, career counseling, careers library, job bank, job interviews. *Major awards:* 1 Fulbright Scholar.
Freshmen 7,490 applied, 4,365 admitted, 1,670 enrolled.

Average high school GPA	3.48	SAT verbal scores above 500	71%
SAT math scores above 500	72%	ACT above 18	100%
From top 10% of their h.s. class	18%	From top quarter	59%
From top half	73%	1998 freshmen returning in 1999	80%

Application *Option:* electronic application. *Application fee:* $45. *Required:* high school transcript.
Standardized tests *Admission: Required:* SAT I or ACT.
Significant dates *Application deadlines:* 2/15 (freshmen), rolling (transfers). *Financial aid deadline:* continuous.
Freshman Application Contact
Mr. Ronald E. Whittaker, Registrar, The University of North Carolina at Wilmington, 601 South College Road, Wilmington, NC 28403-3201. **Phone:** 910-962-3243. **Toll-free phone:** 800-228-5571. **Fax:** 910-962-3038. **E-mail:** admissions@uncwil.edu

North Carolina

Visit CollegeQuest.com for information on majors offered and athletics. College video available at CollegeQuest.com.

WAKE FOREST UNIVERSITY
Winston-Salem, North Carolina

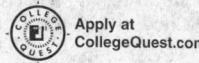

- **Independent**, university, founded 1834, affiliated with North Carolina Baptist State Convention
- **Degrees** bachelor's, master's, doctoral, and first professional
- **Suburban** 340-acre campus
- **Coed**, 3,847 undergraduate students, 99% full-time, 51% women, 49% men
- **Very difficult** entrance level, 49% of applicants were admitted
- **11:1 student-to-undergraduate faculty ratio**
- **81.6% graduate** in 6 years or less
- **$21,452 tuition** and fees
- **$17,451 average financial aid** package, $17,661 average indebtedness upon graduation, $857.9 million endowment

Students *Undergraduates:* 3,793 full-time, 54 part-time. Students come from 50 states and territories, 26 other countries. *The most frequently chosen baccalaureate fields are:* business/marketing, psychology, social sciences and history. *Graduate:* 894 in professional programs, 1,198 in other graduate degree programs.

From out-of-state	72%	Reside on campus	82%
Age 25 or older	3%	Transferred in	2%
International students	1%	African Americans	8%
Asian Americans/Pacific Islanders	2%	Hispanic Americans	1%
Native Americans	0.2%		

Faculty 504 (81% full-time).

Expenses (1999–2000) *Comprehensive fee:* $27,352 includes full-time tuition ($21,420), mandatory fees ($32), and room and board ($5900). *College room only:* $3250. Room and board charges vary according to board plan and housing facility. *Part-time tuition:* $575 per credit. *Payment plan:* installment. *Waivers:* employees or children of employees.

Library Z. Smith Reynolds Library plus 3 others. *Operations spending 1999–2000:* $9.7 million. *Collection:* 886,377 titles, 16,125 serial subscriptions, 19,873 audiovisual materials.

College life *Housing:* on-campus residence required in freshman year. *Options:* coed, women-only. *Social organizations:* national fraternities, national sororities; 37% of eligible men and 51% of eligible women are members. *Most popular organizations:* Student Union Network, Volunteer Service Corps, Intervarsity Christian Fellowship, student government.

Campus security 24-hour emergency response devices and patrols, late-night transport-escort service, controlled dormitory access.

After graduation 180 organizations recruited on campus 1997–98. 62% of class of 1998 had job offers within 6 months. *Career center:* 6 full-time, 1 part-time personnel. Services include job fairs, resume preparation, resume referral, career counseling, careers library, job bank, job interviews.

Freshmen 4,982 applied, 2,465 admitted, 971 enrolled. 74 valedictorians.

SAT verbal scores above 500	97%	SAT math scores above 500	97%
ACT above 18	N/R	From top 10% of their h.s. class	66%
From top quarter	91%	From top half	98%
1998 freshmen returning in 1999	91%		

Application *Options:* eApply at www.CollegeQuest.com, Common Application, early admission, early decision, deferred entrance. *Application fee:* $40. *Required:* essay or personal statement; high school transcript; 1 letter of recommendation.

Standardized tests *Admission: Required:* SAT I. *Recommended:* SAT II Subject Tests.

Significant dates *Application deadlines:* 1/15 (freshmen), 2/15 (transfers). *Early decision:* 11/15. *Notification:* 4/1 (freshmen), 12/15 (early decision). *Financial aid deadline priority date:* 2/1.

Freshman Application Contact
Mr. William G. Starling, Director of Admissions, Wake Forest University, PO Box 7305, Winston-Salem, NC 27109. **Phone:** 336-758-5201. **Fax:** 336-758-6074. **E-mail:** admissions@wfu.edu

Visit CollegeQuest.com for information on majors offered and athletics. College video available at CollegeQuest.com.

WARREN WILSON COLLEGE
Asheville, North Carolina

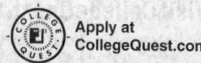

- **Independent**, comprehensive, founded 1894, affiliated with Presbyterian Church (U.S.A.)
- **Degrees** bachelor's and master's
- **Small-town** 1,100-acre campus
- **Coed**, 763 undergraduate students, 98% full-time, 61% women, 39% men
- **Moderately difficult** entrance level, 83% of applicants were admitted
- **12:1 student-to-undergraduate faculty ratio**
- **$13,600 tuition** and fees
- **$11,809 average financial aid** package, $13,880 average indebtedness upon graduation, $30.2 million endowment

Warren Wilson isn't for everyone. Some colleges treat prospective students as if they're all alike. There are very few alike students at Warren Wilson. Balancing academics, working on campus, and performing community service may not be the experience many are looking for. But that's the point—Warren Wilson is not for everyone. Solid academic students who want to make a difference in the world and who are environmentally aware may want to consider applying to Warren Wilson.

Students *Undergraduates:* 746 full-time, 17 part-time. Students come from 42 states and territories, 21 other countries. *The most frequently chosen baccalaureate fields are:* natural resources/environmental science, English, social sciences and history. *Graduate:* 68 in graduate degree programs.

From out-of-state	79%	Reside on campus	93%
Age 25 or older	2%	Transferred in	9%
International students	5%	African Americans	2%
Asian Americans/Pacific Islanders	1%	Hispanic Americans	2%
Native Americans	1%		

Faculty 64 (83% full-time), 67% with terminal degrees.

Expenses (1999–2000) *Comprehensive fee:* $18,044 includes full-time tuition ($13,350), mandatory fees ($250), and room and board ($4444). Full-time tuition and fees vary according to course load. Room and board charges vary according to board plan. Part-time tuition and fees vary according to course load. Full-time students work 15 hours per week to lower the cost of tuition. *Payment plan:* installment. *Waivers:* employees or children of employees.

Library Martha Ellison Library. *Operations spending 1999–2000:* $381,339. *Collection:* 99,000 titles, 950 serial subscriptions, 410 audiovisual materials.

College life *Housing:* on-campus residence required in freshman year. *Options:* coed, men-only, women-only. *Most popular organizations:* Interfaith, Student Caucus, wellness activities, outing club, community service.

Campus security 24-hour emergency response devices and patrols, student patrols, controlled dormitory access.

After graduation 5 organizations recruited on campus 1997–98. *Career center:* 1 part-time personnel. Services include job fairs, resume preparation, interview workshops, resume referral, career/interest testing, career counseling, careers library, job interviews. *Graduate education:* 30% of class of 1999 went directly to graduate and professional school: 23% graduate arts and sciences, 3% veterinary medicine, 1% business, 1% engineering, 1% medicine, 1% theology.

Freshmen 619 applied, 513 admitted, 193 enrolled.

Average high school GPA	3.19	SAT verbal scores above 500	55%
SAT math scores above 500	88%	ACT above 18	100%
From top 10% of their h.s. class	17%	From top quarter	49%
From top half	82%	1998 freshmen returning in 1999	69%

Application *Options:* eApply at www.CollegeQuest.com, Common Application, electronic application, early admission, early decision, deferred entrance. *Application fee:* $0. *Required:* essay or personal statement; high school transcript; minimum 2.5 GPA; 2 letters of recommendation. *Recommended:* interview.

Standardized tests *Admission: Required:* SAT I or ACT.

Significant dates *Application deadlines:* 3/15 (freshmen), 3/15 (transfers). *Early decision:* 11/15. *Notification:* 12/1 (early decision). *Financial aid deadline priority date:* 4/1.

Freshman Application Contact
Mr. Richard Blomgren, Dean of Admission, Warren Wilson College, PO Box 9000, Asheville, NC 28815-9000. **Phone:** 828-298-3325 Ext. 240. **Toll-free phone:** 800-934-3536. **Fax:** 828-298-1440. **E-mail:** admit@warren-wilson.edu

North Carolina

Warren Wilson College (continued)

Visit CollegeQuest.com for information on majors offered and athletics. College video and electronic viewbook available at CollegeQuest.com.

■ *See page 2910 for a narrative description.*

WESTERN CAROLINA UNIVERSITY
Cullowhee, North Carolina

- **State-supported**, comprehensive, founded 1889
- **Degrees** bachelor's, master's, doctoral, and post-master's certificates
- **Rural** 260-acre campus
- **Coed**, 5,254 undergraduate students, 92% full-time, 52% women, 48% men
- **Moderately difficult** entrance level, 82% of applicants were admitted
- **14:1 student-to-undergraduate faculty ratio**
- **49% graduate** in 6 years or less
- **$2082 tuition** and fees (in-state); $9352 (out-of-state)
- **$5107 average financial aid** package, $15,500 average indebtedness upon graduation, $11 million endowment

Part of University of North Carolina System.

Students *Undergraduates:* 4,846 full-time, 408 part-time. Students come from 22 states and territories, 17 other countries. *The most frequently chosen baccalaureate fields are:* business/marketing, education, health professions and related sciences. *Graduate:* 1,001 in graduate degree programs.

From out-of-state	8%	Reside on campus	45%
Age 25 or older	24%	Transferred in	8%
International students	1%	African Americans	5%
Asian Americans/Pacific Islanders	1%	Hispanic Americans	1%
Native Americans	2%		

Faculty 514 (63% full-time), 59% with terminal degrees.

Expenses (1999–2000) *Tuition, state resident:* full-time $962; part-time $241 per term. *Tuition, nonresident:* full-time $8232; part-time $2058 per term. *Required fees:* full-time $1120; $263. Part-time tuition and fees vary according to course load. *College room and board:* $3260; room only: $1540. Room and board charges vary according to board plan and housing facility. *Payment plan:* installment. *Waivers:* senior citizens.

Library Hunter Library. *Operations spending 1999–2000:* $3.5 million. *Collection:* 371,513 titles, 2,952 serial subscriptions, 13,873 audiovisual materials.

College life *Housing:* on-campus residence required in freshman year. *Options:* coed, men-only, women-only. *Social organizations:* national fraternities, national sororities; 15% of eligible men and 11% of eligible women are members. *Most popular organizations:* Last Minute Productions, Student Government Association, Alpha Lambda Delta.

Campus security 24-hour emergency response devices and patrols, controlled dormitory access.

After graduation 150 organizations recruited on campus 1997–98. *Career center:* 6 full-time, 1 part-time personnel. Services include job fairs, resume preparation, interview workshops, resume referral, career/interest testing, career counseling, careers library, job bank, job interviews.

Freshmen 3,408 applied, 2,778 admitted, 1,156 enrolled. 4 National Merit Scholars, 6 valedictorians.

Average high school GPA	3.14	SAT verbal scores above 500	39%
SAT math scores above 500	39%	ACT above 18	N/R
From top 10% of their h.s. class	8%	From top quarter	26%
From top half	56%	1998 freshmen returning in 1999	70%

Application *Option:* early admission. *Application fee:* $35. *Required:* high school transcript; minimum 2.5 GPA.

Standardized tests *Admission: Required:* SAT I.

Significant dates *Application deadlines:* 8/1 (freshmen), 7/1 (transfers). *Financial aid deadline priority date:* 3/31.

Freshman Application Contact
Mr. Philip Cauley, Director of Admissions, Western Carolina University, Cullowhee, NC 28723. **Phone:** 828-227-7317. **E-mail:** cauley@wcu.edu

Visit CollegeQuest.com for information on majors offered and athletics. College video available at CollegeQuest.com.

■ *See page 2944 for a narrative description.*

WINGATE UNIVERSITY
Wingate, North Carolina

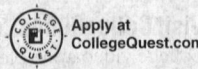
Apply at CollegeQuest.com

- **Independent Baptist**, comprehensive, founded 1896
- **Degrees** bachelor's and master's
- **Small-town** 330-acre campus with easy access to Charlotte
- **Coed**, 1,106 undergraduate students, 96% full-time, 50% women, 50% men
- **Moderately difficult** entrance level, 91% of applicants were admitted
- **12:1 student-to-undergraduate faculty ratio**
- **39% graduate** in 6 years or less
- **$13,050 tuition** and fees
- **$11,500 average financial aid** package, $15,250 average indebtedness upon graduation, $18.1 million endowment

Students *Undergraduates:* 1,060 full-time, 46 part-time. Students come from 34 states and territories, 16 other countries. *The most frequently chosen baccalaureate fields are:* business/marketing, parks and recreation, psychology. *Graduate:* 99 in graduate degree programs.

From out-of-state	42%	Reside on campus	59%
Age 25 or older	8%	Transferred in	6%
International students	2%	African Americans	11%
Asian Americans/Pacific Islanders	1%	Hispanic Americans	1%
Native Americans	0.2%		

Faculty 106 (75% full-time), 65% with terminal degrees.

Expenses (2000–2001) *Comprehensive fee:* $18,250 includes full-time tuition ($12,300), mandatory fees ($750), and room and board ($5200). *Part-time tuition:* $410 per credit hour. *Payment plan:* installment. *Waivers:* employees or children of employees.

Library Ethel K. Smith Library plus 2 others. *Operations spending 1999–2000:* $520,656. *Collection:* 110,000 titles, 600 serial subscriptions.

College life *Housing:* on-campus residence required through senior year. *Options:* men-only, women-only. *Social organizations:* national fraternities, national sororities; 20% of eligible men and 20% of eligible women are members. *Most popular organizations:* Student Community Service Organization, Fellowship of Christian Athletes, Student Government Association, Christian Student Union.

Campus security 24-hour emergency response devices and patrols, late-night transport-escort service.

After graduation 56 organizations recruited on campus 1997–98. 100% of class of 1998 had job offers within 6 months. *Career center:* 1 full-time, 1 part-time personnel. Services include job fairs, resume preparation, resume referral, career counseling, careers library, job bank, job interviews. *Graduate education:* 15% of class of 1999 went directly to graduate and professional school: 10% graduate arts and sciences, 2% theology, 1% business, 1% education, 1% law, 1% medicine.

Freshmen 907 applied, 824 admitted, 303 enrolled. 6 class presidents, 6 valedictorians, 23 student government officers.

Average high school GPA	3.1	SAT verbal scores above 500	50%
SAT math scores above 500	54%	ACT above 18	84%
From top 10% of their h.s. class	18%	From top quarter	38%
From top half	70%	1998 freshmen returning in 1999	67%

Application *Options:* eApply at www.CollegeQuest.com, Common Application, early admission, early decision, deferred entrance. *Application fee:* $25. *Required:* high school transcript; minimum 2.0 GPA. *Required for some:* letters of recommendation; interview. *Recommended:* essay or personal statement; minimum 3.0 GPA.

Standardized tests *Admission: Required:* SAT I or ACT.

Significant dates *Application deadlines:* 8/1 (freshmen), 8/1 (transfers). *Early decision:* 12/1. *Notification:* continuous until 8/1 (freshmen), 1/1 (early decision). *Financial aid deadline priority date:* 3/1.

Freshman Application Contact
Mr. Walter P. Crutchfield III, Dean of Admissions, Wingate University, PO Box 159, Wingate, NC 28174. **Phone:** 704-233-8000. **Toll-free phone:** 800-755-5550. **E-mail:** admit@wingate.edu

Visit CollegeQuest.com for information on majors offered and athletics.

■ *See page 3010 for a narrative description.*

North Carolina–North Dakota

WINSTON-SALEM STATE UNIVERSITY
Winston-Salem, North Carolina

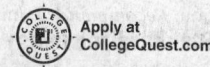 Apply at CollegeQuest.com

- **State-supported**, 4-year, founded 1892
- **Degree** bachelor's
- **Urban** 94-acre campus
- **Coed**, 2,599 undergraduate students, 85% full-time, 66% women, 34% men
- **Minimally difficult** entrance level, 80% of applicants were admitted
- **15:1 student-to-undergraduate faculty ratio**
- **47.8% graduate** in 6 years or less
- **$1704 tuition** and fees (in-state); $8122 (out-of-state)
- **$4580 average financial aid** package, $10,900 average indebtedness upon graduation, $13.8 million endowment

Part of University of North Carolina System.

Students *Undergraduates:* 2,212 full-time, 387 part-time. Students come from 29 states and territories, 2 other countries. *The most frequently chosen baccalaureate fields are:* education, business/marketing, health professions and related sciences.

From out-of-state	7%	Reside on campus	40%
Age 25 or older	31%	Transferred in	7%
African Americans	86%	Asian Americans/Pacific Islanders	1%
Hispanic Americans	1%	Native Americans	0.2%

Faculty 247 (66% full-time), 49% with terminal degrees.

Expenses (1999–2000) *Tuition, state resident:* full-time $806; part-time $202 per term. *Tuition, nonresident:* full-time $7224; part-time $1806 per term. *Required fees:* full-time $898; $235 per term part-time. Full-time tuition and fees vary according to course load. Part-time tuition and fees vary according to course load. *College room and board:* $3503; room only: $1893. Room and board charges vary according to board plan and housing facility. *Payment plan:* installment. *Waivers:* senior citizens and employees or children of employees.

Library O'Kelly Library. *Operations spending 1999–2000:* $1.7 million. *Collection:* 175,982 titles, 1,694 serial subscriptions.

College life *Housing: Option:* coed. *Social organizations:* national fraternities, national sororities, local fraternities, local sororities; 25% of eligible men and 35% of eligible women are members.

Campus security 24-hour emergency response devices and patrols.

After graduation *Career center:* 5 full-time personnel. Services include job fairs, resume preparation, resume referral, career counseling, careers library, job bank, job interviews. *Graduate education:* 15% of class of 1999 went directly to graduate and professional school.

Freshmen 1,435 applied, 1,145 admitted, 489 enrolled.

Average high school GPA	2.8	SAT verbal scores above 500	10%
SAT math scores above 500	N/R	ACT above 18	2%
From top 10% of their h.s. class	1%	From top quarter	10%
From top half	34%	1998 freshmen returning in 1999	75%

Application *Options:* eApply at www.CollegeQuest.com, early admission, deferred entrance. *Application fee:* $20. *Required:* high school transcript. *Recommended:* 1 letter of recommendation.

Standardized tests *Admission: Required:* SAT I or ACT.

Significant dates *Application deadlines:* rolling (freshmen), rolling (transfers). *Financial aid deadline:* 4/1. *Priority date:* 3/1.

Freshman Application Contact
Mr. Van C. Wilson, Director of Admissions, Winston-Salem State University, 601 Martin Luther King Jr Drive, Winston-Salem, NC 27110-0003. **Phone:** 336-750-2070. **Toll-free phone:** 800-257-4052. **Fax:** 336-750-2079. **E-mail:** wilsonv@wssu1adp.wssu.edu

Visit CollegeQuest.com for information on majors offered and athletics. College video available at CollegeQuest.com.

NORTH DAKOTA

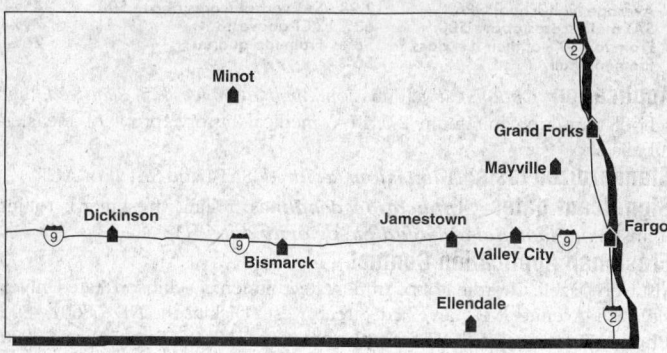

DICKINSON STATE UNIVERSITY
Dickinson, North Dakota

- **State-supported**, 4-year, founded 1918
- **Degrees** associate and bachelor's
- **Small-town** 100-acre campus
- **Coed**, 1,867 undergraduate students, 80% full-time, 56% women, 44% men
- **Noncompetitive** entrance level, 100% of applicants were admitted
- **16:1 student-to-undergraduate faculty ratio**
- **15.5% graduate** in 6 years or less
- **$2302 tuition** and fees (in-state); $5485 (out-of-state)
- **$8932 average indebtedness** upon graduation, $4.2 million endowment

Dickinson State, with an enrollment of approximately 1,800 students, offers Bachelor of Arts and Bachelor of Science degrees. Programs include liberal arts and specialized programs in education, business, nursing, agriculture, and computer science. There is opportunity for preprofessional study and vocational training in selected areas as well.

Part of North Dakota University System.

Students *Undergraduates:* 1,488 full-time, 379 part-time. Students come from 20 states and territories, 6 other countries. *The most frequently chosen baccalaureate fields are:* business/marketing, education, liberal arts/general studies.

From out-of-state	25%	Reside on campus	30%
Age 25 or older	17%	Transferred in	9%
International students	1%	African Americans	0.4%
Asian Americans/Pacific Islanders	0.3%	Hispanic Americans	1%
Native Americans	2%		

Faculty 109 (71% full-time), 58% with terminal degrees.

Expenses (1999–2000) *Tuition, state resident:* full-time $1906; part-time $79 per semester hour. *Tuition, nonresident:* full-time $5089; part-time $212 per semester hour. *Required fees:* full-time $396; $16 per semester hour. Full-time tuition and fees vary according to reciprocity agreements. Part-time tuition and fees vary according to reciprocity agreements. *College room and board:* $2610. Room and board charges vary according to board plan. *Waivers:* minority students and senior citizens.

Library Matilda Stoxen Library. *Operations spending 1999–2000:* $367,757. *Collection:* 73,000 titles, 580 serial subscriptions, 2,270 audiovisual materials.

College life *Housing:* on-campus residence required through sophomore year. *Option:* coed. *Social organizations:* national sororities; 5% of women are members. *Most popular organizations:* rodeo club, Blue Hawk Brigade, chorale, business club, Navigators.

Campus security Late-night transport-escort service.

After graduation 30 organizations recruited on campus 1997–98. 80% of class of 1998 had job offers within 6 months. *Career center:* 1 full-time, 1 part-time personnel. Services include job fairs, resume preparation, resume referral, career counseling, careers library, job bank, job interviews. *Graduate education:* 9% of class of 1999 went directly to graduate and professional school: 5% graduate arts and sciences, 1% dentistry, 1% engineering, 1% law, 1% medicine.

North Dakota

Dickinson State University (continued)

Freshmen 600 applied, 600 admitted, 399 enrolled.

Average high school GPA	2.98	SAT verbal scores above 500	45%
SAT math scores above 500	63%	ACT above 18	79%
From top 10% of their h.s. class	8%	From top quarter	26%
From top half	56%		

Application *Option:* early admission. *Application fee:* $25. *Required:* high school transcript; minimum 2.0 GPA; medical history, proof of measles-rubella shot.

Standardized tests *Admission: Required:* SAT I and SAT II or ACT.

Significant dates *Application deadlines:* rolling (freshmen), rolling (transfers). *Financial aid deadline priority date:* 4/15.

Freshman Application Contact
Ms. Deb Dazell, Coordinator of Student Recruitment, Dickinson State University, 8th Avenue West and 3rd Street West, Dickinson, ND 58601-4896. **Phone:** 701-483-2175. **Toll-free phone:** 800-279-4295. **Fax:** 701-483-2006. **E-mail:** dsuhawk@eagle.dsu.nodak.edu

Visit CollegeQuest.com for information on majors offered and athletics.

■ *See page 1578 for a narrative description.*

JAMESTOWN COLLEGE
Jamestown, North Dakota

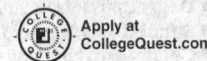
Apply at CollegeQuest.com

- **Independent Presbyterian**, 4-year, founded 1883
- **Degree** bachelor's
- **Small-town** 107-acre campus
- **Coed**, 1,097 undergraduate students, 96% full-time, 56% women, 44% men
- **Minimally difficult** entrance level, 99% of applicants were admitted
- **$7550 tuition** and fees
- **$8632 average financial aid** package, $15,000 average indebtedness upon graduation, $17.9 million endowment

Students *Undergraduates:* 1,050 full-time, 47 part-time. Students come from 26 states and territories, 12 other countries. *The most frequently chosen baccalaureate fields are:* business/marketing, education, health professions and related sciences.

From out-of-state	34%	Reside on campus	70%
Age 25 or older	5%	Transferred in	4%
International students	4%	African Americans	1%
Asian Americans/Pacific Islanders	0.4%	Hispanic Americans	1%
Native Americans	1%		

Faculty 59 full-time.

Expenses (2000–2001) *Comprehensive fee:* $10,850 includes full-time tuition ($7550) and room and board ($3300). *College room only:* $1480. Room and board charges vary according to board plan and housing facility. *Part-time tuition:* $230 per credit hour. Part-time tuition and fees vary according to course load. *Payment plan:* installment. *Waivers:* employees or children of employees.

Library Raugust Library. *Operations spending 1999-2000:* $223,920. *Collection:* 117,620 titles, 6,885 audiovisual materials.

College life *Housing:* on-campus residence required through sophomore year. *Options:* coed, disabled students. *Most popular organizations:* All-Campus Christian Fellowship, Student Education Association, International Students Association, Spurs, Jimmie Janes.

Campus security Late-night transport-escort service, controlled dormitory access.

After graduation 31 organizations recruited on campus 1997-98. 75% of class of 1998 had job offers within 6 months. *Career center:* 1 full-time, 1 part-time personnel. Services include job fairs, resume preparation, interview workshops, resume referral, career/interest testing, career counseling, careers library, job bank, job interviews.

Freshmen 720 applied, 717 admitted, 301 enrolled. 1 National Merit Scholar.

Average high school GPA	3.31	SAT verbal scores above 500	N/R
SAT math scores above 500	N/R	ACT above 18	91%
From top 10% of their h.s. class	15%	From top quarter	37%
From top half	62%	1998 freshmen returning in 1999	80%

Application *Options:* eApply at www.CollegeQuest.com, Common Application, electronic application, deferred entrance. *Application fee:* $20.

Required: high school transcript. *Required for some:* letters of recommendation. *Recommended:* minimum 2.5 GPA.

Standardized tests *Admission: Recommended:* SAT I or ACT. *Required for some:* SAT I or ACT.

Significant dates *Application deadlines:* rolling (freshmen), rolling (transfers). *Financial aid deadline:* continuous.

Freshman Application Contact
Judy Erickson, Director of Admissions, Jamestown College, 6081 College Lane, Jamestown, ND 58405. **Phone:** 701-252-3467 Ext. 2548. **Toll-free phone:** 800-336-2554. **Fax:** 701-253-4318. **E-mail:** admissions@acc.jc.edu

Visit CollegeQuest.com for information on majors offered and athletics.

MAYVILLE STATE UNIVERSITY
Mayville, North Dakota

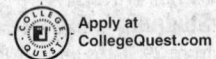
Apply at CollegeQuest.com

- **State-supported**, 4-year, founded 1889
- **Degrees** associate and bachelor's
- **Rural** 60-acre campus
- **Coed**, 851 undergraduate students, 70% full-time, 49% women, 51% men
- **Noncompetitive** entrance level, 99% of applicants were admitted
- **14:1 student-to-undergraduate faculty ratio**
- **38% graduate** in 6 years or less
- **$3106 tuition** and fees (in-state); $6289 (out-of-state)
- **$5394 average financial aid** package, $15,468 average indebtedness upon graduation, $1.5 million endowment

Technology is everywhere at Mayville State. All students receive a notebook computer, with Internet access in classrooms, the library, residence hall rooms, and off campus. A small, personable campus, MSU offers a high-tech liberal arts education. Its teacher education programs are nationally recognized. MSU partners with Great Plains Software to offer an information technology track in business and CIS with internships.

Part of North Dakota University System.

Students *Undergraduates:* 592 full-time, 259 part-time. Students come from 15 states and territories, 2 other countries. *The most frequently chosen baccalaureate fields are:* business/marketing, biological/life sciences, education.

From out-of-state	22%	Reside on campus	32%
Age 25 or older	34%	Transferred in	25%
International students	3%	African Americans	0.5%
Asian Americans/Pacific Islanders	0.5%	Hispanic Americans	1%
Native Americans	1%		

Faculty 61 (66% full-time), 38% with terminal degrees.

Expenses (1999–2000) *Tuition, state resident:* full-time $1906; part-time $79 per credit hour. *Tuition, nonresident:* full-time $5089; part-time $212 per credit hour. *Required fees:* full-time $1200; $50 per credit hour. Full-time tuition and fees vary according to reciprocity agreements. Part-time tuition and fees vary according to reciprocity agreements. *College room and board:* $3042; room only: $1214. Room and board charges vary according to board plan and housing facility. *Waivers:* minority students and senior citizens.

Library Byrnes-Quanbeck Library plus 1 other. *Operations spending 1999-2000:* $302,204. *Collection:* 70,482 titles, 614 serial subscriptions, 20,549 audiovisual materials.

College life *Housing:* on-campus residence required through sophomore year. *Options:* coed, men-only, women-only. *Most popular organizations:* Phi Beta Lambda, Student Education Association, health and physical education club, Campus Crusade, Student Ambassadors.

Campus security Controlled dormitory access.

After graduation 6 organizations recruited on campus 1997–98. 96% of class of 1998 had job offers within 6 months. *Career center:* 2 full-time, 1 part-time personnel. Services include job fairs, resume preparation, interview workshops, resume referral, career/interest testing, career counseling, careers library, job bank, job interviews. *Graduate education:* 3% of class of 1999 went directly to graduate and professional school: 2% education, 1% graduate arts and sciences.

North Dakota

Freshmen 202 applied, 200 admitted, 158 enrolled.

Average high school GPA	2.81	SAT verbal scores above 500	N/R
SAT math scores above 500	N/R	ACT above 18	67%
From top quarter of their h.s. class	23%	From top half	56%
1998 freshmen returning in 1999	53%		

Application *Options:* eApply at www.CollegeQuest.com, electronic application, deferred entrance. *Application fee:* $25. *Required:* high school transcript. *Recommended:* interview.

Standardized tests *Admission: Required:* SAT I or ACT.

Significant dates *Application deadlines:* rolling (freshmen), rolling (transfers). *Financial aid deadline priority date:* 4/15.

Freshman Application Contact Mr. Brian Larson, Director of Enrollment Services, Mayville State University, 330 3rd Street, NE, Mayville, ND 58257-1299. **Phone:** 701-786-2301 Ext. 34768. **Toll-free phone:** 800-437-4104. **Fax:** 701-786-4748. **E-mail:** admit@mail.masu.nodak.edu

Visit CollegeQuest.com for information on majors offered and athletics. College video and electronic viewbook available at CollegeQuest.com.

MEDCENTER ONE COLLEGE OF NURSING
Bismarck, North Dakota

- **Independent**, upper-level, founded 1988
- **Degree** bachelor's
- **Small-town** 15-acre campus
- **Coed**, primarily women, 82 undergraduate students, 98% full-time, 82% women, 18% men
- **Moderately difficult** entrance level
- **9:1 student-to-undergraduate faculty ratio**
- **$3236 tuition** and fees

Students *Undergraduates:* 80 full-time, 2 part-time. Students come from 3 states and territories. *The most frequently chosen baccalaureate field is:* health professions and related sciences.

From out-of-state	4%	Reside on campus	12%
Age 25 or older	36%	Transferred in	50%
Asian Americans/Pacific Islanders	1%	Hispanic Americans	1%
Native Americans	1%		

Faculty 12 (75% full-time).

Expenses (1999–2000) *Tuition:* full-time $2956; part-time $123 per credit. *Required fees:* full-time $280; $5 per credit; $80. Part-time tuition and fees vary according to course load. *College room only:* $900. Room and board charges vary according to housing facility.

Library Q & R/Medcenter One Health Sciences Library plus 1 other. *Collection:* 15,000 titles, 350 serial subscriptions.

College life *Housing: Option:* coed. *Most popular organizations:* student body organization, Student Nurses Association.

Campus security 24-hour patrols.

After graduation 86% of class of 1998 had job offers within 6 months. *Career center:* Services include resume preparation, career counseling, job interviews.

Application *Application fee:* $40.

Significant dates *Application deadline:* 11/7 (transfers). *Financial aid deadline priority date:* 5/1.

Freshman Application Contact Dr. Karen Latham, Dean/Provost, Medcenter One College of Nursing, 512 North 7th Street, Bismarck, ND 58501-4494. **Phone:** 701-323-6832.

Visit CollegeQuest.com for information on majors offered and athletics.

MINOT STATE UNIVERSITY
Minot, North Dakota

- **State-supported**, comprehensive, founded 1913
- **Degrees** bachelor's and master's
- **Small-town** 103-acre campus
- **Coed**, 2,982 undergraduate students, 81% full-time, 62% women, 38% men
- **Minimally difficult** entrance level, 97% of applicants were admitted
- **19:1 student-to-undergraduate faculty ratio**
- **$2331 tuition** and fees (in-state); $5755 (out-of-state)

Part of North Dakota University System.

Students *Undergraduates:* 2,412 full-time, 570 part-time. Students come from 45 states and territories, 11 other countries. *Graduate:* 173 in graduate degree programs.

From out-of-state	18%	Reside on campus	15%
Age 25 or older	30%	Transferred in	11%
International students	7%	African Americans	2%
Asian Americans/Pacific Islanders	1%	Hispanic Americans	1%
Native Americans	5%		

Faculty 207 (82% full-time).

Expenses (1999–2000) *Tuition, state resident:* full-time $2050; part-time $97 per semester hour. *Tuition, nonresident:* full-time $5474; part-time $240 per semester hour. *Required fees:* full-time $281. Full-time tuition and fees vary according to program and reciprocity agreements. Part-time tuition and fees vary according to course load, program, and reciprocity agreements. *College room and board:* $2724; room only: $1021. Room and board charges vary according to board plan, housing facility, and student level. *Waivers:* minority students.

Library Gordon B. Olson Library. *Collection:* 300,000 titles.

College life *Housing: Options:* coed, men-only, women-only. *Most popular organizations:* Student ND Education Association, Minot State Club of Physical Education, Inter-Varsity Christian Fellowship, Residence Hall Association, National Student Speech and Hearing Association.

Campus security Controlled dormitory access, patrols by trained security personnel.

After graduation 100 organizations recruited on campus 1997–98. *Career center:* 3 full-time personnel. Services include job fairs, resume preparation, interview workshops, career/interest testing, career counseling, careers library, job bank, job interviews. *Graduate education:* 10% of class of 1999 went directly to graduate and professional school.

Freshmen 750 applied, 726 admitted, 525 enrolled.

| SAT verbal scores above 500 | N/R | SAT math scores above 500 | N/R |
| ACT above 18 | N/R | | |

Application *Option:* deferred entrance. *Application fee:* $25. *Required:* high school transcript.

Standardized tests *Admission: Required:* SAT I or ACT.

Significant dates *Application deadlines:* rolling (freshmen), rolling (transfers). *Notification:* continuous until 8/20 (freshmen). *Financial aid deadline priority date:* 4/15.

Freshman Application Contact Ms. Ronnie Walker, Administrative Assistant, Records Office, Minot State University, 500 University Avenue West, Minot, ND 58707-0002. **Phone:** 701-858-3340. **Toll-free phone:** 800-777-0750. **Fax:** 701-839-6933. **E-mail:** askmsu@misu.nodak.edu

Visit CollegeQuest.com for information on majors offered and athletics. College video available at CollegeQuest.com.

NORTH DAKOTA STATE UNIVERSITY
Fargo, North Dakota

- **State-supported**, university, founded 1890
- **Degrees** bachelor's, master's, doctoral, and first professional
- **Urban** 2,100-acre campus
- **Coed**, 8,761 undergraduate students, 87% full-time, 42% women, 58% men
- **Moderately difficult** entrance level, 75% of applicants were admitted
- **19:1 student-to-undergraduate faculty ratio**
- **39.5% graduate** in 6 years or less
- **$2886 tuition** and fees (in-state); $7028 (out-of-state)
- **$4926 average financial aid** package, $18,624 average indebtedness upon graduation, $40.9 million endowment

Part of North Dakota University System.

Students *Undergraduates:* 7,612 full-time, 1,149 part-time. Students come from 44 states and territories, 55 other countries. *The most frequently chosen baccalaureate fields are:* business/marketing, engineering/engineering

North Dakota

North Dakota State University (continued)
technologies, health professions and related sciences. **Graduate:** 877 in graduate degree programs.

From out-of-state	42%	Reside on campus	34%
Age 25 or older	12%	Transferred in	9%
International students	1%	African Americans	1%
Asian Americans/Pacific Islanders	1%	Hispanic Americans	0.4%
Native Americans	1%		

Faculty 518 (98% full-time), 77% with terminal degrees.

Expenses (1999–2000) *One-time required fee:* $45. *Tuition, state resident:* full-time $2480; part-time $103 per credit. *Tuition, nonresident:* full-time $6622; part-time $276 per credit. *Required fees:* full-time $406; $17 per credit. Full-time tuition and fees vary according to course load, program, and reciprocity agreements. Part-time tuition and fees vary according to course load, program, and reciprocity agreements. *College room and board:* $3408; room only: $1264. Room and board charges vary according to board plan and housing facility. *Payment plan:* installment. *Waivers:* minority students, senior citizens, and employees or children of employees.

Library North Dakota State University Library plus 3 others. *Operations spending 1999–2000:* $1.4 million. *Collection:* 445,338 titles, 5,300 serial subscriptions.

College life *Housing:* on-campus residence required in freshman year. *Options:* coed, men-only, women-only. *Social organizations:* national fraternities, national sororities; 10% of eligible men and 10% of eligible women are members. *Most popular organizations:* Saddle and Sirloin, Habitat for Humanity, Residence Hall Association, juggling club.

Campus security 24-hour emergency response devices and patrols, student patrols, late-night transport-escort service, controlled dormitory access.

After graduation 158 organizations recruited on campus 1997–98. 77% of class of 1998 had job offers within 6 months. *Career center:* 10 full-time, 2 part-time personnel. Services include job fairs, resume preparation, interview workshops, resume referral, career counseling, careers library, job bank, job interviews. *Graduate education:* 16% of class of 1999 went directly to graduate and professional school: 3% graduate arts and sciences, 1% business, 1% education, 1% engineering, 1% law, 1% medicine, 1% theology, 1% veterinary medicine.

Freshmen 2,864 applied, 2,161 admitted, 1,709 enrolled. 6 National Merit Scholars, 85 valedictorians.

Average high school GPA	3.37	SAT verbal scores above 500	N/R
SAT math scores above 500	N/R	ACT above 18	95%
1998 freshmen returning in 1999	79%		

Application *Option:* electronic application. *Application fee:* $25. *Required:* high school transcript; minimum 2.5 GPA.

Standardized tests *Admission: Required:* SAT I or ACT.

Significant dates *Application deadlines:* 8/15 (freshmen), 8/15 (transfers). *Financial aid deadline priority date:* 4/15.

Freshman Application Contact
Dr. Kate Haugen, Director of Admission, North Dakota State University, PO Box 5454, Fargo, ND 58105-5454. **Phone:** 701-231-8643. **Toll-free phone:** 800-488-NDSU. **Fax:** 701-231-8802. **E-mail:** nuadmiss@plains.nodak.edu

Visit CollegeQuest.com for information on majors offered and athletics. Electronic viewbook available at CollegeQuest.com.

TRINITY BIBLE COLLEGE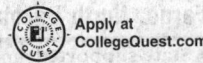
Ellendale, North Dakota

- **Independent**, 4-year, founded 1948, affiliated with Assemblies of God
- **Degrees** associate and bachelor's
- **Rural** 28-acre campus
- **Coed**, 344 undergraduate students, 86% full-time, 54% women, 46% men
- **39% of applicants were admitted**
- **11:1 student-to-undergraduate faculty ratio**
- **29% graduate** in 6 years or less
- **$6294 tuition** and fees
- **$203,119 endowment**

Students *Undergraduates:* 297 full-time, 47 part-time. Students come from 27 states and territories, 1 other country. *The most frequently chosen baccalaureate fields are:* health professions and related sciences, business/marketing, liberal arts/general studies.

From out-of-state	73%	Reside on campus	56%
Age 25 or older	19%	Transferred in	2%
International students	1%	African Americans	0.3%
Asian Americans/Pacific Islanders	1%	Hispanic Americans	3%
Native Americans	2%		

Faculty 33 (58% full-time), 24% with terminal degrees.

Expenses (1999–2000) *Comprehensive fee:* $9974 includes full-time tuition ($5490), mandatory fees ($804), and room and board ($3680). Full-time tuition and fees vary according to course load. Room and board charges vary according to gender and housing facility. *Part-time tuition:* $183 per credit. *Part-time fees:* $175 per term part-time. Part-time tuition and fees vary according to course load. *Payment plans:* installment, deferred payment. *Waivers:* employees or children of employees.

Library Graham Library. *Operations spending 1999–2000:* $65,426. *Collection:* 67,868 titles, 227 serial subscriptions, 2,258 audiovisual materials.

College life *Housing:* on-campus residence required through junior year. *Options:* men-only, women-only. *Most popular organizations:* GAP, Youth Ministry, Inner City Ministry, fine arts club, Children's Ministry.

Campus security 24-hour emergency response devices, student patrols, late-night transport-escort service.

After graduation *Career center:* Services include career counseling. *Graduate education:* 5% of class of 1999 went directly to graduate and professional school: 5% theology.

Freshmen 235 applied, 91 admitted, 91 enrolled. 5 valedictorians.

Average high school GPA	2.87	SAT verbal scores above 500	N/R
SAT math scores above 500	N/R	ACT above 18	61%
From top 10% of their h.s. class	9%	From top quarter	13%
From top half	66%	1998 freshmen returning in 1999	60%

Application *Options:* eApply at www.CollegeQuest.com, Common Application, deferred entrance. *Application fee:* $25. *Required:* essay or personal statement; high school transcript; minimum 2.0 GPA; 2 letters of recommendation; health form, evidence of Christian conversion. *Required for some:* interview.

Standardized tests *Admission: Required:* ACT. *Required for some:* SAT I.

Significant dates *Application deadlines:* rolling (freshmen), rolling (transfers). *Financial aid deadline:* 9/1. *Priority date:* 3/1.

Freshman Application Contact
Rev. Jerry Grimshaw, Enrollment Manager, Trinity Bible College, 50 South Sixth Avenue, Ellendale, ND 58436. **Phone:** 701-349-3621 Ext. 2045. **Toll-free phone:** 800-TBC-2DAY. **Fax:** 701-349-5443. **E-mail:** TBC2DAY.edu

Visit CollegeQuest.com for information on majors offered and athletics.

UNIVERSITY OF MARY
Bismarck, North Dakota

Admissions Office Contact
University of Mary, 7500 University Drive, Bismarck, ND 58504-9652. **Toll-free phone:** 800-288-6279. **Fax:** 701-255-7687. **E-mail:** marauder@umary.edu

UNIVERSITY OF NORTH DAKOTA
Grand Forks, North Dakota

- **State-supported**, university, founded 1883
- **Degrees** bachelor's, master's, doctoral, and first professional
- **Small-town** 570-acre campus
- **Coed**, 8,680 undergraduate students, 90% full-time, 49% women, 51% men
- **Minimally difficult** entrance level, 70% of applicants were admitted
- **14:1 student-to-undergraduate faculty ratio**
- **44% graduate** in 6 years or less
- **$2956 tuition** and fees (in-state); $7098 (out-of-state)
- **$4609 average financial aid** package, $19,143 average indebtedness upon graduation, $19.5 million endowment

Part of North Dakota University System.

Students *Undergraduates:* 7,801 full-time, 879 part-time. Students come from 54 states and territories, 50 other countries. *The most frequently chosen baccalaureate fields are:* business/marketing, health professions and related

North Dakota

sciences, trade and industry. *Graduate:* 418 in professional programs, 1,492 in other graduate degree programs.

From out-of-state	44%	Reside on campus	36%
Age 25 or older	14%	Transferred in	8%
International students	3%	African Americans	1%
Asian Americans/Pacific Islanders	1%	Hispanic Americans	1%
Native Americans	3%		

Faculty 756 (77% full-time), 67% with terminal degrees.

Expenses (1999–2000) *Tuition, state resident:* full-time $2480; part-time $103 per credit hour. *Tuition, nonresident:* full-time $6622; part-time $276 per credit hour. *Required fees:* full-time $476; $15 per credit hour; $32 per term part-time. Full-time tuition and fees vary according to program and reciprocity agreements. Part-time tuition and fees vary according to course load, program, and reciprocity agreements. *College room and board:* $3406; room only: $1346. Room and board charges vary according to board plan and housing facility. *Waivers:* senior citizens and employees or children of employees.

Library Chester Fritz Library plus 2 others. *Operations spending 1999–2000:* $5.6 million. *Collection:* 658,957 titles, 10,438 serial subscriptions, 14,306 audiovisual materials.

College life *Housing: Options:* coed, men-only, women-only. *Social organizations:* national fraternities, national sororities; 15% of eligible men and 10% of eligible women are members. *Most popular organizations:* Student Government, Association of Residence Halls, Mortar Board, Indian Association, Telesis.

Campus security 24-hour emergency response devices and patrols, student patrols, late-night transport-escort service, controlled dormitory access, emergency telephones.

After graduation 349 organizations recruited on campus 1997–98. *Career center:* 7 full-time, 8 part-time personnel. Services include job fairs, resume preparation, interview workshops, resume referral, career/interest testing, career counseling, careers library, job bank, job interviews. *Graduate education:* 12% of class of 1999 went directly to graduate and professional school.

Freshmen 2,928 applied, 2,041 admitted, 1,754 enrolled. 12 National Merit Scholars.

Average high school GPA	3.37	SAT verbal scores above 500	74%
SAT math scores above 500	77%	ACT above 18	93%
From top 10% of their h.s. class	17%	From top quarter	41%
From top half	73%	1998 freshmen returning in 1999	76%

Application *Options:* electronic application, early admission, deferred entrance. *Application fee:* $25. *Required:* high school transcript. *Recommended:* minimum 2.5 GPA.

Standardized tests *Admission: Required:* SAT I or ACT.

Significant dates *Application deadlines:* 7/1 (freshmen), 7/1 (transfers). *Financial aid deadline priority date:* 4/15.

Freshman Application Contact
Ms. Heidi Kippenhan, Assistant Director of Admissions, University of North Dakota, Box 8382, Grand Forks, ND 58202. **Phone:** 701-777-3821. **Toll-free phone:** 800-CALL UND. **Fax:** 701-777-3650. **E-mail:** enrolser@sage.und.nodak.edu

Visit CollegeQuest.com for information on majors offered and athletics. College video and electronic viewbook available at CollegeQuest.com.

VALLEY CITY STATE UNIVERSITY
Valley City, North Dakota

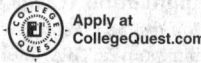
Apply at CollegeQuest.com

- **State-supported**, 4-year, founded 1890
- **Degree** bachelor's
- **Small-town** 55-acre campus
- **Coed**, 1,077 undergraduate students, 74% full-time, 56% women, 44% men
- **Noncompetitive** entrance level, 94% of applicants were admitted
- **14:1 student-to-undergraduate faculty ratio**
- **40.93% graduate** in 6 years or less
- **$3097 tuition** and fees (in-state); $6280 (out-of-state)
- **$5662 average financial aid** package, $617,350 endowment

Part of North Dakota University System.

Students *Undergraduates:* 797 full-time, 280 part-time. Students come from 19 states and territories, 3 other countries. *The most frequently chosen baccalaureate fields are:* business/marketing, education, liberal arts/general studies.

Reside on campus	34%	Age 25 or older	20%
Transferred in	8%	International students	4%
African Americans	2%	Asian Americans/Pacific Islanders	0.4%
Hispanic Americans	1%	Native Americans	1%

Faculty 83 (67% full-time), 33% with terminal degrees.

Expenses (1999–2000) *Tuition, state resident:* full-time $1906; part-time $129 per semester hour. *Tuition, nonresident:* full-time $5089; part-time $262 per semester hour. *Required fees:* full-time $1191. Full-time tuition and fees vary according to reciprocity agreements. Part-time tuition and fees vary according to course load and reciprocity agreements. *College room and board:* $2800; room only: $1050. Room and board charges vary according to board plan and housing facility. *Waivers:* children of alumni and employees or children of employees.

Library Allen Memorial Library. *Operations spending 1999–2000:* $313,426. *Collection:* 90,075 titles, 433 serial subscriptions.

College life *Housing:* on-campus residence required through sophomore year. *Options:* coed, men-only, women-only. *Social organizations:* local fraternities, local sororities; 2% of eligible men and 4% of eligible women are members. *Most popular organizations:* departmental clubs, Greek Organizations.

Campus security Controlled dormitory access.

After graduation 3 organizations recruited on campus 1997–98. 89% of class of 1998 had job offers within 6 months. *Career center:* 2 full-time, 1 part-time personnel. Services include job fairs, resume preparation, resume referral, career counseling, careers library, job bank, job interviews. *Graduate education:* 4% of class of 1999 went directly to graduate and professional school: 3% graduate arts and sciences, 1% law.

Freshmen 295 applied, 277 admitted, 173 enrolled.

Average high school GPA	2.96	SAT verbal scores above 500	N/R
SAT math scores above 500	N/R	ACT above 18	79%
From top 10% of their h.s. class	8%	From top quarter	26%
From top half	64%	1998 freshmen returning in 1999	68%

Application *Options:* eApply at www.CollegeQuest.com, electronic application, early admission, deferred entrance. *Application fee:* $25. *Required:* high school transcript.

Standardized tests *Placement: Required:* SAT I or ACT

Significant dates *Application deadlines:* rolling (freshmen), rolling (transfers). *Financial aid deadline priority date:* 4/15.

Freshman Application Contact
Mr. Monte Johnson, Director of Admissions, Valley City State University, , 101 College Street Southwest, Valley City, ND 58072. **Phone:** 701-845-7101. **Toll-free phone:** 800-532-8641 Ext. 37101. **Fax:** 701-845-7245. **E-mail:** enrollment_services@mail.vcsu.nodak.edu

Visit CollegeQuest.com for information on majors offered and athletics. College video available at CollegeQuest.com.

Peterson's Guide to Four-Year Colleges 2001   www.petersons.com

Ohio

OHIO

The Cleveland area includes the towns of Beachwood, South Euclid, University Heights, and Pepper Pike.

The Columbus area includes the town of Westerville.

The Akron area includes the town of Kent.

The Canton area includes the town of North Canton.

The Newark area includes the town of Granville.

ANTIOCH COLLEGE
Yellow Springs, Ohio

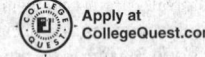 Apply at CollegeQuest.com

- **Independent**, 4-year, founded 1852
- **Degree** bachelor's
- **Small-town** 100-acre campus with easy access to Dayton
- **Coed**, 517 undergraduate students, 99% full-time, 66% women, 34% men
- **Moderately difficult** entrance level, 80% of applicants were admitted
- **9:1 student-to-undergraduate faculty ratio**
- **42% graduate** in 6 years or less
- **$19,231 tuition** and fees
- **$13,927 average indebtedness** upon graduation, $14.9 million endowment

Part of Antioch University.

Students *Undergraduates:* 515 full-time, 2 part-time. Students come from 46 states and territories. *Graduate:* 10 in graduate degree programs.

From out-of-state	80%	Reside on campus	97%
Age 25 or older	4%	Transferred in	8%
International students	0.4%	African Americans	6%
Asian Americans/Pacific Islanders	1%	Hispanic Americans	3%
Native Americans	1%		

Faculty 60 (95% full-time), 100% with terminal degrees.
Expenses (1999–2000) *Comprehensive fee:* $24,107 includes full-time tuition ($17,556), mandatory fees ($1675), and room and board ($4876). *College room only:* $2398. *Part-time tuition:* $375 per credit. *Payment plan:* installment. *Waivers:* employees or children of employees.
Library Olive Kettering Library. *Operations spending 1999–2000:* $450,067. *Collection:* 1,072 serial subscriptions, 4,596 audiovisual materials.
College life *Housing:* on-campus residence required through senior year. *Options:* coed, men-only, women-only. *Most popular organizations:* Third World Alliance, Women's Center, Lesbian/Gay/Bisexual Center, Uni-Dad, Alternative Library.
Campus security 24-hour emergency response devices and patrols, late-night transport-escort service.

After graduation *Career center:* Services include resume preparation. *Major awards:* 1 Fulbright Scholar.
Freshmen 488 applied, 390 admitted, 135 enrolled.

Average high school GPA	3.0	SAT verbal scores above 500	87%
SAT math scores above 500	66%	ACT above 18	97%
From top 10% of their h.s. class	16%	From top quarter	44%
From top half	78%	1998 freshmen returning in 1999	75%

Application *Options:* eApply at www.CollegeQuest.com, Common Application, early action, deferred entrance. *Application fee:* $35. *Required:* essay or personal statement; high school transcript; minimum 2.5 GPA; 2.0 letters of recommendation. *Recommended:* interview.
Significant dates *Application deadlines:* 2/1 (freshmen), rolling (transfers). *Early action:* 11/15. *Notification:* 12/15 (early action). *Financial aid deadline priority date:* 3/1.
Freshman Application Contact
Ms. Cathy Paige, Information Manager, Antioch College, 795 Livermore Street, Yellow Springs, OH 45387-1697. **Phone:** 937-767-6400 Ext. 6559. **Toll-free phone:** 800-543-9436. **Fax:** 937-767-6473. **E-mail:** admissions@antioch-college.edu
Visit CollegeQuest.com for information on majors offered and athletics. College video and electronic viewbook available at CollegeQuest.com.

■ *See page 1178 for a narrative description.*

ART ACADEMY OF CINCINNATI
Cincinnati, Ohio

- **Independent**, comprehensive, founded 1887
- **Degrees** associate, bachelor's, and master's
- **Urban** 184-acre campus
- **Coed**, 209 undergraduate students, 93% full-time, 52% women, 48% men
- **Moderately difficult** entrance level, 86% of applicants were admitted
- **12:1 student-to-undergraduate faculty ratio**
- **$12,200 tuition** and fees
- **$7886 average financial aid** package, $11,290 average indebtedness upon graduation, $6 million endowment

Students *Undergraduates:* 195 full-time, 14 part-time. Students come from 14 states and territories, 5 other countries.

From out-of-state	43%	Age 25 or older	27%
Transferred in	17%	International students	3%
African Americans	2%	Asian Americans/Pacific Islanders	2%
Hispanic Americans	2%	Native Americans	1%

Faculty 37 (41% full-time), 92% with terminal degrees.
Expenses (2000–2001) *Tuition:* full-time $12,200; part-time $465 per credit hour. Part-time tuition and fees vary according to course load. *Payment plan:* installment. *Waivers:* employees or children of employees.
Library Mary Schiff Library. *Collection:* 50,000 titles, 75 serial subscriptions.
College life *Housing:* college housing not available.
Campus security 24-hour emergency response devices and patrols.
After graduation *Career center:* Services include career counseling. *Graduate education:* 6% of class of 1999 went directly to graduate and professional school: 6% graduate arts and sciences.
Freshmen 118 applied, 101 admitted, 50 enrolled.

Average high school GPA	3.1	SAT verbal scores above 500	65%
SAT math scores above 500	36%	ACT above 18	93%
From top 10% of their h.s. class	12%	From top quarter	43%
From top half	45%	1998 freshmen returning in 1999	83%

Application *Options:* Common Application, deferred entrance. *Application fee:* $25. *Required:* essay or personal statement; high school transcript; minimum 2.5 GPA; interview; portfolio. *Recommended:* letters of recommendation.
Standardized tests *Admission: Required:* SAT I or ACT.
Significant dates *Application deadlines:* 6/30 (freshmen), 6/30 (transfers). *Financial aid deadline priority date:* 3/1.
Freshman Application Contact
Ms. Sarah Colby, Director of Enrollment Services, Art Academy of Cincinnati, 1125 Saint Gregory Street, Cincinnati, OH 45202. **Phone:** 513-721-5205. **Fax:** 513-562-8778. **E-mail:** admissions@artacademy.edu

Ohio

VisitCollegeQuest.com for information on majors offered and athletics. College video available at CollegeQuest.com.

■ *See page 1188 for a narrative description.*

ASHLAND UNIVERSITY
Ashland, Ohio

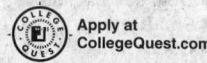 Apply at CollegeQuest.com

- **Independent**, comprehensive, founded 1878, affiliated with Brethren Church
- **Degrees** associate, bachelor's, master's, doctoral, and first professional
- **Small-town** 98-acre campus with easy access to Cleveland
- **Coed**, 2,590 undergraduate students, 80% full-time, 63% women, 37% men
- **Moderately difficult** entrance level, 97% of applicants were admitted
- **15:1 student-to-undergraduate faculty ratio**
- **47.6% graduate** in 6 years or less
- **$14,676 tuition** and fees
- **$14,415 average financial aid** package, $18,100 average indebtedness upon graduation, $36.5 million endowment

Ashland University provides a liberal arts and science curriculum that prepares students for various professions and careers with such distinctive programs as environmental science and toxicology. AU's philosophy of "Accent on the Individual" is evident both in and out of the classroom. The 55,000-square-foot student center and a new technology center are examples of AU's commitment to the future.

Students *Undergraduates:* 2,064 full-time, 526 part-time. Students come from 27 states and territories, 10 other countries. *The most frequently chosen baccalaureate fields are:* business/marketing, education, protective services/public administration. *Graduate:* 239 in professional programs, 3,013 in other graduate degree programs.

From out-of-state	9%	Reside on campus	72%
Age 25 or older	30%	Transferred in	5%
International students	2%	African Americans	3%
Asian Americans/Pacific Islanders	0.3%	Hispanic Americans	1%
Native Americans	0.2%		

Faculty 205 (98% full-time), 80% with terminal degrees.
Expenses (1999–2000) *Comprehensive fee:* $20,126 includes full-time tuition ($14,276), mandatory fees ($400), and room and board ($5450). *College room only:* $2873. Full-time tuition and fees vary according to class time, course load, and program. Room and board charges vary according to board plan and housing facility. *Part-time tuition:* $439 per credit hour. Part-time tuition and fees vary according to class time and program. *Payment plan:* installment. *Waivers:* senior citizens and employees or children of employees.
Library Ashland Library plus 2 others. *Operations spending 1999–2000:* $730,980. *Collection:* 265,229 titles, 950 serial subscriptions.
College life *Housing:* on-campus residence required through senior year. *Options:* coed, men-only, women-only. *Social organizations:* national fraternities, national sororities; 14% of eligible men and 22% of eligible women are members. *Most popular organizations:* Campus Activity Board, Fellowship of Christian Athletes, Hope Fellowship, intramurals, Community Care.
Campus security 24-hour emergency response devices and patrols, student patrols, late-night transport-escort service, controlled dormitory access.
After graduation 29 organizations recruited on campus 1997–98. 85% of class of 1998 had job offers within 6 months. *Career center:* 3 full-time personnel. Services include job fairs, resume preparation, resume referral, career counseling, careers library, job bank, job interviews.
Freshmen 1,792 applied, 1,732 admitted, 543 enrolled.

Average high school GPA	3.23	SAT verbal scores above 500	58%
SAT math scores above 500	57%	ACT above 18	87%
From top 10% of their h.s. class	17%	From top quarter	39%
From top half	71%	1998 freshmen returning in 1999	74%

Application *Options:* eApply at www.CollegeQuest.com, Common Application, electronic application, early admission, deferred entrance. *Application fee:* $25. *Required:* essay or personal statement; high school transcript; minimum 2.5 GPA. *Required for some:* letters of recommendation; interview. *Recommended:* interview.
Standardized tests *Admission: Required:* SAT I or ACT.

Significant dates *Application deadlines:* 8/30 (freshmen), rolling (transfers). *Financial aid deadline:* 3/15.
Freshman Application Contact
Mr. Tom Mansperger, Director of Admissions, Ashland University, 401 College Avenue, Ashland, OH 44805. **Phone:** 419-289-5080. **Toll-free phone:** 800-882-1548. **Fax:** 419-289-5999. **E-mail:** auadmsn@ashland.edu
VisitCollegeQuest.com for information on majors offered and athletics.

■ *See page 1198 for a narrative description.*

BALDWIN-WALLACE COLLEGE
Berea, Ohio

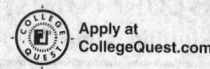 Apply at CollegeQuest.com

- **Independent Methodist**, comprehensive, founded 1845
- **Degrees** bachelor's and master's
- **Suburban** 92-acre campus with easy access to Cleveland
- **Coed**, 3,816 undergraduate students, 77% full-time, 61% women, 39% men
- **Moderately difficult** entrance level, 81% of applicants were admitted
- **13:1 student-to-undergraduate faculty ratio**
- **75.1% graduate** in 6 years or less
- **$15,340 tuition** and fees
- **$11,828 average financial aid** package, $19,768 average indebtedness upon graduation, $123 million endowment

Students *Undergraduates:* 2,948 full-time, 868 part-time. Students come from 34 states and territories. *The most frequently chosen baccalaureate fields are:* business/marketing, education, social sciences and history. *Graduate:* 644 in graduate degree programs.

From out-of-state	7%	Reside on campus	62%
Age 25 or older	5%	Transferred in	5%
International students	0.4%	African Americans	4%
Asian Americans/Pacific Islanders	1%	Hispanic Americans	1%
Native Americans	0.2%		

Faculty 347 (48% full-time), 35% with terminal degrees.
Expenses (2000–2001) *Comprehensive fee:* $20,800 includes full-time tuition ($15,340) and room and board ($5460). *College room only:* $2760. *Part-time tuition:* $490 per hour. Part-time tuition and fees vary according to class time. *Payment plans:* installment, deferred payment. *Waivers:* children of alumni and employees or children of employees.
Library Ritter Library plus 2 others. *Operations spending 1999–2000:* $1.1 million. *Collection:* 160,000 titles, 2,494 serial subscriptions.
College life *Housing: Options:* coed, women-only. *Social organizations:* national fraternities, national sororities; 17% of eligible men and 25% of eligible women are members. *Most popular organizations:* Campus Entertainment Productions, Student Senate, Commuter Activity Board, Campus Crusade, Black Student Alliance.
Campus security 24-hour emergency response devices and patrols, student patrols, late-night transport-escort service, controlled dormitory access.
After graduation 120 organizations recruited on campus 1997–98. 80% of class of 1998 had job offers within 6 months. *Career center:* 6 full-time, 1 part-time personnel. Services include job fairs, resume preparation, interview workshops, resume referral, career/interest testing, career counseling, careers library, job bank, job interviews.
Freshmen 2,115 applied, 1,721 admitted, 714 enrolled.

Average high school GPA	3.4	SAT verbal scores above 500	75%
SAT math scores above 500	80%	ACT above 18	96%
From top 10% of their h.s. class	30%	From top quarter	64%
From top half	91%	1998 freshmen returning in 1999	86%

Application *Options:* eApply at www.CollegeQuest.com, Common Application, electronic application, deferred entrance. *Application fee:* $15. *Required:* essay or personal statement; high school transcript; minimum 2.0 GPA; 1 letter of recommendation. *Recommended:* minimum 3.0 GPA; interview.
Standardized tests *Admission: Required:* SAT I or ACT.
Significant dates *Application deadlines:* rolling (freshmen), rolling (transfers). *Notification:* continuous until 5/1 (freshmen). *Financial aid deadline:* 9/1. *Priority date:* 5/1.

Ohio

Baldwin-Wallace College (continued)
Freshman Application Contact
Mrs. Julie Baker, Director of Undergraduate Admission, Baldwin-Wallace College, 275 Eastland Road, Berea, OH 44017-2088. **Phone:** 440-826-2222. **Toll-free phone:** 877-BWAPPLY. **Fax:** 440-826-3830. **E-mail:** admission@bw.edu

Visit CollegeQuest.com for information on majors offered and athletics. College video available at CollegeQuest.com.

BLUFFTON COLLEGE
Bluffton, Ohio

- **Independent Mennonite**, comprehensive, founded 1899
- **Degrees** bachelor's and master's
- **Small-town** 65-acre campus with easy access to Toledo
- **Coed**, 836 undergraduate students, 98% full-time, 61% women, 39% men
- **Moderately difficult** entrance level, 86% of applicants were admitted
- **13:1 student-to-undergraduate faculty ratio**
- **58% graduate** in 6 years or less
- **$14,306 tuition** and fees
- **$12,395 average financial aid** package, $16,587 average indebtedness upon graduation, $11.8 million endowment

Students *Undergraduates:* 822 full-time, 14 part-time. Students come from 14 states and territories, 11 other countries. *The most frequently chosen baccalaureate fields are:* business/marketing, education, social sciences and history. *Graduate:* 3 in professional programs, 12 in other graduate degree programs.

From out-of-state	8%	Reside on campus	80%
Age 25 or older	9%	Transferred in	4%
International students	1%	African Americans	3%
Asian Americans/Pacific Islanders	1%	Hispanic Americans	2%
Native Americans	0.1%		

Faculty 98 (66% full-time), 79% with terminal degrees.

Expenses (2000–2001, estimated) *Comprehensive fee:* $19,428 includes full-time tuition ($14,056), mandatory fees ($250), and room and board ($5122). *College room only:* $2076. *Part-time tuition:* $414 per semester hour. *Part-time fees:* $125. Part-time tuition and fees vary according to course load. *Payment plan:* installment. *Waivers:* employees or children of employees.

Library Musselman Library. *Operations spending 1999–2000:* $361,313. *Collection:* 146,000 titles, 1,000 serial subscriptions.

College life *Housing:* on-campus residence required through senior year. *Options:* men-only, women-only. *Most popular organizations:* Brothers and Sisters in Christ, campus government, Student Union Board, music groups/chorale, chapel service.

Campus security Late-night transport-escort service, controlled dormitory access, night security guards.

After graduation 200 organizations recruited on campus 1997–98. 73% of class of 1998 had job offers within 6 months. *Career center:* 1 full-time personnel. Services include job fairs, resume preparation, resume referral, career counseling, careers library, job interviews.

Freshmen 743 applied, 637 admitted, 246 enrolled.

Average high school GPA	3.3	SAT verbal scores above 500	66%
SAT math scores above 500	67%	ACT above 18	94%
From top 10% of their h.s. class	16%	From top quarter	51%
From top half	85%	1998 freshmen returning in 1999	72%

Application *Options:* early admission, deferred entrance. *Application fee:* $20. *Required:* high school transcript; 2 letters of recommendation; rank in upper 50% of high school class or 2.3 high school GPA. *Required for some:* essay or personal statement. *Recommended:* interview.

Standardized tests *Admission: Required:* SAT I or ACT.

Significant dates *Application deadlines:* 5/31 (freshmen), rolling (transfers). *Financial aid deadline:* 10/1. *Priority date:* 5/1.

Freshman Application Contact
Mr. Eric Fulcomer, Dean of Admissions, Bluffton College, , 280 West College Avenue, Bluffton, OH 45817. **Phone:** 419-358-3254. **Toll-free phone:** 800-488-3257. **Fax:** 419-358-3232. **E-mail:** admissions@bluffton.edu

Visit CollegeQuest.com for information on majors offered and athletics. College video available at CollegeQuest.com.

■ *See page 1286 for a narrative description.*

BOWLING GREEN STATE UNIVERSITY
Bowling Green, Ohio

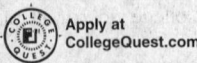
Apply at CollegeQuest.com

- **State-supported**, university, founded 1910
- **Degrees** bachelor's, master's, doctoral, and post-master's certificates
- **Small-town** 1,230-acre campus with easy access to Toledo
- **Coed**, 15,444 undergraduate students, 91% full-time, 57% women, 43% men
- **Moderately difficult** entrance level, 90% of applicants were admitted
- **20:1 student-to-undergraduate faculty ratio**
- **59.4% graduate** in 6 years or less
- **$4874 tuition** and fees (in-state); $10,422 (out-of-state)
- **$5688 average financial aid** package, $15,000 average indebtedness upon graduation, $79.2 million endowment

Bowling Green is a learning community offering the personal attention of a smaller school combined with all the benefits of a large university. A residential campus, BGSU emphasizes first-year student programs, computer technology, and cocurricular activities as vital to its educational program. Sixty percent of students receive financial aid.

Students *Undergraduates:* 14,071 full-time, 1,373 part-time. Students come from 50 states and territories, 30 other countries. *The most frequently chosen baccalaureate fields are:* business/marketing, education, health professions and related sciences. *Graduate:* 2,755 in graduate degree programs.

From out-of-state	6%	Reside on campus	45%
Age 25 or older	8%	Transferred in	4%
International students	1%	African Americans	4%
Asian Americans/Pacific Islanders	1%	Hispanic Americans	2%
Native Americans	0.2%		

Faculty 993 (73% full-time).

Expenses (1999–2000) *Tuition, state resident:* full-time $4058; part-time $200 per credit hour. *Tuition, nonresident:* full-time $9606; part-time $464 per credit hour. *Required fees:* full-time $816; $41 per credit hour. Part-time tuition and fees vary according to course load. *College room and board:* $5494. Room and board charges vary according to board plan and housing facility. *Payment plan:* installment. *Waivers:* senior citizens and employees or children of employees.

Library Jerome Library plus 7 others. *Operations spending 1999–2000:* $4.8 million. *Collection:* 2.2 million titles, 4,520 serial subscriptions, 666,746 audiovisual materials.

College life *Housing:* on-campus residence required through sophomore year. *Options:* coed, disabled students. *Social organizations:* national fraternities, national sororities; 12% of eligible men and 13% of eligible women are members. *Most popular organizations:* University Activities Organization, undergraduate student government, American Marketing Association.

Campus security 24-hour emergency response devices and patrols, student patrols, late-night transport-escort service, controlled dormitory access.

After graduation 475 organizations recruited on campus 1997–98. *Career center:* 12 full-time, 1 part-time personnel. Services include job fairs, resume preparation, resume referral, career counseling, careers library, job bank, job interviews.

Freshmen 9,776 applied, 8,836 admitted, 3,534 enrolled. 15 National Merit Scholars.

Average high school GPA	3.15	SAT verbal scores above 500	56%
SAT math scores above 500	53%	ACT above 18	91%
From top 10% of their h.s. class	13%	From top quarter	35%
From top half	72%	1998 freshmen returning in 1999	78%

Application *Options:* eApply at www.CollegeQuest.com, electronic application, deferred entrance. *Application fee:* $35. *Required:* high school transcript; minimum 2.5 GPA. *Required for some:* interview.

Standardized tests *Admission: Required:* SAT I or ACT.

Significant dates *Application deadlines:* 7/15 (freshmen), 7/15 (transfers). *Financial aid deadline:* continuous.

Freshman Application Contact
Mr. Michael D. Walsh, Director of Admissions, Bowling Green State University, 110 McFall, Bowling Green, OH 43403. **Phone:** 419-372-2086. **E-mail:** admissions@bgnet.bgsu.edu

Visit CollegeQuest.com for information on majors offered and athletics. College video and electronic viewbook available at CollegeQuest.com.

■ *See page 1298 for a narrative description.*

Ohio

BRYANT AND STRATTON COLLEGE
Cleveland, Ohio

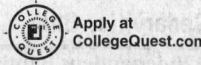 Apply at CollegeQuest.com

- **Proprietary**, 4-year, founded 1929
- **Degrees** associate and bachelor's
- **Urban** campus
- **Coed**, 191 undergraduate students, 59% full-time, 34% women, 66% men
- **Minimally difficult** entrance level, 100% of applicants were admitted
- **10:1 student-to-undergraduate faculty ratio**
- **$9024 tuition** and fees

Part of Bryant and Stratton Business Institute, Inc.

Students *Undergraduates:* 112 full-time, 79 part-time. Students come from 2 states and territories. *The most frequently chosen baccalaureate field is:* engineering/engineering technologies.

| Reside on campus | 10% | Age 25 or older | 48% |
| African Americans | 46% | Hispanic Americans | 2% |

Faculty 21 (24% full-time).

Expenses (1999–2000) *Tuition:* full-time $9024; part-time $282 per semester hour. *College room only:* $3320. *Payment plan:* guaranteed tuition. *Waivers:* employees or children of employees.

Library *Collection:* 4,466 titles, 80 serial subscriptions, 159 audiovisual materials.

College life *Housing: Option:* coed. *Most popular organizations:* student newspaper, student/staff softball.

Campus security Controlled dormitory access.

After graduation 20 organizations recruited on campus 1997–98. 99% of class of 1998 had job offers within 6 months. *Career center:* 2 full-time, 1 part-time personnel. Services include job fairs, resume preparation, resume referral, career counseling, job interviews.

Freshmen 49 applied, 49 admitted, 49 enrolled.

| SAT verbal scores above 500 | N/R | SAT math scores above 500 | N/R |
| ACT above 18 | N/R | 1998 freshmen returning in 1999 | 75% |

Application *Options:* eApply at www.CollegeQuest.com, Common Application, early admission, deferred entrance. *Application fee:* $25. *Required:* essay or personal statement; high school transcript; interview.

Standardized tests *Admission: Required:* TABE. *Recommended:* SAT I or ACT.

Significant dates *Application deadlines:* rolling (freshmen), rolling (transfers). *Financial aid deadline:* continuous.

Freshman Application Contact
Kerry Burton, Director of Admissions, Bryant and Stratton College, 1700 East 13th Street, Cleveland, OH 44114. **Phone:** 216-771-1700. **Fax:** 216-771-1700.

Visit CollegeQuest.com for information on majors offered and athletics.

CAPITAL UNIVERSITY
Columbus, Ohio

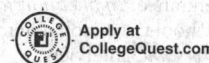 Apply at CollegeQuest.com

- **Independent**, comprehensive, founded 1830, affiliated with Evangelical Lutheran Church in America
- **Degrees** bachelor's, master's, and first professional
- **Suburban** 48-acre campus
- **Coed**, 2,742 undergraduate students, 70% full-time, 63% women, 37% men
- **Moderately difficult** entrance level, 81% of applicants were admitted
- **14:1 student-to-undergraduate faculty ratio**
- **60% graduate** in 6 years or less
- **$16,000 tuition** and fees
- **$14,406 average financial aid** package, $16,200 average indebtedness upon graduation, $36.5 million endowment

Repeated listings in *Barron's 300: Best Buys in College Education*, a Center for Academic Achievement to help each student succeed academically, and a campuswide voice, data, and video network are just a few reasons Capital University is a leader in the Midwest.

Students *Undergraduates:* 1,922 full-time, 820 part-time. Students come from 21 states and territories, 8 other countries. *The most frequently chosen baccalaureate fields are:* business/marketing, education, health professions and related sciences. *Graduate:* 795 in professional programs, 437 in other graduate degree programs.

From out-of-state	8%	Reside on campus	65%
Age 25 or older	6%	Transferred in	2%
International students	1%	African Americans	16%
Asian Americans/Pacific Islanders	1%	Hispanic Americans	1%
Native Americans	0.4%		

Faculty 473 (38% full-time), 50% with terminal degrees.

Expenses (1999–2000) *Comprehensive fee:* $20,900 includes full-time tuition ($16,000) and room and board ($4900). Full-time tuition and fees vary according to program. Room and board charges vary according to board plan and housing facility. *Part-time tuition:* $534 per semester hour. *Part-time fees:* $25 per term part-time. *Payment plan:* installment. *Waivers:* senior citizens and employees or children of employees.

Library Blackmore Library. *Collection:* 175,709 titles, 893 serial subscriptions, 13,253 audiovisual materials.

College life *Housing:* on-campus residence required through sophomore year. *Option:* coed. *Social organizations:* national fraternities, national sororities, local fraternities, local sororities; 25% of eligible men and 25% of eligible women are members. *Most popular organizations:* student government, University Programming, ROTC, Chapel Choir.

Campus security 24-hour patrols, late-night transport-escort service, controlled dormitory access.

After graduation 87% of class of 1998 had job offers within 6 months. *Career center:* 1 full-time, 1 part-time personnel. Services include resume preparation, career counseling, careers library, job interviews. *Graduate education:* 15% of class of 1999 went directly to graduate and professional school: 8% graduate arts and sciences, 4% law, 2% medicine, 1% business, 1% education, 1% theology.

Freshmen 2,151 applied, 1,753 admitted, 542 enrolled. 7 valedictorians.

Average high school GPA	3.3	SAT verbal scores above 500	64%
SAT math scores above 500	67%	ACT above 18	98%
From top 10% of their h.s. class	20%	From top quarter	50%
From top half	82%	1998 freshmen returning in 1999	74%

Application *Options:* eApply at www.CollegeQuest.com, Common Application, deferred entrance. *Application fee:* $25. *Required:* high school transcript; minimum 2.5 GPA; 1 letter of recommendation. *Required for some:* essay or personal statement; audition. *Recommended:* interview.

Standardized tests *Admission: Required:* SAT I or ACT.

Significant dates *Application deadlines:* 4/15 (freshmen), rolling (transfers). *Financial aid deadline priority date:* 2/15.

Freshman Application Contact
Mrs. Kimberly V. Ebbrecht, Director of Admission, Capital University, 2199 East Main Street, Columbus, OH 43209-2394. **Phone:** 614-236-6101. **Toll-free phone:** 800-289-6289. **Fax:** 614-236-6820. **E-mail:** admissions@capital.edu

Visit CollegeQuest.com for information on majors offered and athletics. College video available at CollegeQuest.com.

■ *See page 1354 for a narrative description.*

CASE WESTERN RESERVE UNIVERSITY
Cleveland, Ohio

 Apply at CollegeQuest.com

- **Independent**, university, founded 1826
- **Degrees** bachelor's, master's, doctoral, and first professional
- **Urban** 128-acre campus
- **Coed**, 3,286 undergraduate students, 93% full-time, 39% women, 61% men
- **Very difficult** entrance level, 72% of applicants were admitted
- **8:1 student-to-undergraduate faculty ratio**
- **72% graduate** in 6 years or less
- **$20,260 tuition** and fees
- **$18,549 average financial aid** package, $19,375 average indebtedness upon graduation, $1.4 billion endowment

College-bound students most often list diversity of academic programs as the most important factor in choosing a college. They understand that their academic interests are not fully tested in high school and that a high-quality

Peterson's Guide to Four-Year Colleges 2001 www.petersons.com 623

Ohio

Case Western Reserve University (continued)
college education should offer them the opportunity to explore more varied academic offerings. CWRU has long recognized the importance of academic diversity. At CWRU, regardless of their tentative interest in engineering, liberal arts, management, sciences, or nursing, students apply through a single admission process; admission is not based on academic interest. Once enrolled, students can choose from nearly 60 available majors and can double major across disciplinary lines (engineering and music is a popular combination).

Students *Undergraduates:* 3,054 full-time, 232 part-time. Students come from 54 states and territories, 34 other countries. *The most frequently chosen baccalaureate fields are:* engineering/engineering technologies, biological/life sciences, social sciences and history. *Graduate:* 1,485 in professional programs, 4,435 in other graduate degree programs.

From out-of-state	39%	Reside on campus	73%
Age 25 or older	5%	Transferred in	2%
International students	3%	African Americans	5%
Asian Americans/Pacific Islanders	13%	Hispanic Americans	2%
Native Americans	0.2%		

Faculty 553 (100% full-time), 95% with terminal degrees.
Expenses (2000–2001) *Comprehensive fee:* $26,075 includes full-time tuition ($20,100), mandatory fees ($160), and room and board ($5815). *College room only:* $3580. Room and board charges vary according to board plan and housing facility. *Part-time tuition:* $834 per credit. *Part-time fees:* $5 per credit. Part-time tuition and fees vary according to course load. *Payment plans:* tuition prepayment, installment. *Waivers:* employees or children of employees.
Library University Library plus 6 others. *Operations spending 1999–2000:* $11.6 million. *Collection:* 14,520 serial subscriptions, 106,307 audiovisual materials.
College life *Housing:* on-campus residence required through senior year. *Options:* coed, women-only. *Social organizations:* national fraternities, national sororities, local sororities; 32% of eligible men and 16% of eligible women are members. *Most popular organizations:* fraternities/sororities, student radio station, Habitat for Humanity, international student groups, music/dance groups.
Campus security 24-hour emergency response devices and patrols, student patrols, late-night transport-escort service, controlled dormitory access, crime prevention programs.
After graduation 211 organizations recruited on campus 1997–98. *Career center:* 8 full-time, 2 part-time personnel. Services include job fairs, resume preparation, interview workshops, resume referral, career/interest testing, career counseling, careers library, job bank, job interviews. *Graduate education:* 34% of class of 1999 went directly to graduate and professional school: 9% engineering, 8% medicine, 6% graduate arts and sciences, 3% law, 2% business, 1% dentistry, 1% education.
Freshmen 4,380 applied, 3,135 admitted, 766 enrolled.

SAT verbal scores above 500	93%	SAT math scores above 500	97%
ACT above 18	100%	From top 10% of their h.s. class	67%
From top quarter	89%	From top half	99%
1998 freshmen returning in 1999	92%		

Application *Options:* eApply at www.CollegeQuest.com, Common Application, electronic application, early admission, early decision, deferred entrance. *Application fee:* $0. *Required:* essay or personal statement; high school transcript; 1 letter of recommendation. *Recommended:* interview.
Standardized tests *Admission: Required:* SAT I or ACT. *Recommended:* SAT II Subject Tests.
Significant dates *Application deadlines:* 2/1 (freshmen), 6/30 (transfers). *Early decision:* 1/1. *Notification:* 4/1 (freshmen), 1/15 (early decision). *Financial aid deadline:* 4/15. *Priority date:* 2/1.
Freshman Application Contact
Mr. William T. Conley, Dean of Undergraduate Admission, Case Western Reserve University, 10900 Euclid Avenue, Cleveland, OH 44106. **Phone:** 216-368-4450. **Fax:** 216-368-5111. **E-mail:** admission@po.cwru.edu
Visit CollegeQuest.com for information on majors offered and athletics. College video and electronic viewbook available at CollegeQuest.com.

■ *See page 1376 for a narrative description.*

CEDARVILLE COLLEGE
Cedarville, Ohio

- **Independent Baptist**, 4-year, founded 1887
- **Degrees** associate and bachelor's
- **Rural** 300-acre campus with easy access to Columbus and Dayton
- **Coed**, 2,734 undergraduate students, 97% full-time, 55% women, 45% men
- **Moderately difficult** entrance level, 74% of applicants were admitted
- 17:1 student-to-undergraduate faculty ratio
- 66% graduate in 6 years or less
- **$10,740 tuition** and fees
- **$9452 average financial aid** package, $16,975 average indebtedness upon graduation, $6.7 million endowment

Students *Undergraduates:* 2,642 full-time, 92 part-time. Students come from 54 states and territories. *The most frequently chosen baccalaureate fields are:* education, business/marketing, philosophy.

Reside on campus	80%	Age 25 or older	1%
Transferred in	4%	International students	0.4%
African Americans	1%	Asian Americans/Pacific Islanders	1%
Hispanic Americans	1%	Native Americans	0.2%

Faculty 206 (77% full-time), 50% with terminal degrees.
Expenses (1999–2000) *Comprehensive fee:* $15,528 includes full-time tuition ($10,608), mandatory fees ($132), and room and board ($4788). *Part-time tuition:* $221 per quarter hour. *Part-time fees:* $44 per term part-time. Part-time tuition and fees vary according to course load. *Payment plan:* installment. *Waivers:* senior citizens and employees or children of employees.
Library Centennial Library. *Operations spending 1999–2000:* $1 million. *Collection:* 133,891 titles, 2,878 serial subscriptions.
College life *Housing:* on-campus residence required through senior year. *Options:* men-only, women-only. *Most popular organizations:* Student Government Association, Commuter Crossroads, Mu Kappa, Chi Delta Nu, Society of Automotive Engineers.
Campus security 24-hour emergency response devices and patrols, student patrols, late-night transport-escort service.
After graduation 230 organizations recruited on campus 1997–98. 96% of class of 1998 had job offers within 6 months. *Career center:* 3 full-time personnel. Services include job fairs, resume preparation, interview workshops, resume referral, career/interest testing, career counseling, careers library, job bank, job interviews.
Freshmen 1,814 applied, 1,340 admitted, 722 enrolled. 14 National Merit Scholars, 85 valedictorians.

Average high school GPA	3.59	SAT verbal scores above 500	89%
SAT math scores above 500	87%	ACT above 18	99%
From top 10% of their h.s. class	36%	From top quarter	69%
From top half	85%	1998 freshmen returning in 1999	86%

Application *Options:* electronic application, early admission, deferred entrance. *Application fee:* $30. *Required:* essay or personal statement; high school transcript; minimum 3.0 GPA; 2 letters of recommendation. *Required for some:* interview.
Standardized tests *Admission: Required:* SAT I or ACT.
Significant dates *Application deadlines:* rolling (freshmen), rolling (transfers). *Financial aid deadline priority date:* 3/1.
Freshman Application Contact
Mr. Roscoe Smith, Director of Admissions, Cedarville College, PO Box 601, Cedarville, OH 45314-0601. **Phone:** 937-766-7700. **Toll-free phone:** 800-CEDARVILLE. **Fax:** 937-766-7575. **E-mail:** admiss@cedarville.edu
Visit CollegeQuest.com for information on majors offered and athletics. College video available at CollegeQuest.com.

CENTRAL STATE UNIVERSITY
Wilberforce, Ohio

- **State-supported**, comprehensive, founded 1887
- **Degrees** bachelor's and master's
- **Rural** 60-acre campus with easy access to Dayton
- **Coed**
- **Minimally difficult** entrance level

Ohio

■ **$3443 tuition** and fees (in-state); $7566 (out-of-state)

Expenses (1999–2000) *Tuition, state resident:* full-time $3443; part-time $94 per quarter hour. *Tuition, nonresident:* full-time $7566; part-time $219 per quarter hour. *College room and board:* $4860; room only: $2499.

Institutional Web site http://www.centralstate.edu/

College life *Housing:* on-campus residence required in freshman year. *Options:* coed, men-only, women-only. *Social organizations:* national fraternities, national sororities. *Most popular organizations:* Student Ambassadors, student government.

Campus security 24-hour emergency response devices and patrols.

Application *Options:* Common Application, early admission, deferred entrance. *Application fee:* $15. *Required:* high school transcript; 2.5 high school GPA for nonresidents. *Recommended:* interview.

Standardized tests *Admission: Required:* SAT I or ACT. *Recommended:* ACT.

Admissions Office Contact
Central State University, 1400 Brush Row Road, Wilberforce, OH 45384. **Toll-free phone:** 800-388-CSU1. **Fax:** 937-376-6648. **E-mail:** admissions@csu.ces.edu

Visit CollegeQuest.com for information on athletics. College video available at CollegeQuest.com.

CINCINNATI BIBLE COLLEGE AND SEMINARY
Cincinnati, Ohio

■ **Independent**, comprehensive, founded 1924, affiliated with Church of Christ
■ **Degrees** associate, bachelor's, and master's
■ **Urban** 40-acre campus
■ **Coed**
■ **Minimally difficult** entrance level
■ **$6471 tuition** and fees

Expenses (1999–2000) *Comprehensive fee:* $10,271 includes full-time tuition ($6171), mandatory fees ($300), and room and board ($3800). *College room only:* $1850. Room and board charges vary according to board plan. *Part-time tuition:* $187 per semester hour. *Part-time fees:* $12 per semester hour.

Institutional Web site http://www.cincybible.edu/

College life *Housing:* on-campus residence required through sophomore year. *Options:* men-only, women-only.

Campus security 24-hour emergency response devices and patrols, student patrols.

Application *Options:* early admission, deferred entrance. *Application fee:* $35. *Required:* essay or personal statement; high school transcript; 3 letters of recommendation. *Recommended:* minimum 2.0 GPA; interview.

Standardized tests *Admission: Required:* SAT I or ACT.

Admissions Office Contact
Cincinnati Bible College and Seminary, 2700 Glenway Avenue, Cincinnati, OH 45204-1799. **Toll-free phone:** 800-949-4CBC. **Fax:** 513-244-8140. **E-mail:** admissions@cincybible.edu

Visit CollegeQuest.com for information on athletics. College video available at CollegeQuest.com.

CINCINNATI COLLEGE OF MORTUARY SCIENCE
Cincinnati, Ohio

■ **Independent**, primarily 2-year, founded 1882
■ **Degrees** associate and bachelor's
■ **Urban** 10-acre campus
■ **Coed**, 156 undergraduate students, 100% full-time, 38% women, 62% men
■ **Minimally difficult** entrance level
■ **$12,230 tuition** and fees

Faculty 17.

Admissions Office Contact
Cincinnati College of Mortuary Science, 645 West North Bend Road, Cincinnati, OH 45224-1462. **Fax:** 513-761-3333.

Visit CollegeQuest.com for information on majors offered and athletics.

CIRCLEVILLE BIBLE COLLEGE
Circleville, Ohio

■ **Independent**, 4-year, founded 1948, affiliated with Churches of Christ in Christian Union
■ **Degrees** associate and bachelor's
■ **Small-town** 40-acre campus with easy access to Columbus
■ **Coed**, 212 undergraduate students, 90% full-time, 45% women, 55% men
■ **Minimally difficult** entrance level, 65% of applicants were admitted
■ **12:1 student-to-undergraduate faculty ratio**
■ **17% graduate** in 6 years or less
■ **$6540 tuition** and fees

Students *Undergraduates:* Students come from 15 states and territories, 3 other countries. *The most frequently chosen baccalaureate fields are:* interdisciplinary studies, philosophy, psychology.

From out-of-state	26%	Reside on campus	55%
Age 25 or older	42%	International students	1%
African Americans	3%	Hispanic Americans	1%

Faculty 26 (54% full-time).

Expenses (1999–2000) *Comprehensive fee:* $10,840 includes full-time tuition ($5850), mandatory fees ($690), and room and board ($4300). Full-time tuition and fees vary according to course load, program, and reciprocity agreements. *Part-time tuition:* $250 per semester hour. *Part-time fees:* $258 per term part-time. Part-time tuition and fees vary according to course load, program, and reciprocity agreements. *Payment plan:* installment. *Waivers:* senior citizens and employees or children of employees.

Library Melvin Maxwell Memorial Library. *Operations spending 1999–2000:* $107,466. *Collection:* 28,634 titles, 156 serial subscriptions, 250 audiovisual materials.

College life *Housing:* on-campus residence required through senior year. *Options:* men-only, women-only.

Campus security Security checks after midnight.

After graduation *Career center:* Services include career counseling.

Freshmen 66 applied, 43 admitted.

Average high school GPA	2.9	SAT verbal scores above 500	N/R
SAT math scores above 500	N/R	ACT above 18	70%
From top 10% of their h.s. class	7%	From top quarter	26%
From top half	55%	1998 freshmen returning in 1999	78%

Application *Options:* Common Application, early admission. *Application fee:* $25. *Required:* essay or personal statement; high school transcript; 4 letters of recommendation; medical form. *Required for some:* interview.

Standardized tests *Admission: Recommended:* SAT I. *Required for some:* ACT.

Significant dates *Application deadlines:* rolling (freshmen), rolling (transfers). *Financial aid deadline priority date:* 4/1.

Freshman Application Contact
Rev. Matt Taylor, Director of Enrollment, Circleville Bible College, 1476 Lancaster Pike, PO Box 458, Circleville, OH 43113-9487. **Phone:** 740-477-7701. **Toll-free phone:** 800-701-0222. **Fax:** 740-477-7755. **E-mail:** enroll@biblecollege.edu

Visit CollegeQuest.com for information on majors offered and athletics.

CLEVELAND COLLEGE OF JEWISH STUDIES
Beachwood, Ohio

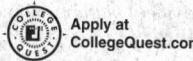

■ **Independent**, comprehensive, founded 1963
■ **Degrees** bachelor's and master's
■ **Suburban** 2-acre campus with easy access to Cleveland

Ohio

Cleveland College of Jewish Studies (continued)
- **Coed**, 14 undergraduate students, 21% full-time, 79% women, 21% men
- **Noncompetitive** entrance level, 20% of applicants were admitted
- **8:1 student-to-undergraduate faculty ratio**
- **$6015 tuition** and fees

Students *Undergraduates:* 3 full-time, 11 part-time. *The most frequently chosen baccalaureate fields are:* education, philosophy. *Graduate:* 67 in graduate degree programs.

| Age 25 or older | 100% | Transferred in | 7% |

Faculty 18 (56% full-time), 39% with terminal degrees.

Expenses (1999–2000) *Tuition:* full-time $6000; part-time $200 per credit. *Required fees:* full-time $15; $15 per year part-time. *Payment plan:* installment. *Waivers:* senior citizens and employees or children of employees.

Library Aaron Garber Library. *Collection:* 28,000 titles, 100 serial subscriptions.

College life *Housing:* college housing not available.

Campus security 24-hour emergency response devices.

Freshmen 5 applied, 1 admitted, 1 enrolled.

| SAT verbal scores above 500 | N/R | SAT math scores above 500 | N/R |
| ACT above 18 | N/R | 1998 freshmen returning in 1999 | 100% |

Application *Options:* eApply at www.CollegeQuest.com, Common Application, deferred entrance. *Application fee:* $25. *Required:* essay or personal statement; high school transcript; 2 letters of recommendation; interview.

Significant dates *Application deadlines:* rolling (freshmen), rolling (transfers). *Financial aid deadline:* continuous.

Freshman Application Contact
Ms. Linda L. Rosen, Director of Enrollment, Cleveland College of Jewish Studies, 26500 Shaker Boulevard, Beachwood, OH 44122-7116. **Phone:** 216-464-4050 Ext. 101. **Toll-free phone:** 888-336-2257. **Fax:** 216-464-5827. **E-mail:** lrosen@ccjs.edu

Visit CollegeQuest.com  for information on majors offered and athletics.

CLEVELAND INSTITUTE OF ART
Cleveland, Ohio

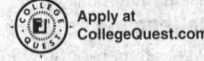 Apply at CollegeQuest.com

- **Independent**, 5-year, founded 1882
- **Degree** bachelor's
- **Urban** 488-acre campus
- **Coed**, 508 undergraduate students, 98% full-time, 47% women, 53% men
- **Moderately difficult** entrance level, 74% of applicants were admitted
- **7:1 student-to-undergraduate faculty ratio**
- **51% graduate** in 6 years or less
- **$15,015 tuition** and fees
- **$11,636 average financial aid** package, $16,253 average indebtedness upon graduation, $21 million endowment

Students *Undergraduates:* 496 full-time, 12 part-time. Students come from 30 states and territories, 12 other countries. *The most frequently chosen baccalaureate fields are:* health professions and related sciences, visual/performing arts.

From out-of-state	30%	Reside on campus	21%
Age 25 or older	14%	Transferred in	10%
International students	4%	African Americans	4%
Asian Americans/Pacific Islanders	2%	Hispanic Americans	2%
Native Americans	0.4%		

Faculty 76 (50% full-time).

Expenses (1999–2000) *Comprehensive fee:* $20,091 includes full-time tuition ($14,175), mandatory fees ($840), and room and board ($5076). *College room only:* $2956. *Part-time tuition:* $525 per credit. *Part-time fees:* $27 per credit. Part-time tuition and fees vary according to course load. *Payment plan:* installment. *Waivers:* employees or children of employees.

Library Jessica R. Gund Memorial Library. *Operations spending 1999–2000:* $228,960. *Collection:* 37,531 titles, 261 serial subscriptions.

College life *Housing:* on-campus residence required in freshman year. *Option:* coed. *Most popular organizations:* nature and hiking club, Student Artist Association, Student Programming Board.

Campus security 24-hour emergency response devices and patrols, late-night transport-escort service, controlled dormitory access.

After graduation 32 organizations recruited on campus 1997–98. 70% of class of 1998 had job offers within 6 months. *Career center:* 1 full-time personnel. Services include job fairs, resume preparation, career counseling, careers library, job bank, job interviews, alumni career counseling. *Graduate education:* 17% of class of 1999 went directly to graduate and professional school: 17% graduate arts and sciences.

Freshmen 562 applied, 415 admitted, 108 enrolled.

Average high school GPA	3.04	SAT verbal scores above 500	78%
SAT math scores above 500	68%	ACT above 18	89%
From top 10% of their h.s. class	15%	From top quarter	40%
From top half	75%	1998 freshmen returning in 1999	80%

Application *Options:* eApply at www.CollegeQuest.com, electronic application, deferred entrance. *Application fee:* $30. *Required:* essay or personal statement; high school transcript; minimum 2.0 GPA; 2 letters of recommendation; portfolio. *Recommended:* interview.

Standardized tests *Admission: Required:* SAT I or ACT.

Significant dates *Application deadlines:* rolling (freshmen), rolling (transfers). *Financial aid deadline priority date:* 3/15.

Freshman Application Contact
Office of Admissions, Cleveland Institute of Art, 11141 East Boulevard, Cleveland, OH 44106. **Phone:** 216-421-7418. **Toll-free phone:** 800-223-4700. **Fax:** 216-421-7438. **E-mail:** admiss@gate.cia.edu

Visit CollegeQuest.com for information on majors offered and athletics. College video and electronic viewbook available at CollegeQuest.com.

■ *See page 1438 for a narrative description.*

CLEVELAND INSTITUTE OF MUSIC
Cleveland, Ohio

- **Independent**, comprehensive, founded 1920
- **Degrees** bachelor's, master's, and doctoral
- **Urban** 488-acre campus
- **Coed**, 222 undergraduate students, 100% full-time, 53% women, 47% men
- **Very difficult** entrance level, 29% of applicants were admitted
- **7:1 student-to-undergraduate faculty ratio**
- **$18,625 tuition** and fees
- **$14,283 average financial aid** package, $12,053 average indebtedness upon graduation, $21 million endowment

Ranked as one of the foremost schools of music in the US, CIM's curriculum is based upon solid, traditional musical values while incorporating liberal arts instruction and new technologies that equip students to meet the challenges of the 21st century. Graduates are admitted routinely to leading graduate schools, are winners of major competitions, and occupy important performance and teaching positions throughout the world.

Students *Undergraduates:* 222 full-time. Students come from 37 states and territories, 13 other countries. *The most frequently chosen baccalaureate field is:* visual/performing arts. *Graduate:* 149 in graduate degree programs.

From out-of-state	83%	Age 25 or older	3%
Transferred in	10%	International students	15%
African Americans	1%	Asian Americans/Pacific Islanders	7%
Hispanic Americans	4%		

Faculty 100 (31% full-time).

Expenses (1999–2000) *One-time required fee:* $500. *Comprehensive fee:* $24,215 includes full-time tuition ($17,875), mandatory fees ($750), and room and board ($5590). *College room only:* $3500. *Part-time tuition:* $800 per credit hour. *Part-time fees:* $750 per year part-time. *Payment plan:* installment. *Waivers:* employees or children of employees.

Library *Operations spending 1999–2000:* $170,000. *Collection:* 47,500 titles, 110 serial subscriptions.

College life *Housing:* on-campus residence required through sophomore year. *Option:* coed.

Campus security 24-hour emergency response devices and patrols, late-night transport-escort service, controlled dormitory access.

After graduation *Career center:* Services include career counseling. *Graduate education:* 90% of class of 1999 went directly to graduate and professional school: 90% graduate arts and sciences.

Freshmen 361 applied, 103 admitted, 52 enrolled.

SAT verbal scores above 500	N/R	SAT math scores above 500	N/R
ACT above 18	N/R	From top 10% of their h.s. class	55%
From top quarter	86%	From top half	96%
1998 freshmen returning in 1999	86%		

Application *Options:* early admission, deferred entrance. *Application fee:* $70. *Required:* essay or personal statement; high school transcript; 2 letters of recommendation; audition. *Recommended:* interview.

Standardized tests *Placement: Required:* SAT I or ACT

Significant dates *Application deadlines:* 12/1 (freshmen), 12/1 (transfers). *Notification:* 4/1 (freshmen). *Financial aid deadline:* 2/15.

Freshman Application Contact Mr. William Fay, Director of Admission, Cleveland Institute of Music, 11021 East Boulevard, Cleveland, OH 44106-1776. **Phone:** 216-795-3107. **Fax:** 216-791-1530. **E-mail:** cimadmission@po.cwru.edu

Visit CollegeQuest.com for information on majors offered and athletics. College video available at CollegeQuest.com.

■ *See page 1440 for a narrative description.*

CLEVELAND STATE UNIVERSITY
Cleveland, Ohio

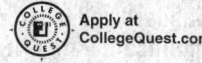 Apply at CollegeQuest.com

- **State-supported**, university, founded 1964
- **Degrees** bachelor's, master's, doctoral, and first professional
- **Urban** 70-acre campus
- **Coed**, 9,405 undergraduate students, 69% full-time, 54% women, 46% men
- **Noncompetitive** entrance level, 82% of applicants were admitted
- **18:1 student-to-undergraduate faculty ratio**
- **$3804 tuition** and fees (in-state); $7608 (out-of-state)
- **$2.6 million endowment**

Students *Undergraduates:* 6,470 full-time, 2,935 part-time. Students come from 24 states and territories, 43 other countries. *The most frequently chosen baccalaureate fields are:* business/marketing, education, social sciences and history. *Graduate:* 808 in professional programs, 4,418 in other graduate degree programs.

From out-of-state	1%	Reside on campus	4%
Age 25 or older	38%	Transferred in	11%
International students	2%	African Americans	19%
Asian Americans/Pacific Islanders	3%	Hispanic Americans	3%
Native Americans	0.4%		

Faculty 942 (56% full-time), 50% with terminal degrees.

Expenses (1999–2000) *Tuition, state resident:* full-time $3804; part-time $161 per semester hour. *Tuition, nonresident:* full-time $7608; part-time $317 per semester hour. Full-time tuition and fees vary according to program. Part-time tuition and fees vary according to program. *College room and board:* $5194; room only: $4198. Room and board charges vary according to board plan and housing facility. *Payment plan:* installment. *Waivers:* senior citizens and employees or children of employees.

Library University Library plus 1 other. *Operations spending 1999–2000:* $7 million. *Collection:* 936,974 titles, 5,050 serial subscriptions, 42,292 audiovisual materials.

College life *Housing: Option:* coed. *Social organizations:* national fraternities, national sororities, local fraternities; 1% of eligible men and 1% of eligible women are members. *Most popular organizations:* honor societies, sororities, fraternities, International Student Association, Chinese Student Association.

Campus security 24-hour emergency response devices and patrols, student patrols, late-night transport-escort service, controlled dormitory access.

After graduation 860 organizations recruited on campus 1997–98. 75% of class of 1998 had job offers within 6 months. *Career center:* 20 full-time, 3 part-time personnel. Services include job fairs, resume preparation, interview workshops, resume referral, career/interest testing, career counseling, careers library, job bank, job interviews, co-op placement. *Major awards:* 1 Fulbright Scholar.

Ohio

Freshmen 2,508 applied, 2,066 admitted, 1,425 enrolled.

SAT verbal scores above 500	39%	SAT math scores above 500	39%
ACT above 18	69%	From top 10% of their h.s. class	1%
From top quarter	31%	From top half	62%
1998 freshmen returning in 1999	57%		

Application *Options:* eApply at www.CollegeQuest.com, early admission, deferred entrance. *Application fee:* $25. *Required:* high school transcript.

Standardized tests *Placement: Recommended:* ACT. *Required for some:* SAT I.

Significant dates *Application deadlines:* 7/15 (freshmen), 7/15 (transfers). *Notification:* continuous until 9/15 (freshmen). *Financial aid deadline priority date:* 4/1.

Freshman Application Contact Mr. Douglas Hartnagel, Director of Admissions, Cleveland State University, East 24th and Euclid Avenue, Cleveland, OH 44115. **Phone:** 216-687-3754. **Fax:** 216-687-9366.

Visit CollegeQuest.com for information on majors offered and athletics. College video and electronic viewbook available at CollegeQuest.com.

COLLEGE OF MOUNT ST. JOSEPH
Cincinnati, Ohio

- **Independent Roman Catholic**, comprehensive, founded 1920
- **Degrees** associate, bachelor's, and master's
- **Suburban** 75-acre campus
- **Coed**, 1,871 undergraduate students, 67% full-time, 70% women, 30% men
- **Moderately difficult** entrance level, 85% of applicants were admitted
- **14:1 student-to-undergraduate faculty ratio**
- **60% graduate** in 6 years or less
- **$13,090 tuition** and fees
- **$11,000 average financial aid** package, $17,125 average indebtedness upon graduation, $19.4 million endowment

The College of Mount St. Joseph is a Catholic, liberal arts college that emphasizes values, integrity, and social responsibility. Graduates are encouraged to become successful professionals and critical thinkers and to lead ethical and civic-minded lives. The College is recognized for its high quality by several national publications, including *U.S. News & World Report* and *The Templeton Guide: Colleges That Encourage Character Development.*

Students *Undergraduates:* 1,262 full-time, 609 part-time. Students come from 14 states and territories, 19 other countries. *The most frequently chosen baccalaureate fields are:* business/marketing, education, health professions and related sciences.

From out-of-state	14%	Reside on campus	18%
Age 25 or older	38%	Transferred in	3%
International students	4%	African Americans	7%
Asian Americans/Pacific Islanders	1%	Hispanic Americans	1%
Native Americans	0.4%		

Faculty 227 (53% full-time), 40% with terminal degrees.

Expenses (1999–2000) *Comprehensive fee:* $18,040 includes full-time tuition ($13,000), mandatory fees ($90), and room and board ($4950). Full-time tuition and fees vary according to course load and program. Room and board charges vary according to board plan and housing facility. *Part-time tuition:* $333 per semester hour. *Part-time fees:* $25 per term part-time. Part-time tuition and fees vary according to course load. *Payment plan:* installment. *Waivers:* senior citizens and employees or children of employees.

Library Archbishop Alter Library. *Operations spending 1999–2000:* $568,495. *Collection:* 96,694 titles, 650 serial subscriptions, 994 audiovisual materials.

College life *Housing: Option:* coed. *Most popular organizations:* Student Government Association, Campus Activity Board, Campus Ambassadors, Dateline (newspaper), Student Physical Therapy Association.

Campus security 24-hour emergency response devices and patrols, late-night transport-escort service.

After graduation 50 organizations recruited on campus 1997–98. 74% of class of 1998 had job offers within 6 months. *Career center:* 6 full-time, 3 part-time personnel. Services include job fairs, resume preparation, interview

Ohio

College of Mount St. Joseph (continued)

workshops, resume referral, career/interest testing, career counseling, careers library, job bank, job interviews. **Graduate education:** 12% of class of 1999 went directly to graduate and professional school.

Freshmen 816 applied, 690 admitted, 330 enrolled. 3 class presidents, 4 valedictorians, 39 student government officers.

Average high school GPA	3.19	SAT verbal scores above 500	55%
SAT math scores above 500	54%	ACT above 18	87%
From top 10% of their h.s. class	20%	From top quarter	50%
From top half	81%	1998 freshmen returning in 1999	87%

Application *Option:* Common Application. *Application fee:* $25. *Required:* high school transcript; minimum 2.25 GPA; minimum SAT score of 960 or ACT score of 19. *Required for some:* essay or personal statement; 1 letter of recommendation; interview. *Recommended:* essay or personal statement; minimum 3.0 GPA; 1 letter of recommendation; interview.

Standardized tests *Admission: Required:* SAT I or ACT.

Significant dates *Application deadlines:* 8/15 (freshmen), 8/15 (transfers). *Financial aid deadline priority date:* 3/1.

Freshman Application Contact
Mr. Edward C. Eckel, Director of Admission, College of Mount St. Joseph, 5701 Delhi Road, Cincinnati, OH 45233-1672. **Phone:** 513-244-4302. **Toll-free phone:** 800-654-9314. **Fax:** 513-244-4629. **E-mail:** edward_eckel@mail.msj.edu

Visit CollegeQuest.com for information on majors offered and athletics. College video available at CollegeQuest.com.

■ *See page 1458 for a narrative description.*

THE COLLEGE OF WOOSTER
Wooster, Ohio

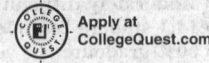 Apply at CollegeQuest.com

■ **Independent**, 4-year, founded 1866, affiliated with Presbyterian Church (U.S.A.)
■ **Degree** bachelor's
■ **Small-town** 320-acre campus with easy access to Cleveland
■ **Coed**, 1,696 undergraduate students, 99% full-time, 53% women, 47% men
■ **Moderately difficult** entrance level, 79% of applicants were admitted
■ **13:1 student-to-undergraduate faculty ratio**
■ **$20,530 tuition** and fees
■ **$17,365 average financial aid** package, $15,800 average indebtedness upon graduation, $206 million endowment

Wooster encourages students to be active participants in their education. First-year seminars; small classes; internships; a required Independent Study (IS) program, which enables each student to work with a faculty mentor on a student-designed research project and which is supported by a new IS library with computer-ready study carrels for each senior; and the Copeland Fund, which allows students to travel or purchase relevant research materials, are central to the curriculum. Wooster also encourages students to be active in areas such as music, theater, student government, athletics, and community service organizations.

Students *Undergraduates:* 1,683 full-time, 13 part-time. Students come from 46 states and territories, 29 other countries. *The most frequently chosen baccalaureate fields are:* English, biological/life sciences, social sciences and history.

From out-of-state	44%	Reside on campus	95%
Age 25 or older	1%	Transferred in	1%
International students	8%	African Americans	4%
Asian Americans/Pacific Islanders	2%	Hispanic Americans	1%
Native Americans	0.1%		

Faculty 160 (77% full-time), 84% with terminal degrees.

Expenses (1999–2000) *Comprehensive fee:* $25,950 includes full-time tuition ($20,530) and room and board ($5420). *College room only:* $2470. Full-time tuition and fees vary according to course load and reciprocity agreements. Part-time tuition and fees vary according to course load. *Payment plan:* installment. *Waivers:* employees or children of employees.

Library The College of Wooster Libraries plus 2 others. *Operations spending 1999–2000:* $2 million. *Collection:* 934,376 titles, 3,746 serial subscriptions.

College life *Housing:* on-campus residence required through senior year. *Options:* coed, men-only, women-only. *Social organizations:* local fraternities, local sororities, coed fraternity; 15% of eligible men and 12% of eligible women are members. *Most popular organizations:* community service, band, International Student Association, Black Student Association, Student Government Association.

Campus security 24-hour emergency response devices and patrols, student patrols, late-night transport-escort service, controlled dormitory access.

After graduation 26 organizations recruited on campus 1997–98. 87% of class of 1998 had job offers within 6 months. *Career center:* 3 full-time personnel. Services include job fairs, resume preparation, interview workshops, resume referral, career/interest testing, career counseling, careers library, job bank, job interviews. **Major awards:** 1 Fulbright Scholar.

Freshmen 2,195 applied, 1,735 admitted, 513 enrolled. 8 National Merit Scholars, 25 valedictorians, 67 student government officers.

Average high school GPA	3.5	SAT verbal scores above 500	91%
SAT math scores above 500	90%	ACT above 18	100%
From top 10% of their h.s. class	64%	From top quarter	71%
From top half	95%	1998 freshmen returning in 1999	80%

Application *Options:* eApply at www.CollegeQuest.com, Common Application, electronic application, early admission, early decision, deferred entrance. *Application fee:* $35. *Required:* essay or personal statement; high school transcript; 2 letters of recommendation. *Recommended:* interview.

Standardized tests *Admission: Required:* SAT I or ACT.

Significant dates *Application deadlines:* 2/15 (freshmen), 6/1 (transfers). *Early decision:* 12/1 (for plan 1), 1/15 (for plan 2). *Notification:* 4/1 (freshmen), 12/15 (early decision plan 1), 2/1 (early decision plan 2). *Financial aid deadline priority date:* 2/15.

Freshman Application Contact
Ms. Carol D. Wheatley, Director of Admissions, The College of Wooster, 1189 Beall Avenue, Wooster, OH 44691-2363. **Phone:** 330-263-2270 Ext. 2118. **Toll-free phone:** 800-877-9905. **Fax:** 330-263-2621. **E-mail:** admissions@wooster.edu

Visit CollegeQuest.com for information on majors offered and athletics. College video and electronic viewbook available at CollegeQuest.com.

■ *See page 1494 for a narrative description.*

COLUMBUS COLLEGE OF ART AND DESIGN
Columbus, Ohio

■ **Independent**, 4-year, founded 1879
■ **Degree** bachelor's
■ **Urban** 7-acre campus
■ **Coed**, 1,354 undergraduate students, 87% full-time, 43% women, 57% men
■ **Moderately difficult** entrance level, 51% of applicants were admitted
■ **9:1 student-to-undergraduate faculty ratio**
■ **$13,440 tuition** and fees

The Joseph V. Canzani Center, opened in 1993, is the focal point of the 17-building campus and houses a large exhibition hall, an auditorium, and a library and resource center. A new student recreation center opened in 1996.

Students *Undergraduates:* 1,184 full-time, 170 part-time. Students come from 41 states and territories, 24 other countries.

Reside on campus	18%	Age 25 or older	10%
Transferred in	6%	International students	3%
African Americans	5%	Asian Americans/Pacific Islanders	3%
Hispanic Americans	2%	Native Americans	0.3%

Expenses (1999–2000) *Comprehensive fee:* $19,440 includes full-time tuition ($13,440) and room and board ($6000). *Part-time tuition:* $560 per semester hour. *Part-time fees:* $60 per term part-time. *Payment plan:* installment. *Waivers:* senior citizens and employees or children of employees.

Library Packard Library. *Collection:* 36,839 titles, 256 serial subscriptions.

College life *Housing:* on-campus residence required in freshman year. *Option:* coed.

Campus security 24-hour emergency response devices and patrols, late-night transport-escort service, controlled dormitory access.

After graduation 130 organizations recruited on campus 1997–98. *Career center:* 1 full-time, 1 part-time personnel. Services include job fairs, resume preparation, interview workshops, resume referral, career counseling, careers library, job bank, job interviews. *Graduate education:* 11% of class of 1999 went directly to graduate and professional school.

Freshmen 665 applied, 341 admitted, 323 enrolled.

Average high school GPA	2.8	SAT verbal scores above 500	N/R
SAT math scores above 500	N/R	ACT above 18	N/R
From top half of their h.s. class	49%	1998 freshmen returning in 1999	76%

Application *Option:* deferred entrance. *Application fee:* $25. *Required:* high school transcript; minimum 2.0 GPA; portfolio. *Required for some:* letters of recommendation. *Recommended:* interview.

Standardized tests *Admission: Required:* SAT I or ACT.

Significant dates *Application deadlines:* rolling (freshmen), rolling (transfers). *Financial aid deadline priority date:* 4/3.

Freshman Application Contact
Mr. Thomas E. Green, Director of Admissions, Columbus College of Art and Design, 107 North Ninth Street, Columbus, OH 43215-1758. **Phone:** 614-224-9101. **E-mail:** brooke@ccad.edu

Visit CollegeQuest.com for information on majors offered and athletics. College video available at CollegeQuest.com.

■ *See page 1518 for a narrative description.*

DAVID N. MYERS COLLEGE
Cleveland, Ohio

- **Independent**, 4-year, founded 1848
- **Degrees** associate and bachelor's
- **Urban** 1-acre campus
- **Coed**, 1,171 undergraduate students, 51% full-time, 70% women, 30% men
- **Minimally difficult** entrance level, 65% of applicants were admitted
- **14:1 student-to-undergraduate faculty ratio**
- **$8760 tuition** and fees
- **$15,906 average indebtedness** upon graduation, $631,558 endowment

Students *Undergraduates:* 593 full-time, 578 part-time. *The most frequently chosen baccalaureate fields are:* engineering/engineering technologies, (pre)law, health professions and related sciences.

Transferred in	12%	African Americans	43%
Asian Americans/Pacific Islanders	1%	Hispanic Americans	2%
Native Americans	0.2%		

Faculty 86 (21% full-time), 22% with terminal degrees.

Expenses (2000–2001, estimated) *Tuition:* full-time $8760; part-time $292 per credit. *Payment plans:* installment, deferred payment. *Waivers:* employees or children of employees.

Library Library Resource Center. *Operations spending 1999–2000:* $159,382. *Collection:* 19,289 titles, 146 serial subscriptions, 309 audiovisual materials.

College life *Housing:* college housing not available. *Most popular organizations:* Students in Free Enterprise, Accounting Association, Mock Trial Association, Delta Club.

Campus security 24-hour patrols, late-night transport-escort service.

After graduation *Career center:* 3 full-time, 1 part-time personnel. Services include job fairs, resume preparation, interview workshops, resume referral, career/interest testing, career counseling, careers library, job bank, job interviews. *Graduate education:* 10% of class of 1999 went directly to graduate and professional school: 8% business, 2% law.

Freshmen 382 applied, 250 admitted, 93 enrolled.

| Average high school GPA | 2.6 | SAT verbal scores above 500 | N/R |
| SAT math scores above 500 | N/R | ACT above 18 | N/R |

Application *Options:* Common Application, early admission, early action, deferred entrance. *Application fee:* $25. *Required:* high school transcript. *Required for some:* essay or personal statement; interview. *Recommended:* letters of recommendation.

Standardized tests *Admission: Required:* SAT I or ACT.

Significant dates *Application deadlines:* rolling (freshmen), rolling (transfers). *Early action:* 5/1. *Notification:* 6/1 (early action). *Financial aid deadline priority date:* 4/30.

Freshman Application Contact
Ms. Tiffiney Payton, Interim Director of Admissions, David N. Myers College, 112 Prospect Avenue, Cleveland, OH 44115. **Phone:** 216-523-3806 Ext. 805. **Toll-free phone:** 800-424-3953. **Fax:** 216-523-3808. **E-mail:** tpayton@dnmyers.edu

Visit CollegeQuest.com for information on majors offered and athletics.

DEFIANCE COLLEGE
Defiance, Ohio

- **Independent**, comprehensive, founded 1850, affiliated with United Church of Christ
- **Degrees** associate, bachelor's, and master's
- **Small-town** 150-acre campus with easy access to Toledo
- **Coed**, 812 undergraduate students, 77% full-time, 53% women, 47% men
- **Moderately difficult** entrance level, 70% of applicants were admitted
- **14:1 student-to-undergraduate faculty ratio**
- **38% graduate** in 6 years or less
- **$14,550 tuition** and fees

Students *Undergraduates:* 626 full-time, 186 part-time. Students come from 11 states and territories, 2 other countries. *Graduate:* 207 in graduate degree programs.

Reside on campus	41%	Age 25 or older	35%
Transferred in	6%	International students	0.2%
African Americans	4%	Asian Americans/Pacific Islanders	0.1%
Hispanic Americans	4%	Native Americans	0.1%

Faculty 69 (57% full-time), 39% with terminal degrees.

Expenses (1999–2000) *Comprehensive fee:* $18,780 includes full-time tuition ($14,350), mandatory fees ($200), and room and board ($4230). *Part-time tuition:* $260 per semester hour. *Part-time fees:* $25 per term. *Payment plan:* installment. *Waivers:* senior citizens and employees or children of employees.

Library Pilgrim Library. *Operations spending 1999–2000:* $278,750. *Collection:* 88,000 titles, 424 serial subscriptions, 25,000 audiovisual materials.

College life *Housing:* on-campus residence required through junior year. *Options:* men-only, women-only. *Social organizations:* national fraternities, national sororities, local fraternities, local sororities; 6% of eligible men and 8% of eligible women are members. *Most popular organizations:* Campus Activities Board, Criminal Justice Society, Greek life, Student Senate.

Campus security Late-night transport-escort service, controlled dormitory access.

After graduation 100 organizations recruited on campus 1997–98. 86% of class of 1998 had job offers within 6 months. *Career center:* 2 full-time personnel. Services include job fairs, resume preparation, interview workshops, resume referral, career/interest testing, career counseling, careers library, job bank, job interviews.

Freshmen 587 applied, 413 admitted, 179 enrolled.

Average high school GPA	2.96	SAT verbal scores above 500	36%
SAT math scores above 500	38%	ACT above 18	88%
From top 10% of their h.s. class	10%	From top quarter	29%
From top half	63%	1998 freshmen returning in 1999	63%

Application *Options:* Common Application, early admission, deferred entrance. *Application fee:* $25. *Required:* high school transcript; minimum 2.0 GPA. *Required for some:* essay or personal statement; letters of recommendation; interview. *Recommended:* interview.

Standardized tests *Admission: Required:* SAT I or ACT.

Significant dates *Application deadlines:* 8/15 (freshmen), 8/15 (transfers). *Financial aid deadline priority date:* 3/1.

Freshman Application Contact
Ms. Sarah Evans Bates, Director of Admissions, Defiance College, 701 North Clinton Street, Defiance, OH 43512-1610. **Phone:** 419-783-2354. **Toll-free phone:** 800-520-4632 Ext. 2359. **Fax:** 419-783-2468. **E-mail:** admissions@defiance.edu

Visit CollegeQuest.com for information on majors offered and athletics.

■ *See page 1566 for a narrative description.*

Ohio

DENISON UNIVERSITY
Granville, Ohio

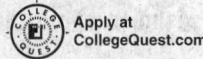 Apply at CollegeQuest.com

- **Independent**, 4-year, founded 1831
- **Degree** bachelor's
- **Small-town** 1,200-acre campus with easy access to Columbus
- **Coed**, 2,082 undergraduate students, 99% full-time, 55% women, 45% men
- **Moderately difficult** entrance level, 69% of applicants were admitted
- **12:1 student-to-undergraduate faculty ratio**
- **$22,210 tuition** and fees
- **$9772 average financial aid** package, $14,021 average indebtedness upon graduation, $353.9 million endowment

Denison University attracts motivated, well-rounded students from throughout the US and 30 other countries. Along with its new Environmental Studies Center, Denison's model Honors Program, exceptional collaborative research opportunities with faculty members, state-of-the-art science facilities, and a new recreation and athletics center provide its students with a challenging and enriching college experience.

Students *Undergraduates:* 2,073 full-time, 9 part-time. Students come from 45 states and territories, 30 other countries. *The most frequently chosen baccalaureate fields are:* biological/life sciences, social sciences and history, visual/performing arts.

From out-of-state	57%	Reside on campus	98%
Age 25 or older	1%	Transferred in	1%
International students	4%	African Americans	4%
Asian Americans/Pacific Islanders	2%	Hispanic Americans	2%
Native Americans	0.2%		

Faculty 174 (96% full-time), 97% with terminal degrees.

Expenses (2000–2001) *Comprehensive fee:* $28,510 includes full-time tuition ($21,710), mandatory fees ($500), and room and board ($6300). Room and board charges vary according to housing facility. *Part-time tuition:* $678 per credit hour. Part-time tuition and fees vary according to course load. *Payment plans:* tuition prepayment, installment. *Waivers:* employees or children of employees.

Library William Howard Doane Library. *Operations spending 1999–2000:* $1.8 million. *Collection:* 339,644 titles, 1,208 serial subscriptions, 18,105 audiovisual materials.

College life *Housing:* on-campus residence required through senior year. *Options:* coed, men-only, women-only. *Social organizations:* national fraternities, national sororities; 30% of eligible men and 32% of eligible women are members. *Most popular organizations:* Denison Community Association, Black Student Union, Denison International Student Association, Student Activities Committee.

Campus security 24-hour emergency response devices and patrols, late-night transport-escort service, controlled dormitory access.

After graduation 60 organizations recruited on campus 1997–98. 72% of class of 1998 had job offers within 6 months. *Career center:* 4 full-time, 1 part-time personnel. Services include job fairs, resume preparation, interview workshops, resume referral, career/interest testing, career counseling, careers library, job bank, job interviews. *Graduate education:* 22% of class of 1999 went directly to graduate and professional school: 8% graduate arts and sciences, 5% medicine, 4% law, 1% business, 1% dentistry, 1% engineering, 1% theology, 1% veterinary medicine.

Freshmen 2,991 applied, 2,054 admitted, 587 enrolled. 16 National Merit Scholars, 29 class presidents, 31 valedictorians, 149 student government officers.

Average high school GPA	3.5	SAT verbal scores above 500	93%
SAT math scores above 500	96%	ACT above 18	100%
From top 10% of their h.s. class	52%	From top quarter	77%
From top half	95%	1998 freshmen returning in 1999	84%

Application *Options:* eApply at www.CollegeQuest.com, Common Application, early admission, early decision, deferred entrance. *Application fee:* $40. *Required:* essay or personal statement; high school transcript; 2 letters of recommendation. *Recommended:* interview.

Standardized tests *Admission: Required:* SAT I or ACT. *Recommended:* SAT II Subject Tests.

Significant dates *Application deadlines:* 2/1 (freshmen), 5/1 (transfers). *Early decision:* 1/1. *Notification:* 4/1 (freshmen), 1/20 (early decision). *Financial aid deadline priority date:* 2/15.

Freshman Application Contact
Ms. Pennie Miller, Communications Coordinator, Denison University, Box H, Granville, OH 43023. **Phone:** 740-587-6618. **Toll-free phone:** 800-DENISON. **Fax:** 740-587-6306. **E-mail:** admissions@denison.edu
Visit CollegeQuest.com for information on majors offered and athletics. College video available at CollegeQuest.com.

- *See page 1570 for a narrative description.*

DeVry Institute of Technology
Columbus, Ohio

- **Proprietary**, 4-year, founded 1952
- **Degrees** associate and bachelor's
- **Urban** 21-acre campus
- **Coed**, 3,332 undergraduate students, 74% full-time, 26% women, 74% men
- **Minimally difficult** entrance level, 62% of applicants were admitted
- **23:1 student-to-undergraduate faculty ratio**
- **$7778 tuition** and fees

Part of DeVry, Inc.

Students *Undergraduates:* 2,464 full-time, 868 part-time. Students come from 37 states and territories, 1 other country. *The most frequently chosen baccalaureate fields are:* business/marketing, computer/information sciences, engineering/engineering technologies.

From out-of-state	21%	Age 25 or older	41%
Transferred in	12%	International students	1%
African Americans	19%	Asian Americans/Pacific Islanders	3%
Hispanic Americans	1%	Native Americans	0.2%

Faculty 128 (54% full-time).

Expenses (1999–2000) *Tuition:* full-time $7778; part-time $290 per credit hour. Part-time tuition and fees vary according to class time and course load. *Payment plan:* installment. *Waivers:* employees or children of employees.

Library Learning Resource Center. *Collection:* 17,830 titles, 50 serial subscriptions.

College life *Housing:* college housing not available. *Most popular organizations:* Institute for Electrical and Electronic Engineers, American Production and Inventory Control Society, Association of Information Technology, Future Accounting Control Society, Black United Students.

Campus security Late-night transport-escort service, security at evening activities.

After graduation 97% of class of 1998 had job offers within 6 months. *Career center:* 9 full-time, 2 part-time personnel. Services include job fairs, resume preparation, career counseling, job bank, job interviews.

Freshmen 1,720 applied, 1,063 admitted, 925 enrolled.

SAT verbal scores above 500	N/R	SAT math scores above 500	N/R
ACT above 18	N/R	1998 freshmen returning in 1999	47%

Application *Options:* electronic application, deferred entrance. *Application fee:* $25. *Required:* high school transcript; interview.

Standardized tests *Admission: Required:* Computerized Placement Test. *Recommended:* SAT I or ACT.

Significant dates *Application deadlines:* rolling (freshmen), rolling (transfers). *Financial aid deadline:* continuous.

Freshman Application Contact
Jody Wasmer, Director of Admissions, DeVry Institute of Technology, 1350 Alum Creek Drive, Columbus, OH 43209-2705. **Phone:** 614-253-7291 Ext. 700. **Toll-free phone:** 800-426-3916 (in-state); 800-426-3090 (out-of-state). **E-mail:** admissions@devrycol5.edu
Visit CollegeQuest.com for information on majors offered and athletics.

Franciscan University of Steubenville
Steubenville, Ohio

- **Independent Roman Catholic**, comprehensive, founded 1946
- **Degrees** associate, bachelor's, and master's

- **Suburban** 116-acre campus with easy access to Pittsburgh
- **Coed**, 1,682 undergraduate students, 91% full-time, 60% women, 40% men
- **Moderately difficult** entrance level, 89% of applicants were admitted
- **16:1 student-to-undergraduate faculty ratio**
- **64% graduate** in 6 years or less
- **$12,270 tuition** and fees
- **$9134 average financial aid** package, $19,692 average indebtedness upon graduation, $15.5 million endowment

Described by the John Templeton Foundation as a liberal arts school where faith and reason are allies, not enemies, Franciscan University of Steubenville has also been included in the *U.S. News & World Report* college guide and *Barron's Best Buys in College Education*. Rigorous academics complemented by dynamic Catholic spirituality create an exciting intellectual and faith community. A residence hall household system, an extensive intramural sports program, and an Austrian study-abroad program enhance the Franciscan University experience.

Students *Undergraduates:* 1,536 full-time, 146 part-time. Students come from 52 states and territories, 39 other countries. *The most frequently chosen baccalaureate fields are:* education, health professions and related sciences, philosophy. *Graduate:* 456 in graduate degree programs.

From out-of-state	77%	Reside on campus	63%
Age 25 or older	8%	Transferred in	12%
International students	3%	African Americans	1%
Asian Americans/Pacific Islanders	2%	Hispanic Americans	4%
Native Americans	0.1%		

Faculty 149 (64% full-time), 42% with terminal degrees.

Expenses (1999–2000) *Comprehensive fee:* $17,240 includes full-time tuition ($11,990), mandatory fees ($280), and room and board ($4970). Room and board charges vary according to board plan. *Part-time tuition:* $400 per credit. *Part-time fees:* $10 per credit. Part-time tuition and fees vary according to class time. *Payment plan:* installment. *Waivers:* employees or children of employees.

Library John Paul II Library. *Operations spending 1999–2000:* $683,466. *Collection:* 221,179 titles, 965 audiovisual materials.

College life *Housing:* on-campus residence required through junior year. *Options:* men-only, women-only. *Social organizations:* national fraternities, national sororities. *Most popular organizations:* Franciscan University Student Association, Student Activities Board, Human Life Concerns, Works of Mercy, Troubadour.

Campus security 24-hour emergency response devices and patrols, student patrols, late-night transport-escort service.

After graduation 25 organizations recruited on campus 1997–98. *Career center:* 1 full-time, 1 part-time personnel. Services include job fairs, resume preparation, interview workshops, resume referral, career counseling, careers library, job bank, job interviews.

Freshmen 717 applied, 640 admitted, 321 enrolled.

Average high school GPA	3.4	SAT verbal scores above 500	85%
SAT math scores above 500	71%	ACT above 18	96%
From top 10% of their h.s. class	24%	From top quarter	46%
From top half	78%	1998 freshmen returning in 1999	83%

Application *Options:* early admission, deferred entrance. *Application fee:* $20. *Required:* essay or personal statement; high school transcript; minimum 2.4 GPA. *Required for some:* letters of recommendation. *Recommended:* interview.

Standardized tests *Admission: Required:* SAT I or ACT.

Significant dates *Application deadlines:* 6/30 (freshmen), 6/30 (transfers). *Financial aid deadline priority date:* 3/15.

Freshman Application Contact
Mrs. Margaret Weber, Director of Admissions, Franciscan University of Steubenville, 1235 University Boulevard, Steubenville, OH 43952-1763. **Phone:** 740-283-6226. **Toll-free phone:** 800-783-6220. **Fax:** 740-283-6472. **E-mail:** admissions@franuniv.edu

Visit CollegeQuest.com for information on majors offered and athletics. College video available at CollegeQuest.com.

- *See page 1690 for a narrative description.*

FRANKLIN UNIVERSITY
Columbus, Ohio

- **Independent**, comprehensive, founded 1902
- **Degrees** associate, bachelor's, and master's
- **Urban** 14-acre campus
- **Coed**, 3,490 undergraduate students, 33% full-time, 58% women, 42% men
- **Noncompetitive** entrance level, 100% of applicants were admitted
- **18:1 student-to-undergraduate faculty ratio**
- **$5531 tuition** and fees
- **$21.4 million endowment**

Students *Undergraduates:* 1,150 full-time, 2,340 part-time. Students come from 14 states and territories, 59 other countries. *The most frequently chosen baccalaureate fields are:* business/marketing, computer/information sciences, health professions and related sciences. *Graduate:* 661 in graduate degree programs.

From out-of-state	1%	Age 25 or older	74%
Transferred in	25%	International students	11%
African Americans	14%	Asian Americans/Pacific Islanders	3%
Hispanic Americans	1%	Native Americans	0.4%

Faculty 255 (18% full-time).

Expenses (1999–2000) *One-time required fee:* $25. *Tuition:* full-time $5456; part-time $176 per credit hour. *Required fees:* full-time $75; $25 per term part-time. Full-time tuition and fees vary according to course load and program. Part-time tuition and fees vary according to program. *Payment plans:* installment, deferred payment. *Waivers:* employees or children of employees.

Library Franklin University Library. *Operations spending 1999–2000:* $505,682. *Collection:* 95,291 titles, 3,878 serial subscriptions, 289 audiovisual materials.

College life *Housing:* college housing not available. *Most popular organizations:* American Marketing Association, American Advertising Federation, African American Student Organization, International Association of Business Communicators, International Student Association.

Campus security Security personnel during operating hours.

After graduation 50 organizations recruited on campus 1997–98. *Career center:* 2 full-time personnel. Services include resume preparation, interview workshops, resume referral, career counseling, careers library, job bank.

Freshmen 327 applied, 327 admitted, 128 enrolled.

SAT verbal scores above 500	N/R	SAT math scores above 500	N/R
ACT above 18	N/R		

Application *Option:* deferred entrance. *Application fee:* $0. *Required:* high school transcript.

Significant dates *Application deadlines:* rolling (freshmen), rolling (transfers). *Financial aid deadline priority date:* 6/30.

Freshman Application Contact
Ms. Linda M. Steele, Vice President for Students and Institutional Initiatives, Franklin University, 201 S. Grant Avenue, Columbus, OH 43215. **Phone:** 614-341-6230. **Toll-free phone:** 877-341-6300. **Fax:** 614-224-8027. **E-mail:** info@franklin.edu

Visit CollegeQuest.com for information on majors offered and athletics. College video available at CollegeQuest.com.

GOD'S BIBLE SCHOOL AND COLLEGE
Cincinnati, Ohio

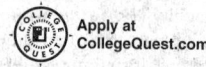
Apply at CollegeQuest.com

- **Independent interdenominational**, 4-year, founded 1900
- **Degrees** associate and bachelor's
- **Urban** 14-acre campus
- **Coed**, 221 undergraduate students, 90% full-time, 57% women, 43% men
- **Minimally difficult** entrance level
- **$3850 tuition** and fees

Students *Undergraduates:* Students come from 24 states and territories, 12 other countries.

Age 25 or older	18%

Ohio

God's Bible School and College (continued)

Faculty 21 (71% full-time).

Expenses (1999–2000) *Comprehensive fee:* $6400 includes full-time tuition ($3560), mandatory fees ($290), and room and board ($2550). *College room only:* $1000. *Part-time tuition:* $135 per semester hour. *Part-time fees:* $290 per year part-time.

Library R. G. Flexon Memorial Library. *Collection:* 28,452 titles, 240 serial subscriptions.

College life On-campus residence required through senior year.

Campus security 24-hour patrols.

After graduation *Graduate education:* 18% of class of 1999 went directly to graduate and professional school: 12% theology, 6% education.

Freshmen

SAT verbal scores above 500	N/R	SAT math scores above 500	N/R
ACT above 18	N/R	1998 freshmen returning in 1999	62%

Application *Options:* eApply at www.CollegeQuest.com, Common Application. *Application fee:* $50. *Required:* high school transcript; 3 letters of recommendation; interview.

Standardized tests *Placement: Required:* SAT I or ACT.

Significant dates *Application deadlines:* rolling (freshmen), rolling (transfers). *Financial aid deadline priority date:* 5/30.

Freshman Application Contact
Mr. Phil Collingsworth, Dean of Enrollment Management, God's Bible School and College, 1810 Young Street, Cincinnati, OH 45210-1599. **Phone:** 513-721-7944 Ext. 270. **Toll-free phone:** 800-486-4637. **Fax:** 513-721-3971. **E-mail:** admissions@gbs.edu

Visit CollegeQuest.com for information on majors offered and athletics.

HEIDELBERG COLLEGE
Tiffin, Ohio

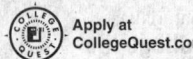

- **Independent**, comprehensive, founded 1850, affiliated with United Church of Christ
- **Degrees** bachelor's and master's
- **Small-town** 110-acre campus with easy access to Toledo
- **Coed**, 1,266 undergraduate students, 76% full-time, 51% women, 49% men
- **Moderately difficult** entrance level, 86% of applicants were admitted
- **13:1** student-to-undergraduate faculty ratio
- **48% graduate** in 6 years or less
- **$16,672 tuition** and fees
- **$14,909 average financial aid** package, $18,725 average indebtedness upon graduation, $32 million endowment

Students *Undergraduates:* 965 full-time, 301 part-time. Students come from 25 states and territories, 8 other countries. *The most frequently chosen baccalaureate fields are:* business/marketing, education, parks and recreation. *Graduate:* 221 in graduate degree programs.

From out-of-state	14%	Reside on campus	83%
Age 25 or older	4%	Transferred in	3%
International students	1%	African Americans	2%
Asian Americans/Pacific Islanders	0.3%	Hispanic Americans	1%
Native Americans	0.4%		

Faculty 122 (61% full-time), 54% with terminal degrees.

Expenses (1999–2000) *Comprehensive fee:* $21,936 includes full-time tuition ($16,422), mandatory fees ($250), and room and board ($5264). *College room only:* $2392. Room and board charges vary according to housing facility. *Part-time tuition:* $380 per semester hour. *Part-time fees:* $50 per term part-time. Part-time tuition and fees vary according to location. *Payment plans:* installment, deferred payment. *Waivers:* employees or children of employees.

Library Beeghly Library plus 1 other. *Operations spending 1999–2000:* $472,000. *Collection:* 260,055 titles, 829 serial subscriptions.

College life *Housing:* on-campus residence required through senior year. *Option:* coed. *Social organizations:* local fraternities, local sororities; 75% of eligible men and 75% of eligible women are members. *Most popular organizations:* concert choir, yearbook, World Student Union, Greek organizations, Alpha Phi Omega.

Campus security 24-hour emergency response devices, student patrols, late-night transport-escort service, controlled dormitory access.

After graduation 30 organizations recruited on campus 1997–98. 95% of class of 1998 had job offers within 6 months. *Career center:* 2 full-time, 1 part-time personnel. Services include job fairs, resume preparation, resume referral, career counseling, careers library, job interviews. *Graduate education:* 20% of class of 1999 went directly to graduate and professional school: 14% graduate arts and sciences, 3% medicine, 1% dentistry, 1% law, 1% veterinary medicine.

Freshmen 1,399 applied, 1,205 admitted, 326 enrolled. 15 valedictorians.

Average high school GPA	3.2	SAT verbal scores above 500	65%
SAT math scores above 500	79%	ACT above 18	89%
From top 10% of their h.s. class	20%	From top quarter	43%
From top half	78%	1998 freshmen returning in 1999	79%

Application *Options:* eApply at www.CollegeQuest.com, Common Application, electronic application, early action, deferred entrance. *Application fee:* $25. *Required:* high school transcript; minimum 2.4 GPA. *Recommended:* 1 letter of recommendation; interview.

Standardized tests *Admission: Required:* SAT I or ACT.

Significant dates *Application deadlines:* 8/1 (freshmen), 8/1 (transfers). *Early action:* 9/1. *Notification:* continuous until 8/1 (freshmen), 9/15 (early action). *Financial aid deadline priority date:* 3/1.

Freshman Application Contact
Ms. Sharon Pugh, Director of Admission, Heidelberg College, 310 East Market Street, Tiffin, OH 44883-2462. **Phone:** 419-448-2330. **Toll-free phone:** 800-434-3352. **Fax:** 419-448-2334. **E-mail:** adminfo@nike.heidelberg.edu

Visit CollegeQuest.com for information on majors offered and athletics. College video available at CollegeQuest.com.

■ *See page 1780 for a narrative description.*

HIRAM COLLEGE
Hiram, Ohio

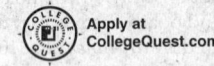

- **Independent**, 4-year, founded 1850, affiliated with Christian Church (Disciples of Christ)
- **Degree** bachelor's
- **Rural** 110-acre campus with easy access to Cleveland
- **Coed**, 1,168 undergraduate students, 81% full-time, 55% women, 45% men
- **Very difficult** entrance level, 86% of applicants were admitted
- **12:1** student-to-undergraduate faculty ratio
- **58.49% graduate** in 6 years or less
- **$17,710 tuition** and fees
- **$16,738 average financial aid** package, $17,125 average indebtedness upon graduation, $69.6 million endowment

Each of Hiram's 15-week semesters is divided into 12- and 3-week terms. During the 3-week terms, students take only 1 course. Hiram supplements classroom study through an extensive study-abroad program. More than 50 percent of students participate, with all courses taught by Hiram faculty members. Hiram opened a $7.2-million library in 1995, and the new $6.2-million Esther and Carl Gerstacker Science Hall opened in January 2000.

Students *Undergraduates:* 948 full-time, 220 part-time. Students come from 23 states and territories, 19 other countries. *The most frequently chosen baccalaureate fields are:* business/marketing, biological/life sciences, social sciences and history.

From out-of-state	21%	Reside on campus	93%
Age 25 or older	26%	Transferred in	2%
International students	2%	African Americans	9%
Asian Americans/Pacific Islanders	1%	Hispanic Americans	2%
Native Americans	0.2%		

Faculty 96 (69% full-time), 67% with terminal degrees.

Expenses (1999–2000) *Comprehensive fee:* $23,734 includes full-time tuition ($17,230), mandatory fees ($480), and room and board ($6024). *College room only:* $2724. Room and board charges vary according to board plan and housing facility. *Part-time tuition:* $575 per credit hour. *Part-time fees:* $30 per term part-time. Part-time tuition and fees vary according to class time. *Payment plan:* installment. *Waivers:* employees or children of employees.

Library Hiram College Library. *Operations spending 1999–2000:* $725,289. *Collection:* 177,282 titles, 908 serial subscriptions, 9,162 audiovisual materials.

Ohio

College life *Housing:* on-campus residence required in freshman year. *Options:* coed, women-only, disabled students. *Social organizations:* vegetarian co-op. *Most popular organizations:* Student Senate, African American Students United, college choir, American Institute of Biological Sciences (AIBS), Organization of Hiram Co-Ops.

Campus security 24-hour emergency response devices and patrols, late-night transport-escort service, controlled dormitory access.

After graduation 24 organizations recruited on campus 1997–98. 53% of class of 1998 had job offers within 6 months. *Career center:* 2 full-time personnel. Services include job fairs, resume preparation, interview workshops, resume referral, career/interest testing, career counseling, careers library, job bank, job interviews.

Freshmen 760 applied, 654 admitted, 286 enrolled. 13 valedictorians.

Average high school GPA	3.4	SAT verbal scores above 500	76%
SAT math scores above 500	73%	ACT above 18	95%
From top 10% of their h.s. class	32%	From top quarter	59%
From top half	87%	1998 freshmen returning in 1999	81%

Application *Options:* eApply at www.CollegeQuest.com, Common Application, electronic application, early admission, deferred entrance. *Application fee:* $25. *Required:* essay or personal statement; high school transcript; 2 letters of recommendation. *Required for some:* interview. *Recommended:* 3 letters of recommendation; interview.

Standardized tests *Admission: Required:* SAT I or ACT.

Significant dates *Application deadlines:* 3/15 (freshmen), 7/15 (transfers). *Financial aid deadline priority date:* 2/15.

Freshman Application Contact
Mr. Monty L. Curtis, Vice President for Admission and College Relations, Hiram College, Box 96, Hiram, OH 44234-0067. **Phone:** 330-569-5169. **Toll-free phone:** 800-362-5280. **Fax:** 330-569-5944. **E-mail:** admission@hiram.edu

Visit CollegeQuest.com for information on majors offered and athletics. College video available at CollegeQuest.com.

■ *See page 1792 for a narrative description.*

JOHN CARROLL UNIVERSITY
University Heights, Ohio

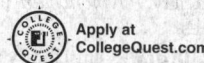 Apply at CollegeQuest.com

- **Independent Roman Catholic (Jesuit)**, comprehensive, founded 1886
- **Degrees** bachelor's and master's
- **Suburban** 60-acre campus with easy access to Cleveland
- **Coed**, 3,442 undergraduate students, 96% full-time, 53% women, 47% men
- **Moderately difficult** entrance level, 88% of applicants were admitted
- **74% graduate** in 6 years or less
- **$16,384 tuition** and fees
- **$13,230 average financial aid** package, $12,695 average indebtedness upon graduation, $131.5 million endowment

From the east side of Cleveland to the Far East, in fall 1998, John Carroll University implemented an undergraduate study program with the Beijing Institute of Language and Culture in Beijing, China. This program offers an exceptional opportunity for students to study in the largest country in the world and gain exposure to its rich cultural heritage.

Students *Undergraduates:* 3,292 full-time, 150 part-time. Students come from 34 states and territories, 17 other countries. *The most frequently chosen baccalaureate fields are:* business/marketing, communications/communication technologies, social sciences and history. *Graduate:* 862 in graduate degree programs.

From out-of-state	27%
Age 25 or older	2%
International students	0.1%
Asian Americans/Pacific Islanders	3%
Native Americans	0.2%
Reside on campus	59%
Transferred in	4%
African Americans	4%
Hispanic Americans	2%

Faculty 410 (57% full-time).

Expenses (2000–2001) *Comprehensive fee:* $22,512 includes full-time tuition ($16,334), mandatory fees ($50), and room and board ($6128). *College room only:* $3310. Room and board charges vary according to board plan.

Part-time tuition: $492 per credit hour. Part-time tuition and fees vary according to course load. *Payment plan:* installment. *Waivers:* employees or children of employees.

Library Grasselli Library. *Operations spending 1999–2000:* $2.4 million. *Collection:* 606,000 titles, 1,859 serial subscriptions, 8,228 audiovisual materials.

College life *Housing:* on-campus residence required in freshman year. *Options:* coed, men-only, women-only. *Social organizations:* local fraternities, local sororities; 32% of eligible men and 35% of eligible women are members. *Most popular organizations:* Volunteer Service Organization, Student Union, Carroll News, band, University Concert Choir.

Campus security 24-hour emergency response devices and patrols, late-night transport-escort service.

After graduation 280 organizations recruited on campus 1997–98. 64% of class of 1998 had job offers within 6 months. *Career center:* 6 full-time, 4 part-time personnel. Services include job fairs, resume preparation, resume referral, career counseling, careers library, job bank, job interviews. *Graduate education:* 27% of class of 1999 went directly to graduate and professional school: 19% graduate arts and sciences, 4% law, 2% medicine, 1% business, 1% dentistry, 1% education. *Major awards:* 1 Fulbright Scholar.

Freshmen 2,612 applied, 2,295 admitted, 834 enrolled. 10 National Merit Scholars, 34 valedictorians.

Average high school GPA	3.27	SAT verbal scores above 500	82%
SAT math scores above 500	83%	ACT above 18	96%
From top 10% of their h.s. class	26%	From top quarter	58%
From top half	88%	1998 freshmen returning in 1999	88%

Application *Options:* eApply at www.CollegeQuest.com, early admission, deferred entrance. *Application fee:* $25. *Required:* high school transcript; 1 letter of recommendation. *Required for some:* interview. *Recommended:* essay or personal statement; interview.

Standardized tests *Admission: Required:* SAT I or ACT. *Recommended:* SAT II Subject Tests.

Significant dates *Application deadlines:* 2/1 (freshmen), rolling (transfers). *Financial aid deadline priority date:* 3/1.

Freshman Application Contact
Mr. Thomas P. Fanning, Director of Admission, John Carroll University, 20700 North Park Boulevard, University Heights, OH 44118-4581. **Phone:** 216-397-4294. **Fax:** 216-397-3098. **E-mail:** admission@jcu.edu

Visit CollegeQuest.com for information on majors offered and athletics. College video available at CollegeQuest.com.

■ *See page 1844 for a narrative description.*

KENT STATE UNIVERSITY
Kent, Ohio

 Apply at CollegeQuest.com

- **State-supported**, university, founded 1910
- **Degrees** associate, bachelor's, master's, and doctoral
- **Small-town** 1,200-acre campus with easy access to Cleveland
- **Coed**, 17,275 undergraduate students, 83% full-time, 59% women, 41% men
- **Moderately difficult** entrance level, 92% of applicants were admitted
- **19:1 student-to-undergraduate faculty ratio**
- **42.3% graduate** in 6 years or less
- **$6016 tuition** and fees (in-state); $10,920 (out-of-state)
- **$5604 average financial aid** package, $16,666 average indebtedness upon graduation, $41.8 million endowment

Part of Kent State University System.

Students *Undergraduates:* 14,275 full-time, 3,000 part-time. Students come from 47 states and territories, 42 other countries. *The most frequently chosen baccalaureate fields are:* business/marketing, education, health professions and related sciences. *Graduate:* 4,378 in graduate degree programs.

From out-of-state	5%
Age 25 or older	16%
International students	1%
Asian Americans/Pacific Islanders	1%
Native Americans	0.2%
Reside on campus	31%
Transferred in	5%
African Americans	8%
Hispanic Americans	1%

Faculty 1,128 (55% full-time).

Expenses (1999–2000) *Tuition, state resident:* full-time $5014; part-time $228 per hour. *Tuition, nonresident:* full-time $9918; part-time $451 per hour.

Ohio

Kent State University *(continued)*

Required fees: full-time $1002. Full-time tuition and fees vary according to course load and program. Part-time tuition and fees vary according to course load and program. *College room and board:* $4530. Room and board charges vary according to board plan and housing facility. *Payment plan:* installment. *Waivers:* employees or children of employees.

Library Kent Library plus 5 others. *Operations spending 1999–2000:* $8.6 million. *Collection:* 3 million titles, 10,310 serial subscriptions, 38,614 audiovisual materials.

College life *Housing:* on-campus residence required through sophomore year. *Options:* coed, men-only, women-only. *Social organizations:* national fraternities, national sororities, local sororities; 7% of eligible men and 5% of eligible women are members. *Most popular organizations:* Kent Student Education Association, Black United Students, May 4th Task Force, Student Recreation Council, Late Night Christian Fellowship.

Campus security 24-hour emergency response devices, late-night transport-escort service, controlled dormitory access, on campus police and fire department.

After graduation 350 organizations recruited on campus 1997–98. *Career center:* 15 full-time, 2 part-time personnel. Services include job fairs, resume preparation, resume referral, career counseling, careers library, job bank, job interviews. *Graduate education:* 20% of class of 1999 went directly to graduate and professional school.

Freshmen 8,594 applied, 7,946 admitted, 3,820 enrolled. 19 valedictorians.

Average high school GPA	2.99	SAT verbal scores above 500	55%
SAT math scores above 500	51%	ACT above 18	83%
From top 10% of their h.s. class	10%	From top quarter	31%
From top half	66%	1998 freshmen returning in 1999	72%

Application *Options:* eApply at www.CollegeQuest.com, electronic application, early admission. *Application fee:* $30. *Required:* high school transcript; minimum 2.5 GPA; rank in upper 50% of high school class for nonresidents.

Standardized tests *Admission: Recommended:* SAT I or ACT. *Required for some:* SAT I or ACT.

Significant dates *Application deadlines:* 3/15 (freshmen), 7/1 (transfers). *Financial aid deadline priority date:* 3/1.

Freshman Application Contact
Mr. Christopher Buttenschon, Assistant Director of Admissions, Kent State University, 161 Michael Schwartz Center, Kent, OH 44242-0001. **Phone:** 330-672-2444. **Toll-free phone:** 800-988-KENT. **Fax:** 330-672-2499. **E-mail:** kentadm@admissions.kent.edu

Visit CollegeQuest.com for information on majors offered and athletics. College video and electronic viewbook available at CollegeQuest.com.

■ *See page 1870 for a narrative description.*

KENT STATE UNIVERSITY, GEAUGA CAMPUS
Burton, Ohio

- **State-supported**, primarily 2-year, founded 1964
- **Degrees** associate and bachelor's
- **Rural** 87-acre campus with easy access to Cleveland
- **Coed**, 526 undergraduate students, 33% full-time, 55% women, 45% men
- **Noncompetitive** entrance level

Part of Kent State University System.
Faculty 51 (16% full-time).
Admissions Office Contact
Kent State University, Geauga Campus, 14111 Claridon-Troy Road, Burton, OH 44021-9500. **Fax:** 440-834-0919. **E-mail:** cbaker@geauga.kent.edu
Visit CollegeQuest.com for information on majors offered and athletics.

KENT STATE UNIVERSITY, STARK CAMPUS
Canton, Ohio

- **State-supported**, primarily 2-year, founded 1967
- **Degrees** associate and bachelor's (also offers some graduate courses)
- **Suburban** 200-acre campus with easy access to Cleveland
- **Coed**, 2,756 undergraduate students
- **Noncompetitive** entrance level

Part of Kent State University System.
Faculty 170 (38% full-time).
Admissions Office Contact
Kent State University, Stark Campus, 6000 Frank Avenue, NW, Canton, OH 44720-7599. **Fax:** 330-494-6121. **E-mail:** ksuinfo@stark.kent.edu
Visit CollegeQuest.com for information on majors offered and athletics.

KENYON COLLEGE
Gambier, Ohio

Apply at CollegeQuest.com

- **Independent**, 4-year, founded 1824
- **Degree** bachelor's
- **Rural** 800-acre campus with easy access to Columbus
- **Coed**, 1,572 undergraduate students, 99% full-time, 56% women, 44% men
- **Very difficult** entrance level, 68% of applicants were admitted
- **11:1 student-to-undergraduate faculty ratio**
- **82.3% graduate** in 6 years or less
- **$24,590 tuition** and fees
- **$18,626 average financial aid** package, $16,650 average indebtedness upon graduation, $110.5 million endowment

Students *Undergraduates:* 1,570 full-time, 2 part-time. Students come from 48 states and territories. *The most frequently chosen baccalaureate fields are:* English, psychology, social sciences and history.

From out-of-state	78%	Reside on campus	99%
International students	1%	African Americans	4%
Asian Americans/Pacific Islanders	3%	Hispanic Americans	3%

Faculty 137 (96% full-time), 96% with terminal degrees.

Expenses (1999–2000) *Comprehensive fee:* $28,750 includes full-time tuition ($23,900), mandatory fees ($690), and room and board ($4160). *College room only:* $1820. Room and board charges vary according to housing facility. *Payment plan:* installment. *Waivers:* employees or children of employees.

Library Olin Library plus 1 other. *Operations spending 1999–2000:* $1.6 million. *Collection:* 362,474 titles, 2,590 serial subscriptions.

College life *Housing:* on-campus residence required through senior year. *Options:* coed, women-only, cooperative, disabled students. *Social organizations:* national fraternities, national sororities, local fraternities, local sororities; 37% of eligible men and 3% of eligible women are members. *Most popular organizations:* student radio station, student theater organization, Environmental Committee, choral music groups, outing club.

Campus security 24-hour emergency response devices and patrols, student patrols, late-night transport-escort service.

After graduation 65 organizations recruited on campus 1997–98. 89% of class of 1998 had job offers within 6 months. *Career center:* 2 full-time, 1 part-time personnel. Services include job fairs, resume preparation, interview workshops, resume referral, career/interest testing, career counseling, careers library, job bank, job interviews. *Graduate education:* 25% of class of 1999 went directly to graduate and professional school: 10% graduate arts and sciences, 5% law, 3% medicine, 1% business.

Freshmen 2,420 applied, 1,644 admitted, 459 enrolled. 34 National Merit Scholars, 1 class president, 24 valedictorians, 13 student government officers.

Average high school GPA	3.63	SAT verbal scores above 500	98%
SAT math scores above 500	96%	ACT above 18	100%
From top 10% of their h.s. class	50%	From top quarter	79%
From top half	96%	1998 freshmen returning in 1999	91%

Application *Options:* eApply at www.CollegeQuest.com, Common Application, early admission, early decision, deferred entrance. *Application fee:* $45. *Required:* essay or personal statement; high school transcript; minimum 2.0 GPA; 1 letter of recommendation. *Recommended:* minimum 3.0 GPA; interview.

Standardized tests *Admission: Required:* SAT I or ACT.

Significant dates *Application deadlines:* 2/1 (freshmen), 4/1 (transfers). *Early decision:* 12/1 (for plan 1), 2/1 (for plan 2). *Notification:* 4/1 (freshmen), 12/15 (early decision plan 1), 2/15 (early decision plan 2). *Financial aid deadline:* 2/15.

Ohio

Freshman Application Contact
Mr. John W. Anderson, Dean of Admissions, Kenyon College, Office of Admissions, Gambier, OH 43022-9623. **Phone:** 740-427-5776. **Toll-free phone:** 800-848-2468. **Fax:** 740-427-2634. **E-mail:** admissions@kenyon.edu
Visit CollegeQuest.com for information on majors offered and athletics. College video and electronic viewbook available at CollegeQuest.com.

KETTERING COLLEGE OF MEDICAL ARTS
Kettering, Ohio

- **Independent Seventh-day Adventist**, primarily 2-year, founded 1967
- **Degrees** associate and bachelor's
- **Suburban** 35-acre campus
- **Coed**, 517 undergraduate students, 59% full-time, 75% women, 25% men
- **Moderately difficult** entrance level

Faculty 44 (52% full-time).
Admissions Office Contact
Kettering College of Medical Arts, 3737 Southern Boulevard, Kettering, OH 45429-1299. **Toll-free phone:** 800-433-5262. **Fax:** 937-297-8106.
Visit CollegeQuest.com for information on majors offered and athletics.

LAKE ERIE COLLEGE
Painesville, Ohio

- **Independent**, comprehensive, founded 1856
- **Degrees** bachelor's and master's
- **Small-town** 57-acre campus with easy access to Cleveland
- **Coed**, 509 undergraduate students
- **Moderately difficult** entrance level, 88% of applicants were admitted
- **12:1 student-to-undergraduate faculty ratio**
- **$15,140 tuition** and fees
- **$9.1 million endowment**

Students *Undergraduates:* Students come from 23 states and territories.

From out-of-state	15%	Reside on campus	40%
Age 25 or older	43%	International students	0.4%
African Americans	4%	Asian Americans/Pacific Islanders	1%
Hispanic Americans	2%	Native Americans	0.2%

Expenses (1999–2000) *Comprehensive fee:* $20,400 includes full-time tuition ($14,280), mandatory fees ($860), and room and board ($5260). *College room only:* $2820. Room and board charges vary according to board plan. *Payment plan:* installment. *Waivers:* senior citizens and employees or children of employees.
Library Lincoln Library plus 2 others. *Operations spending 1999–2000:* $185,219. *Collection:* 85,978 titles, 767 serial subscriptions.
College life *Housing:* on-campus residence required through senior year. *Options:* coed, men-only, women-only. *Most popular organizations:* riding club, Student Government Association, Mortar Board, Pre-Veterinary Medicine Association, Activities Council.
Campus security 24-hour emergency response devices and patrols, late-night transport-escort service.
After graduation *Career center:* 1 full-time personnel. Services include resume preparation, interview workshops, career/interest testing, career counseling, careers library, job bank, job interviews.
Freshmen 457 applied, 401 admitted.

Average high school GPA	3.2	SAT verbal scores above 500	67%
SAT math scores above 500	64%	ACT above 18	88%
From top 10% of their h.s. class	27%	From top quarter	49%
From top half	76%	1998 freshmen returning in 1999	70%

Application *Options:* eApply at www.CollegeQuest.com, early admission, deferred entrance. *Application fee:* $25. *Required:* high school transcript; minimum 2.5 GPA; 1 letter of recommendation. *Required for some:* interview. *Recommended:* interview.
Standardized tests *Admission: Recommended:* SAT I or ACT.
Significant dates *Application deadlines:* 8/1 (freshmen), 8/20 (transfers). *Financial aid deadline:* continuous.

Freshman Application Contact
Ms. Mary Ann Naso, Vice President and Dean of College Services, Lake Erie College, 391 West Washington Street, Painesville, OH 44077-3389. **Phone:** 440-639-7879. **Toll-free phone:** 800-916-0904. **Fax:** 440-352-3533. **E-mail:** lecadmit@lakeerie.edu
Visit CollegeQuest.com for information on majors offered and athletics.

■ *See page 1890 for a narrative description.*

LOURDES COLLEGE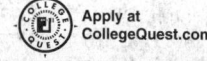
Sylvania, Ohio

- **Independent Roman Catholic**, 4-year, founded 1958
- **Degrees** associate and bachelor's
- **Suburban** 90-acre campus with easy access to Toledo
- **Coed**, 1,046 undergraduate students, 36% full-time, 83% women, 17% men
- **Moderately difficult** entrance level, 47% of applicants were admitted
- **12:1 student-to-undergraduate faculty ratio**
- **36% graduate** in 6 years or less
- **$9368 tuition** and fees

Students *Undergraduates:* 381 full-time, 665 part-time. Students come from 3 states and territories, 4 other countries. *The most frequently chosen baccalaureate fields are:* business/marketing, health professions and related sciences, home economics/vocational home economics.

From out-of-state	8%	Age 25 or older	70%
Transferred in	18%	African Americans	9%
Hispanic Americans	1%	Native Americans	1%

Faculty 104 (63% full-time), 17% with terminal degrees.
Expenses (1999–2000) *Tuition:* full-time $8768; part-time $274 per credit hour. *Required fees:* full-time $600; $25 per credit hour. Full-time tuition and fees vary according to course load and program. Part-time tuition and fees vary according to course load and program. *Payment plans:* installment, deferred payment. *Waivers:* senior citizens and employees or children of employees.
Library Duns Scotus Library plus 1 other. *Collection:* 56,948 titles, 430 serial subscriptions, 1,770 audiovisual materials.
College life *Housing:* college housing not available. *Social organizations:* local sororities; 2% of women are members. *Most popular organizations:* Alpha Kappa Psi, Student Leader Advisory Council, Lourdes College Chorus, Student Nurse Association, Occupational Therapy Club.
Campus security 24-hour emergency response devices, late-night transport-escort service, evening patrols by trained security personnel.
After graduation 125 organizations recruited on campus 1997–98. *Career center:* 1 full-time personnel. Services include job fairs, resume preparation, career counseling, careers library, job bank. *Graduate education:* 24% of class of 1999 went directly to graduate and professional school.
Freshmen 139 applied, 66 admitted, 81 enrolled.

Average high school GPA	2.75	SAT verbal scores above 500	N/R
SAT math scores above 500	N/R	ACT above 18	74%

Application *Options:* eApply at www.CollegeQuest.com, Common Application, early admission, deferred entrance. *Application fee:* $30. *Required:* essay or personal statement; high school transcript; minimum 2.0 GPA. *Required for some:* interview.
Standardized tests *Admission: Required:* SAT I or ACT.
Significant dates *Application deadlines:* rolling (freshmen), rolling (transfers). *Financial aid deadline priority date:* 3/1.
Freshman Application Contact
Ms. Beth Csortos, Director of Admissions, Lourdes College, 6832 Convent Boulevard, Sylvania, OH 43560. **Phone:** 419-885-5291 Ext. 299. **Toll-free phone:** 800-878-3210. **Fax:** 419-882-3987. **E-mail:** btanesky@lourdes.edu
Visit CollegeQuest.com for information on majors offered and athletics.

MALONE COLLEGE
Canton, Ohio

- **Independent**, comprehensive, founded 1892, affiliated with Evangelical Friends Church–Eastern Region

Peterson's Guide to Four-Year Colleges 2001   www.petersons.com   635

Ohio

Malone College (continued)
- **Degrees** bachelor's, master's, and postbachelor's certificates
- **Suburban** 78-acre campus with easy access to Cleveland
- **Coed**, 1,877 undergraduate students, 92% full-time, 61% women, 39% men
- **Moderately difficult** entrance level, 88% of applicants were admitted
- **15:1 student-to-undergraduate faculty ratio**
- **49% graduate** in 6 years or less
- **$12,380 tuition** and fees
- **$10,082 average financial aid** package, $15,114 average indebtedness upon graduation, $5 million endowment

Malone College is a Christian college for the arts, sciences, and professions. It is committed to offering an education of the highest quality in a setting that encourages a solid devotion to God. The combination of strong academics, great location, and spiritual development make Malone an attractive and challenging opportunity for students.

Students *Undergraduates:* 1,730 full-time, 147 part-time. Students come from 20 states and territories, 6 other countries. *The most frequently chosen baccalaureate fields are:* business/marketing, education, health professions and related sciences. *Graduate:* 244 in graduate degree programs.

From out-of-state	9%	Reside on campus	45%
Age 25 or older	23%	Transferred in	3%
International students	1%	African Americans	5%
Asian Americans/Pacific Islanders	0.3%	Hispanic Americans	1%
Native Americans	0.2%		

Faculty 189 (52% full-time), 38% with terminal degrees.
Expenses (1999–2000) *Comprehensive fee:* $17,630 includes full-time tuition ($12,150), mandatory fees ($230), and room and board ($5250). *College room only:* $2940. Room and board charges vary according to board plan. *Part-time tuition:* $305 per semester hour. *Part-time fees:* $58 per term part-time. Part-time tuition and fees vary according to course load. *Payment plan:* installment. *Waivers:* senior citizens and employees or children of employees.
Library Everett L. Cattell Library. *Operations spending 1999–2000:* $668,730. *Collection:* 107,484 titles, 1,658 serial subscriptions, 9,690 audiovisual materials.
College life *Housing:* on-campus residence required through junior year. *Options:* men-only, women-only. *Most popular organizations:* Spiritual Life Committee, student activities committee, student senate, Woolman-Whittier-Fox hall council, intramural athletics.
Campus security 24-hour emergency response devices and patrols, late-night transport-escort service.
After graduation 23 organizations recruited on campus 1997–98. 80% of class of 1998 had job offers within 6 months. *Career center:* 2 full-time, 1 part-time personnel. Services include job fairs, resume preparation, interview workshops, resume referral, career/interest testing, career counseling, careers library, job bank, job interviews. *Graduate education:* 21% of class of 1999 went directly to graduate and professional school: 8% business, 5% education, 2% graduate arts and sciences, 2% law, 1% medicine, 1% theology.
Freshmen 899 applied, 795 admitted, 409 enrolled. 1 National Merit Scholar, 9 valedictorians.

Average high school GPA	3.28	SAT verbal scores above 500	66%
SAT math scores above 500	64%	ACT above 18	96%
From top 10% of their h.s. class	23%	From top quarter	53%
From top half	81%	1998 freshmen returning in 1999	74%

Application *Options:* eApply at www.CollegeQuest.com, Common Application, electronic application, early admission, deferred entrance. *Application fee:* $20. *Required:* essay or personal statement; high school transcript; minimum 2.5 GPA. *Required for some:* interview.
Standardized tests *Admission: Required:* SAT I or ACT.
Significant dates *Application deadlines:* 7/1 (freshmen), 7/1 (transfers). *Notification:* continuous until 7/30 (freshmen). *Financial aid deadline priority date:* 3/1.
Freshman Application Contact
Mr. John Chopka, Dean of Admissions, Malone College, 515 25th Street, NW, Canton, OH 44709-3897. **Phone:** 330-471-8145. **Toll-free phone:** 800-521-1146. **Fax:** 330-454-6977. **E-mail:** admissions@malone.edu
Visit CollegeQuest.com for information on majors offered and athletics. College video available at CollegeQuest.com.

■ *See page 1972 for a narrative description.*

MARIETTA COLLEGE
Marietta, Ohio

Apply at CollegeQuest.com

- **Independent**, comprehensive, founded 1835
- **Degrees** associate, bachelor's, and master's
- **Small-town** 120-acre campus
- **Coed**, 1,133 undergraduate students, 91% full-time, 51% women, 49% men
- **Moderately difficult** entrance level, 92% of applicants were admitted
- **12:1 student-to-undergraduate faculty ratio**
- **54.1% graduate** in 6 years or less
- **$17,510 tuition** and fees
- **$15,800 average financial aid** package, $16,077 average indebtedness upon graduation, $56 million endowment

Students *Undergraduates:* 1,029 full-time, 104 part-time. Students come from 35 states and territories, 11 other countries. *The most frequently chosen baccalaureate fields are:* business/marketing, education, social sciences and history. *Graduate:* 61 in graduate degree programs.

From out-of-state	50%	Reside on campus	85%
Age 25 or older	4%	Transferred in	6%
International students	6%	African Americans	3%
Asian Americans/Pacific Islanders	1%	Hispanic Americans	1%
Native Americans	1%		

Faculty 115 (65% full-time), 59% with terminal degrees.
Expenses (1999–2000) *Comprehensive fee:* $22,480 includes full-time tuition ($17,310), mandatory fees ($200), and room and board ($4970). *College room only:* $2680. *Part-time tuition:* $575 per credit hour. Part-time tuition and fees vary according to class time. *Payment plan:* installment. *Waivers:* employees or children of employees.
Library Dawes Memorial Library. *Operations spending 1999–2000:* $647,737. *Collection:* 146,970 titles, 1,500 serial subscriptions, 7,100 audiovisual materials.
College life *Housing:* on-campus residence required through senior year. *Options:* coed, men-only, women-only. *Social organizations:* national fraternities, national sororities, local sororities; 20% of eligible men and 22% of eligible women are members. *Most popular organizations:* campus newspaper, student government, Great Outdoors Club, Inter-Varsity Christian Fellowship, International Student Organization.
Campus security 24-hour emergency response devices and patrols, student patrols, late-night transport-escort service, controlled dormitory access.
After graduation 23 organizations recruited on campus 1997–98. 77% of class of 1998 had job offers within 6 months. *Career center:* 3 full-time personnel. Services include job fairs, resume preparation, interview workshops, resume referral, career/interest testing, career counseling, careers library, job interviews. *Graduate education:* 22% of class of 1999 went directly to graduate and professional school.
Freshmen 1,065 applied, 978 admitted, 302 enrolled.

Average high school GPA	3.2	SAT verbal scores above 500	66%
SAT math scores above 500	62%	ACT above 18	91%
From top 10% of their h.s. class	24%	From top quarter	50%
From top half	79%	1998 freshmen returning in 1999	69%

Application *Options:* eApply at www.CollegeQuest.com, Common Application, electronic application, early admission, deferred entrance. *Application fee:* $25. *Required:* essay or personal statement; high school transcript; minimum 2.0 GPA; 2 letters of recommendation. *Recommended:* minimum 3.0 GPA; interview.
Standardized tests *Admission: Required:* SAT I or ACT. *Recommended:* SAT II Subject Tests.
Significant dates *Application deadlines:* 4/15 (freshmen), rolling (transfers). *Notification:* continuous until 5/1 (freshmen). *Financial aid deadline priority date:* 3/1.
Freshman Application Contact
Ms. Marke Vickers, Director of Admission, Marietta College, 215 Fifth Street, Marietta, OH 45750-4000. **Phone:** 740-376-4600. **Toll-free phone:** 800-331-7896. **Fax:** 740-376-4896. **E-mail:** admit@marietta.edu
Visit CollegeQuest.com for information on majors offered and athletics. College video and electronic viewbook available at CollegeQuest.com.

Ohio

THE MCGREGOR SCHOOL OF ANTIOCH UNIVERSITY
Yellow Springs, Ohio

- **Independent**, upper-level, founded 1988
- **Degrees** bachelor's and master's
- **Small-town** 100-acre campus with easy access to Dayton
- **Coed**
- **Noncompetitive** entrance level
- **$10,176 tuition** and fees

Part of Antioch University.
Expenses (1999–2000) *Tuition:* full-time $10,176; part-time $212 per credit. Full-time tuition and fees vary according to course load. Part-time tuition and fees vary according to course load.
Institutional Web site http://www.mcgregor.edu/
College life *Housing:* college housing not available.
Campus security 24-hour emergency response devices and patrols.
Application *Option:* deferred entrance. *Application fee:* $45.
Admissions Office Contact
The McGregor School of Antioch University, 800 Livermore Street, Yellow Springs, OH 45387-1609. **Fax:** 937-767-6461. **E-mail:** admiss@mcgregor.edu
Visit CollegeQuest.com for information on athletics. College video and electronic viewbook available at CollegeQuest.com.

MIAMI UNIVERSITY
Oxford, Ohio

- **State-related**, university, founded 1809
- **Degrees** bachelor's, master's, doctoral, and post-master's certificates
- **Small-town** 2,000-acre campus with easy access to Cincinnati
- **Coed**, 15,169 undergraduate students, 94% full-time, 55% women, 45% men
- **Moderately difficult** entrance level, 79% of applicants were admitted
- **18:1** student-to-undergraduate faculty ratio
- **80.4% graduate** in 6 years or less
- **$6112 tuition** and fees (in-state); $12,766 (out-of-state)
- **$5889 average financial aid** package, $16,710 average indebtedness upon graduation, $215.1 million endowment

Part of Miami University System.
Students *Undergraduates:* 14,332 full-time, 837 part-time. Students come from 49 states and territories, 70 other countries. *The most frequently chosen baccalaureate fields are:* business/marketing, education, social sciences and history. *Graduate:* 1,287 in graduate degree programs.

From out-of-state	27%	Reside on campus	45%
Age 25 or older	3%	Transferred in	2%
International students	0.5%	African Americans	4%
Asian Americans/Pacific Islanders	2%	Hispanic Americans	2%
Native Americans	0.4%		

Faculty 1,146 (67% full-time), 66% with terminal degrees.
Expenses (1999–2000) *Tuition, state resident:* full-time $5052; part-time $210 per credit hour. *Tuition, nonresident:* full-time $11,706; part-time $488 per credit hour. *Required fees:* full-time $1060; $44 per credit hour; $18 per term part-time. Full-time tuition and fees vary according to course load. Part-time tuition and fees vary according to course load. *College room and board:* $5330; room only: $2530. Room and board charges vary according to board plan and housing facility. *Payment plan:* installment. *Waivers:* employees or children of employees.
Library King Library plus 3 others. *Operations spending 1999–2000:* $9.4 million. *Collection:* 2.2 million titles.
College life *Housing:* on-campus residence required in freshman year. *Options:* coed, men-only, women-only, disabled students. *Social organizations:* national fraternities, national sororities; 24% of eligible men and 27% of eligible women are members. *Most popular organizations:* student government, Alpha Phi Omega, Miami Marketing Enterprises, Greek system, Campus Crusade for Christ.
Campus security 24-hour emergency response devices and patrols, student patrols, late-night transport-escort service, controlled dormitory access.
After graduation 550 organizations recruited on campus 1997–98. *Career center:* 9 full-time, 5 part-time personnel. Services include job fairs, resume preparation, interview workshops, resume referral, career/interest testing, career counseling, careers library, job bank, job interviews. *Major awards:* 1 Marshall scholar.
Freshmen 11,993 applied, 9,425 admitted, 3,605 enrolled. 38 National Merit Scholars, 180 valedictorians, 252 student government officers.

SAT verbal scores above 500	92%	SAT math scores above 500	93%
ACT above 18	99%	From top 10% of their h.s. class	32%
From top quarter	70%	From top half	96%
1998 freshmen returning in 1999	90%		

Application *Options:* electronic application, early decision, early action. *Application fee:* $35. *Required:* high school transcript. *Recommended:* essay or personal statement; 1 letter of recommendation.
Standardized tests *Admission: Required:* SAT I or ACT.
Significant dates *Application deadlines:* 1/31 (freshmen), 5/1 (transfers). *Early decision:* 11/1, 12/1. *Notification:* 3/15 (freshmen), 12/15 (early decision), 2/1 (early action). *Financial aid deadline priority date:* 2/15.
Freshman Application Contact
Dr. James S. McCoy, Associate Vice President for Enrollment Services, Miami University, Oxford, OH 45056. **Phone:** 513-529-2531. **Fax:** 513-529-1550. **E-mail:** admission@muohio.edu
Visit CollegeQuest.com for information on majors offered and athletics. Electronic viewbook available at CollegeQuest.com.

MIAMI UNIVERSITY–HAMILTON CAMPUS
Hamilton, Ohio

- **State-supported**, primarily 2-year, founded 1968
- **Degrees** associate and bachelor's (also offers up to 2 years of most bachelor's degree programs offered at Miami University main campus)
- **Suburban** 78-acre campus with easy access to Cincinnati
- **Coed**, 2,576 undergraduate students
- **Noncompetitive** entrance level

Part of Miami University System.
Faculty 170 (44% full-time).
Admissions Office Contact
Miami University–Hamilton Campus, 1601 Peck Boulevard, Hamilton, OH 45011-3399. **E-mail:** torgevm@muohio.edu
Visit CollegeQuest.com for information on majors offered and athletics.

MIAMI UNIVERSITY–MIDDLETOWN CAMPUS
Middletown, Ohio

- **State-supported**, primarily 2-year, founded 1966
- **Degrees** associate and bachelor's (also offers up to 2 years of most bachelor's degree programs offered at Miami University main campus)
- **Small-town** 141-acre campus with easy access to Cincinnati and Dayton
- **Coed**, 2,423 undergraduate students, 43% full-time, 59% women, 41% men
- **Noncompetitive** entrance level

Part of Miami University System.
Faculty 158 (53% full-time).
Admissions Office Contact
Miami University–Middletown Campus, 4200 East University Boulevard, Middletown, OH 45042-3497. **Toll-free phone:** 800-622-2262. **Fax:** 513-727-3223. **E-mail:** mlflynn@miavx3.mid.muohio.edu
Visit CollegeQuest.com for information on majors offered and athletics.

MOUNT CARMEL COLLEGE OF NURSING
Columbus, Ohio

Admissions Office Contact
Mount Carmel College of Nursing, 127 South Davis Avenue, Columbus, OH 43222.

Ohio

MOUNT UNION COLLEGE
Alliance, Ohio

- **Independent United Methodist**, 4-year, founded 1846
- **Degree** bachelor's
- **Suburban** 105-acre campus with easy access to Cleveland
- **Coed**, 2,115 undergraduate students, 96% full-time, 53% women, 47% men
- **Moderately difficult** entrance level, 90% of applicants were admitted
- **18:1 student-to-undergraduate faculty ratio**
- **57.9% graduate** in 6 years or less
- **$14,880 tuition** and fees
- **$12,720 average financial aid** package, $15,601 average indebtedness upon graduation, $113 million endowment

There are numerous international education opportunities at Mount Union College. In addition to the cultural interaction with students from about 20 countries who study at the College, many students take advantage of the study-abroad program. The College makes grants available for study overseas, regardless of the student's major.

Students *Undergraduates:* 2,031 full-time, 84 part-time. Students come from 19 states and territories, 15 other countries. *The most frequently chosen baccalaureate fields are:* business/marketing, education, parks and recreation.

From out-of-state	12%	Reside on campus	78%
Age 25 or older	1%	Transferred in	2%
International students	2%	African Americans	4%
Asian Americans/Pacific Islanders	1%	Hispanic Americans	1%
Native Americans	0.3%		

Faculty 186 (60% full-time), 54% with terminal degrees.
Expenses (1999–2000) *Comprehensive fee:* $19,250 includes full-time tuition ($14,080), mandatory fees ($800), and room and board ($4370). *College room only:* $1750. Room and board charges vary according to housing facility. *Part-time tuition:* $595 per semester hour. *Payment plans:* tuition prepayment, installment. *Waivers:* children of alumni, adult students, senior citizens, and employees or children of employees.
Library Mount Union College Library plus 2 others. *Operations spending 1999–2000:* $1.1 million. *Collection:* 223,980 titles, 921 serial subscriptions, 400 audiovisual materials.
College life *Housing:* on-campus residence required through sophomore year. *Options:* coed, men-only, women-only, disabled students. *Social organizations:* national fraternities, national sororities, local sororities; 28% of eligible men and 32% of eligible women are members. *Most popular organizations:* Association of Women Students, Student Senate, Black Student Union, Student Activities Council, Association of International Students.
Campus security 24-hour emergency response devices and patrols, controlled dormitory access, 24-hour locked residence hall entrances, outside phones.
After graduation 40 organizations recruited on campus 1997–98. 94% of class of 1998 had job offers within 6 months. *Career center:* 2 full-time personnel. Services include job fairs, resume preparation, interview workshops, resume referral, career/interest testing, career counseling, careers library, job interviews, online resume. *Graduate education:* 25% of class of 1999 went directly to graduate and professional school.
Freshmen 1,901 applied, 1,705 admitted, 661 enrolled. 15 valedictorians.

SAT verbal scores above 500	N/R	SAT math scores above 500	N/R
ACT above 18	93%	From top 10% of their h.s. class	26%
From top quarter	65%	From top half	93%
1998 freshmen returning in 1999	83%		

Application *Options:* electronic application, early admission, deferred entrance. *Application fee:* $1.50. *Required:* essay or personal statement; high school transcript; minimum 2.0 GPA; 1 letter of recommendation. *Recommended:* interview.
Standardized tests *Admission: Required:* SAT I or ACT.
Significant dates *Application deadlines:* rolling (freshmen), rolling (transfers). *Financial aid deadline:* continuous.
Freshman Application Contact
Mr. Greg King, Director of Admissions and Enrollment Management, Mount Union College, 1972 Clark Avenue, Alliance, OH 44601. **Phone:** 330-823-2590. **Toll-free phone:** 800-334-6682 (in-state); 800-992-6682 (out-of-state). **Fax:** 330-821-0425. **E-mail:** admissn@muc.edu

---

Visit CollegeQuest.com for information on majors offered and athletics. College video and electronic viewbook available at CollegeQuest.com.

- *See page 2126 for a narrative description.*

MOUNT VERNON NAZARENE COLLEGE
Mount Vernon, Ohio

Apply at CollegeQuest.com

- **Independent Nazarene**, comprehensive, founded 1964
- **Degrees** associate, bachelor's, and master's
- **Small-town** 210-acre campus with easy access to Columbus
- **Coed**, 1,798 undergraduate students, 96% full-time, 57% women, 43% men
- **Moderately difficult** entrance level, 89% of applicants were admitted
- **17:1 student-to-undergraduate faculty ratio**
- **$11,926 tuition** and fees
- **$5823 average financial aid** package, $16,253 average indebtedness upon graduation, $7.2 million endowment

Students *Undergraduates:* 1,729 full-time, 69 part-time. Students come from 26 states and territories. *The most frequently chosen baccalaureate fields are:* business/marketing, biological/life sciences, education. *Graduate:* 73 in graduate degree programs.

From out-of-state	17%	Age 25 or older	6%
Transferred in	4%	International students	0.1%
African Americans	1%	Asian Americans/Pacific Islanders	1%
Hispanic Americans	1%	Native Americans	0.2%

Faculty 150 (46% full-time).
Expenses (2000–2001) *Comprehensive fee:* $16,129 includes full-time tuition ($11,468), mandatory fees ($458), and room and board ($4203). *College room only:* $2385. *Part-time tuition:* $410 per credit hour. *Part-time fees:* $14 per credit hour. *Payment plan:* installment. *Waivers:* employees or children of employees.
Library Thorne Library/Learning Resource Center. *Operations spending 1999–2000:* $507,854. *Collection:* 90,045 titles, 560 serial subscriptions, 5,989 audiovisual materials.
College life *Housing:* on-campus residence required through senior year. *Options:* men-only, women-only, disabled students. *Most popular organizations:* Campus Ministry groups, Student Government Association, Student Education Association, drama club, Music Department Ensembles.
Campus security 24-hour emergency response devices and patrols, late-night transport-escort service, controlled dormitory access.
After graduation 28 organizations recruited on campus 1997–98. 73% of class of 1998 had job offers within 6 months. *Career center:* 1 full-time, 1 part-time personnel. Services include job fairs, resume preparation, resume referral, career/interest testing, career counseling, careers library, job bank, job interviews.
Freshmen 708 applied, 627 admitted, 396 enrolled. 1 National Merit Scholar, 13 valedictorians.

Average high school GPA	3.19	SAT verbal scores above 500	N/R
SAT math scores above 500	N/R	ACT above 18	90%
From top 10% of their h.s. class	18%	From top quarter	33%
From top half	53%	1998 freshmen returning in 1999	75%

Application *Options:* eApply at www.CollegeQuest.com, electronic application, early admission, deferred entrance. *Application fee:* $25. *Required:* essay or personal statement; high school transcript; minimum 2.5 GPA; 2 letters of recommendation. *Recommended:* interview.
Standardized tests *Admission: Required:* ACT.
Significant dates *Application deadlines:* 5/30 (freshmen), 5/30 (transfers). *Notification:* continuous until 8/1 (freshmen). *Financial aid deadline priority date:* 3/13.
Freshman Application Contact
Rev. Ron Fox, Director of Admissions and Student Recruitment, Mount Vernon Nazarene College, 800 Martinsburg Road, Mount Vernon, OH 43050-9500. **Phone:** 740-397-6862 Ext. 4510. **Toll-free phone:** 800-782-2435. **E-mail:** admissions@mvnc.edu
Visit CollegeQuest.com for information on majors offered and athletics.

MUSKINGUM COLLEGE
New Concord, Ohio

 Apply at CollegeQuest.com

- **Independent**, comprehensive, founded 1837, affiliated with Presbyterian Church (U.S.A.)
- **Degrees** bachelor's and master's
- **Small-town** 215-acre campus with easy access to Columbus
- **Coed**, 1,496 undergraduate students, 97% full-time, 52% women, 48% men
- **Moderately difficult** entrance level, 85% of applicants were admitted
- **16:1 student-to-undergraduate faculty ratio**
- **61.3% graduate** in 6 years or less
- **$12,665 tuition** and fees
- **$11,954 average financial aid** package, $14,872 average indebtedness upon graduation, $50.2 million endowment

Students *Undergraduates:* 1,457 full-time, 39 part-time. Students come from 26 states and territories, 13 other countries. *The most frequently chosen baccalaureate fields are:* business/marketing, education, social sciences and history. *Graduate:* 309 in graduate degree programs.

From out-of-state	13%	Reside on campus	90%
Age 25 or older	4%	Transferred in	4%
International students	4%	African Americans	2%
Asian Americans/Pacific Islanders	0.2%	Hispanic Americans	1%
Native Americans	0.3%		

Faculty 113 (77% full-time).

Expenses (2000–2001) *One-time required fee:* 125. *Comprehensive fee:* 17,765 includes full-time tuition (12,250), mandatory fees (415), and room and board (5100). *College room only:* 2500. Room and board charges vary according to board plan and housing facility. *Part-time tuition:* 220 per hour. Part-time tuition and fees vary according to course load. *Payment plan:* installment. *Waivers:* senior citizens and employees or children of employees.

Library College Library. *Operations spending 1999–2000:* $451,000. *Collection:* 233,000 titles, 900 serial subscriptions, 6,000 audiovisual materials.

College life *Housing:* on-campus residence required through junior year. *Options:* coed, men-only, women-only. *Social organizations:* national fraternities, national sororities, local fraternities, local sororities; 55% of eligible men and 50% of eligible women are members. *Most popular organizations:* Centerboard, student radio station, BACCHUS, Cable TV 8, Fellowship of Christian Students.

Campus security 24-hour emergency response devices and patrols, student patrols, late-night transport-escort service.

After graduation 16 organizations recruited on campus 1997–98. 80% of class of 1998 had job offers within 6 months. *Career center:* 2 full-time personnel. Services include job fairs, resume preparation, interview workshops, resume referral, career/interest testing, career counseling, careers library, job bank, job interviews. *Graduate education:* 11% of class of 1999 went directly to graduate and professional school.

Freshmen 1,394 applied, 1,187 admitted, 421 enrolled.

Average high school GPA	3.2	SAT verbal scores above 500	69%
SAT math scores above 500	69%	ACT above 18	90%
From top 10% of their h.s. class	26%	From top quarter	53%
From top half	77%	1998 freshmen returning in 1999	76%

Application *Options:* eApply at www.CollegeQuest.com, electronic application, early admission, deferred entrance. *Required:* high school transcript; minimum 2.0 GPA; 1 letter of recommendation. *Recommended:* essay or personal statement; minimum 3.0 GPA; interview.

Standardized tests *Admission: Required:* SAT I or ACT.

Significant dates *Application deadlines:* 6/1 (freshmen), 8/1 (transfers). *Financial aid deadline priority date:* 3/15.

Freshman Application Contact
Mr. Doug Kellar, Director of Admission, Muskingum College, 163 Stormont Street, New Concord, OH 43762. **Phone:** 740-826-8137. **Toll-free phone:** 800-752-6082. **Fax:** 740-826-8404. **E-mail:** adminfo@muskingum.edu

Visit CollegeQuest.com for information on majors offered and athletics.

NORTHWESTERN COLLEGE
Lima, Ohio

- **Independent**, primarily 2-year, founded 1920
- **Degrees** associate and bachelor's
- **Small-town** 35-acre campus with easy access to Dayton and Toledo
- **Coed**, 1,395 undergraduate students, 82% full-time, 38% women, 62% men
- **Noncompetitive** entrance level
- **25:1 student-to-undergraduate faculty ratio**

Admissions Office Contact
- Northwestern College, 1441 North Cable Road, Lima, OH 45805-1498. **Fax:** 419-229-6926. **E-mail:** info@nc.edu

Visit CollegeQuest.com for information on majors offered and athletics. College video available at CollegeQuest.com.

NOTRE DAME COLLEGE OF OHIO
South Euclid, Ohio

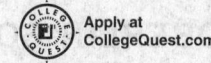 Apply at CollegeQuest.com

- **Independent Roman Catholic**, comprehensive, founded 1922
- **Degrees** associate, bachelor's, and master's
- **Suburban** 53-acre campus with easy access to Cleveland
- **Women** only, 492 undergraduate students, 44% full-time
- **Moderately difficult** entrance level, 55% of applicants were admitted
- **9:1 student-to-undergraduate faculty ratio**
- **48% graduate** in 6 years or less
- **$13,618 tuition** and fees
- **$11,044 average financial aid** package, $15,649 average indebtedness upon graduation, $10.3 million endowment

NDC of Ohio is a special place for women. The focus is on helping women of all ages develop confidence and build self-esteem through a rigorous yet supportive liberal arts environment. NDC of Ohio is large enough to provide many of the opportunities of a large college, yet small enough to give women the individual attention important to their development.

Students *Undergraduates:* 216 full-time, 276 part-time. Students come from 7 states and territories, 1 other country. *The most frequently chosen baccalaureate fields are:* biological/life sciences, business/marketing, communications/communication technologies. *Graduate:* 75 in graduate degree programs.

From out-of-state	2%	Reside on campus	21%
Age 25 or older	75%	Transferred in	14%
International students	1%	African Americans	31%
Asian Americans/Pacific Islanders	1%	Hispanic Americans	1%

Faculty 79 (32% full-time), 91% with terminal degrees.

Expenses (1999–2000) *Comprehensive fee:* $18,866 includes full-time tuition ($13,418), mandatory fees ($200), and room and board ($5248). *College room only:* $2624. Full-time tuition and fees vary according to class time. Room and board charges vary according to board plan. *Part-time tuition:* $338 per credit. Part-time tuition and fees vary according to class time. *Payment plan:* installment. *Waivers:* employees or children of employees.

Library Clara Fritzsche Library. *Operations spending 1999–2000:* $221,806. *Collection:* 9,983 audiovisual materials.

College life *Housing:* on-campus residence required through junior year. *Option:* women-only. *Most popular organizations:* Undergraduate Student Senate, Resident Association Board, Masquers, Commuter Board, gospel choir.

Campus security 24-hour emergency response devices, late-night transport-escort service, controlled dormitory access, residence hall desk attendants.

After graduation 45 organizations recruited on campus 1997–98. *Career center:* 1 full-time personnel. Services include job fairs, resume preparation, resume referral, career/interest testing, career counseling, careers library, job bank, job interviews. *Graduate education:* 7% of class of 1999 went directly to graduate and professional school: 3% graduate arts and sciences, 2% law, 1% business.

Ohio

Notre Dame College of Ohio (continued)

Freshmen 105 applied, 58 admitted, 52 enrolled.

Average high school GPA	3.17	SAT verbal scores above 500	50%
SAT math scores above 500	50%	ACT above 18	88%
From top 10% of their h.s. class	14%	From top quarter	34%
From top half	34%	1998 freshmen returning in 1999	62%

Application *Options:* eApply at www.CollegeQuest.com, deferred entrance. *Application fee:* $30. *Required:* high school transcript; minimum 2.0 GPA. *Recommended:* minimum 2.5 GPA; interview.

Standardized tests *Admission: Required:* SAT I or ACT.

Significant dates *Application deadlines:* rolling (freshmen), rolling (transfers). *Financial aid deadline:* 4/1.

Freshman Application Contact
Ms. Meredith Young, Director of Admissions, Notre Dame College of Ohio, 4545 College Road, South Euclid, OH 44121-4293. **Phone:** 216-381-1680 Ext. 355. **Toll-free phone:** 800-NDC-1680 Ext. 355. **Fax:** 216-381-3802. **E-mail:** admissions@ndc.edu

Visit CollegeQuest.com for information on majors offered and athletics.

■ *See page 2200 for a narrative description.*

OBERLIN COLLEGE
Oberlin, Ohio

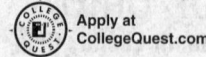
Apply at CollegeQuest.com

- **Independent**, comprehensive, founded 1833
- **Degrees** bachelor's and master's
- **Small-town** 440-acre campus with easy access to Cleveland
- **Coed**, 2,916 undergraduate students, 98% full-time, 59% women, 41% men
- **Very difficult** entrance level, 50% of applicants were admitted
- **10:1 student-to-undergraduate faculty ratio**
- **78.3% graduate** in 6 years or less
- **$24,264 tuition** and fees
- **$22,215 average financial aid** package, $13,926 average indebtedness upon graduation, $508.5 million endowment

Oberlin College is an independent, coeducational liberal arts college of approximately 2,900 students. It comprises 2 divisions, the College of Arts and Sciences and the Conservatory of Music. Oberlin has a history of progressive thinking, a supportive academic community, and a diverse, active student body.

Students *Undergraduates:* 2,848 full-time, 68 part-time. Students come from 52 states and territories, 47 other countries. *The most frequently chosen baccalaureate fields are:* English, social sciences and history, visual/performing arts. *Graduate:* 16 in graduate degree programs.

From out-of-state	91%	Reside on campus	75%
Age 25 or older	1%	Transferred in	3%
International students	6%	African Americans	7%
Asian Americans/Pacific Islanders	7%	Hispanic Americans	3%
Native Americans	1%		

Faculty 323 (75% full-time).

Expenses (1999–2000) *Comprehensive fee:* $30,442 includes full-time tuition ($24,096), mandatory fees ($168), and room and board ($6178). *College room only:* $3200. Room and board charges vary according to housing facility. *Part-time tuition:* $1004 per credit hour. *Part-time fees:* $84 per term part-time. *Payment plan:* installment. *Waivers:* employees or children of employees.

Library Mudd Center Library plus 3 others. *Operations spending 1999–2000:* $3.8 million. *Collection:* 1.5 million titles, 4,560 serial subscriptions, 59,186 audiovisual materials.

College life *Housing:* on-campus residence required through sophomore year. *Option:* coed. *Most popular organizations:* Experimental College, Community Outreach, Black Students Organization, Oberlin Students Cooperative Association, student radio station.

Campus security 24-hour emergency response devices and patrols, late-night transport-escort service, controlled dormitory access, crime prevention programs.

After graduation 20 organizations recruited on campus 1997–98. *Career center:* 7 full-time personnel. Services include job fairs, resume preparation, resume referral, career counseling, careers library, job bank, job interviews. *Graduate education:* 30% of class of 1999 went directly to graduate and professional school.

Freshmen 4,855 applied, 2,433 admitted, 727 enrolled. 37 National Merit Scholars, 33 valedictorians.

Average high school GPA	3.56	SAT verbal scores above 500	100%
SAT math scores above 500	100%	ACT above 18	100%
From top 10% of their h.s. class	56%	From top quarter	88%
From top half	99%	1998 freshmen returning in 1999	88%

Application *Options:* eApply at www.CollegeQuest.com, Common Application, electronic application, early admission, early decision, deferred entrance. *Application fee:* $30. *Required:* essay or personal statement; high school transcript; 2 letters of recommendation. *Required for some:* interview.

Standardized tests *Admission: Required:* SAT I or ACT. *Recommended:* SAT II Subject Tests.

Significant dates *Application deadlines:* 1/15 (freshmen), 3/15 (transfers). *Early decision:* 11/15 (for plan 1), 1/2 (for plan 2). *Notification:* 4/1 (freshmen), 12/15 (early decision plan 1), 1/30 (early decision plan 2). *Financial aid deadline priority date:* 2/15.

Freshman Application Contact
Ms. Debra Chermonte, Director of College Admissions, Oberlin College, Admissions Office, Carnegie Building, Oberlin, OH 44074-1090. **Phone:** 440-775-8411. **Toll-free phone:** 800-622-OBIE. **Fax:** 440-775-8886. **E-mail:** college.admissions@oberlin.edu

Visit CollegeQuest.com for information on majors offered and athletics.

■ *See page 2208 for a narrative description.*

OHIO DOMINICAN COLLEGE
Columbus, Ohio

- **Independent Roman Catholic**, 4-year, founded 1911
- **Degrees** associate and bachelor's
- **Urban** 62-acre campus
- **Coed**, 1,696 undergraduate students, 77% full-time, 66% women, 34% men
- **Moderately difficult** entrance level, 75% of applicants were admitted
- **19:1 student-to-undergraduate faculty ratio**
- **44% graduate** in 6 years or less
- **$10,250 tuition** and fees
- **$9.5 million endowment**

Students *Undergraduates:* 1,300 full-time, 396 part-time. Students come from 12 states and territories, 32 other countries. *The most frequently chosen baccalaureate fields are:* business/marketing, education, social sciences and history.

From out-of-state	2%	Reside on campus	17%
Age 25 or older	48%	Transferred in	10%
International students	4%	African Americans	21%
Asian Americans/Pacific Islanders	1%	Hispanic Americans	2%
Native Americans	0.3%		

Faculty 111 (50% full-time), 53% with terminal degrees.

Expenses (1999–2000) *Comprehensive fee:* $15,320 includes full-time tuition ($10,250) and room and board ($5070). Room and board charges vary according to housing facility. *Part-time tuition:* $321 per credit hour. *Payment plan:* installment. *Waivers:* senior citizens and employees or children of employees.

Library Spangler Library. *Operations spending 1999–2000:* $459,328. *Collection:* 106,939 titles, 545 serial subscriptions, 2,961 audiovisual materials.

College life *Housing:* on-campus residence required through junior year. *Option:* coed. *Most popular organizations:* Campus Ministry, honors program, College Choir, Black Student Union, American-International Membership.

Campus security 24-hour emergency response devices and patrols, late-night transport-escort service, controlled dormitory access.

After graduation *Career center:* 1 full-time, 1 part-time personnel. Services include job fairs, resume preparation, resume referral, career/interest testing, career counseling, careers library, job interviews.

Ohio

Freshmen 777 applied, 584 admitted, 213 enrolled.

Average high school GPA	2.99	SAT verbal scores above 500	N/R
SAT math scores above 500	N/R	ACT above 18	N/R
From top 10% of their h.s. class	12%	From top quarter	31%
From top half	54%	1998 freshmen returning in 1999	71%

Application *Option:* deferred entrance. *Required:* essay or personal statement; high school transcript; minimum 2.0 GPA; interview. *Required for some:* letters of recommendation.

Standardized tests *Admission: Required:* SAT I or ACT.

Significant dates *Application deadlines:* rolling (freshmen), rolling (transfers). *Financial aid deadline priority date:* 4/1.

Freshman Application Contact
Ms. Vicki Thompson-Campbell, Director of Admissions, Ohio Dominican College, 1216 Sunbury Road, Columbus, OH 43219-2099. **Phone:** 614-251-4500. **Toll-free phone:** 800-854-2670. **Fax:** 614-252-0776. **E-mail:** admissions@odc.edu

Visit CollegeQuest.com for information on majors offered and athletics.

■ *See page 2212 for a narrative description.*

OHIO NORTHERN UNIVERSITY
Ada, Ohio

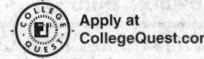

- **Independent United Methodist**, comprehensive, founded 1871
- **Degrees** bachelor's and first professional
- **Small-town** 260-acre campus
- **Coed**, 2,381 undergraduate students, 97% full-time, 49% women, 51% men
- **Moderately difficult** entrance level, 91% of applicants were admitted
- **13:1 student-to-undergraduate faculty ratio**
- **63.1% graduate** in 6 years or less
- **$21,435 tuition** and fees
- **$17,640 average financial aid** package, $16,400 average indebtedness upon graduation, $103.8 million endowment

Students *Undergraduates:* 2,313 full-time, 68 part-time. Students come from 38 states and territories, 15 other countries. *The most frequently chosen baccalaureate fields are:* business/marketing, engineering/engineering technologies, health professions and related sciences. *Graduate:* 778 in professional programs.

From out-of-state	14%	Reside on campus	56%
Age 25 or older	3%	Transferred in	4%
International students	1%	African Americans	3%
Asian Americans/Pacific Islanders	1%	Hispanic Americans	0.5%
Native Americans	0.3%		

Faculty 239 (75% full-time).

Expenses (2000–2001) *Comprehensive fee:* $26,700 includes full-time tuition ($21,435) and room and board ($5265). *College room only:* $2310. Full-time tuition and fees vary according to program. Room and board charges vary according to board plan. *Part-time tuition:* $573 per quarter hour. Part-time tuition and fees vary according to program. *Payment plan:* installment. *Waivers:* employees or children of employees.

Library Heterick Memorial Library plus 1 other. *Operations spending 1999–2000:* $2.8 million. *Collection:* 246,103 titles, 1,038 serial subscriptions, 8,655 audiovisual materials.

College life *Housing:* on-campus residence required through junior year. *Options:* coed, men-only, women-only. *Social organizations:* national fraternities, national sororities; 25% of eligible men and 22% of eligible women are members. *Most popular organizations:* Greek organizations, Good News Bears, Student Planning Committee, Student Senate.

Campus security 24-hour emergency response devices and patrols, late-night transport-escort service, controlled dormitory access.

After graduation 232 organizations recruited on campus 1997–98. 88% of class of 1998 had job offers within 6 months. *Career center:* 2 full-time personnel. Services include job fairs, resume preparation, interview workshops, resume referral, career counseling, careers library, job bank, job interviews.

Freshmen 2,357 applied, 2,145 admitted, 622 enrolled. 84 valedictorians.

Average high school GPA	3.48	SAT verbal scores above 500	N/R
SAT math scores above 500	N/R	ACT above 18	94%
From top 10% of their h.s. class	38%	From top quarter	65%
From top half	87%	1998 freshmen returning in 1999	85%

Application *Options:* eApply at www.CollegeQuest.com, Common Application, electronic application, early admission, deferred entrance. *Application fee:* $30. *Required:* high school transcript; minimum 2.0 GPA. *Recommended:* essay or personal statement; interview.

Standardized tests *Admission: Required:* SAT I or ACT.

Significant dates *Application deadlines:* 8/15 (freshmen), 8/15 (transfers). *Notification:* continuous until 8/31 (freshmen). *Financial aid deadline:* 6/1. *Priority date:* 4/15.

Freshman Application Contact
Ms. Karen Condeni, Vice President of Admissions and Financial Aid, Ohio Northern University, 525 South Main, Ada, OH 45810-1599. **Phone:** 419-772-2260. **Fax:** 419-772-2313. **E-mail:** admissions-ug@onu.edu

Visit CollegeQuest.com for information on majors offered and athletics. College video available at CollegeQuest.com.

■ *See page 2214 for a narrative description.*

THE OHIO STATE UNIVERSITY
Columbus, Ohio

- **State-supported**, university, founded 1870
- **Degrees** bachelor's, master's, doctoral, first professional, and post-master's certificates
- **Urban** campus
- **Coed**, 35,883 undergraduate students, 86% full-time, 48% women, 52% men
- **Moderately difficult** entrance level, 74% of applicants were admitted
- **14:1 student-to-undergraduate faculty ratio**
- **56.4% graduate** in 6 years or less
- **$4137 tuition** and fees (in-state); $12,087 (out-of-state)
- **$7043 average financial aid** package, $11,800 average indebtedness upon graduation, $1.1 billion endowment

Students *Undergraduates:* 30,939 full-time, 4,944 part-time. Students come from 53 states and territories, 87 other countries. *The most frequently chosen baccalaureate fields are:* business/marketing, home economics/vocational home economics, social sciences and history. *Graduate:* 2,758 in professional programs, 9,153 in other graduate degree programs.

From out-of-state	7%	Reside on campus	24%
Age 25 or older	12%	Transferred in	6%
International students	4%	African Americans	8%
Asian Americans/Pacific Islanders	5%	Hispanic Americans	2%
Native Americans	0.4%		

Faculty 3,444 (77% full-time).

Expenses (1999–2000) *Tuition, state resident:* full-time $3780. *Tuition, nonresident:* full-time $11,730. *Required fees:* full-time $357. Part-time tuition and fees vary according to course load. *College room and board:* $5328. Room and board charges vary according to board plan and housing facility. *Payment plan:* installment. *Waivers:* senior citizens and employees or children of employees.

Library Main Library plus 12 others. *Operations spending 1999–2000:* $267.1 million. *Collection:* 5.2 million titles, 36,020 serial subscriptions.

College life *Housing:* on-campus residence required in freshman year. *Options:* coed, women-only, cooperative, disabled students. *Social organizations:* national fraternities, national sororities; 6% of eligible men and 7% of eligible women are members. *Most popular organizations:* Afrikan Student Union, Bisexual, Gay and Lesbian Alliance, Campus Crusade for Christ, University Wide Council of Hispanic Organizations, Asian American Association.

Campus security 24-hour emergency response devices and patrols, student patrols, late-night transport-escort service, controlled dormitory access, dormitory entrances locked after 9 p.m.

After graduation 83% of class of 1998 had job offers within 6 months. *Career center:* Services include job fairs, resume preparation, interview workshops, resume referral, career/interest testing, career counseling, careers

Ohio

The Ohio State University (continued)
library, job bank, job interviews. **Graduate education:** 10% of class of 1999 went directly to graduate and professional school. **Major awards:** 3 Fulbright Scholars.

Freshmen 19,805 applied, 14,566 admitted, 6,119 enrolled. 104 National Merit Scholars, 231 valedictorians.

SAT verbal scores above 500	78%	SAT math scores above 500	82%
ACT above 18	97%	From top 10% of their h.s. class	29%
From top quarter	61%	From top half	93%
1998 freshmen returning in 1999	83%		

Application *Options:* Common Application, electronic application. *Application fee:* $30. *Required:* high school transcript.

Standardized tests *Admission: Required:* SAT I or ACT.

Significant dates *Application deadlines:* 2/15 (freshmen), 6/25 (transfers). *Financial aid deadline priority date:* 2/15.

Freshman Application Contact
Dr. Robin Brown, Director of Undergraduate Admissions, The Ohio State University, 3rd Floor, Lincoln Tower, Columbus, OH 43210-1200. **Phone:** 614-292-3980. **Fax:** 614-292-4818. **E-mail:** telecounseling@fa.adm.ohio-state.edu

Visit CollegeQuest.com for information on majors offered and athletics. College video available at CollegeQuest.com.

THE OHIO STATE UNIVERSITY AT LIMA
Lima, Ohio

- **State-supported**, 4-year, founded 1960
- **Degrees** associate and bachelor's (also offers some graduate courses)
- **Small-town** 565-acre campus
- **Coed**
- **Noncompetitive** entrance level
- **13:1 student-to-undergraduate faculty ratio**
- **$3528 tuition** and fees (in-state); $11,097 (out-of-state)

Part of Ohio State University.

Students *Undergraduates:* Students come from 1 other country.

Age 25 or older	25%

Faculty 91 (62% full-time).

Expenses (1999–2000) *Tuition, area resident:* part-time $99 per hour. *Tuition, state resident:* full-time $3528. *Tuition, nonresident:* full-time $11,097; part-time $210 per hour. Part-time tuition and fees vary according to course load. Part-time tuition per term ranges from $197 to $1079 for state residents, $407 to $3392 for nonresidents. *Payment plan:* installment. *Waivers:* senior citizens and employees or children of employees.

Library Ohio State University-Lima Campus Library. *Collection:* 74,619 titles, 592 serial subscriptions.

College life *Housing:* college housing not available. *Most popular organizations:* Chorus, Psychology Club, Buckeye Scholars, Bucks for Buckeyes, Theatre.

Campus security 24-hour emergency response devices and patrols, late-night transport-escort service.

After graduation *Career center:* Services include resume preparation, career counseling, job bank.

Freshmen

SAT verbal scores above 500	55%	SAT math scores above 500	45%
ACT above 18	N/R	1998 freshmen returning in 1999	57%

Application *Option:* early admission. *Application fee:* $30. *Required:* high school transcript.

Standardized tests *Admission: Required:* ACT.

Significant dates *Application deadlines:* 7/1 (freshmen), 7/1 (transfers). *Notification:* continuous until 9/1 (freshmen).

Freshman Application Contact
Marissa Christoff Snyder, Admissions Counselor, The Ohio State University at Lima, 4240 Campus Drive, Lima, OH 45804. **Phone:** 419-995-8220. **E-mail:** admissions@lima.ohio-state.edu

Visit CollegeQuest.com for information on majors offered and athletics. College video available at CollegeQuest.com.

THE OHIO STATE UNIVERSITY AT MARION
Marion, Ohio

Admissions Office Contact
The Ohio State University at Marion, 1465 Mount Vernon Avenue, Marion, OH 43302-5695.

THE OHIO STATE UNIVERSITY—MANSFIELD CAMPUS
Mansfield, Ohio

Admissions Office Contact
The Ohio State University–Mansfield Campus, 1680 University Drive, Mansfield, OH 44906-1599.

THE OHIO STATE UNIVERSITY—NEWARK CAMPUS
Newark, Ohio

Admissions Office Contact
The Ohio State University–Newark Campus, 1179 University Drive, Newark, OH 43055-1797.

OHIO UNIVERSITY
Athens, Ohio

- **State-supported**, university, founded 1804
- **Degrees** associate, bachelor's, master's, doctoral, and first professional
- **Small-town** 1,700-acre campus
- **Coed**, 16,554 undergraduate students, 93% full-time, 55% women, 45% men
- **Moderately difficult** entrance level, 80% of applicants were admitted
- **21:1 student-to-undergraduate faculty ratio**
- **70% graduate** in 6 years or less
- **$4800 tuition** and fees (in-state); $10,101 (out-of-state)
- **$6528 average financial aid** package, $13,850 average indebtedness upon graduation, $206 million endowment

Part of Ohio Board of Regents.

Students *Undergraduates:* 15,447 full-time, 1,107 part-time. Students come from 52 states and territories, 17 other countries. *The most frequently chosen baccalaureate fields are:* business/marketing, education, English. *Graduate:* 415 in professional programs, 2,669 in other graduate degree programs.

From out-of-state	11%	Reside on campus	41%
Age 25 or older	6%	Transferred in	3%
International students	2%	African Americans	4%
Asian Americans/Pacific Islanders	1%	Hispanic Americans	1%
Native Americans	0.3%		

Faculty 1,233 (68% full-time), 80% with terminal degrees.

Expenses (1999–2000) *Tuition, state resident:* full-time $4800; part-time $154 per quarter hour. *Tuition, nonresident:* full-time $10,101; part-time $329 per quarter hour. *College room and board:* $5484; room only: $2697. Room and board charges vary according to board plan. *Payment plan:* installment. *Waivers:* employees or children of employees.

Library Alden Library. *Collection:* 2.1 million titles, 40,417 serial subscriptions.

College life *Housing:* on-campus residence required through sophomore year. *Options:* coed, men-only, women-only, cooperative, disabled students. *Social organizations:* national fraternities, national sororities; 12% of eligible men and 16% of eligible women are members. *Most popular organizations:* Gamma Pi Delta, Golden Key, International Student Union, Chinese students and visiting scholars club, Campus Crusade for Christ.

Campus security 24-hour emergency response devices and patrols, late-night transport-escort service, controlled dormitory access, security lighting.

After graduation 450 organizations recruited on campus 1997–98. 79% of class of 1998 had job offers within 6 months. *Career center:* 10 full-time, 3 part-time personnel. Services include job fairs, resume preparation, resume referral, career counseling, careers library, job bank, job interviews. ***Graduate education:*** 28% of class of 1999 went directly to graduate and professional school: 7% graduate arts and sciences, 5% education, 3% business, 1% engineering, 1% law, 1% medicine.

Freshmen 11,785 applied, 9,418 admitted, 3,448 enrolled. 6 National Merit Scholars, 62 valedictorians.

Average high school GPA	3.42	SAT verbal scores above 500	76%
SAT math scores above 500	74%	ACT above 18	98%
From top 10% of their h.s. class	18%	From top quarter	49%
From top half	88%	1998 freshmen returning in 1999	84%

Application *Options:* early admission, deferred entrance. *Application fee:* $30. *Required:* high school transcript. *Required for some:* essay or personal statement; interview. *Recommended:* 2 letters of recommendation.

Standardized tests *Admission: Required:* SAT I or ACT.

Significant dates *Application deadlines:* 2/15 (freshmen), 6/1 (transfers). ***Financial aid deadline priority date:*** 3/15.

Freshman Application Contact Shirley Kasler-Thimmes, Director of Admissions, Ohio University, Athens, OH 45701-2979. **Phone:** 740-593-4100. **Fax:** 740-593-4229. **E-mail:** uadmiss1@ohiou.edu

Visit CollegeQuest.com for information on majors offered and athletics. College video available at CollegeQuest.com.

■ *See page 2216 for a narrative description.*

OHIO UNIVERSITY—CHILLICOTHE
Chillicothe, Ohio

- **State-supported**, 4-year, founded 1946
- **Degrees** associate and bachelor's (offers first 2 years of most bachelor's degree programs available at the main campus in Athens; also offers several bachelor's degree programs that can be completed at this campus and several programs exclusive to this campus; also offers some graduate programs)
- **Small-town** 124-acre campus with easy access to Columbus
- **Coed**, 1,509 undergraduate students
- **Noncompetitive** entrance level, 100% of applicants were admitted
- **$3192 tuition** and fees (in-state); $7803 (out-of-state)

Part of Ohio Board of Regents.

Students *Undergraduates:* Students come from 2 states and territories.

Age 25 or older	38%

Faculty 118 (28% full-time).

Expenses (1999–2000) *Tuition, state resident:* full-time $3192; part-time $97 per credit hour. *Tuition, nonresident:* full-time $7803; part-time $250 per credit hour. *Payment plan:* installment. *Waivers:* senior citizens and employees or children of employees.

Library Quinn Library. *Collection:* 47,900 titles, 418 serial subscriptions.

College life *Housing:* college housing not available. *Most popular organizations:* Nursing Student Association, Students In Free Enterprise Club, drama club, Phi Theta Kappa, Gamma Phi Delta.

Campus security 24-hour emergency response devices, patrols by city police.

After graduation *Career center:* 4 full-time personnel. Services include resume preparation, career counseling, careers library. ***Graduate education:*** 10% of class of 1999 went directly to graduate and professional school.

Freshmen 400 applied, 400 admitted.

SAT verbal scores above 500	N/R	SAT math scores above 500	N/R
ACT above 18	N/R	1998 freshmen returning in 1999	55%

Application *Options:* early admission, deferred entrance. *Application fee:* $20. *Required:* high school transcript.

Standardized tests *Placement: Required:* SAT I or ACT

Significant dates *Application deadlines:* 9/1 (freshmen), 9/1 (transfers). ***Financial aid deadline priority date:*** 3/15.

Freshman Application Contact Mr. Richard R. Whitney, Director of Student Services, Ohio University–Chillicothe, 571 West Fifth Street, Chillicothe, OH 45601. **Phone:** 740-774-7242. **Toll-free phone:** 877-462-6824. **Fax:** 740-774-7295.

Visit CollegeQuest.com for information on majors offered and athletics.

OHIO UNIVERSITY—EASTERN
St. Clairsville, Ohio

Admissions Office Contact Ohio University–Eastern, 45425 National Road, St. Clairsville, OH 43950-9724. **Toll-free phone:** 800-648-3331. **E-mail:** hess@ouvaxa.cats.ohiou.edu

OHIO UNIVERSITY—LANCASTER
Lancaster, Ohio

Admissions Office Contact Ohio University–Lancaster, 1570 Granville Pike, Lancaster, OH 43130-1097. **Toll-free phone:** 888-446-4468. **Fax:** 740-687-9497. **E-mail:** shepherd@ouvaxa.cats.ohiou.edu

OHIO UNIVERSITY—SOUTHERN CAMPUS
Ironton, Ohio

- **State-supported**, primarily 2-year, founded 1956
- **Degrees** associate and bachelor's (offers first 2 years of most bachelor's degree programs available at the main campus in Athens; also offers some upper-level and graduate courses)
- **Small-town** 9-acre campus
- **Coed**
- **Noncompetitive** entrance level

Part of Ohio Board of Regents.

Faculty 125 (12% full-time).

Admissions Office Contact Ohio University–Southern Campus, 1804 Liberty Avenue, Ironton, OH 45638-2214. **Fax:** 740-533-4632.

Visit CollegeQuest.com for information on majors offered and athletics.

OHIO UNIVERSITY—ZANESVILLE
Zanesville, Ohio

- **State-supported**, comprehensive, founded 1946
- **Degrees** associate, bachelor's, and master's (offers first 2 years of most bachelor's degree programs available at the main campus in Athens; also offers several bachelor's degree programs that can be completed at this campus; also offers some graduate courses)
- **Rural** 179-acre campus with easy access to Columbus
- **Coed**, 1,178 undergraduate students, 63% full-time, 67% women, 33% men
- **Noncompetitive** entrance level, 100% of applicants were admitted
- **$2128 tuition** and fees (in-state); $8276 (out-of-state)

Part of Ohio Board of Regents.

Students *Undergraduates:* 747 full-time, 431 part-time. Students come from 4 states and territories. *Graduate:* 44 in graduate degree programs.

From out-of-state	1%	Age 25 or older	33%
African Americans	3%	Asian Americans/Pacific Islanders	0.3%
Hispanic Americans	0.3%	Native Americans	0.1%

Faculty 96 (30% full-time), 31% with terminal degrees.

Expenses (1999–2000) *Tuition, state resident:* full-time $2128; part-time $97 per quarter hour. *Tuition, nonresident:* full-time $8276; part-time $250 per quarter hour. *Waivers:* senior citizens and employees or children of employees.

Library Zanesville Campus Library plus 1 other. *Operations spending 1999–2000:* $247,287. *Collection:* 64,227 titles, 489 serial subscriptions.

Ohio

Ohio University–Zanesville (continued)

College life *Housing:* college housing not available. *Most popular organizations:* Student Senate, Student Nurses Association, drama club, chess club.

Campus security Night security.

After graduation *Career center:* 1 part-time personnel. Services include job fairs, resume preparation, career counseling, careers library.

Freshmen 634 applied, 634 admitted, 262 enrolled.

SAT verbal scores above 500	N/R	SAT math scores above 500	N/R
ACT above 18	N/R	1998 freshmen returning in 1999	60%

Application *Options:* Common Application, early admission, deferred entrance. *Application fee:* $20. *Required:* high school transcript.

Standardized tests *Placement: Required for some:* SAT I or ACT, nursing examination.

Significant dates *Application deadlines:* rolling (freshmen), rolling (transfers). *Financial aid deadline priority date:* 4/1.

Freshman Application Contact
Mrs. Karen Ragsdale, Student Services Secretary, Ohio University–Zanesville, 1425 Newark Road, Zanesville, OH 43701-2695. **Phone:** 740-588-1440. **Fax:** 740-453-6161.

Visit CollegeQuest.com for information on majors offered and athletics.

OHIO WESLEYAN UNIVERSITY
Delaware, Ohio

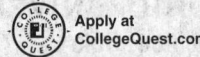 Apply at CollegeQuest.com

- **Independent United Methodist**, 4-year, founded 1842
- **Degree** bachelor's
- **Small-town** 200-acre campus with easy access to Columbus
- **Coed**, 1,913 undergraduate students, 99% full-time, 51% women, 49% men
- **Very difficult** entrance level, 83% of applicants were admitted
- **13:1 student-to-undergraduate faculty ratio**
- **69.3% graduate** in 6 years or less
- **$20,940 tuition** and fees
- **$19,785 average financial aid** package, $19,253 average indebtedness upon graduation, $105.4 million endowment

Personalized honors study offers unusual opportunities to talented students as early as freshman year. Internships and research are encouraged. The University's distinctive commitment to public service and civic involvement is reflected in annual student work trips to Haiti and the South, the acclaimed Sagan National Colloquium, and extensive volunteer and community service opportunities.

Students *Undergraduates:* 1,897 full-time, 16 part-time. Students come from 40 states and territories, 56 other countries. *The most frequently chosen baccalaureate fields are:* business/marketing, psychology, social sciences and history.

From out-of-state	50%	Reside on campus	82%
Age 25 or older	2%	Transferred in	1%
International students	11%	African Americans	4%
Asian Americans/Pacific Islanders	2%	Hispanic Americans	2%
Native Americans	0.2%		

Faculty 175 (72% full-time), 82% with terminal degrees.

Expenses (1999–2000) *Comprehensive fee:* $27,500 includes full-time tuition ($20,940) and room and board ($6560). *College room only:* $3330. Room and board charges vary according to board plan and location. *Part-time tuition:* $2280 per course. *Payment plan:* installment. *Waivers:* children of alumni, senior citizens, and employees or children of employees.

Library L. A. Beeghly Library plus 3 others. *Operations spending 1999–2000:* $1.5 million. *Collection:* 473,193 titles, 1,060 serial subscriptions, 1,553 audiovisual materials.

College life *Housing:* on-campus residence required through senior year. *Options:* coed, men-only, women-only. *Social organizations:* national fraternities, national sororities; 44% of eligible men and 37% of eligible women are members. *Most popular organizations:* community services, student government, academic departments' student boards, President's Club, Fellowship of Christian Athletes.

Campus security 24-hour emergency response devices and patrols, late-night transport-escort service, controlled dormitory access.

After graduation 28 organizations recruited on campus 1997–98. *Career center:* 1 full-time, 2 part-time personnel. Services include job fairs, resume preparation, resume referral, career counseling, careers library, job bank, job interviews.

Freshmen 2,057 applied, 1,714 admitted, 524 enrolled. 6 National Merit Scholars, 21 valedictorians.

Average high school GPA	3.3	SAT verbal scores above 500	89%
SAT math scores above 500	92%	ACT above 18	100%
From top 10% of their h.s. class	30%	From top quarter	56%
From top half	81%	1998 freshmen returning in 1999	77%

Application *Options:* eApply at www.CollegeQuest.com, Common Application, electronic application, early admission, early decision, early action, deferred entrance. *Application fee:* $35. *Required:* essay or personal statement; high school transcript; 2 letters of recommendation. *Recommended:* interview.

Standardized tests *Admission: Required:* SAT I or ACT. *Recommended:* SAT II Subject Tests.

Significant dates *Application deadlines:* 3/1 (freshmen), 8/1 (transfers). *Early decision:* 12/1, 12/15. *Notification:* continuous until 4/1 (freshmen), 12/30 (early decision), 12/30 (early action). *Financial aid deadline priority date:* 3/15.

Freshman Application Contact
Ms. Margaret L. Drugovich, Vice President of Admission and Financial Aid, Ohio Wesleyan University, 61 South Sandusky Street, Delaware, OH 43015. **Phone:** 740-368-3020. **Toll-free phone:** 800-922-8953. **Fax:** 740-368-3314. **E-mail:** owuadmit@cc.owu.edu

Visit CollegeQuest.com for information on majors offered and athletics. Electronic viewbook available at CollegeQuest.com.

- *See page 2218 for a narrative description.*

OTTERBEIN COLLEGE
Westerville, Ohio

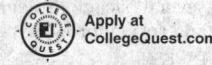 Apply at CollegeQuest.com

- **Independent United Methodist**, comprehensive, founded 1847
- **Degrees** bachelor's and master's
- **Suburban** 140-acre campus with easy access to Columbus
- **Coed**, 2,348 undergraduate students, 73% full-time, 64% women, 36% men
- **Moderately difficult** entrance level, 89% of applicants were admitted
- **13:1 student-to-undergraduate faculty ratio**
- **$16,260 tuition** and fees
- **$51.1 million endowment**

Otterbein continues to offer an excellent combination of a solid liberal arts education with professional/career preparation. Its campus in Westerville provides access to Ohio's capital city, Columbus, for internships as well as cultural and social activities. A student-faculty ratio of 13:1 ensures individual attention for students pursuing one of 73 majors offered. More than $7.2 million in grants and scholarships was awarded last year. Students graduate in 4 years.

Students *Undergraduates:* 1,707 full-time, 641 part-time. Students come from 28 states and territories, 36 other countries. *The most frequently chosen baccalaureate fields are:* business/marketing, communications/communication technologies, education. *Graduate:* 414 in graduate degree programs.

From out-of-state	9%	Reside on campus	60%
Age 25 or older	37%	International students	2%
African Americans	6%	Asian Americans/Pacific Islanders	1%
Hispanic Americans	1%	Native Americans	1%

Faculty 203 (68% full-time).

Expenses (1999–2000) *Comprehensive fee:* $21,381 includes full-time tuition ($16,260) and room and board ($5121). *College room only:* $2262. Room and board charges vary according to housing facility. *Part-time tuition:* $195 per credit hour. *Payment plan:* installment. *Waivers:* employees or children of employees.

Library Courtright Memorial Library. *Operations spending 1999–2000:* $769,462. *Collection:* 182,629 titles, 1,012 serial subscriptions, 8,971 audiovisual materials.

Ohio

College life *Housing:* on-campus residence required through sophomore year. *Options:* men-only, women-only. *Social organizations:* local fraternities, local sororities; 35% of eligible men and 35% of eligible women are members. *Most popular organizations:* musical groups, Greek organizations, honoraries, academic interest clubs.

Campus security 24-hour emergency response devices and patrols, student patrols, late-night transport-escort service, controlled dormitory access, 24-hour locked residence hall entrances.

After graduation 30 organizations recruited on campus 1997–98. 84% of class of 1998 had job offers within 6 months. *Career center:* 2 full-time personnel. Services include resume preparation, resume referral, career counseling, careers library, job bank, job interviews. **Graduate education:** 13% of class of 1999 went directly to graduate and professional school: 6% graduate arts and sciences, 3% medicine, 2% business, 2% law.

Freshmen 1,715 applied, 1,531 admitted, 518 enrolled. 15 valedictorians.

Average high school GPA	3.29	SAT verbal scores above 500	68%
SAT math scores above 500	70%	ACT above 18	91%
From top 10% of their h.s. class	26%	From top quarter	51%
From top half	76%	1998 freshmen returning in 1999	91%

Application *Options:* eApply at www.CollegeQuest.com, Common Application, electronic application, deferred entrance. *Application fee:* $20. *Required:* high school transcript. *Required for some:* letters of recommendation. *Recommended:* interview.

Standardized tests *Admission: Required:* SAT I or ACT.

Significant dates *Application deadlines:* rolling (freshmen), rolling (transfers). *Financial aid deadline priority date:* 4/1.

Freshman Application Contact
Dr. Cass Johnson, Director of Admissions, Otterbein College, One Otterbein College, Westville, OH 43081-9924. **Phone:** 614-823-1500. **Toll-free phone:** 800-488-8144. **Fax:** 614-823-1200. **E-mail:** uotterb@otterbein.edu

Visit CollegeQuest.com for information on majors offered and athletics. College video available at CollegeQuest.com.

■ *See page 2230 for a narrative description.*

PONTIFICAL COLLEGE JOSEPHINUM
Columbus, Ohio

Admissions Office Contact
Pontifical College Josephinum, 7625 North High Street, Columbus, OH 43235-1498.

SHAWNEE STATE UNIVERSITY
Portsmouth, Ohio

- **State-supported**, 4-year, founded 1986
- **Degrees** associate and bachelor's
- **Small-town** campus
- **Coed**, 3,164 undergraduate students, 83% full-time, 64% women, 36% men
- **Noncompetitive** entrance level, 100% of applicants were admitted
- **18:1 student-to-undergraduate faculty ratio**
- **23% graduate** in 6 years or less
- **$4203 tuition** and fees (in-state); $5697 (out-of-state)
- **$3972 average financial aid** package, $10,944 average indebtedness upon graduation, $7.3 million endowment

Shawnee State University offers baccalaureate and associate degrees through the College of Arts and Sciences and the College of Professional Studies. Programs are available in business, health sciences, engineering technologies, arts and sciences, and teacher education. With distinctive student housing and a beautiful new campus, SSU offers a high-quality education with individualized attention.

Part of Ohio Board of Regents.

Students *Undergraduates:* 2,618 full-time, 546 part-time. Students come from 11 states and territories, 7 other countries. *The most frequently chosen baccalaureate fields are:* business/marketing, education, social sciences and history.

From out-of-state	9%	Reside on campus	5%
Age 25 or older	31%	Transferred in	6%
International students	1%	African Americans	2%
Asian Americans/Pacific Islanders	0.4%	Hispanic Americans	0.4%
Native Americans	1%		

Faculty 260 (45% full-time), 35% with terminal degrees.

Expenses (1999–2000) *Tuition, area resident:* full-time $2745; part-time $76 per quarter hour. *Tuition, state resident:* full-time $3654; part-time $102 per quarter hour. *Tuition, nonresident:* full-time $5148; part-time $143 per quarter hour. *Required fees:* full-time $549; $16 per quarter hour. Full-time tuition and fees vary according to reciprocity agreements. Part-time tuition and fees vary according to reciprocity agreements. *College room and board:* $4431; room only: $3015. Room and board charges vary according to board plan and housing facility. *Payment plan:* installment. *Waivers:* senior citizens and employees or children of employees.

Library Shawnee State University Library. *Operations spending 1999–2000:* $1.1 million. *Collection:* 108,973 titles, 1,287 serial subscriptions, 18,523 audiovisual materials.

College life *Housing:* on-campus residence required through sophomore year. *Option:* coed. *Social organizations:* national fraternities, local sororities; 5% of eligible men and 5% of eligible women are members. *Most popular organizations:* campus ministry, Health Executives and Administrators Learning Society, Greek sororities and fraternities, Student Programming Board, SGA.

Campus security 24-hour emergency response devices and patrols.

After graduation 115 organizations recruited on campus 1997–98. *Career center:* 2 full-time personnel. Services include job fairs, resume preparation, interview workshops, resume referral, career/interest testing, career counseling, careers library, job bank, job interviews.

Freshmen 2,188 applied, 2,188 admitted, 564 enrolled.

Average high school GPA	2.0	SAT verbal scores above 500	N/R
SAT math scores above 500	N/R	ACT above 18	57%
1998 freshmen returning in 1999	57%		

Application *Options:* electronic application, deferred entrance. *Application fee:* $30. *Required:* high school transcript. *Required for some:* letters of recommendation; interview.

Standardized tests *Placement: Recommended:* ACT.

Significant dates *Application deadlines:* rolling (freshmen), rolling (transfers). *Financial aid deadline priority date:* 4/1.

Freshman Application Contact
Ms. Suzanne Shelpman, Director of Admission and Retention, Shawnee State University, , 940 Second Street, Portsmouth, OH 45662. **Phone:** 740-355-2610 Ext. 610. **Toll-free phone:** 800-959-2SSU. **Fax:** 740-355-2111. **E-mail:** admsn@shawnee.edu

Visit CollegeQuest.com for information on majors offered and athletics.

■ *See page 2474 for a narrative description.*

TIFFIN UNIVERSITY
Tiffin, Ohio

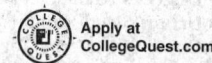
Apply at CollegeQuest.com

- **Independent**, comprehensive, founded 1888
- **Degrees** associate, bachelor's, and master's
- **Small-town** 108-acre campus with easy access to Toledo
- **Coed**, 1,265 undergraduate students, 70% full-time, 51% women, 49% men
- **Minimally difficult** entrance level, 85% of applicants were admitted
- **21:1 student-to-undergraduate faculty ratio**
- **$10,500 tuition** and fees
- **$3790 average financial aid** package, $16,670 average indebtedness upon graduation, $1.4 million endowment

Students *Undergraduates:* 885 full-time, 380 part-time. Students come from 17 states and territories, 13 other countries. *The most frequently chosen baccalaureate fields are:* business/marketing, computer/information sciences, protective services/public administration. *Graduate:* 180 in graduate degree programs.

| From out-of-state | 5% | Reside on campus | 50% |
| Age 25 or older | 22% | Transferred in | 6% |

Faculty 83 (52% full-time), 37% with terminal degrees.

Ohio

Tiffin University (continued)

Expenses (1999–2000) *Comprehensive fee:* $15,350 includes full-time tuition ($10,500) and room and board ($4850). *College room only:* $2450. Room and board charges vary according to board plan and housing facility. *Part-time tuition:* $1050 per course. *Payment plan:* installment. *Waivers:* employees or children of employees.

Library Pfeiffer Library. *Collection:* 20,331 titles, 244 serial subscriptions.

College life *Housing:* on-campus residence required through sophomore year. *Options:* coed, men-only, disabled students. *Social organizations:* national fraternities, national sororities, local fraternities, local sororities, coed fraternity; 16% of eligible men and 15% of eligible women are members. *Most popular organizations:* Hospitality Management Club, Student Government Association, Greek organizations, Black United Students, International Student Association.

Campus security Student patrols, late-night transport-escort service.

After graduation 9 organizations recruited on campus 1997–98. 96% of class of 1998 had job offers within 6 months. *Career center:* 1 full-time personnel. Services include job fairs, resume referral, career counseling, careers library, job interviews. *Graduate education:* 14% of class of 1999 went directly to graduate and professional school: 12% business, 2% law.

Freshmen 1,306 applied, 1,110 admitted, 347 enrolled. 2 class presidents, 3 valedictorians.

Average high school GPA	2.8	SAT verbal scores above 500	N/R
SAT math scores above 500	N/R	ACT above 18	57%
From top 10% of their h.s. class	10%	From top quarter	31%
From top half	60%	1998 freshmen returning in 1999	55%

Application *Options:* eApply at www.CollegeQuest.com, early admission, deferred entrance. *Application fee:* $20. *Required:* essay or personal statement; high school transcript. *Required for some:* letters of recommendation; interview. *Recommended:* minimum 2.0 GPA; interview.

Standardized tests *Placement: Recommended:* SAT I or ACT.

Significant dates *Application deadlines:* rolling (freshmen), rolling (transfers). *Notification:* continuous until 8/15 (freshmen). *Financial aid deadline priority date:* 3/31.

Freshman Application Contact
Mr. Ron Schumacher, Director of Admissions, Tiffin University, 155 Miami Street, Tiffin, OH 44883-2161. **Phone:** 419-448-3425. **Toll-free phone:** 800-968-6446. **Fax:** 419-447-9605. **E-mail:** admiss@tiffin.edu

Visit CollegeQuest.com for information on majors offered and athletics. College video available at CollegeQuest.com.

■ *See page 2624 for a narrative description.*

THE UNION INSTITUTE
Cincinnati, Ohio

- **Independent**, university, founded 1969
- **Degrees** bachelor's and doctoral
- **Urban** 5-acre campus
- **Coed**, 681 undergraduate students, 59% full-time, 63% women, 37% men
- **Moderately difficult** entrance level
- **16:1 student-to-undergraduate faculty ratio**
- **$6288 tuition** and fees
- **$2.5 million endowment**

Students *Undergraduates:* 405 full-time, 276 part-time. Students come from 22 states and territories, 3 other countries. *The most frequently chosen baccalaureate fields are:* business/marketing, protective services/public administration, psychology. *Graduate:* 1,178 in graduate degree programs.

From out-of-state	8%	Age 25 or older	96%
Transferred in	15%	International students	0.4%
African Americans	32%	Asian Americans/Pacific Islanders	1%
Hispanic Americans	9%	Native Americans	1%

Faculty 33 (88% full-time), 85% with terminal degrees.

Expenses (1999–2000) *Tuition:* full-time $6288; part-time $262 per credit. *Payment plan:* installment. *Waivers:* employees or children of employees.

Library *Operations spending 1999–2000:* $41,539. *Collection:* 4,468 titles, 18 audiovisual materials.

College life *Housing:* college housing not available.

Campus security Late-night transport-escort service, security during class hours.

After graduation *Graduate education:* 30% of class of 1999 went directly to graduate and professional school.

Freshmen 14 enrolled.

SAT verbal scores above 500	N/R	SAT math scores above 500	N/R
ACT above 18	N/R	1998 freshmen returning in 1999	50%

Application *Options:* electronic application, deferred entrance. *Application fee:* $50. *Required:* essay or personal statement; high school transcript; 2 letters of recommendation; interview.

Significant dates *Application deadlines:* 10/1 (freshmen), 10/1 (transfers). *Financial aid deadline priority date:* 4/15.

Freshman Application Contact
Mr. Michael Robertson, Associate Registrar, The Union Institute, 440 East McMillan Street, Cincinnati, OH 45206-1925. **Phone:** 513-861-6400. **Toll-free phone:** 800-486-3116. **Fax:** 513-861-0779. **E-mail:** mrobertson@tui.edu

Visit CollegeQuest.com for information on majors offered and athletics.

THE UNIVERSITY OF AKRON
Akron, Ohio

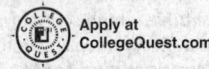
Apply at CollegeQuest.com

- **State-supported**, university, founded 1870
- **Degrees** associate, bachelor's, master's, doctoral, and first professional
- **Urban** 170-acre campus with easy access to Cleveland
- **Coed**, 19,107 undergraduate students, 65% full-time, 55% women, 45% men
- **Noncompetitive** entrance level, 100% of applicants were admitted
- **17:1 student-to-undergraduate faculty ratio**
- **$4152 tuition** and fees (in-state); $9113 (out-of-state)
- **$4495 average financial aid** package, $15,421 average indebtedness upon graduation, $169 million endowment

The University of Akron is a major metropolitan research and teaching institution. It offers more than 200 undergraduate majors and areas of study leading to associate and bachelor's degrees. For advanced study, the University provides 100 master's degree programs and options, 18 doctoral degree programs, and 4 law degree programs.

Students *Undergraduates:* 12,448 full-time, 6,659 part-time. Students come from 30 states and territories, 56 other countries. *The most frequently chosen baccalaureate fields are:* business/marketing, education, engineering/engineering technologies. *Graduate:* 821 in professional programs, 3,195 in other graduate degree programs.

From out-of-state	1%	Reside on campus	9%
Age 25 or older	41%	Transferred in	6%
International students	1%	African Americans	14%
Asian Americans/Pacific Islanders	2%	Hispanic Americans	1%
Native Americans	1%		

Faculty 1,602 (49% full-time), 33% with terminal degrees.

Expenses (1999–2000) *One-time required fee:* $100. *Tuition, state resident:* full-time $3755; part-time $156 per credit. *Tuition, nonresident:* full-time $8716; part-time $363 per credit. *Required fees:* full-time $397; $17 per credit. Full-time tuition and fees vary according to course level and location. Part-time tuition and fees vary according to course level and location. *College room and board:* $5010; room only: $3150. Room and board charges vary according to board plan and housing facility. *Payment plan:* installment. *Waivers:* senior citizens and employees or children of employees.

Library Bierce Library plus 3 others. *Operations spending 1999–2000:* $8.9 million. *Collection:* 725,000 titles, 8,000 serial subscriptions, 40,000 audiovisual materials.

College life *Housing:* on-campus residence required in freshman year. *Options:* coed, men-only, women-only. *Social organizations:* national fraternities, national sororities, local fraternities; 4% of eligible men and 3% of eligible women are members. *Most popular organizations:* Interfraternity Council, Panhellenic Council, Associated Student Government, Residence Hall Program Board, American Society of Mechanical Engineers.

Campus security 24-hour emergency response devices and patrols, student patrols, late-night transport-escort service, controlled dormitory access.

After graduation 240 organizations recruited on campus 1997–98. 85% of class of 1998 had job offers within 6 months. *Career center:* 7 full-time, 5 part-time personnel. Services include job fairs, resume preparation, resume referral, career counseling, careers library, job bank, job interviews.

Freshmen 6,861 applied, 6,861 admitted, 3,423 enrolled. 8 National Merit Scholars.

Average high school GPA	2.75	SAT verbal scores above 500	56%
SAT math scores above 500	56%	ACT above 18	72%
From top 10% of their h.s. class	13%	From top quarter	30%
From top half	57%	1998 freshmen returning in 1999	68%

Application *Options:* eApply at www.CollegeQuest.com, electronic application, early admission, early action, deferred entrance. *Application fee:* $25. *Required:* high school transcript. *Required for some:* essay or personal statement; 3 letters of recommendation; interview.

Standardized tests *Placement: Required:* SAT I or ACT

Significant dates *Application deadlines:* 8/23 (freshmen), 8/23 (transfers). *Early action:* 2/1. *Notification:* 3/15 (early action). *Financial aid deadline priority date:* 3/1.

Freshman Application Contact
Ms. Connie Murray, Interim Director of Admissions, The University of Akron, 381 Buchtel Common, Akron, OH 44325-2001. **Phone:** 330-972-6428. **Toll-free phone:** 800-655-4884. **Fax:** 330-972-7676. **E-mail:** admissions@uakron.edu

Visit CollegeQuest.com for information on majors offered and athletics. College video available at CollegeQuest.com.

■ *See page 2682 for a narrative description.*

UNIVERSITY OF CINCINNATI
Cincinnati, Ohio

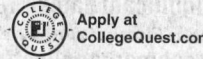 Apply at CollegeQuest.com

- **State-supported**, university, founded 1819
- **Degrees** associate, bachelor's, master's, doctoral, and first professional
- **Urban** 137-acre campus
- **Coed**, 19,451 undergraduate students, 79% full-time, 48% women, 52% men
- **Moderately difficult** entrance level, 86% of applicants were admitted
- **48.9% graduate** in 6 years or less
- **$4998 tuition** and fees (in-state); $12,879 (out-of-state)
- **$5087 average financial aid** package, $807.9 million endowment

Students receive an outstanding education where they can choose from 325 academic programs, exceptional co-op opportunities with 1,400 employers, and 275 student organizations. Rich with opportunity and fascinatingly diverse, the University of Cincinnati prepares students for their future: job, graduate school, and life. Campus tours and information sessions are available daily (telephone: 513-556-1100; e-mail: admissions@uc.edu).

Part of University of Cincinnati System.

Students *Undergraduates:* 15,271 full-time, 4,180 part-time. Students come from 46 states and territories, 50 other countries. *The most frequently chosen baccalaureate fields are:* business/marketing, engineering/engineering technologies, health professions and related sciences. *Graduate:* 974 in professional programs, 6,532 in other graduate degree programs.

Reside on campus	18%	Age 25 or older	16%
Transferred in	6%	International students	1%
African Americans	14%	Asian Americans/Pacific Islanders	3%
Hispanic Americans	1%	Native Americans	0.3%

Faculty 1,939 (100% full-time), 81% with terminal degrees.

Expenses (1999–2000) *Tuition, state resident:* full-time $4257; part-time $139 per credit hour. *Tuition, nonresident:* full-time $12,138; part-time $358 per credit hour. *Required fees:* full-time $741. Full-time tuition and fees vary according to location. Part-time tuition and fees vary according to location. *College room and board:* $6399. *Payment plan:* installment. *Waivers:* employees or children of employees.

Library Langsam Library plus 7 others. *Collection:* 16,363 serial subscriptions, 48,757 audiovisual materials.

College life *Housing:* on-campus residence required in freshman year. *Options:* coed, men-only, women-only. *Social organizations:* national fraternities, national sororities, local sororities.

Campus security 24-hour emergency response devices and patrols, late-night transport-escort service, controlled dormitory access.

After graduation *Career center:* Services include job fairs, resume preparation, career counseling. *Graduate education:* 36% of class of 1999 went directly to graduate and professional school. *Major awards:* 1 Fulbright Scholar.

Freshmen 10,704 applied, 9,169 admitted, 3,846 enrolled.

SAT verbal scores above 500	59%	SAT math scores above 500	63%
ACT above 18	61%	From top 10% of their h.s. class	15%
From top quarter	36%	From top half	65%
1998 freshmen returning in 1999	70%		

Application *Options:* eApply at www.CollegeQuest.com, electronic application. *Preference* given to state residents. *Application fee:* $30. *Required:* high school transcript. *Required for some:* 2 letters of recommendation; audition. *Recommended:* interview.

Standardized tests *Admission: Required:* SAT I or ACT.

Significant dates *Application deadlines:* rolling (freshmen), rolling (transfers). *Financial aid deadline:* continuous.

Freshman Application Contact
Mr. James Williams, Director of Admissions, University of Cincinnati, PO Box 210091, Cincinnati, OH 45221-0091. **Phone:** 513-556-1100. **Toll-free phone:** 800-827-8728. **E-mail:** admissions@uc.edu

Visit CollegeQuest.com for information on majors offered and athletics. College video and electronic viewbook available at CollegeQuest.com.

■ *See page 2712 for a narrative description.*

UNIVERSITY OF DAYTON
Dayton, Ohio

- **Independent Roman Catholic**, university, founded 1850
- **Degrees** bachelor's, master's, doctoral, and first professional
- **Suburban** 110-acre campus with easy access to Cincinnati
- **Coed**, 6,905 undergraduate students, 92% full-time, 51% women, 49% men
- **Moderately difficult** entrance level, 87% of applicants were admitted
- **71% graduate** in 6 years or less
- **$15,530 tuition** and fees
- **$11,032 average financial aid** package, $16,357 average indebtedness upon graduation, $247.5 million endowment

Recognized as one of the nation's leading Catholic universities, the University of Dayton offers the resources and diversity of a comprehensive university and the attention and accessibility of a small college. The impressive campus, challenging academic programs, advanced research facilities, NCAA Division I athletic programs, and access to the Dayton metropolitan community are big-school advantages. Small classes, undergraduate emphasis, student-centered faculty and staff, residential campus, and friendliness are small-school qualities.

Students *Undergraduates:* 6,354 full-time, 551 part-time. Students come from 43 states and territories. *Graduate:* 486 in professional programs, 2,793 in other graduate degree programs.

From out-of-state	38%	Reside on campus	73%
Age 25 or older	6%	Transferred in	2%
International students	1%	African Americans	3%
Asian Americans/Pacific Islanders	1%	Hispanic Americans	2%
Native Americans	0.1%		

Expenses (1999–2000) *Comprehensive fee:* $20,400 includes full-time tuition ($15,020), mandatory fees ($510), and room and board ($4870). *College room only:* $2620. Full-time tuition and fees vary according to program. Room and board charges vary according to board plan, housing facility, and student level. *Part-time tuition:* $501 per semester hour. *Part-time fees:* $25 per term part-time. Part-time tuition and fees vary according to course load and program. *Payment plans:* installment, deferred payment. *Waivers:* senior citizens and employees or children of employees.

Library Roesch Library plus 1 other. *Operations spending 1999–2000:* $6.7 million. *Collection:* 1.7 million titles, 4,196 serial subscriptions, 1,383 audiovisual materials.

College life *Housing:* on-campus residence required through sophomore year. *Options:* coed, men-only, women-only, disabled students. *Social organizations:* national fraternities, national sororities, local fraternities, local

Ohio

University of Dayton (continued)

sororities; 18% of eligible men and 22% of eligible women are members. *Most popular organizations:* Student Government Association, marching band, Habitat for Humanity, Campus Connection, Alpha Phi Omega.

Campus security 24-hour emergency response devices and patrols, student patrols, late-night transport-escort service, controlled dormitory access.

After graduation 195 organizations recruited on campus 1997–98. 88% of class of 1998 had job offers within 6 months. *Career center:* 12 full-time personnel. Services include job fairs, resume preparation, interview workshops, resume referral, career counseling, careers library, job bank, job interviews. *Major awards:* 1 Fulbright Scholar.

Freshmen 6,572 applied, 5,688 admitted, 1,800 enrolled. 13 National Merit Scholars, 39 valedictorians.

SAT verbal scores above 500	79%	SAT math scores above 500	82%
ACT above 18	98%	From top 10% of their h.s. class	22%
From top quarter	48%	From top half	77%
1998 freshmen returning in 1999	86%		

Application *Options:* electronic application, early admission, deferred entrance. *Application fee:* $30. *Required:* high school transcript. *Required for some:* essay or personal statement; 1 letter of recommendation. *Recommended:* interview.

Standardized tests *Admission: Required:* SAT I or ACT.

Significant dates *Application deadlines:* rolling (freshmen), 7/15 (transfers). *Financial aid deadline priority date:* 3/31.

Freshman Application Contact
Mr. Myron H. Achbach, Director of Admission, University of Dayton, 300 College Park, Dayton, OH 45469-1300. **Phone:** 937-229-4411. **Toll-free phone:** 800-837-7433. **Fax:** 937-229-4545. **E-mail:** admission@udayton.edu

Visit CollegeQuest.com for information on majors offered and athletics. College video available at CollegeQuest.com.

■ *See pages 2718 and 2720 for narrative descriptions.*

THE UNIVERSITY OF FINDLAY
Findlay, Ohio

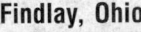 Apply at CollegeQuest.com

- **Independent**, comprehensive, founded 1882, affiliated with Church of God
- **Degrees** associate, bachelor's, and master's
- **Small-town** 160-acre campus with easy access to Toledo
- **Coed**, 3,327 undergraduate students, 80% full-time, 56% women, 44% men
- **Moderately difficult** entrance level, 74% of applicants were admitted
- **18:1 student-to-undergraduate faculty ratio**
- **49% graduate** in 6 years or less
- **$15,260 tuition** and fees
- **$14,200 average financial aid** package, $17,500 average indebtedness upon graduation, $19.3 million endowment

Eleven pre-health profession tracks are offered leading to current and proposed degree programs, including athletic training, nuclear medicine, occupational therapy, physical therapy, and physician assistant studies. Environmental, safety, and occupational health management programs prepare students for these fields. Equestrian studies (English, Western, equine management), pre-veterinary medicine, and bilingual studies in Spanish and Japanese are other programs earning Findlay recognition.

Students *Undergraduates:* 2,673 full-time, 654 part-time. Students come from 35 states and territories, 20 other countries. *The most frequently chosen baccalaureate fields are:* business/marketing, engineering/engineering technologies, health professions and related sciences. *Graduate:* 864 in graduate degree programs.

From out-of-state	20%	Reside on campus	38%
Age 25 or older	31%	Transferred in	4%
International students	1%	African Americans	5%
Asian Americans/Pacific Islanders	4%	Hispanic Americans	3%
Native Americans	1%		

Faculty 310 (42% full-time).

Expenses (1999–2000) *Comprehensive fee:* $21,000 includes full-time tuition ($15,080), mandatory fees ($180), and room and board ($5740). *College room only:* $2800. Full-time tuition and fees vary according to location and program. *Part-time tuition:* $328 per semester hour. *Part-time fees:* $30 per term part-time. Part-time tuition and fees vary according to location and program. *Payment plan:* installment. *Waivers:* senior citizens and employees or children of employees.

Library Shafer Library. *Operations spending 1999–2000:* $869,963. *Collection:* 133,336 titles, 958 serial subscriptions.

College life *Housing:* on-campus residence required through senior year. *Options:* men-only, women-only, disabled students. *Social organizations:* national fraternities, national sororities; 8% of eligible men and 3% of eligible women are members. *Most popular organizations:* Campus Program Board, prevet club, horse club, Circle K, International Club.

Campus security 24-hour emergency response devices and patrols, late-night transport-escort service, controlled dormitory access.

After graduation 316 organizations recruited on campus 1997–98. *Career center:* 2 full-time personnel. Services include job fairs, resume preparation, interview workshops, resume referral, career/interest testing, career counseling, careers library, job bank, job interviews. *Graduate education:* 16% of class of 1999 went directly to graduate and professional school.

Freshmen 2,593 applied, 1,927 admitted, 653 enrolled. 30 valedictorians.

Average high school GPA	3.2	SAT verbal scores above 500	27%
SAT math scores above 500	28%	ACT above 18	100%
From top 10% of their h.s. class	21%	From top quarter	45%
From top half	84%	1998 freshmen returning in 1999	72%

Application *Options:* eApply at www.CollegeQuest.com, Common Application, electronic application, deferred entrance. *Application fee:* $0. *Required:* high school transcript; minimum 2.3 GPA. *Required for some:* essay or personal statement; letters of recommendation; interview.

Standardized tests *Admission: Required:* SAT I or ACT.

Significant dates *Application deadlines:* 7/1 (freshmen), rolling (transfers). *Financial aid deadline:* continuous.

Freshman Application Contact
Mr. Michael Momany, Executive Director of Enrollment Services, The University of Findlay, 1000 North Main Street, Findlay, OH 45840-3653. **Phone:** 419-424-4732. **Toll-free phone:** 800-548-0932. **Fax:** 419-424-4822. **E-mail:** admissions@findlay.edu

Visit CollegeQuest.com for information on majors offered and athletics. Electronic viewbook available at CollegeQuest.com.

■ *See page 2726 for a narrative description.*

UNIVERSITY OF RIO GRANDE
Rio Grande, Ohio

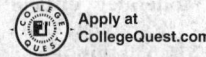 Apply at CollegeQuest.com

- **Independent**, comprehensive, founded 1876
- **Degrees** associate, bachelor's, and master's
- **Rural** 170-acre campus
- **Coed**, 1,851 undergraduate students, 82% full-time, 60% women, 40% men
- **Noncompetitive** entrance level, 100% of applicants were admitted
- **17:1 student-to-undergraduate faculty ratio**
- **$3441 tuition** and fees (in-state); $9225 (out-of-state)
- **$13,750 average indebtedness** upon graduation, $22.6 million endowment

Students *Undergraduates:* Students come from 11 states and territories, 15 other countries. *The most frequently chosen baccalaureate fields are:* business/marketing, communications/communication technologies, education. *Graduate:* 101 in graduate degree programs.

From out-of-state	5%	Reside on campus	27%
Age 25 or older	25%		

Faculty 132 (61% full-time), 33% with terminal degrees.

Expenses (1999–2000) *Tuition, area resident:* full-time $2520; part-time $52 per quarter hour. *Tuition, state resident:* full-time $3000; part-time $62 per quarter hour. *Tuition, nonresident:* full-time $8784; part-time $244 per quarter hour. *Required fees:* full-time $441; $7 per credit hour; $15 per term part-time. Full-time tuition and fees vary according to reciprocity agreements and student level. Part-time tuition and fees vary according to reciprocity agreements and student level. *College room and board:* $4995.

Ohio

Area and state resident tuition rates apply only for the first 2 years. *Payment plans:* installment, deferred payment. *Waivers:* employees or children of employees.
Library Jeanette Albiez Davis Library plus 2 others. *Operations spending 1999–2000:* $353,505. *Collection:* 96,731 titles, 850 serial subscriptions.
College life *Housing:* on-campus residence required through senior year. *Options:* coed, men-only, women-only. *Social organizations:* national fraternities, local fraternities, local sororities; 5% of eligible men and 4% of eligible women are members. *Most popular organizations:* Greek organizations, student government, Honoraries, Bible Studies, Students in Free Enterprise.
Campus security 24-hour emergency response devices and patrols, late-night transport-escort service, controlled dormitory access.
After graduation 40 organizations recruited on campus 1997–98. *Career center:* 1 full-time, 1 part-time personnel. Services include job fairs, resume preparation, interview workshops, resume referral, career/interest testing, career counseling, careers library, job bank, job interviews.
Freshmen 659 applied, 659 admitted.

SAT verbal scores above 500	N/R	SAT math scores above 500	N/R
ACT above 18	63%	From top 10% of their h.s. class	15%
From top quarter	35%	From top half	58%
1998 freshmen returning in 1999	65%		

Application *Options:* eApply at www.CollegeQuest.com, Common Application. *Application fee:* $15. *Required:* high school transcript; medical history.
Standardized tests *Placement: Required:* ACT
Significant dates *Application deadlines:* rolling (freshmen), rolling (transfers). *Financial aid deadline:* continuous.
Freshman Application Contact
Mr. Mark F. Abell, Executive Director of Admissions, University of Rio Grande, PO Box 500, Rio Grande, OH 45674. **Phone:** 740-245-5353 Ext. 7206. **Toll-free phone:** 800-282-7201. **Fax:** 740-245-9220. **E-mail:** mabell@urgrgcc.edu
Visit CollegeQuest.com for information on majors offered and athletics.

■ *See page 2814 for a narrative description.*

UNIVERSITY OF TOLEDO
Toledo, Ohio

- **State-supported**, university, founded 1872
- **Degrees** associate, bachelor's, master's, doctoral, first professional, post-master's, and postbachelor's certificates
- **Suburban** 407-acre campus with easy access to Detroit
- **Coed**
- **Noncompetitive** entrance level
- **$4416 tuition** and fees (in-state); $10,785 (out-of-state)

Expenses (1999–2000) *Tuition, state resident:* full-time $3611; part-time $150 per semester hour. *Tuition, nonresident:* full-time $9980; part-time $416 per semester hour. *Required fees:* full-time $805; $34 per semester hour. *College room and board:* $4538. Room and board charges vary according to board plan and housing facility.
Institutional Web site http://www.utoledo.edu/
College life *Housing:* on-campus residence required in freshman year. *Options:* coed, women-only, disabled students. *Social organizations:* national fraternities, national sororities, local fraternities; 5% of eligible men and 5% of eligible women are members. *Most popular organizations:* student government, University YMCA, Newman Club, International Student Association, Campus Activities and Programming.
Campus security 24-hour emergency response devices and patrols, student patrols, late-night transport-escort service, controlled dormitory access, bicycle patrols by security staff, crime prevention officer.
Application *Options:* electronic application, deferred entrance. *Application fee:* $30. *Required:* high school transcript. *Required for some:* minimum 2.0 GPA.
Standardized tests *Admission: Recommended:* SAT I or ACT. *Required for some:* SAT I or ACT.
Admissions Office Contact
University of Toledo, 2801 West Bancroft, Toledo, OH 43606-3398. **Toll-free phone:** 800-5TOLEDO. **Fax:** 419-530-4504. **E-mail:** enroll@utnet.utoledo.edu

Visit CollegeQuest.com for information on athletics.

URBANA UNIVERSITY
Urbana, Ohio

- **Independent**, comprehensive, founded 1850, affiliated with Church of the New Jerusalem
- **Degrees** associate, bachelor's, and master's
- **Small-town** 128-acre campus with easy access to Columbus and Dayton
- **Coed**, 1,111 undergraduate students, 68% full-time, 49% women, 51% men
- **Moderately difficult** entrance level
- **$11,488 tuition** and fees

The mission of Urbana University is to offer an exemplary liberal arts education in a small college environment emphasizing individual attention, excellence in instruction, career-oriented programs, and affirmation of moral and ethical values. Urbana University operates on the principle that all policies, practices, and decisions must be made in the best interest of the students served.

Students *Undergraduates:* 754 full-time, 357 part-time. Students come from 11 states and territories. *Graduate:* 33 in graduate degree programs.

From out-of-state	2%	Age 25 or older	20%
International students	0.2%	African Americans	20%
Asian Americans/Pacific Islanders	0.2%	Hispanic Americans	2%
Native Americans	0.3%		

Expenses (1999–2000) *Comprehensive fee:* $16,488 includes full-time tuition ($11,388), mandatory fees ($100), and room and board ($5000). *College room only:* $2100. Full-time tuition and fees vary according to location. Room and board charges vary according to student level. *Part-time tuition:* $232 per credit hour. *Part-time fees:* $25 per term part-time. Part-time tuition and fees vary according to location. *Payment plans:* installment, deferred payment. *Waivers:* children of alumni, senior citizens, and employees or children of employees.
Library Swedenborg Memorial Library. *Operations spending 1999–2000:* $105,684. *Collection:* 73,278 titles, 955 serial subscriptions.
College life *Housing:* on-campus residence required through junior year. *Options:* men-only, women-only. *Most popular organizations:* Student government Association, business club, education club, drama club, Student Activities Planning Committee.
Campus security 24-hour patrols, late-night transport-escort service.
After graduation *Career center:* 3 full-time personnel. Services include job fairs, resume preparation, resume referral, career counseling, careers library, job interviews. *Graduate education:* 11% of class of 1999 went directly to graduate and professional school.
Freshmen 167 enrolled. 5 valedictorians.

Average high school GPA	2.8	SAT verbal scores above 500	N/R
SAT math scores above 500	N/R	ACT above 18	N/R
From top 10% of their h.s. class	15%	From top quarter	34%
From top half	66%	1998 freshmen returning in 1999	76%

Application *Options:* electronic application, early admission, deferred entrance. *Application fee:* $25. *Required:* essay or personal statement; high school transcript; minimum 2.0 GPA. *Required for some:* 2 letters of recommendation. *Recommended:* interview.
Standardized tests *Admission: Required:* SAT I or ACT.
Significant dates *Application deadlines:* rolling (freshmen), rolling (transfers). *Financial aid deadline priority date:* 5/1.
Freshman Application Contact
Ms. Mona Newcomer, Admissions Office Manager, Urbana University, 579 College Way, Urbana, OH 43078-2091. **Phone:** 937-484-1356. **Toll-free phone:** 800-787-2262. **Fax:** 937-484-1389. **E-mail:** admiss@urbana.edu
Visit CollegeQuest.com for information on majors offered and athletics.

■ *See page 2868 for a narrative description.*

URSULINE COLLEGE
Pepper Pike, Ohio

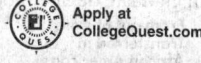

- **Independent Roman Catholic**, comprehensive, founded 1871
- **Degrees** bachelor's and master's

Peterson's Guide to Four-Year Colleges 2001   www.petersons.com   649

Ohio

Ursuline College (continued)
- **Suburban** 112-acre campus with easy access to Cleveland
- **Coed**, primarily women, 1,040 undergraduate students, 48% full-time, 94% women, 6% men
- **Minimally difficult** entrance level, 78% of applicants were admitted
- **14:1 student-to-undergraduate faculty ratio**
- **$13,760 tuition** and fees
- **$17.4 million endowment**

Students *Undergraduates:* Students come from 11 states and territories, 1 other country. *Graduate:* 219 in graduate degree programs.

Reside on campus	8%	Age 25 or older	54%
International students	0.2%	African Americans	18%
Asian Americans/Pacific Islanders	1%	Hispanic Americans	1%
Native Americans	0.3%		

Faculty 153 (42% full-time), 39% with terminal degrees.

Expenses (1999–2000) *Comprehensive fee:* $18,320 includes full-time tuition ($13,760) and room and board ($4560). *Part-time tuition:* $430 per credit hour. *Payment plan:* installment. *Waivers:* employees or children of employees.

Library Ralph M. Besse Library. *Collection:* 115,661 titles, 589 serial subscriptions.

College life *Most popular organizations:* Student Government Association, Student Nurses of Ursuline College, Fashion Focus, Students United for Black Awareness, drama club.

Campus security 24-hour emergency response devices and patrols.

After graduation 40 organizations recruited on campus 1997–98. *Career center:* 4 full-time, 1 part-time personnel. Services include job fairs, resume preparation, resume referral, career counseling, careers library, job bank, job interviews.

Freshmen 212 applied, 165 admitted.

Average high school GPA	2.89	SAT verbal scores above 500	N/R
SAT math scores above 500	N/R	ACT above 18	N/R
1998 freshmen returning in 1999	48%		

Application *Options:* eApply at www.CollegeQuest.com, early admission, deferred entrance. *Application fee:* $25. *Required:* high school transcript. *Recommended:* essay or personal statement; minimum 2.0 GPA; letters of recommendation; interview.

Standardized tests *Admission: Required:* SAT I or ACT.

Significant dates *Application deadlines:* rolling (freshmen), rolling (transfers). *Financial aid deadline priority date:* 4/1.

Freshman Application Contact
Mrs. Colleen C. Sommerfeld, Director of Admissions, Ursuline College, 2550 Lander Road, Pepper Pike, OH 44124-4398. **Phone:** 440-449-4203. **Fax:** 440-449-2235. **E-mail:** dkoeth@ursuline.edu

Visit CollegeQuest.com for information on majors offered and athletics. College video available at CollegeQuest.com.

WALSH UNIVERSITY
North Canton, Ohio

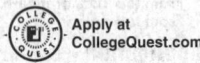

- **Independent Roman Catholic**, comprehensive, founded 1958
- **Degrees** associate, bachelor's, and master's
- **Small-town** 100-acre campus with easy access to Cleveland
- **Coed**, 1,373 undergraduate students, 71% full-time, 56% women, 44% men
- **Moderately difficult** entrance level, 85% of applicants were admitted
- **14:1 student-to-undergraduate faculty ratio**
- **$11,728 tuition** and fees
- **$9972 average financial aid** package, $17,000 average indebtedness upon graduation, $2.1 million endowment

Students *Undergraduates:* 972 full-time, 401 part-time. Students come from 10 states and territories. *The most frequently chosen baccalaureate fields are:* business/marketing, biological/life sciences, education. *Graduate:* 174 in graduate degree programs.

From out-of-state	2%	Reside on campus	50%
Transferred in	16%	International students	1%
African Americans	6%	Asian Americans/Pacific Islanders	1%
Hispanic Americans	1%		

Faculty 165 (36% full-time), 37% with terminal degrees.

Expenses (1999–2000) *Comprehensive fee:* $17,128 includes full-time tuition ($11,350), mandatory fees ($378), and room and board ($5400). Full-time tuition and fees vary according to course load. *Part-time tuition:* $378 per credit hour. *Part-time fees:* $11 per credit hour. *Payment plans:* installment, deferred payment. *Waivers:* children of alumni, senior citizens, and employees or children of employees.

Library Walsh University Library. *Collection:* 130,000 titles, 683 serial subscriptions.

College life *Housing:* on-campus residence required through senior year. *Options:* coed, men-only, women-only. *Most popular organizations:* BACCHUS, Circle K, business club, Student Activities, student government.

Campus security 24-hour emergency response devices and patrols, controlled dormitory access.

After graduation 34 organizations recruited on campus 1997–98. *Career center:* 1 full-time, 1 part-time personnel. Services include job fairs, resume preparation, resume referral, career counseling, careers library, job bank, job interviews.

Freshmen 910 applied, 774 admitted, 319 enrolled.

Average high school GPA	3.1	SAT verbal scores above 500	N/R
SAT math scores above 500	N/R	ACT above 18	89%
From top 10% of their h.s. class	20%	From top quarter	44%
From top half	74%	1998 freshmen returning in 1999	74%

Application *Options:* eApply at www.CollegeQuest.com, Common Application, electronic application, early admission, deferred entrance. *Application fee:* $25. *Required:* high school transcript; minimum 2.0 GPA. *Required for some:* essay or personal statement; minimum 3.0 GPA; 2 letters of recommendation. *Recommended:* interview.

Standardized tests *Admission: Required:* SAT I or ACT.

Significant dates *Application deadlines:* rolling (freshmen), rolling (transfers). *Financial aid deadline:* continuous.

Freshman Application Contact
Mr. Doug Swartz, Director of Admissions, Walsh University, 2020 Easton Street, NW, North Canton, OH 44720-3396. **Phone:** 330-490-7172. **Toll-free phone:** 800-362-9846 (in-state); 800-362-8846 (out-of-state). **Fax:** 330-490-7165. **E-mail:** admissions@alex.walsh.edu

Visit CollegeQuest.com for information on majors offered and athletics. College video and electronic viewbook available at CollegeQuest.com.

- *See page 2906 for a narrative description.*

WILBERFORCE UNIVERSITY
Wilberforce, Ohio

- **Independent**, 4-year, founded 1856, affiliated with African Methodist Episcopal Church
- **Degree** bachelor's
- **Rural** 125-acre campus with easy access to Dayton
- **Coed**
- **Minimally difficult** entrance level
- **$9130 tuition** and fees

For 143 years, Wilberforce University, the nation's oldest historically African-American private college, has provided academically excellent education opportunities. A rigorous curriculum; mandatory cooperative education; study-abroad in England, Egypt, and Israel; cultural and extracurricular programming; and intercollegiate athletic programs are provided to prepare students for careers and graduate and professional studies.

Expenses (1999–2000) *Comprehensive fee:* $13,920 includes full-time tuition ($8200), mandatory fees ($930), and room and board ($4790). *Part-time tuition:* $355 per credit hour. *Part-time fees:* $465 per term part-time.

Institutional Web site http://www.wilberforce.edu/

College life *Housing:* on-campus residence required through junior year. *Options:* men-only, women-only. *Social organizations:* national fraternities, national sororities; 20% of eligible men and 20% of eligible women are members. *Most popular organizations:* campus newspaper, yearbook staff, campus radio station, National Student Business League, Student Government Association.

Ohio

Campus security 24-hour emergency response devices and patrols, controlled dormitory access.
Application *Options:* eApply at www.CollegeQuest.com, Common Application, electronic application, early admission, deferred entrance. *Application fee:* $20. *Required:* essay or personal statement; high school transcript; minimum 2.0 GPA; 2 letters of recommendation. *Recommended:* interview.
Standardized tests *Admission: Required:* SAT I or ACT.
Admissions Office Contact
Wilberforce University, 1055 North Bickett Road, Wilberforce, OH 45384. **Toll-free phone:** 800-367-8568. **Fax:** 937-376-4751. **E-mail:** admissions@shorter.wilberforce.edu
Visit CollegeQuest.com for information on athletics.

■ *See page 2992 for a narrative description.*

WILMINGTON COLLEGE
Wilmington, Ohio

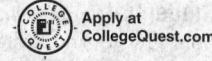

- **Independent Friends**, 4-year, founded 1870
- **Degree** bachelor's
- **Small-town** 1,465-acre campus with easy access to Cincinnati and Columbus
- **Coed**, 1,153 undergraduate students, 99% full-time, 54% women, 46% men
- **Moderately difficult** entrance level, 91% of applicants were admitted
- **17:1 student-to-undergraduate faculty ratio**
- **$14,666 tuition** and fees
- **$12,853 average financial aid** package, $19,800 average indebtedness upon graduation, $20 million endowment

Students *Undergraduates:* 1,140 full-time, 13 part-time. Students come from 12 states and territories, 5 other countries.

From out-of-state	3%	Reside on campus	63%
Transferred in	6%	International students	2%
African Americans	7%		

Expenses (2000–2001) *Comprehensive fee:* $19,886 includes full-time tuition ($14,330), mandatory fees ($336), and room and board ($5220). Room and board charges vary according to housing facility. Part-time tuition and fees vary according to course load. *Payment plan:* installment. *Waivers:* employees or children of employees.
Library Watson Library plus 1 other. *Operations spending 1999–2000:* $326,593. *Collection:* 98,853 titles, 396 serial subscriptions, 1,275 audiovisual materials.
College life *Housing:* on-campus residence required through senior year. *Options:* coed, men-only. *Social organizations:* national fraternities, local fraternities, local sororities; 40% of eligible men and 40% of eligible women are members. *Most popular organizations:* Greek organizations, Aggie Club, Quest, student publications, Commuter Concerns.
Campus security 24-hour emergency response devices and patrols, late-night transport-escort service, controlled dormitory access.
After graduation 32 organizations recruited on campus 1997–98. *Career center:* 2 full-time personnel. Services include job fairs, resume preparation, resume referral, career counseling, careers library, job bank, job interviews.
Freshmen 1,028 applied, 932 admitted, 335 enrolled.

Average high school GPA	3.1	SAT verbal scores above 500	N/R
SAT math scores above 500	N/R	ACT above 18	84%
From top 10% of their h.s. class	15%	From top quarter	40%
From top half	75%	1998 freshmen returning in 1999	72%

Application *Options:* eApply at www.CollegeQuest.com, deferred entrance. *Application fee:* $20. *Required:* high school transcript. *Recommended:* minimum 2.5 GPA; 1 letter of recommendation; interview.
Standardized tests *Admission: Required:* SAT I or ACT.
Significant dates *Application deadlines:* rolling (freshmen), rolling (transfers). *Financial aid deadline:* 6/30. *Priority date:* 3/1.
Freshman Application Contact
Dr. Lawrence T. Lesick, Dean of Admission and Financial Aid, Wilmington College, Pyle Center Box 1185, Wilmington, OH 45177. **Phone:** 937-382-6661 Ext. 260. **Toll-free phone:** 800-341-9318 Ext. 260. **Fax:** 937-382-7077. **E-mail:** admission@wilmington.edu
Visit CollegeQuest.com for information on majors offered and athletics.

WITTENBERG UNIVERSITY
Springfield, Ohio

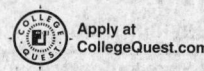

- **Independent**, 4-year, founded 1845, affiliated with Evangelical Lutheran Church
- **Degree** bachelor's
- **Suburban** 71-acre campus with easy access to Columbus and Dayton
- **Coed**, 1,859 undergraduate students, 97% full-time, 56% women, 44% men
- **Moderately difficult** entrance level, 92% of applicants were admitted
- **14:1 student-to-undergraduate faculty ratio**
- **69% graduate** in 6 years or less
- **$20,906 tuition** and fees
- **$19,361 average financial aid** package, $108 million endowment

Students *Undergraduates:* 1,800 full-time, 59 part-time. Students come from 42 states and territories, 36 other countries.

From out-of-state	40%	Reside on campus	98%
Age 25 or older	3%	Transferred in	2%

Faculty 144 (100% full-time), 97% with terminal degrees.
Expenses (1999–2000) *One-time required fee:* $112. *Comprehensive fee:* $26,112 includes full-time tuition ($19,716), mandatory fees ($1190), and room and board ($5206). *College room only:* $2588. Room and board charges vary according to board plan and housing facility. *Part-time tuition:* $657 per credit. *Payment plans:* tuition prepayment, installment, deferred payment. *Waivers:* children of alumni, adult students, senior citizens, and employees or children of employees.
Library Thomas Library plus 2 others. *Collection:* 350,000 titles, 1,200 serial subscriptions.
College life *Housing:* on-campus residence required through sophomore year. *Options:* coed, women-only. *Social organizations:* national fraternities, national sororities; 15% of eligible men and 35% of eligible women are members. *Most popular organizations:* American International Association, East Asian Studies Program, spelunking club, Union Board, marketing club.
Campus security 24-hour emergency response devices and patrols, student patrols, late-night transport-escort service, controlled dormitory access, crime prevention programs.
After graduation 100 organizations recruited on campus 1997–98. 94% of class of 1998 had job offers within 6 months. *Career center:* 4 full-time, 1 part-time personnel. Services include job fairs, resume preparation, interview workshops, resume referral, career/interest testing, career counseling, careers library, job bank, job interviews. *Graduate education:* 24% of class of 1999 went directly to graduate and professional school: 5% business, 5% medicine, 2% education, 2% engineering, 2% graduate arts and sciences, 2% law, 1% dentistry, 1% theology. *Major awards:* 2 Fulbright Scholars.
Freshmen 2,535 applied, 2,332 admitted, 616 enrolled. 3 National Merit Scholars, 40 class presidents, 175 student government officers.

Average high school GPA	3.4	SAT verbal scores above 500	82%
SAT math scores above 500	83%	ACT above 18	99%
From top 10% of their h.s. class	39%	From top quarter	74%
From top half	95%	1998 freshmen returning in 1999	85%

Application *Options:* eApply at www.CollegeQuest.com, Common Application, electronic application, early admission, early decision, early action, deferred entrance. *Preference* given to Lutherans, children of alumni, county residents, minorities. *Application fee:* $40. *Required:* essay or personal statement; high school transcript; 1 letter of recommendation. *Required for some:* interview. *Recommended:* interview.
Standardized tests *Admission: Required:* SAT I or ACT. *Recommended:* SAT II Subject Tests.
Significant dates *Application deadlines:* 3/15 (freshmen), rolling (transfers). *Early decision:* 11/15, 12/1. *Notification:* 1/1 (early decision), 1/1 (early action). *Financial aid deadline:* 3/15. *Priority date:* 2/15.
Freshman Application Contact
Mr. Kenneth G. Benne, Dean of Admissions, Wittenberg University, PO Box 720, Springfield, OH 45501-0720. **Phone:** 937-327-6314 Ext. 6366. **Toll-free phone:** 800-677-7558 Ext. 6314. **Fax:** 937-327-6379. **E-mail:** admission@wittenberg.edu
Visit CollegeQuest.com for information on majors offered and athletics. College video and electronic viewbook available at CollegeQuest.com.

Ohio

WRIGHT STATE UNIVERSITY
Dayton, Ohio

- **State-supported**, university, founded 1964
- **Degrees** associate, bachelor's, master's, doctoral, and first professional
- **Suburban** 557-acre campus with easy access to Cincinnati and Columbus
- **Coed**, 10,662 undergraduate students, 82% full-time, 56% women, 44% men
- **Minimally difficult** entrance level, 91% of applicants were admitted
- **20:1 student-to-undergraduate faculty ratio**
- **30% graduate** in 6 years or less
- **$4128 tuition** and fees (in-state); $8256 (out-of-state)
- **$5.1 million endowment**

Wright State University puts students first, with many small classes, an emphasis on learning outside the classroom, and a rich campus life. Classrooms, research, and extracurricular facilities are state-of-the-art. Modern student housing ranks among the best in the Midwest.

Students *Undergraduates:* 8,743 full-time, 1,919 part-time. Students come from 47 states and territories, 59 other countries. *The most frequently chosen baccalaureate fields are:* business/marketing, education, liberal arts/general studies. *Graduate:* 354 in professional programs, 3,105 in other graduate degree programs.

From out-of-state	3%	Reside on campus	16%
Age 25 or older	31%	Transferred in	8%
International students	1%	African Americans	12%
Asian Americans/Pacific Islanders	2%	Hispanic Americans	1%
Native Americans	0.3%		

Faculty 689.

Expenses (1999–2000) *Tuition, state resident:* full-time $4128; part-time $127 per credit hour. *Tuition, nonresident:* full-time $8256; part-time $254 per credit hour. *College room and board:* $4595. Room and board charges vary according to board plan and housing facility. *Payment plans:* guaranteed tuition, installment. *Waivers:* senior citizens and employees or children of employees.

Library Paul Laurence Dunbar Library plus 2 others. *Operations spending 1999–2000:* $6.4 million. *Collection:* 695,805 titles, 5,312 serial subscriptions.

College life *Housing:* Option: coed. *Social organizations:* national fraternities, national sororities, local fraternities, local sororities; 3% of eligible men and 3% of eligible women are members.

Campus security 24-hour emergency response devices and patrols, late-night transport-escort service.

After graduation *Career center:* 9 full-time personnel. Services include job fairs, resume preparation, resume referral, career counseling, careers library, job bank, job interviews.

Freshmen 4,485 applied, 4,081 admitted, 2,175 enrolled.

Average high school GPA	2.9	SAT verbal scores above 500	N/R
SAT math scores above 500	N/R	ACT above 18	80%
From top 10% of their h.s. class	19%	From top quarter	40%
From top half	65%	1998 freshmen returning in 1999	72%

Application *Options:* early admission, deferred entrance. *Application fee:* $30. *Required:* high school transcript. *Recommended:* minimum 2.0 GPA.

Standardized tests *Admission: Required:* SAT I or ACT.

Significant dates *Application deadlines:* rolling (freshmen), rolling (transfers).

Freshman Application Contact Ms. Cathy Davis, Director of Undergraduate Admissions, Wright State University, 3640 Colonel Glenn Highway, Dayton, OH 45435. **Phone:** 937-775-5700. **Toll-free phone:** 800-247-1770. **Fax:** 937-775-5795. **E-mail:** admissions@wright.edu

Visit CollegeQuest.com for information on majors offered and athletics. College video available at CollegeQuest.com.

- *See page 3020 for a narrative description.*

XAVIER UNIVERSITY
Cincinnati, Ohio

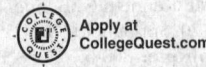 Apply at CollegeQuest.com

- **Independent Roman Catholic**, comprehensive, founded 1831
- **Degrees** associate, bachelor's, master's, doctoral, post-master's, and postbachelor's certificates
- **Suburban** 100-acre campus
- **Coed**, 3,766 undergraduate students, 86% full-time, 60% women, 40% men
- **Moderately difficult** entrance level, 89% of applicants were admitted
- **15:1 student-to-undergraduate faculty ratio**
- **67.03% graduate** in 6 years or less
- **$15,880 tuition** and fees
- **$11,619 average financial aid** package, $10,988 average indebtedness upon graduation, $79.4 million endowment

Founded in 1831, Xavier University is a Jesuit university that seeks to educate the whole person. The Jesuit tradition is evident in Xavier's love of ideas and rigorous intellectual inquiry, respect for life, passion for justice, and sense of community and working together for the common good. With 67 majors and 38 minors, numerous scholarships, and opportunities for leadership and service, Xavier is more than a degree—it's an education for life.

Students *Undergraduates:* 3,245 full-time, 521 part-time. Students come from 43 states and territories, 39 other countries. *The most frequently chosen baccalaureate fields are:* business/marketing, education, liberal arts/general studies. *Graduate:* 2,508 in graduate degree programs.

From out-of-state	35%	Reside on campus	42%
Age 25 or older	16%	Transferred in	3%
International students	1%	African Americans	9%
Asian Americans/Pacific Islanders	2%	Hispanic Americans	1%
Native Americans	0.1%		

Faculty 549 (46% full-time).

Expenses (2000–2001) *Comprehensive fee:* $22,560 includes full-time tuition ($15,680), mandatory fees ($200), and room and board ($6680). *College room only:* $3540. Full-time tuition and fees vary according to program. Room and board charges vary according to board plan and housing facility. *Part-time tuition:* $365 per credit. Part-time tuition and fees vary according to class time and course load. *Payment plans:* installment, deferred payment. *Waivers:* minority students, children of alumni, senior citizens, and employees or children of employees.

Library McDonald Library plus 2 others. *Operations spending 1999–2000:* $1.9 million. *Collection:* 175,293 titles, 1,501 serial subscriptions.

College life *Housing:* on-campus residence required through sophomore year. Option: coed. *Most popular organizations:* Student Government Association, Student Activities Council, Performing Arts Group, Xavier Action (service organization), Residence Hall Association.

Campus security 24-hour emergency response devices and patrols, late-night transport-escort service, controlled dormitory access, campus-wide shuttle service.

After graduation 173 organizations recruited on campus 1997–98. 93% of class of 1998 had job offers within 6 months. *Career center:* 8 full-time personnel. Services include job fairs, resume preparation, interview workshops, resume referral, career counseling, careers library, job bank, job interviews. *Graduate education:* 19% of class of 1999 went directly to graduate and professional school: 7% graduate arts and sciences, 5% medicine, 4% law, 3% education, 0.2% business.

Freshmen 3,247 applied, 2,889 admitted, 774 enrolled. 7 National Merit Scholars, 25 valedictorians.

Average high school GPA	3.46	SAT verbal scores above 500	81%
SAT math scores above 500	76%	ACT above 18	97%
From top 10% of their h.s. class	31%	From top quarter	58%
From top half	83%	1998 freshmen returning in 1999	88%

Application *Options:* eApply at www.CollegeQuest.com, Common Application, early admission, deferred entrance. *Application fee:* $25. *Required:* essay or personal statement; high school transcript; letters of recommendation. *Recommended:* interview.

Standardized tests *Admission: Required:* SAT I or ACT.

Significant dates *Application deadlines:* rolling (freshmen), rolling (transfers). *Financial aid deadline priority date:* 2/15.

Freshman Application Contact Mr. Marc Camille, Dean of Admission, Xavier University, 3800 Victory Parkway, Cincinnati, OH 45207-2111. **Phone:** 513-745-3301. **Toll-free phone:** 800-344-4698. **Fax:** 513-745-4319. **E-mail:** xuadmit@admin.xu.edu

Visit CollegeQuest.com for information on majors offered and athletics. College video and electronic viewbook available at CollegeQuest.com.

- *See page 3022 for a narrative description.*

YOUNGSTOWN STATE UNIVERSITY
Youngstown, Ohio

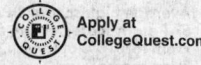
Apply at CollegeQuest.com

- **State-supported**, comprehensive, founded 1908
- **Degrees** associate, bachelor's, master's, doctoral, and postbachelor's certificates
- **Urban** 150-acre campus with easy access to Cleveland and Pittsburgh
- **Coed**, 11,002 undergraduate students, 79% full-time, 54% women, 46% men
- **Noncompetitive** entrance level
- **31.4% graduate** in 6 years or less
- **$3762 tuition** and fees (in-state); $7923 (out-of-state)
- **$3.6 million endowment**

Located on a beautiful campus in northeast Ohio, YSU offers more than 100 major programs at 2-year, 4-year, and graduate levels. A 20:1 student-faculty ratio, flexible curriculum planning, simplified transfer options, and an expanding honors program characterize YSU's academics. A comprehensive scholarship and financial aid program is available. Prospective students are invited to tour the campus and meet with professors in their major.

Students *Undergraduates:* 8,669 full-time, 2,333 part-time. Students come from 40 states and territories, 53 other countries. *The most frequently chosen baccalaureate fields are:* business/marketing, education, protective services/public administration. *Graduate:* 1,197 in graduate degree programs.

From out-of-state	8%	Reside on campus	9%
Age 25 or older	26%	Transferred in	5%
International students	1%	African Americans	8%
Asian Americans/Pacific Islanders	1%	Hispanic Americans	2%
Native Americans	0.3%		

Faculty 801 (51% full-time), 52% with terminal degrees.
Expenses (1999–2000) *Tuition, state resident:* full-time $2940; part-time $79 per credit. *Tuition, nonresident:* full-time $7101; part-time $195 per credit. *Required fees:* full-time $822; $20 per credit; $31 per term part-time. Full-time tuition and fees vary according to course load, reciprocity agreements, and student level. Part-time tuition and fees vary according to course load, reciprocity agreements, and student level. *College room and board:* $4695. Room and board charges vary according to board plan and housing facility. *Payment plan:* installment. *Waivers:* senior citizens and employees or children of employees.
Library Maag Library. *Operations spending 1999–2000:* $3.7 million. *Collection:* 606,417 titles, 3,397 serial subscriptions, 12,460 audiovisual materials.
College life *Housing: Options:* coed, women-only. *Social organizations:* national fraternities, national sororities, local fraternities, local sororities; 3% of eligible men and 2% of eligible women are members. *Most popular organizations:* student government, Panhellenic Council, Interfraternity Council, Omicron Delta Kappa, golden key.
Campus security 24-hour emergency response devices and patrols, student patrols, late-night transport-escort service, controlled dormitory access, residence hall patrols.
After graduation 115 organizations recruited on campus 1997–98. *Career center:* 5 full-time personnel. Services include job fairs, resume preparation, interview workshops, resume referral, career/interest testing, career counseling, careers library, job bank, job interviews.
Freshmen 3,885 applied, 3,436 admitted, 2,104 enrolled.

SAT verbal scores above 500	N/R	SAT math scores above 500	N/R
ACT above 18	73%	From top 10% of their h.s. class	12%
From top quarter	29%	From top half	57%
1998 freshmen returning in 1999	66%		

Application *Options:* eApply at www.CollegeQuest.com, early admission, early action, deferred entrance. *Application fee:* $25. *Required:* high school transcript. *Required for some:* interview.
Standardized tests *Admission: Required:* SAT I or ACT.
Significant dates *Application deadlines:* 8/15 (freshmen), 8/15 (transfers). *Early action:* 2/15. *Financial aid deadline priority date:* 2/15.

Freshman Application Contact
Dr. Jane S. Reid, Director of Undergraduate Recruitment and Admissions, Youngstown State University, One University Plaza, Youngstown, OH 44555-0001. **Phone:** 330-742-2000. **Toll-free phone:** 877-468-6978. **Fax:** 330-742-3674. **E-mail:** enroll@ysu.edu
Visit CollegeQuest.com for information on majors offered and athletics. College video available at CollegeQuest.com.

- *See page 3028 for a narrative description.*

OKLAHOMA

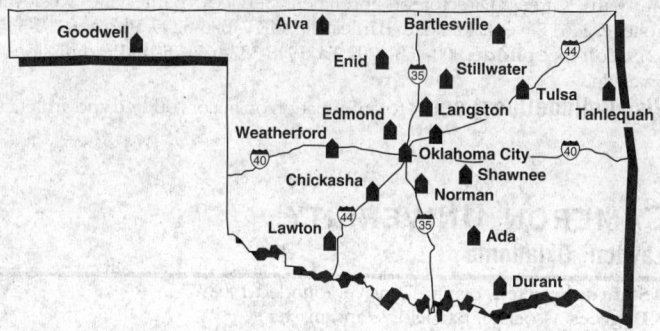

The Oklahoma City area includes the towns of Bethany and Moore.

AMERICAN BIBLE COLLEGE AND SEMINARY
Oklahoma City, Oklahoma

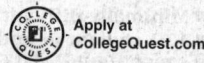
Apply at CollegeQuest.com

Admissions Office Contact
American Bible College and Seminary, 4300 Highline Boulevard, Suite 202, Oklahoma City, OK 73108. **Toll-free phone:** 800-488-2528. **Fax:** 405-945-0311.

BARTLESVILLE WESLEYAN COLLEGE
Bartlesville, Oklahoma

Apply at CollegeQuest.com

- **Independent**, 4-year, founded 1909, affiliated with Wesleyan Church
- **Degrees** associate and bachelor's
- **Small-town** 127-acre campus with easy access to Tulsa
- **Coed**, 603 undergraduate students
- **Minimally difficult** entrance level, 66% of applicants were admitted
- **$9700 tuition** and fees

Students *Undergraduates:* Students come from 28 states and territories, 7 other countries.

From out-of-state	46%	Reside on campus	47%
Age 25 or older	40%		

Expenses (2000–2001) *Comprehensive fee:* $13,800 includes full-time tuition ($9200), mandatory fees ($500), and room and board ($4100). *College room only:* $2000. Room and board charges vary according to housing facility. *Payment plans:* installment, deferred payment. *Waivers:* senior citizens and employees or children of employees.
Library Bartlesville Wesleyan College Library. *Collection:* 124,722 titles, 300 serial subscriptions.
College life On-campus residence required through senior year. *Most popular organizations:* forensics club, Fellowship of Christian Athletes, Teachers Association, theology club, education club.
Campus security 24-hour emergency response devices and patrols, controlled dormitory access.
After graduation *Career center:* 2 full-time, 3 part-time personnel. Services include resume preparation, career counseling, careers library, job bank. *Graduate education:* 10% of class of 1999 went directly to graduate and professional school: 6% theology, 2% graduate arts and sciences, 1% business, 1% medicine.

Oklahoma

Bartlesville Wesleyan College (continued)

Freshmen 489 applied, 321 admitted. 1 National Merit Scholar.

Average high school GPA	3.59	SAT verbal scores above 500	67%
SAT math scores above 500	54%	ACT above 18	88%
From top 10% of their h.s. class	30%	From top quarter	40%
From top half	80%	1998 freshmen returning in 1999	70%

Application *Options:* eApply at www.CollegeQuest.com, early admission, deferred entrance. *Application fee:* $25. *Required:* high school transcript; letters of recommendation. *Recommended:* minimum 2.0 GPA.

Standardized tests *Admission: Required:* SAT I or ACT.

Significant dates *Application deadlines:* rolling (freshmen), rolling (transfers). *Financial aid deadline priority date:* 3/31.

Freshman Application Contact Mr. Marty Carver, Director of Enrollment Services, Bartlesville Wesleyan College, 2201 Silver Lake Road, Bartlesville, OK 74006-6299. **Phone:** 918-335-6219. **Toll-free phone:** 800-468-6292. **Fax:** 918-335-6229. **E-mail:** admissions@bwc.edu

Visit CollegeQuest.com for information on majors offered and athletics.

CAMERON UNIVERSITY
Lawton, Oklahoma

- **State-supported**, comprehensive, founded 1908
- **Degrees** associate, bachelor's, and master's
- **Suburban** 160-acre campus
- **Coed**, 4,381 undergraduate students, 56% full-time, 54% women, 46% men
- **Minimally difficult** entrance level, 90% of applicants were admitted
- **12:1** student-to-undergraduate faculty ratio
- **$2050 tuition** and fees (in-state); $4840 (out-of-state)
- **$3825 average financial aid** package, $6300 average indebtedness upon graduation, $3.8 million endowment

Part of Oklahoma State Regents for Higher Education.

Students *Undergraduates:* 2,441 full-time, 1,940 part-time. Students come from 21 states and territories, 19 other countries. *The most frequently chosen baccalaureate fields are:* business/marketing, education, social sciences and history. *Graduate:* 606 in graduate degree programs.

From out-of-state	2%	Reside on campus	1%
Age 25 or older	46%	Transferred in	8%
International students	2%	African Americans	18%
Asian Americans/Pacific Islanders	3%	Hispanic Americans	7%
Native Americans	5%		

Faculty 436 (47% full-time), 29% with terminal degrees.

Expenses (1999–2000) *Tuition, state resident:* full-time $2000; part-time $67 per semester hour. *Tuition, nonresident:* full-time $4790; part-time $160 per semester hour. *Required fees:* full-time $50; $50 per term part-time. Full-time tuition and fees vary according to course level, course load, degree level, and student level. Part-time tuition and fees vary according to course level, course load, degree level, and student level. *College room and board:* $2830. Room and board charges vary according to board plan. *Payment plan:* installment. *Waivers:* senior citizens and employees or children of employees.

Library Cameron University Library. *Operations spending 1999–2000:* $1.2 million. *Collection:* 170,544 titles, 4,347 serial subscriptions, 4,969 audiovisual materials.

College life *Housing: Options:* men-only, women-only. *Social organizations:* national fraternities, national sororities; 1% of eligible men and 2% of eligible women are members. *Most popular organizations:* Student Government Association, Aggie Club, intramural club, Baptist Student Union, sociology club.

Campus security 24-hour emergency response devices and patrols, student patrols, late-night transport-escort service.

After graduation 75 organizations recruited on campus 1997–98. 20% of class of 1998 had job offers within 6 months. *Career center:* 2 full-time, 3 part-time personnel. Services include job fairs, resume preparation, resume referral, career/interest testing, career counseling, careers library, job bank, job interviews.

Freshmen 1,143 applied, 1,033 admitted, 730 enrolled.

Average high school GPA	3.08	SAT verbal scores above 500	N/R
SAT math scores above 500	N/R	ACT above 18	71%
From top 10% of their h.s. class	12%	From top quarter	32%
From top half	64%	1998 freshmen returning in 1999	37%

Application *Options:* Common Application, early admission, deferred entrance. *Application fee:* $15. *Required:* high school transcript.

Standardized tests *Admission: Required:* SAT I or ACT.

Significant dates *Application deadlines:* rolling (freshmen), rolling (transfers). *Notification:* continuous until 8/10 (freshmen). *Financial aid deadline:* continuous.

Freshman Application Contact Ms. Brenda Dally, Coordinator of Student Recruitment, Cameron University, Cameron University, Attention: Admissions, 2800 West Gore Boulevard, Lawton, OK 73505. **Phone:** 580-581-2837. **Toll-free phone:** 888-454-7600. **Fax:** 580-581-5514. **E-mail:** admiss@cua.cameron.edu

Visit CollegeQuest.com for information on majors offered and athletics.

EAST CENTRAL UNIVERSITY
Ada, Oklahoma

- **State-supported**, comprehensive, founded 1909
- **Degrees** bachelor's and master's
- **Small-town** 140-acre campus with easy access to Oklahoma City
- **Coed**, 3,229 undergraduate students, 87% full-time, 58% women, 42% men
- **Moderately difficult** entrance level, 95% of applicants were admitted
- **19:1** student-to-undergraduate faculty ratio
- **$1962 tuition** and fees (in-state); $4482 (out-of-state)
- **$3697 average financial aid** package, $11,865 average indebtedness upon graduation, $847,022 endowment

Part of Oklahoma State Regents for Higher Education.

Students *Undergraduates:* 2,794 full-time, 435 part-time. Students come from 20 states and territories, 25 other countries. *The most frequently chosen baccalaureate fields are:* business/marketing, education, parks and recreation. *Graduate:* 709 in graduate degree programs.

From out-of-state	3%	Reside on campus	17%
Age 25 or older	39%	Transferred in	9%
International students	2%	African Americans	3%
Asian Americans/Pacific Islanders	0.5%	Hispanic Americans	2%
Native Americans	17%		

Faculty 265 (72% full-time).

Expenses (1999–2000) *One-time required fee:* $21.50. *Tuition, state resident:* full-time $1919; part-time $64 per semester hour. *Tuition, nonresident:* full-time $4439; part-time $148 per semester hour. *Required fees:* full-time $43; $18 per term part-time. Full-time tuition and fees vary according to course level, course load, and student level. Part-time tuition and fees vary according to course level, course load, and student level. *College room and board:* $2226; room only: $726. Room and board charges vary according to board plan and housing facility. *Waivers:* senior citizens and employees or children of employees.

Library Linscheid Library. *Operations spending 1999–2000:* $902,753. *Collection:* 213,000 titles, 800 serial subscriptions.

College life *Housing: Option:* coed. *Social organizations:* national fraternities, national sororities, local fraternities, local sororities; 8% of eligible men and 8% of eligible women are members. *Most popular organizations:* Panhellenic Council, Interfraternity Council, BACCHUS, Fellowship of Christian Athletes.

Campus security 24-hour patrols, controlled dormitory access.

After graduation *Career center:* Services include job fairs, resume preparation, interview workshops, resume referral, career/interest testing, career counseling, job interviews.

Freshmen 665 applied, 630 admitted, 1,119 enrolled.

Average high school GPA	3.3	SAT verbal scores above 500	N/R
SAT math scores above 500	N/R	ACT above 18	43%
From top 10% of their h.s. class	15%	From top quarter	38%
From top half	76%	1998 freshmen returning in 1999	62%

Application *Option:* early admission. *Required:* high school transcript. *Required for some:* minimum 2.7 GPA; rank in upper 50% of high school class.

Standardized tests *Admission: Required:* SAT I or ACT. *Recommended:* ACT.
Significant dates *Application deadlines:* 9/1 (freshmen), 9/1 (transfers). *Financial aid deadline priority date:* 3/1.
Freshman Application Contact
Ms. Pamla Armstrong, Registrar, East Central University, Ada, OK 74820-6899. **Phone:** 580-332-8000 Ext. 239. **Fax:** 580-436-5495. **E-mail:** parmstro@mailclerk.ecok.edu
Visit CollegeQuest.com for information on majors offered and athletics.

HILLSDALE FREE WILL BAPTIST COLLEGE
Moore, Oklahoma

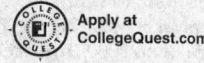
Apply at CollegeQuest.com

- **Independent Free Will Baptist**, 4-year, founded 1959
- **Degrees** associate and bachelor's
- **Suburban** 40-acre campus with easy access to Oklahoma City
- **Coed**, 229 undergraduate students, 93% full-time, 38% women, 62% men
- **Noncompetitive** entrance level, 95% of applicants were admitted
- **15:1 student-to-undergraduate faculty ratio**
- **12% graduate** in 6 years or less
- **$5840 tuition** and fees
- **$272,001 endowment**

Students *Undergraduates:* 212 full-time, 17 part-time. Students come from 12 states and territories, 17 other countries. *The most frequently chosen baccalaureate field is:* philosophy.

From out-of-state	16%	Reside on campus	45%
Age 25 or older	11%	Transferred in	19%
International students	9%	African Americans	7%
Hispanic Americans	2%	Native Americans	6%

Faculty 35 (40% full-time), 34% with terminal degrees.
Expenses (1999–2000) *One-time required fee:* $20. *Comprehensive fee:* $9790 includes full-time tuition ($5250), mandatory fees ($590), and room and board ($3950). *College room only:* $1700. Full-time tuition and fees vary according to course load. Room and board charges vary according to board plan and housing facility. *Part-time tuition:* $175 per credit hour. *Part-time fees:* $130 per term part-time. Part-time tuition and fees vary according to course load. *Payment plan:* deferred payment. *Waivers:* children of alumni, adult students, senior citizens, and employees or children of employees.
Library Geri Ann Hull Learning Resource Center. *Operations spending 1999–2000:* $45,894. *Collection:* 18,110 titles, 350 serial subscriptions, 1,100 audiovisual materials.
College life *Housing:* on-campus residence required through sophomore year. *Options:* men-only, women-only. *Social organizations:* local fraternities, local sororities; 48% of eligible men and 62% of eligible women are members. *Most popular organizations:* Student Mission Fellowship, Ironmen Fellowship, society organizations, Fellowship of Christian Athletes.
Campus security 24-hour emergency response devices, controlled dormitory access.
After graduation 66% of class of 1998 had job offers within 6 months. *Career center:* 1 full-time, 2 part-time personnel. Services include career counseling, job bank. *Graduate education:* 17% of class of 1999 went directly to graduate and professional school: 17% theology.
Freshmen 65 applied, 62 admitted, 62 enrolled. 4 valedictorians.

Average high school GPA	3.07	SAT verbal scores above 500	N/R
SAT math scores above 500	N/R	ACT above 18	66%
From top 10% of their h.s. class	12%	From top quarter	35%
From top half	61%	1998 freshmen returning in 1999	65%

Application *Options:* eApply at www.CollegeQuest.com, Common Application, early admission, deferred entrance. *Application fee:* $20. *Required:* essay or personal statement; high school transcript; 1 letter of recommendation; Biblical foundation statement, student conduct pledge; medical form required for some. *Required for some:* 1 letter of recommendation; interview. *Recommended:* minimum 2.0 GPA; 2 letters of recommendation.
Standardized tests *Placement: Required:* SAT I or ACT
Significant dates *Application deadlines:* rolling (freshmen), rolling (transfers). *Financial aid deadline priority date:* 5/1.

Freshman Application Contact
Ms. Sue Chaffin, Registrar/Assistant Director of Admissions, Hillsdale Free Will Baptist College, PO Box 7208, Moore, OK 73153-1208. **Phone:** 405-912-9005. **Fax:** 405-912-9050. **E-mail:** hillsdale@hc.edu
Visit CollegeQuest.com for information on majors offered and athletics.

LANGSTON UNIVERSITY
Langston, Oklahoma

- **State-supported**, comprehensive, founded 1897
- **Degrees** associate, bachelor's, and master's
- **Rural** 40-acre campus with easy access to Oklahoma City
- **Coed**, 3,206 undergraduate students, 70% full-time, 59% women, 41% men
- **Minimally difficult** entrance level, 33% of applicants were admitted
- **$1704 tuition** and fees (in-state); $3720 (out-of-state)

Part of Oklahoma State Regents for Higher Education.
Students *Undergraduates:* 2,243 full-time, 963 part-time. Students come from 37 states and territories, 8 other countries. *The most frequently chosen baccalaureate fields are:* education, health professions and related sciences, psychology. *Graduate:* 46 in graduate degree programs.

Age 25 or older	20%

Expenses (1999–2000) *Tuition, state resident:* full-time $1176; part-time $49 per credit hour. *Tuition, nonresident:* full-time $3192; part-time $133 per credit hour. *Required fees:* full-time $528; $15 per credit hour; $4 per term part-time. Full-time tuition and fees vary according to course level. Part-time tuition and fees vary according to course level. *College room and board:* $2944.
Library *Collection:* 236,000 titles, 1,732 serial subscriptions.
College life On-campus residence required through sophomore year. *Social organizations:* national fraternities, national sororities.
After graduation *Career center:* Services include career counseling.
Freshmen 2,833 applied, 936 admitted, 508 enrolled.

SAT verbal scores above 500	N/R	SAT math scores above 500	N/R
ACT above 18	N/R		

Application *Options:* electronic application, early admission, deferred entrance. *Required:* high school transcript. *Required for some:* letters of recommendation.
Standardized tests *Placement: Required:* SAT I or ACT
Significant dates *Application deadlines:* rolling (freshmen), rolling (transfers). *Financial aid deadline priority date:* 3/15.
Freshman Application Contact
Ms. La Cressa Trice, Admission Counselor, Langston University, Langston, OK 73050. **Phone:** 405-466-3428. **Fax:** 405-466-3381.
Visit CollegeQuest.com for information on majors offered and athletics.

MID-AMERICA BIBLE COLLEGE
Oklahoma City, Oklahoma

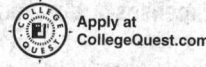
Apply at CollegeQuest.com

- **Independent**, 4-year, founded 1953, affiliated with Church of God
- **Degrees** associate and bachelor's
- **Suburban** 145-acre campus
- **Coed**, 577 undergraduate students, 88% full-time, 49% women, 51% men
- **Noncompetitive** entrance level, 70% of applicants were admitted
- **19:1 student-to-undergraduate faculty ratio**
- **$5552 tuition** and fees

Students *Undergraduates:* 508 full-time, 69 part-time. Students come from 32 states and territories, 4 other countries. *The most frequently chosen baccalaureate fields are:* business/marketing, philosophy, psychology.

From out-of-state	37%	Reside on campus	34%
Age 25 or older	56%	Transferred in	37%
International students	1%	African Americans	6%
Asian Americans/Pacific Islanders	1%	Hispanic Americans	3%
Native Americans	3%		

Faculty 45 (38% full-time), 18% with terminal degrees.

Oklahoma

Mid-America Bible College (continued)

Expenses (1999–2000) *Comprehensive fee:* $8748 includes full-time tuition ($5016), mandatory fees ($536), and room and board ($3196). *College room only:* $1598. *Part-time tuition:* $209 per semester hour. *Payment plan:* installment. *Waivers:* employees or children of employees.

Library Charles Ewing Brown Library. *Operations spending 1999–2000:* $101,656. *Collection:* 53,962 titles, 225 serial subscriptions, 3,906 audiovisual materials.

College life *Housing:* on-campus residence required through senior year. *Options:* men-only, women-only, disabled students. *Most popular organizations:* Christian Women's Organization, Behavioral Science Club, Student Ministers Fellowship, drama club, S.A.C.E.

Campus security 24-hour patrols, student patrols.

After graduation *Career center:* Services include career counseling.

Freshmen 125 applied, 88 admitted, 88 enrolled.

SAT verbal scores above 500	N/R	SAT math scores above 500	N/R
ACT above 18	N/R		

Application *Options:* eApply at www.CollegeQuest.com, Common Application, early admission. *Application fee:* $20. *Required:* high school transcript. *Required for some:* 2 letters of recommendation; interview.

Standardized tests *Admission: Required:* SAT I or ACT. *Placement: Required:* SAT I or ACT. *Recommended:* ACT.

Significant dates *Application deadlines:* rolling (freshmen), rolling (transfers). *Financial aid deadline priority date:* 5/1.

Freshman Application Contact
Director of College Relations, Mid-America Bible College, 3500 Southwest 119th Street, Oklahoma City, OK 73170. **Phone:** 405-691-3800. **E-mail:** mbcinfo@mabc.edu

Visit CollegeQuest.com for information on majors offered and athletics. College video available at CollegeQuest.com.

NORTHEASTERN STATE UNIVERSITY
Tahlequah, Oklahoma

- **State-supported**, comprehensive, founded 1846
- **Degrees** bachelor's, master's, and doctoral
- **Small-town** 160-acre campus with easy access to Tulsa
- **Coed**, 7,254 undergraduate students, 74% full-time, 59% women, 41% men
- **Moderately difficult** entrance level
- **$1865 tuition** and fees (in-state); $4385 (out-of-state)

Part of Oklahoma State Regents for Higher Education.

Students *Undergraduates:* Students come from 28 states and territories, 25 other countries. *Graduate:* 98 in professional programs, 1,110 in other graduate degree programs.

Age 25 or older	43%	International students	1%
African Americans	4%	Asian Americans/Pacific Islanders	0.4%
Hispanic Americans	1%	Native Americans	24%

Faculty 257.

Expenses (1999–2000) *Tuition, state resident:* full-time $1470; part-time $49 per semester hour. *Tuition, nonresident:* full-time $3990; part-time $133 per semester hour. *Required fees:* full-time $395; $13 per semester hour. Full-time tuition and fees vary according to course level, course load, location, and student level. Part-time tuition and fees vary according to course level, course load, and student level. *College room and board:* $2610. Room and board charges vary according to board plan and housing facility.

Library John Vaughn Library. *Collection:* 379,173 titles, 3,442 serial subscriptions.

College life *Housing:* on-campus residence required through sophomore year. *Option:* coed. *Social organizations:* national fraternities, national sororities, local fraternities, local sororities; 3% of eligible men and 2% of eligible women are members.

Campus security 24-hour emergency response devices and patrols, late-night transport-escort service, controlled dormitory access.

After graduation *Career center:* 3 full-time personnel. Services include job fairs, resume preparation, resume referral, career counseling, careers library, job interviews.

Freshmen

Average high school GPA	2.8	SAT verbal scores above 500	N/R
SAT math scores above 500	N/R	ACT above 18	N/R
1998 freshmen returning in 1999	60%		

Application *Options:* early admission, deferred entrance. *Preference* given to state residents. *Application fee:* $0. *Required:* high school transcript. *Required for some:* letters of recommendation; interview.

Standardized tests *Admission: Required:* ACT.

Significant dates *Application deadlines:* 8/5 (freshmen), 8/5 (transfers). *Financial aid deadline priority date:* 3/1.

Freshman Application Contact
Mr. Bill Nowlin, Director of Admissions and Registrar, Northeastern State University, 600 North Grand, Tahlequah, OK 74464-2399. **Phone:** 918-456-5511 Ext. 2200. **Toll-free phone:** 800-722-9614. **Fax:** 918-458-2342. **E-mail:** nsuadmis@cherokee.nsuok.edu

Visit CollegeQuest.com for information on majors offered and athletics.

NORTHWESTERN OKLAHOMA STATE UNIVERSITY
Alva, Oklahoma

- **State-supported**, comprehensive, founded 1897
- **Degrees** bachelor's and master's
- **Small-town** 70-acre campus
- **Coed**, 1,559 undergraduate students, 72% full-time, 56% women, 44% men
- **Moderately difficult** entrance level, 99% of applicants were admitted
- **19:1 student-to-undergraduate faculty ratio**
- **33% graduate** in 6 years or less
- **$1987 tuition** and fees (in-state); $4675 (out-of-state)
- **$6200 average financial aid** package, $9000 average indebtedness upon graduation, $11 million endowment

Part of Oklahoma State Regents for Higher Education.

Students *Undergraduates:* 1,116 full-time, 443 part-time. Students come from 25 states and territories, 18 other countries. *The most frequently chosen baccalaureate fields are:* business/marketing, education, health professions and related sciences. *Graduate:* 323 in graduate degree programs.

From out-of-state	15%	Reside on campus	26%
Age 25 or older	26%	Transferred in	16%
International students	1%	African Americans	4%
Asian Americans/Pacific Islanders	0.3%	Hispanic Americans	1%
Native Americans	3%		

Faculty 113 (71% full-time).

Expenses (1999–2000) *Tuition, state resident:* full-time $1957; part-time $61 per credit hour. *Tuition, nonresident:* full-time $4645; part-time $145 per credit hour. *Required fees:* full-time $30; $15 per term part-time. Full-time tuition and fees vary according to course load, location, and student level. Part-time tuition and fees vary according to course load, location, and student level. *College room and board:* $2316. Room and board charges vary according to board plan. *Waivers:* senior citizens and employees or children of employees.

Library J. W. Martin Library plus 1 other. *Operations spending 1999–2000:* $515,631. *Collection:* 225,000 titles, 1,411 serial subscriptions.

College life *Social organizations:* local fraternities, local sororities. *Most popular organizations:* Student Government Association, Aggie club, Phi Beta Lambda, Baptist student union.

Campus security 24-hour emergency response devices and patrols.

After graduation *Career center:* 2 full-time, 1 part-time personnel. Services include job fairs, resume preparation, resume referral, career counseling, careers library, job bank, job interviews.

Freshmen 475 applied, 469 admitted, 320 enrolled.

Average high school GPA	3.19	SAT verbal scores above 500	N/R
SAT math scores above 500	N/R	ACT above 18	77%
From top 10% of their h.s. class	8%	From top quarter	27%
From top half	59%	1998 freshmen returning in 1999	62%

Application *Option:* early admission. *Application fee:* $15. *Required:* high school transcript. *Required for some:* minimum 2.0 GPA.

Standardized tests *Admission: Required:* SAT I or ACT.

Significant dates *Application deadlines:* rolling (freshmen), rolling (transfers). *Financial aid deadline priority date:* 3/1.

Freshman Application Contact
Mr. Marcus Wallace, Director of Pre-Admissions, Northwestern Oklahoma State University, 709 Oklahoma Boulevard, Alva, OK 73717-2799. **Phone:** 580-327-8545. **Fax:** 580-327-1881. **E-mail:** krschrock@nwosu.edu

Visit CollegeQuest.com for information on majors offered and athletics.

OKLAHOMA BAPTIST UNIVERSITY
Shawnee, Oklahoma

- **Independent Southern Baptist**, comprehensive, founded 1910
- **Degrees** bachelor's and master's
- **Small-town** 125-acre campus with easy access to Oklahoma City
- **Coed**, 2,098 undergraduate students, 76% full-time, 53% women, 47% men
- **Moderately difficult** entrance level, 89% of applicants were admitted
- **14:1 student-to-undergraduate faculty ratio**
- **52% graduate** in 6 years or less
- **$9440 tuition** and fees
- **$65.5 million endowment**

Students *Undergraduates:* Students come from 41 states and territories, 23 other countries. *Graduate:* 25 in graduate degree programs.

From out-of-state	39%	Reside on campus	72%
Age 25 or older	19%	International students	1%
African Americans	3%	Asian Americans/Pacific Islanders	2%
Hispanic Americans	2%	Native Americans	5%

Faculty 165 (67% full-time), 53% with terminal degrees.

Expenses (2000–2001) *Comprehensive fee:* $12,857 includes full-time tuition ($8800), mandatory fees ($640), and room and board ($3417). *College room only:* $1600. Full-time tuition and fees vary according to course load. Room and board charges vary according to board plan and housing facility. *Part-time tuition:* $260 per credit hour. *Part-time fees:* $320 per year part-time. Part-time tuition and fees vary according to course load. *Payment plan:* installment. *Waivers:* senior citizens and employees or children of employees.

Library Mabee Learning Center. *Operations spending 1999–2000:* $785,409. *Collection:* 290,000 titles, 2,000 serial subscriptions, 1,500 audiovisual materials.

College life *Housing:* on-campus residence required through junior year. *Options:* men-only, women-only. *Social organizations:* local fraternities, local sororities; 10% of eligible men and 10% of eligible women are members. *Most popular organizations:* Campus Activities Board, Student Ambassadors, Student Government Association, Baptist Student Union, university concert series.

Campus security 24-hour emergency response devices and patrols, late-night transport-escort service, controlled dormitory access.

After graduation 45 organizations recruited on campus 1997–98. *Career center:* 2 full-time personnel. Services include job fairs, resume preparation, resume referral, career counseling, careers library, job bank, job interviews.

Freshmen 854 applied, 759 admitted. 5 National Merit Scholars, 42 valedictorians.

Average high school GPA	3.65	SAT verbal scores above 500	81%
SAT math scores above 500	72%	ACT above 18	95%
From top 10% of their h.s. class	36%	From top quarter	62%
From top half	87%	1998 freshmen returning in 1999	74%

Application *Options:* early admission, deferred entrance. *Application fee:* $25. *Required:* high school transcript; minimum 2.5 GPA. *Required for some:* essay or personal statement; letters of recommendation; interview.

Standardized tests *Admission: Required:* SAT I or ACT.

Significant dates *Application deadlines:* 8/1 (freshmen), 8/1 (transfers). *Notification:* continuous until 9/1 (freshmen). *Financial aid deadline priority date:* 3/1.

Freshman Application Contact
Mr. Michael Cappo, Dean of Admissions, Oklahoma Baptist University, Box 61174, Shawnee, OK 74804. **Phone:** 405-878-2033. **Toll-free phone:** 800-654-3285. **Fax:** 405-878-2046. **E-mail:** admissions@mail.okbu.edu

Visit CollegeQuest.com for information on majors offered and athletics. Electronic viewbook available at CollegeQuest.com.

- *See page 2220 for a narrative description.*

OKLAHOMA CHRISTIAN UNIVERSITY OF SCIENCE AND ARTS
Oklahoma City, Oklahoma

- **Independent**, comprehensive, founded 1950, affiliated with Church of Christ
- **Degrees** bachelor's and master's
- **Suburban** 200-acre campus
- **Coed**, 1,701 undergraduate students, 91% full-time, 50% women, 50% men
- **Noncompetitive** entrance level, 90% of applicants were admitted
- **19:1 student-to-undergraduate faculty ratio**
- **$9590 tuition** and fees

Students *Undergraduates:* Students come from 59 states and territories. *The most frequently chosen baccalaureate fields are:* communications/communication technologies, education, engineering/engineering technologies. *Graduate:* 33 in graduate degree programs.

From out-of-state	53%	Reside on campus	71%
African Americans	5%	Asian Americans/Pacific Islanders	2%
Hispanic Americans	2%	Native Americans	3%

Faculty 134 (63% full-time), 49% with terminal degrees.

Expenses (1999–2000) *Comprehensive fee:* $13,690 includes full-time tuition ($8850), mandatory fees ($740), and room and board ($4100). *Part-time tuition:* $370 per semester hour. *Part-time fees:* $250 per term part-time. *Payment plan:* tuition prepayment. *Waivers:* employees or children of employees.

Library Mabee Learning Center. *Operations spending 1999–2000:* $410,383. *Collection:* 95,789 titles, 415 serial subscriptions.

College life *Housing:* on-campus residence required through senior year. *Options:* men-only, women-only, disabled students.

Campus security 24-hour emergency response devices and patrols, late-night transport-escort service.

After graduation 75 organizations recruited on campus 1997–98. 82% of class of 1998 had job offers within 6 months. *Career center:* 1 full-time, 2 part-time personnel. Services include job fairs, resume preparation, resume referral, career counseling, careers library, job bank, job interviews.

Freshmen 1,097 applied, 987 admitted.

SAT verbal scores above 500	50%	SAT math scores above 500	70%
ACT above 18	90%	1998 freshmen returning in 1999	67%

Application *Options:* early admission, deferred entrance. *Application fee:* $25. *Required:* high school transcript.

Standardized tests *Admission: Required:* SAT I or ACT.

Significant dates *Application deadlines:* rolling (freshmen), rolling (transfers). *Financial aid deadline:* 8/31. *Priority date:* 3/15.

Freshman Application Contact
Mr. Kyle Ray, Director of Admissions, Oklahoma Christian University of Science and Arts, Box 11000, Oklahoma City, OK 73136-1100. **Phone:** 405-425-5050. **Toll-free phone:** 800-877-5010. **Fax:** 405-425-5208. **E-mail:** info@oc.edu

Visit CollegeQuest.com for information on majors offered and athletics. College video available at CollegeQuest.com.

OKLAHOMA CITY UNIVERSITY
Oklahoma City, Oklahoma

- **Independent United Methodist**, comprehensive, founded 1904
- **Degrees** bachelor's, master's, and first professional
- **Urban** 68-acre campus
- **Coed**, 2,100 undergraduate students, 71% full-time, 57% women, 43% men
- **Moderately difficult** entrance level, 63% of applicants were admitted
- **14:1 student-to-undergraduate faculty ratio**
- **52% graduate** in 6 years or less
- **$9558 tuition** and fees
- **$9956 average financial aid** package, $17,563 average indebtedness upon graduation, $42.9 million endowment

Students *Undergraduates:* 1,497 full-time, 603 part-time. Students come from 44 states and territories, 68 other countries. *The most frequently chosen*

Oklahoma

Oklahoma City University (continued)

baccalaureate fields are: liberal arts/general studies, business/marketing, visual/performing arts. *Graduate:* 508 in professional programs, 1,535 in other graduate degree programs.

From out-of-state	17%	Reside on campus	31%
Age 25 or older	36%	Transferred in	5%
International students	25%	African Americans	5%
Asian Americans/Pacific Islanders	2%	Hispanic Americans	3%
Native Americans	4%		

Faculty 326 (49% full-time), 57% with terminal degrees.

Expenses (1999–2000) *Comprehensive fee:* $18,358 includes full-time tuition ($9320), mandatory fees ($238), and room and board ($8800). *College room only:* $2920. Full-time tuition and fees vary according to program. Room and board charges vary according to board plan and housing facility. *Part-time tuition:* $315 per semester hour. *Part-time fees:* $2 per semester hour; $55 per term part-time. Part-time tuition and fees vary according to program. *Payment plans:* installment, deferred payment. *Waivers:* employees or children of employees.

Library Dulaney Browne Library plus 1 other. *Operations spending 1999–2000:* $2.5 million. *Collection:* 419,329 titles, 5,509 serial subscriptions, 9,649 audiovisual materials.

College life *Housing:* on-campus residence required through senior year. *Options:* men-only, women-only. *Social organizations:* national fraternities, national sororities; 14% of eligible men and 11% of eligible women are members.

Campus security 24-hour emergency response devices and patrols, student patrols, late-night transport-escort service, Operation ID.

After graduation 60 organizations recruited on campus 1997–98. *Career center:* 2 full-time, 1 part-time personnel. Services include job fairs, resume preparation, interview workshops, resume referral, career/interest testing, career counseling, careers library, job bank, job interviews.

Freshmen 1,007 applied, 639 admitted, 346 enrolled.

Average high school GPA	3.53	SAT verbal scores above 500	71%
SAT math scores above 500	59%	ACT above 18	90%
From top 10% of their h.s. class	34%	From top quarter	54%
From top half	84%	1998 freshmen returning in 1999	77%

Application *Options:* Common Application, deferred entrance. *Application fee:* $20. *Required:* high school transcript; minimum 2.5 GPA. *Required for some:* interview; audition for music program.

Standardized tests *Admission: Required:* SAT I or ACT.

Significant dates *Application deadlines:* 8/15 (freshmen), rolling (transfers). *Notification:* continuous until 8/15 (freshmen). *Financial aid deadline:* continuous.

Freshman Application Contact
Laura Lyddon, Dean of Admissions and Enrollment Management, Oklahoma City University, 2501 North Blackwelder, Oklahoma City, OK 73106. **Phone:** 405-521-5050. **Toll-free phone:** 800-633-7242. **E-mail:** uadmissions@okcu.edu

Visit CollegeQuest.com for information on majors offered and athletics. College video available at CollegeQuest.com.

■ *See page 2222 for a narrative description.*

OKLAHOMA PANHANDLE STATE UNIVERSITY
Goodwell, Oklahoma

- **State-supported**, 4-year, founded 1909
- **Degrees** associate and bachelor's
- **Rural** 40-acre campus
- **Coed**, 1,092 undergraduate students, 86% full-time, 52% women, 48% men
- **Noncompetitive** entrance level, 100% of applicants were admitted
- **$1960 tuition** and fees (in-state); $4180 (out-of-state)
- **$4 million endowment**

Part of Oklahoma State Regents for Higher Education.

Students *Undergraduates:* 943 full-time, 149 part-time. Students come from 21 states and territories. *The most frequently chosen baccalaureate fields are:* agriculture, business/marketing, education.

From out-of-state	50%	Reside on campus	17%
Transferred in	7%	African Americans	4%
Asian Americans/Pacific Islanders	0.3%	Hispanic Americans	8%
Native Americans	2%		

Faculty 62 (100% full-time), 10% with terminal degrees.

Expenses (1999–2000) *Tuition, state resident:* full-time $1910; part-time $49 per credit hour. *Tuition, nonresident:* full-time $4130; part-time $133 per credit hour. *Required fees:* full-time $50; $12 per credit hour; $33 per term part-time. Full-time tuition and fees vary according to student level. Part-time tuition and fees vary according to course load and student level. *College room and board:* $2368; room only: $770. Room and board charges vary according to board plan and housing facility. *Waivers:* employees or children of employees.

Library McKee Library. *Collection:* 106,000 titles, 308 serial subscriptions, 2,079 audiovisual materials.

College life *Housing:* on-campus residence required in freshman year. *Option:* coed.

Campus security 24-hour emergency response devices and patrols, student patrols, safety bars over door latches.

After graduation 20 organizations recruited on campus 1997–98. *Career center:* 1 full-time, 2 part-time personnel. Services include job fairs, resume preparation, career counseling, careers library, job bank, job interviews.

Freshmen 817 applied, 817 admitted, 220 enrolled.

SAT verbal scores above 500	N/R	SAT math scores above 500	N/R
ACT above 18	59%		

Application *Option:* Common Application. *Application fee:* $0. *Required:* high school transcript.

Standardized tests *Placement: Required:* SAT I or ACT

Significant dates *Application deadlines:* rolling (freshmen), rolling (transfers). *Financial aid deadline priority date:* 1/1.

Freshman Application Contact
Ms. Melissa Worth, Admissions Counselor, Oklahoma Panhandle State University, PO Box 430, Goodwell, OK 73939-0430. **Phone:** 580-349-2611 Ext. 311. **Toll-free phone:** 800-664-6778. **Fax:** 580-349-2302. **E-mail:** opsu@opsu.edu

Visit CollegeQuest.com for information on majors offered and athletics.

OKLAHOMA STATE UNIVERSITY
Stillwater, Oklahoma

- **State-supported**, university, founded 1890
- **Degrees** bachelor's, master's, doctoral, and first professional
- **Small-town** 840-acre campus with easy access to Oklahoma City and Tulsa
- **Coed**, 16,159 undergraduate students, 90% full-time, 47% women, 53% men
- **Moderately difficult** entrance level, 89% of applicants were admitted
- **18:1 student-to-undergraduate faculty ratio**
- **50.5% graduate** in 6 years or less
- **$2458 tuition** and fees (in-state); $6538 (out-of-state)
- **$7292 average financial aid** package, $14,113 average indebtedness upon graduation, $157.1 million endowment

Part of Oklahoma State University.

Students *Undergraduates:* 14,617 full-time, 1,542 part-time. Students come from 50 states and territories, 119 other countries. *The most frequently chosen baccalaureate fields are:* business/marketing, education, engineering/engineering technologies. *Graduate:* 294 in professional programs, 4,590 in other graduate degree programs.

From out-of-state	12%	Age 25 or older	13%
Transferred in	15%	International students	5%
African Americans	3%	Asian Americans/Pacific Islanders	2%
Hispanic Americans	2%	Native Americans	8%

Faculty 1,023 (87% full-time), 85% with terminal degrees.

Expenses (1999–2000) *Tuition, state resident:* full-time $1830; part-time $61 per credit hour. *Tuition, nonresident:* full-time $5910; part-time $197 per credit hour. *Required fees:* full-time $628; $17 per credit hour; $53 per term part-time. Full-time tuition and fees vary according to course level, program, and reciprocity agreements. Part-time tuition and fees vary according to course level, course load, program, and reciprocity agreements. *College room*

Oklahoma

and board: $4536; room only: $2064. Room and board charges vary according to board plan and housing facility. *Payment plans:* installment, deferred payment. *Waivers:* minority students and children of alumni.

Library Edmon Low Library. *Operations spending 1999–2000:* $9.2 million. *Collection:* 2 million titles, 16,249 serial subscriptions, 350,263 audiovisual materials.

College life *Housing:* on-campus residence required in freshman year. *Options:* coed, men-only, women-only. *Social organizations:* national fraternities, national sororities; 13% of eligible men and 16% of eligible women are members. *Most popular organizations:* Student Government Association, Campus Crusade for Christ, Flying Aggies, Block and Bridle Club, OSU Ski Club.

Campus security 24-hour emergency response devices and patrols, student patrols, controlled dormitory access.

After graduation 363 organizations recruited on campus 1997–98. 70% of class of 1998 had job offers within 6 months. *Career center:* 10 full-time, 20 part-time personnel. Services include job fairs, resume preparation, interview workshops, resume referral, career/interest testing, career counseling, careers library, job bank, job interviews. *Major awards:* 1 Fulbright Scholar.

Freshmen 5,716 applied, 5,081 admitted, 2,929 enrolled. 22 National Merit Scholars, 296 valedictorians.

Average high school GPA	3.55	SAT verbal scores above 500	76%
SAT math scores above 500	78%	ACT above 18	96%
From top 10% of their h.s. class	32%	From top quarter	63%
From top half	91%	1998 freshmen returning in 1999	83%

Application *Option:* early admission. *Application fee:* $25. *Required:* high school transcript; minimum 3.0 GPA; class rank. *Required for some:* interview.

Standardized tests *Admission:* Required: SAT I or ACT.

Significant dates *Application deadlines:* rolling (freshmen), rolling (transfers). *Financial aid deadline:* continuous.

Freshman Application Contact
Ms. Paulette Cundiff, Coordinator of Admissions Processing, Oklahoma State University, Undergraduate Admissions, 324 Student Union, Stillwater, OK 74078. **Phone:** 405-744-6858. **Toll-free phone:** 800-233-5019 (in-state); 800-852-1255 (out-of-state). **Fax:** 405-744-5285. **E-mail:** admit@okstate.edu

Visit CollegeQuest.com for information on majors offered and athletics. Electronic viewbook available at CollegeQuest.com.

ORAL ROBERTS UNIVERSITY
Tulsa, Oklahoma

- **Independent interdenominational**, comprehensive, founded 1963
- **Degrees** bachelor's, master's, and doctoral
- **Urban** 263-acre campus
- **Coed**
- **Moderately difficult** entrance level
- **$10,988 tuition** and fees

Expenses (1999–2000) *Comprehensive fee:* $15,948 includes full-time tuition ($10,668), mandatory fees ($320), and room and board ($4960). Room and board charges vary according to board plan. *Part-time tuition:* $454 per credit hour. *Part-time fees:* $80 per term part-time.

Institutional Web site http://www.oru.edu/

College life *Housing:* on-campus residence required through senior year. *Options:* men-only, women-only. *Most popular organizations:* Missions, Student Nurse Association, American Management Society, Accounting Society.

Campus security 24-hour emergency response devices and patrols, late-night transport-escort service.

Application *Options:* Common Application, early admission, early action, deferred entrance. *Application fee:* $35. *Required:* essay or personal statement; high school transcript; minimum 2.6 GPA; 1 letter of recommendation; proof of immunization. *Required for some:* interview.

Standardized tests *Admission:* Required: SAT I or ACT.

Admissions Office Contact
Oral Roberts University, 7777 South Lewis Avenue, Tulsa, OK 74171-0001. **Toll-free phone:** 800-678-8876. **Fax:** 918-495-6222. **E-mail:** admissions@oru.edu

Visit CollegeQuest.com for information on athletics. College video available at CollegeQuest.com.

ST. GREGORY'S UNIVERSITY
Shawnee, Oklahoma

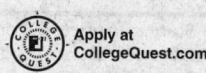
Apply at CollegeQuest.com

- **Independent Roman Catholic**, 4-year, founded 1875
- **Degrees** associate and bachelor's
- **Small-town** 640-acre campus with easy access to Oklahoma City
- **Coed**, 661 undergraduate students, 82% full-time, 53% women, 47% men
- **Minimally difficult** entrance level, 46% of applicants were admitted
- **18:1 student-to-undergraduate faculty ratio**
- **$7866 tuition** and fees
- **$8467 average financial aid** package, $5.8 million endowment

Students *Undergraduates:* 541 full-time, 120 part-time. Students come from 20 states and territories, 17 other countries. *The most frequently chosen baccalaureate fields are:* health professions and related sciences, psychology, visual/performing arts.

Reside on campus	70%	Transferred in	12%
International students	11%	African Americans	6%
Asian Americans/Pacific Islanders	1%	Hispanic Americans	4%
Native Americans	11%		

Faculty 72 (54% full-time).

Expenses (1999–2000) *Comprehensive fee:* $11,936 includes full-time tuition ($7126), mandatory fees ($740), and room and board ($4070). *College room only:* $2290. Full-time tuition and fees vary according to course load. Room and board charges vary according to board plan and housing facility. *Part-time tuition:* $225 per credit hour. *Part-time fees:* $30 per credit hour. Part-time tuition and fees vary according to course load. Additional technology fee: $150 full-time, $75 per term part-time for students who own laptop computers; $400 full-time, $32 per credit hour part-time for students who do not own laptop computers. *Payment plans:* installment, deferred payment. *Waivers:* senior citizens and employees or children of employees.

Library James J. Kelly Library plus 1 other. *Operations spending 1999–2000:* $87,906. *Collection:* 42,574 titles, 284 serial subscriptions.

College life *Housing:* on-campus residence required through junior year. *Options:* men-only, women-only, disabled students. *Social organizations:* local fraternities, local sororities. *Most popular organizations:* Residence Halls Association, Phi Theta Kappa, Campus Ministry, This Is My Environment (TIME).

Campus security 24-hour emergency response devices and patrols, late-night transport-escort service, controlled dormitory access.

After graduation *Career center:* 2 full-time personnel. Services include job fairs, resume preparation, interview workshops, resume referral, career/interest testing, career counseling, careers library, job bank, job interviews.

Freshmen 524 applied, 242 admitted, 173 enrolled.

SAT verbal scores above 500	N/R	SAT math scores above 500	N/R
ACT above 18	83%	From top 10% of their h.s. class	20%
From top quarter	38%	From top half	78%
1998 freshmen returning in 1999	41%		

Application *Options:* eApply at www.CollegeQuest.com, Common Application, electronic application, early admission, deferred entrance. *Application fee:* $25. *Required:* high school transcript; minimum 2.0 GPA. *Required for some:* essay or personal statement; letters of recommendation; interview.

Standardized tests *Admission:* Required: SAT I or ACT.

Significant dates *Application deadlines:* rolling (freshmen), rolling (transfers). *Financial aid deadline:* continuous.

Freshman Application Contact
Mr. Joe Carter, Director of Admissions, St. Gregory's University, 1900 West MacArthur Drive, Shawnee, OK 74804. **Phone:** 405-878-5444 Ext. 447. **Toll-free phone:** 888-STGREGS. **Fax:** 405-878-5198. **E-mail:** admissions@sgc.edu

Visit CollegeQuest.com for information on majors offered and athletics. Electronic viewbook available at CollegeQuest.com.

Oklahoma

SOUTHEASTERN OKLAHOMA STATE UNIVERSITY
Durant, Oklahoma

- **State-supported**, comprehensive, founded 1909
- **Degrees** bachelor's and master's
- **Small-town** 176-acre campus
- **Coed**, 3,371 undergraduate students, 80% full-time, 54% women, 46% men
- **Moderately difficult** entrance level, 93% of applicants were admitted
- **18:1 student-to-undergraduate faculty ratio**
- **37% graduate** in 6 years or less
- **$1964 tuition** and fees (in-state); $4319 (out-of-state)

Part of Oklahoma State Regents for Higher Education.

Students *Undergraduates:* 2,709 full-time, 662 part-time. Students come from 38 states and territories, 17 other countries. *The most frequently chosen baccalaureate fields are:* business/marketing, education, engineering/engineering technologies. *Graduate:* 367 in graduate degree programs.

From out-of-state	22%	Reside on campus	15%
Age 25 or older	26%	Transferred in	11%
International students	1%	African Americans	5%
Asian Americans/Pacific Islanders	1%	Hispanic Americans	1%
Native Americans	32%		

Faculty 213 (73% full-time), 50% with terminal degrees.

Expenses (1999–2000) *Tuition, state resident:* full-time $1470; part-time $49 per semester hour. *Tuition, nonresident:* full-time $3825; part-time $128 per semester hour. *Required fees:* full-time $494; $14 per semester hour; $38 per term part-time. Full-time tuition and fees vary according to course level. Part-time tuition and fees vary according to course level and course load. *College room and board:* $2492; room only: $872. Room and board charges vary according to board plan and housing facility.

Library Henry G. Bennett Memorial Library. *Operations spending 1999–2000:* $655,184. *Collection:* 191,252 titles, 1,341 serial subscriptions, 4,913 audiovisual materials.

College life *Housing: Options:* coed, men-only, women-only. *Social organizations:* national fraternities, national sororities; 3% of eligible men and 3% of eligible women are members. *Most popular organizations:* Baptist Student Union, Alpha Sigma Tau, Kappa Delta Pi, Oklahoma Education Association, Black Student Association.

Campus security 24-hour patrols, late-night transport-escort service.

After graduation 240 organizations recruited on campus 1997–98. *Career center:* 2 full-time personnel. Services include job fairs, resume preparation, interview workshops, resume referral, career counseling, job bank, job interviews.

Freshmen 828 applied, 767 admitted, 579 enrolled. 25 valedictorians.

Average high school GPA	3.24	SAT verbal scores above 500	N/R
SAT math scores above 500	N/R	ACT above 18	81%
From top 10% of their h.s. class	15%	From top quarter	41%
From top half	76%	1998 freshmen returning in 1999	62%

Application *Options:* early admission, deferred entrance. *Application fee:* $0. *Required:* high school transcript.

Standardized tests *Admission: Required:* SAT I or ACT.

Significant dates *Application deadlines:* 8/15 (freshmen), 8/15 (transfers).

Freshman Application Contact
Mr. Rudy Manley, Director of Enrollment Management, Southeastern Oklahoma State University, Box 4225, Durant, OK 74701-0609. **Phone:** 580-924-0121 Ext. 2050. **Toll-free phone:** 800-435-1327 Ext. 2307. **Fax:** 580-920-7472.

Visit CollegeQuest.com for information on majors offered and athletics.

SOUTHERN NAZARENE UNIVERSITY
Bethany, Oklahoma

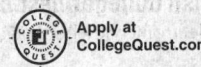 Apply at CollegeQuest.com

- **Independent Nazarene**, comprehensive, founded 1899
- **Degrees** associate, bachelor's, and master's
- **Suburban** 40-acre campus with easy access to Oklahoma City
- **Coed**
- **Noncompetitive** entrance level
- **$9380 tuition** and fees

Expenses (1999–2000) *Comprehensive fee:* $13,696 includes full-time tuition ($8850), mandatory fees ($530), and room and board ($4316). *College room only:* $2096. Room and board charges vary according to board plan and housing facility. *Part-time tuition:* $295 per credit hour. *Part-time fees:* $23 per credit. Part-time tuition and fees vary according to course load.

Institutional Web site http://www.snu.edu/

College life *Housing:* on-campus residence required through senior year. *Options:* men-only, women-only. *Most popular organizations:* Business Gaming Team, Campus Social Life Committee, Intramural Sports Societies, Choral Society, Inter Club.

Campus security 24-hour emergency response devices, controlled dormitory access.

Application *Options:* eApply at www.CollegeQuest.com, deferred entrance. *Application fee:* $25. *Required:* high school transcript. *Recommended:* interview.

Standardized tests *Placement: Required:* SAT I or ACT

Admissions Office Contact
Southern Nazarene University, 6729 Northwest 39th Expressway, Bethany, OK 73008-2694. **Toll-free phone:** 800-648-9899. **Fax:** 405-491-6381. **E-mail:** admiss@snu.edu

Visit CollegeQuest.com for information on athletics.

SOUTHWESTERN COLLEGE OF CHRISTIAN MINISTRIES
Bethany, Oklahoma

- **Independent**, comprehensive, founded 1946, affiliated with Pentecostal Holiness Church
- **Degrees** associate, bachelor's, and master's
- **Suburban** 7-acre campus with easy access to Oklahoma City
- **Coed**, 131 undergraduate students, 100% full-time, 37% women, 63% men
- **Minimally difficult** entrance level
- **15:1 student-to-undergraduate faculty ratio**
- **$5916 tuition** and fees

Students *Undergraduates:* 131 full-time. Students come from 15 states and territories, 3 other countries. *The most frequently chosen baccalaureate field is:* philosophy. *Graduate:* 45 in graduate degree programs.

From out-of-state	30%	Reside on campus	30%
Age 25 or older	20%		

Faculty 17 (29% full-time), 94% with terminal degrees.

Expenses (1999–2000) *Comprehensive fee:* $8916 includes full-time tuition ($5600), mandatory fees ($316), and room and board ($3000). Full-time tuition and fees vary according to course load. *Part-time tuition:* $195 per credit. *Part-time fees:* $3 per credit; $70 per term part-time. Part-time tuition and fees vary according to course load. *Payment plan:* installment. *Waivers:* employees or children of employees.

Library Springer Learning Center. *Collection:* 38,900 titles, 100 serial subscriptions.

College life *Housing:* on-campus residence required through senior year. *Options:* men-only, women-only.

Campus security 24-hour emergency response devices.

After graduation *Career center:* Services include career counseling. *Graduate education:* 20% of class of 1999 went directly to graduate and professional school.

Freshmen 54 enrolled. 2 class presidents, 4 valedictorians, 15 student government officers.

Average high school GPA	2.8	SAT verbal scores above 500	N/R
SAT math scores above 500	N/R	ACT above 18	N/R
From top 10% of their h.s. class	18%	From top quarter	53%
From top half	80%		

Application *Options:* Common Application, early admission, deferred entrance. *Application fee:* $25. *Required:* essay or personal statement; high school transcript; minimum 2.0 GPA; letters of recommendation; minimum ACT score of 19 or SAT score of 910. *Recommended:* interview.

Standardized tests *Admission: Required:* ACT.
Significant dates *Application deadlines:* rolling (freshmen), rolling (transfers). *Financial aid deadline priority date:* 7/15.
Freshman Application Contact
Mr. Steve Ely, Director of Admissions, Southwestern College of Christian Ministries, PO Box 340, Bethany, OK 73008-0340. **Phone:** 405-789-7661 Ext. 3449. **E-mail:** admissions@sccm.edu
Visit CollegeQuest.com for information on majors offered and athletics.

SOUTHWESTERN OKLAHOMA STATE UNIVERSITY
Weatherford, Oklahoma

- **State-supported**, comprehensive, founded 1901
- **Degrees** bachelor's, master's, and first professional
- **Small-town** 73-acre campus with easy access to Oklahoma City
- **Coed**, 3,850 undergraduate students, 89% full-time, 54% women, 46% men
- **Moderately difficult** entrance level, 93% of applicants were admitted
- **19:1** student-to-undergraduate faculty ratio
- **$1873 tuition** and fees (in-state); $4393 (out-of-state)
- **$948 average financial aid** package, $7500 average indebtedness upon graduation, $9.1 million endowment

Part of Southwestern Oklahoma State University.
Students *Undergraduates:* 3,431 full-time, 419 part-time. Students come from 38 states and territories, 36 other countries. *The most frequently chosen baccalaureate fields are:* education, business/marketing, health professions and related sciences. *Graduate:* 204 in professional programs, 317 in other graduate degree programs.

From out-of-state	11%	Reside on campus	23%
Age 25 or older	17%	Transferred in	6%
African Americans	4%	Asian Americans/Pacific Islanders	3%
Hispanic Americans	3%	Native Americans	5%

Faculty 230 (86% full-time), 62% with terminal degrees.
Expenses (1999–2000) *Tuition, state resident:* full-time $1470; part-time $49 per credit hour. *Tuition, nonresident:* full-time $3990; part-time $132 per credit hour. *Required fees:* full-time $403; $13 per credit hour; $10 per term part-time. Full-time tuition and fees vary according to course level and program. Part-time tuition and fees vary according to course level and program. *College room and board:* $2440; room only: $910. Room and board charges vary according to board plan and housing facility. *Payment plan:* installment. *Waivers:* children of alumni, senior citizens, and employees or children of employees.
Library Al Harris Library. *Operations spending 1999–2000:* $1.6 million. *Collection:* 872 audiovisual materials.
College life *Housing: Options:* men-only, women-only. *Social organizations:* national fraternities, local fraternities, local sororities; 1% of eligible men and 2% of eligible women are members. *Most popular organizations:* Student Education Association, Baptist Student Union, Southwestern Pharmaceutical Association, Gamma Delta Kappa, Bible Chair Student Union.
Campus security Late-night transport-escort service, controlled dormitory access, 20-hour campus emergency security.
After graduation 55 organizations recruited on campus 1997–98. *Career center:* 2 full-time, 3 part-time personnel. Services include job fairs, resume preparation, interview workshops, resume referral, career/interest testing, career counseling, careers library, job interviews.
Freshmen 1,236 applied, 1,153 admitted, 790 enrolled.

Average high school GPA	3.35	SAT verbal scores above 500	N/R
SAT math scores above 500	N/R	ACT above 18	82%
From top 10% of their h.s. class	17%	From top quarter	38%
From top half	71%	1998 freshmen returning in 1999	66%

Application *Option:* deferred entrance. *Preference* given to state residents. *Application fee:* $15. *Required:* high school transcript; minimum 2.0 GPA.
Standardized tests *Admission: Required:* ACT.
Significant dates *Financial aid deadline:* 3/1.
Freshman Application Contact
Ms. Connie Phillips, Admission Counselor, Southwestern Oklahoma State University, Registrar's Office, 100 Campus Drive, Weatherford, OK 73096. **Phone:** 580-774-3009. **Fax:** 580-774-3795. **E-mail:** phillic@swosu.edu

Visit CollegeQuest.com for information on majors offered and athletics.

UNIVERSITY OF BIBLICAL STUDIES AND SEMINARY
Oklahoma—See American Bible College and Seminary

UNIVERSITY OF CENTRAL OKLAHOMA
Edmond, Oklahoma

- **State-supported**, comprehensive, founded 1890
- **Degrees** bachelor's and master's
- **Suburban** 200-acre campus with easy access to Oklahoma City
- **Coed**, 11,476 undergraduate students, 65% full-time, 57% women, 43% men
- **Minimally difficult** entrance level, 96% of applicants were admitted
- **21:1** student-to-undergraduate faculty ratio
- **27% graduate** in 6 years or less
- **$1936 tuition** and fees (in-state); $4456 (out-of-state)
- **$4750 average financial aid** package, $10,000 average indebtedness upon graduation, $430,350 endowment

Part of Oklahoma State Regents for Higher Education.
Students *Undergraduates:* 7,405 full-time, 4,071 part-time. Students come from 34 states and territories, 89 other countries. *The most frequently chosen baccalaureate fields are:* business/marketing, education, liberal arts/general studies. *Graduate:* 2,707 in graduate degree programs.

From out-of-state	3%	Reside on campus	10%
Age 25 or older	30%	Transferred in	11%
International students	9%	African Americans	7%
Asian Americans/Pacific Islanders	3%	Hispanic Americans	2%
Native Americans	4%		

Faculty 710 (56% full-time), 51% with terminal degrees.
Expenses (1999–2000) *Tuition, state resident:* full-time $1470; part-time $49 per credit hour. *Tuition, nonresident:* full-time $3990; part-time $133 per credit hour. *Required fees:* full-time $466; $14 per credit hour; $20 per term part-time. Full-time tuition and fees vary according to course level, course load, program, and student level. Part-time tuition and fees vary according to course level, course load, program, and student level. *College room and board:* $2743. Room and board charges vary according to board plan and housing facility. *Waivers:* employees or children of employees.
Library Max Chambers Library. *Operations spending 1999–2000:* $3 million. *Collection:* 254,478 titles, 3,707 serial subscriptions, 37,484 audiovisual materials.
College life *Housing: Options:* coed, men-only, women-only. *Social organizations:* national fraternities, national sororities; 1% of eligible men and 1% of eligible women are members. *Most popular organizations:* Malaysian Student Association, Baptist Student Union, student government association, Association of Women Students, University Center Activities Board.
Campus security 24-hour emergency response devices and patrols, late-night transport-escort service.
After graduation 169 organizations recruited on campus 1997–98. *Career center:* 4 full-time, 6 part-time personnel. Services include job fairs, resume preparation, resume referral, career counseling, careers library, job bank, job interviews.
Freshmen 4,844 applied, 4,641 admitted, 1,626 enrolled.

Average high school GPA	3.17	SAT verbal scores above 500	N/R
SAT math scores above 500	N/R	ACT above 18	88%
From top 10% of their h.s. class	13%	From top quarter	37%
From top half	78%	1998 freshmen returning in 1999	62%

Application *Option:* deferred entrance. *Application fee:* $15. *Required:* high school transcript.
Standardized tests *Admission: Required:* SAT I or ACT.
Significant dates *Application deadlines:* rolling (freshmen), rolling (transfers). *Notification:* continuous until 8/1 (freshmen). *Financial aid deadline priority date:* 3/31.
Freshman Application Contact
Ms. Evelyn Wilson, Dean of Enrollment Services, University of Central Oklahoma, 100 North University Drive, Edmond, OK 73034. **Phone:** 405-974-2338 Ext. 2338. **Toll-free phone:** 800-254-4215. **Fax:** 405-974-4964.

Oklahoma

University of Central Oklahoma (continued)
Visit CollegeQuest.com for information on majors offered and athletics.

UNIVERSITY OF OKLAHOMA
Norman, Oklahoma

- **State-supported**, university, founded 1890
- **Degrees** bachelor's, master's, doctoral, and first professional
- **Suburban** 3,500-acre campus with easy access to Oklahoma City
- **Coed**, 16,990 undergraduate students, 86% full-time, 48% women, 52% men
- **Moderately difficult** entrance level, 89% of applicants were admitted
- **21:1 student-to-undergraduate faculty ratio**
- **45.4% graduate** in 6 years or less
- **$2456 tuition** and fees (in-state); $6791 (out-of-state)
- **$5991 average financial aid** package, $18,976 average indebtedness upon graduation, $483.9 million endowment

Students *Undergraduates:* 14,685 full-time, 2,305 part-time. Students come from 51 states and territories, 93 other countries. *The most frequently chosen baccalaureate fields are:* business/marketing, engineering/engineering technologies, social sciences and history. *Graduate:* 588 in professional programs, 3,487 in other graduate degree programs.

From out-of-state	16%	Reside on campus	20%
Age 25 or older	13%	Transferred in	9%
International students	5%	African Americans	7%
Asian Americans/Pacific Islanders	6%	Hispanic Americans	4%
Native Americans	8%		

Faculty 1,114 (82% full-time).
Expenses (1999–2000) *Tuition, state resident:* full-time $1890; part-time $63 per credit. *Tuition, nonresident:* full-time $6225; part-time $208 per credit. *Required fees:* full-time $566; $13 per credit; $93 per term part-time. Full-time tuition and fees vary according to course level, course load, location, program, and reciprocity agreements. Part-time tuition and fees vary according to course level, course load, location, program, and reciprocity agreements. *College room and board:* $4384. Room and board charges vary according to board plan and housing facility. *Payment plan:* installment. *Waivers:* children of alumni, senior citizens, and employees or children of employees.
Library Bizzell Memorial Library plus 7 others. *Operations spending 1999–2000:* $8.2 million. *Collection:* 4.1 million titles, 16,890 serial subscriptions, 6,235 audiovisual materials.
College life *Housing:* on-campus residence required in freshman year. *Options:* coed, men-only, women-only, disabled students. *Social organizations:* national fraternities, national sororities, international social clubs; 19% of eligible men and 22% of eligible women are members. *Most popular organizations:* intramural sports, international student organizations, OU Cousins, American Indian Student Associations, Black Student Association.
Campus security 24-hour emergency response devices and patrols, student patrols, late-night transport-escort service, controlled dormitory access, crime prevention programs, police bicycle patrols, self-defense classes.
After graduation 372 organizations recruited on campus 1997–98. *Career center:* 9 full-time, 2 part-time personnel. Services include job fairs, resume preparation, interview workshops, resume referral, career counseling, careers library, job bank, job interviews. *Major awards:* 1 Rhodes, 1 Fulbright Scholar.
Freshmen 6,384 applied, 5,687 admitted, 3,298 enrolled. 134 National Merit Scholars, 220 valedictorians.

Average high school GPA	3.48	SAT verbal scores above 500	N/R
SAT math scores above 500	N/R	ACT above 18	96%
From top 10% of their h.s. class	32%	From top quarter	61%
From top half	89%	1998 freshmen returning in 1999	80%

Application *Options:* Common Application, electronic application, early admission. *Application fee:* $25. *Required:* high school transcript; minimum 3.0 GPA. *Required for some:* essay or personal statement.
Standardized tests *Admission: Required:* SAT I or ACT. *Recommended:* SAT I.
Significant dates *Application deadlines:* 7/15 (freshmen), rolling (transfers). *Financial aid deadline:* 6/1. *Priority date:* 3/1.

Freshman Application Contact
Mr. J. P. Audas, Director of Prospective Student Services, University of Oklahoma, 1000 Asp Avenue, Norman, OK 73019-0390. **Phone:** 405-325-2151. **Toll-free phone:** 800-234-6868. **Fax:** 405-325-7478. **E-mail:** admission@ou.edu
Visit CollegeQuest.com for information on majors offered and athletics. College video and electronic viewbook available at CollegeQuest.com.

UNIVERSITY OF OKLAHOMA HEALTH SCIENCES CENTER
Oklahoma City, Oklahoma

- **State-supported**, upper-level, founded 1890
- **Degrees** bachelor's, master's, doctoral, and first professional
- **Urban** 200-acre campus
- **Coed**, 773 undergraduate students, 87% full-time, 85% women, 15% men
- **Moderately difficult** entrance level, 62% of applicants were admitted
- **$2978 tuition** and fees (in-state); $8486 (out-of-state)

Part of University of Oklahoma.
Students *Undergraduates:* 671 full-time, 102 part-time. Students come from 30 states and territories, 5 other countries. *The most frequently chosen baccalaureate field is:* health professions and related sciences. *Graduate:* 1,314 in professional programs, 848 in other graduate degree programs.

From out-of-state	9%	Age 25 or older	45%
Transferred in	51%	International students	2%
African Americans	4%	Asian Americans/Pacific Islanders	5%
Hispanic Americans	3%	Native Americans	9%

Faculty 926 (81% full-time).
Expenses (1999–2000) *One-time required fee:* $40. *Tuition, state resident:* full-time $2340; part-time $65 per credit hour. *Tuition, nonresident:* full-time $7848; part-time $218 per credit hour. *Required fees:* full-time $638; $10 per credit hour; $61 per term part-time. Full-time tuition and fees vary according to student level. Part-time tuition and fees vary according to student level. *Waivers:* minority students, senior citizens, and employees or children of employees.
Library Robert M. Bird Health Sciences Library. *Collection:* 234,000 titles, 2,658 serial subscriptions.
College life *Housing:* college housing not available. *Most popular organizations:* Student Government Association, Public Health Student Association, Student National Medical Association, Graduate Student Council, Student Medical Association.
Campus security 24-hour emergency response devices and patrols, late-night transport-escort service.
After graduation *Career center:* Services include career counseling.
Application *Option:* deferred entrance. *Preference* given to state residents. *Application fee:* $25.
Significant dates *Application deadline:* 10/1 (transfers).
Admissions Office Contact
University of Oklahoma Health Sciences Center, PO Box 26901, Oklahoma City, OK 73190. **Fax:** 405-271-2480. **E-mail:** sophie-mack@uokhsc.edu
Visit CollegeQuest.com for information on majors offered and athletics. College video available at CollegeQuest.com.

UNIVERSITY OF SCIENCE AND ARTS OF OKLAHOMA
Chickasha, Oklahoma

- **State-supported**, 4-year, founded 1908
- **Degree** bachelor's
- **Small-town** 75-acre campus with easy access to Oklahoma City
- **Coed**, 1,205 undergraduate students, 81% full-time, 60% women, 40% men
- **Moderately difficult** entrance level, 66% of applicants were admitted
- **16:1 student-to-undergraduate faculty ratio**
- **24% graduate** in 6 years or less
- **$1878 tuition** and fees (in-state); $4398 (out-of-state)

Oklahoma

- **$6946 average financial aid** package, $11,120 average indebtedness upon graduation, $263,706 endowment

Part of Oklahoma State Regents for Higher Education.

Students *Undergraduates:* 975 full-time, 230 part-time. Students come from 5 states and territories, 23 other countries. *The most frequently chosen baccalaureate fields are:* business/marketing, education, social sciences and history.

From out-of-state	2%	Reside on campus	23%
Age 25 or older	28%	Transferred in	8%
International students	3%	African Americans	4%
Asian Americans/Pacific Islanders	1%	Hispanic Americans	2%
Native Americans	11%		

Faculty 94 (59% full-time), 52% with terminal degrees.

Expenses (1999–2000) *Tuition, state resident:* full-time $1470; part-time $49 per hour. *Tuition, nonresident:* full-time $3990; part-time $133 per hour. *Required fees:* full-time $408; $14 per hour. Full-time tuition and fees vary according to course level and student level. Part-time tuition and fees vary according to course level and student level. *College room and board:* $2320; room only: $690. Room and board charges vary according to board plan and housing facility. *Payment plan:* installment. *Waivers:* senior citizens.

Library Nash Library. *Operations spending 1999–2000:* $135,424. *Collection:* 153,867 titles, 2,975 serial subscriptions, 11,830 audiovisual materials.

College life *Housing: Options:* coed, men-only, women-only. *Most popular organizations:* student activities council, Chi Alpha, Baptist Student Union, Intertribal Heritage Club, Student Bar Association.

Campus security 24-hour emergency response devices and patrols, controlled dormitory access.

After graduation 20 organizations recruited on campus 1997–98. 90% of class of 1998 had job offers within 6 months. *Career center:* 1 full-time personnel. Services include job fairs, resume preparation, resume referral, career counseling, careers library, job bank, job interviews. *Graduate education:* 25% of class of 1999 went directly to graduate and professional school: 20% education, 1% business, 1% law.

Freshmen 561 applied, 372 admitted, 286 enrolled. 6 class presidents, 10 valedictorians, 21 student government officers.

Average high school GPA	3.3	SAT verbal scores above 500	N/R
SAT math scores above 500	N/R	ACT above 18	73%
From top 10% of their h.s. class	11%	From top quarter	34%
From top half	76%	1998 freshmen returning in 1999	56%

Application *Options:* Common Application, electronic application. *Application fee:* $0. *Required:* high school transcript. *Recommended:* minimum 2.7 GPA.

Standardized tests *Admission: Required:* ACT.

Significant dates *Application deadlines:* rolling (freshmen), rolling (transfers). *Financial aid deadline priority date:* 3/15.

Freshman Application Contact
Mr. Joseph Evans, Registrar and Director of Admissions and Records, University of Science and Arts of Oklahoma, PO Box 82345, Chickasha, OK 73018-0001. **Phone:** 405-574-1204. **Toll-free phone:** 800-933-8726 Ext. 1204. **Fax:** 405-521-6244. **E-mail:** registrar@mercur.usao.edu

Visit CollegeQuest.com for information on majors offered and athletics. College video available at CollegeQuest.com.

UNIVERSITY OF TULSA
Tulsa, Oklahoma

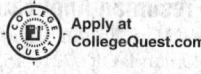

- **Independent**, university, founded 1894, affiliated with Presbyterian Church
- **Degrees** bachelor's, master's, doctoral, and first professional
- **Urban** 160-acre campus
- **Coed**, 2,866 undergraduate students, 92% full-time, 52% women, 48% men
- **Moderately difficult** entrance level, 80% of applicants were admitted
- **11:1 student-to-undergraduate faculty ratio**
- **55% graduate** in 6 years or less
- **$13,480 tuition** and fees
- **$14,439 average financial aid** package, $21,376 average indebtedness upon graduation, $685 million endowment

Students *Undergraduates:* 2,634 full-time, 232 part-time. Students come from 39 states and territories, 61 other countries. *The most frequently chosen baccalaureate fields are:* business/marketing, engineering/engineering technologies, health professions and related sciences. *Graduate:* 564 in professional programs, 704 in other graduate degree programs.

From out-of-state	24%	Reside on campus	46%
Age 25 or older	13%	Transferred in	8%
International students	10%	African Americans	8%
Asian Americans/Pacific Islanders	2%	Hispanic Americans	3%
Native Americans	6%		

Faculty 419 (74% full-time), 96% with terminal degrees.

Expenses (1999–2000) *One-time required fee:* $200. *Comprehensive fee:* $18,140 includes full-time tuition ($13,400), mandatory fees ($80), and room and board ($4660). *College room only:* $2480. Room and board charges vary according to board plan and housing facility. *Part-time tuition:* $480 per credit hour. *Part-time fees:* $3 per credit hour. *Payment plans:* tuition prepayment, installment. *Waivers:* employees or children of employees.

Library McFarlin Library plus 2 others. *Operations spending 1999–2000:* $4.4 million. *Collection:* 890,000 titles, 8,850 serial subscriptions, 17,347 audiovisual materials.

College life *Housing:* on-campus residence required through sophomore year. *Options:* coed, men-only, women-only, disabled students. *Social organizations:* national fraternities, national sororities; 21% of eligible men and 23% of eligible women are members. *Most popular organizations:* Student Association, Residence Hall Association, honor societies, intramural sports, pre-professional clubs.

Campus security 24-hour emergency response devices and patrols, late-night transport-escort service, controlled dormitory access.

After graduation 215 organizations recruited on campus 1997–98. 50% of class of 1998 had job offers within 6 months. *Career center:* 4 full-time, 3 part-time personnel. Services include job fairs, resume preparation, interview workshops, resume referral, career/interest testing, career counseling, careers library, job bank, job interviews. *Major awards:* 1 Marshall scholar.

Freshmen 2,037 applied, 1,623 admitted, 615 enrolled. 21 National Merit Scholars.

Average high school GPA	3.7	SAT verbal scores above 500	91%
SAT math scores above 500	87%	ACT above 18	100%
From top 10% of their h.s. class	49%	From top quarter	76%
From top half	100%	1998 freshmen returning in 1999	81%

Application *Options:* eApply at www.CollegeQuest.com, Common Application, early admission, early action, deferred entrance. *Application fee:* $25. *Required:* high school transcript; 1 letter of recommendation. *Recommended:* essay or personal statement; minimum 3.0 GPA; interview.

Standardized tests *Admission: Required:* SAT I or ACT.

Significant dates *Application deadline:* rolling (transfers). *Notification:* 10/1 (early action). *Financial aid deadline priority date:* 3/1.

Freshman Application Contact
Mr. John C. Corso, Associate VP for Administration/Dean of Admission, University of Tulsa, Office of Admission, The University of Tulsa, 600 South College Avenue, Tulsa, OK 74104. **Phone:** 918-631-2307. **Toll-free phone:** 800-331-3050. **Fax:** 918-631-2247. **E-mail:** admission@utulsa.edu

Visit CollegeQuest.com for information on majors offered and athletics. College video available at CollegeQuest.com.

- *See page 2854 for a narrative description.*

Oregon

OREGON

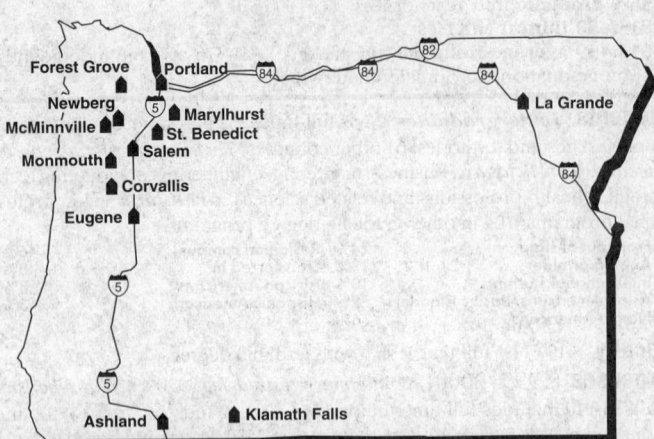

THE ART INSTITUTE OF PORTLAND
Portland, Oregon

- **Proprietary**, 4-year, founded 1963
- **Degrees** associate and bachelor's
- **Urban** 1-acre campus
- **Coed**, 438 undergraduate students, 83% full-time, 56% women, 44% men
- **Minimally difficult** entrance level, 100% of applicants were admitted
- **21:1** student-to-undergraduate faculty ratio
- **$12,060 tuition** and fees

Part of Education Management Corporation.
Students *Undergraduates:* 362 full-time, 76 part-time. Students come from 17 states and territories, 8 other countries. *The most frequently chosen baccalaureate field is:* visual/performing arts.

From out-of-state	77%	Age 25 or older	52%
Transferred in	34%	International students	3%
African Americans	3%	Asian Americans/Pacific Islanders	5%
Hispanic Americans	4%	Native Americans	1%

Faculty 53 (32% full-time), 32% with terminal degrees.
Expenses (1999–2000) *Tuition:* full-time $12,060; part-time $268 per credit. *Payment plans:* guaranteed tuition, installment. *Waivers:* employees or children of employees.
Library AIPD Learning Resource Center. *Collection:* 16,900 titles, 115 serial subscriptions, 300 audiovisual materials.
College life *Housing:* college housing not available. *Most popular organizations:* Fashion Group International, Interior Design Student Chapter.
Campus security 24-hour emergency response devices, security patrol from 4 p.m. to 10 p.m.
After graduation *Career center:* 1 full-time personnel. Services include job fairs, resume preparation, resume referral, career counseling, careers library, job bank.
Freshmen 282 applied, 282 admitted, 81 enrolled.

SAT verbal scores above 500	N/R	SAT math scores above 500	N/R
ACT above 18	N/R	1998 freshmen returning in 1999	57%

Application *Option:* deferred entrance. *Application fee:* $50. *Required:* essay or personal statement; high school transcript; interview. *Recommended:* letters of recommendation.
Significant dates *Application deadlines:* rolling (freshmen), rolling (transfers). *Financial aid deadline:* continuous.
Freshman Application Contact
Ms. Kelly Alston, Director of Admissions, The Art Institute of Portland, 2000 Southwest Fifth Avenue, Portland, OR 97201-4907. **Phone:** 503-228-6528 Ext. 103. **Toll-free phone:** 888-228-6528. **Fax:** 503-228-4227. **E-mail:** alstonk@aii.edu
Visit CollegeQuest.com for information on majors offered and athletics.

- *See page 1192 for a narrative description.*

BASSIST COLLEGE
Oregon—See The Art Institute of Portland

CASCADE COLLEGE
Portland, Oregon

- **Independent**, 4-year, founded 1994, affiliated with Church of Christ
- **Degree** bachelor's
- **Urban** 13-acre campus
- **Coed**, 296 undergraduate students, 97% full-time, 51% women, 49% men
- **Noncompetitive** entrance level, 100% of applicants were admitted
- **17:1** student-to-undergraduate faculty ratio
- **$8590 tuition** and fees
- **$358,467 endowment**

Part of Oklahoma Christian University of Science and Arts.
Students *Undergraduates:* 287 full-time, 9 part-time. Students come from 20 states and territories, 7 other countries. *The most frequently chosen baccalaureate fields are:* liberal arts/general studies, business/marketing, philosophy.

From out-of-state	63%	Reside on campus	68%
Age 25 or older	2%	Transferred in	16%
International students	4%	African Americans	6%
Asian Americans/Pacific Islanders	3%	Hispanic Americans	4%
Native Americans	1%		

Faculty 42 (24% full-time), 21% with terminal degrees.
Expenses (1999–2000) *Comprehensive fee:* $13,290 includes full-time tuition ($8390), mandatory fees ($200), and room and board ($4700). Full-time tuition and fees vary according to course load. Room and board charges vary according to board plan. *Part-time tuition:* $350 per semester hour. *Waivers:* employees or children of employees.
Library E.W. McMillan Library. *Operations spending 1999–2000:* $82,400. *Collection:* 28,050 titles, 104 serial subscriptions.
College life *Housing:* on-campus residence required through senior year. *Options:* coed, men-only, women-only. *Social organizations:* 10% of eligible men and 20% of eligible women are members. *Most popular organizations:* choir, service clubs, drama, Student Government.
Campus security Student patrols, late-night transport-escort service, 8-hour patrols by trained security personnel.
After graduation 2 organizations recruited on campus 1997–98. *Career center:* 3 part-time personnel. Services include job fairs, resume preparation, resume referral, career counseling, careers library, job bank, job interviews. *Graduate education:* 9% of class of 1999 went directly to graduate and professional school: 9% theology.
Freshmen 205 applied, 205 admitted, 104 enrolled.

SAT verbal scores above 500	72%	SAT math scores above 500	63%
ACT above 18	87%	1998 freshmen returning in 1999	60%

Application *Options:* Common Application, early admission, deferred entrance. *Application fee:* $25. *Required:* high school transcript. *Recommended:* essay or personal statement; 1 letter of recommendation.
Standardized tests *Placement:* Required: SAT I or ACT.
Significant dates *Application deadlines:* rolling (freshmen), rolling (transfers). *Financial aid deadline:* continuous.
Freshman Application Contact
Ms. Mary Horton, Director of Admissions, Cascade College, 9101 East Burnside, Portland, OR 97216-1515. **Phone:** 503-257-1202. **Toll-free phone:** 800-550-7678. **E-mail:** admissions@cascade.edu
Visit CollegeQuest.com for information on majors offered and athletics.

CONCORDIA UNIVERSITY
Portland, Oregon

- **Independent**, comprehensive, founded 1905, affiliated with Lutheran Church–Missouri Synod
- **Degrees** associate, bachelor's, master's, and postbachelor's certificates
- **Urban** 13-acre campus
- **Coed**, 910 undergraduate students
- **Minimally difficult** entrance level, 81% of applicants were admitted

Oregon

- **13:1 student-to-undergraduate faculty ratio**
- **37.3% graduate** in 6 years or less
- **$15,500 tuition** and fees
- **$12,000 average financial aid** package, $10,500 average indebtedness upon graduation, $6.8 million endowment

Concordia University, Portland, Oregon, an accredited 4-year Lutheran university, is committed to enlightening students to become competent, experienced, and ethical leaders in society. Degree programs in business, health and social services, theological studies, education, and arts and sciences offer the insights and skills that employers and graduate schools seek. Situated in the beautiful Pacific Northwest, Concordia University utilizes the educational, cultural, and recreational resources of this pristine and progressive region.

Part of Concordia University System.

Students *Undergraduates:* Students come from 27 states and territories, 20 other countries. *The most frequently chosen baccalaureate fields are:* business/marketing, education, health professions and related sciences.

From out-of-state	41%	Age 25 or older	41%
International students	8%	African Americans	4%
Asian Americans/Pacific Islanders	2%	Hispanic Americans	3%
Native Americans	1%		

Faculty 110 (32% full-time), 36% with terminal degrees.

Expenses (2000–2001, estimated) *Comprehensive fee:* $19,320 includes full-time tuition ($15,500) and room and board ($3820). *College room only:* $1110. Full-time tuition and fees vary according to program. Room and board charges vary according to housing facility. *Part-time tuition:* $475 per credit. Part-time tuition and fees vary according to course load and program. *Payment plan:* installment. *Waivers:* employees or children of employees.

Library Concordia Library plus 1 other. *Operations spending 1999–2000:* $264,547. *Collection:* 56,040 titles, 418 serial subscriptions, 7,764 audiovisual materials.

College life *Housing:* on-campus residence required through sophomore year. *Option:* coed. *Most popular organizations:* drama club, business club, Christian Life Ministry, service organization, The Promethean.

Campus security 24-hour emergency response devices and patrols, student patrols, late-night transport-escort service, controlled dormitory access.

After graduation 35 organizations recruited on campus 1997–98. *Career center:* 1 full-time personnel. Services include job fairs, resume preparation, career/interest testing, career counseling, careers library, job interviews.

Freshmen 374 applied, 304 admitted.

Average high school GPA	3.3	SAT verbal scores above 500	61%
SAT math scores above 500	50%	ACT above 18	95%
From top 10% of their h.s. class	19%	From top quarter	48%
From top half	76%	1998 freshmen returning in 1999	74%

Application *Options:* electronic application, deferred entrance. *Application fee:* $20. *Required:* essay or personal statement; high school transcript; minimum 2.5 GPA; 1 letter of recommendation. *Required for some:* interview. *Recommended:* interview.

Standardized tests *Admission: Required:* SAT I or ACT.

Significant dates *Application deadlines:* rolling (freshmen), rolling (transfers). *Financial aid deadline:* continuous.

Freshman Application Contact
Mr. Peter D. Johnson, Director of Admissions, Concordia University, 2811 Northeast Holman, Portland, OR 97211-6099. **Phone:** 503-280-8501. **Toll-free phone:** 800-321-9371. **Fax:** 503-280-8531. **E-mail:** admissions@portland.edu

Visit CollegeQuest.com for information on majors offered and athletics.

- *See page 1524 for a narrative description.*

EASTERN OREGON UNIVERSITY
La Grande, Oregon

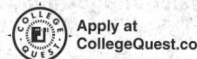
Apply at CollegeQuest.com

- **State-supported**, comprehensive, founded 1929
- **Degrees** associate, bachelor's, and master's
- **Rural** 121-acre campus
- **Coed**, 2,206 undergraduate students, 77% full-time, 60% women, 40% men

- **Moderately difficult** entrance level, 62% of applicants were admitted
- **14:1 student-to-undergraduate faculty ratio**
- **24% graduate** in 6 years or less
- **$3315 tuition** and fees
- **$1.6 million endowment**

Located in the northeast Oregon mountains, this 4-year liberal arts university charges in-state tuition to all undergraduates. Eastern offers 23 baccalaureate degree programs; groundbreaking faculty-student research; teacher preparation; preparatory programs for professional school study; BA, BS, and master's degrees; regional and global internships; and study abroad. Eastern emphasizes faculty-student interaction and research.

Part of Oregon University System.

Students *Undergraduates:* 1,690 full-time, 516 part-time. Students come from 35 states and territories, 21 other countries. *The most frequently chosen baccalaureate fields are:* interdisciplinary studies, business/marketing, liberal arts/general studies. *Graduate:* 212 in graduate degree programs.

From out-of-state	24%	Reside on campus	27%
Age 25 or older	19%	Transferred in	17%
International students	3%	African Americans	1%
Asian Americans/Pacific Islanders	3%	Hispanic Americans	3%
Native Americans	3%		

Faculty 111 (77% full-time), 73% with terminal degrees.

Expenses (1999–2000) *One-time required fee:* $75. *Comprehensive fee:* $7880 includes full-time tuition ($2316), mandatory fees ($999), and room and board ($4565). *College room only:* $3200. Full-time tuition and fees vary according to location. Room and board charges vary according to board plan and housing facility. *Part-time tuition:* $64 per credit. *Part-time fees:* $15 per credit; $85 per term part-time. Part-time tuition and fees vary according to course load and location. *Payment plan:* installment. *Waivers:* employees or children of employees.

Library Walter Pierce Library plus 1 other. *Operations spending 1999–2000:* $1 million. *Collection:* 305,000 titles, 981 serial subscriptions.

College life *Housing:* on-campus residence required in freshman year. *Options:* coed, men-only, women-only. *Most popular organizations:* Outdoor Club, Island Magic, student radio station, intramurals, student government.

Campus security 24-hour emergency response devices and patrols, late-night transport-escort service, controlled dormitory access.

After graduation 139 organizations recruited on campus 1997–98. 61% of class of 1998 had job offers within 6 months. *Career center:* 2 full-time, 1 part-time personnel. Services include job fairs, resume preparation, career/interest testing, career counseling, careers library, job bank, job interviews. *Graduate education:* 15% of class of 1999 went directly to graduate and professional school.

Freshmen 638 applied, 396 admitted, 380 enrolled.

Average high school GPA	3.3	SAT verbal scores above 500	47%
SAT math scores above 500	43%	ACT above 18	85%
From top 10% of their h.s. class	12%	From top quarter	40%
From top half	80%	1998 freshmen returning in 1999	67%

Application *Options:* eApply at www.CollegeQuest.com, early admission, early decision, deferred entrance. *Preference* given to state residents. *Application fee:* $50. *Required:* high school transcript; minimum 3.0 GPA. *Required for some:* essay or personal statement; 2 letters of recommendation.

Standardized tests *Admission: Required:* SAT I or ACT.

Significant dates *Application deadlines:* 9/15 (freshmen), 9/15 (transfers). *Early decision:* 3/15. *Notification:* 4/1 (early decision). *Financial aid deadline priority date:* 1/1.

Freshman Application Contact
Ms. Terral Schut, Director of Enrollment Services, Eastern Oregon University, One University Boulevard, La Grande, OR 97850. **Phone:** 541-962-3393. **Toll-free phone:** 800-452-8639. **Fax:** 541-962-3418. **E-mail:** admissions@eou.edu

Visit CollegeQuest.com for information on majors offered and athletics. Electronic viewbook available at CollegeQuest.com.

Oregon

EUGENE BIBLE COLLEGE
Eugene, Oregon

- **Independent**, 4-year, founded 1925, affiliated with Open Bible Standard Churches
- **Degree** bachelor's
- **Suburban** 40-acre campus
- **Coed**, 175 undergraduate students, 100% full-time, 46% women, 54% men
- **Minimally difficult** entrance level, 65% of applicants were admitted
- **15:1 student-to-undergraduate faculty ratio**
- **33% graduate** in 6 years or less
- **$5913 tuition** and fees
- **$6000 average financial aid** package, $17,500 average indebtedness upon graduation, $546,055 endowment

Eugene Bible College's programs are designed to prepare students for Christian ministries or church vocations through a program of biblical, general, and professional studies. Whether students compete in athletics, perform in music groups, or minister in chapel, they will find opportunity to put their talents to work. Come discover EBC—the college with a view.

Students *Undergraduates:* 175 full-time. Students come from 18 states and territories, 2 other countries.

From out-of-state	49%	Reside on campus	53%
Age 25 or older	19%	Transferred in	11%

Faculty 20 (50% full-time), 25% with terminal degrees.

Expenses (1999–2000) *Comprehensive fee:* $9576 includes full-time tuition ($5325), mandatory fees ($588), and room and board ($3663). Room and board charges vary according to housing facility. *Part-time tuition:* $152 per credit. *Part-time fees:* $106 per term part-time. Part-time tuition and fees vary according to class time and course load. *Payment plans:* tuition prepayment, installment. *Waivers:* senior citizens and employees or children of employees.

Library Flint Memorial Library. *Operations spending 1999–2000:* $58,210. *Collection:* 33,000 titles, 249 serial subscriptions, 288 audiovisual materials.

College life *Housing:* on-campus residence required through junior year. *Options:* men-only, women-only. *Most popular organizations:* Harvesters, Lights of the World.

Campus security 24-hour emergency response devices, student patrols, controlled dormitory access.

After graduation 35 organizations recruited on campus 1997–98. 70% of class of 1998 had job offers within 6 months. *Graduate education:* 12% of class of 1999 went directly to graduate and professional school; 12% theology.

Freshmen 92 applied, 60 admitted, 60 enrolled.

Average high school GPA	2.89	SAT verbal scores above 500	28%
SAT math scores above 500	40%	ACT above 18	60%
1998 freshmen returning in 1999	51%		

Application *Application fee:* $30. *Required:* essay or personal statement; high school transcript; minimum 2.0 GPA; 2 letters of recommendation.

Standardized tests *Admission: Required:* SAT I or ACT.

Significant dates *Application deadlines:* 9/1 (freshmen), 9/1 (transfers). *Notification:* continuous until 9/1 (freshmen). *Financial aid deadline:* 9/1. *Priority date:* 3/1.

Freshman Application Contact
Mr. Trent Combs, Director of Admissions, Eugene Bible College, 2155 Bailey Hill Road, Eugene, OR 97405. **Phone:** 541-485-1780 Ext. 135. **Toll-free phone:** 800-322-2638. **Fax:** 541-343-5801. **E-mail:** admissions@ebc.edu

Visit CollegeQuest.com for information on majors offered and athletics. College video available at CollegeQuest.com.

GEORGE FOX UNIVERSITY
Newberg, Oregon

Apply at CollegeQuest.com

- **Independent Friends**, university, founded 1891
- **Degrees** bachelor's, master's, doctoral, and first professional
- **Small-town** 73-acre campus with easy access to Portland
- **Coed**, 1,631 undergraduate students, 81% full-time, 60% women, 40% men
- **Moderately difficult** entrance level, 93% of applicants were admitted
- **55% graduate** in 6 years or less
- **$17,610 tuition** and fees
- **$14,792 average financial aid** package, $15,708 average indebtedness upon graduation, $15.7 million endowment

George Fox University enjoys a national reputation for academic excellence. Innovative programs such as Juniors Abroad and Computers Across the Curriculum, and facilities such as the new $5.3-million science center, enhance the students' experiences as they pursue their education within an atmosphere of Christian faith.

Students *Undergraduates:* 1,322 full-time, 309 part-time. Students come from 27 states and territories, 15 other countries. *The most frequently chosen baccalaureate fields are:* business/marketing, education, social sciences and history. *Graduate:* 67 in professional programs, 670 in other graduate degree programs.

From out-of-state	35%	Reside on campus	57%
Age 25 or older	19%	Transferred in	5%
International students	1%	African Americans	0.5%
Asian Americans/Pacific Islanders	2%	Hispanic Americans	3%
Native Americans	1%		

Faculty 203 (59% full-time), 50% with terminal degrees.

Expenses (2000–2001) *Comprehensive fee:* $23,160 includes full-time tuition ($17,300), mandatory fees ($310), and room and board ($5550). *College room only:* $2830. Full-time tuition and fees vary according to program. Room and board charges vary according to housing facility. *Part-time tuition:* $535 per semester hour. *Part-time fees:* $100 per term. Part-time tuition and fees vary according to course load. *Payment plan:* installment. *Waivers:* minority students, senior citizens, and employees or children of employees.

Library Murdock Learning Resource Center plus 1 other. *Operations spending 1999–2000:* $1.1 million. *Collection:* 180,272 titles, 1,215 serial subscriptions, 4,498 audiovisual materials.

College life *Housing:* on-campus residence required through junior year. *Options:* men-only, women-only. *Most popular organizations:* student government, student activities, Christian Ministries, Orientation Committee, Chaplain's Committee.

Campus security 24-hour emergency response devices and patrols, student patrols, late-night transport-escort service, controlled dormitory access.

After graduation 200 organizations recruited on campus 1997–98. 64% of class of 1998 had job offers within 6 months. *Career center:* 3 full-time personnel. Services include job fairs, resume preparation, interview workshops, career/interest testing, career counseling, careers library, job bank, job interviews, career courses.

Freshmen 780 applied, 723 admitted, 287 enrolled.

Average high school GPA	3.6	SAT verbal scores above 500	76%
SAT math scores above 500	73%	ACT above 18	91%
From top 10% of their h.s. class	37%	From top quarter	63%
From top half	91%	1998 freshmen returning in 1999	85%

Application *Options:* eApply at www.CollegeQuest.com, Common Application, electronic application, early admission, deferred entrance. *Application fee:* $40. *Required:* essay or personal statement; high school transcript; 2 letters of recommendation. *Required for some:* interview.

Standardized tests *Admission: Required:* SAT I or ACT.

Significant dates *Application deadlines:* 6/1 (freshmen), 6/1 (transfers). *Financial aid deadline priority date:* 3/1.

Freshman Application Contact
Mr. Dale Seipp, Director of Admissions, George Fox University, 414 North Meridian, Newberg, OR 97132-2697. **Phone:** 503-554-2240. **Toll-free phone:** 800-765-4369. **Fax:** 503-554-3830. **E-mail:** admissions@georgefox.edu

Visit CollegeQuest.com for information on majors offered and athletics.

- *See page 1708 for a narrative description.*

ITT TECHNICAL INSTITUTE
Portland, Oregon

- **Proprietary**, primarily 2-year, founded 1971
- **Degrees** associate and bachelor's

Oregon

- **Urban** 4-acre campus
- **Coed**
- **Minimally difficult** entrance level
- **$9190 tuition** and fees

Part of ITT Educational Services, Inc.
Admissions Office Contact
ITT Technical Institute, 6035 Northeast 78th Court, Portland, OR 97218-2854. **Toll-free phone:** 800-234-5488. **Fax:** 503-255-6135.
Visit CollegeQuest.com for information on majors offered and athletics. College video available at CollegeQuest.com.

LEWIS & CLARK COLLEGE
Portland, Oregon

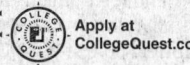
Apply at CollegeQuest.com

- **Independent**, comprehensive, founded 1867
- **Degrees** bachelor's, master's, and first professional
- **Suburban** 115-acre campus
- **Coed**, 1,736 undergraduate students, 98% full-time, 59% women, 41% men
- **Very difficult** entrance level, 69% of applicants were admitted
- **13:1 student-to-undergraduate faculty ratio**
- **66% graduate** in 6 years or less
- **$21,520 tuition** and fees
- **$19,060 average financial aid** package, $134.1 million endowment

Lewis & Clark combines a solid foundation in the liberal arts and sciences with a reputation as a national college with a global reach. Students come from 48 states and 34 countries. More than 55% participate in overseas and off-campus study programs. Portland provides many internship and community service opportunities. Lewis & Clark also offers one of the top-rated outdoors programs in the country.

Students *Undergraduates:* 1,703 full-time, 33 part-time. Students come from 48 states and territories, 34 other countries. *The most frequently chosen baccalaureate fields are:* biological/life sciences, social sciences and history, visual/performing arts. *Graduate:* 671 in professional programs, 790 in other graduate degree programs.

From out-of-state	73%	Reside on campus	57%
Age 25 or older	2%	Transferred in	4%
International students	5%	African Americans	1%
Asian Americans/Pacific Islanders	7%	Hispanic Americans	3%
Native Americans	1%		

Faculty 321 (57% full-time), 76% with terminal degrees.
Expenses (2000–2001) *Comprehensive fee:* $27,620 includes full-time tuition ($21,520) and room and board ($6100). *College room only:* $3280. Room and board charges vary according to board plan and student level. *Part-time tuition:* $1070 per semester hour. *Part-time fees:* $10 per semester hour. Part-time tuition and fees vary according to course load. *Payment plan:* installment. *Waivers:* employees or children of employees.
Library Aubrey Watzek Library plus 1 other. *Operations spending 1999–2000:* $3.7 million. *Collection:* 7,326 serial subscriptions, 8,046 audiovisual materials.
College life *Housing:* on-campus residence required through sophomore year. *Option:* coed. *Most popular organizations:* College Outdoors, Associated Students of Lewis & Clark, Center for Service and Work, musical groups, student radio station.
Campus security 24-hour emergency response devices and patrols, student patrols, late-night transport-escort service, controlled dormitory access.
After graduation 28 organizations recruited on campus 1997–98. *Career center:* 1 full-time, 2 part-time personnel. Services include job fairs, resume preparation, interview workshops, career counseling, careers library, job bank, job interviews. *Graduate education:* 23% of class of 1999 went directly to graduate and professional school: 10% graduate arts and sciences, 2% business, 2% education, 2% law, 2% medicine.
Freshmen 3,008 applied, 2,089 admitted, 512 enrolled. 13 National Merit Scholars, 20 valedictorians.

SAT verbal scores above 500	98%	SAT math scores above 500	95%
ACT above 18	100%	From top 10% of their h.s. class	42%
From top quarter	73%	From top half	94%
1998 freshmen returning in 1999	80%		

Application *Options:* eApply at www.CollegeQuest.com, Common Application, electronic application, early admission, early action, deferred entrance. *Application fee:* $45. *Required:* essay or personal statement; high school transcript; minimum 2.0 GPA; 2 letters of recommendation. *Required for some:* 4 letters of recommendation; portfolio applicants must submit samples of graded work. *Recommended:* minimum 3.0 GPA; interview.
Standardized tests *Admission: Required:* SAT I or ACT or academic portfolio.
Significant dates *Application deadline:* 2/1 (freshmen). *Early action:* 12/1. *Notification:* 4/1 (freshmen), 1/15 (early action). *Financial aid deadline priority date:* 3/1.
Freshman Application Contact
Mr. Michael Sexton, Dean of Admissions, Lewis & Clark College, 0615 SW Palatine Hill Road, Portland, OR 97219-7899. **Phone:** 503-768-7040. **Toll-free phone:** 800-444-4111. **Fax:** 503-768-7055. **E-mail:** admissions@lclark.edu
Visit CollegeQuest.com for information on majors offered and athletics. Electronic viewbook available at CollegeQuest.com.

- *See page 1920 for a narrative description.*

LINFIELD COLLEGE
McMinnville, Oregon

Apply at CollegeQuest.com

- **Independent American Baptist**, 4-year, founded 1849
- **Degree** bachelor's
- **Small-town** 95-acre campus with easy access to Portland
- **Coed**, 1,518 undergraduate students, 98% full-time, 55% women, 45% men
- **Moderately difficult** entrance level, 92% of applicants were admitted
- **13:1 student-to-undergraduate faculty ratio**
- **64% graduate** in 6 years or less
- **$17,720 tuition** and fees
- **$14,800 average financial aid** package, $17,600 average indebtedness upon graduation, $47.9 million endowment

Linfield College, tracing its roots back to 1849, is an independent, 4-year institution nationally recognized for its strong teaching faculty, outstanding science programs, and extensive study-abroad opportunities. Nearly 50 percent of graduating students have spent a January term, a semester, or an academic year in another country. Linfield is located in the heart of the Willamette Valley.

Students *Undergraduates:* 1,494 full-time, 24 part-time. Students come from 30 states and territories, 23 other countries. *The most frequently chosen baccalaureate fields are:* business/marketing, health professions and related sciences, social sciences and history.

From out-of-state	44%	Reside on campus	68%
Age 25 or older	2%	Transferred in	4%
International students	3%	African Americans	2%
Asian Americans/Pacific Islanders	6%	Hispanic Americans	2%
Native Americans	1%		

Faculty 134 (81% full-time).
Expenses (1999–2000) *One-time required fee:* $300. *Comprehensive fee:* $23,020 includes full-time tuition ($17,590), mandatory fees ($130), and room and board ($5300). *College room only:* $2560. Room and board charges vary according to housing facility. *Part-time tuition:* $550 per credit hour. *Part-time fees:* $40 per term part-time. Part-time tuition and fees vary according to course load. *Payment plan:* installment. *Waivers:* senior citizens and employees or children of employees.
Library Emanuel Northup Library. *Operations spending 1999–2000:* $1 million. *Collection:* 155,663 titles, 1,294 serial subscriptions, 9,196 audiovisual materials.
College life *Housing:* on-campus residence required through junior year. *Options:* coed, men-only, women-only. *Social organizations:* national fraternities, national sororities, local fraternities, local sororities; 29% of eligible men and 27% of eligible women are members. *Most popular organizations:* Campus Crusade for Christ, Stars, Hawaiian Club, ski club, Habitat for Humanity.
Campus security 24-hour emergency response devices and patrols, student patrols, late-night transport-escort service.

Peterson's Guide to Four-Year Colleges 2001 www.petersons.com

Oregon

Linfield College (continued)

After graduation 10 organizations recruited on campus 1997–98. 85% of class of 1998 had job offers within 6 months. *Career center:* 1 full-time, 1 part-time personnel. Services include job fairs, resume preparation, interview workshops, career/interest testing, career counseling, careers library, job bank, job interviews. *Graduate education:* 12% of class of 1999 went directly to graduate and professional school: 5% graduate arts and sciences, 2% business, 2% medicine, 1% engineering, 1% law, 1% theology.

Freshmen 1,608 applied, 1,484 admitted, 399 enrolled. 12 class presidents, 28 valedictorians, 110 student government officers.

Average high school GPA	3.5	SAT verbal scores above 500	70%
SAT math scores above 500	75%	ACT above 18	95%
From top 10% of their h.s. class	30%	From top quarter	63%
From top half	91%	1998 freshmen returning in 1999	80%

Application *Options:* eApply at www.CollegeQuest.com, Common Application, electronic application, early decision, deferred entrance. *Application fee:* $40. *Required:* essay or personal statement; high school transcript; 2 letters of recommendation. *Recommended:* interview.

Standardized tests *Admission:* Required: SAT I or ACT.

Significant dates *Application deadlines:* 2/15 (freshmen), 3/15 (transfers). *Early decision:* 12/1. *Notification:* 4/1 (freshmen), 1/15 (early decision). *Financial aid deadline priority date:* 2/1.

Freshman Application Contact
Mr. Ernest Sandlin, Director of Admissions, Linfield College, 900 SE Baker Street, McMinnville, OR 97128-6894. **Phone:** 503-434-2489. **Toll-free phone:** 800-640-2287. **Fax:** 503-434-2472. **E-mail:** admissions@linfield.edu

Visit CollegeQuest.com for information on majors offered and athletics. Electronic viewbook available at CollegeQuest.com.

■ *See page 1932 for a narrative description.*

MARYLHURST UNIVERSITY
Marylhurst, Oregon

- **Independent Roman Catholic**, comprehensive, founded 1893
- **Degrees** bachelor's and master's
- **Suburban** 73-acre campus with easy access to Portland
- **Coed**, 662 undergraduate students, 35% full-time, 79% women, 21% men
- **Noncompetitive** entrance level, 87% of applicants were admitted
- **7:1 student-to-undergraduate faculty ratio**
- **$10,770 tuition** and fees
- **$8.5 million endowment**

Students *Undergraduates:* 232 full-time, 430 part-time. Students come from 5 states and territories, 33 other countries. *The most frequently chosen baccalaureate fields are:* business/marketing, communications/communication technologies, social sciences and history. *Graduate:* 239 in graduate degree programs.

From out-of-state	8%	Age 25 or older	72%
Transferred in	82%		

Faculty 477 (6% full-time).

Expenses (1999–2000) *Comprehensive fee:* $16,698 includes full-time tuition ($10,575), mandatory fees ($195), and room and board ($5928). Full-time tuition and fees vary according to course load. *Part-time tuition:* $235 per credit hour. *Part-time fees:* $4 per credit hour; $17 per term part-time. Part-time tuition and fees vary according to course load. *Payment plan:* deferred payment. *Waivers:* employees or children of employees.

Library Shoen Library. *Operations spending 1999–2000:* $429,000. *Collection:* 1,449 audiovisual materials.

College life *Housing: Options:* coed, men-only, women-only, disabled students. *Most popular organizations:* Association for Women in Communications, Organization Against Social Injustice & Suffering (OASIS), Student Ambassadors, Student Association of Marylhurst Musicians (SAMM).

Campus security 24-hour emergency response devices and patrols, late-night transport-escort service, controlled dormitory access.

After graduation 40 organizations recruited on campus 1997–98. *Career center:* 1 full-time, 1 part-time personnel. Services include job fairs, resume preparation, interview workshops, career/interest testing, career counseling, careers library.

Freshmen 68 applied, 59 admitted, 59 enrolled.

Average high school GPA	3.35	SAT verbal scores above 500	77%
SAT math scores above 500	59%	ACT above 18	N/R
From top 10% of their h.s. class	12%	From top quarter	65%
From top half	88%	1998 freshmen returning in 1999	90%

Application *Option:* deferred entrance. *Application fee:* $50. *Required:* high school transcript. *Required for some:* essay or personal statement; minimum 2.0 GPA; interview.

Standardized tests *Admission:* Required for some: SAT I or ACT.

Significant dates *Application deadlines:* rolling (freshmen), rolling (transfers).

Freshman Application Contact
Ms. Jennifer Damian, Admission Specialist, Marylhurst University, PO Box 261, Marylhurst, OR 97036-0261. **Phone:** 503-699-6268 Ext. 3320. **Toll-free phone:** 800-634-9982 Ext. 3317. **Fax:** 503-636-9526.

Visit CollegeQuest.com for information on majors offered and athletics.

■ *See page 2004 for a narrative description.*

MOUNT ANGEL SEMINARY
Saint Benedict, Oregon

Admissions Office Contact
Mount Angel Seminary, Saint Benedict, OR 97373.

MULTNOMAH BIBLE COLLEGE AND BIBLICAL SEMINARY
Portland, Oregon

- **Independent interdenominational**, comprehensive, founded 1936
- **Degrees** bachelor's, master's, and first professional
- **Urban** 22-acre campus
- **Coed**, 544 undergraduate students, 91% full-time, 46% women, 54% men
- **Moderately difficult** entrance level, 80% of applicants were admitted
- **32.4% graduate** in 6 years or less
- **$8600 tuition** and fees
- **$7090 average financial aid** package, $3.3 million endowment

Students *Undergraduates:* 493 full-time, 51 part-time. Students come from 31 states and territories, 5 other countries. *The most frequently chosen baccalaureate field is:* philosophy. *Graduate:* 66 in professional programs, 164 in other graduate degree programs.

From out-of-state	57%	Reside on campus	53%
Age 25 or older	17%	Transferred in	11%
International students	1%	African Americans	1%
Asian Americans/Pacific Islanders	3%	Hispanic Americans	2%
Native Americans	1%		

Faculty 60 (50% full-time), 33% with terminal degrees.

Expenses (1999–2000) *Comprehensive fee:* $12,320 includes full-time tuition ($8600) and room and board ($3720). *College room only:* $1930. Room and board charges vary according to board plan and housing facility. *Part-time tuition:* $360 per semester hour. Part-time tuition and fees vary according to course load. *Payment plan:* installment. *Waivers:* employees or children of employees.

Library John Mitchell Library. *Operations spending 1999–2000:* $306,672. *Collection:* 64,860 titles, 400 serial subscriptions, 881 audiovisual materials.

College life *Housing:* on-campus residence required through senior year. *Options:* men-only, women-only.

Campus security 24-hour emergency response devices and patrols, late-night transport-escort service, controlled dormitory access.

After graduation 37 organizations recruited on campus 1997–98. *Career center:* 1 full-time personnel. Services include resume preparation, career/interest testing, career counseling, job bank.

Freshmen 377 applied, 303 admitted, 101 enrolled.

SAT verbal scores above 500	N/R	SAT math scores above 500	N/R
ACT above 18	N/R	1998 freshmen returning in 1999	75%

Application *Option:* deferred entrance. *Application fee:* $40. *Required:* essay or personal statement; high school transcript; minimum 2.5 GPA; 4 letters of recommendation.

Oregon

Standardized tests *Admission: Required:* SAT I or ACT.
Significant dates *Application deadlines:* 7/15 (freshmen), 7/15 (transfers). *Notification:* 8/15 (freshmen). *Financial aid deadline priority date:* 3/15.
Freshman Application Contact
Ms. Nancy Gerecz, Admissions Assistant, Multnomah Bible College and Biblical Seminary, 8435 Northeast Glisan Street, Portland, OR 97220-5898. **Phone:** 503-255-0332 Ext. 373. **Toll-free phone:** 800-275-4672. **Fax:** 503-254-1268. **E-mail:** admiss@multnomah.edu
Visit CollegeQuest.com for information on majors offered and athletics. College video available at CollegeQuest.com.

NORTHWEST CHRISTIAN COLLEGE
Eugene, Oregon

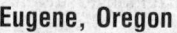
Apply at CollegeQuest.com

Admissions Office Contact
Northwest Christian College, 828 East 11th Avenue, Eugene, OR 97401-3727. **Fax:** 541-684-7317.

OREGON COLLEGE OF ART AND CRAFT
Portland, Oregon

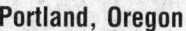
Apply at CollegeQuest.com

- **Independent**, 4-year, founded 1907
- **Degrees** bachelor's and postbachelor's certificates
- **Urban** 7-acre campus
- **Coed**, 87 undergraduate students, 47% full-time, 74% women, 26% men
- **Minimally difficult** entrance level, 67% of applicants were admitted
- **6:1 student-to-undergraduate faculty ratio**
- **$11,710 tuition** and fees
- **$10,286 average financial aid** package, $17,207 average indebtedness upon graduation, $5.2 million endowment

Students *Undergraduates:* 41 full-time, 46 part-time. Students come from 14 states and territories, 2 other countries. *The most frequently chosen baccalaureate field is:* visual/performing arts.

From out-of-state	21%	Age 25 or older	71%
Transferred in	34%	International students	2%
Asian Americans/Pacific Islanders	4%	Native Americans	2%

Faculty 16 (44% full-time), 94% with terminal degrees.
Expenses (2000–2001) *Tuition:* full-time $11,520; part-time $500 per credit hour. *Required fees:* full-time $190; $95 per term part-time. Full-time tuition and fees vary according to course load. *Payment plan:* installment.
Library Oregon College of Art and Craft Library plus 1 other. *Operations spending 1999–2000:* $68,936. *Collection:* 6,500 titles, 90 serial subscriptions, 24,000 audiovisual materials.
College life *Housing:* college housing not available.
Campus security 24-hour emergency response devices, late-night transport-escort service.
Freshmen 3 applied, 2 admitted, 2 enrolled.

Average high school GPA	2.85	SAT verbal scores above 500	N/R
SAT math scores above 500	N/R	ACT above 18	N/R
1998 freshmen returning in 1999	100%		

Application *Options:* eApply at www.CollegeQuest.com, deferred entrance. *Application fee:* $30. *Required:* essay or personal statement; high school transcript; minimum 2.5 GPA; 2 letters of recommendation; interview; portfolio.
Significant dates *Application deadlines:* rolling (freshmen), rolling (transfers). *Financial aid deadline priority date:* 2/1.
Freshman Application Contact
Mr. Paul Krull, Director of Recruitment, Oregon College of Art and Craft, 8245 Southwest Barnes Road, Portland, OR 97225. **Phone:** 503-297-5544 Ext. 131. **Toll-free phone:** 800-390-0632. **Fax:** 503-297-9651. **E-mail:** admissions@ocac.edu
Visit CollegeQuest.com for information on majors offered and athletics.

OREGON HEALTH SCIENCES UNIVERSITY
Portland, Oregon

- **State-related**, upper-level, founded 1974
- **Degrees** bachelor's, master's, doctoral, first professional, post-master's, postbachelor's, and first professional certificates
- **Urban** 116-acre campus
- **Coed**, 653 undergraduate students, 78% full-time, 84% women, 16% men
- **Moderately difficult** entrance level
- **$5747 tuition** and fees (in-state); $12,973 (out-of-state)
- **$9640 average financial aid** package, $13.9 million endowment

Students *Undergraduates:* 509 full-time, 144 part-time. Students come from 31 states and territories, 3 other countries. *The most frequently chosen baccalaureate field is:* health professions and related sciences. *Graduate:* 664 in professional programs, 528 in other graduate degree programs.

From out-of-state	6%	Age 25 or older	64%
International students	1%	African Americans	0.3%
Asian Americans/Pacific Islanders	5%	Hispanic Americans	3%
Native Americans	2%		

Faculty 836 (60% full-time).
Expenses (1999–2000) *Tuition, state resident:* full-time $4647; part-time $109 per credit hour. *Tuition, nonresident:* full-time $11,873; part-time $272 per credit hour. *Required fees:* full-time $1100; $176 per term part-time. Full-time tuition and fees vary according to location, program, and student level. *College room and board:* room only: $2070. *Payment plan:* deferred payment. *Waivers:* employees or children of employees.
Library Bic Bio-Informational Center plus 2 others. *Collection:* 200,771 titles, 2,110 serial subscriptions.
College life *Housing:* Option: coed.
Campus security 24-hour patrols.
After graduation *Career center:* Services include career counseling.
Application *Preference* given to state residents. *Application fee:* $60.
Standardized tests *Admission: Required for some:* SAT I.
Significant dates *Financial aid deadline priority date:* 3/1.
Freshman Application Contact
Ms. Victoria Souza, Registrar and Director of Financial Aid, Oregon Health Sciences University, 3181 Southwest Sam Jackson Park Road, Portland, OR 97201-3098. **Phone:** 503-494-7800.
Visit CollegeQuest.com for information on majors offered and athletics.

OREGON INSTITUTE OF TECHNOLOGY
Klamath Falls, Oregon

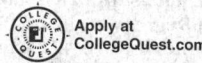
Apply at CollegeQuest.com

- **State-supported**, comprehensive, founded 1947
- **Degrees** associate, bachelor's, and master's
- **Small-town** 173-acre campus
- **Coed**, 2,275 undergraduate students, 76% full-time, 42% women, 58% men
- **Moderately difficult** entrance level, 74% of applicants were admitted
- **14:1 student-to-undergraduate faculty ratio**
- **59% graduate** in 6 years or less
- **$3378 tuition** and fees (in-state); $11,436 (out-of-state)
- **$17,000 average indebtedness** upon graduation, $227,880 endowment

Part of Oregon University System.
Students *Undergraduates:* 1,730 full-time, 545 part-time. Students come from 12 states and territories, 16 other countries. *Graduate:* 3 in graduate degree programs.

Reside on campus	17%	Age 25 or older	38%
Transferred in	11%		

Faculty 176 (63% full-time), 21% with terminal degrees.
Expenses (1999–2000) *One-time required fee:* $25. *Tuition, state resident:* full-time $2592; part-time $72 per credit. *Tuition, nonresident:* full-time $10,650; part-time $72 per credit. *Required fees:* full-time $786; $97 per term part-time. Full-time tuition and fees vary according to course load. Part-time tuition and fees vary according to course load. *College room and board:*

Peterson's Guide to Four-Year Colleges 2001 www.petersons.com

Oregon

Oregon Institute of Technology (continued)

$4866. Room and board charges vary according to board plan. *Payment plans:* installment, deferred payment. *Waivers:* senior citizens and employees or children of employees.

Library Learning Resources Center. *Operations spending 1999–2000:* $886,874. *Collection:* 120,000 titles, 1,270 serial subscriptions.

College life *Housing:* Option: coed. *Social organizations:* national fraternities, local sororities; 1% of men are members. *Most popular organizations:* Phi Delta Theta, Christian Fellowship, International Club, Society of Women Engineers, CELSA.

Campus security 24-hour emergency response devices and patrols, late-night transport-escort service.

After graduation 53 organizations recruited on campus 1997–98. 87% of class of 1998 had job offers within 6 months. *Career center:* 3 full-time personnel. Services include job fairs, resume preparation, resume referral, career counseling, careers library, job bank, job interviews.

Freshmen 660 applied, 491 admitted, 324 enrolled. 1 National Merit Scholar.

Average high school GPA	3.17	SAT verbal scores above 500	64%
SAT math scores above 500	65%	ACT above 18	N/R
1998 freshmen returning in 1999	45%		

Application *Options:* eApply at www.CollegeQuest.com, Common Application, electronic application, deferred entrance. *Application fee:* $50. *Required:* high school transcript; minimum 2.5 GPA. *Required for some:* letters of recommendation.

Standardized tests *Admission: Required for some:* SAT I and SAT II or ACT.

Significant dates *Application deadlines:* 6/1 (freshmen), 6/1 (transfers). *Financial aid deadline:* 3/1.

Freshman Application Contact Director of Admissions, Oregon Institute of Technology, 3201 Campus Drive, Klamath Falls, OR 97601-8801. **Phone:** 541-885-1150. **Toll-free phone:** 800-422-2017 (in-state); 800-343-6653 (out-of-state). **Fax:** 541-885-1115. **E-mail:** oit@oit.edu

Visit CollegeQuest.com for information on majors offered and athletics. College video and electronic viewbook available at CollegeQuest.com.

OREGON STATE UNIVERSITY
Corvallis, Oregon

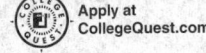

- **State-supported**, university, founded 1868
- **Degrees** bachelor's, master's, doctoral, and first professional
- **Small-town** 422-acre campus with easy access to Portland
- **Coed**, 12,554 undergraduate students, 94% full-time, 46% women, 54% men
- **Moderately difficult** entrance level, 91% of applicants were admitted
- **13:1** student-to-undergraduate faculty ratio
- **62% graduate** in 6 years or less
- **$3549 tuition** and fees (in-state); $12,393 (out-of-state)
- **$208.6 million endowment**

Small classes, motivated students, honors-level instruction, and close interaction with some of Oregon State University's finest faculty members create an exciting, challenging University Honors College atmosphere. In honors classes, colloquia, and other innovative ways, Honors College students explore their majors with an interdisciplinary approach. Students also work with faculty mentors to prepare honors theses. Graduates receive an honors baccalaureate degree in their major, conferred jointly by the Honors College and their academic college.

Part of Oregon University System.

Students *Undergraduates:* 11,747 full-time, 807 part-time. Students come from 50 states and territories, 98 other countries. *The most frequently chosen baccalaureate fields are:* business/marketing, education, natural resources/environmental science. *Graduate:* 151 in professional programs, 3,157 in other graduate degree programs.

From out-of-state	16%	Reside on campus	29%
Age 25 or older	9%	Transferred in	9%
International students	2%	African Americans	1%
Asian Americans/Pacific Islanders	8%	Hispanic Americans	3%
Native Americans	1%		

Faculty 1,347 (79% full-time).

Expenses (1999–2000) *One-time required fee:* $50. *Tuition, state resident:* full-time $3549; part-time $75 per credit. *Tuition, nonresident:* full-time $12,393; part-time $321 per credit. Part-time tuition and fees vary according to course load. *College room and board:* $5394. Room and board charges vary according to board plan and housing facility. *Payment plan:* deferred payment.

Library Valley Library. *Operations spending 1999–2000:* $7 million. *Collection:* 689,119 titles, 11,605 serial subscriptions, 6,225 audiovisual materials.

College life *Housing: Options:* coed, cooperative, disabled students. *Social organizations:* national fraternities, national sororities; 14% of eligible men and 12% of eligible women are members. *Most popular organizations:* Associated Students of OSU, International Students of OSU, graduate students organization, Campus Crusade, MECHA.

Campus security 24-hour emergency response devices and patrols, student patrols, late-night transport-escort service, controlled dormitory access, crime prevention office.

After graduation 293 organizations recruited on campus 1997–98. *Career center:* Services include job fairs, resume preparation, interview workshops, resume referral, career counseling, careers library, job bank, job interviews.

Freshmen 6,494 applied, 5,923 admitted, 2,846 enrolled.

Average high school GPA	3.4	SAT verbal scores above 500	66%
SAT math scores above 500	71%	ACT above 18	91%
1998 freshmen returning in 1999	80%		

Application *Options:* eApply at www.CollegeQuest.com, Common Application, electronic application, early admission, early action, deferred entrance. *Application fee:* $50. *Required:* high school transcript; minimum 3.0 GPA.

Standardized tests *Admission: Required:* SAT I or ACT. *Required for some:* SAT II Subject Tests.

Significant dates *Application deadlines:* 3/1 (freshmen), 5/1 (transfers). *Financial aid deadline priority date:* 2/1.

Freshman Application Contact Ms. Michele Sandlin, Associate Director of Processing, Oregon State University, Corvallis, OR 97331. **Phone:** 541-737-4411. **Toll-free phone:** 800-291-4192. **Fax:** 541-737-6157. **E-mail:** osuadmit@orst.edu

Visit CollegeQuest.com for information on majors offered and athletics. College video available at CollegeQuest.com.

■ *See page 2226 for a narrative description.*

PACIFIC NORTHWEST COLLEGE OF ART
Portland, Oregon

- **Independent**, 4-year, founded 1909
- **Degree** bachelor's
- **Urban** campus
- **Coed**, 316 undergraduate students, 82% full-time, 60% women, 40% men
- **Moderately difficult** entrance level, 99% of applicants were admitted
- **10:1** student-to-undergraduate faculty ratio
- **37% graduate** in 6 years or less
- **$13,200 tuition** and fees
- **$9895 average financial aid** package, $2.8 million endowment

Students *Undergraduates:* 258 full-time, 58 part-time. Students come from 20 states and territories, 4 other countries. *The most frequently chosen baccalaureate field is:* visual/performing arts.

From out-of-state	18%	Reside on campus	4%
Age 25 or older	34%	Transferred in	11%
International students	2%	African Americans	2%
Asian Americans/Pacific Islanders	2%	Hispanic Americans	4%
Native Americans	2%		

Faculty 57 (26% full-time), 58% with terminal degrees.

Expenses (2000–2001) *One-time required fee:* $5. *Tuition:* full-time $12,420; part-time $535 per semester hour. *Required fees:* full-time $780; $12 per term part-time. *College room only:* $3825. *Payment plan:* installment. *Waivers:* employees or children of employees.

Oregon

Library Rex Arragon Library plus 1 other. *Operations spending 1999–2000:* $13,474. *Collection:* 25,000 titles, 82 serial subscriptions.

College life *Housing: Options:* coed, cooperative.

Campus security Entrance security guards during open hours.

After graduation *Career center:* 1 full-time, 1 part-time personnel. Services include resume preparation, interview workshops, resume referral, career/interest testing, career counseling, careers library, job bank, job interviews.

Freshmen 197 applied, 195 admitted, 39 enrolled.

Average high school GPA	2.81	SAT verbal scores above 500	40%
SAT math scores above 500	40%	ACT above 18	100%
From top 10% of their h.s. class	0%	From top quarter	0%
From top half	75%	1998 freshmen returning in 1999	62%

Application *Options:* early action, deferred entrance. *Application fee:* $30. *Required:* essay or personal statement; high school transcript; minimum 2.0 GPA; 2 letters of recommendation; portfolio of artwork. *Recommended:* interview.

Significant dates *Application deadline:* 8/1 (freshmen). *Early action:* 1/15. *Notification:* 2/15 (early action). **Financial aid deadline priority date:** 3/1.

Freshman Application Contact Mr. Clarence Goodman, Enrollment Counselor, Pacific Northwest College of Art, 1241 NW Johnson Street, Portland, OR 97209. **Phone:** 503-821-8975. **Toll-free phone:** 800-818-PNCA. **Fax:** 503-226-3587. **E-mail:** pncainfo@pnca.edu

Visit CollegeQuest.com for information on majors offered and athletics. Electronic viewbook available at CollegeQuest.com.

PACIFIC UNIVERSITY
Forest Grove, Oregon

- **Independent**, comprehensive, founded 1849
- **Degrees** bachelor's, master's, doctoral, and first professional
- **Small-town** 55-acre campus with easy access to Portland
- **Coed**, 1,041 undergraduate students, 96% full-time, 61% women, 39% men
- **Moderately difficult** entrance level, 86% of applicants were admitted
- **10:1** student-to-undergraduate faculty ratio
- **59% graduate** in 6 years or less
- **$17,800 tuition** and fees
- **$15,832 average financial aid** package, $18,500 average indebtedness upon graduation, $23 million endowment

Students *Undergraduates:* 997 full-time, 44 part-time. Students come from 31 states and territories, 7 other countries. *The most frequently chosen baccalaureate fields are:* biological/life sciences, business/marketing, social sciences and history. *Graduate:* 341 in professional programs, 651 in other graduate degree programs.

From out-of-state	50%	Reside on campus	50%
Age 25 or older	7%	Transferred in	6%
International students	2%	African Americans	1%
Asian Americans/Pacific Islanders	18%	Hispanic Americans	2%
Native Americans	1%		

Faculty 271 (60% full-time).

Expenses (2000–2001, estimated) *One-time required fee:* $750. *Comprehensive fee:* $22,703 includes full-time tuition ($17,300), mandatory fees ($500), and room and board ($4903). *College room only:* $2360. Full-time tuition and fees vary according to program. Room and board charges vary according to board plan and housing facility. *Part-time tuition:* $577 per semester hour. Part-time tuition and fees vary according to course load and program. *Payment plans:* installment, deferred payment. *Waivers:* employees or children of employees.

Library Scott Memorial Library. *Operations spending 1999–2000:* $792,000. *Collection:* 1,052 serial subscriptions, 1,026 audiovisual materials.

College life *Housing:* on-campus residence required through sophomore year. *Option:* coed. *Social organizations:* local fraternities, local sororities; 27% of eligible men and 6% of eligible women are members. *Most popular organizations:* Pacific Outback Activities, SOAR (Student Outreach Admissions Representatives), Hawaiian Club, Circle K.

Campus security 24-hour emergency response devices and patrols, late-night transport-escort service.

After graduation 150 organizations recruited on campus 1997–98. *Career center:* 3 full-time personnel. Services include job fairs, resume preparation, interview workshops, resume referral, career/interest testing, career counseling, careers library, job bank, job interviews. **Major awards:** 1 Fulbright Scholar.

Freshmen 989 applied, 853 admitted, 292 enrolled. 18 valedictorians.

Average high school GPA	3.52	SAT verbal scores above 500	79%
SAT math scores above 500	82%	ACT above 18	96%
From top 10% of their h.s. class	40%	From top quarter	71%
From top half	96%	1998 freshmen returning in 1999	80%

Application *Options:* Common Application, electronic application, deferred entrance. *Application fee:* $30. *Required:* essay or personal statement; high school transcript; minimum 3.0 GPA; 2 letters of recommendation. *Recommended:* interview.

Standardized tests *Admission: Required:* SAT I or ACT.

Significant dates *Application deadlines:* rolling (freshmen), rolling (transfers). *Notification:* 4/1 (freshmen). **Financial aid deadline:** continuous.

Freshman Application Contact Ms. Beth Woodward, Director of Undergraduate Admissions, Pacific University, 2043 College Way, Forest Grove, OR 97116-1797. **Phone:** 503-359-2218. **Toll-free phone:** 800-677-6712. **Fax:** 503-359-2975. **E-mail:** admissions@pacificu.edu

Visit CollegeQuest.com for information on majors offered and athletics.

■ *See page 2238 for a narrative description.*

PORTLAND STATE UNIVERSITY
Portland, Oregon

- **State-supported**, university, founded 1946
- **Degrees** bachelor's, master's, doctoral, and postbachelor's certificates
- **Urban** 36-acre campus
- **Coed**, 10,432 undergraduate students, 70% full-time, 56% women, 44% men
- **Minimally difficult** entrance level, 78% of applicants were admitted
- **23:1** student-to-undergraduate faculty ratio
- **33% graduate** in 6 years or less
- **$3468 tuition** and fees (in-state); $11,661 (out-of-state)
- **$6229 average financial aid** package, $13.4 million endowment

Part of Oregon University System.

Students *Undergraduates:* 7,268 full-time, 3,164 part-time. Students come from 54 states and territories, 58 other countries. *The most frequently chosen baccalaureate fields are:* business/marketing, psychology, social sciences and history. *Graduate:* 5,488 in graduate degree programs.

From out-of-state	11%	Reside on campus	9%
Age 25 or older	38%	Transferred in	19%
International students	4%	African Americans	3%
Asian Americans/Pacific Islanders	10%	Hispanic Americans	4%
Native Americans	1%		

Faculty 673 (69% full-time).

Expenses (1999–2000) *Tuition, state resident:* full-time $2694; part-time $673 per term. *Tuition, nonresident:* full-time $10,887; part-time $2723 per term. *Required fees:* full-time $774; $214 per term part-time. Full-time tuition and fees vary according to student level. Part-time tuition and fees vary according to course level and course load. *College room and board:* $6150; room only: $4050. Room and board charges vary according to board plan and housing facility. *Payment plans:* installment, deferred payment. *Waivers:* minority students, senior citizens, and employees or children of employees.

Library Branford P. Millar Library. *Operations spending 1999–2000:* $8.8 million. *Collection:* 681,365 titles, 9,684 serial subscriptions, 102,778 audiovisual materials.

College life *Housing: Options:* coed, disabled students. *Social organizations:* national fraternities, national sororities, local sororities; 2% of eligible men and 2% of eligible women are members. *Most popular organizations:* radio station, Women's Union, Association of African Students, Queers and Allies, OSPERG.

Campus security 24-hour emergency response devices and patrols, late-night transport-escort service, controlled dormitory access, self-defense education.

Oregon

Portland State University (continued)

After graduation 126 organizations recruited on campus 1997–98. *Career center:* 8 full-time, 1 part-time personnel. Services include job fairs, resume preparation, resume referral, career counseling, careers library, job bank, job interviews. *Major awards:* 1 Fulbright Scholar.

Freshmen 2,366 applied, 1,857 admitted, 1,005 enrolled.

Average high school GPA	3.12	SAT verbal scores above 500	58%
SAT math scores above 500	58%	ACT above 18	80%
1998 freshmen returning in 1999	63%		

Application *Options:* electronic application, early admission, deferred entrance. *Application fee:* $50. *Required:* high school transcript; minimum 2.5 GPA.

Standardized tests *Admission: Required:* SAT I or ACT.

Significant dates *Application deadlines:* rolling (freshmen), rolling (transfers). *Financial aid deadline:* continuous.

Freshman Application Contact
Ms. Agnes A. Hoffman, Director of Admissions and Records, Portland State University, PO Box 751, Portland, OR 97207-0751. **Phone:** 503-725-3511. **Toll-free phone:** 800-547-8887. **Fax:** 503-725-5525. **E-mail:** askadm@ess.pdx.edu

Visit CollegeQuest.com for information on majors offered and athletics.

REED COLLEGE
Portland, Oregon

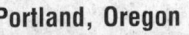

Apply at CollegeQuest.com

- **Independent**, comprehensive, founded 1908
- **Degrees** bachelor's and master's
- **Suburban** 98-acre campus
- **Coed**, 1,309 undergraduate students, 98% full-time, 53% women, 47% men
- **Very difficult** entrance level, 68% of applicants were admitted
- **10:1 student-to-undergraduate faculty ratio**
- **68% graduate** in 6 years or less
- **$24,050 tuition** and fees
- **$21,116 average financial aid** package, $14,010 average indebtedness upon graduation, $267.5 million endowment

Students *Undergraduates:* 1,280 full-time, 29 part-time. Students come from 57 states and territories, 29 other countries. *The most frequently chosen baccalaureate fields are:* biological/life sciences, English, psychology. *Graduate:* 20 in graduate degree programs.

From out-of-state	85%	Reside on campus	65%
Age 25 or older	3%	Transferred in	4%
International students	3%	African Americans	0.4%
Asian Americans/Pacific Islanders	5%	Hispanic Americans	4%
Native Americans	1%		

Faculty 123 (91% full-time), 85% with terminal degrees.

Expenses (1999–2000) *Comprehensive fee:* $30,700 includes full-time tuition ($23,880), mandatory fees ($170), and room and board ($6650). *College room only:* $3450. Room and board charges vary according to board plan. *Part-time tuition:* $4110 per course. Part-time tuition and fees vary according to course load. *Payment plan:* installment. *Waivers:* employees or children of employees.

Library Hauser Library plus 1 other. *Operations spending 1999–2000:* $2.5 million. *Collection:* 438,119 titles, 2,088 serial subscriptions, 13,292 audiovisual materials.

College life *Housing: Options:* coed, women-only, disabled students. *Most popular organizations:* Reed Recycling, Movie Board, Outdoor Club.

Campus security 24-hour emergency response devices and patrols, student patrols, late-night transport-escort service, controlled dormitory access, 24-hour emergency dispatch.

After graduation 24 organizations recruited on campus 1997–98. *Career center:* 2 full-time, 1 part-time personnel. Services include job fairs, resume preparation, interview workshops, resume referral, career counseling, careers library, job bank, job interviews. *Major awards:* 1 Rhodes scholar.

Freshmen 2,018 applied, 1,376 admitted, 334 enrolled. 11 National Merit Scholars, 19 valedictorians.

Average high school GPA	3.7	SAT verbal scores above 500	99%
SAT math scores above 500	99%	ACT above 18	100%
From top 10% of their h.s. class	52%	From top quarter	83%
From top half	98%	1998 freshmen returning in 1999	88%

Application *Options:* eApply at www.CollegeQuest.com, Common Application, electronic application, early admission, early decision, deferred entrance. *Application fee:* $40. *Required:* essay or personal statement; high school transcript; 2 letters of recommendation. *Recommended:* minimum 3.0 GPA; interview.

Standardized tests *Admission: Required:* SAT I or ACT. *Recommended:* SAT II Subject Tests, SAT II: Writing Test.

Significant dates *Application deadlines:* 1/15 (freshmen), 3/1 (transfers). *Early decision:* 11/15 (for plan 1), 1/2 (for plan 2). *Notification:* 4/1 (freshmen), 12/15 (early decision plan 1), 2/1 (early decision plan 2). *Financial aid deadline:* 1/15.

Freshman Application Contact
Dr. Nancy Donehower, Dean of Admission, Reed College, 3203 Southeast Woodstock Boulevard, Portland, OR 97202-8199. **Phone:** 503-777-7511. **Toll-free phone:** 800-547-4750. **Fax:** 503-777-7553. **E-mail:** admission@reed.edu

Visit CollegeQuest.com for information on majors offered and athletics. College video and electronic viewbook available at CollegeQuest.com.

■ *See page 2314 for a narrative description.*

SOUTHERN OREGON UNIVERSITY
Ashland, Oregon

- **State-supported**, comprehensive, founded 1926
- **Degrees** bachelor's and master's
- **Small-town** 175-acre campus
- **Coed**, 4,645 undergraduate students, 78% full-time, 57% women, 43% men
- **Moderately difficult** entrance level, 64% of applicants were admitted
- **18:1 student-to-undergraduate faculty ratio**
- **36.6% graduate** in 6 years or less
- **$3234 tuition** and fees (in-state); $9897 (out-of-state)
- **$6892 average financial aid** package, $13,404 average indebtedness upon graduation, $6.5 million endowment

Part of Oregon University System.

Students *Undergraduates:* 3,637 full-time, 1,008 part-time. Students come from 43 states and territories, 35 other countries. *The most frequently chosen baccalaureate fields are:* business/marketing, communications/communication technologies, social sciences and history. *Graduate:* 665 in graduate degree programs.

From out-of-state	19%	Reside on campus	25%
Age 25 or older	27%	Transferred in	11%
International students	3%	African Americans	1%
Asian Americans/Pacific Islanders	3%	Hispanic Americans	3%
Native Americans	2%		

Faculty 224 (67% full-time), 79% with terminal degrees.

Expenses (1999–2000) *Tuition, state resident:* full-time $3234; part-time $518 per term. *Tuition, nonresident:* full-time $9897; part-time $518 per term. Full-time tuition and fees vary according to course load, location, and reciprocity agreements. Part-time tuition and fees vary according to course load, location, and reciprocity agreements. *College room and board:* $4658. Room and board charges vary according to board plan and housing facility. *Payment plan:* deferred payment. *Waivers:* senior citizens and employees or children of employees.

Library Southern Oregon University Library. *Operations spending 1999–2000:* $1.8 million. *Collection:* 280,000 titles, 2,091 serial subscriptions, 9,301 audiovisual materials.

College life *Housing:* on-campus residence required in freshman year. *Option:* coed. *Most popular organizations:* Native American Student Union, International Student Association, Impact (religious club), Ho'opa'a Hawaii Club, Omicron Delta Kappa.

Campus security 24-hour patrols, student patrols, late-night transport-escort service.

After graduation *Career center:* 2 full-time, 5 part-time personnel. Services include job fairs, resume preparation, resume referral, career counseling, careers library, job bank, job interviews.

Freshmen 1,961 applied, 1,251 admitted, 746 enrolled.

Average high school GPA	3.18	SAT verbal scores above 500	60%
SAT math scores above 500	55%	ACT above 18	N/R
1998 freshmen returning in 1999	65%		

Application *Options:* early admission, deferred entrance. *Application fee:* $50. *Required:* high school transcript; 2.75 high school GPA or minimum SAT score of 1010.

Standardized tests *Admission: Required:* SAT I or ACT. *Required for some:* SAT II Subject Tests.

Significant dates *Application deadlines:* rolling (freshmen), rolling (transfers). *Financial aid deadline priority date:* 3/1.

Freshman Application Contact
Ms. Mara A. Affre, Director of Admissions, Southern Oregon University, Siskiyou Boulevard, Ashland, OR 97520. **Phone:** 541-552-6411. **Toll-free phone:** 800-482-SOSC Ext. 6411. **Fax:** 541-552-6329. **E-mail:** admissions@sou.edu

Visit CollegeQuest.com for information on majors offered and athletics.

■ *See page 2514 for a narrative description.*

UNIVERSITY OF OREGON
Eugene, Oregon

- **State-supported**, university, founded 1872
- **Degrees** bachelor's, master's, doctoral, and first professional
- **Urban** 280-acre campus
- **Coed**, 13,206 undergraduate students, 92% full-time, 53% women, 47% men
- **Moderately difficult** entrance level, 90% of applicants were admitted
- **18:1 student-to-undergraduate faculty ratio**
- **57% graduate** in 6 years or less
- **$3810 tuition** and fees (in-state); $13,197 (out-of-state)
- **$8204 average financial aid** package, $219.6 million endowment

Part of Oregon University System.

Students *Undergraduates:* 12,134 full-time, 1,072 part-time. Students come from 54 states and territories, 82 other countries. *The most frequently chosen baccalaureate fields are:* business/marketing, communications/communication technologies, social sciences and history. *Graduate:* 509 in professional programs, 3,117 in other graduate degree programs.

From out-of-state	27%	Reside on campus	20%
Age 25 or older	2%	Transferred in	10%
International students	7%	African Americans	2%
Asian Americans/Pacific Islanders	6%	Hispanic Americans	3%
Native Americans	1%		

Faculty 1,125 (78% full-time), 94% with terminal degrees.

Expenses (1999–2000) *Tuition, state resident:* full-time $2694; part-time $75 per credit hour. *Tuition, nonresident:* full-time $12,081; part-time $336 per credit hour. *Required fees:* full-time $1116; $255 per term part-time. Part-time tuition and fees vary according to course load. *College room and board:* $5350. Room and board charges vary according to housing facility. *Payment plan:* deferred payment. *Waivers:* minority students.

Library Knight Library plus 5 others. *Operations spending 1999–2000:* $12.5 million. *Collection:* 2.3 million titles, 14,984 serial subscriptions, 60,740 audiovisual materials.

College life *Housing: Options:* coed, men-only, women-only, disabled students. *Social organizations:* national fraternities, national sororities; 11% of eligible men and 11% of eligible women are members. *Most popular organizations:* Political and Environment Action, cultural organizations, student newspaper, Frat Council/Panhellenic, club sports.

Campus security 24-hour emergency response devices and patrols, student patrols, late-night transport-escort service, controlled dormitory access.

After graduation 180 organizations recruited on campus 1997–98. 79% of class of 1998 had job offers within 6 months. *Career center:* 14 full-time, 2 part-time personnel. Services include job fairs, resume preparation, interview workshops, resume referral, career/interest testing, career counseling, careers library, job bank, job interviews. *Graduate education:* 20% of class of 1999 went directly to graduate and professional school: 15% graduate arts and sciences, 2% business, 2% medicine, 1% law. *Major awards:* 7 Fulbright Scholars.

Freshmen 7,157 applied, 6,461 admitted, 2,503 enrolled. 21 National Merit Scholars.

Average high school GPA	3.4	SAT verbal scores above 500	76%
SAT math scores above 500	75%	ACT above 18	N/R
From top 10% of their h.s. class	20%	From top quarter	49%
From top half	83%	1998 freshmen returning in 1999	82%

Application *Options:* electronic application, early admission. *Preference* given to Oregon residents. *Application fee:* $50. *Required:* high school transcript; minimum 3.0 GPA. *Required for some:* essay or personal statement; 2 letters of recommendation.

Standardized tests *Admission: Required:* SAT I or ACT.

Significant dates *Application deadlines:* 2/1 (freshmen), 5/15 (transfers). *Notification:* 3/15 (freshmen). *Financial aid deadline priority date:* 2/1.

Freshman Application Contact
Ms. Martha Pitts, Director of Admissions, University of Oregon, Eugene, OR 97403. **Phone:** 541-346-3201. **Toll-free phone:** 800-232-3825. **Fax:** 541-346-5815. **E-mail:** uoadmit@oregon.uoregon.edu

Visit CollegeQuest.com for information on majors offered and athletics. College video available at CollegeQuest.com.

■ *See page 2798 for a narrative description.*

UNIVERSITY OF PORTLAND
Portland, Oregon

Apply at CollegeQuest.com

- **Independent Roman Catholic**, comprehensive, founded 1901
- **Degrees** bachelor's, master's, and post-master's certificates
- **Suburban** 125-acre campus
- **Coed**, 2,340 undergraduate students, 98% full-time, 57% women, 43% men
- **Moderately difficult** entrance level, 89% of applicants were admitted
- **13:1 student-to-undergraduate faculty ratio**
- **65.1% graduate** in 6 years or less
- **$17,299 tuition** and fees
- **$15,143 average financial aid** package, $19,319 average indebtedness upon graduation, $78.1 million endowment

Students *Undergraduates:* 2,282 full-time, 58 part-time. Students come from 38 states and territories, 42 other countries. *The most frequently chosen baccalaureate fields are:* biological/life sciences, education, foreign language/literature. *Graduate:* 455 in graduate degree programs.

From out-of-state	48%	Reside on campus	48%
Age 25 or older	6%	Transferred in	6%
International students	3%	African Americans	1%
Asian Americans/Pacific Islanders	8%	Hispanic Americans	4%
Native Americans	1%		

Faculty 244 (66% full-time).

Expenses (1999–2000) *Comprehensive fee:* $22,489 includes full-time tuition ($16,930), mandatory fees ($369), and room and board ($5190). Full-time tuition and fees vary according to program. Room and board charges vary according to board plan and housing facility. *Part-time tuition:* $538 per credit hour. Part-time tuition and fees vary according to program. *Payment plans:* installment, deferred payment. *Waivers:* employees or children of employees.

Library Wilson M. Clark Library plus 1 other. *Operations spending 1999–2000:* $1.7 million. *Collection:* 1,446 serial subscriptions, 7,827 audiovisual materials.

College life *Housing: Options:* coed, men-only, women-only. *Most popular organizations:* English Society, international club, Hawaiian club, rugby club, social science club.

Campus security 24-hour patrols, student patrols, late-night transport-escort service, controlled dormitory access.

After graduation 300 organizations recruited on campus 1997–98. *Career center:* 3 full-time, 2 part-time personnel. Services include job fairs, resume preparation, interview workshops, resume referral, career counseling, careers library, job bank, job interviews. *Major awards:* 1 Marshall scholar.

Freshmen 1,813 applied, 1,616 admitted, 626 enrolled. 2 National Merit Scholars, 41 valedictorians.

Oregon

University of Portland (continued)

Average high school GPA	3.58	SAT verbal scores above 500	84%
SAT math scores above 500	83%	ACT above 18	N/R
From top 10% of their h.s. class	33%	From top quarter	67%
From top half	88%	1998 freshmen returning in 1999	82%

Application *Options:* eApply at www.CollegeQuest.com, Common Application, electronic application, early decision, deferred entrance. *Application fee:* $40. *Required:* essay or personal statement; high school transcript; 1 letter of recommendation.
Standardized tests *Admission: Required:* SAT I or ACT.
Significant dates *Application deadlines:* 6/1 (freshmen), rolling (transfers). *Early decision:* 11/15. *Notification:* 1/15 (early decision). *Financial aid deadline priority date:* 3/1.
Freshman Application Contact
Mr. James C. Lyons, Dean of Admissions, University of Portland, 5000 North Willamette Boulevard, Portland, OR 97203-5798. **Phone:** 503-943-7147. **Toll-free phone:** 888-627-5601. **Fax:** 503-943-7399. **E-mail:** admissio@up.edu
Visit CollegeQuest.com for information on majors offered and athletics. College video available at CollegeQuest.com.

WARNER PACIFIC COLLEGE
Portland, Oregon

- **Independent**, comprehensive, founded 1937, affiliated with Church of God
- **Degrees** associate, bachelor's, master's, and first professional certificates
- **Urban** 15-acre campus
- **Coed**, 570 undergraduate students, 92% full-time, 66% women, 34% men
- **Moderately difficult** entrance level, 79% of applicants were admitted
- **14:1 student-to-undergraduate faculty ratio**
- **40% graduate** in 6 years or less
- **$135,000 tuition** and fees
- **$9944 average financial aid** package, $12,908 average indebtedness upon graduation, $1.2 million endowment

Students *Undergraduates:* 522 full-time, 48 part-time. Students come from 17 states and territories, 7 other countries. *The most frequently chosen baccalaureate fields are:* business/marketing, philosophy, psychology. *Graduate:* 5 in graduate degree programs.

From out-of-state	32%	Reside on campus	32%
Age 25 or older	36%	Transferred in	10%
International students	3%	African Americans	3%
Asian Americans/Pacific Islanders	2%	Hispanic Americans	3%
Native Americans	1%		

Faculty 62 (61% full-time), 48% with terminal degrees.
Expenses (2000–2001, estimated) *Comprehensive fee:* $139,567 includes full-time tuition ($135,000) and room and board ($4567). Room and board charges vary according to board plan and housing facility. *Part-time tuition:* $562 per semester hour. Part-time tuition and fees vary according to course load. *Payment plan:* installment. *Waivers:* children of alumni and employees or children of employees.
Library Otto F. Linn Library. *Collection:* 54,000 titles, 400 serial subscriptions.
College life *Housing:* on-campus residence required through sophomore year. *Options:* men-only, women-only. *Most popular organizations:* Associated Students of Warner Pacific College, yearbook, College Activities Board, Fellowship of Christian Athletes.
Campus security 24-hour emergency response devices, student patrols, late-night transport-escort service, controlled dormitory access, 14-hour patrols by trained security personnel.
After graduation *Career center:* 1 full-time personnel. Services include job fairs, resume preparation, resume referral, career counseling, careers library, job bank, job interviews.
Freshmen 159 applied, 126 admitted, 72 enrolled.

Average high school GPA	3.25	SAT verbal scores above 500	59%
SAT math scores above 500	49%	ACT above 18	92%
1998 freshmen returning in 1999	76%		

Application *Application fee:* $25. *Required:* essay or personal statement; high school transcript; minimum 2.5 GPA; 2 letters of recommendation. *Required for some:* interview. *Recommended:* minimum 3.0 GPA; interview.

Standardized tests *Admission: Required:* SAT I or ACT. *Recommended:* SAT II Subject Tests, SAT II: Writing Test.
Significant dates *Application deadlines:* rolling (freshmen), rolling (transfers). *Financial aid deadline priority date:* 5/1.
Freshman Application Contact
Mr. Rick Johnsen, Director of Admissions and Financial Aid, Warner Pacific College, 2219 Southeast 68th Avenue, Portland, OR 97215. **Phone:** 503-517-1020. **Toll-free phone:** 800-582-7885. **Fax:** 503-788-7425. **E-mail:** admiss@warnerpacific.edu
Visit CollegeQuest.com for information on majors offered and athletics. Electronic viewbook available at CollegeQuest.com.

■ *See page 2908 for a narrative description.*

WESTERN BAPTIST COLLEGE
Salem, Oregon

- **Independent religious**, 4-year, founded 1935
- **Degrees** associate and bachelor's
- **Suburban** 107-acre campus with easy access to Portland
- **Coed**, 683 undergraduate students, 91% full-time, 57% women, 43% men
- **Moderately difficult** entrance level
- **17:1 student-to-undergraduate faculty ratio**
- **43.8% graduate** in 6 years or less
- **$13,690 tuition** and fees
- **$10,354 average financial aid** package, $13,498 average indebtedness upon graduation, $581,720 endowment

Students *Undergraduates:* 624 full-time, 59 part-time. Students come from 16 states and territories. *The most frequently chosen baccalaureate fields are:* business/marketing, education, psychology.

From out-of-state	29%	Reside on campus	39%
Age 25 or older	21%	Transferred in	14%
International students	1%	African Americans	1%
Asian Americans/Pacific Islanders	1%	Hispanic Americans	3%
Native Americans	1%		

Faculty 53 (57% full-time).
Expenses (2000–2001) *Comprehensive fee:* $18,630 includes full-time tuition ($13,224), mandatory fees ($466), and room and board ($4940). Room and board charges vary according to board plan. *Part-time tuition:* $551 per credit hour. *Part-time fees:* $30 per term part-time. Part-time tuition and fees vary according to course load. *Payment plan:* installment. *Waivers:* employees or children of employees.
Library *Operations spending 1999–2000:* $190,788. *Collection:* 73,205 titles, 3,869 audiovisual materials.
College life *Housing:* on-campus residence required through sophomore year. *Options:* men-only, women-only.
Campus security 24-hour emergency response devices, student patrols, late-night transport-escort service.
After graduation *Career center:* 1 full-time, 1 part-time personnel. Services include job fairs, resume preparation, interview workshops, resume referral, career/interest testing, career counseling, careers library, job bank, job interviews.
Freshmen 335 applied, 318 admitted, 126 enrolled.

Average high school GPA	3.4	SAT verbal scores above 500	65%
SAT math scores above 500	60%	ACT above 18	100%
From top 10% of their h.s. class	17%	From top quarter	26%
From top half	83%	1998 freshmen returning in 1999	65%

Application *Option:* early admission. *Application fee:* $35. *Required:* essay or personal statement; high school transcript; minimum 2.5 GPA; 3 letters of recommendation.
Standardized tests *Admission: Required:* SAT I or ACT.
Significant dates *Application deadlines:* 8/1 (freshmen), 8/1 (transfers). *Financial aid deadline priority date:* 2/15.
Freshman Application Contact
Mr. Daren Milionis, Dean of Admissions, Western Baptist College, 5000 Deer Park Drive, SE, Salem, OR 97301-9392. **Phone:** 503-375-7005. **Toll-free phone:** 800-845-3005. **Fax:** 503-585-4316. **E-mail:** dmilionis@wbc.edu
Visit CollegeQuest.com for information on majors offered and athletics. College video available at CollegeQuest.com.

Oregon

WESTERN OREGON UNIVERSITY
Monmouth, Oregon

- **State-supported**, comprehensive, founded 1856
- **Degrees** associate, bachelor's, and master's
- **Rural** 157-acre campus with easy access to Portland
- **Coed**, 3,971 undergraduate students, 91% full-time, 60% women, 40% men
- **Moderately difficult** entrance level, 93% of applicants were admitted
- **$3276 tuition** and fees (in-state); $10,293 (out-of-state)

Part of Oregon University System.

Students *Undergraduates:* 3,613 full-time, 358 part-time. Students come from 21 states and territories, 20 other countries. *Graduate:* 470 in graduate degree programs.

From out-of-state	11%	Age 25 or older	25%
Transferred in	13%	International students	2%
African Americans	1%	Asian Americans/Pacific Islanders	3%
Hispanic Americans	4%	Native Americans	2%

Faculty 296 (52% full-time), 61% with terminal degrees.

Expenses (1999–2000) *Tuition, state resident:* full-time $3276; part-time $516 per term. *Tuition, nonresident:* full-time $10,293; part-time $516 per term. Part-time tuition and fees vary according to course load. *College room and board:* $5004. Room and board charges vary according to board plan and housing facility. *Payment plans:* installment, deferred payment. *Waivers:* minority students.

Library Western Library. *Collection:* 177,900 titles, 1,770 serial subscriptions.

College life *Housing:* on-campus residence required in freshman year. *Option:* coed. *Most popular organizations:* Model United Nations, Multicultural Student Union, Oregon Student Association.

Campus security 24-hour emergency response devices and patrols, student patrols, late-night transport-escort service, controlled dormitory access.

After graduation 98 organizations recruited on campus 1997–98. 77% of class of 1998 had job offers within 6 months. *Career center:* 3 full-time personnel. Services include job fairs, resume preparation, resume referral, career counseling, careers library, job interviews.

Freshmen 1,486 applied, 1,377 admitted, 786 enrolled.

Average high school GPA	3.3	SAT verbal scores above 500	46%
SAT math scores above 500	47%	ACT above 18	N/R
1998 freshmen returning in 1999	75%		

Application *Options:* electronic application, deferred entrance. *Application fee:* $50. *Required:* high school transcript; minimum 2.75 GPA.

Standardized tests *Placement: Required:* SAT I or ACT. *Recommended:* SAT I or ACT. *Required for some:* SAT II Subject Tests.

Significant dates *Application deadlines:* rolling (freshmen), rolling (transfers). *Financial aid deadline priority date:* 3/1.

Freshman Application Contact
Ms. Alison Marshall, Director of Admissions, Western Oregon University, 345 North Monmouth Avenue, Monmouth, OR 97361. **Phone:** 503-838-8211. **Toll-free phone:** 877-877-1593. **Fax:** 503-838-8067. **E-mail:** wolfgram@wou.edu

Visit CollegeQuest.com for information on majors offered and athletics.

- *See page 2956 for a narrative description.*

WESTERN STATES CHIROPRACTIC COLLEGE
Portland, Oregon

- **Independent**, upper-level, founded 1904
- **Degrees** incidental bachelor's and first professional
- **Suburban** 22-acre campus
- **Coed**
- **Moderately difficult** entrance level
- **9:1 student-to-undergraduate faculty ratio**
- **$15,777 tuition** and fees
- **$1.2 million endowment**

Students *Undergraduates:* Students come from 40 states and territories, 9 other countries. *Graduate:* 86 in professional programs, 365 in other graduate degree programs.

Age 25 or older	95%	International students	37%
African Americans	1%	Asian Americans/Pacific Islanders	5%
Hispanic Americans	1%	Native Americans	0.4%

Faculty 79 (51% full-time), 94% with terminal degrees.

Expenses (1999–2000) *Tuition:* full-time $15,117. *Required fees:* full-time $660.

Library W. A. Buden Library plus 1 other. *Collection:* 14,700 titles, 365 serial subscriptions.

College life *Housing:* college housing not available. *Most popular organizations:* American Chiropractic Association, Canadian Chiropractic Club, Sports Medicine Club, Gonstead Club, LDS (Latter Day Saints) Club.

Campus security Student patrols, late-night transport-escort service.

After graduation *Graduate education:* 100% of class of 1999 went directly to graduate and professional school.

Application *Option:* Common Application. *Application fee:* $50.

Significant dates *Application deadline:* rolling (transfers).

Freshman Application Contact
Dr. Randell Hand, Dean of Enrollment Management, Western States Chiropractic College, 2900 Northeast 132nd Avenue, Portland, OR 97230-3099. **Phone:** 503-251-5734 Ext. 707. **Toll-free phone:** 800-641-5641. **Fax:** 503-251-5723.

Visit CollegeQuest.com for information on majors offered and athletics. College video available at CollegeQuest.com.

WILLAMETTE UNIVERSITY
Salem, Oregon

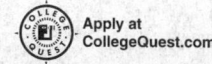
Apply at CollegeQuest.com

- **Independent United Methodist**, comprehensive, founded 1842
- **Degrees** bachelor's, master's, and first professional
- **Urban** 72-acre campus with easy access to Portland
- **Coed**, 1,597 undergraduate students, 98% full-time, 55% women, 45% men
- **Very difficult** entrance level, 90% of applicants were admitted
- **11:1 student-to-undergraduate faculty ratio**
- **74% graduate** in 6 years or less
- **$21,822 tuition** and fees
- **$18,285 average financial aid** package, $16,800 average indebtedness upon graduation, $220 million endowment

Students *Undergraduates:* 1,569 full-time, 28 part-time. Students come from 36 states and territories, 17 other countries. *The most frequently chosen baccalaureate fields are:* biological/life sciences, business/marketing, social sciences and history. *Graduate:* 420 in professional programs, 220 in other graduate degree programs.

From out-of-state	56%	Reside on campus	70%
Transferred in	4%	International students	2%
African Americans	2%	Asian Americans/Pacific Islanders	6%
Hispanic Americans	4%	Native Americans	1%

Faculty 212 (81% full-time), 88% with terminal degrees.

Expenses (1999–2000) *Comprehensive fee:* $27,522 includes full-time tuition ($21,700), mandatory fees ($122), and room and board ($5700). Full-time tuition and fees vary according to course load. Room and board charges vary according to board plan and housing facility. *Part-time tuition:* $2713 per course. Part-time tuition and fees vary according to course load. *Payment plans:* tuition prepayment, installment. *Waivers:* employees or children of employees.

Library Mark O. Hatfield Library plus 1 other. *Operations spending 1999–2000:* $3.5 million. *Collection:* 279,574 titles, 1,569 serial subscriptions, 8,456 audiovisual materials.

College life *Housing:* on-campus residence required through sophomore year. *Option:* coed. *Social organizations:* national fraternities, national sororities; 28% of eligible men and 22% of eligible women are members. *Most popular organizations:* Hawaii club, Bush Mentor Program, outdoors club, Campus Ambassadors, Associated Students of Williamette University.

Campus security 24-hour emergency response devices and patrols, student patrols, late-night transport-escort service, controlled dormitory access.

Oregon–Pennsylvania

Willamette University (continued)

After graduation 150 organizations recruited on campus 1997–98. *Career center:* 2 full-time personnel. Services include job fairs, resume preparation, interview workshops, career/interest testing, career counseling, careers library, job bank, job interviews.

Freshmen 1,541 applied, 1,380 admitted, 363 enrolled. 3 National Merit Scholars, 12 class presidents, 26 valedictorians, 113 student government officers.

Average high school GPA	3.71	SAT verbal scores above 500	88%
SAT math scores above 500	89%	ACT above 18	100%
From top 10% of their h.s. class	48%	From top quarter	75%
From top half	97%	1998 freshmen returning in 1999	88%

Application *Options:* eApply at www.CollegeQuest.com, Common Application, electronic application, early admission, early action, deferred entrance. *Application fee:* $35. *Required:* essay or personal statement; high school transcript; minimum 2.0 GPA; 1 letter of recommendation. *Required for some:* interview. *Recommended:* interview.

Standardized tests *Admission: Required:* SAT I or ACT.

Significant dates *Application deadlines:* 2/1 (freshmen), 2/1 (transfers). *Early action:* 12/1. *Notification:* 4/1 (freshmen), 1/15 (early action). *Financial aid deadline priority date:* 2/1.

Freshman Application Contact
Mr. James M. Sumner, Vice President for Enrollment, Willamette University, 900 State Street, Salem, OR 97301-3931. **Phone:** 503-370-6303. **Toll-free phone:** 877-542-2787. **Fax:** 503-375-5363. **E-mail:** undergrad-admission@willamette.edu

Visit CollegeQuest.com for information on majors offered and athletics.

PENNSYLVANIA

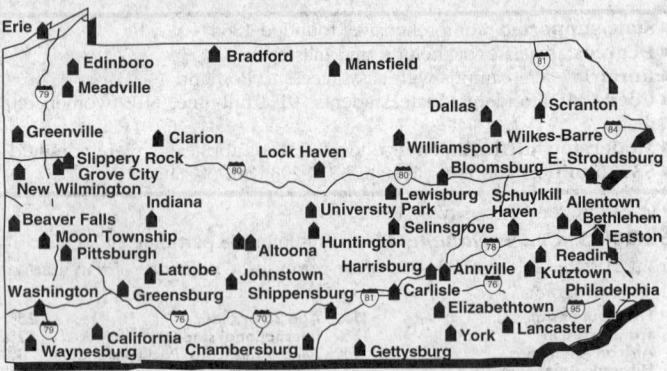

The Philadelphia area includes the towns of Abington, Aston, Bryn Athyn, Bryn Mawr, Chester, Cheyney, Collegeville, Doylestown, Glenside, Gwynedd Valley, Haverford, Immaculata, Langhorne, Media, Melrose Park, Phoenixville, Radnor, Rosemont, St. Davids, Swarthmore, Villanova, West Chester, and Wynnewood.

The Allentown area includes the towns of Center Valley, Fogelsville, and Lincoln University.

The Altoona area includes the towns of Cresson and Loretto.

The Lancaster area includes the town of Millersville.

The Harrisburg area includes the town of Grantham and Middletown.

The Scranton area includes the town of Clarks Summit.

ALBRIGHT COLLEGE
Reading, Pennsylvania

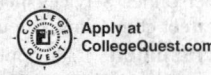

Apply at CollegeQuest.com

- **Independent**, 4-year, founded 1856, affiliated with United Methodist Church
- **Degree** bachelor's
- **Suburban** 110-acre campus with easy access to Philadelphia
- **Coed**, 1,517 undergraduate students, 95% full-time, 57% women, 43% men
- **Moderately difficult** entrance level, 86% of applicants were admitted
- **13:1 student-to-undergraduate faculty ratio**
- **59% graduate** in 6 years or less
- **$19,460 tuition** and fees
- **$16,605 average financial aid** package, $34.5 million endowment

Albright College, is renowned for its openness and warmth. Its motto ought to be "excellence without attitude." For all the accomplishments of its students over the past 144 years, Albright is not a pretentious place. It is an easy place for students to be heard, have an impact, and achieve their dreams.

Students *Undergraduates:* 1,444 full-time, 73 part-time. Students come from 26 states and territories, 21 other countries. *The most frequently chosen baccalaureate fields are:* business/marketing, psychology, social sciences and history.

From out-of-state	30%	Reside on campus	78%
Age 25 or older	2%	Transferred in	5%
International students	5%	African Americans	7%
Asian Americans/Pacific Islanders	2%	Hispanic Americans	3%
Native Americans	0.2%		

Faculty 128 (62% full-time).

Expenses (1999–2000) *Comprehensive fee:* $25,240 includes full-time tuition ($18,910), mandatory fees ($550), and room and board ($5780). *College room only:* $3235. Room and board charges vary according to board plan and housing facility. *Part-time tuition:* $2185 per course. *Part-time fees:* $275 per term part-time. Part-time tuition and fees vary according to class time and program. *Payment plan:* installment. *Waivers:* senior citizens and employees or children of employees.

Pennsylvania

Library Gingrich Library. *Operations spending 1999–2000:* $1 million. *Collection:* 199,408 titles, 875 serial subscriptions, 7,794 audiovisual materials.

College life *Housing:* on-campus residence required in freshman year. *Option:* coed. *Social organizations:* national fraternities, national sororities; 24% of eligible men and 23% of eligible women are members. *Most popular organizations:* Campus Center Board, Student Government Association, yearbook, newspaper, radio station.

Campus security 24-hour emergency response devices and patrols, student patrols, late-night transport-escort service, controlled dormitory access.

After graduation 40 organizations recruited on campus 1997–98. 39% of class of 1998 had job offers within 6 months. *Career center:* 2 full-time personnel. Services include job fairs, resume preparation, resume referral, career counseling, careers library, job bank, job interviews. *Graduate education:* 32% of class of 1999 went directly to graduate and professional school: 12% graduate arts and sciences, 9% law, 5% business, 4% dentistry, 2% medicine, 1% veterinary medicine.

Freshmen 1,752 applied, 1,515 admitted, 393 enrolled. 8 valedictorians.

Average high school GPA	3.38	SAT verbal scores above 500	63%
SAT math scores above 500	55%	ACT above 18	N/R
From top 10% of their h.s. class	20%	From top quarter	46%
From top half	79%	1998 freshmen returning in 1999	89%

Application *Options:* eApply at www.CollegeQuest.com, Common Application, electronic application, early admission, deferred entrance. *Application fee:* $25. *Required:* essay or personal statement; high school transcript; 2 letters of recommendation. *Recommended:* interview.

Standardized tests *Admission: Required:* SAT I or ACT. *Recommended:* SAT II Subject Tests.

Significant dates *Application deadlines:* 2/15 (freshmen), rolling (transfers). *Notification:* continuous until 5/1 (freshmen). *Financial aid deadline priority date:* 3/1.

Freshman Application Contact
Mr. Gregory E. Eichhorn, Dean of Admission, Albright College, 13th and Bern Sts, PO Box 15234, Reading, PA 19612-5234. **Phone:** 610-921-7512. **Toll-free phone:** 800-252-1856. **Fax:** 610-921-7530. **E-mail:** albright@alb.edu

Visit CollegeQuest.com for information on majors offered and athletics.

■ *See page 1146 for a narrative description.*

ALLEGHENY COLLEGE
Meadville, Pennsylvania

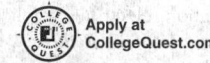
Apply at CollegeQuest.com

■ **Independent**, 4-year, founded 1815, affiliated with United Methodist Church
■ **Degree** bachelor's
■ **Small-town** 254-acre campus
■ **Coed**, 1,860 undergraduate students, 99% full-time, 53% women, 47% men
■ **Very difficult** entrance level, 75% of applicants were admitted
■ **14:1 student-to-undergraduate faculty ratio**
■ **74.6% graduate** in 6 years or less
■ **$20,690 tuition** and fees
■ **$17,415 average financial aid** package, $17,375 average indebtedness upon graduation, $113.1 million endowment

The Allegheny College Center for Experiential Learning (ACCEL) is a vivid symbol of the College's commitment to preparing students for the working world and graduate and professional school. ACCEL gives students one-stop shopping for internships, off-campus study in the US and abroad, service learning opportunities, and leadership development programs.

Students *Undergraduates:* 1,845 full-time, 15 part-time. Students come from 38 states and territories, 17 other countries. *The most frequently chosen baccalaureate fields are:* psychology, biological/life sciences, social sciences and history.

From out-of-state	39%	Reside on campus	73%
Age 25 or older	1%	Transferred in	0.4%
International students	1%	African Americans	2%
Asian Americans/Pacific Islanders	1%	Hispanic Americans	1%
Native Americans	0.5%		

Faculty 152 (86% full-time), 84% with terminal degrees.

Expenses (1999–2000) *One-time required fee:* $200. *Comprehensive fee:* $25,660 includes full-time tuition ($20,410), mandatory fees ($280), and room and board ($4970). *College room only:* $2500. Room and board charges vary according to board plan and housing facility. *Part-time tuition:* $850 per credit hour. *Part-time fees:* $140 per term part-time. Part-time tuition and fees vary according to course load. *Payment plans:* tuition prepayment, installment. *Waivers:* employees or children of employees.

Library Lawrence Lee Pelletier Library. *Operations spending 1999–2000:* $1.3 million. *Collection:* 259,064 titles, 1,265 serial subscriptions, 4,986 audiovisual materials.

College life *Housing:* on-campus residence required through sophomore year. *Options:* coed, men-only, women-only. *Social organizations:* national fraternities, national sororities; 18% of eligible men and 28% of eligible women are members. *Most popular organizations:* student government, gators activity programming, Allegheny Orchesis Dance Company, Playshop Theatre, Allegheny Christian Outreach.

Campus security 24-hour emergency response devices and patrols, student patrols, late-night transport-escort service, local police patrol.

After graduation 59 organizations recruited on campus 1997–98. 60% of class of 1998 had job offers within 6 months. *Career center:* 4 full-time personnel. Services include job fairs, resume preparation, interview workshops, resume referral, career/interest testing, career counseling, careers library, job bank, job interviews, job shadowing.

Freshmen 3,013 applied, 2,250 admitted, 565 enrolled. 11 National Merit Scholars, 24 valedictorians, 390 student government officers.

Average high school GPA	3.64	SAT verbal scores above 500	94%
SAT math scores above 500	93%	ACT above 18	100%
From top 10% of their h.s. class	37%	From top quarter	75%
From top half	94%	1998 freshmen returning in 1999	81%

Application *Options:* eApply at www.CollegeQuest.com, Common Application, electronic application, early admission, early decision, deferred entrance. *Application fee:* $30. *Required:* essay or personal statement; high school transcript; 2 letters of recommendation. *Recommended:* interview.

Standardized tests *Admission: Required:* SAT I or ACT. *Recommended:* SAT II Subject Tests.

Significant dates *Application deadlines:* 2/15 (freshmen), 7/1 (transfers). *Early decision:* 1/15. *Notification:* 4/1 (freshmen), 1/31 (early decision). *Financial aid deadline:* 2/15.

Freshman Application Contact
Ms. Megan K. Murphy, Director of Admissions, Allegheny College, 520 North Main Street, Box 5, Meadville, PA 16335. **Phone:** 814-332-4351. **Toll-free phone:** 800-521-5293. **Fax:** 814-337-0431. **E-mail:** admiss@admin.alleg.edu

Visit CollegeQuest.com for information on majors offered and athletics. College video available at CollegeQuest.com.

■ *See page 1152 for a narrative description.*

ALLEGHENY UNIVERSITY OF THE HEALTH SCIENCES
Pennsylvania—See MCP Hahnemann University

ALLENTOWN COLLEGE OF ST. FRANCIS DE SALES
Center Valley, Pennsylvania

Apply at CollegeQuest.com

■ **Independent Roman Catholic**, comprehensive, founded 1964
■ **Degrees** bachelor's and master's (also offers adult program with significant enrollment not reflected in profile)
■ **Suburban** 300-acre campus with easy access to Philadelphia
■ **Coed**, 1,703 undergraduate students, 73% full-time, 55% women, 45% men
■ **Moderately difficult** entrance level, 75% of applicants were admitted
■ **15:1 student-to-undergraduate faculty ratio**
■ **68% graduate** in 6 years or less
■ **$13,640 tuition** and fees
■ **$23.4 million endowment**

Peterson's Guide to Four-Year Colleges 2001   www.petersons.com

Pennsylvania

Allentown College of St. Francis de Sales (continued)

Students *Undergraduates:* 1,249 full-time, 454 part-time. Students come from 10 states and territories, 12 other countries. *The most frequently chosen baccalaureate fields are:* business/marketing, protective services/public administration, visual/performing arts. *Graduate:* 662 in graduate degree programs.

From out-of-state	22%	Reside on campus	80%
Age 25 or older	1%	Transferred in	3%
International students	1%	African Americans	1%
Asian Americans/Pacific Islanders	1%	Hispanic Americans	2%
Native Americans	0.2%		

Faculty 115 (60% full-time), 54% with terminal degrees.

Expenses (1999–2000) *Comprehensive fee:* $19,500 includes full-time tuition ($13,350), mandatory fees ($290), and room and board ($5860). *College room only:* $3080. Full-time tuition and fees vary according to class time and course load. *Part-time tuition:* $555 per credit. Part-time tuition and fees vary according to class time and course load. *Payment plans:* installment, deferred payment. *Waivers:* employees or children of employees.

Library Trexler Library. *Operations spending 1999–2000:* $600,360. *Collection:* 130,328 titles, 4,500 serial subscriptions, 4,912 audiovisual materials.

College life *Housing:* Options: men-only, women-only. *Social organizations:* local sororities; 8% of women are members. *Most popular organizations:* Sigma Alpha Omega, campus ministry social outreach, Student Nursing Organization, Student Government Association, business club.

Campus security 24-hour emergency response devices and patrols, late-night transport-escort service, controlled dormitory access.

After graduation 46 organizations recruited on campus 1997–98. 93% of class of 1998 had job offers within 6 months. *Career center:* 1 full-time, 2 part-time personnel. Services include job fairs, resume preparation, resume referral, career counseling, careers library, job bank, job interviews. *Graduate education:* 14% of class of 1999 went directly to graduate and professional school: 6% business, 3% law, 2% medicine, 1% education, 1% graduate arts and sciences, 1% theology.

Freshmen 1,286 applied, 965 admitted, 366 enrolled.

SAT verbal scores above 500	62%	SAT math scores above 500	N/R
ACT above 18	N/R	From top 10% of their h.s. class	17%
From top quarter	37%	From top half	64%
1998 freshmen returning in 1999	83%		

Application *Options:* eApply at www.CollegeQuest.com, Common Application, electronic application, early admission, deferred entrance. *Application fee:* $30. *Required:* high school transcript; 2 letters of recommendation. *Recommended:* essay or personal statement; interview.

Standardized tests *Admission: Required:* SAT I or ACT.

Significant dates *Application deadlines:* 8/1 (freshmen), 8/1 (transfers). *Financial aid deadline priority date:* 2/1.

Freshman Application Contact
Ms. Angie Smyth, Director of Admissions, Allentown College of St. Francis de Sales, 2755 Station Avenue, Center Valley, PA 18034-9568. **Phone:** 610-282-1100 Ext. 1206. **Toll-free phone:** 800-228-5114. **Fax:** 610-282-2254. **E-mail:** jgoo@email.allencol.edu

Visit CollegeQuest.com for information on majors offered and athletics.

ALVERNIA COLLEGE
Reading, Pennsylvania

Apply at CollegeQuest.com

- **Independent Roman Catholic**, comprehensive, founded 1958
- **Degrees** associate, bachelor's, and master's
- **Suburban** 85-acre campus with easy access to Philadelphia
- **Coed**, 1,294 undergraduate students, 75% full-time, 64% women, 36% men
- **Moderately difficult** entrance level, 33% of applicants were admitted
- **11:1 student-to-undergraduate faculty ratio**
- **56% graduate** in 6 years or less
- **$12,346 tuition** and fees
- **$12,000 average indebtedness** upon graduation, $10.2 million endowment

Alvernia College, a private Catholic college, blends traditional liberal arts with professional programs. Alvernia offers 27 bachelor's degree programs geared to meet the needs of students and the community. Programs include athletic training, sports management, and forensic science. A new 25,000-square-foot campus center and new residence hall opened in summer 1999.

Students *Undergraduates:* 970 full-time, 324 part-time. Students come from 13 states and territories, 14 other countries. *The most frequently chosen baccalaureate fields are:* business/marketing, health professions and related sciences, protective services/public administration. *Graduate:* 63 in graduate degree programs.

From out-of-state	8%	Reside on campus	25%
Age 25 or older	42%	Transferred in	8%
International students	1%	African Americans	6%
Asian Americans/Pacific Islanders	1%	Hispanic Americans	3%
Native Americans	0.2%		

Faculty 136 (43% full-time), 30% with terminal degrees.

Expenses (1999–2000) *Comprehensive fee:* $17,826 includes full-time tuition ($11,730), mandatory fees ($616), and room and board ($5480). Room and board charges vary according to board plan and housing facility. *Part-time tuition:* $400 per credit. *Part-time fees:* $28 per credit. Part-time tuition and fees vary according to class time and course load. *Payment plans:* installment, deferred payment. *Waivers:* senior citizens and employees or children of employees.

Library Franco Library. *Operations spending 1999–2000:* $475,342. *Collection:* 86,000 titles, 400 serial subscriptions, 7,600 audiovisual materials.

College life *Housing:* Option: coed. *Most popular organizations:* Student Government Association, Phi Beta Lambda, American Criminal Justice Association, Education Association, Society for Human Resource Management.

Campus security 24-hour patrols, late-night transport-escort service, controlled dormitory access.

After graduation 12 organizations recruited on campus 1997–98. 49% of class of 1998 had job offers within 6 months. *Career center:* 1 full-time personnel. Services include job fairs, resume preparation, interview workshops, career/interest testing, career counseling, careers library, job interviews. *Graduate education:* 6% of class of 1999 went directly to graduate and professional school: 4% graduate arts and sciences, 1% business, 1% education, 1% law.

Freshmen 932 applied, 305 admitted, 244 enrolled.

Average high school GPA	2.84	SAT verbal scores above 500	32%
SAT math scores above 500	29%	ACT above 18	N/R
From top 10% of their h.s. class	10%	From top quarter	20%
From top half	80%	1998 freshmen returning in 1999	75%

Application *Options:* eApply at www.CollegeQuest.com, Common Application, electronic application, early admission, deferred entrance. *Application fee:* $25. *Required:* essay or personal statement; high school transcript. *Required for some:* 2 letters of recommendation; interview. *Recommended:* minimum 2.0 GPA; 1 letter of recommendation.

Standardized tests *Admission: Required:* SAT I or ACT.

Significant dates *Application deadlines:* rolling (freshmen), rolling (transfers). *Financial aid deadline priority date:* 4/1.

Freshman Application Contact
Mr. Francis Schodowski, Director of Admissions, Alvernia College, 400 Saint Bernardine Street, Reading, PA 19607. **Phone:** 610-796-8220. **Toll-free phone:** 888-ALVERNIA. **Fax:** 610-796-8336.

Visit CollegeQuest.com for information on majors offered and athletics.

■ *See page 1156 for a narrative description.*

THE ART INSTITUTE OF PHILADELPHIA
Philadelphia, Pennsylvania

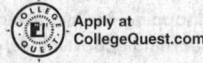
Apply at CollegeQuest.com

- **Proprietary**, primarily 2-year, founded 1966
- **Degrees** associate and bachelor's
- **Urban** campus
- **Coed**, 2,514 undergraduate students, 88% full-time, 39% women, 61% men
- **Minimally difficult** entrance level
- **20:1 student-to-undergraduate faculty ratio**
- **$11,655 tuition** and fees

Part of The Art Institutes International.

Pennsylvania

Admissions Office Contact
The Art Institute of Philadelphia, 1622 Chestnut Street, Philadelphia, PA 19103. **Toll-free phone:** 800-275-2474.
Visit CollegeQuest.com for information on majors offered and athletics. College video available at CollegeQuest.com.

BAPTIST BIBLE COLLEGE OF PENNSYLVANIA
Clarks Summit, Pennsylvania

- **Independent Baptist**, comprehensive, founded 1932
- **Degrees** associate, bachelor's, master's, and doctoral
- **Suburban** 124-acre campus
- **Coed**
- **Minimally difficult** entrance level
- **$8992 tuition** and fees

Expenses (1999–2000) *One-time required fee:* $50. *Comprehensive fee:* $13,706 includes full-time tuition ($8128), mandatory fees ($864), and room and board ($4714). *College room only:* $1860. Full-time tuition and fees vary according to course load. Room and board charges vary according to board plan. *Part-time tuition:* $254 per semester hour. *Part-time fees:* $27 per semester hour. Part-time tuition and fees vary according to course load.
Institutional Web site http://www.bbc.edu/
College life *Housing:* on-campus residence required through senior year. *Options:* men-only, women-only.
Campus security 24-hour patrols, student patrols.
Application *Options:* early admission, deferred entrance. *Application fee:* $30. *Required:* essay or personal statement; high school transcript; 3 letters of recommendation; Christian testimony. *Required for some:* interview.
Standardized tests *Admission: Required:* SAT I or ACT.
Admissions Office Contact
Baptist Bible College of Pennsylvania, PO Box 800, Clarks Summit, PA 18411-1297. **Toll-free phone:** 800-451-7664. **Fax:** 570-585-9400. **E-mail:** gamos@bbc.edu
Visit CollegeQuest.com for information on athletics. College video available at CollegeQuest.com.

BEAVER COLLEGE
Glenside, Pennsylvania

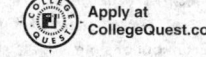
Apply at CollegeQuest.com

- **Independent**, comprehensive, founded 1853, affiliated with Presbyterian Church (U.S.A.)
- **Degrees** bachelor's, master's, and doctoral
- **Suburban** 55-acre campus with easy access to Philadelphia
- **Coed**, 1,551 undergraduate students, 81% full-time, 75% women, 25% men
- **Moderately difficult** entrance level, 63% of applicants were admitted
- **13:1** student-to-undergraduate faculty ratio
- **56.4% graduate** in 6 years or less
- **$17,160 tuition** and fees
- **$15,402 average financial aid** package, $17,125 average indebtedness upon graduation, $23.1 million endowment

Students *Undergraduates:* 1,257 full-time, 294 part-time. Students come from 22 states and territories, 19 other countries. *Graduate:* 1,130 in graduate degree programs.

From out-of-state	27%	Reside on campus	60%
Age 25 or older	29%	Transferred in	7%
International students	2%	African Americans	13%
Asian Americans/Pacific Islanders	3%	Hispanic Americans	2%
Native Americans	0.3%		

Faculty 289 (36% full-time), 85% with terminal degrees.
Expenses (1999–2000) *Comprehensive fee:* $24,470 includes full-time tuition ($16,880), mandatory fees ($280), and room and board ($7310). Room and board charges vary according to board plan. *Part-time tuition:* $320 per credit. *Payment plans:* installment, deferred payment. *Waivers:* employees or children of employees.

Library Eugenia Fuller Atwood Library. *Operations spending 1999–2000:* $770,000. *Collection:* 132,310 titles, 1,069 serial subscriptions, 2,955 audiovisual materials.
College life *Housing: Options:* coed, women-only. *Most popular organizations:* Student Program Board, Residence Hall Council, student government, Beaver College Christian Fellowship, Student Alumni Association.
Campus security 24-hour emergency response devices and patrols, student patrols, late-night transport-escort service, controlled dormitory access.
After graduation 65 organizations recruited on campus 1997–98. 70% of class of 1998 had job offers within 6 months. *Career center:* 2 full-time, 1 part-time personnel. Services include job fairs, resume preparation, interview workshops, resume referral, career/interest testing, career counseling, careers library, job bank, job interviews, career and educational planning software. *Graduate education:* 26% of class of 1999 went directly to graduate and professional school.
Freshmen 1,776 applied, 1,124 admitted, 354 enrolled.

Average high school GPA	2.9	SAT verbal scores above 500	65%
SAT math scores above 500	72%	ACT above 18	N/R
From top 10% of their h.s. class	22%	From top quarter	60%
From top half	88%	1998 freshmen returning in 1999	82%

Application *Options:* eApply at www.CollegeQuest.com, Common Application, electronic application, early admission, early decision, deferred entrance. *Application fee:* $30. *Required:* essay or personal statement; high school transcript; 2 letters of recommendation. *Required for some:* portfolio. *Recommended:* interview.
Standardized tests *Admission: Required:* SAT I or ACT.
Significant dates *Application deadlines:* rolling (freshmen), rolling (transfers). *Early decision:* 11/1. *Notification:* continuous until 9/1 (freshmen), 12/1 (early decision). *Financial aid deadline priority date:* 3/1.
Freshman Application Contact
Mr. Mark Lapreziosa, Director of Enrollment Management, Beaver College, 450 South Easton Road, Glenside, PA 19038. **Phone:** 215-572-2910. **Toll-free phone:** 888-BEAVER3. **Fax:** 215-572-4049. **E-mail:** admiss@beaver.edu
Visit CollegeQuest.com for information on majors offered and athletics. College video available at CollegeQuest.com.

- *See page 1240 for a narrative description.*

BLOOMSBURG UNIVERSITY OF PENNSYLVANIA
Bloomsburg, Pennsylvania

- **State-supported**, comprehensive, founded 1839
- **Degrees** associate, bachelor's, and master's
- **Small-town** 282-acre campus
- **Coed**, 6,554 undergraduate students, 95% full-time, 63% women, 37% men
- **Moderately difficult** entrance level, 57% of applicants were admitted
- **19:1** student-to-undergraduate faculty ratio
- **$4455 tuition** and fees (in-state); $9883 (out-of-state)
- **$6872 average financial aid** package, $13,300 average indebtedness upon graduation, $11.3 million endowment

Part of Pennsylvania State System of Higher Education.
Students *Undergraduates:* 6,202 full-time, 352 part-time. Students come from 22 states and territories, 26 other countries. *The most frequently chosen baccalaureate fields are:* business/marketing, education, social sciences and history. *Graduate:* 689 in graduate degree programs.

From out-of-state	9%	Reside on campus	43%
Age 25 or older	8%	Transferred in	4%
International students	1%	African Americans	3%
Asian Americans/Pacific Islanders	1%	Hispanic Americans	2%
Native Americans	0.2%		

Faculty 394 (90% full-time), 70% with terminal degrees.
Expenses (1999–2000) *Tuition, state resident:* full-time $3618; part-time $150 per credit. *Tuition, nonresident:* full-time $9046; part-time $377 per credit. *Required fees:* full-time $837; $28 per credit; $15 per term part-time. Full-time tuition and fees vary according to course load. Part-time tuition and fees vary according to course load. *College room and board:* $3784. Room and board charges vary according to board plan and housing facility. *Waivers:* minority students and employees or children of employees.

Pennsylvania

Bloomsburg University of Pennsylvania *(continued)*

Library Andruss Library. *Operations spending 1999–2000:* $2.4 million. *Collection:* 278,835 titles, 2,372 serial subscriptions, 6,118 audiovisual materials.

College life *Housing:* on-campus residence required in freshman year. *Options:* coed, men-only, women-only. *Social organizations:* national fraternities, national sororities, local fraternities, local sororities; 3% of eligible men and 4% of eligible women are members.

Campus security 24-hour emergency response devices and patrols, late-night transport-escort service, monitored surveillance cameras.

After graduation 41 organizations recruited on campus 1997–98. *Career center:* 3 full-time, 2 part-time personnel. Services include job fairs, resume preparation, resume referral, career counseling, careers library, job interviews. *Graduate education:* 12% of class of 1999 went directly to graduate and professional school.

Freshmen 6,605 applied, 3,775 admitted, 1,403 enrolled. 4 valedictorians.

SAT verbal scores above 500	58%	SAT math scores above 500	55%
ACT above 18	N/R	From top 10% of their h.s. class	9%
From top quarter	37%	From top half	81%
1998 freshmen returning in 1999	81%		

Application *Options:* electronic application, early admission, early decision. *Preference* given to state residents. *Application fee:* $25. *Required:* high school transcript; letters of recommendation.

Standardized tests *Admission: Required:* SAT I or ACT.

Significant dates *Application deadlines:* rolling (freshmen), rolling (transfers). *Early decision:* 11/15. *Notification:* 12/1 (early decision). *Financial aid deadline priority date:* 3/15.

Freshman Application Contact

Mr. Christopher Keller, Director of Admissions, Bloomsburg University of Pennsylvania, Ben Franklin Building, Room 10, Bloomsburg, PA 17815-1905. **Phone:** 570-389-4316. **E-mail:** buadmiss@bloomu.edu

Visit CollegeQuest.com for information on majors offered and athletics.

BRYN ATHYN COLLEGE OF THE NEW CHURCH
Bryn Athyn, Pennsylvania

- **Independent Swedenborgian**, comprehensive, founded 1876
- **Degrees** associate, bachelor's, master's, and first professional
- **Small-town** 130-acre campus with easy access to Philadelphia
- **Coed**, 139 undergraduate students, 98% full-time, 47% women, 53% men
- **Minimally difficult** entrance level, 82% of applicants were admitted
- **7:1** student-to-undergraduate faculty ratio
- **$5220 tuition** and fees

Students *Undergraduates:* 136 full-time, 3 part-time. Students come from 17 states and territories, 14 other countries. *The most frequently chosen baccalaureate fields are:* education, English, interdisciplinary studies. *Graduate:* 13 in professional programs, 14 in other graduate degree programs.

From out-of-state	24%	Age 25 or older	2%
Transferred in	3%	International students	12%
African Americans	9%	Asian Americans/Pacific Islanders	2%

Faculty 56 (54% full-time).

Expenses (1999–2000) *Comprehensive fee:* $9456 includes full-time tuition ($4431), mandatory fees ($789), and room and board ($4236). *Part-time tuition:* $173 per credit. *Part-time fees:* $28 per credit. *Payment plan:* installment. *Waivers:* senior citizens and employees or children of employees.

Library Swedenborg Library plus 2 others. *Collection:* 90,300 titles, 178 serial subscriptions.

College life On-campus residence required in freshman year. *Most popular organizations:* outing club, community interest activities, drama club.

Campus security 24-hour patrols, controlled dormitory access.

After graduation *Career center:* 1 part-time personnel. Services include resume preparation, career/interest testing, career counseling, careers library. *Graduate education:* 15% of class of 1999 went directly to graduate and professional school.

Freshmen 67 applied, 55 admitted, 55 enrolled.

SAT verbal scores above 500	73%	SAT math scores above 500	83%
ACT above 18	N/R	1998 freshmen returning in 1999	80%

Application *Options:* Common Application, electronic application, deferred entrance. *Application fee:* $30. *Required:* essay or personal statement; high school transcript; 2 letters of recommendation. *Required for some:* interview.

Standardized tests *Admission: Required:* SAT I or ACT.

Significant dates *Application deadlines:* 6/1 (freshmen), rolling (transfers). *Financial aid deadline priority date:* 7/1.

Freshman Application Contact

Dr. Dan Synnestvedt, Director of Admissions, Bryn Athyn College of the New Church, PO Box 717, Bryn Athyn, PA 19009-0717. **Phone:** 215-938-2503. **Fax:** 215-938-2658.

Visit CollegeQuest.com for information on majors offered and athletics. College video available at CollegeQuest.com.

BRYN MAWR COLLEGE
Bryn Mawr, Pennsylvania

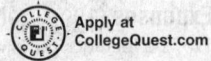
Apply at CollegeQuest.com

- **Independent**, university, founded 1885
- **Degrees** bachelor's, master's, and doctoral
- **Suburban** 135-acre campus with easy access to Philadelphia
- **Women** only, 1,242 undergraduate students, 96% full-time
- **Most difficult** entrance level, 59% of applicants were admitted
- **10:1** student-to-undergraduate faculty ratio
- **77.86% graduate** in 6 years or less
- **$23,360 tuition** and fees
- **$20,802 average financial aid** package, $420.7 million endowment

Bryn Mawr students enjoy a demanding liberal arts education in a small university setting 10 miles from one of the largest cities in the United States—Philadelphia. Distinctive cooperative agreements with nearby Haverford College, Swarthmore College, and the University of Pennsylvania allow for extensive and varied academic, social, and residential exchange. A $22-million chemistry complex and science library opened in 1993, and the Rhys Carpenter Library for Art, Archaeology and Cities was opened to the public in 1997.

Students *Undergraduates:* 1,197 full-time, 45 part-time. Students come from 49 states and territories, 48 other countries. *The most frequently chosen baccalaureate fields are:* biological/life sciences, English, social sciences and history. *Graduate:* 463 in graduate degree programs.

From out-of-state	82%	Reside on campus	97%
Age 25 or older	5%	Transferred in	1%
International students	7%	African Americans	4%
Asian Americans/Pacific Islanders	17%	Hispanic Americans	3%
Native Americans	0.1%		

Faculty 157 (80% full-time), 94% with terminal degrees.

Expenses (1999–2000) *Comprehensive fee:* $31,460 includes full-time tuition ($22,730), mandatory fees ($630), and room and board ($8100). Room and board charges vary according to board plan. *Part-time tuition:* $2850 per course. *Payment plans:* tuition prepayment, installment, deferred payment. *Waivers:* senior citizens and employees or children of employees.

Library Canaday Library plus 3 others. *Operations spending 1999–2000:* $4.3 million. *Collection:* 1 million titles, 3,759 serial subscriptions, 281 audiovisual materials.

College life *Housing:* on-campus residence required in freshman year. *Options:* coed, women-only. *Social organizations:* 85% of eligible undergrads are members. *Most popular organizations:* musical and theater groups, community service, Student Government Association, International Students Association, cultural groups.

Campus security 24-hour emergency response devices and patrols, late-night transport-escort service, controlled dormitory access, shuttle bus service, awareness programs.

After graduation 60 organizations recruited on campus 1997–98. 52% of class of 1998 had job offers within 6 months. *Career center:* 2 full-time, 4 part-time personnel. Services include job fairs, resume preparation, interview workshops, resume referral, career counseling, careers library, job bank, job interviews. *Major awards:* 1 Fulbright Scholar.

Pennsylvania

Freshmen 1,596 applied, 944 admitted, 321 enrolled. 11 National Merit Scholars, 20 valedictorians.

SAT verbal scores above 500	99%	SAT math scores above 500	98%
ACT above 18	100%	From top 10% of their h.s. class	61%
From top quarter	93%	From top half	100%
1998 freshmen returning in 1999	90%		

Application *Options:* eApply at www.CollegeQuest.com, Common Application, early admission, early decision, deferred entrance. *Application fee:* $50. *Required:* essay or personal statement; high school transcript; 3 letters of recommendation. *Recommended:* interview.

Standardized tests *Admission: Required:* SAT I and SAT II or ACT.

Significant dates *Application deadlines:* 1/15 (freshmen), 3/15 (transfers). *Early decision:* 11/15 (for plan 1), 11/1 (for plan 2). *Notification:* 4/1 (freshmen), 12/15 (early decision plan 1), 2/1 (early decision plan 2). *Financial aid deadline:* 1/15.

Freshman Application Contact Ms. Nancy Monnich, Director of Admissions and Financial Aid, Bryn Mawr College, 101 North Merion Avenue, Bryn Mawr, PA 19010. **Phone:** 610-526-5152. **Toll-free phone:** 800-BMC-1885. **Fax:** 610-526-7471. **E-mail:** admissions@brynmawr.edu

Visit CollegeQuest.com for information on majors offered and athletics. Electronic viewbook available at CollegeQuest.com.

■ *See page 1324 for a narrative description.*

BUCKNELL UNIVERSITY
Lewisburg, Pennsylvania

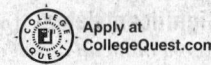
Apply at CollegeQuest.com

- **Independent**, comprehensive, founded 1846
- **Degrees** bachelor's and master's
- **Small-town** 393-acre campus
- **Coed**, 3,370 undergraduate students, 99% full-time, 48% women, 52% men
- **Very difficult** entrance level, 44% of applicants were admitted
- **12:1 student-to-undergraduate faculty ratio**
- **87% graduate** in 6 years or less
- **$22,881 tuition** and fees
- **$17,241 average financial aid** package, $15,500 average indebtedness upon graduation, $392.4 million endowment

Bucknell University is a distinctive university of about 3,300 undergraduates who are enrolled in fields of study that range from foreign languages, performing arts, business administration, and teacher preparation to engineering, research sciences, social sciences, and humanities in an environment that encourages close interaction between faculty members and students.

Students *Undergraduates:* 3,357 full-time, 13 part-time. Students come from 46 states and territories, 33 other countries. *The most frequently chosen baccalaureate fields are:* business/marketing, engineering/engineering technologies, social sciences and history. *Graduate:* 157 in graduate degree programs.

From out-of-state	65%	Reside on campus	86%
Age 25 or older	1%	Transferred in	1%
International students	2%	African Americans	3%
Asian Americans/Pacific Islanders	4%	Hispanic Americans	3%
Native Americans	0.3%		

Faculty 306 (92% full-time), 86% with terminal degrees.

Expenses (1999–2000) *Comprehensive fee:* $28,350 includes full-time tuition ($22,740), mandatory fees ($141), and room and board ($5469). *College room only:* $2925. Room and board charges vary according to board plan and housing facility. *Part-time tuition:* $650 per credit. *Payment plans:* tuition prepayment, installment. *Waivers:* employees or children of employees.

Library Ellen Clarke Bertrand Library. *Operations spending 1999–2000:* $4.2 million. *Collection:* 432,730 titles, 2,789 serial subscriptions, 5,946 audiovisual materials.

College life *Housing:* on-campus residence required through senior year. *Options:* coed, men-only, women-only, disabled students. *Social organizations:* national fraternities, national sororities, local sororities; 51% of eligible men and 57% of eligible women are members. *Most popular organizations:* Alpha Phi Omega, Bucknell Outing Club, Bison Volunteers, International Spectrum, Bucknell Activities Council.

Campus security 24-hour emergency response devices and patrols, student patrols, late-night transport-escort service, well-lit pathways, self-defense education, safety/security orientation.

After graduation 101 organizations recruited on campus 1997–98. 96% of class of 1998 had job offers within 6 months. *Career center:* 5 full-time, 1 part-time personnel. Services include job fairs, resume preparation, interview workshops, resume referral, career/interest testing, career counseling, careers library, job bank, job interviews. *Major awards:* 1 Fulbright Scholar.

Freshmen 7,011 applied, 3,072 admitted, 886 enrolled.

SAT verbal scores above 500	96%	SAT math scores above 500	98%
ACT above 18	N/R	From top 10% of their h.s. class	54%
From top quarter	85%	From top half	99%
1998 freshmen returning in 1999	94%		

Application *Options:* eApply at www.CollegeQuest.com, Common Application, electronic application, early decision, deferred entrance. *Preference given to children of alumni. Application fee:* $50. *Required:* essay or personal statement; high school transcript; minimum 2.5 GPA; letters of recommendation. *Recommended:* interview.

Standardized tests *Admission: Required:* SAT I or ACT.

Significant dates *Application deadlines:* 1/1 (freshmen), 4/1 (transfers). *Early decision:* 11/15 (for plan 1), 1/1 (for plan 2). *Notification:* 4/1 (freshmen), 12/15 (early decision plan 1), 2/1 (early decision plan 2). *Financial aid deadline:* 1/1.

Freshman Application Contact Mr. Mark D. Davies, Dean of Admissions, Bucknell University, Lewisburg, PA 17837. **Phone:** 570-577-1101. **Fax:** 570-577-3760. **E-mail:** admissions@bucknell.edu

Visit CollegeQuest.com for information on majors offered and athletics. College video available at CollegeQuest.com.

■ *See page 1326 for a narrative description.*

CABRINI COLLEGE
Radnor, Pennsylvania

- **Independent Roman Catholic**, comprehensive, founded 1957
- **Degrees** bachelor's and master's
- **Suburban** 112-acre campus with easy access to Philadelphia
- **Coed**, 1,620 undergraduate students, 71% full-time, 67% women, 33% men
- **Minimally difficult** entrance level, 86% of applicants were admitted
- **14:1 student-to-undergraduate faculty ratio**
- **58.5% graduate** in 6 years or less
- **$16,000 tuition** and fees
- **$10.2 million endowment**

Students *Undergraduates:* 1,152 full-time, 468 part-time. Students come from 20 states and territories. *The most frequently chosen baccalaureate fields are:* business/marketing, communications/communication technologies, education. *Graduate:* 382 in graduate degree programs.

From out-of-state	23%	Reside on campus	57%
Age 25 or older	25%	Transferred in	6%
International students	1%	African Americans	6%
Asian Americans/Pacific Islanders	1%	Hispanic Americans	2%
Native Americans	1%		

Faculty 194 (28% full-time), 49% with terminal degrees.

Expenses (1999–2000) *Comprehensive fee:* $23,200 includes full-time tuition ($15,250), mandatory fees ($750), and room and board ($7200). Full-time tuition and fees vary according to course load. Room and board charges vary according to housing facility. *Part-time tuition:* $290 per credit. *Part-time fees:* $45 per term part-time. Part-time tuition and fees vary according to course load. *Payment plan:* installment. *Waivers:* children of alumni, senior citizens, and employees or children of employees.

Library Holy Spirit Library. *Operations spending 1999–2000:* $494,866. *Collection:* 173,144 titles, 584 serial subscriptions, 606 audiovisual materials.

College life *Housing: Options:* coed, women-only, disabled students. *Most popular organizations:* Student Government Association, student newspaper, international club, campus radio station, Council for Exceptional Children.

Campus security 24-hour emergency response devices and patrols, late-night transport-escort service, controlled dormitory access.

Pennsylvania

Cabrini College (continued)

After graduation 72 organizations recruited on campus 1997–98. 80% of class of 1998 had job offers within 6 months. *Career center:* 2 full-time, 1 part-time personnel. Services include job fairs, resume preparation, interview workshops, resume referral, career/interest testing, career counseling, careers library, job bank, job interviews. *Graduate education:* 8% of class of 1999 went directly to graduate and professional school: 2% business, 2% education, 1% law, 1% medicine, 1% theology.

Freshmen 1,470 applied, 1,268 admitted, 295 enrolled.

Average high school GPA	3.04	SAT verbal scores above 500	42%
SAT math scores above 500	35%	ACT above 18	N/R
From top 10% of their h.s. class	8%	From top quarter	28%
From top half	54%	1998 freshmen returning in 1999	76%

Application *Options:* Common Application, electronic application, early admission, deferred entrance. *Application fee:* $25. *Required:* high school transcript; minimum 2.0 GPA. *Recommended:* minimum 3.0 GPA; interview.

Standardized tests *Admission: Required:* SAT I or ACT. *Recommended:* SAT I.

Significant dates *Application deadlines:* rolling (freshmen), rolling (transfers). *Financial aid deadline priority date:* 2/1.

Freshman Application Contact
Ms. Joanne Mayberry, Director of Admissions, Cabrini College, 610 King of Prussia Road, Radnor, PA 19087-3698. **Phone:** 610-902-8552. **Toll-free phone:** 800-848-1003. **Fax:** 610-902-8309. **E-mail:** admit@cabrini.edu

Visit CollegeQuest.com for information on majors offered and athletics. Electronic viewbook available at CollegeQuest.com.

■ *See page 1330 for a narrative description.*

CALIFORNIA UNIVERSITY OF PENNSYLVANIA
California, Pennsylvania

- **State-supported**, comprehensive, founded 1852
- **Degrees** associate, bachelor's, and master's
- **Small-town** 148-acre campus with easy access to Pittsburgh
- **Coed**, 5,013 undergraduate students, 89% full-time, 54% women, 46% men
- **Moderately difficult** entrance level, 81% of applicants were admitted
- **44.48% graduate** in 6 years or less
- **$4742 tuition** and fees (in-state); $10,170 (out-of-state)
- **$328,585 endowment**

Cal U offers more than 100 programs. Offerings in science and technology are the University's special mission. Education and human services programs hold a long tradition of excellence. Liberal arts programs offer outstanding opportunities while providing the general education curriculum. With about 5,000 undergraduate students and a student-faculty ratio of 19:1, education is economical and personal.

Part of Pennsylvania State System of Higher Education.

Students *Undergraduates:* 4,450 full-time, 563 part-time. Students come from 22 states and territories, 17 other countries. *The most frequently chosen baccalaureate fields are:* business/marketing, education, social sciences and history. *Graduate:* 775 in graduate degree programs.

From out-of-state	3%	Reside on campus	25%
Age 25 or older	20%	Transferred in	10%
International students	1%	African Americans	4%
Asian Americans/Pacific Islanders	0.4%	Hispanic Americans	0.3%
Native Americans	1%		

Faculty 335 (85% full-time), 55% with terminal degrees.

Expenses (1999–2000) *Tuition, state resident:* full-time $3618; part-time $150 per credit. *Tuition, nonresident:* full-time $9046; part-time $377 per credit. *Required fees:* full-time $1124; $180 per term part-time. Full-time tuition and fees vary according to location. Part-time tuition and fees vary according to location. *College room and board:* $4526. Room and board charges vary according to board plan. *Payment plan:* installment. *Waivers:* employees or children of employees.

Library Manderino Library. *Operations spending 1999–2000:* $2 million. *Collection:* 415,970 titles, 1,386 serial subscriptions, 59,795 audiovisual materials.

College life *Housing: Options:* men-only, women-only. *Social organizations:* national fraternities, national sororities; 10% of eligible men and 10% of eligible women are members. *Most popular organizations:* student government, In-Res Hall Council, Graduate Student Association, Black Student Union, sports recreation.

Campus security 24-hour emergency response devices and patrols, student patrols, late-night transport-escort service.

After graduation 163 organizations recruited on campus 1997–98. *Career center:* 4 full-time, 3 part-time personnel. Services include job fairs, resume preparation, resume referral, career counseling, careers library, job bank, job interviews. *Graduate education:* 14% of class of 1999 went directly to graduate and professional school: 4% business, 3% graduate arts and sciences, 2% medicine, 1% dentistry, 1% education, 1% engineering, 1% law, 1% theology, 1% veterinary medicine.

Freshmen 2,893 applied, 2,343 admitted, 984 enrolled.

Average high school GPA	2.85	SAT verbal scores above 500	37%
SAT math scores above 500	34%	ACT above 18	N/R
From top 10% of their h.s. class	5%	From top quarter	30%
From top half	62%	1998 freshmen returning in 1999	76%

Application *Options:* Common Application, electronic application, early admission, deferred entrance. *Application fee:* $25. *Required:* high school transcript; minimum 2.0 GPA. *Required for some:* letters of recommendation; interview. *Recommended:* essay or personal statement; minimum 3.0 GPA.

Standardized tests *Admission: Required:* SAT I. *Recommended:* SAT II Subject Tests.

Significant dates *Application deadlines:* 7/30 (freshmen), 7/30 (transfers). *Financial aid deadline priority date:* 5/1.

Freshman Application Contact
Mr. William A. Edmonds, Dean of Enrollment Management and Academic Services, California University of Pennsylvania, 250 University Avenue, California, PA 15419. **Phone:** 724-938-4404. **Fax:** 724-938-4138. **E-mail:** inquiry@cup.edu

Visit CollegeQuest.com for information on majors offered and athletics. College video and electronic viewbook available at CollegeQuest.com.

■ *See page 1344 for a narrative description.*

CARLOW COLLEGE
Pittsburgh, Pennsylvania

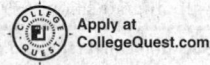
Apply at CollegeQuest.com

- **Independent Roman Catholic**, comprehensive, founded 1929
- **Degrees** bachelor's, master's, and postbachelor's certificates
- **Urban** 13-acre campus
- **Coed**, primarily women, 1,623 undergraduate students, 49% full-time, 93% women, 7% men
- **Moderately difficult** entrance level, 73% of applicants were admitted
- **13:1 student-to-undergraduate faculty ratio**
- **47% graduate** in 6 years or less
- **$12,826 tuition** and fees
- **$11,045 average financial aid** package, $15,000 average indebtedness upon graduation, $3.6 million endowment

Students *Undergraduates:* 802 full-time, 821 part-time. Students come from 14 states and territories. *The most frequently chosen baccalaureate fields are:* health professions and related sciences, education, interdisciplinary studies. *Graduate:* 346 in graduate degree programs.

From out-of-state	2%	Reside on campus	15%
Age 25 or older	63%	Transferred in	16%
International students	1%	African Americans	18%
Asian Americans/Pacific Islanders	1%	Hispanic Americans	1%
Native Americans	1%		

Faculty 191 (35% full-time), 51% with terminal degrees.

Expenses (1999–2000) *Comprehensive fee:* $17,902 includes full-time tuition ($12,450), mandatory fees ($376), and room and board ($5076). Full-time tuition and fees vary according to course load and program. Room and board charges vary according to board plan. *Part-time tuition:* $381 per credit. *Part-time fees:* $24 per credit. Part-time tuition and fees vary according to course load and program. *Payment plans:* installment, deferred payment. *Waivers:* adult students and employees or children of employees.

Library Grace Library. *Operations spending 1999–2000:* $393,026. *Collection:* 117,593 titles, 423 serial subscriptions, 4,464 audiovisual materials.

Pennsylvania

College life *Housing: Option:* women-only. *Social organizations:* coed fraternity. *Most popular organizations:* Commuter Student Association, Resident Student Association, Student Athletic Association, Gospel Choir "Blessed", Student Government Association.
Campus security 24-hour emergency response devices and patrols, late-night transport-escort service, controlled dormitory access.
After graduation 5 organizations recruited on campus 1997–98. *Career center:* 1 full-time personnel. Services include job fairs, resume preparation, interview workshops, career/interest testing, career counseling, careers library, job bank, job interviews.
Freshmen 455 applied, 332 admitted, 171 enrolled.

Average high school GPA	3.1	SAT verbal scores above 500	92%
SAT math scores above 500	83%	ACT above 18	92%
From top 10% of their h.s. class	12%	From top quarter	33%
From top half	71%	1998 freshmen returning in 1999	71%

Application *Options:* eApply at www.CollegeQuest.com, Common Application, electronic application, early admission, early action, deferred entrance. *Application fee:* $20. *Required:* high school transcript. *Recommended:* essay or personal statement; minimum 3.0 GPA; 2 letters of recommendation; interview; rank in upper two-fifths of high school class.
Standardized tests *Admission: Required:* SAT I or ACT.
Significant dates *Application deadlines:* rolling (freshmen), rolling (transfers). *Early action:* 9/30. *Notification:* 10/30 (early action). *Financial aid deadline priority date:* 4/3.
Freshman Application Contact
Ms. Susan Winstel, Assistant Director of Admissions, Carlow College, 3333 Fifth Avenue, Pittsburgh, PA 15213-3165. **Phone:** 412-578-6330. **Toll-free phone:** 800-333-CARLOW. **Fax:** 412-578-6668. **E-mail:** admissions@carlow.edu
Visit CollegeQuest.com for information on majors offered and athletics. College video available at CollegeQuest.com.

■ *See page 1364 for a narrative description.*

CARNEGIE MELLON UNIVERSITY
Pittsburgh, Pennsylvania

- **Independent**, university, founded 1900
- **Degrees** bachelor's, master's, doctoral, post-master's, and postbachelor's certificates
- **Urban** 103-acre campus
- **Coed**, 5,136 undergraduate students, 98% full-time, 36% women, 64% men
- **Very difficult** entrance level, 38% of applicants were admitted
- **6:1** student-to-undergraduate faculty ratio
- **75.37% graduate** in 6 years or less
- **$22,300 tuition** and fees
- **$15,789 average financial aid** package, $17,880 average indebtedness upon graduation, $719.3 million endowment

Students *Undergraduates:* 5,047 full-time, 89 part-time. Students come from 52 states and territories, 54 other countries. *The most frequently chosen baccalaureate fields are:* engineering/engineering technologies, business/marketing, visual/performing arts. *Graduate:* 3,174 in graduate degree programs.

From out-of-state	76%	Reside on campus	59%
Age 25 or older	1%	Transferred in	1%
International students	9%	African Americans	3%
Asian Americans/Pacific Islanders	20%	Hispanic Americans	5%
Native Americans	0.5%		

Faculty 1,254 (83% full-time).
Expenses (1999–2000) *Comprehensive fee:* $29,110 includes full-time tuition ($22,100), mandatory fees ($200), and room and board ($6810). *College room only:* $4105. Room and board charges vary according to board plan, housing facility, and student level. *Part-time tuition:* $307 per unit. *Payment plan:* installment. *Waivers:* employees or children of employees.
Library Hunt Library plus 2 others. *Collection:* 922,337 titles, 5,272 serial subscriptions, 215,813 audiovisual materials.

College life *Housing:* on-campus residence required in freshman year. *Options:* coed, men-only, women-only, disabled students. *Social organizations:* national fraternities, national sororities, local sororities; 13% of eligible men and 9% of eligible women are members. *Most popular organizations:* Student Senate, Alpha Phi Omega, tartan club, spirit club.
Campus security 24-hour emergency response devices and patrols, late-night transport-escort service, controlled dormitory access.
After graduation 945 organizations recruited on campus 1997–98. *Career center:* 13 full-time, 3 part-time personnel. Services include job fairs, resume preparation, interview workshops, resume referral, career/interest testing, career counseling, careers library, job bank, job interviews. **Graduate education:** 20% of class of 1999 went directly to graduate and professional school: 9% graduate arts and sciences, 7% engineering, 2% medicine, 1% business, 1% dentistry, 1% law, 1% veterinary medicine.
Freshmen 14,114 applied, 5,333 admitted, 1,254 enrolled.

Average high school GPA	3.61	SAT verbal scores above 500	96%
SAT math scores above 500	99%	ACT above 18	100%
From top 10% of their h.s. class	67%	From top quarter	93%
From top half	99%	1998 freshmen returning in 1999	92%

Application *Options:* eApply at www.CollegeQuest.com, electronic application, early admission, early decision, deferred entrance. *Application fee:* $50. *Required:* essay or personal statement; high school transcript; 1 letter of recommendation. *Required for some:* portfolio, audition. *Recommended:* interview.
Standardized tests *Admission: Required:* SAT I or ACT, SAT II Subject Tests. *Required for some:* SAT II: Writing Test.
Significant dates *Application deadlines:* 1/1 (freshmen), 3/15 (transfers). *Early decision:* 11/1 (for plan 1), 11/15 (for plan 2). *Notification:* 4/15 (freshmen), 1/15 (early decision plan 1), 1/15 (early decision plan 2). *Financial aid deadline priority date:* 2/15.
Freshman Application Contact
Mr. Michael Steidel, Director of Admissions, Carnegie Mellon University, 5000 Forbes Avenue, Pittsburgh, PA 15213-3891. **Phone:** 412-268-2082. **Fax:** 412-268-7838. **E-mail:** undergraduate-admissions@andrew.cmu.edu
Visit CollegeQuest.com for information on majors offered and athletics. College video available at CollegeQuest.com.

■ *See page 1366 for a narrative description.*

CEDAR CREST COLLEGE
Allentown, Pennsylvania

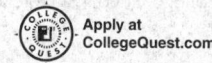

- **Independent**, 4-year, founded 1867, affiliated with United Church of Christ
- **Degrees** associate and bachelor's
- **Suburban** 84-acre campus with easy access to Philadelphia
- **Women** only, 1,468 undergraduate students, 58% full-time
- **Moderately difficult** entrance level, 90% of applicants were admitted
- **11:1** student-to-undergraduate faculty ratio
- **43% graduate** in 6 years or less
- **$17,110 tuition** and fees
- **$15,198 average financial aid** package, $19,095 average indebtedness upon graduation, $13.9 million endowment

U.S. News & World Report named Cedar Crest a top-tier regional liberal arts college for 10 years. New programs in dance, information systems, bioinformatics, and forensic science. Internships; freshmen research and honors program; cross-registration at 5 colleges; academic scholarships and free-tuition senior year to qualified students.

Students *Undergraduates:* 853 full-time, 615 part-time. Students come from 27 states and territories. *The most frequently chosen baccalaureate fields are:* psychology, biological/life sciences, social sciences and history.

From out-of-state	23%	Reside on campus	80%
Age 25 or older	49%	Transferred in	3%

Faculty 142 (47% full-time), 40% with terminal degrees.
Expenses (1999–2000) *Comprehensive fee:* $23,325 includes full-time tuition ($17,110) and room and board ($6215). *College room only:* $3348. Full-time tuition and fees vary according to course load. Room and board charges vary according to board plan. *Part-time tuition:* $487 per credit hour.

Peterson's Guide to Four-Year Colleges 2001

Pennsylvania

Cedar Crest College (continued)

Part-time tuition and fees vary according to class time. *Payment plan:* installment. *Waivers:* employees or children of employees.

Library Cressman Library. *Operations spending 1999–2000:* $767,000. *Collection:* 129,850 titles, 15,888 audiovisual materials.

College life *Housing:* on-campus residence required through junior year. *Options:* women-only, disabled students. *Most popular organizations:* commuter organization, Residence Hall Association, athletes club, Student Activities Board, Student Government Association.

Campus security 24-hour emergency response devices and patrols, late-night transport-escort service, controlled dormitory access, crime prevention programs.

After graduation 47 organizations recruited on campus 1997–98. 81% of class of 1998 had job offers within 6 months. *Career center:* 2 full-time personnel. Services include job fairs, resume preparation, interview workshops, resume referral, career/interest testing, career counseling, careers library, job bank, job interviews, web page. *Graduate education:* 30% of class of 1999 went directly to graduate and professional school: 18% graduate arts and sciences, 5% medicine, 2% engineering, 1% education, 1% law, 1% veterinary medicine.

Freshmen 965 applied, 873 admitted, 244 enrolled.

Average high school GPA	3.12	SAT verbal scores above 500	74%
SAT math scores above 500	62%	ACT above 18	84%
From top 10% of their h.s. class	24%	From top quarter	50%
From top half	84%	1998 freshmen returning in 1999	69%

Application *Options:* eApply at www.CollegeQuest.com, Common Application, electronic application, early admission, deferred entrance. *Application fee:* $30. *Required:* essay or personal statement; high school transcript. *Required for some:* 2 letters of recommendation. *Recommended:* minimum 2.0 GPA; interview.

Standardized tests *Admission: Required:* SAT I or ACT.

Significant dates *Application deadlines:* rolling (freshmen), rolling (transfers). *Financial aid deadline:* continuous.

Freshman Application Contact
Ms. Judith A. Neyhart, Vice President for Enrollment and Advancement, Cedar Crest College, 100 College Drive, Allentown, PA 18104-6196. **Phone:** 610-740-3780. **Toll-free phone:** 800-360-1222. **Fax:** 610-606-4647. **E-mail:** cccadmis@cedarcrest.edu

Visit CollegeQuest.com for information on majors offered and athletics. College video available at CollegeQuest.com.

■ *See page 1386 for a narrative description.*

CHATHAM COLLEGE
Pittsburgh, Pennsylvania

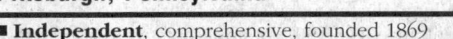 Apply at CollegeQuest.com

- **Independent**, comprehensive, founded 1869
- **Degrees** bachelor's, master's, and postbachelor's certificates
- **Urban** 34-acre campus
- **Women** only, 544 undergraduate students, 88% full-time
- **Moderately difficult** entrance level, 82% of applicants were admitted
- **13:1** student-to-undergraduate faculty ratio
- **54% graduate** in 6 years or less
- **$17,544 tuition** and fees
- **$17,247 average financial aid** package, $17,000 average indebtedness upon graduation, $53.2 million endowment

The Senior Tutorial is the hallmark of the Chatham experience. Seniors pursue independent learning projects on topics related to their majors, interests, and professional aspirations. Many Chatham students continue their education in graduate or professional programs and find the Tutorial is the best possible preparation.

Students *Undergraduates:* 480 full-time, 64 part-time. Students come from 32 states and territories, 16 other countries. *The most frequently chosen baccalaureate fields are:* biological/life sciences, English, psychology. *Graduate:* 429 in graduate degree programs.

From out-of-state	23%	Reside on campus	62%
Age 25 or older	21%	Transferred in	8%
International students	5%	African Americans	11%
Asian Americans/Pacific Islanders	2%	Hispanic Americans	1%
Native Americans	0.4%		

Faculty 81 (95% full-time), 93% with terminal degrees.

Expenses (1999–2000) *Comprehensive fee:* $23,664 includes full-time tuition ($17,388), mandatory fees ($156), and room and board ($6120). *College room only:* $3150. Room and board charges vary according to board plan. *Part-time tuition:* $423 per credit. *Part-time fees:* $39 per term part-time. *Payment plan:* installment. *Waivers:* employees or children of employees.

Library Jennie King Mellon Library. *Operations spending 1999–2000:* $955,694. *Collection:* 95,625 titles, 321 audiovisual materials.

College life *Housing: Options:* coed, women-only. *Most popular organizations:* Activities Board, Chatham Student Government, Chatham Feminist Collective, choir, Students of Community Service.

Campus security 24-hour emergency response devices and patrols, late-night transport-escort service.

After graduation 10 organizations recruited on campus 1997–98. 59% of class of 1998 had job offers within 6 months. *Career center:* 2 full-time, 1 part-time personnel. Services include job fairs, resume preparation, interview workshops, resume referral, career/interest testing, career counseling, careers library, job bank, job interviews. *Graduate education:* 36% of class of 1999 went directly to graduate and professional school: 23% graduate arts and sciences, 5% education, 4% law, 2% dentistry, 2% theology.

Freshmen 580 applied, 478 admitted, 145 enrolled. 1 class president, 5 valedictorians.

Average high school GPA	3.3	SAT verbal scores above 500	75%
SAT math scores above 500	63%	ACT above 18	98%
From top 10% of their h.s. class	31%	From top quarter	51%
From top half	80%	1998 freshmen returning in 1999	71%

Application *Options:* eApply at www.CollegeQuest.com, Common Application, electronic application, early admission, deferred entrance. *Application fee:* $25. *Required:* high school transcript; minimum 2.0 GPA; 3 letters of recommendation. *Recommended:* essay or personal statement; minimum 3.0 GPA; interview.

Standardized tests *Admission: Required:* SAT I or ACT.

Significant dates *Application deadlines:* rolling (freshmen), rolling (transfers). *Financial aid deadline:* 5/1.

Freshman Application Contact
Ms. Karina J. Dayich, Dean of Admissions and Financial Aid, Chatham College, Woodland Road, Pittsburgh, PA 15232-2826. **Phone:** 412-365-1290. **Toll-free phone:** 800-837-1290. **Fax:** 412-365-1609. **E-mail:** admissions@chatham.edu

Visit CollegeQuest.com for information on majors offered and athletics. College video available at CollegeQuest.com.

■ *See page 1408 for a narrative description.*

CHESTNUT HILL COLLEGE
Philadelphia, Pennsylvania

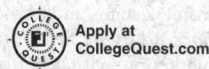 Apply at CollegeQuest.com

- **Independent Roman Catholic**, comprehensive, founded 1924
- **Degrees** associate, bachelor's, master's, doctoral, post-master's, and postbachelor's certificates
- **Suburban** 45-acre campus
- **Women** only, 939 undergraduate students, 67% full-time
- **Moderately difficult** entrance level, 72% of applicants were admitted
- **10:1** student-to-undergraduate faculty ratio
- **61% graduate** in 6 years or less
- **$16,030 tuition** and fees
- **$7824 average financial aid** package, $5.2 million endowment

Students *Undergraduates:* 632 full-time, 307 part-time. Students come from 12 states and territories. *The most frequently chosen baccalaureate fields are:* business/marketing, education, protective services/public administration. *Graduate:* 630 in graduate degree programs.

Pennsylvania

From out-of-state	11%	Reside on campus	24%
Age 25 or older	30%	Transferred in	5%
International students	2%	African Americans	37%
Asian Americans/Pacific Islanders	2%	Hispanic Americans	5%
Native Americans	0.3%		

Faculty 310 (18% full-time).

Expenses (1999-2000) *Comprehensive fee:* $22,540 includes full-time tuition ($15,454), mandatory fees ($576), and room and board ($6510). Full-time tuition and fees vary according to course load. Room and board charges vary according to housing facility. *Part-time tuition:* $305 per hour. *Part-time fees:* $48 per term part-time. *Payment plans:* installment, deferred payment. *Waivers:* senior citizens and employees or children of employees.

Library Logue Library. *Operations spending 1999-2000:* $367,830. *Collection:* 141,430 titles, 596 serial subscriptions, 2,026 audiovisual materials.

College life *Housing: Option:* women-only. *Most popular organizations:* student government, Hispanics in Action, African American Awareness Society, campus ministry community service group, Phi Beta Lambda.

Campus security 24-hour emergency response devices and patrols, late-night transport-escort service, controlled dormitory access.

After graduation 38 organizations recruited on campus 1997-98. 75% of class of 1998 had job offers within 6 months. *Career center:* 2 full-time, 1 part-time personnel. Services include job fairs, resume preparation, interview workshops, resume referral, career counseling, careers library, job bank, job interviews. *Graduate education:* 31% of class of 1999 went directly to graduate and professional school: 18% graduate arts and sciences, 4% education, 4% medicine, 3% business, 2% law.

Freshmen 379 applied, 274 admitted, 117 enrolled.

Average high school GPA	3.1	SAT verbal scores above 500	N/R
SAT math scores above 500	N/R	ACT above 18	N/R
1998 freshmen returning in 1999	74%		

Application *Options:* eApply at www.CollegeQuest.com, Common Application, early admission, early decision, deferred entrance. *Application fee:* $35. *Required:* essay or personal statement; high school transcript; 1 letter of recommendation. *Required for some:* interview. *Recommended:* minimum 2.0 GPA; interview.

Standardized tests *Admission: Required:* SAT I or ACT.

Significant dates *Application deadlines:* rolling (freshmen), rolling (transfers). *Early decision:* 12/1. *Notification:* 1/10 (early decision). *Financial aid deadline priority date:* 4/15.

Freshman Application Contact
Ms. Elizabeth Becker, Director of Admissions, Chestnut Hill College, 9601 Germantown Avenue, Philadelphia, PA 19118-2693. **Phone:** 215-248-7001. **Toll-free phone:** 800-248-0052. **Fax:** 215-248-7056. **E-mail:** chcapply@chc.edu

Visit CollegeQuest.com for information on majors offered and athletics. College video available at CollegeQuest.com.

■ *See page 1410 for a narrative description.*

CHEYNEY UNIVERSITY OF PENNSYLVANIA
Cheyney, Pennsylvania

■ **State-supported**, comprehensive, founded 1837
■ **Degrees** bachelor's and master's
■ **Suburban** 275-acre campus with easy access to Philadelphia
■ **Coed**, 1,103 undergraduate students, 89% full-time, 55% women, 45% men
■ **Minimally difficult** entrance level, 78% of applicants were admitted
■ **13:1 student-to-undergraduate faculty ratio**
■ **$4173 tuition** and fees (in-state); $9601 (out-of-state)
■ **$276,976 endowment**

Cheyney University of Pennsylvania, established in 1837, is America's oldest historically black educational institution. Cheyney strives to develop scholars who are not only well educated but also willing to set priorities that enable them to reach their highest potential in their personal and professional lives. Cheyney graduates are well-prepared to assume leadership roles through which they work for the greater public good.

Part of Pennsylvania State System of Higher Education.

Students *Undergraduates:* 985 full-time, 118 part-time. Students come from 16 states and territories, 3 other countries. *The most frequently chosen baccalaureate fields are:* business/marketing, education, social sciences and history. *Graduate:* 681 in graduate degree programs.

From out-of-state	18%	Reside on campus	66%
Age 25 or older	15%	Transferred in	4%
International students	1%	African Americans	97%
Asian Americans/Pacific Islanders	0.2%	Hispanic Americans	2%
Native Americans	0.1%		

Faculty 119 (85% full-time), 49% with terminal degrees.

Expenses (1999-2000) *Tuition, state resident:* full-time $3618; part-time $150 per credit hour. *Tuition, nonresident:* full-time $9046; part-time $377 per credit hour. *Required fees:* full-time $555; $139 per term part-time. Full-time tuition and fees vary according to reciprocity agreements. Part-time tuition and fees vary according to reciprocity agreements. *College room and board:* $4793; room only: $2410. Room and board charges vary according to board plan. *Payment plan:* deferred payment. *Waivers:* employees or children of employees.

Library Leslie Pickney Hill Library plus 1 other. *Operations spending 1999-2000:* $669,737. *Collection:* 85,536 titles, 1,526 serial subscriptions, 1,379 audiovisual materials.

College life *Housing: Option:* coed. *Social organizations:* national fraternities, national sororities, local fraternities, local sororities; 5% of eligible men and 8% of eligible women are members.

Campus security 24-hour emergency response devices and patrols.

After graduation *Career center:* 3 full-time personnel. Services include job fairs, resume preparation, resume referral, career counseling, careers library, job bank, job interviews.

Freshmen 985 applied, 765 admitted, 276 enrolled.

| SAT verbal scores above 500 | N/R | SAT math scores above 500 | N/R |
| ACT above 18 | N/R | | |

Application *Preference* given to state residents. *Application fee:* $20. *Required:* essay or personal statement; high school transcript. *Required for some:* 3 letters of recommendation. *Recommended:* interview.

Standardized tests *Admission: Required:* SAT I or ACT. *Recommended:* SAT II Subject Tests.

Significant dates *Application deadlines:* rolling (freshmen), rolling (transfers). *Financial aid deadline priority date:* 5/1.

Freshman Application Contact
Mr. James Brown, Interim Director of Admissions, Cheyney University of Pennsylvania, Cheyney and Creek Roads, Cheyney, PA 19319. **Phone:** 610-399-2000. **Toll-free phone:** 800-CHEYNEY. **Fax:** 610-399-2099.

Visit CollegeQuest.com for information on majors offered and athletics. College video available at CollegeQuest.com.

■ *See page 1412 for a narrative description.*

CLARION UNIVERSITY OF PENNSYLVANIA
Clarion, Pennsylvania

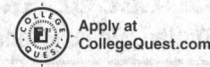
Apply at CollegeQuest.com

■ **State-supported**, comprehensive, founded 1867
■ **Degrees** associate, bachelor's, master's, and post-master's certificates
■ **Rural** 100-acre campus
■ **Coed**, 5,505 undergraduate students, 92% full-time, 61% women, 39% men
■ **Minimally difficult** entrance level, 63% of applicants were admitted
■ **18:1 student-to-undergraduate faculty ratio**
■ **52.5% graduate** in 6 years or less
■ **$4600 tuition** and fees (in-state); $6410 (out-of-state)

Clarion University is located in an inviting environment in central western Pennsylvania. People—students and faculty—are its most valuable resource; students from about 30 states and more than 20 countries specialize in more than 90 different degree programs. Committed to excellence, Clarion's faculty members are outstanding in their respective disciplines and sensitive to the aspirations and needs of students.

Part of Pennsylvania State System of Higher Education.

Pennsylvania

Clarion University of Pennsylvania (continued)

Students *Undergraduates:* 5,052 full-time, 453 part-time. Students come from 28 states and territories, 30 other countries. *The most frequently chosen baccalaureate fields are:* business/marketing, education, health professions and related sciences. *Graduate:* 429 in graduate degree programs.

From out-of-state	4%	Reside on campus	37%
Age 25 or older	14%	Transferred in	5%
International students	1%	African Americans	4%
Asian Americans/Pacific Islanders	0.5%	Hispanic Americans	1%
Native Americans	0.2%		

Faculty 343 (86% full-time), 60% with terminal degrees.

Expenses (1999–2000) *Tuition, state resident:* full-time $3618; part-time $150 per credit. *Tuition, nonresident:* full-time $5428; part-time $226 per credit. *Required fees:* full-time $982; $30 per credit; $70 per term part-time. Full-time tuition and fees vary according to course load and location. Part-time tuition and fees vary according to course load and location. *College room and board:* $3984; room only: $2300. Room and board charges vary according to board plan and housing facility. *Payment plan:* installment. *Waivers:* senior citizens and employees or children of employees.

Library Carlson Library. *Operations spending 1999–2000:* $2.3 million. *Collection:* 268,707 titles, 1,061 serial subscriptions.

College life *Housing:* Options: coed, men-only, women-only. *Social organizations:* national fraternities, national sororities, local fraternities, local sororities; 11% of eligible men and 10% of eligible women are members.

Campus security 24-hour emergency response devices and patrols, student patrols.

After graduation *Career center:* 2 full-time personnel. Services include job fairs, resume preparation, interview workshops, resume referral, career/interest testing, career counseling, careers library, job bank, job interviews.

Freshmen 3,062 applied, 1,927 admitted, 1,352 enrolled.

Average high school GPA	2.91	SAT verbal scores above 500	38%
SAT math scores above 500	35%	ACT above 18	N/R
1998 freshmen returning in 1999	74%		

Application *Options:* eApply at www.CollegeQuest.com, early admission, deferred entrance. *Application fee:* $25. *Required:* high school transcript. *Required for some:* essay or personal statement; interview. *Recommended:* essay or personal statement; letters of recommendation; interview.

Standardized tests *Admission:* Required: SAT I or ACT.

Significant dates *Application deadlines:* rolling (freshmen), rolling (transfers). *Financial aid deadline priority date:* 5/1.

Freshman Application Contact
Mr. John S. Shropshire, Dean of Enrollment Management and Academic Records, Clarion University of Pennsylvania, Clarion, PA 16214. **Phone:** 814-226-2306. **Toll-free phone:** 800-672-7171. **Fax:** 814-393-2030. **E-mail:** smcmille@mail.clarion.edu

Visit CollegeQuest.com for information on majors offered and athletics. College video available at CollegeQuest.com.

■ *See page 1426 for a narrative description.*

COLLEGE MISERICORDIA
Dallas, Pennsylvania

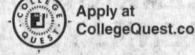 Apply at CollegeQuest.com

- **Independent Roman Catholic**, comprehensive, founded 1924
- **Degrees** bachelor's and master's
- **Small-town** 100-acre campus
- **Coed**, 1,237 undergraduate students, 86% full-time, 73% women, 27% men
- **Moderately difficult** entrance level, 75% of applicants were admitted
- **66% graduate** in 6 years or less
- **$15,250 tuition** and fees
- **$12,709 average financial aid** package, $16,900 average indebtedness upon graduation, $8.3 million endowment

Misericordia's Guaranteed Placement Program integrates academics, cocurricular activities, and internships to fully prepare students for employment. The College guarantees that if a student fulfills the requirements of the program and is not employed in his or her field or enrolled in graduate or professional school within 6 months of graduation, he or she is assured a paid internship.

Students *Undergraduates:* 1,069 full-time, 168 part-time. Students come from 17 states and territories. *The most frequently chosen baccalaureate fields are:* health professions and related sciences, education, liberal arts/general studies. *Graduate:* 157 in graduate degree programs.

From out-of-state	26%	Reside on campus	55%
Age 25 or older	11%	Transferred in	6%

Faculty 166 (51% full-time).

Expenses (1999–2000) *Comprehensive fee:* $21,590 includes full-time tuition ($14,470), mandatory fees ($780), and room and board ($6340). *College room only:* $3470. Room and board charges vary according to board plan and housing facility. *Part-time tuition:* $362 per credit. *Payment plans:* installment, deferred payment. *Waivers:* employees or children of employees.

Library Franceska McLaughlin Memorial Library. *Operations spending 1999–2000:* $538,136. *Collection:* 72,254 titles, 782 serial subscriptions.

College life *Housing:* Option: coed. *Social organizations:* local fraternities. *Most popular organizations:* Circle K, International Club, BACCHUS, Student Nurses Association of Pennsylvania, Commuter Council.

Campus security 24-hour emergency response devices and patrols, late-night transport-escort service, controlled dormitory access.

After graduation 85 organizations recruited on campus 1997–98. 95% of class of 1998 had job offers within 6 months. *Career center:* 3 full-time personnel. Services include job fairs, resume preparation, resume referral, career counseling, careers library, job interviews. *Graduate education:* 17% of class of 1999 went directly to graduate and professional school.

Freshmen 1,019 applied, 760 admitted, 256 enrolled. 3 valedictorians.

Average high school GPA	3.2	SAT verbal scores above 500	60%
SAT math scores above 500	59%	ACT above 18	94%
From top 10% of their h.s. class	27%	From top quarter	50%
From top half	75%	1998 freshmen returning in 1999	83%

Application *Options:* eApply at www.CollegeQuest.com, early admission, deferred entrance. *Application fee:* $25. *Required:* high school transcript. *Required for some:* essay or personal statement; 2 letters of recommendation; interview. *Recommended:* interview.

Standardized tests *Admission:* Required: SAT I or ACT.

Significant dates *Application deadlines:* rolling (freshmen), rolling (transfers). *Financial aid deadline priority date:* 3/1.

Freshman Application Contact
Ms. Jane Dessoye, Executive Director of Admissions and Financial Aid, College Misericordia, 301 Lake Street, Dallas, PA 18612. **Phone:** 570-675-4449. **Toll-free phone:** 800-852-7675. **Fax:** 570-675-2441. **E-mail:** admis@miseri.edu

Visit CollegeQuest.com for information on majors offered and athletics.

■ *See page 1452 for a narrative description.*

THE CURTIS INSTITUTE OF MUSIC
Philadelphia, Pennsylvania

- **Independent**, comprehensive, founded 1924
- **Degrees** bachelor's and master's
- **Urban** campus
- **Coed**, 150 undergraduate students
- **Most difficult** entrance level, 6% of applicants were admitted
- **$795 tuition** and fees

Students *Undergraduates:* Students come from 24 states and territories, 22 other countries. *The most frequently chosen baccalaureate field is:* visual/performing arts.

Faculty 80.

Expenses (1999–2000) *Tuition:* full-time $0. *Required fees:* full-time $795.

Library Curtis Institute of Music Library. *Collection:* 70,000 titles.

College life *Housing:* college housing not available.

Campus security 24-hour patrols.

Freshmen 789 applied, 49 admitted.

SAT verbal scores above 500	N/R	SAT math scores above 500	N/R
ACT above 18	N/R		

Application *Options:* Common Application, early admission. *Application fee:* $60. *Required:* essay or personal statement; high school transcript; letters of recommendation; audition.

Standardized tests *Placement: Required:* SAT I
Significant dates *Application deadlines:* 1/15 (freshmen), 1/15 (transfers).
Freshman Application Contact
Mr. Christopher Hodges, Admissions Officer, The Curtis Institute of Music, 1726 Locust Street, Philadelphia, PA 19103-6107. **Phone:** 215-893-5262. **Fax:** 215-893-7900.
Visit CollegeQuest.com for information on majors offered and athletics.

Freshman Application Contact
Mr. Stephen Zenko, Director of Admissions, Delaware Valley College, 700 East Butler Avenue, Doylestown, PA 18901. **Phone:** 215-489-2211 Ext. 2211. **Toll-free phone:** 800-2DELVAL. **Fax:** 215-345-5277. **E-mail:** admitme@devalcol.edu
Visit CollegeQuest.com for information on majors offered and athletics. College video available at CollegeQuest.com.

■ *See page 1568 for a narrative description.*

DELAWARE VALLEY COLLEGE
Doylestown, Pennsylvania

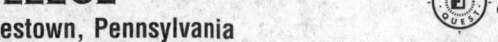

- **Independent**, comprehensive, founded 1896
- **Degrees** associate, bachelor's, and master's
- **Suburban** 600-acre campus with easy access to Philadelphia
- **Coed**, 1,414 undergraduate students, 94% full-time, 49% women, 51% men
- **Moderately difficult** entrance level, 80% of applicants were admitted
- **17:1** student-to-undergraduate faculty ratio
- **$15,687 tuition** and fees
- **$13,935 average financial aid** package, $13.4 million endowment

The distinctive DVC Employment Program gets results. All students complete 24 weeks of hands-on work in jobs related to their academic programs. This on-the-job learning expands resumes, exposes students to real-life work experience in their chosen fields, and allows employers to recognize students' skills and abilities—all before graduation.

Students *Undergraduates:* 1,333 full-time, 81 part-time. Students come from 24 states and territories, 4 other countries. *The most frequently chosen baccalaureate fields are:* agriculture, biological/life sciences, business/marketing. *Graduate:* 26 in graduate degree programs.

From out-of-state	34%	Reside on campus	72%
Age 25 or older	24%	Transferred in	6%
International students	0.3%	African Americans	5%
Asian Americans/Pacific Islanders	0.4%	Hispanic Americans	2%
Native Americans	0.1%		

Faculty 121 (72% full-time), 64% with terminal degrees.
Expenses (1999–2000) *One-time required fee:* $125. *Comprehensive fee:* $21,687 includes full-time tuition ($15,419), mandatory fees ($268), and room and board ($6000). *College room only:* $2687. Room and board charges vary according to board plan. *Part-time tuition:* $375 per credit. Part-time tuition and fees vary according to class time and student level. *Payment plan:* installment. *Waivers:* employees or children of employees.
Library Joseph Krauskopf Memorial Library. *Operations spending 1999–2000:* $522,532. *Collection:* 58,040 titles, 734 serial subscriptions.
College life *Housing: Option:* coed. *Most popular organizations:* student newspaper, Block and Bridle Club, Community Service Corps, student government, Halloween Haunting.
Campus security 24-hour patrols, late-night transport-escort service, controlled dormitory access.
After graduation 135 organizations recruited on campus 1997–98. 94% of class of 1998 had job offers within 6 months. *Career center:* 2 full-time personnel. Services include job fairs, resume preparation, career counseling, careers library, job bank, job interviews. *Graduate education:* 14% of class of 1999 went directly to graduate and professional school: 8% business, 6% veterinary medicine, 3% graduate arts and sciences.
Freshmen 1,358 applied, 1,085 admitted, 323 enrolled.

Average high school GPA	2.85	SAT verbal scores above 500	48%
SAT math scores above 500	47%	ACT above 18	N/R
From top 10% of their h.s. class	12%	From top quarter	34%
From top half	72%	1998 freshmen returning in 1999	75%

Application *Options:* eApply at www.CollegeQuest.com, Common Application, early admission, deferred entrance. *Application fee:* $35. *Required:* high school transcript; 1 letter of recommendation. *Recommended:* interview.
Standardized tests *Admission: Required:* SAT I or ACT.
Significant dates *Application deadlines:* rolling (freshmen), rolling (transfers). *Financial aid deadline priority date:* 4/1.

DICKINSON COLLEGE
Carlisle, Pennsylvania

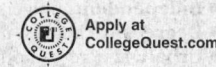

- **Independent**, 4-year, founded 1773
- **Degree** bachelor's
- **Suburban** 103-acre campus with easy access to Harrisburg
- **Coed**, 2,024 undergraduate students, 99% full-time, 60% women, 40% men
- **Very difficult** entrance level, 64% of applicants were admitted
- **13:1** student-to-undergraduate faculty ratio
- **80% graduate** in 6 years or less
- **$24,450 tuition** and fees
- **$20,228 average financial aid** package, $17,752 average indebtedness upon graduation, $159.6 million endowment

Students *Undergraduates:* 2,015 full-time, 9 part-time. Students come from 42 states and territories, 18 other countries. *The most frequently chosen baccalaureate fields are:* foreign language/literature, English, social sciences and history.

From out-of-state	56%	Reside on campus	92%
Age 25 or older	1%	Transferred in	0.5%
International students	1%	African Americans	1%
Asian Americans/Pacific Islanders	3%	Hispanic Americans	2%
Native Americans	0.1%		

Faculty 183 (84% full-time), 81% with terminal degrees.
Expenses (2000–2001) *One-time required fee:* $25. *Comprehensive fee:* $30,900 includes full-time tuition ($24,050), mandatory fees ($400), and room and board ($6450). *College room only:* $3300. *Payment plan:* installment. *Waivers:* employees or children of employees.
Library Boyd Lee Spahr Library plus 6 others. *Operations spending 1999–2000:* $2.3 million. *Collection:* 12,247 audiovisual materials.
College life *Housing:* on-campus residence required in freshman year. *Options:* coed, men-only, women-only, disabled students. *Social organizations:* national fraternities, national sororities, local fraternities, local sororities; 45% of eligible men and 39% of eligible women are members. *Most popular organizations:* Campus Activities Board, Student Senate, volunteer/community service groups, Arts House, Greek organizations.
Campus security 24-hour emergency response devices and patrols, student patrols, late-night transport-escort service, controlled dormitory access.
After graduation 23 organizations recruited on campus 1997–98. 98% of class of 1998 had job offers within 6 months. *Career center:* 3 full-time, 2 part-time personnel. Services include job fairs, resume preparation, resume referral, career counseling, careers library, job bank, job interviews.
Freshmen 3,434 applied, 2,183 admitted, 620 enrolled. 18 National Merit Scholars, 9 class presidents, 19 valedictorians, 77 student government officers.

SAT verbal scores above 500	93%	SAT math scores above 500	92%
ACT above 18	N/R	From top 10% of their h.s. class	47%
From top quarter	80%	From top half	99%
1998 freshmen returning in 1999	89%		

Application *Options:* eApply at www.CollegeQuest.com, Common Application, electronic application, early admission, early decision, early action, deferred entrance. *Application fee:* $40. *Required:* essay or personal statement; high school transcript; 2 letters of recommendation. *Recommended:* minimum 3.0 GPA; interview.
Standardized tests *Admission: Recommended:* SAT I and SAT II or ACT, SAT II Subject Tests.
Significant dates *Application deadlines:* 2/1 (freshmen), 6/1 (transfers). *Early decision:* 11/15 (for plan 1), 1/15 (for plan 2), 12/1. *Notification:* 3/31 (freshmen), 12/15 (early decision plan 1), 2/15 (early decision plan 2), 1/15 (early action). *Financial aid deadline priority date:* 2/1.

Pennsylvania

Dickinson College (continued)
Freshman Application Contact
Mr. Christopher Seth Allen, Director of Admissions, Dickinson College, PO Box 1773, Carlisle, PA 17013-2896. **Phone:** 717-245-1231. **Toll-free phone:** 800-644-1773. **Fax:** 717-245-1442. **E-mail:** admit@dickinson.edu
Visit CollegeQuest.com for information on majors offered and athletics.

DREXEL UNIVERSITY
Philadelphia, Pennsylvania

Apply at CollegeQuest.com

- **Independent**, university, founded 1891
- **Degrees** bachelor's, master's, doctoral, and post-master's certificates
- **Urban** 42-acre campus
- **Coed**, 8,767 undergraduate students, 86% full-time, 37% women, 63% men
- **Moderately difficult** entrance level, 69% of applicants were admitted
- **14:1** student-to-undergraduate faculty ratio
- **63.1% graduate** in 6 years or less
- **$16,150 tuition** and fees
- **$13,622 average financial aid** package, $231.9 million endowment

Drexel is a national leader in curricular innovation and cooperative education. Through Drexel Co-op–The Ultimate Internship, students alternate between periods of classroom study and paid professional employment. By the time they graduate, Drexel students have gained the experience needed to pursue the graduate school or career of their choice.

Students *Undergraduates:* 7,566 full-time, 1,201 part-time. Students come from 44 states and territories, 92 other countries. *The most frequently chosen baccalaureate fields are:* business/marketing, computer/information sciences, engineering/engineering technologies. *Graduate:* 2,483 in graduate degree programs.

From out-of-state	24%	Reside on campus	28%
Age 25 or older	17%	Transferred in	7%
International students	7%	African Americans	8%
Asian Americans/Pacific Islanders	12%	Hispanic Americans	2%
Native Americans	0.3%		

Faculty 888 (52% full-time).
Expenses (1999–2000) *One-time required fee:* $125. *Comprehensive fee:* $23,992 includes full-time tuition ($15,240), mandatory fees ($910), and room and board ($7842). *College room only:* $4800. Full-time tuition and fees vary according to program and student level. Room and board charges vary according to housing facility. *Part-time tuition:* $386 per credit hour. *Part-time fees:* $67 per term part-time. Part-time tuition and fees vary according to class time. *Payment plans:* installment, deferred payment. *Waivers:* senior citizens and employees or children of employees.
Library W. W. Hagerty Library. *Operations spending 1999–2000:* $3.8 million. *Collection:* 32,935 audiovisual materials.
College life *Housing:* on-campus residence required in freshman year. *Options:* coed, disabled students. *Social organizations:* national fraternities, national sororities, local fraternities; 8% of eligible men and 6% of eligible women are members. *Most popular organizations:* Student Government, Black Student Union, Society of Hispanic Professional Engineers, Society of Minority Engineers and Scientists, Campus Activities Board.
Campus security 24-hour emergency response devices and patrols, late-night transport-escort service, controlled dormitory access.
After graduation 265 organizations recruited on campus 1997–98. 82% of class of 1998 had job offers within 6 months. *Career center:* 23 full-time personnel. Services include job fairs, resume preparation, resume referral, career counseling, careers library, job bank, job interviews. *Graduate education:* 13% of class of 1999 went directly to graduate and professional school: 4% engineering, 3% business, 3% graduate arts and sciences, 1% dentistry, 1% law, 1% medicine. *Major awards:* 1 Fulbright Scholar.
Freshmen 9,529 applied, 6,529 admitted, 1,941 enrolled.

Average high school GPA	3.1	SAT verbal scores above 500	83%
SAT math scores above 500	90%	ACT above 18	N/R
From top 10% of their h.s. class	21%	From top quarter	55%
From top half	89%	1998 freshmen returning in 1999	82%

Application *Options:* eApply at www.CollegeQuest.com, Common Application, electronic application, early admission, deferred entrance. *Application fee:* $35. *Required:* essay or personal statement; high school transcript; minimum 2.0 GPA. *Recommended:* 2 letters of recommendation; interview.

Standardized tests *Admission: Required:* SAT I or ACT. *Recommended:* SAT I.
Significant dates *Application deadlines:* 3/1 (freshmen), rolling (transfers). *Financial aid deadline priority date:* 2/15.
Freshman Application Contact
Mr. Gary Hamme, Dean of Enrollment Management and Career Services, Drexel University, Room 220, Philadelphia, PA 19104-2875. **Phone:** 215-895-2400. **Toll-free phone:** 800-2-DREXEL. **Fax:** 215-895-5939. **E-mail:** enroll@drexel.edu
Visit CollegeQuest.com for information on majors offered and athletics. College video available at CollegeQuest.com.

■ *See page 1592 for a narrative description.*

DUQUESNE UNIVERSITY
Pittsburgh, Pennsylvania

- **Independent Roman Catholic**, university, founded 1878
- **Degrees** bachelor's, master's, doctoral, first professional, and postbachelor's certificates
- **Urban** 43-acre campus
- **Coed**, 5,501 undergraduate students, 92% full-time, 58% women, 42% men
- **Moderately difficult** entrance level, 84% of applicants were admitted
- **16:1** student-to-undergraduate faculty ratio
- **71.9% graduate** in 6 years or less
- **$15,588 tuition** and fees
- **$13,444 average financial aid** package, $17,842 average indebtedness upon graduation, $89 million endowment

Students *Undergraduates:* 5,044 full-time, 457 part-time. Students come from 50 states and territories, 77 other countries. *The most frequently chosen baccalaureate fields are:* business/marketing, education, health professions and related sciences. *Graduate:* 1,243 in professional programs, 2,962 in other graduate degree programs.

From out-of-state	19%	Reside on campus	50%
Age 25 or older	13%	Transferred in	3%
International students	4%	African Americans	4%
Asian Americans/Pacific Islanders	2%	Hispanic Americans	3%
Native Americans	0.1%		

Faculty 801 (49% full-time).
Expenses (1999–2000) *Comprehensive fee:* $21,902 includes full-time tuition ($14,378), mandatory fees ($1210), and room and board ($6314). Full-time tuition and fees vary according to program. Room and board charges vary according to board plan. *Part-time tuition:* $485 per credit. *Part-time fees:* $46 per credit. Part-time tuition and fees vary according to program. *Payment plans:* installment, deferred payment. *Waivers:* adult students, senior citizens, and employees or children of employees.
Library Gumberg Library plus 1 other. *Operations spending 1999–2000:* $4 million. *Collection:* 306,540 titles, 1,544 serial subscriptions, 6,844 audiovisual materials.
College life *Housing:* on-campus residence required in freshman year. *Options:* coed, men-only, women-only. *Social organizations:* national fraternities, national sororities, local fraternities, local sororities; 14% of eligible men and 14% of eligible women are members. *Most popular organizations:* Student Government Association, Duquesne University Volunteers, Duquesne Program Council, Commuter Council, Black Student Union.
Campus security 24-hour emergency response devices and patrols, late-night transport-escort service, controlled dormitory access, 24-hour front desk personnel, 24-hour video monitors at residence hall entrances, surveillance cameras throughout the campus.
After graduation 747 organizations recruited on campus 1997–98. 82% of class of 1998 had job offers within 6 months. *Career center:* 8 full-time, 3 part-time personnel. Services include job fairs, resume preparation, interview workshops, resume referral, career counseling, careers library, job bank, job interviews. *Graduate education:* 30% of class of 1999 went directly to graduate and professional school.

Pennsylvania

Freshmen 3,783 applied, 3,180 admitted, 1,211 enrolled.

Average high school GPA	3.4	SAT verbal scores above 500	68%
SAT math scores above 500	69%	ACT above 18	100%
From top 10% of their h.s. class	42%	From top quarter	78%
From top half	96%	1998 freshmen returning in 1999	87%

Application *Options:* Common Application, electronic application, early admission, early decision, early action, deferred entrance. *Application fee:* $50. *Required:* essay or personal statement; high school transcript; 1 letter of recommendation. *Required for some:* minimum 2.5 GPA; interview.

Standardized tests *Admission: Required:* SAT I or ACT.

Significant dates *Application deadlines:* 7/1 (freshmen), 7/1 (transfers). *Early decision:* 11/1, 12/1. *Notification:* 12/15 (early decision), 1/15 (early action). *Financial aid deadline:* 5/1.

Freshman Application Contact
Office of Admissions, Duquesne University, 600 Forbes Avenue, Pittsburgh, PA 15282-0201. **Phone:** 412-396-5000. **Toll-free phone:** 800-456-0590. **Fax:** 412-396-5779. **E-mail:** admissions@duq2.cc.duq.edu

Visit CollegeQuest.com for information on majors offered and athletics. College video and electronic viewbook available at CollegeQuest.com.

EASTERN COLLEGE
St. Davids, Pennsylvania

Apply at CollegeQuest.com

- **Independent American Baptist**, comprehensive, founded 1952
- **Degrees** associate, bachelor's, and master's
- **Small-town** 107-acre campus with easy access to Philadelphia
- **Coed**, 1,878 undergraduate students, 82% full-time, 66% women, 34% men
- **Moderately difficult** entrance level, 84% of applicants were admitted
- **14:1 student-to-undergraduate faculty ratio**
- **55% graduate** in 6 years or less
- **$13,728 tuition** and fees

Eastern College is a Christian college of the arts and sciences dedicated to equipping all students with the ability to make a difference in all areas of society. This is done through a curriculum firmly rooted in a Christian world view and faculty members and students who have a passionate desire to make a difference in the world. In response to recent and dramatic growth, Eastern has increased the size of its faculty, raised the percentage of faculty members with PhDs to 80 percent, improved campus facilities, and raised the standard of admission. Eastern is located near Philadelphia, one of America's educational centers, and is only 2 hours from Washington, D.C., and New York City.

Students *Undergraduates:* 1,549 full-time, 329 part-time. Students come from 38 states and territories, 26 other countries. *The most frequently chosen baccalaureate fields are:* business/marketing, education, philosophy. *Graduate:* 855 in graduate degree programs.

From out-of-state	40%	Reside on campus	47%
Age 25 or older	39%	Transferred in	3%
International students	2%	African Americans	14%
Asian Americans/Pacific Islanders	1%	Hispanic Americans	2%
Native Americans	0.2%		

Faculty 290 (23% full-time), 29% with terminal degrees.

Expenses (1999–2000) *One-time required fee:* $35. *Comprehensive fee:* $19,606 includes full-time tuition ($13,728) and room and board ($5878). Full-time tuition and fees vary according to program. Room and board charges vary according to board plan and housing facility. *Part-time tuition:* $325 per credit. Part-time tuition and fees vary according to course load. *Payment plan:* installment. *Waivers:* employees or children of employees.

Library Warner Library plus 1 other. *Collection:* 143,815 titles, 1,215 serial subscriptions, 11,673 audiovisual materials.

College life *Housing:* on-campus residence required through senior year. *Option:* coed. *Most popular organizations:* Habitat for Humanity, Y.A.C.H.T. club, Angels of Harmony, Black Student League, Fellowship of Christian Athletes.

Campus security 24-hour emergency response devices and patrols, late-night transport-escort service, controlled dormitory access, emergency call boxes.

After graduation 83% of class of 1998 had job offers within 6 months. *Career center:* 2 part-time personnel. Services include job fairs, resume preparation, interview workshops, resume referral, career counseling, careers library, job bank. *Graduate education:* 18% of class of 1999 went directly to graduate and professional school.

Freshmen 908 applied, 761 admitted, 381 enrolled. 17 National Merit Scholars.

Average high school GPA	3.39	SAT verbal scores above 500	78%
SAT math scores above 500	70%	ACT above 18	94%
From top 10% of their h.s. class	25%	From top quarter	55%
From top half	78%	1998 freshmen returning in 1999	79%

Application *Options:* eApply at www.CollegeQuest.com, electronic application, early admission, deferred entrance. *Application fee:* $25. *Required:* essay or personal statement; high school transcript; minimum 2.0 GPA; 1 letter of recommendation. *Recommended:* minimum 3.0 GPA; 3 letters of recommendation; interview.

Standardized tests *Admission: Required:* SAT I or ACT.

Significant dates *Application deadlines:* rolling (freshmen), rolling (transfers). *Financial aid deadline:* continuous.

Freshman Application Contact
Mr. Mark Seymour, Executive Director for Enrollment Management, Eastern College, 1300 Eagle Road, St. Davids, PA 19087-3696. **Phone:** 610-341-5967. **Toll-free phone:** 800-452-0996. **Fax:** 610-341-1723. **E-mail:** ugadm@eastern.edu

Visit CollegeQuest.com for information on majors offered and athletics. College video available at CollegeQuest.com.

■ *See page 1600 for a narrative description.*

EAST STROUDSBURG UNIVERSITY OF PENNSYLVANIA
East Stroudsburg, Pennsylvania

- **State-supported**, comprehensive, founded 1893
- **Degrees** associate, bachelor's, and master's
- **Small-town** 184-acre campus
- **Coed**, 4,641 undergraduate students, 90% full-time, 58% women, 42% men
- **Moderately difficult** entrance level, 67% of applicants were admitted
- **19:1 student-to-undergraduate faculty ratio**
- **50.8% graduate** in 6 years or less
- **$4492 tuition** and fees (in-state); $9920 (out-of-state)
- **$4455 average financial aid** package, $14,139 average indebtedness upon graduation, $5.4 million endowment

Part of Pennsylvania State System of Higher Education.

Students *Undergraduates:* 4,182 full-time, 459 part-time. Students come from 21 states and territories, 20 other countries. *The most frequently chosen baccalaureate fields are:* biological/life sciences, business/marketing, education. *Graduate:* 1,020 in graduate degree programs.

From out-of-state	17%	Reside on campus	44%
Age 25 or older	13%	Transferred in	9%
International students	1%	African Americans	3%
Asian Americans/Pacific Islanders	1%	Hispanic Americans	3%
Native Americans	0.2%		

Faculty 271 (87% full-time), 68% with terminal degrees.

Expenses (1999–2000) *Tuition, state resident:* full-time $3618; part-time $150 per credit. *Tuition, nonresident:* full-time $9046; part-time $388 per credit. *Required fees:* full-time $874; $36 per credit. *College room and board:* $3938; room only: $2432. Room and board charges vary according to board plan and housing facility. *Payment plan:* installment. *Waivers:* senior citizens and employees or children of employees.

Library Kemp Library. *Operations spending 1999–2000:* $2 million. *Collection:* 1,758 serial subscriptions, 12,506 audiovisual materials.

College life *Housing:* on-campus residence required through sophomore year. *Options:* coed, men-only, women-only. *Social organizations:* national fraternities, national sororities; 8% of eligible men and 8% of eligible women are members.

Campus security 24-hour emergency response devices and patrols, student patrols, late-night transport-escort service, controlled dormitory access.

After graduation *Career center:* 2 full-time, 1 part-time personnel. Services include job fairs, resume preparation, resume referral, career counseling, careers library, job bank, job interviews. *Graduate education:* 15% of class of 1999 went directly to graduate and professional school.

Pennsylvania

East Stroudsburg University of Pennsylvania (continued)
Freshmen 4,064 applied, 2,725 admitted, 859 enrolled.

SAT verbal scores above 500	38%	SAT math scores above 500	39%
ACT above 18	N/R	From top 10% of their h.s. class	4%
From top quarter	20%	From top half	64%
1998 freshmen returning in 1999	73%		

Application *Option:* electronic application. *Preference* given to state residents. *Application fee:* $25. *Required:* high school transcript. *Recommended:* 1 letter of recommendation.
Standardized tests *Admission: Required:* SAT I or ACT.
Significant dates *Application deadlines:* 3/1 (freshmen), 6/1 (transfers). *Notification:* 3/1 (freshmen). *Financial aid deadline:* 3/1.
Freshman Application Contact
Mr. Alan T. Chesterton, Director of Admissions, East Stroudsburg University of Pennsylvania, 200 Prospect Street, East Stroudsburg, PA 18301. **Phone:** 570-422-3542. **Toll-free phone:** 877-230-5547. **Fax:** 570-422-3933. **E-mail:** undergrads@po-box.esu.edu

Visit CollegeQuest.com for information on majors offered and athletics.

EDINBORO UNIVERSITY OF PENNSYLVANIA
Edinboro, Pennsylvania

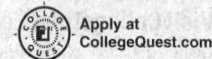

- **State-supported**, comprehensive, founded 1857
- **Degrees** associate, bachelor's, master's, post-master's, and postbachelor's certificates
- **Small-town** 585-acre campus
- **Coed**, 6,323 undergraduate students, 90% full-time, 58% women, 42% men
- **Moderately difficult** entrance level, 77% of applicants were admitted
- **17:1 student-to-undergraduate faculty ratio**
- **46.8% graduate** in 6 years or less
- **$4358 tuition** and fees (in-state); $6168 (out-of-state)
- **$5728 average financial aid** package, $17,500 average indebtedness upon graduation, $2.5 million endowment

Part of Pennsylvania State System of Higher Education.
Students *Undergraduates:* 5,681 full-time, 642 part-time. Students come from 29 states and territories, 39 other countries. *The most frequently chosen baccalaureate fields are:* education, protective services/public administration, visual/performing arts. *Graduate:* 679 in graduate degree programs.

From out-of-state	7%	Reside on campus	31%
Age 25 or older	16%	Transferred in	8%
International students	2%	African Americans	5%
Asian Americans/Pacific Islanders	0.4%	Hispanic Americans	1%
Native Americans	0.3%		

Faculty 375 (93% full-time), 67% with terminal degrees.
Expenses (1999–2000) *Tuition, state resident:* full-time $3618; part-time $150 per credit. *Tuition, nonresident:* full-time $5428; part-time $226 per credit. *Required fees:* full-time $740; $31 per credit. Part-time tuition and fees vary according to course load. *College room and board:* $3788; room only: $2108. Room and board charges vary according to board plan. *Payment plan:* installment. *Waivers:* senior citizens and employees or children of employees.
Library Baron-Forness Library plus 1 other. *Operations spending 1999–2000:* $2.3 million. *Collection:* 468,977 titles, 1,829 serial subscriptions, 12,796 audiovisual materials.
College life *Housing:* on-campus residence required in freshman year. *Options:* coed, women-only, disabled students. *Social organizations:* national fraternities, national sororities, local fraternities, local sororities; 4% of eligible men and 5% of eligible women are members. *Most popular organizations:* Student Government Association, Student Nursing Organization of Edinboro, Alpha Gamma Delta, Future Elementary Educators, Health and Physical Education Majors Club.
Campus security 24-hour emergency response devices and patrols, self-defense education.
After graduation 150 organizations recruited on campus 1997–98. *Career center:* 4 full-time personnel. Services include job fairs, resume preparation, interview workshops, resume referral, career/interest testing, career counseling, careers library, job bank, job interviews.

Freshmen 3,476 applied, 2,669 admitted, 1,372 enrolled.

SAT verbal scores above 500	39%	SAT math scores above 500	35%
ACT above 18	63%	From top 10% of their h.s. class	6%
From top quarter	23%	From top half	59%
1998 freshmen returning in 1999	72%		

Application *Options:* eApply at www.CollegeQuest.com, electronic application, early admission, deferred entrance. *Application fee:* $25. *Required:* high school transcript. *Required for some:* interview; student affairs form. *Recommended:* minimum 2.0 GPA.
Standardized tests *Admission: Required:* SAT I or ACT.
Significant dates *Application deadlines:* rolling (freshmen), rolling (transfers). *Financial aid deadline priority date:* 3/15.
Freshman Application Contact
Mr. Terrence Carlin, Assistant Vice President for Admissions, Edinboro University of Pennsylvania, Biggers House, Edinboro, PA 16444. **Phone:** 814-732-2761. **Toll-free phone:** 888-846-2676 (in-state); 800-626-2203 (out-of-state). **Fax:** 814-732-2420. **E-mail:** carlin@edinboro.edu

Visit CollegeQuest.com for information on majors offered and athletics. Electronic viewbook available at CollegeQuest.com.

■ *See page 1616 for a narrative description.*

ELIZABETHTOWN COLLEGE
Elizabethtown, Pennsylvania

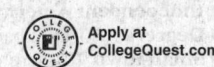

- **Independent**, 4-year, founded 1899, affiliated with Church of the Brethren
- **Degree** bachelor's
- **Small-town** 185-acre campus with easy access to Baltimore and Philadelphia
- **Coed**, 1,778 undergraduate students, 90% full-time, 65% women, 35% men
- **Moderately difficult** entrance level, 78% of applicants were admitted
- **12:1 student-to-undergraduate faculty ratio**
- **67.4% graduate** in 6 years or less
- **$18,220 tuition** and fees
- **$15,036 average financial aid** package, $15,644 average indebtedness upon graduation, $36.2 million endowment

The College, founded in 1899, emphasizes the importance of a strong liberal arts background combined with preprofessional study. A dedicated faculty and a 12:1 student-faculty ratio promote mentoring relationships among students and the faculty. The 19 academic departments collectively offer 40 majors and more than 50 minors and concentrations. The campus community is made up of 1,725 students from 29 states and 25 other countries. Elizabethtown College emphasizes personal attenton and experiential learning. Elizabethtown encourages all interested students to visit the campus.

Students *Undergraduates:* 1,598 full-time, 180 part-time. Students come from 26 states and territories, 25 other countries. *The most frequently chosen baccalaureate fields are:* business/marketing, education, health professions and related sciences.

From out-of-state	32%	Reside on campus	85%
Transferred in	2%		

Faculty 179 (58% full-time), 56% with terminal degrees.
Expenses (1999–2000) *Comprehensive fee:* $23,600 includes full-time tuition ($17,770), mandatory fees ($450), and room and board ($5380). *College room only:* $2680. Room and board charges vary according to board plan and housing facility. *Part-time tuition:* $480 per credit. *Part-time fees:* $40 per term part-time. Part-time tuition and fees vary according to class time, course load, and program. *Payment plan:* installment. *Waivers:* employees or children of employees.
Library High Library plus 1 other. *Operations spending 1999–2000:* $891,000. *Collection:* 141,357 titles, 1,108 serial subscriptions, 30,651 audio-visual materials.
College life *Housing:* on-campus residence required through senior year. *Options:* coed, men-only, women-only. *Most popular organizations:* Activities Planning Board, Student Senate, Residence Hall Association, student newspaper, Habitat for Humanity.

Pennsylvania

Campus security 24-hour emergency response devices and patrols, student patrols, late-night transport-escort service, self-defense workshops, crime prevention program.

After graduation 33 organizations recruited on campus 1997–98. *Career center:* 3 full-time, 1 part-time personnel. Services include job fairs, resume preparation, interview workshops, career/interest testing, career counseling, careers library, job interviews, graduate school fairs. *Graduate education:* 28% of class of 1999 went directly to graduate and professional school.

Freshmen 2,219 applied, 1,724 admitted, 504 enrolled. 8 class presidents, 9 valedictorians, 15 student government officers.

SAT verbal scores above 500	81%	SAT math scores above 500	77%
ACT above 18	81%	From top 10% of their h.s. class	29%
From top quarter	62%	From top half	90%
1998 freshmen returning in 1999	84%		

Application *Options:* eApply at www.CollegeQuest.com, Common Application, electronic application, early admission, deferred entrance. *Application fee:* $20. *Required:* essay or personal statement; high school transcript; minimum 2.0 GPA; 2 letters of recommendation. *Required for some:* interview. *Recommended:* minimum 3.0 GPA; interview.

Standardized tests *Admission: Required:* SAT I or ACT.

Significant dates *Application deadlines:* rolling (freshmen), rolling (transfers). *Financial aid deadline priority date:* 3/15.

Freshman Application Contact
W. Kent Barnds, Director of Admissions, Elizabethtown College, 1 Alpha Drive, Elizabethtown, PA 17022-2298. **Phone:** 717-361-1400. **E-mail:** admissions@acad.etown.edu

Visit CollegeQuest.com for information on majors offered and athletics.

■ *See page 1620 for a narrative description.*

FRANKLIN AND MARSHALL COLLEGE
Lancaster, Pennsylvania

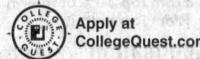

- **Independent**, 4-year, founded 1787
- **Degree** bachelor's
- **Suburban** 125-acre campus with easy access to Philadelphia
- **Coed**, 1,837 undergraduate students, 99% full-time, 50% women, 50% men
- **Very difficult** entrance level, 50% of applicants were admitted
- **11:1 student-to-undergraduate faculty ratio**
- **79% graduate** in 6 years or less
- **$23,720 tuition** and fees
- **$17,860 average financial aid** package, $15,982 average indebtedness upon graduation, $295.3 million endowment

Students *Undergraduates:* 1,831 full-time, 6 part-time. Students come from 39 states and territories, 46 other countries. *The most frequently chosen baccalaureate fields are:* business/marketing, English, social sciences and history.

From out-of-state	59%	Reside on campus	68%
Age 25 or older	1%	Transferred in	1%
International students	6%	African Americans	3%
Asian Americans/Pacific Islanders	4%	Hispanic Americans	3%
Native Americans	0.2%		

Faculty 186 (87% full-time), 87% with terminal degrees.

Expenses (1999–2000) *Comprehensive fee:* $29,450 includes full-time tuition ($23,720) and room and board ($5730). *College room only:* $3686. Full-time tuition and fees vary according to reciprocity agreements. Room and board charges vary according to board plan and housing facility. *Part-time tuition:* $2965 per course. Part-time tuition and fees vary according to course load. *Payment plan:* installment. *Waivers:* employees or children of employees.

Library Shadek-Fackenthal Library plus 1 other. *Operations spending 1999–2000:* $2.2 million. *Collection:* 311,928 titles, 1,596 serial subscriptions, 10,473 audiovisual materials.

College life *Housing:* on-campus residence required through sophomore year. *Options:* coed, men-only, women-only, disabled students. *Most popular organizations:* Women's Center, campus radio station, College Reporter, Ben's Underground, ice hockey club.

Campus security 24-hour emergency response devices and patrols, late-night transport-escort service, controlled dormitory access, residence hall security, campus security connected to city police and fire company.

After graduation 64 organizations recruited on campus 1997–98. 62% of class of 1998 had job offers within 6 months. *Career center:* 4 full-time personnel. Services include job fairs, resume preparation, interview workshops, resume referral, career/interest testing, career counseling, careers library, job bank, job interviews, alumni database.

Freshmen 3,927 applied, 1,956 admitted, 516 enrolled. 6 National Merit Scholars, 21 valedictorians, 123 student government officers.

SAT verbal scores above 500	95%	SAT math scores above 500	99%
ACT above 18	N/R	From top 10% of their h.s. class	64%
From top quarter	88%	From top half	98%
1998 freshmen returning in 1999	96%		

Application *Options:* eApply at www.CollegeQuest.com, Common Application, early admission, early decision, deferred entrance. *Application fee:* $50. *Required:* essay or personal statement; high school transcript; 2 letters of recommendation. *Recommended:* interview.

Standardized tests *Admission: Required for some:* SAT I or ACT.

Significant dates *Application deadlines:* 2/1 (freshmen), 5/15 (transfers). *Early decision:* 11/15 (for plan 1), 1/15 (for plan 2). *Notification:* 4/1 (freshmen), 12/15 (early decision plan 1), 2/15 (early decision plan 2). *Financial aid deadline:* 2/1.

Freshman Application Contact
Gregory Goldsmith, Director of Admissions, Franklin and Marshall College, PO Box 3003, Lancaster, PA 17604-3003. **Phone:** 717-291-3953. **Fax:** 717-291-4389. **E-mail:** admission@fandm.edu

Visit CollegeQuest.com for information on majors offered and athletics.

GANNON UNIVERSITY
Erie, Pennsylvania

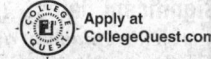

- **Independent Roman Catholic**, comprehensive, founded 1925
- **Degrees** associate, bachelor's, master's, and doctoral
- **Urban** 13-acre campus with easy access to Cleveland
- **Coed**, 2,466 undergraduate students, 86% full-time, 59% women, 41% men
- **Moderately difficult** entrance level, 91% of applicants were admitted
- **11:1 student-to-undergraduate faculty ratio**
- **66.1% graduate** in 6 years or less
- **$13,408 tuition** and fees
- **$11,950 average financial aid** package, $19,005 average indebtedness upon graduation, $27.8 million endowment

At Gannon, students can custom-tailor their education to meet their specific personal, educational, and professional goals for the new millennium. Students can enrich their education with co-ops and internships, honors courses, service learning projects, and campus ministry. At Gannon, students find "the Right Place"—personally, academically, professionally, socially, and spiritually.

Students *Undergraduates:* 2,123 full-time, 343 part-time. Students come from 25 states and territories, 20 other countries. *The most frequently chosen baccalaureate fields are:* business/marketing, education, health professions and related sciences. *Graduate:* 802 in graduate degree programs.

From out-of-state	22%	Reside on campus	38%
Age 25 or older	25%	Transferred in	2%
International students	3%	African Americans	3%
Asian Americans/Pacific Islanders	1%	Hispanic Americans	1%
Native Americans	0.3%		

Faculty 277 (60% full-time), 36% with terminal degrees.

Expenses (1999–2000) *Comprehensive fee:* $18,848 includes full-time tuition ($13,020), mandatory fees ($388), and room and board ($5440). *College room only:* $3020. Full-time tuition and fees vary according to class time and program. Room and board charges vary according to housing facility. *Part-time tuition:* $405 per credit. *Part-time fees:* $12 per credit. Part-time tuition and fees vary according to class time and program. *Payment plan:* installment. *Waivers:* senior citizens and employees or children of employees.

Library Nash Library plus 1 other. *Operations spending 1999–2000:* $1.1 million. *Collection:* 238,681 titles, 962 serial subscriptions, 1,445 audiovisual materials.

Pennsylvania

Gannon University (continued)

College life *Housing:* on-campus residence required through sophomore year. *Option:* coed. *Social organizations:* national fraternities, national sororities; 17% of eligible men and 15% of eligible women are members. *Most popular organizations:* Model United Nations, Vitality Through Exercise, Gannon University Residence Union, Interfraternity Council, Panhellenic Council.

Campus security 24-hour emergency response devices and patrols, student patrols, late-night transport-escort service, controlled dormitory access, security cameras.

After graduation 68 organizations recruited on campus 1997–98. 70% of class of 1998 had job offers within 6 months. *Career center:* 5 full-time personnel. Services include job fairs, resume preparation, interview workshops, resume referral, career/interest testing, career counseling, careers library, job bank, job interviews. *Graduate education:* 22% of class of 1999 went directly to graduate and professional school: 9% graduate arts and sciences, 4% business, 3% engineering, 3% medicine, 2% law, 1% veterinary medicine.

Freshmen 1,587 applied, 1,437 admitted, 520 enrolled.

Average high school GPA	3.18	SAT verbal scores above 500	64%
SAT math scores above 500	59%	ACT above 18	88%
From top 10% of their h.s. class	21%	From top quarter	51%
From top half	79%		

Application *Options:* eApply at www.CollegeQuest.com, Common Application, electronic application, early admission, deferred entrance. *Application fee:* $25. *Required:* high school transcript; minimum 2.0 GPA; counselor's recommendation. *Required for some:* minimum 3.0 GPA; 3 letters of recommendation; interview. *Recommended:* essay or personal statement.

Standardized tests *Admission: Required:* SAT I or ACT.

Significant dates *Application deadlines:* rolling (freshmen), rolling (transfers). *Financial aid deadline priority date:* 3/15.

Freshman Application Contact

Ms. Beth Nemenz, Director of Admissions, Gannon University, University Square, Erie, PA 16541. **Phone:** 814-871-7240. **Toll-free phone:** 800-GANNONU. **Fax:** 814-871-5803. **E-mail:** admissions@gannon.edu

Visit CollegeQuest.com for information on majors offered and athletics.

■ *See page 1702 for a narrative description.*

GENEVA COLLEGE
Beaver Falls, Pennsylvania

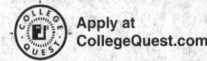
Apply at CollegeQuest.com

- **Independent**, comprehensive, founded 1848, affiliated with Reformed Presbyterian Church of North America
- **Degrees** associate, bachelor's, and master's
- **Small-town** 55-acre campus with easy access to Pittsburgh
- **Coed**, 1,877 undergraduate students, 86% full-time, 54% women, 46% men
- **Moderately difficult** entrance level, 78% of applicants were admitted
- **18:1 student-to-undergraduate faculty ratio**
- **$12,650 tuition** and fees
- **$9000 average financial aid** package, $20,000 average indebtedness upon graduation, $31.7 million endowment

Geneva College is a Christian coeducational liberal arts college whose purpose is to develop servant-leaders. Geneva offers more than 30 undergraduate majors. Innovative offerings include Master of Arts degree programs in professional psychology, higher education, and business; a Master of Science degree in organizational leadership; and an accelerated adult degree-completion program in which students who qualify can transfer 2 years of credit and can earn a bachelor's degree in only 15 months. Cultural diversity in the student body, faculty, and staff is a priority; applications from members of minority groups are especially sought.

Students *Undergraduates:* 1,608 full-time, 269 part-time. Students come from 37 states and territories, 25 other countries. *The most frequently chosen baccalaureate fields are:* business/marketing, education, liberal arts/general studies. *Graduate:* 250 in graduate degree programs.

From out-of-state	23%	Reside on campus	74%
Age 25 or older	4%	Transferred in	5%
International students	3%	African Americans	13%
Asian Americans/Pacific Islanders	1%	Hispanic Americans	1%
Native Americans	0.3%		

Faculty 140 (53% full-time).

Expenses (1999–2000) *Comprehensive fee:* $17,602 includes full-time tuition ($12,350), mandatory fees ($300), and room and board ($4952). *College room only:* $2476. Full-time tuition and fees vary according to course load and reciprocity agreements. Room and board charges vary according to board plan. *Part-time tuition:* $390 per credit. *Part-time fees:* $50 per term part-time. Part-time tuition and fees vary according to course load and reciprocity agreements. *Payment plan:* installment. *Waivers:* employees or children of employees.

Library McCartney Library plus 5 others. *Operations spending 1999–2000:* $670,195. *Collection:* 160,891 titles, 890 serial subscriptions, 23,403 audiovisual materials.

College life *Housing:* on-campus residence required through senior year. *Options:* men-only, women-only. *Most popular organizations:* marching band, Genevans A Capella Choir, ministry groups, International Student Organization, discipleship.

Campus security 24-hour emergency response devices and patrols, late-night transport-escort service, controlled dormitory access.

After graduation 78 organizations recruited on campus 1997–98. 74% of class of 1998 had job offers within 6 months. *Career center:* 2 full-time, 1 part-time personnel. Services include job fairs, resume preparation, interview workshops, resume referral, career/interest testing, career counseling, careers library, job bank, job interviews. *Graduate education:* 17% of class of 1999 went directly to graduate and professional school: 6% graduate arts and sciences, 4% medicine, 3% education, 2% theology, 1% business.

Freshmen 1,027 applied, 803 admitted, 348 enrolled.

Average high school GPA	3.2	SAT verbal scores above 500	76%
SAT math scores above 500	73%	ACT above 18	99%
From top 10% of their h.s. class	15%	From top quarter	44%
From top half	68%	1998 freshmen returning in 1999	80%

Application *Options:* eApply at www.CollegeQuest.com, Common Application, electronic application, early admission, deferred entrance. *Application fee:* $25. *Required:* essay or personal statement; high school transcript; minimum 2.0 GPA; letters of recommendation. *Required for some:* interview. *Recommended:* minimum 3.0 GPA; interview.

Standardized tests *Admission: Required:* SAT I or ACT.

Significant dates *Application deadlines:* rolling (freshmen), rolling (transfers). *Financial aid deadline priority date:* 4/15.

Freshman Application Contact

Mr. David Layton, Director of Admissions, Geneva College, 3200 College Avenue, Beaver Falls, PA 15010-3599. **Phone:** 724-847-6500. **Toll-free phone:** 800-847-8255. **Fax:** 724-847-6687. **E-mail:** admissions@geneva.edu

Visit CollegeQuest.com for information on majors offered and athletics. College video available at CollegeQuest.com.

■ *See page 1706 for a narrative description.*

GETTYSBURG COLLEGE
Gettysburg, Pennsylvania

Apply at CollegeQuest.com

- **Independent**, 4-year, founded 1832, affiliated with Evangelical Lutheran Church in America
- **Degree** bachelor's
- **Small-town** 200-acre campus with easy access to Baltimore and Washington, DC
- **Coed**, 2,156 undergraduate students, 99% full-time, 51% women, 49% men
- **Very difficult** entrance level, 68% of applicants were admitted
- **11:1 student-to-undergraduate faculty ratio**
- **78.45% graduate** in 6 years or less
- **$24,032 tuition** and fees
- **$19,800 average financial aid** package, $13,900 average indebtedness upon graduation, $115.9 million endowment

Students *Undergraduates:* 2,146 full-time, 10 part-time. Students come from 40 states and territories, 25 other countries. *The most frequently chosen*

Pennsylvania

baccalaureate fields are: business/marketing, biological/life sciences, social sciences and history.

From out-of-state	29%	Reside on campus	90%
Transferred in	1%	International students	2%
African Americans	1%	Asian Americans/Pacific Islanders	1%
Hispanic Americans	1%	Native Americans	0.2%

Faculty 228 (71% full-time).
Expenses (1999–2000) *Comprehensive fee:* $29,676 includes full-time tuition ($23,922), mandatory fees ($110), and room and board ($5644). *College room only:* $3012. Room and board charges vary according to board plan and housing facility. *Part-time tuition:* $2658 per course. *Payment plan:* installment.
Library Mussleman Library plus 2 others. *Collection:* 326,328 titles, 1,414 serial subscriptions.
College life *Housing:* on-campus residence required in freshman year. *Options:* coed, women-only. *Social organizations:* national fraternities, national sororities; 42% of eligible men and 38% of eligible women are members.
Campus security 24-hour emergency response devices and patrols, late-night transport-escort service, controlled dormitory access.
After graduation 51 organizations recruited on campus 1997–98. 64% of class of 1998 had job offers within 6 months. *Career center:* 4 full-time, 3 part-time personnel. Services include job fairs, resume preparation, interview workshops, resume referral, career/interest testing, career counseling, careers library, job bank, job interviews. *Major awards:* 1 Fulbright Scholar.
Freshmen 3,871 applied, 2,624 admitted, 689 enrolled.

Average high school GPA	3.5	SAT verbal scores above 500	94%
SAT math scores above 500	95%	ACT above 18	N/R
1998 freshmen returning in 1999	87%		

Application *Options:* eApply at www.CollegeQuest.com, Common Application, electronic application, early admission, early decision, deferred entrance. *Application fee:* $45. *Required:* essay or personal statement; high school transcript; minimum 2.0 GPA; 1 letter of recommendation. *Recommended:* minimum 3.0 GPA; interview.
Standardized tests *Admission: Required:* SAT I or ACT.
Significant dates *Application deadline:* 2/15 (transfers). *Early decision:* 2/1. *Notification:* 4/1 (freshmen), 2/21 (early decision). *Financial aid deadline:* 3/15. *Priority date:* 2/15.
Freshman Application Contact
Ms. Gail Sweezey, Director of Admissions, Gettysburg College, Gettysburg, PA 17325-1483. **Phone:** 717-337-6100. **Toll-free phone:** 800-431-0803. **Fax:** 717-337-6008. **E-mail:** admiss@gettysburg.edu
Visit CollegeQuest.com for information on majors offered and athletics. College video and electronic viewbook available at CollegeQuest.com.

GRATZ COLLEGE
Melrose Park, Pennsylvania

- **Independent Jewish**, comprehensive, founded 1895
- **Degrees** bachelor's and master's
- **Suburban** 28-acre campus with easy access to Philadelphia
- **Coed**, 17 undergraduate students
- **Noncompetitive** entrance level
- **12:1 student-to-undergraduate faculty ratio**
- **$7370 tuition** and fees

Students *Undergraduates:* Students come from 2 states and territories, 4 other countries. *The most frequently chosen baccalaureate field is:* philosophy.

From out-of-state	2%	Age 25 or older	89%

Faculty 13 (62% full-time), 100% with terminal degrees.
Expenses (2000–2001) *Tuition:* full-time $7270. *Required fees:* full-time $100. Part-time tuition and fees vary according to course load. *Payment plan:* installment. *Waivers:* employees or children of employees.
Library Tuttleman Library. *Collection:* 100,000 titles, 145 serial subscriptions.
College life *Housing:* college housing not available.
Campus security 24-hour patrols.

After graduation *Career center:* Services include job fairs.
Freshmen

SAT verbal scores above 500	N/R	SAT math scores above 500	N/R
ACT above 18	N/R		

Application *Options:* early admission, deferred entrance. *Application fee:* $50. *Required:* essay or personal statement; high school transcript. *Required for some:* interview.
Significant dates *Application deadlines:* rolling (freshmen), rolling (transfers).
Freshman Application Contact
Ms. Adena E. Johnston, Director of Admissions, Gratz College, 7605 Old York Road, Melrose Park, PA 19027. **Phone:** 215-635-7300 Ext. 140. **Toll-free phone:** 800-475-4635 Ext. 140. **Fax:** 215-635-7320. **E-mail:** admissions@gratz.edu
Visit CollegeQuest.com for information on majors offered and athletics. College video available at CollegeQuest.com.

GROVE CITY COLLEGE
Grove City, Pennsylvania

Apply at CollegeQuest.com

- **Independent Presbyterian**, comprehensive, founded 1876
- **Degrees** bachelor's and master's
- **Small-town** 150-acre campus with easy access to Pittsburgh
- **Coed**, 2,313 undergraduate students, 99% full-time, 49% women, 51% men
- **Very difficult** entrance level, 44% of applicants were admitted
- **20:1 student-to-undergraduate faculty ratio**
- **76% graduate** in 6 years or less
- **$7506 tuition** and fees

Grove City College has won national acclaim for strong academics, Christian values, and sensible prices. Its humanities and social sciences emphasize classic books and great thinkers proved across the ages to be of value in the quest for knowledge; its excellent professional studies include electrical and mechanical engineering programs, which are accredited by the engineering accreditation commission of the Accreditation Board for Engineering and Technology, Inc. Included in its cost of education, the Grove City College Information Technology Initiative distributes color notebook computers and printers to every freshman.

Students *Undergraduates:* 2,283 full-time, 30 part-time. Students come from 46 states and territories, 11 other countries. *The most frequently chosen baccalaureate fields are:* biological/life sciences, business/marketing, education. *Graduate:* 11 in graduate degree programs.

From out-of-state	44%	Reside on campus	91%
Age 25 or older	1%	Transferred in	1%
International students	1%	African Americans	0.4%
Asian Americans/Pacific Islanders	1%	Hispanic Americans	0.2%

Faculty 153 (74% full-time), 58% with terminal degrees.
Expenses (1999–2000) *Comprehensive fee:* $11,554 includes full-time tuition ($7506) and room and board ($4048). Full-time tuition and fees vary according to course load and program. *Part-time tuition:* $240 per credit hour. *Waivers:* employees or children of employees.
Library Henry Buhl Library. *Collection:* 158,000 titles.
College life *Housing:* on-campus residence required through senior year. *Options:* men-only, women-only. *Social organizations:* local fraternities, local sororities; 9% of eligible men and 19% of eligible women are members. *Most popular organizations:* Salt Company, Warriors for Christ, Orientation Board, Orchesis, Touring Choir.
Campus security 24-hour emergency response devices and patrols, student patrols, late-night transport-escort service, controlled dormitory access, monitored women's residence hall entrances.
After graduation 120 organizations recruited on campus 1997–98. 92% of class of 1998 had job offers within 6 months. *Career center:* 3 full-time personnel. Services include job fairs, resume preparation, interview workshops, resume referral, career/interest testing, career counseling, careers library, job bank, job interviews. *Graduate education:* 18% of class of 1999 went directly to graduate and professional school: 11% graduate arts and sciences, 2% education, 2% medicine, 1% business, 1% engineering, 1% law.

Pennsylvania

Grove City College (continued)

Freshmen 2,163 applied, 957 admitted, 587 enrolled. 13 National Merit Scholars, 76 valedictorians.

Average high school GPA	3.7	SAT verbal scores above 500	96%
SAT math scores above 500	95%	ACT above 18	100%
From top 10% of their h.s. class	59%	From top quarter	88%
From top half	97%	1998 freshmen returning in 1999	91%

Application *Options:* eApply at www.CollegeQuest.com, electronic application, early admission, early decision, deferred entrance. *Application fee:* $30. *Required:* essay or personal statement; high school transcript; 2 letters of recommendation. *Recommended:* interview.

Standardized tests *Admission: Required:* SAT I or ACT.

Significant dates *Application deadlines:* 2/15 (freshmen), rolling (transfers). *Early decision:* 11/15. *Notification:* 3/15 (freshmen), 12/15 (early decision). *Financial aid deadline:* 4/15.

Freshman Application Contact
Mr. Jeffrey C. Mincey, Director of Admissions, Grove City College, 100 Campus Drive, Grove City, PA 16127-2104. **Phone:** 724-458-2100. **Fax:** 724-458-3395. **E-mail:** admissions@gcc.edu

Visit CollegeQuest.com for information on majors offered and athletics. Electronic viewbook available at CollegeQuest.com.

■ *See page 1746 for a narrative description.*

GWYNEDD-MERCY COLLEGE
Gwynedd Valley, Pennsylvania

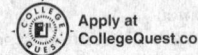 Apply at CollegeQuest.com

- **Independent Roman Catholic**, comprehensive, founded 1948
- **Degrees** associate, bachelor's, master's, post-master's, and postbachelor's certificates
- **Suburban** 170-acre campus with easy access to Philadelphia
- **Coed**, 1,281 undergraduate students, 56% full-time, 79% women, 21% men
- **Moderately difficult** entrance level, 36% of applicants were admitted
- **15:1 student-to-undergraduate faculty ratio**
- **80% graduate** in 6 years or less
- **$13,540 tuition** and fees
- **$12,720 average financial aid** package, $14,282 average indebtedness upon graduation, $5.7 million endowment

Gwynedd-Mercy combines strong academic programs with extensive opportunities for students to gain practical experience through internships, co-ops, and clinicals. With pass rates on national examinations of more than 95%, students are prepared to enter the workforce of the 21st century. The College has affiliations with more than 200 health-care organizations, businesses, and school districts.

Students *Undergraduates:* 715 full-time, 566 part-time. Students come from 4 states and territories. *The most frequently chosen baccalaureate fields are:* education, business/marketing, health professions and related sciences. *Graduate:* 291 in graduate degree programs.

From out-of-state	4%	Reside on campus	14%
Age 25 or older	56%	Transferred in	17%

Faculty 182 (41% full-time), 34% with terminal degrees.

Expenses (1999–2000) *Comprehensive fee:* $20,040 includes full-time tuition ($13,500), mandatory fees ($40), and room and board ($6500). Full-time tuition and fees vary according to program. Room and board charges vary according to board plan. *Part-time tuition:* $290 per credit. *Part-time fees:* $2 per credit; $25 per term part-time. Part-time tuition and fees vary according to program. *Payment plan:* installment. *Waivers:* employees or children of employees.

Library Lourdes Library plus 1 other. *Operations spending 1999–2000:* $429,000. *Collection:* 83,953 titles, 825 serial subscriptions, 52,722 audiovisual materials.

College life *Housing: Option:* coed. *Most popular organizations:* Voices of Gwynedd, Athletic Association, student government, Program Board, Peer Mentors.

Campus security 24-hour emergency response devices and patrols, late-night transport-escort service.

After graduation *Career center:* 1 full-time personnel. Services include job fairs, resume preparation, career counseling, careers library, job bank.

Freshmen 446 applied, 160 admitted, 152 enrolled.

SAT verbal scores above 500	38%	SAT math scores above 500	36%
ACT above 18	N/R	From top 10% of their h.s. class	7%
From top quarter	31%	From top half	67%
1998 freshmen returning in 1999	81%		

Application *Options:* eApply at www.CollegeQuest.com, Common Application, electronic application, early admission, deferred entrance. *Application fee:* $25. *Required:* high school transcript; 1 letter of recommendation. *Required for some:* interview. *Recommended:* interview.

Standardized tests *Admission: Required:* SAT I or ACT.

Significant dates *Application deadlines:* rolling (freshmen), 8/1 (transfers). *Financial aid deadline priority date:* 3/15.

Freshman Application Contact
Mr. Dennis Murphy, Vice President of Enrollment Management, Gwynedd-Mercy College, Sumneytown Pike, Gwynedd Valley, PA 19437-0901. **Phone:** 215-646-7300. **Toll-free phone:** 800-DIAL-GMC. **Fax:** 215-641-5556.

Visit CollegeQuest.com for information on majors offered and athletics.

■ *See page 1752 for a narrative description.*

HAVERFORD COLLEGE
Haverford, Pennsylvania

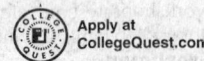 Apply at CollegeQuest.com

- **Independent**, 4-year, founded 1833
- **Degree** bachelor's
- **Suburban** 200-acre campus with easy access to Philadelphia
- **Coed**, 1,118 undergraduate students, 100% full-time, 53% women, 47% men
- **Most difficult** entrance level, 33% of applicants were admitted
- **9:1 student-to-undergraduate faculty ratio**
- **$23,780 tuition** and fees
- **$19,984 average financial aid** package, $13,821 average indebtedness upon graduation, $269.3 million endowment

Students *Undergraduates:* 1,118 full-time. Students come from 47 states and territories, 27 other countries. *The most frequently chosen baccalaureate fields are:* biological/life sciences, English, social sciences and history.

From out-of-state	80%	Reside on campus	98%
Transferred in	0.3%	International students	3%
African Americans	5%	Asian Americans/Pacific Islanders	9%
Hispanic Americans	5%	Native Americans	0.2%

Faculty 118 (86% full-time), 92% with terminal degrees.

Expenses (1999–2000) *Comprehensive fee:* $31,400 includes full-time tuition ($23,556), mandatory fees ($224), and room and board ($7620). *College room only:* $4210. Room and board charges vary according to board plan. *Payment plan:* installment. *Waivers:* employees or children of employees.

Library Magill Library plus 5 others. *Operations spending 1999–2000:* $2.5 million. *Collection:* 386,891 titles; 2,715 serial subscriptions, 9,747 audiovisual materials.

College life *Housing:* on-campus residence required in freshman year. *Options:* coed, men-only, women-only, disabled students. *Most popular organizations:* volunteer programs, student government, choral groups, multicultural groups, orientation team/residential life leaders.

Campus security 24-hour emergency response devices and patrols, late-night transport-escort service.

After graduation 119 organizations recruited on campus 1997–98. 67% of class of 1998 had job offers within 6 months. *Career center:* 5 full-time personnel. Services include job fairs, resume preparation, interview workshops, resume referral, career/interest testing, career counseling, careers library, job bank, job interviews. *Graduate education:* 19% of class of 1999 went directly to graduate and professional school: 8% graduate arts and sciences, 6% medicine, 5% law. *Major awards:* 1 Fulbright Scholar.

Freshmen 2,650 applied, 862 admitted, 302 enrolled.

SAT verbal scores above 500	97%	SAT math scores above 500	97%
ACT above 18	N/R	From top 10% of their h.s. class	76%
From top quarter	95%	From top half	100%
1998 freshmen returning in 1999	95%		

Pennsylvania

Application *Options:* eApply at www.CollegeQuest.com, Common Application, electronic application, early admission, early decision, deferred entrance. *Preference* given to children of alumni. *Application fee:* $50. *Required:* essay or personal statement; high school transcript; 2 letters of recommendation. *Recommended:* interview.
Standardized tests *Admission: Required:* SAT I or ACT, SAT II Subject Tests, SAT II: Writing Test.
Significant dates *Application deadlines:* 1/15 (freshmen), 3/31 (transfers). *Early decision:* 11/15. *Notification:* continuous until 4/15 (freshmen), 12/15 (early decision). *Financial aid deadline:* 1/31.
Freshman Application Contact
Ms. Delsie Z. Phillips, Director of Admissions, Haverford College, 370 Lancaster Avenue, Haverford, PA 19041-1392. **Phone:** 610-896-1350. **Fax:** 610-896-1338. **E-mail:** admitme@haverford.edu
Visit CollegeQuest.com for information on majors offered and athletics.

■ *See page 1776 for a narrative description.*

HOLY FAMILY COLLEGE
Philadelphia, Pennsylvania

- **Independent Roman Catholic**, comprehensive, founded 1954
- **Degrees** associate, bachelor's, master's, and postbachelor's certificates
- **Suburban** 47-acre campus
- **Coed**, 1,927 undergraduate students, 55% full-time, 76% women, 24% men
- **Moderately difficult** entrance level, 73% of applicants were admitted
- **10:1 student-to-undergraduate faculty ratio**
- **75% graduate** in 6 years or less
- **$11,860 tuition** and fees
- **$8632 average financial aid** package, $17,125 average indebtedness upon graduation, $6.6 million endowment

Students *Undergraduates:* 1,058 full-time, 869 part-time. Students come from 4 states and territories, 12 other countries. *The most frequently chosen baccalaureate fields are:* education, business/marketing, health professions and related sciences. *Graduate:* 663 in graduate degree programs.

From out-of-state	8%	Age 25 or older	12%
Transferred in	7%	International students	1%
African Americans	3%	Asian Americans/Pacific Islanders	2%
Hispanic Americans	2%	Native Americans	0.3%

Faculty 234 (34% full-time), 49% with terminal degrees.
Expenses (1999–2000) *Tuition:* full-time $11,500; part-time $260 per credit. *Required fees:* full-time $360; $50 per term part-time. Full-time tuition and fees vary according to course load and program. Part-time tuition and fees vary according to program. *Payment plans:* installment, deferred payment. *Waivers:* employees or children of employees.
Library Holy Family College Library plus 1 other. *Operations spending 1999–2000:* $610,524. *Collection:* 115,000 titles, 840 serial subscriptions, 1,556 audiovisual materials.
College life *Housing:* college housing not available. *Most popular organizations:* Students at your Service (S.A.Y.S.), Rainbow Connections, Campus Ministry Team, Folio, Tri-lite.
Campus security 24-hour emergency response devices and patrols, student patrols, late-night transport-escort service.
After graduation 107 organizations recruited on campus 1997–98. 90% of class of 1998 had job offers within 6 months. *Career center:* 3 full-time personnel. Services include job fairs, resume preparation, interview workshops, resume referral, career/interest testing, career counseling, careers library, job bank, job interviews, job search workshop. *Graduate education:* 14% of class of 1999 went directly to graduate and professional school.
Freshmen 244 applied, 179 admitted, 248 enrolled.

Average high school GPA	2.76	SAT verbal scores above 500	31%
SAT math scores above 500	19%	ACT above 18	N/R
From top 10% of their h.s. class	9%	From top quarter	33%
From top half	68%	1998 freshmen returning in 1999	81%

Application *Options:* Common Application, deferred entrance. *Application fee:* $25. *Required:* essay or personal statement; high school transcript; 1 letter of recommendation. *Recommended:* interview.
Standardized tests *Admission: Required:* SAT I or ACT.

Significant dates *Application deadlines:* rolling (freshmen), rolling (transfers). *Financial aid deadline priority date:* 2/1.
Freshman Application Contact
Mrs. Roberta Nolan, Director of Admissions, Holy Family College, Grant and Frankford Avenues, Philadelphia, PA 19114-2094. **Phone:** 215-637-3050. **Toll-free phone:** 800-637-1191. **Fax:** 215-281-1022. **E-mail:** rnolan@hfc.edu
Visit CollegeQuest.com for information on majors offered and athletics.

IMMACULATA COLLEGE
Immaculata, Pennsylvania

 Apply at CollegeQuest.com

- **Independent Roman Catholic**, comprehensive, founded 1920
- **Degrees** associate, bachelor's, master's, and doctoral
- **Suburban** 400-acre campus with easy access to Philadelphia
- **Women** only, 2,078 undergraduate students, 63% full-time
- **Moderately difficult** entrance level, 83% of applicants were admitted
- **14:1 student-to-undergraduate faculty ratio**
- **61% graduate** in 6 years or less
- **$13,400 tuition** and fees
- **$13,689 average financial aid** package, $17,125 average indebtedness upon graduation, $9.8 million endowment

Immaculata College, The University Within a College™, is a Catholic, comprehensive, liberal arts college dedicated to educating women of all faiths. Founded in 1920, Immaculata has grown to more than 3,000. Immaculata is composed of three areas: the Women's College, the College of Lifelong Learning, and the Graduate Division. Approximately 400 women attend the Women's College; 85% live in campus housing. The evening division includes graduate and undergraduate programs that are open to both men and women. The College is located 20 miles west of Philadelphia.

Students *Undergraduates:* 1,303 full-time, 775 part-time. Students come from 18 states and territories. *The most frequently chosen baccalaureate fields are:* business/marketing, home economics/vocational home economics, psychology. *Graduate:* 645 in graduate degree programs.

From out-of-state	13%	Reside on campus	78%
Age 25 or older	71%	Transferred in	1%

Faculty 247 (31% full-time), 49% with terminal degrees.
Expenses (1999–2000) *Comprehensive fee:* $19,900 includes full-time tuition ($13,100), mandatory fees ($300), and room and board ($6500). *College room only:* $3450. *Part-time tuition:* $255 per credit. *Payment plan:* installment. *Waivers:* senior citizens and employees or children of employees.
Library Gabriele Library. *Operations spending 1999–2000:* $589,595. *Collection:* 1.1 million titles, 766 serial subscriptions, 1,749 audiovisual materials.
College life *Housing: Option:* women-only. *Most popular organizations:* Campus Ministry, Student Association, chorale, Honor Society, Cue and Curtain.
Campus security 24-hour emergency response devices and patrols, late-night transport-escort service, controlled dormitory access.
After graduation 78 organizations recruited on campus 1997–98. 70% of class of 1998 had job offers within 6 months. *Career center:* 2 full-time, 1 part-time personnel. Services include job fairs, resume preparation, interview workshops, resume referral, career counseling, careers library, job bank, job interviews. *Graduate education:* 18% of class of 1999 went directly to graduate and professional school: 6% business, 6% medicine, 4% graduate arts and sciences, 2% law.
Freshmen 479 applied, 399 admitted, 121 enrolled.

Average high school GPA	3.2	SAT verbal scores above 500	53%
SAT math scores above 500	29%	ACT above 18	N/R
From top 10% of their h.s. class	9%	From top quarter	32%
From top half	80%	1998 freshmen returning in 1999	72%

Application *Options:* eApply at www.CollegeQuest.com, early admission, deferred entrance. *Application fee:* $25. *Required:* high school transcript; minimum 2.0 GPA; 1 letter of recommendation. *Recommended:* essay or personal statement; minimum 3.0 GPA; interview.
Standardized tests *Admission: Required:* SAT I or ACT.
Significant dates *Application deadlines:* rolling (freshmen), 7/15 (transfers). *Notification:* continuous until 7/15 (freshmen). *Financial aid deadline:* continuous.

Pennsylvania

Immaculata College (continued)
Freshman Application Contact
Mr. Ken Rasp, Dean of Enrollment Management, Immaculata College, 1145 King Road, Immaculata, PA 19345-0500. **Phone:** 610-647-4400 Ext. 3015. **Toll-free phone:** 877-428-6328. **Fax:** 610-251-1668. **E-mail:** admiss@immaculata.edu
Visit CollegeQuest.com for information on majors offered and athletics. College video available at CollegeQuest.com.

■ *See page 1820 for a narrative description.*

INDIANA UNIVERSITY OF PENNSYLVANIA
Indiana, Pennsylvania

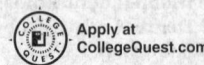

- **State-supported**, university, founded 1875
- **Degrees** associate, bachelor's, master's, and doctoral
- **Small-town** 350-acre campus with easy access to Pittsburgh
- **Coed**, 11,502 undergraduate students, 95% full-time, 56% women, 44% men
- **Moderately difficult** entrance level, 65% of applicants were admitted
- **18:1 student-to-undergraduate faculty ratio**
- **57.4% graduate** in 6 years or less
- **$4397 tuition** and fees (in-state); $9825 (out-of-state)
- **$6483 average financial aid** package, $10,000 average indebtedness upon graduation, $22.4 million endowment

IUP has one of the largest student internship programs in Pennsylvania. More than 50% of its students participate in experiential and cooperative education and student teaching programs prior to graduation. Many graduates are offered a selection of positions by the companies that sponsor their internships. Employers are becoming more interested in graduates who have completed a supervised experience.

Part of Pennsylvania State System of Higher Education.
Students *Undergraduates:* 10,955 full-time, 547 part-time. Students come from 47 states and territories, 80 other countries. *The most frequently chosen baccalaureate fields are:* business/marketing, education, social sciences and history. *Graduate:* 1,550 in graduate degree programs.

From out-of-state	4%	Reside on campus	30%
Age 25 or older	9%	Transferred in	5%
International students	1%	African Americans	6%
Asian Americans/Pacific Islanders	1%	Hispanic Americans	1%
Native Americans	0.1%		

Faculty 803 (89% full-time).
Expenses (1999–2000) *Tuition, state resident:* full-time $3618; part-time $150 per semester hour. *Tuition, nonresident:* full-time $9046; part-time $377 per semester hour. *Required fees:* full-time $779; $186 per term part-time. Full-time tuition and fees vary according to course load and location. Part-time tuition and fees vary according to course load and location. *College room and board:* $3782; room only: $2100. Room and board charges vary according to board plan and housing facility. *Payment plans:* installment, deferred payment. *Waivers:* minority students and employees or children of employees.
Library Stapleton Library. *Operations spending 1999–2000:* $4 million. *Collection:* 835,378 titles, 3,950 serial subscriptions, 198,391 audiovisual materials.
College life *Housing:* on-campus residence required in freshman year. *Option:* coed. *Social organizations:* national fraternities, national sororities; 10% of eligible men and 11% of eligible women are members. *Most popular organizations:* NAACP, Interfraternity Council, Panhellenic Association, Student Congress, Alpha Phi Omega.
Campus security 24-hour emergency response devices and patrols, late-night transport-escort service, controlled dormitory access.
After graduation 109 organizations recruited on campus 1997–98. 76% of class of 1998 had job offers within 6 months. *Career center:* 4 full-time, 12 part-time personnel. Services include job fairs, resume preparation, resume referral, career counseling, careers library, job interviews. *Graduate education:* 15% of class of 1999 went directly to graduate and professional school: 11% graduate arts and sciences, 3% education, 1% business, 1% medicine, 0.4% law.

Freshmen 7,799 applied, 5,044 admitted, 2,575 enrolled. 10 valedictorians.

SAT verbal scores above 500	70%	SAT math scores above 500	62%
ACT above 18	N/R	From top 10% of their h.s. class	22%
From top quarter	50%	From top half	83%
1998 freshmen returning in 1999	75%		

Application *Options:* eApply at www.CollegeQuest.com, Common Application, electronic application, early admission, early action, deferred entrance. *Application fee:* $30. *Required:* high school transcript; letters of recommendation.
Standardized tests *Admission: Required:* SAT I or ACT.
Significant dates *Application deadlines:* rolling (freshmen), rolling (transfers). *Early action:* 10/15. *Notification:* 1/31 (freshmen), 11/30 (early action). *Financial aid deadline:* 4/15.
Freshman Application Contact
Mr. William Nunn, Dean of Admissions, Indiana University of Pennsylvania, 216 Pratt Hall, Indiana, PA 15705. **Phone:** 724-357-2230. **Toll-free phone:** 800-442-6830. **Fax:** 724-357-2685. **E-mail:** admissions_inquiry@grove.iup.edu
Visit CollegeQuest.com for information on majors offered and athletics. College video and electronic viewbook available at CollegeQuest.com.

■ *See page 1824 for a narrative description.*

JUNIATA COLLEGE
Huntingdon, Pennsylvania

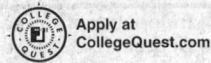

- **Independent**, 4-year, founded 1876, affiliated with Church of the Brethren
- **Degree** bachelor's
- **Small-town** 110-acre campus
- **Coed**, 1,200 undergraduate students, 99% full-time, 56% women, 44% men
- **Moderately difficult** entrance level, 85% of applicants were admitted
- **13:1 student-to-undergraduate faculty ratio**
- **69% graduate** in 6 years or less
- **$19,360 tuition** and fees
- **$16,697 average financial aid** package, $16,395 average indebtedness upon graduation, $72.4 million endowment

Students who welcome academic challenges and are ready to discover who they are and what they are capable of should consider Juniata College. The College's traditions include excellence in academics, small classes, a close-knit community, and many surprises, like Mountain Day.

Students *Undergraduates:* 1,194 full-time, 6 part-time. Students come from 32 states and territories, 21 other countries. *The most frequently chosen baccalaureate fields are:* biological/life sciences, education, social sciences and history.

From out-of-state	24%	Reside on campus	88%
Age 25 or older	4%	Transferred in	2%
International students	3%	African Americans	1%
Asian Americans/Pacific Islanders	1%	Hispanic Americans	1%
Native Americans	0.2%		

Faculty 109 (79% full-time), 72% with terminal degrees.
Expenses (2000–2001) *Comprehensive fee:* $24,650 includes full-time tuition ($18,940), mandatory fees ($420), and room and board ($5290). *College room only:* $2770. *Payment plan:* installment. *Waivers:* adult students and employees or children of employees.
Library Beeghly Library. *Operations spending 1999–2000:* $588,957. *Collection:* 208,000 titles, 1,000 serial subscriptions, 1,300 audiovisual materials.
College life *Housing:* on-campus residence required through junior year. *Options:* coed, men-only, women-only. *Most popular organizations:* student government, Juniata Activities Board, HOSA, International Club, JC Outreach (community service organization).
Campus security 24-hour emergency response devices and patrols, student patrols, late-night transport-escort service.
After graduation 17 organizations recruited on campus 1997–98. 64% of class of 1998 had job offers within 6 months. *Career center:* 2 full-time, 1 part-time personnel. Services include job fairs, resume preparation, interview workshops, resume referral, career/interest testing, career counseling, careers library, job bank, job interviews. *Graduate education:* 33% of class of 1999 went directly to graduate and professional school: 19% graduate arts and

Pennsylvania

sciences, 4% business, 4% medicine, 1% dentistry, 1% education, 1% engineering, 1% law, 1% veterinary medicine.

Freshmen 1,133 applied, 964 admitted, 327 enrolled. 10 valedictorians.

Average high school GPA	3.63	SAT verbal scores above 500	83%
SAT math scores above 500	83%	ACT above 18	N/R
From top 10% of their h.s. class	37%	From top quarter	64%
From top half	98%	1998 freshmen returning in 1999	86%

Application *Options:* eApply at www.CollegeQuest.com, Common Application, electronic application, early admission, early decision, deferred entrance. *Application fee:* $30. *Required:* essay or personal statement; high school transcript; minimum 3.0 GPA; 1 letter of recommendation. *Recommended:* interview.

Standardized tests *Admission: Required:* SAT I or ACT.

Significant dates *Application deadlines:* 3/15 (freshmen), 6/15 (transfers). *Early decision:* 11/15. *Notification:* 12/30 (early decision). *Financial aid deadline priority date:* 3/1.

Freshman Application Contact
Ms. Michelle Bartol, Director of Admissions, Juniata College, 1700 Moore Street, Huntingdon, PA 16652-2119. **Phone:** 814-641-3432. **Toll-free phone:** 877-JUNIATA. **Fax:** 814-641-3100. **E-mail:** info@juniata.edu

Visit CollegeQuest.com for information on majors offered and athletics.

■ *See page 1860 for a narrative description.*

KEYSTONE COLLEGE
La Plume, Pennsylvania

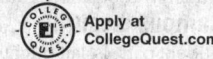

- **Independent**, primarily 2-year, founded 1868
- **Degrees** associate and bachelor's
- **Rural** 270-acre campus
- **Coed**, 914 undergraduate students, 67% full-time, 61% women, 39% men
- **Minimally difficult** entrance level
- **$11,606 tuition** and fees

Faculty 133 (26% full-time).

Admissions Office Contact
Keystone College, One College Green, La Plume, PA 18440-0200. **E-mail:** admissns@keystone.edu

Visit CollegeQuest.com for information on majors offered and athletics. College video and electronic viewbook available at CollegeQuest.com.

KING'S COLLEGE
Wilkes-Barre, Pennsylvania

- **Independent Roman Catholic**, comprehensive, founded 1946
- **Degrees** associate, bachelor's, and master's
- **Suburban** 48-acre campus
- **Coed**, 1,954 undergraduate students, 89% full-time, 53% women, 47% men
- **Moderately difficult** entrance level, 81% of applicants were admitted
- **15:1** student-to-undergraduate faculty ratio
- **70% graduate** in 6 years or less
- **$15,910 tuition** and fees
- **$12,439 average financial aid** package, $15,500 average indebtedness upon graduation, $37.6 million endowment

King's College is a Catholic liberal arts college founded more than 50 years ago by the Holy Cross Fathers of the University of Notre Dame. The William G. McGowan School of Business and the College of Arts and Sciences offer 37 undergraduate majors and graduate programs in education, finance, and health-care administration and a 5-year physician assistant program. Of King's alumni, 99% are employed or attend graduate school within 6 months after graduation, and more than 85% of King's students receive financial aid.

Students *Undergraduates:* 1,731 full-time, 223 part-time. Students come from 28 states and territories, 8 other countries. *The most frequently chosen baccalaureate fields are:* business/marketing, health professions and related sciences, protective services/public administration. *Graduate:* 126 in graduate degree programs.

From out-of-state	27%	Reside on campus	35%
Age 25 or older	14%	Transferred in	5%
International students	1%	African Americans	2%
Asian Americans/Pacific Islanders	1%	Hispanic Americans	1%

Faculty 183 (58% full-time).

Expenses (1999–2000) *Comprehensive fee:* $22,530 includes full-time tuition ($15,240), mandatory fees ($670), and room and board ($6620). *College room only:* $3130. Room and board charges vary according to board plan and housing facility. *Part-time tuition:* $374 per credit hour. *Payment plans:* installment, deferred payment. *Waivers:* senior citizens and employees or children of employees.

Library D. Leonard Corgan Library. *Operations spending 1999–2000:* $990,695. *Collection:* 158,251 titles, 988 serial subscriptions, 6,028 audiovisual materials.

College life *Housing:* on-campus residence required through sophomore year. *Options:* men-only, women-only. *Most popular organizations:* Association of Campus Events, Student Government Association, Accounting Association, international/multicultural club, biology club.

Campus security 24-hour emergency response devices and patrols, student patrols, late-night transport-escort service, bicycle patrols.

After graduation 60 organizations recruited on campus 1997–98. 65% of class of 1998 had job offers within 6 months. *Career center:* 4 full-time personnel. Services include job fairs, resume preparation, interview workshops, resume referral, career/interest testing, career counseling, careers library, job bank, job interviews. *Graduate education:* 17% of class of 1999 went directly to graduate and professional school: 7% graduate arts and sciences, 3% law, 2% medicine, 1% business, 1% education.

Freshmen 1,528 applied, 1,232 admitted, 428 enrolled.

SAT verbal scores above 500	57%	SAT math scores above 500	53%
ACT above 18	N/R	From top 10% of their h.s. class	17%
From top quarter	42%	From top half	75%
1998 freshmen returning in 1999	80%		

Application *Options:* Common Application, early admission, deferred entrance. *Application fee:* $30. *Required:* essay or personal statement; high school transcript. *Recommended:* 2 letters of recommendation; interview.

Standardized tests *Admission: Required:* SAT I or ACT.

Significant dates *Application deadlines:* rolling (freshmen), rolling (transfers). *Financial aid deadline priority date:* 3/1.

Freshman Application Contact
Ms. Susan McGarry-Hannon, Director of Admissions, King's College, 133 North River Street, Wilkes-Barre, PA 18711-0801. **Phone:** 570-208-5858. **Toll-free phone:** 888-KINGSPA. **Fax:** 570-208-5971. **E-mail:** admssns@leo.kings.edu

Visit CollegeQuest.com for information on majors offered and athletics. College video available at CollegeQuest.com.

■ *See page 1878 for a narrative description.*

KUTZTOWN UNIVERSITY OF PENNSYLVANIA
Kutztown, Pennsylvania

- **State-supported**, comprehensive, founded 1866
- **Degrees** bachelor's and master's
- **Rural** 326-acre campus with easy access to Philadelphia
- **Coed**, 6,899 undergraduate students, 92% full-time, 60% women, 40% men
- **Moderately difficult** entrance level, 75% of applicants were admitted
- **19:1** student-to-undergraduate faculty ratio
- **48% graduate** in 6 years or less
- **$4448 tuition** and fees (in-state); $9876 (out-of-state)
- **$5072 average financial aid** package, $12,817 average indebtedness upon graduation, $7.6 million endowment

Kutztown University has completed the following projects recently to enhance the quality of student life: a new addition doubles the size of Rohrbach Library and provides more modern, functional, and comfortable areas and more than 500 personal computer links; all residence hall rooms are now wired for Internet usage, and new multistation computer labs have been opened in buildings across the campus; and historic Old Main has been completely renovated and beautifully restored.

Peterson's Guide to Four-Year Colleges 2001   www.petersons.com   697

Pennsylvania

Kutztown University of Pennsylvania (continued)
Part of Pennsylvania State System of Higher Education.
Students *Undergraduates:* 6,340 full-time, 559 part-time. Students come from 18 states and territories, 45 other countries. *The most frequently chosen baccalaureate fields are:* business/marketing, education, visual/performing arts. *Graduate:* 1,010 in graduate degree programs.

From out-of-state	8%	Reside on campus	40%
Age 25 or older	11%	Transferred in	7%
International students	2%	African Americans	3%
Asian Americans/Pacific Islanders	1%	Hispanic Americans	2%
Native Americans	0.3%		

Faculty 435 (91% full-time), 68% with terminal degrees.
Expenses (1999–2000) *One-time required fee:* $48. *Tuition, state resident:* full-time $3618; part-time $150 per credit. *Tuition, nonresident:* full-time $9046; part-time $377 per credit. *Required fees:* full-time $830; $35 per credit. Part-time tuition and fees vary according to course load. *College room and board:* $4082; room only: $2820. Room and board charges vary according to board plan. *Payment plans:* tuition prepayment, installment, deferred payment. *Waivers:* employees or children of employees.
Library Rohrbach Library. *Operations spending 1999–2000:* $2.5 million. *Collection:* 429,119 titles, 1,892 serial subscriptions, 13,731 audiovisual materials.
College life *Housing: Options:* coed, men-only, women-only. *Social organizations:* national fraternities, national sororities, local sororities; 3% of eligible men and 3% of eligible women are members. *Most popular organizations:* Student Government Board, Student Pennsylvania State Education Association (PSEA), National Art Education Association, Association of Campus Events, Residence Hall Association.
Campus security 24-hour emergency response devices and patrols, late-night transport-escort service, secondary door electronic alarm system in residence halls, 24-hour student desk personnel at main entrance of residence halls.
After graduation 50 organizations recruited on campus 1997–98. *Career center:* 4 full-time, 1 part-time personnel. Services include job fairs, resume preparation, interview workshops, resume referral, career/interest testing, career counseling, careers library, job bank, job interviews. *Graduate education:* 18% of class of 1999 went directly to graduate and professional school.
Freshmen 5,289 applied, 3,989 admitted, 1,554 enrolled.

SAT verbal scores above 500	46%	SAT math scores above 500	43%
ACT above 18	N/R	From top 10% of their h.s. class	4%
From top quarter	20%	From top half	50%
1998 freshmen returning in 1999	76%		

Application *Options:* electronic application, deferred entrance. *Application fee:* $30. *Required:* high school transcript; minimum 2.0 GPA.
Standardized tests *Admission: Required:* SAT I or ACT. *Required for some:* SAT II Subject Tests.
Significant dates *Application deadlines:* rolling (freshmen), rolling (transfers). *Financial aid deadline priority date:* 2/15.
Freshman Application Contact
Dr. Robert McGowan, Director of Admissions, Kutztown University of Pennsylvania, 15200 Kutztown Road, Kutztown, PA 19530. **Phone:** 610-683-4060 Ext. 4053. **Toll-free phone:** 877-628-1915. **Fax:** 610-683-1375. **E-mail:** admission@kutztown.edu
Visit CollegeQuest.com for information on majors offered and athletics. College video and electronic viewbook available at CollegeQuest.com.

■ *See page 1882 for a narrative description.*

LAFAYETTE COLLEGE
Easton, Pennsylvania

Apply at CollegeQuest.com

- **Independent**, 4-year, founded 1826, affiliated with Presbyterian Church (U.S.A.)
- **Degree** bachelor's
- **Suburban** 110-acre campus with easy access to New York City and Philadelphia
- **Coed**, 2,224 undergraduate students, 97% full-time, 49% women, 51% men
- **Very difficult** entrance level, 48% of applicants were admitted
- **11:1** student-to-undergraduate faculty ratio
- **81.8% graduate** in 6 years or less
- **$22,929 tuition** and fees
- **$19,556 average financial aid** package, $13,875 average indebtedness upon graduation, $516.2 million endowment

Students *Undergraduates:* 2,162 full-time, 62 part-time. Students come from 41 states and territories, 53 other countries. *The most frequently chosen baccalaureate fields are:* engineering/engineering technologies, biological/life sciences, social sciences and history.

From out-of-state	71%	Reside on campus	98%
Transferred in	0.2%	International students	3%
African Americans	3%	Asian Americans/Pacific Islanders	1%
Hispanic Americans	1%	Native Americans	0.2%

Faculty 225 (81% full-time), 97% with terminal degrees.
Expenses (1999–2000) *Comprehensive fee:* $30,035 includes full-time tuition ($22,844), mandatory fees ($85), and room and board ($7106). *College room only:* $3900. Room and board charges vary according to board plan. *Part-time tuition:* $990 per course. *Payment plans:* tuition prepayment, deferred payment. *Waivers:* employees or children of employees.
Library Skillman Library plus 1 other. *Collection:* 494,000 titles, 1,837 serial subscriptions.
College life *Housing:* on-campus residence required through senior year. *Option:* coed. *Social organizations:* national fraternities, national sororities, social dorms; 36% of eligible men and 70% of eligible women are members. *Most popular organizations:* Association of Biscer Collegians, International Student Association, Lafayette Activities Forum.
Campus security 24-hour emergency response devices and patrols, student patrols, late-night transport-escort service, controlled dormitory access.
After graduation 250 organizations recruited on campus 1997–98. *Career center:* 4 full-time, 1 part-time personnel. Services include job fairs, resume preparation, resume referral, career counseling, careers library, job bank, job interviews.
Freshmen 4,429 applied, 2,135 admitted, 582 enrolled. 4 National Merit Scholars.

SAT verbal scores above 500	97%	SAT math scores above 500	99%
ACT above 18	N/R	From top 10% of their h.s. class	51%
From top quarter	83%	From top half	99%
1998 freshmen returning in 1999	93%		

Application *Options:* eApply at www.CollegeQuest.com, Common Application, electronic application, early admission, early decision, deferred entrance. *Application fee:* $50. *Required:* essay or personal statement; high school transcript; 1 letter of recommendation. *Recommended:* interview.
Standardized tests *Admission: Required:* SAT I, SAT II Subject Tests. *Recommended:* SAT II: Writing Test.
Significant dates *Application deadlines:* 1/1 (freshmen), 6/1 (transfers). *Early decision:* 12/1. *Notification:* continuous until 4/1 (freshmen), 3/15 (early decision). *Financial aid deadline:* 2/1.
Freshman Application Contact
Ms. Carol Rowlands, Director of Admissions, Lafayette College, Easton, PA 18042-1798. **Phone:** 610-330-5100. **Fax:** 610-330-5127. **E-mail:** admissions@lafayette.edu
Visit CollegeQuest.com for information on majors offered and athletics. College video and electronic viewbook available at CollegeQuest.com.

■ *See page 1886 for a narrative description.*

LANCASTER BIBLE COLLEGE
Lancaster, Pennsylvania

- **Independent nondenominational**, comprehensive, founded 1933
- **Degrees** associate, bachelor's, and master's
- **Suburban** 100-acre campus with easy access to Philadelphia
- **Coed**, 561 undergraduate students, 87% full-time, 53% women, 47% men
- **Minimally difficult** entrance level, 54% of applicants were admitted
- **16:1** student-to-undergraduate faculty ratio
- **42% graduate** in 6 years or less
- **$9430 tuition** and fees
- **$7053 average financial aid** package, $13,071 average indebtedness upon graduation, $2.4 million endowment

Pennsylvania

LBC is a nondenominational Bible college offering BS or AS degrees. Programs prepare students for Christian careers in aviation-missions, Christian education, computer ministries, counseling, education-Bible, Bible music, early childhood and elementary education, missions, music, pastoral studies, secretarial studies, vocational technology, and youth ministry. New programs include women's ministries, guidance counseling/Bible, and physical education/Bible. Two 1-year certificate programs are available. Graduate study is also available.

Students *Undergraduates:* 486 full-time, 75 part-time. Students come from 22 states and territories, 9 other countries. *The most frequently chosen baccalaureate fields are:* education, philosophy. *Graduate:* 52 in graduate degree programs.

From out-of-state	24%	Reside on campus	45%
Age 25 or older		Transferred in	9%
		27%	

Faculty 65 (55% full-time), 32% with terminal degrees.

Expenses (1999–2000) *Comprehensive fee:* $13,730 includes full-time tuition ($9100), mandatory fees ($330), and room and board ($4300). *College room only:* $1800. Full-time tuition and fees vary according to program. Room and board charges vary according to board plan. *Part-time tuition:* $305 per credit hour. *Part-time fees:* $11 per credit hour. Part-time tuition and fees vary according to program. *Payment plan:* installment. *Waivers:* children of alumni, adult students, senior citizens, and employees or children of employees.

Library Lancaster Bible College Library. *Operations spending 1999–2000:* $248,801. *Collection:* 114,753 titles, 502 serial subscriptions, 3,989 audiovisual materials.

College life *Housing:* on-campus residence required through senior year. *Options:* men-only, women-only. *Most popular organizations:* Student Government Association, Student Missionary Fellowship, International Student Fellowship, Resident Affairs Council, Student Intramural Association.

Campus security Student patrols, late-night transport-escort service, controlled dormitory access.

After graduation 70 organizations recruited on campus 1997–98. 60% of class of 1998 had job offers within 6 months. *Career center:* 1 full-time, 1 part-time personnel. Services include resume preparation, resume referral, career counseling, job bank, job interviews.

Freshmen 200 applied, 107 admitted, 107 enrolled. 4 valedictorians.

Average high school GPA	3.57	SAT verbal scores above 500	N/R
SAT math scores above 500	N/R	ACT above 18	N/R
From top 10% of their h.s. class	8%	From top quarter	35%
From top half	70%	1998 freshmen returning in 1999	66%

Application *Options:* early admission, deferred entrance. *Application fee:* $15. *Required:* essay or personal statement; high school transcript; minimum 2.0 GPA; 3 letters of recommendation. *Recommended:* interview.

Standardized tests *Admission:* Recommended: SAT I and SAT II or ACT.

Significant dates *Application deadlines:* rolling (freshmen), rolling (transfers). *Financial aid deadline priority date:* 5/1.

Freshman Application Contact
Mrs. Joanne M. Roper, Director of Admissions, Lancaster Bible College, 901 Eden Road, Lancaster, PA 17601-5036. **Phone:** 717-569-8271. **Toll-free phone:** 888-CALL LBC. **Fax:** 717-560-8213. **E-mail:** admissions@lbc.edu

Visit CollegeQuest.com for information on majors offered and athletics.

LA ROCHE COLLEGE
Pittsburgh, Pennsylvania

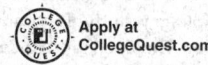 Apply at CollegeQuest.com

- **Independent**, comprehensive, founded 1963, affiliated with Roman Catholic Church
- **Degrees** bachelor's and master's
- **Suburban** 80-acre campus
- **Coed**, 1,380 undergraduate students, 73% full-time, 62% women, 38% men
- **Minimally difficult** entrance level, 88% of applicants were admitted
- **13:1 student-to-undergraduate faculty ratio**
- **42% graduate** in 6 years or less
- **$11,450 tuition** and fees
- **$6.2 million endowment**

Students *Undergraduates:* 1,007 full-time, 373 part-time. Students come from 16 states and territories, 22 other countries. *The most frequently chosen baccalaureate fields are:* business/marketing, psychology, visual/performing arts. *Graduate:* 243 in graduate degree programs.

From out-of-state	7%	Reside on campus	32%
Age 25 or older	32%	Transferred in	13%
International students	9%	African Americans	3%
Asian Americans/Pacific Islanders	1%	Hispanic Americans	0.5%
Native Americans	0.1%		

Faculty 185 (24% full-time), 37% with terminal degrees.

Expenses (1999–2000) *Comprehensive fee:* $15,580 includes full-time tuition ($11,100), mandatory fees ($350), and room and board ($4130). *College room only:* $3760. Full-time tuition and fees vary according to program. *Part-time tuition:* $400 per credit hour. *Part-time fees:* $6 per credit hour; $54 per term part-time. Part-time tuition and fees vary according to program. *Payment plan:* installment. *Waivers:* senior citizens and employees or children of employees.

Library John J. Wright Library. *Operations spending 1999–2000:* $314,351. *Collection:* 71,000 titles, 605 serial subscriptions, 1,350 audiovisual materials.

College life *Housing:* Option: coed. *Most popular organizations:* American Society of Interior Design, Student Government, Visions (environmental club), Helping Hands, Project Achievement.

Campus security 24-hour emergency response devices and patrols, student patrols, late-night transport-escort service, controlled dormitory access.

After graduation *Career center:* 3 full-time personnel. Services include job fairs, resume preparation, interview workshops, resume referral, career/interest testing, career counseling, careers library, job bank, job interviews.

Freshmen 541 applied, 478 admitted, 308 enrolled.

Average high school GPA	3.2	SAT verbal scores above 500	37%
SAT math scores above 500	29%	ACT above 18	50%
From top 10% of their h.s. class	8%	From top quarter	31%
From top half	55%	1998 freshmen returning in 1999	69%

Application *Options:* eApply at www.CollegeQuest.com, Common Application, electronic application, early admission, deferred entrance. *Application fee:* $25. *Required:* high school transcript; minimum 2.0 GPA; letters of recommendation. *Recommended:* essay or personal statement; minimum 3.0 GPA; interview.

Standardized tests *Admission:* Required: SAT I or ACT.

Significant dates *Application deadlines:* rolling (freshmen), rolling (transfers). *Financial aid deadline priority date:* 5/1.

Freshman Application Contact
Ms. Dayna R. McNally, Director of Enrollment Services, La Roche College, 9000 Babcock Boulevard, Pittsburgh, PA 15237. **Phone:** 412-536-1274. **Toll-free phone:** 800-838-4LRC. **Fax:** 412-536-1075. **E-mail:** ad-msns@laroche.edu

Visit CollegeQuest.com for information on majors offered and athletics.

■ *See page 1900 for a narrative description.*

LA SALLE UNIVERSITY
Philadelphia, Pennsylvania

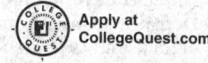 Apply at CollegeQuest.com

- **Independent Roman Catholic**, comprehensive, founded 1863
- **Degrees** associate, bachelor's, master's, and doctoral
- **Urban** 100-acre campus
- **Coed**, 3,794 undergraduate students, 75% full-time, 58% women, 42% men
- **Moderately difficult** entrance level, 39% of applicants were admitted
- **17:1 student-to-undergraduate faculty ratio**
- **64% graduate** in 6 years or less
- **$17,260 tuition** and fees
- **$39.7 million endowment**

Students *Undergraduates:* 2,863 full-time, 931 part-time. Students come from 29 states and territories. *Graduate:* 1,650 in graduate degree programs.

From out-of-state	32%	Reside on campus	61%
Age 25 or older	2%	Transferred in	3%
International students	1%	African Americans	12%
Asian Americans/Pacific Islanders	3%	Hispanic Americans	4%
Native Americans	0.1%		

Faculty 392 (46% full-time), 89% with terminal degrees.

Expenses (1999–2000) *Comprehensive fee:* $23,862 includes full-time tuition ($16,880), mandatory fees ($380), and room and board ($6602).

Pennsylvania

La Salle University *(continued)*
College room only: $3632. Full-time tuition and fees vary according to program. Room and board charges vary according to board plan, housing facility, and location. *Part-time tuition:* $315 per credit hour. *Part-time fees:* $10 per course; $20 per term part-time. Part-time tuition and fees vary according to class time and course load. *Payment plans:* installment, deferred payment. *Waivers:* employees or children of employees.
Library Connelly Library. *Operations spending 1999–2000:* $1.7 million. *Collection:* 365,000 titles, 1,700 serial subscriptions, 5,200 audiovisual materials.
College life *Housing: Option:* coed. *Social organizations:* national fraternities, national sororities, local fraternities, local sororities; 15% of eligible men and 13% of eligible women are members. *Most popular organizations:* Student Government Association, Community Service Organization, La Salle Entertainment Organization, The Explorer (yearbook), The Masque (theater group).
Campus security 24-hour emergency response devices and patrols, student patrols, late-night transport-escort service, controlled dormitory access.
After graduation *Career center:* 4 full-time personnel. Services include job fairs, resume preparation, interview workshops, resume referral, career/interest testing, career counseling, careers library, job bank, job interviews.
Freshmen 3,082 applied, 1,188 admitted, 727 enrolled.

SAT verbal scores above 500	71%	SAT math scores above 500	66%
ACT above 18	N/R	From top 10% of their h.s. class	20%
From top quarter	51%	From top half	78%
1998 freshmen returning in 1999	89%		

Application *Options:* eApply at www.CollegeQuest.com, electronic application, early admission, early action, deferred entrance. *Application fee:* $35. *Required:* essay or personal statement; high school transcript; 1 letter of recommendation. *Recommended:* interview.
Standardized tests *Admission: Required:* SAT I or ACT.
Significant dates *Application deadlines:* 4/1 (freshmen), 8/1 (transfers). *Early action:* 11/15. *Notification:* 12/15 (early action). *Financial aid deadline priority date:* 3/15.
Freshman Application Contact
Mr. Robert G. Voss, Acting Dean of Admission and Financial Aid, La Salle University, 1900 West Olney Avenue, Philadelphia, PA 19141-1199. **Phone:** 215-951-1500. **Toll-free phone:** 800-328-1910. **Fax:** 215-951-1656. **E-mail:** admiss@lasalle.edu
Visit CollegeQuest.com for information on majors offered and athletics. College video available at CollegeQuest.com.

LEBANON VALLEY COLLEGE
Annville, Pennsylvania

- **Independent United Methodist**, comprehensive, founded 1866
- **Degrees** associate, bachelor's, and master's (offers master of business administration degree on a part-time basis only)
- **Small-town** 275-acre campus
- **Coed**, 1,773 undergraduate students, 73% full-time, 59% women, 41% men
- **Moderately difficult** entrance level, 72% of applicants were admitted
- **16:1 student-to-undergraduate faculty ratio**
- **65% graduate** in 6 years or less
- **$17,260 tuition** and fees
- **$13,762 average financial aid** package, $17,462 average indebtedness upon graduation, $26.7 million endowment

Students *Undergraduates:* 1,292 full-time, 481 part-time. Students come from 18 states and territories, 12 other countries. *The most frequently chosen baccalaureate fields are:* biological/life sciences, computer/information sciences, psychology. *Graduate:* 260 in graduate degree programs.

From out-of-state	15%	Reside on campus	76%
Age 25 or older	16%	Transferred in	3%
International students	2%	African Americans	2%
Asian Americans/Pacific Islanders	1%	Hispanic Americans	1%
Native Americans	0.2%		

Faculty 201 (40% full-time), 44% with terminal degrees.
Expenses (1999–2000) *Comprehensive fee:* $22,750 includes full-time tuition ($16,730), mandatory fees ($530), and room and board ($5490).

College room only: $2670. Room and board charges vary according to board plan and housing facility. *Part-time tuition:* $322 per credit. *Part-time fees:* $25 per term part-time. Part-time tuition and fees vary according to class time. *Waivers:* employees or children of employees.
Library Vernon & Bishop Library. *Operations spending 1999–2000:* $804,770. *Collection:* 135,305 titles, 6,160 serial subscriptions, 3,046 audiovisual materials.
College life *Housing:* on-campus residence required through senior year. *Options:* coed, men-only, women-only. *Social organizations:* national fraternities, national sororities, local fraternities, local sororities; 11% of eligible men and 10% of eligible women are members. *Most popular organizations:* LVC PSEA, Council of Religious Organization, International Student Organization, Phi Beta Lambda, Wig and Buckle (theatrical group).
Campus security 24-hour emergency response devices and patrols, late-night transport-escort service, dormitory entrances locked at midnight.
After graduation *Career center:* 1 full-time personnel. Services include job fairs, resume preparation, resume referral, career counseling, careers library, job bank.
Freshmen 2,211 applied, 1,592 admitted, 407 enrolled. 2 valedictorians.

SAT verbal scores above 500	73%	SAT math scores above 500	74%
ACT above 18	90%	From top 10% of their h.s. class	28%
From top quarter	66%	From top half	91%
1998 freshmen returning in 1999	82%		

Application *Options:* electronic application, early admission, deferred entrance. *Application fee:* $25. *Required:* high school transcript. *Required for some:* audition for music majors; interview for physical therapy program. *Recommended:* essay or personal statement; 2 letters of recommendation; interview.
Standardized tests *Admission: Required:* SAT I or ACT.
Significant dates *Application deadlines:* rolling (freshmen), rolling (transfers). *Financial aid deadline priority date:* 3/1.
Freshman Application Contact
William J. Brown Jr., Dean of Admission and Financial Aid, Lebanon Valley College, PO Box R, Annville, PA 17003-0501. **Phone:** 717-867-6181. **Toll-free phone:** 800-445-6181. **Fax:** 717-867-6124. **E-mail:** admiss@lvc.edu
Visit CollegeQuest.com for information on majors offered and athletics.

■ *See page 1908 for a narrative description.*

LEHIGH UNIVERSITY
Bethlehem, Pennsylvania

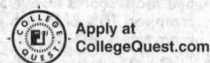

- **Independent**, university, founded 1865
- **Degrees** bachelor's, master's, doctoral, and post-master's certificates
- **Suburban** 1,600-acre campus with easy access to Philadelphia
- **Coed**, 4,526 undergraduate students, 99% full-time, 40% women, 60% men
- **Most difficult** entrance level, 48% of applicants were admitted
- **12:1 student-to-undergraduate faculty ratio**
- **$23,150 tuition** and fees
- **$18,100 average financial aid** package, $15,178 average indebtedness upon graduation, $675.6 million endowment

Lehigh combines a small liberal arts college experience with the strength of a major university. It offers more than 110 majors and minors in 4 colleges. Students and faculty members work closely on hands-on projects and interdisciplinary study. Top undergraduates can receive a 5th year of study tuition-free. The Zoellner Arts Center showcases a dynamic arts program. Alumni and friends create an experience that lasts a lifetime.

Students *Undergraduates:* 4,488 full-time, 38 part-time. Students come from 52 states and territories, 46 other countries. *The most frequently chosen baccalaureate fields are:* business/marketing, engineering/engineering technologies, social sciences and history. *Graduate:* 1,754 in graduate degree programs.

From out-of-state	68%	Reside on campus	69%
Age 25 or older	1%	Transferred in	3%
International students	4%	African Americans	3%
Asian Americans/Pacific Islanders	5%	Hispanic Americans	3%
Native Americans	0.2%		

Faculty 468 (84% full-time), 99% with terminal degrees.

Pennsylvania

Expenses (1999–2000) *Comprehensive fee:* $29,780 includes full-time tuition ($23,150) and room and board ($6630). *College room only:* $3680. Full-time tuition and fees vary according to program. Room and board charges vary according to board plan and housing facility. *Part-time tuition:* $965 per credit hour. Part-time tuition and fees vary according to program. *Payment plans:* tuition prepayment, installment, deferred payment. *Waivers:* senior citizens and employees or children of employees.
Library E. W. Fairchild-Martindale Library plus 1 other. *Collection:* 1.2 million titles, 5,797 serial subscriptions, 3,715 audiovisual materials.
College life *Housing: Options:* coed, disabled students. *Social organizations:* national fraternities, national sororities; 41% of eligible men and 43% of eligible women are members. *Most popular organizations:* Student Senate, University Productions, Black Student Union, Residence Hall Association, Global Union.
Campus security 24-hour emergency response devices and patrols, student patrols, late-night transport-escort service, controlled dormitory access.
After graduation 382 organizations recruited on campus 1997–98. 64% of class of 1998 had job offers within 6 months. *Career center:* 9 full-time, 2 part-time personnel. Services include job fairs, resume preparation, interview workshops, resume referral, career/interest testing, career counseling, careers library, job bank, job interviews. **Graduate education:** 26% of class of 1999 went directly to graduate and professional school.
Freshmen 8,853 applied, 4,228 admitted, 1,078 enrolled. 11 National Merit Scholars.

SAT verbal scores above 500	93%	SAT math scores above 500	98%
ACT above 18	N/R	1998 freshmen returning in 1999	93%

Application *Options:* eApply at www.CollegeQuest.com, Common Application, early admission, early decision, deferred entrance. *Application fee:* $50. *Required:* high school transcript; 1 letter of recommendation; graded writing sample. *Recommended:* essay or personal statement; interview.
Standardized tests *Admission: Required:* SAT I or ACT. *Recommended:* SAT II Subject Tests.
Significant dates *Application deadline:* 1/1 (freshmen). *Early decision:* 11/15. *Notification:* 4/1 (freshmen), 12/15 (early decision). *Financial aid deadline:* 2/1. Priority date: 1/15.
Freshman Application Contact
Mrs. Lorna Hunter, Dean of Admissions and Financial Aid, Lehigh University, 27 Memorial Drive West, Bethlehem, PA 18015. **Phone:** 610-758-3100. **Fax:** 610-758-4361. **E-mail:** inado@lehigh.edu
Visit CollegeQuest.com for information on majors offered and athletics. Electronic viewbook available at CollegeQuest.com.

■ *See page 1910 for a narrative description.*

LINCOLN UNIVERSITY
Lincoln University, Pennsylvania

- **State-related**, comprehensive, founded 1854
- **Degrees** bachelor's and master's
- **Rural** 442-acre campus with easy access to Philadelphia
- **Coed**, 1,447 undergraduate students, 97% full-time, 59% women, 41% men
- **Moderately difficult** entrance level, 53% of applicants were admitted
- **16:1 student-to-undergraduate faculty ratio**
- **50% graduate** in 6 years or less
- **$5208 tuition** and fees (in-state); $7716 (out-of-state)
- **$15.9 million endowment**

Students *Undergraduates:* 1,397 full-time, 50 part-time. Students come from 24 states and territories, 14 other countries. *The most frequently chosen baccalaureate fields are:* business/marketing, education, social sciences and history. *Graduate:* 554 in graduate degree programs.

From out-of-state	56%	Reside on campus	93%
Age 25 or older	4%	Transferred in	1%
International students	5%	African Americans	94%
Asian Americans/Pacific Islanders	0.2%	Hispanic Americans	0.2%

Faculty 134 (73% full-time).
Expenses (1999–2000) *One-time required fee:* $105. *Tuition, state resident:* full-time $3748; part-time $156 per credit hour. *Tuition, nonresident:* full-time $6256; part-time $277 per credit hour. *Required fees:* full-time $1460; $62 per credit hour. Full-time tuition and fees vary according to course load. *College room and board:* $5034; room only: $2756. Room and board charges vary according to board plan. *Payment plans:* installment, deferred payment. *Waivers:* employees or children of employees.
Library Langston Hughes Memorial Library. *Operations spending 1999–2000:* $720,244. *Collection:* 723 serial subscriptions, 2,633 audiovisual materials.
College life *Housing:* on-campus residence required in freshman year. *Options:* coed, men-only, women-only. *Social organizations:* national fraternities, national sororities, local fraternities; 5% of eligible men and 10% of eligible women are members. *Most popular organizations:* The Gospel Ensemble, Ziana Fashion Club, drill team, Militants for Christ, Greek organizations.
Campus security 24-hour emergency response devices and patrols, late-night transport-escort service.
After graduation 204 organizations recruited on campus 1997–98. *Career center:* 3 full-time personnel. Services include job fairs, resume preparation, interview workshops, career counseling, careers library, job bank, job interviews.
Freshmen 2,582 applied, 1,374 admitted, 358 enrolled.

Average high school GPA	2.72	SAT verbal scores above 500	26%
SAT math scores above 500	18%	ACT above 18	27%
From top half of their h.s. class	50%	1998 freshmen returning in 1999	64%

Application *Options:* early admission, deferred entrance. *Preference* given to state residents. *Application fee:* $20. *Required:* essay or personal statement; high school transcript; minimum 2.5 GPA; 2 letters of recommendation; interview.
Standardized tests *Placement: Required for some:* SAT I or ACT, MAPS.
Significant dates *Application deadlines:* rolling (freshmen), rolling (transfers). *Financial aid deadline priority date:* 3/15.
Freshman Application Contact
Dr. Robert Laney Jr., Director of Admissions, Lincoln University, PO Box 179, Lincoln University, PA 19352. **Phone:** 610-932-8300 Ext. 306. **Toll-free phone:** 800-215-4858. **E-mail:** admiss@lu.lincoln.edu
Visit CollegeQuest.com for information on majors offered and athletics. College video available at CollegeQuest.com.

■ *See page 1928 for a narrative description.*

LOCK HAVEN UNIVERSITY OF PENNSYLVANIA
Lock Haven, Pennsylvania

Apply at CollegeQuest.com

- **State-supported**, comprehensive, founded 1870
- **Degrees** associate, bachelor's, and master's
- **Small-town** 165-acre campus
- **Coed**, 3,618 undergraduate students, 94% full-time, 56% women, 44% men
- **Moderately difficult** entrance level, 78% of applicants were admitted
- **17:1 student-to-undergraduate faculty ratio**
- **51.64% graduate** in 6 years or less
- **$4244 tuition** and fees (in-state); $7672 (out-of-state)
- **$5414 average financial aid** package, $16,472 average indebtedness upon graduation, $4.9 million endowment

Lock Haven University pursues a special mission in international education that features diverse student-faculty exchanges and overseas student teaching. Students from all majors have an opportunity to participate in an exchange program during any year of study in Australia, Canada, China, Costa Rica, Croatia, England, Finland, France, Germany, Italy, Japan, Mexico, Morocco, Poland, Russia, Scotland, Spain, Taiwan, Tunisia, or Ukraine.

Part of Pennsylvania State System of Higher Education.
Students *Undergraduates:* 3,383 full-time, 235 part-time. Students come from 26 states and territories, 24 other countries. *The most frequently chosen baccalaureate fields are:* education, health professions and related sciences, parks and recreation. *Graduate:* 117 in graduate degree programs.

Pennsylvania

Lock Haven University of Pennsylvania (continued)

From out-of-state	8%	Reside on campus	55%
Age 25 or older	10%	Transferred in	4%
International students	1%	African Americans	3%
Asian Americans/Pacific Islanders	1%	Hispanic Americans	1%
Native Americans	0.3%		

Faculty 221 (94% full-time), 38% with terminal degrees.
Expenses (1999–2000) *Tuition, state resident:* full-time $3618; part-time $150 per semester hour. *Tuition, nonresident:* full-time $7046; part-time $294 per semester hour. *Required fees:* full-time $626; $17 per semester hour; $36 per term part-time. Part-time tuition and fees vary according to course load. *College room and board:* $4136. Room and board charges vary according to board plan. *Payment plan:* installment. *Waivers:* minority students and employees or children of employees.
Library Stevenson Library. *Operations spending 1999–2000:* $1.3 million. *Collection:* 361,447 titles, 1,558 serial subscriptions, 8,158 audiovisual materials.
College life *Housing:* on-campus residence required through sophomore year. *Options:* coed, women-only. *Social organizations:* national fraternities, national sororities; 10% of eligible men and 10% of eligible women are members. *Most popular organizations:* student government, residence hall association, fraternities, sororities.
Campus security 24-hour emergency response devices and patrols.
After graduation *Career center:* 2 full-time personnel. Services include job fairs, resume preparation, interview workshops, resume referral, career counseling, careers library, job bank, job interviews.
Freshmen 3,215 applied, 2,513 admitted, 941 enrolled.

SAT verbal scores above 500	45%	SAT math scores above 500	43%
ACT above 18	N/R	From top 10% of their h.s. class	9%
From top quarter	30%	From top half	68%
1998 freshmen returning in 1999	80%		

Application *Options:* eApply at www.CollegeQuest.com, Common Application, electronic application, deferred entrance. *Application fee:* $25. *Required:* high school transcript. *Required for some:* letters of recommendation; interview. *Recommended:* minimum 3.0 GPA.
Standardized tests *Admission: Required:* SAT I or ACT.
Significant dates *Application deadlines:* rolling (freshmen), rolling (transfers). *Financial aid deadline priority date:* 3/15.
Freshman Application Contact
Mr. James Reeser, Director of Admissions, Lock Haven University of Pennsylvania, Office of Admission, Akeley Hall, Lock Haven, PA 17745. **Phone:** 570-893-2027. **Toll-free phone:** 800-332-8900 (in-state); 800-233-8978 (out-of-state). **Fax:** 570-893-2201. **E-mail:** admissions@lhup.edu
Visit CollegeQuest.com for information on majors offered and athletics. College video available at CollegeQuest.com.

■ *See page 1934 for a narrative description.*

LYCOMING COLLEGE
Williamsport, Pennsylvania

- **Independent United Methodist**, 4-year, founded 1812
- **Degree** bachelor's
- **Small-town** 35-acre campus
- **Coed**, 1,438 undergraduate students, 99% full-time, 55% women, 45% men
- **Moderately difficult** entrance level, 82% of applicants were admitted
- **14:1 student-to-undergraduate faculty ratio**
- **62% graduate** in 6 years or less
- **$17,600 tuition** and fees
- **$14,323 average financial aid** package, $14,900 average indebtedness upon graduation, $66.8 million endowment

Students *Undergraduates:* 1,424 full-time, 14 part-time. Students come from 20 states and territories, 9 other countries. *The most frequently chosen baccalaureate fields are:* biological/life sciences, business/marketing, psychology.

From out-of-state	21%	Reside on campus	83%
Age 25 or older	7%	Transferred in	3%
International students	1%	African Americans	1%
Asian Americans/Pacific Islanders	1%	Hispanic Americans	1%
Native Americans	0.3%		

Faculty 107 (86% full-time).
Expenses (1999–2000) *Comprehensive fee:* $22,560 includes full-time tuition ($17,520), mandatory fees ($80), and room and board ($4960). *Part-time tuition:* $548 per credit. *Payment plan:* installment. *Waivers:* employees or children of employees.
Library Snowden Library plus 1 other. *Operations spending 1999–2000:* $766,731. *Collection:* 165,000 titles, 950 serial subscriptions.
College life *Housing:* on-campus residence required through senior year. *Options:* coed, women-only. *Social organizations:* national fraternities, national sororities, local sororities; 23% of eligible men and 21% of eligible women are members. *Most popular organizations:* radio club (WRLC), wilderness club, student newspaper, campus ministry, Habitat for Humanity.
Campus security 24-hour emergency response devices and patrols, student patrols, late-night transport-escort service, controlled dormitory access.
After graduation *Career center:* 1 full-time, 1 part-time personnel. Services include job fairs, resume preparation, career counseling, careers library, job bank, job interviews.
Freshmen 1,410 applied, 1,154 admitted, 394 enrolled. 1 National Merit Scholar, 15 class presidents, 15 valedictorians, 70 student government officers.

Average high school GPA	3.2	SAT verbal scores above 500	68%
SAT math scores above 500	63%	ACT above 18	N/R
From top 10% of their h.s. class	27%	From top quarter	54%
From top half	76%	1998 freshmen returning in 1999	83%

Application *Options:* Common Application, electronic application, early admission, deferred entrance. *Application fee:* $25. *Required:* high school transcript; 2 letters of recommendation. *Recommended:* essay or personal statement; minimum 2.0 GPA; interview.
Standardized tests *Admission: Required:* SAT I or ACT.
Significant dates *Application deadlines:* 4/1 (freshmen), 6/1 (transfers). *Financial aid deadline priority date:* 4/15.
Freshman Application Contact
Mr. James Spencer, Dean of Admissions and Financial Aid, Lycoming College, 700 College Place, Williamsport, PA 17701-5192. **Phone:** 570-321-4026. **Toll-free phone:** 800-345-3920. **Fax:** 570-321-4337. **E-mail:** admissions@lycoming.edu
Visit CollegeQuest.com for information on majors offered and athletics.

MANSFIELD UNIVERSITY OF PENNSYLVANIA
Mansfield, Pennsylvania

- **State-supported**, comprehensive, founded 1857
- **Degrees** associate, bachelor's, master's, and postbachelor's certificates
- **Small-town** 205-acre campus
- **Coed**, 2,783 undergraduate students, 91% full-time, 59% women, 41% men
- **Moderately difficult** entrance level, 82% of applicants were admitted
- **16:1 student-to-undergraduate faculty ratio**
- **51% graduate** in 6 years or less
- **$4560 tuition** and fees (in-state); $9988 (out-of-state)

Mansfield University students enjoy a private school environment at a public school price. A small university in the scenic mountains of north-central Pennsylvania, Mansfield prepares students seeking their first employment or graduate school. Mansfield offers more than 70 quality programs of study in the liberal arts tradition. Classes are small, and the learning experience is personalized. A new, technologically advanced library opened in 1996.

Part of Pennsylvania State System of Higher Education.
Students *Undergraduates:* 2,531 full-time, 252 part-time. Students come from 13 states and territories, 16 other countries. *The most frequently chosen baccalaureate fields are:* education, business/marketing, protective services/public administration. *Graduate:* 150 in graduate degree programs.

From out-of-state	16%	Reside on campus	60%
Age 25 or older	18%	Transferred in	7%
International students	1%	African Americans	4%
Asian Americans/Pacific Islanders	1%	Hispanic Americans	1%
Native Americans	1%		

Faculty 183 (82% full-time).

Pennsylvania

Expenses (1999–2000) *Tuition, state resident:* full-time $3618; part-time $150 per credit. *Tuition, nonresident:* full-time $9046; part-time $377 per credit. *Required fees:* full-time $942; $15 per credit; $43 per term part-time. Full-time tuition and fees vary according to reciprocity agreements. Part-time tuition and fees vary according to course load and reciprocity agreements. *College room and board:* $3852. Room and board charges vary according to board plan. *Payment plans:* installment, deferred payment. *Waivers:* senior citizens and employees or children of employees.

Library Main Library. *Operations spending 1999–2000:* $1.3 million. *Collection:* 216,129 titles, 2,200 serial subscriptions.

College life *Housing:* on-campus residence required through senior year. *Options:* coed, women-only. *Social organizations:* national fraternities, national sororities, local fraternities, local sororities; 10% of eligible men and 8% of eligible women are members. *Most popular organizations:* Greek organizations, student government, PSEA, ski club.

Campus security 24-hour emergency response devices and patrols, student patrols, late-night transport-escort service, controlled dormitory access.

After graduation 20 organizations recruited on campus 1997–98. 89% of class of 1998 had job offers within 6 months. *Career center:* 2 full-time personnel. Services include job fairs, resume preparation, resume referral, career/interest testing, career counseling, careers library, job bank, job interviews. *Graduate education:* 8% of class of 1999 went directly to graduate and professional school.

Freshmen 1,861 applied, 1,532 admitted, 632 enrolled.

Average high school GPA	3.2	SAT verbal scores above 500	45%
SAT math scores above 500	43%	ACT above 18	100%
From top 10% of their h.s. class	11%	From top quarter	37%
From top half	80%	1998 freshmen returning in 1999	67%

Application *Options:* eApply at www.CollegeQuest.com, electronic application, early admission, deferred entrance. *Application fee:* $25. *Required:* high school transcript. *Required for some:* interview. *Recommended:* essay or personal statement; minimum 2.5 GPA; letters of recommendation.

Standardized tests *Admission: Required:* SAT I or ACT.

Significant dates *Application deadlines:* rolling (freshmen), rolling (transfers). *Financial aid deadline priority date:* 5/1.

Freshman Application Contact Mr. Brian D. Barden, Director of Admissions, Mansfield University of Pennsylvania, Alumni Hall, Mansfield, PA 16933. **Phone:** 570-662-4813. **Toll-free phone:** 800-577-6826. **Fax:** 570-662-4121. **E-mail:** admissions@mnsfld.edu

Visit CollegeQuest.com for information on majors offered and athletics. Electronic viewbook available at CollegeQuest.com.

■ *See page 1984 for a narrative description.*

MARYWOOD UNIVERSITY
Scranton, Pennsylvania

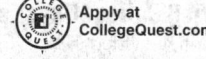

- **Independent Roman Catholic**, comprehensive, founded 1915
- **Degrees** associate, bachelor's, master's, doctoral, post-master's, and postbachelor's certificates
- **Suburban** 115-acre campus
- **Coed**, 1,576 undergraduate students, 88% full-time, 73% women, 27% men
- **Moderately difficult** entrance level, 72% of applicants were admitted
- **11:1 student-to-undergraduate faculty ratio**
- **$15,623 tuition** and fees
- **$13,000 average financial aid** package, $19,170 average indebtedness upon graduation, $24.6 million endowment

Building on its tradition of preparing students from around the world to be successful in professional life and to contribute to the welfare and happiness of others, Marywood continues to strengthen and expand its undergraduate and graduate programs in the arts and sciences. Using its attractive 115-acre campus in northeastern Pennsylvania creatively, Marywood continues to expand its facilities with a new Studio Arts Center and the Center for Graduate and Professional Studies. Marywood is committed to a remarkable scholarship/grant program.

Students *Undergraduates:* 1,392 full-time, 184 part-time. Students come from 24 states and territories, 11 other countries. *The most frequently chosen baccalaureate fields are:* business/marketing, education, health professions and related sciences. *Graduate:* 1,270 in graduate degree programs.

From out-of-state	21%	Reside on campus	28%
Age 25 or older	20%	Transferred in	9%
International students	2%	African Americans	1%
Asian Americans/Pacific Islanders	1%	Hispanic Americans	1%
Native Americans	0.3%		

Faculty 231 (50% full-time).

Expenses (1999–2000) *Comprehensive fee:* $22,163 includes full-time tuition ($15,008), mandatory fees ($615), and room and board ($6540). *College room only:* $3430. Room and board charges vary according to board plan and housing facility. *Part-time tuition:* $469 per credit. *Part-time fees:* $115 per term part-time. Part-time tuition and fees vary according to course load. *Payment plans:* installment, deferred payment. *Waivers:* senior citizens and employees or children of employees.

Library Learning Resources Center. *Operations spending 1999–2000:* $922,447. *Collection:* 209,497 titles, 1,071 serial subscriptions.

College life *Housing:* on-campus residence required through sophomore year. *Options:* coed, men-only, women-only, disabled students. *Most popular organizations:* drama club, student government, outdoor adventure club, Collegiate Volunteers.

Campus security 24-hour emergency response devices and patrols, late-night transport-escort service, controlled dormitory access, apartments with deadbolts.

After graduation 85 organizations recruited on campus 1997–98. 65% of class of 1998 had job offers within 6 months. *Career center:* 3 full-time, 2 part-time personnel. Services include job fairs, resume preparation, interview workshops, resume referral, career/interest testing, career counseling, careers library, job bank, job interviews. *Graduate education:* 19% of class of 1999 went directly to graduate and professional school: 13% graduate arts and sciences, 3% education, 2% business, 0.4% law, 0.4% medicine.

Freshmen 1,170 applied, 838 admitted, 289 enrolled. 9 valedictorians.

Average high school GPA	3.26	SAT verbal scores above 500	63%
SAT math scores above 500	58%	ACT above 18	90%
From top 10% of their h.s. class	16%	From top quarter	49%
From top half	79%	1998 freshmen returning in 1999	81%

Application *Options:* eApply at www.CollegeQuest.com, Common Application, electronic application, early admission, deferred entrance. *Application fee:* $20. *Required:* high school transcript; 1 letter of recommendation. *Required for some:* essay or personal statement; interview. *Recommended:* essay or personal statement; interview.

Standardized tests *Admission: Required:* SAT I or ACT.

Significant dates *Application deadlines:* rolling (freshmen), rolling (transfers). *Financial aid deadline:* continuous.

Freshman Application Contact Ms. Mary Ann Fedrick, Director of Admissions, Marywood University, 2300 Adams Avenue, Scranton, PA 18509-1598. **Phone:** 570-348-6234. **Toll-free phone:** 800-346-5014 (in-state); 800-340-6014 (out-of-state). **Fax:** 570-961-4763. **E-mail:** ugadm@ac.marywood.edu

Visit CollegeQuest.com for information on majors offered and athletics. College video available at CollegeQuest.com.

■ *See page 2018 for a narrative description.*

MCP HAHNEMANN UNIVERSITY
Philadelphia, Pennsylvania

- **Independent**, university, founded 1848
- **Degrees** associate, bachelor's, master's, doctoral, first professional, post-master's, and postbachelor's certificates
- **Urban** campus
- **Coed**, 598 undergraduate students, 62% full-time, 70% women, 30% men
- **Moderately difficult** entrance level, 54% of applicants were admitted
- **10:1 student-to-undergraduate faculty ratio**
- **$10,225 tuition** and fees
- **$55.2 million endowment**

Students *Undergraduates:* 369 full-time, 229 part-time. Students come from 25 states and territories, 3 other countries. *The most frequently chosen baccalaureate fields are:* health professions and related sciences, liberal arts/general studies. *Graduate:* 1,010 in professional programs, 1,051 in

Pennsylvania

MCP Hahnemann University *(continued)*
other graduate degree programs.

From out-of-state	40%	Reside on campus	12%
Age 25 or older	73%	Transferred in	37%
International students	1%	African Americans	21%
Asian Americans/Pacific Islanders	9%	Hispanic Americans	3%
Native Americans	1%		

Faculty 136 (93% full-time), 46% with terminal degrees.
Expenses (1999–2000) *Comprehensive fee:* $18,751 includes full-time tuition ($10,100), mandatory fees ($125), and room and board ($8526). *College room only:* $4926. Full-time tuition and fees vary according to program. Room and board charges vary according to housing facility. *Part-time tuition:* $460 per credit. *Part-time fees:* $32 per term part-time. Part-time tuition and fees vary according to course load and program. *Payment plan:* installment. *Waivers:* employees or children of employees.
Library University Library plus 4 others. *Operations spending 1999–2000:* $3.5 million. *Collection:* 3,238 serial subscriptions, 2,468 audiovisual materials.
College life *Most popular organizations:* Homeless Clinics Project, student government, Minority Student Association, Pre-Med Society, Physician Assistant Club.
Campus security 24-hour emergency response devices and patrols, late-night transport-escort service, controlled dormitory access.
After graduation *Career center:* Services include resume preparation, career counseling.
Freshmen 101 applied, 55 admitted, 28 enrolled.

| SAT verbal scores above 500 | N/R | SAT math scores above 500 | N/R |
| ACT above 18 | N/R | | |

Application *Option:* deferred entrance. *Application fee:* $35. *Required:* essay or personal statement; high school transcript. *Required for some:* minimum 2.0 GPA; letters of recommendation; interview; class rank, community/work experience.
Standardized tests *Admission: Required:* SAT I or ACT, National League of Nursing Exam.
Significant dates *Application deadlines:* 6/1 (freshmen), 6/1 (transfers). *Financial aid deadline priority date:* 5/1.
Freshman Application Contact
Ms. Jarmila H. Force, Associate Director of Enrollment Management, MCP Hahnemann University, 245 North 15th Street, Mail Stop 472, Philadelphia, PA 19102-1192. **Phone:** 215-762-4671. **Toll-free phone:** 800-2-DREXEL Ext. 6333. **E-mail:** enroll@mcphu.edu
Visit CollegeQuest.com for information on majors offered and athletics. College video available at CollegeQuest.com.

■ *See page 2034 for a narrative description.*

MERCYHURST COLLEGE
Erie, Pennsylvania

- **Independent Roman Catholic**, comprehensive, founded 1926
- **Degrees** associate, bachelor's, master's, and postbachelor's certificates
- **Suburban** 88-acre campus with easy access to Buffalo
- **Coed**, 2,667 undergraduate students, 85% full-time, 57% women, 43% men
- **Moderately difficult** entrance level, 79% of applicants were admitted
- **17:1** student-to-undergraduate faculty ratio
- **$14,190 tuition** and fees
- **$8300** average financial aid package, $16,781 average indebtedness upon graduation, $8.8 million endowment

Mercyhurst emphasizes the role of the liberal arts as a basis for sound career preparation and many other life objectives. With this balance in mind, the College supports a wide range of programs. Mercyhurst College strives constantly to remain distinctive in the choice of its academic offerings. For additional information, students should call 814-824-2202 or 800-825-1926 (toll-free) or visit the Web site (www.mercyhurst.edu).

Students *Undergraduates:* 2,278 full-time, 389 part-time. Students come from 37 states and territories, 17 other countries. *The most frequently chosen baccalaureate fields are:* business/marketing, education, social sciences and history. *Graduate:* 166 in graduate degree programs.

From out-of-state	43%	Reside on campus	70%
Age 25 or older	21%	Transferred in	2%
International students	3%	African Americans	4%
Asian Americans/Pacific Islanders	0.5%	Hispanic Americans	1%
Native Americans	0.5%		

Faculty 252 (46% full-time), 51% with terminal degrees.
Expenses (2000–2001) *Comprehensive fee:* $19,296 includes full-time tuition ($13,290), mandatory fees ($900), and room and board ($5106). Room and board charges vary according to board plan and housing facility. *Part-time tuition:* $443 per credit. *Part-time fees:* $300 per term part-time. Part-time tuition and fees vary according to course load and location. *Payment plan:* installment. *Waivers:* employees or children of employees.
Library Hammermill Library plus 1 other. *Operations spending 1999–2000:* $611,509. *Collection:* 123,467 titles, 849 serial subscriptions, 8,051 audiovisual materials.
College life On-campus residence required through sophomore year. *Most popular organizations:* student government, chorus, Admission Ambassadors, Amnesty International, The Merciad.
Campus security 24-hour emergency response devices and patrols, campus-wide camera system.
After graduation 103 organizations recruited on campus 1997–98. 65% of class of 1998 had job offers within 6 months. *Career center:* 3 full-time, 4 part-time personnel. Services include job fairs, resume preparation, interview workshops, resume referral, career/interest testing, career counseling, careers library, job bank, job interviews. *Graduate education:* 16% of class of 1999 went directly to graduate and professional school: 9% graduate arts and sciences, 3% business, 2% medicine, 1% education, 1% law.
Freshmen 1,852 applied, 1,460 admitted, 668 enrolled. 12 class presidents, 9 valedictorians, 246 student government officers.

Average high school GPA	3.2	SAT verbal scores above 500	71%
SAT math scores above 500	69%	ACT above 18	100%
From top 10% of their h.s. class	18%	From top quarter	45%
From top half	78%	1998 freshmen returning in 1999	80%

Application *Options:* Common Application, electronic application, early admission, early action, deferred entrance. *Application fee:* $30. *Required:* high school transcript; minimum 2.5 GPA. *Required for some:* essay or personal statement; interview. *Recommended:* 2 letters of recommendation.
Standardized tests *Admission: Required:* SAT I or ACT.
Significant dates *Application deadlines:* rolling (freshmen), rolling (transfers). *Early action:* 11/15. *Notification:* 12/15 (early action). *Financial aid deadline priority date:* 3/1.
Freshman Application Contact
Mr. Jim Breckenridge, Director of Undergraduate Admissions, Mercyhurst College, 501 East 38th Street, Erie, PA 16546. **Phone:** 814-824-2573. **Toll-free phone:** 800-825-1926. **Fax:** 814-824-2071. **E-mail:** admug@mercyhurst.edu
Visit CollegeQuest.com for information on majors offered and athletics. College video available at CollegeQuest.com.

■ *See page 2044 for a narrative description.*

MESSIAH COLLEGE
Grantham, Pennsylvania

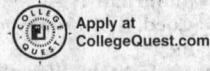
Apply at CollegeQuest.com

- **Independent interdenominational**, 4-year, founded 1909
- **Degree** bachelor's
- **Small-town** 400-acre campus
- **Coed**, 2,695 undergraduate students, 99% full-time, 61% women, 39% men
- **Moderately difficult** entrance level, 81% of applicants were admitted
- **15:1** student-to-undergraduate faculty ratio
- **70.8%** graduate in 6 years or less
- **$15,096 tuition** and fees
- **$11,909** average financial aid package, $16,999 average indebtedness upon graduation, $107.4 million endowment

Students *Undergraduates:* 2,658 full-time, 37 part-time. Students come from 39 states and territories, 22 other countries. *The most frequently chosen baccalaureate fields are:* business/marketing, education, health professions and related sciences.

704   www.petersons.com   Peterson's Guide to Four-Year Colleges 2001

Pennsylvania

From out-of-state	49%	Reside on campus	88%
Age 25 or older	1%	Transferred in	3%
International students	2%	African Americans	1%
Asian Americans/Pacific Islanders	1%	Hispanic Americans	2%
Native Americans	0.2%		

Faculty 245 (58% full-time), 53% with terminal degrees.

Expenses (1999–2000) *Comprehensive fee:* $20,676 includes full-time tuition ($15,000), mandatory fees ($96), and room and board ($5580). *College room only:* $2850. Room and board charges vary according to board plan. *Part-time tuition:* $625 per credit. *Part-time fees:* $4 per credit. *Payment plan:* installment. *Waivers:* minority students, children of alumni, adult students, senior citizens, and employees or children of employees.

Library Murray Library. *Operations spending 1999–2000:* $1.2 million. *Collection:* 233,732 titles, 1,316 serial subscriptions.

College life *Housing:* on-campus residence required through senior year. *Options:* coed, men-only, women-only, disabled students. *Most popular organizations:* Outreach teams, student government, music ensembles, Small Group Program, outdoors club.

Campus security 24-hour emergency response devices and patrols, student patrols, late-night transport-escort service, controlled dormitory access, bicycle patrols.

After graduation 453 organizations recruited on campus 1997–98. 89% of class of 1998 had job offers within 6 months. *Career center:* 4 full-time, 1 part-time personnel. Services include job fairs, resume preparation, interview workshops, resume referral, career/interest testing, career counseling, careers library, job bank, job interviews. *Graduate education:* 8% of class of 1999 went directly to graduate and professional school: 5% graduate arts and sciences, 2% education, 1% medicine.

Freshmen 2,088 applied, 1,681 admitted, 678 enrolled. 13 National Merit Scholars, 43 valedictorians.

Average high school GPA	3.68	SAT verbal scores above 500	88%
SAT math scores above 500	84%	ACT above 18	99%
From top 10% of their h.s. class	34%	From top quarter	66%
From top half	92%	1998 freshmen returning in 1999	86%

Application *Options:* eApply at www.CollegeQuest.com, Common Application, electronic application, early admission, deferred entrance. *Application fee:* $30. *Required:* essay or personal statement; high school transcript; 2 letters of recommendation. *Recommended:* minimum 3.0 GPA; interview.

Standardized tests *Admission: Required:* SAT I or ACT.

Significant dates *Application deadlines:* rolling (freshmen), rolling (transfers). *Financial aid deadline priority date:* 4/1.

Freshman Application Contact
Mr. William G. Strausbaugh, Dean for Enrollment Management, Messiah College, One College Avenue, Grantham, PA 17027-0800. **Phone:** 717-691-6000. **Toll-free phone:** 800-382-1349 (in-state); 800-233-4220 (out-of-state). **Fax:** 717-796-5374. **E-mail:** admiss@messiah.edu
Visit CollegeQuest.com for information on majors offered and athletics. Electronic viewbook available at CollegeQuest.com.

■ *See page 2050 for a narrative description.*

MILLERSVILLE UNIVERSITY OF PENNSYLVANIA
Millersville, Pennsylvania

- **State-supported**, comprehensive, founded 1855
- **Degrees** associate, bachelor's, master's, post-master's, and postbachelor's certificates
- **Suburban** 190-acre campus
- **Coed**, 6,254 undergraduate students, 88% full-time, 58% women, 42% men
- **Moderately difficult** entrance level, 69% of applicants were admitted
- **17:1** student-to-undergraduate faculty ratio
- **65% graduate** in 6 years or less
- **$4595 tuition** and fees (in-state); $10,023 (out-of-state)
- **$6000 average financial aid** package, $12,507 average indebtedness upon graduation, $789,394 endowment

Part of Pennsylvania State System of Higher Education.
Students *Undergraduates:* 5,474 full-time, 780 part-time. Students come from 27 states and territories, 50 other countries. *The most frequently chosen baccalaureate fields are:* business/marketing, education, social sciences and history. *Graduate:* 906 in graduate degree programs.

From out-of-state	4%	Reside on campus	41%
Age 25 or older	14%	Transferred in	6%
International students	1%	African Americans	6%
Asian Americans/Pacific Islanders	2%	Hispanic Americans	2%
Native Americans	0.2%		

Faculty 446 (73% full-time).

Expenses (1999–2000) *Tuition, state resident:* full-time $3618; part-time $150 per credit. *Tuition, nonresident:* full-time $9046; part-time $377 per credit. *Required fees:* full-time $977; $41 per credit. Part-time tuition and fees vary according to course load. *College room and board:* $4730. Room and board charges vary according to board plan. *Payment plan:* installment. *Waivers:* senior citizens and employees or children of employees.

Library Helen A. Ganser Library. *Operations spending 1999–2000:* $2.8 million. *Collection:* 493,347 titles, 2,470 serial subscriptions, 6,831 audiovisual materials.

College life *Housing:* on-campus residence required through sophomore year. *Options:* coed, men-only, women-only. *Social organizations:* national fraternities, national sororities, local fraternities, local sororities; 7% of eligible men and 8% of eligible women are members. *Most popular organizations:* Black Student Union, John Newman Association, Student Ambassadors, Resident Student Association, University Activities Board.

Campus security 24-hour emergency response devices and patrols, student patrols, late-night transport-escort service.

After graduation 47 organizations recruited on campus 1997–98. 71% of class of 1998 had job offers within 6 months. *Career center:* 4 full-time, 2 part-time personnel. Services include job fairs, resume preparation, interview workshops, resume referral, career/interest testing, career counseling, careers library, job interviews. *Graduate education:* 20% of class of 1999 went directly to graduate and professional school.

Freshmen 5,848 applied, 4,041 admitted, 1,284 enrolled.

SAT verbal scores above 500	66%	SAT math scores above 500	67%
ACT above 18	N/R	From top 10% of their h.s. class	12%
From top quarter	45%	From top half	87%
1998 freshmen returning in 1999	81%		

Application *Options:* Common Application, electronic application, early admission, deferred entrance. *Application fee:* $25. *Required:* high school transcript; minimum 2.0 GPA. *Required for some:* letters of recommendation. *Recommended:* letters of recommendation.

Standardized tests *Admission: Required:* SAT I or ACT.

Significant dates *Application deadlines:* rolling (freshmen), rolling (transfers). *Financial aid deadline:* 3/15.

Freshman Application Contact
Mr. Darrell Davis, Director of Admissions, Millersville University of Pennsylvania, PO Box 1002, Millersville, PA 17551-0302. **Phone:** 717-872-3371. **Toll-free phone:** 800-MU-ADMIT. **E-mail:** muadmit@marauder.millersv.edu
Visit CollegeQuest.com for information on majors offered and athletics. College video available at CollegeQuest.com.

■ *See page 2058 for a narrative description.*

MOORE COLLEGE OF ART AND DESIGN
Philadelphia, Pennsylvania

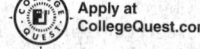 Apply at CollegeQuest.com

- **Independent**, 4-year, founded 1848
- **Degree** bachelor's
- **Urban** 3-acre campus
- **Women** only, 418 undergraduate students, 94% full-time
- **Moderately difficult** entrance level, 59% of applicants were admitted
- **8:1** student-to-undergraduate faculty ratio
- **45% graduate** in 6 years or less
- **$16,025 tuition** and fees
- **$13,345 average financial aid** package, $25,000 average indebtedness upon graduation, $7 million endowment

Moore College of Art and Design, the only fully accredited visual arts college for women in the country, grants BFA degrees in 9 fine and professional arts disciplines. Moore offers small classes taught by practicing artists, designers,

Peterson's Guide to Four-Year Colleges 2001   www.petersons.com

Pennsylvania

Moore College of Art and Design (continued)
and liberal arts scholars, with an emphasis on preparing women for careers in the visual arts.

Students *Undergraduates:* 394 full-time, 24 part-time. Students come from 26 states and territories, 7 other countries. *The most frequently chosen baccalaureate field is:* visual/performing arts.

From out-of-state	30%	Reside on campus	55%
Age 25 or older	15%	Transferred in	11%
International students	4%	African Americans	8%
Asian Americans/Pacific Islanders	5%	Hispanic Americans	5%
Native Americans	0.5%		

Faculty 89 (44% full-time), 34% with terminal degrees.

Expenses (1999–2000) *Comprehensive fee:* $22,175 includes full-time tuition ($15,475), mandatory fees ($550), and room and board ($6150). *Part-time tuition:* $645 per credit. *Part-time fees:* $275 per term part-time. *Payment plan:* installment. *Waivers:* employees or children of employees.

Library Moore College Library. *Operations spending 1999–2000:* $191,070. *Collection:* 33,114 titles, 181 serial subscriptions, 722 audiovisual materials.

College life *Housing: Option:* women-only. *Most popular organizations:* Student Government Association, Into the Streets, Moore Environment Action Now, Black Student Union, Asian Student Union.

Campus security 24-hour patrols, late-night transport-escort service.

After graduation *Career center:* 1 part-time personnel. Services include resume preparation, resume referral, career counseling, careers library, job bank. *Graduate education:* 4% of class of 1999 went directly to graduate and professional school: 4% graduate arts and sciences.

Freshmen 319 applied, 188 admitted, 81 enrolled.

Average high school GPA	3.1	SAT verbal scores above 500	N/R
SAT math scores above 500	N/R	ACT above 18	N/R
1998 freshmen returning in 1999	79%		

Application *Options:* eApply at www.CollegeQuest.com, early admission, early decision, deferred entrance. *Application fee:* $35. *Required:* high school transcript; minimum 2.5 GPA; 1 letter of recommendation; portfolio. *Required for some:* minimum 3.0 GPA. *Recommended:* essay or personal statement; interview.

Standardized tests *Admission: Required:* SAT I or ACT.

Significant dates *Application deadlines:* 8/15 (freshmen), rolling (transfers). *Early decision:* 11/1. *Notification:* 11/15 (early decision). *Financial aid deadline priority date:* 3/1.

Freshman Application Contact
Ms. Deborah Deery, Director of Admissions, Moore College of Art and Design, 20th and the Parkway, Philadelphia, PA 19103. **Phone:** 215-568-4515 Ext. 1108. **Toll-free phone:** 800-523-2025. **Fax:** 215-568-3547. **E-mail:** admiss@access.digex.net

Visit CollegeQuest.com for information on majors offered and athletics.

■ *See page 2092 for a narrative description.*

MORAVIAN COLLEGE
Bethlehem, Pennsylvania

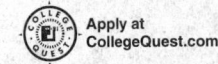
Apply at CollegeQuest.com

■ **Independent**, comprehensive, founded 1742, affiliated with Moravian Church
■ **Degrees** bachelor's, master's, and first professional
■ **Suburban** 70-acre campus with easy access to Philadelphia
■ **Coed**, 1,462 undergraduate students, 87% full-time, 56% women, 44% men
■ **Moderately difficult** entrance level, 73% of applicants were admitted
■ **14:1 student-to-undergraduate faculty ratio**
■ **70% graduate** in 6 years or less
■ **$18,575 tuition** and fees
■ **$15,040 average financial aid** package, $62.3 million endowment

Students *Undergraduates:* 1,266 full-time, 196 part-time. Students come from 23 states and territories, 12 other countries. *The most frequently chosen baccalaureate fields are:* business/marketing, psychology, social sciences and history. *Graduate:* 79 in graduate degree programs.

From out-of-state	40%	Reside on campus	76%
Age 25 or older	15%	Transferred in	5%
International students	1%	African Americans	2%
Asian Americans/Pacific Islanders	2%	Hispanic Americans	3%
Native Americans	0.1%		

Faculty 160 (56% full-time).

Expenses (1999–2000) *Comprehensive fee:* $24,495 includes full-time tuition ($18,245), mandatory fees ($330), and room and board ($5920). *College room only:* $3220. Room and board charges vary according to board plan and housing facility. *Part-time tuition:* $507 per credit. *Part-time fees:* $75 per term part-time. Part-time tuition and fees vary according to class time. *Payment plan:* installment. *Waivers:* employees or children of employees.

Library Reeves Library. *Operations spending 1999–2000:* $1.1 million. *Collection:* 244,787 titles, 1,367 serial subscriptions, 1,098 audiovisual materials.

College life *Housing:* on-campus residence required in freshman year. *Options:* coed, men-only, women-only, disabled students. *Social organizations:* national fraternities, national sororities, local fraternities, local sororities; 18% of eligible men and 24% of eligible women are members. *Most popular organizations:* Student Alumni Association, United Student Government, Moravian College Choir, Twenty-Six Points.

Campus security 24-hour emergency response devices and patrols, late-night transport-escort service, controlled dormitory access.

After graduation 30 organizations recruited on campus 1997–98. 73% of class of 1998 had job offers within 6 months. *Career center:* 1 full-time personnel. Services include job fairs, resume preparation, interview workshops, resume referral, career/interest testing, career counseling, careers library, job bank, job interviews. *Graduate education:* 20% of class of 1999 went directly to graduate and professional school: 9% graduate arts and sciences, 3% business, 3% law, 3% medicine, 1% dentistry, 1% veterinary medicine.

Freshmen 1,356 applied, 995 admitted, 318 enrolled.

SAT verbal scores above 500	77%	SAT math scores above 500	81%
ACT above 18	N/R	From top 10% of their h.s. class	19%
From top quarter	50%	From top half	90%
1998 freshmen returning in 1999	82%		

Application *Options:* eApply at www.CollegeQuest.com, Common Application, electronic application, early decision, deferred entrance. *Application fee:* $30. *Required:* essay or personal statement; high school transcript; minimum 2.5 GPA; 3 letters of recommendation. *Recommended:* interview.

Standardized tests *Admission: Required:* SAT I or ACT.

Significant dates *Application deadlines:* 3/1 (freshmen), 3/1 (transfers). *Early decision:* 1/15. *Notification:* 3/15 (freshmen), 2/1 (early decision). *Financial aid deadline priority date:* 2/15.

Freshman Application Contact
Mr. James P. Mackin, Director of Admission, Moravian College, 1200 Main Street, Bethlehem, PA 18018. **Phone:** 610-861-1320. **Fax:** 610-861-3956. **E-mail:** admissions@moravian.edu

Visit CollegeQuest.com for information on majors offered and athletics. College video and electronic viewbook available at CollegeQuest.com.

■ *See page 2094 for a narrative description.*

MOUNT ALOYSIUS COLLEGE
Cresson, Pennsylvania

Apply at CollegeQuest.com

■ **Independent Roman Catholic**, 4-year, founded 1939
■ **Degrees** associate and bachelor's
■ **Rural** 125-acre campus
■ **Coed**, 999 undergraduate students, 82% full-time, 75% women, 25% men
■ **Minimally difficult** entrance level, 53% of applicants were admitted
■ **13:1 student-to-undergraduate faculty ratio**
■ **$10,980 tuition** and fees
■ **$4650 average financial aid** package, $17,000 average indebtedness upon graduation, $5.7 million endowment

Mount Aloysius College offers merit scholarships that are renewable annually and valued up to $5000. Baccalaureate and associate degrees and certificate programs are offered. All students at Mount Aloysius College receive a broad-based liberal arts education. Committed to excellence, the faculty and staff provide personalized attention.

Students *Undergraduates:* 815 full-time, 184 part-time. Students come from 7 states and territories, 7 other countries. *The most frequently chosen baccalaureate fields are:* health professions and related sciences, interdisciplinary studies, protective services/public administration.

From out-of-state	2%	Reside on campus	11%
Age 25 or older	43%	International students	2%
African Americans	2%	Asian Americans/Pacific Islanders	0.4%
Hispanic Americans	0.1%	Native Americans	0.1%

Faculty 126 (42% full-time), 12% with terminal degrees.

Expenses (2000–2001) *Comprehensive fee:* $15,810 includes full-time tuition ($10,780), mandatory fees ($200), and room and board ($4830). *College room only:* $2140. Full-time tuition and fees vary according to program. Room and board charges vary according to board plan and housing facility. *Part-time tuition:* $385 per credit. *Part-time fees:* $50 per term part-time. Part-time tuition and fees vary according to class time, course level, course load, program, and student level. *Waivers:* employees or children of employees.

Library Mount Aloysius College Library plus 1 other. *Operations spending 1999–2000:* $353,898. *Collection:* 70,000 titles, 350 serial subscriptions.

College life *Housing: Options:* men-only, women-only, disabled students. *Most popular organizations:* Phi Theta Kappa, Student Nursing Association, Student Occupational Therapy Association, Criminology Club, campus ministry.

Campus security 24-hour emergency response devices and patrols, late-night transport-escort service, controlled dormitory access.

After graduation 34 organizations recruited on campus 1997–98. 65% of class of 1998 had job offers within 6 months. *Career center:* 2 full-time personnel. Services include job fairs, resume preparation, resume referral, career counseling, careers library.

Freshmen 647 applied, 344 admitted, 163 enrolled. 2 valedictorians.

Average high school GPA	2.89	SAT verbal scores above 500	17%
SAT math scores above 500	13%	ACT above 18	36%
From top 10% of their h.s. class	5%	From top quarter	21%
From top half	47%	1998 freshmen returning in 1999	73%

Application *Options:* eApply at www.CollegeQuest.com, early admission, deferred entrance. *Application fee:* $25. *Required:* high school transcript; minimum 2.0 GPA. *Required for some:* essay or personal statement; 3 letters of recommendation; interview. *Recommended:* interview.

Standardized tests *Admission: Recommended:* SAT I or ACT. *Required for some:* SAT I or ACT.

Significant dates *Application deadlines:* rolling (freshmen), rolling (transfers). *Financial aid deadline:* 5/1. *Priority date:* 2/15.

Freshman Application Contact
Mr. Mike Macekura, Dean of Enrollment Management, Mount Aloysius College, 7373 Admiral Peary Highway, Cresson, PA 16630. **Phone:** 814-886-6383. **Toll-free phone:** 888-823-2220. **Fax:** 814-886-2978. **E-mail:** admissions@mtaloy.edu

Visit CollegeQuest.com for information on majors offered and athletics. College video and electronic viewbook available at CollegeQuest.com.

■ *See page 2102 for a narrative description.*

MUHLENBERG COLLEGE
Allentown, Pennsylvania

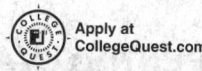
Apply at CollegeQuest.com

- **Independent**, 4-year, founded 1848, affiliated with Lutheran Church
- **Degree** bachelor's
- **Suburban** 75-acre campus with easy access to Philadelphia
- **Coed**, 2,318 undergraduate students, 92% full-time, 57% women, 43% men
- **Very difficult** entrance level, 55% of applicants were admitted
- **13:1 student-to-undergraduate faculty ratio**
- **$20,085 tuition** and fees
- **$14,559 average financial aid** package, $82.3 million endowment

"Friendly" and "challenging" are the words that students use most often to describe Muhlenberg. The educational experience is active and hands-on, with small classes and easy access to faculty members. Internships, field study, study abroad, and a Washington Semester supplement traditional classroom experiences. Students are able to analyze and think critically as well as effectively express themselves in person and in writing—the most prized outcomes of a Muhlenberg education.

Students *Undergraduates:* 2,130 full-time, 188 part-time. Students come from 37 states and territories, 5 other countries. *The most frequently chosen baccalaureate fields are:* biological/life sciences, psychology, social sciences and history.

From out-of-state	66%	Reside on campus	90%
Age 25 or older	4%	Transferred in	0.3%
International students	0.2%	African Americans	2%
Asian Americans/Pacific Islanders	3%	Hispanic Americans	2%
Native Americans	0.05%		

Faculty 213 (62% full-time).

Expenses (1999–2000) *Comprehensive fee:* $25,475 includes full-time tuition ($19,910), mandatory fees ($175), and room and board ($5390). *College room only:* $2795. Room and board charges vary according to board plan, housing facility, and location. *Part-time tuition:* $1405 per course. *Part-time fees:* $88 per term part-time. *Payment plans:* tuition prepayment, installment. *Waivers:* employees or children of employees.

Library Trexler Library. *Operations spending 1999–2000:* $1.2 million. *Collection:* 270,700 titles, 1,700 serial subscriptions, 4,400 audiovisual materials.

College life *Housing:* on-campus residence required in freshman year. *Options:* coed, women-only, disabled students. *Social organizations:* national fraternities, national sororities; 36% of eligible men and 37% of eligible women are members. *Most popular organizations:* Muhlenberg Theater Association, Environmental Action Team, Jefferson School Partnership, Select Choir, Habitat for Humanity.

Campus security 24-hour emergency response devices and patrols, late-night transport-escort service, controlled dormitory access.

After graduation 64 organizations recruited on campus 1997–98. 67% of class of 1998 had job offers within 6 months. *Career center:* 2 full-time, 1 part-time personnel. Services include job fairs, resume preparation, interview workshops, resume referral, career/interest testing, career counseling, careers library, job bank, job interviews.

Freshmen 3,274 applied, 1,808 admitted, 552 enrolled. 1 National Merit Scholar, 24 class presidents, 7 valedictorians, 91 student government officers.

Average high school GPA	3.56	SAT verbal scores above 500	88%
SAT math scores above 500	89%	ACT above 18	N/R
From top 10% of their h.s. class	34%	From top quarter	67%
From top half	94%	1998 freshmen returning in 1999	91%

Application *Options:* eApply at www.CollegeQuest.com, Common Application, electronic application, early admission, early decision, deferred entrance. *Application fee:* $40. *Required:* essay or personal statement; high school transcript; 2 letters of recommendation. *Required for some:* interview. *Recommended:* interview.

Standardized tests *Admission: Required for some:* SAT I or ACT.

Significant dates *Application deadlines:* 2/15 (freshmen), 6/1 (transfers). *Early decision:* 1/15. *Notification:* 4/1 (freshmen), 2/1 (early decision). *Financial aid deadline:* 2/15.

Freshman Application Contact
Mr. Christopher Hooker-Haring, Dean of Admissions, Muhlenberg College, 2400 Chew Street, Allentown, PA 18104-5586. **Phone:** 484-664-3245. **Fax:** 484-664-3234. **E-mail:** adm@muhlenberg.edu

Visit CollegeQuest.com for information on majors offered and athletics.

■ *See page 2128 for a narrative description.*

NEUMANN COLLEGE
Aston, Pennsylvania

- **Independent Roman Catholic**, comprehensive, founded 1965
- **Degrees** associate, bachelor's, and master's
- **Suburban** 28-acre campus with easy access to Philadelphia
- **Coed**, 1,438 undergraduate students, 74% full-time, 67% women, 33% men

Pennsylvania

Neumann College (continued)
- **Moderately difficult** entrance level, 98% of applicants were admitted
- **14:1 student-to-undergraduate faculty ratio**
- **65% graduate** in 6 years or less
- **$13,920 tuition** and fees
- **$13.5 million endowment**

Students *Undergraduates:* 1,068 full-time, 370 part-time. Students come from 17 states and territories. *The most frequently chosen baccalaureate fields are:* health professions and related sciences, education, liberal arts/general studies. *Graduate:* 180 in graduate degree programs.

From out-of-state	25%	Reside on campus	32%
Age 25 or older	33%	Transferred in	5%
African Americans	13%	Asian Americans/Pacific Islanders	1%
Hispanic Americans	2%	Native Americans	0.2%

Faculty 169 (32% full-time), 38% with terminal degrees.
Expenses (1999–2000) *Comprehensive fee:* $20,420 includes full-time tuition ($13,350), mandatory fees ($570), and room and board ($6500). *College room only:* $3600. Full-time tuition and fees vary according to program. *Part-time tuition:* $320 per credit. Part-time tuition and fees vary according to program. *Payment plans:* installment, deferred payment. *Waivers:* employees or children of employees.
Library Neumann College Library. *Operations spending 1999–2000:* $343,348. *Collection:* 95,167 titles, 1,695 serial subscriptions, 52,052 audiovisual materials.
College life *Housing:* Option: coed. *Most popular organizations:* Professional Education Society, Student Nurses Association, theater ensemble, environmental club, community chorus.
Campus security 24-hour emergency response devices and patrols, late-night transport-escort service, controlled dormitory access.
After graduation 55 organizations recruited on campus 1997–98. 89% of class of 1998 had job offers within 6 months. *Career center:* 2 full-time personnel. Services include job fairs, resume preparation, interview workshops, resume referral, career/interest testing, career counseling, careers library, job bank, job interviews. *Graduate education:* 8% of class of 1999 went directly to graduate and professional school.
Freshmen 1,180 applied, 1,158 admitted, 379 enrolled.

Average high school GPA	2.87	SAT verbal scores above 500	36%
SAT math scores above 500	21%	ACT above 18	N/R
1998 freshmen returning in 1999	77%		

Application *Options:* early admission, deferred entrance. *Application fee:* $35. *Required:* high school transcript. *Recommended:* interview.
Standardized tests *Admission: Required:* SAT I or ACT.
Significant dates *Application deadlines:* rolling (freshmen), rolling (transfers). *Financial aid deadline:* continuous.
Freshman Application Contact
Mr. Scott Bogard, Executive Director of Admissions and Financial Aid, Neumann College, One Neumann Drive, Aston, PA 19014-1298. **Phone:** 610-558-5612. **Toll-free phone:** 800-963-8626. **E-mail:** neumann@neumann.edu
Visit CollegeQuest.com for information on majors offered and athletics.

- *See page 2138 for a narrative description.*

PEIRCE COLLEGE
Philadelphia, Pennsylvania

Apply at CollegeQuest.com

- **Independent**, 4-year, founded 1865
- **Degrees** associate, bachelor's, and postbachelor's certificates
- **Urban** 1-acre campus
- **Coed**, primarily women, 2,334 undergraduate students, 39% full-time, 81% women, 19% men
- **Minimally difficult** entrance level, 64% of applicants were admitted
- **12:1 student-to-undergraduate faculty ratio**
- **$8220 tuition** and fees
- **$3500 average financial aid** package, $12,500 average indebtedness upon graduation, $14.7 million endowment

Founded in 1865, Peirce College has a long-standing reputation for providing a leading-edge, high-quality, business-related education that reflects current hiring trends. New IT programs include networking, business information systems, and technology management. The College is located off the Avenue of the Arts at Broad and Pine Streets in Philadelphia.

Students *Undergraduates:* 900 full-time, 1,434 part-time. Students come from 5 states and territories, 10 other countries. *The most frequently chosen baccalaureate field is:* (pre)law.

From out-of-state	9%	Age 25 or older	69%
Transferred in	32%	International students	1%
African Americans	63%	Asian Americans/Pacific Islanders	3%
Hispanic Americans	5%	Native Americans	0.2%

Faculty 394 (8% full-time), 100% with terminal degrees.
Expenses (1999–2000) *Tuition:* full-time $7980; part-time $266 per credit. *Required fees:* full-time $240; $60 per term part-time. *Payment plan:* deferred payment. *Waivers:* children of alumni and employees or children of employees.
Library *Operations spending 1999–2000:* $400,000. *Collection:* 36,900 titles, 159 serial subscriptions, 4,578 audiovisual materials.
College life *Housing:* college housing not available. *Social organizations:* 8% of eligible men and 16% of eligible women are members. *Most popular organization:* Phi Theta Kappa.
Campus security 24-hour emergency response devices and patrols, late-night transport-escort service.
After graduation 75 organizations recruited on campus 1997–98. 68% of class of 1998 had job offers within 6 months. *Career center:* 4 full-time personnel. Services include job fairs, resume preparation, interview workshops, resume referral, career/interest testing, career counseling, careers library, job bank, job interviews. *Graduate education:* 20% of class of 1999 went directly to graduate and professional school.
Freshmen 700 applied, 450 admitted, 362 enrolled. 2 valedictorians, 5 student government officers.

SAT verbal scores above 500	N/R	SAT math scores above 500	N/R
ACT above 18	N/R	1998 freshmen returning in 1999	70%

Application *Options:* eApply at www.CollegeQuest.com, Common Application, electronic application, early admission, deferred entrance. *Application fee:* $20. *Required:* high school transcript. *Recommended:* essay or personal statement; minimum 2.0 GPA; letters of recommendation; interview.
Standardized tests *Placement: Required:* ACT ASSET
Significant dates *Application deadlines:* rolling (freshmen), rolling (transfers). *Financial aid deadline priority date:* 2/15.
Freshman Application Contact
Mr. Jay Pollard, College Representative, Peirce College, 1420 Pine Street, Philadelphia, PA 19102. **Phone:** 215-545-6400 Ext. 292. **Toll-free phone:** 888-467-3472 Ext. 214. **Fax:** 215-546-5996. **E-mail:** info@peirce.edu
Visit CollegeQuest.com for information on majors offered and athletics. Electronic viewbook available at CollegeQuest.com.

- *See page 2250 for a narrative description.*

PENNSYLVANIA COLLEGE OF OPTOMETRY
Elkins Park, Pennsylvania

Admissions Office Contact
Pennsylvania College of Optometry, 8360 Old York Road, Elkins Park, PA 19027-1598. **Toll-free phone:** 800-824-6262.

PENNSYLVANIA COLLEGE OF TECHNOLOGY
Williamsport, Pennsylvania

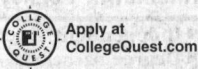
Apply at CollegeQuest.com

- **State-related**, primarily 2-year, founded 1965
- **Degrees** associate and bachelor's
- **Small-town** 927-acre campus
- **Coed**, 5,153 undergraduate students, 81% full-time, 37% women, 63% men
- **Noncompetitive** entrance level

Pennsylvania

Pennsylvania College of Technology is an affiliate of the Pennsylvania State University (Penn State). It is a distinctive institution offering bachelor's and associate degrees and specialized educational opportunities focused on applied technology. Penn College is an integral part of the Penn State System, offering students the opportunity to combine a hands-on, technical education with theory and management education.

Faculty 401 (61% full-time).
Admissions Office Contact
Pennsylvania College of Technology, One College Avenue, Williamsport, PA 17701-5778. **Toll-free phone:** 800-367-9222. **Fax:** 570-321-5536. **E-mail:** cschuman@pct.edu

Visit CollegeQuest.com for information on majors offered and athletics. College video and electronic viewbook available at CollegeQuest.com.

■ *See page 2252 for a narrative description.*

PENNSYLVANIA SCHOOL OF ART & DESIGN
Lancaster, Pennsylvania

- **Independent**, 4-year, founded 1982
- **Degree** bachelor's
- **Coed**, 152 undergraduate students, 88% full-time, 45% women, 55% men
- **50% of applicants were admitted**
- **$9290 tuition** and fees

Students *Undergraduates:* 133 full-time, 19 part-time.
Expenses (1999–2000) *Tuition:* full-time $8940; part-time $298 per credit. *Required fees:* full-time $350; $110 per term part-time. Full-time tuition and fees vary according to course load and program. Part-time tuition and fees vary according to course load and program. *Payment plan:* installment. *Waivers:* employees or children of employees.
Library *Collection:* 7,000 titles, 35 serial subscriptions, 42 audiovisual materials.
College life *Housing:* college housing not available. *Most popular organizations:* student council, yearbook.
Campus security Trained evening/weekend security personnel.
Freshmen 185 applied, 92 admitted, 63 enrolled.

| Average high school GPA | 2.62 | SAT verbal scores above 500 | N/R |
| SAT math scores above 500 | N/R | ACT above 18 | N/R |

Application *Option:* deferred entrance. *Application fee:* $35. *Required:* essay or personal statement; high school transcript; interview; portfolio. *Required for some:* 2 letters of recommendation. *Recommended:* minimum 2.0 GPA; 2 letters of recommendation.
Significant dates *Application deadlines:* 5/1 (freshmen), 5/1 (transfers). *Financial aid deadline priority date:* 8/1.
Freshman Application Contact
Ms. Wendy Sweigart, Director of Admissions, Pennsylvania School of Art & Design, Admissions Office, PO Box 59, Lancaster, PA 17608-0059. **Phone:** 717-396-7833 Ext. 19. **Fax:** 717-396-1339. **E-mail:** term1@psad.edu

Visit CollegeQuest.com for information on majors offered and athletics.

PENNSYLVANIA STATE UNIVERSITY ABINGTON COLLEGE
Abington, Pennsylvania

- **State-related**, 4-year, founded 1950
- **Degrees** associate and bachelor's
- **Small-town** 45-acre campus with easy access to Philadelphia
- **Coed**, 2,477 undergraduate students, 86% full-time, 48% women, 52% men
- **Moderately difficult** entrance level, 83% of applicants were admitted
- **24:1 student-to-undergraduate faculty ratio**
- **43.09% graduate** in 6 years or less
- **$6312 tuition** and fees (in-state); $9672 (out-of-state)

Part of Pennsylvania State University.

Students *Undergraduates:* 2,118 full-time, 359 part-time. The most frequently chosen baccalaureate fields are: liberal arts/general studies, business/marketing, protective services/public administration. *Graduate:* 1 in graduate degree programs.

From out-of-state	2%	Age 25 or older	20%
Transferred in	3%	International students	0.2%
African Americans	10%	Asian Americans/Pacific Islanders	9%
Hispanic Americans	4%	Native Americans	0.2%

Faculty 199 (47% full-time).
Expenses (1999–2000) *Tuition, state resident:* full-time $6058; part-time $243 per credit. *Tuition, nonresident:* full-time $9418; part-time $393 per credit. *Required fees:* full-time $254; $43 per credit. Full-time tuition and fees vary according to course level, location, program, and student level. Part-time tuition and fees vary according to course level, course load, location, program, and student level. *Payment plan:* deferred payment. *Waivers:* senior citizens and employees or children of employees.
Library *Collection:* 58,227 titles, 378 serial subscriptions.
College life *Housing:* college housing not available.
Campus security 24-hour patrols.
After graduation 65 organizations recruited on campus 1997–98. *Career center:* 2 full-time, 1 part-time personnel. Services include job fairs, resume preparation, interview workshops, resume referral, career/interest testing, career counseling, careers library, job bank, job interviews.
Freshmen 2,506 applied, 2,072 admitted, 807 enrolled.

Average high school GPA	3.08	SAT verbal scores above 500	49%
SAT math scores above 500	51%	ACT above 18	N/R
From top 10% of their h.s. class	9%	From top quarter	55%
From top half	80%	1998 freshmen returning in 1999	73%

Application *Options:* electronic application, early admission, deferred entrance. *Application fee:* $50. *Required:* high school transcript.
Standardized tests *Admission: Required:* SAT I or ACT.
Significant dates *Application deadlines:* rolling (freshmen), rolling (transfers). *Financial aid deadline:* continuous.
Freshman Application Contact
Mr. Robert McCaig, Director of Enrollment Management, Pennsylvania State University Abington College, 1600 Woodland Road, Abington, PA 19001-3990. **Phone:** 215-881-7600. **E-mail:** axa43@psu.edu

Visit CollegeQuest.com for information on majors offered and athletics.

■ *See page 2254 for a narrative description.*

PENNSYLVANIA STATE UNIVERSITY ALTOONA COLLEGE
Altoona, Pennsylvania

- **State-related**, 4-year, founded 1939
- **Degrees** associate and bachelor's
- **Suburban** 115-acre campus
- **Coed**, 3,584 undergraduate students, 93% full-time, 51% women, 49% men
- **Moderately difficult** entrance level, 85% of applicants were admitted
- **26:1 student-to-undergraduate faculty ratio**
- **62.02% graduate** in 6 years or less
- **$6332 tuition** and fees (in-state); $9692 (out-of-state)

Part of Pennsylvania State University.

Students *Undergraduates:* 3,340 full-time, 244 part-time. The most frequently chosen baccalaureate fields are: business/marketing, liberal arts/general studies. *Graduate:* 27 in graduate degree programs.

From out-of-state	10%	Reside on campus	23%
Age 25 or older	13%	Transferred in	3%
International students	1%	African Americans	3%
Asian Americans/Pacific Islanders	1%	Hispanic Americans	1%
Native Americans	0.1%		

Faculty 253 (45% full-time).
Expenses (1999–2000) *Tuition, state resident:* full-time $6058; part-time $243 per credit. *Tuition, nonresident:* full-time $9418; part-time $393 per credit. *Required fees:* full-time $274; $46 per credit. Full-time tuition and fees vary according to course level, location, program, and student level. Part-time tuition and fees vary according to course level, course load, location, program, and student level. *College room and board:* $4690; room only:

Pennsylvania

Pennsylvania State University Altoona College (continued)
$2280. Room and board charges vary according to board plan and housing facility. *Payment plan:* deferred payment. *Waivers:* senior citizens and employees or children of employees.

Library *Collection:* 55,703 titles, 200 serial subscriptions.

College life *Housing: Option:* coed.

Campus security 24-hour emergency response devices and patrols, student patrols, late-night transport-escort service, controlled dormitory access.

After graduation *Career center:* Services include career counseling.

Freshmen 3,621 applied, 3,082 admitted, 1,310 enrolled.

Average high school GPA	3.08	SAT verbal scores above 500	49%
SAT math scores above 500	51%	ACT above 18	N/R
From top 10% of their h.s. class	9%	From top quarter	55%
From top half	80%	1998 freshmen returning in 1999	85%

Application *Options:* electronic application, early admission, deferred entrance. *Application fee:* $50. *Required:* high school transcript.

Standardized tests *Admission: Required:* SAT I or ACT.

Significant dates *Application deadlines:* rolling (freshmen), rolling (transfers). *Financial aid deadline:* continuous.

Freshman Application Contact
Ms. Fredina Ingold, Admissions Officer, Pennsylvania State University Altoona College, E108 Smith Building, 3000 Ivyside Park, Altoona, PA 16601-3760. **Phone:** 814-949-5466. **Toll-free phone:** 800-848-9843. **Fax:** 814-949-5011. **E-mail:** aaadmit@psu.edu

Visit CollegeQuest.com for information on majors offered and athletics.

■ *See page 2256 for a narrative description.*

PENNSYLVANIA STATE UNIVERSITY AT ERIE, THE BEHREND COLLEGE
Erie, Pennsylvania

- **State-related**, comprehensive, founded 1948
- **Degrees** associate, bachelor's, and master's
- **Suburban** 727-acre campus
- **Coed**, 3,304 undergraduate students, 93% full-time, 38% women, 62% men
- **Very difficult** entrance level, 83% of applicants were admitted
- **19:1** student-to-undergraduate faculty ratio
- **54.55% graduate** in 6 years or less
- **$6436 tuition** and fees (in-state); $12,110 (out-of-state)

New majors in finance and manufacturing technology complement the physical growth of the campus. A new athletics/recreation center, a new residence hall, and the new Knowledge Park enhance opportunities for students to participate in campus life, undergraduate research, and small classes while they earn an internationally recognized Penn State degree.

Part of Pennsylvania State University.

Students *Undergraduates:* 3,078 full-time, 226 part-time. *The most frequently chosen baccalaureate fields are:* business/marketing, biological/life sciences, engineering/engineering technologies. *Graduate:* 147 in graduate degree programs.

From out-of-state	6%	Reside on campus	42%
Age 25 or older	12%	Transferred in	3%
International students	1%	African Americans	4%
Asian Americans/Pacific Islanders	2%	Hispanic Americans	1%
Native Americans	0.2%		

Faculty 245 (66% full-time).

Expenses (1999–2000) *Tuition, state resident:* full-time $6162; part-time $258 per credit. *Tuition, nonresident:* full-time $11,836; part-time $493 per credit. *Required fees:* full-time $274; $46 per credit. Full-time tuition and fees vary according to course level, location, program, and student level. Part-time tuition and fees vary according to course level, course load, location, program, and student level. *College room and board:* $4690; room only: $2280. Room and board charges vary according to board plan and housing facility. *Payment plan:* deferred payment. *Waivers:* senior citizens and employees or children of employees.

Library *Collection:* 89,907 titles, 835 serial subscriptions.

College life *Housing: Options:* coed, men-only, women-only, disabled students. *Social organizations:* national fraternities, national sororities, local fraternities, local sororities. *Most popular organization:* Student Government Association.

Campus security 24-hour emergency response devices and patrols, student patrols, late-night transport-escort service, controlled dormitory access.

After graduation 70 organizations recruited on campus 1997–98. 93% of class of 1998 had job offers within 6 months. *Career center:* 2 full-time, 1 part-time personnel. Services include job fairs, resume preparation, resume referral, career counseling, careers library, job bank, job interviews.

Freshmen 3,333 applied, 2,774 admitted, 848 enrolled.

Average high school GPA	3.38	SAT verbal scores above 500	64%
SAT math scores above 500	70%	ACT above 18	N/R
From top 10% of their h.s. class	14%	From top quarter	77%
From top half	92%	1998 freshmen returning in 1999	86%

Application *Options:* electronic application, early admission, deferred entrance. *Application fee:* $50. *Required:* high school transcript.

Standardized tests *Admission: Required:* SAT I or ACT.

Significant dates *Application deadlines:* rolling (freshmen), rolling (transfers). *Financial aid deadline:* continuous.

Freshman Application Contact
Ms. Mary-Ellen Madigan, Admissions Director, Pennsylvania State University at Erie, The Behrend College, 5091 Station Road, Erie, PA 16563-0105. **Phone:** 814-898-6100. **E-mail:** behrend.admissions@psu.edu

Visit CollegeQuest.com for information on majors offered and athletics.

■ *See page 2258 for a narrative description.*

PENNSYLVANIA STATE UNIVERSITY BERKS CAMPUS OF THE BERKS—LEHIGH VALLEY COLLEGE
Reading, Pennsylvania

- **State-related**, 4-year, founded 1924
- **Degrees** associate and bachelor's
- **Suburban** 240-acre campus with easy access to Philadelphia
- **Coed**, 1,782 undergraduate students, 92% full-time, 41% women, 59% men
- **Moderately difficult** entrance level, 88% of applicants were admitted
- **22:1** student-to-undergraduate faculty ratio
- **43.36% graduate** in 6 years or less
- **$6332 tuition** and fees (in-state); $9692 (out-of-state)

Part of Pennsylvania State University.

Students *Undergraduates:* 1,631 full-time, 151 part-time. *Graduate:* 18 in graduate degree programs.

From out-of-state	8%	Reside on campus	29%
Age 25 or older	13%	Transferred in	3%
International students	0.4%	African Americans	5%
Asian Americans/Pacific Islanders	3%	Hispanic Americans	3%
Native Americans	0.1%		

Faculty 141 (52% full-time).

Expenses (1999–2000) *Tuition, state resident:* full-time $6058; part-time $243 per credit. *Tuition, nonresident:* full-time $9418; part-time $393 per credit. *Required fees:* full-time $274; $46 per credit. Full-time tuition and fees vary according to course level, location, program, and student level. Part-time tuition and fees vary according to course level, course load, location, program, and student level. *College room and board:* $4690; room only: $2280. Room and board charges vary according to board plan and housing facility. *Payment plan:* deferred payment. *Waivers:* senior citizens and employees or children of employees.

Library *Collection:* 44,544 titles, 287 serial subscriptions.

College life *Housing: Option:* coed.

Campus security 24-hour emergency response devices and patrols, controlled dormitory access.

After graduation *Career center:* Services include career counseling.

Pennsylvania

Freshmen 2,126 applied, 1,877 admitted, 762 enrolled.

Average high school GPA	3.08	SAT verbal scores above 500	49%
SAT math scores above 500	51%	ACT above 18	N/R
From top 10% of their h.s. class	9%	From top quarter	55%
From top half	80%	1998 freshmen returning in 1999	80%

Application *Options:* electronic application, early admission, deferred entrance. *Application fee:* $50. *Required:* high school transcript.

Standardized tests *Admission: Required:* SAT I or ACT.

Significant dates *Application deadlines:* rolling (freshmen), rolling (transfers). *Financial aid deadline:* continuous.

Freshman Application Contact
Mr. Thomas Speakman, Admissions Officer, Pennsylvania State University Berks Campus of the Berks–Lehigh Valley College, 14 Perkins Student Center, Tulpehocken Road, PO Box 7009, Reading, PA 19610-6009. **Phone:** 610-396-6066. **E-mail:** tws7@psu.edu

Visit CollegeQuest.com for information on majors offered and athletics.

PENNSYLVANIA STATE UNIVERSITY DELAWARE COUNTY CAMPUS OF THE COMMONWEALTH COLLEGE
Media, Pennsylvania

- **State-related**, primarily 2-year, founded 1966
- **Degrees** associate and bachelor's (also offers up to 2 years of most bachelor's degree programs offered at University Park campus; of students entering the associate degree program, 25% complete the degree and an additional 35% change to a bachelor's degree program)
- **Small-town** 87-acre campus with easy access to Philadelphia
- **Coed**, 1,356 undergraduate students, 89% full-time, 47% women, 53% men
- **Moderately difficult** entrance level

Part of Pennsylvania State University.

Faculty 117 (48% full-time).

Admissions Office Contact
Pennsylvania State University Delaware County Campus of the Commonwealth College, 25 Yearsley Mill Road, Media, PA 19063-5596. **E-mail:** admissions-delco@psu.edu

Visit CollegeQuest.com for information on majors offered and athletics.

PENNSYLVANIA STATE UNIVERSITY HARRISBURG CAMPUS OF THE CAPITAL COLLEGE
Middletown, Pennsylvania

- **State-related**, comprehensive, founded 1966
- **Degrees** bachelor's, master's, and doctoral
- **Small-town** 218-acre campus
- **Coed**, 1,755 undergraduate students, 69% full-time, 52% women, 48% men
- **Moderately difficult** entrance level
- **13:1 student-to-undergraduate faculty ratio**
- **$6416 tuition** and fees (in-state); $12,090 (out-of-state)

Penn State Harrisburg, Capital College, is an undergraduate transfer college and graduate school of Pennsylvania State University that accepts applications into undergraduate majors from students who have successfully completed most of their freshman- and sophomore-level course work. Penn State Harrisburg offers 26 baccalaureate, 17 master's, and 2 doctoral programs with all the resources of a major research university in a smaller, more intimate setting. Interested students can visit the Web site (www.hbg.psu.edu).

Part of Pennsylvania State University.

Students *Undergraduates:* 1,213 full-time, 542 part-time. *The most frequently chosen baccalaureate fields are:* business/marketing, engineering/engineering technologies, protective services/public administration. *Graduate:* 1,360 in graduate degree programs.

From out-of-state	2%	Reside on campus	19%
Age 25 or older	49%	Transferred in	14%
International students	0.4%	African Americans	6%
Asian Americans/Pacific Islanders	5%	Hispanic Americans	2%
Native Americans	0.2%		

Faculty 253 (56% full-time).

Expenses (1999–2000) *Tuition, state resident:* full-time $6162; part-time $258 per credit. *Tuition, nonresident:* full-time $11,836; part-time $493 per credit. *Required fees:* full-time $254; $43 per credit. Full-time tuition and fees vary according to course level, location, program, and student level. Part-time tuition and fees vary according to course level, course load, location, program, and student level. *College room and board:* $4690; room only: $2280. Room and board charges vary according to board plan and housing facility. *Payment plan:* deferred payment. *Waivers:* senior citizens and employees or children of employees.

Library *Collection:* 246,143 titles, 2,447 serial subscriptions.

Campus security 24-hour patrols, student patrols, late-night transport-escort service.

After graduation 68 organizations recruited on campus 1997–98. *Career center:* 2 full-time personnel. Services include job fairs, resume preparation, resume referral, career counseling, careers library, job bank, job interviews.

Freshmen 2 enrolled.

SAT verbal scores above 500	N/R	SAT math scores above 500	N/R
ACT above 18	N/R		

Application *Options:* electronic application, early admission, deferred entrance. *Application fee:* $50. *Required:* high school transcript.

Standardized tests *Admission: Required:* SAT I or ACT.

Significant dates *Application deadlines:* rolling (freshmen), rolling (transfers). *Financial aid deadline:* continuous.

Freshman Application Contact
Dr. Thomas Streveler, Director of Enrollment Services, Pennsylvania State University Harrisburg Campus of the Capital College, 777 West Harrisburg Pike, Middletown, PA 17057-4898. **Phone:** 717-948-6250. **Toll-free phone:** 800-222-2056. **E-mail:** rrl1@psu.edu

Visit CollegeQuest.com for information on majors offered and athletics.

PENNSYLVANIA STATE UNIVERSITY LEHIGH VALLEY CAMPUS OF THE BERKS-LEHIGH VALLEY COLLEGE
Fogelsville, Pennsylvania

- **State-related**, 4-year, founded 1912
- **Degrees** associate and bachelor's
- **Small-town** 42-acre campus
- **Coed**, 518 undergraduate students, 89% full-time, 39% women, 61% men
- **Moderately difficult** entrance level, 87% of applicants were admitted
- **20:1 student-to-undergraduate faculty ratio**
- **59.84% graduate** in 6 years or less
- **$6242 tuition** and fees (in-state); $9518 (out-of-state)

Part of Pennsylvania State University.

Students *Undergraduates:* 462 full-time, 56 part-time. *Graduate:* 32 in graduate degree programs.

From out-of-state	2%	Age 25 or older	17%
Transferred in	7%	International students	0.4%
African Americans	2%	Asian Americans/Pacific Islanders	7%
Hispanic Americans	6%		

Faculty 62 (39% full-time).

Expenses (1999–2000) *Tuition, state resident:* full-time $5968; part-time $241 per credit. *Tuition, nonresident:* full-time $9244; part-time $386 per credit. *Required fees:* full-time $274; $46 per credit. Full-time tuition and fees vary according to course level, location, program, and student level. Part-time tuition and fees vary according to course level, course load, location, program, and student level. College housing is available through Berks campus only. *Payment plan:* deferred payment. *Waivers:* senior citizens and employees or children of employees.

Library *Collection:* 34,453 titles, 163 serial subscriptions.

College life *Housing:* college housing not available.

After graduation *Career center:* Services include career counseling.

Pennsylvania

Pennsylvania State University Lehigh Valley Campus of the Berks-Lehigh Valley College (continued)

Freshmen 512 applied, 447 admitted, 211 enrolled.

Average high school GPA	3.08	SAT verbal scores above 500	49%
SAT math scores above 500	51%	ACT above 18	N/R
From top 10% of their h.s. class	9%	From top quarter	55%
From top half	80%	1998 freshmen returning in 1999	74%

Application *Options:* electronic application, early admission, deferred entrance. *Application fee:* $50. *Required:* high school transcript.

Standardized tests *Admission: Required:* SAT I or ACT.

Significant dates *Application deadlines:* rolling (freshmen), rolling (transfers). *Financial aid deadline:* continuous.

Freshman Application Contact
Mr. Emory Guffrovich, Admissions Officer, Pennsylvania State University Lehigh Valley Campus of the Berks-Lehigh Valley College, 113 Academic Building, 8400 Mohr Lane, Fogelsville, PA 18051. **Phone:** 610-821-6577. **E-mail:** epg2@psu.edu

Visit CollegeQuest.com for information on majors offered and athletics.

PENNSYLVANIA STATE UNIVERSITY SCHUYLKILL CAMPUS OF THE CAPITAL COLLEGE

Schuylkill Haven, Pennsylvania

- **State-related**, 4-year, founded 1934
- **Degrees** associate and bachelor's (bachelor's degree programs completed at the Harrisburg campus)
- **Small-town** 42-acre campus
- **Coed**, 825 undergraduate students, 86% full-time, 52% women, 48% men
- **Moderately difficult** entrance level, 87% of applicants were admitted
- **18:1 student-to-undergraduate faculty ratio**
- **52.34% graduate** in 6 years or less
- **$6222 tuition** and fees (in-state); $9498 (out-of-state)

Part of Pennsylvania State University.

Students *Undergraduates:* 711 full-time, 114 part-time. *Graduate:* 22 in graduate degree programs.

From out-of-state	10%	Reside on campus	25%
Age 25 or older	18%	Transferred in	3%
International students	0.2%	African Americans	12%
Asian Americans/Pacific Islanders	4%	Hispanic Americans	3%

Faculty 72 (61% full-time).

Expenses (1999–2000) *Tuition, state resident:* full-time $5968; part-time $241 per credit. *Tuition, nonresident:* full-time $9244; part-time $386 per credit. *Required fees:* full-time $254; $43 per credit. Full-time tuition and fees vary according to course level, location, program, and student level. Part-time tuition and fees vary according to course level, course load, location, program, and student level. *College room and board:* $4690; room only: $2280. Room and board charges vary according to board plan and housing facility. *Payment plan:* deferred payment. *Waivers:* senior citizens and employees or children of employees.

Library *Collection:* 35,224 titles, 227 serial subscriptions.

Campus security 24-hour patrols, controlled dormitory access.

After graduation *Career center:* Services include career counseling.

Freshmen 679 applied, 594 admitted, 265 enrolled.

Average high school GPA	3.08	SAT verbal scores above 500	49%
SAT math scores above 500	51%	ACT above 18	N/R
From top 10% of their h.s. class	9%	From top quarter	55%
From top half	80%	1998 freshmen returning in 1999	77%

Application *Options:* electronic application, early admission, deferred entrance. *Application fee:* $50. *Required:* high school transcript.

Standardized tests *Admission: Required:* SAT I or ACT.

Significant dates *Application deadlines:* rolling (freshmen), rolling (transfers). *Financial aid deadline:* continuous.

Freshman Application Contact
Mr. Jerry Bowman, Director of Student Programs and Services, Pennsylvania State University Schuylkill Campus of the Capital College, 200 University Dirve, Schuylkill Haven, PA 17972-2208. **Phone:** 570-385-6252. **E-mail:** jxb25@psu.edu

Visit CollegeQuest.com for information on majors offered and athletics.

PENNSYLVANIA STATE UNIVERSITY SHENANGO CAMPUS OF THE COMMONWEALTH COLLEGE

Sharon, Pennsylvania

- **State-related**, primarily 2-year, founded 1965
- **Degrees** associate and bachelor's (also offers up to 2 years of most bachelor's degree programs offered at University Park campus; of students entering the associate degree program, 25% complete the degree and an additional 35% change to a bachelor's degree program)
- **Small-town** 14-acre campus
- **Coed**, 697 undergraduate students, 61% full-time, 67% women, 33% men
- **Moderately difficult** entrance level

Part of Pennsylvania State University.

Faculty 94 (33% full-time).

Admissions Office Contact
Pennsylvania State University Shenango Campus of the Commonwealth College, 206 Sharon Hall, Sharon, PA 16146-1537. **Fax:** 724-983-2820. **E-mail:** admissions@psu.edu

Visit CollegeQuest.com for information on majors offered and athletics.

PENNSYLVANIA STATE UNIVERSITY UNIVERSITY PARK CAMPUS

State College, Pennsylvania

- **State-related**, university, founded 1855
- **Degrees** associate, bachelor's, master's, and doctoral
- **Small-town** 5,617-acre campus
- **Coed**, 33,209 undergraduate students, 97% full-time, 46% women, 54% men
- **Very difficult** entrance level, 49% of applicants were admitted
- **18:1 student-to-undergraduate faculty ratio**
- **80% graduate** in 6 years or less
- **$6436 tuition** and fees (in-state); $13,552 (out-of-state)
- **$803.1 million endowment**

Part of Pennsylvania State University.

Students *Undergraduates:* 32,093 full-time, 1,116 part-time. Students come from 54 states and territories. *The most frequently chosen baccalaureate fields are:* business/marketing, engineering/engineering technologies, health professions and related sciences. *Graduate:* 6,153 in graduate degree programs.

From out-of-state	19%	Reside on campus	30%
Age 25 or older	5%	Transferred in	1%
International students	1%	African Americans	4%
Asian Americans/Pacific Islanders	5%	Hispanic Americans	3%
Native Americans	0.1%		

Faculty 2,310 (86% full-time), 66% with terminal degrees.

Expenses (1999–2000) *Tuition, state resident:* full-time $6162; part-time $258 per credit. *Tuition, nonresident:* full-time $13,278; part-time $554 per credit. *Required fees:* full-time $274; $46 per credit. Full-time tuition and fees vary according to course level, course load, location, program, and student level. Part-time tuition and fees vary according to course level, course load, location, program, and student level. *College room and board:* $4690; room only: $2280. Room and board charges vary according to board plan. *Payment plan:* deferred payment. *Waivers:* senior citizens and employees or children of employees.

Library Pattee Library plus 7 others. *Collection:* 2.8 million titles, 22,879 serial subscriptions.

College life *Housing:* on-campus residence required in freshman year. *Options:* coed, men-only, women-only, disabled students. *Social organizations:* national fraternities, national sororities; 14% of eligible men and 11% of eligible women are members.

Campus security 24-hour emergency response devices and patrols, student patrols, late-night transport-escort service, controlled dormitory access.

Pennsylvania

After graduation 970 organizations recruited on campus 1997–98. 70% of class of 1998 had job offers within 6 months. *Career center:* 22 full-time, 4 part-time personnel. Services include job fairs, resume preparation, resume referral, career counseling, careers library, job bank, job interviews. *Major awards:* 11 Fulbright Scholars.

Freshmen 26,079 applied, 12,862 admitted, 5,069 enrolled.

Average high school GPA	3.78	SAT verbal scores above 500	89%
SAT math scores above 500	92%	ACT above 18	N/R
From top 10% of their h.s. class	49%	From top quarter	88%
From top half	91%	1998 freshmen returning in 1999	93%

Application *Options:* electronic application, deferred entrance. *Application fee:* $50. *Required:* high school transcript; minimum 2.0 GPA. *Required for some:* 1 letter of recommendation; interview. *Recommended:* essay or personal statement.

Standardized tests *Admission: Required:* SAT I or ACT.

Significant dates *Application deadlines:* rolling (freshmen), rolling (transfers). *Financial aid deadline:* continuous.

Freshman Application Contact
Mr. Geoffrey Harford, Director-Admissions Services and Evaluation, Pennsylvania State University University Park Campus, 201 Old Main, University Park, PA 16802-1503. **Phone:** 814-863-0233. **E-mail:** admissions@psu.edu

Visit CollegeQuest.com for information on majors offered and athletics.

PHILADELPHIA COLLEGE OF BIBLE

Langhorne, Pennsylvania

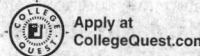

- **Independent nondenominational**, comprehensive, founded 1913
- **Degrees** associate, bachelor's, and master's
- **Suburban** 105-acre campus with easy access to Philadelphia
- **Coed**, 1,007 undergraduate students, 90% full-time, 54% women, 46% men
- **Moderately difficult** entrance level, 92% of applicants were admitted
- **14:1 student-to-undergraduate faculty ratio**
- **$10,355 tuition** and fees
- **$7108 average financial aid** package, $12,170 average indebtedness upon graduation, $4.6 million endowment

PCB is a conservative, evangelical Bible college dedicated to developing leaders for the church and related ministries who possess a foundational knowledge of scripture and a biblical world/life view. Other campuses include Cable, WI, and Liberty Corner, NJ. Friends of Israel Institute of Jewish Studies offers a 1-year program on the main campus.

Students *Undergraduates:* 904 full-time, 103 part-time. Students come from 38 states and territories, 33 other countries. *The most frequently chosen baccalaureate fields are:* education, philosophy, protective services/public administration. *Graduate:* 361 in graduate degree programs.

From out-of-state	52%	Reside on campus	53%
Age 25 or older	26%	Transferred in	12%
International students	4%	African Americans	14%
Asian Americans/Pacific Islanders	3%	Hispanic Americans	1%
Native Americans	0.1%		

Faculty 135 (34% full-time), 42% with terminal degrees.

Expenses (2000–2001) *Comprehensive fee:* $15,428 includes full-time tuition ($10,070), mandatory fees ($285), and room and board ($5073). *College room only:* $2395. Full-time tuition and fees vary according to course load, location, and program. Room and board charges vary according to board plan, housing facility, and location. *Part-time tuition:* $303 per credit. *Part-time fees:* $6 per credit. Part-time tuition and fees vary according to course load, location, and program. *Payment plan:* installment. *Waivers:* children of alumni and employees or children of employees.

Library Masland Learning Resource Center. *Operations spending 1999–2000:* $400,830. *Collection:* 85,229 titles, 567 serial subscriptions, 13,507 audiovisual materials.

College life *Housing:* on-campus residence required through senior year. *Options:* men-only, women-only, disabled students. *Most popular organizations:* Student Theological Society, Student Missionary Fellowship, BASIC (Brothers and Sisters in Christ), All College Social Committee, Student Senate.

Campus security 24-hour emergency response devices and patrols, student patrols, late-night transport-escort service, controlled dormitory access.

After graduation *Career center:* 1 part-time personnel. Services include resume preparation, interview workshops, resume referral, career/interest testing, career counseling, careers library, job bank.

Freshmen 365 applied, 334 admitted, 196 enrolled.

Average high school GPA	3.22	SAT verbal scores above 500	74%
SAT math scores above 500	59%	ACT above 18	100%
From top 10% of their h.s. class	14%	From top quarter	36%
From top half	71%	1998 freshmen returning in 1999	64%

Application *Options:* eApply at www.CollegeQuest.com, Common Application, electronic application, early admission, deferred entrance. *Application fee:* $25. *Required:* essay or personal statement; high school transcript; 1 letter of recommendation. *Required for some:* minimum 2.0 GPA; interview. *Recommended:* minimum 3.0 GPA; interview.

Standardized tests *Admission: Required:* SAT I or ACT.

Significant dates *Application deadlines:* rolling (freshmen), rolling (transfers). *Financial aid deadline priority date:* 5/1.

Freshman Application Contact
Mrs. Fran Emmons, Vice President Admissions and Financial Aid, Philadelphia College of Bible, 200 Manor Avenue, Langhorne, PA 19047-2990. **Phone:** 215-702-4239. **Toll-free phone:** 800-876-5800. **Fax:** 215-752-5812. **E-mail:** admissions@pcb.edu

Visit CollegeQuest.com for information on majors offered and athletics. College video and electronic viewbook available at CollegeQuest.com.

PHILADELPHIA COLLEGE OF PHARMACY AND SCIENCE

Pennsylvania—See University of the Sciences in Philadelphia

PHILADELPHIA COLLEGE OF TEXTILES AND SCIENCE

Pennsylvania—See Philadelphia University

PHILADELPHIA UNIVERSITY

Philadelphia, Pennsylvania

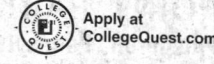

- **Independent**, comprehensive, founded 1884
- **Degrees** bachelor's and master's
- **Suburban** 100-acre campus
- **Coed**, 2,724 undergraduate students, 79% full-time, 64% women, 36% men
- **Moderately difficult** entrance level, 79% of applicants were admitted
- **12:1 student-to-undergraduate faculty ratio**
- **39.3% graduate** in 6 years or less
- **$14,738 tuition** and fees
- **$11,935 average financial aid** package, $19,630 average indebtedness upon graduation, $19.9 million endowment

Students *Undergraduates:* 2,147 full-time, 577 part-time. Students come from 41 states and territories, 41 other countries. *The most frequently chosen baccalaureate fields are:* business/marketing, architecture, visual/performing arts. *Graduate:* 596 in graduate degree programs.

From out-of-state	38%	Reside on campus	52%
Age 25 or older	22%	Transferred in	5%
International students	3%	African Americans	10%
Asian Americans/Pacific Islanders	4%	Hispanic Americans	2%

Faculty 418 (22% full-time).

Expenses (1999–2000) *Comprehensive fee:* $21,314 includes full-time tuition ($14,692), mandatory fees ($46), and room and board ($6576). *College room only:* $3202. Full-time tuition and fees vary according to program. Room and board charges vary according to board plan and housing facility. *Part-time tuition:* $474 per credit. Part-time tuition and fees vary according to class time and program. *Payment plans:* installment, deferred payment. *Waivers:* employees or children of employees.

Peterson's Guide to Four-Year Colleges 2001   www.petersons.com   713

Pennsylvania

Philadelphia University (continued)

Library Paul J. Gutman Library. *Operations spending 1999–2000:* $1 million. *Collection:* 85,700 titles, 1,200 serial subscriptions, 25,500 audiovisual materials.

College life *Housing: Options:* coed, women-only. *Social organizations:* national fraternities, national sororities, local fraternities, local sororities; 7% of eligible men and 3% of eligible women are members. *Most popular organizations:* Gemini Theatre, Delta Phi Epsilon, Black Awareness Society, Textile Volleyball Club.

Campus security 24-hour emergency response devices and patrols, late-night transport-escort service, controlled dormitory access.

After graduation 120 organizations recruited on campus 1997–98. 82% of class of 1998 had job offers within 6 months. *Career center:* 3 full-time personnel. Services include job fairs, resume preparation, interview workshops, resume referral, career/interest testing, career counseling, careers library, job bank, job interviews. *Graduate education:* 11% of class of 1999 went directly to graduate and professional school: 5% business, 3% graduate arts and sciences, 2% education, 1% medicine.

Freshmen 2,594 applied, 2,059 admitted, 623 enrolled.

Average high school GPA	3.25	SAT verbal scores above 500	66%
SAT math scores above 500	66%	ACT above 18	N/R
From top 10% of their h.s. class	14%	From top quarter	43%
From top half	79%	1998 freshmen returning in 1999	71%

Application *Options:* eApply at www.CollegeQuest.com, Common Application, electronic application, early admission, deferred entrance. *Application fee:* $35. *Required:* high school transcript. *Recommended:* 2 letters of recommendation; interview.

Standardized tests *Admission: Required:* SAT I or ACT.

Significant dates *Application deadlines:* rolling (freshmen), rolling (transfers). *Financial aid deadline:* 4/15.

Freshman Application Contact
Ms. Laurie C. Grover, Director of Admissions, Philadelphia University, School House Lane and Henry Avenue, Philadelphia, PA 19144-5497. **Phone:** 215-951-2800. **Fax:** 215-951-2907. **E-mail:** admissions@philau.edu

Visit CollegeQuest.com for information on majors offered and athletics. Electronic viewbook available at CollegeQuest.com.

■ *See page 2266 for a narrative description.*

POINT PARK COLLEGE
Pittsburgh, Pennsylvania

Apply at CollegeQuest.com

- **Independent**, comprehensive, founded 1960
- **Degrees** associate, bachelor's, master's, post-master's, and postbachelor's certificates
- **Urban** campus
- **Coed**, 2,289 undergraduate students, 62% full-time, 54% women, 46% men
- **Moderately difficult** entrance level, 89% of applicants were admitted
- **12:1 student-to-undergraduate faculty ratio**
- **40% graduate** in 6 years or less
- **$12,454 tuition** and fees
- **$8553 average financial aid** package, $5.5 million endowment

Point Park College offers students the opportunity to attend small, intimate classes in a facility located in the midst of vibrant downtown Pittsburgh. Recognized for providing a liberal arts education with career preparation, Point Park's location gives students access to important internships that provide valuable professional-level experience to complement classroom activities.

Students *Undergraduates:* 1,420 full-time, 869 part-time. Students come from 42 states and territories, 32 other countries. *The most frequently chosen baccalaureate fields are:* business/marketing, engineering/engineering technologies, visual/performing arts. *Graduate:* 202 in graduate degree programs.

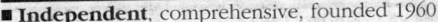

From out-of-state	12%	Reside on campus	16%
Age 25 or older	51%	Transferred in	8%
International students	2%	African Americans	14%
Asian Americans/Pacific Islanders	1%	Hispanic Americans	1%
Native Americans	0.2%		

Faculty 261 (29% full-time).

Expenses (1999–2000) *Comprehensive fee:* $17,788 includes full-time tuition ($12,054), mandatory fees ($400), and room and board ($5334). *College room only:* $2550. Full-time tuition and fees vary according to course load. Room and board charges vary according to board plan. *Part-time tuition:* $321 per credit. *Part-time fees:* $6 per credit. Part-time tuition and fees vary according to course load. *Payment plans:* installment, deferred payment. *Waivers:* senior citizens and employees or children of employees.

Library The Library Center. *Collection:* 269,192 titles, 681 serial subscriptions.

College life *Housing: Option:* coed. *Most popular organizations:* dance club, student radio station, Alpha Phi Omega, BASICS, Gamma Phi Omega.

Campus security 24-hour emergency response devices and patrols, late-night transport-escort service, 24-hour security desk, video security.

After graduation *Career center:* 3 full-time personnel. Services include job fairs, resume preparation, resume referral, career counseling, careers library, job bank, job interviews.

Freshmen 994 applied, 886 admitted, 282 enrolled.

Average high school GPA	3.0	SAT verbal scores above 500	54%
SAT math scores above 500	39%	ACT above 18	85%
From top 10% of their h.s. class	12%	From top quarter	35%
From top half	69%	1998 freshmen returning in 1999	71%

Application *Options:* eApply at www.CollegeQuest.com, Common Application, early admission, deferred entrance. *Application fee:* $20. *Required:* high school transcript. *Required for some:* 2 letters of recommendation; interview; audition. *Recommended:* minimum 2.0 GPA.

Standardized tests *Admission: Required:* SAT I or ACT.

Significant dates *Application deadlines:* rolling (freshmen), rolling (transfers). *Financial aid deadline:* continuous.

Freshman Application Contact
Ms. Michele Lawrence, Director of Admissions, Point Park College, Point Park College, 201 Wood Street, Pittsburgh, PA 15222. **Phone:** 412-392-3430. **Toll-free phone:** 800-321-0129. **Fax:** 412-391-1980. **E-mail:** enroll@ppc.edu

Visit CollegeQuest.com for information on majors offered and athletics.

■ *See page 2278 for a narrative description.*

ROBERT MORRIS COLLEGE
Moon Township, Pennsylvania

- **Independent**, comprehensive, founded 1921
- **Degrees** associate, bachelor's, and master's
- **Suburban** 230-acre campus with easy access to Pittsburgh
- **Coed**, 3,705 undergraduate students, 70% full-time, 50% women, 50% men
- **Moderately difficult** entrance level, 91% of applicants were admitted
- **20:1 student-to-undergraduate faculty ratio**
- **43% graduate** in 6 years or less
- **$9919 tuition** and fees
- **$5600 average financial aid** package, $14.4 million endowment

Robert Morris College, consistently named as one of America's top specialty colleges, offers more than 30 majors. A broad range of business majors lead to a BS in business administration, while excellent programs are offered in elementary education, engineering, sport management, health services management, hospitality management, and communications.

Students *Undergraduates:* 2,611 full-time, 1,094 part-time. Students come from 22 states and territories, 34 other countries. *The most frequently chosen baccalaureate fields are:* business/marketing, computer/information sciences, health professions and related sciences. *Graduate:* 917 in graduate degree programs.

From out-of-state	7%	Reside on campus	22%
Age 25 or older	36%	Transferred in	13%
International students	2%	African Americans	9%
Asian Americans/Pacific Islanders	1%	Hispanic Americans	1%
Native Americans	0.2%		

Faculty 266 (32% full-time), 30% with terminal degrees.

Expenses (1999–2000) *Comprehensive fee:* $15,981 includes full-time tuition ($8940), mandatory fees ($979), and room and board ($6062). *Part-time tuition:* $298 per credit. *Part-time fees:* $16 per credit. *Payment plans:* installment, deferred payment. *Waivers:* senior citizens and employees or children of employees.

Pennsylvania

Library Robert Morris College Library. *Operations spending 1999–2000:* $1.3 million. *Collection:* 114,900 titles, 912 serial subscriptions, 2,904 audio-visual materials.
College life *Housing: Options:* men-only, women-only. *Social organizations:* national fraternities, national sororities; 1% of eligible men and 1% of eligible women are members. *Most popular organizations:* Student Government Association, Residence Hall Association, Interfraternity Council/Panhellenic Council, R-MOVE, Campus Activities Board.
Campus security 24-hour emergency response devices and patrols, controlled dormitory access.
After graduation 59 organizations recruited on campus 1997–98. 90% of class of 1998 had job offers within 6 months. *Career center:* 4 full-time personnel. Services include job fairs, resume preparation, resume referral, career counseling, careers library, job bank, job interviews.
Freshmen 2,353 applied, 2,136 admitted, 567 enrolled.

Average high school GPA	2.75	SAT verbal scores above 500	39%
SAT math scores above 500	39%	ACT above 18	N/R
From top 10% of their h.s. class	10%	From top quarter	20%
From top half	68%	1998 freshmen returning in 1999	75%

Application *Option:* deferred entrance. *Application fee:* $20. *Required:* high school transcript; minimum 2.0 GPA. *Required for some:* interview. *Recommended:* minimum 3.0 GPA; letters of recommendation; interview.
Standardized tests *Admission: Recommended:* SAT I.
Significant dates *Application deadlines:* rolling (freshmen), rolling (transfers). *Financial aid deadline priority date:* 5/1.
Freshman Application Contact
Ms. Diane C. Taylor, Dean of Enrollment Management, Robert Morris College, 881 Narrows Run Road, Moon Township, PA 15108-1189. **Phone:** 412-262-8265. **Toll-free phone:** 800-762-0097. **Fax:** 412-262-8619. **E-mail:** paylo@robert-morris.edu
Visit CollegeQuest.com for information on majors offered and athletics. College video available at CollegeQuest.com.

■ *See page 2340 for a narrative description.*

ROSEMONT COLLEGE
Rosemont, Pennsylvania

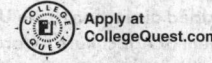 Apply at CollegeQuest.com

- **Independent Roman Catholic**, comprehensive, founded 1921
- **Degrees** bachelor's and master's
- **Suburban** 56-acre campus with easy access to Philadelphia
- **Women** only, 880 undergraduate students, 57% full-time
- **Moderately difficult** entrance level, 83% of applicants were admitted
- **8:1 student-to-undergraduate faculty ratio**
- **70% graduate** in 6 years or less
- **$15,270 tuition** and fees
- **$6.5 million endowment**

Founded in 1921, Rosemont College has been ranked by *U.S. News & World Report* for consecutive years as one of the top regional liberal arts colleges in the North. Rosemont has also been selected for the John Templeton Foundation's Honor Roll for Character Building Colleges and is listed among Barron's "best buys."

Students *Undergraduates:* 503 full-time, 377 part-time. Students come from 19 states and territories, 10 other countries. *The most frequently chosen baccalaureate fields are:* business/marketing, English, psychology. *Graduate:* 221 in graduate degree programs.

From out-of-state	31%	Reside on campus	68%
Age 25 or older	55%	Transferred in	3%
International students	2%	African Americans	19%
Asian Americans/Pacific Islanders	5%	Hispanic Americans	3%
Native Americans	0.2%		

Faculty 172 (26% full-time), 80% with terminal degrees.
Expenses (2000–2001) *Comprehensive fee:* $22,300 includes full-time tuition ($14,580), mandatory fees ($690), and room and board ($7030). *Part-time tuition:* $1680 per course. *Part-time fees:* $64 per course. *Payment plan:* installment. *Waivers:* senior citizens and employees or children of employees.
Library Kistler Library. *Operations spending 1999–2000:* $435,026. *Collection:* 150,000 titles, 690 serial subscriptions, 1,800 audiovisual materials.

College life *Housing:* on-campus residence required through junior year. *Option:* women-only. *Most popular organizations:* student government, Triad, Jest and Gesture, Best Buddies, political science club.
Campus security 24-hour emergency response devices and patrols, late-night transport-escort service, controlled dormitory access.
After graduation 70% of class of 1998 had job offers within 6 months. *Career center:* 1 full-time, 1 part-time personnel. Services include job fairs, resume preparation, interview workshops, resume referral, career/interest testing, career counseling, careers library, job bank, job interviews. *Graduate education:* 26% of class of 1999 went directly to graduate and professional school: 16% graduate arts and sciences, 7% medicine, 3% law.
Freshmen 327 applied, 272 admitted, 116 enrolled.

Average high school GPA	3.1	SAT verbal scores above 500	61%
SAT math scores above 500	52%	ACT above 18	N/R
From top 10% of their h.s. class	21%	From top quarter	44%
From top half	63%	1998 freshmen returning in 1999	74%

Application *Options:* eApply at www.CollegeQuest.com, Common Application, electronic application, early admission, deferred entrance. *Application fee:* $35. *Required:* essay or personal statement; high school transcript; 2 letters of recommendation. *Recommended:* minimum 3.0 GPA; interview.
Standardized tests *Admission: Required:* SAT I.
Significant dates *Application deadlines:* rolling (freshmen), rolling (transfers). *Notification:* continuous until 9/1 (freshmen). *Financial aid deadline priority date:* 3/1.
Freshman Application Contact
Admissions Office, Rosemont College, , 1400 Montgomery Avenue, Rosemont, PA 19010. **Phone:** 610-526-2966. **Toll-free phone:** 800-331-0708. **Fax:** 610-527-1041. **E-mail:** admissions@rosemont.edu
Visit CollegeQuest.com for information on majors offered and athletics. College video available at CollegeQuest.com.

■ *See page 2358 for a narrative description.*

ST. CHARLES BORROMEO SEMINARY, OVERBROOK
Wynnewood, Pennsylvania

- **Independent Roman Catholic**, comprehensive, founded 1832
- **Degrees** bachelor's, master's, and first professional
- **Suburban** 77-acre campus with easy access to Philadelphia
- **Coed**, primarily men, 46 undergraduate students, 100% full-time, 99.9% women, 100% men
- **Moderately difficult** entrance level, 100% of applicants were admitted
- **9:1 student-to-undergraduate faculty ratio**
- **50% graduate** in 6 years or less
- **$7950 tuition** and fees

Students *Undergraduates:* 46 full-time. Students come from 13 states and territories, 1 other country. *The most frequently chosen baccalaureate field is:* philosophy. *Graduate:* 57 in professional programs, 155 in other graduate degree programs.

From out-of-state	43%	Age 25 or older	29%
Transferred in	15%	International students	2%
African Americans	2%	Asian Americans/Pacific Islanders	15%
Hispanic Americans	13%		

Faculty 37 (27% full-time), 59% with terminal degrees.
Expenses (1999–2000) *Comprehensive fee:* $13,500 includes full-time tuition ($7950) and room and board ($5550). *Part-time tuition:* $75 per credit. *Payment plan:* installment. *Waivers:* employees or children of employees.
Library Ryan Memorial Library. *Operations spending 1999–2000:* $365,117. *Collection:* 127,156 titles, 560 serial subscriptions, 8,902 audiovisual materials.
College life *Housing:* on-campus residence required through senior year. *Option:* men-only. *Most popular organizations:* Seminarians for Life, student council.
Campus security 24-hour emergency response devices and patrols.
After graduation *Graduate education:* 100% of class of 1999 went directly to graduate and professional school.

Pennsylvania

St. Charles Borromeo Seminary, Overbrook (continued)
Freshmen 6 applied, 6 admitted, 6 enrolled.

SAT verbal scores above 500	N/R	SAT math scores above 500	N/R
ACT above 18	N/R	From top 10% of their h.s. class	17%
From top quarter	33%	From top half	67%
1998 freshmen returning in 1999	88%		

Application *Option:* deferred entrance. *Required:* essay or personal statement; high school transcript; 3 letters of recommendation; interview; sponsorship by diocese or religious community.
Standardized tests *Admission: Recommended:* SAT I or ACT.
Significant dates *Application deadlines:* 7/15 (freshmen), 7/15 (transfers). *Financial aid deadline priority date:* 4/15.
Freshman Application Contact
Rev. Christopher J. Schreck, Vice Rector for Educational Administration, St. Charles Borromeo Seminary, Overbrook, 100 East Wynnewood Road, Wynnewood, PA 19096. **Phone:** 610-667-3394.
Visit CollegeQuest.com for information on majors offered and athletics.

SAINT FRANCIS COLLEGE
Loretto, Pennsylvania

- **Independent Roman Catholic**, comprehensive, founded 1847
- **Degrees** associate, bachelor's, and master's
- **Rural** 600-acre campus
- **Coed**, 1,417 undergraduate students, 85% full-time, 63% women, 37% men
- **Moderately difficult** entrance level, 89% of applicants were admitted
- **63% graduate** in 6 years or less
- **$15,040 tuition** and fees
- **$15,555 average financial aid** package, $14,075 average indebtedness upon graduation, $11.4 million endowment

Saint Francis College has been nationally recognized for leadership in the field of character development in *The Templeton Guide: Colleges That Encourage Character Development*. The College has been recognized as one of the top 100 character building colleges. Saint Francis continues to improve technological capabilities with the addition of several multimedia facilities on campus.

Students *Undergraduates:* 1,211 full-time, 206 part-time. Students come from 22 states and territories, 12 other countries. *The most frequently chosen baccalaureate fields are:* business/marketing, education, health professions and related sciences. *Graduate:* 509 in graduate degree programs.

From out-of-state	15%	Reside on campus	83%
Age 25 or older	13%	Transferred in	4%
International students	1%	African Americans	2%
Asian Americans/Pacific Islanders	1%	Hispanic Americans	1%
Native Americans	0.2%		

Faculty 120 (68% full-time), 58% with terminal degrees.
Expenses (1999–2000) *Comprehensive fee:* $21,520 includes full-time tuition ($15,040) and room and board ($6480). *College room only:* $3080. Room and board charges vary according to board plan, housing facility, and location. *Part-time tuition:* $470 per credit. Part-time tuition and fees vary according to course load. *Payment plans:* installment, deferred payment. *Waivers:* children of alumni and employees or children of employees.
Library Pasquerella Library. *Operations spending 1999–2000:* $771,030. *Collection:* 155,143 titles, 975 serial subscriptions, 1,957 audiovisual materials.
College life *Housing:* on-campus residence required through junior year. *Options:* men-only, women-only. *Social organizations:* national fraternities, national sororities, local sororities; 17% of eligible men and 12% of eligible women are members. *Most popular organizations:* Student Activities Organization, New Theatre, Student Government Association.
Campus security 24-hour emergency response devices and patrols, late-night transport-escort service, controlled dormitory access.
After graduation 73 organizations recruited on campus 1997–98. 60% of class of 1998 had job offers within 6 months. *Career center:* 2 full-time, 1 part-time personnel. Services include job fairs, resume preparation, interview workshops, resume referral, career/interest testing, career counseling, careers library, job bank, job interviews. *Graduate education:* 39% of class of 1999 went directly to graduate and professional school: 6% graduate arts and sciences, 4% education, 2% law, 1% medicine, 1% veterinary medicine.

Freshmen 1,184 applied, 1,058 admitted, 313 enrolled.

Average high school GPA	3.38	SAT verbal scores above 500	58%
SAT math scores above 500	57%	ACT above 18	94%
From top 10% of their h.s. class	20%	From top quarter	50%
From top half	74%	1998 freshmen returning in 1999	75%

Application *Options:* eApply at www.CollegeQuest.com, electronic application, deferred entrance. *Application fee:* $30. *Required:* high school transcript; 1 letter of recommendation. *Required for some:* 3 letters of recommendation; interview. *Recommended:* essay or personal statement; interview.
Standardized tests *Admission: Required:* SAT I or ACT.
Significant dates *Application deadlines:* rolling (freshmen), rolling (transfers). *Financial aid deadline:* continuous.
Freshman Application Contact
Mr. Evan Lipp, Dean for Enrollment Management, Saint Francis College, PO Box 600, Loretto, PA 15940-0600. **Phone:** 814-472-3100. **Toll-free phone:** 800-342-5732. **Fax:** 814-472-3044. **E-mail:** admission@sfcpa.edu
Visit CollegeQuest.com for information on majors offered and athletics.

■ *See page 2378 for a narrative description.*

SAINT JOSEPH'S UNIVERSITY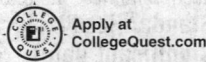
Philadelphia, Pennsylvania

- **Independent Roman Catholic (Jesuit)**, comprehensive, founded 1851
- **Degrees** associate, bachelor's, master's, doctoral, and post-master's certificates
- **Suburban** 60-acre campus
- **Coed**, 4,201 undergraduate students, 81% full-time, 56% women, 44% men
- **Very difficult** entrance level, 74% of applicants were admitted
- **67.7% graduate** in 6 years or less
- **$18,430 tuition** and fees
- **$11,150 average financial aid** package, $39.4 million endowment

Saint Joseph's new international academic center, Mandeville Hall, brings added distinction to the University's Haub School of Business. The US Department of Agriculture awarded Saint Joseph's a $12.4-million matching grant to build this premier educational facility. Mandeville Hall is the most technologically advanced academic center in the Philadelphia region.

Students *Undergraduates:* 3,393 full-time, 808 part-time. Students come from 38 states and territories, 24 other countries.

From out-of-state	50%	Reside on campus	53%
Transferred in	2%		

Expenses (1999–2000) *Comprehensive fee:* $25,944 includes full-time tuition ($18,140), mandatory fees ($290), and room and board ($7514). *College room only:* $4704. Full-time tuition and fees vary according to program. Room and board charges vary according to board plan and housing facility. *Part-time tuition:* $313 per credit. Part-time tuition and fees vary according to class time. *Payment plans:* installment, deferred payment. *Waivers:* employees or children of employees.
Library Francis A. Drexel Library plus 1 other. *Operations spending 1999–2000:* $2 million. *Collection:* 344,801 titles, 1,800 serial subscriptions, 3,295 audiovisual materials.
College life *Housing: Options:* coed, men-only, women-only, disabled students. *Social organizations:* national fraternities, national sororities; 9% of eligible men and 12% of eligible women are members. *Most popular organizations:* Student Government Association, Student Union Board, Cap and Bells Dramatic Arts Society.
Campus security 24-hour emergency response devices and patrols, late-night transport-escort service, controlled dormitory access, 24-hour shuttle/escort service, bicycle patrols.
After graduation 120 organizations recruited on campus 1997–98. 65% of class of 1998 had job offers within 6 months. *Career center:* 4 full-time, 1 part-time personnel. Services include job fairs, resume preparation, interview workshops, resume referral, career/interest testing, career counseling, careers library, job bank, job interviews. *Graduate education:* 24% of class of 1999 went directly to graduate and professional school. *Major awards:* 1 Fulbright Scholar.

Pennsylvania

Freshmen 5,358 applied, 3,977 admitted, 971 enrolled. 15 valedictorians.

Average high school GPA	3.38	SAT verbal scores above 500	84%
SAT math scores above 500	78%	ACT above 18	N/R
From top 10% of their h.s. class	44%	From top quarter	81%
From top half	99%	1998 freshmen returning in 1999	89%

Application *Options:* eApply at www.CollegeQuest.com, Common Application, electronic application, early admission, deferred entrance. *Application fee:* $40. *Required:* essay or personal statement; high school transcript; 1 letter of recommendation. *Required for some:* interview. *Recommended:* minimum 3.0 GPA; interview.
Standardized tests *Admission: Required:* SAT I or ACT. *Recommended:* SAT II Subject Tests.
Significant dates *Application deadlines:* rolling (freshmen), 7/1 (transfers). *Financial aid deadline priority date:* 2/15.
Freshman Application Contact
Mr. David Conway, Assistant Vice President of Enrollment Management, Saint Joseph's University, 5600 City Avenue, Philadelphia, PA 19131-1395. **Phone:** 610-660-1300. **Toll-free phone:** 888-BEAHAWK. **E-mail:** admi@sju.edu
Visit CollegeQuest.com for information on majors offered and athletics. College video and electronic viewbook available at CollegeQuest.com.

■ *See page 2396 for a narrative description.*

SAINT VINCENT COLLEGE
Latrobe, Pennsylvania

Apply at CollegeQuest.com

- **Independent Roman Catholic**, 4-year, founded 1846
- **Degree** bachelor's
- **Suburban** 200-acre campus with easy access to Pittsburgh
- **Coed**, 1,080 undergraduate students, 97% full-time, 50% women, 50% men
- **Moderately difficult** entrance level, 88% of applicants were admitted
- **12:1 student-to-undergraduate faculty ratio**
- **63% graduate** in 6 years or less
- **$14,955 tuition** and fees
- **$11,420 average financial aid** package, $19,842 average indebtedness upon graduation, $34.4 million endowment

Students *Undergraduates:* 1,049 full-time, 31 part-time. Students come from 23 states and territories, 9 other countries. *The most frequently chosen baccalaureate fields are:* business/marketing, psychology, social sciences and history.

From out-of-state	12%	Reside on campus	78%
Age 25 or older	9%	Transferred in	4%
International students	1%	African Americans	3%
Asian Americans/Pacific Islanders	1%	Hispanic Americans	1%

Faculty 117 (69% full-time).
Expenses (1999–2000) *Comprehensive fee:* $20,069 includes full-time tuition ($14,725), mandatory fees ($230), and room and board ($5114). Full-time tuition and fees vary according to course load. Room and board charges vary according to board plan and housing facility. *Part-time tuition:* $475 per credit. *Part-time fees:* $115 per term part-time. Part-time tuition and fees vary according to course load. *Payment plans:* installment, deferred payment. *Waivers:* senior citizens and employees or children of employees.
Library Saint Vincent College Library. *Operations spending 1999–2000:* $765,599. *Collection:* 250,017 titles, 825 serial subscriptions, 1,396 audiovisual materials.
College life *Housing: Option:* coed. *Most popular organizations:* Campus Ministry, prelaw club, The Review (Newspaper), Student Government, SVC Student Education Association.
Campus security 24-hour emergency response devices and patrols, late-night transport-escort service, controlled dormitory access, limited access to residence halls on weekends.
After graduation 140 organizations recruited on campus 1997–98. 66% of class of 1998 had job offers within 6 months. *Career center:* 2 full-time, 1 part-time personnel. Services include job fairs, resume preparation, interview workshops, resume referral, career/interest testing, career counseling, careers library, job bank, job interviews, alumni career night.
Freshmen 743 applied, 653 admitted, 272 enrolled. 7 National Merit Scholars, 8 class presidents, 5 valedictorians, 55 student government officers.

Average high school GPA	3.31	SAT verbal scores above 500	63%
SAT math scores above 500	60%	ACT above 18	81%
From top 10% of their h.s. class	21%	From top quarter	47%
From top half	77%	1998 freshmen returning in 1999	86%

Application *Options:* eApply at www.CollegeQuest.com, early admission, deferred entrance. *Application fee:* $25. *Required:* essay or personal statement; high school transcript; minimum 2.5 GPA. *Required for some:* interview. *Recommended:* minimum 3.2 GPA; 3 letters of recommendation; interview.
Standardized tests *Admission: Required:* SAT I or ACT.
Significant dates *Application deadlines:* 5/1 (freshmen), 7/1 (transfers). *Financial aid deadline priority date:* 2/15.
Freshman Application Contact
Rev. Paul Taylor OSB, Director of Admission and Financial Aid, Saint Vincent College, 300 Fraser Purchase Road, Latrobe, PA 15650. **Phone:** 724-537-4540. **Toll-free phone:** 800-SVC-5549. **Fax:** 724-537-4554. **E-mail:** admission@stvincent.edu
Visit CollegeQuest.com for information on majors offered and athletics. College video available at CollegeQuest.com.

SETON HILL COLLEGE
Greensburg, Pennsylvania

- **Independent Roman Catholic**, comprehensive, founded 1883
- **Degrees** bachelor's, master's, and post-master's certificates
- **Small-town** 200-acre campus with easy access to Pittsburgh
- **Coed**, primarily women, 927 undergraduate students, 74% full-time, 84% women, 16% men
- **Moderately difficult** entrance level, 88% of applicants were admitted
- **13:1 student-to-undergraduate faculty ratio**
- **50% graduate** in 6 years or less
- **$14,500 tuition** and fees
- **$14,350 average financial aid** package, $6.3 million endowment

U.S. News & World Report ranks Seton Hill College in the top tier among regional liberal arts colleges and universities in the northern US. Seton Hill offers 30 undergraduate majors, including a physician assistant program and master's degrees in education, art therapy, management, writing, and counseling psychology.

Students *Undergraduates:* 687 full-time, 240 part-time. Students come from 19 states and territories, 9 other countries. *The most frequently chosen baccalaureate fields are:* business/marketing, social sciences and history, visual/performing arts. *Graduate:* 187 in graduate degree programs.

From out-of-state	16%	Reside on campus	65%
Age 25 or older	13%	Transferred in	8%
International students	1%	African Americans	7%
Asian Americans/Pacific Islanders	1%	Hispanic Americans	2%
Native Americans	1%		

Faculty 69 (84% full-time), 64% with terminal degrees.
Expenses (1999–2000) *Comprehensive fee:* $19,350 includes full-time tuition ($14,500) and room and board ($4850). Room and board charges vary according to board plan. *Part-time tuition:* $360 per credit. *Payment plan:* installment. *Waivers:* employees or children of employees.
Library Reeves Memorial Library. *Operations spending 1999–2000:* $148,129. *Collection:* 6,000 audiovisual materials.
College life *Housing: Options:* coed, men-only, women-only. *Most popular organizations:* Intercultural Student Organization, biology/environmental club, Association of Black Collegians, chemistry club, Pennsylvania Student Education Association.
Campus security 24-hour emergency response devices and patrols, late-night transport-escort service, controlled dormitory access, student personnel at entrances during evening hours, 15-hour overnight patrols by trained police officers.
After graduation 46 organizations recruited on campus 1997–98. 54% of class of 1998 had job offers within 6 months. *Career center:* 2 full-time, 1 part-time personnel. Services include job fairs, resume preparation, interview workshops, resume referral, career/interest testing, career counseling, careers library, job bank, job interviews. *Graduate education:* 20% of class of 1999 went directly to graduate and professional school: 16% graduate arts and sciences, 2% law, 1% education.

Pennsylvania

Seton Hill College (continued)

Freshmen 537 applied, 470 admitted, 165 enrolled.

SAT verbal scores above 500	N/R	SAT math scores above 500	N/R
ACT above 18	N/R	From top 10% of their h.s. class	22%
From top quarter	54%	From top half	85%
1998 freshmen returning in 1999	56%		

Application *Options:* eApply at www.CollegeQuest.com, Common Application, early admission, deferred entrance. *Application fee:* $30. *Required:* high school transcript; minimum 2.0 GPA; portfolio for art program, audition for music and theater programs. *Recommended:* essay or personal statement; letters of recommendation; interview.

Standardized tests *Admission: Required:* SAT I or ACT. *Required for some:* PAA.

Significant dates *Application deadlines:* rolling (freshmen), rolling (transfers). *Financial aid deadline:* continuous.

Freshman Application Contact
Ms. Kathleen Berard, Director of Admissions, Seton Hill College, Seton Hill Drive, Greensburg, PA 15601. **Phone:** 724-838-4255. **Toll-free phone:** 800-826-6234. **Fax:** 724-830-4611. **E-mail:** admit@setonhill.edu

Visit CollegeQuest.com for information on majors offered and athletics. College video and electronic viewbook available at CollegeQuest.com.

■ *See page 2472 for a narrative description.*

SHIPPENSBURG UNIVERSITY OF PENNSYLVANIA
Shippensburg, Pennsylvania

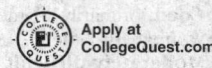
Apply at CollegeQuest.com

- **State-supported**, comprehensive, founded 1871
- **Degrees** bachelor's and master's
- **Rural** 200-acre campus
- **Coed**, 5,672 undergraduate students, 96% full-time, 54% women, 46% men
- **Moderately difficult** entrance level, 64% of applicants were admitted
- **21:1 student-to-undergraduate faculty ratio**
- **58% graduate** in 6 years or less
- **$4550 tuition** and fees (in-state); $9978 (out-of-state)
- **$4962 average financial aid** package, $16.3 million endowment

Recognized for its academic excellence, Shippensburg University has a national reputation for providing students with such opportunities as grant-funded student-faculty research projects and active volunteer community service organizations. The academic quality, stemming from a talented, dedicated faculty, is complemented with the recent opening of 2 new academic buildings.

Part of Pennsylvania State System of Higher Education.

Students *Undergraduates:* 5,453 full-time, 219 part-time. Students come from 17 states and territories. *The most frequently chosen baccalaureate fields are:* business/marketing, education, protective services/public administration. *Graduate:* 941 in graduate degree programs.

From out-of-state	5%	Reside on campus	43%
Age 25 or older	7%	Transferred in	5%
International students	1%	African Americans	4%
Asian Americans/Pacific Islanders	1%	Hispanic Americans	1%
Native Americans	0.2%		

Faculty 343 (87% full-time), 82% with terminal degrees.

Expenses (1999–2000) *Tuition, state resident:* full-time $3618; part-time $150 per credit hour. *Tuition, nonresident:* full-time $9046; part-time $377 per credit hour. *Required fees:* full-time $932; $15 per credit hour; $102 per term part-time. Part-time tuition and fees vary according to course load. *College room and board:* $4120; room only: $2468. Room and board charges vary according to board plan. *Waivers:* senior citizens and employees or children of employees.

Library Ezra Lehman Memorial Library plus 1 other. *Operations spending 1999–2000:* $2.2 million. *Collection:* 438,436 titles, 1,771 serial subscriptions.

College life *Housing:* on-campus residence required in freshman year. *Options:* coed, men-only, women-only. *Social organizations:* national fraternities, national sororities, local fraternities, local sororities; 9% of eligible men and 9% of eligible women are members. *Most popular organizations:* TOUCH, Big Brother/Big Sister, band, Christian Fellowship, Concert Committee.

Campus security 24-hour emergency response devices and patrols, student patrols, late-night transport-escort service, controlled dormitory access, closed circuit TV monitors, bicycle patrols by security officers.

After graduation 100 organizations recruited on campus 1997–98. *Career center:* 5 full-time personnel. Services include job fairs, resume preparation, interview workshops, resume referral, career/interest testing, career counseling, careers library, job interviews, job hotline.

Freshmen 6,100 applied, 3,875 admitted, 1,383 enrolled. 18 class presidents, 157 student government officers.

SAT verbal scores above 500	67%	SAT math scores above 500	67%
ACT above 18	N/R	From top 10% of their h.s. class	10%
From top quarter	39%	From top half	84%
1998 freshmen returning in 1999	75%		

Application *Options:* eApply at www.CollegeQuest.com, Common Application, electronic application, early admission, early action, deferred entrance. *Application fee:* $30. *Required:* high school transcript. *Required for some:* interview. *Recommended:* essay or personal statement; letters of recommendation.

Standardized tests *Admission: Required:* SAT I or ACT.

Significant dates *Application deadlines:* rolling (freshmen), rolling (transfers). *Financial aid deadline:* 5/1. *Priority date:* 3/15.

Freshman Application Contact
Mr. Joseph Cretella, Dean of Admissions, Shippensburg University of Pennsylvania, 1871 Old Main Drive, Shippensburg, PA 17257-2299. **Phone:** 717-477-1231. **Toll-free phone:** 800-822-8028. **Fax:** 717-477-1273. **E-mail:** admiss@ship.edu

Visit CollegeQuest.com for information on majors offered and athletics. College video and electronic viewbook available at CollegeQuest.com.

■ *See page 2482 for a narrative description.*

SLIPPERY ROCK UNIVERSITY OF PENNSYLVANIA
Slippery Rock, Pennsylvania

Apply at CollegeQuest.com

- **State-supported**, comprehensive, founded 1889
- **Degrees** bachelor's, master's, and doctoral
- **Rural** 611-acre campus with easy access to Pittsburgh
- **Coed**, 6,079 undergraduate students, 92% full-time, 57% women, 43% men
- **Moderately difficult** entrance level, 91% of applicants were admitted
- **21:1 student-to-undergraduate faculty ratio**
- **$4484 tuition** and fees (in-state); $9912 (out-of-state)
- **$5619 average financial aid** package, $13,745 average indebtedness upon graduation, $9.3 million endowment

Slippery Rock University's students benefit from more than 100 programs in arts and sciences, business, education, information sciences, and health; 28 study-abroad programs; more than 160 student organizations; athletics; and an online environment linking every student residence hall room to the electronic world. A flexible admission policy and attractive financial aid packages draw 7,000 students from 40 states and more than 70 countries.

Part of Pennsylvania State System of Higher Education.

Students *Undergraduates:* 5,616 full-time, 463 part-time. Students come from 30 states and territories, 61 other countries. *The most frequently chosen baccalaureate fields are:* business/marketing, education, health professions and related sciences. *Graduate:* 673 in graduate degree programs.

From out-of-state	4%	Reside on campus	38%
Age 25 or older	12%	Transferred in	8%
International students	3%	African Americans	3%
Asian Americans/Pacific Islanders	1%	Hispanic Americans	1%
Native Americans	0.2%		

Faculty 385 (91% full-time), 73% with terminal degrees.

Expenses (1999–2000) *Tuition, state resident:* full-time $3618; part-time $150 per credit. *Tuition, nonresident:* full-time $9046; part-time $377 per credit. *Required fees:* full-time $866; $38 per credit; $396 per term part-time. Part-time tuition and fees vary according to course load. *College room and board:* $3810; room only: $2038. Room and board charges vary according to

Pennsylvania

board plan, housing facility, and location. *Payment plan:* installment. *Waivers:* minority students, senior citizens, and employees or children of employees.

Library Bailey Library. *Operations spending 1999–2000:* $2 million. *Collection:* 754,603 titles, 84,054 audiovisual materials.

College life *Housing:* on-campus residence required in freshman year. *Options:* coed, men-only, women-only. *Social organizations:* national fraternities, national sororities; 5% of eligible men and 5% of eligible women are members. *Most popular organizations:* Association of Residence Hall Students, University Program Board, Black Action Society, internations club, Student Government Association.

Campus security 24-hour emergency response devices and patrols, late-night transport-escort service, controlled dormitory access.

After graduation 232 organizations recruited on campus 1997–98. 60% of class of 1998 had job offers within 6 months. *Career center:* 3 full-time personnel. Services include job fairs, resume preparation, interview workshops, resume referral, career/interest testing, career counseling, careers library, job bank, job interviews.

Freshmen 2,984 applied, 2,716 admitted, 1,320 enrolled.

Average high school GPA	3.13	SAT verbal scores above 500	38%
SAT math scores above 500	37%	ACT above 18	77%
From top 10% of their h.s. class	8%	From top quarter	25%
From top half	61%	1998 freshmen returning in 1999	69%

Application *Options:* eApply at www.CollegeQuest.com, Common Application, electronic application, early admission, deferred entrance. *Preference* given to state residents. *Application fee:* $25. *Required:* essay or personal statement; high school transcript. *Required for some:* interview. *Recommended:* letters of recommendation; interview.

Standardized tests *Admission: Required:* SAT I or ACT.

Significant dates *Application deadlines:* 5/1 (freshmen), 5/1 (transfers). *Financial aid deadline priority date:* 5/1.

Freshman Application Contact
Dr. Duncan M. Sargent, Director of Admissions, Slippery Rock University of Pennsylvania, Maltby Center, Slippery Rock, PA 16057. **Phone:** 724-738-2015. **Toll-free phone:** 800-SRU-9111 (in-state); 724-738-2913 (out-of-state). **Fax:** 724-738-2098. **E-mail:** apply@sru.edu

Visit CollegeQuest.com for information on majors offered and athletics. Electronic viewbook available at CollegeQuest.com.

■ *See page 2500 for a narrative description.*

SUSQUEHANNA UNIVERSITY
Selinsgrove, Pennsylvania

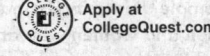

- **Independent**, 4-year, founded 1858, affiliated with Lutheran Church
- **Degree** bachelor's (also offers associate degree through evening program to local students)
- **Small-town** 210-acre campus with easy access to Harrisburg
- **Coed**, 1,681 undergraduate students, 98% full-time, 58% women, 42% men
- **Moderately difficult** entrance level, 75% of applicants were admitted
- **14:1 student-to-undergraduate faculty ratio**
- **71% graduate** in 6 years or less
- **$19,670 tuition** and fees
- **$16,518 average financial aid** package, $17,005 average indebtedness upon graduation, $87.1 million endowment

Students *Undergraduates:* 1,652 full-time, 29 part-time. Students come from 28 states and territories. *The most frequently chosen baccalaureate fields are:* business/marketing, communications/communication technologies, social sciences and history.

From out-of-state	40%	Reside on campus	80%
Age 25 or older	1%	Transferred in	2%
International students	1%	African Americans	2%
Asian Americans/Pacific Islanders	2%	Hispanic Americans	2%
Native Americans	0.3%		

Faculty 161 (60% full-time), 61% with terminal degrees.

Expenses (1999–2000) *Comprehensive fee:* $25,220 includes full-time tuition ($19,380), mandatory fees ($290), and room and board ($5550). *College room only:* $2950. Room and board charges vary according to board plan. *Part-time tuition:* $625 per semester hour. *Payment plans:* tuition prepayment, installment, deferred payment. *Waivers:* employees or children of employees.

Library Blough-Weis Library plus 1 other. *Operations spending 1999–2000:* $1.4 million. *Collection:* 252,000 titles, 2,176 serial subscriptions, 10,800 audiovisual materials.

College life *Housing:* on-campus residence required through junior year. *Options:* coed, women-only. *Social organizations:* national fraternities, national sororities; 25% of eligible men and 25% of eligible women are members. *Most popular organizations:* Student Government Association, community service organizations, music performance groups, theater performance groups, intramurals and outdoor recreation.

Campus security 24-hour patrols, late-night transport-escort service, controlled dormitory access.

After graduation 38 organizations recruited on campus 1997–98. 76% of class of 1998 had job offers within 6 months. *Career center:* 2 full-time, 2 part-time personnel. Services include job fairs, resume preparation, interview workshops, resume referral, career/interest testing, career counseling, careers library, job bank, job interviews. *Graduate education:* 24% of class of 1999 went directly to graduate and professional school: 13% graduate arts and sciences, 3% law, 2% business, 2% medicine, 1% dentistry.

Freshmen 2,143 applied, 1,603 admitted, 464 enrolled. 1 National Merit Scholar, 15 class presidents, 4 valedictorians, 40 student government officers.

SAT verbal scores above 500	86%	SAT math scores above 500	82%
ACT above 18	N/R	From top 10% of their h.s. class	27%
From top quarter	61%	From top half	92%
1998 freshmen returning in 1999	86%		

Application *Options:* eApply at www.CollegeQuest.com, Common Application, electronic application, early admission, early decision, deferred entrance. *Application fee:* $30. *Required:* essay or personal statement; high school transcript; minimum 2.5 GPA; 1 letter of recommendation. *Required for some:* writing portfolio. *Recommended:* minimum 3.0 GPA; interview.

Standardized tests *Admission: Recommended:* SAT II Subject Tests, SAT II: Writing Test. *Required for some:* SAT I or ACT.

Significant dates *Application deadlines:* 3/1 (freshmen), 7/1 (transfers). *Early decision:* 12/15. *Notification:* 1/15 (early decision). *Financial aid deadline priority date:* 3/1.

Freshman Application Contact
Mr. Chris Markle, Director of Admissions, Susquehanna University, 514 University Avenue, Selinsgrove, PA 17870-1040. **Phone:** 570-372-4260. **Toll-free phone:** 800-326-9672. **Fax:** 570-372-2722. **E-mail:** suadmiss@susqu.edu

Visit CollegeQuest.com for information on majors offered and athletics. College video available at CollegeQuest.com.

■ *See page 2582 for a narrative description.*

SWARTHMORE COLLEGE
Swarthmore, Pennsylvania

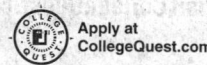

- **Independent**, 4-year, founded 1864
- **Degree** bachelor's
- **Suburban** 330-acre campus with easy access to Philadelphia
- **Coed**, 1,448 undergraduate students, 100% full-time, 53% women, 47% men
- **Most difficult** entrance level, 22% of applicants were admitted
- **8:1 student-to-undergraduate faculty ratio**
- **92% graduate** in 6 years or less
- **$24,190 tuition** and fees
- **$23,515 average financial aid** package, $13,390 average indebtedness upon graduation, $905.7 million endowment

Usually ranked among the top 3 small liberal arts colleges, Swarthmore is half men, half women, more than 30% American students of color, and 8% international students and is located 11 miles from Philadelphia. It has a student-faculty ratio of 8:1, an engineering department, and need-blind admissions.

Students *Undergraduates:* 1,448 full-time. Students come from 50 states and territories, 43 other countries. *The most frequently chosen baccalaureate fields are:* biological/life sciences, English, social sciences and history.

Pennsylvania

Swarthmore College (continued)

From out-of-state	82%	Reside on campus	93%
Transferred in	0.3%	International students	7%
African Americans	9%	Asian Americans/Pacific Islanders	13%
Hispanic Americans	9%	Native Americans	1%

Faculty 193 (86% full-time), 82% with terminal degrees.
Expenses (1999–2000) *Comprehensive fee:* $31,690 includes full-time tuition ($23,964), mandatory fees ($226), and room and board ($7500). *College room only:* $3850. *Payment plan:* installment. *Waivers:* employees or children of employees.
Library McCabe Library plus 4 others. *Operations spending 1999–2000:* $3.4 million. *Collection:* 1 million titles, 6,407 serial subscriptions, 18,147 audiovisual materials.
College life *Housing:* on-campus residence required in freshman year. *Options:* coed, men-only, women-only. *Social organizations:* national fraternities, local fraternities; 4% of men are members. *Most popular organizations:* Civil Liberties Club, International Club, Amnesty International, Cooperative Involvement of Volunteers in Communities, Drama Board.
Campus security 24-hour emergency response devices and patrols, student patrols, late-night transport-escort service.
After graduation 99 organizations recruited on campus 1997–98. *Career center:* 3 full-time, 1 part-time personnel. Services include resume preparation, interview workshops, resume referral, career/interest testing, career counseling, careers library, job bank, job interviews. *Graduate education:* 19% of class of 1999 went directly to graduate and professional school: 11% graduate arts and sciences, 5% law, 2% medicine. *Major awards:* 1 Rhodes, 7 Fulbright Scholars.
Freshmen 4,163 applied, 906 admitted, 368 enrolled. 32 National Merit Scholars, 56 valedictorians.

SAT verbal scores above 500	99%	SAT math scores above 500	99%
ACT above 18	N/R	From top 10% of their h.s. class	82%
From top quarter	97%	From top half	100%
1998 freshmen returning in 1999	95%		

Application *Options:* eApply at www.CollegeQuest.com, Common Application, early admission, early decision, deferred entrance. *Application fee:* $60. *Required:* essay or personal statement; high school transcript; 2 letters of recommendation. *Recommended:* interview.
Standardized tests *Admission: Required:* SAT I or ACT, SAT II Subject Tests, SAT II: Writing Test. *Required for some:* SAT II Subject Test in math.
Significant dates *Application deadlines:* 1/1 (freshmen), 4/1 (transfers). *Early decision:* 11/15 (for plan 1), 1/1 (for plan 2). *Notification:* 4/1 (freshmen), 12/15 (early decision plan 1), 2/1 (early decision plan 2). *Financial aid deadline priority date:* 2/15.
Freshman Application Contact
Office of Admissions, Swarthmore College, 500 College Avenue, Swarthmore, PA 19081-1397. **Phone:** 610-328-8300. **Toll-free phone:** 800-667-3110. **Fax:** 610-328-8673. **E-mail:** admissions@swarthmore.edu
Visit CollegeQuest.com for information on majors offered and athletics.

■ *See page 2584 for a narrative description.*

TALMUDICAL YESHIVA OF PHILADELPHIA
Philadelphia, Pennsylvania

- **Independent Jewish**, 4-year, founded 1953
- **Degree** bachelor's (also offers some graduate courses)
- **Urban** 3-acre campus
- **Men** only, 114 undergraduate students, 100% full-time
- **Moderately difficult** entrance level, 78% of applicants were admitted
- **29:1 student-to-undergraduate faculty ratio**
- **35% graduate** in 6 years or less
- **$5100 tuition** and fees

Students *Undergraduates:* 114 full-time. Students come from 13 states and territories, 5 other countries. *The most frequently chosen baccalaureate field is:* philosophy.

From out-of-state	94%	Reside on campus	100%
International students	24%		

Faculty 5 (60% full-time).

Expenses (1999–2000) *Comprehensive fee:* $9600 includes full-time tuition ($5000), mandatory fees ($100), and room and board ($4500). *Payment plan:* installment. *Waivers:* employees or children of employees.
Library *Collection:* 4,800 titles, 300 serial subscriptions.
College life *Housing:* on-campus residence required through senior year. *Option:* men-only. *Most popular organizations:* Pirchei, Mishmar, Bikur Cholim.
Campus security Controlled dormitory access.
After graduation *Career center:* Services include career counseling. *Graduate education:* 90% of class of 1999 went directly to graduate and professional school: 75% theology, 5% business, 5% law, 5% medicine.
Freshmen 45 applied, 35 admitted, 30 enrolled.

Average high school GPA	3.8	SAT verbal scores above 500	N/R
SAT math scores above 500	N/R	ACT above 18	N/R
From top 10% of their h.s. class	15%	From top quarter	30%
From top half	60%	1998 freshmen returning in 1999	87%

Application *Options:* Common Application, early admission, deferred entrance. *Required:* high school transcript; 1 letter of recommendation; interview; oral examination.
Significant dates *Application deadlines:* 7/15 (freshmen), 7/15 (transfers). *Notification:* 8/5 (freshmen).
Freshman Application Contact
Rabbi Shmuel Kamenetsky, Co-Dean, Talmudical Yeshiva of Philadelphia, 6063 Drexel Road, Philadelphia, PA 19131-1296. **Phone:** 215-473-1212. **Fax:** 215-477-5065.
Visit CollegeQuest.com for information on majors offered and athletics.

TEMPLE UNIVERSITY
Philadelphia, Pennsylvania

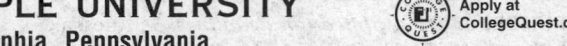
Apply at CollegeQuest.com

- **State-related**, university, founded 1884
- **Degrees** associate, bachelor's, master's, doctoral, first professional, post-master's, and first professional certificates
- **Urban** 76-acre campus
- **Coed**, 17,075 undergraduate students, 83% full-time, 58% women, 42% men
- **Moderately difficult** entrance level, 64% of applicants were admitted
- **11:1 student-to-undergraduate faculty ratio**
- **42% graduate** in 6 years or less
- **$6622 tuition** and fees (in-state); $11,740 (out-of-state)
- **$8947 average financial aid** package, $14,500 average indebtedness upon graduation, $141.5 million endowment

Temple University is a major teaching and research university with a faculty of men and women who are nationally and internationally recognized in their fields. Taking full advantage of its location in Philadelphia, Temple actively promotes programs that help students bridge the worlds of academia and work.

Students *Undergraduates:* 14,187 full-time, 2,888 part-time. Students come from 49 states and territories, 123 other countries. *The most frequently chosen baccalaureate fields are:* business/marketing, education, health professions and related sciences. *Graduate:* 2,808 in professional programs, 7,143 in other graduate degree programs.

From out-of-state	20%	Reside on campus	21%
Age 25 or older	24%	Transferred in	12%
International students	3%	African Americans	28%
Asian Americans/Pacific Islanders	10%	Hispanic Americans	3%
Native Americans	0.2%		

Faculty 2,635 (60% full-time).
Expenses (1999–2000) *Tuition, state resident:* full-time $6332; part-time $224 per semester hour. *Tuition, nonresident:* full-time $11,450; part-time $342 per semester hour. *Required fees:* full-time $290. Full-time tuition and fees vary according to course load and program. Part-time tuition and fees vary according to course load, location, and program. *College room and board:* $6302. Room and board charges vary according to board plan and housing facility. *Payment plan:* installment. *Waivers:* employees or children of employees.
Library Paley Library plus 11 others. *Operations spending 1999–2000:* $13.4 million. *Collection:* 16,755 serial subscriptions, 10.1 million audiovisual materials.

Pennsylvania

College life *Housing: Option:* coed. *Social organizations:* national fraternities, national sororities, local fraternities; 1% of eligible men and 1% of eligible women are members. *Most popular organizations:* African Student Union, India Student Association at Temple, Student Organization for Caribbean Awareness.

Campus security 24-hour emergency response devices and patrols, late-night transport-escort service, controlled dormitory access.

After graduation 500 organizations recruited on campus 1997–98. *Career center:* 13 full-time personnel. Services include job fairs, resume preparation, interview workshops, resume referral, career/interest testing, career counseling, careers library, job bank, job interviews. *Major awards:* 5 Fulbright Scholars.

Freshmen 12,455 applied, 7,955 admitted, 2,777 enrolled. 21 valedictorians.

SAT verbal scores above 500	61%	SAT math scores above 500	54%
ACT above 18	N/R	From top 10% of their h.s. class	17%
From top quarter	42%	From top half	80%
1998 freshmen returning in 1999	77%		

Application *Options:* eApply at www.CollegeQuest.com, early admission, deferred entrance. *Application fee:* $35. *Required:* high school transcript; minimum 2.0 GPA. *Required for some:* letters of recommendation; interview; portfolio, audition. *Recommended:* essay or personal statement.

Standardized tests *Admission: Required:* SAT I or ACT.

Significant dates *Application deadlines:* 4/1 (freshmen), 6/15 (transfers). *Financial aid deadline priority date:* 3/1.

Freshman Application Contact
Dr. Timm Rinehart, Acting Director of Admissions, Temple University, 1801 North Broad Street, Philadelphia, PA 19122-6096. **Phone:** 215-204-8556. **Toll-free phone:** 888-340-2222. **Fax:** 215-204-5694. **E-mail:** tuadm@vm.temple.edu

Visit CollegeQuest.com for information on majors offered and athletics. College video and electronic viewbook available at CollegeQuest.com.

■ *See page 2596 for a narrative description.*

THIEL COLLEGE
Greenville, Pennsylvania

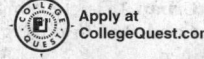
Apply at CollegeQuest.com

■ **Independent**, 4-year, founded 1866, affiliated with Evangelical Lutheran Church in America
■ **Degrees** associate and bachelor's
■ **Rural** 135-acre campus with easy access to Cleveland and Pittsburgh
■ **Coed**, 980 undergraduate students, 88% full-time, 53% women, 47% men
■ **Moderately difficult** entrance level, 83% of applicants were admitted
■ **12:1 student-to-undergraduate faculty ratio**
■ **$10,785 tuition** and fees
■ **$13,740 average financial aid** package, $20,069 average indebtedness upon graduation, $24.3 million endowment

Students *Undergraduates:* 865 full-time, 115 part-time. Students come from 15 states and territories, 18 other countries. *The most frequently chosen baccalaureate fields are:* business/marketing, psychology, social sciences and history.

From out-of-state	12%	Reside on campus	83%
Age 25 or older	10%	Transferred in	6%
International students	5%	African Americans	8%
Asian Americans/Pacific Islanders	0.1%	Hispanic Americans	1%
Native Americans	0.1%		

Expenses (1999–2000) *Comprehensive fee:* $16,275 includes full-time tuition ($9990), mandatory fees ($795), and room and board ($5490). *College room only:* $2798. Full-time tuition and fees vary according to student level. *Part-time tuition:* $270 per credit. *Part-time fees:* $20 per credit. Part-time tuition and fees vary according to course load. *Payment plan:* installment. *Waivers:* senior citizens and employees or children of employees.

Library Langenheim Library. *Operations spending 1999–2000:* $362,471. *Collection:* 189,245 titles, 489 serial subscriptions, 3,533 audiovisual materials.

College life *Housing:* on-campus residence required through senior year. *Options:* coed, men-only, women-only, disabled students. *Social organizations:* national fraternities, national sororities, local fraternities; 38% of eligible men and 30% of eligible women are members. *Most popular organizations:* Thiel Players Theatre Group, Greek organizations, student government, Thiel Choir.

Campus security 24-hour emergency response devices and patrols, student patrols, late-night transport-escort service.

After graduation 30 organizations recruited on campus 1997–98. 98% of class of 1998 had job offers within 6 months. *Career center:* 1 full-time, 2 part-time personnel. Services include job fairs, resume preparation, interview workshops, resume referral, career/interest testing, career counseling, careers library, job bank, job interviews. *Graduate education:* 14% of class of 1999 went directly to graduate and professional school.

Freshmen 1,248 applied, 1,032 admitted, 287 enrolled.

Average high school GPA	2.91	SAT verbal scores above 500	50%
SAT math scores above 500	49%	ACT above 18	67%
From top 10% of their h.s. class	17%	From top quarter	41%
From top half	73%	1998 freshmen returning in 1999	64%

Application *Options:* eApply at www.CollegeQuest.com, Common Application, early admission, deferred entrance. *Application fee:* $25. *Required:* high school transcript; minimum 2.0 GPA. *Required for some:* essay or personal statement; letters of recommendation; interview. *Recommended:* essay or personal statement; letters of recommendation; interview.

Standardized tests *Admission: Required:* SAT I or ACT.

Significant dates *Application deadlines:* 8/15 (freshmen), rolling (transfers). *Financial aid deadline:* continuous.

Freshman Application Contact
Mr. Lindsay Rhodenbaugh, Vice President of Enrollment Management, Thiel College, 75 College Avenue, Greenville, PA 16125-2181. **Phone:** 724-589-2176. **Toll-free phone:** 800-24THIEL. **Fax:** 724-589-2013. **E-mail:** admission@thiel.edu

Visit CollegeQuest.com for information on majors offered and athletics.

■ *See page 2614 for a narrative description.*

THOMAS JEFFERSON UNIVERSITY
Philadelphia, Pennsylvania

■ **Independent**, upper-level, founded 1824
■ **Degrees** bachelor's, master's, and postbachelor's certificates
■ **Urban** 13-acre campus
■ **Coed**, 656 undergraduate students, 64% full-time, 83% women, 17% men
■ **Moderately difficult** entrance level, 57% of applicants were admitted
■ **9:1 student-to-undergraduate faculty ratio**
■ **$16,785 tuition** and fees

Jefferson gives its students the small-college advantage of a 9:1 student-faculty ratio for the entire college plus the resources of one of the nation's leading academic health centers. The University is composed of a medical school, a graduate school, and the College of Health Professions and shares its campus with a 620-bed hospital.

Students *Undergraduates:* 421 full-time, 235 part-time. Students come from 27 states and territories, 7 other countries. *The most frequently chosen baccalaureate field is:* health professions and related sciences. *Graduate:* 894 in professional programs, 541 in other graduate degree programs.

From out-of-state	38%	Reside on campus	30%
Age 25 or older	59%	Transferred in	57%
International students	7%	African Americans	11%
Asian Americans/Pacific Islanders	6%	Hispanic Americans	2%
Native Americans	0.3%		

Faculty 98 (46% full-time), 43% with terminal degrees.

Expenses (1999–2000) *Tuition:* full-time $16,785; part-time $582 per credit. Full-time tuition and fees vary according to course level. Part-time tuition and fees vary according to course level. *College room only:* $2080. Room and board charges vary according to housing facility. *Payment plan:* installment. *Waivers:* employees or children of employees.

Library Scott Memorial Library plus 1 other. *Collection:* 170,000 titles, 2,290 serial subscriptions.

Pennsylvania

Thomas Jefferson University (continued)

College life *Housing: Option:* coed. *Most popular organizations:* Commons Board, student government, choir, Admission Ambassadors, Student Nurses Association of Pennsylvania.

Campus security 24-hour emergency response devices and patrols, late-night transport-escort service, controlled dormitory access.

After graduation 159 organizations recruited on campus 1997–98. 97% of class of 1998 had job offers within 6 months. *Career center:* 4 full-time personnel. Services include job fairs, resume preparation, resume referral, career counseling, careers library, job bank, job interviews.

Application *Option:* deferred entrance. *Application fee:* $45.

Standardized tests *Admission: Recommended:* SAT I or ACT.

Significant dates *Application deadline:* rolling (transfers). *Financial aid deadline priority date:* 5/1.

Freshman Application Contact
Assistant Director of Admissions, Thomas Jefferson University, Edison Building, Suite 1610, 130 South Ninth Street, Philadelphia, PA 19107. **Phone:** 215-503-8890. **Toll-free phone:** 877-533-3247. **Fax:** 215-503-7241. **E-mail:** chp.admissions@mail.tju.edu

Visit CollegeQuest.com for information on majors offered and athletics.

■ *See page 2618 for a narrative description.*

UNIVERSITY OF PENNSYLVANIA
Philadelphia, Pennsylvania

- **Independent**, university, founded 1740
- **Degrees** associate, bachelor's, master's, doctoral, and first professional (also offers evening program with significant enrollment not reflected in profile)
- **Urban** 260-acre campus
- **Coed**, 9,827 undergraduate students, 95% full-time, 49% women, 51% men
- **Most difficult** entrance level, 26% of applicants were admitted
- **7:1 student-to-undergraduate faculty ratio**
- **89.5% graduate** in 6 years or less
- **$24,230 tuition** and fees
- **$21,788 average financial aid** package, $20,200 average indebtedness upon graduation, $3.3 billion endowment

Students *Undergraduates:* 9,323 full-time, 504 part-time. Students come from 50 states and territories, 91 other countries. *The most frequently chosen baccalaureate fields are:* business/marketing, engineering/engineering technologies, social sciences and history. *Graduate:* 2,208 in professional programs, 6,007 in other graduate degree programs.

From out-of-state	81%	Reside on campus	62%
Age 25 or older	1%	Transferred in	3%
International students	9%	African Americans	6%
Asian Americans/Pacific Islanders	19%	Hispanic Americans	4%
Native Americans	0.2%		

Faculty 3,192 (85% full-time), 100% with terminal degrees.

Expenses (1999–2000) *Comprehensive fee:* $31,592 includes full-time tuition ($21,746), mandatory fees ($2484), and room and board ($7362). *College room only:* $4592. Room and board charges vary according to board plan and housing facility. *Part-time tuition:* $2777 per course. *Part-time fees:* $253 per course. Part-time tuition and fees vary according to course load. *Payment plans:* tuition prepayment, installment. *Waivers:* employees or children of employees.

Library Van Pelt-Dietrich Library plus 13 others. *Operations spending 1999–2000:* $28.8 million. *Collection:* 4.7 million titles, 34,276 serial subscriptions.

College life *Housing: Option:* coed. *Social organizations:* national fraternities, national sororities, local fraternities. *Most popular organizations:* Kite and Key Club, Daily Pennsylvania Newspaper, Penn Band.

Campus security 24-hour emergency response devices and patrols, student patrols, late-night transport-escort service.

After graduation 400 organizations recruited on campus 1997–98. 74% of class of 1998 had job offers within 6 months. *Career center:* 25 full-time, 5 part-time personnel. Services include job fairs, resume preparation, resume referral, career counseling, careers library, job bank, job interviews. *Graduate education:* 20% of class of 1999 went directly to graduate and professional school: 7% law, 5% graduate arts and sciences, 5% medicine, 1% business, 1% dentistry, 1% engineering. *Major awards:* 1 Marshall, 9 Fulbright Scholars.

Freshmen 17,666 applied, 4,668 admitted, 2,507 enrolled. 78 class presidents, 235 valedictorians, 264 student government officers.

Average high school GPA	3.79	SAT verbal scores above 500	99%
SAT math scores above 500	100%	ACT above 18	100%
From top 10% of their h.s. class	91%	From top quarter	98%
From top half	100%	1998 freshmen returning in 1999	97%

Application *Options:* early admission, early decision, deferred entrance. *Application fee:* $55. *Required:* essay or personal statement; high school transcript; 2 letters of recommendation. *Recommended:* interview.

Standardized tests *Admission: Required:* SAT I and SAT II or ACT, SAT II: Writing Test.

Significant dates *Application deadlines:* 1/1 (freshmen), 4/1 (transfers). *Early decision:* 11/1. *Notification:* 4/1 (freshmen), 12/15 (early decision). *Financial aid deadline priority date:* 2/15.

Freshman Application Contact
Mr. Willis J. Stetson Jr., Dean of Admissions, University of Pennsylvania, 1 College Hall, Levy Park, Philadelphia, PA 19104. **Phone:** 215-898-7507.

Visit CollegeQuest.com for information on majors offered and athletics. College video available at CollegeQuest.com.

UNIVERSITY OF PITTSBURGH
Pittsburgh, Pennsylvania

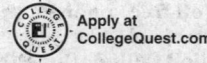
Apply at CollegeQuest.com

- **State-related**, university, founded 1787
- **Degrees** bachelor's, master's, doctoral, first professional, and post-master's certificates
- **Urban** 132-acre campus
- **Coed**, 16,676 undergraduate students, 87% full-time, 52% women, 48% men
- **Moderately difficult** entrance level, 66% of applicants were admitted
- **17:1 student-to-undergraduate faculty ratio**
- **62% graduate** in 6 years or less
- **$6698 tuition** and fees (in-state); $14,014 (out-of-state)
- **$8185 average financial aid** package, $16,000 average indebtedness upon graduation, $854.8 million endowment

The University Honors College combines the educational advantages of a small liberal arts college with the scholarly resources of a major research university. Established for capable and motivated undergraduates as a selective degree-granting school, the Honors College offers a faculty dedicated to teaching, academic rigor, small classes, individualized advising, an intellectual community founded on a reverence for attainment, and special opportunities for independent study and laboratory research.

Part of Commonwealth System of Higher Education.

Students *Undergraduates:* 14,569 full-time, 2,107 part-time. Students come from 54 states and territories, 56 other countries. *The most frequently chosen baccalaureate fields are:* English, health professions and related sciences, social sciences and history. *Graduate:* 1,807 in professional programs, 7,187 in other graduate degree programs.

From out-of-state	13%	Reside on campus	38%
Age 25 or older	15%	Transferred in	7%
International students	1%	African Americans	10%
Asian Americans/Pacific Islanders	4%	Hispanic Americans	1%
Native Americans	0.2%		

Faculty 1,959 (74% full-time).

Expenses (1999–2000) *Tuition, state resident:* full-time $6118; part-time $212 per credit. *Tuition, nonresident:* full-time $13,434; part-time $459 per credit. *Required fees:* full-time $580; $103 per term part-time. Full-time tuition and fees vary according to degree level and program. Part-time tuition and fees vary according to degree level and program. *College room and board:* $5766; room only: $3356. Room and board charges vary according to board plan and housing facility. *Payment plans:* installment, deferred payment. *Waivers:* senior citizens and employees or children of employees.

Pennsylvania

Library Hillman Library plus 26 others. *Operations spending 1999–2000:* $20.4 million. *Collection:* 3.6 million titles, 22,058 serial subscriptions, 926,142 audiovisual materials.

College life *Housing: Options:* coed, women-only. *Social organizations:* national fraternities, national sororities. *Most popular organizations:* Pitt Program Council, Quo Vadis, Black Action Society, crew team, Blue and Gold Society.

Campus security 24-hour emergency response devices and patrols, late-night transport-escort service, controlled dormitory access, on-call van transportation.

After graduation 400 organizations recruited on campus 1997–98. *Career center:* 19 full-time, 1 part-time personnel. Services include job fairs, resume preparation, interview workshops, resume referral, career/interest testing, career counseling, careers library, job bank, job interviews. *Graduate education:* 36% of class of 1999 went directly to graduate and professional school: 6% business, 6% education, 5% graduate arts and sciences, 3% engineering, 2% law, 2% medicine, 1% dentistry. *Major awards:* 1 Marshall, 4 Fulbright Scholars.

Freshmen 12,863 applied, 8,523 admitted, 3,190 enrolled. 18 National Merit Scholars, 64 valedictorians.

SAT verbal scores above 500	85%	SAT math scores above 500	84%
ACT above 18	97%	From top 10% of their h.s. class	28%
From top quarter	62%	From top half	93%
1998 freshmen returning in 1999	85%		

Application *Options:* eApply at www.CollegeQuest.com, Common Application, early admission, deferred entrance. *Application fee:* $35. *Required:* high school transcript. *Recommended:* essay or personal statement; letters of recommendation; interview.

Standardized tests *Admission: Required:* SAT I or ACT. *Recommended:* SAT I.

Significant dates *Application deadlines:* rolling (freshmen), rolling (transfers). *Financial aid deadline priority date:* 3/1.

Freshman Application Contact
Dr. Betsy A. Porter, Director, Office of Admissions and Financial Aid, University of Pittsburgh, 4337 Fifth Avenue, First Floor, Masonic Temple, Pittsburgh, PA 115213. **Phone:** 412-624-7488. **Fax:** 412-648-8815. **E-mail:** oafa@pitt.edu

Visit CollegeQuest.com for information on majors offered and athletics. College video and electronic viewbook available at CollegeQuest.com.

■ *See page 2802 for a narrative description.*

UNIVERSITY OF PITTSBURGH AT BRADFORD

Bradford, Pennsylvania

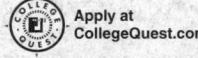
Apply at CollegeQuest.com

- **State-related**, 4-year, founded 1963
- **Degrees** associate and bachelor's
- **Small-town** 145-acre campus with easy access to Buffalo
- **Coed**, 1,087 undergraduate students, 84% full-time, 59% women, 41% men
- **Moderately difficult** entrance level
- **$6598 tuition** and fees (in-state); $13,914 (out-of-state)
- **$16,000 average indebtedness** upon graduation, $15.7 million endowment

Part of University of Pittsburgh System.

Students *Undergraduates:* 915 full-time, 172 part-time. Students come from 17 states and territories, 3 other countries.

From out-of-state	20%	Reside on campus	50%
Age 25 or older	12%	Transferred in	6%
International students	0.5%	African Americans	2%
Asian Americans/Pacific Islanders	1%	Hispanic Americans	0.5%
Native Americans	1%		

Faculty 116 (59% full-time).

Expenses (1999–2000) *Tuition, state resident:* full-time $6118; part-time $212 per credit. *Tuition, nonresident:* full-time $13,434; part-time $459 per credit. *Required fees:* full-time $480; $48 per term part-time. Full-time tuition and fees vary according to course load and program. Part-time tuition and fees vary according to course load and program. *College room and board:*

$5070; room only: $2540. Room and board charges vary according to board plan and housing facility. *Payment plans:* installment, deferred payment. *Waivers:* employees or children of employees.

Library T. Edward and Tullah Hanley Library. *Operations spending 1999–2000:* $469,990. *Collection:* 103,079 titles, 478 serial subscriptions, 2,731 audiovisual materials.

College life *Housing:* on-campus residence required through sophomore year. *Option:* coed. *Social organizations:* local fraternities, local sororities; 10% of eligible men and 10% of eligible women are members. *Most popular organizations:* Student Government Association, Student Activities Board, biology club, ski club, theater club.

Campus security 24-hour emergency response devices and patrols, late-night transport-escort service.

After graduation 92% of class of 1998 had job offers within 6 months. *Career center:* 1 full-time, 1 part-time personnel. Services include job fairs, resume preparation, resume referral, career counseling, careers library, job bank, job interviews. *Graduate education:* 25% of class of 1999 went directly to graduate and professional school.

Freshmen 228 enrolled.

Average high school GPA	3.2	SAT verbal scores above 500	N/R
SAT math scores above 500	N/R	ACT above 18	N/R
From top 10% of their h.s. class	23%	From top quarter	45%
From top half	80%	1998 freshmen returning in 1999	69%

Application *Options:* eApply at www.CollegeQuest.com, Common Application, early admission, deferred entrance. *Application fee:* $35. *Required:* high school transcript; minimum 2.0 GPA. *Required for some:* minimum 3.0 GPA. *Recommended:* essay or personal statement; letters of recommendation; interview.

Standardized tests *Admission: Required:* SAT I or ACT.

Significant dates *Application deadlines:* rolling (freshmen), rolling (transfers). *Financial aid deadline priority date:* 3/1.

Freshman Application Contact
Janet Shade, Administrative Secretary, University of Pittsburgh at Bradford, 300 Campus Drive, Bradford, PA 16701-2812. **Phone:** 814-362-7555. **Toll-free phone:** 800-872-1787. **Fax:** 814-362-7578. **E-mail:** shade@imap.pitt.edu

Visit CollegeQuest.com for information on majors offered and athletics.

■ *See page 2804 for a narrative description.*

UNIVERSITY OF PITTSBURGH AT GREENSBURG

Greensburg, Pennsylvania

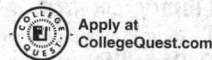
Apply at CollegeQuest.com

- **State-related**, 4-year, founded 1963
- **Degree** bachelor's
- **Small-town** 217-acre campus with easy access to Pittsburgh
- **Coed**
- **Moderately difficult** entrance level
- **$6582 tuition** and fees (in-state); $13,898 (out-of-state)

Many people who visit the University of Pittsburgh at Greensburg wonder why the campus buildings look so new. All of the buildings on the Greensburg campus have been built or totally renovated since 1989. Students can experience the Greensburg campus by scheduling a tour. Tours are provided twice every day.

Part of University of Pittsburgh System.

Expenses (1999–2000) *Tuition, state resident:* full-time $6118; part-time $212 per credit. *Tuition, nonresident:* full-time $13,434; part-time $459 per credit. *Required fees:* full-time $464; $62 per term part-time. *College room and board:* $4380; room only: $2280. Room and board charges vary according to board plan and housing facility.

Institutional Web site http://www.pitt.edu/~upg/

College life *Housing: Option:* coed. *Most popular organizations:* ski club, Activities Board, prelaw club.

Campus security 24-hour emergency response devices and patrols, late-night transport-escort service, controlled dormitory access.

Pennsylvania

University of Pittsburgh at Greensburg (continued)

Application *Options:* eApply at www.CollegeQuest.com, Common Application, electronic application, early admission, deferred entrance. *Application fee:* $35. *Required:* high school transcript; minimum 2.0 GPA. *Required for some:* letters of recommendation. *Recommended:* essay or personal statement; interview.

Standardized tests *Admission: Required:* SAT I or ACT.

Admissions Office Contact
University of Pittsburgh at Greensburg, 1150 Mount Pleasant Road, Greensburg, PA 15601-5860. **Fax:** 724-836-9901. **E-mail:** upgadmit@pitt.edu

Visit CollegeQuest.com for information on athletics.

■ *See page 2806 for a narrative description.*

UNIVERSITY OF PITTSBURGH AT JOHNSTOWN
Johnstown, Pennsylvania

- **State-related**, 4-year, founded 1927
- **Degrees** associate and bachelor's
- **Suburban** 650-acre campus with easy access to Pittsburgh
- **Coed**, 3,102 undergraduate students, 90% full-time, 54% women, 46% men
- **Moderately difficult** entrance level, 84% of applicants were admitted
- **19:1 student-to-undergraduate faculty ratio**
- **$6630 tuition** and fees (in-state); $13,946 (out-of-state)

Part of University of Pittsburgh System.

Students *Undergraduates:* 2,797 full-time, 305 part-time. Students come from 11 states and territories, 1 other country.

Reside on campus	62%	Transferred in	4%
International students	0.1%	African Americans	1%
Asian Americans/Pacific Islanders	1%	Hispanic Americans	0.4%
Native Americans	0.1%		

Faculty 185 (74% full-time).

Expenses (1999–2000) *Tuition, state resident:* full-time $6118; part-time $212 per credit. *Tuition, nonresident:* full-time $13,434; part-time $459 per credit. *Required fees:* full-time $512; $42 per term part-time. Full-time tuition and fees vary according to program. Part-time tuition and fees vary according to program. *College room and board:* $5460; room only: $2930. Room and board charges vary according to board plan and housing facility. *Payment plans:* installment, deferred payment. *Waivers:* employees or children of employees.

Library Owen Library. *Collection:* 136,790 titles, 1,290 serial subscriptions, 1,675 audiovisual materials.

College life *Housing:* Option: coed. *Social organizations:* national fraternities, national sororities, local fraternities, local sororities; 7% of eligible men and 11% of eligible women are members. *Most popular organizations:* student radio station, Student Senate, programming board, dance ensemble, Greek organizations.

Campus security 24-hour patrols, late-night transport-escort service.

After graduation *Career center:* 2 full-time personnel. Services include job fairs, resume preparation, resume referral, career counseling, careers library, job bank, job interviews.

Freshmen 2,089 applied, 1,764 admitted, 740 enrolled. 10 valedictorians.

Average high school GPA	3.0	SAT verbal scores above 500	55%
SAT math scores above 500	54%	ACT above 18	81%
From top 10% of their h.s. class	12%	From top quarter	34%
From top half	70%	1998 freshmen returning in 1999	77%

Application *Options:* eApply at www.CollegeQuest.com, electronic application, early admission, deferred entrance. *Application fee:* $35. *Required:* essay or personal statement; high school transcript; minimum 2.0 GPA. *Required for some:* interview.

Standardized tests *Admission: Required:* SAT I or ACT.

Significant dates *Application deadlines:* rolling (freshmen), rolling (transfers). *Financial aid deadline priority date:* 4/1.

Freshman Application Contact
Mr. James F. Gyure, Director of Admissions, University of Pittsburgh at Johnstown, 157 Blackington Hall, Johnstown, PA 15904-2990. **Phone:** 814-269-7050. **Toll-free phone:** 800-765-4875. **Fax:** 814-269-7044.

Visit CollegeQuest.com for information on majors offered and athletics. Electronic viewbook available at CollegeQuest.com.

THE UNIVERSITY OF SCRANTON
Scranton, Pennsylvania

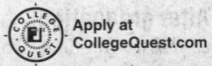

- **Independent Roman Catholic (Jesuit)**, comprehensive, founded 1888
- **Degrees** associate, bachelor's, master's, and post-master's certificates
- **Urban** 50-acre campus
- **Coed**, 4,054 undergraduate students, 90% full-time, 59% women, 41% men
- **Moderately difficult** entrance level, 76% of applicants were admitted
- **14:1 student-to-undergraduate faculty ratio**
- **78.1% graduate** in 6 years or less
- **$17,740 tuition** and fees
- **$12,759 average financial aid** package, $14,800 average indebtedness upon graduation, $57.1 million endowment

The University of Scranton is a community of scholars; the 14:1 student-faculty ratio is the foundation for success. On average, 83 percent of entering freshmen remain to graduate, and 96 percent find employment or attend graduate school within 6 months of graduation. Students are placed in medical schools, law schools, and Fulbright fellowships at rates significantly above the national average, and more than 1,000 alumni are CEOs. With new majors in enterprise management technology and human resources studies and a new building for each of the last 17 years, Scranton maintains a culture of excellence.

Students *Undergraduates:* 3,640 full-time, 414 part-time. Students come from 25 states and territories. *The most frequently chosen baccalaureate fields are:* business/marketing, education, health professions and related sciences. *Graduate:* 674 in graduate degree programs.

From out-of-state	47%	Reside on campus	43%
Age 25 or older	9%	Transferred in	1%
International students	1%	African Americans	1%
Asian Americans/Pacific Islanders	2%	Hispanic Americans	2%
Native Americans	0.1%		

Faculty 380 (64% full-time), 62% with terminal degrees.

Expenses (1999–2000) *One-time required fee:* $20. *Comprehensive fee:* $25,450 includes full-time tuition ($17,540), mandatory fees ($200), and room and board ($7710). *College room only:* $4490. Full-time tuition and fees vary according to degree level, program, and student level. Room and board charges vary according to board plan and housing facility. *Part-time tuition:* $410 per credit hour. *Part-time fees:* $35 per term part-time. Part-time tuition and fees vary according to degree level and student level. *Payment plan:* installment. *Waivers:* senior citizens and employees or children of employees.

Library Harry and Jeanette Weinberg Memorial Library plus 1 other. *Operations spending 1999–2000:* $4.3 million. *Collection:* 375,701 titles, 2,312 serial subscriptions, 11,647 audiovisual materials.

College life *Housing:* on-campus residence required through sophomore year. *Options:* coed, men-only, women-only, disabled students. *Most popular organizations:* Service-Oriented Students Club, Public Relationship Society, Retreat Program, biology/pre-medicine club, pre-law society.

Campus security 24-hour emergency response devices and patrols, student patrols, late-night transport-escort service, controlled dormitory access.

After graduation 61 organizations recruited on campus 1997–98. 59% of class of 1998 had job offers within 6 months. *Career center:* 5 full-time, 1 part-time personnel. Services include job fairs, resume preparation, resume referral, career counseling, careers library, job bank, job interviews. *Major awards:* 4 Fulbright Scholars.

Freshmen 3,640 applied, 2,763 admitted, 969 enrolled. 21 National Merit Scholars, 17 class presidents, 16 valedictorians, 183 student government officers.

Pennsylvania

Average high school GPA	3.27	SAT verbal scores above 500	81%
SAT math scores above 500	80%	ACT above 18	N/R
From top 10% of their h.s. class	27%	From top quarter	62%
From top half	89%	1998 freshmen returning in 1999	91%

Application *Options:* eApply at www.CollegeQuest.com, Common Application, electronic application, early admission, early action, deferred entrance. *Application fee:* $40. *Required:* essay or personal statement; high school transcript; 2 letters of recommendation. *Recommended:* interview.

Standardized tests *Admission: Required:* SAT I or ACT.

Significant dates *Application deadlines:* 3/1 (freshmen), 7/1 (transfers). *Early action:* 11/15. *Notification:* continuous until 5/1 (freshmen), 12/15 (early action). *Financial aid deadline priority date:* 2/15.

Freshman Application Contact
Mr. Raul A. Fonts, Director of Admissions, The University of Scranton, Scranton, PA 18510-4622. **Phone:** 570-941-7540. **Toll-free phone:** 888-SCRANTON. **Fax:** 570-941-5928. **E-mail:** admissions@uofs.edu

Visit CollegeQuest.com for information on majors offered and athletics. College video and electronic viewbook available at CollegeQuest.com.

■ *See page 2828 for a narrative description.*

THE UNIVERSITY OF THE ARTS
Philadelphia, Pennsylvania

- **Independent**, comprehensive, founded 1870
- **Degrees** bachelor's, master's, and postbachelor's certificates
- **Urban** 18-acre campus
- **Coed**, 1,781 undergraduate students, 98% full-time, 52% women, 48% men
- **Moderately difficult** entrance level, 55% of applicants were admitted
- **12:1** student-to-undergraduate faculty ratio
- **$16,800 tuition** and fees
- **$19.5 million endowment**

In addition to many degree programs in the fine arts, performing arts, and visual arts, recent developments include a BFA degree in writing for film and television, a BFA in multimedia, and a BS in communication (with a choice of advertising/public relations, documentary production, and cyber journalism).

Students *Undergraduates:* 1,752 full-time, 29 part-time. Students come from 35 states and territories, 22 other countries. *The most frequently chosen baccalaureate field is:* visual/performing arts. *Graduate:* 132 in graduate degree programs.

From out-of-state	56%	Reside on campus	23%
Age 25 or older	7%	Transferred in	9%
International students	3%	African Americans	9%
Asian Americans/Pacific Islanders	3%	Hispanic Americans	3%
Native Americans	1%		

Faculty 352 (29% full-time), 37% with terminal degrees.

Expenses (1999–2000) *Tuition:* full-time $16,200; part-time $700 per credit. *Required fees:* full-time $600. *College room only:* $4500. Room and board charges vary according to housing facility. *Payment plans:* installment, deferred payment. *Waivers:* children of alumni and employees or children of employees.

Library Greenfield Library plus 2 others. *Operations spending 1999–2000:* $578,000. *Collection:* 184,237 titles, 501 serial subscriptions, 294,075 audiovisual materials.

College life *Housing: Option:* coed. *Most popular organizations:* African-American Student Union, Gaming Society, Outreach, Multimedia Artist Society, Student Council.

Campus security 24-hour emergency response devices and patrols, late-night transport-escort service, crime prevention workshops and seminars.

After graduation 25 organizations recruited on campus 1997–98. *Career center:* 1 full-time, 1 part-time personnel. Services include job fairs, resume preparation, resume referral, career counseling, careers library, job bank, job interviews. *Graduate education:* 14% of class of 1999 went directly to graduate and professional school.

Freshmen 1,634 applied, 891 admitted, 431 enrolled.

Average high school GPA	2.98	SAT verbal scores above 500	63%
SAT math scores above 500	43%	ACT above 18	N/R
From top 10% of their h.s. class	7%	From top half	52%
1998 freshmen returning in 1999	78%		

Application *Options:* Common Application, electronic application, early admission, deferred entrance. *Application fee:* $40. *Required:* essay or personal statement; high school transcript; minimum 2.0 GPA; 1 letter of recommendation; portfolio or audition. *Required for some:* interview. *Recommended:* interview.

Standardized tests *Admission: Required:* SAT I or ACT.

Significant dates *Application deadlines:* rolling (freshmen), rolling (transfers). *Financial aid deadline priority date:* 2/15.

Freshman Application Contact
Ms. Barbara Elliott, Director of Admission, The University of the Arts, 320 South Broad Street, Philadelphia, PA 19102-4944. **Phone:** 215-717-6030. **Toll-free phone:** 800-616-ARTS. **Fax:** 215-875-5458. **E-mail:** admissions@uarts.edu

Visit CollegeQuest.com for information on majors offered and athletics.

■ *See page 2842 for a narrative description.*

UNIVERSITY OF THE SCIENCES IN PHILADELPHIA
Philadelphia, Pennsylvania

- **Independent**, university, founded 1821
- **Degrees** bachelor's, master's, doctoral, and first professional
- **Urban** 35-acre campus
- **Coed**, 966 undergraduate students
- **Moderately difficult** entrance level, 78% of applicants were admitted
- **13:1** student-to-undergraduate faculty ratio
- **$15,204 tuition** and fees
- **$10,481 average financial aid** package, $91.1 million endowment

The University of the Sciences in Philadelphia, formerly known as the Philadelphia College of Pharmacy and Science, is a private university of more than 2,000 students. USP offers 16 majors in 3 colleges: Philadelphia College of Pharmacy, College of Health Sciences, and College of Arts and Sciences. All students are admitted directly into their major of choice for the entire program length and are not required to reapply for admission at a later date.

Students *Undergraduates:* Students come from 33 states and territories.

From out-of-state	56%	Reside on campus	40%
Age 25 or older	6%	International students	1%
African Americans	5%	Asian Americans/Pacific Islanders	31%
Hispanic Americans	2%	Native Americans	0.1%

Faculty 295 (42% full-time).

Expenses (2000–2001, estimated) *Comprehensive fee:* $22,804 includes full-time tuition ($14,700), mandatory fees ($504), and room and board ($7600). *College room only:* $4958. Full-time tuition and fees vary according to program and student level. Room and board charges vary according to board plan and housing facility. *Part-time tuition:* $591 per credit hour. *Part-time fees:* $21 per credit hour. *Payment plans:* installment, deferred payment. *Waivers:* employees or children of employees.

Library Joseph W. England Library. *Operations spending 1999–2000:* $1.3 million. *Collection:* 76,000 titles, 809 serial subscriptions.

College life *Housing:* on-campus residence required through sophomore year. *Option:* coed. *Social organizations:* national fraternities, national sororities, local fraternities, local sororities; 18% of eligible men and 12% of eligible women are members. *Most popular organizations:* student government, Bharat, Academy of Students of Pharmacy, Student Physical Therapy Association, Asian Student Association.

Campus security 24-hour emergency response devices and patrols, late-night transport-escort service, controlled dormitory access.

After graduation 30 organizations recruited on campus 1997–98. 95% of class of 1998 had job offers within 6 months. *Career center:* 1 full-time, 1 part-time personnel. Services include job fairs, resume preparation, interview workshops, resume referral, career counseling, job bank, job interviews. *Graduate education:* 15% of class of 1999 went directly to graduate and

Pennsylvania

University of the Sciences in Philadelphia (continued)
professional school: 8% medicine, 3% graduate arts and sciences, 2% business, 1% dentistry, 1% veterinary medicine.

Freshmen 1,197 applied, 931 admitted.

Average high school GPA	3.4	SAT verbal scores above 500	84%
SAT math scores above 500	95%	ACT above 18	100%
From top 10% of their h.s. class	15%	From top quarter	60%
From top half	89%	1998 freshmen returning in 1999	94%

Application *Options:* electronic application, early admission, deferred entrance. *Application fee:* $45. *Required:* essay or personal statement; high school transcript. *Recommended:* minimum 3.0 GPA.

Standardized tests *Admission: Required:* SAT I or ACT. *Recommended:* SAT I.

Significant dates *Application deadlines:* rolling (freshmen), rolling (transfers). *Financial aid deadline priority date:* 3/15.

Freshman Application Contact
Mr. Louis L. Hegyes, Director of Admission, University of the Sciences in Philadelphia, 600 South 43rd Street, Philadelphia, PA 19104-4495. **Phone:** 215-596-8810. **Toll-free phone:** 888-996-8747. **Fax:** 215-895-1100. **E-mail:** admit@usip.edu

Visit CollegeQuest.com for information on majors offered and athletics. Electronic viewbook available at CollegeQuest.com.

■ *See page 2850 for a narrative description.*

URSINUS COLLEGE
Collegeville, Pennsylvania

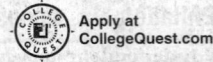
Apply at CollegeQuest.com

- **Independent**, 4-year, founded 1869, affiliated with United Church of Christ
- **Degree** bachelor's
- **Suburban** 140-acre campus with easy access to Philadelphia
- **Coed**, 1,240 undergraduate students, 99% full-time, 53% women, 47% men
- **Very difficult** entrance level, 78% of applicants were admitted
- **12:1** student-to-undergraduate faculty ratio
- **74.6% graduate** in 6 years or less
- **$20,230 tuition** and fees

Ursinus College, founded in 1869, is selective and coeducational and offers a high-quality liberal arts curriculum that prepares students for professional and graduate schools. Ursinus is especially well known for its excellent placement of graduates in advanced schools of medicine, science, law, education, and business. Ursinus holds a distinguished campus chapter of Phi Beta Kappa.

Students *Undergraduates:* 1,226 full-time, 14 part-time. Students come from 25 states and territories, 14 other countries. *The most frequently chosen baccalaureate fields are:* biological/life sciences, business/marketing, social sciences and history.

From out-of-state	35%	Reside on campus	90%
Age 25 or older	1%	Transferred in	1%
International students	2%	African Americans	6%
Asian Americans/Pacific Islanders	3%	Hispanic Americans	2%
Native Americans	0.1%		

Faculty 143 (70% full-time), 73% with terminal degrees.

Expenses (1999–2000) *Comprehensive fee:* $26,200 includes full-time tuition ($19,950), mandatory fees ($280), and room and board ($5970). *Part-time tuition:* $685 per semester hour. Part-time tuition and fees vary according to class time and program. *Payment plan:* installment. *Waivers:* senior citizens and employees or children of employees.

Library Myrin Library. *Operations spending 1999–2000:* $837,357. *Collection:* 200,000 titles, 900 serial subscriptions, 17,500 audiovisual materials.

College life *Housing: Options:* coed, men-only, women-only. *Social organizations:* national fraternities, local fraternities, local sororities; 35% of eligible men and 30% of eligible women are members. *Most popular organizations:* Environmental Action Committee, Habitat for Humanity, Campus Activities Board, Ursinus Christian Fellowship, Multicultural Student Union.

Campus security 24-hour emergency response devices and patrols, late-night transport-escort service.

After graduation 50 organizations recruited on campus 1997–98. 60% of class of 1998 had job offers within 6 months. *Career center:* 1 full-time, 2 part-time personnel. Services include job fairs, resume preparation, interview workshops, resume referral, career/interest testing, career counseling, careers library, job bank, job interviews. *Graduate education:* 32% of class of 1999 went directly to graduate and professional school; 21% graduate arts and sciences, 8% medicine, 2% law, 1% business.

Freshmen 1,491 applied, 1,158 admitted, 353 enrolled. 7 National Merit Scholars, 6 valedictorians, 41 student government officers.

SAT verbal scores above 500	85%	SAT math scores above 500	89%
ACT above 18	N/R	From top 10% of their h.s. class	43%
From top quarter	75%	From top half	94%
1998 freshmen returning in 1999	94%		

Application *Options:* eApply at www.CollegeQuest.com, Common Application, electronic application, early admission, early decision, deferred entrance. *Application fee:* $30. *Required:* essay or personal statement; high school transcript; 2 letters of recommendation. *Recommended:* interview.

Standardized tests *Admission: Required:* SAT I or ACT. *Recommended:* SAT II Subject Tests.

Significant dates *Application deadlines:* 2/15 (freshmen), 8/1 (transfers). *Early decision:* 1/15. *Notification:* 4/1 (freshmen), 2/1 (early decision). *Financial aid deadline priority date:* 2/15.

Freshman Application Contact
Mr. Paul M. Cramer, Director of Admissions, Ursinus College, Box 1000, Collegeville, PA 19426. **Phone:** 610-409-3200. **Fax:** 610-489-0627. **E-mail:** admissions@ursinus.edu

Visit CollegeQuest.com for information on majors offered and athletics.

■ *See page 2870 for a narrative description.*

VALLEY FORGE CHRISTIAN COLLEGE
Phoenixville, Pennsylvania

- **Independent**, 4-year, founded 1938, affiliated with Assemblies of God
- **Degrees** associate and bachelor's
- **Small-town** 77-acre campus with easy access to Philadelphia
- **Coed**
- **Minimally difficult** entrance level
- **$6936 tuition** and fees

Expenses (1999–2000) *Comprehensive fee:* $10,726 includes full-time tuition ($6196), mandatory fees ($740), and room and board ($3790). *College room only:* $1700. Full-time tuition and fees vary according to course load. Room and board charges vary according to board plan and housing facility. *Part-time tuition:* $243 per credit. *Part-time fees:* $210 per term part-time. Part-time tuition and fees vary according to course load.

Institutional Web site http://www.vfcc.edu/

College life *Housing:* on-campus residence required through senior year. *Options:* men-only, women-only. *Most popular organizations:* Prison Ministries Organization, Homeless Outreach Ministry, J.C. Powerhouse.

Campus security Late-night transport-escort service, 16-hour patrols by trained security personnel.

Application *Options:* Common Application, electronic application, early admission, deferred entrance. *Application fee:* $25. *Required:* high school transcript; 2 letters of recommendation. *Required for some:* interview. *Recommended:* essay or personal statement.

Standardized tests *Admission: Required:* SAT I or ACT.

Admissions Office Contact
Valley Forge Christian College, 1401 Charlestown Road, Phoenixville, PA 19460. **Toll-free phone:** 800-432-8322. **E-mail:** admissions@vfcc.edu

Visit CollegeQuest.com for information on athletics. College video available at CollegeQuest.com.

VILLANOVA UNIVERSITY
Villanova, Pennsylvania

- **Independent Roman Catholic**, comprehensive, founded 1842
- **Degrees** associate, bachelor's, master's, doctoral, and first professional
- **Suburban** 222-acre campus with easy access to Philadelphia
- **Coed**, 6,780 undergraduate students, 95% full-time, 51% women, 49% men

- **Moderately difficult** entrance level, 57% of applicants were admitted
- **13:1 student-to-undergraduate faculty ratio**
- **82.4% graduate** in 6 years or less
- **$20,850 tuition** and fees
- **$13,966 average financial aid** package, $16,652 average indebtedness upon graduation, $162.3 million endowment

Students *Undergraduates:* 6,427 full-time, 353 part-time. Students come from 48 states and territories, 30 other countries. *The most frequently chosen baccalaureate fields are:* business/marketing, engineering/engineering technologies, social sciences and history. *Graduate:* 735 in professional programs, 2,089 in other graduate degree programs.

From out-of-state	69%	Reside on campus	65%
Age 25 or older	1%	Transferred in	2%
International students	2%	African Americans	3%
Asian Americans/Pacific Islanders	4%	Hispanic Americans	4%
Native Americans	0.2%		

Faculty 792 (63% full-time), 75% with terminal degrees.

Expenses (1999–2000) *Comprehensive fee:* $28,850 includes full-time tuition ($20,550), mandatory fees ($300), and room and board ($8000). *College room only:* $4400. Full-time tuition and fees vary according to program and student level. Room and board charges vary according to board plan and housing facility. *Part-time tuition:* $475 per credit hour. *Part-time fees:* $150 per term part-time. Part-time tuition and fees vary according to class time and program. *Payment plan:* installment. *Waivers:* employees or children of employees.

Library Falvey Library plus 1 other. *Operations spending 1999–2000:* $6.7 million. *Collection:* 1 million titles, 5,338 serial subscriptions, 7,600 audiovisual materials.

College life *Housing: Options:* coed, men-only, women-only, disabled students. *Social organizations:* national fraternities, national sororities; 18% of eligible men and 34% of eligible women are members. *Most popular organizations:* Blue Key Society, orientation counselor program, Special Olympics, campus activities team, Greek organizations.

Campus security 24-hour emergency response devices and patrols, student patrols, late-night transport-escort service, controlled dormitory access.

After graduation 375 organizations recruited on campus 1997–98. 78% of class of 1998 had job offers within 6 months. *Career center:* 8 full-time personnel. Services include job fairs, resume preparation, interview workshops, resume referral, career/interest testing, career counseling, careers library, job bank, job interviews. *Major awards:* 4 Fulbright Scholars.

Freshmen 9,826 applied, 5,580 admitted, 1,680 enrolled. 5 National Merit Scholars, 27 valedictorians.

SAT verbal scores above 500	93%	SAT math scores above 500	93%
ACT above 18	N/R	From top 10% of their h.s. class	39%
From top quarter	75%	From top half	91%
1998 freshmen returning in 1999	93%		

Application *Options:* electronic application, early admission, early action, deferred entrance. *Application fee:* $50. *Required:* essay or personal statement; high school transcript.

Standardized tests *Admission: Required:* SAT I or ACT.

Significant dates *Application deadlines:* 1/7 (freshmen), 7/15 (transfers). *Early action:* 11/15. *Notification:* 4/1 (freshmen), 1/15 (early action). *Financial aid deadline priority date:* 2/15.

Freshman Application Contact
Mr. James Van Blunk, Director of University Admission, Villanova University, 800 Lancaster Avenue, Villanova, PA 19085-1672. **Phone:** 610-519-4000. **Toll-free phone:** 800-338-7927. **Fax:** 610-519-6450. **E-mail:** gotovu@email.villanova.edu

Visit CollegeQuest.com for information on majors offered and athletics. College video and electronic viewbook available at CollegeQuest.com.

- *See page 2888 for a narrative description.*

WASHINGTON & JEFFERSON COLLEGE
Washington, Pennsylvania

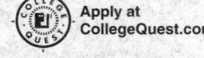
Apply at CollegeQuest.com

- **Independent**, 4-year, founded 1781
- **Degrees** associate and bachelor's

- **Small-town** 40-acre campus with easy access to Pittsburgh
- **Coed**, 1,145 undergraduate students, 99% full-time, 49% women, 51% men
- **Moderately difficult** entrance level, 80% of applicants were admitted
- **12:1 student-to-undergraduate faculty ratio**
- **75% graduate** in 6 years or less
- **$19,000 tuition** and fees
- **$14,489 average financial aid** package, $98 million endowment

Washington & Jefferson College has nationally recognized programs in prehealth, prelaw, and entrepreneurial studies. These attest to the excellence of W&J's liberal arts curriculum. In addition, the Campus Center, renovated in 1999, offers an array of extracurricular opportunities. The academic and social atmospheres combine to produce an outstanding educational environment.

Students *Undergraduates:* 1,135 full-time, 10 part-time. Students come from 27 states and territories, 5 other countries. *The most frequently chosen baccalaureate fields are:* business/marketing, biological/life sciences, psychology.

From out-of-state	15%	Reside on campus	87%
Age 25 or older	1%	Transferred in	2%
International students	1%	African Americans	3%
Asian Americans/Pacific Islanders	2%	Hispanic Americans	1%

Faculty 100 (88% full-time).

Expenses (1999–2000) *One-time required fee:* $30. *Comprehensive fee:* $23,750 includes full-time tuition ($18,675), mandatory fees ($325), and room and board ($4750). *College room only:* $2410. Room and board charges vary according to board plan. *Part-time tuition:* $1850 per course. *Payment plans:* installment, deferred payment. *Waivers:* employees or children of employees.

Library U. Grant Miller Library. *Operations spending 1999–2000:* $536,085. *Collection:* 176,689 titles, 710 serial subscriptions, 6,690 audiovisual materials.

College life *Housing:* on-campus residence required through senior year. *Options:* coed, men-only, women-only. *Social organizations:* national fraternities, national sororities; 50% of eligible men and 40% of eligible women are members. *Most popular organizations:* student government, Saturday Nite Life, George and Tom's, pre-health, pre-law.

Campus security 24-hour emergency response devices and patrols, late-night transport-escort service, controlled dormitory access.

After graduation 55 organizations recruited on campus 1997–98. 60% of class of 1998 had job offers within 6 months. *Career center:* 1 full-time, 1 part-time personnel. Services include job fairs, resume preparation, interview workshops, resume referral, career/interest testing, career counseling, careers library, job bank, job interviews.

Freshmen 1,261 applied, 1,008 admitted, 327 enrolled.

Average high school GPA	3.4	SAT verbal scores above 500	75%
SAT math scores above 500	77%	ACT above 18	95%
From top 10% of their h.s. class	32%	From top quarter	62%
From top half	93%	1998 freshmen returning in 1999	88%

Application *Options:* eApply at www.CollegeQuest.com, electronic application, early admission, early decision, deferred entrance. *Application fee:* $25. *Required:* essay or personal statement; high school transcript. *Recommended:* 3 letters of recommendation; interview.

Standardized tests *Admission: Required:* SAT I and SAT II or ACT, SAT II: Writing Test.

Significant dates *Application deadlines:* 3/1 (freshmen), rolling (transfers). *Early decision:* 11/1. *Notification:* 12/1 (early decision). *Financial aid deadline priority date:* 2/15.

Freshman Application Contact
Mr. Alton E. Newell, Dean of Enrollment, Washington & Jefferson College, 60 South Lincoln Street, Washington, PA 15301-4601. **Phone:** 724-223-6025. **Toll-free phone:** 888-WANDJAY. **Fax:** 724-223-5271. **E-mail:** admission@washjeff.edu

Visit CollegeQuest.com for information on majors offered and athletics. College video and electronic viewbook available at CollegeQuest.com.

- *See page 2914 for a narrative description.*

Pennsylvania

WAYNESBURG COLLEGE
Waynesburg, Pennsylvania

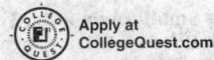
Apply at CollegeQuest.com

- **Independent**, comprehensive, founded 1849, affiliated with Presbyterian Church (U.S.A.)
- **Degrees** associate, bachelor's, and master's
- **Small-town** 30-acre campus with easy access to Pittsburgh
- **Coed**, 1,313 undergraduate students, 91% full-time, 51% women, 49% men
- **Moderately difficult** entrance level, 78% of applicants were admitted
- **20:1 student-to-undergraduate faculty ratio**
- **57% graduate** in 6 years or less
- **$11,430 tuition** and fees
- **$11,425 average financial aid** package, $15,000 average indebtedness upon graduation, $30.3 million endowment

Students *Undergraduates:* 1,192 full-time, 121 part-time. Students come from 17 states and territories, 4 other countries. *The most frequently chosen baccalaureate fields are:* business/marketing, health professions and related sciences, protective services/public administration. *Graduate:* 175 in graduate degree programs.

From out-of-state	17%	Reside on campus	55%
Age 25 or older	13%	Transferred in	4%
International students	0.3%	African Americans	5%
Asian Americans/Pacific Islanders	0.4%	Hispanic Americans	0.4%

Faculty 98 (59% full-time), 34% with terminal degrees.

Expenses (1999–2000) *Comprehensive fee:* $16,020 includes full-time tuition ($11,160), mandatory fees ($270), and room and board ($4590). *College room only:* $2340. Full-time tuition and fees vary according to class time. Room and board charges vary according to board plan. *Part-time tuition:* $465 per credit hour. Part-time tuition and fees vary according to class time, course load, and location. *Payment plan:* installment. *Waivers:* employees or children of employees.

Library Waynesburg College Library. *Operations spending 1999–2000:* $385,000. *Collection:* 91,882 titles, 419 serial subscriptions.

College life *Housing:* on-campus residence required through junior year. *Options:* men-only, women-only. *Most popular organizations:* Student Senate, Student Activities Board (SAB), Student Nurses Association, Christian Fellowship.

Campus security 24-hour emergency response devices and patrols, late-night transport-escort service, controlled dormitory access.

After graduation 45 organizations recruited on campus 1997–98. 90% of class of 1998 had job offers within 6 months. *Career center:* 2 full-time personnel. Services include job fairs, resume preparation, interview workshops, resume referral, career counseling, careers library, job bank, job interviews.

Freshmen 1,261 applied, 985 admitted, 287 enrolled.

Average high school GPA	3.11	SAT verbal scores above 500	N/R
SAT math scores above 500	N/R	ACT above 18	N/R
From top 10% of their h.s. class	14%	From top quarter	35%
From top half	75%	1998 freshmen returning in 1999	77%

Application *Options:* eApply at www.CollegeQuest.com, Common Application, early admission. *Application fee:* $15. *Required:* high school transcript; minimum 2.0 GPA. *Required for some:* essay or personal statement. *Recommended:* minimum 3.0 GPA; 2 letters of recommendation; interview.

Standardized tests *Admission: Required:* SAT I or ACT.

Significant dates *Application deadlines:* rolling (freshmen), rolling (transfers). *Financial aid deadline priority date:* 3/15.

Freshman Application Contact
Ms. Robin L. Moore, Dean of Admissions, Waynesburg College, 51 West College Street, Waynesburg, PA 15070. **Phone:** 724-852-3333. **Toll-free phone:** 800-225-7393. **Fax:** 724-627-8124. **E-mail:** admissions@waynesburg.edu

Visit CollegeQuest.com for information on majors offered and athletics.

- *See page 2922 for a narrative description.*

WEST CHESTER UNIVERSITY OF PENNSYLVANIA
West Chester, Pennsylvania

- **State-supported**, comprehensive, founded 1871
- **Degrees** associate, bachelor's, and master's
- **Suburban** 547-acre campus with easy access to Philadelphia
- **Coed**, 9,505 undergraduate students, 90% full-time, 60% women, 40% men
- **Moderately difficult** entrance level, 58% of applicants were admitted
- **17:1 student-to-undergraduate faculty ratio**
- **55% graduate** in 6 years or less
- **$4422 tuition** and fees (in-state); $9850 (out-of-state)
- **$5931 average financial aid** package, $17,000 average indebtedness upon graduation, $7.7 million endowment

Part of Pennsylvania State System of Higher Education.

Students *Undergraduates:* 8,515 full-time, 990 part-time. Students come from 26 states and territories. *The most frequently chosen baccalaureate fields are:* business/marketing, education, English. *Graduate:* 1,814 in graduate degree programs.

From out-of-state	11%	Reside on campus	35%
Age 25 or older	12%	Transferred in	9%
International students	0.2%	African Americans	8%
Asian Americans/Pacific Islanders	2%	Hispanic Americans	2%
Native Americans	0.2%		

Faculty 745 (76% full-time), 69% with terminal degrees.

Expenses (1999–2000) *Tuition, state resident:* full-time $3618; part-time $150 per credit. *Tuition, nonresident:* full-time $9046; part-time $377 per credit. *Required fees:* full-time $804; $34 per credit. *College room and board:* $4518; room only: $3888. Room and board charges vary according to board plan, housing facility, and location. *Payment plans:* tuition prepayment, installment, deferred payment. *Waivers:* senior citizens and employees or children of employees.

Library Francis Harvey Green Library plus 1 other. *Operations spending 1999–2000:* $3.3 million. *Collection:* 524,976 titles, 2,800 serial subscriptions.

College life *Housing: Options:* coed, women-only. *Social organizations:* national fraternities, national sororities; 11% of eligible men and 7% of eligible women are members. *Most popular organizations:* Abbess Club, Friars Club, University Ambassadors, Inter-Greek Council, Student Government Association.

Campus security 24-hour emergency response devices and patrols, late-night transport-escort service.

After graduation 280 organizations recruited on campus 1997–98. *Career center:* 5 full-time personnel. Services include job fairs, resume preparation, resume referral, career counseling, careers library, job bank, job interviews. *Graduate education:* 19% of class of 1999 went directly to graduate and professional school.

Freshmen 7,827 applied, 4,526 admitted, 1,720 enrolled.

Average high school GPA	3.18	SAT verbal scores above 500	63%
SAT math scores above 500	60%	ACT above 18	N/R
From top 10% of their h.s. class	10%	From top quarter	35%
From top half	92%	1998 freshmen returning in 1999	83%

Application *Options:* early admission, deferred entrance. *Application fee:* $30. *Required:* essay or personal statement; high school transcript; minimum 2.0 GPA. *Required for some:* minimum 3.0 GPA; letters of recommendation; interview. *Recommended:* minimum 3.0 GPA.

Standardized tests *Admission: Required:* SAT I or ACT.

Significant dates *Application deadlines:* rolling (freshmen), rolling (transfers). *Financial aid deadline priority date:* 3/1.

Freshman Application Contact
Ms. Marsha Haug, Director of Admissions, West Chester University of Pennsylvania, Messikomer Hall, Rosedale Avenue, West Chester, PA 19383. **Phone:** 610-436-3411. **E-mail:** ugadmiss@wcupa.edu

Visit CollegeQuest.com for information on majors offered and athletics.

- *See page 2942 for a narrative description.*

Pennsylvania

WESTMINSTER COLLEGE
New Wilmington, Pennsylvania

- **Independent**, comprehensive, founded 1852, affiliated with Presbyterian Church (U.S.A.)
- **Degrees** bachelor's and master's
- **Small-town** 300-acre campus with easy access to Pittsburgh
- **Coed**, 1,448 undergraduate students, 95% full-time, 62% women, 38% men
- **Moderately difficult** entrance level, 89% of applicants were admitted
- **13:1 student-to-undergraduate faculty ratio**
- **$16,270 tuition** and fees
- **$14,503 average financial aid** package, $14,896 average indebtedness upon graduation, $85 million endowment

Westminster College, an independent, coeducational liberal arts college related to the Presbyterian Church (USA), was founded in 1852. Westminster's liberal arts foundation thrives in a caring environment supported by an integrative curriculum featuring state-of-the-art technology and opportunities for involvement to prepare students for a diverse world while choosing from 52 majors.

Students *Undergraduates:* 1,381 full-time, 67 part-time. Students come from 22 states and territories. *The most frequently chosen baccalaureate fields are:* business/marketing, biological/life sciences, social sciences and history. *Graduate:* 149 in graduate degree programs.

From out-of-state	19%	Age 25 or older	1%
Transferred in	2%	International students	0.1%
African Americans	1%	Asian Americans/Pacific Islanders	1%
Hispanic Americans	0.3%		

Faculty 138 (66% full-time).

Expenses (1999–2000) *Comprehensive fee:* $20,800 includes full-time tuition ($15,485), mandatory fees ($785), and room and board ($4530). *College room only:* $2370. Room and board charges vary according to board plan. *Part-time tuition:* $480 per semester hour. *Part-time fees:* $10 per semester hour; $232 per term part-time. *Payment plan:* installment. *Waivers:* children of alumni, adult students, and employees or children of employees.

Library McGill Memorial Library plus 1 other. *Operations spending 1999–2000:* $843,712. *Collection:* 230,000 titles, 827 serial subscriptions.

College life *Housing:* on-campus residence required through junior year. *Options:* men-only, women-only. *Social organizations:* national fraternities, national sororities; 57% of eligible men and 49% of eligible women are members. *Most popular organizations:* student government, Greek life, Habitat for Humanity, established service teams.

Campus security 24-hour patrols, late-night transport-escort service.

After graduation 53 organizations recruited on campus 1997–98. 26% of class of 1998 had job offers within 6 months. *Career center:* 3 full-time personnel. Services include job fairs, resume preparation, resume referral, career counseling, careers library, job bank, job interviews. *Graduate education:* 20% of class of 1999 went directly to graduate and professional school.

Freshmen 975 applied, 865 admitted, 356 enrolled.

Average high school GPA	3.3	SAT verbal scores above 500	62%
SAT math scores above 500	69%	ACT above 18	95%
From top 10% of their h.s. class	22%	From top quarter	70%
From top half	90%	1998 freshmen returning in 1999	89%

Application *Options:* early admission, deferred entrance. *Application fee:* $20. *Required:* essay or personal statement; high school transcript; minimum 2.0 GPA; 2 letters of recommendation. *Recommended:* minimum 3.0 GPA; interview.

Standardized tests *Admission: Required:* SAT I or ACT. *Recommended:* SAT II Subject Tests.

Significant dates *Application deadlines:* rolling (freshmen), rolling (transfers). *Financial aid deadline priority date:* 5/1.

Freshman Application Contact Mr. Doug Swartz, Director of Admissions, Westminster College, South Market Street, New Wilmington, PA 16172-0001. **Phone:** 724-946-7100. **Toll-free phone:** 800-942-8033. **Fax:** 724-946-7171. **E-mail:** swartzdl@westminster.edu

Visit CollegeQuest.com for information on majors offered and athletics. College video available at CollegeQuest.com.

■ *See page 2964 for a narrative description.*

WIDENER UNIVERSITY
Chester, Pennsylvania

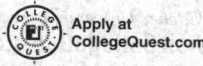
Apply at CollegeQuest.com

- **Independent**, comprehensive, founded 1821
- **Degrees** associate, bachelor's, master's, doctoral, and first professional
- **Suburban** 110-acre campus with easy access to Philadelphia
- **Coed**, 3,526 undergraduate students, 61% full-time, 55% women, 45% men
- **Moderately difficult** entrance level, 89% of applicants were admitted
- **12:1 student-to-undergraduate faculty ratio**
- **$16,750 tuition** and fees
- **$14,388 average financial aid** package, $17,690 average indebtedness upon graduation, $36 million endowment

At Widener, a student's success is the most important thing on the agenda. A small-college atmosphere, a caring attitude, and close attention to student needs characterize the educational atmosphere. Widener is a private, comprehensive university. Emphasis is placed on challenging and motivating students and helping them realize their potential.

Students *Undergraduates:* 2,153 full-time, 1,373 part-time. Students come from 30 states and territories. *The most frequently chosen baccalaureate fields are:* business/marketing, engineering/engineering technologies, health professions and related sciences. *Graduate:* 1,448 in professional programs, 1,964 in other graduate degree programs.

From out-of-state	45%	Reside on campus	63%
Age 25 or older	14%	Transferred in	4%
International students	1%	African Americans	14%
Asian Americans/Pacific Islanders	3%	Hispanic Americans	2%
Native Americans	0.3%		

Faculty 354 (69% full-time).

Expenses (1999–2000) *Comprehensive fee:* $23,670 includes full-time tuition ($16,750) and room and board ($6920). Full-time tuition and fees vary according to course level, course load, program, and student level. Room and board charges vary according to housing facility. *Part-time tuition:* $560 per credit. *Part-time fees:* $15 per term part-time. Part-time tuition and fees vary according to class time, course level, program, and student level. *Payment plan:* installment. *Waivers:* senior citizens and employees or children of employees.

Library Wolfgram Memorial Library. *Operations spending 1999–2000:* $5.4 million. *Collection:* 245,606 titles, 2,256 serial subscriptions, 11,904 audiovisual materials.

College life *Housing:* on-campus residence required through senior year. *Options:* coed, men-only, women-only. *Social organizations:* national fraternities, national sororities; 21% of eligible men and 13% of eligible women are members. *Most popular organizations:* WDNR Radio, Black Student Union, volunteer services, rugby club, Theatre Widener.

Campus security 24-hour emergency response devices and patrols, late-night transport-escort service, controlled dormitory access.

After graduation 79 organizations recruited on campus 1997–98. 82% of class of 1998 had job offers within 6 months. *Career center:* 6 full-time personnel. Services include job fairs, resume preparation, resume referral, career/interest testing, career counseling, careers library, job bank, job interviews, mentoring program, internship assistance. *Graduate education:* 17% of class of 1999 went directly to graduate and professional school.

Freshmen 2,090 applied, 1,850 admitted, 606 enrolled.

Average high school GPA	2.9	SAT verbal scores above 500	44%
SAT math scores above 500	46%	ACT above 18	N/R
From top 10% of their h.s. class	17%	From top quarter	48%
From top half	90%	1998 freshmen returning in 1999	79%

Application *Options:* eApply at www.CollegeQuest.com, Common Application, early admission, deferred entrance. *Application fee:* $30. *Required:* high school transcript; minimum 2.0 GPA. *Recommended:* essay or personal statement; letters of recommendation; interview.

Standardized tests *Admission: Required:* SAT I or ACT.

Significant dates *Application deadlines:* rolling (freshmen), rolling (transfers). *Financial aid deadline priority date:* 2/15.

Freshman Application Contact Dr. Michael L. Mahoney, Vice President of Admissions and Student Services, Widener University, One University Place, Chester, PA 19013-5792. **Phone:** 610-499-4126. **Toll-free phone:** 888-WIDENER. **Fax:** 610-499-4676. **E-mail:** admissions.office@widener.edu

Peterson's Guide to Four-Year Colleges 2001   www.petersons.com

Pennsylvania

Widener University *(continued)*
Visit CollegeQuest.com for information on majors offered and athletics. College video available at CollegeQuest.com.

■ *See page 2990 for a narrative description.*

WILKES UNIVERSITY
Wilkes-Barre, Pennsylvania

- **Independent**, comprehensive, founded 1933
- **Degrees** bachelor's, master's, and first professional
- **Urban** 25-acre campus
- **Coed**, 1,702 undergraduate students, 82% full-time, 47% women, 53% men
- **Moderately difficult** entrance level, 91% of applicants were admitted
- **13:1 student-to-undergraduate faculty ratio**
- **51.2% graduate** in 6 years or less
- **$16,362 tuition** and fees
- **$24 million endowment**

A comprehensive, private university of intimate size, Wilkes University offers high-quality academic programs in business, engineering, sciences, and liberal arts; preprofessional programs in dentistry, medicine, optometry, and law; and a 6-year Doctor of Pharmacy degree. Students have unparalleled access to faculty members and research opportunities, and 99 percent gain employment or attend graduate/professional school within 6 months of graduation.

Students *Undergraduates:* 1,402 full-time, 300 part-time. Students come from 22 states and territories. *The most frequently chosen baccalaureate fields are:* business/marketing, biological/life sciences, psychology. **Graduate:** 252 in professional programs, 1,316 in other graduate degree programs.

From out-of-state	16%	Reside on campus	32%
Age 25 or older	17%	Transferred in	7%
International students	0.4%	African Americans	2%
Asian Americans/Pacific Islanders	2%	Hispanic Americans	1%
Native Americans	0.3%		

Faculty 273 (42% full-time).
Expenses (1999–2000) *Comprehensive fee:* $23,464 includes full-time tuition ($15,652), mandatory fees ($710), and room and board ($7102). Room and board charges vary according to board plan and housing facility. *Part-time tuition:* $434 per credit. *Part-time fees:* $12 per credit. *Payment plan:* installment. *Waivers:* children of alumni, senior citizens, and employees or children of employees.
Library Eugene S. Farley Library. *Collection:* 200,000 titles, 1,150 serial subscriptions.
College life *Housing:* on-campus residence required through sophomore year. *Options:* coed, men-only, women-only.
Campus security 24-hour emergency response devices and patrols, late-night transport-escort service, controlled dormitory access.
After graduation *Career center:* 3 full-time personnel. Services include career counseling. *Graduate education:* 24% of class of 1999 went directly to graduate and professional school: 7% business, 7% medicine, 4% engineering, 3% graduate arts and sciences, 2% dentistry, 2% law.
Freshmen 1,595 applied, 1,458 admitted, 387 enrolled.

SAT verbal scores above 500	59%	SAT math scores above 500	61%
ACT above 18	N/R	From top 10% of their h.s. class	17%
From top quarter	43%	From top half	68%
1998 freshmen returning in 1999	73%		

Application *Options:* Common Application, early admission, deferred entrance. *Application fee:* $30. *Required:* high school transcript. *Required for some:* letters of recommendation. *Recommended:* interview.
Standardized tests *Admission: Required:* SAT I or ACT.
Significant dates *Application deadlines:* rolling (freshmen), rolling (transfers). *Notification:* continuous until 8/30 (freshmen). **Financial aid deadline:** continuous.
Freshman Application Contact
Ms. Deb Erdner, Senior Assistant Director, Wilkes University, PO Box 111, Wilkes-Barre, PA 18766. **Phone:** 570-831-4407. **Toll-free phone:** 800-945-5378 Ext. 4400. **Fax:** 570-408-7820. **E-mail:** admissions@wilkes.edu
Visit CollegeQuest.com for information on majors offered and athletics.

■ *See page 2996 for a narrative description.*

WILSON COLLEGE
Chambersburg, Pennsylvania

- **Independent**, 4-year, founded 1869, affiliated with Presbyterian Church (U.S.A.)
- **Degrees** associate and bachelor's
- **Small-town** 262-acre campus
- **Women** only, 699 undergraduate students, 51% full-time
- **Moderately difficult** entrance level, 93% of applicants were admitted
- **10:1 student-to-undergraduate faculty ratio**
- **41% graduate** in 6 years or less
- **$13,588 tuition** and fees
- **$12,250 average financial aid** package, $14,667 average indebtedness upon graduation, $15.9 million endowment

For 130 years, Wilson has been educating women in a rich tradition of liberal arts. Academic programs allow students to concentrate on interests while receiving a balanced, marketable education. Wilson now offers a major in equine-facilitated therapeutics that combines knowledge of the horse with an in-depth study of the use of the horse as a means of therapy.

Students *Undergraduates:* 354 full-time, 345 part-time. Students come from 20 states and territories, 11 other countries. *The most frequently chosen baccalaureate fields are:* biological/life sciences, agriculture, business/marketing.

From out-of-state	49%	Reside on campus	90%
Age 25 or older	54%	Transferred in	2%

Faculty 99 (38% full-time).
Expenses (1999–2000) *Comprehensive fee:* $19,740 includes full-time tuition ($13,238), mandatory fees ($350), and room and board ($6152). Room and board charges vary according to board plan. *Part-time tuition:* $536 per course. *Payment plans:* tuition prepayment, installment. *Waivers:* children of alumni and employees or children of employees.
Library Stewart Library. *Operations spending 1999–2000:* $182,618. *Collection:* 171,699 titles, 370 serial subscriptions, 1,623 audiovisual materials.
College life *Housing:* on-campus residence required through junior year. *Option:* women-only. *Most popular organizations:* Muhibbah Club, Orchesis Club, student newspaper, student government, Black Student Union.
Campus security 24-hour emergency response devices and patrols, late-night transport-escort service, controlled dormitory access.
After graduation 15 organizations recruited on campus 1997–98. 75% of class of 1998 had job offers within 6 months. *Career center:* 1 part-time personnel. Services include job fairs, resume preparation, interview workshops, resume referral, career counseling, careers library, job bank, job interviews. *Graduate education:* 45% of class of 1999 went directly to graduate and professional school.
Freshmen 326 applied, 303 admitted, 105 enrolled.

Average high school GPA	2.5	SAT verbal scores above 500	67%
SAT math scores above 500	45%	ACT above 18	65%
From top 10% of their h.s. class	26%	From top quarter	45%
From top half	60%	1998 freshmen returning in 1999	85%

Application *Options:* early admission, deferred entrance. *Application fee:* $20. *Required:* essay or personal statement; high school transcript. *Required for some:* letters of recommendation. *Recommended:* minimum 2.7 GPA; interview.
Standardized tests *Admission: Required:* SAT I or ACT.
Significant dates *Application deadlines:* rolling (freshmen), rolling (transfers). *Financial aid deadline:* 4/30.
Freshman Application Contact
Edgerton Deuel II, Director of Admissions, Wilson College, 1015 Philadelphia Avenue, Chambersburg, PA 17201. **Phone:** 717-262-2002. **Toll-free phone:** 800-421-8402. **Fax:** 717-264-1578. **E-mail:** admissions@wilson.edu
Visit CollegeQuest.com for information on majors offered and athletics.

■ *See page 3008 for a narrative description.*

YESHIVA BETH MOSHE
Scranton, Pennsylvania

Admissions Office Contact
Yeshiva Beth Moshe, 930 Hickory Street, PO Box 1141, Scranton, PA 18505-2124.

YORK COLLEGE OF PENNSYLVANIA
York, Pennsylvania

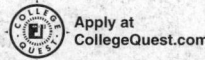 Apply at CollegeQuest.com

- **Independent**, comprehensive, founded 1787
- **Degrees** associate, bachelor's, and master's
- **Suburban** 80-acre campus with easy access to Baltimore
- **Coed**, 4,615 undergraduate students, 83% full-time, 58% women, 42% men
- **Moderately difficult** entrance level, 71% of applicants were admitted
- **59.62% graduate** in 6 years or less
- **$6630 tuition** and fees
- **$5655 average financial aid** package, $14,350 average indebtedness upon graduation, $60.8 million endowment

Students *Undergraduates:* 3,816 full-time, 799 part-time. Students come from 27 states and territories, 29 other countries. *The most frequently chosen baccalaureate fields are:* business/marketing, education, health professions and related sciences. *Graduate:* 189 in graduate degree programs.

From out-of-state	48%	Reside on campus	42%
Age 25 or older	23%	Transferred in	7%
International students	1%	African Americans	1%
Asian Americans/Pacific Islanders	1%	Hispanic Americans	1%
Native Americans	0.1%		

Faculty 347 (39% full-time).

Expenses (1999–2000) *Comprehensive fee:* $11,300 includes full-time tuition ($6280), mandatory fees ($350), and room and board ($4670). *College room only:* $2300. Room and board charges vary according to housing facility. *Part-time tuition:* $200 per credit hour. *Part-time fees:* $76 per term part-time. *Payment plan:* installment. *Waivers:* employees or children of employees.

Library Schmidt Library plus 1 other. *Operations spending 1999–2000:* $1 million. *Collection:* 300,000 titles, 1,400 serial subscriptions, 11,000 audiovisual materials.

College life *Housing:* on-campus residence required in freshman year. *Options:* coed, women-only. *Social organizations:* national fraternities, national sororities, local fraternities, local sororities; 15% of eligible men and 12% of eligible women are members. *Most popular organizations:* Student Senate, Theater Company, ski and outdoor club, marketing club, Student Education Association.

Campus security 24-hour emergency response devices and patrols, late-night transport-escort service.

After graduation 95 organizations recruited on campus 1997–98. 80% of class of 1998 had job offers within 6 months. *Career center:* 1 full-time, 1 part-time personnel. Services include job fairs, resume preparation, interview workshops, resume referral, career/interest testing, career counseling, careers library, job bank, job interviews. *Graduate education:* 28% of class of 1999 went directly to graduate and professional school.

Freshmen 3,669 applied, 2,612 admitted, 741 enrolled. 9 valedictorians.

Average high school GPA	3.0	SAT verbal scores above 500	83%
SAT math scores above 500	80%	ACT above 18	N/R
From top 10% of their h.s. class	28%	From top quarter	64%
From top half	93%	1998 freshmen returning in 1999	82%

Application *Options:* eApply at www.CollegeQuest.com, Common Application, electronic application, early admission, deferred entrance. *Application fee:* $20. *Required:* essay or personal statement; high school transcript. *Required for some:* interview. *Recommended:* 1 letter of recommendation.

Standardized tests *Admission: Required:* SAT I or ACT.

Significant dates *Application deadlines:* rolling (freshmen), rolling (transfers). *Financial aid deadline priority date:* 3/1.

Freshman Application Contact
Mrs. Nancy L. Spataro, Director of Admissions, York College of Pennsylvania, York, PA 17405-7199. **Phone:** 717-849-1600. **Toll-free phone:** 800-455-8018. **E-mail:** admissions@ycp.edu

---

Visit CollegeQuest.com for information on majors offered and athletics. College video and electronic viewbook available at CollegeQuest.com.

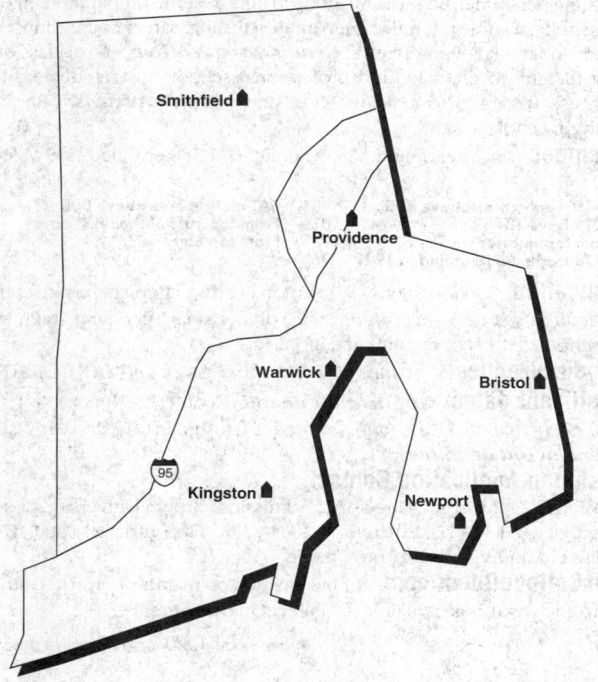

RHODE ISLAND

BROWN UNIVERSITY
Providence, Rhode Island

- **Independent**, university, founded 1764
- **Degrees** bachelor's, master's, doctoral, and first professional
- **Urban** 140-acre campus with easy access to Boston
- **Coed**, 5,868 undergraduate students, 98% full-time, 53% women, 47% men
- **Most difficult** entrance level, 17% of applicants were admitted
- **8:1 student-to-undergraduate faculty ratio**
- **93% graduate** in 6 years or less
- **$25,186 tuition** and fees

Students *Undergraduates:* 5,768 full-time, 100 part-time. Students come from 52 states and territories, 72 other countries. *The most frequently chosen baccalaureate fields are:* liberal arts/general studies, biological/life sciences, social sciences and history. *Graduate:* 316 in professional programs, 1,334 in other graduate degree programs.

From out-of-state	96%	Reside on campus	85%
Age 25 or older	1%	Transferred in	1%
International students	7%	African Americans	6%
Asian Americans/Pacific Islanders	14%	Hispanic Americans	6%
Native Americans	0.4%		

Faculty 715 (98% full-time), 98% with terminal degrees.

Expenses (1999–2000) *One-time required fee:* $186. *Comprehensive fee:* $32,280 includes full-time tuition ($24,624), mandatory fees ($562), and room and board ($7094). *College room only:* $4370. Room and board charges vary according to board plan and housing facility. *Part-time tuition:* $3078 per course. *Payment plans:* tuition prepayment, installment, deferred payment. *Waivers:* employees or children of employees.

Library John D. Rockefeller Library plus 6 others. *Collection:* 3 million titles, 17,000 serial subscriptions.

College life *Housing:* on-campus residence required through junior year. *Options:* coed, women-only, cooperative. *Social organizations:* national fraternities, national sororities, coed fraternity; 10% of eligible men and 2% of

Rhode Island

Brown University (continued)

eligible women are members. *Most popular organizations:* Brown Community Outreach, Bruin Club, Undergraduate Council of Students, Brown Orchestra and Chorus, Brown Daily Herald.

Campus security 24-hour emergency response devices and patrols, late-night transport-escort service, controlled dormitory access.

After graduation 400 organizations recruited on campus 1997–98. 60% of class of 1998 had job offers within 6 months. *Career center:* 5 full-time, 3 part-time personnel. Services include job fairs, resume preparation, interview workshops, resume referral, career/interest testing, career counseling, careers library, job bank, job interviews. *Graduate education:* 30% of class of 1999 went directly to graduate and professional school: 10% graduate arts and sciences, 10% law, 9% medicine, 1% business. *Major awards:* 1 Rhodes, 14 Fulbright Scholars.

Freshmen 14,756 applied, 2,509 admitted, 1,388 enrolled. 159 valedictorians.

SAT verbal scores above 500	98%	SAT math scores above 500	99%
ACT above 18	101%	From top 10% of their h.s. class	86%
From top quarter	97%	From top half	100%
1998 freshmen returning in 1999	96%		

Application *Options:* early admission, early action, deferred entrance. *Application fee:* $55. *Required:* essay or personal statement; high school transcript; 2 letters of recommendation.

Standardized tests *Admission: Required:* SAT I and SAT II or ACT.

Significant dates *Application deadlines:* 1/1 (freshmen), 4/1 (transfers). *Early action:* 11/1. *Notification:* 4/1 (freshmen), 12/15 (early action). *Financial aid deadline:* 3/1.

Freshman Application Contact
Mr. Michael Goldberger, Director of Admission, Brown University, Box 1876, Providence, RI 02912. **Phone:** 401-863-2378. **Fax:** 401-863-9300. **E-mail:** admission_undergraduate@brown.edu

Visit CollegeQuest.com for information on majors offered and athletics. Electronic viewbook available at CollegeQuest.com.

■ *See page 1320 for a narrative description.*

BRYANT COLLEGE
Smithfield, Rhode Island

 Apply at CollegeQuest.com

- **Independent**, comprehensive, founded 1863
- **Degrees** associate, bachelor's, master's, and post-master's certificates
- **Suburban** 387-acre campus with easy access to Boston
- **Coed**, 2,812 undergraduate students, 88% full-time, 41% women, 59% men
- **Moderately difficult** entrance level, 71% of applicants were admitted
- **19:1 student-to-undergraduate faculty ratio**
- **74.4% graduate** in 6 years or less
- **$17,330 tuition** and fees
- **$12,519 average financial aid** package, $19,047 average indebtedness upon graduation, $141.5 million endowment

Students *Undergraduates:* 2,477 full-time, 335 part-time. Students come from 32 states and territories, 43 other countries. *The most frequently chosen baccalaureate fields are:* business/marketing, computer/information sciences, social sciences and history. *Graduate:* 491 in graduate degree programs.

From out-of-state	76%	Reside on campus	70%
Age 25 or older	10%	Transferred in	5%
International students	5%	African Americans	3%
Asian Americans/Pacific Islanders	2%	Hispanic Americans	2%
Native Americans	0.2%		

Faculty 188 (65% full-time), 61% with terminal degrees.

Expenses (2000–2001) *Comprehensive fee:* $24,580 includes full-time tuition ($17,330) and room and board ($7250). *College room only:* $4250. Full-time tuition and fees vary according to course load and program. Room and board charges vary according to board plan and housing facility. *Part-time tuition:* $650 per course. Part-time tuition and fees vary according to course load and program. *Payment plans:* tuition prepayment, installment. *Waivers:* employees or children of employees.

Library Edith M. Hodgson Memorial Library. *Operations spending 1999–2000:* $1.1 million. *Collection:* 132,716 titles, 807 audiovisual materials.

College life *Housing: Options:* coed, women-only. *Social organizations:* national fraternities, national sororities; 10% of eligible men and 11% of eligible women are members. *Most popular organizations:* Student Senate, Student Programming Board, Bryant Outdoor Activities Club, Greek Leadership (Interfraternity/Panhellenic), Finance Association.

Campus security 24-hour emergency response devices and patrols, late-night transport-escort service.

After graduation 301 organizations recruited on campus 1997–98. *Career center:* 6 full-time, 1 part-time personnel. Services include resume preparation, interview workshops, resume referral, career/interest testing, career counseling, careers library, job bank, job interviews, shadowing program. *Graduate education:* 3% of class of 1999 went directly to graduate and professional school: 1% business, 1% graduate arts and sciences, 1% law.

Freshmen 2,967 applied, 2,109 admitted, 652 enrolled. 6 valedictorians.

Average high school GPA	2.97	SAT verbal scores above 500	64%
SAT math scores above 500	77%	ACT above 18	97%
From top 10% of their h.s. class	15%	From top quarter	42%
From top half	86%	1998 freshmen returning in 1999	82%

Application *Options:* eApply at www.CollegeQuest.com, Common Application, electronic application, early admission, early action, deferred entrance. *Application fee:* $50. *Required:* essay or personal statement; high school transcript; minimum 2.5 GPA; 1 letter of recommendation. *Recommended:* minimum 3.0 GPA; interview; senior year first quarter grades.

Standardized tests *Admission: Required:* SAT I or ACT.

Significant dates *Application deadlines:* rolling (freshmen), 8/15 (transfers). *Early action:* 11/1. *Notification:* 12/15 (early action). *Financial aid deadline priority date:* 12/1.

Freshman Application Contact
Ms. Victoria J. LaFore, Dean of Admission and Financial Aid, Bryant College, 1150 Douglas Pike, Smithfield, RI 02917. **Phone:** 401-232-6100. **Toll-free phone:** 800-622-7001. **Fax:** 401-232-6741. **E-mail:** admissions@bryant.edu

Visit CollegeQuest.com for information on majors offered and athletics. College video and electronic viewbook available at CollegeQuest.com.

■ *See page 1322 for a narrative description.*

JOHNSON & WALES UNIVERSITY
Providence, Rhode Island

 Apply at CollegeQuest.com

- **Independent**, comprehensive, founded 1914
- **Degrees** associate, bachelor's, master's, and doctoral (branch locations: Charleston, SC; Vail, CO; Denver, CO; North Miami, FL; Norfolk, VA; Worcester, MA; Gothenberg, Sweden)
- **Urban** 47-acre campus with easy access to Boston
- **Coed**, 8,180 undergraduate students, 84% full-time, 47% women, 53% men
- **Minimally difficult** entrance level, 81% of applicants were admitted
- **30:1 student-to-undergraduate faculty ratio**
- **68.5% graduate** in 6 years or less
- **$13,845 tuition** and fees
- **$10,407 average financial aid** package, $13,431 average indebtedness upon graduation, $148.8 million system endowment

Students *Undergraduates:* 6,832 full-time, 1,348 part-time. Students come from 50 states and territories, 90 other countries. *Graduate:* 575 in graduate degree programs.

Reside on campus	36%	Age 25 or older	11%
Transferred in	5%	International students	7%
African Americans	12%	Asian Americans/Pacific Islanders	3%
Hispanic Americans	5%	Native Americans	0.3%

Expenses (2000–2001) *Comprehensive fee:* $19,815 includes full-time tuition ($13,275), mandatory fees ($570), and room and board ($5970). Full-time tuition and fees vary according to program. Room and board charges vary according to housing facility. Part-time tuition and fees vary according to program. *Payment plans:* guaranteed tuition, installment. *Waivers:* employees or children of employees.

Library Johnson & Wales University Library plus 2 others. *Operations spending 1999–2000:* $812,979. *Collection:* 82,750 titles, 2,429 audiovisual materials.

Rhode Island

College life *Housing:* on-campus residence required in freshman year. *Option:* coed. *Social organizations:* national fraternities, national sororities, local fraternities, local sororities; 10% of eligible men and 10% of eligible women are members. *Most popular organizations:* Delta Epsilon Chi, Vocational Industrial Clubs of America, Phi Beta Lambda, FHA/HERO, FFA.

Campus security 24-hour emergency response devices and patrols, student patrols, late-night transport-escort service.

After graduation 175 organizations recruited on campus 1997–98. *Career center:* 16 full-time personnel. Services include job fairs, resume preparation, interview workshops, resume referral, career/interest testing, career counseling, careers library, job bank, job interviews.

Freshmen 12,317 applied, 9,953 admitted, 2,300 enrolled.

SAT verbal scores above 500	33%	SAT math scores above 500	30%
ACT above 18	N/R	From top 10% of their h.s. class	4%
From top quarter	17%	From top half	43%
1998 freshmen returning in 1999	68%		

Application *Options:* eApply at www.CollegeQuest.com, Common Application, early admission, deferred entrance. *Application fee:* $0. *Required:* high school transcript. *Required for some:* minimum 3.0 GPA; 1 letter of recommendation. *Recommended:* minimum 2.0 GPA; interview.

Standardized tests *Admission: Required for some:* SAT I or ACT.

Significant dates *Application deadlines:* rolling (freshmen), rolling (transfers). *Financial aid deadline:* continuous.

Freshman Application Contact
Mr. Kenneth DiSaia, Dean of Admissions, Johnson & Wales University, 8 Abbott Park Place, Providence, RI 02903-3703. **Phone:** 401-598-2350. **Toll-free phone:** 800-342-5598. **Fax:** 401-598-1835. **E-mail:** admissions@jwu.edu

Visit CollegeQuest.com for information on majors offered and athletics. College video available at CollegeQuest.com.

■ *See page 1852 for a narrative description.*

NEW ENGLAND INSTITUTE OF TECHNOLOGY
Warwick, Rhode Island

- **Independent**, primarily 2-year, founded 1940
- **Degrees** associate and bachelor's
- **Suburban** 10-acre campus with easy access to Boston
- **Coed**, 2,537 undergraduate students
- **Noncompetitive** entrance level

Faculty 208 (52% full-time).

Admissions Office Contact
New England Institute of Technology, 2500 Post Road, Warwick, RI 02886-2244. **E-mail:** neit@ids.net

Visit CollegeQuest.com for information on majors offered and athletics. College video available at CollegeQuest.com.

PROVIDENCE COLLEGE
Providence, Rhode Island

- **Independent Roman Catholic**, comprehensive, founded 1917
- **Degrees** associate, bachelor's, and master's
- **Suburban** 105-acre campus with easy access to Boston
- **Coed**, 4,177 undergraduate students, 91% full-time, 59% women, 41% men
- **Very difficult** entrance level, 60% of applicants were admitted
- **13:1** student-to-undergraduate faculty ratio
- **81% graduate** in 6 years or less
- **$17,945 tuition** and fees
- **$14,350 average financial aid** package, $19,125 average indebtedness upon graduation, $92.7 million endowment

Providence College is the only liberal arts college in the US that was founded and administered by the Dominican Friars, a Catholic teaching order whose heritage spans nearly 800 years. The College is not only concerned with the rigors of intellectual life but also recognizes the importance of students' experiences outside the classroom, including service to others. Scholarship, service, and the exuberant PC spirit—these are the qualities that shape the character of Providence College.

Students *Undergraduates:* 3,791 full-time, 386 part-time. Students come from 38 states and territories, 12 other countries. *The most frequently chosen baccalaureate fields are:* business/marketing, education, social sciences and history. *Graduate:* 937 in graduate degree programs.

From out-of-state	80%	Reside on campus	75%
Age 25 or older	9%	Transferred in	1%
International students	1%	African Americans	2%
Asian Americans/Pacific Islanders	1%	Hispanic Americans	3%
Native Americans	0.1%		

Faculty 324 (79% full-time), 69% with terminal degrees.

Expenses (1999–2000) *Comprehensive fee:* $25,300 includes full-time tuition ($17,640), mandatory fees ($305), and room and board ($7355). *College room only:* $3645. Room and board charges vary according to board plan, housing facility, and student level. *Part-time tuition:* $180 per credit. Part-time tuition and fees vary according to course load. *Payment plan:* installment. *Waivers:* employees or children of employees.

Library Phillips Memorial Library. *Operations spending 1999–2000:* $1.9 million. *Collection:* 229,154 titles, 1,656 serial subscriptions.

College life *Housing:* on-campus residence required through sophomore year. *Options:* coed, men-only, women-only, disabled students. *Most popular organizations:* Board of Programmers, Student Congress, student newspaper, Big Brothers/Big Sisters, Pastoral Council.

Campus security 24-hour emergency response devices and patrols, student patrols, late-night transport-escort service, controlled dormitory access.

After graduation 110 organizations recruited on campus 1997–98. 96% of class of 1998 had job offers within 6 months. *Career center:* 4 full-time, 1 part-time personnel. Services include job fairs, resume preparation, resume referral, career counseling, careers library, job bank. *Graduate education:* 25% of class of 1999 went directly to graduate and professional school: 13% graduate arts and sciences, 5% law, 3% education, 2% business, 2% medicine, 0.2% engineering.

Freshmen 5,331 applied, 3,197 admitted, 978 enrolled. 41 National Merit Scholars, 18 class presidents, 15 valedictorians, 315 student government officers.

Average high school GPA	3.34	SAT verbal scores above 500	92%
SAT math scores above 500	92%	ACT above 18	97%
From top 10% of their h.s. class	37%	From top quarter	77%
From top half	98%	1998 freshmen returning in 1999	90%

Application *Options:* electronic application, early admission, early action, deferred entrance. *Application fee:* $50. *Required:* essay or personal statement; high school transcript; 2 letters of recommendation. *Recommended:* minimum 3.25 GPA; interview.

Standardized tests *Admission: Required:* SAT I or ACT. *Recommended:* SAT II Subject Tests, SAT II: Writing Test.

Significant dates *Application deadlines:* 1/15 (freshmen), 4/15 (transfers). *Early action:* 11/1. *Notification:* 4/1 (freshmen), 1/1 (early action). *Financial aid deadline:* 2/1.

Freshman Application Contact
Mr. Christopher Lydon, Dean of Enrollment Management, Providence College, River Avenue and Eaton Street, Providence, RI 02918. **Phone:** 401-865-2535. **Toll-free phone:** 800-721-6444. **Fax:** 401-865-2826. **E-mail:** pcadmiss@providence.edu

Visit CollegeQuest.com for information on majors offered and athletics.

■ *See page 2294 for a narrative description.*

RHODE ISLAND COLLEGE
Providence, Rhode Island

- **State-supported**, comprehensive, founded 1854
- **Degrees** bachelor's, master's, doctoral, and post-master's certificates
- **Suburban** 170-acre campus with easy access to Boston
- **Coed**
- **Moderately difficult** entrance level

Institutional Web site http://www.ric.edu/

College life *Housing: Options:* coed, women-only, disabled students. *Social organizations:* local fraternities, local sororities; 10% of eligible men

Rhode Island

Rhode Island College (continued)
and 10% of eligible women are members. *Most popular organizations:* ABLE (students with disabilities), newspaper, campus radio station, chess club, coffeehouse.

Campus security 24-hour patrols, late-night transport-escort service.

Application *Options:* Common Application, early admission, deferred entrance. *Application fee:* $25. *Required:* essay or personal statement; high school transcript. *Required for some:* letters of recommendation. *Recommended:* interview.

Standardized tests *Admission: Required:* SAT I or ACT. *Recommended:* SAT II Subject Tests.

Admissions Office Contact
Rhode Island College, 600 Mount Pleasant Avenue, Providence, RI 02908-1924. **Toll-free phone:** 800-669-5760. **E-mail:** admissions@ric.edu

Visit CollegeQuest.com for information on athletics. College video available at CollegeQuest.com.

RHODE ISLAND SCHOOL OF DESIGN
Providence, Rhode Island

- **Independent**, comprehensive, founded 1877
- **Degrees** bachelor's, master's, and first professional
- **Urban** 13-acre campus with easy access to Boston
- **Coed**, 1,861 undergraduate students, 100% full-time, 60% women, 40% men
- **Very difficult** entrance level, 36% of applicants were admitted
- **11:1 student-to-undergraduate faculty ratio**
- **93% graduate** in 6 years or less
- **$21,405 tuition** and fees

Students *Undergraduates:* 1,861 full-time. Students come from 51 states and territories, 52 other countries. *The most frequently chosen baccalaureate fields are:* architecture, visual/performing arts. *Graduate:* 251 in graduate degree programs.

From out-of-state	93%	Reside on campus	39%
Age 25 or older	14%	International students	13%
African Americans	2%	Asian Americans/Pacific Islanders	11%
Hispanic Americans	4%	Native Americans	0.3%

Faculty 342 (41% full-time).

Expenses (1999–2000) *Comprehensive fee:* $27,895 includes full-time tuition ($21,020), mandatory fees ($385), and room and board ($6490). *College room only:* $3490. Room and board charges vary according to board plan. *Payment plan:* installment. *Waivers:* employees or children of employees.

Library RISD Library. *Collection:* 90,000 titles, 393 serial subscriptions.

College life *Housing:* on-campus residence required in freshman year. *Option:* coed. *Most popular organizations:* athletic clubs, industrial design club, Korean Students Association, Lesbian/Gay/Bisexual Alliance.

Campus security 24-hour emergency response devices and patrols, late-night transport-escort service, controlled dormitory access.

After graduation 50 organizations recruited on campus 1997–98. *Career center:* 6 full-time personnel. Services include resume preparation, interview workshops, career counseling, careers library, job bank, job interviews, seminar series. *Graduate education:* 5% of class of 1999 went directly to graduate and professional school: 5% graduate arts and sciences. *Major awards:* 1 Fulbright Scholar.

Freshmen 2,432 applied, 882 admitted, 387 enrolled.

Average high school GPA	3.2	SAT verbal scores above 500	84%
SAT math scores above 500	87%	ACT above 18	N/R
From top 10% of their h.s. class	21%	From top quarter	59%
From top half	88%	1998 freshmen returning in 1999	96%

Application *Options:* early admission, early action, deferred entrance. *Application fee:* $45. *Required:* essay or personal statement; high school transcript; portfolio, drawing assignments. *Recommended:* 3 letters of recommendation.

Standardized tests *Admission: Required:* SAT I or ACT.

Significant dates *Application deadlines:* 2/15 (freshmen), 3/7 (transfers). *Early action:* 12/15. *Notification:* 4/2 (freshmen), 1/25 (early action). *Financial aid deadline priority date:* 2/15.

Freshman Application Contact
Mr. Edward Newhall, Director of Admissions, Rhode Island School of Design, 2 College Street, Providence, RI 02903-2784. **Phone:** 401-454-6300. **Toll-free phone:** 800-364-RISD. **Fax:** 401-454-6309. **E-mail:** admissions@risd.edu

Visit CollegeQuest.com for information on majors offered and athletics.

ROGER WILLIAMS UNIVERSITY
Bristol, Rhode Island

Apply at CollegeQuest.com

- **Independent**, comprehensive, founded 1956
- **Degrees** associate, bachelor's, master's, and first professional
- **Small-town** 140-acre campus with easy access to Boston
- **Coed**, 3,375 undergraduate students, 64% full-time, 50% women, 50% men
- **Moderately difficult** entrance level, 86% of applicants were admitted
- **15:1 student-to-undergraduate faculty ratio**
- **$17,980 tuition** and fees
- **$14,462 average financial aid** package, $17,125 average indebtedness upon graduation, $31.5 million endowment

Students *Undergraduates:* 2,174 full-time, 1,201 part-time. Students come from 46 states and territories, 44 other countries. *The most frequently chosen baccalaureate fields are:* business/marketing, protective services/public administration, social sciences and history. *Graduate:* 394 in professional programs, 64 in other graduate degree programs.

From out-of-state	79%	Reside on campus	74%
Age 25 or older	41%	Transferred in	3%
International students	3%	African Americans	2%
Asian Americans/Pacific Islanders	1%	Hispanic Americans	2%
Native Americans	0.2%		

Faculty 284 (42% full-time), 49% with terminal degrees.

Expenses (2000–2001, estimated) *One-time required fee:* $100. *Comprehensive fee:* $26,180 includes full-time tuition ($17,300), mandatory fees ($680), and room and board ($8200). *College room only:* $4300. Full-time tuition and fees vary according to class time, course load, and program. Room and board charges vary according to board plan and housing facility. *Part-time tuition:* $725 per credit. *Part-time fees:* $350 per term part-time. Part-time tuition and fees vary according to class time. *Payment plans:* installment, deferred payment. *Waivers:* employees or children of employees.

Library Roger Williams University Library plus 2 others. *Operations spending 1999–2000:* $2 million. *Collection:* 155,684 titles, 970 serial subscriptions, 53,129 audiovisual materials.

College life *Housing:* on-campus residence required through sophomore year. *Options:* coed, disabled students. *Most popular organizations:* Entertainment Network, Student Senate, American Institute of Architects, John Jay Society, residence hall councils.

Campus security 24-hour emergency response devices and patrols, student patrols, late-night transport-escort service, controlled dormitory access.

After graduation 60 organizations recruited on campus 1997–98. 89% of class of 1998 had job offers within 6 months. *Career center:* 2 full-time personnel. Services include job fairs, resume preparation, interview workshops, resume referral, career/interest testing, career counseling, careers library, job bank, job interviews.

Freshmen 2,981 applied, 2,576 admitted, 772 enrolled.

Average high school GPA	3.0	SAT verbal scores above 500	69%
SAT math scores above 500	70%	ACT above 18	N/R
From top 10% of their h.s. class	16%	From top quarter	49%
From top half	74%	1998 freshmen returning in 1999	72%

Application *Options:* eApply at www.CollegeQuest.com, Common Application, electronic application, early admission, early decision, deferred entrance. *Application fee:* $35. *Required:* essay or personal statement; high school transcript; minimum 2 GPA; letters of recommendation. *Recommended:* interview.

Standardized tests *Admission: Required:* SAT I. *Required for some:* ACT.

Significant dates *Application deadlines:* rolling (freshmen), rolling (transfers). *Early decision:* 12/1. *Notification:* 12/15 (early decision). *Financial aid deadline priority date:* 3/1.

Rhode Island

Freshman Application Contact
Ms. Julie Cairns, Office of Admissions, Roger Williams University, 1 Old Ferry Road, Bristol, RI 02809. **Phone:** 401-254-3500. **Toll-free phone:** 800-458-7144. **Fax:** 401-254-3557. **E-mail:** admit@alpha.rwu.edu

Visit CollegeQuest.com for information on majors offered and athletics. College video and electronic viewbook available at CollegeQuest.com.

■ *See page 2352 for a narrative description.*

SALVE REGINA UNIVERSITY
Newport, Rhode Island

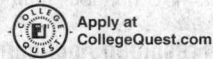
Apply at CollegeQuest.com

- **Independent Roman Catholic**, comprehensive, founded 1934
- **Degrees** associate, bachelor's, master's, doctoral, and post-master's certificates
- **Suburban** 65-acre campus with easy access to Boston
- **Coed**, 1,780 undergraduate students, 91% full-time, 66% women, 34% men
- **Moderately difficult** entrance level, 77% of applicants were admitted
- **13:1 student-to-undergraduate faculty ratio**
- **61.5% graduate** in 6 years or less
- **$16,850 tuition** and fees
- **$13,241 average financial aid** package, $19,125 average indebtedness upon graduation, $12 million endowment

Students *Undergraduates:* 1,621 full-time, 159 part-time. Students come from 28 states and territories, 7 other countries. *The most frequently chosen baccalaureate fields are:* business/marketing, education, protective services/public administration. *Graduate:* 457 in graduate degree programs.

From out-of-state	77%	Reside on campus	60%
Age 25 or older	11%	Transferred in	4%
International students	0.5%	African Americans	2%
Asian Americans/Pacific Islanders	1%	Hispanic Americans	2%
Native Americans	0.3%		

Faculty 232 (47% full-time), 44% with terminal degrees.

Expenses (1999–2000) *Comprehensive fee:* $24,350 includes full-time tuition ($16,500), mandatory fees ($350), and room and board ($7500). *Part-time tuition:* $550 per credit. *Part-time fees:* $35 per term part-time. Part-time tuition and fees vary according to course load. *Waivers:* employees or children of employees.

Library McKillop Library. *Operations spending 1999–2000:* $932,000. *Collection:* 96,235 titles, 3,018 serial subscriptions, 19,655 audiovisual materials.

College life *Housing:* on-campus residence required through sophomore year. *Options:* coed, men-only, women-only, disabled students. *Most popular organizations:* Orpheus Musical Society, Student Government Association, Student Outdoor Adventures, Student Nurse Organization, Stagefright Theatre Company.

Campus security 24-hour emergency response devices and patrols, late-night transport-escort service, controlled dormitory access.

After graduation 108 organizations recruited on campus 1997–98. 87% of class of 1998 had job offers within 6 months. *Career center:* 5 full-time personnel. Services include job fairs, resume preparation, resume referral, career/interest testing, career counseling, careers library, job bank, job interviews.

Freshmen 2,633 applied, 2,034 admitted, 571 enrolled. 5 class presidents, 2 valedictorians, 50 student government officers.

Average high school GPA	2.8	SAT verbal scores above 500	47%
SAT math scores above 500	41%	ACT above 18	N/R
From top 10% of their h.s. class	4%	From top quarter	21%
From top half	51%	1998 freshmen returning in 1999	73%

Application *Options:* eApply at www.CollegeQuest.com, Common Application, electronic application, early admission, early decision, deferred entrance. *Application fee:* $25. *Required:* essay or personal statement; high school transcript; 2 letters of recommendation. *Recommended:* minimum 2.0 GPA; interview.

Standardized tests *Admission: Required:* SAT I or ACT.

Significant dates *Application deadlines:* rolling (freshmen), rolling (transfers). *Early decision:* 11/15. *Notification:* 12/15 (early decision). *Financial aid deadline priority date:* 3/1.

Freshman Application Contact
Laura McPhie Oliveira, Dean of Enrollment Services and Admissions, Salve Regina University, 100 Ochre Point Avenue, Newport, RI 02840-4192. **Phone:** 401-847-6650 Ext. 2908. **Toll-free phone:** 888-GO SALVE. **Fax:** 401-848-2823. **E-mail:** sruadmis@salve.edu

Visit CollegeQuest.com for information on majors offered and athletics. College video available at CollegeQuest.com.

■ *See page 2440 for a narrative description.*

UNIVERSITY OF RHODE ISLAND
Kingston, Rhode Island

Apply at CollegeQuest.com

- **State-supported**, university, founded 1892
- **Degrees** bachelor's, master's, doctoral, first professional, and postbachelor's certificates
- **Small-town** 1,200-acre campus
- **Coed**, 10,223 undergraduate students, 85% full-time, 56% women, 44% men
- **Moderately difficult** entrance level, 75% of applicants were admitted
- **18:1 student-to-undergraduate faculty ratio**
- **$4928 tuition** and fees (in-state); $13,148 (out-of-state)
- **$39.6 million endowment**

Part of Rhode Island State System of Higher Education.

Students *Undergraduates:* 8,710 full-time, 1,513 part-time. Students come from 44 states and territories, 47 other countries. *The most frequently chosen baccalaureate fields are:* business/marketing, education, health professions and related sciences. *Graduate:* 345 in professional programs, 3,593 in other graduate degree programs.

From out-of-state	37%	Reside on campus	42%
Age 25 or older	18%	Transferred in	6%
International students	0.5%	African Americans	4%
Asian Americans/Pacific Islanders	4%	Hispanic Americans	4%
Native Americans	0.4%		

Faculty 669 (99% full-time), 91% with terminal degrees.

Expenses (1999–2000) *Tuition, state resident:* full-time $3372; part-time $226 per credit. *Tuition, nonresident:* full-time $11,592; part-time $568 per credit. *Required fees:* full-time $1556; $42 per credit; $43 per term part-time. Part-time tuition and fees vary according to reciprocity agreements. *College room and board:* $6378; room only: $3592. Room and board charges vary according to board plan and housing facility. *Payment plan:* installment. *Waivers:* minority students, senior citizens, and employees or children of employees.

Library University Library plus 1 other. *Operations spending 1999–2000:* $5.8 million. *Collection:* 783,237 titles, 7,966 serial subscriptions, 9,510 audiovisual materials.

College life *Housing:* Option: coed. *Social organizations:* national fraternities, national sororities, local sororities; 6% of eligible men and 7% of eligible women are members. *Most popular organizations:* Student Entertainment Committee, student radio station, intramural sport clubs, Student Alumni Association, student newspaper.

Campus security 24-hour emergency response devices and patrols, student patrols, late-night transport-escort service, controlled dormitory access.

After graduation 155 organizations recruited on campus 1997–98. *Career center:* 7 full-time personnel. Services include job fairs, resume preparation, career/interest testing, career counseling, careers library, job bank, job interviews.

Freshmen 10,034 applied, 7,476 admitted, 2,150 enrolled.

Average high school GPA	3.4	SAT verbal scores above 500	67%
SAT math scores above 500	70%	ACT above 18	N/R
From top 10% of their h.s. class	17%	From top quarter	52%
From top half	86%	1998 freshmen returning in 1999	79%

Application *Options:* eApply at www.CollegeQuest.com, electronic application, early admission, early action. *Preference* given to state residents. *Application fee:* $45 for nonresidents. *Required:* high school transcript. *Required for some:* minimum 3.0 GPA. *Recommended:* minimum 3.0 GPA; letters of recommendation; interview.

Standardized tests *Admission: Required:* SAT I or ACT.

Rhode Island–South Carolina

University of Rhode Island (continued)
Significant dates *Application deadlines:* 3/1 (freshmen), 5/1 (transfers). *Early action:* 12/15. *Notification:* 1/15 (early action). *Financial aid deadline priority date:* 3/1.
Freshman Application Contact
Ms. Catherine Zeiser, Assistant Dean of Admissions, University of Rhode Island, 8 Ranger Road, Suite 1, Kingston, RI 02881-2020. **Phone:** 401-874-7100. **Fax:** 401-874-5523. **E-mail:** uriadmit@uriacc.uri.edu
Visit CollegeQuest.com for information on majors offered and athletics.

■ *See page 2812 for a narrative description.*

SOUTH CAROLINA

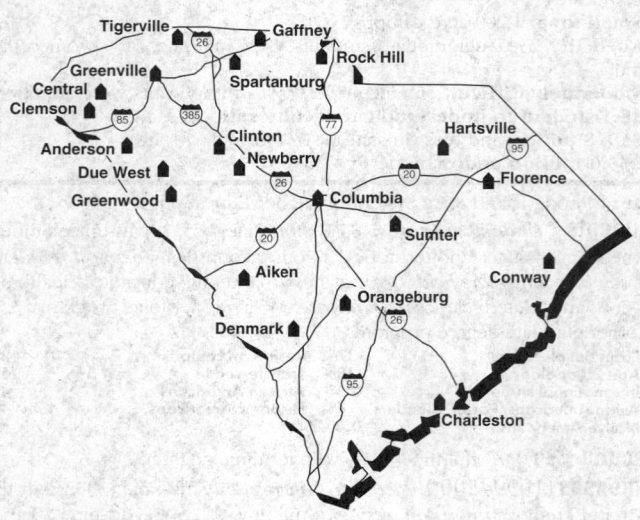

ALLEN UNIVERSITY
Columbia, South Carolina

Apply at CollegeQuest.com

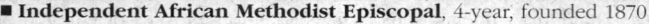

- **Independent African Methodist Episcopal**, 4-year, founded 1870
- **Degree** bachelor's
- **Suburban** campus
- **Coed**, 283 undergraduate students, 81% full-time, 43% women, 57% men
- **Noncompetitive** entrance level, 47% of applicants were admitted
- **15:1 student-to-undergraduate faculty ratio**
- **$4750 tuition** and fees

Students *Undergraduates:* 230 full-time, 53 part-time. Students come from 17 states and territories, 3 other countries. *The most frequently chosen baccalaureate fields are:* business/marketing, liberal arts/general studies, social sciences and history.

Reside on campus	80%	Age 25 or older	2%
Transferred in	2%	International students	5%
African Americans	94%	Asian Americans/Pacific Islanders	0.4%

Faculty 40 (40% full-time), 50% with terminal degrees.
Expenses (1999–2000) *Comprehensive fee:* $9060 includes full-time tuition ($4650), mandatory fees ($100), and room and board ($4310). *Part-time tuition:* $132 per credit hour.
Library J. S. Flipper Library. *Collection:* 50,000 titles, 176 serial subscriptions.
College life *Housing: Options:* men-only, women-only. *Social organizations:* national fraternities, national sororities, local sororities; 1% of eligible men and 2% of eligible women are members. *Most popular organizations:* international students club, social science club, gospel choir.
Campus security 24-hour patrols.
After graduation *Career center:* 2 full-time personnel. Services include job fairs, resume preparation, interview workshops, resume referral, career counseling. *Graduate education:* 1% of class of 1999 went directly to graduate and professional school.

Freshmen 485 applied, 226 admitted, 143 enrolled. 2 student government officers.

SAT verbal scores above 500	N/R	SAT math scores above 500	N/R
ACT above 18	N/R	From top quarter of their h.s. class	2%
From top half	5%	1998 freshmen returning in 1999	68%

Application *Options:* eApply at www.CollegeQuest.com, Common Application. *Application fee:* $15. *Required:* high school transcript; 2 letters of recommendation.
Standardized tests *Placement: Recommended:* SAT I.
Significant dates *Application deadline:* rolling (freshmen). *Notification:* continuous until 8/15 (freshmen). *Financial aid deadline priority date:* 4/15.
Freshman Application Contact
Mr. Kovac Byrum, Director of Admissions, Allen University, 1530 Harden Street, Columbia, SC 29204-1085. **Phone:** 803-376-5716. **Fax:** 803-376-5731. **E-mail:** auniv@mindspring.com
Visit CollegeQuest.com for information on majors offered and athletics.

ANDERSON COLLEGE
Anderson, South Carolina

Apply at CollegeQuest.com

- **Independent Baptist**, 4-year, founded 1911
- **Degrees** associate and bachelor's
- **Suburban** 44-acre campus
- **Coed**, 1,216 undergraduate students, 81% full-time, 57% women, 43% men
- **Moderately difficult** entrance level, 87% of applicants were admitted
- **15:1 student-to-undergraduate faculty ratio**
- **$10,515 tuition** and fees
- **$8229 average financial aid** package, $13,379 average indebtedness upon graduation, $14 million endowment

Students *Undergraduates:* 982 full-time, 234 part-time. Students come from 21 states and territories, 16 other countries. *The most frequently chosen baccalaureate fields are:* business/marketing, education, visual/performing arts.

From out-of-state	18%	Reside on campus	52%
Age 25 or older	25%	Transferred in	4%
International students	1%	African Americans	12%
Asian Americans/Pacific Islanders	0.3%	Hispanic Americans	1%
Native Americans	0.4%		

Faculty 103 (50% full-time).
Expenses (2000–2001) *Comprehensive fee:* $15,120 includes full-time tuition ($9720), mandatory fees ($795), and room and board ($4605). Room and board charges vary according to board plan. *Part-time tuition:* $252 per credit hour. *Payment plan:* installment. *Waivers:* adult students, senior citizens, and employees or children of employees.
Library Olin D. Johnston Library. *Collection:* 55,000 titles, 425 serial subscriptions.
College life *Housing:* on-campus residence required through sophomore year. *Options:* men-only, women-only.
Campus security 24-hour emergency response devices and patrols, late-night transport-escort service, controlled dormitory access.
After graduation *Career center:* 1 full-time, 1 part-time personnel. Services include job fairs, resume preparation, career counseling, careers library, job interviews.
Freshmen 770 applied, 668 admitted, 365 enrolled.

Average high school GPA	3.1	SAT verbal scores above 500	52%
SAT math scores above 500	47%	ACT above 18	N/R
From top 10% of their h.s. class	18%	From top quarter	39%
From top half	72%	1998 freshmen returning in 1999	71%

Application *Options:* eApply at www.CollegeQuest.com, Common Application, electronic application, early admission, early decision, deferred entrance. *Application fee:* $20. *Required:* high school transcript. *Required for some:* essay or personal statement; 2 letters of recommendation; interview. *Recommended:* minimum 2.5 GPA.
Standardized tests *Admission: Required:* SAT I or ACT.
Significant dates *Application deadlines:* 6/30 (freshmen), 8/1 (transfers). *Early decision:* 1/1. *Financial aid deadline:* 7/31.

South Carolina

Freshman Application Contact
Ms. Pam Bryant, Director of Admissions, Anderson College, 316 Boulevard, Anderson, SC 29621. **Phone:** 864-231-2030. **Toll-free phone:** 800-542-3594. **Fax:** 864-231-2004. **E-mail:** apply@anderson-college.edu
Visit CollegeQuest.com for information on majors offered and athletics. College video available at CollegeQuest.com.

■ *See page 1168 for a narrative description.*

BENEDICT COLLEGE
Columbia, South Carolina

Admissions Office Contact
Benedict College, PO Box 98, Columbia, SC 29204. **Toll-free phone:** 800-868-6598. **Fax:** 803-253-5167.

CHARLESTON SOUTHERN UNIVERSITY
Charleston, South Carolina

- **Independent Baptist**, comprehensive, founded 1964
- **Degrees** associate, bachelor's, and master's
- **Suburban** 500-acre campus
- **Coed**, 2,215 undergraduate students, 84% full-time, 61% women, 39% men
- **Moderately difficult** entrance level, 93% of applicants were admitted
- **17:1 student-to-undergraduate faculty ratio**
- **$10,410 tuition** and fees
- **$11,500 average financial aid** package, $17,125 average indebtedness upon graduation, $5.2 million endowment

Located in one of the Southeast's most beautiful regions, Charleston Southern University (CSU) is the second-largest accredited, private university in South Carolina. CSU's enrollment has grown to more than 2,594 students and offers both a traditional liberal arts curriculum and a comprehensive professional program. CSU encourages interested students to schedule a campus visit.

Students *Undergraduates:* 1,851 full-time, 364 part-time. Students come from 27 states and territories. *The most frequently chosen baccalaureate fields are:* business/marketing, education, protective services/public administration. *Graduate:* 235 in graduate degree programs.

From out-of-state	22%	Reside on campus	44%
Age 25 or older	30%	Transferred in	10%
International students	0.3%	African Americans	23%
Asian Americans/Pacific Islanders	1%	Hispanic Americans	2%
Native Americans	0.2%		

Faculty 161 (53% full-time), 42% with terminal degrees.
Expenses (1999–2000) *Comprehensive fee:* $14,412 includes full-time tuition ($10,410) and room and board ($4002). Room and board charges vary according to housing facility. *Part-time tuition:* $170 per credit hour. Part-time tuition and fees vary according to course load.
Library L. Mendel Rivers Library. *Operations spending 1999–2000:* $646,946. *Collection:* 122,867 titles, 1,230 serial subscriptions.
College life *Housing:* on-campus residence required through senior year. *Options:* men-only, women-only. *Most popular organizations:* student government, Baptist Student Union, Fellowship of Christian Athletes.
Campus security 24-hour emergency response devices and patrols, late-night transport-escort service.
After graduation 75 organizations recruited on campus 1997–98. *Career center:* 2 full-time personnel. Services include job fairs, resume preparation, resume referral, career/interest testing, career counseling, careers library, job interviews.
Freshmen 2,734 applied, 2,553 admitted, 557 enrolled.

Average high school GPA	2.51	SAT verbal scores above 500	37%
SAT math scores above 500	36%	ACT above 18	N/R
From top 10% of their h.s. class	7%	From top quarter	25%
From top half	65%	1998 freshmen returning in 1999	67%

Application *Options:* early admission, deferred entrance. *Application fee:* $25. *Required:* high school transcript. *Required for some:* essay or personal statement; 1 letter of recommendation; interview.
Standardized tests *Admission:* Required: SAT I or ACT.

Significant dates *Application deadlines:* rolling (freshmen), rolling (transfers). *Financial aid deadline priority date:* 4/15.
Freshman Application Contact
Mrs. Debbie Williamson, Director of Enrollment Management, Charleston Southern University, PO Box 118087, Charleston, SC 29423-8087. **Phone:** 843-863-7050. **Toll-free phone:** 800-947-7474. **E-mail:** enroll@csuniv.edu
Visit CollegeQuest.com for information on majors offered and athletics. College video available at CollegeQuest.com.

■ *See page 1406 for a narrative description.*

THE CITADEL, THE MILITARY COLLEGE OF SOUTH CAROLINA
Charleston, South Carolina

- **State-supported**, comprehensive, founded 1842
- **Degrees** bachelor's, master's, and post-master's certificates
- **Urban** 130-acre campus
- **Coed**, primarily men, 1,912 undergraduate students, 97% full-time, 5% women, 95% men
- **Moderately difficult** entrance level, 79% of applicants were admitted
- **76.8% graduate** in 6 years or less
- **$4258 tuition** and fees (in-state); $9854 (out-of-state)
- **$7406 average financial aid** package, $14,200 average indebtedness upon graduation, $37.7 million endowment

The Citadel, a comprehensive military college, prepares students for leadership through a challenging curriculum of 20 majors. Graduates participate in all walks of life, from graduate study to private sector and military careers. New barracks and a first-class campuswide computer network are new features. The college actively seeks qualified students regardless of gender or ethnicity.

Students *Undergraduates:* 1,854 full-time, 58 part-time. Students come from 45 states and territories, 31 other countries. *The most frequently chosen baccalaureate fields are:* business/marketing, engineering/engineering technologies, social sciences and history. *Graduate:* 2,013 in graduate degree programs.

From out-of-state	49%	Reside on campus	100%
Age 25 or older	4%	Transferred in	5%
International students	4%	African Americans	8%
Asian Americans/Pacific Islanders	1%	Hispanic Americans	4%
Native Americans	0.4%		

Faculty 182 (80% full-time), 85% with terminal degrees.
Expenses (1999–2000) *Tuition, state resident:* full-time $3396; part-time $132 per credit hour. *Tuition, nonresident:* full-time $8992; part-time $261 per credit hour. *Required fees:* full-time $862. *College room and board:* $4340. Deposit required to defray the cost of books, uniforms and supplies: $4300 for first-year students, $1310 for upperclassmen. *Payment plan:* installment. *Waivers:* senior citizens.
Library Daniel Library. *Operations spending 1999–2000:* $1.4 million. *Collection:* 173,765 titles, 1,318 serial subscriptions, 1,426 audiovisual materials.
College life *Housing:* on-campus residence required through senior year. *Option:* coed.
Campus security 24-hour patrols, student patrols, late-night transport-escort service.
After graduation 96 organizations recruited on campus 1997–98. 95% of class of 1998 had job offers within 6 months. *Career center:* 2 full-time personnel. Services include job fairs, resume preparation, interview workshops, resume referral, career/interest testing, career counseling, careers library, job bank, job interviews. *Graduate education:* 15% of class of 1999 went directly to graduate and professional school: 8% business, 4% law, 2% medicine, 1% graduate arts and sciences.
Freshmen 1,507 applied, 1,198 admitted, 517 enrolled.

Average high school GPA	3.04	SAT verbal scores above 500	63%
SAT math scores above 500	66%	ACT above 18	100%
From top 10% of their h.s. class	10%	From top quarter	36%
From top half	71%	1998 freshmen returning in 1999	77%

Application *Options:* electronic application, deferred entrance. *Preference* given to state residents. *Application fee:* $35. *Required:* high school transcript; minimum 2.0 GPA. *Recommended:* interview.

South Carolina

The Citadel, The Military College of South Carolina (continued)
Standardized tests *Admission:* Required: SAT I or ACT.
Significant dates *Application deadlines:* rolling (freshmen), rolling (transfers). *Notification:* 9/1 (freshmen). *Financial aid deadline priority date:* 3/15.
Freshman Application Contact
Lt. Col. Steven D. Klein, Dean of Enrollment Management, The Citadel, The Military College of South Carolina, 171 Moultrie Street, Charleston, SC 29409. **Phone:** 843-953-5230. **Toll-free phone:** 800-868-1842. **Fax:** 843-953-7084. **E-mail:** admissions@citadel.edu
Visit CollegeQuest.com for information on majors offered and athletics. College video available at CollegeQuest.com.

■ *See page 1418 for a narrative description.*

CLAFLIN UNIVERSITY
Orangeburg, South Carolina

- **Independent United Methodist**, 4-year, founded 1869
- **Degree** bachelor's
- **Small-town** 32-acre campus with easy access to Columbia
- **Coed**, 1,308 undergraduate students, 94% full-time, 59% women, 41% men
- **Minimally difficult** entrance level, 56% of applicants were admitted
- **14:1 student-to-undergraduate faculty ratio**
- **78% graduate** in 6 years or less
- **$7008 tuition** and fees
- **$11,650 average financial aid** package, $13,141 average indebtedness upon graduation, $12 million endowment

Students *Undergraduates:* Students come from 20 states and territories, 12 other countries. *The most frequently chosen baccalaureate fields are:* education, biological/life sciences, social sciences and history.

From out-of-state	11%	Reside on campus	61%
International students	3%	African Americans	97%

Faculty 93 (76% full-time).
Expenses (1999–2000) *One-time required fee:* $100. *Comprehensive fee:* $10,820 includes full-time tuition ($6978), mandatory fees ($30), and room and board ($3812). Room and board charges vary according to gender and housing facility. *Part-time tuition:* $225 per semester hour. *Part-time fees:* $15 per term part-time. *Payment plans:* installment, deferred payment. *Waivers:* employees or children of employees.
Library H. V. Manning Library. *Operations spending 1999–2000:* $388,003. *Collection:* 148,584 titles, 334 serial subscriptions, 469 audiovisual materials.
College life *Housing: Options:* men-only, women-only. *Social organizations:* national fraternities, national sororities; 22% of eligible men and 26% of eligible women are members.
Campus security 24-hour emergency response devices and patrols, student patrols.
After graduation 38 organizations recruited on campus 1997–98. 40% of class of 1998 had job offers within 6 months. *Career center:* 4 full-time personnel. Services include job fairs, resume preparation, interview workshops, resume referral, career counseling, careers library, job interviews.
Freshmen 1,304 applied, 733 admitted. 3 valedictorians.

SAT verbal scores above 500	N/R	SAT math scores above 500	N/R
ACT above 18	N/R	From top 10% of their h.s. class	29%
From top quarter	50%	From top half	81%
1998 freshmen returning in 1999	79%		

Application *Options:* Common Application, early admission, deferred entrance. *Application fee:* $20. *Required:* essay or personal statement; high school transcript; interview. *Recommended:* letters of recommendation.
Standardized tests *Admission:* Required: SAT I or ACT. *Recommended:* SAT II Subject Tests.
Significant dates *Application deadlines:* rolling (freshmen), rolling (transfers). *Financial aid deadline priority date:* 4/15.
Freshman Application Contact
Mr. Michael Zeigler, Director of Admissions, Claflin University, 400 Magnolia Street, Orangeburg, SC 29115. **Phone:** 803-535-5340. **Toll-free phone:** 800-922-1276. **Fax:** 803-531-2860. **E-mail:** zeiglerm@claf1.claflin.edu

Visit CollegeQuest.com for information on majors offered and athletics. College video available at CollegeQuest.com.

CLEMSON UNIVERSITY
Clemson, South Carolina

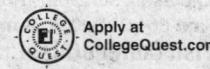 Apply at CollegeQuest.com

- **State-supported**, university, founded 1889
- **Degrees** bachelor's, master's, and doctoral
- **Small-town** 1,400-acre campus
- **Coed**, 13,375 undergraduate students, 95% full-time, 45% women, 55% men
- **Moderately difficult** entrance level, 68% of applicants were admitted
- **16:1 student-to-undergraduate faculty ratio**
- **72.4% graduate** in 6 years or less
- **$3470 tuition** and fees (in-state); $9456 (out-of-state)
- **$7123 average financial aid** package, $13,987 average indebtedness upon graduation, $244 million endowment

Students *Undergraduates:* 12,644 full-time, 731 part-time. Students come from 52 states and territories. *The most frequently chosen baccalaureate fields are:* business/marketing, education, engineering/engineering technologies.
Graduate: 3,456 in graduate degree programs.

From out-of-state	31%	Reside on campus	49%
Age 25 or older	6%	Transferred in	5%
International students	1%	African Americans	8%
Asian Americans/Pacific Islanders	1%	Hispanic Americans	1%
Native Americans	0.2%		

Faculty 1,025 (91% full-time), 84% with terminal degrees.
Expenses (1999–2000) *Tuition, state resident:* full-time $3280; part-time $138 per hour. *Tuition, nonresident:* full-time $9266; part-time $388 per hour. *Required fees:* full-time $190; $5 per term part-time. *College room and board:* $4122; room only: $2202. Room and board charges vary according to board plan and housing facility. *Payment plans:* installment, deferred payment. *Waivers:* senior citizens.
Library Robert Muldrow Cooper Library plus 1 other. *Collection:* 1.6 million titles, 5,978 serial subscriptions, 94,641 audiovisual materials.
College life *Housing:* on-campus residence required in freshman year. *Option:* coed. *Social organizations:* national fraternities, national sororities; 20% of eligible men and 20% of eligible women are members. *Most popular organizations:* student government, Interfraternity Council, Fellowship of Christian Athletes, Panhellenic Council, Tiger Band.
Campus security 24-hour emergency response devices and patrols, late-night transport-escort service, controlled dormitory access.
After graduation 392 organizations recruited on campus 1997–98. 85% of class of 1998 had job offers within 6 months. *Career center:* 14 full-time, 2 part-time personnel. Services include job fairs, resume preparation, interview workshops, resume referral, career/interest testing, career counseling, careers library, job bank, job interviews.
Freshmen 9,501 applied, 6,484 admitted, 2,891 enrolled. 22 National Merit Scholars, 126 valedictorians.

Average high school GPA	3.54	SAT verbal scores above 500	84%
SAT math scores above 500	90%	ACT above 18	99%
From top 10% of their h.s. class	34%	From top quarter	70%
From top half	95%	1998 freshmen returning in 1999	84%

Application *Options:* eApply at www.CollegeQuest.com, electronic application, early admission, deferred entrance. *Preference* given to state residents. *Application fee:* $40. *Required:* high school transcript. *Recommended:* essay or personal statement; letters of recommendation; interview.
Standardized tests *Admission:* Required: SAT I or ACT. *Required for some:* SAT II Subject Tests.
Significant dates *Application deadlines:* 5/1 (freshmen), 8/1 (transfers). *Financial aid deadline priority date:* 4/1.
Freshman Application Contact
Mrs. Audrey Bodell, Assistant Director of Admissions, Clemson University, 105 Sikes Hall, PO Box 345124, Clemson, SC 29634. **Phone:** 864-656-2287. **Fax:** 864-656-2464. **E-mail:** cuadmissions@clemson.edu
Visit CollegeQuest.com for information on majors offered and athletics. College video and electronic viewbook available at CollegeQuest.com.

■ *See page 1436 for a narrative description.*

South Carolina

COASTAL CAROLINA UNIVERSITY
Conway, South Carolina

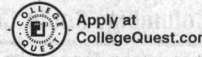 Apply at CollegeQuest.com

- **State-supported**, comprehensive, founded 1954
- **Degrees** bachelor's, master's, and postbachelor's certificates
- **Suburban** 244-acre campus
- **Coed**, 3,998 undergraduate students, 89% full-time, 55% women, 45% men
- **Moderately difficult** entrance level, 75% of applicants were admitted
- **17:1** student-to-undergraduate faculty ratio
- **$3340 tuition** and fees (in-state); $9280 (out-of-state)
- **$6281 average financial aid** package, $12,000 average indebtedness upon graduation, $8.3 million endowment

Students *Undergraduates:* 3,544 full-time, 454 part-time. Students come from 45 states and territories, 36 other countries. *The most frequently chosen baccalaureate fields are:* business/marketing, biological/life sciences, education. *Graduate:* 245 in graduate degree programs.

From out-of-state	38%	Reside on campus	20%
Age 25 or older	18%	Transferred in	12%
International students	2%	African Americans	9%
Asian Americans/Pacific Islanders	1%	Hispanic Americans	1%
Native Americans	0.5%		

Faculty 285 (62% full-time), 56% with terminal degrees.
Expenses (1999–2000) *Tuition, state resident:* full-time $3340; part-time $140 per semester hour. *Tuition, nonresident:* full-time $9280; part-time $385 per semester hour. *Required fees:* $35 per term part-time. Part-time tuition and fees vary according to course load. *College room and board:* $4970. Room and board charges vary according to board plan. *Payment plans:* installment, deferred payment. *Waivers:* senior citizens and employees or children of employees.
Library Kimbel Library. *Operations spending 1999–2000:* $1.1 million. *Collection:* 178,804 titles, 1,279 serial subscriptions, 9,414 audiovisual materials.
College life *Housing:* Option: coed. *Social organizations:* national fraternities, national sororities; 13% of eligible men and 8% of eligible women are members. *Most popular organizations:* Student Government Association, Coastal Productions Board, STAR (Students Taking Active Responsibility), FCA (Fellowship of Christian Athletes), SAM (Society for the Advancement in Management).
Campus security 24-hour emergency response devices and patrols, late-night transport-escort service.
After graduation 45 organizations recruited on campus 1997–98. 62% of class of 1998 had job offers within 6 months. *Career center:* 2 full-time personnel. Services include job fairs, resume preparation, interview workshops, resume referral, career/interest testing, career counseling, careers library, job bank, job interviews. *Graduate education:* 20% of class of 1999 went directly to graduate and professional school.
Freshmen 2,134 applied, 1,607 admitted, 766 enrolled.

Average high school GPA	3.09	SAT verbal scores above 500	59%
SAT math scores above 500	60%	ACT above 18	92%
From top 10% of their h.s. class	11%	From top quarter	48%
From top half	77%	1998 freshmen returning in 1999	66%

Application *Options:* eApply at www.CollegeQuest.com, electronic application, deferred entrance. *Preference* given to state residents. *Application fee:* $25. *Required:* high school transcript; minimum 2.0 GPA. *Recommended:* essay or personal statement; 1 letter of recommendation; interview.
Standardized tests *Admission: Required:* SAT I or ACT.
Significant dates *Application deadlines:* 8/15 (freshmen), 8/15 (transfers). *Notification:* continuous until 8/15 (freshmen). *Financial aid deadline priority date:* 4/1.
Freshman Application Contact
Dr. Judy Vogt, Director of Financial Aid and Admissions, Coastal Carolina University, PO Box 261954, Conway, SC 29528. **Phone:** 843-349-2037. **Toll-free phone:** 800-277-7000. **Fax:** 843-349-2127. **E-mail:** admis@coastal.edu
Visit CollegeQuest.com for information on majors offered and athletics. College video available at CollegeQuest.com.

COKER COLLEGE
Hartsville, South Carolina

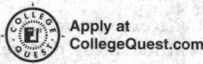 Apply at CollegeQuest.com

- **Independent**, 4-year, founded 1908
- **Degree** bachelor's
- **Small-town** 30-acre campus with easy access to Charlotte
- **Coed**, 975 undergraduate students
- **Moderately difficult** entrance level, 86% of applicants were admitted
- **13:1** student-to-undergraduate faculty ratio
- **$14,552 tuition** and fees
- **$10,996 average financial aid** package, $11,800 average indebtedness upon graduation, $39.9 million endowment

Students *Undergraduates:* Students come from 28 states and territories.

From out-of-state	13%	Reside on campus	31%
Age 25 or older	54%	International students	2%
African Americans	29%	Asian Americans/Pacific Islanders	0.4%
Hispanic Americans	1%	Native Americans	0.3%

Faculty 95 (52% full-time).
Expenses (1999–2000) *Comprehensive fee:* $19,272 includes full-time tuition ($14,352), mandatory fees ($200), and room and board ($4720). *College room only:* $2670. Full-time tuition and fees vary according to location. Room and board charges vary according to housing facility. *Part-time tuition:* $598 per semester hour. *Part-time fees:* $2 per semester hour. Part-time tuition and fees vary according to location. *Payment plan:* installment. *Waivers:* adult students and employees or children of employees.
Library James Lide Coker III Memorial Library plus 1 other. *Operations spending 1999–2000:* $367,013. *Collection:* 80,000 titles, 550 serial subscriptions, 3,400 audiovisual materials.
College life *Housing:* on-campus residence required through junior year. *Options:* coed, men-only, women-only. *Most popular organizations:* Coker College Union, student government, Behavioral Science Club, Sigma Alpha Chi, art club.
Campus security 24-hour patrols, late-night transport-escort service, controlled dormitory access.
After graduation *Career center:* 2 full-time, 1 part-time personnel. Services include job fairs, resume preparation, interview workshops, resume referral, career/interest testing, career counseling, careers library, job bank, job interviews.
Freshmen 459 applied, 394 admitted. 3 valedictorians.

Average high school GPA	3.1	SAT verbal scores above 500	46%
SAT math scores above 500	47%	ACT above 18	N/R
1998 freshmen returning in 1999	73%		

Application *Options:* eApply at www.CollegeQuest.com, Common Application, electronic application, deferred entrance. *Application fee:* $15. *Required:* high school transcript; 1 letter of recommendation. *Required for some:* essay or personal statement; minimum 2.2 GPA; 2 letters of recommendation. *Recommended:* minimum 2.2 GPA; interview.
Standardized tests *Admission: Required:* SAT I or ACT.
Significant dates *Application deadlines:* rolling (freshmen), rolling (transfers). *Notification:* continuous until 8/1 (freshmen). *Financial aid deadline priority date:* 4/1.
Freshman Application Contact
Mr. David Anthony, Director of Admissions, Coker College, 300 East College Avenue, Hartsville, SC 29550. **Phone:** 843-383-8050. **Toll-free phone:** 800-950-1908. **Fax:** 843-383-8056. **E-mail:** admissions@coker.edu
Visit CollegeQuest.com for information on majors offered and athletics. College video available at CollegeQuest.com.

- See page 1446 for a narrative description.

COLLEGE OF CHARLESTON
Charleston, South Carolina

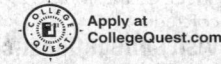 Apply at CollegeQuest.com

- **State-supported**, 4-year, founded 1770
- **Degree** bachelor's (also offers graduate degree programs through University of Charleston, South Carolina)
- **Urban** 52-acre campus
- **Coed**, 9,167 undergraduate students, 93% full-time, 63% women, 37% men

Peterson's Guide to Four-Year Colleges 2001   www.petersons.com

South Carolina

College of Charleston (continued)
- **Moderately difficult** entrance level, 44% of applicants were admitted
- **18:1 student-to-undergraduate faculty ratio**
- **51.8% graduate** in 6 years or less
- **$3520 tuition** and fees (in-state); $7210 (out-of-state)
- **$5644 average financial aid** package, $11,511 average indebtedness upon graduation, $22.9 million endowment

Students at the College of Charleston enjoy one of the most beautiful and historic campuses in the US. It is the oldest institution of higher education in South Carolina and the 13th-oldest in the nation. Specialized and personalized academic programs include an outstanding honors program, preprofessional programs, and national and international exchange programs. Web site: www.cofc.edu.

Students *Undergraduates:* 8,498 full-time, 669 part-time. Students come from 50 states and territories, 65 other countries. *The most frequently chosen baccalaureate fields are:* business/marketing, education, social sciences and history. *Graduate:* 1,911 in graduate degree programs.

From out-of-state	37%	Reside on campus	23%
Age 25 or older	10%	Transferred in	9%
International students	2%	African Americans	8%
Asian Americans/Pacific Islanders	1%	Hispanic Americans	1%
Native Americans	0.2%		

Faculty 743 (66% full-time), 63% with terminal degrees.
Expenses (1999–2000) *Tuition, state resident:* full-time $3520; part-time $147 per semester hour. *Tuition, nonresident:* full-time $7210; part-time $300 per semester hour. *Required fees:* $15 per term part-time. Part-time tuition and fees vary according to course load. *College room and board:* $4070; room only: $2550. Room and board charges vary according to board plan. *Payment plan:* installment. *Waivers:* senior citizens.
Library Robert Scott Small Library plus 1 other. *Operations spending 1999–2000:* $3.4 million. *Collection:* 3,213 serial subscriptions, 3,434 audiovisual materials.
College life *Housing:* Options: coed, men-only, women-only. *Social organizations:* national fraternities, national sororities; 15% of eligible men and 19% of eligible women are members. *Most popular organizations:* Student Government Association, College Activities Board, Black Student Union, Panhellenic Council, Inter-Fraternity Council.
Campus security 24-hour emergency response devices and patrols, student patrols, late-night transport-escort service.
After graduation 164 organizations recruited on campus 1997–98. 95% of class of 1998 had job offers within 6 months. *Career center:* 6 full-time, 1 part-time personnel. Services include job fairs, resume preparation, interview workshops, resume referral, career/interest testing, career counseling, careers library, job bank, job interviews. *Graduate education:* 16% of class of 1999 went directly to graduate and professional school.
Freshmen 7,313 applied, 3,252 admitted, 2,074 enrolled. 20 valedictorians.

Average high school GPA	3.33	SAT verbal scores above 500	90%
SAT math scores above 500	87%	ACT above 18	99%
From top 10% of their h.s. class	28%	From top quarter	59%
From top half	91%	1998 freshmen returning in 1999	81%

Application *Options:* eApply at www.CollegeQuest.com, Common Application, electronic application, early admission, deferred entrance. *Application fee:* $35. *Required:* high school transcript. *Recommended:* essay or personal statement; letters of recommendation.
Standardized tests *Admission: Required:* SAT I or ACT.
Significant dates *Application deadlines:* 6/1 (freshmen), 5/1 (out-of-state freshmen), 6/1 (transfers). *Notification:* continuous until continuous (out-of-state freshmen). *Financial aid deadline priority date:* 3/15.
Freshman Application Contact
Mr. Donald Burkard, Dean of Admissions, College of Charleston, 66 George Street, Charleston, SC 29424-0001. **Phone:** 843-953-5670. **E-mail:** admissions@cofc.edu
Visit CollegeQuest.com for information on majors offered and athletics. College video available at CollegeQuest.com.

COLUMBIA COLLEGE
Columbia, South Carolina

Apply at CollegeQuest.com

- **Independent United Methodist**, comprehensive, founded 1854
- **Degrees** bachelor's and master's
- **Suburban** 33-acre campus
- **Women** only, 1,237 undergraduate students
- **Moderately difficult** entrance level, 80% of applicants were admitted
- **14:1 student-to-undergraduate faculty ratio**
- **58% graduate** in 6 years or less
- **$15,060 tuition** and fees
- **$14,347 average financial aid** package, $22.3 million endowment

Students *Undergraduates:* Students come from 13 states and territories. *The most frequently chosen baccalaureate fields are:* business/marketing, education, personal/miscellaneous services.

From out-of-state	4%	Age 25 or older	23%
International students	0.5%	African Americans	40%
Asian Americans/Pacific Islanders	0.3%	Hispanic Americans	1%

Faculty 171 (54% full-time), 52% with terminal degrees.
Expenses (2000–2001) *Comprehensive fee:* $20,050 includes full-time tuition ($14,760), mandatory fees ($300), and room and board ($4990). Room and board charges vary according to board plan. *Part-time tuition:* $395 per credit. *Part-time fees:* $150 per term. Part-time tuition and fees vary according to course load. *Payment plan:* installment. *Waivers:* employees or children of employees.
Library Edens Library. *Operations spending 1999–2000:* $170,845. *Collection:* 645 serial subscriptions, 8,123 audiovisual materials.
College life *Housing:* Option: women-only.
Campus security 24-hour emergency response devices and patrols, late-night transport-escort service, controlled dormitory access.
After graduation *Career center:* 2 full-time personnel. Services include job fairs, resume preparation, resume referral, career counseling, careers library, job interviews. *Graduate education:* 45% of class of 1999 went directly to graduate and professional school.
Freshmen 891 applied, 714 admitted.

Average high school GPA	3.29	SAT verbal scores above 500	59%
SAT math scores above 500	45%	ACT above 18	N/R
From top 10% of their h.s. class	25%	From top quarter	51%
From top half	82%	1998 freshmen returning in 1999	76%

Application *Options:* eApply at www.CollegeQuest.com, Common Application, early admission, deferred entrance. *Application fee:* $20. *Required:* high school transcript; 3 letters of recommendation. *Required for some:* interview. *Recommended:* minimum 3.0 GPA.
Standardized tests *Admission: Required:* SAT I or ACT.
Significant dates *Application deadlines:* rolling (freshmen), rolling (transfers). *Financial aid deadline priority date:* 4/1.
Freshman Application Contact
Ms. Julie King, Director of Admissions, Columbia College, 1301 Columbia College Drive, Columbia, SC 29203. **Phone:** 803-786-3871. **Toll-free phone:** 800-277-1301. **Fax:** 803-786-3674. **E-mail:** admissions@colacoll.edu
Visit CollegeQuest.com for information on majors offered and athletics. College video available at CollegeQuest.com.

- *See page 1504 for a narrative description.*

COLUMBIA INTERNATIONAL UNIVERSITY
Columbia, South Carolina

- **Independent nondenominational**, comprehensive, founded 1923
- **Degrees** associate, bachelor's, master's, doctoral, and first professional
- **Suburban** 450-acre campus
- **Coed**, 528 undergraduate students, 90% full-time, 56% women, 44% men
- **Minimally difficult** entrance level, 79% of applicants were admitted
- **19:1 student-to-undergraduate faculty ratio**
- **59% graduate** in 6 years or less
- **$8630 tuition** and fees
- **$8.2 million endowment**

Students *Undergraduates:* 477 full-time, 51 part-time. Students come from 39 states and territories, 15 other countries. *The most frequently chosen*

South Carolina

baccalaureate field is: philosophy. **Graduate:** 118 in professional programs, 354 in other graduate degree programs.

From out-of-state	45%	Reside on campus	44%
Age 25 or older	15%	Transferred in	14%
International students	4%	African Americans	4%
Asian Americans/Pacific Islanders	1%	Hispanic Americans	0.2%

Faculty 44 (39% full-time), 25% with terminal degrees.

Expenses (1999–2000) *Comprehensive fee:* $13,010 includes full-time tuition ($8470), mandatory fees ($160), and room and board ($4380). Full-time tuition and fees vary according to course load. Room and board charges vary according to board plan and housing facility. *Part-time tuition:* $355 per semester hour. Part-time tuition and fees vary according to course load. *Payment plan:* installment. *Waivers:* employees or children of employees.

Library G. Allen Fleece Library. *Operations spending 1999–2000:* $415,533. *Collection:* 99,052 titles, 425 serial subscriptions, 6,781 audiovisual materials.

College life *Housing:* Options: men-only, women-only, disabled students. *Most popular organizations:* Student Missions Connection, Student Association, Married Student Association, International Student Organization.

Campus security 24-hour emergency response devices and patrols, late-night transport-escort service.

After graduation *Career center:* 2 part-time personnel. Services include resume preparation, resume referral, career counseling, careers library, job interviews.

Freshmen 235 applied, 185 admitted, 131 enrolled.

Average high school GPA	3.23	SAT verbal scores above 500	N/R
SAT math scores above 500	N/R	ACT above 18	N/R
From top 10% of their h.s. class	18%	From top quarter	40%
From top half	66%	1998 freshmen returning in 1999	67%

Application *Options:* Common Application, electronic application, deferred entrance. *Application fee:* $25. *Required:* essay or personal statement; high school transcript; minimum 2.0 GPA; 4 letters of recommendation. *Required for some:* interview.

Standardized tests *Admission: Required for some:* SAT I, SAT I or ACT.

Significant dates *Application deadlines:* rolling (freshmen), rolling (transfers). **Financial aid deadline priority date:** 3/1.

Freshman Application Contact
Mr. Lawrence M. Dabeck, Director of College Admissions, Columbia International University, P.O. Box 3122, 7435 Monticello Road, Columbia, SC 29230-3122. **Phone:** 803-754-4100 Ext. 3024. **Toll-free phone:** 800-777-2227 Ext. 3024. **Fax:** 803-786-4209. **E-mail:** yesciu@ciu.edu

Visit CollegeQuest.com for information on majors offered and athletics.

■ *See page 1510 for a narrative description.*

CONVERSE COLLEGE
Spartanburg, South Carolina

 Apply at CollegeQuest.com

- **Independent**, comprehensive, founded 1889
- **Degrees** bachelor's, master's, and post-master's certificates
- **Urban** 70-acre campus
- **Women** only, 744 undergraduate students, 89% full-time
- **Moderately difficult** entrance level, 77% of applicants were admitted
- **10:1** student-to-undergraduate faculty ratio
- **53.8% graduate** in 6 years or less
- **$15,230 tuition** and fees
- **$13,770 average financial aid** package, $14,886 average indebtedness upon graduation, $43 million endowment

Students *Undergraduates:* 660 full-time, 84 part-time. Students come from 26 states and territories. *The most frequently chosen baccalaureate fields are:* education, business/marketing, visual/performing arts. **Graduate:** 759 in graduate degree programs.

From out-of-state	29%	Reside on campus	90%
Age 25 or older	19%	Transferred in	5%
International students	0.3%	African Americans	12%
Asian Americans/Pacific Islanders	1%	Hispanic Americans	2%
Native Americans	0.3%		

Faculty 90 (78% full-time), 86% with terminal degrees.

Expenses (1999–2000) *Comprehensive fee:* $19,875 includes full-time tuition ($15,230) and room and board ($4645). Full-time tuition and fees vary according to program. *Part-time tuition:* $490 per credit hour. Part-time tuition and fees vary according to program. *Payment plan:* installment. *Waivers:* adult students, senior citizens, and employees or children of employees.

Library Mickel Library. *Operations spending 1999–2000:* $534,583. *Collection:* 129,411 titles, 1,467 serial subscriptions, 30,132 audiovisual materials.

College life *Housing:* on-campus residence required through senior year. *Option:* women-only. *Most popular organizations:* student government, student volunteer services, Student Christian Organization, Student Activities Committee, Athletic Association.

Campus security 24-hour emergency response devices and patrols, late-night transport-escort service, controlled dormitory access.

After graduation *Career center:* 3 full-time personnel. Services include job fairs, resume preparation, resume referral, career counseling, careers library, job bank, job interviews. **Graduate education:** 27% of class of 1999 went directly to graduate and professional school: 10% education, 5% business, 5% graduate arts and sciences, 3% law, 2% medicine, 1% theology.

Freshmen 622 applied, 477 admitted, 173 enrolled.

Average high school GPA	3.48	SAT verbal scores above 500	88%
SAT math scores above 500	74%	ACT above 18	89%
From top 10% of their h.s. class	46%	From top quarter	71%
From top half	88%	1998 freshmen returning in 1999	71%

Application *Options:* eApply at www.CollegeQuest.com, electronic application, early admission, early decision, early action, deferred entrance. *Application fee:* $35. *Required:* essay or personal statement; high school transcript; minimum 2.00 GPA. *Required for some:* 1 letter of recommendation. *Recommended:* minimum 2.50 GPA; interview.

Standardized tests *Admission: Required:* SAT I or ACT.

Significant dates *Application deadlines:* 8/1 (freshmen), 8/1 (transfers). *Early decision:* 11/15, 6/25. *Notification:* continuous until 8/15 (freshmen), 1/1 (early decision), 7/1 (early action). **Financial aid deadline:** continuous.

Freshman Application Contact
Mr. C. Ray Tatum, Vice President for Enrollment, Converse College, 580 East Main Street, Spartanburg, SC 29302-0006. **Phone:** 864-596-9040 Ext. 9041. **Toll-free phone:** 800-766-1125. **Fax:** 864-596-9158.

Visit CollegeQuest.com for information on majors offered and athletics. College video available at CollegeQuest.com.

■ *See page 1532 for a narrative description.*

ERSKINE COLLEGE
Due West, South Carolina

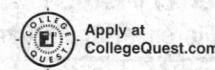 Apply at CollegeQuest.com

- **Independent**, 4-year, founded 1839, affiliated with Associate Reformed Presbyterian Church
- **Degree** bachelor's
- **Rural** 85-acre campus
- **Coed**, 517 undergraduate students, 99% full-time, 59% women, 41% men
- **Moderately difficult** entrance level, 81% of applicants were admitted
- **13:1** student-to-undergraduate faculty ratio
- **67% graduate** in 6 years or less
- **$15,229 tuition** and fees
- **$13,100 average financial aid** package, $13,125 average indebtedness upon graduation, $29 million endowment

Students *Undergraduates:* 510 full-time, 7 part-time. Students come from 9 states and territories, 4 other countries. *The most frequently chosen baccalaureate fields are:* biological/life sciences, business/marketing, social sciences and history.

From out-of-state	22%	Reside on campus	89%
Age 25 or older	1%	Transferred in	4%
International students	1%	African Americans	6%
Asian Americans/Pacific Islanders	1%	Hispanic Americans	1%

Faculty 41 (88% full-time), 78% with terminal degrees.

Expenses (1999–2000) *Comprehensive fee:* $19,998 includes full-time tuition ($14,269), mandatory fees ($960), and room and board ($4769). Room and board charges vary according to board plan and housing facility. *Part-time tuition:* $255 per semester hour. *Payment plan:* installment. *Waivers:* children of alumni and employees or children of employees.

Library McCain Library plus 1 other. *Operations spending 1999–2000:* $333,697. *Collection:* 205,799 titles, 802 serial subscriptions, 916 audiovisual materials.

South Carolina

Erskine College (continued)

College life *Housing:* on-campus residence required through senior year. *Options:* men-only, women-only. *Social organizations:* local fraternities, local sororities, Little Sisters; 22% of eligible men and 20% of eligible women are members. *Most popular organizations:* literary societies, religious organizations, student government organization, publications, honor societies.

Campus security 24-hour patrols, late-night transport-escort service, controlled dormitory access.

After graduation 41 organizations recruited on campus 1997–98. 76% of class of 1998 had job offers within 6 months. *Career center:* 1 full-time, 1 part-time personnel. Services include job fairs, resume preparation, interview workshops, resume referral, career counseling, careers library, job bank, job interviews.

Freshmen 616 applied, 498 admitted, 159 enrolled. 2 National Merit Scholars, 10 valedictorians.

SAT verbal scores above 500	70%	SAT math scores above 500	69%
ACT above 18	N/R	From top 10% of their h.s. class	37%
From top quarter	60%	From top half	88%
1998 freshmen returning in 1999	85%		

Application *Options:* eApply at www.CollegeQuest.com, electronic application. *Preference* given to members of Associate Reformed Presbyterian Church. *Application fee:* $15. *Required:* high school transcript; 1 letter of recommendation. *Required for some:* essay or personal statement; interview. *Recommended:* interview.

Standardized tests *Admission: Required:* SAT I or ACT. *Required for some:* SAT II Subject Tests.

Significant dates *Application deadlines:* rolling (freshmen), rolling (transfers). *Financial aid deadline:* 6/30. *Priority date:* 4/1.

Freshman Application Contact
Mr. Jeff Craft, Director of Admissions, Erskine College, PO Box 176, Due West, SC 29639. **Phone:** 864-379-8830. **Toll-free phone:** 800-241-8721. **Fax:** 864-379-8759. **E-mail:** admissions@erskine.edu

Visit CollegeQuest.com for information on majors offered and athletics.

■ *See page 1642 for a narrative description.*

FRANCIS MARION UNIVERSITY
Florence, South Carolina

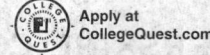 Apply at CollegeQuest.com

- **State-supported**, comprehensive, founded 1970
- **Degrees** bachelor's and master's
- **Rural** 309-acre campus
- **Coed**, 2,923 undergraduate students, 87% full-time, 59% women, 41% men
- **Moderately difficult** entrance level, 80% of applicants were admitted
- **16:1** student-to-undergraduate faculty ratio
- **34% graduate** in 6 years or less
- **$3470 tuition** and fees (in-state); $6730 (out-of-state)

Students *Undergraduates:* Students come from 32 states and territories, 33 other countries. *The most frequently chosen baccalaureate fields are:* business/marketing, education, social sciences and history. *Graduate:* 891 in graduate degree programs.

From out-of-state	9%	Reside on campus	36%
Age 25 or older	15%	International students	2%
African Americans	31%	Asian Americans/Pacific Islanders	1%
Hispanic Americans	1%	Native Americans	0.4%

Faculty 201 (79% full-time).

Expenses (1999–2000) *Tuition, state resident:* full-time $3260; part-time $163 per credit hour. *Tuition, nonresident:* full-time $6520; part-time $326 per credit hour. *Required fees:* full-time $210; $6 per credit hour; $30 per term part-time. Full-time tuition and fees vary according to course load. Part-time tuition and fees vary according to course load. *College room and board:* $3550. Room and board charges vary according to board plan and housing facility. *Waivers:* senior citizens and employees or children of employees.

Library James A. Rogers Library plus 1 other. *Collection:* 305,352 titles, 1,691 serial subscriptions.

College life *Housing:* Option: coed. *Social organizations:* national fraternities, national sororities, local fraternities, local sororities; 12% of eligible men and 9% of eligible women are members. *Most popular organizations:* Baptist Student Union, education club, University Ambassadors.

Campus security 24-hour emergency response devices and patrols, late-night transport-escort service, controlled dormitory access.

After graduation 80 organizations recruited on campus 1997–98. 90% of class of 1998 had job offers within 6 months. *Career center:* 2 full-time, 1 part-time personnel. Services include job fairs, resume preparation, interview workshops, resume referral, career/interest testing, career counseling, careers library, job bank, job interviews.

Freshmen 1,520 applied, 1,216 admitted.

Average high school GPA	2.81	SAT verbal scores above 500	N/R
SAT math scores above 500	N/R	ACT above 18	N/R
From top 10% of their h.s. class	14%	From top quarter	34%
From top half	71%	1998 freshmen returning in 1999	75%

Application *Options:* eApply at www.CollegeQuest.com, Common Application, electronic application, early admission, deferred entrance. *Application fee:* $25. *Required:* high school transcript. *Recommended:* letters of recommendation.

Standardized tests *Admission: Required:* SAT I or ACT.

Significant dates *Application deadlines:* rolling (freshmen), rolling (transfers). *Financial aid deadline priority date:* 3/1.

Freshman Application Contact
Mr. Mark D'Amico, Director of Admissions, Francis Marion University, Box 100547, Florence, SC 29501-0547. **Phone:** 843-661-1231. **Toll-free phone:** 800-368-7551. **Fax:** 843-661-4635. **E-mail:** admission@fmarion.edu

Visit CollegeQuest.com for information on majors offered and athletics. College video available at CollegeQuest.com.

■ *See page 1692 for a narrative description.*

FURMAN UNIVERSITY
Greenville, South Carolina

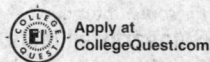 Apply at CollegeQuest.com

- **Independent**, comprehensive, founded 1826
- **Degrees** bachelor's and master's
- **Suburban** 750-acre campus
- **Coed**, 2,812 undergraduate students, 92% full-time, 55% women, 45% men
- **Very difficult** entrance level, 66% of applicants were admitted
- **12:1** student-to-undergraduate faculty ratio
- **75% graduate** in 6 years or less
- **$18,266 tuition** and fees
- **$14,200 average financial aid** package, $11,750 average indebtedness upon graduation, $216.1 million endowment

Students *Undergraduates:* 2,594 full-time, 218 part-time. Students come from 45 states and territories. *The most frequently chosen baccalaureate fields are:* business/marketing, education, social sciences and history. *Graduate:* 613 in graduate degree programs.

From out-of-state	66%	Reside on campus	92%
Age 25 or older	1%	Transferred in	1%
International students	1%	African Americans	5%
Asian Americans/Pacific Islanders	2%	Hispanic Americans	1%
Native Americans	0.1%		

Faculty 210 (95% full-time), 92% with terminal degrees.

Expenses (1999–2000) *Comprehensive fee:* $23,114 includes full-time tuition ($17,888), mandatory fees ($378), and room and board ($4848). *College room only:* $2584. Room and board charges vary according to board plan and housing facility. *Part-time tuition:* $559 per credit hour. *Part-time fees:* $200 per term part-time. Part-time tuition and fees vary according to course load. *Payment plan:* installment. *Waivers:* employees or children of employees.

Library James Buchanan Duke Library plus 2 others. *Operations spending 1999–2000:* $2.1 million. *Collection:* 339,415 titles, 2,464 serial subscriptions, 3,850 audiovisual materials.

College life *Housing:* on-campus residence required through junior year. *Options:* coed, men-only, women-only. *Social organizations:* national fraternities, national sororities; 30% of eligible men and 35% of eligible women are members. *Most popular organizations:* Collegiate Educational Service Corps, Fellowship of Christian Athletes, Baptist Student Union, Furman University Student Activities Board, Furman Singers.

South Carolina

Campus security 24-hour emergency response devices and patrols, student patrols, late-night transport-escort service, controlled dormitory access.
After graduation 89 organizations recruited on campus 1997–98. 64% of class of 1998 had job offers within 6 months. *Career center:* 4 full-time personnel. Services include job fairs, resume preparation, interview workshops, resume referral, career/interest testing, career counseling, careers library, job bank, job interviews. *Graduate education:* 32% of class of 1999 went directly to graduate and professional school; 19% graduate arts and sciences, 5% law, 2% business, 2% medicine, 2% theology, 1% dentistry, 1% veterinary medicine.
Freshmen 3,200 applied, 2,102 admitted, 684 enrolled. 40 National Merit Scholars, 50 valedictorians, 164 student government officers.

Average high school GPA	3.5	SAT verbal scores above 500	97%
SAT math scores above 500	94%	ACT above 18	100%
From top 10% of their h.s. class	64%	From top quarter	87%
From top half	98%	1998 freshmen returning in 1999	92%

Application *Options:* eApply at www.CollegeQuest.com, Common Application, electronic application, early admission, early decision. *Preference* given to children of alumni. *Application fee:* $40. *Required:* essay or personal statement; high school transcript. *Recommended:* minimum 3.0 GPA; 2 letters of recommendation.
Standardized tests *Admission: Required:* SAT I or ACT. *Required for some:* SAT II Subject Tests.
Significant dates *Application deadlines:* 2/1 (freshmen), 8/1 (transfers). *Early decision:* 12/1. *Notification:* 3/15 (freshmen), 12/30 (early decision). *Financial aid deadline priority date:* 2/1.
Freshman Application Contact
Mr. David R. O'Cain, Director of Admissions, Furman University, 3300 Poinsett Highway, Greenville, SC 29613. **Phone:** 864-294-2034. **Fax:** 864-294-3127. **E-mail:** admissions@furman.edu
Visit CollegeQuest.com for information on majors offered and athletics. College video available at CollegeQuest.com.

JOHNSON & WALES UNIVERSITY
Charleston, South Carolina

- **Independent**, 4-year, founded 1984
- **Degrees** associate and bachelor's
- **Urban** campus
- **Coed**
- **Minimally difficult** entrance level

Institutional Web site http://www.jwu.edu/
College life *Housing:* on-campus residence required in freshman year. *Option:* coed. *Most popular organizations:* Delta Epsilon Chi, Black Student Union, Gourmet Club, gospel choir.
Campus security 24-hour emergency response devices, late-night transport-escort service, controlled dormitory access.
Application *Options:* Common Application, early admission, deferred entrance. *Application fee:* $0. *Required:* high school transcript. *Required for some:* minimum 2.0 GPA. *Recommended:* essay or personal statement; letters of recommendation; interview.
Standardized tests *Admission: Required for some:* SAT I or ACT.
Admissions Office Contact
Johnson & Wales University, PCC Box 1409, 701 East Bay Street, Charleston, SC 29403. **Toll-free phone:** 800-868-1522. **Fax:** 843-763-0318. **E-mail:** admissions@jwu.edu
Visit CollegeQuest.com for information on athletics. College video and electronic viewbook available at CollegeQuest.com.

LANDER UNIVERSITY
Greenwood, South Carolina

- **State-supported**, comprehensive, founded 1872
- **Degrees** bachelor's and master's
- **Small-town** 100-acre campus
- **Coed**, 2,385 undergraduate students, 89% full-time, 63% women, 37% men
- **Moderately difficult** entrance level, 85% of applicants were admitted
- **16:1** student-to-undergraduate faculty ratio
- **41.5% graduate** in 6 years or less
- **$3820 tuition** and fees (in-state); $8718 (out-of-state)

Part of South Carolina Commission on Higher Education.
Students *Undergraduates:* 2,125 full-time, 260 part-time. Students come from 27 states and territories, 20 other countries. *Graduate:* 412 in graduate degree programs.

Reside on campus	40%	Age 25 or older	26%
Transferred in	7%	International students	2%
African Americans	19%	Asian Americans/Pacific Islanders	1%
Hispanic Americans	1%	Native Americans	0.2%

Expenses (1999–2000) *Tuition, state resident:* full-time $3770. *Tuition, nonresident:* full-time $8668. *Required fees:* full-time $50. *College room and board:* $3855. Room and board charges vary according to board plan and housing facility. *Payment plan:* installment. *Waivers:* senior citizens.
Library Jackson Library. *Collection:* 148,341 titles, 876 serial subscriptions.
College life *Housing: Option:* coed. *Social organizations:* national fraternities, national sororities, local fraternities, local sororities; 20% of eligible men and 20% of eligible women are members.
Campus security 24-hour emergency response devices, late-night transport-escort service, controlled dormitory access.
After graduation 100 organizations recruited on campus 1997–98. *Career center:* 1 full-time personnel. Services include job fairs, resume preparation, resume referral, career counseling, careers library.
Freshmen 1,438 applied, 1,227 admitted, 497 enrolled.

SAT verbal scores above 500	N/R	SAT math scores above 500	N/R
ACT above 18	N/R	From top 10% of their h.s. class	21%
From top quarter	48%	From top half	87%
1998 freshmen returning in 1999	67%		

Application *Options:* eApply at www.CollegeQuest.com, Common Application, early admission, deferred entrance. *Application fee:* $25. *Required:* high school transcript; 1 letter of recommendation. *Recommended:* interview.
Standardized tests *Admission: Required:* SAT I or ACT.
Significant dates *Application deadlines:* rolling (freshmen), rolling (transfers). *Financial aid deadline:* continuous.
Freshman Application Contact
Mr. Jeffrey A. Constant, Assistant Director of Admissions, Lander University, 320 Stanley Avenue, Greenwood, SC 29649-2099. **Phone:** 864-388-8307. **Toll-free phone:** 888-452-6337. **Fax:** 864-388-8125. **E-mail:** admissions@lander.edu
Visit CollegeQuest.com for information on majors offered and athletics.

LIMESTONE COLLEGE
Gaffney, South Carolina

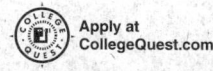

- **Independent**, 4-year, founded 1845
- **Degrees** associate and bachelor's
- **Small-town** 115-acre campus with easy access to Charlotte
- **Coed**, 1,994 undergraduate students, 53% full-time, 50% women, 50% men
- **Minimally difficult** entrance level, 78% of applicants were admitted
- **12:1** student-to-undergraduate faculty ratio
- **28% graduate** in 6 years or less
- **$10,100 tuition** and fees
- **$5659 average financial aid** package, $6339 average indebtedness upon graduation, $5.1 million endowment

Founded in 1845, Limestone is a private, coeducational liberal arts college that maintains a small student body and a well-qualified faculty, creating an atmosphere that assures intellectual, social, ethical, and physical development of students. With a student-faculty ratio of 11:1, Limestone provides the individual attention often lacking in larger institutions.

Students *Undergraduates:* 1,060 full-time, 934 part-time. Students come from 24 states and territories, 3 other countries. *The most frequently chosen baccalaureate fields are:* business/marketing, computer/information sciences, social sciences and history.

Peterson's Guide to Four-Year Colleges 2001 www.petersons.com

South Carolina

Limestone College (continued)

From out-of-state	14%	Reside on campus	52%
Age 25 or older	67%	Transferred in	16%
International students	0.4%	African Americans	29%
Asian Americans/Pacific Islanders	1%	Hispanic Americans	1%
Native Americans	0.4%		

Faculty 191 (26% full-time), 39% with terminal degrees.

Expenses (2000–2001) *Comprehensive fee:* $14,900 includes full-time tuition ($10,100) and room and board ($4800). *College room only:* $2400. Full-time tuition and fees vary according to class time, course load, and program. *Part-time tuition:* $421 per semester hour. Part-time tuition and fees vary according to class time and program. *Payment plan:* installment. *Waivers:* employees or children of employees.

Library A. J. Eastwood Library. *Operations spending 1999–2000:* $126,213. *Collection:* 60,000 titles, 249 serial subscriptions, 2,161 audiovisual materials.

College life *Housing:* on-campus residence required through junior year. *Options:* men-only, women-only. *Social organizations:* local sororities; 6% of women are members. *Most popular organizations:* Fellowship of Christian Athletes, Student Government Association, Delta Chi Sigma, KDK, Student Ambassadors.

Campus security 24-hour emergency response devices and patrols, late-night transport-escort service.

After graduation 8 organizations recruited on campus 1997–98. *Career center:* 1 full-time personnel. Services include job fairs, resume preparation, interview workshops, resume referral, career/interest testing, career counseling, careers library, job bank, job interviews.

Freshmen 482 applied, 374 admitted, 475 enrolled.

Average high school GPA	2.9	SAT verbal scores above 500	68%
SAT math scores above 500	N/R	ACT above 18	63%
From top 10% of their h.s. class	6%	From top quarter	27%
From top half	42%	1998 freshmen returning in 1999	63%

Application *Options:* eApply at www.CollegeQuest.com, Common Application, electronic application. *Application fee:* $25. *Required:* high school transcript; minimum 2.0 GPA. *Recommended:* 2 letters of recommendation; interview.

Standardized tests *Admission: Required:* SAT I or ACT.

Significant dates *Application deadlines:* rolling (freshmen), rolling (transfers). *Financial aid deadline priority date:* 5/1.

Freshman Application Contact
Ms. Terry Capps, Administrative Assistant-Admissions, Limestone College, Limestone College, 1115 College Drive, Gaffney, SC 29340-3799. **Phone:** 864-489-7151 Ext. 554. **Toll-free phone:** 800-795-7151 Ext. 554 (in-state); 800-795-7151 Ext. 553 (out-of-state). **Fax:** 864-487-8706. **E-mail:** cphenicie@limestone.edu

Visit CollegeQuest.com for information on majors offered and athletics.

■ *See page 1926 for a narrative description.*

MEDICAL UNIVERSITY OF SOUTH CAROLINA
Charleston, South Carolina

- **State-supported**, upper-level, founded 1824
- **Degrees** bachelor's, master's, doctoral, first professional, post-master's, and postbachelor's certificates
- **Urban** 61-acre campus
- **Coed**, 422 undergraduate students, 64% full-time, 82% women, 18% men
- **Very difficult** entrance level, 35% of applicants were admitted
- **$4626 tuition** and fees (in-state); $13,150 (out-of-state)

Students *Undergraduates:* 272 full-time, 150 part-time. Students come from 22 states and territories. *The most frequently chosen baccalaureate field is:* health professions and related sciences. *Graduate:* 968 in professional programs, 993 in other graduate degree programs.

From out-of-state	7%	Age 25 or older	67%
Transferred in	34%	African Americans	12%
Asian Americans/Pacific Islanders	1%	Hispanic Americans	0.5%
Native Americans	1%		

Faculty 1,245 (91% full-time).

Expenses (1999–2000) *One-time required fee:* $160. *Tuition, state resident:* full-time $4450; part-time $197 per hour. *Tuition, nonresident:* full-time $12,974; part-time $588 per hour. *Required fees:* full-time $176; $408 per term part-time. Full-time tuition and fees vary according to program. Part-time tuition and fees vary according to program. *Payment plan:* installment. *Waivers:* senior citizens and employees or children of employees.

Library Medical University of South Carolina Library plus 1 other. *Collection:* 204,896 titles, 2,462 serial subscriptions, 6,590 audiovisual materials.

College life *Housing:* college housing not available. *Social organizations:* national fraternities, national sororities.

Campus security 24-hour emergency response devices and patrols, late-night transport-escort service.

After graduation 97% of class of 1998 had job offers within 6 months.

Application *Options:* electronic application, deferred entrance. *Preference* given to state residents. *Application fee:* $55.

Standardized tests *Admission: Recommended:* SAT I or ACT. *Required for some:* SAT I or ACT.

Significant dates *Application deadline:* rolling (transfers). *Financial aid deadline priority date:* 4/1.

Freshman Application Contact
Mr. James F. Menzel, Executive Director, Office of Enrollment Services, Medical University of South Carolina, 171 Ashley Avenue, Charleston, SC 29425-0002. **Phone:** 843-792-5396. **Fax:** 843-792-3764.

Visit CollegeQuest.com for information on majors offered and athletics.

MORRIS COLLEGE
Sumter, South Carolina

- **Independent**, 4-year, founded 1908, affiliated with Baptist Educational and Missionary Convention of South Carolina
- **Degree** bachelor's
- **Small-town** 34-acre campus
- **Coed**, 904 undergraduate students, 97% full-time, 67% women, 33% men
- **Minimally difficult** entrance level, 55% of applicants were admitted
- **17:1 student-to-undergraduate faculty ratio**
- **31% graduate** in 6 years or less
- **$5761 tuition** and fees
- **$4.1 million endowment**

Students *Undergraduates:* 880 full-time, 24 part-time. Students come from 16 states and territories. *The most frequently chosen baccalaureate fields are:* business/marketing, communications/communication technologies, protective services/public administration.

From out-of-state	11%	Reside on campus	76%
Age 25 or older	13%	Transferred in	5%
African Americans	99%		

Faculty 66 (65% full-time), 48% with terminal degrees.

Expenses (1999–2000) *Comprehensive fee:* $8712 includes full-time tuition ($5640), mandatory fees ($121), and room and board ($2951). *Part-time tuition:* $235 per credit hour. *Payment plan:* installment.

Library Richardson-Johnson Learning Resources Center. *Operations spending 1999–2000:* $457,242. *Collection:* 393 serial subscriptions, 2,597 audiovisual materials.

College life *Housing: Options:* men-only, women-only. *Social organizations:* national fraternities, national sororities; 7% of eligible men and 12% of eligible women are members. *Most popular organizations:* Student Government Association, New Emphasis on Nontraditional Students, Block ""M" Club, Students of South Carolina Educational Association, Baptist Student Union.

Campus security 24-hour patrols, controlled dormitory access.

After graduation 73 organizations recruited on campus 1997–98. 40% of class of 1998 had job offers within 6 months. *Career center:* 3 full-time personnel. Services include job fairs, resume preparation, resume referral, career counseling, careers library, job interviews.

Freshmen 1,231 applied, 677 admitted, 264 enrolled.

Average high school GPA	2.35	SAT verbal scores above 500	2%
SAT math scores above 500	0%	ACT above 18	N/R
From top 10% of their h.s. class	2%	From top quarter	13%
From top half	36%	1998 freshmen returning in 1999	55%

Application *Option:* deferred entrance. *Application fee:* $10. *Required:* high school transcript; medical examination.

Standardized tests *Admission: Required for some:* SAT I or ACT.
Significant dates *Application deadlines:* rolling (freshmen), rolling (transfers). *Financial aid deadline priority date:* 3/30.
Freshman Application Contact
Mrs. Queen W. Spann, Director of Admissions and Records, Morris College, 100 West College Street, Sumter, SC 29150-3599. **Phone:** 803-934-3225. **Toll-free phone:** 888-775-1345. **Fax:** 803-773-3687.
Visit CollegeQuest.com for information on majors offered and athletics.

NEWBERRY COLLEGE
Newberry, South Carolina

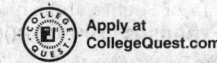 Apply at CollegeQuest.com

- **Independent Lutheran**, 4-year, founded 1856
- **Degree** bachelor's
- **Small-town** 60-acre campus
- **Coed**, 706 undergraduate students, 96% full-time, 45% women, 55% men
- **Moderately difficult** entrance level, 87% of applicants were admitted
- **12:1 student-to-undergraduate faculty ratio**
- **$13,952 tuition** and fees
- **$12 million endowment**

Newberry College has the only bachelor's-level veterinary technology program in the southeastern US, an innovative general honors program, a communications program with a television studio and cable channel, a major in sports management, a professional writing and editing minor, exceptional teacher education and music programs, a beautiful campus, small classes, strong athletic programs, and a family-like environment.

Students *Undergraduates:* 676 full-time, 30 part-time. Students come from 24 states and territories, 4 other countries. *The most frequently chosen baccalaureate fields are:* business/marketing, education, social sciences and history.

From out-of-state	16%	Reside on campus	78%
Age 25 or older	9%	Transferred in	6%
International students	1%	African Americans	18%
Asian Americans/Pacific Islanders	0.3%	Hispanic Americans	1%
Native Americans	0.4%		

Faculty 71 (69% full-time), 59% with terminal degrees.
Expenses (1999–2000) *One-time required fee:* $100. *Comprehensive fee:* $17,952 includes full-time tuition ($13,602), mandatory fees ($350), and room and board ($4000). *College room only:* $1730. Room and board charges vary according to board plan and housing facility. *Part-time tuition:* $185 per semester hour. *Part-time fees:* $30 per term part-time. *Payment plan:* installment. *Waivers:* employees or children of employees.
Library Wessels Library. *Operations spending 1999–2000:* $249,720. *Collection:* 90,763 titles, 422 serial subscriptions.
College life *Housing:* on-campus residence required through sophomore year. *Options:* coed, men-only, women-only. *Social organizations:* national fraternities, national sororities; 30% of eligible men and 31% of eligible women are members. *Most popular organizations:* Fellowship of Christian Athletes (FCA), Metoka Galeda (gospel choir and service group), Lutheran Student Movement (LSM), Baptist Student Union (BSU), Students Organized for Community Service (SOCS).
Campus security 24-hour patrols.
After graduation 28 organizations recruited on campus 1997–98. 95% of class of 1998 had job offers within 6 months. *Career center:* 1 full-time, 1 part-time personnel. Services include job fairs, resume preparation, resume referral, career counseling, careers library, job bank, job interviews. *Graduate education:* 26% of class of 1999 went directly to graduate and professional school: 15% graduate arts and sciences, 3% education, 3% law, 3% theology, 2% business.
Freshmen 685 applied, 593 admitted, 179 enrolled.

SAT verbal scores above 500	37%	SAT math scores above 500	38%
ACT above 18	56%	From top 10% of their h.s. class	13%
From top quarter	37%	From top half	69%
1998 freshmen returning in 1999	65%		

Application *Options:* eApply at www.CollegeQuest.com, early admission, deferred entrance. *Application fee:* $30. *Required:* high school transcript; minimum 2.0 GPA. *Required for some:* essay or personal statement. *Recommended:* 2 letters of recommendation; interview.

Standardized tests *Admission: Required:* SAT I or ACT.
Significant dates *Application deadlines:* rolling (freshmen), rolling (transfers). *Financial aid deadline priority date:* 3/1.
Freshman Application Contact
Mr. Jonathan Reece, Director of Admissions, Newberry College, 2100 College Street, Smeltzer Hall, Newberry, SC 29108. **Phone:** 803-321-5127. **Toll-free phone:** 800-845-4955 Ext. 5127. **E-mail:** admissions@newberry.edu
Visit CollegeQuest.com for information on majors offered and athletics.

■ *See page 2140 for a narrative description.*

NORTH GREENVILLE COLLEGE
Tigerville, South Carolina

- **Independent Southern Baptist**, 4-year, founded 1892
- **Degrees** associate and bachelor's
- **Rural** 500-acre campus with easy access to Greenville
- **Coed**, 1,212 undergraduate students, 91% full-time, 45% women, 55% men
- **Minimally difficult** entrance level, 86% of applicants were admitted
- **$7650 tuition** and fees
- **$8100 average financial aid** package, $9.1 million endowment

Students *Undergraduates:* 1,099 full-time, 113 part-time. Students come from 19 states and territories, 14 other countries. *The most frequently chosen baccalaureate fields are:* education, business/marketing, philosophy.

From out-of-state	11%	Reside on campus	65%
Age 25 or older	13%	Transferred in	10%
International students	1%	African Americans	12%
Asian Americans/Pacific Islanders	0.2%	Hispanic Americans	1%
Native Americans	0.1%		

Faculty 101 (55% full-time).
Expenses (1999–2000) *Comprehensive fee:* $12,150 includes full-time tuition ($7550), mandatory fees ($100), and room and board ($4500). *Part-time tuition:* $175 per hour. *Part-time fees:* $50 per term part-time. Part-time tuition and fees vary according to course load. *Payment plan:* installment. *Waivers:* employees or children of employees.
Library Hester Memorial Library. *Operations spending 1999–2000:* $231,632. *Collection:* 46,870 titles, 500 serial subscriptions, 4,170 audiovisual materials.
College life *Housing:* on-campus residence required through sophomore year. *Options:* men-only, women-only. *Most popular organizations:* Baptist Student Union, Fellowship of Christians in Service, Fellowship of Christian Athletes, Black Student Fellowship, Education Club.
Campus security 24-hour emergency response devices and patrols, controlled dormitory access.
After graduation 8 organizations recruited on campus 1997–98. 75% of class of 1998 had job offers within 6 months. *Career center:* 1 full-time personnel. Services include job fairs, resume preparation, interview workshops, resume referral, career counseling, careers library, job bank, job interviews. *Graduate education:* 16% of class of 1999 went directly to graduate and professional school.
Freshmen 963 applied, 832 admitted, 348 enrolled.

SAT verbal scores above 500	45%	SAT math scores above 500	40%
ACT above 18	61%	From top half of their h.s. class	65%
1998 freshmen returning in 1999	65%		

Application *Options:* electronic application, early admission, deferred entrance. *Preference* given to Baptists. *Application fee:* $20. *Required:* high school transcript. *Recommended:* minimum 2.0 GPA.
Standardized tests *Admission: Required:* SAT I or ACT. *Recommended:* CPT. *Required for some:* CPT.
Significant dates *Application deadlines:* 8/24 (freshmen), 8/24 (transfers). *Notification:* continuous until 8/24 (freshmen). *Financial aid deadline priority date:* 6/30.
Freshman Application Contact
Mr. Buddy Freeman, Executive Director of Admissions, North Greenville College, PO Box 1892, Tigerville, SC 29688-1892. **Phone:** 864-977-7052. **Toll-free phone:** 800-468-6642. **Fax:** 864-977-7177. **E-mail:** bfreeman@ngc.edu
Visit CollegeQuest.com for information on majors offered and athletics. College video and electronic viewbook available at CollegeQuest.com.

South Carolina

PRESBYTERIAN COLLEGE 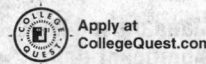 Apply at CollegeQuest.com
Clinton, South Carolina

- **Independent Presbyterian**, 4-year, founded 1880
- **Degree** bachelor's
- **Small-town** 215-acre campus with easy access to Greenville—Spartanburg
- **Coed**, 1,100 undergraduate students, 97% full-time, 52% women, 48% men
- **Very difficult** entrance level, 81% of applicants were admitted
- **12:1 student-to-undergraduate faculty ratio**
- **78% graduate** in 6 years or less
- **$16,524 tuition** and fees
- **$15,331 average financial aid** package, $13,113 average indebtedness upon graduation, $79 million endowment

Students *Undergraduates:* 1,068 full-time, 32 part-time. Students come from 26 states and territories. *The most frequently chosen baccalaureate fields are:* business/marketing, biological/life sciences, social sciences and history.

From out-of-state	43%	Reside on campus	85%
Age 25 or older	1%	Transferred in	1%
African Americans	5%	Asian Americans/Pacific Islanders	0.3%
Hispanic Americans	0.4%	Native Americans	0.1%

Faculty 89 (87% full-time), 83% with terminal degrees.

Expenses (1999–2000) *Comprehensive fee:* $21,174 includes full-time tuition ($15,122), mandatory fees ($1402), and room and board ($4650). *College room only:* $2196. Room and board charges vary according to board plan. *Part-time tuition:* $630 per semester hour. *Part-time fees:* $8 per semester hour; $15 per term part-time. *Payment plans:* tuition prepayment, installment. *Waivers:* senior citizens and employees or children of employees.

Library James H. Thomason Library. *Operations spending 1999–2000:* $658,414. *Collection:* 165,159 titles, 787 serial subscriptions, 6,220 audiovisual materials.

College life *Housing:* on-campus residence required through senior year. *Options:* men-only, women-only. *Social organizations:* national fraternities, national sororities, minority social club; 44% of eligible men and 41% of eligible women are members. *Most popular organizations:* Student Volunteer Services, intramurals, Greek system, Student Union Board, Fellowship of Christian Athletes.

Campus security 24-hour emergency response devices and patrols, late-night transport-escort service, controlled dormitory access.

After graduation 45 organizations recruited on campus 1997–98. 76% of class of 1998 had job offers within 6 months. *Career center:* 3 full-time personnel. Services include job fairs, resume preparation, resume referral, career/interest testing, career counseling, careers library, job bank, job interviews.

Freshmen 994 applied, 807 admitted, 333 enrolled. 19 class presidents, 5 valedictorians, 120 student government officers.

Average high school GPA	3.3	SAT verbal scores above 500	81%
SAT math scores above 500	81%	ACT above 18	100%
From top 10% of their h.s. class	36%	From top quarter	65%
From top half	90%	1998 freshmen returning in 1999	87%

Application *Options:* eApply at www.CollegeQuest.com, electronic application, early action, deferred entrance. *Application fee:* $30. *Required:* essay or personal statement; high school transcript; 1 letter of recommendation. *Recommended:* interview.

Standardized tests *Admission: Required:* SAT I or ACT.

Significant dates *Application deadlines:* 4/1 (freshmen), 7/1 (transfers). *Early action:* 12/5. *Notification:* continuous until 6/1 (freshmen), 1/31 (early action). *Financial aid deadline priority date:* 3/1.

Freshman Application Contact
Mr. Richard Dana Paul, Vice President of Enrollment and Dean of Admissions, Presbyterian College, South Broad Street, Clinton, SC 29325. **Phone:** 864-833-8229. **Toll-free phone:** 800-476-7272. **Fax:** 864-833-8481. **E-mail:** rdpaul@admin.presby.edu

Visit CollegeQuest.com for information on majors offered and athletics. College video available at CollegeQuest.com.

■ *See page 2288 for a narrative description.*

SOUTH CAROLINA STATE UNIVERSITY 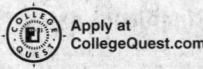 Apply at CollegeQuest.com
Orangeburg, South Carolina

- **State-supported**, comprehensive, founded 1896
- **Degrees** bachelor's, master's, and doctoral
- **Small-town** 160-acre campus
- **Coed**
- **Minimally difficult** entrance level
- **$3410 tuition** and fees (in-state); $6702 (out-of-state)

Part of South Carolina Commission on Higher Education.

Expenses (1999–2000) *Tuition, state resident:* full-time $3410; part-time $142 per semester hour. *Tuition, nonresident:* full-time $6702; part-time $279 per semester hour. *College room and board:* $2976; room only: $1486. Room and board charges vary according to board plan and housing facility.

Institutional Web site http://www.scsu.edu/

College life *Housing: Options:* men-only, women-only. *Social organizations:* national fraternities, national sororities, local fraternities, local sororities; 10% of eligible men and 12% of eligible women are members. *Most popular organizations:* student government, Student Union Board, NAACP.

Campus security 24-hour emergency response devices and patrols, late-night transport-escort service, controlled dormitory access.

Application *Options:* eApply at www.CollegeQuest.com, Common Application, deferred entrance. *Application fee:* $25. *Required:* high school transcript; minimum 2.0 GPA.

Standardized tests *Admission: Required:* SAT I or ACT. *Recommended:* SAT II Subject Tests.

Admissions Office Contact
South Carolina State University, 300 College Street Northeast, Orangeburg, SC 29117-0001. **Toll-free phone:** 800-260-5956. **Fax:** 803-536-8990. **E-mail:** carolyn-free@scsu.scsu.edu

Visit CollegeQuest.com for information on athletics.

SOUTHERN METHODIST COLLEGE
Orangeburg, South Carolina

Admissions Office Contact
Southern Methodist College, 541 Broughton Stret, PO Box 1027, Orangeburg, SC 29116-1027.

SOUTHERN WESLEYAN UNIVERSITY 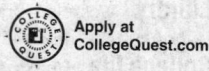 Apply at CollegeQuest.com
Central, South Carolina

- **Independent**, comprehensive, founded 1906, affiliated with Wesleyan Church
- **Degrees** associate, bachelor's, and master's
- **Small-town** 230-acre campus
- **Coed**, 1,472 undergraduate students, 96% full-time, 62% women, 38% men
- **Minimally difficult** entrance level, 34% of applicants were admitted
- **14:1 student-to-undergraduate faculty ratio**
- **$11,498 tuition** and fees
- **$9500 average financial aid** package, $10,000 average indebtedness upon graduation, $1.6 million endowment

Students *Undergraduates:* 1,411 full-time, 61 part-time. Students come from 32 states and territories, 7 other countries. *The most frequently chosen baccalaureate fields are:* business/marketing, education, psychology. **Graduate:** 55 in graduate degree programs.

From out-of-state	16%	Reside on campus	32%
Age 25 or older	67%	Transferred in	2%
International students	1%	African Americans	21%
Asian Americans/Pacific Islanders	0.2%	Hispanic Americans	1%
Native Americans	1%		

Faculty 161 (27% full-time), 40% with terminal degrees.

Expenses (1999–2000) *Comprehensive fee:* $15,350 includes full-time tuition ($11,148), mandatory fees ($350), and room and board ($3852).

College room only: $1320. Full-time tuition and fees vary according to class time, course load, and degree level. Room and board charges vary according to housing facility. *Part-time tuition:* $400 per hour. *Part-time fees:* $50 per term part-time. Part-time tuition and fees vary according to course load and degree level. *Payment plan:* installment. *Waivers:* senior citizens and employees or children of employees.
Library Rickman Library. *Operations spending 1999–2000:* $272,875. *Collection:* 67,823 titles, 440 serial subscriptions.
College life *Housing:* on-campus residence required through senior year. *Options:* men-only, women-only. *Most popular organizations:* Christian Service Organization, Student Missions Fellowship, Rotaract, Minority Awareness Association, Council for Exceptional Children.
Campus security 24-hour emergency response devices, late night security patrols.
After graduation 11 organizations recruited on campus 1997–98. *Career center:* 1 full-time, 1 part-time personnel. Services include job fairs, resume preparation, resume referral, career counseling, careers library, job bank.
Freshmen 468 applied, 159 admitted, 102 enrolled.

Average high school GPA	3.0	SAT verbal scores above 500	46%
SAT math scores above 500	41%	ACT above 18	74%
From top 10% of their h.s. class	12%	From top quarter	39%
From top half	77%	1998 freshmen returning in 1999	66%

Application *Options:* eApply at www.CollegeQuest.com, electronic application, early admission, deferred entrance. *Application fee:* $15. *Required:* high school transcript; minimum 2.0 GPA; 2 letters of recommendation; lifestyle statement. *Required for some:* interview.
Standardized tests *Admission: Required:* SAT I or ACT.
Significant dates *Application deadlines:* 8/10 (freshmen), 8/10 (transfers). *Financial aid deadline priority date:* 6/30.
Freshman Application Contact
Mrs. Joy Bryant, Director of Admissions, Southern Wesleyan University, 907 Wesleyan Drive, PO Box 1020, Central, SC 29630-1020. **Phone:** 864-644-5550. **Toll-free phone:** 800-CUATSWU. **Fax:** 864-639-0826 Ext. 327. **E-mail:** admissions@swu.edu
Visit CollegeQuest.com for information on majors offered and athletics. College video available at CollegeQuest.com.

UNIVERSITY OF SOUTH CAROLINA
Columbia, South Carolina

- **State-supported**, university, founded 1801
- **Degrees** associate, bachelor's, master's, doctoral, first professional, and post-master's certificates
- **Urban** 315-acre campus
- **Coed**, 14,403 undergraduate students, 87% full-time, 55% women, 45% men
- **Moderately difficult** entrance level, 67% of applicants were admitted
- **14:1 student-to-undergraduate faculty ratio**
- **60.2% graduate** in 6 years or less
- **$3740 tuition** and fees (in-state); $9814 (out-of-state)
- **$3211 average financial aid** package, $16,200 average indebtedness upon graduation, $249.7 million endowment

Part of University of South Carolina System.
Students *Undergraduates:* 12,530 full-time, 1,873 part-time. Students come from 52 states and territories, 84 other countries. *The most frequently chosen baccalaureate fields are:* business/marketing, communications/communication technologies, social sciences and history. *Graduate:* 1,209 in professional programs, 6,670 in other graduate degree programs.

From out-of-state	11%	Reside on campus	48%
Age 25 or older	11%	Transferred in	7%
International students	2%	African Americans	19%
Asian Americans/Pacific Islanders	3%	Hispanic Americans	1%
Native Americans	0.2%		

Faculty 1,439 (72% full-time), 81% with terminal degrees.
Expenses (1999–2000) *One-time required fee:* $25. *Tuition, state resident:* full-time $3640; part-time $172 per credit hour. *Tuition, nonresident:* full-time $9714; part-time $442 per credit hour. *Required fees:* full-time $100; $4 per credit hour. Full-time tuition and fees vary according to program and reciprocity agreements. Part-time tuition and fees vary according to course load. *College room and board:* $4167; room only: $2352. Room and board charges vary according to board plan, housing facility, and location. *Payment plans:* installment, deferred payment. *Waivers:* senior citizens and employees or children of employees.
Library Thomas Cooper Library plus 7 others. *Operations spending 1999–2000:* $14.5 million. *Collection:* 3.1 million titles, 18,433 serial subscriptions, 40,921 audiovisual materials.
College life *Housing:* on-campus residence required in freshman year. *Options:* coed, men-only, women-only, disabled students. *Social organizations:* national fraternities, national sororities; 13% of eligible men and 14% of eligible women are members. *Most popular organizations:* Fellowship of Christian Athletes, Association of African-American Students, Carolina for Kids, Fraternity Council, Sorority Council.
Campus security 24-hour emergency response devices and patrols, student patrols, late-night transport-escort service, USC Division of Law Enforcement and Safety.
After graduation 11,980 organizations recruited on campus 1997–98. 80% of class of 1998 had job offers within 6 months. *Career center:* 20 full-time, 15 part-time personnel. Services include job fairs, resume preparation, interview workshops, resume referral, career/interest testing, career counseling, careers library, job bank, job interviews. *Major awards:* 1 Rhodes, 2 Fulbright Scholars.
Freshmen 10,162 applied, 6,844 admitted, 2,668 enrolled. 38 National Merit Scholars, 82 valedictorians.

Average high school GPA	3.47	SAT verbal scores above 500	68%
SAT math scores above 500	72%	ACT above 18	93%
From top 10% of their h.s. class	34%	From top quarter	65%
From top half	92%	1998 freshmen returning in 1999	81%

Application *Option:* electronic application. *Application fee:* $35. *Required:* high school transcript.
Standardized tests *Admission: Required:* SAT I or ACT.
Significant dates *Application deadlines:* rolling (freshmen), rolling (transfers). *Financial aid deadline priority date:* 4/15.
Freshman Application Contact
Ms. Terry L. Davis, Director of Undergraduate Admissions, University of South Carolina, Office of Undergraduate Admissions, University of South Carolina, Columbia, SC 29208. **Phone:** 803-777-7700. **Toll-free phone:** 800-868-5872. **E-mail:** admissions-ugrad@sc.edu
Visit CollegeQuest.com for information on majors offered and athletics. College video and electronic viewbook available at CollegeQuest.com.

■ *See page 2830 for a narrative description.*

UNIVERSITY OF SOUTH CAROLINA AIKEN
Aiken, South Carolina

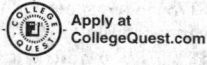
Apply at CollegeQuest.com

- **State-supported**, comprehensive, founded 1961
- **Degrees** associate, bachelor's, and master's
- **Suburban** 453-acre campus with easy access to Columbia
- **Coed**
- **Minimally difficult** entrance level
- **$3358 tuition** and fees (in-state); $7884 (out-of-state)

Part of University of South Carolina System.
Expenses (1999–2000) *One-time required fee:* $50. *Tuition, state resident:* full-time $3218; part-time $141 per semester hour. *Tuition, nonresident:* full-time $7744; part-time $340 per semester hour. *Required fees:* full-time $140; $5 per semester hour; $10 per term part-time. *College room and board:* $3940; room only: $2390. Room and board charges vary according to board plan.
Institutional Web site http://www.usca.sc.edu/
College life *Housing: Option:* coed. *Social organizations:* national fraternities, national sororities; 1% of eligible men and 1% of eligible women are members. *Most popular organizations:* student government, Pacesetters, Student Alumni Ambassadors, African-American Student Alliance, Pacer Union Board.
Campus security 24-hour emergency response devices and patrols, late-night transport-escort service.

South Carolina

University of South Carolina Aiken (continued)
Application *Options:* eApply at www.CollegeQuest.com, electronic application, early admission, deferred entrance. *Application fee:* $25. *Required:* high school transcript. *Recommended:* essay or personal statement; letters of recommendation; interview.
Standardized tests *Admission: Required:* SAT I or ACT.
Admissions Office Contact
University of South Carolina Aiken, 471 University Parkway, Aiken, SC 29801-6309. **Toll-free phone:** 888-WOW-USCA. **Fax:** 803-641-3727. **E-mail:** admit@sc.edu
Visit CollegeQuest.com for information on athletics. College video and electronic viewbook available at CollegeQuest.com.

UNIVERSITY OF SOUTH CAROLINA SPARTANBURG
Spartanburg, South Carolina

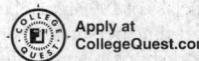
Apply at CollegeQuest.com

- **State-supported**, comprehensive, founded 1967
- **Degrees** associate, bachelor's, and master's
- **Urban** 298-acre campus with easy access to Charlotte
- **Coed**, 3,387 undergraduate students, 73% full-time, 64% women, 36% men
- **Minimally difficult** entrance level, 64% of applicants were admitted
- **16:1 student-to-undergraduate faculty ratio**
- **35% graduate** in 6 years or less
- **$3428 tuition** and fees (in-state); $7954 (out-of-state)
- **$3507 average financial aid** package, $13,597 average indebtedness upon graduation, $1.9 million endowment

Part of University of South Carolina System.
Students *Undergraduates:* 2,477 full-time, 910 part-time. Students come from 41 states and territories, 24 other countries. *The most frequently chosen baccalaureate fields are:* business/marketing, education, interdisciplinary studies. *Graduate:* 286 in graduate degree programs.

From out-of-state	5%	Reside on campus	10%
Age 25 or older	28%	Transferred in	12%
International students	1%	African Americans	21%
Asian Americans/Pacific Islanders	1%	Hispanic Americans	1%
Native Americans	0.1%		

Faculty 226 (62% full-time).
Expenses (1999–2000) *One-time required fee:* $50. *Tuition, state resident:* full-time $3250; part-time $143 per semester hour. *Tuition, nonresident:* full-time $7776; part-time $342 per semester hour. *Required fees:* full-time $178; $5 per semester hour; $20 per term part-time. Part-time tuition and fees vary according to course load. *College room and board:* $3950; room only: $2370. Room and board charges vary according to board plan. *Payment plan:* deferred payment. *Waivers:* senior citizens.
Library University of South Carolina Spartanburg Library. *Operations spending 1999–2000:* $1.3 million. *Collection:* 124,077 titles, 1,166 serial subscriptions.
College life *Housing: Option:* coed. *Social organizations:* national fraternities, national sororities; 4% of eligible men and 4% of eligible women are members. *Most popular organizations:* African American Association, Campus Activity Board, Student Nurses Association, Student Government Association, Association for the Education of Young Children.
Campus security 24-hour emergency response devices and patrols, late-night transport-escort service, campus security cameras.
After graduation 75 organizations recruited on campus 1997–98. 76% of class of 1998 had job offers within 6 months. *Career center:* 2 full-time personnel. Services include job fairs, resume preparation, interview workshops, resume referral, career/interest testing, career counseling, careers library, job bank, job interviews. *Graduate education:* 19% of class of 1999 went directly to graduate and professional school.
Freshmen 1,254 applied, 804 admitted, 601 enrolled.

Average high school GPA	3.0	SAT verbal scores above 500	35%
SAT math scores above 500	34%	ACT above 18	64%
From top 10% of their h.s. class	9%	From top quarter	32%
From top half	68%		

Application *Options:* eApply at www.CollegeQuest.com, deferred entrance. *Application fee:* $25. *Required:* high school transcript.
Standardized tests *Admission: Required:* SAT I or ACT.
Significant dates *Notification:* 8/1 (freshmen). *Financial aid deadline priority date:* 3/1.
Freshman Application Contact
Ms. Donette Stewart, Director of Admissions, University of South Carolina Spartanburg, 800 University Way, Spartanburg, SC 29303. **Phone:** 864-503-5280. **Toll-free phone:** 800-277-8727. **Fax:** 864-503-5201. **E-mail:** uscs.admissions@sc.edu
Visit CollegeQuest.com for information on majors offered and athletics.

VOORHEES COLLEGE
Denmark, South Carolina

- **Independent Episcopal**, 4-year, founded 1897
- **Degree** bachelor's
- **Rural** 350-acre campus
- **Coed**, 943 undergraduate students
- **Minimally difficult** entrance level, 80% of applicants were admitted
- **$5860 tuition** and fees

Voorhees is a small liberal arts college with a friendly, family-like atmosphere and a caring faculty and staff dedicated to excellence. The hub of student activities is the Health and Human Resources Center, which has a sports arena, student center, and swimming pool. Voorhees has a successful intercollegiate and intramural athletic program.

Students *Undergraduates:* Students come from 18 states and territories, 3 other countries.

Reside on campus	85%	Age 25 or older	10%

Faculty 49 (63% full-time).
Expenses (1999–2000) *Comprehensive fee:* $9050 includes full-time tuition ($5860) and room and board ($3190). *Part-time tuition:* $200 per credit hour. *Payment plans:* installment, deferred payment. *Waivers:* employees or children of employees.
Library Wright-Potts Library. *Collection:* 86,261 titles, 408 serial subscriptions.
College life On-campus residence required through sophomore year. *Social organizations:* national fraternities, national sororities; 15% of eligible men and 10% of eligible women are members. *Most popular organizations:* White Rose, Elizabeth Evelyn Wright Culture Club, Panhellenic Council.
Campus security 24-hour emergency response devices and patrols, student patrols, late-night transport-escort service.
After graduation *Career center:* 1 full-time personnel. Services include job fairs, resume preparation, resume referral, career counseling, careers library, job interviews. *Graduate education:* 30% of class of 1999 went directly to graduate and professional school: 18% graduate arts and sciences, 10% business, 1% law, 1% medicine.
Freshmen 1,586 applied, 1,266 admitted.

Average high school GPA	2.5	SAT verbal scores above 500	15%
SAT math scores above 500	11%	ACT above 18	N/R
From top 10% of their h.s. class	3%	From top quarter	9%
From top half	23%	1998 freshmen returning in 1999	58%

Application *Options:* Common Application, electronic application, deferred entrance. *Application fee:* $25. *Required:* high school transcript; letters of recommendation. *Required for some:* essay or personal statement; interview. *Recommended:* minimum 2.0 GPA.
Standardized tests *Admission: Required:* SAT I or ACT.
Significant dates *Application deadlines:* rolling (freshmen), rolling (transfers). *Financial aid deadline priority date:* 4/15.
Freshman Application Contact
Ms. E. E. Phillips, Director of Admissions, Voorhees College, Massachusetts Hall, PO Box 678, Denmark, SC 29042. **Phone:** 803-703-7111 Ext. 7115. **Toll-free phone:** 800-446-6250. **Fax:** 803-793-4584. **E-mail:** elfphi@voorhees.edu
Visit CollegeQuest.com for information on majors offered and athletics. College video and electronic viewbook available at CollegeQuest.com.

- *See page 2902 for a narrative description.*

South Carolina

WINTHROP UNIVERSITY
Rock Hill, South Carolina

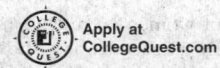 Apply at CollegeQuest.com

- **State-supported**, comprehensive, founded 1886
- **Degrees** bachelor's and master's
- **Suburban** 418-acre campus with easy access to Charlotte
- **Coed**, 4,302 undergraduate students, 91% full-time, 70% women, 30% men
- **Moderately difficult** entrance level, 75% of applicants were admitted
- **14:1 student-to-undergraduate faculty ratio**
- **53% graduate** in 6 years or less
- **$4146 tuition** and fees (in-state); $7454 (out-of-state)
- **$5641 average financial aid** package, $14,751 average indebtedness upon graduation, $693,815 endowment

Part of South Carolina Commission on Higher Education.

Students *Undergraduates:* 3,920 full-time, 382 part-time. Students come from 39 states and territories, 30 other countries. *The most frequently chosen baccalaureate fields are:* business/marketing, education, social sciences and history. *Graduate:* 1,229 in graduate degree programs.

From out-of-state	11%	Reside on campus	50%
Age 25 or older	13%	Transferred in	8%
International students	2%	African Americans	24%
Asian Americans/Pacific Islanders	1%	Hispanic Americans	1%
Native Americans	0.4%		

Faculty 392 (63% full-time), 64% with terminal degrees.

Expenses (1999–2000) *Tuition, state resident:* full-time $4126; part-time $172 per semester hour. *Tuition, nonresident:* full-time $7434; part-time $310 per semester hour. *Required fees:* full-time $20; $10 per term part-time. *College room and board:* $4022. Room and board charges vary according to board plan and housing facility. *Payment plan:* installment. *Waivers:* senior citizens and employees or children of employees.

Library Dacus Library. *Operations spending 1999–2000:* $1.9 million. *Collection:* 633,649 titles, 2,667 serial subscriptions, 1,798 audiovisual materials.

College life *Housing: Options:* coed, men-only, women-only. *Social organizations:* national fraternities, national sororities; 16% of eligible men and 13% of eligible women are members. *Most popular organizations:* Ebonites, Greek organizations, Campus Ministries, student government association, Dinkins Student Union.

Campus security 24-hour emergency response devices and patrols, late-night transport-escort service.

After graduation 24 organizations recruited on campus 1997–98. 80% of class of 1998 had job offers within 6 months. *Career center:* 4 full-time personnel. Services include job fairs, resume preparation, interview workshops, resume referral, career/interest testing, career counseling, careers library, job bank, job interviews. *Graduate education:* 11% of class of 1999 went directly to graduate and professional school.

Freshmen 3,003 applied, 2,251 admitted, 971 enrolled. 12 valedictorians.

Average high school GPA	3.29	SAT verbal scores above 500	62%
SAT math scores above 500	58%	ACT above 18	97%
From top 10% of their h.s. class	24%	From top quarter	55%
From top half	89%	1998 freshmen returning in 1999	77%

Application *Options:* eApply at www.CollegeQuest.com, deferred entrance. *Application fee:* $35. *Required:* high school transcript; 1 letter of recommendation. *Recommended:* essay or personal statement.

Standardized tests *Admission: Required:* SAT I or ACT.

Significant dates *Application deadlines:* 6/1 (freshmen), 7/1 (transfers). *Notification:* continuous until 6/21 (freshmen). *Financial aid deadline priority date:* 3/1.

Freshman Application Contact
Ms. Deborah Barber, Director of Admissions, Winthrop University, 701 Oakland Avenue, Rock Hill, SC 29733. **Phone:** 803-323-2191. **Toll-free phone:** 800-763-0230. **Fax:** 803-323-2137. **E-mail:** admissions@winthrop.edu

Visit CollegeQuest.com for information on majors offered and athletics. College video and electronic viewbook available at CollegeQuest.com.

- See page 3012 for a narrative description.

WOFFORD COLLEGE
Spartanburg, South Carolina

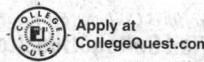 Apply at CollegeQuest.com

- **Independent**, 4-year, founded 1854, affiliated with United Methodist Church
- **Degree** bachelor's
- **Urban** 140-acre campus with easy access to Charlotte
- **Coed**, 1,094 undergraduate students, 99% full-time, 47% women, 53% men
- **Very difficult** entrance level, 85% of applicants were admitted
- **14:1 student-to-undergraduate faculty ratio**
- **$16,975 tuition** and fees
- **$14,278 average financial aid** package, $95.3 million endowment

Long known for Phi Beta Kappa academic standards and efficient management that delivers high-quality programs at reasonable costs, Wofford is the smallest college in the nation with an NCAA Division I football program. In the summer, the NFL's Carolina Panthers use Wofford's excellent athletic and wellness facilities for their training camps.

Students *Undergraduates:* 1,082 full-time, 12 part-time. Students come from 20 states and territories, 3 other countries. *The most frequently chosen baccalaureate fields are:* business/marketing, biological/life sciences, social sciences and history.

Reside on campus	89%	Transferred in	1%
International students	0.3%	African Americans	9%
Asian Americans/Pacific Islanders	1%	Hispanic Americans	1%
Native Americans	1%		

Faculty 102 (70% full-time), 75% with terminal degrees.

Expenses (1999–2000) *Comprehensive fee:* $21,990 includes full-time tuition ($16,410), mandatory fees ($565), and room and board ($5015). *Part-time tuition:* $600 per semester hour. *Payment plan:* installment. *Waivers:* employees or children of employees.

Library Sandor Teszler Library. *Operations spending 1999–2000:* $388,952. *Collection:* 178,874 titles, 642 serial subscriptions, 1,758 audiovisual materials.

College life *Housing:* on-campus residence required through senior year. *Options:* coed, men-only, women-only. *Social organizations:* national fraternities, national sororities; 50% of eligible men and 58% of eligible women are members. *Most popular organizations:* performing arts groups, Twin Towers Student Volunteers, Fellowship of Christian Athletes.

Campus security 24-hour emergency response devices and patrols, late-night transport-escort service, controlled dormitory access.

After graduation 60% of class of 1998 had job offers within 6 months. *Career center:* 2 full-time, 1 part-time personnel. Services include job fairs, resume preparation, interview workshops, resume referral, career/interest testing, career counseling, careers library, job bank, job interviews. *Graduate education:* 31% of class of 1999 went directly to graduate and professional school: 9% graduate arts and sciences, 5% medicine, 4% business, 4% law, 2% dentistry, 1% education, 1% theology.

Freshmen 1,279 applied, 1,085 admitted, 307 enrolled. 4 National Merit Scholars, 9 class presidents, 11 valedictorians, 33 student government officers.

Average high school GPA	3.4	SAT verbal scores above 500	88%
SAT math scores above 500	89%	ACT above 18	100%
From top 10% of their h.s. class	50%	From top quarter	81%
From top half	98%	1998 freshmen returning in 1999	90%

Application *Options:* eApply at www.CollegeQuest.com, Common Application, electronic application, early admission, early decision, early action, deferred entrance. *Application fee:* $35. *Required:* essay or personal statement; high school transcript. *Recommended:* 2 letters of recommendation; interview.

Standardized tests *Admission: Required:* SAT I or ACT. *Recommended:* SAT II: Writing Test.

Significant dates *Application deadlines:* 2/1 (freshmen), rolling (transfers). *Early decision:* 11/15, 12/1. *Notification:* 3/15 (freshmen), 12/1 (early decision), 12/15 (early action). *Financial aid deadline priority date:* 3/15.

Freshman Application Contact
Mr. Brand Stille, Director of Admissions, Wofford College, 429 North Church Street, Spartanburg, SC 29303-3663. **Phone:** 864-597-4130. **Fax:** 864-597-4149. **E-mail:** admissions@wofford.edu

Peterson's Guide to Four-Year Colleges 2001   www.petersons.com

South Carolina–South Dakota

Wofford College (continued)
Visit CollegeQuest.com for information on majors offered and athletics. College video available at CollegeQuest.com.

■ *See page 3014 for a narrative description.*

SOUTH DAKOTA

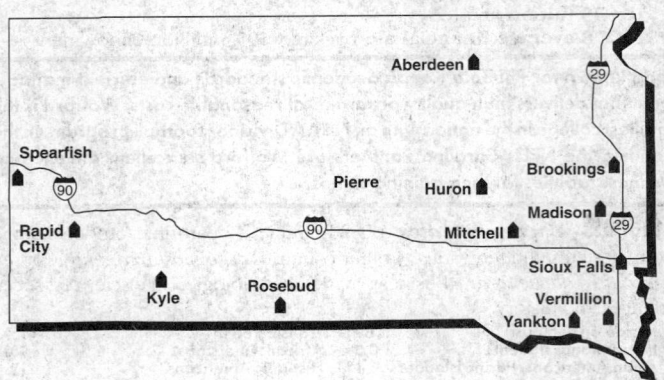

AUGUSTANA COLLEGE
Sioux Falls, South Dakota

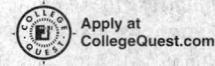 Apply at CollegeQuest.com

- **Independent**, comprehensive, founded 1860, affiliated with Evangelical Lutheran Church in America
- **Degrees** bachelor's and master's
- **Urban** 100-acre campus
- **Coed**, 1,693 undergraduate students, 93% full-time, 65% women, 35% men
- **Moderately difficult** entrance level, 86% of applicants were admitted
- **12:1 student-to-undergraduate faculty ratio**
- **60.5% graduate** in 6 years or less
- **$14,754 tuition** and fees
- **$13,487 average financial aid** package, $17,561 average indebtedness upon graduation, $27.9 million endowment

Nobel Peace Prize Laureate Desmond Tutu, former First Lady Barbara Bush, former British Prime Minister John Major, former Soviet President Mikhail Gorbachev, former President George Bush, and retired General Colin Powell have graced the Augustana campus since 1995 as speakers in the College's Center for Western Studies' distinguished Boe Forum on Public Affairs. The lecture, always a complete "sell-out," is free to Augustana students and to the public.

Students *Undergraduates:* 1,579 full-time, 114 part-time. Students come from 27 states and territories, 10 other countries. *The most frequently chosen baccalaureate fields are:* education, business/marketing, health professions and related sciences. *Graduate:* 46 in graduate degree programs.

From out-of-state	51%	Reside on campus	68%
Age 25 or older	5%	Transferred in	5%
International students	2%	African Americans	1%
Asian Americans/Pacific Islanders	1%	Hispanic Americans	0.2%
Native Americans	0.4%		

Faculty 166 (71% full-time), 69% with terminal degrees.

Expenses (2000–2001) *Comprehensive fee:* $19,014 includes full-time tuition ($14,592), mandatory fees ($162), and room and board ($4260). *College room only:* $2160. Room and board charges vary according to board plan and housing facility. *Part-time tuition:* $200 per credit. Part-time tuition and fees vary according to course load. *Payment plan:* installment. *Waivers:* adult students, senior citizens, and employees or children of employees.

Library Mikkelsen Library plus 1 other. *Operations spending 1999–2000:* $817,109. *Collection:* 295,470 titles, 1,568 serial subscriptions, 5,133 audiovisual materials.

College life *Housing:* on-campus residence required through sophomore year. *Option:* coed. *Social organizations:* local fraternities, local sororities; 2% of women are members. *Most popular organizations:* Community Service Day, Fellowship of Christian Athletes, union board of governors, Augustana Student Association, hall councils.

Campus security 24-hour emergency response devices and patrols, late-night transport-escort service, controlled dormitory access.

After graduation 50 organizations recruited on campus 1997–98. 90% of class of 1998 had job offers within 6 months. *Career center:* 2 full-time, 1 part-time personnel. Services include job fairs, resume preparation, resume referral, career/interest testing, career counseling, careers library, job bank, job interviews.

Freshmen 1,445 applied, 1,242 admitted, 483 enrolled. 38 valedictorians.

Average high school GPA	3.55	SAT verbal scores above 500	91%
SAT math scores above 500	86%	ACT above 18	99%
From top 10% of their h.s. class	27%	From top quarter	61%
From top half	87%	1998 freshmen returning in 1999	80%

Application *Options:* eApply at www.CollegeQuest.com, Common Application, early admission, deferred entrance. *Application fee:* $25. *Required:* high school transcript; minimum 2.5 GPA; 1 letter of recommendation. *Recommended:* interview.

Standardized tests *Admission: Required:* SAT I or ACT.

Significant dates *Application deadlines:* 8/1 (freshmen), rolling (transfers). *Financial aid deadline priority date:* 3/1.

Freshman Application Contact
Robert Preloger, Vice President for Enrollment, Augustana College, 2001 South Summit Avenue, Sioux Falls, SD 57197. **Phone:** 605-336-5518 Ext. 5504. **Toll-free phone:** 800-727-2844. **Fax:** 605-336-5518. **E-mail:** info@inst.augie.edu

Visit CollegeQuest.com for information on majors offered and athletics. College video available at CollegeQuest.com.

■ *See page 1208 for a narrative description.*

BLACK HILLS STATE UNIVERSITY
Spearfish, South Dakota

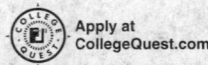 Apply at CollegeQuest.com

- **State-supported**, comprehensive, founded 1883
- **Degrees** associate, bachelor's, master's, and post-master's certificates
- **Small-town** 123-acre campus
- **Coed**, 3,289 undergraduate students, 78% full-time, 60% women, 40% men
- **Minimally difficult** entrance level, 84% of applicants were admitted
- **33:1 student-to-undergraduate faculty ratio**
- **44.85% graduate** in 6 years or less
- **$3363 tuition** and fees (in-state); $7437 (out-of-state)
- **$6.7 million endowment**

Students *Undergraduates:* 2,561 full-time, 728 part-time. Students come from 37 states and territories, 9 other countries. *The most frequently chosen baccalaureate fields are:* business/marketing, education, social sciences and history. *Graduate:* 300 in graduate degree programs.

From out-of-state	17%	Age 25 or older	32%
Transferred in	18%	International students	0.3%
African Americans	1%	Asian Americans/Pacific Islanders	1%
Hispanic Americans	1%	Native Americans	3%

Faculty 105, 74% with terminal degrees.

Expenses (1999–2000) *Tuition, state resident:* full-time $1867; part-time $58 per credit. *Tuition, nonresident:* full-time $5941; part-time $186 per credit. *Required fees:* full-time $1496; $47 per credit. Full-time tuition and fees vary according to course load and reciprocity agreements. Part-time tuition and fees vary according to course load and reciprocity agreements. *College room and board:* $2785; room only: $1472. Room and board charges vary according to board plan. *Payment plan:* installment. *Waivers:* senior citizens and employees or children of employees.

Library E. Y. Berry Library-Learning Center. *Operations spending 1999–2000:* $600,090. *Collection:* 201,952 titles, 2,514 serial subscriptions, 23,364 audiovisual materials.

South Dakota

College life *Housing:* on-campus residence required through sophomore year. *Options:* coed, men-only, women-only, disabled students. *Social organizations:* national fraternities, national sororities; 1% of eligible men and 1% of eligible women are members. *Most popular organizations:* Student Activities Committee, student government.

Campus security 24-hour patrols, late-night transport-escort service, controlled dormitory access.

After graduation 55 organizations recruited on campus 1997–98. *Career center:* 1 full-time, 1 part-time personnel. Services include job fairs, resume preparation, resume referral, career counseling, careers library, job bank, job interviews.

Freshmen 1,323 applied, 1,117 admitted, 876 enrolled.

Average high school GPA	2.99	SAT verbal scores above 500	N/R
SAT math scores above 500	N/R	ACT above 18	79%
From top 10% of their h.s. class	3%	From top quarter	15%
From top half	46%	1998 freshmen returning in 1999	52%

Application *Option:* eApply at www.CollegeQuest.com. *Application fee:* $15. *Required:* high school transcript; minimum 2.0 high school GPA in core curriculum.

Standardized tests *Admission: Required:* SAT I or ACT.

Significant dates *Application deadlines:* rolling (freshmen), rolling (transfers). *Financial aid deadline priority date:* 3/1.

Freshman Application Contact
Ms. Judy Berry, Assistant Director of Admissions, Black Hills State University, University Station Box 9502, Spearfish, SD 57799-9502. **Phone:** 605-642-6343. **Toll-free phone:** 800-255-2478. **E-mail:** jberry@mystic.bhsu.edu

Visit CollegeQuest.com for information on majors offered and athletics. College video available at CollegeQuest.com.

COLORADO TECHNICAL UNIVERSITY SIOUX FALLS CAMPUS
Sioux Falls, South Dakota

- **Proprietary**, comprehensive, founded 1965
- **Degrees** associate, bachelor's, and master's
- **Coed**
- **Minimally difficult** entrance level
- **$7590 tuition** and fees

Expenses (1999–2000) *Tuition:* full-time $7425; part-time $165 per credit hour. *Required fees:* full-time $165; $55 per term part-time. Full-time tuition and fees vary according to course load.

Institutional Web site http://www.colotechu.edu/

College life *Housing:* college housing not available.

Application *Required:* high school transcript.

Standardized tests *Admission: Recommended:* ACT.

Admissions Office Contact
Colorado Technical University Sioux Falls Campus, 3901 West 59th Street, Sioux Falls, SD 57108. **Fax:** 605-361-5954. **E-mail:** ctapallen@midco.net

Visit CollegeQuest.com for information on athletics.

DAKOTA STATE UNIVERSITY
Madison, South Dakota

- **State-supported**, comprehensive, founded 1881
- **Degrees** associate, bachelor's, and master's
- **Rural** 40-acre campus with easy access to Sioux Falls
- **Coed**, 1,309 undergraduate students, 87% full-time, 47% women, 53% men
- **Minimally difficult** entrance level, 70% of applicants were admitted
- **16:1 student-to-undergraduate faculty ratio**
- **$3588 tuition** and fees (in-state); $7661 (out-of-state)
- **$4873 average financial aid** package, $13,840 average indebtedness upon graduation, $3.4 million endowment

Students *Undergraduates:* 1,142 full-time, 167 part-time. Students come from 23 states and territories, 4 other countries. *Graduate:* 403 in graduate degree programs.

Reside on campus	40%

Faculty 82 (88% full-time).

Expenses (1999–2000) *Tuition, state resident:* full-time $3588; part-time $112 per credit hour. *Tuition, nonresident:* full-time $7661; part-time $239 per credit hour. *College room and board:* $2800. *Payment plan:* deferred payment. *Waivers:* senior citizens and employees or children of employees.

Library Karl E. Mundt Library plus 1 other. *Operations spending 1999–2000:* $306,245. *Collection:* 80,027 titles, 6,433 serial subscriptions, 2,536 audiovisual materials.

College life *Housing:* on-campus residence required through sophomore year. *Options:* coed, men-only, women-only, disabled students. *Most popular organizations:* business club, band, computer club.

Campus security 24-hour patrols, controlled dormitory access.

After graduation 22 organizations recruited on campus 1997–98. 90% of class of 1998 had job offers within 6 months. *Career center:* 3 full-time personnel. Services include job fairs, resume preparation, interview workshops, resume referral, career/interest testing, career counseling, careers library, job bank, job interviews. *Graduate education:* 2% of class of 1999 went directly to graduate and professional school: 1% law, 1% medicine.

Freshmen 668 applied, 468 admitted, 353 enrolled. 9 valedictorians.

SAT verbal scores above 500	N/R	SAT math scores above 500	N/R
ACT above 18	84%		

Application *Options:* electronic application, early admission. *Application fee:* $15. *Required:* high school transcript; rank in upper two-thirds of high school class.

Standardized tests *Admission: Required:* ACT.

Significant dates *Application deadlines:* rolling (freshmen), rolling (transfers). *Financial aid deadline priority date:* 3/1.

Freshman Application Contact
Ms. Katy O'Hara, Admissions Secretary, Dakota State University, 820 North Washington, Madison, SD 57042-1799. **Phone:** 605-256-5139. **Toll-free phone:** 888-DSU-9988. **Fax:** 605-256-5316. **E-mail:** dsuinfo@pluto.dsu.edu

Visit CollegeQuest.com for information on majors offered and athletics. Electronic viewbook available at CollegeQuest.com.

DAKOTA WESLEYAN UNIVERSITY
Mitchell, South Dakota

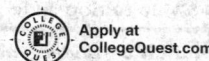
Apply at CollegeQuest.com

- **Independent United Methodist**, 4-year, founded 1885
- **Degrees** associate and bachelor's
- **Small-town** 40-acre campus
- **Coed**, 675 undergraduate students, 94% full-time, 59% women, 41% men
- **Moderately difficult** entrance level, 94% of applicants were admitted
- **16:1 student-to-undergraduate faculty ratio**
- **$9916 tuition** and fees
- **$10,201 average financial aid** package, $16.9 million endowment

Students *Undergraduates:* 634 full-time, 41 part-time. Students come from 29 states and territories, 4 other countries. *The most frequently chosen baccalaureate fields are:* education, protective services/public administration, social sciences and history. *Graduate:* 15 in graduate degree programs.

Reside on campus	38%	Age 25 or older	16%
Transferred in	11%	International students	1%
African Americans	2%	Asian Americans/Pacific Islanders	0.1%
Hispanic Americans	2%	Native Americans	5%

Faculty 67 (66% full-time), 30% with terminal degrees.

Expenses (1999–2000) *Comprehensive fee:* $13,556 includes full-time tuition ($9916) and room and board ($3640). Full-time tuition and fees vary according to program. Room and board charges vary according to board plan. *Part-time tuition:* $202 per credit hour. Part-time tuition and fees vary according to course load and program. *Payment plan:* installment. *Waivers:* senior citizens and employees or children of employees.

Library Layne Library. *Operations spending 1999–2000:* $273,862. *Collection:* 65,000 titles, 412 serial subscriptions.

College life *Housing:* on-campus residence required through sophomore year. *Options:* coed, men-only. *Most popular organizations:* DWU Future Teachers Organization, Student Nurses Association, Culture Club, Human Services Club, Religious Life Council.

South Dakota

Dakota Wesleyan University (continued)

Campus security 24-hour emergency response devices and patrols, student patrols, late-night transport-escort service, controlled dormitory access.

After graduation *Career center:* 1 full-time personnel. Services include job fairs, resume preparation, resume referral, career counseling, careers library, job bank, job interviews. *Graduate education:* 6% of class of 1999 went directly to graduate and professional school: 2% graduate arts and sciences, 2% medicine, 1% theology, 1% veterinary medicine.

Freshmen 385 applied, 363 admitted, 173 enrolled.

Average high school GPA	3.15	SAT verbal scores above 500	N/R
SAT math scores above 500	N/R	ACT above 18	87%
From top 10% of their h.s. class	5%	From top quarter	29%
From top half	60%		

Application *Options:* eApply at www.CollegeQuest.com, early admission. *Application fee:* $15. *Required:* high school transcript. *Recommended:* minimum 2.0 GPA.

Standardized tests *Admission: Required:* SAT I or ACT.

Significant dates *Application deadlines:* 8/26 (freshmen), 8/26 (transfers). *Financial aid deadline priority date:* 3/1.

Freshman Application Contact
Ms. Laura Miller, Director of Enrollment Services, Dakota Wesleyan University, Enrollment Services, Mitchell, SD 57301-4398. **Phone:** 605-995-2650. **Toll-free phone:** 800-333-8506. **Fax:** 605-995-2699. **E-mail:** admissions@dwu.edu.

Visit CollegeQuest.com for information on majors offered and athletics. College video available at CollegeQuest.com.

HURON UNIVERSITY
Huron, South Dakota

- **Proprietary**, 4-year, founded 1883
- **Degrees** associate and bachelor's
- **Small-town** 15-acre campus
- **Coed**, 540 undergraduate students, 81% full-time, 49% women, 51% men
- **Minimally difficult** entrance level, 65% of applicants were admitted
- **13:1 student-to-undergraduate faculty ratio**
- **$7500 tuition** and fees

Students *Undergraduates:* 440 full-time, 100 part-time. Students come from 36 states and territories. *The most frequently chosen baccalaureate fields are:* business/marketing, education, protective services/public administration. *Graduate:* 22 in graduate degree programs.

Reside on campus	50%	Age 25 or older	33%
Transferred in	8%	African Americans	11%
Asian Americans/Pacific Islanders	1%	Hispanic Americans	6%
Native Americans	3%		

Faculty 41 (41% full-time), 20% with terminal degrees.

Expenses (2000–2001, estimated) *Comprehensive fee:* $11,400 includes full-time tuition ($7200), mandatory fees ($300), and room and board ($3900). *College room only:* $1950. Room and board charges vary according to board plan and housing facility. *Part-time tuition:* $200 per quarter hour. *Part-time fees:* $100 per term part-time. *Payment plans:* guaranteed tuition, tuition prepayment, installment, deferred payment. *Waivers:* children of alumni and employees or children of employees.

Library Ella McIntire Library. *Collection:* 50,000 titles, 240 serial subscriptions.

College life *Housing:* on-campus residence required in freshman year. *Options:* coed, men-only, women-only. *Most popular organizations:* Phi Beta Lambda, International Club, computer science club, student government, Fellowship of Christian Athletes.

Campus security 24-hour emergency response devices, student patrols, controlled dormitory access.

After graduation *Career center:* 1 full-time, 1 part-time personnel. Services include job fairs, career counseling, job bank.

Freshmen 509 applied, 333 admitted, 129 enrolled.

Average high school GPA	2.64	SAT verbal scores above 500	N/R
SAT math scores above 500	N/R	ACT above 18	37%
From top 10% of their h.s. class	5%	From top quarter	21%
From top half	62%	1998 freshmen returning in 1999	41%

Application *Options:* Common Application, early admission, deferred entrance. *Application fee:* $35. *Required:* high school transcript; minimum 2.0 GPA; applicants for athletic scholarship programs must meet approved ACT requirement. *Recommended:* interview.

Standardized tests *Admission: Recommended:* SAT I or ACT.

Significant dates *Application deadlines:* rolling (freshmen), rolling (transfers). *Notification:* continuous until 8/30 (freshmen). *Financial aid deadline:* continuous.

Freshman Application Contact
Mr. Richard Shelton, Director of Admissions, Huron University, 333 9th Street Southwest, Huron, SD 57350. **Phone:** 605-352-9465. **Toll-free phone:** 800-710-7159. **Fax:** 605-352-7421.

Visit CollegeQuest.com for information on majors offered and athletics. College video available at CollegeQuest.com.

■ *See page 1812 for a narrative description.*

MOUNT MARTY COLLEGE
Yankton, South Dakota

- **Independent Roman Catholic**, comprehensive, founded 1936
- **Degrees** associate, bachelor's, and master's
- **Small-town** 80-acre campus
- **Coed**, 766 undergraduate students, 70% full-time, 72% women, 28% men
- **Moderately difficult** entrance level, 99% of applicants were admitted
- **11:1 student-to-undergraduate faculty ratio**
- **$10,128 tuition** and fees
- **$10,284 average financial aid** package, $17,285 average indebtedness upon graduation, $6.9 million endowment

Students *Undergraduates:* 540 full-time, 226 part-time. Students come from 18 states and territories, 3 other countries. *The most frequently chosen baccalaureate fields are:* education, business/marketing, health professions and related sciences. *Graduate:* 64 in graduate degree programs.

From out-of-state	35%	Age 25 or older	30%
Transferred in	11%	International students	0.4%
African Americans	1%	Asian Americans/Pacific Islanders	0.4%
Hispanic Americans	1%	Native Americans	1%

Faculty 65 (46% full-time), 25% with terminal degrees.

Expenses (1999–2000) *Comprehensive fee:* $14,148 includes full-time tuition ($9248), mandatory fees ($880), and room and board ($4020). *Part-time tuition:* $160 per credit. *Part-time fees:* $50 per term part-time. Part-time tuition and fees vary according to course load. *Payment plans:* guaranteed tuition, installment. *Waivers:* employees or children of employees.

Library *Operations spending 1999–2000:* $102,550. *Collection:* 77,000 titles, 700 serial subscriptions.

College life *Housing:* on-campus residence required through senior year. *Option:* coed. *Most popular organizations:* Campus Ministry, Student Government Association, nursing club, education club, theater club or SIFE (Students in Free Enterprise).

Campus security 24-hour emergency response devices and patrols, controlled dormitory access.

After graduation *Career center:* 1 full-time personnel. Services include job fairs, resume preparation, resume referral, career counseling, careers library, job bank.

Freshmen 163 applied, 162 admitted, 150 enrolled.

Average high school GPA	3.01	SAT verbal scores above 500	N/R
SAT math scores above 500	N/R	ACT above 18	74%
From top 10% of their h.s. class	6%	From top quarter	26%
From top half	64%	1998 freshmen returning in 1999	72%

Application *Options:* early admission, deferred entrance. *Application fee:* $35. *Required:* high school transcript. *Required for some:* letters of recommendation. *Recommended:* interview.

Standardized tests *Admission: Required:* ACT.

Significant dates *Application deadlines:* rolling (freshmen), rolling (transfers). *Financial aid deadline priority date:* 3/1.

Freshman Application Contact
Ms. Laurie J. Becvar, Dean of Graduate Programs and Enrollment Management, Mount Marty College, 1105 West 8th Street, Yankton, SD 57078. **Phone:** 605-668-1545. **Toll-free phone:** 800-658-4552. **Fax:** 605-668-1607. **E-mail:** mmcadmit@mtmc.edu.

South Dakota

Visit CollegeQuest.com for information on majors offered and athletics.

■ *See page 2108 for a narrative description.*

NATIONAL AMERICAN UNIVERSITY
Rapid City, South Dakota

- **Proprietary**, 4-year, founded 1941
- **Degrees** associate and bachelor's
- **Urban** 8-acre campus
- **Coed**
- **Noncompetitive** entrance level
- **$8880 tuition** and fees

Part of National College.

Expenses (1999–2000) *One-time required fee:* $50. *Comprehensive fee:* $12,420 includes full-time tuition ($8880) and room and board ($3540). *College room only:* $1605. Room and board charges vary according to board plan. *Part-time tuition:* $185 per credit hour.

Institutional Web site http://www.national.edu/

College life *Housing:* on-campus residence required in freshman year. *Option:* coed. *Social organizations:* local fraternities, local sororities; 6% of eligible men and 7% of eligible women are members. *Most popular organizations:* Student Senate, Phi Beta Lambda, Dormitory Council, Student Association of Legal Assistants, President's Advisory Council.

Campus security Part-time security personnel.

Application *Options:* Common Application, electronic application, early admission, deferred entrance. *Application fee:* $25. *Required:* high school transcript. *Recommended:* interview.

Standardized tests *Admission:* Recommended: ACT.

Admissions Office Contact
National American University, PO Box 1780, Rapid City, SD 57709-1780. **Toll-free phone:** 800-843-8892. **Fax:** 605-394-4871. **E-mail:** apply@server1.natcol-rcy.edu

Visit CollegeQuest.com for information on athletics. College video and electronic viewbook available at CollegeQuest.com.

■ *See page 2132 for a narrative description.*

NATIONAL AMERICAN UNIVERSITY– SIOUX FALLS BRANCH
Sioux Falls, South Dakota

- **Proprietary**, 4-year, founded 1941
- **Degrees** associate and bachelor's
- **Urban** campus
- **Coed**
- **Noncompetitive** entrance level

Part of National College.

College life *Housing:* college housing not available.

Campus security 24-hour emergency response devices.

Application *Options:* Common Application, deferred entrance. *Application fee:* $25. *Required:* high school transcript; interview.

Admissions Office Contact
National American University–Sioux Falls Branch, 2801 South Kiwanis Avenue, Suite 100, Sioux Falls, SD 57105-4293. **E-mail:** jmeyer@national.edu

Visit CollegeQuest.com for information on athletics. College video and electronic viewbook available at CollegeQuest.com.

NORTHERN STATE UNIVERSITY
Aberdeen, South Dakota

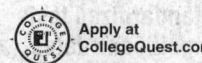
Apply at CollegeQuest.com

- **State-supported**, comprehensive, founded 1901
- **Degrees** associate, bachelor's, and master's
- **Small-town** 52-acre campus

- **Coed**, 2,299 undergraduate students, 78% full-time, 60% women, 40% men
- **Minimally difficult** entrance level, 93% of applicants were admitted
- **31.7% graduate** in 6 years or less
- **$4401 tuition** and fees (in-state); $8219 (out-of-state)
- **$5.8 million endowment**

Northern State University offers the personalized academic atmosphere of a private college at a public school price. Northern has 38 nationally accredited majors in business, education, fine arts, and arts and sciences. Current technology, with superior access, numerous social opportunities, and an almost perfect placement rate, is just one of the benefits that Northern's 3,200 students enjoy. Telephone: 800-NSU-5330 (toll-free).

Part of South Dakota Board of Regents.

Students *Undergraduates:* 1,793 full-time, 506 part-time. Students come from 25 states and territories, 10 other countries. *The most frequently chosen baccalaureate fields are:* business/marketing, education, psychology. **Graduate:** 275 in graduate degree programs.

From out-of-state	19%	Age 25 or older	17%
Transferred in	7%	International students	1%
African Americans	0.5%	Asian Americans/Pacific Islanders	1%
Hispanic Americans	0.3%	Native Americans	10%

Faculty 89 full-time.

Expenses (1999–2000) *Tuition, state resident:* full-time $3076; part-time $58 per credit hour. *Tuition, nonresident:* full-time $6894; part-time $186 per credit hour. *Required fees:* full-time $1325; $44 per credit hour. Full-time tuition and fees vary according to course level, course load, and reciprocity agreements. Part-time tuition and fees vary according to course level, course load, and reciprocity agreements. *College room and board:* $2575; room only: $1312. Room and board charges vary according to board plan. *Payment plan:* installment. *Waivers:* employees or children of employees.

Library Beulah Williams Library. *Operations spending 1999–2000:* $853,323. *Collection:* 179,135 titles, 1,338 serial subscriptions, 5,415 audiovisual materials.

College life *Housing:* on-campus residence required through sophomore year. *Option:* coed. *Most popular organizations:* Student Ambassadors, Choices, Honor Society, Native American Student Association.

Campus security 24-hour emergency response devices, controlled dormitory access, evening patrols.

After graduation *Career center:* 1 full-time personnel. Services include job fairs, resume preparation, resume referral, career counseling, careers library, job bank, job interviews.

Freshmen 1,060 applied, 988 admitted, 579 enrolled. 18 valedictorians.

Average high school GPA	3.06	SAT verbal scores above 500	N/R
SAT math scores above 500	N/R	ACT above 18	80%
From top 10% of their h.s. class	6%	From top quarter	26%
From top half	58%	1998 freshmen returning in 1999	60%

Application *Options:* eApply at www.CollegeQuest.com, Common Application, early admission, deferred entrance. *Application fee:* $15. *Required:* high school transcript; minimum X GPA. *Required for some:* letters of recommendation.

Standardized tests *Admission:* Required: SAT I or ACT.

Significant dates *Application deadlines:* 9/1 (freshmen), 9/1 (transfers).

Freshman Application Contact
Mr. Mike Mutzinger, Director of Admissions, Northern State University, 1200 South Jay Street, Aberdeen, SD 57401-7198. **Phone:** 605-626-2544. **Fax:** 605-626-3022. **E-mail:** admissions1@northern.edu

Visit CollegeQuest.com for information on majors offered and athletics. College video available at CollegeQuest.com.

OGLALA LAKOTA COLLEGE
Kyle, South Dakota

Admissions Office Contact
Oglala Lakota College, PO Box 490, Kyle, SD 57752-0490. **Fax:** 605-455-2787.

Peterson's Guide to Four-Year Colleges 2001  753

South Dakota

Oglala Lakota College (continued)

PRESENTATION COLLEGE
Aberdeen, South Dakota

- **Independent Roman Catholic**, 4-year, founded 1951
- **Degrees** associate and bachelor's
- **Small-town** 100-acre campus
- **Coed**, 421 undergraduate students, 76% full-time, 80% women, 20% men
- **Noncompetitive** entrance level
- **$7762 tuition** and fees

Students *Undergraduates:* 319 full-time, 102 part-time. Students come from 16 states and territories.

| From out-of-state | 27% | Reside on campus | 15% |
| Age 25 or older | 32% | Transferred in | 20% |

Faculty 53 (49% full-time).

Expenses (1999–2000) *Comprehensive fee:* $11,162 includes full-time tuition ($7502), mandatory fees ($260), and room and board ($3400). Full-time tuition and fees vary according to program. Room and board charges vary according to board plan and housing facility. *Part-time tuition:* $286 per credit. *Part-time fees:* $130 per term part-time. Part-time tuition and fees vary according to course load and program. *Payment plan:* installment. *Waivers:* senior citizens and employees or children of employees.

Library Presentation College Library plus 1 other. *Collection:* 40,000 titles, 430 serial subscriptions, 2,900 audiovisual materials.

College life *Housing:* on-campus residence required in freshman year. *Option:* coed. *Most popular organizations:* Wellness, National Student Nursing Association, Social Work Organization, Theatre Production.

Campus security 24-hour emergency response devices and patrols, late-night transport-escort service, controlled dormitory access.

After graduation 40 organizations recruited on campus 1997–98. *Career center:* 1 part-time personnel. Services include job fairs, resume preparation, interview workshops, resume referral, career/interest testing, career counseling, careers library, job bank.

Freshmen 76 enrolled.

Average high school GPA	2.88	SAT verbal scores above 500	N/R
SAT math scores above 500	N/R	ACT above 18	N/R
From top 10% of their h.s. class	1%	From top quarter	18%
From top half	50%		

Application *Application fee:* $15. *Required:* high school transcript. *Required for some:* minimum 2.0 GPA.

Standardized tests *Admission: Required:* ACT ASSET. *Recommended:* ACT.

Significant dates *Application deadlines:* rolling (freshmen), rolling (transfers). *Financial aid deadline priority date:* 4/1.

Freshman Application Contact
Ms. Brenda Schmitt, Director of Admissions and Financial Aid, Presentation College, 1500 North Main Street, Aberdeen, SD 57401-1299. **Phone:** 605-225-8493 Ext. 492. **Toll-free phone:** 800-247-6499 (in-state); 800-437-6060 (out-of-state). **Fax:** 605-229-8518. **E-mail:** admit@presentation.edu

Visit CollegeQuest.com for information on majors offered and athletics.

SINTE GLESKA UNIVERSITY
Rosebud, South Dakota

- **Independent**, comprehensive, founded 1970
- **Degrees** associate, bachelor's, and master's
- **Rural** 52-acre campus
- **Coed**
- **Noncompetitive** entrance level
- **$1770 tuition** and fees

Expenses (1999–2000) *Tuition:* full-time $1632; part-time $68 per credit. *Required fees:* full-time $138; $2 per credit; $45 per term part-time.

College life *Housing:* college housing not available. *Most popular organizations:* Student Association, Lakota Club.

Campus security Late-night transport-escort service.

Application *Application fee:* $0. *Required:* high school transcript.

Admissions Office Contact
Sinte Gleska University, PO Box 490, Rosebud, SD 57570-0490. **Fax:** 605-747-2098.

Visit CollegeQuest.com for information on athletics.

SOUTH DAKOTA SCHOOL OF MINES AND TECHNOLOGY
Rapid City, South Dakota

- **State-supported**, university, founded 1885
- **Degrees** bachelor's, master's, and doctoral
- **Suburban** 120-acre campus
- **Coed**, 1,827 undergraduate students, 86% full-time, 28% women, 72% men
- **Moderately difficult** entrance level, 97% of applicants were admitted
- **15:1** student-to-undergraduate faculty ratio
- **33.3% graduate** in 6 years or less
- **$3850 tuition** and fees (in-state); $7924 (out-of-state)
- **$4058 average financial aid** package, $12,709 average indebtedness upon graduation, $13 million endowment

Students *Undergraduates:* 1,576 full-time, 251 part-time. Students come from 38 states and territories, 23 other countries. *The most frequently chosen baccalaureate fields are:* computer/information sciences, engineering/engineering technologies, mathematics. *Graduate:* 252 in graduate degree programs.

From out-of-state	33%	Reside on campus	28%
Age 25 or older	11%	Transferred in	8%
International students	3%	African Americans	0.4%
Asian Americans/Pacific Islanders	1%	Hispanic Americans	1%
Native Americans	2%		

Faculty 131 (87% full-time), 79% with terminal degrees.

Expenses (1999–2000) *Tuition, state resident:* full-time $1867; part-time $58 per semester hour. *Tuition, nonresident:* full-time $5941; part-time $186 per semester hour. *Required fees:* full-time $1983; $62 per semester hour. Full-time tuition and fees vary according to reciprocity agreements. Part-time tuition and fees vary according to reciprocity agreements. *College room and board:* $3122; room only: $1396. Room and board charges vary according to housing facility. *Payment plan:* installment. *Waivers:* senior citizens.

Library Devereaux Library. *Operations spending 1999–2000:* $652,007. *Collection:* 137,864 titles, 461 serial subscriptions, 2,101 audiovisual materials.

College life *Housing:* on-campus residence required through sophomore year. *Options:* coed, men-only, women-only. *Social organizations:* national fraternities, national sororities; 11% of eligible men and 10% of eligible women are members. *Most popular organizations:* TONITE (Techs Outrageous New Initiative for Total Entertainment), SADD (Students Against Drunk Driving), ASCE (American Society of Civil Engineers), ASME (American Society of Mechanical Engineers), ski club.

Campus security 24-hour emergency response devices and patrols, student patrols, late-night transport-escort service, controlled dormitory access.

After graduation 98 organizations recruited on campus 1997–98. 80% of class of 1998 had job offers within 6 months. *Career center:* 2 full-time, 6 part-time personnel. Services include job fairs, resume preparation, resume referral, career counseling, careers library, job bank, job interviews.

Freshmen 664 applied, 644 admitted, 423 enrolled. 2 National Merit Scholars, 17 class presidents, 11 valedictorians, 31 student government officers.

Average high school GPA	3.44	SAT verbal scores above 500	N/R
SAT math scores above 500	89%	ACT above 18	98%
From top 10% of their h.s. class	21%	From top quarter	53%
From top half	81%	1998 freshmen returning in 1999	68%

Application *Application fee:* $15. *Required:* high school transcript. *Required for some:* minimum 2.6 GPA.

Standardized tests *Admission: Required:* SAT I or ACT.

Significant dates *Application deadlines:* rolling (freshmen), rolling (transfers). *Financial aid deadline priority date:* 4/15.

Freshman Application Contact
Donald Hapward, Director of Admissions, South Dakota School of Mines and Technology, 501 East Saint Joseph, Rapid City, SD 57701-3995. **Phone:**

605-394-2414 Ext. 1266. **Toll-free phone:** 800-544-8162 Ext. 2414. **Fax:** 605-394-2914. **E-mail:** undergraduate_admissions@silver.sdsmt.edu

Visit CollegeQuest.com for information on majors offered and athletics.

SOUTH DAKOTA STATE UNIVERSITY
Brookings, South Dakota

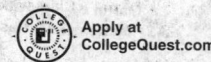
Apply at CollegeQuest.com

- State-supported, university, founded 1881
- Degrees associate, bachelor's, master's, doctoral, and first professional
- Small-town 260-acre campus
- Coed, 7,060 undergraduate students, 88% full-time, 49% women, 51% men
- Moderately difficult entrance level, 94% of applicants were admitted
- 18:1 student-to-undergraduate faculty ratio
- $3357 tuition and fees (in-state); $7431 (out-of-state)
- $6115 average financial aid package, $14,084 average indebtedness upon graduation, $41.3 million endowment

SDSU is a 4-year, comprehensive university ranked by *U.S. News & World Report* as the most efficient university in the Midwest and a best-value university. SDSU offers the largest selection of academic programs within the state. Majors are available in agriculture and biological sciences, arts and science, education, engineering, family and consumer sciences, nursing, and pharmacy.

Students *Undergraduates:* 6,200 full-time, 860 part-time. Students come from 44 states and territories, 27 other countries. *The most frequently chosen baccalaureate fields are:* agriculture, health professions and related sciences, social sciences and history. *Graduate:* 186 in professional programs, 972 in other graduate degree programs.

From out-of-state	33%	Reside on campus	41%
International students	1%	African Americans	0.1%
Asian Americans/Pacific Islanders	0.1%	Hispanic Americans	0.1%
Native Americans	0.3%		

Faculty 530 (96% full-time), 67% with terminal degrees.

Expenses (1999–2000) *Tuition, state resident:* full-time $1867; part-time $58 per credit. *Tuition, nonresident:* full-time $5941; part-time $186 per credit. *Required fees:* full-time $1490; $47 per credit. Full-time tuition and fees vary according to location and reciprocity agreements. Part-time tuition and fees vary according to location and reciprocity agreements. *College room and board:* $2868; room only: $1364. Room and board charges vary according to board plan and housing facility. *Payment plans:* installment, deferred payment. *Waivers:* senior citizens and employees or children of employees.

Library H. M. Briggs Library. *Operations spending 1999–2000:* $2.9 million. *Collection:* 555,523 titles, 6,023 serial subscriptions, 2,504 audiovisual materials.

College life *Housing:* on-campus residence required through sophomore year. *Option:* coed. *Social organizations:* national fraternities, national sororities; 4% of eligible men and 3% of eligible women are members. *Most popular organizations:* Student Association, University Programming Council, Block and Bridle club.

Campus security 24-hour emergency response devices and patrols, student patrols, late-night transport-escort service.

After graduation 125 organizations recruited on campus 1997–98. *Career center:* 4 full-time personnel. Services include job fairs, resume preparation, interview workshops, resume referral, career/interest testing, career counseling, careers library, job bank, job interviews. *Graduate education:* 5% of class of 1999 went directly to graduate and professional school.

Freshmen 2,749 applied, 2,589 admitted, 1,452 enrolled. 6 National Merit Scholars, 77 valedictorians.

Average high school GPA	3.32	SAT verbal scores above 500	N/R
SAT math scores above 500	N/R	ACT above 18	87%
From top 10% of their h.s. class	13%	From top quarter	35%
From top half	70%	1998 freshmen returning in 1999	80%

Application *Options:* eApply at www.CollegeQuest.com, electronic application, early admission, deferred entrance. *Application fee:* $15. *Required:* high school transcript; minimum 2.6 GPA; minimum ACT score of 18.

Standardized tests *Admission:* Required: ACT.
Significant dates *Application deadlines:* rolling (freshmen), rolling (transfers). *Financial aid deadline priority date:* 3/1.
Freshman Application Contact
Ms. Michelle Kuebler, Assistant Director of Admissions, South Dakota State University, PO Box 2201, Brookings, SD 57007. **Phone:** 605-688-4121. **Toll-free phone:** 800-952-3541. **Fax:** 605-688-6384. **E-mail:** sdsuadms@adm.sdstate.edu

Visit CollegeQuest.com for information on majors offered and athletics. College video and electronic viewbook available at CollegeQuest.com.

UNIVERSITY OF SIOUX FALLS
Sioux Falls, South Dakota

- Independent American Baptist, comprehensive, founded 1883
- Degrees associate, bachelor's, and master's
- Suburban 22-acre campus
- Coed, 941 undergraduate students, 81% full-time, 56% women, 44% men
- Moderately difficult entrance level, 97% of applicants were admitted
- 40% graduate in 6 years or less
- $11,500 tuition and fees
- $8.7 million endowment

Students *Undergraduates:* 763 full-time, 178 part-time. Students come from 19 states and territories, 6 other countries. *Graduate:* 161 in graduate degree programs.

From out-of-state	26%	Reside on campus	28%
Age 25 or older	40%	Transferred in	12%
International students	1%	African Americans	1%
Asian Americans/Pacific Islanders	1%	Hispanic Americans	1%
Native Americans	0.4%		

Faculty 76 (47% full-time), 45% with terminal degrees.

Expenses (1999–2000) *Comprehensive fee:* $15,200 includes full-time tuition ($11,500) and room and board ($3700). Room and board charges vary according to board plan. *Part-time tuition:* $195 per semester hour. Part-time tuition and fees vary according to course load. *Payment plan:* installment. *Waivers:* senior citizens and employees or children of employees.

Library Norman B. Mears Library. *Operations spending 1999–2000:* $190,827. *Collection:* 57,399 titles, 364 serial subscriptions, 4,499 audiovisual materials.

College life *Housing:* on-campus residence required through sophomore year. *Options:* coed, men-only, women-only. *Most popular organizations:* Fellowship of Christian Athletes, Campus Ministry Outreach.

Campus security Late-night transport-escort service, controlled dormitory access.

After graduation 188 organizations recruited on campus 1997–98. 94% of class of 1998 had job offers within 6 months. *Career center:* 2 full-time, 1 part-time personnel. Services include job fairs, resume preparation, resume referral, career counseling, careers library, job bank, job interviews. *Graduate education:* 17% of class of 1999 went directly to graduate and professional school.

Freshmen 424 applied, 413 admitted, 181 enrolled.

Average high school GPA	2.98	SAT verbal scores above 500	N/R
SAT math scores above 500	N/R	ACT above 18	80%
From top 10% of their h.s. class	13%	From top quarter	29%
From top half	54%	1998 freshmen returning in 1999	64%

Application *Options:* early admission, deferred entrance. *Application fee:* $25. *Required:* high school transcript. *Required for some:* 2 letters of recommendation; interview. *Recommended:* essay or personal statement; minimum 2.0 GPA.

Standardized tests *Admission:* Required: SAT I and SAT II or ACT.
Significant dates *Application deadlines:* rolling (freshmen), rolling (transfers). *Financial aid deadline priority date:* 3/1.
Freshman Application Contact
Ms. Kathleen Houseman, Director of Admissions, University of Sioux Falls, 1101 West 22nd Street, Sioux Falls, SD 57105-1699. **Phone:** 605-331-6600. **Toll-free phone:** 800-888-1047. **Fax:** 605-331-6615. **E-mail:** admissions@usiouxfalls.edu

Visit CollegeQuest.com for information on majors offered and athletics. College video available at CollegeQuest.com.

South Dakota–Tennessee

UNIVERSITY OF SOUTH DAKOTA
Vermillion, South Dakota

- **State-supported**, university, founded 1862
- **Degrees** associate, bachelor's, master's, doctoral, and first professional
- **Small-town** 216-acre campus
- **Coed**, 4,811 undergraduate students, 85% full-time, 57% women, 43% men
- **Moderately difficult** entrance level, 99% of applicants were admitted
- **14:1** student-to-undergraduate faculty ratio
- **44% graduate** in 6 years or less
- **$3459 tuition** and fees (in-state); $7533 (out-of-state)
- **$5820 average financial aid** package, $37.4 million endowment

Students *Undergraduates:* 4,110 full-time, 701 part-time. Students come from 40 states and territories, 41 other countries: *The most frequently chosen baccalaureate fields are:* business/marketing, education, health professions and related sciences. *Graduate:* 396 in professional programs, 1,370 in other graduate degree programs.

From out-of-state	18%	Reside on campus	32%
Age 25 or older	22%	Transferred in	6%
International students	1%	African Americans	1%
Asian Americans/Pacific Islanders	1%	Hispanic Americans	1%
Native Americans	2%		

Faculty 295 (99% full-time), 83% with terminal degrees.

Expenses (1999–2000) *Tuition, state resident:* full-time $1867; part-time $58 per credit hour. *Tuition, nonresident:* full-time $5941; part-time $186 per credit hour. *Required fees:* full-time $1592; $50 per credit hour. Full-time tuition and fees vary according to course load and reciprocity agreements. Part-time tuition and fees vary according to course load and reciprocity agreements. *College room and board:* $3094; room only: $1408. Room and board charges vary according to board plan and housing facility. *Payment plans:* installment, deferred payment. *Waivers:* children of alumni and senior citizens.

Library I. D. Weeks Library plus 2 others. *Operations spending 1999–2000:* $4.6 million. *Collection:* 1.5 million titles, 2,862 serial subscriptions, 3,766 audiovisual materials.

College life *Housing:* on-campus residence required through sophomore year. *Options:* coed, men-only, women-only. *Social organizations:* national fraternities, national sororities; 20% of eligible men and 15% of eligible women are members. *Most popular organizations:* program council, residence hall association, Interfraternity/Panhellenic Council, Student Ambassadors, Delta Sigma Pi.

Campus security 24-hour emergency response devices and patrols, student patrols, late-night transport-escort service, controlled dormitory access.

After graduation 60 organizations recruited on campus 1997–98. *Career center:* 3 full-time, 1 part-time personnel. Services include job fairs, resume preparation, interview workshops, resume referral, career/interest testing, career counseling, careers library, job bank, job interviews.

Freshmen 2,905 applied, 2,869 admitted, 966 enrolled. 45 valedictorians.

Average high school GPA	3.2	SAT verbal scores above 500	N/R
SAT math scores above 500	N/R	ACT above 18	90%
From top 10% of their h.s. class	14%	From top quarter	36%
From top half	69%	1998 freshmen returning in 1999	72%

Application *Options:* electronic application, early admission, deferred entrance. *Application fee:* $15. *Required:* high school transcript. *Required for some:* letters of recommendation. *Recommended:* minimum 2.6 GPA.

Standardized tests *Admission: Required:* SAT I or ACT.

Significant dates *Application deadlines:* rolling (freshmen), rolling (transfers). *Financial aid deadline priority date:* 3/1.

Freshman Application Contact
Ms. Paula Tacke, Director of Admissions, University of South Dakota, 414 East Clark Street, Vermillion, SD 57069. **Phone:** 605-677-5434. **Toll-free phone:** 877-269-6837. **Fax:** 605-677-6753. **E-mail:** admiss@usd.edu

Visit CollegeQuest.com for information on majors offered and athletics.

TENNESSEE

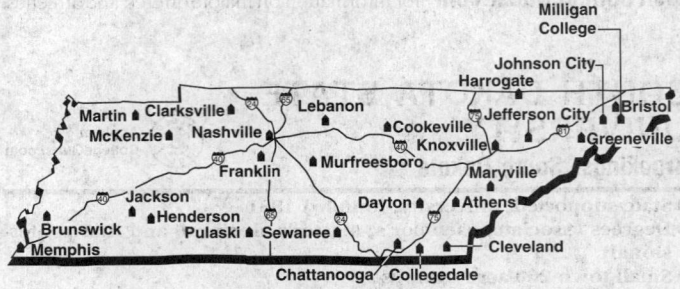

AMERICAN BAPTIST COLLEGE OF AMERICAN BAPTIST THEOLOGICAL SEMINARY
Nashville, Tennessee

- **Independent Baptist**, 4-year, founded 1924
- **Degrees** associate and bachelor's
- **Urban** 52-acre campus
- **Coed**
- **Noncompetitive** entrance level
- **$2860 tuition** and fees

Expenses (1999–2000) *One-time required fee:* $5. *Tuition:* full-time $2780; part-time $140 per credit hour. *Required fees:* full-time $80; $30 per term part-time. *College room only:* $1028. Room and board charges vary according to gender.

College life *Housing: Option:* coed. *Social organizations:* national fraternities; 30% of men are members. *Most popular organizations:* Student Government Association, Vespers Service.

Campus security Student patrols, security patrols from 10 p.m. to 7 a.m.

Application *Options:* electronic application, deferred entrance. *Application fee:* $20. *Required:* high school transcript; 3 letters of recommendation; interview. *Recommended:* essay or personal statement.

Standardized tests *Admission: Recommended:* SAT I or ACT.

Admissions Office Contact
American Baptist College of American Baptist Theological Seminary, 1800 Baptist World Center Drive, Nashville, TN 37207.

Visit CollegeQuest.com for information on athletics.

AQUINAS COLLEGE
Nashville, Tennessee

- **Independent Roman Catholic**, 4-year, founded 1961
- **Degrees** associate and bachelor's
- **Urban** 92-acre campus
- **Coed**, 410 undergraduate students
- **Moderately difficult** entrance level
- **15:1** student-to-undergraduate faculty ratio
- **$8800 tuition** and fees
- **$2.3 million** endowment

Students *Undergraduates:* Students come from 5 states and territories, 2 other countries.

From out-of-state	10%	Age 25 or older	61%

Faculty 54.

Expenses (1999–2000) *Tuition:* full-time $8500; part-time $300 per semester hour. *Required fees:* full-time $300; $140 per term part-time. Full-time tuition and fees vary according to program. Part-time tuition and fees vary according to program. *Payment plan:* installment.

Library Aquinas College Library plus 1 other. *Operations spending 1999–2000:* $133,167. *Collection:* 45,762 titles, 301 serial subscriptions.

College life *Housing:* college housing not available. *Most popular organization:* Student Council.

Tennessee

Campus security 24-hour emergency response devices, patrols by security after class hours.
After graduation 2 organizations recruited on campus 1997–98. *Career center:* 1 part-time personnel. Services include job fairs, resume preparation, career/interest testing, career counseling, careers library, job bank.
Freshmen

SAT verbal scores above 500	N/R	SAT math scores above 500	N/R
ACT above 18	56%	From top 10% of their h.s. class	5%
From top quarter	21%	From top half	38%

Application *Option:* deferred entrance. *Application fee:* $10. *Required:* essay or personal statement; high school transcript; minimum 2.0 GPA; interview.
Standardized tests *Admission: Required:* SAT I or ACT.
Significant dates *Application deadlines:* rolling (freshmen), rolling (transfers). *Financial aid deadline priority date:* 5/1.
Freshman Application Contact
Mr. Neil J. Devine, Director of Planning and Admissions, Aquinas College, 4210 Harding Road, Nashville, TN 37205-2005. **Phone:** 615-297-7545 Ext. 426. **Fax:** 615-297-7970.
Visit CollegeQuest.com for information on majors offered and athletics.

AUSTIN PEAY STATE UNIVERSITY
Clarksville, Tennessee

- **State-supported**, comprehensive, founded 1927
- **Degrees** associate, bachelor's, master's, and post-master's certificates
- **Suburban** 200-acre campus with easy access to Nashville
- **Coed**, 6,233 undergraduate students, 70% full-time, 59% women, 41% men
- **Moderately difficult** entrance level, 58% of applicants were admitted
- **17:1 student-to-undergraduate faculty ratio**
- **$2584 tuition** and fees (in-state); $7700 (out-of-state)
- **$6924 average financial aid** package, $16,108 average indebtedness upon graduation, $3.1 million endowment

Part of Tennessee Board of Regents.
Students *Undergraduates:* 4,367 full-time, 1,866 part-time. Students come from 37 states and territories, 17 other countries. *The most frequently chosen baccalaureate fields are:* business/marketing, health professions and related sciences, interdisciplinary studies. *Graduate:* 455 in graduate degree programs.

From out-of-state	3%	Reside on campus	15%
Age 25 or older	42%	Transferred in	12%
International students	0.3%	African Americans	18%
Asian Americans/Pacific Islanders	3%	Hispanic Americans	5%
Native Americans	1%		

Faculty 486 (56% full-time), 56% with terminal degrees.
Expenses (1999–2000) *Tuition, state resident:* full-time $2020; part-time $90 per semester hour. *Tuition, nonresident:* full-time $7136; part-time $314 per semester hour. *Required fees:* full-time $564; $20 per credit; $64 per term part-time. Part-time tuition and fees vary according to course load. *College room and board:* $3230; room only: $1800. Room and board charges vary according to board plan and housing facility. *Payment plans:* installment, deferred payment. *Waivers:* senior citizens and employees or children of employees.
Library Felix G. Woodward Library. *Operations spending 1999–2000:* $2.2 million. *Collection:* 174,474 titles, 1,787 serial subscriptions, 7,374 audiovisual materials.
College life *Housing:* on-campus residence required in freshman year. *Options:* coed, men-only, women-only. *Social organizations:* national fraternities, national sororities; 6% of eligible men and 4% of eligible women are members.
Campus security 24-hour patrols, late-night transport-escort service, controlled dormitory access.
After graduation *Career center:* 3 full-time, 1 part-time personnel. Services include job fairs, resume preparation, resume referral, career counseling, careers library, job bank, job interviews.

Freshmen 2,967 applied, 1,713 admitted, 915 enrolled.

Average high school GPA	2.94	SAT verbal scores above 500	50%
SAT math scores above 500	41%	ACT above 18	82%
From top 10% of their h.s. class	10%	From top quarter	26%
From top half	60%	1998 freshmen returning in 1999	64%

Application *Options:* early admission, deferred entrance. *Application fee:* $15. *Required:* high school transcript; 2.75 high school GPA, minimum ACT composite score of 19, or SAT I combined score of 720.
Standardized tests *Admission: Required:* SAT I or ACT.
Significant dates *Application deadlines:* 8/15 (freshmen), rolling (transfers). *Financial aid deadline priority date:* 4/1.
Freshman Application Contact
Mr. Charles McCorkle, Director of Admissions, Austin Peay State University, PO Box 4548, Clarksville, TN 37044-4548. **Phone:** 931-221-7661. **Toll-free phone:** 800-844-2778. **Fax:** 931-221-5994. **E-mail:** admissions@apsu01.apsu.edu
Visit CollegeQuest.com for information on majors offered and athletics.

BAPTIST MEMORIAL COLLEGE OF HEALTH SCIENCES
Memphis, Tennessee

Admissions Office Contact
Baptist Memorial College of Health Sciences, 1003 Monroe Avenue, Memphis, TN 38104. **Toll-free phone:** 800-796-7171.

BELMONT UNIVERSITY
Nashville, Tennessee

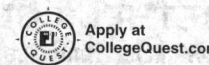
Apply at CollegeQuest.com

- **Independent Baptist**, comprehensive, founded 1951
- **Degrees** bachelor's, master's, and postbachelor's certificates
- **Urban** 34-acre campus
- **Coed**, 2,521 undergraduate students, 84% full-time, 61% women, 39% men
- **Moderately difficult** entrance level, 78% of applicants were admitted
- **10:1 student-to-undergraduate faculty ratio**
- **43% graduate** in 6 years or less
- **$11,600 tuition** and fees
- **$11,764 average financial aid** package, $20,469 average indebtedness upon graduation, $38.2 million endowment

Students *Undergraduates:* 2,130 full-time, 391 part-time. Students come from 48 states and territories, 12 other countries. *The most frequently chosen baccalaureate fields are:* business/marketing, health professions and related sciences, visual/performing arts. *Graduate:* 505 in graduate degree programs.

From out-of-state	37%	Reside on campus	50%
Age 25 or older	17%	Transferred in	12%
International students	1%	African Americans	3%
Asian Americans/Pacific Islanders	1%	Hispanic Americans	1%
Native Americans	0.5%		

Faculty 380 (51% full-time).
Expenses (1999–2000) *Comprehensive fee:* $16,600 includes full-time tuition ($11,300), mandatory fees ($300), and room and board ($5000). *College room only:* $2390. Full-time tuition and fees vary according to class time and course load. Room and board charges vary according to board plan, housing facility, and location. *Part-time tuition:* $425 per semester hour. *Part-time fees:* $90 per term part-time. Part-time tuition and fees vary according to course load. *Payment plans:* installment, deferred payment. *Waivers:* senior citizens and employees or children of employees.
Library Lila D. Bunch Library. *Operations spending 1999–2000:* $1.4 million. *Collection:* 166,194 titles, 1,381 serial subscriptions, 20,958 audiovisual materials.
College life *Housing:* on-campus residence required through sophomore year. *Options:* men-only, women-only. *Social organizations:* national fraternities, national sororities, local fraternities, local sororities; 6% of eligible men and 8% of eligible women are members.
Campus security 24-hour emergency response devices and patrols, late-night transport-escort service, controlled dormitory access.

Tennessee

Belmont University (continued)

After graduation 160 organizations recruited on campus 1997–98. *Career center:* 4 full-time personnel. Services include job fairs, resume preparation, interview workshops, resume referral, career/interest testing, career counseling, careers library, job bank, job interviews. *Graduate education:* 20% of class of 1999 went directly to graduate and professional school.

Freshmen 1,130 applied, 884 admitted, 507 enrolled. 18 valedictorians.

Average high school GPA	3.43	SAT verbal scores above 500	82%
SAT math scores above 500	80%	ACT above 18	99%
From top 10% of their h.s. class	26%	From top quarter	51%
From top half	70%	1998 freshmen returning in 1999	76%

Application *Options:* eApply at www.CollegeQuest.com, Common Application, deferred entrance. *Application fee:* $35. *Required:* essay or personal statement; high school transcript; minimum 3.0 GPA; letters of recommendation; resume of activities. *Required for some:* interview.

Standardized tests *Admission: Required:* SAT I or ACT.

Significant dates *Application deadlines:* 8/1 (freshmen), 8/1 (transfers). *Financial aid deadline priority date:* 3/1.

Freshman Application Contact
Dr. Kathryn Baugher, Dean of Enrollment Services, Belmont University, 1900 Belmont Boulevard, Nashville, TN 37212. **Phone:** 615-460-6785. **Toll-free phone:** 800-56E-NROL. **E-mail:** buadmission@mail.belmont.edu

Visit CollegeQuest.com for information on majors offered and athletics. College video available at CollegeQuest.com.

■ *See page 1246 for a narrative description.*

BETHEL COLLEGE
McKenzie, Tennessee

Apply at CollegeQuest.com

- **Independent Cumberland Presbyterian**, comprehensive, founded 1842
- **Degrees** bachelor's and master's
- **Small-town** 100-acre campus
- **Coed**, 715 undergraduate students, 88% full-time, 49% women, 51% men
- **Minimally difficult** entrance level, 65% of applicants were admitted
- **16:1 student-to-undergraduate faculty ratio**
- **$7800 tuition** and fees
- **$8614 average financial aid** package, $6.6 million endowment

Students *Undergraduates:* 629 full-time, 86 part-time. Students come from 28 states and territories, 2 other countries. *The most frequently chosen baccalaureate fields are:* business/marketing, biological/life sciences, education. *Graduate:* 46 in graduate degree programs.

From out-of-state	19%	Reside on campus	50%
Age 25 or older	50%	Transferred in	8%
International students	1%	African Americans	13%
Asian Americans/Pacific Islanders	0.4%	Hispanic Americans	1%
Native Americans	1%		

Faculty 72 (44% full-time), 33% with terminal degrees.

Expenses (1999–2000) *Comprehensive fee:* $12,180 includes full-time tuition ($7550), mandatory fees ($250), and room and board ($4380). *Part-time tuition:* $225 per semester hour. *Part-time fees:* $10 per semester hour. Part-time tuition and fees vary according to course load. *Payment plan:* installment. *Waivers:* employees or children of employees.

Library Burroughs Learning Center. *Operations spending 1999–2000:* $530,995. *Collection:* 73,288 titles, 254 serial subscriptions.

College life *Housing:* on-campus residence required through senior year. *Options:* coed, men-only, women-only, disabled students. *Social organizations:* local fraternities, local sororities; 50% of eligible men and 50% of eligible women are members. *Most popular organizations:* FCA, SETA (Education), Black Student Union, Honor Club.

Campus security Night patrols by trained security personnel.

After graduation 7 organizations recruited on campus 1997–98. *Career center:* 1 full-time personnel. Services include job fairs, resume preparation, resume referral, career/interest testing, career counseling, careers library, job bank, job interviews. *Graduate education:* 1% of class of 1999 went directly to graduate and professional school; 1% education.

Freshmen 516 applied, 333 admitted, 147 enrolled.

Average high school GPA	2.85	SAT verbal scores above 500	N/R
SAT math scores above 500	N/R	ACT above 18	80%
From top 10% of their h.s. class	7%	From top quarter	19%
From top half	62%	1998 freshmen returning in 1999	54%

Application *Options:* eApply at www.CollegeQuest.com, Common Application, early admission. *Application fee:* $30. *Required:* high school transcript; minimum 2.5 GPA. *Required for some:* essay or personal statement; 1 letter of recommendation; interview.

Standardized tests *Admission: Required:* SAT I or ACT.

Significant dates *Application deadlines:* 9/1 (freshmen), 9/1 (transfers). *Financial aid deadline priority date:* 2/15.

Freshman Application Contact
Ms. Darla Zakowicz, Director of Recruitment and Retention, Bethel College, 325 Cherry Avenue, McKenzie, TN 38201. **Phone:** 901-352-4030. **Fax:** 901-352-4069. **E-mail:** zakowiczd@bethel-college.edu

Visit CollegeQuest.com for information on majors offered and athletics.

BRYAN COLLEGE
Dayton, Tennessee

- **Independent interdenominational**, 4-year, founded 1930
- **Degrees** associate and bachelor's
- **Small-town** 100-acre campus
- **Coed**, 519 undergraduate students, 96% full-time, 56% women, 44% men
- **Moderately difficult** entrance level, 74% of applicants were admitted
- **47% graduate** in 6 years or less
- **$11,200 tuition** and fees
- **$7457 average financial aid** package, $10,952 average indebtedness upon graduation, $2 million endowment

Bryan College is a 4-year, interdenominational, Christian liberal arts college. High-quality academics, spiritual atmosphere, and close interpersonal relationships highlight the reasons students choose Bryan College. BryanNET, an innovative campuswide computer network, provides students with Internet, library research resources, and cutting-edge software. Visits to the Bryan campus are encouraged.

Students *Undergraduates:* 498 full-time, 21 part-time. Students come from 33 states and territories, 15 other countries.

Reside on campus	74%	Age 25 or older	1%
Transferred in	6%	International students	4%
African Americans	2%	Asian Americans/Pacific Islanders	0.4%
Hispanic Americans	1%	Native Americans	0.2%

Faculty 50 (62% full-time).

Expenses (1999–2000) *Comprehensive fee:* $15,200 includes full-time tuition ($11,200) and room and board ($4000). *College room only:* $1800. *Part-time tuition:* $450 per semester hour.

Library Ironside Memorial Library. *Operations spending 1999–2000:* $156,248. *Collection:* 119,348 titles, 949 serial subscriptions, 3,786 audiovisual materials.

College life *Housing:* on-campus residence required through senior year. *Options:* men-only, women-only. *Most popular organizations:* Practical Christian Involvement, Student Government Association, Fellowship of Christian Athletes, Hilltop Players, chorale.

Campus security Student patrols, late-night transport-escort service, controlled dormitory access, police patrols.

After graduation *Career center:* 1 part-time personnel. Services include job fairs, resume preparation, resume referral, career counseling, careers library, job bank, job interviews.

Freshmen 427 applied, 316 admitted, 140 enrolled. 4 valedictorians.

Average high school GPA	3.4	SAT verbal scores above 500	76%
SAT math scores above 500	68%	ACT above 18	87%
From top 10% of their h.s. class	21%	From top quarter	50%
From top half	91%	1998 freshmen returning in 1999	77%

Application *Options:* electronic application, early admission, deferred entrance. *Application fee:* $20. *Required:* essay or personal statement; high school transcript; minimum 2.0 GPA; 3 letters of recommendation. *Required for some:* interview.

Standardized tests *Admission: Required:* ACT. *Recommended:* SAT I.

Significant dates *Application deadlines:* rolling (freshmen), rolling (transfers). *Financial aid deadline priority date:* 5/1.
Freshman Application Contact
Mr. Ronald D. Petitte, Registrar, Bryan College, PO Box 7000, Dayton, TN 37321-7000. **Phone:** 423-775-7237. **Toll-free phone:** 800-277-9522. **Fax:** 423-775-7330. **E-mail:** admiss@bryannet.bryan.edu
Visit CollegeQuest.com for information on majors offered and athletics. College video available at CollegeQuest.com.

CARSON-NEWMAN COLLEGE
Jefferson City, Tennessee

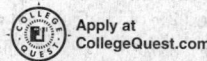
Apply at CollegeQuest.com

- **Independent Southern Baptist**, comprehensive, founded 1851
- **Degrees** associate, bachelor's, and master's
- **Small-town** 90-acre campus with easy access to Knoxville
- **Coed**, 1,908 undergraduate students, 93% full-time, 58% women, 42% men
- **Moderately difficult** entrance level, 88% of applicants were admitted
- **13:1 student-to-undergraduate faculty ratio**
- **54% graduate** in 6 years or less
- **$11,640 tuition** and fees
- **$10,643 average financial aid** package, $14,591 average indebtedness upon graduation, $19.2 million endowment

Students *Undergraduates:* 1,767 full-time, 141 part-time. Students come from 40 states and territories, 23 other countries. *The most frequently chosen baccalaureate fields are:* business/marketing, biological/life sciences, education. *Graduate:* 259 in graduate degree programs.

From out-of-state	40%	Reside on campus	51%
Age 25 or older	13%	Transferred in	7%
International students	2%	African Americans	6%
Asian Americans/Pacific Islanders	0.3%	Hispanic Americans	0.4%
Native Americans	0.1%		

Faculty 177 (67% full-time), 46% with terminal degrees.
Expenses (1999–2000) *Comprehensive fee:* $15,550 includes full-time tuition ($10,960), mandatory fees ($680), and room and board ($3910). *College room only:* $1560. Full-time tuition and fees vary according to class time. Room and board charges vary according to board plan. *Part-time tuition:* $450 per semester hour. *Part-time fees:* $200 per term part-time. Part-time tuition and fees vary according to class time. *Payment plan:* installment. *Waivers:* senior citizens and employees or children of employees.
Library Stephens-Burnett Library plus 1 other. *Operations spending 1999–2000:* $655,997. *Collection:* 2,245 serial subscriptions, 14,008 audiovisual materials.
College life *Housing:* on-campus residence required through junior year. *Options:* men-only, women-only. *Social organizations:* national fraternities, national sororities, local fraternities, local sororities; 5% of eligible men and 5% of eligible women are members. *Most popular organizations:* Baptist Student Union, Fellowship of Christian Athletes, Student Government Association, Student Ambassadors Association, Columbians.
Campus security 24-hour emergency response devices and patrols, late-night transport-escort service, controlled dormitory access.
After graduation 24 organizations recruited on campus 1997–98. *Career center:* 2 full-time, 1 part-time personnel. Services include job fairs, resume preparation, resume referral, career counseling, careers library, job bank, job interviews. *Graduate education:* 25% of class of 1999 went directly to graduate and professional school.
Freshmen 1,220 applied, 1,074 admitted, 384 enrolled.

Average high school GPA	3.25	SAT verbal scores above 500	68%
SAT math scores above 500	70%	ACT above 18	93%
From top 10% of their h.s. class	27%	From top quarter	52%
From top half	80%	1998 freshmen returning in 1999	75%

Application *Options:* eApply at www.CollegeQuest.com, electronic application, deferred entrance. *Application fee:* $25. *Required:* high school transcript; minimum 2.25 GPA; medical history. *Required for some:* essay or personal statement; letters of recommendation; interview. *Recommended:* interview.
Standardized tests *Admission: Required:* SAT I or ACT.

Significant dates *Application deadlines:* 8/1 (freshmen), 8/1 (transfers). *Financial aid deadline priority date:* 4/1.
Freshman Application Contact
Mrs. Sheryl M. Gray, Director of Undergraduate Admissions, Carson-Newman College, PO Box 72025, Jefferson City, TN 37760. **Phone:** 423-471-3223. **Toll-free phone:** 800-678-9061. **Fax:** 423-471-3502. **E-mail:** cnadmiss@cncacc.cn.edu
Visit CollegeQuest.com for information on majors offered and athletics. College video available at CollegeQuest.com.

■ *See page 1372 for a narrative description.*

CHRISTIAN BROTHERS UNIVERSITY
Memphis, Tennessee

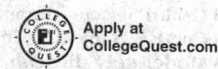
Apply at CollegeQuest.com

- **Independent Roman Catholic**, comprehensive, founded 1871
- **Degrees** bachelor's and master's
- **Urban** 70-acre campus
- **Coed**, 1,485 undergraduate students, 81% full-time, 53% women, 47% men
- **Moderately difficult** entrance level, 77% of applicants were admitted
- **13:1 student-to-undergraduate faculty ratio**
- **$13,490 tuition** and fees
- **$17.3 million endowment**

Students *Undergraduates:* 1,201 full-time, 284 part-time. Students come from 27 states and territories, 44 other countries. *The most frequently chosen baccalaureate fields are:* business/marketing, engineering/engineering technologies, psychology. *Graduate:* 394 in graduate degree programs.

From out-of-state	28%	Reside on campus	31%
Age 25 or older	24%	Transferred in	4%
International students	7%	African Americans	21%
Asian Americans/Pacific Islanders	3%	Hispanic Americans	2%
Native Americans	0.3%		

Faculty 191 (61% full-time).
Expenses (1999–2000) *Comprehensive fee:* $17,440 includes full-time tuition ($13,140), mandatory fees ($350), and room and board ($3950). Room and board charges vary according to board plan and housing facility. *Part-time tuition:* $390 per semester hour. *Part-time fees:* $25 per term part-time. Part-time tuition and fees vary according to class time. *Payment plans:* installment, deferred payment. *Waivers:* children of alumni and employees or children of employees.
Library Plough Memorial Library and Media Center. *Collection:* 100,000 titles, 537 serial subscriptions.
College life *Housing:* on-campus residence required in freshman year. *Option:* coed. *Social organizations:* national fraternities, national sororities, local sororities; 24% of eligible men and 20% of eligible women are members. *Most popular organizations:* Black Student Association, BACCHUS Alcohol Awareness Group, Intercultural Club, College Republicans, Beta Beta Beta.
Campus security 24-hour emergency response devices and patrols, student patrols, late-night transport-escort service, controlled dormitory access.
After graduation 211 organizations recruited on campus 1997–98. 86% of class of 1998 had job offers within 6 months. *Career center:* 3 full-time personnel. Services include job fairs, resume preparation, interview workshops, resume referral, career/interest testing, career counseling, careers library, job bank, job interviews. *Graduate education:* 30% of class of 1999 went directly to graduate and professional school.
Freshmen 859 applied, 659 admitted, 245 enrolled.

Average high school GPA	3.47	SAT verbal scores above 500	69%
SAT math scores above 500	88%	ACT above 18	99%
From top 10% of their h.s. class	28%	From top quarter	55%
From top half	65%	1998 freshmen returning in 1999	73%

Application *Options:* eApply at www.CollegeQuest.com, Common Application, electronic application, early admission, deferred entrance. *Application fee:* $25. *Required:* essay or personal statement; high school transcript; minimum 2.25 GPA. *Required for some:* letters of recommendation. *Recommended:* interview.
Standardized tests *Admission: Required:* SAT I or ACT.
Significant dates *Application deadlines:* 8/23 (freshmen), 8/23 (transfers). *Financial aid deadline priority date:* 3/15.

Tennessee

Christian Brothers University (continued)
Freshman Application Contact
Ms. Courtney Fee, Dean of Admission, Christian Brothers University, 650 East Parkway South, Memphis, TN 38104. **Phone:** 901-321-3205. **Toll-free phone:** 800-288-7576. **Fax:** 901-321-3202. **E-mail:** admissions@cbu.edu
Visit CollegeQuest.com for information on majors offered and athletics.

CRICHTON COLLEGE
Memphis, Tennessee

- **Independent**, 4-year, founded 1941
- **Degree** bachelor's
- **Urban** 55-acre campus
- **Coed**, 875 undergraduate students, 80% full-time, 58% women, 42% men
- **Moderately difficult** entrance level, 67% of applicants were admitted
- **15:1 student-to-undergraduate faculty ratio**
- **23% graduate** in 6 years or less
- **$7152 tuition** and fees
- **$4162 average financial aid** package, $14,000 average indebtedness upon graduation, $500,000 endowment

Students *Undergraduates:* 700 full-time, 175 part-time. Students come from 8 states and territories, 3 other countries. *The most frequently chosen baccalaureate fields are:* business/marketing, education, psychology.

From out-of-state	10%	Reside on campus	5%
Age 25 or older	80%	Transferred in	43%
African Americans	46%	Asian Americans/Pacific Islanders	1%
Hispanic Americans	1%	Native Americans	0.1%

Faculty 92 (28% full-time), 22% with terminal degrees.
Expenses (1999–2000) *One-time required fee:* $5. *Tuition:* full-time $7152; part-time $298 per semester hour. Full-time tuition and fees vary according to program. Part-time tuition and fees vary according to program. *College room only:* $2800. *Waivers:* minority students, children of alumni, adult students, and employees or children of employees.
Library Crichton College Library. *Operations spending 1999–2000:* $178,948. *Collection:* 42,767 titles, 435 serial subscriptions, 360 audiovisual materials.
College life *Housing: Options:* men-only, women-only. *Most popular organizations:* Student Council, Orientation staff, Presidential Ambassadors, Psychology club, Crichton Student Teacher Education Association.
Campus security 24-hour patrols, controlled dormitory access, security alarms in campus apartments.
After graduation *Career center:* Services include resume preparation, career counseling, careers library.
Freshmen 436 applied, 293 admitted, 60 enrolled.

Average high school GPA	2.7	SAT verbal scores above 500	N/R
SAT math scores above 500	N/R	ACT above 18	80%
1998 freshmen returning in 1999	59%		

Application *Options:* early admission, deferred entrance. *Application fee:* $25. *Required:* high school transcript; 3 letters of recommendation. *Required for some:* essay or personal statement. *Recommended:* minimum 2.0 GPA; interview.
Standardized tests *Admission: Required:* SAT I or ACT.
Significant dates *Application deadlines:* 8/31 (freshmen), 8/31 (transfers). *Financial aid deadline priority date:* 3/31.
Freshman Application Contact
Mr. John G. Smith, Director of Student Recruitment, Crichton College, 6655 Winchester Road, PO Box 757830, Memphis, TN 38175-7830. **Phone:** 901-367-3888. **Toll-free phone:** 800-960-9777. **E-mail:** jgsmith@crichton.edu
Visit CollegeQuest.com for information on majors offered and athletics.

CUMBERLAND UNIVERSITY
Lebanon, Tennessee

Apply at CollegeQuest.com

- **Independent**, comprehensive, founded 1842
- **Degrees** associate, bachelor's, and master's
- **Small-town** 44-acre campus with easy access to Nashville
- **Coed**
- **Moderately difficult** entrance level
- **$9900 tuition** and fees

Expenses (1999–2000) *Comprehensive fee:* $13,400 includes full-time tuition ($9850), mandatory fees ($50), and room and board ($3500). *College room only:* $1370. Room and board charges vary according to board plan and housing facility. *Part-time tuition:* $410 per semester hour. *Part-time fees:* $25 per term part-time. Part-time tuition and fees vary according to location.
Institutional Web site http://www.cumberland.edu/
College life *Housing: Options:* coed, men-only, women-only. *Social organizations:* national fraternities, national sororities; 8% of eligible men and 2% of eligible women are members. *Most popular organizations:* Alpha Chi Honor Society, Alpha Lambda Delta Honor Society, Baptist Student Union, campus radio station, Student Government Association.
Campus security 24-hour patrols.
Application *Options:* eApply at www.CollegeQuest.com, deferred entrance. *Application fee:* $25. *Required:* high school transcript. *Required for some:* 3 letters of recommendation. *Recommended:* minimum 2.0 GPA.
Standardized tests *Admission: Required:* SAT I or ACT.
Admissions Office Contact
Cumberland University, One Cumberland Square, Lebanon, TN 37087-3554. **Toll-free phone:** 800-467-0562. **Fax:** 615-444-2569. **E-mail:** admissions@cumberland.edu
Visit CollegeQuest.com for information on athletics.

DAVID LIPSCOMB UNIVERSITY
Nashville, Tennessee

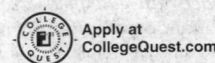
Apply at CollegeQuest.com

- **Independent**, comprehensive, founded 1891, affiliated with Church of Christ
- **Degrees** bachelor's, master's, and first professional
- **Urban** 65-acre campus
- **Coed**, 2,315 undergraduate students, 86% full-time, 56% women, 44% men
- **Moderately difficult** entrance level, 93% of applicants were admitted
- **49.35% graduate** in 6 years or less
- **$9689 tuition** and fees
- **$9040 average financial aid** package, $13,750 average indebtedness upon graduation, $53.9 million endowment

Founded in 1891, Lipscomb University is a distinctly Christian university with a sterling academic reputation. More than 100 major programs of study are offered. Lipscomb's 21st-century, campuswide fiber-optic network provides PC connections in every dorm room and many other locations for Internet access to resources worldwide.

Students *Undergraduates:* 1,984 full-time, 331 part-time. Students come from 40 states and territories, 38 other countries. *The most frequently chosen baccalaureate fields are:* business/marketing, communications/communication technologies, education. *Graduate:* 36 in professional programs, 151 in other graduate degree programs.

From out-of-state	36%	Reside on campus	49%
Age 25 or older	10%	Transferred in	6%
International students	1%	African Americans	4%
Asian Americans/Pacific Islanders	1%	Hispanic Americans	0.4%
Native Americans	0.3%		

Faculty 207 (45% full-time), 59% with terminal degrees.
Expenses (1999–2000) *Comprehensive fee:* $14,033 includes full-time tuition ($9345), mandatory fees ($344), and room and board ($4344). *College room only:* $2184. Full-time tuition and fees vary according to degree level and location. Room and board charges vary according to board plan, housing facility, and location. *Part-time tuition:* $312 per hour. *Part-time fees:* $10 per hour; $14. Part-time tuition and fees vary according to degree level and location. *Payment plan:* installment. *Waivers:* minority students and employees or children of employees.
Library Beaman Library plus 1 other.
College life *Housing:* on-campus residence required through senior year. *Options:* men-only, women-only. *Social organizations:* local fraternities,

local sororities; 15% of eligible men and 20% of eligible women are members. *Most popular organizations:* social clubs, Sigma Pi Beta, Circle K, business fraternities, intramural program.

Campus security 24-hour emergency response devices and patrols, late-night transport-escort service, controlled dormitory access.

After graduation 271 organizations recruited on campus 1997–98. *Career center:* 2 full-time personnel. Services include job fairs, resume preparation, resume referral, career/interest testing, career counseling, careers library, job bank, job interviews.

Freshmen 1,598 applied, 1,481 admitted, 598 enrolled. 1 National Merit Scholar, 23 valedictorians.

Average high school GPA	3.17	SAT verbal scores above 500	77%
SAT math scores above 500	72%	ACT above 18	92%
From top 10% of their h.s. class	26%	From top quarter	53%
From top half	78%	1998 freshmen returning in 1999	79%

Application *Options:* eApply at www.CollegeQuest.com, Common Application, electronic application, early admission, early action. *Application fee:* $50. *Required:* high school transcript; minimum 2.25 GPA; 2 letters of recommendation. *Recommended:* essay or personal statement; interview.

Standardized tests *Admission: Required:* SAT I or ACT.

Significant dates *Application deadlines:* rolling (freshmen), rolling (transfers). *Early action:* 11/15. *Notification:* 12/15 (early action). *Financial aid deadline priority date:* 2/28.

Freshman Application Contact
Mr. Scott Gilman, Director of Admissions, David Lipscomb University, 3901 Granny White Pike, Nashville, TN 37204-3951. **Phone:** 615-269-1776. **Toll-free phone:** 800-333-4358 Ext. 1776. **Fax:** 615-269-1804. **E-mail:** admissions@dlu.edu

Visit CollegeQuest.com for information on majors offered and athletics. College video and electronic viewbook available at CollegeQuest.com.

■ *See page 1560 for a narrative description.*

EAST TENNESSEE STATE UNIVERSITY
Johnson City, Tennessee

- **State-supported**, university, founded 1911
- **Degrees** associate, bachelor's, master's, doctoral, first professional, and post-master's certificates
- **Small-town** 366-acre campus
- **Coed**, 9,097 undergraduate students, 84% full-time, 58% women, 42% men
- **Moderately difficult** entrance level, 77% of applicants were admitted
- **14:1 student-to-undergraduate faculty ratio**
- **$2532 tuition** and fees (in-state); $7648 (out-of-state)
- **$7082 average financial aid** package, $38.2 million endowment

East Tennessee State University serves 12,000 students and is located in the beautiful Appalachian region of northeast Tennessee. Programs in the Colleges of Arts and Sciences, Business, Medicine, Education, Applied Science and Technology, Public and Allied Health, and Nursing are available. Extensive graduate study is available, including a master's degree in physical therapy. A new $28-million library opened in January 1999. Unique programs include bluegrass music and Appalachian studies.

Part of State University and Community College System of Tennessee.

Students *Undergraduates:* 7,662 full-time, 1,435 part-time. Students come from 38 states and territories, 39 other countries. *The most frequently chosen baccalaureate fields are:* business/marketing, health professions and related sciences, protective services/public administration. *Graduate:* 236 in professional programs, 1,784 in other graduate degree programs.

From out-of-state	11%	Reside on campus	20%
Age 25 or older	30%	Transferred in	8%
International students	1%	African Americans	4%
Asian Americans/Pacific Islanders	1%	Hispanic Americans	1%
Native Americans	0.4%		

Faculty 923 (63% full-time), 62% with terminal degrees.

Expenses (1999–2000) *Tuition, state resident:* full-time $2020; part-time $90 per credit. *Tuition, nonresident:* full-time $7136; part-time $314 per credit. *Required fees:* full-time $512; $31 per credit; $4 per term part-time. *College room and board:* $3070; room only: $1750. Room and board charges vary according to board plan and housing facility. *Payment plan:* deferred payment. *Waivers:* senior citizens and employees or children of employees.

Library Sherrod Library plus 2 others. *Collection:* 594,080 titles, 3,403 serial subscriptions.

College life *Housing: Options:* men-only, women-only. *Social organizations:* national fraternities, national sororities; 10% of eligible men and 10% of eligible women are members. *Most popular organizations:* honor societies, Volunteer ETSU, Greek organizations, religious groups, Residence Hall Councils.

Campus security 24-hour emergency response devices and patrols, student patrols, late-night transport-escort service, controlled dormitory access.

After graduation 238 organizations recruited on campus 1997–98. 96% of class of 1998 had job offers within 6 months. *Career center:* 5 full-time personnel. Services include job fairs, resume preparation, resume referral, career counseling, careers library, job bank, job interviews.

Freshmen 4,853 applied, 3,725 admitted, 1,511 enrolled.

Average high school GPA	3.11	SAT verbal scores above 500	53%
SAT math scores above 500	53%	ACT above 18	84%
From top 10% of their h.s. class	16%	From top quarter	37%
From top half	66%	1998 freshmen returning in 1999	66%

Application *Options:* electronic application, early admission. *Application fee:* $15. *Required:* high school transcript; minimum 2.3 GPA.

Standardized tests *Admission: Required:* SAT I or ACT.

Significant dates *Financial aid deadline priority date:* 4/15.

Freshman Application Contact
Mr. Mike Pitts, Director of Admissions, East Tennessee State University, PO Box 70731, Johnson City, TN 37614-0734. **Phone:** 423-439-6861. **Toll-free phone:** 800-462-3878. **Fax:** 423-439-5770. **E-mail:** go2etsu@etsu.edu

Visit CollegeQuest.com for information on majors offered and athletics. College video available at CollegeQuest.com.

FISK UNIVERSITY
Nashville, Tennessee

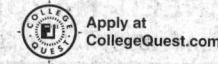
Apply at CollegeQuest.com

- **Independent**, comprehensive, founded 1866, affiliated with United Church of Christ
- **Degrees** bachelor's and master's
- **Urban** 40-acre campus
- **Coed**, 812 undergraduate students, 98% full-time, 72% women, 28% men
- **Moderately difficult** entrance level, 97% of applicants were admitted
- **12:1 student-to-undergraduate faculty ratio**
- **52% graduate** in 6 years or less
- **$8770 tuition** and fees
- **$12,500 average financial aid** package, $20,000 average indebtedness upon graduation, $14 million endowment

Historic rehabilitation has overtaken the Fisk University campus. The recently restored Carnegie Building, originally built in 1908, features 3 state-of-the-art computer laboratories equipped with 44 PCs, 6 Sun Workstations, 1 Macintosh computer, and 12 dot-matrix and laser printers. All 3 labs are completely networked so that students may access a LAN and the Internet. A primary facility for the computer science and mathematics programs, the labs are also available for general University use and student and faculty research. New undergraduate studies include the women's and gender studies program and a concentration in materials science as part of a BS in physics.

Students *Undergraduates:* 794 full-time, 18 part-time. Students come from 41 states and territories, 3 other countries. *The most frequently chosen baccalaureate fields are:* business/marketing, biological/life sciences, psychology. *Graduate:* 74 in graduate degree programs.

From out-of-state	71%	Age 25 or older	5%
Transferred in	2%	International students	2%
African Americans	98%	Asian Americans/Pacific Islanders	0.1%

Faculty 83 (76% full-time), 65% with terminal degrees.

Expenses (1999–2000) *Comprehensive fee:* $13,700 includes full-time tuition ($8480), mandatory fees ($290), and room and board ($4930). *Part-time tuition:* $353 per credit hour. *Part-time fees:* $145 per term part-time. *Payment plan:* installment. *Waivers:* employees or children of employees.

Library Fisk University Main Library. *Operations spending 1999–2000:* $706,413. *Collection:* 202,636 titles, 380 serial subscriptions.

Tennessee

Fisk University (continued)

College life On-campus residence required through senior year. *Social organizations:* national fraternities, national sororities; 25% of eligible men and 35% of eligible women are members. *Most popular organizations:* Student Government Association, state clubs, Panhellenic Council.

Campus security 24-hour patrols, late-night transport-escort service.

After graduation 63 organizations recruited on campus 1997–98. *Career center:* 2 full-time personnel. Services include job fairs, resume preparation, resume referral, career counseling, careers library, job bank, job interviews.

Freshmen 730 applied, 707 admitted, 262 enrolled. 12 class presidents, 2 valedictorians, 10 student government officers.

Average high school GPA	3.03	SAT verbal scores above 500	28%
SAT math scores above 500	28%	ACT above 18	59%
From top 10% of their h.s. class	18%	From top quarter	37%
From top half	67%	1998 freshmen returning in 1999	88%

Application *Options:* eApply at www.CollegeQuest.com, Common Application, electronic application, early admission. *Application fee:* $25. *Required:* essay or personal statement; high school transcript; minimum 2.0 GPA; 2 letters of recommendation; medical history.

Standardized tests *Placement: Required:* SAT I or ACT. *Recommended:* SAT II Subject Tests.

Significant dates *Application deadlines:* 6/15 (freshmen), 6/15 (transfers). *Financial aid deadline priority date:* 2/15.

Freshman Application Contact
Mr. Anthony E. Jones, Director of Admissions, Fisk University, 1000 17th Avenue North, Nashville, TN 37208-3051. **Phone:** 615-329-8665. **Toll-free phone:** 800-443-FISK. **Fax:** 615-329-8576. **E-mail:** lcampbel@dubois.fisk.edu

Visit CollegeQuest.com for information on majors offered and athletics.

■ *See page 1664 for a narrative description.*

FREED-HARDEMAN UNIVERSITY
Henderson, Tennessee

- **Independent**, comprehensive, founded 1869, affiliated with Church of Christ
- **Degrees** bachelor's and master's
- **Small-town** 96-acre campus
- **Coed**, 1,387 undergraduate students, 94% full-time, 55% women, 45% men
- **Moderately difficult** entrance level, 72% of applicants were admitted
- **49.3% graduate** in 6 years or less
- **$8558 tuition** and fees
- **$18.8 million endowment**

Students *Undergraduates:* 1,310 full-time, 77 part-time. Students come from 32 states and territories, 16 other countries. *The most frequently chosen baccalaureate fields are:* business/marketing, education, philosophy. *Graduate:* 411 in graduate degree programs.

From out-of-state	51%	Reside on campus	72%
Age 25 or older	11%	Transferred in	10%

Faculty 113 (84% full-time), 63% with terminal degrees.

Expenses (1999–2000) *Comprehensive fee:* $12,958 includes full-time tuition ($7328), mandatory fees ($1230), and room and board ($4400). *College room only:* $2180. Full-time tuition and fees vary according to course load. Room and board charges vary according to board plan. *Part-time tuition:* $280 per semester hour. *Part-time fees:* $46 per semester hour. Part-time tuition and fees vary according to course load. *Payment plan:* installment. *Waivers:* senior citizens and employees or children of employees.

Library Loden-Daniel Library. *Operations spending 1999–2000:* $536,688. *Collection:* 154,800 titles, 1,571 serial subscriptions, 40,160 audiovisual materials.

College life *Housing:* on-campus residence required through senior year. *Options:* men-only, women-only. *Social organizations:* coed social clubs. *Most popular organizations:* Student Alumni Association, University Program Council, University Student Ambassadors.

Campus security 24-hour emergency response devices and patrols, late-night transport-escort service.

After graduation 60 organizations recruited on campus 1997–98. *Career center:* 2 full-time personnel. Services include job fairs, resume preparation, interview workshops, career/interest testing, career counseling, careers library, job bank, job interviews. *Major awards:* 1 Fulbright Scholar.

Freshmen 872 applied, 631 admitted, 324 enrolled.

Average high school GPA	3.31	SAT verbal scores above 500	75%
SAT math scores above 500	66%	ACT above 18	84%
1998 freshmen returning in 1999	75%		

Application *Options:* electronic application, early admission, deferred entrance. *Application fee:* $0. *Required:* high school transcript; minimum 2.25 GPA. *Required for some:* interview. *Recommended:* essay or personal statement; letters of recommendation.

Standardized tests *Admission: Required:* ACT.

Significant dates *Application deadlines:* rolling (freshmen), rolling (transfers). *Notification:* continuous until 9/1 (freshmen). *Financial aid deadline priority date:* 4/1.

Freshman Application Contact
Ms. Kimberlie Helton, Director of Admissions, Freed-Hardeman University, 158 East Main Street, Henderson, TN 38340-2399. **Phone:** 901-989-6651. **Toll-free phone:** 800-630-3480. **Fax:** 901-989-6047. **E-mail:** admissions@fhu.edu

Visit CollegeQuest.com for information on majors offered and athletics. College video available at CollegeQuest.com.

FREE WILL BAPTIST BIBLE COLLEGE
Nashville, Tennessee

- **Independent Free Will Baptist**, 4-year, founded 1942
- **Degrees** associate and bachelor's
- **Suburban** 10-acre campus
- **Coed**, 334 undergraduate students
- **Noncompetitive** entrance level
- **$6442 tuition** and fees

Students *Undergraduates:* Students come from 28 states and territories, 8 other countries.

From out-of-state	80%	Reside on campus	71%
Age 25 or older	7%		

Faculty 37 (54% full-time).

Expenses (1999–2000) *Comprehensive fee:* $10,120 includes full-time tuition ($6040), mandatory fees ($402), and room and board ($3678). *College room only:* $1418. *Part-time tuition:* $189 per semester hour. *Part-time fees:* $100 per term part-time. Part-time tuition and fees vary according to course load. *Payment plans:* installment, deferred payment. *Waivers:* employees or children of employees.

Library Welch Library. *Collection:* 64,473 titles, 394 serial subscriptions.

College life On-campus residence required through senior year.

Campus security 24-hour emergency response devices, student patrols, late-night transport-escort service, controlled dormitory access.

After graduation *Graduate education:* 11% of class of 1999 went directly to graduate and professional school: 6% graduate arts and sciences, 3% theology.

Freshmen

Average high school GPA	3.1	SAT verbal scores above 500	N/R
SAT math scores above 500	N/R	ACT above 18	N/R
From top 10% of their h.s. class	16%	From top quarter	42%
From top half	79%	1998 freshmen returning in 1999	57%

Application *Options:* early admission, deferred entrance. *Preference* given to Free Will Baptists. *Application fee:* $25. *Required:* essay or personal statement; high school transcript; 3 letters of recommendation; medical history.

Standardized tests *Admission: Required:* ACT.

Significant dates *Application deadline:* rolling (freshmen). *Financial aid deadline priority date:* 4/15.

Freshman Application Contact
Dr. Charles E. Hampton, Registrar/Chairman of Department of General Education, Free Will Baptist Bible College, 3606 West End Avenue, Nashville, TN 37205-2498. **Phone:** 615-383-1340 Ext. 5233. **Toll-free phone:** 800-763-9222. **Fax:** 615-269-6028.

Visit CollegeQuest.com for information on majors offered and athletics.

Tennessee

ITT TECHNICAL INSTITUTE
Knoxville, Tennessee

- **Proprietary**, primarily 2-year, founded 1988
- **Degrees** associate and bachelor's
- **Suburban** 5-acre campus
- **Coed**
- **Minimally difficult** entrance level
- **$9190 tuition** and fees

Part of ITT Educational Services, Inc.
Admissions Office Contact
ITT Technical Institute, 10208 Technology Drive, Knoxville, TN 37932. **Toll-free phone:** 800-952-9004. **Fax:** 423-691-0337.
Visit CollegeQuest.com for information on majors offered and athletics. College video available at CollegeQuest.com.

ITT TECHNICAL INSTITUTE
Nashville, Tennessee

- **Proprietary**, primarily 2-year, founded 1984
- **Degrees** associate and bachelor's
- **Urban** 21-acre campus
- **Coed**
- **Minimally difficult** entrance level
- **$9190 tuition** and fees

Part of ITT Educational Services, Inc.
Admissions Office Contact
ITT Technical Institute, 441 Donelson Pike, PO Box 148029, Nashville, TN 37214-8029. **Toll-free phone:** 800-331-8386. **Fax:** 615-872-7209.
Visit CollegeQuest.com for information on majors offered and athletics. College video available at CollegeQuest.com.

JOHNSON BIBLE COLLEGE
Knoxville, Tennessee

- **Independent**, comprehensive, founded 1893, affiliated with Christian Churches and Churches of Christ
- **Degrees** associate, bachelor's, and master's
- **Rural** 75-acre campus
- **Coed**, 486 undergraduate students, 96% full-time, 47% women, 53% men
- **Minimally difficult** entrance level, 67% of applicants were admitted
- **15:1 student-to-undergraduate faculty ratio**
- **37% graduate** in 6 years or less
- **$5280 tuition** and fees

Students *Undergraduates:* 465 full-time, 21 part-time. Students come from 30 states and territories, 8 other countries. *The most frequently chosen baccalaureate fields are:* education, philosophy. *Graduate:* 89 in graduate degree programs.

From out-of-state	73%	Reside on campus	80%
Age 25 or older	29%	Transferred in	11%
International students	2%	African Americans	2%
Asian Americans/Pacific Islanders	0.4%	Hispanic Americans	1%
Native Americans	0.2%		

Faculty 41 (56% full-time), 44% with terminal degrees.
Expenses (2000–2001) *Comprehensive fee:* $8650 includes full-time tuition ($4740), mandatory fees ($540), and room and board ($3370). Room and board charges vary according to housing facility. *Part-time tuition:* $198 per semester hour. *Part-time fees:* $17 per semester hour. Part-time tuition and fees vary according to course load. *Payment plan:* installment. *Waivers:* employees or children of employees.
Library Glass Memorial Library plus 1 other. *Operations spending 1999–2000:* $309,391. *Collection:* 55,922 titles, 455 serial subscriptions, 10,578 audiovisual materials.
College life *Housing:* on-campus residence required through senior year. *Options:* men-only, women-only. *Most popular organizations:* Quest, Timothy club, International Harvesters.
Campus security 24-hour emergency response devices, student patrols.

After graduation 66% of class of 1998 had job offers within 6 months. *Career center:* 1 full-time personnel. Services include resume preparation, resume referral, career counseling. *Graduate education:* 20% of class of 1999 went directly to graduate and professional school: 10% education, 10% theology.
Freshmen 158 applied, 106 admitted, 106 enrolled.

Average high school GPA	3.01	SAT verbal scores above 500	62%
SAT math scores above 500	56%	ACT above 18	88%
From top 10% of their h.s. class	13%	From top quarter	34%
From top half	68%	1998 freshmen returning in 1999	66%

Application *Option:* deferred entrance. *Application fee:* $35. *Required:* essay or personal statement; high school transcript; 3 letters of recommendation; medical history. *Required for some:* interview.
Standardized tests *Admission: Required:* SAT I or ACT. *Required for some:* ACT.
Significant dates *Application deadlines:* 8/1 (freshmen), 8/1 (transfers). *Financial aid deadline:* continuous.
Freshman Application Contact
Mr. Tim Wingfield, Director of Admissions, Johnson Bible College, 7900 Johnson Drive, Knoxville, TN 37998. **Phone:** 865-251-2346. **Toll-free phone:** 800-827-2122. **Fax:** 865-579-2336. **E-mail:** twingfield@jbc.edu
Visit CollegeQuest.com for information on majors offered and athletics. College video available at CollegeQuest.com.

KING COLLEGE
Bristol, Tennessee

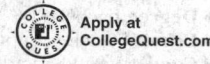
Apply at CollegeQuest.com

- **Independent**, 4-year, founded 1867, affiliated with Presbyterian Church (U.S.A.)
- **Degree** bachelor's
- **Suburban** 135-acre campus
- **Coed**, 518 undergraduate students, 95% full-time, 60% women, 40% men
- **Moderately difficult** entrance level, 79% of applicants were admitted
- **10:1 student-to-undergraduate faculty ratio**
- **39% graduate** in 6 years or less
- **$10,750 tuition** and fees
- **$11,005 average financial aid** package, $14,636 average indebtedness upon graduation, $17 million endowment

Students *Undergraduates:* 490 full-time, 28 part-time. Students come from 27 states and territories, 29 other countries. *The most frequently chosen baccalaureate fields are:* English, biological/life sciences, social sciences and history.

From out-of-state	57%	Reside on campus	63%
Age 25 or older	9%	Transferred in	10%
International students	8%	African Americans	2%
Asian Americans/Pacific Islanders	0.4%	Hispanic Americans	1%

Faculty 68 (53% full-time), 43% with terminal degrees.
Expenses (1999–2000) *Comprehensive fee:* $14,600 includes full-time tuition ($10,030), mandatory fees ($720), and room and board ($3850). *College room only:* $1900. *Part-time tuition:* $285 per semester hour. *Part-time fees:* $70 per term part-time. Part-time tuition and fees vary according to course load and program. *Payment plans:* guaranteed tuition, tuition prepayment, installment. *Waivers:* employees or children of employees.
Library E. W. King Library. *Collection:* 95,136 titles, 605 serial subscriptions, 4,296 audiovisual materials.
College life *Housing:* on-campus residence required in freshman year. *Options:* men-only, women-only, disabled students. *Most popular organizations:* Student Government Association, campus life committee, World Christian Fellowship, Fellowship of Christian Athletes, drama club.
Campus security Late-night transport-escort service.
After graduation 15 organizations recruited on campus 1997–98. 65% of class of 1998 had job offers within 6 months. *Career center:* 1 full-time, 1 part-time personnel. Services include job fairs, resume preparation, interview workshops, resume referral, career/interest testing, career counseling, careers library, job bank, job interviews. *Graduate education:* 31% of class of 1999 went directly to graduate and professional school.

Tennessee

King College (continued)

Freshmen 428 applied, 340 admitted, 133 enrolled.

Average high school GPA	3.19	SAT verbal scores above 500	69%
SAT math scores above 500	69%	ACT above 18	89%
From top 10% of their h.s. class	34%	From top quarter	62%
From top half	82%	1998 freshmen returning in 1999	74%

Application *Options:* eApply at www.CollegeQuest.com, Common Application, electronic application, early admission, deferred entrance. *Application fee:* $20. *Required:* essay or personal statement; high school transcript; minimum 2.4 GPA. *Required for some:* letters of recommendation; interview. *Recommended:* letters of recommendation; interview.

Standardized tests *Admission: Required:* SAT I or ACT.

Significant dates *Application deadlines:* rolling (freshmen), rolling (transfers). *Financial aid deadline priority date:* 3/1.

Freshman Application Contact
Ms. Mindy Clark, Director of Admissions, King College, 1350 King College Road, Bristol, TN 37620-2699. **Phone:** 423-652-4861. **Toll-free phone:** 800-362-0014. **Fax:** 423-968-4456. **E-mail:** admissions@king.edu

Visit CollegeQuest.com for information on majors offered and athletics.

LAMBUTH UNIVERSITY
Jackson, Tennessee

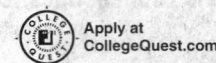

- **Independent United Methodist**, 4-year, founded 1843
- **Degree** bachelor's
- **Urban** 50-acre campus with easy access to Memphis
- **Coed**, 936 undergraduate students, 91% full-time, 57% women, 43% men
- **Moderately difficult** entrance level, 70% of applicants were admitted
- **16:1** student-to-undergraduate faculty ratio
- **34.6% graduate** in 6 years or less
- **$7918 tuition** and fees
- **$5912 average financial aid** package, $11,000 average indebtedness upon graduation, $10.4 million endowment

Students *Undergraduates:* 850 full-time, 86 part-time. Students come from 29 states and territories, 16 other countries. *The most frequently chosen baccalaureate fields are:* business/marketing, education, social sciences and history.

From out-of-state	19%	Reside on campus	50%
Age 25 or older	17%	Transferred in	11%
International students	4%	African Americans	14%
Asian Americans/Pacific Islanders	1%	Hispanic Americans	0.4%
Native Americans	0.1%		

Faculty 94 (51% full-time), 48% with terminal degrees.

Expenses (1999–2000) *Comprehensive fee:* $12,138 includes full-time tuition ($7818), mandatory fees ($100), and room and board ($4220). *College room only:* $1900. Room and board charges vary according to board plan and housing facility. *Part-time tuition:* $260 per credit hour. *Part-time fees:* $50 per term part-time. Part-time tuition and fees vary according to class time and course load. *Payment plans:* installment, deferred payment. *Waivers:* adult students, senior citizens, and employees or children of employees.

Library Luther L. Gobbel Library. *Operations spending 1999–2000:* $236,089. *Collection:* 174,185 titles, 100 audiovisual materials.

College life *Housing:* on-campus residence required through senior year. *Options:* coed, men-only, women-only. *Social organizations:* national fraternities, national sororities; 25% of eligible men and 25% of eligible women are members. *Most popular organizations:* Student Government, Student Activities Committee, Gamma Beta Phi, Black Student Union, International Students Organization.

Campus security 24-hour emergency response devices and patrols, late-night transport-escort service.

After graduation 45 organizations recruited on campus 1997–98. 80% of class of 1998 had job offers within 6 months. *Career center:* 1 full-time personnel. Services include job fairs, resume preparation, interview workshops, resume referral, career counseling, careers library, job bank, job interviews. *Graduate education:* 18% of class of 1999 went directly to graduate and professional school.

Freshmen 830 applied, 578 admitted, 224 enrolled. 13 valedictorians.

Average high school GPA	3.2	SAT verbal scores above 500	74%
SAT math scores above 500	47%	ACT above 18	97%
From top 10% of their h.s. class	19%	From top quarter	42%
From top half	75%	1998 freshmen returning in 1999	66%

Application *Options:* eApply at www.CollegeQuest.com, Common Application, electronic application, early admission, deferred entrance. *Application fee:* $25. *Required:* essay or personal statement; high school transcript; minimum 2.0 GPA. *Required for some:* 3 letters of recommendation.

Standardized tests *Admission: Required:* SAT I or ACT.

Significant dates *Application deadlines:* rolling (freshmen), rolling (transfers). *Financial aid deadline priority date:* 2/15.

Freshman Application Contact
Barkley Thompson, Director of Admissions, Lambuth University, 705 Lambuth Boulevard, Jackson, TN 38301. **Phone:** 901-425-3223. **Toll-free phone:** 800-526-2884. **Fax:** 901-988-4600. **E-mail:** admit@lambuth.edu

Visit CollegeQuest.com for information on majors offered and athletics.

■ *See page 1898 for a narrative description.*

LANE COLLEGE
Jackson, Tennessee

- **Independent**, 4-year, founded 1882, affiliated with Christian Methodist Episcopal Church
- **Degree** bachelor's
- **Suburban** 25-acre campus with easy access to Memphis
- **Coed**, 661 undergraduate students, 98% full-time, 50% women, 50% men
- **Minimally difficult** entrance level, 65% of applicants were admitted
- **15:1** student-to-undergraduate faculty ratio
- **49% graduate** in 6 years or less
- **$6150 tuition** and fees
- **$2.2 million endowment**

Students *Undergraduates:* 646 full-time, 15 part-time. Students come from 25 states and territories. *The most frequently chosen baccalaureate fields are:* business/marketing, education, protective services/public administration.

From out-of-state	40%	Reside on campus	64%
Age 25 or older	5%	Transferred in	6%
African Americans	99%	Hispanic Americans	0.2%

Faculty 45 (100% full-time), 62% with terminal degrees.

Expenses (1999–2000) *Comprehensive fee:* $9950 includes full-time tuition ($5600), mandatory fees ($550), and room and board ($3800). Full-time tuition and fees vary according to course load. *Part-time tuition:* $250 per semester hour. Part-time tuition and fees vary according to course load. *Payment plans:* installment, deferred payment. *Waivers:* employees or children of employees.

Library Chambers-McClure Resource Center. *Operations spending 1999–2000:* $220,000. *Collection:* 128,000 titles, 350 serial subscriptions.

College life *Housing: Options:* men-only, women-only. *Social organizations:* national fraternities, national sororities; 65% of eligible men and 60% of eligible women are members. *Most popular organizations:* student government association, pre-law club, Student Christian Association, drama club.

Campus security 24-hour emergency response devices and patrols, surveillance cameras, lighted parking areas.

After graduation 20 organizations recruited on campus 1997–98. 35% of class of 1998 had job offers within 6 months. *Career center:* 1 full-time personnel. Services include job fairs, resume preparation, interview workshops, resume referral, career counseling, careers library, job bank, job interviews.

Freshmen 1,038 applied, 675 admitted, 202 enrolled. 12 valedictorians.

Average high school GPA	2.5	SAT verbal scores above 500	N/R
SAT math scores above 500	N/R	ACT above 18	19%
From top 10% of their h.s. class	5%	From top quarter	14%
From top half	61%	1998 freshmen returning in 1999	74%

Application *Options:* Common Application, early admission. *Application fee:* $0. *Required:* high school transcript; minimum 2.0 GPA; 2 letters of recommendation.

Standardized tests *Admission: Required:* SAT I or ACT.

Significant dates *Application deadlines:* rolling (freshmen), rolling (transfers). *Financial aid deadline priority date:* 4/1.

Freshman Application Contact
Ms. E. Brown, Director of Admissions, Lane College, 545 Lane Avenue, Jackson, TN 38301-4598. **Phone:** 901-426-7532. **Toll-free phone:** 800-960-7533. **Fax:** 901-426-7559.

Visit CollegeQuest.com for information on majors offered and athletics. College video available at CollegeQuest.com.

LEE UNIVERSITY
Cleveland, Tennessee

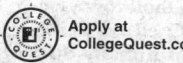

- **Independent**, comprehensive, founded 1918, affiliated with Church of God
- **Degrees** bachelor's and master's
- **Small-town** 45-acre campus
- **Coed**, 3,155 undergraduate students, 93% full-time, 56% women, 44% men
- **Minimally difficult** entrance level, 90% of applicants were admitted
- **20:1 student-to-undergraduate faculty ratio**
- **36% graduate** in 6 years or less
- **$6862 tuition** and fees
- **$6644 average financial aid** package, $10,982 average indebtedness upon graduation, $6.4 million endowment

Students *Undergraduates:* 2,920 full-time, 235 part-time. Students come from 46 states and territories, 30 other countries. *The most frequently chosen baccalaureate fields are:* education, business/marketing, philosophy. *Graduate:* 104 in graduate degree programs.

From out-of-state	63%	Reside on campus	43%
Age 25 or older	11%	Transferred in	13%
International students	2%	African Americans	2%
Asian Americans/Pacific Islanders	1%	Hispanic Americans	3%
Native Americans	0.4%		

Faculty 237 (48% full-time), 40% with terminal degrees.

Expenses (2000–2001) *Comprehensive fee:* $10,882 includes full-time tuition ($6700), mandatory fees ($162), and room and board ($4020). *College room only:* $1990. Full-time tuition and fees vary according to program. Room and board charges vary according to board plan and housing facility. *Part-time tuition:* $280 per semester hour. *Part-time fees:* $10 per term part-time. Part-time tuition and fees vary according to program. *Payment plan:* deferred payment. *Waivers:* employees or children of employees.

Library William G. Squires Library. *Operations spending 1999–2000:* $803,364. *Collection:* 148,179 titles, 1,100 serial subscriptions, 12,708 audio-visual materials.

College life *Housing:* on-campus residence required in freshman year. *Options:* men-only, women-only, disabled students. *Social organizations:* local fraternities, local sororities; 13% of eligible men and 10% of eligible women are members. *Most popular organizations:* campus choir, Pi Delta Gamma: Education Club, Pioneers for Christ, theatre company, Greek Council.

Campus security 24-hour emergency response devices and patrols, late-night transport-escort service.

After graduation 40 organizations recruited on campus 1997–98. *Career center:* 1 part-time personnel. Services include job fairs, career/interest testing, job bank.

Freshmen 1,175 applied, 1,060 admitted, 618 enrolled.

Average high school GPA	2.93	SAT verbal scores above 500	62%
SAT math scores above 500	55%	ACT above 18	81%
From top 10% of their h.s. class	20%	From top quarter	44%
From top half	72%	1998 freshmen returning in 1999	67%

Application *Options:* eApply at www.CollegeQuest.com, electronic application, early admission, deferred entrance. *Application fee:* $25. *Required:* high school transcript; minimum 2.0 GPA; MMR immunization record. *Required for some:* 1 letter of recommendation. *Recommended:* 3 letters of recommendation.

Standardized tests *Admission: Required:* SAT I or ACT. *Recommended:* ACT.

Significant dates *Application deadlines:* 9/1 (freshmen), rolling (transfers). *Financial aid deadline priority date:* 4/15.

Freshman Application Contact
Admissions Coordinator, Lee University, PO Box 3450, Cleveland, TN 37311. **Phone:** 423-614-8500. **Toll-free phone:** 800-LEE-9930. **Fax:** 423-614-8533. **E-mail:** admissions@leeuniversity.edu

Visit CollegeQuest.com for information on majors offered and athletics. College video available at CollegeQuest.com.

LEMOYNE-OWEN COLLEGE
Memphis, Tennessee

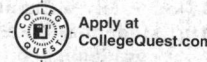

- **Independent**, comprehensive, founded 1862, affiliated with United Church of Christ
- **Degrees** bachelor's and master's
- **Urban** 15-acre campus
- **Coed**, 974 undergraduate students, 83% full-time, 66% women, 34% men
- **Minimally difficult** entrance level, 100% of applicants were admitted
- **$6900 tuition** and fees
- **$7513 average financial aid** package, $10,500 average indebtedness upon graduation, $13.2 million endowment

Students *Undergraduates:* 807 full-time, 167 part-time. Students come from 23 states and territories. *The most frequently chosen baccalaureate fields are:* business/marketing, education, social sciences and history. *Graduate:* 39 in graduate degree programs.

From out-of-state	13%	Reside on campus	19%
Age 25 or older	42%	Transferred in	28%
African Americans	98%	Hispanic Americans	0.1%

Faculty 94 (63% full-time), 41% with terminal degrees.

Expenses (1999–2000) *Comprehensive fee:* $10,950 includes full-time tuition ($6900) and room and board ($4050). *College room only:* $2100. Room and board charges vary according to housing facility. *Part-time tuition:* $288 per credit hour. *Payment plans:* tuition prepayment, installment, deferred payment. *Waivers:* employees or children of employees.

Library Hollis F. Price Library. *Operations spending 1999–2000:* $162,000. *Collection:* 90,000 titles, 350 serial subscriptions.

College life *Housing: Options:* men-only, women-only. *Social organizations:* national fraternities, national sororities; 35% of eligible men and 65% of eligible women are members. *Most popular organizations:* Students in Free Enterprise, National Black Student Accountant Club, Gospel Choir, Pre-Alumni, National Panhellenic Council.

Campus security 24-hour patrols, late-night transport-escort service, controlled dormitory access.

After graduation 200 organizations recruited on campus 1997–98. 30% of class of 1998 had job offers within 6 months. *Career center:* 2 full-time personnel. Services include job fairs, resume preparation, resume referral, career counseling, careers library, job bank, job interviews.

Freshmen 459 applied, 459 admitted, 320 enrolled.

Average high school GPA	2.64	SAT verbal scores above 500	14%
SAT math scores above 500	21%	ACT above 18	33%
1998 freshmen returning in 1999	65%		

Application *Options:* eApply at www.CollegeQuest.com, Common Application, early admission, deferred entrance. *Application fee:* $25. *Required:* essay or personal statement; high school transcript; minimum 2.0 GPA; 2 letters of recommendation; interview.

Standardized tests *Admission: Required:* SAT I or ACT.

Significant dates *Application deadlines:* 4/1 (freshmen), rolling (transfers). *Financial aid deadline priority date:* 5/1.

Freshman Application Contact
Ms. Frankie Jeffries, Assistant Director Admissions/Recruitment, LeMoyne-Owen College, 807 Walker Avenue, Memphis, TN 38126-6595. **Phone:** 901-942-7302 Ext. 214. **Toll-free phone:** 800-737-7778. **Fax:** 901-942-6272. **E-mail:** admissions@locness.lemoyne-owen.edu

Visit CollegeQuest.com for information on majors offered and athletics. College video and electronic viewbook available at CollegeQuest.com.

Tennessee

LINCOLN MEMORIAL UNIVERSITY
Harrogate, Tennessee

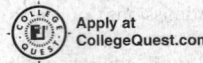

- **Independent**, comprehensive, founded 1897
- **Degrees** associate, bachelor's, master's, and post-master's certificates
- **Small-town** 1,000-acre campus
- **Coed**, 869 undergraduate students, 77% full-time, 67% women, 33% men
- **Moderately difficult** entrance level, 84% of applicants were admitted
- **9:1 student-to-undergraduate faculty ratio**
- **46% graduate** in 6 years or less
- **$9600 tuition** and fees
- **$7201 average financial aid** package, $11,200 average indebtedness upon graduation, $30.4 million endowment

Students *Undergraduates:* 667 full-time, 202 part-time. Students come from 26 states and territories, 14 other countries. *The most frequently chosen baccalaureate fields are:* business/marketing, education, parks and recreation. *Graduate:* 826 in graduate degree programs.

From out-of-state	54%	Reside on campus	32%
Age 25 or older	28%	Transferred in	14%
International students	5%	African Americans	3%
Asian Americans/Pacific Islanders	0.3%	Hispanic Americans	0.2%

Faculty 152 (57% full-time), 53% with terminal degrees.

Expenses (2000–2001) *Comprehensive fee:* $13,500 includes full-time tuition ($9600) and room and board ($3900). *College room only:* $1680. Room and board charges vary according to board plan and housing facility. *Part-time tuition:* $400 per semester hour. *Payment plans:* installment, deferred payment. *Waivers:* senior citizens and employees or children of employees.

Library Carnegie Library. *Operations spending 1999–2000:* $217,353. *Collection:* 66,195 titles, 2,375 serial subscriptions, 3,700 audiovisual materials.

College life *Housing: Options:* coed, men-only, women-only. *Social organizations:* local fraternities, local sororities; 5% of eligible men and 10% of eligible women are members. *Most popular organizations:* Baptist Student Association, Wesleyan Association, Student Nurses Association, Student National Education Association, Student Alumni Association.

Campus security 24-hour emergency response devices and patrols.

After graduation *Career center:* Services include job fairs, resume preparation, resume referral, career counseling, careers library, job bank, job interviews.

Freshmen 806 applied, 679 admitted, 142 enrolled. 14 valedictorians, 10 student government officers.

Average high school GPA	2.8	SAT verbal scores above 500	N/R
SAT math scores above 500	N/R	ACT above 18	91%
From top 10% of their h.s. class	36%	From top quarter	58%
From top half	94%	1998 freshmen returning in 1999	54%

Application *Options:* eApply at www.CollegeQuest.com, Common Application. *Application fee:* $25. *Required:* high school transcript; minimum 2.3 GPA. *Required for some:* essay or personal statement. *Recommended:* interview.

Standardized tests *Admission: Required:* SAT I or ACT.

Significant dates *Application deadlines:* rolling (freshmen), rolling (transfers). *Financial aid deadline priority date:* 4/1.

Freshman Application Contact Mr. Conrad Daniels, Dean of Admissions and Recruitment, Lincoln Memorial University, Cumberland Gap Parkway, Harrogate, TN 37752-1901. **Phone:** 423-869-6280. **Toll-free phone:** 800-325-0900. **Fax:** 423-869-6370. **E-mail:** admissions@inetlmu.lmunet.edu

Visit CollegeQuest.com for information on majors offered and athletics.

LIPSCOMB UNIVERSITY
Tennessee—See David Lipscomb University

MARTIN METHODIST COLLEGE
Pulaski, Tennessee

- **Independent United Methodist**, 4-year, founded 1870
- **Degrees** associate and bachelor's
- **Small-town** 6-acre campus with easy access to Nashville
- **Coed**, 550 undergraduate students, 69% full-time, 60% women, 40% men
- **Minimally difficult** entrance level, 98% of applicants were admitted
- **15:1 student-to-undergraduate faculty ratio**
- **7% graduate** in 6 years or less
- **$8520 tuition** and fees
- **$5610 average financial aid** package, $7985 average indebtedness upon graduation, $6.6 million endowment

Students *Undergraduates:* 379 full-time, 171 part-time. Students come from 22 states and territories, 12 other countries. *The most frequently chosen baccalaureate fields are:* business/marketing, education, social sciences and history.

From out-of-state	14%	Reside on campus	35%
Age 25 or older	29%	Transferred in	11%
International students	11%	African Americans	11%
Asian Americans/Pacific Islanders	0.4%	Hispanic Americans	1%
Native Americans	1%		

Faculty 51 (43% full-time), 31% with terminal degrees.

Expenses (1999–2000) *Comprehensive fee:* $11,920 includes full-time tuition ($8500), mandatory fees ($20), and room and board ($3400). Room and board charges vary according to housing facility. *Part-time tuition:* $355 per hour. Part-time tuition and fees vary according to class time. *Payment plan:* installment. *Waivers:* employees or children of employees.

Library Warden Memorial Library. *Operations spending 1999–2000:* $215,868. *Collection:* 67,040 titles, 243 serial subscriptions, 340 audiovisual materials.

College life *Housing:* on-campus residence required through sophomore year. *Options:* men-only, women-only. *Most popular organizations:* Student Christian Association, Fellowship of Christian Athletes, drama club, International Club, Students for Environment Awareness.

Campus security Controlled dormitory access.

After graduation 25 organizations recruited on campus 1997–98. *Career center:* 1 part-time personnel. Services include resume preparation, resume referral, career counseling, careers library, job bank, job interviews. **Graduate education:** 5% of class of 1999 went directly to graduate and professional school: 5% graduate arts and sciences.

Freshmen 356 applied, 350 admitted, 132 enrolled. 5 class presidents, 2 valedictorians, 20 student government officers.

Average high school GPA	2.8	SAT verbal scores above 500	N/R
SAT math scores above 500	N/R	ACT above 18	N/R
From top 10% of their h.s. class	12%	From top quarter	30%
From top half	80%	1998 freshmen returning in 1999	45%

Application *Options:* eApply at www.CollegeQuest.com, Common Application, early admission, deferred entrance. *Application fee:* $25. *Required:* high school transcript; minimum 2.0 GPA. *Recommended:* essay or personal statement; interview.

Standardized tests *Admission: Required:* SAT I or ACT.

Significant dates *Application deadlines:* 8/30 (freshmen), 8/30 (transfers). *Financial aid deadline priority date:* 2/1.

Freshman Application Contact Mr. Robby Shelton, Director of Admissions and Enrollment Management, Martin Methodist College, 433 West Madison Street, Pulaski, TN 38478-2716. **Phone:** 931-363-9807. **Toll-free phone:** 800-467-1273. **Fax:** 931-363-9818.

Visit CollegeQuest.com for information on majors offered and athletics. College video available at CollegeQuest.com.

Tennessee

MARYVILLE COLLEGE
Maryville, Tennessee

- **Independent Presbyterian**, 4-year, founded 1819
- **Degree** bachelor's
- **Suburban** 350-acre campus with easy access to Knoxville
- **Coed**, 1,001 undergraduate students, 97% full-time, 56% women, 44% men
- **Moderately difficult** entrance level, 81% of applicants were admitted
- **13:1 student-to-undergraduate faculty ratio**
- **48.2% graduate** in 6 years or less
- **$16,025 tuition** and fees
- **$15,168 average financial aid** package, $16,397 average indebtedness upon graduation, $23.8 million endowment

Students *Undergraduates:* 972 full-time, 29 part-time. Students come from 30 states and territories, 11 other countries. *The most frequently chosen baccalaureate fields are:* business/marketing, education, social sciences and history.

From out-of-state	30%	Reside on campus	74%
Age 25 or older	6%	Transferred in	4%
International students	3%	African Americans	5%
Asian Americans/Pacific Islanders	2%	Hispanic Americans	1%
Native Americans	0.3%		

Faculty 100 (63% full-time), 66% with terminal degrees.

Expenses (1999–2000) *Comprehensive fee:* $21,105 includes full-time tuition ($15,600), mandatory fees ($425), and room and board ($5080). *College room only:* $2400. Room and board charges vary according to board plan and housing facility. *Part-time tuition:* $650 per semester hour. *Part-time fees:* $425 per year part-time. *Payment plans:* installment, deferred payment. *Waivers:* employees or children of employees.

Library Lamar Memorial Library plus 1 other. *Operations spending 1999–2000:* $538,375. *Collection:* 672 serial subscriptions, 672 audiovisual materials.

College life *Housing:* on-campus residence required through senior year. *Options:* coed, men-only, women-only, disabled students. *Most popular organizations:* Fellowship of Christian Athletes, student government, Student Programming Board, international club, Peer Mentors.

Campus security 24-hour emergency response devices and patrols, late-night transport-escort service, controlled dormitory access.

After graduation 80 organizations recruited on campus 1997–98. 62% of class of 1998 had job offers within 6 months. *Career center:* 2 full-time personnel. Services include job fairs, resume preparation, interview workshops, resume referral, career/interest testing, career counseling, careers library, job bank, job interviews. *Graduate education:* 18% of class of 1999 went directly to graduate and professional school: 11% graduate arts and sciences, 3% law, 2% business, 1% education, 1% medicine, 1% theology.

Freshmen 1,744 applied, 1,416 admitted, 313 enrolled. 6 valedictorians.

Average high school GPA	3.49	SAT verbal scores above 500	68%
SAT math scores above 500	65%	ACT above 18	93%
From top 10% of their h.s. class	23%	From top quarter	68%
From top half	91%	1998 freshmen returning in 1999	73%

Application *Options:* eApply at www.CollegeQuest.com, electronic application, early admission, early decision, early action, deferred entrance. *Application fee:* $25. *Required:* high school transcript; minimum 2.5 GPA. *Required for some:* essay or personal statement; letters of recommendation; interview. *Recommended:* minimum 3.0 GPA.

Standardized tests *Admission: Required:* SAT I or ACT.

Significant dates *Application deadlines:* 3/1 (freshmen), 8/1 (transfers). *Early decision:* 11/15, 9/15. *Notification:* 4/1 (freshmen), 12/1 (early decision), 10/1 (early action). *Financial aid deadline priority date:* 3/1.

Freshman Application Contact
Ms. Linda L. Moore, Administrative Assistant of Admissions, Maryville College, 502 East Lamar Alexander Parkway, Maryville, TN 37804-5907. **Phone:** 865-981-8092. **Toll-free phone:** 800-597-2687. **Fax:** 865-983-0581. **E-mail:** admissions@maryvillecollege.edu

Visit CollegeQuest.com for information on majors offered and athletics. College video and electronic viewbook available at CollegeQuest.com.

- *See page 2012 for a narrative description.*

MEMPHIS COLLEGE OF ART
Memphis, Tennessee

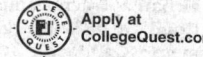

- **Independent**, comprehensive, founded 1936
- **Degrees** bachelor's and master's
- **Urban** 200-acre campus
- **Coed**, 236 undergraduate students
- **Moderately difficult** entrance level, 80% of applicants were admitted
- **10:1 student-to-undergraduate faculty ratio**
- **$11,990 tuition** and fees

For more than half a century, Memphis College of Art has been a small, distinctive community of artists. Students of diverse backgrounds work together in the shared pursuit of a challenging professional education in the visual arts. The College is situated in 340-acre Overton Park in midtown Memphis. Students have access to excellent equipment—from looms and presses to the latest in computer technology. Degrees are offered in both fine arts and applied arts.

Students *Undergraduates:* Students come from 30 states and territories, 10 other countries. *The most frequently chosen baccalaureate field is:* visual/performing arts. *Graduate:* 54 in graduate degree programs.

From out-of-state	56%	Reside on campus	11%
Age 25 or older	30%	International students	6%
African Americans	14%	Asian Americans/Pacific Islanders	1%
Hispanic Americans	0.4%	Native Americans	0.4%

Faculty 18 full-time.

Expenses (1999–2000) *Tuition:* full-time $11,940; part-time $500 per credit hour. *Required fees:* full-time $50; $25 per term part-time. Part-time tuition and fees vary according to course load. *College room only:* $3070. Room and board charges vary according to housing facility. *Payment plans:* installment, deferred payment. *Waivers:* employees or children of employees.

Library G. Pillow Lewis Library. *Collection:* 14,500 titles, 102 serial subscriptions.

College life *Housing: Option:* coed. *Most popular organization:* student government.

Campus security Late-night transport-escort service, late night security patrols by trained personnel.

After graduation 20 organizations recruited on campus 1997–98. *Career center:* 1 full-time personnel. Services include job fairs, resume preparation, career counseling, careers library. *Graduate education:* 20% of class of 1999 went directly to graduate and professional school: 20% graduate arts and sciences.

Freshmen 192 applied, 154 admitted.

Average high school GPA	2.5	SAT verbal scores above 500	N/R
SAT math scores above 500	N/R	ACT above 18	62%
1998 freshmen returning in 1999	54%		

Application *Options:* eApply at www.CollegeQuest.com, Common Application, electronic application, early admission, deferred entrance. *Application fee:* $25. *Required:* essay or personal statement; high school transcript; portfolio. *Recommended:* interview.

Standardized tests *Admission: Required:* SAT I or ACT.

Significant dates *Application deadlines:* rolling (freshmen), rolling (transfers). *Financial aid deadline priority date:* 3/1.

Freshman Application Contact
Ms. Annette Moore, Director of Admission, Memphis College of Art, 1930 Poplar Avenue, Memphis, TN 38104. **Phone:** 901-272-5153. **Toll-free phone:** 800-727-1088. **Fax:** 901-272-5104. **E-mail:** info@mca.edu

Visit CollegeQuest.com for information on majors offered and athletics.

MIDDLE TENNESSEE STATE UNIVERSITY
Murfreesboro, Tennessee

- **State-supported**, university, founded 1911
- **Degrees** associate, bachelor's, master's, doctoral, and post-master's certificates

Tennessee

Middle Tennessee State University *(continued)*
- **Urban** 500-acre campus with easy access to Nashville
- **Coed**, 16,957 undergraduate students, 83% full-time, 53% women, 47% men
- **Moderately difficult** entrance level, 77% of applicants were admitted
- **23:1** student-to-undergraduate faculty ratio
- **38% graduate** in 6 years or less
- **$2516 tuition** and fees (in-state); $7632 (out-of-state)
- **$4450 average financial aid** package, $17,372 average indebtedness upon graduation, $890,591 endowment

Part of Tennessee Board of Regents.

Students *Undergraduates:* 14,139 full-time, 2,818 part-time. Students come from 47 states and territories, 64 other countries. *The most frequently chosen baccalaureate fields are:* business/marketing, communications/communication technologies, interdisciplinary studies. *Graduate:* 1,956 in graduate degree programs.

From out-of-state	5%	Reside on campus	20%
Age 25 or older	23%	Transferred in	11%
International students	1%	African Americans	11%
Asian Americans/Pacific Islanders	2%	Hispanic Americans	1%
Native Americans	0.5%		

Faculty 923 (72% full-time).
Expenses (1999–2000) *Tuition, state resident:* full-time $2020; part-time $90 per semester hour. *Tuition, nonresident:* full-time $7136; part-time $314 per semester hour. *Required fees:* full-time $496; $17 per semester hour; $25 per term part-time. Part-time tuition and fees vary according to course load. *College room and board:* $3096; room only: $1920. Room and board charges vary according to board plan and housing facility. *Payment plan:* deferred payment. *Waivers:* senior citizens and employees or children of employees.
Library University Library. *Operations spending 1999–2000:* $4.4 million. *Collection:* 642,018 titles, 3,436 serial subscriptions.
College life *Housing: Options:* men-only, women-only. *Social organizations:* national fraternities, national sororities, local sororities; 15% of eligible men and 20% of eligible women are members. *Most popular organizations:* African American Student Association, Student Tennessee Education Association, Gamma Beta Phi, Golden Key National Honor Society, Inter-Fraternity Council.
Campus security 24-hour emergency response devices and patrols, student patrols, late-night transport-escort service, controlled dormitory access.
After graduation 211 organizations recruited on campus 1997–98. *Career center:* 5 full-time personnel. Services include job fairs, resume preparation, interview workshops, resume referral, career counseling, careers library, job bank, job interviews. *Graduate education:* 19% of class of 1999 went directly to graduate and professional school.
Freshmen 5,529 applied, 4,259 admitted, 2,612 enrolled.

Average high school GPA	3.1	SAT verbal scores above 500	N/R
SAT math scores above 500	N/R	ACT above 18	91%
From top 10% of their h.s. class	15%	From top half	73%
1998 freshmen returning in 1999	69%		

Application *Options:* electronic application, early admission, deferred entrance. *Application fee:* $15. *Required:* high school transcript; minimum 2.8 GPA. *Required for some:* essay or personal statement.
Standardized tests *Admission: Required:* SAT I or ACT.
Significant dates *Application deadlines:* rolling (freshmen), rolling (transfers). *Financial aid deadline priority date:* 5/15.
Freshman Application Contact
Ms. Lynn Palmer, Director of Admissions, Middle Tennessee State University, Murfreesboro, TN 37132. **Phone:** 615-898-2111. **E-mail:** admissions@mtsu.edu
Visit CollegeQuest.com for information on majors offered and athletics. College video available at CollegeQuest.com.

MILLIGAN COLLEGE
Milligan College, Tennessee

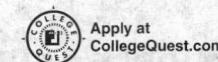 Apply at CollegeQuest.com

- **Independent Christian**, comprehensive, founded 1866
- **Degrees** bachelor's and master's
- **Suburban** 145-acre campus
- **Coed**, 783 undergraduate students, 98% full-time, 60% women, 40% men
- **Moderately difficult** entrance level, 69% of applicants were admitted
- **13:1** student-to-undergraduate faculty ratio
- **$11,480 tuition** and fees
- **$9896 average financial aid** package, $19,275 average indebtedness upon graduation, $7.2 million endowment

Students *Undergraduates:* 770 full-time, 13 part-time. Students come from 40 states and territories, 17 other countries. *The most frequently chosen baccalaureate fields are:* business/marketing, education, health professions and related sciences. *Graduate:* 118 in graduate degree programs.

From out-of-state	64%	Reside on campus	68%
Age 25 or older	13%	Transferred in	6%
International students	3%	African Americans	2%
Asian Americans/Pacific Islanders	0.4%	Hispanic Americans	1%
Native Americans	0.3%		

Faculty 109 (61% full-time), 50% with terminal degrees.
Expenses (1999–2000) *Comprehensive fee:* $15,480 includes full-time tuition ($11,100), mandatory fees ($380), and room and board ($4000). *College room only:* $1900. Full-time tuition and fees vary according to class time. Room and board charges vary according to board plan and housing facility. *Part-time tuition:* $460 per hour. *Part-time fees:* $95 per term part-time. Part-time tuition and fees vary according to class time and course load. *Payment plan:* installment. *Waivers:* employees or children of employees.
Library P. H. Welshimer Memorial Library. *Operations spending 1999–2000:* $287,107. *Collection:* 78,727 titles, 620 serial subscriptions, 2,348 audiovisual materials.
College life *Housing:* on-campus residence required through senior year. *Options:* men-only, women-only. *Most popular organizations:* Social Affairs Committee, Buffalo Ramblers, Concert Council, Volunteer Milligan, Milligan Students for Life.
Campus security 24-hour patrols, late-night transport-escort service.
After graduation 10 organizations recruited on campus 1997–98. *Career center:* 1 part-time personnel. Services include job fairs, resume preparation, career counseling, careers library, job bank, job interviews.
Freshmen 762 applied, 527 admitted, 214 enrolled.

Average high school GPA	3.4	SAT verbal scores above 500	76%
SAT math scores above 500	74%	ACT above 18	98%
1998 freshmen returning in 1999	70%		

Application *Options:* eApply at www.CollegeQuest.com, deferred entrance. *Application fee:* $30. *Required:* essay or personal statement; high school transcript; minimum 2.0 GPA; 2 letters of recommendation. *Required for some:* interview. *Recommended:* minimum 3.0 GPA.
Standardized tests *Admission: Required:* SAT I or ACT.
Significant dates *Application deadlines:* rolling (freshmen), rolling (transfers). *Financial aid deadline priority date:* 3/1.
Freshman Application Contact
Mr. Michael A. Johnson, Vice President for Enrollment Management, Milligan College, PO Box 210, Milligan College, TN 37682. **Phone:** 423-461-8730. **Toll-free phone:** 800-262-8337. **Fax:** 423-461-8960.
Visit CollegeQuest.com for information on majors offered and athletics.

■ *See page 2060 for a narrative description.*

O'MORE COLLEGE OF DESIGN
Franklin, Tennessee

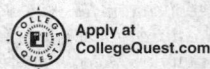 Apply at CollegeQuest.com

- **Independent**, 4-year, founded 1970
- **Degree** bachelor's
- **Small-town** 6-acre campus with easy access to Nashville
- **Coed**, 145 undergraduate students
- **Moderately difficult** entrance level
- **$8505 tuition** and fees

Students *Undergraduates:* Students come from 7 states and territories, 2 other countries.

From out-of-state	11%	Reside on campus	30%
Age 25 or older	29%		

Faculty 42 (17% full-time).
Expenses (1999–2000) *Tuition:* full-time $8500; part-time $375 per semester hour. *Required fees:* full-time $5; $5 per year part-time. *Payment plans:* installment, deferred payment.

Tennessee

Library Fleming-Farrar Hall. *Collection:* 4,000 titles, 60 serial subscriptions.
College life *Housing: Option:* cooperative.
Campus security 24-hour emergency response devices.
After graduation 90% of class of 1998 had job offers within 6 months. *Career center:* Services include resume referral, job interviews.
Freshmen 88 applied.

Average high school GPA	2.69	SAT verbal scores above 500	N/R
SAT math scores above 500	N/R	ACT above 18	N/R
From top 10% of their h.s. class	5%	From top quarter	15%
From top half	50%	1998 freshmen returning in 1999	85%

Application *Options:* eApply at www.CollegeQuest.com, Common Application, deferred entrance. *Application fee:* $25. *Required:* essay or personal statement; high school transcript; minimum 2.5 GPA; interview. *Required for some:* 3 letters of recommendation; portfolio.
Standardized tests *Admission: Required:* ACT.
Significant dates *Application deadlines:* 8/1 (freshmen), 8/1 (transfers). *Notification:* continuous until 8/1 (freshmen). *Financial aid deadline priority date:* 5/1.
Freshman Application Contact
Ms. Amy Shelton, Vice President for Admissions and Records, O'More College of Design, 423 South Margin Street, Franklin, TN 37064-2816. **Phone:** 615-794-4254 Ext. 25. **Fax:** 615-790-1662.
Visit CollegeQuest.com for information on majors offered and athletics.

RHODES COLLEGE
Memphis, Tennessee

 Apply at CollegeQuest.com

- **Independent Presbyterian**, comprehensive, founded 1848
- **Degrees** bachelor's and master's (master's degree in accounting only)
- **Suburban** 100-acre campus
- **Coed**, 1,484 undergraduate students, 99% full-time, 54% women, 46% men
- **Very difficult** entrance level, 78% of applicants were admitted
- **12:1 student-to-undergraduate faculty ratio**
- **$19,303 tuition** and fees

Students *Undergraduates:* 1,470 full-time, 14 part-time. Students come from 45 states and territories, 17 other countries. *The most frequently chosen baccalaureate fields are:* business/marketing, biological/life sciences, social sciences and history. *Graduate:* 11 in graduate degree programs.

From out-of-state	72%	Reside on campus	70%
Age 25 or older	1%	Transferred in	2%
International students	2%	African Americans	4%
Asian Americans/Pacific Islanders	3%	Hispanic Americans	1%
Native Americans	0.1%		

Faculty 159 (76% full-time).
Expenses (2000–2001) *Comprehensive fee:* $24,656 includes full-time tuition ($19,303) and room and board ($5353). Room and board charges vary according to board plan. *Part-time tuition:* $780 per credit hour. *Part-time fees:* $155 per year part-time. *Payment plan:* installment. *Waivers:* employees or children of employees.
Library Burrow Library plus 3 others. *Operations spending 1999–2000:* $1.2 million. *Collection:* 250,000 titles, 1,200 serial subscriptions, 9,000 audiovisual materials.
College life *Housing:* on-campus residence required through sophomore year. *Options:* men-only, women-only. *Social organizations:* national fraternities, national sororities; 57% of eligible men and 55% of eligible women are members. *Most popular organizations:* Greek organizations, Kinney Volunteer Program, Habitat for Humanity, Adopt A Friend, Foster.
Campus security 24-hour emergency response devices and patrols, student patrols, late-night transport-escort service, 24-hour monitored security cameras in parking areas, fenced campus with monitored access at night.
After graduation 55 organizations recruited on campus 1997–98. *Career center:* 3 full-time personnel. Services include job fairs, resume preparation, interview workshops, resume referral, career/interest testing, career counseling, careers library, job bank, job interviews. *Graduate education:* 33% of class of 1999 went directly to graduate and professional school: 15% graduate arts and sciences, 6% law, 5% medicine, 4% business, 1% veterinary medicine.
Major awards: 2 Fulbright Scholars.

Freshmen 2,247 applied, 1,748 admitted, 439 enrolled. 25 National Merit Scholars, 29 class presidents, 34 valedictorians, 26 student government officers.

Average high school GPA	3.51	SAT verbal scores above 500	98%
SAT math scores above 500	97%	ACT above 18	100%
From top 10% of their h.s. class	56%	From top quarter	80%
From top half	96%	1998 freshmen returning in 1999	90%

Application *Options:* eApply at www.CollegeQuest.com, Common Application, electronic application, early admission, early decision, deferred entrance. *Application fee:* $40. *Required:* essay or personal statement; high school transcript; 2 letters of recommendation. *Recommended:* interview.
Standardized tests *Admission: Required:* SAT I or ACT.
Significant dates *Application deadlines:* 2/1 (freshmen), 2/1 (transfers). *Early decision:* 12/1. *Notification:* 4/1 (freshmen), 12/15 (early decision). *Financial aid deadline priority date:* 3/1.
Freshman Application Contact
Mr. David J. Wottle, Dean of Admissions and Financial Aid, Rhodes College, 2000 North Parkway, Memphis, TN 38112-1690. **Phone:** 901-843-3700. **Toll-free phone:** 800-844-5969. **Fax:** 901-843-3719. **E-mail:** adminfo@rhodes.edu
Visit CollegeQuest.com for information on majors offered and athletics. College video and electronic viewbook available at CollegeQuest.com.

■ *See page 2324 for a narrative description.*

SOUTHERN ADVENTIST UNIVERSITY
Collegedale, Tennessee

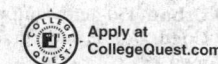 Apply at CollegeQuest.com

- **Independent Seventh-day Adventist**, comprehensive, founded 1892
- **Degrees** associate, bachelor's, and master's
- **Small-town** 1,000-acre campus with easy access to Chattanooga
- **Coed**, 1,707 undergraduate students, 89% full-time, 55% women, 45% men
- **Moderately difficult** entrance level, 80% of applicants were admitted
- **14:1 student-to-undergraduate faculty ratio**
- **$10,620 tuition** and fees
- **$9894 average financial aid** package, $15,600 average indebtedness upon graduation, $19.4 million endowment

Students *Undergraduates:* 1,515 full-time, 192 part-time. Students come from 50 states and territories, 50 other countries. *The most frequently chosen baccalaureate fields are:* business/marketing, education, health professions and related sciences. *Graduate:* 74 in graduate degree programs.

From out-of-state	76%	Reside on campus	74%
Age 25 or older	10%	Transferred in	10%
International students	5%	African Americans	5%
Asian Americans/Pacific Islanders	4%	Hispanic Americans	10%
Native Americans	1%		

Faculty 159 (67% full-time), 45% with terminal degrees.
Expenses (1999–2000) *Comprehensive fee:* $14,350 includes full-time tuition ($10,300), mandatory fees ($320), and room and board ($3730). *College room only:* $1780. Full-time tuition and fees vary according to program. Room and board charges vary according to housing facility. *Part-time tuition:* $445 per semester hour. *Part-time fees:* $160 per term part-time. Part-time tuition and fees vary according to course load and program. *Payment plans:* tuition prepayment, installment, deferred payment. *Waivers:* adult students, senior citizens, and employees or children of employees.
Library McKee Library. *Operations spending 1999–2000:* $835,997. *Collection:* 109,077 titles, 1,931 serial subscriptions, 3,250 audiovisual materials.
College life *Housing:* on-campus residence required through senior year. *Options:* men-only, women-only. *Most popular organizations:* student association, Black Christian Union, campus ministries.
Campus security 24-hour patrols, late-night transport-escort service, controlled dormitory access.
After graduation 30 organizations recruited on campus 1997–98. *Career center:* 3 full-time personnel. Services include job fairs, resume preparation, interview workshops, career/interest testing, career counseling, careers library, job bank, job interviews.

Tennessee

Southern Adventist University (continued)

Freshmen 1,053 applied, 845 admitted, 421 enrolled.

Average high school GPA	3.2	SAT verbal scores above 500	N/R
SAT math scores above 500	N/R	ACT above 18	87%
1998 freshmen returning in 1999	70%		

Application *Options:* eApply at www.CollegeQuest.com, early admission, deferred entrance. *Application fee:* $25. *Required:* high school transcript; minimum 2.0 GPA; 2 letters of recommendation. *Required for some:* essay or personal statement; interview.

Standardized tests *Admission: Required:* SAT I or ACT.

Significant dates *Application deadlines:* rolling (freshmen), rolling (transfers). *Financial aid deadline priority date:* 3/1.

Freshman Application Contact
Mr. Victor Czerkasij, Director of Admissions and Recruitment, Southern Adventist University, PO Box 370, Collegedale, TN 37315-0370. **Phone:** 423-238-2843. **Toll-free phone:** 800-768-8437. **Fax:** 423-238-3005. **E-mail:** admissions@southern.edu

Visit CollegeQuest.com for information on majors offered and athletics. College video available at CollegeQuest.com.

TENNESSEE STATE UNIVERSITY
Nashville, Tennessee

- **State-supported**, comprehensive, founded 1912
- **Degrees** associate, bachelor's, master's, and doctoral
- **Urban** 450-acre campus
- **Coed**, 7,061 undergraduate students, 86% full-time, 63% women, 37% men
- **Minimally difficult** entrance level, 61% of applicants were admitted
- **29:1 student-to-undergraduate faculty ratio**
- **40.94% graduate** in 6 years or less
- **$2730 tuition** and fees (in-state); $7556 (out-of-state)

Part of Tennessee Board of Regents.

Students *Undergraduates:* 6,093 full-time, 968 part-time. Students come from 45 states and territories. *The most frequently chosen baccalaureate fields are:* health professions and related sciences, business/marketing, interdisciplinary studies. *Graduate:* 1,559 in graduate degree programs.

From out-of-state	39%	Reside on campus	39%
Age 25 or older	36%	Transferred in	7%
African Americans	83%	Asian Americans/Pacific Islanders	1%
Hispanic Americans	0.4%	Native Americans	0.03%

Faculty 507 (67% full-time).

Expenses (1999–2000) *Tuition, state resident:* full-time $2308; part-time $138 per semester hour. *Tuition, nonresident:* full-time $7134; part-time $349 per semester hour. *Required fees:* full-time $422. Full-time tuition and fees vary according to course load. Part-time tuition and fees vary according to course load. *College room and board:* $3600; room only: $2090. Room and board charges vary according to board plan and housing facility. *Payment plan:* deferred payment. *Waivers:* minority students and employees or children of employees.

Library Martha M. Brown/Lois H. Daniel Library plus 1 other. *Operations spending 1999–2000:* $2.1 million. *Collection:* 580,650 titles, 23,668 audiovisual materials.

College life *Housing: Options:* coed, men-only, women-only. *Social organizations:* national fraternities, national sororities; 12% of eligible men and 12% of eligible women are members. *Most popular organizations:* SADD, Pre Alumni Council, Baptist Student Union, T. E. Poag Players.

Campus security 24-hour patrols, controlled dormitory access.

After graduation 142 organizations recruited on campus 1997–98. *Career center:* 7 full-time personnel. Services include job fairs, resume preparation, resume referral, career counseling, careers library, job bank, job interviews.

Freshmen 5,344 applied, 3,283 admitted, 1,368 enrolled.

Average high school GPA	2.98	SAT verbal scores above 500	N/R
SAT math scores above 500	N/R	ACT above 18	68%
1998 freshmen returning in 1999	79%		

Application *Option:* electronic application. *Preference* given to state residents. *Application fee:* $15. *Required:* high school transcript. *Required for some:* 3 letters of recommendation.

Standardized tests *Admission: Required:* SAT I or ACT.

Significant dates *Application deadlines:* 8/1 (freshmen), 8/1 (transfers). *Notification:* continuous until 8/15 (freshmen). *Financial aid deadline priority date:* 4/1.

Freshman Application Contact
Ms. Vernella Smith, Admissions Coordinator, Tennessee State University, 3500 John A Merritt Boulevard, Nashville, TN 37209-1561. **Phone:** 615-963-5104. **Fax:** 615-963-5108. **E-mail:** jcade@picard.tnstate.edu

Visit CollegeQuest.com for information on majors offered and athletics. Electronic viewbook available at CollegeQuest.com.

■ *See page 2598 for a narrative description.*

TENNESSEE TECHNOLOGICAL UNIVERSITY
Cookeville, Tennessee

- **State-supported**, university, founded 1915
- **Degrees** bachelor's, master's, and doctoral
- **Small-town** 235-acre campus
- **Coed**, 6,927 undergraduate students, 88% full-time, 46% women, 54% men
- **Moderately difficult** entrance level, 89% of applicants were admitted
- **17:1 student-to-undergraduate faculty ratio**
- **41% graduate** in 6 years or less
- **$2390 tuition** and fees (in-state); $8028 (out-of-state)
- **$2992 average financial aid** package, $25 million endowment

Part of Tennessee Board of Regents.

Students *Undergraduates:* 6,091 full-time, 836 part-time. Students come from 41 states and territories, 25 other countries. *The most frequently chosen baccalaureate fields are:* business/marketing, engineering/engineering technologies, interdisciplinary studies. *Graduate:* 1,541 in graduate degree programs.

From out-of-state	4%	Reside on campus	25%
Age 25 or older	25%	Transferred in	11%
International students	1%	African Americans	3%
Asian Americans/Pacific Islanders	1%	Hispanic Americans	1%
Native Americans	0.3%		

Faculty 483 (76% full-time), 70% with terminal degrees.

Expenses (1999–2000) *Tuition, state resident:* full-time $2390; part-time $111 per semester hour. *Tuition, nonresident:* full-time $8028; part-time $335 per semester hour. Part-time tuition and fees vary according to course load. *College room and board:* $4170; room only: $1784. Room and board charges vary according to board plan and housing facility. *Waivers:* employees or children of employees.

Library *Operations spending 1999–2000:* $1.3 million. *Collection:* 390,915 titles, 3,828 serial subscriptions.

College life *Housing:* on-campus residence required through sophomore year. *Options:* coed, men-only, women-only. *Social organizations:* national fraternities, national sororities; 18% of eligible men and 12% of eligible women are members. *Most popular organizations:* Baptist Student Union, Fellowship of Christian Athletes, University Christian Student Center, Interfraternity Council, Residence Hall Association.

Campus security 24-hour emergency response devices and patrols, late-night transport-escort service, student safety organization, lighted pathways.

After graduation 270 organizations recruited on campus 1997–98. *Career center:* 4 full-time personnel. Services include job fairs, resume preparation, interview workshops, resume referral, career counseling, careers library, job bank, job interviews.

Freshmen 2,375 applied, 2,121 admitted, 1,183 enrolled. 5 National Merit Scholars, 32 valedictorians.

Average high school GPA	3.02	SAT verbal scores above 500	N/R
SAT math scores above 500	N/R	ACT above 18	87%
From top 10% of their h.s. class	23%	From top quarter	52%
From top half	80%	1998 freshmen returning in 1999	71%

Application *Options:* early admission, deferred entrance. *Preference* given to state residents. *Application fee:* $15. *Required:* high school transcript; 2.35 high school GPA or ACT composite score of 19. *Recommended:* interview.

Standardized tests *Admission: Required:* ACT.

Tennessee

Significant dates *Application deadlines:* rolling (freshmen), rolling (transfers). *Financial aid deadline priority date:* 3/15.
Freshman Application Contact
Mr. Jim Rose, Associate Vice President for Enrollment and Records, Tennessee Technological University, TTU Box 5006, Cookeville, TN 38505. **Phone:** 931-372-3888. **Toll-free phone:** 800-255-8881. **Fax:** 931-372-6250. **E-mail:** u_admissions@tntech.edu
Visit CollegeQuest.com for information on majors offered and athletics.

■ *See pages 2600 and 2602 for narrative descriptions.*

TENNESSEE TEMPLE UNIVERSITY
Chattanooga, Tennessee

- **Independent Baptist**, comprehensive, founded 1946
- **Degrees** associate, bachelor's, and master's
- **Urban** 55-acre campus
- **Coed**
- **Minimally difficult** entrance level
- **$5250 tuition** and fees

Expenses (1999–2000) *Comprehensive fee:* $10,000 includes full-time tuition ($4650), mandatory fees ($600), and room and board ($4750). *Part-time tuition:* $210 per credit hour.
Institutional Web site http://www.tntemple.edu/
College life *Housing:* on-campus residence required through senior year. *Options:* men-only, women-only. *Social organizations:* societies for men and women.
Campus security 24-hour emergency response devices and patrols, late-night transport-escort service.
Application *Options:* electronic application, deferred entrance. *Application fee:* $30. *Required:* high school transcript; minimum 2.0 GPA; 3 letters of recommendation; interview. *Required for some:* essay or personal statement.
Standardized tests *Placement: Required:* SAT I or ACT
Admissions Office Contact
Tennessee Temple University, 1815 Union Avenue, Chattanooga, TN 37404-3587. **Toll-free phone:** 800-553-4050. **Fax:** 423-493-4497. **E-mail:** ttuinfo@tntemple.edu
Visit CollegeQuest.com for information on athletics.

TENNESSEE WESLEYAN COLLEGE
Athens, Tennessee

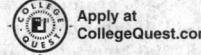

- **Independent United Methodist**, 4-year, founded 1857
- **Degree** bachelor's (all information given is for both main and branch campuses)
- **Small-town** 40-acre campus
- **Coed**, 797 undergraduate students, 77% full-time, 65% women, 35% men
- **Moderately difficult** entrance level, 31% of applicants were admitted
- **14:1 student-to-undergraduate faculty ratio**
- **$7550 tuition** and fees
- **$7668 average financial aid** package, $11,746 average indebtedness upon graduation, $5.9 million endowment

Students *Undergraduates:* 615 full-time, 182 part-time. Students come from 15 states and territories, 11 other countries. *The most frequently chosen baccalaureate fields are:* business/marketing, protective services/public administration, psychology.

From out-of-state	9%	Reside on campus	27%
Age 25 or older	30%	Transferred in	19%
International students	7%	African Americans	4%
Asian Americans/Pacific Islanders	0.1%	Hispanic Americans	0.3%

Faculty 96 (44% full-time).
Expenses (1999–2000) *Comprehensive fee:* $11,630 includes full-time tuition ($7400), mandatory fees ($150), and room and board ($4080). *College room only:* $1580. *Part-time tuition:* $205 per semester hour. Part-time tuition and fees vary according to class time and location. *Payment plan:* deferred payment. *Waivers:* minority students and employees or children of employees.

Library Merner-Pfeifer Library. *Operations spending 1999–2000:* $200,798. *Collection:* 75,752 titles, 408 serial subscriptions, 4,239 audiovisual materials.
College life *Housing:* on-campus residence required through senior year. *Options:* men-only, women-only. *Social organizations:* national fraternities, national sororities, local sororities; 39% of eligible men and 39% of eligible women are members. *Most popular organizations:* Wesleyan Christian Fellowship, Circle K, Baptist Student Union, Student Government Association, choir.
Campus security Controlled dormitory access, night patrols by trained security personnel.
After graduation 6 organizations recruited on campus 1997–98. 30% of class of 1998 had job offers within 6 months. *Career center:* 1 full-time personnel. Services include job fairs, resume preparation, interview workshops, resume referral, career counseling, careers library, job bank, job interviews. *Graduate education:* 26% of class of 1999 went directly to graduate and professional school.
Freshmen 452 applied, 140 admitted, 145 enrolled. 2 class presidents, 9 valedictorians, 15 student government officers.

Average high school GPA	3.3	SAT verbal scores above 500	N/R
SAT math scores above 500	N/R	ACT above 18	N/R
From top 10% of their h.s. class	15%	From top quarter	43%
From top half	71%	1998 freshmen returning in 1999	65%

Application *Options:* eApply at www.CollegeQuest.com, early admission, deferred entrance. *Application fee:* $25. *Required:* high school transcript; minimum 2.25 GPA; 1 letter of recommendation. *Required for some:* interview. *Recommended:* essay or personal statement.
Standardized tests *Admission: Required:* SAT I or ACT.
Significant dates *Application deadlines:* rolling (freshmen), rolling (transfers). *Financial aid deadline:* 5/1. *Priority date:* 2/28.
Freshman Application Contact
Mrs. Ruthie Cawood, Director of Admission, Tennessee Wesleyan College, PO Box 40, Athens, TN 37371-0040. **Phone:** 423-746-5287. **Toll-free phone:** 800-PICK-TWC. **Fax:** 423-744-9968.
Visit CollegeQuest.com for information on majors offered and athletics. College video available at CollegeQuest.com.

TREVECCA NAZARENE UNIVERSITY
Nashville, Tennessee

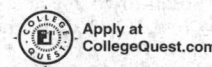

- **Independent Nazarene**, comprehensive, founded 1901
- **Degrees** associate, bachelor's, master's, doctoral, and post-master's certificates
- **Urban** 65-acre campus
- **Coed**, 945 undergraduate students, 79% full-time, 56% women, 44% men
- **Noncompetitive** entrance level, 84% of applicants were admitted
- **13:1 student-to-undergraduate faculty ratio**
- **$10,656 tuition** and fees
- **$9584 average financial aid** package, $19,532 average indebtedness upon graduation, $8.3 million endowment

Students *Undergraduates:* 744 full-time, 201 part-time. Students come from 36 states and territories. *The most frequently chosen baccalaureate fields are:* business/marketing, education, health professions and related sciences. *Graduate:* 611 in graduate degree programs.

From out-of-state	41%	Reside on campus	75%
Age 25 or older	10%	Transferred in	6%

Faculty 139 (46% full-time).
Expenses (1999–2000) *Comprehensive fee:* $15,104 includes full-time tuition ($10,016), mandatory fees ($640), and room and board ($4448). *College room only:* $1926. Full-time tuition and fees vary according to course load. Room and board charges vary according to board plan. *Part-time tuition:* $313 per semester hour. Part-time tuition and fees vary according to course load. *Payment plan:* installment. *Waivers:* senior citizens and employees or children of employees.
Library Mackey Library. *Operations spending 1999–2000:* $567,014. *Collection:* 102,419 titles, 2,353 serial subscriptions, 3,731 audiovisual materials.
College life *Housing:* on-campus residence required through junior year. *Options:* men-only, women-only.

Tennessee

Trevecca Nazarene University (continued)

Campus security 24-hour patrols, student patrols, late-night transport-escort service.

After graduation 31 organizations recruited on campus 1997–98. *Career center:* 3 full-time, 3 part-time personnel. Services include job fairs, resume preparation, interview workshops, resume referral, career counseling, careers library, job bank, job interviews. *Graduate education:* 22% of class of 1999 went directly to graduate and professional school.

Freshmen 424 applied, 356 admitted, 200 enrolled. 2 valedictorians, 33 student government officers.

Average high school GPA	3.07	SAT verbal scores above 500	N/R
SAT math scores above 500	N/R	ACT above 18	86%
From top 10% of their h.s. class	13%	From top quarter	37%
From top half	66%	1998 freshmen returning in 1999	58%

Application *Options:* eApply at www.CollegeQuest.com, early admission, deferred entrance. *Application fee:* $25. *Required:* high school transcript; minimum 2.5 GPA; medical history and immunization records. *Recommended:* letters of recommendation.

Standardized tests *Admission: Required:* SAT I or ACT. *Recommended:* ACT.

Significant dates *Application deadlines:* rolling (freshmen), rolling (transfers). *Financial aid deadline priority date:* 3/1.

Freshman Application Contact Ms. Patricia D. Cook, Director of Admissions, Trevecca Nazarene University, 333 Murfreesboro Road, Nashville, TN 37210-2834. *Phone:* 615-248-1700. *Toll-free phone:* 888-210-4TNU. *Fax:* 615-248-7728. *E-mail:* admissions_und@trevecca.edu

Visit CollegeQuest.com for information on majors offered and athletics. College video available at CollegeQuest.com.

■ See page 2636 for a narrative description.

TUSCULUM COLLEGE
Greeneville, Tennessee

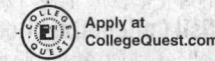 Apply at CollegeQuest.com

- **Independent Presbyterian**, comprehensive, founded 1794
- **Degrees** bachelor's and master's
- **Small-town** 140-acre campus
- **Coed**, 1,285 undergraduate students, 98% full-time, 55% women, 45% men
- **Moderately difficult** entrance level, 79% of applicants were admitted
- **13:1 student-to-undergraduate faculty ratio**
- **$12,500 tuition** and fees
- **$7150 average financial aid** package, $12,675 average indebtedness upon graduation, $8.8 million endowment

Imagine an education that goes far beyond the 4 walls of a classroom. Tusculum believes that to actually learn something, students need to experience it. With the focused calendar (1 course at a time for 3½ weeks), students have hands-on experiences that allow them to travel to such places as Costa Rica, England, Mexico, Scotland, and Spain.

Students *Undergraduates:* 1,262 full-time, 23 part-time. Students come from 29 states and territories, 10 other countries. *The most frequently chosen baccalaureate fields are:* business/marketing, education, health professions and related sciences. *Graduate:* 277 in graduate degree programs.

From out-of-state	21%	Reside on campus	23%
Age 25 or older	6%	Transferred in	5%
International students	2%	African Americans	8%
Asian Americans/Pacific Islanders	0.3%	Hispanic Americans	0.4%
Native Americans	0.4%		

Faculty 36 (92% full-time), 61% with terminal degrees.

Expenses (1999–2000) *Comprehensive fee:* $16,600 includes full-time tuition ($12,500) and room and board ($4100). Full-time tuition and fees vary according to course load and reciprocity agreements. *Part-time tuition:* $500 per credit hour. Part-time tuition and fees vary according to course load and reciprocity agreements. *Payment plan:* installment. *Waivers:* employees or children of employees.

Library Albert Columbus Tate Library plus 2 others. *Operations spending 1999–2000:* $239,600. *Collection:* 67,841 titles, 1,000 serial subscriptions, 672 audiovisual materials.

College life *Housing:* on-campus residence required through senior year. *Options:* coed, men-only, women-only. *Most popular organizations:* Pioneer Newspaper, Bonwondi, Campus Activities Board, Fellowship of Christian Athletes, "Tusculana" (yearbook).

Campus security 24-hour patrols, student patrols, trained security personnel on duty.

After graduation *Career center:* 1 full-time personnel. Services include job fairs, resume preparation, interview workshops, resume referral, career counseling, careers library, job bank, job interviews. *Graduate education:* 10% of class of 1999 went directly to graduate and professional school: 3% business, 2% graduate arts and sciences, 2% medicine, 1% dentistry, 1% law, 1% veterinary medicine.

Freshmen 640 applied, 505 admitted, 183 enrolled. 3 valedictorians.

Average high school GPA	2.8	SAT verbal scores above 500	35%
SAT math scores above 500	33%	ACT above 18	86%
From top 10% of their h.s. class	15%	From top quarter	37%
From top half	73%	1998 freshmen returning in 1999	62%

Application *Options:* eApply at www.CollegeQuest.com, early admission, deferred entrance. *Application fee:* $0. *Required:* essay or personal statement; high school transcript; minimum 2.0 GPA; letters of recommendation. *Recommended:* interview.

Standardized tests *Admission: Required:* SAT I or ACT.

Significant dates *Application deadlines:* rolling (freshmen), rolling (transfers). *Financial aid deadline priority date:* 3/1.

Freshman Application Contact Ms. Amy Yeazel, Director of Admissions, Tusculum College, PO Box 5047, Greeneville, TN 37743-9997. *Phone:* 423-636-7300 Ext. 611. *Toll-free phone:* 800-729-0256. *Fax:* 423-638-7166 Ext. 312. *E-mail:* admissions@tusculum.edu

Visit CollegeQuest.com for information on majors offered and athletics.

■ See page 2654 for a narrative description.

UNION UNIVERSITY
Jackson, Tennessee

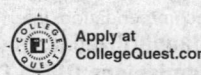 Apply at CollegeQuest.com

- **Independent Southern Baptist**, comprehensive, founded 1823
- **Degrees** associate, bachelor's, and master's
- **Small-town** 290-acre campus with easy access to Memphis
- **Coed**, 1,930 undergraduate students, 78% full-time, 59% women, 41% men
- **Moderately difficult** entrance level, 85% of applicants were admitted
- **13:1 student-to-undergraduate faculty ratio**
- **59.84% graduate** in 6 years or less
- **$11,900 tuition** and fees
- **$7800 average financial aid** package, $7800 average indebtedness upon graduation, $14.5 million endowment

Students *Undergraduates:* 1,501 full-time, 429 part-time. Students come from 40 states and territories, 26 other countries. *The most frequently chosen baccalaureate fields are:* education, business/marketing, health professions and related sciences. *Graduate:* 366 in graduate degree programs.

From out-of-state	27%	Reside on campus	65%
Age 25 or older	22%	Transferred in	10%
International students	2%	African Americans	7%
Asian Americans/Pacific Islanders	1%	Hispanic Americans	1%
Native Americans	0.2%		

Faculty 198 (64% full-time).

Expenses (2000–2001) *Comprehensive fee:* $15,750 includes full-time tuition ($11,550), mandatory fees ($350), and room and board ($3850). Full-time tuition and fees vary according to class time, course load, location, and program. Room and board charges vary according to board plan and location. *Part-time tuition:* $385 per credit hour. *Part-time fees:* $150 per term part-time. *Payment plans:* installment, deferred payment. *Waivers:* employees or children of employees.

Library Emma Waters Summar Library. *Operations spending 1999–2000:* $731,048. *Collection:* 129,678 titles, 2,653 serial subscriptions.

College life *Housing:* on-campus residence required through senior year. *Options:* men-only, women-only, disabled students. *Social organizations:* national fraternities, national sororities; 26% of eligible men and 23% of eligible women are members. *Most popular organizations:* Campus Ministries, Student Government Association, Student Activities Council, SIFE.

Campus security 24-hour emergency response devices and patrols, student patrols, late-night transport-escort service.

After graduation 85 organizations recruited on campus 1997–98. *Career center:* 2 full-time personnel. Services include job fairs, resume preparation, interview workshops, resume referral, career/interest testing, career counseling, careers library, job bank, job interviews. *Graduate education:* 40% of class of 1999 went directly to graduate and professional school.

Freshmen 913 applied, 774 admitted, 424 enrolled. 4 National Merit Scholars, 44 valedictorians.

Average high school GPA	3.48	SAT verbal scores above 500	N/R
SAT math scores above 500	N/R	ACT above 18	96%
From top 10% of their h.s. class	36%	From top quarter	64%
From top half	85%	1998 freshmen returning in 1999	93%

Application *Options:* eApply at www.CollegeQuest.com, electronic application, early admission, early decision. *Application fee:* $25. *Required:* high school transcript; minimum 2.5 GPA. *Required for some:* letters of recommendation. *Recommended:* essay or personal statement; interview.

Standardized tests *Admission: Required:* SAT I or ACT.

Significant dates *Application deadlines:* rolling (freshmen), rolling (transfers). *Early decision:* 11/15. *Notification:* continuous until 8/15 (freshmen). *Financial aid deadline priority date:* 2/15.

Freshman Application Contact
Ms. Robbie Graves, Director of Enrollment Services, Union University, 1050 Union University Drive, Jackson, TN 38305-3697. **Phone:** 901-661-5008. **Toll-free phone:** 800-33-UNION. **Fax:** 901-661-5187. **E-mail:** info@uu.edu

Visit CollegeQuest.com for information on majors offered and athletics.

THE UNIVERSITY OF MEMPHIS
Memphis, Tennessee

- **State-supported**, university, founded 1912
- **Degrees** bachelor's, master's, doctoral, first professional, post-master's, postbachelor's, and first professional certificates
- **Urban** 1,100-acre campus
- **Coed**, 14,528 undergraduate students, 74% full-time, 59% women, 41% men
- **Moderately difficult** entrance level, 71% of applicants were admitted
- **15:1** student-to-undergraduate faculty ratio
- **31.2% graduate** in 6 years or less
- **$2818 tuition** and fees (in-state); $8078 (out-of-state)
- **$4118 average financial aid** package, $17,257 average indebtedness upon graduation, $144.6 million endowment

Part of Tennessee Board of Regents.

Students *Undergraduates:* 10,782 full-time, 3,746 part-time. Students come from 46 states and territories, 49 other countries. *The most frequently chosen baccalaureate fields are:* business/marketing, education, social sciences and history. *Graduate:* 439 in professional programs, 4,434 in other graduate degree programs.

From out-of-state	9%	Reside on campus	10%
Age 25 or older	31%	Transferred in	9%
International students	2%	African Americans	33%
Asian Americans/Pacific Islanders	2%	Hispanic Americans	1%
Native Americans	0.3%		

Faculty 1,321 (58% full-time), 48% with terminal degrees.

Expenses (1999–2000) *Tuition, state resident:* full-time $2730; part-time $130 per credit hour. *Tuition, nonresident:* full-time $7990; part-time $360 per credit hour. *Required fees:* full-time $88; $6 per credit hour. Part-time tuition and fees vary according to course load. *College room and board:* $3320; room only: $1820. Room and board charges vary according to housing facility. *Payment plan:* installment. *Waivers:* senior citizens and employees or children of employees.

Library McWherter Library plus 6 others. *Operations spending 1999–2000:* $8.5 million. *Collection:* 1.5 million titles, 8,802 serial subscriptions.

College life *Housing: Options:* coed, men-only, women-only, disabled students. *Social organizations:* national fraternities, national sororities.

Campus security 24-hour emergency response devices and patrols, student patrols, late-night transport-escort service.

After graduation 125 organizations recruited on campus 1997–98. *Career center:* 4 full-time, 2 part-time personnel. Services include job fairs, resume preparation, resume referral, career counseling, careers library, job bank, job interviews.

Freshmen 4,602 applied, 3,279 admitted, 1,939 enrolled.

Average high school GPA	3.03	SAT verbal scores above 500	70%
SAT math scores above 500	62%	ACT above 18	89%
1998 freshmen returning in 1999	74%		

Application *Option:* early admission. *Application fee:* $15. *Required:* high school transcript. *Required for some:* minimum 2.0 GPA; 2 letters of recommendation; interview.

Standardized tests *Admission: Required:* SAT I or ACT.

Significant dates *Application deadlines:* 8/1 (freshmen), 8/1 (transfers). *Financial aid deadline priority date:* 3/1.

Freshman Application Contact
Mr. David Wallace, Director of Admissions, The University of Memphis, Memphis, TN 38152. **Phone:** 901-678-2101. **Fax:** 901-678-3053. **E-mail:** dwallace@memphis.edu

Visit CollegeQuest.com for information on majors offered and athletics. College video available at CollegeQuest.com.

■ *See page 2770 for a narrative description.*

THE UNIVERSITY OF TENNESSEE AT CHATTANOOGA
Chattanooga, Tennessee

- **State-supported**, comprehensive, founded 1886
- **Degrees** bachelor's, master's, and post-master's certificates
- **Urban** 102-acre campus with easy access to Atlanta
- **Coed**, 7,011 undergraduate students, 82% full-time, 57% women, 43% men
- **Moderately difficult** entrance level, 85% of applicants were admitted
- **17:1** student-to-undergraduate faculty ratio
- **40.3% graduate** in 6 years or less
- **$2660 tuition** and fees (in-state); $7920 (out-of-state)
- **$7853 average financial aid** package, $12,445 average indebtedness upon graduation, $93 million endowment

Part of University of Tennessee System.

Students *Undergraduates:* 5,731 full-time, 1,280 part-time. Students come from 41 states and territories, 45 other countries. *The most frequently chosen baccalaureate fields are:* business/marketing, education, health professions and related sciences. *Graduate:* 1,388 in graduate degree programs.

From out-of-state	9%	Reside on campus	21%
Age 25 or older	23%	Transferred in	8%
International students	1%	African Americans	17%
Asian Americans/Pacific Islanders	2%	Hispanic Americans	1%
Native Americans	1%		

Faculty 610 (56% full-time), 55% with terminal degrees.

Expenses (1999–2000) *Tuition, state resident:* full-time $2660; part-time $115 per semester hour. *Tuition, nonresident:* full-time $7920; part-time $319 per semester hour. *College room and board:* room only: $2000. Room and board charges vary according to housing facility. *Payment plan:* deferred payment. *Waivers:* senior citizens and employees or children of employees.

Library Lupton Library. *Collection:* 467,684 titles, 2,737 serial subscriptions, 14,062 audiovisual materials.

College life *Housing: Option:* coed. *Social organizations:* national fraternities, national sororities; 6% of eligible men and 5% of eligible women are members. *Most popular organizations:* student government association, black student association, Association for Campus Entertainment, international student association, Baptist Student Union.

Campus security 24-hour emergency response devices and patrols, late-night transport-escort service.

After graduation *Career center:* 10 full-time personnel. Services include job fairs, resume preparation, interview workshops, resume referral, career counseling.

Tennessee

The University of Tennessee at Chattanooga (continued)

Freshmen 2,368 applied, 2,017 admitted, 1,106 enrolled.

Average high school GPA	3.2	SAT verbal scores above 500	N/R
SAT math scores above 500	N/R	ACT above 18	87%
1998 freshmen returning in 1999	74%		

Application *Options:* early admission, deferred entrance. *Application fee:* $25. *Required:* high school transcript; 1 letter of recommendation. *Recommended:* essay or personal statement.

Standardized tests *Admission: Required:* SAT I or ACT.

Significant dates *Application deadlines:* rolling (freshmen), rolling (transfers). *Financial aid deadline priority date:* 4/1.

Freshman Application Contact
Ms. Patsy Reynolds, Director of Admissions, The University of Tennessee at Chattanooga, 131 Hooper Hall, Chattanooga, TN 37403-2598. **Phone:** 423-755-4662. **Toll-free phone:** 800-UTC-6627. **Fax:** 423-755-4157. **E-mail:** patsy-reynolds@utc.edu

Visit CollegeQuest.com for information on majors offered and athletics.

THE UNIVERSITY OF TENNESSEE AT MARTIN

Martin, Tennessee

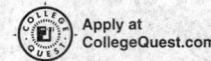

- **State-supported**, comprehensive, founded 1900
- **Degrees** bachelor's and master's
- **Small-town** 250-acre campus
- **Coed**, 5,014 undergraduate students, 91% full-time, 57% women, 43% men
- **Moderately difficult** entrance level, 80% of applicants were admitted
- **21:1** student-to-undergraduate faculty ratio
- **33% graduate** in 6 years or less
- **$2656 tuition** and fees (in-state); $7916 (out-of-state)
- **$5867 average financial aid** package, $10,500 average indebtedness upon graduation, $12.2 million endowment

Part of University of Tennessee System.

Students *Undergraduates:* 4,577 full-time, 437 part-time. Students come from 38 states and territories, 32 other countries. *The most frequently chosen baccalaureate fields are:* business/marketing, education, interdisciplinary studies. *Graduate:* 356 in graduate degree programs.

From out-of-state	6%	Reside on campus	40%
Age 25 or older	25%	Transferred in	7%
International students	4%	African Americans	14%
Asian Americans/Pacific Islanders	1%	Hispanic Americans	1%
Native Americans	0.2%		

Faculty 291 (81% full-time), 66% with terminal degrees.

Expenses (1999–2000) *Tuition, state resident:* full-time $2656; part-time $112 per semester hour. *Tuition, nonresident:* full-time $7916; part-time $332 per semester hour. *College room and board:* $3606; room only: $1760. Room and board charges vary according to board plan and housing facility. *Payment plan:* deferred payment. *Waivers:* senior citizens and employees or children of employees.

Library Paul Meek Library plus 1 other. *Operations spending 1999–2000:* $1.5 million. *Collection:* 436,366 titles, 2,654 serial subscriptions, 10,858 audiovisual materials.

College life *Housing:* on-campus residence required through sophomore year. *Options:* coed, men-only, women-only, disabled students. *Social organizations:* national fraternities, national sororities; 18% of eligible men and 13% of eligible women are members. *Most popular organizations:* Student Government Association, Greek organizations, religious affiliated groups, Student Activities Council, Black Student Association (BSA).

Campus security 24-hour emergency response devices and patrols, student patrols, late-night transport-escort service, controlled dormitory access.

After graduation 145 organizations recruited on campus 1997–98. 73% of class of 1998 had job offers within 6 months. *Career center:* 1 full-time personnel. Services include job fairs, resume preparation, interview workshops, resume referral, career/interest testing, career counseling, careers library, job bank, job interviews. *Graduate education:* 16% of class of 1999 went directly to graduate and professional school.

Freshmen 2,114 applied, 1,689 admitted, 948 enrolled. 19 valedictorians.

Average high school GPA	3.15	SAT verbal scores above 500	N/R
SAT math scores above 500	N/R	ACT above 18	81%
From top 10% of their h.s. class	17%	From top quarter	41%
From top half	65%	1998 freshmen returning in 1999	60%

Application *Options:* eApply at www.CollegeQuest.com, Common Application, electronic application, deferred entrance. *Application fee:* $25. *Required:* high school transcript; minimum 2.25 GPA.

Standardized tests *Admission: Required:* SAT I or ACT.

Significant dates *Application deadlines:* rolling (freshmen), rolling (transfers). *Notification:* continuous until 8/1 (freshmen). *Financial aid deadline priority date:* 3/1.

Freshman Application Contact
Ms. Judy Rayburn, Director of Admission, The University of Tennessee at Martin, 200 Hall-Moody Administration Building, Martin, TN 38238. **Phone:** 901-587-7032. **Toll-free phone:** 800-829-8861. **Fax:** 901-587-7029. **E-mail:** jrayburn@utm.edu

Visit CollegeQuest.com for information on majors offered and athletics. College video available at CollegeQuest.com.

■ *See page 2838 for a narrative description.*

THE UNIVERSITY OF TENNESSEE KNOXVILLE

Knoxville, Tennessee

- **State-supported**, university, founded 1794
- **Degrees** bachelor's, master's, doctoral, and first professional
- **Urban** 533-acre campus
- **Coed**, 19,830 undergraduate students, 90% full-time, 51% women, 49% men
- **Moderately difficult** entrance level, 67% of applicants were admitted
- **14:1** student-to-undergraduate faculty ratio
- **57% graduate** in 6 years or less
- **$3104 tuition** and fees (in-state); $9172 (out-of-state)
- **$5892 average financial aid** package, $19,624 average indebtedness upon graduation, $213.7 million endowment

Part of University of Tennessee System.

Students *Undergraduates:* 17,896 full-time, 1,934 part-time. Students come from 50 states and territories, 100 other countries. *The most frequently chosen baccalaureate fields are:* business/marketing, engineering/engineering technologies, social sciences and history. *Graduate:* 728 in professional programs, 5,450 in other graduate degree programs.

From out-of-state	11%	Reside on campus	37%
Age 25 or older	19%	Transferred in	7%
International students	1%	African Americans	6%
Asian Americans/Pacific Islanders	2%	Hispanic Americans	1%
Native Americans	0.3%		

Faculty 1,475 (96% full-time), 75% with terminal degrees.

Expenses (1999–2000) *Tuition, state resident:* full-time $2604; part-time $109 per semester hour. *Tuition, nonresident:* full-time $8672; part-time $362 per semester hour. *Required fees:* full-time $500; $22 per semester hour. *College room and board:* $4030; room only: $2030. Room and board charges vary according to board plan and housing facility. *Payment plans:* installment, deferred payment. *Waivers:* senior citizens and employees or children of employees.

Library John C. Hodges Library plus 6 others. *Operations spending 1999–2000:* $12.7 million. *Collection:* 1.1 million titles, 11,156 serial subscriptions, 36,009 audiovisual materials.

College life *Housing:* on-campus residence required in freshman year. *Option:* coed. *Social organizations:* national fraternities, national sororities; 8% of eligible men and 8% of eligible women are members. *Most popular organizations:* Central Program Council, religious organizations, Volunteer Outreach for Leadership and Service, Student Government Association, International Student Council.

Campus security 24-hour emergency response devices and patrols, late-night transport-escort service.

After graduation 503 organizations recruited on campus 1997–98. *Career center:* 15 full-time, 2 part-time personnel. Services include job fairs, resume preparation, resume referral, career counseling, careers library, job bank, job interviews.

Freshmen 10,605 applied, 7,130 admitted, 4,155 enrolled. 44 National Merit Scholars.

Average high school GPA	3.34	SAT verbal scores above 500	75%
SAT math scores above 500	74%	ACT above 18	99%
From top 10% of their h.s. class	26%	From top quarter	52%
From top half	83%	1998 freshmen returning in 1999	79%

Application *Options:* early admission, deferred entrance. *Preference* given to state residents, children of alumni. *Application fee:* $25. *Required:* high school transcript; minimum 2.0 GPA.

Standardized tests *Admission: Required:* SAT I or ACT.

Significant dates *Application deadlines:* 6/1 (freshmen), 6/1 (transfers). *Financial aid deadline priority date:* 3/1.

Freshman Application Contact
Ms. Kathy Keebler, Acting Director of Admissions, The University of Tennessee Knoxville, 320 Student Services Building, Knoxville, TN 37996-0230. **Phone:** 865-974-2184. **Toll-free phone:** 800-221-8657. **E-mail:** admissions@utk.edu

Visit CollegeQuest.com for information on majors offered and athletics.

THE UNIVERSITY OF TENNESSEE MEMPHIS
Memphis, Tennessee

Admissions Office Contact
The University of Tennessee Memphis, 800 Madison Avenue, Memphis, TN 38163-0002. **Fax:** 901-448-7585. **E-mail:** jpeoples@utmem.edu

UNIVERSITY OF THE SOUTH
Sewanee, Tennessee

 Apply at CollegeQuest.com

- **Independent Episcopal**, comprehensive, founded 1857
- **Degrees** bachelor's, master's, doctoral, and first professional
- **Small-town** 10,000-acre campus
- **Coed**, 1,308 undergraduate students, 100% full-time, 54% women, 46% men
- **Very difficult** entrance level, 73% of applicants were admitted
- **11:1** student-to-undergraduate faculty ratio
- **$19,080 tuition** and fees
- **$16,600 average financial aid** package, $13,103 average indebtedness upon graduation, $206.3 million endowment

Students *Undergraduates:* 1,308 full-time. Students come from 46 states and territories, 20 other countries. *The most frequently chosen baccalaureate fields are:* English, foreign language/literature, social sciences and history. *Graduate:* 91 in professional programs, 15 in other graduate degree programs.

From out-of-state	79%
Age 25 or older	1%
International students	2%
Asian Americans/Pacific Islanders	1%
Native Americans	0.2%
Reside on campus	92%
Transferred in	1%
African Americans	4%
Hispanic Americans	1%

Faculty 140 (82% full-time), 90% with terminal degrees.

Expenses (1999–2000) *Comprehensive fee:* $24,310 includes full-time tuition ($18,900), mandatory fees ($180), and room and board ($5230). *College room only:* $2680. *Part-time tuition:* $705 per semester hour. *Payment plans:* installment, deferred payment. *Waivers:* employees or children of employees.

Library Jessie Ball duPont Library. *Operations spending 1999–2000:* $2 million. *Collection:* 469,120 titles, 2,478 serial subscriptions.

College life *Housing:* on-campus residence required through senior year. *Option:* coed. *Social organizations:* national fraternities, local sororities; 65% of eligible men and 55% of eligible women are members. *Most popular organizations:* Sewanee Outing Program, Community Service Council, Student Activities Programming Board, student radio station, BACCHUS (Alcohol and Drug Education).

Campus security 24-hour emergency response devices and patrols, late-night transport-escort service, security lighting.

After graduation 17 organizations recruited on campus 1997–98. 74% of class of 1998 had job offers within 6 months. *Career center:* 2 full-time, 3 part-time personnel. Services include job fairs, resume preparation, resume referral, career counseling, careers library, job bank, job interviews. *Graduate education:* 38% of class of 1999 went directly to graduate and professional school: 14% graduate arts and sciences, 6% law, 4% business, 3% education, 3% medicine, 3% theology, 1% dentistry, 1% engineering, 1% veterinary medicine.

Freshmen 1,642 applied, 1,200 admitted, 392 enrolled. 13 National Merit Scholars.

Average high school GPA	3.31	SAT verbal scores above 500	98%
SAT math scores above 500	96%	ACT above 18	100%
From top 10% of their h.s. class	49%	From top quarter	81%
From top half	99%	1998 freshmen returning in 1999	88%

Application *Options:* eApply at www.CollegeQuest.com, Common Application, electronic application, early admission, early decision, deferred entrance. *Application fee:* $45. *Required:* essay or personal statement; high school transcript; 2 letters of recommendation. *Recommended:* interview.

Standardized tests *Admission: Required:* SAT I or ACT. *Recommended:* SAT II Subject Tests.

Significant dates *Application deadlines:* 2/1 (freshmen), 4/1 (transfers). *Early decision:* 11/15. *Notification:* 4/1 (freshmen), 12/15 (early decision). *Financial aid deadline priority date:* 3/1.

Freshman Application Contact
Mr. Robert M. Hedrick, Director of Admission, University of the South, 735 University Avenue, Sewanee, TN 37383-1000. **Phone:** 931-598-1238. **Toll-free phone:** 800-522-2234. **Fax:** 931-598-1145. **E-mail:** admiss@sewanee.edu

Visit CollegeQuest.com for information on majors offered and athletics. College video and electronic viewbook available at CollegeQuest.com.

VANDERBILT UNIVERSITY
Nashville, Tennessee

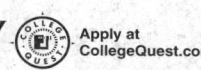 Apply at CollegeQuest.com

- **Independent**, university, founded 1873
- **Degrees** bachelor's, master's, doctoral, and first professional
- **Urban** 330-acre campus
- **Coed**, 5,752 undergraduate students, 99% full-time, 53% women, 47% men
- **Very difficult** entrance level, 61% of applicants were admitted
- **8:1** student-to-undergraduate faculty ratio
- **82% graduate** in 6 years or less
- **$23,598 tuition** and fees
- **$23,905 average financial aid** package, $19,900 average indebtedness upon graduation, $1.4 billion endowment

Vanderbilt University enrolls talented students who are challenged daily to expand their intellectual horizons and free their imaginations. Dialogue, service, the Honor Code, the search for knowledge and personal fulfillment—a Vanderbilt education enhances the life of every student. Vanderbilt alumni carry with them not only knowledge gained in classes but also a lifelong connection to a special community of learners. Vanderbilt is committed to enrolling talented, motivated students from diverse backgrounds. The University offers a full range of financial aid and financing options for those who need assistance.

Students *Undergraduates:* 5,716 full-time, 36 part-time. Students come from 54 states and territories, 36 other countries. *The most frequently chosen baccalaureate fields are:* engineering/engineering technologies, psychology, social sciences and history. *Graduate:* 1,140 in professional programs, 3,102 in other graduate degree programs.

From out-of-state	85%
Age 25 or older	1%
International students	3%
Asian Americans/Pacific Islanders	6%
Native Americans	0.2%
Reside on campus	85%
Transferred in	1%
African Americans	4%
Hispanic Americans	3%

Faculty 1,046 (67% full-time).

Expenses (1999–2000) *Comprehensive fee:* $31,630 includes full-time tuition ($22,990), mandatory fees ($608), and room and board ($8032). *College room only:* $5172. Room and board charges vary according to board plan and housing facility. *Part-time tuition:* $958 per credit hour. *Part-time fees:* $300 per term part-time. Part-time tuition and fees vary according to

Tennessee

Vanderbilt University (continued)

course load. *Payment plans:* tuition prepayment, installment, deferred payment. *Waivers:* employees or children of employees.

Library Jean and Alexander Heard Library plus 7 others. *Collection:* 2.5 million titles, 21,608 serial subscriptions, 29,364 audiovisual materials.

College life *Housing:* on-campus residence required through senior year. *Options:* coed, men-only, women-only, disabled students. *Social organizations:* national fraternities, national sororities; 34% of eligible men and 48% of eligible women are members.

Campus security 24-hour emergency response devices and patrols, student patrols, late-night transport-escort service, controlled dormitory access.

After graduation 250 organizations recruited on campus 1997–98. 63% of class of 1998 had job offers within 6 months. *Career center:* 10 full-time, 4 part-time personnel. Services include job fairs, resume preparation, interview workshops, resume referral, career/interest testing, career counseling, careers library, job bank, job interviews. *Graduate education:* 32% of class of 1999 went directly to graduate and professional school: 20% graduate arts and sciences, 7% law, 4% medicine, 1% business. *Major awards:* 2 Fulbright Scholars.

Freshmen 8,494 applied, 5,216 admitted, 1,633 enrolled. 85 National Merit Scholars, 30 class presidents, 101 valedictorians.

Average high school GPA	3.57	SAT verbal scores above 500	98%
SAT math scores above 500	98%	ACT above 18	100%
From top 10% of their h.s. class	66%	From top quarter	93%
From top half	99%	1998 freshmen returning in 1999	92%

Application *Options:* eApply at www.CollegeQuest.com, Common Application, electronic application, early admission, early decision, deferred entrance. *Application fee:* $50. *Required:* essay or personal statement; high school transcript; 2 letters of recommendation.

Standardized tests *Admission: Required:* SAT I or ACT. *Recommended:* SAT II Subject Tests, SAT II: Writing Test.

Significant dates *Application deadlines:* 1/7 (freshmen), 2/1 (transfers). *Early decision:* 11/1 (for plan 1), 1/7 (for plan 2). *Notification:* 4/1 (freshmen), 12/15 (early decision plan 1), 2/15 (early decision plan 2). *Financial aid deadline priority date:* 2/1.

Freshman Application Contact

Mr. Bill Shain, Dean of Undergraduate Admissions, Vanderbilt University, Nashville, TN 37203-1727. **Phone:** 615-322-2561. **Toll-free phone:** 800-288-0432. **Fax:** 615-343-7765. **E-mail:** admissions@vanderbilt.edu

Visit CollegeQuest.com for information on majors offered and athletics. College video available at CollegeQuest.com.

■ *See page 2876 for a narrative description.*

Texas

TEXAS

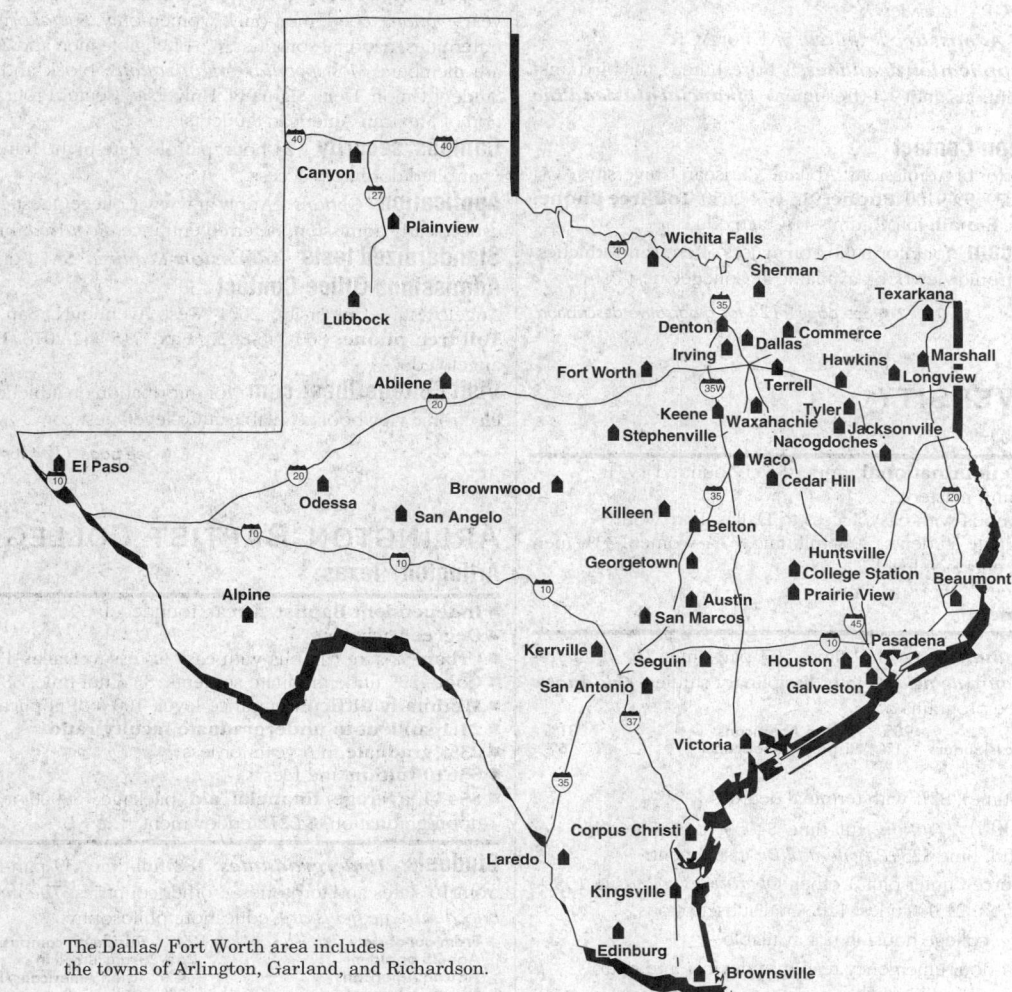

The Dallas/Fort Worth area includes the towns of Arlington, Garland, and Richardson.

ABILENE CHRISTIAN UNIVERSITY
Abilene, Texas

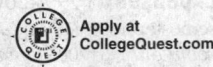 Apply at CollegeQuest.com

- **Independent**, comprehensive, founded 1906, affiliated with Church of Christ
- **Degrees** associate, bachelor's, master's, doctoral, and first professional
- **Urban** 208-acre campus
- **Coed**, 4,029 undergraduate students, 92% full-time, 55% women, 45% men
- **Moderately difficult** entrance level, 79% of applicants were admitted
- **18:1 student-to-undergraduate faculty ratio**
- **50.53% graduate** in 6 years or less
- **$10,290 tuition** and fees
- **$10,694 average financial aid** package, $115 million endowment

Students *Undergraduates:* 3,699 full-time, 330 part-time. Students come from 47 states and territories, 61 other countries. *The most frequently chosen baccalaureate fields are:* business/marketing, education, interdisciplinary studies. *Graduate:* 59 in professional programs, 513 in other graduate degree programs.

From out-of-state	23%	Reside on campus	54%
Age 25 or older	8%	Transferred in	7%
International students	4%	African Americans	5%
Asian Americans/Pacific Islanders	1%	Hispanic Americans	5%
Native Americans	0.4%		

Faculty 307 (67% full-time), 54% with terminal degrees.
Expenses (1999–2000) *Comprehensive fee:* $14,480 includes full-time tuition ($9810), mandatory fees ($480), and room and board ($4190). *College room only:* $1750. Full-time tuition and fees vary according to course load.

Room and board charges vary according to board plan and housing facility. *Part-time tuition:* $327 per semester hour. *Part-time fees:* $16 per semester hour; $5 per term part-time. Part-time tuition and fees vary according to course load. *Payment plans:* tuition prepayment, installment. *Waivers:* employees or children of employees.

Library Brown Library. *Operations spending 1999–2000:* $1.4 million. *Collection:* 49,864 audiovisual materials.

College life *Housing:* on-campus residence required through sophomore year. *Options:* men-only, women-only. *Social organizations:* local fraternities, local sororities; 22% of eligible men and 23% of eligible women are members. *Most popular organizations:* Student Association, Alpha Phi Omega, "'W' Club, Spring Break Campaign, Student Alumni Association.

Campus security 24-hour emergency response devices and patrols, late-night transport-escort service.

After graduation 150 organizations recruited on campus 1997–98. 70% of class of 1998 had job offers within 6 months. *Career center:* 2 full-time, 1 part-time personnel. Services include job fairs, resume preparation, resume referral, career counseling, careers library, job bank, job interviews. *Graduate education:* 30% of class of 1999 went directly to graduate and professional school.

Freshmen 2,292 applied, 1,802 admitted, 924 enrolled. 5 National Merit Scholars, 21 valedictorians.

Average high school GPA	3.4	SAT verbal scores above 500	69%
SAT math scores above 500	69%	ACT above 18	92%
From top 10% of their h.s. class	24%	From top quarter	48%
From top half	78%	1998 freshmen returning in 1999	73%

Application *Options:* eApply at www.CollegeQuest.com, Common Application, electronic application, deferred entrance. *Application fee:* $25.

Peterson's Guide to Four-Year Colleges 2001   www.petersons.com   777

Texas

Abilene Christian University (continued)
Required: high school transcript; 2 letters of recommendation. *Recommended:* minimum 2.0 GPA; interview.

Standardized tests *Admission: Required:* SAT I or ACT.

Significant dates *Application deadlines:* 8/1 (freshmen), rolling (transfers). *Notification:* continuous until 9/1 (freshmen). *Financial aid deadline priority date:* 3/1.

Freshman Application Contact
Mr. Tim Johnston, Director of Admissions, Abilene Christian University, ACU Box 29100, Abilene, TX 79699-9100. **Phone:** 915-674-2650. **Toll-free phone:** 800-460-6228 Ext. 2650. **E-mail:** info@admissions.acu.edu

Visit CollegeQuest.com for information on majors offered and athletics. College video and electronic viewbook available at CollegeQuest.com.

■ *See page 1124 for a narrative description.*

AMBER UNIVERSITY
Garland, Texas

- **Independent nondenominational**, upper-level, founded 1971
- **Degrees** bachelor's and master's
- **Suburban** 5-acre campus with easy access to Dallas–Fort Worth
- **Coed**, 633 undergraduate students, 20% full-time, 67% women, 33% men
- **Minimally difficult** entrance level
- **$4075 tuition** and fees
- **$5 million endowment**

Students *Undergraduates:* 126 full-time, 507 part-time. *The most frequently chosen baccalaureate field is:* interdisciplinary studies. **Graduate:** 1,015 in graduate degree programs.

Age 25 or older	98%	African Americans	31%
Asian Americans/Pacific Islanders	1%	Hispanic Americans	6%
Native Americans	1%		

Faculty 39 (36% full-time), 82% with terminal degrees.

Expenses (1999–2000) *Tuition:* full-time $4050; part-time $450 per course. *Required fees:* full-time $25. *Payment plan:* installment.

Library Library Resource Center plus 1 other. *Operations spending 1999–2000:* $100,000. *Collection:* 21,000 titles, 120 serial subscriptions.

College life *Housing:* college housing not available.

Campus security 24-hour emergency response devices and patrols.

Application *Options:* Common Application, deferred entrance. *Application fee:* $25.

Significant dates *Application deadline:* rolling (transfers).

Freshman Application Contact
Dr. Algia Allen, Vice President for Academic Services, Amber University, 1700 Eastgate Drive, Garland, TX 75041-5595. **Phone:** 972-279-6511 Ext. 135. **E-mail:** webteam@amberu.edu

Visit CollegeQuest.com for information on majors offered and athletics.

ANGELO STATE UNIVERSITY
San Angelo, Texas

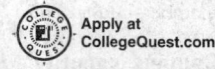

- **State-supported**, comprehensive, founded 1928
- **Degrees** associate, bachelor's, and master's
- **Urban** 268-acre campus
- **Coed**
- **Moderately difficult** entrance level
- **$2320 tuition** and fees (in-state); $8800 (out-of-state)

Part of Texas State University System.

Expenses (1999–2000) *Tuition, state resident:* full-time $1140; part-time $38 per semester hour. *Tuition, nonresident:* full-time $7620; part-time $254 per semester hour. *Required fees:* full-time $1180; $41 per semester hour; $71 per term part-time. Full-time tuition and fees vary according to course load. Part-time tuition and fees vary according to course load. *College room and board:* $4066; room only: $2566. Room and board charges vary according to board plan and housing facility.

Institutional Web site http://www.angelo.edu/

College life *Housing:* on-campus residence required through sophomore year. *Options:* coed, men-only, women-only. *Social organizations:* national fraternities, national sororities; 3% of eligible men and 2% of eligible women are members. *Most popular organizations:* block and bridle club, Baptist Student Union, Delta Sigma Pi, University Center Program Council, Association of Mexican-American Students.

Campus security 24-hour patrols, late-night transport-escort service, controlled dormitory access.

Application *Options:* eApply at www.CollegeQuest.com, electronic application, early admission, deferred entrance. *Required:* high school transcript.

Standardized tests *Admission: Required:* SAT I or ACT.

Admissions Office Contact
Angelo State University, 2601 West Avenue N, San Angelo, TX 76909. **Toll-free phone:** 800-946-8627. **Fax:** 915-942-2078. **E-mail:** admissions@angelo.edu

Visit CollegeQuest.com for information on athletics. College video and electronic viewbook available at CollegeQuest.com.

■ *See page 1174 for a narrative description.*

ARLINGTON BAPTIST COLLEGE
Arlington, Texas

- **Independent Baptist**, 4-year, founded 1939
- **Degree** bachelor's
- **Urban** 32-acre campus with easy access to Dallas–Fort Worth
- **Coed**, 227 undergraduate students, 83% full-time, 38% women, 62% men
- **Minimally difficult** entrance level, 100% of applicants were admitted
- **21:1 student-to-undergraduate faculty ratio**
- **23% graduate** in 6 years or less
- **$3610 tuition** and fees
- **$5434 average financial aid** package, $8000 average indebtedness upon graduation, $4,212 endowment

Students *Undergraduates:* 188 full-time, 39 part-time. Students come from 16 states and territories, 3 other countries. *The most frequently chosen baccalaureate fields are:* education, philosophy.

From out-of-state	24%	Reside on campus	54%
Age 25 or older	26%	Transferred in	13%
African Americans	4%	Asian Americans/Pacific Islanders	0.4%
Hispanic Americans	3%		

Faculty 25 (28% full-time), 16% with terminal degrees.

Expenses (1999–2000) *Tuition:* full-time $3360; part-time $105 per semester hour. *Required fees:* full-time $250; $125 per term part-time. *College room only:* $1700. *Payment plans:* installment, deferred payment. *Waivers:* employees or children of employees.

Library Dr. Earl K. Oldham Library. *Operations spending 1999–2000:* $55,988. *Collection:* 25,534 titles, 214 serial subscriptions.

College life *Housing:* on-campus residence required through senior year. *Options:* men-only, women-only. *Most popular organizations:* Preachers Fellowship, Student Missionary Association, L.I.F.T., International Students Association, 4-12 Group.

Campus security Student patrols, controlled dormitory access.

After graduation 6 organizations recruited on campus 1997–98. 90% of class of 1998 had job offers within 6 months. *Career center:* 1 part-time personnel. Services include career counseling, job interviews. **Graduate education:** 12% of class of 1999 went directly to graduate and professional school: 6% theology, 3% education.

Freshmen 96 applied, 96 admitted, 61 enrolled. 1 valedictorian.

Average high school GPA	3.04	SAT verbal scores above 500	N/R
SAT math scores above 500	N/R	ACT above 18	88%
From top 10% of their h.s. class	3%	From top quarter	17%
From top half	39%	1998 freshmen returning in 1999	64%

Application *Options:* Common Application, electronic application, early admission, deferred entrance. *Preference* given to professing Christians. *Application fee:* $15. *Required:* essay or personal statement; high school transcript; 1 letter of recommendation; pastoral recommendation, medical examination. *Required for some:* interview.

Standardized tests *Placement: Recommended:* SAT I and SAT II or ACT.

Significant dates *Application deadlines:* rolling (freshmen), rolling (transfers). *Financial aid deadline priority date:* 8/1.
Freshman Application Contact
Ms. Janie Hall, Registrar/Admissions, Arlington Baptist College, 3001 West Division, Arlington, TX 76012-3425. **Phone:** 817-461-8741 Ext. 105. **Fax:** 817-274-1138.
Visit CollegeQuest.com for information on majors offered and athletics. Electronic viewbook available at CollegeQuest.com.

AUSTIN COLLEGE
Sherman, Texas

- **Independent Presbyterian**, comprehensive, founded 1849
- **Degrees** bachelor's and master's
- **Suburban** 60-acre campus with easy access to Dallas–Fort Worth
- **Coed**, 1,225 undergraduate students, 99% full-time, 54% women, 46% men
- **Very difficult** entrance level, 78% of applicants were admitted
- **13:1 student-to-undergraduate faculty ratio**
- **64% graduate** in 6 years or less
- **$15,219 tuition** and fees
- **$15,654 average financial aid** package, $21,550 average indebtedness upon graduation, $111.6 million endowment

Students *Undergraduates:* 1,216 full-time, 9 part-time. Students come from 25 states and territories, 14 other countries. *The most frequently chosen baccalaureate fields are:* area/ethnic studies, biological/life sciences, social sciences and history. *Graduate:* 24 in graduate degree programs.

From out-of-state	7%	Reside on campus	74%
Age 25 or older	2%	International students	2%
African Americans	4%	Asian Americans/Pacific Islanders	8%
Hispanic Americans	6%	Native Americans	1%

Faculty 114 (69% full-time), 96% with terminal degrees.
Expenses (2000–2001) *Comprehensive fee:* $21,110 includes full-time tuition ($15,094), mandatory fees ($125), and room and board ($5891). *College room only:* $2678. Room and board charges vary according to board plan. *Payment plan:* installment. *Waivers:* employees or children of employees.
Library Abell Library. *Collection:* 156,268 titles, 7,971 serial subscriptions, 6,089 audiovisual materials.
College life *Housing:* on-campus residence required through junior year. *Options:* coed, men-only, women-only. *Social organizations:* local fraternities, local sororities; 33% of eligible men and 30% of eligible women are members. *Most popular organizations:* Fellowship of Christian Athletes, Campus Activity Board, Indian Cultural Association, Student Development Board, International Relations Club.
Campus security 24-hour emergency response devices and patrols, late-night transport-escort service, controlled dormitory access.
After graduation 18 organizations recruited on campus 1997–98. 45% of class of 1998 had job offers within 6 months. *Career center:* 2 full-time, 1 part-time personnel. Services include job fairs, resume preparation, career counseling, careers library, job interviews. *Graduate education:* 36% of class of 1999 went directly to graduate and professional school. *Major awards:* 1 Fulbright Scholar.
Freshmen 1,003 applied, 782 admitted, 324 enrolled. 5 National Merit Scholars, 14 valedictorians.

SAT verbal scores above 500	94%	SAT math scores above 500	91%
ACT above 18	100%	From top 10% of their h.s. class	61%
From top quarter	77%	From top half	95%
1998 freshmen returning in 1999	83%		

Application *Options:* Common Application, electronic application, early admission, early decision, early action, deferred entrance. *Application fee:* $35. *Required:* essay or personal statement; high school transcript; 2 letters of recommendation. *Required for some:* interview. *Recommended:* minimum 3.0 GPA; interview.
Standardized tests *Admission:* Required: SAT I or ACT.
Significant dates *Application deadlines:* 8/15 (freshmen), 8/15 (transfers). *Early decision:* 12/1, 1/15. *Notification:* 1/10 (early decision), 2/10 (early action). *Financial aid deadline priority date:* 4/1.
Freshman Application Contact
Ms. Nan Massingill, Vice President for Institutional Enrollment, Austin College, 900 North Grand Avenue, Sherman, TX 75090-4400. **Phone:** 903-813-3000. **Toll-free phone:** 800-442-5363. **Fax:** 903-813-3198. **E-mail:** admissions@austinc.edu
Visit CollegeQuest.com for information on majors offered and athletics. College video and electronic viewbook available at CollegeQuest.com.

■ *See page 1214 for a narrative description.*

BAPTIST MISSIONARY ASSOCIATION THEOLOGICAL SEMINARY
Jacksonville, Texas

- **Independent Baptist**, comprehensive, founded 1955
- **Degrees** associate, bachelor's, master's, and first professional
- **Small-town** 17-acre campus
- **Coed**, primarily men, 26 undergraduate students, 27% full-time, 8% women, 92% men
- **Noncompetitive** entrance level, 100% of applicants were admitted
- **14:1 student-to-undergraduate faculty ratio**
- **$2220 tuition** and fees
- **$1098 average financial aid** package, $448,505 endowment

Students *Undergraduates:* 7 full-time, 19 part-time. Students come from 3 states and territories, 2 other countries. *The most frequently chosen baccalaureate field is:* philosophy. *Graduate:* 17 in professional programs, 6 in other graduate degree programs.

From out-of-state	8%	Reside on campus	36%
Age 25 or older	80%	Transferred in	8%
International students	4%	African Americans	11%
Hispanic Americans	7%	Native Americans	7%

Faculty 7 (71% full-time), 86% with terminal degrees.
Expenses (1999–2000) *Tuition:* full-time $2100; part-time $70 per semester hour. *Required fees:* full-time $120; $30 per term part-time. *College room only:* $3580. *Payment plan:* installment. *Waivers:* employees or children of employees.
Library Kellar Library. *Operations spending 1999–2000:* $115,325. *Collection:* 59,615 titles, 526 serial subscriptions, 5,307 audiovisual materials.
After graduation 63% of class of 1998 had job offers within 6 months. *Career center:* Services include career counseling. *Graduate education:* 50% of class of 1999 went directly to graduate and professional school: 50% theology.
Freshmen 7 applied, 7 admitted, 10 enrolled.

SAT verbal scores above 500	N/R	SAT math scores above 500	N/R
ACT above 18	N/R	1998 freshmen returning in 1999	100%

Application *Application fee:* $20. *Required:* 3 letters of recommendation; interview.
Significant dates *Application deadlines:* 7/17 (freshmen), 8/1 (transfers). *Financial aid deadline priority date:* 8/1.
Freshman Application Contact
Dr. W. K. Benningfield, Dean and Registrar, Baptist Missionary Association Theological Seminary, 1530 East Pine Street, Jacksonville, TX 75766-5407. **Phone:** 903-586-2501. **E-mail:** bmatsem@flash.net
Visit CollegeQuest.com for information on majors offered and athletics.

BAYLOR COLLEGE OF DENTISTRY
Texas—See Texas A&M University System Health Science Center

BAYLOR UNIVERSITY
Waco, Texas

- **Independent Baptist**, university, founded 1845
- **Degrees** bachelor's, master's, doctoral, and first professional
- **Urban** 432-acre campus with easy access to Dallas–Fort Worth

Texas

Baylor University (continued)
- **Coed**, 11,394 undergraduate students, 97% full-time, 58% women, 42% men
- **Moderately difficult** entrance level, 87% of applicants were admitted
- **18:1 student-to-undergraduate faculty ratio**
- **66.9% graduate** in 6 years or less
- **$11,938 tuition** and fees
- **$8805 average financial aid** package, $539.8 million endowment

The oldest university in Texas, Baylor is proud of its strong Christian heritage. Teaching, scholarly attention to discovery, and service to others are emphasized. Baylor University is the largest Baptist institution of higher education in the world. Students can choose from 118 baccalaureate, 75 master's, 16 doctoral, and 4 professional programs with the assurance of individual attention due to the low student-faculty ratio and small classes.

Students *Undergraduates:* 11,004 full-time, 390 part-time. Students come from 50 states and territories, 75 other countries. *Graduate:* 587 in professional programs, 1,275 in other graduate degree programs.

From out-of-state	18%	Reside on campus	32%
Age 25 or older	3%	Transferred in	4%
International students	2%	African Americans	6%
Asian Americans/Pacific Islanders	5%	Hispanic Americans	8%
Native Americans	1%		

Faculty 764 (85% full-time), 67% with terminal degrees.

Expenses (2000–2001) *One-time required fee:* $850. *Comprehensive fee:* $17,176 includes full-time tuition ($10,650), mandatory fees ($1288), and room and board ($5238). *College room only:* $2248. Room and board charges vary according to board plan and housing facility. *Part-time tuition:* $355 per semester hour. *Part-time fees:* $37 per semester hour; $1 per term part-time. *Payment plans:* guaranteed tuition, installment. *Waivers:* employees or children of employees.

Library Moody Memorial Library plus 8 others. *Operations spending 1999–2000:* $8.6 million. *Collection:* 1.5 million titles, 20,555 serial subscriptions.

College life *Housing: Options:* men-only, women-only, disabled students. *Social organizations:* national fraternities, national sororities, local fraternities, local sororities; 20% of eligible men and 30% of eligible women are members. *Most popular organizations:* Alpha Phi Omega, College Republicans, Gamma Beta Phi, student government.

Campus security 24-hour emergency response devices and patrols, late-night transport-escort service, controlled dormitory access, bicycle patrols.

After graduation 265 organizations recruited on campus 1997–98. *Career center:* 8 full-time, 11 part-time personnel. Services include job fairs, resume preparation, resume referral, career counseling, careers library, job bank, job interviews. *Major awards:* 1 Fulbright Scholar.

Freshmen 7,209 applied, 6,262 admitted, 2,772 enrolled. 51 National Merit Scholars.

SAT verbal scores above 500	87%	SAT math scores above 500	89%
ACT above 18	100%	From top 10% of their h.s. class	38%
From top quarter	65%	From top half	92%
1998 freshmen returning in 1999	82%		

Application *Options:* electronic application, early admission, deferred entrance. *Application fee:* $35. *Required:* essay or personal statement; high school transcript. *Recommended:* interview.

Standardized tests *Admission: Required:* SAT I or ACT.

Significant dates *Application deadlines:* rolling (freshmen), rolling (transfers). *Financial aid deadline priority date:* 3/1.

Freshman Application Contact
Ms. Teri Tippit, Director of Recruitment, Baylor University, PO Box 97056, Waco, TX 76798-7056. **Phone:** 254-710-3435. **Toll-free phone:** 800-BAYLOR U. **E-mail:** admissions_office@baylor.edu

Visit CollegeQuest.com for information on majors offered and athletics. College video and electronic viewbook available at CollegeQuest.com.

■ *See page 1236 for a narrative description.*

CONCORDIA UNIVERSITY AT AUSTIN
Austin, Texas

- **Independent**, comprehensive, founded 1926, affiliated with Lutheran Church–Missouri Synod
- **Degrees** associate, bachelor's, and master's
- **Urban** 20-acre campus with easy access to San Antonio
- **Coed**, 664 undergraduate students, 76% full-time, 55% women, 45% men
- **Moderately difficult** entrance level, 83% of applicants were admitted
- **33.9% graduate** in 6 years or less
- **$11,570 tuition** and fees
- **$10,258 average financial aid** package, $15,472 average indebtedness upon graduation, $6.1 million endowment

Part of Concordia University System.

Students *Undergraduates:* 505 full-time, 159 part-time. Students come from 22 states and territories, 7 other countries. *The most frequently chosen baccalaureate fields are:* business/marketing, education, psychology. *Graduate:* 12 in graduate degree programs.

From out-of-state	8%	Reside on campus	32%
Age 25 or older	22%	International students	3%
African Americans	5%	Asian Americans/Pacific Islanders	0.5%
Hispanic Americans	13%	Native Americans	0.5%

Faculty 43 full-time.

Expenses (1999–2000) *Comprehensive fee:* $16,770 includes full-time tuition ($11,500), mandatory fees ($70), and room and board ($5200). Room and board charges vary according to board plan and housing facility. *Part-time tuition:* $385 per semester hour. *Waivers:* employees or children of employees.

Library Founders Library. *Operations spending 1999–2000:* $215,406. *Collection:* 104,038 titles, 583 serial subscriptions, 3,838 audiovisual materials.

College life *Housing:* on-campus residence required in freshman year. *Options:* coed, men-only, women-only. *Most popular organizations:* student government, education club, Lutheran Student Fellowship, Students Active for the Environment, accounting club.

Campus security 24-hour emergency response devices, student patrols, late-night transport-escort service.

After graduation *Career center:* 1 part-time personnel. Services include resume preparation, career/interest testing, career counseling, careers library, job bank.

Freshmen 422 applied, 352 admitted, 156 enrolled.

Average high school GPA	3.1	SAT verbal scores above 500	43%
SAT math scores above 500	40%	ACT above 18	75%
From top 10% of their h.s. class	5%	From top quarter	31%
From top half	66%	1998 freshmen returning in 1999	55%

Application *Option:* early admission. *Application fee:* $25. *Required:* high school transcript; minimum 2.5 GPA. *Required for some:* letters of recommendation; interview.

Standardized tests *Admission: Required:* SAT I or ACT.

Significant dates *Application deadlines:* 8/15 (freshmen), 8/1 (transfers). *Financial aid deadline priority date:* 4/15.

Freshman Application Contact
Mr. Jay Krause, Vice President for Enrollment Services, Concordia University at Austin, 3400 Interstate 35 North, Austin, TX 78705-2799. **Phone:** 512-486-2000 Ext. 1107. **Toll-free phone:** 800-285-4252. **Fax:** 512-459-8517. **E-mail:** ctxadmis@crf.cuis.edu

Visit CollegeQuest.com for information on majors offered and athletics.

THE CRISWELL COLLEGE
Dallas, Texas

- **Independent Baptist**, comprehensive, founded 1970
- **Degrees** associate, bachelor's, master's, and first professional
- **Urban** 1-acre campus
- **Coed**
- **Minimally difficult** entrance level
- **$3910 tuition** and fees

Expenses (1999–2000) *Tuition:* full-time $3750; part-time $125 per credit hour. *Required fees:* full-time $160; $80 per term part-time. Part-time tuition and fees vary according to course load.

Institutional Web site http://www.criswell.edu/

College life *Housing:* college housing not available. *Most popular organizations:* International Student Ministry, Women's Fellowship, Mission Awareness Fellowship, The Torchbearer, Student Life Cabinet.

Campus security 24-hour emergency response devices and patrols, late-night transport-escort service.
Application *Options:* early admission, deferred entrance. *Application fee:* $30. *Required:* essay or personal statement; high school transcript; 2 letters of recommendation; church recommendation. *Recommended:* minimum 2.0 GPA; interview.
Standardized tests *Admission: Required for some:* SAT I or ACT.
Admissions Office Contact
The Criswell College, 4010 Gaston Avenue, Dallas, TX 75246-1537. **Toll-free phone:** 800-899-0012. **Fax:** 214-818-1310.
Visit CollegeQuest.com for information on athletics. College video available at CollegeQuest.com.

DALLAS BAPTIST UNIVERSITY
Dallas, Texas

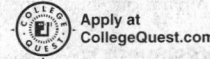
Apply at CollegeQuest.com

- **Independent**, comprehensive, founded 1965, affiliated with Baptist Church
- **Degrees** associate, bachelor's, and master's
- **Urban** 288-acre campus
- **Coed**, 3,150 undergraduate students, 43% full-time, 61% women, 39% men
- **Moderately difficult** entrance level
- **20:1 student-to-undergraduate faculty ratio**
- **$8700 tuition** and fees
- **$8905 average financial aid** package, $18.6 million endowment

Students *Undergraduates:* 1,360 full-time, 1,790 part-time. Students come from 30 states and territories, 37 other countries. *The most frequently chosen baccalaureate fields are:* business/marketing, education, liberal arts/general studies. *Graduate:* 771 in graduate degree programs.

From out-of-state	5%	Reside on campus	22%
Age 25 or older	47%	Transferred in	6%
International students	5%	African Americans	19%
Asian Americans/Pacific Islanders	2%	Hispanic Americans	7%
Native Americans	3%		

Faculty 283 (29% full-time), 48% with terminal degrees.
Expenses (1999–2000) *Comprehensive fee:* $12,380 includes full-time tuition ($8700) and room and board ($3680). *College room only:* $1500. Room and board charges vary according to board plan. *Part-time tuition:* $290 per credit hour. *Payment plan:* installment. *Waivers:* employees or children of employees.
Library Vance Memorial Library. *Operations spending 1999–2000:* $615,931. *Collection:* 205,724 titles, 739 serial subscriptions, 5,216 audiovisual materials.
College life *Housing:* on-campus residence required through senior year. *Options:* men-only, women-only. *Most popular organizations:* Student Activities Board, Baptist Student Ministry, Student Government Association, Student Education Association, Alpha Delta Kappa.
Campus security 24-hour emergency response devices and patrols, late-night transport-escort service, controlled dormitory access.
After graduation 50 organizations recruited on campus 1997–98. *Career center:* 1 full-time, 1 part-time personnel. Services include job fairs, interview workshops, resume referral, career/interest testing, career counseling, careers library, job bank.
Freshmen 478 applied, 261 admitted, 261 enrolled. 1 valedictorian.

Average high school GPA	3.4	SAT verbal scores above 500	57%
SAT math scores above 500	57%	ACT above 18	90%
From top 10% of their h.s. class	15%	From top quarter	40%
From top half	63%		

Application *Options:* eApply at www.CollegeQuest.com, early admission, deferred entrance. *Application fee:* $25. *Required:* essay or personal statement; high school transcript; rank in upper 50% of high school class or 3.0 high school GPA. *Recommended:* letters of recommendation; interview.
Standardized tests *Admission: Required:* SAT I or ACT.
Significant dates *Application deadlines:* rolling (freshmen), rolling (transfers). *Financial aid deadline priority date:* 3/15.

Freshman Application Contact
Mr. Jeremy Dutschke, Director of Admissions, Dallas Baptist University, 3000 Mountain Creek Parkway, Dallas, TX 75211-9299. **Phone:** 214-333-5360. **Toll-free phone:** 800-460-1328. **Fax:** 214-333-5447. **E-mail:** admiss@dbu.edu
Visit CollegeQuest.com for information on majors offered and athletics. College video available at CollegeQuest.com.

DALLAS CHRISTIAN COLLEGE
Dallas, Texas

- **Independent**, 4-year, founded 1950, affiliated with Christian Churches and Churches of Christ
- **Degree** bachelor's
- **Urban** 22-acre campus with easy access to Fort Worth
- **Coed**, 253 undergraduate students, 88% full-time, 46% women, 54% men
- **Minimally difficult** entrance level, 56% of applicants were admitted
- **21% graduate** in 6 years or less
- **$5690 tuition** and fees
- **$4461 average financial aid** package, $96,583 endowment

Students *Undergraduates:* 222 full-time, 31 part-time. Students come from 10 states and territories, 4 other countries. *The most frequently chosen baccalaureate fields are:* business/marketing, philosophy.

From out-of-state	17%	Reside on campus	37%
Age 25 or older	37%	Transferred in	16%
International students	3%	African Americans	15%
Asian Americans/Pacific Islanders	0.4%	Hispanic Americans	7%
Native Americans	0.4%		

Expenses (1999–2000) *Comprehensive fee:* $9390 includes full-time tuition ($5440), mandatory fees ($250), and room and board ($3700). Full-time tuition and fees vary according to course load and program. *Part-time tuition:* $170 per semester hour. *Part-time fees:* $125 per term part-time. Part-time tuition and fees vary according to course load and program. *Payment plan:* installment. *Waivers:* employees or children of employees.
Library C. C. Crawford Memorial Library. *Operations spending 1999–2000:* $70,527. *Collection:* 24,853 titles, 325 serial subscriptions.
College life *Housing:* on-campus residence required through senior year. *Options:* men-only, women-only.
Campus security Controlled dormitory access.
After graduation 71% of class of 1998 had job offers within 6 months.
Freshmen 145 applied, 81 admitted, 41 enrolled. 1 student government officer.

Average high school GPA	2.8	SAT verbal scores above 500	59%
SAT math scores above 500	66%	ACT above 18	59%
From top 10% of their h.s. class	10%	From top quarter	10%
From top half	33%	1998 freshmen returning in 1999	71%

Application *Option:* deferred entrance. *Preference* given to Christians. *Application fee:* $20. *Required:* high school transcript; 2 letters of recommendation. *Required for some:* essay or personal statement; interview.
Standardized tests *Admission: Required:* SAT I or ACT.
Significant dates *Application deadlines:* rolling (freshmen), rolling (transfers). *Financial aid deadline priority date:* 4/15.
Freshman Application Contact
Mr. Michael Frisbie, Director of Student Recruitment, Dallas Christian College, 2700 Christian Parkway, Dallas, TX 75234-7299. **Phone:** 972-241-3371 Ext. 151. **Fax:** 972-241-8021. **E-mail:** dcc@dallas.edu
Visit CollegeQuest.com for information on majors offered and athletics.

- *See page 1554 for a narrative description.*

DEVRY INSTITUTE OF TECHNOLOGY
Irving, Texas

- **Proprietary**, 4-year, founded 1969
- **Degrees** associate and bachelor's
- **Suburban** 13-acre campus with easy access to Dallas
- **Coed**, 3,032 undergraduate students, 58% full-time, 27% women, 73% men
- **Minimally difficult** entrance level, 64% of applicants were admitted
- **18:1 student-to-undergraduate faculty ratio**

Texas

DeVry Institute of Technology *(continued)*
- **$7778 tuition** and fees

Part of DeVry, Inc.

Students *Undergraduates:* 1,762 full-time, 1,270 part-time. Students come from 41 states and territories, 6 other countries. *The most frequently chosen baccalaureate fields are:* business/marketing, computer/information sciences, engineering/engineering technologies.

From out-of-state	11%	Age 25 or older	55%
Transferred in	9%	International students	1%
African Americans	26%	Asian Americans/Pacific Islanders	7%
Hispanic Americans	14%	Native Americans	1%

Faculty 168 (39% full-time).
Expenses (1999–2000) *Tuition:* full-time $7778; part-time $290 per credit hour. Part-time tuition and fees vary according to class time and course load. *Payment plan:* installment. *Waivers:* employees or children of employees.
Library Learning Resource Center. *Collection:* 10,000 titles, 125 serial subscriptions.
College life *Housing:* college housing not available. *Most popular organizations:* Institute for Electrical and Electronic Engineers, Association of Information Systems, Minority Student Union, Institute of Management Accounts, American Production and Inventory Control Society.
Campus security 24-hour emergency response devices.
After graduation 94% of class of 1998 had job offers within 6 months. *Career center:* 7 full-time, 2 part-time personnel. Services include job fairs, resume preparation, career counseling, job bank, job interviews.
Freshmen 1,581 applied, 1,015 admitted, 945 enrolled.

SAT verbal scores above 500	N/R	SAT math scores above 500	N/R
ACT above 18	N/R	1998 freshmen returning in 1999	38%

Application *Options:* electronic application, deferred entrance. *Application fee:* $25. *Required:* high school transcript; interview.
Standardized tests *Admission: Required:* Computerized Placement Test. *Recommended:* SAT I or ACT.
Significant dates *Application deadlines:* rolling (freshmen), rolling (transfers). *Financial aid deadline:* continuous.
Freshman Application Contact
Mr. Daniel Millan, Director of Admissions, DeVry Institute of Technology, 4800 Regent Boulevard, Irving, TX 75063-2439. **Phone:** 972-929-6777. **Toll-free phone:** 800-443-3879 (in-state); 800-633-3879 (out-of-state).
Visit CollegeQuest.com for information on majors offered and athletics.

EAST TEXAS BAPTIST UNIVERSITY
Marshall, Texas

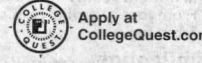 Apply at CollegeQuest.com

- **Independent Baptist**, 4-year, founded 1912
- **Degrees** associate and bachelor's
- **Small-town** 200-acre campus
- **Coed**, 1,175 undergraduate students, 92% full-time, 59% women, 41% men
- **Moderately difficult** entrance level, 80% of applicants were admitted
- **15:1 student-to-undergraduate faculty ratio**
- **30% graduate** in 6 years or less
- **$8450 tuition** and fees
- **$47.8 million endowment**

Students *Undergraduates:* 1,079 full-time, 96 part-time. Students come from 17 states and territories, 23 other countries. *The most frequently chosen baccalaureate fields are:* business/marketing, education, philosophy.

From out-of-state	8%	Reside on campus	69%
Age 25 or older	12%	Transferred in	9%
International students	3%	African Americans	6%
Asian Americans/Pacific Islanders	0.3%	Hispanic Americans	4%
Native Americans	1%		

Faculty 107 (58% full-time), 48% with terminal degrees.
Expenses (2000–2001) *Comprehensive fee:* $11,652 includes full-time tuition ($7650), mandatory fees ($800), and room and board ($3202). *College room only:* $1350. Room and board charges vary according to board plan and housing facility. *Part-time tuition:* $255 per semester hour. *Part-time fees:* $35 per semester hour. *Payment plan:* installment. *Waivers:* employees or children of employees.
Library Mamye Jarrett Library. *Operations spending 1999–2000:* $517,832. *Collection:* 113,124 titles, 672 serial subscriptions.
College life *Housing:* on-campus residence required through senior year. *Options:* men-only, women-only, disabled students. *Social organizations:* national fraternities, local sororities; 5% of eligible men and 6% of eligible women are members. *Most popular organizations:* Baptist Student Ministries, Phi Beta Lambda, Student Government Association.
Campus security 24-hour emergency response devices, controlled dormitory access.
After graduation 69 organizations recruited on campus 1997–98. *Career center:* 1 full-time, 1 part-time personnel. Services include job fairs, resume preparation, career/interest testing, career counseling, careers library, job bank.
Freshmen 796 applied, 640 admitted, 307 enrolled.

SAT verbal scores above 500	61%	SAT math scores above 500	57%
ACT above 18	83%	From top 10% of their h.s. class	22%
From top quarter	55%	From top half	85%
1998 freshmen returning in 1999	65%		

Application *Options:* eApply at www.CollegeQuest.com, Common Application, deferred entrance. *Application fee:* $25. *Required:* essay or personal statement; high school transcript; minimum 2.0 GPA. *Required for some:* interview.
Standardized tests *Admission: Required:* ACT.
Significant dates *Application deadlines:* rolling (freshmen), rolling (transfers). *Financial aid deadline priority date:* 6/1.
Freshman Application Contact
Director of Admissions, East Texas Baptist University, 1209 North Grove, Marshall, TX 75670-1498. **Phone:** 903-935-7963 Ext. 225. **Toll-free phone:** 800-804-3828. **Fax:** 903-938-1705. **E-mail:** mbender@etbu.edu
Visit CollegeQuest.com for information on majors offered and athletics. College video available at CollegeQuest.com.

HARDIN-SIMMONS UNIVERSITY
Abilene, Texas

- **Independent Baptist**, comprehensive, founded 1891
- **Degrees** bachelor's, master's, and first professional
- **Urban** 40-acre campus
- **Coed**, 1,914 undergraduate students, 87% full-time, 54% women, 46% men
- **Moderately difficult** entrance level
- **17:1 student-to-undergraduate faculty ratio**
- **40% graduate** in 6 years or less
- **$9330 tuition** and fees
- **$10,773 average financial aid** package, $12,080 average indebtedness upon graduation, $42.9 million endowment

Students *Undergraduates:* 1,669 full-time, 245 part-time. Students come from 28 states and territories, 3 other countries. *The most frequently chosen baccalaureate fields are:* business/marketing, education, health professions and related sciences. *Graduate:* 54 in professional programs, 313 in other graduate degree programs.

From out-of-state	6%	Reside on campus	43%
Age 25 or older	11%	Transferred in	9%
International students	0.2%	African Americans	3%
Asian Americans/Pacific Islanders	1%	Hispanic Americans	7%
Native Americans	1%		

Faculty 180 (66% full-time), 56% with terminal degrees.
Expenses (1999–2000) *Comprehensive fee:* $12,666 includes full-time tuition ($8700), mandatory fees ($630), and room and board ($3336). *College room only:* $1730. Full-time tuition and fees vary according to program. Room and board charges vary according to board plan and housing facility. *Part-time tuition:* $290 per semester hour. Part-time tuition and fees vary according to course load and program. *Payment plans:* guaranteed tuition, installment, deferred payment. *Waivers:* employees or children of employees.

Library Richardson Library plus 1 other. *Operations spending 1999–2000:* $913,023. *Collection:* 178,071 titles, 2,207 serial subscriptions, 15,844 audiovisual materials.

College life *Housing:* on-campus residence required through junior year. *Options:* men-only, women-only. *Social organizations:* national fraternities, local fraternities, local sororities; 10% of eligible men and 15% of eligible women are members. *Most popular organizations:* Baptist Student Union, Student Foundation, Student Congress, Fellowship Christian Athletes.

Campus security 24-hour patrols, controlled dormitory access.

After graduation 6 organizations recruited on campus 1997–98. 95% of class of 1998 had job offers within 6 months. *Career center:* 1 full-time, 1 part-time personnel. Services include job fairs, resume preparation, interview workshops, resume referral, career/interest testing, career counseling, careers library, job bank, job interviews.

Freshmen 945 applied, 501 admitted, 365 enrolled. 13 valedictorians.

Average high school GPA	3.4	SAT verbal scores above 500	61%
SAT math scores above 500	59%	ACT above 18	91%
From top 10% of their h.s. class	20%	From top quarter	49%
From top half	79%	1998 freshmen returning in 1999	67%

Application *Options:* early admission, deferred entrance. *Application fee:* $25. *Required:* high school transcript; minimum 2.0 GPA.

Standardized tests *Admission: Required:* SAT I or ACT.

Significant dates *Application deadlines:* rolling (freshmen), rolling (transfers). *Financial aid deadline priority date:* 3/15.

Freshman Application Contact Ms. Stacey Vaughn, Enrollment Services Counselor, Hardin-Simmons University, Box 16050, Abilene, TX 79698-6050. **Phone:** 915-670-5813. **Toll-free phone:** 800-568-2692. **Fax:** 915-670-1527. **E-mail:** enroll.services@hsutx.edu

Visit CollegeQuest.com for information on majors offered and athletics. College video available at CollegeQuest.com.

HOUSTON BAPTIST UNIVERSITY
Houston, Texas

- **Independent Baptist**, comprehensive, founded 1960
- **Degrees** associate, bachelor's, and master's
- **Urban** 158-acre campus
- **Coed**, 1,779 undergraduate students, 85% full-time, 70% women, 30% men
- **Moderately difficult** entrance level, 48% of applicants were admitted
- **$10,828 tuition** and fees
- **$47.1 million endowment**

Students *Undergraduates:* 1,514 full-time, 265 part-time. Students come from 17 states and territories, 36 other countries. *Graduate:* 583 in graduate degree programs.

From out-of-state	4%	Reside on campus	30%
Age 25 or older	21%	Transferred in	20%
International students	4%	African Americans	17%
Asian Americans/Pacific Islanders	16%	Hispanic Americans	12%

Faculty 189 (65% full-time).

Expenses (2000–2001) *Comprehensive fee:* $14,728 includes full-time tuition ($10,048), mandatory fees ($780), and room and board ($3900). Full-time tuition and fees vary according to course load and student level. Room and board charges vary according to board plan. *Part-time tuition:* $298 per credit hour. *Part-time fees:* $240 per term part-time. Part-time tuition and fees vary according to course load and student level. *Payment plans:* guaranteed tuition, installment, deferred payment. *Waivers:* senior citizens and employees or children of employees.

Library Moody Library. *Operations spending 1999–2000:* $782,517. *Collection:* 188,000 titles, 1,025 serial subscriptions.

College life *Housing:* on-campus residence required in freshman year. *Options:* men-only, women-only. *Social organizations:* national fraternities, national sororities, local fraternities; 15% of eligible men and 20% of eligible women are members. *Most popular organizations:* Christian Life on Campus, International Friends, Amnesty International, Students in Free Enterprise, Alpha Phi Omega.

Campus security 24-hour emergency response devices and patrols, late-night transport-escort service.

After graduation *Career center:* 1 full-time personnel. Services include job fairs, resume preparation, resume referral, career counseling, careers library, job bank, job interviews.

Freshmen 865 applied, 413 admitted, 599 enrolled.

SAT verbal scores above 500	70%	SAT math scores above 500	73%
ACT above 18	90%	From top 10% of their h.s. class	10%
From top quarter	40%	From top half	68%
1998 freshmen returning in 1999	72%		

Application *Options:* early admission, deferred entrance. *Application fee:* $25. *Required:* essay or personal statement; high school transcript; 1 letter of recommendation. *Recommended:* interview.

Standardized tests *Admission: Required:* SAT I or ACT.

Significant dates *Application deadlines:* rolling (freshmen), rolling (transfers). *Financial aid deadline priority date:* 2/15.

Freshman Application Contact Mr. David Melton, Director of Admissions, Houston Baptist University, 7502 Fondren Road, Houston, TX 77074. **Phone:** 281-649-3211 Ext. 3208. **Toll-free phone:** 800-969-3210. **Fax:** 281-649-3209. **E-mail:** unadm@hbu.edu

Visit CollegeQuest.com for information on majors offered and athletics.

HOWARD PAYNE UNIVERSITY
Brownwood, Texas

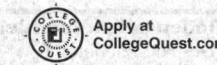

- **Independent Southern Baptist**, 4-year, founded 1889
- **Degree** bachelor's
- **Small-town** 30-acre campus
- **Coed**, 1,496 undergraduate students, 80% full-time, 50% women, 50% men
- **Minimally difficult** entrance level, 100% of applicants were admitted
- **17:1 student-to-undergraduate faculty ratio**
- **35.8% graduate** in 6 years or less
- **$9000 tuition** and fees
- **$9419 average indebtedness** upon graduation, $37 million endowment

Students *Undergraduates:* 1,194 full-time, 302 part-time. Students come from 19 states and territories, 10 other countries. *The most frequently chosen baccalaureate fields are:* business/marketing, education, philosophy.

From out-of-state	4%	Reside on campus	44%
Age 25 or older	22%	Transferred in	6%
International students	1%	African Americans	7%
Asian Americans/Pacific Islanders	3%	Hispanic Americans	9%
Native Americans	1%		

Faculty 106 (79% full-time), 41% with terminal degrees.

Expenses (1999–2000) *Comprehensive fee:* $12,830 includes full-time tuition ($8400), mandatory fees ($600), and room and board ($3830). *College room only:* $1720. Full-time tuition and fees vary according to course load. Room and board charges vary according to board plan, gender, and housing facility. *Part-time tuition:* $175 per semester hour. *Part-time fees:* $100 per term part-time. *Payment plan:* installment. *Waivers:* senior citizens and employees or children of employees.

Library Walker Memorial Library. *Operations spending 1999–2000:* $473,939. *Collection:* 140,000 titles, 2,369 serial subscriptions, 54 audiovisual materials.

College life *Housing:* on-campus residence required through junior year. *Options:* men-only, women-only. *Social organizations:* local fraternities, local sororities; 15% of eligible men and 20% of eligible women are members. *Most popular organizations:* BSM, Zeta Zeta Zeta, Delta Chi Rho, Students Foundations, Iota Chi Alpha.

Campus security 24-hour emergency response devices, controlled dormitory access, 12-hour patrols by trained security personnel.

After graduation 15 organizations recruited on campus 1997–98. *Career center:* 1 full-time, 1 part-time personnel. Services include job fairs, resume preparation, interview workshops, resume referral, career/interest testing, career counseling, careers library, job bank, job interviews. *Graduate education:* 41% of class of 1999 went directly to graduate and professional school: 21% theology.

Texas

Howard Payne University (continued)

Freshmen 530 applied, 530 admitted, 364 enrolled. 7 valedictorians.

Average high school GPA	3.31	SAT verbal scores above 500	53%
SAT math scores above 500	45%	ACT above 18	78%
From top 10% of their h.s. class	10%	From top quarter	34%
From top half	59%	1998 freshmen returning in 1999	60%

Application *Options:* eApply at www.CollegeQuest.com, early admission. *Application fee:* $25. *Required:* high school transcript; minimum 3.0 GPA. *Required for some:* letters of recommendation; interview.

Standardized tests *Admission: Required:* SAT I or ACT.

Significant dates *Application deadlines:* rolling (freshmen), rolling (transfers). *Financial aid deadline priority date:* 3/15.

Freshman Application Contact Ms. Cheryl Mangrum, Coordinator of Admission Services, Howard Payne University, HPU Station Box 828, Brownwood, TX 76801. **Phone:** 915-649-8027. **Toll-free phone:** 800-880-4478. **Fax:** 915-649-8900. **E-mail:** enroll@hputx.edu

Visit CollegeQuest.com for information on majors offered and athletics. College video available at CollegeQuest.com.

HUSTON-TILLOTSON COLLEGE
Austin, Texas

- **Independent interdenominational**, 4-year, founded 1875
- **Degree** bachelor's
- **Urban** 23-acre campus
- **Coed**, 518 undergraduate students, 92% full-time, 52% women, 48% men
- **Moderately difficult** entrance level, 82% of applicants were admitted
- **14:1 student-to-undergraduate faculty ratio**
- **31% graduate** in 6 years or less
- **$6350 tuition** and fees
- **$9852 average financial aid** package, $6.1 million endowment

Students *Undergraduates:* 475 full-time, 43 part-time. Students come from 17 states and territories, 26 other countries. *The most frequently chosen baccalaureate fields are:* business/marketing, interdisciplinary studies, social sciences and history.

From out-of-state	9%	Reside on campus	40%
Age 25 or older	32%	Transferred in	9%
International students	7%	African Americans	75%
Asian Americans/Pacific Islanders	4%	Hispanic Americans	7%

Faculty 62 (56% full-time), 48% with terminal degrees.

Expenses (1999–2000) *Comprehensive fee:* $11,032 includes full-time tuition ($6350) and room and board ($4682). Room and board charges vary according to housing facility. *Part-time tuition:* $175 per credit hour. *Part-time fees:* $225 per term part-time. Part-time tuition and fees vary according to course load. *Payment plan:* installment. *Waivers:* employees or children of employees.

Library Downs–Jones Library. *Operations spending 1999–2000:* $227,934. *Collection:* 84,200 titles, 349 serial subscriptions.

College life *Housing: Options:* men-only, women-only. *Social organizations:* national fraternities, national sororities; 4% of eligible men and 4% of eligible women are members. *Most popular organizations:* Student Government Association, Campus Pals.

Campus security 24-hour patrols.

After graduation 80 organizations recruited on campus 1997–98. *Career center:* 4 full-time personnel. Services include job fairs, resume preparation, interview workshops, resume referral, career/interest testing, career counseling, careers library, job bank, job interviews. *Graduate education:* 18% of class of 1999 went directly to graduate and professional school.

Freshmen 170 applied, 140 admitted, 118 enrolled.

Average high school GPA	2.53	SAT verbal scores above 500	N/R
SAT math scores above 500	N/R	ACT above 18	20%
1998 freshmen returning in 1999	49%		

Application *Option:* Common Application. *Application fee:* $25. *Required:* essay or personal statement; high school transcript; minimum 2.5 GPA. *Required for some:* interview.

Standardized tests *Admission: Required:* SAT I and SAT II or ACT.

Significant dates *Application deadlines:* 3/1 (freshmen), 3/1 (transfers). *Financial aid deadline priority date:* 3/15.

Freshman Application Contact Tmitria A. Glenn, Admissions Counselor, Huston-Tillotson College, 900 Chicon Street, Austin, TX 78702. **Phone:** 512-505-3029. **Fax:** 512-505-3190. **E-mail:** taglenn@htc.edu

Visit CollegeQuest.com for information on majors offered and athletics. College video available at CollegeQuest.com.

INSTITUTE FOR CHRISTIAN STUDIES
Austin, Texas

- **Independent**, upper-level, founded 1917, affiliated with Church of Christ
- **Degree** bachelor's
- **Urban** campus
- **Coed**, 27 undergraduate students, 41% full-time, 44% women, 56% men
- **Minimally difficult** entrance level, 100% of applicants were admitted
- **10:1 student-to-undergraduate faculty ratio**
- **$1560 tuition** and fees
- **$5500 average indebtedness** upon graduation, $4 million endowment

Students *Undergraduates:* 11 full-time, 16 part-time. Students come from 5 states and territories. *The most frequently chosen baccalaureate field is:* philosophy.

Age 25 or older	65%	Transferred in	26%
African Americans	30%		

Faculty 10 (40% full-time), 60% with terminal degrees.

Expenses (1999–2000) *Tuition:* full-time $1560; part-time $195 per course. *College room only:* $1500. *Payment plan:* installment.

Library ICS Library plus 1 other. *Collection:* 25,000 titles, 93 serial subscriptions.

College life *Housing: Option:* coed. *Most popular organization:* student government.

Campus security 24-hour emergency response devices.

After graduation *Career center:* Services include career counseling.

Standardized tests *Admission: Required for some:* SAT I or ACT.

Significant dates *Application deadline:* rolling (transfers). *Financial aid deadline priority date:* 4/15.

Freshman Application Contact Mr. Bob Burgess, Director of Admissions and Registrar, Institute for Christian Studies, 1909 University Avenue, Austin, TX 78705-5610. **Phone:** 512-476-2772. **Toll-free phone:** 800-ICS-AUSTIN. **Fax:** 512-476-3919. **E-mail:** burgess@mail.ics.edu

Visit CollegeQuest.com for information on majors offered and athletics.

JARVIS CHRISTIAN COLLEGE
Hawkins, Texas

- **Independent**, 4-year, founded 1912, affiliated with Christian Church (Disciples of Christ)
- **Degree** bachelor's
- **Rural** 465-acre campus
- **Coed**, 517 undergraduate students, 97% full-time, 57% women, 43% men
- **Minimally difficult** entrance level
- **14:1 student-to-undergraduate faculty ratio**
- **$5200 tuition** and fees
- **$14 million endowment**

Students *Undergraduates:* 499 full-time, 18 part-time. Students come from 25 states and territories, 7 other countries. *The most frequently chosen baccalaureate fields are:* business/marketing, philosophy, social sciences and history.

Age 25 or older	2%	Transferred in	6%
International students	3%	African Americans	94%
Hispanic Americans	1%		

Faculty 68 (57% full-time), 44% with terminal degrees.

Expenses (1999–2000) *Comprehensive fee:* $8950 includes full-time tuition ($5200) and room and board ($3750). *College room only:* $1610. *Part-time tuition:* $173 per semester hour. *Payment plans:* tuition prepayment, deferred payment. *Waivers:* employees or children of employees.

Library Olin Library. *Operations spending 1999–2000:* $102,723. *Collection:* 74,002 titles, 495 serial subscriptions.

College life On-campus residence required through senior year. *Social organizations:* national fraternities, national sororities. *Most popular organizations:* Student Government Association, SIFE.

Campus security 24-hour patrols.

After graduation 104 organizations recruited on campus 1997–98. 54% of class of 1998 had job offers within 6 months. *Career center:* 2 full-time, 1 part-time personnel. Services include job fairs, resume preparation, resume referral, career counseling, careers library, job interviews.

Freshmen 115 enrolled.

Average high school GPA	2.75	SAT verbal scores above 500	N/R
SAT math scores above 500	N/R	ACT above 18	N/R
From top 10% of their h.s. class	7%	From top quarter	18%
From top half	29%	1998 freshmen returning in 1999	50%

Application *Options:* Common Application, early admission, deferred entrance. *Application fee:* $25. *Required:* high school transcript. *Recommended:* minimum 2.0 GPA.

Standardized tests *Placement: Required:* ACT. *Recommended:* SAT I.

Significant dates *Application deadlines:* rolling (freshmen), rolling (transfers). *Financial aid deadline priority date:* 4/1.

Freshman Application Contact Ms. Serena Sentell, Admissions Counselor, Jarvis Christian College, PO Drawer G, Hawkins, TX 75765-9989. **Phone:** 903-769-0417. **Toll-free phone:** 800-292-9517. **Fax:** 903-769-4842.

Visit CollegeQuest.com for information on majors offered and athletics. College video available at CollegeQuest.com.

LAMAR UNIVERSITY
Beaumont, Texas

- **State-supported**, university, founded 1923
- **Degrees** associate, bachelor's, master's, and doctoral
- **Suburban** 200-acre campus with easy access to Houston
- **Coed**, 7,382 undergraduate students, 65% full-time, 61% women, 39% men
- **Minimally difficult** entrance level, 76% of applicants were admitted
- **$2161 tuition** and fees (in-state); $7681 (out-of-state)

Part of Texas State University System.

Students *Undergraduates:* Students come from 39 states and territories, 61 other countries. *Graduate:* 767 in graduate degree programs.

Age 25 or older	39%	International students	1%
African Americans	18%	Asian Americans/Pacific Islanders	3%
Hispanic Americans	4%	Native Americans	1%

Faculty 398 (82% full-time).

Expenses (1999–2000) *Tuition, state resident:* full-time $1584; part-time $396 per term. *Tuition, nonresident:* full-time $7104; part-time $1776 per term. *Required fees:* full-time $577; $204 per term part-time. Part-time tuition and fees vary according to course load. *College room and board:* $3516. Room and board charges vary according to board plan and housing facility. *Payment plan:* installment. *Waivers:* senior citizens.

Library Mary and John Gray Library. *Collection:* 600,000 titles, 2,900 serial subscriptions.

College life *Housing: Option:* coed. *Social organizations:* national fraternities, national sororities; 5% of eligible men and 5% of eligible women are members.

Campus security 24-hour patrols, student patrols, late-night transport-escort service.

After graduation 135 organizations recruited on campus 1997–98. 60% of class of 1998 had job offers within 6 months. *Career center:* 4 full-time, 4 part-time personnel. Services include job fairs, resume preparation, resume referral, career counseling, careers library, job bank, job interviews. *Graduate education:* 30% of class of 1999 went directly to graduate and professional school.

Freshmen 951 applied, 727 admitted.

Average high school GPA	3.0	SAT verbal scores above 500	40%
SAT math scores above 500	34%	ACT above 18	N/R
From top 10% of their h.s. class	10%	From top quarter	30%
From top half	75%	1998 freshmen returning in 1999	67%

Application *Options:* electronic application, early admission. *Required:* high school transcript.

Standardized tests *Admission: Required:* SAT I or ACT. *Required for some:* SAT II Subject Tests.

Significant dates *Application deadlines:* 8/1 (freshmen), 8/1 (transfers). *Financial aid deadline priority date:* 4/1.

Freshman Application Contact Ms. Melissa Chesser, Director of Recruitment, Lamar University, PO Box 10009, Beaumont, TX 77710. **Phone:** 409-880-8888. **Fax:** 409-880-8463. **E-mail:** admissions@hal.lamar.edu

Visit CollegeQuest.com for information on majors offered and athletics. College video available at CollegeQuest.com.

LETOURNEAU UNIVERSITY
Longview, Texas

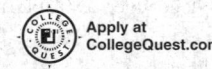

- **Independent nondenominational**, comprehensive, founded 1946
- **Degrees** associate, bachelor's, and master's
- **Suburban** 162-acre campus
- **Coed**, 2,491 undergraduate students, 98% full-time, 47% women, 53% men
- **Moderately difficult** entrance level, 85% of applicants were admitted
- **15:1 student-to-undergraduate faculty ratio**
- **50.27% graduate** in 6 years or less
- **$12,240 tuition** and fees
- **$11,748 average financial aid** package, $17,263 average indebtedness upon graduation, $6.5 million endowment

At LeTourneau, solutions are a specialty. Nationally recognized programs, from engineering and aeronautical science to education and business, focus on ingenuity and problem solving. Everything is also solidly founded in the ageless principles of God's Word. At LeTourneau, "Faith brings us together. Ingenuity sets us apart."

Students *Undergraduates:* 2,435 full-time, 56 part-time. Students come from 49 states and territories, 24 other countries. *The most frequently chosen baccalaureate fields are:* business/marketing, biological/life sciences, engineering/engineering technologies. *Graduate:* 282 in graduate degree programs.

From out-of-state	50%	Reside on campus	67%
Age 25 or older	10%	Transferred in	4%
International students	2%	African Americans	13%
Asian Americans/Pacific Islanders	1%	Hispanic Americans	6%
Native Americans	1%		

Faculty 199 (30% full-time).

Expenses (2000–2001) *One-time required fee:* $75. *Comprehensive fee:* $17,490 includes full-time tuition ($12,090), mandatory fees ($150), and room and board ($5250). Room and board charges vary according to board plan. Part-time tuition and fees vary according to course load. *Payment plan:* installment. *Waivers:* employees or children of employees.

Library Margaret Estes Resource Center. *Operations spending 1999–2000:* $580,384. *Collection:* 260,000 titles, 600 serial subscriptions, 4,563 audiovisual materials.

College life *Housing:* on-campus residence required through junior year. *Options:* men-only, women-only. *Social organizations:* 3 societies for men, 1 society for women; 8% of eligible men and 3% of eligible women are members. *Most popular organizations:* LeTourneau Student Ministries, Themelios, Student Foundation, Student Senate, roller hockey club.

Campus security 24-hour emergency response devices and patrols, late-night transport-escort service, controlled dormitory access.

After graduation 60 organizations recruited on campus 1997–98. 91% of class of 1998 had job offers within 6 months. *Career center:* 1 full-time, 2 part-time personnel. Services include job fairs, resume preparation, interview workshops, resume referral, career/interest testing, career counseling, careers library, job bank, job interviews.

Texas

LeTourneau University (continued)

Freshmen 953 applied, 806 admitted, 263 enrolled. 6 National Merit Scholars, 11 valedictorians.

Average high school GPA	3.5	SAT verbal scores above 500	83%
SAT math scores above 500	89%	ACT above 18	99%
From top 10% of their h.s. class	27%	From top quarter	54%
From top half	82%	1998 freshmen returning in 1999	79%

Application *Options:* eApply at www.CollegeQuest.com, early admission, deferred entrance. *Application fee:* $25. *Required:* essay or personal statement; high school transcript; minimum 2.5 GPA; 2 letters of recommendation. *Required for some:* interview.

Standardized tests *Admission: Required:* SAT I or ACT.

Significant dates *Application deadlines:* 8/1 (freshmen), 8/1 (transfers). *Financial aid deadline priority date:* 2/15.

Freshman Application Contact
Mr. Rodney Stanford, Director of Admissions, LeTourneau University, PO Box 7001, Admissions Office, Longview, TX 75607-7001. **Phone:** 903-233-3400. **Toll-free phone:** 800-759-8811. **Fax:** 903-233-3411. **E-mail:** admissions@letu.edu

Visit CollegeQuest.com for information on majors offered and athletics. College video available at CollegeQuest.com.

LUBBOCK CHRISTIAN UNIVERSITY
Lubbock, Texas

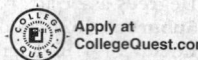

- **Independent**, comprehensive, founded 1957, affiliated with Church of Christ
- **Degrees** bachelor's and master's
- **Suburban** 120-acre campus
- **Coed**, 1,368 undergraduate students, 82% full-time, 59% women, 41% men
- **Moderately difficult** entrance level, 90% of applicants were admitted
- **17:1 student-to-undergraduate faculty ratio**
- **30.5% graduate** in 6 years or less
- **$9316 tuition** and fees
- **$10,924 average financial aid** package, $8.5 million endowment

Students *Undergraduates:* 1,120 full-time, 248 part-time. Students come from 23 states and territories, 17 other countries. *The most frequently chosen baccalaureate fields are:* business/marketing, education, liberal arts/general studies. *Graduate:* 93 in graduate degree programs.

From out-of-state	15%	Age 25 or older	27%
Transferred in	12%	International students	2%
African Americans	4%	Asian Americans/Pacific Islanders	1%
Hispanic Americans	10%	Native Americans	1%

Faculty 117 (61% full-time).

Expenses (1999–2000) *Comprehensive fee:* $13,016 includes full-time tuition ($8760), mandatory fees ($556), and room and board ($3700). Full-time tuition and fees vary according to program. Room and board charges vary according to board plan and housing facility. *Part-time tuition:* $129 per credit hour. *Part-time fees:* $148 per term part-time. Part-time tuition and fees vary according to course load and program. *Payment plans:* tuition prepayment, installment.

Library University Library. *Collection:* 100,000 titles, 556 serial subscriptions.

College life *Housing:* on-campus residence required through sophomore year. *Options:* men-only, women-only. *Social organizations:* local fraternities, local sororities; 29% of eligible men and 45% of eligible women are members. *Most popular organization:* Primary Ministry Groups.

Campus security 24-hour patrols.

After graduation 25 organizations recruited on campus 1997–98. *Career center:* 1 full-time, 5 part-time personnel. Services include job fairs, resume preparation, interview workshops, resume referral, career/interest testing, career counseling, careers library, job bank, job interviews.

Freshmen 592 applied, 534 admitted, 352 enrolled. 1 National Merit Scholar, 15 class presidents, 25 valedictorians, 62 student government officers.

Average high school GPA	3.12	SAT verbal scores above 500	65%
SAT math scores above 500	63%	ACT above 18	79%
From top 10% of their h.s. class	18%	From top quarter	46%
From top half	62%	1998 freshmen returning in 1999	76%

Application *Options:* eApply at www.CollegeQuest.com, Common Application, electronic application, early admission, deferred entrance. *Application fee:* $20. *Required:* high school transcript.

Standardized tests *Admission: Required:* SAT I or ACT.

Significant dates *Application deadlines:* rolling (freshmen), rolling (transfers). *Financial aid deadline priority date:* 6/15.

Freshman Application Contact
Office of Admissions, Lubbock Christian University, 5601 19th Street, Lubbock, TX 79407-2099. **Phone:** 806-796-8800 Ext. 260. **Toll-free phone:** 800-933-7601 Ext. 260. **Fax:** 806-796-8917. **E-mail:** admissions@lcu.edu

Visit CollegeQuest.com for information on majors offered and athletics. Electronic viewbook available at CollegeQuest.com.

MCMURRY UNIVERSITY
Abilene, Texas

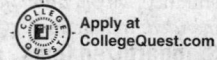

- **Independent United Methodist**, 4-year, founded 1923
- **Degree** bachelor's
- **Urban** 41-acre campus
- **Coed**, 1,339 undergraduate students, 80% full-time, 49% women, 51% men
- **Moderately difficult** entrance level, 68% of applicants were admitted
- **13:1 student-to-undergraduate faculty ratio**
- **37% graduate** in 6 years or less
- **$9695 tuition** and fees
- **$9226 average financial aid** package, $14,250 average indebtedness upon graduation, $32 million endowment

Students *Undergraduates:* 1,070 full-time, 269 part-time. Students come from 12 states and territories, 7 other countries. *The most frequently chosen baccalaureate fields are:* business/marketing, education, social sciences and history.

From out-of-state	6%	Reside on campus	41%
Age 25 or older	25%	Transferred in	10%
International students	1%	African Americans	8%
Asian Americans/Pacific Islanders	2%	Hispanic Americans	11%
Native Americans	1%		

Faculty 114 (66% full-time), 67% with terminal degrees.

Expenses (1999–2000) *Comprehensive fee:* $13,939 includes full-time tuition ($8670), mandatory fees ($1025), and room and board ($4244). *College room only:* $1990. Full-time tuition and fees vary according to course load. Room and board charges vary according to board plan. *Part-time tuition:* $289 per semester hour. *Part-time fees:* $32 per semester hour. Part-time tuition and fees vary according to course load. *Payment plans:* guaranteed tuition, installment. *Waivers:* employees or children of employees.

Library Jay-Rollins Library. *Operations spending 1999–2000:* $294,437. *Collection:* 145,724 titles, 566 serial subscriptions.

College life *Housing:* on-campus residence required through junior year. *Options:* men-only, women-only. *Social organizations:* local fraternities, local sororities; 33% of eligible men and 42% of eligible women are members. *Most popular organizations:* Alpha Phi Omega, McMurry Christian Ministries, Indian Insight Service Club, Students Against Drunk Driving.

Campus security 24-hour emergency response devices and patrols, late-night transport-escort service, controlled dormitory access.

After graduation 7 organizations recruited on campus 1997–98. 86% of class of 1998 had job offers within 6 months. *Career center:* 3 full-time personnel. Services include job fairs, resume preparation, resume referral, career/interest testing, career counseling, careers library, job bank, job interviews.

Freshmen 931 applied, 637 admitted, 306 enrolled. 8 valedictorians.

Average high school GPA	3.35	SAT verbal scores above 500	54%
SAT math scores above 500	59%	ACT above 18	87%
From top 10% of their h.s. class	20%	From top quarter	53%
From top half	84%	1998 freshmen returning in 1999	64%

Application *Options:* eApply at www.CollegeQuest.com, Common Application, electronic application, deferred entrance. *Application fee:* $20.

Required: high school transcript; minimum 2.0 GPA. *Required for some:* essay or personal statement; 3 letters of recommendation. *Recommended:* interview.

Standardized tests *Admission: Required:* SAT I or ACT.
Significant dates *Application deadlines:* 8/15 (freshmen), 8/15 (transfers). *Financial aid deadline priority date:* 3/15.
Freshman Application Contact
Mr. L. Russell Watjen, Vice President, Enrollment Management and Student Relations, McMurry University, Box 947, Abilene, TX 79697. **Phone:** 915-793-4720. **Toll-free phone:** 800-477-0077. **Fax:** 915-691-6599. **E-mail:** admissions@mcm.edu

Visit CollegeQuest.com for information on majors offered and athletics.

■ *See page 2032 for a narrative description.*

MIDWESTERN STATE UNIVERSITY
Wichita Falls, Texas

Apply at CollegeQuest.com

- **State-supported**, comprehensive, founded 1922
- **Degrees** associate, bachelor's, and master's
- **Urban** 172-acre campus
- **Coed**, 5,090 undergraduate students, 72% full-time, 57% women, 43% men
- **Minimally difficult** entrance level
- **20:1** student-to-undergraduate faculty ratio
- **29% graduate** in 6 years or less
- **$2426 tuition** and fees (in-state); $8906 (out-of-state)
- **$5.4 million endowment**

Students *Undergraduates:* 3,643 full-time, 1,447 part-time. Students come from 43 states and territories, 56 other countries. *The most frequently chosen baccalaureate fields are:* business/marketing, health professions and related sciences, interdisciplinary studies. *Graduate:* 675 in graduate degree programs.

From out-of-state	7%	Reside on campus	12%
Age 25 or older	29%	Transferred in	11%
International students	6%	African Americans	7%
Asian Americans/Pacific Islanders	3%	Hispanic Americans	7%
Native Americans	1%		

Faculty 287 (64% full-time), 46% with terminal degrees.
Expenses (1999–2000) *Tuition, state resident:* full-time $1860; part-time $62 per credit hour. *Tuition, nonresident:* full-time $8340; part-time $278 per credit hour. *Required fees:* full-time $566; $17 per credit hour; $58 per term part-time. Full-time tuition and fees vary according to course load. Part-time tuition and fees vary according to course load. *College room and board:* $3728; room only: $1894. Room and board charges vary according to board plan and housing facility. *Payment plan:* installment. *Waivers:* employees or children of employees.
Library Moffett Library. *Operations spending 1999–2000:* $1.2 million. *Collection:* 366,350 titles, 1,100 serial subscriptions.
College life *Housing:* on-campus residence required through sophomore year. *Option:* coed. *Social organizations:* national fraternities, national sororities; 14% of eligible men and 12% of eligible women are members. *Most popular organizations:* honor societies, Greek Organizations, political groups.
Campus security 24-hour emergency response devices and patrols, controlled dormitory access.
After graduation *Career center:* 2 full-time, 1 part-time personnel. Services include job fairs, resume preparation, resume referral, career counseling, careers library, job bank, job interviews.
Freshmen 850 enrolled.

Average high school GPA	3.05	SAT verbal scores above 500	N/R
SAT math scores above 500	N/R	ACT above 18	N/R
From top 10% of their h.s. class	6%	From top quarter	26%
From top half	60%	1998 freshmen returning in 1999	60%

Application *Options:* eApply at www.CollegeQuest.com, Common Application, early admission, deferred entrance. *Required:* high school transcript.
Standardized tests *Admission: Required:* SAT I or ACT.
Significant dates *Application deadlines:* 8/7 (freshmen), 8/7 (transfers). *Notification:* continuous until 8/31 (freshmen). *Financial aid deadline priority date:* 6/1.

Freshman Application Contact
Ms. Billye Tims, Registrar and Director of Admissions, Midwestern State University, 3410 Taft Boulevard, Wichita Falls, TX 76308-2096. **Phone:** 940-397-4321. **Toll-free phone:** 800-842-1922. **Fax:** 940-397-4302. **E-mail:** school.relations@nexus.mwsu.edu

Visit CollegeQuest.com for information on majors offered and athletics. College video available at CollegeQuest.com.

NORTHWOOD UNIVERSITY, TEXAS CAMPUS
Cedar Hill, Texas

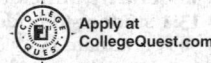
Apply at CollegeQuest.com

- **Independent**, 4-year, founded 1966
- **Degrees** associate and bachelor's
- **Small-town** 360-acre campus with easy access to Dallas
- **Coed**, 1,007 undergraduate students, 71% full-time, 52% women, 48% men
- **Minimally difficult** entrance level, 95% of applicants were admitted
- **35:1** student-to-undergraduate faculty ratio
- **$11,625 tuition** and fees
- **$9982 average financial aid** package, $17,125 average indebtedness upon graduation, $42 million system endowment

Students *Undergraduates:* 719 full-time, 288 part-time. Students come from 13 states and territories, 14 other countries. *The most frequently chosen baccalaureate fields are:* business/marketing, computer/information sciences.

From out-of-state	7%	Reside on campus	17%
Age 25 or older	5%	Transferred in	6%
International students	5%	African Americans	28%
Asian Americans/Pacific Islanders	3%	Hispanic Americans	14%
Native Americans	0.2%		

Faculty 22 (50% full-time), 32% with terminal degrees.
Expenses (1999–2000) *Comprehensive fee:* $16,771 includes full-time tuition ($11,325), mandatory fees ($300), and room and board ($5146). Room and board charges vary according to board plan. *Part-time tuition:* $235 per credit hour. Part-time tuition and fees vary according to course load. *Payment plan:* installment. *Waivers:* children of alumni and employees or children of employees.
Library Texas Campus Library. *Operations spending 1999–2000:* $105,000. *Collection:* 13,000 titles, 160 serial subscriptions.
College life *Housing:* on-campus residence required in freshman year. *Options:* men-only, women-only. *Most popular organizations:* student senate, Students in Free Enterprise, Student Programming Board, Black Student Alliance, Hispanic Students Association.
Campus security 24-hour patrols, student patrols.
After graduation 30 organizations recruited on campus 1997–98. *Career center:* 1 part-time personnel. Services include job fairs, resume preparation, interview workshops, resume referral, career counseling, careers library, job bank, job interviews.
Freshmen 486 applied, 460 admitted, 212 enrolled.

Average high school GPA	3.1	SAT verbal scores above 500	40%
SAT math scores above 500	41%	ACT above 18	61%
From top 10% of their h.s. class	7%	From top quarter	25%
From top half	78%	1998 freshmen returning in 1999	74%

Application *Options:* eApply at www.CollegeQuest.com, Common Application, electronic application, deferred entrance. *Application fee:* $15. *Required:* high school transcript. *Recommended:* essay or personal statement; minimum 2.0 GPA; 1 letter of recommendation; interview.
Standardized tests *Admission: Required:* SAT I or ACT.
Significant dates *Application deadlines:* 9/1 (freshmen), 9/1 (transfers). *Financial aid deadline:* continuous.
Freshman Application Contact
Mr. James R. Hickerson, Director of Admissions, Northwood University, Texas Campus, 1114 W FM 1382, PO Box 58, Cedar Hill, TX 75104-1204. **Phone:** 972-293-5400. **Toll-free phone:** 800-927-9663. **Fax:** 972-291-3824. **E-mail:** txadmit@northwood.edu

Visit CollegeQuest.com for information on majors offered and athletics. College video available at CollegeQuest.com.

Texas

OUR LADY OF THE LAKE UNIVERSITY OF SAN ANTONIO
San Antonio, Texas

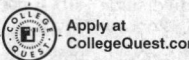 Apply at CollegeQuest.com

- **Independent Roman Catholic**, comprehensive, founded 1895
- **Degrees** bachelor's, master's, and doctoral
- **Urban** 75-acre campus
- **Coed**, 2,306 undergraduate students, 59% full-time, 77% women, 23% men
- **Moderately difficult** entrance level, 68% of applicants were admitted
- **13:1 student-to-undergraduate faculty ratio**
- **30% graduate** in 6 years or less
- **$11,408 tuition** and fees
- **$12,060 average financial aid** package, $16,649 average indebtedness upon graduation, $25.9 million endowment

Students *Undergraduates:* 1,352 full-time, 954 part-time. Students come from 28 states and territories, 17 other countries. *The most frequently chosen baccalaureate fields are:* business/marketing, liberal arts/general studies, psychology. *Graduate:* 1,234 in graduate degree programs.

From out-of-state	2%	Reside on campus	19%
Age 25 or older	48%	Transferred in	6%
International students	1%	African Americans	7%
Asian Americans/Pacific Islanders	1%	Hispanic Americans	64%
Native Americans	0.2%		

Faculty 269 (48% full-time).
Expenses (1999–2000) *Comprehensive fee:* $15,760 includes full-time tuition ($11,150), mandatory fees ($258), and room and board ($4352). *College room only:* $2412. Room and board charges vary according to board plan and housing facility. *Part-time tuition:* $362 per credit hour. *Part-time fees:* $4 per credit hour; $38 per term part-time. *Payment plan:* installment. *Waivers:* employees or children of employees.
Library Saint Florence Library plus 2 others. *Operations spending 1999–2000:* $1.1 million. *Collection:* 120,521 titles, 29,588 serial subscriptions.
College life *Housing:* Options: coed, men-only, women-only, disabled students.
Campus security 24-hour emergency response devices and patrols, late-night transport-escort service, controlled dormitory access.
After graduation 85 organizations recruited on campus 1997–98. *Career center:* 2 full-time, 1 part-time personnel. Services include job fairs, resume preparation, resume referral, career counseling, careers library, job bank, job interviews. *Graduate education:* 30% of class of 1999 went directly to graduate and professional school.
Freshmen 1,848 applied, 1,255 admitted, 308 enrolled.

Average high school GPA	3.29	SAT verbal scores above 500	42%
SAT math scores above 500	34%	ACT above 18	79%
From top 10% of their h.s. class	19%	From top quarter	52%
From top half	82%	1998 freshmen returning in 1999	64%

Application *Options:* eApply at www.CollegeQuest.com, Common Application, deferred entrance. *Application fee:* $25. *Required:* high school transcript. *Required for some:* interview.
Standardized tests *Admission: Required:* SAT I or ACT.
Significant dates *Application deadlines:* rolling (freshmen), rolling (transfers). *Financial aid deadline:* continuous.
Freshman Application Contact
Mr. Michael Boatner, Acting Director of Admissions, Our Lady of the Lake University of San Antonio, 411 Southwest 24th Street, San Antonio, TX 78207-4689. **Phone:** 210-434-6711 Ext. 314. **Toll-free phone:** 800-436-6558. **Fax:** 210-436-0824. **E-mail:** admission@lake.ollusa.edu
Visit CollegeQuest.com for information on majors offered and athletics.

■ *See page 2232 for a narrative description.*

PAUL QUINN COLLEGE
Dallas, Texas

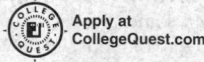 Apply at CollegeQuest.com

Admissions Office Contact
Paul Quinn College, 3837 Simpson-Stuart Road, Dallas, TX 75241-4331. **Toll-free phone:** 800-237-2648. **Fax:** 214-302-3559.

PRAIRIE VIEW A&M UNIVERSITY
Prairie View, Texas

- **State-supported**, comprehensive, founded 1878
- **Degrees** bachelor's and master's
- **Small-town** 1,440-acre campus with easy access to Houston
- **Coed**, 4,963 undergraduate students, 92% full-time, 54% women, 46% men
- **Moderately difficult** entrance level, 96% of applicants were admitted
- **19:1 student-to-undergraduate faculty ratio**

Prairie View A&M University is the 2nd-oldest public institution of higher education in Texas, originating in the Texas Constitution of 1876. The University opened in 1878 as the Agricultural and Mechanical College of Texas for Colored Youth, with 8 students and 2 professors. Today, it enrolls more than 6,000 students and offers undergraduate and graduate degrees. Its most prominent programs are in accounting, computer science, criminal justice, education, engineering, nursing, and premedicine. Major academic units include the School of Architecture, the College of Agriculture and Human Sciences, the College of Arts and Sciences, the College of Business, the College of Education, the College of Engineering, The School of Juvenile Justice, the College of Nursing, and the Graduate School. The University is fully accredited by the Southern Association of Colleges and Schools and has specialized accreditation in several areas, including computer science, education, engineering, nursing, nutrition, and social work.

Part of Texas A&M University System.
Students *Undergraduates:* 4,557 full-time, 406 part-time. Students come from 44 states and territories, 39 other countries. *The most frequently chosen baccalaureate fields are:* engineering/engineering technologies, business/marketing, health professions and related sciences. *Graduate:* 1,308 in graduate degree programs.

From out-of-state	9%	Age 25 or older	16%
International students	2%	African Americans	92%
Asian Americans/Pacific Islanders	1%	Hispanic Americans	1%
Native Americans	0.04%		

Faculty 357 (82% full-time).
Library John B. Coleman Library. *Operations spending 1999–2000:* $939,376.
College life *Housing:* on-campus residence required through senior year. *Options:* coed, men-only, women-only. *Social organizations:* national fraternities, national sororities, local fraternities, local sororities; 10% of eligible men and 10% of eligible women are members. *Most popular organizations:* National Society of Black Engineers, National Association of Black Accountants, National Organization of Black Chemists and Chemical Engineers, Toastmasters International, Baptist Student Movement.
Campus security 24-hour emergency response devices and patrols.
After graduation 410 organizations recruited on campus 1997–98. 77% of class of 1998 had job offers within 6 months. *Career center:* 7 full-time, 2 part-time personnel. Services include job fairs, resume preparation, interview workshops, resume referral, career counseling, careers library, job interviews. *Graduate education:* 21% of class of 1999 went directly to graduate and professional school.
Freshmen 2,025 applied, 1,943 admitted, 1,094 enrolled. 4 valedictorians.

Average high school GPA	2.72	SAT verbal scores above 500	15%
SAT math scores above 500	15%	ACT above 18	38%
From top 10% of their h.s. class	7%	From top quarter	21%
From top half	47%	1998 freshmen returning in 1999	69%

Application *Options:* Common Application, electronic application, early admission, deferred entrance. *Application fee:* $15. *Required:* high school transcript; minimum 2.0 GPA; letters of recommendation.
Standardized tests *Admission: Required:* SAT I or ACT.
Significant dates *Application deadline:* 7/1 (transfers). *Financial aid deadline priority date:* 4/1.
Freshman Application Contact
Ms. Mary Gooch, Director of Admissions, Prairie View A&M University, PO Box 3089, Prairie View, TX 77446-0188. **Phone:** 409-857-2626. **Fax:** 409-857-2699. **E-mail:** mary_gooch@pvamu.edu
Visit CollegeQuest.com for information on majors offered and athletics.

■ *See page 2284 for a narrative description.*

Texas

RICE UNIVERSITY
Houston, Texas

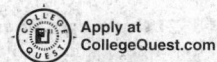 Apply at CollegeQuest.com

- **Independent**, university, founded 1912
- **Degrees** bachelor's, master's, and doctoral
- **Urban** 300-acre campus
- **Coed**, 2,769 undergraduate students, 97% full-time, 47% women, 53% men
- **Most difficult** entrance level, 28% of applicants were admitted
- **$15,796 tuition** and fees
- **$2.9 billion endowment**

Students *Undergraduates:* Students come from 50 states and territories, 28 other countries.

From out-of-state	50%	Reside on campus	63%
Age 25 or older	1%	International students	3%
African Americans	7%	Asian Americans/Pacific Islanders	15%
Hispanic Americans	10%	Native Americans	1%

Expenses (1999–2000) *Comprehensive fee:* $22,396 includes full-time tuition ($15,350), mandatory fees ($446), and room and board ($6600). *College room only:* $3700. Full-time tuition and fees vary according to student level. Room and board charges vary according to board plan. *Part-time tuition:* $607 per semester hour. *Part-time fees:* $110 per term part-time. Part-time tuition and fees vary according to student level. *Payment plan:* installment. *Waivers:* employees or children of employees.

Library Fondren Library. *Operations spending 1999–2000:* $8.8 million. *Collection:* 1.9 million titles, 14,000 serial subscriptions.

College life *Housing: Option:* coed. *Most popular organizations:* drama club, volunteer program, marching band, college government, intramural sports.

Campus security 24-hour emergency response devices and patrols, late-night transport-escort service, controlled dormitory access.

After graduation *Career center:* 5 full-time, 1 part-time personnel. Services include job fairs, resume preparation, resume referral, career counseling, careers library, job bank, job interviews. *Major awards:* 2 Fulbright Scholars.

Freshmen 5,740 applied, 1,595 admitted. 244 National Merit Scholars, 132 valedictorians.

SAT verbal scores above 500	99%	SAT math scores above 500	99%
ACT above 18	100%	From top 10% of their h.s. class	93%
From top quarter	96%	From top half	99%
1998 freshmen returning in 1999	95%		

Application *Options:* eApply at www.CollegeQuest.com, Common Application, electronic application, early admission, early decision, early action, deferred entrance. *Application fee:* $35. *Required:* essay or personal statement; high school transcript; 2 letters of recommendation. *Recommended:* interview.

Standardized tests *Admission: Required:* SAT I or ACT, SAT II Subject Tests, SAT II: Writing Test.

Significant dates *Application deadlines:* 1/2 (freshmen), 4/1 (transfers). *Early decision:* 11/1, 12/1. *Notification:* 4/1 (freshmen), 12/15 (early decision), 2/10 (early action). *Financial aid deadline priority date:* 3/1.

Freshman Application Contact
Ms. Julie M. Browning, Dean for Undergraduate Admission, Rice University, PO Box 1892, MS 17, Houston, TX 77251-1892. **Phone:** 713-348-RICE. **Toll-free phone:** 800-527-OWLS. **E-mail:** admission@rice.edu

Visit CollegeQuest.com for information on majors offered and athletics. College video available at CollegeQuest.com.

- *See page 2326 for a narrative description.*

ST. EDWARD'S UNIVERSITY
Austin, Texas

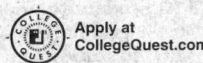 Apply at CollegeQuest.com

- **Independent Roman Catholic**, comprehensive, founded 1885
- **Degrees** bachelor's, master's, and postbachelor's certificates
- **Urban** 180-acre campus
- **Coed**, 2,906 undergraduate students, 68% full-time, 56% women, 44% men
- **Moderately difficult** entrance level, 79% of applicants were admitted
- **15:1 student-to-undergraduate faculty ratio**
- **38% graduate** in 6 years or less
- **$11,438 tuition** and fees
- **$9587 average financial aid** package, $33.1 million endowment

Students *Undergraduates:* 1,967 full-time, 939 part-time. Students come from 32 states and territories, 44 other countries. *The most frequently chosen baccalaureate fields are:* business/marketing, liberal arts/general studies, social sciences and history. *Graduate:* 712 in graduate degree programs.

From out-of-state	4%	Reside on campus	34%
Age 25 or older	10%	Transferred in	10%
International students	4%	African Americans	5%
Asian Americans/Pacific Islanders	2%	Hispanic Americans	29%
Native Americans	0.4%		

Faculty 255 (39% full-time), 54% with terminal degrees.

Expenses (1999–2000) *Comprehensive fee:* $16,438 includes full-time tuition ($11,438) and room and board ($5000). Room and board charges vary according to housing facility. *Part-time tuition:* $381 per credit hour. *Payment plan:* installment. *Waivers:* employees or children of employees.

Library Scarborough–Phillips Library. *Operations spending 1999–2000:* $893,824. *Collection:* 103,712 titles, 24,617 serial subscriptions, 1,884 audiovisual materials.

College life *Housing:* on-campus residence required in freshman year. *Options:* coed, men-only, women-only. *Most popular organizations:* Student Government Association, University Programming Board, Student Leadership Training Program, Academy of Science, Residence Housing Association.

Campus security 24-hour emergency response devices and patrols, late-night transport-escort service, controlled dormitory access.

After graduation 130 organizations recruited on campus 1997–98. *Career center:* 5 full-time, 2 part-time personnel. Services include job fairs, resume preparation, interview workshops, resume referral, career/interest testing, career counseling, careers library, job bank, job interviews, career course. *Graduate education:* 19% of class of 1999 went directly to graduate and professional school.

Freshmen 1,014 applied, 797 admitted, 381 enrolled. 3 valedictorians.

SAT verbal scores above 500	61%	SAT math scores above 500	59%
ACT above 18	93%	From top 10% of their h.s. class	16%
From top quarter	43%	From top half	77%
1998 freshmen returning in 1999	71%		

Application *Options:* eApply at www.CollegeQuest.com, Common Application, deferred entrance. *Application fee:* $30. *Required:* essay or personal statement; high school transcript. *Recommended:* letters of recommendation; interview.

Standardized tests *Admission: Required:* SAT I or ACT.

Significant dates *Application deadlines:* 8/1 (freshmen), 8/1 (transfers). *Financial aid deadline priority date:* 4/15.

Freshman Application Contact
Ms. Elizabeth Stanley, Director of Admission, St. Edward's University, 3001 South Congress Avenue, Austin, TX 78704-6489. **Phone:** 512-448-8500. **Toll-free phone:** 800-555-0164. **Fax:** 512-448-8492. **E-mail:** seu.admit@admin.stedwards.edu

Visit CollegeQuest.com for information on majors offered and athletics.

- *See page 2374 for a narrative description.*

ST. MARY'S UNIVERSITY OF SAN ANTONIO
San Antonio, Texas

 Apply at CollegeQuest.com

- **Independent Roman Catholic**, comprehensive, founded 1852
- **Degrees** bachelor's, master's, doctoral, and first professional
- **Urban** 135-acre campus
- **Coed**, 2,500 undergraduate students, 88% full-time, 58% women, 42% men
- **Moderately difficult** entrance level, 86% of applicants were admitted
- **14:1 student-to-undergraduate faculty ratio**
- **59.2% graduate** in 6 years or less
- **$11,880 tuition** and fees
- **$12,100 average financial aid** package, $16,415 average indebtedness upon graduation, $72.9 million endowment

Peterson's Guide to Four-Year Colleges 2001   www.petersons.com   789

Texas

St. Mary's University of San Antonio *(continued)*

Students *Undergraduates:* 2,210 full-time, 290 part-time. Students come from 35 states and territories, 50 other countries. *The most frequently chosen baccalaureate fields are:* biological/life sciences, business/marketing, social sciences and history. *Graduate:* 760 in professional programs, 762 in other graduate degree programs.

From out-of-state	4%	Reside on campus	44%
Age 25 or older	17%	Transferred in	6%
International students	4%	African Americans	3%
Asian Americans/Pacific Islanders	3%	Hispanic Americans	66%
Native Americans	0.4%		

Faculty 298 (65% full-time).

Expenses (1999–2000) *Comprehensive fee:* $17,131 includes full-time tuition ($11,500), mandatory fees ($380), and room and board ($5251). *College room only:* $3096. Room and board charges vary according to board plan and housing facility. *Part-time tuition:* $377 per semester hour. *Part-time fees:* $61 per term part-time. *Payment plans:* tuition prepayment, installment, deferred payment. *Waivers:* employees or children of employees.

Library Academic Library plus 1 other. *Operations spending 1999–2000:* $2.7 million. *Collection:* 391,700 titles, 1,331 serial subscriptions, 14,224 audiovisual materials.

College life *Housing:* on-campus residence required in freshman year. *Options:* coed, men-only, women-only, disabled students. *Social organizations:* national fraternities, national sororities, local fraternities; 16% of eligible men and 15% of eligible women are members. *Most popular organizations:* Alpha Phi Omega, Rotoract, Student Government Association, International Student Association, Delta Sigma Pi.

Campus security 24-hour emergency response devices and patrols, late-night transport-escort service, controlled dormitory access.

After graduation 124 organizations recruited on campus 1997–98. *Career center:* 6 full-time, 1 part-time personnel. Services include job fairs, resume preparation, interview workshops, resume referral, career/interest testing, career counseling, careers library, job bank, job interviews. *Graduate education:* 50% of class of 1999 went directly to graduate and professional school.

Freshmen 1,359 applied, 1,174 admitted, 489 enrolled. 19 student government officers.

SAT verbal scores above 500	72%	SAT math scores above 500	72%
ACT above 18	96%	From top 10% of their h.s. class	33%
From top quarter	59%	From top half	80%
1998 freshmen returning in 1999	79%		

Application *Options:* eApply at www.CollegeQuest.com, Common Application, deferred entrance. *Application fee:* $30. *Required:* essay or personal statement; high school transcript. *Required for some:* letters of recommendation. *Recommended:* interview.

Standardized tests *Admission: Required:* SAT I or ACT.

Significant dates *Application deadlines:* rolling (freshmen), rolling (transfers). *Financial aid deadline priority date:* 4/1.

Freshman Application Contact
Mr. Richard Castillo, Director of Admissions, St. Mary's University of San Antonio, 1 Camino Santa Maria, San Antonio, TX 78228-8503. **Phone:** 210-436-3126. **Toll-free phone:** 800-FOR-STMU. **Fax:** 210-431-6742. **E-mail:** uadm@stmarytx.edu

Visit CollegeQuest.com for information on majors offered and athletics. College video available at CollegeQuest.com.

■ *See page 2420 for a narrative description.*

SAM HOUSTON STATE UNIVERSITY
Huntsville, Texas

- **State-supported**, comprehensive, founded 1879
- **Degrees** bachelor's, master's, and doctoral
- **Small-town** 2,143-acre campus with easy access to Houston
- **Coed**, 10,825 undergraduate students, 80% full-time, 56% women, 44% men
- **Moderately difficult** entrance level, 78% of applicants were admitted
- **22:1** student-to-undergraduate faculty ratio
- **39.18% graduate** in 6 years or less
- **$1988 tuition** and fees (in-state); $7172 (out-of-state)
- **$5718 average financial aid** package, $8530 average indebtedness upon graduation, $19.2 million endowment

Part of Texas State University System.

Students *Undergraduates:* 8,614 full-time, 2,211 part-time. Students come from 38 states and territories, 24 other countries. *The most frequently chosen baccalaureate fields are:* business/marketing, education, protective services/public administration. *Graduate:* 1,390 in graduate degree programs.

From out-of-state	1%	Reside on campus	25%
Age 25 or older	19%	Transferred in	13%
International students	0.4%	African Americans	14%
Asian Americans/Pacific Islanders	1%	Hispanic Americans	8%
Native Americans	1%		

Faculty 520 (72% full-time), 68% with terminal degrees.

Expenses (1999–2000) *Tuition, state resident:* full-time $912; part-time $38 per semester hour. *Tuition, nonresident:* full-time $6096; part-time $254 per semester hour. *Required fees:* full-time $1076; $54 per semester hour; $97 per term part-time. Full-time tuition and fees vary according to course load. Part-time tuition and fees vary according to course load. *College room and board:* $3390; room only: $1750. Room and board charges vary according to board plan and housing facility. *Payment plan:* installment.

Library Newton Gresham Library. *Operations spending 1999–2000:* $2.5 million. *Collection:* 1.8 million titles, 3,297 serial subscriptions, 18,427 audiovisual materials.

College life *Housing:* on-campus residence required in freshman year. *Option:* coed. *Social organizations:* national fraternities, national sororities, local fraternities, local sororities; 9% of eligible men and 8% of eligible women are members. *Most popular organizations:* Residence Hall Association, Inter-Fraternal Council, Pan-Hellenic Council, NAACP, Baptist student ministry.

Campus security 24-hour emergency response devices and patrols, student patrols, late-night transport-escort service.

After graduation 413 organizations recruited on campus 1997–98. *Career center:* 5 full-time, 10 part-time personnel. Services include job fairs, resume preparation, resume referral, career counseling, careers library, job interviews.

Freshmen 4,171 applied, 3,253 admitted, 1,608 enrolled.

SAT verbal scores above 500	42%	SAT math scores above 500	37%
ACT above 18	74%	From top 10% of their h.s. class	9%
From top quarter	34%	From top half	82%
1998 freshmen returning in 1999	63%		

Application *Options:* Common Application, early admission. *Application fee:* $20. *Required:* high school transcript.

Standardized tests *Admission: Required for some:* SAT I or ACT.

Significant dates *Application deadlines:* rolling (freshmen), rolling (transfers). *Financial aid deadline priority date:* 3/31.

Freshman Application Contact
Ms. Joey Chandler, Director of Admissions and Recruitment, Sam Houston State University, PO Box 2418, Huntsville, TX 77341. **Phone:** 409-294-1828.

Visit CollegeQuest.com for information on majors offered and athletics. College video available at CollegeQuest.com.

SCHREINER COLLEGE
Kerrville, Texas

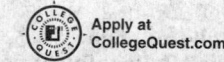
Apply at CollegeQuest.com

- **Independent Presbyterian**, comprehensive, founded 1923
- **Degrees** associate, bachelor's, and master's
- **Small-town** 175-acre campus with easy access to San Antonio and Austin
- **Coed**, 762 undergraduate students, 85% full-time, 60% women, 40% men
- **Moderately difficult** entrance level, 72% of applicants were admitted
- **17:1** student-to-undergraduate faculty ratio
- **30.3% graduate** in 6 years or less
- **$11,740 tuition** and fees
- **$10,720 average financial aid** package, $9476 average indebtedness upon graduation, $9.5 million endowment

Students *Undergraduates:* 649 full-time, 113 part-time. Students come from 21 states and territories. *The most frequently chosen baccalaureate fields are:* business/marketing, English, parks and recreation. *Graduate:* 41 in graduate degree programs.

Texas

From out-of-state	3%	Reside on campus	57%
Age 25 or older	23%	Transferred in	10%
International students	1%	African Americans	3%
Asian Americans/Pacific Islanders	1%	Hispanic Americans	14%
Native Americans	1%		

Faculty 68 (59% full-time), 54% with terminal degrees.
Expenses (2000–2001) *Comprehensive fee:* $18,260 includes full-time tuition ($11,540), mandatory fees ($200), and room and board ($6520). *College room only:* $3340. Room and board charges vary according to board plan and housing facility. *Part-time tuition:* $492 per credit hour. *Payment plan:* installment. *Waivers:* employees or children of employees.
Library W. M. Logan Library. *Operations spending 1999–2000:* $255,707. *Collection:* 73,335 titles, 702 serial subscriptions, 613 audiovisual materials.
College life *Housing:* on-campus residence required through junior year. *Option:* coed. *Most popular organizations:* student senate, Back on Campus Again (nontraditional student organization), Campus Ministry, International Club, Best Buddies.
Campus security 18-hour patrols by trained security personnel.
After graduation 4 organizations recruited on campus 1997–98. 85% of class of 1998 had job offers within 6 months. *Career center:* 1 full-time, 2 part-time personnel. Services include job fairs, resume preparation, interview workshops, resume referral, career/interest testing, career counseling, careers library, job bank, job interviews. *Graduate education:* 9% of class of 1999 went directly to graduate and professional school: 5% graduate arts and sciences, 1% business, 1% law.
Freshmen 530 applied, 383 admitted, 230 enrolled. 5 valedictorians.

SAT verbal scores above 500	48%	SAT math scores above 500	48%
ACT above 18	84%	From top 10% of their h.s. class	22%
From top quarter	45%	From top half	75%
1998 freshmen returning in 1999	70%		

Application *Options:* eApply at www.CollegeQuest.com, Common Application. *Application fee:* $20. *Required:* high school transcript. *Required for some:* essay or personal statement; 1 letter of recommendation. *Recommended:* essay or personal statement; minimum 2.0 GPA; interview.
Standardized tests *Admission: Required:* SAT I or ACT.
Significant dates *Application deadlines:* 8/1 (freshmen), 8/15 (transfers). *Financial aid deadline priority date:* 4/15.
Freshman Application Contact
Mr. Todd Brown, Dean of Admission and Financial Aid, Schreiner College, 2100 Memorial Boulevard, Kerrville, TX 78028-5697. **Phone:** 830-792-7217. **Toll-free phone:** 800-343-4919. **Fax:** 830-792-7226. **E-mail:** admissions@schreiner.edu
Visit CollegeQuest.com for information on majors offered and athletics.

■ *See page 2462 for a narrative description.*

SOUTHERN METHODIST UNIVERSITY
Dallas, Texas

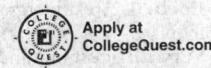 Apply at CollegeQuest.com

- **Independent**, university, founded 1911, affiliated with United Methodist Church
- **Degrees** bachelor's, master's, doctoral, first professional, and postbachelor's certificates
- **Suburban** 163-acre campus
- **Coed**, 5,426 undergraduate students, 96% full-time, 53% women, 47% men
- **Moderately difficult** entrance level, 89% of applicants were admitted
- **11:1 student-to-undergraduate faculty ratio**
- **70% graduate** in 6 years or less
- **$18,510 tuition** and fees
- **$19,298 average financial aid** package, $790.1 million endowment

Students *Undergraduates:* 5,190 full-time, 236 part-time. Students come from 48 states and territories, 54 other countries. *The most frequently chosen baccalaureate fields are:* business/marketing, communications/communication technologies, social sciences and history. *Graduate:* 1,123 in professional programs, 3,686 in other graduate degree programs.

From out-of-state	35%	Reside on campus	48%
Age 25 or older	5%	Transferred in	5%
International students	3%	African Americans	7%
Asian Americans/Pacific Islanders	6%	Hispanic Americans	9%
Native Americans	1%		

Faculty 697 (74% full-time).
Expenses (1999–2000) *Comprehensive fee:* $25,411 includes full-time tuition ($16,422), mandatory fees ($2088), and room and board ($6901). Room and board charges vary according to board plan and housing facility. *Part-time tuition:* $686 per credit hour. *Part-time fees:* $88 per credit hour. Part-time tuition and fees vary according to class time and course load. *Payment plans:* tuition prepayment, installment. *Waivers:* employees or children of employees.
Library Central University Library plus 7 others. *Operations spending 1999–2000:* $7.5 million. *Collection:* 3.1 million titles, 11,216 serial subscriptions.
College life *Housing:* on-campus residence required in freshman year. *Options:* coed, disabled students. *Social organizations:* national fraternities, national sororities; 36% of eligible men and 37% of eligible women are members. *Most popular organizations:* Program Council, student senate, student foundation, Residence Hall Association, United Methodist Campus Ministries.
Campus security 24-hour emergency response devices and patrols, late-night transport-escort service, controlled dormitory access.
After graduation 210 organizations recruited on campus 1997–98. 80% of class of 1998 had job offers within 6 months. *Career center:* 6 full-time, 1 part-time personnel. Services include job fairs, resume preparation, interview workshops, resume referral, career/interest testing, career counseling, careers library, job bank, job interviews. *Graduate education:* 16% of class of 1999 went directly to graduate and professional school: 5% graduate arts and sciences, 4% engineering, 3% law, 3% medicine, 1% business, 1% education. *Major awards:* 4 Fulbright Scholars.
Freshmen 4,280 applied, 3,809 admitted, 1,331 enrolled. 16 National Merit Scholars.

Average high school GPA	3.19	SAT verbal scores above 500	82%
SAT math scores above 500	84%	ACT above 18	97%
From top 10% of their h.s. class	31%	From top quarter	61%
From top half	87%	1998 freshmen returning in 1999	84%

Application *Options:* eApply at www.CollegeQuest.com, Common Application, early admission, early action, deferred entrance. *Application fee:* $40. *Required:* essay or personal statement; high school transcript; 1 letter of recommendation.
Standardized tests *Admission: Required:* SAT I or ACT. *Required for some:* SAT II Subject Tests.
Significant dates *Application deadlines:* 4/1 (freshmen), 7/1 (transfers). *Early action:* 11/1. *Notification:* 12/30 (early action). **Financial aid deadline priority date:** 2/1.
Freshman Application Contact
Mr. Ron W. Moss, Director of Admission and Enrollment Management, Southern Methodist University, PO Box 750296, Dallas, TX 75275. **Phone:** 214-768-2058. **Toll-free phone:** 800-323-0672. **E-mail:** ugadmission@smu.edu
Visit CollegeQuest.com for information on majors offered and athletics. College video and electronic viewbook available at CollegeQuest.com.

■ *See page 2512 for a narrative description.*

SOUTHWESTERN ADVENTIST UNIVERSITY
Keene, Texas

- **Independent Seventh-day Adventist**, comprehensive, founded 1894
- **Degrees** associate, bachelor's, and master's
- **Rural** 150-acre campus with easy access to Dallas–Fort Worth
- **Coed**, 1,119 undergraduate students, 75% full-time, 58% women, 42% men
- **Minimally difficult** entrance level, 92% of applicants were admitted
- **18:1 student-to-undergraduate faculty ratio**
- **23% graduate** in 6 years or less
- **$9062 tuition** and fees
- **$8694 average financial aid** package, $17,375 average indebtedness upon graduation, $34.1 million endowment

Texas

Southwestern Adventist University (continued)

Students *Undergraduates:* 835 full-time, 284 part-time. Students come from 45 states and territories, 45 other countries. *The most frequently chosen baccalaureate fields are:* business/marketing, education, philosophy. *Graduate:* 30 in graduate degree programs.

From out-of-state	38%	Reside on campus	31%
Age 25 or older	35%	Transferred in	24%
International students	9%	African Americans	15%
Asian Americans/Pacific Islanders	4%	Hispanic Americans	15%
Native Americans	1%		

Faculty 93 (52% full-time), 46% with terminal degrees.

Expenses (1999–2000) *Comprehensive fee:* $13,396 includes full-time tuition ($8962), mandatory fees ($100), and room and board ($4334). Room and board charges vary according to board plan. *Part-time tuition:* $374 per semester hour. Part-time tuition and fees vary according to course load. *Payment plan:* installment. *Waivers:* employees or children of employees.

Library Chan Shun Centennial Library. *Operations spending 1999–2000:* $404,932. *Collection:* 108,481 titles, 457 serial subscriptions.

College life *Housing:* on-campus residence required in freshman year. *Options:* men-only, women-only, cooperative. *Most popular organizations:* student association, BOSS, education/psychology club, theology club, nursing club.

Campus security 24-hour emergency response devices, student patrols.

After graduation 9 organizations recruited on campus 1997–98. *Career center:* 2 full-time personnel. Services include resume preparation, resume referral, career counseling, careers library, job bank.

Freshmen 422 applied, 389 admitted, 197 enrolled. 2 National Merit Scholars, 6 class presidents, 9 valedictorians, 33 student government officers.

Average high school GPA	3.2	SAT verbal scores above 500	46%
SAT math scores above 500	33%	ACT above 18	77%
From top 10% of their h.s. class	12%	From top quarter	32%
From top half	55%	1998 freshmen returning in 1999	68%

Application *Option:* deferred entrance. *Application fee:* $0. *Required:* high school transcript; minimum 2.0 GPA. *Required for some:* essay or personal statement; 1 letter of recommendation; interview.

Standardized tests *Admission: Required:* SAT I or ACT.

Significant dates *Application deadlines:* 8/31 (freshmen), 8/31 (transfers). *Notification:* 9/1 (freshmen). *Financial aid deadline priority date:* 3/15.

Freshman Application Contact
Mrs. Danna Burt, Admissions Counselor, Southwestern Adventist University, PO Box 567, Keene, TX 76059. **Phone:** 817-645-3921. **Toll-free phone:** 800-433-2240. **Fax:** 817-556-4744. **E-mail:** burtd@swau.edu

Visit CollegeQuest.com for information on majors offered and athletics. College video available at CollegeQuest.com.

SOUTHWESTERN ASSEMBLIES OF GOD UNIVERSITY
Waxahachie, Texas

- **Independent**, comprehensive, founded 1927, affiliated with Assemblies of God
- **Degrees** associate, bachelor's, and master's
- **Small-town** 70-acre campus with easy access to Dallas
- **Coed**
- **Noncompetitive** entrance level
- **$5858 tuition** and fees
- **$5156 average financial aid** package, $13,321 average indebtedness upon graduation, $853,777 endowment

Students *Undergraduates:* Students come from 42 states and territories, 11 other countries.

From out-of-state	35%	Reside on campus	55%
Age 25 or older	24%		

Faculty 70 (59% full-time).

Expenses (1999–2000) *Comprehensive fee:* $9804 includes full-time tuition ($5320), mandatory fees ($538), and room and board ($3946). *Part-time tuition:* $190 per hour. *Part-time fees:* $30 per hour; $19 per term part-time. Part-time tuition and fees vary according to course load. *Payment plans:* guaranteed tuition, installment. *Waivers:* employees or children of employees.

Library P. C. Nelson Memorial Library plus 1 other. *Operations spending 1999–2000:* $110,773. *Collection:* 110,000 titles, 600 serial subscriptions.

College life *Housing:* on-campus residence required through senior year. *Option:* coed. *Most popular organizations:* Gold Jackets/Blazers, intramurals, Mission Association, Student Congress, SOCS.

Campus security Student patrols, late-night transport-escort service.

After graduation *Career center:* 1 full-time personnel. Services include job fairs, resume preparation, resume referral, career counseling, job bank, job interviews.

Freshmen

Average high school GPA	2.8	SAT verbal scores above 500	56%
SAT math scores above 500	48%	ACT above 18	70%
From top 10% of their h.s. class	9%	From top quarter	19%
From top half	40%	1998 freshmen returning in 1999	61%

Application *Options:* early admission, deferred entrance. *Application fee:* $35. *Required:* essay or personal statement; high school transcript; 2 letters of recommendation; medical history, evidence of approved Christian character.

Standardized tests *Admission: Required:* SAT I or ACT.

Significant dates *Application deadlines:* rolling (freshmen), rolling (transfers). *Financial aid deadline:* 7/1. *Priority date:* 3/1.

Freshman Application Contact
Ms. Becky McDonald, Admissions Counselor, Southwestern Assemblies of God University, 1200 Sycamore Street, Waxahachie, TX 75165-2397. **Phone:** 972-937-4010 Ext. 1121. **Toll-free phone:** 800-262-SAGU.

Visit CollegeQuest.com for information on majors offered and athletics. College video available at CollegeQuest.com.

SOUTHWESTERN CHRISTIAN COLLEGE
Terrell, Texas

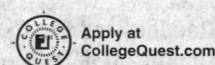
Apply at CollegeQuest.com

Admissions Office Contact
Southwestern Christian College, Box 10, Terrell, TX 75160-0010.

SOUTHWESTERN UNIVERSITY
Georgetown, Texas

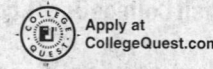
Apply at CollegeQuest.com

- **Independent Methodist**, 4-year, founded 1840
- **Degree** bachelor's
- **Suburban** 500-acre campus with easy access to Austin
- **Coed**, 1,256 undergraduate students, 98% full-time, 58% women, 42% men
- **Very difficult** entrance level, 67% of applicants were admitted
- **11:1 student-to-undergraduate faculty ratio**
- **69% graduate** in 6 years or less
- **$15,750 tuition** and fees
- **$14,024 average financial aid** package, $18,879 average indebtedness upon graduation, $336 million endowment

Students *Undergraduates:* 1,231 full-time, 25 part-time. Students come from 35 states and territories. *The most frequently chosen baccalaureate fields are:* biological/life sciences, business/marketing, social sciences and history.

From out-of-state	10%	Reside on campus	82%
Age 25 or older	2%	Transferred in	2%
International students	1%	African Americans	3%
Asian Americans/Pacific Islanders	3%	Hispanic Americans	9%
Native Americans	0.2%		

Faculty 152 (66% full-time), 62% with terminal degrees.

Expenses (2000–2001) *Comprehensive fee:* $22,070 includes full-time tuition ($15,750) and room and board ($6320). *College room only:* $3090. Room and board charges vary according to board plan, housing facility, and student level. *Part-time tuition:* $650 per semester hour. *Payment plans:* tuition prepayment, installment, deferred payment. *Waivers:* employees or children of employees.

Texas

Library A. Frank Smith Jr. Library Center. *Operations spending 1999–2000:* $1.8 million. *Collection:* 288,010 titles, 1,404 serial subscriptions, 9,122 audiovisual materials.

College life *Housing:* on-campus residence required in freshman year. *Options:* coed, men-only, women-only. *Social organizations:* national fraternities, national sororities; 31% of eligible men and 32% of eligible women are members. *Most popular organizations:* Alpha Phi Omega, International Club, Latinos Unidos.

Campus security 24-hour emergency response devices and patrols, student patrols, late-night transport-escort service, controlled dormitory access.

After graduation 23 organizations recruited on campus 1997–98. 63% of class of 1998 had job offers within 6 months. *Career center:* 2 full-time, 1 part-time personnel. Services include job fairs, resume preparation, interview workshops, resume referral, career/interest testing, career counseling, careers library, job bank, job interviews. *Graduate education:* 31% of class of 1999 went directly to graduate and professional school: 8% medicine, 7% graduate arts and sciences, 7% law, 4% business, 3% education, 1% dentistry, 1% engineering.

Freshmen 1,495 applied, 995 admitted, 354 enrolled. 10 National Merit Scholars, 73 class presidents, 21 valedictorians, 241 student government officers.

Average high school GPA	3.5	SAT verbal scores above 500	96%
SAT math scores above 500	97%	ACT above 18	100%
From top 10% of their h.s. class	58%	From top quarter	89%
From top half	99%	1998 freshmen returning in 1999	88%

Application *Options:* eApply at www.CollegeQuest.com, Common Application, electronic application, early admission, early decision, deferred entrance. *Application fee:* $40. *Required:* essay or personal statement; high school transcript; 1 letter of recommendation. *Required for some:* interview. *Recommended:* interview.

Standardized tests *Admission: Required:* SAT I or ACT.

Significant dates *Application deadlines:* 2/15 (freshmen), 6/1 (transfers). *Early decision:* 11/1 (for plan 1), 1/1 (for plan 2). *Notification:* 3/31 (freshmen), 12/1 (early decision plan 1), 2/1 (early decision plan 2). *Financial aid deadline priority date:* 3/1.

Freshman Application Contact
Mr. John W. Lind, Vice President for Enrollment Management, Southwestern University, 1001 East University Avenue, Georgetown, TX 78626. **Phone:** 512-863-1200. **Toll-free phone:** 800-252-3166. **Fax:** 512-863-6511. **E-mail:** admission@southwestern.edu

Visit CollegeQuest.com for information on majors offered and athletics.

SOUTHWEST TEXAS STATE UNIVERSITY
San Marcos, Texas

- **State-supported**, comprehensive, founded 1899
- **Degrees** bachelor's, master's, and doctoral
- **Small-town** 423-acre campus with easy access to San Antonio and Austin
- **Coed**, 18,856 undergraduate students, 81% full-time, 55% women, 45% men
- **Moderately difficult** entrance level, 65% of applicants were admitted
- **22:1 student-to-undergraduate faculty ratio**
- **37% graduate** in 6 years or less
- **$2756 tuition** and fees (in-state); $7940 (out-of-state)
- **$6217 average financial aid** package, $13,511 average indebtedness upon graduation, $26.5 million endowment

Part of Texas State University System.

Students *Undergraduates:* 15,187 full-time, 3,669 part-time. Students come from 49 states and territories, 48 other countries. *The most frequently chosen baccalaureate fields are:* business/marketing, interdisciplinary studies, social sciences and history. *Graduate:* 2,913 in graduate degree programs.

From out-of-state	1%	Reside on campus	25%
Age 25 or older	20%	Transferred in	13%
International students	1%	African Americans	5%
Asian Americans/Pacific Islanders	2%	Hispanic Americans	19%
Native Americans	1%		

Faculty 992 (64% full-time), 58% with terminal degrees.

Expenses (2000–2001, estimated) *Tuition, state resident:* full-time $960; part-time $40 per semester hour. *Tuition, nonresident:* full-time $6144; part-time $256 per semester hour. *Required fees:* full-time $1796; $62 per semester hour; $159 per term part-time. Full-time tuition and fees vary according to course load. Part-time tuition and fees vary according to course load. *College room and board:* $4583; room only: $2818. Room and board charges vary according to board plan and housing facility. *Payment plan:* installment. *Waivers:* employees or children of employees.

Library Alkek Library. *Operations spending 1999–2000:* $3.8 million. *Collection:* 667,840 titles, 5,495 serial subscriptions, 188,245 audiovisual materials.

College life *Housing:* on-campus residence required through sophomore year. *Options:* coed, men-only, women-only. *Social organizations:* national fraternities, national sororities, local sororities; 7% of eligible men and 6% of eligible women are members. *Most popular organizations:* Non-traditional Students Association (NTSO), Panhellenic Council (PC), Student Association for Campus Activities (SACA), Association Student Government (ASG), Interfraternity Council (IFC).

Campus security 24-hour emergency response devices and patrols, late-night transport-escort service, controlled dormitory access.

After graduation 995 organizations recruited on campus 1997–98. 95% of class of 1998 had job offers within 6 months. *Career center:* 11 full-time personnel. Services include job fairs, resume preparation, interview workshops, resume referral, career/interest testing, career counseling, careers library, job bank, job interviews.

Freshmen 7,294 applied, 4,747 admitted, 2,568 enrolled. 19 valedictorians.

Average high school GPA	3.53	SAT verbal scores above 500	59%
SAT math scores above 500	59%	ACT above 18	90%
From top 10% of their h.s. class	16%	From top quarter	51%
From top half	94%	1998 freshmen returning in 1999	70%

Application *Options:* early admission, deferred entrance. *Application fee:* $25. *Required:* essay or personal statement; high school transcript. *Required for some:* minimum 2.0 GPA; interview.

Standardized tests *Admission: Required:* SAT I or ACT.

Significant dates *Application deadlines:* 7/1 (freshmen), 7/1 (transfers). *Financial aid deadline priority date:* 4/1.

Freshman Application Contact
Mr. Scott Smiley, Acting Director of Admissions, Southwest Texas State University, Admissions and Visitors Center, San Marcos, TX 78666. **Phone:** 512-245-2364 Ext. 2803. **Fax:** 512-245-8044. **E-mail:** admissions@swt.edu

Visit CollegeQuest.com for information on majors offered and athletics.

■ *See page 2522 for a narrative description.*

STEPHEN F. AUSTIN STATE UNIVERSITY
Nacogdoches, Texas

- **State-supported**, comprehensive, founded 1923
- **Degrees** bachelor's, master's, and doctoral
- **Small-town** 400-acre campus
- **Coed**, 10,508 undergraduate students, 88% full-time, 57% women, 43% men
- **Moderately difficult** entrance level, 68% of applicants were admitted
- **19:1 student-to-undergraduate faculty ratio**
- **37.1% graduate** in 6 years or less
- **$2578 tuition** and fees (in-state); $9058 (out-of-state)

Students *Undergraduates:* 9,267 full-time, 1,241 part-time. Students come from 32 states and territories, 44 other countries. *The most frequently chosen baccalaureate fields are:* business/marketing, health professions and related sciences, interdisciplinary studies. *Graduate:* 1,411 in graduate degree programs.

From out-of-state	1%	Reside on campus	34%
Age 25 or older	14%	Transferred in	9%
International students	0.2%	African Americans	12%
Asian Americans/Pacific Islanders	1%	Hispanic Americans	5%
Native Americans	0.5%		

Faculty 657 (66% full-time), 55% with terminal degrees.

Expenses (1999–2000) *Tuition, state resident:* full-time $1860; part-time $62 per semester hour. *Tuition, nonresident:* full-time $8340; part-time $278 per semester hour. *Required fees:* full-time $718; $21 per semester hour; $10 per term part-time. Full-time tuition and fees vary according to course load and reciprocity agreements. Part-time tuition and fees vary according to

Texas

Stephen F. Austin State University (continued)
course load and reciprocity agreements. *College room and board:* $4168. Room and board charges vary according to board plan and housing facility. *Payment plan:* installment.

Library Ralph W. Steen Library plus 1 other. *Collection:* 4,083 serial subscriptions, 48,902 audiovisual materials.

College life *Housing:* on-campus residence required through sophomore year. *Options:* coed, men-only, women-only. *Social organizations:* national fraternities, national sororities; 17% of eligible men and 10% of eligible women are members. *Most popular organizations:* Texas Student Education Association, American Marketing Association, Baptist Student Union.

Campus security 24-hour emergency response devices and patrols, student patrols, late-night transport-escort service, controlled dormitory access.

After graduation 180 organizations recruited on campus 1997–98. 85% of class of 1998 had job offers within 6 months. *Career center:* 5 full-time, 5 part-time personnel. Services include job fairs, resume preparation, resume referral, career/interest testing, career counseling, careers library, job bank, job interviews. *Graduate education:* 10% of class of 1999 went directly to graduate and professional school: 5% graduate arts and sciences, 1% business, 1% dentistry, 1% education, 1% law, 1% medicine.

Freshmen 8,432 applied, 5,756 admitted, 2,257 enrolled.

SAT verbal scores above 500	48%	SAT math scores above 500	47%
ACT above 18	81%	From top 10% of their h.s. class	14%
From top quarter	37%	From top half	79%
1998 freshmen returning in 1999	59%		

Application *Option:* early admission. *Application fee:* $0. *Required:* high school transcript.

Standardized tests *Admission: Required:* SAT I or ACT.

Significant dates *Application deadlines:* rolling (freshmen), rolling (transfers). *Financial aid deadline priority date:* 4/15.

Freshman Application Contact
Mr. Roger Bilow, Director of Admission, Stephen F. Austin State University, SFA Box 13051, Nacogdoches, TX 75962. **Phone:** 409-468-2504. **Toll-free phone:** 800-731-2902. **Fax:** 409-468-3849. **E-mail:** mbsmith@sfasu.edu

Visit CollegeQuest.com for information on majors offered and athletics.

SUL ROSS STATE UNIVERSITY
Alpine, Texas

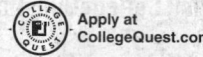
Apply at CollegeQuest.com

- **State-supported**, comprehensive, founded 1920
- **Degrees** associate, bachelor's, and master's
- **Small-town** 640-acre campus
- **Coed**, 1,459 undergraduate students, 78% full-time, 48% women, 52% men
- **Noncompetitive** entrance level, 99% of applicants were admitted
- **17:1 student-to-undergraduate faculty ratio**
- **20.86% graduate** in 6 years or less
- **$2150 tuition** and fees (in-state); $8630 (out-of-state)
- **$5.9 million endowment**

Part of Texas State University System.

Students *Undergraduates:* 1,132 full-time, 327 part-time. Students come from 12 states and territories, 2 other countries. *The most frequently chosen baccalaureate fields are:* agriculture, business/marketing, education. *Graduate:* 660 in graduate degree programs.

From out-of-state	2%	Age 25 or older	24%
Transferred in	8%	International students	0.5%
African Americans	4%	Asian Americans/Pacific Islanders	0.5%
Hispanic Americans	46%	Native Americans	1%

Faculty 113 (75% full-time), 69% with terminal degrees.

Expenses (1999–2000) *Tuition, state resident:* full-time $1140; part-time $38 per semester hour. *Tuition, nonresident:* full-time $7620; part-time $254 per semester hour. *Required fees:* full-time $1010; $41 per semester hour. Full-time tuition and fees vary according to course load. Part-time tuition and fees vary according to course load. *College room and board:* $3530; room only: $1690. Room and board charges vary according to board plan and housing facility. *Payment plan:* installment.

Library Bryan Wildenthal Memorial Library. *Operations spending 1999–2000:* $1.2 million. *Collection:* 262,466 titles.

College life *Housing:* on-campus residence required through sophomore year. *Option:* coed. *Most popular organizations:* Baptist Student Union, Wesley Center, rodeo club, Wildlife Society, MECHA.

Campus security 24-hour patrols, late-night transport-escort service.

After graduation 40 organizations recruited on campus 1997–98. *Career center:* 2 part-time personnel. Services include job fairs, resume preparation, interview workshops, resume referral, career/interest testing, career counseling, careers library, job bank, job interviews.

Freshmen 448 applied, 443 admitted, 268 enrolled.

SAT verbal scores above 500	19%	SAT math scores above 500	19%
ACT above 18	54%	From top 10% of their h.s. class	5%
From top quarter	21%	From top half	46%
1998 freshmen returning in 1999	49%		

Application *Options:* eApply at www.CollegeQuest.com; early admission, deferred entrance. *Application fee:* $0. *Required:* high school transcript. *Recommended:* interview.

Standardized tests *Admission: Required:* SAT I or ACT.

Significant dates *Application deadlines:* rolling (freshmen), rolling (transfers). *Financial aid deadline:* continuous.

Freshman Application Contact
Mr. Robert Cullins, Dean of Admissions and Records, Sul Ross State University, Box C-2, Alpine, TX 79832. **Phone:** 915-837-8052. **Fax:** 915-837-8046. **E-mail:** rcullins@sulross.edu

Visit CollegeQuest.com for information on majors offered and athletics.

TARLETON STATE UNIVERSITY
Stephenville, Texas

- **State-supported**, comprehensive, founded 1899
- **Degrees** bachelor's and master's
- **Small-town** 165-acre campus with easy access to Dallas–Fort Worth
- **Coed**
- **Moderately difficult** entrance level
- **$2638 tuition** and fees (in-state); $9550 (out-of-state)

Part of Texas A&M University System.

Expenses (1999–2000) *Tuition, state resident:* full-time $1984; part-time $66 per semester hour. *Tuition, nonresident:* full-time $8896; part-time $278 per semester hour. *Required fees:* full-time $654; $24 per semester hour; $16 per term part-time. Full-time tuition and fees vary according to course load. Part-time tuition and fees vary according to course load. *College room and board:* $3480; room only: $1800. Room and board charges vary according to board plan and housing facility.

Institutional Web site http://www.tarleton.edu/

College life *Housing:* on-campus residence required through sophomore year. *Option:* coed. *Social organizations:* national fraternities, national sororities; 7% of eligible men and 5% of eligible women are members. *Most popular organizations:* Student Government Association, Student Programming Association, Plowboys Association, Student Organizational Forum, Tarleton Association of Student Leaders.

Campus security 24-hour emergency response devices and patrols, late-night transport-escort service.

Application *Options:* early admission, deferred entrance. *Application fee:* $20. *Required:* high school transcript. *Required for some:* interview.

Standardized tests *Admission: Required:* SAT I or ACT.

Admissions Office Contact
Tarleton State University, Stephenville, TX 76402. **Toll-free phone:** 800-687-4878. **Fax:** 254-968-9389.

Visit CollegeQuest.com for information on athletics.

TEXAS A&M INTERNATIONAL UNIVERSITY
Laredo, Texas

- **State-supported**, comprehensive, founded 1969
- **Degrees** bachelor's and master's
- **Urban** 300-acre campus

Texas

- **Coed**, 2,241 undergraduate students, 62% full-time, 63% women, 37% men
- **Moderately difficult** entrance level, 93% of applicants were admitted
- **20:1 student-to-undergraduate faculty ratio**
- **$2579 tuition** and fees (in-state); $8905 (out-of-state)
- **$3932 average financial aid** package, $10,000 average indebtedness upon graduation, $3.7 million endowment

Part of Texas A&M University System.

Students *Undergraduates:* 1,389 full-time, 852 part-time. Students come from 25 states and territories, 8 other countries. *The most frequently chosen baccalaureate fields are:* business/marketing, English, liberal arts/general studies. *Graduate:* 968 in graduate degree programs.

From out-of-state	1%	Age 25 or older	20%
Transferred in	11%	International students	2%
African Americans	0.1%	Asian Americans/Pacific Islanders	0.3%
Hispanic Americans	92%	Native Americans	0.1%

Faculty 160, 84% with terminal degrees.

Expenses (2000–2001) *One-time required fee:* $10. *Tuition, state resident:* full-time $1984; part-time $62 per semester hour. *Tuition, nonresident:* full-time $8310; part-time $277 per semester hour. *Required fees:* full-time $595; $20 per semester hour; $34 per term part-time. Full-time tuition and fees vary according to course load. Part-time tuition and fees vary according to course load. *Payment plan:* installment. *Waivers:* senior citizens and employees or children of employees.

Library Sue and Radcliff Killam Library. *Operations spending 1999–2000:* $1.4 million. *Collection:* 128,845 titles, 1,728 serial subscriptions, 136 audiovisual materials.

College life *Most popular organizations:* TAMIU Ambassadors, Electronic Commerce Association, Rainbow Education Association of Laredo, Student Finance Society, psychology club.

Campus security 24-hour emergency response devices and patrols.

After graduation 5 organizations recruited on campus 1997–98. *Career center:* 3 full-time personnel. Services include job fairs, resume preparation, interview workshops, resume referral, career/interest testing, career counseling, careers library, job interviews.

Freshmen 446 applied, 414 admitted, 268 enrolled.

SAT verbal scores above 500	N/R	SAT math scores above 500	N/R
ACT above 18	N/R	From top 10% of their h.s. class	14%
From top quarter	38%	From top half	67%
1998 freshmen returning in 1999	57%		

Application *Options:* Common Application, electronic application, early admission, deferred entrance. *Application fee:* $0. *Required:* high school transcript.

Standardized tests *Admission: Required:* SAT I or ACT.

Significant dates *Application deadlines:* 7/1 (freshmen), 7/1 (transfers). *Notification:* 7/15 (freshmen). *Financial aid deadline priority date:* 3/15.

Freshman Application Contact
Ms. Veronica Gonzalez, Director of Enrollment Management and School Relations, Texas A&M International University, 5201 University Boulevard, Laredo, TX 78041-1900. **Phone:** 956-326-2270. **Fax:** 956-326-2348. **E-mail:** enroll@tamiu.edu

Visit CollegeQuest.com for information on majors offered and athletics.

TEXAS A&M UNIVERSITY
College Station, Texas

- **State-supported**, university, founded 1876
- **Degrees** bachelor's, master's, doctoral, first professional, and postbachelor's certificates
- **Suburban** 5,200-acre campus with easy access to Houston
- **Coed**, 36,045 undergraduate students, 94% full-time, 48% women, 52% men
- **Moderately difficult** entrance level, 74% of applicants were admitted
- **21:1 student-to-undergraduate faculty ratio**
- **71% graduate** in 6 years or less
- **$2639 tuition** and fees (in-state); $7823 (out-of-state)
- **$6959 average financial aid** package, $12,401 average indebtedness upon graduation, $3.6 billion endowment

Part of Texas A&M University System.

Students *Undergraduates:* 33,755 full-time, 2,290 part-time. Students come from 52 states and territories, 110 other countries. *The most frequently chosen baccalaureate fields are:* business/marketing, education, home economics/vocational home economics. *Graduate:* 499 in professional programs, 6,861 in other graduate degree programs.

From out-of-state	6%	Reside on campus	29%
Age 25 or older	4%	Transferred in	6%
International students	1%	African Americans	3%
Asian Americans/Pacific Islanders	3%	Hispanic Americans	9%
Native Americans	0.5%		

Faculty 2,143 (88% full-time), 87% with terminal degrees.

Expenses (1999–2000) *Tuition, state resident:* full-time $1824; part-time $76 per credit hour. *Tuition, nonresident:* full-time $7008; part-time $292 per credit hour. *Required fees:* full-time $815; $23 per credit hour; $132 per term part-time. Full-time tuition and fees vary according to course load, location, and program. *College room and board:* $4898; room only: $2970. Room and board charges vary according to board plan and housing facility. *Payment plan:* installment.

Library Sterling C. Evans Library plus 4 others. *Operations spending 1999–2000:* $9.5 million. *Collection:* 2.4 million titles, 26,625 serial subscriptions, 253,951 audiovisual materials.

College life *Housing: Options:* coed, men-only, women-only, disabled students. *Social organizations:* national fraternities, national sororities, local fraternities, local sororities; 6% of eligible men and 14% of eligible women are members. *Most popular organizations:* Memorial Student Center, Corps of Cadets, Greek organizations, Fish Camp, student government.

Campus security 24-hour emergency response devices and patrols, late-night transport-escort service, controlled dormitory access, student escorts.

After graduation 1,501 organizations recruited on campus 1997–98. 52% of class of 1998 had job offers within 6 months. *Career center:* 38 full-time, 7 part-time personnel. Services include job fairs, resume preparation, interview workshops, resume referral, career counseling, careers library, job bank, job interviews. *Graduate education:* 17% of class of 1999 went directly to graduate and professional school. *Major awards:* 1 Marshall, 1 Fulbright Scholar.

Freshmen 14,453 applied, 10,748 admitted, 6,695 enrolled. 149 National Merit Scholars.

SAT verbal scores above 500	86%	SAT math scores above 500	92%
ACT above 18	99%	From top 10% of their h.s. class	49%
From top quarter	82%	From top half	98%
1998 freshmen returning in 1999	88%		

Application *Application fee:* $50. *Required:* high school transcript.

Standardized tests *Admission: Required:* SAT I or ACT.

Significant dates *Application deadlines:* 2/15 (freshmen), 4/1 (transfers). *Financial aid deadline priority date:* 4/1.

Freshman Application Contact
Ms. Stephanie D. Hays, Associate Director of Admissions, Texas A&M University, 217 John J. Koldus Building, College Station, TX 77843-1265. **Phone:** 409-845-3741. **E-mail:** admissions@tamu.edu

Visit CollegeQuest.com for information on majors offered and athletics.

TEXAS A&M UNIVERSITY AT GALVESTON
Galveston, Texas

- **State-supported**, 4-year, founded 1962
- **Degree** bachelor's
- **Suburban** 100-acre campus with easy access to Houston
- **Coed**, 1,288 undergraduate students
- **Moderately difficult** entrance level, 89% of applicants were admitted
- **14:1 student-to-undergraduate faculty ratio**
- **43.5% graduate** in 6 years or less
- **$2855 tuition** and fees (in-state); $9335 (out-of-state)
- **$150,396 endowment**

Part of Texas A&M University System.

Students *Undergraduates:* Students come from 48 states and territories. *The most frequently chosen baccalaureate fields are:* biological/life sciences, business/marketing, interdisciplinary studies.

Peterson's Guide to Four-Year Colleges 2001   www.petersons.com   795

Texas

Texas A&M University at Galveston (continued)

From out-of-state	23%	Reside on campus	54%
Age 25 or older	11%	International students	1%
African Americans	1%	Asian Americans/Pacific Islanders	2%
Hispanic Americans	8%	Native Americans	1%

Faculty 123, 88% with terminal degrees.

Expenses (1999–2000) *Tuition, state resident:* full-time $1140; part-time $38 per credit hour. *Tuition, nonresident:* full-time $7620; part-time $254 per credit hour. *Required fees:* full-time $1715; $56 per credit hour; $42 per term part-time. Part-time tuition and fees vary according to program. *College room and board:* $3977; room only: $1780. Room and board charges vary according to board plan. *Payment plan:* installment.

Library Jack K. Williams Library. *Operations spending 1999–2000:* $607,007. *Collection:* 61,436 titles.

College life *Housing:* on-campus residence required through sophomore year. *Options:* coed, men-only, women-only, disabled students. *Most popular organizations:* sail club, caving club, dive club, rowing club, drill team.

Campus security 24-hour emergency response devices and patrols.

After graduation 180 organizations recruited on campus 1997–98. 78% of class of 1998 had job offers within 6 months. *Career center:* 1 full-time, 1 part-time personnel. Services include job fairs, resume preparation, resume referral, career counseling, careers library, job bank, job interviews. *Graduate education:* 35% of class of 1999 went directly to graduate and professional school: 35% graduate arts and sciences.

Freshmen 779 applied, 692 admitted. 3 National Merit Scholars, 9 valedictorians.

SAT verbal scores above 500	70%	SAT math scores above 500	74%
ACT above 18	98%	From top 10% of their h.s. class	17%
From top quarter	53%	From top half	82%
1998 freshmen returning in 1999	68%		

Application *Options:* electronic application, early admission, deferred entrance. *Application fee:* $35. *Required:* high school transcript. *Required for some:* interview. *Recommended:* essay or personal statement; letters of recommendation.

Standardized tests *Admission: Required:* SAT I or ACT, TASP. *Recommended:* SAT II Subject Tests, SAT II: Writing Test.

Significant dates *Application deadlines:* rolling (freshmen), rolling (transfers). *Financial aid deadline priority date:* 4/1.

Freshman Application Contact
Ms. Cheryl Moon, Director of Admissions, Texas A&M University at Galveston, PO Box 1675, Galveston, TX 77553-1675. **Phone:** 409-740-4415. **Toll-free phone:** 800-850-6376. **Fax:** 409-740-4709. **E-mail:** seaaggie@tamug.tamu.edu

Visit CollegeQuest.com for information on majors offered and athletics. College video available at CollegeQuest.com.

■ *See page 2604 for a narrative description.*

TEXAS A&M UNIVERSITY—COMMERCE
Commerce, Texas

- **State-supported**, university, founded 1889
- **Degrees** bachelor's, master's, and doctoral
- **Small-town** 140-acre campus with easy access to Dallas–Fort Worth
- **Coed**, 4,574 undergraduate students, 76% full-time, 56% women, 44% men
- **Moderately difficult** entrance level, 67% of applicants were admitted
- **$2526 tuition** and fees (in-state); $9006 (out-of-state)
- **$4.2 million endowment**

Part of Texas A&M University System.

Students *Undergraduates:* 3,491 full-time, 1,083 part-time. Students come from 29 states and territories, 25 other countries. *The most frequently chosen baccalaureate fields are:* business/marketing, interdisciplinary studies, protective services/public administration. *Graduate:* 3,334 in graduate degree programs.

From out-of-state	3%	Reside on campus	24%
Age 25 or older	26%	Transferred in	11%
International students	1%	African Americans	14%
Asian Americans/Pacific Islanders	1%	Hispanic Americans	4%
Native Americans	1%		

Faculty 396 (60% full-time).

Expenses (1999–2000) *Tuition, state resident:* full-time $1980. *Tuition, nonresident:* full-time $8460. *Required fees:* full-time $546. Full-time tuition and fees vary according to course load. Part-time tuition and fees vary according to course load. *College room and board:* $4055; room only: $2125. Room and board charges vary according to board plan and housing facility. *Payment plan:* installment. *Waivers:* senior citizens.

Library Gee Library. *Operations spending 1999–2000:* $1.2 million. *Collection:* 1.2 million titles, 1,817 serial subscriptions, 24,494 audiovisual materials.

College life *Housing:* on-campus residence required in freshman year. *Options:* coed, men-only, women-only, disabled students. *Social organizations:* national fraternities, national sororities; 15% of eligible men and 12% of eligible women are members.

Campus security 24-hour emergency response devices and patrols, controlled dormitory access.

After graduation 318 organizations recruited on campus 1997–98. *Career center:* 3 full-time, 3 part-time personnel. Services include job fairs, resume preparation, interview workshops, resume referral, career counseling, careers library, job bank, job interviews.

Freshmen 1,974 applied, 1,313 admitted, 481 enrolled.

Average high school GPA	3.23	SAT verbal scores above 500	47%
SAT math scores above 500	51%	ACT above 18	87%
From top 10% of their h.s. class	15%	From top quarter	38%
From top half	68%	1998 freshmen returning in 1999	69%

Application *Options:* Common Application, early admission. *Application fee:* $0. *Required:* high school transcript.

Standardized tests *Admission: Required:* SAT I or ACT.

Significant dates *Application deadlines:* 8/6 (freshmen), rolling (transfers). *Financial aid deadline priority date:* 5/1.

Freshman Application Contact
Mr. Randy McDonald, Director of School Relations, Texas A&M University–Commerce, PO Box 3011, Commerce, TX 75429-3011. **Phone:** 903-886-5072. **Toll-free phone:** 800-331-3878. **Fax:** 903-886-5888. **E-mail:** sheri_humphries@tamu-commerce.edu

Visit CollegeQuest.com for information on majors offered and athletics.

TEXAS A&M UNIVERSITY—CORPUS CHRISTI
Corpus Christi, Texas

- **State-supported**, comprehensive, founded 1947
- **Degrees** bachelor's, master's, and doctoral
- **Suburban** 240-acre campus
- **Coed**
- **Moderately difficult** entrance level
- **$2138 tuition** and fees (in-state); $7322 (out-of-state)

Part of Texas A&M University System.

Expenses (1999–2000) *Tuition, state resident:* full-time $912; part-time $38 per semester hour. *Tuition, nonresident:* full-time $6096; part-time $254 per semester hour. *Required fees:* full-time $1226; $50 per semester hour; $55 per term part-time. Full-time tuition and fees vary according to course load. Part-time tuition and fees vary according to course load. *College room and board:* room only: $3141. Room and board charges vary according to housing facility.

Institutional Web site http://www.tamucc.edu/

College life *Housing: Option:* coed. *Social organizations:* national fraternities. *Most popular organizations:* Student Accounting Society, Student Art Association, science clubs.

Campus security 24-hour emergency response devices and patrols, late-night transport-escort service, security gate access with card after 10 p.m.

Application *Application fee:* $10. *Required:* high school transcript; minimum 2.0 GPA.

Standardized tests *Admission: Required:* SAT I or ACT.

Admissions Office Contact
Texas A&M University–Corpus Christi, 6300 Ocean Drive, Corpus Christi, TX 78412-5503. **Toll-free phone:** 800-482-6822. **Fax:** 361-825-5810. **E-mail:** jperales@tamucc.edu

Visit CollegeQuest.com for information on athletics. College video and electronic viewbook available at CollegeQuest.com.

TEXAS A&M UNIVERSITY–KINGSVILLE
Kingsville, Texas

- **State-supported**, university, founded 1925
- **Degrees** bachelor's, master's, and doctoral
- **Small-town** 255-acre campus
- **Coed**, 4,644 undergraduate students, 79% full-time, 47% women, 53% men
- **Moderately difficult** entrance level, 74% of applicants were admitted
- **15:1 student-to-undergraduate faculty ratio**
- **20.53% graduate** in 6 years or less
- **$2542 tuition** and fees (in-state); $8962 (out-of-state)

Part of Texas A&M University System.
Students *Undergraduates:* 3,672 full-time, 972 part-time. Students come from 37 states and territories, 58 other countries. *The most frequently chosen baccalaureate fields are:* engineering/engineering technologies, business/marketing, interdisciplinary studies. *Graduate:* 1,199 in graduate degree programs.

From out-of-state	2%	Reside on campus	25%
Age 25 or older	30%	Transferred in	6%
International students	2%	African Americans	6%
Asian Americans/Pacific Islanders	1%	Hispanic Americans	66%
Native Americans	0.4%		

Faculty 311 (98% full-time), 70% with terminal degrees.
Expenses (1999–2000) *Tuition, state resident:* full-time $1200; part-time $38 per credit. *Tuition, nonresident:* full-time $7620; part-time $254 per credit. *Required fees:* full-time $1342; $48 per credit; $41 per term part-time. Full-time tuition and fees vary according to course load. Part-time tuition and fees vary according to course load. *College room and board:* $3484. Room and board charges vary according to board plan. *Payment plan:* installment. *Waivers:* senior citizens and employees or children of employees.
Library James C. Jernigan Library. *Operations spending 1999–2000:* $1 million. *Collection:* 358,466 titles, 2,304 serial subscriptions, 3,229 audiovisual materials.
College life *Housing:* on-campus residence required through sophomore year. *Options:* coed, men-only, women-only, disabled students. *Social organizations:* national fraternities, national sororities, local sororities; 2% of eligible men and 2% of eligible women are members. *Most popular organizations:* Aggie Club, rodeo club, educational association, child development club, resident's hall club.
Campus security 24-hour emergency response devices and patrols, late-night transport-escort service.
After graduation 125 organizations recruited on campus 1997–98. *Career center:* 2 full-time, 5 part-time personnel. Services include job fairs, resume preparation, career counseling, careers library, job bank, job interviews.
Freshmen 1,716 applied, 1,263 admitted, 720 enrolled.

Average high school GPA	3.28	SAT verbal scores above 500	31%
SAT math scores above 500	35%	ACT above 18	58%
From top 10% of their h.s. class	12%	From top quarter	32%
From top half	63%	1998 freshmen returning in 1999	54%

Application *Options:* early admission, deferred entrance. *Application fee:* $15. *Required:* high school transcript. *Required for some:* interview. *Recommended:* minimum 2.0 GPA.
Standardized tests *Admission: Required:* SAT I or ACT.
Significant dates *Application deadlines:* rolling (freshmen), rolling (transfers). *Financial aid deadline priority date:* 4/15.
Freshman Application Contact
Mr. Ray Broglie, Director, School Relations, Texas A&M University–Kingsville, Campus Box 105, Kingsville, TX 78363. **Phone:** 512-593-2315. **Toll-free phone:** 800-687-6000.
Visit CollegeQuest.com for information on majors offered and athletics.

TEXAS A&M UNIVERSITY SYSTEM HEALTH SCIENCE CENTER
College Station, Texas

- **State-supported**, upper-level, founded 1999
- **Degrees** bachelor's, master's, and first professional
- **Coed**, 60 undergraduate students, 93% full-time, 97% women, 3% men
- **$3248 tuition** and fees (in-state); $11,168 (out-of-state)

Students *Undergraduates:* 56 full-time, 4 part-time. *The most frequently chosen baccalaureate field is:* health professions and related sciences. *Graduate:* 341 in professional programs, 100 in other graduate degree programs.

From out-of-state	1%	Age 25 or older	36%
African Americans	2%	Asian Americans/Pacific Islanders	7%
Hispanic Americans	8%	Native Americans	2%

Expenses (1999–2000) *One-time required fee:* 15. *Tuition, state resident:* full-time 1393. *Tuition, nonresident:* full-time 9313. *Required fees:* full-time 1855. Full-time tuition and fees vary according to course level, course load, and student level.
College life *Housing:* college housing not available.
Campus security 24-hour emergency response devices and patrols, late-night transport-escort service, electronically operated building access.
Application *Application fee:* 35.
Significant dates *Application deadline:* rolling (transfers).
Freshman Application Contact
Dr. Jack L. Long, Director of Admissions and Records, Texas A&M University System Health Science Center, PO Box 660677, Dallas, TX 75266-0677. **Phone:** 214-828-8230. **Fax:** 409-458-6477.
Visit CollegeQuest.com for information on majors offered and athletics.

TEXAS A&M UNIVERSITY–TEXARKANA
Texarkana, Texas

- **State-supported**, upper-level, founded 1971
- **Degrees** bachelor's and master's
- **Small-town** 1-acre campus
- **Coed**, 761 undergraduate students, 40% full-time, 67% women, 33% men
- **Noncompetitive** entrance level
- **17:1 student-to-undergraduate faculty ratio**
- **$1692 tuition** and fees (in-state); $6876 (out-of-state)

Part of Texas A&M University System.
Students *Undergraduates:* 304 full-time, 457 part-time. Students come from 4 states and territories. *The most frequently chosen baccalaureate fields are:* business/marketing, health professions and related sciences, liberal arts/general studies. *Graduate:* 371 in graduate degree programs.

Transferred in	20%	African Americans	11%
Asian Americans/Pacific Islanders	0.3%	Hispanic Americans	2%
Native Americans	1%		

Faculty 63 (49% full-time), 65% with terminal degrees.
Expenses (1999–2000) *Tuition, state resident:* full-time $1392; part-time $58 per semester hour. *Tuition, nonresident:* full-time $6576; part-time $274 per semester hour. *Required fees:* full-time $300; $12 per semester hour; $6 per term part-time. Part-time tuition and fees vary according to course load. *Payment plan:* installment. *Waivers:* senior citizens.
Library John F. Moss Library plus 1 other. *Operations spending 1999–2000:* $397,805. *Collection:* 174,305 titles, 2,037 serial subscriptions.
College life *Housing:* college housing not available. *Most popular organizations:* education club, psychology club, science club, Multi-cultural Association, reading club.
Campus security 24-hour patrols.
After graduation 65 organizations recruited on campus 1997–98. *Career center:* 1 full-time, 1 part-time personnel. Services include job fairs, resume preparation, resume referral, career/interest testing, career counseling, careers library, job interviews.
Application *Options:* Common Application, electronic application. *Application fee:* $0.
Standardized tests *Admission: Required:* TASP.

Texas

Texas A&M University–Texarkana (continued)
Significant dates *Application deadline:* rolling (transfers). *Financial aid deadline priority date:* 5/1.
Freshman Application Contact
Mrs. Patricia Black, Director of Admissions and Registrar, Texas A&M University–Texarkana, PO Box 5518, Texarkana, TX 75505-5518. **Phone:** 903-223-3068. **Fax:** 903-832-8890. **E-mail:** admissions@tamut.edu
Visit CollegeQuest.com for information on majors offered and athletics.

TEXAS CHIROPRACTIC COLLEGE
Pasadena, Texas

- **Independent**, upper-level, founded 1908
- **Degrees** incidental bachelor's and first professional
- **Suburban** 18-acre campus with easy access to Houston
- **Coed**
- **Moderately difficult** entrance level
- **$13,935 tuition** and fees

Expenses (1999–2000) *Tuition:* full-time $13,800. *Required fees:* full-time $135.
Institutional Web site http://www.txchiro.edu/
College life *Housing:* college housing not available. *Social organizations:* local fraternities, local women's organization; 20% of eligible men and 20% of eligible women are members.
Application *Option:* deferred entrance. *Application fee:* $50.
Admissions Office Contact
Texas Chiropractic College, 5912 Spencer Highway, Pasadena, TX 77505-1699. **Toll-free phone:** 800-468-6839.
Visit CollegeQuest.com for information on athletics.

TEXAS CHRISTIAN UNIVERSITY
Fort Worth, Texas

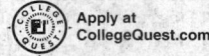

- **Independent**, university, founded 1873, affiliated with Christian Church (Disciples of Christ)
- **Degrees** bachelor's, master's, doctoral, and first professional
- **Suburban** 237-acre campus
- **Coed**, 6,267 undergraduate students, 93% full-time, 59% women, 41% men
- **Moderately difficult** entrance level, 75% of applicants were admitted
- **15:1 student-to-undergraduate faculty ratio**
- **63% graduate** in 6 years or less
- **$12,290 tuition** and fees
- **$12,006 average financial aid** package, $834.4 million endowment

TCU is about people. From National Merit Scholars to those just realizing their potential, TCU attracts and serves leaders and thinkers who will contribute to and succeed in society. Embracing values and celebrating differences, TCU offers 140 undergraduate and graduate programs in a challenging, friendly, affordable, private atmosphere.

Students *Undergraduates:* 5,843 full-time, 424 part-time. Students come from 49 states and territories, 75 other countries. *The most frequently chosen baccalaureate fields are:* business/marketing, communications/communication technologies, education. *Graduate:* 183 in professional programs, 912 in other graduate degree programs.

From out-of-state	25%	Reside on campus	50%
Age 25 or older	6%	Transferred in	6%
International students	4%	African Americans	4%
Asian Americans/Pacific Islanders	2%	Hispanic Americans	5%
Native Americans	1%		

Faculty 569 (65% full-time).
Expenses (1999–2000) *One-time required fee:* $200. *Comprehensive fee:* $16,260 includes full-time tuition ($10,950), mandatory fees ($1340), and room and board ($3970). *College room only:* $2770. Room and board charges vary according to board plan and housing facility. *Part-time tuition:* $365 per semester hour. *Part-time fees:* $55 per semester hour. *Payment plan:* installment. *Waivers:* employees or children of employees.
Library Mary Couts Burnett Library. *Collection:* 797,419 titles, 5,374 serial subscriptions, 54,700 audiovisual materials.
College life *Housing:* on-campus residence required in freshman year. *Options:* coed, men-only, women-only, disabled students. *Social organizations:* national fraternities, national sororities, local fraternities, local sororities, local coed music fraternities.
Campus security 24-hour emergency response devices and patrols, student patrols, late-night transport-escort service, controlled dormitory access, emergency call boxes, video camera surveillance in parking lots.
After graduation 247 organizations recruited on campus 1997–98. *Career center:* 5 full-time, 6 part-time personnel. Services include job fairs, resume preparation, interview workshops, resume referral, career/interest testing, career counseling, careers library, job bank, job interviews.
Freshmen 5,028 applied, 3,769 admitted, 1,424 enrolled.

Average high school GPA	3.0	SAT verbal scores above 500	N/R
SAT math scores above 500	N/R	ACT above 18	N/R
From top 10% of their h.s. class	33%	From top quarter	65%
From top half	96%	1998 freshmen returning in 1999	82%

Application *Options:* eApply at www.CollegeQuest.com, Common Application, electronic application, early admission, early action, deferred entrance. *Application fee:* $30. *Required:* essay or personal statement; high school transcript; minimum 2.0 GPA; 2 letters of recommendation. *Recommended:* minimum 3.0 GPA; interview.
Standardized tests *Admission: Required:* SAT I or ACT. *Recommended:* SAT II Subject Tests, SAT II: Writing Test.
Significant dates *Application deadlines:* 1/15 (freshmen), 6/15 (transfers). *Early action:* 11/15. *Notification:* 3/1 (freshmen), 1/1 (early action). *Financial aid deadline priority date:* 5/1.
Freshman Application Contact
Ms. Sandra J. Ware, Dean of Admissions, Texas Christian University, TCU Box 297013, Fort Worth, TX 76129-0002. **Phone:** 817-257-7490. **Toll-free phone:** 800-828-3764. **Fax:** 817-257-7333. **E-mail:** frogmail@tcu.edu
Visit CollegeQuest.com for information on majors offered and athletics. College video and electronic viewbook available at CollegeQuest.com.

■ *See page 2606 for a narrative description.*

TEXAS COLLEGE
Tyler, Texas

Admissions Office Contact
Texas College, 2404 North Grand Avenue, PO Box 4500, Tyler, TX 75712-4500.

TEXAS LUTHERAN UNIVERSITY
Seguin, Texas

- **Independent**, 4-year, founded 1891, affiliated with Evangelical Lutheran Church
- **Degree** bachelor's
- **Suburban** 196-acre campus with easy access to San Antonio
- **Coed**, 1,420 undergraduate students, 88% full-time, 51% women, 49% men
- **Moderately difficult** entrance level, 83% of applicants were admitted
- **20:1 student-to-undergraduate faculty ratio**
- **43.7% graduate** in 6 years or less
- **$11,444 tuition** and fees
- **$11,319 average financial aid** package, $18,519 average indebtedness upon graduation, $28.9 million endowment

TLU was named by *US News & World Report* as a best value among regional liberal arts colleges in the western US for the 4th consecutive year. TLU has been ranked among the 10 best regional liberal arts colleges in the West for 11 of the last 12 years. This recognition affirms the quality of education offered at Texas Lutheran.

Students *Undergraduates:* 1,243 full-time, 177 part-time. Students come from 27 states and territories, 15 other countries. *The most frequently chosen baccalaureate fields are:* business/marketing, biological/life sciences, education.

From out-of-state	5%	Reside on campus	70%
Age 25 or older	8%	Transferred in	8%
International students	3%	African Americans	6%
Asian Americans/Pacific Islanders	1%	Hispanic Americans	18%
Native Americans	1%		

Faculty 146 (46% full-time).

Expenses (1999–2000) *Comprehensive fee:* $15,810 includes full-time tuition ($11,374), mandatory fees ($70), and room and board ($4366). *College room only:* $1786. Room and board charges vary according to board plan and housing facility. *Part-time tuition:* $380 per credit hour. *Part-time fees:* $35 per term part-time. *Payment plan:* installment. *Waivers:* employees or children of employees.

Library Blumberg Memorial Library. *Operations spending 1999–2000:* $550,000. *Collection:* 144,248 titles, 717 serial subscriptions, 10,208 audiovisual materials.

College life *Housing:* on-campus residence required through senior year. *Options:* coed, men-only, women-only. *Social organizations:* local fraternities, local sororities; 19% of eligible men and 17% of eligible women are members. *Most popular organizations:* Campus Ministry, Amnesty International, Student Government Association.

Campus security 24-hour emergency response devices and patrols, late-night transport-escort service, controlled dormitory access.

After graduation *Career center:* 1 full-time, 1 part-time personnel. Services include job fairs, resume preparation, interview workshops, resume referral, career counseling, careers library, job bank, job interviews. *Major awards:* 1 Fulbright Scholar.

Freshmen 948 applied, 789 admitted, 386 enrolled. 3 valedictorians, 34 student government officers.

Average high school GPA	3.2	SAT verbal scores above 500	68%
SAT math scores above 500	60%	ACT above 18	N/R
From top 10% of their h.s. class	34%	From top quarter	64%
From top half	92%	1998 freshmen returning in 1999	67%

Application *Options:* eApply at www.CollegeQuest.com, Common Application, electronic application, deferred entrance. *Application fee:* $25. *Required:* essay or personal statement; high school transcript. *Required for some:* minimum 2.0 GPA; 2 letters of recommendation; interview.

Standardized tests *Admission: Required:* SAT I or ACT.

Significant dates *Application deadlines:* rolling (freshmen), rolling (transfers). *Notification:* continuous until 8/1 (freshmen). *Financial aid deadline priority date:* 4/1.

Freshman Application Contact
Mr. E. Norman Jones, Vice President for Enrollment Services, Texas Lutheran University, 1000 West Court Street, Seguin, TX 78155-5999. **Phone:** 830-372-8050. **Toll-free phone:** 800-771-8521. **Fax:** 830-372-8096. **E-mail:** admissions@txlutheran.edu

Visit CollegeQuest.com for information on majors offered and athletics.

■ *See page 2608 for a narrative description.*

TEXAS SOUTHERN UNIVERSITY
Houston, Texas

- **State-supported**, university, founded 1947
- **Degrees** bachelor's, master's, doctoral, and first professional
- **Urban** 147-acre campus
- **Coed**, 4,423 undergraduate students, 77% full-time, 55% women, 45% men
- **Noncompetitive** entrance level, 95% of applicants were admitted
- **$3964 tuition** and fees (in-state); $9148 (out-of-state)
- **$799 million endowment**

Part of Texas Higher Education Coordinating Board.

Students *Undergraduates:* 3,420 full-time, 1,003 part-time. Students come from 48 states and territories, 56 other countries. *The most frequently chosen baccalaureate fields are:* business/marketing, biological/life sciences, health professions and related sciences. *Graduate:* 1,150 in professional programs, 949 in other graduate degree programs.

From out-of-state	15%	Reside on campus	10%
Age 25 or older	43%	Transferred in	13%
International students	4%	African Americans	90%
Asian Americans/Pacific Islanders	2%	Hispanic Americans	2%
Native Americans	0.02%		

Faculty 385 (88% full-time).

Expenses (1999–2000) *Tuition, state resident:* full-time $1982; part-time $38 per semester hour. *Tuition, nonresident:* full-time $7166; part-time $254 per semester hour. *Required fees:* full-time $1982. Full-time tuition and fees vary according to course load and program. Part-time tuition and fees vary according to course load and program. *College room and board:* $4000; room only: $2092. *Payment plan:* installment. *Waivers:* minority students and senior citizens.

Library Robert J. Terry Library plus 2 others. *Operations spending 1999–2000:* $1.6 million. *Collection:* 473,499 titles, 1,597 serial subscriptions, 15,259 audiovisual materials.

College life *Housing:* on-campus residence required in freshman year. *Options:* men-only, women-only. *Social organizations:* national fraternities, national sororities, local fraternities, local sororities; 15% of eligible men and 20% of eligible women are members. *Most popular organizations:* debate team, University Program Council, Student Government Association.

Campus security 24-hour emergency response devices and patrols, student patrols.

After graduation 73 organizations recruited on campus 1997–98. *Career center:* 4 full-time, 3 part-time personnel. Services include job fairs, resume preparation, resume referral, career counseling, careers library, job bank, job interviews.

Freshmen 2,308 applied, 2,182 admitted, 807 enrolled.

SAT verbal scores above 500	N/R	SAT math scores above 500	N/R
ACT above 18	N/R	From top 10% of their h.s. class	10%
From top half	50%	1998 freshmen returning in 1999	48%

Application *Options:* Common Application, electronic application. *Application fee:* $25. *Required:* high school transcript.

Standardized tests *Placement: Required:* SAT I or ACT

Significant dates *Application deadlines:* 8/10 (freshmen), 8/10 (transfers). *Notification:* continuous until 8/28 (freshmen).

Freshman Application Contact
Ms. Georgia Cooley, Coordinator of Recruitment, Texas Southern University, 3100 Cleburne, Houston, TX 77004-4598. **Phone:** 713-313-7474. **Fax:** 713-527-7842.

Visit CollegeQuest.com for information on majors offered and athletics.

TEXAS TECH UNIVERSITY
Lubbock, Texas

- **State-supported**, university, founded 1923
- **Degrees** bachelor's, master's, doctoral, and first professional
- **Urban** 1,839-acre campus
- **Coed**, 20,227 undergraduate students, 89% full-time, 46% women, 54% men
- **Moderately difficult** entrance level, 75% of applicants were admitted
- **21:1 student-to-undergraduate faculty ratio**
- **48% graduate** in 6 years or less
- **$3107 tuition** and fees (in-state); $9587 (out-of-state)
- **$5322 average financial aid** package, $134.2 million endowment

Students *Undergraduates:* 18,035 full-time, 2,192 part-time. Students come from 54 states and territories, 84 other countries. *The most frequently chosen baccalaureate fields are:* business/marketing, engineering/engineering technologies, interdisciplinary studies. *Graduate:* 598 in professional programs, 3,424 in other graduate degree programs.

From out-of-state	5%	Reside on campus	25%
Age 25 or older	11%	Transferred in	8%
International students	1%	African Americans	3%
Asian Americans/Pacific Islanders	2%	Hispanic Americans	10%
Native Americans	0.4%		

Faculty 939 (89% full-time), 88% with terminal degrees.

Expenses (1999–2000) *Tuition, state resident:* full-time $1140; part-time $38 per credit hour. *Tuition, nonresident:* full-time $7620; part-time $254 per credit hour. *Required fees:* full-time $1967; $38 per credit hour. Full-time tuition and fees vary according to course load. Part-time tuition and fees vary

Texas

Texas Tech University (continued)

according to course load. *College room and board:* $4787; room only: $2633. Room and board charges vary according to board plan and housing facility. *Payment plan:* installment.

Library Texas Tech Library plus 3 others. *Operations spending 1999–2000:* $8.4 million. *Collection:* 2.1 million titles, 21,357 serial subscriptions, 79,471 audiovisual materials.

College life *Housing:* on-campus residence required in freshman year. *Options:* coed, men-only, women-only. *Social organizations:* national fraternities, national sororities, local fraternities, local sororities; 14% of eligible men and 19% of eligible women are members.

Campus security 24-hour emergency response devices and patrols, late-night transport-escort service, controlled dormitory access.

After graduation 811 organizations recruited on campus 1997–98. 83% of class of 1998 had job offers within 6 months. *Career center:* 10 full-time, 7 part-time personnel. Services include job fairs, resume preparation, interview workshops, resume referral, career counseling, careers library, job bank, job interviews, computerized career guidance program.

Freshmen 8,114 applied, 6,090 admitted, 3,536 enrolled. 13 National Merit Scholars, 79 valedictorians.

SAT verbal scores above 500	70%	SAT math scores above 500	74%
ACT above 18	96%	From top 10% of their h.s. class	23%
From top quarter	52%	From top half	85%
1998 freshmen returning in 1999	78%		

Application *Options:* electronic application, early admission, deferred entrance. *Application fee:* $25. *Required:* high school transcript; minimum 2.0 GPA.

Standardized tests *Admission: Required:* SAT I or ACT.

Significant dates *Application deadlines:* rolling (freshmen), rolling (transfers). *Financial aid deadline priority date:* 5/1.

Freshman Application Contact
Mrs. Marty Grassel, Director Admissions and School Relations, Texas Tech University, Box 45005, Lubbock, TX 79409-5005. **Phone:** 806-742-1482. **Fax:** 806-742-3055. **E-mail:** martyg@ttu.edu

Visit CollegeQuest.com for information on majors offered and athletics. College video and electronic viewbook available at CollegeQuest.com.

■ *See page 2610 for a narrative description.*

TEXAS WESLEYAN UNIVERSITY
Fort Worth, Texas

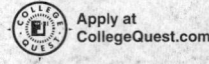 Apply at CollegeQuest.com

- **Independent United Methodist**, comprehensive, founded 1890
- **Degrees** bachelor's, master's, and first professional
- **Urban** 74-acre campus
- **Coed**, 1,758 undergraduate students, 74% full-time, 64% women, 36% men
- **Moderately difficult** entrance level, 84% of applicants were admitted
- **15:1 student-to-undergraduate faculty ratio**
- **$9250 tuition** and fees
- **$44.7 million endowment**

Students *Undergraduates:* 1,294 full-time, 464 part-time. Students come from 24 states and territories, 40 other countries. *The most frequently chosen baccalaureate fields are:* education, communications/communication technologies, psychology. *Graduate:* 575 in professional programs, 440 in other graduate degree programs.

From out-of-state	4%	Reside on campus	10%
Age 25 or older	31%	Transferred in	19%
International students	3%	African Americans	17%
Asian Americans/Pacific Islanders	3%	Hispanic Americans	16%
Native Americans	2%		

Faculty 238 (47% full-time).

Expenses (1999–2000) *Comprehensive fee:* $13,136 includes full-time tuition ($8500), mandatory fees ($750), and room and board ($3886). *College room only:* $1500. Full-time tuition and fees vary according to program. Room and board charges vary according to board plan and student level. *Part-time tuition:* $280 per credit hour. *Part-time fees:* $30 per credit hour. Part-time tuition and fees vary according to program. *Payment plans:* installment, deferred payment. *Waivers:* employees or children of employees.

Library Eunice and James L. West Library plus 1 other. *Operations spending 1999–2000:* $2.4 million. *Collection:* 180,192 titles, 5,804 audiovisual materials.

College life *Housing:* Options: coed, men-only, women-only. *Social organizations:* national fraternities, national sororities; 5% of eligible men and 5% of eligible women are members.

Campus security 24-hour emergency response devices and patrols, student patrols, late-night transport-escort service, controlled dormitory access.

After graduation *Career center:* 1 full-time, 1 part-time personnel. Services include job fairs, resume preparation, resume referral, career counseling, job bank, job interviews.

Freshmen 640 applied, 536 admitted, 281 enrolled.

Average high school GPA	3.54	SAT verbal scores above 500	49%
SAT math scores above 500	47%	ACT above 18	75%
From top 10% of their h.s. class	17%	From top quarter	44%
From top half	81%	1998 freshmen returning in 1999	58%

Application *Options:* eApply at www.CollegeQuest.com, Common Application, deferred entrance. *Application fee:* $25. *Required:* high school transcript; minimum 2.5 GPA. *Required for some:* interview. *Recommended:* essay or personal statement.

Standardized tests *Admission: Required:* SAT I or ACT.

Significant dates *Application deadlines:* rolling (freshmen), rolling (transfers). *Financial aid deadline:* continuous.

Freshman Application Contact
Ms. Stephanie Lewis-Boatner, Director of Freshman Admissions, Texas Wesleyan University, 1201 Wesleyan Street, Fort Worth, TX 76105-1536. **Phone:** 817-531-4422. **Toll-free phone:** 800-580-8980. **Fax:** 817-531-7515. **E-mail:** freshman@txwesleyan.edu

Visit CollegeQuest.com for information on majors offered and athletics. College video available at CollegeQuest.com.

TEXAS WOMAN'S UNIVERSITY
Denton, Texas

- **State-supported**, university, founded 1901
- **Degrees** bachelor's, master's, and doctoral
- **Suburban** 270-acre campus with easy access to Dallas–Fort Worth
- **Coed**, primarily women, 4,606 undergraduate students, 72% full-time, 94% women, 6% men
- **Minimally difficult** entrance level, 87% of applicants were admitted
- **12:1 student-to-undergraduate faculty ratio**
- **36.3% graduate** in 6 years or less
- **$2072 tuition** and fees (in-state); $7256 (out-of-state)
- **$7571 average financial aid** package, $18,912 average indebtedness upon graduation, $6.4 million endowment

TWU, a comprehensive public university primarily for women, offers bachelor's, master's, and doctoral degree programs to approximately 8,600 students. A teaching and research institution, TWU emphasizes liberal arts and specialized or professional study in most major career fields, including health sciences. TWU offers a university experience focusing not only on the priorities and potential of women but also on the needs and goals of every student.

Students *Undergraduates:* 3,325 full-time, 1,281 part-time. Students come from 31 states and territories, 30 other countries. *The most frequently chosen baccalaureate fields are:* health professions and related sciences, home economics/vocational home economics, interdisciplinary studies. *Graduate:* 3,894 in graduate degree programs.

From out-of-state	2%	Reside on campus	22%
Age 25 or older	43%	Transferred in	13%
International students	2%	African Americans	18%
Asian Americans/Pacific Islanders	6%	Hispanic Americans	10%
Native Americans	1%		

Faculty 821 (54% full-time).

Expenses (1999–2000) *Tuition, state resident:* full-time $912; part-time $38 per semester hour. *Tuition, nonresident:* full-time $6096; part-time $254 per semester hour. *Required fees:* full-time $1160; $43 per semester hour; $120 per term part-time. Full-time tuition and fees vary according to course load and location. Part-time tuition and fees vary according to course load.

Texas

College room and board: $3872. Room and board charges vary according to board plan and housing facility. *Payment plan:* installment. *Waivers:* senior citizens.

Library Blagg-Huey Library. *Operations spending 1999–2000:* $2.2 million. *Collection:* 711,462 titles, 10,224 audiovisual materials.

College life *Housing:* on-campus residence required through sophomore year. *Option:* coed. *Social organizations:* national sororities, local sororities; 2% of women are members.

Campus security 24-hour emergency response devices and patrols, late-night transport-escort service, controlled dormitory access.

After graduation *Career center:* 8 full-time, 1 part-time personnel. Services include job fairs, resume preparation, resume referral, career counseling, careers library, job bank.

Freshmen 776 applied, 677 admitted, 340 enrolled.

Average high school GPA	3.2	SAT verbal scores above 500	N/R
SAT math scores above 500	N/R	ACT above 18	N/R
1998 freshmen returning in 1999	74%		

Application *Options:* early admission, deferred entrance. *Application fee:* $30. *Required:* high school transcript; minimum 2.0 GPA.

Standardized tests *Admission: Required:* SAT I or ACT.

Significant dates *Application deadlines:* 7/15 (freshmen), 7/15 (transfers). *Notification:* continuous until 8/15 (freshmen). *Financial aid deadline priority date:* 4/1.

Freshman Application Contact
Director of Undergraduate Admissions, Texas Woman's University, PO Box 425589, Denton, TX 76204-5589. **Phone:** 940-898-3040. **Toll-free phone:** 888-948-9984. **Fax:** 940-898-3198. **E-mail:** admissions@twu.edu

Visit CollegeQuest.com for information on majors offered and athletics. College video available at CollegeQuest.com.

■ *See page 2612 for a narrative description.*

TRINITY UNIVERSITY
San Antonio, Texas

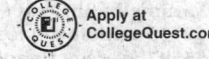 Apply at CollegeQuest.com

- **Independent**, comprehensive, founded 1869, affiliated with Presbyterian Church
- **Degrees** bachelor's and master's
- **Urban** 113-acre campus
- **Coed**, 2,264 undergraduate students, 99% full-time, 51% women, 49% men
- **Very difficult** entrance level, 76% of applicants were admitted
- **11:1 student-to-undergraduate faculty ratio**
- **72% graduate** in 6 years or less
- **$15,804 tuition** and fees
- **$15,745 average financial aid** package, $14,272 average indebtedness upon graduation, $584.4 million endowment

Students *Undergraduates:* 2,231 full-time, 33 part-time. Students come from 49 states and territories, 21 other countries. *The most frequently chosen baccalaureate fields are:* business/marketing, biological/life sciences, social sciences and history. *Graduate:* 237 in graduate degree programs.

From out-of-state	27%	Reside on campus	77%
Age 25 or older	1%	Transferred in	1%
International students	1%	African Americans	2%
Asian Americans/Pacific Islanders	8%	Hispanic Americans	10%
Native Americans	0.5%		

Faculty 263 (80% full-time).

Expenses (2000–2001, estimated) *Comprehensive fee:* $22,134 includes full-time tuition ($15,660), mandatory fees ($144), and room and board ($6330). *College room only:* $4070. Room and board charges vary according to board plan. *Part-time tuition:* $653 per semester hour. *Part-time fees:* $6 per semester hour. *Payment plans:* tuition prepayment, installment. *Waivers:* employees or children of employees.

Library Elizabeth Huth Coates Library. *Operations spending 1999–2000:* $3.6 million. *Collection:* 838,262 titles, 3,476 serial subscriptions, 58,146 audiovisual materials.

College life *Housing:* on-campus residence required through junior year. *Option:* coed. *Social organizations:* local fraternities, local sororities; 26% of eligible men and 28% of eligible women are members. *Most popular organizations:* Trinity University Voluntary Action Center, Alpha Phi Omega, Association of Student Representatives, Trinity Activities Council, Trinity Multicultural Network.

Campus security 24-hour emergency response devices and patrols, student patrols, late-night transport-escort service.

After graduation 82 organizations recruited on campus 1997–98. 39% of class of 1998 had job offers within 6 months. *Career center:* 5 full-time personnel. Services include job fairs, resume preparation, interview workshops, resume referral, career/interest testing, career counseling, careers library, job bank, job interviews. *Major awards:* 1 Fulbright Scholar.

Freshmen 2,743 applied, 2,076 admitted, 637 enrolled. 22 National Merit Scholars.

Average high school GPA	3.7	SAT verbal scores above 500	98%
SAT math scores above 500	99%	ACT above 18	100%
From top 10% of their h.s. class	53%	From top quarter	82%
From top half	98%	1998 freshmen returning in 1999	86%

Application *Options:* eApply at www.CollegeQuest.com, Common Application, electronic application, early decision, early action, deferred entrance. *Application fee:* $30. *Required:* essay or personal statement; high school transcript; 2 letters of recommendation. *Recommended:* interview.

Standardized tests *Admission: Required:* SAT I or ACT.

Significant dates *Application deadlines:* 2/1 (freshmen), 4/15 (transfers). *Early decision:* 11/15, 12/15. *Notification:* 4/1 (freshmen), 12/15 (early decision), 2/1 (early action). *Financial aid deadline priority date:* 2/1.

Freshman Application Contact
Dr. George Boyd, Director of Admissions, Trinity University, 715 Stadium Drive, San Antonio, TX 78212-7200. **Phone:** 210-999-7207. **Toll-free phone:** 800-TRINITY. **Fax:** 210-999-7696. **E-mail:** admissions@trinity.edu

Visit CollegeQuest.com for information on majors offered and athletics. College video and electronic viewbook available at CollegeQuest.com.

■ *See page 2646 for a narrative description.*

UNIVERSITY OF DALLAS
Irving, Texas

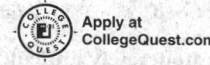 Apply at CollegeQuest.com

- **Independent Roman Catholic**, university, founded 1955
- **Degrees** bachelor's, master's, and doctoral
- **Suburban** 750-acre campus with easy access to Dallas–Fort Worth
- **Coed**, 1,143 undergraduate students, 97% full-time, 59% women, 41% men
- **Very difficult** entrance level, 76% of applicants were admitted
- **13:1 student-to-undergraduate faculty ratio**
- **60% graduate** in 6 years or less
- **$14,420 tuition** and fees
- **$13,365 average financial aid** package, $15,300 average indebtedness upon graduation, $48.7 million endowment

Students *Undergraduates:* 1,106 full-time, 37 part-time. Students come from 46 states and territories, 20 other countries. *The most frequently chosen baccalaureate fields are:* social sciences and history, philosophy, visual/performing arts. *Graduate:* 2,027 in graduate degree programs.

From out-of-state	41%	Reside on campus	51%
Age 25 or older	7%	Transferred in	4%
International students	3%	African Americans	2%
Asian Americans/Pacific Islanders	6%	Hispanic Americans	14%
Native Americans	1%		

Faculty 239 (52% full-time).

Expenses (1999–2000) *Comprehensive fee:* $19,866 includes full-time tuition ($14,354), mandatory fees ($66), and room and board ($5446). *College room only:* $2764. Room and board charges vary according to board plan and housing facility. *Part-time tuition:* $600 per credit. *Part-time fees:* $33 per term part-time. *Payment plans:* installment, deferred payment. *Waivers:* employees or children of employees.

Library William A. Blakley Library. *Operations spending 1999–2000:* $1 million. *Collection:* 192,468 titles, 1,819 serial subscriptions, 1,223 audiovisual materials.

College life *Housing:* on-campus residence required through junior year. *Options:* coed, men-only, women-only. *Most popular organizations:* student government, Student Foundation, Program Board, Crusaders for Life, Residence Hall Association.

Texas

University of Dallas (continued)
Campus security 24-hour emergency response devices and patrols, late-night transport-escort service, controlled dormitory access.
After graduation 50 organizations recruited on campus 1997–98. *Career center:* 1 full-time personnel. Services include job fairs, resume preparation, resume referral, career counseling, careers library, job bank, job interviews.
Freshmen 1,213 applied, 927 admitted, 310 enrolled. 17 National Merit Scholars, 27 valedictorians.

Average high school GPA	3.8	SAT verbal scores above 500	95%
SAT math scores above 500	89%	ACT above 18	98%
From top 10% of their h.s. class	55%	From top quarter	78%
From top half	93%	1998 freshmen returning in 1999	85%

Application *Options:* eApply at www.CollegeQuest.com, early admission, early action, deferred entrance. *Application fee:* $40. *Required:* essay or personal statement; high school transcript; 1 letter of recommendation. *Required for some:* interview. *Recommended:* interview.
Standardized tests *Admission: Required:* SAT I or ACT.
Significant dates *Application deadlines:* 2/15 (freshmen), 7/1 (transfers). *Early action:* 12/1. *Notification:* 1/15 (early action). *Financial aid deadline priority date:* 3/1.
Freshman Application Contact
Mr. Larry Webb, Director of Enrollment, University of Dallas, 1845 East Northgate Drive, Irving, TX 75062-4799. **Phone:** 972-721-5266. **Toll-free phone:** 800-628-6999. **Fax:** 972-721-5017. **E-mail:** undadmis@acad.udallas.edu
Visit CollegeQuest.com for information on majors offered and athletics.

UNIVERSITY OF HOUSTON
Houston, Texas

- **State-supported**, university, founded 1927
- **Degrees** bachelor's, master's, doctoral, and first professional
- **Urban** 550-acre campus
- **Coed**, 23,629 undergraduate students, 69% full-time, 54% women, 46% men
- **Moderately difficult** entrance level, 70% of applicants were admitted
- **21:1 student-to-undergraduate faculty ratio**
- **35% graduate** in 6 years or less
- **$2444 tuition** and fees (in-state); $7604 (out-of-state)
- **$134.4 million endowment**

Part of University of Houston System.
Students *Undergraduates:* 16,406 full-time, 7,223 part-time. Students come from 48 states and territories, 108 other countries. *The most frequently chosen baccalaureate fields are:* business/marketing, engineering/engineering technologies, psychology. *Graduate:* 1,472 in professional programs, 6,507 in other graduate degree programs.

From out-of-state	2%	Reside on campus	9%
Age 25 or older	25%	Transferred in	11%
International students	4%	African Americans	15%
Asian Americans/Pacific Islanders	20%	Hispanic Americans	19%
Native Americans	1%		

Faculty 1,613 (60% full-time), 58% with terminal degrees.
Expenses (2000–2001, estimated) *Tuition, state resident:* full-time $960; part-time $40 per credit hour. *Tuition, nonresident:* full-time $6120; part-time $255 per credit hour. *Required fees:* full-time $1484; $696 per term part-time. Full-time tuition and fees vary according to program. Part-time tuition and fees vary according to course load and program. *College room and board:* $4513; room only: $2553. Room and board charges vary according to board plan and housing facility. *Payment plan:* installment.
Library M.D. Anderson Library plus 5 others. *Operations spending 1999–2000:* $10.5 million. *Collection:* 2 million titles, 18,103 serial subscriptions, 5,515 audiovisual materials.
College life *Housing:* Option: coed. *Social organizations:* national fraternities, national sororities; 34% of eligible men and 36% of eligible women are members. *Most popular organizations:* Council of Ethnic Organizations, Greek Life, Frontier Fiesta Association, intramural sports, Golden Key National Honor Society.
Campus security 24-hour emergency response devices and patrols, student patrols, late-night transport-escort service, controlled dormitory access, vehicle assistance.

After graduation 641 organizations recruited on campus 1997–98. 93% of class of 1998 had job offers within 6 months. *Career center:* 11 full-time, 5 part-time personnel. Services include job fairs, resume preparation, interview workshops, resume referral, career counseling, careers library, job bank, job interviews.
Freshmen 8,306 applied, 5,787 admitted, 3,303 enrolled.

Average high school GPA	3.1	SAT verbal scores above 500	53%
SAT math scores above 500	60%	ACT above 18	82%
From top 10% of their h.s. class	20%	From top quarter	48%
From top half	80%	1998 freshmen returning in 1999	76%

Application *Options:* Common Application, electronic application. *Application fee:* $40. *Required:* high school transcript; minimum 2.0 GPA. *Recommended:* letters of recommendation.
Standardized tests *Admission: Required:* SAT I or ACT. *Recommended:* SAT I, SAT II Subject Tests.
Significant dates *Application deadlines:* 5/15 (freshmen), 6/2 (transfers). *Financial aid deadline priority date:* 4/1.
Freshman Application Contact
Ms. Tyene Houston, Assistant Director of Admissions, University of Houston, 4800 Calhoun, Houston, TX 77204-2161. **Phone:** 713-743-9632. **Fax:** 713-743-9633. **E-mail:** admissions@uh.edu
Visit CollegeQuest.com for information on majors offered and athletics.

■ *See page 2734 for a narrative description.*

UNIVERSITY OF HOUSTON—CLEAR LAKE
Houston, Texas

- **State-supported**, upper-level, founded 1974
- **Degrees** bachelor's and master's
- **Suburban** 487-acre campus
- **Coed**, 3,484 undergraduate students, 48% full-time, 63% women, 37% men
- **Minimally difficult** entrance level, 81% of applicants were admitted
- **$2138 tuition** and fees (in-state); $7322 (out-of-state)
- **$5597 average financial aid** package, $97,487 endowment

Part of University of Houston System.
Students *Undergraduates:* Students come from 19 states and territories, 31 other countries. *The most frequently chosen baccalaureate fields are:* business/marketing, computer/information sciences, education. *Graduate:* 3,322 in graduate degree programs.

Age 25 or older	66%	International students	3%
African Americans	6%	Asian Americans/Pacific Islanders	5%
Hispanic Americans	13%	Native Americans	0.3%

Faculty 179 (87% full-time).
Expenses (1999–2000) *Tuition, state resident:* full-time $912; part-time $38 per semester hour. *Tuition, nonresident:* full-time $6096; part-time $254 per semester hour. *Required fees:* full-time $1226; $428 per term part-time. Part-time tuition and fees vary according to course load. *Payment plan:* installment. *Waivers:* senior citizens.
Library Neumann Library. *Operations spending 1999–2000:* $1.7 million. *Collection:* 374,981 titles, 3,539 serial subscriptions.
College life *Housing:* college housing not available. *Most popular organizations:* Beta Alpha Psi, International Student Organization, Family Therapy Student Association, Texas Student Education Association, Accounting Association.
Campus security 24-hour emergency response devices and patrols, late-night transport-escort service.
After graduation 80 organizations recruited on campus 1997–98. *Career center:* 9 full-time, 6 part-time personnel. Services include job fairs, resume preparation, interview workshops, resume referral, career/interest testing, career counseling, careers library, job bank, job interviews.
Application *Options:* Common Application, electronic application, deferred entrance. *Application fee:* $30.
Standardized tests *Admission: Required:* TASP.
Significant dates *Application deadline:* rolling (transfers). *Financial aid deadline priority date:* 6/1.

Freshman Application Contact
Ms. Darella L. Banks, Executive Director of Enrollment Services, University of Houston–Clear Lake, 2700 Bay Area Boulevard, Box 13, Houston, TX 77058-1098. **Phone:** 281-283-2517. **Fax:** 281-283-2530. **E-mail:** admissions@cl.uh.edu
Visit CollegeQuest.com for information on majors offered and athletics.

UNIVERSITY OF HOUSTON—DOWNTOWN
Houston, Texas

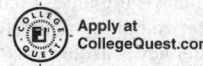
Apply at CollegeQuest.com

- **State-supported**, 4-year, founded 1974
- **Degree** bachelor's
- **Urban** 20-acre campus
- **Coed**, 8,712 undergraduate students, 48% full-time, 58% women, 42% men
- **Noncompetitive** entrance level, 99% of applicants were admitted
- **25:1 student-to-undergraduate faculty ratio**
- **9.32% graduate** in 6 years or less
- **$2316 tuition** and fees (in-state); $8796 (out-of-state)
- **$5201 average financial aid** package, $7 million endowment

Part of University of Houston System.
Students *Undergraduates:* 4,200 full-time, 4,512 part-time. Students come from 14 states and territories, 74 other countries. *The most frequently chosen baccalaureate fields are:* business/marketing, liberal arts/general studies, protective services/public administration.

From out-of-state	1%	Age 25 or older	47%
Transferred in	12%	International students	2%
African Americans	29%	Asian Americans/Pacific Islanders	12%
Hispanic Americans	32%	Native Americans	0.2%

Faculty 458 (44% full-time), 49% with terminal degrees.
Expenses (1999–2000) *Tuition, state resident:* full-time $1140; part-time $38 per credit hour. *Tuition, nonresident:* full-time $7620; part-time $254 per credit hour. *Required fees:* full-time $1176; $275 per term part-time. Full-time tuition and fees vary according to course load. Part-time tuition and fees vary according to course load. *Payment plan:* installment. *Waivers:* senior citizens.
Library W. I. Dykes Library. *Collection:* 231,600 titles, 1,600 serial subscriptions.
College life *Housing:* college housing not available. *Social organizations:* national fraternities, national sororities. *Most popular organizations:* Latin-American student services organization, Chinese student association, Indo-Pakistan student association, Professional Accounting Society, Student Government Association.
Campus security 24-hour emergency response devices and patrols, late-night transport-escort service.
After graduation *Career center:* 4 full-time, 3 part-time personnel. Services include job fairs, resume preparation, interview workshops, resume referral, career/interest testing, career counseling, careers library, job bank, job interviews.
Freshmen 950 applied, 949 admitted, 970 enrolled.

SAT verbal scores above 500	N/R	SAT math scores above 500	N/R
ACT above 18	N/R		

Application *Options:* eApply at www.CollegeQuest.com, Common Application, early admission, deferred entrance. *Application fee:* $10. *Required:* high school transcript.
Significant dates *Application deadlines:* 8/7 (freshmen), 8/7 (transfers). *Notification:* continuous until 8/21 (freshmen). *Financial aid deadline priority date:* 4/1.
Freshman Application Contact
Dr. Carol Duckworth, Director, Admissions and Records, University of Houston–Downtown, One Main Street, Houston, TX 77002-1001. **Phone:** 713-221-8931. **Fax:** 713-221-8157. **E-mail:** uhdadmit@dt.uh.edu
Visit CollegeQuest.com for information on majors offered and athletics.

UNIVERSITY OF HOUSTON—VICTORIA
Victoria, Texas

- **State-supported**, upper-level, founded 1973
- **Degrees** bachelor's and master's
- **Small-town** campus
- **Coed**, 710 undergraduate students, 37% full-time, 73% women, 27% men
- **Minimally difficult** entrance level, 84% of applicants were admitted
- **20:1 student-to-undergraduate faculty ratio**
- **$2004 tuition** and fees (in-state); $7188 (out-of-state)
- **$6709 average financial aid** package, $12,530 average indebtedness upon graduation, $5.7 million endowment

Part of University of Houston System.
Students *Undergraduates:* 261 full-time, 449 part-time. Students come from 3 other countries. *The most frequently chosen baccalaureate fields are:* business/marketing, computer/information sciences, education. *Graduate:* 694 in graduate degree programs.

Age 25 or older	59%	Transferred in	34%
International students	0.4%	African Americans	6%
Asian Americans/Pacific Islanders	2%	Hispanic Americans	18%

Faculty 86 (44% full-time), 53% with terminal degrees.
Expenses (1999–2000) *Tuition, state resident:* full-time $912; part-time $38 per credit hour. *Tuition, nonresident:* full-time $6096; part-time $254 per credit hour. *Required fees:* full-time $1092; $46 per credit hour. Full-time tuition and fees vary according to course load. Part-time tuition and fees vary according to course load. *Payment plans:* tuition prepayment, installment. *Waivers:* senior citizens.
Library *Operations spending 1999–2000:* $667,046. *Collection:* 202,484 titles, 1,051 serial subscriptions, 7,477 audiovisual materials.
College life *Housing:* college housing not available. *Most popular organization:* Texas Student Education Association.
Campus security 24-hour emergency response devices and patrols.
After graduation 90 organizations recruited on campus 1997–98. *Career center:* 1 full-time personnel. Services include job fairs, resume preparation, interview workshops, resume referral, career/interest testing, career counseling, careers library, job bank, job interviews.
Significant dates *Application deadline:* rolling (transfers). *Financial aid deadline priority date:* 4/15.
Freshman Application Contact
Mr. Richard Phillips, Director of Enrollment Management, University of Houston–Victoria, 2506 East Red River, Victoria, TX 77901-4450. **Phone:** 361-570-4110. **Toll-free phone:** 800-687-8648. **Fax:** 361-572-9377. **E-mail:** urbanom@jade.vic.uh.edu
Visit CollegeQuest.com for information on majors offered and athletics.

UNIVERSITY OF MARY HARDIN-BAYLOR
Belton, Texas

- **Independent Southern Baptist**, comprehensive, founded 1845
- **Degrees** bachelor's and master's
- **Small-town** 100-acre campus with easy access to Austin
- **Coed**, 2,303 undergraduate students, 85% full-time, 64% women, 36% men
- **Minimally difficult** entrance level, 60% of applicants were admitted
- **15:1 student-to-undergraduate faculty ratio**
- **34.4% graduate** in 6 years or less
- **$8430 tuition** and fees
- **$7477 average financial aid** package, $15,300 average indebtedness upon graduation, $39.7 million endowment

Students *Undergraduates:* 1,953 full-time, 350 part-time. Students come from 25 states and territories, 11 other countries. *The most frequently chosen baccalaureate fields are:* education, health professions and related sciences, liberal arts/general studies. *Graduate:* 224 in graduate degree programs.

From out-of-state	2%	Reside on campus	42%
Age 25 or older	26%	Transferred in	14%
International students	1%	African Americans	10%
Asian Americans/Pacific Islanders	2%	Hispanic Americans	10%
Native Americans	1%		

Faculty 203 (55% full-time).
Expenses (1999–2000) *Comprehensive fee:* $11,972 includes full-time tuition ($7950), mandatory fees ($480), and room and board ($3542). *College room only:* $1550. Full-time tuition and fees vary according to degree level. Room and board charges vary according to housing facility. *Part-time tuition:* $265 per semester hour. *Part-time fees:* $16 per semester hour. Part-time

Texas

University of Mary Hardin-Baylor (continued)
tuition and fees vary according to degree level. *Payment plan:* installment. *Waivers:* employees or children of employees.
Library Townsend Memorial Library. *Operations spending 1999–2000:* $947,540. *Collection:* 86,545 titles, 1,663 serial subscriptions, 4,982 audiovisual materials.
College life *Housing:* on-campus residence required through junior year. *Options:* men-only, women-only, disabled students. *Most popular organizations:* Baptist Student Ministry, Student Government Association, Residence Hall Association, Campus Activities Board, Crusaders for Christ.
Campus security 24-hour emergency response devices and patrols, controlled dormitory access.
After graduation 100 organizations recruited on campus 1997–98. *Career center:* 1 full-time, 1 part-time personnel. Services include job fairs, resume preparation, interview workshops, resume referral, career/interest testing, career counseling, careers library, job bank, job interviews.
Freshmen 906 applied, 540 admitted, 473 enrolled. 6 valedictorians.

SAT verbal scores above 500	50%	SAT math scores above 500	47%
ACT above 18	81%	From top 10% of their h.s. class	15%
From top quarter	40%	From top half	76%
1998 freshmen returning in 1999	54%		

Application *Options:* early admission, deferred entrance. *Application fee:* $35. *Required:* high school transcript. *Required for some:* essay or personal statement. *Recommended:* interview.
Standardized tests *Admission: Required:* SAT I or ACT. *Recommended:* ACT.
Significant dates *Application deadlines:* rolling (freshmen), rolling (transfers). *Financial aid deadline priority date:* 3/1.
Freshman Application Contact
Ms. Diane Stanford, Associate Director of Admissions, University of Mary Hardin-Baylor, 900 College Street, Belton, TX 76513. **Phone:** 254-295-4520. **Toll-free phone:** 800-727-8642. **Fax:** 254-295-4535.
Visit CollegeQuest.com for information on majors offered and athletics. College video available at CollegeQuest.com.

■ *See page 2752 for a narrative description.*

UNIVERSITY OF NORTH TEXAS
Denton, Texas

- **State-supported**, university, founded 1890
- **Degrees** bachelor's, master's, and doctoral
- **Urban** 500-acre campus with easy access to Dallas–Fort Worth
- **Coed**, 20,452 undergraduate students
- **Moderately difficult** entrance level, 74% of applicants were admitted
- **16:1 student-to-undergraduate faculty ratio**
- **36.6% graduate** in 6 years or less
- **$2769 tuition** and fees (in-state); $9249 (out-of-state)
- **$5145 average financial aid** package, $14,955 average indebtedness upon graduation, $8.4 million endowment

Students *Undergraduates:* Students come from 49 states and territories, 115 other countries. *The most frequently chosen baccalaureate fields are:* business/marketing, communications/communication technologies, home economics/vocational home economics.

From out-of-state	5%	Reside on campus	16%
Age 25 or older	33%	International students	2%
African Americans	10%	Asian Americans/Pacific Islanders	4%
Hispanic Americans	8%	Native Americans	1%

Faculty 1,009 (73% full-time).
Expenses (1999–2000) *Tuition, state resident:* full-time $2070; part-time $69 per credit. *Tuition, nonresident:* full-time $8550; part-time $285 per credit. *Required fees:* full-time $699; $18 per credit; $80 per term part-time. Full-time tuition and fees vary according to course load. Part-time tuition and fees vary according to course load. *College room and board:* $4096; room only: $2100. Room and board charges vary according to board plan. *Payment plan:* installment. *Waivers:* senior citizens and employees or children of employees.
Library Willis Library plus 4 others. *Operations spending 1999–2000:* $8.1 million. *Collection:* 1.8 million titles, 12,243 serial subscriptions, 61,850 audiovisual materials.

College life *Housing:* on-campus residence required in freshman year. *Options:* coed, women-only, disabled students. *Social organizations:* national fraternities, national sororities; 3% of eligible men and 3% of eligible women are members.
Campus security 24-hour emergency response devices, late-night transport-escort service, controlled dormitory access.
After graduation 183 organizations recruited on campus 1997–98. *Career center:* 7 full-time, 4 part-time personnel. Services include job fairs, resume preparation, resume referral, career counseling, careers library, job bank, job interviews. *Major awards:* 1 Fulbright Scholar.
Freshmen 7,189 applied, 5,350 admitted. 10 National Merit Scholars.

SAT verbal scores above 500	68%	SAT math scores above 500	67%
ACT above 18	93%	From top 10% of their h.s. class	13%
From top quarter	44%	From top half	82%
1998 freshmen returning in 1999	68%		

Application *Options:* Common Application, electronic application, early admission, deferred entrance. *Application fee:* $25. *Required:* high school transcript. *Required for some:* essay or personal statement; 3 letters of recommendation; interview.
Standardized tests *Admission: Required:* SAT I or ACT.
Significant dates *Application deadlines:* 6/15 (freshmen), 6/15 (transfers). *Financial aid deadline priority date:* 6/1.
Freshman Application Contact
Mr. Joel Daboub, Senior Assistant Director of Admissions and Director of Freshman Orientation, University of North Texas, Box 311277, Denton, TX 76203-9988. **Phone:** 940-565-2681. **Toll-free phone:** 800-868-8211. **Fax:** 940-565-2408. **E-mail:** undergrad@abn.unt.edu
Visit CollegeQuest.com for information on majors offered and athletics. College video available at CollegeQuest.com.

UNIVERSITY OF ST. THOMAS
Houston, Texas

- **Independent Roman Catholic**, comprehensive, founded 1947
- **Degrees** bachelor's, master's, doctoral, and first professional
- **Urban** 20-acre campus
- **Coed**, 1,520 undergraduate students, 78% full-time, 65% women, 35% men
- **Moderately difficult** entrance level, 81% of applicants were admitted
- **14:1 student-to-undergraduate faculty ratio**
- **45% graduate** in 6 years or less
- **$12,416 tuition** and fees
- **$11,667 average financial aid** package, $42.6 million endowment

Students *Undergraduates:* 1,192 full-time, 328 part-time. Students come from 22 states and territories, 57 other countries. *The most frequently chosen baccalaureate fields are:* business/marketing, liberal arts/general studies, social sciences and history. *Graduate:* 130 in professional programs, 1,549 in other graduate degree programs.

From out-of-state	4%	Reside on campus	13%
Age 25 or older	29%	Transferred in	18%
International students	6%	African Americans	6%
Asian Americans/Pacific Islanders	12%	Hispanic Americans	27%
Native Americans	0.5%		

Faculty 235 (43% full-time), 38% with terminal degrees.
Expenses (2000–2001) *Comprehensive fee:* $17,466 includes full-time tuition ($12,300), mandatory fees ($116), and room and board ($5050). *College room only:* $2900. Full-time tuition and fees vary according to degree level. Room and board charges vary according to board plan and housing facility. *Part-time tuition:* $418 per credit hour. Part-time tuition and fees vary according to degree level. *Payment plans:* installment, deferred payment. *Waivers:* senior citizens and employees or children of employees.
Library Doherty Library plus 1 other. *Collection:* 200,000 titles, 2,300 serial subscriptions, 1,091 audiovisual materials.
College life *Housing:* on-campus residence required in freshman year. *Option:* coed. *Most popular organizations:* Asian Students Association, Filipino Students Association, science club, Student Organization of Latinos, Texas Student Education Association.

Campus security 24-hour emergency response devices and patrols, late-night transport-escort service.

After graduation 6 organizations recruited on campus 1997–98. *Career center:* 2 full-time personnel. Services include job fairs, resume preparation, resume referral, career counseling, careers library, job bank, job interviews.

Freshmen 547 applied, 445 admitted, 225 enrolled.

SAT verbal scores above 500	84%	SAT math scores above 500	76%
ACT above 18	89%	From top 10% of their h.s. class	47%
From top quarter	73%	From top half	91%
1998 freshmen returning in 1999	88%		

Application *Options:* eApply at www.CollegeQuest.com, early admission, deferred entrance. *Application fee:* $35. *Required:* high school transcript; minimum 2.0 GPA. *Required for some:* essay or personal statement; 2 letters of recommendation. *Recommended:* interview.

Standardized tests *Admission: Required:* SAT I or ACT.

Significant dates *Application deadlines:* rolling (freshmen), rolling (transfers). *Financial aid deadline priority date:* 2/1.

Freshman Application Contact
Mrs. Elsie Biron, Dean of Admissions, University of St. Thomas, 3800 Montrose Boulevard, Houston, TX 77006-4696. **Phone:** 713-525-3500. **Toll-free phone:** 800-856-8565. **Fax:** 713-525-3558. **E-mail:** admissions@stthom.edu

Visit CollegeQuest.com for information on majors offered and athletics. College video and electronic viewbook available at CollegeQuest.com.

■ *See page 2822 for a narrative description.*

THE UNIVERSITY OF TEXAS AT ARLINGTON
Arlington, Texas

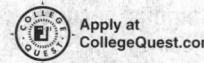

- **State-supported**, university, founded 1895
- **Degrees** bachelor's, master's, doctoral, post-master's, and postbachelor's certificates
- **Urban** 395-acre campus with easy access to Dallas–Fort Worth
- **Coed**, 15,266 undergraduate students, 64% full-time, 53% women, 47% men
- **Moderately difficult** entrance level, 97% of applicants were admitted
- **20:1 student-to-undergraduate faculty ratio**
- **27.7% graduate** in 6 years or less
- **$2670 tuition** and fees (in-state); $7854 (out-of-state)
- **$7149 average financial aid** package, $13,055 average indebtedness upon graduation, $29.8 million endowment

Part of University of Texas System.

Students *Undergraduates:* 9,836 full-time, 5,430 part-time. Students come from 46 states and territories, 89 other countries. *The most frequently chosen baccalaureate fields are:* business/marketing, health professions and related sciences, social sciences and history. *Graduate:* 3,883 in graduate degree programs.

From out-of-state	4%	Reside on campus	16%
Age 25 or older	37%	Transferred in	17%
International students	3%	African Americans	12%
Asian Americans/Pacific Islanders	12%	Hispanic Americans	11%
Native Americans	1%		

Faculty 891 (66% full-time).

Expenses (1999–2000) *Tuition, state resident:* full-time $1824. *Tuition, nonresident:* full-time $7008. *Required fees:* full-time $846. Full-time tuition and fees vary according to course load. Part-time tuition and fees vary according to course load. *College room and board:* room only: $1686. Room and board charges vary according to housing facility. *Payment plan:* installment.

Library Central Library plus 2 others. *Operations spending 1999–2000:* $5.8 million. *Collection:* 1.1 million titles, 6,819 serial subscriptions, 2,165 audiovisual materials.

College life *Housing: Options:* coed, men-only, women-only. *Social organizations:* national fraternities, national sororities; 5% of eligible men and 3% of eligible women are members. *Most popular organizations:* Alpha Chi honor society, Golden Key, Baptist Student Ministry, Chinese Students Association, Beta Gamma Sigma.

Campus security 24-hour emergency response devices and patrols, late-night transport-escort service, controlled dormitory access, remote emergency telephones, bicycle patrols, crime prevention program, student shuttle service from 7:30 a.m. to 4:30 p.m.

After graduation 400 organizations recruited on campus 1997–98. *Career center:* 5 full-time, 1 part-time personnel. Services include job fairs, resume preparation, interview workshops, resume referral, career/interest testing, career counseling, careers library, job bank, job interviews.

Freshmen 2,514 applied, 2,446 admitted, 1,481 enrolled.

SAT verbal scores above 500	58%	SAT math scores above 500	66%
ACT above 18	88%	From top 10% of their h.s. class	21%
From top quarter	53%	From top half	85%
1998 freshmen returning in 1999	68%		

Application *Options:* eApply at www.CollegeQuest.com, early admission, deferred entrance. *Application fee:* $25. *Required:* high school transcript; class rank.

Standardized tests *Admission: Required:* SAT I or ACT. *Required for some:* SAT II Subject Tests.

Significant dates *Application deadlines:* rolling (freshmen), rolling (transfers). *Financial aid deadline priority date:* 6/1.

Freshman Application Contact
Mr. George E. Norton, Associate Director of Admissions, The University of Texas at Arlington, PO Box 19111, 701 South Nedderman Drive, Room 110, Davis Hall, Arlington, TX 76019-0088. **Phone:** 817-272-3254. **Fax:** 817-272-5656. **E-mail:** admissions@uta.edu

Visit CollegeQuest.com for information on majors offered and athletics.

THE UNIVERSITY OF TEXAS AT AUSTIN
Austin, Texas

- **State-supported**, university, founded 1883
- **Degrees** bachelor's, master's, doctoral, and first professional
- **Urban** 350-acre campus with easy access to San Antonio
- **Coed**, 36,164 undergraduate students, 89% full-time, 50% women, 50% men
- **Very difficult** entrance level, 63% of applicants were admitted
- **19:1 student-to-undergraduate faculty ratio**
- **66.48% graduate** in 6 years or less
- **$3128 tuition** and fees (in-state); $9608 (out-of-state)
- **$7452 average financial aid** package, $17,000 average indebtedness upon graduation, $1.4 billion endowment

Part of University of Texas System.

Students *Undergraduates:* 32,118 full-time, 4,046 part-time. Students come from 52 states and territories, 100 other countries. *The most frequently chosen baccalaureate fields are:* business/marketing, communications/communication technologies, social sciences and history. *Graduate:* 1,572 in professional programs, 10,278 in other graduate degree programs.

From out-of-state	5%	Reside on campus	14%
Age 25 or older	8%	Transferred in	6%
International students	3%	African Americans	3%
Asian Americans/Pacific Islanders	15%	Hispanic Americans	14%
Native Americans	0.5%		

Faculty 2,544 (91% full-time), 90% with terminal degrees.

Expenses (1999–2000) *Tuition, state resident:* full-time $2280; part-time $76 per semester hour. *Tuition, nonresident:* full-time $8760; part-time $292 per semester hour. *Required fees:* full-time $848; $21 per semester hour; $142 per term part-time. Full-time tuition and fees vary according to course load and program. Part-time tuition and fees vary according to course load and program. *College room and board:* $4854; room only: $2521. Room and board charges vary according to board plan and housing facility. *Payment plan:* installment.

Library Perry-Castañeda Library plus 18 others. *Operations spending 1999–2000:* $20.1 million. *Collection:* 52,515 serial subscriptions, 132,365 audiovisual materials.

College life *Housing: Options:* coed, men-only, women-only, cooperative. *Social organizations:* national fraternities, national sororities; 10% of eligible men and 13% of eligible women are members. *Most popular organizations:* Alpha Phi Omega, Orange Jackets, Baptist Student Ministry, Longhorn Band Student Organization.

Texas

The University of Texas at Austin (continued)
Campus security 24-hour emergency response devices and patrols, student patrols, late-night transport-escort service, controlled dormitory access.
After graduation *Career center:* 7 full-time, 22 part-time personnel. Services include job fairs, resume preparation, interview workshops, resume referral, career/interest testing, career counseling, careers library, job bank, job interviews. *Major awards:* 9 Fulbright Scholars.
Freshmen 18,919 applied, 11,948 admitted, 7,040 enrolled. 238 National Merit Scholars.

SAT verbal scores above 500	88%	SAT math scores above 500	91%
ACT above 18	99%	From top 10% of their h.s. class	48%
From top quarter	83%	From top half	98%
1998 freshmen returning in 1999	89%		

Application *Options:* electronic application, deferred entrance. *Application fee:* $50. *Required:* high school transcript. *Required for some:* essay or personal statement.
Standardized tests *Admission: Required:* SAT I or ACT.
Significant dates *Application deadlines:* 2/1 (freshmen), rolling (transfers). *Financial aid deadline priority date:* 4/1.
Freshman Application Contact
Freshman Admissions Center, The University of Texas at Austin, John Hargis Hall, Austin, TX 78712-1111. **Phone:** 512-475-7440. **Fax:** 512-475-7475. **E-mail:** frmn@uts.cc.utexas.edu
Visit CollegeQuest.com for information on majors offered and athletics.

THE UNIVERSITY OF TEXAS AT BROWNSVILLE
Brownsville, Texas

- **State-supported**, upper-level, founded 1973
- **Degrees** bachelor's and master's
- **Urban** 65-acre campus
- **Coed**
- **Noncompetitive** entrance level
- **$2322 tuition** and fees (in-state); $8682 (out-of-state)

Part of University of Texas System.
Expenses (1999–2000) *Tuition, area resident:* full-time $660; part-time $22 per credit. *Tuition, state resident:* full-time $1260; part-time $42 per credit. *Tuition, nonresident:* full-time $7620; part-time $254 per credit. *Required fees:* full-time $1062; $32 per credit; $49 per term part-time. Full-time tuition and fees vary according to student level. Part-time tuition and fees vary according to course load and student level.
Institutional Web site http://www.utb.edu/
College life *Housing:* college housing not available. *Social organizations:* national fraternities, local fraternities, local sororities. *Most popular organizations:* Student Activities Programming Board, Criminal Justice Club, Gorgas Science Club, Club Cultural Latinoamericano, Ballet Follclorico Tizatlan.
Campus security 24-hour emergency response devices and patrols.
Application *Option:* Common Application. *Application fee:* $0.
Standardized tests *Admission: Required:* TASP.
Admissions Office Contact
The University of Texas at Brownsville, 80 Fort Brown, Brownsville, TX 78520-4991. **Fax:** 956-544-8832.
Visit CollegeQuest.com for information on athletics. College video available at CollegeQuest.com.

THE UNIVERSITY OF TEXAS AT DALLAS
Richardson, Texas

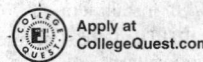
Apply at CollegeQuest.com

- **State-supported**, university, founded 1969
- **Degrees** bachelor's, master's, and doctoral
- **Suburban** 455-acre campus with easy access to Dallas
- **Coed**, 5,974 undergraduate students
- **Very difficult** entrance level, 62% of applicants were admitted
- **18:1 student-to-undergraduate faculty ratio**
- **47.3% graduate** in 6 years or less
- **$2912 tuition** and fees (in-state); $8096 (out-of-state)
- **$4072 average financial aid** package, $82.1 million endowment

Part of University of Texas System.
Students *Undergraduates:* Students come from 45 states and territories, 95 other countries. *The most frequently chosen baccalaureate fields are:* business/marketing, computer/information sciences, social sciences and history. *Graduate:* 4,123 in graduate degree programs.

From out-of-state	1%	Reside on campus	30%
Age 25 or older	44%		

Faculty 531 (65% full-time).
Expenses (1999–2000) *One-time required fee:* $10. *Tuition, state resident:* full-time $912; part-time $38 per semester hour. *Tuition, nonresident:* full-time $6096; part-time $254 per semester hour. *Required fees:* full-time $2000; $67 per semester hour; $118 per term part-time. Full-time tuition and fees vary according to course level, course load, degree level, and program. Part-time tuition and fees vary according to course level, course load, degree level, and program. *College room and board:* room only: $1700. Room and board charges vary according to board plan and housing facility. *Payment plan:* installment. *Waivers:* senior citizens.
Library Eugene McDermott Library plus 2 others. *Operations spending 1999–2000:* $3.8 million. *Collection:* 435,618 titles, 3,163 serial subscriptions, 2,695 audiovisual materials.
College life *Housing: Option:* coed. *Social organizations:* national fraternities, national sororities, local sororities; 5% of eligible men and 5% of eligible women are members.
Campus security 24-hour emergency response devices and patrols, late-night transport-escort service.
After graduation 210 organizations recruited on campus 1997–98. 74% of class of 1998 had job offers within 6 months. *Career center:* 14 full-time, 9 part-time personnel. Services include job fairs, resume preparation, interview workshops, resume referral, career/interest testing, career counseling, careers library, job bank, job interviews.
Freshmen 1,974 applied, 1,230 admitted. 10 National Merit Scholars, 13 valedictorians.

SAT verbal scores above 500	85%	SAT math scores above 500	92%
ACT above 18	100%	From top 10% of their h.s. class	34%
From top quarter	69%	From top half	95%
1998 freshmen returning in 1999	74%		

Application *Options:* eApply at www.CollegeQuest.com, deferred entrance. *Application fee:* $25. *Required:* essay or personal statement; high school transcript.
Standardized tests *Admission: Required:* SAT I and SAT II or ACT. *Recommended:* SAT II: Writing Test. *Required for some:* TASP.
Significant dates *Application deadline:* 8/1 (freshmen). **Financial aid deadline:** 4/30. Priority date: 3/4.
Freshman Application Contact
Admissions Office, The University of Texas at Dallas, PO Box 830688 Mail Station MC11, Richardson, TX 75083-0688. **Phone:** 972-883-2342. **Toll-free phone:** 800-889-2443. **Fax:** 972-883-6803. **E-mail:** ugrad-admissions@utdallas.edu
Visit CollegeQuest.com for information on majors offered and athletics. College video available at CollegeQuest.com.

■ *See page 2840 for a narrative description.*

THE UNIVERSITY OF TEXAS AT EL PASO
El Paso, Texas

- **State-supported**, university, founded 1913
- **Degrees** bachelor's, master's, and doctoral
- **Urban** 360-acre campus
- **Coed**
- **Minimally difficult** entrance level
- **$2244 tuition** and fees (in-state); $7428 (out-of-state)

Part of University of Texas System.
Expenses (1999–2000) *Tuition, state resident:* full-time $912; part-time $38 per semester hour. *Tuition, nonresident:* full-time $6096; part-time $254

per semester hour. *Required fees:* full-time $1332; $50 per semester hour; $60 per term part-time. Full-time tuition and fees vary according to course load and reciprocity agreements. Part-time tuition and fees vary according to reciprocity agreements. *College room and board:* room only: $2058. Room and board charges vary according to housing facility.

Institutional Web site http://www.utep.edu/

College life *Housing: Options:* coed, disabled students. *Social organizations:* national fraternities, national sororities.

Campus security 24-hour emergency response devices and patrols, late-night transport-escort service.

Application *Application fee:* $0. *Required:* high school transcript.

Standardized tests *Admission: Required for some:* SAT I and SAT II or ACT, PAA.

Admissions Office Contact
The University of Texas at El Paso, 500 West University Avenue, El Paso, TX 79968-0001. **Fax:** 915-747-5122. **E-mail:** admission@utep.edu

Visit CollegeQuest.com for information on athletics.

THE UNIVERSITY OF TEXAS AT SAN ANTONIO
San Antonio, Texas

- **State-supported**, comprehensive, founded 1969
- **Degrees** bachelor's, master's, and doctoral
- **Suburban** 600-acre campus
- **Coed**, 15,499 undergraduate students, 69% full-time, 55% women, 45% men
- **Moderately difficult** entrance level, 99% of applicants were admitted
- **27% graduate** in 6 years or less
- **$2974 tuition** and fees (in-state); $9454 (out-of-state)

Part of University of Texas System.

Students *Undergraduates:* 10,695 full-time, 4,804 part-time. Students come from 50 states and territories, 66 other countries. *The most frequently chosen baccalaureate fields are:* business/marketing, biological/life sciences, interdisciplinary studies. *Graduate:* 2,812 in graduate degree programs.

From out-of-state	1%	Reside on campus	13%
Age 25 or older	35%	Transferred in	15%
International students	2%	African Americans	5%
Asian Americans/Pacific Islanders	4%	Hispanic Americans	46%
Native Americans	0.4%		

Faculty 905 (42% full-time), 99% with terminal degrees.

Expenses (1999–2000) *Tuition, state resident:* full-time $2160; part-time $72 per semester hour. *Tuition, nonresident:* full-time $8640; part-time $288 per semester hour. *Required fees:* full-time $814; $34 per semester hour; $24 per term part-time. Full-time tuition and fees vary according to course load. Part-time tuition and fees vary according to course load. *College room and board:* room only: $2832. Room and board charges vary according to housing facility. *Payment plan:* installment.

Library John Peace Library plus 1 other. *Collection:* 521,009 titles, 2,665 serial subscriptions, 24,752 audiovisual materials.

College life *Housing: Option:* coed. *Social organizations:* national fraternities, national sororities, local fraternities; 1% of eligible men and 1% of eligible women are members. *Most popular organizations:* Pre-Med Society, MPA Student Association, Intervarsity Christian Fellowship, Catholic Student Association.

Campus security 24-hour emergency response devices and patrols, student patrols, late-night transport-escort service, controlled dormitory access.

After graduation 300 organizations recruited on campus 1997–98. *Career center:* 9 full-time, 14 part-time personnel. Services include job fairs, resume preparation, interview workshops, resume referral, career/interest testing, career counseling, careers library, job bank, job interviews. *Graduate education:* 6% of class of 1999 went directly to graduate and professional school.

Freshmen 3,917 applied, 3,874 admitted, 2,098 enrolled.

Average high school GPA	2.23	SAT verbal scores above 500	49%
SAT math scores above 500	47%	ACT above 18	81%
From top 10% of their h.s. class	20%	From top quarter	46%
From top half	79%	1998 freshmen returning in 1999	60%

Application *Option:* early admission. *Application fee:* $25. *Required:* high school transcript.

Standardized tests *Admission: Required:* SAT I or ACT.

Significant dates *Application deadlines:* 7/1 (freshmen), 7/1 (transfers). *Financial aid deadline priority date:* 3/31.

Freshman Application Contact
Ms. Sandy Speed, Interim Director, The University of Texas at San Antonio, 6900 North Loop 1604 West, San Antonio, TX 78249-0617. **Phone:** 210-458-4530. **Toll-free phone:** 800-669-0919.

Visit CollegeQuest.com for information on majors offered and athletics.

THE UNIVERSITY OF TEXAS AT TYLER
Tyler, Texas

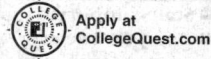
Apply at CollegeQuest.com

- **State-supported**, comprehensive, founded 1971
- **Degrees** bachelor's and master's
- **Urban** 200-acre campus
- **Coed**, 2,455 undergraduate students, 59% full-time, 67% women, 33% men
- **28% of applicants were admitted**
- **$2240 tuition** and fees (in-state); $7424 (out-of-state)

The University of Texas at Tyler, a broad-spectrum liberal arts university, also offers academic programs that support professional and specialized careers. Seventy-four bachelor's and master's degree programs are offered through the University's 6 schools, which include the Schools of Business Administration, Education and Psychology, Engineering, Liberal Arts, Nursing, and Sciences and Mathematics. For more information, students should call 903-566-7202.

Part of University of Texas System.

Students *Undergraduates:* 1,438 full-time, 1,017 part-time. Students come from 13 states and territories, 14 other countries. *The most frequently chosen baccalaureate fields are:* health professions and related sciences, business/marketing, interdisciplinary studies. *Graduate:* 938 in graduate degree programs.

From out-of-state	1%	Age 25 or older	59%
International students	1%	African Americans	9%
Asian Americans/Pacific Islanders	1%	Hispanic Americans	3%
Native Americans	1%		

Faculty 264 (59% full-time), 56% with terminal degrees.

Expenses (1999–2000) *Tuition, state resident:* full-time $912; part-time $38 per semester hour. *Tuition, nonresident:* full-time $6096; part-time $254 per semester hour. *Required fees:* full-time $1328; $49 per semester hour; $76 per term part-time. Full-time tuition and fees vary according to course load. *College room and board:* room only: $3199. Room and board charges vary according to board plan and housing facility. *Payment plan:* installment.

Library Robert Muntz Library. *Collection:* 193,519 titles, 1,282 serial subscriptions.

College life *Housing: Option:* coed.

After graduation *Career center:* Services include career counseling.

Freshmen 335 applied, 93 admitted, 103 enrolled.

SAT verbal scores above 500	N/R	SAT math scores above 500	N/R
ACT above 18	N/R		

Application *Option:* eApply at www.CollegeQuest.com.

Standardized tests *Admission: Required:* SAT I or ACT. *Required for some:* TASP.

Significant dates *Application deadline:* 4/1 (freshmen). *Financial aid deadline priority date:* 4/1.

Freshman Application Contact
Ms. Shawnda Kennedy, Director of Admissions, The University of Texas at Tyler, 3900 University Boulevard, Tyler, TX 75799-0001. **Phone:** 903-566-7207. **Toll-free phone:** 800-UTTYLER. **Fax:** 903-566-7068.

Texas

The University of Texas at Tyler (continued)
Visit CollegeQuest.com for information on majors offered and athletics.

THE UNIVERSITY OF TEXAS HEALTH SCIENCE CENTER AT SAN ANTONIO
San Antonio, Texas

Admissions Office Contact
The University of Texas Health Science Center at San Antonio, 7703 Floyd Curl Drive, San Antonio, TX 78284-6200. **Fax:** 210-567-2685.

THE UNIVERSITY OF TEXAS–HOUSTON HEALTH SCIENCE CENTER
Houston, Texas

- **State-supported**, upper-level, founded 1972
- **Degrees** bachelor's, master's, doctoral, first professional, and post-master's certificates
- **Urban** campus
- **Coed**, 262 undergraduate students, 89% full-time, 93% women, 7% men
- **Moderately difficult** entrance level
- **$3477 tuition** and fees (in-state); $13,107 (out-of-state)
- **$9371 average financial aid** package, $15,504 average indebtedness upon graduation, $77.1 million endowment

Part of University of Texas System.
Students *Undergraduates:* 232 full-time, 30 part-time. Students come from 6 states and territories, 2 other countries. *The most frequently chosen baccalaureate field is:* health professions and related sciences. **Graduate:** 1,080 in professional programs, 1,828 in other graduate degree programs.

From out-of-state	5%	Age 25 or older	51%
Transferred in	100%	International students	2%
African Americans	10%	Asian Americans/Pacific Islanders	13%
Hispanic Americans	14%		

Faculty 1,084 (82% full-time).
Expenses (2000–2001) *Tuition, state resident:* full-time $2880; part-time $58 per semester hour. *Tuition, nonresident:* full-time $12,510; part-time $274 per semester hour. *Required fees:* full-time $597; $13 per semester hour; $20 per term part-time. Part-time tuition and fees vary according to course load. *Payment plan:* installment.
Library Houston Academy of Medicine-Texas Medical Center Library plus 3 others. *Operations spending 1999–2000:* $2.7 million. *Collection:* 270,649 titles, 2,778 serial subscriptions.
College life *Housing: Option:* coed.
Campus security 24-hour emergency response devices and patrols, late-night transport-escort service, controlled access to all buildings.
Application *Option:* electronic application. *Preference* given to state residents. *Application fee:* $10.
Significant dates *Application deadline:* rolling (transfers). *Financial aid deadline:* continuous.
Freshman Application Contact
Mr. Robert L. Jenkins, Associate Registrar, The University of Texas–Houston Health Science Center, PO Box 20036, Houston, TX 77225-0036. **Phone:** 713-500-3333 Ext. 2203. **Fax:** 713-500-3026. **E-mail:** uthschro@admin4.hsc.uth.tmc.edu
Visit CollegeQuest.com for information on majors offered and athletics.

THE UNIVERSITY OF TEXAS MEDICAL BRANCH AT GALVESTON
Galveston, Texas

- **State-supported**, upper-level, founded 1891
- **Degrees** bachelor's, master's, doctoral, and first professional
- **Small-town** 100-acre campus with easy access to Houston
- **Coed**, 652 undergraduate students, 80% full-time, 79% women, 21% men
- **Most difficult** entrance level, 36% of applicants were admitted

- **$1832 tuition** and fees (in-state); $9608 (out-of-state)
- **$19,674 average indebtedness** upon graduation, $302.1 million endowment

Part of University of Texas System.
Students *Undergraduates:* 523 full-time, 129 part-time. Students come from 7 states and territories, 2 other countries. *The most frequently chosen baccalaureate field is:* health professions and related sciences. **Graduate:** 820 in professional programs, 479 in other graduate degree programs.

From out-of-state	2%	Reside on campus	20%
Age 25 or older	57%	Transferred in	45%
International students	0.5%	African Americans	10%
Asian Americans/Pacific Islanders	11%	Hispanic Americans	16%
Native Americans	0.2%		

Faculty 151 (77% full-time), 97% with terminal degrees.
Expenses (1999–2000) *One-time required fee:* $10. *Tuition, state resident:* full-time $1368; part-time $38 per semester hour. *Tuition, nonresident:* full-time $9144; part-time $254 per semester hour. *Required fees:* full-time $464; $12 per semester hour; $45 per term part-time. Full-time tuition and fees vary according to course load and program. Part-time tuition and fees vary according to course load and program. *College room and board:* room only: $1755. Room and board charges vary according to housing facility. *Payment plan:* installment.
Library Moody Medical Library. *Operations spending 1999–2000:* $3.8 million. *Collection:* 245,619 titles, 2,265 serial subscriptions.
College life *Housing: Option:* coed. *Social organizations:* national fraternities; 20% of men are members. *Most popular organizations:* Texas Medical Association, American Medical Student Association, American Medical Women's Association, Texas Association Latin American Medical Students, National Medical Student Association.
Campus security 24-hour emergency response devices and patrols, late-night transport-escort service.
After graduation *Career center:* Services include career counseling.
Application *Option:* electronic application. *Preference* given to state residents. *Application fee:* $30.
Significant dates *Financial aid deadline priority date:* 3/1.
Freshman Application Contact
Mr. Richard Lewis, University Registrar, The University of Texas Medical Branch at Galveston, 1212 Ashbel Smith, Galveston, TX 77555-1305. **Phone:** 409-772-1215. **Fax:** 409-772-5056. **E-mail:** student.admissions@utmb.edu
Visit CollegeQuest.com for information on majors offered and athletics.

THE UNIVERSITY OF TEXAS OF THE PERMIAN BASIN
Odessa, Texas

Admissions Office Contact
The University of Texas of the Permian Basin, 4901 East University, Odessa, TX 79762-0001. **Fax:** 915-552-2374. **E-mail:** gomez-v@gusher.pb.utexas.edu

THE UNIVERSITY OF TEXAS–PAN AMERICAN
Edinburg, Texas

- **State-supported**, comprehensive, founded 1927
- **Degrees** bachelor's, master's, and doctoral
- **Rural** 200-acre campus
- **Coed**, 10,922 undergraduate students, 65% full-time, 57% women, 43% men
- **Noncompetitive** entrance level, 100% of applicants were admitted
- **33:1 student-to-undergraduate faculty ratio**
- **17.96% graduate** in 6 years or less
- **$2017 tuition** and fees (in-state); $8917 (out-of-state)
- **$2650 average financial aid** package, $18.4 million endowment

Part of University of Texas System.
Students *Undergraduates:* 7,122 full-time, 3,800 part-time. Students come from 30 states and territories, 10 other countries. *The most frequently*

chosen baccalaureate fields are: business/marketing, interdisciplinary studies, protective services/public administration. **Graduate:** 1,647 in graduate degree programs.

From out-of-state	1%	Age 25 or older	26%
Transferred in	25%	International students	1%
African Americans	0.5%	Asian Americans/Pacific Islanders	1%
Hispanic Americans	85%	Native Americans	0.1%

Faculty 833 (48% full-time), 35% with terminal degrees.
Expenses (1999–2000) *Tuition, state resident:* full-time $1800; part-time $60 per semester hour. *Tuition, nonresident:* full-time $8700; part-time $290 per semester hour. *Required fees:* full-time $217; $16 per semester hour; $19 per term part-time. Part-time tuition and fees vary according to course load. *College room and board:* $2663; room only: $1540. Room and board charges vary according to board plan and housing facility.
Library Learning Resource Library. *Operations spending 1999–2000:* $2.8 million. *Collection:* 224,012 titles, 2,454 serial subscriptions.
College life *Social organizations:* national fraternities, national sororities; 5% of eligible men and 6% of eligible women are members. *Most popular organizations:* Accounting Society, American Marketing Association, Pre-Medical/Bio Medical Society, Association of Texas Professional Educators, Financial Management Association.
Campus security 24-hour emergency response devices and patrols, late-night transport-escort service.
After graduation *Career center:* Services include job fairs, resume referral, career counseling, careers library, job interviews.
Freshmen 3,335 applied, 3,335 admitted, 1,464 enrolled. 1 valedictorian.

SAT verbal scores above 500	N/R	SAT math scores above 500	N/R
ACT above 18	49%	From top 10% of their h.s. class	21%
From top quarter	50%	From top half	79%
1998 freshmen returning in 1999	58%		

Application *Options:* Common Application, electronic application, early admission. *Application fee:* $0. *Required:* high school transcript. *Required for some:* interview.
Standardized tests *Admission: Required:* SAT I or ACT.
Significant dates *Application deadlines:* 7/15 (freshmen), 7/15 (transfers). *Financial aid deadline:* 4/15. Priority date: 2/28.
Freshman Application Contact
Mr. David Zuniga, Director of Admissions, The University of Texas–Pan American, Office of Admissions and Records, 1201 West University Drive, Edinburg, TX 78539. **Phone:** 956-381-2201.
Visit CollegeQuest.com for information on majors offered and athletics.

THE UNIVERSITY OF TEXAS SOUTHWESTERN MEDICAL CENTER AT DALLAS
Dallas, Texas

Admissions Office Contact
The University of Texas Southwestern Medical Center at Dallas, 5323 Harry Hines Boulevard, Dallas, TX 75235. **Fax:** 214-648-3289. **E-mail:** admissions@mednet.swmed.edu

UNIVERSITY OF THE INCARNATE WORD
San Antonio, Texas

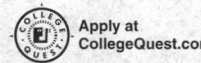
Apply at CollegeQuest.com

- **Independent Roman Catholic**, comprehensive, founded 1881
- **Degrees** bachelor's, master's, and doctoral
- **Urban** 200-acre campus
- **Coed**
- **Moderately difficult** entrance level
- **$11,950 tuition** and fees

Expenses (1999–2000) *One-time required fee:* $130. *Comprehensive fee:* $16,420 includes full-time tuition ($11,850), mandatory fees ($100), and room and board ($4470). *College room only:* $2730. *Part-time tuition:* $370 per semester hour. *Part-time fees:* $92 per term part-time. Part-time tuition and fees vary according to course load.
Institutional Web site http://www.uiw.edu/
College life *Housing: Options:* coed, men-only, women-only. *Social organizations:* national fraternities, national sororities, local sororities; 2% of women are members. *Most popular organizations:* Alpha Phi Omega, dietetics club, Red Alert, Student Nurses Association, Crusaders Seeking Christ.
Campus security 24-hour emergency response devices and patrols, late-night transport-escort service, controlled dormitory access.
Application *Options:* eApply at www.CollegeQuest.com, electronic application, early admission, deferred entrance. *Application fee:* $20. *Required:* high school transcript. *Required for some:* essay or personal statement; interview. *Recommended:* minimum 2.0 GPA; 1 letter of recommendation; interview.
Standardized tests *Admission: Required:* SAT I or ACT.
Admissions Office Contact
University of the Incarnate Word, Box 285, San Antonio, TX 78209-6397. **Toll-free phone:** 800-749-WORD. **Fax:** 210-829-3921. **E-mail:** admis@universe.uiwtx.edu
Visit CollegeQuest.com for information on athletics. College video available at CollegeQuest.com.

■ *See page 2846 for a narrative description.*

WAYLAND BAPTIST UNIVERSITY
Plainview, Texas

- **Independent Baptist**, comprehensive, founded 1908
- **Degrees** associate, bachelor's, and master's (branch locations: Anchorage, AK; Amarillo, TX; Luke Airforce Base, AZ; Glorieta, NM; Aiea, HI; Lubbock, TX; San Antonio, TX; Wichita Falls, TX)
- **Small-town** 80-acre campus
- **Coed**, 3,791 undergraduate students, 23% full-time, 45% women, 55% men
- **Minimally difficult** entrance level, 100% of applicants were admitted
- **13:1 student-to-undergraduate faculty ratio**
- **26% graduate** in 6 years or less
- **$7400 tuition** and fees
- **$8485 average financial aid** package, $33.8 million endowment

Students *Undergraduates:* 870 full-time, 2,921 part-time. Students come from 24 states and territories, 14 other countries. *The most frequently chosen baccalaureate fields are:* business/marketing, education, social sciences and history. **Graduate:** 456 in graduate degree programs.

From out-of-state	33%	Reside on campus	49%
Age 25 or older	73%	Transferred in	2%
International students	1%	African Americans	16%
Asian Americans/Pacific Islanders	2%	Hispanic Americans	14%
Native Americans	1%		

Faculty 282 (30% full-time).
Expenses (1999–2000) *Comprehensive fee:* $10,521 includes full-time tuition ($7050), mandatory fees ($350), and room and board ($3121). *College room only:* $1216. Room and board charges vary according to board plan and housing facility. *Part-time tuition:* $235 per semester hour. *Part-time fees:* $40 per term part-time. Part-time tuition and fees vary according to course load. *Payment plan:* installment. *Waivers:* employees or children of employees.
Library J.E. and L.E. Mabee Learning Resource Center. *Operations spending 1999–2000:* $403,184. *Collection:* 101,455 titles, 497 serial subscriptions.
College life *Housing:* on-campus residence required through junior year. *Options:* men-only, women-only. *Social organizations:* national fraternities, national sororities, local fraternities, local sororities; 9% of eligible men and 10% of eligible women are members. *Most popular organization:* student government.
Campus security 24-hour emergency response devices and patrols, security lighting.
After graduation *Career center:* 1 full-time, 1 part-time personnel. Services include job fairs, resume preparation, career counseling, careers library, job bank.

Texas

Wayland Baptist University (continued)

Freshmen 322 applied, 322 admitted, 221 enrolled.

Average high school GPA	3.32	SAT verbal scores above 500	48%
SAT math scores above 500	53%	ACT above 18	71%
From top 10% of their h.s. class	18%	From top quarter	46%
From top half	77%	1998 freshmen returning in 1999	60%

Application *Application fee:* $35. *Required:* high school transcript. *Recommended:* interview.

Standardized tests *Admission: Required:* SAT I or ACT.

Significant dates *Application deadlines:* rolling (freshmen), rolling (transfers). *Financial aid deadline priority date:* 5/1.

Freshman Application Contact
Mr. Shawn Thomas, Director of Student Admissions, Wayland Baptist University, 1900 West 7th Street #712, Plainview, TX 79072. **Phone:** 806-296-4709. **Toll-free phone:** 800-588-1-WBU. **E-mail:** admityou@mail.wbu.edu

Visit CollegeQuest.com for information on majors offered and athletics.

WEST TEXAS A&M UNIVERSITY
Canyon, Texas

- **State-supported**, comprehensive, founded 1909
- **Degrees** bachelor's and master's
- **Small-town** 128-acre campus
- **Coed**, 5,521 undergraduate students, 80% full-time, 54% women, 46% men
- **Moderately difficult** entrance level, 77% of applicants were admitted
- **23:1 student-to-undergraduate faculty ratio**
- **27.56% graduate** in 6 years or less
- **$1974 tuition** and fees (in-state); $7158 (out-of-state)
- **$7425 average financial aid** package, $17,125 average indebtedness upon graduation, $12.5 million endowment

Part of Texas A&M University System.

Students *Undergraduates:* 4,438 full-time, 1,083 part-time. Students come from 32 states and territories, 24 other countries. *The most frequently chosen baccalaureate fields are:* business/marketing, health professions and related sciences, interdisciplinary studies. *Graduate:* 1,130 in graduate degree programs.

From out-of-state	7%	Reside on campus	29%
Age 25 or older	21%	Transferred in	12%
International students	1%	African Americans	3%
Asian Americans/Pacific Islanders	1%	Hispanic Americans	11%
Native Americans	1%		

Faculty 299 (63% full-time), 54% with terminal degrees.

Expenses (1999–2000) *Tuition, state resident:* full-time $1404; part-time $58 per semester hour. *Tuition, nonresident:* full-time $6588; part-time $274 per semester hour. *Required fees:* full-time $570; $55 per term part-time. Full-time tuition and fees vary according to course load and reciprocity agreements. Part-time tuition and fees vary according to course load and reciprocity agreements. *College room and board:* $3310; room only: $1484. Room and board charges vary according to board plan and housing facility. *Payment plan:* installment. *Waivers:* senior citizens.

Library Cornette Library. *Operations spending 1999–2000:* $858,775. *Collection:* 2,836 audiovisual materials.

College life *Housing:* on-campus residence required through sophomore year. *Options:* coed, men-only, women-only, disabled students. *Social organizations:* national fraternities, national sororities, local fraternities, local sororities; 7% of eligible men and 5% of eligible women are members. *Most popular organizations:* Residence Hall Association, Greek System, Dean's Roundtable, student government, Students in Free Enterprise.

Campus security 24-hour emergency response devices and patrols, student patrols, late-night transport-escort service, controlled dormitory access.

After graduation 42 organizations recruited on campus 1997–98. 86% of class of 1998 had job offers within 6 months. *Career center:* 6 full-time personnel. Services include job fairs, resume preparation, interview workshops, resume referral, career/interest testing, career counseling, careers library, job bank, job interviews.

Freshmen 2,128 applied, 1,642 admitted, 980 enrolled. 1 National Merit Scholar, 34 valedictorians.

Average high school GPA	2.61	SAT verbal scores above 500	54%
SAT math scores above 500	57%	ACT above 18	89%
From top 10% of their h.s. class	13%	From top quarter	38%
From top half	77%	1998 freshmen returning in 1999	67%

Application *Options:* Common Application, electronic application. *Required:* high school transcript.

Standardized tests *Admission: Required:* SAT I or ACT.

Significant dates *Application deadlines:* rolling (freshmen), rolling (transfers). *Financial aid deadline priority date:* 5/1.

Freshman Application Contact
Ms. Lila Vars, Director of Admissions, West Texas A&M University, WT Box 60907, Canyon, TX 79016-0001. **Phone:** 806-651-2020. **Toll-free phone:** 800-99-WTAMU (in-state); 800-99-WTAMU (out-of-state). **Fax:** 806-651-2126. **E-mail:** lvars@mail.wtamu.edu

Visit CollegeQuest.com for information on majors offered and athletics. College video available at CollegeQuest.com.

WILEY COLLEGE
Marshall, Texas

- **Independent**, 4-year, founded 1873, affiliated with United Methodist Church
- **Degrees** associate and bachelor's
- **Small-town** 58-acre campus
- **Coed**
- **Noncompetitive** entrance level
- **$5176 tuition** and fees

Expenses (1999–2000) *Comprehensive fee:* $8730 includes full-time tuition ($4500), mandatory fees ($676), and room and board ($3554). *College room only:* $1708. *Part-time tuition:* $150 per credit hour. *Part-time fees:* $50 per term part-time.

Institutional Web site http://www.wileyc.edu/

College life *Social organizations:* national fraternities, national sororities.

Application *Options:* early admission, deferred entrance. *Application fee:* $10. *Required:* high school transcript; 1 letter of recommendation.

Standardized tests *Placement: Recommended:* SAT I or ACT.

Admissions Office Contact
Wiley College, 711 Wiley Avenue, Marshall, TX 75670-5199. **Toll-free phone:** 800-658-6889. **Fax:** 903-938-8100.

Visit CollegeQuest.com for information on athletics.

UTAH

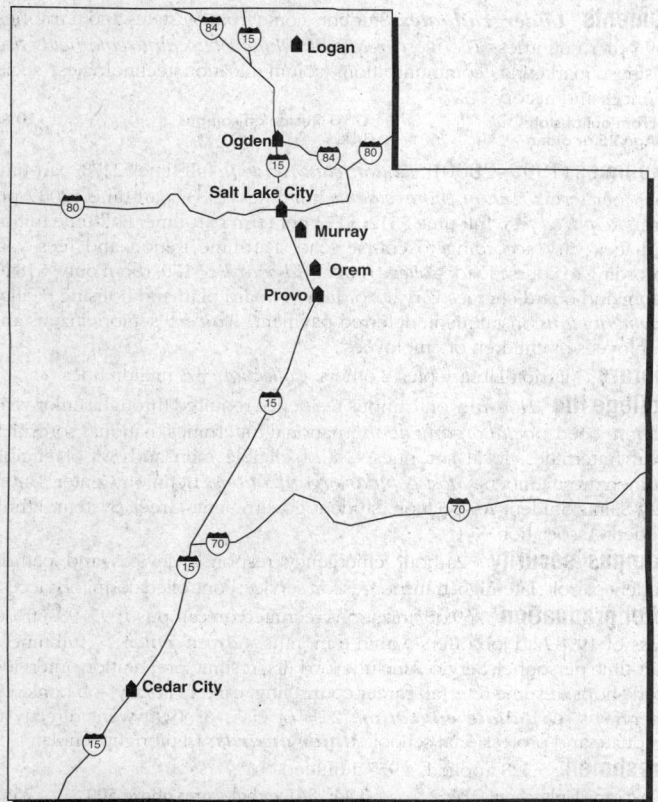

BRIGHAM YOUNG UNIVERSITY
Provo, Utah

- **Independent**, university, founded 1875, affiliated with Church of Jesus Christ of Latter-day Saints
- **Degrees** bachelor's, master's, doctoral, and first professional
- **Suburban** 638-acre campus with easy access to Salt Lake City
- **Coed**, 29,919 undergraduate students, 88% full-time, 53% women, 47% men
- **Moderately difficult** entrance level, 64% of applicants were admitted
- **20:1 student-to-undergraduate faculty ratio**
- **67% graduate** in 6 years or less
- **$2830 tuition** and fees

Students *Undergraduates:* 26,473 full-time, 3,446 part-time. Students come from 53 states and territories, 107 other countries. *The most frequently chosen baccalaureate fields are:* education, business/marketing, social sciences and history. *Graduate:* 471 in professional programs, 2,223 in other graduate degree programs.

From out-of-state	71%	Reside on campus	20%
Age 25 or older	8%	Transferred in	6%
International students	3%	African Americans	0.3%
Asian Americans/Pacific Islanders	2%	Hispanic Americans	2%
Native Americans	1%		

Faculty 1,795 (78% full-time), 63% with terminal degrees.
Expenses (1999–2000) *Comprehensive fee:* $7284 includes full-time tuition ($2830) and room and board ($4454). *College room only:* $1846. Full-time tuition and fees vary according to reciprocity agreements. Room and board charges vary according to board plan and housing facility. *Part-time tuition:* $145 per credit hour. Part-time tuition and fees vary according to course load and reciprocity agreements. *Waivers:* employees or children of employees.
Library Harold B. Lee Library plus 2 others. *Collection:* 2.5 million titles, 16,029 serial subscriptions.
College life *Housing: Options:* men-only, women-only. *Most popular organizations:* Swing Kids, Adaptive Aquatics, ACCESS, Young Republicans.

Campus security 24-hour emergency response devices and patrols, late-night transport-escort service, controlled dormitory access.
After graduation 600 organizations recruited on campus 1997–98. 79% of class of 1998 had job offers within 6 months. *Career center:* 7 full-time, 9 part-time personnel. Services include job fairs, resume preparation, interview workshops, resume referral, career/interest testing, career counseling, careers library, job bank, job interviews. *Graduate education:* 23% of class of 1999 went directly to graduate and professional school. *Major awards:* 2 Fulbright Scholars.
Freshmen 8,078 applied, 5,181 admitted, 4,857 enrolled. 133 National Merit Scholars.

Average high school GPA	3.74	SAT verbal scores above 500	N/R
SAT math scores above 500	N/R	ACT above 18	99%
From top 10% of their h.s. class	54%	From top quarter	88%
From top half	98%	1998 freshmen returning in 1999	87%

Application *Options:* electronic application, early admission, deferred entrance. *Application fee:* $25. *Required:* essay or personal statement; high school transcript; 1 letter of recommendation; interview.
Standardized tests *Admission: Required:* ACT.
Significant dates *Application deadlines:* 2/15 (freshmen), 3/15 (transfers). *Financial aid deadline priority date:* 4/15.
Freshman Application Contact
Mr. Erlend D. Peterson, Dean of Admissions and Records, Brigham Young University, Provo, UT 84602-1110. **Phone:** 801-378-2539. **E-mail:** admissions@byu.edu
Visit CollegeQuest.com for information on majors offered and athletics. College video and electronic viewbook available at CollegeQuest.com.

DIXIE STATE COLLEGE OF UTAH
St. George, Utah

- **State-supported**, primarily 2-year, founded 1911
- **Degrees** associate and bachelor's
- **Small-town** 60-acre campus
- **Coed**, 3,505 undergraduate students, 76% full-time, 54% women, 46% men
- **Noncompetitive** entrance level
- **33:1 student-to-undergraduate faculty ratio**
- **$1435 tuition** and fees (in-state); $5284 (out-of-state)

Faculty 183 (45% full-time), 70% with terminal degrees.
Admissions Office Contact
Dixie State College of Utah, 225 South 700 East, St. George, UT 84770-3876. **Fax:** 435-656-4005. **E-mail:** rollins@cc.dixie.edu
Visit CollegeQuest.com for information on majors offered and athletics. College video and electronic viewbook available at CollegeQuest.com.

ITT TECHNICAL INSTITUTE
Murray, Utah

- **Proprietary**, primarily 2-year, founded 1984
- **Degrees** associate and bachelor's
- **Suburban** 3-acre campus with easy access to Salt Lake City
- **Coed**
- **Minimally difficult** entrance level
- **$9190 tuition** and fees

Part of ITT Educational Services, Inc.
Admissions Office Contact
ITT Technical Institute, 920 West Levoy Drive, Murray, UT 84123-2500. **Toll-free phone:** 800-365-2136.
Visit CollegeQuest.com for information on majors offered and athletics. College video available at CollegeQuest.com.

SOUTHERN UTAH UNIVERSITY
Cedar City, Utah

- **State-supported**, comprehensive, founded 1897
- **Degrees** associate, bachelor's, and master's

Utah

Southern Utah University (continued)
- **Small-town** 113-acre campus
- **Coed,** 4,166 undergraduate students, 87% full-time, 58% women, 42% men
- **Moderately difficult** entrance level, 84% of applicants were admitted
- **21:1 student-to-undergraduate faculty ratio**
- **37.9% graduate** in 6 years or less
- **$1965 tuition** and fees (in-state); $6195 (out-of-state)
- **$5148 average financial aid** package, $10,712 average indebtedness upon graduation, $5.1 million endowment

Part of Utah System of Higher Education.

Students *Undergraduates:* 3,607 full-time, 559 part-time. Students come from 40 states and territories, 14 other countries. *The most frequently chosen baccalaureate fields are:* business/marketing, education, social sciences and history. *Graduate:* 158 in graduate degree programs.

From out-of-state	12%	Reside on campus	7%
Age 25 or older	15%	Transferred in	14%
International students	2%	African Americans	1%
Asian Americans/Pacific Islanders	1%	Hispanic Americans	2%
Native Americans	1%		

Faculty 321 (64% full-time), 41% with terminal degrees.

Expenses (1999–2000) *Tuition, state resident:* full-time $1524; part-time $78 per credit hour. *Tuition, nonresident:* full-time $5754; part-time $1729 per term. *Required fees:* full-time $441; $148 per term part-time. Part-time tuition and fees vary according to course load. *College room and board:* $2520. Room and board charges vary according to board plan and housing facility. *Waivers:* senior citizens and employees or children of employees.

Library Southern Utah University Library. *Operations spending 1999–2000:* $1.1 million. *Collection:* 222,873 titles, 6,165 serial subscriptions, 13,352 audiovisual materials.

College life *Housing: Options:* coed, men-only, women-only, disabled students. *Social organizations:* national fraternities, national sororities, local sororities; 2% of eligible men and 3% of eligible women are members. *Most popular organizations:* Outdoor Club, Intertribal Club, Latter Day Saints Student Association, Ski Club, Residence Halls Association.

Campus security 24-hour emergency response devices, student patrols, late-night transport-escort service, controlled dormitory access.

After graduation 49 organizations recruited on campus 1997–98. 75% of class of 1998 had job offers within 6 months. *Career center:* 4 full-time personnel. Services include job fairs, resume preparation, resume referral, career counseling, careers library, job bank, job interviews.

Freshmen 2,423 applied, 2,047 admitted, 841 enrolled.

Average high school GPA	3.39	SAT verbal scores above 500	43%
SAT math scores above 500	43%	ACT above 18	80%
From top 10% of their h.s. class	16%	From top quarter	40%
From top half	75%	1998 freshmen returning in 1999	47%

Application *Options:* eApply at www.CollegeQuest.com, electronic application, early admission, deferred entrance. *Application fee:* $25. *Required:* high school transcript; minimum 2.0 GPA.

Standardized tests *Admission: Required:* SAT I or ACT. *Recommended:* ACT.

Significant dates *Application deadlines:* 7/1 (freshmen), rolling (transfers). *Financial aid deadline:* continuous.

Freshman Application Contact
Mr. Dale S. Orton, Director of Admissions, Southern Utah University, 351 West Center Street, Cedar City, UT 84720-2498. **Phone:** 801-586-7740. **Fax:** 435-586-5475. **E-mail:** adminfo@suu.edu

Visit CollegeQuest.com for information on majors offered and athletics. College video available at CollegeQuest.com.

UNIVERSITY OF UTAH
Salt Lake City, Utah

- **State-supported,** university, founded 1850
- **Degrees** bachelor's, master's, doctoral, and first professional
- **Urban** 1,500-acre campus
- **Coed,** 21,956 undergraduate students, 59% full-time, 44% women, 56% men
- **Moderately difficult** entrance level, 93% of applicants were admitted
- **37% graduate** in 6 years or less
- **$2790 tuition** and fees (in-state); $8495 (out-of-state)

Part of Utah System of Higher Education.

Students *Undergraduates:* Students come from 54 states and territories, 109 other countries. *The most frequently chosen baccalaureate fields are:* business/marketing, communications/communication technologies, social sciences and history.

From out-of-state	17%	Reside on campus	10%
Age 25 or older	34%		

Expenses (1999–2000) *Tuition, state resident:* full-time $2278; part-time $563 per term. *Tuition, nonresident:* full-time $7983; part-time $2009 per term. *Required fees:* full-time $512; $173 per term part-time. Full-time tuition and fees vary according to course load. Part-time tuition and fees vary according to course load. *College room and board:* $5179; room only: $1840. Room and board charges vary according to board plan and housing facility. *Payment plans:* installment, deferred payment. *Waivers:* senior citizens and employees or children of employees.

Library Marriott Library plus 2 others. *Collection:* 3.3 million titles.

College life *Housing:* on-campus residence required through senior year. *Option:* coed. *Social organizations:* national fraternities, national sororities, local fraternities, local sororities; 2% of eligible men and 3% of eligible women are members. *Most popular organizations:* Bennion Center, Latter-Day Saints Student Association, student government, Greek System, Ethnic Student Association.

Campus security 24-hour emergency response devices and patrols, student patrols, late-night transport-escort service, controlled dormitory access.

After graduation 269 organizations recruited on campus 1997–98. 60% of class of 1998 had job offers within 6 months. *Career center:* 17 full-time, 7 part-time personnel. Services include job fairs, resume preparation, interview workshops, resume referral, career counseling, careers library, job bank, job interviews. *Graduate education:* 24% of class of 1999 went directly to graduate and professional school. *Major awards:* 1 Fulbright Scholar.

Freshmen 5,328 applied, 4,957 admitted.

Average high school GPA	3.44	SAT verbal scores above 500	75%
SAT math scores above 500	77%	ACT above 18	94%
From top 10% of their h.s. class	27%	From top quarter	54%
From top half	80%	1998 freshmen returning in 1999	59%

Application *Options:* Common Application, electronic application, early admission, deferred entrance. *Application fee:* $30. *Required:* high school transcript; minimum 2.0 GPA. *Recommended:* minimum 3.0 GPA.

Standardized tests *Admission: Required:* SAT I or ACT.

Significant dates *Application deadlines:* 7/1 (freshmen), 7/1 (transfers). *Financial aid deadline priority date:* 3/15.

Freshman Application Contact
Ms. Suzanne Espinoza, Director of High School Services, University of Utah, 250 South Student Services Building, Salt Lake City, UT 84112. **Phone:** 801-581-8761. **Toll-free phone:** 800-444-8638. **Fax:** 801-585-3034.

Visit CollegeQuest.com for information on majors offered and athletics. College video available at CollegeQuest.com.

UTAH STATE UNIVERSITY
Logan, Utah

- **State-supported,** university, founded 1888
- **Degrees** associate, bachelor's, master's, and doctoral
- **Urban** 456-acre campus
- **Coed,** 14,888 undergraduate students, 78% full-time, 52% women, 48% men
- **Moderately difficult** entrance level, 86% of applicants were admitted
- **23:1 student-to-undergraduate faculty ratio**
- **$2314 tuition** and fees (in-state); $7003 (out-of-state)
- **$5400 average financial aid** package, $13,400 average indebtedness upon graduation, $66.7 million endowment

Part of Utah System of Higher Education.

Students *Undergraduates:* 11,594 full-time, 3,294 part-time. Students come from 53 states and territories, 65 other countries. *The most frequently chosen baccalaureate fields are:* business/marketing, education, engineering/engineering technologies. *Graduate:* 3,637 in graduate degree programs.

Utah

From out-of-state	30%	Age 25 or older	19%
Transferred in	10%	International students	3%
African Americans	0.4%	Asian Americans/Pacific Islanders	1%
Hispanic Americans	1%	Native Americans	1%

Faculty 689 (93% full-time), 82% with terminal degrees.

Expenses (1999–2000) *Tuition, state resident:* full-time $1871. *Tuition, nonresident:* full-time $6560. *Required fees:* full-time $443. Full-time tuition and fees vary according to course load. Part-time tuition and fees vary according to course load. *College room and board:* $3938; room only: $1558. Room and board charges vary according to board plan and housing facility. *Payment plan:* deferred payment. *Waivers:* minority students, children of alumni, adult students, senior citizens, and employees or children of employees.

Library Merrill Library plus 4 others. *Operations spending 1999–2000:* $6.7 million. *Collection:* 34,796 audiovisual materials.

College life *Housing: Options:* coed, men-only, women-only, disabled students. *Social organizations:* national fraternities, national sororities; 3% of eligible men and 3% of eligible women are members. *Most popular organizations:* Latter-Day Saints Student Association, Greek organizations, multicultural clubs, volunteer groups, college councils.

Campus security 24-hour emergency response devices and patrols, student patrols, late-night transport-escort service, video monitor in pedestrian tunnels.

After graduation 161 organizations recruited on campus 1997–98. 66% of class of 1998 had job offers within 6 months. *Career center:* 11 full-time, 2 part-time personnel. Services include job fairs, resume preparation, interview workshops, resume referral, career/interest testing, career counseling, careers library, job bank, job interviews. *Graduate education:* 20% of class of 1999 went directly to graduate and professional school. *Major awards:* 1 Fulbright Scholar.

Freshmen 5,744 applied, 4,934 admitted, 2,564 enrolled. 26 National Merit Scholars.

| Average high school GPA | 3.39 | SAT verbal scores above 500 | 62% |
| SAT math scores above 500 | 64% | ACT above 18 | 87% |

Application *Options:* early admission, deferred entrance. *Preference* given to state residents. *Application fee:* $35. *Required:* high school transcript; minimum 2.5 GPA; 2.7 high school GPA for elementary education program. *Required for some:* minimum 3.0 GPA.

Standardized tests *Admission: Required:* SAT I or ACT. *Recommended:* ACT.

Significant dates *Application deadlines:* rolling (freshmen), rolling (transfers). *Financial aid deadline:* continuous.

Freshman Application Contact
Mr. Lynn Poulsen, Associate Vice President, Student Services, Utah State University, 1600 Old Main Hill, Logan, UT 84322-1600. **Phone:** 435-797-1107. **Fax:** 435-797-3900. **E-mail:** admit@admissions.usu.edu

Visit CollegeQuest.com for information on majors offered and athletics. College video available at CollegeQuest.com.

UTAH VALLEY STATE COLLEGE
Orem, Utah

- **State-supported**, primarily 2-year, founded 1941
- **Degrees** associate and bachelor's
- **Suburban** 200-acre campus with easy access to Salt Lake City
- **Coed**, 14,361 undergraduate students, 53% full-time, 44% women, 56% men
- **Noncompetitive** entrance level
- **$1630 tuition** and fees (in-state); $5070 (out-of-state)

Part of Utah System of Higher Education.
Faculty 967.
Admissions Office Contact
Utah Valley State College, 800 West 1200 South Street, Orem, UT 84058-5999. **Fax:** 801-225-4677. **E-mail:** info@uvsc.edu

Visit CollegeQuest.com for information on majors offered and athletics.

WEBER STATE UNIVERSITY
Ogden, Utah

- **State-supported**, comprehensive, founded 1889
- **Degrees** associate, bachelor's, and master's
- **Urban** 526-acre campus with easy access to Salt Lake City
- **Coed**, 14,813 undergraduate students, 60% full-time, 52% women, 48% men
- **Noncompetitive** entrance level, 100% of applicants were admitted
- **19:1 student-to-undergraduate faculty ratio**
- **$2042 tuition** and fees (in-state); $6058 (out-of-state)
- **$21.8 million endowment**

Part of Utah System of Higher Education.

Students *Undergraduates:* 8,920 full-time, 5,893 part-time. Students come from 46 states and territories, 40 other countries. *The most frequently chosen baccalaureate fields are:* business/marketing, education, protective services/public administration. *Graduate:* 171 in graduate degree programs.

From out-of-state	5%	Reside on campus	4%
Age 25 or older	32%	Transferred in	9%
International students	2%	African Americans	1%
Asian Americans/Pacific Islanders	2%	Hispanic Americans	3%
Native Americans	1%		

Faculty 749 (57% full-time).

Expenses (1999–2000) *Tuition, state resident:* full-time $1606; part-time $485 per term. *Tuition, nonresident:* full-time $5622; part-time $1698 per term. *Required fees:* full-time $436; $143 per term part-time. Part-time tuition and fees vary according to course load. *College room and board:* $3878; room only: $1680. Room and board charges vary according to board plan and housing facility. *Payment plans:* installment, deferred payment. *Waivers:* senior citizens and employees or children of employees.

Library Stewart Library plus 1 other. *Operations spending 1999–2000:* $2.7 million. *Collection:* 599,210 titles, 2,399 serial subscriptions.

College life *Housing: Options:* men-only, women-only, disabled students. *Social organizations:* national fraternities, national sororities, local fraternities, local sororities; 2% of eligible men and 3% of eligible women are members. *Most popular organizations:* LDSSA, mountaineering club, rodeo club, Beta Alpha Psi, Student Nurses.

Campus security 24-hour emergency response devices and patrols, student patrols, late-night transport-escort service, controlled dormitory access.

After graduation 2,624 organizations recruited on campus 1997–98. 94% of class of 1998 had job offers within 6 months. *Career center:* 13 full-time, 4 part-time personnel. Services include job fairs, resume preparation, interview workshops, resume referral, career/interest testing, career counseling, careers library, job bank, job interviews. *Graduate education:* 46% of class of 1999 went directly to graduate and professional school.

Freshmen 2,712 applied, 2,712 admitted, 2,712 enrolled.

Average high school GPA	3.3	SAT verbal scores above 500	53%
SAT math scores above 500	59%	ACT above 18	88%
From top quarter of their h.s. class	56%	From top half	89%
1998 freshmen returning in 1999	64%		

Application *Options:* electronic application, early admission, deferred entrance. *Application fee:* $30. *Required:* high school transcript.

Standardized tests *Placement: Required:* SAT I or ACT

Significant dates *Application deadline:* rolling (transfers). *Financial aid deadline priority date:* 3/1.

Freshman Application Contact
Mr. John Allred, Admissions Advisor, Weber State University, 1137 University Circle, Ogden, UT 84408-1137. **Phone:** 801-626-6050. **Toll-free phone:** 800-634-6568. **Fax:** 801-626-6747. **E-mail:** admissions@weber.edu

Visit CollegeQuest.com for information on majors offered and athletics. Electronic viewbook available at CollegeQuest.com.

WESTMINSTER COLLEGE
Salt Lake City, Utah

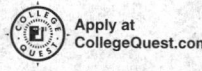 Apply at CollegeQuest.com

- **Independent**, comprehensive, founded 1875
- **Degrees** bachelor's, master's, and postbachelor's certificates
- **Suburban** 27-acre campus
- **Coed**, 1,722 undergraduate students, 81% full-time, 62% women, 38% men

Utah–Vermont

Westminster College (continued)
- **Moderately difficult** entrance level, 86% of applicants were admitted
- **17:1 student-to-undergraduate faculty ratio**
- **49.2% graduate** in 6 years or less
- **$12,726 tuition** and fees
- **$10,686 average financial aid** package, $45.7 million endowment

Students *Undergraduates:* 1,387 full-time, 335 part-time. Students come from 25 states and territories, 21 other countries. *The most frequently chosen baccalaureate fields are:* business/marketing, communications/communication technologies, education. *Graduate:* 537 in graduate degree programs.

From out-of-state	6%	Reside on campus	18%
Age 25 or older	28%	Transferred in	16%
International students	1%	African Americans	0.5%
Asian Americans/Pacific Islanders	3%	Hispanic Americans	5%
Native Americans	1%		

Faculty 229 (48% full-time), 58% with terminal degrees.

Expenses (1999–2000) *Comprehensive fee:* $17,476 includes full-time tuition ($12,456), mandatory fees ($270), and room and board ($4750). Full-time tuition and fees vary according to course load. Room and board charges vary according to board plan and housing facility. *Part-time tuition:* $492 per credit hour. *Part-time fees:* $100 per term. Part-time tuition and fees vary according to course load. *Payment plans:* installment, deferred payment. *Waivers:* employees or children of employees.

Library Ginger Gore Giovale Library. *Operations spending 1999–2000:* $744,526. *Collection:* 88,086 titles, 1,456 serial subscriptions, 3,145 audiovisual materials.

College life *Housing:* on-campus residence required in freshman year. *Option:* coed. *Most popular organizations:* outdoor club, Pre-Med Society, English club, Westminster Theatre Society, Students Educators Association of Westminster College.

Campus security 24-hour emergency response devices and patrols, student patrols, late-night transport-escort service, controlled dormitory access.

After graduation 80 organizations recruited on campus 1997–98. *Career center:* 3 full-time personnel. Services include job fairs, resume preparation, resume referral, career/interest testing, career counseling, careers library, job bank, job interviews. *Graduate education:* 48% of class of 1999 went directly to graduate and professional school: 14% business, 3% education, 2% graduate arts and sciences, 2% law, 2% medicine.

Freshmen 876 applied, 756 admitted, 320 enrolled.

Average high school GPA	3.64	SAT verbal scores above 500	71%
SAT math scores above 500	71%	ACT above 18	100%
From top 10% of their h.s. class	30%	From top quarter	63%
From top half	91%	1998 freshmen returning in 1999	77%

Application *Options:* eApply at www.CollegeQuest.com, Common Application, electronic application, early admission, deferred entrance. *Application fee:* $25. *Required:* high school transcript; minimum 2.5 GPA. *Recommended:* essay or personal statement; minimum 3.0 GPA; 1 letter of recommendation; interview.

Standardized tests *Admission: Required:* SAT I or ACT.

Significant dates *Application deadlines:* rolling (freshmen), rolling (transfers). *Financial aid deadline:* continuous.

Freshman Application Contact
Mr. Philip J. Alletto, Vice President of Student Development and Enrollment Management, Westminster College, 1840 South 1300 East, Salt Lake City, UT 84105-3697. **Phone:** 801-832-2200. **Toll-free phone:** 800-748-4753. **Fax:** 801-484-3252. **E-mail:** admispub@wsclc.edu

Visit CollegeQuest.com for information on majors offered and athletics.

■ *See page 2966 for a narrative description.*

VERMONT

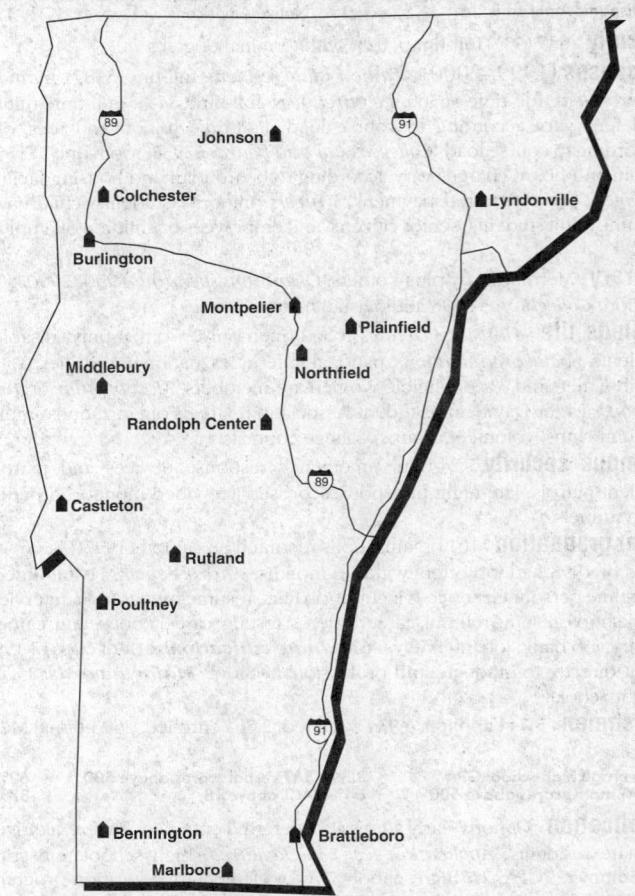

BENNINGTON COLLEGE
Bennington, Vermont

 Apply at CollegeQuest.com

- **Independent**, comprehensive, founded 1932
- **Degrees** bachelor's, master's, and postbachelor's certificates
- **Small-town** 550-acre campus with easy access to Albany
- **Coed**, 447 undergraduate students, 100% full-time, 70% women, 30% men
- **Very difficult** entrance level, 83% of applicants were admitted
- **7:1 student-to-undergraduate faculty ratio**
- **44% graduate** in 6 years or less
- **$22,500 tuition** and fees
- **$17,610 average financial aid** package, $19,300 average indebtedness upon graduation, $9.1 million endowment

Bennington regards education as a sensual and ethical, no less than intellectual, process. It seeks to liberate and nurture the individuality, the creative intelligence, and the ethical and aesthetic sensibility of its students, to the end that their richly varied natural endowments will be directed toward self-fulfillment and toward constructive social purposes.

Students *Undergraduates:* 447 full-time. Students come from 37 states and territories, 10 other countries. *The most frequently chosen baccalaureate fields are:* interdisciplinary studies, English, visual/performing arts. *Graduate:* 124 in graduate degree programs.

From out-of-state	92%	Reside on campus	98%
Age 25 or older	1%	Transferred in	6%
International students	9%	African Americans	2%
Asian Americans/Pacific Islanders	2%	Hispanic Americans	2%
Native Americans	0.2%		

Faculty 76 (76% full-time), 74% with terminal degrees.

Expenses (1999–2000) *Comprehensive fee:* $28,150 includes full-time tuition ($22,200), mandatory fees ($300), and room and board ($5650). *College room only:* $2950. *Part-time tuition:* $2775 per course. *Payment plan:* installment. *Waivers:* employees or children of employees.

Vermont

Library Crossett Library plus 2 others. *Operations spending 1999–2000:* $495,774. *Collection:* 119,804 titles, 600 serial subscriptions, 26,884 audiovisual materials.
College life *Housing:* on-campus residence required through senior year. *Option:* coed. *Most popular organizations:* literary magazine, Amnesty International, Campus Activities Board, film society, student newspaper.
Campus security 24-hour emergency response devices and patrols, late-night transport-escort service.
After graduation *Career center:* 1 full-time, 1 part-time personnel. Services include resume preparation, resume referral, career counseling, careers library, job bank, job interviews.
Freshmen 524 applied, 436 admitted, 142 enrolled.

Average high school GPA	3.5	SAT verbal scores above 500	98%
SAT math scores above 500	80%	ACT above 18	N/R
From top 10% of their h.s. class	34%	From top quarter	63%
From top half	90%	1998 freshmen returning in 1999	78%

Application *Options:* eApply at www.CollegeQuest.com, Common Application, early admission, early decision, deferred entrance. *Application fee:* $50. *Required:* essay or personal statement; high school transcript; 2 letters of recommendation. *Recommended:* interview.
Standardized tests *Admission: Required:* SAT I or ACT.
Significant dates *Application deadlines:* 1/1 (freshmen), 3/1 (transfers). *Early decision:* 11/15. *Notification:* 4/1 (freshmen), 12/1 (early decision). *Financial aid deadline priority date:* 3/1.
Freshman Application Contact
Mr. Deane Bogardus, Director of Admissions, Bennington College, Bennington, VT 05201. **Phone:** 802-440-4312. **Toll-free phone:** 800-833-6845. **Fax:** 802-447-4269. **E-mail:** admissions@bennington.edu
Visit CollegeQuest.com for information on majors offered and athletics. Electronic viewbook available at CollegeQuest.com.

■ *See page 1254 for a narrative description.*

BURLINGTON COLLEGE
Burlington, Vermont

 Apply at CollegeQuest.com

- **Independent**, 4-year, founded 1972
- **Degrees** associate and bachelor's
- **Urban** 1-acre campus
- **Coed**, 163 undergraduate students, 57% full-time, 60% women, 40% men
- **Noncompetitive** entrance level, 65% of applicants were admitted
- **8:1 student-to-undergraduate faculty ratio**
- **$9066 tuition** and fees
- **$7526 average financial aid** package, $16,508 average indebtedness upon graduation, $134,180 endowment

A small, progressive liberal arts college offering flexible learning options within a friendly, supportive environment. A third of students self-design their liberal arts majors. A distance learning degree program is also offered. New paralegal, cinema studies, and film production programs enhance a curriculum already strong in social sciences and the humanities.

Students *Undergraduates:* 93 full-time, 70 part-time. Students come from 20 states and territories, 8 other countries. *The most frequently chosen baccalaureate fields are:* English, psychology, social sciences and history.

From out-of-state	8%	Age 25 or older	66%
Transferred in	36%		

Faculty 68, 26% with terminal degrees.
Expenses (1999–2000) *Tuition:* full-time $8850; part-time $295 per credit. *Required fees:* full-time $216; $108 per term part-time. Full-time tuition and fees vary according to program. Part-time tuition and fees vary according to program. *Payment plan:* installment. *Waivers:* senior citizens and employees or children of employees.
Library Burlington College Library. *Collection:* 43,500 titles, 1,650 serial subscriptions, 1,754 audiovisual materials.
College life *Housing: Options:* coed, cooperative. *Most popular organization:* Student Association.
Campus security 24-hour emergency response devices.
After graduation *Career center:* 2 part-time personnel. Services include resume preparation, interview workshops, career counseling, careers library, job bank, job interviews. *Graduate education:* 40% of class of 1999 went directly to graduate and professional school: 40% graduate arts and sciences.
Freshmen 40 applied, 26 admitted, 28 enrolled.

SAT verbal scores above 500	N/R	SAT math scores above 500	N/R
ACT above 18	N/R	1998 freshmen returning in 1999	60%

Application *Options:* eApply at www.CollegeQuest.com, Common Application, electronic application, deferred entrance. *Application fee:* $30. *Required:* essay or personal statement; high school transcript; 2 letters of recommendation; interview.
Significant dates *Application deadlines:* 8/16 (freshmen), rolling (transfers). *Financial aid deadline:* continuous.
Freshman Application Contact
Ms. Cathleen Sullivan, Assistant Director of Admissions, Burlington College, 95 North Avenue, Burlington, VT 05401-2998. **Phone:** 802-862-9616 Ext. 24. **Toll-free phone:** 800-862-9616. **Fax:** 802-658-0071. **E-mail:** admissions@burlcol.edu
Visit CollegeQuest.com for information on majors offered and athletics. College video available at CollegeQuest.com.

CASTLETON STATE COLLEGE
Castleton, Vermont

- **State-supported**, comprehensive, founded 1787
- **Degrees** associate, bachelor's, master's, and post-master's certificates
- **Rural** 130-acre campus
- **Coed**, 1,517 undergraduate students, 92% full-time, 57% women, 43% men
- **Moderately difficult** entrance level, 79% of applicants were admitted
- **16:1 student-to-undergraduate faculty ratio**
- **40% graduate** in 6 years or less
- **$4870 tuition** and fees (in-state); $10,366 (out-of-state)
- **$2.9 million endowment**

Located in a historic Vermont village close to skiing, Castleton is small enough to be a community where individuals matter yet large enough to offer 30 academic programs in career preparation and the liberal arts, 12 intercollegiate sports, and more than 40 clubs and student organizations. Castleton provides exceptional programs for first-year students.

Part of Vermont State Colleges System.
Students *Undergraduates:* 1,393 full-time, 124 part-time. Students come from 25 states and territories. *The most frequently chosen baccalaureate fields are:* business/marketing, communications/communication technologies, social sciences and history. *Graduate:* 112 in graduate degree programs.

From out-of-state	34%	Reside on campus	41%
Age 25 or older	15%	Transferred in	10%
International students	0.1%	African Americans	0.1%
Asian Americans/Pacific Islanders	1%	Hispanic Americans	1%
Native Americans	0.1%		

Faculty 177 (50% full-time), 59% with terminal degrees.
Expenses (1999–2000) *Tuition, state resident:* full-time $4092; part-time $171 per credit. *Tuition, nonresident:* full-time $9588; part-time $400 per credit. *Required fees:* full-time $778; $27 per credit. Full-time tuition and fees vary according to reciprocity agreements. Part-time tuition and fees vary according to course load and reciprocity agreements. *College room and board:* $5298; room only: $3108. Room and board charges vary according to board plan. *Payment plan:* installment. *Waivers:* senior citizens and employees or children of employees.
Library Calvin Coolidge Library. *Operations spending 1999–2000:* $606,266. *Collection:* 126,000 titles, 3,250 audiovisual materials.
College life *Housing:* on-campus residence required in freshman year. *Option:* coed. *Most popular organizations:* Student Radio Station, community service, women's issues, rugby, snowboarding.
Campus security 24-hour emergency response devices and patrols, student patrols, late-night transport-escort service, controlled dormitory access.
After graduation 50 organizations recruited on campus 1997–98. *Career center:* 1 full-time personnel. Services include job fairs, resume preparation, interview workshops, resume referral, career counseling, careers library, job bank, job interviews.

Peterson's Guide to Four-Year Colleges 2001 — www.petersons.com — 815

Vermont

Castleton State College (continued)

Freshmen 941 applied, 743 admitted, 314 enrolled.

SAT verbal scores above 500	35%	SAT math scores above 500	29%
ACT above 18	100%	From top 10% of their h.s. class	3%
From top quarter	16%	From top half	48%
1998 freshmen returning in 1999	64%		

Application *Options:* Common Application, electronic application, deferred entrance. *Application fee:* $30. *Required:* essay or personal statement; high school transcript; minimum 2.5 GPA; letters of recommendation. *Recommended:* interview.

Standardized tests *Admission: Required:* SAT I or ACT.

Significant dates *Application deadlines:* rolling (freshmen), rolling (transfers). *Financial aid deadline priority date:* 3/15.

Freshman Application Contact
Mr. Bill Allen, Dean of Enrollment, Castleton State College, Seminary Street, Castleton, VT 05735. **Phone:** 802-468-1214. **Toll-free phone:** 800-639-8521. **Fax:** 802-468-1476. **E-mail:** info@castleton.edu

Visit CollegeQuest.com for information on majors offered and athletics.

■ *See page 1378 for a narrative description.*

CHAMPLAIN COLLEGE
Burlington, Vermont

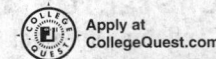

- **Independent**, 4-year, founded 1878
- **Degrees** associate and bachelor's (the baccalaureate programs are part of the 2+2 curriculum)
- **Suburban** 19-acre campus
- **Coed**, 2,114 undergraduate students, 66% full-time, 55% women, 45% men
- **Minimally difficult** entrance level, 81% of applicants were admitted
- **23:1 student-to-undergraduate faculty ratio**
- **83.3% graduate** in 6 years or less
- **$10,585 tuition** and fees
- **$8532 average financial aid** package, $4.4 million endowment

Since 1878, Champlain College has celebrated the Vermont ideal of practical, independent thinking by teaching students the skills and knowledge they need to be successful. Students can earn their bachelor's or associate degrees in 23 career-oriented majors at a college that is located within an hour's drive of world-class skiing, hiking, and mountain biking.

Students *Undergraduates:* 1,386 full-time, 728 part-time. Students come from 25 states and territories.

From out-of-state	45%	Reside on campus	40%
Age 25 or older	16%	Transferred in	9%

Faculty 117 (52% full-time).

Expenses (1999–2000) *Comprehensive fee:* $18,035 includes full-time tuition ($10,485), mandatory fees ($100), and room and board ($7450). *College room only:* $4445. Room and board charges vary according to board plan. *Part-time tuition:* $318 per credit hour. *Payment plan:* installment. *Waivers:* senior citizens and employees or children of employees.

Library Champlain College Library plus 1 other. *Operations spending 1999–2000:* $311,410. *Collection:* 43,500 titles, 1,900 serial subscriptions, 350 audiovisual materials.

College life *Housing: Options:* coed, men-only, women-only. *Most popular organizations:* outing club, community service dorm programs, theater club, international club, snowboarding club.

Campus security 24-hour emergency response devices and patrols, late-night transport-escort service, controlled dormitory access.

After graduation 50 organizations recruited on campus 1997–98. 98% of class of 1998 had job offers within 6 months. *Career center:* 5 full-time, 1 part-time personnel. Services include job fairs, resume preparation, interview workshops, resume referral, career/interest testing, career counseling, careers library, job bank, job interviews. *Graduate education:* 3% of class of 1999 went directly to graduate and professional school: 3% business.

Freshmen 1,817 applied, 1,473 admitted, 462 enrolled.

Average high school GPA	2.8	SAT verbal scores above 500	34%
SAT math scores above 500	32%	ACT above 18	72%
From top 10% of their h.s. class	15%	From top quarter	25%
From top half	60%	1998 freshmen returning in 1999	78%

Application *Options:* eApply at www.CollegeQuest.com, Common Application, early admission, deferred entrance. *Application fee:* $35. *Required:* essay or personal statement; high school transcript. *Required for some:* minimum 3.0 GPA. *Recommended:* minimum 2.0 GPA; 1 letter of recommendation; interview.

Standardized tests *Admission: Required:* SAT I or ACT.

Significant dates *Application deadlines:* rolling (freshmen), rolling (transfers). *Financial aid deadline priority date:* 5/1.

Freshman Application Contact
Ms. Josephine H. Churchill, Director of Admissions, Champlain College, 163 South Willard Street, Burlington, VT 05401. **Phone:** 802-860-2727. **Toll-free phone:** 800-570-5858. **Fax:** 802-862-2772. **E-mail:** admission@champlain.edu

Visit CollegeQuest.com for information on majors offered and athletics. College video available at CollegeQuest.com.

■ *See page 1402 for a narrative description.*

COLLEGE OF ST. JOSEPH
Rutland, Vermont

- **Independent Roman Catholic**, comprehensive, founded 1950
- **Degrees** associate, bachelor's, master's, and postbachelor's certificates
- **Small-town** 90-acre campus
- **Coed**, 385 undergraduate students
- **Minimally difficult** entrance level, 88% of applicants were admitted
- **18:1 student-to-undergraduate faculty ratio**
- **42% graduate** in 6 years or less
- **$11,350 tuition** and fees
- **$9956 average financial aid** package, $14,585 average indebtedness upon graduation, $657,000 endowment

Students *Undergraduates:* Students come from 15 states and territories. *The most frequently chosen baccalaureate fields are:* business/marketing, psychology, social sciences and history.

From out-of-state	30%	Reside on campus	29%
Age 25 or older	53%	International students	1%
African Americans	3%	Asian Americans/Pacific Islanders	1%
Hispanic Americans	1%	Native Americans	1%

Faculty 66 (20% full-time), 42% with terminal degrees.

Expenses (1999–2000) *Comprehensive fee:* $17,400 includes full-time tuition ($11,250), mandatory fees ($100), and room and board ($6050). Full-time tuition and fees vary according to program. Room and board charges vary according to housing facility. *Part-time tuition:* $200 per credit. *Part-time fees:* $32 per term part-time. Part-time tuition and fees vary according to program. *Payment plan:* installment. *Waivers:* senior citizens and employees or children of employees.

Library St. Joseph Library plus 1 other. *Operations spending 1999–2000:* $170,000. *Collection:* 38,756 titles, 255 serial subscriptions, 5,235 audiovisual materials.

College life *Housing:* on-campus residence required through sophomore year. *Options:* men-only, women-only. *Most popular organizations:* Human Services Club, Campus Ministry Club, Psi Chi, Ambassadors, chorus.

Campus security 24-hour emergency response devices.

After graduation *Career center:* 1 full-time, 1 part-time personnel. Services include job fairs, resume preparation, interview workshops, resume referral, career counseling, careers library.

Freshmen 103 applied, 91 admitted. 3 class presidents, 12 student government officers.

Average high school GPA	2.6	SAT verbal scores above 500	28%
SAT math scores above 500	20%	ACT above 18	N/R
From top 10% of their h.s. class	5%	From top quarter	20%
From top half	57%	1998 freshmen returning in 1999	65%

Application *Options:* eApply at www.CollegeQuest.com, early admission, deferred entrance. *Application fee:* $25. *Required:* essay or personal statement; high school transcript; minimum 2.0 GPA; 2 letters of recommendation. *Recommended:* interview.

Vermont

Standardized tests *Admission: Required:* SAT I or ACT.
Significant dates *Application deadlines:* rolling (freshmen), rolling (transfers). *Financial aid deadline:* continuous.
Freshman Application Contact
Mr. Steven Soba, Director of Admissions, College of St. Joseph, 71 Clement Road, Rutland, VT 05701-3899. **Phone:** 802-773-5900 Ext. 205. **E-mail:** admissions@csj.edu

Visit CollegeQuest.com for information on majors offered and athletics.

■ *See page 1478 for a narrative description.*

GODDARD COLLEGE
Plainfield, Vermont

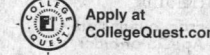

- **Independent**, comprehensive, founded 1938
- **Degrees** bachelor's and master's
- **Rural** 250-acre campus
- **Coed**, 346 undergraduate students, 100% full-time, 59% women, 41% men
- **Moderately difficult** entrance level, 97% of applicants were admitted
- **11:1** student-to-undergraduate faculty ratio
- **29% graduate** in 6 years or less
- **$15,470 tuition** and fees
- **$17,100 average financial aid** package, $17,125 average indebtedness upon graduation, $351,764 endowment

Students *Undergraduates:* 346 full-time. Students come from 28 states and territories, 2 other countries. *Graduate:* 214 in graduate degree programs.

From out-of-state	82%	Reside on campus	80%
Age 25 or older	36%	International students	1%
African Americans	4%	Asian Americans/Pacific Islanders	1%
Hispanic Americans	3%	Native Americans	1%

Faculty 91 (27% full-time), 27% with terminal degrees.
Expenses (1999–2000) *Comprehensive fee:* $20,758 includes full-time tuition ($15,218), mandatory fees ($252), and room and board ($5288). *College room only:* $2318. *Payment plan:* installment. *Waivers:* employees or children of employees.
Library Eliot Pratt Center. *Operations spending 1999–2000:* $176,287. *Collection:* 70,000 titles, 280 serial subscriptions, 175 audiovisual materials.
College life *Housing:* on-campus residence required through sophomore year. *Options:* coed, women-only, cooperative. *Most popular organizations:* women's center, student newspaper, student art group, multicultural center, student theatre.
Campus security Patrols by trained security personnel 9 p.m. to 6 a.m.
After graduation 23 organizations recruited on campus 1997–98. *Career center:* 1 full-time personnel. Services include resume preparation, career counseling, careers library.
Freshmen 128 applied, 124 admitted, 37 enrolled. 20 student government officers.

Average high school GPA	2.98	SAT verbal scores above 500	78%
SAT math scores above 500	59%	ACT above 18	N/R
From top 10% of their h.s. class	9%	From top quarter	27%
From top half	57%	1998 freshmen returning in 1999	62%

Application *Options:* eApply at www.CollegeQuest.com, electronic application, deferred entrance. *Application fee:* $40. *Required:* essay or personal statement; high school transcript; 2 letters of recommendation; interview.
Standardized tests *Admission: Recommended:* SAT I and SAT II or ACT.
Significant dates *Application deadlines:* rolling (freshmen), rolling (transfers). *Financial aid deadline priority date:* 3/1.
Freshman Application Contact
Ms. Susan M. Batchelder, Admissions Counselor, Goddard College, 123 Pitkin Road, Plainfield, VT 05667-9432. **Phone:** 802-454-8311 Ext. 322. **Toll-free phone:** 800-468-4888 Ext. 307. **Fax:** 802-454-1029. **E-mail:** admissions@earth.goddard.edu

Visit CollegeQuest.com for information on majors offered and athletics.

■ *See page 1722 for a narrative description.*

GREEN MOUNTAIN COLLEGE
Poultney, Vermont

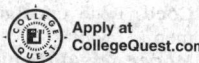

- **Independent**, 4-year, founded 1834, affiliated with United Methodist Church
- **Degree** bachelor's
- **Small-town** 155-acre campus
- **Coed**, 641 undergraduate students, 97% full-time, 47% women, 53% men
- **Moderately difficult** entrance level, 70% of applicants were admitted
- **40% graduate** in 6 years or less
- **$17,200 tuition** and fees
- **$3.1 million endowment**

Students *Undergraduates:* 624 full-time, 17 part-time. Students come from 23 states and territories, 19 other countries. *The most frequently chosen baccalaureate fields are:* education, health professions and related sciences, parks and recreation.

From out-of-state	92%	Reside on campus	85%
Age 25 or older	5%	Transferred in	7%
International students	8%	African Americans	2%
Asian Americans/Pacific Islanders	0.5%	Hispanic Americans	1%
Native Americans	1%		

Faculty 64 (66% full-time).
Expenses (1999–2000) *Comprehensive fee:* $21,500 includes full-time tuition ($17,000), mandatory fees ($200), and room and board ($4300). *Part-time tuition:* $567 per credit. *Part-time fees:* $100 per term part-time. Part-time tuition and fees vary according to course load. *Payment plan:* installment. *Waivers:* employees or children of employees.
Library Griswold Library. *Operations spending 1999–2000:* $257,373. *Collection:* 60,000 titles, 224 serial subscriptions, 4,387 audiovisual materials.
College life *Housing:* on-campus residence required through junior year. *Options:* coed, cooperative. *Most popular organizations:* Student National Education Association, Student Government Association, outing club, intercultural club, peer majors club.
Campus security 24-hour emergency response devices and patrols, student patrols, late-night transport-escort service, controlled dormitory access.
After graduation *Career center:* 1 full-time, 1 part-time personnel. Services include job fairs, resume preparation, career counseling, careers library, job bank.
Freshmen 935 applied, 658 admitted, 196 enrolled.

Average high school GPA	2.72	SAT verbal scores above 500	N/R
SAT math scores above 500	N/R	ACT above 18	N/R
1998 freshmen returning in 1999	65%		

Application *Options:* eApply at www.CollegeQuest.com, Common Application, electronic application, early admission, deferred entrance. *Application fee:* $30. *Required:* high school transcript. *Recommended:* essay or personal statement; minimum 2.4 GPA; 2 letters of recommendation; interview.
Standardized tests *Admission: Recommended:* SAT I or ACT. *Required for some:* SAT I or ACT.
Significant dates *Application deadlines:* rolling (freshmen), rolling (transfers). *Notification:* continuous until 8/1 (freshmen). *Financial aid deadline priority date:* 2/15.
Freshman Application Contact
Ms. Merrilyn Tatarczuch-Koft, Dean of Enrollment Services, Green Mountain College, One College Circle, Poultney, VT 05764. **Phone:** 802-287-8000 Ext. 8305. **Toll-free phone:** 800-776-6675. **Fax:** 802-287-8099. **E-mail:** admiss@greenmtn.edu

Visit CollegeQuest.com for information on majors offered and athletics. College video and electronic viewbook available at CollegeQuest.com.

JOHNSON STATE COLLEGE
Johnson, Vermont

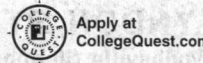

- **State-supported**, comprehensive, founded 1828
- **Degrees** associate, bachelor's, and master's
- **Rural** 350-acre campus with easy access to Montreal

Vermont

Johnson State College (continued)
- **Coed**, 1,345 undergraduate students, 78% full-time, 55% women, 45% men
- **Moderately difficult** entrance level, 85% of applicants were admitted
- **17:1 student-to-undergraduate faculty ratio**
- **29% graduate** in 6 years or less
- **$5009 tuition** and fees (in-state); $10,505 (out-of-state)

Some people come to Johnson wanting to change the world. Others come not knowing what they want. Every student brings a different dream. All are welcomed and warmly received to a wealth of academic opportunities. At Johnson State College, it is called Education by Engagement—getting involved with the world and putting ideas into practice.

Part of Vermont State Colleges System.
Students *Undergraduates:* 1,054 full-time, 291 part-time. Students come from 23 states and territories, 6 other countries. *The most frequently chosen baccalaureate fields are:* business/marketing, education, liberal arts/general studies. *Graduate:* 143 in graduate degree programs.

From out-of-state	37%	Reside on campus	57%
Age 25 or older	12%	Transferred in	8%
International students	2%	African Americans	0.2%
Asian Americans/Pacific Islanders	0.4%	Hispanic Americans	1%
Native Americans	2%		

Faculty 126 (49% full-time).
Expenses (1999–2000) *Tuition, state resident:* full-time $4092; part-time $171 per credit. *Tuition, nonresident:* full-time $9588; part-time $400 per credit. *Required fees:* full-time $917; $16 per credit; $98 per term part-time. Full-time tuition and fees vary according to reciprocity agreements. Part-time tuition and fees vary according to course load and reciprocity agreements. *College room and board:* $5298; room only: $3108. Room and board charges vary according to board plan and housing facility. *Payment plans:* installment, deferred payment. *Waivers:* senior citizens and employees or children of employees.
Library Library and Learning Center. *Collection:* 133,087 titles, 760 serial subscriptions, 7,200 audiovisual materials.
College life *Housing:* on-campus residence required through sophomore year. *Option:* coed. *Most popular organizations:* SERVE, Hospitality Association, WJSC, Earth awareness club, snowboarding.
Campus security 24-hour emergency response devices and patrols, student patrols, late-night transport-escort service, controlled dormitory access.
After graduation *Career center:* 1 full-time, 2 part-time personnel. Services include resume preparation, interview workshops, career/interest testing, career counseling, careers library, job bank.
Freshmen 725 applied, 618 admitted, 234 enrolled.

SAT verbal scores above 500	54%	SAT math scores above 500	37%
ACT above 18	N/R	From top 10% of their h.s. class	5%
From top quarter	17%	From top half	29%
1998 freshmen returning in 1999	60%		

Application *Options:* eApply at www.CollegeQuest.com, electronic application, deferred entrance. *Application fee:* $30. *Required:* essay or personal statement; high school transcript; minimum 2.0 GPA; 1 letter of recommendation. *Recommended:* minimum 2.5 GPA; interview.
Standardized tests *Admission: Required:* SAT I or ACT.
Significant dates *Application deadlines:* rolling (freshmen), rolling (transfers). *Financial aid deadline priority date:* 3/1.
Freshman Application Contact
Ms. Gwyneth Harris, Associate Director of Admissions, Johnson State College, 337 College Hill, Johnson, VT 05656-9405. **Phone:** 802-635-1219. **Toll-free phone:** 800-635-2356. **Fax:** 802-635-1230. **E-mail:** jscapply@badger.jsc.vsc.edu
Visit CollegeQuest.com for information on majors offered and athletics.

■ *See page 1856 for a narrative description.*

LYNDON STATE COLLEGE
Lyndonville, Vermont

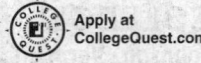
Apply at CollegeQuest.com

- **State-supported**, comprehensive, founded 1911
- **Degrees** associate, bachelor's, and master's
- **Rural** 175-acre campus
- **Coed**, 1,098 undergraduate students, 90% full-time, 44% women, 56% men
- **Moderately difficult** entrance level, 93% of applicants were admitted
- **39% graduate** in 6 years or less
- **$4864 tuition** and fees (in-state); $10,360 (out-of-state)

Part of Vermont State Colleges System.
Students *Undergraduates:* 985 full-time, 113 part-time. Students come from 20 states and territories, 3 other countries. *The most frequently chosen baccalaureate fields are:* business/marketing, communications/communication technologies, parks and recreation. *Graduate:* 101 in graduate degree programs.

From out-of-state	44%	Reside on campus	50%
Age 25 or older	14%	International students	1%
African Americans	0.4%	Asian Americans/Pacific Islanders	0.2%
Hispanic Americans	1%	Native Americans	0.3%

Faculty 119 (47% full-time), 33% with terminal degrees.
Expenses (1999–2000) *One-time required fee:* $150. *Tuition, state resident:* full-time $4092; part-time $171 per credit hour. *Tuition, nonresident:* full-time $9588; part-time $400 per credit hour. *Required fees:* full-time $772; $32 per credit hour. Full-time tuition and fees vary according to reciprocity agreements. Part-time tuition and fees vary according to reciprocity agreements. *College room and board:* $5298. Room and board charges vary according to board plan and housing facility. *Waivers:* senior citizens and employees or children of employees.
Library Samuel Read Hall Library. *Collection:* 100,000 titles, 542 serial subscriptions.
College life *Housing:* on-campus residence required through sophomore year. *Option:* coed. *Most popular organizations:* drama club, Rescue Squad, Student Senate, Campus Activities Board.
Campus security Student patrols, late-night transport-escort service, controlled dormitory access.
After graduation *Career center:* Services include resume preparation, career counseling, careers library, job bank.
Freshmen 899 applied, 835 admitted, 276 enrolled.

Average high school GPA	2.5	SAT verbal scores above 500	42%
SAT math scores above 500	39%	ACT above 18	N/R
From top 10% of their h.s. class	12%	From top quarter	22%
From top half	69%	1998 freshmen returning in 1999	57%

Application *Options:* eApply at www.CollegeQuest.com, Common Application, early admission, deferred entrance. *Application fee:* $30. *Required:* essay or personal statement; high school transcript; minimum 2.0 GPA; 1 letter of recommendation. *Required for some:* minimum 3.0 GPA. *Recommended:* minimum 3.0 GPA; interview.
Standardized tests *Admission: Required:* SAT I or ACT.
Significant dates *Application deadlines:* rolling (freshmen), rolling (transfers). *Financial aid deadline priority date:* 2/11.
Freshman Application Contact
Ms. Michelle Keenan, Associate Director of Admissions, Lyndon State College, PO Box 919, Lyndonville, VT 05851-0919. **Phone:** 802-626-6413. **Toll-free phone:** 800-225-1998. **Fax:** 802-626-6335. **E-mail:** butlers@mail.lsc.vsc.edu
Visit CollegeQuest.com for information on majors offered and athletics.

■ *See page 1964 for a narrative description.*

MARLBORO COLLEGE
Marlboro, Vermont

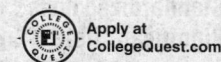
Apply at CollegeQuest.com

- **Independent**, comprehensive, founded 1946
- **Degrees** bachelor's and master's
- **Rural** 350-acre campus
- **Coed**, 283 undergraduate students, 97% full-time, 58% women, 42% men
- **Moderately difficult** entrance level, 80% of applicants were admitted
- **7:1 student-to-undergraduate faculty ratio**
- **37% graduate** in 6 years or less
- **$19,560 tuition** and fees
- **$19,450 average financial aid** package, $15,906 average indebtedness upon graduation, $1.8 million endowment

Students *Undergraduates:* 275 full-time, 8 part-time. Students come from 32 states and territories, 5 other countries. *The most frequently chosen*

baccalaureate fields are: social sciences and history, biological/life sciences, visual/performing arts.

From out-of-state	82%	Reside on campus	78%
Age 25 or older	10%	Transferred in	10%
International students	2%	African Americans	1%
Asian Americans/Pacific Islanders	1%	Hispanic Americans	2%
Native Americans	1%		

Faculty 40 (83% full-time), 83% with terminal degrees.
Expenses (2000–2001) *Comprehensive fee:* $26,310 includes full-time tuition ($18,800), mandatory fees ($760), and room and board ($6750). *College room only:* $3300. *Part-time tuition:* $630 per credit. *Part-time fees:* $165 per term part-time.
Library Rice Memorial Library. *Operations spending 1999–2000:* $342,481. *Collection:* 54,289 titles, 250 serial subscriptions, 746 audiovisual materials.
College life *Housing:* on-campus residence required in freshman year. *Options:* coed, women-only. *Most popular organizations:* theater club, outdoor program, fencing club, Gay/Lesbian/Bisexual Alliance, student newspaper.
Campus security 24-hour emergency response devices.
After graduation *Career center:* 1 full-time personnel. Services include resume preparation, career counseling, careers library.
Freshmen 308 applied, 247 admitted, 93 enrolled.

Average high school GPA	3.2	SAT verbal scores above 500	95%
SAT math scores above 500	76%	ACT above 18	N/R
From top 10% of their h.s. class	31%	From top quarter	51%
From top half	79%	1998 freshmen returning in 1999	78%

Application *Options:* eApply at www.CollegeQuest.com, Common Application, electronic application, early admission, early decision, early action, deferred entrance. *Application fee:* $30. *Required:* essay or personal statement; high school transcript; 1 letter of recommendation; interview; graded expository essay. *Recommended:* minimum 3.0 GPA.
Standardized tests *Admission: Required:* SAT I or ACT. *Recommended:* SAT II Subject Tests.
Significant dates *Application deadlines:* 3/1 (freshmen), 4/1 (transfers). *Early decision:* 11/15, 1/15. *Notification:* 4/1 (freshmen), 12/15 (early decision), 2/1 (early action). *Financial aid deadline priority date:* 3/1.
Freshman Application Contact
Ms. Katherine S. Hallas, Director of Admissions, Marlboro College, PO Box A, South Road, Marlboro, VT 05344. **Phone:** 802-257-4333 Ext. 237. **Toll-free phone:** 800-343-0049. **E-mail:** admissions@marlboro.edu
Visit CollegeQuest.com for information on majors offered and athletics. College video and electronic viewbook available at CollegeQuest.com.

■ *See page 1992 for a narrative description.*

MIDDLEBURY COLLEGE
Middlebury, Vermont

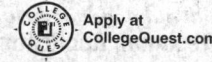

- **Independent**, comprehensive, founded 1800
- **Degrees** bachelor's, master's, and doctoral
- **Small-town** 350-acre campus
- **Coed**, 2,265 undergraduate students, 98% full-time, 51% women, 49% men
- **Very difficult** entrance level, 26% of applicants were admitted
- **10:1 student-to-undergraduate faculty ratio**
- **87% graduate** in 6 years or less
- **$31,790 comprehensive fee**
- **$23,538 average financial aid** package, $18,731 average indebtedness upon graduation, $639 million endowment

Students *Undergraduates:* 2,225 full-time, 40 part-time. Students come from 50 states and territories, 71 other countries. *The most frequently chosen baccalaureate fields are:* English, foreign language/literature, social sciences and history. *Graduate:* 5 in graduate degree programs.

From out-of-state	95%	Reside on campus	94%
Age 25 or older	0.4%	Transferred in	0.4%
International students	7%	African Americans	2%
Asian Americans/Pacific Islanders	4%	Hispanic Americans	5%
Native Americans	1%		

Faculty 238 (92% full-time), 89% with terminal degrees.
Expenses (1999–2000) *Comprehensive fee:* $31,790. *Payment plans:* tuition prepayment, installment. *Waivers:* children of alumni and employees or children of employees.
Library Egbert Starr Library plus 3 others. *Collection:* 774,993 titles, 1,923 serial subscriptions.
College life *Housing:* on-campus residence required through junior year. *Options:* coed, disabled students. *Social organizations:* social houses, commons system. *Most popular organizations:* Environmental Quality, international students organization, mountain club, Middlebury College activities board, feminist action at Middlebury.
Campus security Student patrols, late-night transport-escort service.
After graduation 65 organizations recruited on campus 1997–98. *Career center:* 7 full-time personnel. Services include job fairs, resume preparation, interview workshops, resume referral, career/interest testing, career counseling, careers library, job bank, job interviews. *Graduate education:* 12% of class of 1999 went directly to graduate and professional school: 3% graduate arts and sciences, 2% law, 1% medicine.
Freshmen 4,869 applied, 1,247 admitted, 524 enrolled.

SAT verbal scores above 500	99%	SAT math scores above 500	99%
ACT above 18	N/R	From top 10% of their h.s. class	72%
From top quarter	92%	From top half	99%
1998 freshmen returning in 1999	96%		

Application *Options:* eApply at www.CollegeQuest.com, Common Application, early admission, early decision, deferred entrance. *Application fee:* $55. *Required:* essay or personal statement; high school transcript; 3 letters of recommendation. *Recommended:* interview.
Standardized tests *Admission: Required:* ACT or 3 SAT II Subject Tests (including SAT II: Writing Test and 1 quantitative SAT II Test) or 3 Advanced Placement Tests (including AP English and 1 quantitative AP Test) or 3 I.B. Subsidiary Tests (including I.B. Languages and 1 quantitative I.B. Test).
Significant dates *Application deadlines:* 12/15 (freshmen), 3/1 (transfers). *Early decision:* 11/15 (for plan 1), 12/15 (for plan 2). *Notification:* 4/1 (freshmen), 12/15 (early decision plan 1), 1/31 (early decision plan 2). *Financial aid deadline priority date:* 12/31.
Freshman Application Contact
Mr. John Hanson, Director of Admissions, Middlebury College, Emma Willard House, Middlebury, VT 05753-6002. **Phone:** 802-443-3000. **Fax:** 802-443-2056. **E-mail:** admissions@middlebury.edu
Visit CollegeQuest.com for information on majors offered and athletics. Electronic viewbook available at CollegeQuest.com.

■ *See page 2052 for a narrative description.*

NEW ENGLAND CULINARY INSTITUTE
Montpelier, Vermont

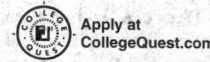

- **Proprietary**, primarily 2-year, founded 1980
- **Degrees** associate and bachelor's
- **Small-town** campus
- **Coed**, 589 undergraduate students, 100% full-time, 33% women, 67% men
- **Moderately difficult** entrance level

Faculty 65 (88% full-time).
Admissions Office Contact
New England Culinary Institute, 250 Main Street, Montpelier, VT 05602-9720. **Fax:** 802-223-0634. **E-mail:** amyh@plainfield.bypass.com
Visit CollegeQuest.com for information on majors offered and athletics.

NORWICH UNIVERSITY
Northfield, Vermont

- **Independent**, comprehensive, founded 1819
- **Degrees** bachelor's, master's, and post-master's certificates
- **Small-town** 1,125-acre campus
- **Coed**, 2,098 undergraduate students, 96% full-time, 38% women, 62% men
- **Moderately difficult** entrance level, 94% of applicants were admitted
- **$15,156 tuition** and fees
- **$88.1 million endowment**

Vermont

Norwich University (continued)

Students *Undergraduates:* 2,019 full-time, 79 part-time. Students come from 51 states and territories, 26 other countries. *Graduate:* 523 in graduate degree programs.

From out-of-state	77%	Reside on campus	84%
Age 25 or older	23%	International students	3%
African Americans	3%	Asian Americans/Pacific Islanders	3%
Hispanic Americans	4%	Native Americans	1%

Faculty 272 (51% full-time).

Expenses (1999–2000) *Comprehensive fee:* $20,874 includes full-time tuition ($15,000), mandatory fees ($156), and room and board ($5718). Full-time tuition and fees vary according to degree level, location, and program. Room and board charges vary according to board plan and location. *Part-time tuition:* $425 per credit hour. *Part-time fees:* $25 per term part-time. Part-time tuition and fees vary according to course load, degree level, location, and program. *Payment plan:* installment. *Waivers:* employees or children of employees.

Library Kreitzberg Library. *Operations spending 1999–2000:* $837,080. *Collection:* 256,530 titles, 904 serial subscriptions, 1,501 audiovisual materials.

College life *Housing:* on-campus residence required through senior year. *Option:* coed. *Most popular organizations:* rugby club, National Eagle Scout Association, Mountain and Cold Weather Company, outing club, band.

Campus security 24-hour emergency response devices and patrols, late-night transport-escort service.

After graduation 5 organizations recruited on campus 1997–98. 79% of class of 1998 had job offers within 6 months. *Career center:* 2 full-time personnel. Services include job fairs, interview workshops, resume referral, career counseling, careers library, job bank, job interviews.

Freshmen 1,605 applied, 1,514 admitted, 492 enrolled.

Average high school GPA	2.5	SAT verbal scores above 500	56%
SAT math scores above 500	55%	ACT above 18	N/R
From top 10% of their h.s. class	10%	From top quarter	25%
From top half	65%	1998 freshmen returning in 1999	68%

Application *Options:* eApply at www.CollegeQuest.com, electronic application, early admission, early decision, deferred entrance. *Application fee:* $35. *Required:* high school transcript. *Required for some:* portfolio. *Recommended:* essay or personal statement; minimum 2.0 GPA; 2 letters of recommendation; interview.

Standardized tests *Admission: Required:* SAT I or ACT. *Recommended:* SAT II Subject Tests.

Significant dates *Application deadlines:* rolling (freshmen), rolling (transfers). *Early decision:* 11/15. *Notification:* 12/15 (early decision). *Financial aid deadline priority date:* 3/1.

Freshman Application Contact
Ms. Karen McGrath, Dean of Enrollment Management, Norwich University, Northfield, VT 05663. **Phone:** 802-485-2001. **Toll-free phone:** 800-468-6679. **Fax:** 802-485-2580. **E-mail:** nuadm@norwich.edu

Visit CollegeQuest.com for information on majors offered and athletics. Electronic viewbook available at CollegeQuest.com.

■ *See page 2196 for a narrative description.*

SAINT MICHAEL'S COLLEGE
Colchester, Vermont

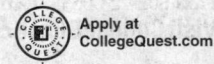
Apply at CollegeQuest.com

- **Independent Roman Catholic**, comprehensive, founded 1904
- **Degrees** bachelor's and master's
- **Small-town** 440-acre campus with easy access to Montreal
- **Coed**, 1,939 undergraduate students, 97% full-time, 53% women, 47% men
- **Moderately difficult** entrance level, 71% of applicants were admitted
- **13:1 student-to-undergraduate faculty ratio**
- **75% graduate** in 6 years or less
- **$17,662 tuition** and fees
- **$12,032 average financial aid** package, $58.9 million endowment

Students *Undergraduates:* 1,874 full-time, 65 part-time. Students come from 26 states and territories, 17 other countries. *The most frequently chosen baccalaureate fields are:* business/marketing, psychology, social sciences and history. *Graduate:* 624 in graduate degree programs.

From out-of-state	81%	Reside on campus	89%
Age 25 or older	2%	Transferred in	3%
International students	2%	African Americans	1%
Asian Americans/Pacific Islanders	1%	Hispanic Americans	1%
Native Americans	0.1%		

Faculty 199 (70% full-time), 70% with terminal degrees.

Expenses (1999–2000) *Comprehensive fee:* $24,915 includes full-time tuition ($17,500), mandatory fees ($162), and room and board ($7253). *College room only:* $4508. Room and board charges vary according to board plan and housing facility. *Part-time tuition:* $585 per semester hour. *Payment plan:* installment. *Waivers:* employees or children of employees.

Library Saint Michael's College Library. *Operations spending 1999–2000:* $1.1 million. *Collection:* 195,000 titles, 1,134 serial subscriptions, 3,000 audio-visual materials.

College life *Housing:* on-campus residence required through senior year. *Options:* coed, men-only, women-only, disabled students. *Most popular organizations:* Student Association, Mobilization of Volunteer Efforts (MOVE), student radio station, wilderness program, student newspaper.

Campus security 24-hour emergency response devices and patrols, student patrols, late-night transport-escort service, controlled dormitory access, bicycle patrols.

After graduation 79 organizations recruited on campus 1997–98. 84% of class of 1998 had job offers within 6 months. *Career center:* 3 full-time personnel. Services include job fairs, resume preparation, interview workshops, resume referral, career/interest testing, career counseling, careers library, job bank, job interviews. *Graduate education:* 11% of class of 1999 went directly to graduate and professional school.

Freshmen 2,267 applied, 1,616 admitted, 506 enrolled. 6 valedictorians.

SAT verbal scores above 500	82%	SAT math scores above 500	82%
ACT above 18	N/R	From top 10% of their h.s. class	18%
From top quarter	49%	From top half	84%
1998 freshmen returning in 1999	85%		

Application *Options:* eApply at www.CollegeQuest.com, Common Application, electronic application, early admission, early action, deferred entrance. *Application fee:* $45. *Required:* essay or personal statement; high school transcript. *Recommended:* minimum 3.0 GPA; letters of recommendation; interview.

Standardized tests *Admission: Required:* SAT I or ACT.

Significant dates *Application deadlines:* 2/1 (freshmen), 2/1 (transfers). *Early action:* 11/15. *Notification:* 4/1 (freshmen), 12/30 (early action). *Financial aid deadline priority date:* 3/15.

Freshman Application Contact
Ms. Jacqueline Murphy, Director of Admission, Saint Michael's College, One Winooski Park, Colchester, VT 05439. **Phone:** 802-654-3000. **Toll-free phone:** 800-762-8000. **Fax:** 802-654-2242. **E-mail:** admission@smcvt.edu

Visit CollegeQuest.com for information on majors offered and athletics. College video and electronic viewbook available at CollegeQuest.com.

■ *See page 2422 for a narrative description.*

SOUTHERN VERMONT COLLEGE
Bennington, Vermont

Apply at CollegeQuest.com

- **Independent**, 4-year, founded 1926
- **Degrees** associate and bachelor's
- **Small-town** 371-acre campus with easy access to Albany
- **Coed**, 498 undergraduate students, 63% full-time, 64% women, 36% men
- **Minimally difficult** entrance level, 82% of applicants were admitted
- **18:1 student-to-undergraduate faculty ratio**
- **$10,990 tuition** and fees
- **$11,505 average financial aid** package, $13,507 average indebtedness upon graduation, $1.2 million endowment

Students *Undergraduates:* 314 full-time, 184 part-time. Students come from 15 states and territories. *The most frequently chosen baccalaureate fields are:* business/marketing, protective services/public administration, psychology.

820 www.petersons.com Peterson's Guide to Four-Year Colleges 2001

Vermont

From out-of-state	60%	Reside on campus	32%
Age 25 or older	35%	Transferred in	7%
African Americans	1%	Asian Americans/Pacific Islanders	1%
Hispanic Americans	1%	Native Americans	0.4%

Faculty 61 (34% full-time), 10% with terminal degrees.
Expenses (1999–2000) *Comprehensive fee:* $16,340 includes full-time tuition ($10,990) and room and board ($5350). *College room only:* $2560. Room and board charges vary according to board plan. *Part-time tuition:* $265 per credit. Part-time tuition and fees vary according to course load. *Payment plans:* installment, deferred payment. *Waivers:* senior citizens and employees or children of employees.
Library Southern Vermont College Library. *Operations spending 1999–2000:* $121,850. *Collection:* 26,000 titles, 201 serial subscriptions.
College life *Housing:* on-campus residence required in freshman year. *Option:* coed. *Most popular organizations:* Student Association, Environmental Association, business club, Criminal Justice Association, Madhatters (drama club).
Campus security 24-hour patrols, late-night transport-escort service, controlled dormitory access.
After graduation 71% of class of 1998 had job offers within 6 months. *Career center:* 1 full-time, 1 part-time personnel. Services include resume preparation, interview workshops, resume referral, career/interest testing, career counseling, careers library, job bank, job interviews. *Graduate education:* 13% of class of 1999 went directly to graduate and professional school.
Freshmen 271 applied, 222 admitted, 83 enrolled.

Average high school GPA	2.8	SAT verbal scores above 500	39%
SAT math scores above 500	45%	ACT above 18	75%
From top 10% of their h.s. class	3%	From top quarter	15%
From top half	41%	1998 freshmen returning in 1999	57%

Application *Options:* eApply at www.CollegeQuest.com, Common Application, electronic application, early admission, deferred entrance. *Application fee:* $25. *Required:* essay or personal statement; high school transcript; 2 letters of recommendation. *Required for some:* interview. *Recommended:* minimum 2.0 GPA; interview.
Standardized tests *Admission: Required:* SAT I or ACT.
Significant dates *Application deadlines:* rolling (freshmen), rolling (transfers). *Financial aid deadline priority date:* 5/1.
Freshman Application Contact
Dr. Bobbi Gabrenya, Director of Admissions, Southern Vermont College, 982 Foothills Road, Bennington, VT 05201. **Phone:** 802-447-6304. **Toll-free phone:** 800-378-2782. **Fax:** 802-447-4695. **E-mail:** admis@svc.edu
Visit CollegeQuest.com for information on majors offered and athletics. Electronic viewbook available at CollegeQuest.com.

■ *See page 2518 for a narrative description.*

STERLING COLLEGE
Craftsbury Common, Vermont

Apply at CollegeQuest.com

- **Independent**, 4-year, founded 1958
- **Degrees** associate and bachelor's
- **Rural** 150-acre campus
- **Coed**, 90 undergraduate students, 99% full-time, 42% women, 58% men
- **Moderately difficult** entrance level, 97% of applicants were admitted
- **8:1 student-to-undergraduate faculty ratio**
- **$13,355 tuition** and fees
- **$8000 average financial aid** package, $590,476 endowment

Students *Undergraduates:* 89 full-time, 1 part-time. Students come from 12 states and territories, 1 other country.

From out-of-state	77%	Reside on campus	90%
Age 25 or older	42%	Transferred in	4%
International students	2%		

Faculty 21 (38% full-time), 14% with terminal degrees.
Expenses (2000–2001, estimated) *Comprehensive fee:* $19,025 includes full-time tuition ($13,230), mandatory fees ($125), and room and board ($5670). Full-time tuition and fees vary according to course load, program, and reciprocity agreements. Room and board charges vary according to board plan, housing facility, and student level. *Payment plan:* installment. *Waivers:* employees or children of employees.

Library Brown Library plus 1 other. *Operations spending 1999–2000:* $58,280. *Collection:* 8,619 titles, 124 serial subscriptions, 305 audiovisual materials.
College life *Housing:* on-campus residence required in freshman year. *Options:* coed, men-only, women-only. *Most popular organizations:* outing club, timbersports team, Student Life.
Campus security Student patrols.
After graduation 63% of class of 1998 had job offers within 6 months. *Career center:* 2 full-time, 1 part-time personnel. Services include resume preparation, interview workshops, resume referral, career counseling, careers library, job bank.
Freshmen 99 applied, 96 admitted, 28 enrolled. 1 National Merit Scholar, 1 class president, 1 student government officer.

Average high school GPA	3.0	SAT verbal scores above 500	48%
SAT math scores above 500	44%	ACT above 18	N/R
1998 freshmen returning in 1999	88%		

Application *Options:* eApply at www.CollegeQuest.com, Common Application, early admission, deferred entrance. *Application fee:* $35. *Required:* essay or personal statement; high school transcript; 3 letters of recommendation; interview. *Recommended:* minimum 2.0 GPA.
Standardized tests *Admission: Recommended:* SAT I and SAT II or ACT, SAT II: Writing Test.
Significant dates *Application deadlines:* rolling (freshmen), rolling (transfers). *Notification:* continuous until 8/30 (freshmen). *Financial aid deadline:* continuous.
Freshman Application Contact
Mr. John Zaber, Director of Admissions, Sterling College, PO Box 72, Craftsbury Common, VT 05827. **Phone:** 802-586-7711 Ext. 40. **Toll-free phone:** 800-648-3591 (in-state); 800-802-2596 (out-of-state). **E-mail:** admissions@sterlingcollege.edu
Visit CollegeQuest.com for information on majors offered and athletics.

■ *See page 2572 for a narrative description.*

TRINITY COLLEGE OF VERMONT
Burlington, Vermont

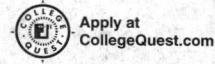

Apply at CollegeQuest.com

- **Independent Roman Catholic**, comprehensive, founded 1925
- **Degrees** associate, bachelor's, master's, post-master's, and postbachelor's certificates
- **Suburban** 24-acre campus
- **Coed**, primarily women, 569 undergraduate students, 57% full-time, 92% women, 8% men
- **Moderately difficult** entrance level, 99% of applicants were admitted
- **10:1 student-to-undergraduate faculty ratio**
- **47% graduate** in 6 years or less
- **$14,120 tuition** and fees
- **$13,993 average financial aid** package, $16,462 average indebtedness upon graduation, $1.8 million endowment

The student-faculty mentoring relationships are one of the most outstanding aspects of Trinity. Of a recent graduating class, 91% were employed and 8% enrolled in graduate school within 1 year of graduation. More than 80% of full-time undergraduates receive financial assistance. The Community Service Learning Program is nationally recognized for its campuswide participation levels.

Students *Undergraduates:* 327 full-time, 242 part-time. Students come from 16 states and territories. *The most frequently chosen baccalaureate fields are:* business/marketing, education, protective services/public administration. *Graduate:* 60 in graduate degree programs.

From out-of-state	24%	Reside on campus	35%
Age 25 or older	51%	Transferred in	4%
International students	1%	African Americans	3%
Asian Americans/Pacific Islanders	1%	Hispanic Americans	1%
Native Americans	1%		

Faculty 74 (30% full-time), 39% with terminal degrees.
Expenses (1999–2000) *Comprehensive fee:* $20,820 includes full-time tuition ($13,620), mandatory fees ($500), and room and board ($6700).

Vermont

Trinity College of Vermont (continued)
College room only: $3800. Room and board charges vary according to board plan. *Part-time tuition:* $454 per credit. *Part-time fees:* $20 per credit. Part-time tuition and fees vary according to class time and program. *Payment plans:* installment, deferred payment. *Waivers:* senior citizens and employees or children of employees.
Library Farrell Family Library. *Operations spending 1999–2000:* $262,202. *Collection:* 56,962 titles, 360 serial subscriptions, 1,406 audiovisual materials.
College life *Housing:* on-campus residence required through junior year. *Option:* women-only. *Most popular organizations:* GIVE (community service), Student Senate, S.T.A.R.S. (Students Taking Action Against Rape and Sexual Assault), Triple Key Society, Trinity Times.
Campus security 24-hour patrols, late-night transport-escort service, vehicle assistance.
After graduation 10 organizations recruited on campus 1997–98. 70% of class of 1998 had job offers within 6 months. *Career center:* 1 full-time, 1 part-time personnel. Services include job fairs, resume preparation, interview workshops, resume referral, career/interest testing, career counseling, careers library, job bank, job interviews. **Graduate education:** 17% of class of 1999 went directly to graduate and professional school.
Freshmen 557 applied, 551 admitted, 77 enrolled.

Average high school GPA	2.76	SAT verbal scores above 500	38%
SAT math scores above 500	27%	ACT above 18	N/R
1998 freshmen returning in 1999	60%		

Application *Options:* eApply at www.CollegeQuest.com, deferred entrance. *Application fee:* $40. *Required:* high school transcript. *Recommended:* minimum 2.0 GPA; interview.
Standardized tests *Admission: Required:* SAT I or ACT.
Significant dates *Application deadlines:* rolling (freshmen), rolling (transfers). *Financial aid deadline:* continuous.
Freshman Application Contact
Ms. Cristin Chafe, Admissions, Trinity College of Vermont, 208 Colchester Avenue, Burlington, VT 05401-1470. **Phone:** 802-846-7234. **Toll-free phone:** 888-277-5975. **Fax:** 802-846-7001. **E-mail:** cchafe@charity.trinityvt.edu
Visit CollegeQuest.com for information on majors offered and athletics.

■ *See page 2644 for a narrative description.*

UNIVERSITY OF VERMONT
Burlington, Vermont

- **State-supported**, university, founded 1791
- **Degrees** associate, bachelor's, master's, doctoral, first professional, post-master's, and postbachelor's certificates
- **Suburban** 425-acre campus
- **Coed**, 7,470 undergraduate students, 95% full-time, 55% women, 45% men
- **Moderately difficult** entrance level, 80% of applicants were admitted
- **14:1 student-to-undergraduate faculty ratio**
- **69% graduate** in 6 years or less
- **$8044 tuition** and fees (in-state); $19,252 (out-of-state)
- **$16,500 average financial aid** package, $21,500 average indebtedness upon graduation, $208.1 million endowment

Students *Undergraduates:* 7,085 full-time, 385 part-time. Students come from 49 states and territories, 26 other countries. *The most frequently chosen baccalaureate fields are:* natural resources/environmental science, business/marketing, social sciences and history. *Graduate:* 380 in professional programs, 1,087 in other graduate degree programs.

From out-of-state	59%	Reside on campus	48%
Age 25 or older	5%	Transferred in	4%
International students	1%	African Americans	0.5%
Asian Americans/Pacific Islanders	2%	Hispanic Americans	1%
Native Americans	0.3%		

Faculty 697 (79% full-time), 76% with terminal degrees.
Expenses (1999–2000) *Tuition, state resident:* full-time $7464; part-time $311 per credit. *Tuition, nonresident:* full-time $18,672; part-time $778 per credit. *Required fees:* full-time $580; $130 per term part-time. Part-time tuition and fees vary according to course load and program. *College room and board:* $5620; room only: $3700. Room and board charges vary according to board plan. *Payment plans:* installment, deferred payment. *Waivers:* senior citizens and employees or children of employees.
Library Bailey-Howe Library plus 3 others. *Operations spending 1999–2000:* $8.4 million. *Collection:* 1.8 million titles, 20,278 serial subscriptions, 45,299 audiovisual materials.
College life *Housing:* on-campus residence required through sophomore year. *Option:* coed. *Social organizations:* national fraternities, national sororities, local fraternities. *Most popular organizations:* Vermont Cynic, club sports, Outing Club, Volunteers in Action.
Campus security 24-hour emergency response devices and patrols, late-night transport-escort service, controlled dormitory access.
After graduation 234 organizations recruited on campus 1997–98. 64% of class of 1998 had job offers within 6 months. *Career center:* 11 full-time, 1 part-time personnel. Services include job fairs, resume preparation, interview workshops, resume referral, career/interest testing, career counseling, careers library, job bank, job interviews. **Graduate education:** 18% of class of 1999 went directly to graduate and professional school: 7% graduate arts and sciences, 2% education, 2% law, 2% medicine, 1% business, 1% engineering, 1% veterinary medicine.
Freshmen 7,564 applied, 6,088 admitted, 1,818 enrolled. 14 valedictorians.

SAT verbal scores above 500	82%	SAT math scores above 500	82%
ACT above 18	95%	From top 10% of their h.s. class	16%
From top quarter	47%	From top half	88%
1998 freshmen returning in 1999	81%		

Application *Options:* electronic application, early admission, early decision, early action, deferred entrance. *Preference* given to state residents. *Application fee:* $45. *Required:* essay or personal statement; high school transcript. *Recommended:* 2 letters of recommendation; interview.
Standardized tests *Admission: Required:* SAT I or ACT.
Significant dates *Application deadlines:* 1/15 (freshmen), 4/1 (transfers). *Early decision:* 11/1, 11/1. *Notification:* continuous until 3/31 (freshmen), 12/15 (early decision), 12/30 (early action). *Financial aid deadline priority date:* 2/10.
Freshman Application Contact
Mr. Donald M. Honeman, Director of Admissions, University of Vermont, Office of Admissions, Burlington, VT 05401-3596. **Phone:** 802-656-3370. **Fax:** 802-656-8611.
Visit CollegeQuest.com for information on majors offered and athletics.

■ *See page 2856 for a narrative description.*

VERMONT TECHNICAL COLLEGE
Randolph Center, Vermont

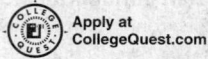
Apply at CollegeQuest.com

- **State-supported**, primarily 2-year, founded 1866
- **Degrees** associate and bachelor's
- **Rural** 544-acre campus
- **Coed**, 1,002 undergraduate students, 77% full-time, 31% women, 69% men
- **Minimally difficult** entrance level

Vermont Tech offers education for careers in today's technology-driven workplace. A residential, coeducational college offering both associate and bachelor's degree programs on its 544-acre campus in central Vermont, VTC has state-of-the-art laboratories and equipment, one of the most sophisticated microcomputer networks in Vermont, and an outstanding 65-member full-time faculty.

Part of Vermont State Colleges System.
Faculty 107 (61% full-time).
Admissions Office Contact
Vermont Technical College, PO Box 500, Randolph Center, VT 05061-0500. **Toll-free phone:** 800-442-VTC1. **Fax:** 802-728-1390 Ext. 390. **E-mail:** admissions@vtc.vsc.edu
Visit CollegeQuest.com for information on majors offered and athletics.

■ *See page 2884 for a narrative description.*

VIRGINIA

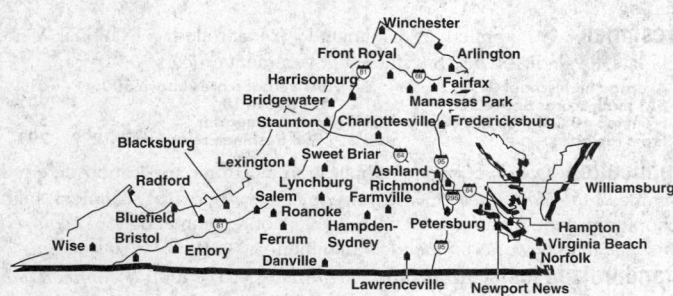

AMERICAN MILITARY UNIVERSITY
Manassas Park, Virginia

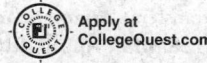 Apply at CollegeQuest.com

- **Proprietary**, comprehensive, founded 1991
- **Degrees** associate, bachelor's, and master's
- **Coed**, 351 undergraduate students
- **Noncompetitive** entrance level, 98% of applicants were admitted
- **5:1 student-to-undergraduate faculty ratio**
- **$9000 tuition** and fees

Students *Undergraduates:* Students come from 29 states and territories. *The most frequently chosen baccalaureate field is:* military science/technologies.

| From out-of-state | 76% | Age 25 or older | 72% |

Faculty 48, 25% with terminal degrees.
Expenses (1999–2000) *Tuition:* full-time $9000; part-time $750 per course. Full-time tuition and fees vary according to course load.
College life *Housing:* college housing not available.
Freshmen 153 applied, 150 admitted.

| SAT verbal scores above 500 | N/R | SAT math scores above 500 | N/R |
| ACT above 18 | N/R | 1998 freshmen returning in 1999 | 68% |

Application *Options:* eApply at www.CollegeQuest.com, Common Application, deferred entrance. *Application fee:* $50. *Required:* high school transcript.
Significant dates *Application deadline:* rolling (transfers).
Freshman Application Contact
Ms. Bonnie Struckholz, Director of Admissions, American Military University, 9104-P Manassas Drive, Manassas Park, VA 20111. **Phone:** 703-330-5398 Ext. 105. **Fax:** 703-330-5109. **E-mail:** amugen@amunet.edu
Visit CollegeQuest.com for information on majors offered and athletics. College video available at CollegeQuest.com.

THE ART INSTITUTE OF WASHINGTON
Arlington, Virginia

Admissions Office Contact
The Art Institute of Washington, 1820 North Fort Meyer Drive, Ground Floor, Arlington, VA 22209. **Toll-free phone:** 877-303-3771. **Fax:** 703-528-2487.

AVERETT COLLEGE
Danville, Virginia

 Apply at CollegeQuest.com

- **Independent Baptist**, comprehensive, founded 1859
- **Degrees** associate, bachelor's, and master's
- **Suburban** 25-acre campus
- **Coed**, 1,564 undergraduate students, 53% full-time, 61% women, 39% men
- **Moderately difficult** entrance level, 76% of applicants were admitted
- **14:1 student-to-undergraduate faculty ratio**
- **33% graduate** in 6 years or less
- **$13,595 tuition** and fees
- **$10,359 average financial aid** package, $19.9 million endowment

Students *Undergraduates:* 827 full-time, 737 part-time. Students come from 25 states and territories, 9 other countries. *The most frequently chosen baccalaureate fields are:* business/marketing, education, psychology. **Graduate:** 657 in graduate degree programs.

From out-of-state	12%	Reside on campus	44%
Age 25 or older	61%	Transferred in	13%
International students	2%	African Americans	19%
Asian Americans/Pacific Islanders	1%	Hispanic Americans	1%
Native Americans	1%		

Faculty 247 (24% full-time).
Expenses (1999–2000) *Comprehensive fee:* $17,980 includes full-time tuition ($13,145), mandatory fees ($450), and room and board ($4385). *Part-time tuition:* $245 per credit. Part-time tuition and fees vary according to course load. *Payment plan:* installment. *Waivers:* senior citizens and employees or children of employees.
Library Mary B. Blount Library. *Operations spending 1999–2000:* $447,264. *Collection:* 310,000 titles, 563 serial subscriptions.
College life *Housing:* on-campus residence required through junior year. *Option:* coed. *Social organizations:* national fraternities, national sororities; 15% of eligible men and 12% of eligible women are members. *Most popular organization:* Baptist Student Union.
Campus security 24-hour emergency response devices and patrols.
After graduation 2 organizations recruited on campus 1997–98. 91% of class of 1998 had job offers within 6 months. *Career center:* 1 full-time personnel. Services include job fairs, resume preparation, interview workshops, career counseling, careers library, job interviews. **Graduate education:** 25% of class of 1999 went directly to graduate and professional school.
Freshmen 695 applied, 526 admitted, 272 enrolled.

Average high school GPA	3.02	SAT verbal scores above 500	49%
SAT math scores above 500	38%	ACT above 18	93%
From top 10% of their h.s. class	13%	From top quarter	31%
From top half	58%	1998 freshmen returning in 1999	58%

Application *Options:* eApply at www.CollegeQuest.com, electronic application, early admission, deferred entrance. *Required:* essay or personal statement; high school transcript; 1 letter of recommendation. *Recommended:* interview.
Standardized tests *Admission:* Required: SAT I or ACT.
Significant dates *Application deadlines:* 8/15 (freshmen), 8/15 (transfers). *Notification:* continuous until 9/1 (freshmen). **Financial aid deadline priority date:** 4/1.
Freshman Application Contact
Mr. Gary Sherman, Dean of Enrollment Management, Averett College, 420 West Main Street, Danville, VA 24541-3692. **Phone:** 804-791-5660. **Toll-free phone:** 800-AVERETT. **Fax:** 804-791-5637. **E-mail:** admit@averett.edu
Visit CollegeQuest.com for information on majors offered and athletics. College video available at CollegeQuest.com.

BLUEFIELD COLLEGE
Bluefield, Virginia

- **Independent Southern Baptist**, 4-year, founded 1922
- **Degrees** associate and bachelor's
- **Small-town** 85-acre campus
- **Coed**
- **Moderately difficult** entrance level
- **$7280 tuition** and fees

Expenses (1999–2000) *Comprehensive fee:* $12,170 includes full-time tuition ($6900), mandatory fees ($380), and room and board ($4890). Room and board charges vary according to board plan. Part-time tuition and fees vary according to course load.
Institutional Web site http://www.bluefield.edu/
College life *Housing:* on-campus residence required through sophomore year. *Options:* men-only, women-only. *Social organizations:* local fraternities, local sororities; 2% of eligible men and 2% of eligible women are members. *Most popular organizations:* Baptist Student Union, Fellowship of Christian Athletes, Student Union Board, Student Government Association, Bluefield Singers.
Campus security Controlled dormitory access, night security patrols.

Virginia

Bluefield College (continued)
Application *Option:* deferred entrance. *Application fee:* $15. *Required:* essay or personal statement; high school transcript; minimum 2.0 GPA. *Required for some:* letters of recommendation; interview. *Recommended:* interview.
Standardized tests *Admission: Required:* SAT I or ACT.
Admissions Office Contact
Bluefield College, 3000 College Drive, Bluefield, VA 24605-1799. **Toll-free phone:** 800-872-0175. **Fax:** 540-326-4288. **E-mail:** admissions@mail.bluefield.edu
Visit CollegeQuest.com for information on athletics. College video and electronic viewbook available at CollegeQuest.com.

BRIDGEWATER COLLEGE
Bridgewater, Virginia

- **Independent**, 4-year, founded 1880, affiliated with Church of the Brethren
- **Degree** bachelor's
- **Small-town** 190-acre campus
- **Coed**, 1,090 undergraduate students, 99% full-time, 57% women, 43% men
- **Moderately difficult** entrance level, 89% of applicants were admitted
- **14:1** student-to-undergraduate faculty ratio
- **55% graduate** in 6 years or less
- **$14,970 tuition** and fees
- **$14,900 average financial aid** package, $17,630 average indebtedness upon graduation, $45 million endowment

Bridgewater College offers a balanced liberal arts and sciences program in a challenging and supportive environment. Excellent academic facilities include the McKinney Center for Science and Mathematics, new classroom facilities, advanced information technology capabilities, and a fully automated library. Outstanding academic scholarships are available, based solely on high school class standing. A scholarship based on SAT scores is also available. The College has implemented a Personal Development Portfolio Program that helps students address the dimensions of academics, leadership, wellness, aesthetics, citizenship, cultural awareness, ethical development, and social proficiency. In this program, students are paired with a faculty mentor for 4 years. The program culminates in an enhanced resume, supplementing the academic transcript and documenting achievement in these 8 dimensions.

Students *Undergraduates:* 1,077 full-time, 13 part-time. Students come from 17 states and territories, 7 other countries. *The most frequently chosen baccalaureate fields are:* business/marketing, psychology, social sciences and history.

From out-of-state	24%	Reside on campus	85%
Age 25 or older	1%	Transferred in	3%
International students	1%	African Americans	4%
Asian Americans/Pacific Islanders	1%	Hispanic Americans	1%
Native Americans	0.4%		

Faculty 84 (88% full-time), 68% with terminal degrees.
Expenses (2000–2001) *Comprehensive fee:* $21,940 includes full-time tuition ($14,470), mandatory fees ($500), and room and board ($6970). *College room only:* $3420. *Payment plan:* installment. *Waivers:* employees or children of employees.
Library Alexander Mack Memorial Library. *Operations spending 1999–2000:* $603,603. *Collection:* 123,461 titles, 4,893 serial subscriptions, 7,675 audiovisual materials.
College life *Housing:* on-campus residence required through senior year. *Options:* men-only, women-only, disabled students. *Most popular organizations:* Habitat for Humanity, pep band, Oratorio Choir, Baptist Student Union, Brethren Student Fellowship.
Campus security 24-hour emergency response devices, controlled dormitory access, evening and early morning security patrols.
After graduation 23 organizations recruited on campus 1997–98. *Career center:* 1 full-time, 1 part-time personnel. Services include job fairs, resume preparation, interview workshops, resume referral, career/interest testing, career counseling, careers library, job bank, job interviews. *Graduate*

education: 29% of class of 1999 went directly to graduate and professional school: 9% graduate arts and sciences, 4% education, 4% medicine, 2% theology.
Freshmen 992 applied, 886 admitted, 324 enrolled. 5 National Merit Scholars, 8 valedictorians, 100 student government officers.

Average high school GPA	3.4	SAT verbal scores above 500	61%
SAT math scores above 500	61%	ACT above 18	90%
From top 10% of their h.s. class	31%	From top quarter	57%
From top half	88%	1998 freshmen returning in 1999	79%

Application *Options:* Common Application, electronic application, deferred entrance. *Application fee:* $30. *Required:* essay or personal statement; high school transcript; minimum 2.0 GPA; 2 letters of recommendation. *Required for some:* interview. *Recommended:* minimum 3.0 GPA.
Standardized tests *Admission: Required:* SAT I or ACT. *Recommended:* SAT I.
Significant dates *Application deadlines:* rolling (freshmen), rolling (transfers). *Financial aid deadline priority date:* 3/1.
Freshman Application Contact
Mr. Brian C. Hildebrand, Dean for Enrollment Management, Bridgewater College, 402 East College Street, Bridgewater, VA 22812-1599. **Phone:** 540-828-5375. **Toll-free phone:** 800-759-8328. **Fax:** 540-828-5481. **E-mail:** admissions@bridgewater.edu
Visit CollegeQuest.com for information on majors offered and athletics.

■ *See page 1312 for a narrative description.*

BRYANT AND STRATTON COLLEGE, VIRGINIA BEACH
Virginia Beach, Virginia

- **Proprietary**, primarily 2-year, founded 1952
- **Degrees** associate and bachelor's
- **Suburban** campus
- **Coed**, 177 undergraduate students, 85% full-time, 81% women, 19% men
- **Minimally difficult** entrance level
- **8:1** student-to-undergraduate faculty ratio
- **$9024 tuition** and fees

Part of Bryant and Stratton Business Institute, Inc.
Faculty 32 (22% full-time), 19% with terminal degrees.
Admissions Office Contact
Bryant and Stratton College, Virginia Beach, 301 Centre Pointe Drive, Virginia Beach, VA 23462-4417. **Fax:** 757-499-7799.
Visit CollegeQuest.com for information on majors offered and athletics.

CHRISTENDOM COLLEGE
Front Royal, Virginia

- **Independent Roman Catholic**, comprehensive, founded 1977
- **Degrees** associate, bachelor's, and master's
- **Rural** 100-acre campus with easy access to Washington, DC
- **Coed**, 259 undergraduate students, 97% full-time, 53% women, 47% men
- **Moderately difficult** entrance level, 85% of applicants were admitted
- **12:1** student-to-undergraduate faculty ratio
- **51% graduate** in 6 years or less
- **$11,530 tuition** and fees
- **$9085 average financial aid** package, $8980 average indebtedness upon graduation, $3.3 million endowment

Students *Undergraduates:* 252 full-time, 7 part-time. Students come from 48 states and territories, 4 other countries. *The most frequently chosen baccalaureate fields are:* philosophy, English, social sciences and history. *Graduate:* 85 in graduate degree programs.

From out-of-state	79%	Reside on campus	92%
Age 25 or older	4%	Transferred in	7%
International students	4%	African Americans	1%
Asian Americans/Pacific Islanders	2%	Hispanic Americans	2%

Faculty 30 (70% full-time), 67% with terminal degrees.
Expenses (2000–2001) *Comprehensive fee:* $16,100 includes full-time tuition ($11,300), mandatory fees ($230), and room and board ($4570).

Part-time tuition: $495 per credit. *Part-time fees:* $115 per term part-time. *Payment plans:* tuition prepayment, installment. *Waivers:* employees or children of employees.

Library O'Reilly Memorial Library. *Operations spending 1999–2000:* $159,830. *Collection:* 61,787 titles, 249 serial subscriptions, 840 audiovisual materials.

College life *Housing:* on-campus residence required through senior year. *Options:* men-only, women-only. *Most popular organizations:* drama, choir, Shield of Roses, Legion of Mary, debate.

Campus security 24-hour emergency response devices, late-night transport-escort service, night patrols by trained security personnel.

After graduation 4 organizations recruited on campus 1997–98. 80% of class of 1998 had job offers within 6 months. *Career center:* 1 part-time personnel. Services include job fairs, resume preparation, resume referral, career counseling, careers library, job bank, job interviews. *Graduate education:* 20% of class of 1999 went directly to graduate and professional school: 8% graduate arts and sciences, 6% theology, 4% law, 2% education.

Freshmen 162 applied, 138 admitted, 74 enrolled.

Average high school GPA	3.45	SAT verbal scores above 500	98%
SAT math scores above 500	84%	ACT above 18	100%
From top 10% of their h.s. class	30%	From top quarter	60%
From top half	100%	1998 freshmen returning in 1999	84%

Application *Options:* eApply at www.CollegeQuest.com, Common Application, early admission, early action. *Application fee:* $25. *Required:* essay or personal statement; high school transcript; 2 letters of recommendation. *Recommended:* minimum 3.0 GPA; interview.

Standardized tests *Admission: Required:* SAT I or ACT.

Significant dates *Application deadlines:* rolling (freshmen), rolling (transfers). *Early action:* 12/1. *Notification:* 12/15 (early action). *Financial aid deadline priority date:* 4/1.

Freshman Application Contact
Mr. Paul Heisler, Director of Admissions, Christendom College, 134 Christendom Drive, Front Royal, VA 22630-5103. **Phone:** 540-636-2900 Ext. 290. **Toll-free phone:** 800-877-5456 Ext. 290. **Fax:** 540-636-1655. **E-mail:** admissions@christendom.edu

Visit CollegeQuest.com for information on majors offered and athletics.

CHRISTOPHER NEWPORT UNIVERSITY
Newport News, Virginia

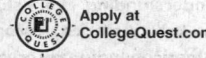

- **State-supported**, comprehensive, founded 1960
- **Degrees** bachelor's and master's
- **Suburban** 113-acre campus with easy access to Norfolk
- **Coed**, 4,545 undergraduate students, 77% full-time, 61% women, 39% men
- **Moderately difficult** entrance level, 61% of applicants were admitted
- **17:1 student-to-undergraduate faculty ratio**
- **33.7% graduate** in 6 years or less
- **$3048 tuition** and fees (in-state); $8816 (out-of-state)
- **$4645 average financial aid** package, $2.7 million endowment

Students *Undergraduates:* 3,497 full-time, 1,048 part-time. Students come from 37 states and territories, 20 other countries. *The most frequently chosen baccalaureate fields are:* business/marketing, psychology, social sciences and history. *Graduate:* 186 in graduate degree programs.

From out-of-state	6%	Reside on campus	13%
Age 25 or older	31%	Transferred in	11%
International students	1%	African Americans	17%
Asian Americans/Pacific Islanders	3%	Hispanic Americans	3%
Native Americans	1%		

Faculty 326 (57% full-time).

Expenses (1999–2000) *Tuition, state resident:* full-time $1888; part-time $126 per semester hour. *Tuition, nonresident:* full-time $7656; part-time $366 per semester hour. *Required fees:* full-time $1160; $20 per term part-time. Full-time tuition and fees vary according to course load. Part-time tuition and fees vary according to course load. *College room and board:* $4950. *Payment plan:* installment. *Waivers:* senior citizens and employees or children of employees.

Library Captain John Smith Library. *Operations spending 1999–2000:* $2.5 million. *Collection:* 178,055 titles, 1,551 serial subscriptions.

College life *Housing:* on-campus residence required in freshman year. *Option:* coed. *Social organizations:* national fraternities, national sororities; 3% of eligible men and 4% of eligible women are members. *Most popular organizations:* Student Virginia Education Association, Student Government Association.

Campus security 24-hour emergency response devices and patrols, late-night transport-escort service, controlled dormitory access, campus police.

After graduation 240 organizations recruited on campus 1997–98. *Career center:* 6 full-time personnel. Services include job fairs, resume preparation, interview workshops, resume referral, career/interest testing, career counseling, careers library, job bank, job interviews. *Graduate education:* 15% of class of 1999 went directly to graduate and professional school.

Freshmen 2,443 applied, 1,494 admitted, 823 enrolled. 8 class presidents, 8 valedictorians, 20 student government officers.

Average high school GPA	3.0	SAT verbal scores above 500	66%
SAT math scores above 500	54%	ACT above 18	50%
From top 10% of their h.s. class	9%	From top quarter	38%
From top half	83%	1998 freshmen returning in 1999	71%

Application *Options:* eApply at www.CollegeQuest.com, Common Application, electronic application, early admission, early action, deferred entrance. *Application fee:* $25. *Required:* high school transcript; minimum 3.0 GPA. *Required for some:* essay or personal statement; 3 letters of recommendation; interview.

Standardized tests *Admission: Required:* SAT I or ACT.

Significant dates *Application deadlines:* 3/1 (freshmen), 7/1 (transfers). *Early action:* 12/1. *Financial aid deadline priority date:* 3/1.

Freshman Application Contact
Ms. Angela Boyd, Associate Director of Admissions, Christopher Newport University, 1 University Place, Newport News, VA 23606-2998. **Phone:** 757-594-7045. **Toll-free phone:** 800-333-4CNU. **Fax:** 757-594-7333. **E-mail:** admit@cnu.edu

Visit CollegeQuest.com for information on majors offered and athletics. Electronic viewbook available at CollegeQuest.com.

■ *See page 1416 for a narrative description.*

CLINCH VALLEY COLLEGE OF THE UNIVERSITY OF VIRGINIA
Virginia—See University of Virginia's College at Wise

THE COLLEGE OF WILLIAM AND MARY
Williamsburg, Virginia

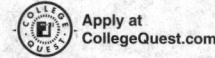

- **State-supported**, university, founded 1693
- **Degrees** bachelor's, master's, doctoral, and first professional
- **Small-town** 1,200-acre campus with easy access to Richmond
- **Coed**, 5,469 undergraduate students, 99% full-time, 58% women, 42% men
- **Very difficult** entrance level, 45% of applicants were admitted
- **12:1 student-to-undergraduate faculty ratio**
- **88% graduate** in 6 years or less
- **$4610 tuition** and fees (in-state); $16,434 (out-of-state)
- **$7965 average financial aid** package, $354.6 million endowment

Students *Undergraduates:* 5,389 full-time, 80 part-time. Students come from 50 states and territories, 52 other countries. *The most frequently chosen baccalaureate fields are:* business/marketing, biological/life sciences, social sciences and history. *Graduate:* 536 in professional programs, 1,465 in other graduate degree programs.

From out-of-state	36%	Reside on campus	76%
Age 25 or older	2%	Transferred in	3%
International students	1%	African Americans	4%
Asian Americans/Pacific Islanders	7%	Hispanic Americans	3%
Native Americans	0.4%		

Faculty 711 (81% full-time), 85% with terminal degrees.

Expenses (1999–2000) *Tuition, state resident:* full-time $4610; part-time $122 per credit hour. *Tuition, nonresident:* full-time $16,434; part-time $510

Virginia

The College of William and Mary *(continued)*
per credit hour. *College room and board:* $4897; room only: $2857. Room and board charges vary according to board plan and housing facility. *Payment plan:* installment. *Waivers:* senior citizens and employees or children of employees.

Library Swem Library plus 9 others. *Operations spending 1999–2000:* $7.2 million. *Collection:* 2 million titles, 11,462 serial subscriptions, 5,864 audiovisual materials.

College life *Housing:* on-campus residence required in freshman year. *Options:* coed, women-only. *Social organizations:* national fraternities, national sororities; 32% of eligible men and 24% of eligible women are members. *Most popular organizations:* Alpha Phi Omega, College Partnership for Kids, student assembly, Flat Hat (student newspaper), Resident Housing Association.

Campus security 24-hour emergency response devices and patrols, student patrols, late-night transport-escort service, controlled dormitory access.

After graduation 150 organizations recruited on campus 1997–98. 47% of class of 1998 had job offers within 6 months. *Career center:* 8 full-time, 1 part-time personnel. Services include job fairs, resume preparation, resume referral, career counseling, careers library, job bank, job interviews. **Major awards:** 2 Rhodes, 1 Fulbright Scholar.

Freshmen 6,878 applied, 3,090 admitted, 1,301 enrolled. 13 National Merit Scholars, 33 class presidents, 117 valedictorians, 683 student government officers.

Average high school GPA	3.9	SAT verbal scores above 500	99%
SAT math scores above 500	98%	ACT above 18	100%
From top 10% of their h.s. class	74%	From top quarter	97%
From top half	100%	1998 freshmen returning in 1999	95%

Application *Options:* eApply at www.CollegeQuest.com, electronic application, early admission, early decision, deferred entrance. *Preference* given to state residents. *Application fee:* $40. *Required:* essay or personal statement; high school transcript. *Required for some:* interview. *Recommended:* 1 letter of recommendation.

Standardized tests *Admission: Required:* SAT I or ACT. *Recommended:* SAT II Subject Tests, SAT II: Writing Test.

Significant dates *Application deadlines:* 1/5 (freshmen), 2/15 (transfers). *Early decision:* 11/1. *Notification:* 4/1 (freshmen), 12/1 (early decision). *Financial aid deadline:* 3/15. *Priority date:* 2/15.

Freshman Application Contact
Ms. Virginia Carey, Dean of Admission, The College of William and Mary, Office of Admission, PO Box 8795, Williamsburg, VA 23187-8795. **Phone:** 757-221-4223. **Fax:** 757-221-1242. **E-mail:** admiss@facstaff.wm.edu

Visit CollegeQuest.com for information on majors offered and athletics. College video available at CollegeQuest.com.

COMMONWEALTH COLLEGE, VIRGINIA BEACH
Virginia—See Bryant and Stratton College, Virginia Beach

COMMUNITY HOSPITAL OF ROANOKE VALLEY—COLLEGE OF HEALTH SCIENCES
Roanoke, Virginia

- **Independent**, 4-year, founded 1982
- **Degrees** associate and bachelor's
- **Urban** 1-acre campus
- **Coed**
- **Moderately difficult** entrance level
- **$11,100 tuition** and fees

Expenses (1999–2000) *Comprehensive fee:* $15,260 includes full-time tuition ($11,100) and room and board ($4160). *College room only:* $2000. Full-time tuition and fees vary according to course level, course load, degree level, and program. Room and board charges vary according to board plan. *Part-time tuition:* $370 per credit hour. Part-time tuition and fees vary according to course level, course load, degree level, and program.

Institutional Web site http://www.chs.edu/

College life *Housing: Option:* coed. *Most popular organizations:* student government association, Student Nurse Association.

Campus security 24-hour emergency response devices and patrols, late-night transport-escort service, controlled dormitory access.

Application *Option:* early decision. *Application fee:* $25. *Required:* essay or personal statement; high school transcript; minimum 2.0 GPA. *Required for some:* letters of recommendation; interview; volunteer experience.

Standardized tests *Admission: Recommended:* SAT I. *Required for some:* SAT I or ACT, ACT ASSET.

Admissions Office Contact
Community Hospital of Roanoke Valley–College of Health Sciences, PO Box 13186, Roanoke, VA 24031-3186. **Toll-free phone:** 888-985-8483. **Fax:** 540-985-9773. **E-mail:** jbailey@health.chs.edu

Visit CollegeQuest.com for information on athletics.

EASTERN MENNONITE UNIVERSITY
Harrisonburg, Virginia

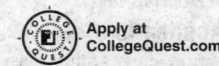
Apply at CollegeQuest.com

- **Independent Mennonite**, comprehensive, founded 1917
- **Degrees** associate, bachelor's, master's, first professional, postbachelor's, and first professional certificates
- **Small-town** 92-acre campus
- **Coed**, 1,075 undergraduate students, 97% full-time, 60% women, 40% men
- **Moderately difficult** entrance level, 85% of applicants were admitted
- **13:1 student-to-undergraduate faculty ratio**
- **$13,480 tuition** and fees
- **$12,247 average financial aid** package, $16,668 average indebtedness upon graduation, $15.5 million endowment

International education is a special mission of Eastern Mennonite University. The University's distinctive Global Village curriculum builds an outstanding liberal arts education on a foundation of Christian values and cross-cultural understanding. Every student engages in cross-cultural study in locations such as Latin America, Europe, the Middle East, Russia, China, Africa, and an American Indian reservation.

Students *Undergraduates:* 1,044 full-time, 31 part-time. Students come from 35 states and territories, 14 other countries. *The most frequently chosen baccalaureate fields are:* business/marketing, education, health professions and related sciences. *Graduate:* 81 in professional programs, 169 in other graduate degree programs.

From out-of-state	60%	Reside on campus	61%
Age 25 or older	4%	Transferred in	6%
International students	5%	African Americans	5%
Asian Americans/Pacific Islanders	2%	Hispanic Americans	2%
Native Americans	0.4%		

Faculty 124 (61% full-time), 52% with terminal degrees.

Expenses (1999–2000) *Comprehensive fee:* $18,430 includes full-time tuition ($13,480) and room and board ($4950). *College room only:* $2500. Full-time tuition and fees vary according to program. Room and board charges vary according to board plan and housing facility. *Part-time tuition:* $565 per semester hour. Part-time tuition and fees vary according to program. *Payment plan:* installment. *Waivers:* employees or children of employees.

Library Sadie Hartzler Library. *Operations spending 1999–2000:* $709,282. *Collection:* 175,147 titles, 1,112 serial subscriptions, 10,072 audiovisual materials.

College life *Housing:* on-campus residence required through junior year. *Options:* coed, men-only, women-only. *Most popular organizations:* YPCA, Campus Activities Council, Celebration Committee, Student Government Association.

Campus security 24-hour emergency response devices, controlled dormitory access, night watchman.

After graduation 12 organizations recruited on campus 1997–98. 76% of class of 1998 had job offers within 6 months. *Career center:* 1 full-time

Virginia

personnel. Services include job fairs, resume preparation, interview workshops, resume referral, career/interest testing, career counseling, careers library, job bank, job interviews. **Graduate education:** 10% of class of 1999 went directly to graduate and professional school.

Freshmen 619 applied, 526 admitted, 219 enrolled. 2 National Merit Scholars, 11 valedictorians.

Average high school GPA	3.4	SAT verbal scores above 500	71%
SAT math scores above 500	63%	ACT above 18	69%
From top 10% of their h.s. class	21%	From top quarter	49%
From top half	76%	1998 freshmen returning in 1999	76%

Application *Options:* eApply at www.CollegeQuest.com, Common Application, electronic application, early admission, deferred entrance. *Application fee:* $25. *Required:* high school transcript; minimum 2.0 GPA; 1 letter of recommendation; statement of commitment. *Recommended:* interview.

Standardized tests *Admission: Required:* SAT I or ACT.

Significant dates *Application deadlines:* 8/1 (freshmen), 8/1 (transfers). *Financial aid deadline priority date:* 3/15.

Freshman Application Contact
Ms. Ellen B. Miller, Director of Admissions, Eastern Mennonite University, 1200 Park Road, Harrisonburg, VA 22802-2462. **Phone:** 540-432-4118. **Toll-free phone:** 800-368-2665. **Fax:** 540-432-4444. **E-mail:** admiss@emu.edu

Visit CollegeQuest.com for information on majors offered and athletics. College video available at CollegeQuest.com.

■ *See page 1604 for a narrative description.*

EMORY & HENRY COLLEGE
Emory, Virginia

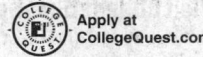

- **Independent United Methodist**, comprehensive, founded 1836
- **Degrees** bachelor's and master's
- **Rural** 163-acre campus
- **Coed**, 981 undergraduate students, 99% full-time, 50% women, 50% men
- **Moderately difficult** entrance level, 80% of applicants were admitted
- **14:1 student-to-undergraduate faculty ratio**
- **63% graduate** in 6 years or less
- **$13,150 tuition** and fees
- **$11,729 average financial aid** package, $18,000 average indebtedness upon graduation, $64 million endowment

Excellence is a long-standing tradition at Emory & Henry. *Money* magazine consistently ranks it among the top 100 college buys in the nation. *U.S. News & World Report* lists Emory & Henry among the top 5 regional liberal arts colleges in the South. In addition, Loren Pope, a college placement expert, claims in his book *Colleges That Change Lives*, that Emory & Henry doubles the talents of most of its students. Founded in 1836, the College offers small classes, a 14:1 student-faculty ratio, a wide range of academic programs, and a variety of student life activities in one of the nation's most beautiful settings.

Students *Undergraduates:* 968 full-time, 13 part-time. Students come from 23 states and territories, 6 other countries. *The most frequently chosen baccalaureate fields are:* business/marketing, communications/communication technologies, social sciences and history. *Graduate:* 9 in graduate degree programs.

From out-of-state	26%	Reside on campus	69%
Age 25 or older	4%	Transferred in	6%
International students	1%	African Americans	6%
Asian Americans/Pacific Islanders	1%	Hispanic Americans	0.4%
Native Americans	0.2%		

Faculty 83 (75% full-time), 65% with terminal degrees.

Expenses (2000–2001) *Comprehensive fee:* $18,472 includes full-time tuition ($12,950), mandatory fees ($200), and room and board ($5322). Full-time tuition and fees vary according to course load. Room and board charges vary according to board plan. *Part-time tuition:* $540 per semester hour. Part-time tuition and fees vary according to course load. *Payment plan:* installment. *Waivers:* employees or children of employees.

Library Kelly Library. *Operations spending 1999–2000:* $885,073. *Collection:* 297,281 titles, 1,109 serial subscriptions, 3,388 audiovisual materials.

College life *Housing:* on-campus residence required through senior year. *Options:* men-only, women-only. *Social organizations:* local fraternities, local sororities; 19% of eligible men and 24% of eligible women are members. *Most popular organizations:* Alpha Phi Omega, Student Virginia Education Association, student radio station, Campus Christian Fellowship, Greek organizations.

Campus security 24-hour emergency response devices and patrols, student patrols, late-night transport-escort service.

After graduation 65 organizations recruited on campus 1997–98. 75% of class of 1998 had job offers within 6 months. *Career center:* 1 full-time, 1 part-time personnel. Services include job fairs, resume preparation, resume referral, career/interest testing, career counseling, careers library, job bank, job interviews. **Graduate education:** 25% of class of 1999 went directly to graduate and professional school: 8% graduate arts and sciences, 4% law, 4% medicine, 3% education, 2% business, 2% theology, 1% dentistry, 1% veterinary medicine.

Freshmen 1,001 applied, 800 admitted, 277 enrolled. 9 valedictorians.

Average high school GPA	3.14	SAT verbal scores above 500	55%
SAT math scores above 500	54%	ACT above 18	94%
From top 10% of their h.s. class	19%	From top quarter	47%
From top half	79%	1998 freshmen returning in 1999	70%

Application *Options:* eApply at www.CollegeQuest.com, Common Application, electronic application, early admission, early decision, deferred entrance. *Application fee:* $25. *Required:* essay or personal statement; high school transcript. *Required for some:* 2 letters of recommendation. *Recommended:* interview.

Standardized tests *Admission: Required:* SAT I or ACT.

Significant dates *Application deadlines:* rolling (freshmen), rolling (transfers). *Early decision:* 12/1. *Notification:* 12/20 (early decision). *Financial aid deadline:* 8/1. *Priority date:* 4/1.

Freshman Application Contact
Ms. Debbie Jones Thompson, Dean of Admissions and Financial Aid, Emory & Henry College, 30479 Armbrister Drive, Emory, VA 24327. **Phone:** 540-944-6133. **Toll-free phone:** 800-848-5493. **Fax:** 540-944-6935. **E-mail:** ehadmiss@ehc.edu

Visit CollegeQuest.com for information on majors offered and athletics. College video available at CollegeQuest.com.

■ *See page 1636 for a narrative description.*

FERRUM COLLEGE
Ferrum, Virginia

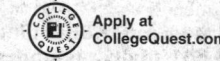

- **Independent United Methodist**, 4-year, founded 1913
- **Degree** bachelor's
- **Rural** 720-acre campus
- **Coed**, 938 undergraduate students, 96% full-time, 39% women, 61% men
- **Minimally difficult** entrance level, 81% of applicants were admitted
- **13:1 student-to-undergraduate faculty ratio**
- **37% graduate** in 6 years or less
- **$10,990 tuition** and fees
- **$10,022 average financial aid** package, $17,093 average indebtedness upon graduation, $41.3 million endowment

Students *Undergraduates:* 903 full-time, 35 part-time. Students come from 26 states and territories. *The most frequently chosen baccalaureate fields are:* business/marketing, natural resources/environmental science, protective services/public administration.

From out-of-state	16%	Reside on campus	81%
Age 25 or older	8%	Transferred in	7%
African Americans	16%	Asian Americans/Pacific Islanders	1%
Hispanic Americans	1%	Native Americans	0.2%

Faculty 98 (69% full-time), 47% with terminal degrees.

Expenses (1999–2000) *Comprehensive fee:* $15,990 includes full-time tuition ($10,990) and room and board ($5000). *Part-time tuition:* $250 per credit hour. Part-time tuition and fees vary according to course load. *Payment plan:* installment. *Waivers:* senior citizens and employees or children of employees.

Library Stanley Library. *Operations spending 1999–2000:* $423,642. *Collection:* 7,739 serial subscriptions, 1,610 audiovisual materials.

College life *Housing:* on-campus residence required through senior year. *Options:* coed, women-only. *Most popular organizations:* Student Government Association, agriculture club, BACCHUS, Panther Productions, African American Student Association, Students in Free Enterprise.

Virginia

Ferrum College (continued)

Campus security 24-hour emergency response devices and patrols, student patrols, late-night transport-escort service, controlled dormitory access.

After graduation 60 organizations recruited on campus 1997–98. *Career center:* 2 full-time personnel. Services include job fairs, resume preparation, interview workshops, resume referral, career/interest testing, career counseling, careers library, job bank, job interviews. *Graduate education:* 17% of class of 1999 went directly to graduate and professional school.

Freshmen 1,031 applied, 835 admitted, 328 enrolled.

Average high school GPA	2.6	SAT verbal scores above 500	28%
SAT math scores above 500	27%	ACT above 18	N/R
From top 10% of their h.s. class	4%	From top quarter	16%
From top half	41%	1998 freshmen returning in 1999	56%

Application *Options:* eApply at www.CollegeQuest.com, Common Application, electronic application, early admission, deferred entrance. *Application fee:* $25. *Required:* high school transcript. *Required for some:* interview. *Recommended:* essay or personal statement; minimum 2.0 GPA; 2 letters of recommendation; interview.

Standardized tests *Admission: Required for some:* SAT I or ACT.

Significant dates *Application deadlines:* rolling (freshmen), rolling (transfers). *Financial aid deadline priority date:* 4/1.

Freshman Application Contact
Ms. Gilda Q. Woods, Director of Admissions, Ferrum College, Spilman-Daniel House, PO Box 1000, Ferrum, VA 24088-9001. **Phone:** 540-365-4290. **Toll-free phone:** 800-868-9797. **Fax:** 540-365-4266. **E-mail:** admissions@ferrum.edu

Visit CollegeQuest.com for information on majors offered and athletics.

■ *See page 1658 for a narrative description.*

GEORGE MASON UNIVERSITY
Fairfax, Virginia

- **State-supported**, university, founded 1957
- **Degrees** bachelor's, master's, doctoral, first professional, and postbachelor's certificates
- **Suburban** 677-acre campus with easy access to Washington, DC
- **Coed**, 14,547 undergraduate students, 73% full-time, 55% women, 45% men
- **Moderately difficult** entrance level, 59% of applicants were admitted
- **17:1 student-to-undergraduate faculty ratio**
- **49% graduate** in 6 years or less
- **$3756 tuition** and fees (in-state); $12,516 (out-of-state)
- **$6049 average financial aid** package, $13,826 average indebtedness upon graduation, $32.3 million endowment

Students *Undergraduates:* 10,669 full-time, 3,878 part-time. Students come from 54 states and territories, 118 other countries. *The most frequently chosen baccalaureate fields are:* business/marketing, education, social sciences and history. *Graduate:* 728 in professional programs, 8,190 in other graduate degree programs.

From out-of-state	9%	Reside on campus	19%
Age 25 or older	29%	Transferred in	15%
International students	4%	African Americans	9%
Asian Americans/Pacific Islanders	16%	Hispanic Americans	7%
Native Americans	0.4%		

Faculty 1,973 (45% full-time), 37% with terminal degrees.

Expenses (1999–2000) *One-time required fee:* $100. *Tuition, state resident:* full-time $3756; part-time $156 per credit hour. *Tuition, nonresident:* full-time $12,516; part-time $522 per credit hour. Full-time tuition and fees vary according to course load. Part-time tuition and fees vary according to course load. *College room and board:* $5298; room only: $3300. Room and board charges vary according to board plan and housing facility. *Payment plans:* installment, deferred payment. *Waivers:* senior citizens and employees or children of employees.

Library Fenwick Library plus 1 other. *Operations spending 1999–2000:* $11 million. *Collection:* 947,288 titles, 18,820 serial subscriptions, 233,891 audiovisual materials.

College life *Housing: Options:* coed, men-only, women-only, disabled students. *Social organizations:* national fraternities, national sororities; 10% of eligible men and 8% of eligible women are members. *Most popular organizations:* intramurals, Greek life, student government, club sports, volunteer and community service.

Campus security 24-hour emergency response devices and patrols, student patrols, late-night transport-escort service, controlled dormitory access.

After graduation 181 organizations recruited on campus 1997–98. *Career center:* 8 full-time, 11 part-time personnel. Services include job fairs, resume preparation, resume referral, career counseling, careers library, job bank, job interviews. *Graduate education:* 3% of class of 1999 went directly to graduate and professional school.

Freshmen 6,508 applied, 3,858 admitted, 2,130 enrolled.

Average high school GPA	3.13	SAT verbal scores above 500	65%
SAT math scores above 500	66%	ACT above 18	79%
1998 freshmen returning in 1999	71%		

Application *Options:* Common Application, electronic application, early admission, early action, deferred entrance. *Application fee:* $30. *Required:* essay or personal statement; high school transcript; minimum 2.0 GPA; interview. *Recommended:* minimum 3.0 GPA; letters of recommendation.

Standardized tests *Admission: Required:* SAT I or ACT. *Recommended:* SAT II Subject Tests.

Significant dates *Application deadlines:* 2/1 (freshmen), 3/15 (transfers). *Early action:* 12/1. *Notification:* 4/1 (freshmen), 1/15 (early action). *Financial aid deadline priority date:* 3/1.

Freshman Application Contact
Mr. Eddie Tallent, Director of Admissions, George Mason University, 4400 University Drive, MSN 3A4, Fairfax, VA 22030-4444. **Phone:** 703-993-2398. **E-mail:** admissions@gmu.edu

Visit CollegeQuest.com for information on majors offered and athletics. College video and electronic viewbook available at CollegeQuest.com.

■ *See page 1710 for a narrative description.*

HAMPDEN-SYDNEY COLLEGE
Hampden-Sydney, Virginia

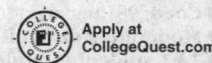
Apply at CollegeQuest.com

- **Independent Presbyterian**, 4-year, founded 1776
- **Degree** bachelor's
- **Rural** 660-acre campus with easy access to Richmond
- **Men** only, 976 undergraduate students, 100% full-time
- **Moderately difficult** entrance level, 74% of applicants were admitted
- **13:1 student-to-undergraduate faculty ratio**
- **64.1% graduate** in 6 years or less
- **$16,531 tuition** and fees
- **$12,638 average financial aid** package, $10,400 average indebtedness upon graduation, $116.3 million endowment

Students *Undergraduates:* 976 full-time. Students come from 34 states and territories, 3 other countries. *The most frequently chosen baccalaureate fields are:* business/marketing, psychology, social sciences and history.

From out-of-state	40%	Reside on campus	94%
Transferred in	1%	International students	0.3%
African Americans	4%	Asian Americans/Pacific Islanders	1%
Hispanic Americans	1%	Native Americans	0.2%

Faculty 100 (62% full-time), 80% with terminal degrees.

Expenses (1999–2000) *Comprehensive fee:* $22,429 includes full-time tuition ($16,048), mandatory fees ($483), and room and board ($5898). *College room only:* $2464. Room and board charges vary according to housing facility. *Part-time tuition:* $536 per semester hour. *Payment plan:* installment. *Waivers:* employees or children of employees.

Library Eggleston Library. *Operations spending 1999–2000:* $914,287. *Collection:* 219,221 titles, 948 serial subscriptions.

College life *Housing:* on-campus residence required through senior year. *Option:* men-only. *Social organizations:* national fraternities; 37% of eligible undergrads are members. *Most popular organizations:* Good Men-Good Citizens, Fellowship of Christian Athletes, Rugby Club, College Republicans, Society for the Preservation of Southern Heritage.

Campus security 24-hour emergency response devices and patrols.

After graduation 30 organizations recruited on campus 1997–98. 75% of class of 1998 had job offers within 6 months. *Career center:* 2 full-time

Virginia

personnel. Services include job fairs, resume preparation, interview workshops, resume referral, career/interest testing, career counseling, careers library, job bank, job interviews. *Graduate education:* 30% of class of 1999 went directly to graduate and professional school: 8% law, 7% graduate arts and sciences, 3% business, 2% medicine, 1% dentistry, 1% education, 1% engineering, 1% theology, 1% veterinary medicine.

Freshmen 991 applied, 738 admitted, 307 enrolled. 6 class presidents, 6 valedictorians, 64 student government officers.

Average high school GPA	3.1	SAT verbal scores above 500	75%
SAT math scores above 500	79%	ACT above 18	85%
From top 10% of their h.s. class	14%	From top quarter	37%
From top half	72%	1998 freshmen returning in 1999	80%

Application *Options:* eApply at www.CollegeQuest.com, Common Application, electronic application, early admission, early decision. *Application fee:* $30. *Required:* essay or personal statement; high school transcript; minimum 2.0 GPA; 2 letters of recommendation. *Recommended:* minimum 3.0 GPA; interview.

Standardized tests *Admission: Required:* SAT I or ACT. *Recommended:* SAT II Subject Tests, SAT II: Writing Test.

Significant dates *Application deadlines:* 3/1 (freshmen), 7/1 (transfers). *Early decision:* 11/15. *Notification:* continuous until 4/15 (freshmen), 12/15 (early decision). *Financial aid deadline priority date:* 3/1.

Freshman Application Contact
Ms. Anita H. Garland, Dean of Admissions, Hampden-Sydney College, PO Box 667, Hampden-Sydney, VA 23943-0667. **Phone:** 804-223-6120. **Toll-free phone:** 800-755-0733. **Fax:** 804-223-6346. **E-mail:** hsapp@tiger.hsc.edu

Visit CollegeQuest.com for information on majors offered and athletics. Electronic viewbook available at CollegeQuest.com.

■ *See page 1756 for a narrative description.*

HAMPTON UNIVERSITY
Hampton, Virginia

- **Independent**, comprehensive, founded 1868
- **Degrees** associate, bachelor's, master's, doctoral, and post-master's certificates
- **Urban** 210-acre campus with easy access to Norfolk
- **Coed**, 4,622 undergraduate students, 97% full-time, 62% women, 38% men
- **Moderately difficult** entrance level, 64% of applicants were admitted
- **16:1 student-to-undergraduate faculty ratio**
- **$10,580 tuition** and fees
- **$122.4 million endowment**

Students *Undergraduates:* 4,474 full-time, 148 part-time. *The most frequently chosen baccalaureate fields are:* business/marketing, psychology, social sciences and history. *Graduate:* 389 in graduate degree programs.

From out-of-state	63%	Reside on campus	55%
Age 25 or older	5%	Transferred in	3%

Faculty 452 (72% full-time), 57% with terminal degrees.

Expenses (1999–2000) *Comprehensive fee:* $15,334 includes full-time tuition ($9490), mandatory fees ($1090), and room and board ($4754). Full-time tuition and fees vary according to program. Room and board charges vary according to housing facility. *Part-time tuition:* $230 per hour. *Part-time fees:* $545 per term part-time. Part-time tuition and fees vary according to program. *Payment plan:* installment. *Waivers:* employees or children of employees.

Library William R. and Norma B. Harvey Library. *Collection:* 317,902 titles, 1,326 serial subscriptions.

College life *Housing: Option:* coed. *Social organizations:* national fraternities, national sororities. *Most popular organizations:* student government, Student Leaders, Student Union Board, student recruitment team.

Campus security 24-hour emergency response devices and patrols, controlled dormitory access, emergency call boxes.

After graduation 360 organizations recruited on campus 1997–98. 72% of class of 1998 had job offers within 6 months. *Career center:* 5 full-time, 6 part-time personnel. Services include job fairs, resume preparation, resume referral, career counseling, careers library, job bank, job interviews.

Freshmen 7,192 applied, 4,598 admitted, 1,376 enrolled.

Average high school GPA	3.0	SAT verbal scores above 500	52%
SAT math scores above 500	45%	ACT above 18	74%
From top 10% of their h.s. class	25%	From top quarter	68%
From top half	93%	1998 freshmen returning in 1999	85%

Application *Options:* Common Application, early admission, deferred entrance. *Application fee:* $25. *Required:* high school transcript; minimum 2.0 GPA; 2 letters of recommendation.

Standardized tests *Admission: Required:* SAT I or ACT.

Significant dates *Application deadlines:* 3/15 (freshmen), 3/15 (transfers). *Notification:* continuous until 7/31 (freshmen). *Financial aid deadline priority date:* 3/1.

Freshman Application Contact
Mr. Leonard M. Jones Jr., Director of Admissions, Hampton University, , Office of Admissions, Hampton, VA 23668. **Phone:** 757-727-5328. **Toll-free phone:** 800-624-3328. **Fax:** 757-727-5084. **E-mail:** admit@hamptonu.edu

Visit CollegeQuest.com for information on majors offered and athletics. College video available at CollegeQuest.com.

■ *See page 1760 for a narrative description.*

HOLLINS UNIVERSITY
Roanoke, Virginia

- **Independent**, comprehensive, founded 1842
- **Degrees** bachelor's, master's, and post-master's certificates
- **Suburban** 475-acre campus
- **Women** only, 808 undergraduate students, 96% full-time
- **Moderately difficult** entrance level, 86% of applicants were admitted
- **10:1 student-to-undergraduate faculty ratio**
- **66% graduate** in 6 years or less
- **$16,710 tuition** and fees
- **$14,846 average financial aid** package, $14,809 average indebtedness upon graduation, $89.8 million endowment

Students *Undergraduates:* 772 full-time, 36 part-time. Students come from 43 states and territories, 8 other countries. *The most frequently chosen baccalaureate fields are:* social sciences and history, psychology, visual/performing arts. *Graduate:* 258 in graduate degree programs.

From out-of-state	61%	Reside on campus	83%
Age 25 or older	11%	Transferred in	3%
International students	1%	African Americans	6%
Asian Americans/Pacific Islanders	2%	Hispanic Americans	2%
Native Americans	0.2%		

Faculty 98 (76% full-time), 85% with terminal degrees.

Expenses (1999–2000) *Comprehensive fee:* $22,835 includes full-time tuition ($16,460), mandatory fees ($250), and room and board ($6125). *College room only:* $3640. *Part-time tuition:* $514 per credit. *Part-time fees:* $125 per year part-time. *Payment plans:* tuition prepayment, installment. *Waivers:* employees or children of employees.

Library Fishburn Library plus 1 other. *Operations spending 1999–2000:* $744,177. *Collection:* 195,376 titles, 2,980 audiovisual materials.

College life *Housing:* on-campus residence required through senior year. *Option:* women-only. *Most popular organizations:* Student Government Association, SHARE (volunteer group), Religious Life Association, Student Athletic Association, campus political organizations.

Campus security 24-hour emergency response devices and patrols, late-night transport-escort service, controlled dormitory access, emergency call boxes.

After graduation 10 organizations recruited on campus 1997–98. 83% of class of 1998 had job offers within 6 months. *Career center:* 3 full-time personnel. Services include job fairs, resume preparation, interview workshops, resume referral, career/interest testing, career counseling, careers library, job bank, job interviews. *Graduate education:* 29% of class of 1999 went directly to graduate and professional school: 23% graduate arts and sciences, 4% law, 1% business, 1% veterinary medicine.

Freshmen 722 applied, 619 admitted, 238 enrolled. 6 National Merit Scholars, 1 class president, 1 valedictorian, 3 student government officers.

Virginia

Hollins University (continued)

Average high school GPA	3.42	SAT verbal scores above 500	88%
SAT math scores above 500	75%	ACT above 18	99%
From top 10% of their h.s. class	25%	From top quarter	58%
From top half	87%	1998 freshmen returning in 1999	80%

Application *Options:* eApply at www.CollegeQuest.com, Common Application, early admission, early decision, deferred entrance. *Application fee:* $25. *Required:* essay or personal statement; high school transcript; 1 letter of recommendation. *Recommended:* interview.

Standardized tests *Admission: Required:* SAT I or ACT. *Recommended:* SAT II Subject Tests.

Significant dates *Application deadlines:* 2/15 (freshmen), 7/1 (transfers). *Early decision:* 12/1. *Notification:* 12/15 (early decision). *Financial aid deadline:* 2/15. *Priority date:* 2/1.

Freshman Application Contact
Ms. Terri Reddings, Dean of Admissions, Hollins University, PO Box 9707, Roanoke, VA 24020-1707. **Phone:** 540-362-6401. **Toll-free phone:** 800-456-9595. **Fax:** 540-362-6218. **E-mail:** huadm@hollins.edu

Visit CollegeQuest.com for information on majors offered and athletics. College video available at CollegeQuest.com.

■ *See page 1798 for a narrative description.*

ITT TECHNICAL INSTITUTE
Norfolk, Virginia

- **Proprietary**, primarily 2-year, founded 1988
- **Degrees** associate and bachelor's
- **Suburban** 2-acre campus
- **Coed**
- **Minimally difficult** entrance level
- **$9190 tuition** and fees

Part of ITT Educational Services, Inc.

Admissions Office Contact
ITT Technical Institute, 863 Glenrock Road, Suite 100, Norfolk, VA 23502-3701.

Visit CollegeQuest.com for information on majors offered and athletics. College video available at CollegeQuest.com.

JAMES MADISON UNIVERSITY
Harrisonburg, Virginia

- **State-supported**, comprehensive, founded 1908
- **Degrees** bachelor's, master's, and doctoral (also offers specialist in education degree)
- **Small-town** 472-acre campus
- **Coed**, 13,668 undergraduate students, 96% full-time, 57% women, 43% men
- **Very difficult** entrance level, 65% of applicants were admitted
- **18:1 student-to-undergraduate faculty ratio**
- **80.3% graduate** in 6 years or less
- **$3926 tuition** and fees (in-state); $9532 (out-of-state)
- **$5036 average financial aid** package, $12,000 average indebtedness upon graduation, $23.3 million endowment

Students *Undergraduates:* 13,185 full-time, 483 part-time. Students come from 49 states and territories, 51 other countries. *The most frequently chosen baccalaureate fields are:* business/marketing, psychology, social sciences and history. *Graduate:* 1,067 in graduate degree programs.

From out-of-state	29%	Reside on campus	43%
Age 25 or older	3%	Transferred in	4%
International students	1%	African Americans	5%
Asian Americans/Pacific Islanders	4%	Hispanic Americans	2%
Native Americans	0.2%		

Faculty 874 (73% full-time), 61% with terminal degrees.

Expenses (1999–2000) *Tuition, state resident:* full-time $3926; part-time $1085 per term. *Tuition, nonresident:* full-time $9532; part-time $2770 per term. Part-time tuition and fees vary according to course load. *College room and board:* $5182; room only: $2788. *Payment plan:* installment. *Waivers:* senior citizens and employees or children of employees.

Library Carrier Library plus 1 other. *Operations spending 1999–2000:* $4.4 million. *Collection:* 26,300 audiovisual materials.

College life *Housing:* on-campus residence required in freshman year. *Option:* coed. *Social organizations:* national fraternities, national sororities; 14% of eligible men and 17% of eligible women are members. *Most popular organizations:* Student Ambassadors, sports clubs, Greek organizations, service organizations, special interest groups.

Campus security 24-hour emergency response devices and patrols, student patrols, late-night transport-escort service, controlled dormitory access, lighted pathways.

After graduation 208 organizations recruited on campus 1997–98. 74% of class of 1998 had job offers within 6 months. *Career center:* Services include job fairs, resume preparation, interview workshops, resume referral, career/interest testing, career counseling, careers library, job bank, job interviews.

Freshmen 12,980 applied, 8,494 admitted, 3,039 enrolled.

Average high school GPA	3.53	SAT verbal scores above 500	89%
SAT math scores above 500	89%	ACT above 18	N/R
From top 10% of their h.s. class	33%	From top quarter	80%
From top half	99%	1998 freshmen returning in 1999	90%

Application *Option:* early action. *Preference* given to state residents. *Application fee:* $30. *Required:* essay or personal statement; high school transcript. *Recommended:* minimum 3.0 GPA.

Standardized tests *Admission: Required:* SAT I or ACT. *Recommended:* SAT I. *Required for some:* SAT II Subject Tests.

Significant dates *Application deadlines:* 1/15 (freshmen), 3/1 (transfers). *Early action:* 11/1. *Notification:* 4/7 (freshmen), 1/15 (early action). *Financial aid deadline:* 2/15.

Freshman Application Contact
Ms. Laika Tamny, Associate Director of Admission, James Madison University, Office of Admission, Sonner Hall MSC 0101, Harrisonburg, VA 22807. **Phone:** 540-568-6147. **Fax:** 540-568-3332. **E-mail:** gotojmu@jmu.edu

Visit CollegeQuest.com for information on majors offered and athletics.

LIBERTY UNIVERSITY
Lynchburg, Virginia

- **Independent nondenominational**, comprehensive, founded 1971
- **Degrees** associate, bachelor's, master's, doctoral, and first professional (also offers external degree program with significant enrollment not reflected in profile)
- **Suburban** 160-acre campus
- **Coed**, 5,889 undergraduate students, 81% full-time, 49% women, 51% men
- **Minimally difficult** entrance level, 52% of applicants were admitted
- **25:1 student-to-undergraduate faculty ratio**
- **$8750 tuition** and fees

Students *Undergraduates:* 4,769 full-time, 1,120 part-time. Students come from 52 states and territories, 47 other countries. *The most frequently chosen baccalaureate fields are:* business/marketing, philosophy, psychology. *Graduate:* 52 in professional programs, 685 in other graduate degree programs.

From out-of-state	67%	Reside on campus	62%
Age 25 or older	21%	International students	3%
African Americans	8%	Asian Americans/Pacific Islanders	1%
Hispanic Americans	3%	Native Americans	1%

Faculty 254 (69% full-time), 50% with terminal degrees.

Expenses (2000–2001) *Comprehensive fee:* $13,550 includes full-time tuition ($8550), mandatory fees ($200), and room and board ($4800). Full-time tuition and fees vary according to course load. *Part-time tuition:* $285 per semester hour. *Part-time fees:* $50 per term part-time. Part-time tuition and fees vary according to course load. *Payment plan:* installment. *Waivers:* employees or children of employees.

Library A. Pierre Guillermin Library plus 1 other. *Operations spending 1999–2000:* $933,928. *Collection:* 193,242 titles, 1,701 serial subscriptions, 5,171 audiovisual materials.

College life *Housing:* on-campus residence required through junior year. *Options:* men-only, women-only. *Most popular organizations:* College Republicans, Youthquest, Circle K.

Virginia

Campus security 24-hour patrols, late-night transport-escort service, 24-hour emergency dispatch.
After graduation 145 organizations recruited on campus 1997–98. *Career center:* 3 full-time, 5 part-time personnel. Services include job fairs, resume preparation, interview workshops, resume referral, career/interest testing, career counseling, careers library, job bank, job interviews. *Graduate education:* 10% of class of 1999 went directly to graduate and professional school.
Freshmen 4,689 applied, 2,453 admitted, 1,118 enrolled.

Average high school GPA	2.8	SAT verbal scores above 500	N/R
SAT math scores above 500	N/R	ACT above 18	N/R

Application *Options:* early admission, deferred entrance. *Application fee:* $35. *Required:* essay or personal statement; high school transcript. *Required for some:* 1 letter of recommendation; interview. *Recommended:* minimum 2.0 GPA; 1 letter of recommendation.
Standardized tests *Admission: Required:* SAT I or ACT. *Required for some:* ACT.
Significant dates *Application deadlines:* 6/30 (freshmen), 6/30 (transfers). *Notification:* continuous until 8/15 (freshmen). *Financial aid deadline priority date:* 4/15.
Freshman Application Contact
Mr. Mark Camper, Director of Admissions, Liberty University, 1971 University Boulevard, Lynchburg, VA 24502. **Phone:** 804-582-2778. **Toll-free phone:** 800-543-5317. **E-mail:** admissions@liberty.edu
Visit CollegeQuest.com for information on majors offered and athletics. College video available at CollegeQuest.com.

■ *See page 1924 for a narrative description.*

LONGWOOD COLLEGE
Farmville, Virginia

Apply at CollegeQuest.com

- **State-supported**, comprehensive, founded 1839
- **Degrees** bachelor's and master's
- **Small-town** 160-acre campus with easy access to Richmond
- **Coed**, 3,161 undergraduate students, 97% full-time, 65% women, 35% men
- **Moderately difficult** entrance level, 76% of applicants were admitted
- **18:1 student-to-undergraduate faculty ratio**
- **60% graduate** in 6 years or less
- **$3924 tuition** and fees (in-state); $9370 (out-of-state)
- **$6420 average financial aid** package, $14,197 average indebtedness upon graduation, $21.6 million endowment

Part of Commonwealth of Virginia Council of Higher Education.
Students *Undergraduates:* 3,070 full-time, 91 part-time. Students come from 19 states and territories. *The most frequently chosen baccalaureate fields are:* business/marketing, education, social sciences and history. *Graduate:* 501 in graduate degree programs.

From out-of-state	10%	Reside on campus	77%
Age 25 or older	3%	Transferred in	7%
International students	0.4%	African Americans	9%
Asian Americans/Pacific Islanders	2%	Hispanic Americans	2%
Native Americans	0.2%		

Faculty 166 full-time.
Expenses (1999–2000) *Tuition, state resident:* full-time $2020; part-time $84 per credit hour. *Tuition, nonresident:* full-time $7466; part-time $311 per credit hour. *Required fees:* full-time $1904; $31 per credit hour. *College room and board:* $4620; room only: $2710. Room and board charges vary according to board plan. *Payment plan:* installment. *Waivers:* senior citizens and employees or children of employees.
Library Longwood Library. *Operations spending 1999–2000:* $1.7 million. *Collection:* 2,147 serial subscriptions, 7,730 audiovisual materials.
College life *Housing:* on-campus residence required through junior year. *Options:* coed, men-only, women-only. *Social organizations:* national fraternities, national sororities; 21% of eligible men and 23% of eligible women are members. *Most popular organizations:* Student Government Association, Alpha Phi Omega, Intervarsity Christian, Longwood Ambassadors, Wellness Advocates.

Campus security 24-hour emergency response devices and patrols, late-night transport-escort service, controlled dormitory access, security lighting.
After graduation 59 organizations recruited on campus 1997–98. *Career center:* 4 full-time personnel. Services include job fairs, resume preparation, resume referral, career/interest testing, career counseling, careers library, job bank, job interviews. *Graduate education:* 18% of class of 1999 went directly to graduate and professional school.
Freshmen 2,762 applied, 2,108 admitted, 816 enrolled. 79 student government officers.

Average high school GPA	3.1	SAT verbal scores above 500	76%
SAT math scores above 500	67%	ACT above 18	N/R
From top 10% of their h.s. class	11%	From top quarter	38%
From top half	81%	1998 freshmen returning in 1999	79%

Application *Options:* eApply at www.CollegeQuest.com, Common Application, electronic application, early admission, early action, deferred entrance. *Application fee:* $25. *Required:* essay or personal statement; high school transcript. *Required for some:* interview. *Recommended:* minimum 2.6 GPA; letters of recommendation.
Standardized tests *Admission: Required:* SAT I or ACT. *Required for some:* SAT II Subject Tests.
Significant dates *Application deadlines:* 3/1 (freshmen), 6/1 (transfers). *Early action:* 12/10. *Notification:* continuous until 6/1 (freshmen), 1/1 (early action). *Financial aid deadline priority date:* 3/1.
Freshman Application Contact
Mr. Robert J. Chonko, Director of Admissions, Longwood College, 201 High Street, Farmville, VA 23909. **Phone:** 804-395-2060. **Toll-free phone:** 800-281-4677. **Fax:** 804-395-2332. **E-mail:** lcadmit@longwood.lwc.edu
Visit CollegeQuest.com for information on majors offered and athletics.

LYNCHBURG COLLEGE
Lynchburg, Virginia

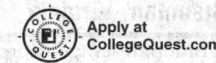

Apply at CollegeQuest.com

- **Independent**, comprehensive, founded 1903, affiliated with Christian Church (Disciples of Christ)
- **Degrees** bachelor's and master's
- **Suburban** 214-acre campus
- **Coed**, 1,669 undergraduate students, 93% full-time, 61% women, 39% men
- **Moderately difficult** entrance level, 82% of applicants were admitted
- **15:1 student-to-undergraduate faculty ratio**
- **55% graduate** in 6 years or less
- **$18,105 tuition** and fees
- **$13,127 average financial aid** package, $17,992 average indebtedness upon graduation, $67.8 million endowment

Students *Undergraduates:* 1,555 full-time, 114 part-time. Students come from 31 states and territories, 10 other countries. *The most frequently chosen baccalaureate fields are:* business/marketing, education, social sciences and history. *Graduate:* 304 in graduate degree programs.

From out-of-state	43%	Reside on campus	72%
Age 25 or older	15%	International students	1%
African Americans	9%	Asian Americans/Pacific Islanders	1%
Hispanic Americans	2%	Native Americans	1%

Faculty 190 (57% full-time), 53% with terminal degrees.
Expenses (2000–2001) *Comprehensive fee:* $22,505 includes full-time tuition ($17,980), mandatory fees ($125), and room and board ($4400). *College room only:* $2600. Room and board charges vary according to board plan. *Part-time tuition:* $280 per credit hour. Part-time tuition and fees vary according to course load. *Payment plan:* installment. *Waivers:* adult students, senior citizens, and employees or children of employees.
Library Knight-Capron Library. *Operations spending 1999–2000:* $700,876. *Collection:* 287,601 titles, 636 serial subscriptions, 9,360 audiovisual materials.
College life *Housing:* on-campus residence required through junior year. *Option:* coed. *Social organizations:* national fraternities, national sororities; 23% of eligible men and 12% of eligible women are members. *Most popular organizations:* Student Activities Board, SGA, Black Student Association, Habitat for Humanity, gospel ensemble.
Campus security 24-hour emergency response devices and patrols, late-night transport-escort service, controlled dormitory access.

Virginia

Lynchburg College (continued)

After graduation 143 organizations recruited on campus 1997–98. 70% of class of 1998 had job offers within 6 months. *Career center:* 2 full-time, 2 part-time personnel. Services include job fairs, resume preparation, career counseling, careers library, job interviews. *Graduate education:* 22% of class of 1999 went directly to graduate and professional school.

Freshmen 1,872 applied, 1,542 admitted, 474 enrolled.

Average high school GPA	3.0	SAT verbal scores above 500	54%
SAT math scores above 500	53%	ACT above 18	81%
From top 10% of their h.s. class	12%	From top quarter	40%
From top half	72%	1998 freshmen returning in 1999	75%

Application *Options:* eApply at www.CollegeQuest.com, Common Application, electronic application, early admission, early decision, deferred entrance. *Application fee:* $30. *Required:* essay or personal statement; high school transcript. *Recommended:* 2 letters of recommendation; interview.

Standardized tests *Admission: Required:* SAT I or ACT. *Recommended:* SAT II Subject Tests, SAT II: Writing Test.

Significant dates *Application deadlines:* rolling (freshmen), rolling (transfers). *Early decision:* 11/15. *Notification:* 12/15 (early decision). *Financial aid deadline priority date:* 3/1.

Freshman Application Contact
Ms. Sharon Walters-Bower, Director of Recruitment, Lynchburg College, 1501 Lakeside Drive, Lynchburg, VA 24501-3199. **Phone:** 804-544-8300. **Toll-free phone:** 800-426-8101. **Fax:** 804-544-8653. **E-mail:** admissions@lynchburg.edu

Visit CollegeQuest.com for information on majors offered and athletics.

■ *See page 1962 for a narrative description.*

MARY BALDWIN COLLEGE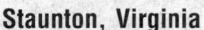
Staunton, Virginia

- **Independent**, comprehensive, founded 1842, affiliated with Presbyterian Church (U.S.A.)
- **Degrees** bachelor's and master's
- **Small-town** 54-acre campus
- **Coed**, primarily women, 1,356 undergraduate students, 74% full-time, 97% women, 3% men
- **Moderately difficult** entrance level, 87% of applicants were admitted
- **11:1** student-to-undergraduate faculty ratio
- **54.5% graduate** in 6 years or less
- **$14,645 tuition** and fees
- **$14,459 average financial aid** package, $31.9 million endowment

Students *Undergraduates:* 998 full-time, 358 part-time. Students come from 32 states and territories, 3 other countries. *The most frequently chosen baccalaureate fields are:* business/marketing, psychology, social sciences and history. *Graduate:* 78 in graduate degree programs.

From out-of-state	35%	Reside on campus	87%
Age 25 or older	35%	Transferred in	3%
International students	1%	African Americans	13%
Asian Americans/Pacific Islanders	2%	Hispanic Americans	2%
Native Americans	0.3%		

Faculty 114 (62% full-time), 56% with terminal degrees.

Expenses (1999–2000) *Comprehensive fee:* $22,095 includes full-time tuition ($14,475), mandatory fees ($170), and room and board ($7450). Room and board charges vary according to housing facility. *Part-time tuition:* $290 per semester hour. *Payment plan:* installment. *Waivers:* employees or children of employees.

Library Grafton Library. *Operations spending 1999–2000:* $360,488. *Collection:* 165,000 titles, 1,540 serial subscriptions, 4,640 audiovisual materials.

College life *Housing:* on-campus residence required through senior year. *Option:* women-only. *Most popular organizations:* Student Government Association, Baldwin Program Board, Black Student Alliance, President's Society, Students in Free Enterprise.

Campus security 24-hour emergency response devices and patrols, late-night transport-escort service, controlled dormitory access.

After graduation 20 organizations recruited on campus 1997–98. 83% of class of 1998 had job offers within 6 months. *Career center:* 3 full-time, 1 part-time personnel. Services include job fairs, resume preparation, interview workshops, resume referral, career/interest testing, career counseling, careers library, job bank, job interviews. *Graduate education:* 20% of class of 1999 went directly to graduate and professional school: 9% education, 3% business, 2% graduate arts and sciences, 2% law, 2% medicine, 2% theology.

Freshmen 1,185 applied, 1,027 admitted, 295 enrolled.

Average high school GPA	3.12	SAT verbal scores above 500	60%
SAT math scores above 500	41%	ACT above 18	90%
1998 freshmen returning in 1999	71%		

Application *Options:* eApply at www.CollegeQuest.com, Common Application, electronic application, early admission, early decision, deferred entrance. *Application fee:* $25. *Required:* high school transcript; minimum 2.0 GPA; 1 letter of recommendation. *Recommended:* interview.

Standardized tests *Admission: Required:* SAT I or ACT.

Significant dates *Application deadlines:* rolling (freshmen), rolling (transfers). *Early decision:* 11/15. *Notification:* 12/1 (early decision). *Financial aid deadline priority date:* 6/1.

Freshman Application Contact
Mr. Douglas E. Clark, Vice President for Enrollment Management, Mary Baldwin College, Frederick and New Streets, Staunton, VA 24401. **Phone:** 540-887-7019. **Toll-free phone:** 800-468-2262. **Fax:** 540-886-6634. **E-mail:** admit@mbc.edu

Visit CollegeQuest.com for information on majors offered and athletics.

MARYMOUNT UNIVERSITY
Arlington, Virginia

- **Independent**, comprehensive, founded 1950, affiliated with Roman Catholic Church
- **Degrees** associate, bachelor's, and master's
- **Suburban** 21-acre campus with easy access to Washington, DC
- **Coed**
- **Moderately difficult** entrance level
- **$13,870 tuition** and fees

Marymount is a comprehensive, coeducational Catholic university that emphasizes excellence in teaching, attention to the individual, and values and ethics across the curriculum. The University offers 38 undergraduate majors and 25 graduate degree programs. It serves approximately 2,100 undergraduate and 1,600 graduate students. With its main campus in Arlington, Virginia, Marymount University is just minutes from the resources of Washington, DC.

Expenses (1999–2000) *Comprehensive fee:* $20,030 includes full-time tuition ($13,750), mandatory fees ($120), and room and board ($6160). *Part-time tuition:* $450 per credit hour. *Part-time fees:* $5 per credit hour.

Institutional Web site http://www.marymount.edu/

College life *Housing:* on-campus residence required through sophomore year. *Options:* coed, men-only, women-only. *Most popular organizations:* American Society of Interior Design, Student Nurses Association, fashion club, International Club, No Exit (drama club).

Campus security 24-hour emergency response devices and patrols, late-night transport-escort service, controlled dormitory access.

Application *Options:* Common Application, electronic application, early admission, deferred entrance. *Application fee:* $35. *Required:* high school transcript; minimum 2.0 GPA; 1 letter of recommendation. *Recommended:* essay or personal statement; interview.

Standardized tests *Admission: Required:* SAT I or ACT.

Admissions Office Contact
Marymount University, 2807 North Glebe Road, Arlington, VA 22207-4299. **Toll-free phone:** 800-548-7638. **Fax:** 703-522-0349. **E-mail:** admissions@marymount.edu

Visit CollegeQuest.com for information on athletics. College video available at CollegeQuest.com.

■ *See page 2010 for a narrative description.*

MARY WASHINGTON COLLEGE
Fredericksburg, Virginia

- **State-supported**, comprehensive, founded 1908
- **Degrees** bachelor's and master's

Virginia

- **Small-town** 176-acre campus with easy access to Richmond and Washington, DC
- **Coed**, 3,761 undergraduate students, 86% full-time, 69% women, 31% men
- **Very difficult** entrance level, 56% of applicants were admitted
- **17:1 student-to-undergraduate faculty ratio**
- **74% graduate** in 6 years or less
- **$3204 tuition** and fees (in-state); $9634 (out-of-state)
- **$4690 average financial aid** package, $11,000 average indebtedness upon graduation, $27 million endowment

Students *Undergraduates:* 3,227 full-time, 534 part-time. Students come from 44 states and territories, 7 other countries. *The most frequently chosen baccalaureate fields are:* liberal arts/general studies, business/marketing, social sciences and history. *Graduate:* 35 in graduate degree programs.

From out-of-state	26%	Reside on campus	70%
Age 25 or older	24%	Transferred in	7%
International students	0.4%	African Americans	4%
Asian Americans/Pacific Islanders	3%	Hispanic Americans	2%
Native Americans	0.2%		

Faculty 262 (69% full-time), 57% with terminal degrees.

Expenses (1999–2000) *Tuition, state resident:* full-time $1550; part-time $101 per credit hour. *Tuition, nonresident:* full-time $7980; part-time $320 per credit hour. *Required fees:* full-time $1654. Part-time tuition and fees vary according to course load. *College room and board:* $5298; room only: $2994. Room and board charges vary according to board plan. *Payment plan:* installment. *Waivers:* minority students.

Library Simpson Library. *Operations spending 1999–2000:* $1.5 million. *Collection:* 335,061 titles, 1,715 serial subscriptions, 2,210 audiovisual materials.

College life *Housing: Options:* coed, men-only, women-only. *Most popular organizations:* Community Outreach, debate team, Washington Guides, trek club, entertainment committee.

Campus security 24-hour emergency response devices and patrols, student patrols, late-night transport-escort service, controlled dormitory access, self-defense and safety classes.

After graduation 64 organizations recruited on campus 1997–98. 70% of class of 1998 had job offers within 6 months. *Career center:* 4 full-time personnel. Services include job fairs, resume preparation, interview workshops, resume referral, career/interest testing, career counseling, careers library, job bank, job interviews. *Graduate education:* 18% of class of 1999 went directly to graduate and professional school: 8% graduate arts and sciences, 4% medicine, 2% education, 1% business, 1% law, 1% theology.

Freshmen 4,405 applied, 2,450 admitted, 837 enrolled. 1 National Merit Scholar, 12 valedictorians, 260 student government officers.

Average high school GPA	3.67	SAT verbal scores above 500	97%
SAT math scores above 500	94%	ACT above 18	N/R
From top 10% of their h.s. class	46%	From top quarter	88%
From top half	99%	1998 freshmen returning in 1999	83%

Application *Options:* eApply at www.CollegeQuest.com, electronic application, early decision, deferred entrance. *Preference* given to state residents. *Application fee:* $35. *Required:* essay or personal statement; high school transcript.

Standardized tests *Admission: Required:* SAT I or ACT. *Recommended:* SAT II Subject Tests.

Significant dates *Application deadlines:* 2/1 (freshmen), 3/1 (transfers). *Early decision:* 11/1. *Notification:* 4/1 (freshmen), 12/15 (early decision). *Financial aid deadline:* 3/1.

Freshman Application Contact Dr. Martin A. Wilder Jr., Vice President for Admissions and Financial Aid, Mary Washington College, 1301 College Avenue, Fredericksburg, VA 22401-5358. **Phone:** 540-654-2000. **Toll-free phone:** 800-468-5614. **E-mail:** admit@mwc.edu

Visit CollegeQuest.com for information on majors offered and athletics. College video available at CollegeQuest.com.

- *See page 2016 for a narrative description.*

NATIONAL BUSINESS COLLEGE
Salem, Virginia

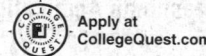
Apply at CollegeQuest.com

- **Proprietary**, primarily 2-year, founded 1886
- **Degrees** associate and bachelor's
- **Urban** 3-acre campus
- **Coed**, 355 undergraduate students
- **Noncompetitive** entrance level

Part of National Business College.

Faculty 37 (19% full-time).

Admissions Office Contact National Business College, PO Box 6400, Roanoke, VA 24017. **Toll-free phone:** 800-666-6221. **Fax:** 540-986-1344. **E-mail:** adm@nbc.educorp.edu

Visit CollegeQuest.com for information on majors offered and athletics. College video available at CollegeQuest.com.

NORFOLK STATE UNIVERSITY
Norfolk, Virginia

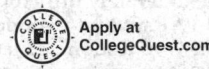
Apply at CollegeQuest.com

- **State-supported**, comprehensive, founded 1935
- **Degrees** associate, bachelor's, master's, and doctoral
- **Urban** 130-acre campus
- **Coed**, 5,861 undergraduate students, 86% full-time, 61% women, 39% men
- **Moderately difficult** entrance level, 93% of applicants were admitted
- **14:1 student-to-undergraduate faculty ratio**
- **19.6% graduate** in 6 years or less
- **$2708 tuition** and fees (in-state); $7172 (out-of-state)

Part of Commonwealth of Virginia Council of Higher Education.

Students *Undergraduates:* 5,061 full-time, 800 part-time. Students come from 31 states and territories, 3 other countries. *The most frequently chosen baccalaureate fields are:* interdisciplinary studies, business/marketing, social sciences and history. *Graduate:* 848 in graduate degree programs.

From out-of-state	8%	Age 25 or older	30%
Transferred in	19%	International students	0.5%
African Americans	92%	Asian Americans/Pacific Islanders	1%
Hispanic Americans	1%	Native Americans	0.3%

Faculty 508 (64% full-time).

Expenses (1999–2000) *One-time required fee:* $35. *Tuition, state resident:* full-time $2708; part-time $45 per credit. *Tuition, nonresident:* full-time $7172; part-time $230 per credit. *Required fees:* $6 per credit; $53 per term part-time. *College room and board:* $5494; room only: $3552. Room and board charges vary according to board plan and housing facility.

Library Lymon Beecher Brooks Library. *Operations spending 1999–2000:* $2.4 million. *Collection:* 393,119 titles, 1,426 serial subscriptions.

College life *Housing: Options:* men-only, women-only. *Social organizations:* national fraternities, national sororities, local fraternities, local sororities.

Campus security 24-hour patrols, late-night transport-escort service, campus call boxes.

After graduation *Career center:* 4 full-time personnel. Services include job fairs, resume preparation, interview workshops, resume referral, career/interest testing, career counseling, careers library, job bank, job interviews.

Freshmen 3,172 applied, 2,961 admitted, 1,166 enrolled.

Average high school GPA	2.5	SAT verbal scores above 500	N/R
SAT math scores above 500	N/R	ACT above 18	N/R
1998 freshmen returning in 1999	65%		

Application *Options:* eApply at www.CollegeQuest.com, Common Application, deferred entrance. *Application fee:* $25. *Required:* high school transcript; minimum 2.0 GPA. *Required for some:* letters of recommendation.

Standardized tests *Admission: Required:* SAT I or ACT.

Significant dates *Application deadlines:* rolling (freshmen), rolling (transfers). *Financial aid deadline priority date:* 3/15.

Virginia

Norfolk State University *(continued)*
Freshman Application Contact
Ms. Michelle Marable, Director of Admissions, Norfolk State University, 2401 Corprew Avenue, Norfolk, VA 23504-3907. **Phone:** 757-823-8396. **Fax:** 757-823-9435.
Visit CollegeQuest.com for information on majors offered and athletics. College video available at CollegeQuest.com.

OLD DOMINION UNIVERSITY
Norfolk, Virginia

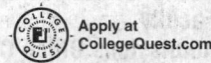 Apply at CollegeQuest.com

- **State-supported**, university, founded 1930
- **Degrees** bachelor's, master's, doctoral, and post-master's certificates
- **Urban** 186-acre campus with easy access to Virginia Beach
- **Coed**, 11,730 undergraduate students, 72% full-time, 58% women, 42% men
- **Moderately difficult** entrance level, 94% of applicants were admitted
- **17:1 student-to-undergraduate faculty ratio**
- **$3796 tuition** and fees (in-state); $11,386 (out-of-state)
- **$6550 average financial aid** package, $16,500 average indebtedness upon graduation, $61 million endowment

Students *Undergraduates:* 8,466 full-time, 3,264 part-time. Students come from 49 states and territories, 109 other countries. *The most frequently chosen baccalaureate fields are:* engineering/engineering technologies, business/marketing, health professions and related sciences. *Graduate:* 5,808 in graduate degree programs.

From out-of-state	5%	Reside on campus	23%
Age 25 or older	34%	Transferred in	11%
International students	3%	African Americans	22%
Asian Americans/Pacific Islanders	6%	Hispanic Americans	3%
Native Americans	1%		

Faculty 940 (65% full-time), 55% with terminal degrees.
Expenses (1999–2000) *Tuition, state resident:* full-time $2184; part-time $73 per semester hour. *Tuition, nonresident:* full-time $9774; part-time $326 per semester hour. *Required fees:* full-time $1612; $49 per semester hour. Full-time tuition and fees vary according to course level and location. Part-time tuition and fees vary according to course level and location. *College room and board:* $5114; room only: $3100. Room and board charges vary according to board plan and housing facility. *Payment plans:* installment, deferred payment. *Waivers:* senior citizens and employees or children of employees.
Library Douglas and Patricia Perry Library plus 1 other. *Operations spending 1999–2000:* $6 million. *Collection:* 923,462 titles, 12,526 serial subscriptions, 34,596 audiovisual materials.
College life *Housing: Option:* coed. *Social organizations:* national fraternities, national sororities; 6% of eligible men and 4% of eligible women are members. *Most popular organizations:* Ebony Impact Gospel Choir, WODU Radio, Habitat for Humanity, Circle K, International Student Association.
Campus security 24-hour emergency response devices and patrols, late-night transport-escort service.
After graduation 265 organizations recruited on campus 1997–98. *Career center:* 15 full-time, 1 part-time personnel. Services include job fairs, resume preparation, interview workshops, resume referral, career counseling, careers library, job bank, job interviews.
Freshmen 2,675 applied, 2,503 admitted, 1,578 enrolled.

Average high school GPA	3.15	SAT verbal scores above 500	59%
SAT math scores above 500	56%	ACT above 18	N/R
From top 10% of their h.s. class	19%	From top quarter	53%
From top half	90%	1998 freshmen returning in 1999	76%

Application *Options:* eApply at www.CollegeQuest.com, Common Application, early admission, early action, deferred entrance. *Application fee:* $30. *Required:* high school transcript; minimum 2.5 GPA. *Required for some:* essay or personal statement; interview. *Recommended:* essay or personal statement; 3 letters of recommendation; interview.
Standardized tests *Admission: Required:* SAT I or ACT.
Significant dates *Application deadlines:* 2/15 (freshmen), rolling (transfers). *Early action:* 12/15. *Notification:* 3/15 (freshmen), 1/15 (early action). *Financial aid deadline priority date:* 2/15.

Freshman Application Contact
Mr. Michael T. O'Connor, Director of Admissions, Old Dominion University, 108 Rollins Hall, Norfolk, VA 23529-0050. **Phone:** 757-683-3637. **Toll-free phone:** 800-348-7926. **Fax:** 757-683-5357. **E-mail:** admit@odu.edu
Visit CollegeQuest.com for information on majors offered and athletics. College video and electronic viewbook available at CollegeQuest.com.

RADFORD UNIVERSITY
Radford, Virginia

- **State-supported**, comprehensive, founded 1910
- **Degrees** bachelor's, master's, and post-master's certificates
- **Small-town** 177-acre campus
- **Coed**, 7,339 undergraduate students, 93% full-time, 61% women, 39% men
- **Moderately difficult** entrance level, 75% of applicants were admitted
- **19:1 student-to-undergraduate faculty ratio**
- **$2887 tuition** and fees (in-state); $8642 (out-of-state)
- **$6738 average financial aid** package, $13,727 average indebtedness upon graduation, $19.8 million endowment

Students *Undergraduates:* 6,831 full-time, 508 part-time. Students come from 49 states and territories, 66 other countries. *The most frequently chosen baccalaureate fields are:* business/marketing, interdisciplinary studies, protective services/public administration. *Graduate:* 1,173 in graduate degree programs.

From out-of-state	13%	Reside on campus	40%
Age 25 or older	10%	Transferred in	9%
International students	1%	African Americans	7%
Asian Americans/Pacific Islanders	2%	Hispanic Americans	1%
Native Americans	0.3%		

Faculty 524 (68% full-time), 66% with terminal degrees.
Expenses (1999–2000) *Tuition, state resident:* full-time $1629; part-time $120 per semester hour. *Tuition, nonresident:* full-time $7384; part-time $360 per semester hour. *Required fees:* full-time $1258. *College room and board:* $4770; room only: $2614. Room and board charges vary according to board plan and housing facility. *Payment plan:* installment. *Waivers:* employees or children of employees.
Library McConnell Library. *Operations spending 1999–2000:* $2.5 million. *Collection:* 527,789 titles, 14,914 audiovisual materials.
College life *Housing:* on-campus residence required in freshman year. *Options:* coed, women-only. *Social organizations:* national fraternities, national sororities; 18% of eligible men and 19% of eligible women are members. *Most popular organizations:* Student Government Association, Student Education Association, international club, ski club, Student Life Committee.
Campus security 24-hour emergency response devices and patrols, student patrols, late-night transport-escort service, controlled dormitory access.
After graduation 210 organizations recruited on campus 1997–98. 71% of class of 1998 had job offers within 6 months. *Career center:* 4 full-time personnel. Services include job fairs, resume preparation, interview workshops, resume referral, career counseling, careers library, job bank, job interviews. *Graduate education:* 26% of class of 1999 went directly to graduate and professional school.
Freshmen 5,730 applied, 4,317 admitted, 1,664 enrolled.

Average high school GPA	2.93	SAT verbal scores above 500	49%
SAT math scores above 500	41%	ACT above 18	85%
From top 10% of their h.s. class	1%	From top quarter	24%
From top half	70%	1998 freshmen returning in 1999	76%

Application *Options:* Common Application, electronic application, early admission. *Application fee:* $20. *Required:* high school transcript; minimum 2.0 GPA. *Required for some:* essay or personal statement. *Recommended:* 1 letter of recommendation; interview.
Standardized tests *Admission: Required:* SAT I or ACT.
Significant dates *Application deadlines:* 5/1 (freshmen), rolling (transfers). *Notification:* continuous until 6/1 (freshmen). *Financial aid deadline priority date:* 3/1.
Freshman Application Contact
Dr. David Kraus, Director of Admissions and Records, Radford University, PO Box 6903, RU Station, Radford, VA 24142. **Phone:** 540-831-5371. **Toll-free phone:** 800-890-4265. **Fax:** 540-831-5138. **E-mail:** ruadmiss@runet.edu

Virginia

Visit CollegeQuest.com for information on majors offered and athletics. College video available at CollegeQuest.com.

■ *See page 2306 for a narrative description.*

RANDOLPH-MACON COLLEGE
Ashland, Virginia

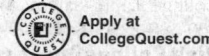
Apply at CollegeQuest.com

- **Independent United Methodist**, 4-year, founded 1830
- **Degree** bachelor's
- **Suburban** 110-acre campus with easy access to Richmond
- **Coed**, 1,109 undergraduate students, 99% full-time, 52% women, 48% men
- **Moderately difficult** entrance level
- **11:1** student-to-undergraduate faculty ratio
- **66% graduate** in 6 years or less
- **$17,660 tuition** and fees
- **$13,627 average financial aid** package, $16,832 average indebtedness upon graduation, $66.6 million endowment

Students *Undergraduates:* 1,095 full-time, 14 part-time. Students come from 31 states and territories, 14 other countries. *The most frequently chosen baccalaureate fields are:* business/marketing, English, social sciences and history.

From out-of-state	40%	Reside on campus	90%
Age 25 or older	1%	Transferred in	2%
International students	1%	African Americans	5%
Asian Americans/Pacific Islanders	2%	Hispanic Americans	1%
Native Americans	0.4%		

Faculty 147 (63% full-time), 70% with terminal degrees.

Expenses (1999–2000) *Comprehensive fee:* $22,180 includes full-time tuition ($17,160), mandatory fees ($500), and room and board ($4520). *College room only:* $2305. Room and board charges vary according to board plan and housing facility. *Part-time tuition:* $175 per credit hour. Part-time tuition and fees vary according to course load. *Payment plan:* installment. *Waivers:* employees or children of employees.

Library McGraw-Page Library. *Operations spending 1999–2000:* $424,649. *Collection:* 167,489 titles, 1,455 serial subscriptions, 7,819 audiovisual materials.

College life *Housing:* on-campus residence required through junior year. *Options:* coed, men-only, women-only. *Social organizations:* national fraternities, national sororities; 45% of eligible men and 45% of eligible women are members. *Most popular organizations:* Christian Fellowship, Student Activities Board/Student Government Association, Drama Guild, Business/Economics Society, Amnesty International.

Campus security 24-hour emergency response devices and patrols, late-night transport-escort service, controlled dormitory access.

After graduation 75% of class of 1998 had job offers within 6 months. *Career center:* 3 full-time personnel. Services include job fairs, resume preparation, interview workshops, resume referral, career/interest testing, career counseling, careers library, job bank, job interviews. **Graduate education:** 25% of class of 1999 went directly to graduate and professional school: 7% graduate arts and sciences, 3% education, 2% business, 2% law, 2% medicine, 2% theology, 1% engineering.

Freshmen 360 enrolled. 51 student government officers.

Average high school GPA	3.1	SAT verbal scores above 500	79%
SAT math scores above 500	75%	ACT above 18	N/R
From top 10% of their h.s. class	14%	From top quarter	45%
From top half	83%	1998 freshmen returning in 1999	75%

Application *Options:* eApply at www.CollegeQuest.com, Common Application, electronic application, early admission, early decision, deferred entrance. *Application fee:* $30. *Required:* essay or personal statement; high school transcript; 1 letter of recommendation. *Recommended:* interview.

Standardized tests *Admission: Required:* SAT I or ACT. *Recommended:* SAT II Subject Tests, SAT II: Writing Test.

Significant dates *Application deadlines:* 3/1 (freshmen), 3/1 (transfers). *Early decision:* 12/1. *Notification:* continuous until 4/1 (freshmen), 12/20 (early decision). *Financial aid deadline priority date:* 2/1.

Freshman Application Contact
Mr. John C. Conkright, Dean of Admissions and Financial Aid, Randolph-Macon College, PO Box 5005, Ashland, VA 23005-5505. **Phone:** 804-752-7305. **Toll-free phone:** 800-888-1762. **Fax:** 804-752-4707. **E-mail:** admissions_office@rmc.edu

Visit CollegeQuest.com for information on majors offered and athletics. College video available at CollegeQuest.com.

■ *See page 2310 for a narrative description.*

RANDOLPH-MACON WOMAN'S COLLEGE
Lynchburg, Virginia

Apply at CollegeQuest.com

- **Independent Methodist**, 4-year, founded 1891
- **Degree** bachelor's
- **Suburban** 100-acre campus
- **Women** only, 661 undergraduate students, 98% full-time
- **Moderately difficult** entrance level, 84% of applicants were admitted
- **9:1** student-to-undergraduate faculty ratio
- **64% graduate** in 6 years or less
- **$17,080 tuition** and fees
- **$15,515 average financial aid** package, $15,495 average indebtedness upon graduation, $128.9 million endowment

Students *Undergraduates:* 645 full-time, 16 part-time. Students come from 48 states and territories, 34 other countries. *The most frequently chosen baccalaureate fields are:* psychology, biological/life sciences, social sciences and history.

From out-of-state	60%	Reside on campus	83%
Age 25 or older	10%	Transferred in	6%
International students	9%	African Americans	7%
Asian Americans/Pacific Islanders	3%	Hispanic Americans	3%
Native Americans	0.4%		

Faculty 91 (80% full-time), 81% with terminal degrees.

Expenses (1999–2000) *Comprehensive fee:* $24,090 includes full-time tuition ($16,730), mandatory fees ($350), and room and board ($7010). *Part-time tuition:* $700 per semester hour. Part-time tuition and fees vary according to course load. *Payment plan:* installment. *Waivers:* adult students and employees or children of employees.

Library Lipscomb Library. *Operations spending 1999–2000:* $587,629. *Collection:* 115,222 titles, 1,680 serial subscriptions, 500 audiovisual materials.

College life *Housing:* on-campus residence required through senior year. *Option:* women-only. *Most popular organizations:* Believe It or Not, I Care (volunteer organization), Macon Activities Council, Pan World Club, Sock and Buskin (Theater Group), class organizations.

Campus security 24-hour emergency response devices and patrols, late-night transport-escort service.

After graduation 15 organizations recruited on campus 1997–98. 60% of class of 1998 had job offers within 6 months. *Career center:* 3 full-time personnel. Services include job fairs, resume preparation, interview workshops, resume referral, career/interest testing, career counseling, careers library, job bank, job interviews.

Freshmen 719 applied, 604 admitted, 201 enrolled. 1 National Merit Scholar, 2 valedictorians, 37 student government officers.

Average high school GPA	3.4	SAT verbal scores above 500	88%
SAT math scores above 500	76%	ACT above 18	99%
From top 10% of their h.s. class	39%	From top quarter	70%
From top half	95%	1998 freshmen returning in 1999	73%

Application *Options:* eApply at www.CollegeQuest.com, Common Application, electronic application, early admission, early decision, deferred entrance. *Application fee:* $25. *Required:* essay or personal statement; high school transcript; 2 letters of recommendation. *Recommended:* interview.

Standardized tests *Admission: Required:* SAT I or ACT.

Significant dates *Application deadline:* 2/15 (freshmen). *Early decision:* 11/15. *Notification:* 12/15 (early decision). *Financial aid deadline:* 3/1. *Priority date:* 2/1.

Virginia

Randolph-Macon Woman's College *(continued)*
Freshman Application Contact
Pat LeDonne, Director of Admissions, Randolph-Macon Woman's College, 2500 Rivermont Avenue, Lynchburg, VA 24503-1526. **Phone:** 804-947-8100. **Toll-free phone:** 800-745-7692. **Fax:** 804-947-8996. **E-mail:** admissions@rmwc.edu

Visit CollegeQuest.com for information on majors offered and athletics. College video available at CollegeQuest.com.

■ *See page 2312 for a narrative description.*

ROANOKE COLLEGE
Salem, Virginia

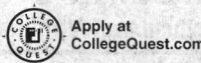

- **Independent**, 4-year, founded 1842, affiliated with Evangelical Lutheran Church in America
- **Degree** bachelor's
- **Suburban** 68-acre campus
- **Coed**, 1,670 undergraduate students, 95% full-time, 60% women, 40% men
- **Moderately difficult** entrance level, 81% of applicants were admitted
- **14:1 student-to-undergraduate faculty ratio**
- **60% graduate** in 6 years or less
- **$17,095 tuition** and fees
- **$14,784 average financial aid** package, $14,784 average indebtedness upon graduation, $79.1 million endowment

Students *Undergraduates:* 1,590 full-time, 80 part-time. Students come from 40 states and territories, 18 other countries. *The most frequently chosen baccalaureate fields are:* business/marketing, English, social sciences and history.

From out-of-state	44%	Reside on campus	57%
Age 25 or older	6%	Transferred in	5%
International students	1%	African Americans	3%
Asian Americans/Pacific Islanders	1%	Hispanic Americans	1%
Native Americans	0.4%		

Faculty 175 (65% full-time), 68% with terminal degrees.
Expenses (1999–2000) *Comprehensive fee:* $22,545 includes full-time tuition ($16,655), mandatory fees ($440), and room and board ($5450). *College room only:* $2645. *Part-time tuition:* $830 per course. *Part-time fees:* $25 per term part-time. *Payment plan:* installment. *Waivers:* senior citizens and employees or children of employees.
Library Fintel Library plus 1 other. *Operations spending 1999–2000:* $862,738. *Collection:* 424,539 titles, 15,197 serial subscriptions, 5,890 audiovisual materials.
College life *Housing:* on-campus residence required through senior year. *Options:* coed, men-only, women-only. *Social organizations:* national fraternities, national sororities, local fraternities, local sororities; 35% of eligible men and 40% of eligible women are members. *Most popular organizations:* Alpha Phi Omega, Habitat for Humanity, Earthbound Environment Group, Campus Activities Board, BACCHUS.
Campus security 24-hour emergency response devices and patrols, late-night transport-escort service, controlled dormitory access.
After graduation 32 organizations recruited on campus 1997–98. 97% of class of 1998 had job offers within 6 months. *Career center:* 2 full-time personnel. Services include job fairs, resume preparation, interview workshops, resume referral, career/interest testing, career counseling, careers library, job bank, job interviews. *Graduate education:* 20% of class of 1999 went directly to graduate and professional school.
Freshmen 2,560 applied, 2,079 admitted, 450 enrolled. 9 class presidents, 10 valedictorians, 75 student government officers.

Average high school GPA	3.3	SAT verbal scores above 500	82%
SAT math scores above 500	75%	ACT above 18	N/R
From top 10% of their h.s. class	26%	From top quarter	57%
From top half	88%	1998 freshmen returning in 1999	75%

Application *Options:* eApply at www.CollegeQuest.com, Common Application, electronic application, early admission, early decision, early action, deferred entrance. *Application fee:* $30. *Required:* high school transcript. *Recommended:* essay or personal statement; 3 letters of recommendation; interview.
Standardized tests *Admission: Required:* SAT I or ACT.

Significant dates *Application deadlines:* 3/1 (freshmen), 8/1 (transfers). *Early decision:* 11/15, 9/15. *Notification:* 4/1 (freshmen), 11/30 (early decision), 10/15 (early action). *Financial aid deadline priority date:* 3/1.
Freshman Application Contact
Mr. Michael C. Maxey, Vice President of Admissions, Roanoke College, 221 College Lane, Salem, VA 24153. **Phone:** 540-375-2270. **Toll-free phone:** 800-388-2276. **Fax:** 540-375-2267. **E-mail:** admissions@roanoke.edu

Visit CollegeQuest.com for information on majors offered and athletics. College video and electronic viewbook available at CollegeQuest.com.

SAINT PAUL'S COLLEGE
Lawrenceville, Virginia

- **Independent Episcopal**, 4-year, founded 1888
- **Degree** bachelor's
- **Small-town** 75-acre campus with easy access to Richmond
- **Coed**
- **Minimally difficult** entrance level, 88% of applicants were admitted
- **20:1 student-to-undergraduate faculty ratio**
- **$8200 tuition** and fees

Students *Undergraduates:* Students come from 12 states and territories, 5 other countries.

Age 25 or older	1%

Faculty 39 (77% full-time), 46% with terminal degrees.
Expenses (1999–2000) *Comprehensive fee:* $12,460 includes full-time tuition ($7760), mandatory fees ($440), and room and board ($4260). *Part-time tuition:* $323 per credit. *Part-time fees:* $220 per term part-time.
Library *Collection:* 100,000 titles, 275 serial subscriptions.
College life *Housing:* on-campus residence required through senior year. *Options:* men-only, women-only. *Social organizations:* national fraternities, national sororities; 2% of eligible men and 2% of eligible women are members. *Most popular organizations:* dance troupe, Literary Society, college choir, drama club.
Campus security 24-hour emergency response devices and patrols, late-night transport-escort service, alarms on doors.
After graduation *Career center:* 1 part-time personnel. Services include job fairs, resume preparation, resume referral, career counseling, careers library, job bank, job interviews.
Freshmen 408 applied, 359 admitted.

Average high school GPA	2.56	SAT verbal scores above 500	N/R
SAT math scores above 500	N/R	ACT above 18	N/R
1998 freshmen returning in 1999	57%		

Application *Options:* Common Application, deferred entrance. *Application fee:* $20. *Required:* high school transcript; 1 letter of recommendation. *Recommended:* essay or personal statement; interview.
Standardized tests *Placement: Required:* SAT I or ACT
Significant dates *Notification:* continuous until 8/15 (freshmen). *Financial aid deadline:* continuous.
Freshman Application Contact
Mr. Lyndon Elliot, Director of Admissions and Recruitment, Saint Paul's College, 115 College Drive, Lawrenceville, VA 23868. **Phone:** 804-848-3984. **Toll-free phone:** 800-678-7071. **E-mail:** 115 College Drive

Visit CollegeQuest.com for information on majors offered and athletics. College video available at CollegeQuest.com.

SHENANDOAH UNIVERSITY
Winchester, Virginia

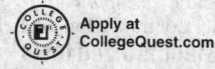

- **Independent United Methodist**, comprehensive, founded 1875
- **Degrees** associate, bachelor's, master's, doctoral, first professional, and postbachelor's certificates
- **Small-town** 100-acre campus with easy access to Baltimore and Washington, DC
- **Coed**, 1,202 undergraduate students, 91% full-time, 65% women, 35% men

Virginia

- **Moderately difficult** entrance level, 80% of applicants were admitted
- **8:1 student-to-undergraduate faculty ratio**
- **40% graduate** in 6 years or less
- **$15,700 tuition** and fees
- **$10,544 average financial aid** package, $13,618 average indebtedness upon graduation, $37 million endowment

Students *Undergraduates:* 1,094 full-time, 108 part-time. Students come from 32 states and territories, 19 other countries. *The most frequently chosen baccalaureate fields are:* business/marketing, education, health professions and related sciences. *Graduate:* 299 in professional programs, 685 in other graduate degree programs.

From out-of-state	40%	Reside on campus	42%
Age 25 or older	21%	Transferred in	12%
International students	4%	African Americans	6%
Asian Americans/Pacific Islanders	1%	Hispanic Americans	2%
Native Americans	0.4%		

Faculty 278 (55% full-time), 49% with terminal degrees.
Expenses (1999–2000) *Comprehensive fee:* $21,000 includes full-time tuition ($15,700) and room and board ($5300). Full-time tuition and fees vary according to course load. Room and board charges vary according to board plan. *Part-time tuition:* $490 per semester hour. Part-time tuition and fees vary according to course load. *Payment plan:* deferred payment. *Waivers:* employees or children of employees.
Library Alson H. Smith Jr. Library plus 1 other. *Operations spending 1999–2000:* $771,608. *Collection:* 16,564 audiovisual materials.
College life *Housing:* on-campus residence required through senior year. *Options:* coed, women-only, disabled students. *Most popular organizations:* Harambee Singers, Alpha Psi Omega, Music Educators National Conference, Student Government Association, Intervarsity Student Council.
Campus security 24-hour emergency response devices and patrols, controlled dormitory access, side door alarms, guard gate house.
After graduation 40 organizations recruited on campus 1997–98. *Career center:* 1 full-time personnel. Services include job fairs, resume preparation, interview workshops, career/interest testing, career counseling, careers library, job bank, job interviews. *Graduate education:* 40% of class of 1999 went directly to graduate and professional school.
Freshmen 1,154 applied, 918 admitted, 296 enrolled.

Average high school GPA	3.0	SAT verbal scores above 500	63%
SAT math scores above 500	53%	ACT above 18	81%
From top 10% of their h.s. class	10%	From top quarter	29%
From top half	66%	1998 freshmen returning in 1999	69%

Application *Options:* eApply at www.CollegeQuest.com, electronic application, early admission, deferred entrance. *Application fee:* $30. *Required:* high school transcript. *Required for some:* interview; audition. *Recommended:* minimum 2.0 GPA.
Standardized tests *Admission: Required:* SAT I or ACT.
Significant dates *Application deadlines:* rolling (freshmen), rolling (transfers). *Financial aid deadline priority date:* 3/1.
Freshman Application Contact
Mr. Michael Carpenter, Director of Admissions, Shenandoah University, 1460 University Drive, Winchester, VA 22601-5195. **Phone:** 540-665-4581. **Toll-free phone:** 800-432-2266. **Fax:** 540-665-4627. **E-mail:** admit@su.edu
Visit CollegeQuest.com for information on majors offered and athletics. Electronic viewbook available at CollegeQuest.com.

■ *See page 2476 for a narrative description.*

SWEET BRIAR COLLEGE
Sweet Briar, Virginia

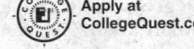
Apply at CollegeQuest.com

- **Independent**, 4-year, founded 1901
- **Degree** bachelor's
- **Rural** 3,300-acre campus
- **Women** only, 582 undergraduate students, 98% full-time
- **Moderately difficult** entrance level, 89% of applicants were admitted
- **7:1 student-to-undergraduate faculty ratio**
- **$17,150 tuition** and fees
- **$14,621 average financial aid** package, $17,689 average indebtedness upon graduation, $125.6 million endowment

Students *Undergraduates:* 569 full-time, 13 part-time. Students come from 43 states and territories, 12 other countries. *The most frequently chosen baccalaureate fields are:* psychology, English, social sciences and history.

From out-of-state	63%	Reside on campus	93%
Age 25 or older	4%	Transferred in	3%
International students	2%	African Americans	5%
Asian Americans/Pacific Islanders	2%	Hispanic Americans	4%
Native Americans	1%		

Faculty 104 (66% full-time), 82% with terminal degrees.
Expenses (2000–2001, estimated) *Comprehensive fee:* $24,150 includes full-time tuition ($17,000), mandatory fees ($150), and room and board ($7000). *College room only:* $2850. Full-time tuition and fees vary according to program. *Part-time tuition:* $575 per semester hour. Part-time tuition and fees vary according to program. *Payment plan:* installment. *Waivers:* adult students, senior citizens, and employees or children of employees.
Library Mary Helen Cochran Library plus 3 others. *Operations spending 1999–2000:* $911,000. *Collection:* 474,818 titles, 9,792 serial subscriptions, 6,634 audiovisual materials.
College life *Housing:* on-campus residence required through senior year. *Option:* women-only. *Most popular organizations:* Paint and Patches, Nations United, Riding Council, Campus Events Organization, Sweet Briar Voice.
Campus security 24-hour emergency response devices and patrols, late-night transport-escort service, controlled dormitory access, front gate security.
After graduation 13 organizations recruited on campus 1997–98. 67% of class of 1998 had job offers within 6 months. *Career center:* 2 full-time, 1 part-time personnel. Services include job fairs, resume preparation, interview workshops, resume referral, career/interest testing, career counseling, careers library, job bank, job interviews.
Freshmen 499 applied, 445 admitted, 188 enrolled. 1 class president, 5 valedictorians, 23 student government officers.

Average high school GPA	3.36	SAT verbal scores above 500	83%
SAT math scores above 500	64%	ACT above 18	94%
From top 10% of their h.s. class	26%	From top quarter	59%
From top half	92%	1998 freshmen returning in 1999	80%

Application *Options:* eApply at www.CollegeQuest.com, Common Application, electronic application, early admission, early decision, deferred entrance. *Application fee:* $25. *Required:* essay or personal statement; high school transcript; 2 letters of recommendation. *Recommended:* interview.
Standardized tests *Admission: Required:* SAT I or ACT. *Recommended:* SAT II Subject Tests.
Significant dates *Application deadlines:* 2/15 (freshmen), 7/1 (transfers). *Early decision:* 12/1. *Notification:* continuous until 4/1 (freshmen); 12/15 (early decision). *Financial aid deadline priority date:* 3/1.
Freshman Application Contact
Ms. Nancy E. Church, Dean of Admissions, Sweet Briar College, PO Box B, Sweet Briar, VA 24595. **Phone:** 804-381-6142. **Toll-free phone:** 800-381-6142. **Fax:** 804-381-6152. **E-mail:** admissions@sbc.edu
Visit CollegeQuest.com for information on majors offered and athletics. College video available at CollegeQuest.com.

■ *See page 2586 for a narrative description.*

UNIVERSITY OF RICHMOND
Richmond, Virginia

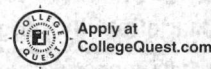
Apply at CollegeQuest.com

- **Independent**, comprehensive, founded 1830
- **Degrees** associate, bachelor's, master's, and first professional
- **Suburban** 350-acre campus
- **Coed**, 3,004 undergraduate students, 100% full-time, 50% women, 50% men
- **Very difficult** entrance level, 45% of applicants were admitted
- **11:1 student-to-undergraduate faculty ratio**
- **$19,610 tuition** and fees
- **$15,111 average financial aid** package, $14,300 average indebtedness upon graduation, $803 million endowment

Students *Undergraduates:* 3,004 full-time. Students come from 47 states and territories, 60 other countries. *The most frequently chosen baccalaureate fields are:* business/marketing, area/ethnic studies, social sciences and history. *Graduate:* 474 in professional programs, 269 in other graduate degree programs.

Virginia

University of Richmond (continued)

From out-of-state	83%	Reside on campus	92%
Transferred in	1%	International students	3%
African Americans	5%	Asian Americans/Pacific Islanders	2%
Hispanic Americans	1%	Native Americans	0.1%

Faculty 363 (70% full-time), 77% with terminal degrees.

Expenses (1999–2000) *Comprehensive fee:* $23,660 includes full-time tuition ($19,340), mandatory fees ($270), and room and board ($4050). *College room only:* $1716. Room and board charges vary according to board plan and housing facility. *Part-time tuition:* $965 per semester hour. Part-time tuition and fees vary according to class time. *Payment plan:* installment. *Waivers:* employees or children of employees.

Library Boatwright Memorial Library plus 4 others. *Operations spending 1999–2000:* $7.6 million. *Collection:* 684,704 titles, 4,322 serial subscriptions, 8,825 audiovisual materials.

College life *Housing: Options:* coed, men-only, women-only. *Social organizations:* national fraternities, national sororities; 39% of eligible men and 50% of eligible women are members. *Most popular organizations:* Volunteer Action Council, Student Government Association, Campus Activities Board, Multicultural Student Union, intramurals.

Campus security 24-hour emergency response devices and patrols, late-night transport-escort service, controlled dormitory access, campus police.

After graduation 280 organizations recruited on campus 1997–98. *Career center:* 7 full-time, 2 part-time personnel. Services include job fairs, resume preparation, interview workshops, resume referral, career/interest testing, career counseling, careers library, job bank, job interviews. *Graduate education:* 20% of class of 1999 went directly to graduate and professional school: 10% graduate arts and sciences, 5% medicine, 4% law, 1% business.

Freshmen 6,234 applied, 2,787 admitted, 854 enrolled. 9 National Merit Scholars, 36 valedictorians, 146 student government officers.

SAT verbal scores above 500	99%	SAT math scores above 500	99%
ACT above 18	100%	From top 10% of their h.s. class	53%
From top quarter	91%	From top half	99%
1998 freshmen returning in 1999	92%		

Application *Options:* eApply at www.CollegeQuest.com, Common Application, early admission, early decision, deferred entrance. *Application fee:* $40. *Required:* essay or personal statement; high school transcript; minimum 2.0 GPA; 1 letter of recommendation; signed character statement.

Standardized tests *Admission: Required:* SAT I and SAT II or ACT, SAT II: Writing Test, SAT II Subject Test in math.

Significant dates *Application deadlines:* 1/15 (freshmen), 2/15 (transfers). *Early decision:* 11/15 (for plan 1), 1/15 (for plan 2). *Notification:* 4/1 (freshmen), 12/15 (early decision plan 1), 2/15 (early decision plan 2). *Financial aid deadline:* 2/25.

Freshman Application Contact
Ms. Pamela Spence, Dean of Admission, University of Richmond, 28 Westhampton Way, University of Richmond, VA 23173. **Phone:** 804-289-8640. **Toll-free phone:** 800-700-1662. **Fax:** 804-287-6003.

Visit CollegeQuest.com for information on majors offered and athletics. College video available at CollegeQuest.com.

UNIVERSITY OF VIRGINIA
Charlottesville, Virginia

- **State-supported**, university, founded 1819
- **Degrees** bachelor's, master's, doctoral, first professional, and post-master's certificates
- **Suburban** 1,133-acre campus with easy access to Richmond
- **Coed**, 12,467 undergraduate students, 99% full-time, 55% women, 45% men
- **Most difficult** entrance level, 34% of applicants were admitted
- **14:1 student-to-undergraduate faculty ratio**
- **92% graduate** in 6 years or less
- **$4130 tuition** and fees (in-state); $16,603 (out-of-state)
- **$10,042 average financial aid** package, $13,913 average indebtedness upon graduation, $1.3 billion endowment

Students *Undergraduates:* 12,381 full-time, 86 part-time. Students come from 52 states and territories, 106 other countries. *The most frequently chosen baccalaureate fields are:* business/marketing, engineering/engineering technologies, social sciences and history. *Graduate:* 1,645 in professional programs, 7,218 in other graduate degree programs.

From out-of-state	31%	Reside on campus	47%
Age 25 or older	2%	Transferred in	4%
International students	4%	African Americans	10%
Asian Americans/Pacific Islanders	10%	Hispanic Americans	2%
Native Americans	0.3%		

Faculty 1,219 (84% full-time), 86% with terminal degrees.

Expenses (1999–2000) *Tuition, state resident:* full-time $3046. *Tuition, nonresident:* full-time $15,519. *Required fees:* full-time $1084. Full-time tuition and fees vary according to program. *College room and board:* $4589; room only: $2059. Room and board charges vary according to board plan and housing facility. *Payment plan:* installment. *Waivers:* senior citizens and employees or children of employees.

Library Alderman Library plus 14 others. *Collection:* 4.5 million titles, 47,479 serial subscriptions, 71,523 audiovisual materials.

College life *Housing:* on-campus residence required in freshman year. *Option:* coed. *Social organizations:* national fraternities, national sororities, local fraternities; 30% of eligible men and 30% of eligible women are members. *Most popular organizations:* Madison House, student government, university guides, University Union, The Cavalier Daily.

Campus security 24-hour emergency response devices and patrols, late-night transport-escort service, controlled dormitory access.

After graduation 450 organizations recruited on campus 1997–98. *Career center:* 15 full-time, 1 part-time personnel. Services include job fairs, resume preparation, resume referral, career counseling, careers library, job bank, job interviews. *Graduate education:* 32% of class of 1999 went directly to graduate and professional school. *Major awards:* 8 Fulbright Scholars.

Freshmen 16,461 applied, 5,588 admitted, 2,924 enrolled. 211 valedictorians.

Average high school GPA	3.78	SAT verbal scores above 500	97%
SAT math scores above 500	98%	ACT above 18	99%
From top 10% of their h.s. class	82%	From top quarter	96%
From top half	99%	1998 freshmen returning in 1999	96%

Application *Options:* early decision, deferred entrance. *Preference* given to state residents, children of alumni. *Required:* essay or personal statement; high school transcript; 1 letter of recommendation.

Standardized tests *Admission: Required:* SAT I or ACT, SAT II Subject Tests, SAT II: Writing Test.

Significant dates *Application deadlines:* 1/2 (freshmen), 3/1 (transfers). *Early decision:* 11/1. *Notification:* 4/1 (freshmen), 12/1 (early decision). *Financial aid deadline priority date:* 3/1.

Freshman Application Contact
Mr. John A. Blackburn, Dean of Admission, University of Virginia, PO Box 9017, Charlottesville, VA 22906. **Phone:** 804-982-3200. **Fax:** 804-924-3587. **E-mail:** undergrad-admission@virginia.edu

Visit CollegeQuest.com for information on majors offered and athletics. Electronic viewbook available at CollegeQuest.com.

UNIVERSITY OF VIRGINIA'S COLLEGE AT WISE
Wise, Virginia

- **State-supported**, 4-year, founded 1954
- **Degrees** bachelor's and postbachelor's certificates
- **Small-town** 350-acre campus
- **Coed**, 1,377 undergraduate students, 87% full-time, 55% women, 45% men
- **Moderately difficult** entrance level, 73% of applicants were admitted
- **18:1 student-to-undergraduate faculty ratio**
- **35% graduate** in 6 years or less
- **$3192 tuition** and fees (in-state); $9286 (out-of-state)
- **$10.3 million endowment**

Part of University of Virginia.

Students *Undergraduates:* 1,198 full-time, 179 part-time. Students come from 7 states and territories, 2 other countries. *The most frequently chosen baccalaureate fields are:* business/marketing, psychology, social sciences and history.

Virginia

From out-of-state	7%	Reside on campus	30%
Age 25 or older	24%	Transferred in	12%
International students	0.1%	African Americans	4%
Asian Americans/Pacific Islanders	1%	Hispanic Americans	1%
Native Americans	0.1%		

Faculty 97 (69% full-time), 55% with terminal degrees.
Expenses (1999–2000) *Tuition, state resident:* full-time $3192; part-time $77 per semester hour. *Tuition, nonresident:* full-time $9286; part-time $330 per semester hour. *Required fees:* $5 per semester hour. Part-time tuition and fees vary according to course load. *College room and board:* $4938; room only: $2774. Room and board charges vary according to board plan and housing facility. *Payment plan:* installment. *Waivers:* senior citizens.
Library Wyllie Library. *Operations spending 1999–2000:* $1 million. *Collection:* 10,733 serial subscriptions, 4,562 audiovisual materials.
College life *Housing: Options:* coed, men-only, women-only. *Social organizations:* national fraternities, national sororities, local sororities; 10% of eligible men and 7% of eligible women are members. *Most popular organizations:* student government, Phi Beta Lambda, Inter Greek Council, Comtra, Baptist Student Union.
Campus security 24-hour emergency response devices and patrols, student patrols, late-night transport-escort service.
After graduation 20 organizations recruited on campus 1997–98. *Career center:* 1 full-time personnel. Services include job fairs, resume preparation, interview workshops, resume referral, career/interest testing, career counseling, careers library, job bank, job interviews. *Graduate education:* 24% of class of 1999 went directly to graduate and professional school: 8% graduate arts and sciences, 7% education, 2% business, 2% law, 2% medicine.
Freshmen 935 applied, 685 admitted, 299 enrolled. 18 valedictorians.

Average high school GPA	3.2	SAT verbal scores above 500	48%
SAT math scores above 500	41%	ACT above 18	64%
From top 10% of their h.s. class	22%	From top quarter	50%
From top half	88%	1998 freshmen returning in 1999	68%

Application *Option:* early admission. *Application fee:* $15. *Required:* high school transcript; minimum 2.0 GPA. *Required for some:* interview. *Recommended:* 2 letters of recommendation.
Standardized tests *Admission: Required:* SAT I or ACT.
Significant dates *Application deadlines:* 8/1 (freshmen), 8/15 (transfers). *Notification:* continuous until 8/20 (freshmen). *Financial aid deadline priority date:* 4/1.
Freshman Application Contact
Mr. Russell Necessary, Director of Enrollment Management, University of Virginia's College at Wise, 1 College Avenue, Wise, VA 24293. **Phone:** 540-328-0102. **Toll-free phone:** 888-282-9324. **Fax:** 540-328-0251. **E-mail:** admissions@wise.virginia.edu
Visit CollegeQuest.com for information on majors offered and athletics. College video available at CollegeQuest.com.

VIRGINIA COMMONWEALTH UNIVERSITY
Richmond, Virginia

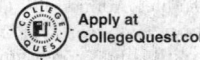

- **State-supported**, university, founded 1838
- **Degrees** bachelor's, master's, doctoral, first professional, post-master's, and postbachelor's certificates
- **Urban** 126-acre campus
- **Coed**, 13,550 undergraduate students, 80% full-time, 59% women, 41% men
- **Moderately difficult** entrance level, 74% of applicants were admitted
- **12:1** student-to-undergraduate faculty ratio
- **42% graduate** in 6 years or less
- **$3587 tuition** and fees (in-state); $13,041 (out-of-state)
- **$5377 average financial aid** package, $22,379 average indebtedness upon graduation, $135.8 million endowment

VCU is noted for excellent programs in the arts, business, health sciences, education, mass communications, and others and its diverse student body. Honors freshmen are encouraged to investigate distinctive curricula, including the 4-year MBA program and guaranteed admission programs in medicine,

dentistry, and other medical and professional fields. The School of Engineering, offering degrees in biomedical, chemical, mechanical, and electrical engineering, graduates its first class in spring 2000.

Students *Undergraduates:* 10,868 full-time, 2,682 part-time. Students come from 35 states and territories, 60 other countries. *The most frequently chosen baccalaureate fields are:* business/marketing, health professions and related sciences, visual/performing arts. *Graduate:* 1,395 in professional programs, 6,262 in other graduate degree programs.

From out-of-state	5%	Reside on campus	10%
Age 25 or older	28%	Transferred in	10%
International students	2%	African Americans	23%
Asian Americans/Pacific Islanders	8%	Hispanic Americans	2%
Native Americans	1%		

Faculty 2,212 (43% full-time).
Expenses (1999–2000) *Tuition, state resident:* full-time $2492; part-time $104 per credit. *Tuition, nonresident:* full-time $11,946; part-time $498 per credit. *Required fees:* full-time $1095; $40 per credit. Full-time tuition and fees vary according to location and program. Part-time tuition and fees vary according to course load and location. *College room and board:* $4839; room only: $2824. Room and board charges vary according to board plan and housing facility. *Payment plan:* installment. *Waivers:* senior citizens.
Library James Branch Cabell and Tompkins-McCaw Library. *Operations spending 1999–2000:* $10.3 million. *Collection:* 1.5 million titles, 18,315 serial subscriptions, 39,090 audiovisual materials.
College life *Housing: Options:* coed, men-only, women-only, disabled students. *Social organizations:* national fraternities, national sororities, local fraternities, local sororities; 3% of eligible men and 4% of eligible women are members. *Most popular organizations:* Student Government Organization, Black Caucus, International Student Union, Activities Programming Board, Greek Council.
Campus security 24-hour emergency response devices and patrols, late-night transport-escort service, security personnel in residence halls.
After graduation 150 organizations recruited on campus 1997–98. *Career center:* 7 full-time, 3 part-time personnel. Services include job fairs, resume preparation, interview workshops, resume referral, career/interest testing, career counseling, careers library, job bank, job interviews.
Freshmen 6,748 applied, 4,960 admitted, 2,460 enrolled.

Average high school GPA	3.03	SAT verbal scores above 500	60%
SAT math scores above 500	51%	ACT above 18	74%
From top 10% of their h.s. class	13%	From top quarter	37%
From top half	74%	1998 freshmen returning in 1999	74%

Application *Options:* eApply at www.CollegeQuest.com, Common Application, electronic application, early admission, early decision, deferred entrance. *Preference* given to state residents for allied health programs. *Application fee:* $25. *Required:* high school transcript. *Required for some:* essay or personal statement; minimum 3.0 GPA; letters of recommendation; interview. *Recommended:* interview.
Standardized tests *Admission: Required:* SAT I or ACT.
Significant dates *Application deadlines:* 2/1 (freshmen), 8/1 (transfers). *Early decision:* 11/1. *Notification:* continuous until 4/1 (freshmen), 12/1 (early decision). *Financial aid deadline priority date:* 4/1.
Freshman Application Contact
Counseling Staff, Virginia Commonwealth University, 821 West Franklin Street, Box 842526, Richmond, VA 23284-9005. **Phone:** 804-828-1222. **Toll-free phone:** 800-841-3638. **Fax:** 804-828-1899. **E-mail:** vcuinfo@vcu.edu
Visit CollegeQuest.com for information on majors offered and athletics. Electronic viewbook available at CollegeQuest.com.

■ *See page 2890 for a narrative description.*

VIRGINIA INTERMONT COLLEGE
Bristol, Virginia

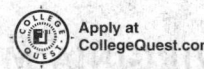

- **Independent**, 4-year, founded 1884, affiliated with Baptist Church
- **Degrees** associate and bachelor's
- **Small-town** 27-acre campus
- **Coed**, 789 undergraduate students, 58% full-time, 76% women, 24% men
- **Minimally difficult** entrance level, 76% of applicants were admitted

Peterson's Guide to Four-Year Colleges 2001   www.petersons.com   839

Virginia

Virginia Intermont College (continued)
- **11:1 student-to-undergraduate faculty ratio**
- **37% graduate** in 6 years or less
- **$11,750 tuition** and fees
- **$5054 average financial aid** package, $17,125 average indebtedness upon graduation, $2 million endowment

Students from all over the United States who are looking for a solid liberal arts background with a variety of academic majors come to Virginia Intermont. They appreciate the individualized instruction and challenging academic atmosphere. Specialized areas, such as photography, equine studies, paralegal studies, and sports management, are invaluable assets to the educational background and practical experience that Virginia Intermont College has to offer.

Students *Undergraduates:* 457 full-time, 332 part-time. Students come from 36 states and territories, 7 other countries. *The most frequently chosen baccalaureate fields are:* business/marketing, agriculture, education.

From out-of-state	32%	Reside on campus	62%
Age 25 or older	43%	Transferred in	21%
International students	3%	African Americans	4%
Asian Americans/Pacific Islanders	1%	Hispanic Americans	0.4%
Native Americans	1%		

Faculty 70 (56% full-time), 49% with terminal degrees.

Expenses (2000–2001) *Comprehensive fee:* $16,950 includes full-time tuition ($11,430), mandatory fees ($320), and room and board ($5200). *College room only:* $2600. *Part-time tuition:* $150 per credit. *Part-time fees:* $60 per term part-time. Part-time tuition and fees vary according to course load. *Payment plan:* installment. *Waivers:* employees or children of employees.

Library J. F. Hicks Library. *Operations spending 1999–2000:* $270,933. *Collection:* 62,000 titles, 336 serial subscriptions.

College life *Housing:* on-campus residence required through junior year. *Options:* coed, men-only, women-only. *Most popular organizations:* Student Government Association, Student Activities Committee, Baptist Student Union, equestrian club, Business Organization for Student Success.

Campus security Late-night transport-escort service, 17-hour patrols by trained security personnel.

After graduation 90 organizations recruited on campus 1997–98. 49% of class of 1998 had job offers within 6 months. *Career center:* 1 full-time personnel. Services include job fairs, resume preparation, resume referral, career counseling, careers library, job bank, job interviews. *Graduate education:* 3% of class of 1999 went directly to graduate and professional school.

Freshmen 495 applied, 376 admitted, 116 enrolled.

Average high school GPA	2.87	SAT verbal scores above 500	41%
SAT math scores above 500	23%	ACT above 18	67%
From top 10% of their h.s. class	14%	From top quarter	31%
From top half	55%	1998 freshmen returning in 1999	63%

Application *Options:* eApply at www.CollegeQuest.com, Common Application, electronic application, early admission, deferred entrance. *Application fee:* $15. *Required:* high school transcript; minimum 2.0 GPA. *Required for some:* essay or personal statement. *Recommended:* interview.

Standardized tests *Admission: Required:* SAT I or ACT.

Significant dates *Application deadlines:* rolling (freshmen), rolling (transfers). *Financial aid deadline:* continuous.

Freshman Application Contact
Ms. Robin B. Cozart, Director of Admissions, Virginia Intermont College, 1013 Moore Street, Bristol, VA 24201-4298. **Phone:** 540-466-7854. **Toll-free phone:** 800-451-1842. **Fax:** 540-669-5763. **E-mail:** viadmit@vic.edu

Visit CollegeQuest.com for information on majors offered and athletics. College video available at CollegeQuest.com.

- *See page 2892 for a narrative description.*

VIRGINIA MILITARY INSTITUTE
Lexington, Virginia

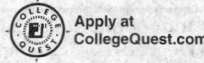
Apply at CollegeQuest.com

- **State-supported**, 4-year, founded 1839
- **Degree** bachelor's
- **Small-town** 140-acre campus
- **Coed,** primarily men, 1,335 undergraduate students, 100% full-time, 5% women, 95% men
- **Moderately difficult** entrance level, 74% of applicants were admitted
- **12:1 student-to-undergraduate faculty ratio**
- **62.4% graduate** in 6 years or less
- **$5014 tuition** and fees (in-state); $14,454 (out-of-state)
- **$8873 average financial aid** package, $14,000 average indebtedness upon graduation, $278 million endowment

Students *Undergraduates:* 1,335 full-time. Students come from 46 states and territories, 22 other countries. *The most frequently chosen baccalaureate fields are:* engineering/engineering technologies, English, social sciences and history.

From out-of-state	45%	Reside on campus	100%
Transferred in	2%	International students	2%
African Americans	6%	Asian Americans/Pacific Islanders	5%
Hispanic Americans	3%	Native Americans	0.3%

Faculty 143 (70% full-time), 75% with terminal degrees.

Expenses (1999–2000) *Tuition, state resident:* full-time $2924. *Tuition, nonresident:* full-time $12,364. *Required fees:* full-time $2090. *College room and board:* $4376. Additional mandatory fees per year: $1000 quartermaster charge. *Payment plan:* installment.

Library Preston Library plus 1 other. *Operations spending 1999–2000:* $1.2 million. *Collection:* 468,508 titles, 9,629 serial subscriptions, 4,258 audiovisual materials.

College life *Housing:* on-campus residence required through senior year. *Option:* coed. *Most popular organizations:* Newman Club, Officers Christian Fellowship, Strength & Fitness, Promaji, Pre-law Society.

Campus security 24-hour emergency response devices and patrols, student patrols.

After graduation 36 organizations recruited on campus 1997–98. 80% of class of 1998 had job offers within 6 months. *Career center:* 3 full-time personnel. Services include job fairs, resume preparation, interview workshops, resume referral, career/interest testing, career counseling, careers library, job interviews.

Freshmen 1,071 applied, 788 admitted, 374 enrolled. 60 student government officers.

Average high school GPA	3.14	SAT verbal scores above 500	83%
SAT math scores above 500	86%	ACT above 18	96%
From top 10% of their h.s. class	11%	From top quarter	42%
From top half	81%	1998 freshmen returning in 1999	84%

Application *Options:* eApply at www.CollegeQuest.com, early decision. Preference given to state residents. *Application fee:* $25. *Required:* high school transcript. *Recommended:* essay or personal statement; 2 letters of recommendation; interview.

Standardized tests *Admission: Required:* SAT I or ACT.

Significant dates *Application deadlines:* 4/1 (freshmen), 4/1 (transfers). *Early decision:* 11/15. *Notification:* 12/15 (early decision). *Financial aid deadline:* 4/1. *Priority date:* 3/1.

Freshman Application Contact
Lt. Col. Tom Mortenson, Associate Director of Admissions, Virginia Military Institute, Admissions Office, 309 Letcher Avenue, Lexington, VA 24450. **Phone:** 540-464-7211. **Toll-free phone:** 800-767-4207. **Fax:** 540-464-7746. **E-mail:** admissions@vmi.edu

Visit CollegeQuest.com for information on majors offered and athletics. College video available at CollegeQuest.com.

- *See page 2894 for a narrative description.*

VIRGINIA POLYTECHNIC INSTITUTE AND STATE UNIVERSITY
Blacksburg, Virginia

- **State-supported**, university, founded 1872
- **Degrees** associate, bachelor's, master's, doctoral, and first professional
- **Small-town** 2,600-acre campus
- **Coed,** 21,479 undergraduate students, 98% full-time, 41% women, 59% men
- **Moderately difficult** entrance level, 73% of applicants were admitted
- **19:1 student-to-undergraduate faculty ratio**

Virginia

- **72% graduate** in 6 years or less
- **$3620 tuition** and fees (in-state); $11,844 (out-of-state)
- **$6015 average financial aid** package, $14,530 average indebtedness upon graduation, $340.6 million endowment

Students *Undergraduates:* 21,017 full-time, 462 part-time. Students come from 52 states and territories, 104 other countries. *The most frequently chosen baccalaureate fields are:* business/marketing, engineering/engineering technologies, home economics/vocational home economics. *Graduate:* 355 in professional programs, 3,618 in other graduate degree programs.

From out-of-state	25%	Reside on campus	44%
Age 25 or older	4%	Transferred in	4%
International students	2%	African Americans	4%
Asian Americans/Pacific Islanders	7%	Hispanic Americans	2%
Native Americans	0.3%		

Faculty 1,491 (83% full-time).

Expenses (1999–2000) *Tuition, state resident:* full-time $2792; part-time $116 per credit hour. *Tuition, nonresident:* full-time $11,016; part-time $459 per credit hour. *Required fees:* full-time $828; $107 per term part-time. Full-time tuition and fees vary according to location. Part-time tuition and fees vary according to course load. *College room and board:* $3722; room only: $1838. Room and board charges vary according to board plan and housing facility. *Payment plan:* installment. *Waivers:* employees or children of employees.

Library Newman Library plus 4 others. *Operations spending 1999–2000:* $12.1 million. *Collection:* 2 million titles, 18,281 serial subscriptions, 17,510 audiovisual materials.

College life *Housing:* on-campus residence required in freshman year. *Options:* coed, men-only, women-only. *Social organizations:* national fraternities, national sororities, local fraternities; 13% of eligible men and 23% of eligible women are members. *Most popular organizations:* Virginia Tech Union, Greek organizations, Student Government Association, international student organizations.

Campus security 24-hour emergency response devices and patrols, student patrols, late-night transport-escort service, controlled dormitory access.

After graduation 468 organizations recruited on campus 1997–98. 79% of class of 1998 had job offers within 6 months. *Career center:* 22 full-time, 5 part-time personnel. Services include job fairs, resume preparation, interview workshops, resume referral, career/interest testing, career counseling, careers library, job bank, job interviews. *Graduate education:* 13% of class of 1999 went directly to graduate and professional school.

Freshmen 15,883 applied, 11,616 admitted, 4,613 enrolled. 36 National Merit Scholars.

Average high school GPA	3.5	SAT verbal scores above 500	86%
SAT math scores above 500	90%	ACT above 18	N/R
From top 10% of their h.s. class	33%	From top quarter	63%
From top half	98%	1998 freshmen returning in 1999	90%

Application *Options:* electronic application, early admission, early decision, deferred entrance. *Application fee:* $25. *Required:* high school transcript; minimum 2.0 GPA. *Recommended:* minimum 3.0 GPA.

Standardized tests *Admission: Required:* SAT I or ACT.

Significant dates *Application deadlines:* 2/1 (freshmen), 3/1 (transfers). *Early decision:* 11/1. *Notification:* 4/15 (freshmen), 12/15 (early decision). *Financial aid deadline priority date:* 3/1.

Freshman Application Contact Mr. Shelley Blumenthal, Associate Director for Freshmen Admissions, Virginia Polytechnic Institute and State University, 201 Burruss Hall, Blacksburg, VA 24061-0202. **Phone:** 540-231-6267. **Fax:** 540-231-3242. **E-mail:** vtadmiss@vt.edu

Visit CollegeQuest.com for information on majors offered and athletics. College video and electronic viewbook available at CollegeQuest.com.

VIRGINIA STATE UNIVERSITY
Petersburg, Virginia

- **State-supported**, comprehensive, founded 1882
- **Degrees** bachelor's, master's, and post-master's certificates
- **Suburban** 236-acre campus with easy access to Richmond
- **Coed**
- **Minimally difficult** entrance level
- **$3086 tuition** and fees (in-state); $8630 (out-of-state)

Part of Commonwealth of Virginia Council of Higher Education.

Expenses (1999–2000) *Tuition, state resident:* full-time $1588; part-time $69 per credit hour. *Tuition, nonresident:* full-time $7132; part-time $311 per credit hour. *Required fees:* full-time $1498; $29 per credit hour. Full-time tuition and fees vary according to course level, course load, and program. Part-time tuition and fees vary according to course level, course load, and program. *College room and board:* $5096. Room and board charges vary according to board plan and housing facility.

Institutional Web site http://www.vsu.edu/

College life *Housing:* on-campus residence required in freshman year. *Options:* men-only, women-only. *Social organizations:* national fraternities, national sororities, local fraternities, local sororities; 10% of eligible men and 10% of eligible women are members. *Most popular organizations:* NAACP, Betterment of Brothers/Sisters, Student Government Association, dormitory cabinets, pre-alumni associations.

Campus security 24-hour emergency response devices and patrols.

Application *Options:* Common Application, electronic application. *Application fee:* $25. *Required:* high school transcript. *Recommended:* 2 letters of recommendation.

Standardized tests *Admission: Required:* SAT I or ACT.

Admissions Office Contact Virginia State University, PO Box 9018, Petersburg, VA 23806-2096. **Toll-free phone:** 800-871-7611. **Fax:** 804-524-5055. **E-mail:** lwinn@vsu.edu

Visit CollegeQuest.com for information on athletics. College video available at CollegeQuest.com.

VIRGINIA UNION UNIVERSITY
Richmond, Virginia

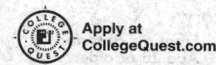
Apply at CollegeQuest.com

- **Independent Baptist**, comprehensive, founded 1865
- **Degrees** bachelor's, doctoral, and first professional
- **Urban** 72-acre campus
- **Coed**, 1,500 undergraduate students
- **Moderately difficult** entrance level
- **$9580 tuition** and fees

Students *Undergraduates:* Students come from 21 states and territories, 2 other countries.

Faculty 104 (86% full-time).

Expenses (1999–2000) *Comprehensive fee:* $13,830 includes full-time tuition ($8780), mandatory fees ($800), and room and board ($4250). *Part-time tuition:* $366 per semester hour. *Part-time fees:* $400 per term part-time. *Payment plans:* installment, deferred payment. *Waivers:* employees or children of employees.

Library L. Douglas Wilder Learning Resource Center and Library. *Collection:* 147,611 titles, 311 serial subscriptions.

College life *Housing: Option:* coed. *Social organizations:* national fraternities, national sororities; 10% of eligible men and 10% of eligible women are members.

Campus security 24-hour emergency response devices and patrols, controlled dormitory access.

After graduation 105 organizations recruited on campus 1997–98. *Career center:* 2 full-time personnel. Services include job fairs, resume preparation, resume referral, career counseling, careers library, job bank, job interviews. *Graduate education:* 42% of class of 1999 went directly to graduate and professional school: 29% graduate arts and sciences, 7% education, 3% law, 2% business, 1% theology.

Freshmen

Average high school GPA	2.45	SAT verbal scores above 500	N/R
SAT math scores above 500	N/R	ACT above 18	N/R
From top 10% of their h.s. class	13%	From top quarter	42%
From top half	54%	1998 freshmen returning in 1999	70%

Application *Options:* eApply at www.CollegeQuest.com, Common Application, early admission, deferred entrance. *Application fee:* $15. *Required:* high school transcript. *Recommended:* essay or personal statement; 3 letters of recommendation.

Virginia

Virginia Union University *(continued)*
Standardized tests *Placement: Required:* SAT I or ACT
Significant dates *Application deadlines:* rolling (freshmen), rolling (transfers). *Financial aid deadline priority date:* 5/1.
Freshman Application Contact
Mr. Gil Powell, Director of Admissions, Virginia Union University, 1500 North Lombardy Street, Richmond, VA 23220-1170. **Phone:** 804-257-5881. **Toll-free phone:** 800-368-3227.
Visit CollegeQuest.com for information on majors offered and athletics. College video available at CollegeQuest.com.

■ *See page 2896 for a narrative description.*

VIRGINIA WESLEYAN COLLEGE
Norfolk, Virginia

- **Independent United Methodist**, 4-year, founded 1961
- **Degree** bachelor's
- **Urban** 300-acre campus
- **Coed**, 1,337 undergraduate students, 78% full-time, 66% women, 34% men
- **Moderately difficult** entrance level, 77% of applicants were admitted
- **14:1 student-to-undergraduate faculty ratio**
- **54.47% graduate** in 6 years or less
- **$14,050 tuition** and fees
- **$10,874 average financial aid** package, $16,292 average indebtedness upon graduation, $18.8 million endowment

Students *Undergraduates:* 1,038 full-time, 299 part-time. Students come from 27 states and territories. *The most frequently chosen baccalaureate fields are:* business/marketing, interdisciplinary studies, social sciences and history.

From out-of-state	25%	Reside on campus	37%
Age 25 or older	35%	Transferred in	12%
International students	0.1%	African Americans	12%
Asian Americans/Pacific Islanders	2%	Hispanic Americans	3%
Native Americans	1%		

Faculty 111 (59% full-time), 58% with terminal degrees.
Expenses (1999–2000) *Comprehensive fee:* $19,700 includes full-time tuition ($14,050) and room and board ($5650). Full-time tuition and fees vary according to class time. Room and board charges vary according to board plan and housing facility. *Part-time tuition:* $586 per semester hour. Part-time tuition and fees vary according to class time and course load. *Payment plans:* installment, deferred payment. *Waivers:* senior citizens and employees or children of employees.
Library H. C. Hofheimer II Library. *Operations spending 1999–2000:* $468,701. *Collection:* 92,000 titles, 650 serial subscriptions, 3,750 audiovisual materials.
College life *Housing:* on-campus residence required through senior year. *Option:* coed. *Social organizations:* national fraternities, national sororities; 12% of eligible men and 12% of eligible women are members. *Most popular organizations:* student government, Religious Life Council, student radio station, student newspaper, Habitat for Humanity.
Campus security 24-hour emergency response devices and patrols, late-night transport-escort service, controlled dormitory access, self-defense education, well-lit pathways.
After graduation 120 organizations recruited on campus 1997–98. 81% of class of 1998 had job offers within 6 months. *Career center:* 2 full-time, 1 part-time personnel. Services include job fairs, resume preparation, interview workshops, resume referral, career/interest testing, career counseling, careers library, job bank, job interviews, graduate school advising.
Freshmen 1,050 applied, 808 admitted, 292 enrolled. 4 National Merit Scholars, 8 valedictorians.

Average high school GPA	3.0	SAT verbal scores above 500	49%
SAT math scores above 500	40%	ACT above 18	N/R
From top 10% of their h.s. class	13%	From top quarter	33%
From top half	61%	1998 freshmen returning in 1999	64%

Application *Options:* Common Application, electronic application, early admission, deferred entrance. *Application fee:* $35. *Required:* essay or personal statement; high school transcript; minimum 2.0 GPA. *Required for some:* 1 letter of recommendation. *Recommended:* minimum 2.5 GPA; 1 letter of recommendation; interview.

Standardized tests *Admission: Required:* SAT I or ACT.
Significant dates *Application deadlines:* rolling (freshmen), rolling (transfers). *Financial aid deadline:* continuous.
Freshman Application Contact
Mr. Richard T. Hinshaw, Vice President for Enrollment Management, Dean of Admissions, Virginia Wesleyan College, Office of Admissions, Virginia Wesleyan College, 1584 Wesleyan Drive, Norfolk, VA 23502-5599. **Phone:** 757-455-3208. **Toll-free phone:** 800-737-8684. **Fax:** 757-461-5238. **E-mail:** admissions@vwc.edu
Visit CollegeQuest.com for information on majors offered and athletics. Electronic viewbook available at CollegeQuest.com.

■ *See page 2898 for a narrative description.*

WASHINGTON AND LEE UNIVERSITY
Lexington, Virginia

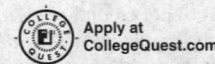
Apply at CollegeQuest.com

- **Independent**, comprehensive, founded 1749
- **Degrees** bachelor's and first professional
- **Small-town** 322-acre campus
- **Coed**, 1,726 undergraduate students, 100% full-time, 44% women, 56% men
- **Most difficult** entrance level, 36% of applicants were admitted
- **10:1 student-to-undergraduate faculty ratio**
- **84% graduate** in 6 years or less
- **$17,105 tuition** and fees
- **$13,560 average financial aid** package, $736.8 million endowment

Students *Undergraduates:* 1,726 full-time. Students come from 47 states and territories, 29 other countries. *The most frequently chosen baccalaureate fields are:* business/marketing, biological/life sciences, social sciences and history. *Graduate:* 367 in professional programs.

From out-of-state	88%	Reside on campus	61%
Age 25 or older	0.2%	Transferred in	0.4%
International students	3%	African Americans	3%
Asian Americans/Pacific Islanders	1%	Hispanic Americans	1%
Native Americans	0.1%		

Expenses (1999–2000) *Comprehensive fee:* $22,652 includes full-time tuition ($16,950), mandatory fees ($155), and room and board ($5547). *College room only:* $3000. Room and board charges vary according to board plan and housing facility. *Part-time tuition:* $565 per credit hour. *Waivers:* employees or children of employees.
Library James G. Leyburn Library plus 1 other. *Operations spending 1999–2000:* $3.1 million. *Collection:* 702,532 titles, 6,807 serial subscriptions, 10,487 audiovisual materials.
College life *Housing:* on-campus residence required through sophomore year. *Option:* coed. *Social organizations:* national fraternities, national sororities, local sororities; 80% of eligible men and 71% of eligible women are members. *Most popular organizations:* Outing Club, Student Activities Board, music groups, Freshman Orientation Committee, student recruitment.
Campus security 24-hour emergency response devices, late-night transport-escort service, controlled dormitory access.
After graduation *Career center:* 4 full-time personnel. Services include job fairs, resume preparation, interview workshops, resume referral, career/interest testing, career counseling, careers library, job bank, job interviews. *Graduate education:* 25% of class of 1999 went directly to graduate and professional school: 8% law, 5% medicine, 1% business, 1% dentistry, 1% veterinary medicine. *Major awards:* 1 Fulbright Scholar.
Freshmen 3,082 applied, 1,102 admitted, 467 enrolled. 36 National Merit Scholars, 60 valedictorians.

SAT verbal scores above 500	98%	SAT math scores above 500	100%
ACT above 18	100%	From top 10% of their h.s. class	69%
From top quarter	95%	From top half	100%
1998 freshmen returning in 1999	94%		

Application *Options:* eApply at www.CollegeQuest.com, Common Application, early decision, deferred entrance. *Application fee:* $40. *Required:* essay or personal statement; high school transcript; 3 letters of recommendation. *Recommended:* interview.
Standardized tests *Admission: Required:* SAT I or ACT, 3 unrelated SAT II Subject Tests (including SAT II: Writing Test).

Virginia-Washington

Significant dates *Application deadlines:* 1/15 (freshmen), 4/1 (transfers). *Early decision:* 12/1. *Notification:* 4/1 (freshmen), 12/22 (early decision). *Financial aid deadline priority date:* 2/1.

Freshman Application Contact
Mr. William M. Hartog, Dean of Admissions and Financial Aid, Washington and Lee University, Lexington, VA 24450-0303. **Phone:** 540-463-8710. **Fax:** 540-463-8062. **E-mail:** admissions@wlu.edu

Visit CollegeQuest.com for information on majors offered and athletics. College video available at CollegeQuest.com.

■ *See page 2916 for a narrative description.*

WORLD COLLEGE
Virginia Beach, Virginia

Students *Undergraduates:* Students come from 50 states and territories, 25 other countries.

Age 25 or older	92%

Faculty 6 (83% full-time).

Expenses (1999–2000) *Tuition:* part-time $2990 per term. Full-time tuition and fees vary according to course level, course load, and program. Part-time tuition and fees vary according to course level, course load, and program. *Payment plans:* installment, deferred payment.

College life *Housing:* college housing not available.

Freshmen

SAT verbal scores above 500	N/R	SAT math scores above 500	N/R
ACT above 18	N/R	1998 freshmen returning in 1999	80%

Application *Options:* Common Application, early admission. *Required:* high school transcript.

Significant dates *Application deadline:* rolling (freshmen).

Freshman Application Contact
Mr. Michael Smith, Director of Operations and Registrar, World College, 5193 Shore Drive, Suite 105, Virginia Beach, VA 23455. **Phone:** 757-464-4600. **Toll-free phone:** 800-696-7532. **E-mail:** instruct@cie-wc.edu

Visit CollegeQuest.com for information on majors offered and athletics.

WASHINGTON

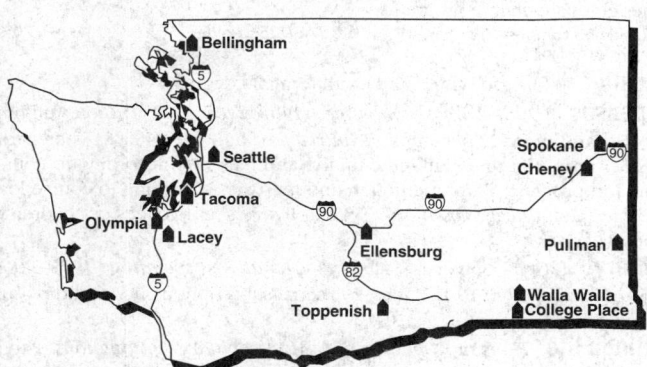

The Seattle area includes the towns of Bothell, Bellevue, Edmonds, Everett, Issaquah, Kirkland, and Poulsbo.

ANTIOCH UNIVERSITY SEATTLE
Seattle, Washington

- **Independent**, upper-level, founded 1975
- **Degrees** bachelor's and master's
- **Urban** campus
- **Coed**, 156 undergraduate students, 25% full-time, 78% women, 22% men
- **Noncompetitive** entrance level, 90% of applicants were admitted
- **8:1 student-to-undergraduate faculty ratio**
- **$10,710 tuition** and fees

Part of Antioch University.

Students *Undergraduates:* 39 full-time, 117 part-time. Students come from 6 states and territories. *Graduate:* 678 in graduate degree programs.

Age 25 or older	95%	Transferred in	100%
International students	3%	African Americans	8%
Asian Americans/Pacific Islanders	1%	Hispanic Americans	3%
Native Americans	3%		

Faculty 15 (53% full-time), 47% with terminal degrees.

Expenses (1999–2000) *Tuition:* full-time $10,620; part-time $295 per credit hour. *Required fees:* full-time $90; $15 per term part-time. Full-time tuition and fees vary according to course load. Part-time tuition and fees vary according to course load and program. *Payment plan:* installment. *Waivers:* employees or children of employees.

Library Antioch Seattle Library. *Collection:* 4,750 titles, 85 serial subscriptions.

College life *Housing:* college housing not available.

Application *Options:* electronic application, deferred entrance. *Application fee:* $50.

Significant dates *Application deadline:* 9/15 (transfers). *Notification:* continuous until 10/1 (transfers). *Financial aid deadline:* continuous.

Freshman Application Contact
Mr. Steve Bangs, Admissions Director, Antioch University Seattle, 2326 Sixth Avenue, Seattle, WA 98121-1814. **Phone:** 206-441-5352 Ext. 5200.

Visit CollegeQuest.com for information on majors offered and athletics.

BASTYR UNIVERSITY
Kenmore, Washington

- **Independent**, upper-level, founded 1978
- **Degrees** bachelor's, master's, and first professional
- **Suburban** 50-acre campus with easy access to Seattle
- **Coed**, 143 undergraduate students, 81% full-time, 82% women, 18% men
- **Moderately difficult** entrance level, 79% of applicants were admitted
- **4:1 student-to-undergraduate faculty ratio**
- **$9825 tuition** and fees
- **$326,031 endowment**

Students *Undergraduates:* 116 full-time, 27 part-time. Students come from 5 other countries. *The most frequently chosen baccalaureate field is:*

Peterson's Guide to Four-Year Colleges 2001   www.petersons.com   843

Washington

Bastyr University (continued)
biological/life sciences. **Graduate:** 529 in professional programs, 207 in other graduate degree programs.

| Reside on campus | 6% | Age 25 or older | 70% |
| Transferred in | 57% | | |

Faculty 50 (38% full-time), 90% with terminal degrees.
Expenses (1999–2000) *One-time required fee:* $300. *Tuition:* full-time $9345; part-time $192 per credit. *Required fees:* full-time $480; $15 per credit; $35 per term part-time. Full-time tuition and fees vary according to course load and program. Part-time tuition and fees vary according to course load and program. *College room only:* $3500. *Waivers:* employees or children of employees.
Library Bastyr University Library. *Operations spending 1999–2000:* $159,407. *Collection:* 10,125 titles, 293 serial subscriptions, 1,200 audiovisual materials.
College life *Housing:* Option: coed. *Most popular organizations:* Parent Resource Center, nature club, Spirituality in Focus, Environmental Action Team, Toastmasters.
Campus security Student patrols, late-night transport-escort service.
After graduation *Career center:* Services include career counseling.
Application *Option:* deferred entrance. *Application fee:* $60.
Significant dates *Application deadline:* 3/15 (transfers). *Notification:* continuous until 9/1 (transfers). *Financial aid deadline priority date:* 5/1.
Freshman Application Contact
Mr. Richard Dent, Director of Student Enrollment, Bastyr University, 14500 Juanita Drive, NE, Kenmore, WA 98028-4966. **Phone:** 425-602-3080. **Fax:** 425-823-6222.
Visit CollegeQuest.com for information on majors offered and athletics. Electronic viewbook available at CollegeQuest.com.

CENTRAL WASHINGTON UNIVERSITY
Ellensburg, Washington

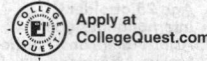
Apply at CollegeQuest.com

- **State-supported**, comprehensive, founded 1891
- **Degrees** bachelor's and master's
- **Small-town** 380-acre campus
- **Coed**
- **Moderately difficult** entrance level

Institutional Web site http://www.cwu.edu/
College life *Housing:* on-campus residence required in freshman year. *Options:* coed, disabled students. *Most popular organizations:* International Business Club, Marketing Club, Associated Students of CWU.
Campus security 24-hour emergency response devices and patrols, controlled dormitory access.
Application *Options:* eApply at www.CollegeQuest.com, Common Application, electronic application, early admission. *Application fee:* $35. *Required:* high school transcript; minimum 2.0 GPA. *Required for some:* essay or personal statement; interview.
Standardized tests *Admission: Required:* SAT I or ACT.
Admissions Office Contact
Central Washington University, Mitchell Hall, Ellensburg, WA 98926-7463. **Fax:** 509-963-3022. **E-mail:** cwuadmis@cwu.edu
Visit CollegeQuest.com for information on athletics. College video available at CollegeQuest.com.

CITY UNIVERSITY
Bellevue, Washington

- **Independent**, upper-level, founded 1973
- **Degrees** associate, bachelor's, master's, and postbachelor's certificates
- **Suburban** campus with easy access to Seattle
- **Coed**, 2,151 undergraduate students, 58% full-time, 46% women, 54% men
- **Noncompetitive** entrance level, 100% of applicants were admitted
- **$6600 tuition** and fees

Students *Undergraduates:* 1,246 full-time, 905 part-time. Students come from 43 states and territories, 33 other countries. *The most frequently chosen baccalaureate fields are:* business/marketing, computer/information sciences, liberal arts/general studies. **Graduate:** 2,862 in graduate degree programs.

From out-of-state	52%	Age 25 or older	90%
International students	5%	African Americans	4%
Asian Americans/Pacific Islanders	7%	Hispanic Americans	2%
Native Americans	1%		

Faculty 1,095 (5% full-time), 98% with terminal degrees.
Expenses (1999–2000) *Tuition:* full-time $6600; part-time $165 per credit. *Payment plan:* deferred payment. *Waivers:* employees or children of employees.
Library City University Library. *Operations spending 1999–2000:* $774,136. *Collection:* 32,329 titles, 1,518 serial subscriptions, 5,184 audiovisual materials.
College life *Housing:* college housing not available.
Campus security 24-hour emergency response devices.
After graduation 3 organizations recruited on campus 1997–98. *Career center:* 2 full-time personnel. Services include job fairs, career counseling, careers library, job bank.
Application *Options:* Common Application, electronic application, deferred entrance. *Application fee:* $75.
Significant dates *Application deadline:* rolling (transfers). *Financial aid deadline:* continuous.
Freshman Application Contact
Mr. Nabil El-Khatib, Vice President of Admissions and Student Affairs, City University, 919 SW Grady Way, Renton, WA 98055. **Phone:** 425-637-1010. **Toll-free phone:** 800-426-5596. **Fax:** 425-277-2437. **E-mail:** info@cityu.edu
Visit CollegeQuest.com for information on majors offered and athletics. Electronic viewbook available at CollegeQuest.com.

■ *See page 1422 for a narrative description.*

CORNISH COLLEGE OF THE ARTS
Seattle, Washington

- **Independent**, 4-year, founded 1914
- **Degree** bachelor's
- **Urban** 4-acre campus
- **Coed**, 659 undergraduate students, 94% full-time, 61% women, 39% men
- **Moderately difficult** entrance level, 78% of applicants were admitted
- **9:1** student-to-undergraduate faculty ratio
- **$13,900 tuition** and fees
- **$12,061 average financial aid** package, $24,000 average indebtedness upon graduation, $636,870 endowment

Students *Undergraduates:* 619 full-time, 40 part-time. Students come from 27 states and territories, 14 other countries. *The most frequently chosen baccalaureate field is:* visual/performing arts.

| Age 25 or older | 24% | Transferred in | 2% |

Faculty 158 (68% full-time).
Expenses (1999–2000) *Tuition:* full-time $13,700; part-time $575 per credit. *Required fees:* full-time $200; $100 per term part-time. Part-time tuition and fees vary according to program. *Payment plan:* installment. *Waivers:* employees or children of employees.
Library Cornish College of the Arts Library plus 1 other. *Operations spending 1999–2000:* $100,000. *Collection:* 12,000 titles, 100 serial subscriptions.
College life *Housing:* college housing not available. *Most popular organization:* student union.
Campus security 24-hour emergency response devices and patrols, late-night transport-escort service.
After graduation *Career center:* Services include job fairs, resume preparation, career counseling, careers library, job bank. **Graduate education:** 5% of class of 1999 went directly to graduate and professional school.

Washington

Freshmen 612 applied, 476 admitted, 112 enrolled.
Average high school GPA	2.87	SAT verbal scores above 500	N/R
SAT math scores above 500	N/R	ACT above 18	N/R
1998 freshmen returning in 1999	72%		

Application *Option:* deferred entrance. *Application fee:* $35. *Required:* essay or personal statement; high school transcript; minimum 2.0 GPA; portfolio or audition. *Required for some:* 2 letters of recommendation. *Recommended:* 2 letters of recommendation; interview.

Standardized tests *Admission: Recommended:* SAT I or ACT.

Significant dates *Application deadlines:* 8/15 (freshmen), 8/15 (transfers). *Financial aid deadline priority date:* 2/1.

Freshman Application Contact
Ms. Sharron Starling, Associate Director of Admissions, Cornish College of the Arts, 710 East Roy Street, Seattle, WA 98102-4696. **Phone:** 206-726-5017. **Toll-free phone:** 800-726-ARTS.

Visit CollegeQuest.com for information on majors offered and athletics. Electronic viewbook available at CollegeQuest.com.

CROWN COLLEGE
Tacoma, Washington

- **Proprietary**, primarily 2-year, founded 1969
- **Degrees** associate and bachelor's (bachelor's degree in public administration only)
- **Urban** campus with easy access to Seattle
- **232 undergraduate students**, 100% full-time, 51% women, 49% men
- **20:1 student-to-undergraduate faculty ratio**

Admissions Office Contact
- Crown College, 8739 South Hosmer, Tacoma, WA 98444-1836. **Toll-free phone:** 800-755-9525. **Fax:** 253-531-3521. **E-mail:** admissions@crowncollege.edu

Visit CollegeQuest.com for information on majors offered and athletics.

EASTERN WASHINGTON UNIVERSITY
Cheney, Washington

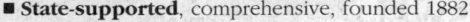
Apply at CollegeQuest.com

- **State-supported**, comprehensive, founded 1882
- **Degrees** bachelor's and master's
- **Small-town** 335-acre campus
- **Coed**, 7,225 undergraduate students, 88% full-time, 58% women, 42% men
- **Moderately difficult** entrance level, 88% of applicants were admitted
- **19:1 student-to-undergraduate faculty ratio**
- **48% graduate** in 6 years or less
- **$2907 tuition** and fees (in-state); $9801 (out-of-state)
- **$13,003 average financial aid** package, $14,509 average indebtedness upon graduation, $4.2 million endowment

Students *Undergraduates:* 6,377 full-time, 848 part-time. Students come from 44 states and territories, 35 other countries. *The most frequently chosen baccalaureate fields are:* business/marketing, education, social sciences and history. *Graduate:* 1,036 in graduate degree programs.
From out-of-state	7%	Reside on campus	18%
Age 25 or older	27%	Transferred in	15%
International students	3%	African Americans	2%
Asian Americans/Pacific Islanders	3%	Hispanic Americans	4%
Native Americans	3%		

Faculty 506 (68% full-time), 48% with terminal degrees.

Expenses (1999–2000) *Tuition, state resident:* full-time $2700; part-time $90 per quarter hour. *Tuition, nonresident:* full-time $9594; part-time $320 per quarter hour. *Required fees:* full-time $207. Full-time tuition and fees vary according to reciprocity agreements. Part-time tuition and fees vary according to course load and reciprocity agreements. *College room and board:* $4399; room only: $2276. Room and board charges vary according to board plan and housing facility. *Payment plan:* installment. *Waivers:* employees or children of employees.

Library John F. Kennedy Library plus 2 others. *Operations spending 1999–2000:* $3.7 million. *Collection:* 759,977 titles, 499,989 serial subscriptions, 27,595 audiovisual materials.

College life *Housing: Options:* coed, men-only, women-only, disabled students. *Social organizations:* national fraternities, national sororities; 6% of eligible men and 4% of eligible women are members. *Most popular organizations:* International Student Association, cultural heritage groups, Eagle Ambassadors, business/honor fraternities, religious organizations.

Campus security 24-hour emergency response devices and patrols, student patrols, late-night transport-escort service, controlled dormitory access, emergency call boxes.

After graduation 110 organizations recruited on campus 1997–98. *Career center:* 6 full-time, 1 part-time personnel. Services include job fairs, resume preparation, interview workshops, resume referral, career/interest testing, career counseling, careers library, job bank, job interviews. *Graduate education:* 14% of class of 1999 went directly to graduate and professional school.

Freshmen 2,680 applied, 2,368 admitted, 1,079 enrolled.
Average high school GPA	3.28	SAT verbal scores above 500	48%
SAT math scores above 500	51%	ACT above 18	83%
From top 10% of their h.s. class	21%	From top quarter	51%
From top half	81%	1998 freshmen returning in 1999	87%

Application *Options:* eApply at www.CollegeQuest.com, electronic application, early admission, deferred entrance. *Application fee:* $35. *Required:* high school transcript; minimum 2.0 GPA. *Required for some:* essay or personal statement; letters of recommendation; interview. *Recommended:* minimum 3.0 GPA.

Standardized tests *Admission: Required:* SAT I or ACT.

Significant dates *Application deadlines:* rolling (freshmen), rolling (transfers). *Financial aid deadline priority date:* 2/15.

Freshman Application Contact
Ms. Michelle Whittingham, Director of Admissions, Eastern Washington University, 526 Fifth Street, MS-148, Cheney, WA 99004-2431. **Phone:** 509-359-6582. **Toll-free phone:** 888-740-1914. **Fax:** 509-359-4330. **E-mail:** admissions@mail.ewu.edu

Visit CollegeQuest.com for information on majors offered and athletics. College video available at CollegeQuest.com.

■ *See page 1610 for a narrative description.*

THE EVERGREEN STATE COLLEGE
Olympia, Washington

- **State-supported**, comprehensive, founded 1967
- **Degrees** bachelor's and master's
- **Small-town** 1,000-acre campus with easy access to Seattle
- **Coed**, 3,855 undergraduate students, 86% full-time, 58% women, 42% men
- **Moderately difficult** entrance level, 85% of applicants were admitted
- **22:1 student-to-undergraduate faculty ratio**
- **$2898 tuition** and fees (in-state); $9900 (out-of-state)
- **$9472 average financial aid** package, $12,000 average indebtedness upon graduation, $1.1 million endowment

Students *Undergraduates:* Students come from 40 states and territories, 15 other countries. *Graduate:* 247 in graduate degree programs.
From out-of-state	25%	Reside on campus	26%
Age 25 or older	37%	International students	1%
African Americans	3%	Asian Americans/Pacific Islanders	5%
Hispanic Americans	4%	Native Americans	4%

Faculty 223 (69% full-time).

Expenses (1999–2000) *Tuition, state resident:* full-time $2757; part-time $92 per quarter hour. *Tuition, nonresident:* full-time $9759; part-time $325 per quarter hour. *Required fees:* full-time $141. *College room and board:* $4645. Room and board charges vary according to board plan and housing facility. *Payment plan:* installment.

Library Daniel J. Evans Library. *Operations spending 1999–2000:* $2.9 million. *Collection:* 376,703 titles, 4,748 serial subscriptions, 81,390 audiovisual materials.

Peterson's Guide to Four-Year Colleges 2001 www.petersons.com 845

Washington

The Evergreen State College (continued)

College life *Housing: Option:* coed. *Most popular organizations:* Evergreen Political Information Committee, Environmental Resource Center, Women's Resource Center, Washpirg.

Campus security 24-hour emergency response devices and patrols, student patrols, late-night transport-escort service.

After graduation 87% of class of 1998 had job offers within 6 months. *Career center:* 4 full-time, 1 part-time personnel. Services include job fairs, resume preparation, interview workshops, resume referral, career/interest testing, career counseling, careers library, job bank, job interviews. *Graduate education:* 17% of class of 1999 went directly to graduate and professional school: 6% business, 4% graduate arts and sciences, 3% medicine, 1% engineering, 1% law, 1% theology, 1% veterinary medicine. *Major awards:* 1 Fulbright Scholar.

Freshmen 1,539 applied, 1,305 admitted.

Average high school GPA	3.1	SAT verbal scores above 500	84%
SAT math scores above 500	68%	ACT above 18	N/R

Application *Options:* electronic application, early admission. *Preference* given to state residents. *Application fee:* $35. *Required:* high school transcript; minimum 2.0 GPA. *Required for some:* interview. *Recommended:* essay or personal statement.

Standardized tests *Admission: Required:* SAT I or ACT.

Significant dates *Application deadlines:* 3/1 (freshmen), 3/1 (transfers). *Notification:* 4/1 (freshmen). *Financial aid deadline priority date:* 3/15.

Freshman Application Contact
Ms. Christine Licht, Senior Admissions Officer, The Evergreen State College, 2700 Evergreen Parkway, NW, Olympia, WA 98505. **Phone:** 360-866-6000 Ext. 6170. **Fax:** 360-866-6680. **E-mail:** admissions@evergreen.edu

Visit CollegeQuest.com for information on majors offered and athletics. College video available at CollegeQuest.com.

■ *See page 1646 for a narrative description.*

GONZAGA UNIVERSITY
Spokane, Washington

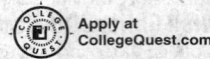
Apply at CollegeQuest.com

- **Independent Roman Catholic**, comprehensive, founded 1887
- **Degrees** bachelor's, master's, doctoral, first professional, and post-master's certificates
- **Urban** 94-acre campus
- **Coed**, 2,721 undergraduate students, 93% full-time, 54% women, 46% men
- **Moderately difficult** entrance level, 87% of applicants were admitted
- **12:1 student-to-undergraduate faculty ratio**
- **66% graduate** in 6 years or less
- **$16,860 tuition** and fees
- **$11,510 average financial aid** package, $19,731 average indebtedness upon graduation, $96.8 million endowment

Gonzaga's nationally dominant debate team, exceptional medical school acceptance rate, and CPA examination pass rates exemplify Gonzaga's commitment to academic excellence. Outstanding facilities supporting these programs include Foley Center Library, featuring 782,000 volumes and microform titles, and Jundt Art Center and Museum, with modern classroom studios and a gallery that attracts national exhibits.

Students *Undergraduates:* 2,543 full-time, 178 part-time. Students come from 47 states and territories, 41 other countries. *The most frequently chosen baccalaureate fields are:* business/marketing, engineering/engineering technologies, social sciences and history. *Graduate:* 455 in professional programs, 969 in other graduate degree programs.

From out-of-state	49%	Reside on campus	44%
Age 25 or older	21%	Transferred in	7%
International students	5%	African Americans	1%
Asian Americans/Pacific Islanders	5%	Hispanic Americans	2%
Native Americans	1%		

Faculty 273 (97% full-time), 86% with terminal degrees.

Expenses (1999–2000) *Comprehensive fee:* $22,210 includes full-time tuition ($16,710), mandatory fees ($150), and room and board ($5350). Full-time tuition and fees vary according to course load, degree level, location, program, and reciprocity agreements. Room and board charges vary according to board plan and housing facility. *Part-time tuition:* $480 per credit hour. *Part-time fees:* $25 per term part-time. Part-time tuition and fees vary according to course load, degree level, location, program, and reciprocity agreements. *Payment plans:* installment, deferred payment. *Waivers:* senior citizens and employees or children of employees.

Library Ralph E. and Helen Higgins Foley Center plus 1 other. *Operations spending 1999–2000:* $3.7 million. *Collection:* 2,552 audiovisual materials.

College life *Housing:* on-campus residence required through sophomore year. *Options:* coed, men-only, women-only. *Most popular organizations:* Gonzaga Student Body Association, Search, Circle K, Encore, Knights and Setons.

Campus security 24-hour emergency response devices and patrols, late-night transport-escort service, controlled dormitory access.

After graduation 85 organizations recruited on campus 1997–98. 65% of class of 1998 had job offers within 6 months. *Career center:* 3 full-time personnel. Services include job fairs, resume preparation, interview workshops, resume referral, career counseling, careers library, job bank, job interviews.

Freshmen 2,067 applied, 1,800 admitted, 682 enrolled. 4 National Merit Scholars.

Average high school GPA	3.56	SAT verbal scores above 500	77%
SAT math scores above 500	80%	ACT above 18	100%
From top 10% of their h.s. class	32%	From top quarter	63%
From top half	89%	1998 freshmen returning in 1999	88%

Application *Options:* eApply at www.CollegeQuest.com, Common Application, electronic application, early admission, early action, deferred entrance. *Application fee:* $40. *Required:* essay or personal statement; high school transcript; minimum 2.0 GPA; 1 letter of recommendation. *Recommended:* interview.

Standardized tests *Admission: Required:* SAT I or ACT.

Significant dates *Application deadlines:* 4/1 (freshmen), 6/1 (transfers). *Early action:* 11/15. *Notification:* 12/24 (early action). *Financial aid deadline priority date:* 2/1.

Freshman Application Contact
Ms. Julie McCulloh, Associate Dean of Admission, Gonzaga University, Ad Box 102, Spokane, WA 99258-0102. **Phone:** 509-323-6591. **Toll-free phone:** 800-322-2584 Ext. 6572. **Fax:** 509-324-5780. **E-mail:** ballinger@gu.gonzaga.edu

Visit CollegeQuest.com for information on majors offered and athletics. College video available at CollegeQuest.com.

■ *See page 1724 for a narrative description.*

HENRY COGSWELL COLLEGE
Everett, Washington

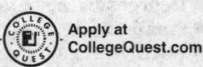
Apply at CollegeQuest.com

- **Independent**, 4-year, founded 1979
- **Degree** bachelor's
- **Urban** 1-acre campus with easy access to Seattle
- **Coed**, primarily men, 252 undergraduate students, 36% full-time, 13% women, 87% men
- **Noncompetitive** entrance level, 100% of applicants were admitted
- **8:1 student-to-undergraduate faculty ratio**
- **$10,800 tuition** and fees
- **$3708 average financial aid** package, $16,432 average indebtedness upon graduation, $97,000 endowment

Students *Undergraduates:* 90 full-time, 162 part-time. Students come from 2 states and territories. *The most frequently chosen baccalaureate fields are:* computer/information sciences, engineering/engineering technologies.

From out-of-state	1%	Age 25 or older	82%
Transferred in	91%	International students	1%
African Americans	3%	Asian Americans/Pacific Islanders	14%
Hispanic Americans	4%	Native Americans	0.4%

Faculty 11 full-time.

Expenses (1999–2000) *Tuition:* full-time $10,800; part-time $450 per credit. *Payment plans:* guaranteed tuition, installment, deferred payment. *Waivers:* employees or children of employees.

Washington

Library Henry Cogswell College Library. *Operations spending 1999–2000:* $93,783. *Collection:* 6,000 titles, 60 serial subscriptions, 85 audiovisual materials.
College life *Housing:* college housing not available. *Most popular organization:* Student Senate.
After graduation *Career center:* Services include resume preparation, resume referral, career counseling.
Freshmen 23 applied, 23 admitted, 65 enrolled. 1 valedictorian.

Average high school GPA	2.98	SAT verbal scores above 500	75%
SAT math scores above 500	50%	ACT above 18	N/R
1998 freshmen returning in 1999	86%		

Application *Options:* eApply at www.CollegeQuest.com, Common Application, early decision, deferred entrance. *Application fee:* $50. *Required:* essay or personal statement; high school transcript. *Required for some:* 3 letters of recommendation; portfolio. *Recommended:* interview.
Standardized tests *Admission: Required:* SAT I or ACT.
Significant dates *Application deadlines:* 3/1 (freshmen), rolling (transfers). *Early decision:* 11/15. *Notification:* 4/1 (freshmen), 12/15 (early decision). *Financial aid deadline:* continuous.
Freshman Application Contact
Ms. Cristy Null, Assistant for Recruitment and Enrollment, Henry Cogswell College, 2802 Wetmore Avenue, Suite 100, Everett, WA 98201. **Phone:** 425-258-3351. **E-mail:** information@henrycogswell.edu
Visit CollegeQuest.com for information on majors offered and athletics.

HERITAGE COLLEGE
Toppenish, Washington

- **Independent**, comprehensive, founded 1982
- **Degrees** associate, bachelor's, and master's
- **Rural** 10-acre campus
- **Coed**, 635 undergraduate students, 51% full-time, 71% women, 29% men
- **Noncompetitive** entrance level
- **9:1 student-to-undergraduate faculty ratio**
- **$5190 tuition** and fees

Students *Undergraduates:* 322 full-time, 313 part-time. Students come from 1 other country. *The most frequently chosen baccalaureate fields are:* (pre)law, education, protective services/public administration. *Graduate:* 487 in graduate degree programs.

Age 25 or older	79%	International students	0.2%
African Americans	1%	Asian Americans/Pacific Islanders	1%
Hispanic Americans	40%	Native Americans	15%

Faculty 165, 53% with terminal degrees.
Expenses (1999–2000) *One-time required fee:* $30. *Tuition:* full-time $5160; part-time $215 per credit hour. *Required fees:* full-time $30. *Payment plans:* installment, deferred payment. *Waivers:* senior citizens and employees or children of employees.
Library Library and Resource Center. *Collection:* 57,550 titles, 203 serial subscriptions.
College life *Housing:* college housing not available.
Campus security 24-hour emergency response devices.
After graduation *Career center:* Services include job fairs, resume preparation, career counseling, job interviews.
Freshmen 27 admitted, 30 enrolled.

| SAT verbal scores above 500 | N/R | SAT math scores above 500 | N/R |
| ACT above 18 | N/R | 1998 freshmen returning in 1999 | 38% |

Application *Options:* Common Application, early admission, deferred entrance. *Required:* high school transcript.
Standardized tests *Placement: Recommended:* SAT I or ACT.
Significant dates *Application deadlines:* rolling (freshmen), rolling (transfers). *Financial aid deadline priority date:* 2/10.
Freshman Application Contact
Mr. Norberto T. Espindola, Director of Admissions and Recruitment, Heritage College, 3240 Fort Road, Toppenish, WA 98948-9599. **Phone:** 509-865-8500 Ext. 2002. **Toll-free phone:** 509-865-8508. **Fax:** 509-865-4469. **E-mail:** espindola_b@heritage.edu
Visit CollegeQuest.com for information on majors offered and athletics.

ITT TECHNICAL INSTITUTE
Seattle, Washington

- **Proprietary**, primarily 2-year, founded 1932
- **Degrees** associate and bachelor's
- **Urban** campus
- **Coed**
- **Minimally difficult** entrance level
- **$9190 tuition** and fees

Part of ITT Educational Services, Inc.
Admissions Office Contact
ITT Technical Institute, 12720 Gateway Drive, Suite 100, Seattle, WA 98168-3333.
Visit CollegeQuest.com for information on majors offered and athletics. College video available at CollegeQuest.com.

THE LEADERSHIP INSTITUTE OF SEATTLE
Bellevue, Washington

- **Independent**, upper-level, founded 1973
- **Degrees** bachelor's and master's
- **Suburban** campus with easy access to Seattle
- **Coed**
- **Minimally difficult** entrance level
- **$10,285 tuition** and fees

Expenses (1999–2000) *Comprehensive fee:* $11,795 includes full-time tuition ($9855), mandatory fees ($430), and room and board ($1510).
Institutional Web site http://www.lios.org/
Application *Option:* deferred entrance. *Application fee:* $65.
Admissions Office Contact
The Leadership Institute of Seattle, 1450 114th Avenue SE, Suite 230, Bellevue, WA 98004-6934. **Toll-free phone:** 800-789-5467. **E-mail:** lios@lios.org
Visit CollegeQuest.com for information on athletics.

LUTHERAN BIBLE INSTITUE OF SEATTLE
Washington—See Trinity Lutheran College

NORTHWEST COLLEGE
Kirkland, Washington

- **Independent**, 4-year, founded 1934, affiliated with Assemblies of God
- **Degrees** associate and bachelor's
- **Suburban** 65-acre campus with easy access to Seattle
- **Coed**, 939 undergraduate students, 94% full-time, 55% women, 45% men
- **Moderately difficult** entrance level, 99% of applicants were admitted
- **17:1 student-to-undergraduate faculty ratio**
- **46.6% graduate** in 6 years or less
- **$9870 tuition** and fees
- **$9996 average financial aid** package, $10,722 average indebtedness upon graduation, $7.7 million endowment

Students *Undergraduates:* 879 full-time, 60 part-time. Students come from 26 states and territories, 15 other countries. *The most frequently chosen baccalaureate fields are:* business/marketing, education, philosophy.

From out-of-state	24%	Reside on campus	61%
Age 25 or older	25%	Transferred in	21%
International students	3%	African Americans	4%
Asian Americans/Pacific Islanders	4%	Hispanic Americans	3%
Native Americans	1%		

Faculty 81 (56% full-time), 35% with terminal degrees.
Expenses (1999–2000) *Comprehensive fee:* $14,900 includes full-time tuition ($9672), mandatory fees ($198), and room and board ($5030). Room and board charges vary according to board plan. *Part-time tuition:* $403 per

Washington

Northwest College (continued)
credit hour. *Part-time fees:* $21 per credit hour. *Payment plans:* installment, deferred payment. *Waivers:* senior citizens and employees or children of employees.
Library D. V. Hurst Library. *Collection:* 61,334 titles, 1,007 serial subscriptions, 16,887 audiovisual materials.
College life *Housing:* on-campus residence required through sophomore year. *Options:* men-only, women-only. *Most popular organizations:* environmental club, psychology club, Association of Business Students, drama club, student ministries.
Campus security 24-hour emergency response devices and patrols, late-night transport-escort service, controlled dormitory access.
After graduation *Career center:* 1 full-time personnel. Services include job fairs, resume preparation, interview workshops, resume referral, career/interest testing, career counseling, careers library, job bank, job interviews.
Freshmen 199 applied, 198 admitted, 210 enrolled. 1 National Merit Scholar, 10 class presidents, 30 student government officers.

Average high school GPA	3.1	SAT verbal scores above 500	74%
SAT math scores above 500	26%	ACT above 18	78%
1998 freshmen returning in 1999	65%		

Application *Options:* Common Application, early admission, early action, deferred entrance. *Application fee:* $30. *Required:* essay or personal statement; high school transcript; minimum 2.3 GPA; 2 letters of recommendation. *Required for some:* interview.
Standardized tests *Placement: Required:* SAT I or ACT
Significant dates *Application deadlines:* 8/1 (freshmen), 8/1 (transfers). *Early action:* 11/15. *Notification:* 12/31 (early action). *Financial aid deadline priority date:* 3/1.
Freshman Application Contact
Mr. Myles Corrigan, Director of Enrollment Services, Northwest College, PO Box 579, Kirkland, WA 98083-0579. **Phone:** 425-889-5209. **Toll-free phone:** 800-669-3781. **Fax:** 425-425-0148. **E-mail:** admissions@ncag.edu
Visit CollegeQuest.com for information on majors offered and athletics. College video available at CollegeQuest.com.

NORTHWEST COLLEGE OF ART
Poulsbo, Washington

- **Proprietary**, 4-year, founded 1982
- **Degree** bachelor's
- **Small-town** 26-acre campus with easy access to Seattle
- **Coed**
- **Moderately difficult** entrance level
- **$8200 tuition** and fees

Expenses (1999–2000) *Tuition:* full-time $8000; part-time $330 per credit. *Required fees:* full-time $200; $100 per term part-time. Part-time tuition and fees vary according to course load.
Institutional Web site http://www.nca.edu/
College life *Housing:* college housing not available.
Application *Option:* deferred entrance. *Application fee:* $50. *Required:* essay or personal statement; high school transcript; minimum 2.0 GPA; 3 letters of recommendation; interview; portfolio.
Admissions Office Contact
Northwest College of Art, 16464 State Highway 305, Poulsbo, WA 98370. **Toll-free phone:** 800-769-ARTS. **Fax:** 360-779-9533. **E-mail:** kimatnca@silverlink.net
Visit CollegeQuest.com for information on athletics.

PACIFIC LUTHERAN UNIVERSITY
Tacoma, Washington

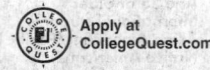

- **Independent**, comprehensive, founded 1890, affiliated with Evangelical Lutheran Church in America
- **Degrees** bachelor's and master's
- **Suburban** 126-acre campus with easy access to Seattle
- **Coed**, 3,302 undergraduate students, 91% full-time, 60% women, 40% men
- **Moderately difficult** entrance level, 84% of applicants were admitted
- **15:1 student-to-undergraduate faculty ratio**
- **70% graduate** in 6 years or less
- **$16,224 tuition** and fees
- **$14,990 average financial aid** package, $19,267 average indebtedness upon graduation, $37.3 million endowment

A keener understanding of the global community is vital to the future. At Pacific Lutheran, highly acclaimed international programs—from Chinese and Scandinavian studies to a new CD-ROM-based Language Resource Center—encourage a world focus in studies across the curriculum.

Students *Undergraduates:* 2,999 full-time, 303 part-time. Students come from 44 states and territories, 26 other countries. *The most frequently chosen baccalaureate fields are:* business/marketing, education, health professions and related sciences. *Graduate:* 300 in graduate degree programs.

From out-of-state	28%	Reside on campus	50%
Age 25 or older	16%	Transferred in	10%
International students	7%	African Americans	2%
Asian Americans/Pacific Islanders	5%	Hispanic Americans	2%
Native Americans	1%		

Faculty 327 (72% full-time), 64% with terminal degrees.
Expenses (1999–2000) *Comprehensive fee:* $21,262 includes full-time tuition ($16,224) and room and board ($5038). *College room only:* $2472. Room and board charges vary according to board plan. *Part-time tuition:* $507 per semester hour. *Payment plan:* installment. *Waivers:* senior citizens and employees or children of employees.
Library Mortvedt Library. *Operations spending 1999–2000:* $1.9 million. *Collection:* 353,766 titles, 2,255 serial subscriptions, 11,166 audiovisual materials.
College life *Housing:* on-campus residence required through sophomore year. *Options:* coed, women-only. *Most popular organizations:* Rejoice, Circle K, adult students club, Residence Hall Government, Inter-varsity Fellowship.
Campus security 24-hour emergency response devices and patrols, student patrols, late-night transport-escort service.
After graduation 69 organizations recruited on campus 1997–98. 69% of class of 1998 had job offers within 6 months. *Career center:* 1 full-time, 2 part-time personnel. Services include job fairs, resume preparation, interview workshops, resume referral, career/interest testing, career counseling, careers library, job bank, job interviews. *Graduate education:* 9% of class of 1999 went directly to graduate and professional school. *Major awards:* 3 Fulbright Scholars.
Freshmen 1,685 applied, 1,413 admitted, 568 enrolled. 5 National Merit Scholars, 32 valedictorians.

Average high school GPA	3.61	SAT verbal scores above 500	74%
SAT math scores above 500	73%	ACT above 18	94%
From top 10% of their h.s. class	35%	From top quarter	63%
From top half	82%	1998 freshmen returning in 1999	81%

Application *Options:* eApply at www.CollegeQuest.com, Common Application, early admission, early action, deferred entrance. *Application fee:* $35. *Required:* essay or personal statement; high school transcript; minimum 2.5 GPA; 1 letter of recommendation. *Required for some:* interview.
Standardized tests *Admission: Required:* SAT I or ACT.
Significant dates *Application deadlines:* rolling (freshmen), rolling (transfers). *Early action:* 11/15. *Notification:* 12/1 (early action). *Financial aid deadline priority date:* 3/1.
Freshman Application Contact
Office of Admissions, Pacific Lutheran University, Tacoma, WA 98447. **Phone:** 253-535-7151. **Toll-free phone:** 800-274-6758. **Fax:** 253-536-5136. **E-mail:** admissions@plu.edu
Visit CollegeQuest.com for information on majors offered and athletics. College video and electronic viewbook available at CollegeQuest.com.

■ *See page 2236 for a narrative description.*

Washington

PUGET SOUND CHRISTIAN COLLEGE
Edmonds, Washington

- **Independent Christian**, 4-year, founded 1950
- **Degrees** associate and bachelor's
- **Suburban** 4-acre campus with easy access to Seattle
- **Coed**
- **Minimally difficult** entrance level
- **$6420 tuition** and fees

Expenses (1999–2000) *Comprehensive fee:* $10,570 includes full-time tuition ($6250), mandatory fees ($170), and room and board ($4150). *College room only:* $2550. Full-time tuition and fees vary according to class time. Room and board charges vary according to board plan. *Part-time tuition:* $290 per semester hour. *Part-time fees:* $40 per term part-time. Part-time tuition and fees vary according to class time and course load.

College life *Housing:* on-campus residence required in freshman year. *Options:* men-only, women-only. *Most popular organizations:* Team Macedonia, ASB Outreach Committee.

Campus security 24-hour emergency response devices, student patrols.

Application *Option:* deferred entrance. *Preference* given to members of Christian Church or Church of Christ. *Application fee:* $25. *Required:* essay or personal statement; high school transcript; minimum 2.0 GPA; letters of recommendation. *Required for some:* interview.

Standardized tests *Placement: Recommended:* SAT I and SAT II or ACT, SAT II: Writing Test. *Required for some:* SAT I and SAT II or ACT.

Admissions Office Contact
Puget Sound Christian College, 410 4th Avenue North, Edmonds, WA 98020-3171. **Fax:** 425-775-8688. **E-mail:** psccdeve@ricochet.net

Visit CollegeQuest.com for information on athletics.

SAINT MARTIN'S COLLEGE
Lacey, Washington

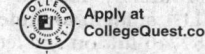

- **Independent Roman Catholic**, comprehensive, founded 1895
- **Degrees** associate, bachelor's, and master's
- **Suburban** 380-acre campus with easy access to Tacoma
- **Coed**, 1,215 undergraduate students
- **Moderately difficult** entrance level, 94% of applicants were admitted
- **12:1 student-to-undergraduate faculty ratio**
- **48% graduate** in 6 years or less
- **$14,180 tuition** and fees
- **$14,336 average financial aid** package, $12,813 average indebtedness upon graduation, $4 million endowment

Students *Undergraduates:* Students come from 12 states and territories, 11 other countries. *The most frequently chosen baccalaureate fields are:* business/marketing, education, psychology.

Reside on campus	16%	Age 25 or older	47%
International students	3%	African Americans	8%
Asian Americans/Pacific Islanders	6%	Hispanic Americans	4%
Native Americans	1%		

Faculty 69 (77% full-time), 57% with terminal degrees.

Expenses (1999–2000) *Comprehensive fee:* $18,948 includes full-time tuition ($14,050), mandatory fees ($130), and room and board ($4768). *Part-time tuition:* $468 per credit. *Payment plan:* installment. *Waivers:* employees or children of employees.

Library Saint Martin's College Library. *Operations spending 1999–2000:* $522,925. *Collection:* 86,738 titles, 990 serial subscriptions.

College life *Housing:* on-campus residence required through sophomore year. *Option:* coed. *Social organizations:* local fraternities, local sororities; 5% of eligible men and 5% of eligible women are members. *Most popular organizations:* Hawaiian Club, Education Club, NUTS (non-traditional students club).

Campus security 24-hour emergency response devices and patrols, late-night transport-escort service, night patrols by security personnel.

After graduation 150 organizations recruited on campus 1997–98. 93% of class of 1998 had job offers within 6 months. *Career center:* 2 full-time, 4 part-time personnel. Services include job fairs, resume preparation, interview workshops, resume referral, career/interest testing, career counseling, careers library, job bank, job interviews. *Graduate education:* 8% of class of 1999 went directly to graduate and professional school: 2% graduate arts and sciences, 2% medicine, 2% veterinary medicine, 1% business, 1% law.

Freshmen 248 applied, 234 admitted. 3 class presidents, 4 valedictorians, 15 student government officers.

Average high school GPA	3.25	SAT verbal scores above 500	62%
SAT math scores above 500	61%	ACT above 18	89%
From top 10% of their h.s. class	17%	From top quarter	42%
From top half	71%	1998 freshmen returning in 1999	69%

Application *Options:* eApply at www.CollegeQuest.com, Common Application, electronic application, deferred entrance. *Application fee:* $0. *Required:* essay or personal statement; high school transcript; minimum 2.5 GPA; 1 letter of recommendation. *Required for some:* interview.

Standardized tests *Admission: Required:* SAT I or ACT.

Significant dates *Application deadlines:* 8/1 (freshmen), 8/1 (transfers). *Notification:* continuous until 8/15 (freshmen). *Financial aid deadline priority date:* 3/1.

Freshman Application Contact
Ms. Carleen Jackson, Director of Enrollment Management and Marketing, Saint Martin's College, 5300 Pacific Avenue, SE, Lacey, WA 98503-7500. **Phone:** 360-491-4700. **Toll-free phone:** 800-368-8803. **Fax:** 360-459-4124. **E-mail:** admissions@stmartin.edu

Visit CollegeQuest.com for information on majors offered and athletics.

- *See page 2404 for a narrative description.*

SEATTLE PACIFIC UNIVERSITY
Seattle, Washington

- **Independent Free Methodist**, comprehensive, founded 1891
- **Degrees** bachelor's, master's, doctoral, and post-master's certificates
- **Urban** 35-acre campus
- **Coed**, 2,531 undergraduate students, 94% full-time, 66% women, 34% men
- **Moderately difficult** entrance level, 93% of applicants were admitted
- **16:1 student-to-undergraduate faculty ratio**
- **52% graduate** in 6 years or less
- **$14,934 tuition** and fees
- **$12,576 average financial aid** package, $16,550 average indebtedness upon graduation, $24 million endowment

All Seattle Pacific University residence halls have been wired to allow students dedicated online connections to e-mail, the Internet, and the campus computer network. Students may also access holdings in SPU's new 62,000-square-foot library, a spacious 4-level facility offering the latest technology for study and research.

Students *Undergraduates:* 2,377 full-time, 154 part-time. Students come from 39 states and territories, 34 other countries. *The most frequently chosen baccalaureate fields are:* business/marketing, health professions and related sciences, psychology. *Graduate:* 791 in graduate degree programs.

From out-of-state	36%	Reside on campus	59%
Age 25 or older	10%	Transferred in	9%
International students	3%	African Americans	2%
Asian Americans/Pacific Islanders	5%	Hispanic Americans	2%
Native Americans	1%		

Faculty 231 (66% full-time), 59% with terminal degrees.

Expenses (1999–2000) *Comprehensive fee:* $20,658 includes full-time tuition ($14,934) and room and board ($5724). *College room only:* $2982. Room and board charges vary according to board plan and housing facility. *Part-time tuition:* $238 per credit. Part-time tuition and fees vary according to course load. *Payment plan:* installment. *Waivers:* senior citizens and employees or children of employees.

Library Seattle Pacific University Library. *Operations spending 1999–2000:* $1.3 million. *Collection:* 128,506 titles, 1,356 serial subscriptions.

College life *Housing:* on-campus residence required through senior year. *Options:* coed, women-only. *Most popular organizations:* Centurions, Falconettes, Forensics, Amnesty International, University Players.

Campus security 24-hour emergency response devices and patrols, student patrols, late-night transport-escort service, closed circuit TV monitors.

Washington

Seattle Pacific University (continued)

After graduation 56 organizations recruited on campus 1997–98. 86% of class of 1998 had job offers within 6 months. *Career center:* 4 full-time, 3 part-time personnel. Services include job fairs, resume preparation, career/interest testing, career counseling, careers library, job bank, job interviews. *Graduate education:* 12% of class of 1999 went directly to graduate and professional school.

Freshmen 1,442 applied, 1,334 admitted, 571 enrolled. 8 National Merit Scholars, 41 valedictorians.

Average high school GPA	3.58	SAT verbal scores above 500	87%
SAT math scores above 500	76%	ACT above 18	97%
From top 10% of their h.s. class	42%	From top quarter	79%
From top half	97%	1998 freshmen returning in 1999	80%

Application *Options:* Common Application, electronic application, early admission, early action. *Application fee:* $35. *Required:* essay or personal statement; high school transcript; minimum 2.5 GPA; 2 letters of recommendation.

Standardized tests *Admission: Required:* SAT I or ACT. *Recommended:* SAT I.

Significant dates *Application deadlines:* 6/1 (freshmen), 8/1 (transfers). *Early action:* 12/1. *Notification:* 2/15 (early action). *Financial aid deadline priority date:* 1/31.

Freshman Application Contact
Mr. Ken Cornell, Director of Admissions, Seattle Pacific University, 3307 Third Avenue West, Seattle, WA 98119-1997. **Phone:** 206-281-2021. **Toll-free phone:** 800-366-3344. **E-mail:** admissions@spu.edu

Visit CollegeQuest.com for information on majors offered and athletics. Electronic viewbook available at CollegeQuest.com.

■ *See page 2466 for a narrative description.*

SEATTLE UNIVERSITY
Seattle, Washington

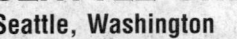

Apply at CollegeQuest.com

- **Independent Roman Catholic**, comprehensive, founded 1891
- **Degrees** bachelor's, master's, doctoral, first professional, post-master's, and postbachelor's certificates
- **Urban** 46-acre campus
- **Coed**, 3,208 undergraduate students, 89% full-time, 59% women, 41% men
- **Moderately difficult** entrance level, 80% of applicants were admitted
- **14:1** student-to-undergraduate faculty ratio
- **54% graduate** in 6 years or less
- **$16,110 tuition** and fees
- **$17,567 average financial aid** package, $122.4 million endowment

Students *Undergraduates:* 2,863 full-time, 345 part-time. Students come from 45 states and territories, 69 other countries. *The most frequently chosen baccalaureate fields are:* business/marketing, health professions and related sciences, psychology. *Graduate:* 982 in professional programs, 1,602 in other graduate degree programs.

From out-of-state	26%	Reside on campus	33%
Age 25 or older	19%	Transferred in	10%
International students	10%	African Americans	4%
Asian Americans/Pacific Islanders	20%	Hispanic Americans	5%
Native Americans	1%		

Faculty 454 (69% full-time).

Expenses (1999–2000) *One-time required fee:* $75. *Comprehensive fee:* $21,980 includes full-time tuition ($16,110) and room and board ($5870). *College room only:* $3825. Full-time tuition and fees vary according to course load. Room and board charges vary according to board plan and housing facility. *Part-time tuition:* $358 per credit hour. Part-time tuition and fees vary according to course load. *Payment plan:* installment. *Waivers:* employees or children of employees.

Library Lemieux Library. *Operations spending 1999–2000:* $3.1 million. *Collection:* 210,091 titles, 6,777 serial subscriptions.

College life *Housing:* on-campus residence required through sophomore year. *Options:* coed, disabled students. *Most popular organizations:* student government, volunteer center, Hawaiian Club, International Student Club.

Campus security 24-hour emergency response devices and patrols, late-night transport-escort service, controlled dormitory access, bicycle patrols.

After graduation 98 organizations recruited on campus 1997–98. *Career center:* 5 full-time, 3 part-time personnel. Services include job fairs, resume preparation, resume referral, career counseling, careers library, job bank, job interviews. *Major awards:* 1 Fulbright Scholar.

Freshmen 2,596 applied, 2,087 admitted, 579 enrolled.

Average high school GPA	3.43	SAT verbal scores above 500	80%
SAT math scores above 500	79%	ACT above 18	97%
From top 10% of their h.s. class	30%	From top quarter	56%
From top half	86%	1998 freshmen returning in 1999	83%

Application *Options:* eApply at www.CollegeQuest.com, Common Application, electronic application, early admission, deferred entrance. *Application fee:* $50. *Required:* essay or personal statement; high school transcript; minimum 2.5 GPA; 2 letters of recommendation.

Standardized tests *Admission: Required:* SAT I or ACT.

Significant dates *Application deadlines:* 7/1 (freshmen), 8/1 (transfers). *Financial aid deadline priority date:* 2/1.

Freshman Application Contact
Mr. Michael K. McKeon, Dean of Admissions, Seattle University, 900 Broadway, Seattle, WA 98122-4340. **Phone:** 206-296-5800. **Toll-free phone:** 800-542-0833 (in-state); 800-426-7123 (out-of-state). **Fax:** 206-296-5656. **E-mail:** admissions@seattleu.edu

Visit CollegeQuest.com for information on majors offered and athletics. College video and electronic viewbook available at CollegeQuest.com.

■ *See page 2468 for a narrative description.*

TRINITY LUTHERAN COLLEGE
Issaquah, Washington

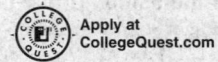

Apply at CollegeQuest.com

- **Independent Lutheran**, 4-year, founded 1944
- **Degrees** associate, bachelor's, and postbachelor's certificates
- **Suburban** 46-acre campus with easy access to Seattle
- **Coed**, 116 undergraduate students, 88% full-time, 64% women, 36% men
- **Minimally difficult** entrance level, 100% of applicants were admitted
- **11:1** student-to-undergraduate faculty ratio
- **$7746 tuition** and fees
- **$1.2 million endowment**

Students *Undergraduates:* 102 full-time, 14 part-time. Students come from 16 states and territories. *The most frequently chosen baccalaureate field is:* philosophy.

From out-of-state	43%	Age 25 or older	22%
Transferred in	15%	African Americans	7%
Asian Americans/Pacific Islanders	9%		

Expenses (1999–2000) *Comprehensive fee:* $12,271 includes full-time tuition ($6900), mandatory fees ($846), and room and board ($4525). *Part-time tuition:* $198 per credit. *Part-time fees:* $27 per credit. *Payment plan:* installment. *Waivers:* senior citizens and employees or children of employees.

Library Lutheran Bible Institute Library. *Operations spending 1999–2000:* $147,806. *Collection:* 31,000 titles, 217 serial subscriptions.

College life *Housing: Option:* coed. *Most popular organizations:* Environmental Commission, Student government, Worship Commission, Global Concerns, Activities Commission.

Campus security 24-hour emergency response devices, student patrols, controlled dormitory access.

After graduation 91% of class of 1998 had job offers within 6 months. *Career center:* 1 part-time personnel. Services include resume preparation, interview workshops, career/interest testing, career counseling, careers library, job bank. *Graduate education:* 8% of class of 1999 went directly to graduate and professional school: 8% theology.

Freshmen 32 applied, 32 admitted, 14 enrolled. 2 student government officers.

Average high school GPA	3.31	SAT verbal scores above 500	47%
SAT math scores above 500	53%	ACT above 18	93%
From top 10% of their h.s. class	25%	From top quarter	50%
From top half	50%	1998 freshmen returning in 1999	88%

Application *Options:* eApply at www.CollegeQuest.com, early admission, deferred entrance. *Application fee:* $30. *Required:* essay or personal statement; high school transcript; minimum 2.0 GPA; 2 letters of recommendation. *Required for some:* interview. *Recommended:* interview.
Standardized tests *Admission: Required:* SAT I or ACT.
Significant dates *Application deadlines:* 8/15 (freshmen), 8/15 (transfers). *Financial aid deadline priority date:* 3/1.
Freshman Application Contact
Ms. Sigrid Olsen Cutler, Director of Admission, Trinity Lutheran College, 4221 228th Avenue, SE, Issaquah, WA 98029-9299. **Phone:** 425-961-5516. **Toll-free phone:** 800-843-5659. **Fax:** 425-392-0404. **E-mail:** admission@tlc.edu
Visit CollegeQuest.com for information on majors offered and athletics.

UNIVERSITY OF PUGET SOUND
Tacoma, Washington

Apply at CollegeQuest.com

- **Independent**, comprehensive, founded 1888
- **Degrees** bachelor's and master's
- **Suburban** 97-acre campus with easy access to Seattle
- **Coed**, 2,695 undergraduate students, 96% full-time, 61% women, 39% men
- **Very difficult** entrance level, 74% of applicants were admitted
- **12:1** student-to-undergraduate faculty ratio
- **71.6% graduate** in 6 years or less
- **$20,605 tuition** and fees
- **$16,939 average financial aid** package, $20,259 average indebtedness upon graduation, $190.4 million endowment

Students *Undergraduates:* 2,597 full-time, 98 part-time. Students come from 48 states and territories, 16 other countries. *The most frequently chosen baccalaureate fields are:* business/marketing, English, social sciences and history. *Graduate:* 278 in graduate degree programs.

From out-of-state	68%	Reside on campus	54%
Age 25 or older	6%	Transferred in	4%
International students	1%	African Americans	2%
Asian Americans/Pacific Islanders	11%	Hispanic Americans	2%
Native Americans	1%		

Faculty 257 (82% full-time), 74% with terminal degrees.
Expenses (1999–2000) *Comprehensive fee:* $25,875 includes full-time tuition ($20,450), mandatory fees ($155), and room and board ($5270). *College room only:* $2880. Room and board charges vary according to board plan. *Part-time tuition:* $2580 per unit. *Payment plans:* installment, deferred payment. *Waivers:* employees or children of employees.
Library Collins Memorial Library. *Operations spending 1999–2000:* $2.6 million. *Collection:* 298,447 titles, 1,874 serial subscriptions, 19,423 audiovisual materials.
College life *Housing: Options:* coed, women-only, disabled students. *Social organizations:* national fraternities, national sororities; 25% of eligible men and 24% of eligible women are members. *Most popular organizations:* Hui-O-Hawaii, Repertory Dance Group, Circle K, outdoor programs, Lighthouse.
Campus security 24-hour emergency response devices and patrols, student patrols, late-night transport-escort service, controlled dormitory access, 24-hour locked residence hall entrances.
After graduation 141 organizations recruited on campus 1997–98. 70% of class of 1998 had job offers within 6 months. *Career center:* 8 full-time, 1 part-time personnel. Services include job fairs, resume preparation, interview workshops, resume referral, career/interest testing, career counseling, careers library, job bank, job interviews, job newsletter, alumni network, web page. *Graduate education:* 30% of class of 1999 went directly to graduate and professional school: 9% graduate arts and sciences, 5% business, 5% education, 5% law, 3% medicine, 1% dentistry, 1% engineering, 1% veterinary medicine.
Freshmen 4,138 applied, 3,069 admitted, 684 enrolled. 28 National Merit Scholars.

Average high school GPA	3.61	SAT verbal scores above 500	97%
SAT math scores above 500	96%	ACT above 18	100%
From top 10% of their h.s. class	47%	From top quarter	77%
From top half	96%	1998 freshmen returning in 1999	83%

Application *Options:* eApply at www.CollegeQuest.com, Common Application, electronic application, early admission, early decision, deferred entrance. *Application fee:* $40. *Required:* essay or personal statement; high school transcript; 2 letters of recommendation. *Recommended:* minimum 3.0 GPA; interview.
Standardized tests *Admission: Required:* SAT I or ACT.
Significant dates *Application deadlines:* 2/1 (freshmen), 6/1 (transfers). *Early decision:* 11/15 (for plan 1), 12/15 (for plan 2). *Notification:* 12/15 (early decision plan 1), 1/15 (early decision plan 2). *Financial aid deadline priority date:* 2/1.
Freshman Application Contact
Dr. George H. Mills, Vice President for Enrollment, University of Puget Sound, 1500 North Warner Street, Tacoma, WA 98416-0005. **Phone:** 253-879-3211. **Toll-free phone:** 800-396-7191. **Fax:** 253-879-3500. **E-mail:** admission@ups.edu
Visit CollegeQuest.com for information on majors offered and athletics. College video available at CollegeQuest.com.

■ *See page 2808 for a narrative description.*

UNIVERSITY OF WASHINGTON
Seattle, Washington

- **State-supported**, university, founded 1861
- **Degrees** bachelor's, master's, doctoral, and first professional
- **Urban** 703-acre campus
- **Coed**, 25,346 undergraduate students, 86% full-time, 52% women, 48% men
- **Moderately difficult** entrance level, 77% of applicants were admitted
- **11:1** student-to-undergraduate faculty ratio
- **71% graduate** in 6 years or less
- **$3638 tuition** and fees (in-state); $12,029 (out-of-state)
- **$8167 average financial aid** package, $963 million endowment

Students *Undergraduates:* 21,672 full-time, 3,674 part-time. Students come from 52 states and territories, 59 other countries. *The most frequently chosen baccalaureate fields are:* business/marketing, engineering/engineering technologies, social sciences and history. *Graduate:* 1,709 in professional programs, 8,212 in other graduate degree programs.

From out-of-state	11%	Reside on campus	17%
Age 25 or older	16%	Transferred in	8%
International students	2%	African Americans	3%
Asian Americans/Pacific Islanders	22%	Hispanic Americans	4%
Native Americans	1%		

Faculty 3,181 (82% full-time), 73% with terminal degrees.
Expenses (1999–2000) *Tuition, state resident:* full-time $3638. *Tuition, nonresident:* full-time $12,029. Part-time tuition and fees vary according to course load. *College room and board:* $4905. Room and board charges vary according to board plan. Part-time tuition per term ranges from $242 to $1092 for state residents, $802 to $3609 for nonresidents. *Payment plan:* installment. *Waivers:* employees or children of employees.
Library Suzzallo/Allen Library plus 21 others. *Operations spending 1999–2000:* $26.5 million. *Collection:* 5.8 million titles, 50,245 serial subscriptions, 1.4 million audiovisual materials.
College life *Housing: Options:* coed, disabled students. *Social organizations:* national fraternities, national sororities; 12% of eligible men and 11% of eligible women are members.
Campus security 24-hour emergency response devices and patrols, late-night transport-escort service, controlled dormitory access.
After graduation 450 organizations recruited on campus 1997–98. *Career center:* 17 full-time, 14 part-time personnel. Services include job fairs, resume preparation, resume referral, career counseling, careers library, job bank, job interviews. *Major awards:* 9 Fulbright Scholars.

Washington

University of Washington (continued)

Freshmen 12,785 applied, 9,817 admitted, 4,353 enrolled.

Average high school GPA	3.63	SAT verbal scores above 500	79%
SAT math scores above 500	86%	ACT above 18	96%
From top 10% of their h.s. class	39%	From top quarter	76%
From top half	97%	1998 freshmen returning in 1999	90%

Application *Options:* electronic application, early admission. *Preference* given to state residents, children of alumni. *Application fee:* $35. *Required:* essay or personal statement; high school transcript; minimum 2.0 GPA.

Standardized tests *Admission: Required:* SAT I or ACT.

Significant dates *Application deadlines:* 1/15 (freshmen), 4/15 (transfers). *Notification:* continuous until 4/15 (freshmen). *Financial aid deadline priority date:* 2/28.

Freshman Application Contact
Ms. Stephanie Preston, Assistant Director of Admissions, University of Washington, Office of Admissions, Box 355840, Seattle, WA 98195-5840. **Phone:** 206-543-9686. **E-mail:** askuwadm@u.washington.edu

Visit CollegeQuest.com for information on majors offered and athletics.

WALLA WALLA COLLEGE
College Place, Washington

- **Independent Seventh-day Adventist**, comprehensive, founded 1892
- **Degrees** associate, bachelor's, and master's
- **Small-town** 77-acre campus
- **Coed**, 1,519 undergraduate students, 87% full-time, 49% women, 51% men
- **Moderately difficult** entrance level, 73% of applicants were admitted
- **12:1 student-to-undergraduate faculty ratio**
- **$13,941 tuition** and fees
- **$14,166 average financial aid** package, $18,876 average indebtedness upon graduation, $9.1 million endowment

Students *Undergraduates:* 1,315 full-time, 204 part-time. Students come from 49 states and territories. *The most frequently chosen baccalaureate fields are:* engineering/engineering technologies, education, health professions and related sciences. *Graduate:* 247 in graduate degree programs.

From out-of-state	53%	Transferred in	10%
International students	3%	African Americans	2%
Asian Americans/Pacific Islanders	5%	Hispanic Americans	5%
Native Americans	0.3%		

Faculty 200 (61% full-time), 45% with terminal degrees.

Expenses (1999–2000) *Comprehensive fee:* $16,962 includes full-time tuition ($13,806), mandatory fees ($135), and room and board ($3021). *College room only:* $2034. Full-time tuition and fees vary according to course load, degree level, and location. Room and board charges vary according to gender, housing facility, and location. *Part-time tuition:* $365 per quarter hour. *Part-time fees:* $45 per term part-time. *Payment plan:* installment. *Waivers:* senior citizens and employees or children of employees.

Library Peterson Memorial Library plus 3 others. *Operations spending 1999–2000:* $1.8 million. *Collection:* 123,282 titles, 2,313 serial subscriptions, 2,935 audiovisual materials.

College life *Housing:* on-campus residence required through junior year. *Options:* men-only, women-only. *Most popular organizations:* Aleph Gimel Ain (women's club), Amnesty International, Associated Students of Walla Walla College (ASWWC), Omicron Pi Sigma (men's club), Village Singles' Club.

Campus security 24-hour emergency response devices and patrols, student patrols, late-night transport-escort service, controlled dormitory access.

After graduation 10 organizations recruited on campus 1997–98. *Career center:* 3 full-time, 2 part-time personnel. Services include job fairs, resume preparation, resume referral, career/interest testing, career counseling, careers library, job bank, job interviews.

Freshmen 518 applied, 378 admitted, 321 enrolled. 9 National Merit Scholars.

Average high school GPA	3.37	SAT verbal scores above 500	N/R
SAT math scores above 500	N/R	ACT above 18	86%
From top 10% of their h.s. class	10%	From top quarter	31%
From top half	59%		

Application *Options:* Common Application, electronic application, early admission, deferred entrance. *Application fee:* $30. *Required:* high school transcript; minimum 2.0 GPA; 3 letters of recommendation.

Standardized tests *Admission: Required:* SAT I or ACT.

Significant dates *Application deadlines:* rolling (freshmen), rolling (transfers). *Financial aid deadline:* continuous.

Freshman Application Contact
Mr. Dallas Weis, Director of Admissions, Walla Walla College, 204 South College Avenue, College Place, WA 99324. **Phone:** 509-527-2327. **Toll-free phone:** 800-541-8900. **Fax:** 509-527-2397. **E-mail:** info@wwc.edu

Visit CollegeQuest.com for information on majors offered and athletics. College video and electronic viewbook available at CollegeQuest.com.

WASHINGTON STATE UNIVERSITY
Pullman, Washington

- **State-supported**, university, founded 1890
- **Degrees** bachelor's, master's, doctoral, and first professional
- **Rural** 620-acre campus
- **Coed**, 16,585 undergraduate students, 86% full-time, 51% women, 49% men
- **Moderately difficult** entrance level, 84% of applicants were admitted
- **16:1 student-to-undergraduate faculty ratio**
- **59% graduate** in 6 years or less
- **$3662 tuition** and fees (in-state); $10,696 (out-of-state)
- **$10,500 average financial aid** package, $15,000 average indebtedness upon graduation, $417.9 million endowment

Students *Undergraduates:* 14,254 full-time, 2,331 part-time. Students come from 55 states and territories, 68 other countries. *The most frequently chosen baccalaureate fields are:* business/marketing, communications/communication technologies, social sciences and history. *Graduate:* 679 in professional programs, 3,033 in other graduate degree programs.

From out-of-state	9%	Reside on campus	49%
Age 25 or older	20%	Transferred in	12%
International students	3%	African Americans	2%
Asian Americans/Pacific Islanders	5%	Hispanic Americans	3%
Native Americans	2%		

Faculty 1,230 (87% full-time), 83% with terminal degrees.

Expenses (1999–2000) *Tuition, state resident:* full-time $3233; part-time $177 per credit. *Tuition, nonresident:* full-time $10,267; part-time $528 per credit. *Required fees:* full-time $429. Full-time tuition and fees vary according to reciprocity agreements. Part-time tuition and fees vary according to course load and reciprocity agreements. *College room and board:* $4618. Room and board charges vary according to board plan and housing facility. *Payment plans:* tuition prepayment, installment. *Waivers:* children of alumni, senior citizens, and employees or children of employees.

Library Holland Library plus 5 others. *Operations spending 1999–2000:* $12.4 million. *Collection:* 2 million titles, 27,377 serial subscriptions.

College life *Housing:* on-campus residence required in freshman year. *Options:* coed, men-only, women-only. *Social organizations:* national fraternities, national sororities; 17% of eligible men and 16% of eligible women are members.

Campus security 24-hour patrols, late-night transport-escort service.

After graduation 225 organizations recruited on campus 1997–98. *Career center:* 16 full-time, 1 part-time personnel. Services include job fairs, resume preparation, interview workshops, resume referral, career/interest testing, career counseling, careers library, job bank, job interviews. *Major awards:* 1 Fulbright Scholar.

Freshmen 7,132 applied, 6,009 admitted, 2,487 enrolled.

Average high school GPA	3.41	SAT verbal scores above 500	63%
SAT math scores above 500	64%	ACT above 18	N/R
1998 freshmen returning in 1999	83%		

Application *Options:* Common Application, electronic application, early admission. *Application fee:* $35. *Required:* high school transcript; minimum 2.0 GPA. *Required for some:* 3 letters of recommendation.

Standardized tests *Admission: Required:* SAT I or ACT.

Significant dates *Application deadlines:* 5/1 (freshmen), 5/1 (transfers). *Financial aid deadline priority date:* 3/1.

Freshman Application Contact
Kenneth Vreeland, Interim Director of Admissions, Washington State University, PO Box 641067, Pullman, WA 99164. **Phone:** 509-335-5586. **E-mail:** admiss@wsu.edu

Visit CollegeQuest.com for information on majors offered and athletics.

WESTERN WASHINGTON UNIVERSITY
Bellingham, Washington

- **State-supported**, comprehensive, founded 1893
- **Degrees** bachelor's, master's, and postbachelor's certificates
- **Small-town** 223-acre campus with easy access to Seattle and Vancouver
- **Coed**, 11,042 undergraduate students, 95% full-time, 56% women, 44% men
- **Moderately difficult** entrance level, 87% of applicants were admitted
- **20:1 student-to-undergraduate faculty ratio**
- **63% graduate** in 6 years or less
- **$2992 tuition** and fees (in-state); $9994 (out-of-state)
- **$6370 average financial aid** package, $3.6 million endowment

Western Washington University is an innovative public university considered to be among the foremost institutions in the Pacific Northwest. Western is recognized for excellence in undergraduate education, an increasingly diverse and multicultural learning environment, and a strong sense of community. Primary reasons for attending Western are academic reputation, location, size, job placement, and cost.

Students *Undergraduates:* 10,512 full-time, 530 part-time. Students come from 51 states and territories, 37 other countries. *The most frequently chosen baccalaureate fields are:* business/marketing, education, social sciences and history. *Graduate:* 658 in graduate degree programs.

From out-of-state	6%	Reside on campus	33%
Age 25 or older	13%	Transferred in	11%
International students	1%	African Americans	2%
Asian Americans/Pacific Islanders	7%	Hispanic Americans	3%
Native Americans	2%		

Faculty 615 (72% full-time), 73% with terminal degrees.

Expenses (1999–2000) *Tuition, state resident:* full-time $2738; part-time $91 per quarter hour. *Tuition, nonresident:* full-time $9740; part-time $325 per quarter hour. *Required fees:* full-time $254; $84 per term part-time. Part-time tuition and fees vary according to course load. *College room and board:* $5076. Room and board charges vary according to board plan and housing facility. *Payment plan:* installment. *Waivers:* senior citizens and employees or children of employees.

Library Wilson Library plus 3 others. *Operations spending 1999–2000:* $5.9 million. *Collection:* 786,760 titles, 4,995 serial subscriptions, 23,947 audiovisual materials.

College life *Housing: Option:* coed. *Most popular organizations:* Intramurals, Residence Hall Association, Associated Students, Outdoor Center, Ethnic Student Center.

Campus security 24-hour emergency response devices and patrols, student patrols, late-night transport-escort service, controlled dormitory access.

After graduation 60 organizations recruited on campus 1997–98. *Career center:* 7 full-time, 4 part-time personnel. Services include job fairs, resume preparation, interview workshops, resume referral, career/interest testing, career counseling, careers library, job bank, job interviews.

Freshmen 6,160 applied, 5,344 admitted, 2,086 enrolled. 7 National Merit Scholars, 59 valedictorians.

Average high school GPA	3.47	SAT verbal scores above 500	76%
SAT math scores above 500	76%	ACT above 18	96%
From top 10% of their h.s. class	23%	From top quarter	56%
From top half	89%	1998 freshmen returning in 1999	79%

Application *Option:* electronic application. *Application fee:* $35. *Required:* high school transcript; minimum 2.5 GPA. *Recommended:* essay or personal statement.

Standardized tests *Admission: Required:* SAT I or ACT.

Significant dates *Application deadlines:* 3/1 (freshmen), 4/1 (transfers). *Notification:* continuous until 4/15 (freshmen). **Financial aid deadline priority date:** 2/15.

Freshman Application Contact
Ms. Karen Copetas, Director of Admissions, Western Washington University, 516 High Street, Bellingham, WA 98225-9009. **Phone:** 360-650-3440 Ext. 3440. **E-mail:** admit@cc.wwu.edu

Visit CollegeQuest.com for information on majors offered and athletics. Electronic viewbook available at CollegeQuest.com.

WHITMAN COLLEGE
Walla Walla, Washington

Apply at CollegeQuest.com

- **Independent**, 4-year, founded 1859
- **Degree** bachelor's
- **Small-town** 55-acre campus
- **Coed**, 1,368 undergraduate students, 99% full-time, 57% women, 43% men
- **Very difficult** entrance level, 50% of applicants were admitted
- **10:1 student-to-undergraduate faculty ratio**
- **74.4% graduate** in 6 years or less
- **$21,742 tuition** and fees
- **$13,533 average financial aid** package, $12,431 average indebtedness upon graduation, $240.4 million endowment

Whitman College is committed to providing an excellent, well-rounded liberal arts and sciences undergraduate education. A concentration on basic disciplines combined with a supportive residential life program that encourages personal and social development is intended to foster intellectual vitality, confidence, leadership, and the flexibility to succeed in a changing technological and multicultural world. An active student-faculty research program, required senior projects, and comprehensive examinations challenge students in all areas of the arts and sciences. Whitman's location in Walla Walla, Washington, offers an ideal setting in the Pacific Northwest for a rigorous education, an active campus life, and a strong sense of community.

Students *Undergraduates:* 1,350 full-time, 18 part-time. Students come from 37 states and territories, 16 other countries. *The most frequently chosen baccalaureate fields are:* biological/life sciences, English, social sciences and history.

From out-of-state	53%	Reside on campus	71%
Age 25 or older	1%	Transferred in	2%
International students	2%	African Americans	1%
Asian Americans/Pacific Islanders	7%	Hispanic Americans	3%
Native Americans	1%		

Faculty 159 (67% full-time), 82% with terminal degrees.

Expenses (2000–2001) *Comprehensive fee:* $27,832 includes full-time tuition ($21,550), mandatory fees ($192), and room and board ($6090). *College room only:* $2790. Room and board charges vary according to board plan and housing facility. *Part-time tuition:* $900 per credit. *Payment plan:* deferred payment. *Waivers:* employees or children of employees.

Library Penrose Library plus 1 other. *Operations spending 1999–2000:* $1.7 million. *Collection:* 282,540 titles, 1,916 serial subscriptions, 1,754 audiovisual materials.

College life *Housing:* on-campus residence required through sophomore year. *Options:* coed, women-only. *Social organizations:* national fraternities, national sororities, local sororities; 37% of eligible men and 34% of eligible women are members. *Most popular organizations:* Associated Students of Whitman College, Interfraternity Council, Panhellenic, outing program, Center for Community Service.

Campus security 24-hour emergency response devices and patrols, student patrols, late-night transport-escort service, controlled dormitory access.

After graduation 25 organizations recruited on campus 1997–98. *Career center:* 3 full-time, 1 part-time personnel. Services include job fairs, resume preparation, interview workshops, resume referral, career/interest testing, career counseling, careers library, job bank, job interviews.

Freshmen 2,151 applied, 1,072 admitted, 368 enrolled. 22 National Merit Scholars, 42 valedictorians.

Average high school GPA	3.75	SAT verbal scores above 500	99%
SAT math scores above 500	99%	ACT above 18	100%
From top 10% of their h.s. class	63%	From top quarter	92%
From top half	100%	1998 freshmen returning in 1999	91%

Application *Options:* eApply at www.CollegeQuest.com, Common Application, electronic application, early admission, early decision, deferred

Washington–West Virginia

Whitman College (continued)
entrance. *Application fee:* $45. *Required:* essay or personal statement; high school transcript; 1 letter of recommendation. *Recommended:* interview.
Standardized tests *Admission: Required:* SAT I or ACT. *Recommended:* SAT II Subject Tests.
Significant dates *Application deadlines:* 2/1 (freshmen), 2/1 (transfers). *Early decision:* 11/15 (for plan 1), 1/1 (for plan 2). *Notification:* 4/1 (freshmen), 12/15 (early decision plan 1), 1/25 (early decision plan 2). *Financial aid deadline priority date:* 11/15.
Freshman Application Contact
Mr. John Bogley, Dean of Admission and Financial Aid, Whitman College, 345 Boyer Avenue, Walla Walla, WA 99362-2083. **Phone:** 509-527-5176. **Fax:** 509-527-4967. **E-mail:** admission@whitman.edu
Visit CollegeQuest.com for information on majors offered and athletics. College video available at CollegeQuest.com.

■ *See page 2984 for a narrative description.*

WHITWORTH COLLEGE
Spokane, Washington

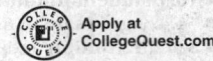 Apply at CollegeQuest.com

- **Independent Presbyterian**, comprehensive, founded 1890
- **Degrees** bachelor's and master's
- **Suburban** 200-acre campus
- **Coed**, 1,735 undergraduate students, 94% full-time, 61% women, 39% men
- **Very difficult** entrance level, 86% of applicants were admitted
- **15:1** student-to-undergraduate faculty ratio
- **60% graduate** in 6 years or less
- **$16,924 tuition** and fees
- **$14,550 average financial aid** package, $45 million endowment

Students *Undergraduates:* 1,625 full-time, 110 part-time. Students come from 27 states and territories, 26 other countries. *The most frequently chosen baccalaureate fields are:* business/marketing, education, visual/performing arts.

From out-of-state	45%	Reside on campus	60%
Age 25 or older	15%	Transferred in	7%
International students	2%	African Americans	1%
Asian Americans/Pacific Islanders	6%	Hispanic Americans	2%
Native Americans	1%		

Faculty 110 (84% full-time), 77% with terminal degrees.
Expenses (2000–2001) *Comprehensive fee:* $22,424 includes full-time tuition ($16,700), mandatory fees ($224), and room and board ($5500). Room and board charges vary according to board plan and housing facility. Part-time tuition and fees vary according to class time. *Payment plans:* tuition prepayment, installment. *Waivers:* children of alumni and employees or children of employees.
Library Harriet Cheney Cowles Library. *Operations spending 1999–2000:* $593,152. *Collection:* 135,373 titles, 725 serial subscriptions.
College life *Housing:* on-campus residence required through sophomore year. *Option:* coed. *Most popular organizations:* international club, Habitat for Humanity, En Christo, Hawaiian club, ski club.
Campus security 24-hour emergency response devices and patrols, late-night transport-escort service.
After graduation 125 organizations recruited on campus 1997–98. *Career center:* 3 full-time, 4 part-time personnel. Services include job fairs, resume preparation, resume referral, career counseling, careers library, job bank, job interviews. *Graduate education:* 20% of class of 1999 went directly to graduate and professional school.
Freshmen 1,291 applied, 1,106 admitted, 404 enrolled. 30 valedictorians.

Average high school GPA	3.56	SAT verbal scores above 500	50%
SAT math scores above 500	69%	ACT above 18	N/R
From top 10% of their h.s. class	44%	From top quarter	65%
From top half	95%	1998 freshmen returning in 1999	83%

Application *Options:* eApply at www.CollegeQuest.com, Common Application, electronic application, early admission, early action, deferred entrance. *Application fee:* $25. *Required:* essay or personal statement; high school transcript; letters of recommendation. *Required for some:* interview.
Standardized tests *Admission: Required:* SAT I or ACT.

Significant dates *Application deadlines:* 3/1 (freshmen), 7/1 (transfers). *Early action:* 11/30. *Notification:* 12/15 (early action). *Financial aid deadline priority date:* 3/1.
Freshman Application Contact
Mr. Fred Pfursich, Dean of Enrollment Services, Whitworth College, 300 West Hawthorne Road, Spokane, WA 99251-0001. **Phone:** 509-777-4348. **Toll-free phone:** 800-533-4668. **Fax:** 509-777-3773. **E-mail:** admission@whitworth.edu
Visit CollegeQuest.com for information on majors offered and athletics. College video available at CollegeQuest.com.

■ *See page 2988 for a narrative description.*

WEST VIRGINIA

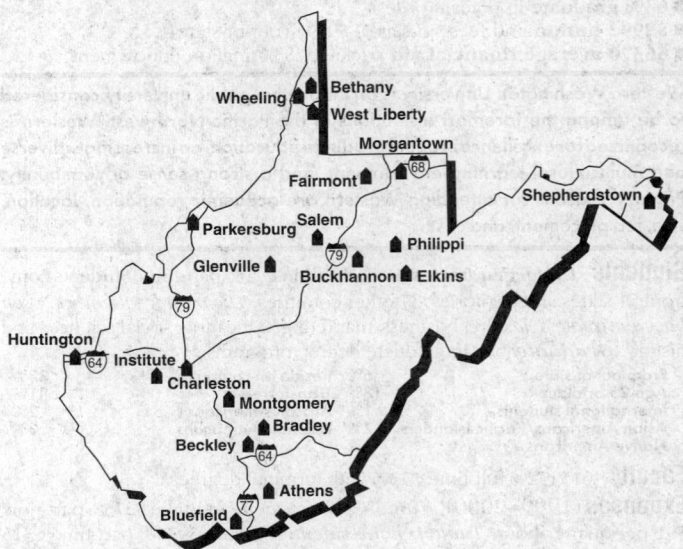

ALDERSON-BROADDUS COLLEGE
Philippi, West Virginia

- **Independent**, comprehensive, founded 1871, affiliated with American Baptist Churches in the U.S.A.
- **Degrees** associate, bachelor's, and master's
- **Rural** 170-acre campus
- **Coed**, 666 undergraduate students, 98% full-time, 61% women, 39% men
- **Moderately difficult** entrance level, 70% of applicants were admitted
- **13:1** student-to-undergraduate faculty ratio
- **$13,380 tuition** and fees
- **$12 million endowment**

Students *Undergraduates:* 656 full-time, 10 part-time. Students come from 35 states and territories, 4 other countries. *The most frequently chosen baccalaureate fields are:* education, health professions and related sciences, social sciences and history. *Graduate:* 56 in graduate degree programs.

From out-of-state	43%	Age 25 or older	33%
Transferred in	10%	International students	1%
African Americans	3%	Asian Americans/Pacific Islanders	3%
Hispanic Americans	1%	Native Americans	1%

Faculty 96 (61% full-time), 44% with terminal degrees.
Expenses (1999–2000) *Comprehensive fee:* $18,480 includes full-time tuition ($13,230), mandatory fees ($150), and room and board ($5100). *College room only:* $2490. Room and board charges vary according to housing facility. *Part-time tuition:* $437 per credit hour. *Part-time fees:* $38 per term part-time. *Payment plans:* installment, deferred payment. *Waivers:* employees or children of employees.
Library Pickett Library. *Collection:* 82,685 titles, 270 serial subscriptions.
College life *Housing:* on-campus residence required through senior year. *Options:* coed, women-only. *Social organizations:* local fraternities, local sororities; 10% of eligible men and 12% of eligible women are members. *Most popular organizations:* Baptist Campus Ministry, Collegiate 4-H, American

West Virginia

Academy of Physician Assistants, S.L.I.C.E. (Students Learning in Community Education), Association of Women Students.
Campus security 24-hour patrols, late-night transport-escort service, controlled dormitory access.
After graduation 10 organizations recruited on campus 1997–98. 69% of class of 1998 had job offers within 6 months. *Career center:* 1 full-time personnel. Services include job fairs, resume preparation, career/interest testing, career counseling, careers library. *Graduate education:* 15% of class of 1999 went directly to graduate and professional school: 6% law, 6% medicine, 3% theology.
Freshmen 916 applied, 637 admitted, 240 enrolled. 3 valedictorians.

Average high school GPA	3.1	SAT verbal scores above 500	60%
SAT math scores above 500	53%	ACT above 18	96%
From top 10% of their h.s. class	21%	From top quarter	48%
From top half	81%	1998 freshmen returning in 1999	69%

Application *Options:* early admission, deferred entrance. *Application fee:* $10. *Required:* high school transcript; minimum 2.0 GPA. *Required for some:* 3 letters of recommendation; interview.
Standardized tests *Admission: Required:* SAT I or ACT.
Significant dates *Application deadlines:* rolling (freshmen), rolling (transfers). *Notification:* continuous until 8/31 (freshmen). *Financial aid deadline priority date:* 3/1.
Freshman Application Contact
Kimberly Klaus, Assistant Director of Admissions, Alderson-Broaddus College, PO Box 2003, Philippi, WV 26416. **Phone:** 304-457-1700 Ext. 6255. **Toll-free phone:** 800-263-1549. **Fax:** 304-457-6239. **E-mail:** admissions@ab.edu
Visit CollegeQuest.com for information on majors offered and athletics. College video available at CollegeQuest.com.

■ *See page 1148 for a narrative description.*

APPALACHIAN BIBLE COLLEGE
Bradley, West Virginia

- **Independent nondenominational**, 4-year, founded 1950
- **Degrees** associate and bachelor's
- **Small-town** 110-acre campus
- **Coed**, 303 undergraduate students, 75% full-time, 48% women, 52% men
- **Minimally difficult** entrance level, 95% of applicants were admitted
- **17:1** student-to-undergraduate faculty ratio
- **29% graduate** in 6 years or less
- **$6132 tuition** and fees
- **$3116 average financial aid** package, $89,642 endowment

Students *Undergraduates:* 228 full-time, 75 part-time. Students come from 35 states and territories. *The most frequently chosen baccalaureate field is:* philosophy.

From out-of-state	58%	Age 25 or older	21%
Transferred in	11%	International students	1%
African Americans	1%	Asian Americans/Pacific Islanders	2%
Hispanic Americans	2%	Native Americans	1%

Faculty 24 (33% full-time), 29% with terminal degrees.
Expenses (2000–2001) *Comprehensive fee:* $9442 includes full-time tuition ($5112), mandatory fees ($1020), and room and board ($3310). *Part-time tuition:* $213 per credit hour. *Part-time fees:* $26 per credit hour. *Payment plan:* installment. *Waivers:* employees or children of employees.
Library John Van Pufflen Library. *Collection:* 42,409 titles, 349 serial subscriptions.
College life *Housing:* on-campus residence required through senior year. *Options:* men-only, women-only. *Most popular organization:* Campus Missionary Fellowship.
Campus security 24-hour emergency response devices, patrols by trained security personnel.
After graduation *Career center:* 1 full-time personnel. Services include resume referral, career counseling, job interviews.
Freshmen 106 applied, 101 admitted, 48 enrolled.

SAT verbal scores above 500	N/R	SAT math scores above 500	N/R
ACT above 18	N/R		

Application *Options:* early admission, deferred entrance. *Application fee:* $10. *Required:* essay or personal statement; high school transcript; 3 letters of recommendation. *Recommended:* minimum 2.0 GPA; interview.
Standardized tests *Admission: Required:* SAT I or ACT.
Significant dates *Application deadlines:* rolling (freshmen), rolling (transfers). *Notification:* continuous until 8/23 (freshmen). *Financial aid deadline priority date:* 3/1.
Freshman Application Contact
Ms. Angela Harding, Admissions Counselor, Appalachian Bible College, PO Box ABC, Bradley, WV 25818. **Phone:** 800-678-9ABC Ext. 3213. **Toll-free phone:** 800-678-9ABC. **E-mail:** admissions@appbibco.edu
Visit CollegeQuest.com for information on majors offered and athletics. College video available at CollegeQuest.com.

BETHANY COLLEGE
Bethany, West Virginia

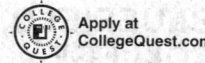
Apply at CollegeQuest.com

- **Independent**, 4-year, founded 1840, affiliated with Christian Church (Disciples of Christ)
- **Degree** bachelor's
- **Rural** 1,600-acre campus with easy access to Pittsburgh
- **Coed**, 707 undergraduate students, 99% full-time, 46% women, 54% men
- **Moderately difficult** entrance level, 70% of applicants were admitted
- **12:1** student-to-undergraduate faculty ratio
- **$18,574 tuition** and fees
- **$16,302 average financial aid** package, $16,500 average indebtedness upon graduation, $63.8 million endowment

Students *Undergraduates:* 706 full-time, 1 part-time. Students come from 30 states and territories, 23 other countries. *The most frequently chosen baccalaureate fields are:* education, psychology, social sciences and history.

From out-of-state	72%	Reside on campus	88%
Age 25 or older	3%	Transferred in	3%
International students	7%	African Americans	4%
Asian Americans/Pacific Islanders	0.3%	Hispanic Americans	1%
Native Americans	0.1%		

Faculty 66 (86% full-time), 71% with terminal degrees.
Expenses (1999–2000) *Comprehensive fee:* $24,696 includes full-time tuition ($18,230), mandatory fees ($344), and room and board ($6122). *College room only:* $2397. *Part-time tuition:* $686 per credit hour. *Part-time fees:* $344 per year part-time. *Payment plan:* installment. *Waivers:* employees or children of employees.
Library T. W. Phillips Memorial Library. *Operations spending 1999–2000:* $411,165. *Collection:* 123,699 titles, 514 serial subscriptions, 1,531 audiovisual materials.
College life *Housing:* on-campus residence required through senior year. *Options:* coed, men-only, women-only, disabled students. *Social organizations:* national fraternities, national sororities; 55% of eligible men and 50% of eligible women are members. *Most popular organizations:* Student Board of Governors, outdoor club, Model United Nations, Public Relations Society, International Student Association.
Campus security 24-hour emergency response devices and patrols, late-night transport-escort service.
After graduation 13 organizations recruited on campus 1997–98. 66% of class of 1998 had job offers within 6 months. *Career center:* 1 full-time, 2 part-time personnel. Services include job fairs, resume preparation, interview workshops, resume referral, career/interest testing, career counseling, careers library, job bank, job interviews.
Freshmen 802 applied, 562 admitted, 178 enrolled. 17 class presidents, 4 valedictorians, 131 student government officers.

Average high school GPA	3.2	SAT verbal scores above 500	56%
SAT math scores above 500	57%	ACT above 18	97%
From top 10% of their h.s. class	15%	From top quarter	46%
From top half	95%	1998 freshmen returning in 1999	81%

Application *Options:* eApply at www.CollegeQuest.com, Common Application, electronic application. *Application fee:* $25. *Required:* essay or personal statement; high school transcript; minimum 2.0 GPA; 1 letter of recommendation. *Required for some:* interview. *Recommended:* interview.
Standardized tests *Admission: Required:* SAT I or ACT.

West Virginia

Bethany College (continued)

Significant dates *Application deadlines:* 8/15 (freshmen), rolling (transfers). *Notification:* continuous until 8/15 (freshmen). *Financial aid deadline priority date:* 3/1.

Freshman Application Contact
Mr. Brian C. Ralph, Vice President for Enrollment Management, Bethany College, Office of Admission, Bethany, WV 26032. **Phone:** 304-829-7611. **Toll-free phone:** 800-922-7611. **Fax:** 304-829-7142. **E-mail:** admission@mail.bethanywv.edu

Visit CollegeQuest.com for information on majors offered and athletics. College video available at CollegeQuest.com.

■ *See page 1266 for a narrative description.*

BLUEFIELD STATE COLLEGE
Bluefield, West Virginia

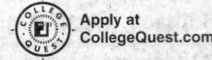
Apply at CollegeQuest.com

- **State-supported**, 4-year, founded 1895
- **Degrees** associate and bachelor's
- **Small-town** 45-acre campus
- **Coed**, 2,339 undergraduate students, 63% full-time, 59% women, 41% men
- **Noncompetitive** entrance level, 96% of applicants were admitted
- **16:1** student-to-undergraduate faculty ratio
- **41.3% graduate** in 6 years or less
- **$2178 tuition** and fees (in-state); $5290 (out-of-state)
- **$4500 average financial aid** package, $6800 average indebtedness upon graduation, $5.1 million endowment

Part of State College System of West Virginia.
Students *Undergraduates:* 1,465 full-time, 874 part-time. Students come from 8 states and territories, 6 other countries. *The most frequently chosen baccalaureate fields are:* business/marketing, engineering/engineering technologies, protective services/public administration.

From out-of-state	5%	Age 25 or older	39%
Transferred in	12%	International students	1%
African Americans	9%	Asian Americans/Pacific Islanders	0.3%
Hispanic Americans	0.3%	Native Americans	0.3%

Faculty 172 (48% full-time).
Expenses (1999–2000) *Tuition, state resident:* full-time $2178; part-time $91 per credit hour. *Tuition, nonresident:* full-time $5290; part-time $222 per credit hour. Full-time tuition and fees vary according to program and reciprocity agreements. Part-time tuition and fees vary according to course load, program, and reciprocity agreements. *Payment plan:* deferred payment. *Waivers:* senior citizens.
Library Hardway Library. *Operations spending 1999–2000:* $448,986. *Collection:* 90,436 titles, 462 serial subscriptions, 341 audiovisual materials.
College life *Housing:* college housing not available. *Social organizations:* national fraternities, national sororities, local fraternities, local sororities; 5% of eligible men and 8% of eligible women are members. *Most popular organizations:* Phi Eta Sigma, Student Nurses Association, Student Government Association, Minorities on the Move.
Campus security 24-hour emergency response devices and patrols, student patrols.
After graduation 53 organizations recruited on campus 1997–98. 67% of class of 1998 had job offers within 6 months. *Career center:* 2 full-time personnel. Services include job fairs, resume preparation, interview workshops, resume referral, career/interest testing, career counseling, careers library, job bank, job interviews. *Graduate education:* 7% of class of 1999 went directly to graduate and professional school: 4% business, 1% engineering, 1% law, 1% medicine.
Freshmen 1,319 applied, 1,270 admitted, 472 enrolled. 3 class presidents, 6 valedictorians, 32 student government officers.

Average high school GPA	2.85	SAT verbal scores above 500	N/R
SAT math scores above 500	N/R	ACT above 18	62%
From top 10% of their h.s. class	8%	From top quarter	25%
From top half	70%	1998 freshmen returning in 1999	53%

Application *Options:* eApply at www.CollegeQuest.com, Common Application, electronic application, deferred entrance. *Application fee:* $0. *Required:* high school transcript; minimum 2.0 GPA.

Standardized tests *Admission: Recommended:* SAT I or ACT.
Significant dates *Application deadlines:* rolling (freshmen), rolling (transfers). *Financial aid deadline priority date:* 3/1.
Freshman Application Contact
Mr. John C. Cardwell, Director of Enrollment Management, Bluefield State College, 219 Rock Street, Bluefield, WV 24701-2198. **Phone:** 304-327-4068. **Toll-free phone:** 800-344-8892 Ext. 4065 (in-state); 800-654-7798 Ext. 4065 (out-of-state). **Fax:** 304-327-7747. **E-mail:** bscadmit@bscvax.wvnet.edu
Visit CollegeQuest.com for information on majors offered and athletics. College video available at CollegeQuest.com.

THE COLLEGE OF WEST VIRGINIA
Beckley, West Virginia

- **Independent**, comprehensive, founded 1933
- **Degrees** associate, bachelor's, and master's
- **Small-town** 7-acre campus
- **Coed**, 1,948 undergraduate students, 77% full-time, 68% women, 32% men
- **Noncompetitive** entrance level, 50% of applicants were admitted
- **14:1** student-to-undergraduate faculty ratio
- **$3840 tuition** and fees
- **$8124 average financial aid** package, $11,423 average indebtedness upon graduation, $3.4 million endowment

Students *Undergraduates:* 1,495 full-time, 453 part-time. *The most frequently chosen baccalaureate fields are:* business/marketing, health professions and related sciences, interdisciplinary studies. *Graduate:* 29 in graduate degree programs.

From out-of-state	2%	Age 25 or older	44%
Transferred in	8%	African Americans	8%
Asian Americans/Pacific Islanders	3%	Hispanic Americans	1%
Native Americans	0.4%		

Faculty 146 (40% full-time).
Expenses (1999–2000) *Comprehensive fee:* $8216 includes full-time tuition ($3240), mandatory fees ($600), and room and board ($4376). *College room only:* $2160. Full-time tuition and fees vary according to program. Room and board charges vary according to board plan. *Part-time tuition:* $135 per semester hour. *Part-time fees:* $25 per semester hour. Part-time tuition and fees vary according to program. *Payment plan:* installment. *Waivers:* adult students and employees or children of employees.
Library Robert C. Byrd Learning Resource Center plus 1 other. *Operations spending 1999–2000:* $287,074. *Collection:* 75,000 titles, 1,162 audiovisual materials.
College life *Housing:* on-campus residence required through sophomore year. *Option:* coed. *Most popular organizations:* Student Christian Organization, astronomy club, Creative Writing Group, Gay, Lesbian, and Bisexual Student Support Group, Student Government Association.
Campus security 24-hour emergency response devices, late-night transport-escort service, controlled dormitory access, night patrols by security.
After graduation 55 organizations recruited on campus 1997–98. *Career center:* 1 full-time, 1 part-time personnel. Services include job fairs, resume preparation, interview workshops, resume referral, career/interest testing, career counseling, careers library, job bank.
Freshmen 732 applied, 363 admitted, 226 enrolled. 1 National Merit Scholar, 2 valedictorians.

| SAT verbal scores above 500 | 42% | SAT math scores above 500 | 21% |
| ACT above 18 | 50% | 1998 freshmen returning in 1999 | 65% |

Application *Options:* Common Application, electronic application, early admission, deferred entrance. *Required:* high school transcript.
Standardized tests *Placement: Required:* SAT I or ACT.
Significant dates *Application deadlines:* rolling (freshmen), rolling (transfers). *Financial aid deadline priority date:* 3/1.
Freshman Application Contact
Marketing Department, The College of West Virginia, P.O. Box A6, Beckley, WV 25802. **Phone:** 304-253-7351 Ext. 1433. **Toll-free phone:** 800-766-6067. **Fax:** 304-253-5072. **E-mail:** gocwv@@cwv.edu
Visit CollegeQuest.com for information on majors offered and athletics.

■ *See page 1492 for a narrative description.*

West Virginia

CONCORD COLLEGE
Athens, West Virginia

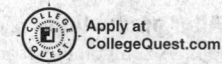
Apply at CollegeQuest.com

- **State-supported**, 4-year, founded 1872
- **Degrees** associate and bachelor's
- **Rural** 100-acre campus
- **Coed**, 2,630 undergraduate students, 87% full-time, 57% women, 43% men
- **Minimally difficult** entrance level, 74% of applicants were admitted
- **21:1 student-to-undergraduate faculty ratio**
- **80% graduate** in 6 years or less
- **$2538 tuition** and fees (in-state); $5580 (out-of-state)
- **$4800 average financial aid** package, $10,000 average indebtedness upon graduation, $14 million endowment

Part of State College System of West Virginia.

Students *Undergraduates:* 2,278 full-time, 352 part-time. Students come from 26 states and territories, 26 other countries. *The most frequently chosen baccalaureate fields are:* business/marketing, education, social sciences and history.

From out-of-state	11%	Reside on campus	35%
Age 25 or older	16%	Transferred in	7%
International students	0.3%	African Americans	6%
Asian Americans/Pacific Islanders	1%	Hispanic Americans	1%
Native Americans	0.3%		

Faculty 191 (46% full-time), 31% with terminal degrees.

Expenses (1999–2000) *One-time required fee:* $40. *Tuition, state resident:* full-time $2538; part-time $106 per semester hour. *Tuition, nonresident:* full-time $5580; part-time $233 per semester hour. Full-time tuition and fees vary according to program. Part-time tuition and fees vary according to program. *College room and board:* $4018; room only: $1844. Room and board charges vary according to board plan and housing facility. *Payment plans:* installment, deferred payment. *Waivers:* employees or children of employees.

Library J. Frank Marsh Library. *Operations spending 1999–2000:* $627,845. *Collection:* 142,876 titles, 542 serial subscriptions.

College life *Housing:* on-campus residence required through senior year. *Options:* coed, men-only, women-only. *Social organizations:* national fraternities, national sororities, local fraternities, local sororities; 20% of eligible men and 25% of eligible women are members. *Most popular organizations:* Student Union Board, student government, student-run publications, Greek organizations, music groups.

Campus security 24-hour patrols, late-night transport-escort service.

After graduation 25 organizations recruited on campus 1997–98. 40% of class of 1998 had job offers within 6 months. *Career center:* 3 full-time personnel. Services include job fairs, resume preparation, resume referral, career counseling, careers library, job interviews.

Freshmen 1,672 applied, 1,231 admitted, 632 enrolled. 22 valedictorians.

Average high school GPA	3.75	SAT verbal scores above 500	52%
SAT math scores above 500	48%	ACT above 18	74%
From top 10% of their h.s. class	21%	From top quarter	46%
From top half	77%	1998 freshmen returning in 1999	64%

Application *Options:* eApply at www.CollegeQuest.com, Common Application, early admission. *Application fee:* $0. *Required:* high school transcript; minimum 2.0 GPA. *Recommended:* interview.

Standardized tests *Admission: Required:* SAT I or ACT. *Recommended:* ACT.

Significant dates *Application deadlines:* rolling (freshmen), rolling (transfers). *Financial aid deadline priority date:* 4/15.

Freshman Application Contact
Mr. Michael Curry, Vice President of Admissions and Financial Aid, Concord College, 1000 Vermillion Street, Athens, WV 24712. **Phone:** 304-384-5248. **Toll-free phone:** 888-384-5249. **Fax:** 304-384-9044. **E-mail:** admissions@concord.edu

Visit CollegeQuest.com for information on majors offered and athletics. College video available at CollegeQuest.com.

■ *See page 1520 for a narrative description.*

DAVIS & ELKINS COLLEGE
Elkins, West Virginia

- **Independent Presbyterian**, 4-year, founded 1904
- **Degrees** associate and bachelor's
- **Small-town** 170-acre campus
- **Coed**
- **Minimally difficult** entrance level
- **$12,280 tuition** and fees

Expenses (1999–2000) *Comprehensive fee:* $17,610 includes full-time tuition ($12,080), mandatory fees ($200), and room and board ($5330). *College room only:* $2370. *Part-time tuition:* $485 per credit. *Part-time fees:* $50 per term part-time. Part-time tuition and fees vary according to course load.

Institutional Web site http://www.dne.edu/

College life *Housing:* on-campus residence required through senior year. *Options:* coed, men-only, women-only, disabled students. *Social organizations:* national fraternities, national sororities; 16% of eligible men and 16% of eligible women are members. *Most popular organizations:* Beta Alpha Beta, campus radio station, Student Nurses Association, Student Education Association, International Student Organization.

Campus security Late-night transport-escort service, controlled dormitory access, late night security personnel.

Application *Options:* Common Application, electronic application, early admission, deferred entrance. *Application fee:* $25. *Required:* high school transcript; minimum 2.0 GPA. *Recommended:* interview.

Standardized tests *Admission: Required:* SAT I or ACT.

Admissions Office Contact
Davis & Elkins College, 100 Campus Drive, Elkins, WV 26241-3996. **Toll-free phone:** 800-624-3157. **Fax:** 304-637-1800. **E-mail:** admiss@dne.wvnet.edu

Visit CollegeQuest.com for information on athletics. College video and electronic viewbook available at CollegeQuest.com.

■ *See page 1564 for a narrative description.*

FAIRMONT STATE COLLEGE
Fairmont, West Virginia

- **State-supported**, 4-year, founded 1865
- **Degrees** associate and bachelor's
- **Small-town** 80-acre campus
- **Coed**, 6,645 undergraduate students, 68% full-time, 56% women, 44% men
- **Minimally difficult** entrance level, 99.9% of applicants were admitted
- **18:1 student-to-undergraduate faculty ratio**
- **22% graduate** in 6 years or less
- **$2244 tuition** and fees (in-state); $5228 (out-of-state)
- **$4090 average financial aid** package, $6.4 million endowment

Part of State College System of West Virginia.

Students *Undergraduates:* 4,498 full-time, 2,147 part-time. Students come from 24 states and territories, 17 other countries. *The most frequently chosen baccalaureate fields are:* business/marketing, education, protective services/public administration.

From out-of-state	6%	Reside on campus	6%
Age 25 or older	26%	Transferred in	5%
International students	1%	African Americans	3%
Asian Americans/Pacific Islanders	0.5%	Hispanic Americans	1%
Native Americans	0.2%		

Faculty 437 (45% full-time), 28% with terminal degrees.

Expenses (1999–2000) *One-time required fee:* $29. *Tuition, state resident:* full-time $2244; part-time $94 per credit. *Tuition, nonresident:* full-time $5228; part-time $218 per credit. Full-time tuition and fees vary according to program. Part-time tuition and fees vary according to program. *College room and board:* $3882; room only: $1786. Room and board charges vary according to board plan. *Payment plans:* installment, deferred payment. *Waivers:* employees or children of employees.

Library Musick Library. *Operations spending 1999–2000:* $936,519. *Collection:* 1,175 serial subscriptions, 7,298 audiovisual materials.

College life *Housing: Options:* coed, men-only, women-only. *Social organizations:* national fraternities, national sororities, local fraternities; 1%

West Virginia

Fairmont State College (continued)

of eligible men and 2% of eligible women are members. *Most popular organizations:* Alpha Phi Omega, Circle K, Society for Non-traditional Students, Criminal Justice Club, Honors Association.

Campus security 24-hour emergency response devices and patrols, student patrols, controlled dormitory access.

After graduation 105 organizations recruited on campus 1997–98. 86% of class of 1998 had job offers within 6 months. *Career center:* 2 full-time, 1 part-time personnel. Services include job fairs, resume preparation, resume referral, career counseling, careers library, job bank, job interviews.

Freshmen 2,140 applied, 2,138 admitted, 1,111 enrolled. 12 valedictorians.

Average high school GPA	2.6	SAT verbal scores above 500	N/R
SAT math scores above 500	N/R	ACT above 18	61%
From top 10% of their h.s. class	12%	From top quarter	25%
From top half	66%	1998 freshmen returning in 1999	64%

Application *Options:* Common Application, electronic application, early admission. *Application fee:* $0. *Required:* high school transcript. *Recommended:* minimum 2.0 GPA.

Standardized tests *Admission: Required:* SAT I or ACT.

Significant dates *Application deadlines:* 6/15 (freshmen), 6/15 (transfers). *Financial aid deadline priority date:* 3/1.

Freshman Application Contact
Dr. John G. Conaway, Director of Admissions, Fairmont State College, 1201 Locust Avenue, Fairmont, WV 26554. **Phone:** 304-367-4141. **Toll-free phone:** 800-641-5678. **Fax:** 304-367-4789. **E-mail:** admit@fscvax.fairmont.wvnet.edu

Visit CollegeQuest.com for information on majors offered and athletics.

■ *See page 1650 for a narrative description.*

GLENVILLE STATE COLLEGE
Glenville, West Virginia

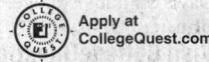
Apply at CollegeQuest.com

- **State-supported**, 4-year, founded 1872
- **Degrees** associate and bachelor's
- **Rural** 331-acre campus
- **Coed**, 2,260 undergraduate students
- **Noncompetitive** entrance level, 99.9% of applicants were admitted
- **$2208 tuition** and fees (in-state); $5208 (out-of-state)
- **$5885 average financial aid** package, $12,116 average indebtedness upon graduation, $1.1 million endowment

Glenville State is a small state-assisted college located in rural central West Virginia. Although the major academic emphasis is on traditional 4-year baccalaureate degree programs such as education, behavioral science, and business administration, Glenville State also offers highly successful associate-level programs in a variety of technical fields. The campus setting is tranquil, picturesque, and safe.

Part of State College System of West Virginia.

Students *Undergraduates:* Students come from 10 states and territories, 6 other countries. *The most frequently chosen baccalaureate fields are:* business/marketing, education, psychology.

From out-of-state	5%	Reside on campus	30%
Age 25 or older	27%		

Faculty 201 (36% full-time), 19% with terminal degrees.

Expenses (1999–2000) *Tuition, state resident:* full-time $2208; part-time $92 per credit hour. *Tuition, nonresident:* full-time $5208; part-time $217 per credit hour. *College room and board:* $3710. Room and board charges vary according to board plan and housing facility. *Payment plan:* installment.

Library Robert F. Kidd Library. *Operations spending 1999–2000:* $448,781. *Collection:* 120,540 titles, 1,448 serial subscriptions.

College life *Housing:* Option: coed. *Social organizations:* national fraternities, national sororities; 2% of eligible men and 2% of eligible women are members. *Most popular organizations:* percussion ensemble, student government, band, choir, Fellowship of Christian Athletes.

Campus security 24-hour patrols.

After graduation 22 organizations recruited on campus 1997–98. *Career center:* 2 full-time personnel. Services include job fairs, resume preparation, interview workshops, career/interest testing, career counseling, careers library, job bank, job interviews.

Freshmen 1,153 applied, 1,152 admitted.

SAT verbal scores above 500	37%	SAT math scores above 500	30%
ACT above 18	N/R		

Application *Options:* eApply at www.CollegeQuest.com, Common Application, electronic application, early admission. *Application fee:* $0. *Required:* high school transcript; minimum 2.0 GPA.

Standardized tests *Admission: Required:* SAT I or ACT.

Significant dates *Application deadlines:* 8/1 (freshmen), 6/1 (transfers). *Financial aid deadline priority date:* 3/1.

Freshman Application Contact
Ms. Brenda McCartney, Records Assistant, Glenville State College, 200 High Street, Glenville, WV 26351-1200. **Phone:** 304-462-4117. **Toll-free phone:** 800-924-2010. **Fax:** 304-462-8619. **E-mail:** simon@glenville.wvnet.edu

Visit CollegeQuest.com for information on majors offered and athletics.

MARSHALL UNIVERSITY
Huntington, West Virginia

- **State-supported**, comprehensive, founded 1837
- **Degrees** associate, bachelor's, master's, doctoral, first professional, and post-master's certificates
- **Urban** 70-acre campus
- **Coed**, 9,169 undergraduate students, 86% full-time, 55% women, 45% men
- **Minimally difficult** entrance level, 98% of applicants were admitted
- **22:1 student-to-undergraduate faculty ratio**
- **$2886 tuition** and fees (in-state); $6958 (out-of-state)
- **$5358 average financial aid** package, $13,020 average indebtedness upon graduation, $41 million endowment

Part of University System of West Virginia.

Students *Undergraduates:* 7,888 full-time, 1,281 part-time. Students come from 41 states and territories, 37 other countries. *The most frequently chosen baccalaureate fields are:* business/marketing, education, liberal arts/general studies. *Graduate:* 207 in professional programs, 3,738 in other graduate degree programs.

From out-of-state	15%	Reside on campus	20%
Age 25 or older	17%	Transferred in	6%
International students	1%	African Americans	4%
Asian Americans/Pacific Islanders	1%	Hispanic Americans	0.5%
Native Americans	1%		

Faculty 735 (59% full-time), 53% with terminal degrees.

Expenses (1999–2000) *Tuition, state resident:* full-time $2440; part-time $83 per semester hour. *Tuition, nonresident:* full-time $6512; part-time $253 per semester hour. *Required fees:* full-time $446; $19 per semester hour. Full-time tuition and fees vary according to program and reciprocity agreements. Part-time tuition and fees vary according to program and reciprocity agreements. *College room and board:* $4652; room only: $2432. Room and board charges vary according to board plan and housing facility. *Payment plans:* installment, deferred payment.

Library John Deaver Drinko Library plus 2 others. *Operations spending 1999–2000:* $4.5 million. *Collection:* 397,958 titles, 2,921 serial subscriptions, 18,935 audiovisual materials.

College life *Housing:* on-campus residence required through sophomore year. *Options:* coed, men-only, women-only, disabled students. *Social organizations:* national fraternities, national sororities; 6% of eligible men and 3% of eligible women are members. *Most popular organizations:* Gamma Beta Phi, MUEMS, Newman Center Student Organization, Phi Eta Sigma, Campus Crusade for Christ.

Campus security 24-hour emergency response devices and patrols, student patrols, late-night transport-escort service.

After graduation 410 organizations recruited on campus 1997–98. *Career center:* 4 full-time, 3 part-time personnel. Services include job fairs, resume preparation, interview workshops, resume referral, career/interest testing, career counseling, careers library, job bank, job interviews.

West Virginia

Freshmen 2,278 applied, 2,241 admitted, 1,847 enrolled.

Average high school GPA	3.23	SAT verbal scores above 500	N/R
SAT math scores above 500	N/R	ACT above 18	83%
From top quarter of their h.s. class	48%	From top half	81%
1998 freshmen returning in 1999	72%		

Application *Options:* Common Application, electronic application, early admission, deferred entrance. *Application fee:* $30 for nonresidents. *Required:* high school transcript; minimum 2.0 GPA.
Standardized tests *Admission: Required:* SAT I or ACT.
Significant dates *Application deadlines:* rolling (freshmen), rolling (transfers). *Financial aid deadline priority date:* 3/1.
Freshman Application Contact
Dr. James W. Harless, Admissions Director, Marshall University, 400 Hal Greer Boulevard, Huntington, WV 25755. **Phone:** 304-696-3160. **Toll-free phone:** 800-642-3499. **Fax:** 304-696-3135. **E-mail:** admissions@marshall.edu
Visit CollegeQuest.com for information on majors offered and athletics. College video available at CollegeQuest.com.

■ *See page 1994 for a narrative description.*

OHIO VALLEY COLLEGE
Parkersburg, West Virginia

- **Independent**, 4-year, founded 1960, affiliated with Church of Christ
- **Degrees** associate and bachelor's
- **Small-town** 299-acre campus
- **Coed**, 407 undergraduate students, 94% full-time, 52% women, 48% men
- **Minimally difficult** entrance level, 100% of applicants were admitted
- **15:1 student-to-undergraduate faculty ratio**
- **26% graduate** in 6 years or less
- **$7528 tuition** and fees
- **$8251 average financial aid** package, $17,780 average indebtedness upon graduation, $6 million endowment

Students *Undergraduates:* 383 full-time, 24 part-time. Students come from 19 states and territories, 8 other countries. *The most frequently chosen baccalaureate fields are:* business/marketing, education, psychology.

From out-of-state	42%	Reside on campus	55%
Age 25 or older	27%	Transferred in	15%
International students	3%	African Americans	5%
Asian Americans/Pacific Islanders	1%	Hispanic Americans	1%

Faculty 35 (46% full-time), 89% with terminal degrees.
Expenses (1999–2000) *One-time required fee:* $37. *Comprehensive fee:* $11,528 includes full-time tuition ($6860), mandatory fees ($668), and room and board ($4000). Full-time tuition and fees vary according to course load. Room and board charges vary according to board plan. *Part-time tuition:* $215 per credit hour. Part-time tuition and fees vary according to course load. *Payment plan:* installment. *Waivers:* senior citizens and employees or children of employees.
Library Icy Belle Library. *Operations spending 1999–2000:* $121,061. *Collection:* 30,913 titles, 406 serial subscriptions, 5,869 audiovisual materials.
College life *Housing:* on-campus residence required through junior year. *Options:* men-only, women-only. *Social organizations:* local fraternities, local sororities; 78% of eligible men and 80% of eligible women are members. *Most popular organizations:* Mission Club, Women for Christ, Timothy Club, Ambassador.
Campus security 24-hour emergency response devices, late-night transport-escort service.
After graduation *Career center:* 1 full-time personnel. Services include resume preparation, interview workshops, career/interest testing, career counseling, careers library.
Freshmen 245 applied, 245 admitted, 88 enrolled. 6 valedictorians, 23 student government officers.

Average high school GPA	3.0	SAT verbal scores above 500	57%
SAT math scores above 500	40%	ACT above 18	80%
From top 10% of their h.s. class	13%	From top quarter	23%
From top half	66%	1998 freshmen returning in 1999	55%

Application *Options:* Common Application, electronic application, early admission, early action, deferred entrance. *Application fee:* $20. *Required:* high school transcript.
Standardized tests *Admission: Required:* SAT I or ACT.

Significant dates *Application deadlines:* rolling (freshmen), rolling (transfers). *Early action:* 9/1. *Notification:* 10/1 (early action). *Financial aid deadline priority date:* 3/1.
Freshman Application Contact
Mr. Larry R. Lyons, Director of Admissions, Vice President for Enrollment, Ohio Valley College, 4501 College Parkway, Parkersburg, WV 26101-8100. **Phone:** 304-485-7384 Ext. 123. **Toll-free phone:** 800-678-6780. **Fax:** 304-485-3106. **E-mail:** admissions@juno.com
Visit CollegeQuest.com for information on majors offered and athletics. College video available at CollegeQuest.com.

SALEM-TEIKYO UNIVERSITY
Salem, West Virginia

- **Independent**, comprehensive, founded 1888
- **Degrees** associate, bachelor's, and master's
- **Rural** 300-acre campus
- **Coed**
- **Minimally difficult** entrance level
- **$12,840 tuition** and fees

Expenses (1999–2000) *Comprehensive fee:* $17,168 includes full-time tuition ($12,800), mandatory fees ($40), and room and board ($4328). Full-time tuition and fees vary according to course load and program. *Part-time tuition:* $264 per credit. *Part-time fees:* $5 per term part-time. Part-time tuition and fees vary according to course load and program.
Institutional Web site http://www.salem-teikyo.wvnet.edu/
College life *Housing:* on-campus residence required through junior year. *Options:* coed, men-only, women-only. *Social organizations:* national fraternities, national sororities, local fraternities, local sororities; 30% of eligible men and 30% of eligible women are members. *Most popular organizations:* National Honor Society, Humanics Student Association, equestrian club, Alpha Phi Omega service fraternity, LIGHT.
Campus security 24-hour emergency response devices and patrols, late-night transport-escort service, controlled dormitory access.
Application *Options:* eApply at www.CollegeQuest.com, electronic application, deferred entrance. *Application fee:* $25. *Required:* high school transcript. *Required for some:* interview. *Recommended:* essay or personal statement; interview.
Standardized tests *Placement: Required:* SAT I or ACT
Admissions Office Contact
Salem-Teikyo University, PO Box 500, Salem, WV 26426-0500. **Toll-free phone:** 800-283-4562. **E-mail:** admiss_new@salem.wvnet.edu
Visit CollegeQuest.com for information on athletics.

■ *See page 2436 for a narrative description.*

SHEPHERD COLLEGE
Shepherdstown, West Virginia

- **State-supported**, 4-year, founded 1871
- **Degrees** associate and bachelor's
- **Small-town** 320-acre campus with easy access to Washington, DC
- **Coed**, 3,379 undergraduate students, 82% full-time, 58% women, 42% men
- **Moderately difficult** entrance level, 84% of applicants were admitted
- **19:1 student-to-undergraduate faculty ratio**
- **40% graduate** in 6 years or less
- **$2430 tuition** and fees (in-state); $5754 (out-of-state)
- **$6609 average financial aid** package, $12,381 average indebtedness upon graduation, $14 million endowment

Shepherd College, a National Liberal Arts College, has a long-standing reputation for providing high-quality education at a reasonable cost. Recently, the College was number 12 on *Money* magazine's list of the 25 public schools providing the best buys in education, marking the 5th time Shepherd has been named to one of *Money*'s best buys in education lists.

Peterson's Guide to Four-Year Colleges 2001 www.petersons.com 859

West Virginia

Shepherd College (continued)
Part of State College System of West Virginia.
Students *Undergraduates:* 2,765 full-time, 614 part-time. Students come from 50 states and territories. *The most frequently chosen baccalaureate fields are:* business/marketing, education, liberal arts/general studies.

From out-of-state	34%	Reside on campus	25%
Age 25 or older	26%	Transferred in	10%
African Americans	5%	Asian Americans/Pacific Islanders	1%
Hispanic Americans	1%	Native Americans	1%

Faculty 274 (38% full-time), 40% with terminal degrees.
Expenses (1999–2000) *Tuition, state resident:* full-time $2430; part-time $101 per semester hour. *Tuition, nonresident:* full-time $5754; part-time $240 per semester hour. Full-time tuition and fees vary according to location and reciprocity agreements. Part-time tuition and fees vary according to location. *College room and board:* $4432; room only: $2316. Room and board charges vary according to board plan and housing facility. *Payment plan:* installment. *Waivers:* minority students and employees or children of employees.
Library Ruth Scarborough Library. *Operations spending 1999–2000:* $904,454. *Collection:* 176,061 titles, 2,408 serial subscriptions, 11,510 audiovisual materials.
College life *Housing:* on-campus residence required through senior year. *Option:* coed. *Social organizations:* national fraternities, national sororities; 10% of eligible men and 10% of eligible women are members. *Most popular organizations:* Student Government Association, Outdoors Club, Christian Student Union, NAACP, Living Learning Center.
Campus security 24-hour emergency response devices and patrols, late-night transport-escort service, controlled dormitory access.
After graduation 250 organizations recruited on campus 1997–98. 72% of class of 1998 had job offers within 6 months. *Career center:* 4 full-time personnel. Services include job fairs, resume preparation, interview workshops, resume referral, career/interest testing, career counseling, careers library, job bank, job interviews. *Graduate education:* 15% of class of 1999 went directly to graduate and professional school.
Freshmen 1,668 applied, 1,401 admitted, 714 enrolled.

Average high school GPA	3.13	SAT verbal scores above 500	55%
SAT math scores above 500	54%	ACT above 18	71%
1998 freshmen returning in 1999	66%		

Application *Options:* early admission, early action, deferred entrance. *Application fee:* $25. *Required:* high school transcript; minimum 2.5 GPA. *Recommended:* essay or personal statement; minimum 3.0 GPA; 3 letters of recommendation; interview.
Standardized tests *Admission: Required:* SAT I or ACT.
Significant dates *Application deadlines:* 2/1 (freshmen), 3/15 (transfers). *Early action:* 11/15. *Notification:* continuous until 7/15 (freshmen), 12/15 (early action). *Financial aid deadline priority date:* 3/1.
Freshman Application Contact
Mr. Karl L. Wolf, Director of Admissions, Shepherd College, King Street, Shepherdstown, WV 25443-3210. **Phone:** 304-876-5212. **Toll-free phone:** 800-344-5231. **Fax:** 304-876-5165. **E-mail:** admoff@shepherd.edu
Visit CollegeQuest.com for information on majors offered and athletics.

■ *See page 2478 for a narrative description.*

UNIVERSITY OF CHARLESTON
Charleston, West Virginia

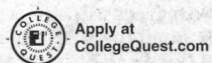 Apply at CollegeQuest.com

- **Independent**, comprehensive, founded 1888
- **Degrees** associate, bachelor's, and master's
- **Urban** 40-acre campus
- **Coed**, 1,037 undergraduate students, 81% full-time, 67% women, 33% men
- **Moderately difficult** entrance level, 73% of applicants were admitted
- **12:1 student-to-undergraduate faculty ratio**
- **47.5% graduate** in 6 years or less
- **$13,200 tuition** and fees
- **$33.7 million endowment**

Students *Undergraduates:* 839 full-time, 198 part-time. Students come from 29 states and territories, 27 other countries. *The most frequently chosen baccalaureate fields are:* business/marketing, biological/life sciences, health professions and related sciences. *Graduate:* 52 in graduate degree programs.

From out-of-state	16%	Reside on campus	28%
Age 25 or older	29%	Transferred in	8%
International students	5%	African Americans	4%
Asian Americans/Pacific Islanders	2%	Hispanic Americans	1%
Native Americans	1%		

Faculty 120 (59% full-time), 58% with terminal degrees.
Expenses (2000–2001) *Comprehensive fee:* $18,730 includes full-time tuition ($13,200) and room and board ($5530). Room and board charges vary according to board plan and housing facility. *Part-time tuition:* $275 per credit. Part-time tuition and fees vary according to course load and program. *Payment plan:* installment. *Waivers:* senior citizens and employees or children of employees.
Library Schoenbaum Library. *Operations spending 1999–2000:* $344,778. *Collection:* 111,264 titles, 2,011 serial subscriptions, 2,505 audiovisual materials.
College life *Housing:* on-campus residence required in freshman year. *Option:* coed. *Social organizations:* national fraternities, local sororities; 15% of eligible men and 12% of eligible women are members. *Most popular organizations:* Student Activities Board, American Society of Interior Designers, Student Government Association, Capito Association of Nursing Students, International Student Organization.
Campus security 24-hour emergency response devices and patrols, student patrols, late-night transport-escort service, controlled dormitory access, radio connection to city police and ambulance.
After graduation 60 organizations recruited on campus 1997–98. 90% of class of 1998 had job offers within 6 months. *Career center:* 1 full-time, 1 part-time personnel. Services include job fairs, resume preparation, interview workshops, resume referral, career/interest testing, career counseling, careers library, job bank, job interviews. *Graduate education:* 14% of class of 1999 went directly to graduate and professional school: 7% graduate arts and sciences, 3% medicine, 2% business, 1% law.
Freshmen 1,322 applied, 971 admitted, 184 enrolled.

Average high school GPA	3.32	SAT verbal scores above 500	48%
SAT math scores above 500	46%	ACT above 18	89%
From top 10% of their h.s. class	21%	From top half	80%
1998 freshmen returning in 1999	64%		

Application *Options:* eApply at www.CollegeQuest.com, electronic application, early admission, early decision, deferred entrance. *Application fee:* $25. *Required:* high school transcript; minimum 2.25 GPA. *Recommended:* essay or personal statement; letters of recommendation.
Standardized tests *Admission: Required:* SAT I or ACT.
Significant dates *Application deadlines:* rolling (freshmen), rolling (transfers). *Early decision:* 12/15. *Notification:* 2/1 (early decision). *Financial aid deadline priority date:* 3/1.
Freshman Application Contact
Ms. Lynn Jackson, Director of Admissions, University of Charleston, 2300 MacCorkle Avenue, SE, Charleston, WV 25304-1099. **Phone:** 304-357-4750. **Toll-free phone:** 800-995-GOUC. **Fax:** 304-357-4781. **E-mail:** admissions@uchaswv.edu
Visit CollegeQuest.com for information on majors offered and athletics.

■ *See page 2708 for a narrative description.*

WEST LIBERTY STATE COLLEGE
West Liberty, West Virginia

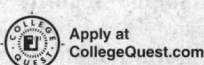 Apply at CollegeQuest.com

- **State-supported**, 4-year, founded 1837
- **Degrees** associate and bachelor's
- **Rural** 290-acre campus with easy access to Pittsburgh
- **Coed**, 2,579 undergraduate students, 89% full-time, 54% women, 46% men
- **Minimally difficult** entrance level, 98% of applicants were admitted
- **19:1 student-to-undergraduate faculty ratio**
- **42% graduate** in 6 years or less
- **$2320 tuition** and fees (in-state); $5760 (out-of-state)
- **$4235 average financial aid** package, $10,890 average indebtedness upon graduation, $4.2 million endowment

Part of State College System of West Virginia.

Students *Undergraduates:* 2,292 full-time, 287 part-time. Students come from 20 states and territories, 9 other countries. *The most frequently chosen baccalaureate fields are:* business/marketing, education, health professions and related sciences.

From out-of-state	28%	Reside on campus	43%
Age 25 or older	18%	Transferred in	11%
International students	1%	African Americans	2%
Asian Americans/Pacific Islanders	1%	Hispanic Americans	1%
Native Americans	0.2%		

Faculty 157 (69% full-time), 35% with terminal degrees.

Expenses (1999–2000) *Tuition, state resident:* full-time $2320; part-time $97 per semester hour. *Tuition, nonresident:* full-time $5760; part-time $240 per semester hour. *College room and board:* $3200. Room and board charges vary according to board plan and housing facility. *Payment plans:* installment, deferred payment.

Library Paul N. Elbin Library plus 1 other. *Operations spending 1999–2000:* $581,616. *Collection:* 200,322 titles, 853 serial subscriptions, 13,431 audiovisual materials.

College life *Housing: Options:* coed, men-only, women-only, disabled students. *Social organizations:* national fraternities, national sororities, local fraternities, local sororities; 10% of eligible men and 11% of eligible women are members. *Most popular organizations:* Delta Sigma Pi, Student Senate, Drama Club, Students in Free Enterprise, Chi Omega Sorority.

Campus security 24-hour emergency response devices and patrols, late-night transport-escort service.

After graduation 19 organizations recruited on campus 1997–98. *Career center:* 1 full-time personnel. Services include job fairs, resume preparation, interview workshops, resume referral, career/interest testing, career counseling, job bank, job interviews.

Freshmen 1,130 applied, 1,106 admitted, 503 enrolled. 4 valedictorians.

Average high school GPA	2.99	SAT verbal scores above 500	37%
SAT math scores above 500	34%	ACT above 18	71%
From top 10% of their h.s. class	10%	From top quarter	23%
From top half	60%	1998 freshmen returning in 1999	71%

Application *Options:* eApply at www.CollegeQuest.com, electronic application, early admission, deferred entrance. *Application fee:* $0. *Required:* high school transcript; minimum 2.0 GPA. *Recommended:* interview.

Standardized tests *Admission: Required:* SAT I or ACT.

Significant dates *Application deadlines:* 8/1 (freshmen), 8/1 (transfers). *Financial aid deadline priority date:* 3/1.

Freshman Application Contact
Ms. Stephanie North, Admissions Counselor, West Liberty State College, PO Box 295, West Liberty, WV 26074. **Phone:** 304-336-8078. **Toll-free phone:** 800-732-6204 Ext. 8076. **Fax:** 304-336-8285. **E-mail:** wladmsn1@wlsc.wvnet.edu

Visit CollegeQuest.com for information on majors offered and athletics.

WEST VIRGINIA STATE COLLEGE
Institute, West Virginia

Apply at CollegeQuest.com

- **State-supported**, 4-year, founded 1891
- **Degrees** associate, bachelor's, and postbachelor's certificates
- **Suburban** 90-acre campus
- **Coed**, 4,794 undergraduate students, 61% full-time, 58% women, 42% men
- **Minimally difficult** entrance level, 100% of applicants were admitted
- **$2836 tuition** and fees (in-state); $5588 (out-of-state)

Part of State College System of West Virginia.

Students *Undergraduates:* 2,938 full-time, 1,856 part-time. Students come from 34 states and territories, 8 other countries. *The most frequently chosen baccalaureate fields are:* education, business/marketing, liberal arts/general studies.

From out-of-state	3%	Reside on campus	7%
Age 25 or older	30%	Transferred in	6%
African Americans	13%	Asian Americans/Pacific Islanders	1%
Hispanic Americans	0.4%	Native Americans	0.5%

Faculty 140 (13% full-time).

Expenses (1999–2000) *One-time required fee:* $5. *Tuition, state resident:* full-time $2836; part-time $99 per semester hour. *Tuition, nonresident:* full-time $5588; part-time $233 per semester hour. Full-time tuition and fees vary according to program. Part-time tuition and fees vary according to course load and program. *College room and board:* $3600; room only: $1700. *Payment plans:* tuition prepayment, installment.

Library Drain-Jordan Library. *Collection:* 194,706 titles, 1,678 serial subscriptions, 3,290 audiovisual materials.

College life *Housing:* on-campus residence required in freshman year. *Options:* men-only, women-only. *Social organizations:* national fraternities, national sororities; 1% of eligible men and 1% of eligible women are members.

Campus security 24-hour emergency response devices and patrols, late-night transport-escort service.

After graduation *Career center:* 2 full-time, 3 part-time personnel. Services include job fairs, resume preparation, resume referral, career counseling, careers library, job bank, job interviews.

Freshmen 2,372 applied, 2,372 admitted, 715 enrolled.

Average high school GPA	2.65	SAT verbal scores above 500	N/R
SAT math scores above 500	N/R	ACT above 18	N/R

Application *Options:* eApply at www.CollegeQuest.com, Common Application, early admission. *Application fee:* $0. *Required:* high school transcript.

Standardized tests *Placement: Required:* SAT I or ACT

Significant dates *Application deadlines:* 8/11 (freshmen), 8/11 (transfers). *Financial aid deadline:* 6/30.

Freshman Application Contact
Ms. Alice Ruhnke, Interim Director of Admissions, West Virginia State College, Campus Box 188, PO Box 1000, Institute, WV 25112-1000. **Phone:** 304-766-3221. **Toll-free phone:** 800-987-2112. **Fax:** 304-766-4158. **E-mail:** ruhnkeam@mail.wvsc.edu

Visit CollegeQuest.com for information on majors offered and athletics. College video available at CollegeQuest.com.

WEST VIRGINIA UNIVERSITY
Morgantown, West Virginia

- **State-supported**, university, founded 1867
- **Degrees** bachelor's, master's, doctoral, and first professional
- **Small-town** 541-acre campus with easy access to Pittsburgh
- **Coed**, 15,417 undergraduate students, 94% full-time, 46% women, 54% men
- **Moderately difficult** entrance level, 94% of applicants were admitted
- **19:1** student-to-undergraduate faculty ratio
- **55% graduate** in 6 years or less
- **$2748 tuition** and fees (in-state); $8100 (out-of-state)
- **$4590 average financial aid** package, $15,864 average indebtedness upon graduation, $220 million endowment

Part of University of West Virginia System.

Students *Undergraduates:* 14,566 full-time, 851 part-time. Students come from 51 states and territories, 100 other countries. *The most frequently chosen baccalaureate fields are:* business/marketing, engineering/engineering technologies, health professions and related sciences. *Graduate:* 1,167 in professional programs, 5,731 in other graduate degree programs.

From out-of-state	39%	Reside on campus	20%
Age 25 or older	9%	Transferred in	5%
International students	2%	African Americans	4%
Asian Americans/Pacific Islanders	2%	Hispanic Americans	1%
Native Americans	0.4%		

Faculty 1,579 (82% full-time), 78% with terminal degrees.

Expenses (1999–2000) *Tuition, state resident:* full-time $2748; part-time $109 per credit hour. *Tuition, nonresident:* full-time $8100; part-time $332 per credit hour. Full-time tuition and fees vary according to location, program, and reciprocity agreements. Part-time tuition and fees vary according to course load, location, program, and reciprocity agreements. *College room and board:* $4990. Room and board charges vary according to board plan, housing facility, and location. *Payment plans:* installment, deferred payment. *Waivers:* employees or children of employees.

West Virginia

West Virginia University (continued)

Library Wise Library plus 9 others. *Operations spending 1999–2000:* $8.3 million. *Collection:* 1.6 million titles, 11,500 serial subscriptions, 40,000 audiovisual materials.

College life *Housing:* on-campus residence required in freshman year. *Options:* coed, men-only, women-only, disabled students. *Social organizations:* national fraternities, national sororities. *Most popular organizations:* Residential Hall Association, Gamma Beta Phi, Alpha Beta Phi.

Campus security 24-hour emergency response devices and patrols, student patrols, late-night transport-escort service.

After graduation 735 organizations recruited on campus 1997–98. *Career center:* 13 full-time, 6 part-time personnel. Services include job fairs, resume preparation, resume referral, career counseling, careers library, job bank, job interviews. *Major awards:* 1 Marshall, 1 Fulbright Scholar.

Freshmen 8,124 applied, 7,641 admitted, 3,567 enrolled.

Average high school GPA	3.2	SAT verbal scores above 500	54%
SAT math scores above 500	58%	ACT above 18	92%
From top 10% of their h.s. class	23%	From top quarter	49%
From top half	81%	1998 freshmen returning in 1999	78%

Application *Options:* Common Application, electronic application, early admission, deferred entrance. *Preference* given to state residents. *Application fee:* $35 for nonresidents. *Required:* high school transcript; minimum 2.0 GPA; audition for music program, portfolio for art program. *Required for some:* essay or personal statement; minimum 2.25 GPA.

Standardized tests *Admission: Required:* SAT I or ACT.

Significant dates *Application deadlines:* rolling (freshmen), rolling (transfers). *Financial aid deadline:* 3/1. *Priority date:* 2/15.

Freshman Application Contact
Mr. Cheng H. Khoo, Director of Admissions and Records, West Virginia University, Box 6009, Morgantown, WV 26506-6009. **Phone:** 304-293-2121 Ext. 1511. **Toll-free phone:** 800-344-9881. **Fax:** 304-293-3080. **E-mail:** wvuadmissions@arc.wvu.edu

Visit CollegeQuest.com for information on majors offered and athletics. College video available at CollegeQuest.com.

WEST VIRGINIA UNIVERSITY AT PARKERSBURG
Parkersburg, West Virginia

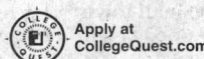

- **State-supported**, primarily 2-year, founded 1971
- **Degrees** associate and bachelor's
- **Small-town** 140-acre campus
- **Coed**, 3,500 undergraduate students
- **Noncompetitive** entrance level

Part of University System of West Virginia.

Faculty 176 (43% full-time).

Admissions Office Contact
West Virginia University at Parkersburg, 300 Campus Drive, Parkersburg, WV 26101-9577. **Toll-free phone:** 800-WVA-WVUP.

Visit CollegeQuest.com for information on majors offered and athletics.

WEST VIRGINIA UNIVERSITY INSTITUTE OF TECHNOLOGY
Montgomery, West Virginia

- **State-supported**, comprehensive, founded 1895
- **Degrees** associate, bachelor's, and master's
- **Small-town** 200-acre campus
- **Coed**, 2,587 undergraduate students, 65% full-time, 39% women, 61% men
- **Noncompetitive** entrance level, 99.9% of applicants were admitted
- **16:1** student-to-undergraduate faculty ratio
- **39% graduate** in 6 years or less
- **$2646 tuition** and fees (in-state); $6458 (out-of-state)

Tech's home is in scenic, wild-and-wonderful West Virginia, with opportunities for snow skiing and white-water rafting nearby. Tech offers more than 35 majors, including engineering, engineering technologies, business, computer science, social sciences, nursing, dental hygiene, health service administration, and printing. In addition, Tech offers an optional 5-year program in cooperative education and a practicum experience in social science. The low student-faculty ratio ensures a personalized education for Tech students.

Part of University System of West Virginia.

Students *Undergraduates:* 1,682 full-time, 905 part-time. Students come from 23 states and territories, 22 other countries. *The most frequently chosen baccalaureate fields are:* business/marketing, engineering/engineering technologies, interdisciplinary studies. *Graduate:* 6 in graduate degree programs.

From out-of-state	9%	Reside on campus	26%
Age 25 or older	27%	Transferred in	8%
International students	3%	African Americans	5%
Asian Americans/Pacific Islanders	2%	Hispanic Americans	1%
Native Americans	0.4%		

Faculty 173 (70% full-time), 41% with terminal degrees.

Expenses (1999–2000) *Tuition, state resident:* full-time $2646; part-time $110 per semester hour. *Tuition, nonresident:* full-time $6458; part-time $269 per semester hour. Full-time tuition and fees vary according to location and program. Part-time tuition and fees vary according to location. *College room and board:* $4048; room only: $2090. Room and board charges vary according to board plan. *Payment plan:* installment. *Waivers:* employees or children of employees.

Library Vining Library plus 1 other. *Operations spending 1999–2000:* $747,000. *Collection:* 153,167 titles, 763 serial subscriptions.

College life *Housing:* on-campus residence required through sophomore year. *Option:* coed. *Social organizations:* national fraternities, national sororities; 9% of eligible men and 8% of eligible women are members. *Most popular organizations:* Student Government Association, Christian Student Union, Alpha Phi Omega.

Campus security 24-hour emergency response devices and patrols, late-night transport-escort service.

After graduation 45 organizations recruited on campus 1997–98. 80% of class of 1998 had job offers within 6 months. *Career center:* 2 full-time personnel. Services include job fairs, resume preparation, interview workshops, resume referral, career/interest testing, career counseling, careers library, job bank, job interviews.

Freshmen 1,021 applied, 1,020 admitted, 440 enrolled. 12 valedictorians.

Average high school GPA	2.97	SAT verbal scores above 500	N/R
SAT math scores above 500	N/R	ACT above 18	71%
From top 10% of their h.s. class	10%	From top half	60%
1998 freshmen returning in 1999	62%		

Application *Options:* Common Application, electronic application, early admission. *Required:* high school transcript. *Required for some:* minimum 2.0 GPA.

Standardized tests *Admission: Required:* SAT I or ACT.

Significant dates *Application deadlines:* rolling (freshmen), rolling (transfers). *Notification:* continuous until 8/15 (freshmen). *Financial aid deadline priority date:* 3/1.

Freshman Application Contact
Ms. Donna Varney, Director of Admissions, West Virginia University Institute of Technology, 405 Fayette Pike, Montgomery, WV 25136. **Phone:** 304-442-3167. **Toll-free phone:** 888-554-8324. **Fax:** 304-442-3097. **E-mail:** wvutech@wvit.wvnet.edu

Visit CollegeQuest.com for information on majors offered and athletics. College video available at CollegeQuest.com.

■ *See page 2970 for a narrative description.*

WEST VIRGINIA WESLEYAN COLLEGE
Buckhannon, West Virginia

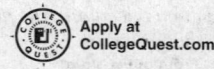

- **Independent**, comprehensive, founded 1890, affiliated with United Methodist Church
- **Degrees** bachelor's and master's

West Virginia

- **Small-town** 80-acre campus
- **Coed**, 1,601 undergraduate students, 95% full-time, 57% women, 43% men
- **Moderately difficult** entrance level, 84% of applicants were admitted
- **15:1** student-to-undergraduate faculty ratio
- **48% graduate** in 6 years or less
- **$18,050 tuition** and fees
- **$16,796 average financial aid** package, $15,787 average indebtedness upon graduation, $32.4 million endowment

As part of a partnership with IBM, all entering students at West Virginia Wesleyan College are provided with a ThinkPad laptop computer for academic and personal use. The campus fiber-optic system ensures rapid Internet and e-mail access from all academic buildings and residence hall rooms.

Students *Undergraduates:* 1,518 full-time, 83 part-time. Students come from 35 states and territories, 26 other countries. *The most frequently chosen baccalaureate fields are:* business/marketing, education, social sciences and history. *Graduate:* 47 in graduate degree programs.

From out-of-state	48%	Reside on campus	85%
Age 25 or older	3%	Transferred in	3%
International students	4%	African Americans	6%
Asian Americans/Pacific Islanders	1%	Hispanic Americans	1%
Native Americans	0.1%		

Faculty 134 (60% full-time).

Expenses (1999–2000) *One-time required fee:* $250. *Comprehensive fee:* $22,400 includes full-time tuition ($16,800), mandatory fees ($1250), and room and board ($4350). Full-time tuition and fees vary according to student level. Room and board charges vary according to board plan and housing facility. Part-time tuition and fees vary according to course load. *Payment plan:* installment. *Waivers:* employees or children of employees.

Library A. M. Pfeiffer Library. *Operations spending 1999–2000:* $648,400. *Collection:* 7,605 audiovisual materials.

College life *Housing:* on-campus residence required through senior year. *Options:* coed, men-only, women-only, disabled students. *Social organizations:* national fraternities, national sororities; 24% of eligible men and 25% of eligible women are members. *Most popular organizations:* Campus Activities Board, environmental club, American Marketing Club, Wesleyan Ambassadors.

Campus security 24-hour emergency response devices and patrols, student patrols, late-night transport-escort service, controlled dormitory access.

After graduation 72% of class of 1998 had job offers within 6 months. *Career center:* 5 full-time, 1 part-time personnel. Services include job fairs, resume preparation, resume referral, career counseling, careers library, job bank, job interviews. *Graduate education:* 26% of class of 1999 went directly to graduate and professional school: 9% business, 7% graduate arts and sciences, 5% law, 3% medicine, 2% dentistry.

Freshmen 1,504 applied, 1,269 admitted, 472 enrolled. 1 National Merit Scholar, 9 valedictorians.

Average high school GPA	3.28	SAT verbal scores above 500	56%
SAT math scores above 500	56%	ACT above 18	92%
From top 10% of their h.s. class	23%	From top quarter	50%
From top half	80%	1998 freshmen returning in 1999	78%

Application *Options:* eApply at www.CollegeQuest.com, Common Application, electronic application, early admission, deferred entrance. *Application fee:* $25. *Required:* high school transcript. *Recommended:* essay or personal statement; letters of recommendation; interview.

Standardized tests *Admission: Required:* SAT I or ACT.

Significant dates *Application deadlines:* 8/1 (freshmen), rolling (transfers). *Notification:* continuous until 9/1 (freshmen). *Financial aid deadline priority date:* 2/15.

Freshman Application Contact
Mr. Robert N. Skinner II, Director of Admission, West Virginia Wesleyan College, 59 College Avenue, Buckhannon, WV 26201. **Phone:** 304-473-8510. **Toll-free phone:** 800-722-9933. **Fax:** 304-472-2571. **E-mail:** admissions@academ.wvwc.edu

Visit CollegeQuest.com for information on majors offered and athletics. College video available at CollegeQuest.com.

- *See page 2972 for a narrative description.*

WHEELING JESUIT UNIVERSITY
Wheeling, West Virginia

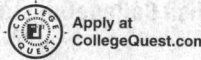
Apply at CollegeQuest.com

- **Independent Roman Catholic (Jesuit)**, comprehensive, founded 1954
- Degrees **bachelor's and master's**
- **Suburban** 70-acre campus with easy access to Pittsburgh
- **Coed**, 1,254 undergraduate students, 82% full-time, 60% women, 40% men
- **Moderately difficult** entrance level, 94% of applicants were admitted
- **12:1** student-to-undergraduate faculty ratio
- **58% graduate** in 6 years or less
- **$15,220 tuition** and fees
- **$15,840 average financial aid** package, $15,000 average indebtedness upon graduation, $18.3 million endowment

WJU, the youngest school of the 60 best regional universities recognized by *U.S. News & World Report*, will break ground in spring 2000 for a new $8.5 million science center. The 50,000 square foot building will house several faculty offices, classrooms, research rooms, and a computer science center.

Students *Undergraduates:* 1,034 full-time, 220 part-time. Students come from 26 states and territories, 19 other countries. *The most frequently chosen baccalaureate fields are:* business/marketing, health professions and related sciences, psychology. *Graduate:* 218 in graduate degree programs.

From out-of-state	65%	Reside on campus	80%
Age 25 or older	25%	Transferred in	10%
International students	2%	African Americans	2%
Asian Americans/Pacific Islanders	1%	Hispanic Americans	1%
Native Americans	0.2%		

Faculty 91 (90% full-time), 70% with terminal degrees.

Expenses (1999–2000) *Comprehensive fee:* $20,420 includes full-time tuition ($15,000), mandatory fees ($220), and room and board ($5200). Full-time tuition and fees vary according to program. Room and board charges vary according to board plan, gender, and housing facility. *Part-time tuition:* $405 per credit hour. *Part-time fees:* $55 per term part-time. Part-time tuition and fees vary according to class time and program. *Payment plan:* guaranteed tuition. *Waivers:* senior citizens and employees or children of employees.

Library Bishop Hodges Learning Center. *Operations spending 1999–2000:* $547,599. *Collection:* 139,500 titles, 570 serial subscriptions.

College life *Housing:* on-campus residence required through sophomore year. *Options:* men-only, women-only, disabled students.

Campus security 24-hour patrols, student patrols, late-night transport-escort service, controlled dormitory access.

After graduation 80% of class of 1998 had job offers within 6 months. *Career center:* 1 full-time, 1 part-time personnel. Services include job fairs, resume preparation, resume referral, career counseling, careers library, job interviews. *Graduate education:* 25% of class of 1999 went directly to graduate and professional school: 15% graduate arts and sciences, 5% business, 2% law, 2% medicine, 1% dentistry.

Freshmen 804 applied, 758 admitted, 323 enrolled. 1 National Merit Scholar, 3 valedictorians.

Average high school GPA	3.2	SAT verbal scores above 500	59%
SAT math scores above 500	56%	ACT above 18	91%
From top 10% of their h.s. class	27%	From top quarter	44%
From top half	84%	1998 freshmen returning in 1999	75%

Application *Options:* eApply at www.CollegeQuest.com, electronic application, early admission, deferred entrance. *Application fee:* $25. *Required:* high school transcript; minimum 2.0 GPA. *Required for some:* minimum 3.0 GPA; letters of recommendation; interview. *Recommended:* letters of recommendation; interview.

Standardized tests *Admission: Required:* SAT I or ACT.

Significant dates *Application deadlines:* rolling (freshmen), rolling (transfers). *Financial aid deadline priority date:* 3/1.

Freshman Application Contact
Mr. Thomas M. Pie, Director of Admissions, Wheeling Jesuit University, 316 Washington Avenue, Wheeling, WV 26003-6295. **Phone:** 304-243-2359. **Toll-free phone:** 800-624-6992. **Fax:** 304-243-2397. **E-mail:** admis@wju.edu

West Virginia–Wisconsin

Wheeling Jesuit University (continued)
Visit CollegeQuest.com for information on majors offered and athletics. College video available at CollegeQuest.com.

■ See page 2978 for a narrative description.

WISCONSIN

ALVERNO COLLEGE
Milwaukee, Wisconsin

Apply at CollegeQuest.com

- **Independent Roman Catholic**, comprehensive, founded 1887
- **Degrees** associate, bachelor's, and master's (also offers weekend program with significant enrollment not reflected in profile)
- **Suburban** 46-acre campus
- **Women** only, 1,585 undergraduate students, 56% full-time
- **Moderately difficult** entrance level, 66% of applicants were admitted
- **14:1 student-to-undergraduate faculty ratio**
- **49% graduate** in 6 years or less
- **$10,900 tuition** and fees
- **$20.8 million endowment**

Students *Undergraduates:* 883 full-time, 702 part-time. Students come from 10 states and territories. *The most frequently chosen baccalaureate fields are:* business/marketing, communications/communication technologies, health professions and related sciences. *Graduate:* 118 in graduate degree programs.

From out-of-state	3%	Reside on campus	8%
Age 25 or older	14%	Transferred in	1%
International students	0.4%	African Americans	25%
Asian Americans/Pacific Islanders	2%	Hispanic Americans	9%
Native Americans	1%		

Faculty 185 (55% full-time), 82% with terminal degrees.

Expenses (1999–2000) *One-time required fee:* $15. *Comprehensive fee:* $15,150 includes full-time tuition ($10,800), mandatory fees ($100), and room and board ($4250). *College room only:* $1470. Full-time tuition and fees vary according to class time and program. Room and board charges vary according to board plan. *Part-time tuition:* $450 per credit hour. *Part-time fees:* $50 per term part-time. Part-time tuition and fees vary according to class time and program. *Payment plans:* installment, deferred payment. *Waivers:* employees or children of employees.

Library Library Media Center. *Operations spending 1999–2000:* $910,592. *Collection:* 104,019 titles, 1,407 serial subscriptions, 3,628 audiovisual materials.

College life *Housing:* on-campus residence required in freshman year. *Option:* women-only. *Most popular organizations:* Student Nurses Association, Women in Communication, Pi Sigma Epsilon, Students in Free Enterprise, Alverno Student Educators Organization.

Campus security 24-hour emergency response devices and patrols, late-night transport-escort service, controlled dormitory access, video camera surveillance at entrances of residence halls, emergency telephones, well-lit parking lots and pathways, security personnel.

After graduation 35 organizations recruited on campus 1997–98. *Career center:* 7 full-time, 5 part-time personnel. Services include job fairs, resume preparation, interview workshops, resume referral, career/interest testing, career counseling, careers library, job bank.

Freshmen 333 applied, 219 admitted, 156 enrolled.

SAT verbal scores above 500	N/R	SAT math scores above 500	N/R
ACT above 18	N/R	From top 10% of their h.s. class	8%
1998 freshmen returning in 1999	76%		

Application *Options:* eApply at www.CollegeQuest.com, Common Application, electronic application, deferred entrance. *Application fee:* $20. *Required:* essay or personal statement; high school transcript. *Required for some:* letters of recommendation; Alverno Communication Placement Assessment. *Recommended:* interview.

Standardized tests *Admission: Required:* ACT.

Significant dates *Application deadlines:* 8/1 (freshmen), 8/1 (transfers). *Financial aid deadline priority date:* 4/15.

Freshman Application Contact
Mr. Owen Smith, Director of Admissions, Alverno College, 3400 South 43 Street, PO Box 343922, Milwaukee, WI 53234-3922. **Phone:** 414-382-6113. **Toll-free phone:** 800-933-3401. **Fax:** 414-382-6354. **E-mail:** admissions@alverno.edu

Visit CollegeQuest.com for information on majors offered and athletics. College video and electronic viewbook available at CollegeQuest.com.

■ See page 1158 for a narrative description.

BELLIN COLLEGE OF NURSING
Green Bay, Wisconsin

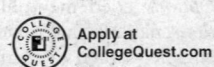

- **Independent**, 4-year, founded 1909
- **Degree** bachelor's
- **Urban** campus
- **Coed**, primarily women, 160 undergraduate students, 90% full-time, 92% women, 8% men
- **Moderately difficult** entrance level, 57% of applicants were admitted
- **9:1 student-to-undergraduate faculty ratio**
- **70% graduate** in 6 years or less
- **$9455 tuition** and fees
- **$10,030 average financial aid** package, $18,961 average indebtedness upon graduation, $8 million endowment

Students *Undergraduates:* 144 full-time, 16 part-time. Students come from 4 states and territories. *The most frequently chosen baccalaureate field is:* health professions and related sciences.

From out-of-state	2%	Age 25 or older	21%
Transferred in	16%	African Americans	1%
Asian Americans/Pacific Islanders	1%	Native Americans	3%

Faculty 18 (83% full-time), 6% with terminal degrees.

Expenses (1999–2000) *Tuition:* full-time $9289; part-time $464 per credit. *Required fees:* full-time $166. Full-time tuition and fees vary according to student level. *Payment plan:* installment.

Library Meredith B. and John M. Rose Library. *Operations spending 1999–2000:* $92,936. *Collection:* 5,000 titles, 233 serial subscriptions.

College life *Housing:* college housing not available. *Most popular organizations:* Student Senate, Student Nurses Association.

Campus security 24-hour patrols, late-night transport-escort service, electronically operated building access after hours.

After graduation 10 organizations recruited on campus 1997–98. 90% of class of 1998 had job offers within 6 months. *Career center:* Services include job fairs, resume preparation, career counseling.

Wisconsin

Freshmen 123 applied, 70 admitted, 26 enrolled. 2 valedictorians.

Average high school GPA	3.44	SAT verbal scores above 500	N/R
SAT math scores above 500	N/R	ACT above 18	100%
From top 10% of their h.s. class	12%	From top quarter	44%
From top half	100%	1998 freshmen returning in 1999	86%

Application *Options:* eApply at www.CollegeQuest.com, electronic application. *Application fee:* $20. *Required:* high school transcript; 3 letters of recommendation; interview. *Recommended:* minimum 3.0 GPA.

Standardized tests *Admission: Required:* ACT.

Significant dates *Application deadlines:* rolling (freshmen), rolling (transfers). *Financial aid deadline priority date:* 3/1.

Freshman Application Contact
Dr. Penny Croghan, Admissions Director, Bellin College of Nursing, 725 South Webster Ave, PO Box 23400, Green Bay, WI 54305-3400. **Phone:** 920-433-5803. **Toll-free phone:** 800-236-8707. **Fax:** 920-433-7416. **E-mail:** admissio@bcon.edu

Visit CollegeQuest.com for information on majors offered and athletics. College video available at CollegeQuest.com.

BELOIT COLLEGE
Beloit, Wisconsin

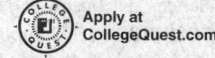
Apply at CollegeQuest.com

- **Independent**, 4-year, founded 1846
- **Degree** bachelor's
- **Small-town** 65-acre campus with easy access to Chicago and Milwaukee
- **Coed**, 1,128 undergraduate students, 99% full-time, 57% women, 43% men
- **Very difficult** entrance level, 67% of applicants were admitted
- **11:1 student-to-undergraduate faculty ratio**
- **66.3% graduate** in 6 years or less
- **$20,440 tuition** and fees
- **$16,256 average financial aid** package, $12,896 average indebtedness upon graduation, $84.9 million endowment

Beloit College is an uncommonly diverse academic, residential, and international community where, through investigation and scholarship, students invent themselves. Featuring an extraordinary teaching faculty, Beloit's curriculum combines a rigorous academic program with interdisciplinary studies and hands-on learning expectations. Beloit students compliment classroom activities by studying abroad, conducting independent research, participating in internships, and engaging in student government and a host of other campus clubs and activities. With enthusiastic faculty advisers and the College's extensive resources, students tailor their Beloit experience to reach their fullest intellectual, professional, and personal development.

Students *Undergraduates:* 1,123 full-time, 5 part-time. Students come from 49 states and territories, 52 other countries. *The most frequently chosen baccalaureate fields are:* social sciences and history, English, visual/performing arts.

From out-of-state	78%	Reside on campus	91%
Age 25 or older	5%	Transferred in	3%
International students	11%	African Americans	5%
Asian Americans/Pacific Islanders	4%	Hispanic Americans	4%
Native Americans	0.4%		

Faculty 108 (84% full-time), 91% with terminal degrees.

Expenses (1999–2000) *Comprehensive fee:* $25,068 includes full-time tuition ($20,220), mandatory fees ($220), and room and board ($4628). *College room only:* $2258. Room and board charges vary according to board plan and housing facility. *Part-time tuition:* $2530 per course. *Payment plan:* installment. *Waivers:* adult students, senior citizens, and employees or children of employees.

Library Morse Library and Black Information Center. *Collection:* 243,779 titles, 980 serial subscriptions.

College life *Housing:* on-campus residence required through junior year. *Options:* coed, men-only, women-only. *Social organizations:* national fraternities, local sororities; 15% of eligible men and 5% of eligible women are members. *Most popular organizations:* Beloit Science Fiction and Fantasy Association, anthropology club, International Club, WBEL (student radio station), Outdoor Environmental Club.

Campus security 24-hour emergency response devices and patrols, late-night transport-escort service.

After graduation 70% of class of 1998 had job offers within 6 months. *Career center:* 4 full-time, 6 part-time personnel. Services include job fairs, resume preparation, interview workshops, resume referral, career/interest testing, career counseling, careers library, job bank, job interviews. **Graduate education:** 30% of class of 1999 went directly to graduate and professional school: 20% graduate arts and sciences, 5% medicine, 3% business, 2% law.

Freshmen 1,495 applied, 1,001 admitted, 302 enrolled. 4 National Merit Scholars, 3 class presidents, 12 valedictorians.

Average high school GPA	3.5	SAT verbal scores above 500	94%
SAT math scores above 500	91%	ACT above 18	100%
From top 10% of their h.s. class	40%	From top quarter	62%
From top half	93%	1998 freshmen returning in 1999	93%

Application *Options:* eApply at www.CollegeQuest.com, Common Application, electronic application, early admission, early decision, deferred entrance. *Application fee:* $25. *Required:* essay or personal statement; high school transcript; 1 letter of recommendation. *Required for some:* interview. *Recommended:* interview.

Standardized tests *Admission: Required:* SAT I or ACT.

Significant dates *Application deadlines:* rolling (freshmen), rolling (transfers). *Early decision:* 12/1. *Notification:* 12/15 (early decision). **Financial aid deadline:** 2/1.

Freshman Application Contact
Mr. James Zielinski, Director of Admissions, Beloit College, 700 College Street, Beloit, WI 53511-5596. **Phone:** 608-363-2500. **Toll-free phone:** 800-356-0751. **Fax:** 608-363-2075. **E-mail:** admiss@beloit.edu

Visit CollegeQuest.com for information on majors offered and athletics. College video and electronic viewbook available at CollegeQuest.com.

- *See page 1248 for a narrative description.*

CARDINAL STRITCH UNIVERSITY
Milwaukee, Wisconsin

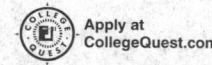
Apply at CollegeQuest.com

- **Independent Roman Catholic**, comprehensive, founded 1937
- **Degrees** associate, bachelor's, master's, and doctoral
- **Suburban** 40-acre campus
- **Coed**, 2,934 undergraduate students, 95% full-time, 66% women, 34% men
- **Moderately difficult** entrance level, 70% of applicants were admitted
- **17:1 student-to-undergraduate faculty ratio**
- **54% graduate** in 6 years or less
- **$11,120 tuition** and fees
- **$17.3 million endowment**

Cardinal Stritch University is a Catholic, coeducational institution rooted in the liberal arts. The University provides all of the resources associated with a large university yet offers the benefits of personal attention and 1-on-1 instruction associated with a smaller institution. Graduate and undergraduate programs, offered in traditional and nontraditional formats, range from business and education to religious studies and art.

Students *Undergraduates:* 2,779 full-time, 155 part-time. Students come from 25 states and territories. *The most frequently chosen baccalaureate fields are:* business/marketing, education, health professions and related sciences. *Graduate:* 2,703 in graduate degree programs.

From out-of-state	20%	Reside on campus	9%
Age 25 or older	5%	Transferred in	4%
International students	0.03%	African Americans	10%
Asian Americans/Pacific Islanders	1%	Hispanic Americans	2%
Native Americans	0.5%		

Faculty 607 (15% full-time).

Expenses (1999–2000) *One-time required fee:* $20. *Comprehensive fee:* $15,600 includes full-time tuition ($11,000), mandatory fees ($120), and room and board ($4480). Full-time tuition and fees vary according to program. Room and board charges vary according to board plan. *Part-time tuition:* $344 per credit. *Part-time fees:* $42 per term part-time. Part-time tuition and fees vary according to course load and program. *Payment plan:* installment. *Waivers:* employees or children of employees.

Library Cardinal Stritch University Library. *Operations spending 1999–2000:* $604,642. *Collection:* 117,712 titles, 1,312 serial subscriptions.

Wisconsin

Cardinal Stritch University (continued)

College life *Housing: Option:* coed. *Most popular organizations:* Residence Hall Association, Student Government Association, Student Activities Board.

Campus security 24-hour emergency response devices and patrols, late-night transport-escort service.

After graduation 24 organizations recruited on campus 1997–98. 86% of class of 1998 had job offers within 6 months. *Career center:* 3 full-time personnel. Services include job fairs, resume preparation, interview workshops, resume referral, career/interest testing, career counseling, careers library, job bank, job interviews.

Freshmen 316 applied, 220 admitted, 177 enrolled.

Average high school GPA	3.01	SAT verbal scores above 500	N/R
SAT math scores above 500	N/R	ACT above 18	98%
From top 10% of their h.s. class	11%	From top quarter	32%
From top half	62%	1998 freshmen returning in 1999	90%

Application *Options:* eApply at www.CollegeQuest.com, Common Application, electronic application, early admission, deferred entrance. *Application fee:* $20. *Required:* essay or personal statement; high school transcript; minimum 2.0 GPA. *Required for some:* letters of recommendation. *Recommended:* interview.

Standardized tests *Admission: Required:* SAT I or ACT.

Significant dates *Application deadlines:* rolling (freshmen), rolling (transfers). *Financial aid deadline priority date:* 4/1.

Freshman Application Contact
Mr. David Wegener, Director of Admissions, Cardinal Stritch University, 6801 North Yates Road, Milwaukee, WI 53217-3985. **Phone:** 414-410-4040. **Toll-free phone:** 800-347-8822 Ext. 4040. **Fax:** 414-410-4239. **E-mail:** admityou@stritch.edu

Visit CollegeQuest.com for information on majors offered and athletics. College video and electronic viewbook available at CollegeQuest.com.

■ *See page 1358 for a narrative description.*

CARROLL COLLEGE
Waukesha, Wisconsin

Apply at CollegeQuest.com

- **Independent Presbyterian**, comprehensive, founded 1846
- **Degrees** bachelor's and master's (master's degrees in education and physical therapy)
- **Suburban** 52-acre campus with easy access to Milwaukee
- **Coed**, 2,436 undergraduate students, 74% full-time, 66% women, 34% men
- **Moderately difficult** entrance level, 90% of applicants were admitted
- **18:1 student-to-undergraduate faculty ratio**
- **49% graduate** in 6 years or less
- **$15,000 tuition** and fees
- **$13,219 average financial aid** package, $15,772 average indebtedness upon graduation, $37.2 million endowment

Carroll College gives its students the support they need to learn and grow—small classes and individual attention provide a quality educational experience at Wisconsin's oldest college. Students are encouraged to explore the world around them by studying in other countries or participating in internships. An Honors Program is available to academically talented students.

Students *Undergraduates:* 1,794 full-time, 642 part-time. Students come from 30 states and territories, 8 other countries. *The most frequently chosen baccalaureate fields are:* business/marketing, health professions and related sciences, psychology. *Graduate:* 170 in graduate degree programs.

From out-of-state	18%	Reside on campus	58%
Age 25 or older	29%	Transferred in	6%
International students	2%	African Americans	3%
Asian Americans/Pacific Islanders	1%	Hispanic Americans	2%
Native Americans	0.2%		

Faculty 242 (43% full-time).

Expenses (1999–2000) *One-time required fee:* $69. *Comprehensive fee:* $19,600 includes full-time tuition ($14,740), mandatory fees ($260), and room and board ($4600). *College room only:* $2470. Full-time tuition and fees vary according to program. Room and board charges vary according to board plan and housing facility. *Part-time tuition:* $185 per semester hour. Part-time tuition and fees vary according to course load and program. *Payment plan:* installment. *Waivers:* employees or children of employees.

Library Todd Wehr Memorial Library. *Operations spending 1999–2000:* $580,945. *Collection:* 195,578 titles, 633 serial subscriptions, 353 audiovisual materials.

College life *Housing:* on-campus residence required through sophomore year. *Options:* coed, women-only. *Social organizations:* national sororities, local fraternities; 8% of eligible men and 9% of eligible women are members. *Most popular organizations:* College Activities Board, Student Senate, Black Student Union, Carroll College Christian Fellowship, Residence Hall Association.

Campus security 24-hour emergency response devices and patrols, student patrols, late-night transport-escort service, controlled dormitory access.

After graduation 13 organizations recruited on campus 1997–98. 93% of class of 1998 had job offers within 6 months. *Career center:* 3 full-time, 1 part-time personnel. Services include job fairs, resume preparation, interview workshops, resume referral, career/interest testing, career counseling, careers library, job bank, job interviews. *Graduate education:* 10% of class of 1999 went directly to graduate and professional school: 7% graduate arts and sciences, 1% business, 1% law, 1% medicine.

Freshmen 1,772 applied, 1,595 admitted, 504 enrolled.

SAT verbal scores above 500	N/R	SAT math scores above 500	N/R
ACT above 18	91%	From top 10% of their h.s. class	20%
From top quarter	57%	From top half	80%
1998 freshmen returning in 1999	78%		

Application *Options:* eApply at www.CollegeQuest.com, Common Application, electronic application, early admission, deferred entrance. *Application fee:* $0. *Required:* high school transcript; minimum 2.0 GPA; 1 letter of recommendation. *Required for some:* essay or personal statement. *Recommended:* interview.

Standardized tests *Admission: Required:* SAT I and SAT II or ACT.

Significant dates *Application deadlines:* rolling (freshmen), rolling (transfers). *Notification:* continuous until 8/20 (freshmen). *Financial aid deadline:* continuous.

Freshman Application Contact
Mr. James V. Wiseman III, Vice President of Enrollment, Carroll College, 100 North East Avenue, Waukesha, WI 53186-5593. **Phone:** 262-524-7221. **Toll-free phone:** 800-CARROLL. **Fax:** 262-524-7139. **E-mail:** cc.info@ccadmin.cc.edu

Visit CollegeQuest.com for information on majors offered and athletics.

■ *See page 1370 for a narrative description.*

CARTHAGE COLLEGE
Kenosha, Wisconsin

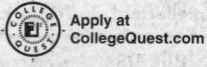
Apply at CollegeQuest.com

- **Independent**, comprehensive, founded 1847, affiliated with Evangelical Lutheran Church in America
- **Degrees** bachelor's and master's
- **Suburban** 72-acre campus with easy access to Chicago and Milwaukee
- **Coed**, 1,888 undergraduate students, 80% full-time, 56% women, 44% men
- **Moderately difficult** entrance level, 91% of applicants were admitted
- **55% graduate** in 6 years or less
- **$16,690 tuition** and fees
- **$14,384 average financial aid** package, $37.6 million endowment

Students *Undergraduates:* 1,515 full-time, 373 part-time. Students come from 23 states and territories. *The most frequently chosen baccalaureate fields are:* business/marketing, education, social sciences and history. *Graduate:* 89 in graduate degree programs.

From out-of-state	60%	Reside on campus	74%
Age 25 or older	11%	Transferred in	4%
International students	0.1%	African Americans	5%
Asian Americans/Pacific Islanders	1%	Hispanic Americans	3%
Native Americans	0.2%		

Faculty 144 (68% full-time), 63% with terminal degrees.

Expenses (1999–2000) *Comprehensive fee:* $21,500 includes full-time tuition ($16,690) and room and board ($4810). Room and board charges vary according to board plan. *Part-time tuition:* $250 per credit hour. Part-time tuition and fees vary according to class time. *Payment plan:* installment. *Waivers:* children of alumni and employees or children of employees.

Wisconsin

Library Ruthrauff Library. *Operations spending 1999–2000:* $968,132. *Collection:* 141,187 titles, 615 serial subscriptions, 2,371 audiovisual materials.

College life *Housing:* on-campus residence required through senior year. *Options:* coed, women-only. *Social organizations:* national fraternities, national sororities, local fraternities, local sororities; 25% of eligible men and 23% of eligible women are members. *Most popular organizations:* Residence Life Council, Alpha Lambda Delta, Circle K, Intervarsity Christian Fellowship.

Campus security 24-hour emergency response devices and patrols, student patrols, late-night transport-escort service, controlled dormitory access.

After graduation 30 organizations recruited on campus 1997–98. 75% of class of 1998 had job offers within 6 months. *Career center:* 3 full-time personnel. Services include job fairs, resume preparation, interview workshops, resume referral, career/interest testing, career counseling, careers library, job bank, job interviews. *Graduate education:* 13% of class of 1999 went directly to graduate and professional school: 7% graduate arts and sciences, 2% medicine, 2% theology, 1% business, 1% law.

Freshmen 2,075 applied, 1,883 admitted, 436 enrolled.

Average high school GPA	3.11	SAT verbal scores above 500	69%
SAT math scores above 500	67%	ACT above 18	N/R
From top 10% of their h.s. class	19%	From top quarter	39%
From top half	65%	1998 freshmen returning in 1999	73%

Application *Options:* eApply at www.CollegeQuest.com, electronic application, early action, deferred entrance. *Application fee:* $25. *Required:* high school transcript; minimum 2.0 GPA. *Required for some:* essay or personal statement; 2 letters of recommendation. *Recommended:* essay or personal statement; minimum 3.0 GPA; interview.

Standardized tests *Admission: Required:* SAT I or ACT.

Significant dates *Application deadlines:* rolling (freshmen), rolling (transfers). *Early action:* 7/1. *Notification:* 7/15 (early action). *Financial aid deadline priority date:* 2/15.

Freshman Application Contact
Mr. Tom Augustine, Director of Admission, Carthage College, 2001 Alford Park Drive, Kenosha, WI 53140-1994. **Phone:** 262-551-6000. **Toll-free phone:** 800-351-4058. **Fax:** 414-551-5762. **E-mail:** admissions@carthage.edu

Visit CollegeQuest.com for information on majors offered and athletics.

■ *See page 1374 for a narrative description.*

COLUMBIA COLLEGE OF NURSING
Milwaukee, Wisconsin

- **Independent**, 4-year, founded 1901
- **Degree** bachelor's
- **Urban** campus
- **Coed**, 242 undergraduate students, 70% full-time, 93% women, 7% men
- **Moderately difficult** entrance level, 82% of applicants were admitted
- **12:1 student-to-undergraduate faculty ratio**
- **$15,720 tuition** and fees
- **$1.4 million endowment**

Students *Undergraduates:* 170 full-time, 72 part-time. Students come from 10 states and territories, 2 other countries. *The most frequently chosen baccalaureate field is:* health professions and related sciences.

From out-of-state	13%	Reside on campus	18%
Age 25 or older	32%	Transferred in	10%
International students	1%	African Americans	4%
Asian Americans/Pacific Islanders	0.4%	Hispanic Americans	2%
Native Americans	0.4%		

Faculty 16 (63% full-time), 31% with terminal degrees.

Expenses (2000–2001) *Comprehensive fee:* $18,915 includes full-time tuition ($15,250), mandatory fees ($470), and room and board ($3195). *College room only:* $2326. Room and board charges vary according to board plan, housing facility, location, and student level. *Part-time tuition:* $255 per credit. *Part-time fees:* $296 per term part-time. *Payment plan:* installment. *Waivers:* employees or children of employees.

Library Ellen Bacon Library. *Operations spending 1999–2000:* $84,000. *Collection:* 6,293 titles, 248 serial subscriptions, 469 audiovisual materials.

College life *Housing:* on-campus residence required through sophomore year. *Option:* coed. *Most popular organizations:* Student Senate, Student Nurses Association.

Campus security 24-hour emergency response devices and patrols, student patrols, late-night transport-escort service, controlled dormitory access.

After graduation 6 organizations recruited on campus 1997–98. 85% of class of 1998 had job offers within 6 months. *Career center:* 1 full-time personnel. Services include job fairs, resume preparation, interview workshops, resume referral, career counseling, careers library, job bank. *Graduate education:* 18% of class of 1999 went directly to graduate and professional school.

Freshmen 111 applied, 91 admitted, 33 enrolled.

Average high school GPA	3.5	SAT verbal scores above 500	N/R
SAT math scores above 500	N/R	ACT above 18	97%
From top 10% of their h.s. class	9%	From top quarter	58%
From top half	94%	1998 freshmen returning in 1999	63%

Application *Option:* Common Application. *Application fee:* $0. *Required:* high school transcript. *Required for some:* essay or personal statement. *Recommended:* essay or personal statement; 1 letter of recommendation; interview.

Standardized tests *Admission: Required:* SAT I or ACT.

Significant dates *Application deadlines:* rolling (freshmen), rolling (transfers).

Freshman Application Contact
Mr. James Wiseman, Dean of Admissions, Columbia College of Nursing, Carroll College, 100 North East Avenue, Milwaukee, WI 53186. **Phone:** 262-524-7220.

Visit CollegeQuest.com for information on majors offered and athletics. College video available at CollegeQuest.com.

CONCORDIA UNIVERSITY WISCONSIN
Mequon, Wisconsin

- **Independent**, comprehensive, founded 1881, affiliated with Lutheran Church–Missouri Synod
- **Degrees** bachelor's and master's
- **Suburban** 155-acre campus with easy access to Milwaukee
- **Coed**, 3,787 undergraduate students, 67% full-time, 63% women, 37% men
- **Moderately difficult** entrance level, 79% of applicants were admitted
- **11:1 student-to-undergraduate faculty ratio**
- **$12,460 tuition** and fees

Students *Undergraduates:* 2,555 full-time, 1,232 part-time. *Graduate:* 670 in graduate degree programs.

Reside on campus	69%	International students	1%
African Americans	7%	Asian Americans/Pacific Islanders	0.3%
Hispanic Americans	0.5%	Native Americans	0.4%

Faculty 168 (55% full-time).

Expenses (1999–2000) *Comprehensive fee:* $16,660 includes full-time tuition ($12,400), mandatory fees ($60), and room and board ($4200). Full-time tuition and fees vary according to program. *Part-time tuition:* $520 per credit. Part-time tuition and fees vary according to class time and program. *Payment plans:* guaranteed tuition, installment, deferred payment. *Waivers:* employees or children of employees.

Library Rinker Memorial Library. *Collection:* 110,929 titles, 1,411 serial subscriptions, 4,645 audiovisual materials.

College life *Housing: Options:* men-only, women-only. *Most popular organizations:* Fellowship of Christian Athletes, Kammerchor, Youth Ministry, band.

Campus security Student patrols, controlled dormitory access.

After graduation *Career center:* 2 full-time, 3 part-time personnel. Services include job fairs, resume preparation, career counseling, careers library, job interviews.

Freshmen 921 applied, 730 admitted, 277 enrolled.

Average high school GPA	3.1	SAT verbal scores above 500	N/R
SAT math scores above 500	N/R	ACT above 18	83%
1998 freshmen returning in 1999	75%		

Application *Option:* deferred entrance. *Application fee:* $25. *Required:* high school transcript; minimum 2.0 GPA. *Required for some:* essay or personal statement; minimum 3.0 GPA; 3 letters of recommendation. *Recommended:* interview.

Wisconsin

Concordia University Wisconsin *(continued)*

Standardized tests *Admission: Required:* SAT I or ACT.

Significant dates *Application deadlines:* 8/15 (freshmen), 8/15 (transfers). *Notification:* continuous until 8/15 (freshmen). **Financial aid deadline priority date:** 5/1.

Freshman Application Contact

Mr. Andrew Locke, Director of Admissions, Concordia University Wisconsin, 12800 North Lake Shore Drive, Mequon, WI 53097-2402. **Phone:** 262-243-4304 Ext. 305. **Fax:** 262-243-4351. **E-mail:** kgaschk@bach.cuw.edu

Visit CollegeQuest.com for information on majors offered and athletics. Electronic viewbook available at CollegeQuest.com.

■ *See page 1528 for a narrative description.*

EDGEWOOD COLLEGE
Madison, Wisconsin

- **Independent Roman Catholic**, comprehensive, founded 1927
- **Degrees** associate, bachelor's, and master's
- **Urban** 55-acre campus
- **Coed**, 1,286 undergraduate students, 72% full-time, 72% women, 28% men
- **Moderately difficult** entrance level, 77% of applicants were admitted
- **13:1 student-to-undergraduate faculty ratio**
- **45% graduate** in 6 years or less
- **$11,650 tuition** and fees
- **$9940 average financial aid** package, $18,318 average indebtedness upon graduation, $3.8 million endowment

Edgewood College, which promotes personal challenges and professional success, is in an exciting period of fresh facilities, new faculty members, and a growing student body. Students are encouraged to visit by appointment or during one of the Edgewood Event days on campus in fall and spring. Students should call the Admissions Office at 800-444-4861.

Students *Undergraduates:* 930 full-time, 356 part-time. Students come from 11 states and territories, 10 other countries. *The most frequently chosen baccalaureate fields are:* business/marketing, education, home economics/vocational home economics. *Graduate:* 508 in graduate degree programs.

From out-of-state	10%	Reside on campus	15%
Age 25 or older	30%	Transferred in	12%
International students	4%	African Americans	1%
Asian Americans/Pacific Islanders	1%	Hispanic Americans	1%
Native Americans	0.5%		

Faculty 173, 32% with terminal degrees.

Expenses (1999–2000) *Comprehensive fee:* $16,030 includes full-time tuition ($11,450), mandatory fees ($200), and room and board ($4380). *College room only:* $2196. Full-time tuition and fees vary according to program. Room and board charges vary according to board plan and housing facility. *Part-time tuition:* $340 per credit. *Part-time fees:* $55 per term part-time. Part-time tuition and fees vary according to course load and program. *Payment plans:* installment, deferred payment. *Waivers:* employees or children of employees.

Library Oscar Rennebohm Library. *Operations spending 1999–2000:* $432,370. *Collection:* 534 serial subscriptions, 4,156 audiovisual materials.

College life *Housing: Options:* coed, women-only, disabled students. *Most popular organizations:* Student Government Association, Student Programming Board, Resident Life Association, Chalk Talk, Student Nurses Association.

Campus security 24-hour emergency response devices and patrols, student patrols, late-night transport-escort service, controlled dormitory access.

After graduation 23 organizations recruited on campus 1997–98. 86% of class of 1998 had job offers within 6 months. *Career center:* 2 full-time, 1 part-time personnel. Services include resume preparation, interview workshops, resume referral, career counseling, careers library, job bank, job interviews. *Graduate education:* 8% of class of 1999 went directly to graduate and professional school.

Freshmen 703 applied, 541 admitted, 200 enrolled.

Average high school GPA	3.23	SAT verbal scores above 500	67%
SAT math scores above 500	66%	ACT above 18	90%
From top 10% of their h.s. class	13%	From top quarter	33%
From top half	70%	1998 freshmen returning in 1999	68%

Application *Options:* eApply at www.CollegeQuest.com, deferred entrance. *Application fee:* $25. *Required:* high school transcript; minimum 2.5 GPA. *Required for some:* essay or personal statement; 2 letters of recommendation; interview.

Standardized tests *Admission: Required:* SAT I or ACT.

Significant dates *Application deadlines:* rolling (freshmen), rolling (transfers). *Financial aid deadline priority date:* 3/15.

Freshman Application Contact

Mr. Scott Flanagan, Dean of Admissions and Financial Aid, Edgewood College, 855 Woodrow Street, Madison, WI 53711-1997. **Phone:** 608-663-2254. **Toll-free phone:** 800-444-4861. **Fax:** 608-663-3291. **E-mail:** admissions@edgewood.edu

Visit CollegeQuest.com for information on majors offered and athletics.

■ *See page 1614 for a narrative description.*

HERZING COLLEGE
Madison, Wisconsin

- **Proprietary**, primarily 2-year, founded 1948
- **Degrees** associate and bachelor's
- **Suburban** campus with easy access to Milwaukee
- **Coed**, primarily men, 550 undergraduate students
- **Moderately difficult** entrance level

Part of Herzing Institutes, Inc.

Faculty 28 (71% full-time).

Admissions Office Contact

Herzing College, 1227 North Sherman Avenue, Madison, WI 53704-4236. **E-mail:** faculty@wse.tec.wi.us

Visit CollegeQuest.com for information on majors offered and athletics. College video available at CollegeQuest.com.

ITT TECHNICAL INSTITUTE
Greenfield, Wisconsin

- **Proprietary**, primarily 2-year, founded 1968
- **Degrees** associate and bachelor's
- **Suburban** campus with easy access to Milwaukee
- **Coed**
- **Minimally difficult** entrance level
- **$9190 tuition** and fees

Part of ITT Educational Services, Inc.

Admissions Office Contact

ITT Technical Institute, 6300 West Layton Avenue, Greenfield, WI 53220-4612.

Visit CollegeQuest.com for information on majors offered and athletics. College video available at CollegeQuest.com.

LAKELAND COLLEGE
Sheboygan, Wisconsin

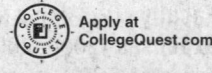

- **Independent**, comprehensive, founded 1862, affiliated with United Church of Christ
- **Degrees** bachelor's and master's
- **Rural** 240-acre campus with easy access to Milwaukee
- **Coed**, 2,920 undergraduate students, 38% full-time, 62% women, 38% men
- **Moderately difficult** entrance level, 74% of applicants were admitted
- **15:1 student-to-undergraduate faculty ratio**
- **65.6% graduate** in 6 years or less
- **$12,480 tuition** and fees

Wisconsin

- **$10,004 average financial aid** package, $10,301 average indebtedness upon graduation, $4.7 million endowment

Students *Undergraduates:* 1,115 full-time, 1,805 part-time. Students come from 14 states and territories, 19 other countries. *The most frequently chosen baccalaureate fields are:* business/marketing, computer/information sciences, education. *Graduate:* 154 in graduate degree programs.

From out-of-state	15%	Reside on campus	65%
Age 25 or older	22%	International students	3%
African Americans	5%	Asian Americans/Pacific Islanders	2%
Hispanic Americans	1%	Native Americans	1%

Faculty 42 full-time.

Expenses (1999–2000) *Comprehensive fee:* $17,160 includes full-time tuition ($11,980), mandatory fees ($500), and room and board ($4680). *College room only:* $2260. Full-time tuition and fees vary according to location. Room and board charges vary according to board plan and housing facility. *Part-time tuition:* $1140 per course. Part-time tuition and fees vary according to class time and location. *Payment plan:* installment. *Waivers:* senior citizens and employees or children of employees.

Library Esch Memorial Library. *Operations spending 1999–2000:* $189,283. *Collection:* 116,171 titles, 298 serial subscriptions, 587 audiovisual materials.

College life *Housing:* on-campus residence required through senior year. *Options:* coed, men-only, women-only. *Social organizations:* local fraternities, local sororities; 17% of eligible men and 11% of eligible women are members. *Most popular organizations:* Lakeland College Activities Board, Student Association, Habitat for Humanity, Mortar Board, PSI Alpha Kappa business fraternity.

Campus security Student patrols, late-night transport-escort service, controlled dormitory access.

After graduation 52% of class of 1998 had job offers within 6 months. *Career center:* 1 full-time, 1 part-time personnel. Services include job fairs, resume preparation, interview workshops, resume referral, career/interest testing, career counseling, careers library, job bank, job interviews. *Graduate education:* 14% of class of 1999 went directly to graduate and professional school: 10% business, 2% law, 1% graduate arts and sciences, 1% theology.

Freshmen 580 applied, 430 admitted, 179 enrolled.

Average high school GPA	2.76	SAT verbal scores above 500	N/R
SAT math scores above 500	N/R	ACT above 18	72%
From top 10% of their h.s. class	9%	From top quarter	27%
From top half	53%	1998 freshmen returning in 1999	75%

Application *Options:* eApply at www.CollegeQuest.com, Common Application, electronic application, deferred entrance. *Application fee:* $20. *Required:* essay or personal statement; high school transcript; minimum 2.0 GPA. *Required for some:* interview. *Recommended:* letters of recommendation.

Standardized tests *Admission: Required:* ACT.

Significant dates *Application deadlines:* rolling (freshmen), rolling (transfers). *Financial aid deadline priority date:* 5/1.

Freshman Application Contact
Mr. Leo Gavrilos, Director of Admissions, Lakeland College, PO Box 359, Sheboygan, WI 53082-0359. **Phone:** 920-565-1217. **Toll-free phone:** 800-242-3347. **Fax:** 920-565-1206. **E-mail:** admissions@lakeland.edu

Visit CollegeQuest.com for information on majors offered and athletics. College video available at CollegeQuest.com.

LAWRENCE UNIVERSITY
Appleton, Wisconsin

 Apply at CollegeQuest.com

- **Independent**, 4-year, founded 1847
- **Degree** bachelor's
- **Small-town** 84-acre campus
- **Coed**, 1,191 undergraduate students, 96% full-time, 54% women, 46% men
- **Very difficult** entrance level, 81% of applicants were admitted
- **11:1 student-to-undergraduate faculty ratio**
- **72% graduate** in 6 years or less
- **$21,012 tuition** and fees
- **$19,124 average financial aid** package, $17,727 average indebtedness upon graduation, $147.4 million endowment

Lawrence is committed to development of intellect and talent, acquisition of knowledge and understanding, and cultivation of judgment and values. Research opportunities and independent study with faculty members, an academic honor code, a conservatory of music, a freshman seminar that focuses on developing communication and analysis skills, and weekend retreats to the college's 400-acre estate on Lake Michigan are among the programs that contribute to "the Lawrence Difference."

Students *Undergraduates:* 1,144 full-time, 47 part-time. Students come from 45 states and territories, 35 other countries. *The most frequently chosen baccalaureate fields are:* biological/life sciences, psychology, social sciences and history.

From out-of-state	47%	Reside on campus	98%
Age 25 or older	1%	Transferred in	1%
International students	7%	African Americans	1%
Asian Americans/Pacific Islanders	3%	Hispanic Americans	1%
Native Americans	0.3%		

Faculty 163 (75% full-time), 78% with terminal degrees.

Expenses (1999–2000) *Comprehensive fee:* $25,709 includes full-time tuition ($20,880), mandatory fees ($132), and room and board ($4697). *College room only:* $2085. Room and board charges vary according to board plan. *Payment plan:* installment. *Waivers:* employees or children of employees.

Library Seeley G. Mudd Library. *Operations spending 1999–2000:* $1.2 million. *Collection:* 367,112 titles, 1,346 serial subscriptions, 15,900 audiovisual materials.

College life *Housing:* on-campus residence required through senior year. *Option:* coed. *Social organizations:* national fraternities, national sororities; 35% of eligible men and 20% of eligible women are members. *Most popular organizations:* Psychology Student Association, outdoor recreation club, Lawrence International, Lawrence Christian Fellowship, political science club.

Campus security 24-hour emergency response devices, student patrols, late-night transport-escort service, controlled dormitory access, evening patrols by trained security personnel.

After graduation 25 organizations recruited on campus 1997–98. 59% of class of 1998 had job offers within 6 months. *Career center:* 3 full-time, 1 part-time personnel. Services include job fairs, resume preparation, interview workshops, resume referral, career/interest testing, career counseling, careers library, job bank, job interviews. *Graduate education:* 27% of class of 1999 went directly to graduate and professional school: 20% graduate arts and sciences, 4% medicine, 3% law. *Major awards:* 1 Fulbright Scholar.

Freshmen 1,348 applied, 1,096 admitted, 327 enrolled. 19 valedictorians.

Average high school GPA	3.62	SAT verbal scores above 500	91%
SAT math scores above 500	93%	ACT above 18	100%
From top 10% of their h.s. class	49%	From top quarter	78%
From top half	97%	1998 freshmen returning in 1999	85%

Application *Options:* eApply at www.CollegeQuest.com, Common Application, electronic application, early admission, early decision, early action, deferred entrance. *Application fee:* $30. *Required:* essay or personal statement; high school transcript; 2 letters of recommendation; audition for music program. *Recommended:* minimum 3.0 GPA; interview.

Standardized tests *Admission: Required:* SAT I or ACT.

Significant dates *Application deadlines:* 1/15 (freshmen), rolling (transfers). *Early decision:* 11/15, 12/1. *Notification:* 4/1 (freshmen), 12/1 (early decision), 1/15 (early action). *Financial aid deadline priority date:* 3/1.

Freshman Application Contact
Mr. Steven T. Syverson, Dean of Admissions and Financial Aid, Lawrence University, PO Box 599, Appleton, WI 54912-0599. **Phone:** 920-832-6500. **Toll-free phone:** 800-227-0982. **Fax:** 920-832-6606. **E-mail:** excel@lawrence.edu

Visit CollegeQuest.com for information on majors offered and athletics. College video and electronic viewbook available at CollegeQuest.com.

- *See page 1906 for a narrative description.*

Wisconsin

MARANATHA BAPTIST BIBLE COLLEGE
Watertown, Wisconsin

- **Independent Baptist**, comprehensive, founded 1968
- **Degrees** associate, bachelor's, and master's
- **Small-town** 60-acre campus with easy access to Milwaukee
- **Coed**, 715 undergraduate students, 89% full-time, 54% women, 46% men
- **Noncompetitive** entrance level
- **18:1 student-to-undergraduate faculty ratio**
- **$6370 tuition** and fees
- **$5104 average financial aid** package, $10,829 average indebtedness upon graduation, $151,276 endowment

Students *Undergraduates:* 633 full-time, 82 part-time. Students come from 35 states and territories, 8 other countries. *Graduate:* 31 in graduate degree programs.

From out-of-state	58%	Reside on campus	80%
Age 25 or older	8%	Transferred in	5%
International students	2%	African Americans	1%
Asian Americans/Pacific Islanders	1%	Hispanic Americans	2%
Native Americans	0.4%		

Faculty 41 (83% full-time), 27% with terminal degrees.
Expenses (1999–2000) *Comprehensive fee:* $10,170 includes full-time tuition ($5760), mandatory fees ($610), and room and board ($3800). *Part-time tuition:* $180 per semester hour. *Part-time fees:* $6 per semester hour; $125 per term part-time. *Payment plan:* installment. *Waivers:* children of alumni and employees or children of employees.
Library Cedarholm Library and Resource Center plus 1 other. *Operations spending 1999–2000:* $247,516. *Collection:* 99,390 titles, 515 serial subscriptions, 3,441 audiovisual materials.
College life *Housing:* on-campus residence required through senior year. *Options:* men-only, women-only. *Social organizations:* Married Students Society; 100% of eligible men and 100% of eligible women are members.
Campus security Student patrols, late-night transport-escort service, controlled dormitory access.
After graduation *Career center:* 1 full-time, 1 part-time personnel. Services include resume referral, career counseling. *Graduate education:* 28% of class of 1999 went directly to graduate and professional school.
Freshmen 358 applied, 209 admitted, 219 enrolled.

SAT verbal scores above 500	N/R	SAT math scores above 500	N/R
ACT above 18	78%	1998 freshmen returning in 1999	64%

Application *Options:* Common Application, early admission, deferred entrance. *Preference* given to Christians. *Application fee:* $25. *Required:* essay or personal statement; high school transcript; 3 letters of recommendation.
Standardized tests *Admission: Recommended:* ACT.
Significant dates *Application deadlines:* rolling (freshmen), rolling (transfers). *Financial aid deadline priority date:* 3/1.
Freshman Application Contact
James H. Harrison, Director of Admissions, Maranatha Baptist Bible College, 745 West Main Street, Watertown, WI 53094. **Phone:** 920-206-2327. **Toll-free phone:** 800-622-2947. **Fax:** 920-261-9109 Ext. 308. **E-mail:** admissions@mbbc.edu
Visit CollegeQuest.com for information on majors offered and athletics.

MARIAN COLLEGE OF FOND DU LAC
Fond du Lac, Wisconsin

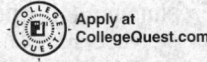 Apply at CollegeQuest.com

- **Independent Roman Catholic**, comprehensive, founded 1936
- **Degrees** bachelor's and master's
- **Small-town** 50-acre campus with easy access to Milwaukee
- **Coed**, 1,484 undergraduate students, 65% full-time, 67% women, 33% men
- **Moderately difficult** entrance level, 44% of applicants were admitted
- **14:1 student-to-undergraduate faculty ratio**
- **49% graduate** in 6 years or less
- **$12,256 tuition** and fees
- **$10,635 average financial aid** package, $14,500 average indebtedness upon graduation, $3.3 million endowment

Marian College distinguishes itself from other institutions with extensive clinical, internship, and cooperative education experiences. As a result of these experiences, students develop the knowledge and skills necessary to be competent and marketable in their chosen fields. In fact, 97 percent of Marian graduates find employment or enter graduate schools of their choice. Marian students enjoy the benefits of a truly personal education and make their home away from home in unique housing options, including residence halls, townhouses, and courtyard suites.

Students *Undergraduates:* 963 full-time, 521 part-time. Students come from 13 states and territories, 8 other countries. *The most frequently chosen baccalaureate fields are:* business/marketing, education, health professions and related sciences. *Graduate:* 807 in graduate degree programs.

From out-of-state	20%	Reside on campus	55%
Age 25 or older	22%	Transferred in	7%

Faculty 125 (65% full-time), 27% with terminal degrees.
Expenses (1999–2000) *Comprehensive fee:* $16,620 includes full-time tuition ($11,966), mandatory fees ($290), and room and board ($4364). *College room only:* $2036. Room and board charges vary according to board plan, housing facility, and location. *Part-time tuition:* $255 per credit. *Part-time fees:* $290 per year part-time. Part-time tuition and fees vary according to class time, course load, and program. *Payment plan:* installment. *Waivers:* senior citizens and employees or children of employees.
Library Cardinal Meyer Library. *Operations spending 1999–2000:* $349,000. *Collection:* 100,000 titles, 700 serial subscriptions.
College life *Housing:* on-campus residence required through sophomore year. *Option:* coed. *Social organizations:* national fraternities, national sororities; 15% of eligible men and 15% of eligible women are members. *Most popular organizations:* student senate, Student Nurses Association, Student Education Association, arts and humanities club, music performance organization.
Campus security 24-hour emergency response devices and patrols, student patrols, late-night transport-escort service, controlled dormitory access.
After graduation 25 organizations recruited on campus 1997–98. 98% of class of 1998 had job offers within 6 months. *Career center:* 4 full-time, 2 part-time personnel. Services include job fairs, resume preparation, interview workshops, resume referral, career/interest testing, career counseling, careers library, job bank, job interviews. *Graduate education:* 5% of class of 1999 went directly to graduate and professional school.
Freshmen 485 applied, 212 admitted, 227 enrolled. 6 class presidents, 8 valedictorians, 20 student government officers.

Average high school GPA	3.02	SAT verbal scores above 500	N/R
SAT math scores above 500	N/R	ACT above 18	16%
From top 10% of their h.s. class	15%	From top quarter	25%
From top half	85%	1998 freshmen returning in 1999	71%

Application *Options:* eApply at www.CollegeQuest.com, Common Application, electronic application, early admission, deferred entrance. *Application fee:* $15. *Required:* high school transcript. *Required for some:* interview. *Recommended:* minimum 2.0 GPA; letters of recommendation.
Standardized tests *Admission: Required:* SAT I or ACT.
Significant dates *Application deadlines:* rolling (freshmen), rolling (transfers). *Notification:* continuous until 8/15 (freshmen). *Financial aid deadline priority date:* 3/1.
Freshman Application Contact
Ms. Stacey Akey, Dean of Admissions, Marian College of Fond du Lac, 45 South National Avenue, Fond du Lac, WI 54935. **Phone:** 920-923-7652. **Toll-free phone:** 800-2-MARIAN. **Fax:** 920-923-8755. **E-mail:** admit@mariancollege.edu
Visit CollegeQuest.com for information on majors offered and athletics. College video and electronic viewbook available at CollegeQuest.com.

- *See page 1988 for a narrative description.*

MARQUETTE UNIVERSITY
Milwaukee, Wisconsin

  Apply at CollegeQuest.com

- **Independent Roman Catholic (Jesuit)**, university, founded 1881
- **Degrees** associate, bachelor's, master's, doctoral, and first professional
- **Urban** 80-acre campus

Wisconsin

- **Coed**, 7,238 undergraduate students, 93% full-time, 54% women, 46% men
- **Moderately difficult** entrance level, 84% of applicants were admitted
- **14:1 student-to-undergraduate faculty ratio**
- **70.3% graduate** in 6 years or less
- **$17,336 tuition** and fees
- **$15,461 average financial aid** package, $205.2 million endowment

Students *Undergraduates:* 6,713 full-time, 525 part-time. Students come from 54 states and territories, 62 other countries. *The most frequently chosen baccalaureate fields are:* business/marketing, engineering/engineering technologies, health professions and related sciences. *Graduate:* 1,104 in professional programs, 2,239 in other graduate degree programs.

From out-of-state	54%	Reside on campus	55%
Transferred in	2%	International students	2%
African Americans	5%	Asian Americans/Pacific Islanders	4%
Hispanic Americans	4%	Native Americans	0.3%

Faculty 956 (56% full-time).
Expenses (1999–2000) *Comprehensive fee:* $23,422 includes full-time tuition ($17,080), mandatory fees ($256), and room and board ($6086). Full-time tuition and fees vary according to program and student level. Room and board charges vary according to board plan and housing facility. *Part-time tuition:* $350 per credit. Part-time tuition and fees vary according to program. *Payment plans:* tuition prepayment, installment. *Waivers:* senior citizens and employees or children of employees.
Library Memorial Library plus 2 others. *Operations spending 1999–2000:* $7.8 million. *Collection:* 1.2 million titles, 9,225 serial subscriptions, 7,276 audiovisual materials.
College life *Housing:* on-campus residence required through sophomore year. *Options:* coed, men-only, women-only, disabled students. *Social organizations:* national fraternities, national sororities; 9% of eligible men and 8% of eligible women are members. *Most popular organizations:* Marquette University Student Government, club sports, Marquette University Community Action Program, student publications, band/jazz/orchestra.
Campus security 24-hour emergency response devices and patrols, student patrols, late-night transport-escort service, 24-hour desk attendants in residence halls.
After graduation 400 organizations recruited on campus 1997–98. 66% of class of 1998 had job offers within 6 months. *Career center:* 4 full-time personnel. Services include job fairs, resume preparation, interview workshops, resume referral, career/interest testing, career counseling, careers library, job bank, job interviews. *Graduate education:* 30% of class of 1999 went directly to graduate and professional school.
Freshmen 6,925 applied, 5,795 admitted, 1,718 enrolled. 75 valedictorians.

SAT verbal scores above 500	86%	SAT math scores above 500	86%
ACT above 18	100%	From top 10% of their h.s. class	36%
From top quarter	68%	From top half	94%
1998 freshmen returning in 1999	88%		

Application *Options:* eApply at www.CollegeQuest.com, Common Application, electronic application, deferred entrance. *Application fee:* $30. *Required:* essay or personal statement; high school transcript; minimum 2.0 GPA. *Recommended:* minimum 3.0 GPA; 1 letter of recommendation; interview.
Standardized tests *Admission: Required:* SAT I or ACT.
Significant dates *Application deadlines:* rolling (freshmen), rolling (transfers). *Financial aid deadline:* continuous.
Freshman Application Contact
Mr. Raymond A. Brown, Dean of Admissions, Marquette University, PO Box 1881, Milwaukee, WI 53201-1881. **Phone:** 414-288-7302. **Toll-free phone:** 800-222-6544. **E-mail:** go2marquette@marquette.edu
Visit CollegeQuest.com for information on majors offered and athletics. Electronic viewbook available at CollegeQuest.com.

MILWAUKEE INSTITUTE OF ART AND DESIGN
Milwaukee, Wisconsin

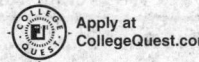
Apply at CollegeQuest.com

- **Independent**, 4-year, founded 1974
- **Degree** bachelor's
- **Urban** campus
- **Coed**, 611 undergraduate students, 90% full-time, 45% women, 55% men
- **Moderately difficult** entrance level, 84% of applicants were admitted
- **11:1 student-to-undergraduate faculty ratio**
- **$15,080 tuition** and fees
- **$13,210 average financial aid** package, $21,053 average indebtedness upon graduation, $1.5 million endowment

Students *Undergraduates:* 548 full-time, 63 part-time. Students come from 20 states and territories, 2 other countries. *The most frequently chosen baccalaureate field is:* visual/performing arts.

From out-of-state	29%	Reside on campus	22%
Age 25 or older	15%	Transferred in	10%
International students	0.2%	African Americans	3%
Asian Americans/Pacific Islanders	2%	Hispanic Americans	8%
Native Americans	0.3%		

Faculty 101 (26% full-time), 67% with terminal degrees.
Expenses (1999–2000) *Comprehensive fee:* $21,538 includes full-time tuition ($14,950), mandatory fees ($130), and room and board ($6458). Full-time tuition and fees vary according to student level. Room and board charges vary according to board plan. *Part-time tuition:* $500 per credit. *Part-time fees:* $65 per term part-time. Part-time tuition and fees vary according to course load. *Payment plan:* deferred payment. *Waivers:* employees or children of employees.
Library *Operations spending 1999–2000:* $157,371. *Collection:* 23,000 titles, 84 serial subscriptions, 360 audiovisual materials.
College life *Housing:* on-campus residence required in freshman year. *Option:* coed. *Most popular organizations:* student government, Student Gallery Committee, Student Activities Committee, Minority Student Organization, community service.
Campus security 24-hour emergency response devices, late-night transport-escort service.
After graduation 10 organizations recruited on campus 1997–98. 87% of class of 1998 had job offers within 6 months. *Career center:* 1 full-time personnel. Services include resume preparation, resume referral, career counseling, careers library, job bank. *Graduate education:* 1% of class of 1999 went directly to graduate and professional school; 1% graduate arts and sciences.
Freshmen 290 applied, 244 admitted, 139 enrolled.

Average high school GPA	2.9	SAT verbal scores above 500	N/R
SAT math scores above 500	N/R	ACT above 18	N/R
1998 freshmen returning in 1999	73%		

Application *Options:* eApply at www.CollegeQuest.com, Common Application, deferred entrance. *Application fee:* $25. *Required:* essay or personal statement; high school transcript; interview; portfolio. *Required for some:* letters of recommendation. *Recommended:* minimum 2.0 GPA.
Standardized tests *Placement: Recommended:* SAT I or ACT.
Significant dates *Application deadlines:* rolling (freshmen), rolling (transfers). *Financial aid deadline:* 3/1.
Freshman Application Contact
Ms. Mary Schopp, Executive Director of Enrollment Services, Milwaukee Institute of Art and Design, 273 East Erie Street, Milwaukee, WI 53202. **Phone:** 414-291-8070. **Toll-free phone:** 888-749-MIAD. **Fax:** 414-291-8077.
Visit CollegeQuest.com for information on majors offered and athletics. College video available at CollegeQuest.com.

MILWAUKEE SCHOOL OF ENGINEERING
Milwaukee, Wisconsin

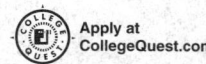
Apply at CollegeQuest.com

- **Independent**, comprehensive, founded 1903
- **Degrees** associate, bachelor's, and master's
- **Urban** 12-acre campus
- **Coed**, primarily men, 2,343 undergraduate students, 72% full-time, 17% women, 83% men
- **Moderately difficult** entrance level, 71% of applicants were admitted
- **12:1 student-to-undergraduate faculty ratio**
- **48% graduate** in 6 years or less
- **$19,845 tuition** and fees

Wisconsin

Milwaukee School of Engineering (continued)

- **$12,400 average financial aid** package, $21,500 average indebtedness upon graduation, $10.1 million endowment

Students *Undergraduates:* 1,694 full-time, 649 part-time. Students come from 34 states and territories, 27 other countries. *The most frequently chosen baccalaureate fields are:* business/marketing, engineering/engineering technologies, health professions and related sciences. *Graduate:* 368 in graduate degree programs.

From out-of-state	20%	Reside on campus	34%
Age 25 or older	27%	Transferred in	7%
International students	4%	African Americans	3%
Asian Americans/Pacific Islanders	3%	Hispanic Americans	2%
Native Americans	0.4%		

Faculty 229 (51% full-time), 33% with terminal degrees.

Expenses (2000–2001) *One-time required fee:* $1140. *Comprehensive fee:* $24,555 includes full-time tuition ($19,845) and room and board ($4710). *College room only:* $2850. Full-time tuition and fees vary according to student level. Room and board charges vary according to board plan and housing facility. *Part-time tuition:* $345 per quarter hour. Part-time tuition and fees vary according to course load. *Payment plan:* installment. *Waivers:* employees or children of employees.

Library Walter Schroeder Library. *Operations spending 1999–2000:* $456,863. *Collection:* 55,310 titles, 565 serial subscriptions, 565 audiovisual materials.

College life *Housing:* on-campus residence required through sophomore year. *Options:* coed, disabled students. *Social organizations:* national fraternities, national sororities, local fraternities, local sororities; 11% of eligible men and 9% of eligible women are members. *Most popular organizations:* Architectural Engineering Society, Society of Automotive Engineers, Student Government Association, Circle K, Student Union Board.

Campus security 24-hour emergency response devices and patrols, late-night transport-escort service, controlled dormitory access.

After graduation 194 organizations recruited on campus 1997–98. 95% of class of 1998 had job offers within 6 months. *Career center:* 3 full-time, 2 part-time personnel. Services include job fairs, resume preparation, interview workshops, resume referral, career/interest testing, career counseling, careers library, job bank, job interviews.

Freshmen 1,837 applied, 1,312 admitted, 511 enrolled.

Average high school GPA	3.4	SAT verbal scores above 500	80%
SAT math scores above 500	89%	ACT above 18	99%
From top 10% of their h.s. class	26%	From top quarter	59%
From top half	89%	1998 freshmen returning in 1999	76%

Application *Options:* eApply at www.CollegeQuest.com, electronic application, deferred entrance. *Application fee:* $25. *Required:* high school transcript; minimum 2.0 GPA. *Required for some:* essay or personal statement; interview.

Standardized tests *Admission: Required:* SAT I or ACT.

Significant dates *Application deadlines:* rolling (freshmen), rolling (transfers). *Financial aid deadline priority date:* 3/15.

Freshman Application Contact
Mr. Tim A. Valley, Dean of Enrollment Management, Milwaukee School of Engineering, 1025 North Broadway, Milwaukee, WI 53202-3109. **Phone:** 414-277-6763. **Toll-free phone:** 800-332-6763. **Fax:** 414-277-7475. **E-mail:** explore@msoe.edu

Visit CollegeQuest.com for information on majors offered and athletics. Electronic viewbook available at CollegeQuest.com.

- *See page 2064 for a narrative description.*

MOUNT MARY COLLEGE
Milwaukee, Wisconsin

Apply at CollegeQuest.com

- **Independent Roman Catholic**, comprehensive, founded 1913
- **Degrees** bachelor's and master's
- **Suburban** 80-acre campus
- **Women** only, 922 undergraduate students, 64% full-time
- **Moderately difficult** entrance level, 83% of applicants were admitted
- **8:1** student-to-undergraduate faculty ratio
- **62.8% graduate** in 6 years or less
- **$12,270 tuition** and fees
- **$10,005 average financial aid** package, $16.8 million endowment

Students *Undergraduates:* 587 full-time, 335 part-time. Students come from 14 states and territories. *The most frequently chosen baccalaureate fields are:* business/marketing, education, protective services/public administration. *Graduate:* 152 in graduate degree programs.

Reside on campus	27%	Age 25 or older	31%
Transferred in	21%	International students	1%
African Americans	11%	Asian Americans/Pacific Islanders	2%
Hispanic Americans	4%	Native Americans	0.5%

Faculty 157 (49% full-time).

Expenses (1999–2000) *Comprehensive fee:* $16,460 includes full-time tuition ($12,120), mandatory fees ($150), and room and board ($4190). Room and board charges vary according to board plan and housing facility. *Part-time tuition:* $365 per credit. *Part-time fees:* $40 per term part-time. Part-time tuition and fees vary according to course load. *Payment plan:* installment. *Waivers:* senior citizens and employees or children of employees.

Library Haggerty Library. *Operations spending 1999–2000:* $463,874. *Collection:* 104,400 titles, 1,340 serial subscriptions, 5,650 audiovisual materials.

College life *Housing: Option:* women-only. *Most popular organizations:* Student Association, campus ministry, Student Occupational Therapy Association, ARTS Organization.

Campus security 24-hour patrols, late-night transport-escort service, controlled dormitory access.

After graduation 3 organizations recruited on campus 1997–98. *Career center:* 1 full-time, 3 part-time personnel. Services include job fairs, resume preparation, interview workshops, career/interest testing, career counseling, careers library. *Graduate education:* 6% of class of 1999 went directly to graduate and professional school: 4% graduate arts and sciences, 2% business.

Freshmen 232 applied, 193 admitted, 110 enrolled.

Average high school GPA	3.14	SAT verbal scores above 500	67%
SAT math scores above 500	67%	ACT above 18	91%
From top 10% of their h.s. class	12%	From top quarter	40%
From top half	75%	1998 freshmen returning in 1999	86%

Application *Options:* eApply at www.CollegeQuest.com, Common Application, electronic application, early admission. *Application fee:* $25. *Required:* high school transcript; minimum 2.3 GPA. *Required for some:* essay or personal statement; 2 letters of recommendation.

Standardized tests *Admission: Required:* SAT I or ACT.

Significant dates *Application deadlines:* 8/15 (freshmen), 8/15 (transfers). *Financial aid deadline priority date:* 3/1.

Freshman Application Contact
Ms. Yvonne Hennigan, Dean of Enrollment Management, Mount Mary College, 2900 North Menomonee River Parkway, Milwaukee, WI 53222-4597. **Phone:** 414-258-4810 Ext. 360. **Fax:** 414-256-1224. **E-mail:** admiss@mtmary.edu

Visit CollegeQuest.com for information on majors offered and athletics.

- *See page 2110 for a narrative description.*

MOUNT SENARIO COLLEGE
Ladysmith, Wisconsin

- **Independent**, 4-year, founded 1962
- **Degrees** associate and bachelor's
- **Small-town** 110-acre campus
- **Coed**, 917 undergraduate students, 48% full-time, 35% women, 65% men
- **Minimally difficult** entrance level, 75% of applicants were admitted
- **11:1** student-to-undergraduate faculty ratio
- **33% graduate** in 6 years or less
- **$12,250 tuition** and fees
- **$10,598 average financial aid** package, $275,000 endowment

Students *Undergraduates:* 436 full-time, 481 part-time. Students come from 13 states and territories, 20 other countries. *The most frequently chosen baccalaureate fields are:* business/marketing, education, protective services/public administration.

Wisconsin

From out-of-state	9%	Age 25 or older	56%
Transferred in	4%	International students	5%
African Americans	12%	Asian Americans/Pacific Islanders	2%
Hispanic Americans	3%	Native Americans	1%

Faculty 69 (55% full-time), 20% with terminal degrees.
Expenses (2000–2001) *Comprehensive fee:* $16,990 includes full-time tuition ($12,250) and room and board ($4740). *College room only:* $2150. Full-time tuition and fees vary according to course load. *Part-time tuition:* $525 per credit. Part-time tuition and fees vary according to course load. *Payment plan:* installment. *Waivers:* employees or children of employees.
Library Mount Senario College Library plus 1 other. *Collection:* 38,796 titles, 4,150 serial subscriptions.
College life *Housing:* on-campus residence required through junior year. *Option:* coed. *Most popular organizations:* Student Senate, Hmong Student Association, Black Student Association, business club, social work club.
Campus security Student patrols, late-night transport-escort service, controlled dormitory access, security lighting.
After graduation 3 organizations recruited on campus 1997–98. *Career center:* 1 full-time personnel. Services include job fairs, resume preparation, career counseling, job bank.
Freshmen 238 applied, 179 admitted, 99 enrolled.

Average high school GPA	2.55	SAT verbal scores above 500	N/R
SAT math scores above 500	N/R	ACT above 18	54%
From top 10% of their h.s. class	10%	From top quarter	33%
From top half	68%	1998 freshmen returning in 1999	44%

Application *Options:* Common Application, electronic application, early admission. *Application fee:* $10. *Required:* essay or personal statement; high school transcript; 1 letter of recommendation; interview.
Standardized tests *Admission: Required:* SAT I or ACT.
Significant dates *Application deadline:* 8/20 (freshmen). *Financial aid deadline priority date:* 5/15.
Freshman Application Contact
Mr. Max M. Waits, Admissions Consultant/Foreign Student Advisor, Mount Senario College, 1500 College Avenue West, Ladysmith, WI 54848-2128. **Phone:** 715-532-5511 Ext. 110. **Toll-free phone:** 800-281-6514. **Fax:** 715-532-7690. **E-mail:** admissions@mscfs.edu
Visit CollegeQuest.com for information on majors offered and athletics.

NORTHLAND COLLEGE
Ashland, Wisconsin

- **Independent**, 4-year, founded 1892, affiliated with United Church of Christ
- **Degree** bachelor's
- **Small-town** 130-acre campus
- **Coed**, 776 undergraduate students, 95% full-time, 59% women, 41% men
- **Moderately difficult** entrance level, 89% of applicants were admitted
- **14:1** student-to-undergraduate faculty ratio
- **$14,675 tuition** and fees
- **$12,185 average financial aid** package, $17.6 million endowment

Students *Undergraduates:* 737 full-time, 39 part-time. Students come from 47 states and territories, 10 other countries.

From out-of-state	67%	Reside on campus	64%
Age 25 or older	17%	Transferred in	7%
International students	2%	African Americans	1%
Asian Americans/Pacific Islanders	2%	Hispanic Americans	2%
Native Americans	2%		

Faculty 87 (53% full-time).
Expenses (2000–2001) *Comprehensive fee:* $19,145 includes full-time tuition ($14,415), mandatory fees ($260), and room and board ($4470). *College room only:* $1860. Room and board charges vary according to board plan and housing facility. *Payment plans:* tuition prepayment, installment. *Waivers:* employees or children of employees.
Library Dexter Library. *Collection:* 81,000 titles, 340 serial subscriptions.
College life *Housing:* on-campus residence required through sophomore year. *Options:* coed, men-only, women-only. *Social organizations:* local sororities. *Most popular organizations:* Let's Go Boatin', Northland College student association, Native American student association, Northland Greens, "N" Club.
Campus security 24-hour emergency response devices, controlled dormitory access.
After graduation 90 organizations recruited on campus 1997–98. *Career center:* 1 full-time, 1 part-time personnel. Services include job fairs, resume preparation, interview workshops, career/interest testing, career counseling, careers library, job bank, job interviews. *Graduate education:* 26% of class of 1999 went directly to graduate and professional school: 16% graduate arts and sciences, 6% business, 2% veterinary medicine, 1% engineering, 1% medicine.
Freshmen 1,133 applied, 1,012 admitted, 203 enrolled.

SAT verbal scores above 500	N/R	SAT math scores above 500	N/R
ACT above 18	N/R	From top 10% of their h.s. class	22%
From top quarter	47%	From top half	77%
1998 freshmen returning in 1999	67%		

Application *Options:* Common Application, electronic application, early admission, deferred entrance. *Application fee:* $0. *Required:* essay or personal statement; high school transcript; 1 letter of recommendation. *Required for some:* interview. *Recommended:* minimum 2.0 GPA.
Standardized tests *Admission: Required:* SAT I or ACT.
Significant dates *Application deadlines:* 8/1 (freshmen), 8/1 (transfers). *Financial aid deadline priority date:* 4/15.
Freshman Application Contact
Mr. Eric A. Peterson, Director of Admission, Northland College, 1411 Ellis Avenue, Ashland, WI 54806. **Phone:** 715-682-1224. **Toll-free phone:** 800-753-1840. **Fax:** 715-682-1258. **E-mail:** admit@northland.edu
Visit CollegeQuest.com for information on majors offered and athletics. College video available at CollegeQuest.com.

RIPON COLLEGE
Ripon, Wisconsin

Apply at CollegeQuest.com

- **Independent**, 4-year, founded 1851
- **Degree** bachelor's
- **Small-town** 250-acre campus with easy access to Milwaukee
- **Coed**, 710 undergraduate students, 99% full-time, 51% women, 49% men
- **Moderately difficult** entrance level, 87% of applicants were admitted
- **10:1** student-to-undergraduate faculty ratio
- **56.1%** graduate in 6 years or less
- **$18,240 tuition** and fees
- **$16,798 average financial aid** package, $15,507 average indebtedness upon graduation, $30.6 million endowment

Students *Undergraduates:* 704 full-time, 6 part-time. Students come from 35 states and territories, 11 other countries. *The most frequently chosen baccalaureate fields are:* biological/life sciences, English, social sciences and history.

From out-of-state	29%	Reside on campus	94%
Age 25 or older	1%	Transferred in	2%
International students	2%	African Americans	1%
Asian Americans/Pacific Islanders	2%	Hispanic Americans	3%
Native Americans	1%		

Faculty 91 (67% full-time).
Expenses (1999–2000) *Comprehensive fee:* $22,640 includes full-time tuition ($18,000), mandatory fees ($240), and room and board ($4400). *College room only:* $2000. *Part-time tuition:* $775 per credit. *Payment plans:* guaranteed tuition, installment. *Waivers:* children of alumni and employees or children of employees.
Library Lane Library. *Operations spending 1999–2000:* $536,665. *Collection:* 161,396 titles, 710 serial subscriptions, 8,200 audiovisual materials.
College life *Housing:* on-campus residence required through senior year. *Options:* coed, men-only, women-only. *Social organizations:* national fraternities, national sororities, local fraternities, local sororities; 59% of eligible men and 33% of eligible women are members. *Most popular organizations:* Environmental Group of Ripon, Student Senate, Community Service Coalition, SMAC (Student Media and Activities Committee).
Campus security 24-hour emergency response devices and patrols, student patrols, late-night transport-escort service, controlled dormitory access.
After graduation 20 organizations recruited on campus 1997–98. 74% of class of 1998 had job offers within 6 months. *Career center:* 2 full-time personnel. Services include job fairs, resume preparation, resume referral, career counseling, careers library, job bank, job interviews.

Wisconsin

Ripon College (continued)

Freshmen 824 applied, 718 admitted, 283 enrolled. 15 valedictorians.

Average high school GPA	3.4	SAT verbal scores above 500	91%
SAT math scores above 500	91%	ACT above 18	97%
From top 10% of their h.s. class	28%	From top quarter	57%
From top half	86%	1998 freshmen returning in 1999	85%

Application *Options:* eApply at www.CollegeQuest.com, Common Application, electronic application. *Application fee:* $25. *Required:* high school transcript; minimum 2.0 GPA; 1 letter of recommendation. *Recommended:* essay or personal statement; interview.

Standardized tests *Admission: Required:* SAT I or ACT.

Significant dates *Application deadlines:* 3/15 (freshmen), rolling (transfers). *Financial aid deadline:* continuous.

Freshman Application Contact
Mr. Scott J. Goplin, Vice President and Dean of Admission and Financial Aid, Ripon College, 300 Seward Street, PO Box 248, Ripon, WI 54971. **Phone:** 920-748-8185. **Toll-free phone:** 800-947-4766. **Fax:** 920-748-7243. **E-mail:** adminfo@ripon.edu

Visit CollegeQuest.com for information on majors offered and athletics. College video available at CollegeQuest.com.

■ *See page 2334 for a narrative description.*

ST. NORBERT COLLEGE
De Pere, Wisconsin

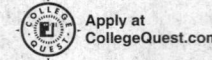
Apply at CollegeQuest.com

- **Independent Roman Catholic**, comprehensive, founded 1898
- **Degrees** bachelor's and master's
- **Suburban** 84-acre campus
- **Coed**, 1,938 undergraduate students, 97% full-time, 59% women, 41% men
- **Moderately difficult** entrance level, 90% of applicants were admitted
- **15:1 student-to-undergraduate faculty ratio**
- **74.8% graduate** in 6 years or less
- **$16,770 tuition** and fees
- **$13,045 average financial aid** package, $14,088 average indebtedness upon graduation, $43.5 million endowment

To firmly address the concern of private school affordability, St. Norbert College offers a 4-year cost guarantee upon payment of a premium, a 4-year graduation guarantee, and guaranteed campus employment to all students regardless of need.

Students *Undergraduates:* 1,872 full-time, 66 part-time. Students come from 27 states and territories, 28 other countries. *The most frequently chosen baccalaureate fields are:* business/marketing, education, social sciences and history. *Graduate:* 9 in graduate degree programs.

From out-of-state	28%	Reside on campus	86%
Age 25 or older	3%	Transferred in	4%
International students	4%	African Americans	1%
Asian Americans/Pacific Islanders	1%	Hispanic Americans	1%
Native Americans	1%		

Faculty 167 (69% full-time), 65% with terminal degrees.

Expenses (2000–2001) *Comprehensive fee:* $21,932 includes full-time tuition ($16,570), mandatory fees ($200), and room and board ($5162). *College room only:* $2742. Full-time tuition and fees vary according to course load. Room and board charges vary according to board plan and housing facility. *Part-time tuition:* $518 per credit hour. *Part-time fees:* $12 per course; $20 per term part-time. Part-time tuition and fees vary according to course load. *Payment plans:* guaranteed tuition, installment, deferred payment. *Waivers:* employees or children of employees.

Library Todd Wehr Library. *Operations spending 1999–2000:* $472,800. *Collection:* 134,203 titles, 698 serial subscriptions, 2,362 audiovisual materials.

College life *Housing:* on-campus residence required through senior year. *Options:* coed, women-only, disabled students. *Social organizations:* national fraternities, national sororities, local fraternities, local sororities; 20% of eligible men and 20% of eligible women are members. *Most popular organizations:* Yes! Your Entertainment Service, social organizations, student newspaper, student government, Residence Hall Association.

Campus security 24-hour emergency response devices and patrols, student patrols, late-night transport-escort service, crime prevention programs.

After graduation 38 organizations recruited on campus 1997–98. 76% of class of 1998 had job offers within 6 months. *Career center:* 5 full-time personnel. Services include job fairs, resume preparation, interview workshops, resume referral, career/interest testing, career counseling, careers library, job bank, job interviews.

Freshmen 1,396 applied, 1,251 admitted, 519 enrolled. 3 National Merit Scholars, 15 class presidents, 19 valedictorians.

Average high school GPA	3.4	SAT verbal scores above 500	N/R
SAT math scores above 500	N/R	ACT above 18	98%
From top 10% of their h.s. class	31%	From top quarter	60%
From top half	92%	1998 freshmen returning in 1999	83%

Application *Options:* eApply at www.CollegeQuest.com, Common Application, electronic application, early decision, deferred entrance. *Preference* given to children of alumni, siblings of current or former students, dependents of employees. *Application fee:* $25. *Required:* essay or personal statement; high school transcript; 1 letter of recommendation. *Recommended:* interview.

Standardized tests *Admission: Required:* SAT I or ACT.

Significant dates *Application deadlines:* rolling (freshmen), rolling (transfers). *Early decision:* 12/1. *Notification:* 12/15 (early decision). *Financial aid deadline priority date:* 3/1.

Freshman Application Contact
Mr. Daniel L. Meyer, Dean of Admission and Enrollment Management, St. Norbert College, 100 Grant Street, Office of Admission, De Pere, WI 54115-2099. **Phone:** 920-403-3005. **Toll-free phone:** 800-236-4878. **E-mail:** admit@mail.snc.edu

Visit CollegeQuest.com for information on majors offered and athletics. Electronic viewbook available at CollegeQuest.com.

■ *See page 2424 for a narrative description.*

SILVER LAKE COLLEGE
Manitowoc, Wisconsin

- **Independent Roman Catholic**, comprehensive, founded 1869
- **Degrees** associate, bachelor's, and master's
- **Rural** 30-acre campus with easy access to Milwaukee
- **Coed**, 516 undergraduate students, 51% full-time, 67% women, 33% men
- **Minimally difficult** entrance level, 44% of applicants were admitted
- **8:1 student-to-undergraduate faculty ratio**
- **44% graduate** in 6 years or less
- **$11,150 tuition** and fees
- **$10,398 average financial aid** package, $15,344 average indebtedness upon graduation, $4.3 million endowment

In a recent survey of SLC graduates, 98% of those responding said they are very satisfied or satisfied with their education. For information about programs of study likely to satisfy students' needs, contact the College's admissions office at 800-236-4SLC Ext. 175 (toll-free) or visit the College's Web site at www.sl.edu.

Students *Undergraduates:* 264 full-time, 252 part-time. Students come from 3 states and territories, 2 other countries. *The most frequently chosen baccalaureate fields are:* business/marketing, education, engineering/engineering technologies. *Graduate:* 241 in graduate degree programs.

From out-of-state	3%	Reside on campus	3%
Age 25 or older	70%	Transferred in	16%
International students	0.2%	African Americans	0.2%
Asian Americans/Pacific Islanders	1%	Hispanic Americans	2%
Native Americans	0.4%		

Faculty 120 (31% full-time), 20% with terminal degrees.

Expenses (1999–2000) *Comprehensive fee:* $15,515 includes full-time tuition ($11,150) and room and board ($4365). *College room only:* $2400. Full-time tuition and fees vary according to location and program. Room and board charges vary according to board plan and housing facility. *Part-time tuition:* $275 per credit. Part-time tuition and fees vary according to course load, location, and program. *Payment plan:* installment. *Waivers:* senior citizens and employees or children of employees.

Wisconsin

Library The Erma M. and Theodore M. Zigmunt Library. *Operations spending 1999–2000:* $186,726. *Collection:* 64,362 titles, 312 serial subscriptions, 15,965 audiovisual materials.

College life *Housing: Option:* coed.

Campus security 24-hour emergency response devices.

After graduation *Career center:* 1 full-time, 1 part-time personnel. Services include job fairs, resume preparation, interview workshops, career/interest testing, career counseling, job bank, job interviews, web page.

Freshmen 62 applied, 27 admitted, 27 enrolled.

Average high school GPA	3.05	SAT verbal scores above 500	N/R
SAT math scores above 500	N/R	ACT above 18	100%
From top 10% of their h.s. class	11%	From top quarter	21%
From top half	31%	1998 freshmen returning in 1999	84%

Application *Options:* electronic application, early admission, deferred entrance. *Application fee:* $25. *Required:* high school transcript; minimum 2.0 GPA. *Required for some:* interview; audition.

Standardized tests *Admission: Required for some:* ACT.

Significant dates *Application deadlines:* 8/31 (freshmen), 8/31 (transfers). *Financial aid deadline priority date:* 4/15.

Freshman Application Contact
Ms. Janis Algozine, Vice President, Dean of Students, Silver Lake College, 2406 South Alverno Road, Manitowoc, WI 54220-9319. **Phone:** 920-684-5955 Ext. 175. **Toll-free phone:** 800-236-4752 Ext. 175. **Fax:** 920-684-7082. **E-mail:** admslc@silver.sl.edu

Visit CollegeQuest.com for information on majors offered and athletics.

UNIVERSITY OF WISCONSIN–EAU CLAIRE
Eau Claire, Wisconsin

- **State-supported**, comprehensive, founded 1916
- **Degrees** associate, bachelor's, master's, post-master's, and postbachelor's certificates
- **Urban** 333-acre campus
- **Coed**, 9,678 undergraduate students, 94% full-time, 60% women, 40% men
- **Moderately difficult** entrance level, 74% of applicants were admitted
- **21:1 student-to-undergraduate faculty ratio**
- **53% graduate** in 6 years or less
- **$3210 tuition** and fees (in-state); $10,074 (out-of-state)
- **$5225 average financial aid** package, $13,252 average indebtedness upon graduation, $16.3 million endowment

Part of University of Wisconsin System.

Students *Undergraduates:* 9,059 full-time, 619 part-time. Students come from 27 states and territories, 46 other countries. *The most frequently chosen baccalaureate fields are:* business/marketing, education, health professions and related sciences. *Graduate:* 476 in graduate degree programs.

From out-of-state	24%	Reside on campus	35%
Age 25 or older	8%	Transferred in	4%
International students	1%	African Americans	1%
Asian Americans/Pacific Islanders	2%	Hispanic Americans	1%
Native Americans	1%		

Faculty 495 (84% full-time), 79% with terminal degrees.

Expenses (1999–2000) *Tuition, state resident:* full-time $3210; part-time $136 per credit. *Tuition, nonresident:* full-time $10,074; part-time $422 per credit. Full-time tuition and fees vary according to reciprocity agreements. Part-time tuition and fees vary according to reciprocity agreements. *College room and board:* $3301; room only: $1985. Room and board charges vary according to board plan. *Payment plan:* installment. *Waivers:* minority students and senior citizens.

Library William D. McIntyre Library plus 1 other. *Operations spending 1999–2000:* $2.7 million. *Collection:* 534,922 titles, 5,258 serial subscriptions, 11,307 audiovisual materials.

College life *Housing:* on-campus residence required in freshman year. *Options:* coed, men-only, women-only. *Social organizations:* national fraternities, national sororities; 1% of eligible men and 1% of eligible women are members. *Most popular organizations:* American Marketing Association, Beta Upsilon Sigma, International Greek Association, Student Information Management Society, Hobnailers.

Campus security 24-hour emergency response devices and patrols, late-night transport-escort service, controlled dormitory access.

After graduation 305 organizations recruited on campus 1997–98. 75% of class of 1998 had job offers within 6 months. *Career center:* 4 full-time, 1 part-time personnel. Services include job fairs, resume preparation, interview workshops, resume referral, career/interest testing, career counseling, careers library, job bank, job interviews. *Major awards:* 1 Fulbright Scholar.

Freshmen 5,690 applied, 4,195 admitted, 2,016 enrolled. 4 National Merit Scholars, 52 valedictorians.

SAT verbal scores above 500	80%	SAT math scores above 500	85%
ACT above 18	99%	From top 10% of their h.s. class	21%
From top quarter	54%	From top half	93%
1998 freshmen returning in 1999	79%		

Application *Options:* Common Application, electronic application, early admission. *Application fee:* $35. *Required:* high school transcript; rank in upper 50% of high school class.

Standardized tests *Admission: Recommended:* SAT I or ACT.

Significant dates *Application deadlines:* rolling (freshmen), 7/1 (transfers). *Financial aid deadline priority date:* 4/15.

Freshman Application Contact
Mr. Roger GroeneWold, Director of Admissions, University of Wisconsin–Eau Claire, PO Box 4004, Eau Claire, WI 54702-4004. **Phone:** 715-836-5415. **Fax:** 715-836-2380. **E-mail:** ask-uwec@uwec.edu

Visit CollegeQuest.com for information on majors offered and athletics. College video and electronic viewbook available at CollegeQuest.com.

UNIVERSITY OF WISCONSIN–GREEN BAY
Green Bay, Wisconsin

- **State-supported**, comprehensive, founded 1968
- **Degrees** associate, bachelor's, master's, and postbachelor's certificates
- **Suburban** 700-acre campus
- **Coed**, 5,110 undergraduate students, 81% full-time, 64% women, 36% men
- **Moderately difficult** entrance level, 82% of applicants were admitted
- **21:1 student-to-undergraduate faculty ratio**
- **47% graduate** in 6 years or less
- **$3184 tuition** and fees (in-state); $10,048 (out-of-state)
- **$5477 average financial aid** package, $7.7 million endowment

Part of University of Wisconsin System.

Students *Undergraduates:* 4,139 full-time, 971 part-time. Students come from 23 states and territories, 32 other countries. *The most frequently chosen baccalaureate fields are:* business/marketing, biological/life sciences, interdisciplinary studies. *Graduate:* 154 in graduate degree programs.

From out-of-state	5%	Reside on campus	31%
Age 25 or older	22%	Transferred in	9%
International students	2%	African Americans	1%
Asian Americans/Pacific Islanders	2%	Hispanic Americans	1%
Native Americans	2%		

Faculty 297 (60% full-time), 63% with terminal degrees.

Expenses (1999–2000) *Tuition, state resident:* full-time $2594; part-time $109 per credit. *Tuition, nonresident:* full-time $9458; part-time $395 per credit. *Required fees:* full-time $590; $20 per credit. Full-time tuition and fees vary according to reciprocity agreements. Part-time tuition and fees vary according to reciprocity agreements. *College room and board:* room only: $2035. Room and board charges vary according to housing facility. *Payment plan:* installment. *Waivers:* senior citizens.

Library Cofrin Library. *Operations spending 1999–2000:* $1.2 million. *Collection:* 281,750 titles, 7,000 serial subscriptions, 3,415 audiovisual materials.

College life *Housing: Option:* coed. *Social organizations:* national fraternities, national sororities, local fraternities, local sororities; 1% of eligible men and 1% of eligible women are members. *Most popular organizations:* Good Times, Concerned, Ambassadors, SUFAC, 4th Estate.

Campus security 24-hour emergency response devices and patrols, late-night transport-escort service, controlled dormitory access.

After graduation 50 organizations recruited on campus 1997–98. 90% of class of 1998 had job offers within 6 months. *Career center:* 2 full-time, 3

Wisconsin

University of Wisconsin–Green Bay (continued)
part-time personnel. Services include job fairs, resume preparation, interview workshops, resume referral, career counseling, careers library, job bank, job interviews. **Graduate education:** 10% of class of 1999 went directly to graduate and professional school: 2% business, 2% education, 2% graduate arts and sciences, 1% dentistry, 1% law, 1% medicine, 1% veterinary medicine.

Freshmen 2,484 applied, 2,044 admitted, 918 enrolled. 15 valedictorians.

Average high school GPA	3.27	SAT verbal scores above 500	N/R
SAT math scores above 500	N/R	ACT above 18	95%
From top 10% of their h.s. class	17%	From top quarter	50%
From top half	94%	1998 freshmen returning in 1999	69%

Application *Options:* electronic application, deferred entrance. *Application fee:* $35. *Required:* essay or personal statement; high school transcript; rank in upper 50% of high school class. *Required for some:* letters of recommendation; interview.
Standardized tests *Placement: Required:* SAT I or ACT
Significant dates *Application deadlines:* 2/1 (freshmen), 4/15 (transfers). *Notification:* continuous until 8/15 (freshmen). **Financial aid deadline priority date:** 4/15.
Freshman Application Contact
Ms. Pam Harvey-Jacobs, Interim Director of Admissions, University of Wisconsin–Green Bay, 2420 Nicolet Drive, Green Bay, WI 54311-7001. **Phone:** 920-465-2111. **Toll-free phone:** 888-367-8942. **Fax:** 920-465-2032. **E-mail:** admissns@uwgb.edu
Visit CollegeQuest.com for information on majors offered and athletics. College video and electronic viewbook available at CollegeQuest.com.

■ *See page 2864 for a narrative description.*

UNIVERSITY OF WISCONSIN–LA CROSSE
La Crosse, Wisconsin

- **State-supported**, comprehensive, founded 1909
- **Degrees** associate, bachelor's, and master's
- **Suburban** 121-acre campus
- **Coed**, 8,362 undergraduate students, 94% full-time, 58% women, 42% men
- **Moderately difficult** entrance level, 70% of applicants were admitted
- **21:1 student-to-undergraduate faculty ratio**
- **51% graduate** in 6 years or less
- **$3242 tuition** and fees (in-state); $10,106 (out-of-state)

Part of University of Wisconsin System.
Students *Undergraduates:* 7,854 full-time, 508 part-time. Students come from 33 states and territories, 43 other countries. *The most frequently chosen baccalaureate fields are:* biological/life sciences, business/marketing, education. *Graduate:* 659 in graduate degree programs.

From out-of-state	18%	Reside on campus	32%
Age 25 or older	6%	Transferred in	5%
International students	1%	African Americans	1%
Asian Americans/Pacific Islanders	2%	Hispanic Americans	1%
Native Americans	1%		

Faculty 511 (70% full-time), 68% with terminal degrees.
Expenses (1999–2000) *Tuition, state resident:* full-time $3242; part-time $153 per credit. *Tuition, nonresident:* full-time $10,106; part-time $439 per credit. Full-time tuition and fees vary according to program and reciprocity agreements. Part-time tuition and fees vary according to course load and reciprocity agreements. *College room and board:* $3300; room only: $1740. *Payment plan:* installment. *Waivers:* minority students and senior citizens.
Library Murphy Library. *Operations spending 1999–2000:* $2 million. *Collection:* 926,554 titles, 5,705 serial subscriptions, 1,358 audiovisual materials.
College life *Housing: Options:* coed, men-only, women-only. *Social organizations:* national fraternities, national sororities; 2% of eligible men and 2% of eligible women are members. *Most popular organizations:* Greek Organization Council, Sports and Activities Club, Residential Hall Council.
Campus security 24-hour emergency response devices and patrols, late-night transport-escort service.
After graduation 95 organizations recruited on campus 1997–98. 94% of class of 1998 had job offers within 6 months. *Career center:* 4 full-time personnel. Services include job fairs, resume preparation, resume referral, career counseling, careers library, job bank, job interviews. **Graduate education:** 21% of class of 1999 went directly to graduate and professional school.

Freshmen 4,925 applied, 3,470 admitted, 1,639 enrolled. 2 National Merit Scholars, 38 valedictorians.

Average high school GPA	3.5	SAT verbal scores above 500	N/R
SAT math scores above 500	N/R	ACT above 18	99%
From top 10% of their h.s. class	23%	From top quarter	65%
From top half	98%	1998 freshmen returning in 1999	82%

Application *Options:* electronic application, early admission, deferred entrance. *Application fee:* $35. *Required:* high school transcript.
Standardized tests *Admission: Required:* SAT I or ACT.
Significant dates *Application deadlines:* rolling (freshmen), rolling (transfers). **Financial aid deadline priority date:** 3/15.
Freshman Application Contact
Mr. Tim Lewis, Director of Admissions, University of Wisconsin–La Crosse, 1725 State Street, LaCrosse, WI 54601. **Phone:** 608-785-8939. **Fax:** 608-785-6695. **E-mail:** admissions@uwlax.edu
Visit CollegeQuest.com for information on majors offered and athletics.

UNIVERSITY OF WISCONSIN–MADISON
Madison, Wisconsin

- **State-supported**, university, founded 1848
- **Degrees** bachelor's, master's, doctoral, and first professional
- **Urban** 1,050-acre campus
- **Coed**, 27,293 undergraduate students, 93% full-time, 52% women, 48% men
- **Very difficult** entrance level, 73% of applicants were admitted
- **14:1 student-to-undergraduate faculty ratio**
- **$3738 tuition** and fees (in-state); $13,052 (out-of-state)
- **$15,813 average indebtedness** upon graduation, $454.8 million endowment

Part of University of Wisconsin System.
Students *Undergraduates:* 25,383 full-time, 1,910 part-time. Students come from 52 states and territories, 99 other countries.

From out-of-state	35%	Age 25 or older	3%
Transferred in	4%	International students	4%
African Americans	2%	Asian Americans/Pacific Islanders	4%
Hispanic Americans	2%	Native Americans	0.4%

Expenses (1999–2000) *Tuition, state resident:* full-time $3290; part-time $828 per term. *Tuition, nonresident:* full-time $12,604; part-time $3156 per term. *Required fees:* full-time $448; $113 per term part-time. Full-time tuition and fees vary according to reciprocity agreements. Part-time tuition and fees vary according to course load and reciprocity agreements. *College room and board:* $4206.
Library Memorial Library plus 40 others. *Collection:* 5.8 million titles, 62,000 serial subscriptions.
College life *Housing: Options:* coed, men-only, women-only, cooperative, disabled students. *Social organizations:* national fraternities, national sororities, eating clubs; 20% of eligible men and 20% of eligible women are members.
Campus security 24-hour emergency response devices and patrols, late-night transport-escort service, controlled dormitory access, free cab rides throughout city.
After graduation *Career center:* Services include job fairs, resume preparation, resume referral, career counseling, careers library, job bank, job interviews. **Graduate education:** 69% of class of 1999 went directly to graduate and professional school. *Major awards:* 1 Rhodes, 14 Fulbright Scholars.
Freshmen 16,456 applied, 12,008 admitted, 5,880 enrolled. 141 National Merit Scholars, 442 valedictorians.

Average high school GPA	3.74	SAT verbal scores above 500	93%
SAT math scores above 500	93%	ACT above 18	99%
From top 10% of their h.s. class	47%	From top quarter	89%
From top half	99%	1998 freshmen returning in 1999	96%

Application *Options:* electronic application, early admission, deferred entrance. *Application fee:* $35. *Required:* essay or personal statement; high school transcript.

Standardized tests *Admission: Required:* SAT I or ACT. *Required for some:* SAT II Subject Tests.
Significant dates *Application deadlines:* 2/1 (freshmen), 2/1 (transfers). *Financial aid deadline:* continuous.
Freshman Application Contact
Mr. Thomas Reason, Office of Admissions, University of Wisconsin–Madison, 716 Langdon Street, Madison, WI 53706-1400. **Phone:** 608-262-3961. **Fax:** 608-262-1429. **E-mail:** on.wisconsin@mail.admin.wisc.edu
Visit CollegeQuest.com for information on majors offered and athletics.

UNIVERSITY OF WISCONSIN–MILWAUKEE
Milwaukee, Wisconsin

- **State-supported**, university, founded 1956
- **Degrees** bachelor's, master's, and doctoral
- **Urban** 90-acre campus
- **Coed**, 15,224 undergraduate students, 75% full-time, 53% women, 47% men
- **Moderately difficult** entrance level, 82% of applicants were admitted
- **37.7% graduate** in 6 years or less
- **$3741 tuition** and fees (in-state); $12,361 (out-of-state)

Part of University of Wisconsin System.
Students *Undergraduates:* 11,374 full-time, 3,850 part-time. Students come from 53 states and territories. *The most frequently chosen baccalaureate fields are:* business/marketing, education, health professions and related sciences. *Graduate:* 4,493 in graduate degree programs.

| From out-of-state | 3% | Transferred in | 10% |

Expenses (1999–2000) *Tuition, state resident:* full-time $3741; part-time $134 per credit. *Tuition, nonresident:* full-time $12,361; part-time $493 per credit. Full-time tuition and fees vary according to location and reciprocity agreements. Part-time tuition and fees vary according to course load, location, and reciprocity agreements. *College room and board:* room only: $2542. Room and board charges vary according to board plan. *Payment plan:* installment.
Library Golda Meir Library. *Collection:* 1 million titles, 7,821 serial subscriptions.
College life *Housing: Option:* coed. *Social organizations:* national fraternities, national sororities, local fraternities.
Campus security 24-hour emergency response devices, late-night transport-escort service.
After graduation 104 organizations recruited on campus 1997–98. *Career center:* 7 full-time, 5 part-time personnel. Services include job fairs, resume preparation, resume referral, career counseling, careers library, job bank, job interviews. *Major awards:* 1 Fulbright Scholar.
Freshmen 6,413 applied, 5,248 admitted, 2,248 enrolled.

SAT verbal scores above 500	71%	SAT math scores above 500	65%
ACT above 18	87%	From top 10% of their h.s. class	8%
From top quarter	28%	From top half	67%
1998 freshmen returning in 1999	69%		

Application *Option:* deferred entrance. *Application fee:* $35. *Required:* high school transcript.
Standardized tests *Admission: Required:* SAT I or ACT, ACT for state residents.
Significant dates *Application deadlines:* rolling (freshmen), rolling (transfers). *Financial aid deadline priority date:* 3/1.
Freshman Application Contact
Ms. Jan Ford, Director, Recruitment and Outreach, University of Wisconsin–Milwaukee, PO Box 413, Milwaukee, WI 53201-0413. **Phone:** 414-229-4397. **Fax:** 414-229-6940. **E-mail:** uwmlook@des.uwm.edu
Visit CollegeQuest.com for information on majors offered and athletics.

UNIVERSITY OF WISCONSIN–OSHKOSH
Oshkosh, Wisconsin

Admissions Office Contact
University of Wisconsin–Oshkosh, 800 Algoma Boulevard, Oshkosh, WI 54901-8602. **Fax:** 920-424-1098. **E-mail:** oshadmuw@uwosh.edu

UNIVERSITY OF WISCONSIN–PARKSIDE
Kenosha, Wisconsin

- **State-supported**, comprehensive, founded 1968
- **Degrees** bachelor's and master's
- **Suburban** 700-acre campus with easy access to Chicago and Milwaukee
- **Coed**, 4,207 undergraduate students, 75% full-time, 58% women, 42% men
- **Moderately difficult** entrance level, 95% of applicants were admitted
- **21.96% graduate** in 6 years or less
- **$3200 tuition** and fees (in-state); $10,400 (out-of-state)

Part of University of Wisconsin System.
Students *Undergraduates:* 3,151 full-time, 1,056 part-time. Students come from 22 states and territories. *The most frequently chosen baccalaureate fields are:* business/marketing, psychology, social sciences and history. *Graduate:* 140 in graduate degree programs.

From out-of-state	7%	Reside on campus	17%
Age 25 or older	78%	Transferred in	12%
International students	1%	African Americans	8%
Asian Americans/Pacific Islanders	2%	Hispanic Americans	6%
Native Americans	1%		

Faculty 262 (58% full-time).
Expenses (1999–2000) *Tuition, state resident:* full-time $3200; part-time $777 per term. *Tuition, nonresident:* full-time $10,400; part-time $2,493 per term. Full-time tuition and fees vary according to course load and reciprocity agreements. Part-time tuition and fees vary according to course load. *College room and board:* $4230; room only: $2860. Room and board charges vary according to board plan and housing facility. *Payment plan:* installment. *Waivers:* minority students and employees or children of employees.
Library Library-Learning Center. *Collection:* 265,110 titles, 4,096 serial subscriptions, 18,007 audiovisual materials.
College life *Housing:* on-campus residence required through sophomore year. *Options:* coed, disabled students. *Social organizations:* national fraternities, national sororities; 1% of eligible men and 0.4% of eligible women are members. *Most popular organizations:* Black Student Union, Latinos Unidos, Parkside Student Government Association, Asian American Club.
Campus security 24-hour emergency response devices and patrols, late-night transport-escort service, controlled dormitory access.
After graduation *Career center:* 4 full-time personnel. Services include job fairs, resume preparation, resume referral, career/interest testing, career counseling, careers library, job bank.
Freshmen 2,108 applied, 2,000 admitted, 888 enrolled.

SAT verbal scores above 500	N/R	SAT math scores above 500	N/R
ACT above 18	N/R	From top 10% of their h.s. class	8%
From top quarter	29%	From top half	59%
1998 freshmen returning in 1999	72%		

Application *Options:* electronic application, deferred entrance. *Application fee:* $35. *Required:* high school transcript.
Standardized tests *Admission: Required:* SAT I or ACT for nonresidents, ACT for state residents.
Significant dates *Application deadlines:* 8/15 (freshmen), rolling (transfers). *Financial aid deadline priority date:* 4/1.
Freshman Application Contact
Mr. Charles Murphy, Director of Admissions, University of Wisconsin–Parkside, 900 Wood Road, PO Box 2000, Kenosha, WI 53141-2000. **Phone:** 262-595-2355. **Toll-free phone:** 877-633-3897. **E-mail:** charles.murphy@uwp.edu
Visit CollegeQuest.com for information on majors offered and athletics.

UNIVERSITY OF WISCONSIN–PLATTEVILLE
Platteville, Wisconsin

- **State-supported**, comprehensive, founded 1866
- **Degrees** associate, bachelor's, and master's
- **Small-town** 380-acre campus
- **Coed**, 5,240 undergraduate students, 88% full-time, 38% women, 62% men
- **Moderately difficult** entrance level, 65% of applicants were admitted

Wisconsin

University of Wisconsin–Platteville (continued)
- **53.6% graduate** in 6 years or less
- **$3132 tuition** and fees (in-state); $9996 (out-of-state)
- **$8500 average indebtedness** upon graduation, $3 million endowment

Part of University of Wisconsin System.

Students *Undergraduates:* 4,625 full-time, 615 part-time. Students come from 15 states and territories, 14 other countries. *Graduate:* 254 in graduate degree programs.

Reside on campus	50%	Age 25 or older	18%
Transferred in	5%	International students	0.5%
African Americans	1%	Asian Americans/Pacific Islanders	1%
Hispanic Americans	1%	Native Americans	0.2%

Expenses (1999–2000) *Tuition, state resident:* full-time $2594; part-time $109 per credit. *Tuition, nonresident:* full-time $9458. *Required fees:* full-time $538; $27 per credit. Full-time tuition and fees vary according to reciprocity agreements. Part-time tuition and fees vary according to course load and reciprocity agreements. *College room and board:* $3338; room only: $1608. Room and board charges vary according to board plan. *Payment plan:* installment.

Library Karrmann Library. *Collection:* 257,566 titles, 1,499 serial subscriptions.

College life *Housing:* on-campus residence required through sophomore year. *Option:* coed. *Social organizations:* national fraternities, national sororities, local fraternities, local sororities; 8% of eligible men and 6% of eligible women are members.

Campus security 24-hour emergency response devices and patrols, student patrols, late-night transport-escort service.

After graduation 184 organizations recruited on campus 1997–98. 88% of class of 1998 had job offers within 6 months. *Career center:* 3 full-time personnel. Services include job fairs, resume preparation, resume referral, career counseling, careers library, job bank, job interviews. *Graduate education:* 12% of class of 1999 went directly to graduate and professional school.

Freshmen 2,073 applied, 1,348 admitted, 1,157 enrolled. 21 valedictorians.

SAT verbal scores above 500	N/R	SAT math scores above 500	N/R
ACT above 18	N/R	From top 10% of their h.s. class	15%
From top half	84%	1998 freshmen returning in 1999	49%

Application *Option:* electronic application. *Application fee:* $35. *Required:* high school transcript. *Required for some:* letters of recommendation.

Standardized tests *Admission: Required:* ACT.

Significant dates *Application deadlines:* rolling (freshmen), rolling (transfers). *Financial aid deadline priority date:* 3/15.

Freshman Application Contact
Dr. Richard Schumacher, Dean of Admissions and Enrollment Management, University of Wisconsin–Platteville, 1 University Plaza, Platteville, WI 53818-3099. **Phone:** 608-342-1125. **Toll-free phone:** 800-362-5515. **E-mail:** admit@uwplatt.edu

Visit CollegeQuest.com for information on majors offered and athletics. College video available at CollegeQuest.com.

UNIVERSITY OF WISCONSIN–RIVER FALLS
River Falls, Wisconsin

- **State-supported**, comprehensive, founded 1874
- **Degrees** bachelor's and master's
- **Suburban** 225-acre campus with easy access to Minneapolis–St. Paul
- **Coed**, 5,399 undergraduate students, 90% full-time, 62% women, 38% men
- **Moderately difficult** entrance level, 74% of applicants were admitted
- **19:1 student-to-undergraduate faculty ratio**
- **$3102 tuition** and fees (in-state); $9936 (out-of-state)

Part of University of Wisconsin System.

Students *Undergraduates:* Students come from 24 states and territories, 13 other countries. *Graduate:* 329 in graduate degree programs.

From out-of-state	45%	Reside on campus	38%
Age 25 or older	10%	International students	1%
African Americans	1%	Asian Americans/Pacific Islanders	3%
Native Americans	0.4%		

Faculty 216.

Expenses (1999–2000) *Tuition, state resident:* full-time $3102; part-time $840 per term. *Tuition, nonresident:* full-time $9936; part-time $2,556 per term. Full-time tuition and fees vary according to reciprocity agreements. Part-time tuition and fees vary according to course load and reciprocity agreements. *College room and board:* $3350; room only: $1800. Room and board charges vary according to board plan. *Payment plan:* installment.

Library Davee Library. *Collection:* 295,291 titles.

College life *Housing:* on-campus residence required through sophomore year. *Options:* coed, women-only. *Social organizations:* national fraternities, national sororities; 5% of eligible men and 3% of eligible women are members. *Most popular organizations:* Bushwackers (High Adventure Club), Habitat for Humanity, Agricultural Education Society, Dairy Club, Rodeo Club.

Campus security 24-hour emergency response devices and patrols, student patrols, late-night transport-escort service, controlled dormitory access.

After graduation 100 organizations recruited on campus 1997–98. *Career center:* 2 full-time, 1 part-time personnel. Services include job fairs, resume preparation, interview workshops, resume referral, career/interest testing, career counseling, careers library, job bank, job interviews. *Graduate education:* 22% of class of 1999 went directly to graduate and professional school: 6% graduate arts and sciences, 4% veterinary medicine, 3% business, 2% education, 2% engineering, 2% law, 2% medicine, 1% dentistry.

Freshmen 2,762 applied, 2,033 admitted.

SAT verbal scores above 500	N/R	SAT math scores above 500	N/R
ACT above 18	97%	From top 10% of their h.s. class	17%
From top quarter	48%	From top half	88%
1998 freshmen returning in 1999	70%		

Application *Options:* Common Application, electronic application, deferred entrance. *Application fee:* $35. *Required:* high school transcript. *Recommended:* rank in upper 40% of high school class.

Standardized tests *Admission: Required:* ACT.

Significant dates *Application deadlines:* 1/1 (freshmen), 1/1 (transfers). *Financial aid deadline priority date:* 3/15.

Freshman Application Contact
Mr. Alan Tuchtenhagen, Director of Admissions, University of Wisconsin–River Falls, 410 South Third Street, 112 South Hall, River Falls, WI 54022-5001. **Phone:** 715-425-3500. **Fax:** 715-425-0678. **E-mail:** admit@uwrf.edu

Visit CollegeQuest.com for information on majors offered and athletics. Electronic viewbook available at CollegeQuest.com.

UNIVERSITY OF WISCONSIN–STEVENS POINT
Stevens Point, Wisconsin

- **State-supported**, comprehensive, founded 1894
- **Degrees** associate, bachelor's, and master's
- **Small-town** 335-acre campus
- **Coed**, 8,400 undergraduate students, 90% full-time, 56% women, 44% men
- **Moderately difficult** entrance level, 60% of applicants were admitted
- **21:1 student-to-undergraduate faculty ratio**
- **54% graduate** in 6 years or less
- **$3140 tuition** and fees (in-state); $10,004 (out-of-state)
- **$5152 average financial aid** package, $12,921 average indebtedness upon graduation, $10.2 million endowment

Part of University of Wisconsin System.

Students *Undergraduates:* 7,561 full-time, 839 part-time. Students come from 30 states and territories, 30 other countries. *The most frequently chosen baccalaureate fields are:* education, business/marketing, natural resources/environmental science. *Graduate:* 568 in graduate degree programs.

Reside on campus	38%	Age 25 or older	14%
Transferred in	8%	International students	2%
African Americans	0.5%	Asian Americans/Pacific Islanders	1%
Hispanic Americans	1%	Native Americans	1%

Wisconsin

Faculty 426 (86% full-time), 71% with terminal degrees.
Expenses (1999–2000) *Tuition, state resident:* full-time $3140; part-time $158 per credit. *Tuition, nonresident:* full-time $10,004; part-time $444 per credit. Full-time tuition and fees vary according to reciprocity agreements. Part-time tuition and fees vary according to course load and reciprocity agreements. *College room and board:* $3524; room only: $2076. Room and board charges vary according to board plan. *Payment plan:* deferred payment.
Library Learning Resources Center. *Operations spending 1999–2000:* $2.1 million. *Collection:* 362,788 titles, 1,816 serial subscriptions.
College life *Housing:* on-campus residence required through sophomore year. *Options:* coed, men-only, women-only. *Social organizations:* national fraternities, national sororities; 2% of eligible men and 1% of eligible women are members.
Campus security 24-hour emergency response devices and patrols, student patrols, late-night transport-escort service, controlled dormitory access.
After graduation *Career center:* 2 full-time, 1 part-time personnel. Services include job fairs, resume preparation, interview workshops, resume referral, career/interest testing, career counseling, careers library, job interviews. *Graduate education:* 15% of class of 1999 went directly to graduate and professional school.
Freshmen 3,918 applied, 2,345 admitted, 1,492 enrolled. 40 valedictorians.

Average high school GPA	3.35	SAT verbal scores above 500	N/R
SAT math scores above 500	N/R	ACT above 18	95%
From top 10% of their h.s. class	17%	From top quarter	47%
From top half	95%	1998 freshmen returning in 1999	76%

Application *Option:* deferred entrance. *Application fee:* $35. *Required:* high school transcript. *Recommended:* campus visit.
Standardized tests *Admission: Required:* SAT I or ACT.
Significant dates *Application deadlines:* rolling (freshmen), rolling (transfers). *Financial aid deadline priority date:* 6/15.
Freshman Application Contact
Dr. David Eckholm, Director of Admissions, University of Wisconsin–Stevens Point, 2100 Main Street, Stevens Point, WI 54481-3897. **Phone:** 715-346-2441. **Fax:** 715-346-2561. **E-mail:** admiss@uwsp.edu
Visit CollegeQuest.com for information on majors offered and athletics.

UNIVERSITY OF WISCONSIN–STOUT
Menomonie, Wisconsin

- **State-supported**, comprehensive, founded 1891
- **Degrees** bachelor's and master's
- **Small-town** 120-acre campus with easy access to Minneapolis–St. Paul
- **Coed**, 6,932 undergraduate students
- **Moderately difficult** entrance level, 62% of applicants were admitted
- **21:1 student-to-undergraduate faculty ratio**
- **46% graduate** in 6 years or less
- **$3256 tuition** and fees (in-state); $10,120 (out-of-state)
- **$5865 average financial aid** package, $234,466 endowment

Part of University of Wisconsin System.
Students *Undergraduates:* Students come from 23 states and territories, 23 other countries. *The most frequently chosen baccalaureate fields are:* business/marketing, education, engineering/engineering technologies.

From out-of-state	26%	Reside on campus	35%
Age 25 or older	15%	International students	1%
African Americans	1%	Asian Americans/Pacific Islanders	2%
Hispanic Americans	1%	Native Americans	0.3%

Faculty 399 (76% full-time), 65% with terminal degrees.
Expenses (1999–2000) *Tuition, state resident:* full-time $2594; part-time $114 per credit. *Tuition, nonresident:* full-time $9458; part-time $400 per credit. *Required fees:* full-time $662; $24 per credit. Full-time tuition and fees vary according to reciprocity agreements. Part-time tuition and fees vary according to reciprocity agreements. *College room and board:* $3284; room only: $1816. Room and board charges vary according to board plan. *Payment plan:* installment.
Library Library Learning Center. *Operations spending 1999–2000:* $2.2 million. *Collection:* 221,738 titles, 5,380 serial subscriptions, 14,921 audiovisual materials.

College life *Housing:* on-campus residence required through sophomore year. *Option:* coed. *Social organizations:* national fraternities, national sororities, local fraternities; 2% of eligible men and 4% of eligible women are members. *Most popular organizations:* Hotel/Motel Management Association, Intergreek Council, DECA-District Educational Clubs of America, Recreation Commission, OASIS.
Campus security 24-hour emergency response devices and patrols, student patrols, late-night transport-escort service.
After graduation 677 organizations recruited on campus 1997–98. 95% of class of 1998 had job offers within 6 months. *Career center:* 7 full-time, 4 part-time personnel. Services include job fairs, resume preparation, interview workshops, resume referral, career counseling, careers library, job bank, job interviews. *Graduate education:* 6% of class of 1999 went directly to graduate and professional school.
Freshmen 2,757 applied, 1,713 admitted.

Average high school GPA	3.1	SAT verbal scores above 500	N/R
SAT math scores above 500	N/R	ACT above 18	N/R
From top 10% of their h.s. class	9%	From top quarter	27%
From top half	78%	1998 freshmen returning in 1999	73%

Application *Options:* electronic application, early admission, deferred entrance. *Application fee:* $35. *Required:* high school transcript. *Required for some:* minimum 2.75 GPA.
Standardized tests *Admission: Required:* SAT I or ACT. *Recommended:* ACT.
Significant dates *Application deadlines:* rolling (freshmen), rolling (transfers). *Financial aid deadline priority date:* 4/1.
Freshman Application Contact
Ms. Cynthia Jenkins, Director of Admissions, University of Wisconsin–Stout, Menomonie, WI 54751. **Phone:** 715-232-2639. **Toll-free phone:** 800-HI-STOUT. **Fax:** 715-232-1667. **E-mail:** admissions@uwstout.edu
Visit CollegeQuest.com for information on majors offered and athletics. College video and electronic viewbook available at CollegeQuest.com.

UNIVERSITY OF WISCONSIN–SUPERIOR
Superior, Wisconsin

- **State-supported**, comprehensive, founded 1893
- **Degrees** associate, bachelor's, and master's
- **Small-town** 230-acre campus
- **Coed**, 2,264 undergraduate students
- **Moderately difficult** entrance level, 84% of applicants were admitted
- **16:1 student-to-undergraduate faculty ratio**
- **$2974 tuition** and fees (in-state); $9838 (out-of-state)
- **$5026 average financial aid** package, $12,500 average indebtedness upon graduation, $5.5 million endowment

Part of University of Wisconsin System.
Students *Undergraduates:* Students come from 29 states and territories, 18 other countries. *The most frequently chosen baccalaureate fields are:* business/marketing, biological/life sciences, education.

From out-of-state	38%	Reside on campus	24%
Age 25 or older	28%		

Faculty 140 (74% full-time), 73% with terminal degrees.
Expenses (1999–2000) *Tuition, state resident:* full-time $2594; part-time $109 per credit hour. *Tuition, nonresident:* full-time $9458; part-time $395 per credit hour. *Required fees:* full-time $380. Full-time tuition and fees vary according to course load and reciprocity agreements. Part-time tuition and fees vary according to course load and reciprocity agreements. *College room and board:* $3426; room only: $1740. *Payment plan:* installment. *Waivers:* minority students, children of alumni, adult students, and employees or children of employees.
Library Jim Dan Hill Library. *Operations spending 1999–2000:* $867,034.
College life *Housing:* on-campus residence required through sophomore year. *Options:* coed, men-only, women-only, disabled students. *Most popular organizations:* Student Senate, Student Activities Board, Residence Hall Association, Intervarsity Christian Fellowship.
Campus security 24-hour emergency response devices and patrols, student patrols, late-night transport-escort service, controlled dormitory access.
After graduation 26 organizations recruited on campus 1997–98. *Career center:* 1 full-time, 2 part-time personnel. Services include job fairs, resume

Wisconsin

University of Wisconsin–Superior (continued)
preparation, interview workshops, resume referral, career/interest testing, career counseling, careers library, job bank, job interviews. **Graduate education:** 18% of class of 1999 went directly to graduate and professional school.

Freshmen 831 applied, 694 admitted. 1 National Merit Scholar, 20 class presidents, 11 valedictorians, 43 student government officers.

Average high school GPA	3.1	SAT verbal scores above 500	N/R
SAT math scores above 500	N/R	ACT above 18	N/R
From top 10% of their h.s. class	13%	From top quarter	34%
From top half	79%	1998 freshmen returning in 1999	65%

Application *Options:* electronic application, deferred entrance. *Application fee:* $35. *Required:* high school transcript. *Required for some:* minimum 2.6 GPA; letters of recommendation. *Recommended:* interview.
Standardized tests *Admission: Required:* ACT.
Significant dates *Application deadlines:* 6/1 (freshmen), 5/1 (transfers). *Financial aid deadline priority date:* 1/3.
Freshman Application Contact
Ms. Lorraine Washa, Student Application Contact, University of Wisconsin–Superior, Belknap and Catlin, PO Box 2000, Superior, WI 54880-4500. **Phone:** 715-394-8230. **Fax:** 715-394-8407. **E-mail:** admissions@uwsuper.edu
Visit CollegeQuest.com for information on majors offered and athletics. College video available at CollegeQuest.com.

UNIVERSITY OF WISCONSIN–WHITEWATER
Whitewater, Wisconsin

- **State-supported**, comprehensive, founded 1868
- **Degrees** associate, bachelor's, and master's
- **Small-town** 385-acre campus with easy access to Milwaukee
- **Coed**, 9,583 undergraduate students
- **Moderately difficult** entrance level, 84% of applicants were admitted
- **21:1 student-to-undergraduate faculty ratio**
- **49.71% graduate** in 6 years or less
- **$3105 tuition** and fees (in-state); $9969 (out-of-state)
- **$5729 average financial aid** package, $10,451 average indebtedness upon graduation, $3.2 million endowment

Part of University of Wisconsin System.
Students *Undergraduates:* Students come from 27 states and territories, 38 other countries. *The most frequently chosen baccalaureate fields are:* business/marketing, education, social sciences and history.

From out-of-state	5%	Reside on campus	40%
Age 25 or older	10%	International students	1%
African Americans	2%	Asian Americans/Pacific Islanders	1%
Hispanic Americans	1%	Native Americans	0.3%

Faculty 465 (85% full-time), 78% with terminal degrees.
Expenses (1999–2000) *Tuition, state resident:* full-time $3105; part-time $130 per credit. *Tuition, nonresident:* full-time $9969; part-time $416 per credit. Full-time tuition and fees vary according to reciprocity agreements. Part-time tuition and fees vary according to reciprocity agreements. *College room and board:* $3204; room only: $1810. Room and board charges vary according to board plan. *Payment plan:* installment.
Library Andersen Library. *Operations spending 1999–2000:* $1.8 million. *Collection:* 436,521 titles.
College life *Housing:* on-campus residence required through sophomore year. *Option:* coed. *Social organizations:* national fraternities, national sororities, local fraternities, local sororities; 4% of eligible men and 3% of eligible women are members. *Most popular organizations:* Finance Association, American Marketing Association, Black Student Union, P.S.E., Wisconsin Education Association.
Campus security 24-hour emergency response devices, late-night transport-escort service.
After graduation 210 organizations recruited on campus 1997–98. 85% of class of 1998 had job offers within 6 months. *Career center:* 7 full-time personnel. Services include job fairs, resume preparation, resume referral, career counseling, careers library, job bank, job interviews. **Graduate education:** 10% of class of 1999 went directly to graduate and professional school.

Freshmen 4,142 applied, 3,474 admitted.

Average high school GPA	2.66	SAT verbal scores above 500	N/R
SAT math scores above 500	N/R	ACT above 18	89%
From top 10% of their h.s. class	11%	From top quarter	35%
From top half	80%	1998 freshmen returning in 1999	75%

Application *Option:* early admission. *Application fee:* $35. *Required:* high school transcript. *Required for some:* letters of recommendation.
Standardized tests *Admission: Required:* ACT. *Required for some:* SAT I.
Significant dates *Application deadlines:* rolling (freshmen), rolling (transfers). *Financial aid deadline priority date:* 3/15.
Freshman Application Contact
Dr. Tori A. McGuire, Executive Director of Admissions, University of Wisconsin–Whitewater, 800 West Main Street, Whitewater, WI 53190-1790. **Phone:** 414-472-1440 Ext. 1512. **Fax:** 414-472-1515. **E-mail:** uwwadmit@uwwvax.uww.edu
Visit CollegeQuest.com for information on majors offered and athletics. College video available at CollegeQuest.com.

VITERBO UNIVERSITY
La Crosse, Wisconsin

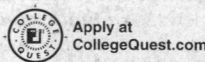

- **Independent Roman Catholic**, comprehensive, founded 1890
- **Degrees** bachelor's and master's
- **Urban** 5-acre campus
- **Coed**
- **Moderately difficult** entrance level
- **$12,490 tuition** and fees

Expenses (1999–2000) *Comprehensive fee:* $16,890 includes full-time tuition ($12,220), mandatory fees ($270), and room and board ($4400). *College room only:* $1930. *Part-time tuition:* $355 per credit. *Part-time fees:* $14 per credit. Part-time tuition and fees vary according to course load.
Institutional Web site http://www.viterbo.edu/
College life *Housing:* on-campus residence required through sophomore year. *Option:* coed.
Campus security 24-hour emergency response devices and patrols, late-night transport-escort service, controlled dormitory access.
Application *Options:* eApply at www.CollegeQuest.com, early admission, deferred entrance. *Application fee:* $15. *Required:* high school transcript. *Required for some:* letters of recommendation; interview.
Standardized tests *Admission: Required:* ACT.
Admissions Office Contact
Viterbo University, 815 South Ninth Street, La Crosse, WI 54601-4797. **Toll-free phone:** 800-VIT-ERBO. **Fax:** 608-796-3050. **E-mail:** admission@viterbo.edu
Visit CollegeQuest.com for information on athletics. College video available at CollegeQuest.com.

- *See page 2900 for a narrative description.*

WISCONSIN LUTHERAN COLLEGE
Milwaukee, Wisconsin

- **Independent**, 4-year, founded 1973, affiliated with Wisconsin Evangelical Lutheran Synod
- **Degree** bachelor's
- **Suburban** 16-acre campus
- **Coed**, 551 undergraduate students, 94% full-time, 58% women, 42% men
- **Moderately difficult** entrance level, 90% of applicants were admitted
- **11:1 student-to-undergraduate faculty ratio**
- **44% graduate** in 6 years or less
- **$13,106 tuition** and fees
- **$12,046 average financial aid** package, $13,830 average indebtedness upon graduation, $3.8 million endowment

Students *Undergraduates:* 519 full-time, 32 part-time. Students come from 25 states and territories, 9 other countries. *The most frequently chosen*

baccalaureate fields are: business/marketing, communications/communication technologies, education.

From out-of-state	23%	Reside on campus	74%
Age 25 or older	6%	Transferred in	3%
International students	2%	African Americans	1%
Asian Americans/Pacific Islanders	1%	Hispanic Americans	1%

Faculty 71 (54% full-time), 48% with terminal degrees.

Expenses (2000–2001) *Comprehensive fee:* $17,856 includes full-time tuition ($12,980), mandatory fees ($126), and room and board ($4750). *College room only:* $2300. Room and board charges vary according to board plan and housing facility. *Part-time tuition:* $400 per credit. *Part-time fees:* $30 per term part-time. *Payment plan:* installment. *Waivers:* employees or children of employees.

Library Marvin M. Schwan Library. *Operations spending 1999–2000:* $301,533. *Collection:* 58,026 titles, 585 serial subscriptions, 3,929 audiovisual materials.

College life *Housing:* on-campus residence required through senior year. *Options:* men-only, women-only.

Campus security 24-hour emergency response devices and patrols, late-night transport-escort service, closed circuit TV monitors.

After graduation 10 organizations recruited on campus 1997–98. 78% of class of 1998 had job offers within 6 months. *Career center:* 1 full-time, 1 part-time personnel. Services include job fairs, resume preparation, interview workshops, career/interest testing, career counseling, careers library, job bank, job interviews. *Graduate education:* 17% of class of 1999 went directly to graduate and professional school: 13% graduate arts and sciences, 2% law, 2% medicine.

Freshmen 352 applied, 318 admitted, 161 enrolled. 7 valedictorians.

Average high school GPA	3.41	SAT verbal scores above 500	N/R
SAT math scores above 500	N/R	ACT above 18	99%
From top 10% of their h.s. class	29%	From top quarter	54%
From top half	81%	1998 freshmen returning in 1999	82%

Application *Options:* eApply at www.CollegeQuest.com, electronic application, early admission. *Application fee:* $20. *Required:* high school transcript; minimum 2.50 GPA; 1 letter of recommendation; minimum ACT score of 20. *Required for some:* interview.

Standardized tests *Admission: Required:* SAT I or ACT.

Significant dates *Application deadlines:* 9/1 (freshmen), 9/1 (transfers). *Notification:* continuous until 9/1 (freshmen). *Financial aid deadline priority date:* 3/1.

Freshman Application Contact
Mr. Jeff Weber, Director of Admissions, Wisconsin Lutheran College, 8800 West Bluemound Road, Milwaukee, WI 53226-9942. **Phone:** 414-443-8819. **Toll-free phone:** 888-WIS LUTH. **Fax:** 414-443-8514. **E-mail:** admissions@wlc.edu

Visit CollegeQuest.com for information on majors offered and athletics. College video and electronic viewbook available at CollegeQuest.com.

WYOMING

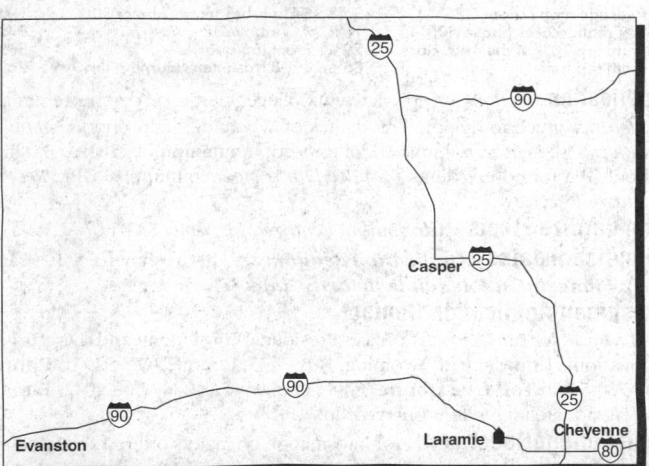

UNIVERSITY OF WYOMING
Laramie, Wyoming

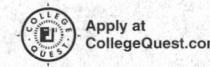
Apply at CollegeQuest.com

- **State-supported**, university, founded 1886
- **Degrees** bachelor's, master's, doctoral, first professional, and post-master's certificates
- **Small-town** campus
- **Coed**, 8,221 undergraduate students, 87% full-time, 53% women, 47% men
- **Moderately difficult** entrance level, 97% of applicants were admitted
- **14:1 student-to-undergraduate faculty ratio**
- **47.7% graduate** in 6 years or less
- **$2416 tuition** and fees (in-state); $7684 (out-of-state)
- **$5814 average financial aid** package, $16,168 average indebtedness upon graduation, $138.3 million endowment

Students *Undergraduates:* 7,137 full-time, 1,084 part-time. Students come from 52 states and territories, 59 other countries. *The most frequently chosen baccalaureate fields are:* business/marketing, education, engineering/engineering technologies. *Graduate:* 429 in professional programs, 2,073 in other graduate degree programs.

From out-of-state	22%	Reside on campus	79%
Age 25 or older	21%	Transferred in	13%
International students	1%	African Americans	1%
Asian Americans/Pacific Islanders	1%	Hispanic Americans	4%
Native Americans	1%		

Faculty 649 (93% full-time), 84% with terminal degrees.

Expenses (1999–2000) *Tuition, state resident:* full-time $2016; part-time $84 per semester hour. *Tuition, nonresident:* full-time $7284; part-time $304 per semester hour. *Required fees:* full-time $400; $7 per semester hour. *College room and board:* $4618; room only: $1846. Room and board charges vary according to board plan. *Payment plans:* installment, deferred payment. *Waivers:* children of alumni, senior citizens, and employees or children of employees.

Library Coe Library plus 7 others. *Operations spending 1999–2000:* $5.6 million. *Collection:* 14,737 serial subscriptions, 3,701 audiovisual materials.

College life *Housing:* on-campus residence required in freshman year. *Options:* coed, women-only, disabled students. *Social organizations:* national fraternities, national sororities; 6% of eligible men and 4% of eligible women are members. *Most popular organizations:* MECHA, Golden Key (Honoraries), SAC, Fly Casters, SPURS.

Campus security 24-hour emergency response devices and patrols, student patrols, late-night transport-escort service, controlled dormitory access.

After graduation 120 organizations recruited on campus 1997–98. 55% of class of 1998 had job offers within 6 months. *Career center:* 5 full-time, 4 part-time personnel. Services include job fairs, resume preparation, interview workshops, resume referral, career/interest testing, career counseling, careers library, job bank, job interviews. *Graduate education:* 22% of class of 1999 went directly to graduate and professional school. *Major awards:* 1 Rhodes scholar.

Wyoming–Puerto Rico

University of Wyoming (continued)

Freshmen 2,466 applied, 2,396 admitted, 1,225 enrolled.

Average high school GPA	3.48	SAT verbal scores above 500	N/R
SAT math scores above 500	N/R	ACT above 18	94%
From top 10% of their h.s. class	29%	From top quarter	56%
From top half	85%	1998 freshmen returning in 1999	76%

Application *Options:* eApply at www.CollegeQuest.com, deferred entrance. *Preference* given to qualified graduates of Wyoming high schools. *Application fee:* $30. *Required:* high school transcript; minimum 2.75 GPA; 3.0 high school GPA for nonresidents. *Required for some:* minimum 3.0 GPA. *Recommended:* interview.

Standardized tests *Admission: Required for some:* SAT I or ACT.

Significant dates *Application deadlines:* 8/10 (freshmen), 8/10 (transfers). *Financial aid deadline priority date:* 3/1.

Freshman Application Contact
Ms. Sara Axelson, Associate Vice President Enrollment and Director of Admissions, University of Wyoming, Box 3435, Laramie, WY 82071. **Phone:** 307-766-5160. **Toll-free phone:** 800-342-5996. **Fax:** 307-766-4042. **E-mail:** undergraduate.admissions@uwyo.edu

Visit CollegeQuest.com for information on majors offered and athletics. College video and electronic viewbook available at CollegeQuest.com.

■ *See page 2866 for a narrative description.*

GUAM

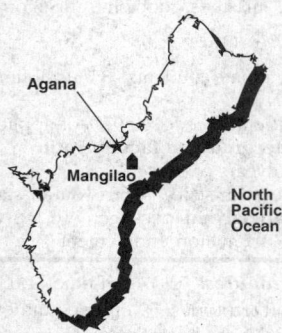

University of Guam
Mangilao, Guam

Admissions Office Contact
University of Guam, University Drive, UOG Station, Mangilao, GU 96923. **Fax:** 671-734-6005. **E-mail:** admrecs@uog.edu

PUERTO RICO

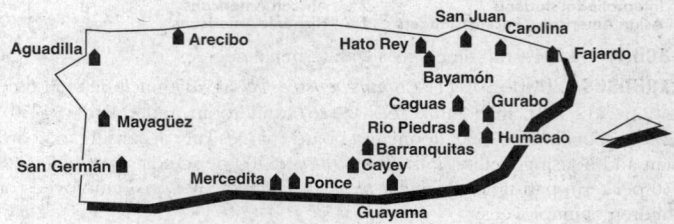

American University of Puerto Rico
Bayamón, Puerto Rico

Students *Undergraduates:* Students come from 1 other country.
Age 25 or older 5%

Faculty 206 (26% full-time).

Expenses (1999–2000) *Payment plan:* guaranteed tuition.

Library Loida Figueroa Meacado. *Collection:* 46,009 titles, 231 serial subscriptions, 2,091 audiovisual materials.

College life *Housing:* college housing not available.

Campus security 24-hour patrols.

After graduation 3 organizations recruited on campus 1997–98. *Career center:* Services include job fairs, resume preparation, interview workshops, career/interest testing, career counseling, job bank, job interviews.

Freshmen 800 applied, 800 admitted.

SAT verbal scores above 500	N/R	SAT math scores above 500	N/R
ACT above 18	N/R	From top 10% of their h.s. class	3%
From top quarter	15%	From top half	25%

Application *Option:* deferred entrance. *Application fee:* $15. *Required:* high school transcript.

Standardized tests *Placement: Required:* SAT I, CEEB

Significant dates *Application deadlines:* 7/1 (freshmen), 7/1 (transfers). *Financial aid deadline:* 5/30. *Priority date:* 4/15.

Freshman Application Contact
Ms. Margarita Cruz, Director of Admissions, American University of Puerto Rico, PO Box 2037, Bayamón, PR 00960-2037. **Phone:** 787-740-6410. **Fax:** 787-785-7377.

Visit CollegeQuest.com for information on majors offered and athletics. College video available at CollegeQuest.com.

Atlantic College
Guaynabo, Puerto Rico

Admissions Office Contact
Atlantic College, PO Box 3918, Guaynabo, PR 00970. **Fax:** 787-720-1092.

Bayamón Central University
Bayamón, Puerto Rico

- **Independent Roman Catholic**, comprehensive, founded 1970
- **Degrees** associate, bachelor's, and master's
- **Suburban** 55-acre campus with easy access to San Juan
- **Coed**, 2,863 undergraduate students, 82% full-time, 65% women, 35% men
- **Moderately difficult** entrance level, 55% of applicants were admitted
- **22:1 student-to-undergraduate faculty ratio**
- **26% graduate** in 6 years or less
- **$3570 tuition** and fees
- **$7500 average indebtedness** upon graduation, $6.6 million endowment

Students *Undergraduates:* 2,359 full-time, 504 part-time. *The most frequently chosen baccalaureate fields are:* business/marketing, education, health professions and related sciences. *Graduate:* 263 in graduate degree programs.

| Age 25 or older | 25% | Transferred in | 8% |
| Hispanic Americans | 100% | | |

Faculty 252 (25% full-time), 26% with terminal degrees.

Expenses (1999–2000) *Tuition:* full-time $3330; part-time $110 per credit. *Required fees:* full-time $240; $140 per term part-time. Full-time tuition and fees vary according to program. Part-time tuition and fees vary according to program. *Payment plan:* deferred payment. *Waivers:* employees or children of employees.

Library BCU Library plus 1 other. *Operations spending 1999–2000:* $420,590. *Collection:* 51,011 titles, 3,027 serial subscriptions, 900 audiovisual materials.

College life *Housing:* college housing not available.

Campus security 24-hour patrols.

After graduation 5 organizations recruited on campus 1997–98. *Career center:* 6 full-time personnel. Services include job fairs, resume preparation, interview workshops, resume referral, career/interest testing, career counseling, careers library, job bank, job interviews.

Freshmen 1,005 applied, 553 admitted, 507 enrolled.

Average high school GPA	2.55	SAT verbal scores above 500	N/R
SAT math scores above 500	N/R	ACT above 18	N/R
1998 freshmen returning in 1999	66%		

Application *Option:* Common Application. *Application fee:* $15. *Required:* high school transcript; medical history. *Required for some:* letters of recommendation; interview.

Standardized tests *Admission: Required:* SAT I, SAT II Subject Tests.

Significant dates *Application deadlines:* 6/15 (freshmen), 6/15 (transfers). *Financial aid deadline priority date:* 4/15.

Freshman Application Contact
Mrs. Christine M. Hernandez, Director of Admissions, Bayamón Central University, PO Box 1725, Bayamón, PR 00960-1725. **Phone:** 787-786-3030 Ext. 2100.

Visit CollegeQuest.com for information on majors offered and athletics.

BAYAMÓN TECHNOLOGICAL UNIVERSITY COLLEGE
Bayamón, Puerto Rico

Admissions Office Contact
Bayamón Technological University College, 170 Carr 174 Parque Indust Minillas, Bayamón, PR 00959-1919. **E-mail:** e_velez@cutb.upr.clu.edu

CARIBBEAN UNIVERSITY
Bayamón, Puerto Rico

Admissions Office Contact
Caribbean University, Box 493, Bayamón, PR 00960-0493.

COLEGIO BIBLICO PENTECOSTAL
St. Just, Puerto Rico

Admissions Office Contact
Colegio Biblico Pentecostal, PO Box 901, St. Just, PR 00978-0901.

COLEGIO PENTECOSTAL MIZPA
Río Piedras, Puerto Rico

Admissions Office Contact
Colegio Pentecostal Mizpa, Km. 0 Hm. 2, Bo. Caimito, Apartado 20966, Río Piedras, PR 00928-0966. **Fax:** 787-720-2012.

COLEGIO UNIVERSITARIO DEL ESTE
Carolina, Puerto Rico

- **Independent**, 4-year, founded 1949
- **Degrees** associate and bachelor's
- **Small-town** campus with easy access to San Juan
- **Coed**, 7,077 undergraduate students, 77% full-time, 66% women, 34% men
- **Noncompetitive** entrance level, 54% of applicants were admitted
- **$3780 tuition** and fees

Part of Ana G. Méndez University System.

Students *Undergraduates:* 5,423 full-time, 1,654 part-time. *The most frequently chosen baccalaureate fields are:* business/marketing, education, protective services/public administration.

| Age 25 or older | 36% | Transferred in | 6% |
| Hispanic Americans | 100% | | |

Faculty 439 (14% full-time).

Expenses (1999–2000) *Tuition:* full-time $3480; part-time $116 per credit. *Required fees:* full-time $300; $150 per term. *Payment plan:* installment. *Waivers:* employees or children of employees.

Library *Collection:* 13,856 titles, 223 serial subscriptions.

College life *Housing:* college housing not available.

Campus security 24-hour patrols.

After graduation *Career center:* Services include career counseling.

Freshmen 4,172 applied, 2,244 admitted, 1,746 enrolled.

| SAT verbal scores above 500 | N/R | SAT math scores above 500 | N/R |
| ACT above 18 | N/R | 1998 freshmen returning in 1999 | 65% |

Application *Option:* deferred entrance. *Application fee:* $15. *Required:* high school transcript. *Required for some:* interview.

Standardized tests *Admission: Required:* CEEB.

Significant dates *Application deadlines:* 3/15 (freshmen), 3/15 (transfers).

Freshman Application Contact
Carmen Rodríguez, Associate Director, Colegio Universitario del Este, PO Box 2010, Carolina, PR 00984-2010. **Phone:** 787-257-7373 Ext. 3300. **Fax:** 787-257-7373 Ext. 4000.

Visit CollegeQuest.com for information on majors offered and athletics.

COLUMBIA COLLEGE
Caguas, Puerto Rico

- **Proprietary**, 4-year, founded 1966
- **Degrees** associate and bachelor's
- **Rural** 6-acre campus with easy access to San Juan
- **Coed**
- **Noncompetitive** entrance level

College life *Housing:* college housing not available.

Campus security 24-hour patrols.

Application *Option:* Common Application. *Application fee:* $50. *Required:* high school transcript. *Recommended:* essay or personal statement.

Admissions Office Contact
Columbia College, PO Box 8517, Caguas, PR 00726. **Toll-free phone:** 800-981-4877 Ext. 239. **Fax:** 787-744-7931. **E-mail:** columbia@loqui.net

Visit CollegeQuest.com for information on athletics.

CONSERVATORY OF MUSIC OF PUERTO RICO
San Juan, Puerto Rico

Admissions Office Contact
Conservatory of Music of Puerto Rico, 350 Rafael Lamar St at FDR Ave, San Juan, PR 00918.

Puerto Rico

ELECTRONIC DATA PROCESSING COLLEGE OF PUERTO RICO
San Juan, Puerto Rico

Admissions Office Contact
Electronic Data Processing College of Puerto Rico, 555 Munoz Rivera Avenue, San Juan, PR 00919-2303.

ESCUELA DE ARTES PLASTICAS DE PUERTO RICO
San Juan, Puerto Rico

- **Commonwealth-supported**, 4-year, founded 1966
- **Degree** bachelor's
- **Urban** campus
- **Coed**, 309 undergraduate students, 72% full-time, 38% women, 62% men
- **Moderately difficult** entrance level, 43% of applicants were admitted
- **11:1 student-to-undergraduate faculty ratio**
- **41% graduate** in 6 years or less
- **$4650 tuition** and fees

Students *Undergraduates:* 222 full-time, 87 part-time. *The most frequently chosen baccalaureate fields are:* education, visual/performing arts.

| Age 25 or older | 62% | Transferred in | 7% |
| Hispanic Americans | 100% | | |

Faculty 57 (25% full-time), 35% with terminal degrees.
Expenses (1999–2000) *Tuition:* full-time $3150. *Required fees:* full-time $1500. *Payment plan:* deferred payment. *Waivers:* employees or children of employees.
Library Francisco Oller Library. *Operations spending 1999–2000:* $88,900. *Collection:* 19,883 titles, 49 serial subscriptions.
College life *Housing:* college housing not available.
Campus security 24-hour patrols.
After graduation 10 organizations recruited on campus 1997–98. *Career center:* 1 full-time, 1 part-time personnel. Services include job fairs, resume preparation, resume referral, career counseling, careers library, job bank.
Freshmen 174 applied, 74 admitted, 72 enrolled.

Average high school GPA	2.72	SAT verbal scores above 500	37%
SAT math scores above 500	51%	ACT above 18	N/R
1998 freshmen returning in 1999	86%		

Application *Option:* Common Application. *Application fee:* $20. *Required:* essay or personal statement; high school transcript; minimum 2.0 GPA; interview; portfolio.
Standardized tests *Placement: Required:* SAT I
Significant dates *Application deadlines:* 4/1 (freshmen), 5/1 (transfers). *Notification:* 5/1 (freshmen). *Financial aid deadline priority date:* 7/11.

Freshman Application Contact
Milagros Lugo, Admission Assistant, Escuela de Artes Plasticas de Puerto Rico, PO Box 9021112, San Juan, PR 00902-1112. **Phone:** 787-725-8120 Ext. 233. **E-mail:** eap@coqui.net
Visit CollegeQuest.com for information on majors offered and athletics.

INTER AMERICAN UNIVERSITY OF PUERTO RICO, AGUADILLA CAMPUS
Aguadilla, Puerto Rico

- **Independent**, 4-year, founded 1957
- **Degrees** associate and bachelor's
- **Small-town** 50-acre campus
- **Coed**, 2,873 undergraduate students, 86% full-time, 63% women, 37% men
- **Moderately difficult** entrance level, 89% of applicants were admitted
- **$2954 tuition** and fees
- **$100.3 million system endowment**

Part of Inter American University of Puerto Rico.

Students *Undergraduates:* 2,482 full-time, 391 part-time. *The most frequently chosen baccalaureate fields are:* biological/life sciences, education, protective services/public administration.

| Transferred in | 3% | Hispanic Americans | 100% |

Faculty 196 (39% full-time), 13% with terminal degrees.
Expenses (1999–2000) *Tuition:* full-time $2640; part-time $110 per credit hour. *Required fees:* full-time $314; $119 per term part-time. Full-time tuition and fees vary according to course load. Part-time tuition and fees vary according to course load. *Payment plan:* deferred payment. *Waivers:* employees or children of employees.
Library *Operations spending 1999–2000:* $498,340. *Collection:* 39,847 titles, 545 serial subscriptions.
College life *Housing:* college housing not available. *Most popular organizations:* Criminal Justice Association, Secretarial Sciences Association, Future Teachers Association, Psychosocial Human Services Association, IPDAS (Drugs, Alcohol and Aids Prevention Institute).
Campus security 24-hour emergency response devices and patrols.
After graduation *Career center:* Services include career counseling.
Freshmen 602 applied, 535 admitted, 731 enrolled.

| Average high school GPA | 2.33 | SAT verbal scores above 500 | N/R |
| SAT math scores above 500 | N/R | ACT above 18 | N/R |

Application *Option:* deferred entrance. *Required:* high school transcript; minimum 2.00 GPA.
Standardized tests *Admission: Required:* SAT I, PAA.
Significant dates *Application deadlines:* rolling (freshmen), rolling (transfers).

Freshman Application Contact
Ms. Doris Pérez, Director of Admissions, Inter American University of Puerto Rico, Aguadilla Campus, PO Box 20,000, Aguadilla, PR 00605. **Phone:** 787-891-0925 Ext. 207.
Visit CollegeQuest.com for information on majors offered and athletics.

INTER AMERICAN UNIVERSITY OF PUERTO RICO, ARECIBO CAMPUS
Arecibo, Puerto Rico

- **Independent**, comprehensive, founded 1957
- **Degrees** associate, bachelor's, and master's
- **Urban** 20-acre campus with easy access to San Juan
- **Coed**, 3,603 undergraduate students, 81% full-time, 68% women, 32% men
- **Moderately difficult** entrance level, 90% of applicants were admitted
- **24:1 student-to-undergraduate faculty ratio**
- **$2940 tuition** and fees
- **$40.5 million endowment**

Part of Inter American University of Puerto Rico.

Students *Undergraduates:* 2,906 full-time, 697 part-time. *The most frequently chosen baccalaureate fields are:* business/marketing, education, protective services/public administration. *Graduate:* 20 in graduate degree programs.

| Age 25 or older | 29% | Transferred in | 4% |
| Hispanic Americans | 100% | | |

Faculty 232 (37% full-time), 13% with terminal degrees.
Expenses (1999–2000) *Tuition:* full-time $2640; part-time $110 per credit hour. *Required fees:* full-time $300; $150 per term part-time. *Payment plan:* guaranteed tuition. *Waivers:* employees or children of employees.
Library René Marqués Library. *Operations spending 1999–2000:* $38,297. *Collection:* 74,991 titles, 739 serial subscriptions.
College life *Housing:* college housing not available. *Social organizations:* local fraternities, local sororities; 5% of eligible men and 5% of eligible women are members. *Most popular organizations:* theatrical group "Ciclorama," Association of Student Advisers Youth Against Drugs, literary circle "René Marqués," Future Social Workers Association, Student Counseling Association.
Campus security 24-hour emergency response devices and patrols.
After graduation 60 organizations recruited on campus 1997–98. 29% of class of 1998 had job offers within 6 months. *Career center:* 1 full-time

Puerto Rico

personnel. Services include job fairs, resume preparation, resume referral, career counseling, careers library, job interviews.

Freshmen 872 applied, 786 admitted, 463 enrolled.

Average high school GPA	2.7	SAT verbal scores above 500	N/R
SAT math scores above 500	N/R	ACT above 18	N/R
1998 freshmen returning in 1999	80%		

Application *Options:* early admission, deferred entrance. *Application fee:* $19. *Required:* high school transcript; minimum 2.0 GPA. *Required for some:* interview. *Recommended:* minimum 3.0 GPA.

Standardized tests *Admission: Required:* PAA, CEEB.

Significant dates *Application deadlines:* rolling (freshmen), rolling (transfers).

Freshman Application Contact
Ms. Provi Montalvo, Admission Director, Inter American University of Puerto Rico, Arecibo Campus, PO Box 4050, Arecibo, PR 00614-4050. **Phone:** 787-878-5475 Ext. 2268. **Fax:** 787-880-1624.

Visit CollegeQuest.com for information on majors offered and athletics.

INTER AMERICAN UNIVERSITY OF PUERTO RICO, BARRANQUITAS CAMPUS
Barranquitas, Puerto Rico

- **Independent**, 4-year, founded 1957
- **Degrees** associate and bachelor's
- **Small-town** campus with easy access to San Juan
- **Coed**
- **Moderately difficult** entrance level

Part of Inter American University of Puerto Rico.

College life *Housing:* college housing not available.

Campus security 24-hour patrols.

Application *Options:* Common Application, deferred entrance. *Application fee:* $19. *Required:* high school transcript; interview.

Standardized tests *Admission: Required:* SAT I or ACT.

Admissions Office Contact
Inter American University of Puerto Rico, Barranquitas Campus, PO Box 517, Barranquitas, PR 00794. **Fax:** 787-857-9244.

Visit CollegeQuest.com for information on athletics.

INTER AMERICAN UNIVERSITY OF PUERTO RICO, BAYAMÓN CAMPUS
Bayamón, Puerto Rico

- **Independent**, 4-year, founded 1912
- **Degrees** associate and bachelor's
- **Urban** 51-acre campus with easy access to San Juan
- **Coed**

Part of Inter American University of Puerto Rico.

Institutional Web site http://bc.inter.edu/

College life *Housing:* college housing not available. *Most popular organizations:* Associacion de Estudiantes de Administracion de Empresas, Estudiantes Unidos por la Ciencia, Associacion Estudiantes de Aviacion, Associacion Estudiantes de Programacion, Asociacion Estudiantes de Ingenieria.

Campus security 24-hour patrols.

Application *Option:* Common Application. *Application fee:* $25. *Required:* high school transcript; minimum 2.0 GPA; 2.50 GPA for engineering programs. *Recommended:* interview.

Standardized tests *Admission: Required:* CEEB. *Required for some:* SAT I.

Admissions Office Contact
Inter American University of Puerto Rico, Bayamón Campus, 500 Road 830, Bayamón, PR 00957. **Fax:** 787-279-2205 Ext. 2017. **E-mail:** cdehoyos@bc.inter.edu

Visit CollegeQuest.com for information on athletics.

INTER AMERICAN UNIVERSITY OF PUERTO RICO, FAJARDO CAMPUS
Fajardo, Puerto Rico

- **Independent**, 4-year, founded 1965
- **Degrees** associate and bachelor's
- **Small-town** campus with easy access to San Juan
- **Coed**
- **Moderately difficult** entrance level, 77% of applicants were admitted

Part of Inter American University of Puerto Rico.

Faculty 124 (33% full-time), 8% with terminal degrees.

Library Antonio S. Belaval Library. *Collection:* 39,951 titles, 686 serial subscriptions.

College life *Housing:* college housing not available. *Most popular organizations:* Future Teachers Association, Criminal Justice Student Association, Student Counseling Association, Practical Teaching Association.

Campus security 24-hour patrols.

After graduation *Career center:* 6 full-time personnel. Services include job fairs, resume preparation, resume referral, career counseling, careers library, job interviews.

Freshmen 429 applied, 329 admitted.

Average high school GPA	2.0	SAT verbal scores above 500	N/R
SAT math scores above 500	N/R	ACT above 18	N/R
1998 freshmen returning in 1999	65%		

Application *Options:* early admission, deferred entrance. *Required:* high school transcript; minimum 2.0 GPA. *Required for some:* letters of recommendation.

Standardized tests *Admission: Required:* SAT I, PAA.

Significant dates *Application deadlines:* rolling (freshmen), rolling (transfers). *Notification:* 5/1 (freshmen).

Freshman Application Contact
Ms. Ada Caraballo, Technician, Inter American University of Puerto Rico, Fajardo Campus, Call Box 70003, Fajardo, PR 00738-7003. **Phone:** 787-863-2390 Ext. 2210. **E-mail:** evrivera@ns.inter.edu

Visit CollegeQuest.com for information on majors offered and athletics.

INTER AMERICAN UNIVERSITY OF PUERTO RICO, GUAYAMA CAMPUS
Guayama, Puerto Rico

- **Independent**, 4-year, founded 1958
- **Degrees** associate and bachelor's
- **Small-town** 50-acre campus
- **Coed**
- **Moderately difficult** entrance level
- **$3700 tuition** and fees

Part of Inter American University of Puerto Rico.

Expenses (1999–2000) *Tuition:* full-time $3300; part-time $110 per credit. *Required fees:* full-time $400; $100 per term part-time.

Institutional Web site http://www.inter.edu/guayama.html

College life *Housing:* college housing not available. *Most popular organizations:* nursing club, CONFRA Inter, sciences club, AFPO Association.

Application *Options:* Common Application, early admission, deferred entrance.

Standardized tests *Admission: Required:* SAT I, PAA.

Admissions Office Contact
Inter American University of Puerto Rico, Guayama Campus, Call Box 10004, Guayama, PR 00785.

Visit CollegeQuest.com for information on athletics.

INTER AMERICAN UNIVERSITY OF PUERTO RICO, METROPOLITAN CAMPUS
San Juan, Puerto Rico

- **Independent**, comprehensive, founded 1960

Puerto Rico

Inter American University of Puerto Rico, Metropolitan Campus (continued)
- **Degrees** associate, bachelor's, master's, doctoral, and postbachelor's certificates
- **Coed**, 6,788 undergraduate students, 74% full-time, 60% women, 40% men
- **Moderately difficult** entrance level, 83% of applicants were admitted
- **42:1 student-to-undergraduate faculty ratio**
- **$3830 tuition** and fees

Part of Inter American University of Puerto Rico.
Students *Undergraduates:* 4,996 full-time, 1,792 part-time. Students come from 5 states and territories, 14 other countries. *The most frequently chosen baccalaureate fields are:* business/marketing, education, protective services/public administration. *Graduate:* 2,081 in graduate degree programs.

| Age 25 or older | 24% | Hispanic Americans | 100% |

Faculty 643 (43% full-time), 37% with terminal degrees.
Expenses (2000–2001, estimated) *Tuition:* full-time $3300; part-time $110 per credit. *Required fees:* full-time $530; $183 per term part-time. *Payment plans:* installment, deferred payment. *Waivers:* employees or children of employees.
College life *Housing:* college housing not available. *Most popular organizations:* Association of Future Social Workers, Accounting Students Association, Golden Key National Honor Society, Association of Arabes and Musulmanic, Human Resources Management Association.
Campus security 24-hour emergency response devices and patrols, video security system.
After graduation *Career center:* Services include career counseling.
Freshmen 1,491 applied, 1,243 admitted, 1,193 enrolled.

| Average high school GPA | 2.68 | SAT verbal scores above 500 | N/R |
| SAT math scores above 500 | N/R | ACT above 18 | N/R |

Application *Option:* early admission. *Application fee:* $0. *Required:* high school transcript; 2.0 letters of recommendation.
Standardized tests *Admission: Required:* SAT I, PAA. *Required for some:* SAT II Subject Tests.
Significant dates *Application deadlines:* rolling (freshmen), rolling (transfers).
Freshman Application Contact
Ms. Ida G. Betancourt, Official Admission, Inter American University of Puerto Rico, Metropolitan Campus, Metropolitan Campus—Admission Ofc, PO Box 191293, San Juan, PR 00919-1293. **Phone:** 787-250-1912 Ext. 2100.
Visit CollegeQuest.com for information on majors offered and athletics.

INTER AMERICAN UNIVERSITY OF PUERTO RICO, PONCE CAMPUS
Mercedita, Puerto Rico

Admissions Office Contact
Inter American University of Puerto Rico, Ponce Campus, Street # 1, Km 123.2, Mercedita, PR 00715-2201. **E-mail:** fldiaz@acpon1.ponce.inter.edu

INTER AMERICAN UNIVERSITY OF PUERTO RICO, SAN GERMÁN CAMPUS
San Germán, Puerto Rico

- **Independent**, comprehensive, founded 1912
- **Degrees** associate, bachelor's, and master's
- **Small-town** 260-acre campus
- **Coed**, 4,619 undergraduate students, 86% full-time, 55% women, 45% men
- **Moderately difficult** entrance level, 72% of applicants were admitted
- **31:1 student-to-undergraduate faculty ratio**
- **$3996 tuition** and fees

Part of Inter American University of Puerto Rico.
Students *Undergraduates:* Students come from 15 states and territories, 17 other countries. *Graduate:* 806 in graduate degree programs.

| From out-of-commonwealth | 1% | Reside on campus | 10% |
| Age 25 or older | 19% | | |

Faculty 332 (39% full-time), 21% with terminal degrees.
Expenses (1999–2000) *Comprehensive fee:* $6196 includes full-time tuition ($3630), mandatory fees ($366), and room and board ($2200). *College room only:* $900. Room and board charges vary according to housing facility. *Part-time tuition:* $110 per credit. *Part-time fees:* $183 per term part-time. *Payment plan:* deferred payment. *Waivers:* employees or children of employees.
Library Juan Cancio Ortiz Library. *Collection:* 119,887 titles, 1,818 serial subscriptions, 4,356 audiovisual materials.
College life *Housing: Options:* men-only, women-only. *Social organizations:* national fraternities, national sororities; 10% of eligible men and 9% of eligible women are members. *Most popular organizations:* Olympic Movement 2004, PolyNature, Association for Computer Machinery, Secretarial Collegiate International, Biology Honor Society.
Campus security 24-hour patrols.
After graduation *Career center:* 3 full-time personnel. Services include job fairs, resume preparation, resume referral, career counseling, careers library, job bank, job interviews.
Freshmen 1,660 applied, 1,195 admitted.

| Average high school GPA | 2.76 | SAT verbal scores above 500 | N/R |
| SAT math scores above 500 | N/R | ACT above 18 | N/R |

Application *Options:* early admission, early decision. *Application fee:* $0. *Required:* high school transcript; medical history. *Required for some:* 1 letter of recommendation; interview. *Recommended:* essay or personal statement; minimum 2.0 GPA.
Standardized tests *Admission: Required:* CEEB.
Significant dates *Application deadlines:* 5/13 (freshmen), 5/15 (transfers). *Financial aid deadline priority date:* 4/26.
Freshman Application Contact
Mrs. Mildred Camacho, Director of Admissions, Inter American University of Puerto Rico, San Germán Campus, PO Box 5100, San Germán, PR 00683-5008. **Phone:** 787-264-1912 Ext. 7283. **Fax:** 787-892-6350. **E-mail:** milcama@sg.inter.edu
Visit CollegeQuest.com for information on majors offered and athletics.

POLYTECHNIC UNIVERSITY OF PUERTO RICO
Hato Rey, Puerto Rico

- **Independent**, comprehensive, founded 1966
- **Degrees** bachelor's and master's
- **Urban** 10-acre campus with easy access to San Juan
- **Coed**, 4,544 undergraduate students, 41% full-time, 20% women, 80% men
- **Minimally difficult** entrance level, 87% of applicants were admitted
- **98% graduate** in 6 years or less
- **$4485 tuition** and fees
- **$11.6 million endowment**

Students *Undergraduates:* 1,862 full-time, 2,682 part-time. *The most frequently chosen baccalaureate fields are:* business/marketing, engineering/engineering technologies. *Graduate:* 445 in graduate degree programs.

| Age 25 or older | 16% | Transferred in | 6% |
| Hispanic Americans | 100% | | |

Faculty 265 (45% full-time), 14% with terminal degrees.
Expenses (1999–2000) *One-time required fee:* $10. *Tuition:* full-time $4200; part-time $115 per credit hour. *Required fees:* full-time $285; $95 per credit hour. Full-time tuition and fees vary according to program. Part-time tuition and fees vary according to program. *Payment plan:* deferred payment. *Waivers:* employees or children of employees.
Library Main library plus 1 other. *Operations spending 1999–2000:* $954,250. *Collection:* 58,622 titles, 1,715 serial subscriptions.
College life *Housing:* college housing not available.
Campus security 24-hour patrols.
After graduation 50 organizations recruited on campus 1997–98. *Career center:* 5 full-time personnel. Services include job fairs, resume preparation,

Puerto Rico

resume referral, career counseling, careers library, job bank, job interviews. **Graduate education:** 4% of class of 1999 went directly to graduate and professional school: 4% engineering.

Freshmen 1,024 applied, 893 admitted, 658 enrolled. 36 valedictorians.

Average high school GPA	3.0	SAT verbal scores above 500	N/R
SAT math scores above 500	N/R	ACT above 18	N/R
1998 freshmen returning in 1999	70%		

Application *Options:* early admission, deferred entrance. *Application fee:* $30. *Required:* high school transcript.

Standardized tests *Admission: Required for some:* SAT I.

Significant dates *Application deadline:* 8/15 (freshmen).

Freshman Application Contact
Ms. Teresa Cardona, Director of Admissions, Polytechnic University of Puerto Rico, PO Box 192017, San Juan, PR 00919-2017. **Phone:** 787-754-8000 Ext. 240. **E-mail:** rbelvis@pupr.edu

Visit CollegeQuest.com for information on majors offered and athletics. College video available at CollegeQuest.com.

PONTIFICAL CATHOLIC UNIVERSITY OF PUERTO RICO
Ponce, Puerto Rico

- **$4961 average financial aid** package, $14.3 million endowment

Students *Undergraduates:* 5,395 full-time, 655 part-time. *The most frequently chosen baccalaureate fields are:* business/marketing, education, health professions and related sciences. **Graduate:** 536 in professional programs, 1,108 in other graduate degree programs.

From out-of-commonwealth	1%	Reside on campus	4%
Age 25 or older	9%	Transferred in	4%
Hispanic Americans	100%		

Faculty 355 (78% full-time), 100% with terminal degrees.

Expenses (1999–2000) *Waivers:* employees or children of employees.

Library Encarnacion Valdes Library plus 1 other. *Operations spending 1999–2000:* $2.4 million. *Collection:* 47,322 serial subscriptions.

College life *Housing: Options:* men-only, women-only. *Social organizations:* national fraternities, national sororities, local fraternities, local sororities; 1% of eligible men and 1% of eligible women are members. *Most popular organizations:* Accounting Students Club, Foreign Students Club, Christ Heralds.

Campus security 24-hour emergency response devices and patrols.

After graduation 20 organizations recruited on campus 1997–98. *Career center:* Services include career counseling.

Freshmen 1,599 applied, 1,342 admitted, 1,228 enrolled.

SAT verbal scores above 500	36%	SAT math scores above 500	43%
ACT above 18	N/R	1998 freshmen returning in 1999	98%

Application *Options:* early admission, deferred entrance. *Application fee:* $15. *Required:* high school transcript; minimum 2.0 GPA. *Required for some:* essay or personal statement; minimum 3.0 GPA; 1 letter of recommendation; interview.

Standardized tests *Admission: Required:* SAT I.

Significant dates *Application deadlines:* 4/15 (freshmen), 4/15 (transfers). *Financial aid deadline priority date:* 5/14.

Freshman Application Contact
Sra. Ana O. Bonilla, Director of Admissions, Pontifical Catholic University of Puerto Rico, 2250 Avenida Las Americas, Ponce, PR 00717-0777. **Phone:** 787-841-2000 Ext. 1004. **Toll-free phone:** 800-981-5040. **Fax:** 787-840-4295. **E-mail:** admissions@pucpr.edu

Visit CollegeQuest.com for information on majors offered and athletics. College video available at CollegeQuest.com.

UNIVERSIDAD ADVENTISTA DE LAS ANTILLAS
Mayagüez, Puerto Rico

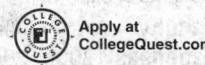
Apply at CollegeQuest.com

- **Independent Seventh-day Adventist**, 4-year, founded 1957
- **Degrees** associate and bachelor's
- **Rural** 284-acre campus
- **Coed**, 710 undergraduate students, 89% full-time, 62% women, 38% men
- **Minimally difficult** entrance level, 69% of applicants were admitted
- **$3690 tuition** and fees

Students *Undergraduates:* 629 full-time, 81 part-time. Students come from 10 states and territories, 21 other countries. **Graduate:** 31 in graduate degree programs.

From out-of-commonwealth	21%	Reside on campus	27%
Age 25 or older	23%	Transferred in	11%
African Americans	2%	Hispanic Americans	95%

Faculty 69 (65% full-time), 14% with terminal degrees.

Expenses (1999–2000) *One-time required fee:* $75. *Comprehensive fee:* $5840 includes full-time tuition ($3150), mandatory fees ($540), and room and board ($2150). Full-time tuition and fees vary according to course load. Room and board charges vary according to board plan. *Part-time tuition:* $110 per credit. Part-time tuition and fees vary according to course load. *Payment plans:* tuition prepayment, installment, deferred payment. *Waivers:* employees or children of employees.

Library *Operations spending 1999–2000:* $97,659. *Collection:* 84,842 titles, 434 serial subscriptions.

College life *Housing:* on-campus residence required in freshman year. *Options:* coed, men-only, women-only. *Social organizations:* men's and women's associations; 9% of eligible men and 13% of eligible women are members. *Most popular organizations:* Score Group, gymnastic club, Student Council, Group Life.

Campus security 24-hour emergency response devices and patrols, student patrols, controlled dormitory access.

After graduation *Career center:* Services include career counseling.

Freshmen 187 applied, 129 admitted, 327 enrolled.

SAT verbal scores above 500	N/R	SAT math scores above 500	N/R
ACT above 18	N/R	1998 freshmen returning in 1999	69%

Application *Options:* eApply at www.CollegeQuest.com, Common Application, deferred entrance. *Application fee:* $20. *Required:* high school transcript; minimum 2.0 GPA; letters of recommendation. *Required for some:* interview.

Standardized tests *Admission: Required:* SAT I, PAA.

Significant dates *Application deadlines:* 7/8 (freshmen), 8/10 (transfers). *Notification:* continuous until 8/23 (freshmen). *Financial aid deadline:* continuous.

Freshman Application Contact
Ms. Evelyn del Valle, Recluter, Universidad Adventista de las Antillas, Universidad Adventista de las Antillas oficina de Admisiones, PO Box 118, Mayaguez, PR 00681. **Phone:** 787-834-9595 Ext. 2208. **Fax:** 787-834-9597. **E-mail:** admissions@uaa.edu

Visit CollegeQuest.com for information on majors offered and athletics.

UNIVERSIDAD DEL TURABO
Turabo, Puerto Rico

- **Independent**, comprehensive, founded 1972
- **Degrees** associate, bachelor's, and master's
- **Urban** 140-acre campus with easy access to San Juan
- **Coed**, 6,987 undergraduate students, 83% full-time, 56% women, 44% men
- **Minimally difficult** entrance level, 66% of applicants were admitted
- **$3324 tuition** and fees

Part of Ana G. Méndez University System.

Students *Undergraduates:* 5,787 full-time, 1,200 part-time. *The most frequently chosen baccalaureate fields are:* business/marketing, education,

Puerto Rico

Universidad del Turabo (continued)
social sciences and history. **Graduate:** 1,078 in graduate degree programs.

| Age 25 or older | 35% | Hispanic Americans | 100% |

Faculty 410 (25% full-time).
Expenses (2000–2001) *Tuition:* full-time $3024; part-time $116 per credit. *Required fees:* full-time $300; $150 per term part-time.
Library *Collection:* 90,020 titles, 655 serial subscriptions.
College life *Housing:* college housing not available. *Most popular organizations:* Social Work Students Association, Honor's Student Association, Drama Club, Chorus, Computerized Sciences Organization.
Campus security 24-hour patrols.
After graduation *Career center:* Services include job fairs, career counseling, careers library, job interviews.
Freshmen 3,147 applied, 2,091 admitted, 1,660 enrolled.

Average high school GPA	2.42	SAT verbal scores above 500	N/R
SAT math scores above 500	N/R	ACT above 18	N/R
1998 freshmen returning in 1999	69%		

Application *Option:* deferred entrance. *Application fee:* $15. *Required:* high school transcript.
Standardized tests *Placement: Required:* CEEB
Significant dates *Application deadlines:* rolling (freshmen), rolling (transfers). *Notification:* continuous until 8/1 (freshmen).
Freshman Application Contact
Sr. Jesús Torres, Director of Admissions, Universidad del Turabo, PO Box 3030, Turabo, PR 00778-3030. **Phone:** 787-743-7979 Ext. 201.
Visit CollegeQuest.com for information on majors offered and athletics.

UNIVERSIDAD METROPOLITANA
Río Piedras, Puerto Rico

- **Independent**, comprehensive, founded 1980
- **Degrees** associate, bachelor's, and master's
- **Small-town** campus with easy access to San Juan
- **Coed**, 5,319 undergraduate students, 77% full-time, 65% women, 35% men
- **Moderately difficult** entrance level, 57% of applicants were admitted
- **$3324 tuition** and fees

Part of Ana G. Méndez University System.
Students *Undergraduates:* 4,103 full-time, 1,216 part-time. *The most frequently chosen baccalaureate fields are:* business/marketing, education, health professions and related sciences. **Graduate:** 538 in graduate degree programs.

| Age 25 or older | 33% | Transferred in | 6% |
| Hispanic Americans | 100% | | |

Faculty 358 (25% full-time).
Expenses (2000–2001) *Tuition:* full-time $3024; part-time $116 per credit. *Required fees:* full-time $300.
College life *Housing:* college housing not available. *Social organizations:* national fraternities.
Campus security 24-hour patrols.
After graduation *Career center:* 2 full-time personnel. Services include job fairs, resume preparation, resume referral, career counseling, careers library, job bank, job interviews.
Freshmen 3,406 applied, 1,929 admitted, 1,335 enrolled.

| SAT verbal scores above 500 | N/R | SAT math scores above 500 | N/R |
| ACT above 18 | N/R | 1998 freshmen returning in 1999 | 65% |

Application *Option:* Common Application. *Application fee:* $15. *Required:* high school transcript. *Required for some:* interview.
Standardized tests *Admission: Required:* PAA.
Significant dates *Application deadlines:* 7/30 (freshmen), 7/30 (transfers).
Freshman Application Contact
Ms. Carmen Rosado, Director of Admissions, Universidad Metropolitana, Call Box 21150, Río Piedras, PR 00928-1150. **Phone:** 787-766-1717 Ext. 540.
E-mail: um_frivera@suagm1.suagm.edu
Visit CollegeQuest.com for information on majors offered and athletics. College video available at CollegeQuest.com.

UNIVERSIDAD POLITÉCNICA DE PUERTO RICO
Puerto Rico—See Polytechnic University of Puerto Rico

UNIVERSITY OF PUERTO RICO, AGUADILLA UNIVERSITY COLLEGE
Aguadilla, Puerto Rico

- **Commonwealth-supported**, 4-year, founded 1972
- **Degrees** associate and bachelor's
- **Suburban** 32-acre campus
- **Coed**
- **Moderately difficult** entrance level

Part of University of Puerto Rico System.
College life *Housing:* college housing not available. *Social organizations:* local fraternities.
Campus security 24-hour patrols.
Application *Options:* Common Application, early admission, deferred entrance. *Required:* high school transcript.
Standardized tests *Admission: Required:* SAT I, SAT II Subject Tests, PAA.
Admissions Office Contact
University of Puerto Rico, Aguadilla University College, PO Box 250-160, Aguadilla, PR 00604-0160.
Visit CollegeQuest.com for information on athletics.

UNIVERSITY OF PUERTO RICO AT ARECIBO
Arecibo, Puerto Rico

- **Commonwealth-supported**, 4-year, founded 1967
- **Degrees** associate and bachelor's
- **Urban** 44-acre campus with easy access to San Juan
- **Coed**
- **Very difficult** entrance level

Part of University of Puerto Rico System.
College life *Housing:* college housing not available. *Social organizations:* local fraternities, local sororities; 10% of eligible men and 17% of eligible women are members. *Most popular organizations:* Club Rotaract, CONFRA, Student Counselors, band/ATUC, ACTRE.
Campus security 24-hour emergency response devices and patrols.
Application *Required:* high school transcript.
Standardized tests *Admission: Required:* SAT II Subject Tests, PAA or SAT I, CEEB.
Admissions Office Contact
University of Puerto Rico at Arecibo, PO Box 4010, Arecibo, PR 00614-4010.
E-mail: m_saenz@cuta.upr.clu.edu
Visit CollegeQuest.com for information on athletics.

UNIVERSITY OF PUERTO RICO AT PONCE
Ponce, Puerto Rico

- **Commonwealth-supported**, 4-year, founded 1970
- **Degrees** associate and bachelor's
- **Urban** 86-acre campus with easy access to San Juan
- **Coed**, 4,049 undergraduate students, 91% full-time, 63% women, 37% men
- **Moderately difficult** entrance level, 69% of applicants were admitted
- **20:1 student-to-undergraduate faculty ratio**
- **44% graduate** in 6 years or less
- **$1815 tuition** and fees (in-commonwealth)

Puerto Rico

Part of University of Puerto Rico System.
Students *Undergraduates:* 3,688 full-time, 361 part-time. *The most frequently chosen baccalaureate fields are:* business/marketing, education, personal/miscellaneous services.

| Age 25 or older | 3% | Transferred in | 1% |

Faculty 190 (78% full-time), 12% with terminal degrees.
Expenses (1999–2000) *Tuition, state resident:* full-time $1020. *Required fees:* full-time $795. Nonresidents who are U.S. citizens pay an amount equal to the rate for nonresidents at a state university in their home state. *Payment plan:* installment. *Waivers:* employees or children of employees.
Library *Operations spending 1999–2000:* $660,456. *Collection:* 53,000 titles, 1,643 serial subscriptions.
College life *Housing:* college housing not available. *Most popular organizations:* American Marketing Association, Secretarial Sciences Association, drama club, Alfa Computer Club.
Campus security 24-hour patrols.
After graduation *Career center:* 1 full-time personnel. Services include job fairs, career counseling, careers library.
Freshmen 1,622 applied, 1,117 admitted, 1,054 enrolled.

Average high school GPA	3.2	SAT verbal scores above 500	N/R
SAT math scores above 500	N/R	ACT above 18	N/R
1998 freshmen returning in 1999	88%		

Application *Options:* Common Application, early admission, early decision. *Application fee:* $15. *Required:* high school transcript.
Standardized tests *Admission: Required:* SAT I, PAA.
Significant dates *Application deadlines:* 11/15 (freshmen), 2/23 (transfers). *Early decision:* 1/15. *Notification:* 3/4 (freshmen), 1/20 (early decision). *Financial aid deadline:* 6/30. *Priority date:* 5/29.
Freshman Application Contact
Mr. William Rodriguez Mercado, Admissions Officer, University of Puerto Rico at Ponce, PO Box 7186, Ponce, PR 00732-7186. **Phone:** 787-844-8181 Ext. 2530. **Fax:** 787-844-8679.
Visit **CollegeQuest.com** for information on majors offered and athletics.

UNIVERSITY OF PUERTO RICO, CAROLINA REGIONAL COLLEGE
Carolina, Puerto Rico

- **Commonwealth-supported**, primarily 2-year, founded 1974
- **Degrees** associate and bachelor's
- **Urban** 60-acre campus with easy access to San Juan
- **Coed**
- **Moderately difficult** entrance level

Part of University of Puerto Rico System.
Faculty 87 (84% full-time).
Admissions Office Contact
University of Puerto Rico, Carolina Regional College, PO Box 4800, Carolina, PR 00984-4800.
Visit **CollegeQuest.com** for information on majors offered and athletics.

UNIVERSITY OF PUERTO RICO, CAYEY UNIVERSITY COLLEGE
Cayey, Puerto Rico

Admissions Office Contact
University of Puerto Rico, Cayey University College, Antonio Barcelo, Cayey, PR 00737.

UNIVERSITY OF PUERTO RICO, COLEGIO REGIONAL DE LA MONTAÑA
Utuado, Puerto Rico

- **Commonwealth-supported**, primarily 2-year, founded 1979
- **Degrees** associate and bachelor's
- **Small-town** 180-acre campus with easy access to San Juan
- **Coed**, 1,330 undergraduate students, 91% full-time, 57% women, 43% men
- **Moderately difficult** entrance level

Part of University of Puerto Rico System.
Faculty 76 (82% full-time).
Admissions Office Contact
University of Puerto Rico, Colegio Regional de la Montaña, PO Box 2500, Utuado, PR 00641-2500.
Visit **CollegeQuest.com** for information on majors offered and athletics.

UNIVERSITY OF PUERTO RICO, HUMACAO UNIVERSITY COLLEGE
Humacao, Puerto Rico

- **Commonwealth-supported**, 4-year, founded 1962
- **Degrees** associate and bachelor's
- **Suburban** 62-acre campus with easy access to San Juan
- **Coed**, 4,019 undergraduate students, 87% full-time, 70% women, 30% men
- **Moderately difficult** entrance level, 62% of applicants were admitted
- **15:1 student-to-undergraduate faculty ratio**
- **48% graduate** in 6 years or less
- **$1095 tuition** and fees (in-commonwealth)

Part of University of Puerto Rico System.
Students *Undergraduates:* 3,503 full-time, 516 part-time. Students come from 5 states and territories. *The most frequently chosen baccalaureate fields are:* business/marketing, biological/life sciences, physical sciences.

| Age 25 or older | 10% | Transferred in | 1% |
| Hispanic Americans | 100% | | |

Faculty 284 (92% full-time), 33% with terminal degrees.
Expenses (1999–2000) *Tuition, state resident:* full-time $1020; part-time $30 per credit. *Required fees:* full-time $75; $38 per term part-time. Full-time tuition and fees vary according to course load, program, and reciprocity agreements. Part-time tuition and fees vary according to program. Nonresidents who are U.S. citizens pay an amount equal to the rate for nonresidents at a state university in their home state. *Payment plan:* deferred payment. *Waivers:* employees or children of employees.
Library *Operations spending 1999–2000:* $1.5 million. *Collection:* 99,956 titles, 1,333 serial subscriptions, 164 audiovisual materials.
College life *Housing:* college housing not available. *Most popular organizations:* Recreational Organization, Accounting Students Association, Management Students Association, Microbiology Students Association, Human Resources Students Association.
Campus security 24-hour patrols, 24-hour gate security.
After graduation 20 organizations recruited on campus 1997–98. *Career center:* 1 full-time personnel. Services include job fairs, resume preparation, interview workshops, resume referral, career/interest testing, career counseling, careers library, job bank, job interviews.
Freshmen 1,517 applied, 945 admitted, 889 enrolled.

Average high school GPA	3.44	SAT verbal scores above 500	N/R
SAT math scores above 500	N/R	ACT above 18	N/R
1998 freshmen returning in 1999	87%		

Application *Option:* deferred entrance. *Application fee:* $15. *Required:* high school transcript; minimum 2.0 GPA.
Standardized tests *Admission: Required:* CEEB for Puerto Rican applicants. *Required for some:* SAT I, SAT II Subject Tests.
Significant dates *Application deadlines:* 11/16 (freshmen), 2/15 (transfers). *Notification:* continuous until 3/30 (freshmen). *Financial aid deadline:* 6/30.
Freshman Application Contact
Mrs. Inara Ferrer, Director of Admissions, University of Puerto Rico, Humacao University College, HUC Station, Humacao, PR 00791. **Phone:** 787-850-9301. **E-mail:** i_ferrer@cuhac.upr.clu.edu
Visit **CollegeQuest.com** for information on majors offered and athletics. Electronic viewbook available at CollegeQuest.com.

Puerto Rico

UNIVERSITY OF PUERTO RICO, MAYAGÜEZ CAMPUS
Mayagüez, Puerto Rico

- **Commonwealth-supported**, university, founded 1911
- **Degrees** bachelor's, master's, and doctoral
- **Urban** 315-acre campus
- **Coed**, 12,019 undergraduate students
- **Very difficult** entrance level, 70% of applicants were admitted

Part of University of Puerto Rico System.
Students *Undergraduates: The most frequently chosen baccalaureate fields are:* biological/life sciences, agriculture, business/marketing.

Hispanic Americans 100%

Library General Library plus 3 others. *Collection:* 1.1 million titles, 47,784 audiovisual materials.
College life *Social organizations:* national fraternities, national sororities, local fraternities, local sororities.
Campus security 24-hour emergency response devices and patrols.
After graduation *Career center:* 20 full-time, 2 part-time personnel. Services include job fairs, resume preparation, resume referral, career counseling, job interviews.
Freshmen 3,780 applied, 2,636 admitted. 1 Westinghouse recipient.

Average high school GPA	3.28	SAT verbal scores above 500	89%
SAT math scores above 500	93%	ACT above 18	N/R
1998 freshmen returning in 1999	91%		

Application *Option:* early decision. *Application fee:* $15. *Required:* high school transcript.
Standardized tests *Admission: Required:* SAT I, SAT II Subject Tests, PAA.
Significant dates *Application deadlines:* 12/15 (freshmen), 2/15 (transfers). *Early decision:* 12/15. *Notification:* 3/15 (freshmen), 2/15 (early decision).
Freshman Application Contact
Ms. Norma Torres, Acting Director of Admissions, University of Puerto Rico, Mayagüez Campus, PO Box 9021, Mayaguez, PR 00681-9021. **Phone:** 787-265-3811. **E-mail:** norma_t@dediego.uprm.edu
Visit CollegeQuest.com for information on majors offered and athletics.

UNIVERSITY OF PUERTO RICO, MEDICAL SCIENCES CAMPUS
San Juan, Puerto Rico

- **Commonwealth-supported**, upper-level, founded 1950
- **Degrees** associate, bachelor's, master's, doctoral, first professional, postbachelor's, and first professional certificates (bachelor's degree is upper-level)
- **Urban** 11-acre campus
- **Coed**, primarily women
- **Moderately difficult** entrance level

Part of University of Puerto Rico System.
Institutional Web site http://wwwrcm.upr.clu.edu/
College life *Housing:* college housing not available. *Social organizations:* national fraternities, national sororities, local fraternities, local sororities. *Most popular organizations:* general council of students, Association of Biomedical Sciences Graduate Students, council of medicine students, council of public health students, American Medical Association-Puerto Rico Chapter-Student Section.
Campus security 24-hour emergency response devices.
Application *Preference* given to commonwealth residents. *Application fee:* $25.
Standardized tests *Placement: Required:* SAT I *Required for some:* PCAT, MCAT, DAT.
Admissions Office Contact
University of Puerto Rico, Medical Sciences Campus, PO Box 365067, San Juan, PR 00936-5067. **Fax:** 787-754-0474. **E-mail:** raponte@rcmad.upr.clu.edu

Visit CollegeQuest.com for information on athletics.

UNIVERSITY OF PUERTO RICO, RÍO PIEDRAS
San Juan, Puerto Rico

- **Commonwealth-supported**, university, founded 1903
- **Degrees** bachelor's, master's, doctoral, first professional, and post-master's certificates
- **Urban** 281-acre campus
- **Coed**, 17,616 undergraduate students, 84% full-time, 69% women, 31% men
- **Very difficult** entrance level, 59% of applicants were admitted
- **17:1 student-to-undergraduate faculty ratio**
- **$790 tuition** and fees (in-commonwealth)

Part of University of Puerto Rico System.
Students *Undergraduates:* 14,857 full-time, 2,759 part-time. Students come from 4 states and territories, 24 other countries. *The most frequently chosen baccalaureate fields are:* business/marketing, biological/life sciences, education. *Graduate:* 568 in professional programs, 3,056 in other graduate degree programs.

From out-of-commonwealth	1%	Age 25 or older	0.1%
Transferred in	1%	International students	0.2%
Hispanic Americans	99%		

Faculty 1,293 (81% full-time), 50% with terminal degrees.
Expenses (1999–2000) *Tuition, state resident:* full-time $720. *Required fees:* full-time $70. *College room and board:* $3320. Nonresidents who are U.S. citizens pay an amount equal to the rate for nonresidents at a state university in their home state.
Library Jose M. Lazaro Library plus 10 others. *Collection:* 1.8 million titles, 5,599 serial subscriptions, 5,599 audiovisual materials.
College life *Housing: Option:* coed. *Social organizations:* national fraternities, national sororities, local fraternities, local sororities.
Campus security 24-hour emergency response devices, late-night transport-escort service.
After graduation *Career center:* Services include job fairs, career/interest testing, career counseling.
Freshmen 6,470 applied, 3,798 admitted, 3,301 enrolled.

| Average high school GPA | 3.5 | SAT verbal scores above 500 | 87% |
| SAT math scores above 500 | 84% | ACT above 18 | N/R |

Application *Option:* Common Application. *Application fee:* $15. *Required:* high school transcript; minimum 2.0 GPA. *Required for some:* interview.
Standardized tests *Admission: Required:* SAT I, SAT II Subject Tests, CEEB.
Significant dates *Application deadlines:* 2/15 (freshmen), 9/21 (transfers).
Freshman Application Contact
Mrs. Cruz B. Valentin, Director of Admissions, University of Puerto Rico, Río Piedras, PO Box 21907, San Juan, PR 00931-1907. **Phone:** 787-764-0000 Ext. 5666.
Visit CollegeQuest.com for information on majors offered and athletics.

UNIVERSITY OF THE SACRED HEART
San Juan, Puerto Rico

- **Independent Roman Catholic**, comprehensive, founded 1935
- **Degrees** associate, bachelor's, and master's
- **Urban** 33-acre campus
- **Coed**, 4,552 undergraduate students, 79% full-time, 64% women, 36% men
- **Moderately difficult** entrance level, 66% of applicants were admitted
- **22:1 student-to-undergraduate faculty ratio**
- **36% graduate** in 6 years or less
- **$4660 tuition** and fees
- **$15.3 million endowment**

Puerto Rico–Virgin Islands

Students *Undergraduates:* 3,614 full-time, 938 part-time. Students come from 30 other countries. *The most frequently chosen baccalaureate fields are:* business/marketing, communications/communication technologies, psychology. *Graduate:* 27 in professional programs, 385 in other graduate degree programs.

| From out-of-commonwealth | 2% | Age 25 or older | 14% |
| Transferred in | 6% | Hispanic Americans | 100% |

Faculty 324 (35% full-time), 29% with terminal degrees.

Expenses (1999–2000) *One-time required fee:* $10. *Tuition:* full-time $4280; part-time $130 per credit. *Required fees:* full-time $380. Full-time tuition and fees vary according to student level. Part-time tuition and fees vary according to student level. *College room only:* $1800. Room and board charges vary according to student level. *Payment plan:* deferred payment. *Waivers:* employees or children of employees.

Library Maria Teresa Guevara Library plus 1 other. *Operations spending 1999–2000:* $713,551. *Collection:* 1,525 serial subscriptions, 58,149 audiovisual materials.

College life *Housing: Options:* men-only, women-only. *Most popular organizations:* La Red (personal development center), Student Council, Judo Club, Athletic Association.

Campus security 24-hour patrols.

After graduation *Career center:* 1 full-time, 1 part-time personnel. Services include resume preparation, career/interest testing, career counseling, careers library, job bank, job interviews.

Freshmen 2,252 applied, 1,497 admitted, 841 enrolled.

Average high school GPA	2.86	SAT verbal scores above 500	N/R
SAT math scores above 500	N/R	ACT above 18	N/R
1998 freshmen returning in 1999	77%		

Application *Options:* Common Application, early admission. *Application fee:* $15. *Required:* high school transcript; minimum 2.5 GPA; 1 letter of recommendation.

Standardized tests *Admission: Required:* PAA, CEEB.

Significant dates *Application deadlines:* 6/30 (freshmen), 6/30 (transfers). *Financial aid deadline priority date:* 5/30.

Freshman Application Contact
Mr. Josué González, Coordinator of Admissions, University of the Sacred Heart, Admissions Office, PO Box 12383, San Juan, PR 00914-0383. **Phone:** 787-728-1515 Ext. 3237.

Visit CollegeQuest.com for information on majors offered and athletics.

VIRGIN ISLANDS

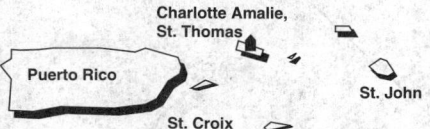

UNIVERSITY OF THE VIRGIN ISLANDS
Charlotte Amalie, Virgin Islands

- **Territory-supported**, comprehensive, founded 1962
- **Degrees** associate, bachelor's, and master's
- **Small-town** 175-acre campus
- **Coed**, 1,973 undergraduate students, 59% full-time, 80% women, 20% men
- **Minimally difficult** entrance level, 76% of applicants were admitted
- **28:1 student-to-undergraduate faculty ratio**
- **$4946 tuition** and fees (in-territory); $10,406 (out-of-territory)
- **$4.9 million endowment**

Students *Undergraduates:* 1,157 full-time, 816 part-time. Students come from 26 states and territories, 19 other countries. *The most frequently chosen baccalaureate fields are:* business/marketing, education, health professions and related sciences. *Graduate:* 203 in graduate degree programs.

From out-of-territory	2%	Age 25 or older	58%
Transferred in	2%	International students	7%
African Americans	71%	Asian Americans/Pacific Islanders	0.5%
Hispanic Americans	3%		

Faculty 222 (45% full-time), 41% with terminal degrees.

Expenses (1999–2000) *Tuition, state resident:* full-time $2730; part-time $91 per credit. *Tuition, nonresident:* full-time $8190; part-time $273 per credit. *Required fees:* full-time $2216; $55 per term part-time. *College room and board:* $5830. *Waivers:* senior citizens and employees or children of employees.

Library Ralph M. Paiewonsky Library. *Operations spending 1999–2000:* $795,153. *Collection:* 106,361 titles, 940 serial subscriptions.

College life *Housing: Options:* men-only, women-only. *Social organizations:* national fraternities, national sororities.

Campus security 24-hour patrols.

After graduation *Career center:* 3 full-time personnel. Services include job fairs, resume preparation, career counseling, careers library, job bank, job interviews.

Freshmen 617 applied, 470 admitted, 316 enrolled.

| SAT verbal scores above 500 | 19% | SAT math scores above 500 | 3% |
| ACT above 18 | N/R | | |

Application *Options:* early admission, deferred entrance. *Application fee:* $20. *Required:* essay or personal statement; high school transcript; 2 letters of recommendation.

Standardized tests *Admission: Required:* SAT I and SAT II or ACT.

Significant dates *Application deadlines:* 4/15 (freshmen), 4/15 (transfers). *Financial aid deadline:* 3/1.

Freshman Application Contact
Ms. Carolyn Cook, Director of Admissions & New Student Services, University of the Virgin Islands, 2 John Brewers Bay, Charlotte Amalie, VI 00802-9990. **Phone:** 340-693-1224. **E-mail:** admissions@uvi.edu

Visit CollegeQuest.com for information on majors offered and athletics.

- *See page 2852 for a narrative description.*

Canada

CANADA

[Map of Canada showing locations of cities with colleges: Prince George, Athabasca, Edmonton, Camrose, Vancouver, Kamloops, Langley, Burnaby, Three Hills, Victoria, Abbotsford, Calgary, Saskatoon, Kelowna, Lethbridge, Caronport, Regina, Brandon, Saint-Boniface, Winnipeg, Otterburne, Steinbach, Hull, North Bay, Thunder Bay, Sudbury, Chicoutimi, Rimouski, Sainte-Foy, Québec, Charlottetown, New Brunswick, Nova Scotia, St. John's, Newfoundland, Ottawa, Montréal, Waterloo, Kingston, London, Peterborough, Toronto, Hamilton, Windsor]

The Toronto area includes the towns of Ancaster, Cambridge, Guelph, Kitchener, Thornhill, North York, and St. Catharines.

Quebec includes the towns of Lennoxville, Rouyn-Noranda, Sherbrooke, and Trois-Riviéres.

Nova Scotia includes the towns of Antigonish, Church Point, Halifax, Sydney, Truro, and Wolfville.

The New Brunswick area includes the towns of Fredericton, Moncton, Sackville, Saint John, and Sussex.

ACADIA UNIVERSITY
Wolfville, Nova Scotia, Canada

- **Province-supported**, comprehensive, founded 1838
- **Degrees** bachelor's and master's
- **Small-town** 250-acre campus
- **Coed**, 3,155 undergraduate students, 96% full-time, 54% women, 46% men
- **Moderately difficult** entrance level, 45% of applicants were admitted
- **13:1** student-to-undergraduate faculty ratio
- **$5597** tuition and fees (out-of-province)
- **$22 million** endowment

Students *Undergraduates:* 3,043 full-time, 112 part-time. Students come from 12 provinces and territories, 39 other countries. *The most frequently chosen baccalaureate fields are:* business/marketing, education, social sciences and history. *Graduate:* 258 in professional programs, 256 in other graduate degree programs.

From out-of-province	42%	Reside on campus	40%
Age 25 or older	5%	Transferred in	5%

Faculty 288 (63% full-time).

Expenses (1999–2000) Tuition, fee, and room and board charges are reported in Canadian dollars. *Tuition, nonresident:* full-time $5450; part-time $452 per course. *International tuition:* $9700 full-time. *Required fees:* full-time $147; $5 per course. *College room and board:* $4955; room only: $2475. Room and board charges vary according to board plan and housing facility. *Payment plan:* installment. *Waivers:* employees or children of employees.

Library Vaughan Memorial Library. *Operations spending 1999–2000:* $1.5 million. *Collection:* 810,393 titles, 2,233 serial subscriptions, 4,169 audiovisual materials.

College life *Housing: Options:* coed, men-only, women-only. *Most popular organizations:* Acadia Recreation Club, Acadia Ski Club, Education Society, computer science club, Caricom.

Campus security 24-hour emergency response devices and patrols, student patrols, late-night transport-escort service, controlled dormitory access.

After graduation *Career center:* 1 full-time, 5 part-time personnel. Services include job fairs, resume preparation, interview workshops, resume referral, career counseling, careers library, job bank, job interviews.

Canada

Freshmen 2,091 applied, 939 admitted, 737 enrolled.

SAT verbal scores above 500	N/R	SAT math scores above 500	N/R
ACT above 18	N/R	1998 freshmen returning in 1999	86%

Application *Options:* electronic application, deferred entrance. *Application fee:* $25. *Required:* high school transcript; minimum 2.5 GPA. *Required for some:* essay or personal statement; letters of recommendation; interview.

Standardized tests *Admission: Required:* SAT I. *Required for some:* SAT II Subject Tests.

Significant dates *Application deadlines:* 7/1 (freshmen), 5/31 (out-of-state freshmen), 7/1 (transfers).

Freshman Application Contact
Ms. Anne Scott, Manager of Admissions, Acadia University, Wolfville, NS B0P 1X0, Canada. **Phone:** 902-585-1222. **Fax:** 902-585-1081. **E-mail:** admissions@acadiau.ca

Visit CollegeQuest.com for information on majors offered and athletics. College video and electronic viewbook available at CollegeQuest.com.

■ *See page 1128 for a narrative description.*

ALBERTA COLLEGE OF ART AND DESIGN
Calgary, Alberta, Canada

- **Province-supported**, 4-year, founded 1926
- **Degree** bachelor's
- **Urban** 1-acre campus
- **Coed**, 785 undergraduate students
- **Moderately difficult** entrance level, 57% of applicants were admitted
- **$2759 tuition and fees (out-of-province)**

Students *Undergraduates:* Students come from 9 provinces and territories, 12 other countries.

Faculty 87 (40% full-time).

Expenses (1999–2000) Tuition and fee charges are reported in Canadian dollars. *Tuition, nonresident:* full-time $2472; part-time $988 per course. *International tuition:* $8700 full-time. *Required fees:* full-time $287. *Payment plan:* installment. *Waivers:* senior citizens and employees or children of employees.

Library Luke Lindo Library. *Collection:* 20,000 titles, 85 serial subscriptions.

College life *Housing:* college housing not available.

Campus security 24-hour emergency response devices and patrols, late-night transport-escort service.

After graduation *Career center:* 3 full-time personnel. Services include resume preparation, interview workshops, resume referral, career/interest testing, career counseling, careers library, job bank.

Freshmen 472 applied, 267 admitted.

SAT verbal scores above 500	N/R	SAT math scores above 500	N/R
ACT above 18	N/R	1998 freshmen returning in 1999	92%

Application *Options:* early admission, early decision, early action. *Application fee:* $25. *Required:* essay or personal statement; high school transcript; portfolio of artwork. *Recommended:* minimum 2.0 GPA.

Significant dates *Application deadlines:* 4/15 (freshmen), 4/15 (transfers). *Early decision:* 3/1, 3/1. *Notification:* 6/15 (freshmen), 4/1 (early decision), 4/30 (early action).

Freshman Application Contact
Mr. Kevin Bird, Admissions/Recruitment Officer, Alberta College of Art and Design, 1407 14 Avenue NW, Calgary, AB T2N 4R3, Canada. **Phone:** 403-284-7678. **Toll-free phone:** 800-251-8290. **E-mail:** admissions@acad.ab.ca

Visit CollegeQuest.com for information on majors offered and athletics.

ATHABASCA UNIVERSITY
Athabasca, Alberta, Canada

- **Province-supported**, comprehensive, founded 1970
- **Degrees** bachelor's and master's (offers only external degree programs)
- **Small-town** 480-acre campus
- **Coed**, 14,200 undergraduate students
- **Noncompetitive** entrance level
- **$3636 tuition** and fees (in-province); $4176 (out-of-province)
- **$1.1 million endowment**

Students *Undergraduates:* Students come from 12 provinces and territories, 30 other countries.

Age 25 or older	69%

Faculty 275.

Expenses (1999–2000) Tuition charges are reported in Canadian dollars. *Tuition, state resident:* full-time $3636; part-time $404 per course. *Tuition, nonresident:* full-time $4176; part-time $464 per course. *International tuition:* $5436 full-time. *Waivers:* senior citizens and employees or children of employees.

Library Athabasca University Library plus 1 other. *Collection:* 113,000 titles, 800 serial subscriptions.

College life *Housing:* college housing not available.

Campus security 24-hour emergency response devices.

Freshmen

SAT verbal scores above 500	N/R	SAT math scores above 500	N/R
ACT above 18	N/R		

Application *Application fee:* $50.

Significant dates *Application deadlines:* rolling (freshmen), rolling (transfers). *Financial aid deadline:* continuous.

Freshman Application Contact
Ms. Margaret Carmichael, Assistant Registrar, Admissions, Athabasca University, 1 University Drive, Athabasca, AB T9S 3A3, Canada. **Phone:** 780-675-6377. **Toll-free phone:** 800-788-9041. **Fax:** 780-675-6174. **E-mail:** auinfo@athabascau.ca

Visit CollegeQuest.com for information on majors offered and athletics.

ATLANTIC BAPTIST UNIVERSITY
Moncton, New Brunswick, Canada

- **Independent Baptist**, 4-year, founded 1949
- **Degree** bachelor's
- **Urban** campus
- **Coed**, 381 undergraduate students, 83% full-time, 61% women, 39% men
- **Minimally difficult** entrance level, 82% of applicants were admitted
- **$4605 tuition** and fees
- **$890,870 endowment**

Students *Undergraduates:* 316 full-time, 65 part-time. Students come from 6 provinces and territories, 2 other countries.

From out-of-province	30%	Reside on campus	34%
Age 25 or older	85%	Transferred in	5%

Faculty 24 (67% full-time).

Expenses (1999–2000) Tuition, fee, and room and board charges are reported in Canadian dollars. *Comprehensive fee:* $8645 includes full-time tuition ($4100), mandatory fees ($505), and room and board ($4040). *College room only:* $1750. Room and board charges vary according to board plan and student level. *Part-time tuition:* $450 per course. Part-time tuition and fees vary according to course load. *Payment plan:* installment. *Waivers:* senior citizens and employees or children of employees.

Library George A. Rawlyk Library. *Operations spending 1999–2000:* $146,571. *Collection:* 40,000 titles, 150 serial subscriptions.

College life *Housing: Options:* men-only, women-only.

Campus security 24-hour emergency response devices.

After graduation *Career center:* 1 full-time, 1 part-time personnel. Services include career counseling, careers library. *Graduate education:* 33% of class of 1999 went directly to graduate and professional school: 25% graduate arts and sciences, 4% education, 4% theology.

Freshmen 176 applied, 145 admitted, 110 enrolled.

SAT verbal scores above 500	N/R	SAT math scores above 500	N/R
ACT above 18	N/R	1998 freshmen returning in 1999	60%

Application *Options:* Common Application, deferred entrance. *Required:* essay or personal statement; high school transcript; 3 letters of recommendation. *Required for some:* interview.

Significant dates *Application deadlines:* rolling (freshmen), rolling (transfers). *Financial aid deadline priority date:* 8/1.

Canada

Atlantic Baptist University (continued)
Freshman Application Contact
Ms. Shawna Peverill, Admissions Officer, Atlantic Baptist University, Box 6004, Moncton, NB E1C 9L7, Canada. **Phone:** 506-858-8970 Ext. 106. **Toll-free phone:** 888-YOU-N-ABU. **Fax:** 506-858-9694. **E-mail:** admissions@abu.nb.ca
Visit CollegeQuest.com for information on majors offered and athletics. College video available at CollegeQuest.com.

AUGUSTANA UNIVERSITY COLLEGE
Camrose, Alberta, Canada

Admissions Office Contact
Augustana University College, 4901 46th Avenue, Camrose, AB T4V 2R3, Canada. **Fax:** 780-679-1129.

BETHANY BIBLE COLLEGE
Sussex, New Brunswick, Canada

- **Independent**, 4-year, founded 1945, affiliated with Wesleyan Church
- **Degree** bachelor's
- **Small-town** 55-acre campus
- **Coed**, 200 undergraduate students, 97% full-time, 43% women, 57% men
- **Moderately difficult** entrance level, 67% of applicants were admitted
- **34% graduate** in 6 years or less
- **$94,150 endowment**

Students *Undergraduates:* 194 full-time, 6 part-time. Students come from 5 provinces and territories.

| From out-of-province | 21% | Reside on campus | 77% |
| Age 25 or older | 14% | Transferred in | 4% |

Faculty 21 (48% full-time).
Library Rogers Memorial Library. *Operations spending 1999–2000:* $53,538. *Collection:* 27,319 titles, 124 serial subscriptions, 347 audiovisual materials.
College life On-campus residence required through senior year. *Most popular organizations:* Ministerial Association, Athletic Association, Student Mission Fellowship, Social Committee, Drama Club.
Campus security Controlled dormitory access.
Freshmen 136 applied, 91 admitted, 65 enrolled.

| SAT verbal scores above 500 | N/R | SAT math scores above 500 | N/R |
| ACT above 18 | N/R | 1998 freshmen returning in 1999 | 80% |

Application *Options:* eApply at www.CollegeQuest.com, Common Application, electronic application. *Application fee:* $20. *Required:* high school transcript; 2 letters of recommendation. *Recommended:* interview.
Standardized tests *Admission: Required for some:* SAT I or ACT.
Significant dates *Application deadlines:* rolling (freshmen), rolling (transfers). *Financial aid deadline:* 10/15.
Freshman Application Contact
Rev. Jon Steppe, Director of Admissions and Marketing, Bethany Bible College, 26 Western Street, Sussex, NB E4E 1E6, Canada. **Phone:** 506-432-4402. **Toll-free phone:** 888-432-4422. **Fax:** 506-432-4425. **E-mail:** steppej@bethany-ca.edu
Visit CollegeQuest.com for information on majors offered and athletics. College video available at CollegeQuest.com.

BETHANY BIBLE INSTITUTE
Hepburn, Saskatchewan, Canada

Admissions Office Contact
Bethany Bible Institute, Box 160, Hepburn, SK S0K 1Z0, Canada. **Fax:** 306-947-4229.

BISHOP'S UNIVERSITY
Lennoxville, Quebec, Canada

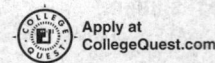

- **Province-supported**, comprehensive, founded 1843
- **Degrees** bachelor's and master's
- **Small-town** 500-acre campus
- **Coed**, 1,981 undergraduate students, 96% full-time, 54% women, 46% men
- **Moderately difficult** entrance level, 83% of applicants were admitted
- **18:1** student-to-undergraduate faculty ratio
- **$4,131 tuition and fees** (out-of-province)
- **$13 million endowment**

Students *Undergraduates:* Students come from 10 provinces and territories, 32 other countries. *The most frequently chosen baccalaureate fields are:* business/marketing, psychology, social sciences and history.

| From out-of-province | 47% | Reside on campus | 27% |
| Age 25 or older | 10% | | |

Faculty 74 (92% full-time), 100% with terminal degrees.
Expenses (1999–2000) Tuition, fee, and room and board charges are reported in Canadian dollars. *Tuition, nonresident:* full-time $3438; part-time $115 per credit. *International tuition:* $9168 full-time. *Required fees:* full-time $692. Full-time tuition and fees vary according to program. Part-time tuition and fees vary according to program. *College room and board:* $5500. Room and board charges vary according to board plan, housing facility, and location. *Payment plan:* installment. *Waivers:* senior citizens and employees or children of employees.
Library John Bassett Memorial Library plus 1 other. *Operations spending 1999–2000:* $1.7 million. *Collection:* 443,345 titles, 1,742 serial subscriptions, 15,356 audiovisual materials.
College life *Housing: Options:* coed, women-only. *Social organizations:* national fraternities, national sororities; 3% of eligible men and 3% of eligible women are members. *Most popular organizations:* Big Buddies, The Campus, psychology club, student patrol, Intervarsity Christian Fellowship.
Campus security 24-hour emergency response devices and patrols, student patrols, late-night transport-escort service, controlled dormitory access.
After graduation 60 organizations recruited on campus 1997–98. *Career center:* 1 full-time personnel. Services include job fairs, resume preparation, interview workshops, resume referral, career/interest testing, career counseling, careers library, job bank, job interviews.
Freshmen 1,776 applied, 1,472 admitted.

| SAT verbal scores above 500 | 74% | SAT math scores above 500 | 77% |
| ACT above 18 | N/R | 1998 freshmen returning in 1999 | 89% |

Application *Option:* eApply at www.CollegeQuest.com. *Application fee:* $55. *Required:* high school transcript; minimum 3.0 GPA; birth certificate, copy of student visa. *Required for some:* 1 letter of recommendation.
Standardized tests *Admission: Recommended:* SAT II Subject Tests. *Required for some:* SAT I or ACT.
Significant dates *Application deadlines:* 3/1 (freshmen), 3/1 (transfers). *Notification:* continuous until 8/31 (freshmen).
Freshman Application Contact
Mr. David McBride, Director of Enrollment Management, Bishop's University, Lennoxville, PQ J1M 1Z7, Canada. **Phone:** 819-822-9600 Ext. 2217. **Toll-free phone:** 800-567-2792 Ext. 2681. **Fax:** 819-822-9661. **E-mail:** liaison@ubishops.ca
Visit CollegeQuest.com for information on majors offered and athletics. Electronic viewbook available at CollegeQuest.com.

- *See page 1280 for a narrative description.*

BRANDON UNIVERSITY
Brandon, Manitoba, Canada

- **Province-supported**, comprehensive, founded 1899
- **Degrees** bachelor's and master's
- **Small-town** 30-acre campus
- **Coed**, 2,566 undergraduate students, 66% full-time, 66% women, 34% men
- **Noncompetitive** entrance level, 80% of applicants were admitted
- **10:1** student-to-undergraduate faculty ratio
- **$3218 tuition and fees** (out-of-province)
- **$22.4 million endowment**

Students *Undergraduates:* Students come from 32 other countries. *Graduate:* 100 in graduate degree programs.

Canada

From out-of-province	29%	Reside on campus	16%
Age 25 or older	34%		

Faculty 144 full-time.

Expenses (1999–2000) Tuition and room and board charges are reported in Canadian dollars. *Tuition, nonresident:* full-time $3218. *International tuition:* $5493 full-time. Full-time tuition and fees vary according to class time, location, program, and reciprocity agreements. Part-time tuition and fees vary according to class time, location, program, and reciprocity agreements. *College room and board:* $4853. Room and board charges vary according to board plan and housing facility. *Waivers:* senior citizens.

Library John E. Robbins Library. *Collection:* 236,937 titles, 866 serial subscriptions, 12,233 audiovisual materials.

College life *Housing: Options:* coed, men-only, women-only. *Most popular organizations:* psychology club, zoology club, Intervarsity Christian Fellowship, international students club, business administration club.

Campus security 24-hour emergency response devices, late-night transport-escort service, controlled dormitory access, night residence hall security personnel.

After graduation *Career center:* 1 full-time personnel. Services include job fairs, resume preparation, resume referral, career counseling, careers library, job bank, job interviews. *Graduate education:* 44% of class of 1999 went directly to graduate and professional school.

Freshmen 1,606 applied, 1,292 admitted.

Average high school GPA	3.0	SAT verbal scores above 500	N/R
SAT math scores above 500	N/R	ACT above 18	N/R
1998 freshmen returning in 1999	47%		

Application *Options:* Common Application, deferred entrance. *Application fee:* $35. *Required:* high school transcript. *Required for some:* letters of recommendation.

Significant dates *Application deadlines:* rolling (freshmen), rolling (transfers). *Notification:* continuous until 9/30 (freshmen). *Financial aid deadline priority date:* 6/30.

Freshman Application Contact
Ms. Faye Douglas, Director of Admissions, Brandon University, 270 18th Street, Brandon, MB R7A 6A9, Canada. **Phone:** 204-727-7352. **Toll-free phone:** 800-852-2704. **E-mail:** douglas@brandonu.ca

Visit CollegeQuest.com for information on majors offered and athletics. College video available at CollegeQuest.com.

BRIERCREST BIBLE COLLEGE
Caronport, Saskatchewan, Canada

- **Independent interdenominational**, 4-year, founded 1935
- **Degrees** associate and bachelor's
- **Rural** 300-acre campus
- **Coed**, 677 undergraduate students
- **Noncompetitive** entrance level
- **24:1 student-to-undergraduate faculty ratio**
- **$4808 tuition** and fees
- **$667,580 endowment**

Part of Briercrest Family of Schools.

Students *Undergraduates:* Students come from 9 provinces and territories, 7 other countries. *The most frequently chosen baccalaureate fields are:* business/marketing, parks and recreation, philosophy.

From out-of-province	70%	Reside on campus	75%
Age 25 or older	14%		

Faculty 38 (45% full-time).

Expenses (1999–2000) Tuition and room and board charges are reported in Canadian dollars. *Comprehensive fee:* $8148 includes full-time tuition ($4808) and room and board ($3340). *College room only:* $1670. Room and board charges vary according to housing facility. *Part-time tuition:* $150 per credit. *Payment plan:* installment. *Waivers:* senior citizens and employees or children of employees.

Library Archibald Library. *Operations spending 1999–2000:* $270,768. *Collection:* 56,764 titles, 396 serial subscriptions, 1,791 audiovisual materials.

College life *Housing:* on-campus residence required through senior year. *Options:* men-only, women-only. *Most popular organizations:* Student Missions Fellowship, Titus II, Student Families Association, Yearbook Committee, Weekend Activities Committee.

Campus security 24-hour patrols.

After graduation 120 organizations recruited on campus 1997–98. 48% of class of 1998 had job offers within 6 months. *Career center:* 2 full-time personnel. Services include resume preparation, interview workshops, resume referral, career/interest testing, career counseling, careers library.

Freshmen 338 admitted.

Average high school GPA	2.88	SAT verbal scores above 500	N/R
SAT math scores above 500	N/R	ACT above 18	N/R
1998 freshmen returning in 1999	55%		

Application *Options:* Common Application, electronic application, early admission, deferred entrance. *Preference* given to applicants interested in religious studies or ministries. *Application fee:* $25. *Required:* essay or personal statement; high school transcript; 2 letters of recommendation. *Required for some:* interview.

Significant dates *Application deadlines:* 8/15 (freshmen), 8/15 (transfers). *Notification:* continuous until 9/1 (freshmen). *Financial aid deadline priority date:* 1/5.

Freshman Application Contact
Mr. Michael Penner, Director of Enrollment Management, Briercrest Bible College, 510 College Drive, Caronport, SK S0H 0S0, Canada. **Phone:** 306-756-3200 Ext. 309. **Toll-free phone:** 800-667-5199. **E-mail:** enrollment@briercrest.ca

Visit CollegeQuest.com for information on majors offered and athletics. College video and electronic viewbook available at CollegeQuest.com.

BROCK UNIVERSITY
St. Catharines, Ontario, Canada

- **Province-supported**, comprehensive, founded 1964
- **Degrees** bachelor's, master's, and doctoral
- **Urban** 540-acre campus with easy access to Toronto
- **Coed**, 10,346 undergraduate students
- **Moderately difficult** entrance level
- **$4073 tuition** and fees (in-province); $4073 (out-of-province)

Students *Undergraduates:* Students come from 10 provinces and territories, 18 other countries.

Reside on campus	16%

Faculty 335 full-time.

Expenses (1999–2000) Tuition and room and board charges are reported in Canadian dollars. *Tuition, area resident:* full-time $4073; part-time $815 per credit. *Tuition, state resident:* full-time $4073; part-time $815 per credit. *Tuition, nonresident:* full-time $4073; part-time $815 per credit. *International tuition:* $9525 full-time. Full-time tuition and fees vary according to course load. Part-time tuition and fees vary according to course load. *College room and board:* $5120; room only: $2445. Room and board charges vary according to board plan and housing facility. *Payment plan:* installment. *Waivers:* senior citizens and employees or children of employees.

Library Brock University Library plus 1 other. *Collection:* 2,900 serial subscriptions.

College life *Housing: Option:* coed. *Most popular organizations:* International Students Association, Brock University Student Association, Business Administration Association.

Campus security 24-hour emergency response devices and patrols, student patrols, late-night transport-escort service, controlled dormitory access.

After graduation *Career center:* 2 full-time, 9 part-time personnel. Services include job fairs, resume preparation, career counseling, careers library, job bank, job interviews.

Freshmen

Average high school GPA	3.0	SAT verbal scores above 500	N/R
SAT math scores above 500	N/R	ACT above 18	N/R

Application *Options:* Common Application, electronic application. *Application fee:* $90. *Required:* high school transcript; minimum 3.0 GPA. *Required for some:* essay or personal statement; interview; audition; portfolio.

Standardized tests *Admission: Recommended:* SAT I and SAT II or ACT.

Significant dates *Application deadlines:* 6/1 (freshmen), 6/1 (transfers).

Canada

Brock University (continued)
Freshman Application Contact
Mrs. Barbara Anderson, Associate Registrar/Admissions, Brock University, 500 Glenridge Avenue, St. Catharines, St. Catharines, ON L2T 3A1, Canada. **Phone:** 905-688-5550 Ext. 3566. **Fax:** 905-988-5488. **E-mail:** barb@spartan.ac.brocku.ca
Visit CollegeQuest.com for information on majors offered and athletics. College video available at CollegeQuest.com.

■ *See page 1316 for a narrative description.*

CANADIAN BIBLE COLLEGE
Regina, Saskatchewan, Canada

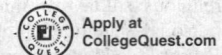
Apply at CollegeQuest.com

- **Independent**, 4-year, founded 1941, affiliated with The Christian and Missionary Alliance
- **Degree** bachelor's
- **Urban** 16-acre campus
- **Coed**, 294 undergraduate students, 77% full-time, 47% women, 53% men
- **Noncompetitive** entrance level, 98% of applicants were admitted
- **17:1 student-to-undergraduate faculty ratio**
- **40% graduate** in 6 years or less
- **$5006 tuition** and fees
- **$349,450 endowment**

Canadian Bible College is the only denominational college of the Christian and Missionary Alliance in Canada. It trains students for Christian ministry professions and provides foundational studies in Christian life and thought for students entering other professions. Distinctive features are its 1-year foundational program, vocational and personal counselling services, practical internship program, spiritual formation activities, overseas study opportunities, personal atmosphere, and emphasis on developing the whole person.

Students *Undergraduates:* 225 full-time, 69 part-time. Students come from 9 provinces and territories, 7 other countries. *The most frequently chosen baccalaureate field is:* philosophy.

From out-of-province	67%	Reside on campus	65%
Age 25 or older	16%	Transferred in	11%

Faculty 28 (61% full-time), 50% with terminal degrees.
Expenses (1999–2000) Tuition, fee, and room and board charges are reported in Canadian dollars. *Comprehensive fee:* $8776 includes full-time tuition ($4410), mandatory fees ($596), and room and board ($3770). Full-time tuition and fees vary according to course load. Room and board charges vary according to board plan. *Part-time tuition:* $147 per credit. *Part-time fees:* $18 per credit; $28 per term part-time. Part-time tuition and fees vary according to course load. *Payment plans:* installment, deferred payment. *Waivers:* employees or children of employees.
Library Archibald Foundation Library. *Operations spending 1999–2000:* $124,277. *Collection:* 65,000 titles, 546 serial subscriptions.
College life *Housing:* on-campus residence required through sophomore year. *Options:* men-only, women-only. *Most popular organizations:* International Students Fellowship, Missions Group.
Campus security 24-hour emergency response devices, student patrols, controlled dormitory access.
After graduation 20 organizations recruited on campus 1997–98. 80% of class of 1998 had job offers within 6 months. *Career center:* 1 full-time, 1 part-time personnel. Services include resume preparation, resume referral, career/interest testing, career counseling, careers library, job bank, job interviews.
Freshmen 61 applied, 60 admitted, 52 enrolled.

SAT verbal scores above 500	N/R	SAT math scores above 500	N/R
ACT above 18	N/R	1998 freshmen returning in 1999	64%

Application *Options:* eApply at www.CollegeQuest.com, Common Application, electronic application, early admission, deferred entrance. *Application fee:* $30. *Required:* essay or personal statement; high school transcript; 2 letters of recommendation. *Required for some:* interview. *Recommended:* medical history.

Significant dates *Application deadlines:* rolling (freshmen), rolling (transfers). *Notification:* continuous until 9/1 (freshmen). **Financial aid deadline priority date:** 7/31.
Freshman Application Contact
Tamela Friesen, Admissions Officer, Canadian Bible College, , 440 Fourth Avenue, Regina, SK S4T 0H8, Canada. **Phone:** 306-545-1515 Ext. 305. **Toll-free phone:** 800-461-1222. **Fax:** 306-545-0210. **E-mail:** enrollment@cbccts.sk.ca
Visit CollegeQuest.com for information on majors offered and athletics. College video and electronic viewbook available at CollegeQuest.com.

CARLETON UNIVERSITY
Ottawa, Ontario, Canada

- **Province-supported**, university, founded 1942
- **Degrees** bachelor's, master's, and doctoral
- **Urban** 152-acre campus
- **Coed**, 12,876 undergraduate students, 86% full-time, 47% women, 53% men
- **Moderately difficult** entrance level, 82% of applicants were admitted
- **26:1 student-to-undergraduate faculty ratio**
- **$4290 tuition and fees** (out-of-province)
- **$23.8 million endowment**

Students *Undergraduates:* 11,118 full-time, 1,758 part-time. Students come from 13 provinces and territories, 115 other countries. *The most frequently chosen baccalaureate fields are:* psychology, (pre)law, social sciences and history. *Graduate:* 2,411 in graduate degree programs.

From out-of-province	11%	Reside on campus	10%
Age 25 or older	22%	Transferred in	4%

Faculty 604 (98% full-time), 82% with terminal degrees.
Expenses (1999–2000) Tuition, fee, and room and board charges are reported in Canadian dollars. *Tuition, nonresident:* full-time $3780; part-time $750 per credit. *International tuition:* $8500 full-time. *Required fees:* full-time $510; $76 per credit. Full-time tuition and fees vary according to program. Part-time tuition and fees vary according to program. *College room and board:* $5261. Room and board charges vary according to board plan. *Payment plans:* installment, deferred payment. *Waivers:* senior citizens and employees or children of employees.
Library MacOdrum Library. *Operations spending 1999–2000:* $4.9 million. *Collection:* 10,174 serial subscriptions, 19,994 audiovisual materials.
College life *Housing:* Option: coed.
Campus security 24-hour emergency response devices and patrols, student patrols, late-night transport-escort service, controlled dormitory access.
After graduation *Career center:* 6 full-time personnel. Services include job fairs, resume preparation, interview workshops, resume referral, career/interest testing, career counseling, careers library, job bank, job interviews.
Freshmen 11,794 applied, 9,679 admitted, 3,158 enrolled.

SAT verbal scores above 500	N/R	SAT math scores above 500	N/R
ACT above 18	N/R	1998 freshmen returning in 1999	83%

Application *Options:* Common Application, deferred entrance. *Application fee:* $85. *Required:* high school transcript; minimum 2.0 GPA. *Required for some:* minimum 3.0 GPA; letters of recommendation; interview.
Standardized tests *Admission: Required for some:* SAT I and SAT II or ACT.
Significant dates *Application deadlines:* 6/1 (freshmen), 4/1 (out-of-state freshmen), 6/1 (transfers). *Notification:* continuous until continuous (out-of-state freshmen).
Freshman Application Contact
Mr. Jean Mullan, Manager, Undergraduate Recruitment Office, Carleton University, 1125 Colonel By Drive, Ottawa, ON K1S 5B6, Canada. **Phone:** 613-520-3663. **Toll-free phone:** 888-354-4414. **Fax:** 613-520-7455. **E-mail:** liaison@admissions.carleton.ca
Visit CollegeQuest.com for information on majors offered and athletics. College video and electronic viewbook available at CollegeQuest.com.

■ *See page 1362 for a narrative description.*

CATHERINE BOOTH BIBLE COLLEGE
Manitoba, Canada—See William and Catherine Booth College

CENTRAL PENTECOSTAL COLLEGE
Saskatoon, Saskatchewan, Canada

- **Independent**, 4-year, founded 1930, affiliated with Pentecostal Assemblies of Canada
- **Degree** bachelor's
- **Urban** 5-acre campus
- **Coed**, 62 undergraduate students, 100% full-time, 32% women, 68% men
- **Minimally difficult** entrance level, 89% of applicants were admitted
- **$4146 tuition** and fees

Students *Undergraduates:* 62 full-time. Students come from 5 provinces and territories, 2 other countries.

| Reside on campus | 50% | Age 25 or older | 7% |
| Transferred in | 6% | | |

Expenses (2000–2001) Tuition, fee, and room and board charges are reported in Canadian dollars. *Comprehensive fee:* $7196 includes full-time tuition ($3776), mandatory fees ($370), and room and board ($3050). *Part-time tuition:* $118 per credit hour. *Part-time fees:* $12 per credit hour. *Payment plans:* installment, deferred payment. *Waivers:* children of alumni, senior citizens, and employees or children of employees.

Library A. C. Schindel Library. *Collection:* 20,000 titles, 130 serial subscriptions.

College life On-campus residence required through sophomore year.

Campus security Late-night transport-escort service.

Freshmen 27 applied, 24 admitted, 20 enrolled.

| SAT verbal scores above 500 | N/R | SAT math scores above 500 | N/R |
| ACT above 18 | | 1998 freshmen returning in 1999 | 58% |

Application *Options:* Common Application, deferred entrance. *Application fee:* $35. *Required:* essay or personal statement; high school transcript; 3 letters of recommendation.

Significant dates *Application deadline:* 8/15 (freshmen).

Freshman Application Contact
Mrs. Betty Krohn, Assistant Registrar, Central Pentecostal College, 1303 Jackson Avenue, Saskatoon, SK S7H 2M9, Canada. **Phone:** 306-374-6655. **Fax:** 306-373-6968. **E-mail:** rkadyschuk@sk.sympatico.ca

Visit CollegeQuest.com for information on majors offered and athletics.

COLLÈGE DOMINICAIN DE PHILOSOPHIE ET DE THÉOLOGIE
Ottawa, Ontario, Canada

- **Independent Roman Catholic**, comprehensive, founded 1909
- **Degrees** bachelor's, master's, and doctoral
- **Urban** campus
- **Coed**, 178 undergraduate students, 38% full-time, 53% women, 47% men
- **Noncompetitive** entrance level, 100% of applicants were admitted
- **$2455 tuition** and fees

Students *Undergraduates:* 68 full-time, 110 part-time. Students come from 8 provinces and territories, 8 other countries. *The most frequently chosen baccalaureate field is:* philosophy. *Graduate:* 46 in graduate degree programs.

| Age 25 or older | 82% |

Faculty 63 (38% full-time), 35% with terminal degrees.

Expenses (1999–2000) Tuition and fee charges are reported in Canadian dollars. *Tuition:* full-time $2400; part-time $80 per credit. *International tuition:* $8800 full-time. *Required fees:* full-time $55. Part-time tuition and fees vary according to course load. *Payment plan:* installment. *Waivers:* senior citizens.

Library Bibliothéque du College Dominicain. *Collection:* 85,000 titles, 500 serial subscriptions.

College life *Most popular organization:* Association Etudiant College Dominicain.

Campus security Late-night transport-escort service.

Freshmen 24 applied, 24 admitted, 49 enrolled.

SAT verbal scores above 500	N/R	SAT math scores above 500	N/R
ACT above 18	N/R	From top half of their h.s. class	100%
1998 freshmen returning in 1999	65%		

Application *Option:* Common Application. *Application fee:* $20. *Required:* high school transcript. *Recommended:* interview.

Significant dates *Application deadlines:* 7/15 (freshmen), rolling (transfers).

Freshman Application Contact
Fr. Jacques Lison OP, Registrar, Collège Dominicain de Philosophie et de Théologie, 96, Avenue Empress, Ottawa, ON K1R 7G3, Canada. **Phone:** 613-233-5696.

Visit CollegeQuest.com for information on majors offered and athletics.

COLLEGE OF EMMANUEL AND ST. CHAD
Saskatoon, Saskatchewan, Canada

Admissions Office Contact
College of Emmanuel and St. Chad, 1337 College Drive, Saskatoon, SK S7N 0W6, Canada.

COLLÉGE UNIVERSITAIRE DE SAINT-BONIFACE
Saint-Boniface, Manitoba, Canada

Admissions Office Contact
Collége universitaire de Saint-Boniface, 200 avenue de la Cathèdrale, Saint-Boniface, MB R2H 0H7, Canada. **Fax:** 204-237-3240.

COLUMBIA BIBLE COLLEGE
Abbotsford, British Columbia, Canada

Admissions Office Contact
Columbia Bible College, 2940 Clearbrook Road, Abbotsford, BC V2T 2Z8, Canada. **Toll-free phone:** 800-283-0881. **Fax:** 604-853-3063. **E-mail:** admissions@columbiabc.edu

CONCORD COLLEGE
Winnipeg, Manitoba, Canada

- **Independent Mennonite Brethren**, 4-year, founded 1943
- **Degree** bachelor's
- **Urban** 2-acre campus
- **Coed**
- **Moderately difficult** entrance level

College life *Housing:* Option: coed. *Most popular organizations:* Oratorio Choir, Fellowship Groups, Christian Emphasis Committee, Peace and Social Concerns, Witness and Service Committee.

Campus security Student patrols, late-night transport-escort service, controlled dormitory access, combination door locks to sections of the campus.

Application *Options:* Common Application, deferred entrance. *Application fee:* $20. *Required:* high school transcript; minimum 2.0 GPA. *Required for some:* essay or personal statement.

Admissions Office Contact
Concord College, 169 Riverton Avenue, Winnipeg, MB R2L 2E5, Canada. **E-mail:** recruitment@concordcollege.mb.ca

Visit CollegeQuest.com for information on athletics.

Canada

CONCORDIA UNIVERSITY
Montréal, Quebec, Canada
Apply at CollegeQuest.com

- **Province-supported**, university, founded 1974
- **Degrees** bachelor's, master's, doctoral, and postbachelor's certificates
- **Urban** 110-acre campus
- **Coed**, 21,135 undergraduate students, 54% full-time, 51% women, 49% men
- **Moderately difficult** entrance level, 67% of applicants were admitted
- **16:1** student-to-undergraduate faculty ratio
- **$2430 tuition** and fees (in-province); $4200 (out-of-province)
- **$32.2 million endowment**

Students *Undergraduates:* 11,482 full-time, 9,653 part-time. Students come from 10 provinces and territories, 101 other countries. *Graduate:* 3,273 in graduate degree programs.

Reside on campus	1%	Age 25 or older	34%
Transferred in	3%		

Faculty 1,654 (42% full-time).

Expenses (2000–2001) Tuition, fee, and room only charges are reported in Canadian dollars. *Tuition, state resident:* full-time $1668; part-time $56 per credit. *Tuition, nonresident:* full-time $3438; part-time $115 per credit. *International tuition:* $9200 full-time. *Required fees:* full-time $762; $25 per credit. Full-time tuition and fees vary according to program. Part-time tuition and fees vary according to program. *College room and board:* room only: $2300. Room and board charges vary according to housing facility. *Payment plan:* installment. *Waivers:* senior citizens and employees or children of employees.

Library Webster Library plus 2 others. *Operations spending 1999–2000:* $10.3 million. *Collection:* 1.3 million titles, 5,894 serial subscriptions.

College life *Housing:* Option: coed. *Social organizations:* national fraternities, national sororities, local fraternities, local sororities. *Most popular organizations:* ethnic clubs, student media, departmental clubs.

Campus security 24-hour emergency response devices and patrols, student patrols, late-night transport-escort service, controlled dormitory access.

After graduation 428 organizations recruited on campus 1997–98. *Career center:* 4 full-time, 4 part-time personnel. Services include job fairs, resume preparation, resume referral, career counseling, careers library, job bank, job interviews.

Freshmen 12,581 applied, 8,468 admitted, 5,575 enrolled.

Average high school GPA	2.75	SAT verbal scores above 500	52%
SAT math scores above 500	79%	ACT above 18	N/R
1998 freshmen returning in 1999	78%		

Application *Options:* eApply at www.CollegeQuest.com, Common Application, electronic application, early action. *Preference* given to graduates of Collèges d'Enseignement Général et Professionnel (CEGEP). *Application fee:* $50. *Required:* high school transcript. *Required for some:* essay or personal statement; 3 letters of recommendation; interview; CEGEP transcript.

Standardized tests *Placement: Recommended:* SAT I and SAT II or ACT, SAT II: Writing Test.

Significant dates *Application deadlines:* 3/1 (freshmen), 3/1 (transfers). *Early action:* 2/1. *Notification:* continuous until 9/1 (freshmen), 4/15 (early action).

Freshman Application Contact
Assunta Fargnoli, Admissions Coordinator, Concordia University, Admissions Application Center, PO Box 2900, Montréal, PQ H3G 2S2, Canada. **Phone:** 514-848-2628. **Toll-free phone:** 514-848-2668. **E-mail:** admreg@alcor.concordia.ca

Visit CollegeQuest.com for information on majors offered and athletics. Electronic viewbook available at CollegeQuest.com.

▪ *See page 1526 for a narrative description.*

CONCORDIA UNIVERSITY COLLEGE OF ALBERTA
Edmonton, Alberta, Canada

- **Independent religious**, 4-year, founded 1921
- **Degree** bachelor's
- **Coed**, 1,220 undergraduate students
- **61%** of applicants were admitted
- **18:1** student-to-undergraduate faculty ratio
- **$4732 tuition** and fees
- **$525,000 endowment**

Students *Undergraduates:* Students come from 6 provinces and territories, 4 other countries. *The most frequently chosen baccalaureate fields are:* education, biological/life sciences, psychology.

Reside on campus	3%

Faculty 111 full-time.

Expenses (1999–2000) Tuition, fee, and room and board charges are reported in Canadian dollars. *Comprehensive fee:* $8932 includes full-time tuition ($4470), mandatory fees ($262), and room and board ($4200). Full-time tuition and fees vary according to class time, course load, and program. Room and board charges vary according to board plan. *Part-time tuition:* $186 per credit. *Part-time fees:* $80 per term part-time. Part-time tuition and fees vary according to class time, course load, and program. *Payment plan:* installment. *Waivers:* employees or children of employees.

Library *Operations spending 1999–2000:* $642,200.

College life *Housing:* Options: men-only, women-only. *Most popular organizations:* orchestra, community chorus, Toastmasters.

Campus security 24-hour patrols, late-night transport-escort service.

Freshmen 1,205 applied, 735 admitted.

SAT verbal scores above 500	N/R	SAT math scores above 500	N/R
ACT above 18	N/R		

Application *Application fee:* 0. *Required:* high school transcript; minimum 1.7 GPA. *Required for some:* essay or personal statement; 2 letters of recommendation; interview.

Significant dates *Application deadline:* 6/30 (freshmen). *Notification:* 9/1 (freshmen).

Freshman Application Contact
Mr. Tony Norrad, Dean of Admissions and Financial Aid, Concordia University College of Alberta, 7128 Ada Boulevard, Edmonton, AB T5B 4E4, Canada. **Phone:** 780-479-9224. **Fax:** 403-474-1933. **E-mail:** admits@concordia.ab.ca

Visit CollegeQuest.com for information on majors offered and athletics.

DALHOUSIE UNIVERSITY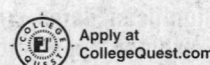
Halifax, Nova Scotia, Canada
Apply at CollegeQuest.com

- **Province-supported**, university, founded 1818
- **Degrees** bachelor's, master's, doctoral, and first professional
- **Urban** 80-acre campus
- **Coed**, 10,869 undergraduate students
- **Moderately difficult** entrance level, 67% of applicants were admitted
- **12:1** student-to-undergraduate faculty ratio
- **$4454 tuition** and fees (out-of-province)
- **$230.3 million endowment**

Serving Canada and the international community, Dalhousie University has a worldwide reputation and offers undergraduate, graduate, and professional programs. With an enrollment of 13,000, the University offers a unique combination of personal attention with a variety of programs at the undergraduate and graduate levels. For further information about programs in the arts, social sciences, science, engineering, architecture, computer science, health professions, law, medicine, and dentistry, students should contact the Registrar's Office, Dalhousie University, Halifax, NS Canada B3H 4H6 (e-mail: admissions@dal.ca; Web site: http://www.dal.ca).

Students *Undergraduates:* Students come from 12 provinces and territories, 98 other countries.

Reside on campus	14%	Age 25 or older	40%

Expenses (2000–2001, estimated) Tuition and room and board charges are reported in Canadian dollars. *Tuition, nonresident:* full-time $4454. *International tuition:* $7544 full-time. Full-time tuition and fees vary according to course load, degree level, and program. Part-time tuition and fees vary according to course load, degree level, and program. *College room and board:* $5220. Room and board charges vary according to board plan and housing facility. *Payment plan:* installment. *Waivers:* senior citizens and employees or children of employees.

Library The Killam Memorial Library plus 4 others. *Operations spending 1999–2000:* $7.6 million. *Collection:* 1.7 million titles, 8,306 serial subscriptions, 6,001 audiovisual materials.

College life *Housing: Options:* coed, men-only, women-only, disabled students. *Social organizations:* national fraternities, national sororities, local fraternities, local sororities. *Most popular organizations:* International Students Association, Arts Society, Science Society, Commerce Society, Dalhousie outdoors club.

Campus security 24-hour emergency response devices and patrols, student patrols, late-night transport-escort service.

After graduation *Career center:* 1 full-time, 2 part-time personnel. Services include job fairs, resume preparation, career/interest testing, career counseling, careers library, job bank.

Freshmen 8,382 applied, 5,575 admitted.

SAT verbal scores above 500	82%	SAT math scores above 500	88%
ACT above 18	N/R	1998 freshmen returning in 1999	74%

Application *Options:* eApply at www.CollegeQuest.com, electronic application, deferred entrance. *Application fee:* $35. *Required:* high school transcript; minimum 3.0 GPA. *Required for some:* essay or personal statement; 1 letter of recommendation; interview; minimum 1100 comprehensive score on SAT I for U.S. applicants.

Standardized tests *Admission: Required:* SAT I.

Significant dates *Application deadlines:* 6/1 (freshmen), 6/1 (transfers). *Financial aid deadline:* continuous.

Freshman Application Contact
Ms. Susan Tanner, Associate Registrar/Admissions and Awards, Dalhousie University, Halifax, NS B3H 4H6, Canada. **Phone:** 902-494-2148. **Fax:** 902-494-1630. **E-mail:** admissions@dal.ca

Visit CollegeQuest.com for information on majors offered and athletics. Electronic viewbook available at CollegeQuest.com.

■ *See page 1552 for a narrative description.*

EASTERN PENTECOSTAL BIBLE COLLEGE
Peterborough, Ontario, Canada

- **Independent Pentecostal**, 4-year, founded 1939
- **Degree** bachelor's
- **Small-town** 7-acre campus with easy access to Toronto
- **Coed**, 463 undergraduate students
- **Noncompetitive** entrance level, 97% of applicants were admitted
- **20:1 student-to-undergraduate faculty ratio**
- **$4831 tuition** and fees

Students *Undergraduates:* Students come from 7 provinces and territories, 7 other countries. *The most frequently chosen baccalaureate field is:* philosophy.

Faculty 34 (35% full-time), 18% with terminal degrees.

Expenses (1999–2000) Tuition, fee, and room and board charges are reported in Canadian dollars. *Comprehensive fee:* $8892 includes full-time tuition ($4440), mandatory fees ($391), and room and board ($4061). Full-time tuition and fees vary according to course load. *Part-time tuition:* $148 per credit hour. *Part-time fees:* $36 per course. Part-time tuition and fees vary according to course load. *Payment plan:* installment. *Waivers:* employees or children of employees.

Library *Collection:* 41,676 titles, 314 serial subscriptions, 2,428 audiovisual materials.

College life *Housing:* on-campus residence required through junior year. *Options:* men-only, women-only.

Campus security Student patrols.

Freshmen 183 applied, 178 admitted.

SAT verbal scores above 500	N/R	SAT math scores above 500	N/R
ACT above 18	N/R	1998 freshmen returning in 1999	77%

Application *Option:* deferred entrance. *Application fee:* $50. *Required:* essay or personal statement; high school transcript; 3 letters of recommendation; medical history, Christian commitment. *Required for some:* interview. *Recommended:* minimum 2.0 GPA.

Significant dates *Application deadlines:* 8/31 (freshmen), 8/31 (transfers).

Freshman Application Contact
Mrs. Joan Mann, Director of Enrollment Management, Eastern Pentecostal Bible College, 780 Argyle Street, Peterborough, ON K9H 5T2, Canada. **Phone:** 705-748-9111 Ext. 145. **Toll-free phone:** 800-295-6368. **E-mail:** jmann@epbc.edu

Visit CollegeQuest.com for information on majors offered and athletics.

ÉCOLE DES HAUTES ÉTUDES COMMERCIALES
Montréal, Quebec, Canada

- **Province-supported**, comprehensive, founded 1910
- **Degrees** bachelor's, master's, and doctoral
- **Urban** 9-acre campus
- **Coed**, 6,971 undergraduate students, 51% full-time, 50% women, 50% men
- **Moderately difficult** entrance level, 41% of applicants were admitted
- **77% graduate** in 6 years or less
- **$1989 tuition** and fees (in-province); $3759 (out-of-province)

Part of Université de Montréal.

Students *Undergraduates:* 3,563 full-time, 3,408 part-time. Students come from 4 provinces and territories, 69 other countries. *The most frequently chosen baccalaureate field is:* business/marketing. *Graduate:* 2,504 in graduate degree programs.

From out-of-province	0.5%	Age 25 or older	49%
Transferred in	3%		

Faculty 475 (36% full-time).

Expenses (1999–2000) Tuition and fee charges are reported in Canadian dollars. *Tuition, state resident:* full-time $1680; part-time $56 per credit. *Tuition, nonresident:* full-time $3450; part-time $115 per credit. *International tuition:* $9180 full-time. *Required fees:* full-time $309; $3 per credit; $42 per term part-time. Full-time tuition and fees vary according to program. Part-time tuition and fees vary according to program. *Payment plan:* installment. *Waivers:* employees or children of employees.

Library Myriam et J.-Robert Ouimet Library plus 1 other. *Collection:* 325,661 titles, 5,969 serial subscriptions.

College life *Housing:* college housing not available. *Social organizations:* Student Associations.

Campus security 24-hour emergency response devices and patrols.

After graduation 95% of class of 1998 had job offers within 6 months. *Career center:* 6 full-time personnel. Services include job fairs, resume preparation, resume referral, career counseling, careers library, job bank, job interviews. *Graduate education:* 14% of class of 1999 went directly to graduate and professional school: 14% business.

Freshmen 2,395 applied, 977 admitted, 921 enrolled.

SAT verbal scores above 500	N/R	SAT math scores above 500	N/R
ACT above 18	N/R	1998 freshmen returning in 1999	80%

Application *Option:* deferred entrance. *Application fee:* $40. *Required:* high school transcript. *Required for some:* cote de rendement collégial.

Significant dates *Application deadlines:* 3/1 (freshmen), 5/1 (out-of-state freshmen), 3/1 (transfers). *Notification:* 3/15 (freshmen), 6/1 (out-of-state freshmen).

Freshman Application Contact
Ms. Lyne Héroux, Administrative Director of Bachelor Program, École des Hautes Études Commerciales, 3000, chemin de la Côte-Sainte-Catherine, Montréal, QC H3T 2A7, Canada. **Phone:** 514-340-6139. **Fax:** 514-340-5640. **E-mail:** registraire.info@hec.ca

Visit CollegeQuest.com for information on majors offered and athletics.

EMMANUEL BIBLE COLLEGE
Kitchener, Ontario, Canada

Admissions Office Contact
Emmanuel Bible College, 100 Fergus Avenue, Kitchener, ON N2A 2H2, Canada. **Fax:** 519-894-9430.

Canada

HERITAGE BAPTIST COLLEGE AND HERITAGE THEOLOGICAL SEMINARY
Cambridge, Ontario, Canada

- **Independent Baptist**, comprehensive, founded 1993
- **Degrees** bachelor's and master's
- **Urban** 7-acre campus with easy access to Toronto
- **Coed**, 217 undergraduate students
- **Noncompetitive** entrance level, 80% of applicants were admitted
- **$5120 tuition** and fees

Students *Undergraduates:* Students come from 4 provinces and territories, 2 other countries. *The most frequently chosen baccalaureate field is:* philosophy.

Age 25 or older — 25%

Faculty 30 (37% full-time), 73% with terminal degrees.

Expenses (1999–2000) Tuition and room and board charges are reported in Canadian dollars. *Comprehensive fee:* $8120 includes full-time tuition ($5120) and room and board ($3000). *Part-time tuition:* $160 per credit hour. *Payment plan:* installment. *Waivers:* senior citizens and employees or children of employees.

Library Heritage Library. *Collection:* 40,430 titles, 173 serial subscriptions, 1,809 audiovisual materials.

College life *Housing: Options:* men-only, women-only.

Campus security Controlled dormitory access.

Freshmen 99 applied, 79 admitted.

| SAT verbal scores above 500 | N/R | SAT math scores above 500 | N/R |
| ACT above 18 | N/R | 1998 freshmen returning in 1999 | 76% |

Application *Option:* deferred entrance. *Application fee:* $30. *Required:* essay or personal statement; high school transcript; 3 letters of recommendation. *Required for some:* interview.

Standardized tests *Admission: Required for some:* SAT I, ACT.

Significant dates *Application deadlines:* rolling (freshmen), rolling (transfers).

Freshman Application Contact
Mr. Alan Wiseman, Registrar/Director of Admissions, Heritage Baptist College and Heritage Theological Seminary, 175 Holiday Inn Drive, Cambridge, ON N3C 3T2, Canada. **Phone:** 519-651-2869 Ext. 227. **E-mail:** admissions@heritage-theo.edu

Visit CollegeQuest.com for information on majors offered and athletics.

THE KING'S UNIVERSITY COLLEGE
Edmonton, Alberta, Canada

- **Independent interdenominational**, 4-year, founded 1979
- **Degree** bachelor's
- **Suburban** 20-acre campus
- **Coed**, 526 undergraduate students, 90% full-time, 61% women, 39% men
- **Moderately difficult** entrance level, 70% of applicants were admitted
- **37% graduate** in 6 years or less
- **$5665 tuition** and fees
- **$281,914 endowment**

Students *Undergraduates:* 472 full-time, 54 part-time. Students come from 6 provinces and territories, 6 other countries. *The most frequently chosen baccalaureate fields are:* education, natural resources/environmental science, social sciences and history.

| From out-of-province | 20% | Reside on campus | 17% |
| Age 25 or older | 18% | Transferred in | 19% |

Faculty 85 (33% full-time), 45% with terminal degrees.

Expenses (2000–2001, estimated) Tuition, fee, and room and board charges are reported in Canadian dollars. *Comprehensive fee:* $10,548 includes full-time tuition ($5425), mandatory fees ($240), and room and board ($4883). Full-time tuition and fees vary according to course load and program. Room and board charges vary according to board plan. *Part-time tuition:* $175 per credit. *Part-time fees:* $120 per term part-time. Part-time tuition and fees vary according to course load and program. *Payment plan:* installment. *Waivers:* employees or children of employees.

Library The King's University College Library. *Operations spending 1999–2000:* $243,169. *Collection:* 62,000 titles, 350 serial subscriptions, 3,250 audiovisual materials.

College life *Housing: Options:* coed, women-only. *Most popular organizations:* The Outdoors Club, The King's Players (drama club), chamber and concert choirs, men's and women's soccer clubs, The Political Studies Club.

Campus security 24-hour emergency response devices, student patrols, controlled dormitory access.

After graduation *Career center:* 1 full-time personnel. Services include career counseling, careers library.

Freshmen 394 applied, 275 admitted, 111 enrolled.

| SAT verbal scores above 500 | N/R | SAT math scores above 500 | N/R |
| ACT above 18 | N/R | 1998 freshmen returning in 1999 | 69% |

Application *Option:* electronic application. *Application fee:* $35. *Required:* high school transcript; 1 letter of recommendation. *Required for some:* essay or personal statement; interview.

Standardized tests *Admission: Recommended:* SAT I and SAT II or ACT.

Significant dates *Application deadlines:* rolling (freshmen), rolling (transfers). *Notification:* continuous until 8/15 (freshmen). *Financial aid deadline:* 3/31.

Freshman Application Contact
Mr. Glenn J. Keeler, Registrar/Director of Admissions, The King's University College, 9125-50 Street, Edmonton, AB T6B 2H3, Canada. **Phone:** 780-465-8330. **Toll-free phone:** 800-661-8582. **Fax:** 780-465-3534. **E-mail:** registrar@kingsu.ab.ca

Visit CollegeQuest.com for information on majors offered and athletics.

LAKEHEAD UNIVERSITY
Thunder Bay, Ontario, Canada

- **Province-supported**, comprehensive, founded 1965
- **Degrees** bachelor's, master's, and doctoral
- **Suburban** 345-acre campus
- **Coed**, 6,267 undergraduate students, 81% full-time, 54% women, 46% men
- **Moderately difficult** entrance level, 59% of applicants were admitted
- **$4232 tuition and fees (out-of-province)**
- **$6.6 million endowment**

Students *Undergraduates:* Students come from 10 provinces and territories, 34 other countries. *Graduate:* 318 in graduate degree programs.

| From out-of-province | 6% | Reside on campus | 22% |
| Age 25 or older | 30% | | |

Expenses (1999–2000) Tuition, fee, and room and board charges are reported in Canadian dollars. *Tuition, nonresident:* full-time $3800; part-time $760 per course. *International tuition:* $7900 full-time. *Required fees:* full-time $432; $62 per course. *College room and board:* $4917; room only: $2852. Room and board charges vary according to housing facility. *Payment plans:* installment, deferred payment. *Waivers:* senior citizens and employees or children of employees.

Library Chancellor Norman M. Paterson Library plus 1 other. *Operations spending 1999–2000:* $3 million. *Collection:* 704,637 titles, 2,460 serial subscriptions, 260 audiovisual materials.

College life *Housing: Options:* coed, women-only. *Most popular organizations:* Outdoor Recreation Students Association, Engineering Students Society, Business Association, ECHO/LUFROG, Educational Students Association.

Campus security 24-hour emergency response devices and patrols, student patrols, late-night transport-escort service, controlled dormitory access.

After graduation *Career center:* 3 full-time, 3 part-time personnel. Services include job fairs, resume preparation, interview workshops, resume referral, career counseling, careers library, job bank, job interviews.

Freshmen 6,052 applied, 3,570 admitted.

| Average high school GPA | 3.1 | SAT verbal scores above 500 | N/R |
| SAT math scores above 500 | N/R | ACT above 18 | N/R |

Application *Options:* Common Application, early admission, deferred entrance. *Application fee:* $85. *Required for some:* high school transcript; letters of recommendation.

Significant dates *Application deadlines:* rolling (freshmen), rolling (transfers). *Notification:* continuous until 9/23 (freshmen).
Freshman Application Contact
Ms. Sarena Knapik, Assistant Registrar, Lakehead University, 955 Oliver Road, Thunder Bay, ON P7B 5E1, Canada. **Phone:** 807-343-8500. **Toll-free phone:** 800-465-3959. **Fax:** 807-343-8156. **E-mail:** liaison@lakeheadu.ca
Visit CollegeQuest.com for information on majors offered and athletics. College video and electronic viewbook available at CollegeQuest.com.

■ *See page 1894 for a narrative description.*

LAURENTIAN UNIVERSITY
Sudbury, Ontario, Canada

Admissions Office Contact
Laurentian University, Ramsey Lake Road, Sudbury, ON P3E 2C6, Canada. **Fax:** 705-675-4891. **E-mail:** admissions@nickel.laurentian.ca

LAVAL UNIVERSITY
Quebec, Canada—See Université Laval

MCGILL UNIVERSITY
Montréal, Quebec, Canada

- **Independent**, university, founded 1821
- **Degrees** bachelor's, master's, doctoral, first professional, and postbachelor's certificates
- **Urban** 80-acre campus
- **Coed**, 20,510 undergraduate students, 72% full-time, 59% women, 41% men
- **Very difficult** entrance level, 60% of applicants were admitted
- **13:1 student-to-undergraduate faculty ratio**
- **$2527 tuition** and fees (in-province); $4027 (out-of-province)
- **$441.8 million endowment**

Students *Undergraduates:* Students come from 12 provinces and territories, 138 other countries. *Graduate:* 1,100 in professional programs, 6,637 in other graduate degree programs.

| From out-of-province | 26% | Reside on campus | 7% |
| Age 25 or older | 11% | | |

Faculty 2,238 (63% full-time).
Expenses (1999–2000) Tuition, fee, and room and board charges are reported in Canadian dollars. *Tuition, state resident:* full-time $1668; part-time $56 per credit. *Tuition, nonresident:* full-time $3168; part-time $106 per credit. *International tuition:* $8268 full-time. *Required fees:* full-time $859; $306 per term part-time. Full-time tuition and fees vary according to course load and program. Part-time tuition and fees vary according to course load and program. *College room and board:* $5404. Room and board charges vary according to board plan, gender, housing facility, and location. *Payment plan:* installment. *Waivers:* senior citizens and employees or children of employees.
Library Humanities and Social Sciences Library plus 16 others. *Operations spending 1999–2000:* $12.5 million. *Collection:* 3 million titles, 15,919 serial subscriptions, 553,469 audiovisual materials.
College life *Housing: Options:* coed, women-only, cooperative. *Social organizations:* national fraternities, national sororities, local fraternities; 4% of eligible men and 2% of eligible women are members. *Most popular organizations:* Debating Union, UNSAM (Model United Nations), Sexual Assault Centre, Walksafe, Queer McGill.
Campus security 24-hour emergency response devices and patrols, student patrols, late-night transport-escort service, controlled dormitory access.
After graduation 4,000 organizations recruited on campus 1997–98. *Career center:* 11 full-time, 7 part-time personnel. Services include job fairs, resume preparation, interview workshops, career/interest testing, career counseling, careers library, job bank, job interviews.

Freshmen 13,405 applied, 8,086 admitted.

SAT verbal scores above 500	N/R	SAT math scores above 500	N/R
ACT above 18	N/R	From top quarter of their h.s. class	90%
From top half	100%		

Application *Options:* electronic application, deferred entrance. *Application fee:* $60. *Required:* high school transcript; minimum 3.0 GPA. *Required for some:* letters of recommendation; audition for music program, portfolio for architecture program.
Standardized tests *Admission: Required:* SAT I and SAT II or ACT.
Significant dates *Application deadlines:* 1/15 (freshmen), 3/1 (transfers).
Freshman Application Contact
Ms. Robin Geller, Registrar and Director of Admissions, Recruitment and Registrar's Office, McGill University, 845 Sherbrooke Street West, Montreal, PQ H3A 2T5, Canada. **Phone:** 514-398-3910. **Fax:** 514-398-4193. **E-mail:** admissions@aro.lan.mcgill.ca
Visit CollegeQuest.com for information on majors offered and athletics. College video available at CollegeQuest.com.

■ *See page 2028 for a narrative description.*

MCMASTER UNIVERSITY
Hamilton, Ontario, Canada

- **Province-supported**, university, founded 1887
- **Degrees** bachelor's, master's, and doctoral
- **Suburban** 300-acre campus with easy access to Toronto
- **Coed**
- **Very difficult** entrance level

Institutional Web site http://www.mcmaster.ca/
College life *Housing: Options:* coed, men-only, women-only. *Most popular organizations:* Inter-Varsity Christian Fellowship Club, African-Caribbean Student Association, Chinese Students' Association, AIESEC (international leadership organization), South East Asian Society.
Campus security 24-hour emergency response devices and patrols, student patrols, late-night transport-escort service, controlled dormitory access.
Application *Option:* early action. *Application fee:* $90. *Required:* high school transcript. *Required for some:* essay or personal statement; interview.
Admissions Office Contact
McMaster University, 1280 Main Street West, Hamilton, ON L8S 4M2, Canada. **Fax:** 905-527-1105. **E-mail:** macadmit@mcmaster.ca
Visit CollegeQuest.com for information on athletics.

MEMORIAL UNIVERSITY OF NEWFOUNDLAND
St. John's, Newfoundland, Canada

- **Province-supported**, university, founded 1925
- **Degrees** bachelor's, master's, and doctoral
- **Urban** 220-acre campus
- **Coed**, 13,191 undergraduate students
- **Moderately difficult** entrance level, 76% of applicants were admitted
- **12:1 student-to-undergraduate faculty ratio**
- **$3360 tuition and fees (out-of-province)**

Students *Undergraduates:* Students come from 12 provinces and territories. *The most frequently chosen baccalaureate fields are:* education, business/marketing, social sciences and history.

| From out-of-province | 5% | Reside on campus | 10% |
| Age 25 or older | 20% | | |

Faculty 1,526 (61% full-time), 50% with terminal degrees.
Expenses (1999–2000) Tuition, fee, and room and board charges are reported in Canadian dollars. *Tuition, nonresident:* full-time $3300; part-time $110 per credit hour. *International tuition:* $6600 full-time. *Required fees:* full-time $60; $5 per term part-time. *College room and board:* $3826; room only: $1344. Room and board charges vary according to board plan, housing facility, and location. *Waivers:* employees or children of employees.

Canada

Memorial University of Newfoundland (continued)

Library Queen Elizabeth II Library plus 2 others. *Operations spending 1999–2000:* $7.1 million. *Collection:* 1.2 million titles, 17,000 serial subscriptions.

College life *Housing: Options:* coed, men-only, women-only, disabled students. *Most popular organizations:* International Student Center, Students Older Than Average, Memorial's Organization for the Disabled, Biology Society, Student Parents at MUN.

Campus security 24-hour emergency response devices and patrols, student patrols, late-night transport-escort service.

After graduation 15 organizations recruited on campus 1997–98. *Career center:* 3 full-time, 12 part-time personnel. Services include job fairs, resume preparation, resume referral, career counseling, careers library, job bank, job interviews. *Graduate education:* 24% of class of 1999 went directly to graduate and professional school.

Freshmen 2,981 applied, 2,269 admitted.

SAT verbal scores above 500	N/R	SAT math scores above 500	N/R
ACT above 18	N/R		

Application *Option:* electronic application. *Application fee:* $80. *Required:* high school transcript. *Required for some:* essay or personal statement; 2 letters of recommendation; interview; audition, portfolio.

Significant dates *Application deadlines:* rolling (freshmen), 3/1 (out-of-state freshmen), 3/1 (transfers). *Notification:* continuous until continuous (out-of-state freshmen).

Freshman Application Contact Ms. Phyllis McCann, Admissions Manager, Memorial University of Newfoundland, Elizabeth Avenue, St. John's, NF A1C 5S7, Canada. **Phone:** 709-737-3705. **E-mail:** sturecru@morgan.ucs.mun.ca

Visit CollegeQuest.com for information on majors offered and athletics. College video available at CollegeQuest.com.

■ *See page 2036 for a narrative description.*

MOUNT ALLISON UNIVERSITY
Sackville, New Brunswick, Canada

- **Province-supported**, comprehensive, founded 1839
- **Degrees** bachelor's and master's
- **Small-town** 50-acre campus
- **Coed**, 2,538 undergraduate students, 89% full-time, 60% women, 40% men
- **Moderately difficult** entrance level
- **18:1** student-to-undergraduate faculty ratio
- **$4400** tuition and fees (out-of-province)
- **$65 million** endowment

Students *Undergraduates:* Students come from 13 provinces and territories, 48 other countries. *The most frequently chosen baccalaureate fields are:* business/marketing, biological/life sciences, social sciences and history. *Graduate:* 7 in graduate degree programs.

From out-of-province	5%	Reside on campus	65%
Age 25 or older	4%		

Expenses (1999–2000) Tuition, fee, and room and board charges are reported in Canadian dollars. *Tuition, nonresident:* full-time $4220; part-time $844 per course. *International tuition:* $8440 full-time. *Required fees:* full-time $180. Full-time tuition and fees vary according to course load. Part-time tuition and fees vary according to course load. *College room and board:* $5675; room only: $3475. Room and board charges vary according to board plan and housing facility. *Payment plan:* installment. *Waivers:* senior citizens and employees or children of employees.

Library Ralph Pickard Bell Library plus 3 others. *Collection:* 400,000 titles, 1,700 serial subscriptions.

College life *Housing:* on-campus residence required through senior year. *Options:* coed, women-only. *Most popular organizations:* Commerce Society, Windsor Theatre, President's Leadership Development Certificate, Newfoundland Society, Garnet and Gold Society.

Campus security 24-hour emergency response devices, late-night transport-escort service.

After graduation *Career center:* 1 full-time personnel. Services include job fairs, resume preparation, career counseling, careers library, job bank, job interviews.

Freshmen 1,733 applied, 709 admitted.

Average high school GPA	3.7	SAT verbal scores above 500	N/R
SAT math scores above 500	N/R	ACT above 18	N/R
From top 10% of their h.s. class	25%	From top quarter	50%
From top half	95%	1998 freshmen returning in 1999	89%

Application *Option:* deferred entrance. *Application fee:* $40. *Required:* high school transcript; minimum 3.0 GPA. *Required for some:* essay or personal statement; interview. *Recommended:* 2 letters of recommendation.

Standardized tests *Admission: Required for some:* SAT I and SAT II or ACT, SAT II: Writing Test.

Significant dates *Application deadlines:* rolling (freshmen), rolling (transfers). *Financial aid deadline:* continuous.

Freshman Application Contact Ms. Kristine George, Admissions Counselor, Mount Allison University, Centennial Hall, 65 York Street, Sackville, NB E4L1E4, Canada. **Phone:** 506-364-2269. **Fax:** 506-364-2272. **E-mail:** swallace@mta.ca

Visit CollegeQuest.com for information on majors offered and athletics. Electronic viewbook available at CollegeQuest.com.

MOUNT SAINT VINCENT UNIVERSITY
Halifax, Nova Scotia, Canada

- **Province-supported**, comprehensive, founded 1873
- **Degrees** bachelor's, master's, first professional, and postbachelor's certificates
- **Suburban** 40-acre campus
- **Coed**, primarily women, 2,998 undergraduate students, 63% full-time, 84% women, 16% men
- **Moderately difficult** entrance level, 89% of applicants were admitted
- **12:1** student-to-undergraduate faculty ratio
- **$4041** tuition and fees (out-of-province)
- **$13.2 million** endowment

Students *Undergraduates:* Students come from 10 provinces and territories, 30 other countries. *Graduate:* 210 in professional programs, 520 in other graduate degree programs.

From out-of-province	13%	Reside on campus	6%
Age 25 or older	40%		

Faculty 363 (40% full-time), 32% with terminal degrees.

Expenses (1999–2000) Tuition, fee, and room and board charges are reported in Canadian dollars. *Tuition, nonresident:* full-time $3915; part-time $783 per unit. *International tuition:* $6615 full-time. *Required fees:* full-time $126; $25 per unit. Full-time tuition and fees vary according to course load, degree level, location, and program. Part-time tuition and fees vary according to course load, degree level, location, and program. *College room and board:* $5050; room only: $3160. Room and board charges vary according to board plan and housing facility. *Payment plan:* installment. *Waivers:* senior citizens and employees or children of employees.

Library E. Margaret Fulton Communications Centre Library plus 3 others. *Operations spending 1999–2000:* $1.2 million. *Collection:* 192,000 titles, 1,550 serial subscriptions, 1,285 audiovisual materials.

College life *Housing: Options:* men-only, women-only. *Most popular organizations:* Business Society, Information Technology Society, Athletic Recreation Society, International Students' Society, Student Alumni Association.

Campus security 24-hour emergency response devices and patrols, late-night transport-escort service, controlled dormitory access.

After graduation 592 organizations recruited on campus 1997–98. *Career center:* 1 full-time personnel. Services include job fairs, resume preparation, interview workshops, career/interest testing, career counseling, careers library, job bank, job interviews, internet workstations for job searches.

Freshmen 1,468 applied, 1,302 admitted.

SAT verbal scores above 500	N/R	SAT math scores above 500	N/R
ACT above 18	N/R	From top 10% of their h.s. class	25%
From top quarter	70%	From top half	100%

Application *Options:* Common Application, electronic application, deferred entrance. *Application fee:* $30. *Required:* high school transcript; minimum 2.0 GPA. *Required for some:* essay or personal statement; minimum 3.0 GPA; 2 letters of recommendation; interview.
Standardized tests *Admission: Required for some:* SAT I and SAT II or ACT.
Significant dates *Application deadlines:* 8/14 (freshmen), 5/30 (out-of-state freshmen), 8/14 (transfers). *Notification:* continuous until 9/1 (freshmen), 6/1 (out-of-state freshmen). *Financial aid deadline:* continuous.
Freshman Application Contact
Ms. Tara Wigglesunth-Hines, Assistant Registrar/Admissions, Mount Saint Vincent University, 166 Bedford Highway, Halifax, NS B3M 2J6, Canada. **Phone:** 902-457-6128. **Fax:** 902-457-6455. **E-mail:** admissions@msvu.ca
Visit CollegeQuest.com for information on majors offered and athletics. College video and electronic viewbook available at CollegeQuest.com.

■ *See page 2124 for a narrative description.*

NER ISRAEL YESHIVA COLLEGE OF TORONTO
Thornhill, Ontario, Canada

Admissions Office Contact
Ner Israel Yeshiva College of Toronto, 8950 Bathurst Street, Thornhill, ON L4J 8A7, Canada.

NIPISSING UNIVERSITY
North Bay, Ontario, Canada

- **Province-supported**, comprehensive, founded 1992
- **Degrees** bachelor's and master's
- **Suburban** 290-hectare campus
- **Coed**, 1,824 undergraduate students, 67% full-time, 67% women, 33% men
- **70% of applicants were admitted**
- **17:1 student-to-undergraduate faculty ratio**
- **61% graduate** in 6 years or less
- **$3981 tuition and fees (out-of-province)**
- **$3.5 million endowment**

Students *Undergraduates:* Students come from 9 provinces and territories, 15 other countries. *The most frequently chosen baccalaureate fields are:* education, liberal arts/general studies, trade and industry. *Graduate:* 1,597 in professional programs, 243 in other graduate degree programs.

| Reside on campus | 20% | Age 25 or older | 43% |

Faculty 119 (57% full-time), 47% with terminal degrees.
Expenses (1999–2000) Tuition, fee, and room only charges are reported in Canadian dollars. *Tuition, nonresident:* full-time $3510; part-time $702 per course. *International tuition:* $6500 full-time. *Required fees:* full-time $471; $60 per course. Full-time tuition and fees vary according to course load. Part-time tuition and fees vary according to course load and location. *College room and board:* room only: $3320. Room and board charges vary according to housing facility and location. *Payment plan:* installment. *Waivers:* employees or children of employees.
Library Education Centre Library. *Operations spending 1999–2000:* $1.1 million. *Collection:* 161,856 titles, 1,313 serial subscriptions, 99 audiovisual materials.
College life *Housing: Options:* coed, disabled students. *Most popular organizations:* BACCHUS, NUSAC (Nipissing University Student Athletic Counsel), Business Society, drama club, ski club.
Campus security 24-hour emergency response devices and patrols, student patrols, late-night transport-escort service, controlled dormitory access.
After graduation 25 organizations recruited on campus 1997–98. 40% of class of 1998 had job offers within 6 months. *Career center:* 1 full-time personnel. Services include job fairs, resume preparation, interview workshops, resume referral, career/interest testing, career counseling, careers library, job bank, job interviews. *Graduate education:* 40% of class of 1999 went directly to graduate and professional school: 36% education, 4% graduate arts and sciences.
Freshmen 1,800 applied, 1,265 admitted.

| SAT verbal scores above 500 | N/R | SAT math scores above 500 | N/R |
| ACT above 18 | N/R | 1998 freshmen returning in 1999 | 82% |

Application *Application fee:* $40. *Required:* high school transcript.
Significant dates *Application deadlines:* 8/30 (freshmen), 8/30 (transfers). *Notification:* continuous until 9/24 (freshmen).
Freshman Application Contact
Ms. Andrea Robinson, Associate Registrar, Nipissing University, Box 5002, Station Main, North Bay, ON P1B 8L7, Canada. **Phone:** 705-474-3461 Ext. 4516. **Fax:** 705-474-1947. **E-mail:** nipureg@unipissing.ca
Visit CollegeQuest.com for information on majors offered and athletics. College video available at CollegeQuest.com.

NORTH AMERICAN BAPTIST COLLEGE AND EDMONTON BAPTIST SEMINARY
Edmonton, Alberta, Canada

- **Independent North American Baptist**, comprehensive, founded 1940
- **Degrees** bachelor's and master's
- **Urban** 27-acre campus
- **Coed**, 241 undergraduate students
- **Minimally difficult** entrance level
- **$4890 tuition** and fees
- **$1.2 million endowment**

Students *Undergraduates:* Students come from 4 provinces and territories, 4 other countries.

| From out-of province | 28% | Reside on campus | 55% |

Faculty 44 (36% full-time).
Expenses (2000–2001) Tuition, fee, and room and board charges are reported in Canadian dollars. *Comprehensive fee:* $7890 includes full-time tuition ($4850), mandatory fees ($40), and room and board ($3000). Room and board charges vary according to board plan and housing facility. *Part-time tuition:* $199 per credit hour. *Part-time fees:* $10 per term part-time. *Waivers:* senior citizens and employees or children of employees.
Library Schalm Library. *Operations spending 1999–2000:* $92,400. *Collection:* 50,083 titles, 303 serial subscriptions.
College life *Housing:* on-campus residence required in freshman year. *Option:* coed. *Most popular organizations:* Choristers (choral group), Student Union, prayer groups, Sacrifice of Praise (band).
Campus security Evening and late night patrols by security.
After graduation *Career center:* 1 part-time personnel. Services include job fairs, resume preparation, career counseling, careers library, job bank. *Graduate education:* 10% of class of 1999 went directly to graduate and professional school: 10% theology.
Freshmen

| SAT verbal scores above 500 | N/R | SAT math scores above 500 | N/R |
| ACT above 18 | N/R | 1998 freshmen returning in 1999 | 88% |

Application *Options:* Common Application, deferred entrance. *Application fee:* $25. *Required:* essay or personal statement; high school transcript; 3 letters of recommendation. *Required for some:* minimum 3.0 GPA; interview.
Standardized tests *Admission: Recommended:* SAT I or ACT.
Significant dates *Application deadlines:* 8/1 (freshmen), 8/1 (transfers). *Notification:* continuous until 8/31 (freshmen). *Financial aid deadline:* 7/1.
Freshman Application Contact
Mr. Todd Liske, Admissions Counselor, North American Baptist College and Edmonton Baptist Seminary, 11525 Twenty-third Avenue, AB T6J 4T3, Canada. **Phone:** 780-431-5200 Ext. 215. **Toll-free phone:** 800-567-4988. **Fax:** 780-436-9416. **E-mail:** nabc@nabcebs.ab.ca
Visit CollegeQuest.com for information on majors offered and athletics. College video available at CollegeQuest.com.

Canada

NORTHWEST BIBLE COLLEGE
Edmonton, Alberta, Canada

- **Independent**, 4-year, founded 1946, affiliated with Pentecostal Assemblies of Canada
- **Degree** bachelor's
- **Coed**, 212 undergraduate students
- **99% of applicants were admitted**
- **12:1 student-to-undergraduate faculty ratio**
- **$4030 tuition** and fees

Students *Undergraduates:* Students come from 9 provinces and territories, 5 other countries. *The most frequently chosen baccalaureate field is:* philosophy.

From out-of-province — 24%

Faculty 27 (37% full-time), 96% with terminal degrees.
Expenses (1999–2000) *Tuition:* full-time 3680; part-time 115 per credit hour. *Required fees:* full-time 350. Full-time tuition and fees vary according to program.
College life *Housing:* college housing not available.
Freshmen 127 applied, 126 admitted.

SAT verbal scores above 500	N/R	SAT math scores above 500	N/R
ACT above 18	N/R	1998 freshmen returning in 1999	77%

Application *Application fee:* $50. *Required:* essay or personal statement; high school transcript; letters of recommendation.
Significant dates *Application deadline:* 8/20 (freshmen).
Freshman Application Contact
Registrar, Northwest Bible College, 11617-106 Avenue, Edmonton, AB T5H 0S1, Canada. **Phone:** 780-452-0808. **Fax:** 780-452-5803. **E-mail:** info@nwbc.ab.ca
Visit CollegeQuest.com for information on majors offered and athletics.

NOVA SCOTIA AGRICULTURAL COLLEGE
Truro, Nova Scotia, Canada

- **Province-supported**, comprehensive, founded 1905
- **Degrees** bachelor's and master's
- **Small-town** 408-acre campus with easy access to Halifax
- **Coed**, 545 undergraduate students, 93% full-time, 61% women, 39% men
- **Minimally difficult** entrance level, 63% of applicants were admitted
- **7:1 student-to-undergraduate faculty ratio**
- **$4118 tuition and fees (out-of-province)**

Students *Undergraduates:* 505 full-time, 40 part-time. Students come from 14 provinces and territories. *The most frequently chosen baccalaureate fields are:* agriculture, engineering/engineering technologies, natural resources/environmental science. *Graduate:* 51 in graduate degree programs.

From out-of-province	25%	Age 25 or older	16%
International students	1%	Black Canadians	0.4%
Asian Canadian	1%	Native Americans	0.4%

Faculty 79 (82% full-time), 62% with terminal degrees.
Expenses (2000–2001) Tuition, fee, and room and board charges are reported in Canadian dollars. *Tuition, nonresident:* full-time $4000. *International tuition:* $8000 full-time. *Required fees:* full-time $118. *College room and board:* $4476. Room and board charges vary according to board plan. *Payment plan:* installment.
Library MacRae Library. *Collection:* 23,000 titles, 800 serial subscriptions.
College life *Housing: Option:* coed.
Campus security 24-hour patrols, student patrols.
After graduation *Career center:* 2 full-time, 1 part-time personnel. Services include job fairs, resume referral, career counseling, careers library, job bank, job interviews. *Graduate education:* 20% of class of 1999 went directly to graduate and professional school: 12% graduate arts and sciences, 4% business, 2% education, 2% veterinary medicine.
Freshmen 563 applied, 352 admitted, 168 enrolled.

SAT verbal scores above 500	N/R	SAT math scores above 500	N/R
ACT above 18	N/R	1998 freshmen returning in 1999	85%

Application *Option:* Common Application. *Application fee:* $25. *Required:* high school transcript. *Required for some:* interview.
Standardized tests *Admission: Required:* SAT I and SAT II or ACT.
Significant dates *Application deadline:* 8/1 (freshmen).
Freshman Application Contact
Ms. Elizabeth Johnson, Admissions Officer, Nova Scotia Agricultural College, PO Box 550, Truro, NS B2N 5E3, Canada. **Phone:** 902-893-8212. **E-mail:** reg_info@nsac.ns.ca
Visit CollegeQuest.com for information on majors offered and athletics. Electronic viewbook available at CollegeQuest.com.

NOVA SCOTIA COLLEGE OF ART AND DESIGN
Halifax, Nova Scotia, Canada

- **Province-supported**, comprehensive, founded 1887
- **Degrees** bachelor's and master's
- **Urban** 1-acre campus
- **Coed**, 682 undergraduate students, 92% full-time, 66% women, 34% men
- **Very difficult** entrance level, 58% of applicants were admitted
- **$3986 tuition and fees (out-of-province)**
- **$867,300 endowment**

Students *Undergraduates:* 626 full-time, 56 part-time. Students come from 10 provinces and territories, 11 other countries. *The most frequently chosen baccalaureate field is:* visual/performing arts. *Graduate:* 32 in graduate degree programs.

Age 25 or older — 19%   Transferred in — 16%

Faculty 50 (72% full-time), 90% with terminal degrees.
Expenses (1999–2000) Tuition and fee charges are reported in Canadian dollars. *Tuition, nonresident:* full-time $3986; part-time $157 per credit. *International tuition:* $7390 full-time. *Required fees:* $17 per term part-time. Full-time tuition and fees vary according to course load. Part-time tuition and fees vary according to course load. *Payment plans:* installment, deferred payment. *Waivers:* senior citizens and employees or children of employees.
Library Nova Scotia College of Art and Design Library. *Operations spending 1999–2000:* $420,798. *Collection:* 32,000 titles, 235 serial subscriptions, 118,080 audiovisual materials.
College life *Housing:* college housing not available.
Campus security Evening patrols by trained security personnel.
After graduation *Career center:* Services include resume preparation, career counseling, careers library.
Freshmen 238 applied, 139 admitted, 95 enrolled.

SAT verbal scores above 500	N/R	SAT math scores above 500	N/R
ACT above 18	N/R		

Application *Option:* deferred entrance. *Application fee:* $25. *Required:* essay or personal statement; high school transcript; portfolio. *Required for some:* 2 letters of recommendation; interview.
Significant dates *Application deadlines:* 5/15 (freshmen), 5/1 (transfers). *Notification:* 6/15 (freshmen). *Financial aid deadline:* continuous.
Freshman Application Contact
Mr. Terry Bailey, Coordinator of Admissions, Off Campus and Recruitment, Nova Scotia College of Art and Design, 5163 Duke Street, Halifax, NS B3J 3J6, Canada. **Phone:** 902-494-8129. **Fax:** 902-425-2420. **E-mail:** tbailey@nscad.ns.ca
Visit CollegeQuest.com for information on majors offered and athletics.

- *See page 2202 for a narrative description.*

OKANAGAN UNIVERSITY COLLEGE
Kelowna, British Columbia, Canada

- **Province-supported**, 4-year
- **Degree** bachelor's
- **3,118 undergraduate students, 83% full-time, 65% women, 35% men**
- **88% of applicants were admitted**
- **15:1 student-to-undergraduate faculty ratio**
- **$895 tuition and fees (out-of-province)**

Students *Undergraduates:* 2,588 full-time, 530 part-time. Students come from 12 provinces and territories, 9 other countries. *The most frequently chosen baccalaureate fields are:* liberal arts/general studies, health professions and related sciences, physical sciences.

| From out-of-province | 6% | Age 25 or older | 28% |

Faculty 475.

Expenses (1999–2000) Tuition, fee, and room and board charges are reported in Canadian dollars. *Tuition, nonresident:* full-time $705; part-time $150 per course. *International tuition:* $3350 full-time. *Required fees:* full-time $190; $120 per term part-time. Full-time tuition and fees vary according to course load and location. Part-time tuition and fees vary according to course load and location. *College room and board:* $3880; room only: $2380. Room and board charges vary according to board plan, housing facility, and location. *Waivers:* senior citizens and employees or children of employees.

Library *Operations spending 1999–2000:* $1.1 million.

Campus security 24-hour emergency response devices and patrols, controlled dormitory access.

Freshmen 2,645 applied, 2,325 admitted, 689 enrolled.

| SAT verbal scores above 500 | N/R | SAT math scores above 500 | N/R |
| ACT above 18 | N/R | | |

Application *Application fee:* $20. *Required for some:* essay or personal statement; high school transcript; minimum 2.0 GPA; interview.

Significant dates *Application deadlines:* 3/30 (freshmen), 10/30 (transfers).

Freshman Application Contact
Ms. Deborah Matheson, Manager of Admissions, Okanagan University College, 1000 Klo Road, Kelowna, BC V14 4X8, Canada. **Phone:** 250-862-5417 Ext. 4213. **Fax:** 250-862-5470.

Visit CollegeQuest.com for information on majors offered and athletics.

ONTARIO BIBLE COLLEGE
Ontario, Canada—See Tyndale College & Seminary

OPEN LEARNING AGENCY
Burnaby, British Columbia, Canada

- $570,662 endowment

Students

| | Age 25 or older | 70% |

Expenses (1999–2000) Tuition charges are reported in Canadian dollars. *Tuition, nonresident:* part-time $51 per credit. Part-time tuition and fees vary according to course level, program, and reciprocity agreements. *Payment plan:* deferred payment. *Waivers:* senior citizens and employees or children of employees.

Library Open Learning Agency Library plus 1 other. *Operations spending 1999–2000:* $281,000. *Collection:* 5,000 titles, 200 serial subscriptions.

College life *Housing:* college housing not available.

Freshmen

| SAT verbal scores above 500 | N/R | SAT math scores above 500 | N/R |
| ACT above 18 | N/R | | |

Application *Options:* Common Application, deferred entrance. *Application fee:* $0.

Significant dates *Application deadlines:* rolling (freshmen), rolling (transfers). *Financial aid deadline:* continuous.

Freshman Application Contact
Ms. Norma Macovi, Director of Student Services/Registrar, Open Learning Agency, 4355 Mathissi Place, Burnaby, BC V5G 4S8, Canada. **Phone:** 604-431-3000 Ext. 3055. **Toll-free phone:** 800-663-9711. **Fax:** 604-431-3381. **E-mail:** student@ola.bc.ca

Visit CollegeQuest.com for information on majors offered and athletics.

PRAIRIE BIBLE COLLEGE
Three Hills, Alberta, Canada

- **Independent interdenominational**, 4-year, founded 1922
- **Degree** bachelor's
- **Small-town** 130-acre campus with easy access to Calgary
- **Coed**, 448 undergraduate students
- **Minimally difficult** entrance level, 89% of applicants were admitted

Students *Undergraduates:* Students come from 7 other countries.

| | Reside on campus | 78% |

Faculty 30 (67% full-time).

Library T. S. Rendall Library. *Operations spending 1999–2000:* $177,886. *Collection:* 60,745 titles, 458 serial subscriptions.

College life *Housing:* on-campus residence required in freshman year. *Options:* men-only, women-only. *Most popular organizations:* WIN, SMF, student government, Off-Campus.

Campus security 24-hour emergency response devices and patrols, late-night transport-escort service, controlled dormitory access.

After graduation 50 organizations recruited on campus 1997–98.

Freshmen 180 applied, 160 admitted.

| SAT verbal scores above 500 | N/R | SAT math scores above 500 | N/R |
| ACT above 18 | N/R | 1998 freshmen returning in 1999 | 43% |

Application *Options:* Common Application, electronic application, early decision. *Application fee:* $0. *Required:* essay or personal statement; high school transcript; 2 letters of recommendation. *Required for some:* minimum 3.0 GPA. *Recommended:* minimum 2.0 GPA.

Significant dates *Application deadlines:* 8/15 (freshmen), 8/15 (transfers). *Early decision:* 3/1.

Freshman Application Contact
Mr. Vance Neudorf, Director of Enrollment, Prairie Bible College, 319 Fifth Avenue North, PO Box 4000, Three Hills, AB T0M 2N0, Canada. **Phone:** 403-443-5511 Ext. 3421. **Toll-free phone:** 800-661-2425. **Fax:** 403-443-5540. **E-mail:** vance.neudorf@pbi.ab.ca

Visit CollegeQuest.com for information on majors offered and athletics. Electronic viewbook available at CollegeQuest.com.

PROVIDENCE COLLEGE AND THEOLOGICAL SEMINARY
Otterburne, Manitoba, Canada

- **Independent interdenominational**, comprehensive, founded 1925
- **Degrees** bachelor's, master's, and doctoral
- **Rural** 100-acre campus with easy access to Winnipeg
- **Coed**, 417 undergraduate students
- **Noncompetitive** entrance level, 88% of applicants were admitted
- **$4736 tuition** and fees
- **$687,655 endowment**

Students *Undergraduates:* Students come from 4 provinces and territories, 18 other countries.

| From out-of-province | 30% | Reside on campus | 60% |

Faculty 54 (37% full-time).

Expenses (2000–2001) Tuition, fee, and room and board charges are reported in Canadian dollars. *Comprehensive fee:* $8136 includes full-time tuition ($4400), mandatory fees ($336), and room and board ($3400). *Part-time tuition:* $155 per semester hour. *Part-time fees:* $12 per credit hour. *Payment plan:* installment. *Waivers:* children of alumni and employees or children of employees.

Library *Operations spending 1999–2000:* $233,204. *Collection:* 47,756 titles, 635 serial subscriptions.

College life *Housing:* on-campus residence required in freshman year. *Options:* men-only, women-only.

Campus security Student patrols, controlled dormitory access.

After graduation *Career center:* 1 part-time personnel. Services include resume preparation, career counseling, job bank. *Graduate education:* 28% of class of 1999 went directly to graduate and professional school.

Freshmen 230 applied, 202 admitted.

| SAT verbal scores above 500 | N/R | SAT math scores above 500 | N/R |
| ACT above 18 | N/R | 1998 freshmen returning in 1999 | 72% |

Application *Option:* deferred entrance. *Application fee:* $25. *Required:* high school transcript; 4 letters of recommendation.

Canada

Providence College and Theological Seminary (continued)
Standardized tests *Placement: Recommended:* SAT I or ACT.
Significant dates *Application deadlines:* rolling (freshmen), rolling (transfers).
Freshman Application Contact
Mr. Mark Little, Dean of Admissions and Records, Providence College and Theological Seminary, General Delivery, Otterburne, MB R0A 1G0, Canada. **Phone:** 204-433-7488 Ext. 249. **Toll-free phone:** 800-668-7768. **E-mail:** mlittle@providence.mb.ca
Visit CollegeQuest.com for information on majors offered and athletics. College video available at CollegeQuest.com.

QUEEN'S UNIVERSITY AT KINGSTON
Kingston, Ontario, Canada

- **Province-supported**, university, founded 1841
- **Degrees** bachelor's, master's, and doctoral
- **Urban** 160-acre campus
- **Coed**, 14,394 undergraduate students
- **Most difficult** entrance level, 63% of applicants were admitted
- **11:1 student-to-undergraduate faculty ratio**
- **$4539 tuition and fees (out-of-province)**

Students *Undergraduates:* Students come from 13 provinces and territories, 86 other countries.

From out-of province	11%	Reside on campus	25%
Age 25 or older	8%		

Faculty 965 (100% full-time).
Expenses (1999–2000) Tuition, fee, and room and board charges are reported in Canadian dollars. *Tuition, nonresident:* full-time $3874; part-time $775 per course. *International tuition:* $10,300 full-time. *Required fees:* full-time $665. Full-time tuition and fees vary according to program. Part-time tuition and fees vary according to course load and program. *College room and board:* $6234; room only: $3487. Room and board charges vary according to board plan and housing facility. *Waivers:* senior citizens and employees or children of employees.
Library Joseph S. Stauffer Library. *Operations spending 1999–2000:* $10.4 million. *Collection:* 3.2 million titles, 10,825 serial subscriptions.
College life *Housing: Options:* coed, men-only, women-only, cooperative. *Most popular organizations:* Arts and Sciences Undergraduate Society, Alma Mater Society, Engineering Society, Commerce Society.
Campus security 24-hour emergency response devices and patrols, student patrols, late-night transport-escort service, controlled dormitory access.
After graduation 325 organizations recruited on campus 1997–98. *Career center:* 6 full-time, 5 part-time personnel. Services include job fairs, resume preparation, interview workshops, career/interest testing, career counseling, careers library, job bank, job interviews.
Freshmen 19,012 applied, 11,977 admitted.

Average high school GPA	3.48	SAT verbal scores above 500	83%
SAT math scores above 500	85%	ACT above 18	N/R

Application *Options:* Common Application, deferred entrance. *Application fee:* $85. *Required:* high school transcript; minimum 2.0 GPA. *Required for some:* essay or personal statement; 1 letter of recommendation; interview.
Standardized tests *Admission: Required:* SAT I. *Required for some:* SAT II Subject Tests.
Significant dates *Application deadlines:* 3/31 (freshmen), 6/1 (transfers). *Notification:* 5/15 (freshmen). *Financial aid deadline:* continuous.
Freshman Application Contact
Mr. Nicholas Snider, Manager, Student Recruitment, Queen's University at Kingston, , 110 Alfred Street, Kingston, ON K7L 3N6, Canada. **Phone:** 613-533-2217. **Fax:** 613-533-6300. **E-mail:** admissn@post.queensu.ca
Visit CollegeQuest.com for information on majors offered and athletics. College video and electronic viewbook available at CollegeQuest.com.

■ *See page 2300 for a narrative description.*

REDEEMER COLLEGE
Ancaster, Ontario, Canada

- **Independent interdenominational**, 4-year, founded 1980
- **Degrees** bachelor's and postbachelor's certificates
- **Small-town** 78-acre campus with easy access to Toronto
- **Coed**, 580 undergraduate students, 95% full-time, 61% women, 39% men
- **Moderately difficult** entrance level, 80% of applicants were admitted
- **15:1 student-to-undergraduate faculty ratio**
- **53% graduate** in 6 years or less
- **$8963 tuition** and fees
- **$507,705 endowment**

Students *Undergraduates:* 550 full-time, 30 part-time. Students come from 8 provinces and territories, 17 other countries. *The most frequently chosen baccalaureate fields are:* education, English, social sciences and history.

Reside on campus	59%	Age 25 or older	4%
Transferred in	2%		

Faculty 59 (58% full-time), 58% with terminal degrees.
Expenses (1999–2000) Tuition, fee, and room and board charges are reported in Canadian dollars. *Comprehensive fee:* $13,323 includes full-time tuition ($8600), mandatory fees ($363), and room and board ($4360). Room and board charges vary according to student level. *Part-time tuition:* $875 per course. Part-time tuition and fees vary according to course load. *Payment plans:* installment, deferred payment. *Waivers:* senior citizens and employees or children of employees.
Library Redeemer College Library. *Operations spending 1999–2000:* $332,890. *Collection:* 93,500 titles, 419 serial subscriptions.
College life *Housing:* on-campus residence required through sophomore year. *Options:* men-only, women-only. *Most popular organizations:* Church in the Box, mission trips, Bible study groups, choir, intramurals.
Campus security 24-hour emergency response devices, student patrols, late-night transport-escort service.
After graduation 25 organizations recruited on campus 1997–98. 61% of class of 1998 had job offers within 6 months. *Career center:* 1 full-time personnel. Services include resume preparation, interview workshops, career/interest testing, career counseling, careers library, job bank. **Graduate education:** 19% of class of 1999 went directly to graduate and professional school: 11% education, 5% theology, 1% graduate arts and sciences, 1% medicine.
Freshmen 424 applied, 341 admitted, 207 enrolled.

Average high school GPA	3.3	SAT verbal scores above 500	N/R
SAT math scores above 500	N/R	ACT above 18	100%
1998 freshmen returning in 1999	82%		

Application *Option:* deferred entrance. *Preference* given to Christians. *Application fee:* $30. *Required:* high school transcript; 2 letters of recommendation; pastoral reference. *Required for some:* essay or personal statement; interview.
Standardized tests *Admission: Required for some:* SAT I or ACT.
Significant dates *Application deadlines:* 8/1 (freshmen), 8/1 (transfers).
Freshman Application Contact
Office of Admissions, Redeemer College, 777 Garner Road East, Ancaster, ON L9K 1J4, Canada. **Phone:** 905-648-2131 Ext. 4280. **Toll-free phone:** 800-263-6467 Ext. 4280. **Fax:** 905-648-2134. **E-mail:** adm@redeemer.on.ca
Visit CollegeQuest.com for information on majors offered and athletics.

ROCKY MOUNTAIN COLLEGE
Calgary, Alberta, Canada

- **Independent**, 4-year, founded 1992, affiliated with Missionary Church
- **Degree** bachelor's
- **Suburban** 1-acre campus
- **Coed**, 300 undergraduate students
- **Noncompetitive** entrance level, 96% of applicants were admitted
- **$4710 tuition** and fees
- **$238,300 endowment**

Students *Undergraduates:* Students come from 6 provinces and territories, 2 other countries. *The most frequently chosen baccalaureate field is:*

philosophy.

| Reside on campus | 20% | Age 25 or older | 32% |

Faculty 27 (44% full-time), 22% with terminal degrees.

Expenses (1999–2000) *Tuition:* full-time $4590; part-time $153 per semester hour. *Required fees:* full-time $120. *College room only:* $1600.

Library Main library plus 1 other. *Operations spending 1999–2000:* $51,890. *Collection:* 25,280 titles, 135 serial subscriptions.

College life *Housing: Option:* coed. *Social organizations:* missions fellowship; 40% of eligible men and 40% of eligible women are members.

Campus security 24-hour emergency response devices.

After graduation 20 organizations recruited on campus 1997–98. *Career center:* 2 part-time personnel. Services include career counseling, careers library.

Freshmen 169 applied, 163 admitted.

| SAT verbal scores above 500 | N/R | SAT math scores above 500 | N/R |
| ACT above 18 | N/R | 1998 freshmen returning in 1999 | 62% |

Application *Option:* deferred entrance. *Application fee:* $25. *Required:* essay or personal statement; high school transcript; 2 letters of recommendation. *Required for some:* interview.

Significant dates *Application deadlines:* rolling (freshmen), rolling (transfers). *Financial aid deadline:* continuous.

Freshman Application Contact
Mr. Randy Young, Rocky Mountain College, , 4039 Brentwood Drive NW, Calgary, AB T2L 1L1, Canada. **Phone:** 403-284-5100 Ext. 222. **E-mail:** rockymc@telusplanet.net

Visit CollegeQuest.com for information on majors offered and athletics.

ROYAL MILITARY COLLEGE OF CANADA
Kingston, Ontario, Canada

- **Federally supported**, comprehensive, founded 1876
- **Degrees** bachelor's, master's, and doctoral
- **Suburban** 90-acre campus
- **Coed**
- **Most difficult** entrance level

Institutional Web site http://www.rmc.ca/

College life *Housing:* on-campus residence required through senior year. *Option:* coed. *Most popular organization:* band.

Campus security 24-hour emergency response devices and patrols.

Application *Application fee:* $0. *Required:* high school transcript; letters of recommendation; interview; medical, aptitude and physical fitness testing for full-time students.

Admissions Office Contact
Royal Military College of Canada, PO Box 17000, Station Forces, Kingston, ON K7K 7B4, Canada. **Fax:** 613-542-3565. **E-mail:** registrar@rmc.ca

Visit CollegeQuest.com for information on athletics. College video and electronic viewbook available at CollegeQuest.com.

ROYAL ROADS UNIVERSITY
Victoria, British Columbia, Canada

- **Province-supported**, upper-level, founded 1996
- **Degrees** bachelor's and master's
- **Suburban** 125-acre campus
- **Coed**, 199 undergraduate students, 75% full-time, 43% women, 57% men
- **Moderately difficult** entrance level
- **$6160 tuition and fees (out-of-province)**
- **$746,000 endowment**

Students *Undergraduates:* 149 full-time, 50 part-time. Students come from 4 provinces and territories, 5 other countries. *The most frequently chosen baccalaureate fields are:* business/marketing, natural resources/environmental science. *Graduate:* 543 in graduate degree programs.

| From out-of-province | 17% | Reside on campus | 45% |
| Age 25 or older | 53% | Transferred in | 82% |

Faculty 20.

Canada

Expenses (2000–2001) Tuition, fee, and room and board charges are reported in Canadian dollars. *Tuition, nonresident:* full-time $5800; part-time $485 per course. *International tuition:* $11,600 full-time. *Required fees:* full-time $360; $30 per course. Full-time tuition and fees vary according to course load and program. Part-time tuition and fees vary according to course load and program. *College room and board:* $7000. Room and board charges vary according to board plan. *Payment plans:* guaranteed tuition, tuition prepayment, installment.

Library Learning Resource Centre plus 1 other. *Operations spending 1999–2000:* $1.3 million.

College life *Housing: Option:* coed. *Most popular organizations:* rowing, mountain biking, recycling club.

Campus security 24-hour emergency response devices and patrols, late-night transport-escort service, controlled dormitory access.

After graduation *Career center:* 1 part-time personnel. Services include resume preparation, interview workshops, career/interest testing, career counseling, careers library, job interviews.

Application *Option:* Common Application. *Application fee:* $50.

Significant dates *Application deadline:* rolling (transfers). *Notification:* 5/30 (transfers).

Freshman Application Contact
Ms. Ann Nightingale, Registrar and Director, Learner Services, Royal Roads University, Office of Learner Services and Registrar, 2005 Sooke Road, Victoria, BC V9B 5Y2, Canada. **Phone:** 250-391-2552. **Toll-free phone:** 800-788-8028. **Fax:** 250-391-2500. **E-mail:** rruregistrar@royalroads.ca

Visit CollegeQuest.com for information on majors offered and athletics.

RYERSON POLYTECHNIC UNIVERSITY
Toronto, Ontario, Canada

- **Province-supported**, 4-year, founded 1948
- **Degrees** bachelor's and master's
- **Urban** 20-acre campus
- **Coed**, 14,296 undergraduate students, 72% full-time, 54% women, 46% men
- **Moderately difficult** entrance level
- **$4324 tuition and fees (out-of-province)**

Students *Undergraduates:* 10,266 full-time, 4,030 part-time. Students come from 68 other countries.

| Reside on campus | 6% |

Faculty 814 (67% full-time).

Expenses (1999–2000) Tuition and fee charges are reported in Canadian dollars. *Tuition, nonresident:* full-time $3941. *International tuition:* $11,250 full-time. *Required fees:* full-time $383. Full-time tuition and fees vary according to course load and program. Part-time tuition and fees vary according to course load and program. Room and board charges vary according to board plan and housing facility. Full-time mandatory fees: $119 for Canadian residents, $546 for nonresidents. *Payment plans:* installment, deferred payment. *Waivers:* senior citizens and employees or children of employees.

Library Ryerson Library plus 1 other. *Collection:* 403,897 titles, 2,914 serial subscriptions, 10,402 audiovisual materials.

College life *Housing: Option:* coed.

Campus security 24-hour emergency response devices and patrols, late-night transport-escort service, controlled dormitory access.

After graduation *Career center:* 4 full-time, 2 part-time personnel. Services include job fairs, resume preparation, career counseling, careers library, job bank, job interviews.

Freshmen 3,369 enrolled.

| SAT verbal scores above 500 | N/R | SAT math scores above 500 | N/R |
| ACT above 18 | N/R | | |

Application *Option:* electronic application. *Application fee:* $85. *Required:* high school transcript. *Required for some:* essay or personal statement; letters of recommendation; interview; portfolio, audition, entrance examination.

Significant dates *Application deadlines:* 3/1 (freshmen), 3/1 (transfers). *Financial aid deadline:* 1/15.

Canada

Ryerson Polytechnic University (continued)
Freshman Application Contact
Office of Admissions, Ryerson Polytechnic University, 350 Victoria Street, Toronto, ON M5B 2K3, Canada. **Phone:** 416-979-5036. **E-mail:** inquire@acs.ryerson.ca
Visit CollegeQuest.com for information on majors offered and athletics.

ST. FRANCIS XAVIER UNIVERSITY
Antigonish, Nova Scotia, Canada

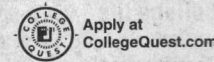
Apply at CollegeQuest.com

- **Independent Roman Catholic**, comprehensive, founded 1853
- **Degrees** bachelor's and master's
- **Small-town** 100-acre campus
- **Coed**, 3,801 undergraduate students, 86% full-time, 58% women, 42% men
- **Moderately difficult** entrance level, 66% of applicants were admitted
- **17:1** student-to-undergraduate faculty ratio
- **68% graduate** in 6 years or less
- **$4283 tuition** and fees
- **$20.3 million endowment**

Students *Undergraduates:* Students come from 12 provinces and territories, 18 other countries. *The most frequently chosen baccalaureate fields are:* biological/life sciences, business/marketing, education. *Graduate:* 206 in professional programs, 184 in other graduate degree programs.

From out-of-province	30%	Reside on campus	43%
Age 25 or older	7%		

Faculty 229 (86% full-time), 74% with terminal degrees.
Expenses (1999–2000) Tuition, fee, and room and board charges are reported in Canadian dollars. *Comprehensive fee:* $9388 includes full-time tuition ($4160), mandatory fees ($123), and room and board ($5105). Full-time tuition and fees vary according to course load. Room and board charges vary according to board plan and housing facility. *Part-time tuition:* $890 per course. *Part-time fees:* $13 per course. Part-time tuition and fees vary according to course load. *International tuition:* $7160 full-time. *Payment plan:* installment. *Waivers:* senior citizens and employees or children of employees.
Library Angus L. MacDonald Library plus 1 other. *Operations spending 1999–2000:* $1.4 million. *Collection:* 623,348 titles, 2,308 serial subscriptions, 5,356 audiovisual materials.
College life *Housing: Options:* coed, men-only, women-only, disabled students. *Most popular organizations:* X-Project, Walkhome Program, orientation committee, Exekoi Tutoring, Off-Campus Society.
Campus security 24-hour emergency response devices and patrols, student patrols, late-night transport-escort service, controlled dormitory access.
After graduation 27 organizations recruited on campus 1997–98. *Career center:* 1 full-time, 1 part-time personnel. Services include resume preparation, interview workshops, career counseling, job bank, job interviews.
Freshmen 1,935 applied, 1,274 admitted.

SAT verbal scores above 500	N/R	SAT math scores above 500	N/R
ACT above 18	N/R	1998 freshmen returning in 1999	88%

Application *Options:* eApply at www.CollegeQuest.com, Common Application. *Application fee:* $30. *Required:* high school transcript.
Standardized tests *Admission: Recommended:* SAT I or ACT, SAT II Subject Tests, SAT II: Writing Test. *Required for some:* SAT I or ACT, SAT II: Writing Test.
Significant dates *Application deadlines:* rolling (freshmen), rolling (transfers). *Notification:* continuous until 8/15 (freshmen).
Freshman Application Contact
Ms. Rose Ann Septon, Admissions Officer, St. Francis Xavier University, Box 5000, Antigonish, NS B2G 2W5, Canada. **Phone:** 902-867-2219. **Fax:** 902-867-2329. **E-mail:** admit@stfx.ca
Visit CollegeQuest.com for information on majors offered and athletics. Electronic viewbook available at CollegeQuest.com.

■ *See page 2380 for a narrative description.*

SAINT MARY'S UNIVERSITY
Halifax, Nova Scotia, Canada

- **Province-supported**, comprehensive, founded 1802
- **Degrees** bachelor's and master's
- **Urban** 30-acre campus
- **Coed**, 6,101 undergraduate students, 80% full-time, 52% women, 48% men
- **Moderately difficult** entrance level
- **24:1** student-to-undergraduate faculty ratio
- **$4123 tuition** and fees (out-of-province)

Students *Undergraduates:* 4,880 full-time, 1,221 part-time. Students come from 56 other countries. *The most frequently chosen baccalaureate fields are:* business/marketing, psychology, social sciences and history. *Graduate:* 446 in graduate degree programs.

From out-of-province	11%	Reside on campus	15%

Faculty 443 (48% full-time), 57% with terminal degrees.
Expenses (1999–2000) Tuition, fee, and room and board charges are reported in Canadian dollars. *Tuition, nonresident:* full-time $4010; part-time $802 per course. *International tuition:* $7650 full-time. *Required fees:* full-time $113; $35 per term part-time. Full-time tuition and fees vary according to course level and course load. Part-time tuition and fees vary according to course level and course load. *College room and board:* $4530; room only: $2365. Room and board charges vary according to board plan and housing facility. *Payment plan:* installment. *Waivers:* senior citizens and employees or children of employees.
Library Patrick Power Library plus 1 other. *Operations spending 1999–2000:* $2 million. *Collection:* 385,310 titles, 1,973 serial subscriptions.
College life *Housing: Options:* coed, women-only. *Most popular organizations:* International Students Organization, commerce society, AIESEC, journal society, political science society.
Campus security 24-hour emergency response devices and patrols, student patrols, late-night transport-escort service, controlled dormitory access, electronic surveillance of labs and key areas.
After graduation *Career center:* 2 full-time personnel. Services include job fairs, resume preparation, interview workshops, resume referral, career/interest testing, career counseling, careers library, job bank, job interviews.
Freshmen 1,506 enrolled.

SAT verbal scores above 500	N/R	SAT math scores above 500	N/R
ACT above 18	N/R		

Application *Option:* early action. *Application fee:* $35. *Required:* high school transcript; minimum 2.0 GPA. *Required for some:* interview.
Significant dates *Application deadlines:* 7/1 (freshmen), 6/1 (transfers). *Early action:* 1/1. *Notification:* 4/1 (early action). *Financial aid deadline priority date:* 6/30.
Freshman Application Contact
Mr. Greg Ferguson, Director of Admissions, Saint Mary's University, Halifax, NS B3H 3C3, Canada. **Phone:** 902-420-5415. **Fax:** 902-496-8100. **E-mail:** jim.dunn@stmarys.edu
Visit CollegeQuest.com for information on majors offered and athletics. College video available at CollegeQuest.com.

■ *See page 2416 for a narrative description.*

SAINT PAUL UNIVERSITY
Ottawa, Ontario, Canada

- **Province-supported**, university, founded 1848
- **Degrees** bachelor's, master's, and doctoral
- **Urban** 4-acre campus
- **Coed**, 439 undergraduate students, 32% full-time, 62% women, 38% men
- **Moderately difficult** entrance level
- **$2800 tuition** and fees (out-of-province)

Students *Undergraduates:* Students come from 40 other countries. *The most frequently chosen baccalaureate fields are:* communications/communication technologies, philosophy. *Graduate:* 269 in graduate degree programs.
Faculty 151 (42% full-time).

Expenses (1999–2000) Tuition charges are reported in Canadian dollars. *Tuition, nonresident:* full-time $2800. *International tuition:* $7000 full-time.
Library Saint Paul University Library. *Collection:* 400,000 titles, 1,100 serial subscriptions.
College life *Housing: Option:* coed.
Freshmen

| SAT verbal scores above 500 | N/R | SAT math scores above 500 | N/R |
| ACT above 18 | N/R | | |

Application *Options:* Common Application, deferred entrance. *Application fee:* $20. *Required:* high school transcript.
Standardized tests *Admission: Recommended:* SAT I.
Significant dates *Application deadline:* 8/15 (freshmen). *Notification:* continuous until 9/4 (freshmen).
Freshman Application Contact
Ms. Evelyn G. Dutrisac, Registrar, Saint Paul University, 223 Main Street, Ottawa, ON K1S 1C4, Canada. **Phone:** 613-236-1393 Ext. 2238. **Fax:** 613-782-3033. **E-mail:** edutrisac@ustpaul.ca
Visit CollegeQuest.com for information on majors offered and athletics. College video available at CollegeQuest.com.

ST. THOMAS UNIVERSITY
Fredericton, New Brunswick, Canada

Admissions Office Contact
St. Thomas University, Fredericton, NB E3B 5G3, Canada. **Fax:** 506-450-9615. **E-mail:** admissions@stthomasu.ca

SIMON FRASER UNIVERSITY
Burnaby, British Columbia, Canada

- **Province-supported**, university, founded 1965
- **Degrees** bachelor's, master's, and doctoral
- **Suburban** 1,200-acre campus with easy access to Vancouver
- **Coed**, 15,315 undergraduate students, 52% full-time, 57% women, 43% men
- **Moderately difficult** entrance level, 47% of applicants were admitted
- **22:1 student-to-undergraduate faculty ratio**
- **55% graduate** in 6 years or less
- **$2517 tuition and fees (out-of-province)**
- **$54.6 million endowment**

Students *Undergraduates:* 8,015 full-time, 7,300 part-time. Students come from 11 provinces and territories, 63 other countries. *The most frequently chosen baccalaureate fields are:* business/marketing, liberal arts/general studies, social sciences and history. *Graduate:* 2,358 in graduate degree programs.

| From out-of province | 7% | Reside on campus | 8% |
| Age 25 or older | 25% | Transferred in | 5% |

Faculty 609, 90% with terminal degrees.
Expenses (1999–2000) Tuition, fee, and room only charges are reported in Canadian dollars. *Tuition, nonresident:* full-time $2310; part-time $77 per credit. *International tuition:* $6930 full-time. *Required fees:* full-time $207; $121 per term part-time. *College room and board:* room only: $3465. Room and board charges vary according to housing facility. *Waivers:* senior citizens and employees or children of employees.
Library W. A. C. Bennett Library. *Operations spending 1999–2000:* $8.2 million. *Collection:* 1.4 million titles, 8,335 serial subscriptions, 135,675 audiovisual materials.
College life *Housing: Options:* coed, women-only, disabled students. *Most popular organizations:* The Peak Newspaper, orientation leaders, crisis line, Women's Centre, Simon Fraser Public Interest Research Group.
Campus security 24-hour emergency response devices and patrols, student patrols, late-night transport-escort service, controlled dormitory access, safe-walk stations, 24-hour safe study area.
After graduation 400 organizations recruited on campus 1997–98. *Career center:* 2 full-time, 2 part-time personnel. Services include job fairs, resume preparation, interview workshops, resume referral, career/interest testing, career counseling, careers library, job bank, job interviews.
Freshmen 14,621 applied, 6,912 admitted, 2,076 enrolled.

Average high school GPA	3.42	SAT verbal scores above 500	N/R
SAT math scores above 500	N/R	ACT above 18	N/R
1998 freshmen returning in 1999	81%		

Application *Options:* electronic application, early admission, deferred entrance. *Application fee:* $25. *Required:* high school transcript; minimum 3.2 GPA. *Required for some:* essay or personal statement; interview.
Standardized tests *Admission: Required:* SAT I or ACT.
Significant dates *Application deadlines:* 4/30 (freshmen), rolling (transfers). *Financial aid deadline priority date:* 7/1.
Freshman Application Contact
Mr. Nick Heath, Director of Admissions, Simon Fraser University, 8888 University Drive, Burnaby, BC V5A 1S6, Canada. **Phone:** 604-291-3224. **Fax:** 604-291-4969. **E-mail:** undergraduate-admissions@sfu.ca/
Visit CollegeQuest.com for information on majors offered and athletics.

STEINBACH BIBLE COLLEGE
Steinbach, Manitoba, Canada

- **Independent Mennonite**, 4-year, founded 1936
- **Degree** bachelor's
- **Small-town** campus with easy access to Winnipeg
- **Coed**, 82 undergraduate students, 95% full-time, 51% women, 49% men
- **Minimally difficult** entrance level, 100% of applicants were admitted
- **$3442 tuition** and fees

Students *Undergraduates: The most frequently chosen baccalaureate field is:* philosophy.
Faculty 14 (7% full-time), 29% with terminal degrees.
Expenses (1999–2000) Tuition and room and board charges are reported in Canadian dollars. *Comprehensive fee:* $6662 includes full-time tuition ($3442) and room and board ($3220).
Freshmen 38 applied, 38 admitted.

| SAT verbal scores above 500 | N/R | SAT math scores above 500 | N/R |
| ACT above 18 | N/R | 1998 freshmen returning in 1999 | 75% |

Freshman Application Contact
Dr. Terry Hiebert, Registrar, Steinbach Bible College, PO Box 1420, Steinbach, MB R0A 2A0, Canada. **Phone:** 204-326-6451. **E-mail:** inof@sbcollege.mb.ca
Visit CollegeQuest.com for information on majors offered and athletics.

TECHNICAL UNIVERSITY OF BRITISH COLUMBIA
Surrey, British Columbia, Canada

- **Province-supported**, comprehensive
- **Degrees** bachelor's and master's
- **Coed**, primarily men, 89 undergraduate students, 100% full-time, 20% women, 80% men
- **24% of applicants were admitted**
- **8:1 student-to-undergraduate faculty ratio**
- **$2980 tuition and fees (out-of-province)**

Students *Undergraduates:* 89 full-time. *Graduate:* 3 in graduate degree programs.

| Age 25 or older | 12% |

Faculty 18 (100% full-time), 67% with terminal degrees.
Expenses (1999–2000) Tuition and fee charges are reported in Canadian dollars. *Tuition, nonresident:* full-time $2880. *International tuition:* $8560 full-time. *Required fees:* full-time $100. Full-time tuition and fees vary according to course load and degree level. *Waivers:* employees or children of employees.
College life *Housing:* college housing not available. *Most popular organizations:* Chinese Association, martial arts club, women in technology, activity group, film society.
Campus security 24-hour patrols.

Canada

Technical University of British Columbia (continued)
After graduation *Graduate education:* 99% of class of 1999 went directly to graduate and professional school.
Freshmen 400 applied, 96 admitted, 68 enrolled.
  SAT verbal scores above 500   N/R   SAT math scores above 500   N/R
  ACT above 18   N/R
Application *Option:* early decision. *Application fee:* $25. *Required:* essay or personal statement; high school transcript; minimum 2.5 GPA.
Significant dates *Application deadlines:* 4/15 (freshmen), 4/15 (transfers). *Early decision:* 2/15.
Freshman Application Contact
Ms. Kathleen Pettman, Coordinator, Registrar Services, Technical University of British Columbia, 1063 Surrey Place Mall, Surrey, BC V3T 2W1, Canada. **Phone:** 604-586-6004. **Toll-free phone:** 604-586-6000. **Fax:** 604-586-5237. **E-mail:** admissions@techbc.ca
Visit CollegeQuest.com for information on majors offered and athletics.

TECHNICAL UNIVERSITY OF NOVA SCOTIA
Nova Scotia, Canada—See Dalhousie University

TÉLÉ-UNIVERSITÉ
Sainte-Foy, Quebec, Canada

- **Province-supported**, comprehensive, founded 1972
- **Degrees** bachelor's and master's (offers only distance learning degree programs)
- **Coed**
- **Noncompetitive** entrance level

Part of Université du Québec.
Institutional Web site http://www.telug.uquebec.ca/
College life *Housing:* college housing not available.
Application *Option:* Common Application. *Application fee:* $30. *Required:* Diploma of Collegiate Studies (and transcript) or equivalent.
Admissions Office Contact
Télé-université, 2600, Blvd Laurier, PO Box 10700, Sainte-Foy, PQ G1V 4V9, Canada. **Fax:** 418-657-2094. **E-mail:** info@teluq.uquebec.ca
Visit CollegeQuest.com for information on athletics. Electronic viewbook available at CollegeQuest.com.

TRENT UNIVERSITY
Peterborough, Ontario, Canada

- **Province-supported**, comprehensive, founded 1963
- **Degrees** bachelor's, master's, and doctoral
- **Suburban** 1,400-acre campus with easy access to Toronto
- **Coed**
- **Moderately difficult** entrance level, 80% of applicants were admitted
- **22:1 student-to-undergraduate faculty ratio**
- **$3874 tuition and fees (out-of-province)**

Students *Undergraduates:* Students come from 13 provinces and territories, 62 other countries.
Expenses (1999–2000) Tuition and room and board charges are reported in Canadian dollars. *Tuition, nonresident:* full-time $3874; part-time $775 per course. *International tuition:* $10,439 full-time. Part-time tuition and fees vary according to course load. *College room and board:* $6200. Room and board charges vary according to board plan and housing facility. Mandatory fees per year for nonresidents: $570.43. *Payment plan:* installment. *Waivers:* senior citizens and employees or children of employees.
Library Thomas J. Bata Library plus 2 others. *Collection:* 579,557 titles, 2,312 serial subscriptions.

College life *Housing: Options:* coed, women-only. *Most popular organizations:* Trent Radio, Trent International Program, Trent Central Student Association, Arthur (student newspaper), Excalibur (yearbook).
Campus security 24-hour emergency response devices and patrols, student patrols, late-night transport-escort service.
After graduation 50% of class of 1998 had job offers within 6 months. *Career center:* 1 full-time, 3 part-time personnel. Services include resume preparation, resume referral, career counseling, careers library, job interviews.
Freshmen 4,212 applied, 3,362 admitted.
  Average high school GPA   3.04   SAT verbal scores above 500   N/R
  SAT math scores above 500   N/R   ACT above 18   N/R
  1998 freshmen returning in 1999   85%
Application *Option:* deferred entrance. *Application fee:* $95. *Required:* high school transcript; minimum 2.8 GPA. *Required for some:* essay or personal statement; letters of recommendation; interview.
Standardized tests *Admission: Required for some:* SAT I or ACT.
Significant dates *Application deadlines:* 6/1 (freshmen), 6/1 (transfers).
Freshman Application Contact
Mrs. Carol Murray, Admissions Officer, Trent University, Office of the Registrar, Peterborough, ON K9J 7B8, Canada. **Phone:** 705-748-1215. **Fax:** 705-748-1629. **E-mail:** leaders@trentu.ca
Visit CollegeQuest.com for information on majors offered and athletics.

■ *See page 2634 for a narrative description.*

TRINITY WESTERN UNIVERSITY
Langley, British Columbia, Canada

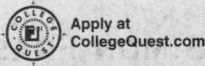

- **Independent**, comprehensive, founded 1962, affiliated with Evangelical Free Church of America
- **Degrees** bachelor's and master's
- **Suburban** 110-acre campus with easy access to Vancouver
- **Coed**, 2,379 undergraduate students
- **Moderately difficult** entrance level, 78% of applicants were admitted
- **18:1 student-to-undergraduate faculty ratio**
- **$10,460 tuition** and fees
- **$3 million endowment**

Students *Undergraduates:* Students come from 10 provinces and territories, 29 other countries. *The most frequently chosen baccalaureate fields are:* liberal arts/general studies, biological/life sciences, psychology.
  From out-of-province   33%   Reside on campus   40%
  Age 25 or older   15%
Faculty 138 (56% full-time), 61% with terminal degrees.
Expenses (2000–2001) Tuition, fee, and room and board charges are reported in Canadian dollars. *Comprehensive fee:* $16,450 includes full-time tuition ($10,350), mandatory fees ($110), and room and board ($5990). Full-time tuition and fees vary according to course load and program. Room and board charges vary according to board plan, housing facility, and student level. *Part-time tuition:* $345 per semester hour. *Part-time fees:* $30. Part-time tuition and fees vary according to course load and program. *Payment plan:* installment. *Waivers:* employees or children of employees.
Library Norma Marion Alloway Library. *Collection:* 115,626 titles, 2,316 serial subscriptions, 3,002 audiovisual materials.
College life *Housing:* on-campus residence required through sophomore year. *Options:* coed, men-only, women-only, disabled students. *Most popular organizations:* Campus Ministries, choir, student newspaper, discipleship program.
Campus security 24-hour emergency response devices and patrols, late-night transport-escort service, controlled dormitory access.
After graduation *Career center:* 4 full-time, 1 part-time personnel. Services include job fairs, resume preparation, resume referral, career counseling, careers library, job bank, job interviews. *Graduate education:* 15% of class of 1999 went directly to graduate and professional school.

Freshmen 1,371 applied, 1,065 admitted.

Average high school GPA	3.0	SAT verbal scores above 500	N/R
SAT math scores above 500	N/R	ACT above 18	N/R
1998 freshmen returning in 1999	80%		

Application *Options:* eApply at www.CollegeQuest.com, Common Application, electronic application, deferred entrance. *Application fee:* $35. *Required:* essay or personal statement; high school transcript; minimum 2.5 GPA; 2 letters of recommendation; community standards document. *Required for some:* interview.

Standardized tests *Admission: Required for some:* SAT I or ACT.

Significant dates *Application deadlines:* 6/15 (freshmen), 6/15 (transfers). *Financial aid deadline priority date:* 3/15.

Freshman Application Contact
Mr. Cam Lee, Director of Admissions, Trinity Western University, 7600 Glover Road, Langley, BC V2Y 1Y1, Canada. **Phone:** 604-513-2019 Ext. 3015. **Toll-free phone:** 888-468-6898. **Fax:** 604-513-2061. **E-mail:** admissions@twu.ca

Visit CollegeQuest.com for information on majors offered and athletics. Electronic viewbook available at CollegeQuest.com.

TYNDALE COLLEGE & SEMINARY
Toronto, Ontario, Canada

- **Independent interdenominational**, comprehensive, founded 1894
- **Degrees** bachelor's, master's, and first professional
- **Urban** 10-acre campus with easy access to Toronto
- **Coed**, 346 undergraduate students, 52% full-time, 51% women, 49% men
- **Moderately difficult** entrance level
- **10:1** student-to-undergraduate faculty ratio
- **$6095 tuition** and fees

Students *Undergraduates:* 181 full-time, 165 part-time. Students come from 7 provinces and territories. *The most frequently chosen baccalaureate field is:* philosophy. *Graduate:* 437 in professional programs, 316 in other graduate degree programs.

| Reside on campus | 30% | Black Canadians | 13% |
| Asian Canadian | 23% | Hispanic Americans | 2% |

Faculty 44 (27% full-time), 100% with terminal degrees.

Expenses (2000–2001) Tuition, fee, and room and board charges are reported in Canadian dollars. *Comprehensive fee:* $10,205 includes full-time tuition ($5600), mandatory fees ($495), and room and board ($4110). *Part-time tuition:* $176 per credit hour. *Part-time fees:* $16 per credit hour. *Payment plan:* installment. *Waivers:* employees or children of employees.

Library J. William Horsey Library. *Collection:* 65,013 titles, 410 serial subscriptions.

College life *Housing: Option:* coed. *Most popular organizations:* Choir, Student Government, Urban Ministry Team, "'Steadfast" Drama Team.

Campus security Student patrols, late-night transport-escort service, controlled dormitory access.

After graduation *Career center:* Services include career counseling, job bank, job interviews.

Freshmen 94 enrolled.

| SAT verbal scores above 500 | N/R | SAT math scores above 500 | N/R |
| ACT above 18 | N/R | 1998 freshmen returning in 1999 | 49% |

Application *Option:* deferred entrance. *Application fee:* $50. *Required:* essay or personal statement; high school transcript; 3 letters of recommendation. *Required for some:* interview.

Significant dates *Application deadlines:* 8/15 (freshmen), 8/15 (transfers). *Financial aid deadline priority date:* 5/31.

Freshman Application Contact
Mr. Kevin Kirk, Assistant Director of Admissions, Tyndale College & Seminary, 25 Ballyconnor Court, Toronto, ON M2M 4B3, Canada. **Phone:** 416-226-6380 Ext. 6701. **Toll-free phone:** 800-663-6052. **Fax:** 416-226-4210. **E-mail:** admissions@obcots.on.ca

Visit CollegeQuest.com for information on majors offered and athletics.

UNIVERSITÉ DE MONCTON
Moncton, New Brunswick, Canada

- **Province-supported**, comprehensive, founded 1963
- **Degrees** bachelor's, master's, doctoral, and first professional (doctoral degree in French studies only)
- **Urban** 400-acre campus
- **Coed**
- **Moderately difficult** entrance level

Institutional Web site http://www.umoncton.ca/

College life *Housing: Options:* coed, women-only, disabled students. *Most popular organizations:* Amnesty International, student radio station, business clubs, Improvisational League, WSC.

Campus security 24-hour emergency response devices and patrols, controlled dormitory access, student security attendants in residences 8 p.m. to 2 a.m.

Application *Options:* Common Application, deferred entrance. *Application fee:* $30. *Required:* high school transcript; French examination. *Required for some:* essay or personal statement; minimum 2.0 GPA; 1 letter of recommendation; interview.

Admissions Office Contact
Université de Moncton, Moncton, NB E1A 3E9, Canada. **Toll-free phone:** 800-363-8336. **Fax:** 506-858-4544. **E-mail:** registrariat@umoncton.ca

Visit CollegeQuest.com for information on athletics. College video available at CollegeQuest.com.

UNIVERSITÉ DE MONTRÉAL
Montréal, Quebec, Canada

- **Independent**, university, founded 1920
- **Degrees** bachelor's, master's, and doctoral
- **Urban** 150-acre campus
- **Coed**, 23,733 undergraduate students, 65% full-time, 68% women, 32% men
- **Moderately difficult** entrance level
- **66.5% graduate** in 6 years or less
- **$1800 tuition** and fees (in-province); $3039 (out-of-province)

Expenses (1999–2000) Tuition and room only charges are reported in Canadian dollars. *Tuition, state resident:* full-time $1800; part-time $61 per credit. *Tuition, nonresident:* full-time $3039; part-time $101 per credit. *International tuition:* $9200 full-time. Full-time tuition and fees vary according to program. Part-time tuition and fees vary according to program. *College room and board:* room only: $1890. *Payment plan:* installment. *Waivers:* employees or children of employees.

Library Main library plus 18 others. *Collection:* 15,300 serial subscriptions, 164,079 audiovisual materials.

College life *Housing: Option:* coed. *Most popular organization:* Federation des Associations Etudiantes du Campus.

Campus security 24-hour emergency response devices and patrols, student patrols, late-night transport-escort service, controlled dormitory access, cameras, alarm systems, crime prevention programs.

After graduation 1,200 organizations recruited on campus 1997–98. *Career center:* 5 full-time, 3 part-time personnel. Services include job fairs, resume preparation, interview workshops, resume referral, career counseling, careers library, job bank, job interviews. *Graduate education:* 23% of class of 1999 went directly to graduate and professional school.

Freshmen

| SAT verbal scores above 500 | N/R | SAT math scores above 500 | N/R |
| ACT above 18 | N/R | 1998 freshmen returning in 1999 | 83% |

Application *Option:* Common Application. *Application fee:* $30. *Required:* Diploma of Collegiate Studies (and transcript) or equivalent. *Required for some:* interview.

Significant dates *Application deadlines:* 3/1 (freshmen), 3/1 (transfers). *Notification:* 5/15 (freshmen).

Freshman Application Contact
Mr. Fernand Boucher, Registrar, Université de Montréal, Case postale 6205, Succursale Centre-ville, Montréal, PQ H3C 3T5, Canada. **Phone:** 514-343-7076. **Fax:** 514-343-5788. **E-mail:** fernand.boucher@umontreal.ca

Canada

Université de Montréal (continued)
Visit CollegeQuest.com for information on majors offered and athletics. Electronic viewbook available at CollegeQuest.com.

UNIVERSITÉ DE SHERBROOKE
Sherbrooke, Quebec, Canada

- **Independent**, university, founded 1954
- **Degrees** bachelor's, master's, doctoral, and first professional
- **Urban** 800-acre campus with easy access to Montreal
- **Coed**
- **Moderately difficult** entrance level
- **$2861 tuition** and fees (in-province); $5111 (out-of-province)

Students *Undergraduates:* Students come from 3 provinces and territories, 62 other countries.
Expenses (2000–2001) Tuition, fee, and room only charges are reported in Canadian dollars. *Tuition, state resident:* full-time $2801; part-time $62 per credit. *Tuition, nonresident:* full-time $5051; part-time $112 per credit. *International tuition:* $13,752 full-time. *Required fees:* full-time $60; $20 per term part-time. *College room and board:* room only: $1488. Room and board charges vary according to housing facility. *Waivers:* employees or children of employees.
Library Bibliothéque Generale plus 3 others. *Collection:* 1.2 million titles, 5,937 serial subscriptions.
College life *Housing:* Option: coed.
Campus security 24-hour emergency response devices and patrols.
After graduation *Career center:* 3 full-time personnel. Services include resume preparation, career counseling, careers library, job interviews.
Freshmen
  SAT verbal scores above 500   N/R   SAT math scores above 500   N/R
  ACT above 18   N/R
Application *Option:* early admission. *Preference* given to province residents. *Application fee:* $30. *Required:* high school transcript. *Required for some:* letters of recommendation; interview.
Significant dates *Application deadline:* 3/1 (freshmen). *Notification:* continuous until 5/15 (freshmen). *Financial aid deadline:* 3/31.
Freshman Application Contact
Ms. Lisa Bedard, Admissions Officer, Université de Sherbrooke, 2500, Boulevard de l'Université, Sherbrooke, PQ J1K 2R1, Canada. **Phone:** 819-821-7681. **Toll-free phone:** 800-267-UDES. **Fax:** 819-821-7966. **E-mail:** information@courrier.usherb.ca
Visit CollegeQuest.com for information on majors offered and athletics. College video available at CollegeQuest.com.

UNIVERSITÉ DU QUÉBEC À CHICOUTIMI
Chicoutimi, Quebec, Canada

- **Province-supported**, university, founded 1969
- **Degrees** bachelor's, master's, and doctoral
- **Urban** 100-acre campus
- **Coed**
- **Noncompetitive** entrance level

Part of Université du Québec.
Faculty 394 (56% full-time).
Library *Collection:* 689,214 titles, 5,092 serial subscriptions.
College life *Housing:* Option: coed.
Campus security 24-hour emergency response devices and patrols.
After graduation *Career center:* Services include career counseling.
Freshmen
  SAT verbal scores above 500   N/R   SAT math scores above 500   N/R
  ACT above 18   N/R
Application *Required:* Diploma of Collegiate Studies (and transcript) or equivalent. *Required for some:* interview.
Significant dates *Application deadline:* 3/1 (freshmen). *Notification:* 5/15 (freshmen).
Freshman Application Contact
Mr. Claudio Zoccastello, Admissions Officer, Université du Québec à Chicoutimi, 555, boulevard de L'Université, Chicoutimi, PQ G7H 2B1, Canada. **Phone:** 418-545-5005. **Fax:** 418-545-5012. **E-mail:** czoccast@uqac.uquebec.ca
Visit CollegeQuest.com for information on majors offered and athletics. College video available at CollegeQuest.com.

UNIVERSITÉ DU QUÉBEC À HULL
Hull, Quebec, Canada

- **Province-supported**, comprehensive, founded 1981
- **Degrees** bachelor's, master's, and doctoral
- **Small-town** campus with easy access to Ottawa
- **Coed**
- **Noncompetitive** entrance level, 85% of applicants were admitted

Part of Université du Québec.
Library *Collection:* 169,289 titles, 4,458 serial subscriptions.
College life *Housing:* on-campus residence required through senior year. Option: coed. *Most popular organizations:* AGE, AIESEC, AEME, REMAA.
Campus security 24-hour emergency response devices and patrols, late-night transport-escort service.
After graduation *Career center:* 1 full-time, 1 part-time personnel. Services include job fairs, resume referral, career counseling, job bank, job interviews.
Freshmen 3,166 applied, 2,691 admitted.
  SAT verbal scores above 500   N/R   SAT math scores above 500   N/R
  ACT above 18   N/R   1998 freshmen returning in 1999 90%
Application *Required:* Diploma of Collegiate Studies (and transcript) or equivalent. *Required for some:* interview.
Significant dates *Application deadline:* 8/19 (freshmen). *Notification:* 5/15 (freshmen).
Freshman Application Contact
Ms. Lene Blais, Admissions Officer, Université du Québec à Hull, C.P. 1250, Station "B" Hull, Quebec, PQ J8X 3X7, Canada. **Phone:** 819-595-3900 Ext. 1841. **E-mail:** lene_blais@uqah.uquebec.ca
Visit CollegeQuest.com for information on majors offered and athletics. College video available at CollegeQuest.com.

UNIVERSITÉ DU QUÉBEC À MONTRÉAL
Montréal, Quebec, Canada

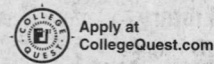

Admissions Office Contact
Université du Québec à Montréal, CP 8888, Succursale Centre-ville, Montréal, PQ H2L 4S8, Canada. **Fax:** 514-987-7728. **E-mail:** admission@uqam.ca

UNIVERSITÉ DU QUÉBEC À RIMOUSKI
Rimouski, Quebec, Canada

Admissions Office Contact
Université du Québec à Rimouski, 300, Allee des Ursulines, CP 3300, Rimouski, PQ G5L 3A1, Canada. **Fax:** 418-724-1525. **E-mail:** raymond_cote@uqar.uquebec.ca

UNIVERSITÉ DU QUÉBEC À TROIS-RIVIÈRES
Trois-Rivières, Quebec, Canada

- **Province-supported**, university, founded 1969
- **Degrees** bachelor's, master's, and doctoral
- **Urban** campus with easy access to Montreal
- **Coed**, 8,711 undergraduate students
- **Noncompetitive** entrance level
- **$1,881 tuition** and fees (in-province); $3,921 (out-of-province)

- $3.3 million endowment

Part of Université du Québec.
Students *Undergraduates:* Students come from 33 other countries.
Faculty 730 (43% full-time).
Expenses (2000–2001) Tuition and room only charges are reported in Canadian dollars. *Tuition, area resident:* part-time $56 per credit hour. *Tuition, state resident:* full-time $1,881; part-time $124 per credit hour. *Tuition, nonresident:* full-time $3,921; part-time $303 per credit hour. *International tuition:* $9,881 full-time. *College room and board:* room only: $3200. *Payment plan:* installment.
Library Main library plus 1 other. *Operations spending 1999–2000:* $2.2 million. *Collection:* 464,338 titles.
College life *Housing: Option:* coed.
Campus security 24-hour emergency response devices and patrols, late-night transport-escort service, controlled dormitory access.
After graduation *Career center:* 2 full-time, 1 part-time personnel. Services include job fairs, resume preparation, interview workshops, career counseling, careers library, job bank, job interviews.
Freshmen
SAT verbal scores above 500 N/R SAT math scores above 500 N/R
ACT above 18 N/R
Application *Application fee:* $30. *Required:* Diploma of Collegiate Studies (and transcript) or equivalent. *Required for some:* interview.
Significant dates *Application deadline:* 3/1 (freshmen). *Notification:* 6/1 (freshmen).
Freshman Application Contact
Mrs. Suzanne Camirand, Admissions Officer, Université du Québec à Trois-Rivières, , Bureau du registraire, Service des admissions, 3350 Boulevard Des Forges, Trois Rivieres, PQ G9A 5H7, Canada. **Phone:** 819-376-5045. **Toll-free phone:** 800-365-0922. **Fax:** 819-376-5210. **E-mail:** registraire@uqtr.uquebec.ca
Visit CollegeQuest.com for information on majors offered and athletics. College video available at CollegeQuest.com.

UNIVERSITÉ DU QUÉBEC, ÉCOLE DE TECHNOLOGIE SUPÉRIEURE
Montréal, Quebec, Canada

Admissions Office Contact
Université du Québec, École de technologie supérieure, 1100, rue Notre Dame Ouest, Montréal, PQ H3C 1K3, Canada. **Fax:** 514-289-8950. **E-mail:** admission@ets.mtl.ca

UNIVERSITÉ DU QUÉBEC EN ABITIBI-TÉMISCAMINGUE
Rouyn-Noranda, Quebec, Canada

- **Province-supported**, comprehensive, founded 1983
- **Degrees** bachelor's, master's, and doctoral
- **Small-town** 5-acre campus
- **Coed**, 748 undergraduate students
- **Noncompetitive** entrance level

Part of Université du Québec.
Students *Undergraduates:* Students come from 8 other countries.
Faculty 159 (45% full-time).
Library *Collection:* 135,882 titles, 302 serial subscriptions.
College life *Housing:* college housing not available.
Campus security 24-hour patrols.
After graduation *Career center:* 1 full-time personnel. Services include job fairs, resume preparation, career counseling, careers library, job bank, job interviews.
Freshmen
SAT verbal scores above 500 N/R SAT math scores above 500 N/R
ACT above 18 N/R

Application *Application fee:* $30. *Required:* Diploma of Collegiate Studies (and transcript) or equivalent. *Required for some:* interview.
Significant dates *Application deadline:* rolling (freshmen). *Notification:* 5/15 (freshmen).
Freshman Application Contact
Mrs. Monique Fay, Admissions Officer, Université du Québec en Abitibi-Témiscamingue, 445 boulevard de l'Université, Rouyn-Noranda, PQ J9X 5E4, Canada. **Phone:** 819-762-0971. **Fax:** 819-797-4727. **E-mail:** micheline.chevalier@uqat.uquebec.ca
Visit CollegeQuest.com for information on majors offered and athletics. College video and electronic viewbook available at CollegeQuest.com.

UNIVERSITÉ DU QUÉBEC, TÉLÉ-UNIVERSITÉ
Quebec, Canada—See Télé-université

UNIVERSITÉ LAVAL
Sainte-Foy, Quebec, Canada

- **Independent**, university, founded 1852
- **Degrees** bachelor's, master's, and doctoral
- **Urban** 465-acre campus with easy access to Québec City
- **Coed**, 28,789 undergraduate students, 66% full-time, 59% women, 41% men
- **Moderately difficult** entrance level, 82% of applicants were admitted
- **11:1** student-to-undergraduate faculty ratio
- **$1893 tuition** and fees (in-province); $3663 (out-of-province)
- **$33.8 million endowment**

Students *Undergraduates:* Students come from 12 provinces and territories, 83 other countries. *The most frequently chosen baccalaureate fields are:* engineering/engineering technologies, education, liberal arts/general studies. *Graduate:* 6,490 in graduate degree programs.
From out-of-province 4% Reside on campus 7%
Age 25 or older 35%
Faculty 1,528 (98% full-time), 87% with terminal degrees.
Expenses (2000–2001) Tuition, fee, and room and board charges are reported in Canadian dollars. *Tuition, state resident:* full-time $1743; part-time $56 per credit. *Tuition, nonresident:* full-time $3513; part-time $115 per credit. *International tuition:* $9702 full-time. *Required fees:* full-time $150; $6 per credit. Full-time tuition and fees vary according to program. Part-time tuition and fees vary according to program. *College room and board:* $6500; room only: $1568. Room and board charges vary according to housing facility. *Payment plan:* deferred payment. *Waivers:* employees or children of employees.
Library Bibliothéque Générale plus 2 others. *Operations spending 1999–2000:* $11.3 million. *Collection:* 2.2 million titles, 13,655 serial subscriptions, 19,700 audiovisual materials.
College life *Housing: Option:* coed. *Social organizations:* national fraternities. *Most popular organizations:* drama club, Improvisation Ligue, Création Littéraire, Chorale de L'uviversit&, e Laval.
Campus security 24-hour emergency response devices and patrols, student patrols, late-night transport-escort service, controlled dormitory access, video cameras in most buildings, underground walkways.
After graduation 602 organizations recruited on campus 1997–98. *Career center:* 33 full-time, 5 part-time personnel. Services include job fairs, resume preparation, resume referral, career counseling, careers library, job bank, job interviews.
Freshmen 13,594 applied, 11,086 admitted.
SAT verbal scores above 500 N/R SAT math scores above 500 N/R
ACT above 18 N/R 1998 freshmen returning in 1999 73%
Application *Option:* Common Application. *Application fee:* $30. *Required:* high school transcript; general knowledge of French language. *Required for some:* interview.
Significant dates *Application deadlines:* 3/1 (freshmen), 5/1 (transfers).

Canada

Université Laval (continued)
Freshman Application Contact
Mrs. Claire Sormany, Responsable des Communications, Université Laval, C. P. 2208, Sainte-Foy, QC G1K 7P4, Canada. **Phone:** 418-656-3080 Ext. 2119. **Toll-free phone:** 877-785-2825 Ext. 3080 (in-state); 877-7ULAVAL Ext. 3080 (out-of-state). **Fax:** 418-656-2809. **E-mail:** reg@reg.ulaval.ca
Visit CollegeQuest.com for information on majors offered and athletics. Electronic viewbook available at CollegeQuest.com.

■ *See page 2674 for a narrative description.*

UNIVERSITÉ SAINTE-ANNE
Church Point, Nova Scotia, Canada

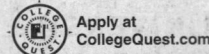
Apply at CollegeQuest.com

- **Province-supported**, 4-year, founded 1890
- **Degree** bachelor's
- **Rural** 115-acre campus
- **Coed**
- **Minimally difficult** entrance level

Institutional Web site http://ustanne-59.ustanne.ednet.ns.ca/
College life *Housing: Option:* coed. *Most popular organizations:* Student Organization, Amnesty International, Club de Plein Air, Education Committee, Commerce Committee.
Campus security Student patrols, late-night transport-escort service, 14-hour patrols by trained security personnel.
Application *Options:* eApply at www.CollegeQuest.com, Common Application, electronic application. *Application fee:* $30. *Required:* high school transcript. *Required for some:* essay or personal statement; 3 letters of recommendation.
Admissions Office Contact
Université Sainte-Anne, Church Point, NS B0W 1M0, Canada. **Fax:** 902-769-2930. **E-mail:** admission@ustanne.ednet.ns.ca
Visit CollegeQuest.com for information on athletics. Electronic viewbook available at CollegeQuest.com.

■ *See page 2676 for a narrative description.*

UNIVERSITY COLLEGE OF CAPE BRETON
Sydney, Nova Scotia, Canada

- **Province-supported**, comprehensive, founded 1974
- **Degrees** bachelor's, master's, and postbachelor's certificates
- **Small-town** 57-hectare campus
- **Coed**, 2,682 undergraduate students, 84% full-time, 58% women, 42% men
- **Moderately difficult** entrance level, 89% of applicants were admitted
- **15:1** student-to-undergraduate faculty ratio
- **79% graduate** in 6 years or less
- **$3950 tuition and fees (out-of-province)**

Students *Undergraduates:* 2,242 full-time, 440 part-time. Students come from 10 provinces and territories, 23 other countries. *The most frequently chosen baccalaureate fields are:* psychology, business/marketing, social sciences and history. *Graduate:* 23 in graduate degree programs.

From out-of province	11%	Reside on campus	5%
Age 25 or older	28%	Transferred in	9%

Faculty 257 (74% full-time), 36% with terminal degrees.
Expenses (1999–2000) Tuition, fee, and room and board charges are reported in Canadian dollars. *Tuition, nonresident:* full-time $3700; part-time $740 per course. *International tuition:* $6817 full-time. *Required fees:* full-time $250; $23 per course. Full-time tuition and fees vary according to course load and program. Part-time tuition and fees vary according to course load. *College room and board:* $5630. Room and board charges vary according to board plan and housing facility. *Payment plan:* installment. *Waivers:* senior citizens and employees or children of employees.

Library University College Library. *Collection:* 344,987 titles, 800 serial subscriptions, 1,850 audiovisual materials.
College life *Housing: Option:* coed. *Most popular organizations:* Business Society, Mature Student Association, International Students Association, Honours Society, Dramagroup.
Campus security 24-hour patrols, controlled dormitory access, security for social events, escort service.
After graduation 150 organizations recruited on campus 1997–98. *Career center:* 11 full-time personnel. Services include resume preparation, interview workshops, resume referral, career counseling, careers library, job bank, job interviews.
Freshmen 1,679 applied, 1,497 admitted, 1,014 enrolled.

SAT verbal scores above 500	N/R	SAT math scores above 500	N/R
ACT above 18	N/R	1998 freshmen returning in 1999	55%

Application *Application fee:* $20. *Required:* high school transcript. *Required for some:* essay or personal statement; 3 letters of recommendation; interview.
Significant dates *Application deadline:* 8/1 (freshmen).
Freshman Application Contact
Ms. Moira Ross, Admissions/PLA Coordinator, University College of Cape Breton, PO Box 5300, Sydney, NS B1P 6L2, Canada. **Phone:** 902-563-1117. **Toll-free phone:** 888-959-9995. **Fax:** 902-563-1371. **E-mail:** mross@uccb.ns.ca
Visit CollegeQuest.com for information on majors offered and athletics. College video available at CollegeQuest.com.

■ *See page 2678 for a narrative description.*

UNIVERSITY COLLEGE OF THE CARIBOO
Kamloops, British Columbia, Canada

Admissions Office Contact
University College of the Cariboo, PO Box 3010, Station Terminal, Kamloops, BC V2C 5N3, Canada. **Fax:** 250-828-5086.

UNIVERSITY COLLEGE OF THE FRASER VALLEY
Abbotsford, British Columbia, Canada

- **Province-supported**, 4-year, founded 1974
- **Degree** bachelor's
- **Urban** campus with easy access to Vancouver
- **Coed**, 6,000 undergraduate students
- **$1400 tuition and fees (out-of-province)**

Students *Undergraduates:* The most frequently chosen baccalaureate fields are: health professions and related sciences, home economics/vocational home economics, social sciences and history.
Faculty 314 (96% full-time).
Expenses (1999–2000) Tuition and fee charges are reported in Canadian dollars. *Tuition, area resident:* part-time $120 per course. *Tuition, nonresident:* full-time $1200. *Required fees:* full-time $200; $2 per credit; $12 per term part-time. Full-time tuition and fees vary according to course level and course load. Part-time tuition and fees vary according to course level and course load. *Payment plan:* deferred payment. *Waivers:* senior citizens and employees or children of employees.
Library Peter Jones Library plus 3 others.
College life *Housing:* college housing not available.
Campus security Late-night transport-escort service.
After graduation *Career center:* Services include career counseling.
Freshmen

SAT verbal scores above 500	N/R	SAT math scores above 500	N/R
ACT above 18	N/R		

Application *Options:* electronic application, deferred entrance. *Application fee:* $15. *Required for some:* essay or personal statement; high school transcript; 1 letter of recommendation; interview.

Significant dates *Application deadline:* 2/28 (freshmen). *Notification:* 6/1 (freshmen).

Freshman Application Contact
Ms. Elaine Harris, Associate Registrar, University College of the Fraser Valley, 33844 King Road, Abbotsford, BC V2S 7M8, Canada. **Phone:** 604-864-4645. **Fax:** 604-853-9990. **E-mail:** reginfo@ucfv.bc.ca

Visit CollegeQuest.com for information on majors offered and athletics.

UNIVERSITY OF ALBERTA
Edmonton, Alberta, Canada

- **Province-supported**, university, founded 1906
- **Degrees** bachelor's, master's, doctoral, and first professional
- **Urban** 154-acre campus
- **Coed**, 25,893 undergraduate students
- **Moderately difficult** entrance level, 64% of applicants were admitted
- **13:1 student-to-undergraduate faculty ratio**
- **$4203 tuition and fees (out-of-province)**
- **$476.1 million endowment**

Students *Undergraduates:* Students come from 12 provinces and territories, 110 other countries. *The most frequently chosen baccalaureate fields are:* education, area/ethnic studies, health professions and related sciences.

| From out-of province | 5% | Reside on campus | 15% |
| Age 25 or older | 16% | | |

Faculty 2,239 (74% full-time).

Expenses (2000–2001, estimated) Tuition, fee, and room and board charges are reported in Canadian dollars. *Tuition, nonresident:* full-time $3764; part-time $376 per course. *International tuition:* $7528 full-time. *Required fees:* full-time $439; $121. Full-time tuition and fees vary according to course load and program. Part-time tuition and fees vary according to course load and program. *College room and board:* $3345. Room and board charges vary according to board plan, housing facility, and location. *Payment plan:* installment.

Library Cameron Library plus 10 others. *Operations spending 1999–2000:* $24.1 million. *Collection:* 4.6 million titles, 25,673 serial subscriptions.

College life *Housing: Options:* coed, disabled students. *Social organizations:* national fraternities, national sororities, local fraternities, local sororities.

Campus security 24-hour emergency response devices, student patrols, late-night transport-escort service.

After graduation 186 organizations recruited on campus 1997–98. *Career center:* 9 full-time, 30 part-time personnel. Services include job fairs, resume preparation, interview workshops, resume referral, career/interest testing, career counseling, careers library, job bank, job interviews.

Freshmen 20,508 applied, 13,156 admitted.

| Average high school GPA | 3.16 | SAT verbal scores above 500 | N/R |
| SAT math scores above 500 | N/R | ACT above 18 | N/R |

Application *Options:* electronic application, deferred entrance. *Preference* given to province residents. *Application fee:* $60. *Required:* high school transcript. *Required for some:* essay or personal statement; letters of recommendation; interview. *Recommended:* minimum 2.0 GPA.

Significant dates *Application deadlines:* 5/1 (freshmen), 5/1 (transfers). *Notification:* continuous until 9/1 (freshmen).

Freshman Application Contact
Ms. Carole Byrne, Associate Registrar/Director of Admissions, University of Alberta, 201 Administration Building, Edmonton, AB T6G 2M7, Canada. **Phone:** 780-492-3113. **Fax:** 780-492-7172. **E-mail:** registrar@ualberta.ca

Visit CollegeQuest.com for information on majors offered and athletics. Electronic viewbook available at CollegeQuest.com.

UNIVERSITY OF BRITISH COLUMBIA
Vancouver, British Columbia, Canada

- **Province-supported**, university, founded 1915
- **Degrees** bachelor's, master's, doctoral, and postbachelor's certificates
- **Urban** 1,000-acre campus
- **Coed**, 29,146 undergraduate students
- **Very difficult** entrance level, 42% of applicants were admitted
- **15:1 student-to-undergraduate faculty ratio**
- **$2489 tuition and fees (out-of-province)**
- **$411.7 million endowment**

Students *Undergraduates:* Students come from 12 provinces and territories, 114 other countries.

| From out-of province | 11% | Reside on campus | 23% |
| Age 25 or older | 25% | | |

Faculty 1,753 full-time.

Expenses (1999–2000) Tuition, fee, and room and board charges are reported in Canadian dollars. *Tuition, nonresident:* full-time $2295. *International tuition:* $13,830 full-time. *Required fees:* full-time $194. Full-time tuition and fees vary according to course load, program, and reciprocity agreements. Part-time tuition and fees vary according to course load, program, and reciprocity agreements. *College room and board:* $5160; room only: $2451. Room and board charges vary according to board plan and housing facility. *Payment plan:* deferred payment. *Waivers:* senior citizens and employees or children of employees.

Library Walter C. Koerner Library plus 16 others. *Operations spending 1999–2000:* $16.4 million. *Collection:* 3.7 million titles, 18,124 serial subscriptions.

College life *Housing: Options:* coed, men-only, women-only, disabled students. *Social organizations:* national fraternities, national sororities, local fraternities, local sororities; 4% of eligible men and 4% of eligible women are members. *Most popular organizations:* ski club, dance club, AIESEC club, Chinese Collegiate Society, varsity outdoors club.

Campus security 24-hour emergency response devices and patrols, student patrols, late-night transport-escort service, 24-hour desk attendants in residence halls.

After graduation 2,800 organizations recruited on campus 1997–98. *Career center:* 4 full-time, 2 part-time personnel. Services include resume preparation, interview workshops, career counseling, careers library, job bank, job interviews.

Freshmen 18,464 applied, 7,732 admitted.

| SAT verbal scores above 500 | N/R | SAT math scores above 500 | N/R |
| ACT above 18 | N/R | | |

Application *Options:* electronic application, early admission. *Application fee:* $100. *Required:* high school transcript; minimum 2.6 GPA. *Required for some:* letters of recommendation.

Standardized tests *Admission: Recommended:* SAT I.

Significant dates *Application deadlines:* 4/30 (freshmen), 4/30 (out-of-state freshmen), 4/30 (transfers). *Notification:* continuous until 8/31 (freshmen), continuous until 8/15 (out-of-state freshmen). *Financial aid deadline:* 10/1. *Priority date:* 4/15.

Freshman Application Contact
Ms. Mary Cooney, Associate Registrar/Admissions, University of British Columbia, 1874 East Mall, Vancouver, BC V6T 1Z1, Canada. **Phone:** 604-822-9325. **Toll-free phone:** 877-272-1422. **Fax:** 604-822-3599. **E-mail:** student.information@ubc.ca

Visit CollegeQuest.com for information on majors offered and athletics.

■ *See page 2700 for a narrative description.*

UNIVERSITY OF CALGARY
Calgary, Alberta, Canada

- **Province-supported**, university, founded 1945
- **Degrees** bachelor's, master's, and doctoral
- **Urban** 304-acre campus
- **Coed**, 21,744 undergraduate students, 85% full-time, 56% women, 44% men
- **Moderately difficult** entrance level, 54% of applicants were admitted
- **$4245 tuition and fees (out-of-province)**

Students *Undergraduates:* Students come from 83 other countries. *The most frequently chosen baccalaureate fields are:* education, business/marketing, social sciences and history. *Graduate:* 3,623 in graduate degree programs.

Canada

University of Calgary (continued)

Age 25 or older	20%

Expenses (2000–2001) Tuition, fee, and room and board charges are reported in Canadian dollars. *Tuition, nonresident:* full-time $3834; part-time $383 per course. *International tuition:* $7668 full-time. *Required fees:* full-time $411; $68 per term part-time. Full-time tuition and fees vary according to course load. Part-time tuition and fees vary according to course load. *College room and board:* $3255. Room and board charges vary according to board plan and housing facility. *Waivers:* senior citizens and employees or children of employees.

Library MacKimmie Library plus 4 others. *Collection:* 2.1 million titles, 14,413 serial subscriptions.

College life *Housing: Options:* coed, disabled students.

Campus security 24-hour emergency response devices and patrols, late-night transport-escort service, controlled dormitory access.

After graduation 2,398 organizations recruited on campus 1997–98. *Career center:* 4 full-time personnel. Services include job fairs, resume preparation, interview workshops, career counseling, careers library, job bank, job interviews.

Freshmen 5,687 applied, 3,076 admitted.

SAT verbal scores above 500	N/R	SAT math scores above 500	N/R
ACT above 18	N/R		

Application *Option:* electronic application. *Application fee:* $65. *Required:* high school transcript.

Standardized tests *Admission: Required for some:* SAT I, SAT II Subject Tests, SAT II: Writing Test.

Significant dates *Application deadline:* 6/1 (freshmen).

Freshman Application Contact
Director of Recruitment and Admissions, University of Calgary, Office of Admissions, Calgary, AB T2N 1N4, Canada. **Phone:** 403-220-6645. **Fax:** 403-289-1253. **E-mail:** applinfo@ucalgary.ca

Visit CollegeQuest.com for information on majors offered and athletics.

UNIVERSITY OF GUELPH
Guelph, Ontario, Canada

- **Province-supported**, university, founded 1964
- **Degrees** bachelor's, master's, doctoral, and first professional
- **Urban** 817-acre campus with easy access to Toronto
- **Coed**, 12,390 undergraduate students, 88% full-time, 63% women, 37% men
- **Moderately difficult** entrance level, 61% of applicants were admitted
- **20:1 student-to-undergraduate faculty ratio**
- **79% graduate** in 6 years or less
- **$4394 tuition and fees (out-of-province)**

Students *Undergraduates:* 10,911 full-time, 1,479 part-time. Students come from 12 provinces and territories, 85 other countries. *Graduate:* 126 in professional programs, 1,711 in other graduate degree programs.

Reside on campus	38%	Age 25 or older	11%

Faculty 791 (79% full-time).

Expenses (1999–2000) Tuition, fee, and room and board charges are reported in Canadian dollars. *Tuition, nonresident:* full-time $3794; part-time $379 per course. *International tuition:* $8000 full-time. *Required fees:* full-time $600; $13 per course; $125 per term part-time. Full-time tuition and fees vary according to program. Part-time tuition and fees vary according to course load. *College room and board:* $5766; room only: $2896. Room and board charges vary according to board plan and housing facility. *Waivers:* senior citizens and employees or children of employees.

Library McLaughlin Library plus 1 other. *Collection:* 2.1 million titles, 7,294 serial subscriptions, 16,437 audiovisual materials.

College life *Housing: Options:* coed, men-only, women-only, cooperative.

Campus security 24-hour emergency response devices and patrols, late-night transport-escort service, video camera surveillance in parking lots, alarms in women's locker room.

After graduation 140 organizations recruited on campus 1997–98. *Career center:* 7 full-time, 20 part-time personnel. Services include job fairs, resume preparation, interview workshops, resume referral, career/interest testing, career counseling, careers library, job bank, job interviews.

Freshmen 16,832 applied, 10,316 admitted, 3,241 enrolled.

SAT verbal scores above 500	N/R	SAT math scores above 500	N/R
ACT above 18	N/R	1998 freshmen returning in 1999	92%

Application *Option:* early admission. *Application fee:* $85. *Required:* high school transcript. *Required for some:* essay or personal statement; interview. *Recommended:* minimum 3.0 GPA; letters of recommendation.

Standardized tests *Admission: Required for some:* SAT I or ACT.

Significant dates *Application deadlines:* 4/1 (freshmen), 12/1 (transfers). *Notification:* continuous until 9/1 (freshmen). *Financial aid deadline priority date:* 7/1.

Freshman Application Contact
Mr. Jock Phippen, Admissions Coordinator, University of Guelph, Admission Services, L-3 University Centre, Guelph, ON N1G 2W1, Canada. **Phone:** 519-824-4120 Ext. 6066. **E-mail:** info@registrar.uoguelph.ca

Visit CollegeQuest.com for information on majors offered and athletics. College video and electronic viewbook available at CollegeQuest.com.

■ *See page 2730 for a narrative description.*

UNIVERSITY OF KING'S COLLEGE
Halifax, Nova Scotia, Canada

- **Province-supported**, 4-year, founded 1789
- **Degree** bachelor's
- **Urban** 4-acre campus
- **Coed**, 886 undergraduate students, 98% full-time, 55% women, 45% men
- **Moderately difficult** entrance level, 77% of applicants were admitted
- **$4455 tuition and fees (out-of-province)**
- **$16 million endowment**

Students *Undergraduates:* Students come from 10 provinces and territories, 6 other countries.

From out-of province	52%	Reside on campus	26%

Faculty 38 (100% full-time).

Expenses (1999–2000) Tuition, fee, and room and board charges are reported in Canadian dollars. *Tuition, nonresident:* full-time $4050; part-time $135 per credit. *International tuition:* $7140 full-time. *Required fees:* full-time $405; $315 per year part-time. Full-time tuition and fees vary according to course load and program. Part-time tuition and fees vary according to course load and program. *College room and board:* $5080. Room and board charges vary according to housing facility. *Payment plan:* installment. *Waivers:* employees or children of employees.

Library University of King's College Library. *Operations spending 1999–2000:* $190,000. *Collection:* 80,000 titles, 192 serial subscriptions, 74 audiovisual materials.

College life *Housing: Options:* coed, men-only, women-only. *Most popular organizations:* King's Theatrical Society, student newspaper, King's College Dance Collective, St. Andrew's Missionary Society, King's Independent Film-Makers Society.

Campus security Student patrols, late-night transport-escort service.

After graduation *Career center:* 1 full-time, 2 part-time personnel. Services include job fairs, resume preparation, career/interest testing, career counseling, careers library, job bank.

Freshmen 853 applied, 661 admitted.

SAT verbal scores above 500	N/R	SAT math scores above 500	N/R
ACT above 18	N/R		

Application *Application fee:* $35. *Required:* high school transcript; minimum 3.0 GPA. *Required for some:* essay or personal statement; letters of recommendation; writing sample.

Standardized tests *Admission: Required for some:* SAT I.

Significant dates *Application deadlines:* 6/1 (freshmen), 6/1 (transfers). *Financial aid deadline:* continuous.

Freshman Application Contact
Karl Turner, Admissions Officer, University of King's College, Registrar's Office, Halifax, NS B3H 2A1, Canada. **Phone:** 902-422-1271 Ext. 193. **Fax:** 902-423-3357. **E-mail:** admissions@ukings.ns.ca

Canada

Visit CollegeQuest.com for information on majors offered and athletics.

THE UNIVERSITY OF LETHBRIDGE
Lethbridge, Alberta, Canada

- **Province-supported**, comprehensive, founded 1967
- **Degrees** bachelor's and master's
- **Urban** 576-acre campus
- **Coed**, 5,774 undergraduate students, 89% full-time, 57% women, 43% men
- **Moderately difficult** entrance level, 59% of applicants were admitted
- 18:1 student-to-undergraduate faculty ratio
- $3995 tuition and fees (out-of-province)
- $8.2 million endowment

Students *Undergraduates:* Students come from 16 provinces and territories, 30 other countries. *The most frequently chosen baccalaureate fields are:* business/marketing, liberal arts/general studies, social sciences and history. *Graduate:* 235 in graduate degree programs.

From out-of province	12%	Reside on campus	10%
Age 25 or older	33%		

Faculty 278, 79% with terminal degrees.

Expenses (1999–2000) Tuition, fee, and room and board charges are reported in Canadian dollars. *Tuition, nonresident:* full-time $3470. *International tuition:* $6940 full-time. *Required fees:* full-time $525. Part-time tuition and fees vary according to course load. *College room and board:* $4370; room only: $2270. Room and board charges vary according to board plan, housing facility, and student level. *Payment plan:* deferred payment. *Waivers:* senior citizens and employees or children of employees.

Library The University of Lethbridge Library. *Operations spending 1999–2000:* $4 million. *Collection:* 482,278 titles, 3,297 audiovisual materials.

College life *Housing:* on-campus residence required through senior year. *Option:* coed. *Most popular organizations:* Management Students Society, Inter-Varsity Christian Fellowship, Organization of Residence Students, The University of Lethbridge Geography Club, Education Undergraduate Society.

Campus security 24-hour emergency response devices and patrols, student patrols, late-night transport-escort service, video camera monitored entrances, hallways.

After graduation *Career center:* 1 full-time, 1 part-time personnel. Services include job fairs, resume preparation, interview workshops, resume referral, career counseling, careers library, job bank, job interviews. *Graduate education:* 9% of class of 1999 went directly to graduate and professional school: 5% education, 2% graduate arts and sciences, 1% business.

Freshmen 1,417 applied, 842 admitted.

Average high school GPA	3.3	SAT verbal scores above 500	N/R
SAT math scores above 500	N/R	ACT above 18	N/R
From top 10% of their h.s. class	6%	From top quarter	56%
From top half	100%		

Application *Options:* Common Application, electronic application, early admission, early decision, deferred entrance. *Application fee:* $50. *Required:* high school transcript; minimum 2.0 GPA. *Required for some:* minimum 3.0 GPA; letters of recommendation; interview.

Standardized tests *Admission:* Required for some: SAT I and SAT II or ACT, SAT II: Writing Test.

Significant dates *Application deadlines:* 8/26 (freshmen), 8/26 (transfers). *Early decision:* 4/1. *Notification:* 4/22 (early decision).

Freshman Application Contact
Mr. Peter Haney, Assistant Registrar, The University of Lethbridge, 4401 University Drive, Lethbridge, AB T1K 3M4, Canada. **Phone:** 403-382-7134. **Toll-free phone:** 403-320-5700. **E-mail:** inquiries@uleth.ca

Visit CollegeQuest.com for information on majors offered and athletics.

UNIVERSITY OF MANITOBA
Winnipeg, Manitoba, Canada

- **Province-supported**, university, founded 1877
- **Degrees** bachelor's, master's, and doctoral
- **Suburban** 685-acre campus
- **Coed**, 18,154 undergraduate students, 76% full-time, 55% women, 45% men
- **Moderately difficult** entrance level, 69% of applicants were admitted
- $3082 tuition and fees (out-of-province)

Students *Undergraduates:* 13,844 full-time, 4,310 part-time. *Graduate:* 2,970 in graduate degree programs.

Faculty 1,096.

Expenses (1999–2000) Tuition, fee, and room and board charges are reported in Canadian dollars. *Tuition, nonresident:* full-time $2872. *International tuition:* $5026 full-time. *Required fees:* full-time $210. Full-time tuition and fees vary according to program. Part-time tuition and fees vary according to program. *College room and board:* $4057; room only: $2357. Room and board charges vary according to board plan, housing facility, and location. *Waivers:* senior citizens and employees or children of employees.

Library Elizabeth Dafoe Library plus 12 others. *Collection:* 1.6 million titles, 12,800 serial subscriptions.

College life *Housing: Option:* coed. *Social organizations:* national fraternities, local fraternities, eating clubs.

Campus security 24-hour emergency response devices, student patrols, late-night transport-escort service.

After graduation *Career center:* Services include resume referral, career counseling, job bank.

Freshmen 4,301 applied, 2,950 admitted, 6,201 enrolled.

SAT verbal scores above 500	N/R	SAT math scores above 500	N/R
ACT above 18		N/R	

Application *Preference* given to province residents for some programs. *Application fee:* $35. *Required:* high school transcript.

Significant dates *Application deadlines:* 7/1 (freshmen), 7/1 (transfers). *Financial aid deadline priority date:* 6/30.

Freshman Application Contact
Mr. Peter Dueck, Acting Director of Admissions, University of Manitoba, Winnipeg, MB R3T 2N2, Canada. **Phone:** 204-474-6382.

Visit CollegeQuest.com for information on majors offered and athletics.

UNIVERSITY OF NEW BRUNSWICK
Fredericton, New Brunswick, Canada

- **Province-supported**, university, founded 1785
- **Degrees** bachelor's, master's, and doctoral
- **Urban** 7,100-acre campus
- **Coed**, 6,539 undergraduate students, 100% full-time, 48% women, 52% men
- **Moderately difficult** entrance level, 82% of applicants were admitted
- 15:1 student-to-undergraduate faculty ratio
- $3660 tuition and fees (out-of-province)

Students *Undergraduates:* 6,539 full-time. Students come from 12 provinces and territories, 65 other countries. *Graduate:* 819 in graduate degree programs.

Reside on campus	20%	Age 25 or older	32%

Faculty 645 (78% full-time).

Expenses (1999–2000) Tuition, fee, and room and board charges are reported in Canadian dollars. *Tuition, nonresident:* full-time $3430; part-time $343 per course. *International tuition:* $5980 full-time. *Required fees:* full-time $230; $8 per course. *College room and board:* $4620. Room and board charges vary according to board plan. *Payment plan:* installment. *Waivers:* senior citizens and employees or children of employees.

Library Harriet Irving Library plus 3 others. *Collection:* 1.1 million titles, 4,817 serial subscriptions, 65,000 audiovisual materials.

College life *Housing: Option:* coed.

Campus security Late-night transport-escort service.

After graduation *Career center:* 2 full-time personnel. Services include resume preparation, resume referral, career counseling, careers library, job bank, job interviews.

Canada

University of New Brunswick (continued)

Freshmen 2,414 applied, 1,978 admitted, 1,157 enrolled.

SAT verbal scores above 500	N/R	SAT math scores above 500	N/R
ACT above 18	N/R	From top 10% of their h.s. class	15%
From top quarter	40%	From top half	75%
1998 freshmen returning in 1999	75%		

Application *Options:* early admission, deferred entrance. *Application fee:* $35. *Required:* high school transcript. *Required for some:* essay or personal statement; 1 letter of recommendation; interview.

Standardized tests *Admission: Required for some:* SAT I.

Significant dates *Application deadlines:* rolling (freshmen), rolling (out-of-state freshmen), rolling (transfers). *Notification:* continuous until 8/31 (freshmen), continuous until continuous (out-of-state freshmen). *Financial aid deadline:* continuous.

Freshman Application Contact
Ms. Kathryn E. Monti, Assistant Registrar/Admissions, University of New Brunswick, PO Box 4400, Sir Howard Douglas Hall, Fredericton, NB E3B 5Z8, Canada. **Phone:** 506-453-4865. **Fax:** 506-453-5016. **E-mail:** unbfacts@unb.ca

Visit CollegeQuest.com for information on majors offered and athletics.

UNIVERSITY OF NEW BRUNSWICK
Saint John, New Brunswick, Canada

- **Province-supported**, comprehensive, founded 1964
- **Degrees** bachelor's, master's, and doctoral
- **Urban** 250-acre campus
- **Coed**, 2,483 undergraduate students, 75% full-time, 58% women, 42% men
- **Moderately difficult** entrance level, 71% of applicants were admitted
- **10:1** student-to-undergraduate faculty ratio
- **$3594** tuition and fees (out-of-province)

Students *Undergraduates:* 1,862 full-time, 621 part-time. Students come from 8 provinces and territories, 45 other countries. *The most frequently chosen baccalaureate fields are:* business/marketing, biological/life sciences, psychology. *Graduate:* 70 in graduate degree programs.

From out-of province	6%	Reside on campus	5%

Faculty 128 full-time.

Expenses (1999–2000) Tuition, fee, and room and board charges are reported in Canadian dollars. *Tuition, nonresident:* full-time $3594; part-time $343 per course. *International tuition:* $6144 full-time. *Required fees:* $8 per course. *College room and board:* $5010. Room and board charges vary according to board plan. *Payment plan:* installment. *Waivers:* employees or children of employees.

Library Ward Chipman Library. *Operations spending 1999–2000:* $270,000. *Collection:* 155,500 titles, 700 serial subscriptions.

College life *Housing: Option:* coed. *Most popular organizations:* Business Administration Society, OPTAMUS, International Student Association, Chinese Cultural Association, Muslim Student Association.

Campus security 24-hour emergency response devices and patrols, student patrols, late-night transport-escort service, controlled dormitory access.

After graduation 330 organizations recruited on campus 1997–98. *Career center:* 2 full-time, 5 part-time personnel. Services include job fairs, resume preparation, interview workshops, resume referral, career/interest testing, career counseling, careers library, job bank, job interviews. *Graduate education:* 10% of class of 1999 went directly to graduate and professional school.

Freshmen 1,541 applied, 1,092 admitted, 688 enrolled.

SAT verbal scores above 500	N/R	SAT math scores above 500	N/R
ACT above 18	N/R	From top 10% of their h.s. class	15%
From top quarter	45%	From top half	70%
1998 freshmen returning in 1999	85%		

Application *Options:* electronic application, early admission, deferred entrance. *Application fee:* $35. *Required:* high school transcript. *Required for some:* letters of recommendation.

Standardized tests *Admission: Required:* SAT I.

Significant dates *Application deadlines:* rolling (freshmen), 3/31 (out-of-state freshmen), rolling (transfers). *Notification:* continuous until 8/31 (freshmen), continuous until continuous (out-of-state freshmen).

Freshman Application Contact
Ms. Sue Ellis Loparco, Admissions Officer, University of New Brunswick, PO Box 5050, Tucker Park Road, Saint John, NB E2L 4L5, Canada. **Phone:** 506-648-5674. **Toll-free phone:** 800-743-4333 (in-state); 800-743-5691 (out-of-state). **E-mail:** apply@unbsj.ca

Visit CollegeQuest.com for information on majors offered and athletics. Electronic viewbook available at CollegeQuest.com.

UNIVERSITY OF NORTHERN BRITISH COLUMBIA
Prince George, British Columbia, Canada

Admissions Office Contact
University of Northern British Columbia, 3333 University Way, Prince George, BC V2N 4Z9, Canada. **Fax:** 250-960-5791.

UNIVERSITY OF OTTAWA
Ottawa, Ontario, Canada

- **Province-supported**, university, founded 1848
- **Degrees** bachelor's, master's, and doctoral
- **Urban** 70-acre campus
- **Coed**
- **Moderately difficult** entrance level

Institutional Web site http://www.uottawa.ca/

College life *Housing: Option:* coed. *Most popular organization:* Student Federation.

Campus security 24-hour emergency response devices and patrols, student patrols, late-night transport-escort service, controlled dormitory access.

Application *Option:* early admission. *Application fee:* $95. *Required:* high school transcript; minimum 3.0 GPA. *Required for some:* interview.

Standardized tests *Admission: Required:* SAT I.

Admissions Office Contact
University of Ottawa, PO Box 450, Station A, Ottawa, ON K1N 6N5, Canada. **E-mail:** liaison@uottawa.ca

Visit CollegeQuest.com for information on athletics. Electronic viewbook available at CollegeQuest.com.

- *See page 2800 for a narrative description.*

UNIVERSITY OF PRINCE EDWARD ISLAND
Charlottetown, Prince Edward Island, Canada

- **Province-supported**, comprehensive, founded 1834
- **Degrees** bachelor's, master's, doctoral, and first professional
- **Small-town** 130-acre campus
- **Coed**, 2,516 undergraduate students, 82% full-time, 61% women, 39% men
- **Moderately difficult** entrance level, 63% of applicants were admitted
- **$3873** tuition and fees (out-of-province)

Students *Undergraduates:* Students come from 8 provinces and territories, 6 other countries. *Graduate:* 494 in professional programs, 96 in other graduate degree programs.

Reside on campus	14%	Age 25 or older	24%

Faculty 177 full-time.

Expenses (1999–2000) Tuition, fee, and room and board charges are reported in Canadian dollars. *Tuition, nonresident:* full-time $3480; part-time $348 per course. *International tuition:* $6880 full-time. *Required fees:* full-time $393; $5 per course. *College room and board:* $5870; room only: $3284. Room and board charges vary according to board plan. *Waivers:* senior citizens.

Library Robertson Library. *Collection:* 394,000 titles, 1,700 serial subscriptions.

Canada

College life *Housing: Option:* coed. *Most popular organizations:* Business Society, biology club, Music Society, intramurals, Theatre Society.
Campus security 24-hour emergency response devices and patrols, late-night transport-escort service, controlled dormitory access, late night residence hall security personnel.
After graduation 15 organizations recruited on campus 1997–98. *Career center:* 1 part-time personnel. Services include resume preparation, interview workshops, resume referral, career/interest testing, career counseling, careers library, job bank, job interviews.
Freshmen 1,575 applied, 997 admitted.

| SAT verbal scores above 500 | N/R | SAT math scores above 500 | N/R |
| ACT above 18 | N/R | 1998 freshmen returning in 1999 | 69% |

Application *Options:* Common Application, early admission. *Application fee:* $35. *Required:* high school transcript; minimum 2.0 GPA. *Required for some:* 3 letters of recommendation; interview.
Significant dates *Application deadlines:* 8/15 (freshmen), 4/1 (out-of-state freshmen), 8/15 (transfers). *Notification:* continuous until 8/31 (freshmen), continuous until 6/30 (out-of-state freshmen).
Freshman Application Contact
Dr. Marion Hannaford, Associate Registrar, University of Prince Edward Island, , Registrar's Office, Charlottetown, PE C1A 4D3, Canada. **Phone:** 902-566-0361. **Fax:** 902-566-0795. **E-mail:** registrar@upei.ca
Visit CollegeQuest.com for information on majors offered and athletics.

UNIVERSITY OF REGINA
Regina, Saskatchewan, Canada

- **Province-supported**, university, founded 1974
- **Degrees** bachelor's, master's, and doctoral
- **Urban** 330-acre campus
- **Coed**
- **Minimally difficult** entrance level
- **$3066 tuition and fees (out-of-province)**
- **$62.8 million endowment**

Students *Undergraduates:* Students come from 12 provinces and territories, 57 other countries.

| Age 25 or older | 34% |

Faculty 1,800 (56% full-time).
Expenses (1999–2000) *Tuition, nonresident:* full-time $2813; part-time $94 per credit hour. *International tuition:* $5625 full-time. *Required fees:* full-time $253; $2 per credit hour; $54 per term part-time. Part-time tuition and fees vary according to course load. *College room and board:* $3680. *Waivers:* senior citizens and employees or children of employees.
Library University of Regina Main Library plus 6 others. *Collection:* 2.3 million titles.
College life *Housing: Option:* coed. *Most popular organizations:* Administration Students' Society, Education Students' Society, Engineering Students Society.
Campus security 24-hour emergency response devices, student patrols, late-night transport-escort service, controlled dormitory access.
After graduation *Career center:* 10 full-time personnel. Services include resume preparation, resume referral, career counseling, job bank, job interviews.
Freshmen

| SAT verbal scores above 500 | N/R | SAT math scores above 500 | N/R |
| ACT above 18 | N/R | | |

Application *Options:* early admission, deferred entrance. *Preference* given to province residents. *Application fee:* $25. *Required:* high school transcript; minimum 2.0 GPA. *Required for some:* essay or personal statement; letters of recommendation; interview.
Standardized tests *Admission: Required for some:* CELT, Michigan Test of English Language Proficiency.
Significant dates *Application deadlines:* 8/15 (freshmen), 6/15 (out-of-state freshmen). *Financial aid deadline:* continuous.

Freshman Application Contact
Mr. Clarence Gray, Assistant Registrar/Admissions and Awards, University of Regina, Regina, SK S4S 0A2, Canada. **Phone:** 306-585-4591. **Fax:** 306-585-5203. **E-mail:** admissions.office@uregina.ca
Visit CollegeQuest.com for information on majors offered and athletics.

UNIVERSITY OF SASKATCHEWAN
Saskatoon, Saskatchewan, Canada

Admissions Office Contact
University of Saskatchewan, Office of the Registrar, Saskatoon, SK S7N 5A2, Canada. **Fax:** 306-966-7026. **E-mail:** admissions@usask.ca

UNIVERSITY OF TORONTO
Toronto, Ontario, Canada

- **Province-supported**, university, founded 1827
- **Degrees** bachelor's, master's, doctoral, and first professional
- **Urban** 900-acre campus
- **Coed**, 35,258 undergraduate students, 79% full-time, 57% women, 43% men
- **Very difficult** entrance level
- **$4521 tuition and fees (out-of-province)**
- **$382.5 million endowment**

Students *Undergraduates:* 27,982 full-time, 7,276 part-time. Students come from 12 provinces and territories, 120 other countries. *Graduate:* 2,469 in professional programs, 9,675 in other graduate degree programs.

| Age 25 or older | 27% |

Expenses (1999–2000) Tuition, fee, and room and board charges are reported in Canadian dollars. *Tuition, nonresident:* full-time $3835; part-time $767 per course. *International tuition:* $8639 full-time. *Required fees:* full-time $686; $223 per term part-time. Full-time tuition and fees vary according to program. Part-time tuition and fees vary according to program. *College room and board:* $6000; room only: $3600. *Payment plan:* installment. *Waivers:* senior citizens and employees or children of employees.
Library Robart's Library plus 31 others. *Operations spending 1999–2000:* $27.5 million. *Collection:* 8.3 million titles, 35,558 serial subscriptions.
College life *Housing: Option:* coed. *Social organizations:* national fraternities, national sororities, local sororities.
Campus security 24-hour emergency response devices and patrols, student patrols, late-night transport-escort service.
After graduation *Career center:* 33 full-time personnel. Services include job fairs, resume preparation, career counseling, careers library.
Freshmen 8,870 enrolled.

| SAT verbal scores above 500 | N/R | SAT math scores above 500 | N/R |
| ACT above 18 | N/R | 1998 freshmen returning in 1999 | 94% |

Application *Option:* deferred entrance. *Preference* given to province residents for pharmacy program; Canadian residents for dentistry, physical and occupational therapy, rehabilitation medicine programs. *Required:* high school transcript. *Required for some:* interview.
Standardized tests *Admission: Required for some:* SAT I, SAT II Subject Tests.
Significant dates *Application deadlines:* 7/1 (freshmen), 7/1 (transfers).
Freshman Application Contact
Admissions and Awards, University of Toronto, Toronto, ON M5S 1A1, Canada. **Phone:** 416-978-2190. **E-mail:** ask@adm.utoronto.ca
Visit CollegeQuest.com for information on majors offered and athletics.

UNIVERSITY OF VICTORIA
Victoria, British Columbia, Canada

- **Province-supported**, university, founded 1963
- **Degrees** bachelor's, master's, doctoral, and first professional
- **Suburban** 380-acre campus with easy access to Vancouver

Canada

University of Victoria (continued)
- **Coed**, 14,771 undergraduate students, 63% full-time, 60% women, 40% men
- **Moderately difficult** entrance level, 59% of applicants were admitted
- **$2624 tuition and fees (out-of-province)**

Students *Undergraduates:* 9,273 full-time, 5,498 part-time. Students come from 11 provinces and territories, 93 other countries. *Graduate:* 371 in professional programs, 1,867 in other graduate degree programs.

| From out-of province | 13% | Reside on campus | 12% |
| Age 25 or older | 30% | Transferred in | 7% |

Faculty 947 (69% full-time).

Expenses (2000–2001, estimated) Tuition, fee, and room and board charges are reported in Canadian dollars. *Tuition, nonresident:* full-time $2265. *International tuition:* $6795 full-time. *Required fees:* full-time $359. Part-time tuition and fees vary according to course load. *College room and board:* $4600; room only: $3072. Room and board charges vary according to board plan and housing facility. *Payment plan:* installment.

Library McPherson Library plus 2 others. *Operations spending 1999–2000:* $10 million. *Collection:* 1.6 million titles, 12,000 serial subscriptions.

College life *Housing: Option:* coed.

Campus security 24-hour emergency response devices and patrols, student patrols, late-night transport-escort service.

After graduation 1,000 organizations recruited on campus 1997–98. *Career center:* 8 full-time personnel. Services include job fairs, resume preparation, interview workshops, career counseling, careers library, job bank, job interviews.

Freshmen 6,150 applied, 3,640 admitted, 1,789 enrolled.

| SAT verbal scores above 500 | N/R | SAT math scores above 500 | N/R |
| ACT above 18 | N/R | | |

Application *Options:* electronic application, early admission, early action, deferred entrance. *Application fee:* $65 for nonresidents. *Required:* high school transcript; minimum 2.5 GPA. *Required for some:* essay or personal statement; minimum 3.0 GPA; interview; audition, portfolio.

Significant dates *Application deadlines:* 4/30 (freshmen), 4/30 (transfers). *Early action:* 2/28. *Notification:* 5/1 (early action). *Financial aid deadline priority date:* 6/30.

Freshman Application Contact
Mr. Bruno Rocca, Admission Services Office, University of Victoria, PO Box 3025, Victoria, BC V8W 3P2, Canada. **Phone:** 250-721-8121 Ext. 8109. **Fax:** 250-721-6225. **E-mail:** srsad13@uvvm.uvic.ca

Visit CollegeQuest.com for information on majors offered and athletics.

UNIVERSITY OF WATERLOO
Waterloo, Ontario, Canada

- **Province-supported**, university, founded 1957
- **Degrees** bachelor's, master's, doctoral, and first professional
- **Suburban** 900-acre campus with easy access to Toronto
- **Coed**, 18,842 undergraduate students, 85% full-time, 48% women, 52% men
- **Moderately difficult** entrance level, 59% of applicants were admitted
- **20:1 student-to-undergraduate faculty ratio**
- **$4298 tuition and fees (out-of-province)**

Students *Undergraduates:* Students come from 12 provinces and territories, 34 other countries. *The most frequently chosen baccalaureate fields are:* engineering/engineering technologies, liberal arts/general studies, mathematics. *Graduate:* 1,825 in graduate degree programs.

| From out-of province | 1% | Reside on campus | 39% |

Faculty 1,364 (55% full-time).

Expenses (1999–2000) Tuition, fee, and room and board charges are reported in Canadian dollars. *Tuition, nonresident:* full-time $3874; part-time $435 per course. *International tuition:* $20,848 full-time. *Required fees:* full-time $424. Full-time tuition and fees vary according to program. Part-time tuition and fees vary according to program. *College room and board:* $5139; room only: $2889. Room and board charges vary according to board plan and housing facility. *Waivers:* senior citizens and employees or children of employees.

Library Dana Porter Library plus 7 others. *Collection:* 2.9 million titles, 13,228 serial subscriptions.

College life *Housing: Option:* coed. *Social organizations:* national fraternities, national sororities; 1% of eligible men and 1% of eligible women are members. *Most popular organizations:* Chinese Students Association, swing and social dance club, The Hindi Movie Club, Canadian Asian Students Association, UW Breakers.

Campus security 24-hour emergency response devices and patrols, student patrols, late-night transport-escort service.

After graduation *Career center:* 3 full-time personnel. Services include job fairs, resume preparation, interview workshops, career/interest testing, career counseling, careers library, job bank, job interviews.

Freshmen 23,279 applied, 13,665 admitted.

Average high school GPA	3.5	SAT verbal scores above 500	N/R
SAT math scores above 500	N/R	ACT above 18	N/R
From top half of their h.s. class	100%	1998 freshmen returning in 1999	98%

Application *Options:* electronic application, early admission. *Application fee:* $80. *Required:* high school transcript. *Required for some:* essay or personal statement; minimum 3.0 GPA; letters of recommendation; interview.

Standardized tests *Admission: Required for some:* SAT I or ACT, SAT II Subject Tests.

Significant dates *Notification:* continuous until 7/30 (freshmen). *Financial aid deadline priority date:* 7/1.

Freshman Application Contact
Mr. P. Burroughs, Director of Admissions, University of Waterloo, 200 University Avenue West, Waterloo, ON N2L 3G1, Canada. **Phone:** 519-888-4567 Ext. 2265. **Fax:** 519-746-2882 Ext. 5378. **E-mail:** watquest@uwaterloo.ca

Visit CollegeQuest.com for information on majors offered and athletics.

THE UNIVERSITY OF WESTERN ONTARIO
London, Ontario, Canada

- **Province-supported**, university, founded 1878
- **Degrees** bachelor's, master's, and doctoral
- **Suburban** 420-acre campus
- **Coed**, 19,335 undergraduate students
- **Very difficult** entrance level, 46% of applicants were admitted
- **$4598 tuition and fees (out-of-province)**

Students *Undergraduates:* Students come from 12 provinces and territories, 71 other countries.

| Reside on campus | 13% | Age 25 or older | 26% |

Faculty 1,241 full-time.

Expenses (1999–2000) Tuition and fee charges are reported in Canadian dollars. *Tuition, nonresident:* full-time $3845; part-time $769 per course. *International tuition:* $9436 full-time. *Required fees:* full-time $753; $116 per course. Full-time tuition and fees vary according to program. Part-time tuition and fees vary according to program. Room and board charges vary according to board plan and housing facility. *Payment plans:* installment, deferred payment. *Waivers:* children of alumni, senior citizens, and employees or children of employees.

Library The University of Western Ontario Library System plus 7 others. *Operations spending 1999–2000:* $8.5 million. *Collection:* 2.1 million titles, 15,698 serial subscriptions.

College life *Housing: Option:* coed. *Social organizations:* national fraternities, national sororities; 10% of eligible men and 3% of eligible women are members.

Campus security 24-hour emergency response devices and patrols, student patrols, late-night transport-escort service.

After graduation 140 organizations recruited on campus 1997–98. *Career center:* 7 full-time, 10 part-time personnel. Services include job fairs, resume preparation, career counseling, careers library, job interviews.

Freshmen 28,191 applied, 12,903 admitted.

| SAT verbal scores above 500 | N/R | SAT math scores above 500 | N/R |
| ACT above 18 | N/R | 1998 freshmen returning in 1999 | 93% |

Application *Option:* deferred entrance. *Application fee:* $85. *Required:* high school transcript; minimum 3.0 GPA.

Standardized tests *Admission: Required for some:* SAT I.
Significant dates *Application deadlines:* 6/1 (freshmen), 5/15 (out-of-state freshmen), 6/1 (transfers).
Freshman Application Contact
Mr. R. J. Tiffin, Deputy Registrar, The University of Western Ontario, London, ON N6A 5B8, Canada. **Phone:** 519-661-2100. **E-mail:** reg-admissions@julian.uwo.ca
Visit CollegeQuest.com for information on majors offered and athletics. College video available at CollegeQuest.com.

UNIVERSITY OF WINDSOR
Windsor, Ontario, Canada

- **Province-supported**, university, founded 1857
- **Degrees** bachelor's, master's, doctoral, and first professional
- **Urban** 125-acre campus with easy access to Detroit
- **Coed**, 10,488 undergraduate students, 78% full-time, 54% women, 46% men
- **Moderately difficult** entrance level, 67% of applicants were admitted
- **22:1** student-to-undergraduate faculty ratio
- **$4420** tuition and fees (out-of-province)
- **$13.1 million** endowment

Students *Undergraduates:* 8,226 full-time, 2,262 part-time. Students come from 11 provinces and territories, 46 other countries. *Graduate:* 436 in professional programs, 936 in other graduate degree programs.

| Reside on campus | 16% | Age 25 or older | 26% |

Faculty 581 (74% full-time).
Expenses (1999–2000) Tuition, fee, and room and board charges are reported in Canadian dollars. *Tuition, nonresident:* full-time $4000; part-time $373 per course. *International tuition:* $9400 full-time. *Required fees:* full-time $420; $52 per course. Full-time tuition and fees vary according to program. Part-time tuition and fees vary according to program. *College room and board:* $6500; room only: $3,598. Room and board charges vary according to board plan and housing facility. *Payment plan:* installment. *Waivers:* senior citizens and employees or children of employees.
Library Leddy Library plus 2 others. *Operations spending 1999–2000:* $5.5 million. *Collection:* 2.4 million titles, 9,104 serial subscriptions, 1,920 audio-visual materials.
College life *Housing: Option:* coed. *Social organizations:* national fraternities, national sororities; 2% of eligible men and 2% of eligible women are members. *Most popular organizations:* University of Windsor Student Alliance, Environmental Awareness Association, Social Science Society, Commerce Society, Science Society.
Campus security 24-hour emergency response devices and patrols, student patrols, late-night transport-escort service, controlled dormitory access.
After graduation 300 organizations recruited on campus 1997–98. *Career center:* 3 full-time personnel. Services include job fairs, resume preparation, interview workshops, career/interest testing, career counseling, careers library, job bank, job interviews.
Freshmen 9,864 applied, 6,635 admitted, 3,023 enrolled.

| SAT verbal scores above 500 | N/R | SAT math scores above 500 | N/R |
| ACT above 18 | N/R | 1998 freshmen returning in 1999 | 77% |

Application *Option:* early admission. *Application fee:* $30. *Required:* high school transcript; minimum 2.3 GPA. *Required for some:* essay or personal statement; minimum 3.3 GPA; 1 letter of recommendation; interview. *Recommended:* minimum 2.7 GPA.
Standardized tests *Admission: Required for some:* SAT I, SAT I and SAT II or ACT.
Significant dates *Application deadlines:* rolling (freshmen), 7/1 (out-of-state freshmen), rolling (transfers). *Financial aid deadline:* continuous.
Freshman Application Contact
Ms. Charlene Yates, Assistant Registrar, University of Windsor, 401 Sunset Avenue, Windsor, ON N9B 3P4, Canada. **Phone:** 519-253-3000 Ext. 3332. **Toll-free phone:** 800-864-2860. **Fax:** 519-973-7050. **E-mail:** registr@uwindsor.ca
Visit CollegeQuest.com for information on majors offered and athletics. College video available at CollegeQuest.com.

■ *See page 2862 for a narrative description.*

THE UNIVERSITY OF WINNIPEG
Winnipeg, Manitoba, Canada

- **Province-supported**, comprehensive, founded 1967
- **Degrees** bachelor's and master's
- **Urban** 2-acre campus
- **Coed**, 1,565 undergraduate students
- **Moderately difficult** entrance level

Students *Undergraduates:* Students come from 5 provinces and territories, 32 other countries.
Faculty 378 (63% full-time).
Library *Collection:* 442,614 titles, 1,840 serial subscriptions.
College life *Housing:* college housing not available.
Campus security 24-hour emergency response devices and patrols, student patrols, video controlled external access.
After graduation *Career center:* Services include resume preparation, career counseling, careers library.
Freshmen

| SAT verbal scores above 500 | N/R | SAT math scores above 500 | N/R |
| ACT above 18 | N/R | | |

Application *Options:* early admission, deferred entrance. *Application fee:* $55 for nonresidents. *Required:* high school transcript. *Required for some:* interview.
Significant dates *Application deadlines:* 8/9 (freshmen), 7/15 (out-of-state freshmen), 8/9 (transfers). *Notification:* continuous until continuous (out-of-state freshmen).
Freshman Application Contact
Ms. Nancy LaTocki, Director of Admissions, The University of Winnipeg, 515 Portage Avenue, Winnipeg, MB R3B 2E9, Canada. **Phone:** 204-786-9740. **E-mail:** admissions@uwinnipeg.ca
Visit CollegeQuest.com for information on majors offered and athletics.

WESTERN PENTECOSTAL BIBLE COLLEGE
Abbotsford, British Columbia, Canada

Admissions Office Contact
Western Pentecostal Bible College, Box 1700, Abbotsford, BC V2S 7E7, Canada. **Toll-free phone:** 800-976-8388. **Fax:** 604-853-8951.

WILFRID LAURIER UNIVERSITY
Waterloo, Ontario, Canada

- **Province-supported**, comprehensive, founded 1911
- **Degrees** bachelor's, master's, and doctoral
- **Urban** 40-acre campus with easy access to Toronto
- **Coed**, 7,845 undergraduate students, 83% full-time, 57% women, 43% men
- **Moderately difficult** entrance level, 68% of applicants were admitted
- **$4214** tuition and fees (out-of-province)

Students *Undergraduates:* 6,488 full-time, 1,357 part-time. Students come from 12 provinces and territories, 37 other countries. *Graduate:* 903 in graduate degree programs.

| Age 25 or older | 2% |

Faculty 283.
Expenses (1999–2000) Tuition, fee, and room and board charges are reported in Canadian dollars. *Tuition, nonresident:* full-time $3834; part-time $860 per course. *International tuition:* $8500 full-time. *Required fees:* full-time $380; $55 per course. *College room and board:* $5820; room only: $3350. Room and board charges vary according to board plan and housing facility. *Payment plan:* installment. *Waivers:* senior citizens and employees or children of employees.
Library Wilfrid Laurier University Library. *Collection:* 580,000 titles, 4,500 serial subscriptions.

Canada

Wilfrid Laurier University *(continued)*

College life *Housing: Option:* coed. *Most popular organizations:* Water Buffaloes, TAMIAE, ski club, Musicians' Network, Laurier Christian Fellowship.

Campus security 24-hour emergency response devices and patrols, student patrols, late-night transport-escort service, controlled dormitory access.

After graduation 1,500 organizations recruited on campus 1997–98. *Career center:* 8 full-time, 10 part-time personnel. Services include job fairs, resume preparation, resume referral, career counseling, careers library, job bank, job interviews.

Freshmen 10,471 applied, 7,120 admitted, 2,087 enrolled.

| SAT verbal scores above 500 | N/R | SAT math scores above 500 | N/R |
| ACT above 18 | N/R | | |

Application *Option:* Common Application. *Application fee:* $80. *Required:* high school transcript. *Required for some:* letters of recommendation; interview.

Standardized tests *Admission: Required for some:* SAT I.

Significant dates *Application deadlines:* 4/1 (freshmen), 4/1 (transfers).

Freshman Application Contact
Ms. Gail Forsyth, Manager of Admissions, Wilfrid Laurier University, 75 University Avenue West, Waterloo, ON N2L 3C5, Canada. **Phone:** 519-884-0710 Ext. 6099. **Fax:** 519-884-8826. **E-mail:** admissions@mach1.wlu.ca

Visit CollegeQuest.com for information on majors offered and athletics. College video available at CollegeQuest.com.

■ *See page 2994 for a narrative description.*

WILLIAM AND CATHERINE BOOTH COLLEGE
Winnipeg, Manitoba, Canada

Admissions Office Contact
William and Catherine Booth College, 447 Webb Place, Winnipeg, MB R3B 2P2, Canada. **Toll-free phone:** 800-781-6044. **Fax:** 204-942-3856.

YORK UNIVERSITY
Toronto, Ontario, Canada

- **Province-supported**, university, founded 1959
- **Degrees** bachelor's, master's, doctoral, first professional, post-master's, and postbachelor's certificates
- **Urban** 650-acre campus
- **Coed**, 33,990 undergraduate students, 77% full-time, 61% women, 39% men
- **Moderately difficult** entrance level, 26% of applicants were admitted
- **$5135 tuition and fees (out-of-province)**
- **$88 million endowment**

Students *Undergraduates:* Students come from 150 other countries. *Graduate:* 3,910 in graduate degree programs.

| From out-of province | 2% | Reside on campus | 6% |
| Age 25 or older | 29% | | |

Faculty 2,899 (39% full-time), 94% with terminal degrees.

Expenses (1999–2000) Tuition, fee, and room and board charges are reported in Canadian dollars. *Tuition, area resident:* part-time $889 per course. *Tuition, state resident:* part-time $889 per course. *Tuition, nonresident:* full-time $4445; part-time $889 per course. *International tuition:* $10,800 full-time. *Required fees:* full-time $690. Full-time tuition and fees vary according to course load, degree level, and program. Part-time tuition and fees vary according to course load, degree level, and program. *College room and board:* $4650; room only: $2850. Room and board charges vary according to board plan and housing facility. *Payment plans:* installment, deferred payment. *Waivers:* senior citizens and employees or children of employees.

Library Scott Library plus 4 others. *Operations spending 1999–2000:* $18.4 million. *Collection:* 2.2 million titles, 13,651 serial subscriptions.

College life *Housing: Options:* coed, disabled students. *Most popular organizations:* college student councils, York Federation of Students, Jewish Student Association, First Nations and Aboriginal Student Association, International and Exchange Students Club.

Campus security 24-hour emergency response devices and patrols, student patrols, late-night transport-escort service, controlled dormitory access.

After graduation 30 organizations recruited on campus 1997–98. *Career center:* 6 full-time, 11 part-time personnel. Services include job fairs, resume preparation, interview workshops, career counseling, careers library, job bank, job interviews, internet job placement, career planning workshops.

Freshmen 33,147 applied, 8,681 admitted.

| Average high school GPA | 3.0 | SAT verbal scores above 500 | N/R |
| SAT math scores above 500 | N/R | ACT above 18 | N/R |

Application *Options:* electronic application, early admission, early action, deferred entrance. *Preference* given to students with identified learning disabilities, extenuating circumstances. *Application fee:* $60. *Required:* high school transcript; minimum 3.0 GPA; audition/evaluation for fine arts program, supplemental applications for business and environmental studies. *Required for some:* 1 letter of recommendation; interview.

Standardized tests *Admission: Required:* SAT I or ACT.

Significant dates *Application deadlines:* 6/1 (freshmen), 6/1 (transfers). *Early action:* 2/1. *Notification:* 7/1 (early action). **Financial aid deadline:** continuous.

Freshman Application Contact
Vanessa Grafi, International Recruitment Officer, York University, 140 Atkinson Building, Toronto, ON M3J 1P3, Canada. **Phone:** 416-736-5825. **Fax:** 416-736-5741. **E-mail:** intlenq@yorku.ca

Visit CollegeQuest.com for information on majors offered and athletics.

■ *See page 3026 for a narrative description.*

CAYMAN ISLANDS

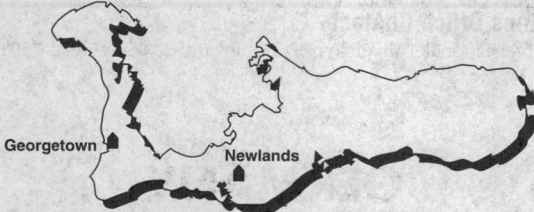

INTERNATIONAL COLLEGE OF THE CAYMAN ISLANDS
Newlands, Cayman Islands

- **Independent**, comprehensive, founded 1970
- **Degrees** associate, bachelor's, and master's
- **Rural** 3-acre campus
- **Coed**, 103 undergraduate students, 42% full-time, 67% women, 33% men
- **Moderately difficult** entrance level, 85% of applicants were admitted
- **15:1 student-to-undergraduate faculty ratio**
- **$3581 tuition** and fees

Students *Undergraduates:* 43 full-time, 60 part-time. Students come from 26 other countries. *The most frequently chosen baccalaureate fields are:* business/marketing, liberal arts/general studies, protective services/public administration. *Graduate:* 21 in graduate degree programs.

| Reside on campus | 3% | Transferred in | 3% |

Faculty 45 (13% full-time), 13% with terminal degrees.

Expenses (1999–2000) *One-time required fee:* $15. *Tuition:* full-time $3375; part-time $75 per quarter hour. *Required fees:* full-time $206; $62 per term part-time. Full-time tuition and fees vary according to course level and location. Part-time tuition and fees vary according to course level and location. *College room only:* $2438. *Payment plan:* installment. *Waivers:* employees or children of employees.

Library ICCI Library. *Operations spending 1999–2000:* $66,245. *Collection:* 16,677 titles, 140 serial subscriptions.

College life *Housing: Option:* coed. *Most popular organizations:* Student Activities Committee, graduation celebration planning committee, Academic Council Student Representation, student representation on various self study committees for accreditation review.

Campus security 24-hour emergency response devices.

After graduation 85% of class of 1998 had job offers within 6 months. *Career center:* 1 part-time personnel. Services include job fairs, resume preparation, resume referral, career counseling, careers library, job bank, job interviews.

Freshmen 116 applied, 99 admitted, 53 enrolled.

| SAT verbal scores above 500 | N/R | SAT math scores above 500 | N/R |
| ACT above 18 | N/R | | |

Application *Options:* Common Application, deferred entrance. *Application fee:* $37.50. *Required:* essay or personal statement; high school transcript; minimum 2.0 GPA; 2 letters of recommendation; rank in upper 50% of high school class. *Required for some:* interview.

Standardized tests *Admission: Required for some:* SAT I or ACT.

Significant dates *Application deadlines:* 7/1 (freshmen), 5/1 (out-of-state freshmen), 7/1 (transfers). *Notification:* continuous until continuous (out-of-state freshmen). *Financial aid deadline:* 8/15.

Freshman Application Contact
Ms. Dianne Levy, Admissions Representative, International College of the Cayman Islands, PO Box 136, Savannah Post Office, Newlands, Grand Cayman, Cayman Islands. **Phone:** 345-947-1100 Ext. 301. **Fax:** 947-1210. **E-mail:** icci@candw.ky

Visit CollegeQuest.com for information on majors offered and athletics. College video available at CollegeQuest.com.

- *See page 1828 for a narrative description.*

EGYPT

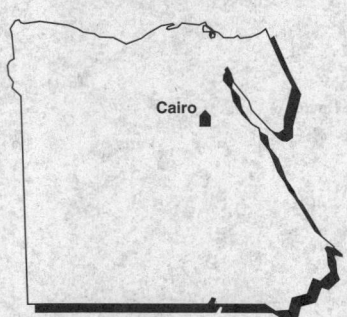

AMERICAN UNIVERSITY IN CAIRO
Cairo, Egypt

- **Independent**, comprehensive, founded 1919
- **Degrees** bachelor's and master's (majority of students are Egyptians; enrollment open to all nationalities)
- **Urban** 26-acre campus
- **Coed**, 3,661 undergraduate students, 85% full-time, 52% women, 48% men
- **Very difficult** entrance level, 48% of applicants were admitted
- **11:1 student-to-undergraduate faculty ratio**
- **74.6% graduate** in 6 years or less
- **$10,860 tuition** and fees
- **$358.6 million endowment**

Students *Undergraduates:* 3,111 full-time, 550 part-time. Students come from 64 other countries. *The most frequently chosen baccalaureate fields are:* engineering/engineering technologies, business/marketing, social sciences and history. *Graduate:* 776 in graduate degree programs.

| Reside on campus | 6% | Age 25 or older | 1% |

Faculty 474 (63% full-time).

Expenses (1999–2000) *Tuition:* full-time $10,750; part-time $448 per credit. *Required fees:* full-time $110; $55 per term part-time. Part-time tuition and fees vary according to course load. *College room only:* $2720. Room and board charges vary according to housing facility. *Payment plan:* deferred payment. *Waivers:* employees or children of employees.

Library American University in Cairo Library plus 2 others. *Operations spending 1999–2000:* $3.2 million. *Collection:* 289,000 titles, 2,500 audiovisual materials.

College life *Housing: Options:* men-only, women-only. *Most popular organizations:* Folklore Dancing Group, choral groups, Student Union, International Association for Students in Economics and Business, soccer.

Campus security 24-hour emergency response devices and patrols, controlled dormitory access.

After graduation 450 organizations recruited on campus 1997–98. 80% of class of 1998 had job offers within 6 months. *Career center:* 8 full-time, 1 part-time personnel. Services include job fairs, resume preparation, interview workshops, resume referral, career counseling, careers library, job bank, job interviews, job shadowing, career seminars.

Freshmen 2,048 applied, 986 admitted, 625 enrolled.

| SAT verbal scores above 500 | N/R | SAT math scores above 500 | N/R |
| ACT above 18 | N/R | 1998 freshmen returning in 1999 | 96% |

Application *Options:* early admission, early decision. *Preference* given to residents of Egypt. *Application fee:* $50. *Required:* essay or personal statement; high school transcript; minimum 2.00 GPA.

Standardized tests *Admission: Required for some:* SAT I or ACT.

Significant dates *Application deadlines:* 6/1 (freshmen), 6/1 (transfers). *Early decision:* 3/15.

Freshman Application Contact
Randa Kamel, Associate Director of Admissions, American University in Cairo, The Office of Student Affairs, 420 Fifth Avenue, 3rd Floor, New York, NY 10018-2728. **Phone:** 202-357-5199. **Fax:** 2-355-7565. **E-mail:** davidson@aucnyu.edu

Visit CollegeQuest.com for information on majors offered and athletics.

France-Germany

FRANCE

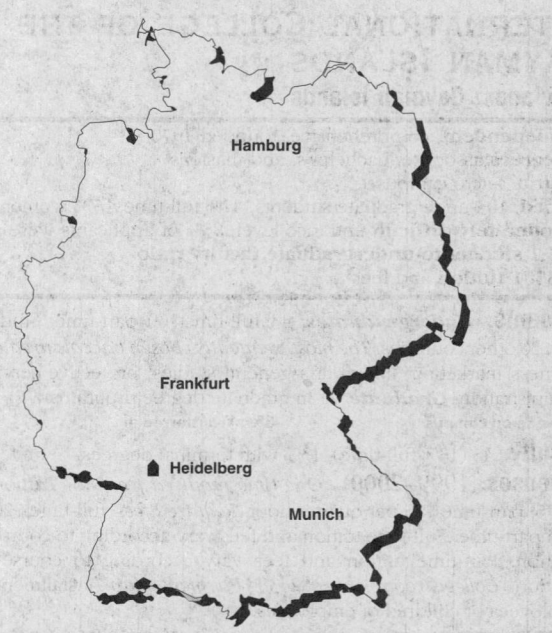

THE AMERICAN UNIVERSITY OF PARIS
Paris, France

- **Independent**, 4-year, founded 1962
- **Degree** bachelor's
- **Urban** campus
- **Coed**, 731 undergraduate students
- **Moderately difficult** entrance level, 80% of applicants were admitted
- **8:1 student-to-undergraduate faculty ratio**
- **$19,940 tuition** and fees

Students *Undergraduates:* Students come from 92 other countries. *The most frequently chosen baccalaureate fields are:* business/marketing, communications/communication technologies, social sciences and history.
Faculty 84, 71% with terminal degrees.
Expenses (1999–2000) *Tuition:* full-time $18,440; part-time $584 per credit. *Required fees:* full-time $1500. Part-time tuition and fees vary according to course load. *Payment plan:* installment. *Waivers:* children of alumni and employees or children of employees.
Library The American University of Paris Library. *Collection:* 65,000 titles, 1,000 serial subscriptions.
College life *Housing:* college housing not available. *Most popular organizations:* Safe Haven Aids Information, Publications Board, Student Senate, International Business Student Association, Sports Association.
Campus security 24-hour emergency response devices.
After graduation *Career center:* 1 full-time personnel. Services include resume preparation, resume referral, career counseling, careers library.
Freshmen 502 applied, 403 admitted.

SAT verbal scores above 500	74%	SAT math scores above 500	68%
ACT above 18	N/R	From top 10% of their h.s. class	5%
From top quarter	10%	From top half	85%

Application *Option:* deferred entrance. *Application fee:* $50. *Required:* essay or personal statement; high school transcript; minimum 2.8 GPA; 2 letters of recommendation. *Recommended:* minimum 3.0 GPA; interview.
Standardized tests *Admission: Recommended:* SAT II Subject Tests. *Required for some:* SAT I or ACT.
Significant dates *Application deadlines:* 5/1 (freshmen), 5/1 (transfers). *Financial aid deadline:* continuous.
Freshman Application Contact
Ms. Candace McLaughlin, New York Office, The American University of Paris, 60 East 42nd Street, Suite 1463, New York, NY 10017. **Phone:** 212-983-1414. **Fax:** 212-983-0444. **E-mail:** nyoffice@aup.fr
Visit CollegeQuest.com for information on majors offered and athletics.

SCHILLER INTERNATIONAL UNIVERSITY
Paris, France

Admissions Office Contact
Schiller International University, 32 Boulevard de Vaugirard, 75015 Paris, France.

GERMANY

SCHILLER INTERNATIONAL UNIVERSITY
Heidelberg, Germany

Part of Schiller International University.
Students *Undergraduates:* Students come from 130 other countries.
Faculty 28 (29% full-time).
Expenses (2000–2001) *Payment plan:* deferred payment. *Waivers:* employees or children of employees.
Library *Collection:* 8,000 titles, 94 serial subscriptions.
College life *Housing: Option:* coed. *Most popular organizations:* student government, student newspaper, yearbook staff.
Campus security 24-hour emergency response devices.
After graduation *Career center:* Services include resume preparation, career counseling. *Graduate education:* 21% of class of 1999 went directly to graduate and professional school.
Freshmen

| SAT verbal scores above 500 | N/R | SAT math scores above 500 | N/R |
| ACT above 18 | N/R | | |

Application *Options:* Common Application, deferred entrance. *Application fee:* $35. *Required:* essay or personal statement; high school transcript. *Recommended:* minimum 2.0 GPA.
Significant dates *Application deadlines:* rolling (freshmen), rolling (transfers). *Financial aid deadline:* 6/1. *Priority date:* 4/1.
Freshman Application Contact
Dr. Nicolle Macho, Campus Director, Schiller International University, Bergstrasse 106, 69121 Heidelberg, Germany. **Phone:** 49-6221-45810 Ext. 35. **E-mail:** siu_hd@compuserve.com
Visit CollegeQuest.com for information on majors offered and athletics. College video available at CollegeQuest.com.

GREECE

AMERICAN COLLEGE OF THESSALONIKI
Thessaloniki, Greece

 Apply at CollegeQuest.com

- **Independent**, 4-year
- **Degree** bachelor's
- **Suburban** 40-acre campus
- **Coed**, 719 undergraduate students, 77% full-time, 66% women, 34% men
- **Minimally difficult** entrance level, 86% of applicants were admitted
- **10:1 student-to-undergraduate faculty ratio**
- **$3785 tuition** and fees

Students *Undergraduates:* 555 full-time, 164 part-time. Students come from 19 other countries. *The most frequently chosen baccalaureate fields are:* business/marketing, English, psychology.

Reside on campus	1%	Age 25 or older	2%
Transferred in	1%		

Faculty 68 (28% full-time), 37% with terminal degrees.

Expenses (1999–2000) *Comprehensive fee:* $8785 includes full-time tuition ($3700), mandatory fees ($85), and room and board ($5000). *College room only:* $2500. *Part-time tuition:* $450 per course. *Part-time fees:* $22 per term part-time. *Payment plan:* installment. *Waivers:* employees or children of employees.

Library Eleftheriadis Library. *Operations spending 1999–2000:* $150,000. *Collection:* 35,000 titles, 142 serial subscriptions.

College life *Most popular organizations:* drama club, marketing club, sailing club, investments club, student newspaper.

Campus security 24-hour patrols.

After graduation 20 organizations recruited on campus 1997–98. *Career center:* 1 full-time, 1 part-time personnel. Services include job fairs, resume preparation, interview workshops, resume referral, career counseling, job bank, job interviews. *Graduate education:* 40% of class of 1999 went directly to graduate and professional school.

Freshmen 273 applied, 235 admitted, 135 enrolled.

Average high school GPA	2.5	SAT verbal scores above 500	N/R
SAT math scores above 500	N/R	ACT above 18	N/R
From top 10% of their h.s. class	10%	From top quarter	25%
From top half	40%	1998 freshmen returning in 1999	90%

Application *Options:* eApply at www.CollegeQuest.com, Common Application, early admission, deferred entrance. *Application fee:* $42. *Required:* high school transcript; proficiency in English. *Required for some:* essay or personal statement; interview. *Recommended:* minimum 2.0 GPA.

Significant dates *Application deadlines:* 9/1 (freshmen), 9/1 (transfers). *Notification:* 9/10 (freshmen). *Financial aid deadline priority date:* 8/30.

Freshman Application Contact
Ms. Roula Lebetli, Admissions Officer, American College of Thessaloniki, PO Box 21021, Pylea, Thessaloniki 55510, Greece. **Phone:** 30-31398239. **E-mail:** rleb@ac.antolia.edu.gr

Visit CollegeQuest.com for information on majors offered and athletics.

THE COLLEGE OF SOUTHEASTERN EUROPE, THE AMERICAN UNIVERSITY OF ATHENS
Athens, Greece

- **Independent**, 4-year, founded 1982
- **Degree** bachelor's
- **Urban** campus
- **Coed**, 315 undergraduate students, 83% full-time, 42% women, 58% men
- **Moderately difficult** entrance level, 64% of applicants were admitted
- **$4687 tuition** and fees
- **$5.6 million endowment**

Students *Undergraduates:* 261 full-time, 54 part-time. Students come from 12 other countries.

Transferred in	22%

Faculty 61 (90% full-time), 64% with terminal degrees.

Expenses (1999–2000) *Tuition:* full-time $4530; part-time $186 per credit. *Required fees:* full-time $157. All figures are in U.S. dollars. Actual costs will vary with the rate of exchange. *Payment plan:* deferred payment.

Library The College of Southeastern Europe Library. *Operations spending 1999–2000:* $252,737. *Collection:* 35,000 titles, 213 serial subscriptions, 35 audiovisual materials.

College life *Housing:* college housing not available. *Most popular organizations:* Poetry & Literature Society, journalism association, drama club, political science association, Parliamentary Debating Society.

Campus security 24-hour emergency response devices.

After graduation 12 organizations recruited on campus 1997–98. 86% of class of 1998 had job offers within 6 months. *Career center:* 1 full-time, 2 part-time personnel. Services include job fairs, resume preparation, interview workshops, resume referral, career counseling, job bank, job interviews. *Graduate education:* 13% of class of 1999 went directly to graduate and professional school.

Freshmen 110 applied, 70 admitted, 72 enrolled.

SAT verbal scores above 500	N/R	SAT math scores above 500	N/R
ACT above 18	N/R	1998 freshmen returning in 1999	90%

Application *Option:* Common Application. *Application fee:* $50. *Required:* essay or personal statement; high school transcript; 2 letters of recommendation; interview.

Significant dates *Application deadline:* rolling (freshmen).

Freshman Application Contact
Ms. Thalia Poulos, Director of Admissions, The College of Southeastern Europe, The American University of Athens, 17 Patriarchou Ieremiou Street, GR-114 75 Athens, Greece. **Phone:** 30-1-6454403. **Toll-free phone:** 30-1-725-9301-2. **Fax:** 1-725-9304. **E-mail:** admissions@southeastern.edu.gr

Visit CollegeQuest.com for information on majors offered and athletics. College video available at CollegeQuest.com.

DEREE COLLEGE
Aghia Paraskevi, Greece

- **Independent**, 4-year, founded 1875
- **Degrees** associate and bachelor's
- **Urban** 60-acre campus
- **Coed**, 8,992 undergraduate students, 47% full-time, 76% women, 24% men
- **Moderately difficult** entrance level, 82% of applicants were admitted
- **25:1 student-to-undergraduate faculty ratio**
- **99% graduate** in 6 years or less
- **$3956 tuition** and fees

Part of American College of Greece.

Students *Undergraduates:* 4,183 full-time, 4,809 part-time. Students come from 30 other countries. *The most frequently chosen baccalaureate fields are:* business/marketing, communications/communication technologies, liberal arts/general studies.

Transferred in	2%

Faculty 292 (39% full-time).

Greece–Ireland

Deree College (continued)

Expenses (1999–2000) *Tuition:* full-time $3516; part-time $138 per credit. *Required fees:* full-time $440; $400 per year part-time. All figures are in U.S. dollars. Actual costs will vary with the rate of exchange. *Payment plan:* deferred payment. *Waivers:* employees or children of employees.

Library The College Learning Center plus 2 others. *Collection:* 78,000 titles, 300 serial subscriptions.

College life *Housing:* college housing not available. *Most popular organizations:* Ballroom Dance Club, aerobics club, photography club, debate club, student union.

Campus security 24-hour emergency response devices and patrols.

After graduation 160 organizations recruited on campus 1997–98. 40% of class of 1998 had job offers within 6 months. *Career center:* 3 full-time personnel. Services include job fairs, resume preparation, interview workshops, resume referral, career counseling, careers library, job bank, job interviews. *Graduate education:* 11% of class of 1999 went directly to graduate and professional school: 7% business, 4% graduate arts and sciences.

Freshmen 1,401 applied, 1,146 admitted, 3,611 enrolled.

| SAT verbal scores above 500 | 55% | SAT math scores above 500 | 55% |
| ACT above 18 | N/R | 1998 freshmen returning in 1999 | 81% |

Application *Option:* deferred entrance. *Application fee:* $110. *Required:* high school transcript; minimum 2.0 GPA; 3 letters of recommendation; interview; medical certificate. *Required for some:* essay or personal statement. *Recommended:* essay or personal statement.

Standardized tests *Admission: Required for some:* SAT I and SAT II or ACT, General Certificate of Education—Ordinary Level in English, Michigan Test of English Language Proficiency, or Cambridge Proficiency in English Examination.

Significant dates *Application deadlines:* 7/10 (freshmen), 7/1 (transfers). *Financial aid deadline:* 1/15.

Freshman Application Contact
Mrs. Konstantina Founta, Director of Admissions, Deree College, 6 Gravias Street, GR-153 42 Aghia Paraskevi, Athens, Greece. **Phone:** 301-600-9814. **Fax:** 1-600-9811. **E-mail:** dereeadm@hol.gr

Visit CollegeQuest.com for information on majors offered and athletics.

IRELAND

INSTITUTE OF PUBLIC ADMINISTRATION
Dublin, Ireland

Students *Undergraduates:* 951 part-time. *The most frequently chosen baccalaureate fields are:* business/marketing, health professions and related sciences, protective services/public administration. *Graduate:* 139 in graduate degree programs.

| Age 25 or older | 93% | Transferred in | 2% |

Faculty 55 (4% full-time), 49% with terminal degrees.

Expenses (1999–2000) Tuition charges are reported in Irish punt. *Tuition:* part-time 1300 per year.

Library *Operations spending 1999–2000:* $255,000.

College life *Housing:* college housing not available.

Campus security 24-hour emergency response devices.

Freshmen 279 applied, 279 admitted, 212 enrolled.

| SAT verbal scores above 500 | N/R | SAT math scores above 500 | N/R |
| ACT above 18 | N/R | | |

Significant dates *Application deadline:* 9/27 (freshmen). *Notification:* 9/30 (freshmen).

Freshman Application Contact
Ms. Mary T. Coolahan, Registrar, Institute of Public Administration, 52-61 Lansdowne Road, Dublin 4, Ireland. **Phone:** 1-668-6233. **Fax:** 1-668-9135.

Visit CollegeQuest.com for information on majors offered and athletics.

ITALY

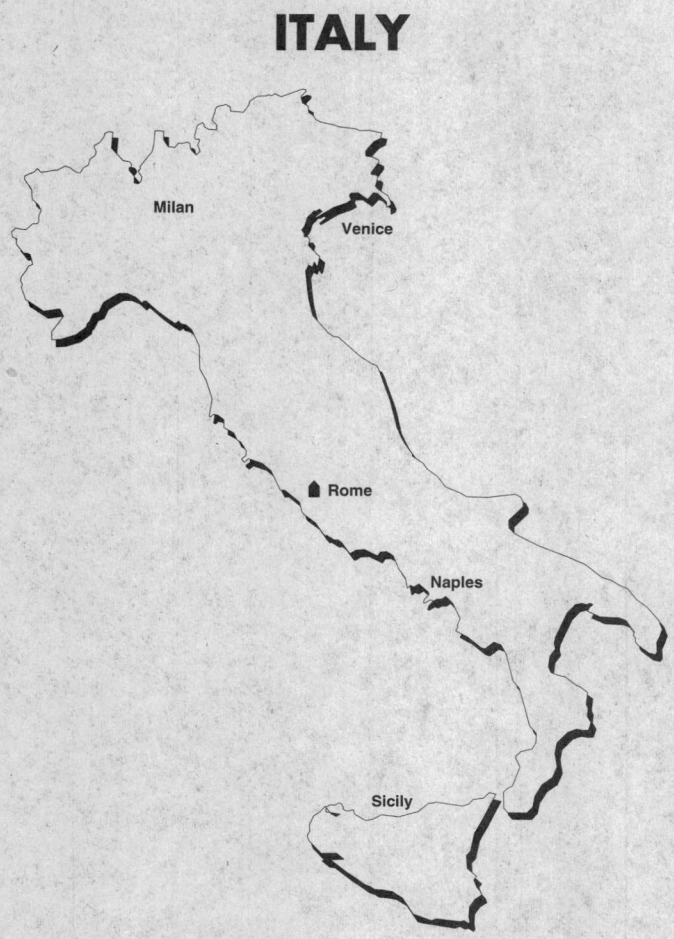

AMERICAN UNIVERSITY OF ROME
Rome, Italy

- **Independent**, 4-year, founded 1969
- **Degrees** associate and bachelor's
- **Urban** 1-acre campus
- **Coed**, 98 undergraduate students, 88% full-time, 62% women, 38% men
- **Moderately difficult** entrance level
- **9:1 student-to-undergraduate faculty ratio**
- **$9768 tuition** and fees

Students *Undergraduates:* 86 full-time, 12 part-time. *The most frequently chosen baccalaureate fields are:* business/marketing, foreign language/literature, social sciences and history.

Reside on campus 57% Age 25 or older 10%

Faculty 32 (56% full-time), 41% with terminal degrees.

Expenses (1999–2000) *One-time required fee:* $55. *Tuition:* full-time $9536; part-time $1192 per course. *Required fees:* full-time $232. Full-time tuition and fees vary according to course load and reciprocity agreements. Part-time tuition and fees vary according to course load. *College room only:* $5900. Room and board charges vary according to housing facility and location.

Library American University of Rome Library. *Collection:* 5,000 titles, 15 serial subscriptions.

College life *Housing: Options:* men-only, women-only. *Most popular organizations:* International Business Clubs, International Liberal Arts Club, drama club.

After graduation *Career center:* 1 full-time personnel. Services include resume preparation, career counseling, careers library, job interviews. ***Graduate education:*** 14% of class of 1999 went directly to graduate and professional school.

Freshmen 46 enrolled.

| SAT verbal scores above 500 | N/R | SAT math scores above 500 | N/R |
| ACT above 18 | N/R | 1998 freshmen returning in 1999 | 52% |

Application *Options:* Common Application, deferred entrance. *Application fee:* $55. *Required:* essay or personal statement; high school transcript; minimum 2.0 GPA; letters of recommendation. *Recommended:* minimum 2.5 GPA; interview.

Standardized tests *Admission: Required for some:* SAT I.

Significant dates *Application deadline:* 7/30 (freshmen). *Notification:* 8/15 (freshmen).

Freshman Application Contact
Mrs. Mary B. Handley, Director of Administration, American University of Rome, Via Pietro Roselli 4, 00153 Rome, Italy. **Phone:** 39-06-58330919. **Fax:** 202-966-3215. **E-mail:** aurinfo@aur.edu

Visit CollegeQuest.com for information on majors offered and athletics.

■ *See page 1166 for a narrative description.*

JOHN CABOT UNIVERSITY
Rome, Italy

Admissions Office Contact
John Cabot University, Via Della Lungara 233, 00165 Rome, Italy. **Fax:** 6-6832088.

KENYA

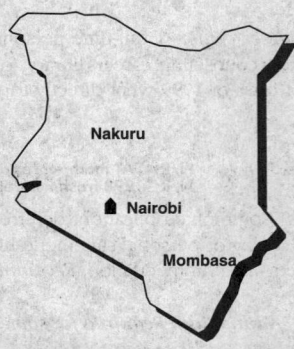

UNITED STATES INTERNATIONAL UNIVERSITY–AFRICA
Nairobi, Kenya

Admissions Office Contact
United States International University–Africa, 10455 Pomerado Road, San Diego, CA 92131-1799. **Fax:** 619-635-4739. **E-mail:** admission@usiu.edu

LEBANON

LEBANESE AMERICAN UNIVERSITY
Beirut, Lebanon

Admissions Office Contact
Lebanese American University, PO Box 13-5053, Beirut, Lebanon. **Fax:** 1-867098.

MEXICO

The Mexico City area includes the towns of Atizapan de Zaragoza, Col Tizapan A. Obregon, and Pachuca.

INSTITUTO TECNOLÓGICO Y DE ESTUDIOS SUPERIORES DE MONTERREY, CAMPUS CENTRAL DE VERACRUZ
Córdoba, Mexico

- **Independent**, comprehensive, founded 1981
- **Degrees** bachelor's and master's
- **Urban** 63-acre campus with easy access to Puebla
- **Coed**
- **Very difficult** entrance level

Part of Sistema Instituto Tecnológico y de Estudios Superiores de Monterrey.
Institutional Web site http://www.ver.itesm.mx/
College life *Housing:* college housing not available.
Campus security 24-hour emergency response devices.
Application *Option:* deferred entrance. *Preference* given to graduates from a high school in the ITESM system. *Required:* high school transcript. *Recommended:* essay or personal statement.
Standardized tests *Admission: Required:* SAT I.
Admissions Office Contact
Instituto Tecnológico y de Estudios Superiores de Monterrey, Campus Central de Veracruz, Avenida Eugenio Garza Sada 1, Apartado Postal 314, 94500 Córdoba, Veracruz, Mexico. **Fax:** 271-3-23-20.
Visit CollegeQuest.com for information on athletics. College video available at CollegeQuest.com.

INSTITUTO TECNOLÓGICO Y DE ESTUDIOS SUPERIORES DE MONTERREY, CAMPUS CHIAPAS
Tuxtla Gutiérrez, Mexico

- **Independent**, comprehensive, founded 1980
- **Degrees** bachelor's and master's
- **Suburban** 50-acre campus
- **Coed**
- **Very difficult** entrance level

Part of Sistema Instituto Tecnológico y de Estudios Superiores de Monterrey.
Institutional Web site http://www.sistema.itesm.mx/
College life *Housing:* college housing not available.
Campus security 24-hour emergency response devices and patrols, late-night transport-escort service.
Application *Option:* deferred entrance. *Preference* given to graduates from a high school in the ITESM system. *Required:* high school transcript. *Recommended:* essay or personal statement.
Standardized tests *Admission: Required:* SAT I.
Admissions Office Contact
Instituto Tecnológico y de Estudios Superiores de Monterrey, Campus Chiapas, Carretera a Tapanatepec Km 149&746, Apartado Postal 312, 29000 Tuxtla Gutiérrez, Chiapas, Mexico. **Fax:** 961-5-02-41.
Visit CollegeQuest.com for information on athletics. College video available at CollegeQuest.com.

Mexico

INSTITUTO TECNOLÓGICO Y DE ESTUDIOS SUPERIORES DE MONTERREY, CAMPUS CHIHUAHUA
Chihuahua, Mexico

- **Independent**, comprehensive, founded 1976
- **Degrees** bachelor's and master's
- **Urban** 28-acre campus
- **Coed**
- **Very difficult** entrance level

Part of Sistema Instituto Tecnológico y de Estudios Superiores de Monterrey.
Institutional Web site http://www.sistema.itesm.mx/
Campus security 24-hour emergency response devices and patrols.
Application *Options:* Common Application, deferred entrance. *Preference* given to graduates from a high school in the ITESM system. *Required:* high school transcript. *Recommended:* essay or personal statement.
Standardized tests *Admission: Required:* SAT I.
Admissions Office Contact
Instituto Tecnológico y de Estudios Superiores de Monterrey, Campus Chihuahua, Colegio Militar 2011, Colonia Nombre de Dios, Apartado Postal 28-B, 31110 Chihuahua, Chihuahua, Mexico. **Fax:** 14-24-07-07.
Visit CollegeQuest.com for information on athletics. College video available at CollegeQuest.com.

INSTITUTO TECNOLÓGICO Y DE ESTUDIOS SUPERIORES DE MONTERREY, CAMPUS CIUDAD DE MÉXICO
Ciudad de Mexico, Mexico

- **Independent**, comprehensive, founded 1973
- **Degrees** bachelor's, master's, and doctoral
- **Urban** 25-acre campus
- **Coed**
- **Very difficult** entrance level

Part of Sistema Instituto Tecnológico y de Estudios Superiores de Monterrey.
Institutional Web site http://www.ccm.itesm.mx/
College life *Housing:* college housing not available.
Campus security 24-hour emergency response devices and patrols.
Application *Option:* deferred entrance. *Preference* given to graduates from a high school in the ITESM system. *Required:* high school transcript. *Recommended:* essay or personal statement.
Standardized tests *Admission: Required:* SAT I.
Admissions Office Contact
Instituto Tecnológico y de Estudios Superiores de Monterrey, Campus Ciudad de México, Calle del Puente #222 esquina con Periférico, 14380 Colonia Huipulco, Tlalpan, MDF, Mexico. **Fax:** 5-673-25-00.
Visit CollegeQuest.com for information on athletics. College video available at CollegeQuest.com.

INSTITUTO TECNOLÓGICO Y DE ESTUDIOS SUPERIORES DE MONTERREY, CAMPUS CIUDAD JUÁREZ
Ciudad Juárez, Mexico

- **Independent**, comprehensive, founded 1983
- **Degrees** bachelor's and master's
- **Suburban** 25-acre campus
- **Coed**
- **Very difficult** entrance level

Part of Sistema Instituto Tecnológico y de Estudios Superiores de Monterrey.
Institutional Web site http://www.sistema.itesm.mx/
College life *Housing:* college housing not available.
Campus security 24-hour emergency response devices and patrols.
Application *Option:* deferred entrance. *Preference* given to graduates from a high school in the ITESM system. *Required:* high school transcript. *Recommended:* essay or personal statement.
Standardized tests *Admission: Required:* SAT I.
Admissions Office Contact
Instituto Tecnológico y de Estudios Superiores de Monterrey, Campus Ciudad Juárez, Boulevard Tomas Fernandez y Avenida A J Bermudez, Apartado Postal 3105-J, 32320 Ciudad Juárez, Chihuahua, Mexico. **Fax:** 16-25-17-73.
Visit CollegeQuest.com for information on athletics. College video and electronic viewbook available at CollegeQuest.com.

INSTITUTO TECNOLÓGICO Y DE ESTUDIOS SUPERIORES DE MONTERREY, CAMPUS CIUDAD OBREGÓN
Ciudad Obregón, Mexico

- **Independent**, comprehensive, founded 1973
- **Degrees** bachelor's and master's
- **Suburban** 180-acre campus with easy access to Hermosillo
- **Coed**
- **Very difficult** entrance level

Part of Sistema Instituto Tecnológico y de Estudios Superiores de Monterrey.
Institutional Web site http://www.cob.itesm.mx/
College life *Housing:* college housing not available.
Campus security 24-hour emergency response devices.
Application *Option:* deferred entrance. *Preference* given to graduates from a high school in the ITESM system. *Required:* high school transcript. *Recommended:* essay or personal statement.
Standardized tests *Admission: Required:* SAT I.
Admissions Office Contact
Instituto Tecnológico y de Estudios Superiores de Monterrey, Campus Ciudad Obregón, Dr Norman E Bourlaugh Km 14, Apartado Postal 662, 85000 Ciudad Obregón, Sonora, Mexico. **Fax:** 641-4-12-20.
Visit CollegeQuest.com for information on athletics. College video available at CollegeQuest.com.

INSTITUTO TECNOLÓGICO Y DE ESTUDIOS SUPERIORES DE MONTERREY, CAMPUS COLIMA
Colima, Mexico

- **Independent**, comprehensive, founded 1980
- **Degrees** bachelor's and master's
- **Suburban** 13-acre campus with easy access to Guadalajara
- **Coed**
- **Very difficult** entrance level

Part of Sistema Instituto Tecnológico y de Estudios Superiores de Monterrey.
Institutional Web site http://www.sistema.itesm.mx/
College life *Housing:* college housing not available.
Campus security 24-hour patrols.
Application *Option:* deferred entrance. *Preference* given to graduates from a high school in the ITESM system. *Required:* high school transcript. *Recommended:* essay or personal statement.
Standardized tests *Admission: Required:* SAT I.

Mexico

Admissions Office Contact
Instituto Tecnológico y de Estudios Superiores de Monterrey, Campus Colima, Prolongacion Ignacio Sandoval s/n, Fraccionamiento Jardines de Vista Hermosa, Apartado Postal 190, 28010 Colima, Colima, Mexico. **Fax:** 331-4-26-05.
Visit CollegeQuest.com for information on athletics. College video available at CollegeQuest.com.

INSTITUTO TECNOLÓGICO Y DE ESTUDIOS SUPERIORES DE MONTERREY, CAMPUS ESTADO DE MÉXICO
Atizapán de Zaragoza, Mexico

- **Independent**, comprehensive, founded 1978
- **Degrees** bachelor's, master's, and doctoral
- **Urban** 50-acre campus
- **Coed**
- **Very difficult** entrance level

Part of Sistema Instituto Tecnológico y de Estudios Superiores de Monterrey.
Institutional Web site http://www.cem.itesm.mx/
College life *Housing:* college housing not available.
Campus security 24-hour emergency response devices and patrols, late-night transport-escort service, closed circuit TV monitors, seismic alarm devices.
Application *Option:* deferred entrance. *Preference* given to graduates from a high school in the ITESM system. *Required:* high school transcript. *Recommended:* essay or personal statement.
Standardized tests *Admission: Required:* SAT I.
Admissions Office Contact
Instituto Tecnológico y de Estudios Superiores de Monterrey, Campus Estado de México, Camino al Lago de Guadalupe Km 4, Apartado Postal 214, 52500 Atizapán de Zaragoza, Mexico. **Fax:** 5-379-08-80.
Visit CollegeQuest.com for information on athletics. College video available at CollegeQuest.com.

INSTITUTO TECNOLÓGICO Y DE ESTUDIOS SUPERIORES DE MONTERREY, CAMPUS GUADALAJARA
Zapopan, Mexico

- **Independent**, comprehensive, founded 1991
- **Degrees** bachelor's and master's
- **Urban** 47-acre campus
- **Coed**
- **Very difficult** entrance level

Part of Sistema Instituto Tecnológico y de Estudios Superiores de Monterrey.
Institutional Web site http://www.gda.itesm.mx/
College life *Housing: Option:* coed.
Campus security 24-hour emergency response devices and patrols, student patrols.
Application *Option:* deferred entrance. *Preference* given to graduates from a high school in the ITESM system. *Required:* high school transcript. *Recommended:* essay or personal statement.
Standardized tests *Admission: Required:* SAT I.
Admissions Office Contact
Instituto Tecnológico y de Estudios Superiores de Monterrey, Campus Guadalajara, Avenida General Ramón Corona 2514, 44100 Zapopan, Jalisco, Mexico. **Fax:** 3-669-30-61.
Visit CollegeQuest.com for information on athletics. College video available at CollegeQuest.com.

INSTITUTO TECNOLÓGICO Y DE ESTUDIOS SUPERIORES DE MONTERREY, CAMPUS HIDALGO
Pachuca, Mexico

- **Independent**, comprehensive, founded 1980
- **Degrees** bachelor's and master's
- **Suburban** 50-acre campus with easy access to Mexico City
- **Coed**
- **Very difficult** entrance level

Part of Sistema Instituto Tecnológico y de Estudios Superiores de Monterrey.
Institutional Web site http://www.sistema.itesm.mx/
College life *Housing:* college housing not available.
Application *Option:* deferred entrance. *Preference* given to graduates from a high school in the ITESM system. *Required:* high school transcript. *Recommended:* essay or personal statement.
Standardized tests *Admission: Required:* SAT I.
Admissions Office Contact
Instituto Tecnológico y de Estudios Superiores de Monterrey, Campus Hidalgo, Apartado Postal 237, 42090 Pachuca, Hidalgo, Mexico. **Fax:** 771-4-25-22.
E-mail: lizmelo@campus.hgo.itesm.mx
Visit CollegeQuest.com for information on athletics. College video available at CollegeQuest.com.

INSTITUTO TECNOLÓGICO Y DE ESTUDIOS SUPERIORES DE MONTERREY, CAMPUS IRAPUATO
Irapuato, Mexico

- **Independent**, comprehensive, founded 1976
- **Degrees** bachelor's, master's, and doctoral
- **Suburban** campus with easy access to León
- **Coed**
- **Very difficult** entrance level

Part of Sistema Instituto Tecnológico y de Estudios Superiores de Monterrey.
Institutional Web site http://www.sistema.itesm.mx/
College life *Housing:* college housing not available.
Campus security 24-hour patrols.
Application *Option:* deferred entrance. *Preference* given to graduates from a high school in the ITESM system. *Required:* high school transcript. *Recommended:* essay or personal statement.
Standardized tests *Admission: Required:* SAT I.
Admissions Office Contact
Instituto Tecnológico y de Estudios Superiores de Monterrey, Campus Irapuato, Paseo Mirador del Valle No. 445, Col. Villas de Irapuato, Apartado Postal 568, 36660 Irapuato, Guanajuato, Mexico. **Fax:** 462-3-05-80.
Visit CollegeQuest.com for information on athletics. College video available at CollegeQuest.com.

INSTITUTO TECNOLÓGICO Y DE ESTUDIOS SUPERIORES DE MONTERREY, CAMPUS LAGUNA
Torreón, Mexico

- **Independent**, comprehensive, founded 1976
- **Degrees** bachelor's and master's
- **Urban** 17-acre campus
- **Coed**
- **Very difficult** entrance level

Part of Sistema Instituto Tecnológico y de Estudios Superiores de Monterrey.

Mexico

Instituto Tecnológico y de Estudios Superiores de Monterrey, Campus Laguna (continued)
Institutional Web site http://www.lag.itesm.mx/
College life *Housing:* college housing not available.
Campus security 24-hour emergency response devices and patrols.
Application *Option:* deferred entrance. *Preference* given to graduates from a high school in the ITESM system. *Required:* high school transcript. *Recommended:* essay or personal statement.
Standardized tests *Admission: Required:* SAT I.
Admissions Office Contact
Instituto Tecnológico y de Estudios Superiores de Monterrey, Campus Laguna, Paseo del Tecnologico s/n Ampliacion La Rosita, Apartado Postal 506, 27250 Torreón, Coahuila, Mexico. **Fax:** 17-20-63-63.
Visit CollegeQuest.com for information on athletics. College video available at CollegeQuest.com.

INSTITUTO TECNOLÓGICO Y DE ESTUDIOS SUPERIORES DE MONTERREY, CAMPUS LEÓN
León, Mexico

- **Independent**, comprehensive, founded 1978
- **Degrees** bachelor's and master's
- **Urban** 40-acre campus
- **Coed**, 1,003 undergraduate students, 96% full-time, 41% women, 59% men
- **Very difficult** entrance level, 63% of applicants were admitted

Part of Sistema Instituto Tecnológico y de Estudios Superiores de Monterrey.
Students *Undergraduates:* 966 full-time, 37 part-time. *Graduate:* 133 in graduate degree programs.
Faculty 159 (43% full-time).
Library *Collection:* 34,969 titles, 179 serial subscriptions.
College life *Housing:* college housing not available.
Campus security 24-hour emergency response devices and patrols.
After graduation *Career center:* Services include career counseling, job bank.
Freshmen 326 applied, 206 admitted, 164 enrolled.
SAT verbal scores above 500 N/R SAT math scores above 500 N/R
ACT above 18 N/R
Application *Option:* deferred entrance. *Preference* given to graduates from a high school in the ITESM system. *Required:* high school transcript. *Recommended:* essay or personal statement.
Standardized tests *Admission: Required:* SAT I.
Significant dates *Application deadline:* 3/21 (freshmen). *Notification:* continuous until 4/5 (freshmen).
Freshman Application Contact
Lic. Eddie Villegas, Registrar, Instituto Tecnológico y de Estudios Superiores de Monterrey, Campus León, Apdo. Postal No. 872, 37120 León, Guanajuato, Mexico. **Phone:** 47-17-10-00 Ext. 131. **Fax:** 47-17-79-32.
Visit CollegeQuest.com for information on majors offered and athletics. College video available at CollegeQuest.com.

INSTITUTO TECNOLÓGICO Y DE ESTUDIOS SUPERIORES DE MONTERREY, CAMPUS MAZATLÁN
Mazatlán, Mexico

- **Independent**, comprehensive, founded 1983
- **Degrees** bachelor's and master's
- **Suburban** 50-acre campus with easy access to Hermosillo
- **Coed**
- **Very difficult** entrance level

Part of Sistema Instituto Tecnológico y de Estudios Superiores de Monterrey.
Institutional Web site http://www.muz.itesm.mx/
College life *Housing:* college housing not available.
Campus security 24-hour emergency response devices and patrols.
Application *Option:* deferred entrance. *Preference* given to graduates from a high school in the ITESM system. *Required:* high school transcript. *Recommended:* essay or personal statement.
Standardized tests *Admission: Required:* SAT I.
Admissions Office Contact
Instituto Tecnológico y de Estudios Superiores de Monterrey, Campus Mazatlán, Carretera Mazatlan-Higueras, Km 3, Camino al Conchi, Apartado Postal 799, 82000 Mazatlán, Sinaloa, Mexico. **Fax:** 69-80-11-95.
Visit CollegeQuest.com for information on athletics. College video available at CollegeQuest.com.

INSTITUTO TECNOLÓGICO Y DE ESTUDIOS SUPERIORES DE MONTERREY, CAMPUS MONTERREY
Monterrey, Mexico

- **Independent**, university, founded 1943
- **Degrees** bachelor's, master's, and doctoral
- **Urban** 86-acre campus
- **Coed**, 14,275 undergraduate students, 82% full-time, 37% women, 63% men
- **Very difficult** entrance level, 69% of applicants were admitted
- **$6900 tuition** and fees

Part of Sistema Instituto Tecnológico y de Estudios Superiores de Monterrey.
Students *Undergraduates:* 11,688 full-time, 2,587 part-time. Students come from 25 other countries. *The most frequently chosen baccalaureate fields are:* business/marketing, engineering/engineering technologies, trade and industry. *Graduate:* 2,352 in graduate degree programs.
Faculty 1,134 (46% full-time), 100% with terminal degrees.
Expenses (2000–2001) *Tuition:* full-time $6900; part-time $288 per credit hour. Full-time tuition and fees vary according to course load. Part-time tuition and fees vary according to course load. *College room only:* $2333. Room and board charges vary according to housing facility. All figures are in U.S. dollars. Actual costs will vary with the rate of exchange. *Payment plans:* installment, deferred payment. *Waivers:* employees or children of employees.
Library *Collection:* 315,012 titles, 2,300 serial subscriptions.
College life *Housing: Options:* men-only, women-only. *Most popular organizations:* care, feitesm, difusion cultural, sociedades de alumnos.
Campus security 24-hour patrols, late-night transport-escort service.
After graduation *Career center:* 5 full-time, 2 part-time personnel. Services include job fairs, resume preparation, interview workshops, career counseling, job bank, job interviews.
Freshmen 2,636 applied, 1,813 admitted, 1,505 enrolled.
SAT verbal scores above 500 N/R SAT math scores above 500 N/R
ACT above 18 N/R
Application *Option:* deferred entrance. *Preference* given to graduates from a high school in the ITESM system. *Required:* high school transcript. *Recommended:* essay or personal statement.
Standardized tests *Admission: Required:* SAT I.
Significant dates *Application deadline:* 3/21 (freshmen). *Notification:* continuous until 4/5 (freshmen).
Freshman Application Contact
Lic. Julieta Miery Teran, Director of Admissions, Instituto Tecnológico y de Estudios Superiores de Monterrey, Campus Monterrey, Avenida Eugenio Garza Sada 2501 Sur Colonia Tecnnologico, Sucursal de Correos J, 64849 Monterrey, Nuevo León, Mexico. **Phone:** 83-58-46-50. **Fax:** 83-58-89-31.
Visit CollegeQuest.com for information on majors offered and athletics. College video and electronic viewbook available at CollegeQuest.com.

Mexico

INSTITUTO TECNOLÓGICO Y DE ESTUDIOS SUPERIORES DE MONTERREY, CAMPUS MORELOS
Temixco, Mexico

- **Independent**, comprehensive, founded 1980
- **Degrees** bachelor's and master's
- **Suburban** 5-acre campus with easy access to Mexico City
- **Coed**
- **Very difficult** entrance level

Part of Sistema Instituto Tecnológico y de Estudios Superiores de Monterrey.

Institutional Web site http://www.mor.itesm.mx/
College life *Housing:* college housing not available.
Campus security 24-hour emergency response devices and patrols.
Application *Option:* deferred entrance. *Preference* given to graduates from a high school in the ITESM system. *Required:* high school transcript. *Recommended:* essay or personal statement.
Standardized tests *Placement: Required:* SAT I
Admissions Office Contact
Instituto Tecnológico y de Estudios Superiores de Monterrey, Campus Morelos, Paseo de la Reforma 182-A, Colonia Lomas de Cuernavaca, 62000 Temixco, Morelos, Mexico. **Fax:** 73-18-49-51.
Visit CollegeQuest.com for information on athletics. College video available at CollegeQuest.com.

INSTITUTO TECNOLÓGICO Y DE ESTUDIOS SUPERIORES DE MONTERREY, CAMPUS QUERÉTARO
Querétaro, Mexico

- **Independent**, comprehensive, founded 1975
- **Degrees** bachelor's and master's
- **Urban** 205-acre campus with easy access to Mexico City
- **Coed**, 2,540 undergraduate students, 94% full-time, 42% women, 58% men
- **Very difficult** entrance level, 75% of applicants were admitted
- **$6500 tuition** and fees

Part of Sistema Instituto Tecnológico y de Estudios Superiores de Monterrey.

Students *Undergraduates:* 2,378 full-time, 162 part-time. *Graduate:* 263 in graduate degree programs.
Faculty 324 (42% full-time).
Expenses (1999–2000) *Tuition:* full-time $6500; part-time $170 per credit hour. Full-time tuition and fees vary according to course load. Part-time tuition and fees vary according to course load. All figures are in U.S. dollars. Actual costs will vary with the rate of exchange. *Payment plans:* tuition prepayment, installment, deferred payment. *Waivers:* employees or children of employees.
Library *Collection:* 95,201 titles, 613 serial subscriptions.
College life *Housing:* college housing not available.
Campus security 24-hour emergency response devices and patrols.
After graduation *Career center:* Services include career counseling, job bank.
Freshmen 1,032 applied, 774 admitted, 370 enrolled.

SAT verbal scores above 500	N/R	SAT math scores above 500	N/R
ACT above 18	N/R		

Application *Option:* deferred entrance. *Preference* given to graduates from a high school in the ITESM system. *Required:* high school transcript. *Recommended:* essay or personal statement.
Standardized tests *Admission: Required:* SAT I.
Significant dates *Application deadline:* 3/21 (freshmen). *Notification:* continuous until 4/5 (freshmen).

Freshman Application Contact
Lic. Marco Vinicio Lopez, Registrar, Instituto Tecnológico y de Estudios Superiores de Monterrey, Campus Querétaro, Avenida Epigmenio Gonzalez #500, Fracc. San Pablo, 76000 Querétaro, Querétaro, Mexico. **Phone:** 42-17-38-25 Ext. 156. **Fax:** 42-17-35-23.
Visit CollegeQuest.com for information on majors offered and athletics. College video available at CollegeQuest.com.

INSTITUTO TECNOLÓGICO Y DE ESTUDIOS SUPERIORES DE MONTERREY, CAMPUS SALTILLO
Saltillo, Mexico

- **Independent**, comprehensive, founded 1974
- **Degrees** bachelor's and master's
- **Suburban** 14-acre campus with easy access to Monterrey
- **Coed**
- **Very difficult** entrance level

Part of Sistema Instituto Tecnológico y de Estudios Superiores de Monterrey.

Institutional Web site http://www.sal.itesm.mx/
College life *Housing:* college housing not available.
Campus security 24-hour emergency response devices and patrols.
Application *Option:* deferred entrance. *Preference* given to graduates from a high school in the ITESM system. *Required:* high school transcript. *Recommended:* essay or personal statement.
Standardized tests *Admission: Required:* SAT I.
Admissions Office Contact
Instituto Tecnológico y de Estudios Superiores de Monterrey, Campus Saltillo, Prolongacion Juan de la Barrera 1241 Ote, Apartado Postal 539, 25270 Saltillo, Coahuila, Mexico. **Fax:** 84-16-53-22.
Visit CollegeQuest.com for information on athletics. College video available at CollegeQuest.com.

INSTITUTO TECNOLÓGICO Y DE ESTUDIOS SUPERIORES DE MONTERREY, CAMPUS SAN LUIS POTOSÍ
San Luis Potosí, Mexico

- **Independent**, comprehensive, founded 1975
- **Degrees** bachelor's and master's
- **Suburban** 17-acre campus
- **Coed**
- **Very difficult** entrance level

Part of Sistema Instituto Tecnológico y de Estudios Superiores de Monterrey.

Institutional Web site http://www.slp.itesm.mx/
College life *Housing:* college housing not available.
Campus security 24-hour emergency response devices and patrols.
Application *Option:* deferred entrance. *Preference* given to graduates from a high school in the ITESM system. *Required:* high school transcript. *Recommended:* essay or personal statement.
Standardized tests *Admission: Required:* SAT I.
Admissions Office Contact
Instituto Tecnológico y de Estudios Superiores de Monterrey, Campus San Luis Potosí, Avenida Robles 600, Colonia Jacarandas, Apartado Postal 1473 Suc E, 78140 San Luis Potosí, SLP, Mexico. **Fax:** 48-11-93-44.
Visit CollegeQuest.com for information on athletics. College video available at CollegeQuest.com.

Mexico

INSTITUTO TECNOLÓGICO Y DE ESTUDIOS SUPERIORES DE MONTERREY, CAMPUS SINALOA
Culiacán, Mexico

- **Independent**, comprehensive, founded 1983
- **Degrees** bachelor's and master's
- **Suburban** 50-acre campus with easy access to Hermosillo
- **Coed**
- **Very difficult** entrance level

Part of Sistema Instituto Tecnológico y de Estudios Superiores de Monterrey.
Institutional Web site http://www.sin.itesm.mx/
College life *Housing:* college housing not available.
Campus security 24-hour emergency response devices.
Application *Option:* deferred entrance. *Preference* given to graduates from a high school in the ITESM system. *Required:* high school transcript. *Recommended:* essay or personal statement.
Standardized tests *Admission: Required:* SAT I.
Admissions Office Contact
Instituto Tecnológico y de Estudios Superiores de Monterrey, Campus Sinaloa, Boulevard Culiacán 3773, Apartado Postal 69-F, 80800 Culiacán, Sinaloa, Mexico. **Fax:** 67-17-03-59.
Visit CollegeQuest.com for information on athletics. College video available at CollegeQuest.com.

INSTITUTO TECNOLÓGICO Y DE ESTUDIOS SUPERIORES DE MONTERREY, CAMPUS SONORA NORTE
Hermosillo, Mexico

- **Independent**, comprehensive, founded 1983
- **Degrees** bachelor's and master's
- **Suburban** 44-acre campus
- **Coed**
- **Very difficult** entrance level

Part of Sistema Instituto Tecnológico y de Estudios Superiores de Monterrey.
Institutional Web site http://www.her.itesm.mx/
College life *Housing:* college housing not available.
Campus security 24-hour emergency response devices and patrols.
Application *Option:* deferred entrance. *Preference* given to graduates from a high school in the ITESM system. *Required:* high school transcript. *Recommended:* essay or personal statement.
Standardized tests *Admission: Required:* SAT I.
Admissions Office Contact
Instituto Tecnológico y de Estudios Superiores de Monterrey, Campus Sonora Norte, Carretera Hermosillo-Nogales Km 9, Apartado Postal 216, 83000 Hermosillo, Sonora, Mexico. **Fax:** 62-80-04-15.
Visit CollegeQuest.com for information on athletics. College video available at CollegeQuest.com.

INSTITUTO TECNOLÓGICO Y DE ESTUDIOS SUPERIORES DE MONTERREY, CAMPUS TAMPICO
Altimira, Mexico

- **Independent**, comprehensive, founded 1981
- **Degrees** bachelor's and master's
- **Suburban** 53-acre campus
- **Coed**, 641 undergraduate students, 90% full-time, 45% women, 55% men
- **Very difficult** entrance level, 84% of applicants were admitted
- **$6500 tuition** and fees

Part of Sistema Instituto Tecnológico y de Estudios Superiores de Monterrey.
Students *Undergraduates:* 575 full-time, 66 part-time. Students come from 1 other country. *Graduate:* 215 in graduate degree programs.
Faculty 118 (23% full-time).
Expenses (1999–2000) *Tuition:* full-time $6500; part-time $170 per credit hour. Full-time tuition and fees vary according to course load. Part-time tuition and fees vary according to course load. All figures are in U.S. dollars. Actual costs will vary with the rate of exchange. *Payment plan:* tuition prepayment. *Waivers:* employees or children of employees.
Library *Collection:* 25,348 titles, 115 serial subscriptions.
College life *Housing:* college housing not available.
Campus security 24-hour emergency response devices and patrols.
After graduation *Career center:* Services include career counseling, job bank.
Freshmen 222 applied, 186 admitted, 153 enrolled.
SAT verbal scores above 500 N/R SAT math scores above 500 N/R
ACT above 18 N/R
Application *Option:* deferred entrance. *Preference* given to graduates from a high school in the ITESM system. *Required:* high school transcript. *Recommended:* essay or personal statement.
Standardized tests *Admission: Required:* SAT I.
Significant dates *Application deadline:* 3/21 (freshmen). *Notification:* continuous until 4/5 (freshmen).
Freshman Application Contact
Ing. Javier Ponce, Registrar, Instituto Tecnológico y de Estudios Superiores de Monterrey, Campus Tampico, Apdo. Postal 7, Conedor Industrial, Canekra Tampico-Mark, 89120 Altimira, Tamaulipas, Mexico. **Phone:** 126-4-19-79. **Fax:** 12-64-19-79.
Visit CollegeQuest.com for information on majors offered and athletics. College video available at CollegeQuest.com.

INSTITUTO TECNOLÓGICO Y DE ESTUDIOS SUPERIORES DE MONTERREY, CAMPUS TOLUCA
Toluca, Mexico

- **Independent**, comprehensive, founded 1982
- **Degrees** bachelor's and master's
- **Suburban** 25-acre campus with easy access to Mexico City
- **Coed**
- **Very difficult** entrance level

Part of Sistema Instituto Tecnológico y de Estudios Superiores de Monterrey.
Institutional Web site http://www.tol.itesm.mx/
College life *Housing:* college housing not available.
Campus security 24-hour patrols.
Application *Option:* deferred entrance. *Preference* given to graduates from a high school in the ITESM system. *Required:* high school transcript. *Recommended:* essay or personal statement.
Standardized tests *Admission: Required:* SAT I.
Admissions Office Contact
Instituto Tecnológico y de Estudios Superiores de Monterrey, Campus Toluca, Ex-hacienda La Pila, 100 metros al norte de San Antonio Buenavista, 50252 Toluca, Estado de Mexico, Mexico. **Fax:** 72-74-11-78.
Visit CollegeQuest.com for information on athletics. College video available at CollegeQuest.com.

INSTITUTO TECNOLÓGICO Y DE ESTUDIOS SUPERIORES DE MONTERREY, CAMPUS ZACATECAS
Zacatecas, Mexico

- **Independent**, comprehensive, founded 1985
- **Degrees** bachelor's and master's

- **Suburban** 30-acre campus with easy access to San Luis Potosi
- **Coed**
- **Very difficult** entrance level

Part of Sistema Instituto Tecnológico y de Estudios Superiores de Monterrey.
Institutional Web site http://www.zac.itesm.mx/
College life *Housing:* college housing not available.
Campus security 24-hour emergency response devices and patrols.
Application *Option:* deferred entrance. *Preference* given to graduates from a high school in the ITESM system. *Required:* high school transcript. *Recommended:* essay or personal statement.
Standardized tests *Admission: Required:* SAT I.
Admissions Office Contact
Instituto Tecnológico y de Estudios Superiores de Monterrey, Campus Zacatecas, Calzada Pedro Coronel #16, Frente al Club Bernades, Municipio de Guadalupe, 98000 Zacatecas, Zacatecas, Mexico. **Fax:** 492-3-04-60.
Visit CollegeQuest.com for information on athletics. College video available at CollegeQuest.com.

UNITED STATES INTERNATIONAL UNIVERSITY—MEXICO
Mexico City, Mexico
Admissions Office Contact
United States International University–Mexico, 10455 Pomerado Road, San Diego, CA 92131-1799. **Fax:** 619-635-4739. **E-mail:** admissions@usiu.edu

UNIVERSIDAD DE LAS AMERICAS, A.C.
Mexico City, Mexico
Admissions Office Contact
Universidad de las Americas, A.C., Calle de Puebla 223, Col. Roma, Mexico City 06700, Mexico. **Fax:** 5-511-6040.

UNIVERSIDAD DE LAS AMÉRICAS—PUEBLA
Cholula, Mexico
Admissions Office Contact
Universidad de las Américas–Puebla, Cholula Apartado 359, 72820 Cholula, Mexico. **Fax:** 22-29-20-18. **E-mail:** jvarela@udlapvms.pue.udlap.mx

NICARAGUA

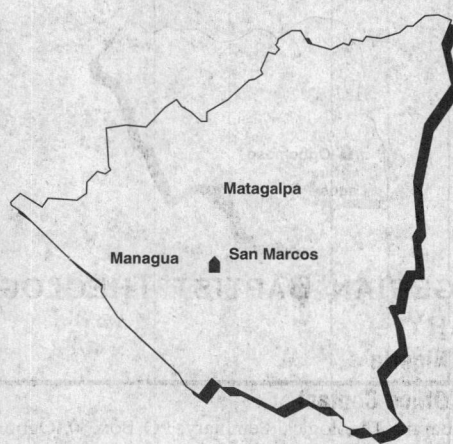

UNIVERSITY OF MOBILE—LATIN AMERICAN BRANCH CAMPUS
San Marcos, Nicaragua
- **Independent Southern Baptist**, 4-year, founded 1993
- **Degree** bachelor's
- **Small-town** 2-acre campus with easy access to Managua
- **Coed**
- **Moderately difficult** entrance level

Part of University of Mobile.
Institutional Web site http://www.mobile.edu.ni/
College life *Most popular organizations:* Humanities Club, Science Club, Computer Science Club, Drama Club, Business Association.
Campus security 24-hour patrols.
Application *Options:* early admission, deferred entrance. *Application fee:* $50. *Required:* high school transcript; minimum 2.0 GPA.
Standardized tests *Admission: Required:* SAT I or ACT, Michigan Test of English Language Proficiency.
Admissions Office Contact
University of Mobile–Latin American Branch Campus, San Marcos, Carazo, Nicaragua.
Visit CollegeQuest.com for information on athletics. College video available at CollegeQuest.com.

NIGERIA

THE NIGERIAN BAPTIST THEOLOGICAL SEMINARY
Ogbomoso, Nigeria

Admissions Office Contact
The Nigerian Baptist Theological Seminary, PO Box 30, Ogbomoso, Oyo, Nigeria.

SPAIN

SCHILLER INTERNATIONAL UNIVERSITY
Madrid, Spain

Admissions Office Contact
Schiller International University, San Bernardo 97-99, Edif. Colomina, 28015 Madrid, Spain. **Fax:** 91-445-2110.

SWITZERLAND

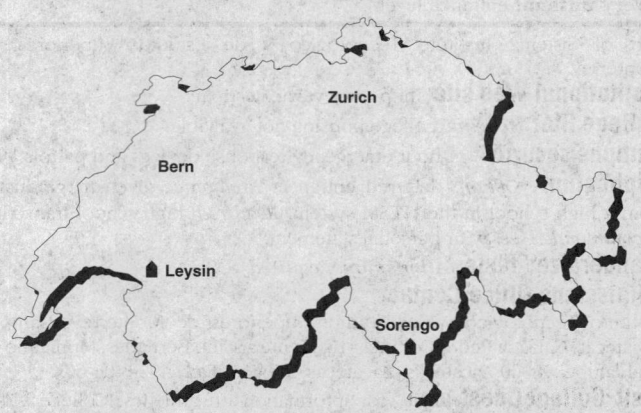

ECOLE HÔTELIÈRE DE LAUSANNE
Lausanne, Switzerland

Admissions Office Contact
Ecole Hôtelière de Lausanne, 1000 Lausanne 25, Switzerland. **Fax:** 21-784-1407.

FRANKLIN COLLEGE SWITZERLAND
Sorengo, Switzerland

- **Independent**, 4-year, founded 1969
- **Degrees** associate and bachelor's
- **Suburban** 5-acre campus
- **Coed**, 242 undergraduate students, 96% full-time, 62% women, 38% men
- **Moderately difficult** entrance level, 91% of applicants were admitted
- **10:1 student-to-undergraduate faculty ratio**
- **45.24% graduate** in 6 years or less
- **$19,320 tuition** and fees

Franklin College is a 4-year, coeducational, residential American liberal arts college located in southern Switzerland and specializing in international studies. Students from more than 50 countries attend. Semester and Year Abroad students are welcome. Summer sessions are offered May–July. Every semester, students take faculty-led Academic Travel trips to destinations worldwide.

Students *Undergraduates:* 232 full-time, 10 part-time. Students come from 25 states and territories, 48 other countries. *The most frequently chosen baccalaureate fields are:* business/marketing, communications/communication technologies, social sciences and history.

Reside on campus	70%	Age 25 or older	3%
Transferred in	6%		

Faculty 38 (45% full-time), 100% with terminal degrees.

Expenses (1999–2000) *Comprehensive fee:* $27,170 includes full-time tuition ($18,200), mandatory fees ($1120), and room and board ($7850). *College room only:* $5500. Room and board charges vary according to housing facility. *Part-time tuition:* $1770 per course. *Part-time fees:* $110 per course. *Payment plans:* installment, deferred payment. *Waivers:* employees or children of employees.

Library David R. Grace Library. *Operations spending 1999–2000:* $181,320. *Collection:* 28,690 titles, 155 serial subscriptions, 1,506 audiovisual materials.

College life *Housing:* on-campus residence required through sophomore year. *Options:* coed, men-only, women-only.

After graduation *Career center:* Services include resume preparation, interview workshops, career counseling, careers library, job interviews. *Graduate education:* 30% of class of 1999 went directly to graduate and professional school: 20% business, 10% graduate arts and sciences.

Freshmen 249 applied, 226 admitted, 100 enrolled.

SAT verbal scores above 500	95%	SAT math scores above 500	85%
ACT above 18	N/R	From top 10% of their h.s. class	11%
From top quarter	28%	From top half	60%
1998 freshmen returning in 1999	42%		

Application *Options:* Common Application, early admission, early decision, early action, deferred entrance. *Application fee:* $40. *Required:* essay or personal statement; high school transcript; minimum 2.0 GPA; 3 letters of recommendation. *Recommended:* interview.
Standardized tests *Admission: Required:* SAT I or ACT. *Recommended:* SAT II Subject Tests, SAT II: Writing Test.
Significant dates *Application deadlines:* 3/15 (freshmen), 6/15 (transfers). *Early decision:* 12/1, 12/1. *Notification:* 1/1 (early decision), 1/15 (early action). *Financial aid deadline priority date:* 2/15.
Freshman Application Contact
Ms. Karen Ballard, Director of Admissions, Franklin College Switzerland, 135 East 65th Street, New York, NY 10021. **Phone:** 212-772-2090. **Fax:** 212-772-2718. **E-mail:** info@fc.edu
Visit CollegeQuest.com for information on majors offered and athletics. College video available at CollegeQuest.com.

■ *See page 1696 for a narrative description.*

HOTEL MANAGEMENT SCHOOL, "LES ROCHES"
Valais, Switzerland

Admissions Office Contact
Hotel Management School, "Les Roches", CH-3975 Bluch-Crans-Montana, Valais, Switzerland. **Fax:** 27-41-9246.

SCHILLER INTERNATIONAL UNIVERSITY, AMERICAN COLLEGE OF SWITZERLAND
Leysin, Switzerland

Admissions Office Contact
Schiller International University, American College of Switzerland, 453 Edgewater Drive, Dunedin, FL 34698. **Toll-free phone:** 800-336-4133. **Fax:** 813-734-0359.

UNITED ARAB EMIRATES

THE AMERICAN UNIVERSITY IN DUBAI
Dubai, United Arab Emirates

- **Proprietary**, comprehensive
- **Degrees** associate, bachelor's, and master's
- **Coed**, 663 undergraduate students, 73% full-time, 55% women, 45% men
- **$10,218 tuition** and fees

Students *Undergraduates:* Students come from 51 other countries. *The most frequently chosen baccalaureate fields are:* business/marketing, visual/performing arts. *Graduate:* 24 in graduate degree programs.

Reside on campus	15%

Expenses (1999–2000) *Tuition:* full-time 10,218; part-time 1145 per course. Full-time tuition and fees vary according to course load. Part-time tuition and fees vary according to course load. *College room only:* 3863. *Payment plan:* installment. *Waivers:* employees or children of employees.
College life *Housing: Options:* men-only, women-only. *Most popular organizations:* Student Government Association, community service club, drama club, music club, debate club.
Campus security 24-hour patrols.
Freshmen

SAT verbal scores above 500	N/R	SAT math scores above 500	N/R
ACT above 18	N/R		

Application *Application fee:* 35. *Required:* essay or personal statement; high school transcript; minimum 2.0 GPA; 2 letters of recommendation. *Recommended:* essay or personal statement; interview.
Standardized tests *Admission: Recommended:* SAT I.
Admissions Office Contact
The American University in Dubai, PO Box 28282, Dubai, United Arab Emirates. **Fax:** 4-388-899. **E-mail:** info@aud.edu
Visit CollegeQuest.com for information on majors offered and athletics.

United Kingdom

UNITED KINGDOM

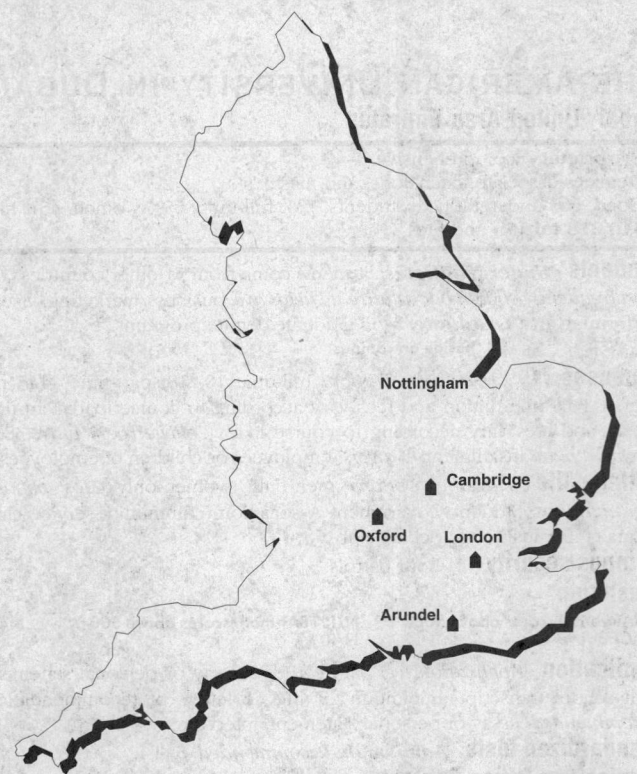

The London area includes the borough of Richmond.

THE AMERICAN COLLEGE
United Kingdom—See American InterContinental University

AMERICAN INTERCONTINENTAL UNIVERSITY
London, United Kingdom

- **Proprietary**, comprehensive, founded 1970
- **Degrees** associate, bachelor's, and master's
- **Urban** campus
- **Coed**, 729 undergraduate students, 84% full-time, 61% women, 39% men
- **Noncompetitive** entrance level, 87% of applicants were admitted
- **12:1** student-to-undergraduate faculty ratio
- **$13,725 tuition** and fees

Students *Undergraduates:* Students come from 34 states and territories, 83 other countries. The most frequently chosen baccalaureate fields are: business/marketing, communications/communication technologies. *Graduate:* 42 in graduate degree programs.

| From out-of-state | 100% | Reside on campus | 40% |

Faculty 88 (19% full-time).

Expenses (1999–2000) *Tuition:* full-time $13,725; part-time $1525 per course. *International tuition:* $15,192 full-time. Full-time tuition and fees vary according to course load. Part-time tuition and fees vary according to course load. *College room only:* $7200. Room and board charges vary according to housing facility. *Payment plan:* installment. *Waivers:* employees or children of employees.

Library Niklaus Weibel Library plus 1 other. *Operations spending 1999–2000:* $149,000. *Collection:* 26,000 titles, 350 serial subscriptions, 15,000 audiovisual materials.

College life *Housing: Options:* men-only, women-only. *Most popular organizations:* Student Government Association, drama group, International Interior Designers Association.

Campus security 24-hour emergency response devices.

After graduation 12 organizations recruited on campus 1997–98. *Career center:* 1 full-time, 2 part-time personnel. Services include resume preparation, interview workshops, resume referral, career/interest testing, career counseling, careers library, job bank, job interviews.

Freshmen 243 applied, 211 admitted.

| SAT verbal scores above 500 | N/R | SAT math scores above 500 | N/R |
| ACT above 18 | N/R | | |

Application *Options:* early admission, deferred entrance. *Application fee:* $35. *Required:* essay or personal statement; high school transcript; 2 letters of recommendation; interview.

Significant dates *Application deadlines:* rolling (freshmen), rolling (transfers). *Financial aid deadline:* continuous.

Freshman Application Contact
Mr. Geoff Hazell, Director of Admissions, American InterContinental University, 110 Marylebone High Street, London W1M 3DB, United Kingdom. **Phone:** 171-467-5640. **Fax:** 171-935-8144. **E-mail:** admissions@aiulondon.ac.uk

Visit CollegeQuest.com for information on majors offered and athletics. College video available at CollegeQuest.com.

HURON UNIVERSITY USA IN LONDON
London, United Kingdom

Admissions Office Contact
Huron University USA in London, 58 Princes Gate-Exhibition Road, London SW7 2PG, United Kingdom. **Fax:** 171-589-9406.

RICHMOND, THE AMERICAN INTERNATIONAL UNIVERSITY IN LONDON
Richmond, United Kingdom

 Apply at CollegeQuest.com

- **Independent**, comprehensive, founded 1972
- **Degrees** associate, bachelor's, master's, and post-master's certificates
- **Urban** 5-acre campus with easy access to London
- **Coed**, 1,110 undergraduate students, 100% full-time, 56% women, 44% men
- **Moderately difficult** entrance level, 57% of applicants were admitted
- **17:1** student-to-undergraduate faculty ratio
- **$15,310 tuition** and fees

Students *Undergraduates:* 1,110 full-time. Students come from 110 other countries. *Graduate:* 104 in graduate degree programs.

Faculty 135 (36% full-time), 81% with terminal degrees.

Expenses (2000–2001) *Comprehensive fee:* $23,770 includes full-time tuition ($14,230), mandatory fees ($1080), and room and board ($8460). *Part-time tuition:* $2000 per course. *Part-time fees:* $550 per term part-time. *Waivers:* employees or children of employees.

Library Richmond College Library plus 2 others. *Collection:* 80,000 titles, 277 serial subscriptions.

College life *Housing: Option:* coed. *Most popular organizations:* international club, computer club, ethnic clubs, Debate Society, sports clubs.

Campus security 24-hour patrols.

After graduation *Career center:* 2 full-time personnel. Services include career counseling, job bank. *Graduate education:* 25% of class of 1999 went directly to graduate and professional school.

Freshmen 868 applied, 492 admitted, 336 enrolled.

Average high school GPA	3.2	SAT verbal scores above 500	75%
SAT math scores above 500	80%	ACT above 18	100%
From top 10% of their h.s. class	12%	From top quarter	35%
From top half	53%	1998 freshmen returning in 1999	73%

Application *Options:* eApply at www.CollegeQuest.com, Common Application, deferred entrance. *Application fee:* $60. *Required:* essay or personal statement; high school transcript; 1 letter of recommendation.

United Kingdom

Standardized tests *Admission: Required:* SAT I or ACT.
Significant dates *Application deadline:* rolling (freshmen). *Financial aid deadline:* continuous.

Freshman Application Contact
Mr. Brian E. Davis, Director of United States Admissions, Richmond, The American International University in London, 19 Bay State Road, Richmond, Boston, MA 02215. **Phone:** 617-954-9942. **Fax:** 617-236-4703. **E-mail:** us_admissions@richmond.ac.uk

Visit CollegeQuest.com for information on majors offered and athletics. College video available at CollegeQuest.com.

■ *See page 2330 for a narrative description.*

SCHILLER INTERNATIONAL UNIVERSITY
London, United Kingdom

Admissions Office Contact
Schiller International University, 51-55 Waterloo Road, London SE1 8TX, United Kingdom.

Quick-Reference College Search Indexes

Entrance Difficulty Index   **943**
Shows how the colleges rank themselves—by percentage of applicants accepted, high school class rank, and test scores.

Cost Ranges Index   **951**
Groups colleges into eleven price ranges, from under $2000 to $20,000 and over.

Majors Index   **959**
Shows all the colleges that offer each major.

1998–99 Changes in Institutions   **1103**

Alphabetical Index   **1105**

Geographic Index of In-Depth Descriptions   **1117**

ENTRANCE DIFFICULTY INDEX

This index groups colleges by their own assessment of their entrance difficulty level. The colleges were asked to select the level that most closely corresponds to their entrance difficulty, according to the guidelines below. Institutions for which high school class rank and/or standardized test scores do not apply as admission criteria were asked to select the level that best indicates their entrance difficulty as compared to other institutions.

Most Difficult

More than 75% of the freshmen were in the top 10% of their high school class and scored over 1310 on the SAT I (verbal and mathematical combined) or over 29 on the ACT (composite); about 30% or fewer of the applicants were accepted.

Amherst College, MA
Barnard College, NY
Bates College, ME
Bowdoin College, ME
Brandeis University, MA
Brown University, RI
Bryn Mawr College, PA
California Institute of Technology, CA
Colby College, ME
Columbia College, NY
Columbia University, School of General Studies, NY
Columbia University, The Fu Foundation School of Engineering and Applied Science, NY
Cooper Union for the Advancement of Science and Art, NY
Cornell University, NY
The Curtis Institute of Music, PA
Dartmouth College, NH
Des Moines University Osteopathic Medical Center, IA
Duke University, NC
Emory University, GA
Georgetown University, DC
Harvard University, MA
Harvey Mudd College, CA
Haverford College, PA
Johns Hopkins University, MD
The Juilliard School, NY
Lehigh University, PA
Massachusetts Institute of Technology, MA
New World School of the Arts, FL
New York University, NY
Northwestern University, IL
Pomona College, CA
Princeton University, NJ
Queen's University at Kingston, ON, Canada
Rice University, TX
Rutgers, The State University of New Jersey, College of Pharmacy, NJ
Stanford University, CA
Swarthmore College, PA
Tufts University, MA
United States Air Force Academy, CO
United States Military Academy, NY
University of Chicago, IL
University of Notre Dame, IN
University of Pennsylvania, PA
The University of Texas Medical Branch at Galveston, TX
University of Virginia, VA
Washington and Lee University, VA
Webb Institute, NY
Wellesley College, MA
Wesleyan University, CT
Williams College, MA
Yale University, CT

Very Difficult

More than 50% of the freshmen were in the top 10% of their high school class and scored over 1230 on the SAT I or over 26 on the ACT; about 60% or fewer applicants were accepted.

Agnes Scott College, GA
Allegheny College, PA
American University in Cairo, Egypt
Art Center College of Design, CA
Austin College, TX
Babson College, MA
Bard College, NY
Beloit College, WI
Bennington College, VT
Boston College, MA
Boston University, MA
Bucknell University, PA
California Institute of the Arts, CA
Carleton College, MN
Carnegie Mellon University, PA
Case Western Reserve University, OH
Centre College, KY
Claremont McKenna College, CA
Clarkson University, NY
Cleveland Institute of Music, OH
Colgate University, NY
College of Insurance, NY
The College of New Jersey, NJ
College of the Atlantic, ME
College of the Holy Cross, MA
The College of William and Mary, VA
The Colorado College, CO
Colorado School of Mines, CO
Connecticut College, CT
Davidson College, NC
Dickinson College, PA
Drew University, NJ
Florida State University, FL
Fordham University, NY
Franklin and Marshall College, PA
Furman University, SC
The George Washington University, DC
Georgia Institute of Technology, GA
Gettysburg College, PA
Grinnell College, IA
Grove City College, PA
Gustavus Adolphus College, MN
Hamilton College, NY
Hendrix College, AR
Hillsdale College, MI
Hiram College, OH
Illinois Institute of Technology, IL
Illinois Wesleyan University, IL
Instituto Tecnológico y de Estudios Superiores de Monterrey, Campus León, Mexico
Instituto Tecnológico y de Estudios Superiores de Monterrey, Campus Monterrey, Mexico
Instituto Tecnológico y de Estudios Superiores de Monterrey, Campus Querétaro, Mexico
Instituto Tecnológico y de Estudios Superiores de Monterrey, Campus Tampico, Mexico
James Madison University, VA
Jewish Theological Seminary of America, NY
Kalamazoo College, MI
Kenyon College, OH
Kettering University, MI
Knox College, IL
Lafayette College, PA
Lake Forest College, IL
Lawrence University, WI
Lewis & Clark College, OR
Lyon College, AR
Macalester College, MN
Manhattan School of Music, NY
Mannes College of Music, New School University, NY
Maryland Institute, College of Art, MD
Mary Washington College, VA
Massachusetts College of Art, MA
McGill University, PQ, Canada
Medical University of South Carolina, SC
Middlebury College, VT
Mount Holyoke College, MA
Muhlenberg College, PA
New College of the University of South Florida, FL
New England Conservatory of Music, MA
North Carolina School of the Arts, NC
North Carolina State University, NC
Nova Scotia College of Art and Design, NS, Canada
Oberlin College, OH
Occidental College, CA
Oglethorpe University, GA
Ohio Wesleyan University, OH
Parsons School of Design, New School University, NY
Peabody Conservatory of Music of The Johns Hopkins University, MD
Pennsylvania State University at Erie, The Behrend College, PA
Pennsylvania State University University Park Campus, PA
Pepperdine University, Malibu, CA
Polytechnic University, Brooklyn Campus, NY
Polytechnic University, Farmingdale Campus, NY
Presbyterian College, SC
Providence College, RI
Queens College of the City University of New York, NY
Rabbinical Seminary of America, NY
Reed College, OR
Rensselaer Polytechnic Institute, NY
Rhode Island School of Design, RI
Rhodes College, TN
The Richard Stockton College of New Jersey, NJ
Rollins College, FL
Rose-Hulman Institute of Technology, IN
Rutgers, The State University of New Jersey, Cook College, NJ
Rutgers, The State University of New Jersey, Mason Gross School of the Arts, NJ
Rutgers, The State University of New Jersey, Rutgers College, NJ
Rutgers, The State University of New Jersey, School of Engineering, NJ
Saint Joseph's University, PA
St. Lawrence University, NY
Saint Luke's College, MO
St. Olaf College, MN
Sarah Lawrence College, NY
Scripps College, CA
Simon's Rock College of Bard, MA
Skidmore College, NY
Smith College, MA
Southwestern University, TX
Spelman College, GA
State University of New York at Binghamton, NY
State University of New York at Stony Brook, NY
State University of New York College at Geneseo, NY
State University of New York College of Environmental Science and Forestry, NY
Stevens Institute of Technology, NJ
Syracuse University, NY
Taylor University, IN
Thomas Aquinas College, CA
Transylvania University, KY
Trinity College, CT
Trinity University, TX
Tulane University, LA
Union College, NY
United States Coast Guard Academy, CT
United States Merchant Marine Academy, NY
United States Naval Academy, MD
University of Arkansas for Medical Sciences, AR
University of British Columbia, BC, Canada
University of California, Berkeley, CA
University of California, Davis, CA
University of California, Los Angeles, CA
University of California, Riverside, CA
University of California, San Diego, CA
University of California, Santa Barbara, CA
University of California, Santa Cruz, CA
University of Dallas, TX
University of Florida, FL
University of Illinois at Urbana–Champaign, IL
University of Michigan, MI
University of Missouri–Rolla, MO
The University of North Carolina at Chapel Hill, NC
University of North Florida, FL
University of Puerto Rico, Mayagüez Campus, PR
University of Puerto Rico, Río Piedras, PR
University of Puget Sound, WA
University of Richmond, VA
University of Rochester, NY
University of Southern California, CA
The University of Texas at Austin, TX
The University of Texas at Dallas, TX
University of the South, TN
University of Toronto, ON, Canada
The University of Western Ontario, ON, Canada
University of Wisconsin–Madison, WI
Ursinus College, PA
Vanderbilt University, TN
Vassar College, NY

Entrance Difficulty Index
Very Difficult–Moderately Difficult

Wake Forest University, NC
Washington University in St. Louis, MO
Wheaton College, IL
Whitman College, WA
Whitworth College, WA
Willamette University, OR
Wofford College, SC
Worcester Polytechnic Institute, MA
Yeshiva Karlin Stolin Rabbinical Institute, NY

Moderately Difficult

More than 75% of the freshmen were in the top half of their high school class and scored over 1010 on the SAT I or over 18 on the ACT; about 85% or fewer of the applicants were accepted.

Abilene Christian University, TX
Acadia University, NS, Canada
Adams State College, CO
Adelphi University, NY
Adrian College, MI
Alaska Pacific University, AK
Alberta College of Art and Design, AB, Canada
Albertson College of Idaho, ID
Albertus Magnus College, CT
Albion College, MI
Albright College, PA
Alderson-Broaddus College, WV
Alfred University, NY
Alice Lloyd College, KY
Allen College, IA
Allentown College of St. Francis de Sales, PA
Alma College, MI
Alvernia College, PA
Alverno College, WI
American Academy of Art, IL
American College of Prehospital Medicine, FL
American International College, MA
American University, DC
The American University of Paris, France
American University of Rome, Italy
Anderson College, SC
Anderson University, IN
Andrews University, MI
Anna Maria College, MA
Antioch College, OH
Antioch Southern California/ Los Angeles, CA
Appalachian State University, NC
Aquinas College, MI
Aquinas College, TN
Arizona State University, AZ
Arizona State University East, AZ
Arizona State University West, AZ
Arkansas State University, AR
Art Academy of Cincinnati, OH
The Art Institute of Boston at Lesley, MA
Art Institute of Southern California, CA
Art Institutes International at San Francisco, CA
Asbury College, KY
Ashland University, OH
Assumption College, MA
Atlanta College of Art, GA
Atlantic Union College, MA
Auburn University, AL
Auburn University Montgomery, AL
Audrey Cohen College, NY
Augsburg College, MN
Augustana College, IL
Augustana College, SD
Austin Peay State University, TN
Averett College, VA
Azusa Pacific University, CA
Baker University, KS
Baldwin-Wallace College, OH
Ball State University, IN
Barat College, IL
Barry University, FL
Bastyr University, WA
Bayamón Central University, PR
Baylor University, TX
Bay Path College, MA
Beaver College, PA
Belhaven College, MS
Bellarmine College, KY
Bellin College of Nursing, WI
Belmont Abbey College, NC
Belmont University, TN
Bemidji State University, MN
Benedictine College, KS
Benedictine University, IL
Bennett College, NC
Bentley College, MA
Berea College, KY
Berklee College of Music, MA
Bernard M. Baruch College of the City University of New York, NY
Berry College, GA
Bethany Bible College, NB, Canada
Bethany College, KS
Bethany College, WV
Bethel College, IN
Bethel College, KS
Bethel College, MN
Biola University, CA
Birmingham-Southern College, AL
Bishop's University, PQ, Canada
Blackburn College, IL
Blessing-Rieman College of Nursing, IL
Bloomsburg University of Pennsylvania, PA
Bluffton College, OH
Bowling Green State University, OH
Bradley University, IL
Brenau University, GA
Brescia University, KY
Briar Cliff College, IA
Bridgewater College, VA
Bridgewater State College, MA
Brigham Young University, UT
Brigham Young University–Hawaii Campus, HI
Brock University, ON, Canada
Brooklyn College of the City University of New York, NY
Brooks Institute of Photography, CA
Bryan College, TN
Bryant College, RI
Buena Vista University, IA
Butler University, IN
Caldwell College, NJ
California College of Arts and Crafts, CA
California Lutheran University, CA
California Maritime Academy, CA
California Polytechnic State University, San Luis Obispo, CA
California State Polytechnic University, Pomona, CA
California State University, Chico, CA
California State University, Dominguez Hills, CA
California State University, Fresno, CA
California State University, Fullerton, CA
California State University, Hayward, CA
California State University, Long Beach, CA
California State University, Los Angeles, CA
California State University, Northridge, CA
California State University, Sacramento, CA
California State University, San Bernardino, CA
California State University, San Marcos, CA
California State University, Stanislaus, CA
California University of Pennsylvania, PA
Calvin College, MI
Campbellsville University, KY
Campbell University, NC
Canisius College, NY
Capital University, OH
Cardinal Stritch University, WI
Carleton University, ON, Canada
Carlow College, PA
Carroll College, MT
Carroll College, WI
Carson-Newman College, TN
Carthage College, WI
Castleton State College, VT
Catawba College, NC
The Catholic University of America, DC
Cedar Crest College, PA
Cedarville College, OH
Centenary College, NJ
Centenary College of Louisiana, LA
Center for Creative Studies— College of Art and Design, MI
Central Bible College, MO
Central College, IA
Central Connecticut State University, CT
Central Methodist College, MO
Central Michigan University, MI
Central Missouri State University, MO
Chaminade University of Honolulu, HI
Chapman University, CA
Charleston Southern University, SC
Chatham College, PA
Chestnut Hill College, PA
Chicago State University, IL
Christendom College, VA
Christian Brothers University, TN
Christopher Newport University, VA
The Citadel, The Military College of South Carolina, SC
City College of the City University of New York, NY
Clark Atlanta University, GA
Clarke College, IA
Clarkson College, NE
Clark University, MA
Clemson University, SC
Cleveland Institute of Art, OH
Coastal Carolina University, SC
Coe College, IA
Cogswell Polytechnical College, CA
Coker College, SC
Colby-Sawyer College, NH
Coleman College, CA
College Misericordia, PA
College of Charleston, SC
College of Mount St. Joseph, OH
College of Mount Saint Vincent, NY
The College of New Rochelle, NY
College of Notre Dame, CA
College of Notre Dame of Maryland, MD
College of Our Lady of the Elms, MA
College of Saint Benedict, MN
College of St. Catherine, MN
College of Saint Elizabeth, NJ
College of Saint Mary, NE
The College of Saint Rose, NY
The College of St. Scholastica, MN
College of Santa Fe, NM
The College of Southeastern Europe, The American University of Athens, Greece
College of the Ozarks, MO
College of the Southwest, NM
The College of Wooster, OH
Colorado Christian University, CO
Colorado State University, CO
Colorado Technical University, CO
Columbia College, MO
Columbia College, SC
Columbia College of Nursing, WI
Columbus College of Art and Design, OH
Concordia College, MI
Concordia College, MN
Concordia College, NY
Concordia University, CA
Concordia University, IL
Concordia University, NE
Concordia University, PQ, Canada
Concordia University at Austin, TX
Concordia University Wisconsin, WI
Converse College, SC
Coppin State College, MD
The Corcoran College of Art and Design, DC
Cornell College, IA
Cornerstone University, MI
Cornish College of the Arts, WA
Covenant College, GA
Creighton University, NE
Crichton College, TN
The Culinary Institute of America, NY
Culver-Stockton College, MO
Cumberland College, KY
Curry College, MA
Daemen College, NY
Dakota Wesleyan University, SD
Dalhousie University, NS, Canada
Dallas Baptist University, TX
Dana College, NE
Daniel Webster College, NH
David Lipscomb University, TN
Deaconess College of Nursing, MO
Defiance College, OH
Delaware State University, DE
Delaware Valley College, PA
Denison University, OH
DePaul University, IL
DePauw University, IN
Deree College, Greece
Doane College, NE
Dr. William M. Scholl College of Podiatric Medicine, IL
Dominican College of Blauvelt, NY
Dominican University, IL
Dominican University of California, CA
Dordt College, IA
Dowling College, NY
Drake University, IA
Drexel University, PA
Drury University, MO
Duquesne University, PA
D'Youville College, NY
Earlham College, IN
East Carolina University, NC
East Central University, OK
Eastern College, PA
Eastern Connecticut State University, CT
Eastern Illinois University, IL
Eastern Mennonite University, VA
Eastern Michigan University, MI
Eastern Nazarene College, MA
Eastern Oregon University, OR
Eastern Washington University, WA
East Stroudsburg University of Pennsylvania, PA
East Tennessee State University, TN
East Texas Baptist University, TX
Eckerd College, FL
École des Hautes Études Commerciales, PQ, Canada
Edgewood College, WI
Edinboro University of Pennsylvania, PA

Entrance Difficulty Index
Moderately Difficult

Elizabeth City State University, NC
Elizabethtown College, PA
Elmhurst College, IL
Elmira College, NY
Elon College, NC
Embry-Riddle Aeronautical University, AZ
Embry-Riddle Aeronautical University, FL
Emerson College, MA
Emmanuel College, MA
Emory & Henry College, VA
Endicott College, MA
Erskine College, SC
Escuela de Artes Plasticas de Puerto Rico, PR
Eugene Lang College, New School University, NY
Evangel University, MO
The Evergreen State College, WA
Fairfield University, CT
Fairleigh Dickinson University, Florham-Madison Campus, NJ
Fairleigh Dickinson University, Teaneck–Hackensack Campus, NJ
Fashion Institute of Technology, NY
Faulkner University, AL
Felician College, NJ
Fisk University, TN
Fitchburg State College, MA
Flagler College, FL
Florida Agricultural and Mechanical University, FL
Florida Atlantic University, FL
Florida College, FL
Florida Gulf Coast University, FL
Florida Institute of Technology, FL
Florida International University, FL
Florida Southern College, FL
Fontbonne College, MO
Fort Lewis College, CO
Fort Valley State University, GA
Framingham State College, MA
Franciscan University of Steubenville, OH
Francis Marion University, SC
Franklin College of Indiana, IN
Franklin College Switzerland, Switzerland
Franklin Pierce College, NH
Freed-Hardeman University, TN
Fresno Pacific University, CA
Friends University, KS
Frostburg State University, MD
Gallaudet University, DC
Gannon University, PA
Gardner-Webb University, NC
Geneva College, PA
George Fox University, OR
George Mason University, VA
Georgetown College, KY
Georgia Baptist College of Nursing, GA
Georgia College and State University, GA
Georgian Court College, NJ
Georgia Southern University, GA
Georgia Southwestern State University, GA
Georgia State University, GA
Goddard College, VT
Golden Gate University, CA
Goldey-Beacom College, DE
Gonzaga University, WA
Gordon College, MA
Goshen College, IN
Goucher College, MD
Grace College, IN
Graceland College, IA
Grand Canyon University, AZ
Grand Valley State University, MI
Green Mountain College, VT
Greensboro College, NC
Greenville College, IL
Guilford College, NC
Gwynedd-Mercy College, PA
Hamline University, MN
Hampden-Sydney College, VA
Hampshire College, MA
Hampton University, VA
Hannibal-LaGrange College, MO
Hanover College, IN
Harding University, AR
Hardin-Simmons University, TX
Harris-Stowe State College, MO
Hartwick College, NY
Hastings College, NE
Hawaii Pacific University, HI
Hebrew Theological College, IL
Heidelberg College, OH
Henderson State University, AR
Herzing College, GA
Herzing College, WI
Hesser College, NH
High Point University, NC
Hobart and William Smith Colleges, NY
Hofstra University, NY
Hollins University, VA
Holy Family College, PA
Holy Names College, CA
Hood College, MD
Hope College, MI
Hope International University, CA
Houghton College, NY
Houston Baptist University, TX
Howard University, DC
Humboldt State University, CA
Hunter College of the City University of New York, NY
Huntingdon College, AL
Huntington College, IN
Husson College, ME
Huston-Tillotson College, TX
Illinois College, IL
Illinois State University, IL
Immaculata College, PA
Indiana Institute of Technology, IN
Indiana State University, IN
Indiana University Bloomington, IN
Indiana University East, IN
Indiana University of Pennsylvania, PA
Indiana University–Purdue University Indianapolis, IN
Indiana University South Bend, IN
Indiana Wesleyan University, IN
Inter American University of Puerto Rico, Aguadilla Campus, PR
Inter American University of Puerto Rico, Arecibo Campus, PR
Inter American University of Puerto Rico, Fajardo Campus, PR
Inter American University of Puerto Rico, Metropolitan Campus, PR
Inter American University of Puerto Rico, San Germán Campus, PR
International College of the Cayman Islands, Cayman Islands
International Fine Arts College, FL
Iona College, NY
Iowa State University of Science and Technology, IA
Iowa Wesleyan College, IA
Ithaca College, NY
Jacksonville University, FL
Jewish Hospital College of Nursing and Allied Health, MO
John Brown University, AR
John Carroll University, OH
John Jay College of Criminal Justice of the City University of New York, NY
Johnson State College, VT
Judson College, AL
Judson College, IL
Juniata College, PA
Kansas City Art Institute, MO
Kean University, NJ
Keene State College, NH
Kendall College, IL
Kent State University, OH
Kentucky Christian College, KY
Kentucky Wesleyan College, KY
Keuka College, NY
King College, TN
King's College, PA
The King's University College, AB, Canada
Kutztown University of Pennsylvania, PA
Laboratory Institute of Merchandising, NY
LaGrange College, GA
Lake Erie College, OH
Lakehead University, ON, Canada
Lakeland College, WI
Lake Superior State University, MI
Lakeview College of Nursing, IL
Lambuth University, TN
Lander University, SC
La Salle University, PA
Lasell College, MA
Lawrence Technological University, MI
Lebanon Valley College, PA
Lehman College of the City University of New York, NY
Le Moyne College, NY
Lenoir-Rhyne College, NC
Lesley College, MA
LeTourneau University, TX
Lewis University, IL
Lincoln Christian College, IL
Lincoln Memorial University, TN
Lincoln University, PA
Lindenwood University, MO
Linfield College, OR
Lock Haven University of Pennsylvania, PA
Logan University of Chiropractic, MO
Long Island University, C.W. Post Campus, NY
Long Island University, Southampton College, NY
Longwood College, VA
Loras College, IA
Louisiana College, LA
Louisiana State University and Agricultural and Mechanical College, LA
Louisiana Tech University, LA
Lourdes College, OH
Loyola College in Maryland, MD
Loyola Marymount University, CA
Loyola University Chicago, IL
Loyola University New Orleans, LA
Lubbock Christian University, TX
Luther College, IA
Lycoming College, PA
Lyme Academy of Fine Arts, CT
Lynchburg College, VA
Lyndon State College, VT
Machzikei Hadath Rabbinical College, NY
MacMurray College, IL
Madonna University, MI
Maharishi University of Management, IA
Maine College of Art, ME
Maine Maritime Academy, ME
Malone College, OH
Manchester College, IN
Manhattan College, NY
Manhattanville College, NY
Mansfield University of Pennsylvania, PA
Marian College, IN
Marian College of Fond du Lac, WI
Marietta College, OH
Marist College, NY
Marlboro College, VT
Marquette University, WI
Mars Hill College, NC
Martin Luther College, MN
Mary Baldwin College, VA
Marycrest International University, IA
Marygrove College, MI
Marymount College, NY
Marymount Manhattan College, NY
Maryville College, TN
Maryville University of Saint Louis, MO
Marywood University, PA
Massachusetts College of Liberal Arts, MA
Massachusetts College of Pharmacy and Health Sciences, MA
Massachusetts Maritime Academy, MA
McKendree College, IL
McMurry University, TX
MCP Hahnemann University, PA
McPherson College, KS
Medaille College, NY
Medcenter One College of Nursing, ND
Medical College of Georgia, GA
Memorial University of Newfoundland, NF, Canada
Memphis College of Art, TN
Mercer University, GA
Mercyhurst College, PA
Meredith College, NC
Merrimack College, MA
Mesivta Torah Vodaath Rabbinical Seminary, NY
Messenger College, MO
Messiah College, PA
Methodist College, NC
Metropolitan State University, MN
Miami University, OH
Michigan State University, MI
Michigan Technological University, MI
Middle Tennessee State University, TN
Midland Lutheran College, NE
Millersville University of Pennsylvania, PA
Milligan College, TN
Millikin University, IL
Millsaps College, MS
Mills College, CA
Milwaukee Institute of Art and Design, WI
Milwaukee School of Engineering, WI
Minneapolis College of Art and Design, MN
Minnesota State University, Mankato, MN
Minnesota State University Moorhead, MN
Mississippi College, MS
Mississippi State University, MS
Mississippi University for Women, MS
Missouri Baptist College, MO
Missouri Southern State College, MO
Missouri Valley College, MO
Molloy College, NY
Monmouth College, IL
Monmouth University, NJ
Monroe College, Bronx, NY
Monroe College, New Rochelle, NY
Montana State University–Billings, MT
Montana State University–Bozeman, MT
Montana State University–Northern, MT
Montana Tech of The University of Montana, MT
Monterey Institute of International Studies, CA
Montreat College, NC
Montserrat College of Art, MA
Moody Bible Institute, IL
Moore College of Art and Design, PA
Moravian College, PA
Morehouse College, GA
Morgan State University, MD
Morningside College, IA

Entrance Difficulty Index
Moderately Difficult

Mount Allison University, NB, Canada
Mount Marty College, SD
Mount Mary College, WI
Mount Mercy College, IA
Mount Saint Mary College, NY
Mount St. Mary's College, CA
Mount Saint Mary's College and Seminary, MD
Mount Saint Vincent University, NS, Canada
Mount Union College, OH
Mount Vernon Nazarene College, OH
Multnomah Bible College and Biblical Seminary, OR
Murray State University, KY
Muskingum College, OH
Naropa University, CO
The National College of Chiropractic, IL
Nazarene Indian Bible College, NM
Nazareth College of Rochester, NY
Nebraska Methodist College of Nursing and Allied Health, NE
Nebraska Wesleyan University, NE
Neumann College, PA
Newberry College, SC
New England College, NH
New England Culinary Institute, VT
New Hampshire College, NH
New Jersey City University, NJ
New Jersey Institute of Technology, NJ
New Mexico Institute of Mining and Technology, NM
New Mexico State University, NM
New School Bachelor of Arts, New School University, NY
New York Institute of Technology, NY
New York School of Interior Design, NY
Niagara University, NY
Nichols College, MA
Norfolk State University, VA
North Carolina Agricultural and Technical State University, NC
North Carolina Wesleyan College, NC
North Central College, IL
North Dakota State University, ND
Northeastern State University, OK
Northeastern University, MA
Northern Arizona University, AZ
Northern Illinois University, IL
North Georgia College & State University, GA
Northland College, WI
North Park University, IL
Northwest College, WA
Northwestern College, IA
Northwestern College, MN
Northwestern Oklahoma State University, OK
Northwest Missouri State University, MO
Northwest Nazarene University, ID

Northwood University, MI
Northwood University, Florida Campus, FL
Norwich University, VT
Notre Dame College, NH
Notre Dame College of Ohio, OH
Nova Southeastern University, FL
Nyack College, NY
Oakland University, MI
Ohio Dominican College, OH
Ohio Northern University, OH
The Ohio State University, OH
Ohio University, OH
Oklahoma Baptist University, OK
Oklahoma City University, OK
Oklahoma State University, OK
Old Dominion University, VA
Olivet Nazarene University, IL
O'More College of Design, TN
Oregon Health Sciences University, OR
Oregon Institute of Technology, OR
Oregon State University, OR
Otis College of Art and Design, CA
Ottawa University, KS
Otterbein College, OH
Ouachita Baptist University, AR
Our Lady of the Lake University of San Antonio, TX
Pace University, New York City Campus, NY
Pacific Lutheran University, WA
Pacific Northwest College of Art, OR
Pacific Union College, CA
Pacific University, OR
Palm Beach Atlantic College, FL
Palmer College of Chiropractic, IA
Park University, MO
Peace College, NC
Pennsylvania State University Abington College, PA
Pennsylvania State University Altoona College, PA
Pennsylvania State University Berks Campus of the Berks–Lehigh Valley College, PA
Pennsylvania State University Delaware County Campus of the Commonwealth College, PA
Pennsylvania State University Harrisburg Campus of the Capital College, PA
Pennsylvania State University Lehigh Valley Campus of the Berks-Lehigh Valley College, PA
Pennsylvania State University Schuylkill Campus of the Capital College, PA
Pennsylvania State University Shenango Campus of the Commonwealth College, PA
Pfeiffer University, NC
Philadelphia College of Bible, PA
Philadelphia University, PA

Piedmont College, GA
Pine Manor College, MA
Pitzer College, CA
Plattsburgh State University of New York, NY
Plymouth State College, NH
Point Loma Nazarene University, CA
Point Park College, PA
Pontifical Catholic University of Puerto Rico, PR
Prairie View A&M University, TX
Pratt Institute, NY
Principia College, IL
Purchase College, State University of New York, NY
Purdue University, IN
Queens College, NC
Quincy University, IL
Quinnipiac University, CT
Radford University, VA
Ramapo College of New Jersey, NJ
Randolph-Macon College, VA
Randolph-Macon Woman's College, VA
Redeemer College, ON, Canada
Reformed Bible College, MI
Regis College, MA
Regis University, CO
Reinhardt College, GA
Richmond, The American International University in London, United Kingdom
Rider University, NJ
Ringling School of Art and Design, FL
Ripon College, WI
Rivier College, NH
Roanoke College, VA
Robert Morris College, PA
Roberts Wesleyan College, NY
Rochester Institute of Technology, NY
Rockford College, IL
Rockhurst University, MO
Rocky Mountain College, MT
Rocky Mountain College of Art & Design, CO
Roger Williams University, RI
Rosemont College, PA
Rowan University, NJ
Royal Roads University, BC, Canada
Rush University, IL
Russell Sage College, NY
Rust College, MS
Rutgers, The State University of New Jersey, Camden College of Arts and Sciences, NJ
Rutgers, The State University of New Jersey, College of Nursing, NJ
Rutgers, The State University of New Jersey, Douglass College, NJ
Rutgers, The State University of New Jersey, Livingston College, NJ
Rutgers, The State University of New Jersey, Newark College of Arts and Sciences, NJ
Rutgers, The State University of New Jersey, University College–Camden, NJ

Rutgers, The State University of New Jersey, University College–Newark, NJ
Rutgers, The State University of New Jersey, University College–New Brunswick, NJ
Ryerson Polytechnic University, ON, Canada
Sacred Heart Major Seminary, MI
Sacred Heart University, CT
Saginaw Valley State University, MI
St. Ambrose University, IA
St. Andrews Presbyterian College, NC
Saint Anselm College, NH
Saint Anthony College of Nursing, IL
St. Bonaventure University, NY
St. Charles Borromeo Seminary, Overbrook, PA
St. Cloud State University, MN
St. Edward's University, TX
St. Francis College, NY
Saint Francis College, PA
Saint Francis Medical Center College of Nursing, IL
St. Francis Xavier University, NS, Canada
St. John Fisher College, NY
St. John's College, IL
St. John's College, MD
St. John's College, NM
St. John's Seminary College, CA
Saint John's University, MN
St. John's University, NY
Saint Joseph College, CT
Saint Joseph's College, IN
Saint Joseph's College, ME
St. Joseph's College, New York, NY
St. Joseph's College, Suffolk Campus, NY
Saint Leo University, FL
St. Louis College of Pharmacy, MO
Saint Louis University, MO
Saint Martin's College, WA
Saint Mary College, KS
Saint Mary-of-the-Woods College, IN
Saint Mary's College, IN
Saint Mary's College, MI
Saint Mary's College of California, CA
St. Mary's College of Maryland, MD
Saint Mary's University, NS, Canada
Saint Mary's University of Minnesota, MN
St. Mary's University of San Antonio, TX
Saint Michael's College, VT
St. Norbert College, WI
Saint Paul University, ON, Canada
Saint Peter's College, NJ
St. Thomas University, FL
Saint Vincent College, PA
Saint Xavier University, IL
Salem College, NC
Salisbury State University, MD
Salve Regina University, RI
Samford University, AL
Sam Houston State University, TX

San Diego State University, CA
San Francisco Art Institute, CA
San Francisco Conservatory of Music, CA
San Francisco State University, CA
San Jose State University, CA
Santa Clara University, CA
Savannah College of Art and Design, GA
School of the Art Institute of Chicago, IL
School of the Museum of Fine Arts, MA
School of Visual Arts, NY
Schreiner College, TX
Seattle Pacific University, WA
Seattle University, WA
Seton Hall University, NJ
Seton Hill College, PA
Shenandoah University, VA
Shepherd College, WV
Shimer College, IL
Shippensburg University of Pennsylvania, PA
Shorter College, GA
Siena College, NY
Siena Heights University, MI
Sierra Nevada College, NV
Simmons College, MA
Simon Fraser University, BC, Canada
Simpson College, IA
Simpson College and Graduate School, CA
Slippery Rock University of Pennsylvania, PA
Sonoma State University, CA
South Dakota School of Mines and Technology, SD
South Dakota State University, SD
Southeastern Oklahoma State University, OK
Southeast Missouri State University, MO
Southern Adventist University, TN
Southern Illinois University Carbondale, IL
Southern Illinois University Edwardsville, IL
Southern Methodist University, TX
Southern Oregon University, OR
Southern Polytechnic State University, GA
Southern Utah University, UT
Southwest Baptist University, MO
Southwestern College, KS
Southwestern Oklahoma State University, OK
Southwest Missouri State University, MO
Southwest State University, MN
Southwest Texas State University, TX
Spalding University, KY
Spring Arbor College, MI
Spring Hill College, AL
State University of New York at Albany, NY
State University of New York at Buffalo, NY

Entrance Difficulty Index
Moderately Difficult

State University of New York at Farmingdale, NY
State University of New York at New Paltz, NY
State University of New York at Oswego, NY
State University of New York College at Brockport, NY
State University of New York College at Buffalo, NY
State University of New York College at Cortland, NY
State University of New York College at Fredonia, NY
State University of New York College at Oneonta, NY
State University of New York College at Potsdam, NY
State University of New York College of Agriculture and Technology at Cobleskill, NY
State University of New York College of Technology at Alfred, NY
State University of New York Institute of Technology at Utica/Rome, NY
State University of New York Maritime College, NY
State University of New York Upstate Medical University, NY
Stephen F. Austin State University, TX
Stephens College, MO
Sterling College, VT
Stetson University, FL
Stonehill College, MA
Suffolk University, MA
Susquehanna University, PA
Sweet Briar College, VA
Tabor College, KS
Talmudical Yeshiva of Philadelphia, PA
Taylor University, Fort Wayne Campus, IN
Temple University, PA
Tennessee Technological University, TN
Tennessee Wesleyan College, TN
Texas A&M International University, TX
Texas A&M University, TX
Texas A&M University at Galveston, TX
Texas A&M University–Commerce, TX
Texas A&M University–Kingsville, TX
Texas Christian University, TX
Texas Lutheran University, TX
Texas Tech University, TX
Texas Wesleyan University, TX
Thiel College, PA
Thomas Jefferson University, PA
Thomas More College, KY
Thomas More College of Liberal Arts, NH
Toccoa Falls College, GA
Touro College, NY
Towson University, MD
Trent University, ON, Canada
Trinity Baptist College, FL
Trinity Christian College, IL
Trinity College of Vermont, VT
Trinity Western University, BC, Canada
Tri-State University, IN
Troy State University, AL
Truman State University, MO
Tusculum College, TN
Tuskegee University, AL
Tyndale College & Seminary, ON, Canada
Union College, KY
The Union Institute, OH
Union University, TN
United States International University, CA
Unity College, ME
Universidad Metropolitana, PR
Université de Montréal, PQ, Canada
Université de Sherbrooke, PQ, Canada
Université Laval, PQ, Canada
University College of Cape Breton, NS, Canada
The University of Alabama, AL
The University of Alabama at Birmingham, AL
The University of Alabama in Huntsville, AL
University of Alaska Fairbanks, AK
University of Alberta, AB, Canada
The University of Arizona, AZ
University of Arkansas, AR
University of Bridgeport, CT
University of Calgary, AB, Canada
University of California, Irvine, CA
University of Central Arkansas, AR
University of Central Florida, FL
University of Charleston, WV
University of Cincinnati, OH
University of Colorado at Boulder, CO
University of Colorado at Colorado Springs, CO
University of Colorado at Denver, CO
University of Colorado Health Sciences Center, CO
University of Connecticut, CT
University of Dayton, OH
University of Delaware, DE
University of Denver, CO
University of Detroit Mercy, MI
University of Dubuque, IA
University of Evansville, IN
The University of Findlay, OH
University of Georgia, GA
University of Guelph, ON, Canada
University of Hartford, CT
University of Hawaii at Manoa, HI
University of Houston, TX
University of Idaho, ID
University of Illinois at Chicago, IL
University of Indianapolis, IN
The University of Iowa, IA
University of Judaism, CA
University of Kansas, KS
University of Kentucky, KY
University of King's College, NS, Canada
University of La Verne, CA
The University of Lethbridge, AB, Canada
University of Louisville, KY
University of Maine, ME
University of Maine at Farmington, ME
University of Maine at Fort Kent, ME
University of Maine at Machias, ME
University of Manitoba, MB, Canada
University of Maryland, Baltimore County, MD
University of Maryland, College Park, MD
University of Massachusetts Amherst, MA
University of Massachusetts Boston, MA
University of Massachusetts Dartmouth, MA
University of Massachusetts Lowell, MA
The University of Memphis, TN
University of Miami, FL
University of Michigan–Dearborn, MI
University of Michigan–Flint, MI
University of Minnesota, Duluth, MN
University of Minnesota, Morris, MN
University of Minnesota, Twin Cities Campus, MN
University of Mississippi, MS
University of Mississippi Medical Center, MS
University of Missouri–Columbia, MO
University of Missouri–Kansas City, MO
University of Missouri–St. Louis, MO
University of Mobile, AL
The University of Montana–Missoula, MT
University of Montevallo, AL
University of Nebraska at Kearney, NE
University of Nebraska–Lincoln, NE
University of Nebraska Medical Center, NE
University of Nevada, Las Vegas, NV
University of Nevada, Reno, NV
University of New Brunswick, Fredericton, NB, Canada
University of New Brunswick, Saint John, NB, Canada
University of New England, ME
University of New Hampshire, NH
University of New Hampshire at Manchester, NH
University of New Haven, CT
University of New Mexico, NM
University of New Orleans, LA
The University of North Carolina at Asheville, NC
The University of North Carolina at Charlotte, NC
The University of North Carolina at Greensboro, NC
The University of North Carolina at Pembroke, NC
The University of North Carolina at Wilmington, NC
University of Northern Colorado, CO
University of Northern Iowa, IA
University of North Texas, TX
University of Oklahoma, OK
University of Oklahoma Health Sciences Center, OK
University of Oregon, OR
University of Pittsburgh, PA
University of Pittsburgh at Bradford, PA
University of Pittsburgh at Johnstown, PA
University of Portland, OR
University of Prince Edward Island, PE, Canada
University of Puerto Rico at Ponce, PR
University of Puerto Rico, Humacao University College, PR
University of Redlands, CA
University of Rhode Island, RI
University of St. Francis, IL
University of Saint Francis, IN
University of St. Thomas, MN
University of St. Thomas, TX
University of San Diego, CA
University of San Francisco, CA
University of Science and Arts of Oklahoma, OK
The University of Scranton, PA
University of Sioux Falls, SD
University of South Alabama, AL
University of South Carolina, SC
University of South Dakota, SD
University of Southern Colorado, CO
University of Southern Maine, ME
University of Southern Mississippi, MS
University of South Florida, FL
The University of Tampa, FL
The University of Tennessee at Chattanooga, TN
The University of Tennessee at Martin, TN
The University of Tennessee Knoxville, TN
The University of Texas at Arlington, TX
The University of Texas at San Antonio, TX
The University of Texas–Houston Health Science Center, TX
The University of the Arts, PA
University of the Ozarks, AR
University of the Pacific, CA
University of the Sacred Heart, PR
University of the Sciences in Philadelphia, PA
University of Tulsa, OK
University of Utah, UT
University of Vermont, VT
University of Victoria, BC, Canada
University of Virginia's College at Wise, VA
University of Washington, WA
University of Waterloo, ON, Canada
University of West Florida, FL
University of Windsor, ON, Canada
The University of Winnipeg, MB, Canada
University of Wisconsin–Eau Claire, WI
University of Wisconsin–Green Bay, WI
University of Wisconsin–La Crosse, WI
University of Wisconsin–Milwaukee, WI
University of Wisconsin–Parkside, WI
University of Wisconsin–Platteville, WI
University of Wisconsin–River Falls, WI
University of Wisconsin–Stevens Point, WI
University of Wisconsin–Stout, WI
University of Wisconsin–Superior, WI
University of Wisconsin–Whitewater, WI
University of Wyoming, WY
Upper Iowa University, IA
Urbana University, OH
Utah State University, UT
Utica College of Syracuse University, NY
Valdosta State University, GA
Valparaiso University, IN
VanderCook College of Music, IL
Vanguard University of Southern California, CA
Villa Julie College, MD
Villanova University, PA
Virginia Commonwealth University, VA
Virginia Military Institute, VA
Virginia Polytechnic Institute and State University, VA
Virginia Union University, VA
Virginia Wesleyan College, VA
Wabash College, IN
Wadhams Hall Seminary-College, NY
Wagner College, NY
Waldorf College, IA
Walla Walla College, WA
Walsh University, OH
Warner Pacific College, OR
Warren Wilson College, NC
Wartburg College, IA
Washington & Jefferson College, PA
Washington Bible College, MD
Washington College, MD
Washington State University, WA
Waynesburg College, PA
Wayne State University, MI
Webber College, FL
Webster University, MO
Wells College, NY
Wentworth Institute of Technology, MA
Wesleyan College, GA
Wesley College, DE
West Chester University of Pennsylvania, PA
Western Baptist College, OR
Western Carolina University, NC
Western Connecticut State University, CT

Entrance Difficulty Index
Moderately Difficult–Minimally Difficult

Western Illinois University, IL
Western Kentucky University, KY
Western Maryland College, MD
Western Michigan University, MI
Western Montana College of The University of Montana, MT
Western New England College, MA
Western Oregon University, OR
Western State College of Colorado, CO
Western States Chiropractic College, OR
Western Washington University, WA
Westfield State College, MA
Westminster Choir College of Rider University, NJ
Westminster College, MO
Westminster College, PA
Westminster College, UT
Westmont College, CA
West Texas A&M University, TX
West Virginia University, WV
West Virginia Wesleyan College, WV
Westwood College of Technology, CO
Wheaton College, MA
Wheeling Jesuit University, WV
Wheelock College, MA
Whittier College, CA
Widener University, PA
Wilfrid Laurier University, ON, Canada
Wilkes University, PA
William Jewell College, MO
William Paterson University of New Jersey, NJ
William Penn University, IA
William Woods University, MO
Wilmington College, OH
Wilson College, PA
Wingate University, NC
Winona State University, MN
Winthrop University, SC
Wisconsin Lutheran College, WI
Wittenberg University, OH
Woodbury University, CA
Worcester State College, MA
Xavier University, OH
Xavier University of Louisiana, LA
Yeshiva Ohr Elchonon Chabad/West Coast Talmudical Seminary, CA
Yeshiva University, NY
York College, NE
York College of Pennsylvania, PA
York University, ON, Canada

Minimally Difficult

Most freshmen were not in the top half of their high school class and scored somewhat below 1010 on the SAT I or below 19 on the ACT; up to 95% of the applicants were accepted.

The Advertising Arts College, CA
Alabama Agricultural and Mechanical University, AL
Alabama State University, AL
Alaska Bible College, AK
Albany State University, GA
Amber University, TX
American College of Thessaloniki, Greece
American Indian College of the Assemblies of God, Inc., AZ
Antioch Southern California/Santa Barbara, CA
Appalachian Bible College, WV
Arkansas Tech University, AR
Arlington Baptist College, TX
Armstrong Atlantic State University, GA
The Art Institute of Atlanta, GA
The Art Institute of Colorado, CO
The Art Institute of Philadelphia, PA
The Art Institute of Phoenix, AZ
The Art Institute of Portland, OR
Atlanta Christian College, GA
Atlantic Baptist University, NB, Canada
Augusta State University, GA
Avila College, MO
Baltimore International College, MD
Barber-Scotia College, NC
Barclay College, KS
Bartlesville Wesleyan College, OK
Barton College, NC
Becker College, MA
Berkeley College, New York, NY
Berkeley College, White Plains, NY
Bethany College of the Assemblies of God, CA
Bethel College, TN
Bethune-Cookman College, FL
Black Hills State University, SD
Bloomfield College, NJ
Boise Bible College, ID
Boise State University, ID
Bowie State University, MD
Brevard College, NC
Briarcliffe College, NY
Bryant and Stratton College, Cleveland, OH
Bryant and Stratton College, Virginia Beach, VA
Bryn Athyn College of the New Church, PA
Cabrini College, PA
California Baptist University, CA
California State University, Monterey Bay, CA
Calumet College of Saint Joseph, IN
Calvary Bible College and Theological Seminary, MO
Cambridge College, MA
Cameron University, OK
Capitol College, MD
Cazenovia College, NY

Central Baptist College, AR
Central Christian College of Kansas, KS
Central Pentecostal College, SK, Canada
Champlain College, VT
Cheyney University of Pennsylvania, PA
Chowan College, NC
Cincinnati College of Mortuary Science, OH
Circleville Bible College, OH
Claflin University, SC
Clarion University of Pennsylvania, PA
Clayton College & State University, GA
College of Aeronautics, NY
College of St. Catherine–Minneapolis, MN
College of St. Joseph, VT
College of Visual Arts, MN
Colorado Technical University Denver Campus, CO
Columbia College–Hollywood, CA
Columbia International University, SC
Columbia Union College, MD
Columbus State University, GA
Concord College, WV
Concordia University, OR
Concordia University at St. Paul, MN
Crown College, MN
Dakota State University, SD
Dallas Christian College, TX
David N. Myers College, OH
Delta State University, MS
DeVry Institute, NJ
DeVry Institute of Technology, AZ
DeVry Institute of Technology, Fremont, CA
DeVry Institute of Technology, Long Beach, CA
DeVry Institute of Technology, Pomona, CA
DeVry Institute of Technology, Alpharetta, GA
DeVry Institute of Technology, Decatur, GA
DeVry Institute of Technology, Addison, IL
DeVry Institute of Technology, Chicago, IL
DeVry Institute of Technology, MO
DeVry Institute of Technology, NY
DeVry Institute of Technology, OH
DeVry Institute of Technology, TX
Eastern New Mexico University, NM
Embry-Riddle Aeronautical University, Extended Campus, FL
Emmanuel College, GA
Eugene Bible College, OR
Fairmont State College, WV
Faith Baptist Bible College and Theological Seminary, IA
Ferris State University, MI
Ferrum College, VA

Finch University of Health Sciences/The Chicago Medical School, IL
Finlandia University, MI
Fisher College, MA
Five Towns College, NY
Florida Christian College, FL
Florida Metropolitan University–Tampa College, Brandon, FL
Franklin Institute of Boston, MA
God's Bible School and College, OH
Governors State University, IL
Grace Bible College, MI
Griggs University, MD
Hellenic College, MA
Heritage Bible College, NC
Hilbert College, NY
Howard Payne University, TX
Huron University, SD
Idaho State University, ID
Indiana University Kokomo, IN
Indiana University Northwest, IN
Indiana University–Purdue University Fort Wayne, IN
Indiana University Southeast, IN
Institute for Christian Studies, TX
International Academy of Merchandising & Design, Ltd., IL
International College, FL
Jacksonville State University, AL
Jamestown College, ND
Jarvis Christian College, TX
Johnson & Wales University, RI
Johnson Bible College, TN
Johnson C. Smith University, NC
John Wesley College, NC
Kendall College of Art and Design, MI
Kentucky Mountain Bible College, KY
Kentucky State University, KY
Kol Yaakov Torah Center, NY
Lamar University, TX
Lancaster Bible College, PA
Lane College, TN
Langston University, OK
La Roche College, PA
La Sierra University, CA
Lees-McRae College, NC
Lee University, TN
LeMoyne-Owen College, TN
Lewis-Clark State College, ID
Liberty University, VA
LIFE Bible College, CA
Limestone College, SC
Lincoln University, CA
Lindsey Wilson College, KY
Long Island University, Brooklyn Campus, NY
Lynn University, FL
Macon State College, GA
Manhattan Christian College, KS
Marshall University, WV
Martin Methodist College, TN
Menlo College, CA
Mesa State College, CO
Metropolitan State College of Denver, CO

MidAmerica Nazarene University, KS
Midway College, KY
Midwestern State University, TX
Minot State University, ND
Mississippi Valley State University, MS
Mitchell College, CT
Morehead State University, KY
Morris College, SC
Mount Aloysius College, PA
Mount Ida College, MA
Mount Olive College, NC
Mount St. Clare College, IA
Mount Senario College, WI
National-Louis University, IL
Nebraska Christian College, NE
Newbury College, MA
Newman University, KS
New Mexico Highlands University, NM
North American Baptist College and Edmonton Baptist Seminary, AB, Canada
North Carolina Central University, NC
Northeastern Illinois University, IL
Northern Michigan University, MI
Northern State University, SD
North Greenville College, SC
Northwood University, Texas Campus, TX
Nova Scotia Agricultural College, NS, Canada
Oak Hills Christian College, MN
Oakland City University, IN
Oakwood College, AL
Ohio Valley College, WV
Oregon College of Art and Craft, OR
Our Lady of Holy Cross College, LA
Paier College of Art, Inc., CT
Paine College, GA
Peirce College, PA
Polytechnic University of Puerto Rico, PR
Portland State University, OR
Practical Bible College, NY
Prairie Bible College, AB, Canada
Robert Morris College, IL
Rochester College, MI
Saint Augustine's College, NC
St. Gregory's University, OK
Saint John's Seminary College of Liberal Arts, MA
St. Louis Christian College, MO
Saint Paul's College, VA
Salem State College, MA
Savannah State University, GA
Shaw University, NC
Silver Lake College, WI
South College, AL
South College, FL
Southeastern College of the Assemblies of God, FL
Southern Arkansas University–Magnolia, AR
Southern Christian University, AL

Entrance Difficulty Index
Minimally Difficult–Noncompetitive

Southern Vermont College, VT
Southern Wesleyan University, SC
Southwestern Adventist University, TX
Southwestern College of Christian Ministries, OK
State University of New York College at Old Westbury, NY
State University of New York College of Agriculture and Technology at Morrisville, NY
State University of New York College of Technology at Canton, NY
State University of West Georgia, GA
Steinbach Bible College, MB, Canada
Sterling College, KS
Stillman College, AL
Talladega College, AL
Teikyo Post University, CT
Tennessee State University, TN
Texas Woman's University, TX
Thomas College, ME
Tiffin University, OH
Tougaloo College, MS
Trinity College of Florida, FL
Trinity Lutheran College, WA
Troy State University Dothan, AL
Union College, NE
Universidad Adventista de las Antillas, PR
Universidad del Turabo, PR
University of Arkansas at Little Rock, AR
University of Arkansas at Pine Bluff, AR
University of Central Oklahoma, OK
University of Houston–Clear Lake, TX
University of Houston–Victoria, TX
University of Illinois at Springfield, IL
University of Louisiana at Lafayette, LA
University of Maine at Presque Isle, ME
University of Mary Hardin-Baylor, TX
University of Nebraska at Omaha, NE
University of North Alabama, AL
University of North Dakota, ND
University of Regina, SK, Canada
University of South Carolina Spartanburg, SC
University of the Virgin Islands, VI
The University of West Alabama, AL
University of West Los Angeles, CA
Ursuline College, OH
Vermont Technical College, VT
Virginia Intermont College, VA
Voorhees College, SC
Warner Southern College, FL

Wayland Baptist University, TX
West Liberty State College, WV
West Virginia State College, WV
White Pines College, NH
Williams Baptist College, AR
William Tyndale College, MI
Winston-Salem State University, NC
Wright State University, OH

Noncompetitive

Virtually all applicants were accepted regardless of high school rank or test scores.

Academy of Art College, CA
Allen University, SC
American InterContinental University, CA
American InterContinental University, Atlanta, GA
American InterContinental University, United Kingdom
American Military University, VA
American University of Puerto Rico, PR
Antioch University Seattle, WA
Arkansas Baptist College, AR
The Art Institute of Fort Lauderdale, FL
Athabasca University, AB, Canada
Athens State University, AL
Baker College of Auburn Hills, MI
Baker College of Flint, MI
Baker College of Jackson, MI
Baker College of Muskegon, MI
Baker College of Owosso, MI
Baker College of Port Huron, MI
Baptist Missionary Association Theological Seminary, TX
Bellevue University, NE
Beulah Heights Bible College, GA
Bluefield State College, WV
Blue Mountain College, MS
Boston Architectural Center, MA
Brandon University, MB, Canada
Briercrest Bible College, SK, Canada
Burlington College, VT
California Christian College, CA
California College for Health Sciences, CA
Canadian Bible College, SK, Canada
Cascade College, OR
Chadron State College, NE
Chaparral College, AZ
Charter Oak State College, CT
City University, WA
Cleary College, MI
Cleveland College of Jewish Studies, OH
Cleveland State University, OH

Colegio Universitario del Este, PR
Collège Dominicain de Philosophie et de Théologie, ON, Canada
College of Staten Island of the City University of New York, NY
The College of West Virginia, WV
Columbia College Chicago, IL
Conception Seminary College, MO
Dalton State College, GA
Davenport College of Business, MI
Davenport College of Business, Kalamazoo Campus, MI
Davenport College of Business, Lansing Campus, MI
Design Institute of San Diego, CA
Detroit College of Business, MI
Detroit College of Business–Flint, MI
Detroit College of Business, Warren Campus, MI
Dickinson State University, ND
Dixie State College of Utah, UT
Eastern Kentucky University, KY
Eastern Pentecostal Bible College, ON, Canada
Emmaus Bible College, IA
Emporia State University, KS
Florida Baptist Theological College, FL
Fort Hays State University, KS
Franklin University, OH
Free Will Baptist Bible College, TN
Glenville State College, WV
Global University of the Assemblies of God, MO
Grand View College, IA
Grantham College of Engineering, LA
Gratz College, PA
Hamilton Technical College, IA
Harrington Institute of Interior Design, IL
Henry Cogswell College, WA
Heritage Baptist College and Heritage Theological Seminary, ON, Canada
Heritage College, WA
Hillsdale Free Will Baptist College, OK
Hobe Sound Bible College, FL
Holy Trinity Orthodox Seminary, NY
Humphreys College, CA
Institute of Computer Technology, CA
International Academy of Design, FL
International Bible College, AL
John F. Kennedy University, CA
Jones College, FL
Jones International University, CO
Kansas State University, KS
Kent State University, Geauga Campus, OH

Kent State University, Stark Campus, OH
Lincoln University, MO
Long Island University, Southampton College, Friends World Program, NY
Louisiana State University in Shreveport, LA
Magnolia Bible College, MS
Maranatha Baptist Bible College, WI
Marylhurst University, OR
Mayville State University, ND
McNeese State University, LA
Medgar Evers College of the City University of New York, NY
Mercy College, NY
Miami University–Hamilton Campus, OH
Mid-America Bible College, OK
Mid-Continent College, KY
Minnesota Bible College, MN
Missouri Western State College, MO
NAES College, IL
National American University, MO
National American University–St. Paul Campus, MN
National Business College, Salem, VA
National University, CA
Nazarene Bible College, CO
New England College of Finance, MA
New York City Technical College of the City University of New York, NY
Nicholls State University, LA
North Central University, MN
Northern Kentucky University, KY
Northwestern College, OH
Northwestern State University of Louisiana, LA
The Ohio State University at Lima, OH
Ohio University–Chillicothe, OH
Ohio University–Zanesville, OH
Oklahoma Christian University of Science and Arts, OK
Oklahoma Panhandle State University, OK
Open Learning Agency, BC, Canada
Our Lady of the Lake College, LA
Ozark Christian College, MO
Patten College, CA
Pennsylvania College of Technology, PA
Peru State College, NE
Philander Smith College, AR
Piedmont Baptist College, NC
Pikeville College, KY
Pittsburg State University, KS
Presentation College, SD
Providence College and Theological Seminary, MB, Canada
Purdue University Calumet, IN
Purdue University North Central, IN
Regents College, NY

Rocky Mountain College, AB, Canada
St. Augustine College, IL
Salish Kootenai College, MT
San Jose Christian College, CA
Schiller International University, Germany
Shawnee State University, OH
Sheldon Jackson College, AK
Southeastern Louisiana University, LA
Southeastern University, DC
Southwestern Assemblies of God University, TX
Sul Ross State University, TX
Texas A&M University–Texarkana, TX
Texas Southern University, TX
Thomas Edison State College, NJ
Thomas University, GA
Trevecca Nazarene University, TN
Troy State University Montgomery, AL
Université du Québec à Chicoutimi, PQ, Canada
Université du Québec à Hull, PQ, Canada
Université du Québec à Trois-Rivières, PQ, Canada
Université du Québec en Abitibi-Témiscamingue, PQ, Canada
The University of Akron, OH
University of Arkansas at Monticello, AR
University of Baltimore, MD
University of Great Falls, MT
University of Houston–Downtown, TX
University of Louisiana at Monroe, LA
The University of Maine at Augusta, ME
University of Maryland University College, MD
University of Minnesota, Crookston, MN
University of Phoenix, AZ
University of Rio Grande, OH
University of Southern Indiana, IN
The University of Texas–Pan American, TX
University of the District of Columbia, DC
University System College for Lifelong Learning, NH
Valley City State University, ND
Walsh College of Accountancy and Business Administration, MI
Wayne State College, NE
Weber State University, UT
Wesley College, MS
West Virginia University Institute of Technology, WV
Wichita State University, KS
Wilmington College, DE
World College, VA
York College of the City University of New York, NY
Youngstown State University, OH

COST RANGES INDEX

Less than $2000

Colleges with No Room and Board or with Room Only

The Curtis Institute of Music, PA
Dalton State College, GA
Embry-Riddle Aeronautical University, Extended Campus, FL
Global University of the Assemblies of God, MO
Macon State College, GA
New World School of the Arts, FL
Texas A&M University–Texarkana, TX
University of Puerto Rico at Ponce, PR
University of Puerto Rico, Humacao University College, PR

Colleges with Room and Board

United States Air Force Academy, CO
United States Coast Guard Academy, CT
United States Merchant Marine Academy, NY
United States Military Academy, NY
United States Naval Academy, MD

$2000–$3999

Colleges with No Room and Board or with Room Only

Arizona State University West, AZ
Athens State University, AL (room only)
Auburn University, AL
Augusta State University, GA
Bayamón Central University, PR
Bernard M. Baruch College of the City University of New York, NY
Bluefield State College, WV
Brooklyn College of the City University of New York, NY
City College of the City University of New York, NY
Clayton College & State University, GA
Colegio Universitario del Este, PR
College of Staten Island of the City University of New York, NY
Deree College,
Georgia Baptist College of Nursing, GA (room only)
Governors State University, IL
Harris-Stowe State College, MO
Hunter College of the City University of New York, NY
Indiana University East, IN
Indiana University Kokomo, IN
Indiana University Northwest, IN
Indiana University–Purdue University Fort Wayne, IN
Indiana University South Bend, IN
Indiana University Southeast, IN
Institute for Christian Studies, TX (room only)
Inter American University of Puerto Rico, Aguadilla Campus, PR
Inter American University of Puerto Rico, Arecibo Campus, PR
Inter American University of Puerto Rico, Metropolitan Campus, PR
John Jay College of Criminal Justice of the City University of New York, NY
Jones International University, CO
Lehman College of the City University of New York, NY
Medgar Evers College of the City University of New York, NY
Metropolitan State College of Denver, CO
Metropolitan State University, MN
Northeastern Illinois University, IL
The Ohio State University at Lima, OH
Ohio University–Chillicothe, OH
Ohio University–Zanesville, OH
Purdue University Calumet, IN
Purdue University North Central, IN
Queens College of the City University of New York, NY
Texas A&M International University, TX
Troy State University Dothan, AL
Troy State University Montgomery, AL
Universidad del Turabo, PR
Universidad Metropolitana, PR
University of Colorado at Denver, CO
University of Houston–Clear Lake, TX
University of Houston–Downtown, TX
University of Houston–Victoria, TX
The University of Maine at Augusta, ME
University of Michigan–Flint, MI
University of Missouri–Kansas City, MO
University of Nebraska Medical Center, NE
University of Oklahoma Health Sciences Center, OK
The University of Texas–Houston Health Science Center, TX
The University of Texas Medical Branch at Galveston, TX (room only)
University of the District of Columbia, DC
University System College for Lifelong Learning, NH
York College of the City University of New York, NY

Colleges with Room and Board

Alice Lloyd College, KY
Berea College, KY
College of the Ozarks, MO

$4000–$5999

Colleges with No Room and Board or with Room Only

Amber University, TX
Arizona State University East, AZ (room only)
Arlington Baptist College, TX (room only)
Auburn University Montgomery, AL (room only)
Baptist Missionary Association Theological Seminary, TX (room only)
Bellevue University, NE
Beulah Heights Bible College, GA (room only)
California State University, Dominguez Hills, CA (room only)
California State University, Fullerton, CA (room only)
California State University, Hayward, CA (room only)
California State University, Los Angeles, CA (room only)
California State University, San Marcos, CA (room only)
The College of Southeastern Europe, The American University of Athens,
Detroit College of Business–Flint, MI
Escuela de Artes Plasticas de Puerto Rico, PR
Franklin University, OH
Grantham College of Engineering, LA
Griggs University, MD
Hamilton Technical College, IA
Heritage College, WA
Jones College, FL
Medcenter One College of Nursing, ND (room only)
Medical College of Georgia, GA (room only)
Medical University of South Carolina, SC
NAES College, IL
Nazarene Bible College, CO
Our Lady of Holy Cross College, LA
Our Lady of the Lake College, LA
Polytechnic University of Puerto Rico, PR
The University of Alabama at Birmingham, AL (room only)
University of Arkansas at Little Rock, AR (room only)
University of Baltimore, MD
University of Illinois at Springfield, IL (room only)
University of Maryland University College, MD
University of Massachusetts Boston, MA
University of Michigan–Dearborn, MI
University of Mississippi Medical Center, MS (room only)
University of New Hampshire at Manchester, NH
University of Southern Indiana, IN (room only)
The University of Tennessee at Chattanooga, TN (room only)
The University of Texas at Arlington, TX (room only)
The University of Texas at Dallas, TX (room only)
The University of Texas at San Antonio, TX (room only)
The University of Texas at Tyler, TX (room only)
University of West Florida, FL (room only)
University of Wisconsin–Green Bay, WI (room only)
Walsh College of Accountancy and Business Administration, MI

Colleges with Room and Board

Alabama Agricultural and Mechanical University, AL
Albany State University, GA
Appalachian State University, NC
Arkansas Baptist College, AR
Arkansas State University, AR
Arkansas Tech University, AR
Austin Peay State University, TN
Boise State University, ID
California State University, Monterey Bay, CA
Cameron University, OK
Chadron State College, NE
Delta State University, MS
Dickinson State University, ND
Dixie State College of Utah, UT
East Central University, OK
Eastern New Mexico University, NM
East Tennessee State University, TN
Elizabeth City State University, NC
Emporia State University, KS
Fort Hays State University, KS
Fort Valley State University, GA
Georgia Southwestern State University, GA
Glenville State College, WV
Henderson State University, AR
Holy Trinity Orthodox Seminary, NY
Jacksonville State University, AL
Kentucky State University, KY
Lamar University, TX
Langston University, OK
Lewis-Clark State College, ID
Louisiana Tech University, LA
McNeese State University, LA
Mid-Continent College, KY
Middle Tennessee State University, TN
Minot State University, ND
Mississippi University for Women, MS
Mississippi Valley State University, MS
Moody Bible Institute, IL
Morehead State University, KY
Nazarene Indian Bible College, NM
New Mexico Highlands University, NM
New Mexico Institute of Mining and Technology, NM
Nicholls State University, LA
North Carolina Agricultural and Technical State University, NC
North Carolina Central University, NC
Northeastern State University, OK
Northern Arizona University, AZ
North Georgia College & State University, GA
Northwestern Oklahoma State University, OK
Northwestern State University of Louisiana, LA
Oklahoma Panhandle State University, OK
Peru State College, NE
Pittsburg State University, KS
Sam Houston State University, TX
Southeastern Louisiana University, LA
Southeastern Oklahoma State University, OK
Southern Arkansas University–Magnolia, AR
Southern Utah University, UT
Southwestern Oklahoma State University, OK
Sul Ross State University, TX
Texas Woman's University, TX
Universidad Adventista de las Antillas, PR

Peterson's Guide to Four-Year Colleges 2001   www.petersons.com

Cost Ranges Index
$6000–$7999

University of Arkansas at Monticello, AR
University of Central Oklahoma, OK
University of Louisiana at Lafayette, LA
University of Louisiana at Monroe, LA
University of New Orleans, LA
The University of North Carolina at Charlotte, NC
The University of North Carolina at Pembroke, NC
University of Puerto Rico, Río Piedras, PR
University of Science and Arts of Oklahoma, OK
University of South Alabama, AL
The University of Texas–Pan American, TX
The University of West Alabama, AL
Valley City State University, ND
Wayne State College, NE
Weber State University, UT
Wesley College, MS
Western Carolina University, NC
Western Kentucky University, KY
West Liberty State College, WV
West Texas A&M University, TX
Winston-Salem State University, NC

$6000–$7999

Colleges with No Room and Board or with Room Only

Baker College of Auburn Hills, MI
Baker College of Flint, MI **(room only)**
Baker College of Jackson, MI
Baker College of Port Huron, MI
Boston Architectural Center, MA
Calumet College of Saint Joseph, IN
Cambridge College, MA
Carlos Albizu University, FL
Chaparral College, AZ
City University, WA
Cleary College, MI
Cleveland College of Jewish Studies, OH
Colorado Technical University, CO
Colorado Technical University Denver Campus, CO
Detroit College of Business, MI
Detroit College of Business, Warren Campus, MI
DeVry Institute, NJ
DeVry Institute of Technology, AZ
DeVry Institute of Technology, Long Beach, CA
DeVry Institute of Technology, Pomona, CA
DeVry Institute of Technology, Alpharetta, GA

DeVry Institute of Technology, Decatur, GA
DeVry Institute of Technology, Addison, IL
DeVry Institute of Technology, Chicago, IL
DeVry Institute of Technology, MO
DeVry Institute of Technology, OH
DeVry Institute of Technology, TX
Florida Christian College, FL **(room only)**
Florida Metropolitan University–Tampa College, Brandon, FL
Georgia State University, GA **(room only)**
Gratz College, PA
Herzing College, GA
Instituto Tecnológico y de Estudios Superiores de Monterrey, Campus Querétaro,
Instituto Tecnológico y de Estudios Superiores de Monterrey, Campus Tampico,
International Bible College, AL **(room only)**
International College, FL
International College of the Cayman Islands, **(room only)**
John Wesley College, NC **(room only)**
Lakeview College of Nursing, IL
Lincoln University, CA
Louisiana State University in Shreveport, LA **(room only)**
Minnesota Bible College, MN **(room only)**
National University, CA
Oregon Health Sciences University, OR **(room only)**
Pennsylvania State University Abington College, PA
Pennsylvania State University Lehigh Valley Campus of the Berks-Lehigh Valley College, PA
Rocky Mountain College, AB **(room only)**
St. Augustine College, IL
St. John's College, IL
Shasta Bible College, CA **(room only)**
Sheldon Jackson College, AK
Southeastern University, DC
Thomas University, GA
The Union Institute, OH
University of Colorado Health Sciences Center, CO
University of Phoenix, AZ
University of the Sacred Heart, PR **(room only)**
University of West Los Angeles, CA
University of Wisconsin–Milwaukee, WI **(room only)**
Wayne State University, MI **(room only)**
Wilmington College, DE

Colleges with Room and Board

Adams State College, CO
Alabama State University, AL
American Indian College of the Assemblies of God, Inc., AZ
Arizona State University, AZ
Armstrong Atlantic State University, GA
Bemidji State University, MN
Black Hills State University, SD
Bowie State University, MD
Bridgewater State College, MA
Brigham Young University, UT
California Christian College, CA
California Polytechnic State University, San Luis Obispo, CA
California State University, Chico, CA
California State University, Fresno, CA
California State University, Northridge, CA
California State University, Sacramento, CA
Central Missouri State University, MO
Christopher Newport University, VA
Clemson University, SC
College of Charleston, SC
Columbus State University, GA
Concord College, WV
Dakota State University, SD
East Carolina University, NC
Eastern Kentucky University, KY
Eastern Oregon University, OR
Eastern Washington University, WA
The Evergreen State College, WA
Fairmont State College, WV
Fitchburg State College, MA
Florida Agricultural and Mechanical University, FL
Florida Atlantic University, FL
Florida Baptist Theological College, FL
Florida Gulf Coast University, FL
Florida International University, FL
Florida State University, FL
Fort Lewis College, CO
Framingham State College, MA
Francis Marion University, SC
Georgia College and State University, GA
Georgia Southern University, GA
God's Bible School and College, OH
Heritage Bible College, NC
Hobe Sound Bible College, FL
Humboldt State University, CA
Idaho State University, ID
Indiana State University, IN
Indiana University–Purdue University Indianapolis, IN
Inter American University of Puerto Rico, San Germán Campus, PR
International Baptist College, AZ

Iowa State University of Science and Technology, IA
Kansas State University, KS
Kentucky Mountain Bible College, KY
Lander University, SC
Lincoln University, MO
Louisiana State University and Agricultural and Mechanical College, LA
Magnolia Bible College, MS
Marshall University, WV
Martin Luther College, MN
Massachusetts College of Liberal Arts, MA
Massachusetts Maritime Academy, MA
Mayville State University, ND
Mesa State College, CO
Messenger College, MO
Midwestern State University, TX
Minnesota State University Moorhead, MN
Mississippi State University, MS
Missouri Southern State College, MO
Missouri Western State College, MO
Montana State University–Billings, MT
Montana State University–Bozeman, MT
Montana State University–Northern, MT
Montana Tech of The University of Montana, MT
Murray State University, KY
Nebraska Christian College, NE
New College of the University of South Florida, FL
New Mexico State University, NM
North Carolina School of the Arts, NC
North Carolina State University, NC
North Dakota State University, ND
Northern Kentucky University, KY
Northern Michigan University, MI
Northern State University, SD
Northwest Missouri State University, MO
Oklahoma State University, OK
Philander Smith College, AR
Radford University, VA
Rust College, MS
St. Cloud State University, MN
Salem State College, MA
Savannah State University, GA
Shawnee State University, OH
Shepherd College, WV
South Dakota School of Mines and Technology, SD
South Dakota State University, SD
Southeast Missouri State University, MO
Southern Illinois University Carbondale, IL
Southern Illinois University Edwardsville, IL

Southern Oregon University, OR
Southern Polytechnic State University, GA
Southwest Missouri State University, MO
Southwest State University, MN
Southwest Texas State University, TX
State University of West Georgia, GA
Stephen F. Austin State University, TX
Tennessee State University, TN
Tennessee Technological University, TN
Texas A&M University, TX
Texas A&M University at Galveston, TX
Texas A&M University–Commerce, TX
Texas A&M University–Kingsville, TX
Texas Southern University, TX
Texas Tech University, TX
Trinity Baptist College, FL
Trinity College of Florida, FL
Troy State University, AL
Truman State University, MO
The University of Alabama, AL
The University of Alabama in Huntsville, AL
University of Alaska Fairbanks, AK
The University of Arizona, AZ
University of Arkansas, AR
University of Arkansas at Pine Bluff, AR
University of Central Arkansas, AR
University of Central Florida, FL
University of Florida, FL
University of Georgia, GA
University of Houston, TX
University of Idaho, ID
The University of Iowa, IA
University of Kansas, KS
University of Kentucky, KY
University of Louisville, KY
University of Maine at Fort Kent, ME
University of Maine at Machias, ME
University of Maine at Presque Isle, ME
The University of Memphis, TN
University of Mississippi, MS
The University of Montana–Missoula, MT
University of Montevallo, AL
University of Nebraska at Kearney, NE
University of Nebraska–Lincoln, NE
University of Nevada, Reno, NV
University of New Mexico, NM
University of North Alabama, AL
The University of North Carolina at Asheville, NC
The University of North Carolina at Chapel Hill, NC
The University of North Carolina at Greensboro, NC

Cost Ranges Index
$10,000–$11,999

The University of North Carolina at Wilmington, NC
University of North Dakota, ND
University of Northern Colorado, CO
University of Northern Iowa, IA
University of North Florida, FL
University of North Texas, TX
University of Oklahoma, OK
University of Regina, SK
University of Rio Grande, OH
University of South Carolina, SC
University of South Carolina Spartanburg, SC
University of South Dakota, SD
University of Southern Colorado, CO
University of Southern Mississippi, MS
University of South Florida, FL
The University of Tennessee at Martin, TN
The University of Tennessee Knoxville, TN
The University of Texas at Austin, TX
University of Utah, UT
University of Wisconsin–Eau Claire, WI
University of Wisconsin–La Crosse, WI
University of Wisconsin–Madison, WI
University of Wisconsin–Parkside, WI
University of Wisconsin–Platteville, WI
University of Wisconsin–River Falls, WI
University of Wisconsin–Stevens Point, WI
University of Wisconsin–Stout, WI
University of Wisconsin–Superior, WI
University of Wisconsin–Whitewater, WI
University of Wyoming, WY
Utah State University, UT
Valdosta State University, GA
Virginia Polytechnic Institute and State University, VA
Webb Institute, NY
Western Montana College of The University of Montana, MT
Western State College of Colorado, CO
Westfield State College, MA
West Virginia State College, WV
West Virginia University, WV
West Virginia University Institute of Technology, WV
Wichita State University, KS
Winona State University, MN
Worcester State College, MA

$8000–$9999

Colleges with No Room and Board or with Room Only

The Advertising Arts College, CA
Allen College, IA
American Military University, VA
Antioch Southern California/Santa Barbara, CA
Aquinas College, TN
Baker College of Muskegon, MI **(room only)**
Baker College of Owosso, MI **(room only)**
Bellin College of Nursing, WI
Briarcliffe College, NY
Bryant and Stratton College, Virginia Beach, VA
Burlington College, VT
Clarkson College, NE **(room only)**
Cogswell Polytechnical College, CA
College of Aeronautics, NY
Crichton College, TN **(room only)**
Davenport College of Business, Kalamazoo Campus, MI
Davenport College of Business, Lansing Campus, MI
David N. Myers College, OH
DeVry Institute of Technology, Fremont, CA
DeVry Institute of Technology, NY
Five Towns College, NY
Golden Gate University, CA
Humphreys College, CA **(room only)**
Instituto Tecnológico y de Estudios Superiores de Monterrey, Campus Monterrey, **(room only)**
Kean University, NJ **(room only)**
Logan University of Chiropractic, MO
Lourdes College, OH
Monroe College, Bronx, NY **(room only)**
National American University, MO
O'More College of Design, TN
Peirce College, PA
Pennsylvania School of Art & Design, PA
St. Francis College, NY
St. Joseph's College, New York, NY
St. Joseph's College, Suffolk Campus, NY
Southern Christian University, AL
Touro College, NY
University of Great Falls, MT **(room only)**
Westwood College of Technology, CO

Colleges with Room and Board

Alaska Bible College, AK
Allen University, SC
American College of Thessaloniki
Appalachian Bible College, WV
Ball State University, IN
Barclay College, KS
Bloomsburg University of Pennsylvania, PA
Blue Mountain College, MS
Boise Bible College, ID
Brigham Young University–Hawaii Campus, HI
Bryn Athyn College of the New Church, PA
California Maritime Academy, CA
California State Polytechnic University, Pomona, CA
California State University, Stanislaus, CA
California University of Pennsylvania, PA
Calvary Bible College and Theological Seminary, MO
Central Baptist College, AR
Central Bible College, MO
Central Connecticut State University, CT
Central Michigan University, MI
Cheyney University of Pennsylvania, PA
Chicago State University, IL
The Citadel, The Military College of South Carolina, SC
Clarion University of Pennsylvania, PA
Cleveland State University, OH
Coastal Carolina University, SC
College of the Southwest, NM
The College of West Virginia, WV
The College of William and Mary, VA
Colorado State University, CO
Coppin State College, MD
Dallas Christian College, TX
Delaware State University, DE
Eastern Connecticut State University, CT
Eastern Illinois University, IL
Eastern Michigan University, MI
East Stroudsburg University of Pennsylvania, PA
Edinboro University of Pennsylvania, PA
Emmaus Bible College, IA
Eugene Bible College, OR
Ferris State University, MI
Flagler College, FL
Frostburg State University, MD
George Mason University, VA
Georgia Institute of Technology, GA
Grand Valley State University, MI
Hillsdale Free Will Baptist College, OK
Illinois State University, IL
Indiana University Bloomington, IN
Indiana University of Pennsylvania, PA
James Madison University, VA
Jarvis Christian College, TX
Johnson Bible College, TN
Keene State College, NH
Kutztown University of Pennsylvania, PA
Lake Superior State University, MI
Lane College, TN
LIFE Bible College, CA
Lock Haven University of Pennsylvania, PA
Longwood College, VA
Mansfield University of Pennsylvania, PA
Mary Washington College, VA
Michigan State University, MI
Michigan Technological University, MI
Mid-America Bible College, OK
Millersville University of Pennsylvania, PA
Minnesota State University, Mankato, MN
Morgan State University, MD
Morris College, SC
New Jersey City University, NJ
Norfolk State University, VA
Northern Illinois University, IL
Oakland University, MI
The Ohio State University, OH
Old Dominion University, VA
Oregon Institute of Technology, OR
Oregon State University, OR
Ozark Christian College, MO
Park University, MO
Piedmont Baptist College, NC
Plattsburgh State University of New York, NY
Portland State University, OR
Purchase College, State University of New York, NY
Purdue University, IN
The Richard Stockton College of New Jersey, NJ
Saginaw Valley State University, MI
Saint John's Seminary College of Liberal Arts, MA
St. Louis Christian College, MO
Salisbury State University, MD
San Francisco State University, CA
San Jose State University, CA
Shippensburg University of Pennsylvania, PA
Slippery Rock University of Pennsylvania, PA
Southeastern College of the Assemblies of God, FL
Southwestern Assemblies of God University, TX
Southwestern College of Christian Ministries, OK
State University of New York at Binghamton, NY
State University of New York at New Paltz, NY
State University of New York College at Buffalo, NY
State University of New York College at Cortland, NY
State University of New York College at Geneseo, NY
State University of New York College at Old Westbury, NY
State University of New York College at Oneonta, NY
State University of New York College at Potsdam, NY
State University of New York College of Technology at Alfred, NY
State University of New York Maritime College, NY
Stillman College, AL
Talladega College, AL
Talmudical Yeshiva of Philadelphia, PA
Trinity Bible College, ND
The University of Akron, OH
University of Colorado at Boulder, CO
University of Colorado at Colorado Springs, CO
University of Delaware, DE
University of Hawaii at Manoa, HI
University of Maine, ME
University of Maine at Farmington, ME
University of Massachusetts Dartmouth, MA
University of Massachusetts Lowell, MA
University of Minnesota, Crookston, MN
University of Minnesota, Duluth, MN
University of Minnesota, Morris, MN
University of Minnesota, Twin Cities Campus, MN
University of Missouri–Columbia, MO
University of Missouri–Rolla, MO
University of Missouri–St. Louis, MO
University of Nebraska at Omaha, NE
University of Nevada, Las Vegas, NV
University of Oregon, OR
University of Southern Maine, ME
University of Virginia, VA
University of Virginia's College at Wise, VA
University of Washington, WA
Virginia Commonwealth University, VA
Virginia Military Institute, VA
Voorhees College, SC
Washington State University, WA
West Chester University of Pennsylvania, PA
Western Connecticut State University, CT
Western Illinois University, IL
Western Michigan University, MI
Western Oregon University, OR
Western Washington University, WA
Williams Baptist College, AR
William Tyndale College, MI
Winthrop University, SC
Wright State University, OH
Yeshiva Karlin Stolin Rabbinical Institute, NY
Youngstown State University, OH

$10,000–$11,999

Colleges with No Room and Board or with Room Only

Antioch Southern California/Los Angeles, CA
Antioch University Seattle, WA
College of Visual Arts, MN

Cost Ranges Index

$12,000–$13,999

Columbia College–Hollywood, CA
Design Institute of San Diego, CA
Franklin Institute of Boston, MA
Harrington Institute of Interior Design, IL
Henry Cogswell College, WA
Holy Family College, PA
International Academy of Design, FL
International Academy of Merchandising & Design, Ltd., IL
John F. Kennedy University, CA
Kendall College of Art and Design, MI
Lyme Academy of Fine Arts, CT
National American University–St. Paul Campus, MN
Nebraska Methodist College of Nursing and Allied Health, NE **(room only)**
Oregon College of Art and Craft, OR
Paier College of Art, Inc., CT
Robert Morris College, IL
Saint Anthony College of Nursing, IL
Saint Francis Medical Center College of Nursing, IL **(room only)**
Union College, KY

Colleges with Room and Board

Barber-Scotia College, NC
Blackburn College, IL
Bowling Green State University, OH
Castleton State College, VT
Circleville Bible College, OH
Claflin University, SC
Colorado School of Mines, CO
East Texas Baptist University, TX
Emmanuel College, GA
Faith Baptist Bible College and Theological Seminary, IA
Fashion Institute of Technology, NY
Faulkner University, AL
Free Will Baptist Bible College, TN
Grace Bible College, MI
Grove City College, PA
Hannibal-LaGrange College, MO
Huron University, SD
Huston-Tillotson College, TX
Jamestown College, ND
Johnson State College, VT
Kent State University, OH
Kentucky Christian College, KY
Lee University, TN
LeMoyne-Owen College, TN
Lincoln Christian College, IL
Lincoln University, PA
Louisiana College, LA
Lyndon State College, VT
Madonna University, MI
Maine Maritime Academy, ME
Manhattan Christian College, KS
Maranatha Baptist Bible College, WI
Martin Methodist College, TN
Massachusetts College of Art, MA
Miami University, OH
North Central University, MN
Oak Hills Christian College, MN
Ohio University, OH
Ohio Valley College, WV
Paine College, GA
Patten College, CA
Pennsylvania State University Altoona College, PA
Pennsylvania State University at Erie, The Behrend College, PA
Pennsylvania State University Berks Campus of the Berks–Lehigh Valley College, PA
Pennsylvania State University Harrisburg Campus of the Capital College, PA
Pennsylvania State University Schuylkill Campus of the Capital College, PA
Pennsylvania State University University Park Campus, PA
Pikeville College, KY
Plymouth State College, NH
Practical Bible College, NY
Presentation College, SD
Ramapo College of New Jersey, NJ
Reformed Bible College, MI
Rowan University, NJ
Rutgers, The State University of New Jersey, Camden College of Arts and Sciences, NJ
Rutgers, The State University of New Jersey, College of Nursing, NJ
Rutgers, The State University of New Jersey, Newark College of Arts and Sciences, NJ
Sacred Heart Major Seminary, MI
Saint Augustine's College, NC
St. Gregory's University, OK
St. John's Seminary College, CA
Saint Luke's College, MO
San Jose Christian College, CA
Shaw University, NC
State University of New York at Albany, NY
State University of New York at Buffalo, NY
State University of New York at Farmingdale, NY
State University of New York at Oswego, NY
State University of New York at Stony Brook, NY
State University of New York Institute of Technology at Utica/Rome, NY
State University of New York Upstate Medical University, NY
Tennessee Wesleyan College, TN
Tougaloo College, MS
Towson University, MD
University of California, Davis, CA
University of California, Irvine, CA
University of California, Los Angeles, CA
University of California, Riverside, CA
University of California, San Diego, CA
University of California, Santa Barbara, CA
University of California, Santa Cruz, CA
University of Cincinnati, OH
University of Connecticut, CT
University of Illinois at Chicago, IL
University of Illinois at Urbana–Champaign, IL
University of Mary Hardin-Baylor, TX
University of Maryland, Baltimore County, MD
University of Maryland, College Park, MD
University of Massachusetts Amherst, MA
University of Michigan, MI
University of New Hampshire, NH
University of Pittsburgh at Bradford, PA
University of Rhode Island, RI
University of the Virgin Islands, VI
Wadhams Hall Seminary-College, NY
Washington Bible College, MD
Wayland Baptist University, TX
Webber College, FL
William Paterson University of New Jersey, NJ
Yeshiva Ohr Elchonon Chabad/West Coast Talmudical Seminary, CA
York College, NE
York College of Pennsylvania, PA

$12,000–$13,999

Colleges with No Room and Board or with Room Only

American University in Cairo, **(room only)**
Art Academy of Cincinnati, OH
The Art Institute of Portland, OR
Art Institute of Southern California, CA
Bastyr University, WA **(room only)**
Berkeley College, New York, NY
Bryant and Stratton College, Cleveland, OH **(room only)**
Cincinnati College of Mortuary Science, OH
College of St. Catherine–Minneapolis, MN **(room only)**
Cornish College of the Arts, WA
Davenport College of Business, MI **(room only)**
Des Moines University Osteopathic Medical Center, IA
Finch University of Health Sciences/The Chicago Medical School, IL
Goldey-Beacom College, DE **(room only)**
Jewish Hospital College of Nursing and Allied Health, MO **(room only)**
Jewish Theological Seminary of America, NY **(room only)**
Laboratory Institute of Merchandising, NY
Lawrence Technological University, MI **(room only)**
Molloy College, NY
Naropa University, CO
National-Louis University, IL
Pacific Oaks College, CA

Colleges with Room and Board

Atlanta Christian College, GA
Bartlesville Wesleyan College, OK
Bennett College, NC
Bethel College, TN
Brescia University, KY
Campbellsville University, KY
Cascade College, OR
The College of New Jersey, NJ
Columbia International University, SC
Conception Seminary College, MO
Dakota Wesleyan University, SD
Dallas Baptist University, TX
Deaconess College of Nursing, MO
Evangel University, MO
Fisk University, TN
Florida College, FL
Freed-Hardeman University, TN
Grand Canyon University, AZ
Harding University, AR
Hardin-Simmons University, TX
Hesser College, NH
Howard Payne University, TX
Howard University, DC
Johnson C. Smith University, NC
Judson College, AL
Lambuth University, TN
Lancaster Bible College, PA
Liberty University, VA
Lincoln Memorial University, TN
Lubbock Christian University, TX
McMurry University, TX
Midway College, KY
Mississippi College, MS
Missouri Baptist College, MO
Mount Olive College, NC
Multnomah Bible College and Biblical Seminary, OR
New Jersey Institute of Technology, NJ
North Greenville College, SC
Oakland City University, IN
Oklahoma Baptist University, OK
Oklahoma Christian University of Science and Arts, OK
Ouachita Baptist University, AR
Piedmont College, GA
Reinhardt College, GA
Rochester College, MI
Rutgers, The State University of New Jersey, College of Pharmacy, NJ
Rutgers, The State University of New Jersey, Cook College, NJ
Rutgers, The State University of New Jersey, Douglass College, NJ
Rutgers, The State University of New Jersey, Livingston College, NJ
Rutgers, The State University of New Jersey, Mason Gross School of the Arts, NJ
Rutgers, The State University of New Jersey, Rutgers College, NJ
Rutgers, The State University of New Jersey, School of Engineering, NJ
St. Charles Borromeo Seminary, Overbrook, PA
Saint Mary's College, MI
St. Mary's College of Maryland, MD
Saint Paul's College, VA
Shorter College, GA
Southwest Baptist University, MO
Southwestern Adventist University, TX
Spalding University, KY
State University of New York College of Environmental Science and Forestry, NY
Temple University, PA
Texas Wesleyan University, TX
Toccoa Falls College, GA
Trinity Lutheran College, WA
Union College, NE
University of California, Berkeley, CA
University of Mobile, AL
University of Pittsburgh, PA
University of Pittsburgh at Johnstown, PA
University of the Ozarks, AR
University of Vermont, VT
Virginia Union University, VA
Warner Southern College, FL

$14,000–$15,999

Colleges with No Room and Board or with Room Only

American Academy of Art, IL
American University of Rome, **(room only)**
The Art Institute of Fort Lauderdale, FL **(room only)**
Art Institutes International at San Francisco, CA
Audrey Cohen College, NY
California Institute of Integral Studies, CA
Capitol College, MD **(room only)**
Columbia College Chicago, IL **(room only)**
The Corcoran College of Art and Design, DC

Cost Ranges Index
$16,000–$17,999

Memphis College of Art, TN **(room only)**
Palmer College of Chiropractic, IA
Rocky Mountain College of Art & Design, CO
Villa Julie College, MD **(room only)**
Western States Chiropractic College, OR

Colleges with Room and Board

Abilene Christian University, TX
Alaska Pacific University, AK
Alverno College, WI
American InterContinental University, Atlanta, GA
Anderson College, SC
Barton College, NC
Belhaven College, MS
Bethany College of the Assemblies of God, CA
Bethel College, IN
Bethune-Cookman College, FL
Blessing-Rieman College of Nursing, IL
Bloomfield College, NJ
Bryan College, TN
California Baptist University, CA
California State University, Long Beach, CA
Campbell University, NC
Cardinal Stritch University, WI
Carson-Newman College, TN
Cedarville College, OH
Central Christian College of Kansas, KS
Charleston Southern University, SC
Colorado Christian University, CO
Columbia College, MO
Concordia University, NE
Cornerstone University, MI
Crown College, MN
Culver-Stockton College, MO
Cumberland College, KY
David Lipscomb University, TN
Drury University, MO
Embry-Riddle Aeronautical University, AZ
Ferrum College, VA
Friends University, KS
Gallaudet University, DC
Grace College, IN
Graceland College, IA
Hampton University, VA
Hanover College, IN
Hellenic College, MA
Hilbert College, NY
Hope International University, CA
Houston Baptist University, TX
Husson College, ME
Illinois College, IL
International Fine Arts College, FL
John Brown University, AR
Kentucky Wesleyan College, KY
King College, TN
LaGrange College, GA
La Roche College, PA
Lees-McRae College, NC
Limestone College, SC
Lindsey Wilson College, KY
Lyon College, AR
Mars Hill College, NC
Marygrove College, MI
McKendree College, IL
Mercy College, NY
Meredith College, NC
MidAmerica Nazarene University, KS
Milligan College, TN
Montreat College, NC
Mount Aloysius College, PA
Mount Marty College, SD
Newman University, KS
North Carolina Wesleyan College, NC
Northwest College, WA
Northwestern College, IA
Oakwood College, AL
Ohio Dominican College, OH
Ottawa University, KS
Our Lady of the Lake University of San Antonio, TX
Palm Beach Atlantic College, FL
Peace College, NC
Pfeiffer University, NC
Philadelphia College of Bible, PA
Robert Morris College, PA
Saint Mary College, KS
Samford University, AL
Silver Lake College, WI
Simpson College and Graduate School, CA
Sonoma State University, CA
Southern Adventist University, TN
Southern Wesleyan University, SC
Southwestern College, KS
State University of New York College at Brockport, NY
Sterling College, KS
Texas Lutheran University, TX
Tiffin University, OH
Trevecca Nazarene University, TN
Tuskegee University, AL
Union University, TN
University of Sioux Falls, SD
Upper Iowa University, IA
White Pines College, NH
Xavier University of Louisiana, LA

$16,000–$17,999

Colleges with No Room and Board or with Room Only

Academy of Art College, CA **(room only)**
American InterContinental University, CA **(room only)**
The Art Institute of Atlanta, GA **(room only)**
The Art Institute of Philadelphia, PA **(room only)**
Brooks Institute of Photography, CA
Loma Linda University, CA **(room only)**
Montserrat College of Art, MA **(room only)**
New York School of Interior Design, NY
Pacific Northwest College of Art, OR **(room only)**
Shimer College, IL **(room only)**
University of La Verne, CA

Colleges with Room and Board

Alvernia College, PA
Andrews University, MI
Asbury College, KY
Atlantic Union College, MA
Averett College, VA
Avila College, MO
Baker University, KS
Baylor University, TX
Becker College, MA
Bellarmine College, KY
Belmont University, TN
Benedictine College, KS
Berry College, GA
Bethany College, KS
Bethel College, KS
Brevard College, NC
Carlow College, PA
Carroll College, MT
Catawba College, NC
Central Methodist College, MO
Chaminade University of Honolulu, HI
Chowan College, NC
Christendom College, VA
Christian Brothers University, TN
Clark Atlanta University, GA
The College of New Rochelle, NY
College of St. Joseph, VT
College of Saint Mary, NE
Columbia Union College, MD
Concordia College, MN
Concordia University at Austin, TX
Concordia University Wisconsin, WI
Dana College, NE
Doane College, NE
Dordt College, IA
D'Youville College, NY
Edgewood College, WI
Elon College, NC
Embry-Riddle Aeronautical University, FL
Felician College, NJ
Finlandia University, MI
Fontbonne College, MO
Franciscan University of Steubenville, OH
Franklin College of Indiana, IN
Gardner-Webb University, NC
Geneva College, PA
Georgetown College, KY
Georgian Court College, NJ
Goshen College, IN
Grand View College, IA
Greensboro College, NC
Greenville College, IL
Hastings College, NE
Hawaii Pacific University, HI
Hendrix College, AR
Huntingdon College, AL
Indiana Institute of Technology, IN
Indiana Wesleyan University, IN
Iowa Wesleyan College, IA
Kendall College, IL
Lakeland College, WI
LeTourneau University, TX
Lindenwood University, MO
MacMurray College, IL
Malone College, OH
Marian College of Fond du Lac, WI
Marycrest International University, IA
Marylhurst University, OR
Maryville University of Saint Louis, MO
McPherson College, KS
Medaille College, NY
Methodist College, NC
Midland Lutheran College, NE
Missouri Valley College, MO
Morningside College, IA
Mount Mary College, WI
Mount St. Clare College, IA
Mount Saint Mary College, NY
Mount Senario College, WI
Mount Vernon Nazarene College, OH
Nebraska Wesleyan University, NE
Newberry College, SC
Northwest Nazarene University, ID
Northwood University, MI
Northwood University, Florida Campus, FL
Northwood University, Texas Campus, TX
Olivet Nazarene University, IL
Point Park College, PA
Queens College, NC
Rocky Mountain College, MT
St. Edward's University, TX
Saint Leo University, FL
St. Mary's University of San Antonio, TX
St. Thomas University, FL
San Diego State University, CA
Siena Heights University, MI
Sierra Nevada College, NV
Southern Vermont College, VT
Spelman College, GA
Spring Arbor College, MI
Tabor College, KS
Taylor University, Fort Wayne Campus, IN
Texas Christian University, TX
Thiel College, PA
Thomas College, ME
Thomas More College, KY
Thomas More College of Liberal Arts, NH
Trinity Christian College, IL
Tusculum College, TN
University of Dubuque, IA
University of Saint Francis, IN
University of St. Thomas, TX
Urbana University, OH
VanderCook College of Music, IL
Virginia Intermont College, VA
Walla Walla College, WA
Walsh University, OH
Waynesburg College, PA
Webster University, MO
Wesley College, DE
Westminster College, UT
William Jewell College, MO
William Penn University, IA
Wisconsin Lutheran College, WI

$18,000–$19,999

Colleges with No Room and Board or with Room Only

The American University of Paris,
Art Center College of Design, CA
The Art Institute of Phoenix, AZ **(room only)**
Center for Creative Studies—College of Art and Design, MI **(room only)**
Dowling College, NY **(room only)**
Monterey Institute of International Studies, CA
New School Bachelor of Arts, New School University, NY **(room only)**
Otis College of Art and Design, CA
Rush University, IL **(room only)**
San Francisco Art Institute, CA
San Francisco Conservatory of Music, CA
School of the Museum of Fine Arts, MA
Thomas Jefferson University, PA **(room only)**

Colleges with Room and Board

Adrian College, MI
Alderson-Broaddus College, WV
Allentown College of St. Francis de Sales, PA
American International College, MA
Anderson University, IN
Anna Maria College, MA
Aquinas College, MI
The Art Institute of Colorado, CO
Augustana College, SD
Azusa Pacific University, CA
Barat College, IL
Bay Path College, MA
Belmont Abbey College, NC
Benedictine University, IL
Bluffton College, OH
Bradley University, IL
Brenau University, GA
Briar Cliff College, IA
Caldwell College, NJ
Calvin College, MI
Carroll College, WI
Cazenovia College, NY
Centenary College of Louisiana, LA
Central College, IA
Champlain College, VT
Clarke College, IA
Coker College, SC
College of Mount St. Joseph, OH
The College of Saint Rose, NY
Columbia College of Nursing, WI
Columbus College of Art and Design, OH

Cost Ranges Index
$18,000–$19,999

Concordia College, MI
Concordia University, IL
Concordia University, OR
Concordia University at St. Paul, MN
Converse College, SC
Creighton University, NE
Daemen College, NY
Defiance College, OH
Dominican College of Blauvelt, NY
Dominican University, IL
Eastern College, PA
Eastern Mennonite University, VA
Eastern Nazarene College, MA
Elmhurst College, IL
Emory & Henry College, VA
Erskine College, SC
Florida Southern College, FL
Fresno Pacific University, CA
Gannon University, PA
High Point University, NC
Hillsdale College, MI
Huntington College, IN
Immaculata College, PA
Johnson & Wales University, RI
Judson College, IL
Kettering University, MI
Keuka College, NY
La Sierra University, CA
Lenoir-Rhyne College, NC
Lewis University, IL
Manchester College, IN
Marian College, IN
MCP Hahnemann University, PA
Mercyhurst College, PA
Morehouse College, GA
Mount Mercy College, IA
Mount Union College, OH
New York Institute of Technology, NY
Northland College, WI
Northwestern College, MN
Notre Dame College of Ohio, OH
Nova Southeastern University, FL
Nyack College, NY
Oklahoma City University, OK
Pacific Union College, CA
Pine Manor College, MA
Point Loma Nazarene University, CA
Quincy University, IL
Rivier College, NH
Roberts Wesleyan College, NY
Rockhurst University, MO
St. Ambrose University, IA
St. Andrews Presbyterian College, NC
Saint Joseph's College, IN
Saint Joseph's College, ME
St. Louis College of Pharmacy, MO
Saint Martin's College, WA
Saint Mary's University of Minnesota, MN
Saint Xavier University, IL
Schreiner College, TX
Seton Hill College, PA
Simpson College, IA
Sterling College, VT
Taylor University, IN
Teikyo Post University, CT
Thomas Aquinas College, CA

Transylvania University, KY
Tri-State University, IN
United States International University, CA
Unity College, ME
University of Charleston, WV
University of Dallas, TX
University of Detroit Mercy, MI
University of Indianapolis, IN
University of St. Francis, IL
University of Tulsa, OK
Ursuline College, OH
Vanguard University of Southern California, CA
Virginia Wesleyan College, VA
Warren Wilson College, NC
Wells College, NY
Wentworth Institute of Technology, MA
Western Baptist College, OR
Westminster College, MO
William Woods University, MO
Wilmington College, OH
Wilson College, PA
Wingate University, NC

$20,000 and over

Colleges with No Room and Board or with Room Only

American InterContinental University, (room only)
Dr. William M. Scholl College of Podiatric Medicine, IL
Manhattan School of Music, NY (room only)
Mannes College of Music, New School University, NY (room only)
Maryland Institute, College of Art, MD (room only)
Marymount Manhattan College, NY (room only)
Minneapolis College of Art and Design, MN (room only)
The National College of Chiropractic, IL (room only)
Parsons School of Design, New School University, NY
School of the Art Institute of Chicago, IL (room only)
School of Visual Arts, NY (room only)
The University of the Arts, PA (room only)

Colleges with Room and Board

Adelphi University, NY
Agnes Scott College, GA
Albertson College of Idaho, ID
Albertus Magnus College, CT
Albion College, MI
Albright College, PA
Alfred University, NY
Allegheny College, PA
Alma College, MI
American University, DC
Amherst College, MA
Antioch College, OH
The Art Institute of Boston at Lesley, MA
Ashland University, OH
Assumption College, MA
Augsburg College, MN
Augustana College, IL
Austin College, TX
Babson College, MA

Baldwin-Wallace College, OH
Baltimore International College, MD
Bard College, NY
Barnard College, NY
Barry University, FL
Bates College, ME
Beaver College, PA
Beloit College, WI
Bennington College, VT
Bentley College, MA
Berkeley College, White Plains, NY
Berklee College of Music, MA
Bethany College, WV
Bethel College, MN
Biola University, CA
Birmingham-Southern College, AL
Boston College, MA
Boston University, MA
Bowdoin College, ME
Brandeis University, MA
Bridgewater College, VA
Brown University, RI
Bryant College, RI
Bryn Mawr College, PA
Bucknell University, PA
Buena Vista University, IA
Butler University, IN
Cabrini College, PA
California College of Arts and Crafts, CA
California Institute of Technology, CA
California Institute of the Arts, CA
California Lutheran University, CA
Canisius College, NY
Capital University, OH
Carleton College, MN
Carnegie Mellon University, PA
Carthage College, WI
Case Western Reserve University, OH
The Catholic University of America, DC
Cedar Crest College, PA
Centenary College, NJ
Centre College, KY
Chapman University, CA
Chatham College, PA
Chestnut Hill College, PA
Claremont McKenna College, CA
Clarkson University, NY
Clark University, MA
Cleveland Institute of Art, OH
Cleveland Institute of Music, OH
Coe College, IA
Colby College, ME
Colby-Sawyer College, NH
Colgate University, NY
College Misericordia, PA
College of Insurance, NY
College of Mount Saint Vincent, NY
College of Notre Dame, CA
College of Notre Dame of Maryland, MD
College of Our Lady of the Elms, MA
College of Saint Benedict, MN
College of St. Catherine, MN
College of Saint Elizabeth, NJ
The College of St. Scholastica, MN

College of Santa Fe, NM
College of the Atlantic, ME
College of the Holy Cross, MA
The College of Wooster, OH
The Colorado College, CO
Columbia College, NY
Columbia College, SC
Columbia University, School of General Studies, NY
Columbia University, The Fu Foundation School of Engineering and Applied Science, NY
Concordia College, NY
Concordia University, CA
Connecticut College, CT
Cornell College, IA
Cornell University, NY
Covenant College, GA
The Culinary Institute of America, NY
Curry College, MA
Daniel Webster College, NH
Dartmouth College, NH
Davidson College, NC
Delaware Valley College, PA
Denison University, OH
DePaul University, IL
DePauw University, IN
Dickinson College, PA
Dominican University of California, CA
Drake University, IA
Drew University, NJ
Drexel University, PA
Duke University, NC
Duquesne University, PA
Earlham College, IN
Eckerd College, FL
Elizabethtown College, PA
Elmira College, NY
Emerson College, MA
Emmanuel College, MA
Emory University, GA
Endicott College, MA
Eugene Lang College, New School University, NY
Fairfield University, CT
Fairleigh Dickinson University, Florham-Madison Campus, NJ
Fairleigh Dickinson University, Teaneck–Hackensack Campus, NJ
Fisher College, MA
Florida Institute of Technology, FL
Fordham University, NY
Franklin and Marshall College, PA
Franklin College Switzerland,
Franklin Pierce College, NH
Furman University, SC
George Fox University, OR
Georgetown University, DC
The George Washington University, DC
Gettysburg College, PA
Goddard College, VT
Gonzaga University, WA
Gordon College, MA
Goucher College, MD
Green Mountain College, VT
Grinnell College, IA
Guilford College, NC
Gustavus Adolphus College, MN
Gwynedd-Mercy College, PA
Hamilton College, NY
Hamline University, MN

Hampden-Sydney College, VA
Hampshire College, MA
Hartwick College, NY
Harvard University, MA
Harvey Mudd College, CA
Haverford College, PA
Heidelberg College, OH
Hiram College, OH
Hobart and William Smith Colleges, NY
Hofstra University, NY
Hollins University, VA
Holy Names College, CA
Hood College, MD
Hope College, MI
Houghton College, NY
Illinois Institute of Technology, IL
Illinois Wesleyan University, IL
Iona College, NY
Ithaca College, NY
Jacksonville University, FL
John Carroll University, OH
Johns Hopkins University, MD
The Juilliard School, NY
Juniata College, PA
Kalamazoo College, MI
Kansas City Art Institute, MO
Kenyon College, OH
King's College, PA
Knox College, IL
Lafayette College, PA
Lake Erie College, OH
Lake Forest College, IL
La Salle University, PA
Lasell College, MA
Lawrence University, WI
Lebanon Valley College, PA
Lehigh University, PA
Le Moyne College, NY
Lesley College, MA
Lewis & Clark College, OR
Linfield College, OR
Long Island University, Brooklyn Campus, NY
Long Island University, Southampton College, NY
Long Island University, Southampton College, Friends World Program, NY
Loras College, IA
Loyola College in Maryland, MD
Loyola Marymount University, CA
Loyola University Chicago, IL
Loyola University New Orleans, LA
Luther College, IA
Lycoming College, PA
Lynchburg College, VA
Lynn University, FL
Macalester College, MN
Maharishi University of Management, IA
Maine College of Art, ME
Manhattan College, NY
Manhattanville College, NY
Marietta College, OH
Marist College, NY
Marlboro College, VT
Marquette University, WI
Mary Baldwin College, VA
Marymount College, NY
Maryville College, TN
Marywood University, PA
Massachusetts College of Pharmacy and Health Sciences, MA

Cost Ranges Index
$20,000 and over

Massachusetts Institute of Technology, MA
Menlo College, CA
Mercer University, GA
Merrimack College, MA
Messiah College, PA
Middlebury College, VT
Millikin University, IL
Millsaps College, MS
Mills College, CA
Milwaukee Institute of Art and Design, WI
Milwaukee School of Engineering, WI
Mitchell College, CT
Monmouth College, IL
Monmouth University, NJ
Moore College of Art and Design, PA
Moravian College, PA
Mount Holyoke College, MA
Mount Ida College, MA
Mount St. Mary's College, CA
Mount Saint Mary's College and Seminary, MD
Muhlenberg College, PA
Nazareth College of Rochester, NY
Neumann College, PA
Newbury College, MA
New England College, NH
New England Conservatory of Music, MA
New Hampshire College, NH
New York University, NY
Niagara University, NY
Nichols College, MA
North Central College, IL
Northeastern University, MA
North Park University, IL
Northwestern University, IL
Norwich University, VT
Notre Dame College, NH
Oberlin College, OH
Occidental College, CA
Oglethorpe University, GA
Ohio Northern University, OH
Ohio Wesleyan University, OH
Otterbein College, OH
Pace University, New York City Campus, NY

Pacific Lutheran University, WA
Pacific University, OR
Peabody Conservatory of Music of The Johns Hopkins University, MD
Pepperdine University, Malibu, CA
Philadelphia University, PA
Pitzer College, CA
Polytechnic University, Brooklyn Campus, NY
Polytechnic University, Farmingdale Campus, NY
Pomona College, CA
Pratt Institute, NY
Presbyterian College, SC
Princeton University, NJ
Principia College, IL
Providence College, RI
Quinnipiac University, CT
Randolph-Macon College, VA
Randolph-Macon Woman's College, VA
Reed College, OR
Regis College, MA
Regis University, CO
Rensselaer Polytechnic Institute, NY
Rhode Island School of Design, RI
Rhodes College, TN
Rice University, TX
Richmond, The American International University in London,
Rider University, NJ
Ringling School of Art and Design, FL
Ripon College, WI
Roanoke College, VA
Rochester Institute of Technology, NY
Rockford College, IL
Roger Williams University, RI
Rollins College, FL
Rose-Hulman Institute of Technology, IN

Rosemont College, PA
Russell Sage College, NY
Sacred Heart University, CT
Saint Anselm College, NH
St. Bonaventure University, NY
Saint Francis College, PA
St. John Fisher College, NY
St. John's College, MD
St. John's College, NM
Saint John's University, MN
St. John's University, NY
Saint Joseph College, CT
Saint Joseph's University, PA
St. Lawrence University, NY
Saint Louis University, MO
Saint Mary-of-the-Woods College, IN
Saint Mary's College, IN
Saint Mary's College of California, CA
Saint Michael's College, VT
St. Norbert College, WI
St. Olaf College, MN
Saint Peter's College, NJ
Saint Vincent College, PA
Salem College, NC
Salve Regina University, RI
Santa Clara University, CA
Sarah Lawrence College, NY
Savannah College of Art and Design, GA
Scripps College, CA
Seattle Pacific University, WA
Seattle University, WA
Seton Hall University, NJ
Shenandoah University, VA
Siena College, NY
Simmons College, MA
Simon's Rock College of Bard, MA
Skidmore College, NY
Smith College, MA
Southern Methodist University, TX
Southwestern University, TX
Spring Hill College, AL
Stanford University, CA

Stephens College, MO
Stetson University, FL
Stevens Institute of Technology, NJ
Stonehill College, MA
Suffolk University, MA
Susquehanna University, PA
Swarthmore College, PA
Sweet Briar College, VA
Syracuse University, NY
Trinity College, CT
Trinity College of Vermont, VT
Trinity University, TX
Tufts University, MA
Tulane University, LA
Union College, NY
University of Bridgeport, CT
University of Chicago, IL
University of Dayton, OH
University of Denver, CO
The University of Findlay, OH
University of Hartford, CT
University of Miami, FL
University of New England, ME
University of New Haven, CT
University of Notre Dame, IN
University of Pennsylvania, PA
University of Portland, OR
University of Puget Sound, WA
University of Redlands, CA
University of Richmond, VA
University of Rochester, NY
University of St. Thomas, MN
University of San Diego, CA
University of San Francisco, CA
The University of Scranton, PA
University of Southern California, CA
The University of Tampa, FL
University of the Pacific, CA
University of the Sciences in Philadelphia, PA
University of the South, TN
Ursinus College, PA
Utica College of Syracuse University, NY

Valparaiso University, IN
Vanderbilt University, TN
Vassar College, NY
Villanova University, PA
Wabash College, IN
Wagner College, NY
Wake Forest University, NC
Warner Pacific College, OR
Wartburg College, IA
Washington & Jefferson College, PA
Washington and Lee University, VA
Washington College, MD
Washington University in St. Louis, MO
Wellesley College, MA
Wesleyan College, GA
Wesleyan University, CT
Western Maryland College, MD
Western New England College, MA
Westminster Choir College of Rider University, NJ
Westminster College, PA
Westmont College, CA
West Virginia Wesleyan College, WV
Wheaton College, IL
Wheaton College, MA
Wheeling Jesuit University, WV
Wheelock College, MA
Whitman College, WA
Whittier College, CA
Whitworth College, WA
Widener University, PA
Wilkes University, PA
Willamette University, OR
Williams College, MA
Wittenberg University, OH
Wofford College, SC
Woodbury University, CA
Worcester Polytechnic Institute, MA
Xavier University, OH
Yale University, CT
Yeshiva University, NY

Majors Index

ACCOUNTING TECHNICIAN
Bryant Coll (RI)
Peirce Coll (PA)
Robert Morris Coll (IL)

ACTING/DIRECTING
Bard Coll (NY)
Barry U (FL)
Baylor U (TX)
Boston U (MA)
Carroll Coll (MT)
Columbia Coll Chicago (IL)
Concordia U (PQ, Canada)
Emerson Coll (MA)
Florida State U (FL)
Greensboro Coll (NC)
Ithaca Coll (NY)
Johnson State Coll (VT)
Kent State U (OH)
Maharishi U of Management (IA)
Marymount Manhattan Coll (NY)
Memorial U of Newfoundland (NF, Canada)
The Ohio State U (OH)
Ohio U (OH)
Penn State U Univ Park Campus (PA)
Ryerson Polytechnic U (ON, Canada)
Seton Hill Coll (PA)
Simon's Rock Coll of Bard (MA)
Texas Tech U (TX)
Trinity U (TX)
The U of Akron (OH)
U of Connecticut (CT)
U of Northern Iowa (IA)
U of Southern California (CA)
York U (ON, Canada)

ACTUARIAL SCIENCE
Ball State U (IN)
Bellarmine Coll (KY)
Baruch Coll of the City U of NY (NY)
Bradley U (IL)
Bryant Coll (RI)
Butler U (IN)
Carroll Coll (WI)
Central Connecticut State U (CT)
Central Michigan U (MI)
Central Missouri State U (MO)
Coll of Insurance (NY)
Colorado State U (CO)
Concordia U (PQ, Canada)
DePaul U (IL)
Dominican Coll of Blauvelt (NY)
Drake U (IA)
Eastern Michigan U (MI)
Elmhurst Coll (IL)
Florida A&M U (FL)
Florida State U (FL)
Frostburg State U (MD)
Georgia State U (GA)
Indiana U Northwest (IN)
Jamestown Coll (ND)
Lebanon Valley Coll (PA)
Lincoln U (PA)
Lycoming Coll (PA)
Mansfield U of Pennsylvania (PA)
Maryville U of Saint Louis (MO)
Mercy Coll (NY)
Mercyhurst Coll (PA)
Millersville U of Pennsylvania (PA)
Missouri Valley Coll (MO)
New Jersey Inst of Technology (NJ)
New York U (NY)
North Central Coll (IL)
North Dakota State U (ND)
Northern Arizona U (AZ)
The Ohio State U (OH)
Ohio U (OH)
Oregon State U (OR)
Penn State U Univ Park Campus (PA)
Plymouth State Coll (NH)
Quinnipiac U (CT)
Rider U (NJ)
St. Cloud State U (MN)
Saint Xavier U (IL)
Seton Hill Coll (PA)
Simon Fraser U (BC, Canada)
Southern Adventist U (TN)
State U of NY at Albany (NY)
Tabor Coll (KS)
Temple U (PA)
Thiel Coll (PA)
Université de Montréal (PQ, Canada)
Université Laval (PQ, Canada)
U of Calgary (AB, Canada)
U of Central Oklahoma (OK)
U of Connecticut (CT)
U of Hartford (CT)
U of Illinois at Urbana–Champaign (IL)
The U of Iowa (IA)
U of Manitoba (MB, Canada)
U of Michigan–Flint (MI)
U of Minnesota, Duluth (MN)
U of Minnesota, Twin Cities Campus (MN)
U of Nebraska–Lincoln (NE)
U of Northern Iowa (IA)
U of Pennsylvania (PA)
U of Pittsburgh at Bradford (PA)
U of St. Francis (IL)
U of St. Thomas (MN)
U of Toronto (ON, Canada)
U of Waterloo (ON, Canada)
The U of Western Ontario (ON, Canada)
U of Wisconsin–Madison (WI)
U of Wisconsin–Stevens Point (WI)
Worcester Polytechnic Inst (MA)
York U (ON, Canada)

ADAPTED PHYSICAL EDUCATION
Bridgewater State Coll (MA)
Central Michigan U (MI)
Eastern Michigan U (MI)
Ithaca Coll (NY)
Messiah Coll (PA)
St. Ambrose U (IA)
San Jose State U (CA)
Shaw U (NC)
U of Nebraska at Kearney (NE)

ADULT/CONTINUING EDUCATION
American International Coll (MA)
Andrews U (MI)
Arkansas Baptist Coll (AR)
Atlantic Union Coll (MA)
Auburn U (AL)
Bethel Coll (MN)
Biola U (CA)
Brock U (ON, Canada)
Colorado Christian U (CO)
Cornerstone U (MI)
Delaware Valley Coll (PA)
DePaul U (IL)
Franklin Pierce Coll (NH)
Immaculata Coll (PA)
Iona Coll (NY)
Iowa Wesleyan Coll (IA)
Lenoir-Rhyne Coll (NC)
Long Island U, Southampton Coll, Friends World Program (NY)
Louisiana Coll (LA)
Lynn U (FL)
Mars Hill Coll (NC)
Massachusetts Coll of Liberal Arts (MA)
Memorial U of Newfoundland (NF, Canada)
Milligan Coll (TN)
Morehouse Coll (GA)
Norwich U (VT)
Pittsburg State U (KS)
Pratt Inst (NY)
St. Joseph's Coll, Suffolk Campus (NY)
San Diego State U (CA)
Tabor Coll (KS)
Tennessee State U (TN)
Université de Sherbrooke (PQ, Canada)
U du Québec à Trois-Rivières (PQ, Canada)
U Coll of the Fraser Valley (BC, Canada)
U of Alberta (AB, Canada)
U of British Columbia (BC, Canada)
U of La Verne (CA)
U of Nevada, Las Vegas (NV)
U of New Brunswick, Fredericton (NB, Canada)
U of New Hampshire (NH)
U of Regina (SK, Canada)
U of San Francisco (CA)
Urbana U (OH)

ADULT/CONTINUING EDUCATION ADMINISTRATION
Penn State U Univ Park Campus (PA)
U Coll of the Fraser Valley (BC, Canada)

ADVERTISING
Abilene Christian U (TX)
Academy of Art Coll (CA)
Adams State Coll (CO)
The Advertising Arts Coll (CA)
American Academy of Art (IL)
Appalachian State U (NC)
Art Center Coll of Design (CA)
The Art Inst of Colorado (CO)
Ball State U (IN)
Barry U (FL)
Belmont U (TN)
Baruch Coll of the City U of NY (NY)
Boise State U (ID)
California State U, Fullerton (CA)
California State U, Hayward (CA)
Campbell U (NC)
Central Michigan U (MI)
Chapman U (CA)
Clarke Coll (IA)
Coll of Notre Dame (CA)
Columbia Coll Chicago (IL)
Columbus Coll of Art and Design (OH)
Concordia Coll (MN)
DePaul U (IL)
Drake U (IA)
Eastern Nazarene Coll (MA)
East Tennessee State U (TN)
Emerson Coll (MA)
Fairleigh Dickinson U, Teaneck-Hackensack Campus (NJ)
Fashion Inst of Technology (NY)
Ferris State U (MI)
Florida Southern Coll (FL)
Florida State U (FL)
Franklin Pierce Coll (NH)
Gannon U (PA)
Grand Valley State U (MI)
Hampton U (VA)
Harding U (AR)
Hastings Coll (NE)
Hawaii Pacific U (HI)
Howard U (DC)
Iona Coll (NY)
Iowa State U of Science and Technology (IA)
Johnson & Wales U (RI)
Kent State U (OH)
Lock Haven U of Pennsylvania (PA)
Louisiana Coll (LA)
Marietta Coll (OH)
Marist Coll (NY)
Marquette U (WI)
Marshall U (WV)
Mary Baldwin Coll (VA)
Memphis Coll of Art (TN)
Mercyhurst Coll (PA)
Michigan State U (MI)
Milligan Coll (TN)
Minneapolis Coll of Art and Design (MN)
Minnesota State U Moorhead (MN)
Murray State U (KY)
New England Coll (NH)
New Hampshire Coll (NH)
New York Inst of Technology (NY)
Northeastern U (MA)
Northern Arizona U (AZ)
Northwest Missouri State U (MO)
The Ohio State U (OH)
Ohio U (OH)
Oklahoma Baptist U (OK)
Oklahoma Christian U of Science and Arts (OK)
Oklahoma City U (OK)
Oklahoma State U (OK)
Pacific Union Coll (CA)
Penn State U Univ Park Campus (PA)
Pepperdine U, Malibu (CA)
Pittsburg State U (KS)
Point Park Coll (PA)
Portland State U (OR)
Quinnipiac U (CT)
Rider U (NJ)
Rochester Inst of Technology (NY)
Rowan U (NJ)
St. Ambrose U (IA)
St. Cloud State U (MN)
Sam Houston State U (TX)
San Jose State U (CA)
School of Visual Arts (NY)
Simpson Coll (IA)
Southeast Missouri State U (MO)
Southern Methodist U (TX)
Southwest Texas State U (TX)
Spring Hill Coll (AL)
Stephens Coll (MO)
Syracuse U (NY)
Temple U (PA)
Texas A&M U–Commerce (TX)
Texas Christian U (TX)
Texas Tech U (TX)
Texas Wesleyan U (TX)
Thomas Edison State Coll (NJ)
Union U (TN)
The U of Akron (OH)
The U of Alabama (AL)
U of Arkansas at Little Rock (AR)
U of Central Florida (FL)
U of Central Oklahoma (OK)
U of Colorado at Boulder (CO)
U of Florida (FL)
U of Georgia (GA)
U of Illinois at Urbana–Champaign (IL)
U of Kansas (KS)
U of Kentucky (KY)
U of Miami (FL)
U of Mississippi (MS)
U of Missouri–Columbia (MO)
U of Nebraska at Omaha (NE)
U of Nebraska–Lincoln (NE)
U of Nevada, Reno (NV)
U of North Texas (TX)
U of Oklahoma (OK)
U of Oregon (OR)
U of San Francisco (CA)
U of South Carolina (SC)
U of South Dakota (SD)
U of Southern Colorado (CO)
U of Southern Mississippi (MS)
The U of Tennessee Knoxville (TN)
The U of Texas at Austin (TX)
U of the Sacred Heart (PR)
U of Wisconsin–Madison (WI)
Virginia Commonwealth U (VA)
Washington State U (WA)
Washington U in St. Louis (MO)
Waynesburg Coll (PA)
Wayne State Coll (NE)
Webster U (MO)
Western Kentucky U (KY)
Western Michigan U (MI)
Western New England Coll (MA)
Westminster Coll (MO)
West Texas A&M U (TX)
West Virginia U (WV)
Widener U (PA)
Winona State U (MN)
Xavier U (OH)
Youngstown State U (OH)

AEROSPACE ENGINEERING TECHNOLOGY
Arizona State U East (AZ)
Central Missouri State U (MO)
Eastern Michigan U (MI)
Embry-Riddle Aeronautical U (FL)
Massachusetts Inst of Technology (MA)
New York Inst of Technology (NY)
Northeastern U (MA)
Purdue U (IN)
Saint Louis U (MO)
Utah State U (UT)

AEROSPACE SCIENCE
Augsburg Coll (MN)
Bishop's U (PQ, Canada)
Daniel Webster Coll (NH)
Dowling Coll (NY)
Indiana State U (IN)
U of the District of Columbia (DC)
York U (ON, Canada)

AFRICAN-AMERICAN (BLACK) STUDIES
Amherst Coll (MA)
Antioch Coll (OH)
Bowdoin Coll (ME)
Brandeis U (MA)
Brown U (RI)
California State U, Dominguez Hills (CA)
California State U, Fresno (CA)
California State U, Fullerton (CA)
California State U, Hayward (CA)
California State U, Long Beach (CA)
California State U, Los Angeles (CA)
California State U, Northridge (CA)
California State U, San Bernardino (CA)
City Coll of the City U of NY (NY)
Claflin U (SC)
Claremont McKenna Coll (CA)
Coe Coll (IA)
Colby Coll (ME)
Colgate U (NY)
Coll of Staten Island of the City U of NY (NY)
Coll of the Holy Cross (MA)
The Coll of William and Mary (VA)
The Coll of Wooster (OH)
Columbia Coll (NY)
Columbia U, School of General Studies (NY)
Cornell U (NY)
Dartmouth Coll (NH)
Denison U (OH)
DePaul U (IL)
Duke U (NC)
Earlham Coll (IN)

Majors Index
African-American (Black) Studies–Agricultural Education

Eastern Illinois U (IL)
Eastern Michigan U (MI)
Emory U (GA)
Florida A&M U (FL)
Fordham U (NY)
Georgia State U (GA)
Gettysburg Coll (PA)
Goddard Coll (VT)
Grinnell Coll (IA)
Guilford Coll (NC)
Hampshire Coll (MA)
Harvard U (MA)
Hobart and William Smith Colls (NY)
Hofstra U (NY)
Howard U (DC)
Hunter Coll of the City U of NY (NY)
Indiana State U (IN)
Indiana U Bloomington (IN)
Indiana U Northwest (IN)
Kent State U (OH)
Kenyon Coll (OH)
Knox Coll (IL)
Lehman Coll of the City U of NY (NY)
Lincoln U (PA)
Long Island U, Southampton Coll, Friends World Program (NY)
Loyola Marymount U (CA)
Luther Coll (IA)
Marquette U (WI)
Mercer U (GA)
Metropolitan State Coll of Denver (CO)
Miami U (OH)
Morehouse Coll (GA)
Morgan State U (MD)
Mount Holyoke Coll (MA)
New York U (NY)
Northeastern U (MA)
Northwestern U (IL)
Oakland U (MI)
Oberlin Coll (OH)
The Ohio State U (OH)
Ohio U (OH)
Ohio Wesleyan U (OH)
Penn State U Univ Park Campus (PA)
Pitzer Coll (CA)
Pomona Coll (CA)
Purdue U (IN)
Rutgers, State U of NJ, Camden Coll of Arts & Scis (NJ)
Rutgers, State U of NJ, Newark Coll of Arts & Scis (NJ)
Rutgers, State U of NJ, U Coll–Camden (NJ)
Saint Augustine's Coll (NC)
St. Olaf Coll (MN)
San Diego State U (CA)
San Francisco State U (CA)
San Jose State U (CA)
Sarah Lawrence Coll (NY)
Savannah State U (GA)
Scripps Coll (CA)
Seton Hall U (NJ)
Simmons Coll (MA)
Simon's Rock Coll of Bard (MA)
Smith Coll (MA)
Sonoma State U (CA)
Southern Methodist U (TX)
Stanford U (CA)
State U of NY at Albany (NY)
State U of NY at Binghamton (NY)
State U of NY at Buffalo (NY)
State U of NY at New Paltz (NY)
State U of NY Coll at Brockport (NY)
State U of NY Coll at Cortland (NY)
State U of NY Coll at Geneseo (NY)
State U of NY Coll at Oneonta (NY)
Suffolk U (MA)
Syracuse U (NY)
Temple U (PA)
Tougaloo Coll (MS)
Tufts U (MA)
U of Calif, Berkeley (CA)
U of Calif, Davis (CA)
U of Calif, Los Angeles (CA)
U of Calif, Riverside (CA)
U of Calif, Santa Barbara (CA)
U of Chicago (IL)
U of Cincinnati (OH)
U of Delaware (DE)

U of Georgia (GA)
U of Illinois at Chicago (IL)
The U of Iowa (IA)
U of Kansas (KS)
U of Louisville (KY)
U of Maryland, Baltimore County (MD)
U of Maryland, Coll Park (MD)
U of Massachusetts Amherst (MA)
U of Massachusetts Boston (MA)
U of Miami (FL)
U of Michigan (MI)
U of Michigan–Flint (MI)
U of Minnesota, Twin Cities Campus (MN)
The U of Montana–Missoula (MT)
U of Nebraska at Omaha (NE)
The U of North Carolina at Chapel Hill (NC)
The U of North Carolina at Charlotte (NC)
The U of North Carolina at Greensboro (NC)
U of Northern Colorado (CO)
U of Oklahoma (OK)
U of Pennsylvania (PA)
U of Pittsburgh (PA)
U of South Carolina (SC)
U of Southern California (CA)
U of South Florida (FL)
U of Virginia (VA)
U of Washington (WA)
U of Wisconsin–Madison (WI)
U of Wisconsin–Milwaukee (WI)
Vanderbilt U (TN)
Washington U in St. Louis (MO)
Wayne State U (MI)
Wellesley Coll (MA)
Wesleyan U (CT)
Western Michigan U (MI)
William Paterson U of New Jersey (NJ)
Yale U (CT)
York Coll of the City U of New York (NY)
Youngstown State U (OH)

AFRICAN LANGUAGES
Harvard U (MA)
Lincoln U (PA)
Long Island U, Southampton Coll, Friends World Program (NY)
U of Calif, Los Angeles (CA)
U of Wisconsin–Madison (WI)

AFRICAN STUDIES
Antioch Coll (OH)
Bard Coll (NY)
Barnard Coll (NY)
Bates Coll (ME)
Bloomfield Coll (NJ)
Bowdoin Coll (ME)
Brandeis U (MA)
Brooklyn Coll of the City U of NY (NY)
California State U, Northridge (CA)
Carleton Coll (MN)
Carleton U (ON, Canada)
Chicago State U (IL)
Colgate U (NY)
The Coll of Wooster (OH)
Columbia Coll (NY)
Connecticut Coll (CT)
Cornell U (NY)
Dartmouth Coll (NH)
DePaul U (IL)
Emory U (GA)
Fordham U (NY)
Franklin and Marshall Coll (PA)
Hamilton Coll (NY)
Hampshire Coll (MA)
Harvard U (MA)
Haverford Coll (PA)
Hobart and William Smith Colls (NY)
Indiana U (IN)
Indiana U Bloomington (IN)
Lake Forest Coll (IL)
Lehigh U (PA)
Long Island U, Southampton Coll, Friends World Program (NY)
Luther Coll (IA)
Marlboro Coll (VT)
McGill U (PQ, Canada)
Morgan State U (MD)
Oakland U (MI)
The Ohio State U (OH)

Ohio U (OH)
Portland State U (OR)
Queens Coll of the City U of NY (NY)
Rutgers, State U of NJ, Douglass Coll (NJ)
Rutgers, State U of NJ, Livingston Coll (NJ)
Rutgers, State U of NJ, Newark Coll of Arts & Scis (NJ)
Rutgers, State U of NJ, Rutgers Coll (NJ)
Rutgers, State U of NJ, U Coll–New Brunswick (NJ)
San Diego State U (CA)
Stanford U (CA)
State U of NY at Binghamton (NY)
State U of NY at Stony Brook (NY)
State U of NY Coll at Brockport (NY)
Tennessee State U (TN)
Tulane U (LA)
U of Calif, Davis (CA)
U of Chicago (IL)
The U of Iowa (IA)
U of Kansas (KS)
U of Michigan (MI)
U of Minnesota, Twin Cities Campus (MN)
U of Pennsylvania (PA)
U of Toronto (ON, Canada)
U of Wisconsin–Madison (WI)
Vanderbilt U (TN)
Vassar Coll (NY)
Washington U in St. Louis (MO)
Wellesley Coll (MA)
Western Michigan U (MI)
William Paterson U of New Jersey (NJ)
York U (ON, Canada)

AGRIBUSINESS
Abilene Christian U (TX)
Arkansas State U (AR)
Central Missouri State U (MO)
Coll of the Ozarks (MO)
Colorado State U (CO)
Cornell U (NY)
Illinois State U (IL)
McGill U (PQ, Canada)
Michigan State U (MI)
Middle Tennessee State U (TN)
Mississippi State U (MS)
North Carolina State U (NC)
Penn State U Univ Park Campus (PA)
South Dakota State U (SD)
Southwest Missouri State U (MO)
Southwest Texas State U (TX)
Stephen F. Austin State U (TX)
Texas A&M U (TX)
U of Delaware (DE)
U of Illinois at Urbana–Champaign (IL)
The U of Tennessee Knoxville (TN)
U of Wyoming (WY)

AGRICULTURAL AND FOOD PRODUCTS PROCESSING
Kansas State U (KS)
McGill U (PQ, Canada)
Michigan State U (MI)
The Ohio State U (OH)
Texas A&M U (TX)
U of Illinois at Urbana–Champaign (IL)

AGRICULTURAL ANIMAL HEALTH
Sul Ross State U (TX)

AGRICULTURAL BUSINESS
Andrews U (MI)
Arizona State U East (AZ)
Arkansas Tech U (AR)
Berea Coll (KY)
California Polytechnic State U, San Luis Obispo (CA)
California State Polytechnic U, Pomona (CA)
California State U, Chico (CA)
California State U, Fresno (CA)
Cameron U (OK)
Central Missouri State U (MO)
Clemson U (SC)
Concordia U Wisconsin (WI)
Cornell U (NY)

Delaware State U (DE)
Delaware Valley Coll (PA)
Dickinson State U (ND)
Dordt Coll (IA)
Eastern Kentucky U (KY)
Eastern New Mexico U (NM)
Eastern Oregon U (OR)
Florida A&M U (FL)
Florida Southern Coll (FL)
Fort Hays State U (KS)
Fort Lewis Coll (CO)
Freed-Hardeman U (TN)
Insto Tecno Estudios Sups Monterrey (Mexico)
Iowa State U of Science and Technology (IA)
Kansas State U (KS)
Lincoln U (MO)
Louisiana State U and A&M Coll (LA)
Louisiana Tech U (LA)
Lubbock Christian U (TX)
McPherson Coll (KS)
Michigan State U (MI)
MidAmerica Nazarene U (KS)
Missouri Valley Coll (MO)
Montana State U–Bozeman (MT)
Murray State U (KY)
New Mexico State U (NM)
Nicholls State U (LA)
North Carolina Ag and Tech State U (NC)
Northwestern Oklahoma State U (OK)
Northwest Missouri State U (MO)
Nova Scotia Ag Coll (NS, Canada)
The Ohio State U (OH)
Oklahoma Panhandle State U (OK)
Oklahoma State U (OK)
Oregon State U (OR)
Rocky Mountain Coll (MT)
Sam Houston State U (TX)
Simon's Rock Coll of Bard (MA)
Southeast Missouri State U (MO)
Southern Arkansas U–Magnolia (AR)
Southwest State U (MN)
State U of NY Coll of A&T at Cobleskill (NY)
Sul Ross State U (TX)
Tabor Coll (KS)
Tennessee Technological U (TN)
Texas A&M U–Kingsville (TX)
Texas Tech U (TX)
Tuskegee U (AL)
U of Alberta (AB, Canada)
U of Calif, Davis (CA)
U of Delaware (DE)
U of Georgia (GA)
U of Guelph (ON, Canada)
U of Idaho (ID)
The U of Lethbridge (AB, Canada)
U of Louisiana at Monroe (LA)
U of Maryland, Coll Park (MD)
U of Minnesota, Crookston (MN)
U of Minnesota, Twin Cities Campus (MN)
U of Missouri–Columbia (MO)
U of Nebraska at Kearney (NE)
U of Nebraska–Lincoln (NE)
U of New Hampshire (NH)
U of Puerto Rico, Mayagüez Campus (PR)
The U of Tennessee at Martin (TN)
The U of Tennessee Knoxville (TN)
U of Vermont (VT)
U of Wisconsin–Madison (WI)
U of Wisconsin–Platteville (WI)
U of Wisconsin–River Falls (WI)
Utah State U (UT)
Washington State U (WA)
Wayne State Coll (NE)
Western Michigan U (MI)
West Texas A&M U (TX)
Wilmington Coll (OH)

AGRICULTURAL ECONOMICS
Alabama A&M U (AL)
Auburn U (AL)
Central Missouri State U (MO)
Clemson U (SC)
Colorado State U (CO)
Cornell U (NY)
Eastern Oregon U (OR)
Fort Valley State U (GA)
Kansas State U (KS)
Langston U (OK)

McGill U (PQ, Canada)
McPherson Coll (KS)
Michigan State U (MI)
Mississippi State U (MS)
Murray State U (KY)
New Mexico State U (NM)
North Carolina Ag and Tech State U (NC)
North Dakota State U (ND)
Northwest Missouri State U (MO)
Nova Scotia Ag Coll (NS, Canada)
The Ohio State U (OH)
Oklahoma State U (OK)
Oregon State U (OR)
Purdue U (IN)
Rutgers, State U of NJ, Cook Coll (NJ)
South Dakota State U (SD)
Southern Illinois U Carbondale (IL)
Texas A&M U (TX)
Texas A&M U–Commerce (TX)
Texas Tech U (TX)
Truman State U (MO)
Université Laval (PQ, Canada)
U of Alberta (AB, Canada)
The U of Arizona (AZ)
U of Arkansas at Pine Bluff (AR)
U of British Columbia (BC, Canada)
U of Calif, Davis (CA)
U of Connecticut (CT)
U of Delaware (DE)
U of Florida (FL)
U of Georgia (GA)
U of Guelph (ON, Canada)
U of Hawaii at Manoa (HI)
U of Idaho (ID)
U of Illinois at Urbana–Champaign (IL)
U of Kentucky (KY)
U of Maine (ME)
U of Manitoba (MB, Canada)
U of Maryland, Coll Park (MD)
U of Missouri–Columbia (MO)
U of Nebraska–Lincoln (NE)
U of Nevada, Reno (NV)
U of Puerto Rico, Mayagüez Campus (PR)
The U of Tennessee Knoxville (TN)
U of Vermont (VT)
U of Wisconsin–Madison (WI)
Utah State U (UT)
Virginia Polytechnic Inst and State U (VA)
Washington State U (WA)

AGRICULTURAL EDUCATION
Andrews U (MI)
Arkansas State U (AR)
Auburn U (AL)
California State Polytechnic U, Pomona (CA)
California State U, Chico (CA)
California State U, Fresno (CA)
Central Missouri State U (MO)
Clemson U (SC)
Coll of the Ozarks (MO)
Colorado State U (CO)
Cornell U (NY)
Delaware State U (DE)
Iowa State U of Science and Technology (IA)
Langston U (OK)
Michigan State U (MI)
Mississippi State U (MS)
Montana State U–Bozeman (MT)
Morehead State U (KY)
Murray State U (KY)
New Mexico State U (NM)
North Carolina Ag and Tech State U (NC)
North Carolina State U (NC)
North Dakota State U (ND)
Northwest Missouri State U (MO)
The Ohio State U (OH)
Oklahoma Panhandle State U (OK)
Oklahoma State U (OK)
Penn State U Univ Park Campus (PA)
Prairie View A&M U (TX)
Purdue U (IN)
Rutgers, State U of NJ, Cook Coll (NJ)
Sam Houston State U (TX)
South Dakota State U (SD)
Southern Arkansas U–Magnolia (AR)

Majors Index
Agricultural Education–American Studies

Southwest Missouri State U (MO)
Tennessee Technological U (TN)
Texas A&M U–Commerce (TX)
Texas A&M U–Kingsville (TX)
The U of Arizona (AZ)
U of Arkansas (AR)
U of Arkansas at Pine Bluff (AR)
U of Calif, Davis (CA)
U of Connecticut (CT)
U of Delaware (DE)
U of Florida (FL)
U of Georgia (GA)
U of Idaho (ID)
U of Illinois at Urbana–Champaign (IL)
U of Minnesota, Twin Cities Campus (MN)
U of Missouri–Columbia (MO)
U of Nebraska–Lincoln (NE)
U of Nevada, Reno (NV)
U of Puerto Rico, Mayagüez Campus (PR)
The U of Tennessee at Martin (TN)
The U of Tennessee Knoxville (TN)
U of Wisconsin–Madison (WI)
U of Wisconsin–River Falls (WI)
U of Wyoming (WY)
Utah State U (UT)
Virginia Polytechnic Inst and State U (VA)
Washington State U (WA)
Western Kentucky U (KY)
West Virginia U (WV)
Wilmington Coll (OH)

AGRICULTURAL ENGINEERING
Auburn U (AL)
California Polytechnic State U, San Luis Obispo (CA)
California State Polytechnic U, Pomona (CA)
Clemson U (SC)
Colorado State U (CO)
Cornell U (NY)
Dalhousie U (NS, Canada)
Fort Valley State U (GA)
Iowa State U of Science and Technology (IA)
Kansas State U (KS)
McGill U (PQ, Canada)
Michigan State U (MI)
Mississippi State U (MS)
Murray State U (KY)
New Mexico State U (NM)
North Carolina State U (NC)
North Dakota State U (ND)
The Ohio State U (OH)
Penn State U Univ Park Campus (PA)
Purdue U (IN)
Rutgers, State U of NJ, Cook Coll (NJ)
Rutgers, State U of NJ, Coll of Engineering (NJ)
Saint Augustine's Coll (NC)
South Dakota State U (SD)
Tennessee Technological U (TN)
Texas A&M U (TX)
The U of Arizona (AZ)
U of Arkansas (AR)
U of British Columbia (BC, Canada)
U of Calif, Davis (CA)
U of Delaware (DE)
U of Florida (FL)
U of Georgia (GA)
U of Idaho (ID)
U of Illinois at Urbana–Champaign (IL)
U of Kentucky (KY)
U of Manitoba (MB, Canada)
U of Maryland, Coll Park (MD)
U of Minnesota, Twin Cities Campus (MN)
U of Nebraska–Lincoln (NE)
The U of Tennessee Knoxville (TN)
U of Wisconsin–Madison (WI)
U of Wisconsin–River Falls (WI)
Utah State U (UT)
Washington State U (WA)

AGRICULTURAL MECHANIZATION
Andrews U (MI)
Cameron U (OK)
Central Missouri State U (MO)
Clemson U (SC)

Coll of the Ozarks (MO)
Cornell U (NY)
Eastern Kentucky U (KY)
Iowa State U of Science and Technology (IA)
Kansas State U (KS)
Lewis-Clark State Coll (ID)
Montana State U–Bozeman (MT)
North Carolina Ag and Tech State U (NC)
North Dakota State U (ND)
Northwest Missouri State U (MO)
Nova Scotia Ag Coll (NS, Canada)
Penn State U Univ Park Campus (PA)
Purdue U (IN)
Sam Houston State U (TX)
South Dakota State U (SD)
Southwest Texas State U (TX)
State U of NY Coll of A&T at Cobleskill (NY)
Stephen F. Austin State U (TX)
The U of Arizona (AZ)
U of Arkansas (AR)
U of Idaho (ID)
U of Illinois at Urbana–Champaign (IL)
U of Missouri–Columbia (MO)
U of Nebraska–Lincoln (NE)
U of Puerto Rico, Mayagüez Campus (PR)
Washington State U (WA)

AGRICULTURAL PRODUCTION
The Ohio State U (OH)
Stephen F. Austin State U (TX)
Texas Tech U (TX)
U of Hawaii at Manoa (HI)
Washington State U (WA)

AGRICULTURAL SCIENCES
Andrews U (MI)
Arkansas State U (AR)
Auburn U (AL)
Austin Peay State U (TN)
Berea Coll (KY)
California Polytechnic State U, San Luis Obispo (CA)
California State Polytechnic U, Pomona (CA)
Cameron U (OK)
Clemson U (SC)
Colorado State U (CO)
Cornell U (NY)
Delaware State U (DE)
Dordt Coll (IA)
Eastern Kentucky U (KY)
Eastern Mennonite U (VA)
The Evergreen State Coll (WA)
Ferrum Coll (VA)
Florida A&M U (FL)
Fort Hays State U (KS)
Hampshire Coll (MA)
Hardin-Simmons U (TX)
Illinois State U (IL)
Iowa State U of Science and Technology (IA)
Lincoln U (MO)
Lubbock Christian U (TX)
Maharishi U of Management (IA)
McGill U (PQ, Canada)
McNeese State U (LA)
Michigan State U (MI)
Mississippi State U (MS)
Morehead State U (KY)
Murray State U (KY)
New Mexico State U (NM)
North Carolina Ag and Tech State U (NC)
North Dakota State U (ND)
Northwest Missouri State U (MO)
Nova Scotia Ag Coll (NS, Canada)
Oklahoma State U (OK)
Oregon State U (OR)
Penn State U Univ Park Campus (PA)
Prairie View A&M U (TX)
Purdue U (IN)
Rutgers, State U of NJ, Cook Coll (NJ)
Sam Houston State U (TX)
South Dakota State U (SD)
Southeast Missouri State U (MO)
Southern Arkansas U–Magnolia (AR)
Southern Illinois U Carbondale (IL)
Southwest Missouri State U (MO)

Southwest Texas State U (TX)
State U of NY Coll of A&T at Cobleskill (NY)
Stephen F. Austin State U (TX)
Sterling Coll (VT)
Tennessee State U (TN)
Texas A&M U (TX)
Texas A&M U–Commerce (TX)
Texas A&M U–Kingsville (TX)
Texas Tech U (TX)
Truman State U (MO)
Tuskegee U (AL)
U of Alaska Fairbanks (AK)
U of Alberta (AB, Canada)
The U of Arizona (AZ)
U of Arkansas at Monticello (AR)
U of Arkansas at Pine Bluff (AR)
U of British Columbia (BC, Canada)
U of Connecticut (CT)
U of Delaware (DE)
U of Idaho (ID)
U of Illinois at Urbana–Champaign (IL)
The U of Lethbridge (AB, Canada)
U of Louisiana at Lafayette (LA)
U of Manitoba (MB, Canada)
U of Maryland, Coll Park (MD)
U of Minnesota, Crookston (MN)
U of Minnesota, Twin Cities Campus (MN)
U of Missouri–Columbia (MO)
U of New Hampshire (NH)
U of Puerto Rico, Mayagüez Campus (PR)
The U of Tennessee at Martin (TN)
U of Vermont (VT)
U of Wisconsin–Madison (WI)
U of Wisconsin–River Falls (WI)
U of Wyoming (WY)
Utah State U (UT)
Warren Wilson Coll (NC)
Western Illinois U (IL)
Western Kentucky U (KY)
West Texas A&M U (TX)
Wilmington Coll (OH)

AGRONOMY/CROP SCIENCE
Andrews U (MI)
Brigham Young U (UT)
California Polytechnic State U, San Luis Obispo (CA)
California State Polytechnic U, Pomona (CA)
California State U, Chico (CA)
California State U, Fresno (CA)
Cameron U (OK)
Clemson U (SC)
Coll of the Ozarks (MO)
Colorado State U (CO)
Cornell U (NY)
Delaware Valley Coll (PA)
Eastern Oregon U (OR)
Fort Hays State U (KS)
Fort Valley State U (GA)
Insto Tecno Estudios Sups Monterrey (Mexico)
Insto Tecno Estudios Sups Monterrey, Querétaro (Mexico)
Iowa State U of Science and Technology (IA)
Kansas State U (KS)
McGill U (PQ, Canada)
Michigan State U (MI)
Mississippi State U (MS)
Murray State U (KY)
New Mexico State U (NM)
North Carolina State U (NC)
North Dakota State U (ND)
Northwest Missouri State U (MO)
The Ohio State U (OH)
Oklahoma Panhandle State U (OK)
Oregon State U (OR)
Penn State U Univ Park Campus (PA)
Purdue U (IN)
South Dakota State U (SD)
Southeast Missouri State U (MO)
Southwest Missouri State U (MO)
Southwest State U (MN)
Stephen F. Austin State U (TX)
Tennessee Technological U (TN)
Texas A&M U (TX)
Texas A&M U–Commerce (TX)
Texas A&M U–Kingsville (TX)
Texas Tech U (TX)
Truman State U (MO)

Tuskegee U (AL)
Université Laval (PQ, Canada)
U of Alaska Fairbanks (AK)
U of Alberta (AB, Canada)
U of Arkansas (AR)
U of Arkansas at Pine Bluff (AR)
U of Connecticut (CT)
U of Delaware (DE)
U of Florida (FL)
U of Georgia (GA)
U of Guelph (ON, Canada)
U of Illinois at Urbana–Champaign (IL)
U of Kentucky (KY)
U of Maine (ME)
U of Manitoba (MB, Canada)
U of Maryland, Coll Park (MD)
U of Minnesota, Crookston (MN)
U of Minnesota, Twin Cities Campus (MN)
U of Nebraska–Lincoln (NE)
U of New Hampshire (NH)
U of Puerto Rico, Mayagüez Campus (PR)
The U of Tennessee at Martin (TN)
U of Wisconsin–Madison (WI)
U of Wisconsin–Platteville (WI)
U of Wisconsin–River Falls (WI)
Utah State U (UT)
Virginia Polytechnic Inst and State U (VA)
Washington State U (WA)
West Virginia U (WV)

AIRCRAFT MECHANIC/AIRFRAME
Coll of Aeronautics (NY)
Dowling Coll (NY)
Inter American U of PR, Metropolitan Campus (PR)
LeTourneau U (TX)
Lewis U (IL)
Saint Louis U (MO)
Utah State U (UT)
Wilmington Coll (DE)

AIRCRAFT MECHANIC/POWERPLANT
Calvary Bible Coll and Theological Seminary (MO)
Thomas Edison State Coll (NJ)

AIRCRAFT PILOT (PRIVATE)
Calvary Bible Coll and Theological Seminary (MO)

AIRCRAFT PILOT (PROFESSIONAL)
Andrews U (MI)
Averett Coll (VA)
Baylor U (TX)
Bowling Green State U (OH)
Bridgewater State Coll (MA)
Calvary Bible Coll and Theological Seminary (MO)
Concordia Coll (MI)
Concordia U Wisconsin (WI)
Cornerstone U (MI)
Daniel Webster Coll (NH)
Delaware State U (DE)
Delta State U (MS)
Eastern Kentucky U (KY)
Embry-Riddle Aeronautical U (AZ)
Embry-Riddle Aeronautical U (FL)
Embry-Riddle Aeronautical U, Extended Campus (FL)
Florida Inst of Technology (FL)
Henderson State U (AR)
Indiana State U (IN)
Inter American U of PR, Metropolitan Campus (PR)
Jacksonville U (FL)
Kansas State U (KS)
LeTourneau U (TX)
Lewis U (IL)
Lynn U (FL)
Ohio U (OH)
Oklahoma State U (OK)
Piedmont Baptist Coll (NC)
Providence Coll and Theological Seminary (MB, Canada)
Purdue U (IN)
Rocky Mountain Coll (MT)
St. Cloud State U (MN)
Saint Louis U (MO)

Southeastern Oklahoma State U (OK)
State U of NY at Farmingdale (NY)
Thomas Edison State Coll (NJ)
Trinity Western U (BC, Canada)
U of Dubuque (IA)
U of Minnesota, Crookston (MN)
U of North Dakota (ND)
U of Oklahoma (OK)
Western Michigan U (MI)
Westminster Coll (UT)

AIR SCIENCE
La Salle U (PA)
Rensselaer Polytechnic Inst (NY)
The U of Iowa (IA)
U of Washington (WA)
Weber State U (UT)
York Coll (NE)

AIR TRAFFIC CONTROL
Averett Coll (VA)
Daniel Webster Coll (NH)
Hampton U (VA)
Kent State U (OH)
St. Cloud State U (MN)
Thomas Edison State Coll (NJ)
U of North Dakota (ND)

ALCOHOL/DRUG ABUSE COUNSELING
Alvernia Coll (PA)
Bethany Coll of the Assemblies of God (CA)
Calumet Coll of Saint Joseph (IN)
Cedar Crest Coll (PA)
Graceland Coll (IA)
Indiana Wesleyan U (IN)
MCP Hahnemann U (PA)
Minot State U (ND)
National-Louis U (IL)
Newman U (KS)
St. Cloud State U (MN)
Sheldon Jackson Coll (AK)
State U of NY Coll at Brockport (NY)
U of Detroit Mercy (MI)
U of South Dakota (SD)

AMERICAN GOVERNMENT
Bard Coll (NY)
Bridgewater State Coll (MA)
Daemen Coll (NY)
Dartmouth Coll (NH)
David Lipscomb U (TN)
Gallaudet U (DC)
Huston-Tillotson Coll (TX)
Rivier Coll (NH)
United States Coast Guard Academy (CT)
U of Maryland University Coll (MD)
The U of Montana–Missoula (MT)

AMERICAN HISTORY
Bard Coll (NY)
Brevard Coll (NC)
Bridgewater Coll (VA)
Calvin Coll (MI)
North Central Coll (IL)
Salve Regina U (RI)
The U of Iowa (IA)
U of Puerto Rico, Río Piedras (PR)

AMERICAN LITERATURE
Castleton State Coll (VT)
The Coll of Southeastern Europe, The American U of Athens (Greece)
Queens Coll (NC)
U of Calif, Los Angeles (CA)
U of Southern California (CA)
Washington U in St. Louis (MO)

AMERICAN STUDIES
Albion Coll (MI)
Albright Coll (PA)
American U (DC)
Amherst Coll (MA)
Arizona State U West (AZ)
Ashland U (OH)
Austin Coll (TX)
Bard Coll (NY)
Barnard Coll (NY)
Bates Coll (ME)
Baylor U (TX)
Boston U (MA)
Bowling Green State U (OH)

Majors Index
American Studies–Anthropology

Brandeis U (MA)
Brigham Young U (UT)
Brooklyn Coll of the City U of NY (NY)
Brown U (RI)
Cabrini Coll (PA)
California State U, Chico (CA)
California State U, Fullerton (CA)
California State U, San Bernardino (CA)
Carleton Coll (MN)
Case Western Reserve U (OH)
Cedarville Coll (OH)
Chapman U (CA)
Claremont McKenna Coll (CA)
Coe Coll (IA)
Colby Coll (ME)
Coll of Our Lady of the Elms (MA)
Coll of Saint Elizabeth (NJ)
Coll of St. Joseph (VT)
The Coll of Saint Rose (NY)
Coll of Staten Island of the City U of NY (NY)
The Coll of William and Mary (VA)
Colorado State U (CO)
Cornell U (NY)
Creighton U (NE)
David Lipscomb U (TN)
DePaul U (IL)
Dickinson Coll (PA)
Dominican Coll of Blauvelt (NY)
Dominican U (IL)
Drew U (NJ)
Eckerd Coll (FL)
Elmhurst Coll (IL)
Elmira Coll (NY)
Erskine Coll (SC)
The Evergreen State Coll (WA)
Fairfield U (CT)
Florida State U (FL)
Fordham U (NY)
Franklin and Marshall Coll (PA)
Franklin Coll of Indiana (IN)
Freed-Hardeman U (TN)
George Mason U (VA)
Georgetown Coll (KY)
Georgetown U (DC)
The George Washington U (DC)
Gettysburg Coll (PA)
Goddard Coll (VT)
Goucher Coll (MD)
Grinnell Coll (IA)
Hamilton Coll (NY)
Hampshire Coll (MA)
Harding U (AR)
Harvard U (MA)
High Point U (NC)
Hillsdale Coll (MI)
Hobart and William Smith Colls (NY)
Hofstra U (NY)
Howard Payne U (TX)
Huntingdon Coll (AL)
Idaho State U (ID)
Iona Coll (NY)
Johns Hopkins U (MD)
Keene State Coll (NH)
Kendall Coll (IL)
Kent State U (OH)
Kenyon Coll (OH)
King Coll (TN)
Knox Coll (IL)
Lafayette Coll (PA)
Lake Forest Coll (IL)
Lehigh U (PA)
Lehman Coll of the City U of NY (NY)
Lindsey Wilson Coll (KY)
Long Island U, Southampton Coll, Friends World Program (NY)
Lycoming Coll (PA)
Manhattanville Coll (NY)
Marist Coll (NY)
Marlboro Coll (VT)
Marymount Coll (NY)
Mary Washington Coll (VA)
Massachusetts Inst of Technology (MA)
Meredith Coll (NC)
Miami U (OH)
Middlebury Coll (VT)
Millikin U (IL)
Mills Coll (CA)
Minnesota State U Moorhead (MN)
Mississippi Coll (MS)
Montreat Coll (NC)
Mount Allison U (NB, Canada)

Mount Holyoke Coll (MA)
Mount St. Mary's Coll (CA)
Mount Union Coll (OH)
Muhlenberg Coll (PA)
Muskingum Coll (OH)
Nazareth Coll of Rochester (NY)
New Hampshire Coll (NH)
Northwestern U (IL)
Occidental Coll (CA)
Oglethorpe U (GA)
The Ohio State U (OH)
Oklahoma City U (OK)
Oregon State U (OR)
Our Lady of the Lake U of San Antonio (TX)
Penn State U Abington Coll (PA)
Penn State U Delaware County Campus of the Commonwealth Coll (PA)
Penn State U Harrisburg Campus of the Capital Coll (PA)
Penn State U Univ Park Campus (PA)
Pfeiffer U (NC)
Pine Manor Coll (MA)
Pitzer Coll (CA)
Pomona Coll (CA)
Providence Coll (RI)
Queens Coll (NC)
Queens Coll of the City U of NY (NY)
Ramapo Coll of New Jersey (NJ)
Reed Coll (OR)
Rider U (NJ)
Roger Williams U (RI)
Rosemont Coll (PA)
Rutgers, State U of NJ, Douglass Coll (NJ)
Rutgers, State U of NJ, Livingston Coll (NJ)
Rutgers, State U of NJ, Newark Coll of Arts & Scis (NJ)
Rutgers, State U of NJ, Rutgers Coll (NJ)
Rutgers, State U of NJ, U Coll–New Brunswick (NJ)
St. Cloud State U (MN)
Saint Francis Coll (PA)
St. John's U (NY)
Saint Joseph Coll (CT)
Saint Louis U (MO)
Saint Michael's Coll (VT)
St. Olaf Coll (MN)
Saint Peter's Coll (NJ)
Salem Coll (NC)
Salve Regina U (RI)
San Diego State U (CA)
San Francisco State U (CA)
San Jose State U (CA)
Sarah Lawrence Coll (NY)
Scripps Coll (CA)
Shenandoah U (VA)
Siena Coll (NY)
Simon's Rock Coll of Bard (MA)
Skidmore Coll (NY)
Smith Coll (MA)
Sonoma State U (CA)
Southeast Missouri State U (MO)
Southwestern U (TX)
Southwest Texas State U (TX)
Stanford U (CA)
State U of NY at Buffalo (NY)
State U of NY at Oswego (NY)
State U of NY Coll at Fredonia (NY)
State U of NY Coll at Geneseo (NY)
State U of NY Coll at Old Westbury (NY)
Stetson U (FL)
Stonehill Coll (MA)
Syracuse U (NY)
Temple U (PA)
Tennessee Wesleyan Coll (TN)
Trinity Coll (CT)
Tufts U (MA)
Tulane U (LA)
Union Coll (NY)
United States Military Academy (NY)
The U of Alabama (AL)
U of Alaska Fairbanks (AK)
U of Calif, Berkeley (CA)
U of Calif, Davis (CA)
U of Calif, Santa Cruz (CA)
U of Chicago (IL)
U of Colorado at Boulder (CO)

U of Dayton (OH)
U of Florida (FL)
U of Hawaii at Manoa (HI)
U of Idaho (ID)
The U of Iowa (IA)
U of Kansas (KS)
U of Maryland, Baltimore County (MD)
U of Maryland, Coll Park (MD)
U of Massachusetts Boston (MA)
U of Massachusetts Lowell (MA)
U of Miami (FL)
U of Michigan (MI)
U of Michigan–Dearborn (MI)
U of Minnesota, Twin Cities Campus (MN)
U of Mississippi (MS)
U of Missouri–Kansas City (MO)
U of New England (ME)
U of New Hampshire (NH)
U of New Mexico (NM)
The U of North Carolina at Chapel Hill (NC)
U of Northern Iowa (IA)
U of Notre Dame (IN)
U of Pennsylvania (PA)
U of Pittsburgh at Bradford (PA)
U of Pittsburgh at Johnstown (PA)
U of Richmond (VA)
U of Rio Grande (OH)
U of San Diego (CA)
U of Southern California (CA)
U of Southern Mississippi (MS)
U of South Florida (FL)
The U of Texas at Austin (TX)
The U of Texas at Dallas (TX)
The U of Texas at San Antonio (TX)
The U of Texas–Pan American (TX)
U of the South (TN)
U of Toronto (ON, Canada)
U of Wisconsin–Madison (WI)
U of Wyoming (WY)
Upper Iowa U (IA)
Ursuline Coll (OH)
Utah State U (UT)
Valparaiso U (IN)
Vanderbilt U (TN)
Vassar Coll (NY)
Virginia Wesleyan Coll (VA)
Warner Pacific Coll (OR)
Warren Wilson Coll (NC)
Washington Coll (MD)
Washington State U (WA)
Washington U in St. Louis (MO)
Wayne State U (MI)
Wellesley Coll (MA)
Wells Coll (NY)
Wesleyan Coll (GA)
Wesleyan U (CT)
Wesley Coll (DE)
West Chester U of Pennsylvania (PA)
Western Connecticut State U (CT)
Western Michigan U (MI)
Western New England Coll (MA)
Western State Coll of Colorado (CO)
Western Washington U (WA)
Wheaton Coll (MA)
Whitworth Coll (WA)
Willamette U (OR)
Williams Coll (MA)
Wingate U (NC)
Wittenberg U (OH)
Yale U (CT)
Youngstown State U (OH)

ANALYTICAL CHEMISTRY
Florida State U (FL)
McGill U (PQ, Canada)

ANATOMY
Andrews U (MI)
Cornell U (NY)
Duke U (NC)
Hampshire Coll (MA)
Howard U (DC)
McGill U (PQ, Canada)
Minnesota State U, Mankato (MN)
U of Indianapolis (IN)
U of Regina (SK, Canada)
U of Toronto (ON, Canada)

ANIMAL SCIENCES
Abilene Christian U (TX)
Alabama A&M U (AL)

Arkansas State U (AR)
Auburn U (AL)
Berry Coll (GA)
Brigham Young U (UT)
California Polytechnic State U, San Luis Obispo (CA)
California State Polytechnic U, Pomona (CA)
California State U, Chico (CA)
California State U, Fresno (CA)
Cameron U (OK)
Clemson U (SC)
Coll of the Ozarks (MO)
Colorado State U (CO)
Cornell U (NY)
Delaware State U (DE)
Delaware Valley Coll (PA)
Dordt Coll (IA)
Florida A&M U (FL)
Fort Hays State U (KS)
Fort Valley State U (GA)
Hampshire Coll (MA)
Insto Tecno Estudios Sups Monterrey (Mexico)
Insto Tecno Estudios Sups Monterrey, Querétaro (Mexico)
Iowa State U of Science and Technology (IA)
Kansas State U (KS)
Langston U (OK)
Louisiana State U and A&M Coll (LA)
Louisiana Tech U (LA)
McGill U (PQ, Canada)
Michigan State U (MI)
Middle Tennessee State U (TN)
Mississippi State U (MS)
Montana State U–Bozeman (MT)
Mount Ida Coll (MA)
New Mexico State U (NM)
North Carolina Ag and Tech State U (NC)
North Carolina State U (NC)
North Dakota State U (ND)
Northwest Missouri State U (MO)
Nova Scotia Ag Coll (NS, Canada)
The Ohio State U (OH)
Oklahoma Panhandle State U (OK)
Oklahoma State U (OK)
Oregon State U (OR)
Penn State U Univ Park Campus (PA)
Purdue U (IN)
Rutgers, State U of NJ, Cook Coll (NJ)
Sam Houston State U (TX)
South Dakota State U (SD)
Southeast Missouri State U (MO)
Southern Illinois U Carbondale (IL)
Southwestern U (TX)
Southwest Missouri State U (MO)
Southwest Texas State U (TX)
State U of NY Coll of A&T at Cobleskill (NY)
Stephen F. Austin State U (TX)
Sul Ross State U (TX)
Tennessee State U (TN)
Tennessee Technological U (TN)
Texas A&M U (TX)
Texas A&M U–Commerce (TX)
Texas A&M U–Kingsville (TX)
Texas Tech U (TX)
Truman State U (MO)
Tuskegee U (AL)
U of Alaska Fairbanks (AK)
U of Alberta (AB, Canada)
The U of Arizona (AZ)
U of Arkansas (AR)
U of Arkansas at Pine Bluff (AR)
U of British Columbia (BC, Canada)
U of Calif, Davis (CA)
U of Connecticut (CT)
U of Delaware (DE)
U of Denver (CO)
U of Florida (FL)
U of Georgia (GA)
U of Guelph (ON, Canada)
U of Hawaii at Manoa (HI)
U of Idaho (ID)
U of Illinois at Urbana–Champaign (IL)
U of Kentucky (KY)
U of Maine (ME)
U of Manitoba (MB, Canada)
U of Maryland, Coll Park (MD)
U of Massachusetts Amherst (MA)

U of Minnesota, Crookston (MN)
U of Minnesota, Twin Cities Campus (MN)
U of Missouri–Columbia (MO)
U of Nebraska–Lincoln (NE)
U of Nevada, Reno (NV)
U of New Hampshire (NH)
U of Puerto Rico, Mayagüez Campus (PR)
U of Rhode Island (RI)
U of Southern California (CA)
The U of Tennessee at Martin (TN)
The U of Tennessee Knoxville (TN)
U of Vermont (VT)
U of Wisconsin–Madison (WI)
U of Wisconsin–Platteville (WI)
U of Wisconsin–River Falls (WI)
U of Wyoming (WY)
Utah State U (UT)
Virginia Polytechnic Inst and State U (VA)
Washington State U (WA)
West Virginia U (WV)

ANTHROPOLOGY
Adelphi U (NY)
Agnes Scott Coll (GA)
Albertson Coll of Idaho (ID)
Albion Coll (MI)
American U (DC)
American U in Cairo (Egypt)
Amherst Coll (MA)
Antioch Coll (OH)
Appalachian State U (NC)
Arizona State U (AZ)
Athabasca U (AB, Canada)
Auburn U (AL)
Augustana Coll (IL)
Ball State U (IN)
Bard Coll (NY)
Barnard Coll (NY)
Bates Coll (ME)
Baylor U (TX)
Beloit Coll (WI)
Bennington Coll (VT)
Berry Coll (GA)
Biola U (CA)
Bishop's U (PQ, Canada)
Bloomsburg U of Pennsylvania (PA)
Boise State U (ID)
Boston U (MA)
Bowdoin Coll (ME)
Brandeis U (MA)
Bridgewater State Coll (MA)
Brigham Young U (UT)
Brooklyn Coll of the City U of NY (NY)
Brown U (RI)
Bryn Mawr Coll (PA)
Bucknell U (PA)
Butler U (IN)
California State Polytechnic U, Pomona (CA)
California State U, Chico (CA)
California State U, Dominguez Hills (CA)
California State U, Fresno (CA)
California State U, Fullerton (CA)
California State U, Hayward (CA)
California State U, Long Beach (CA)
California State U, Los Angeles (CA)
California State U, Northridge (CA)
California State U, Sacramento (CA)
California State U, San Bernardino (CA)
California State U, Stanislaus (CA)
California U of Pennsylvania (PA)
Canisius Coll (NY)
Carleton Coll (MN)
Carleton U (ON, Canada)
Case Western Reserve U (OH)
The Catholic U of America (DC)
Central Connecticut State U (CT)
Central Michigan U (MI)
Centre Coll (KY)
Chicago State U (IL)
City Coll of the City U of NY (NY)
Clarion U of Pennsylvania (PA)
Cleveland State U (OH)
Colby Coll (ME)
Colgate U (NY)
Coll of Charleston (SC)

Majors Index
Anthropology–Applied Art

Coll of Staten Island of the City U of NY (NY)
The Coll of William and Mary (VA)
The Colorado Coll (CO)
Colorado State U (CO)
Columbia Coll (NY)
Columbia U, School of General Studies (NY)
Concordia U (PQ, Canada)
Connecticut Coll (CT)
Cornell Coll (IA)
Cornell U (NY)
Dalhousie U (NS, Canada)
Dartmouth Coll (NH)
Davidson Coll (NC)
Denison U (OH)
DePaul U (IL)
DePauw U (IN)
Dickinson Coll (PA)
Dowling Coll (NY)
Drake U (IA)
Drew U (NJ)
Duke U (NC)
East Carolina U (NC)
Eastern Kentucky U (KY)
Eastern Michigan U (MI)
Eastern New Mexico U (NM)
Eastern Oregon U (OR)
Eastern Washington U (WA)
Eckerd Coll (FL)
Edinboro U of Pennsylvania (PA)
Elizabethtown Coll (PA)
Elmira Coll (NY)
Emory U (GA)
Eugene Lang Coll, New School U (NY)
The Evergreen State Coll (WA)
Florida Atlantic U (FL)
Florida State U (FL)
Fordham U (NY)
Fort Lewis Coll (CO)
Framingham State Coll (MA)
Franciscan U of Steubenville (OH)
Franklin and Marshall Coll (PA)
Franklin Pierce Coll (NH)
George Mason U (VA)
The George Washington U (DC)
Georgia Southern U (GA)
Georgia State U (GA)
Gettysburg Coll (PA)
Goddard Coll (VT)
Grand Valley State U (MI)
Grinnell Coll (IA)
Guilford Coll (NC)
Gustavus Adolphus Coll (MN)
Hamilton Coll (NY)
Hamline U (MN)
Hampshire Coll (MA)
Hanover Coll (IN)
Hartwick Coll (NY)
Harvard U (MA)
Haverford Coll (PA)
Hawaii Pacific U (HI)
Heidelberg Coll (OH)
Hendrix Coll (AR)
Hobart and William Smith Colls (NY)
Hofstra U (NY)
Howard U (DC)
Humboldt State U (CA)
Hunter Coll of the City U of NY (NY)
Idaho State U (ID)
Illinois State U (IL)
Indiana State U (IN)
Indiana U Bloomington (IN)
Indiana U of Pennsylvania (PA)
Indiana U–Purdue U Fort Wayne (IN)
Indiana U–Purdue U Indianapolis (IN)
Iowa State U of Science and Technology (IA)
Ithaca Coll (NY)
Jacksonville State U (AL)
James Madison U (VA)
Johns Hopkins U (MD)
Johnson State Coll (VT)
Judson Coll (IL)
Juniata Coll (PA)
Kalamazoo Coll (MI)
Kansas State U (KS)
Kent State U (OH)
Kenyon Coll (OH)
Knox Coll (IL)
Kutztown U of Pennsylvania (PA)
Lafayette Coll (PA)

Lake Forest Coll (IL)
Lakehead U (ON, Canada)
Lawrence U (WI)
Lehigh U (PA)
Lehman Coll of the City U of NY (NY)
Lewis & Clark Coll (OR)
Lincoln U (PA)
Linfield Coll (OR)
Lock Haven U of Pennsylvania (PA)
Long Island U, Brooklyn Campus (NY)
Long Island U, Southampton Coll, Friends World Program (NY)
Longwood Coll (VA)
Louisiana State U and A&M Coll (LA)
Loyola U Chicago (IL)
Luther Coll (IA)
Lycoming Coll (PA)
Macalester Coll (MN)
Mansfield U of Pennsylvania (PA)
Marlboro Coll (VT)
Marquette U (WI)
Marshall U (WV)
Massachusetts Coll of Liberal Arts (MA)
Massachusetts Inst of Technology (MA)
McGill U (PQ, Canada)
Memorial U of Newfoundland (NF, Canada)
Mercyhurst Coll (PA)
Mesa State Coll (CO)
Metropolitan State Coll of Denver (CO)
Miami U (OH)
Michigan State U (MI)
Middlebury Coll (VT)
Middle Tennessee State U (TN)
Millersville U of Pennsylvania (PA)
Millsaps Coll (MS)
Mills Coll (CA)
Minnesota State U, Mankato (MN)
Minnesota State U Moorhead (MN)
Mississippi State U (MS)
Monmouth U (NJ)
Mount Allison U (NB, Canada)
Mount Holyoke Coll (MA)
Mount Saint Vincent U (NS, Canada)
National-Louis U (IL)
New Coll of the U of South Florida (FL)
New Mexico Highlands U (NM)
New Mexico State U (NM)
New York U (NY)
North Carolina Wesleyan Coll (NC)
North Central Coll (IL)
North Dakota State U (ND)
Northeastern Illinois U (IL)
Northeastern U (MA)
Northern Arizona U (AZ)
Northern Illinois U (IL)
Northern Kentucky U (KY)
North Park U (IL)
Northwestern State U of Louisiana (LA)
Northwestern U (IL)
Oakland U (MI)
Oberlin Coll (OH)
Occidental Coll (CA)
The Ohio State U (OH)
Ohio U (OH)
Ohio Wesleyan U (OH)
Okanagan U Coll (BC, Canada)
Oregon State U (OR)
Pace U, Pleasantville/Briarcliff Campus (NY)
Pacific Lutheran U (WA)
Penn State U Univ Park Campus (PA)
Pitzer Coll (CA)
Plattsburgh State U of NY (NY)
Plymouth State Coll (NH)
Pomona Coll (CA)
Portland State U (OR)
Princeton U (NJ)
Principia Coll (IL)
Purchase Coll, State U of NY (NY)
Queens Coll of the City U of NY (NY)
Radford U (VA)
Reed Coll (OR)
Rhodes Coll (TN)
Rice U (TX)

Richmond, The American International U in London (United Kingdom)
Ripon Coll (WI)
Rockford Coll (IL)
Rollins Coll (FL)
Rutgers, State U of NJ, Douglass Coll (NJ)
Rutgers, State U of NJ, Livingston Coll (NJ)
Rutgers, State U of NJ, Newark Coll of Arts & Scis (NJ)
Rutgers, State U of NJ, Rutgers Coll (NJ)
Rutgers, State U of NJ, U Coll–New Brunswick (NJ)
St. Cloud State U (MN)
Saint Francis Coll (PA)
St. Francis Xavier U (NS, Canada)
St. John Fisher Coll (NY)
St. John's U (NY)
St. Lawrence U (NY)
Saint Mary's Coll (IN)
Saint Mary's Coll of California (CA)
St. Mary's Coll of Maryland (MD)
Saint Mary's U (NS, Canada)
Saint Vincent Coll (PA)
Salve Regina U (RI)
San Diego State U (CA)
San Francisco State U (CA)
San Jose State U (CA)
Santa Clara U (CA)
Sarah Lawrence Coll (NY)
Scripps Coll (CA)
Seton Hall U (NJ)
Simon Fraser U (BC, Canada)
Simon's Rock Coll of Bard (MA)
Skidmore Coll (NY)
Slippery Rock U of Pennsylvania (PA)
Smith Coll (MA)
Sonoma State U (CA)
Southeast Missouri State U (MO)
Southern Illinois U Carbondale (IL)
Southern Illinois U Edwardsville (IL)
Southern Methodist U (TX)
Southern Oregon U (OR)
Southwest Missouri State U (MO)
Southwest Texas State U (TX)
Stanford U (CA)
State U of NY at Albany (NY)
State U of NY at Binghamton (NY)
State U of NY at Buffalo (NY)
State U of NY at New Paltz (NY)
State U of NY at Oswego (NY)
State U of NY at Stony Brook (NY)
State U of NY Coll at Brockport (NY)
State U of NY Coll at Buffalo (NY)
State U of NY Coll at Cortland (NY)
State U of NY Coll at Geneseo (NY)
State U of NY Coll at Oneonta (NY)
State U of NY Coll at Potsdam (NY)
State U of West Georgia (GA)
Swarthmore Coll (PA)
Sweet Briar Coll (VA)
Syracuse U (NY)
Temple U (PA)
Texas A&M U (TX)
Texas A&M U–Commerce (TX)
Texas A&M U–Kingsville (TX)
Texas Tech U (TX)
Thomas Edison State Coll (NJ)
Thomas U (GA)
Towson U (MD)
Transylvania U (KY)
Trent U (ON, Canada)
Trinity Coll (CT)
Trinity U (TX)
Tufts U (MA)
Tulane U (LA)
Union Coll (NY)
Université de Montréal (PQ, Canada)
Université Laval (PQ, Canada)
U Coll of Cape Breton (NS, Canada)
U Coll of the Fraser Valley (BC, Canada)
The U of Alabama (AL)
The U of Alabama at Birmingham (AL)
U of Alaska Fairbanks (AK)
U of Alberta (AB, Canada)

The U of Arizona (AZ)
U of Arkansas (AR)
U of Arkansas at Little Rock (AR)
U of British Columbia (BC, Canada)
U of Calgary (AB, Canada)
U of Calif, Berkeley (CA)
U of Calif, Davis (CA)
U of Calif, Irvine (CA)
U of Calif, Los Angeles (CA)
U of Calif, Riverside (CA)
U of Calif, San Diego (CA)
U of Calif, Santa Barbara (CA)
U of Calif, Santa Cruz (CA)
U of Central Florida (FL)
U of Chicago (IL)
U of Cincinnati (OH)
U of Colorado at Boulder (CO)
U of Colorado at Colorado Springs (CO)
U of Colorado at Denver (CO)
U of Connecticut (CT)
U of Delaware (DE)
U of Denver (CO)
U of Evansville (IN)
U of Florida (FL)
U of Georgia (GA)
U of Guelph (ON, Canada)
U of Hawaii at Manoa (HI)
U of Houston (TX)
U of Houston–Clear Lake (TX)
U of Idaho (ID)
U of Illinois at Chicago (IL)
U of Illinois at Springfield (IL)
U of Illinois at Urbana–Champaign (IL)
U of Indianapolis (IN)
The U of Iowa (IA)
U of Kansas (KS)
U of Kentucky (KY)
U of King's Coll (NS, Canada)
U of La Verne (CA)
The U of Lethbridge (AB, Canada)
U of Louisiana at Lafayette (LA)
U of Louisville (KY)
U of Maine (ME)
U of Maine at Farmington (ME)
U of Manitoba (MB, Canada)
U of Maryland, Baltimore County (MD)
U of Maryland, Coll Park (MD)
U of Maryland University Coll (MD)
U of Massachusetts Amherst (MA)
U of Massachusetts Boston (MA)
The U of Memphis (TN)
U of Miami (FL)
U of Michigan (MI)
U of Michigan–Dearborn (MI)
U of Michigan–Flint (MI)
U of Minnesota, Duluth (MN)
U of Minnesota, Twin Cities Campus (MN)
U of Mississippi (MS)
U of Missouri–Columbia (MO)
U of Missouri–St. Louis (MO)
The U of Montana–Missoula (MT)
U of Nebraska–Lincoln (NE)
U of Nevada, Las Vegas (NV)
U of Nevada, Reno (NV)
U of New Brunswick, Fredericton (NB, Canada)
U of New Hampshire (NH)
U of New Mexico (NM)
U of New Orleans (LA)
The U of North Carolina at Chapel Hill (NC)
The U of North Carolina at Charlotte (NC)
The U of North Carolina at Greensboro (NC)
The U of North Carolina at Wilmington (NC)
U of North Dakota (ND)
U of Northern Iowa (IA)
U of North Texas (TX)
U of Notre Dame (IN)
U of Oklahoma (OK)
U of Oregon (OR)
U of Pennsylvania (PA)
U of Pittsburgh (PA)
U of Prince Edward Island (PE, Canada)
U of Puerto Rico, Río Piedras (PR)
U of Redlands (CA)
U of Regina (SK, Canada)
U of Rhode Island (RI)
U of Rochester (NY)

U of San Diego (CA)
U of South Alabama (AL)
U of South Carolina (SC)
U of South Dakota (SD)
U of Southern California (CA)
U of Southern Maine (ME)
U of Southern Mississippi (MS)
U of South Florida (FL)
The U of Texas at Arlington (TX)
The U of Texas at Austin (TX)
The U of Texas at San Antonio (TX)
The U of Texas–Pan American (TX)
U of the District of Columbia (DC)
U of the South (TN)
U of Toronto (ON, Canada)
U of Tulsa (OK)
U of Utah (UT)
U of Vermont (VT)
U of Victoria (BC, Canada)
U of Virginia (VA)
U of Washington (WA)
U of Waterloo (ON, Canada)
The U of Western Ontario (ON, Canada)
U of West Florida (FL)
U of Windsor (ON, Canada)
The U of Winnipeg (MB, Canada)
U of Wisconsin–Madison (WI)
U of Wisconsin–Milwaukee (WI)
U of Wisconsin–Parkside (WI)
U of Wyoming (WY)
Ursinus Coll (PA)
Utah State U (UT)
Utica Coll of Syracuse U (NY)
Valdosta State U (GA)
Vanderbilt U (TN)
Vanguard U of Southern California (CA)
Vassar Coll (NY)
Virginia Commonwealth U (VA)
Wagner Coll (NY)
Wake Forest U (NC)
Warren Wilson Coll (NC)
Washington and Lee U (VA)
Washington Coll (MD)
Washington State U (WA)
Washington U in St. Louis (MO)
Wayne State U (MI)
Webster U (MO)
Wellesley Coll (MA)
Wells Coll (NY)
Wesleyan U (CT)
West Chester U of Pennsylvania (PA)
Western Carolina U (NC)
Western Connecticut State U (CT)
Western Kentucky U (KY)
Western Michigan U (MI)
Western Oregon U (OR)
Western State Coll of Colorado (CO)
Western Washington U (WA)
Westminster Coll (MO)
Westmont Coll (CA)
West Virginia U (WV)
Wheaton Coll (IL)
Wheaton Coll (MA)
Whitman Coll (WA)
Wichita State U (KS)
Widener U (PA)
Wilfrid Laurier U (ON, Canada)
William Paterson U of New Jersey (NJ)
Williams Coll (MA)
Wright State U (OH)
Yale U (CT)
York Coll of the City U of New York (NY)
York U (ON, Canada)
Youngstown State U (OH)

APPAREL MARKETING
Concordia Coll (MN)
U of Massachusetts Amherst (MA)
U of Rhode Island (RI)

APPLIED ART
Academy of Art Coll (CA)
Alfred U (NY)
American Academy of Art (IL)
Athabasca U (AB, Canada)
Azusa Pacific U (CA)
Bemidji State U (MN)
Berry Coll (GA)
Brevard Coll (NC)

Majors Index
Applied Art–Architectural Environmental Design

California Coll of Arts and Crafts (CA)
California Polytechnic State U, San Luis Obispo (CA)
California State U, Dominguez Hills (CA)
California State U, Northridge (CA)
Carthage Coll (WI)
Ctr for Creative Studies—Coll of Art and Design (MI)
Chicago State U (IL)
Cleveland State U (OH)
The Coll of New Rochelle (NY)
Coll of Our Lady of the Elms (MA)
Coll of Staten Island of the City U of NY (NY)
Columbia Coll (MO)
Columbia Coll (SC)
Columbia U, School of General Studies (NY)
Columbus Coll of Art and Design (OH)
Converse Coll (SC)
The Corcoran Coll of Art and Design (DC)
Cornell U (NY)
Daemen Coll (NY)
DePaul U (IL)
Dowling Coll (NY)
Elizabeth City State U (NC)
Fashion Inst of Technology (NY)
Franklin Pierce Coll (NH)
Friends U (KS)
Georgia Southwestern State U (GA)
Goddard Coll (VT)
Howard Payne U (TX)
Howard U (DC)
Huntingdon Coll (AL)
Illinois Wesleyan U (IL)
Indiana State U (IN)
Indiana U Bloomington (IN)
Indiana U of Pennsylvania (PA)
Inter American U of PR, San Germán Campus (PR)
Iowa Wesleyan Coll (IA)
Kutztown U of Pennsylvania (PA)
Lakeland Coll (WI)
Lamar U (TX)
Lindenwood U (MO)
Long Island U, C.W. Post Campus (NY)
Long Island U, Southampton Coll, Friends World Program (NY)
Lubbock Christian U (TX)
Mansfield U of Pennsylvania (PA)
Marygrove Coll (MI)
Marylhurst U (OR)
Maryville Coll (TN)
Marywood U (PA)
McNeese State U (LA)
Memphis Coll of Art (TN)
Mesa State Coll (CO)
Midwestern State U (TX)
Minnesota State U, Mankato (MN)
Minnesota State U Moorhead (MN)
Mississippi Coll (MS)
Moore Coll of Art and Design (PA)
Mount Vernon Nazarene Coll (OH)
Muskingum Coll (OH)
New World School of the Arts (FL)
Northern Michigan U (MI)
Oakland City U (IN)
Oklahoma Baptist U (OK)
Oregon State U (OR)
Otis Coll of Art and Design (CA)
Peru State Coll (NE)
Point Park Coll (PA)
Portland State U (OR)
Pratt Inst (NY)
Rochester Inst of Technology (NY)
St. Cloud State U (MN)
Savannah Coll of Art and Design (GA)
School of the Museum of Fine Arts (MA)
School of Visual Arts (NY)
Seton Hill Coll (PA)
State U of NY Coll at Buffalo (NY)
State U of NY Coll at Fredonia (NY)
Syracuse U (NY)
Truman State U (MO)
The U of Akron (OH)
U of Calif, Los Angeles (CA)
U of Dayton (OH)
U of Delaware (DE)
U of Houston–Clear Lake (TX)
U of Michigan (MI)
U of North Texas (TX)
U of Oregon (OR)
U of Sioux Falls (SD)
U of South Dakota (SD)
U of Southern Colorado (CO)
The U of Tennessee Knoxville (TN)
The U of the Arts (PA)
U of the South (TN)
U of Wisconsin–Madison (WI)
Virginia Commonwealth U (VA)
Washington U in St. Louis (MO)
Western Montana Coll of The U of Montana (MT)
William Paterson U of New Jersey (NJ)
Winona State U (MN)
York Coll (NE)
York U (ON, Canada)
Youngstown State U (OH)

APPLIED ECONOMICS
Cornell U (NY)
École des Hautes Études Commerciales (PQ, Canada)
Florida State U (FL)
Ithaca Coll (NY)
Penn State U Univ Park Campus (PA)
Plymouth State Coll (NH)
Saint Joseph's Coll (IN)
Southern Methodist U (TX)
U of Massachusetts Amherst (MA)
U of Northern Iowa (IA)
U of Rhode Island (RI)
U of San Francisco (CA)

APPLIED HISTORY
East Carolina U (NC)
Meredith Coll (NC)
U of Calif, Santa Barbara (CA)
Western Michigan U (MI)

APPLIED MATHEMATICS
Alderson-Broaddus Coll (WV)
American U (DC)
Asbury Coll (KY)
Auburn U (AL)
Barnard Coll (NY)
Baylor U (TX)
Belmont U (TN)
Bethel Coll (TN)
Brescia U (KY)
Brock U (ON, Canada)
Brown U (RI)
California Inst of Technology (CA)
California State Polytechnic U, Pomona (CA)
California State U, Chico (CA)
California State U, Fullerton (CA)
California State U, Hayward (CA)
California State U, Long Beach (CA)
California State U, Los Angeles (CA)
California State U, Northridge (CA)
Carleton U (ON, Canada)
Carnegie Mellon U (PA)
Case Western Reserve U (OH)
Chapman U (CA)
Charleston Southern U (SC)
Coastal Carolina U (SC)
Coll of Our Lady of the Elms (MA)
Colorado State U (CO)
Columbia U, School of General Studies (NY)
Columbia U, School of Engineering & Applied Sci (NY)
Concordia U (PQ, Canada)
DePaul U (IL)
Dowling Coll (NY)
Drew U (NJ)
Eastern Kentucky U (KY)
Elizabeth City State U (NC)
Emory & Henry Coll (VA)
Ferris State U (MI)
Florida Inst of Technology (FL)
Florida International U (FL)
Florida State U (FL)
Fresno Pacific U (CA)
Geneva Coll (PA)
The George Washington U (DC)
Grand Valley State U (MI)
Grand View Coll (IA)
Hampshire Coll (MA)
Harvard U (MA)
Hofstra U (NY)
Humboldt State U (CA)
Illinois Inst of Technology (IL)
Indiana State U (IN)
Indiana U of Pennsylvania (PA)
Indiana U South Bend (IN)
Inter American U of PR, Metropolitan Campus (PR)
Inter American U of PR, San Germán Campus (PR)
Ithaca Coll (NY)
Johnson C. Smith U (NC)
Kent State U (OH)
Kettering U (MI)
Lakeland Coll (WI)
Lamar U (TX)
La Roche Coll (PA)
La Salle U (PA)
La Sierra U (CA)
Le Moyne Coll (NY)
Limestone Coll (SC)
Long Island U, C.W. Post Campus (NY)
Longwood Coll (VA)
Loyola Coll in Maryland (MD)
Marlboro Coll (VT)
Mary Baldwin Coll (VA)
Massachusetts Inst of Technology (MA)
McGill U (PQ, Canada)
Memorial U of Newfoundland (NF, Canada)
Mesa State Coll (CO)
Michigan Technological U (MI)
Montana Tech of The U of Montana (MT)
Mount Allison U (NB, Canada)
Mount Saint Vincent U (NS, Canada)
Murray State U (KY)
New Jersey Inst of Technology (NJ)
New Mexico Inst of Mining and Technology (NM)
North Carolina Ag and Tech State U (NC)
North Carolina State U (NC)
North Central Coll (IL)
Northern Arizona U (AZ)
Northland Coll (WI)
Northwestern U (IL)
Oakland City U (IN)
Oakwood Coll (AL)
Ohio U (OH)
Oregon State U (OR)
Pace U, New York City Campus (NY)
Pace U, Pleasantville/Briarcliff Campus (NY)
Pacific Union Coll (CA)
Penn State U Harrisburg Campus of the Capital Coll (PA)
Penn State U Univ Park Campus (PA)
Plymouth State Coll (NH)
Queens Coll (NC)
Queens Coll of the City U of NY (NY)
Quinnipiac U (CT)
Rensselaer Polytechnic Inst (NY)
Robert Morris Coll (PA)
Rochester Inst of Technology (NY)
Rutgers, State U of NJ, Newark Coll of Arts & Scis (NJ)
Rutgers, State U of NJ, U Coll–Newark (NJ)
Saint Joseph's Coll (IN)
Saint Mary's Coll (IN)
Salem State Coll (MA)
San Diego State U (CA)
San Francisco State U (CA)
San Jose State U (CA)
Seattle U (WA)
Shawnee State U (OH)
Simon Fraser U (BC, Canada)
Simon's Rock Coll of Bard (MA)
Sonoma State U (CA)
State U of NY at Albany (NY)
State U of NY at New Paltz (NY)
State U of NY at Stony Brook (NY)
State U of NY Inst of Tech at Utica/Rome (NY)
Tabor Coll (KS)
Texas A&M U (TX)
Trent U (ON, Canada)
Trinity Western U (BC, Canada)
United States Military Academy (NY)
Universidad del Turabo (PR)
Universidad Metropolitana (PR)
Université de Montréal (PQ, Canada)
Université de Sherbrooke (PQ, Canada)
The U of Akron (OH)
U of Alberta (AB, Canada)
U of British Columbia (BC, Canada)
U of Calgary (AB, Canada)
U of Calif, Berkeley (CA)
U of Calif, Los Angeles (CA)
U of Calif, San Diego (CA)
U of Central Oklahoma (OK)
U of Chicago (IL)
U of Colorado at Boulder (CO)
U of Colorado at Colorado Springs (CO)
U of Colorado at Denver (CO)
U of Connecticut (CT)
U of Guelph (ON, Canada)
U of Houston (TX)
U of Houston–Downtown (TX)
U of Idaho (ID)
U of Manitoba (MB, Canada)
U of Maryland, Baltimore County (MD)
U of Massachusetts Boston (MA)
U of Massachusetts Lowell (MA)
U of Michigan (MI)
U of Missouri–Rolla (MO)
U of Missouri–St. Louis (MO)
The U of Montana–Missoula (MT)
U of Nevada, Las Vegas (NV)
U of New Brunswick, Fredericton (NB, Canada)
U of New Brunswick, Saint John (NB, Canada)
The U of North Carolina at Greensboro (NC)
U of Pittsburgh (PA)
U of Pittsburgh at Bradford (PA)
U of Rochester (NY)
U of Sioux Falls (SD)
The U of Tennessee at Chattanooga (TN)
The U of Texas at Dallas (TX)
U of Toronto (ON, Canada)
U of Tulsa (OK)
U of Vermont (VT)
U of Virginia (VA)
U of Washington (WA)
U of Waterloo (ON, Canada)
The U of Western Ontario (ON, Canada)
U of Windsor (ON, Canada)
The U of Winnipeg (MB, Canada)
U of Wisconsin–Madison (WI)
U of Wisconsin–Milwaukee (WI)
U of Wisconsin–Stout (WI)
Ursinus Coll (PA)
Valdosta State U (GA)
Virginia Commonwealth U (VA)
Wake Forest U (NC)
Washington U in St. Louis (MO)
Wayne State Coll (NE)
Weber State U (UT)
Western Michigan U (MI)
Western Montana Coll of The U of Montana (MT)
West Virginia State Coll (WV)
William Paterson U of New Jersey (NJ)
Winona State U (MN)
Worcester Polytechnic Inst (MA)
Wright State U (OH)
Yale U (CT)
York U (ON, Canada)

ARABIC
Georgetown U (DC)
Harvard U (MA)
Johns Hopkins U (MD)
Long Island U, Southampton Coll, Friends World Program (NY)
The Ohio State U (OH)
State U of NY at Binghamton (NY)
United States Military Academy (NY)
U of Alberta (AB, Canada)
U of Calif, Los Angeles (CA)
U of Chicago (IL)
U of Michigan (MI)
The U of Texas at Austin (TX)
U of Toronto (ON, Canada)
U of Utah (UT)
Washington U in St. Louis (MO)

ARCHITECTURAL DRAFTING
U of Advancing Computer Technology (AZ)

ARCHITECTURAL ENGINEERING
Andrews U (MI)
Auburn U (AL)
California Polytechnic State U, San Luis Obispo (CA)
The Coll of Southeastern Europe, The American U of Athens (Greece)
Drexel U (PA)
Harvard U (MA)
Illinois Inst of Technology (IL)
Kansas State U (KS)
Milwaukee School of Engineering (WI)
North Carolina Ag and Tech State U (NC)
Oklahoma State U (OK)
Penn State U Univ Park Campus (PA)
Tennessee State U (TN)
Tufts U (MA)
U of Cincinnati (OH)
U of Colorado at Boulder (CO)
U of Kansas (KS)
U of Miami (FL)
U of Nebraska–Lincoln (NE)
U of Southern California (CA)
The U of Texas at Austin (TX)
U of Wyoming (WY)

ARCHITECTURAL ENGINEERING TECHNOLOGY
Abilene Christian U (TX)
Andrews U (MI)
Bluefield State Coll (WV)
California State U, Chico (CA)
Central Missouri State U (MO)
Cornell U (NY)
Delaware State U (DE)
Florida A&M U (FL)
Indiana U–Purdue U Indianapolis (IN)
Louisiana State U and A&M Coll (LA)
New York Inst of Technology (NY)
Purdue U (IN)
Southern Polytechnic State U (GA)
State U of NY Coll of Technology at Alfred (NY)
Texas Southern U (TX)
Texas Tech U (TX)
Thomas Edison State Coll (NJ)
U of Cincinnati (OH)
U of Hartford (CT)
The U of Memphis (TN)
U of Southern Mississippi (MS)
Vermont Tech Coll (VT)
Washington U in St. Louis (MO)
Wentworth Inst of Technology (MA)

ARCHITECTURAL ENVIRONMENTAL DESIGN
Art Center Coll of Design (CA)
Auburn U (AL)
Ball State U (IN)
Bowling Green State U (OH)
California State U, Fullerton (CA)
Ctr for Creative Studies—Coll of Art and Design (MI)
Coll of the Atlantic (ME)
Cornell U (NY)
Florida International U (FL)
Hampshire Coll (MA)
Harvard U (MA)
Miami U (OH)
Montana State U–Bozeman (MT)
North Dakota State U (ND)
Nova Scotia Coll of Art and Design (NS, Canada)
Otis Coll of Art and Design (CA)
Parsons School of Design, New School U (NY)
Rutgers, State U of NJ, Cook Coll (NJ)
State U of NY at Buffalo (NY)
State U of NY Coll of Environ Sci and Forestry (NY)
Syracuse U (NY)
Texas A&M U (TX)
U of Colorado at Boulder (CO)

Majors Index
Architectural Environmental Design–Art

U of Houston (TX)
U of Manitoba (MB, Canada)
U of Massachusetts Amherst (MA)
U of New Mexico (NM)
U of Oklahoma (OK)
U of Pennsylvania (PA)
U of Puerto Rico, Río Piedras (PR)

ARCHITECTURAL HISTORY
Coll of Charleston (SC)
Goucher Coll (MD)
Mary Washington Coll (VA)
Roger Williams U (RI)
Savannah Coll of Art and Design (GA)
Southeast Missouri State U (MO)
U of Delaware (DE)

ARCHITECTURAL URBAN DESIGN
U of Nevada, Las Vegas (NV)
U of Washington (WA)

ARCHITECTURE
Andrews U (MI)
Arizona State U (AZ)
Auburn U (AL)
Ball State U (IN)
Barnard Coll (NY)
Baylor U (TX)
Bennington Coll (VT)
Boston Architectural Center (MA)
Brown U (RI)
California Coll of Arts and Crafts (CA)
California Polytechnic State U, San Luis Obispo (CA)
California State Polytechnic U, Pomona (CA)
Carleton U (ON, Canada)
Carnegie Mellon U (PA)
The Catholic U of America (DC)
City Coll of the City U of NY (NY)
Clemson U (SC)
Columbia Coll (NY)
Columbia U, School of General Studies (NY)
Connecticut Coll (CT)
Cooper Union for the Advancement of Science & Art (NY)
Cornell Coll (IA)
Cornell U (NY)
Dalhousie U (NS, Canada)
Drexel U (PA)
Drury U (MO)
Eastern Michigan U (MI)
Florida A&M U (FL)
Florida Atlantic U (FL)
Georgia Inst of Technology (GA)
Hampshire Coll (MA)
Hampton U (VA)
Hobart and William Smith Colls (NY)
Howard U (DC)
Illinois Inst of Technology (IL)
Insto Tecno Estudios Sups Monterrey (Mexico)
Insto Tecno Estudios Sups Monterrey, Querétaro (Mexico)
Iowa State U of Science and Technology (IA)
Judson Coll (IL)
Kansas State U (KS)
Kent State U (OH)
Lawrence Technological U (MI)
Lehigh U (PA)
Louisiana State U and A&M Coll (LA)
Louisiana Tech U (LA)
Massachusetts Coll of Art (MA)
Massachusetts Inst of Technology (MA)
McGill U (PQ, Canada)
Miami U (OH)
Mississippi State U (MS)
New Jersey Inst of Technology (NJ)
New York Inst of Technology (NY)
North Carolina State U (NC)
North Dakota State U (ND)
Northeastern U (MA)
Norwich U (VT)
The Ohio State U (OH)
Oklahoma State U (OK)
Parsons School of Design, New School U (NY)
Penn State U Univ Park Campus (PA)

Philadelphia U (PA)
Polytechnic U of Puerto Rico (PR)
Portland State U (OR)
Prairie View A&M U (TX)
Pratt Inst (NY)
Princeton U (NJ)
Rensselaer Polytechnic Inst (NY)
Rhode Island School of Design (RI)
Rice U (TX)
Roger Williams U (RI)
Ryerson Polytechnic U (ON, Canada)
Savannah Coll of Art and Design (GA)
Smith Coll (MA)
Southern Illinois U Carbondale (IL)
Southern Polytechnic State U (GA)
State U of NY at Buffalo (NY)
Syracuse U (NY)
Temple U (PA)
Texas Tech U (TX)
Tulane U (LA)
Tuskegee U (AL)
United States International U (CA)
Université de Montréal (PQ, Canada)
Université Laval (PQ, Canada)
The U of Arizona (AZ)
U of Arkansas (AR)
U of Calif, Berkeley (CA)
U of Cincinnati (OH)
U of Detroit Mercy (MI)
U of Florida (FL)
U of Hawaii at Manoa (HI)
U of Houston (TX)
U of Idaho (ID)
U of Illinois at Chicago (IL)
U of Illinois at Urbana–Champaign (IL)
U of Kansas (KS)
U of Kentucky (KY)
U of Louisiana at Lafayette (LA)
U of Manitoba (MB, Canada)
U of Maryland, Coll Park (MD)
U of Miami (FL)
U of Michigan (MI)
U of Minnesota, Twin Cities Campus (MN)
U of Nebraska–Lincoln (NE)
U of Nevada, Las Vegas (NV)
U of New Mexico (NM)
The U of North Carolina at Charlotte (NC)
U of Notre Dame (IN)
U of Oklahoma (OK)
U of Oregon (OR)
U of San Francisco (CA)
U of Southern California (CA)
The U of Tennessee Knoxville (TN)
The U of Texas at Arlington (TX)
The U of Texas at Austin (TX)
The U of Texas at San Antonio (TX)
U of the District of Columbia (DC)
U of Toronto (ON, Canada)
U of Utah (UT)
U of Virginia (VA)
U of Washington (WA)
U of Waterloo (ON, Canada)
U of Wisconsin–Milwaukee (WI)
Virginia Polytechnic Inst and State U (VA)
Washington State U (WA)
Washington U in St. Louis (MO)
Wellesley Coll (MA)
Wentworth Inst of Technology (MA)
Woodbury U (CA)
Yale U (CT)

AREA STUDIES
Abilene Christian U (TX)
American U in Cairo (Egypt)
Bard Coll (NY)
Eastern Michigan U (MI)
Gettysburg Coll (PA)
Hawaii Pacific U (HI)
Marymount Coll (NY)
McGill U (PQ, Canada)
Memorial U of Newfoundland (NF, Canada)
Regents Coll (NY)
United States Air Force Academy (CO)
U of Maryland University Coll (MD)
The U of Montana–Missoula (MT)
U of Oklahoma (OK)

ART
Abilene Christian U (TX)
Academy of Art Coll (CA)
Adams State Coll (CO)
Adelphi U (NY)
Adrian Coll (MI)
Agnes Scott Coll (GA)
Alabama State U (AL)
Albany State U (GA)
Alberta Coll of Art and Design (AB, Canada)
Albertson Coll of Idaho (ID)
Albertus Magnus Coll (CT)
Albion Coll (MI)
Alfred U (NY)
Allegheny Coll (PA)
Alma Coll (MI)
Alverno Coll (WI)
American Academy of Art (IL)
American U (DC)
Amherst Coll (MA)
Anderson Coll (SC)
Andrews U (MI)
Anna Maria Coll (MA)
Appalachian State U (NC)
Aquinas Coll (MI)
Arizona State U (AZ)
Arkansas State U (AR)
Arkansas Tech U (AR)
Armstrong Atlantic State U (GA)
Art Academy of Cincinnati (OH)
Art Center Coll of Design (CA)
The Art Inst of Boston at Lesley (MA)
The Art Inst of Colorado (CO)
Art Inst of Southern California (CA)
Ashland U (OH)
Athens State U (AL)
Atlantic Union Coll (MA)
Auburn U (AL)
Auburn U Montgomery (AL)
Augsburg Coll (MN)
Augustana Coll (IL)
Augustana Coll (SD)
Austin Coll (TX)
Austin Peay State U (TN)
Averett Coll (VA)
Azusa Pacific U (CA)
Baldwin-Wallace Coll (OH)
Ball State U (IN)
Barat Coll (IL)
Bard Coll (NY)
Bates Coll (ME)
Baylor U (TX)
Beaver Coll (PA)
Belhaven Coll (MS)
Bellarmine Coll (KY)
Bellevue U (NE)
Belmont U (TN)
Bemidji State U (MN)
Bennett Coll (NC)
Bennington Coll (VT)
Berea Coll (KY)
Berry Coll (GA)
Bethany Coll (KS)
Bethany Coll (WV)
Bethel Coll (IN)
Bethel Coll (KS)
Bethel Coll (MN)
Biola U (CA)
Birmingham-Southern Coll (AL)
Bishop's U (PQ, Canada)
Blackburn Coll (IL)
Black Hills State U (SD)
Bloomfield Coll (NJ)
Bluffton Coll (OH)
Boise State U (ID)
Bowdoin Coll (ME)
Bowie State U (MD)
Bowling Green State U (OH)
Brandeis U (MA)
Brenau U (GA)
Brescia U (KY)
Brevard Coll (NC)
Briar Cliff Coll (IA)
Bridgewater Coll (VA)
Bridgewater State Coll (MA)
Brigham Young U (UT)
Brigham Young U–Hawaii Campus (HI)
Brock U (ON, Canada)
Brooklyn Coll of the City U of NY (NY)
Brown U (RI)
Bryn Mawr Coll (PA)
Bucknell U (PA)
Buena Vista U (IA)

Burlington Coll (VT)
Caldwell Coll (NJ)
California Baptist U (CA)
California Coll of Arts and Crafts (CA)
California Inst of the Arts (CA)
California Lutheran U (CA)
California Polytechnic State U, San Luis Obispo (CA)
California State Polytechnic U, Pomona (CA)
California State U, Chico (CA)
California State U, Dominguez Hills (CA)
California State U, Fresno (CA)
California State U, Fullerton (CA)
California State U, Long Beach (CA)
California State U, Monterey Bay (CA)
California State U, Northridge (CA)
California State U, Sacramento (CA)
California State U, San Bernardino (CA)
California State U, Stanislaus (CA)
California U of Pennsylvania (PA)
Calvin Coll (MI)
Cameron U (OK)
Campbellsville U (KY)
Campbell U (NC)
Capital U (OH)
Cardinal Stritch U (WI)
Carlow Coll (PA)
Carnegie Mellon U (PA)
Carroll Coll (WI)
Carson-Newman Coll (TN)
Castleton State Coll (VT)
The Cathol c U of America (DC)
Cedar Crest Coll (PA)
Centenary Coll of Louisiana (LA)
Ctr for Creative Studies—Coll of Art and Design (MI)
Central Coll (IA)
Central Connecticut State U (CT)
Central Michigan U (MI)
Centre Coll (KY)
Chadron State Coll (NE)
Chapman U (CA)
Chatham Coll (PA)
Cheyney U of Pennsylvania (PA)
Chowan Coll (NC)
Christopher Newport U (VA)
City Coll of the City U of NY (NY)
Claflin U (SC)
Claremont McKenna Coll (CA)
Clarion U of Pennsylvania (PA)
Clark Atlanta U (GA)
Clarke Coll (IA)
Clark U (MA)
Cleveland State U (OH)
Coastal Carolina U (SC)
Coe Coll (IA)
Coker Coll (SC)
Colby Coll (ME)
Colby-Sawyer Coll (NH)
Colgate U (NY)
Coll of Mount St. Joseph (OH)
The Coll of New Jersey (NJ)
Coll of Notre Dame (CA)
Coll of Notre Dame of Maryland (MD)
Coll of Our Lady of the Elms (MA)
Coll of Saint Benedict (MN)
Coll of St. Catherine (MN)
Coll of Saint Elizabeth (NJ)
Coll of Staten Island of the City U of NY (NY)
Coll of the Atlantic (ME)
Coll of Visual Arts (MN)
The Coll of William and Mary (VA)
The Coll of Wooster (OH)
Colorado Christian U (CO)
Colorado State U (CO)
Columbia Coll (MO)
Columbia Coll (NY)
Columbia Coll (SC)
Columbia Coll Chicago (IL)
Columbus Coll of Art and Design (OH)
Columbus State U (GA)
Concordia Coll (MI)
Concordia Coll (MN)
Concordia U (CA)
Concordia U (IL)
Concordia U (NE)
Concordia U (PQ, Canada)

Concordia U Wisconsin (WI)
Connecticut Coll (CT)
Converse Coll (SC)
Cooper Union for the Advancement of Science & Art (NY)
The Corcoran Coll of Art and Design (DC)
Cornell Coll (IA)
Cornell U (NY)
Cornish Coll of the Arts (WA)
Creighton U (NE)
Culver-Stockton Coll (MO)
Cumberland Coll (KY)
Curry Coll (MA)
Daemen Coll (NY)
Dakota Wesleyan U (SD)
Dallas Baptist U (TX)
Dana Coll (NE)
David Lipscomb U (TN)
Defiance Coll (OH)
Delaware State U (DE)
Denison U (OH)
Dickinson State U (ND)
Doane Coll (NE)
Dominican U (IL)
Dominican U of California (CA)
Dordt Coll (IA)
Dowling Coll (NY)
Drake U (IA)
Drew U (NJ)
Drury U (MO)
Duke U (NC)
Earlham Coll (IN)
East Carolina U (NC)
East Central U (OK)
Eastern Connecticut State U (CT)
Eastern Illinois U (IL)
Eastern Kentucky U (KY)
Eastern Mennonite U (VA)
Eastern Michigan U (MI)
Eastern New Mexico U (NM)
Eastern Oregon U (OR)
Eastern Washington U (WA)
East Tennessee State U (TN)
Eckerd Coll (FL)
Edgewood Coll (WI)
Elizabeth City State U (NC)
Elizabethtown Coll (PA)
Elmhurst Coll (IL)
Elmira Coll (NY)
Elon Coll (NC)
Emmanuel Coll (MA)
Emory & Henry Coll (VA)
Emporia State U (KS)
Evangel U (MO)
The Evergreen State Coll (WA)
Fairfield U (CT)
Fairleigh Dickinson U, Florham-Madison Campus (NJ)
Fairleigh Dickinson U, Teaneck-Hackensack Campus (NJ)
Felician Coll (NJ)
Ferrum Coll (VA)
Finlandia U (MI)
Fisk U (TN)
Florida A&M U (FL)
Florida Atlantic U (FL)
Florida Southern Coll (FL)
Florida State U (FL)
Fontbonne Coll (MO)
Fordham U (NY)
Fort Hays State U (KS)
Fort Lewis Coll (CO)
Francis Marion U (SC)
Franklin and Marshall Coll (PA)
Franklin Pierce Coll (NH)
Freed-Hardeman U (TN)
Friends U (KS)
Furman U (SC)
Gallaudet U (DC)
Gardner-Webb U (NC)
George Fox U (OR)
George Mason U (VA)
Georgetown Coll (KY)
Georgetown U (DC)
The George Washington U (DC)
Georgia Coll and State U (GA)
Georgian Court Coll (NJ)
Georgia Southern U (GA)
Georgia Southwestern State U (GA)
Gettysburg Coll (PA)
Goddard Coll (VT)
Gonzaga U (WA)
Gordon Coll (MA)
Goshen Coll (IN)
Goucher Coll (MD)

Majors Index
Art

Governors State U (IL)
Grace Coll (IN)
Graceland Coll (IA)
Grand Canyon U (AZ)
Grand Valley State U (MI)
Grand View Coll (IA)
Green Mountain Coll (VT)
Greensboro Coll (NC)
Greenville Coll (IL)
Grinnell Coll (IA)
Guilford Coll (NC)
Gustavus Adolphus Coll (MN)
Hamilton Coll (NY)
Hamline U (MN)
Hampshire Coll (MA)
Hampton U (VA)
Hannibal-LaGrange Coll (MO)
Hanover Coll (IN)
Harding U (AR)
Hardin-Simmons U (TX)
Hartwick Coll (NY)
Harvard U (MA)
Hastings Coll (NE)
Haverford Coll (PA)
Henderson State U (AR)
Hendrix Coll (AR)
Hillsdale Coll (MI)
Hiram Coll (OH)
Hobart and William Smith Colls (NY)
Holy Family Coll (PA)
Hood Coll (MD)
Houghton Coll (NY)
Houston Baptist U (TX)
Howard Payne U (TX)
Howard U (DC)
Humboldt State U (CA)
Hunter Coll of the City U of NY (NY)
Huntingdon Coll (AL)
Huntington Coll (IN)
Idaho State U (ID)
Illinois Coll (IL)
Illinois State U (IL)
Illinois Wesleyan U (IL)
Indiana State U (IN)
Indiana U Bloomington (IN)
Indiana U Northwest (IN)
Indiana U of Pennsylvania (PA)
Indiana U South Bend (IN)
Indiana U Southeast (IN)
Indiana Wesleyan U (IN)
Inter American U of PR, Metropolitan Campus (PR)
Inter American U of PR, San Germán Campus (PR)
Iona Coll (NY)
Iowa State U of Science and Technology (IA)
Iowa Wesleyan Coll (IA)
Ithaca Coll (NY)
Jacksonville State U (AL)
Jacksonville U (FL)
James Madison U (VA)
Jamestown Coll (ND)
Johnson State Coll (VT)
Judson Coll (AL)
Judson Coll (IL)
Kalamazoo Coll (MI)
Kansas State U (KS)
Kean U (NJ)
Keene State Coll (NH)
Kentucky Wesleyan Coll (KY)
Kenyon Coll (OH)
Knox Coll (IL)
Kutztown U of Pennsylvania (PA)
Lafayette Coll (PA)
LaGrange Coll (GA)
Lake Erie Coll (OH)
Lakehead U (ON, Canada)
Lakeland Coll (WI)
Lamar U (TX)
Lambuth U (TN)
Lander U (SC)
Langston U (OK)
La Salle U (PA)
La Sierra U (CA)
Lehigh U (PA)
Lehman Coll of the City U of NY (NY)
LeMoyne-Owen Coll (TN)
Lewis & Clark Coll (OR)
Lewis U (IL)
Lincoln Memorial U (TN)
Lincoln U (MO)
Lindenwood U (MO)
Lindsey Wilson Coll (KY)

Linfield Coll (OR)
Lock Haven U of Pennsylvania (PA)
Long Island U, Brooklyn Campus (NY)
Long Island U, C.W. Post Campus (NY)
Long Island U, Southampton Coll (NY)
Long Island U, Southampton Coll, Friends World Program (NY)
Longwood Coll (VA)
Loras Coll (IA)
Louisiana Coll (LA)
Louisiana State U in Shreveport (LA)
Louisiana Tech U (LA)
Lourdes Coll (OH)
Loyola Coll in Maryland (MD)
Loyola U Chicago (IL)
Loyola U New Orleans (LA)
Luther Coll (IA)
Lycoming Coll (PA)
Lyon Coll (AR)
MacMurray Coll (IL)
Madonna U (MI)
Maharishi U of Management (IA)
Malone Coll (OH)
Manchester Coll (IN)
Manhattanville Coll (NY)
Mansfield U of Pennsylvania (PA)
Marian Coll (IN)
Marian Coll of Fond du Lac (WI)
Marietta Coll (OH)
Marist Coll (NY)
Marlboro Coll (VT)
Marshall U (WV)
Mars Hill Coll (NC)
Mary Baldwin Coll (VA)
Marygrove Coll (MI)
Maryland Inst, Coll of Art (MD)
Marylhurst U (OR)
Marymount Coll (NY)
Marymount Manhattan Coll (NY)
Maryville Coll (TN)
Mary Washington Coll (VA)
Massachusetts Coll of Liberal Arts (MA)
Massachusetts Inst of Technology (MA)
McKendree Coll (IL)
McMurry U (TX)
McPherson Coll (KS)
Memorial U of Newfoundland (NF, Canada)
Memphis Coll of Art (TN)
Mercer U (GA)
Mercy Coll (NY)
Mercyhurst Coll (PA)
Meredith Coll (NC)
Mesa State Coll (CO)
Methodist Coll (NC)
Metropolitan State Coll of Denver (CO)
Miami U (OH)
Michigan State U (MI)
Middlebury Coll (VT)
Middle Tennessee State U (TN)
Midland Lutheran Coll (NE)
Midwestern State U (TX)
Millersville U of Pennsylvania (PA)
Milligan Coll (TN)
Millsaps Coll (MS)
Mills Coll (CA)
Milwaukee Inst of Art and Design (WI)
Minnesota State U, Mankato (MN)
Minnesota State U Moorhead (MN)
Minot State U (ND)
Mississippi Coll (MS)
Mississippi State U (MS)
Mississippi U for Women (MS)
Mississippi Valley State U (MS)
Missouri Valley Coll (MO)
Missouri Western State Coll (MO)
Molloy Coll (NY)
Monmouth Coll (IL)
Monmouth U (NJ)
Montana State U–Billings (MT)
Montana State U–Bozeman (MT)
Montserrat Coll of Art (MA)
Moore Coll of Art and Design (PA)
Moravian Coll (PA)
Morehouse Coll (GA)
Morgan State U (MD)
Morningside Coll (IA)
Mount Mary Coll (WI)

Mount Mercy Coll (IA)
Mount Olive Coll (NC)
Mount St. Mary's Coll (CA)
Mount Senario Coll (WI)
Mount Union Coll (OH)
Mount Vernon Nazarene Coll (OH)
Muhlenberg Coll (PA)
Murray State U (KY)
Muskingum Coll (OH)
Naropa U (CO)
National-Louis U (IL)
Nazareth Coll of Rochester (NY)
Nebraska Wesleyan U (NE)
Newberry Coll (SC)
New Coll of the U of South Florida (FL)
New England Coll (NH)
New Jersey City U (NJ)
New Mexico Highlands U (NM)
New Mexico State U (NM)
New World School of the Arts (FL)
New York Inst of Technology (NY)
New York U (NY)
Nicholls State U (LA)
Norfolk State U (VA)
North Carolina Central U (NC)
North Central Coll (IL)
North Dakota State U (ND)
Northeastern Illinois U (IL)
Northeastern State U (OK)
Northeastern U (MA)
Northern Arizona U (AZ)
Northern Illinois U (IL)
Northern Kentucky U (KY)
Northern Michigan U (MI)
Northern State U (SD)
North Georgia Coll & State U (GA)
Northland Coll (WI)
North Park U (IL)
Northwestern Coll (IA)
Northwestern State U of Louisiana (LA)
Northwestern U (IL)
Northwest Missouri State U (MO)
Northwest Nazarene U (ID)
Notre Dame Coll (NH)
Notre Dame Coll of Ohio (OH)
Nova Scotia Coll of Art and Design (NS, Canada)
Oakland City U (IN)
Oberlin Coll (OH)
Oglethorpe U (GA)
Ohio Northern U (OH)
The Ohio State U (OH)
Ohio U (OH)
Okanagan U Coll (BC, Canada)
Oklahoma Baptist U (OK)
Oklahoma Christian U of Science and Arts (OK)
Oklahoma City U (OK)
Oklahoma State U (OK)
Old Dominion U (VA)
Olivet Nazarene U (IL)
Oregon State U (OR)
Otis Coll of Art and Design (CA)
Ottawa U (KS)
Otterbein Coll (OH)
Ouachita Baptist U (AR)
Our Lady of the Lake U of San Antonio (TX)
Pace U, New York City Campus (NY)
Pace U, Pleasantville/Briarcliff Campus (NY)
Pacific Lutheran U (WA)
Pacific Northwest Coll of Art (OR)
Pacific Union Coll (CA)
Pacific U (OR)
Paier Coll of Art, Inc. (CT)
Palm Beach Atlantic Coll (FL)
Parsons School of Design, New School U (NY)
Penn State U Univ Park Campus (PA)
Pepperdine U, Malibu (CA)
Peru State Coll (NE)
Pikeville Coll (KY)
Pine Manor Coll (MA)
Pittsburg State U (KS)
Pitzer Coll (CA)
Point Loma Nazarene U (CA)
Pomona Coll (CA)
Pontifical Catholic U of Puerto Rico (PR)
Portland State U (OR)
Pratt Inst (NY)
Presbyterian Coll (SC)

Purchase Coll, State U of NY (NY)
Purdue U (IN)
Queens Coll (NC)
Queens Coll of the City U of NY (NY)
Quincy U (IL)
Radford U (VA)
Ramapo Coll of New Jersey (NJ)
Randolph-Macon Coll (VA)
Randolph-Macon Woman's Coll (VA)
Redeemer Coll (ON, Canada)
Reed Coll (OR)
Regis Coll (MA)
Rhode Island School of Design (RI)
Rhodes Coll (TN)
Rice U (TX)
Richmond, The American International U in London (United Kingdom)
Ripon Coll (WI)
Rivier Coll (NH)
Roanoke Coll (VA)
Roberts Wesleyan Coll (NY)
Rochester Inst of Technology (NY)
Rockford Coll (IL)
Rocky Mountain Coll (MT)
Rollins Coll (FL)
Rowan U (NJ)
Rutgers, State U of NJ, Camden Coll of Arts & Scis (NJ)
Rutgers, State U of NJ, Douglass Coll (NJ)
Rutgers, State U of NJ, Livingston Coll (NJ)
Rutgers, State U of NJ, Mason Gross School of Arts (NJ)
Rutgers, State U of NJ, Newark Coll of Arts & Scis (NJ)
Rutgers, State U of NJ, Rutgers Coll (NJ)
Rutgers, State U of NJ, U Coll–Camden (NJ)
Rutgers, State U of NJ, U Coll–New Brunswick (NJ)
Sacred Heart U (CT)
Saginaw Valley State U (MI)
St. Ambrose U (IA)
St. Andrews Presbyterian Coll (NC)
Saint Anselm Coll (NH)
St. Cloud State U (MN)
St. Edward's U (TX)
Saint John's U (MN)
Saint Joseph's U (PA)
St. Lawrence U (NY)
Saint Mary Coll (KS)
Saint Mary-of-the-Woods Coll (IN)
Saint Mary's Coll (IN)
Saint Mary's Coll of California (CA)
St. Mary's Coll of Maryland (MD)
Saint Michael's Coll (VT)
St. Norbert Coll (WI)
St. Olaf Coll (MN)
Saint Peter's Coll (NJ)
Saint Xavier U (IL)
Salem State Coll (MA)
Salisbury State U (MD)
Samford U (AL)
Sam Houston State U (TX)
San Diego State U (CA)
San Francisco Art Inst (CA)
San Francisco State U (CA)
San Jose State U (CA)
Santa Clara U (CA)
Sarah Lawrence Coll (NY)
Savannah Coll of Art and Design (GA)
School of the Art Inst of Chicago (IL)
School of the Museum of Fine Arts (MA)
School of Visual Arts (NY)
Schreiner Coll (TX)
Scripps Coll (CA)
Seattle Pacific U (WA)
Seattle U (WA)
Seton Hall U (NJ)
Seton Hill Coll (PA)
Shawnee State U (OH)
Shepherd Coll (WV)
Shippensburg U of Pennsylvania (PA)
Shorter Coll (GA)
Siena Heights U (MI)
Sierra Nevada Coll (NV)
Silver Lake Coll (WI)
Simmons Coll (MA)

Simon Fraser U (BC, Canada)
Simpson Coll (IA)
Skidmore Coll (NY)
Slippery Rock U of Pennsylvania (PA)
Smith Coll (MA)
Sonoma State U (CA)
South Dakota State U (SD)
Southeastern Louisiana U (LA)
Southeastern Oklahoma State U (OK)
Southeast Missouri State U (MO)
Southern Adventist U (TN)
Southern Arkansas U–Magnolia (AR)
Southern Illinois U Carbondale (IL)
Southern Illinois U Edwardsville (IL)
Southern Oregon U (OR)
Southern Utah U (UT)
Southwest Baptist U (MO)
Southwestern U (TX)
Southwest Missouri State U (MO)
Southwest State U (MN)
Southwest Texas State U (TX)
Spalding U (KY)
Spelman Coll (GA)
Spring Arbor Coll (MI)
Stanford U (CA)
State U of NY at Albany (NY)
State U of NY at Binghamton (NY)
State U of NY at Buffalo (NY)
State U of NY at New Paltz (NY)
State U of NY at Oswego (NY)
State U of NY Coll at Brockport (NY)
State U of NY Coll at Buffalo (NY)
State U of NY Coll at Fredonia (NY)
State U of NY Coll at Geneseo (NY)
State U of NY Coll at Old Westbury (NY)
State U of NY Coll at Oneonta (NY)
State U of NY Coll at Potsdam (NY)
State U of West Georgia (GA)
Stephen F. Austin State U (TX)
Sterling Coll (KS)
Stetson U (FL)
Suffolk U (MA)
Sul Ross State U (TX)
Susquehanna U (PA)
Syracuse U (NY)
Taylor U (IN)
Temple U (PA)
Tennessee State U (TN)
Tennessee Technological U (TN)
Texas A&M U–Commerce (TX)
Texas A&M U–Kingsville (TX)
Texas Lutheran U (TX)
Texas Southern U (TX)
Texas Tech U (TX)
Texas Wesleyan U (TX)
Texas Woman's U (TX)
Thiel Coll (PA)
Thomas Edison State Coll (NJ)
Thomas More Coll (KY)
Thomas U (GA)
Tougaloo Coll (MS)
Towson U (MD)
Transylvania U (KY)
Trinity Christian Coll (IL)
Trinity Coll (CT)
Trinity U (TX)
Troy State U (AL)
Truman State U (MO)
Tulane U (LA)
Tusculum Coll (TN)
Union U (TN)
Université de Montréal (PQ, Canada)
U du Québec à Chicoutimi (PQ, Canada)
U du Québec à Hull (PQ, Canada)
U du Québec à Trois-Rivières (PQ, Canada)
The U of Akron (OH)
The U of Alabama in Huntsville (AL)
U of Alaska Fairbanks (AK)
U of Alberta (AB, Canada)
The U of Arizona (AZ)
U of Arkansas (AR)
U of Arkansas at Little Rock (AR)
U of Arkansas at Monticello (AR)
U of Arkansas at Pine Bluff (AR)

Majors Index
Art–Art Education

U of Bridgeport (CT)
U of Calgary (AB, Canada)
U of Calif, Berkeley (CA)
U of Calif, Davis (CA)
U of Calif, Irvine (CA)
U of Calif, Los Angeles (CA)
U of Calif, San Diego (CA)
U of Calif, Santa Cruz (CA)
U of Central Arkansas (AR)
U of Central Florida (FL)
U of Central Oklahoma (OK)
U of Charleston (WV)
U of Chicago (IL)
U of Cincinnati (OH)
U of Colorado at Boulder (CO)
U of Colorado at Colorado Springs (CO)
U of Dallas (TX)
U of Dayton (OH)
U of Delaware (DE)
U of Denver (CO)
U of Evansville (IN)
The U of Findlay (OH)
U of Georgia (GA)
U of Great Falls (MT)
U of Hawaii at Manoa (HI)
U of Houston (TX)
U of Idaho (ID)
U of Illinois at Springfield (IL)
U of Indianapolis (IN)
The U of Iowa (IA)
U of Kansas (KS)
U of La Verne (CA)
The U of Lethbridge (AB, Canada)
U of Louisiana at Lafayette (LA)
U of Louisiana at Monroe (LA)
U of Maine (ME)
U of Maine at Farmington (ME)
U of Maine at Presque Isle (ME)
U of Manitoba (MB, Canada)
U of Mary Hardin-Baylor (TX)
U of Maryland, Baltimore County (MD)
U of Maryland University Coll (MD)
U of Massachusetts Boston (MA)
U of Massachusetts Dartmouth (MA)
The U of Memphis (TN)
U of Miami (FL)
U of Michigan–Flint (MI)
U of Minnesota, Duluth (MN)
U of Minnesota, Twin Cities Campus (MN)
U of Mississippi (MS)
U of Missouri–Columbia (MO)
U of Missouri–Kansas City (MO)
U of Missouri–St. Louis (MO)
U of Mobile (AL)
The U of Montana–Missoula (MT)
U of Montevallo (AL)
U of Nebraska at Kearney (NE)
U of Nebraska at Omaha (NE)
U of Nevada, Las Vegas (NV)
U of Nevada, Reno (NV)
U of New Hampshire (NH)
U of New Haven (CT)
U of New Mexico (NM)
The U of North Carolina at Asheville (NC)
The U of North Carolina at Charlotte (NC)
The U of North Carolina at Greensboro (NC)
The U of North Carolina at Pembroke (NC)
U of North Dakota (ND)
U of Northern Colorado (CO)
U of Northern Iowa (IA)
U of North Florida (FL)
U of North Texas (TX)
U of Oklahoma (OK)
U of Oregon (OR)
U of Pennsylvania (PA)
U of Puerto Rico, Mayagüez Campus (PR)
U of Puerto Rico, Río Piedras (PR)
U of Puget Sound (WA)
U of Regina (SK, Canada)
U of Rhode Island (RI)
U of Richmond (VA)
U of Rio Grande (OH)
U of Saint Francis (IN)
U of San Diego (CA)
U of Science and Arts of Oklahoma (OK)
U of South Alabama (AL)
U of South Dakota (SD)

U of Southern California (CA)
U of Southern Colorado (CO)
U of Southern Indiana (IN)
U of Southern Maine (ME)
U of Southern Mississippi (MS)
U of South Florida (FL)
The U of Tampa (FL)
The U of Tennessee at Chattanooga (TN)
The U of Texas at Arlington (TX)
The U of Texas at Austin (TX)
The U of Texas at Dallas (TX)
The U of Texas at San Antonio (TX)
The U of Texas at Tyler (TX)
The U of Texas–Pan American (TX)
The U of the Arts (PA)
U of the Ozarks (AR)
U of the Pacific (CA)
U of the Sacred Heart (PR)
U of the South (TN)
U of Toronto (ON, Canada)
U of Tulsa (OK)
U of Utah (UT)
U of Virginia (VA)
U of Virginia's Coll at Wise (VA)
U of Washington (WA)
The U of Western Ontario (ON, Canada)
U of West Florida (FL)
U of Windsor (ON, Canada)
U of Wisconsin–Eau Claire (WI)
U of Wisconsin–Green Bay (WI)
U of Wisconsin–La Crosse (WI)
U of Wisconsin–Madison (WI)
U of Wisconsin–Milwaukee (WI)
U of Wisconsin–Parkside (WI)
U of Wisconsin–Platteville (WI)
U of Wisconsin–River Falls (WI)
U of Wisconsin–Stevens Point (WI)
U of Wisconsin–Whitewater (WI)
U of Wyoming (WY)
Upper Iowa U (IA)
Ursinus Coll (PA)
Ursuline Coll (OH)
Utah State U (UT)
Valdosta State U (GA)
Valley City State U (ND)
Valparaiso U (IN)
Vanderbilt U (TN)
Virginia Commonwealth U (VA)
Virginia Intermont Coll (VA)
Virginia Polytechnic Inst and State U (VA)
Virginia Wesleyan Coll (VA)
Wabash Coll (IN)
Wagner Coll (NY)
Wake Forest U (NC)
Walla Walla Coll (WA)
Warren Wilson Coll (NC)
Wartburg Coll (IA)
Washington & Jefferson Coll (PA)
Washington Coll (MD)
Washington State U (WA)
Washington U in St. Louis (MO)
Wayland Baptist U (TX)
Waynesburg Coll (PA)
Wayne State Coll (NE)
Wayne State U (MI)
Weber State U (UT)
Webster U (MO)
Wells Coll (NY)
West Chester U of Pennsylvania (PA)
Western Carolina U (NC)
Western Connecticut State U (CT)
Western Illinois U (IL)
Western Maryland Coll (MD)
Western Michigan U (MI)
Western Montana Coll of The U of Montana (MT)
Western Oregon U (OR)
Western State Coll of Colorado (CO)
Western Washington U (WA)
Westfield State Coll (MA)
Westminster Coll (PA)
Westminster Coll (UT)
Westmont Coll (CA)
West Texas A&M U (TX)
West Virginia State Coll (WV)
West Virginia U (WV)
West Virginia Wesleyan Coll (WV)
Wheaton Coll (IL)
Wheaton Coll (MA)
White Pines Coll (NH)
Whitman Coll (WA)

Whittier Coll (CA)
Whitworth Coll (WA)
Wichita State U (KS)
Wilfrid Laurier U (ON, Canada)
Willamette U (OR)
William Jewell Coll (MO)
William Paterson U of New Jersey (NJ)
Williams Baptist Coll (AR)
William Woods U (MO)
Wilson Coll (PA)
Wingate U (NC)
Winona State U (MN)
Winston-Salem State U (NC)
Winthrop U (SC)
Wisconsin Lutheran Coll (WI)
Wittenberg U (OH)
Wright State U (OH)
Xavier U (OH)
Xavier U of Louisiana (LA)
Yale U (CT)
York Coll of Pennsylvania (PA)
York Coll of the City U of New York (NY)
York U (ON, Canada)
Youngstown State U (OH)

ART EDUCATION

Abilene Christian U (TX)
Adams State Coll (CO)
Adelphi U (NY)
Adrian Coll (MI)
Alabama State U (AL)
Alfred U (NY)
Allen U (SC)
Alma Coll (MI)
Alverno Coll (WI)
Anderson Coll (SC)
Anderson U (IN)
Andrews U (MI)
Anna Maria Coll (MA)
Appalachian State U (NC)
Aquinas Coll (MI)
Arkansas State U (AR)
Arkansas Tech U (AR)
Armstrong Atlantic State U (GA)
Asbury Coll (KY)
Ashland U (OH)
Atlantic Union Coll (MA)
Augsburg Coll (MN)
Augustana Coll (IL)
Augustana Coll (SD)
Averett Coll (VA)
Avila Coll (MO)
Baker U (KS)
Baldwin-Wallace Coll (OH)
Ball State U (IN)
Barton Coll (NC)
Baylor U (TX)
Beaver Coll (PA)
Belmont U (TN)
Beloit Coll (WI)
Bemidji State U (MN)
Berea Coll (KY)
Berry Coll (GA)
Bethany Coll (KS)
Bethel Coll (MN)
Birmingham-Southern Coll (AL)
Bluffton Coll (OH)
Boise State U (ID)
Boston U (MA)
Bowie State U (MD)
Bowling Green State U (OH)
Brenau U (GA)
Brescia U (KY)
Briar Cliff Coll (IA)
Bridgewater Coll (VA)
Brigham Young U (UT)
Brigham Young U–Hawaii Campus (HI)
Brooklyn Coll of the City U of NY (NY)
California Lutheran U (CA)
California State U, Chico (CA)
California State U, Fullerton (CA)
California State U, Long Beach (CA)
California State U, Northridge (CA)
Calumet Coll of Saint Joseph (IN)
Calvin Coll (MI)
Cameron U (OK)
Campbellsville U (KY)
Capital U (OH)
Cardinal Stritch U (WI)
Carlow Coll (PA)
Carroll Coll (WI)
Carson-Newman Coll (TN)

Case Western Reserve U (OH)
The Catholic U of America (DC)
Centenary Coll of Louisiana (LA)
Central Connecticut State U (CT)
Central Michigan U (MI)
Central Missouri State U (MO)
Chicago State U (IL)
City Coll of the City U of NY (NY)
Claflin U (SC)
Clark Atlanta U (GA)
Clarke Coll (IA)
Cleveland State U (OH)
Coastal Carolina U (SC)
Coe Coll (IA)
Coker Coll (SC)
Colby-Sawyer Coll (NH)
Coll of Mount St. Joseph (OH)
The Coll of New Jersey (NJ)
The Coll of New Rochelle (NY)
Coll of Our Lady of the Elms (MA)
Coll of Saint Benedict (MN)
Coll of St. Catherine (MN)
The Coll of Saint Rose (NY)
Coll of the Ozarks (MO)
Colorado State U (CO)
Columbia Coll (MO)
Columbia Coll (SC)
Columbus State U (GA)
Concord Coll (WV)
Concordia Coll (MN)
Concordia U (IL)
Concordia U (NE)
Concordia U (PQ, Canada)
Concordia U Wisconsin (WI)
Converse Coll (SC)
Cornell Coll (IA)
Creighton U (NE)
Culver-Stockton Coll (MO)
Cumberland Coll (KY)
Daemen Coll (NY)
Dakota State U (SD)
Dakota Wesleyan U (SD)
Dana Coll (NE)
Defiance Coll (OH)
Delaware State U (DE)
Delta State U (MS)
Dickinson State U (ND)
Drury U (MO)
East Carolina U (NC)
East Central U (OK)
Eastern Illinois U (IL)
Eastern Kentucky U (KY)
Eastern Michigan U (MI)
Eastern Washington U (WA)
Edgewood Coll (WI)
Edinboro U of Pennsylvania (PA)
Elmhurst Coll (IL)
Elmira Coll (NY)
Emmanuel Coll (MA)
Emporia State U (KS)
Escuela de Artes Plasticas de Puerto Rico (PR)
Evangel U (MO)
The Evergreen State Coll (WA)
Fairmont State Coll (WV)
Flagler Coll (FL)
Florida A&M U (FL)
Florida International U (FL)
Florida Southern Coll (FL)
Florida State U (FL)
Fontbonne Coll (MO)
Fort Hays State U (KS)
Fort Lewis Coll (CO)
Framingham State Coll (MA)
Francis Marion U (SC)
Franklin Pierce Coll (NH)
Freed-Hardeman U (TN)
Friends U (KS)
Frostburg State U (MD)
Gallaudet U (DC)
Georgia Coll and State U (GA)
Georgian Court Coll (NJ)
Georgia Southern U (GA)
Georgia Southwestern State U (GA)
Georgia State U (GA)
Glenville State Coll (WV)
Goddard Coll (VT)
Goshen Coll (IN)
Grace Coll (IN)
Graceland Coll (IA)
Grand Canyon U (AZ)
Grand Valley State U (MI)
Grand View Coll (IA)
Greensboro Coll (NC)
Greenville Coll (IL)
Gustavus Adolphus Coll (MN)

Hampton U (VA)
Hannibal-LaGrange Coll (MO)
Harding U (AR)
Hardin-Simmons U (TX)
Hastings Coll (NE)
Henderson State U (AR)
High Point U (NC)
Hofstra U (NY)
Houghton Coll (NY)
Houston Baptist U (TX)
Howard Payne U (TX)
Humboldt State U (CA)
Huntingdon Coll (AL)
Huntington Coll (IN)
Indiana State U (IN)
Indiana U Bloomington (IN)
Indiana U of Pennsylvania (PA)
Indiana U–Purdue U Indianapolis (IN)
Indiana Wesleyan U (IN)
Inter American U of PR, Fajardo Campus (PR)
Inter American U of PR, Metropolitan Campus (PR)
Inter American U of PR, San Germán Campus (PR)
Iowa Wesleyan Coll (IA)
Jacksonville U (FL)
Johnson State Coll (VT)
Kent State U (OH)
Kentucky State U (KY)
Kentucky Wesleyan Coll (KY)
Kutztown U of Pennsylvania (PA)
LaGrange Coll (GA)
Lakeland Coll (WI)
Lamar U (TX)
Lambuth U (TN)
Lander U (SC)
Langston U (OK)
Lenoir-Rhyne Coll (NC)
Lewis U (IL)
Limestone Coll (SC)
Lincoln U (MO)
Lincoln U (PA)
Lindenwood U (MO)
Long Island U, Brooklyn Campus (NY)
Long Island U, C.W. Post Campus (NY)
Long Island U, Southampton Coll (NY)
Long Island U, Southampton Coll, Friends World Program (NY)
Longwood Coll (VA)
Loras Coll (IA)
Louisiana Coll (LA)
Louisiana State U in Shreveport (LA)
Louisiana Tech U (LA)
Luther Coll (IA)
Lycoming Coll (PA)
Madonna U (MI)
Malone Coll (OH)
Manchester Coll (IN)
Manhattanville Coll (NY)
Mansfield U of Pennsylvania (PA)
Marian Coll (IN)
Marian Coll of Fond du Lac (WI)
Marshall U (WV)
Mars Hill Coll (NC)
Maryland Inst, Coll of Art (MD)
Marymount Coll (NY)
Maryville Coll (TN)
Maryville U of Saint Louis (MO)
Marywood U (PA)
Massachusetts Coll of Art (MA)
McKendree Coll (IL)
McMurry U (TX)
McPherson Coll (KS)
Mercer U (GA)
Mercyhurst Coll (PA)
Meredith Coll (NC)
Messiah Coll (PA)
Methodist Coll (NC)
Miami U (OH)
Michigan State U (MI)
Middle Tennessee State U (TN)
Midland Lutheran Coll (NE)
Midwestern State U (TX)
Millersville U of Pennsylvania (PA)
Millikin U (IL)
Minnesota State U, Mankato (MN)
Minnesota State U Moorhead (MN)
Minot State U (ND)
Mississippi Coll (MS)
Mississippi U for Women (MS)
Missouri Southern State Coll (MO)

Majors Index
Art Education–Art History

Missouri Western State Coll (MO)
Montana State U–Billings (MT)
Montserrat Coll of Art (MA)
Moore Coll of Art and Design (PA)
Moravian Coll (PA)
Morningside Coll (IA)
Mount Mary Coll (WI)
Mount Mercy Coll (IA)
Mount St. Mary's Coll (CA)
Mount Saint Vincent U (NS, Canada)
Mount Senario Coll (WI)
Mount Vernon Nazarene Coll (OH)
Murray State U (KY)
Muskingum Coll (OH)
Nazareth Coll of Rochester (NY)
New Jersey City U (NJ)
New Mexico Highlands U (NM)
New York Inst of Technology (NY)
Nicholls State U (LA)
North Carolina Ag and Tech State U (NC)
North Carolina Central U (NC)
North Central Coll (IL)
Northeastern State U (OK)
Northern Arizona U (AZ)
Northern Illinois U (IL)
Northern Michigan U (MI)
Northern State U (SD)
North Georgia Coll & State U (GA)
Northland Coll (WI)
North Park U (IL)
Northwestern Coll (IA)
Northwestern Coll (MN)
Northwestern State U of Louisiana (LA)
Northwest Missouri State U (MO)
Northwest Nazarene U (ID)
Notre Dame Coll (NH)
Nova Scotia Coll of Art and Design (NS, Canada)
Oakland City U (IN)
Ohio Dominican Coll (OH)
Ohio Northern U (OH)
The Ohio State U (OH)
Ohio U (OH)
Ohio Wesleyan U (OH)
Oklahoma Baptist U (OK)
Oklahoma Christian U of Science and Arts (OK)
Oklahoma City U (OK)
Olivet Nazarene U (IL)
Ottawa U (KS)
Otterbein Coll (OH)
Ouachita Baptist U (AR)
Pacific Lutheran U (WA)
Pacific Oaks Coll (CA)
Pacific U (OR)
Palm Beach Atlantic Coll (FL)
Parsons School of Design, New School U (NY)
Penn State U Univ Park Campus (PA)
Peru State Coll (NE)
Piedmont Coll (GA)
Pittsburg State U (KS)
Plymouth State Coll (NH)
Pontifical Catholic U of Puerto Rico (PR)
Pratt Inst (NY)
Queens Coll of the City U of NY (NY)
Queen's U at Kingston (ON, Canada)
Quincy U (IL)
Rivier Coll (NH)
Roberts Wesleyan Coll (NY)
Rockford Coll (IL)
Rocky Mountain Coll (MT)
Rowan U (NJ)
St. Ambrose U (IA)
St. Bonaventure U (NY)
St. Cloud State U (MN)
Saint John's U (MN)
St. John's U (NY)
Saint Joseph Coll (CT)
Saint Mary-of-the-Woods Coll (IN)
Saint Mary's Coll (IN)
Saint Mary's Coll of California (CA)
St. Mary's U of San Antonio (TX)
Saint Michael's Coll (VT)
St. Olaf Coll (MN)
Saint Vincent Coll (PA)
Salem State Coll (MA)
School of the Art Inst of Chicago (IL)

School of the Museum of Fine Arts (MA)
School of Visual Arts (NY)
Seattle Pacific U (WA)
Seton Hall U (NJ)
Seton Hill Coll (PA)
Shorter Coll (GA)
Siena Heights U (MI)
Silver Lake Coll (WI)
Simpson Coll (IA)
South Dakota State U (SD)
Southeastern Louisiana U (LA)
Southeastern Oklahoma State U (OK)
Southeast Missouri State U (MO)
Southern Arkansas U–Magnolia (AR)
Southern Utah U (UT)
Southwest Baptist U (MO)
Southwestern Oklahoma State U (OK)
Southwestern U (TX)
Southwest Missouri State U (MO)
Southwest State U (MN)
State U of NY at New Paltz (NY)
State U of NY Coll at Buffalo (NY)
State U of NY Coll at Potsdam (NY)
State U of West Georgia (GA)
Syracuse U (NY)
Tabor Coll (KS)
Taylor U (IN)
Temple U (PA)
Tennessee Technological U (TN)
Texas A&M U–Commerce (TX)
Texas Christian U (TX)
Texas Lutheran U (TX)
Texas Southern U (TX)
Texas Wesleyan U (TX)
Thomas More Coll (KY)
Towson U (MD)
Transylvania U (KY)
Trinity Christian Coll (IL)
Troy State U (AL)
Tusculum Coll (TN)
Union Coll (NE)
Union U (TN)
U du Québec à Chicoutimi (PQ, Canada)
U du Québec à Trois-Rivières (PQ, Canada)
Université Laval (PQ, Canada)
The U of Akron (OH)
The U of Alabama (AL)
The U of Alabama at Birmingham (AL)
U of Alaska Fairbanks (AK)
U of Alberta (AB, Canada)
The U of Arizona (AZ)
U of Arkansas at Pine Bluff (AR)
U of British Columbia (BC, Canada)
U of Calgary (AB, Canada)
U of Central Arkansas (AR)
U of Central Florida (FL)
U of Central Oklahoma (OK)
U of Cincinnati (OH)
U of Dallas (TX)
U of Dayton (OH)
U of Denver (CO)
U of Evansville (IN)
The U of Findlay (OH)
U of Florida (FL)
U of Georgia (GA)
U of Idaho (ID)
U of Illinois at Chicago (IL)
U of Illinois at Urbana–Champaign (IL)
U of Indianapolis (IN)
The U of Iowa (IA)
U of Kansas (KS)
U of Kentucky (KY)
The U of Lethbridge (AB, Canada)
U of Louisiana at Monroe (LA)
U of Maine (ME)
U of Mary Hardin-Baylor (TX)
U of Maryland, Coll Park (MD)
U of Massachusetts Dartmouth (MA)
U of Michigan (MI)
U of Michigan–Dearborn (MI)
U of Michigan–Flint (MI)
U of Minnesota, Duluth (MN)
U of Minnesota, Twin Cities Campus (MN)
U of Missouri–Columbia (MO)
The U of Montana–Missoula (MT)

U of Montevallo (AL)
U of Nebraska–Lincoln (NE)
U of Nevada, Reno (NV)
U of New Brunswick, Fredericton (NB, Canada)
U of New Hampshire (NH)
U of New Mexico (NM)
The U of North Carolina at Charlotte (NC)
The U of North Carolina at Greensboro (NC)
The U of North Carolina at Pembroke (NC)
U of Northern Iowa (IA)
U of North Florida (FL)
U of North Texas (TX)
U of Regina (SK, Canada)
U of Richmond (VA)
U of Rio Grande (OH)
U of Saint Francis (IN)
U of Sioux Falls (SD)
U of South Alabama (AL)
U of South Carolina (SC)
U of South Dakota (SD)
U of Southern Colorado (CO)
U of Southern Maine (ME)
U of South Florida (FL)
The U of Tennessee at Chattanooga (TN)
The U of Tennessee at Martin (TN)
The U of Tennessee Knoxville (TN)
The U of Texas–Pan American (TX)
The U of the Arts (PA)
U of the District of Columbia (DC)
U of the Ozarks (AR)
U of Toronto (ON, Canada)
U of Vermont (VT)
U of Victoria (BC, Canada)
The U of Western Ontario (ON, Canada)
U of West Florida (FL)
U of Windsor (ON, Canada)
U of Wisconsin–La Crosse (WI)
U of Wisconsin–Madison (WI)
U of Wisconsin–Milwaukee (WI)
U of Wisconsin–Parkside (WI)
U of Wisconsin–River Falls (WI)
U of Wisconsin–Stout (WI)
U of Wisconsin–Superior (WI)
U of Wisconsin–Whitewater (WI)
Upper Iowa U (IA)
Ursuline Coll (OH)
Utah State U (UT)
Valdosta State U (GA)
Valley City State U (ND)
Valparaiso U (IN)
Virginia Commonwealth U (VA)
Virginia Intermont Coll (VA)
Virginia Wesleyan Coll (VA)
Walla Walla Coll (WA)
Wartburg Coll (IA)
Washington & Jefferson Coll (PA)
Washington U in St. Louis (MO)
Wayne State U (MI)
Weber State U (UT)
Western Carolina U (NC)
Western Kentucky U (KY)
Western Maryland Coll (MD)
Western Michigan U (MI)
Western Montana Coll of The U of Montana (MT)
Western State Coll of Colorado (CO)
Western Washington U (WA)
Westfield State Coll (MA)
West Liberty State Coll (WV)
Westmont Coll (CA)
West Virginia State Coll (WV)
West Virginia Wesleyan Coll (WV)
Whitworth Coll (WA)
Wichita State U (KS)
Wilkes U (PA)
William Paterson U of New Jersey (NJ)
Williams Baptist Coll (AR)
William Woods U (MO)
Wilmington Coll (OH)
Wingate U (NC)
Winona State U (MN)
Winston-Salem State U (NC)
Wittenberg U (OH)
Wright State U (OH)
Xavier U of Louisiana (LA)
York U (ON, Canada)
Youngstown State U (OH)

ART HISTORY

Adams State Coll (CO)
Adelphi U (NY)
Albertus Magnus Coll (CT)
Alfred U (NY)
Allegheny Coll (PA)
American U (DC)
The American U of Paris (France)
Andrews U (MI)
Appalachian State U (NC)
Aquinas Coll (MI)
Arizona State U (AZ)
Art Academy of Cincinnati (OH)
Assumption Coll (MA)
Augsburg Coll (MN)
Augustana Coll (IL)
Baker U (KS)
Baldwin-Wallace Coll (OH)
Barat Coll (IL)
Bard Coll (NY)
Barnard Coll (NY)
Baylor U (TX)
Beaver Coll (PA)
Beloit Coll (WI)
Berea Coll (KY)
Berry Coll (GA)
Bethel Coll (MN)
Birmingham-Southern Coll (AL)
Blackburn Coll (IL)
Bloomsburg U of Pennsylvania (PA)
Boise State U (ID)
Boston Coll (MA)
Boston U (MA)
Bowdoin Coll (ME)
Bowling Green State U (OH)
Bradley U (IL)
Brandeis U (MA)
Brevard Coll (NC)
Brigham Young U (UT)
Brooklyn Coll of the City U of NY (NY)
Brown U (RI)
Bryn Mawr Coll (PA)
Bucknell U (PA)
California State U, Chico (CA)
California State U, Dominguez Hills (CA)
California State U, Fullerton (CA)
California State U, Hayward (CA)
California State U, Long Beach (CA)
California State U, Los Angeles (CA)
California State U, Northridge (CA)
California State U, San Bernardino (CA)
Calvin Coll (MI)
Canisius Coll (NY)
Carleton Coll (MN)
Carleton U (ON, Canada)
Carlow Coll (PA)
Case Western Reserve U (OH)
The Catholic U of America (DC)
Centre Coll (KY)
Chapman U (CA)
Chatham Coll (PA)
Chestnut Hill Coll (PA)
Chicago State U (IL)
City Coll of the City U of NY (NY)
Clarke Coll (IA)
Clark U (MA)
Cleveland State U (OH)
Colby Coll (ME)
Colgate U (NY)
Coll of Charleston (SC)
The Coll of New Rochelle (NY)
Coll of Saint Benedict (MN)
Coll of St. Catherine (MN)
Coll of Santa Fe (NM)
The Coll of Southeastern Europe, The American U of Athens (Greece)
Coll of the Holy Cross (MA)
The Coll of William and Mary (VA)
The Coll of Wooster (OH)
The Colorado Coll (CO)
Colorado State U (CO)
Columbia Coll (NY)
Columbia Coll (SC)
Columbia U, School of General Studies (NY)
Concordia Coll (MN)
Concordia U (PQ, Canada)
Concordia U at St. Paul (MN)
Connecticut Coll (CT)
Converse Coll (SC)

Cornell Coll (IA)
Cornell U (NY)
Creighton U (NE)
Dartmouth Coll (NH)
Davidson Coll (NC)
Denison U (OH)
DePaul U (IL)
DePauw U (IN)
Deree Coll (Greece)
Dominican U (IL)
Dominican U of California (CA)
Drake U (IA)
Drew U (NJ)
Drury U (MO)
Duke U (NC)
East Carolina U (NC)
Eastern Coll (PA)
Eastern Michigan U (MI)
Eastern Washington U (WA)
Edinboro U of Pennsylvania (PA)
Emmanuel Coll (MA)
Emory U (GA)
The Evergreen State Coll (WA)
Florida International U (FL)
Florida State U (FL)
Fordham U (NY)
Framingham State Coll (MA)
Franklin Coll Switzerland (Switzerland)
Furman U (SC)
Gallaudet U (DC)
George Mason U (VA)
The George Washington U (DC)
Georgian Court Coll (NJ)
Gettysburg Coll (PA)
Goddard Coll (VT)
Governors State U (IL)
Grand Valley State U (MI)
Gustavus Adolphus Coll (MN)
Hamilton Coll (NY)
Hamline U (MN)
Hampshire Coll (MA)
Hanover Coll (IN)
Hartwick Coll (NY)
Harvard U (MA)
Hastings Coll (NE)
Haverford Coll (PA)
Hiram Coll (OH)
Hobart and William Smith Colls (NY)
Hofstra U (NY)
Hollins U (VA)
Hope Coll (MI)
Humboldt State U (CA)
Hunter Coll of the City U of NY (NY)
Illinois Wesleyan U (IL)
Indiana State U (IN)
Indiana U Bloomington (IN)
Indiana U–Purdue U Indianapolis (IN)
Inter American U of PR, San Germán Campus (PR)
Ithaca Coll (NY)
Jacksonville U (FL)
James Madison U (VA)
John Carroll U (OH)
Johns Hopkins U (MD)
Juniata Coll (PA)
Kalamazoo Coll (MI)
Kansas City Art Inst (MO)
Kean U (NJ)
Kendall Coll of Art and Design (MI)
Kent State U (OH)
Kenyon Coll (OH)
Knox Coll (IL)
Lafayette Coll (PA)
Lake Forest Coll (IL)
Lambuth U (TN)
La Salle U (PA)
Lawrence U (WI)
Lehman Coll of the City U of NY (NY)
Lindenwood U (MO)
Long Island U, C.W. Post Campus (NY)
Long Island U, Southampton Coll, Friends World Program (NY)
Longwood Coll (VA)
Lourdes Coll (OH)
Loyola Marymount U (CA)
Lycoming Coll (PA)
Macalester Coll (MN)
MacMurray Coll (IL)
Manhattanville Coll (NY)
Mansfield U of Pennsylvania (PA)
Marian Coll (IN)

Majors Index
Art History–Astronomy

Marlboro Coll (VT)
Mars Hill Coll (NC)
Mary Baldwin Coll (VA)
Marymount Coll (NY)
Marymount Manhattan Coll (NY)
Mary Washington Coll (VA)
Massachusetts Coll of Art (MA)
McGill U (PQ, Canada)
Memorial U of Newfoundland (NF, Canada)
Meredith Coll (NC)
Messiah Coll (PA)
Miami U (OH)
Michigan State U (MI)
Middlebury Coll (VT)
Mills Coll (CA)
Minnesota State U, Mankato (MN)
Minnesota State U Moorhead (MN)
Mississippi Coll (MS)
Monmouth U (NJ)
Moore Coll of Art and Design (PA)
Moravian Coll (PA)
Morgan State U (MD)
Mount Allison U (NB, Canada)
Mount Holyoke Coll (MA)
Muhlenberg Coll (PA)
Nazareth Coll of Rochester (NY)
New England Coll (NH)
New York U (NY)
Northern Arizona U (AZ)
Northern Illinois U (IL)
Northwestern U (IL)
Notre Dame Coll of Ohio (OH)
Nova Scotia Coll of Art and Design (NS, Canada)
Oakland U (MI)
Oberlin Coll (OH)
Occidental Coll (CA)
The Ohio State U (OH)
Ohio U (OH)
Ohio Wesleyan U (OH)
Oklahoma City U (OK)
Old Dominion U (VA)
Oregon State U (OR)
Pace U, New York City Campus (NY)
Pace U, Pleasantville/Briarcliff Campus (NY)
Pacific Lutheran U (WA)
Pacific Union Coll (CA)
Penn State U Univ Park Campus (PA)
Piedmont Coll (GA)
Pine Manor Coll (MA)
Plattsburgh State U of NY (NY)
Plymouth State Coll (NH)
Pomona Coll (CA)
Portland State U (OR)
Pratt Inst (NY)
Princeton U (NJ)
Principia Coll (IL)
Providence Coll (RI)
Purchase Coll, State U of NY (NY)
Queens Coll (NC)
Queens Coll of the City U of NY (NY)
Queen's U at Kingston (ON, Canada)
Randolph-Macon Coll (VA)
Randolph-Macon Woman's Coll (VA)
Rhodes Coll (TN)
Rice U (TX)
Richmond, The American International U in London (United Kingdom)
Rockford Coll (IL)
Roger Williams U (RI)
Rollins Coll (FL)
Rosemont Coll (PA)
Rutgers, State U of NJ, Camden Coll of Arts & Scis (NJ)
Rutgers, State U of NJ, Douglass Coll (NJ)
Rutgers, State U of NJ, Livingston Coll (NJ)
Rutgers, State U of NJ, Newark Coll of Arts & Scis (NJ)
Rutgers, State U of NJ, Rutgers Coll (NJ)
Rutgers, State U of NJ, U Coll–Camden (NJ)
Rutgers, State U of NJ, U Coll–New Brunswick (NJ)
St. Cloud State U (MN)
Saint John's U (MN)
Saint Joseph Coll (CT)

St. Lawrence U (NY)
Saint Louis U (MO)
Saint Mary's Coll of California (CA)
St. Olaf Coll (MN)
Saint Vincent Coll (PA)
Salem Coll (NC)
San Diego State U (CA)
San Jose State U (CA)
Santa Clara U (CA)
Sarah Lawrence Coll (NY)
Savannah Coll of Art and Design (GA)
School of the Art Inst of Chicago (IL)
Scripps Coll (CA)
Seton Hall U (NJ)
Seton Hill Coll (PA)
Simon's Rock Coll of Bard (MA)
Skidmore Coll (NY)
Smith Coll (MA)
Sonoma State U (CA)
Southern Methodist U (TX)
Southwestern U (TX)
State U of NY at Albany (NY)
State U of NY at Binghamton (NY)
State U of NY at Buffalo (NY)
State U of NY at New Paltz (NY)
State U of NY at Stony Brook (NY)
State U of NY Coll at Buffalo (NY)
State U of NY Coll at Cortland (NY)
State U of NY Coll at Fredonia (NY)
State U of NY Coll at Geneseo (NY)
State U of NY Coll at Oneonta (NY)
State U of NY Coll at Potsdam (NY)
Stephen F. Austin State U (TX)
Susquehanna U (PA)
Swarthmore Coll (PA)
Sweet Briar Coll (VA)
Syracuse U (NY)
Temple U (PA)
Texas A&M U–Commerce (TX)
Texas Christian U (TX)
Texas Tech U (TX)
Texas Woman's U (TX)
Trinity Coll (CT)
Trinity U (TX)
Troy State U (AL)
Truman State U (MO)
Tufts U (MA)
Tulane U (LA)
Université de Montréal (PQ, Canada)
Université Laval (PQ, Canada)
The U of Akron (OH)
The U of Alabama (AL)
The U of Alabama at Birmingham (AL)
U of Alberta (AB, Canada)
The U of Arizona (AZ)
U of Arkansas at Little Rock (AR)
U of British Columbia (BC, Canada)
U of Calgary (AB, Canada)
U of Calif, Berkeley (CA)
U of Calif, Davis (CA)
U of Calif, Irvine (CA)
U of Calif, Los Angeles (CA)
U of Calif, Riverside (CA)
U of Calif, San Diego (CA)
U of Calif, Santa Barbara (CA)
U of Calif, Santa Cruz (CA)
U of Chicago (IL)
U of Cincinnati (OH)
U of Connecticut (CT)
U of Dallas (TX)
U of Dayton (OH)
U of Delaware (DE)
U of Denver (CO)
U of Evansville (IN)
U of Florida (FL)
U of Georgia (GA)
U of Guelph (ON, Canada)
U of Hartford (CT)
U of Houston (TX)
U of Illinois at Chicago (IL)
U of Illinois at Urbana–Champaign (IL)
U of Indianapolis (IN)
The U of Iowa (IA)
U of Kansas (KS)
U of Kentucky (KY)
U of Louisville (KY)
U of Maine (ME)

U of Manitoba (MB, Canada)
U of Maryland, Baltimore County (MD)
U of Maryland, Coll Park (MD)
U of Massachusetts Amherst (MA)
U of Massachusetts Dartmouth (MA)
The U of Memphis (TN)
U of Miami (FL)
U of Michigan (MI)
U of Michigan–Dearborn (MI)
U of Minnesota, Duluth (MN)
U of Minnesota, Morris (MN)
U of Minnesota, Twin Cities Campus (MN)
U of Mississippi (MS)
U of Missouri–Kansas City (MO)
U of Missouri–St. Louis (MO)
The U of Montana–Missoula (MT)
U of Nebraska at Omaha (NE)
U of Nebraska–Lincoln (NE)
U of Nevada, Las Vegas (NV)
U of Nevada, Reno (NV)
U of New Hampshire (NH)
U of New Mexico (NM)
U of New Orleans (LA)
The U of North Carolina at Chapel Hill (NC)
The U of North Carolina at Greensboro (NC)
U of Northern Iowa (IA)
U of North Texas (TX)
U of Notre Dame (IN)
U of Oklahoma (OK)
U of Oregon (OR)
U of Pennsylvania (PA)
U of Pittsburgh (PA)
U of Puerto Rico, Río Piedras (PR)
U of Redlands (CA)
U of Regina (SK, Canada)
U of Rhode Island (RI)
U of Richmond (VA)
U of Rochester (NY)
U of St. Thomas (MN)
U of South Alabama (AL)
U of South Carolina (SC)
U of Southern California (CA)
The U of Tennessee Knoxville (TN)
The U of Texas at Arlington (TX)
The U of Texas at Austin (TX)
The U of Texas–Pan American (TX)
U of the Pacific (CA)
U of the South (TN)
U of Toronto (ON, Canada)
U of Tulsa (OK)
U of Utah (UT)
U of Vermont (VT)
U of Victoria (BC, Canada)
U of Washington (WA)
U of Waterloo (ON, Canada)
The U of Western Ontario (ON, Canada)
U of West Florida (FL)
U of Windsor (ON, Canada)
The U of Winnipeg (MB, Canada)
U of Wisconsin–Madison (WI)
U of Wisconsin–Milwaukee (WI)
U of Wisconsin–Parkside (WI)
U of Wisconsin–Superior (WI)
U of Wisconsin–Whitewater (WI)
Valparaiso U (IN)
Vassar Coll (NY)
Villanova U (PA)
Virginia Commonwealth U (VA)
Wake Forest U (NC)
Washington and Lee U (VA)
Washington U in St. Louis (MO)
Wayne State U (MI)
Webster U (MO)
Wellesley Coll (MA)
Wells Coll (NY)
Wesleyan Coll (GA)
Wesleyan U (CT)
Western Maryland Coll (MD)
Western Michigan U (MI)
Western Washington U (WA)
West Virginia Wesleyan Coll (WV)
Wheaton Coll (IL)
Wheaton Coll (MA)
Whitman Coll (WA)
Whitworth Coll (WA)
Wichita State U (KS)
Willamette U (OR)
William Paterson U of New Jersey (NJ)
Williams Coll (MA)
Winthrop U (SC)

Wittenberg U (OH)
Wofford Coll (SC)
Wright State U (OH)
Yale U (CT)
York U (ON, Canada)
Youngstown State U (OH)

ARTS MANAGEMENT
Adrian Coll (MI)
American U (DC)
Appalachian State U (NC)
Baldwin-Wallace Coll (OH)
Bellarmine Coll (KY)
Benedictine Coll (KS)
Bennett Coll (NC)
Baruch Coll of the City U of NY (NY)
Bishop's U (PQ, Canada)
Brenau U (GA)
Brevard Coll (NC)
Buena Vista U (IA)
Butler U (IN)
Cabrini Coll (PA)
California State U, Hayward (CA)
Centenary Coll of Louisiana (LA)
Chatham Coll (PA)
Coll of Charleston (SC)
Coll of Santa Fe (NM)
Columbia Coll (SC)
Columbia Coll Chicago (IL)
Concordia Coll (NY)
Culver-Stockton Coll (MO)
Dakota State U (SD)
DePaul U (IL)
Eastern Michigan U (MI)
The Evergreen State Coll (WA)
Fontbonne Coll (MO)
Georgia Coll and State U (GA)
Green Mountain Coll (VT)
Illinois Wesleyan U (IL)
Ithaca Coll (NY)
Lakeland Coll (WI)
Long Island U, C.W. Post Campus (NY)
Long Island U, Southampton Coll, Friends World Program (NY)
Luther Coll (IA)
Mary Baldwin Coll (VA)
Marywood U (PA)
Mercyhurst Coll (PA)
Millikin U (IL)
Newberry Coll (SC)
North Carolina State U (NC)
Northern Arizona U (AZ)
Oklahoma City U (OK)
Pfeiffer U (NC)
Piedmont Coll (GA)
Point Park Coll (PA)
Quincy U (IL)
Randolph-Macon Coll (VA)
Salem Coll (NC)
Seton Hill Coll (PA)
Shenandoah U (VA)
Simmons Coll (MA)
Southeastern Louisiana U (LA)
Spring Hill Coll (AL)
State U of NY Coll at Brockport (NY)
State U of NY Coll at Fredonia (NY)
U of Evansville (IN)
The U of Iowa (IA)
U of Kentucky (KY)
U of Michigan–Dearborn (MI)
U of Portland (OR)
U of South Dakota (SD)
U of the Pacific (CA)
U of Toronto (ON, Canada)
U of Waterloo (ON, Canada)
U of Wisconsin–Stevens Point (WI)
Upper Iowa U (IA)
Ursuline Coll (OH)
Wagner Coll (NY)
Wartburg Coll (IA)
Waynesburg Coll (PA)
Whitworth Coll (WA)

ART THERAPY
Albertus Magnus Coll (CT)
Alverno Coll (WI)
Anna Maria Coll (MA)
Avila Coll (MO)
Barat Coll (IL)
Beaver Coll (PA)
Bowling Green State U (OH)
Brescia U (KY)
Capital U (OH)

The Coll of New Rochelle (NY)
Coll of Our Lady of the Elms (MA)
Coll of Santa Fe (NM)
Concordia U (PQ, Canada)
Converse Coll (SC)
Edgewood Coll (WI)
Emmanuel Coll (MA)
Endicott Coll (MA)
Goshen Coll (IN)
Harding U (AR)
Howard U (DC)
Long Island U, C.W. Post Campus (NY)
Long Island U, Southampton Coll, Friends World Program (NY)
Marygrove Coll (MI)
Marymount Coll (NY)
Marywood U (PA)
Mercyhurst Coll (PA)
Millikin U (IL)
Mount Mary Coll (WI)
Nazareth Coll of Rochester (NY)
Ohio Wesleyan U (OH)
Piedmont Coll (GA)
Pittsburg State U (KS)
Russell Sage Coll (NY)
School of the Art Inst of Chicago (IL)
School of Visual Arts (NY)
Seton Hill Coll (PA)
Spring Hill Coll (AL)
U of Indianapolis (IN)
The U of the Arts (PA)
U of Wisconsin–Superior (WI)
Webster U (MO)

ASIAN-AMERICAN STUDIES
California State U, Hayward (CA)
Columbia Coll (NY)
The Ohio State U (OH)
Pitzer Coll (CA)
Scripps Coll (CA)
U of Calif, Berkeley (CA)
U of Calif, Los Angeles (CA)
U of Calif, Riverside (CA)
U of Calif, Santa Barbara (CA)
U of Denver (CO)
U of Southern California (CA)

ASTRONOMY
Amherst Coll (MA)
Barnard Coll (NY)
Benedictine Coll (KS)
Boston U (MA)
Bryn Mawr Coll (PA)
California Inst of Technology (CA)
Case Western Reserve U (OH)
Central Michigan U (MI)
Colgate U (NY)
Columbia Coll (NY)
Columbia U, School of General Studies (NY)
Cornell U (NY)
Dartmouth Coll (NH)
Drake U (IA)
Eastern Coll (PA)
Hampshire Coll (MA)
Harvard U (MA)
Haverford Coll (PA)
Indiana U Bloomington (IN)
Johns Hopkins U (MD)
Lycoming Coll (PA)
Marlboro Coll (VT)
Minnesota State U, Mankato (MN)
Mount Holyoke Coll (MA)
Mount Union Coll (OH)
Northern Arizona U (AZ)
Northwestern U (IL)
The Ohio State U (OH)
Ohio Wesleyan U (OH)
Pomona Coll (CA)
Saint Mary's U (NS, Canada)
San Diego State U (CA)
San Francisco State U (CA)
Smith Coll (MA)
State U of NY at Stony Brook (NY)
State U of NY Coll at Brockport (NY)
Swarthmore Coll (PA)
Tufts U (MA)
The U of Arizona (AZ)
U of British Columbia (BC, Canada)
U of Delaware (DE)
U of Florida (FL)
U of Georgia (GA)

Majors Index
Astronomy–Biblical Languages/Literatures

U of Illinois at Urbana–Champaign (IL)
The U of Iowa (IA)
U of Kansas (KS)
U of Manitoba (MB, Canada)
U of Maryland, Coll Park (MD)
U of Massachusetts Amherst (MA)
U of Michigan (MI)
U of Minnesota, Twin Cities Campus (MN)
The U of Montana–Missoula (MT)
U of Oklahoma (OK)
U of Regina (SK, Canada)
U of Rochester (NY)
U of Southern California (CA)
The U of Texas at Austin (TX)
U of Toronto (ON, Canada)
U of Victoria (BC, Canada)
U of Virginia (VA)
U of Washington (WA)
The U of Western Ontario (ON, Canada)
U of Wisconsin–Madison (WI)
U of Wyoming (WY)
Valdosta State U (GA)
Valparaiso U (IN)
Vanderbilt U (TN)
Vassar Coll (NY)
Villanova U (PA)
Wellesley Coll (MA)
Wesleyan U (CT)
Wheaton Coll (MA)
Whitman Coll (WA)
Williams Coll (MA)
Yale U (CT)
York U (ON, Canada)
Youngstown State U (OH)

ASTROPHYSICS
Agnes Scott Coll (GA)
Augsburg Coll (MN)
Brigham Young U (UT)
California Inst of Technology (CA)
California State U, Northridge (CA)
Colgate U (NY)
Columbia Coll (NY)
Connecticut Coll (CT)
Florida Inst of Technology (FL)
Hampshire Coll (MA)
Harvard U (MA)
Indiana U Bloomington (IN)
Johns Hopkins U (MD)
Marlboro Coll (VT)
Michigan State U (MI)
New Mexico Inst of Mining and Technology (NM)
Pacific Union Coll (CA)
Princeton U (NJ)
Queen's U at Kingston (ON, Canada)
Saint Mary's U (NS, Canada)
San Francisco State U (CA)
Swarthmore Coll (PA)
Texas Christian U (TX)
U of Calgary (AB, Canada)
U of Calif, Berkeley (CA)
U of Calif, Los Angeles (CA)
U of Delaware (DE)
U of Minnesota, Twin Cities Campus (MN)
U of Missouri–St. Louis (MO)
U of New Mexico (NM)
U of Oklahoma (OK)
U of Wyoming (WY)
Villanova U (PA)
Williams Coll (MA)
Yale U (CT)

ATMOSPHERIC SCIENCES
Cornell U (NY)
Creighton U (NE)
Florida Inst of Technology (FL)
Florida State U (FL)
Harvard U (MA)
Iowa State U of Science and Technology (IA)
Lyndon State Coll (VT)
McGill U (PQ, Canada)
Metropolitan State Coll of Denver (CO)
Millersville U of Pennsylvania (PA)
New Mexico Inst of Mining and Technology (NM)
North Carolina State U (NC)
Northern Arizona U (AZ)
Northern Illinois U (IL)
Northland Coll (WI)
The Ohio State U (OH)
Ohio U (OH)
Penn State U Univ Park Campus (PA)
Plymouth State Coll (NH)
Rutgers, State U of NJ, Cook Coll (NJ)
Rutgers, State U of NJ, Douglass Coll (NJ)
St. Cloud State U (MN)
Saint Louis U (MO)
San Francisco State U (CA)
San Jose State U (CA)
State U of NY at Albany (NY)
State U of NY at Oswego (NY)
State U of NY at Stony Brook (NY)
State U of NY Coll at Brockport (NY)
State U of NY Coll at Oneonta (NY)
State U of NY Maritime Coll (NY)
Texas A&M U (TX)
United States Air Force Academy (CO)
U of Alberta (AB, Canada)
The U of Arizona (AZ)
U of British Columbia (BC, Canada)
U of Calif, Davis (CA)
U of Calif, Los Angeles (CA)
U of Hawaii at Manoa (HI)
U of Kansas (KS)
U of Louisiana at Monroe (LA)
U of Miami (FL)
U of Michigan (MI)
U of Missouri–Columbia (MO)
U of Nebraska–Lincoln (NE)
The U of North Carolina at Asheville (NC)
U of North Dakota (ND)
U of Oklahoma (OK)
U of South Alabama (AL)
U of Utah (UT)
U of Victoria (BC, Canada)
U of Washington (WA)
U of Wisconsin–Milwaukee (WI)
Valparaiso U (IN)
Western Connecticut State U (CT)
York U (ON, Canada)

AUDIO ENGINEERING
American U (DC)
Berklee Coll of Music (MA)
Cleveland Inst of Music (OH)
Cogswell Polytechnical Coll (CA)
DePaul U (IL)
The Evergreen State Coll (WA)
Five Towns Coll (NY)
Lebanon Valley Coll (PA)
Peabody Conserv of Music of Johns Hopkins U (MD)
State U of NY Coll at Fredonia (NY)
U of Hartford (CT)
U of Miami (FL)
U of Southern California (CA)
Webster U (MO)

AUTO MECHANIC/TECHNICIAN
Andrews U (MI)
Ferris State U (MI)
Franklin Inst of Boston (MA)
Indiana State U (IN)
Lewis-Clark State Coll (ID)
Montana State U–Northern (MT)
Pennsylvania Coll of Technology (PA)
Pittsburg State U (KS)
U of Arkansas at Pine Bluff (AR)
U of Southern Colorado (CO)
Walla Walla Coll (WA)
Weber State U (UT)

AUTOMOTIVE ENGINEERING TECHNOLOGY
Central Michigan U (MI)
Central Missouri State U (MO)
Franklin Inst of Boston (MA)
Minnesota State U, Mankato (MN)
Pennsylvania Coll of Technology (PA)
Rochester Inst of Technology (NY)
Southern Illinois U Carbondale (IL)
Weber State U (UT)
Western Michigan U (MI)
Western Washington U (WA)

AVIATION MANAGEMENT
Averett Coll (VA)
Baker Coll of Muskegon (MI)
Bowling Green State U (OH)
Bridgewater State Coll (MA)
Coll of Aeronautics (NY)
Daniel Webster Coll (NH)
Delaware State U (DE)
Dowling Coll (NY)
Eastern Kentucky U (KY)
Embry-Riddle Aeronautical U (AZ)
Embry-Riddle Aeronautical U (FL)
Embry-Riddle Aeronautical U, Extended Campus (FL)
Fairmont State Coll (WV)
Florida Inst of Technology (FL)
Geneva Coll (PA)
Hampton U (VA)
Indiana State U (IN)
Inter American U of PR, Fajardo Campus (PR)
Inter American U of PR, Metropolitan Campus (PR)
Jacksonville U (FL)
Lewis U (IL)
Lynn U (FL)
Marywood U (PA)
Metropolitan State Coll of Denver (CO)
Minnesota State U, Mankato (MN)
The Ohio State U (OH)
Ohio U (OH)
Oklahoma State U (OK)
Robert Morris Coll (PA)
Rocky Mountain Coll (MT)
St. Cloud State U (MN)
St. Francis Coll (NY)
Saint Louis U (MO)
Salem State Coll (MA)
San Jose State U (CA)
Southeastern Oklahoma State U (OK)
Southern Illinois U Carbondale (IL)
State U of NY at Farmingdale (NY)
Texas Southern U (TX)
U Coll of the Fraser Valley (BC, Canada)
U of Dubuque (IA)
U of Nebraska at Kearney (NE)
U of Nebraska at Omaha (NE)
U of New Haven (CT)
U of North Dakota (ND)
Westminster Coll (UT)
Wheeling Jesuit U (WV)
Wilmington Coll (DE)
Winona State U (MN)

AVIATION TECHNOLOGY
Andrews U (MI)
Coll of Aeronautics (NY)
Coll of the Ozarks (MO)
Elizabeth City State U (NC)
Fairmont State Coll (WV)
Hampton U (VA)
Indiana State U (IN)
Inter American U of PR, Fajardo Campus (PR)
Inter American U of PR, Metropolitan Campus (PR)
LeTourneau U (TX)
Lewis U (IL)
Moody Bible Inst (IL)
Northwestern State U of Louisiana (LA)
The Ohio State U (OH)
Oklahoma State U (OK)
Piedmont Baptist Coll (NC)
Providence Coll and Theological Seminary (MB, Canada)
San Jose State U (CA)
Southern Illinois U Carbondale (IL)
Walla Walla Coll (WA)
Western Michigan U (MI)
Wilmington Coll (DE)

BAKER/PASTRY CHEF
Johnson & Wales U (RI)

BANKING
Central Michigan U (MI)
Delaware State U (DE)
Husson Coll (ME)
Mississippi State U (MS)
National U (CA)
North Carolina Central U (NC)
The Ohio State U (OH)
Southeastern U (DC)
Thomas Edison State Coll (NJ)
U of Indianapolis (IN)
U of Nebraska at Omaha (NE)
U of North Florida (FL)
West Liberty State Coll (WV)

BEHAVIORAL SCIENCES
Andrews U (MI)
Anna Maria Coll (MA)
Antioch Coll (OH)
Athens State U (AL)
Augsburg Coll (MN)
Averett Coll (VA)
Barat Coll (IL)
Bartlesville Wesleyan Coll (OK)
Belmont U (TN)
Bemidji State U (MN)
Bowie State U (MD)
Brown U (RI)
California Baptist U (CA)
California State Polytechnic U, Pomona (CA)
California State U, Dominguez Hills (CA)
California State U, Monterey Bay (CA)
Cedar Crest Coll (PA)
Chaminade U of Honolulu (HI)
Circleville Bible Coll (OH)
Coker Coll (SC)
Coll of Notre Dame (CA)
The Coll of West Virginia (WV)
Columbia Coll (MO)
Concordia U (CA)
Concordia U (NE)
Concordia U (PQ, Canada)
Concordia U at Austin (TX)
Cornell U (NY)
Dakota Wesleyan U (SD)
Drew U (NJ)
Drury U (MO)
East Texas Baptist U (TX)
Erskine Coll (SC)
Evangel U (MO)
Felician Coll (NJ)
Freed-Hardeman U (TN)
Georgia Southwestern State U (GA)
Glenville State Coll (WV)
Goddard Coll (VT)
Grand Valley State U (MI)
Green Mountain Coll (VT)
Gwynedd-Mercy Coll (PA)
Hampshire Coll (MA)
Harvard U (MA)
Hawaii Pacific U (HI)
Howard Payne U (TX)
Huntingdon Coll (AL)
Indiana U Kokomo (IN)
Inter American U of PR, Metropolitan Campus (PR)
Inter American U of PR, San Germán Campus (PR)
Iona Coll (NY)
John Jay Coll of Criminal Justice, the City U of NY (NY)
Johns Hopkins U (MD)
King Coll (TN)
Lakeland Coll (WI)
Lincoln U (PA)
Long Island U, Southampton Coll (NY)
Long Island U, Southampton Coll, Friends World Program (NY)
Loyola U New Orleans (LA)
Marist Coll (NY)
Marlboro Coll (VT)
Mars Hill Coll (NC)
McPherson Coll (KS)
Mercy Coll (NY)
Mesa State Coll (CO)
Methodist Coll (NC)
Metropolitan State Coll of Denver (CO)
Mid-America Bible Coll (OK)
Midland Lutheran Coll (NE)
Minnesota State U, Mankato (MN)
Morgan State U (MD)
Mount Aloysius Coll (PA)
Mount Marty Coll (SD)
Mount Mary Coll (WI)
National-Louis U (IL)
National U (CA)
New Mexico Inst of Mining and Technology (NM)
New York Inst of Technology (NY)
New York U (NY)

Northeastern U (MA)
Northwest Coll (WA)
Northwest Missouri State U (MO)
Notre Dame Coll (OH)
Our Lady of Holy Cross Coll (LA)
Our Lady of the Lake U of San Antonio (TX)
Pacific Union Coll (CA)
Penn State U Harrisburg Campus of the Capital Coll (PA)
Point Park Coll (PA)
Purdue U Calumet (IN)
Redeemer Coll (ON, Canada)
Rice U (TX)
Rochester Coll (MI)
St. Cloud State U (MN)
St. Joseph's Coll, Suffolk Campus (NY)
San Jose State U (CA)
Southwestern Coll of Christian Ministries (OK)
Sterling Coll (KS)
Syracuse U (NY)
Tennessee Wesleyan Coll (TN)
Texas Wesleyan U (TX)
Trevecca Nazarene U (TN)
Tufts U (MA)
United States Air Force Academy (CO)
United States Military Academy (NY)
U du Québec en Abitibi-Témiscamingue (PQ, Canada)
The U of Akron (OH)
U of Chicago (IL)
U of Detroit Mercy (MI)
U of Houston–Clear Lake (TX)
U of La Verne (CA)
U of Maine at Fort Kent (ME)
U of Maine at Machias (ME)
U of Maine at Presque Isle (ME)
U of Maryland University Coll (MD)
U of Michigan–Dearborn (MI)
U of Missouri–St. Louis (MO)
U of Mobile (AL)
U of New England (ME)
U of North Texas (TX)
U of Pennsylvania (PA)
U of St. Thomas (MN)
U of San Diego (CA)
U of Sioux Falls (SD)
U of Utah (UT)
U System Coll for Lifelong Learning (NH)
Ursuline Coll (OH)
Walsh U (OH)
Westminster Coll (PA)
Widener U (PA)
William Paterson U of New Jersey (NJ)
Wilmington Coll (DE)
Wittenberg U (OH)
York Coll of Pennsylvania (PA)
York U (ON, Canada)

BIBLICAL LANGUAGES/LITERATURES
Baylor U (TX)
Belmont U (TN)
Bethany Coll of the Assemblies of God (CA)
Carson-Newman Coll (TN)
Central Bible Coll (MO)
Cleveland Coll of Jewish Studies (OH)
Columbia International U (SC)
Concordia Coll (MI)
Concordia U (IL)
Concordia U Wisconsin (WI)
Cornerstone U (MI)
David Lipscomb U (TN)
Harding U (AR)
Harvard U (MA)
Howard Payne U (TX)
Indiana Wesleyan U (IN)
Long Island U, Southampton Coll, Friends World Program (NY)
Lubbock Christian U (TX)
Luther Coll (IA)
Mid-Continent Coll (KY)
Multnomah Bible Coll and Biblical Seminary (OR)
North Central U (MN)
North Greenville Coll (SC)
Northwest Nazarene U (ID)
Oklahoma Baptist U (OK)
Ozark Christian Coll (MO)

Majors Index
Biblical Languages/Literatures–Biochemistry

Prairie Bible Coll (AB, Canada)
Southern Christian U (AL)
Southwestern Assemblies of God U (TX)
Taylor U (IN)
Toccoa Falls Coll (GA)
Union U (TN)
U of Chicago (IL)
U of Toronto (ON, Canada)
Walla Walla Coll (WA)
Wheaton Coll (IL)
York Coll (NE)
York U (ON, Canada)

BIBLICAL STUDIES
Abilene Christian U (TX)
Alaska Bible Coll (AK)
Anderson U (IN)
Andrews U (MI)
Appalachian Bible Coll (WV)
Arlington Baptist Coll (TX)
Asbury Coll (KY)
Atlanta Christian Coll (GA)
Atlantic Baptist U (NB, Canada)
Azusa Pacific U (CA)
Barclay Coll (KS)
Beacon Coll (GA)
Belhaven Coll (MS)
Belmont U (TN)
Bethany Bible Coll (NB, Canada)
Bethany Coll of the Assemblies of God (CA)
Bethel Coll (IN)
Bethel Coll (MN)
Bethesda Christian U (CA)
Beulah Heights Bible Coll (GA)
Biola U (CA)
Blue Mountain Coll (MS)
Boise Bible Coll (ID)
Briercrest Bible Coll (SK, Canada)
Bryan Coll (TN)
California Christian Coll (CA)
Calvary Bible Coll and Theological Seminary (MO)
Calvin Coll (MI)
Campbellsville U (KY)
Canadian Bible Coll (SK, Canada)
Carson-Newman Coll (TN)
Cascade Coll (OR)
Cedarville Coll (OH)
Centenary Coll of Louisiana (LA)
Central Baptist Coll (AR)
Central Bible Coll (MO)
Central Christian Coll of Kansas (KS)
Circleville Bible Coll (OH)
Cleveland Coll of Jewish Studies (OH)
Colorado Christian U (CO)
Columbia International U (SC)
Concordia U at Austin (TX)
Cornerstone U (MI)
Covenant Coll (GA)
Crichton Coll (TN)
Crown Coll (MN)
Dallas Baptist U (TX)
Dallas Christian Coll (TX)
David Lipscomb U (TN)
Eastern Coll (PA)
Eastern Mennonite U (VA)
Emmanuel Bible Coll (CA)
Emmanuel Coll (GA)
Emmaus Bible Coll (IA)
Erskine Coll (SC)
Eugene Bible Coll (OR)
Evangel U (MO)
Faith Baptist Bible Coll and Theological Seminary (IA)
Faulkner U (AL)
Florida Baptist Theological Coll (FL)
Florida Christian Coll (FL)
Florida Coll (FL)
Freed-Hardeman U (TN)
Free Will Baptist Bible Coll (TN)
Fresno Pacific U (CA)
Friends U (KS)
Geneva Coll (PA)
George Fox U (OR)
Global U of the Assemblies of God (MO)
God's Bible School and Coll (OH)
Gordon Coll (MA)
Goshen Coll (IN)
Grace Bible Coll (MI)
Grace Coll (IN)
Grand Canyon U (AZ)

Hannibal-LaGrange Coll (MO)
Harding U (AR)
Hardin-Simmons U (TX)
Harvard U (MA)
Heritage Baptist Coll & Heritage Theological Sem (ON, Canada)
Hobe Sound Bible Coll (FL)
Hope International U (CA)
Houghton Coll (NY)
Houston Baptist U (TX)
Howard Payne U (TX)
Huntington Coll (IN)
Indiana Wesleyan U (IN)
Inst for Christian Studies (TX)
International Baptist Coll (AZ)
International Bible Coll (AL)
Jewish Theological Seminary of America (NY)
John Brown U (AR)
Johnson Bible Coll (TN)
John Wesley Coll (NC)
Judson Coll (IL)
Kentucky Christian Coll (KY)
King Coll (TN)
Lancaster Bible Coll (PA)
Lee U (TN)
LeTourneau U (TX)
LIFE Bible Coll (CA)
Lincoln Christian Coll (IL)
Long Island U, Southampton Coll, Friends World Program (NY)
Lubbock Christian U (TX)
Magnolia Bible Coll (MS)
Malone Coll (OH)
Manhattan Christian Coll (KS)
Maranatha Baptist Bible Coll (WI)
Marlboro Coll (VT)
Messenger Coll (MO)
Messiah Coll (PA)
Methodist Coll (NC)
Mid-America Bible Coll (OK)
Mid-Continent Coll (KY)
Milligan Coll (TN)
Minnesota Bible Coll (MN)
Montreat Coll (NC)
Moody Bible Inst (IL)
Mount Vernon Nazarene Coll (OH)
Multnomah Bible Coll and Biblical Seminary (OR)
Nazarene Bible Coll (CO)
Nazarene Indian Bible Coll (NM)
North American Baptist Coll & Edmonton Baptist Sem (AB, Canada)
North Greenville Coll (SC)
North Park U (IL)
Northwest Bible Coll (AB, Canada)
Northwest Coll (WA)
Northwestern Coll (MN)
Nyack Coll (NY)
Oak Hills Christian Coll (MN)
Oakland City U (IN)
Ohio Valley Coll (WV)
Oklahoma Baptist U (OK)
Oklahoma Christian U of Science and Arts (OK)
Olivet Nazarene U (IL)
Ouachita Baptist U (AR)
Ozark Christian Coll (MO)
Patten Coll (CA)
Philadelphia Coll of Bible (PA)
Piedmont Baptist Coll (NC)
Point Loma Nazarene U (CA)
Practical Bible Coll (NY)
Providence Coll and Theological Seminary (MB, Canada)
Redeemer Coll (ON, Canada)
Reformed Bible Coll (MI)
Rochester Coll (MI)
Rocky Mountain Coll (AB, Canada)
St. Louis Christian Coll (MO)
Saint Paul U (ON, Canada)
San Jose Christian Coll (CA)
Shasta Bible Coll (CA)
Simpson Coll and Graduate School (CA)
Southeastern Coll of the Assemblies of God (FL)
Southern Christian U (AL)
Southwest Baptist U (MO)
Southwestern Assemblies of God U (TX)
Southwestern Coll of Christian Ministries (OK)
Steinbach Bible Coll (MB, Canada)
Tabor Coll (KS)
Taylor U (IN)

Taylor U, Fort Wayne Campus (IN)
Toccoa Falls Coll (GA)
Touro Coll (NY)
Trinity Baptist Coll (FL)
Trinity Bible Coll (ND)
Trinity Coll of Florida (FL)
Trinity Lutheran Coll (WA)
Trinity Western U (BC, Canada)
Tyndale Coll & Seminary (ON, Canada)
Union U (TN)
Universidad Adventista de las Antillas (PR)
Université de Montréal (PQ, Canada)
U of Evansville (IN)
U of Michigan (MI)
Vanguard U of Southern California (CA)
Warner Pacific Coll (OR)
Warner Southern Coll (FL)
Washington Bible Coll (MD)
Wesley Coll (MS)
Western Baptist Coll (OR)
Wheaton Coll (IL)
William Tyndale Coll (MI)
Yeshiva Karlin Stolin Rabbinical Inst (NY)
York Coll (NE)

BILINGUAL/BICULTURAL EDUCATION
Adrian Coll (MI)
Alfred U (NY)
Belmont U (TN)
Biola U (CA)
Boise State U (ID)
Boston U (MA)
Brooklyn Coll of the City U of NY (NY)
California State Polytechnic U, Pomona (CA)
California State U, Dominguez Hills (CA)
California State U, Sacramento (CA)
Calvin Coll (MI)
Chicago State U (IL)
Coll of Our Lady of the Elms (MA)
Coll of the Southwest (NM)
Eastern Michigan U (MI)
Eastern Nazarene Coll (MA)
Fordham U (NY)
Fresno Pacific U (CA)
Goshen Coll (IN)
Hardin-Simmons U (TX)
Heritage Coll (WA)
Houston Baptist U (TX)
Indiana U Bloomington (IN)
Long Island U, Southampton Coll, Friends World Program (NY)
Marquette U (WI)
McGill U (PQ, Canada)
McMurry U (TX)
Mercy Coll (NY)
Mount Mary Coll (WI)
New Mexico Highlands U (NM)
Northeastern Illinois U (IL)
Our Lady of the Lake U of San Antonio (TX)
Pacific Oaks Coll (CA)
Rider U (NJ)
St. Edward's U (TX)
State U of NY Coll at Old Westbury (NY)
Texas A&M International U (TX)
Texas A&M U–Kingsville (TX)
Texas Southern U (TX)
Texas Wesleyan U (TX)
Universidad Metropolitana (PR)
The U of Akron (OH)
U of Alberta (AB, Canada)
The U of Findlay (OH)
U of Michigan–Dearborn (MI)
U of Regina (SK, Canada)
U of San Francisco (CA)
The U of Texas at San Antonio (TX)
U of the Pacific (CA)
U of the Sacred Heart (PR)
U of Washington (WA)
U of Wisconsin–Milwaukee (WI)
Weber State U (UT)
Western Illinois U (IL)
York U (ON, Canada)

BIOCHEMICAL TECHNOLOGY
Norwich U (VT)

BIOCHEMISTRY
Abilene Christian U (TX)
Adelphi U (NY)
Agnes Scott Coll (GA)
Albright Coll (PA)
Alma Coll (MI)
Alvernia Coll (PA)
American International Coll (MA)
Andrews U (MI)
Arizona State U (AZ)
Asbury Coll (KY)
Atlantic Union Coll (MA)
Auburn U (AL)
Averett Coll (VA)
Azusa Pacific U (CA)
Bard Coll (NY)
Barnard Coll (NY)
Bates Coll (ME)
Baylor U (TX)
Belmont U (TN)
Beloit Coll (WI)
Benedictine Coll (KS)
Benedictine U (IL)
Bennington Coll (VT)
Berry Coll (GA)
Bethel Coll (MN)
Biola U (CA)
Bishop's U (PQ, Canada)
Bloomfield Coll (NJ)
Boston Coll (MA)
Boston U (MA)
Bowdoin Coll (ME)
Bowling Green State U (OH)
Bradley U (IL)
Brandeis U (MA)
Bridgewater State Coll (MA)
Brigham Young U (UT)
Brock U (ON, Canada)
Brown U (RI)
Bucknell U (PA)
California Inst of Technology (CA)
California Lutheran U (CA)
California Polytechnic State U, San Luis Obispo (CA)
California State U, Chico (CA)
California State U, Dominguez Hills (CA)
California State U, Fullerton (CA)
California State U, Hayward (CA)
California State U, Long Beach (CA)
California State U, Los Angeles (CA)
California State U, Northridge (CA)
California State U, San Bernardino (CA)
California State U, San Marcos (CA)
Calvin Coll (MI)
Campbell U (NC)
Canisius Coll (NY)
Carleton U (ON, Canada)
Carnegie Mellon U (PA)
Case Western Reserve U (OH)
The Catholic U of America (DC)
Cedar Crest Coll (PA)
Centenary Coll of Louisiana (LA)
Centre Coll (KY)
Chapman U (CA)
Charleston Southern U (SC)
Chatham Coll (PA)
Chestnut Hill Coll (PA)
City Coll of the City U of NY (NY)
Claremont McKenna Coll (CA)
Clarkson U (NY)
Clark U (MA)
Clemson U (SC)
Coe Coll (IA)
Colby Coll (ME)
Colgate U (NY)
Coll Misericordia (PA)
Coll of Charleston (SC)
Coll of Mount St. Joseph (OH)
Coll of Mount Saint Vincent (NY)
Coll of Notre Dame (CA)
Coll of St. Catherine (MN)
Coll of Saint Elizabeth (NJ)
The Coll of Saint Rose (NY)
The Coll of St. Scholastica (MN)
The Coll of Southeastern Europe, The American U of Athens (Greece)
Coll of Staten Island of the City U of NY (NY)

Coll of the Holy Cross (MA)
The Coll of Wooster (OH)
The Colorado Coll (CO)
Colorado State U (CO)
Columbia Coll (NY)
Columbia Union Coll (MD)
Concordia U (PQ, Canada)
Connecticut Coll (CT)
Converse Coll (SC)
Cornell Coll (IA)
Cornell U (NY)
Dalhousie U (NS, Canada)
Dartmouth Coll (NH)
David Lipscomb U (TN)
Denison U (OH)
DePaul U (IL)
Dickinson Coll (PA)
Dominican U (IL)
Drew U (NJ)
Duquesne U (PA)
East Carolina U (NC)
Eastern Coll (PA)
Eastern Kentucky U (KY)
Eastern Mennonite U (VA)
Eastern Michigan U (MI)
Eastern Washington U (WA)
East Stroudsburg U of Pennsylvania (PA)
Edinboro U of Pennsylvania (PA)
Elizabethtown Coll (PA)
Elmira Coll (NY)
Emmanuel Coll (MA)
The Evergreen State Coll (WA)
Fairleigh Dickinson U, Florham-Madison Campus (NJ)
Fairleigh Dickinson U, Teaneck-Hackensack Campus (NJ)
Felician Coll (NJ)
Florida Inst of Technology (FL)
Florida State U (FL)
Fort Lewis Coll (CO)
Furman U (SC)
Georgetown U (DC)
Georgian Court Coll (NJ)
Gettysburg Coll (PA)
Gonzaga U (WA)
Grove City Coll (PA)
Gustavus Adolphus Coll (MN)
Hamilton Coll (NY)
Hampden-Sydney Coll (VA)
Hampshire Coll (MA)
Harding U (AR)
Hartwick Coll (NY)
Harvard U (MA)
Haverford Coll (PA)
Hobart and William Smith Colls (NY)
Hofstra U (NY)
Holy Family Coll (PA)
Hood Coll (MD)
Hope Coll (MI)
Humboldt State U (CA)
Idaho State U (ID)
Immaculata Coll (PA)
Indiana State U (IN)
Indiana U Bloomington (IN)
Indiana U of Pennsylvania (PA)
Insto Tecno Estudios Sups Monterrey (Mexico)
Insto Tecno Estudios Sups Monterrey, Querétaro (Mexico)
Iona Coll (NY)
Iowa State U of Science and Technology (IA)
Ithaca Coll (NY)
Jamestown Coll (ND)
John Brown U (AR)
Juniata Coll (PA)
Kansas State U (KS)
Kenyon Coll (OH)
Keuka Coll (NY)
King Coll (TN)
Knox Coll (IL)
Lafayette Coll (PA)
LaGrange Coll (GA)
La Salle U (PA)
La Sierra U (CA)
Lebanon Valley Coll (PA)
Lehigh U (PA)
Lehman Coll of the City U of NY (NY)
Lewis & Clark Coll (OR)
Lewis U (IL)
Loras Coll (IA)
Louisiana State U and A&M Coll (LA)

Majors Index
Biochemistry–Biological and Physical Sciences

Louisiana State U in Shreveport (LA)
Loyola Marymount U (CA)
Madonna U (MI)
Maharishi U of Management (IA)
Manhattan Coll (NY)
Manhattanville Coll (NY)
Mansfield U of Pennsylvania (PA)
Marietta Coll (OH)
Marist Coll (NY)
Marlboro Coll (VT)
Marquette U (WI)
Mary Baldwin Coll (VA)
Maryville Coll (TN)
McGill U (PQ, Canada)
McMurry U (TX)
Memorial U of Newfoundland (NF, Canada)
Merrimack Coll (MA)
Messiah Coll (PA)
Miami U (OH)
Michigan State U (MI)
Michigan Technological U (MI)
Middlebury Coll (VT)
Millersville U of Pennsylvania (PA)
Mills Coll (CA)
Minnesota State U, Mankato (MN)
Mississippi State U (MS)
Mount Allison U (NB, Canada)
Mount Holyoke Coll (MA)
Mount St. Mary's Coll (CA)
Mount Saint Mary's Coll and Seminary (MD)
Mount Vernon Nazarene Coll (OH)
Muhlenberg Coll (PA)
Nazareth Coll of Rochester (NY)
Nebraska Wesleyan U (NE)
New Mexico State U (NM)
New York U (NY)
Niagara U (NY)
North Carolina State U (NC)
North Central Coll (IL)
North Dakota State U (ND)
Northeastern U (MA)
Northern Michigan U (MI)
Northwestern U (IL)
Notre Dame Coll of Ohio (OH)
Oakland U (MI)
Oakwood Coll (AL)
Oberlin Coll (OH)
Occidental Coll (CA)
Ohio Northern U (OH)
The Ohio State U (OH)
Oklahoma Christian U of Science and Arts (OK)
Oklahoma City U (OK)
Oklahoma State U (OK)
Old Dominion U (VA)
Olivet Nazarene U (IL)
Oregon State U (OR)
Pace U, New York City Campus (NY)
Pace U, Pleasantville/Briarcliff Campus (NY)
Pacific Lutheran U (WA)
Pacific Union Coll (CA)
Penn State U Univ Park Campus (PA)
Philadelphia U (PA)
Plattsburgh State U of NY (NY)
Point Loma Nazarene U (CA)
Pomona Coll (CA)
Portland State U (OR)
Purdue U (IN)
Queens Coll (NC)
Queens Coll of the City U of NY (NY)
Queen's U at Kingston (ON, Canada)
Quinnipiac U (CT)
Ramapo Coll of New Jersey (NJ)
Reed Coll (OR)
Regis Coll (MA)
Regis U (CO)
Rensselaer Polytechnic Inst (NY)
Rhodes Coll (TN)
Rice U (TX)
The Richard Stockton Coll of New Jersey (NJ)
Rider U (NJ)
Ripon Coll (WI)
Roanoke Coll (VA)
Roberts Wesleyan Coll (NY)
Rochester Inst of Technology (NY)
Rockford Coll (IL)
Rosemont Coll (PA)
Russell Sage Coll (NY)

Rutgers, State U of NJ, Camden Coll of Arts & Scis (NJ)
Rutgers, State U of NJ, Cook Coll (NJ)
Rutgers, State U of NJ, U Coll–Camden (NJ)
Sacred Heart U (CT)
Saginaw Valley State U (MI)
St. Andrews Presbyterian Coll (NC)
Saint Anselm Coll (NH)
St. Bonaventure U (NY)
St. Edward's U (TX)
St. John Fisher Coll (NY)
Saint Joseph Coll (CT)
Saint Joseph's Coll (IN)
Saint Mary's Coll (IN)
St. Mary's U of San Antonio (TX)
Saint Michael's Coll (VT)
Saint Peter's Coll (NJ)
Saint Vincent Coll (PA)
Samford U (AL)
San Francisco State U (CA)
San Jose State U (CA)
Schreiner Coll (TX)
Scripps Coll (CA)
Seattle Pacific U (WA)
Seattle U (WA)
Seton Hall U (NJ)
Seton Hill Coll (PA)
Simmons Coll (MA)
Simon Fraser U (BC, Canada)
Simpson Coll (IA)
Skidmore Coll (NY)
Smith Coll (MA)
South Dakota State U (SD)
Southern Adventist U (TN)
Southern Methodist U (TX)
Southern Oregon U (OR)
Southwestern Coll (KS)
Spelman Coll (GA)
Spring Arbor Coll (MI)
Spring Hill Coll (AL)
State U of NY at Albany (NY)
State U of NY at Binghamton (NY)
State U of NY at Buffalo (NY)
State U of NY at New Paltz (NY)
State U of NY at Stony Brook (NY)
State U of NY Coll at Brockport (NY)
State U of NY Coll at Fredonia (NY)
State U of NY Coll at Geneseo (NY)
State U of NY Coll of Environ Sci and Forestry (NY)
Stetson U (FL)
Stevens Inst of Technology (NJ)
Suffolk U (MA)
Susquehanna U (PA)
Swarthmore Coll (PA)
Sweet Briar Coll (VA)
Syracuse U (NY)
Temple U (PA)
Tennessee Technological U (TN)
Texas A&M U (TX)
Texas Christian U (TX)
Texas Tech U (TX)
Texas Wesleyan U (TX)
Trent U (ON, Canada)
Trinity Coll (CT)
Trinity U (TX)
Tulane U (LA)
Union Coll (NE)
Union Coll (NY)
United States Air Force Academy (CO)
Université de Montréal (PQ, Canada)
Université de Sherbrooke (PQ, Canada)
U du Québec à Trois-Rivières (PQ, Canada)
Université Laval (PQ, Canada)
U of Alberta (AB, Canada)
The U of Arizona (AZ)
U of British Columbia (BC, Canada)
U of Calgary (AB, Canada)
U of Calif, Davis (CA)
U of Calif, Los Angeles (CA)
U of Calif, Riverside (CA)
U of Calif, San Diego (CA)
U of Calif, Santa Barbara (CA)
U of Calif, Santa Cruz (CA)
U of Chicago (IL)
U of Cincinnati (OH)
U of Colorado at Boulder (CO)

U of Dallas (TX)
U of Dayton (OH)
U of Delaware (DE)
U of Denver (CO)
U of Detroit Mercy (MI)
U of Evansville (IN)
U of Georgia (GA)
U of Guelph (ON, Canada)
U of Houston (TX)
U of Illinois at Chicago (IL)
U of Illinois at Urbana–Champaign (IL)
The U of Iowa (IA)
U of Kansas (KS)
U of King's Coll (NS, Canada)
The U of Lethbridge (AB, Canada)
U of Maine (ME)
U of Maryland, Baltimore County (MD)
U of Maryland, Coll Park (MD)
U of Massachusetts Amherst (MA)
U of Massachusetts Boston (MA)
U of Miami (FL)
U of Michigan (MI)
U of Michigan–Dearborn (MI)
U of Minnesota, Duluth (MN)
U of Minnesota, Twin Cities Campus (MN)
U of Missouri–Columbia (MO)
U of Missouri–St. Louis (MO)
The U of Montana–Missoula (MT)
U of Nebraska–Lincoln (NE)
U of Nevada, Reno (NV)
U of New Brunswick, Fredericton (NB, Canada)
U of New Hampshire (NH)
U of New Mexico (NM)
U of Northern Iowa (IA)
U of North Texas (TX)
U of Notre Dame (IN)
U of Oklahoma (OK)
U of Oregon (OR)
U of Pennsylvania (PA)
U of Pittsburgh (PA)
U of Regina (SK, Canada)
U of Rochester (NY)
U of San Francisco (CA)
U of Southern California (CA)
The U of Tampa (FL)
The U of Tennessee Knoxville (TN)
The U of Texas at Arlington (TX)
The U of Texas at Austin (TX)
U of the Pacific (CA)
U of the Sciences in Philadelphia (PA)
U of Toronto (ON, Canada)
U of Tulsa (OK)
U of Vermont (VT)
U of Victoria (BC, Canada)
U of Washington (WA)
U of Waterloo (ON, Canada)
The U of Western Ontario (ON, Canada)
U of Windsor (ON, Canada)
U of Wisconsin–Eau Claire (WI)
U of Wisconsin–Madison (WI)
U of Wisconsin–Milwaukee (WI)
U of Wisconsin–Parkside (WI)
U of Wisconsin–River Falls (WI)
Ursinus Coll (PA)
Vassar Coll (NY)
Virginia Polytechnic Inst and State U (VA)
Warren Wilson Coll (NC)
Wartburg Coll (IA)
Washington State U (WA)
Washington U in St. Louis (MO)
Wellesley Coll (MA)
Wells Coll (NY)
Wesleyan U (CT)
West Chester U of Pennsylvania (PA)
Western Kentucky U (KY)
Western Maryland Coll (MD)
Western Michigan U (MI)
Western Washington U (WA)
Wheaton Coll (MA)
Whittier Coll (CA)
Wilkes U (PA)
William Jewell Coll (MO)
Wittenberg U (OH)
Worcester Polytechnic Inst (MA)
Xavier U of Louisiana (LA)

BIOLOGICAL AND PHYSICAL SCIENCES

Adams State Coll (CO)
Albertus Magnus Coll (CT)
Alfred U (NY)
Alice Lloyd Coll (KY)
Alma Coll (MI)
Alvernia Coll (PA)
Antioch Coll (OH)
Athabasca U (AB, Canada)
Atlantic Union Coll (MA)
Augsburg Coll (MN)
Averett Coll (VA)
Avila Coll (MO)
Bard Coll (NY)
Bartlesville Wesleyan Coll (OK)
Bayamón Central U (PR)
Belmont U (TN)
Bemidji State U (MN)
Benedictine Coll (KS)
Bennington Coll (VT)
Bethel Coll (IN)
Bishop's U (PQ, Canada)
Bluefield State Coll (WV)
Bowie State U (MD)
Brandeis U (MA)
Brescia U (KY)
Brock U (ON, Canada)
Buena Vista U (IA)
California State U, Fresno (CA)
California U of Pennsylvania (PA)
Calvin Coll (MI)
Cameron U (OK)
Carleton U (ON, Canada)
Case Western Reserve U (OH)
Castleton State Coll (VT)
Cedar Crest Coll (PA)
Cedarville Coll (OH)
Cheyney U of Pennsylvania (PA)
Chowan Coll (NC)
Clarion U of Pennsylvania (PA)
Coe Coll (IA)
Coll of Santa Fe (NM)
Coll of the Atlantic (ME)
Concordia Coll (MI)
Concordia U (IL)
Concordia U (OR)
Delta State U (MS)
Dowling Coll (NY)
Drexel U (PA)
Eastern Michigan U (MI)
Eastern Nazarene Coll (MA)
Eastern Oregon U (OR)
Eastern Washington U (WA)
Edinboro U of Pennsylvania (PA)
Erskine Coll (SC)
The Evergreen State Coll (WA)
Fairleigh Dickinson U, Florham-Madison Campus (NJ)
Fairleigh Dickinson U, Teaneck-Hackensack Campus (NJ)
Florida Gulf Coast U (FL)
Fordham U (NY)
Fort Hays State U (KS)
Framingham State Coll (MA)
Freed-Hardeman U (TN)
Gannon U (PA)
Georgia Southwestern State U (GA)
Gettysburg Coll (PA)
Goddard Coll (VT)
Grand Valley State U (MI)
Grand View Coll (IA)
Grinnell Coll (IA)
Hampshire Coll (MA)
Harding U (AR)
Hardin-Simmons U (TX)
Harvard U (MA)
Heritage Coll (WA)
Hofstra U (NY)
Houghton Coll (NY)
Huntington Coll (IN)
Indiana U Kokomo (IN)
Indiana U of Pennsylvania (PA)
Iowa Wesleyan Coll (IA)
John Carroll U (OH)
Johnson C. Smith U (NC)
Judson Coll (IL)
Juniata Coll (PA)
Kent State U (OH)
King Coll (TN)
King's Coll (PA)
Kutztown U of Pennsylvania (PA)
Lakehead U (ON, Canada)
Lees-McRae Coll (NC)
Lee U (TN)
Le Moyne Coll (NY)

Lewis-Clark State Coll (ID)
Linfield Coll (OR)
Lock Haven U of Pennsylvania (PA)
Long Island U, Brooklyn Campus (NY)
Loras Coll (IA)
Lyndon State Coll (VT)
Madonna U (MI)
Mansfield U of Pennsylvania (PA)
Marian Coll of Fond du Lac (WI)
Mars Hill Coll (NC)
Marygrove Coll (MI)
Marylhurst U (OR)
Marymount Coll (NY)
Maryville U of Saint Louis (MO)
Massachusetts Coll of Liberal Arts (MA)
Massachusetts Inst of Technology (MA)
McGill U (PQ, Canada)
Memorial U of Newfoundland (NF, Canada)
Methodist Coll (NC)
Michigan State U (MI)
Middlebury Coll (VT)
Middle Tennessee State U (TN)
Midland Lutheran Coll (NE)
Milligan Coll (TN)
Minnesota State U, Mankato (MN)
Minot State U (ND)
Mississippi State U (MS)
Mississippi U for Women (MS)
Montana State U–Northern (MT)
Montana Tech of The U of Montana (MT)
Mount Allison U (NB, Canada)
Mount Saint Vincent U (NS, Canada)
Mount Vernon Nazarene Coll (OH)
National-Louis U (IL)
New Mexico Inst of Mining and Technology (NM)
North Dakota State U (ND)
Northern State U (SD)
Northland Coll (WI)
North Park U (IL)
Northwest Missouri State U (MO)
Northwest Nazarene U (ID)
Oakland City U (IN)
Oklahoma Baptist U (OK)
Oklahoma Christian U of Science and Arts (OK)
Oklahoma City U (OK)
Oklahoma Panhandle State U (OK)
Olivet Nazarene U (IL)
Open Learning Agency (BC, Canada)
Oregon State U (OR)
Pace U, New York City Campus (NY)
Pace U, Pleasantville/Briarcliff Campus (NY)
Palmer Coll of Chiropractic (IA)
Penn State U Abington Coll (PA)
Penn State U Univ Park Campus (PA)
Peru State Coll (NE)
Philander Smith Coll (AR)
Point Park Coll (PA)
Pontifical Catholic U of Puerto Rico (PR)
Portland State U (OR)
Purdue U (IN)
Purdue U Calumet (IN)
Quinnipiac U (CT)
Redeemer Coll (ON, Canada)
Rensselaer Polytechnic Inst (NY)
Roberts Wesleyan Coll (NY)
Rochester Coll (MI)
Rochester Inst of Technology (NY)
Rockford Coll (IL)
Rocky Mountain Coll (MT)
Rutgers, State U of NJ, Camden Coll of Arts & Scis (NJ)
Rutgers, State U of NJ, U Coll–Camden (NJ)
Saginaw Valley State U (MI)
St. Francis Xavier U (NS, Canada)
Saint Mary-of-the-Woods Coll (IN)
St. Norbert Coll (WI)
Saint Peter's Coll (NJ)
Saint Xavier U (IL)
San Francisco State U (CA)
Santa Clara U (CA)
Sarah Lawrence Coll (NY)
Seattle U (WA)

Majors Index
Biological and Physical Sciences–Biology

Shawnee State U (OH)
Sierra Nevada Coll (NV)
Simon Fraser U (BC, Canada)
Simpson Coll (IA)
Southern Arkansas U–Magnolia (AR)
State U of NY Coll at Fredonia (NY)
State U of NY Coll of Environ Sci and Forestry (NY)
Tabor Coll (KS)
Texas Tech U (TX)
Towson U (MD)
Trent U (ON, Canada)
Trevecca Nazarene U (TN)
Trinity Western U (BC, Canada)
Union Coll (NY)
Union U (TN)
United States Air Force Academy (CO)
United States Military Academy (NY)
U Coll of Cape Breton (NS, Canada)
The U of Alabama at Birmingham (AL)
U of Alaska Fairbanks (AK)
U of Alberta (AB, Canada)
U of Central Arkansas (AR)
U of Central Oklahoma (OK)
U of Charleston (WV)
U of Denver (CO)
U of Dubuque (IA)
The U of Findlay (OH)
U of Georgia (GA)
U of Great Falls (MT)
U of Guelph (ON, Canada)
U of Houston–Clear Lake (TX)
U of Houston–Downtown (TX)
U of Kansas (KS)
U of La Verne (CA)
The U of Lethbridge (AB, Canada)
The U of Maine at Augusta (ME)
U of Massachusetts Amherst (MA)
U of Michigan–Dearborn (MI)
U of Mobile (AL)
U of Nebraska at Omaha (NE)
U of New Brunswick, Fredericton (NB, Canada)
U of New Hampshire (NH)
U of New Orleans (LA)
U of Northern Iowa (IA)
U of North Florida (FL)
U of Oregon (OR)
U of Pittsburgh (PA)
U of Puerto Rico, Río Piedras (PR)
U of Regina (SK, Canada)
U of Rochester (NY)
U of Saint Francis (IN)
U of Southern Indiana (IN)
U of South Florida (FL)
The U of Texas at San Antonio (TX)
U of the Pacific (CA)
U of Toronto (ON, Canada)
U of Tulsa (OK)
U of Waterloo (ON, Canada)
The U of Western Ontario (ON, Canada)
U of West Florida (FL)
U of Windsor (ON, Canada)
U of Wisconsin–Platteville (WI)
U of Wisconsin–Superior (WI)
U of Wisconsin–Whitewater (WI)
Upper Iowa U (IA)
Vanguard U of Southern California (CA)
Villa Julie Coll (MD)
Virginia Commonwealth U (VA)
Virginia Wesleyan Coll (VA)
Walsh U (OH)
Warner Pacific Coll (OR)
Washington State U (WA)
West Chester U of Pennsylvania (PA)
Western Montana Coll of The U of Montana (MT)
Western Washington U (WA)
Wilmington Coll (OH)
Winona State U (MN)
Wittenberg U (OH)
Worcester Polytechnic Inst (MA)
Worcester State Coll (MA)
York Coll (NE)
York U (ON, Canada)
Youngstown State U (OH)

BIOLOGICAL TECHNOLOGY
Arizona State U East (AZ)
California State Polytechnic U, Pomona (CA)
Carleton U (ON, Canada)
Harvard U (MA)
Indiana State U (IN)
Manhattan Coll (NY)
Michigan Technological U (MI)
Millersville U of Pennsylvania (PA)
Minnesota State U, Mankato (MN)
Niagara U (NY)
Northeastern U (MA)
Penn State U Univ Park Campus (PA)
Purdue U Calumet (IN)
St. Cloud State U (MN)
State U of NY Coll at Brockport (NY)
State U of NY Coll at Fredonia (NY)
State U of NY Coll at Oneonta (NY)
Suffolk U (MA)
Texas A&M U (TX)
Université de Sherbrooke (PQ, Canada)
U of Alberta (AB, Canada)
U of Delaware (DE)
U of Missouri–St. Louis (MO)
U of Nebraska at Omaha (NE)
U of New Haven (CT)
U of Puerto Rico, Mayagüez Campus (PR)
U of Windsor (ON, Canada)
Villa Julie Coll (MD)
Westminster Coll (PA)
Worcester Polytechnic Inst (MA)
Worcester State Coll (MA)
York Coll of the City U of New York (NY)

BIOLOGY
Abilene Christian U (TX)
Acadia U (NS, Canada)
Adams State Coll (CO)
Adelphi U (NY)
Adrian Coll (MI)
Agnes Scott Coll (GA)
Alabama A&M U (AL)
Alabama State U (AL)
Albany State U (GA)
Albertson Coll of Idaho (ID)
Albertus Magnus Coll (CT)
Albion Coll (MI)
Albright Coll (PA)
Alderson-Broaddus Coll (WV)
Alfred U (NY)
Alice Lloyd Coll (KY)
Allegheny Coll (PA)
Allentown Coll of St. Francis de Sales (PA)
Allen U (SC)
Alma Coll (MI)
Alvernia Coll (PA)
Alverno Coll (WI)
American International Coll (MA)
American U (DC)
American U in Cairo (Egypt)
Amherst Coll (MA)
Anderson Coll (SC)
Anderson U (IN)
Andrews U (MI)
Anna Maria Coll (MA)
Antioch Coll (OH)
Appalachian State U (NC)
Aquinas Coll (MI)
Arizona State U (AZ)
Arizona State U West (AZ)
Arkansas State U (AR)
Arkansas Tech U (AR)
Armstrong Atlantic State U (GA)
Asbury Coll (KY)
Ashland U (OH)
Assumption Coll (MA)
Athens State U (AL)
Atlantic Baptist U (NB, Canada)
Atlantic Union Coll (MA)
Auburn U (AL)
Auburn U Montgomery (AL)
Augsburg Coll (MN)
Augustana Coll (IL)
Augustana Coll (SD)
Augusta State U (GA)
Austin Coll (TX)
Austin Peay State U (TN)
Avila Coll (MO)
Azusa Pacific U (CA)
Baker U (KS)
Baldwin-Wallace Coll (OH)
Ball State U (IN)
Barber-Scotia Coll (NC)
Bard Coll (NY)
Barnard Coll (NY)
Barry U (FL)
Bartlesville Wesleyan Coll (OK)
Barton Coll (NC)
Bates Coll (ME)
Bayamón Central U (PR)
Baylor U (TX)
Beaver Coll (PA)
Belhaven Coll (MS)
Bellarmine Coll (KY)
Belmont Abbey Coll (NC)
Belmont U (TN)
Beloit Coll (WI)
Bemidji State U (MN)
Benedictine Coll (KS)
Benedictine U (IL)
Bennett Coll (NC)
Bennington Coll (VT)
Berea Coll (KY)
Berry Coll (GA)
Bethany Coll (KS)
Bethany Coll (WV)
Bethel Coll (IN)
Bethel Coll (KS)
Bethel Coll (MN)
Bethel Coll (TN)
Bethune-Cookman Coll (FL)
Biola U (CA)
Birmingham-Southern Coll (AL)
Bishop's U (PQ, Canada)
Blackburn Coll (IL)
Black Hills State U (SD)
Bloomfield Coll (NJ)
Bloomsburg U of Pennsylvania (PA)
Blue Mountain Coll (MS)
Bluffton Coll (OH)
Boise State U (ID)
Boston Coll (MA)
Boston U (MA)
Bowdoin Coll (ME)
Bowie State U (MD)
Bowling Green State U (OH)
Bradley U (IL)
Brandeis U (MA)
Brandon U (MB, Canada)
Brenau U (GA)
Brescia U (KY)
Briar Cliff Coll (IA)
Bridgewater Coll (VA)
Bridgewater State Coll (MA)
Brigham Young U (UT)
Brigham Young U–Hawaii Campus (HI)
Brock U (ON, Canada)
Brooklyn Coll of the City U of NY (NY)
Brown U (RI)
Bryan Coll (TN)
Bryn Athyn Coll of the New Church (PA)
Bryn Mawr Coll (PA)
Bucknell U (PA)
Buena Vista U (IA)
Butler U (IN)
Cabrini Coll (PA)
Caldwell Coll (NJ)
California Baptist U (CA)
California Inst of Technology (CA)
California Lutheran U (CA)
California Polytechnic State U, San Luis Obispo (CA)
California State Polytechnic U, Pomona (CA)
California State U, Chico (CA)
California State U, Dominguez Hills (CA)
California State U, Fresno (CA)
California State U, Fullerton (CA)
California State U, Hayward (CA)
California State U, Long Beach (CA)
California State U, Los Angeles (CA)
California State U, Northridge (CA)
California State U, Sacramento (CA)
California State U, San Bernardino (CA)
California State U, San Marcos (CA)
California State U, Stanislaus (CA)
California U of Pennsylvania (PA)
Calvin Coll (MI)
Cameron U (OK)
Campbellsville U (KY)
Campbell U (NC)
Canisius Coll (NY)
Capital U (OH)
Cardinal Stritch U (WI)
Carleton Coll (MN)
Carleton U (ON, Canada)
Carlow Coll (PA)
Carnegie Mellon U (PA)
Carroll Coll (MT)
Carroll Coll (WI)
Carson-Newman Coll (TN)
Carthage Coll (WI)
Case Western Reserve U (OH)
Castleton State Coll (VT)
Catawba Coll (NC)
The Catholic U of America (DC)
Cedar Crest Coll (PA)
Cedarville Coll (OH)
Centenary Coll of Louisiana (LA)
Central Coll (IA)
Central Connecticut State U (CT)
Central Methodist Coll (MO)
Central Michigan U (MI)
Central Missouri State U (MO)
Centre Coll (KY)
Chadron State Coll (NE)
Chaminade U of Honolulu (HI)
Chapman U (CA)
Charleston Southern U (SC)
Chatham Coll (PA)
Chestnut Hill Coll (PA)
Cheyney U of Pennsylvania (PA)
Chicago State U (IL)
Chowan Coll (NC)
Christian Brothers U (TN)
Christopher Newport U (VA)
Citadel, The Military Coll of South Carolina (SC)
City Coll of the City U of NY (NY)
Claflin U (SC)
Claremont McKenna Coll (CA)
Clarion U of Pennsylvania (PA)
Clark Atlanta U (GA)
Clarke Coll (IA)
Clarkson U (NY)
Clark U (MA)
Clemson U (SC)
Cleveland State U (OH)
Coastal Carolina U (SC)
Coe Coll (IA)
Coker Coll (SC)
Colby Coll (ME)
Colby-Sawyer Coll (NH)
Colgate U (NY)
Coll Misericordia (PA)
Coll of Charleston (SC)
Coll of Mount St. Joseph (OH)
Coll of Mount Saint Vincent (NY)
The Coll of New Jersey (NJ)
The Coll of New Rochelle (NY)
Coll of Notre Dame (CA)
Coll of Notre Dame of Maryland (MD)
Coll of Our Lady of the Elms (MA)
Coll of Saint Benedict (MN)
Coll of St. Catherine (MN)
Coll of Saint Elizabeth (NJ)
Coll of Saint Mary (NE)
The Coll of Saint Rose (NY)
The Coll of St. Scholastica (MN)
Coll of Santa Fe (NM)
The Coll of Southeastern Europe, The American U of Athens (Greece)
Coll of Staten Island of the City U of NY (NY)
Coll of the Atlantic (ME)
Coll of the Holy Cross (MA)
Coll of the Ozarks (MO)
Coll of the Southwest (NM)
The Coll of William and Mary (VA)
The Coll of Wooster (OH)
Colorado Christian U (CO)
The Colorado Coll (CO)
Colorado State U (CO)
Columbia Coll (MO)
Columbia Coll (NY)
Columbia Coll (SC)
Columbia Union Coll (MD)
Columbia U, School of General Studies (NY)
Columbus State U (GA)
Concord Coll (WV)
Concordia Coll (MI)
Concordia Coll (MN)
Concordia Coll (NY)
Concordia U (CA)
Concordia U (IL)
Concordia U (NE)
Concordia U (OR)
Concordia U (PQ, Canada)
Concordia U at Austin (TX)
Concordia U at St. Paul (MN)
Concordia U Coll of Alberta (AB, Canada)
Concordia U Wisconsin (WI)
Connecticut Coll (CT)
Converse Coll (SC)
Coppin State Coll (MD)
Cornell Coll (IA)
Cornell U (NY)
Cornerstone U (MI)
Covenant Coll (GA)
Creighton U (NE)
Crichton Coll (TN)
Culver-Stockton Coll (MO)
Cumberland Coll (KY)
Curry Coll (MA)
Daemen Coll (NY)
Dakota State U (SD)
Dakota Wesleyan U (SD)
Dalhousie U (NS, Canada)
Dallas Baptist U (TX)
Dana Coll (NE)
Dartmouth Coll (NH)
David Lipscomb U (TN)
Davidson Coll (NC)
Defiance Coll (OH)
Delaware State U (DE)
Delaware Valley Coll (PA)
Delta State U (MS)
Denison U (OH)
DePaul U (IL)
DePauw U (IN)
Dickinson Coll (PA)
Dickinson State U (ND)
Doane Coll (NE)
Dr. William M. Scholl Coll of Podiatric Medicine (IL)
Dominican Coll of Blauvelt (NY)
Dominican U (IL)
Dominican U of California (CA)
Dordt Coll (IA)
Dowling Coll (NY)
Drake U (IA)
Drew U (NJ)
Drexel U (PA)
Drury U (MO)
Duke U (NC)
Duquesne U (PA)
D'Youville Coll (NY)
Earlham Coll (IN)
East Carolina U (NC)
East Central U (OK)
Eastern Coll (PA)
Eastern Connecticut State U (CT)
Eastern Illinois U (IL)
Eastern Kentucky U (KY)
Eastern Mennonite U (VA)
Eastern Michigan U (MI)
Eastern Nazarene Coll (MA)
Eastern New Mexico U (NM)
Eastern Oregon U (OR)
Eastern Washington U (WA)
East Stroudsburg U of Pennsylvania (PA)
East Tennessee State U (TN)
East Texas Baptist U (TX)
Eckerd Coll (FL)
Edgewood Coll (WI)
Edinboro U of Pennsylvania (PA)
Elizabeth City State U (NC)
Elizabethtown Coll (PA)
Elmhurst Coll (IL)
Elmira Coll (NY)
Elon Coll (NC)
Emmanuel Coll (MA)
Emory & Henry Coll (VA)
Emory U (GA)
Emporia State U (KS)
Erskine Coll (SC)
Evangel U (MO)
The Evergreen State Coll (WA)
Fairfield U (CT)
Fairleigh Dickinson U, Florham-Madison Campus (NJ)
Fairleigh Dickinson U, Teaneck-Hackensack Campus (NJ)
Fairmont State Coll (WV)

Majors Index
Biology

Faulkner U (AL)
Felician Coll (NJ)
Ferris State U (MI)
Ferrum Coll (VA)
Fisk U (TN)
Fitchburg State Coll (MA)
Florida A&M U (FL)
Florida Atlantic U (FL)
Florida Gulf Coast U (FL)
Florida Inst of Technology (FL)
Florida International U (FL)
Florida Southern Coll (FL)
Florida State U (FL)
Fontbonne Coll (MO)
Fordham U (NY)
Fort Hays State U (KS)
Fort Lewis Coll (CO)
Fort Valley State U (GA)
Framingham State Coll (MA)
Franciscan U of Steubenville (OH)
Francis Marion U (SC)
Franklin and Marshall Coll (PA)
Franklin Coll of Indiana (IN)
Franklin Pierce Coll (NH)
Freed-Hardeman U (TN)
Fresno Pacific U (CA)
Friends U (KS)
Frostburg State U (MD)
Furman U (SC)
Gallaudet U (DC)
Gannon U (PA)
Gardner-Webb U (NC)
Geneva Coll (PA)
George Fox U (OR)
George Mason U (VA)
Georgetown Coll (KY)
Georgetown U (DC)
The George Washington U (DC)
Georgia Coll and State U (GA)
Georgia Inst of Technology (GA)
Georgian Court Coll (NJ)
Georgia Southern U (GA)
Georgia Southwestern State U (GA)
Georgia State U (GA)
Gettysburg Coll (PA)
Glenville State Coll (WV)
Goddard Coll (VT)
Gonzaga U (WA)
Gordon Coll (MA)
Goshen Coll (IN)
Goucher Coll (MD)
Governors State U (IL)
Grace Coll (IN)
Graceland Coll (IA)
Grand Canyon U (AZ)
Grand Valley State U (MI)
Grand View Coll (IA)
Green Mountain Coll (VT)
Greensboro Coll (NC)
Greenville Coll (IL)
Grinnell Coll (IA)
Grove City Coll (PA)
Guilford Coll (NC)
Gustavus Adolphus Coll (MN)
Gwynedd-Mercy Coll (PA)
Hamilton Coll (NY)
Hamline U (MN)
Hampden-Sydney Coll (VA)
Hampshire Coll (MA)
Hampton U (VA)
Hannibal-LaGrange Coll (MO)
Hanover Coll (IN)
Harding U (AR)
Hardin-Simmons U (TX)
Hartwick Coll (NY)
Harvard U (MA)
Harvey Mudd Coll (CA)
Hastings Coll (NE)
Haverford Coll (PA)
Hawaii Pacific U (HI)
Heidelberg Coll (OH)
Henderson State U (AR)
Hendrix Coll (AR)
Heritage Coll (WA)
High Point U (NC)
Hillsdale Coll (MI)
Hiram Coll (OH)
Hobart and William Smith Colls (NY)
Hofstra U (NY)
Hollins U (VA)
Holy Family Coll (PA)
Hood Coll (MD)
Hope Coll (MI)
Houghton Coll (NY)
Houston Baptist U (TX)

Howard Payne U (TX)
Howard U (DC)
Humboldt State U (CA)
Hunter Coll of the City U of NY (NY)
Huntingdon Coll (AL)
Huntington Coll (IN)
Husson Coll (ME)
Huston-Tillotson Coll (TX)
Idaho State U (ID)
Illinois Coll (IL)
Illinois Inst of Technology (IL)
Illinois State U (IL)
Illinois Wesleyan U (IL)
Immaculata Coll (PA)
Indiana State U (IN)
Indiana U Bloomington (IN)
Indiana U East (IN)
Indiana U Kokomo (IN)
Indiana U Northwest (IN)
Indiana U of Pennsylvania (PA)
Indiana U–Purdue U Fort Wayne (IN)
Indiana U–Purdue U Indianapolis (IN)
Indiana U South Bend (IN)
Indiana U Southeast (IN)
Indiana Wesleyan U (IN)
Inter American U of PR, Aguadilla Campus (PR)
Inter American U of PR, Arecibo Campus (PR)
Inter American U of PR, Fajardo Campus (PR)
Inter American U of PR, Metropolitan Campus (PR)
Inter American U of PR, San Germán Campus (PR)
Iona Coll (NY)
Iowa State U of Science and Technology (IA)
Iowa Wesleyan Coll (IA)
Ithaca Coll (NY)
Jacksonville State U (AL)
Jacksonville U (FL)
James Madison U (VA)
Jamestown Coll (ND)
Jarvis Christian Coll (TX)
John Brown U (AR)
John Carroll U (OH)
Johns Hopkins U (MD)
Johnson C. Smith U (NC)
Johnson State Coll (VT)
Judson Coll (AL)
Judson Coll (IL)
Juniata Coll (PA)
Kalamazoo Coll (MI)
Kansas State U (KS)
Kean U (NJ)
Keene State Coll (NH)
Kent State U (OH)
Kentucky State U (KY)
Kentucky Wesleyan Coll (KY)
Kenyon Coll (OH)
Keuka Coll (NY)
King Coll (TN)
King's Coll (PA)
The King's U Coll (AB, Canada)
Knox Coll (IL)
Kutztown U of Pennsylvania (PA)
Lafayette Coll (PA)
LaGrange Coll (GA)
Lake Erie Coll (OH)
Lake Forest Coll (IL)
Lakehead U (ON, Canada)
Lakeland Coll (WI)
Lake Superior State U (MI)
Lamar U (TX)
Lambuth U (TN)
Lander U (SC)
Lane Coll (TN)
Langston U (OK)
La Roche Coll (PA)
La Salle U (PA)
La Sierra U (CA)
Lawrence U (WI)
Lebanon Valley Coll (PA)
Lees-McRae Coll (NC)
Lee U (TN)
Lehigh U (PA)
Lehman Coll of the City U of NY (NY)
Le Moyne Coll (NY)
LeMoyne-Owen Coll (TN)
Lenoir-Rhyne Coll (NC)
LeTourneau U (TX)
Lewis & Clark Coll (OR)

Lewis-Clark State Coll (ID)
Lewis U (IL)
Liberty U (VA)
Limestone Coll (SC)
Lincoln Memorial U (TN)
Lincoln U (MO)
Lincoln U (PA)
Lindenwood U (MO)
Lindsey Wilson Coll (KY)
Linfield Coll (OR)
Lock Haven U of Pennsylvania (PA)
Logan U of Chiropractic (MO)
Long Island U, Brooklyn Campus (NY)
Long Island U, C.W. Post Campus (NY)
Long Island U, Southampton Coll (NY)
Longwood Coll (VA)
Loras Coll (IA)
Louisiana Coll (LA)
Louisiana State U and A&M Coll (LA)
Louisiana State U in Shreveport (LA)
Louisiana Tech U (LA)
Lourdes Coll (OH)
Loyola Coll in Maryland (MD)
Loyola Marymount U (CA)
Loyola U Chicago (IL)
Loyola U New Orleans (LA)
Lubbock Christian U (TX)
Luther Coll (IA)
Lycoming Coll (PA)
Lynchburg Coll (VA)
Lyon Coll (AR)
Macalester Coll (MN)
MacMurray Coll (IL)
Madonna U (MI)
Maharishi U of Management (IA)
Malone Coll (OH)
Manchester Coll (IN)
Manhattan Coll (NY)
Manhattanville Coll (NY)
Mansfield U of Pennsylvania (PA)
Marian Coll (IN)
Marian Coll of Fond du Lac (WI)
Marietta Coll (OH)
Marist Coll (NY)
Marlboro Coll (VT)
Marquette U (WI)
Marshall U (WV)
Mars Hill Coll (NC)
Mary Baldwin Coll (VA)
Marycrest International U (IA)
Marygrove Coll (MI)
Marymount Coll (NY)
Marymount Manhattan Coll (NY)
Maryville Coll (TN)
Maryville U of Saint Louis (MO)
Mary Washington Coll (VA)
Marywood U (PA)
Massachusetts Coll of Liberal Arts (MA)
Massachusetts Inst of Technology (MA)
Mayville State U (ND)
McGill U (PQ, Canada)
McKendree Coll (IL)
McMurry U (TX)
McNeese State U (LA)
McPherson Coll (KS)
Medaille Coll (NY)
Medgar Evers Coll of the City U of NY (NY)
Memorial U of Newfoundland (NF, Canada)
Mercer U (GA)
Mercy Coll (NY)
Mercyhurst Coll (PA)
Meredith Coll (NC)
Merrimack Coll (MA)
Mesa State Coll (CO)
Messiah Coll (PA)
Methodist Coll (NC)
Metropolitan State Coll of Denver (CO)
Miami U (OH)
Michigan State U (MI)
Michigan Technological U (MI)
MidAmerica Nazarene U (KS)
Middlebury Coll (VT)
Middle Tennessee State U (TN)
Midland Lutheran Coll (NE)
Midway Coll (KY)
Midwestern State U (TX)

Millersville U of Pennsylvania (PA)
Milligan Coll (TN)
Millikin U (IL)
Millsaps Coll (MS)
Mills Coll (CA)
Minnesota State U, Mankato (MN)
Minnesota State U Moorhead (MN)
Minot State U (ND)
Mississippi Coll (MS)
Mississippi State U (MS)
Mississippi U for Women (MS)
Mississippi Valley State U (MS)
Missouri Baptist Coll (MO)
Missouri Southern State Coll (MO)
Missouri Valley Coll (MO)
Missouri Western State Coll (MO)
Molloy Coll (NY)
Monmouth Coll (IL)
Monmouth U (NJ)
Montana State U–Billings (MT)
Montana State U–Bozeman (MT)
Montana State U–Northern (MT)
Montana Tech of The U of Montana (MT)
Moravian Coll (PA)
Morehead State U (KY)
Morehouse Coll (GA)
Morgan State U (MD)
Morningside Coll (IA)
Morris Coll (SC)
Mount Allison U (NB, Canada)
Mount Holyoke Coll (MA)
Mount Marty Coll (SD)
Mount Mary Coll (WI)
Mount Mercy Coll (IA)
Mount Olive Coll (NC)
Mount St. Clare Coll (IA)
Mount Saint Mary Coll (NY)
Mount St. Mary's Coll (CA)
Mount Saint Mary's Coll and Seminary (MD)
Mount Saint Vincent U (NS, Canada)
Mount Senario Coll (WI)
Mount Union Coll (OH)
Mount Vernon Nazarene Coll (OH)
Muhlenberg Coll (PA)
Murray State U (KY)
Muskingum Coll (OH)
The National Coll of Chiropractic (IL)
National-Louis U (IL)
Nazareth Coll of Rochester (NY)
Nebraska Wesleyan U (NE)
Neumann Coll (PA)
Newberry Coll (SC)
New Coll of the U of South Florida (FL)
New England Coll (NH)
New Jersey City U (NJ)
Newman U (KS)
New Mexico Highlands U (NM)
New Mexico Inst of Mining and Technology (NM)
New Mexico State U (NM)
New York Inst of Technology (NY)
New York U (NY)
Niagara U (NY)
Nicholls State U (LA)
Nipissing U (ON, Canada)
Norfolk State U (VA)
North Carolina Ag and Tech State U (NC)
North Carolina Central U (NC)
North Carolina State U (NC)
North Carolina Wesleyan Coll (NC)
North Central Coll (IL)
North Dakota State U (ND)
Northeastern Illinois U (IL)
Northeastern State U (OK)
Northeastern U (MA)
Northern Arizona U (AZ)
Northern Illinois U (IL)
Northern Kentucky U (KY)
Northern Michigan U (MI)
Northern State U (SD)
North Georgia Coll & State U (GA)
Northland Coll (WI)
North Park U (IL)
Northwestern Coll (IA)
Northwestern Coll (MN)
Northwestern Oklahoma State U (OK)
Northwestern State U of Louisiana (LA)
Northwestern U (IL)
Northwest Missouri State U (MO)

Northwest Nazarene U (ID)
Norwich U (VT)
Notre Dame Coll (NH)
Notre Dame Coll of Ohio (OH)
Nova Southeastern U (FL)
Oakland City U (IN)
Oakland U (MI)
Oakwood Coll (AL)
Oberlin Coll (OH)
Occidental Coll (CA)
Oglethorpe U (GA)
Ohio Dominican Coll (OH)
Ohio Northern U (OH)
The Ohio State U (OH)
Ohio U (OH)
Ohio Wesleyan U (OH)
Okanagan U Coll (BC, Canada)
Oklahoma Baptist U (OK)
Oklahoma Christian U of Science and Arts (OK)
Oklahoma City U (OK)
Oklahoma Panhandle State U (OK)
Oklahoma State U (OK)
Old Dominion U (VA)
Olivet Nazarene U (IL)
Open Learning Agency (BC, Canada)
Oregon State U (OR)
Ottawa U (KS)
Otterbein Coll (OH)
Ouachita Baptist U (AR)
Our Lady of Holy Cross Coll (LA)
Our Lady of the Lake U of San Antonio (TX)
Pace U, New York City Campus (NY)
Pace U, Pleasantville/Briarcliff Campus (NY)
Pacific Lutheran U (WA)
Pacific Union Coll (CA)
Pacific U (OR)
Paine Coll (GA)
Palm Beach Atlantic Coll (FL)
Park U (MO)
Peace Coll (NC)
Penn State U at Erie, The Behrend Coll (PA)
Penn State U Univ Park Campus (PA)
Pepperdine U, Malibu (CA)
Peru State Coll (NE)
Pfeiffer U (NC)
Philadelphia U (PA)
Philander Smith Coll (AR)
Piedmont Coll (GA)
Pikeville Coll (KY)
Pine Manor Coll (MA)
Pittsburg State U (KS)
Pitzer Coll (CA)
Plattsburgh State U of NY (NY)
Plymouth State Coll (NH)
Point Loma Nazarene U (CA)
Point Park Coll (PA)
Pomona Coll (CA)
Pontifical Catholic U of Puerto Rico (PR)
Portland State U (OR)
Prairie View A&M U (TX)
Presbyterian Coll (SC)
Principia Coll (IL)
Providence Coll (RI)
Purchase Coll, State U of NY (NY)
Purdue U (IN)
Purdue U Calumet (IN)
Purdue U North Central (IN)
Queens Coll (NC)
Queens Coll of the City U of NY (NY)
Queen's U at Kingston (ON, Canada)
Quincy U (IL)
Quinnipiac U (CT)
Radford U (VA)
Ramapo Coll of New Jersey (NJ)
Randolph-Macon Coll (VA)
Randolph-Macon Woman's Coll (VA)
Redeemer Coll (ON, Canada)
Reed Coll (OR)
Regents Coll (NY)
Regis Coll (MA)
Regis U (CO)
Reinhardt Coll (GA)
Rensselaer Polytechnic Inst (NY)
Rhodes Coll (TN)
Rice U (TX)

Majors Index
Biology

The Richard Stockton Coll of New Jersey (NJ)
Rider U (NJ)
Ripon Coll (WI)
Rivier Coll (NH)
Roanoke Coll (VA)
Roberts Wesleyan Coll (NY)
Rochester Inst of Technology (NY)
Rockford Coll (IL)
Rockhurst U (MO)
Rocky Mountain Coll (MT)
Roger Williams U (RI)
Rollins Coll (FL)
Rosemont Coll (PA)
Rowan U (NJ)
Russell Sage Coll (NY)
Rust Coll (MS)
Rutgers, State U of NJ, Camden Coll of Arts & Scis (NJ)
Rutgers, State U of NJ, Cook Coll (NJ)
Rutgers, State U of NJ, Douglass Coll (NJ)
Rutgers, State U of NJ, Livingston Coll (NJ)
Rutgers, State U of NJ, Newark Coll of Arts & Scis (NJ)
Rutgers, State U of NJ, Rutgers Coll (NJ)
Rutgers, State U of NJ, U Coll–Camden (NJ)
Rutgers, State U of NJ, U Coll–New Brunswick (NJ)
Ryerson Polytechnic U (ON, Canada)
Sacred Heart U (CT)
Saginaw Valley State U (MI)
St. Ambrose U (IA)
St. Andrews Presbyterian Coll (NC)
Saint Anselm Coll (NH)
Saint Augustine's Coll (NC)
St. Bonaventure U (NY)
St. Cloud State U (MN)
St. Edward's U (TX)
St. Francis Coll (NY)
Saint Francis Coll (PA)
St. Francis Xavier U (NS, Canada)
St. John Fisher Coll (NY)
Saint John's U (MN)
St. John's U (NY)
Saint Joseph Coll (CT)
Saint Joseph's Coll (IN)
Saint Joseph's Coll (ME)
St. Joseph's Coll, New York (NY)
St. Joseph's Coll, Suffolk Campus (NY)
Saint Joseph's U (PA)
St. Lawrence U (NY)
Saint Leo U (FL)
Saint Louis U (MO)
Saint Martin's Coll (WA)
Saint Mary Coll (KS)
Saint Mary-of-the-Woods Coll (IN)
Saint Mary's Coll (IN)
Saint Mary's Coll (MI)
Saint Mary's Coll of California (CA)
St. Mary's Coll of Maryland (MD)
Saint Mary's U (NS, Canada)
Saint Mary's U of Minnesota (MN)
St. Mary's U of San Antonio (TX)
Saint Michael's Coll (VT)
St. Norbert Coll (WI)
St. Olaf Coll (MN)
Saint Paul's Coll (VA)
Saint Peter's Coll (NJ)
St. Thomas U (FL)
Saint Vincent Coll (PA)
Saint Xavier U (IL)
Salem Coll (NC)
Salem State Coll (MA)
Salisbury State U (MD)
Salve Regina U (RI)
Samford U (AL)
Sam Houston State U (TX)
San Diego State U (CA)
San Francisco State U (CA)
San Jose State U (CA)
Santa Clara U (CA)
Sarah Lawrence Coll (NY)
Savannah State U (GA)
Schreiner Coll (TX)
Scripps Coll (CA)
Seattle Pacific U (WA)
Seattle U (WA)
Seton Hall U (NJ)
Seton Hill Coll (PA)
Shawnee State U (OH)

Shaw U (NC)
Shenandoah U (VA)
Shepherd Coll (WV)
Shippensburg U of Pennsylvania (PA)
Shorter Coll (GA)
Siena Coll (NY)
Siena Heights U (MI)
Silver Lake Coll (WI)
Simmons Coll (MA)
Simon Fraser U (BC, Canada)
Simon's Rock Coll of Bard (MA)
Simpson Coll (IA)
Skidmore Coll (NY)
Slippery Rock U of Pennsylvania (PA)
Smith Coll (MA)
Sonoma State U (CA)
South Dakota State U (SD)
Southeastern Louisiana U (LA)
Southeastern Oklahoma State U (OK)
Southeast Missouri State U (MO)
Southern Adventist U (TN)
Southern Arkansas U–Magnolia (AR)
Southern Illinois U Carbondale (IL)
Southern Illinois U Edwardsville (IL)
Southern Methodist U (TX)
Southern Oregon U (OR)
Southern Utah U (UT)
Southern Wesleyan U (SC)
Southwest Baptist U (MO)
Southwestern Adventist U (TX)
Southwestern Coll (KS)
Southwestern Oklahoma State U (OK)
Southwestern U (TX)
Southwest Missouri State U (MO)
Southwest State U (MN)
Southwest Texas State U (TX)
Spalding U (KY)
Spelman Coll (GA)
Spring Arbor Coll (MI)
Stanford U (CA)
State U of NY at Albany (NY)
State U of NY at Binghamton (NY)
State U of NY at Buffalo (NY)
State U of NY at New Paltz (NY)
State U of NY at Oswego (NY)
State U of NY at Stony Brook (NY)
State U of NY Coll at Brockport (NY)
State U of NY Coll at Buffalo (NY)
State U of NY Coll at Cortland (NY)
State U of NY Coll at Fredonia (NY)
State U of NY Coll at Geneseo (NY)
State U of NY Coll at Old Westbury (NY)
State U of NY Coll at Oneonta (NY)
State U of NY Coll at Potsdam (NY)
State U of NY Coll of Environ Sci and Forestry (NY)
State U of West Georgia (GA)
Stephen F. Austin State U (TX)
Stephens Coll (MO)
Sterling Coll (KS)
Stetson U (FL)
Stillman Coll (AL)
Stonehill Coll (MA)
Suffolk U (MA)
Sul Ross State U (TX)
Susquehanna U (PA)
Swarthmore Coll (PA)
Sweet Briar Coll (VA)
Syracuse U (NY)
Tabor Coll (KS)
Talladega Coll (AL)
Taylor U (IN)
Temple U (PA)
Tennessee State U (TN)
Tennessee Technological U (TN)
Tennessee Wesleyan Coll (TN)
Texas A&M International U (TX)
Texas A&M U (TX)
Texas A&M U–Commerce (TX)
Texas A&M U–Kingsville (TX)
Texas Christian U (TX)
Texas Lutheran U (TX)
Texas Southern U (TX)
Texas Tech U (TX)
Texas Wesleyan U (TX)
Texas Woman's U (TX)

Thiel Coll (PA)
Thomas Edison State Coll (NJ)
Thomas More Coll (KY)
Thomas More Coll of Liberal Arts (NH)
Thomas U (GA)
Tougaloo Coll (MS)
Touro Coll (NY)
Towson U (MD)
Transylvania U (KY)
Trent U (ON, Canada)
Trevecca Nazarene U (TN)
Trinity Christian Coll (IL)
Trinity Coll (CT)
Trinity Coll of Vermont (VT)
Trinity U (TX)
Trinity Western U (BC, Canada)
Tri-State U (IN)
Troy State U (AL)
Troy State U Dothan (AL)
Truman State U (MO)
Tufts U (MA)
Tulane U (LA)
Tusculum Coll (TN)
Tuskegee U (AL)
Union Coll (KY)
Union Coll (NE)
Union Coll (NY)
Union U (TN)
United States Air Force Academy (CO)
United States Military Academy (NY)
Universidad Adventista de las Antillas (PR)
Universidad del Turabo (PR)
Universidad Metropolitana (PR)
Université de Montréal (PQ, Canada)
Université de Sherbrooke (PQ, Canada)
U du Québec à Chicoutimi (PQ, Canada)
U du Québec à Trois-Rivières (PQ, Canada)
Université Laval (PQ, Canada)
U Coll of Cape Breton (NS, Canada)
U Coll of the Fraser Valley (BC, Canada)
The U of Akron (OH)
The U of Alabama (AL)
The U of Alabama at Birmingham (AL)
The U of Alabama in Huntsville (AL)
U of Alaska Fairbanks (AK)
U of Alberta (AB, Canada)
The U of Arizona (AZ)
U of Arkansas (AR)
U of Arkansas at Little Rock (AR)
U of Arkansas at Monticello (AR)
U of Arkansas at Pine Bluff (AR)
U of Bridgeport (CT)
U of British Columbia (BC, Canada)
U of Calgary (AB, Canada)
U of Calif, Davis (CA)
U of Calif, Irvine (CA)
U of Calif, Los Angeles (CA)
U of Calif, Riverside (CA)
U of Calif, San Diego (CA)
U of Calif, Santa Barbara (CA)
U of Calif, Santa Cruz (CA)
U of Central Arkansas (AR)
U of Central Florida (FL)
U of Central Oklahoma (OK)
U of Charleston (WV)
U of Chicago (IL)
U of Cincinnati (OH)
U of Colorado at Boulder (CO)
U of Colorado at Colorado Springs (CO)
U of Colorado at Denver (CO)
U of Connecticut (CT)
U of Dallas (TX)
U of Dayton (OH)
U of Delaware (DE)
U of Denver (CO)
U of Detroit Mercy (MI)
U of Dubuque (IA)
U of Evansville (IN)
The U of Findlay (OH)
U of Georgia (GA)
U of Great Falls (MT)
U of Guelph (ON, Canada)
U of Hartford (CT)

U of Hawaii at Manoa (HI)
U of Houston (TX)
U of Houston–Clear Lake (TX)
U of Houston–Downtown (TX)
U of Idaho (ID)
U of Illinois at Chicago (IL)
U of Illinois at Springfield (IL)
U of Illinois at Urbana–Champaign (IL)
U of Indianapolis (IN)
The U of Iowa (IA)
U of Kansas (KS)
U of Kentucky (KY)
U of King's Coll (NS, Canada)
U of La Verne (CA)
The U of Lethbridge (AB, Canada)
U of Louisiana at Lafayette (LA)
U of Louisiana at Monroe (LA)
U of Louisville (KY)
U of Maine (ME)
U of Maine at Farmington (ME)
U of Maine at Fort Kent (ME)
U of Maine at Machias (ME)
U of Maine at Presque Isle (ME)
U of Manitoba (MB, Canada)
U of Mary Hardin-Baylor (TX)
U of Maryland, Baltimore County (MD)
U of Maryland, Coll Park (MD)
U of Massachusetts Amherst (MA)
U of Massachusetts Boston (MA)
U of Massachusetts Dartmouth (MA)
U of Massachusetts Lowell (MA)
The U of Memphis (TN)
U of Miami (FL)
U of Michigan (MI)
U of Michigan–Dearborn (MI)
U of Michigan–Flint (MI)
U of Minnesota, Duluth (MN)
U of Minnesota, Morris (MN)
U of Minnesota, Twin Cities Campus (MN)
U of Mississippi (MS)
U of Missouri–Columbia (MO)
U of Missouri–Kansas City (MO)
U of Missouri–Rolla (MO)
U of Missouri–St. Louis (MO)
U of Mobile (AL)
The U of Montana–Missoula (MT)
U of Montevallo (AL)
U of Nebraska at Kearney (NE)
U of Nebraska at Omaha (NE)
U of Nebraska–Lincoln (NE)
U of Nevada, Las Vegas (NV)
U of Nevada, Reno (NV)
U of New Brunswick, Fredericton (NB, Canada)
U of New Brunswick, Saint John (NB, Canada)
U of New England (ME)
U of New Hampshire (NH)
U of New Haven (CT)
U of New Mexico (NM)
U of New Orleans (LA)
U of North Alabama (AL)
The U of North Carolina at Asheville (NC)
The U of North Carolina at Chapel Hill (NC)
The U of North Carolina at Charlotte (NC)
The U of North Carolina at Greensboro (NC)
The U of North Carolina at Pembroke (NC)
The U of North Carolina at Wilmington (NC)
U of North Dakota (ND)
U of Northern Colorado (CO)
U of Northern Iowa (IA)
U of North Florida (FL)
U of North Texas (TX)
U of Notre Dame (IN)
U of Oregon (OR)
U of Pennsylvania (PA)
U of Pittsburgh (PA)
U of Pittsburgh at Bradford (PA)
U of Pittsburgh at Johnstown (PA)
U of Portland (OR)
U of Prince Edward Island (PE, Canada)
U of Puerto Rico, Humacao U Coll (PR)
U of Puerto Rico, Mayagüez Campus (PR)
U of Puerto Rico, Río Piedras (PR)

U of Puget Sound (WA)
U of Redlands (CA)
U of Regina (SK, Canada)
U of Rhode Island (RI)
U of Richmond (VA)
U of Rio Grande (OH)
U of Rochester (NY)
U of St. Francis (IL)
U of Saint Francis (IN)
U of St. Thomas (MN)
U of St. Thomas (TX)
U of San Diego (CA)
U of San Francisco (CA)
U of Science and Arts of Oklahoma (OK)
The U of Scranton (PA)
U of Sioux Falls (SD)
U of South Alabama (AL)
U of South Carolina (SC)
U of South Carolina Spartanburg (SC)
U of South Dakota (SD)
U of Southern California (CA)
U of Southern Colorado (CO)
U of Southern Indiana (IN)
U of Southern Maine (ME)
U of Southern Mississippi (MS)
U of South Florida (FL)
The U of Tampa (FL)
The U of Tennessee at Chattanooga (TN)
The U of Tennessee at Martin (TN)
The U of Tennessee Knoxville (TN)
The U of Texas at Arlington (TX)
The U of Texas at Austin (TX)
The U of Texas at Dallas (TX)
The U of Texas at San Antonio (TX)
The U of Texas at Tyler (TX)
The U of Texas–Pan American (TX)
U of the District of Columbia (DC)
U of the Ozarks (AR)
U of the Pacific (CA)
U of the Sacred Heart (PR)
U of the Sciences in Philadelphia (PA)
U of the South (TN)
U of the Virgin Islands (VI)
U of Toronto (ON, Canada)
U of Tulsa (OK)
U of Utah (UT)
U of Vermont (VT)
U of Victoria (BC, Canada)
U of Virginia (VA)
U of Virginia's Coll at Wise (VA)
U of Washington (WA)
U of Waterloo (ON, Canada)
The U of West Alabama (AL)
The U of Western Ontario (ON, Canada)
U of West Florida (FL)
U of Windsor (ON, Canada)
The U of Winnipeg (MB, Canada)
U of Wisconsin–Eau Claire (WI)
U of Wisconsin–Green Bay (WI)
U of Wisconsin–La Crosse (WI)
U of Wisconsin–Madison (WI)
U of Wisconsin–Milwaukee (WI)
U of Wisconsin–Parkside (WI)
U of Wisconsin–Platteville (WI)
U of Wisconsin–River Falls (WI)
U of Wisconsin–Stevens Point (WI)
U of Wisconsin–Superior (WI)
U of Wisconsin–Whitewater (WI)
U of Wyoming (WY)
Upper Iowa U (IA)
Urbana U (OH)
Ursinus Coll (PA)
Ursuline Coll (OH)
Utah State U (UT)
Utica Coll of Syracuse U (NY)
Valdosta State U (GA)
Valley City State U (ND)
Valparaiso U (IN)
Vanderbilt U (TN)
Vanguard U of Southern California (CA)
Vassar Coll (NY)
Villa Julie Coll (MD)
Villanova U (PA)
Virginia Commonwealth U (VA)
Virginia Intermont Coll (VA)
Virginia Military Inst (VA)
Virginia Polytechnic Inst and State U (VA)
Virginia Union U (VA)
Virginia Wesleyan Coll (VA)

Majors Index
Biology–Botany

Voorhees Coll (SC)
Wabash Coll (IN)
Wagner Coll (NY)
Wake Forest U (NC)
Walla Walla Coll (WA)
Walsh U (OH)
Warner Pacific Coll (OR)
Warner Southern Coll (FL)
Warren Wilson Coll (NC)
Wartburg Coll (IA)
Washington & Jefferson Coll (PA)
Washington and Lee U (VA)
Washington Coll (MD)
Washington State U (WA)
Washington U in St. Louis (MO)
Wayland Baptist U (TX)
Waynesburg Coll (PA)
Wayne State Coll (NE)
Wayne State U (MI)
Webster U (MO)
Wellesley Coll (MA)
Wells Coll (NY)
Wesleyan Coll (GA)
Wesleyan U (CT)
Wesley Coll (DE)
West Chester U of Pennsylvania (PA)
Western Carolina U (NC)
Western Connecticut State U (CT)
Western Illinois U (IL)
Western Kentucky U (KY)
Western Maryland Coll (MD)
Western Michigan U (MI)
Western Montana Coll of The U of Montana (MT)
Western New England Coll (MA)
Western Oregon U (OR)
Western State Coll of Colorado (CO)
Western States Chiropractic Coll (OR)
Western Washington U (WA)
Westfield State Coll (MA)
West Liberty State Coll (WV)
Westminster Coll (MO)
Westminster Coll (PA)
Westminster Coll (UT)
Westmont Coll (CA)
West Texas A&M U (TX)
West Virginia State Coll (WV)
West Virginia U (WV)
West Virginia U Inst of Technology (WV)
West Virginia Wesleyan Coll (WV)
Wheaton Coll (IL)
Wheaton Coll (MA)
Wheeling Jesuit U (WV)
Whitman Coll (WA)
Whittier Coll (CA)
Whitworth Coll (WA)
Wichita State U (KS)
Widener U (PA)
Wilfrid Laurier U (ON, Canada)
Wilkes U (PA)
Willamette U (OR)
William Jewell Coll (MO)
William Paterson U of New Jersey (NJ)
William Penn U (IA)
Williams Baptist Coll (AR)
Williams Coll (MA)
William Woods U (MO)
Wilmington Coll (OH)
Wilson Coll (PA)
Wingate U (NC)
Winona State U (MN)
Winston-Salem State U (NC)
Winthrop U (SC)
Wisconsin Lutheran Coll (WI)
Wittenberg U (OH)
Wofford Coll (SC)
Worcester Polytechnic Inst (MA)
Worcester State Coll (MA)
Wright State U (OH)
Xavier U (OH)
Xavier U of Louisiana (LA)
Yale U (CT)
Yeshiva U (NY)
York Coll of Pennsylvania (PA)
York Coll of the City U of New York (NY)
York U (ON, Canada)
Youngstown State U (OH)

BIOLOGY EDUCATION
Abilene Christian U (TX)
Adams State Coll (CO)

Alvernia Coll (PA)
Arkansas State U (AR)
Arkansas Tech U (AR)
Baylor U (TX)
Berea Coll (KY)
Berry Coll (GA)
Bethany Coll (KS)
Bethel Coll (IN)
Bethel Coll (TN)
Bethune-Cookman Coll (FL)
Blue Mountain Coll (MS)
Bowling Green State U (OH)
Bridgewater Coll (VA)
Brigham Young U–Hawaii Campus (HI)
Cabrini Coll (PA)
Campbell U (NC)
Canisius Coll (NY)
Carroll Coll (MT)
The Catholic U of America (DC)
Cedarville Coll (OH)
Central Michigan U (MI)
Central Missouri State U (MO)
Christian Brothers U (TN)
Citadel, The Military Coll of South Carolina (SC)
Colby-Sawyer Coll (NH)
The Coll of New Jersey (NJ)
Coll of St. Catherine (MN)
Coll of the Ozarks (MO)
Colorado State U (CO)
Concordia Coll (MN)
Concordia U (IL)
Concordia U (NE)
Crichton Coll (TN)
Daemen Coll (NY)
David Lipscomb U (TN)
Delta State U (MS)
Dominican Coll of Blauvelt (NY)
Duquesne U (PA)
Eastern Michigan U (MI)
East Texas Baptist U (TX)
Elmhurst Coll (IL)
Elmira Coll (NY)
Florida Inst of Technology (FL)
Framingham State Coll (MA)
Freed-Hardeman U (TN)
George Fox U (OR)
Greensboro Coll (NC)
Greenville Coll (IL)
Gustavus Adolphus Coll (MN)
Hardin-Simmons U (TX)
Hastings Coll (NE)
Husson Coll (ME)
Indiana U Bloomington (IN)
Indiana U Northwest (IN)
Indiana U–Purdue U Fort Wayne (IN)
Indiana U South Bend (IN)
Indiana U Southeast (IN)
Inter American U of PR, Aguadilla Campus (PR)
Ithaca Coll (NY)
Johnson State Coll (VT)
Juniata Coll (PA)
Keuka Coll (NY)
King Coll (TN)
La Roche Coll (PA)
Liberty U (VA)
Limestone Coll (SC)
Long Island U, C.W. Post Campus (NY)
Luther Coll (IA)
Manhattanville Coll (NY)
Mansfield U of Pennsylvania (PA)
Marymount Coll (NY)
Maryville Coll (TN)
Mayville State U (ND)
McGill U (PQ, Canada)
McKendree Coll (IL)
McMurry U (TX)
Messiah Coll (PA)
Miami U (OH)
Molloy Coll (NY)
Nazareth Coll of Rochester (NY)
New York Inst of Technology (NY)
New York U (NY)
Niagara U (NY)
North Carolina Central U (NC)
North Carolina State U (NC)
North Dakota State U (ND)
Northwest Nazarene U (ID)
Ohio U (OH)
Oklahoma Baptist U (OK)
Philander Smith Coll (AR)
Pikeville Coll (KY)
Plymouth State Coll (NH)

Rivier Coll (NH)
St. Ambrose U (IA)
Saint Augustine's Coll (NC)
St. John's U (NY)
Salve Regina U (RI)
Seattle Pacific U (WA)
Seton Hill Coll (PA)
Shaw U (NC)
Southeastern Coll of the Assemblies of God (FL)
Southern Arkansas U–Magnolia (AR)
Southwest Missouri State U (MO)
Southwest State U (MN)
State U of NY Coll of Environ Sci and Forestry (NY)
Tennessee Wesleyan Coll (TN)
Texas A&M International U (TX)
Texas Wesleyan U (TX)
Trevecca Nazarene U (TN)
Trinity Christian Coll (IL)
Union Coll (NE)
The U of Arizona (AZ)
U of Central Arkansas (AR)
U of Delaware (DE)
U of Illinois at Chicago (IL)
U of Illinois at Urbana–Champaign (IL)
U of Maine at Farmington (ME)
U of Nebraska–Lincoln (NE)
U of North Texas (TX)
U of Rio Grande (OH)
The U of Tennessee at Martin (TN)
U of Washington (WA)
U of Waterloo (ON, Canada)
U of Wisconsin–River Falls (WI)
U of Wisconsin–Superior (WI)
Utah State U (UT)
Virginia Intermont Coll (VA)
Washington U in St. Louis (MO)
Weber State U (UT)
Westminster Coll (UT)
Wheeling Jesuit U (WV)
York U (ON, Canada)
Youngstown State U (OH)

BIOMEDICAL ENGINEERING-RELATED TECHNOLOGY
Texas Southern U (TX)
Thomas Edison State Coll (NJ)
The U of Akron (OH)

BIOMEDICAL SCIENCE
Antioch Coll (OH)
Brown U (RI)
Cedar Crest Coll (PA)
City Coll of the City U of NY (NY)
Emory U (GA)
Framingham State Coll (MA)
Grand Valley State U (MI)
Harvard U (MA)
Howard U (DC)
Immaculata Coll (PA)
Inter American U of PR, San Germán Campus (PR)
Marquette U (WI)
MCP Hahnemann U (PA)
Ohio U (OH)
Rutgers, State U of NJ, Douglass Coll (NJ)
Rutgers, State U of NJ, Livingston Coll (NJ)
Rutgers, State U of NJ, Rutgers Coll (NJ)
Rutgers, State U of NJ, U Coll–New Brunswick (NJ)
St. Cloud State U (MN)
St. Francis Coll (NY)
State U of NY Coll at Fredonia (NY)
Stephens Coll (MO)
Suffolk U (MA)
Texas A&M U (TX)
Union Coll (NY)
Université de Montréal (PQ, Canada)
U du Québec à Trois-Rivières (PQ, Canada)
U of Calif, Riverside (CA)
U of Guelph (ON, Canada)
U of Michigan (MI)
U of Mississippi (MS)
The U of North Carolina at Pembroke (NC)
U of South Alabama (AL)
U of Utah (UT)
Worcester Polytechnic Inst (MA)

BIOMEDICAL TECHNOLOGY
Alfred U (NY)
Alvernia Coll (PA)
Andrews U (MI)
California State U, Hayward (CA)
Cedar Crest Coll (PA)
Cleveland State U (OH)
George Mason U (VA)
New York Inst of Technology (NY)
Northwest Missouri State U (MO)
Suffolk U (MA)
U of New Hampshire (NH)
U of Southern Colorado (CO)
Walla Walla Coll (WA)

BIOMETRICS
Cornell U (NY)
Harvard U (MA)
Rutgers, State U of NJ, Douglass Coll (NJ)
Rutgers, State U of NJ, Livingston Coll (NJ)
Rutgers, State U of NJ, Rutgers Coll (NJ)
Rutgers, State U of NJ, U Coll–New Brunswick (NJ)
U of Michigan (MI)

BIOPHYSICS
Andrews U (MI)
Brandeis U (MA)
Brown U (RI)
California State U, Los Angeles (CA)
Carnegie Mellon U (PA)
Centenary Coll of Louisiana (LA)
Claremont McKenna Coll (CA)
Clarkson U (NY)
Columbia Coll (NY)
Hampden-Sydney Coll (VA)
Hampshire Coll (MA)
Harvard U (MA)
Haverford Coll (PA)
Howard U (DC)
Illinois Inst of Technology (IL)
Iowa State U of Science and Technology (IA)
Johns Hopkins U (MD)
La Sierra U (CA)
Longwood Coll (VA)
The Ohio State U (OH)
Oregon State U (OR)
Pacific Union Coll (CA)
Rensselaer Polytechnic Inst (NY)
St. Bonaventure U (NY)
St. Lawrence U (NY)
Saint Mary's U of Minnesota (MN)
Southwestern Oklahoma State U (OK)
State U of NY at Buffalo (NY)
State U of NY Coll at Geneseo (NY)
Suffolk U (MA)
U du Québec à Trois-Rivières (PQ, Canada)
U of Calif, San Diego (CA)
U of Connecticut (CT)
U of Guelph (ON, Canada)
U of Illinois at Urbana–Champaign (IL)
U of Michigan (MI)
U of New Brunswick, Fredericton (NB, Canada)
U of Pennsylvania (PA)
U of San Francisco (CA)
U of Southern California (CA)
U of Southern Indiana (IN)
U of Toronto (ON, Canada)
The U of Western Ontario (ON, Canada)
U of Windsor (ON, Canada)
Walla Walla Coll (WA)
Washington State U (WA)
Washington U in St. Louis (MO)

BIOPSYCHOLOGY
Barnard Coll (NY)
Coll of the Holy Cross (MA)
The Coll of William and Mary (VA)
Morningside Coll (IA)
Mount Allison U (NB, Canada)
Philadelphia U (PA)
Pine Manor Coll (MA)
Rider U (NJ)
Russell Sage Coll (NY)
U of Calif, Santa Barbara (CA)
U of Denver (CO)

U of Pittsburgh at Johnstown (PA)
Washington U in St. Louis (MO)

BIOSTATISTICS
Cornell U (NY)
The U of North Carolina at Chapel Hill (NC)
U of Washington (WA)

BIOTECHNOLOGY RESEARCH
Assumption Coll (MA)
Brock U (ON, Canada)
Clarkson U (NY)
Elizabethtown Coll (PA)
Missouri Southern State Coll (MO)
Montana State U–Bozeman (MT)
North Dakota State U (ND)
The Ohio State U (OH)
Pine Manor Coll (MA)
Plymouth State Coll (NH)
Rochester Inst of Technology (NY)
Rutgers, State U of NJ, Cook Coll (NJ)
Rutgers, State U of NJ, Douglass Coll (NJ)
State U of NY Coll of Environ Sci and Forestry (NY)
Thomas Jefferson U (PA)
U of Calif, San Diego (CA)
U of Delaware (DE)
U of Nebraska at Omaha (NE)
U of Southern Maine (ME)
U of Waterloo (ON, Canada)
U of Wisconsin–River Falls (WI)
York U (ON, Canada)

BLOOD BANK TECHNOLOGY
Louisiana Tech U (LA)

BOTANY
Andrews U (MI)
Arizona State U (AZ)
Arkansas State U (AR)
Ball State U (IN)
Brandon U (MB, Canada)
Brigham Young U (UT)
California State Polytechnic U, Pomona (CA)
California State U, Fullerton (CA)
Carleton U (ON, Canada)
Coll of the Atlantic (ME)
Colorado State U (CO)
Concordia U (PQ, Canada)
Connecticut Coll (CT)
Cornell U (NY)
Eastern Washington U (WA)
Fort Valley State U (GA)
Hampshire Coll (MA)
Howard U (DC)
Humboldt State U (CA)
Idaho State U (ID)
Iowa State U of Science and Technology (IA)
Juniata Coll (PA)
Kent State U (OH)
Marlboro Coll (VT)
Mars Hill Coll (NC)
McGill U (PQ, Canada)
Miami U (OH)
Michigan State U (MI)
Millersville U of Pennsylvania (PA)
Minnesota State U, Mankato (MN)
North Carolina State U (NC)
North Dakota State U (ND)
Northern Arizona U (AZ)
Northern Michigan U (MI)
Northwest Missouri State U (MO)
The Ohio State U (OH)
Ohio U (OH)
Ohio Wesleyan U (OH)
Oklahoma State U (OK)
Oregon State U (OR)
Purdue U (IN)
Purdue U Calumet (IN)
Rutgers, State U of NJ, Camden Coll of Arts & Scis (NJ)
Rutgers, State U of NJ, Newark Coll of Arts & Scis (NJ)
Rutgers, State U of NJ, U Coll–Camden (NJ)
St. Cloud State U (MN)
Saint Xavier U (IL)
San Diego State U (CA)
San Francisco State U (CA)
Sonoma State U (CA)
Southeastern Oklahoma State U (OK)

Majors Index
Botany–Business Administration

Southern Illinois U Carbondale (IL)
Southern Utah U (UT)
Southwest Texas State U (TX)
State U of NY Coll of A&T at Cobleskill (NY)
State U of NY Coll of Environ Sci and Forestry (NY)
Texas A&M U (TX)
The U of Akron (OH)
U of Alberta (AB, Canada)
U of Arkansas (AR)
U of Calgary (AB, Canada)
U of Calif, Davis (CA)
U of Calif, Riverside (CA)
U of Calif, Santa Cruz (CA)
U of Delaware (DE)
U of Florida (FL)
U of Georgia (GA)
U of Guelph (ON, Canada)
U of Hawaii at Manoa (HI)
U of Idaho (ID)
U of Illinois at Urbana–Champaign (IL)
U of Maine (ME)
U of Manitoba (MB, Canada)
U of Michigan (MI)
U of Minnesota, Twin Cities Campus (MN)
The U of Montana–Missoula (MT)
U of Nevada, Las Vegas (NV)
U of Nevada, Reno (NV)
U of New Brunswick, Fredericton (NB, Canada)
U of New Hampshire (NH)
U of Oklahoma (OK)
The U of Tennessee Knoxville (TN)
The U of Texas at Austin (TX)
U of Toronto (ON, Canada)
U of Vermont (VT)
U of Victoria (BC, Canada)
U of Washington (WA)
U of Wisconsin–Madison (WI)
U of Wyoming (WY)
Utah State U (UT)
Weber State U (UT)
Wittenberg U (OH)

BRITISH LITERATURE
The Coll of Southeastern Europe, The American U of Athens (Greece)
Gannon U (PA)
Maharishi U of Management (IA)
Point Loma Nazarene U (CA)
U of Pittsburgh (PA)
U of Southern California (CA)
Washington U in St. Louis (MO)

BROADCAST JOURNALISM
Adrian Coll (MI)
Alderson-Broaddus Coll (WV)
American U (DC)
Auburn U (AL)
Avila Coll (MO)
Baldwin-Wallace Coll (OH)
Barry U (FL)
Barton Coll (NC)
Belmont U (TN)
Bemidji State U (MN)
Berry Coll (GA)
Bowie State U (MD)
Bowling Green State U (OH)
Brooklyn Coll of the City U of NY (NY)
California State U, Hayward (CA)
California State U, Long Beach (CA)
California State U, Northridge (CA)
Calvary Bible Coll and Theological Seminary (MO)
Carson-Newman Coll (TN)
Cedarville Coll (OH)
Chapman U (CA)
Chicago State U (IL)
The Coll of New Rochelle (NY)
Coll of the Ozarks (MO)
Colorado Christian U (CO)
Columbia Coll Chicago (IL)
Columbia Coll–Hollywood (CA)
Columbia Union Coll (MD)
Concordia Coll (MN)
Drake U (IA)
Duquesne U (PA)
East Carolina U (NC)
Eastern Kentucky U (KY)
Eastern Michigan U (MI)
Eastern Washington U (WA)

East Tennessee State U (TN)
Elizabeth City State U (NC)
Elon Coll (NC)
Emerson Coll (MA)
Evangel U (MO)
Fairleigh Dickinson U, Teaneck-Hackensack Campus (NJ)
Florida International U (FL)
Florida Southern Coll (FL)
Fontbonne Coll (MO)
Fordham U (NY)
Franklin Coll of Indiana (IN)
Gonzaga U (WA)
Goshen Coll (IN)
Grand Valley State U (MI)
Hampton U (VA)
Hofstra U (NY)
Houston Baptist U (TX)
Howard U (DC)
Humboldt State U (CA)
Huntington Coll (IN)
Indiana State U (IN)
Indiana U Bloomington (IN)
Iona Coll (NY)
Ithaca Coll (NY)
John Brown U (AR)
Kent State U (OH)
Lamar U (TX)
Langston U (OK)
La Salle U (PA)
Lewis U (IL)
Lindenwood U (MO)
Lock Haven U of Pennsylvania (PA)
Louisiana Coll (LA)
Malone Coll (OH)
Manhattan Coll (NY)
Mansfield U of Pennsylvania (PA)
Marist Coll (NY)
Marquette U (WI)
Marshall U (WV)
Massachusetts Coll of Liberal Arts (MA)
Mercyhurst Coll (PA)
Mesa State Coll (CO)
Midland Lutheran Coll (NE)
Millersville U of Pennsylvania (PA)
Milligan Coll (TN)
Minnesota State U Moorhead (MN)
Minot State U (ND)
Morris Coll (SC)
Mount Vernon Nazarene Coll (OH)
New York U (NY)
North Central Coll (IL)
North Central U (MN)
Northern Arizona U (AZ)
Northern Michigan U (MI)
Northwestern State U of Louisiana (LA)
Northwest Missouri State U (MO)
Ohio Northern U (OH)
The Ohio State U (OH)
Ohio U (OH)
Ohio Wesleyan U (OH)
Oklahoma Baptist U (OK)
Oklahoma Christian U of Science and Arts (OK)
Oklahoma City U (OK)
Oklahoma State U (OK)
Olivet Nazarene U (IL)
Otterbein Coll (OH)
Pacific Lutheran U (WA)
Pacific U (OR)
Pittsburg State U (KS)
Plattsburgh State U of NY (NY)
Point Park Coll (PA)
Quinnipiac U (CT)
Reformed Bible Coll (MI)
Ryerson Polytechnic U (ON, Canada)
St. Cloud State U (MN)
St. Francis Coll (NY)
Saint Joseph's Coll (ME)
San Jose State U (CA)
Shorter Coll (GA)
Southern Adventist U (TN)
Southern Arkansas U–Magnolia (AR)
Southern Methodist U (TX)
Southwestern Adventist U (TX)
Southwest Texas State U (TX)
State U of NY at New Paltz (NY)
State U of NY at Oswego (NY)
State U of NY Coll at Brockport (NY)
State U of NY Coll at Buffalo (NY)

State U of NY Coll at Fredonia (NY)
Stephens Coll (MO)
Suffolk U (MA)
Susquehanna U (PA)
Syracuse U (NY)
Temple U (PA)
Texas Christian U (TX)
Toccoa Falls Coll (GA)
Troy State U (AL)
Union U (TN)
The U of Akron (OH)
U of Alaska Fairbanks (AK)
U of Central Oklahoma (OK)
U of Cincinnati (OH)
U of Colorado at Boulder (CO)
U of Dayton (OH)
U of Detroit Mercy (MI)
The U of Findlay (OH)
U of Georgia (GA)
U of Illinois at Urbana–Champaign (IL)
The U of Iowa (IA)
U of Kansas (KS)
U of La Verne (CA)
U of Maryland, Coll Park (MD)
U of Miami (FL)
U of Missouri–Columbia (MO)
U of Montevallo (AL)
U of Nebraska at Omaha (NE)
U of Nebraska–Lincoln (NE)
U of Nevada, Reno (NV)
The U of North Carolina at Pembroke (NC)
U of Northern Iowa (IA)
U of North Texas (TX)
U of Oklahoma (OK)
U of Oregon (OR)
U of Pittsburgh at Bradford (PA)
U of St. Francis (IL)
U of St. Thomas (MN)
U of San Francisco (CA)
U of South Carolina (SC)
U of South Dakota (SD)
U of Southern California (CA)
U of Southern Colorado (CO)
The U of Tennessee at Chattanooga (TN)
The U of Tennessee at Martin (TN)
U of the Pacific (CA)
U of Utah (UT)
U of Windsor (ON, Canada)
U of Wisconsin–Madison (WI)
U of Wisconsin–Milwaukee (WI)
U of Wisconsin–Platteville (WI)
U of Wisconsin–River Falls (WI)
U of Wisconsin–Superior (WI)
U of Wyoming (WY)
Valdosta State U (GA)
Valparaiso U (IN)
Virginia Commonwealth U (VA)
Waldorf Coll (IA)
Wartburg Coll (IA)
Webster U (MO)
Western Washington U (WA)
Westminster Coll (PA)
West Texas A&M U (TX)
William Woods U (MO)
Winona State U (MN)
Youngstown State U (OH)

BUSINESS ADMINISTRATION
Abilene Christian U (TX)
Acadia U (NS, Canada)
Adams State Coll (CO)
Adelphi U (NY)
Adrian Coll (MI)
Alabama A&M U (AL)
Alabama State U (AL)
Alaska Pacific U (AK)
Albany State U (GA)
Albertson Coll of Idaho (ID)
Albion Coll (MI)
Albright Coll (PA)
Alderson-Broaddus Coll (WV)
Alfred U (NY)
Alice Lloyd Coll (KY)
Allentown Coll of St. Francis de Sales (PA)
Allen U (SC)
Alma Coll (MI)
Alvernia Coll (PA)
Alverno Coll (WI)
Amber U (TX)
American Coll of Thessaloniki (Greece)
American InterContinental U (CA)

American InterContinental U, Atlanta (GA)
American InterContinental U, Atlanta (GA)
American InterContinental U (United Kingdom)
American International Coll (MA)
American U (DC)
American U in Cairo (Egypt)
The American U in Dubai (United Arab Emirates)
American U of Puerto Rico (PR)
American U of Rome (Italy)
Anderson Coll (SC)
Anderson U (IN)
Andrews U (MI)
Anna Maria Coll (MA)
Antioch Coll (OH)
Appalachian State U (NC)
Aquinas Coll (MI)
Arizona State U (AZ)
Arizona State U West (AZ)
Arkansas Baptist Coll (AR)
Arkansas State U (AR)
Arkansas Tech U (AR)
Ashland U (OH)
Assumption Coll (MA)
Athabasca U (AB, Canada)
Athens State U (AL)
Atlanta Christian Coll (GA)
Atlantic Baptist U (NB, Canada)
Atlantic Union Coll (MA)
Auburn U (AL)
Auburn U Montgomery (AL)
Audrey Cohen Coll (NY)
Augsburg Coll (MN)
Augustana Coll (IL)
Augustana Coll (SD)
Augusta State U (GA)
Austin Coll (TX)
Averett Coll (VA)
Avila Coll (MO)
Azusa Pacific U (CA)
Babson Coll (MA)
Baker Coll of Auburn Hills (MI)
Baker Coll of Flint (MI)
Baker Coll of Jackson (MI)
Baker Coll of Muskegon (MI)
Baker Coll of Owosso (MI)
Baker Coll of Port Huron (MI)
Baker U (KS)
Baldwin-Wallace Coll (OH)
Ball State U (IN)
Barat Coll (IL)
Barber-Scotia Coll (NC)
Barclay Coll (KS)
Barry U (FL)
Bartlesville Wesleyan Coll (OK)
Barton Coll (NC)
Bayamón Central U (PR)
Baylor U (TX)
Beaver Coll (PA)
Becker Coll (MA)
Belhaven Coll (MS)
Bellarmine Coll (KY)
Bellevue U (NE)
Belmont Abbey Coll (NC)
Belmont U (TN)
Beloit Coll (WI)
Bemidji State U (MN)
Benedictine Coll (KS)
Bennett Coll (NC)
Bentley Coll (MA)
Berea Coll (KY)
Berkeley Coll, New York (NY)
Berkeley Coll, White Plains (NY)
Baruch Coll of the City U of NY (NY)
Berry Coll (GA)
Bethany Coll (KS)
Bethel Coll (IN)
Bethel Coll (KS)
Bethel Coll (MN)
Bethel Coll (TN)
Bethune-Cookman Coll (FL)
Biola U (CA)
Birmingham-Southern Coll (AL)
Bishop's U (PQ, Canada)
Blackburn Coll (IL)
Black Hills State U (SD)
Bloomfield Coll (NJ)
Bloomsburg U of Pennsylvania (PA)
Bluefield State Coll (WV)
Blue Mountain Coll (MS)
Bluffton Coll (OH)
Boise State U (ID)

Boston Coll (MA)
Boston U (MA)
Bowie State U (MD)
Bowling Green State U (OH)
Bradley U (IL)
Brandon U (MB, Canada)
Brenau U (GA)
Briar Cliff Coll (IA)
Bridgewater Coll (VA)
Bridgewater State Coll (MA)
Briercrest Bible Coll (SK, Canada)
Brigham Young U (UT)
Brigham Young U–Hawaii Campus (HI)
Brock U (ON, Canada)
Brooklyn Coll of the City U of NY (NY)
Bryan Coll (TN)
Bryant Coll (RI)
Bucknell U (PA)
Buena Vista U (IA)
Butler U (IN)
Cabrini Coll (PA)
Caldwell Coll (NJ)
California Baptist U (CA)
California Lutheran U (CA)
California Maritime Academy (CA)
California Polytechnic State U, San Luis Obispo (CA)
California State Polytechnic U, Pomona (CA)
California State U, Chico (CA)
California State U, Dominguez Hills (CA)
California State U, Fresno (CA)
California State U, Fullerton (CA)
California State U, Hayward (CA)
California State U, Long Beach (CA)
California State U, Los Angeles (CA)
California State U, Monterey Bay (CA)
California State U, Northridge (CA)
California State U, Sacramento (CA)
California State U, San Bernardino (CA)
California State U, San Marcos (CA)
California State U, Stanislaus (CA)
California U of Pennsylvania (PA)
Calumet Coll of Saint Joseph (IN)
Calvary Bible Coll and Theological Seminary (MO)
Calvin Coll (MI)
Cameron U (OK)
Campbellsville U (KY)
Canisius Coll (NY)
Capital U (OH)
Cardinal Stritch U (WI)
Carleton U (ON, Canada)
Carnegie Mellon U (PA)
Carroll Coll (MT)
Carroll Coll (WI)
Carson-Newman Coll (TN)
Carthage Coll (WI)
Cascade Coll (OR)
Case Western Reserve U (OH)
Castleton State Coll (VT)
Catawba Coll (NC)
The Catholic U of America (DC)
Cazenovia Coll (NY)
Cedar Crest Coll (PA)
Cedarville Coll (OH)
Centenary Coll (NJ)
Centenary Coll of Louisiana (LA)
Central Christian Coll of Kansas (KS)
Central Coll (IA)
Central Connecticut State U (CT)
Central Methodist Coll (MO)
Central Michigan U (MI)
Central Missouri State U (MO)
Chadron State Coll (NE)
Chaminade U of Honolulu (HI)
Champlain Coll (VT)
Chaparral Coll (AZ)
Chapman U (CA)
Charleston Southern U (SC)
Chatham Coll (PA)
Chestnut Hill Coll (PA)
Cheyney U of Pennsylvania (PA)
Chicago State U (IL)
Chowan Coll (NC)
Christian Brothers U (TN)
Christopher Newport U (VA)

Majors Index
Business Administration

Citadel, The Military Coll of South Carolina (SC)
City Coll of the City U of NY (NY)
City U (WA)
Claflin U (SC)
Clarion U of Pennsylvania (PA)
Clark Atlanta U (GA)
Clarke Coll (IA)
Clarkson Coll (NE)
Clarkson U (NY)
Clark U (MA)
Clayton Coll & State U (GA)
Cleary Coll (MI)
Clemson U (SC)
Coastal Carolina U (SC)
Coe Coll (IA)
Coker Coll (SC)
Colby-Sawyer Coll (NH)
Coleman Coll (CA)
Coll Misericordia (PA)
Coll of Charleston (SC)
Coll of Insurance (NY)
Coll of Mount St. Joseph (OH)
Coll of Mount Saint Vincent (NY)
The Coll of New Jersey (NJ)
The Coll of New Rochelle (NY)
Coll of Notre Dame (CA)
Coll of Notre Dame of Maryland (MD)
Coll of Our Lady of the Elms (MA)
Coll of Saint Benedict (MN)
Coll of St. Catherine (MN)
Coll of Saint Elizabeth (NJ)
Coll of St. Joseph (VT)
Coll of Saint Mary (NE)
The Coll of Saint Rose (NY)
Coll of Santa Fe (NM)
The Coll of Southeastern Europe, The American U of Athens (Greece)
Coll of Staten Island of the City U of NY (NY)
Coll of the Ozarks (MO)
Coll of the Southwest (NM)
The Coll of William and Mary (VA)
Colorado Christian U (CO)
Colorado State U (CO)
Colorado Tech U (CO)
Colorado Tech U Denver Campus (CO)
Columbia Coll (MO)
Columbia Coll (SC)
Columbia Coll Chicago (IL)
Columbia Union Coll (MD)
Columbus State U (GA)
Concord Coll (WV)
Concordia Coll (MI)
Concordia Coll (MN)
Concordia Coll (NY)
Concordia U (CA)
Concordia U (IL)
Concordia U (NE)
Concordia U (OR)
Concordia U (PQ, Canada)
Concordia U at Austin (TX)
Concordia U at St. Paul (MN)
Concordia U Wisconsin (WI)
Converse Coll (SC)
Coppin State Coll (MD)
Cornell U (NY)
Cornerstone U (MI)
Covenant Coll (GA)
Crichton Coll (TN)
Crown Coll (MN)
Culver-Stockton Coll (MO)
Cumberland Coll (KY)
Curry Coll (MA)
Daemen Coll (NY)
Dakota State U (SD)
Dakota Wesleyan U (SD)
Dalhousie U (NS, Canada)
Dallas Baptist U (TX)
Dallas Christian Coll (TX)
Dana Coll (NE)
Daniel Webster Coll (NH)
Davenport Coll of Business (MI)
Davenport Coll of Business, Kalamazoo Campus (MI)
Davenport Coll of Business, Lansing Campus (MI)
David Lipscomb U (TN)
David N. Myers Coll (OH)
Defiance Coll (OH)
Delaware State U (DE)
Delaware Valley Coll (PA)
Delta State U (MS)
DePaul U (IL)

Deree Coll (Greece)
Detroit Coll of Business (MI)
Detroit Coll of Business–Flint (MI)
Detroit Coll of Business, Warren Campus (MI)
DeVry Inst of Technology (AZ)
DeVry Inst of Technology, Fremont (CA)
DeVry Inst of Technology, Long Beach (CA)
DeVry Inst of Technology, Pomona (CA)
DeVry Inst of Technology, West Hills (CA)
DeVry Inst of Technology, Alpharetta (GA)
DeVry Inst of Technology, Decatur (GA)
DeVry Inst of Technology, Addison (IL)
DeVry Inst of Technology, Chicago (IL)
DeVry Inst of Technology (MO)
DeVry Inst of Technology (NY)
DeVry Inst of Technology (OH)
DeVry Inst of Technology (TX)
Dickinson State U (ND)
Dixie State Coll of Utah (UT)
Doane Coll (NE)
Dominican Coll of Blauvelt (NY)
Dominican U (IL)
Dominican U of California (CA)
Dordt Coll (IA)
Dowling Coll (NY)
Drake U (IA)
Drexel U (PA)
Drury U (MO)
D'Youville Coll (NY)
Earlham Coll (IN)
East Carolina U (NC)
East Central U (OK)
Eastern Connecticut State U (CT)
Eastern Kentucky U (KY)
Eastern Mennonite U (VA)
Eastern Michigan U (MI)
Eastern Nazarene Coll (MA)
Eastern New Mexico U (NM)
Eastern Washington U (WA)
East Stroudsburg U of Pennsylvania (PA)
East Tennessee State U (TN)
East Texas Baptist U (TX)
Eckerd Coll (FL)
École des Hautes Études Commerciales (PQ, Canada)
Edgewood Coll (WI)
Edinboro U of Pennsylvania (PA)
Elizabeth City State U (NC)
Elizabethtown Coll (PA)
Elmhurst Coll (IL)
Elmira Coll (NY)
Elon Coll (NC)
Embry-Riddle Aeronautical U (AZ)
Embry-Riddle Aeronautical U (FL)
Embry-Riddle Aeronautical U, Extended Campus (FL)
Emmanuel Coll (GA)
Emmanuel Coll (MA)
Emory & Henry Coll (VA)
Emory U (GA)
Emporia State U (KS)
Endicott Coll (MA)
Erskine Coll (SC)
Evangel U (MO)
The Evergreen State Coll (WA)
Fairfield U (CT)
Fairleigh Dickinson U, Florham-Madison Campus (NJ)
Fairleigh Dickinson U, Teaneck-Hackensack Campus (NJ)
Fairmont State Coll (WV)
Fashion Inst of Technology (NY)
Faulkner U (AL)
Felician Coll (NJ)
Ferris State U (MI)
Ferrum Coll (VA)
Finlandia U (MI)
Fisher Coll (MA)
Fisk U (TN)
Fitchburg State Coll (MA)
Five Towns Coll (NY)
Flagler Coll (FL)
Florida A&M U (FL)
Florida Atlantic U (FL)
Florida Gulf Coast U (FL)
Florida Inst of Technology (FL)
Florida International U (FL)

Florida Metropolitan U-Tampa Coll, Brandon (FL)
Florida Southern Coll (FL)
Florida State U (FL)
Fontbonne Coll (MO)
Fordham U (NY)
Fort Hays State U (KS)
Fort Lewis Coll (CO)
Fort Valley State U (GA)
Framingham State Coll (MA)
Franciscan U of Steubenville (OH)
Francis Marion U (SC)
Franklin and Marshall Coll (PA)
Franklin Coll of Indiana (IN)
Franklin Pierce Coll (NH)
Franklin U (OH)
Freed-Hardeman U (TN)
Free Will Baptist Bible Coll (TN)
Fresno Pacific U (CA)
Friends U (KS)
Frostburg State U (MD)
Furman U (SC)
Gallaudet U (DC)
Gannon U (PA)
Gardner-Webb U (NC)
Geneva Coll (PA)
George Fox U (OR)
George Mason U (VA)
Georgetown Coll (KY)
Georgetown U (DC)
The George Washington U (DC)
Georgia Coll and State U (GA)
Georgia Inst of Technology (GA)
Georgian Court Coll (NJ)
Georgia Southern U (GA)
Georgia Southwestern State U (GA)
Georgia State U (GA)
Gettysburg Coll (PA)
Glenville State Coll (WV)
Golden Gate U (CA)
Goldey-Beacom Coll (DE)
Gonzaga U (WA)
Gordon Coll (MA)
Goshen Coll (IN)
Governors State U (IL)
Grace Bible Coll (MI)
Grace Coll (IN)
Graceland Coll (IA)
Grand Canyon U (AZ)
Grand Valley State U (MI)
Grand View Coll (IA)
Green Mountain Coll (VT)
Greenville Coll (IL)
Griggs U (MD)
Grove City Coll (PA)
Guilford Coll (NC)
Gustavus Adolphus Coll (MN)
Gwynedd-Mercy Coll (PA)
Hamline U (MN)
Hampton U (VA)
Hannibal-LaGrange Coll (MO)
Hanover Coll (IN)
Harding U (AR)
Hardin-Simmons U (TX)
Harris-Stowe State Coll (MO)
Hartwick Coll (NY)
Hastings Coll (NE)
Hawaii Pacific U (HI)
Heidelberg Coll (OH)
Henry Cogswell Coll (WA)
Heritage Coll (WA)
Herzing Coll (GA)
Hesser Coll (NH)
High Point U (NC)
Hilbert Coll (NY)
Hillsdale Coll (MI)
Hiram Coll (OH)
Hofstra U (NY)
Holy Family Coll (PA)
Holy Names Coll (CA)
Hood Coll (MD)
Hope Coll (MI)
Hope International U (CA)
Houghton Coll (NY)
Houston Baptist U (TX)
Howard Payne U (TX)
Howard U (DC)
Humboldt State U (CA)
Humphreys Coll (CA)
Huntingdon Coll (AL)
Huntington Coll (IN)
Huron U (SD)
Husson Coll (ME)
Huston-Tillotson Coll (TX)
Idaho State U (ID)
Illinois Coll (IL)

Illinois State U (IL)
Illinois Wesleyan U (IL)
Immaculata Coll (PA)
Indiana Inst of Technology (IN)
Indiana State U (IN)
Indiana U Bloomington (IN)
Indiana U Northwest (IN)
Indiana U of Pennsylvania (PA)
Indiana U–Purdue U Fort Wayne (IN)
Indiana Wesleyan U (IN)
Inst of Computer Technology (CA)
Insto Tecno Estudios Sups Monterrey, León (Mexico)
Insto Tecno Estudios Sups Monterrey (Mexico)
Insto Tecno Estudios Sups Monterrey, Querétaro (Mexico)
Insto Tecno Estudios Sups Monterrey, Tampico (Mexico)
Inter American U of PR, Aguadilla Campus (PR)
Inter American U of PR, Arecibo Campus (PR)
Inter American U of PR, Fajardo Campus (PR)
Inter American U of PR, Metropolitan Campus (PR)
Inter American U of PR, San Germán Campus (PR)
International Coll (FL)
International Coll of the Cayman Islands (Cayman Islands)
Iona Coll (NY)
Iowa State U of Science and Technology (IA)
Iowa Wesleyan Coll (IA)
Ithaca Coll (NY)
Jacksonville State U (AL)
Jacksonville U (FL)
James Madison U (VA)
Jamestown Coll (ND)
Jarvis Christian Coll (TX)
John Brown U (AR)
John Carroll U (OH)
John F. Kennedy U (CA)
Johnson & Wales U (RI)
Johnson C. Smith U (NC)
Johnson State Coll (VT)
John Wesley Coll (NC)
Jones Coll (FL)
Judson Coll (IL)
Juniata Coll (PA)
Kansas State U (KS)
Keene State Coll (NH)
Kendall Coll (IL)
Kent State U (OH)
Kent State U, Geauga Campus (OH)
Kentucky Christian Coll (KY)
Kentucky State U (KY)
Kentucky Wesleyan Coll (KY)
Kettering U (MI)
Keuka Coll (NY)
King Coll (TN)
King's Coll (PA)
The King's U Coll (AB, Canada)
Kutztown U of Pennsylvania (PA)
LaGrange Coll (GA)
Lake Erie Coll (OH)
Lakehead U (ON, Canada)
Lakeland Coll (WI)
Lake Superior State U (MI)
Lamar U (TX)
Lambuth U (TN)
Lane Coll (TN)
Langston U (OK)
Lander U (SC)
La Roche Coll (PA)
La Salle U (PA)
Lasell Coll (MA)
La Sierra U (CA)
Lawrence Technological U (MI)
Lebanon Valley Coll (PA)
Lees-McRae Coll (NC)
Lee U (TN)
Lehigh U (PA)
Lehman Coll of the City U of NY (NY)
Le Moyne Coll (NY)
LeMoyne-Owen Coll (TN)
Lenoir-Rhyne Coll (NC)
Lesley Coll (MA)
LeTourneau U (TX)
Lewis & Clark Coll (OR)
Lewis-Clark State Coll (ID)
Lewis U (IL)

Liberty U (VA)
Limestone Coll (SC)
Lincoln Christian Coll (IL)
Lincoln Memorial U (TN)
Lincoln U (CA)
Lincoln U (MO)
Lincoln U (PA)
Lindenwood U (MO)
Lindsey Wilson Coll (KY)
Lock Haven U of Pennsylvania (PA)
Long Island U, Brentwood Campus (NY)
Long Island U, Brooklyn Campus (NY)
Long Island U, C.W. Post Campus (NY)
Long Island U, Southampton Coll (NY)
Longwood Coll (VA)
Loras Coll (IA)
Louisiana Coll (LA)
Louisiana State U and A&M Coll (LA)
Louisiana State U in Shreveport (LA)
Louisiana Tech U (LA)
Lourdes Coll (OH)
Loyola Marymount U (CA)
Loyola U Chicago (IL)
Loyola U New Orleans (LA)
Lubbock Christian U (TX)
Luther Coll (IA)
Lycoming Coll (PA)
Lynchburg Coll (VA)
Lyndon State Coll (VT)
Lynn U (FL)
Lyon Coll (AR)
MacMurray Coll (IL)
Madonna U (MI)
Maharishi U of Management (IA)
Maine Maritime Academy (ME)
Malone Coll (OH)
Manchester Coll (IN)
Manhattan Christian Coll (KS)
Manhattan Coll (NY)
Manhattanville Coll (NY)
Mansfield U of Pennsylvania (PA)
Maranatha Baptist Bible Coll (WI)
Marian Coll (IN)
Marian Coll of Fond du Lac (WI)
Marietta Coll (OH)
Marist Coll (NY)
Marquette U (WI)
Marshall U (WV)
Mars Hill Coll (NC)
Martin Methodist Coll (TN)
Mary Baldwin Coll (VA)
Marycrest International U (IA)
Marygrove Coll (MI)
Marylhurst U (OR)
Marymount Coll (NY)
Marymount Manhattan Coll (NY)
Maryville Coll (TN)
Maryville U of Saint Louis (MO)
Mary Washington Coll (VA)
Marywood U (PA)
Massachusetts Coll of Liberal Arts (MA)
Massachusetts Inst of Technology (MA)
Mayville State U (ND)
McGill U (PQ, Canada)
McKendree Coll (IL)
McMurry U (TX)
McNeese State U (LA)
McPherson Coll (KS)
Medaille Coll (NY)
Medgar Evers Coll of the City U of NY (NY)
Memorial U of Newfoundland (NF, Canada)
Menlo Coll (CA)
Mercer U (GA)
Mercy Coll (NY)
Mercyhurst Coll (PA)
Meredith Coll (NC)
Merrimack Coll (MA)
Mesa State Coll (CO)
Messiah Coll (PA)
Methodist Coll (NC)
Metropolitan State U (MN)
Miami U (OH)
Michigan State U (MI)
Michigan Technological U (MI)
Mid-America Bible Coll (OK)
MidAmerica Nazarene U (KS)

Majors Index
Business Administration

Middle Tennessee State U (TN)
Midland Lutheran Coll (NE)
Midway Coll (KY)
Midwestern State U (TX)
Millersville U of Pennsylvania (PA)
Milligan Coll (TN)
Millikin U (IL)
Millsaps Coll (MS)
Milwaukee School of Engineering (WI)
Minnesota State U, Mankato (MN)
Minnesota State U Moorhead (MN)
Minot State U (ND)
Mississippi Coll (MS)
Mississippi State U (MS)
Mississippi U for Women (MS)
Mississippi Valley State U (MS)
Missouri Baptist Coll (MO)
Missouri Southern State Coll (MO)
Missouri Valley Coll (MO)
Missouri Western State Coll (MO)
Molloy Coll (NY)
Monmouth Coll (IL)
Monmouth U (NJ)
Monroe Coll, Bronx (NY)
Monroe Coll, New Rochelle (NY)
Montana State U–Billings (MT)
Montana State U–Northern (MT)
Montana Tech of The U of Montana (MT)
Montreat Coll (NC)
Moravian Coll (PA)
Morehead State U (KY)
Morehouse Coll (GA)
Morgan State U (MD)
Morningside Coll (IA)
Morris Coll (SC)
Mount Allison U (NB, Canada)
Mount Aloysius Coll (PA)
Mount Ida Coll (MA)
Mount Marty Coll (SD)
Mount Mary Coll (WI)
Mount Mercy Coll (IA)
Mount Olive Coll (NC)
Mount St. Clare Coll (IA)
Mount Saint Mary Coll (NY)
Mount St. Mary's Coll (CA)
Mount Saint Mary's Coll and Seminary (MD)
Mount Saint Vincent U (NS, Canada)
Mount Senario Coll (WI)
Mount Union Coll (OH)
Mount Vernon Nazarene Coll (OH)
Muhlenberg Coll (PA)
Murray State U (KY)
Muskingum Coll (OH)
National American U (MO)
National American U–St. Paul Campus (MN)
National-Louis U (IL)
National U (CA)
Nazareth Coll of Rochester (NY)
Nebraska Wesleyan U (NE)
Neumann Coll (PA)
Newberry Coll (SC)
Newbury Coll (MA)
New England Coll (NH)
New Hampshire Coll (NH)
New Jersey City U (NJ)
New Jersey Inst of Technology (NJ)
Newman U (KS)
New Mexico Highlands U (NM)
New Mexico Inst of Mining and Technology (NM)
New Mexico State U (NM)
New York Inst of Technology (NY)
New York U (NY)
Niagara U (NY)
Nicholls State U (LA)
Nichols Coll (MA)
Nipissing U (ON, Canada)
Norfolk State U (VA)
North Carolina Ag and Tech State U (NC)
North Carolina Central U (NC)
North Carolina State U (NC)
North Carolina Wesleyan Coll (NC)
North Central Coll (IL)
North Central U (MN)
North Dakota State U (ND)
Northeastern State U (OK)
Northeastern U (MA)
Northern Arizona U (AZ)
Northern Illinois U (IL)
Northern Kentucky U (KY)
Northern Michigan U (MI)

Northern State U (SD)
North Georgia Coll & State U (GA)
North Greenville Coll (SC)
Northland Coll (WI)
North Park U (IL)
Northwest Coll (WA)
Northwestern Coll (IA)
Northwestern Coll (MN)
Northwestern Oklahoma State U (OK)
Northwestern State U of Louisiana (LA)
Northwest Missouri State U (MO)
Northwest Nazarene U (ID)
Northwood U (MI)
Northwood U, Florida Campus (FL)
Northwood U, Texas Campus (TX)
Norwich U (VT)
Notre Dame Coll (NH)
Notre Dame Coll of Ohio (OH)
Nova Southeastern U (FL)
Nyack Coll (NY)
Oak Hills Christian Coll (MN)
Oakland City U (IN)
Oakland U (MI)
Oakwood Coll (AL)
Oglethorpe U (GA)
Ohio Dominican Coll (OH)
Ohio Northern U (OH)
The Ohio State U (OH)
Ohio U (OH)
Ohio U–Chillicothe (OH)
Ohio Valley Coll (WV)
Ohio Wesleyan U (OH)
Okanagan U Coll (BC, Canada)
Oklahoma Baptist U (OK)
Oklahoma Christian U of Science and Arts (OK)
Oklahoma City U (OK)
Oklahoma Panhandle State U (OK)
Old Dominion U (VA)
Olivet Nazarene U (IL)
Open Learning Agency (BC, Canada)
Oregon Inst of Technology (OR)
Oregon State U (OR)
Ottawa U (KS)
Otterbein Coll (OH)
Ouachita Baptist U (AR)
Our Lady of Holy Cross Coll (LA)
Our Lady of the Lake U of San Antonio (TX)
Pacific Lutheran U (WA)
Pacific Union Coll (CA)
Pacific U (OR)
Paine Coll (GA)
Palm Beach Atlantic Coll (FL)
Park U (MO)
Patten Coll (CA)
Peace Coll (NC)
Peirce Coll (PA)
Pennsylvania Coll of Technology (PA)
Penn State U at Erie, The Behrend Coll (PA)
Penn State U Harrisburg Campus of the Capital Coll (PA)
Penn State U Univ Park Campus (PA)
Pepperdine U, Malibu (CA)
Peru State Coll (NE)
Pfeiffer U (NC)
Philadelphia Coll of Bible (PA)
Philadelphia U (PA)
Philander Smith Coll (AR)
Piedmont Coll (GA)
Pikeville Coll (KY)
Pine Manor Coll (MA)
Pittsburg State U (KS)
Pitzer Coll (CA)
Plattsburgh State U of NY (NY)
Plymouth State Coll (NH)
Point Loma Nazarene U (CA)
Point Park Coll (PA)
Polytechnic U of Puerto Rico (PR)
Pontifical Catholic U of Puerto Rico (PR)
Portland State U (OR)
Prairie View A&M U (TX)
Presbyterian Coll (SC)
Presentation Coll (SD)
Principia Coll (IL)
Providence Coll (RI)
Providence Coll and Theological Seminary (MB, Canada)
Purdue U (IN)
Purdue U Calumet (IN)

Purdue U North Central (IN)
Queens Coll (NC)
Queen's U at Kingston (ON, Canada)
Quincy U (IL)
Quinnipiac U (CT)
Radford U (VA)
Ramapo Coll of New Jersey (NJ)
Redeemer Coll (ON, Canada)
Reformed Bible Coll (MI)
Regents Coll (NY)
Regis U (CO)
Reinhardt Coll (GA)
Rensselaer Polytechnic Inst (NY)
Rhodes Coll (TN)
Rice U (TX)
The Richard Stockton Coll of New Jersey (NJ)
Richmond, The American International U in London (United Kingdom)
Rider U (NJ)
Ripon Coll (WI)
Rivier Coll (NH)
Roanoke Coll (VA)
Robert Morris Coll (IL)
Robert Morris Coll (PA)
Roberts Wesleyan Coll (NY)
Rochester Coll (MI)
Rochester Inst of Technology (NY)
Rockford Coll (IL)
Rockhurst U (MO)
Rocky Mountain Coll (MT)
Roger Williams U (RI)
Rosemont Coll (PA)
Rowan U (NJ)
Royal Roads U (BC, Canada)
Russell Sage Coll (NY)
Rust Coll (MS)
Rutgers, State U of NJ, Camden Coll of Arts & Scis (NJ)
Rutgers, State U of NJ, Douglass Coll (NJ)
Rutgers, State U of NJ, Livingston Coll (NJ)
Rutgers, State U of NJ, Newark Coll of Arts & Scis (NJ)
Rutgers, State U of NJ, Rutgers Coll (NJ)
Rutgers, State U of NJ, U Coll–Camden (NJ)
Rutgers, State U of NJ, U Coll–Newark (NJ)
Rutgers, State U of NJ, U Coll–New Brunswick (NJ)
Ryerson Polytechnic U (ON, Canada)
Sacred Heart U (CT)
Saginaw Valley State U (MI)
St. Ambrose U (IA)
St. Andrews Presbyterian Coll (NC)
Saint Augustine's Coll (NC)
St. Bonaventure U (NY)
St. Cloud State U (MN)
St. Edward's U (TX)
St. Francis Coll (NY)
Saint Francis Coll (PA)
St. Francis Xavier U (NS, Canada)
St. Gregory's U (OK)
St. John Fisher Coll (NY)
Saint John's U (MN)
St. John's U (NY)
Saint Joseph Coll (CT)
Saint Joseph's Coll (IN)
Saint Joseph's Coll (ME)
St. Joseph's Coll, New York (NY)
St. Joseph's Coll, Suffolk Campus (NY)
Saint Joseph's U (PA)
Saint Leo U (FL)
Saint Louis U (MO)
Saint Martin's Coll (WA)
Saint Mary Coll (KS)
Saint Mary-of-the-Woods Coll (IN)
Saint Mary's Coll (IN)
Saint Mary's Coll (MI)
Saint Mary's Coll of California (CA)
Saint Mary's U (NS, Canada)
Saint Mary's U of Minnesota (MN)
St. Mary's U of San Antonio (TX)
Saint Michael's Coll (VT)
Saint Paul's Coll (VA)
Saint Peter's Coll (NJ)
St. Thomas U (FL)
Saint Vincent Coll (PA)
Salem Coll (NC)
Salem State Coll (MA)

Salisbury State U (MD)
Salve Regina U (RI)
Samford U (AL)
Sam Houston State U (TX)
San Diego State U (CA)
San Francisco State U (CA)
San Jose State U (CA)
Santa Clara U (CA)
Savannah State U (GA)
Schiller International U (Germany)
Schreiner Coll (TX)
Seattle Pacific U (WA)
Seattle U (WA)
Seton Hall U (NJ)
Seton Hill Coll (PA)
Shawnee State U (OH)
Shaw U (NC)
Sheldon Jackson Coll (AK)
Shenandoah U (VA)
Shepherd Coll (WV)
Shippensburg U of Pennsylvania (PA)
Shorter Coll (GA)
Siena Heights U (MI)
Sierra Nevada Coll (NV)
Silver Lake Coll (WI)
Simmons Coll (MA)
Simon Fraser U (BC, Canada)
Simpson Coll (IA)
Simpson Coll and Graduate School (CA)
Skidmore Coll (NY)
Slippery Rock U of Pennsylvania (PA)
Sonoma State U (CA)
South Coll (FL)
Southeastern Coll of the Assemblies of God (FL)
Southeastern Louisiana U (LA)
Southeastern Oklahoma State U (OK)
Southeastern U (DC)
Southeast Missouri State U (MO)
Southern Adventist U (TN)
Southern Illinois U Carbondale (IL)
Southern Methodist U (TX)
Southern Oregon U (OR)
Southern Utah U (UT)
Southern Vermont Coll (VT)
Southern Wesleyan U (SC)
Southwest Baptist U (MO)
Southwestern Adventist U (TX)
Southwestern Assemblies of God U (TX)
Southwestern Coll (KS)
Southwestern Oklahoma State U (OK)
Southwestern U (TX)
Southwest Missouri State U (MO)
Southwest State U (MN)
Southwest Texas State U (TX)
Spalding U (KY)
Spring Arbor Coll (MI)
Spring Hill Coll (AL)
State U of NY at Albany (NY)
State U of NY at Buffalo (NY)
State U of NY at New Paltz (NY)
State U of NY at Oswego (NY)
State U of NY at Stony Brook (NY)
State U of NY Coll at Brockport (NY)
State U of NY Coll at Buffalo (NY)
State U of NY Coll at Fredonia (NY)
State U of NY Coll at Geneseo (NY)
State U of NY Coll at Old Westbury (NY)
State U of NY Inst of Tech at Utica/Rome (NY)
State U of NY Maritime Coll (NY)
State U of West Georgia (GA)
Stephen F. Austin State U (TX)
Stephens Coll (MO)
Sterling Coll (KS)
Stetson U (FL)
Stillman Coll (AL)
Stonehill Coll (MA)
Suffolk U (MA)
Sul Ross State U (TX)
Susquehanna U (PA)
Syracuse U (NY)
Tabor Coll (KS)
Talladega Coll (AL)
Taylor U (IN)
Taylor U, Fort Wayne Campus (IN)
Teikyo Post U (CT)

Temple U (PA)
Tennessee State U (TN)
Tennessee Technological U (TN)
Tennessee Wesleyan Coll (TN)
Texas A&M International U (TX)
Texas A&M U (TX)
Texas A&M U–Commerce (TX)
Texas A&M U–Kingsville (TX)
Texas A&M U–Texarkana (TX)
Texas Christian U (TX)
Texas Lutheran U (TX)
Texas Southern U (TX)
Texas Tech U (TX)
Texas Wesleyan U (TX)
Texas Woman's U (TX)
Thiel Coll (PA)
Thomas Coll (ME)
Thomas Edison State Coll (NJ)
Thomas More Coll (KY)
Thomas U (GA)
Tiffin U (OH)
Toccoa Falls Coll (GA)
Tougaloo Coll (MS)
Touro Coll (NY)
Towson U (MD)
Trent U (ON, Canada)
Trevecca Nazarene U (TN)
Trinity Bible Coll (ND)
Trinity Christian Coll (IL)
Trinity Coll of Vermont (VT)
Trinity U (TX)
Trinity Western U (BC, Canada)
Tri-State U (IN)
Troy State U (AL)
Troy State U Dothan (AL)
Troy State U Montgomery (AL)
Truman State U (MO)
Tulane U (LA)
Tusculum Coll (TN)
Tuskegee U (AL)
Union Coll (KY)
Union Coll (NE)
Union U (TN)
United States Air Force Academy (CO)
United States International U (CA)
United States Military Academy (NY)
Universidad Adventista de las Antillas (PR)
Universidad del Turabo (PR)
Universidad Metropolitana (PR)
Université de Sherbrooke (PQ, Canada)
U du Québec à Chicoutimi (PQ, Canada)
U du Québec à Hull (PQ, Canada)
U du Québec à Trois-Rivières (PQ, Canada)
U du Québec en Abitibi-Témiscamingue (PQ, Canada)
Université Laval (PQ, Canada)
U Coll of Cape Breton (NS, Canada)
U Coll of the Fraser Valley (BC, Canada)
The U of Akron (OH)
The U of Alabama (AL)
The U of Alabama at Birmingham (AL)
The U of Alabama in Huntsville (AL)
U of Alaska Fairbanks (AK)
U of Alberta (AB, Canada)
U of Arkansas (AR)
U of Arkansas at Little Rock (AR)
U of Arkansas at Monticello (AR)
U of Arkansas at Pine Bluff (AR)
U of Baltimore (MD)
U of Bridgeport (CT)
U of British Columbia (BC, Canada)
U of Calgary (AB, Canada)
U of Calif, Berkeley (CA)
U of Calif, Riverside (CA)
U of Central Arkansas (AR)
U of Central Florida (FL)
U of Central Oklahoma (OK)
U of Charleston (WV)
U of Cincinnati (OH)
U of Colorado at Boulder (CO)
U of Colorado at Colorado Springs (CO)
U of Colorado at Denver (CO)
U of Connecticut (CT)
U of Dayton (OH)
U of Delaware (DE)

Majors Index
Business Administration–Business Economics

U of Denver (CO)
U of Detroit Mercy (MI)
U of Dubuque (IA)
U of Evansville (IN)
The U of Findlay (OH)
U of Florida (FL)
U of Georgia (GA)
U of Great Falls (MT)
U of Hartford (CT)
U of Hawaii at Manoa (HI)
U of Houston (TX)
U of Houston–Clear Lake (TX)
U of Houston–Downtown (TX)
U of Houston–Victoria (TX)
U of Illinois at Chicago (IL)
U of Illinois at Springfield (IL)
U of Illinois at Urbana–Champaign (IL)
U of Indianapolis (IN)
The U of Iowa (IA)
U of La Verne (CA)
The U of Lethbridge (AB, Canada)
U of Louisiana at Lafayette (LA)
U of Louisiana at Monroe (LA)
U of Louisville (KY)
U of Maine (ME)
The U of Maine at Augusta (ME)
U of Maine at Fort Kent (ME)
U of Maine at Machias (ME)
U of Maine at Presque Isle (ME)
U of Manitoba (MB, Canada)
U of Mary Hardin-Baylor (TX)
U of Maryland, Coll Park (MD)
U of Maryland University Coll (MD)
U of Massachusetts Amherst (MA)
U of Massachusetts Boston (MA)
U of Massachusetts Dartmouth (MA)
U of Massachusetts Lowell (MA)
The U of Memphis (TN)
U of Miami (FL)
U of Michigan (MI)
U of Michigan–Dearborn (MI)
U of Michigan–Flint (MI)
U of Minnesota, Crookston (MN)
U of Minnesota, Duluth (MN)
U of Minnesota, Morris (MN)
U of Mississippi (MS)
U of Missouri–Columbia (MO)
U of Missouri–Kansas City (MO)
U of Missouri–St. Louis (MO)
U of Mobile (AL)
U of Montevallo (AL)
U of Nebraska at Kearney (NE)
U of Nebraska–Lincoln (NE)
U of Nevada, Las Vegas (NV)
U of New Brunswick, Fredericton (NB, Canada)
U of New Brunswick, Saint John (NB, Canada)
U of New England (ME)
U of New Hampshire (NH)
U of New Hampshire at Manchester (NH)
U of New Haven (CT)
U of New Mexico (NM)
U of New Orleans (LA)
U of North Alabama (AL)
The U of North Carolina at Asheville (NC)
The U of North Carolina at Chapel Hill (NC)
The U of North Carolina at Charlotte (NC)
The U of North Carolina at Greensboro (NC)
The U of North Carolina at Pembroke (NC)
The U of North Carolina at Wilmington (NC)
U of Northern Colorado (CO)
U of Northern Iowa (IA)
U of North Florida (FL)
U of Oklahoma (OK)
U of Oregon (OR)
U of Pennsylvania (PA)
U of Phoenix (AZ)
U of Pittsburgh at Bradford (PA)
U of Pittsburgh at Johnstown (PA)
U of Portland (OR)
U of Prince Edward Island (PE, Canada)
U of Puerto Rico at Ponce (PR)
U of Puerto Rico, Humacao U Coll (PR)
U of Puerto Rico, Mayagüez Campus (PR)

U of Puerto Rico, Río Piedras (PR)
U of Redlands (CA)
U of Regina (SK, Canada)
U of Rhode Island (RI)
U of Richmond (VA)
U of Rio Grande (OH)
U of St. Francis (IL)
U of Saint Francis (IN)
U of St. Thomas (MN)
U of St. Thomas (TX)
U of San Diego (CA)
U of San Francisco (CA)
U of Science and Arts of Oklahoma (OK)
The U of Scranton (PA)
U of Sioux Falls (SD)
U of South Alabama (AL)
U of South Carolina (SC)
U of South Carolina Spartanburg (SC)
U of South Dakota (SD)
U of Southern California (CA)
U of Southern Colorado (CO)
U of Southern Indiana (IN)
U of Southern Maine (ME)
U of Southern Mississippi (MS)
U of South Florida (FL)
The U of Tampa (FL)
The U of Tennessee at Chattanooga (TN)
The U of Tennessee at Martin (TN)
The U of Tennessee Knoxville (TN)
The U of Texas at Arlington (TX)
The U of Texas at Austin (TX)
The U of Texas at Dallas (TX)
The U of Texas at San Antonio (TX)
The U of Texas at Tyler (TX)
The U of Texas–Pan American (TX)
U of the District of Columbia (DC)
U of the Ozarks (AR)
U of the Pacific (CA)
U of the Sacred Heart (PR)
U of the Virgin Islands (VI)
U of Toronto (ON, Canada)
U of Tulsa (OK)
U of Utah (UT)
U of Vermont (VT)
U of Virginia's Coll at Wise (VA)
U of Washington (WA)
U of Waterloo (ON, Canada)
The U of West Alabama (AL)
The U of Western Ontario (ON, Canada)
U of West Florida (FL)
U of Windsor (ON, Canada)
The U of Winnipeg (MB, Canada)
U of Wisconsin–Eau Claire (WI)
U of Wisconsin–Green Bay (WI)
U of Wisconsin–La Crosse (WI)
U of Wisconsin–Madison (WI)
U of Wisconsin–Milwaukee (WI)
U of Wisconsin–Parkside (WI)
U of Wisconsin–Platteville (WI)
U of Wisconsin–River Falls (WI)
U of Wisconsin–Stevens Point (WI)
U of Wisconsin–Stout (WI)
U of Wisconsin–Superior (WI)
U of Wisconsin–Whitewater (WI)
U of Wyoming (WY)
U System Coll for Lifelong Learning (NH)
Upper Iowa U (IA)
Urbana U (OH)
Ursinus Coll (PA)
Ursuline Coll (OH)
Utah State U (UT)
Utica Coll of Syracuse U (NY)
Valdosta State U (GA)
Valley City State U (ND)
Valparaiso U (IN)
Vanguard U of Southern California (CA)
Villa Julie Coll (MD)
Villanova U (PA)
Virginia Commonwealth U (VA)
Virginia Intermont Coll (VA)
Virginia Polytechnic Inst and State U (VA)
Virginia Union U (VA)
Virginia Wesleyan Coll (VA)
Voorhees Coll (SC)
Wagner Coll (NY)
Waldorf Coll (IA)
Walla Walla Coll (WA)
Walsh Coll of Accountancy and Business Admin (MI)

Walsh U (OH)
Warner Pacific Coll (OR)
Warner Southern Coll (FL)
Warren Wilson Coll (NC)
Wartburg Coll (IA)
Washington & Jefferson Coll (PA)
Washington and Lee U (VA)
Washington Coll (MD)
Washington State U (WA)
Washington U in St. Louis (MO)
Wayland Baptist U (TX)
Waynesburg Coll (PA)
Wayne State Coll (NE)
Wayne State U (MI)
Webber Coll (FL)
Weber State U (UT)
Webster U (MO)
Wells Coll (NY)
Wentworth Inst of Technology (MA)
Wesleyan Coll (GA)
Wesley Coll (DE)
West Chester U of Pennsylvania (PA)
Western Baptist Coll (OR)
Western Carolina U (NC)
Western Connecticut State U (CT)
Western Kentucky U (KY)
Western Maryland Coll (MD)
Western Michigan U (MI)
Western New England Coll (MA)
Western State Coll of Colorado (CO)
Western Washington U (WA)
Westfield State Coll (MA)
West Liberty State Coll (WV)
Westminster Coll (MO)
Westminster Coll (PA)
Westminster Coll (UT)
West Virginia State Coll (WV)
West Virginia U (WV)
West Virginia U Inst of Technology (WV)
West Virginia Wesleyan Coll (WV)
Westwood Coll of Technology (CO)
Wheeling Jesuit U (WV)
Whittier Coll (CA)
Whitworth Coll (WA)
Wichita State U (KS)
Widener U (PA)
Wilfrid Laurier U (ON, Canada)
Wilkes U (PA)
William Jewell Coll (MO)
William Paterson U of New Jersey (NJ)
William Penn U (IA)
Williams Baptist Coll (AR)
William Tyndale Coll (MI)
William Woods U (MO)
Wilmington Coll (DE)
Wilmington Coll (OH)
Wilson Coll (PA)
Wingate U (NC)
Winona State U (MN)
Winston-Salem State U (NC)
Winthrop U (SC)
Wisconsin Lutheran Coll (WI)
Wittenberg U (OH)
Woodbury U (CA)
Worcester Polytechnic Inst (MA)
Worcester State Coll (MA)
Wright State U (OH)
Xavier U (OH)
Xavier U of Louisiana (LA)
Yeshiva U (NY)
York Coll (NE)
York Coll of Pennsylvania (PA)
York Coll of the City U of New York (NY)
York U (ON, Canada)
Youngstown State U (OH)

BUSINESS COMMUNICATIONS
Assumption Coll (MA)
Augustana Coll (SD)
Babson Coll (MA)
Bentley Coll (MA)
Brock U (ON, Canada)
Calvin Coll (MI)
Central Michigan U (MI)
Chestnut Hill Coll (PA)
The Coll of St. Scholastica (MN)
Elon Coll (NC)
Florida State U (FL)
Grove City Coll (PA)
Jones International U (CO)
King's Coll (PA)
Marietta Coll (OH)

Morningside Coll (IA)
Point Loma Nazarene U (CA)
Point Park Coll (PA)
Simpson Coll (IA)
Spring Hill Coll (AL)
Susquehanna U (PA)
The U of Findlay (OH)
U of Houston (TX)
U of Rio Grande (OH)
U of St. Thomas (MN)
U of Southern California (CA)

BUSINESS COMPUTER FACILITIES OPERATOR
Eastern Illinois U (IL)
Seattle Pacific U (WA)
Southwest Texas State U (TX)

BUSINESS COMPUTER PROGRAMMING
Husson Coll (ME)
Inst of Public Administration (Ireland)
Kent State U (OH)
Limestone Coll (SC)
Luther Coll (IA)
Milwaukee School of Engineering (WI)
Oklahoma Baptist U (OK)
Robert Morris Coll (IL)
Saint Anselm Coll (NH)
St. Norbert Coll (WI)
U of North Texas (TX)
U of Puget Sound (WA)
U of Windsor (ON, Canada)

BUSINESS ECONOMICS
Alabama A&M U (AL)
Albertus Magnus Coll (CT)
Alfred U (NY)
American International Coll (MA)
Anderson U (IN)
Andrews U (MI)
Arkansas State U (AR)
Auburn U (AL)
Auburn U Montgomery (AL)
Augsburg Coll (MN)
Ball State U (IN)
Baylor U (TX)
Bellarmine Coll (KY)
Belmont U (TN)
Beloit Coll (WI)
Benedictine U (IL)
Bentley Coll (MA)
Baruch Coll of the City U of NY (NY)
Berry Coll (GA)
Bethany Coll (KS)
Bethany Coll (WV)
Bishop's U (PQ, Canada)
Bloomsburg U of Pennsylvania (PA)
Bluffton Coll (OH)
Boise State U (ID)
Bowie State U (MD)
Bradley U (IL)
Bridgewater Coll (VA)
Brock U (ON, Canada)
Buena Vista U (IA)
Butler U (IN)
California Lutheran U (CA)
California State U, Fullerton (CA)
California State U, Hayward (CA)
California State U, Long Beach (CA)
California State U, Los Angeles (CA)
California State U, San Bernardino (CA)
Cameron U (OK)
Campbellsville U (KY)
Cardinal Stritch U (WI)
Carnegie Mellon U (PA)
Carroll Coll (MT)
Carson-Newman Coll (TN)
Catawba Coll (NC)
Cedar Crest Coll (PA)
Centenary Coll of Louisiana (LA)
Chapman U (CA)
Charleston Southern U (SC)
Christopher Newport U (VA)
Clarion U of Pennsylvania (PA)
Clarkson U (NY)
Cleveland State U (OH)
Coll of Mount Saint Vincent (NY)
The Coll of New Jersey (NJ)
Coll of Notre Dame (CA)

The Coll of Southeastern Europe, The American U of Athens (Greece)
The Coll of Wooster (OH)
Columbus State U (GA)
Concordia U (PQ, Canada)
Cornell Coll (IA)
Creighton U (NE)
Dallas Baptist U (TX)
David Lipscomb U (TN)
Delaware State U (DE)
DePaul U (IL)
Dominican Coll of Blauvelt (NY)
Drexel U (PA)
East Central U (OK)
Eastern Kentucky U (KY)
Eastern Michigan U (MI)
Eastern Oregon U (OR)
Eastern Washington U (WA)
École des Hautes Études Commerciales (PQ, Canada)
Elmira Coll (NY)
Emmanuel Coll (MA)
Emory U (GA)
Fairleigh Dickinson U, Florham-Madison Campus (NJ)
Fairleigh Dickinson U, Teaneck-Hackensack Campus (NJ)
Ferris State U (MI)
Fordham U (NY)
Fort Hays State U (KS)
Framingham State Coll (MA)
Francis Marion U (SC)
Freed-Hardeman U (TN)
George Fox U (OR)
The George Washington U (DC)
Georgia Coll and State U (GA)
Georgia Inst of Technology (GA)
Georgia Southern U (GA)
Georgia State U (GA)
Gonzaga U (WA)
Grand Canyon U (AZ)
Green Mountain Coll (VT)
Greensboro Coll (NC)
Grove City Coll (PA)
Gustavus Adolphus Coll (MN)
Hampden-Sydney Coll (VA)
Hampshire Coll (MA)
Hawaii Pacific U (HI)
Hendrix Coll (AR)
Houston Baptist U (TX)
Huntingdon Coll (AL)
Huntington Coll (IN)
Illinois Coll (IL)
Immaculata Coll (PA)
Indiana State U (IN)
Indiana U Bloomington (IN)
Indiana U Southeast (IN)
Inter American U of PR, Metropolitan Campus (PR)
Inter American U of PR, San Germán Campus (PR)
Iona Coll (NY)
Ithaca Coll (NY)
James Madison U (VA)
Jamestown Coll (ND)
Kalamazoo Coll (MI)
Kent State U (OH)
Kentucky State U (KY)
Kutztown U of Pennsylvania (PA)
Lafayette Coll (PA)
LaGrange Coll (GA)
Lake Forest Coll (IL)
Lakeland Coll (WI)
Lake Superior State U (MI)
Lander U (SC)
La Salle U (PA)
Lehigh U (PA)
Lewis U (IL)
Limestone Coll (SC)
Lincoln Memorial U (TN)
Lock Haven U of Pennsylvania (PA)
Longwood Coll (VA)
Louisiana State U and A&M Coll (LA)
Louisiana Tech U (LA)
Loyola U Chicago (IL)
Loyola U New Orleans (LA)
Manhattan Coll (NY)
Marian Coll of Fond du Lac (WI)
Marquette U (WI)
Marshall U (WV)
Mars Hill Coll (NC)
Mary Baldwin Coll (VA)
Marycrest International U (IA)
Marymount Coll (NY)

Majors Index
Business Economics–Business Education

McGill U (PQ, Canada)
McMurry U (TX)
Mercy Coll (NY)
Meredith Coll (NC)
Merrimack Coll (MA)
Mesa State Coll (CO)
Messiah Coll (PA)
Miami U (OH)
Michigan Technological U (MI)
Middle Tennessee State U (TN)
Milligan Coll (TN)
Mills Coll (CA)
Mississippi State U (MS)
Montana State U–Billings (MT)
Montreat Coll (NC)
Morehead State U (KY)
Morgan State U (MD)
Mount Allison U (NB, Canada)
Mount Senario Coll (WI)
Newberry Coll (SC)
New Hampshire Coll (NH)
New Mexico State U (NM)
New York U (NY)
Niagara U (NY)
Northern Arizona U (AZ)
Northern State U (SD)
North Georgia Coll & State U (GA)
North Greenville Coll (SC)
Northland Coll (WI)
Northwest Missouri State U (MO)
Northwood U (MI)
Occidental Coll (CA)
Oglethorpe U (GA)
Ohio U (OH)
Oklahoma City U (OK)
Oklahoma State U (OK)
Old Dominion U (VA)
Olivet Nazarene U (IL)
Otterbein Coll (OH)
Pace U, New York City Campus (NY)
Pace U, Pleasantville/Briarcliff Campus (NY)
Park U (MO)
Penn State U at Erie, The Behrend Coll (PA)
Penn State U Univ Park Campus (PA)
Pittsburg State U (KS)
Plattsburgh State U of NY (NY)
Providence Coll (RI)
Quinnipiac U (CT)
Randolph-Macon Coll (VA)
Rider U (NJ)
Robert Morris Coll (PA)
Rockford Coll (IL)
Rocky Mountain Coll (MT)
Rutgers, State U of NJ, Cook Coll (NJ)
Ryerson Polytechnic U (ON, Canada)
Sacred Heart U (CT)
Saginaw Valley State U (MI)
St. Andrews Presbyterian Coll (NC)
Saint Anselm Coll (NH)
St. Bonaventure U (NY)
St. John's U (NY)
Saint Louis U (MO)
St. Mary's Coll of Maryland (MD)
Saint Mary's U (NS, Canada)
Saint Peter's Coll (NJ)
Salem State Coll (MA)
Sam Houston State U (TX)
Santa Clara U (CA)
Seattle Pacific U (WA)
Seattle U (WA)
Seton Hall U (NJ)
Seton Hill Coll (PA)
Siena Coll (NY)
Skidmore Coll (NY)
Sonoma State U (CA)
Southeastern Oklahoma State U (OK)
Southern Illinois U Carbondale (IL)
Southern Illinois U Edwardsville (IL)
Southwest Texas State U (TX)
Spring Arbor Coll (MI)
State U of NY at New Paltz (NY)
State U of NY Coll at Oneonta (NY)
State U of NY Coll at Potsdam (NY)
State U of West Georgia (GA)
Stephen F. Austin State U (TX)
Stetson U (FL)
Stonehill Coll (MA)
Susquehanna U (PA)

Temple U (PA)
Tennessee State U (TN)
Texas A&M International U (TX)
Texas A&M U–Kingsville (TX)
Texas Wesleyan U (TX)
Union U (TN)
U du Québec à Trois-Rivières (PQ, Canada)
U Coll of Cape Breton (NS, Canada)
The U of Alabama (AL)
The U of Alabama at Birmingham (AL)
U of Alaska Fairbanks (AK)
The U of Arizona (AZ)
U of Arkansas (AR)
U of Arkansas at Pine Bluff (AR)
U of Calif, Los Angeles (CA)
U of Calif, Riverside (CA)
U of Calif, Santa Barbara (CA)
U of Calif, Santa Cruz (CA)
U of Central Florida (FL)
U of Central Oklahoma (OK)
U of Dayton (OH)
U of Delaware (DE)
U of Denver (CO)
U of Evansville (IN)
U of Georgia (GA)
U of Guelph (ON, Canada)
U of Hartford (CT)
U of Hawaii at Manoa (HI)
U of Indianapolis (IN)
The U of Iowa (IA)
U of Judaism (CA)
U of Kentucky (KY)
U of La Verne (CA)
U of Louisiana at Lafayette (LA)
U of Louisiana at Monroe (LA)
U of Louisville (KY)
U of Maine at Farmington (ME)
U of Manitoba (MB, Canada)
The U of Memphis (TN)
U of Miami (FL)
U of Mississippi (MS)
U of Missouri–Columbia (MO)
U of Nebraska at Omaha (NE)
U of Nebraska–Lincoln (NE)
U of Nevada, Reno (NV)
U of New Brunswick, Fredericton (NB, Canada)
U of New Haven (CT)
U of New Orleans (LA)
U of North Alabama (AL)
The U of North Carolina at Charlotte (NC)
The U of North Carolina at Wilmington (NC)
U of North Dakota (ND)
U of North Florida (FL)
U of Oklahoma (OK)
U of Pittsburgh at Johnstown (PA)
U of Puerto Rico, Río Piedras (PR)
U of Richmond (VA)
U of San Diego (CA)
U of South Alabama (AL)
U of South Carolina (SC)
U of South Dakota (SD)
U of Southern California (CA)
U of Southern Mississippi (MS)
U of South Florida (FL)
The U of Tennessee at Martin (TN)
The U of Tennessee Knoxville (TN)
The U of Texas at San Antonio (TX)
U of West Florida (FL)
U of Windsor (ON, Canada)
U of Wisconsin–Platteville (WI)
U of Wisconsin–Superior (WI)
U of Wisconsin–Whitewater (WI)
U of Wyoming (WY)
Urbana U (OH)
Utica Coll of Syracuse U (NY)
Valdosta State U (GA)
Villanova U (PA)
Virginia Commonwealth U (VA)
Washington U in St. Louis (MO)
Wayne State U (NE)
Weber State U (UT)
West Chester U of Pennsylvania (PA)
Western Carolina U (NC)
Western Illinois U (IL)
Western Kentucky U (KY)
Western Washington U (WA)
West Liberty State Coll (WV)
Westminster Coll (UT)
Westmont Coll (CA)

West Texas A&M U (TX)
West Virginia Wesleyan Coll (WV)
Wheaton Coll (IL)
Widener U (PA)
William Paterson U of New Jersey (NJ)
Wilmington Coll (OH)
Wingate U (NC)
Winona State U (MN)
Wittenberg U (OH)
Wofford Coll (SC)
Wright State U (OH)
Xavier U of Louisiana (LA)
York Coll of Pennsylvania (PA)
York U (ON, Canada)

BUSINESS EDUCATION
Abilene Christian U (TX)
Adams State Coll (CO)
Adrian Coll (MI)
Alabama State U (AL)
Albany State U (GA)
Albertus Magnus Coll (CT)
Alfred U (NY)
Allen U (SC)
American International Coll (MA)
Appalachian State U (NC)
Arkansas State U (AR)
Arkansas Tech U (AR)
Armstrong Atlantic State U (GA)
Atlantic Union Coll (MA)
Auburn U (AL)
Baldwin-Wallace Coll (OH)
Ball State U (IN)
Bartlesville Wesleyan Coll (OK)
Baylor U (TX)
Belmont U (TN)
Bethany Coll (KS)
Bethel Coll (IN)
Bethune-Cookman Coll (FL)
Black Hills State U (SD)
Bloomsburg U of Pennsylvania (PA)
Blue Mountain Coll (MS)
Bluffton Coll (OH)
Boise State U (ID)
Bowling Green State U (OH)
Briar Cliff Coll (IA)
Brigham Young U–Hawaii Campus (HI)
Buena Vista U (IA)
California State U, Chico (CA)
California State U, Fresno (CA)
California State U, Northridge (CA)
California State U, Sacramento (CA)
Campbellsville U (KY)
Canisius Coll (NY)
Carson-Newman Coll (TN)
Central Michigan U (MI)
Central Missouri State U (MO)
Chicago State U (IL)
Clark Atlanta U (GA)
Coll of Santa Fe (NM)
Coll of the Ozarks (MO)
Coll of the Southwest (NM)
Colorado State U (CO)
Columbia Coll (MO)
Concord Coll (WV)
Concordia Coll (MN)
Concordia Coll (NY)
Concordia Coll (NE)
Concordia U Wisconsin (WI)
Cornell Coll (IA)
Cornerstone U (MI)
Cumberland Coll (KY)
Daemen Coll (NY)
Dakota State U (SD)
Dakota Wesleyan U (SD)
Dana Coll (NE)
Defiance Coll (OH)
Delaware State U (DE)
Delta State U (MS)
Dickinson State U (ND)
Doane Coll (NE)
Dordt Coll (IA)
Drake U (IA)
D'Youville Coll (NY)
East Carolina U (NC)
East Central U (OK)
Eastern Illinois U (IL)
Eastern Kentucky U (KY)
Eastern Michigan U (MI)
Eastern New Mexico U (NM)
Eastern Washington U (WA)
East Texas Baptist U (TX)
Elizabeth City State U (NC)

Emporia State U (KS)
Evangel U (MO)
Fairmont State Coll (WV)
Ferris State U (MI)
Florida A&M U (FL)
Fort Hays State U (KS)
Friends U (KS)
Frostburg State U (MD)
Geneva Coll (PA)
Georgia Southern U (GA)
Georgia Southwestern State U (GA)
Glenville State Coll (WV)
Goshen Coll (IN)
Grand Canyon U (AZ)
Grand View Coll (IA)
Gwynedd-Mercy Coll (PA)
Hampton U (VA)
Hardin-Simmons U (TX)
Hastings Coll (NE)
Henderson State U (AR)
Hofstra U (NY)
Howard Payne U (TX)
Huntington Coll (IN)
Husson Coll (ME)
Illinois State U (IL)
Indiana State U (IN)
Indiana U of Pennsylvania (PA)
Inter American U of PR, Fajardo Campus (PR)
International Coll of the Cayman Islands (Cayman Islands)
James Madison U (VA)
Jarvis Christian Coll (TX)
John Brown U (AR)
Kent State U (OH)
Lakeland Coll (WI)
La Salle U (PA)
Lee U (TN)
Lehman Coll of the City U of NY (NY)
Lenoir-Rhyne Coll (NC)
Lincoln Memorial U (TN)
Lincoln U (MO)
Lindenwood U (MO)
Louisiana Coll (LA)
Maranatha Baptist Bible Coll (WI)
Marshall U (WV)
Marycrest International U (IA)
Mayville State U (ND)
McGill U (PQ, Canada)
McKendree Coll (IL)
McMurry U (TX)
McPherson Coll (KS)
Mercyhurst Coll (PA)
MidAmerica Nazarene U (KS)
Middle Tennessee State U (TN)
Midland Lutheran Coll (NE)
Midwestern State U (TX)
Minot State U (ND)
Mississippi Coll (MS)
Mississippi State U (MS)
Missouri Southern State Coll (MO)
Montana State U–Northern (MT)
Morehead State U (KY)
Morgan State U (MD)
Morningside Coll (IA)
Mount Mary Coll (WI)
Mount St. Mary's Coll (CA)
Mount Vernon Nazarene Coll (OH)
Murray State U (KY)
Muskingum Coll (OH)
Nazareth Coll of Rochester (NY)
New Hampshire Coll (NH)
New York Inst of Technology (NY)
Niagara U (NY)
Nicholls State U (LA)
Norfolk State U (VA)
North Carolina Ag and Tech State U (NC)
North Central Coll (IL)
Northeastern State U (OK)
Northern Arizona U (AZ)
Northern Illinois U (IL)
Northern Kentucky U (KY)
Northern Michigan U (MI)
Northern State U (SD)
Northwestern Coll (IA)
Northwestern Oklahoma State U (OK)
Northwestern State U of Louisiana (LA)
Northwest Missouri State U (MO)
Oakland City U (IN)
Oakwood Coll (AL)
Ohio U (OH)
Oklahoma Panhandle State U (OK)

Otterbein Coll (OH)
Ouachita Baptist U (AR)
Our Lady of Holy Cross Coll (LA)
Pace U, New York City Campus (NY)
Pace U, Pleasantville/Briarcliff Campus (NY)
Pacific Union Coll (CA)
Philander Smith Coll (AR)
Pontifical Catholic U of Puerto Rico (PR)
Rider U (NJ)
Robert Morris Coll (PA)
Rust Coll (MS)
St. Ambrose U (IA)
Saint Augustine's Coll (NC)
St. Bonaventure U (NY)
St. Francis Coll (NY)
Saint Joseph's Coll (IN)
Saint Mary's Coll (IN)
St. Mary's U of San Antonio (TX)
Salem State Coll (MA)
Sam Houston State U (TX)
Shippensburg U of Pennsylvania (PA)
Siena Heights U (MI)
Southeastern Oklahoma State U (OK)
Southeast Missouri State U (MO)
Southern Arkansas U–Magnolia (AR)
Southern Utah U (UT)
Southwest Baptist U (MO)
Southwest Missouri State U (MO)
Spalding U (KY)
State U of NY Coll at Buffalo (NY)
State U of NY Coll at Oneonta (NY)
State U of West Georgia (GA)
Suffolk U (MA)
Tabor Coll (KS)
Temple U (PA)
Tennessee State U (TN)
Texas A&M U–Commerce (TX)
Texas Southern U (TX)
Texas Wesleyan U (TX)
Thomas Coll (ME)
Thomas More Coll (KY)
Trinity Christian Coll (IL)
Troy State U (AL)
Union Coll (KY)
Union Coll (NE)
Union U (TN)
U du Québec à Chicoutimi (PQ, Canada)
U du Québec en Abitibi-Témiscamingue (PQ, Canada)
The U of Akron (OH)
U of Alberta (AB, Canada)
U of Arkansas at Monticello (AR)
U of Arkansas at Pine Bluff (AR)
U of British Columbia (BC, Canada)
U of Central Arkansas (AR)
U of Central Florida (FL)
U of Central Oklahoma (OK)
The U of Findlay (OH)
U of Georgia (GA)
U of Idaho (ID)
U of Illinois at Urbana–Champaign (IL)
U of Indianapolis (IN)
The U of Lethbridge (AB, Canada)
U of Maine at Machias (ME)
U of Mary Hardin-Baylor (TX)
U of Minnesota, Twin Cities Campus (MN)
U of Missouri–St. Louis (MO)
The U of Montana–Missoula (MT)
U of Nebraska at Kearney (NE)
U of Nebraska–Lincoln (NE)
U of Nevada, Reno (NV)
U of New Brunswick, Fredericton (NB, Canada)
U of New Mexico (NM)
The U of North Carolina at Greensboro (NC)
U of North Dakota (ND)
U of Northern Iowa (IA)
U of North Texas (TX)
U of Pittsburgh (PA)
U of Regina (SK, Canada)
U of Rio Grande (OH)
U of Saint Francis (IN)
U of Southern Indiana (IN)
U of South Florida (FL)
The U of Tennessee at Martin (TN)

Majors Index
Business Education–Business Marketing and Marketing Management

The U of Tennessee Knoxville (TN)
U of the District of Columbia (DC)
U of the Ozarks (AR)
The U of Western Ontario (ON, Canada)
U of Wisconsin–Superior (WI)
U of Wisconsin–Whitewater (WI)
U of Wyoming (WY)
Upper Iowa U (IA)
Utah State U (UT)
Valdosta State U (GA)
Valley City State U (ND)
Virginia Intermont Coll (VA)
Virginia Polytechnic Inst and State U (VA)
Virginia Union U (VA)
Walla Walla Coll (WA)
Walsh U (OH)
Warner Southern Coll (FL)
Wayne State Coll (NE)
Weber State U (UT)
Western Kentucky U (KY)
Western Michigan U (MI)
Western Montana Coll of The U of Montana (MT)
Westfield State Coll (MA)
West Virginia State Coll (WV)
William Penn U (IA)
Wilmington Coll (OH)
Winona State U (MN)
Winston-Salem State U (NC)
Winthrop U (SC)
Wright State U (OH)
Youngstown State U (OH)

BUSINESS HOME ECONOMICS
The Ohio State U (OH)
Point Loma Nazarene U (CA)
U of Houston (TX)

BUSINESS MARKETING AND MARKETING MANAGEMENT
Abilene Christian U (TX)
Adams State Coll (CO)
Alabama A&M U (AL)
Alabama State U (AL)
Albany State U (GA)
Albertus Magnus Coll (CT)
Albright Coll (PA)
Alderson-Broaddus Coll (WV)
Alfred U (NY)
Allentown Coll of St. Francis de Sales (PA)
Alma Coll (MI)
Alvernia Coll (PA)
Amber U (TX)
American InterContinental U (CA)
American InterContinental U, Atlanta (GA)
American InterContinental U, Atlanta (GA)
American InterContinental U (United Kingdom)
American International Coll (MA)
American U (DC)
Anderson U (IN)
Andrews U (MI)
Appalachian State U (NC)
Arizona State U (AZ)
Arkansas State U (AR)
The Art Inst of Colorado (CO)
Art Insts International at San Francisco (CA)
Ashland U (OH)
Assumption Coll (MA)
Auburn U (AL)
Auburn U Montgomery (AL)
Augsburg Coll (MN)
Augustana Coll (IL)
Augusta State U (GA)
Averett Coll (VA)
Avila Coll (MO)
Azusa Pacific U (CA)
Babson Coll (MA)
Baker Coll of Auburn Hills (MI)
Baker Coll of Flint (MI)
Baker Coll of Jackson (MI)
Baker Coll of Muskegon (MI)
Baker Coll of Owosso (MI)
Baker Coll of Port Huron (MI)
Baldwin-Wallace Coll (OH)
Ball State U (IN)
Barat Coll (IL)
Barber-Scotia Coll (NC)
Barry U (FL)
Bayamón Central U (PR)
Baylor U (TX)

Beaver Coll (PA)
Becker Coll (MA)
Bellevue U (NE)
Belmont U (TN)
Benedictine Coll (KS)
Bentley Coll (MA)
Berkeley Coll, New York (NY)
Berkeley Coll, White Plains (NY)
Baruch Coll of the City U of NY (NY)
Berry Coll (GA)
Bishop's U (PQ, Canada)
Black Hills State U (SD)
Bluefield State Coll (WV)
Boise State U (ID)
Boston Coll (MA)
Boston U (MA)
Bowling Green State U (OH)
Bradley U (IL)
Brenau U (GA)
Brescia U (KY)
Briar Cliff Coll (IA)
Bridgewater State Coll (MA)
Brigham Young U (UT)
Brock U (ON, Canada)
Bryant Coll (RI)
Buena Vista U (IA)
Butler U (IN)
Cabrini Coll (PA)
Caldwell Coll (NJ)
California Lutheran U (CA)
California State Polytechnic U, Pomona (CA)
California State U, Chico (CA)
California State U, Dominguez Hills (CA)
California State U, Fresno (CA)
California State U, Fullerton (CA)
California State U, Hayward (CA)
California State U, Long Beach (CA)
California State U, Los Angeles (CA)
California State U, Northridge (CA)
California State U, San Bernardino (CA)
California State U, Stanislaus (CA)
Cameron U (OK)
Campbellsville U (KY)
Canisius Coll (NY)
Capital U (OH)
Carleton U (ON, Canada)
Carroll Coll (WI)
Carson-Newman Coll (TN)
Castleton State Coll (VT)
Catawba Coll (NC)
Cedarville Coll (OH)
Centenary Coll (NJ)
Central Connecticut State U (CT)
Central Michigan U (MI)
Central Missouri State U (MO)
Chaminade U of Honolulu (HI)
Champlain Coll (VT)
Chapman U (CA)
Charleston Southern U (SC)
Chatham Coll (PA)
Chestnut Hill Coll (PA)
Chicago State U (IL)
Chowan Coll (NC)
Christian Brothers U (TN)
Christopher Newport U (VA)
City U (WA)
Clarion U of Pennsylvania (PA)
Clarke Coll (IA)
Clarkson U (NY)
Cleary Coll (MI)
Clemson U (SC)
Cleveland State U (OH)
Coastal Carolina U (SC)
Coker Coll (SC)
Coll Misericordia (PA)
Coll of Notre Dame (CA)
Coll of Our Lady of the Elms (MA)
Coll of St. Catherine (MN)
Coll of Saint Elizabeth (NJ)
The Coll of Southeastern Europe, The American U of Athens (Greece)
Coll of the Ozarks (MO)
Coll of the Southwest (NM)
Colorado State U (CO)
Columbia Coll (MO)
Columbia Coll (SC)
Columbia Coll Chicago (IL)
Columbus State U (GA)
Concordia U (PQ, Canada)
Concordia U Wisconsin (WI)

Converse Coll (SC)
Cornerstone U (MI)
Creighton U (NE)
Dakota State U (SD)
Dakota Wesleyan U (SD)
Dallas Baptist U (TX)
Davenport Coll of Business (MI)
Davenport Coll of Business, Kalamazoo Campus (MI)
David Lipscomb U (TN)
David N. Myers Coll (OH)
Defiance Coll (OH)
Delaware State U (DE)
Delaware Valley Coll (PA)
Delta State U (MS)
DePaul U (IL)
Deree Coll (Greece)
Detroit Coll of Business (MI)
Detroit Coll of Business, Warren Campus (MI)
Dickinson State U (ND)
Dowling Coll (NY)
Drake U (IA)
Drexel U (PA)
Duquesne U (PA)
D'Youville Coll (NY)
East Carolina U (NC)
East Central U (OK)
Eastern Coll (PA)
Eastern Illinois U (IL)
Eastern Kentucky U (KY)
Eastern Michigan U (MI)
Eastern Nazarene Coll (MA)
Eastern New Mexico U (NM)
Eastern Washington U (WA)
East Tennessee State U (TN)
East Texas Baptist U (TX)
École des Hautes Études Commerciales (PQ, Canada)
Elmhurst Coll (IL)
Elmira Coll (NY)
Emerson Coll (MA)
Emory U (GA)
Emporia State U (KS)
Evangel U (MO)
Fairfield U (CT)
Fairleigh Dickinson U, Florham-Madison Campus (NJ)
Fairleigh Dickinson U, Teaneck-Hackensack Campus (NJ)
Fashion Inst of Technology (NY)
Faulkner U (AL)
Felician Coll (NJ)
Ferris State U (MI)
Fitchburg State Coll (MA)
Florida Atlantic U (FL)
Florida Gulf Coast U (FL)
Florida International U (FL)
Florida Metropolitan U-Tampa Coll, Brandon (FL)
Florida Southern Coll (FL)
Florida State U (FL)
Fontbonne Coll (MO)
Fordham U (NY)
Fort Hays State U (KS)
Fort Lewis Coll (CO)
Fort Valley State U (GA)
Framingham State Coll (MA)
Francis Marion U (SC)
Franklin Coll of Indiana (IN)
Franklin Pierce Coll (NH)
Franklin U (OH)
Freed-Hardeman U (TN)
Fresno Pacific U (CA)
Gannon U (PA)
George Mason U (VA)
Georgetown Coll (KY)
Georgetown U (DC)
The George Washington U (DC)
Georgia Coll and State U (GA)
Georgia Southern U (GA)
Georgia Southwestern State U (GA)
Georgia State U (GA)
Glenville State Coll (WV)
Golden Gate U (CA)
Goldey-Beacom Coll (DE)
Gonzaga U (WA)
Governors State U (IL)
Grand Canyon U (AZ)
Grand Valley State U (MI)
Green Mountain Coll (VT)
Greenville Coll (IL)
Grove City Coll (PA)
Gwynedd-Mercy Coll (PA)
Hampton U (VA)
Hannibal-LaGrange Coll (MO)

Harding U (AR)
Hardin-Simmons U (TX)
Hastings Coll (NE)
Hawaii Pacific U (HI)
Hesser Coll (NH)
High Point U (NC)
Hillsdale Coll (MI)
Hofstra U (NY)
Holy Family Coll (PA)
Houston Baptist U (TX)
Howard Payne U (TX)
Howard U (DC)
Humboldt State U (CA)
Huntingdon Coll (AL)
Husson Coll (ME)
Huston-Tillotson Coll (TX)
Idaho State U (ID)
Illinois State U (IL)
Immaculata Coll (PA)
Indiana Inst of Technology (IN)
Indiana State U (IN)
Indiana U Bloomington (IN)
Indiana U of Pennsylvania (PA)
Indiana U–Purdue U Fort Wayne (IN)
Indiana U South Bend (IN)
Indiana Wesleyan U (IN)
Inst of Public Administration (Ireland)
Insto Tecno Estudios Sups Monterrey, León (Mexico)
Insto Tecno Estudios Sups Monterrey (Mexico)
Insto Tecno Estudios Sups Monterrey, Querétaro (Mexico)
Inter American U of PR, Aguadilla Campus (PR)
Inter American U of PR, Arecibo Campus (PR)
Inter American U of PR, Metropolitan Campus (PR)
Inter American U of PR, San Germán Campus (PR)
Iona Coll (NY)
Iowa State U of Science and Technology (IA)
Ithaca Coll (NY)
Jacksonville State U (AL)
Jacksonville U (FL)
James Madison U (VA)
Jarvis Christian Coll (TX)
John Carroll U (OH)
Johnson & Wales U (RI)
Johnson C. Smith U (NC)
Johnson State Coll (VT)
Juniata Coll (PA)
Kansas State U (KS)
Kean U (NJ)
Kendall Coll (IL)
Kent State U (OH)
Kentucky State U (KY)
Kettering U (MI)
Keuka Coll (NY)
King's Coll (PA)
Kutztown U of Pennsylvania (PA)
Laboratory Inst of Merchandising (NY)
Lakehead U (ON, Canada)
Lakeland Coll (WI)
Lamar U (TX)
Lambuth U (TN)
La Salle U (PA)
Lasell Coll (MA)
Lehigh U (PA)
LeTourneau U (TX)
Lewis U (IL)
Limestone Coll (SC)
Lincoln Memorial U (TN)
Lincoln U (MO)
Lindenwood U (MO)
Long Island U, Brentwood Campus (NY)
Long Island U, Brooklyn Campus (NY)
Long Island U, C.W. Post Campus (NY)
Longwood Coll (VA)
Loras Coll (IA)
Louisiana Coll (LA)
Louisiana State U and A&M Coll (LA)
Louisiana State U in Shreveport (LA)
Louisiana Tech U (LA)
Loyola U Chicago (IL)
Loyola U New Orleans (LA)
Luther Coll (IA)

Lycoming Coll (PA)
Lynchburg Coll (VA)
Lynn U (FL)
MacMurray Coll (IL)
Madonna U (MI)
Manchester Coll (IN)
Manhattan Coll (NY)
Mansfield U of Pennsylvania (PA)
Marian Coll of Fond du Lac (WI)
Marietta Coll (OH)
Marquette U (WI)
Marshall U (WV)
Mars Hill Coll (NC)
Marygrove Coll (MI)
Marymount Coll (NY)
Maryville U of Saint Louis (MO)
Marywood U (PA)
Massachusetts Coll of Liberal Arts (MA)
McKendree Coll (IL)
McMurry U (TX)
McNeese State U (LA)
Medaille Coll (NY)
Memorial U of Newfoundland (NF, Canada)
Mercer U (GA)
Mercy Coll (NY)
Mercyhurst Coll (PA)
Meredith Coll (NC)
Merrimack Coll (MA)
Mesa State Coll (CO)
Messiah Coll (PA)
Metropolitan State U (MN)
Miami U (OH)
Michigan State U (MI)
Michigan Technological U (MI)
Middle Tennessee State U (TN)
Midland Lutheran Coll (NE)
Midwestern State U (TX)
Millersville U of Pennsylvania (PA)
Millikin U (IL)
Minnesota State U, Mankato (MN)
Minnesota State U Moorhead (MN)
Minot State U (ND)
Mississippi Coll (MS)
Mississippi State U (MS)
Mississippi U for Women (MS)
Missouri Baptist Coll (MO)
Missouri Southern State Coll (MO)
Missouri Valley Coll (MO)
Missouri Western State Coll (MO)
Monmouth U (NJ)
Montana State U–Billings (MT)
Montreat Coll (NC)
Morehead State U (KY)
Morehouse Coll (GA)
Morgan State U (MD)
Morningside Coll (IA)
Mount Ida Coll (MA)
Mount Mercy Coll (IA)
Mount St. Mary's Coll (CA)
Mount Saint Vincent U (NS, Canada)
Mount Vernon Nazarene Coll (OH)
Murray State U (KY)
National U (CA)
Nazareth Coll of Rochester (NY)
Neumann Coll (PA)
Newbury Coll (MA)
New England Coll (NH)
New Hampshire Coll (NH)
Newman U (KS)
New Mexico Highlands U (NM)
New Mexico State U (NM)
New York Inst of Technology (NY)
New York U (NY)
Niagara U (NY)
Nicholls State U (LA)
Nichols Coll (MA)
North Carolina Central U (NC)
North Carolina State U (NC)
North Central Coll (IL)
Northeastern Illinois U (IL)
Northeastern State U (OK)
Northeastern U (MA)
Northern Arizona U (AZ)
Northern Illinois U (IL)
Northern Kentucky U (KY)
Northern Michigan U (MI)
Northern State U (SD)
North Georgia Coll & State U (GA)
North Park U (IL)
Northwestern Coll (MN)
Northwest Missouri State U (MO)
Northwest Nazarene U (ID)
Northwood U (MI)
Northwood U, Florida Campus (FL)

Majors Index
Business Marketing and Marketing Management–Canadian Studies

Northwood U, Texas Campus (TX)
Notre Dame Coll of Ohio (OH)
Oakland U (MI)
The Ohio State U (OH)
Ohio U (OH)
Oklahoma Baptist U (OK)
Oklahoma Christian U of Science and Arts (OK)
Oklahoma City U (OK)
Oklahoma State U (OK)
Old Dominion U (VA)
Olivet Nazarene U (IL)
Oregon State U (OR)
Otterbein Coll (OH)
Ouachita Baptist U (AR)
Our Lady of the Lake U of San Antonio (TX)
Pace U, New York City Campus (NY)
Pace U, Pleasantville/Briarcliff Campus (NY)
Pacific Lutheran U (WA)
Pacific Union Coll (CA)
Pacific U (OR)
Palm Beach Atlantic Coll (FL)
Penn State U at Erie, The Behrend Coll (PA)
Penn State U Harrisburg Campus of the Capital Coll (PA)
Penn State U Univ Park Campus (PA)
Peru State Coll (NE)
Philadelphia U (PA)
Pine Manor Coll (MA)
Pittsburg State U (KS)
Plattsburgh State U of NY (NY)
Plymouth State Coll (NH)
Pontifical Catholic U of Puerto Rico (PR)
Portland State U (OR)
Prairie View A&M U (TX)
Providence Coll (RI)
Purdue U Calumet (IN)
Quincy U (IL)
Quinnipiac U (CT)
Radford U (VA)
Regents Coll (NY)
Rider U (NJ)
Robert Morris Coll (PA)
Rochester Coll (MI)
Rochester Inst of Technology (NY)
Rockford Coll (IL)
Rockhurst U (MO)
Roger Williams U (RI)
Rowan U (NJ)
Rutgers, State U of NJ, Camden Coll of Arts & Scis (NJ)
Rutgers, State U of NJ, Douglass Coll (NJ)
Rutgers, State U of NJ, Livingston Coll (NJ)
Rutgers, State U of NJ, Newark Coll of Arts & Scis (NJ)
Rutgers, State U of NJ, Rutgers Coll (NJ)
Rutgers, State U of NJ, U Coll–Camden (NJ)
Rutgers, State U of NJ, U Coll–Newark (NJ)
Rutgers, State U of NJ, U Coll–New Brunswick (NJ)
Ryerson Polytechnic U (ON, Canada)
Sacred Heart U (CT)
St. Ambrose U (IA)
St. Bonaventure U (NY)
St. Cloud State U (MN)
Saint Francis Coll (PA)
St. John Fisher Coll (NY)
Saint Joseph's Coll (IN)
Saint Joseph's Coll (ME)
Saint Joseph's U (PA)
Saint Leo U (FL)
Saint Louis U (MO)
Saint Martin's Coll (WA)
Saint Mary-of-the-Woods Coll (IN)
Saint Mary's Coll (IN)
Saint Mary's U (NS, Canada)
Saint Mary's U of Minnesota (MN)
St. Mary's U of San Antonio (TX)
Saint Peter's Coll (NJ)
St. Thomas U (FL)
Salem State Coll (MA)
Salisbury State U (MD)
Sam Houston State U (TX)
San Diego State U (CA)
San Francisco State U (CA)

San Jose State U (CA)
Santa Clara U (CA)
Savannah State U (GA)
Schiller International U (Germany)
Schreiner Coll (TX)
Seattle U (WA)
Seton Hall U (NJ)
Seton Hill Coll (PA)
Shippensburg U of Pennsylvania (PA)
Siena Coll (NY)
Siena Heights U (MI)
Simmons Coll (MA)
Slippery Rock U of Pennsylvania (PA)
Southeastern Louisiana U (LA)
Southeastern Oklahoma State U (OK)
Southeastern U (DC)
Southeast Missouri State U (MO)
Southern Adventist U (TN)
Southern Illinois U Carbondale (IL)
Southern Illinois U Edwardsville (IL)
Southern Methodist U (TX)
Southern Oregon U (OR)
Southwestern Oklahoma State U (OK)
Southwest Missouri State U (MO)
Southwest State U (MN)
Southwest Texas State U (TX)
Spring Hill Coll (AL)
State U of NY at New Paltz (NY)
State U of NY at Oswego (NY)
State U of NY Coll at Brockport (NY)
State U of NY Coll at Fredonia (NY)
State U of NY Coll at Old Westbury (NY)
State U of West Georgia (GA)
Stephen F. Austin State U (TX)
Stephens Coll (MO)
Stetson U (FL)
Stonehill Coll (MA)
Suffolk U (MA)
Susquehanna U (PA)
Syracuse U (NY)
Tabor Coll (KS)
Teikyo Post U (CT)
Temple U (PA)
Tennessee Technological U (TN)
Texas A&M International U (TX)
Texas A&M U (TX)
Texas A&M U–Commerce (TX)
Texas A&M U–Kingsville (TX)
Texas A&M U–Texarkana (TX)
Texas Christian U (TX)
Texas Southern U (TX)
Texas Tech U (TX)
Texas Wesleyan U (TX)
Texas Woman's U (TX)
Thomas Coll (ME)
Thomas Edison State Coll (NJ)
Tiffin U (OH)
Towson U (MD)
Trevecca Nazarene U (TN)
Trinity Christian Coll (IL)
Trinity U (TX)
Tri-State U (IN)
Tulane U (LA)
Tuskegee U (AL)
Union U (TN)
United States International U (CA)
Universidad Metropolitana (PR)
Université de Sherbrooke (PQ, Canada)
U Coll of Cape Breton (NS, Canada)
The U of Akron (OH)
The U of Alabama (AL)
The U of Alabama at Birmingham (AL)
The U of Alabama in Huntsville (AL)
U of Alaska Fairbanks (AK)
U of Alberta (AB, Canada)
The U of Arizona (AZ)
U of Arkansas (AR)
U of Arkansas at Little Rock (AR)
U of Baltimore (MD)
U of Bridgeport (CT)
U of British Columbia (BC, Canada)
U of Calgary (AB, Canada)
U of Central Arkansas (AR)
U of Central Florida (FL)
U of Central Oklahoma (OK)

U of Charleston (WV)
U of Cincinnati (OH)
U of Colorado at Boulder (CO)
U of Colorado at Colorado Springs (CO)
U of Connecticut (CT)
U of Dayton (OH)
U of Delaware (DE)
U of Denver (CO)
U of Detroit Mercy (MI)
U of Evansville (IN)
The U of Findlay (OH)
U of Florida (FL)
U of Georgia (GA)
U of Great Falls (MT)
U of Guelph (ON, Canada)
U of Hartford (CT)
U of Hawaii at Manoa (HI)
U of Houston–Clear Lake (TX)
U of Houston–Downtown (TX)
U of Idaho (ID)
U of Illinois at Chicago (IL)
U of Indianapolis (IN)
The U of Iowa (IA)
U of Kentucky (KY)
U of La Verne (CA)
The U of Lethbridge (AB, Canada)
U of Louisiana at Lafayette (LA)
U of Louisiana at Monroe (LA)
U of Louisville (KY)
U of Maine at Machias (ME)
U of Mary Hardin-Baylor (TX)
U of Maryland, Coll Park (MD)
U of Massachusetts Amherst (MA)
U of Massachusetts Dartmouth (MA)
The U of Memphis (TN)
U of Miami (FL)
U of Michigan–Dearborn (MI)
U of Minnesota, Duluth (MN)
U of Minnesota, Twin Cities Campus (MN)
U of Mississippi (MS)
U of Missouri–Columbia (MO)
U of Missouri–St. Louis (MO)
The U of Montana–Missoula (MT)
U of Montevallo (AL)
U of Nebraska at Omaha (NE)
U of Nebraska–Lincoln (NE)
U of Nevada, Las Vegas (NV)
U of Nevada, Reno (NV)
U of New Brunswick, Fredericton (NB, Canada)
U of New Haven (CT)
U of New Orleans (LA)
U of North Alabama (AL)
The U of North Carolina at Charlotte (NC)
The U of North Carolina at Greensboro (NC)
The U of North Carolina at Wilmington (NC)
U of North Dakota (ND)
U of Northern Iowa (IA)
U of North Florida (FL)
U of North Texas (TX)
U of Notre Dame (IN)
U of Oklahoma (OK)
U of Oregon (OR)
U of Pennsylvania (PA)
U of Phoenix (AZ)
U of Pittsburgh (PA)
U of Pittsburgh at Bradford (PA)
U of Portland (OR)
U of Puerto Rico, Mayagüez Campus (PR)
U of Puerto Rico, Río Piedras (PR)
U of Regina (SK, Canada)
U of Rhode Island (RI)
U of Richmond (VA)
U of Rio Grande (OH)
U of St. Francis (IL)
U of Saint Francis (IN)
U of St. Thomas (MN)
U of St. Thomas (TX)
U of San Francisco (CA)
U of Scranton (PA)
U of Sioux Falls (SD)
U of South Alabama (AL)
U of South Carolina (SC)
U of South Dakota (SD)
U of Southern California (CA)
U of Southern Colorado (CO)
U of Southern Indiana (IN)
U of Southern Mississippi (MS)
U of South Florida (FL)
The U of Tampa (FL)

The U of Tennessee at Chattanooga (TN)
The U of Tennessee at Martin (TN)
The U of Tennessee Knoxville (TN)
The U of Texas at Arlington (TX)
The U of Texas at Austin (TX)
The U of Texas at San Antonio (TX)
The U of Texas at Tyler (TX)
The U of Texas–Pan American (TX)
U of the District of Columbia (DC)
U of the Ozarks (AR)
U of the Pacific (CA)
U of the Sacred Heart (PR)
U of Tulsa (OK)
U of Utah (UT)
U of West Florida (FL)
U of Windsor (ON, Canada)
U of Wisconsin–Eau Claire (WI)
U of Wisconsin–La Crosse (WI)
U of Wisconsin–Milwaukee (WI)
U of Wisconsin–Parkside (WI)
U of Wisconsin–River Falls (WI)
U of Wisconsin–Stout (WI)
U of Wisconsin–Superior (WI)
U of Wisconsin–Whitewater (WI)
U of Wyoming (WY)
Upper Iowa U (IA)
Urbana U (OH)
Ursuline Coll (OH)
Utah State U (UT)
Valdosta State U (GA)
Valparaiso U (IN)
Vanguard U of Southern California (CA)
Villanova U (PA)
Virginia Commonwealth U (VA)
Virginia Intermont Coll (VA)
Virginia Polytechnic Inst and State U (VA)
Virginia Union U (VA)
Walla Walla Coll (WA)
Walsh Coll of Accountancy and Business Admin (MI)
Walsh U (OH)
Warner Southern Coll (FL)
Wartburg Coll (IA)
Washington State U (WA)
Washington U in St. Louis (MO)
Waynesburg Coll (PA)
Wayne State U (MI)
Webber Coll (FL)
Weber State U (UT)
Webster U (MO)
Wesley Coll (DE)
West Chester U of Pennsylvania (PA)
Western Carolina U (NC)
Western Connecticut State U (CT)
Western Illinois U (IL)
Western Kentucky U (KY)
Western Michigan U (MI)
Western New England Coll (MA)
Western State Coll of Colorado (CO)
Western Washington U (WA)
Westfield State Coll (MA)
West Liberty State Coll (WV)
Westminster Coll (MO)
Westminster Coll (UT)
West Texas A&M U (TX)
West Virginia U (WV)
West Virginia Wesleyan Coll (WV)
Wheeling Jesuit U (WV)
Wichita State U (KS)
Wilmington Coll (OH)
Wingate U (NC)
Winona State U (MN)
Wittenberg U (OH)
Woodbury U (CA)
Worcester State Coll (MA)
Wright State U (OH)
Xavier U (OH)
Xavier U of Louisiana (LA)
Yeshiva U (NY)
York Coll of Pennsylvania (PA)
York Coll of the City U of New York (NY)
York U (ON, Canada)
Youngstown State U (OH)

BUSINESS SERVICES MARKETING
American Military U (VA)
New Hampshire Coll (NH)

BUSINESS STATISTICS
Alabama A&M U (AL)
Baylor U (TX)
École des Hautes Études Commerciales (PQ, Canada)
Southern Oregon U (OR)
U of Houston (TX)
U of Puerto Rico, Río Piedras (PR)
York U (ON, Canada)

BUSINESS SYSTEMS ANALYSIS AND DESIGN
Cameron U (OK)
Detroit Coll of Business, Warren Campus (MI)
École des Hautes Études Commerciales (PQ, Canada)
Kent State U (OH)
Mount Saint Vincent U (NS, Canada)
Pennsylvania Coll of Technology (PA)
Seattle Pacific U (WA)
Shippensburg U of Pennsylvania (PA)
Southern Illinois U Carbondale (IL)
U of Southern California (CA)

BUSINESS SYSTEMS NETWORKING AND TELECOMMUNICATIONS
California State U, Hayward (CA)
Crown Coll (MN)
Detroit Coll of Business (MI)
Detroit Coll of Business, Warren Campus (MI)
DeVry Inst of Technology, Fremont (CA)
DeVry Inst of Technology, Long Beach (CA)
DeVry Inst of Technology, Pomona (CA)
DeVry Inst of Technology, West Hills (CA)
DeVry Inst of Technology, Alpharetta (GA)
DeVry Inst of Technology, Decatur (GA)
DeVry Inst of Technology, Addison (IL)
DeVry Inst of Technology (MO)
DeVry Inst of Technology (TX)
Illinois State U (IL)
Our Lady of the Lake U of San Antonio (TX)
Peirce Coll (PA)
Pennsylvania Coll of Technology (PA)
Robert Morris Coll (IL)
Ryerson Polytechnic U (ON, Canada)
The U of Findlay (OH)
U of Wisconsin–Stout (WI)
Weber State U (UT)

CANADIAN STUDIES
Acadia U (NS, Canada)
Athabasca U (AB, Canada)
Bishop's U (PQ, Canada)
Brandon U (MB, Canada)
Brock U (ON, Canada)
Carleton U (ON, Canada)
Concordia U Coll of Alberta (AB, Canada)
Dalhousie U (NS, Canada)
Franklin Coll of Indiana (IN)
George Mason U (VA)
Hampshire Coll (MA)
Long Island U, Southampton Coll, Friends World Program (NY)
McGill U (PQ, Canada)
Memorial U of Newfoundland (NF, Canada)
Mount Allison U (NB, Canada)
Mount Saint Vincent U (NS, Canada)
Plattsburgh State U of NY (NY)
Queen's U at Kingston (ON, Canada)
St. Francis Xavier U (NS, Canada)
St. Lawrence U (NY)
Saint Mary's U (NS, Canada)
Simon Fraser U (BC, Canada)
State U of NY Coll at Brockport (NY)
Trent U (ON, Canada)

Majors Index
Canadian Studies–Chemical Engineering

U of Alberta (AB, Canada)
U of British Columbia (BC, Canada)
U of Calgary (AB, Canada)
U of Guelph (ON, Canada)
The U of Lethbridge (AB, Canada)
U of Manitoba (MB, Canada)
U of New Brunswick, Fredericton (NB, Canada)
U of Prince Edward Island (PE, Canada)
U of Regina (SK, Canada)
U of Toronto (ON, Canada)
U of Vermont (VT)
U of Washington (WA)
U of Waterloo (ON, Canada)
U of Windsor (ON, Canada)
The U of Winnipeg (MB, Canada)
Western Washington U (WA)
Wilfrid Laurier U (ON, Canada)
York U (ON, Canada)

CARDIOVASCULAR TECHNOLOGY
Nebraska Methodist Coll of Nursing & Allied Health (NE)
Northeastern U (MA)
State U of New York Upstate Medical University (NY)
Thomas Jefferson U (PA)

CARPENTRY
Andrews U (MI)

CARTOGRAPHY
Appalachian State U (NC)
Ball State U (IN)
California State U, Northridge (CA)
East Central U (OK)
Frostburg State U (MD)
Memorial U of Newfoundland (NF, Canada)
The Ohio State U (OH)
Ohio U (OH)
Salem State Coll (MA)
Samford U (AL)
San Jose State U (CA)
Southwest Missouri State U (MO)
State U of NY Coll at Oneonta (NY)
The U of Akron (OH)
U of Alberta (AB, Canada)
U of Idaho (ID)
U of Maryland, Coll Park (MD)
U of Wisconsin–Madison (WI)
U of Wisconsin–Platteville (WI)
Wittenberg U (OH)

CELL BIOLOGY
Ball State U (IN)
Beloit Coll (WI)
Bucknell U (PA)
California Inst of Technology (CA)
California State U, Fresno (CA)
California State U, Fullerton (CA)
California State U, Long Beach (CA)
California State U, Northridge (CA)
California State U, San Marcos (CA)
Clarkson U (NY)
Colby Coll (ME)
Concordia U (PQ, Canada)
Cornell U (NY)
Florida State U (FL)
Fort Lewis Coll (CO)
Hampshire Coll (MA)
Harvard U (MA)
Humboldt State U (CA)
Juniata Coll (PA)
Lindenwood U (MO)
Lock Haven U of Pennsylvania (PA)
Mansfield U of Pennsylvania (PA)
Marlboro Coll (VT)
McGill U (PQ, Canada)
Memorial U of Newfoundland (NF, Canada)
Northeastern State U (OK)
Northwestern U (IL)
Ohio U (OH)
Okanagan U Coll (BC, Canada)
Oklahoma State U (OK)
Oregon State U (OR)
Pomona Coll (CA)
Rutgers, State U of NJ, Camden Coll of Arts & Scis (NJ)
Rutgers, State U of NJ, Douglass Coll (NJ)
Rutgers, State U of NJ, Livingston Coll (NJ)
Rutgers, State U of NJ, Rutgers Coll (NJ)
Rutgers, State U of NJ, U Coll–Camden (NJ)
Rutgers, State U of NJ, U Coll–New Brunswick (NJ)
San Francisco State U (CA)
Sonoma State U (CA)
Southwest Missouri State U (MO)
Spring Hill Coll (AL)
State U of NY Coll at Brockport (NY)
Texas A&M U (TX)
Texas Tech U (TX)
Tulane U (LA)
U of Alberta (AB, Canada)
The U of Arizona (AZ)
U of British Columbia (BC, Canada)
U of Calgary (AB, Canada)
U of Calif, Davis (CA)
U of Calif, Los Angeles (CA)
U of Calif, San Diego (CA)
U of Calif, Santa Barbara (CA)
U of Calif, Santa Cruz (CA)
U of Colorado at Boulder (CO)
U of Connecticut (CT)
U of Georgia (GA)
U of Illinois at Urbana–Champaign (IL)
U of Kansas (KS)
U of Maryland, Coll Park (MD)
U of Michigan (MI)
U of Minnesota, Duluth (MN)
U of Minnesota, Twin Cities Campus (MN)
U of New Hampshire (NH)
U of Rochester (NY)
U of Vermont (VT)
U of Washington (WA)
The U of Western Ontario (ON, Canada)
U of Wisconsin–Madison (WI)
U of Wisconsin–Superior (WI)
West Chester U of Pennsylvania (PA)
Western Washington U (WA)
William Jewell Coll (MO)
Wittenberg U (OH)
Worcester Polytechnic Inst (MA)
Yale U (CT)

CERAMIC ARTS
Adams State Coll (CO)
Alberta Coll of Art and Design (AB, Canada)
Alfred U (NY)
Arizona State U (AZ)
Ball State U (IN)
Barat Coll (IL)
Barton Coll (NC)
Beaver Coll (PA)
Bennington Coll (VT)
Bethany Coll (KS)
Bowling Green State U (OH)
California Coll of Arts and Crafts (CA)
California State U, Fullerton (CA)
California State U, Hayward (CA)
California State U, Long Beach (CA)
California State U, Los Angeles (CA)
California State U, Northridge (CA)
Carnegie Mellon U (PA)
Ctr for Creative Studies—Coll of Art and Design (MI)
Chicago State U (IL)
Cleveland Inst of Art (OH)
Coll of the Atlantic (ME)
Colorado State U (CO)
Columbus Coll of Art and Design (OH)
Concord Coll (WV)
Concordia U (PQ, Canada)
The Corcoran Coll of Art and Design (DC)
Eastern Kentucky U (KY)
The Evergreen State Coll (WA)
Finlandia U (MI)
Franklin Pierce Coll (NH)
Friends U (KS)
Georgia Southwestern State U (GA)
Goddard Coll (VT)
Grand Valley State U (MI)
Hampton U (VA)
Howard U (DC)
Indiana U Bloomington (IN)
Indiana Wesleyan U (IN)
Inter American U of PR, Metropolitan Campus (PR)
Inter American U of PR, San Germán Campus (PR)
Kansas City Art Inst (MO)
Long Island U, Southampton Coll, Friends World Program (NY)
Maharishi U of Management (IA)
Maine Coll of Art (ME)
Marlboro Coll (VT)
Maryland Inst, Coll of Art (MD)
Massachusetts Coll of Art (MA)
McMurry U (TX)
McNeese State U (LA)
Memphis Coll of Art (TN)
Minnesota State U, Mankato (MN)
Minnesota State U Moorhead (MN)
Moore Coll of Art and Design (PA)
Mount Senario Coll (WI)
Nazareth Coll of Rochester (NY)
Northern Arizona U (AZ)
Northern Michigan U (MI)
Nova Scotia Coll of Art and Design (NS, Canada)
Ohio Northern U (OH)
The Ohio State U (OH)
Ohio U (OH)
Pacific Northwest Coll of Art (OR)
Plymouth State Coll (NH)
Pratt Inst (NY)
Rhode Island School of Design (RI)
Rochester Inst of Technology (NY)
Rutgers, State U of NJ, Mason Gross School of Arts (NJ)
St. Cloud State U (MN)
San Francisco Art Inst (CA)
School of the Museum of Fine Arts (MA)
Seton Hill Coll (PA)
Simon's Rock Coll of Bard (MA)
State U of NY at New Paltz (NY)
State U of NY Coll at Brockport (NY)
Syracuse U (NY)
Temple U (PA)
Texas Woman's U (TX)
Trinity Christian Coll (IL)
The U of Akron (OH)
U of Dallas (TX)
U of Evansville (IN)
U of Hartford (CT)
The U of Iowa (IA)
U of Massachusetts Dartmouth (MA)
U of Miami (FL)
U of Michigan (MI)
U of Montevallo (AL)
U of North Texas (TX)
U of Oklahoma (OK)
U of Oregon (OR)
U of South Alabama (AL)
U of South Dakota (SD)
The U of Texas at Arlington (TX)
The U of the Arts (PA)
U of the District of Columbia (DC)
U of Washington (WA)
U of Wisconsin–Milwaukee (WI)
Washington U in St. Louis (MO)
Webster U (MO)
Western Washington U (WA)
West Virginia Wesleyan Coll (WV)
Wittenberg U (OH)
Youngstown State U (OH)

CERAMIC SCIENCES/ENGINEERING
Alfred U (NY)
Clemson U (SC)
Iowa State U of Science and Technology (IA)
The Ohio State U (OH)
Rutgers, State U of NJ, Coll of Engineering (NJ)
U of Illinois at Urbana–Champaign (IL)
U of Missouri–Rolla (MO)
U of Washington (WA)

CHEMICAL AND ATOMIC/MOLECULAR PHYSICS
The Catholic U of America (DC)
Columbia Coll (NY)
Maryville Coll (TN)
Queen's U at Kingston (ON, Canada)
Saint Mary's U of Minnesota (MN)
Simon Fraser U (BC, Canada)
U of Calif, San Diego (CA)
U of Guelph (ON, Canada)
U of Waterloo (ON, Canada)

CHEMICAL ENGINEERING
Arizona State U (AZ)
Auburn U (AL)
Bethel Coll (IN)
Brigham Young U (UT)
Brown U (RI)
Bucknell U (PA)
California Inst of Technology (CA)
California State Polytechnic U, Pomona (CA)
California State U, Long Beach (CA)
California State U, Northridge (CA)
Calvin Coll (MI)
Carlow Coll (PA)
Carnegie Mellon U (PA)
Case Western Reserve U (OH)
Christian Brothers U (TN)
City Coll of the City U of NY (NY)
Clarkson U (NY)
Clemson U (SC)
Cleveland State U (OH)
Colorado School of Mines (CO)
Colorado State U (CO)
Columbia U, School of Engineering & Applied Sci (NY)
Cooper Union for the Advancement of Science & Art (NY)
Cornell U (NY)
Dalhousie U (NS, Canada)
Drexel U (PA)
Florida A&M U (FL)
Florida Inst of Technology (FL)
Florida International U (FL)
Florida State U (FL)
Geneva Coll (PA)
Georgia Inst of Technology (GA)
Hampton U (VA)
Harvard U (MA)
Howard U (DC)
Illinois Inst of Technology (IL)
Insto Tecno Estudios Sups Monterrey (Mexico)
Iowa State U of Science and Technology (IA)
Johns Hopkins U (MD)
Kansas State U (KS)
Lafayette Coll (PA)
Lakehead U (ON, Canada)
Lamar U (TX)
Lehigh U (PA)
Louisiana State U and A&M Coll (LA)
Louisiana Tech U (LA)
Manhattan Coll (NY)
Massachusetts Inst of Technology (MA)
McGill U (PQ, Canada)
Memorial U of Newfoundland (NF, Canada)
Michigan State U (MI)
Michigan Technological U (MI)
Mississippi State U (MS)
Montana State U–Bozeman (MT)
New Jersey Inst of Technology (NJ)
New Mexico Inst of Mining and Technology (NM)
New Mexico State U (NM)
New York U (NY)
North Carolina Ag and Tech State U (NC)
North Carolina State U (NC)
Northeastern U (MA)
Northwestern U (IL)
The Ohio State U (OH)
Ohio U (OH)
Oklahoma State U (OK)
Oregon State U (OR)
Penn State U Univ Park Campus (PA)
Polytechnic U, Brooklyn Campus (NY)
Polytechnic U of Puerto Rico (PR)
Prairie View A&M U (TX)
Princeton U (NJ)
Purdue U (IN)
Queen's U at Kingston (ON, Canada)
Rensselaer Polytechnic Inst (NY)
Rice U (TX)
Rose-Hulman Inst of Technology (IN)
Rowan U (NJ)
Rutgers, State U of NJ, Coll of Engineering (NJ)
Ryerson Polytechnic U (ON, Canada)
Saint Augustine's Coll (NC)
San Diego State U (CA)
San Jose State U (CA)
South Dakota School of Mines and Technology (SD)
Stanford U (CA)
State U of NY at Buffalo (NY)
State U of NY Coll of Environ Sci and Forestry (NY)
Stevens Inst of Technology (NJ)
Syracuse U (NY)
Tennessee Technological U (TN)
Texas A&M U (TX)
Texas A&M U–Kingsville (TX)
Texas Tech U (TX)
Thiel Coll (PA)
Tri-State U (IN)
Tufts U (MA)
Tulane U (LA)
Tuskegee U (AL)
United States Military Academy (NY)
Université de Montréal (PQ, Canada)
Université de Sherbrooke (PQ, Canada)
U du Québec à Trois-Rivières (PQ, Canada)
Université Laval (PQ, Canada)
The U of Akron (OH)
The U of Alabama (AL)
The U of Alabama in Huntsville (AL)
U of Alberta (AB, Canada)
The U of Arizona (AZ)
U of Arkansas (AR)
U of British Columbia (BC, Canada)
U of Calgary (AB, Canada)
U of Calif, Berkeley (CA)
U of Calif, Davis (CA)
U of Calif, Irvine (CA)
U of Calif, Los Angeles (CA)
U of Calif, Riverside (CA)
U of Calif, San Diego (CA)
U of Calif, Santa Barbara (CA)
U of Cincinnati (OH)
U of Colorado at Boulder (CO)
U of Connecticut (CT)
U of Dayton (OH)
U of Delaware (DE)
U of Detroit Mercy (MI)
U of Florida (FL)
U of Houston (TX)
U of Idaho (ID)
U of Illinois at Chicago (IL)
U of Illinois at Urbana–Champaign (IL)
The U of Iowa (IA)
U of Kansas (KS)
U of Kentucky (KY)
U of Louisiana at Lafayette (LA)
U of Louisville (KY)
U of Maine (ME)
U of Maryland, Baltimore County (MD)
U of Maryland, Coll Park (MD)
U of Massachusetts Amherst (MA)
U of Massachusetts Lowell (MA)
U of Michigan (MI)
U of Minnesota, Duluth (MN)
U of Minnesota, Twin Cities Campus (MN)
U of Mississippi (MS)
U of Missouri–Columbia (MO)
U of Missouri–Rolla (MO)
U of Nebraska–Lincoln (NE)
U of Nevada, Reno (NV)
U of New Brunswick, Fredericton (NB, Canada)
U of New Brunswick, Saint John (NB, Canada)
U of New Hampshire (NH)
U of New Haven (CT)

Majors Index
Chemical Engineering–Chemistry

U of New Mexico (NM)
U of North Dakota (ND)
U of Notre Dame (IN)
U of Oklahoma (OK)
U of Pennsylvania (PA)
U of Pittsburgh (PA)
U of Pittsburgh at Bradford (PA)
U of Puerto Rico, Mayagüez Campus (PR)
U of Regina (SK, Canada)
U of Rhode Island (RI)
U of Rochester (NY)
U of South Alabama (AL)
U of South Carolina (SC)
U of Southern California (CA)
U of South Florida (FL)
The U of Tennessee at Chattanooga (TN)
The U of Tennessee Knoxville (TN)
The U of Texas at Austin (TX)
U of Toronto (ON, Canada)
U of Tulsa (OK)
U of Utah (UT)
U of Virginia (VA)
U of Washington (WA)
U of Waterloo (ON, Canada)
The U of Western Ontario (ON, Canada)
U of Wisconsin–Madison (WI)
U of Wyoming (WY)
Vanderbilt U (TN)
Villanova U (PA)
Virginia Commonwealth U (VA)
Virginia Polytechnic Inst and State U (VA)
Washington and Lee U (VA)
Washington State U (WA)
Washington U in St. Louis (MO)
Wayne State U (MI)
Western Michigan U (MI)
West Virginia U (WV)
West Virginia U Inst of Technology (WV)
Widener U (PA)
Winona State U (MN)
Worcester Polytechnic Inst (MA)
Yale U (CT)
Youngstown State U (OH)

CHEMICAL ENGINEERING TECHNOLOGY
Gallaudet U (DC)
Inter American U of PR, Metropolitan Campus (PR)
Lakehead U (ON, Canada)
Midwestern State U (TX)
Regents Coll (NY)
Savannah State U (GA)
State U of NY at Stony Brook (NY)
The U of Akron (OH)
U of Hartford (CT)

CHEMICAL TECHNOLOGY
U Coll of Cape Breton (NS, Canada)
U of Massachusetts Lowell (MA)

CHEMISTRY
Abilene Christian U (TX)
Acadia U (NS, Canada)
Adams State Coll (CO)
Adelphi U (NY)
Adrian Coll (MI)
Agnes Scott Coll (GA)
Alabama A&M U (AL)
Alabama State U (AL)
Albany State U (GA)
Albertson Coll of Idaho (ID)
Albertus Magnus Coll (CT)
Albion Coll (MI)
Albright Coll (PA)
Alderson-Broaddus Coll (WV)
Alfred U (NY)
Allegheny Coll (PA)
Allentown Coll of St. Francis de Sales (PA)
Alma Coll (MI)
Alvernia Coll (PA)
Alverno Coll (WI)
American International Coll (MA)
American U (DC)
American U in Cairo (Egypt)
Amherst Coll (MA)
Anderson U (IN)
Andrews U (MI)
Antioch Coll (OH)
Appalachian State U (NC)

Aquinas Coll (MI)
Arizona State U (AZ)
Arkansas State U (AR)
Arkansas Tech U (AR)
Armstrong Atlantic State U (GA)
Asbury Coll (KY)
Ashland U (OH)
Assumption Coll (MA)
Athens State U (AL)
Atlantic Union Coll (MA)
Auburn U (AL)
Augsburg Coll (MN)
Augustana Coll (IL)
Augustana Coll (SD)
Augusta State U (GA)
Austin Coll (TX)
Austin Peay State U (TN)
Averett Coll (VA)
Avila Coll (MO)
Azusa Pacific U (CA)
Baker U (KS)
Baldwin-Wallace Coll (OH)
Ball State U (IN)
Barat Coll (IL)
Bard Coll (NY)
Barnard Coll (NY)
Barry U (FL)
Bartlesville Wesleyan Coll (OK)
Barton Coll (NC)
Bates Coll (ME)
Bayamón Central U (PR)
Baylor U (TX)
Beaver Coll (PA)
Belhaven Coll (MS)
Bellarmine Coll (KY)
Belmont U (TN)
Beloit Coll (WI)
Bemidji State U (MN)
Benedictine Coll (KS)
Benedictine U (IL)
Bennett Coll (NC)
Bennington Coll (VT)
Berea Coll (KY)
Berry Coll (GA)
Bethany Coll (KS)
Bethany Coll (WV)
Bethel Coll (IN)
Bethel Coll (KS)
Bethel Coll (MN)
Bethel Coll (TN)
Bethune-Cookman Coll (FL)
Birmingham-Southern Coll (AL)
Bishop's U (PQ, Canada)
Blackburn Coll (IL)
Black Hills State U (SD)
Bloomfield Coll (NJ)
Bloomsburg U of Pennsylvania (PA)
Blue Mountain Coll (MS)
Bluffton Coll (OH)
Boise State U (ID)
Boston Coll (MA)
Boston U (MA)
Bowdoin Coll (ME)
Bowling Green State U (OH)
Bradley U (IL)
Brandeis U (MA)
Brandon U (MB, Canada)
Brescia U (KY)
Briar Cliff Coll (IA)
Bridgewater Coll (VA)
Bridgewater State Coll (MA)
Brigham Young U (UT)
Brigham Young U–Hawaii Campus (HI)
Brock U (ON, Canada)
Brooklyn Coll of the City U of NY (NY)
Brown U (RI)
Bryn Athyn Coll of the New Church (PA)
Bryn Mawr Coll (PA)
Bucknell U (PA)
Buena Vista U (IA)
Butler U (IN)
Cabrini Coll (PA)
Caldwell Coll (NJ)
California Inst of Technology (CA)
California Lutheran U (CA)
California Polytechnic State U, San Luis Obispo (CA)
California State Polytechnic U, Pomona (CA)
California State U, Chico (CA)
California State U, Dominguez Hills (CA)
California State U, Fresno (CA)

California State U, Fullerton (CA)
California State U, Hayward (CA)
California State U, Long Beach (CA)
California State U, Los Angeles (CA)
California State U, Northridge (CA)
California State U, Sacramento (CA)
California State U, San Bernardino (CA)
California State U, San Marcos (CA)
California State U, Stanislaus (CA)
California U of Pennsylvania (PA)
Calvin Coll (MI)
Cameron U (OK)
Campbellsville U (KY)
Campbell U (NC)
Canisius Coll (NY)
Capital U (OH)
Cardinal Stritch U (WI)
Carleton Coll (MN)
Carleton U (ON, Canada)
Carlow Coll (PA)
Carnegie Mellon U (PA)
Carroll Coll (MT)
Carroll Coll (WI)
Carson-Newman Coll (TN)
Carthage Coll (WI)
Case Western Reserve U (OH)
Catawba Coll (NC)
The Catholic U of America (DC)
Cedar Crest Coll (PA)
Cedarville Coll (OH)
Centenary Coll of Louisiana (LA)
Central Coll (IA)
Central Connecticut State U (CT)
Central Methodist Coll (MO)
Central Michigan U (MI)
Central Missouri State U (MO)
Centre Coll (KY)
Chadron State Coll (NE)
Chaminade U of Honolulu (HI)
Chapman U (CA)
Charleston Southern U (SC)
Chatham Coll (PA)
Chestnut Hill Coll (PA)
Cheyney U of Pennsylvania (PA)
Chicago State U (IL)
Christian Brothers U (TN)
Citadel, The Military Coll of South Carolina (SC)
City Coll of the City U of NY (NY)
Claflin U (SC)
Claremont McKenna Coll (CA)
Clarion U of Pennsylvania (PA)
Clark Atlanta U (GA)
Clarke Coll (IA)
Clarkson U (NY)
Clark U (MA)
Clemson U (SC)
Cleveland State U (OH)
Coastal Carolina U (SC)
Coe Coll (IA)
Coker Coll (SC)
Colby Coll (ME)
Colgate U (NY)
Coll Misericordia (PA)
Coll of Charleston (SC)
Coll of Mount St. Joseph (OH)
Coll of Mount Saint Vincent (NY)
The Coll of New Jersey (NJ)
The Coll of New Rochelle (NY)
Coll of Notre Dame of Maryland (MD)
Coll of Our Lady of the Elms (MA)
Coll of Saint Benedict (MN)
Coll of St. Catherine (MN)
Coll of Saint Elizabeth (NJ)
Coll of Saint Mary (NE)
The Coll of Saint Rose (NY)
The Coll of St. Scholastica (MN)
The Coll of Southeastern Europe, The American U of Athens (Greece)
Coll of Staten Island of the City U of NY (NY)
Coll of the Holy Cross (MA)
Coll of the Ozarks (MO)
The Coll of William and Mary (VA)
The Coll of Wooster (OH)
The Colorado Coll (CO)
Colorado School of Mines (CO)
Colorado State U (CO)
Columbia Coll (MO)
Columbia Coll (NY)

Columbia Coll (SC)
Columbia Union Coll (MD)
Columbia U, School of General Studies (NY)
Columbus State U (GA)
Concord Coll (WV)
Concordia Coll (MN)
Concordia U (IL)
Concordia U (NE)
Concordia U (OR)
Concordia U (PQ, Canada)
Concordia U Coll of Alberta (AB, Canada)
Connecticut Coll (CT)
Converse Coll (SC)
Coppin State Coll (MD)
Cornell Coll (IA)
Cornell U (NY)
Covenant Coll (GA)
Creighton U (NE)
Crichton Coll (TN)
Culver-Stockton Coll (MO)
Cumberland Coll (KY)
Curry Coll (MA)
Daemen Coll (NY)
Dakota State U (SD)
Dalhousie U (NS, Canada)
Dana Coll (NE)
Dartmouth Coll (NH)
David Lipscomb U (TN)
Davidson Coll (NC)
Defiance Coll (OH)
Delaware State U (DE)
Delaware Valley Coll (PA)
Delta State U (MS)
Denison U (OH)
DePaul U (IL)
DePauw U (IN)
Dickinson Coll (PA)
Dickinson State U (ND)
Doane Coll (NE)
Dominican U (IL)
Dordt Coll (IA)
Drake U (IA)
Drew U (NJ)
Drexel U (PA)
Drury U (MO)
Duke U (NC)
Duquesne U (PA)
Earlham Coll (IN)
East Carolina U (NC)
East Central U (OK)
Eastern Coll (PA)
Eastern Illinois U (IL)
Eastern Kentucky U (KY)
Eastern Mennonite U (VA)
Eastern Michigan U (MI)
Eastern Nazarene Coll (MA)
Eastern New Mexico U (NM)
Eastern Oregon U (OR)
Eastern Washington U (WA)
East Stroudsburg U of Pennsylvania (PA)
East Tennessee State U (TN)
East Texas Baptist U (TX)
Eckerd Coll (FL)
Edgewood Coll (WI)
Edinboro U of Pennsylvania (PA)
Elizabeth City State U (NC)
Elizabethtown Coll (PA)
Elmhurst Coll (IL)
Elmira Coll (NY)
Elon Coll (NC)
Emmanuel Coll (MA)
Emory & Henry Coll (VA)
Emory U (GA)
Emporia State U (KS)
Erskine Coll (SC)
Evangel U (MO)
The Evergreen State Coll (WA)
Fairfield U (CT)
Fairleigh Dickinson U, Florham-Madison Campus (NJ)
Fairleigh Dickinson U, Teaneck-Hackensack Campus (NJ)
Fairmont State Coll (WV)
Ferrum Coll (VA)
Fisk U (TN)
Fitchburg State Coll (MA)
Florida A&M U (FL)
Florida Atlantic U (FL)
Florida Inst of Technology (FL)
Florida International U (FL)
Florida Southern Coll (FL)
Florida State U (FL)
Fordham U (NY)
Fort Hays State U (KS)

Fort Lewis Coll (CO)
Fort Valley State U (GA)
Framingham State Coll (MA)
Franciscan U of Steubenville (OH)
Francis Marion U (SC)
Franklin and Marshall Coll (PA)
Franklin Coll of Indiana (IN)
Freed-Hardeman U (TN)
Fresno Pacific U (CA)
Friends U (KS)
Frostburg State U (MD)
Furman U (SC)
Gallaudet U (DC)
Gannon U (PA)
Gardner-Webb U (NC)
Geneva Coll (PA)
George Fox U (OR)
George Mason U (VA)
Georgetown Coll (KY)
Georgetown U (DC)
The George Washington U (DC)
Georgia Coll and State U (GA)
Georgia Inst of Technology (GA)
Georgian Court Coll (NJ)
Georgia Southern U (GA)
Georgia Southwestern State U (GA)
Georgia State U (GA)
Gettysburg Coll (PA)
Glenville State Coll (WV)
Gonzaga U (WA)
Gordon Coll (MA)
Goshen Coll (IN)
Goucher Coll (MD)
Governors State U (IL)
Graceland Coll (IA)
Grand Canyon U (AZ)
Grand Valley State U (MI)
Greensboro Coll (NC)
Greenville Coll (IL)
Grinnell Coll (IA)
Grove City Coll (PA)
Guilford Coll (NC)
Gustavus Adolphus Coll (MN)
Hamilton Coll (NY)
Hamline U (MN)
Hampden-Sydney Coll (VA)
Hampshire Coll (MA)
Hampton U (VA)
Hanover Coll (IN)
Harding U (AR)
Hardin-Simmons U (TX)
Hartwick Coll (NY)
Harvard U (MA)
Harvey Mudd Coll (CA)
Hastings Coll (NE)
Haverford Coll (PA)
Heidelberg Coll (OH)
Henderson State U (AR)
Hendrix Coll (AR)
High Point U (NC)
Hillsdale Coll (MI)
Hiram Coll (OH)
Hobart and William Smith Colls (NY)
Hofstra U (NY)
Hollins U (VA)
Holy Family Coll (PA)
Hood Coll (MD)
Hope Coll (MI)
Houghton Coll (NY)
Houston Baptist U (TX)
Howard Payne U (TX)
Howard U (DC)
Humboldt State U (CA)
Hunter Coll of the City U of NY (NY)
Huntingdon Coll (AL)
Huntington Coll (IN)
Huston-Tillotson Coll (TX)
Idaho State U (ID)
Illinois Coll (IL)
Illinois Inst of Technology (IL)
Illinois State U (IL)
Illinois Wesleyan U (IL)
Immaculata Coll (PA)
Indiana State U (IN)
Indiana U Bloomington (IN)
Indiana U Northwest (IN)
Indiana U of Pennsylvania (PA)
Indiana U–Purdue U Fort Wayne (IN)
Indiana U–Purdue U Indianapolis (IN)
Indiana U South Bend (IN)
Indiana U Southeast (IN)
Indiana Wesleyan U (IN)

Majors Index
Chemistry

Insto Tecno Estudios Sups Monterrey (Mexico)
Inter American U of PR, Arecibo Campus (PR)
Inter American U of PR, Metropolitan Campus (PR)
Inter American U of PR, San Germán Campus (PR)
Iona Coll (NY)
Iowa State U of Science and Technology (IA)
Iowa Wesleyan Coll (IA)
Ithaca Coll (NY)
Jacksonville State U (AL)
Jacksonville U (FL)
James Madison U (VA)
Jamestown Coll (ND)
Jarvis Christian Coll (TX)
John Brown U (AR)
John Carroll U (OH)
Johns Hopkins U (MD)
Johnson C. Smith U (NC)
Judson Coll (AL)
Judson Coll (IL)
Juniata Coll (PA)
Kalamazoo Coll (MI)
Kansas State U (KS)
Kean U (NJ)
Keene State Coll (NH)
Kent State U (OH)
Kentucky State U (KY)
Kentucky Wesleyan Coll (KY)
Kenyon Coll (OH)
Kettering U (MI)
King Coll (TN)
King's Coll (PA)
The King's U Coll (AB, Canada)
Knox Coll (IL)
Kutztown U of Pennsylvania (PA)
Lafayette Coll (PA)
LaGrange Coll (GA)
Lake Erie Coll (OH)
Lake Forest Coll (IL)
Lakehead U (ON, Canada)
Lakeland Coll (WI)
Lamar U (TX)
Lambuth U (TN)
Lander U (SC)
Lane Coll (TN)
Langston U (OK)
La Roche Coll (PA)
La Salle U (PA)
La Sierra U (CA)
Lawrence Technological U (MI)
Lawrence U (WI)
Lebanon Valley Coll (PA)
Lee U (TN)
Lehigh U (PA)
Lehman Coll of the City U of NY (NY)
Le Moyne Coll (NY)
LeMoyne-Owen Coll (TN)
Lenoir-Rhyne Coll (NC)
LeTourneau U (TX)
Lewis & Clark Coll (OR)
Lewis-Clark State Coll (ID)
Lewis U (IL)
Limestone Coll (SC)
Lincoln Memorial U (TN)
Lincoln U (MO)
Lincoln U (PA)
Lindenwood U (MO)
Linfield Coll (OR)
Lock Haven U of Pennsylvania (PA)
Long Island U, Brooklyn Campus (NY)
Long Island U, C.W. Post Campus (NY)
Long Island U, Southampton Coll (NY)
Longwood Coll (VA)
Loras Coll (IA)
Louisiana Coll (LA)
Louisiana State U and A&M Coll (LA)
Louisiana State U in Shreveport (LA)
Louisiana Tech U (LA)
Lourdes Coll (OH)
Loyola Coll in Maryland (MD)
Loyola Marymount U (CA)
Loyola U Chicago (IL)
Loyola U New Orleans (LA)
Lubbock Christian U (TX)
Luther Coll (IA)
Lycoming Coll (PA)

Lynchburg Coll (VA)
Lyon Coll (AR)
Macalester Coll (MN)
MacMurray Coll (IL)
Madonna U (MI)
Maharishi U of Management (IA)
Malone Coll (OH)
Manchester Coll (IN)
Manhattan Coll (NY)
Manhattanville Coll (NY)
Mansfield U of Pennsylvania (PA)
Marian Coll (IN)
Marian Coll of Fond du Lac (WI)
Marietta Coll (OH)
Marist Coll (NY)
Marlboro Coll (VT)
Marquette U (WI)
Marshall U (WV)
Mars Hill Coll (NC)
Mary Baldwin Coll (VA)
Marygrove Coll (MI)
Marymount Coll (NY)
Maryville Coll (TN)
Maryville U of Saint Louis (MO)
Mary Washington Coll (VA)
Massachusetts Coll of Liberal Arts (MA)
Mass Coll of Pharmacy and Allied Health Sciences (MA)
Massachusetts Inst of Technology (MA)
Mayville State U (ND)
McKendree Coll (IL)
McMurry U (TX)
McNeese State U (LA)
McPherson Coll (KS)
Memorial U of Newfoundland (NF, Canada)
Mercer U (GA)
Mercyhurst Coll (PA)
Meredith Coll (NC)
Merrimack Coll (MA)
Mesa State Coll (CO)
Messiah Coll (PA)
Methodist Coll (NC)
Metropolitan State Coll of Denver (CO)
Miami U (OH)
Michigan State U (MI)
Michigan Technological U (MI)
MidAmerica Nazarene U (KS)
Middlebury Coll (VT)
Middle Tennessee State U (TN)
Midland Lutheran Coll (NE)
Midwestern State U (TX)
Millersville U of Pennsylvania (PA)
Milligan Coll (TN)
Millikin U (IL)
Millsaps Coll (MS)
Mills Coll (CA)
Minnesota State U, Mankato (MN)
Minnesota State U Moorhead (MN)
Minot State U (ND)
Mississippi Coll (MS)
Mississippi State U (MS)
Mississippi U for Women (MS)
Mississippi Valley State U (MS)
Missouri Baptist Coll (MO)
Missouri Southern State Coll (MO)
Missouri Western State Coll (MO)
Monmouth Coll (IL)
Monmouth U (NJ)
Montana State U–Billings (MT)
Montana State U–Bozeman (MT)
Montana Tech of The U of Montana (MT)
Moravian Coll (PA)
Morehead State U (KY)
Morehouse Coll (GA)
Morgan State U (MD)
Morningside Coll (IA)
Mount Allison U (NB, Canada)
Mount Holyoke Coll (MA)
Mount Marty Coll (SD)
Mount Mary Coll (WI)
Mount Saint Mary Coll (NY)
Mount St. Mary's Coll (CA)
Mount Saint Mary's Coll and Seminary (MD)
Mount Saint Vincent U (NS, Canada)
Mount Union Coll (OH)
Mount Vernon Nazarene Coll (OH)
Muhlenberg Coll (PA)
Murray State U (KY)
Muskingum Coll (OH)

Nazareth Coll of Rochester (NY)
Nebraska Wesleyan U (NE)
Newberry Coll (SC)
New Coll of the U of South Florida (FL)
New Jersey City U (NJ)
New Jersey Inst of Technology (NJ)
Newman U (KS)
New Mexico Highlands U (NM)
New Mexico Inst of Mining and Technology (NM)
New Mexico State U (NM)
New York Inst of Technology (NY)
New York U (NY)
Niagara U (NY)
Nicholls State U (LA)
Norfolk State U (VA)
North Carolina Ag and Tech State U (NC)
North Carolina Central U (NC)
North Carolina State U (NC)
North Carolina Wesleyan Coll (NC)
North Central Coll (IL)
North Dakota State U (ND)
Northeastern Illinois U (IL)
Northeastern State U (OK)
Northeastern U (MA)
Northern Arizona U (AZ)
Northern Illinois U (IL)
Northern Kentucky U (KY)
Northern Michigan U (MI)
Northern State U (SD)
North Georgia Coll & State U (GA)
Northland Coll (WI)
North Park U (IL)
Northwestern Coll (IA)
Northwestern Oklahoma State U (OK)
Northwestern State U of Louisiana (LA)
Northwestern U (IL)
Northwest Missouri State U (MO)
Northwest Nazarene U (ID)
Norwich U (VT)
Notre Dame Coll of Ohio (OH)
Oakland City U (IN)
Oakland U (MI)
Oberlin Coll (OH)
Occidental Coll (CA)
Oglethorpe U (GA)
Ohio Dominican Coll (OH)
Ohio Northern U (OH)
The Ohio State U (OH)
Ohio U (OH)
Ohio Wesleyan U (OH)
Okanagan U Coll (BC, Canada)
Oklahoma Baptist U (OK)
Oklahoma Christian U of Science and Arts (OK)
Oklahoma City U (OK)
Oklahoma Panhandle State U (OK)
Oklahoma State U (OK)
Old Dominion U (VA)
Olivet Nazarene U (IL)
Open Learning Agency (BC, Canada)
Oregon State U (OR)
Otterbein Coll (OH)
Ouachita Baptist U (AR)
Our Lady of the Lake U of San Antonio (TX)
Pace U, New York City Campus (NY)
Pace U, Pleasantville/Briarcliff Campus (NY)
Pacific Lutheran U (WA)
Pacific Union Coll (CA)
Pacific U (OR)
Paine Coll (GA)
Park U (MO)
Penn State U at Erie, The Behrend Coll (PA)
Penn State U Univ Park Campus (PA)
Pepperdine U, Malibu (CA)
Peru State Coll (NE)
Pfeiffer U (NC)
Philadelphia U (PA)
Philander Smith Coll (AR)
Piedmont Coll (GA)
Pikeville Coll (KY)
Pittsburg State U (KS)
Pitzer Coll (CA)
Plattsburgh State U of NY (NY)
Plymouth State Coll (NH)
Point Loma Nazarene U (CA)

Polytechnic U, Brooklyn Campus (NY)
Pomona Coll (CA)
Pontifical Catholic U of Puerto Rico (PR)
Portland State U (OR)
Prairie View A&M U (TX)
Presbyterian Coll (SC)
Princeton U (NJ)
Principia Coll (IL)
Providence Coll (RI)
Purchase Coll, State U of NY (NY)
Purdue U (IN)
Purdue U Calumet (IN)
Queens Coll of the City U of NY (NY)
Queen's U at Kingston (ON, Canada)
Quincy U (IL)
Quinnipiac U (CT)
Radford U (VA)
Ramapo Coll of New Jersey (NJ)
Randolph-Macon Coll (VA)
Randolph-Macon Woman's Coll (VA)
Reed Coll (OR)
Regents Coll (NY)
Regis Coll (MA)
Regis U (CO)
Rensselaer Polytechnic Inst (NY)
Rhodes Coll (TN)
Rice U (TX)
The Richard Stockton Coll of New Jersey (NJ)
Rider U (NJ)
Ripon Coll (WI)
Rivier Coll (NH)
Roanoke Coll (VA)
Roberts Wesleyan Coll (NY)
Rochester Inst of Technology (NY)
Rockford Coll (IL)
Rockhurst U (MO)
Rocky Mountain Coll (MT)
Roger Williams U (RI)
Rollins Coll (FL)
Rose-Hulman Inst of Technology (IN)
Rosemont Coll (PA)
Rowan U (NJ)
Russell Sage Coll (NY)
Rust Coll (MS)
Rutgers, State U of NJ, Camden Coll of Arts & Scis (NJ)
Rutgers, State U of NJ, Cook Coll (NJ)
Rutgers, State U of NJ, Douglass Coll (NJ)
Rutgers, State U of NJ, Livingston Coll (NJ)
Rutgers, State U of NJ, Newark Coll of Arts & Scis (NJ)
Rutgers, State U of NJ, Rutgers Coll (NJ)
Rutgers, State U of NJ, U Coll– Camden (NJ)
Rutgers, State U of NJ, U Coll– New Brunswick (NJ)
Ryerson Polytechnic U (ON, Canada)
Sacred Heart U (CT)
Saginaw Valley State U (MI)
St. Ambrose U (IA)
St. Andrews Presbyterian Coll (NC)
St. Anselm Coll (NH)
Saint Augustine's Coll (NC)
St. Bonaventure U (NY)
St. Cloud State U (MN)
St. Edward's U (TX)
Saint Francis Coll (PA)
St. Francis Xavier U (NS, Canada)
St. John Fisher Coll (NY)
Saint John's U (MN)
St. John's U (NY)
Saint Joseph Coll (CT)
Saint Joseph's Coll (IN)
St. Joseph's Coll, New York (NY)
Saint Joseph's U (PA)
St. Lawrence U (NY)
Saint Louis U (MO)
Saint Martin's Coll (WA)
Saint Mary Coll (KS)
Saint Mary's Coll (IN)
Saint Mary's Coll (MI)
Saint Mary's Coll of California (CA)
St. Mary's Coll of Maryland (MD)
Saint Mary's U (NS, Canada)
Saint Mary's U of Minnesota (MN)

St. Mary's U of San Antonio (TX)
Saint Michael's Coll (VT)
St. Norbert Coll (WI)
St. Olaf Coll (MN)
Saint Peter's Coll (NJ)
St. Thomas U (FL)
Saint Vincent Coll (PA)
Saint Xavier U (IL)
Salem Coll (NC)
Salem State Coll (MA)
Salisbury State U (MD)
Salve Regina U (RI)
Samford U (AL)
Sam Houston State U (TX)
San Diego State U (CA)
San Francisco State U (CA)
San Jose State U (CA)
Santa Clara U (CA)
Sarah Lawrence Coll (NY)
Savannah State U (GA)
Schreiner Coll (TX)
Scripps Coll (CA)
Seattle Pacific U (WA)
Seattle U (WA)
Seton Hall U (NJ)
Seton Hill Coll (PA)
Shawnee State U (OH)
Shaw U (NC)
Shenandoah U (VA)
Shepherd Coll (WV)
Shippensburg U of Pennsylvania (PA)
Shorter Coll (GA)
Siena Coll (NY)
Siena Heights U (MI)
Simmons Coll (MA)
Simon Fraser U (BC, Canada)
Simon's Rock Coll of Bard (MA)
Simpson Coll (IA)
Skidmore Coll (NY)
Slippery Rock U of Pennsylvania (PA)
Smith Coll (MA)
Sonoma State U (CA)
South Dakota School of Mines and Technology (SD)
South Dakota State U (SD)
Southeastern Louisiana U (LA)
Southeastern Oklahoma State U (OK)
Southeast Missouri State U (MO)
Southern Adventist U (TN)
Southern Arkansas U–Magnolia (AR)
Southern Illinois U Carbondale (IL)
Southern Illinois U Edwardsville (IL)
Southern Methodist U (TX)
Southern Oregon U (OR)
Southern Utah U (UT)
Southern Wesleyan U (SC)
Southwest Baptist U (MO)
Southwestern Adventist U (TX)
Southwestern Coll (KS)
Southwestern Oklahoma State U (OK)
Southwestern U (TX)
Southwest Missouri State U (MO)
Southwest State U (MN)
Southwest Texas State U (TX)
Spalding U (KY)
Spelman Coll (GA)
Spring Arbor Coll (MI)
Spring Hill Coll (AL)
Stanford U (CA)
State U of NY at Albany (NY)
State U of NY at Binghamton (NY)
State U of NY at Buffalo (NY)
State U of NY at New Paltz (NY)
State U of NY at Oswego (NY)
State U of NY at Stony Brook (NY)
State U of NY Coll at Brockport (NY)
State U of NY Coll at Buffalo (NY)
State U of NY Coll at Cortland (NY)
State U of NY Coll at Fredonia (NY)
State U of NY Coll at Geneseo (NY)
State U of NY Coll at Old Westbury (NY)
State U of NY Coll at Oneonta (NY)
State U of NY Coll at Potsdam (NY)
State U of NY Coll of Environ Sci and Forestry (NY)
State U of West Georgia (GA)

Majors Index
Chemistry–Chemistry Education

Stephen F. Austin State U (TX)
Stetson U (FL)
Stevens Inst of Technology (NJ)
Stillman Coll (AL)
Stonehill Coll (MA)
Suffolk U (MA)
Sul Ross State U (TX)
Susquehanna U (PA)
Swarthmore Coll (PA)
Sweet Briar Coll (VA)
Syracuse U (NY)
Tabor Coll (KS)
Talladega Coll (AL)
Taylor U (IN)
Temple U (PA)
Tennessee State U (TN)
Tennessee Technological U (TN)
Tennessee Wesleyan Coll (TN)
Texas A&M International U (TX)
Texas A&M U (TX)
Texas A&M U–Commerce (TX)
Texas A&M U–Kingsville (TX)
Texas Christian U (TX)
Texas Lutheran U (TX)
Texas Southern U (TX)
Texas Tech U (TX)
Texas Wesleyan U (TX)
Texas Woman's U (TX)
Thiel Coll (PA)
Thomas Edison State Coll (NJ)
Thomas More Coll (KY)
Tougaloo Coll (MS)
Touro Coll (NY)
Towson U (MD)
Transylvania U (KY)
Trent U (ON, Canada)
Trevecca Nazarene U (TN)
Trinity Christian Coll (IL)
Trinity Coll (CT)
Trinity U (TX)
Trinity Western U (BC, Canada)
Tri-State U (IN)
Troy State U (AL)
Truman State U (MO)
Tufts U (MA)
Tulane U (LA)
Tuskegee U (AL)
Union Coll (KY)
Union Coll (NE)
Union Coll (NY)
Union U (TN)
United States Air Force Academy (CO)
United States Military Academy (NY)
United States Naval Academy (MD)
Universidad Adventista de las Antillas (PR)
Universidad del Turabo (PR)
Université de Montréal (PQ, Canada)
Université de Sherbrooke (PQ, Canada)
U du Québec à Chicoutimi (PQ, Canada)
U du Québec à Trois-Rivières (PQ, Canada)
Université Laval (PQ, Canada)
U Coll of Cape Breton (NS, Canada)
U Coll of the Fraser Valley (BC, Canada)
The U of Akron (OH)
The U of Alabama (AL)
The U of Alabama at Birmingham (AL)
The U of Alabama in Huntsville (AL)
U of Alaska Fairbanks (AK)
U of Alberta (AB, Canada)
The U of Arizona (AZ)
U of Arkansas (AR)
U of Arkansas at Little Rock (AR)
U of Arkansas at Monticello (AR)
U of Arkansas at Pine Bluff (AR)
U of British Columbia (BC, Canada)
U of Calgary (AB, Canada)
U of Calif, Berkeley (CA)
U of Calif, Davis (CA)
U of Calif, Irvine (CA)
U of Calif, Los Angeles (CA)
U of Calif, Riverside (CA)
U of Calif, San Diego (CA)
U of Calif, Santa Barbara (CA)
U of Calif, Santa Cruz (CA)
U of Central Arkansas (AR)

U of Central Florida (FL)
U of Central Oklahoma (OK)
U of Charleston (WV)
U of Chicago (IL)
U of Cincinnati (OH)
U of Colorado at Boulder (CO)
U of Colorado at Colorado Springs (CO)
U of Colorado at Denver (CO)
U of Connecticut (CT)
U of Dallas (TX)
U of Dayton (OH)
U of Delaware (DE)
U of Denver (CO)
U of Detroit Mercy (MI)
U of Evansville (IN)
U of Florida (FL)
U of Georgia (GA)
U of Great Falls (MT)
U of Guelph (ON, Canada)
U of Hartford (CT)
U of Hawaii at Manoa (HI)
U of Houston (TX)
U of Houston–Clear Lake (TX)
U of Houston–Downtown (TX)
U of Idaho (ID)
U of Illinois at Chicago (IL)
U of Illinois at Springfield (IL)
U of Illinois at Urbana–Champaign (IL)
U of Indianapolis (IN)
The U of Iowa (IA)
U of Kansas (KS)
U of Kentucky (KY)
U of King's Coll (NS, Canada)
U of La Verne (CA)
The U of Lethbridge (AB, Canada)
U of Louisiana at Lafayette (LA)
U of Louisiana at Monroe (LA)
U of Louisville (KY)
U of Maine (ME)
U of Maine at Farmington (ME)
U of Manitoba (MB, Canada)
U of Mary Hardin-Baylor (TX)
U of Maryland, Baltimore County (MD)
U of Maryland, Coll Park (MD)
U of Massachusetts Amherst (MA)
U of Massachusetts Boston (MA)
U of Massachusetts Dartmouth (MA)
U of Massachusetts Lowell (MA)
The U of Memphis (TN)
U of Miami (FL)
U of Michigan (MI)
U of Michigan–Dearborn (MI)
U of Michigan–Flint (MI)
U of Minnesota, Duluth (MN)
U of Minnesota, Morris (MN)
U of Minnesota, Twin Cities Campus (MN)
U of Mississippi (MS)
U of Missouri–Columbia (MO)
U of Missouri–Kansas City (MO)
U of Missouri–Rolla (MO)
U of Missouri–St. Louis (MO)
U of Mobile (AL)
The U of Montana–Missoula (MT)
U of Montevallo (AL)
U of Nebraska at Kearney (NE)
U of Nebraska at Omaha (NE)
U of Nebraska–Lincoln (NE)
U of Nevada, Las Vegas (NV)
U of Nevada, Reno (NV)
U of New Brunswick, Fredericton (NB, Canada)
U of New Hampshire (NH)
U of New Haven (CT)
U of New Mexico (NM)
U of New Orleans (LA)
U of North Alabama (AL)
The U of North Carolina at Asheville (NC)
The U of North Carolina at Chapel Hill (NC)
The U of North Carolina at Charlotte (NC)
The U of North Carolina at Greensboro (NC)
The U of North Carolina at Pembroke (NC)
The U of North Carolina at Wilmington (NC)
U of North Dakota (ND)
U of Northern Colorado (CO)
U of Northern Iowa (IA)
U of North Florida (FL)

U of North Texas (TX)
U of Notre Dame (IN)
U of Oklahoma (OK)
U of Oregon (OR)
U of Pennsylvania (PA)
U of Pittsburgh (PA)
U of Pittsburgh at Bradford (PA)
U of Pittsburgh at Johnstown (PA)
U of Portland (OR)
U of Prince Edward Island (PE, Canada)
U of Puerto Rico, Humacao U Coll (PR)
U of Puerto Rico, Mayagüez Campus (PR)
U of Puerto Rico, Río Piedras (PR)
U of Puget Sound (WA)
U of Redlands (CA)
U of Regina (SK, Canada)
U of Rhode Island (RI)
U of Richmond (VA)
U of Rio Grande (OH)
U of Rochester (NY)
U of Saint Francis (IN)
U of St. Thomas (MN)
U of St. Thomas (TX)
U of San Diego (CA)
U of San Francisco (CA)
U of Science and Arts of Oklahoma (OK)
The U of Scranton (PA)
U of Sioux Falls (SD)
U of South Alabama (AL)
U of South Carolina (SC)
U of South Carolina Spartanburg (SC)
U of South Dakota (SD)
U of Southern California (CA)
U of Southern Colorado (CO)
U of Southern Indiana (IN)
U of Southern Maine (ME)
U of Southern Mississippi (MS)
U of South Florida (FL)
The U of Tampa (FL)
The U of Tennessee at Chattanooga (TN)
The U of Tennessee at Martin (TN)
The U of Tennessee Knoxville (TN)
The U of Texas at Arlington (TX)
The U of Texas at Austin (TX)
The U of Texas at Dallas (TX)
The U of Texas at San Antonio (TX)
The U of Texas at Tyler (TX)
The U of Texas–Pan American (TX)
U of the District of Columbia (DC)
U of the Ozarks (AR)
U of the Pacific (CA)
U of the Sacred Heart (PR)
U of the Sciences in Philadelphia (PA)
U of the South (TN)
U of the Virgin Islands (VI)
U of Toronto (ON, Canada)
U of Tulsa (OK)
U of Utah (UT)
U of Vermont (VT)
U of Victoria (BC, Canada)
U of Virginia (VA)
U of Virginia's Coll at Wise (VA)
U of Washington (WA)
U of Waterloo (ON, Canada)
The U of West Alabama (AL)
The U of Western Ontario (ON, Canada)
U of West Florida (FL)
U of Windsor (ON, Canada)
The U of Winnipeg (MB, Canada)
U of Wisconsin–Eau Claire (WI)
U of Wisconsin–Green Bay (WI)
U of Wisconsin–La Crosse (WI)
U of Wisconsin–Madison (WI)
U of Wisconsin–Milwaukee (WI)
U of Wisconsin–Parkside (WI)
U of Wisconsin–River Falls (WI)
U of Wisconsin–Stevens Point (WI)
U of Wisconsin–Superior (WI)
U of Wisconsin–Whitewater (WI)
U of Wyoming (WY)
Upper Iowa U (IA)
Urbana U (OH)
Ursinus Coll (PA)
Utah State U (UT)
Utica Coll of Syracuse U (NY)
Valdosta State U (GA)
Valley City State U (ND)
Valparaiso U (IN)

Vanderbilt U (TN)
Vanguard U of Southern California (CA)
Vassar Coll (NY)
Villa Julie Coll (MD)
Villanova U (PA)
Virginia Commonwealth U (VA)
Virginia Military Inst (VA)
Virginia Polytechnic Inst and State U (VA)
Virginia Union U (VA)
Virginia Wesleyan Coll (VA)
Voorhees Coll (SC)
Wabash Coll (IN)
Wagner Coll (NY)
Wake Forest U (NC)
Walla Walla Coll (WA)
Walsh U (OH)
Warren Wilson Coll (NC)
Wartburg Coll (IA)
Washington & Jefferson Coll (PA)
Washington and Lee U (VA)
Washington Coll (MD)
Washington State U (WA)
Washington U in St. Louis (MO)
Wayland Baptist U (TX)
Waynesburg Coll (PA)
Wayne State Coll (NE)
Wayne State U (MI)
Weber State U (UT)
Wellesley Coll (MA)
Wells Coll (NY)
Wesleyan Coll (GA)
Wesleyan U (CT)
West Chester U of Pennsylvania (PA)
Western Carolina U (NC)
Western Connecticut State U (CT)
Western Illinois U (IL)
Western Kentucky U (KY)
Western Maryland Coll (MD)
Western Michigan U (MI)
Western Montana Coll of The U of Montana (MT)
Western New England Coll (MA)
Western Oregon U (OR)
Western State Coll of Colorado (CO)
Western Washington U (WA)
West Liberty State Coll (WV)
Westminster Coll (MO)
Westminster Coll (PA)
Westminster Coll (UT)
Westmont Coll (CA)
West Texas A&M U (TX)
West Virginia State Coll (WV)
West Virginia U (WV)
West Virginia U Inst of Technology (WV)
West Virginia Wesleyan Coll (WV)
Wheaton Coll (IL)
Wheaton Coll (MA)
Wheeling Jesuit U (WV)
Whitman Coll (WA)
Whittier Coll (CA)
Whitworth Coll (WA)
Wichita State U (KS)
Widener U (PA)
Wilfrid Laurier U (ON, Canada)
Wilkes U (PA)
Willamette U (OR)
William Jewell Coll (MO)
Williams Coll (MA)
Wilmington Coll (OH)
Wilson Coll (PA)
Wingate U (NC)
Winona State U (MN)
Winston-Salem State U (NC)
Winthrop U (SC)
Wisconsin Lutheran Coll (WI)
Wittenberg U (OH)
Wofford Coll (SC)
Worcester Polytechnic Inst (MA)
Worcester State Coll (MA)
Wright State U (OH)
Xavier U (OH)
Xavier U of Louisiana (LA)
Yale U (CT)
Yeshiva U (NY)
York Coll of Pennsylvania (PA)
York Coll of the City U of New York (NY)
York U (ON, Canada)
Youngstown State U (OH)

CHEMISTRY EDUCATION
Abilene Christian U (TX)
Adams State Coll (CO)
Alvernia Coll (PA)
Appalachian State U (NC)
Arkansas State U (AR)
Arkansas Tech U (AR)
Baylor U (TX)
Berry Coll (GA)
Bethany Coll (KS)
Bethel Coll (IN)
Bethune-Cookman Coll (FL)
Blue Mountain Coll (MS)
Boston U (MA)
Bowling Green State U (OH)
Bridgewater Coll (VA)
Brigham Young U (UT)
Cabrini Coll (PA)
Canisius Coll (NY)
The Catholic U of America (DC)
Central Missouri State U (MO)
Christian Brothers U (TN)
The Coll of New Jersey (NJ)
Coll of St. Catherine (MN)
Coll of the Ozarks (MO)
Colorado State U (CO)
Concordia Coll (MN)
Concordia U (NE)
Delta State U (MS)
Duquesne U (PA)
Eastern Michigan U (MI)
East Texas Baptist U (TX)
Elmhurst Coll (IL)
Elmira Coll (NY)
Florida Inst of Technology (FL)
Framingham State Coll (MA)
George Fox U (OR)
Greenville Coll (IL)
Gustavus Adolphus Coll (MN)
Hardin-Simmons U (TX)
Hastings Coll (NE)
Huntingdon Coll (AL)
Indiana U Bloomington (IN)
Indiana U Northwest (IN)
Indiana U–Purdue U Fort Wayne (IN)
Indiana U South Bend (IN)
Ithaca Coll (NY)
Juniata Coll (PA)
Kent State U (OH)
King Coll (TN)
La Roche Coll (PA)
Long Island U, C.W. Post Campus (NY)
Luther Coll (IA)
Manhattanville Coll (NY)
Mansfield U of Pennsylvania (PA)
Marymount Coll (NY)
Maryville Coll (TN)
Mayville State U (ND)
McGill U (PQ, Canada)
Messiah Coll (PA)
MidAmerica Nazarene U (KS)
Mount Marty Coll (SD)
Nazareth Coll of Rochester (NY)
New York Inst of Technology (NY)
New York U (NY)
Niagara U (NY)
North Carolina Central U (NC)
North Carolina State U (NC)
North Dakota State U (ND)
Northwest Nazarene U (ID)
Ohio U (OH)
Oklahoma Baptist U (OK)
Rivier Coll (NH)
Rocky Mountain Coll (MT)
St. Ambrose U (IA)
St. John's U (NY)
Salve Regina U (RI)
Seton Hill Coll (PA)
Southern Arkansas U–Magnolia (AR)
Southwest Missouri State U (MO)
Southwest State U (MN)
State U of NY Coll of Environ Sci and Forestry (NY)
Tennessee Wesleyan Coll (TN)
Trevecca Nazarene U (TN)
Trinity Christian Coll (IL)
Union Coll (KY)
The U of Arizona (AZ)
U of Calif, San Diego (CA)
U of Central Arkansas (AR)
U of Delaware (DE)
U of Illinois at Chicago (IL)
U of Illinois at Urbana–Champaign (IL)

Majors Index
Chemistry Education–Civil Engineering

The U of Iowa (IA)
U of Nebraska–Lincoln (NE)
The U of North Carolina at Charlotte (NC)
U of North Texas (TX)
The U of Tennessee at Martin (TN)
U of Waterloo (ON, Canada)
U of Wisconsin–River Falls (WI)
U of Wisconsin–Superior (WI)
Washington U in St. Louis (MO)
Weber State U (UT)
Wheeling Jesuit U (WV)
York U (ON, Canada)
Youngstown State U (OH)

CHILD CARE AND GUIDANCE
Central Michigan U (MI)
Kent State U (OH)
U Coll of the Fraser Valley (BC, Canada)

CHILD CARE/DEVELOPMENT
Albertus Magnus Coll (CT)
Albright Coll (PA)
Ashland U (OH)
Auburn U (AL)
Becker Coll (MA)
Berea Coll (KY)
Bethel Coll (MN)
Bluffton Coll (OH)
Bowling Green State U (OH)
Briercrest Bible Coll (SK, Canada)
California State U, Dominguez Hills (CA)
California State U, Fresno (CA)
California State U, Hayward (CA)
California State U, Long Beach (CA)
California State U, Los Angeles (CA)
California State U, Northridge (CA)
Cameron U (OK)
Carleton U (ON, Canada)
Carson-Newman Coll (TN)
Coll of the Ozarks (MO)
Concordia Coll (MN)
Cornell U (NY)
Crown Coll (MN)
East Carolina U (NC)
Eastern Kentucky U (KY)
East Tennessee State U (TN)
Florida State U (FL)
Freed-Hardeman U (TN)
Friends U (KS)
Gallaudet U (DC)
Goddard Coll (VT)
Goshen Coll (IN)
Hampshire Coll (MA)
Hampton U (VA)
Harding U (AR)
Hope International U (CA)
Humboldt State U (CA)
Indiana State U (IN)
Indiana U Bloomington (IN)
Kansas State U (KS)
Lasell Coll (MA)
Lesley Coll (MA)
Lincoln Christian Coll (IL)
Long Island U, Southampton Coll, Friends World Program (NY)
Louisiana Tech U (LA)
Madonna U (MI)
McNeese State U (LA)
Medaille Coll (NY)
Meredith Coll (NC)
Miami U (OH)
Minnesota State U, Mankato (MN)
Missouri Baptist Coll (MO)
Mitchell Coll (CT)
Montreat Coll (NC)
Mount Ida Coll (MA)
Mount Saint Vincent U (NS, Canada)
Norfolk State U (VA)
North Carolina Ag and Tech State U (NC)
North Dakota State U (ND)
Northern Michigan U (MI)
Northwestern Coll (MN)
Northwest Missouri State U (MO)
The Ohio State U (OH)
Ohio U (OH)
Oklahoma Baptist U (OK)
Oklahoma Christian U of Science and Arts (OK)
Oklahoma State U (OK)
Olivet Nazarene U (IL)

Oregon State U (OR)
Pacific Oaks Coll (CA)
Park U (MO)
Pittsburg State U (KS)
Plattsburgh State U of NY (NY)
Point Loma Nazarene U (CA)
Portland State U (OR)
Quinnipiac U (CT)
Reformed Bible Coll (MI)
Ryerson Polytechnic U (ON, Canada)
St. Cloud State U (MN)
Saint Joseph Coll (CT)
San Jose State U (CA)
Seton Hill Coll (PA)
South Dakota State U (SD)
Southern Vermont Coll (VT)
State U of NY Coll at Oneonta (NY)
Stephens Coll (MO)
Syracuse U (NY)
Tennessee Technological U (TN)
Texas A&M U–Kingsville (TX)
Texas Southern U (TX)
Texas Tech U (TX)
Texas Woman's U (TX)
Tufts U (MA)
The U of Akron (OH)
U of Alberta (AB, Canada)
U of Arkansas (AR)
U of British Columbia (BC, Canada)
U of Central Oklahoma (OK)
U of Delaware (DE)
U of Guelph (ON, Canada)
U of Idaho (ID)
U of Illinois at Springfield (IL)
U of La Verne (CA)
U of Maine (ME)
U of Manitoba (MB, Canada)
U of Michigan–Dearborn (MI)
U of Missouri–St. Louis (MO)
U of New England (ME)
U of New Hampshire (NH)
The U of North Carolina at Chapel Hill (NC)
U of Pittsburgh (PA)
U of Pittsburgh at Bradford (PA)
U of Puerto Rico, Río Piedras (PR)
The U of Tennessee at Martin (TN)
The U of Texas at Arlington (TX)
U of Utah (UT)
U of Vermont (VT)
U of Victoria (BC, Canada)
U of Wisconsin–Madison (WI)
Ursuline Coll (OH)
Utah State U (UT)
Villa Julie Coll (MD)
Weber State U (UT)
Wheelock Coll (MA)
Youngstown State U (OH)

CHILD GUIDANCE
California State U, Stanislaus (CA)
Coll of the Ozarks (MO)
Oklahoma Baptist U (OK)
Reformed Bible Coll (MI)
Rochester Coll (MI)
Siena Heights U (MI)
Thomas Edison State Coll (NJ)
Tougaloo Coll (MS)
U of North Texas (TX)

CHINESE
Arizona State U (AZ)
Bard Coll (NY)
Bates Coll (ME)
Bennington Coll (VT)
Brigham Young U (UT)
Brown U (RI)
Claremont McKenna Coll (CA)
Colgate U (NY)
Connecticut Coll (CT)
Cornell U (NY)
Georgetown U (DC)
The George Washington U (DC)
Grinnell Coll (IA)
Harvard U (MA)
Hobart and William Smith Colls (NY)
Hunter Coll of the City U of NY (NY)
Indiana U Bloomington (IN)
Long Island U, Southampton Coll, Friends World Program (NY)
Middlebury Coll (VT)
The Ohio State U (OH)

Pacific Lutheran U (WA)
Pacific U (OR)
Pomona Coll (CA)
Portland State U (OR)
Queens Coll of the City U of NY (NY)
Reed Coll (OR)
Rutgers, State U of NJ, Douglass Coll (NJ)
Rutgers, State U of NJ, Livingston Coll (NJ)
Rutgers, State U of NJ, Rutgers Coll (NJ)
Rutgers, State U of NJ, U Coll–New Brunswick (NJ)
San Francisco State U (CA)
San Jose State U (CA)
Scripps Coll (CA)
Stanford U (CA)
State U of NY at Albany (NY)
Swarthmore Coll (PA)
Trinity U (TX)
Tufts U (MA)
United States Military Academy (NY)
U of Alberta (AB, Canada)
U of British Columbia (BC, Canada)
U of Calif, Berkeley (CA)
U of Calif, Davis (CA)
U of Calif, Los Angeles (CA)
U of Calif, Riverside (CA)
U of Calif, San Diego (CA)
U of Calif, Santa Barbara (CA)
U of Calif, Santa Cruz (CA)
U of Chicago (IL)
U of Colorado at Boulder (CO)
U of Hawaii at Manoa (HI)
The U of Iowa (IA)
U of Kansas (KS)
U of Maryland, Coll Park (MD)
U of Massachusetts Amherst (MA)
U of Michigan (MI)
U of Minnesota, Twin Cities Campus (MN)
The U of Montana–Missoula (MT)
U of Oregon (OR)
U of Pittsburgh (PA)
U of Regina (SK, Canada)
U of Southern California (CA)
U of Toronto (ON, Canada)
U of Utah (UT)
U of Victoria (BC, Canada)
U of Washington (WA)
U of Wisconsin–Madison (WI)
Washington U in St. Louis (MO)
Wellesley Coll (MA)
Williams Coll (MA)

CITY/COMMUNITY/REGIONAL PLANNING
Alabama A&M U (AL)
Appalachian State U (NC)
Arizona State U (AZ)
Ball State U (IN)
Bard Coll (NY)
Bridgewater State Coll (MA)
Bryn Mawr Coll (PA)
California Polytechnic State U, San Luis Obispo (CA)
California State Polytechnic U, Pomona (CA)
California State U, Chico (CA)
Carleton U (ON, Canada)
Clemson U (SC)
Cornell U (NY)
DePaul U (IL)
East Carolina U (NC)
Eastern Kentucky U (KY)
Eastern Michigan U (MI)
Eastern Oregon U (OR)
Eastern Washington U (WA)
Florida Atlantic U (FL)
Framingham State Coll (MA)
George Mason U (VA)
Hampshire Coll (MA)
Harvard U (MA)
Indiana State U (IN)
Indiana U Bloomington (IN)
Indiana U of Pennsylvania (PA)
Iowa State U of Science and Technology (IA)
Long Island U, Southampton Coll, Friends World Program (NY)
Mansfield U of Pennsylvania (PA)
Massachusetts Inst of Technology (MA)

Miami U (OH)
Michigan State U (MI)
Minnesota State U, Mankato (MN)
New Mexico State U (NM)
New York U (NY)
Northern Arizona U (AZ)
Northern Michigan U (MI)
Nova Scotia Coll of Art and Design (NS, Canada)
The Ohio State U (OH)
Plymouth State Coll (NH)
Portland State U (OR)
Pratt Inst (NY)
Ryerson Polytechnic U (ON, Canada)
St. Cloud State U (MN)
Salem State Coll (MA)
San Diego State U (CA)
Southwest Missouri State U (MO)
Southwest Texas State U (TX)
State U of NY at New Paltz (NY)
State U of NY Coll at Buffalo (NY)
State U of NY Coll of Environ Sci and Forestry (NY)
Texas Southern U (TX)
The U of Alabama (AL)
U of Alaska Fairbanks (AK)
The U of Arizona (AZ)
U of Cincinnati (OH)
U of Illinois at Urbana–Champaign (IL)
U of Michigan–Flint (MI)
The U of Montana–Missoula (MT)
U of Nevada, Las Vegas (NV)
U of New Hampshire (NH)
U of Oregon (OR)
U of Southern California (CA)
U of Southern Mississippi (MS)
U of the District of Columbia (DC)
U of Virginia (VA)
U of Washington (WA)
U of Waterloo (ON, Canada)
The U of Western Ontario (ON, Canada)
U of Windsor (ON, Canada)
Virginia Commonwealth U (VA)
Western Washington U (WA)
Westfield State Coll (MA)
West Virginia U Inst of Technology (WV)
Winona State U (MN)
Worcester Polytechnic Inst (MA)
Wright State U (OH)

CIVIL ENGINEERING
Alabama A&M U (AL)
Arizona State U (AZ)
Auburn U (AL)
Bethel Coll (IN)
Boise State U (ID)
Bradley U (IL)
Brigham Young U (UT)
Brown U (RI)
Bucknell U (PA)
California Inst of Technology (CA)
California Polytechnic State U, San Luis Obispo (CA)
California State Polytechnic U, Pomona (CA)
California State U, Chico (CA)
California State U, Fresno (CA)
California State U, Fullerton (CA)
California State U, Long Beach (CA)
California State U, Los Angeles (CA)
California State U, Northridge (CA)
Calvin Coll (MI)
Carleton U (ON, Canada)
Carnegie Mellon U (PA)
Carroll Coll (MT)
Case Western Reserve U (OH)
The Catholic U of America (DC)
Christian Brothers U (TN)
Citadel, The Military Coll of South Carolina (SC)
City Coll of the City U of NY (NY)
Clarkson U (NY)
Clemson U (SC)
Cleveland State U (OH)
The Coll of Southeastern Europe, The American U of Athens (Greece)
Colorado School of Mines (CO)
Colorado State U (CO)
Columbia U, School of Engineering & Applied Sci (NY)

Concordia U (PQ, Canada)
Cooper Union for the Advancement of Science & Art (NY)
Cornell U (NY)
Dalhousie U (NS, Canada)
Delaware State U (DE)
Drexel U (PA)
Duke U (NC)
Embry-Riddle Aeronautical U (FL)
Florida A&M U (FL)
Florida Inst of Technology (FL)
Florida International U (FL)
Florida State U (FL)
Gallaudet U (DC)
The George Washington U (DC)
Georgia Inst of Technology (GA)
Gonzaga U (WA)
Harvard U (MA)
Howard U (DC)
Illinois Inst of Technology (IL)
Indiana Inst of Technology (IN)
Insto Tecno Estudios Sups Monterrey (Mexico)
Iowa State U of Science and Technology (IA)
Johns Hopkins U (MD)
Kansas State U (KS)
Lafayette Coll (PA)
Lakehead U (ON, Canada)
Lamar U (TX)
Lawrence Technological U (MI)
Lehigh U (PA)
Louisiana State U and A&M Coll (LA)
Louisiana Tech U (LA)
Loyola Marymount U (CA)
Manhattan Coll (NY)
Marquette U (WI)
Massachusetts Inst of Technology (MA)
Memorial U of Newfoundland (NF, Canada)
Merrimack Coll (MA)
Messiah Coll (PA)
Michigan State U (MI)
Michigan Technological U (MI)
Mississippi State U (MS)
Montana State U–Bozeman (MT)
Montana Tech of The U of Montana (MT)
Morgan State U (MD)
New Jersey Inst of Technology (NJ)
New Mexico State U (NM)
New York U (NY)
North Carolina Ag and Tech State U (NC)
North Carolina State U (NC)
North Dakota State U (ND)
Northeastern U (MA)
Northern Arizona U (AZ)
Northwestern U (IL)
Norwich U (VT)
Ohio Northern U (OH)
The Ohio State U (OH)
Ohio U (OH)
Oklahoma State U (OK)
Old Dominion U (VA)
Oregon Inst of Technology (OR)
Oregon State U (OR)
Penn State U Univ Park Campus (PA)
Polytechnic U, Brooklyn Campus (NY)
Polytechnic U, Farmingdale Campus (NY)
Polytechnic U of Puerto Rico (PR)
Portland State U (OR)
Prairie View A&M U (TX)
Princeton U (NJ)
Purdue U (IN)
Queen's U at Kingston (ON, Canada)
Rensselaer Polytechnic Inst (NY)
Rice U (TX)
Rose-Hulman Inst of Technology (IN)
Rowan U (NJ)
Rutgers, State U of NJ, Coll of Engineering (NJ)
Ryerson Polytechnic U (ON, Canada)
Saint Augustine's Coll (NC)
Saint Martin's Coll (WA)
San Diego State U (CA)
San Francisco State U (CA)
San Jose State U (CA)
Santa Clara U (CA)

Majors Index
Civil Engineering–Classics

Savannah State U (GA)
Seattle U (WA)
South Dakota School of Mines and Technology (SD)
South Dakota State U (SD)
Southern Illinois U Carbondale (IL)
Southern Illinois U Edwardsville (IL)
Stanford U (CA)
State U of NY at Buffalo (NY)
Stevens Inst of Technology (NJ)
Syracuse U (NY)
Temple U (PA)
Tennessee State U (TN)
Tennessee Technological U (TN)
Texas A&M U (TX)
Texas A&M U–Kingsville (TX)
Texas Tech U (TX)
Tri-State U (IN)
Tufts U (MA)
Tulane U (LA)
Union Coll (NY)
United States Air Force Academy (CO)
United States Coast Guard Academy (CT)
United States Military Academy (NY)
Université de Sherbrooke (PQ, Canada)
Université Laval (PQ, Canada)
The U of Akron (OH)
The U of Alabama (AL)
The U of Alabama at Birmingham (AL)
The U of Alabama in Huntsville (AL)
U of Alaska Fairbanks (AK)
U of Alberta (AB, Canada)
The U of Arizona (AZ)
U of Arkansas (AR)
U of British Columbia (BC, Canada)
U of Calgary (AB, Canada)
U of Calif, Berkeley (CA)
U of Calif, Davis (CA)
U of Calif, Irvine (CA)
U of Calif, Los Angeles (CA)
U of Central Florida (FL)
U of Cincinnati (OH)
U of Colorado at Boulder (CO)
U of Colorado at Denver (CO)
U of Connecticut (CT)
U of Dayton (OH)
U of Delaware (DE)
U of Detroit Mercy (MI)
U of Evansville (IN)
U of Florida (FL)
U of Hartford (CT)
U of Hawaii at Manoa (HI)
U of Houston (TX)
U of Idaho (ID)
U of Illinois at Chicago (IL)
U of Illinois at Urbana–Champaign (IL)
The U of Iowa (IA)
U of Kansas (KS)
U of Kentucky (KY)
U of Louisiana at Lafayette (LA)
U of Louisville (KY)
U of Maine (ME)
U of Manitoba (MB, Canada)
U of Maryland, Coll Park (MD)
U of Massachusetts Amherst (MA)
U of Massachusetts Dartmouth (MA)
U of Massachusetts Lowell (MA)
The U of Memphis (TN)
U of Miami (FL)
U of Michigan (MI)
U of Minnesota, Twin Cities Campus (MN)
U of Mississippi (MS)
U of Missouri–Columbia (MO)
U of Missouri–Kansas City (MO)
U of Missouri–Rolla (MO)
U of Missouri–St. Louis (MO)
U of Nebraska at Omaha (NE)
U of Nebraska–Lincoln (NE)
U of Nevada, Las Vegas (NV)
U of Nevada, Reno (NV)
U of New Brunswick, Fredericton (NB, Canada)
U of New Brunswick, Saint John (NB, Canada)
U of New Hampshire (NH)
U of New Haven (CT)
U of New Mexico (NM)

U of New Orleans (LA)
The U of North Carolina at Charlotte (NC)
U of North Dakota (ND)
U of Notre Dame (IN)
U of Oklahoma (OK)
U of Pennsylvania (PA)
U of Pittsburgh (PA)
U of Pittsburgh at Bradford (PA)
U of Portland (OR)
U of Puerto Rico, Mayagüez Campus (PR)
U of Regina (SK, Canada)
U of Rhode Island (RI)
U of South Alabama (AL)
U of South Carolina (SC)
U of Southern California (CA)
U of South Florida (FL)
The U of Tennessee at Chattanooga (TN)
The U of Tennessee Knoxville (TN)
The U of Texas at Arlington (TX)
The U of Texas at Austin (TX)
The U of Texas at San Antonio (TX)
U of the District of Columbia (DC)
U of the Pacific (CA)
U of Toronto (ON, Canada)
U of Utah (UT)
U of Vermont (VT)
U of Virginia (VA)
U of Washington (WA)
U of Waterloo (ON, Canada)
The U of Western Ontario (ON, Canada)
U of Windsor (ON, Canada)
U of Wisconsin–Madison (WI)
U of Wisconsin–Milwaukee (WI)
U of Wisconsin–Platteville (WI)
U of Wyoming (WY)
Utah State U (UT)
Valparaiso U (IN)
Vanderbilt U (TN)
Villanova U (PA)
Virginia Military Inst (VA)
Virginia Polytechnic Inst and State U (VA)
Walla Walla Coll (WA)
Washington State U (WA)
Washington U in St. Louis (MO)
Wayne State U (MI)
West Virginia U (WV)
West Virginia U Inst of Technology (WV)
Widener U (PA)
Worcester Polytechnic Inst (MA)
Youngstown State U (OH)

CIVIL ENGINEERING TECHNOLOGY
Alabama A&M U (AL)
Bluefield State Coll (WV)
Central Connecticut State U (CT)
Delaware State U (DE)
Fairleigh Dickinson U, Teaneck-Hackensack Campus (NJ)
Fairmont State Coll (WV)
Florida A&M U (FL)
Fontbonne Coll (MO)
Francis Marion U (SC)
Georgia Southern U (GA)
Lakehead U (ON, Canada)
Louisiana Tech U (LA)
Metropolitan State Coll of Denver (CO)
Missouri Western State Coll (MO)
Montana State U–Northern (MT)
Murray State U (KY)
New Jersey Inst of Technology (NJ)
Point Park Coll (PA)
Purdue U Calumet (IN)
Rochester Inst of Technology (NY)
Savannah State U (GA)
Southern Polytechnic State U (GA)
State U of NY Inst of Tech at Utica/Rome (NY)
Temple U (PA)
Texas Southern U (TX)
Thomas Edison State Coll (NJ)
U of Cincinnati (OH)
U of Houston (TX)
U of Houston–Downtown (TX)
U of Massachusetts Lowell (MA)
The U of North Carolina at Charlotte (NC)
U of North Texas (TX)
U of Pittsburgh at Johnstown (PA)

U of Southern Colorado (CO)
Washington U in St. Louis (MO)
Wentworth Inst of Technology (MA)
Western Kentucky U (KY)
West Virginia U Inst of Technology (WV)
Youngstown State U (OH)

CIVIL/STRUCTURAL DRAFTING
U of Advancing Computer Technology (AZ)

CLASSICS
Acadia U (NS, Canada)
Agnes Scott Coll (GA)
Albertus Magnus Coll (CT)
Amherst Coll (MA)
Asbury Coll (KY)
Assumption Coll (MA)
Augustana Coll (IL)
Austin Coll (TX)
Ball State U (IN)
Bard Coll (NY)
Barnard Coll (NY)
Bates Coll (ME)
Baylor U (TX)
Beloit Coll (WI)
Berea Coll (KY)
Bishop's U (PQ, Canada)
Boston Coll (MA)
Boston U (MA)
Bowdoin Coll (ME)
Bowling Green State U (OH)
Brandeis U (MA)
Brigham Young U (UT)
Brock U (ON, Canada)
Brooklyn Coll of the City U of NY (NY)
Brown U (RI)
Bryn Mawr Coll (PA)
Bucknell U (PA)
California State U, Northridge (CA)
Calvin Coll (MI)
Carleton Coll (MN)
Carleton U (ON, Canada)
Case Western Reserve U (OH)
The Catholic U of America (DC)
Centre Coll (KY)
Christendom Coll (VA)
Claremont McKenna Coll (CA)
Clark U (MA)
Coe Coll (IA)
Colby Coll (ME)
Colgate U (NY)
Coll of Charleston (SC)
The Coll of New Rochelle (NY)
Coll of Notre Dame of Maryland (MD)
Coll of Saint Benedict (MN)
Coll of the Holy Cross (MA)
The Coll of William and Mary (VA)
The Coll of Wooster (OH)
The Colorado Coll (CO)
Columbia Coll (NY)
Columbia U, School of General Studies (NY)
Concordia Coll (MN)
Concordia U (PQ, Canada)
Connecticut Coll (CT)
Cornell Coll (IA)
Cornell U (NY)
Creighton U (NE)
Dalhousie U (NS, Canada)
Dartmouth Coll (NH)
Davidson Coll (NC)
Denison U (OH)
DePauw U (IN)
Dickinson Coll (PA)
Drew U (NJ)
Duke U (NC)
Duquesne U (PA)
Earlham Coll (IN)
Elmira Coll (NY)
Emory U (GA)
The Evergreen State Coll (WA)
Florida State U (FL)
Fordham U (NY)
Franciscan U of Steubenville (OH)
Franklin and Marshall Coll (PA)
George Mason U (VA)
Georgetown U (DC)
The George Washington U (DC)
Georgia State U (GA)
Gettysburg Coll (PA)
Grinnell Coll (IA)
Gustavus Adolphus Coll (MN)
Hamilton Coll (NY)

Hampden-Sydney Coll (VA)
Hanover Coll (IN)
Harvard U (MA)
Haverford Coll (PA)
Hellenic Coll (MA)
Hillsdale Coll (MI)
Hiram Coll (OH)
Hobart and William Smith Colls (NY)
Hofstra U (NY)
Hollins U (VA)
Hope Coll (MI)
Howard U (DC)
Hunter Coll of the City U of NY (NY)
Indiana U Bloomington (IN)
John Carroll U (OH)
Johns Hopkins U (MD)
Kalamazoo Coll (MI)
Kent State U (OH)
Kenyon Coll (OH)
Knox Coll (IL)
La Salle U (PA)
Lawrence U (WI)
Lehigh U (PA)
Lehman Coll of the City U of NY (NY)
Lenoir-Rhyne Coll (NC)
Loras Coll (IA)
Loyola Coll in Maryland (MD)
Loyola Marymount U (CA)
Loyola U Chicago (IL)
Loyola U New Orleans (LA)
Luther Coll (IA)
Macalester Coll (MN)
Manhattanville Coll (NY)
Marlboro Coll (VT)
Marquette U (WI)
Mary Washington Coll (VA)
McGill U (PQ, Canada)
Memorial U of Newfoundland (NF, Canada)
Miami U (OH)
Middlebury Coll (VT)
Millsaps Coll (MS)
Monmouth Coll (IL)
Mount Allison U (NB, Canada)
Mount Holyoke Coll (MA)
Muhlenberg Coll (PA)
New Coll of the U of South Florida (FL)
New York U (NY)
Nipissing U (ON, Canada)
North Central Coll (IL)
Northwestern U (IL)
Oberlin Coll (OH)
The Ohio State U (OH)
Ohio U (OH)
Ohio Wesleyan U (OH)
Pacific Lutheran U (WA)
Penn State U Univ Park Campus (PA)
Pitzer Coll (CA)
Pomona Coll (CA)
Princeton U (NJ)
Queens Coll of the City U of NY (NY)
Queen's U at Kingston (ON, Canada)
Randolph-Macon Coll (VA)
Randolph-Macon Woman's Coll (VA)
Reed Coll (OR)
Regis Coll (MA)
Rhodes Coll (TN)
Rice U (TX)
Rockford Coll (IL)
Rollins Coll (FL)
Rutgers, State U of NJ, Douglass Coll (NJ)
Rutgers, State U of NJ, Livingston Coll (NJ)
Rutgers, State U of NJ, Rutgers Coll (NJ)
Rutgers, State U of NJ, U Coll–New Brunswick (NJ)
Saint Anselm Coll (NH)
St. Bonaventure U (NY)
St. Francis Xavier U (NS, Canada)
St. John's Coll (NM)
Saint John's U (MN)
Saint Louis U (MO)
Saint Mary's U (NS, Canada)
Saint Michael's Coll (VT)
St. Olaf Coll (MN)
Saint Peter's Coll (NJ)

Samford U (AL)
San Diego State U (CA)
San Francisco State U (CA)
Santa Clara U (CA)
Sarah Lawrence Coll (NY)
Scripps Coll (CA)
Seattle Pacific U (WA)
Seton Hall U (NJ)
Siena Coll (NY)
Skidmore Coll (NY)
Smith Coll (MA)
Southern Illinois U Carbondale (IL)
Stanford U (CA)
State U of NY at Albany (NY)
State U of NY at Binghamton (NY)
State U of NY at Buffalo (NY)
Swarthmore Coll (PA)
Sweet Briar Coll (VA)
Syracuse U (NY)
Temple U (PA)
Trent U (ON, Canada)
Trinity Coll (CT)
Trinity U (TX)
Truman State U (MO)
Tufts U (MA)
Tulane U (LA)
Union Coll (NY)
Université de Montréal (PQ, Canada)
The U of Akron (OH)
The U of Alabama (AL)
U of Alberta (AB, Canada)
The U of Arizona (AZ)
U of Arkansas (AR)
U of British Columbia (BC, Canada)
U of Calgary (AB, Canada)
U of Calif, Berkeley (CA)
U of Calif, Irvine (CA)
U of Calif, Los Angeles (CA)
U of Calif, Riverside (CA)
U of Calif, San Diego (CA)
U of Calif, Santa Barbara (CA)
U of Chicago (IL)
U of Cincinnati (OH)
U of Colorado at Boulder (CO)
U of Connecticut (CT)
U of Dallas (TX)
U of Delaware (DE)
U of Evansville (IN)
U of Florida (FL)
U of Georgia (GA)
U of Guelph (ON, Canada)
U of Hawaii at Manoa (HI)
U of Houston (TX)
U of Idaho (ID)
U of Illinois at Chicago (IL)
U of Illinois at Urbana–Champaign (IL)
The U of Iowa (IA)
U of Kansas (KS)
U of Kentucky (KY)
U of King's Coll (NS, Canada)
U of Maine (ME)
U of Manitoba (MB, Canada)
U of Maryland, Baltimore County (MD)
U of Maryland, Coll Park (MD)
U of Massachusetts Amherst (MA)
U of Massachusetts Boston (MA)
U of Michigan (MI)
U of Mississippi (MS)
U of Missouri–Columbia (MO)
The U of Montana–Missoula (MT)
U of Nebraska–Lincoln (NE)
U of New Brunswick, Fredericton (NB, Canada)
U of New Hampshire (NH)
U of New Mexico (NM)
The U of North Carolina at Asheville (NC)
The U of North Carolina at Chapel Hill (NC)
The U of North Carolina at Greensboro (NC)
U of Notre Dame (IN)
U of Oklahoma (OK)
U of Oregon (OR)
U of Pennsylvania (PA)
U of Pittsburgh (PA)
U of Puget Sound (WA)
U of Regina (SK, Canada)
U of Rhode Island (RI)
U of Richmond (VA)
U of Rochester (NY)
U of St. Thomas (MN)
U of South Carolina (SC)

Majors Index
Classics–Communications

U of South Dakota (SD)
U of Southern California (CA)
U of Southern Maine (ME)
U of South Florida (FL)
The U of Tennessee Knoxville (TN)
The U of Texas at Arlington (TX)
The U of Texas at Austin (TX)
U of the Pacific (CA)
U of the South (TN)
U of Toronto (ON, Canada)
U of Utah (UT)
U of Vermont (VT)
U of Victoria (BC, Canada)
U of Virginia (VA)
U of Washington (WA)
U of Waterloo (ON, Canada)
The U of Western Ontario (ON, Canada)
U of Windsor (ON, Canada)
The U of Winnipeg (MB, Canada)
U of Wisconsin–Madison (WI)
U of Wisconsin–Milwaukee (WI)
Ursinus Coll (PA)
Valparaiso U (IN)
Vanderbilt U (TN)
Vassar Coll (NY)
Villanova U (PA)
Wabash Coll (IN)
Wake Forest U (NC)
Washington and Lee U (VA)
Washington State U (WA)
Washington U in St. Louis (MO)
Wayne State U (MI)
Wellesley Coll (MA)
Wesleyan U (CT)
Western Washington U (WA)
Westminster Coll (MO)
Westminster Coll (PA)
Wheaton Coll (MA)
Whitman Coll (WA)
Wilfrid Laurier U (ON, Canada)
Willamette U (OR)
Williams Coll (MA)
Wright State U (OH)
Xavier U (OH)
Yale U (CT)
Yeshiva U (NY)
York U (ON, Canada)

CLINICAL AND MEDICAL SOCIAL WORK
William Woods U (MO)

CLINICAL PSYCHOLOGY
Alfred U (NY)
Averett Coll (VA)
Barat Coll (IL)
Biola U (CA)
Bridgewater State Coll (MA)
Crichton Coll (TN)
Eastern Nazarene Coll (MA)
Eastern Washington U (WA)
Fairfield U (CT)
Florida State U (FL)
Franklin Pierce Coll (NH)
George Fox U (OR)
Husson Coll (ME)
Lakehead U (ON, Canada)
Lamar U (TX)
La Sierra U (CA)
Long Island U, Brooklyn Campus (NY)
Mansfield U of Pennsylvania (PA)
Moravian Coll (PA)
Point Park Coll (PA)
Purdue U Calumet (IN)
Ramapo Coll of New Jersey (NJ)
Redeemer Coll (ON, Canada)
San Diego State U (CA)
Tennessee State U (TN)
Toccoa Falls Coll (GA)
U of Alberta (AB, Canada)
U of British Columbia (BC, Canada)
U of Michigan–Flint (MI)
U of Missouri–St. Louis (MO)
U of New Brunswick, Fredericton (NB, Canada)
U of Southern Colorado (CO)
Western State Coll of Colorado (CO)
Westminster Coll (MO)

CLOTHING AND TEXTILES
Albright Coll (PA)
Appalachian State U (NC)
Bluffton Coll (OH)
Bowling Green State U (OH)
California State U, Long Beach (CA)
California State U, Northridge (CA)
Cheyney U of Pennsylvania (PA)
Concordia Coll (MN)
Cornell U (NY)
Delaware State U (DE)
Eastern Kentucky U (KY)
Fashion Inst of Technology (NY)
Florida State U (FL)
Framingham State Coll (MA)
Indiana State U (IN)
Indiana U Bloomington (IN)
Jacksonville State U (AL)
Long Island U, Southampton Coll, Friends World Program (NY)
Marymount Coll (NY)
Mercyhurst Coll (PA)
Minnesota State U, Mankato (MN)
Mississippi U for Women (MS)
New Mexico State U (NM)
North Carolina Ag and Tech State U (NC)
North Dakota State U (ND)
Northwest Missouri State U (MO)
Ohio Dominican Coll (OH)
The Ohio State U (OH)
Oklahoma State U (OK)
Olivet Nazarene U (IL)
Oregon State U (OR)
Philadelphia U (PA)
Queens Coll of the City U of NY (NY)
Rhode Island School of Design (RI)
San Francisco State U (CA)
Syracuse U (NY)
Tennessee Technological U (TN)
Texas Southern U (TX)
The U of Akron (OH)
U of Alberta (AB, Canada)
U of Arkansas at Pine Bluff (AR)
U of Central Oklahoma (OK)
U of Idaho (ID)
U of Manitoba (MB, Canada)
U of Minnesota, Twin Cities Campus (MN)
U of Nebraska at Omaha (NE)
The U of North Carolina at Greensboro (NC)
U of the District of Columbia (DC)
The U of Western Ontario (ON, Canada)
U of Wisconsin–Madison (WI)
Virginia Polytechnic Inst and State U (VA)
Western Michigan U (MI)

CLOTHING/APPAREL/TEXTILE
Concordia Coll (MN)
Wayne State U (MI)

CLOTHING/APPAREL/TEXTILE STUDIES
Appalachian State U (NC)
Auburn U (AL)
Baylor U (TX)
Central Missouri State U (MO)
Coll of the Ozarks (MO)
Colorado State U (CO)
East Carolina U (NC)
Freed-Hardeman U (TN)
Gallaudet U (DC)
Georgia Southern U (GA)
Indiana U Bloomington (IN)
Iowa State U of Science and Technology (IA)
Kansas State U (KS)
Kent State U (OH)
Kentucky State U (KY)
Michigan State U (MI)
Middle Tennessee State U (TN)
Murray State U (KY)
North Dakota State U (ND)
Northern Illinois U (IL)
The Ohio State U (OH)
Purdue U (IN)
Seattle Pacific U (WA)
Southern Illinois U Carbondale (IL)
Southwest Missouri State U (MO)
Texas Tech U (TX)
Texas Woman's U (TX)
The U of Alabama (AL)
U of Calif, Davis (CA)
U of Georgia (GA)
U of Hawaii at Manoa (HI)
U of Illinois at Urbana–Champaign (IL)
U of Kentucky (KY)
U of Missouri–Columbia (MO)
U of Nebraska–Lincoln (NE)
U of Northern Iowa (IA)
U of Rhode Island (RI)
U of Southern Mississippi (MS)
The U of Texas at Austin (TX)
U of Wisconsin–Stout (WI)
U of Wyoming (WY)
Washington State U (WA)
Western Kentucky U (KY)
Youngstown State U (OH)

COGNITIVE PSYCHOLOGY AND PSYCHOLINGUISTICS
Albright Coll (PA)
Brandeis U (MA)
Brown U (RI)
California State U, Stanislaus (CA)
Carleton U (ON, Canada)
Carnegie Mellon U (PA)
George Fox U (OR)
Hampshire Coll (MA)
Harvard U (MA)
Indiana U Bloomington (IN)
Johns Hopkins U (MD)
Lawrence U (WI)
Lehigh U (PA)
Massachusetts Inst of Technology (MA)
Occidental Coll (CA)
Queen's U at Kingston (ON, Canada)
Rice U (TX)
Simon's Rock Coll of Bard (MA)
State U of NY at Oswego (NY)
Tulane U (LA)
U of Calif, Irvine (CA)
U of Calif, Los Angeles (CA)
U of Georgia (GA)
U of Kansas (KS)
U of Rochester (NY)
The U of Texas at Dallas (TX)
Vanderbilt U (TN)
Vassar Coll (NY)
Washington and Lee U (VA)
Washington U in St. Louis (MO)
Wellesley Coll (MA)

COLLEGE/POSTSECONDARY STUDENT COUNSELING
Bowling Green State U (OH)

COMMERCIAL PHOTOGRAPHY
Memphis Coll of Art (TN)
Minnesota State U Moorhead (MN)
Rochester Inst of Technology (NY)

COMMUNICATION DISORDERS
Baylor U (TX)
Biola U (CA)
Boston U (MA)
Bowling Green State U (OH)
Bridgewater State Coll (MA)
Brock U (ON, Canada)
California State U, Chico (CA)
California State U, Fresno (CA)
Case Western Reserve U (OH)
The Coll of Saint Rose (NY)
Edinboro U of Pennsylvania (PA)
Emerson Coll (MA)
Harding U (AR)
Kansas State U (KS)
Longwood Coll (VA)
Minnesota State U, Mankato (MN)
Northern Illinois U (IL)
Oklahoma State U (OK)
Plattsburgh State U of NY (NY)
Radford U (VA)
Southern Illinois U Carbondale (IL)
State U of NY at Buffalo (NY)
State U of NY Coll at Fredonia (NY)
Syracuse U (NY)
Truman State U (MO)
The U of Akron (OH)
The U of Arizona (AZ)
U of Arkansas (AR)
U of Colorado at Boulder (CO)
U of Georgia (GA)
U of Kansas (KS)
U of Maine (ME)
U of Massachusetts Amherst (MA)
U of Nebraska at Kearney (NE)
U of Rhode Island (RI)
The U of Texas at Austin (TX)
U of Vermont (VT)
U of Wisconsin–Eau Claire (WI)
U of Wisconsin–River Falls (WI)
Western Carolina U (NC)
Western Illinois U (IL)
West Texas A&M U (TX)
Winthrop U (SC)

COMMUNICATION EQUIPMENT TECHNOLOGY
California State U, Sacramento (CA)
Cedarville Coll (OH)
Chestnut Hill Coll (PA)
Cheyney U of Pennsylvania (PA)
Columbia Coll Chicago (IL)
Eastern Michigan U (MI)
Ferris State U (MI)
Hastings Coll (NE)
Insto Tecno Estudios Sups Monterrey (Mexico)
Insto Tecno Estudios Sups Monterrey, Querétaro (Mexico)
Saint Mary-of-the-Woods Coll (IN)
State U of NY at Farmingdale (NY)
U of Michigan–Dearborn (MI)
Wilmington Coll (DE)
Xavier U (OH)

COMMUNICATIONS
Adams State Coll (CO)
Allegheny Coll (PA)
Alverno Coll (WI)
American U of Rome (Italy)
Antioch Coll (OH)
Aquinas Coll (MI)
Arizona State U (AZ)
Arizona State U West (AZ)
Auburn U Montgomery (AL)
Augusta State U (GA)
Azusa Pacific U (CA)
Barry U (FL)
Baylor U (TX)
Belhaven Coll (MS)
Bellarmine Coll (KY)
Benedictine U (IL)
Berry Coll (GA)
Bethany Coll (KS)
Bethany Coll (WV)
Bethel Coll (IN)
Bethel Coll (KS)
Bloomsburg U of Pennsylvania (PA)
Boston U (MA)
Bowling Green State U (OH)
Bradley U (IL)
Brigham Young U (UT)
Brock U (ON, Canada)
Bryant Coll (RI)
Buena Vista U (IA)
Cabrini Coll (PA)
Caldwell Coll (NJ)
California State U, Chico (CA)
California State U, Monterey Bay (CA)
California State U, San Marcos (CA)
California U of Pennsylvania (PA)
Campbell U (NC)
Carlow Coll (PA)
Carroll Coll (MT)
Carroll Coll (WI)
Castleton State Coll (VT)
The Catholic U of America (DC)
Cedar Crest Coll (PA)
Cedarville Coll (OH)
Central Coll (IA)
Central Connecticut State U (CT)
Central Methodist Coll (MO)
Chatham Coll (PA)
Christopher Newport U (VA)
Clarion U of Pennsylvania (PA)
Clarkson U (NY)
Clemson U (SC)
Colby-Sawyer Coll (NH)
Coll Misericordia (PA)
Coll of Charleston (SC)
Coll of Mount St. Joseph (OH)
Coll of Saint Elizabeth (NJ)
Coll of St. Joseph (VT)
The Coll of Saint Rose (NY)
The Coll of St. Scholastica (MN)
The Coll of Wooster (OH)
Colorado Christian U (CO)
Columbia International U (SC)
Concordia Coll (MI)
Concordia Coll (MN)
Concordia U (CA)
Concordia U (IL)
Concordia U (NE)
Concordia U (PQ, Canada)
Cornell U (NY)
Crichton Coll (TN)
Cumberland Coll (KY)
Dana Coll (NE)
Delaware Valley Coll (PA)
Doane Coll (NE)
Dominican U of California (CA)
Dowling Coll (NY)
Duquesne U (PA)
East Carolina U (NC)
Eastern Coll (PA)
Eastern Connecticut State U (CT)
Eastern Mennonite U (VA)
Eastern New Mexico U (NM)
East Stroudsburg U of Pennsylvania (PA)
Edinboro U of Pennsylvania (PA)
Elizabethtown Coll (PA)
Elmhurst Coll (IL)
Elon Coll (NC)
Embry-Riddle Aeronautical U (FL)
Emerson Coll (MA)
Emmanuel Coll (GA)
Emporia State U (KS)
Endicott Coll (MA)
Fitchburg State Coll (MA)
Flagler Coll (FL)
Florida Inst of Technology (FL)
Florida International U (FL)
Florida Southern Coll (FL)
Florida State U (FL)
Franciscan U of Steubenville (OH)
Franklin Coll Switzerland (Switzerland)
Franklin U (OH)
Freed-Hardeman U (TN)
Friends U (KS)
Furman U (SC)
Gallaudet U (DC)
Gannon U (PA)
Geneva Coll (PA)
George Fox U (OR)
George Mason U (VA)
Georgia Southern U (GA)
Gordon Coll (MA)
Hastings Coll (NE)
Hawaii Pacific U (HI)
Hollins U (VA)
Holy Family Coll (PA)
Hope Coll (MI)
Howard Payne U (TX)
Huntingdon Coll (AL)
Idaho State U (ID)
Indiana U Bloomington (IN)
Indiana U East (IN)
Indiana U Kokomo (IN)
Indiana U of Pennsylvania (PA)
Indiana U–Purdue U Indianapolis (IN)
Indiana U Southeast (IN)
Indiana Wesleyan U (IN)
Insto Tecno Estudios Sups Monterrey (Mexico)
Jacksonville State U (AL)
Jacksonville U (FL)
James Madison U (VA)
Jamestown Coll (ND)
Juniata Coll (PA)
Kansas State U (KS)
Kean U (NJ)
Kent State U (OH)
Kentucky Wesleyan Coll (KY)
Keuka Coll (NY)
King's Coll (PA)
Lake Forest Coll (IL)
La Roche Coll (PA)
La Sierra U (CA)
Le Moyne Coll (NY)
Liberty U (VA)
Linfield Coll (OR)
Long Island U, C.W. Post Campus (NY)
Longwood Coll (VA)
Loyola Coll in Maryland (MD)
Loyola U Chicago (IL)
Loyola U New Orleans (LA)
Macalester Coll (MN)
Malone Coll (OH)
Manhattan Coll (NY)
Marietta Coll (OH)
Marist Coll (NY)
Marquette U (WI)

Majors Index
Communications–Computer Education

Mary Baldwin Coll (VA)
Maryville U of Saint Louis (MO)
Mercer U (GA)
Merrimack Coll (MA)
Messiah Coll (PA)
Michigan Technological U (MI)
Millersville U of Pennsylvania (PA)
Millikin U (IL)
Mississippi Coll (MS)
Mississippi State U (MS)
Mississippi U for Women (MS)
Missouri Baptist Coll (MO)
Molloy Coll (NY)
Monmouth U (NJ)
Montana Tech of The U of Montana (MT)
Moody Bible Inst (IL)
Morehead State U (KY)
Mount Mary Coll (WI)
Mount Saint Mary's Coll and Seminary (MD)
Mount Union Coll (OH)
Multnomah Bible Coll and Biblical Seminary (OR)
National U (CA)
Neumann Coll (PA)
New Hampshire Coll (NH)
New Jersey City U (NJ)
North Carolina State U (NC)
Northeastern U (MA)
Northwestern Coll (MN)
Norwich U (VT)
Notre Dame Coll of Ohio (OH)
Nyack Coll (NY)
Oakland U (MI)
Ohio Dominican Coll (OH)
The Ohio State U (OH)
Ohio U (OH)
Our Lady of the Lake U of San Antonio (TX)
Park U (MO)
Peace Coll (NC)
Penn State U at Erie, The Behrend Coll (PA)
Penn State U Harrisburg Campus of the Capital Coll (PA)
Penn State U Univ Park Campus (PA)
Pepperdine U, Malibu (CA)
Pikeville Coll (KY)
Pine Manor Coll (MA)
Plattsburgh State U of NY (NY)
Plymouth State Coll (NH)
Point Loma Nazarene U (CA)
Purdue U (IN)
Quincy U (IL)
Radford U (VA)
Ramapo Coll of New Jersey (NJ)
Reformed Bible Coll (MI)
Regis Coll (MA)
Regis U (CO)
The Richard Stockton Coll of New Jersey (NJ)
Rivier Coll (NH)
Roberts Wesleyan Coll (NY)
Rochester Coll (MI)
Rochester Inst of Technology (NY)
Rocky Mountain Coll (MT)
Roger Williams U (RI)
Rutgers, State U of NJ, Cook Coll (NJ)
Rutgers, State U of NJ, Douglass Coll (NJ)
Rutgers, State U of NJ, Livingston Coll (NJ)
Rutgers, State U of NJ, Rutgers Coll (NJ)
Rutgers, State U of NJ, U Coll–New Brunswick (NJ)
Saginaw Valley State U (MI)
Saint Augustine's Coll (NC)
St. Edward's U (TX)
St. Francis Coll (NY)
St. John's U (NY)
Saint Joseph's Coll (IN)
Saint Louis U (MO)
Saint Mary's Coll (IN)
St. Mary's U of San Antonio (TX)
St. Norbert Coll (WI)
Saint Peter's Coll (NJ)
Saint Vincent Coll (PA)
Saint Xavier U (IL)
Salisbury State U (MD)
Santa Clara U (CA)
Seattle Pacific U (WA)
Seton Hall U (NJ)
Seton Hill Coll (PA)

Shenandoah U (VA)
Simon Fraser U (BC, Canada)
Simpson Coll and Graduate School (CA)
Southeastern Coll of the Assemblies of God (FL)
Southeastern Oklahoma State U (OK)
Southern Oregon U (OR)
Southern Vermont Coll (VT)
Southwest Baptist U (MO)
Southwestern Coll (KS)
Southwest Missouri State U (MO)
Southwest State U (MN)
Stanford U (CA)
State U of NY Coll at Cortland (NY)
State U of NY Coll at Geneseo (NY)
State U of NY Coll at Old Westbury (NY)
Stephen F. Austin State U (TX)
Stonehill Coll (MA)
Susquehanna U (PA)
Tabor Coll (KS)
Texas A&M International U (TX)
Texas A&M U (TX)
Thiel Coll (PA)
Thomas Edison State Coll (NJ)
Thomas U (GA)
Towson U (MD)
Trevecca Nazarene U (TN)
Trinity Christian Coll (IL)
Trinity U (TX)
Trinity Western U (BC, Canada)
Tri-State U (IN)
The Union Inst (OH)
United States International U (CA)
U Coll of Cape Breton (NS, Canada)
The U of Alabama at Birmingham (AL)
The U of Arizona (AZ)
U of Calgary (AB, Canada)
U of Calif, Los Angeles (CA)
U of Calif, Santa Barbara (CA)
U of Central Florida (FL)
U of Colorado at Boulder (CO)
U of Colorado at Colorado Springs (CO)
U of Colorado at Denver (CO)
U of Connecticut (CT)
U of Delaware (DE)
U of Denver (CO)
U of Hartford (CT)
U of Hawaii at Manoa (HI)
U of Houston (TX)
U of Houston–Clear Lake (TX)
U of Idaho (ID)
U of Indianapolis (IN)
U of Kentucky (KY)
U of La Verne (CA)
U of Louisiana at Lafayette (LA)
U of Louisville (KY)
U of Maine (ME)
U of Maine at Presque Isle (ME)
U of Mary Hardin-Baylor (TX)
U of Maryland, Coll Park (MD)
U of Maryland University Coll (MD)
U of Massachusetts Amherst (MA)
U of Miami (FL)
U of Missouri–Columbia (MO)
U of Missouri–St. Louis (MO)
U of Nebraska at Omaha (NE)
U of Nebraska–Lincoln (NE)
U of Nevada, Las Vegas (NV)
U of Nevada, Reno (NV)
U of New Brunswick, Saint John (NB, Canada)
U of New Haven (CT)
U of New Orleans (LA)
The U of North Carolina at Chapel Hill (NC)
The U of North Carolina at Charlotte (NC)
U of North Dakota (ND)
U of Northern Colorado (CO)
U of Northern Iowa (IA)
U of North Florida (FL)
U of North Texas (TX)
U of Oklahoma (OK)
U of Pennsylvania (PA)
U of Pittsburgh (PA)
U of Puget Sound (WA)
U of Rhode Island (RI)
U of Rio Grande (OH)
U of Saint Francis (IN)
U of St. Thomas (MN)

U of St. Thomas (TX)
U of San Francisco (CA)
U of Science and Arts of Oklahoma (OK)
The U of Scranton (PA)
U of South Carolina Spartanburg (SC)
U of Southern Indiana (IN)
U of Southern Maine (ME)
U of Southern Mississippi (MS)
U of South Florida (FL)
The U of Texas at Arlington (TX)
The U of Texas at San Antonio (TX)
The U of Texas–Pan American (TX)
U of the Ozarks (AR)
U of the Sacred Heart (PR)
U of Virginia's Coll at Wise (VA)
U of Washington (WA)
U of West Florida (FL)
U of Wisconsin–Eau Claire (WI)
U of Wisconsin–Green Bay (WI)
U of Wisconsin–La Crosse (WI)
U of Wisconsin–Parkside (WI)
U of Wisconsin–Stevens Point (WI)
U of Wisconsin–Superior (WI)
U of Wyoming (WY)
Valparaiso U (IN)
Virginia Polytechnic Inst and State U (VA)
Virginia Wesleyan Coll (VA)
Wake Forest U (NC)
Warner Southern Coll (FL)
Waynesburg Coll (PA)
Wayne State U (MI)
Wesleyan Coll (GA)
Western Carolina U (NC)
Western Illinois U (IL)
Western Kentucky U (KY)
Western Maryland Coll (MD)
Western Michigan U (MI)
Western Washington U (WA)
Westminster Coll (UT)
Westmont Coll (CA)
Wichita State U (KS)
William Penn U (IA)
William Woods U (MO)
Wisconsin Lutheran Coll (WI)
Wittenberg U (OH)
Woodbury U (CA)
York U (ON, Canada)

COMMUNITY HEALTH LIAISON
California State U, Chico (CA)
Florida State U (FL)
Hofstra U (NY)
James Madison U (VA)
Marymount Coll (NY)
Minnesota State U Moorhead (MN)
Northern Illinois U (IL)
Prairie View A&M U (TX)
Sam Houston State U (TX)
Southwest Texas State U (TX)
Texas Tech U (TX)
Texas Woman's U (TX)
U of Houston (TX)
U of Nebraska–Lincoln (NE)
U of Northern Iowa (IA)
The U of Texas at Austin (TX)
The U of Texas at San Antonio (TX)
The U of Texas–Pan American (TX)
U of West Florida (FL)
Western Kentucky U (KY)
Western Michigan U (MI)
Worcester State Coll (MA)
Youngstown State U (OH)

COMMUNITY PSYCHOLOGY
New York Inst of Technology (NY)
Saint Mary Coll (KS)

COMMUNITY SERVICES
Alverno Coll (WI)
Aquinas Coll (MI)
Barat Coll (IL)
Beaver Coll (PA)
Bellarmine Coll (KY)
Bemidji State U (MN)
Brandon U (MB, Canada)
Cazenovia Coll (NY)
Central Michigan U (MI)
Cornell U (NY)
Eastern Mennonite U (VA)
Emory & Henry Coll (VA)
The Evergreen State Coll (WA)
Framingham State Coll (MA)

Goddard Coll (VT)
Hampshire Coll (MA)
High Point U (NC)
Humphreys Coll (CA)
International Coll of the Cayman Islands (Cayman Islands)
Iowa State U of Science and Technology (IA)
Long Island U, Southampton Coll, Friends World Program (NY)
Maryville Coll (TN)
Michigan State U (MI)
Missouri Baptist Coll (MO)
Montana State U–Northern (MT)
NAES Coll (IL)
Northern State U (SD)
North Park U (IL)
Ohio U (OH)
Oklahoma Christian U of Science and Arts (OK)
Providence Coll (RI)
St. John's U (NY)
Saint Martin's Coll (WA)
Saint Mary Coll (KS)
Siena Heights U (MI)
Southern Arkansas U–Magnolia (AR)
Thomas Edison State Coll (NJ)
U Coll of Cape Breton (NS, Canada)
U of Delaware (DE)
U of Hartford (CT)
U of Massachusetts Boston (MA)
U of Oregon (OR)
Virginia Commonwealth U (VA)
Western Baptist Coll (OR)
West Virginia U Inst of Technology (WV)

COMPARATIVE LITERATURE
American U in Cairo (Egypt)
The American U of Paris (France)
Antioch Coll (OH)
Bard Coll (NY)
Barnard Coll (NY)
Beloit Coll (WI)
Bennington Coll (VT)
Brandeis U (MA)
Brigham Young U (UT)
Brooklyn Coll of the City U of NY (NY)
Brown U (RI)
Bryn Mawr Coll (PA)
California State U, Fullerton (CA)
California State U, Long Beach (CA)
Carleton U (ON, Canada)
Case Western Reserve U (OH)
Cedar Crest Coll (PA)
Chapman U (CA)
Clark U (MA)
The Coll of Wooster (OH)
The Colorado Coll (CO)
Columbia Coll (NY)
Columbia U, School of General Studies (NY)
Cornell U (NY)
Dartmouth Coll (NH)
DePaul U (IL)
Eckerd Coll (FL)
Emory U (GA)
The Evergreen State Coll (WA)
Fordham U (NY)
Georgetown U (DC)
Goddard Coll (VT)
Hamilton Coll (NY)
Hampshire Coll (MA)
Harvard U (MA)
Haverford Coll (PA)
Hillsdale Coll (MI)
Hobart and William Smith Colls (NY)
Hunter Coll of the City U of NY (NY)
Indiana U Bloomington (IN)
Inter American U of PR, Metropolitan Campus (PR)
Long Island U, Southampton Coll, Friends World Program (NY)
Marlboro Coll (VT)
Millersville U of Pennsylvania (PA)
Mills Coll (CA)
New York U (NY)
Northwestern U (IL)
Oberlin Coll (OH)
Occidental Coll (CA)
The Ohio State U (OH)

Oregon State U (OR)
Penn State U Univ Park Campus (PA)
Princeton U (NJ)
Queens Coll of the City U of NY (NY)
Ramapo Coll of New Jersey (NJ)
Rutgers, State U of NJ, Douglass Coll (NJ)
Rutgers, State U of NJ, Livingston Coll (NJ)
Rutgers, State U of NJ, Rutgers Coll (NJ)
Rutgers, State U of NJ, U Coll–New Brunswick (NJ)
St. Cloud State U (MN)
Salem State Coll (MA)
San Diego State U (CA)
San Francisco State U (CA)
Sarah Lawrence Coll (NY)
Simmons Coll (MA)
Smith Coll (MA)
Stanford U (CA)
State U of NY at Binghamton (NY)
State U of NY at New Paltz (NY)
State U of NY at Stony Brook (NY)
State U of NY Coll at Geneseo (NY)
Swarthmore Coll (PA)
Trinity Coll (CT)
U of Alberta (AB, Canada)
U of Calif, Berkeley (CA)
U of Calif, Davis (CA)
U of Calif, Irvine (CA)
U of Calif, Los Angeles (CA)
U of Calif, Riverside (CA)
U of Calif, Santa Barbara (CA)
U of Cincinnati (OH)
U of Delaware (DE)
U of Georgia (GA)
U of Illinois at Urbana–Champaign (IL)
The U of Iowa (IA)
U of La Verne (CA)
U of Massachusetts Amherst (MA)
U of Michigan (MI)
U of Michigan–Dearborn (MI)
U of Minnesota, Twin Cities Campus (MN)
U of Nevada, Las Vegas (NV)
U of New Brunswick, Fredericton (NB, Canada)
U of New Mexico (NM)
The U of North Carolina at Chapel Hill (NC)
U of Oregon (OR)
U of Pennsylvania (PA)
U of Puerto Rico, Mayagüez Campus (PR)
U of Puerto Rico, Río Piedras (PR)
U of Rhode Island (RI)
U of Rochester (NY)
U of St. Thomas (MN)
U of Southern California (CA)
U of the South (TN)
U of Virginia (VA)
U of Washington (WA)
U of Windsor (ON, Canada)
U of Wisconsin–Madison (WI)
U of Wisconsin–Milwaukee (WI)
Virginia Commonwealth U (VA)
Washington U in St. Louis (MO)
Wellesley Coll (MA)
West Chester U of Pennsylvania (PA)
Western Washington U (WA)
Willamette U (OR)
Wittenberg U (OH)
Yale U (CT)

COMPUTER EDUCATION
Abilene Christian U (TX)
Baylor U (TX)
Bowling Green State U (OH)
Bridgewater Coll (VA)
Central Michigan U (MI)
Concordia U (IL)
Concordia U (NE)
Eastern Michigan U (MI)
East Texas Baptist U (TX)
Florida Inst of Technology (FL)
Hardin-Simmons U (TX)
Johnson Bible Coll (TN)
McGill U (PQ, Canada)
Pontifical Catholic U of Puerto Rico (PR)
South Dakota State U (SD)

Majors Index
Computer Education–Computer/Information Sciences

Union Coll (NE)
U of Illinois at Urbana–Champaign (IL)
U of Nebraska–Lincoln (NE)
U of North Texas (TX)
U of Wisconsin–River Falls (WI)
Youngstown State U (OH)

COMPUTER ENGINEERING
Arizona State U (AZ)
Auburn U (AL)
Bellarmine Coll (KY)
Boston U (MA)
Brigham Young U (UT)
Brown U (RI)
Bucknell U (PA)
California Inst of Technology (CA)
California Polytechnic State U, San Luis Obispo (CA)
California State Polytechnic U, Pomona (CA)
California State U, Chico (CA)
California State U, Fresno (CA)
California State U, Long Beach (CA)
California State U, Northridge (CA)
California State U, Sacramento (CA)
Capitol Coll (MD)
Carleton U (ON, Canada)
Carnegie Mellon U (PA)
Case Western Reserve U (OH)
The Catholic U of America (DC)
Christian Brothers U (TN)
Christopher Newport U (VA)
Clarkson U (NY)
Clemson U (SC)
Colorado State U (CO)
Colorado Tech U (CO)
Columbia U, School of Engineering & Applied Sci (NY)
Concordia U (PQ, Canada)
Dalhousie U (NS, Canada)
Dominican U (IL)
Drexel U (PA)
Eastern Michigan U (MI)
Eastern Nazarene Coll (MA)
Elizabethtown Coll (PA)
Embry-Riddle Aeronautical U (AZ)
Embry-Riddle Aeronautical U (FL)
Florida Atlantic U (FL)
Florida Inst of Technology (FL)
Florida International U (FL)
Florida State U (FL)
Gallaudet U (DC)
George Mason U (VA)
The George Washington U (DC)
Georgia Inst of Technology (GA)
Gonzaga U (WA)
Grantham Coll of Engineering (LA)
Harding U (AR)
Harvard U (MA)
Illinois Inst of Technology (IL)
Indiana Inst of Technology (IN)
Indiana U–Purdue U Indianapolis (IN)
Insto Tecno Estudios Sups Monterrey, León (Mexico)
Insto Tecno Estudios Sups Monterrey (Mexico)
Insto Tecno Estudios Sups Monterrey, Querétaro (Mexico)
Iona Coll (NY)
Iowa State U of Science and Technology (IA)
Johns Hopkins U (MD)
Johnson & Wales U (RI)
Johnson C. Smith U (NC)
Kansas State U (KS)
Kettering U (MI)
Lakehead U (ON, Canada)
Lehigh U (PA)
LeTourneau U (TX)
Louisiana State U and A&M Coll (LA)
Manhattan Coll (NY)
Marquette U (WI)
Massachusetts Inst of Technology (MA)
McGill U (PQ, Canada)
Mercer U (GA)
Merrimack Coll (MA)
Michigan State U (MI)
Michigan Technological U (MI)
Milwaukee School of Engineering (WI)
Mississippi State U (MS)
Montana State U–Bozeman (MT)
Montana Tech of The U of Montana (MT)
New Jersey Inst of Technology (NJ)
New York U (NY)
North Carolina State U (NC)
North Dakota State U (ND)
Northeastern U (MA)
Northern Arizona U (AZ)
Northwestern U (IL)
Oakland U (MI)
Ohio Northern U (OH)
The Ohio State U (OH)
Ohio U (OH)
Oklahoma Christian U of Science and Arts (OK)
Oklahoma State U (OK)
Old Dominion U (VA)
Oregon State U (OR)
Pacific Lutheran U (WA)
Penn State U at Erie, The Behrend Coll (PA)
Penn State U Univ Park Campus (PA)
Polytechnic U, Brooklyn Campus (NY)
Polytechnic U, Farmingdale Campus (NY)
Portland State U (OR)
Purdue U (IN)
Purdue U Calumet (IN)
Queen's U at Kingston (ON, Canada)
Rensselaer Polytechnic Inst (NY)
Rice U (TX)
Richmond, The American International U in London (United Kingdom)
Rochester Inst of Technology (NY)
Rose-Hulman Inst of Technology (IN)
Rutgers, State U of NJ, Coll of Engineering (NJ)
St. Mary's U of San Antonio (TX)
San Jose State U (CA)
Santa Clara U (CA)
Savannah State U (GA)
South Dakota School of Mines and Technology (SD)
Southern Illinois U Carbondale (IL)
Southern Illinois U Edwardsville (IL)
Southern Methodist U (TX)
State U of NY at Binghamton (NY)
State U of NY at New Paltz (NY)
Stevens Inst of Technology (NJ)
Stonehill Coll (MA)
Suffolk U (MA)
Syracuse U (NY)
Taylor U (IN)
Tennessee Technological U (TN)
Texas A&M U (TX)
Texas Tech U (TX)
Tufts U (MA)
Tulane U (LA)
United States Military Academy (NY)
Université de Sherbrooke (PQ, Canada)
U du Québec à Chicoutimi (PQ, Canada)
U du Québec à Trois-Rivières (PQ, Canada)
Université Laval (PQ, Canada)
The U of Akron (OH)
The U of Alabama in Huntsville (AL)
U of Alberta (AB, Canada)
The U of Arizona (AZ)
U of Arkansas (AR)
U of Bridgeport (CT)
U of British Columbia (BC, Canada)
U of Calgary (AB, Canada)
U of Calif, Davis (CA)
U of Calif, Irvine (CA)
U of Calif, Los Angeles (CA)
U of Calif, San Diego (CA)
U of Calif, Santa Cruz (CA)
U of Central Florida (FL)
U of Cincinnati (OH)
U of Colorado at Boulder (CO)
U of Colorado at Colorado Springs (CO)
U of Connecticut (CT)
U of Dayton (OH)
U of Delaware (DE)
U of Denver (CO)
U of Detroit Mercy (MI)
U of Evansville (IN)
U of Florida (FL)
U of Hartford (CT)
U of Houston–Clear Lake (TX)
U of Idaho (ID)
U of Illinois at Chicago (IL)
U of Illinois at Urbana–Champaign (IL)
The U of Iowa (IA)
U of Kansas (KS)
U of Louisiana at Lafayette (LA)
U of Louisville (KY)
U of Maine (ME)
U of Manitoba (MB, Canada)
U of Maryland, Baltimore County (MD)
U of Maryland, Coll Park (MD)
U of Massachusetts Amherst (MA)
U of Massachusetts Dartmouth (MA)
The U of Memphis (TN)
U of Miami (FL)
U of Michigan (MI)
U of Minnesota, Duluth (MN)
U of Missouri–Columbia (MO)
U of Missouri–Rolla (MO)
U of Nebraska–Lincoln (NE)
U of Nevada, Las Vegas (NV)
U of New Brunswick, Fredericton (NB, Canada)
U of New Hampshire (NH)
U of New Mexico (NM)
The U of North Carolina at Charlotte (NC)
U of Notre Dame (IN)
U of Oklahoma (OK)
U of Pennsylvania (PA)
U of Pittsburgh (PA)
U of Pittsburgh at Bradford (PA)
U of Portland (OR)
U of Puerto Rico, Mayagüez Campus (PR)
U of Rhode Island (RI)
U of South Alabama (AL)
U of South Carolina (SC)
U of Southern California (CA)
U of South Florida (FL)
The U of Tennessee Knoxville (TN)
The U of Texas at Arlington (TX)
U of the Pacific (CA)
U of Toronto (ON, Canada)
U of Utah (UT)
U of Victoria (BC, Canada)
U of Washington (WA)
U of Waterloo (ON, Canada)
U of West Florida (FL)
U of Wisconsin–Madison (WI)
U of Wisconsin–Parkside (WI)
Utah State U (UT)
Vanderbilt U (TN)
Villanova U (PA)
Virginia Polytechnic Inst and State U (VA)
Washington State U (WA)
Washington U in St. Louis (MO)
Western Michigan U (MI)
West Virginia U (WV)
Wichita State U (KS)
Worcester Polytechnic Inst (MA)
Wright State U (OH)

COMPUTER ENGINEERING TECHNOLOGY
Andrews U (MI)
Arizona State U East (AZ)
Bennington Coll (VT)
Brock U (ON, Canada)
California State U, Long Beach (CA)
Capitol Coll (MD)
Central Michigan U (MI)
Coleman Coll (CA)
DePaul U (IL)
DeVry Inst of Technology (AZ)
DeVry Inst of Technology, Fremont (CA)
DeVry Inst of Technology, Long Beach (CA)
DeVry Inst of Technology, Pomona (CA)
DeVry Inst of Technology (MO)
DeVry Inst of Technology (OH)
DeVry Inst of Technology (TX)
East Carolina U (NC)
Eastern Washington U (WA)
Georgia Southwestern State U (GA)
Grantham Coll of Engineering (LA)
Harvard U (MA)
Indiana State U (IN)
Inter American U of PR, Metropolitan Campus (PR)
Iona Coll (NY)
Lake Superior State U (MI)
LeTourneau U (TX)
Lewis-Clark State Coll (ID)
Loras Coll (IA)
Marist Coll (NY)
Murray State U (KY)
Norfolk State U (VA)
Northeastern U (MA)
Oregon Inst of Technology (OR)
Pace U, New York City Campus (NY)
Pace U, Pleasantville/Briarcliff Campus (NY)
Peirce Coll (PA)
Prairie View A&M U (TX)
Purdue U Calumet (IN)
Regents Coll (NY)
Rochester Inst of Technology (NY)
Savannah State U (GA)
Shawnee State U (OH)
Southern Polytechnic State U (GA)
State U of NY at Buffalo (NY)
State U of NY at Farmingdale (NY)
State U of NY at Stony Brook (NY)
State U of NY Inst of Tech at Utica/Rome (NY)
Texas Southern U (TX)
U of Arkansas at Little Rock (AR)
U of Dayton (OH)
U of Guelph (ON, Canada)
U of Hartford (CT)
U of Houston (TX)
U of Houston–Clear Lake (TX)
U of Houston–Downtown (TX)
The U of Memphis (TN)
U of New Brunswick, Saint John (NB, Canada)
U of Rochester (NY)
U of Southern Colorado (CO)
U of Southern Mississippi (MS)
Utah State U (UT)
Wentworth Inst of Technology (MA)

COMPUTER GRAPHICS
Academy of Art Coll (CA)
The Advertising Arts Coll (CA)
Alberta Coll of Art and Design (AB, Canada)
American Academy of Art (IL)
The Art Inst of Atlanta (GA)
The Art Inst of Boston at Lesley (MA)
The Art Inst of Colorado (CO)
The Art Inst of Fort Lauderdale (FL)
The Art Inst of Portland (OR)
Art Insts International at San Francisco (CA)
Atlanta Coll of Art (GA)
Baker Coll of Flint (MI)
California Inst of the Arts (CA)
California State U, Hayward (CA)
California State U, Los Angeles (CA)
Ctr for Creative Studies—Coll of Art and Design (MI)
Cogswell Polytechnical Coll (CA)
Coll of Aeronautics (NY)
Coll of Saint Mary (NE)
Coll of the Atlantic (ME)
Columbia Coll (MO)
Columbia Coll Chicago (IL)
DePaul U (IL)
Dominican U (IL)
Hampshire Coll (MA)
Harvard U (MA)
Henry Cogswell Coll (WA)
Huntington Coll (AL)
Indiana Wesleyan U (IN)
John Brown U (AR)
Judson Coll (IL)
Long Island U, C.W. Post Campus (NY)
Maharishi U of Management (IA)
Marycrest International U (IA)
Memphis Coll of Art (TN)
Millersville U of Pennsylvania (PA)
Northern Michigan U (MI)
Oakland City U (IN)
Pine Manor Coll (MA)
Pratt Inst (NY)
Ringling School of Art and Design (FL)
Rochester Inst of Technology (NY)
Savannah Coll of Art and Design (GA)
School of the Art Inst of Chicago (IL)
School of the Museum of Fine Arts (MA)
School of Visual Arts (NY)
Simon's Rock Coll of Bard (MA)
Southern Adventist U (TN)
State U of NY Coll at Fredonia (NY)
Stetson U (FL)
Syracuse U (NY)
U of Advancing Computer Technology (AZ)
U of Dubuque (IA)
U of Mary Hardin-Baylor (TX)
The U of the Arts (PA)
Villa Julie Coll (MD)
Wingate U (NC)
Wittenberg U (OH)

COMPUTER/INFORMATION SCIENCES
Abilene Christian U (TX)
Alabama A&M U (AL)
Allegheny Coll (PA)
Amber U (TX)
Andrews U (MI)
Arkansas State U (AR)
Asbury Coll (KY)
Athabasca U (AB, Canada)
Augusta State U (GA)
Austin Peay State U (TN)
Avila Coll (MO)
Baker Coll of Muskegon (MI)
Bellarmine Coll (KY)
Bentley Coll (MA)
Berry Coll (GA)
Bethel Coll (IN)
Biola U (CA)
Bishop's U (PQ, Canada)
Bloomsburg U of Pennsylvania (PA)
Bluefield State Coll (WV)
Boise State U (ID)
Bowling Green State U (OH)
Bradley U (IL)
Brooklyn Coll of the City U of NY (NY)
Bryant Coll (RI)
Bucknell U (PA)
Cabrini Coll (PA)
Caldwell Coll (NJ)
California State Polytechnic U, Pomona (CA)
California State U, Chico (CA)
California State U, Sacramento (CA)
California State U, San Bernardino (CA)
California State U, Stanislaus (CA)
Cameron U (OK)
Campbell U (NC)
Carnegie Mellon U (PA)
Carroll Coll (WI)
Castleton State Coll (VT)
Cedar Crest Coll (PA)
Central Connecticut State U (CT)
Central Michigan U (MI)
Central Missouri State U (MO)
Chatham Coll (PA)
Christopher Newport U (VA)
Clarion U of Pennsylvania (PA)
Clarkson U (NY)
Cleveland State U (OH)
Coleman Coll (CA)
Coll of Charleston (SC)
Coll of St. Catherine (MN)
Coll of Saint Elizabeth (NJ)
The Coll of St. Scholastica (MN)
The Coll of Southeastern Europe, The American U of Athens (Greece)
Coll of the Ozarks (MO)
Colorado Christian U (CO)
Colorado Tech U Denver Campus (CO)
Concordia U (NE)
Cumberland Coll (KY)
Dallas Baptist U (TX)
Delaware State U (DE)
DePaul U (IL)

Majors Index
Computer/Information Sciences–Computer Science

Deree Coll (Greece)
Detroit Coll of Business–Flint (MI)
Detroit Coll of Business, Warren Campus (MI)
DeVry Inst of Technology, West Hills (CA)
Doane Coll (NE)
Drexel U (PA)
Drury U (MO)
Eastern Connecticut State U (CT)
Eastern Michigan U (MI)
Eastern New Mexico U (NM)
Eastern Washington U (WA)
East Stroudsburg U of Pennsylvania (PA)
East Tennessee State U (TN)
East Texas Baptist U (TX)
Edinboro U of Pennsylvania (PA)
Embry-Riddle Aeronautical U (AZ)
Embry-Riddle Aeronautical U (FL)
Emmaus Bible Coll (IA)
Emporia State U (KS)
Fairleigh Dickinson U, Florham-Madison Campus (NJ)
Fairleigh Dickinson U, Teaneck-Hackensack Campus (NJ)
Florida Atlantic U (FL)
Florida Gulf Coast U (FL)
Florida International U (FL)
Florida State U (FL)
Fordham U (NY)
Franciscan U of Steubenville (OH)
Franklin Coll of Indiana (IN)
Freed-Hardeman U (TN)
Fresno Pacific U (CA)
Friends U (KS)
Frostburg State U (MD)
Gallaudet U (DC)
Gannon U (PA)
George Fox U (OR)
George Mason U (VA)
The George Washington U (DC)
Georgia Coll and State U (GA)
Georgia Inst of Technology (GA)
Georgia Southern U (GA)
Georgia State U (GA)
Grand Valley State U (MI)
Hampshire Coll (MA)
Hartwick Coll (NY)
Harvard U (MA)
Hastings Coll (NE)
Hawaii Pacific U (HI)
Henderson State U (AR)
Herzing Coll (WI)
High Point U (NC)
Hofstra U (NY)
Holy Family Coll (PA)
Hood Coll (MD)
Idaho State U (ID)
Immaculata Coll (PA)
Indiana State U (IN)
Indiana U Bloomington (IN)
Indiana U of Pennsylvania (PA)
Indiana U–Purdue U Indianapolis (IN)
Indiana Wesleyan U (IN)
Insto Tecno Estudios Sups Monterrey (Mexico)
Insto Tecno Estudios Sups Monterrey, Querétaro (Mexico)
International Coll (FL)
Ithaca Coll (NY)
Jacksonville State U (AL)
Jacksonville U (FL)
James Madison U (VA)
Johnson & Wales U (RI)
Juniata Coll (PA)
Kansas State U (KS)
Kean U (NJ)
Kentucky State U (KY)
King's Coll (PA)
Knox Coll (IL)
La Roche Coll (PA)
La Salle U (PA)
Liberty U (VA)
Long Island U, Brooklyn Campus (NY)
Loyola Coll in Maryland (MD)
Loyola U New Orleans (LA)
Luther Coll (IA)
Lyndon State Coll (VT)
Mansfield U of Pennsylvania (PA)
Marygrove Coll (MI)
Marymount Coll (NY)
Marywood U (PA)
McGill U (PQ, Canada)
McMurry U (TX)

Medaille Coll (NY)
Mercer U (GA)
Messiah Coll (PA)
Metropolitan State Coll of Denver (CO)
Michigan State U (MI)
Millikin U (IL)
Minnesota State U Moorhead (MN)
Mississippi Coll (MS)
Mississippi State U (MS)
Missouri Baptist Coll (MO)
Missouri Southern State Coll (MO)
Missouri Western State Coll (MO)
Monmouth U (NJ)
Montana Tech of The U of Montana (MT)
Morehouse Coll (GA)
Mount St. Clare Coll (IA)
Mount Saint Vincent U (NS, Canada)
Murray State U (KY)
Neumann Coll (PA)
New Hampshire Coll (NH)
New Jersey City U (NJ)
New Jersey Inst of Technology (NJ)
New York U (NY)
Northeastern Illinois U (IL)
Northern Kentucky U (KY)
North Georgia Coll & State U (GA)
Oakland U (MI)
The Ohio State U (OH)
Oklahoma Baptist U (OK)
Oklahoma State U (OK)
Old Dominion U (VA)
Oregon Inst of Technology (OR)
Our Lady of the Lake U of San Antonio (TX)
Pace U, New York City Campus (NY)
Pace U, Pleasantville/Briarcliff Campus (NY)
Pacific Union Coll (CA)
Park U (MO)
Penn State U Harrisburg Campus of the Capital Coll (PA)
Penn State U Univ Park Campus (PA)
Portland State U (OR)
Principia Coll (IL)
Purdue U (IN)
Purdue U Calumet (IN)
Queen's U at Kingston (ON, Canada)
Ramapo Coll of New Jersey (NJ)
Reformed Bible Coll (MI)
Rensselaer Polytechnic Inst (NY)
The Richard Stockton Coll of New Jersey (NJ)
Robert Morris Coll (PA)
Rochester Inst of Technology (NY)
Sacred Heart U (CT)
Saginaw Valley State U (MI)
St. Andrews Presbyterian Coll (NC)
Saint Augustine's Coll (NC)
St. Edward's U (TX)
St. Francis Xavier U (NS, Canada)
St. John's U (NY)
Saint Joseph's Coll (IN)
Saint Louis U (MO)
Saint Mary-of-the-Woods Coll (IN)
Saint Peter's Coll (NJ)
Saint Vincent Coll (PA)
Saint Xavier U (IL)
Sam Houston State U (TX)
San Diego State U (CA)
Seton Hall U (NJ)
Seton Hill Coll (PA)
Shaw U (NC)
Shippensburg U of Pennsylvania (PA)
Silver Lake Coll (WI)
South Dakota State U (SD)
Southeastern Oklahoma State U (OK)
Southern Arkansas U–Magnolia (AR)
Southern Illinois U Carbondale (IL)
Southern Illinois U Edwardsville (IL)
Southern Polytechnic State U (GA)
Southwestern Oklahoma State U (OK)
Southwest Texas State U (TX)
State U of NY at Albany (NY)
Stephen F. Austin State U (TX)
Sterling Coll (KS)
Suffolk U (MA)
Syracuse U (NY)

Tech U of British Columbia (BC, Canada)
Texas Tech U (TX)
Texas Woman's U (TX)
Thomas Coll (ME)
Thomas Edison State Coll (NJ)
Towson U (MD)
Trinity U (TX)
Troy State U (AL)
Troy State U Montgomery (AL)
Tulane U (LA)
Union Coll (NY)
U Coll of Cape Breton (NS, Canada)
U Coll of the Fraser Valley (BC, Canada)
The U of Alabama (AL)
The U of Alabama at Birmingham (AL)
The U of Alabama in Huntsville (AL)
The U of Arizona (AZ)
U of Arkansas (AR)
U of Baltimore (MD)
U of Calif, Berkeley (CA)
U of Calif, Irvine (CA)
U of Central Florida (FL)
U of Charleston (WV)
U of Cincinnati (OH)
U of Colorado at Boulder (CO)
U of Colorado at Colorado Springs (CO)
U of Delaware (DE)
U of Denver (CO)
U of Detroit Mercy (MI)
U of Florida (FL)
U of Georgia (GA)
U of Hartford (CT)
U of Hawaii at Manoa (HI)
U of Houston (TX)
U of Houston–Downtown (TX)
U of Illinois at Chicago (IL)
U of Illinois at Urbana–Champaign (IL)
U of Kansas (KS)
U of Kentucky (KY)
U of Louisiana at Monroe (LA)
U of Mary Hardin-Baylor (TX)
U of Maryland, Coll Park (MD)
U of Maryland University Coll (MD)
U of Massachusetts Dartmouth (MA)
U of Michigan–Dearborn (MI)
U of Mississippi (MS)
The U of Montana–Missoula (MT)
U of Nebraska at Kearney (NE)
U of Nebraska at Omaha (NE)
U of Nevada, Reno (NV)
U of New Haven (CT)
U of New Mexico (NM)
U of North Alabama (AL)
The U of North Carolina at Greensboro (NC)
The U of North Carolina at Wilmington (NC)
U of North Dakota (ND)
U of Northern Iowa (IA)
U of North Florida (FL)
U of North Texas (TX)
U of Notre Dame (IN)
U of Puerto Rico, Río Piedras (PR)
U of Rhode Island (RI)
U of St. Thomas (MN)
U of San Francisco (CA)
U of South Carolina (SC)
U of South Carolina Spartanburg (SC)
U of Southern Indiana (IN)
U of South Florida (FL)
The U of Texas at Austin (TX)
The U of Texas at San Antonio (TX)
The U of Texas–Pan American (TX)
U of Virginia (VA)
U of Virginia's Coll at Wise (VA)
U of Washington (WA)
The U of Western Ontario (ON, Canada)
U of West Florida (FL)
U of Wisconsin–Eau Claire (WI)
U of Wisconsin–River Falls (WI)
U of Wisconsin–Stevens Point (WI)
U of Wisconsin–Superior (WI)
U of Wyoming (WY)
Utah State U (UT)
Virginia Commonwealth U (VA)
Wake Forest U (NC)

Walsh Coll of Accountancy and Business Admin (MI)
Waynesburg Coll (PA)
Wayne State U (MI)
Weber State U (UT)
Western Illinois U (IL)
Western Kentucky U (KY)
Western Michigan U (MI)
West Texas A&M U (TX)
Wichita State U (KS)
Williams Baptist Coll (AR)
Winona State U (MN)
Worcester Polytechnic Inst (MA)
Yale U (CT)

COMPUTER MAINTENANCE TECHNOLOGY
Peirce Coll (PA)
Wayne State U (MI)

COMPUTER MANAGEMENT
American InterContinental U (CA)
American InterContinental U, Atlanta (GA)
American InterContinental U (United Kingdom)
Barat Coll (IL)
Belmont U (TN)
Champlain Coll (VT)
Coll of Saint Mary (NE)
Columbus State U (GA)
Daniel Webster Coll (NH)
École des Hautes Études Commerciales (PQ, Canada)
Faulkner U (AL)
Fordham U (NY)
Grove City Coll (PA)
Holy Family Coll (PA)
Insto Tecno Estudios Sups Monterrey (Mexico)
Insto Tecno Estudios Sups Monterrey, Querétaro (Mexico)
Inter American U of PR, Metropolitan Campus (PR)
Lehman Coll of the City U of NY (NY)
Luther Coll (IA)
Mary Baldwin Coll (VA)
Minot State U (ND)
National American U (MO)
National-Louis U (IL)
New England Coll (NH)
Northwest Missouri State U (MO)
Northwood U (MI)
Oakland City U (IN)
Oklahoma Baptist U (OK)
Oklahoma State U (OK)
Pacific Union Coll (CA)
Pontifical Catholic U of Puerto Rico (PR)
Rochester Coll (MI)
St. Mary's U of San Antonio (TX)
Simpson Coll (IA)
Tiffin U (OH)
Université de Sherbrooke (PQ, Canada)
U of Cincinnati (OH)
U of Great Falls (MT)
Webster U (MO)
West Chester U of Pennsylvania (PA)
Western Washington U (WA)
West Virginia U Inst of Technology (WV)
Worcester Polytechnic Inst (MA)
York Coll of the City U of New York (NY)

COMPUTER PROGRAMMING
Andrews U (MI)
Baker Coll of Flint (MI)
Baker Coll of Owosso (MI)
Beaver Coll (PA)
Belmont U (TN)
Brigham Young U–Hawaii Campus (HI)
Brock U (ON, Canada)
Carleton U (ON, Canada)
Champlain Coll (VT)
Charleston Southern U (SC)
City U (WA)
Columbus State U (GA)
Daniel Webster Coll (NH)
Davenport Coll of Business (MI)
Davenport Coll of Business, Kalamazoo Campus (MI)
DePaul U (IL)

Ferris State U (MI)
Florida Metropolitan U-Tampa Coll, Brandon (FL)
Fontbonne Coll (MO)
Franklin Pierce Coll (NH)
Grand Valley State U (MI)
Hampshire Coll (MA)
Hannibal-LaGrange Coll (MO)
Harvard U (MA)
Humphreys Coll (CA)
Husson Coll (ME)
Indiana State U (IN)
Inter American U of PR, Metropolitan Campus (PR)
Inter American U of PR, San Germán Campus (PR)
Iowa Wesleyan Coll (IA)
Lamar U (TX)
La Salle U (PA)
Limestone Coll (SC)
Luther Coll (IA)
McPherson Coll (KS)
Memorial U of Newfoundland (NF, Canada)
Michigan Technological U (MI)
Midland Lutheran Coll (NE)
Minnesota State U, Mankato (MN)
Montana Tech of The U of Montana (MT)
Newbury Coll (MA)
New Mexico Highlands U (NM)
New Mexico Inst of Mining and Technology (NM)
Northern Michigan U (MI)
Northwest Missouri State U (MO)
The Ohio State U (OH)
Oklahoma State U (OK)
Oregon Inst of Technology (OR)
Pacific Union Coll (CA)
Pittsburg State U (PA)
Richmond, The American International U in London (United Kingdom)
Rochester Inst of Technology (NY)
Rockhurst U (MO)
Saint Peter's Coll (NJ)
Taylor U (IN)
Texas Southern U (TX)
U du Québec à Trois-Rivières (PQ, Canada)
U of Advancing Computer Technology (AZ)
U of Central Oklahoma (OK)
U of Cincinnati (OH)
U of Detroit Mercy (MI)
U of Regina (SK, Canada)
U of St. Francis (IL)
U of Southern Colorado (CO)
The U of Tampa (FL)
Villa Julie Coll (MD)
West Chester U of Pennsylvania (PA)
Western Washington U (WA)
West Virginia U Inst of Technology (WV)
Wheeling Jesuit U (WV)
Winona State U (MN)
York U (ON, Canada)
Youngstown State U (OH)

COMPUTER SCIENCE
Abilene Christian U (TX)
Acadia U (NS, Canada)
Adams State Coll (CO)
Adelphi U (NY)
Alabama State U (AL)
Albany State U (GA)
Albertson Coll of Idaho (ID)
Albion Coll (MI)
Albright Coll (PA)
Alderson-Broaddus Coll (WV)
Alfred U (NY)
Allegheny Coll (PA)
Allentown Coll of St. Francis de Sales (PA)
Alma Coll (MI)
American Military U (VA)
American U (DC)
American U in Cairo (Egypt)
The American U of Paris (France)
Amherst Coll (MA)
Anderson U (IN)
Andrews U (MI)
Antioch Coll (OH)
Appalachian State U (NC)
Arizona State U (AZ)
Arkansas Baptist Coll (AR)

Peterson's Guide to Four-Year Colleges 2001 — www.petersons.com

Majors Index
Computer Science

Arkansas Tech U (AR)
Armstrong Atlantic State U (GA)
Ashland U (OH)
Assumption Coll (MA)
Athens State U (AL)
Atlantic Union Coll (MA)
Augsburg Coll (MN)
Augustana Coll (IL)
Augustana Coll (SD)
Azusa Pacific U (CA)
Baker Coll of Muskegon (MI)
Baker Coll of Owosso (MI)
Baker U (KS)
Baldwin-Wallace Coll (OH)
Ball State U (IN)
Barat Coll (IL)
Barber-Scotia Coll (NC)
Barnard Coll (NY)
Barry U (FL)
Baylor U (TX)
Beaver Coll (PA)
Belhaven Coll (MS)
Bellarmine U (KY)
Belmont U (TN)
Beloit Coll (WI)
Bemidji State U (MN)
Benedictine Coll (KS)
Benedictine U (IL)
Bennett Coll (NC)
Bennington Coll (VT)
Berry Coll (GA)
Bethany Coll (WV)
Bethel Coll (IN)
Bethel Coll (MN)
Bethune-Cookman Coll (FL)
Birmingham-Southern Coll (AL)
Bishop's U (PQ, Canada)
Blackburn Coll (IL)
Bluffton Coll (OH)
Boise State U (ID)
Boston Coll (MA)
Boston U (MA)
Bowdoin Coll (ME)
Bowie State U (MD)
Brandeis U (MA)
Brandon U (MB, Canada)
Brevard Coll (NC)
Briar Cliff Coll (IA)
Bridgewater Coll (VA)
Bridgewater State Coll (MA)
Brigham Young U (UT)
Brock U (ON, Canada)
Brooklyn Coll of the City U of NY (NY)
Brown U (RI)
Bryan Coll (TN)
Buena Vista U (IA)
Butler U (IN)
Caldwell Coll (NJ)
California Inst of Technology (CA)
California Lutheran U (CA)
California Polytechnic State U, San Luis Obispo (CA)
California State Polytechnic U, Pomona (CA)
California State U, Dominguez Hills (CA)
California State U, Fresno (CA)
California State U, Fullerton (CA)
California State U, Hayward (CA)
California State U, Long Beach (CA)
California State U, Los Angeles (CA)
California State U, Northridge (CA)
California State U, San Bernardino (CA)
California State U, San Marcos (CA)
California State U, Stanislaus (CA)
Calvary Bible Coll and Theological Seminary (MO)
Calvin Coll (MI)
Cameron U (OK)
Canisius Coll (NY)
Capital U (OH)
Cardinal Stritch U (WI)
Carleton Coll (MN)
Carleton U (ON, Canada)
Carlow Coll (PA)
Carnegie Mellon U (PA)
Carroll Coll (MT)
Carroll Coll (WI)
Carson-Newman Coll (TN)
Carthage Coll (WI)
Case Western Reserve U (OH)
Catawba Coll (NC)

The Catholic U of America (DC)
Cedarville Coll (OH)
Central Coll (IA)
Central Methodist Coll (MO)
Centre Coll (KY)
Chapman U (CA)
Charleston Southern U (SC)
Chestnut Hill Coll (PA)
Cheyney U of Pennsylvania (PA)
Chicago State U (IL)
Christian Brothers U (TN)
Christopher Newport U (VA)
Citadel, The Military Coll of South Carolina (SC)
City Coll of the City U of NY (NY)
Claflin U (SC)
Claremont McKenna Coll (CA)
Clarke Coll (IA)
Clarkson U (NY)
Clark U (MA)
Clemson U (SC)
Cleveland State U (OH)
Coastal Carolina U (SC)
Coe Coll (IA)
Colby Coll (ME)
Colgate U (NY)
Coll Misericordia (PA)
Coll of Mount St. Joseph (OH)
Coll of Mount Saint Vincent (NY)
The Coll of New Jersey (NJ)
Coll of Notre Dame (CA)
Coll of Notre Dame of Maryland (MD)
Coll of Our Lady of the Elms (MA)
Coll of Saint Benedict (MN)
Coll of Santa Fe (NM)
The Coll of Southeastern Europe, The American U of Athens (Greece)
Coll of Staten Island of the City U of NY (NY)
Coll of the Ozarks (MO)
The Coll of West Virginia (WV)
The Coll of William and Mary (VA)
The Coll of Wooster (OH)
Colorado School of Mines (CO)
Colorado State U (CO)
Colorado Tech U (CO)
Colorado Tech U Denver Campus (CO)
Columbia Coll (NY)
Columbia Union Coll (MD)
Columbia U, School of General Studies (NY)
Columbia U, School of Engineering & Applied Sci (NY)
Columbus State U (GA)
Concord Coll (WV)
Concordia Coll (MN)
Concordia U (IL)
Concordia U (NE)
Concordia U (PQ, Canada)
Concordia U at Austin (TX)
Concordia U Wisconsin (WI)
Converse Coll (SC)
Coppin State Coll (MD)
Cornell Coll (IA)
Cornell U (NY)
Covenant Coll (GA)
Creighton U (NE)
Dakota State U (SD)
Dalhousie U (NS, Canada)
Dallas Baptist U (TX)
Dana Coll (NE)
Daniel Webster Coll (NH)
Dartmouth Coll (NH)
David Lipscomb U (TN)
Defiance Coll (OH)
Delaware State U (DE)
Denison U (OH)
DePaul U (IL)
DePauw U (IN)
Dickinson Coll (PA)
Dickinson State U (ND)
Dixie State Coll of Utah (UT)
Doane Coll (NE)
Dominican U (IL)
Dordt Coll (IA)
Dowling Coll (NY)
Drake U (IA)
Drew U (NJ)
Drexel U (PA)
Drury U (MO)
Duke U (NC)
Duquesne U (PA)
Earlham Coll (IN)
East Carolina U (NC)

East Central U (OK)
Eastern Illinois U (IL)
Eastern Kentucky U (KY)
Eastern Mennonite U (VA)
Eastern Nazarene Coll (MA)
Eastern Oregon U (OR)
Eastern Washington U (WA)
East Tennessee State U (TN)
Eckerd Coll (FL)
Elizabeth City State U (NC)
Elizabethtown Coll (PA)
Elmhurst Coll (IL)
Elon Coll (NC)
Emory & Henry Coll (VA)
Emory U (GA)
Evangel U (MO)
The Evergreen State Coll (WA)
Fairfield U (CT)
Fairleigh Dickinson U, Florham-Madison Campus (NJ)
Fairleigh Dickinson U, Teaneck-Hackensack Campus (NJ)
Fairmont State Coll (WV)
Felician Coll (NJ)
Ferrum Coll (VA)
Fisk U (TN)
Fitchburg State Coll (MA)
Florida Inst of Technology (FL)
Florida International U (FL)
Florida Metropolitan U-Tampa Coll, Brandon (FL)
Florida Southern Coll (FL)
Florida State U (FL)
Fontbonne Coll (MO)
Fordham U (NY)
Fort Lewis Coll (CO)
Fort Valley State U (GA)
Framingham State Coll (MA)
Franciscan U of Steubenville (OH)
Francis Marion U (SC)
Franklin Coll of Indiana (IN)
Franklin Pierce Coll (NH)
Franklin U (OH)
Freed-Hardeman U (TN)
Friends U (KS)
Furman U (SC)
Gallaudet U (DC)
Gardner-Webb U (NC)
Geneva Coll (PA)
George Mason U (VA)
Georgetown Coll (KY)
Georgetown U (DC)
The George Washington U (DC)
Georgia Southwestern State U (GA)
Gettysburg Coll (PA)
Glenville State Coll (WV)
Gonzaga U (WA)
Gordon Coll (MA)
Goshen Coll (IN)
Goucher Coll (MD)
Governors State U (IL)
Graceland Coll (IA)
Grand Valley State U (MI)
Grand View Coll (IA)
Grantham Coll of Engineering (LA)
Greenville Coll (IL)
Grinnell Coll (IA)
Gustavus Adolphus Coll (MN)
Hamilton Coll (NY)
Hampden-Sydney Coll (VA)
Hampshire Coll (MA)
Hampton U (VA)
Hanover Coll (IN)
Harding U (AR)
Hardin-Simmons U (TX)
Hartwick Coll (NY)
Harvard U (MA)
Harvey Mudd Coll (CA)
Hastings Coll (NE)
Haverford Coll (PA)
Hawaii Pacific U (HI)
Heidelberg Coll (OH)
Hendrix Coll (AR)
Henry Cogswell Coll (WA)
Heritage Coll (WA)
High Point U (NC)
Hillsdale Coll (MI)
Hiram Coll (OH)
Hobart and William Smith Colls (NY)
Hofstra U (NY)
Hollins U (VA)
Hood Coll (MD)
Hope Coll (MI)
Houghton Coll (NY)
Houston Baptist U (TX)

Humphreys Coll (CA)
Hunter Coll of the City U of NY (NY)
Huntingdon Coll (AL)
Huntington Coll (IN)
Huron U (SD)
Huston-Tillotson Coll (TX)
Illinois Coll (IL)
Illinois Inst of Technology (IL)
Illinois Wesleyan U (IL)
Immaculata Coll (PA)
Indiana Inst of Technology (IN)
Indiana State U (IN)
Indiana U–Purdue U Fort Wayne (IN)
Indiana U South Bend (IN)
Indiana U Southeast (IN)
Inst of Computer Technology (CA)
Insto Tecno Estudios Sups Monterrey (Mexico)
Inter American U of PR, Aguadilla Campus (PR)
Inter American U of PR, Arecibo Campus (PR)
Inter American U of PR, Fajardo Campus (PR)
Inter American U of PR, Metropolitan Campus (PR)
Inter American U of PR, San Germán Campus (PR)
Iona Coll (NY)
Iowa State U of Science and Technology (IA)
Iowa Wesleyan Coll (IA)
Ithaca Coll (NY)
Jamestown Coll (ND)
Jarvis Christian Coll (TX)
John Carroll U (OH)
Johns Hopkins U (MD)
Johnson & Wales U (RI)
Johnson C. Smith U (NC)
Judson Coll (IL)
Kalamazoo Coll (MI)
Keene State Coll (NH)
Kendall Coll (IL)
Kentucky Wesleyan Coll (KY)
Kettering U (MI)
King's Coll (PA)
Kutztown U of Pennsylvania (PA)
Lafayette Coll (PA)
LaGrange Coll (GA)
Lake Forest Coll (IL)
Lakehead U (ON, Canada)
Lakeland Coll (WI)
Lake Superior State U (MI)
Lamar U (TX)
Lander U (SC)
Lane Coll (TN)
Langston U (OK)
La Salle U (PA)
La Sierra U (CA)
Lawrence Technological U (MI)
Lawrence U (WI)
Lebanon Valley Coll (PA)
Lehigh U (PA)
Lehman Coll of the City U of NY (NY)
LeMoyne-Owen Coll (TN)
Lenoir-Rhyne Coll (NC)
LeTourneau U (TX)
Lewis & Clark Coll (OR)
Lewis U (IL)
Limestone Coll (SC)
Lincoln U (CA)
Lincoln U (PA)
Lindenwood U (MO)
Linfield Coll (OR)
Lock Haven U of Pennsylvania (PA)
Long Island U, Brooklyn Campus (NY)
Long Island U, C.W. Post Campus (NY)
Longwood Coll (VA)
Loras Coll (IA)
Louisiana State U and A&M Coll (LA)
Louisiana State U in Shreveport (LA)
Louisiana Tech U (LA)
Loyola Marymount U (CA)
Loyola U Chicago (IL)
Lubbock Christian U (TX)
Luther Coll (IA)
Lycoming Coll (PA)
Lynchburg Coll (VA)
Lyon Coll (AR)

Macalester Coll (MN)
MacMurray Coll (IL)
Madonna U (MI)
Maharishi U of Management (IA)
Malone Coll (OH)
Manchester Coll (IN)
Manhattan Coll (NY)
Manhattanville Coll (NY)
Mansfield U of Pennsylvania (PA)
Marietta Coll (OH)
Marist Coll (NY)
Marlboro Coll (VT)
Marquette U (WI)
Marshall U (WV)
Mars Hill Coll (NC)
Marycrest International U (IA)
Maryville Coll (TN)
Mary Washington Coll (VA)
Massachusetts Coll of Liberal Arts (MA)
Massachusetts Inst of Technology (MA)
McGill U (PQ, Canada)
McKendree Coll (IL)
McMurry U (TX)
McNeese State U (LA)
McPherson Coll (KS)
Memorial U of Newfoundland (NF, Canada)
Mercer U (GA)
Mercy Coll (NY)
Mercyhurst Coll (PA)
Meredith Coll (NC)
Merrimack Coll (MA)
Mesa State Coll (CO)
Methodist Coll (NC)
Metropolitan State Coll of Denver (CO)
Michigan State U (MI)
Michigan Technological U (MI)
MidAmerica Nazarene U (KS)
Middlebury Coll (VT)
Middle Tennessee State U (TN)
Midland Lutheran Coll (NE)
Midwestern State U (TX)
Millersville U of Pennsylvania (PA)
Milligan Coll (TN)
Millsaps Coll (MS)
Mills Coll (CA)
Minnesota State U, Mankato (MN)
Minnesota State U Moorhead (MN)
Minot State U (ND)
Mississippi Coll (MS)
Mississippi Valley State U (MS)
Missouri Southern State Coll (MO)
Missouri Valley Coll (MO)
Molloy Coll (NY)
Monmouth Coll (IL)
Montana State U–Bozeman (MT)
Montana Tech of The U of Montana (MT)
Moravian Coll (PA)
Morgan State U (MD)
Morningside Coll (IA)
Mount Allison U (NB, Canada)
Mount Holyoke Coll (MA)
Mount Marty Coll (SD)
Mount Mercy Coll (IA)
Mount Saint Mary Coll (NY)
Mount Saint Mary's Coll and Seminary (MD)
Mount Union Coll (OH)
Mount Vernon Nazarene Coll (OH)
Muhlenberg Coll (PA)
Muskingum Coll (OH)
National U (CA)
Nebraska Wesleyan U (NE)
Newberry Coll (SC)
Newbury Coll (MA)
New Jersey Inst of Technology (NJ)
New Mexico Highlands U (NM)
New Mexico Inst of Mining and Technology (NM)
New Mexico State U (NM)
New York Inst of Technology (NY)
New York U (NY)
Niagara U (NY)
Nicholls State U (LA)
Nipissing U (ON, Canada)
Norfolk State U (VA)
North Carolina Ag and Tech State U (NC)
North Carolina Central U (NC)
North Carolina State U (NC)
North Central Coll (IL)
North Dakota State U (ND)
Northeastern State U (OK)

Majors Index
Computer Science

Northeastern U (MA)
Northern Arizona U (AZ)
Northern Illinois U (IL)
Northern Kentucky U (KY)
Northern Michigan U (MI)
North Georgia Coll & State U (GA)
Northwestern Coll (IA)
Northwestern Oklahoma State U (OK)
Northwestern U (IL)
Northwest Missouri State U (MO)
Northwest Nazarene U (ID)
Norwich U (VT)
Nova Southeastern U (FL)
Nyack Coll (NY)
Oakwood Coll (AL)
Oberlin Coll (OH)
Oglethorpe U (GA)
Ohio Dominican Coll (OH)
Ohio Northern U (OH)
The Ohio State U (OH)
Ohio U (OH)
Ohio Wesleyan U (OH)
Oklahoma Baptist U (OK)
Oklahoma Christian U of Science and Arts (OK)
Oklahoma City U (OK)
Oklahoma State U (OK)
Olivet Nazarene U (IL)
Oregon State U (OR)
Otterbein Coll (OH)
Ouachita Baptist U (AR)
Pace U, New York City Campus (NY)
Pace U, Pleasantville/Briarcliff Campus (NY)
Pacific Lutheran U (WA)
Pacific Union Coll (CA)
Pacific U (OR)
Park U (MO)
Pepperdine U, Malibu (CA)
Peru State Coll (NE)
Philadelphia U (PA)
Philander Smith Coll (AR)
Piedmont Coll (GA)
Pikeville Coll (KY)
Pittsburg State U (KS)
Plattsburgh State U of NY (NY)
Plymouth State Coll (NH)
Point Loma Nazarene U (CA)
Point Park Coll (PA)
Polytechnic U, Brooklyn Campus (NY)
Polytechnic U, Farmingdale Campus (NY)
Pomona Coll (CA)
Portland State U (OR)
Prairie View A&M U (TX)
Princeton U (NJ)
Providence Coll (RI)
Purdue U Calumet (IN)
Queens Coll of the City U of NY (NY)
Queen's U at Kingston (ON, Canada)
Quincy U (IL)
Quinnipiac U (CT)
Radford U (VA)
Randolph-Macon Coll (VA)
Redeemer Coll (ON, Canada)
Regents Coll (NY)
Regis U (CO)
Rensselaer Polytechnic Inst (NY)
Rhodes Coll (TN)
Rice U (TX)
The Richard Stockton Coll of New Jersey (NJ)
Richmond, The American International U in London (United Kingdom)
Rider U (NJ)
Ripon Coll (WI)
Rivier Coll (NH)
Roanoke Coll (VA)
Roberts Wesleyan Coll (NY)
Rochester Inst of Technology (NY)
Rockford Coll (IL)
Rockhurst U (MO)
Rocky Mountain Coll (MT)
Roger Williams U (RI)
Rollins Coll (FL)
Rose-Hulman Inst of Technology (IN)
Rowan U (NJ)
Russell Sage Coll (NY)
Rust Coll (MS)

Rutgers, State U of NJ, Camden Coll of Arts & Scis (NJ)
Rutgers, State U of NJ, Cook Coll (NJ)
Rutgers, State U of NJ, Douglass Coll (NJ)
Rutgers, State U of NJ, Livingston Coll (NJ)
Rutgers, State U of NJ, Newark Coll of Arts & Scis (NJ)
Rutgers, State U of NJ, Rutgers Coll (NJ)
Rutgers, State U of NJ, U Coll–Camden (NJ)
Rutgers, State U of NJ, U Coll–Newark (NJ)
Rutgers, State U of NJ, U Coll–New Brunswick (NJ)
Ryerson Polytechnic U (ON, Canada)
Sacred Heart U (CT)
St. Ambrose U (IA)
Saint Anselm Coll (NH)
Saint Augustine's Coll (NC)
St. Bonaventure U (NY)
St. Cloud State U (MN)
St. Edward's U (TX)
Saint Francis Coll (PA)
St. John Fisher Coll (NY)
Saint John's U (MN)
Saint Joseph Coll (CT)
Saint Joseph's Coll (IN)
St. Joseph's Coll, Suffolk Campus (NY)
Saint Joseph's U (PA)
St. Lawrence U (NY)
Saint Louis U (MO)
Saint Martin's Coll (WA)
St. Mary's Coll of Maryland (MD)
Saint Mary's U (NS, Canada)
Saint Mary's U of Minnesota (MN)
St. Mary's U of San Antonio (TX)
Saint Michael's Coll (VT)
Saint Paul's Coll (VA)
St. Thomas U (FL)
Saint Xavier U (IL)
Salem State Coll (MA)
Samford U (AL)
San Diego State U (CA)
San Francisco State U (CA)
San Jose State U (CA)
Santa Clara U (CA)
Sarah Lawrence Coll (NY)
Schreiner Coll (TX)
Scripps Coll (CA)
Seattle Pacific U (WA)
Seattle U (WA)
Seton Hill Coll (PA)
Shaw U (NC)
Shepherd Coll (WV)
Siena Coll (NY)
Simmons Coll (MA)
Simon Fraser U (BC, Canada)
Simon's Rock Coll of Bard (MA)
Simpson Coll (IA)
Skidmore Coll (NY)
Slippery Rock U of Pennsylvania (PA)
Smith Coll (MA)
Sonoma State U (CA)
South Dakota School of Mines and Technology (SD)
Southeastern Louisiana U (LA)
Southeastern U (DC)
Southeast Missouri State U (MO)
Southern Adventist U (TN)
Southern Methodist U (TX)
Southern Oregon U (OR)
Southern Utah U (UT)
Southwest Baptist U (MO)
Southwestern Adventist U (TX)
Southwestern Oklahoma State U (OK)
Southwestern U (TX)
Southwest Missouri State U (MO)
Southwest State U (MN)
Spalding U (KY)
Spelman Coll (GA)
Spring Arbor Coll (MI)
Stanford U (CA)
State U of NY at Albany (NY)
State U of NY at Binghamton (NY)
State U of NY at Buffalo (NY)
State U of NY at New Paltz (NY)
State U of NY at Oswego (NY)
State U of NY at Stony Brook (NY)

State U of NY Coll at Brockport (NY)
State U of NY Coll at Fredonia (NY)
State U of NY Coll at Geneseo (NY)
State U of NY Coll at Oneonta (NY)
State U of NY Coll at Potsdam (NY)
State U of NY Inst of Tech at Utica/Rome (NY)
State U of West Georgia (GA)
Stetson U (FL)
Stevens Inst of Technology (NJ)
Stillman Coll (AL)
Stonehill Coll (MA)
Suffolk U (MA)
Susquehanna U (PA)
Swarthmore Coll (PA)
Sweet Briar Coll (VA)
Syracuse U (NY)
Tabor Coll (KS)
Talladega Coll (AL)
Taylor U (IN)
Taylor U, Fort Wayne Campus (IN)
Temple U (PA)
Tennessee State U (TN)
Tennessee Technological U (TN)
Texas A&M U (TX)
Texas A&M U–Commerce (TX)
Texas A&M U–Kingsville (TX)
Texas Christian U (TX)
Texas Lutheran U (TX)
Texas Southern U (TX)
Texas Wesleyan U (TX)
Thiel Coll (PA)
Thomas Edison State Coll (NJ)
Tougaloo Coll (MS)
Touro Coll (NY)
Transylvania U (KY)
Trent U (ON, Canada)
Trinity Christian Coll (IL)
Trinity Coll (CT)
Trinity Western U (BC, Canada)
Tri-State U (IN)
Troy State U Dothan (AL)
Truman State U (MO)
Tufts U (MA)
Tulane U (LA)
Tusculum Coll (TN)
Tuskegee U (AL)
Union Coll (NE)
Union U (TN)
United States Air Force Academy (CO)
United States Military Academy (NY)
United States Naval Academy (MD)
Universidad Adventista de las Antillas (PR)
Universidad Metropolitana (PR)
Université de Montréal (PQ, Canada)
Université de Sherbrooke (PQ, Canada)
U du Québec à Chicoutimi (PQ, Canada)
U du Québec à Hull (PQ, Canada)
U du Québec à Trois-Rivières (PQ, Canada)
Université Laval (PQ, Canada)
U Coll of Cape Breton (NS, Canada)
The U of Akron (OH)
U of Alaska Fairbanks (AK)
U of Alberta (AB, Canada)
U of Arkansas at Little Rock (AR)
U of Arkansas at Pine Bluff (AR)
U of Bridgeport (CT)
U of British Columbia (BC, Canada)
U of Calgary (AB, Canada)
U of Calif, Irvine (CA)
U of Calif, Los Angeles (CA)
U of Calif, Riverside (CA)
U of Calif, San Diego (CA)
U of Calif, Santa Barbara (CA)
U of Calif, Santa Cruz (CA)
U of Central Oklahoma (OK)
U of Chicago (IL)
U of Cincinnati (OH)
U of Colorado at Boulder (CO)
U of Colorado at Colorado Springs (CO)
U of Colorado at Denver (CO)
U of Dallas (TX)

U of Dayton (OH)
U of Delaware (DE)
U of Detroit Mercy (MI)
U of Dubuque (IA)
U of Evansville (IN)
The U of Findlay (OH)
U of Great Falls (MT)
U of Guelph (ON, Canada)
U of Houston–Clear Lake (TX)
U of Houston–Victoria (TX)
U of Idaho (ID)
U of Illinois at Springfield (IL)
U of Indianapolis (IN)
The U of Iowa (IA)
U of King's Coll (NS, Canada)
U of La Verne (CA)
The U of Lethbridge (AB, Canada)
U of Louisiana at Lafayette (LA)
U of Louisiana at Monroe (LA)
U of Maine (ME)
U of Maine at Farmington (ME)
U of Maine at Fort Kent (ME)
U of Manitoba (MB, Canada)
U of Mary Hardin-Baylor (TX)
U of Maryland, Baltimore County (MD)
U of Maryland, Coll Park (MD)
U of Maryland University Coll (MD)
U of Massachusetts Amherst (MA)
U of Massachusetts Boston (MA)
U of Massachusetts Lowell (MA)
The U of Memphis (TN)
U of Miami (FL)
U of Michigan (MI)
U of Michigan–Dearborn (MI)
U of Michigan–Flint (MI)
U of Minnesota, Duluth (MN)
U of Minnesota, Morris (MN)
U of Minnesota, Twin Cities Campus (MN)
U of Missouri–Columbia (MO)
U of Missouri–Kansas City (MO)
U of Missouri–Rolla (MO)
U of Missouri–St. Louis (MO)
U of Mobile (AL)
The U of Montana–Missoula (MT)
U of Nebraska at Omaha (NE)
U of Nebraska–Lincoln (NE)
U of Nevada, Las Vegas (NV)
U of Nevada, Reno (NV)
U of New Brunswick, Fredericton (NB, Canada)
U of New Brunswick, Saint John (NB, Canada)
U of New Hampshire (NH)
U of New Mexico (NM)
U of New Orleans (LA)
The U of North Carolina at Asheville (NC)
The U of North Carolina at Charlotte (NC)
The U of North Carolina at Pembroke (NC)
U of Northern Iowa (IA)
U of Oklahoma (OK)
U of Oregon (OR)
U of Pittsburgh (PA)
U of Pittsburgh at Bradford (PA)
U of Pittsburgh at Johnstown (PA)
U of Portland (OR)
U of Prince Edward Island (PE, Canada)
U of Puerto Rico at Ponce (PR)
U of Puerto Rico, Mayagüez Campus (PR)
U of Puerto Rico, Río Piedras (PR)
U of Puget Sound (WA)
U of Redlands (CA)
U of Regina (SK, Canada)
U of Richmond (VA)
U of Rio Grande (OH)
U of Rochester (NY)
U of St. Francis (IL)
U of San Diego (CA)
U of San Francisco (CA)
U of Science and Arts of Oklahoma (OK)
The U of Scranton (PA)
U of Sioux Falls (SD)
U of South Alabama (AL)
U of South Dakota (SD)
U of Southern California (CA)
U of Southern Colorado (CO)
U of Southern Maine (ME)
U of Southern Mississippi (MS)
The U of Tennessee at Chattanooga (TN)

The U of Tennessee at Martin (TN)
The U of Tennessee Knoxville (TN)
The U of Texas at Dallas (TX)
The U of Texas at Tyler (TX)
The U of Texas–Pan American (TX)
U of the District of Columbia (DC)
U of the Pacific (CA)
U of the Sacred Heart (PR)
U of the South (TN)
U of Toronto (ON, Canada)
U of Tulsa (OK)
U of Utah (UT)
U of Vermont (VT)
U of Victoria (BC, Canada)
U of Washington (WA)
U of Waterloo (ON, Canada)
The U of Western Ontario (ON, Canada)
U of Windsor (ON, Canada)
U of Wisconsin–Green Bay (WI)
U of Wisconsin–La Crosse (WI)
U of Wisconsin–Madison (WI)
U of Wisconsin–Milwaukee (WI)
U of Wisconsin–Parkside (WI)
U of Wisconsin–Platteville (WI)
U of Wisconsin–River Falls (WI)
U of Wisconsin–Superior (WI)
U of Wisconsin–Whitewater (WI)
U of Wyoming (WY)
Ursinus Coll (PA)
Utica Coll of Syracuse U (NY)
Valdosta State U (GA)
Valparaiso U (IN)
Vanderbilt U (TN)
Vassar Coll (NY)
Villanova U (PA)
Virginia Commonwealth U (VA)
Virginia Military Inst (VA)
Virginia Polytechnic Inst and State U (VA)
Virginia Wesleyan Coll (VA)
Voorhees Coll (SC)
Wagner Coll (NY)
Walla Walla Coll (WA)
Walsh U (OH)
Wartburg Coll (IA)
Washington and Lee U (VA)
Washington State U (WA)
Washington U in St. Louis (MO)
Waynesburg Coll (PA)
Wayne State Coll (NE)
Weber State U (UT)
Webster U (MO)
Wellesley Coll (MA)
Wells Coll (NY)
Wentworth Inst of Technology (MA)
Wesleyan U (CT)
West Chester U of Pennsylvania (PA)
Western Baptist Coll (OR)
Western Carolina U (NC)
Western Connecticut State U (CT)
Western Michigan U (MI)
Western New England Coll (MA)
Western Oregon U (OR)
Western State Coll of Colorado (CO)
Western Washington U (WA)
Westfield State Coll (MA)
Westminster Coll (MO)
Westminster Coll (PA)
Westminster Coll (UT)
Westmont Coll (CA)
West Virginia U (WV)
West Virginia U Inst of Technology (WV)
West Virginia Wesleyan Coll (WV)
Wheaton Coll (IL)
Wheaton Coll (MA)
Wheeling Jesuit U (WV)
Whitworth Coll (WA)
Widener U (PA)
Wilfrid Laurier U (ON, Canada)
Wilkes U (PA)
Willamette U (OR)
William Jewell Coll (MO)
William Paterson U of New Jersey (NJ)
William Penn U (IA)
Williams Coll (MA)
Wilmington Coll (OH)
Winona State U (MN)
Winston-Salem State U (NC)
Winthrop U (SC)
Wittenberg U (OH)
Wofford Coll (SC)
Worcester Polytechnic Inst (MA)

Majors Index
Computer Science–Criminal Justice Studies

Worcester State Coll (MA)
Wright State U (OH)
Xavier U (OH)
Xavier U of Louisiana (LA)
Yeshiva U (NY)
York U (ON, Canada)
Youngstown State U (OH)

COMPUTER SYSTEMS ANALYSIS
Baker Coll of Flint (MI)
Kent State U (OH)
McGill U (PQ, Canada)
Miami U (OH)
Montana Tech of The U of Montana (MT)
Oklahoma Baptist U (OK)
Rockhurst U (MO)
Saginaw Valley State U (MI)
St. Ambrose U (IA)
U du Québec à Trois-Rivières (PQ, Canada)
U Coll of the Fraser Valley (BC, Canada)
U of Houston (TX)
U of Miami (FL)

COMPUTER TYPOGRAPHY/COMPOSITION
David N. Myers Coll (OH)

CONSTRUCTION ENGINEERING
American U in Cairo (Egypt)
Andrews U (MI)
California State U, Chico (CA)
The Catholic U of America (DC)
Concordia U (PQ, Canada)
Fitchburg State Coll (MA)
Iowa State U of Science and Technology (IA)
John Brown U (AR)
Lawrence Technological U (MI)
Michigan Technological U (MI)
North Carolina State U (NC)
North Dakota State U (ND)
The Ohio State U (OH)
Oregon State U (OR)
State U of NY Coll of Environ Sci and Forestry (NY)
State U of NY Coll of Technology at Alfred (NY)
Temple U (PA)
Texas A&M U–Commerce (TX)
U of Alberta (AB, Canada)
U of Cincinnati (OH)
U of Nevada, Las Vegas (NV)
U of New Brunswick, Fredericton (NB, Canada)
U of Southern Mississippi (MS)
Western Michigan U (MI)
Worcester Polytechnic Inst (MA)

CONSTRUCTION MANAGEMENT
Andrews U (MI)
Boise State U (ID)
Brigham Young U (UT)
California State U, Long Beach (CA)
Clemson U (SC)
Drexel U (PA)
Ferris State U (MI)
Hampton U (VA)
Indiana State U (IN)
John Brown U (AR)
Michigan State U (MI)
Milwaukee School of Engineering (WI)
Minnesota State U, Mankato (MN)
Mississippi State U (MS)
North Carolina Ag and Tech State U (NC)
North Dakota State U (ND)
Northern Arizona U (AZ)
Oklahoma State U (OK)
Oregon State U (OR)
Pittsburg State U (KS)
Pratt Inst (NY)
Roger Williams U (RI)
Sam Houston State U (TX)
State U of NY at Farmingdale (NY)
U of Cincinnati (OH)
U of Denver (CO)
U of Minnesota, Twin Cities Campus (MN)
U of Nebraska–Lincoln (NE)
U of the District of Columbia (DC)
U of Washington (WA)

U of Wisconsin–Madison (WI)
U of Wisconsin–Platteville (WI)
Wentworth Inst of Technology (MA)
Western Michigan U (MI)
Worcester Polytechnic Inst (MA)

CONSTRUCTION TECHNOLOGY
Andrews U (MI)
Arizona State U (AZ)
Bemidji State U (MN)
Bowling Green State U (OH)
Bradley U (IL)
California State Polytechnic U, Pomona (CA)
California State U, Fresno (CA)
California State U, Long Beach (CA)
California State U, Sacramento (CA)
Central Missouri State U (MO)
Colorado State U (CO)
Eastern Kentucky U (KY)
Eastern Washington U (WA)
East Tennessee State U (TN)
Fairleigh Dickinson U, Teaneck-Hackensack Campus (NJ)
Fitchburg State Coll (MA)
Florida A&M U (FL)
Florida International U (FL)
Georgia Inst of Technology (GA)
Georgia Southern U (GA)
Hampton U (VA)
Indiana State U (IN)
Indiana U–Purdue U Fort Wayne (IN)
Minnesota State U Moorhead (MN)
Montana State U–Bozeman (MT)
Murray State U (KY)
Norfolk State U (VA)
North Dakota State U (ND)
Northern Michigan U (MI)
Oklahoma State U (OK)
Penn State U Harrisburg Campus of the Capital Coll (PA)
Peru State Coll (NE)
Pittsburg State U (KS)
Purdue U Calumet (IN)
South Dakota State U (SD)
Southern Illinois U Edwardsville (IL)
Southern Polytechnic State U (GA)
Southern Utah U (UT)
Southwest Missouri State U (MO)
Southwest Texas State U (TX)
Texas A&M U (TX)
Texas Southern U (TX)
Thomas Edison State Coll (NJ)
Tuskegee U (AL)
The U of Akron (OH)
U of Arkansas at Little Rock (AR)
U of Central Oklahoma (OK)
U of Cincinnati (OH)
U of Florida (FL)
U of Houston (TX)
U of Louisiana at Monroe (LA)
U of Maine (ME)
U of Nebraska at Omaha (NE)
U of Nebraska–Lincoln (NE)
U of New Mexico (NM)
U of North Florida (FL)
U of Oklahoma (OK)
U of Southern Colorado (CO)
U of Southern Mississippi (MS)
U of Wisconsin–Stout (WI)
Virginia Polytechnic Inst and State U (VA)
Washington State U (WA)
Wentworth Inst of Technology (MA)

CONSUMER AND HOMEMAKING EDUCATION
North Dakota State U (ND)
Virginia Polytechnic Inst and State U (VA)

CONSUMER ECONOMICS
Bradley U (IL)
Indiana U of Pennsylvania (PA)
Louisiana Tech U (LA)
Mount Mary Coll (WI)
Southeastern Louisiana U (LA)
Texas Woman's U (TX)
The U of Alabama (AL)
The U of Arizona (AZ)
U of Delaware (DE)
U of Georgia (GA)
U of Illinois at Urbana–Champaign (IL)

U of Kentucky (KY)
U of Rhode Island (RI)
The U of Tennessee Knoxville (TN)

CONSUMER SERVICES
Carson-Newman Coll (TN)
Coll of the Ozarks (MO)
Cornell U (NY)
Iowa State U of Science and Technology (IA)
Mount Saint Vincent U (NS, Canada)
Norfolk State U (VA)
Oklahoma State U (OK)
Pacific Union Coll (CA)
South Dakota State U (SD)
State U of NY Coll at Oneonta (NY)
Syracuse U (NY)
Tennessee State U (TN)
Université Laval (PQ, Canada)
U of Wisconsin–Madison (WI)

CORRECTIONS
Averett Coll (VA)
Bluefield State Coll (WV)
California State U, Hayward (CA)
Chicago State U (IL)
Coll of the Ozarks (MO)
Eastern Kentucky U (KY)
Eastern Washington U (WA)
Hardin-Simmons U (TX)
Jacksonville State U (AL)
John Jay Coll of Criminal Justice, the City U of NY (NY)
Lake Superior State U (MI)
Lamar U (TX)
Langston U (OK)
Marshall U (WV)
Mercyhurst Coll (PA)
Minnesota State U, Mankato (MN)
Murray State U (KY)
Northeastern U (MA)
Oklahoma City U (OK)
St. Cloud State U (MN)
Saint Louis U (MO)
Sam Houston State U (TX)
Southeast Missouri State U (MO)
Southwest Texas State U (TX)
State U of NY Coll at Brockport (NY)
Stephen F. Austin State U (TX)
Tiffin U (OH)
Troy State U (AL)
Troy State U Dothan (AL)
The U of Akron (OH)
U of Arkansas at Pine Bluff (AR)
U of Indianapolis (IN)
U of New Mexico (NM)
U of Pittsburgh (PA)
U of Regina (SK, Canada)
U of Southern Colorado (CO)
The U of Tennessee at Chattanooga (TN)
The U of Texas at San Antonio (TX)
The U of Texas–Pan American (TX)
Utica Coll of Syracuse U (NY)
Virginia Commonwealth U (VA)
Weber State U (UT)
Western Oregon U (OR)
Westfield State Coll (MA)
Winona State U (MN)
York Coll of Pennsylvania (PA)

COUNSELING PSYCHOLOGY
Atlanta Christian Coll (GA)
Crichton Coll (TN)
George Fox U (OR)
Grace Coll (IN)
Mid-Continent Coll (KY)
Morningside Coll (IA)
Oregon Inst of Technology (OR)
Samford U (AL)
Texas Wesleyan U (TX)
Toccoa Falls Coll (GA)
U of North Alabama (AL)

COUNSELOR EDUCATION/GUIDANCE
Amber U (TX)
Belmont U (TN)
Bowling Green State U (OH)
Brandon U (MB, Canada)
California State Polytechnic U, Pomona (CA)
Circleville Bible Coll (OH)

DePaul U (IL)
East Central U (OK)
The Evergreen State Coll (WA)
Franklin Pierce Coll (NH)
Houston Baptist U (TX)
Howard U (DC)
Lamar U (TX)
Limestone Coll (SC)
Loras Coll (IA)
Memorial U of Newfoundland (NF, Canada)
Mesa State Coll (CO)
Northwest Missouri State U (MO)
Pittsburg State U (KS)
Purdue U Calumet (IN)
St. Cloud State U (MN)
San Diego State U (CA)
Southern Christian U (AL)
Texas A&M U–Commerce (TX)
Texas Southern U (TX)
Toccoa Falls Coll (GA)
Université de Sherbrooke (PQ, Canada)
U of British Columbia (BC, Canada)
U of Central Arkansas (AR)
U of Central Oklahoma (OK)
U of New Brunswick, Fredericton (NB, Canada)
U of North Texas (TX)
U of Toronto (ON, Canada)
U of Windsor (ON, Canada)
U of Wisconsin–Superior (WI)
Valdosta State U (GA)
Wayne State Coll (NE)
Western Washington U (WA)
Westfield State Coll (MA)

COURT REPORTING
Central Michigan U (MI)
Johnson & Wales U (RI)
Northwood U, Texas Campus (TX)
U of Mississippi (MS)

CRAFT/FOLK ART
Bowling Green State U (OH)
Bridgewater State Coll (MA)
Cleveland Inst of Art (OH)
Kent State U (OH)
Kutztown U of Pennsylvania (PA)
Oregon Coll of Art and Craft (OR)
Rochester Inst of Technology (NY)
U of Illinois at Urbana–Champaign (IL)
The U of the Arts (PA)
Virginia Commonwealth U (VA)

CRIMINAL JUSTICE STUDIES
Alfred U (NY)
Allentown Coll of St. Francis de Sales (PA)
American Military U (VA)
American U (DC)
Appalachian State U (NC)
Arizona State U (AZ)
Auburn U Montgomery (AL)
Augsburg Coll (MN)
Augusta State U (GA)
Barton Coll (NC)
Bellarmine Coll (KY)
Bethany Coll (KS)
Bloomsburg U of Pennsylvania (PA)
Bluefield State Coll (WV)
Butler U (IN)
Caldwell Coll (NJ)
California Baptist U (CA)
Cazenovia Coll (NY)
Central Methodist Coll (MO)
Chowan Coll (NC)
The Coll of West Virginia (WV)
Colorado State U (CO)
Delta State U (MS)
East Carolina U (NC)
Eastern New Mexico U (NM)
Edinboro U of Pennsylvania (PA)
Endicott Coll (MA)
Ferrum Coll (VA)
Florida Gulf Coast U (FL)
Florida International U (FL)
Florida Southern Coll (FL)
Fort Hays State U (KS)
Frostburg State U (MD)
Gannon U (PA)
Georgia Southern U (GA)
Georgia State U (GA)
Harding U (AR)

Hesser Coll (NH)
High Point U (NC)
Illinois State U (IL)
Indiana U Bloomington (IN)
Indiana U Kokomo (IN)
Indiana U–Purdue U Fort Wayne (IN)
Indiana U–Purdue U Indianapolis (IN)
Indiana Wesleyan U (IN)
Inter American U of PR, Aguadilla Campus (PR)
International Coll (FL)
Jamestown Coll (ND)
Judson Coll (AL)
Judson Coll (IL)
Kendall Coll (IL)
Kent State U (OH)
Kentucky State U (KY)
Kentucky Wesleyan Coll (KY)
King's Coll (PA)
La Roche Coll (PA)
La Salle U (PA)
Lasell Coll (MA)
Long Island U, Brentwood Campus (NY)
Loyola U Chicago (IL)
Loyola U New Orleans (LA)
McNeese State U (LA)
Medaille Coll (NY)
Millersville U of Pennsylvania (PA)
Minnesota State U Moorhead (MN)
Missouri Baptist Coll (MO)
Missouri Western State Coll (MO)
Molloy Coll (NY)
Monmouth U (NJ)
Morningside Coll (IA)
Mount Aloysius Coll (PA)
Mount Marty Coll (SD)
Murray State U (KY)
National U (CA)
New Jersey City U (NJ)
Northeastern Illinois U (IL)
Northern Kentucky U (KY)
Northwestern Coll (MN)
Northwestern State U of Louisiana (LA)
The Ohio State U (OH)
Penn State U Altoona Coll (PA)
Penn State U Harrisburg Campus of the Capital Coll (PA)
Penn State U Schuylkill Campus of the Capital Coll (PA)
Penn State U Univ Park Campus (PA)
Pikeville Coll (KY)
Pine Manor Coll (MA)
Pittsburg State U (KS)
Point Park Coll (PA)
Prairie View A&M U (TX)
Quinnipiac U (CT)
Roanoke Coll (VA)
Rochester Inst of Technology (NY)
Rutgers, State U of NJ, Camden Coll of Arts & Scis (NJ)
Rutgers, State U of NJ, U Coll–Camden (NJ)
Saginaw Valley State U (MI)
St. Ambrose U (IA)
Saint Joseph's Coll (IN)
Saint Mary's U of Minnesota (MN)
Saint Peter's Coll (NJ)
Saint Xavier U (IL)
Sam Houston State U (TX)
Seton Hall U (NJ)
Seton Hill Coll (PA)
Shaw U (NC)
Shippensburg U of Pennsylvania (PA)
Southeastern Louisiana U (LA)
Southeastern Oklahoma State U (OK)
Southwestern Coll (KS)
Southwest Missouri State U (MO)
Southwest State U (MN)
Southwest Texas State U (TX)
Stephen F. Austin State U (TX)
Stonehill Coll (MA)
Taylor U, Fort Wayne Campus (IN)
Texas A&M International U (TX)
Texas A&M–Texarkana (TX)
Texas Christian U (TX)
Texas Woman's U (TX)
Universidad Metropolitana (PR)
U Coll of the Fraser Valley (BC, Canada)
The U of Akron (OH)

Majors Index
Criminal Justice Studies–Dance

The U of Alabama (AL)
U of Arkansas at Monticello (AR)
U of Central Florida (FL)
U of Florida (FL)
U of Georgia (GA)
U of Houston–Downtown (TX)
U of Illinois at Chicago (IL)
U of Louisiana at Lafayette (LA)
U of Louisiana at Monroe (LA)
U of Massachusetts Boston (MA)
U of Nebraska at Kearney (NE)
U of Nebraska at Omaha (NE)
The U of North Carolina at Charlotte (NC)
U of North Dakota (ND)
U of North Florida (FL)
U of Portland (OR)
The U of Scranton (PA)
U of Southern Mississippi (MS)
U of South Florida (FL)
The U of Texas at Arlington (TX)
U of the Sacred Heart (PR)
U of Virginia's Coll at Wise (VA)
U of West Florida (FL)
U of Wisconsin–Eau Claire (WI)
U of Wisconsin–Superior (WI)
Virginia Wesleyan Coll (VA)
Wayland Baptist U (TX)
Wayne State U (MI)
Weber State U (UT)
Western Carolina U (NC)
Western Michigan U (MI)
Wichita State U (KS)
Youngstown State U (OH)

CRIMINOLOGY
Adams State Coll (CO)
Arkansas State U (AR)
Auburn U (AL)
Ball State U (IN)
Barry U (FL)
Bridgewater State Coll (MA)
California State U, Fresno (CA)
Capital U (OH)
Carleton U (ON, Canada)
Castleton State Coll (VT)
Centenary Coll (NJ)
Central Connecticut State U (CT)
Central Michigan U (MI)
Coll of the Ozarks (MO)
Dominican U (IL)
Drury U (MO)
Eastern Michigan U (MI)
Florida State U (FL)
Gallaudet U (DC)
Husson Coll (ME)
Indiana State U (IN)
Indiana U of Pennsylvania (PA)
Kent State U (OH)
Lindenwood U (MO)
Marquette U (WI)
Memorial U of Newfoundland (NF, Canada)
Mesa State Coll (CO)
Midland Lutheran Coll (NE)
New Mexico Highlands U (NM)
Niagara U (NY)
The Ohio State U (OH)
Ohio U (OH)
Old Dominion U (VA)
Plattsburgh State U of NY (NY)
The Richard Stockton Coll of New Jersey (NJ)
Saint Augustine's Coll (NC)
St. Cloud State U (MN)
Saint Leo U (FL)
Saint Mary's U (NS, Canada)
St. Mary's U of San Antonio (TX)
San Jose State U (CA)
Simon Fraser U (BC, Canada)
Southern Oregon U (OR)
State U of NY Coll at Brockport (NY)
State U of NY Coll at Old Westbury (NY)
Texas A&M U–Kingsville (TX)
Universidad del Turabo (PR)
Université de Montréal (PQ, Canada)
U of Alberta (AB, Canada)
U of Calif, Irvine (CA)
U of La Verne (CA)
U of Maryland, Coll Park (MD)
U of Maryland University Coll (MD)
U of Miami (FL)
U of Minnesota, Duluth (MN)
U of Missouri–St. Louis (MO)

U of Nevada, Reno (NV)
U of Northern Iowa (IA)
U of Oklahoma (OK)
U of St. Thomas (MN)
U of Southern Colorado (CO)
U of Southern Maine (ME)
The U of Tampa (FL)
The U of Texas at Dallas (TX)
U of Windsor (ON, Canada)
Upper Iowa U (IA)
Valparaiso U (IN)
Virginia Union U (VA)
Western Michigan U (MI)
William Penn U (IA)

CROP PRODUCTION MANAGEMENT
Cornell U (NY)

CULTURAL STUDIES
Azusa Pacific U (CA)
Bard Coll (NY)
Bethel Coll (MN)
Boise State U (ID)
Bridgewater Coll (VA)
Briercrest Bible Coll (SK, Canada)
Brigham Young U–Hawaii Campus (HI)
California State Polytechnic U, Pomona (CA)
California State U, Chico (CA)
California State U, Fullerton (CA)
California State U, Hayward (CA)
California State U, Northridge (CA)
California State U, Sacramento (CA)
Chatham Coll (PA)
Clark U (MA)
Coll of the Holy Cross (MA)
The Coll of William and Mary (VA)
Columbia International U (SC)
Concordia U (PQ, Canada)
Cornell Coll (IA)
The Evergreen State Coll (WA)
Fort Lewis Coll (CO)
Goddard Coll (VT)
Hampshire Coll (MA)
Harvard U (MA)
Indiana State U (IN)
Indiana Wesleyan U (IN)
Kent State U (OH)
Long Island U, Southampton Coll, Friends World Program (NY)
Marlboro Coll (VT)
Mills Coll (CA)
Minnesota State U, Mankato (MN)
The Ohio State U (OH)
Ohio Wesleyan U (OH)
Oregon State U (OR)
Penn State U Berks Cmps of Berks-Lehigh Valley Coll (PA)
Penn State U Lehigh Valley Cmps of Berks-Lehigh Valley Coll (PA)
Queens Coll of the City U of NY (NY)
Reformed Bible Coll (MI)
St. Francis Xavier U (NS, Canada)
Saint Mary-of-the-Woods Coll (IN)
St. Olaf Coll (MN)
Simon's Rock Coll of Bard (MA)
Sonoma State U (CA)
U of British Columbia (BC, Canada)
U of Calif, Berkeley (CA)
U of Calif, Irvine (CA)
U of Calif, Riverside (CA)
U of Calif, San Diego (CA)
U of Colorado at Boulder (CO)
U of Hawaii at Manoa (HI)
U of Nevada, Las Vegas (NV)
U of Oregon (OR)
U of Regina (SK, Canada)
U of Southern California (CA)
The U of Tennessee Knoxville (TN)
The U of Texas–Pan American (TX)
U of Toronto (ON, Canada)
U of Virginia (VA)
U of Washington (WA)
U of Wisconsin–Milwaukee (WI)
Washington U in St. Louis (MO)
Western Washington U (WA)
Yale U (CT)
York U (ON, Canada)

CURRICULUM AND INSTRUCTION
George Fox U (OR)
McGill U (PQ, Canada)
Texas Southern U (TX)
The U of Montana–Missoula (MT)
Utah State U (UT)
York U (ON, Canada)

CYTOTECHNOLOGY
Alderson-Broaddus Coll (WV)
Augustana Coll (IL)
Barry U (FL)
Bloomfield Coll (NJ)
California State U, Dominguez Hills (CA)
Coll of Saint Elizabeth (NJ)
The Coll of Saint Rose (NY)
Eastern Kentucky U (KY)
Eastern Michigan U (MI)
Edgewood Coll (WI)
Elmhurst Coll (IL)
Fairleigh Dickinson U, Teaneck-Hackensack Campus (NJ)
Felician Coll (NJ)
Illinois Coll (IL)
Indiana U–Purdue U Indianapolis (IN)
Indiana U Southeast (IN)
Jewish Hospital Coll of Nursing and Allied Health (MO)
Loma Linda U (CA)
Long Island U, Brooklyn Campus (NY)
Luther Coll (IA)
Marian Coll of Fond du Lac (WI)
Marshall U (WV)
Minnesota State U Moorhead (MN)
Monmouth U (NJ)
Mount St. Clare Coll (IA)
Northern Michigan U (MI)
Oakland U (MI)
Rockhurst U (MO)
St. John's U (NY)
Saint Mary's Coll (IN)
Saint Mary's U of Minnesota (MN)
Salve Regina U (RI)
Slippery Rock U of Pennsylvania (PA)
State U of NY at Stony Brook (NY)
State U of New York Upstate Medical University (NY)
Suffolk U (MA)
Thiel Coll (PA)
Thomas Edison State Coll (NJ)
Thomas Jefferson U (PA)
The U of Akron (OH)
The U of Alabama at Birmingham (AL)
U of Arkansas for Medical Sciences (AR)
U of Connecticut (CT)
U of Kansas (KS)
U of Louisville (KY)
U of Mississippi Medical Center (MS)
U of Missouri–St. Louis (MO)
U of North Dakota (ND)
U of North Texas (TX)
Ursuline Coll (OH)
Winona State U (MN)

DAIRY SCIENCE
California Polytechnic State U, San Luis Obispo (CA)
Clemson U (SC)
Cornell U (NY)
Delaware Valley Coll (PA)
Eastern Kentucky U (KY)
Iowa State U of Science and Technology (IA)
Louisiana State U and A&M Coll (LA)
Oregon State U (OR)
South Dakota State U (SD)
Texas A&M U (TX)
U of Alberta (AB, Canada)
U of Florida (FL)
U of Georgia (GA)
U of New Hampshire (NH)
U of Vermont (VT)
U of Wisconsin–Madison (WI)
U of Wisconsin–River Falls (WI)
Utah State U (UT)
Virginia Polytechnic Inst and State U (VA)

DANCE
Adelphi U (NY)
Allentown Coll of St. Francis de Sales (PA)
Alma Coll (MI)
Amherst Coll (MA)
Antioch Coll (OH)
Arizona State U (AZ)
Baldwin-Wallace Coll (OH)
Ball State U (IN)
Barat Coll (IL)
Bard Coll (NY)
Barnard Coll (NY)
Belhaven Coll (MS)
Bennington Coll (VT)
Birmingham-Southern Coll (AL)
Bowling Green State U (OH)
Brenau U (GA)
Brigham Young U (UT)
Butler U (IN)
California Inst of the Arts (CA)
California State U, Fresno (CA)
California State U, Fullerton (CA)
California State U, Hayward (CA)
California State U, Long Beach (CA)
California State U, Los Angeles (CA)
California State U, Northridge (CA)
Cedar Crest Coll (PA)
Centenary Coll of Louisiana (LA)
Chapman U (CA)
Coker Coll (SC)
The Colorado Coll (CO)
Colorado State U (CO)
Columbia Coll (NY)
Columbia Coll (SC)
Columbia Coll Chicago (IL)
Columbia U, School of General Studies (NY)
Concordia U (PQ, Canada)
Connecticut Coll (CT)
Cornell U (NY)
Cornish Coll of the Arts (WA)
Denison U (OH)
Deree Coll (Greece)
Dickinson Coll (PA)
East Carolina U (NC)
Eastern Kentucky U (KY)
Eastern Michigan U (MI)
Eastern Washington U (WA)
Emerson Coll (MA)
Emory U (GA)
The Evergreen State Coll (WA)
Florida International U (FL)
Florida State U (FL)
Fordham U (NY)
Friends U (KS)
George Mason U (VA)
The George Washington U (DC)
Goucher Coll (MD)
Gustavus Adolphus Coll (MN)
Hamilton Coll (NY)
Hampshire Coll (MA)
Hobart and William Smith Colls (NY)
Hofstra U (NY)
Hollins U (VA)
Hope Coll (MI)
Hunter Coll of the City U of NY (NY)
Huntingdon Coll (AL)
Indiana U Bloomington (IN)
Ithaca Coll (NY)
Jacksonville U (FL)
Johnson State Coll (VT)
The Juilliard School (NY)
Kent State U (OH)
Kenyon Coll (OH)
Kutztown U of Pennsylvania (PA)
Lake Erie Coll (OH)
Lamar U (TX)
La Roche Coll (PA)
Lees-McRae Coll (NC)
Lehman Coll of the City U of NY (NY)
Lindenwood U (MO)
Long Island U, Brooklyn Campus (NY)
Long Island U, C.W. Post Campus (NY)
Long Island U, Southampton Coll, Friends World Program (NY)
Longwood Coll (VA)
Loyola Marymount U (CA)
Luther Coll (IA)
Manhattanville Coll (NY)

Marlboro Coll (VT)
Marygrove Coll (MI)
Marymount Manhattan Coll (NY)
Mercyhurst Coll (PA)
Meredith Coll (NC)
Middlebury Coll (VT)
Mills Coll (CA)
Mount Holyoke Coll (MA)
Muhlenberg Coll (PA)
Naropa U (CO)
New Mexico State U (NM)
New World School of the Arts (FL)
New York U (NY)
North Carolina School of the Arts (NC)
Northwestern U (IL)
Oakland U (MI)
Oberlin Coll (OH)
The Ohio State U (OH)
Ohio U (OH)
Oklahoma City U (OK)
Otterbein Coll (OH)
Point Park Coll (PA)
Pomona Coll (CA)
Purchase Coll, State U of NY (NY)
Queens Coll of the City U of NY (NY)
Radford U (VA)
Randolph-Macon Woman's Coll (VA)
Reed Coll (OR)
Roger Williams U (RI)
Rutgers, State U of NJ, Douglass Coll (NJ)
Rutgers, State U of NJ, Livingston Coll (NJ)
Rutgers, State U of NJ, Mason Gross School of Arts (NJ)
Rutgers, State U of NJ, Rutgers Coll (NJ)
Rutgers, State U of NJ, U Coll–New Brunswick (NJ)
Ryerson Polytechnic U (ON, Canada)
Saint Mary's Coll of California (CA)
St. Olaf Coll (MN)
Sam Houston State U (TX)
San Diego State U (CA)
San Francisco State U (CA)
San Jose State U (CA)
Sarah Lawrence Coll (NY)
Scripps Coll (CA)
Shenandoah U (VA)
Simon Fraser U (BC, Canada)
Simon's Rock Coll of Bard (MA)
Skidmore Coll (NY)
Slippery Rock U of Pennsylvania (PA)
Smith Coll (MA)
Southern Illinois U Edwardsville (IL)
Southern Methodist U (TX)
Southern Utah U (UT)
Southwest Missouri State U (MO)
State U of NY Coll at Brockport (NY)
State U of NY Coll at Fredonia (NY)
State U of NY Coll at Potsdam (NY)
Stephen F. Austin State U (TX)
Stephens Coll (MO)
Swarthmore Coll (PA)
Sweet Briar Coll (VA)
Temple U (PA)
Texas Christian U (TX)
Texas Tech U (TX)
Texas Woman's U (TX)
Thomas Edison State Coll (NJ)
Towson U (MD)
Trinity Coll (CT)
The U of Akron (OH)
The U of Alabama (AL)
U of Alberta (AB, Canada)
The U of Arizona (AZ)
U of Calgary (AB, Canada)
U of Calif, Irvine (CA)
U of Calif, Riverside (CA)
U of Calif, San Diego (CA)
U of Calif, Santa Barbara (CA)
U of Cincinnati (OH)
U of Colorado at Boulder (CO)
U of Florida (FL)
U of Hartford (CT)
U of Hawaii at Manoa (HI)
U of Idaho (ID)
U of Illinois at Urbana–Champaign (IL)

Majors Index
Dance–Dietetics

The U of Iowa (IA)
U of Kansas (KS)
U of Maryland, Baltimore County (MD)
U of Maryland, Coll Park (MD)
U of Massachusetts Amherst (MA)
U of Michigan (MI)
U of Minnesota, Twin Cities Campus (MN)
U of Missouri–Kansas City (MO)
The U of Montana–Missoula (MT)
U of Nebraska–Lincoln (NE)
U of Nevada, Las Vegas (NV)
U of New Mexico (NM)
The U of North Carolina at Charlotte (NC)
The U of North Carolina at Greensboro (NC)
U of North Texas (TX)
U of Oklahoma (OK)
U of Oregon (OR)
U of Regina (SK, Canada)
U of Southern Mississippi (MS)
U of South Florida (FL)
The U of Texas at Austin (TX)
The U of the Arts (PA)
U of Utah (UT)
U of Washington (WA)
U of Wisconsin–Milwaukee (WI)
U of Wisconsin–Stevens Point (WI)
U of Wyoming (WY)
Utah State U (UT)
Virginia Commonwealth U (VA)
Virginia Intermont Coll (VA)
Washington U in St. Louis (MO)
Wayne State U (MI)
Weber State U (UT)
Webster U (MO)
Wells Coll (NY)
Wesleyan U (CT)
Western Michigan U (MI)
Western Oregon U (OR)
Westmont Coll (CA)
West Texas A&M U (TX)
Winthrop U (SC)
Wright State U (OH)
York U (ON, Canada)

DANCE THERAPY
Barat Coll (IL)
Long Island U, Southampton Coll, Friends World Program (NY)
Mercyhurst Coll (PA)
Naropa U (CO)

DATA PROCESSING
East Carolina U (NC)
Eastern Michigan U (MI)
Peirce Coll (PA)

DATA PROCESSING TECHNOLOGY
Arkansas State U (AR)
Bemidji State U (MN)
Champlain Coll (VT)
Chicago State U (IL)
Cleary Coll (MI)
Gardner-Webb U (NC)
Hannibal-LaGrange Coll (MO)
Harding U (AR)
Indiana U Kokomo (IN)
Indiana U Northwest (IN)
Minnesota State U, Mankato (MN)
Mount Vernon Nazarene Coll (OH)
Murray State U (KY)
Northern Michigan U (MI)
Northwest Missouri State U (MO)
Pacific Union Coll (CA)
Peirce Coll (PA)
Saint Mary's U (NS, Canada)
Stephen F. Austin State U (TX)
U of Advancing Computer Technology (AZ)
U of New Brunswick, Fredericton (NB, Canada)
U of New Haven (CT)
U of Washington (WA)
The U of Winnipeg (MB, Canada)
West Virginia U Inst of Technology (WV)

DENTAL HYGIENE
Armstrong Atlantic State U (GA)
Dalhousie U (NS, Canada)
Eastern Washington U (WA)
Howard U (DC)
Idaho State U (ID)

Indiana U–Purdue U Indianapolis (IN)
Loma Linda U (CA)
Louisiana State U Health Sciences Center (LA)
Marquette U (WI)
Mars Hill Coll (NC)
Medical Coll of Georgia (GA)
Midwestern State U (TX)
New York U (NY)
Northeastern U (MA)
Northern Arizona U (AZ)
The Ohio State U (OH)
Old Dominion U (VA)
Oregon Health Sciences U (OR)
Oregon Inst of Technology (OR)
Pennsylvania Coll of Technology (PA)
Southern Illinois U Carbondale (IL)
Tennessee State U (TN)
Texas A&M U System Health Science Center (TX)
Texas Woman's U (TX)
Thomas Edison State Coll (NJ)
U of Alberta (AB, Canada)
U of Arkansas for Medical Sciences (AR)
U of Bridgeport (CT)
U of Colorado Health Sciences Center (CO)
U of Detroit Mercy (MI)
U of Hawaii at Manoa (HI)
U of Louisiana at Monroe (LA)
U of Louisville (KY)
U of Manitoba (MB, Canada)
U of Michigan (MI)
U of Minnesota, Twin Cities Campus (MN)
U of Mississippi Medical Center (MS)
U of Missouri–Kansas City (MO)
U of Nebraska Medical Center (NE)
U of New England (ME)
U of New Haven (CT)
U of New Mexico (NM)
The U of North Carolina at Chapel Hill (NC)
U of Oklahoma Health Sciences Center (OK)
U of Pittsburgh (PA)
U of Rhode Island (RI)
U of South Dakota (SD)
U of Southern California (CA)
U of Washington (WA)
U of Wyoming (WY)
Virginia Commonwealth U (VA)
Weber State U (UT)
Western Kentucky U (KY)
West Liberty State Coll (WV)
West Virginia U (WV)
Wichita State U (KS)

DENTAL LABORATORY TECHNICIAN
Boston U (MA)
Louisiana State U Health Sciences Center (LA)

DESIGN/VISUAL COMMUNICATIONS
Adams State Coll (CO)
Al Collins Graphic Design School (AZ)
American Academy of Art (IL)
American InterContinental U, Atlanta (GA)
The American U in Dubai (United Arab Emirates)
Atlanta Coll of Art (GA)
Bowling Green State U (OH)
Brigham Young U (UT)
California State U, Chico (CA)
Carlow Coll (PA)
Carroll Coll (WI)
Cazenovia Coll (NY)
The Illinois Inst of Art at Schaumburg (IL)
International Academy of Design (FL)
International Acad of Merchandising & Design, Ltd (IL)
Iowa State U of Science and Technology (IA)
Jacksonville U (FL)
Kean U (NJ)
Kendall Coll of Art and Design (MI)
Kent State U (OH)

Maharishi U of Management (IA)
Marywood U (PA)
North Carolina Central U (NC)
North Carolina State U (NC)
Ohio Dominican Coll (OH)
Ohio U (OH)
Open Learning Agency (BC, Canada)
Paier Coll of Art, Inc. (CT)
Peace Coll (NC)
Purdue U (IN)
Rochester Inst of Technology (NY)
Saginaw Valley State U (MI)
St. Ambrose U (IA)
Southern Illinois U Carbondale (IL)
Southwest Missouri State U (MO)
Syracuse U (NY)
Texas Woman's U (TX)
U of Calif, Davis (CA)
U of Calif, Los Angeles (CA)
U of Kansas (KS)
U of Massachusetts Dartmouth (MA)
U of Michigan (MI)
U of Notre Dame (IN)
The U of Texas at Austin (TX)
U of Wisconsin–Stout (WI)
Washington U in St. Louis (MO)
Weber State U (UT)
York U (ON, Canada)

DEVELOPMENTAL/CHILD PSYCHOLOGY
Appalachian State U (NC)
Auburn U (AL)
Barat Coll (IL)
Becker Coll (MA)
Belmont U (TN)
Bennington Coll (VT)
Berea Coll (KY)
Bluffton Coll (OH)
California Polytechnic State U, San Luis Obispo (CA)
California State U, Fullerton (CA)
California State U, Hayward (CA)
California State U, Northridge (CA)
California State U, San Bernardino (CA)
Carson-Newman Coll (TN)
Castleton State Coll (VT)
Christopher Newport U (VA)
Clark Atlanta U (GA)
Colby-Sawyer Coll (NH)
Concordia U (PQ, Canada)
Cornell U (NY)
Eastern Nazarene Coll (MA)
Eastern Washington U (WA)
Edgewood Coll (WI)
Fitchburg State Coll (MA)
Fort Valley State U (GA)
Framingham State Coll (MA)
Fresno Pacific U (CA)
Goddard Coll (VT)
Hampshire Coll (MA)
Hampton U (VA)
Houston Baptist U (TX)
Humboldt State U (CA)
Indiana State U (IN)
Iowa State U of Science and Technology (IA)
Langston U (OK)
Long Island U, Southampton Coll, Friends World Program (NY)
Longwood Coll (VA)
Lynchburg Coll (VA)
Madonna U (MI)
Marlboro Coll (VT)
Maryville Coll (TN)
Michigan State U (MI)
Mills Coll (CA)
Minnesota State U, Mankato (MN)
Mount St. Mary's Coll (CA)
Mount Saint Vincent U (NS, Canada)
Northwest Missouri State U (MO)
Oklahoma Baptist U (OK)
Olivet Nazarene U (IL)
Pine Manor Coll (MA)
Plymouth State Coll (NH)
Point Park Coll (PA)
Queens Coll of the City U of NY (NY)
Quinnipiac U (CT)
Rockford Coll (IL)
St. Joseph's Coll, New York (NY)
St. Joseph's Coll, Suffolk Campus (NY)

San Diego State U (CA)
San Jose State U (CA)
Sarah Lawrence Coll (NY)
Seton Hill Coll (PA)
Simon's Rock Coll of Bard (MA)
Southeast Missouri State U (MO)
Spelman Coll (GA)
Suffolk U (MA)
Tufts U (MA)
Université de Montréal (PQ, Canada)
The U of Akron (OH)
U of Alberta (AB, Canada)
U of British Columbia (BC, Canada)
U of Central Oklahoma (OK)
U of Delaware (DE)
U of Detroit Mercy (MI)
U of Kansas (KS)
U of La Verne (CA)
U of Michigan–Dearborn (MI)
U of Minnesota, Twin Cities Campus (MN)
U of Missouri–Columbia (MO)
U of New Brunswick, Fredericton (NB, Canada)
U of New England (ME)
U of Southern Colorado (CO)
U of the District of Columbia (DC)
U of Utah (UT)
The U of Winnipeg (MB, Canada)
U of Wisconsin–Green Bay (WI)
U of Wisconsin–Madison (WI)
Utica Coll of Syracuse U (NY)
Villa Julie Coll (MD)
Virginia Commonwealth U (VA)
Western Washington U (WA)
Whittier Coll (CA)
Wittenberg U (OH)

DEVELOPMENT ECONOMICS
Arkansas State U (AR)
Brown U (RI)
Clark U (MA)
Eastern Mennonite U (VA)
Georgia Southern U (GA)
U of Calgary (AB, Canada)
U of Guelph (ON, Canada)
U of King's Coll (NS, Canada)
York U (ON, Canada)

DIAGNOSTIC MEDICAL SONOGRAPHY
The Coll of West Virginia (WV)
Medical Coll of Georgia (GA)
Nebraska Methodist Coll of Nursing & Allied Health (NE)
Rochester Inst of Technology (NY)
Seattle U (WA)
U of Nebraska Medical Center (NE)
Weber State U (UT)

DIETETICS
Abilene Christian U (TX)
Acadia U (NS, Canada)
Andrews U (MI)
Arizona State U East (AZ)
Ashland U (OH)
Ball State U (IN)
Bastyr U (WA)
Baylor U (TX)
Bennett Coll (NC)
Berea Coll (KY)
Bluffton Coll (OH)
Bowling Green State U (OH)
Brigham Young U (UT)
California State Polytechnic U, Pomona (CA)
California State U, Fresno (CA)
California State U, Long Beach (CA)
California State U, Northridge (CA)
California State U, San Bernardino (CA)
Carson-Newman Coll (TN)
Case Western Reserve U (OH)
Central Michigan U (MI)
Central Missouri State U (MO)
Coll of Saint Benedict (MN)
Coll of St. Catherine (MN)
The Coll of St. Scholastica (MN)
Coll of the Ozarks (MO)
Colorado State U (CO)
Concordia Coll (MN)
Cornell U (NY)
David Lipscomb U (TN)
Dominican U (IL)

Drexel U (PA)
D'Youville Coll (NY)
East Carolina U (NC)
Eastern Illinois U (IL)
Eastern Kentucky U (KY)
Eastern Michigan U (MI)
East Tennessee State U (TN)
Florida International U (FL)
Florida State U (FL)
Fontbonne Coll (MO)
Framingham State Coll (MA)
Gannon U (PA)
Georgia State U (GA)
Harding U (AR)
Immaculata Coll (PA)
Indiana State U (IN)
Indiana U Bloomington (IN)
Indiana U of Pennsylvania (PA)
Iowa State U of Science and Technology (IA)
Jacksonville State U (AL)
Kansas State U (KS)
Keene State Coll (NH)
Lamar U (TX)
Langston U (OK)
Lehman Coll of the City U of NY (NY)
Loma Linda U (CA)
Louisiana State U and A&M Coll (LA)
Louisiana Tech U (LA)
Madonna U (MI)
Mansfield U of Pennsylvania (PA)
Marian Coll (IN)
Marshall U (WV)
Marymount Coll (NY)
Marywood U (PA)
McGill U (PQ, Canada)
Memorial U of Newfoundland (NF, Canada)
Mercyhurst Coll (PA)
Meredith Coll (NC)
Messiah Coll (PA)
Miami U (OH)
Michigan State U (MI)
Minnesota State U, Mankato (MN)
Morgan State U (MD)
Mount Mary Coll (WI)
Mount Saint Vincent U (NS, Canada)
Nicholls State U (LA)
North Carolina Ag and Tech State U (NC)
North Dakota State U (ND)
Northern Michigan U (MI)
Northwest Missouri State U (MO)
Notre Dame Coll of Ohio (OH)
Oakwood Coll (AL)
The Ohio State U (OH)
Ohio U (OH)
Olivet Nazarene U (IL)
Oregon State U (OR)
Ouachita Baptist U (AR)
Pacific Union Coll (CA)
Point Loma Nazarene U (CA)
Queens Coll of the City U of NY (NY)
Radford U (VA)
Rochester Inst of Technology (NY)
Saint John's U (MN)
Saint Joseph Coll (CT)
Samford U (AL)
San Francisco State U (CA)
San Jose State U (CA)
Seton Hill Coll (PA)
Simmons Coll (MA)
South Dakota State U (SD)
Southeast Missouri State U (MO)
Southwest Missouri State U (MO)
Spalding U (KY)
State U of NY Coll at Buffalo (NY)
State U of NY Coll at Oneonta (NY)
Syracuse U (NY)
Tennessee Technological U (TN)
Texas A&M U–Kingsville (TX)
Texas Christian U (TX)
Texas Southern U (TX)
Texas Tech U (TX)
Texas Woman's U (TX)
Tuskegee U (AL)
The U of Akron (OH)
U of Arkansas at Pine Bluff (AR)
U of British Columbia (BC, Canada)
U of Central Oklahoma (OK)
U of Connecticut (CT)

Majors Index
Dietetics–Early Childhood Education

U of Dayton (OH)
U of Delaware (DE)
U of Georgia (GA)
U of Guelph (ON, Canada)
U of Illinois at Urbana–Champaign (IL)
U of Louisiana at Lafayette (LA)
U of Maryland, Coll Park (MD)
U of Missouri–Columbia (MO)
U of Montevallo (AL)
U of Nebraska at Kearney (NE)
U of Nebraska at Omaha (NE)
U of New Hampshire (NH)
U of New Haven (CT)
The U of North Carolina at Greensboro (NC)
U of North Dakota (ND)
U of Northern Colorado (CO)
U of Northern Iowa (IA)
U of Oklahoma Health Sciences Center (OK)
U of Pittsburgh (PA)
U of Puerto Rico, Río Piedras (PR)
U of Rhode Island (RI)
U of Southern Mississippi (MS)
The U of Tennessee at Martin (TN)
The U of Texas–Pan American (TX)
U of Vermont (VT)
The U of Western Ontario (ON, Canada)
U of Wisconsin–Madison (WI)
U of Wisconsin–Stevens Point (WI)
U of Wisconsin–Stout (WI)
Virginia Polytechnic Inst and State U (VA)
Wayne State U (MI)
Western Carolina U (NC)
Western Michigan U (MI)
Youngstown State U (OH)

DIVINITY/MINISTRY
Arlington Baptist Coll (TX)
Atlantic Union Coll (MA)
Azusa Pacific U (CA)
Barclay Coll (KS)
Bartlesville Wesleyan Coll (OK)
Belmont U (TN)
Bethany Bible Coll (NB, Canada)
Bethany Coll of the Assemblies of God (CA)
Bethel Coll (IN)
Biola U (CA)
Bluffton Coll (OH)
Boise Bible Coll (ID)
Briercrest Bible Coll (SK, Canada)
Calvary Bible Coll and Theological Seminary (MO)
Campbellsville U (KY)
Cardinal Stritch U (WI)
Central Baptist Coll (AR)
Central Christian Coll of Kansas (KS)
Colorado Christian U (CO)
Concordia U (CA)
Cornerstone U (MI)
Creighton U (NE)
David Lipscomb U (TN)
Eastern Mennonite U (VA)
Eastern Nazarene Coll (MA)
Eastern Pentecostal Bible Coll (ON, Canada)
Emmanuel Coll (GA)
Eugene Bible Coll (OR)
Faith Baptist Bible Coll and Theological Seminary (IA)
Faulkner U (AL)
Florida Christian Coll (FL)
Fresno Pacific U (CA)
Friends U (KS)
George Fox U (OR)
Global U of the Assemblies of God (MO)
Grace Coll (IN)
Grand Canyon U (AZ)
Greenville Coll (IL)
Grove City Coll (PA)
Hannibal-LaGrange Coll (MO)
Hardin-Simmons U (TX)
Houghton Coll (NY)
Huntington Coll (IN)
Indiana Wesleyan U (IN)
International Baptist Coll (AZ)
John Brown U (AR)
John Wesley Coll (NC)
Lincoln Christian Coll (IL)
Manhattan Christian Coll (KS)
Martin Methodist Coll (TN)

Marylhurst U (OR)
Merrimack Coll (MA)
Messenger Coll (MO)
Mid-America Bible Coll (OK)
Mount Olive Coll (NC)
Multnomah Bible Coll and Biblical Seminary (OR)
Nebraska Christian Coll (NE)
North American Baptist Coll & Edmonton Baptist Sem (AB, Canada)
North Central U (MN)
North Park U (IL)
Northwest Coll (WA)
Northwest Nazarene U (ID)
Oakland City U (IN)
Oklahoma Baptist U (OK)
Oklahoma Christian U of Science and Arts (OK)
Patten Coll (CA)
Providence Coll and Theological Seminary (MB, Canada)
Reformed Bible Coll (MI)
Roberts Wesleyan Coll (NY)
St. Louis Christian Coll (MO)
Saint Paul U (ON, Canada)
San Jose Christian Coll (CA)
Shorter Coll (GA)
Simpson Coll and Graduate School (CA)
Southeastern Coll of the Assemblies of God (FL)
Southern Wesleyan U (SC)
Southwestern Assemblies of God U (TX)
Southwestern Coll of Christian Ministries (OK)
Spring Arbor Coll (MI)
Tabor Coll (KS)
Taylor U, Fort Wayne Campus (IN)
Trinity Western U (BC, Canada)
Tyndale Coll & Seminary (ON, Canada)
Union Coll (KY)
U of Saint Francis (IN)
Warner Pacific Coll (OR)
Western Baptist Coll (OR)
Williams Baptist Coll (AR)
York Coll (NE)

DRAFTING
Baker Coll of Flint (MI)
Baker Coll of Owosso (MI)
Central Missouri State U (MO)
Columbus Coll of Art and Design (OH)
East Central U (OK)
Herzing Coll (WI)
Indiana State U (IN)
Keene State Coll (NH)
Lewis-Clark State Coll (ID)
Lynn U (FL)
Montana State U–Northern (MT)
Murray State U (KY)
Norfolk State U (VA)
Northern Michigan U (MI)
Northern State U (SD)
Pace U, Pleasantville/Briarcliff Campus (NY)
Pacific Union Coll (CA)
Prairie View A&M U (TX)
Robert Morris Coll (IL)
Sam Houston State U (TX)
Southwest Missouri State U (MO)
Texas Southern U (TX)
Thomas Edison State Coll (NJ)
Tri-State U (IN)
U of Houston (TX)
U of Nebraska at Omaha (NE)
U of Rio Grande (OH)
Western Michigan U (MI)

DRAMA AND DANCE EDUCATION
Abilene Christian U (TX)
Appalachian State U (NC)
Baylor U (TX)
Boston U (MA)
Bowling Green State U (OH)
Brenau U (GA)
Bridgewater State Coll (MA)
Brigham Young U (UT)
The Catholic U of America (DC)
Coll of St. Catherine (MN)
Concordia U (PQ, Canada)
Dana Coll (NE)
East Carolina U (NC)

Eastern Michigan U (MI)
East Texas Baptist U (TX)
Emerson Coll (MA)
Greensboro Coll (NC)
Greenville Coll (IL)
Hastings Coll (NE)
Huntingdon Coll (AL)
Indiana U–Purdue U Fort Wayne (IN)
Jacksonville U (FL)
Johnson State Coll (VT)
Luther Coll (IA)
Marywood U (PA)
Meredith Coll (NC)
Minnesota State U Moorhead (MN)
New York U (NY)
The Ohio State U (OH)
Oklahoma Baptist U (OK)
Piedmont Coll (GA)
Point Park Coll (PA)
Ryerson Polytechnic U (ON, Canada)
Saint Mary's U of Minnesota (MN)
St. Olaf Coll (MN)
Salve Regina U (RI)
Southwestern Coll (KS)
Southwest State U (MN)
Texas Wesleyan U (TX)
The U of Arizona (AZ)
U of Calgary (AB, Canada)
U of Georgia (GA)
The U of Iowa (IA)
U of Maryland, Coll Park (MD)
The U of North Carolina at Charlotte (NC)
U of South Florida (FL)
The U of the Arts (PA)
Washington U in St. Louis (MO)
Weber State U (UT)
William Jewell Coll (MO)
York Coll (NE)
York U (ON, Canada)
Youngstown State U (OH)

DRAMA/THEATER LITERATURE
Averett Coll (VA)
Bard Coll (NY)
Barnard Coll (NY)
Boston U (MA)
Marymount Manhattan Coll (NY)
Memorial U of Newfoundland (NF, Canada)
Spring Hill Coll (AL)
U of Northern Iowa (IA)
Virginia Wesleyan Coll (VA)
Washington U in St. Louis (MO)

DRAMA THERAPY
Howard U (DC)
Long Island U, Southampton Coll, Friends World Program (NY)
Longwood Coll (VA)
Virginia Union U (VA)

DRAWING
Academy of Art Coll (CA)
Adams State Coll (CO)
Alberta Coll of Art and Design (AB, Canada)
Alfred U (NY)
Alma Coll (MI)
American Academy of Art (IL)
Anderson Coll (SC)
Antioch Coll (OH)
Aquinas Coll (MI)
Arizona State U (AZ)
Art Academy of Cincinnati (OH)
The Art Inst of Boston at Lesley (MA)
Art Inst of Southern California (CA)
Atlanta Coll of Art (GA)
Ball State U (IN)
Barat Coll (IL)
Bard Coll (NY)
Beaver Coll (PA)
Bennington Coll (VT)
Bethany Coll (KS)
Biola U (CA)
Birmingham-Southern Coll (AL)
Boise State U (ID)
Boston U (MA)
Bowling Green State U (OH)
Brenau U (GA)
Brevard Coll (NC)
Brock U (ON, Canada)
California Coll of Arts and Crafts (CA)

California State U, Fullerton (CA)
California State U, Hayward (CA)
California State U, Long Beach (CA)
California State U, Northridge (CA)
Carson-Newman Coll (TN)
Centenary Coll of Louisiana (LA)
Ctr for Creative Studies—Coll of Art and Design (MI)
Chicago State U (IL)
Cleveland Inst of Art (OH)
The Coll of Southeastern Europe, The American U of Athens (Greece)
Coll of the Atlantic (ME)
Coll of Visual Arts (MN)
Colorado State U (CO)
Columbia Coll (MO)
Columbus Coll of Art and Design (OH)
Concordia U (PQ, Canada)
The Corcoran Coll of Art and Design (DC)
Cornell U (NY)
DePaul U (IL)
Drake U (IA)
Eastern Kentucky U (KY)
Framingham State Coll (MA)
Georgia Southwestern State U (GA)
Georgia State U (GA)
Goddard Coll (VT)
Governors State U (IL)
Grace Coll (IN)
Grand Valley State U (MI)
Hampshire Coll (MA)
Hampton U (VA)
Illinois Wesleyan U (IL)
Indiana U Bloomington (IN)
Inter American U of PR, Metropolitan Campus (PR)
Inter American U of PR, San Germán Campus (PR)
Judson Coll (IL)
Kent State U (OH)
Lewis U (IL)
Lindenwood U (MO)
Long Island U, Southampton Coll, Friends World Program (NY)
Longwood Coll (VA)
Lyme Academy of Fine Arts (CT)
Maharishi U of Management (IA)
Marlboro Coll (VT)
Marshall U (WV)
Maryland Inst, Coll of Art (MD)
McMurry U (TX)
McNeese State U (LA)
Memorial U of Newfoundland (NF, Canada)
Memphis Coll of Art (TN)
Middlebury Coll (VT)
Milwaukee Inst of Art and Design (WI)
Minneapolis Coll of Art and Design (MN)
Minnesota State U, Mankato (MN)
Mississippi U for Women (MS)
Montserrat Coll of Art (MA)
Moore Coll of Art and Design (PA)
Mount Allison U (NB, Canada)
Nazareth Coll of Rochester (NY)
New England Coll (NH)
New York U (NY)
Northern Arizona U (AZ)
Northern Michigan U (MI)
Northwest Missouri State U (MO)
Northwest Nazarene U (ID)
Nova Scotia Coll of Art and Design (NS, Canada)
The Ohio State U (OH)
Otis Coll of Art and Design (CA)
Pacific Northwest Coll of Art (OR)
Parsons School of Design, New School U (NY)
Plymouth State Coll (NH)
Portland State U (OR)
Pratt Inst (NY)
Queens Coll of the City U of NY (NY)
Rhode Island School of Design (RI)
Rivier Coll (NH)
Rocky Mountain Coll of Art & Design (CO)
Rowan U (NJ)
Rutgers, State U of NJ, Mason Gross School of Arts (NJ)
Sacred Heart U (CT)

St. Cloud State U (MN)
Salem State Coll (MA)
Samford U (AL)
San Francisco Art Inst (CA)
Sarah Lawrence Coll (NY)
School of the Art Inst of Chicago (IL)
School of the Museum of Fine Arts (MA)
School of Visual Arts (NY)
Seton Hill Coll (PA)
Shawnee State U (OH)
Simon's Rock Coll of Bard (MA)
Sonoma State U (CA)
State U of NY at Binghamton (NY)
State U of NY at New Paltz (NY)
State U of NY Coll at Brockport (NY)
State U of NY Coll at Buffalo (NY)
State U of NY Coll at Fredonia (NY)
State U of NY Coll at Potsdam (NY)
Temple U (PA)
Texas A&M U–Commerce (TX)
Trinity Christian Coll (IL)
The U of Akron (OH)
U of Alberta (AB, Canada)
U of Calif, Santa Cruz (CA)
U of Evansville (IN)
U of Hartford (CT)
The U of Iowa (IA)
U of Michigan (MI)
The U of Montana–Missoula (MT)
U of Montevallo (AL)
U of North Texas (TX)
U of Oregon (OR)
U of Puerto Rico, Río Piedras (PR)
U of Regina (SK, Canada)
U of San Francisco (CA)
U of South Dakota (SD)
The U of the Arts (PA)
U of the South (TN)
U of Windsor (ON, Canada)
Washington U in St. Louis (MO)
Webster U (MO)
West Virginia Wesleyan Coll (WV)
Wingate U (NC)
Winona State U (MN)
Wittenberg U (OH)
Wright State U (OH)
York U (ON, Canada)
Youngstown State U (OH)

DRIVER AND SAFETY EDUCATION
Bridgewater Coll (VA)
William Penn U (IA)

EARLY CHILDHOOD EDUCATION
Alabama A&M U (AL)
Alabama State U (AL)
Albany State U (GA)
Allen U (SC)
Alma Coll (MI)
Alvernia Coll (PA)
American International Coll (MA)
American U (DC)
Anderson Coll (SC)
Anna Maria Coll (MA)
Appalachian State U (NC)
Arizona State U (AZ)
Arkansas State U (AR)
Arkansas Tech U (AR)
Armstrong Atlantic State U (GA)
Ashland U (OH)
Athens State U (AL)
Atlanta Christian Coll (GA)
Atlantic Union Coll (MA)
Auburn U (AL)
Augsburg Coll (MN)
Augusta State U (GA)
Averett Coll (VA)
Ball State U (IN)
Barry U (FL)
Bayamón Central U (PR)
Baylor U (TX)
Bay Path Coll (MA)
Beaver Coll (PA)
Becker Coll (MA)
Belmont U (TN)
Bennett Coll (NC)
Bennington Coll (VT)
Berea Coll (KY)
Berry Coll (GA)
Bethany Coll of the Assemblies of God (CA)

Majors Index
Early Childhood Education

Bethel Coll (MN)
Bethesda Christian U (CA)
Birmingham-Southern Coll (AL)
Black Hills State U (SD)
Bloomsburg U of Pennsylvania (PA)
Bluffton Coll (OH)
Boise State U (ID)
Boston Coll (MA)
Boston U (MA)
Bowie State U (MD)
Bowling Green State U (OH)
Bradley U (IL)
Brandon U (MB, Canada)
Brenau U (GA)
Brescia U (KY)
Bridgewater State Coll (MA)
Brigham Young U (UT)
Brooklyn Coll of the City U of NY (NY)
Bryan Coll (TN)
Bucknell U (PA)
Cabrini Coll (PA)
California Polytechnic State U, San Luis Obispo (CA)
California State U, Chico (CA)
California State U, Sacramento (CA)
California U of Pennsylvania (PA)
Cardinal Stritch U (WI)
Carlow Coll (PA)
Carroll Coll (WI)
Carson-Newman Coll (TN)
The Catholic U of America (DC)
Cedarville Coll (OH)
Centenary Coll of Louisiana (LA)
Central Connecticut State U (CT)
Central Methodist Coll (MO)
Chaminade U of Honolulu (HI)
Champlain Coll (VT)
Charleston Southern U (SC)
Chestnut Hill Coll (PA)
Cheyney U of Pennsylvania (PA)
Chicago State U (IL)
City Coll of the City U of NY (NY)
Clarion U of Pennsylvania (PA)
Clark Atlanta U (GA)
Clarke Coll (IA)
Clemson U (SC)
Cleveland State U (OH)
Coastal Carolina U (SC)
Coker Coll (SC)
Coll Misericordia (PA)
Coll of Mount St. Joseph (OH)
The Coll of New Jersey (NJ)
Coll of Notre Dame of Maryland (MD)
Coll of Our Lady of the Elms (MA)
Coll of St. Catherine (MN)
Coll of Saint Elizabeth (NJ)
Coll of St. Joseph (VT)
Coll of Saint Mary (NE)
Coll of Santa Fe (NM)
Columbia Coll (SC)
Columbia Coll Chicago (IL)
Columbia International U (SC)
Columbia Union Coll (MD)
Columbus State U (GA)
Concord Coll (WV)
Concordia Coll (MN)
Concordia U (CA)
Concordia U (IL)
Concordia U (NE)
Concordia U (OR)
Concordia U (PQ, Canada)
Concordia U at Austin (TX)
Concordia U at St. Paul (MN)
Concordia U Wisconsin (WI)
Converse Coll (SC)
Coppin State Coll (MD)
Cornerstone U (MI)
Crown Coll (MN)
Cumberland Coll (KY)
Curry Coll (MA)
Dallas Baptist U (TX)
Delaware State U (DE)
Delta State U (MS)
DePaul U (IL)
Duquesne U (PA)
East Carolina U (NC)
East Central U (OK)
Eastern Connecticut State U (CT)
Eastern Illinois U (IL)
Eastern Kentucky U (KY)
Eastern Mennonite U (VA)
Eastern Nazarene Coll (MA)
Eastern New Mexico U (NM)

East Stroudsburg U of Pennsylvania (PA)
East Texas Baptist U (TX)
Edgewood Coll (WI)
Edinboro U of Pennsylvania (PA)
Elizabeth City State U (NC)
Elizabethtown Coll (PA)
Elmhurst Coll (IL)
Endicott Coll (MA)
Erskine Coll (SC)
Evangel U (MO)
Faulkner U (AL)
Fitchburg State Coll (MA)
Florida A&M U (FL)
Florida Gulf Coast U (FL)
Florida Southern Coll (FL)
Florida State U (FL)
Fontbonne Coll (MO)
Fort Hays State U (KS)
Fort Lewis Coll (CO)
Fort Valley State U (GA)
Framingham State Coll (MA)
Francis Marion U (SC)
Franklin Pierce Coll (NH)
Friends U (KS)
Frostburg State U (MD)
Furman U (SC)
Gallaudet U (DC)
Gannon U (PA)
Gardner-Webb U (NC)
Georgetown Coll (KY)
Georgia Coll and State U (GA)
Georgia Southern U (GA)
Georgia Southwestern State U (GA)
Georgia State U (GA)
Glenville State Coll (WV)
Goddard Coll (VT)
Gordon Coll (MA)
Goshen Coll (IN)
Governors State U (IL)
Grace Bible Coll (MI)
Greensboro Coll (NC)
Greenville Coll (IL)
Grove City Coll (PA)
Gwynedd-Mercy Coll (PA)
Hampshire Coll (MA)
Hampton U (VA)
Hannibal-LaGrange Coll (MO)
Harding U (AR)
Harris-Stowe State Coll (MO)
High Point U (NC)
Hillsdale Coll (MI)
Holy Family Coll (PA)
Hood Coll (MD)
Houston Baptist U (TX)
Howard Payne U (TX)
Howard U (DC)
Humboldt State U (CA)
Hunter Coll of the City U of NY (NY)
Huntingdon Coll (AL)
Idaho State U (ID)
Illinois State U (IL)
Immaculata Coll (PA)
Indiana State U (IN)
Indiana U Bloomington (IN)
Indiana U of Pennsylvania (PA)
Inter American U of PR, Aguadilla Campus (PR)
Inter American U of PR, Arecibo Campus (PR)
Inter American U of PR, Metropolitan Campus (PR)
Inter American U of PR, San Germán Campus (PR)
Iowa State U of Science and Technology (IA)
Iowa Wesleyan Coll (IA)
Jacksonville State U (AL)
James Madison U (VA)
Jarvis Christian Coll (TX)
John Brown U (AR)
John Carroll U (OH)
Johnson Bible Coll (TN)
Johnson C. Smith U (NC)
Judson Coll (IL)
Juniata Coll (PA)
Kean U (NJ)
Keene State Coll (NH)
Kendall Coll (IL)
Kent State U (OH)
King Coll (TN)
King's Coll (PA)
Kutztown U of Pennsylvania (PA)
LaGrange Coll (GA)
Lakeland Coll (WI)

Lamar U (TX)
Lander U (SC)
Langston U (OK)
La Roche Coll (PA)
Lasell Coll (MA)
Lenoir-Rhyne Coll (NC)
Lesley Coll (MA)
Lincoln Christian Coll (IL)
Lincoln Memorial U (TN)
Lincoln U (PA)
Lindenwood U (MO)
Lock Haven U of Pennsylvania (PA)
Long Island U, Brooklyn Campus (NY)
Long Island U, C.W. Post Campus (NY)
Long Island U, Southampton Coll, Friends World Program (NY)
Longwood Coll (VA)
Loras Coll (IA)
Louisiana Coll (LA)
Louisiana Tech U (LA)
Lourdes Coll (OH)
Luther Coll (IA)
Lynchburg Coll (VA)
Lynn U (FL)
Malone Coll (OH)
Mansfield U of Pennsylvania (PA)
Maranatha Baptist Bible Coll (WI)
Marian Coll (IN)
Marian Coll of Fond du Lac (WI)
Marshall U (WV)
Mars Hill Coll (NC)
Martin Luther Coll (MN)
Marygrove Coll (MI)
Maryville U of Saint Louis (MO)
Massachusetts Coll of Liberal Arts (MA)
McNeese State U (LA)
McPherson Coll (KS)
Medaille Coll (NY)
Mercer U (GA)
Mercy Coll (NY)
Mercyhurst Coll (PA)
Messiah Coll (PA)
Methodist Coll (NC)
Miami U (OH)
Michigan State U (MI)
Middle Tennessee State U (TN)
Midland Lutheran Coll (NE)
Midway Coll (KY)
Millersville U of Pennsylvania (PA)
Milligan Coll (TN)
Mills Coll (CA)
Minnesota State U, Mankato (MN)
Minnesota State U Moorhead (MN)
Missouri Baptist Coll (MO)
Missouri Southern State Coll (MO)
Montana State U–Billings (MT)
Morehead State U (KY)
Morningside Coll (IA)
Morris Coll (SC)
Mount Aloysius Coll (PA)
Mount Ida Coll (MA)
Mount Mary Coll (WI)
Mount St. Clare Coll (IA)
Mount Saint Vincent U (NS, Canada)
Mount Union Coll (OH)
Mount Vernon Nazarene Coll (OH)
Muskingum Coll (OH)
Naropa U (CO)
National-Louis U (IL)
Neumann Coll (PA)
Newberry Coll (SC)
New Jersey City U (NJ)
New Mexico Highlands U (NM)
New Mexico State U (NM)
New York U (NY)
Nicholls State U (LA)
Norfolk State U (VA)
North Carolina Ag and Tech State U (NC)
North Carolina Central U (NC)
North Central Coll (IL)
Northeastern Illinois U (IL)
Northeastern State U (OK)
Northeastern U (MA)
Northern Arizona U (AZ)
Northern Illinois U (IL)
Northern Kentucky U (KY)
North Georgia Coll & State U (GA)
North Greenville Coll (SC)
Northland Coll (WI)
North Park U (IL)

Northwestern Oklahoma State U (OK)
Northwestern State U of Louisiana (LA)
Northwest Missouri State U (MO)
Notre Dame Coll (NH)
Notre Dame Coll of Ohio (OH)
Nova Southeastern U (FL)
Oglethorpe U (GA)
Ohio Northern U (OH)
Ohio U (OH)
Oklahoma Baptist U (OK)
Oklahoma Christian U of Science and Arts (OK)
Oklahoma City U (OK)
Oklahoma State U (OK)
Olivet Nazarene U (IL)
Oregon State U (OR)
Ouachita Baptist U (AR)
Our Lady of the Lake U of San Antonio (TX)
Pace U, New York City Campus (NY)
Pace U, Pleasantville/Briarcliff Campus (NY)
Pacific Lutheran U (WA)
Pacific Oaks Coll (CA)
Pacific Union Coll (CA)
Pacific U (OR)
Paine Coll (GA)
Palm Beach Atlantic Coll (FL)
Park U (MO)
Patten Coll (CA)
Peru State Coll (NE)
Philadelphia Coll of Bible (PA)
Piedmont Coll (GA)
Pine Manor Coll (MA)
Pittsburg State U (KS)
Plymouth State Coll (NH)
Point Park Coll (PA)
Pontifical Catholic U of Puerto Rico (PR)
Presbyterian Coll (SC)
Purdue U (IN)
Queens Coll (NC)
Queens Coll of the City U of NY (NY)
Reinhardt Coll (GA)
Rider U (NJ)
Rivier Coll (NH)
Rowan U (NJ)
Rust Coll (MS)
Ryerson Polytechnic U (ON, Canada)
Sacred Heart U (CT)
St. Ambrose U (IA)
St. Andrews Presbyterian Coll (NC)
St. Cloud State U (MN)
Saint Joseph Coll (CT)
Saint Joseph's Coll (ME)
St. Joseph's Coll, New York (NY)
St. Joseph's Coll, Suffolk Campus (NY)
Saint Louis U (MO)
Saint Mary-of-the-Woods Coll (IN)
Saint Xavier U (IL)
Salem State Coll (MA)
Salve Regina U (RI)
Samford U (AL)
San Diego State U (CA)
Sarah Lawrence Coll (NY)
Seton Hill Coll (PA)
Siena Heights U (MI)
Silver Lake Coll (WI)
Simmons Coll (MA)
Simpson Coll (IA)
Slippery Rock U of Pennsylvania (PA)
South Dakota State U (SD)
Southeastern Coll of the Assemblies of God (FL)
Southeastern Oklahoma State U (OK)
Southeast Missouri State U (MO)
Southern Adventist U (TN)
Southern Arkansas U–Magnolia (AR)
Southern Illinois U Carbondale (IL)
Southern Illinois U Edwardsville (IL)
Southern Wesleyan U (SC)
Southwestern Coll (KS)
Southwest Missouri State U (MO)
Southwest State U (MN)
Spalding U (KY)
Spring Arbor Coll (MI)
Spring Hill Coll (AL)
State U of NY at New Paltz (NY)

State U of NY Coll at Buffalo (NY)
State U of NY Coll at Cortland (NY)
State U of NY Coll at Fredonia (NY)
State U of NY Coll at Geneseo (NY)
State U of West Georgia (GA)
Stephens Coll (MO)
Stonehill Coll (MA)
Susquehanna U (PA)
Syracuse U (NY)
Tabor Coll (KS)
Temple U (PA)
Tennessee State U (TN)
Tennessee Technological U (TN)
Texas A&M International U (TX)
Texas A&M U–Commerce (TX)
Texas A&M U–Kingsville (TX)
Texas Southern U (TX)
Texas Wesleyan U (TX)
Thomas U (GA)
Toccoa Falls Coll (GA)
Tougaloo Coll (MS)
Touro Coll (NY)
Towson U (MD)
Trevecca Nazarene U (TN)
Trinity Coll of Vermont (VT)
Troy State U (AL)
Troy State U Dothan (AL)
Tufts U (MA)
Tusculum Coll (TN)
Tuskegee U (AL)
Union U (TN)
Universidad Metropolitana (PR)
Université de Montréal (PQ, Canada)
Université de Sherbrooke (PQ, Canada)
U du Québec à Chicoutimi (PQ, Canada)
U du Québec à Hull (PQ, Canada)
U du Québec à Trois-Rivières (PQ, Canada)
U du Québec en Abitibi-Témiscamingue (PQ, Canada)
The U of Akron (OH)
The U of Alabama (AL)
The U of Alabama at Birmingham (AL)
U of Alberta (AB, Canada)
The U of Arizona (AZ)
U of Arkansas at Little Rock (AR)
U of Arkansas at Pine Bluff (AR)
U of British Columbia (BC, Canada)
U of Calgary (AB, Canada)
U of Calif, Davis (CA)
U of Central Arkansas (AR)
U of Central Florida (FL)
U of Central Oklahoma (OK)
U of Cincinnati (OH)
U of Dayton (OH)
U of Delaware (DE)
U of Detroit Mercy (MI)
U of Georgia (GA)
U of Hartford (CT)
U of Illinois at Urbana–Champaign (IL)
U of Kentucky (KY)
U of La Verne (CA)
U of Louisiana at Monroe (LA)
U of Maine (ME)
U of Maine at Farmington (ME)
U of Manitoba (MB, Canada)
U of Mary Hardin-Baylor (TX)
U of Maryland, Coll Park (MD)
U of Michigan–Dearborn (MI)
U of Michigan–Flint (MI)
U of Minnesota, Crookston (MN)
U of Minnesota, Duluth (MN)
U of Minnesota, Twin Cities Campus (MN)
U of Missouri–Columbia (MO)
U of Missouri–Kansas City (MO)
U of Missouri–St. Louis (MO)
U of Mobile (AL)
U of Montevallo (AL)
U of Nevada, Las Vegas (NV)
U of New Brunswick, Fredericton (NB, Canada)
U of New England (ME)
U of New Hampshire (NH)
U of New Mexico (NM)
U of North Alabama (AL)
The U of North Carolina at Charlotte (NC)

Majors Index
Early Childhood Education–Ecology

The U of North Carolina at Pembroke (NC)
The U of North Carolina at Wilmington (NC)
U of North Dakota (ND)
U of Northern Iowa (IA)
U of North Texas (TX)
U of Oklahoma (OK)
U of Pittsburgh at Bradford (PA)
U of Regina (SK, Canada)
U of Science and Arts of Oklahoma (OK)
The U of Scranton (PA)
U of South Alabama (AL)
U of South Carolina Spartanburg (SC)
The U of Tennessee at Chattanooga (TN)
The U of Tennessee at Martin (TN)
The U of Texas at San Antonio (TX)
The U of Texas–Pan American (TX)
U of the District of Columbia (DC)
U of the Ozarks (AR)
U of the Pacific (CA)
U of Utah (UT)
U of Vermont (VT)
U of Victoria (BC, Canada)
The U of West Alabama (AL)
The U of Western Ontario (ON, Canada)
U of West Florida (FL)
U of Windsor (ON, Canada)
U of Wisconsin–La Crosse (WI)
U of Wisconsin–Madison (WI)
U of Wisconsin–Milwaukee (WI)
U of Wisconsin–Platteville (WI)
U of Wisconsin–Stevens Point (WI)
U of Wisconsin–Stout (WI)
U of Wisconsin–Whitewater (WI)
U System Coll for Lifelong Learning (NH)
Utah State U (UT)
Valdosta State U (GA)
Vanderbilt U (TN)
Villa Julie Coll (MD)
Virginia Commonwealth U (VA)
Virginia Polytechnic Inst and State U (VA)
Virginia Union U (VA)
Voorhees Coll (SC)
Wagner Coll (NY)
Walsh U (OH)
Warner Pacific Coll (OR)
Wartburg Coll (IA)
Washington Bible Coll (MD)
Wayne State U (NE)
Weber State U (UT)
Webster U (MO)
Wesleyan Coll (GA)
West Chester U of Pennsylvania (PA)
Western Carolina U (NC)
Western Kentucky U (KY)
Western Washington U (WA)
Westfield State Coll (MA)
West Liberty State Coll (WV)
Westminster Coll (MO)
Westminster Coll (UT)
West Virginia State Coll (WV)
West Virginia Wesleyan Coll (WV)
Wheelock Coll (MA)
Whittier Coll (CA)
Williams Baptist Coll (AR)
William Woods U (MO)
Wingate U (NC)
Winona State U (MN)
Winthrop U (SC)
Worcester State Coll (MA)
Wright State U (OH)
Xavier U of Louisiana (LA)
Yeshiva U (NY)
York U (ON, Canada)
Youngstown State U (OH)

EARTH SCIENCES
Adams State Coll (CO)
Adelphi U (NY)
Adrian Coll (MI)
Alfred U (NY)
Antioch Coll (OH)
Augustana Coll (IL)
Baylor U (TX)
Bemidji State U (MN)
Bloomsburg U of Pennsylvania (PA)
Boise State U (ID)
Boston U (MA)
Bridgewater State Coll (MA)
Brigham Young U (UT)
Brock U (ON, Canada)
Brooklyn Coll of the City U of NY (NY)
California Inst of Technology (CA)
California State Polytechnic U, Pomona (CA)
California State U, Chico (CA)
California State U, Dominguez Hills (CA)
California State U, Long Beach (CA)
California State U, Los Angeles (CA)
California State U, Monterey Bay (CA)
California State U, Northridge (CA)
California U of Pennsylvania (PA)
Carleton U (ON, Canada)
Centenary Coll of Louisiana (LA)
Central Connecticut State U (CT)
Central Michigan U (MI)
Central Missouri State U (MO)
City Coll of the City U of NY (NY)
Clarion U of Pennsylvania (PA)
Clark U (MA)
Colby Coll (ME)
Dalhousie U (NS, Canada)
Dartmouth Coll (NH)
DePauw U (IN)
Dickinson State U (ND)
Eastern Kentucky U (KY)
Eastern Michigan U (MI)
Eastern Washington U (WA)
East Stroudsburg U of Pennsylvania (PA)
Edinboro U of Pennsylvania (PA)
Emporia State U (KS)
The Evergreen State Coll (WA)
Fitchburg State Coll (MA)
Framingham State Coll (MA)
Frostburg State U (MD)
Gannon U (PA)
George Mason U (VA)
Georgia Southwestern State U (GA)
Grand Valley State U (MI)
Hampshire Coll (MA)
Harvard U (MA)
Indiana State U (IN)
Indiana U of Pennsylvania (PA)
Iowa State U of Science and Technology (IA)
Johns Hopkins U (MD)
Kean U (NJ)
Kent State U (OH)
Kutztown U of Pennsylvania (PA)
Lewis-Clark State Coll (ID)
Lock Haven U of Pennsylvania (PA)
Longwood Coll (VA)
Mansfield U of Pennsylvania (PA)
Massachusetts Inst of Technology (MA)
McGill U (PQ, Canada)
Memorial U of Newfoundland (NF, Canada)
Mercer U (GA)
Mercyhurst Coll (PA)
Miami U (OH)
Michigan State U (MI)
Michigan Technological U (MI)
Millersville U of Pennsylvania (PA)
Minnesota State U, Mankato (MN)
Minot State U (ND)
Montana State U–Bozeman (MT)
Murray State U (KY)
Muskingum Coll (OH)
North Dakota State U (ND)
Northeastern Illinois U (IL)
Northern Arizona U (AZ)
Northern Michigan U (MI)
Northland Coll (WI)
Northwest Missouri State U (MO)
Ohio Wesleyan U (OH)
Olivet Nazarene U (IL)
Pacific Lutheran U (WA)
Penn State U Univ Park Campus (PA)
Queens Coll of the City U of NY (NY)
St. Cloud State U (MN)
Saint Louis U (MO)
St. Mary's U of San Antonio (TX)
Salem State Coll (MA)
Shippensburg U of Pennsylvania (PA)
Simon Fraser U (BC, Canada)
Slippery Rock U of Pennsylvania (PA)
Sonoma State U (CA)
Southeast Missouri State U (MO)
Stanford U (CA)
State U of NY at Albany (NY)
State U of NY at New Paltz (NY)
State U of NY at Stony Brook (NY)
State U of NY Coll at Brockport (NY)
State U of NY Coll at Buffalo (NY)
State U of NY Coll at Cortland (NY)
State U of NY Coll at Fredonia (NY)
State U of NY Coll at Oneonta (NY)
State U of West Georgia (GA)
Texas A&M U (TX)
Texas A&M U–Commerce (TX)
Tulane U (LA)
U of Alaska Fairbanks (AK)
U of Alberta (AB, Canada)
The U of Arizona (AZ)
U of Arkansas (AR)
U of British Columbia (BC, Canada)
U of Calgary (AB, Canada)
U of Calif, Berkeley (CA)
U of Calif, Los Angeles (CA)
U of Calif, San Diego (CA)
U of Calif, Santa Cruz (CA)
U of Guelph (ON, Canada)
U of Indianapolis (IN)
The U of Iowa (IA)
U of King's Coll (NS, Canada)
The U of Lethbridge (AB, Canada)
U of Manitoba (MB, Canada)
U of Massachusetts Amherst (MA)
U of Michigan–Flint (MI)
U of Missouri–Kansas City (MO)
U of Nebraska at Omaha (NE)
U of Nevada, Las Vegas (NV)
U of New Hampshire (NH)
The U of North Carolina at Charlotte (NC)
U of Northern Colorado (CO)
U of Pittsburgh at Bradford (PA)
U of Rochester (NY)
U of South Dakota (SD)
U of Toronto (ON, Canada)
U of Victoria (BC, Canada)
U of Waterloo (ON, Canada)
The U of Western Ontario (ON, Canada)
U of Windsor (ON, Canada)
U of Wisconsin–Green Bay (WI)
U of Wisconsin–Madison (WI)
U of Wisconsin–Milwaukee (WI)
Washington U in St. Louis (MO)
Wesleyan U (CT)
West Chester U of Pennsylvania (PA)
Western Connecticut State U (CT)
Western Michigan U (MI)
Western Washington U (WA)
Winona State U (MN)
Wittenberg U (OH)
York U (ON, Canada)
Youngstown State U (OH)

EAST ASIAN STUDIES
Augsburg Coll (MN)
Barnard Coll (NY)
Bates Coll (ME)
Boston U (MA)
Brown U (RI)
Bryn Mawr Coll (PA)
Bucknell U (PA)
Carleton U (ON, Canada)
Colby Coll (ME)
Colgate U (NY)
The Coll of William and Mary (VA)
Columbia Coll (NY)
Columbia U, School of General Studies (NY)
Cornell U (NY)
Denison U (OH)
DePauw U (IN)
Dickinson Coll (PA)
Emory & Henry Coll (VA)
The George Washington U (DC)
Hamilton Coll (NY)
Hamline U (MN)
Hampshire Coll (MA)
Harvard U (MA)
Haverford Coll (PA)
Indiana U Bloomington (IN)
John Carroll U (OH)
Johns Hopkins U (MD)
Lawrence U (WI)
Lewis & Clark Coll (OR)
Long Island U, Southampton Coll, Friends World Program (NY)
Macalester Coll (MN)
Marlboro Coll (VT)
Massachusetts Inst of Technology (MA)
McGill U (PQ, Canada)
Michigan State U (MI)
Middlebury Coll (VT)
New York U (NY)
Oakland U (MI)
Oberlin Coll (OH)
The Ohio State U (OH)
Ohio Wesleyan U (OH)
Penn State U Univ Park Campus (PA)
Pomona Coll (CA)
Portland State U (OR)
Princeton U (NJ)
Queens Coll of the City U of NY (NY)
Rutgers, State U of NJ, Douglass Coll (NJ)
Rutgers, State U of NJ, Livingston Coll (NJ)
Rutgers, State U of NJ, Rutgers Coll (NJ)
Rutgers, State U of NJ, U Coll–New Brunswick (NJ)
San Jose State U (CA)
Scripps Coll (CA)
Seattle U (WA)
Simmons Coll (MA)
Smith Coll (MA)
Stanford U (CA)
State U of NY at Albany (NY)
United States Military Academy (NY)
Université de Montréal (PQ, Canada)
U of Alberta (AB, Canada)
The U of Arizona (AZ)
U of Calgary (AB, Canada)
U of Calif, Davis (CA)
U of Calif, Irvine (CA)
U of Calif, Los Angeles (CA)
U of Calif, Santa Cruz (CA)
U of Chicago (IL)
U of Colorado at Boulder (CO)
U of Delaware (DE)
U of Minnesota, Twin Cities Campus (MN)
The U of Montana–Missoula (MT)
U of Oregon (OR)
U of Pennsylvania (PA)
U of Southern California (CA)
U of Toronto (ON, Canada)
U of Washington (WA)
Ursinus Coll (PA)
Valparaiso U (IN)
Vanderbilt U (TN)
Washington and Lee U (VA)
Washington U in St. Louis (MO)
Wesleyan U (CT)
Western Washington U (WA)
Wittenberg U (OH)
Yale U (CT)
York U (ON, Canada)

EASTERN EUROPEAN AREA STUDIES
Bard Coll (NY)
Barnard Coll (NY)
California State U, Fullerton (CA)
Carleton U (ON, Canada)
Columbia Coll (NY)
Cornell U (NY)
Emory U (GA)
Florida State U (FL)
Fordham U (NY)
Hamline U (MN)
Hampshire Coll (MA)
Harvard U (MA)
Indiana U Bloomington (IN)
Kent State U (OH)
Long Island U, Southampton Coll, Friends World Program (NY)
Marlboro Coll (VT)
Middlebury Coll (VT)
The Ohio State U (OH)
Portland State U (OR)
Princeton U (NJ)
Rutgers, State U of NJ, Douglass Coll (NJ)
Rutgers, State U of NJ, Livingston Coll (NJ)
Rutgers, State U of NJ, Rutgers Coll (NJ)
Rutgers, State U of NJ, U Coll–New Brunswick (NJ)
Salem State Coll (MA)
San Diego State U (CA)
Sarah Lawrence Coll (NY)
State U of NY at Albany (NY)
United States Military Academy (NY)
U of Alberta (AB, Canada)
U of Chicago (IL)
U of Colorado at Boulder (CO)
The U of Iowa (IA)
U of Massachusetts Amherst (MA)
U of Oregon (OR)
U of Richmond (VA)
U of Toronto (ON, Canada)
U of Vermont (VT)
U of Victoria (BC, Canada)
Wesleyan U (CT)
Western Michigan U (MI)

ECOLOGY
Alma Coll (MI)
Appalachian State U (NC)
Averett Coll (VA)
Ball State U (IN)
Bard Coll (NY)
Barry U (FL)
Bemidji State U (MN)
Bennington Coll (VT)
Boston U (MA)
Bradley U (IL)
Brevard Coll (NC)
California State U, Fresno (CA)
California State U, Fullerton (CA)
California State U, Hayward (CA)
California State U, Sacramento (CA)
California State U, San Marcos (CA)
Carleton U (ON, Canada)
Carlow Coll (PA)
Clark U (MA)
Coll of the Atlantic (ME)
Concordia Coll (NY)
Concordia U (PQ, Canada)
Cornell U (NY)
Defiance Coll (OH)
DePaul U (IL)
East Central U (OK)
Eastern Kentucky U (KY)
East Stroudsburg U of Pennsylvania (PA)
The Evergreen State Coll (WA)
Florida Inst of Technology (FL)
Florida State U (FL)
Franklin Pierce Coll (NH)
Friends U (KS)
Frostburg State U (MD)
Georgetown Coll (KY)
Goddard Coll (VT)
Hampshire Coll (MA)
Harvard U (MA)
Idaho State U (ID)
Indiana State U (IN)
Iona Coll (NY)
Iowa State U of Science and Technology (IA)
Jacksonville State U (AL)
Juniata Coll (PA)
Keene State Coll (NH)
Lawrence U (WI)
Lenoir-Rhyne Coll (NC)
Lock Haven U of Pennsylvania (PA)
Long Island U, Southampton Coll, Friends World Program (NY)
Maharishi U of Management (IA)
Manchester Coll (IN)
Marlboro Coll (VT)
McGill U (PQ, Canada)
Memorial U of Newfoundland (NF, Canada)
Michigan Technological U (MI)
Millersville U of Pennsylvania (PA)
Minnesota State U, Mankato (MN)
Missouri Southern State Coll (MO)
Montreat Coll (NC)
Morehead State U (KY)

Majors Index
Ecology–Education

Naropa U (CO)
New England Coll (NH)
Northern Arizona U (AZ)
Northern Michigan U (MI)
Northland Coll (WI)
Northwest Missouri State U (MO)
Oberlin Coll (OH)
Okanagan U Coll (BC, Canada)
Oklahoma State U (OK)
Pomona Coll (CA)
Princeton U (NJ)
Queens Coll of the City U of NY (NY)
Rice U (TX)
Rutgers, State U of NJ, Camden Coll of Arts & Scis (NJ)
Rutgers, State U of NJ, Douglass Coll (NJ)
Rutgers, State U of NJ, Livingston Coll (NJ)
Rutgers, State U of NJ, Rutgers Coll (NJ)
Rutgers, State U of NJ, U Coll–Camden (NJ)
Rutgers, State U of NJ, U Coll–New Brunswick (NJ)
St. Bonaventure U (NY)
St. Cloud State U (MN)
St. John's U (NY)
St. Lawrence U (NY)
San Francisco State U (CA)
San Jose State U (CA)
Sarah Lawrence Coll (NY)
Sierra Nevada Coll (NV)
Simon's Rock Coll of Bard (MA)
Slippery Rock U of Pennsylvania (PA)
Sonoma State U (CA)
State U of NY Coll of Environ Sci and Forestry (NY)
Sterling Coll (VT)
Tufts U (MA)
Tulane U (LA)
Unity Coll (ME)
Université de Montréal (PQ, Canada)
Université de Sherbrooke (PQ, Canada)
The U of Akron (OH)
The U of Arizona (AZ)
U of Calgary (AB, Canada)
U of Calif, Irvine (CA)
U of Calif, Los Angeles (CA)
U of Calif, San Diego (CA)
U of Calif, Santa Barbara (CA)
U of Calif, Santa Cruz (CA)
U of Colorado at Colorado Springs (CO)
U of Connecticut (CT)
U of Delaware (DE)
U of Georgia (GA)
U of Guelph (ON, Canada)
U of Illinois at Urbana–Champaign (IL)
U of Kansas (KS)
U of Maine at Machias (ME)
U of Manitoba (MB, Canada)
U of Maryland, Coll Park (MD)
U of Michigan (MI)
U of Minnesota, Twin Cities Campus (MN)
U of Missouri–St. Louis (MO)
U of New Brunswick, Fredericton (NB, Canada)
U of New England (ME)
U of New Hampshire (NH)
U of Pittsburgh (PA)
U of Pittsburgh at Bradford (PA)
U of Pittsburgh at Johnstown (PA)
U of Rio Grande (OH)
The U of Tennessee Knoxville (TN)
The U of Texas at Austin (TX)
U of Toronto (ON, Canada)
U of Vermont (VT)
U of Victoria (BC, Canada)
The U of Western Ontario (ON, Canada)
The U of Winnipeg (MB, Canada)
U of Wisconsin–Milwaukee (WI)
Ursinus Coll (PA)
Vanderbilt U (TN)
West Chester U of Pennsylvania (PA)
Western Washington U (WA)
William Paterson U of New Jersey (NJ)
Winona State U (MN)

Yale U (CT)
York U (ON, Canada)

EDUCATION
Acadia U (NS, Canada)
Adrian Coll (MI)
Alabama State U (AL)
Albertus Magnus Coll (CT)
Albion Coll (MI)
Alderson-Broaddus Coll (WV)
Alfred U (NY)
Allen U (SC)
Alma Coll (MI)
Alvernia Coll (PA)
American International Coll (MA)
American U (DC)
American U of Puerto Rico (PR)
Anderson Coll (SC)
Anderson U (IN)
Andrews U (MI)
Antioch Coll (OH)
Arlington Baptist Coll (TX)
Armstrong Atlantic State U (GA)
Ashland U (OH)
Assumption Coll (MA)
Athens State U (AL)
Atlantic Baptist U (NB, Canada)
Atlantic Union Coll (MA)
Augsburg Coll (MN)
Augustana Coll (IL)
Averett Coll (VA)
Baldwin-Wallace Coll (OH)
Ball State U (IN)
Barat Coll (IL)
Barry U (FL)
Bartlesville Wesleyan Coll (OK)
Barton Coll (NC)
Baylor U (TX)
Beaver Coll (PA)
Bellarmine Coll (KY)
Belmont Abbey Coll (NC)
Belmont U (TN)
Beloit Coll (WI)
Bemidji State U (MN)
Benedictine U (IL)
Berea Coll (KY)
Baruch Coll of the City U of NY (NY)
Berry Coll (GA)
Bethany Coll (KS)
Bethany Coll (WV)
Bethany Coll of the Assemblies of God (CA)
Bethel Coll (IN)
Bethel Coll (MN)
Bethel Coll (TN)
Biola U (CA)
Birmingham-Southern Coll (AL)
Bishop's U (PQ, Canada)
Bluffton Coll (OH)
Boise State U (ID)
Boston U (MA)
Bowie State U (MD)
Bowling Green State U (OH)
Brandon U (MB, Canada)
Brenau U (GA)
Brescia U (KY)
Briar Cliff Coll (IA)
Bridgewater State Coll (MA)
Brigham Young U–Hawaii Campus (HI)
Brock U (ON, Canada)
Brooklyn Coll of the City U of NY (NY)
Brown U (RI)
Bryan Coll (TN)
Bucknell U (PA)
Buena Vista U (IA)
Cabrini Coll (PA)
California Lutheran U (CA)
California State U, Sacramento (CA)
California U of Pennsylvania (PA)
Calvary Bible Coll and Theological Seminary (MO)
Cameron U (OK)
Campbell U (NC)
Canisius Coll (NY)
Capital U (OH)
Cardinal Stritch U (WI)
Carroll Coll (MT)
Carroll Coll (WI)
Carson-Newman Coll (TN)
Carthage Coll (WI)
Catawba Coll (NC)
The Catholic U of America (DC)
Cedar Crest Coll (PA)

Cedarville Coll (OH)
Centenary Coll (NJ)
Centenary Coll of Louisiana (LA)
Central Methodist Coll (MO)
Central Missouri State U (MO)
Chadron State Coll (NE)
Charleston Southern U (SC)
Cheyney U of Pennsylvania (PA)
Chicago State U (IL)
Christian Brothers U (TN)
Christopher Newport U (VA)
Circleville Bible Coll (OH)
City Coll of the City U of NY (NY)
Clarion U of Pennsylvania (PA)
Clark Atlanta U (GA)
Clarke Coll (IA)
Clark U (MA)
Clemson U (SC)
Cleveland Coll of Jewish Studies (OH)
Cleveland State U (OH)
Coe Coll (IA)
Coker Coll (SC)
Colgate U (NY)
Coll of Mount Saint Vincent (NY)
The Coll of New Jersey (NJ)
The Coll of New Rochelle (NY)
Coll of Notre Dame (CA)
Coll of Notre Dame of Maryland (MD)
Coll of Our Lady of the Elms (MA)
Coll of Saint Benedict (MN)
Coll of St. Catherine (MN)
Coll of St. Joseph (VT)
Coll of Saint Mary (NE)
The Coll of Saint Rose (NY)
The Coll of St. Scholastica (MN)
Coll of Staten Island of the City U of NY (NY)
Coll of the Atlantic (ME)
Coll of the Ozarks (MO)
Coll of the Southwest (NM)
Columbia Coll (MO)
Columbia Coll (SC)
Columbus State U (GA)
Concord Coll (WV)
Concordia Coll (MN)
Concordia Coll (NY)
Concordia U (CA)
Concordia U (IL)
Concordia U (NE)
Concordia U (OR)
Concordia U at St. Paul (MN)
Concordia U Coll of Alberta (AB, Canada)
Concordia U Wisconsin (WI)
Converse Coll (SC)
Coppin State Coll (MD)
Cornell Coll (IA)
Cornell U (NY)
Cornerstone U (MI)
Creighton U (NE)
Cumberland Coll (KY)
Curry Coll (MA)
Dakota State U (SD)
Dakota Wesleyan U (SD)
Dallas Baptist U (TX)
Dallas Christian Coll (TX)
Dana Coll (NE)
Dartmouth Coll (NH)
David Lipscomb U (TN)
Defiance Coll (OH)
Delaware State U (DE)
Delta State U (MS)
DePaul U (IL)
Dickinson State U (ND)
Dominican Coll of Blauvelt (NY)
Dordt Coll (IA)
Dowling Coll (NY)
Drexel U (PA)
Drury U (MO)
Duquesne U (PA)
D'Youville Coll (NY)
Earlham Coll (IN)
East Central U (OK)
Eastern Kentucky U (KY)
Eastern Mennonite U (VA)
Eastern Nazarene Coll (MA)
Eastern Oregon U (OR)
Eastern Washington U (WA)
Edgewood Coll (WI)
Elizabeth City State U (NC)
Elizabethtown Coll (PA)
Elmhurst Coll (IL)
Elmira Coll (NY)
Elon Coll (NC)
Emmanuel Coll (MA)

Emory U (GA)
Endicott Coll (MA)
Eugene Lang Coll, New School U (NY)
Evangel U (MO)
The Evergreen State Coll (WA)
Fairleigh Dickinson U, Teaneck-Hackensack Campus (NJ)
Fairmont State Coll (WV)
Faulkner U (AL)
Felician Coll (NJ)
Ferris State U (MI)
Ferrum Coll (VA)
Fitchburg State Coll (MA)
Florida A&M U (FL)
Florida Atlantic U (FL)
Florida Baptist Theological Coll (FL)
Florida Southern Coll (FL)
Fontbonne Coll (MO)
Fordham U (NY)
Fort Lewis Coll (CO)
Framingham State Coll (MA)
Franklin Pierce Coll (NH)
Freed-Hardeman U (TN)
Free Will Baptist Bible Coll (TN)
Fresno Pacific U (CA)
Friends U (KS)
Frostburg State U (MD)
Furman U (SC)
Gallaudet U (DC)
Gardner-Webb U (NC)
Georgetown Coll (KY)
Georgia Southwestern State U (GA)
Gettysburg Coll (PA)
Glenville State Coll (WV)
Goddard Coll (VT)
Gordon Coll (MA)
Goshen Coll (IN)
Goucher Coll (MD)
Graceland Coll (IA)
Grand Valley State U (MI)
Grand View Coll (IA)
Greensboro Coll (NC)
Greenville Coll (IL)
Guilford Coll (NC)
Gustavus Adolphus Coll (MN)
Gwynedd-Mercy Coll (PA)
Hamline U (MN)
Hampshire Coll (MA)
Hampton U (VA)
Hannibal-LaGrange Coll (MO)
Hardin-Simmons U (TX)
Hastings Coll (NE)
Haverford Coll (PA)
Heidelberg Coll (OH)
Heritage Coll (WA)
High Point U (NC)
Hillsdale Coll (MI)
Hofstra U (NY)
Holy Family Coll (PA)
Houghton Coll (NY)
Houston Baptist U (TX)
Howard Payne U (TX)
Howard U (DC)
Humboldt State U (CA)
Huntingdon Coll (AL)
Huntington Coll (IN)
Huston-Tillotson Coll (TX)
Idaho State U (ID)
Illinois Coll (IL)
Illinois Wesleyan U (IL)
Immaculata Coll (PA)
Indiana State U (IN)
Indiana U Bloomington (IN)
Indiana U East (IN)
Indiana U Northwest (IN)
Indiana U–Purdue U Fort Wayne (IN)
Indiana U–Purdue U Indianapolis (IN)
Indiana U South Bend (IN)
Indiana U Southeast (IN)
Indiana Wesleyan U (IN)
Inter American U of PR, Arecibo Campus (PR)
Inter American U of PR, Fajardo Campus (PR)
Inter American U of PR, Metropolitan Campus (PR)
Inter American U of PR, San Germán Campus (PR)
Iona Coll (NY)
Iowa State U of Science and Technology (IA)
Iowa Wesleyan Coll (IA)

Jacksonville State U (AL)
Jacksonville U (FL)
John Brown U (AR)
John Carroll U (OH)
Johnson C. Smith U (NC)
Johnson State Coll (VT)
Judson Coll (AL)
Judson Coll (IL)
Juniata Coll (PA)
Keene State Coll (NH)
Kent State U (OH)
King Coll (TN)
Knox Coll (IL)
Kutztown U of Pennsylvania (PA)
LaGrange Coll (GA)
Lake Forest Coll (IL)
Lakehead U (ON, Canada)
Lakeland Coll (WI)
Lake Superior State U (MI)
Lamar U (TX)
Lambuth U (TN)
Lancaster Bible Coll (PA)
Lander U (SC)
Lane Coll (TN)
Langston U (OK)
La Salle U (PA)
Lasell Coll (MA)
Lees-McRae Coll (NC)
Lee U (TN)
LeMoyne-Owen Coll (TN)
Lenoir-Rhyne Coll (NC)
Lesley Coll (MA)
Lewis-Clark State Coll (ID)
Lewis U (IL)
Limestone Coll (SC)
Lincoln Memorial U (TN)
Lincoln U (PA)
Lindenwood U (MO)
Lindsey Wilson Coll (KY)
Lock Haven U of Pennsylvania (PA)
Long Island U, Brooklyn Campus (NY)
Long Island U, C.W. Post Campus (NY)
Long Island U, Southampton Coll, Friends World Program (NY)
Longwood Coll (VA)
Loras Coll (IA)
Louisiana Coll (LA)
Louisiana State U in Shreveport (LA)
Loyola Coll in Maryland (MD)
Loyola U New Orleans (LA)
Lubbock Christian U (TX)
Luther Coll (IA)
Lycoming Coll (PA)
Lynchburg Coll (VA)
Lynn U (FL)
Madonna U (MI)
Maharishi U of Management (IA)
Manchester Coll (IN)
Manhattan Coll (NY)
Manhattanville Coll (NY)
Mansfield U of Pennsylvania (PA)
Maranatha Baptist Bible Coll (WI)
Marian Coll (IN)
Marian Coll of Fond du Lac (WI)
Marietta Coll (OH)
Marquette U (WI)
Marshall U (WV)
Mars Hill Coll (NC)
Marycrest International U (IA)
Marymount Coll (NY)
Maryville Coll (TN)
Maryville U of Saint Louis (MO)
Marywood U (PA)
Massachusetts Coll of Liberal Arts (MA)
Mayville State U (ND)
McGill U (PQ, Canada)
McMurry U (TX)
McNeese State U (LA)
McPherson Coll (KS)
Medaille Coll (NY)
Medgar Evers Coll of the City U of NY (NY)
Memorial U of Newfoundland (NF, Canada)
Mercy Coll (NY)
Mercyhurst Coll (PA)
Mesa State Coll (CO)
Methodist Coll (NC)
Michigan State U (MI)
Middlebury Coll (VT)
Midland Lutheran Coll (NE)
Midway Coll (KY)

Majors Index
Education–Education (Multiple Levels)

Milligan Coll (TN)
Millsaps Coll (MS)
Mills Coll (CA)
Minnesota State U, Mankato (MN)
Minot State U (ND)
Mississippi Coll (MS)
Mississippi U for Women (MS)
Mississippi Valley State U (MS)
Missouri Southern State Coll (MO)
Missouri Valley Coll (MO)
Molloy Coll (NY)
Monmouth Coll (IL)
Monmouth U (NJ)
Montana State U–Billings (MT)
Montana State U–Northern (MT)
Montreat Coll (NC)
Moravian Coll (PA)
Morgan State U (MD)
Morningside Coll (IA)
Mount Holyoke Coll (MA)
Mount Marty Coll (SD)
Mount Mary Coll (WI)
Mount Mercy Coll (IA)
Mount St. Clare Coll (IA)
Mount Saint Mary Coll (NY)
Mount St. Mary's Coll (CA)
Mount Saint Vincent U (NS, Canada)
Mount Senario Coll (WI)
Mount Vernon Nazarene Coll (OH)
Muskingum Coll (OH)
Nazareth Coll of Rochester (NY)
Newberry Coll (SC)
New England Coll (NH)
Newman U (KS)
New Mexico Highlands U (NM)
New York Inst of Technology (NY)
New York U (NY)
Niagara U (NY)
Nicholls State U (LA)
Nipissing U (ON, Canada)
North American Baptist Coll & Edmonton Baptist Sem (AB, Canada)
North Carolina Ag and Tech State U (NC)
North Carolina State U (NC)
North Carolina Wesleyan Coll (NC)
North Central Coll (IL)
North Dakota State U (ND)
Northeastern State U (OK)
Northeastern U (MA)
Northern Arizona U (AZ)
Northern Illinois U (IL)
Northern Kentucky U (KY)
Northern Michigan U (MI)
Northern State U (SD)
North Georgia Coll & State U (GA)
Northland Coll (WI)
North Park U (IL)
Northwest Coll (WA)
Northwestern Coll (IA)
Northwestern State U of Louisiana (LA)
Northwest Missouri State U (MO)
Notre Dame Coll (NH)
Nova Scotia Coll of Art and Design (NS, Canada)
Oakland City U (IN)
Oglethorpe U (GA)
Ohio Dominican Coll (OH)
Ohio Valley Coll (WV)
Ohio Wesleyan U (OH)
Okanagan U Coll (BC, Canada)
Oklahoma Baptist U (OK)
Oklahoma City U (OK)
Oklahoma State U (OK)
Olivet Nazarene U (IL)
Otterbein Coll (OH)
Ouachita Baptist U (AR)
Our Lady of Holy Cross Coll (LA)
Our Lady of the Lake U of San Antonio (TX)
Pace U, New York City Campus (NY)
Pace U, Pleasantville/Briarcliff Campus (NY)
Pacific Lutheran U (WA)
Pacific Union Coll (CA)
Pacific U (OR)
Palm Beach Atlantic Coll (FL)
Pepperdine U, Malibu (CA)
Peru State Coll (NE)
Pfeiffer U (NC)
Piedmont Baptist Coll (NC)
Pikeville Coll (KY)
Pittsburg State U (KS)

Plattsburgh State U of NY (NY)
Point Park Coll (PA)
Pontifical Catholic U of Puerto Rico (PR)
Presbyterian Coll (SC)
Providence Coll and Theological Seminary (MB, Canada)
Purdue U (IN)
Purdue U Calumet (IN)
Queens Coll (NC)
Queens Coll of the City U of NY (NY)
Queen's U at Kingston (ON, Canada)
Quinnipiac U (CT)
Redeemer Coll (ON, Canada)
Regis U (CO)
Rider U (NJ)
Ripon Coll (WI)
Rivier Coll (NH)
Roberts Wesleyan Coll (NY)
Rockford Coll (IL)
Rockhurst U (MO)
Rocky Mountain Coll (MT)
Rocky Mountain Coll (AB, Canada)
Rollins Coll (FL)
Rust Coll (MS)
Sacred Heart U (CT)
St. Ambrose U (IA)
St. Cloud State U (MN)
Saint Francis Coll (PA)
St. Francis Xavier U (NS, Canada)
Saint John's U (MN)
Saint Joseph Coll (CT)
Saint Joseph's Coll (ME)
St. Joseph's Coll, New York (NY)
St. Joseph's Coll, Suffolk Campus (NY)
Saint Joseph's U (PA)
Saint Leo U (FL)
Saint Louis U (MO)
Saint Martin's Coll (WA)
Saint Mary-of-the-Woods Coll (IN)
Saint Mary's Coll (IN)
Saint Mary's Coll of California (CA)
Saint Mary's U (NS, Canada)
St. Mary's U of San Antonio (TX)
Saint Michael's Coll (VT)
St. Olaf Coll (MN)
Saint Xavier U (IL)
Salem Coll (NC)
Salem State Coll (MA)
Salisbury State U (MD)
San Diego State U (CA)
San Jose Christian Coll (CA)
Sarah Lawrence Coll (NY)
Schreiner Coll (TX)
Seton Hill Coll (PA)
Shasta Bible Coll (CA)
Shawnee State U (OH)
Sheldon Jackson Coll (AK)
Simmons Coll (MA)
Simon Fraser U (BC, Canada)
Simpson Coll (IA)
Simpson Coll and Graduate School (CA)
Slippery Rock U of Pennsylvania (PA)
Smith Coll (MA)
South Dakota State U (SD)
Southeastern Oklahoma State U (OK)
Southeast Missouri State U (MO)
Southern Utah U (UT)
Southern Wesleyan U (SC)
Southwestern Oklahoma State U (OK)
Southwest State U (MN)
Spalding U (KY)
State U of NY at New Paltz (NY)
State U of NY at Oswego (NY)
State U of NY Coll at Brockport (NY)
State U of NY Coll at Fredonia (NY)
State U of NY Coll at Geneseo (NY)
State U of NY Coll at Oneonta (NY)
State U of NY Coll at Potsdam (NY)
State U of West Georgia (GA)
Stetson U (FL)
Stillman Coll (AL)
Stonehill Coll (MA)
Suffolk U (MA)
Swarthmore Coll (PA)

Syracuse U (NY)
Tabor Coll (KS)
Talladega Coll (AL)
Taylor U (IN)
Temple U (PA)
Tennessee State U (TN)
Tennessee Technological U (TN)
Tennessee Wesleyan Coll (TN)
Texas A&M U–Commerce (TX)
Texas A&M U–Kingsville (TX)
Texas Lutheran U (TX)
Texas Southern U (TX)
Texas Wesleyan U (TX)
Thomas More Coll (KY)
Tougaloo Coll (MS)
Touro Coll (NY)
Towson U (MD)
Trent U (ON, Canada)
Trinity Christian Coll (IL)
Trinity Coll (CT)
Trinity Western U (BC, Canada)
Tri-State U (IN)
Troy State U (AL)
Troy State U Dothan (AL)
Tusculum Coll (TN)
Union Coll (KY)
Union Coll (NE)
The Union Inst (OH)
Union U (TN)
Universidad del Turabo (PR)
Université de Montréal (PQ, Canada)
Université de Sherbrooke (PQ, Canada)
U du Québec à Hull (PQ, Canada)
U du Québec à Trois-Rivières (PQ, Canada)
U du Québec en Abitibi-Témiscamingue (PQ, Canada)
The U of Akron (OH)
U of Alaska Fairbanks (AK)
U of Alberta (AB, Canada)
The U of Arizona (AZ)
U of Arkansas at Little Rock (AR)
U of Arkansas at Monticello (AR)
U of British Columbia (BC, Canada)
U of Calgary (AB, Canada)
U of Central Oklahoma (OK)
U of Charleston (WV)
U of Cincinnati (OH)
U of Connecticut (CT)
U of Dallas (TX)
U of Dayton (OH)
U of Delaware (DE)
U of Detroit Mercy (MI)
The U of Findlay (OH)
U of Great Falls (MT)
U of Houston–Clear Lake (TX)
U of Houston–Victoria (TX)
U of Indianapolis (IN)
The U of Iowa (IA)
U of La Verne (CA)
The U of Lethbridge (AB, Canada)
U of Maine (ME)
U of Maine at Fort Kent (ME)
U of Maine at Machias (ME)
U of Maine at Presque Isle (ME)
U of Manitoba (MB, Canada)
U of Mary Hardin-Baylor (TX)
U of Maryland, Coll Park (MD)
U of Massachusetts Amherst (MA)
U of Michigan (MI)
U of Michigan–Dearborn (MI)
U of Michigan–Flint (MI)
U of Minnesota, Duluth (MN)
U of Minnesota, Morris (MN)
U of Minnesota, Twin Cities Campus (MN)
U of Missouri–Columbia (MO)
U of Missouri–Kansas City (MO)
U of Missouri–St. Louis (MO)
The U of Montana–Missoula (MT)
U of Nebraska at Omaha (NE)
U of Nebraska–Lincoln (NE)
U of Nevada, Las Vegas (NV)
U of New Brunswick, Fredericton (NB, Canada)
U of New Brunswick, Saint John (NB, Canada)
U of New England (ME)
U of New Mexico (NM)
The U of North Carolina at Pembroke (NC)
U of Pennsylvania (PA)
U of Pittsburgh at Bradford (PA)
U of Pittsburgh at Johnstown (PA)

U of Portland (OR)
U of Prince Edward Island (PE, Canada)
U of Redlands (CA)
U of Regina (SK, Canada)
U of Richmond (VA)
U of Rio Grande (OH)
U of Saint Francis (IN)
U of St. Thomas (TX)
U of San Diego (CA)
U of San Francisco (CA)
U of Science and Arts of Oklahoma (OK)
U of Sioux Falls (SD)
U of South Alabama (AL)
U of South Dakota (SD)
U of Southern California (CA)
U of Southern Colorado (CO)
U of South Florida (FL)
The U of Tennessee at Chattanooga (TN)
The U of Tennessee Knoxville (TN)
The U of the Arts (PA)
U of the Pacific (CA)
U of the Sacred Heart (PR)
U of Toronto (ON, Canada)
U of Vermont (VT)
U of Victoria (BC, Canada)
U of Washington (WA)
The U of Western Ontario (ON, Canada)
U of Windsor (ON, Canada)
The U of Winnipeg (MB, Canada)
U of Wisconsin–La Crosse (WI)
U of Wisconsin–Milwaukee (WI)
U of Wisconsin–Platteville (WI)
U of Wisconsin–River Falls (WI)
U of Wisconsin–Stevens Point (WI)
U of Wisconsin–Superior (WI)
U of Wisconsin–Whitewater (WI)
Upper Iowa U (IA)
Urbana U (OH)
Ursinus Coll (PA)
Ursuline Coll (OH)
Valdosta State U (GA)
Valley City State U (ND)
Valparaiso U (IN)
Vanderbilt U (TN)
Vanguard U of Southern California (CA)
Villanova U (PA)
Virginia Commonwealth U (VA)
Virginia Wesleyan Coll (VA)
Voorhees Coll (SC)
Wagner Coll (NY)
Wake Forest U (NC)
Walsh U (OH)
Warner Pacific Coll (OR)
Warren Wilson Coll (NC)
Washington State U (WA)
Washington U in St. Louis (MO)
Wayland Baptist U (TX)
Wayne State Coll (NE)
Webster U (MO)
Wells Coll (NY)
Wesleyan Coll (GA)
Wesley Coll (DE)
West Chester U of Pennsylvania (PA)
Western Baptist Coll (OR)
Western Connecticut State U (CT)
Western Montana Coll of The U of Montana (MT)
Western State Coll of Colorado (CO)
Western Washington U (WA)
Westfield State Coll (MA)
West Liberty State Coll (WV)
Westminster Coll (MO)
Westminster Coll (PA)
Westmont Coll (CA)
West Virginia State Coll (WV)
West Virginia Wesleyan Coll (WV)
Wheeling Jesuit U (WV)
Wheelock Coll (MA)
Wilkes U (PA)
William Jewell Coll (MO)
William Paterson U of New Jersey (NJ)
William Penn U (IA)
Williams Baptist Coll (AR)
William Woods U (MO)
Wilmington Coll (OH)
Wingate U (NC)
Winona State U (MN)
Winston-Salem State U (NC)
Wittenberg U (OH)

Wright State U (OH)
Xavier U (OH)
Xavier U of Louisiana (LA)
Yeshiva U (NY)
York Coll (NE)
York Coll of Pennsylvania (PA)
York U (ON, Canada)
Youngstown State U (OH)

EDUCATION ADMINISTRATION
Campbell U (NC)
Cleveland Coll of Jewish Studies (OH)
Lamar U (TX)
Lindenwood U (MO)
Long Island U, Brooklyn Campus (NY)
McNeese State U (LA)
Northwest Missouri State U (MO)
Purdue U Calumet (IN)
St. Cloud State U (MN)
Saint Mary's U (NS, Canada)
Tennessee State U (TN)
Texas Southern U (TX)
U of British Columbia (BC, Canada)
U of Central Arkansas (AR)
U of Central Oklahoma (OK)
The U of Lethbridge (AB, Canada)
U of Nebraska at Omaha (NE)
U of Oregon (OR)
U of Regina (SK, Canada)
U of San Francisco (CA)
U of Windsor (ON, Canada)
U of Wisconsin–Superior (WI)
Valdosta State U (GA)
Western Washington U (WA)

EDUCATIONAL MEDIA DESIGN
Ball State U (IN)
Bayamón Central U (PR)
California State U, Chico (CA)
Chadron State Coll (NE)
Indiana State U (IN)
Ithaca Coll (NY)
Jacksonville State U (AL)
James Madison U (VA)
Norwich U (VT)
St. Cloud State U (MN)
Texas Southern U (TX)
U of Central Arkansas (AR)
U of Central Oklahoma (OK)
U of Nebraska at Omaha (NE)
Western Illinois U (IL)
Western Oregon U (OR)
Widener U (PA)

EDUCATIONAL MEDIA TECHNOLOGY
Duquesne U (PA)
Seton Hill Coll (PA)
U of Wisconsin–Superior (WI)

EDUCATIONAL PSYCHOLOGY
Christian Brothers U (TN)
Jacksonville State U (AL)
Mississippi State U (MS)
St. Mary's Coll of Maryland (MD)

EDUCATIONAL STATISTICS/RESEARCH METHODS
Bucknell U (PA)

EDUCATION (MULTIPLE LEVELS)
California State U, Sacramento (CA)
East Texas Baptist U (TX)
George Fox U (OR)
Howard Payne U (TX)
International Baptist Coll (AZ)
Ithaca Coll (NY)
Lake Superior State U (MI)
Martin Luther Coll (MN)
The Richard Stockton Coll of New Jersey (NJ)
U of Nebraska–Lincoln (NE)
U of North Alabama (AL)
U of Rio Grande (OH)
U of Washington (WA)
Western Washington U (WA)
York Coll (NE)
Youngstown State U (OH)

Majors Index
Education of the Emotionally Handicapped–Electrical/Electronics Engineering

EDUCATION OF THE EMOTIONALLY HANDICAPPED
Bradley U (IL)
Central Michigan U (MI)
East Carolina U (NC)
Eastern Michigan U (MI)
Florida International U (FL)
Florida State U (FL)
Greensboro Coll (NC)
Hope Coll (MI)
Johnson Bible Coll (TN)
Marygrove Coll (MI)
Minnesota State U Moorhead (MN)
Ohio U (OH)
Oklahoma Baptist U (OK)
Trinity Christian Coll (IL)
U of Maine at Farmington (ME)
U of Nebraska at Omaha (NE)
U of South Florida (FL)
Western Michigan U (MI)

EDUCATION OF THE HEARING IMPAIRED
Augustana Coll (SD)
Barton Coll (NC)
Boston U (MA)
Bowling Green State U (OH)
The Coll of New Jersey (NJ)
Duquesne U (PA)
Eastern Michigan U (MI)
Flagler Coll (FL)
Indiana U of Pennsylvania (PA)
Lambuth U (TN)
Long Island U, C.W. Post Campus (NY)
New York U (NY)
Ohio U (OH)
Texas Christian U (TX)
U of Arkansas at Little Rock (AR)
U of Nebraska at Omaha (NE)
U of Nebraska–Lincoln (NE)
The U of North Carolina at Greensboro (NC)
U of Science and Arts of Oklahoma (OK)

EDUCATION OF THE MENTALLY HANDICAPPED
Augusta State U (GA)
Bowling Green State U (OH)
Central Michigan U (MI)
East Carolina U (NC)
Eastern Michigan U (MI)
Flagler Coll (FL)
Florida International U (FL)
Florida State U (FL)
Greensboro Coll (NC)
Johnson Bible Coll (TN)
Minnesota State U Moorhead (MN)
Oklahoma Baptist U (OK)
Shaw U (NC)
Silver Lake Coll (WI)
Trinity Christian Coll (IL)
U du Québec à Trois-Rivières (PQ, Canada)
U of Maine at Farmington (ME)
The U of North Carolina at Charlotte (NC)
U of Northern Iowa (IA)
U of Rio Grande (OH)
U of South Florida (FL)
Western Michigan U (MI)
York Coll (NE)

EDUCATION OF THE MULTIPLE HANDICAPPED
Bowling Green State U (OH)
Johnson Bible Coll (TN)
Ohio U (OH)
The U of Akron (OH)
U of Northern Iowa (IA)

EDUCATION OF THE PHYSICALLY HANDICAPPED
Eastern Michigan U (MI)
Indiana U of Pennsylvania (PA)
Johnson Bible Coll (TN)

EDUCATION OF THE SPECIFIC LEARNING DISABLED
Appalachian State U (NC)
Aquinas Coll (MI)
Bethune-Cookman Coll (FL)
Bowling Green State U (OH)
Bradley U (IL)
East Carolina U (NC)
Flagler Coll (FL)
Florida International U (FL)
Florida Southern Coll (FL)
Florida State U (FL)
Greensboro Coll (NC)
Harding U (AR)
Hope Coll (MI)
Johnson Bible Coll (TN)
Kent State U (OH)
Malone Coll (OH)
Mercer U (GA)
Minnesota State U Moorhead (MN)
Ohio U (OH)
Oklahoma Baptist U (OK)
Silver Lake Coll (WI)
Trinity Christian Coll (IL)
U of Maine at Farmington (ME)
U of Rio Grande (OH)
U of South Florida (FL)
Wheeling Jesuit U (WV)

EDUCATION OF THE SPEECH IMPAIRED
Alabama A&M U (AL)
Baylor U (TX)
Bloomsburg U of Pennsylvania (PA)
Eastern Michigan U (MI)
Emerson Coll (MA)
Indiana U of Pennsylvania (PA)
Ithaca Coll (NY)
Kent State U (OH)
Louisiana Tech U (LA)
New York U (NY)
Ohio U (OH)
St. John's U (NY)
Southeastern Louisiana U (LA)
State U of NY Coll at Cortland (NY)
U of Central Arkansas (AR)
Wayne State U (MI)
Western Kentucky U (KY)

EDUCATION OF THE VISUALLY HANDICAPPED
Auburn U (AL)
Dominican Coll of Blauvelt (NY)
Eastern Michigan U (MI)
Florida State U (FL)
Western Michigan U (MI)

ELECTRICAL/ELECTRONIC ENGINEERING TECHNOLOGY
Andrews U (MI)
Appalachian State U (NC)
Arizona State U East (AZ)
Athens State U (AL)
Baker Coll of Muskegon (MI)
Baker Coll of Owosso (MI)
Bluefield State Coll (WV)
Bowling Green State U (OH)
Brigham Young U (UT)
Bryant and Stratton Coll, Cleveland (OH)
California State Polytechnic U, Pomona (CA)
California State U, Long Beach (CA)
California U of Pennsylvania (PA)
Cameron U (OK)
Capitol Coll (MD)
Central Michigan U (MI)
Central Missouri State U (MO)
Cleveland State U (OH)
Cogswell Polytechnical Coll (CA)
Colorado Tech U (CO)
Delaware State U (DE)
DePaul U (IL)
DeVry Inst (NJ)
DeVry Inst of Technology (AZ)
DeVry Inst of Technology, Fremont (CA)
DeVry Inst of Technology, Long Beach (CA)
DeVry Inst of Technology, Pomona (CA)
DeVry Inst of Technology, West Hills (CA)
DeVry Inst of Technology, Alpharetta (GA)
DeVry Inst of Technology, Decatur (GA)
DeVry Inst of Technology, Addison (IL)
DeVry Inst of Technology, Chicago (IL)
DeVry Inst of Technology (MO)
DeVry Inst of Technology (NY)
DeVry Inst of Technology (OH)
DeVry Inst of Technology (TX)
East Central U (OK)
Eastern Washington U (WA)
East Tennessee State U (TN)
Elizabeth City State U (NC)
Embry-Riddle Aeronautical U (FL)
Fairleigh Dickinson U, Teaneck-Hackensack Campus (NJ)
Fairmont State Coll (WV)
Ferris State U (MI)
Fitchburg State Coll (MA)
Florida A&M U (FL)
Fort Valley State U (GA)
Francis Marion U (SC)
Georgia Southern U (GA)
Grantham Coll of Engineering (LA)
Hamilton Tech Coll (IA)
Hampton U (VA)
Herzing Coll (GA)
Herzing Coll (WI)
Indiana State U (IN)
Indiana U–Purdue U Fort Wayne (IN)
Indiana U–Purdue U Indianapolis (IN)
Inter American U of PR, Aguadilla Campus (PR)
Inter American U of PR, Metropolitan Campus (PR)
Inter American U of PR, San Germán Campus (PR)
Jacksonville State U (AL)
Johnson & Wales U (RI)
Kansas State U (KS)
Keene State Coll (NH)
Kent State U (OH)
Lakehead U (ON, Canada)
Lake Superior State U (MI)
LeTourneau U (TX)
Lewis-Clark State Coll (ID)
Louisiana Tech U (LA)
Maharishi U of Management (IA)
McNeese State U (LA)
Metropolitan State Coll of Denver (CO)
Michigan Technological U (MI)
Midwestern State U (TX)
Millersville U of Pennsylvania (PA)
Milwaukee School of Engineering (WI)
Minnesota State U, Mankato (MN)
Missouri Western State Coll (MO)
Montana State U–Bozeman (MT)
Montana State U–Northern (MT)
Murray State U (KY)
New Jersey Inst of Technology (NJ)
New York Inst of Technology (NY)
Norfolk State U (VA)
Northeastern State U (OK)
Northeastern U (MA)
Northern Kentucky U (KY)
Northern Michigan U (MI)
Northern State U (SD)
Oklahoma State U (OK)
Oregon Inst of Technology (OR)
Pacific Union Coll (CA)
Pennsylvania Coll of Technology (PA)
Penn State U at Erie, The Behrend Coll (PA)
Penn State U Harrisburg Campus of the Capital Coll (PA)
Pittsburg State U (KS)
Point Park Coll (PA)
Prairie View A&M U (TX)
Purdue U (IN)
Purdue U Calumet (IN)
Regents Coll (NY)
Rochester Inst of Technology (NY)
St. Cloud State U (MN)
Sam Houston State U (TX)
Savannah State U (GA)
South Dakota State U (SD)
Southeastern Oklahoma State U (OK)
Southeast Missouri State U (MO)
Southern Polytechnic State U (GA)
Southern Utah U (UT)
Southwest Missouri State U (MO)
State U of NY at Farmingdale (NY)
State U of NY Coll at Buffalo (NY)
State U of NY Coll of Technology at Alfred (NY)
State U of NY Inst of Tech at Utica/Rome (NY)
Temple U (PA)
Texas Southern U (TX)
Texas Tech U (TX)
Thomas Edison State Coll (NJ)
The U of Akron (OH)
U of Arkansas at Little Rock (AR)
U of Central Florida (FL)
U of Cincinnati (OH)
U of Dayton (OH)
U of Hartford (CT)
U of Maine (ME)
U of Massachusetts Dartmouth (MA)
U of Massachusetts Lowell (MA)
The U of Memphis (TN)
U of Nebraska at Omaha (NE)
U of New Hampshire (NH)
U of New Hampshire at Manchester (NH)
The U of North Carolina at Charlotte (NC)
U of North Texas (TX)
U of Pittsburgh at Johnstown (PA)
U of Regina (SK, Canada)
U of Southern Colorado (CO)
U of Southern Mississippi (MS)
The U of Texas at Dallas (TX)
Wayne State U (MI)
Weber State U (UT)
Wentworth Inst of Technology (MA)
Western Carolina U (NC)
Western Kentucky U (KY)
Western Washington U (WA)
Westwood Coll of Technology (CO)
World Coll (VA)
Youngstown State U (OH)

ELECTRICAL/ELECTRONICS DRAFTING
Idaho State U (ID)

ELECTRICAL/ELECTRONICS ENGINEERING
Abilene Christian U (TX)
Alabama A&M U (AL)
Alfred U (NY)
Arizona State U (AZ)
Arkansas Tech U (AR)
Auburn U (AL)
Bethel Coll (IN)
Boise State U (ID)
Boston U (MA)
Bradley U (IL)
Brigham Young U (UT)
Brown U (RI)
Bucknell U (PA)
California Inst of Technology (CA)
California Polytechnic State U, San Luis Obispo (CA)
California State Polytechnic U, Pomona (CA)
California State U, Chico (CA)
California State U, Fresno (CA)
California State U, Fullerton (CA)
California State U, Long Beach (CA)
California State U, Los Angeles (CA)
California State U, Northridge (CA)
California State U, Sacramento (CA)
Calvin Coll (MI)
Capitol Coll (MD)
Carleton U (ON, Canada)
Carnegie Mellon U (PA)
Case Western Reserve U (OH)
The Catholic U of America (DC)
Cedarville Coll (OH)
Christian Brothers U (TN)
Citadel, The Military Coll of South Carolina (SC)
City Coll of the City U of NY (NY)
Clarkson U (NY)
Clemson U (SC)
Cleveland State U (OH)
Cogswell Polytechnical Coll (CA)
The Coll of Southeastern Europe, The American U of Athens (Greece)
Colorado School of Mines (CO)
Colorado State U (CO)
Colorado Tech U (CO)
Columbia U, School of Engineering & Applied Sci (NY)
Concordia U (PQ, Canada)
Cooper Union for the Advancement of Science & Art (NY)
Cornell U (NY)
Dominican U (IL)
Dordt Coll (IA)
Drexel U (PA)
Duke U (NC)
Eastern Nazarene Coll (MA)
Embry-Riddle Aeronautical U (AZ)
Fairleigh Dickinson U, Teaneck-Hackensack Campus (NJ)
Florida A&M U (FL)
Florida Atlantic U (FL)
Florida Inst of Technology (FL)
Florida International U (FL)
Florida State U (FL)
Frostburg State U (MD)
Gallaudet U (DC)
Gannon U (PA)
George Mason U (VA)
The George Washington U (DC)
Georgia Inst of Technology (GA)
Gonzaga U (WA)
Grand Valley State U (MI)
Grantham Coll of Engineering (LA)
Grove City Coll (PA)
Hampton U (VA)
Harvard U (MA)
Henry Cogswell Coll (WA)
Hofstra U (NY)
Howard U (DC)
Illinois Inst of Technology (IL)
Indiana Inst of Technology (IN)
Indiana U–Purdue U Indianapolis (IN)
Insto Tecno Estudios Sups Monterrey (Mexico)
Insto Tecno Estudios Sups Monterrey, Querétaro (Mexico)
Inter American U of PR, Fajardo Campus (PR)
Iowa State U of Science and Technology (IA)
Jacksonville U (FL)
John Brown U (AR)
Johns Hopkins U (MD)
Johnson & Wales U (RI)
Kansas State U (KS)
Kettering U (MI)
Lafayette Coll (PA)
Lakehead U (ON, Canada)
Lake Superior State U (MI)
Lamar U (TX)
Lawrence Technological U (MI)
Lehigh U (PA)
LeTourneau U (TX)
Louisiana State U and A&M Coll (LA)
Louisiana Tech U (LA)
Loyola Coll in Maryland (MD)
Loyola Marymount U (CA)
Maharishi U of Management (IA)
Manhattan Coll (NY)
Marquette U (WI)
Massachusetts Inst of Technology (MA)
McGill U (PQ, Canada)
McNeese State U (LA)
Memorial U of Newfoundland (NF, Canada)
Mercer U (GA)
Merrimack Coll (MA)
Michigan State U (MI)
Michigan Technological U (MI)
Milwaukee School of Engineering (WI)
Minnesota State U, Mankato (MN)
Mississippi State U (MS)
Montana State U–Bozeman (MT)
Morgan State U (MD)
New Jersey Inst of Technology (NJ)
New Mexico Inst of Mining and Technology (NM)
New Mexico State U (NM)
New York Inst of Technology (NY)
New York U (NY)
Norfolk State U (VA)
North Carolina Ag and Tech State U (NC)
North Carolina State U (NC)
North Dakota State U (ND)
Northeastern U (MA)
Northern Arizona U (AZ)
Northern Illinois U (IL)
Northwestern U (IL)
Norwich U (VT)
Oakland U (MI)
Ohio Northern U (OH)
The Ohio State U (OH)

1004   www.petersons.com   Peterson's Guide to Four-Year Colleges 2001

Majors Index
Electrical/Electronics Engineering–Elementary Education

Ohio U (OH)
Oklahoma Christian U of Science and Arts (OK)
Oklahoma State U (OK)
Old Dominion U (VA)
Oregon State U (OR)
Pace U, New York City Campus (NY)
Pace U, Pleasantville/Briarcliff Campus (NY)
Pacific Lutheran U (WA)
Pennsylvania Coll of Technology (PA)
Penn State U at Erie, The Behrend Coll (PA)
Penn State U Harrisburg Campus of the Capital Coll (PA)
Penn State U Univ Park Campus (PA)
Polytechnic U, Brooklyn Campus (NY)
Polytechnic U, Farmingdale Campus (NY)
Polytechnic U of Puerto Rico (PR)
Portland State U (OR)
Prairie View A&M U (TX)
Princeton U (NJ)
Purdue U (IN)
Purdue U Calumet (IN)
Queen's U at Kingston (ON, Canada)
Rensselaer Polytechnic Inst (NY)
Rice U (TX)
Rochester Inst of Technology (NY)
Rose-Hulman Inst of Technology (IN)
Rowan U (NJ)
Rutgers, State U of NJ, Coll of Engineering (NJ)
Ryerson Polytechnic U (ON, Canada)
Saginaw Valley State U (MI)
St. Cloud State U (MN)
Saint Louis U (MO)
St. Mary's U of San Antonio (TX)
San Diego State U (CA)
San Francisco State U (CA)
San Jose State U (CA)
Santa Clara U (CA)
Seattle Pacific U (WA)
Seattle U (WA)
South Dakota School of Mines and Technology (SD)
South Dakota State U (SD)
Southern Illinois U Carbondale (IL)
Southern Illinois U Edwardsville (IL)
Southern Methodist U (TX)
Stanford U (CA)
State U of NY at Binghamton (NY)
State U of NY at Buffalo (NY)
State U of NY at New Paltz (NY)
State U of NY at Stony Brook (NY)
State U of NY Maritime Coll (NY)
Stevens Inst of Technology (NJ)
Suffolk U (MA)
Syracuse U (NY)
Temple U (PA)
Tennessee State U (TN)
Tennessee Technological U (TN)
Texas A&M U (TX)
Texas A&M U–Kingsville (TX)
Texas Tech U (TX)
Tri-State U (IN)
Tufts U (MA)
Tulane U (LA)
Tuskegee U (AL)
Union Coll (NY)
United States Air Force Academy (CO)
United States Coast Guard Academy (CT)
United States Military Academy (NY)
United States Naval Academy (MD)
Universidad del Turabo (PR)
Université de Sherbrooke (PQ, Canada)
U du Québec à Trois-Rivières (PQ, Canada)
U du Québec en Abitibi-Témiscamingue (PQ, Canada)
Université Laval (PQ, Canada)
The U of Akron (OH)
The U of Alabama (AL)
The U of Alabama at Birmingham (AL)

The U of Alabama in Huntsville (AL)
U of Alaska Fairbanks (AK)
U of Alberta (AB, Canada)
The U of Arizona (AZ)
U of Arkansas (AR)
U of British Columbia (BC, Canada)
U of Calgary (AB, Canada)
U of Calif, Berkeley (CA)
U of Calif, Davis (CA)
U of Calif, Irvine (CA)
U of Calif, Los Angeles (CA)
U of Calif, Riverside (CA)
U of Calif, San Diego (CA)
U of Calif, Santa Barbara (CA)
U of Calif, Santa Cruz (CA)
U of Central Florida (FL)
U of Cincinnati (OH)
U of Colorado at Boulder (CO)
U of Colorado at Colorado Springs (CO)
U of Colorado at Denver (CO)
U of Connecticut (CT)
U of Dayton (OH)
U of Delaware (DE)
U of Denver (CO)
U of Detroit Mercy (MI)
U of Evansville (IN)
U of Florida (FL)
U of Hartford (CT)
U of Hawaii at Manoa (HI)
U of Houston (TX)
U of Idaho (ID)
U of Illinois at Chicago (IL)
U of Illinois at Urbana–Champaign (IL)
U of Indianapolis (IN)
The U of Iowa (IA)
U of Kansas (KS)
U of Kentucky (KY)
U of Louisiana at Lafayette (LA)
U of Louisville (KY)
U of Maine (ME)
U of Manitoba (MB, Canada)
U of Maryland, Coll Park (MD)
U of Massachusetts Amherst (MA)
U of Massachusetts Dartmouth (MA)
U of Massachusetts Lowell (MA)
The U of Memphis (TN)
U of Miami (FL)
U of Michigan (MI)
U of Michigan–Dearborn (MI)
U of Minnesota, Duluth (MN)
U of Minnesota, Twin Cities Campus (MN)
U of Mississippi (MS)
U of Missouri–Columbia (MO)
U of Missouri–Kansas City (MO)
U of Missouri–Rolla (MO)
U of Missouri–St. Louis (MO)
U of Nebraska–Lincoln (NE)
U of Nevada, Las Vegas (NV)
U of Nevada, Reno (NV)
U of New Brunswick, Fredericton (NB, Canada)
U of New Brunswick, Saint John (NB, Canada)
U of New Hampshire (NH)
U of New Haven (CT)
U of New Mexico (NM)
U of New Orleans (LA)
The U of North Carolina at Charlotte (NC)
U of North Dakota (ND)
U of North Florida (FL)
U of Notre Dame (IN)
U of Oklahoma (OK)
U of Pennsylvania (PA)
U of Pittsburgh (PA)
U of Pittsburgh at Bradford (PA)
U of Portland (OR)
U of Puerto Rico, Mayagüez Campus (PR)
U of Regina (SK, Canada)
U of Rhode Island (RI)
U of Rochester (NY)
U of San Diego (CA)
The U of Scranton (PA)
U of South Alabama (AL)
U of South Carolina (SC)
U of Southern California (CA)
U of Southern Maine (ME)
U of South Florida (FL)
The U of Tennessee at Chattanooga (TN)

The U of Tennessee Knoxville (TN)
The U of Texas at Arlington (TX)
The U of Texas at Austin (TX)
The U of Texas at Dallas (TX)
The U of Texas at San Antonio (TX)
The U of Texas at Tyler (TX)
The U of Texas–Pan American (TX)
U of the District of Columbia (DC)
U of the Pacific (CA)
U of Toronto (ON, Canada)
U of Tulsa (OK)
U of Utah (UT)
U of Vermont (VT)
U of Victoria (BC, Canada)
U of Virginia (VA)
U of Washington (WA)
U of Waterloo (ON, Canada)
The U of Western Ontario (ON, Canada)
U of Windsor (ON, Canada)
U of Wisconsin–Madison (WI)
U of Wisconsin–Milwaukee (WI)
U of Wisconsin–Platteville (WI)
U of Wyoming (WY)
Utah State U (UT)
Valparaiso U (IN)
Vanderbilt U (TN)
Villanova U (PA)
Virginia Commonwealth U (VA)
Virginia Military Inst (VA)
Virginia Polytechnic Inst and State U (VA)
Walla Walla Coll (WA)
Washington State U (WA)
Washington U in St. Louis (MO)
Wayne State U (MI)
Wentworth Inst of Technology (MA)
Western Michigan U (MI)
Western New England Coll (MA)
West Virginia U (WV)
West Virginia U Inst of Technology (WV)
Wichita State U (KS)
Widener U (PA)
Wilkes U (PA)
Worcester Polytechnic Inst (MA)
Wright State U (OH)
Yale U (CT)
Youngstown State U (OH)

ELECTROMECHANICAL TECHNOLOGY
Insto Tecno Estudios Sups Monterrey (Mexico)
Loras Coll (IA)
New York City Tech Coll of the City U of NY (NY)
New York Inst of Technology (NY)
Penn State U Altoona Coll (PA)
Penn State U Berks Cmps of Berks-Lehigh Valley Coll (PA)
Regents Coll (NY)
State U of NY Coll of Technology at Alfred (NY)
U du Québec en Abitibi-Témiscamingue (PQ, Canada)
U of Houston (TX)
U of the District of Columbia (DC)
Vermont Tech Coll (VT)
Wayne State U (MI)
Western Kentucky U (KY)

ELEMENTARY EDUCATION
Abilene Christian U (TX)
Acadia U (NS, Canada)
Adams State Coll (CO)
Adelphi U (NY)
Adrian Coll (MI)
Alabama A&M U (AL)
Alabama State U (AL)
Alaska Pacific U (AK)
Albertson Coll of Idaho (ID)
Albion Coll (MI)
Albright Coll (PA)
Alderson-Broaddus Coll (WV)
Alfred U (NY)
Alice Lloyd Coll (KY)
Allentown Coll of St. Francis de Sales (PA)
Allen U (SC)
Alma Coll (MI)
Alvernia Coll (PA)
Alverno Coll (WI)
American Indian Coll of the Assemblies of God, Inc (AZ)
American International Coll (MA)

American U (DC)
American U of Puerto Rico (PR)
Anderson Coll (SC)
Anderson U (IN)
Andrews U (MI)
Anna Maria Coll (MA)
Aquinas Coll (MI)
Aquinas Coll (TN)
Arizona State U (AZ)
Arizona State U East (AZ)
Arizona State U West (AZ)
Arkansas Baptist Coll (AR)
Arkansas State U (AR)
Arkansas Tech U (AR)
Armstrong Atlantic State U (GA)
Asbury Coll (KY)
Ashland U (OH)
Assumption Coll (MA)
Athens State U (AL)
Atlantic Union Coll (MA)
Auburn U (AL)
Auburn U Montgomery (AL)
Augsburg Coll (MN)
Augustana Coll (IL)
Augustana Coll (SD)
Augusta State U (GA)
Averett Coll (VA)
Avila Coll (MO)
Baker U (KS)
Baldwin-Wallace Coll (OH)
Ball State U (IN)
Barat Coll (IL)
Barber-Scotia Coll (NC)
Barry U (FL)
Bartlesville Wesleyan Coll (OK)
Barton Coll (NC)
Bayamón Central U (PR)
Baylor U (TX)
Bay Path Coll (MA)
Beaver Coll (PA)
Becker Coll (MA)
Belhaven Coll (MS)
Bellarmine Coll (KY)
Belmont Abbey Coll (NC)
Belmont U (TN)
Beloit Coll (WI)
Bemidji State U (MN)
Benedictine Coll (KS)
Benedictine U (IL)
Bennett Coll (NC)
Berea Coll (KY)
Berry Coll (GA)
Bethany Bible Coll (NB, Canada)
Bethany Coll (KS)
Bethany Coll (WV)
Bethany Coll of the Assemblies of God (CA)
Bethel Coll (IN)
Bethel Coll (KS)
Bethel Coll (MN)
Bethel Coll (TN)
Bethune-Cookman Coll (FL)
Biola U (CA)
Birmingham-Southern Coll (AL)
Blackburn Coll (IL)
Black Hills State U (SD)
Bloomsburg U of Pennsylvania (PA)
Bluefield State Coll (WV)
Blue Mountain Coll (MS)
Bluffton Coll (OH)
Boise State U (ID)
Boston Coll (MA)
Boston U (MA)
Bowie State U (MD)
Bowling Green State U (OH)
Bradley U (IL)
Brandon U (MB, Canada)
Brenau U (GA)
Briar Cliff Coll (IA)
Bridgewater Coll (VA)
Bridgewater State Coll (MA)
Brigham Young U (UT)
Brigham Young U–Hawaii Campus (HI)
Brock U (ON, Canada)
Brooklyn Coll of the City U of NY (NY)
Bryan Coll (TN)
Bryn Athyn Coll of the New Church (PA)
Bucknell U (PA)
Buena Vista U (IA)
Butler U (IN)
Cabrini Coll (PA)
Caldwell Coll (NJ)
California Lutheran U (CA)

California State U, Fresno (CA)
California U of Pennsylvania (PA)
Calumet Coll of Saint Joseph (IN)
Calvary Bible Coll and Theological Seminary (MO)
Calvin Coll (MI)
Cameron U (OK)
Campbellsville U (KY)
Campbell U (NC)
Canisius Coll (NY)
Capital U (OH)
Cardinal Stritch U (WI)
Carlow Coll (PA)
Carroll Coll (MT)
Carroll Coll (WI)
Carson-Newman Coll (TN)
Carthage Coll (WI)
Catawba Coll (NC)
The Catholic U of America (DC)
Cedar Crest Coll (PA)
Cedarville Coll (OH)
Centenary Coll (NJ)
Centenary Coll of Louisiana (LA)
Central Coll (IA)
Central Connecticut State U (CT)
Central Methodist Coll (MO)
Central Michigan U (MI)
Central Missouri State U (MO)
Centre Coll (KY)
Chadron State Coll (NE)
Chaminade U of Honolulu (HI)
Champlain Coll (VT)
Charleston Southern U (SC)
Chestnut Hill Coll (PA)
Cheyney U of Pennsylvania (PA)
Chicago State U (IL)
Chowan Coll (NC)
Christian Brothers U (TN)
Christopher Newport U (VA)
Circleville Bible Coll (OH)
City Coll of the City U of NY (NY)
Claflin U (SC)
Clarion U of Pennsylvania (PA)
Clark Atlanta U (GA)
Clarke Coll (IA)
Clark U (MA)
Clemson U (SC)
Cleveland State U (OH)
Coastal Carolina U (SC)
Coe Coll (IA)
Coker Coll (SC)
Colby-Sawyer Coll (NH)
Coll Misericordia (PA)
Coll of Charleston (SC)
Coll of Mount Saint Vincent (NY)
The Coll of New Jersey (NJ)
The Coll of New Rochelle (NY)
Coll of Notre Dame (CA)
Coll of Notre Dame of Maryland (MD)
Coll of Our Lady of the Elms (MA)
Coll of Saint Benedict (MN)
Coll of St. Catherine (MN)
Coll of Saint Elizabeth (NJ)
Coll of St. Joseph (VT)
Coll of Saint Mary (NE)
The Coll of Saint Rose (NY)
Coll of Santa Fe (NM)
Coll of the Atlantic (ME)
Coll of the Ozarks (MO)
Coll of the Southwest (NM)
Colorado Christian U (CO)
Columbia Coll (MO)
Columbia Coll (SC)
Columbia International U (SC)
Columbia Union Coll (MD)
Columbus State U (GA)
Concord Coll (WV)
Concordia Coll (MI)
Concordia Coll (MN)
Concordia Coll (NY)
Concordia U (CA)
Concordia U (IL)
Concordia U (NE)
Concordia U (OR)
Concordia U (PQ, Canada)
Concordia U at Austin (TX)
Concordia U at St. Paul (MN)
Concordia U Wisconsin (WI)
Converse Coll (SC)
Coppin State Coll (MD)
Cornell Coll (IA)
Cornerstone U (MI)
Covenant Coll (GA)
Creighton U (NE)
Crichton Coll (TN)
Crown Coll (MN)

Majors Index
Elementary Education

Culver-Stockton Coll (MO)
Cumberland Coll (KY)
Curry Coll (MA)
Daemen Coll (NY)
Dakota State U (SD)
Dakota Wesleyan U (SD)
Dallas Baptist U (TX)
Dana Coll (NE)
David Lipscomb U (TN)
Defiance Coll (OH)
Delaware State U (DE)
Delta State U (MS)
DePaul U (IL)
DePauw U (IN)
Dickinson State U (ND)
Doane Coll (NE)
Dominican Coll of Blauvelt (NY)
Dominican U (IL)
Dordt Coll (IA)
Dowling Coll (NY)
Drake U (IA)
Drury U (MO)
Duquesne U (PA)
D'Youville Coll (NY)
East Carolina U (NC)
East Central U (OK)
Eastern Coll (PA)
Eastern Connecticut State U (CT)
Eastern Illinois U (IL)
Eastern Kentucky U (KY)
Eastern Mennonite U (VA)
Eastern Michigan U (MI)
Eastern Nazarene Coll (MA)
Eastern New Mexico U (NM)
Eastern Washington U (WA)
East Stroudsburg U of Pennsylvania (PA)
East Texas Baptist U (TX)
Edgewood Coll (WI)
Edinboro U of Pennsylvania (PA)
Elizabeth City State U (NC)
Elizabethtown Coll (PA)
Elmhurst Coll (IL)
Elmira Coll (NY)
Elon Coll (NC)
Emmanuel Coll (GA)
Emmanuel Coll (MA)
Emmaus Bible Coll (IA)
Emory U (GA)
Emporia State U (KS)
Endicott Coll (MA)
Erskine Coll (SC)
Evangel U (MO)
The Evergreen State Coll (WA)
Fairleigh Dickinson U, Florham-Madison Campus (NJ)
Fairleigh Dickinson U, Teaneck-Hackensack Campus (NJ)
Fairmont State Coll (WV)
Faith Baptist Bible Coll and Theological Seminary (IA)
Faulkner U (AL)
Felician Coll (NJ)
Fitchburg State Coll (MA)
Flagler Coll (FL)
Florida A&M U (FL)
Florida Atlantic U (FL)
Florida Baptist Theological Coll (FL)
Florida Coll (FL)
Florida Gulf Coast U (FL)
Florida International U (FL)
Florida Southern Coll (FL)
Florida State U (FL)
Fontbonne Coll (MO)
Fordham U (NY)
Fort Hays State U (KS)
Fort Lewis Coll (CO)
Framingham State Coll (MA)
Franciscan U of Steubenville (OH)
Francis Marion U (SC)
Franklin Coll of Indiana (IN)
Franklin Pierce Coll (NH)
Freed-Hardeman U (TN)
Free Will Baptist Bible Coll (TN)
Fresno Pacific U (CA)
Friends U (KS)
Frostburg State U (MD)
Furman U (SC)
Gallaudet U (DC)
Gannon U (PA)
Gardner-Webb U (NC)
Geneva Coll (PA)
George Fox U (OR)
Georgetown Coll (KY)
Georgian Court Coll (NJ)
Georgia Southwestern State U (GA)
Gettysburg Coll (PA)
Glenville State Coll (WV)
Goddard Coll (VT)
Gonzaga U (WA)
Gordon Coll (MA)
Goshen Coll (IN)
Goucher Coll (MD)
Governors State U (IL)
Grace Bible Coll (MI)
Grace Coll (IN)
Graceland Coll (IA)
Grand Canyon U (AZ)
Grand Valley State U (MI)
Grand View Coll (IA)
Green Mountain Coll (VT)
Greensboro Coll (NC)
Greenville Coll (IL)
Grove City Coll (PA)
Guilford Coll (NC)
Gustavus Adolphus Coll (MN)
Gwynedd-Mercy Coll (PA)
Hamline U (MN)
Hampshire Coll (MA)
Hampton U (VA)
Hannibal-LaGrange Coll (MO)
Hanover Coll (IN)
Harding U (AR)
Hardin-Simmons U (TX)
Harris-Stowe State Coll (MO)
Hastings Coll (NE)
Heidelberg Coll (OH)
Hellenic Coll (MA)
Henderson State U (AR)
Hendrix Coll (AR)
Heritage Coll (WA)
High Point U (NC)
Hillsdale Coll (MI)
Hiram Coll (OH)
Hobe Sound Bible Coll (FL)
Hofstra U (NY)
Holy Family Coll (PA)
Hope International U (CA)
Houghton Coll (NY)
Houston Baptist U (TX)
Howard Payne U (TX)
Humboldt State U (CA)
Hunter Coll of the City U of NY (NY)
Huntingdon Coll (AL)
Huntington Coll (IN)
Huron U (SD)
Husson Coll (ME)
Huston-Tillotson Coll (TX)
Idaho State U (ID)
Illinois Coll (IL)
Illinois State U (IL)
Illinois Wesleyan U (IL)
Immaculata Coll (PA)
Indiana State U (IN)
Indiana U Bloomington (IN)
Indiana U East (IN)
Indiana U Kokomo (IN)
Indiana U Northwest (IN)
Indiana U of Pennsylvania (PA)
Indiana U–Purdue U Fort Wayne (IN)
Indiana U–Purdue U Indianapolis (IN)
Indiana U South Bend (IN)
Indiana U Southeast (IN)
Indiana Wesleyan U (IN)
Inter American U of PR, Aguadilla Campus (PR)
Inter American U of PR, Arecibo Campus (PR)
Inter American U of PR, Fajardo Campus (PR)
Inter American U of PR, Metropolitan Campus (PR)
Inter American U of PR, San Germán Campus (PR)
International Coll of the Cayman Islands (Cayman Islands)
Iona Coll (NY)
Iowa State U of Science and Technology (IA)
Iowa Wesleyan Coll (IA)
Jacksonville State U (AL)
Jacksonville U (FL)
James Madison U (VA)
Jamestown Coll (ND)
Jarvis Christian Coll (TX)
John Brown U (AR)
John Carroll U (OH)
Johnson Bible Coll (TN)
Johnson C. Smith U (NC)
Johnson State Coll (VT)
John Wesley Coll (NC)
Judson Coll (AL)
Judson Coll (IL)
Juniata Coll (PA)
Kansas State U (KS)
Kean U (NJ)
Keene State Coll (NH)
Kent State U (OH)
Kentucky Christian Coll (KY)
Kentucky State U (KY)
Kentucky Wesleyan Coll (KY)
Keuka Coll (NY)
King Coll (TN)
King's Coll (PA)
The King's U Coll (AB, Canada)
Kutztown U of Pennsylvania (PA)
LaGrange Coll (GA)
Lake Erie Coll (OH)
Lake Forest Coll (IL)
Lakehead U (ON, Canada)
Lakeland Coll (WI)
Lake Superior State U (MI)
Lamar U (TX)
Lambuth U (TN)
Lander U (SC)
Langston U (OK)
La Roche Coll (PA)
La Salle U (PA)
Lasell Coll (MA)
La Sierra U (CA)
Lebanon Valley Coll (PA)
Lees-McRae Coll (NC)
Lee U (TN)
Le Moyne Coll (NY)
LeMoyne-Owen Coll (TN)
Lenoir-Rhyne Coll (NC)
Lesley Coll (MA)
LeTourneau U (TX)
Lewis-Clark State Coll (ID)
Lewis U (IL)
Liberty U (VA)
Limestone Coll (SC)
Lincoln Christian Coll (IL)
Lincoln Memorial U (TN)
Lincoln U (MO)
Lincoln U (PA)
Lindenwood U (MO)
Lindsey Wilson Coll (KY)
Linfield Coll (OR)
Lock Haven U of Pennsylvania (PA)
Long Island U, Brooklyn Campus (NY)
Long Island U, C.W. Post Campus (NY)
Long Island U, Southampton Coll (NY)
Long Island U, Southampton Coll, Friends World Program (NY)
Longwood Coll (VA)
Loras Coll (IA)
Louisiana Coll (LA)
Louisiana State U and A&M Coll (LA)
Louisiana State U in Shreveport (LA)
Louisiana Tech U (LA)
Loyola Coll in Maryland (MD)
Loyola U Chicago (IL)
Loyola U New Orleans (LA)
Lubbock Christian U (TX)
Luther Coll (IA)
Lycoming Coll (PA)
Lynchburg Coll (VA)
Lyndon State Coll (VT)
Lynn U (FL)
MacMurray Coll (IL)
Madonna U (MI)
Malone Coll (OH)
Manchester Coll (IN)
Manhattan Coll (NY)
Manhattanville Coll (NY)
Mansfield U of Pennsylvania (PA)
Maranatha Baptist Bible Coll (WI)
Marian Coll (IN)
Marian Coll of Fond du Lac (WI)
Marietta Coll (OH)
Marist Coll (NY)
Marquette U (WI)
Marshall U (WV)
Mars Hill Coll (NC)
Martin Luther Coll (MN)
Martin Methodist Coll (TN)
Marycrest International U (IA)
Marymount Coll (NY)
Maryville U of Saint Louis (MO)
Mary Washington Coll (VA)
Marywood U (PA)
Massachusetts Coll of Liberal Arts (MA)
Mayville State U (ND)
McGill U (PQ, Canada)
McKendree Coll (IL)
McMurry U (TX)
McNeese State U (LA)
McPherson Coll (KS)
Medaille Coll (NY)
Memorial U of Newfoundland (NF, Canada)
Mercer U (GA)
Mercy Coll (NY)
Mercyhurst Coll (PA)
Merrimack Coll (MA)
Mesa State Coll (CO)
Messiah Coll (PA)
Methodist Coll (NC)
Miami U (OH)
Michigan State U (MI)
Mid-America Bible Coll (OK)
MidAmerica Nazarene U (KS)
Midland Lutheran Coll (NE)
Midway Coll (KY)
Midwestern State U (TX)
Millersville U of Pennsylvania (PA)
Milligan Coll (TN)
Millikin U (IL)
Mills Coll (CA)
Minnesota State U, Mankato (MN)
Minnesota State U Moorhead (MN)
Minot State U (ND)
Mississippi Coll (MS)
Mississippi State U (MS)
Mississippi U for Women (MS)
Mississippi Valley State U (MS)
Missouri Baptist Coll (MO)
Missouri Southern State Coll (MO)
Missouri Valley Coll (MO)
Missouri Western State Coll (MO)
Molloy Coll (NY)
Monmouth Coll (IL)
Montana State U–Billings (MT)
Montana State U–Bozeman (MT)
Montana State U–Northern (MT)
Montreat Coll (NC)
Moravian Coll (PA)
Morehead State U (KY)
Morehouse Coll (GA)
Morgan State U (MD)
Morningside Coll (IA)
Morris Coll (SC)
Mount Marty Coll (SD)
Mount Mary Coll (WI)
Mount Mercy Coll (IA)
Mount St. Clare Coll (IA)
Mount Saint Mary Coll (NY)
Mount St. Mary's Coll (CA)
Mount Saint Mary's Coll and Seminary (MD)
Mount Saint Vincent U (NS, Canada)
Mount Senario Coll (WI)
Mount Vernon Nazarene Coll (OH)
Muhlenberg Coll (PA)
Murray State U (KY)
Muskingum Coll (OH)
National-Louis U (IL)
Nazareth Coll of Rochester (NY)
Nebraska Christian Coll (NE)
Nebraska Wesleyan U (NE)
Neumann Coll (PA)
Newberry Coll (SC)
New England Coll (NH)
New Jersey City U (NJ)
Newman U (KS)
New Mexico Highlands U (NM)
New Mexico State U (NM)
New York Inst of Technology (NY)
New York U (NY)
Niagara U (NY)
Nicholls State U (LA)
Norfolk State U (VA)
North Carolina Ag and Tech State U (NC)
North Carolina Central U (NC)
North Carolina Wesleyan Coll (NC)
North Central Coll (IL)
North Central U (MN)
Northeastern Illinois U (IL)
Northeastern State U (OK)
Northeastern U (MA)
Northern Arizona U (AZ)
Northern Illinois U (IL)
Northern Kentucky U (KY)
Northern Michigan U (MI)
Northern State U (SD)
North Georgia Coll & State U (GA)
North Greenville Coll (SC)
Northland Coll (WI)
North Park U (IL)
Northwest Coll (WA)
Northwestern Coll (IA)
Northwestern Coll (MN)
Northwestern Oklahoma State U (OK)
Northwestern State U of Louisiana (LA)
Northwest Missouri State U (MO)
Northwest Nazarene U (ID)
Notre Dame Coll (NH)
Notre Dame Coll of Ohio (OH)
Nova Southeastern U (FL)
Nyack Coll (NY)
Oakland City U (IN)
Oakland U (MI)
Oakwood Coll (AL)
Oglethorpe U (GA)
Ohio Dominican Coll (OH)
Ohio Northern U (OH)
The Ohio State U at Lima (OH)
Ohio U (OH)
Ohio U–Chillicothe (OH)
Ohio U–Zanesville (OH)
Ohio Valley Coll (WV)
Ohio Wesleyan U (OH)
Oklahoma Baptist U (OK)
Oklahoma Christian U of Science and Arts (OK)
Oklahoma City U (OK)
Oklahoma Panhandle State U (OK)
Oklahoma State U (OK)
Olivet Nazarene U (IL)
Ottawa U (KS)
Otterbein Coll (OH)
Our Lady of Holy Cross Coll (LA)
Pace U, New York City Campus (NY)
Pace U, Pleasantville/Briarcliff Campus (NY)
Pacific Lutheran U (WA)
Pacific Oaks Coll (CA)
Pacific Union Coll (CA)
Pacific U (OR)
Paine Coll (GA)
Palm Beach Atlantic Coll (FL)
Park U (MO)
Penn State U Harrisburg Campus of the Capital Coll (PA)
Penn State U Univ Park Campus (PA)
Pepperdine U, Malibu (CA)
Peru State Coll (NE)
Pfeiffer U (NC)
Philadelphia Coll of Bible (PA)
Philander Smith Coll (AR)
Piedmont Baptist Coll (NC)
Pikeville Coll (KY)
Pine Manor Coll (MA)
Pittsburg State U (KS)
Plattsburgh State U of NY (NY)
Plymouth State Coll (NH)
Point Park Coll (PA)
Pontifical Catholic U of Puerto Rico (PR)
Presbyterian Coll (SC)
Principia Coll (IL)
Purdue U (IN)
Purdue U Calumet (IN)
Purdue U North Central (IN)
Queens Coll (NC)
Queens Coll of the City U of NY (NY)
Queen's U at Kingston (ON, Canada)
Quincy U (IL)
Redeemer Coll (ON, Canada)
Reformed Bible Coll (MI)
Regis U (CO)
Rider U (NJ)
Ripon Coll (WI)
Rivier Coll (NH)
Roberts Wesleyan Coll (NY)
Rockford Coll (IL)
Rockhurst U (MO)
Rocky Mountain Coll (MT)
Roger Williams U (RI)
Rollins Coll (FL)
Rowan U (NJ)
Russell Sage Coll (NY)
Rust Coll (MS)

Majors Index
Elementary Education–Engineering

Sacred Heart U (CT)
Saginaw Valley State U (MI)
St. Ambrose U (IA)
Saint Augustine's Coll (NC)
St. Bonaventure U (NY)
St. Cloud State U (MN)
St. Edward's U (TX)
St. Francis Coll (NY)
Saint Francis Coll (PA)
St. Francis Xavier U (NS, Canada)
St. John Fisher Coll (NY)
Saint John's U (MN)
St. John's U (NY)
Saint Joseph Coll (CT)
Saint Joseph's Coll (IN)
Saint Joseph's Coll (ME)
St. Joseph's Coll, New York (NY)
St. Joseph's Coll, Suffolk Campus (NY)
Saint Joseph's U (PA)
Saint Leo U (FL)
Saint Louis U (MO)
Saint Martin's Coll (WA)
Saint Mary Coll (KS)
Saint Mary-of-the-Woods Coll (IN)
Saint Mary's Coll (IN)
Saint Mary's U (NS, Canada)
Saint Mary's U of Minnesota (MN)
Saint Michael's Coll (VT)
St. Norbert Coll (WI)
Saint Paul's Coll (VA)
Saint Peter's Coll (NJ)
St. Thomas U (FL)
Saint Xavier U (IL)
Salem State Coll (MA)
Salisbury State U (MD)
Salve Regina U (RI)
Samford U (AL)
San Diego State U (CA)
Seton Hall U (NJ)
Seton Hill Coll (PA)
Shawnee State U (OH)
Shaw U (NC)
Sheldon Jackson Coll (AK)
Shepherd Coll (WV)
Shippensburg U of Pennsylvania (PA)
Shorter Coll (GA)
Siena Heights U (MI)
Silver Lake Coll (WI)
Simmons Coll (MA)
Simpson Coll (IA)
Simpson Coll and Graduate School (CA)
Skidmore Coll (NY)
Slippery Rock U of Pennsylvania (PA)
Southeastern Coll of the Assemblies of God (FL)
Southeastern Louisiana U (LA)
Southeastern Oklahoma State U (OK)
Southeast Missouri State U (MO)
Southern Adventist U (TN)
Southern Arkansas U–Magnolia (AR)
Southern Illinois U Carbondale (IL)
Southern Illinois U Edwardsville (IL)
Southern Utah U (UT)
Southern Wesleyan U (SC)
Southwest Baptist U (MO)
Southwestern Adventist U (TX)
Southwestern Assemblies of God U (TX)
Southwestern Coll (KS)
Southwestern Oklahoma State U (OK)
Southwest Missouri State U (MO)
Southwest State U (MN)
Southwest Texas State U (TX)
Spalding U (KY)
Spring Arbor Coll (MI)
Spring Hill Coll (AL)
State U of NY at New Paltz (NY)
State U of NY at Oswego (NY)
State U of NY Coll at Brockport (NY)
State U of NY Coll at Buffalo (NY)
State U of NY Coll at Cortland (NY)
State U of NY Coll at Fredonia (NY)
State U of NY Coll at Geneseo (NY)
State U of NY Coll at Old Westbury (NY)
State U of NY Coll at Oneonta (NY)

State U of NY Coll at Potsdam (NY)
State U of West Georgia (GA)
Stephens Coll (MO)
Sterling Coll (KS)
Stetson U (FL)
Stonehill Coll (MA)
Suffolk U (MA)
Sul Ross State U (TX)
Susquehanna U (PA)
Syracuse U (NY)
Tabor Coll (KS)
Taylor U (IN)
Taylor U, Fort Wayne Campus (IN)
Temple U (PA)
Tennessee State U (TN)
Tennessee Technological U (TN)
Tennessee Wesleyan Coll (TN)
Texas A&M U–Commerce (TX)
Texas A&M U–Kingsville (TX)
Texas Christian U (TX)
Texas Lutheran U (TX)
Texas Southern U (TX)
Texas Wesleyan U (TX)
Thiel Coll (PA)
Thomas More Coll (KY)
Toccoa Falls Coll (GA)
Tougaloo Coll (MS)
Towson U (MD)
Transylvania U (KY)
Trent U (ON, Canada)
Trevecca Nazarene U (TN)
Trinity Baptist Coll (FL)
Trinity Bible Coll (ND)
Trinity Christian Coll (IL)
Trinity Coll of Florida (FL)
Trinity Coll of Vermont (VT)
Trinity Western U (BC, Canada)
Tri-State U (IN)
Troy State U (AL)
Troy State U Dothan (AL)
Tufts U (MA)
Tusculum Coll (TN)
Tuskegee U (AL)
Union Coll (KY)
Union Coll (NE)
Union U (TN)
United States International U (CA)
Universidad Adventista de las Antillas (PR)
Universidad del Turabo (PR)
Universidad Metropolitana (PR)
Université de Montréal (PQ, Canada)
Université de Sherbrooke (PQ, Canada)
U du Québec à Chicoutimi (PQ, Canada)
U du Québec à Hull (PQ, Canada)
U du Québec à Trois-Rivières (PQ, Canada)
U du Québec en Abitibi-Témiscamingue (PQ, Canada)
Université Laval (PQ, Canada)
The U of Akron (OH)
The U of Alabama (AL)
The U of Alabama at Birmingham (AL)
The U of Alabama in Huntsville (AL)
U of Alaska Fairbanks (AK)
U of Alberta (AB, Canada)
The U of Arizona (AZ)
U of Arkansas (AR)
U of Arkansas at Little Rock (AR)
U of Arkansas at Monticello (AR)
U of Arkansas at Pine Bluff (AR)
U of British Columbia (BC, Canada)
U of Calgary (AB, Canada)
U of Central Arkansas (AR)
U of Central Florida (FL)
U of Central Oklahoma (OK)
U of Charleston (WV)
U of Cincinnati (OH)
U of Connecticut (CT)
U of Dallas (TX)
U of Dayton (OH)
U of Delaware (DE)
U of Detroit Mercy (MI)
U of Dubuque (IA)
U of Evansville (IN)
The U of Findlay (OH)
U of Florida (FL)
U of Great Falls (MT)
U of Hartford (CT)
U of Hawaii at Manoa (HI)

U of Idaho (ID)
U of Illinois at Chicago (IL)
U of Illinois at Springfield (IL)
U of Illinois at Urbana–Champaign (IL)
U of Indianapolis (IN)
The U of Iowa (IA)
U of Kansas (KS)
U of Kentucky (KY)
U of La Verne (CA)
U of Louisiana at Lafayette (LA)
U of Louisiana at Monroe (LA)
U of Maine (ME)
U of Maine at Farmington (ME)
U of Maine at Fort Kent (ME)
U of Maine at Machias (ME)
U of Maine at Presque Isle (ME)
U of Manitoba (MB, Canada)
U of Mary Hardin-Baylor (TX)
U of Maryland, Coll Park (MD)
U of Miami (FL)
U of Michigan (MI)
U of Michigan–Dearborn (MI)
U of Michigan–Flint (MI)
U of Minnesota, Duluth (MN)
U of Minnesota, Morris (MN)
U of Minnesota, Twin Cities Campus (MN)
U of Mississippi (MS)
U of Missouri–Columbia (MO)
U of Missouri–Kansas City (MO)
U of Missouri–St. Louis (MO)
U of Mobile (AL)
The U of Montana–Missoula (MT)
U of Montevallo (AL)
U of Nebraska at Kearney (NE)
U of Nebraska at Omaha (NE)
U of Nebraska–Lincoln (NE)
U of Nevada, Las Vegas (NV)
U of Nevada, Reno (NV)
U of New Brunswick, Fredericton (NB, Canada)
U of New Brunswick, Saint John (NB, Canada)
U of New England (ME)
U of New Mexico (NM)
U of New Orleans (LA)
U of North Alabama (AL)
The U of North Carolina at Chapel Hill (NC)
The U of North Carolina at Charlotte (NC)
The U of North Carolina at Greensboro (NC)
The U of North Carolina at Pembroke (NC)
The U of North Carolina at Wilmington (NC)
U of North Dakota (ND)
U of Northern Iowa (IA)
U of North Florida (FL)
U of Oklahoma (OK)
U of Pennsylvania (PA)
U of Pittsburgh at Bradford (PA)
U of Pittsburgh at Johnstown (PA)
U of Portland (OR)
U of Prince Edward Island (PE, Canada)
U of Puerto Rico at Ponce (PR)
U of Puerto Rico, Humacao U Coll (PR)
U of Puerto Rico, Río Piedras (PR)
U of Redlands (CA)
U of Regina (SK, Canada)
U of Rhode Island (RI)
U of Richmond (VA)
U of Rio Grande (OH)
U of St. Francis (IL)
U of Saint Francis (IN)
U of St. Thomas (MN)
U of St. Thomas (TX)
U of San Francisco (CA)
U of Science and Arts of Oklahoma (OK)
The U of Scranton (PA)
U of Sioux Falls (SD)
U of South Alabama (AL)
U of South Carolina Spartanburg (SC)
U of South Dakota (SD)
U of Southern Colorado (CO)
U of Southern Indiana (IN)
U of Southern Mississippi (MS)
U of South Florida (FL)
The U of Tampa (FL)
The U of Tennessee at Chattanooga (TN)

The U of Tennessee at Martin (TN)
The U of Texas–Pan American (TX)
U of the District of Columbia (DC)
U of the Pacific (CA)
U of the Sacred Heart (PR)
U of the Virgin Islands (VI)
U of Tulsa (OK)
U of Utah (UT)
U of Vermont (VT)
U of Victoria (BC, Canada)
U of Washington (WA)
The U of West Alabama (AL)
The U of Western Ontario (ON, Canada)
U of West Florida (FL)
U of Windsor (ON, Canada)
The U of Winnipeg (MB, Canada)
U of Wisconsin–Eau Claire (WI)
U of Wisconsin–Green Bay (WI)
U of Wisconsin–La Crosse (WI)
U of Wisconsin–Madison (WI)
U of Wisconsin–Milwaukee (WI)
U of Wisconsin–Parkside (WI)
U of Wisconsin–Platteville (WI)
U of Wisconsin–River Falls (WI)
U of Wisconsin–Stevens Point (WI)
U of Wisconsin–Superior (WI)
U of Wisconsin–Whitewater (WI)
U of Wyoming (WY)
Upper Iowa U (IA)
Urbana U (OH)
Ursuline Coll (OH)
Utah State U (UT)
Utica Coll of Syracuse U (NY)
Valdosta State U (GA)
Valley City State U (ND)
Valparaiso U (IN)
Vanderbilt U (TN)
Vassar Coll (NY)
Villa Julie Coll (MD)
Villanova U (PA)
Virginia Commonwealth U (VA)
Virginia Intermont Coll (VA)
Virginia Union U (VA)
Virginia Wesleyan Coll (VA)
Voorhees Coll (SC)
Wagner Coll (NY)
Wake Forest U (NC)
Walla Walla Coll (WA)
Walsh U (OH)
Warner Pacific Coll (OR)
Warner Southern Coll (FL)
Warren Wilson Coll (NC)
Wartburg Coll (IA)
Washington Bible Coll (MD)
Washington State U (WA)
Washington U in St. Louis (MO)
Wayland Baptist U (TX)
Waynesburg Coll (PA)
Wayne State Coll (NE)
Wayne State U (MI)
Weber State U (UT)
Webster U (MO)
Wells Coll (NY)
Wesley Coll (DE)
West Chester U of Pennsylvania (PA)
Western Baptist Coll (OR)
Western Carolina U (NC)
Western Connecticut State U (CT)
Western Illinois U (IL)
Western Kentucky U (KY)
Western Michigan U (MI)
Western Montana Coll of The U of Montana (MT)
Western State Coll of Colorado (CO)
Western Washington U (WA)
Westfield State Coll (MA)
West Liberty State Coll (WV)
Westminster Coll (MO)
Westminster Coll (PA)
Westminster Coll (UT)
Westmont Coll (CA)
West Virginia State Coll (WV)
West Virginia U (WV)
West Virginia Wesleyan Coll (WV)
Wheaton Coll (IL)
Wheeling Jesuit U (WV)
Wheelock Coll (MA)
Whitworth Coll (WA)
Wichita State U (KS)
William Jewell Coll (MO)
William Paterson U of New Jersey (NJ)
William Penn U (IA)
Williams Baptist Coll (AR)

William Woods U (MO)
Wilmington Coll (DE)
Wilmington Coll (OH)
Wilson Coll (PA)
Wingate U (NC)
Winona State U (MN)
Winston-Salem State U (NC)
Winthrop U (SC)
Wisconsin Lutheran Coll (WI)
Wittenberg U (OH)
Worcester State Coll (MA)
Wright State U (OH)
Xavier U of Louisiana (LA)
Yeshiva U (NY)
York Coll (NE)
York Coll of Pennsylvania (PA)
York U (ON, Canada)
Youngstown State U (OH)

ELEMENTARY/MIDDLE/SECONDARY EDUCATION ADMINISTRATION
Campbell U (NC)
Marquette U (WI)

EMERGENCY MEDICAL TECHNOLOGY
American Coll of Prehospital Medicine (FL)
Creighton U (NE)
The George Washington U (DC)
Loma Linda U (CA)
MCP Hahnemann U (PA)
Nebraska Methodist Coll of Nursing & Allied Health (NE)
Oklahoma Christian U of Science and Arts (OK)
U of Maryland, Baltimore County (MD)
U of Minnesota, Twin Cities Campus (MN)
U of the District of Columbia (DC)
Western Carolina U (NC)

ENERGY MANAGEMENT TECHNOLOGY
Eastern Michigan U (MI)
The Evergreen State Coll (WA)
Ferris State U (MI)
Lamar U (TX)

ENGINEERING
Arkansas State U (AR)
Arkansas Tech U (AR)
Auburn U (AL)
Baker U (KS)
Barry U (FL)
Baylor U (TX)
Beloit Coll (WI)
Boston U (MA)
Brigham Young U (UT)
Brown U (RI)
California Inst of Technology (CA)
California State U, Long Beach (CA)
California State U, Los Angeles (CA)
California State U, Northridge (CA)
California State U, Sacramento (CA)
Calvin Coll (MI)
Carleton U (ON, Canada)
Carnegie Mellon U (PA)
Carroll Coll (MT)
Carthage Coll (WI)
Case Western Reserve U (OH)
The Catholic U of America (DC)
Centenary Coll of Louisiana (LA)
Clark Atlanta U (GA)
Clarkson U (NY)
Clark U (MA)
Clemson U (SC)
Cogswell Polytechnical Coll (CA)
Colorado School of Mines (CO)
Cooper Union for the Advancement of Science & Art (NY)
Cornell U (NY)
Dalhousie U (NS, Canada)
Dartmouth Coll (NH)
Dordt Coll (IA)
Drexel U (PA)
Eastern Illinois U (IL)
Elizabethtown Coll (PA)
Elon Coll (NC)
Embry-Riddle Aeronautical U (AZ)
Embry-Riddle Aeronautical U (FL)

Majors Index
Engineering–Engineering Technology

Fontbonne Coll (MO)
Gallaudet U (DC)
Gannon U (PA)
Geneva Coll (PA)
George Fox U (OR)
The George Washington U (DC)
Gonzaga U (WA)
Grand Valley State U (MI)
Harvard U (MA)
Harvey Mudd Coll (CA)
Hofstra U (NY)
Hood Coll (MD)
Hope Coll (MI)
Houston Baptist U (TX)
Idaho State U (ID)
Indiana U–Purdue U Fort Wayne (IN)
Indiana U–Purdue U Indianapolis (IN)
Iowa State U of Science and Technology (IA)
John Brown U (AR)
Johns Hopkins U (MD)
Lafayette Coll (PA)
Lakehead U (ON, Canada)
Lehigh U (PA)
LeTourneau U (TX)
Lock Haven U of Pennsylvania (PA)
Loyola Coll in Maryland (MD)
Maharishi U of Management (IA)
Maine Maritime Academy (ME)
Manhattan Coll (NY)
Marietta Coll (OH)
Marquette U (WI)
Maryville Coll (TN)
Massachusetts Inst of Technology (MA)
Massachusetts Maritime Academy (MA)
McNeese State U (LA)
Memorial U of Newfoundland (NF, Canada)
Messiah Coll (PA)
Michigan State U (MI)
Michigan Technological U (MI)
Milligan Coll (TN)
Montana Tech of The U of Montana (MT)
Morehouse Coll (GA)
Morgan State U (MD)
New Jersey Inst of Technology (NJ)
New Mexico Highlands U (NM)
New Mexico Inst of Mining and Technology (NM)
New York U (NY)
North Carolina State U (NC)
North Dakota State U (ND)
Northeastern U (MA)
Northwestern U (IL)
Nova Scotia Ag Coll (NS, Canada)
Oakwood Coll (AL)
Oklahoma Christian U of Science and Arts (OK)
Oklahoma State U (OK)
Olivet Nazarene U (IL)
Oregon State U (OR)
Pace U, New York City Campus (NY)
Pace U, Pleasantville/Briarcliff Campus (NY)
Pacific Union Coll (CA)
Pitzer Coll (CA)
Purdue U (IN)
Purdue U Calumet (IN)
Queen's U at Kingston (ON, Canada)
Rensselaer Polytechnic Inst (NY)
Rochester Inst of Technology (NY)
Roger Williams U (RI)
Rowan U (NJ)
Russell Sage Coll (NY)
Rutgers, State U of NJ, Coll of Engineering (NJ)
St. Cloud State U (MN)
Saint Mary's Coll of California (CA)
Saint Mary's (NS, Canada)
St. Mary's U of San Antonio (TX)
Saint Vincent Coll (PA)
San Diego State U (CA)
San Jose State U (CA)
Santa Clara U (CA)
Seton Hill Coll (PA)
Shaw U (NC)
Spelman Coll (GA)
Stanford U (CA)
State U of NY Coll at Buffalo (NY)

Swarthmore Coll (PA)
Tennessee State U (TN)
Texas Christian U (TX)
Texas Tech U (TX)
Texas Wesleyan U (TX)
Trinity Coll (CT)
Tufts U (MA)
United States Air Force Academy (CO)
United States Military Academy (NY)
United States Naval Academy (MD)
Université de Sherbrooke (PQ, Canada)
U du Québec à Chicoutimi (PQ, Canada)
U du Québec en Abitibi-Témiscamingue (PQ, Canada)
U Coll of Cape Breton (NS, Canada)
The U of Akron (OH)
U of Alaska Fairbanks (AK)
U of Alberta (AB, Canada)
U of Calif, Berkeley (CA)
U of Calif, Davis (CA)
U of Calif, Irvine (CA)
U of Calif, San Diego (CA)
U of Cincinnati (OH)
U of Delaware (DE)
U of Denver (CO)
U of Detroit Mercy (MI)
U of Florida (FL)
U of Hartford (CT)
U of Idaho (ID)
U of Illinois at Urbana–Champaign (IL)
The U of Iowa (IA)
U of Louisville (KY)
U of Maryland, Coll Park (MD)
U of Michigan (MI)
U of Michigan–Dearborn (MI)
U of Michigan–Flint (MI)
U of Mississippi (MS)
U of New Brunswick, Fredericton (NB, Canada)
U of New Haven (CT)
U of New Mexico (NM)
U of Oklahoma (OK)
U of Pittsburgh at Bradford (PA)
U of Portland (OR)
U of Regina (SK, Canada)
U of Rochester (NY)
U of South Florida (FL)
The U of Tennessee at Chattanooga (TN)
The U of Tennessee at Martin (TN)
U of the Pacific (CA)
U of Toronto (ON, Canada)
U of Tulsa (OK)
U of Virginia (VA)
U of Washington (WA)
U of Waterloo (ON, Canada)
U of Windsor (ON, Canada)
U of Wisconsin–Madison (WI)
U of Wisconsin–Milwaukee (WI)
Valparaiso U (IN)
Vanderbilt U (TN)
Virginia Polytechnic Inst and State U (VA)
Walla Walla Coll (WA)
Washington U in St. Louis (MO)
Wells Coll (NY)
Western New England Coll (MA)
West Virginia U Inst of Technology (WV)
Wheaton Coll (IL)
Wilkes U (PA)
Winona State U (MN)
Worcester Polytechnic Inst (MA)
Youngstown State U (OH)

(PRE)ENGINEERING
Azusa Pacific U (CA)
Columbia Coll (MO)
McPherson Coll (KS)
The Ohio State U (OH)
Saint Anselm Coll (NH)
St. Norbert Coll (WI)
Spring Hill Coll (AL)
The U of Montana–Missoula (MT)
Valley City State U (ND)

ENGINEERING DESIGN
Cameron U (OK)
Carnegie Mellon U (PA)
Lawrence Technological U (MI)
Pacific Union Coll (CA)

Tufts U (MA)
U of Houston–Downtown (TX)
Western Washington U (WA)
Worcester Polytechnic Inst (MA)

ENGINEERING/INDUSTRIAL MANAGEMENT
California State U, Long Beach (CA)
Claremont McKenna Coll (CA)
Columbia U, School of Engineering & Applied Sci (NY)
Fashion Inst of Technology (NY)
Fort Lewis Coll (CO)
Grand Valley State U (MI)
Idaho State U (ID)
Insto Tecno Estudios Sups Monterrey (Mexico)
John Brown U (AR)
Kettering U (MI)
Lake Superior State U (MI)
Mercer U (GA)
Miami U (OH)
New York Inst of Technology (NY)
North Dakota State U (ND)
Pitzer Coll (CA)
Princeton U (NJ)
Rensselaer Polytechnic Inst (NY)
Saint Louis U (MO)
Stevens Inst of Technology (NJ)
Texas A&M U (TX)
Tri-State U (IN)
United States Merchant Marine Academy (NY)
United States Military Academy (NY)
U du Québec à Trois-Rivières (PQ, Canada)
U of Evansville (IN)
U of Illinois at Chicago (IL)
The U of Iowa (IA)
U of Missouri–Rolla (MO)
U of Portland (OR)
U of Southern California (CA)
The U of Tennessee at Chattanooga (TN)
U of the Pacific (CA)
U of Vermont (VT)
Western Michigan U (MI)
Widener U (PA)
Wilkes U (PA)
Worcester Polytechnic Inst (MA)
York Coll of Pennsylvania (PA)

ENGINEERING MECHANICS
California State U, Fullerton (CA)
Columbia U, School of Engineering & Applied Sci (NY)
Dordt Coll (IA)
Johns Hopkins U (MD)
Lehigh U (PA)
Michigan State U (MI)
Michigan Technological U (MI)
New Mexico Inst of Mining and Technology (NM)
United States Air Force Academy (CO)
Universidad del Turabo (PR)
U du Québec à Trois-Rivières (PQ, Canada)
U du Québec en Abitibi-Témiscamingue (PQ, Canada)
U of Cincinnati (OH)
U of Illinois at Urbana–Champaign (IL)
U of Southern California (CA)
U of Windsor (ON, Canada)
U of Wisconsin–Madison (WI)
Wentworth Inst of Technology (MA)
West Virginia Wesleyan Coll (WV)
Worcester Polytechnic Inst (MA)

ENGINEERING PHYSICS
Abilene Christian U (TX)
Arkansas Tech U (AR)
Augustana Coll (IL)
Augustana Coll (SD)
Bemidji State U (MN)
Bradley U (IL)
Brandeis U (MA)
California Inst of Technology (CA)
California State U, Northridge (CA)
Case Western Reserve U (OH)
Christian Brothers U (TN)
Colorado School of Mines (CO)
Colorado State U (CO)
Connecticut Coll (CT)

Cornell U (NY)
Dartmouth Coll (NH)
Eastern Nazarene Coll (MA)
Elizabethtown Coll (PA)
Embry-Riddle Aeronautical U (FL)
Harvard U (MA)
Hope Coll (MI)
Houston Baptist U (TX)
Insto Tecno Estudios Sups Monterrey (Mexico)
Jacksonville U (FL)
John Carroll U (OH)
Lehigh U (PA)
Loyola Marymount U (CA)
Merrimack Coll (MA)
Miami U (OH)
Michigan Technological U (MI)
Morgan State U (MD)
Morningside Coll (IA)
Murray State U (KY)
New York U (NY)
North Carolina Ag and Tech State U (NC)
North Dakota State U (ND)
Northeastern State U (OK)
Northwest Nazarene U (ID)
Oakland U (MI)
The Ohio State U (OH)
Oklahoma Christian U of Science and Arts (OK)
Oregon State U (OR)
Otterbein Coll (OH)
Pacific Lutheran U (WA)
Point Loma Nazarene U (CA)
Queen's U at Kingston (ON, Canada)
Rensselaer Polytechnic Inst (NY)
St. Ambrose U (IA)
St. Bonaventure U (NY)
Saint Louis U (MO)
Saint Mary's U of Minnesota (MN)
Samford U (AL)
Santa Clara U (CA)
South Dakota State U (SD)
Southeast Missouri State U (MO)
Southern Arkansas U–Magnolia (AR)
Southwestern Oklahoma State U (OK)
Southwest Missouri State U (MO)
State U of NY at Buffalo (NY)
State U of NY at New Paltz (NY)
Syracuse U (NY)
Taylor U (IN)
Texas Tech U (TX)
Thiel Coll (PA)
Tufts U (MA)
United States Military Academy (NY)
U of Alberta (AB, Canada)
The U of Arizona (AZ)
U of British Columbia (BC, Canada)
U of Calif, Berkeley (CA)
U of Calif, San Diego (CA)
U of Colorado at Boulder (CO)
U of Illinois at Chicago (IL)
U of Illinois at Urbana–Champaign (IL)
U of Kansas (KS)
U of Maine (ME)
U of Massachusetts Boston (MA)
U of Michigan (MI)
U of Nevada, Reno (NV)
U of Northern Iowa (IA)
U of Oklahoma (OK)
U of Pittsburgh (PA)
The U of Tennessee Knoxville (TN)
U of the Pacific (CA)
U of Toronto (ON, Canada)
U of Tulsa (OK)
U of Wisconsin–Madison (WI)
Washington and Lee U (VA)
Washington U in St. Louis (MO)
Westmont Coll (CA)
West Virginia U Inst of Technology (WV)
West Virginia Wesleyan Coll (WV)
Worcester Polytechnic Inst (MA)
Wright State U (OH)
Yale U (CT)

ENGINEERING SCIENCE
Abilene Christian U (TX)
Appalachian State U (NC)
Baldwin-Wallace Coll (OH)
Belmont U (TN)

Benedictine U (IL)
Bethel Coll (IN)
Brown U (RI)
California Polytechnic State U, San Luis Obispo (CA)
California State U, Fullerton (CA)
Case Western Reserve U (OH)
The Coll of New Jersey (NJ)
Coll of Notre Dame of Maryland (MD)
Coll of Staten Island of the City U of NY (NY)
Colorado School of Mines (CO)
Colorado State U (CO)
Cornell U (NY)
Dartmouth Coll (NH)
David Lipscomb U (TN)
Franciscan U of Steubenville (OH)
Gallaudet U (DC)
Harvard U (MA)
Hofstra U (NY)
Houston Baptist U (TX)
Iowa State U of Science and Technology (IA)
Lamar U (TX)
Lock Haven U of Pennsylvania (PA)
Manchester Coll (IN)
Montana Tech of The U of Montana (MT)
New Jersey Inst of Technology (NJ)
Ohio Wesleyan U (OH)
Otterbein Coll (OH)
Pacific Lutheran U (WA)
Penn State U Univ Park Campus (PA)
Pfeiffer U (NC)
Queen's U at Kingston (ON, Canada)
Rensselaer Polytechnic Inst (NY)
Rutgers, State U of NJ, Coll of Engineering (NJ)
St. Mary's U of San Antonio (TX)
Seattle Pacific U (WA)
Simon Fraser U (BC, Canada)
State U of NY at Stony Brook (NY)
State U of NY Coll at Oneonta (NY)
Trinity U (TX)
Tufts U (MA)
Tulane U (LA)
United States Air Force Academy (CO)
U of Calif, San Diego (CA)
U of Cincinnati (OH)
U of Manitoba (MB, Canada)
U of Maryland, Baltimore County (MD)
U of Miami (FL)
U of Michigan (MI)
U of Michigan–Flint (MI)
U of New Mexico (NM)
U of Portland (OR)
U of Rochester (NY)
The U of Tennessee Knoxville (TN)
U of Toronto (ON, Canada)
Vanderbilt U (TN)
Virginia Polytechnic Inst and State U (VA)
Washington U in St. Louis (MO)
Worcester Polytechnic Inst (MA)
Yale U (CT)

ENGINEERING TECHNOLOGY
Andrews U (MI)
Arkansas State U (AR)
Austin Peay State U (TN)
Brigham Young U (UT)
California State Polytechnic U, Pomona (CA)
California State U, Long Beach (CA)
Central Connecticut State U (CT)
Delaware State U (DE)
East Carolina U (NC)
East Tennessee State U (TN)
Embry-Riddle Aeronautical U (AZ)
Embry-Riddle Aeronautical U (FL)
Fairmont State Coll (WV)
Gallaudet U (DC)
Grantham Coll of Engineering (LA)
Lawrence Technological U (MI)
LeTourneau U (TX)
Maine Maritime Academy (ME)
Massachusetts Maritime Academy (MA)
Miami U (OH)

Majors Index
Engineering Technology–English

Miami U–Hamilton Campus (OH)
Michigan State U (MI)
Middle Tennessee State U (TN)
Midwestern State U (TX)
New Jersey Inst of Technology (NJ)
New Mexico State U (NM)
New York Inst of Technology (NY)
Northeastern U (MA)
Northern Illinois U (IL)
Oklahoma State U (OK)
Pacific Union Coll (CA)
Pittsburg State U (KS)
Prairie View A&M U (TX)
Purdue U Calumet (IN)
Rochester Inst of Technology (NY)
St. Cloud State U (MN)
Southern Illinois U Carbondale (IL)
Southwestern Oklahoma State U (OK)
Southwest Texas State U (TX)
State U of NY Coll at Buffalo (NY)
State U of NY Inst of Tech at Utica/Rome (NY)
Temple U (PA)
Texas A&M U (TX)
Texas Tech U (TX)
U of Central Florida (FL)
U of Hartford (CT)
U of Maine (ME)
U of New Hampshire (NH)
U of North Texas (TX)
U of Pittsburgh at Johnstown (PA)
U of Southern Colorado (CO)
U of Southern Indiana (IN)
U of the District of Columbia (DC)
The U of West Alabama (AL)
U of Wisconsin–River Falls (WI)
Wentworth Inst of Technology (MA)
Western Washington U (WA)
West Texas A&M U (TX)
West Virginia U Inst of Technology (WV)
William Penn U (IA)
Youngstown State U (OH)

ENGLISH

Abilene Christian U (TX)
Acadia U (NS, Canada)
Adams State Coll (CO)
Adelphi U (NY)
Adrian Coll (MI)
Agnes Scott Coll (GA)
Alabama A&M U (AL)
Alabama State U (AL)
Albany State U (GA)
Albertson Coll of Idaho (ID)
Albertus Magnus Coll (CT)
Albion Coll (MI)
Albright Coll (PA)
Alfred U (NY)
Alice Lloyd Coll (KY)
Allegheny Coll (PA)
Allentown Coll of St. Francis de Sales (PA)
Allen U (SC)
Alma Coll (MI)
Alvernia Coll (PA)
Alverno Coll (WI)
American Coll of Thessaloniki (Greece)
American International Coll (MA)
American U in Cairo (Egypt)
Amherst Coll (MA)
Anderson Coll (SC)
Anderson U (IN)
Andrews U (MI)
Anna Maria Coll (MA)
Antioch Coll (OH)
Appalachian State U (NC)
Aquinas Coll (MI)
Arizona State U (AZ)
Arizona State U West (AZ)
Arkansas State U (AR)
Arkansas Tech U (AR)
Armstrong Atlantic State U (GA)
Asbury Coll (KY)
Ashland U (OH)
Assumption Coll (MA)
Athabasca U (AB, Canada)
Athens State U (AL)
Atlantic Baptist U (NB, Canada)
Atlantic Union Coll (MA)
Auburn U (AL)
Auburn U Montgomery (AL)
Augsburg Coll (MN)
Augustana Coll (IL)
Augustana Coll (SD)

Augusta State U (GA)
Austin Coll (TX)
Austin Peay State U (TN)
Averett Coll (VA)
Avila Coll (MO)
Azusa Pacific U (CA)
Baker U (KS)
Baldwin-Wallace Coll (OH)
Ball State U (IN)
Barat Coll (IL)
Barber-Scotia Coll (NC)
Bard Coll (NY)
Barnard Coll (NY)
Barry U (FL)
Bartlesville Wesleyan Coll (OK)
Barton Coll (NC)
Bates Coll (ME)
Baylor U (TX)
Beaver Coll (PA)
Belhaven Coll (MS)
Bellarmine Coll (KY)
Bellevue U (NE)
Belmont Abbey Coll (NC)
Belmont U (TN)
Beloit Coll (WI)
Bemidji State U (MN)
Benedictine Coll (KS)
Benedictine U (IL)
Bennett Coll (NC)
Bennington Coll (VT)
Bentley Coll (MA)
Berea Coll (KY)
Baruch Coll of the City U of NY (NY)
Berry Coll (GA)
Bethany Coll (KS)
Bethany Coll (WV)
Bethany Coll of the Assemblies of God (CA)
Bethel Coll (IN)
Bethel Coll (KS)
Bethel Coll (MN)
Bethel Coll (TN)
Bethune-Cookman Coll (FL)
Biola U (CA)
Birmingham-Southern Coll (AL)
Bishop's U (PQ, Canada)
Blackburn Coll (IL)
Black Hills State U (SD)
Bloomfield Coll (NJ)
Bloomsburg U of Pennsylvania (PA)
Blue Mountain Coll (MS)
Bluffton Coll (OH)
Boise State U (ID)
Boston Coll (MA)
Boston U (MA)
Bowdoin Coll (ME)
Bowie State U (MD)
Bowling Green State U (OH)
Bradley U (IL)
Brandeis U (MA)
Brandon U (MB, Canada)
Brenau U (GA)
Brescia U (KY)
Brevard Coll (NC)
Briar Cliff Coll (IA)
Bridgewater Coll (VA)
Bridgewater State Coll (MA)
Brigham Young U (UT)
Brigham Young U–Hawaii Campus (HI)
Brock U (ON, Canada)
Brooklyn Coll of the City U of NY (NY)
Brown U (RI)
Bryan Coll (TN)
Bryant Coll (RI)
Bryn Athyn Coll of the New Church (PA)
Bryn Mawr Coll (PA)
Bucknell U (PA)
Buena Vista U (IA)
Butler U (IN)
Cabrini Coll (PA)
Caldwell Coll (NJ)
California Baptist U (CA)
California Lutheran U (CA)
California Polytechnic State U, San Luis Obispo (CA)
California State Polytechnic U, Pomona (CA)
California State U, Chico (CA)
California State U, Dominguez Hills (CA)
California State U, Fresno (CA)
California State U, Fullerton (CA)

California State U, Hayward (CA)
California State U, Long Beach (CA)
California State U, Los Angeles (CA)
California State U, Northridge (CA)
California State U, Sacramento (CA)
California State U, San Bernardino (CA)
California State U, San Marcos (CA)
California State U, Stanislaus (CA)
California U of Pennsylvania (PA)
Calumet Coll of Saint Joseph (IN)
Calvin Coll (MI)
Cameron U (OK)
Campbellsville U (KY)
Campbell U (NC)
Canisius Coll (NY)
Capital U (OH)
Cardinal Stritch U (WI)
Carleton Coll (MN)
Carleton U (ON, Canada)
Carlow Coll (PA)
Carnegie Mellon U (PA)
Carroll Coll (MT)
Carroll Coll (WI)
Carson-Newman Coll (TN)
Carthage Coll (WI)
Case Western Reserve U (OH)
Catawba Coll (NC)
The Catholic U of America (DC)
Cedar Crest Coll (PA)
Cedarville Coll (OH)
Centenary Coll (NJ)
Centenary Coll of Louisiana (LA)
Central Coll (IA)
Central Connecticut State U (CT)
Central Methodist Coll (MO)
Central Michigan U (MI)
Central Missouri State U (MO)
Centre Coll (KY)
Chadron State Coll (NE)
Chaminade U of Honolulu (HI)
Chapman U (CA)
Charleston Southern U (SC)
Chatham Coll (PA)
Chestnut Hill Coll (PA)
Cheyney U of Pennsylvania (PA)
Chicago State U (IL)
Chowan Coll (NC)
Christian Brothers U (TN)
Christopher Newport U (VA)
Citadel, The Military Coll of South Carolina (SC)
City Coll of the City U of NY (NY)
Claflin U (SC)
Claremont McKenna Coll (CA)
Clarion U of Pennsylvania (PA)
Clark Atlanta U (GA)
Clarke Coll (IA)
Clark U (MA)
Clemson U (SC)
Cleveland State U (OH)
Coastal Carolina U (SC)
Coe Coll (IA)
Coker Coll (SC)
Colby Coll (ME)
Colby-Sawyer Coll (NH)
Colgate U (NY)
Coll Misericordia (PA)
Coll of Charleston (SC)
Coll of Mount St. Joseph (OH)
Coll of Mount Saint Vincent (NY)
The Coll of New Jersey (NJ)
The Coll of New Rochelle (NY)
Coll of Notre Dame (CA)
Coll of Notre Dame of Maryland (MD)
Coll of Our Lady of the Elms (MA)
Coll of Saint Benedict (MN)
Coll of St. Catherine (MN)
Coll of Saint Elizabeth (NJ)
Coll of St. Joseph (VT)
Coll of Saint Mary (NE)
The Coll of Saint Rose (NY)
Coll of Santa Fe (NM)
Coll of Staten Island of the City U of NY (NY)
Coll of the Atlantic (ME)
Coll of the Holy Cross (MA)
Coll of the Ozarks (MO)
Coll of the Southwest (NM)
The Coll of William and Mary (VA)
The Coll of Wooster (OH)
Colorado Christian U (CO)

The Colorado Coll (CO)
Colorado State U (CO)
Columbia Coll (MO)
Columbia Coll (NY)
Columbia Coll (SC)
Columbia Union Coll (MD)
Columbia U, School of General Studies (NY)
Columbus State U (GA)
Concord Coll (WV)
Concordia Coll (MI)
Concordia Coll (MN)
Concordia Coll (NY)
Concordia U (CA)
Concordia U (IL)
Concordia U (NE)
Concordia U (OR)
Concordia U (PQ, Canada)
Concordia U at Austin (TX)
Concordia U at St. Paul (MN)
Concordia U Coll of Alberta (AB, Canada)
Concordia U Wisconsin (WI)
Connecticut Coll (CT)
Converse Coll (SC)
Coppin State Coll (MD)
Cornell Coll (IA)
Cornell U (NY)
Cornerstone U (MI)
Covenant Coll (GA)
Creighton U (NE)
Crichton Coll (TN)
Crown Coll (MN)
Culver-Stockton Coll (MO)
Cumberland Coll (KY)
Curry Coll (MA)
Daemen Coll (NY)
Dakota State U (SD)
Dakota Wesleyan U (SD)
Dalhousie U (NS, Canada)
Dallas Baptist U (TX)
Dana Coll (NE)
Dartmouth Coll (NH)
David Lipscomb U (TN)
Davidson Coll (NC)
Defiance Coll (OH)
Delaware State U (DE)
Delaware Valley Coll (PA)
Delta State U (MS)
Denison U (OH)
DePaul U (IL)
DePauw U (IN)
Deree Coll (Greece)
Dickinson Coll (PA)
Dickinson State U (ND)
Doane Coll (NE)
Dominican Coll of Blauvelt (NY)
Dominican U (IL)
Dominican U of California (CA)
Dordt Coll (IA)
Dowling Coll (NY)
Drake U (IA)
Drew U (NJ)
Drury U (MO)
Duke U (NC)
Duquesne U (PA)
D'Youville Coll (NY)
Earlham Coll (IN)
East Carolina U (NC)
East Central U (OK)
Eastern Coll (PA)
Eastern Connecticut State U (CT)
Eastern Illinois U (IL)
Eastern Kentucky U (KY)
Eastern Mennonite U (VA)
Eastern Michigan U (MI)
Eastern Nazarene Coll (MA)
Eastern New Mexico U (NM)
Eastern Oregon U (OR)
Eastern Washington U (WA)
East Stroudsburg U of Pennsylvania (PA)
East Tennessee State U (TN)
East Texas Baptist U (TX)
Eckerd Coll (FL)
Edgewood Coll (WI)
Edinboro U of Pennsylvania (PA)
Elizabeth City State U (NC)
Elizabethtown Coll (PA)
Elmhurst Coll (IL)
Elmira Coll (NY)
Elon Coll (NC)
Emmanuel Coll (GA)
Emmanuel Coll (MA)
Emory & Henry Coll (VA)
Emory U (GA)
Emporia State U (KS)

Erskine Coll (SC)
Eugene Lang Coll, New School U (NY)
Evangel U (MO)
The Evergreen State Coll (WA)
Fairfield U (CT)
Fairleigh Dickinson U, Florham-Madison Campus (NJ)
Fairleigh Dickinson U, Teaneck-Hackensack Campus (NJ)
Fairmont State Coll (WV)
Faulkner U (AL)
Felician Coll (NJ)
Ferrum Coll (VA)
Fisk U (TN)
Fitchburg State Coll (MA)
Flagler Coll (FL)
Florida A&M U (FL)
Florida Atlantic U (FL)
Florida Gulf Coast U (FL)
Florida International U (FL)
Florida Southern Coll (FL)
Florida State U (FL)
Fontbonne Coll (MO)
Fordham U (NY)
Fort Hays State U (KS)
Fort Lewis Coll (CO)
Framingham State Coll (MA)
Franciscan U of Steubenville (OH)
Francis Marion U (SC)
Franklin and Marshall Coll (PA)
Franklin Coll of Indiana (IN)
Franklin Pierce Coll (NH)
Freed-Hardeman U (TN)
Free Will Baptist Bible Coll (TN)
Fresno Pacific U (CA)
Friends U (KS)
Frostburg State U (MD)
Furman U (SC)
Gallaudet U (DC)
Gardner-Webb U (NC)
Geneva Coll (PA)
George Fox U (OR)
George Mason U (VA)
Georgetown Coll (KY)
Georgetown U (DC)
The George Washington U (DC)
Georgia Coll and State U (GA)
Georgian Court Coll (NJ)
Georgia Southern U (GA)
Georgia Southwestern State U (GA)
Georgia State U (GA)
Gettysburg Coll (PA)
Glenville State Coll (WV)
Goddard Coll (VT)
Gonzaga U (WA)
Gordon Coll (MA)
Goshen Coll (IN)
Goucher Coll (MD)
Governors State U (IL)
Grace Coll (IN)
Graceland Coll (IA)
Grand Canyon U (AZ)
Grand Valley State U (MI)
Grand View Coll (IA)
Green Mountain Coll (VT)
Greensboro Coll (NC)
Greenville Coll (IL)
Grinnell Coll (IA)
Grove City Coll (PA)
Guilford Coll (NC)
Gustavus Adolphus Coll (MN)
Gwynedd-Mercy Coll (PA)
Hamilton Coll (NY)
Hamline U (MN)
Hampden-Sydney Coll (VA)
Hampshire Coll (MA)
Hampton U (VA)
Hannibal-LaGrange Coll (MO)
Hanover Coll (IN)
Harding U (AR)
Hardin-Simmons U (TX)
Hartwick Coll (NY)
Harvard U (MA)
Hastings Coll (NE)
Haverford Coll (PA)
Heidelberg Coll (OH)
Henderson State U (AR)
Hendrix Coll (AR)
Heritage Coll (WA)
High Point U (NC)
Hilbert Coll (NY)
Hillsdale Coll (MI)
Hiram Coll (OH)
Hobart and William Smith Colls (NY)

Majors Index
English

Hofstra U (NY)
Hollins U (VA)
Holy Family Coll (PA)
Holy Names Coll (CA)
Hood Coll (MD)
Hope Coll (MI)
Houghton Coll (NY)
Houston Baptist U (TX)
Howard Payne U (TX)
Howard U (DC)
Humboldt State U (CA)
Hunter Coll of the City U of NY (NY)
Huntingdon Coll (AL)
Huntington Coll (IN)
Huston-Tillotson Coll (TX)
Idaho State U (ID)
Illinois Coll (IL)
Illinois State U (IL)
Illinois Wesleyan U (IL)
Immaculata Coll (PA)
Indiana State U (IN)
Indiana U Bloomington (IN)
Indiana U East (IN)
Indiana U Kokomo (IN)
Indiana U Northwest (IN)
Indiana U of Pennsylvania (PA)
Indiana U–Purdue U Fort Wayne (IN)
Indiana U–Purdue U Indianapolis (IN)
Indiana U South Bend (IN)
Indiana U Southeast (IN)
Indiana Wesleyan U (IN)
Inter American U of PR, Metropolitan Campus (PR)
Inter American U of PR, San Germán Campus (PR)
Iona Coll (NY)
Iowa State U of Science and Technology (IA)
Iowa Wesleyan Coll (IA)
Ithaca Coll (NY)
Jacksonville State U (AL)
Jacksonville U (FL)
James Madison U (VA)
Jamestown Coll (ND)
Jarvis Christian Coll (TX)
John Brown U (AR)
John Carroll U (IN)
Johns Hopkins U (MD)
Johnson C. Smith U (NC)
Johnson State Coll (VT)
Judson Coll (AL)
Judson Coll (IL)
Juniata Coll (PA)
Kalamazoo Coll (MI)
Kansas State U (KS)
Kean U (NJ)
Keene State Coll (NH)
Kent State U (OH)
Kentucky State U (KY)
Kentucky Wesleyan Coll (KY)
Kenyon Coll (OH)
Keuka Coll (NY)
King Coll (TN)
King's Coll (PA)
The King's U Coll (AB, Canada)
Knox Coll (IL)
Kutztown U of Pennsylvania (PA)
Lafayette Coll (PA)
LaGrange Coll (GA)
Lake Erie Coll (OH)
Lake Forest Coll (IL)
Lakehead U (ON, Canada)
Lakeland Coll (WI)
Lake Superior State U (MI)
Lamar U (TX)
Lambuth U (TN)
Lander U (SC)
Lane Coll (TN)
Langston U (OK)
La Roche Coll (PA)
La Salle U (PA)
La Sierra U (CA)
Lawrence U (WI)
Lebanon Valley Coll (PA)
Lees-McRae Coll (NC)
Lee U (TN)
Lehigh U (PA)
Lehman Coll of the City U of NY (NY)
Le Moyne Coll (NY)
LeMoyne-Owen Coll (TN)
Lenoir-Rhyne Coll (NC)
LeTourneau U (TX)
Lewis & Clark Coll (OR)

Lewis-Clark State Coll (ID)
Lewis U (IL)
Liberty U (VA)
Limestone Coll (SC)
Lincoln Memorial U (TN)
Lincoln U (MO)
Lincoln U (PA)
Lindenwood U (MO)
Lindsey Wilson Coll (KY)
Linfield Coll (OR)
Lock Haven U of Pennsylvania (PA)
Long Island U, Brooklyn Campus (NY)
Long Island U, C.W. Post Campus (NY)
Long Island U, Southampton Coll (NY)
Long Island U, Southampton Coll, Friends World Program (NY)
Longwood Coll (VA)
Loras Coll (IA)
Louisiana Coll (LA)
Louisiana State U and A&M Coll (LA)
Louisiana State U in Shreveport (LA)
Louisiana Tech U (LA)
Lourdes Coll (OH)
Loyola Coll in Maryland (MD)
Loyola Marymount U (CA)
Loyola U Chicago (IL)
Loyola U New Orleans (LA)
Lubbock Christian U (TX)
Luther Coll (IA)
Lycoming Coll (PA)
Lynchburg Coll (VA)
Lyndon State Coll (VT)
Lynn U (FL)
Lyon Coll (AR)
Macalester Coll (MN)
MacMurray Coll (IL)
Madonna U (MI)
Maharishi U of Management (IA)
Malone Coll (OH)
Manchester Coll (IN)
Manhattan Coll (NY)
Manhattanville Coll (NY)
Mansfield U of Pennsylvania (PA)
Marian Coll (IN)
Marian Coll of Fond du Lac (WI)
Marietta Coll (OH)
Marist Coll (NY)
Marlboro Coll (VT)
Marquette U (WI)
Marshall U (WV)
Mars Hill Coll (NC)
Martin Methodist Coll (TN)
Mary Baldwin Coll (VA)
Marycrest International U (IA)
Marygrove Coll (MI)
Marymount Coll (NY)
Marymount Manhattan Coll (NY)
Maryville Coll (TN)
Maryville U of Saint Louis (MO)
Mary Washington Coll (VA)
Marywood U (PA)
Massachusetts Coll of Liberal Arts (MA)
Mayville State U (ND)
McGill U (PQ, Canada)
McKendree Coll (IL)
McMurry U (TX)
McNeese State U (LA)
McPherson Coll (KS)
Memorial U of Newfoundland (NF, Canada)
Mercer U (GA)
Mercy Coll (NY)
Mercyhurst Coll (PA)
Meredith Coll (NC)
Merrimack Coll (MA)
Mesa State Coll (CO)
Messiah Coll (PA)
Methodist Coll (NC)
Metropolitan State Coll of Denver (CO)
Metropolitan State U (MN)
Miami U (OH)
Michigan State U (MI)
Michigan Technological U (MI)
Mid-America Bible Coll (OK)
MidAmerica Nazarene U (KS)
Mid-Continent Coll (KY)
Middlebury Coll (VT)
Middle Tennessee State U (TN)
Midland Lutheran Coll (NE)

Midway Coll (KY)
Midwestern State U (TX)
Millersville U of Pennsylvania (PA)
Milligan Coll (TN)
Millikin U (IL)
Millsaps Coll (MS)
Mills Coll (CA)
Minnesota State U, Mankato (MN)
Minnesota State U Moorhead (MN)
Minot State U (ND)
Mississippi Coll (MS)
Mississippi State U (MS)
Mississippi U for Women (MS)
Mississippi Valley State U (MS)
Missouri Baptist Coll (MO)
Missouri Southern State Coll (MO)
Missouri Valley Coll (MO)
Missouri Western State Coll (MO)
Molloy Coll (NY)
Monmouth Coll (IL)
Monmouth U (NJ)
Montana State U–Billings (MT)
Montana State U–Bozeman (MT)
Montreat Coll (NC)
Moravian Coll (PA)
Morehead State U (KY)
Morehouse Coll (GA)
Morgan State U (MD)
Morningside Coll (IA)
Morris Coll (SC)
Mount Allison U (NB, Canada)
Mount Holyoke Coll (MA)
Mount Marty Coll (SD)
Mount Mary Coll (WI)
Mount Mercy Coll (IA)
Mount Olive Coll (NC)
Mount St. Clare Coll (IA)
Mount Saint Mary Coll (NY)
Mount St. Mary's Coll (CA)
Mount Saint Mary's Coll and Seminary (MD)
Mount Saint Vincent U (NS, Canada)
Mount Senario Coll (WI)
Mount Union Coll (OH)
Mount Vernon Nazarene Coll (OH)
Muhlenberg Coll (PA)
Murray State U (KY)
Muskingum Coll (OH)
National-Louis U (IL)
Nazareth Coll of Rochester (NY)
Nebraska Wesleyan U (NE)
Neumann Coll (PA)
Newberry Coll (SC)
New England Coll (NH)
New Hampshire Coll (NH)
New Jersey City U (NJ)
Newman U (KS)
New Mexico Highlands U (NM)
New Mexico State U (NM)
New York Inst of Technology (NY)
New York U (NY)
Niagara U (NY)
Nicholls State U (LA)
Nichols Coll (MA)
Nipissing U (ON, Canada)
Norfolk State U (VA)
North Carolina Ag and Tech State U (NC)
North Carolina Central U (NC)
North Carolina State U (NC)
North Carolina Wesleyan Coll (NC)
North Central Coll (IL)
North Central U (MN)
North Dakota State U (ND)
Northeastern Illinois U (IL)
Northeastern State U (OK)
Northeastern U (MA)
Northern Arizona U (AZ)
Northern Illinois U (IL)
Northern Kentucky U (KY)
Northern Michigan U (MI)
Northern State U (SD)
North Georgia Coll & State U (GA)
Northland Coll (WI)
North Park U (IL)
Northwest Coll (WA)
Northwestern Coll (IA)
Northwestern Coll (MN)
Northwestern Oklahoma State U (OK)
Northwestern State U of Louisiana (LA)
Northwestern U (IL)
Northwest Missouri State U (MO)
Northwest Nazarene U (ID)
Norwich U (VT)

Notre Dame Coll (NH)
Notre Dame Coll of Ohio (OH)
Nyack Coll (NY)
Oakland City U (IN)
Oakland U (MI)
Oakwood Coll (AL)
Oberlin Coll (OH)
Oglethorpe U (GA)
Ohio Dominican Coll (OH)
Ohio Northern U (OH)
The Ohio State U (OH)
The Ohio State U at Lima (OH)
Ohio U (OH)
Ohio Wesleyan U (OH)
Okanagan U Coll (BC, Canada)
Oklahoma Baptist U (OK)
Oklahoma Christian U of Science and Arts (OK)
Oklahoma City U (OK)
Oklahoma Panhandle State U (OK)
Oklahoma State U (OK)
Old Dominion U (VA)
Olivet Nazarene U (IL)
Open Learning Agency (BC, Canada)
Oregon State U (OR)
Ottawa U (KS)
Otterbein Coll (OH)
Ouachita Baptist U (AR)
Our Lady of Holy Cross Coll (LA)
Our Lady of the Lake U of San Antonio (TX)
Pace U, New York City Campus (NY)
Pace U, Pleasantville/Briarcliff Campus (NY)
Pacific Lutheran U (WA)
Pacific Union Coll (CA)
Pacific U (OR)
Paine Coll (GA)
Palm Beach Atlantic Coll (FL)
Park U (MO)
Peace Coll (NC)
Penn State U Abington Coll (PA)
Penn State U Altoona Coll (PA)
Penn State U at Erie, The Behrend Coll (PA)
Penn State U Univ Park Campus (PA)
Pepperdine U, Malibu (CA)
Peru State Coll (NE)
Pfeiffer U (NC)
Philander Smith Coll (AR)
Piedmont Baptist Coll (NC)
Piedmont Coll (GA)
Pikeville Coll (KY)
Pine Manor Coll (MA)
Pittsburg State U (KS)
Pitzer Coll (CA)
Plattsburgh State U of NY (NY)
Plymouth State Coll (NH)
Point Park Coll (PA)
Pomona Coll (CA)
Pontifical Catholic U of Puerto Rico (PR)
Portland State U (OR)
Prairie View A&M U (TX)
Presbyterian Coll (SC)
Princeton U (NJ)
Principia Coll (IL)
Providence Coll (RI)
Purdue U (IN)
Purdue U Calumet (IN)
Purdue U North Central (IN)
Queens Coll (NC)
Queens Coll of the City U of NY (NY)
Queen's U at Kingston (ON, Canada)
Quincy U (IL)
Quinnipiac U (CT)
Radford U (VA)
Randolph-Macon Coll (VA)
Randolph-Macon Woman's Coll (VA)
Redeemer Coll (ON, Canada)
Reed Coll (OR)
Regis Coll (MA)
Regis U (CO)
Rhodes Coll (TN)
Rice U (TX)
The Richard Stockton Coll of New Jersey (NJ)
Richmond, The American International U in London (United Kingdom)
Rider U (NJ)

Ripon Coll (WI)
Rivier Coll (NH)
Roanoke Coll (VA)
Robert Morris Coll (PA)
Roberts Wesleyan Coll (NY)
Rochester Coll (MI)
Rockford Coll (IL)
Rockhurst U (MO)
Rocky Mountain Coll (MT)
Roger Williams U (RI)
Rollins Coll (FL)
Rosemont Coll (PA)
Rowan U (NJ)
Russell Sage Coll (NY)
Rust Coll (MS)
Rutgers, State U of NJ, Camden Coll of Arts & Scis (NJ)
Rutgers, State U of NJ, Douglass Coll (NJ)
Rutgers, State U of NJ, Livingston Coll (NJ)
Rutgers, State U of NJ, Newark Coll of Arts & Scis (NJ)
Rutgers, State U of NJ, Rutgers Coll (NJ)
Rutgers, State U of NJ, U Coll–Camden (NJ)
Rutgers, State U of NJ, U Coll–Newark (NJ)
Rutgers, State U of NJ, U Coll–New Brunswick (NJ)
Sacred Heart U (CT)
Saginaw Valley State U (MI)
St. Ambrose U (IA)
St. Andrews Presbyterian Coll (NC)
Saint Anselm Coll (NH)
Saint Augustine's Coll (NC)
St. Bonaventure U (NY)
St. Cloud State U (MN)
St. Edward's U (TX)
St. Francis Coll (NY)
Saint Francis Coll (PA)
St. Francis Xavier U (NS, Canada)
St. John Fisher Coll (NY)
St. John's Seminary Coll (CA)
Saint John's U (MN)
St. John's U (NY)
Saint Joseph Coll (CT)
Saint Joseph's Coll (IN)
Saint Joseph's Coll (ME)
St. Joseph's Coll, New York (NY)
St. Joseph's Coll, Suffolk Campus (NY)
Saint Joseph's U (PA)
St. Lawrence U (NY)
Saint Leo U (FL)
Saint Louis U (MO)
Saint Martin's Coll (WA)
Saint Mary Coll (KS)
Saint Mary-of-the-Woods Coll (IN)
Saint Mary's Coll (IN)
Saint Mary's Coll (MI)
Saint Mary's Coll of California (CA)
St. Mary's Coll of Maryland (MD)
Saint Mary's U (NS, Canada)
Saint Mary's U of Minnesota (MN)
St. Mary's U of San Antonio (TX)
Saint Michael's Coll (VT)
St. Norbert Coll (WI)
St. Olaf Coll (MN)
Saint Paul's Coll (VA)
Saint Peter's Coll (NJ)
St. Thomas U (FL)
Saint Vincent Coll (PA)
Saint Xavier U (IL)
Salem Coll (NC)
Salem State Coll (MA)
Salisbury State U (MD)
Salve Regina U (RI)
Samford U (AL)
Sam Houston State U (TX)
San Diego State U (CA)
San Francisco State U (CA)
San Jose State U (CA)
Santa Clara U (CA)
Sarah Lawrence Coll (NY)
Savannah State U (GA)
Schreiner Coll (TX)
Scripps Coll (CA)
Seattle Pacific U (WA)
Seattle U (WA)
Seton Hall U (NJ)
Seton Hill Coll (PA)
Shawnee State U (OH)
Shaw U (NC)
Sheldon Jackson Coll (AK)
Shenandoah U (VA)

Majors Index
English–English Composition

Shepherd Coll (WV)
Shippensburg U of Pennsylvania (PA)
Shorter Coll (GA)
Siena Coll (NY)
Siena Heights U (MI)
Silver Lake Coll (WI)
Simmons Coll (MA)
Simon Fraser U (BC, Canada)
Simpson Coll (IA)
Simpson Coll and Graduate School (CA)
Skidmore Coll (NY)
Slippery Rock U of Pennsylvania (PA)
Smith Coll (MA)
Sonoma State U (CA)
South Dakota State U (SD)
Southeastern Louisiana U (LA)
Southeastern Oklahoma State U (OK)
Southeast Missouri State U (MO)
Southern Adventist U (TN)
Southern Arkansas U–Magnolia (AR)
Southern Illinois U Carbondale (IL)
Southern Illinois U Edwardsville (IL)
Southern Methodist U (TX)
Southern Oregon U (OR)
Southern Utah U (UT)
Southern Vermont Coll (VT)
Southern Wesleyan U (SC)
Southwest Baptist U (MO)
Southwestern Adventist U (TX)
Southwestern Coll (KS)
Southwestern Oklahoma State U (OK)
Southwestern U (TX)
Southwest Missouri State U (MO)
Southwest State U (MN)
Southwest Texas State U (TX)
Spalding U (KY)
Spelman Coll (GA)
Spring Arbor Coll (MI)
Spring Hill Coll (AL)
Stanford U (CA)
State U of NY at Albany (NY)
State U of NY at Binghamton (NY)
State U of NY at Buffalo (NY)
State U of NY at New Paltz (NY)
State U of NY at Oswego (NY)
State U of NY at Stony Brook (NY)
State U of NY Coll at Brockport (NY)
State U of NY Coll at Buffalo (NY)
State U of NY Coll at Cortland (NY)
State U of NY Coll at Fredonia (NY)
State U of NY Coll at Geneseo (NY)
State U of NY Coll at Oneonta (NY)
State U of NY Coll at Potsdam (NY)
State U of West Georgia (GA)
Stephen F. Austin State U (TX)
Stephens Coll (MO)
Sterling Coll (KS)
Stetson U (FL)
Stevens Inst of Technology (NJ)
Stillman Coll (AL)
Stonehill Coll (MA)
Suffolk U (MA)
Sul Ross State U (TX)
Susquehanna U (PA)
Swarthmore Coll (PA)
Sweet Briar Coll (VA)
Syracuse U (NY)
Tabor Coll (KS)
Talladega Coll (AL)
Taylor U (IN)
Taylor U, Fort Wayne Campus (IN)
Teikyo Post U (CT)
Temple U (PA)
Tennessee State U (TN)
Tennessee Technological U (TN)
Tennessee Wesleyan Coll (TN)
Texas A&M International (TX)
Texas A&M U (TX)
Texas A&M U–Commerce (TX)
Texas A&M U–Kingsville (TX)
Texas A&M U–Texarkana (TX)
Texas Christian U (TX)
Texas Lutheran U (TX)
Texas Southern U (TX)
Texas Tech U (TX)
Texas Wesleyan U (TX)

Texas Woman's U (TX)
Thiel Coll (PA)
Thomas Edison State Coll (NJ)
Thomas More Coll (KY)
Thomas U (GA)
Toccoa Falls Coll (GA)
Tougaloo Coll (MS)
Touro Coll (NY)
Towson U (MD)
Transylvania U (KY)
Trent U (ON, Canada)
Trevecca Nazarene U (TN)
Trinity Christian Coll (IL)
Trinity Coll (CT)
Trinity U (TX)
Trinity Western U (BC, Canada)
Troy State U (AL)
Troy State U Dothan (AL)
Troy State U Montgomery (AL)
Truman State U (MO)
Tufts U (MA)
Tulane U (LA)
Tusculum Coll (TN)
Tuskegee U (AL)
Union Coll (KY)
Union Coll (NE)
Union Coll (NY)
Union U (TN)
United States Air Force Academy (CO)
United States International U (CA)
United States Naval Academy (MD)
Universidad del Turabo (PR)
Université de Montréal (PQ, Canada)
Université de Sherbrooke (PQ, Canada)
U du Québec à Chicoutimi (PQ, Canada)
Université Laval (PQ, Canada)
U Coll of Cape Breton (NS, Canada)
The U of Akron (OH)
The U of Alabama (AL)
The U of Alabama at Birmingham (AL)
The U of Alabama in Huntsville (AL)
U of Alaska Fairbanks (AK)
U of Alberta (AB, Canada)
The U of Arizona (AZ)
U of Arkansas (AR)
U of Arkansas at Little Rock (AR)
U of Arkansas at Monticello (AR)
U of Arkansas at Pine Bluff (AR)
U of Baltimore (MD)
U of Bridgeport (CT)
U of British Columbia (BC, Canada)
U of Calgary (AB, Canada)
U of Calif, Berkeley (CA)
U of Calif, Davis (CA)
U of Calif, Irvine (CA)
U of Calif, Los Angeles (CA)
U of Calif, Riverside (CA)
U of Calif, San Diego (CA)
U of Calif, Santa Barbara (CA)
U of Central Arkansas (AR)
U of Central Florida (FL)
U of Central Oklahoma (OK)
U of Charleston (WV)
U of Chicago (IL)
U of Cincinnati (OH)
U of Colorado at Boulder (CO)
U of Colorado at Colorado Springs (CO)
U of Colorado at Denver (CO)
U of Connecticut (CT)
U of Dallas (TX)
U of Dayton (OH)
U of Delaware (DE)
U of Denver (CO)
U of Detroit Mercy (MI)
U of Dubuque (IA)
U of Evansville (IN)
The U of Findlay (OH)
U of Florida (FL)
U of Georgia (GA)
U of Great Falls (MT)
U of Guelph (ON, Canada)
U of Hartford (CT)
U of Hawaii at Manoa (HI)
U of Houston (TX)
U of Houston–Downtown (TX)
U of Idaho (ID)
U of Illinois at Chicago (IL)
U of Illinois at Springfield (IL)

U of Illinois at Urbana–Champaign (IL)
U of Indianapolis (IN)
The U of Iowa (IA)
U of Kansas (KS)
U of Kentucky (KY)
U of King's Coll (NS, Canada)
U of La Verne (CA)
The U of Lethbridge (AB, Canada)
U of Louisiana at Lafayette (LA)
U of Louisiana at Monroe (LA)
U of Louisville (KY)
U of Maine (ME)
The U of Maine at Augusta (ME)
U of Maine at Farmington (ME)
U of Maine at Fort Kent (ME)
U of Maine at Machias (ME)
U of Maine at Presque Isle (ME)
U of Manitoba (MB, Canada)
U of Mary Hardin-Baylor (TX)
U of Maryland, Baltimore County (MD)
U of Maryland, Coll Park (MD)
U of Maryland University Coll (MD)
U of Massachusetts Amherst (MA)
U of Massachusetts Boston (MA)
U of Massachusetts Dartmouth (MA)
U of Massachusetts Lowell (MA)
The U of Memphis (TN)
U of Miami (FL)
U of Michigan (MI)
U of Michigan–Dearborn (MI)
U of Michigan–Flint (MI)
U of Minnesota, Duluth (MN)
U of Minnesota, Morris (MN)
U of Minnesota, Twin Cities Campus (MN)
U of Mississippi (MS)
U of Missouri–Columbia (MO)
U of Missouri–Kansas City (MO)
U of Missouri–Rolla (MO)
U of Missouri–St. Louis (MO)
U of Mobile (AL)
The U of Montana–Missoula (MT)
U of Montevallo (AL)
U of Nebraska at Kearney (NE)
U of Nebraska at Omaha (NE)
U of Nebraska–Lincoln (NE)
U of Nevada, Las Vegas (NV)
U of Nevada, Reno (NV)
U of New Brunswick, Fredericton (NB, Canada)
U of New Brunswick, Saint John (NB, Canada)
U of New Hampshire (NH)
U of New Hampshire at Manchester (NH)
U of New Haven (CT)
U of New Mexico (NM)
U of New Orleans (LA)
U of North Alabama (AL)
The U of North Carolina at Asheville (NC)
The U of North Carolina at Chapel Hill (NC)
The U of North Carolina at Charlotte (NC)
The U of North Carolina at Greensboro (NC)
The U of North Carolina at Pembroke (NC)
The U of North Carolina at Wilmington (NC)
U of North Dakota (ND)
U of Northern Colorado (CO)
U of Northern Iowa (IA)
U of North Florida (FL)
U of North Texas (TX)
U of Notre Dame (IN)
U of Oklahoma (OK)
U of Oregon (OR)
U of Pennsylvania (PA)
U of Pittsburgh (PA)
U of Pittsburgh at Bradford (PA)
U of Pittsburgh at Johnstown (PA)
U of Portland (OR)
U of Prince Edward Island (PE, Canada)
U of Puerto Rico, Mayagüez Campus (PR)
U of Puerto Rico, Río Piedras (PR)
U of Puget Sound (WA)
U of Redlands (CA)
U of Regina (SK, Canada)
U of Rhode Island (RI)
U of Richmond (VA)

U of Rio Grande (OH)
U of Rochester (NY)
U of St. Francis (IL)
U of Saint Francis (IN)
U of St. Thomas (MN)
U of St. Thomas (TX)
U of San Diego (CA)
U of San Francisco (CA)
U of Science and Arts of Oklahoma (OK)
The U of Scranton (PA)
U of Sioux Falls (SD)
U of South Alabama (AL)
U of South Carolina (SC)
U of South Carolina Spartanburg (SC)
U of South Dakota (SD)
U of Southern California (CA)
U of Southern Colorado (CO)
U of Southern Indiana (IN)
U of Southern Maine (ME)
U of Southern Mississippi (MS)
U of South Florida (FL)
The U of Tampa (FL)
The U of Tennessee at Chattanooga (TN)
The U of Tennessee at Martin (TN)
The U of Tennessee Knoxville (TN)
The U of Texas at Arlington (TX)
The U of Texas at Austin (TX)
The U of Texas at San Antonio (TX)
The U of Texas at Tyler (TX)
The U of Texas–Pan American (TX)
U of the District of Columbia (DC)
U of the Ozarks (AR)
U of the Pacific (CA)
U of the Sacred Heart (PR)
U of the South (TN)
U of the Virgin Islands (VI)
U of Toronto (ON, Canada)
U of Tulsa (OK)
U of Utah (UT)
U of Vermont (VT)
U of Victoria (BC, Canada)
U of Virginia (VA)
U of Virginia's Coll at Wise (VA)
U of Washington (WA)
U of Waterloo (ON, Canada)
The U of West Alabama (AL)
U of West Florida (FL)
U of Windsor (ON, Canada)
The U of Winnipeg (MB, Canada)
U of Wisconsin–Eau Claire (WI)
U of Wisconsin–Green Bay (WI)
U of Wisconsin–La Crosse (WI)
U of Wisconsin–Madison (WI)
U of Wisconsin–Milwaukee (WI)
U of Wisconsin–Parkside (WI)
U of Wisconsin–Platteville (WI)
U of Wisconsin–River Falls (WI)
U of Wisconsin–Stevens Point (WI)
U of Wisconsin–Superior (WI)
U of Wisconsin–Whitewater (WI)
U of Wyoming (WY)
Upper Iowa U (IA)
Urbana U (OH)
Ursinus Coll (PA)
Ursuline Coll (OH)
Utah State U (UT)
Utica Coll of Syracuse U (NY)
Valdosta State U (GA)
Valley City State U (ND)
Valparaiso U (IN)
Vanderbilt U (TN)
Vanguard U of Southern California (CA)
Vassar Coll (NY)
Villa Julie Coll (MD)
Villanova U (PA)
Virginia Commonwealth U (VA)
Virginia Intermont Coll (VA)
Virginia Military Inst (VA)
Virginia Polytechnic Inst and State U (VA)
Virginia Union U (VA)
Virginia Wesleyan Coll (VA)
Voorhees Coll (SC)
Wabash Coll (IN)
Wagner Coll (NY)
Wake Forest U (NC)
Walla Walla Coll (WA)
Walsh U (OH)
Warner Pacific Coll (OR)
Warner Southern Coll (FL)

Warren Wilson Coll (NC)
Wartburg Coll (IA)
Washington & Jefferson Coll (PA)
Washington and Lee U (VA)
Washington Coll (MD)
Washington State U (WA)
Washington U in St. Louis (MO)
Wayland Baptist U (TX)
Waynesburg Coll (PA)
Wayne State Coll (NE)
Wayne State U (MI)
Weber State U (UT)
Webster U (MO)
Wellesley Coll (MA)
Wells Coll (NY)
Wesleyan Coll (GA)
Wesleyan U (CT)
Wesley Coll (DE)
West Chester U of Pennsylvania (PA)
Western Baptist Coll (OR)
Western Carolina U (NC)
Western Connecticut State U (CT)
Western Illinois U (IL)
Western Kentucky U (KY)
Western Maryland Coll (MD)
Western Michigan U (MI)
Western Montana Coll of The U of Montana (MT)
Western New England Coll (MA)
Western Oregon U (OR)
Western State Coll of Colorado (CO)
Western Washington U (WA)
Westfield State Coll (MA)
West Liberty State Coll (WV)
Westminster Coll (MO)
Westminster Coll (PA)
Westminster Coll (UT)
Westmont Coll (CA)
West Texas A&M U (TX)
West Virginia State Coll (WV)
West Virginia U (WV)
West Virginia Wesleyan Coll (WV)
Wheaton Coll (IL)
Wheaton Coll (MA)
Wheeling Jesuit U (WV)
Whitman Coll (WA)
Whittier Coll (CA)
Whitworth Coll (WA)
Wichita State U (KS)
Widener U (PA)
Wilfrid Laurier U (ON, Canada)
Wilkes U (PA)
Willamette U (OR)
William Jewell Coll (MO)
William Paterson U of New Jersey (NJ)
Williams Baptist Coll (AR)
Williams Coll (MA)
William Tyndale Coll (MI)
William Woods U (MO)
Wilmington Coll (OH)
Wilson Coll (PA)
Wingate U (NC)
Winona State U (MN)
Winston-Salem State U (NC)
Winthrop U (SC)
Wisconsin Lutheran Coll (WI)
Wittenberg U (OH)
Wofford Coll (SC)
Worcester State Coll (MA)
Wright State U (OH)
Xavier U (OH)
Xavier U of Louisiana (LA)
Yale U (CT)
Yeshiva U (NY)
York Coll (NE)
York Coll of Pennsylvania (PA)
York Coll of the City U of New York (NY)
York U (ON, Canada)
Youngstown State U (OH)

ENGLISH COMPOSITION

Baylor U (TX)
The Coll of St. Scholastica (MN)
DePauw U (IN)
Eastern Michigan U (MI)
Florida Southern Coll (FL)
Gallaudet U (DC)
Luther Coll (IA)
Mount Union Coll (OH)
Oklahoma Baptist U (OK)
Rochester Coll (MI)
U of Colorado at Denver (CO)

Majors Index
English Composition–Environmental Education

U of Illinois at Urbana–Champaign (IL)
U of Nevada, Reno (NV)
U of North Texas (TX)
U of Pittsburgh (PA)
U of Tulsa (OK)
Wartburg Coll (IA)

ENGLISH EDUCATION
Abilene Christian U (TX)
Adams State Coll (CO)
Alvernia Coll (PA)
Anderson U (IN)
Appalachian State U (NC)
Arkansas State U (AR)
Arkansas Tech U (AR)
Barry U (FL)
Bayamón Central U (PR)
Baylor U (TX)
Berea Coll (KY)
Berry Coll (GA)
Bethany Coll (KS)
Bethel Coll (IN)
Bethel Coll (TN)
Bethune-Cookman Coll (FL)
Blue Mountain Coll (MS)
Boston U (MA)
Bowling Green State U (OH)
Bridgewater Coll (VA)
Brigham Young U (UT)
Brigham Young U–Hawaii Campus (HI)
Cabrini Coll (PA)
California State U, Chico (CA)
Canisius Coll (NY)
Carroll Coll (MT)
The Catholic U of America (DC)
Cedarville Coll (OH)
Central Michigan U (MI)
Central Missouri State U (MO)
Chowan Coll (NC)
Christian Brothers U (TN)
Citadel, The Military Coll of South Carolina (SC)
Colby-Sawyer Coll (NH)
The Coll of New Jersey (NJ)
Coll of Our Lady of the Elms (MA)
Coll of St. Catherine (MN)
Coll of Santa Fe (NM)
Coll of the Ozarks (MO)
Colorado Christian U (CO)
Colorado State U (CO)
Concordia Coll (MN)
Concordia U (IL)
Concordia U (NE)
Concordia U (OR)
Crichton Coll (TN)
Crown Coll (MN)
Culver-Stockton Coll (MO)
Cumberland Coll (KY)
Daemen Coll (NY)
Dana Coll (NE)
Delta State U (MS)
Dominican Coll of Blauvelt (NY)
Duquesne U (PA)
East Carolina U (NC)
Eastern Coll (PA)
Eastern Michigan U (MI)
East Texas Baptist U (TX)
Elmhurst Coll (IL)
Elmira Coll (NY)
Faith Baptist Bible Coll and Theological Seminary (IA)
Florida Atlantic U (FL)
Florida International U (FL)
Florida State U (FL)
Framingham State Coll (MA)
Freed-Hardeman U (TN)
Gallaudet U (DC)
George Fox U (OR)
Georgia Southern U (GA)
Grace Coll (IN)
Greensboro Coll (NC)
Greenville Coll (IL)
Hardin-Simmons U (TX)
Hastings Coll (NE)
Hope International U (CA)
Huntingdon Coll (AL)
Indiana U Bloomington (IN)
Indiana U Northwest (IN)
Indiana U–Purdue U Indianapolis (IN)
Indiana U South Bend (IN)
Indiana U Southeast (IN)
Indiana Wesleyan U (IN)
Ithaca Coll (NY)
Johnson State Coll (VT)

Judson Coll (AL)
Juniata Coll (PA)
Keuka Coll (NY)
King Coll (TN)
La Roche Coll (PA)
Le Moyne Coll (NY)
Liberty U (VA)
Limestone Coll (SC)
Lincoln U (PA)
Long Island U, C.W. Post Campus (NY)
Luther Coll (IA)
Manhattanville Coll (NY)
Mansfield U of Pennsylvania (PA)
Maryville Coll (TN)
Mayville State U (ND)
McGill U (PQ, Canada)
McKendree Coll (IL)
Mercer U (GA)
Messiah Coll (PA)
Miami U (OH)
MidAmerica Nazarene U (KS)
Minnesota State U Moorhead (MN)
Mississippi Valley State U (MS)
Missouri Western State Coll (MO)
Molloy Coll (NY)
Mount Marty Coll (SD)
Nazareth Coll of Rochester (NY)
New Hampshire Coll (NH)
New York Inst of Technology (NY)
New York U (NY)
North Carolina State U (NC)
North Dakota State U (ND)
Northwest Coll (WA)
Northwestern Coll (MN)
Northwest Nazarene U (ID)
Oakland City U (IN)
Ohio U (OH)
Oklahoma Baptist U (OK)
Penn State U Harrisburg Campus of the Capital Coll (PA)
Philadelphia Coll of Bible (PA)
Pikeville Coll (KY)
Plymouth State Coll (NH)
Queens Coll (NC)
Rivier Coll (NH)
Rocky Mountain Coll (MT)
St. Ambrose U (IA)
Saint Augustine's Coll (NC)
St. Edward's U (TX)
St. John's U (NY)
Saint Mary's U of Minnesota (MN)
St. Olaf Coll (MN)
Salve Regina U (RI)
Seattle Pacific U (WA)
Seton Hill Coll (PA)
Shaw U (NC)
Simpson Coll and Graduate School (CA)
Southeastern Coll of the Assemblies of God (FL)
Southeastern Louisiana U (LA)
Southeastern Oklahoma State U (OK)
Southern Adventist U (TN)
Southern Arkansas U–Magnolia (AR)
Southwest Baptist U (MO)
Southwestern Coll (KS)
Southwestern Oklahoma State U (OK)
Southwest Missouri State U (MO)
Southwest State U (MN)
Syracuse U (NY)
Tennessee Wesleyan Coll (TN)
Texas A&M International U (TX)
Texas Wesleyan U (TX)
Trevecca Nazarene U (TN)
Trinity Christian Coll (IL)
Tri-State U (IN)
Union Coll (NE)
United States International U (CA)
U du Québec à Trois-Rivières (PQ, Canada)
The U of Arizona (AZ)
U of Arkansas (AR)
U of Central Arkansas (AR)
U of Central Florida (FL)
U of Delaware (DE)
U of Georgia (GA)
U of Illinois at Chicago (IL)
U of Illinois at Urbana–Champaign (IL)
U of Indianapolis (IN)
U of Louisiana at Monroe (LA)
U of Maine at Farmington (ME)
U of Maryland, Coll Park (MD)

U of Minnesota, Twin Cities Campus (MN)
U of Mississippi (MS)
U of Nebraska–Lincoln (NE)
U of Nevada, Reno (NV)
U of New Orleans (LA)
The U of North Carolina at Chapel Hill (NC)
The U of North Carolina at Charlotte (NC)
U of Northern Iowa (IA)
U of North Texas (TX)
U of Oklahoma (OK)
U of Rio Grande (OH)
U of Southern California (CA)
U of South Florida (FL)
The U of Tennessee at Martin (TN)
U of Vermont (VT)
U of West Florida (FL)
U of Wisconsin–River Falls (WI)
U of Wisconsin–Superior (WI)
Virginia Intermont Coll (VA)
Warner Southern Coll (FL)
Warren Wilson Coll (NC)
Wayne State U (MI)
Weber State U (UT)
Western Carolina U (NC)
Western Montana Coll of The U of Montana (MT)
Westmont Coll (CA)
Wheeling Jesuit U (WV)
William Penn U (IA)
York U (ON, Canada)
Youngstown State U (OH)

ENTERPRISE MANAGEMENT
American U (DC)
Baylor U (TX)
Bridgewater State Coll (MA)
Concordia U (PQ, Canada)
Detroit Coll of Business (MI)
Detroit Coll of Business–Flint (MI)
Detroit Coll of Business, Warren Campus (MI)
École des Hautes Études Commerciales (PQ, Canada)
Gannon U (PA)
Iowa State U of Science and Technology (IA)
Lyndon State Coll (VT)
Morris Coll (SC)
Northwood U (MI)
Northwood U, Texas Campus (TX)
Ohio U (OH)
Southern Polytechnic State U (GA)
Syracuse U (NY)
Transylvania U (KY)
Union Coll (NE)
U du Québec à Trois-Rivières (PQ, Canada)
The U of Arizona (AZ)
U of Massachusetts Lowell (MA)
U of Miami (FL)
U of Nebraska at Omaha (NE)
U of Nevada, Reno (NV)
U of Puerto Rico, Río Piedras (PR)
U of St. Thomas (MN)
U of Southern California (CA)

ENTOMOLOGY
California State U, Long Beach (CA)
Colorado State U (CO)
Cornell U (NY)
Florida A&M U (FL)
Harvard U (MA)
Iowa State U of Science and Technology (IA)
McGill U (PQ, Canada)
Memorial U of Newfoundland (NF, Canada)
Michigan State U (MI)
The Ohio State U (OH)
Oklahoma State U (OK)
Oregon State U (OR)
Purdue U (IN)
Rutgers, State U of NJ, Cook Coll (NJ)
San Jose State U (CA)
State U of NY Coll of Environ Sci and Forestry (NY)
Texas A&M U (TX)
U of Alberta (AB, Canada)
U of Arkansas (AR)
U of Calif, Davis (CA)
U of Calif, Riverside (CA)
U of Delaware (DE)

U of Florida (FL)
U of Georgia (GA)
U of Hawaii at Manoa (HI)
U of Idaho (ID)
U of Illinois at Urbana–Champaign (IL)
U of Manitoba (MB, Canada)
U of New Brunswick, Fredericton (NB, Canada)
U of Wisconsin–Madison (WI)
U of Wyoming (WY)
Utah State U (UT)
Washington State U (WA)

ENTREPRENEURSHIP
Babson Coll (MA)
Black Hills State U (SD)
Brock U (ON, Canada)
Canisius Coll (NY)
Chatham Coll (PA)
Clarkson U (NY)
Columbia Coll (SC)
École des Hautes Études Commerciales (PQ, Canada)
Florida State U (FL)
Hawaii Pacific U (HI)
Howard Payne U (TX)
Husson Coll (ME)
Johnson & Wales U (RI)
Kendall Coll (IL)
McGill U (PQ, Canada)
New England Coll (NH)
Ryerson Polytechnic U (ON, Canada)
St. Mary's U of San Antonio (TX)
Seton Hill Coll (PA)
Sierra Nevada Coll (NV)
Syracuse U (NY)
Thomas Coll (ME)
Thomas Edison State Coll (NJ)
Trinity Christian Coll (IL)
U of Baltimore (MD)
The U of Findlay (OH)
U of Hartford (CT)
U of Houston (TX)
The U of Iowa (IA)
U of North Texas (TX)
U of Pennsylvania (PA)
Wichita State U (KS)
Xavier U (OH)
York U (ON, Canada)

ENVIRONMENTAL BIOLOGY
Antioch Coll (OH)
Bard Coll (NY)
Beaver Coll (PA)
Beloit Coll (WI)
Bennington Coll (VT)
Bethel Coll (IN)
Bloomfield Coll (NJ)
Bridgewater State Coll (MA)
California Polytechnic State U, San Luis Obispo (CA)
California State U, Monterey Bay (CA)
California State U, Northridge (CA)
Capital U (OH)
Carlow Coll (PA)
Cedar Crest Coll (PA)
Cedarville Coll (OH)
Central Methodist Coll (MO)
Chowan Coll (NC)
Colgate U (NY)
Coll of the Atlantic (ME)
Concordia U (PQ, Canada)
Concordia U Coll of Alberta (AB, Canada)
Eastern Kentucky U (KY)
Eastern Washington U (WA)
The Evergreen State Coll (WA)
Fort Lewis Coll (CO)
Framingham State Coll (MA)
Franklin Pierce Coll (NH)
Georgia Southwestern State U (GA)
Grand Canyon U (AZ)
Greenville Coll (IL)
Hampshire Coll (MA)
Harvard U (MA)
Heidelberg Coll (OH)
Humboldt State U (CA)
Iowa Wesleyan Coll (IA)
Jacksonville State U (AL)
Lakehead U (ON, Canada)
Lewis-Clark State Coll (ID)
Lock Haven U of Pennsylvania (PA)

Long Island U, Southampton Coll (NY)
Luther Coll (IA)
Maharishi U of Management (IA)
Manhattan Coll (NY)
Mansfield U of Pennsylvania (PA)
Marist Coll (NY)
Marlboro Coll (VT)
McGill U (PQ, Canada)
Memorial U of Newfoundland (NF, Canada)
Michigan State U (MI)
Midway Coll (KY)
Minnesota State U, Mankato (MN)
Mount Union Coll (OH)
New Mexico Inst of Mining and Technology (NM)
New York Inst of Technology (NY)
Nipissing U (ON, Canada)
Northland Coll (WI)
Northwest Coll (WA)
Ohio U (OH)
Oregon State U (OR)
Otterbein Coll (OH)
Pittsburg State U (KS)
Plymouth State Coll (NH)
Queens Coll (NC)
Sacred Heart U (CT)
St. Cloud State U (MN)
Saint Mary's U of Minnesota (MN)
Simpson Coll (IA)
State U of NY Coll at Brockport (NY)
State U of NY Coll at Cortland (NY)
State U of NY Coll of Environ Sci and Forestry (NY)
Suffolk U (MA)
Tabor Coll (KS)
Taylor U (IN)
Trinity Western U (BC, Canada)
Tulane U (LA)
Unity Coll (ME)
U of Alberta (AB, Canada)
U of Arkansas at Pine Bluff (AR)
U of British Columbia (BC, Canada)
U of Calif, Davis (CA)
U of Charleston (WV)
U of Dayton (OH)
U of Dubuque (IA)
U of Guelph (ON, Canada)
U of La Verne (CA)
U of Maryland, Coll Park (MD)
U of Nebraska at Omaha (NE)
U of New England (ME)
U of Pittsburgh at Johnstown (PA)
U of Southern Colorado (CO)
The U of Tampa (FL)
U of Vermont (VT)
U of Windsor (ON, Canada)
Western Washington U (WA)
Westfield State Coll (MA)
William Penn U (IA)
Wingate U (NC)
Winona State U (MN)
Wittenberg U (OH)
York U (ON, Canada)

ENVIRONMENTAL EDUCATION
Coll of the Atlantic (ME)
Concordia U at St. Paul (MN)
The Evergreen State Coll (WA)
Goddard Coll (VT)
Johnson State Coll (VT)
Long Island U, Southampton Coll (NY)
Long Island U, Southampton Coll, Friends World Program (NY)
Neumann Coll (PA)
Northland Coll (WI)
The Ohio State U (OH)
Queens Coll of the City U of NY (NY)
Rutgers, State U of NJ, Cook Coll (NJ)
Slippery Rock U of Pennsylvania (PA)
Sonoma State U (CA)
State U of NY Coll of Environ Sci and Forestry (NY)
Unity Coll (ME)
U of Maine at Machias (ME)
The U of Montana–Missoula (MT)
U of Pittsburgh (PA)
U of Vermont (VT)
Western Washington U (WA)
York U (ON, Canada)

Majors Index
Environmental Engineering–Exercise Sciences

ENVIRONMENTAL ENGINEERING
Bradley U (IL)
California Inst of Technology (CA)
California Polytechnic State U, San Luis Obispo (CA)
California State U, Northridge (CA)
Carleton U (ON, Canada)
Carnegie Mellon U (PA)
Christian Brothers U (TN)
Clarkson U (NY)
Colorado School of Mines (CO)
Colorado State U (CO)
Columbia U, School of Engineering & Applied Sci (NY)
Concordia U (PQ, Canada)
Cornell U (NY)
Florida State U (FL)
Gannon U (PA)
The George Washington U (DC)
Harvard U (MA)
Humboldt State U (CA)
Illinois Inst of Technology (IL)
Johns Hopkins U (MD)
Lafayette Coll (PA)
Louisiana State U and A&M Coll (LA)
Manhattan Coll (NY)
Marietta Coll (OH)
Marquette U (WI)
Massachusetts Inst of Technology (MA)
Massachusetts Maritime Academy (MA)
Mercer U (GA)
Michigan Technological U (MI)
Montana Tech of The U of Montana (MT)
New Mexico Inst of Mining and Technology (NM)
North Carolina State U (NC)
Northern Arizona U (AZ)
The Ohio State U (OH)
Old Dominion U (VA)
Oregon State U (OR)
Penn State U Harrisburg Campus of the Capital Coll (PA)
Penn State U Univ Park Campus (PA)
Polytechnic U of Puerto Rico (PR)
Rensselaer Polytechnic Inst (NY)
Rice U (TX)
Roger Williams U (RI)
Seattle U (WA)
South Dakota School of Mines and Technology (SD)
South Dakota State U (SD)
Southern Methodist U (TX)
Stanford U (CA)
State U of NY Coll of Environ Sci and Forestry (NY)
Stevens Inst of Technology (NJ)
Syracuse U (NY)
Texas A&M U (TX)
Texas A&M U–Kingsville (TX)
Texas Tech U (TX)
Tufts U (MA)
Tulane U (LA)
United States Air Force Academy (CO)
United States Military Academy (NY)
U of Alberta (AB, Canada)
U of Calif, Berkeley (CA)
U of Calif, Irvine (CA)
U of Calif, Riverside (CA)
U of Central Florida (FL)
U of Colorado at Boulder (CO)
U of Delaware (DE)
U of Florida (FL)
U of Guelph (ON, Canada)
U of Hartford (CT)
The U of Iowa (IA)
U of Miami (FL)
U of Michigan (MI)
U of Nevada, Reno (NV)
U of New Hampshire (NH)
U of North Dakota (ND)
U of Notre Dame (IN)
U of Oklahoma (OK)
U of Regina (SK, Canada)
U of Southern California (CA)
U of Utah (UT)
U of Waterloo (ON, Canada)
U of Windsor (ON, Canada)
U of Wisconsin–Madison (WI)
Utah State U (UT)
Wentworth Inst of Technology (MA)
Western Michigan U (MI)
Wilkes U (PA)
Worcester Polytechnic Inst (MA)

ENVIRONMENTAL HEALTH
Boise State U (ID)
Bowling Green State U (OH)
California State U, Los Angeles (CA)
California State U, Northridge (CA)
California State U, Sacramento (CA)
Clarkson U (NY)
Colorado State U (CO)
Delaware State U (DE)
East Carolina U (NC)
East Central U (OK)
Eastern Kentucky U (KY)
East Tennessee State U (TN)
Ferris State U (MI)
Hampshire Coll (MA)
Illinois State U (IL)
Indiana State U (IN)
Indiana U of Pennsylvania (PA)
Iowa Wesleyan Coll (IA)
Massachusetts Inst of Technology (MA)
MCP Hahnemann U (PA)
Missouri Southern State Coll (MO)
Oakland U (MI)
Ohio U (OH)
Oregon State U (OR)
Rutgers, State U of NJ, Cook Coll (NJ)
Ryerson Polytechnic U (ON, Canada)
Salisbury State U (MD)
San Diego State U (CA)
San Jose State U (CA)
Texas Southern U (TX)
U Coll of Cape Breton (NS, Canada)
U of Arkansas at Little Rock (AR)
U of Georgia (GA)
U of Michigan–Flint (MI)
U of Southern Colorado (CO)
U of Southern Maine (ME)
U of Washington (WA)
U of Wisconsin–Eau Claire (WI)
West Chester U of Pennsylvania (PA)
Western Carolina U (NC)
Wright State U (OH)
York Coll of the City U of New York (NY)

ENVIRONMENTAL TECHNOLOGY
Arizona State U East (AZ)
Baker U (KS)
California State U, Long Beach (CA)
Lake Superior State U (MI)
Middle Tennessee State U (TN)
New York Inst of Technology (NY)
San Jose State U (CA)
Shawnee State U (OH)
Texas Southern U (TX)
Unity Coll (ME)
U Coll of Cape Breton (NS, Canada)
U of Delaware (DE)
U of Guelph (ON, Canada)
U of North Dakota (ND)
Western Kentucky U (KY)

EQUESTRIAN STUDIES
Averett Coll (VA)
Cazenovia Coll (NY)
Centenary Coll (NJ)
Colorado State U (CO)
Delaware Valley Coll (PA)
Johnson & Wales U (RI)
Lake Erie Coll (OH)
Midway Coll (KY)
Mount Ida Coll (MA)
The Ohio State U (OH)
Oregon State U (OR)
Otterbein Coll (OH)
Rocky Mountain Coll (MT)
St. Andrews Presbyterian Coll (NC)
Saint Mary-of-the-Woods Coll (IN)
State U of NY Coll of A&T at Morrisville (NY)
Stephens Coll (MO)
Sul Ross State U (TX)
Teikyo Post U (CT)
Truman State U (MO)
The U of Findlay (OH)
U of Louisville (KY)
U of Minnesota, Crookston (MN)
U of New Hampshire (NH)
U of Wisconsin–River Falls (WI)
Virginia Intermont Coll (VA)
William Woods U (MO)
Wilson Coll (PA)

EUROPEAN HISTORY
Bard Coll (NY)
Brevard Coll (NC)
Calvin Coll (MI)
Salve Regina U (RI)
U of Puerto Rico, Río Piedras (PR)

EUROPEAN STUDIES
American U (DC)
The American U of Paris (France)
Amherst Coll (MA)
Antioch Coll (OH)
Bard Coll (NY)
Barnard Coll (NY)
Beloit Coll (WI)
Bennington Coll (VT)
Brandeis U (MA)
Brigham Young U (UT)
Brock U (ON, Canada)
Canisius Coll (NY)
Carleton U (ON, Canada)
Carnegie Mellon U (PA)
Case Western Reserve U (OH)
Chapman U (CA)
Chatham Coll (PA)
Claremont McKenna Coll (CA)
The Coll of William and Mary (VA)
The Coll of Wooster (OH)
Connecticut Coll (CT)
Cornell U (NY)
Elmira Coll (NY)
The Evergreen State Coll (WA)
Fort Lewis Coll (CO)
George Mason U (VA)
Georgetown Coll (KY)
The George Washington U (DC)
Hamline U (MN)
Hampshire Coll (MA)
Harvard U (MA)
Hillsdale Coll (MI)
Hobart and William Smith Colls (NY)
Howard Payne U (TX)
Huntingdon Coll (AL)
Illinois Wesleyan U (IL)
Lake Forest Coll (IL)
Long Island U, Southampton Coll, Friends World Program (NY)
Loyola Marymount U (CA)
Marlboro Coll (VT)
Millsaps Coll (MS)
Mount Holyoke Coll (MA)
New York U (NY)
Ohio U (OH)
Pitzer Coll (CA)
Richmond, The American International U in London (United Kingdom)
Salem State Coll (MA)
San Diego State U (CA)
San Jose State U (CA)
Sarah Lawrence Coll (NY)
Schiller International U (Germany)
Scripps Coll (CA)
Seattle Pacific U (WA)
Simon's Rock Coll of Bard (MA)
Southern Methodist U (TX)
Southwest Texas State U (TX)
State U of NY Coll at Brockport (NY)
Trinity U (TX)
United States Military Academy (NY)
U of British Columbia (BC, Canada)
U of Calif, Los Angeles (CA)
U of Guelph (ON, Canada)
U of Kansas (KS)
U of Michigan (MI)
U of Minnesota, Morris (MN)
U of Minnesota, Twin Cities Campus (MN)
U of New Mexico (NM)
The U of North Carolina at Chapel Hill (NC)
The U of North Carolina at Greensboro (NC)
U of Northern Iowa (IA)
U of Richmond (VA)
U of San Diego (CA)
U of South Carolina (SC)
U of the South (TN)
U of Toronto (ON, Canada)
U of Vermont (VT)
U of Washington (WA)
Valparaiso U (IN)
Vanderbilt U (TN)
Washington U in St. Louis (MO)
Western Michigan U (MI)

EVOLUTIONARY BIOLOGY
Coll of the Atlantic (ME)
Dartmouth Coll (NH)
Florida State U (FL)
Hampshire Coll (MA)
Harvard U (MA)
Oregon State U (OR)
Rice U (TX)
Rutgers, State U of NJ, Camden Coll of Arts & Scis (NJ)
Rutgers, State U of NJ, Cook Coll (NJ)
Rutgers, State U of NJ, Douglass Coll (NJ)
Rutgers, State U of NJ, Livingston Coll (NJ)
Rutgers, State U of NJ, Rutgers Coll (NJ)
Rutgers, State U of NJ, U Coll–Camden (NJ)
Rutgers, State U of NJ, U Coll–New Brunswick (NJ)
Tulane U (LA)
U of Maryland, Coll Park (MD)
U of New Hampshire (NH)
U of Rochester (NY)
The U of Texas at Austin (TX)
Yale U (CT)

EXECUTIVE ASSISTANT
Eastern Michigan U (MI)
Robert Morris Coll (IL)
U of Central Arkansas (AR)

EXERCISE SCIENCES
Abilene Christian U (TX)
Acadia U (NS, Canada)
Adams State Coll (CO)
Adrian Coll (MI)
Albertson Coll of Idaho (ID)
Alma Coll (MI)
Andrews U (MI)
Arizona State U (AZ)
Augustana Coll (SD)
Ball State U (IN)
Barry U (FL)
Bartlesville Wesleyan Coll (OK)
Bastyr U (WA)
Becker Coll (MA)
Bethel Coll (TN)
Biola U (CA)
Bloomsburg U of Pennsylvania (PA)
Bluffton Coll (OH)
Boise State U (ID)
Boston U (MA)
Bowling Green State U (OH)
Brevard Coll (NC)
Bridgewater State Coll (MA)
Brock U (ON, Canada)
Cabrini Coll (PA)
California Baptist U (CA)
California State U, Chico (CA)
California State U, Hayward (CA)
California State U, Long Beach (CA)
Calvin Coll (MI)
Carroll Coll (WI)
Carson-Newman Coll (TN)
Castleton State Coll (VT)
Central Coll (IA)
Chapman U (CA)
Chowan Coll (NC)
Coker Coll (SC)
Colby-Sawyer Coll (NH)
Coll of Mount Saint Vincent (NY)
The Coll of St. Scholastica (MN)
Colorado State U (CO)
Columbia Union Coll (MD)
Columbus State U (GA)
Concordia Coll (MN)
Concordia U (CA)
Concordia U (IL)
Concordia U (NE)
Concordia U (PQ, Canada)
Cornell Coll (IA)
Creighton U (NE)
Dakota State U (SD)
Dalhousie U (NS, Canada)
David Lipscomb U (TN)
Defiance Coll (OH)
Dordt Coll (IA)
Drury U (MO)
East Carolina U (NC)
Eastern Kentucky U (KY)
Eastern Washington U (WA)
East Stroudsburg U of Pennsylvania (PA)
Elmhurst Coll (IL)
Emmanuel Coll (GA)
Fitchburg State Coll (MA)
Florida Atlantic U (FL)
Furman U (SC)
The George Washington U (DC)
Georgia Southern U (GA)
Gonzaga U (WA)
Gordon Coll (MA)
Grand Canyon U (AZ)
Hamline U (MN)
Hampshire Coll (MA)
Harding U (AR)
Hardin-Simmons U (TX)
High Point U (NC)
Hofstra U (NY)
Hope Coll (MI)
Houston Baptist U (TX)
Howard Payne U (TX)
Humboldt State U (CA)
Huntingdon Coll (AL)
Huntington Coll (IN)
Indiana State U (IN)
Inter American U of PR, San Germán Campus (PR)
Iowa Wesleyan Coll (IA)
Ithaca Coll (NY)
Jacksonville State U (AL)
John Brown U (AR)
Johnson State Coll (VT)
Judson Coll (AL)
Kansas State U (KS)
Kent State U (OH)
Lakeland Coll (WI)
Lake Superior State U (MI)
Lander U (SC)
Lasell Coll (MA)
La Sierra U (CA)
Lenoir-Rhyne Coll (NC)
Lewis-Clark State Coll (ID)
Liberty U (VA)
Limestone Coll (SC)
Linfield Coll (OR)
Longwood Coll (VA)
Louisiana Coll (LA)
Lynchburg Coll (VA)
Malone Coll (OH)
Marshall U (WV)
Memorial U of Newfoundland (NF, Canada)
Meredith Coll (NC)
Mesa State Coll (CO)
Messiah Coll (PA)
Metropolitan State Coll of Denver (CO)
Miami U (OH)
Michigan State U (MI)
MidAmerica Nazarene U (KS)
Midwestern State U (TX)
Milligan Coll (TN)
Mississippi U for Women (MS)
Missouri Southern State Coll (MO)
Missouri Western State Coll (MO)
Mount Senario Coll (WI)
Mount Union Coll (OH)
Nebraska Wesleyan U (NE)
New Mexico Highlands U (NM)
North Central Coll (IL)
Northeastern U (MA)
Northern Arizona U (AZ)
Northern Kentucky U (KY)
Northern Michigan U (MI)
North Park U (IL)
Northwestern Coll (IA)
Notre Dame Coll (NH)
Oakland U (MI)
Occidental Coll (CA)
The Ohio State U (OH)
Ohio U (OH)
Oklahoma Baptist U (OK)
Oregon State U (OR)
Pacific Union Coll (CA)
Pacific U (OR)
Piedmont Coll (GA)

Peterson's Guide to Four-Year Colleges 2001   www.petersons.com   1013

Majors Index
Exercise Sciences–Fine/Studio Arts

Plymouth State Coll (NH)
Redeemer Coll (ON, Canada)
Rivier Coll (NH)
Rocky Mountain Coll (MT)
Rutgers, State U of NJ, Cook Coll (NJ)
Rutgers, State U of NJ, Douglass Coll (NJ)
Rutgers, State U of NJ, Livingston Coll (NJ)
Rutgers, State U of NJ, Rutgers Coll (NJ)
Rutgers, State U of NJ, U Coll–New Brunswick (NJ)
St. Cloud State U (MN)
St. Francis Xavier U (NS, Canada)
Saint Louis U (MO)
St. Mary's U of San Antonio (TX)
Salem State Coll (MA)
Sam Houston State U (TX)
San Jose State U (CA)
Schreiner Coll (TX)
Seattle Pacific U (WA)
Simon Fraser U (BC, Canada)
Skidmore Coll (NY)
Slippery Rock U of Pennsylvania (PA)
Southern Adventist U (TN)
Southwestern Adventist U (TX)
State U of NY at Buffalo (NY)
State U of NY Coll at Brockport (NY)
State U of NY Coll at Buffalo (NY)
Stetson U (FL)
Syracuse U (NY)
Tennessee Wesleyan Coll (TN)
Texas Wesleyan U (TX)
Transylvania U (KY)
Trevecca Nazarene U (TN)
Truman State U (MO)
Tulane U (LA)
Université de Sherbrooke (PQ, Canada)
U of Alaska Fairbanks (AK)
U of Alberta (AB, Canada)
U of Calgary (AB, Canada)
U of Calif, Los Angeles (CA)
U of Dayton (OH)
U of Delaware (DE)
U of Evansville (IN)
U of Florida (FL)
U of Houston (TX)
U of Houston–Clear Lake (TX)
The U of Iowa (IA)
U of Maryland, Coll Park (MD)
U of Massachusetts Amherst (MA)
U of Massachusetts Lowell (MA)
U of Miami (FL)
U of Michigan (MI)
U of Minnesota, Duluth (MN)
U of Mississippi (MS)
U of Nebraska–Lincoln (NE)
U of Nevada, Las Vegas (NV)
U of New Brunswick, Fredericton (NB, Canada)
U of New Brunswick, Saint John (NB, Canada)
U of New Hampshire (NH)
U of Northern Colorado (CO)
U of North Texas (TX)
U of Oregon (OR)
U of Puget Sound (WA)
U of Regina (SK, Canada)
U of San Francisco (CA)
U of Sioux Falls (SD)
U of South Carolina (SC)
U of Southern California (CA)
U of Southern Colorado (CO)
U of Southern Indiana (IN)
The U of Tampa (FL)
The U of Tennessee Knoxville (TN)
The U of Texas at Tyler (TX)
U of the Sacred Heart (PR)
U of Tulsa (OK)
U of Utah (UT)
U of Victoria (BC, Canada)
U of Windsor (ON, Canada)
U of Wisconsin–Eau Claire (WI)
U of Wisconsin–La Crosse (WI)
U of Wyoming (WY)
Upper Iowa U (IA)
Voorhees Coll (SC)
Wake Forest U (NC)
Walla Walla Coll (WA)
Warner Pacific Coll (OR)
Warner Southern Coll (FL)
Washington State U (WA)

Wayne State Coll (NE)
Weber State U (UT)
Wesley Coll (DE)
West Chester U of Pennsylvania (PA)
Western Michigan U (MI)
Western State Coll of Colorado (CO)
Western Washington U (WA)
West Liberty State Coll (WV)
Westmont Coll (CA)
West Virginia U (WV)
Wheaton Coll (IL)
Willamette U (OR)
William Paterson U of New Jersey (NJ)
Winona State U (MN)
Youngstown State U (OH)

EXPERIMENTAL PSYCHOLOGY
Alfred U (NY)
Cedar Crest Coll (PA)
Embry-Riddle Aeronautical U (FL)
Florida State U (FL)
La Sierra U (CA)
Longwood Coll (VA)
Marlboro Coll (VT)
Millikin U (IL)
Moravian Coll (PA)
New Mexico Inst of Mining and Technology (NM)
Queens Coll of the City U of NY (NY)
Redeemer Coll (ON, Canada)
Southwestern U (TX)
Tufts U (MA)
U of Alberta (AB, Canada)
U of British Columbia (BC, Canada)
U of Regina (SK, Canada)
U of South Carolina (SC)
U of Southern Colorado (CO)
U of Wisconsin–Madison (WI)

FAMILY/COMMUNITY STUDIES
Andrews U (MI)
Bowling Green State U (OH)
Brandon U (MB, Canada)
Brigham Young U (UT)
Cornell U (NY)
Eastern Illinois U (IL)
Eastern Kentucky U (KY)
Goshen Coll (IN)
Iowa State U of Science and Technology (IA)
Kent State U (OH)
Liberty U (VA)
Long Island U, Southampton Coll, Friends World Program (NY)
Messiah Coll (PA)
Michigan State U (MI)
Ohio U (OH)
Oklahoma Christian U of Science and Arts (OK)
Oklahoma State U (OK)
Olivet Nazarene U (IL)
Oregon State U (OR)
Pacific Union Coll (CA)
Prairie View A&M U (TX)
Saint Paul U (ON, Canada)
Seton Hill Coll (PA)
Southern Utah U (UT)
Syracuse U (NY)
Toccoa Falls Coll (GA)
Union U (TN)
U of Calif, Santa Cruz (CA)
U of Delaware (DE)
U of Florida (FL)
U of Maryland, Coll Park (MD)
U of Minnesota, Twin Cities Campus (MN)
The U of North Carolina at Greensboro (NC)
U of Northern Iowa (IA)
U of Vermont (VT)
Utah State U (UT)
Youngstown State U (OH)

FAMILY/CONSUMER STUDIES
Alabama A&M U (AL)
Andrews U (MI)
Ashland U (OH)
Baldwin-Wallace Coll (OH)
Ball State U (IN)
Berea Coll (KY)
Bradley U (IL)
California State U, Fresno (CA)

California State U, Northridge (CA)
California State U, Sacramento (CA)
Carson-Newman Coll (TN)
Chadron State Coll (NE)
Concordia Coll (MN)
Cornell U (NY)
David Lipscomb U (TN)
Fairmont State Coll (WV)
Florida State U (FL)
Framingham State Coll (MA)
Hampshire Coll (MA)
Harding U (AR)
Howard U (DC)
Illinois State U (IL)
Indiana State U (IN)
Indiana U Bloomington (IN)
Iowa State U of Science and Technology (IA)
Lambuth U (TN)
Louisiana Coll (LA)
Miami U (OH)
Michigan State U (MI)
Minnesota State U, Mankato (MN)
Mississippi Coll (MS)
Mount Saint Vincent U (NS, Canada)
Murray State U (KY)
New Mexico State U (NM)
North Carolina Central U (NC)
North Dakota State U (ND)
Northern Michigan U (MI)
Northwest Missouri State U (MO)
Ohio U (OH)
Oklahoma State U (OK)
Oregon State U (OR)
Pacific Union Coll (CA)
Ryerson Polytechnic U (ON, Canada)
Saint Joseph Coll (CT)
St. Olaf Coll (MN)
Seattle Pacific U (WA)
Seton Hill Coll (PA)
Shepherd Coll (WV)
Southeast Missouri State U (MO)
Tennessee State U (TN)
The U of Akron (OH)
U of Alberta (AB, Canada)
U of British Columbia (BC, Canada)
U of Delaware (DE)
U of Hawaii at Manoa (HI)
The U of Memphis (TN)
U of Missouri–Columbia (MO)
U of Montevallo (AL)
U of Nebraska at Kearney (NE)
U of Nebraska–Lincoln (NE)
U of New Hampshire (NH)
U of Northern Iowa (IA)
U of Prince Edward Island (PE, Canada)
The U of Tennessee at Chattanooga (TN)
U of Utah (UT)
U of Vermont (VT)
U of Windsor (ON, Canada)
U of Wisconsin–Madison (WI)
U of Wisconsin–Stevens Point (WI)
U of Wyoming (WY)
Wayne State Coll (NE)

FAMILY LIVING/PARENTHOOD
U of North Texas (TX)

FAMILY RESOURCE MANAGEMENT STUDIES
Arizona State U (AZ)
Central Michigan U (MI)
Cornell U (NY)
Eastern Michigan U (MI)
George Fox U (OR)
Iowa State U of Science and Technology (IA)
Michigan State U (MI)
Middle Tennessee State U (TN)
New Mexico State U (NM)
Ohio U (OH)
U of Connecticut (CT)
U of Massachusetts Amherst (MA)

FAMILY STUDIES
Anderson U (IN)
Brigham Young U (UT)
Central Michigan U (MI)
Gallaudet U (DC)
Michigan State U (MI)
The Ohio State U (OH)

Park U (MO)
Point Loma Nazarene U (CA)
Southern Adventist U (TN)
Syracuse U (NY)
Texas Tech U (TX)
U of Guelph (ON, Canada)
The U of North Carolina at Chapel Hill (NC)
U of Southern Mississippi (MS)
The U of Tennessee Knoxville (TN)
Weber State U (UT)
Western Michigan U (MI)

FARM/RANCH MANAGEMENT
California Polytechnic State U, San Luis Obispo (CA)
California State Polytechnic U, Pomona (CA)
Cazenovia Coll (NY)
Colorado State U (CO)
Cornell U (NY)
Dickinson State U (ND)
Eastern Kentucky U (KY)
Iowa State U of Science and Technology (IA)
Johnson & Wales U (RI)
North Dakota State U (ND)
Northwest Missouri State U (MO)
The Ohio State U (OH)
Oklahoma State U (OK)
U of Alberta (AB, Canada)
The U of Findlay (OH)
U of Wisconsin–Madison (WI)
U of Wyoming (WY)

FILM/VIDEO PRODUCTION
Academy of Art Coll (CA)
The Advertising Arts Coll (CA)
Allentown Coll of St. Francis de Sales (PA)
American InterContinental U (CA)
American InterContinental U, Atlanta (GA)
American InterContinental U (United Kingdom)
American U (DC)
Antioch Coll (OH)
Atlanta Coll of Art (GA)
Bard Coll (NY)
Boston U (MA)
Brooks Inst of Photography (CA)
Brown U (RI)
Burlington Coll (VT)
California State U, Long Beach (CA)
California State U, Northridge (CA)
Chapman U (CA)
City Coll of the City U of NY (NY)
Coll of Santa Fe (NM)
Columbia Coll Chicago (IL)
Columbia Coll–Hollywood (CA)
Concordia U (PQ, Canada)
Drexel U (PA)
Emerson Coll (MA)
The Evergreen State Coll (WA)
Fairleigh Dickinson U, Florham-Madison Campus (NJ)
Fitchburg State Coll (MA)
Five Towns Coll (NY)
Florida State U (FL)
Grand Valley State U (MI)
Hampshire Coll (MA)
Hofstra U (NY)
The Illinois Inst of Art at Schaumburg (IL)
Iowa Wesleyan Coll (IA)
Ithaca Coll (NY)
Kent State U (OH)
Long Island U, Southampton Coll, Friends World Program (NY)
Loyola Marymount U (CA)
Maharishi U of Management (IA)
Massachusetts Coll of Art (MA)
Minneapolis Coll of Art and Design (MN)
Montana State U–Bozeman (MT)
New York U (NY)
North Carolina School of the Arts (NC)
Northern Michigan U (MI)
Oklahoma City U (OK)
Point Park Coll (PA)
Pratt Inst (NY)
Quinnipiac U (CT)
Rochester Inst of Technology (NY)
Sacred Heart U (CT)
St. Cloud State U (MN)

San Diego State U (CA)
Sarah Lawrence Coll (NY)
Savannah Coll of Art and Design (GA)
School of the Art Inst of Chicago (IL)
School of the Museum of Fine Arts (MA)
School of Visual Arts (NY)
Southern Adventist U (TN)
Syracuse U (NY)
Temple U (PA)
U of Calif, Berkeley (CA)
U of Calif, Santa Cruz (CA)
U of Central Florida (FL)
U of Hartford (CT)
U of Illinois at Chicago (IL)
The U of Iowa (IA)
U of Miami (FL)
The U of North Carolina at Greensboro (NC)
U of Oklahoma (OK)
U of Regina (SK, Canada)
U of South Dakota (SD)
U of Southern California (CA)
U of Southern Colorado (CO)
The U of Texas at Arlington (TX)
The U of the Arts (PA)
Vanguard U of Southern California (CA)
Villa Julie Coll (MD)
Waldorf Coll (IA)
Webster U (MO)
York U (ON, Canada)
Youngstown State U (OH)

FINANCIAL PLANNING
Baylor U (TX)
Bethany Coll (KS)
Bryant Coll (RI)
Central Michigan U (MI)
Marywood U (PA)
Medaille Coll (NY)
The Ohio State U at Lima (OH)
Roger Williams U (RI)
Trinity Christian Coll (IL)

FINANCIAL SERVICES MARKETING
Nipissing U (ON, Canada)

FINE/STUDIO ARTS
Abilene Christian U (TX)
Academy of Art Coll (CA)
Adams State Coll (CO)
Adelphi U (NY)
Alberta Coll of Art and Design (AB, Canada)
Albertus Magnus Coll (CT)
Alfred U (NY)
Allegheny Coll (PA)
American Academy of Art (IL)
American U (DC)
Amherst Coll (MA)
Anderson Coll (SC)
Anderson U (IN)
Anna Maria Coll (MA)
Appalachian State U (NC)
Aquinas Coll (MI)
Arizona State U (AZ)
Art Academy of Cincinnati (OH)
Asbury Coll (KY)
Ashland U (OH)
Assumption Coll (MA)
Atlanta Coll of Art (GA)
Auburn U (AL)
Augsburg Coll (MN)
Augustana Coll (IL)
Avila Coll (MO)
Baker U (KS)
Baldwin-Wallace Coll (OH)
Ball State U (IN)
Barat Coll (IL)
Bard Coll (NY)
Barton Coll (NC)
Baylor U (TX)
Bay Path Coll (MA)
Beaver Coll (PA)
Belmont U (TN)
Beloit Coll (WI)
Bemidji State U (MN)
Bennington Coll (VT)
Berea Coll (KY)
Berry Coll (GA)
Bethany Coll (WV)
Bethel Coll (KS)
Bethel Coll (MN)

1014   www.petersons.com   Peterson's Guide to Four-Year Colleges 2001

Majors Index
Fine/Studio Arts

Biola U (CA)
Birmingham-Southern Coll (AL)
Bloomsburg U of Pennsylvania (PA)
Boston Coll (MA)
Bowdoin Coll (ME)
Bradley U (IL)
Brandeis U (MA)
Brenau U (GA)
Brevard Coll (NC)
Bridgewater State Coll (MA)
Brock U (ON, Canada)
Brown U (RI)
Cabrini Coll (PA)
California Baptist U (CA)
California Coll of Arts and Crafts (CA)
California Inst of the Arts (CA)
California State U, Chico (CA)
California State U, Dominguez Hills (CA)
California State U, Fullerton (CA)
California State U, Hayward (CA)
California State U, Long Beach (CA)
California State U, Los Angeles (CA)
California State U, Northridge (CA)
Calvin Coll (MI)
Campbell U (NC)
Capital U (OH)
Cardinal Stritch U (WI)
Carleton Coll (MN)
Carnegie Mellon U (PA)
Carroll Coll (WI)
Carthage Coll (WI)
Cedar Crest Coll (PA)
Centenary Coll of Louisiana (LA)
Ctr for Creative Studies—Coll of Art and Design (MI)
Central Missouri State U (MO)
Chapman U (CA)
Chatham Coll (PA)
Chestnut Hill Coll (PA)
Chicago State U (IL)
Chowan Coll (NC)
Clarke Coll (IA)
Clark U (MA)
Clemson U (SC)
Coe Coll (IA)
Coker Coll (SC)
Coll of Charleston (SC)
Coll of Mount St. Joseph (OH)
The Coll of New Jersey (NJ)
The Coll of New Rochelle (NY)
Coll of Notre Dame (CA)
Coll of Saint Benedict (MN)
Coll of St. Catherine (MN)
The Coll of Saint Rose (NY)
Coll of Santa Fe (NM)
Coll of the Holy Cross (MA)
Coll of the Ozarks (MO)
The Coll of Wooster (OH)
The Colorado Coll (CO)
Colorado State U (CO)
Columbia Coll (MO)
Columbia Coll (SC)
Columbia Coll Chicago (IL)
Columbus Coll of Art and Design (OH)
Concordia Coll (MN)
Concordia Coll (NE)
Concordia U (PQ, Canada)
Converse Coll (SC)
The Corcoran Coll of Art and Design (DC)
Cornell U (NY)
Cornish Coll of the Arts (WA)
Daemen Coll (NY)
Dartmouth Coll (NH)
David Lipscomb U (TN)
Davidson Coll (NC)
Denison U (OH)
DePaul U (IL)
DePauw U (IN)
Dickinson Coll (PA)
Dominican U (IL)
Drake U (IA)
Drury U (MO)
Duquesne U (PA)
East Carolina U (NC)
Eastern Illinois U (IL)
Eastern Washington U (WA)
East Tennessee State U (TN)
Edinboro U of Pennsylvania (PA)
Elmira Coll (NY)
Emmanuel Coll (MA)

Endicott Coll (MA)
The Evergreen State Coll (WA)
Fairleigh Dickinson U, Florham-Madison Campus (NJ)
Fairleigh Dickinson U, Teaneck-Hackensack Campus (NJ)
Fashion Inst of Technology (NY)
Felician Coll (NJ)
Ferrum Coll (VA)
Finlandia U (MI)
Flagler Coll (FL)
Florida Gulf Coast U (FL)
Florida International U (FL)
Florida Southern Coll (FL)
Florida State U (FL)
Fontbonne Coll (MO)
Fordham U (NY)
Fort Lewis Coll (CO)
Framingham State Coll (MA)
Franklin Pierce Coll (NH)
Furman U (SC)
Gallaudet U (DC)
George Mason U (VA)
The George Washington U (DC)
Georgia Southwestern State U (GA)
Gettysburg Coll (PA)
Goddard Coll (VT)
Governors State U (IL)
Graceland Coll (IA)
Grand Canyon U (AZ)
Grand Valley State U (MI)
Grand View Coll (IA)
Green Mountain Coll (VT)
Hamilton Coll (NY)
Hamline U (MN)
Hampden-Sydney Coll (VA)
Hampshire Coll (MA)
Harvard U (MA)
High Point U (NC)
Hiram Coll (OH)
Hobart and William Smith Colls (NY)
Hofstra U (NY)
Hollins U (VA)
Hope Coll (MI)
Howard Payne U (TX)
Humboldt State U (CA)
Hunter Coll of the City U of NY (NY)
Illinois Wesleyan U (IL)
Indiana State U (IN)
Indiana U Bloomington (IN)
Indiana U–Purdue U Fort Wayne (IN)
Indiana U–Purdue U Indianapolis (IN)
Indiana U South Bend (IN)
Indiana U Southeast (IN)
Iowa Wesleyan Coll (IA)
Ithaca Coll (NY)
Jacksonville U (FL)
Johnson State Coll (VT)
Judson Coll (IL)
Juniata Coll (PA)
Kean U (NJ)
Kendall Coll of Art and Design (MI)
Kent State U (OH)
Kentucky State U (KY)
Kenyon Coll (OH)
King Coll (TN)
Kutztown U of Pennsylvania (PA)
Lafayette Coll (PA)
Lake Erie Coll (OH)
Lake Forest Coll (IL)
Lamar U (TX)
Lambuth U (TN)
La Sierra U (CA)
Lawrence U (WI)
Lewis U (IL)
Limestone Coll (SC)
Lindenwood U (MO)
Long Island U, C.W. Post Campus (NY)
Long Island U, Southampton Coll (NY)
Long Island U, Southampton Coll, Friends World Program (NY)
Longwood Coll (VA)
Loras Coll (IA)
Louisiana Coll (LA)
Louisiana State U and A&M Coll (LA)
Loyola Marymount U (CA)
Lycoming Coll (PA)
Lynchburg Coll (VA)
Macalester Coll (MN)

MacMurray Coll (IL)
Manchester Coll (IN)
Manhattanville Coll (NY)
Mansfield U of Pennsylvania (PA)
Marian Coll (IN)
Marietta Coll (OH)
Marist Coll (NY)
Marlboro Coll (VT)
Mary Baldwin Coll (VA)
Marygrove Coll (MI)
Maryland Inst, Coll of Art (MD)
Marymount Coll (NY)
Marymount Manhattan Coll (NY)
Maryville Coll (TN)
Maryville U of Saint Louis (MO)
Mary Washington Coll (VA)
Marywood U (PA)
Massachusetts Coll of Art (MA)
Memphis Coll of Art (TN)
Mercyhurst Coll (PA)
Meredith Coll (NC)
Merrimack Coll (MA)
Messiah Coll (PA)
Miami U (OH)
Michigan State U (MI)
Middlebury Coll (VT)
Millikin U (IL)
Mills Coll (CA)
Minneapolis Coll of Art and Design (MN)
Minnesota State U, Mankato (MN)
Minnesota State U Moorhead (MN)
Monmouth U (NJ)
Montana State U–Bozeman (MT)
Montserrat Coll of Art (MA)
Moore Coll of Art and Design (PA)
Moravian Coll (PA)
Morehead State U (KY)
Morningside Coll (IA)
Mount Allison U (NB, Canada)
Mount Holyoke Coll (MA)
Mount Senario Coll (WI)
Muhlenberg Coll (PA)
Murray State U (KY)
Nazareth Coll of Rochester (NY)
New Coll of the U of South Florida (FL)
New England Coll (NH)
New Mexico State U (NM)
New World School of the Arts (FL)
New York Inst of Technology (NY)
New York U (NY)
North Carolina Central U (NC)
Northeastern State U (OK)
Northern Arizona U (AZ)
Northern Illinois U (IL)
Northern Kentucky U (KY)
Northern Michigan U (MI)
Northland Coll (WI)
North Park U (IL)
Northwestern Coll (MN)
Northwest Missouri State U (MO)
Notre Dame Coll of Ohio (OH)
Nova Scotia Coll of Art and Design (NS, Canada)
Oberlin Coll (OH)
Occidental Coll (CA)
Ohio Dominican Coll (OH)
The Ohio State U (OH)
Ohio Wesleyan U (OH)
Oklahoma Baptist U (OK)
Oklahoma City U (OK)
Oklahoma State U (OK)
Open Learning Agency (BC, Canada)
Oregon State U (OR)
Otis Coll of Art and Design (CA)
Pacific Lutheran U (WA)
Pacific Northwest Coll of Art (OR)
Pacific Union Coll (CA)
Paier Coll of Art, Inc. (CT)
Park U (MO)
Pennsylvania School of Art & Design (PA)
Piedmont Coll (GA)
Pine Manor Coll (MA)
Pittsburg State U (KS)
Plattsburgh State U of NY (NY)
Plymouth State Coll (NH)
Pomona Coll (CA)
Pratt Inst (NY)
Principia Coll (IL)
Providence Coll (RI)
Queens Coll (NC)
Queens Coll of the City U of NY (NY)

Queen's U at Kingston (ON, Canada)
Quincy U (IL)
Ramapo Coll of New Jersey (NJ)
Randolph-Macon Coll (VA)
Randolph-Macon Woman's Coll (VA)
Reed Coll (OR)
Rhodes Coll (TN)
Richmond, The American International U in London (United Kingdom)
Ringling School of Art and Design (FL)
River Coll (NH)
Roberts Wesleyan Coll (NY)
Rochester Inst of Technology (NY)
Rockford Coll (IL)
Rollins Coll (FL)
Rosemont Coll (PA)
Rowan U (NJ)
Saginaw Valley State U (MI)
St. Ambrose U (IA)
St. Andrews Presbyterian Coll (NC)
St. Cloud State U (MN)
Saint John's U (MN)
St. John's U (NY)
Saint Louis U (MO)
Saint Mary-of-the-Woods Coll (IN)
Saint Mary's U of Minnesota (MN)
Saint Peter's Coll (NJ)
Saint Vincent Coll (PA)
Salem Coll (NC)
Salve Regina U (RI)
San Francisco Art Inst (CA)
San Jose State U (CA)
Sarah Lawrence Coll (NY)
School of the Art Inst of Chicago (IL)
School of the Museum of Fine Arts (MA)
School of Visual Arts (NY)
Scripps Coll (CA)
Seattle U (WA)
Seton Hill Coll (PA)
Shawnee State U (OH)
Shorter Coll (GA)
Sierra Nevada Coll (NV)
Simon's Rock Coll of Bard (MA)
Skidmore Coll (NY)
Smith Coll (MA)
Sonoma State U (CA)
Southern Illinois U Carbondale (IL)
Southern Illinois U Edwardsville (IL)
Southern Methodist U (TX)
Southwestern U (TX)
Southwest State U (MN)
Southwest Texas State U (TX)
Spring Hill Coll (AL)
State U of NY at Binghamton (NY)
State U of NY at Buffalo (NY)
State U of NY at New Paltz (NY)
State U of NY at Stony Brook (NY)
State U of NY Coll at Brockport (NY)
State U of NY Coll at Buffalo (NY)
State U of NY Coll at Cortland (NY)
State U of NY Coll at Fredonia (NY)
State U of NY Coll at Geneseo (NY)
State U of NY Coll at Oneonta (NY)
State U of NY Coll at Potsdam (NY)
Stonehill Coll (MA)
Swarthmore Coll (PA)
Sweet Briar Coll (VA)
Syracuse U (NY)
Texas Christian U (TX)
Texas Tech U (TX)
Texas Woman's U (TX)
Thomas More Coll (KY)
Transylvania U (KY)
Trinity Coll (CT)
Troy State U (AL)
Truman State U (MO)
Tulane U (LA)
Union Coll (NE)
Union Coll (NY)
Université Laval (PQ, Canada)
U Coll of the Fraser Valley (BC, Canada)
The U of Akron (OH)
The U of Alabama (AL)
The U of Alabama at Birmingham (AL)

U of Alberta (AB, Canada)
The U of Arizona (AZ)
U of British Columbia (BC, Canada)
U of Calif, Irvine (CA)
U of Calif, Riverside (CA)
U of Calif, San Diego (CA)
U of Calif, Santa Barbara (CA)
U of Central Florida (FL)
U of Chicago (IL)
U of Colorado at Boulder (CO)
U of Colorado at Colorado Springs (CO)
U of Colorado at Denver (CO)
U of Connecticut (CT)
U of Dallas (TX)
U of Dayton (OH)
U of Denver (CO)
U of Florida (FL)
U of Georgia (GA)
U of Guelph (ON, Canada)
U of Houston (TX)
U of Illinois at Chicago (IL)
U of Indianapolis (IN)
The U of Iowa (IA)
U of Kansas (KS)
U of Kentucky (KY)
U of Louisville (KY)
U of Maine (ME)
U of Maine at Presque Isle (ME)
U of Maryland, Coll Park (MD)
U of Massachusetts Amherst (MA)
U of Minnesota, Duluth (MN)
U of Minnesota, Morris (MN)
U of Missouri–Kansas City (MO)
U of Missouri–St. Louis (MO)
U of Montevallo (AL)
U of Nebraska at Omaha (NE)
U of Nebraska–Lincoln (NE)
U of New Hampshire (NH)
U of North Alabama (AL)
The U of North Carolina at Asheville (NC)
The U of North Carolina at Chapel Hill (NC)
The U of North Carolina at Charlotte (NC)
The U of North Carolina at Greensboro (NC)
U of Northern Iowa (IA)
U of North Florida (FL)
U of Notre Dame (IN)
U of Oklahoma (OK)
U of Pittsburgh (PA)
U of Redlands (CA)
U of Richmond (VA)
U of Rochester (NY)
U of St. Thomas (TX)
U of San Francisco (CA)
U of South Alabama (AL)
U of South Carolina (SC)
U of South Dakota (SD)
U of Southern California (CA)
The U of Tennessee Knoxville (TN)
The U of Texas at Arlington (TX)
The U of Texas at Austin (TX)
The U of Texas–Pan American (TX)
The U of the Arts (PA)
U of the District of Columbia (DC)
U of the Pacific (CA)
U of the South (TN)
U of Toronto (ON, Canada)
U of Tulsa (OK)
U of Vermont (VT)
U of Victoria (BC, Canada)
U of Waterloo (ON, Canada)
The U of Western Ontario (ON, Canada)
U of West Florida (FL)
U of Windsor (ON, Canada)
U of Wisconsin–Milwaukee (WI)
U of Wisconsin–Stevens Point (WI)
U of Wisconsin–Superior (WI)
U of Wyoming (WY)
Valdosta State U (GA)
Valparaiso U (IN)
Vassar Coll (NY)
Virginia Commonwealth U (VA)
Washington and Lee U (VA)
Washington U in St. Louis (MO)
Webster U (MO)
Wellesley Coll (MA)
Wells Coll (NY)
Wesleyan Coll (GA)
Wesleyan U (CT)
West Chester U of Pennsylvania (PA)

Majors Index
Fine/Studio Arts–Forestry

Western Carolina U (NC)
Western Illinois U (IL)
Western Kentucky U (KY)
Western Maryland Coll (MD)
Western State Coll of Colorado (CO)
Western Washington U (WA)
West Texas A&M U (TX)
West Virginia Wesleyan Coll (WV)
Wheaton Coll (MA)
Whitworth Coll (WA)
Willamette U (OR)
William Paterson U of New Jersey (NJ)
Williams Baptist Coll (AR)
Williams Coll (MA)
William Woods U (MO)
Wingate U (NC)
Winona State U (MN)
Wittenberg U (OH)
Xavier U (OH)
York U (ON, Canada)
Youngstown State U (OH)

FIRE PROTECTION/SAFETY TECHNOLOGY
California State U, Los Angeles (CA)
Eastern Kentucky U (KY)
Oklahoma State U (OK)
Thomas Edison State Coll (NJ)
U of Cincinnati (OH)
U of Maryland, Coll Park (MD)
U of New Haven (CT)
West Texas A&M U (TX)
Worcester Polytechnic Inst (MA)

FIRE SCIENCE
Anna Maria Coll (MA)
Cogswell Polytechnical Coll (CA)
Eastern Kentucky U (KY)
Eastern Oregon U (OR)
Hampton U (VA)
Holy Family Coll (PA)
John Jay Coll of Criminal Justice, the City U of NY (NY)
Lake Superior State U (MI)
Madonna U (MI)
Mercy Coll (NY)
U of Maryland University Coll (MD)
U of New Brunswick, Fredericton (NB, Canada)
U of the District of Columbia (DC)
Wright State U (OH)

FIRE SERVICES ADMINISTRATION
Southern Illinois U Carbondale (IL)
Western Oregon U (OR)

FISH/GAME MANAGEMENT
Delaware State U (DE)
The Evergreen State Coll (WA)
Humboldt State U (CA)
Iowa State U of Science and Technology (IA)
Lake Superior State U (MI)
Lincoln Memorial U (TN)
Michigan State U (MI)
New Mexico State U (NM)
North Dakota State U (ND)
Northern Arizona U (AZ)
Northland Coll (WI)
Oklahoma State U (OK)
Oregon State U (OR)
Pittsburg State U (KS)
Rutgers, State U of NJ, Cook Coll (NJ)
Sheldon Jackson Coll (AK)
South Dakota State U (SD)
Southeastern Oklahoma State U (OK)
State U of NY Coll of Environ Sci and Forestry (NY)
Texas A&M U (TX)
Texas A&M U at Galveston (TX)
Texas A&M U–Kingsville (TX)
U of Alaska Fairbanks (AK)
U of Arkansas at Pine Bluff (AR)
U of British Columbia (BC, Canada)
U of Idaho (ID)
U of Minnesota, Duluth (MN)
U of Minnesota, Twin Cities Campus (MN)
U of Missouri–Columbia (MO)

U of New Brunswick, Fredericton (NB, Canada)
U of South Dakota (SD)
U of Vermont (VT)
Utah State U (UT)
West Virginia U (WV)

FISHING SCIENCES AND MANAGEMENT
Colorado State U (CO)
Mansfield U of Pennsylvania (PA)
Murray State U (KY)
The Ohio State U (OH)
State U of NY Coll of Environ Sci and Forestry (NY)
Texas A&M U (TX)
Texas Tech U (TX)
Unity Coll (ME)
U of Georgia (GA)
U of Nebraska–Lincoln (NE)
U of Rhode Island (RI)
U of Washington (WA)
U of Wyoming (WY)

FLUID AND THERMAL SCIENCES
Harvard U (MA)
Worcester Polytechnic Inst (MA)

FOLKLORE
Harvard U (MA)
Indiana State U (IN)
Indiana U Bloomington (IN)
Long Island U, Southampton Coll, Friends World Program (NY)
Marlboro Coll (VT)
Memorial U of Newfoundland (NF, Canada)
The Ohio State U (OH)
U of Alberta (AB, Canada)
U of Oregon (OR)
U of Pennsylvania (PA)

FOOD PRODUCTS RETAILING
Ball State U (IN)
California State U, Chico (CA)
California State U, Northridge (CA)
Concord Coll (WV)
David Lipscomb U (TN)
Delaware Valley Coll (PA)
Dominican U (IL)
Immaculata Coll (PA)
Indiana State U (IN)
Iowa State U of Science and Technology (IA)
Johnson & Wales U (RI)
Lindenwood U (MO)
Lynn U (FL)
Madonna U (MI)
Marshall U (WV)
Michigan State U (MI)
Mount Saint Vincent U (NS, Canada)
New England Culinary Inst (VT)
North Carolina Wesleyan Coll (NC)
Northern Michigan U (MI)
Ohio U (OH)
Oregon State U (OR)
Otterbein Coll (OH)
Rochester Inst of Technology (NY)
San Francisco State U (CA)
Southeast Missouri State U (MO)
State U of NY Coll at Buffalo (NY)
Syracuse U (NY)
U of Alberta (AB, Canada)
U of Central Oklahoma (OK)
Wayne State Coll (NE)

FOOD SALES OPERATIONS
Immaculata Coll (PA)
Johnson & Wales U (RI)
Northwest Missouri State U (MO)
Rochester Inst of Technology (NY)
Saint Joseph's U (PA)
U of Delaware (DE)

FOOD SCIENCES
Acadia U (NS, Canada)
Alabama A&M U (AL)
Arizona State U East (AZ)
Auburn U (AL)
Brigham Young U (UT)
California Polytechnic State U, San Luis Obispo (CA)
California State U, Los Angeles (CA)
California State U, Northridge (CA)
Chapman U (CA)

Clemson U (SC)
Cornell U (NY)
Delaware Valley Coll (PA)
Dominican U (IL)
Drexel U (PA)
Framingham State Coll (MA)
Indiana State U (IN)
Insto Tecno Estudios Sups Monterrey (Mexico)
Insto Tecno Estudios Sups Monterrey, Querétaro (Mexico)
Kansas State U (KS)
Lamar U (TX)
Louisiana State U and A&M Coll (LA)
Marymount Coll (NY)
McGill U (PQ, Canada)
Memorial U of Newfoundland (NF, Canada)
Michigan State U (MI)
Mississippi State U (MS)
Mount Saint Vincent U (NS, Canada)
North Carolina Ag and Tech State U (NC)
North Carolina State U (NC)
North Dakota State U (ND)
Northwest Missouri State U (MO)
The Ohio State U (OH)
Olivet Nazarene U (IL)
Oregon State U (OR)
Penn State U Univ Park Campus (PA)
Purdue U (IN)
Rutgers, State U of NJ, Cook Coll (NJ)
Rutgers, State U of NJ, Douglass Coll (NJ)
Rutgers, State U of NJ, U Coll–New Brunswick (NJ)
San Jose State U (CA)
South Dakota State U (SD)
Texas A&M U (TX)
Texas A&M U–Kingsville (TX)
Texas Tech U (TX)
Tuskegee U (AL)
Université Laval (PQ, Canada)
The U of Akron (OH)
U of Alberta (AB, Canada)
U of Arkansas (AR)
U of British Columbia (BC, Canada)
U of Calif, Davis (CA)
U of Delaware (DE)
U of Florida (FL)
U of Georgia (GA)
U of Idaho (ID)
U of Illinois at Urbana–Champaign (IL)
U of Kentucky (KY)
The U of Lethbridge (AB, Canada)
U of Manitoba (MB, Canada)
U of Maryland, Coll Park (MD)
U of Massachusetts Amherst (MA)
U of Missouri–Columbia (MO)
U of Nebraska–Lincoln (NE)
The U of Tennessee Knoxville (TN)
U of the District of Columbia (DC)
U of Utah (UT)
U of Wisconsin–Madison (WI)
U of Wisconsin–River Falls (WI)
Virginia Polytechnic Inst and State U (VA)

FOOD SERVICES TECHNOLOGY
California State U, Northridge (CA)
Delaware Valley Coll (PA)
Iowa State U of Science and Technology (IA)
Johnson & Wales U (RI)
Madonna U (MI)
Mansfield U of Pennsylvania (PA)
Meredith Coll (NC)
Ohio U (OH)
San Jose State U (CA)
Tennessee State U (TN)

FOREIGN LANGUAGES EDUCATION
Arkansas Tech U (AR)
Baylor U (TX)
Berea Coll (KY)
Bethune-Cookman Coll (FL)
Boston U (MA)
Bowling Green State U (OH)
Brigham Young U (UT)
Central Methodist Coll (MO)

Dana Coll (NE)
Delta State U (MS)
Duquesne U (PA)
Eastern Michigan U (MI)
Elmira Coll (NY)
Florida International U (FL)
Florida State U (FL)
Gannon U (PA)
Greenville Coll (IL)
Hastings Coll (NE)
Juniata Coll (PA)
Le Moyne Coll (NY)
Lincoln U (PA)
Luther Coll (IA)
Mercer U (GA)
Nazareth Coll of Rochester (NY)
New York U (NY)
Rivier Coll (NH)
St. John's U (NY)
St. Olaf Coll (MN)
Seton Hill Coll (PA)
Southwestern Coll (KS)
Southwest Missouri State U (MO)
Texas Wesleyan U (TX)
The U of Arizona (AZ)
U of Arkansas (AR)
U of Central Florida (FL)
U of Delaware (DE)
U of Georgia (GA)
U of Illinois at Chicago (IL)
U of Illinois at Urbana–Champaign (IL)
U of Louisiana at Monroe (LA)
U of Maryland, Coll Park (MD)
U of Minnesota, Twin Cities Campus (MN)
U of Nebraska–Lincoln (NE)
U of Nevada, Reno (NV)
U of New Orleans (LA)
U of Northern Iowa (IA)
U of Oklahoma (OK)
U of South Florida (FL)
U of Vermont (VT)
U of West Florida (FL)
Wheeling Jesuit U (WV)
Youngstown State U (OH)

FOREIGN LANGUAGES/LITERATURES
Arkansas Tech U (AR)
Assumption Coll (MA)
Auburn U Montgomery (AL)
Augustana Coll (SD)
Austin Peay State U (TN)
Bethune-Cookman Coll (FL)
Boston U (MA)
California State U, Monterey Bay (CA)
Central Methodist Coll (MO)
The Coll of Southeastern Europe, The American U of Athens (Greece)
Delta State U (MS)
Duquesne U (PA)
Eastern Illinois U (IL)
East Tennessee State U (TN)
Elmira Coll (NY)
Elon Coll (NC)
Emporia State U (KS)
Frostburg State U (MD)
Gannon U (PA)
Gordon Coll (MA)
Graceland Coll (IA)
Hastings Coll (NE)
James Madison U (VA)
Kansas State U (KS)
Kent State U (OH)
Knox Coll (IL)
Massachusetts Inst of Technology (MA)
McGill U (PQ, Canada)
Metropolitan State Coll of Denver (CO)
Middle Tennessee State U (TN)
Millikin U (IL)
Minnesota State U Moorhead (MN)
Mississippi Coll (MS)
Mississippi State U (MS)
Monmouth U (NJ)
Montana State U–Bozeman (MT)
Mount Saint Mary's Coll and Seminary (MD)
New Mexico State U (NM)
Norfolk State U (VA)
Old Dominion U (VA)
Principia Coll (IL)
Purdue U (IN)

Radford U (VA)
Regents Coll (NY)
The Richard Stockton Coll of New Jersey (NJ)
Roger Williams U (RI)
Rutgers, State U of NJ, Douglass Coll (NJ)
Rutgers, State U of NJ, Livingston Coll (NJ)
Rutgers, State U of NJ, Rutgers Coll (NJ)
Rutgers, State U of NJ, U Coll–New Brunswick (NJ)
St. Lawrence U (NY)
Saint Peter's Coll (NJ)
Samford U (AL)
Scripps Coll (CA)
Seton Hall U (NJ)
Simon's Rock Coll of Bard (MA)
Southern Adventist U (TN)
Southern Illinois U Edwardsville (IL)
Southern Methodist U (TX)
Southwestern Coll (KS)
Stonehill Coll (MA)
Syracuse U (NY)
Thomas Edison State Coll (NJ)
Union Coll (NY)
Union U (TN)
U of Calif, San Diego (CA)
U of Calif, Santa Cruz (CA)
U of Central Florida (FL)
U of Delaware (DE)
U of Georgia (GA)
U of Hartford (CT)
U of Idaho (ID)
U of Massachusetts Lowell (MA)
The U of Memphis (TN)
The U of Montana–Missoula (MT)
U of North Alabama (AL)
U of North Dakota (ND)
U of Northern Iowa (IA)
U of Puerto Rico, Río Piedras (PR)
The U of Scranton (PA)
U of Southern Mississippi (MS)
U of Virginia's Coll at Wise (VA)
Virginia Wesleyan Coll (VA)
Washington and Lee U (VA)
Wayne State U (MI)
West Virginia U (WV)
Wilson Coll (PA)

FOREIGN LANGUAGE TRANSLATION
Concordia U (PQ, Canada)
York U (ON, Canada)

FOREST ENGINEERING
Oregon State U (OR)
State U of NY Coll of Environ Sci and Forestry (NY)
U of Maine (ME)
U of New Brunswick, Fredericton (NB, Canada)
U of New Brunswick, Saint John (NB, Canada)
U of Washington (WA)

FOREST HARVESTING PRODUCTION TECHNOLOGY
Lakehead U (ON, Canada)

FOREST MANAGEMENT
Louisiana State U and A&M Coll (LA)
North Carolina State U (NC)
State U of NY Coll of Environ Sci and Forestry (NY)
Stephen F. Austin State U (TX)
Université Laval (PQ, Canada)
U of Minnesota, Twin Cities Campus (MN)
The U of Montana–Missoula (MT)
U of Washington (WA)
Warren Wilson Coll (NC)

FORESTRY
Albright Coll (PA)
Baylor U (TX)
California Polytechnic State U, San Luis Obispo (CA)
Clemson U (SC)
Coll of Saint Benedict (MN)
Humboldt State U (CA)
Iowa State U of Science and Technology (IA)
Lakehead U (ON, Canada)
Lees-McRae Coll (NC)

Majors Index
Forestry–French

Louisiana Tech U (LA)
Michigan State U (MI)
Michigan Technological U (MI)
Mississippi State U (MS)
North Dakota State U (ND)
Northern Arizona U (AZ)
Northland Coll (WI)
Northwest Missouri State U (MO)
The Ohio State U (OH)
Oklahoma State U (OK)
Oregon State U (OR)
Purdue U (IN)
Rutgers, State U of NJ, Cook Coll (NJ)
Saint John's U (MN)
Southern Illinois U Carbondale (IL)
State U of NY Coll of Environ Sci and Forestry (NY)
Stephen F. Austin State U (TX)
Sterling Coll (VT)
Texas A&M U (TX)
Thomas Edison State Coll (NJ)
Unity Coll (ME)
U of Alaska Fairbanks (AK)
U of Alberta (AB, Canada)
U of Arkansas at Monticello (AR)
U of British Columbia (BC, Canada)
U of Florida (FL)
U of Georgia (GA)
U of Idaho (ID)
U of Illinois at Urbana–Champaign (IL)
U of Maine (ME)
U of Massachusetts Amherst (MA)
U of Minnesota, Twin Cities Campus (MN)
U of Missouri–Columbia (MO)
The U of Montana–Missoula (MT)
U of Nevada, Reno (NV)
U of New Brunswick, Fredericton (NB, Canada)
U of New Brunswick, Saint John (NB, Canada)
U of New Hampshire (NH)
The U of Tennessee Knoxville (TN)
U of the District of Columbia (DC)
U of the South (TN)
U of Toronto (ON, Canada)
U of Vermont (VT)
U of Washington (WA)
U of Wisconsin–Madison (WI)
U of Wisconsin–Milwaukee (WI)
U of Wisconsin–Stevens Point (WI)
Utah State U (UT)
Virginia Polytechnic Inst and State U (VA)
Washington and Lee U (VA)
Washington State U (WA)
West Virginia U (WV)

FORESTRY SCIENCES
Auburn U (AL)
Brevard Coll (NC)
Colorado State U (CO)
Memorial U of Newfoundland (NF, Canada)
Penn State U Univ Park Campus (PA)
Samford U (AL)
U of Calif, Berkeley (CA)
U of Georgia (GA)
U of Kentucky (KY)
U of Washington (WA)

FRENCH
Abilene Christian U (TX)
Acadia U (NS, Canada)
Adelphi U (NY)
Adrian Coll (MI)
Agnes Scott Coll (GA)
Alabama State U (AL)
Albany State U (GA)
Albertson Coll of Idaho (ID)
Albertus Magnus Coll (CT)
Albion Coll (MI)
Albright Coll (PA)
Alfred U (NY)
Allegheny Coll (PA)
Alma Coll (MI)
American U (DC)
The American U of Paris (France)
Amherst Coll (MA)
Anderson U (IN)
Andrews U (MI)
Antioch Coll (OH)
Appalachian State U (NC)

Aquinas Coll (MI)
Arizona State U (AZ)
Arkansas State U (AR)
Arkansas Tech U (AR)
Asbury Coll (KY)
Ashland U (OH)
Assumption Coll (MA)
Athabasca U (AB, Canada)
Atlantic Union Coll (MA)
Auburn U (AL)
Augsburg Coll (MN)
Augustana Coll (IL)
Augustana Coll (SD)
Augusta State U (GA)
Austin Coll (TX)
Baker U (KS)
Baldwin-Wallace Coll (OH)
Ball State U (IN)
Bard Coll (NY)
Barnard Coll (NY)
Barry U (FL)
Bates Coll (ME)
Baylor U (TX)
Bellarmine Coll (KY)
Beloit Coll (WI)
Bemidji State U (MN)
Benedictine Coll (KS)
Bennington Coll (VT)
Berea Coll (KY)
Berry Coll (GA)
Bethany Coll (WV)
Birmingham-Southern Coll (AL)
Bishop's U (PQ, Canada)
Bloomfield Coll (NJ)
Bloomsburg U of Pennsylvania (PA)
Blue Mountain Coll (MS)
Boston Coll (MA)
Boston U (MA)
Bowdoin Coll (ME)
Bowling Green State U (OH)
Bradley U (IL)
Brandeis U (MA)
Brandon U (MB, Canada)
Bridgewater Coll (VA)
Brigham Young U (UT)
Brock U (ON, Canada)
Brooklyn Coll of the City U of NY (NY)
Brown U (RI)
Bryn Mawr Coll (PA)
Bucknell U (PA)
Butler U (IN)
Cabrini Coll (PA)
Caldwell Coll (NJ)
California Lutheran U (CA)
California State U, Chico (CA)
California State U, Dominguez Hills (CA)
California State U, Fresno (CA)
California State U, Fullerton (CA)
California State U, Hayward (CA)
California State U, Long Beach (CA)
California State U, Los Angeles (CA)
California State U, Northridge (CA)
California State U, Sacramento (CA)
California State U, San Bernardino (CA)
California State U, Stanislaus (CA)
California U of Pennsylvania (PA)
Calvin Coll (MI)
Campbell U (NC)
Canisius Coll (NY)
Capital U (OH)
Cardinal Stritch U (WI)
Carleton Coll (MN)
Carleton U (ON, Canada)
Carnegie Mellon U (PA)
Carroll Coll (MT)
Carson-Newman Coll (TN)
Carthage Coll (WI)
Case Western Reserve U (OH)
Catawba Coll (NC)
The Catholic U of America (DC)
Cedar Crest Coll (PA)
Centenary Coll of Louisiana (LA)
Central Coll (IA)
Central Connecticut State U (CT)
Central Methodist Coll (MO)
Central Michigan U (MI)
Central Missouri State U (MO)
Centre Coll (KY)
Chapman U (CA)
Chatham Coll (PA)

Chestnut Hill Coll (PA)
Cheyney U of Pennsylvania (PA)
Christendom Coll (VA)
Christopher Newport U (VA)
Citadel, The Military Coll of South Carolina (SC)
City Coll of the City U of NY (NY)
Claremont McKenna Coll (CA)
Clarion U of Pennsylvania (PA)
Clark Atlanta U (GA)
Clarke Coll (IA)
Clark U (MA)
Clemson U (SC)
Cleveland State U (OH)
Coe Coll (IA)
Coker Coll (SC)
Colby Coll (ME)
Colgate U (NY)
Coll of Charleston (SC)
Coll of Mount Saint Vincent (NY)
The Coll of New Rochelle (NY)
Coll of Notre Dame (CA)
Coll of Our Lady of the Elms (MA)
Coll of Saint Benedict (MN)
Coll of St. Catherine (MN)
Coll of Saint Elizabeth (NJ)
Coll of the Holy Cross (MA)
Coll of the Ozarks (MO)
The Coll of William and Mary (VA)
The Coll of Wooster (OH)
The Colorado Coll (CO)
Colorado State U (CO)
Columbia Coll (NY)
Columbia Coll (SC)
Columbia U, School of General Studies (NY)
Concordia Coll (MN)
Concordia U (PQ, Canada)
Concordia U Coll of Alberta (AB, Canada)
Connecticut Coll (CT)
Converse Coll (SC)
Cornell Coll (IA)
Cornell U (NY)
Creighton U (NE)
Daemen Coll (NY)
Dalhousie U (NS, Canada)
Dartmouth Coll (NH)
David Lipscomb U (TN)
Davidson Coll (NC)
Delaware State U (DE)
Denison U (OH)
DePaul U (IL)
DePauw U (IN)
Dickinson Coll (PA)
Doane Coll (NE)
Dominican U (IL)
Drake U (IA)
Drew U (NJ)
Drury U (MO)
Duke U (NC)
Duquesne U (PA)
Earlham Coll (IN)
East Carolina U (NC)
Eastern Coll (PA)
Eastern Kentucky U (KY)
Eastern Mennonite U (VA)
Eastern Michigan U (MI)
Eastern Nazarene Coll (MA)
Eastern Washington U (WA)
East Stroudsburg U of Pennsylvania (PA)
East Tennessee State U (TN)
Eckerd Coll (FL)
Edgewood Coll (WI)
Elizabethtown Coll (PA)
Elmhurst Coll (IL)
Elmira Coll (NY)
Elon Coll (NC)
Emory & Henry Coll (VA)
Emory U (GA)
Erskine Coll (SC)
The Evergreen State Coll (WA)
Fairfield U (CT)
Fairleigh Dickinson U, Florham-Madison Campus (NJ)
Fairleigh Dickinson U, Teaneck-Hackensack Campus (NJ)
Fairmont State Coll (WV)
Ferrum Coll (VA)
Fisk U (TN)
Florida A&M U (FL)
Florida Atlantic U (FL)
Florida International U (FL)
Florida State U (FL)
Fordham U (NY)
Fort Hays State U (KS)

Fort Valley State U (GA)
Framingham State Coll (MA)
Franciscan U of Steubenville (OH)
Francis Marion U (SC)
Franklin and Marshall Coll (PA)
Franklin Coll of Indiana (IN)
Furman U (SC)
Gallaudet U (DC)
Gardner-Webb U (NC)
George Mason U (VA)
Georgetown Coll (KY)
Georgetown U (DC)
The George Washington U (DC)
Georgia Coll and State U (GA)
Georgian Court Coll (NJ)
Georgia Southern U (GA)
Georgia Southwestern State U (GA)
Georgia State U (GA)
Gettysburg Coll (PA)
Gonzaga U (WA)
Gordon Coll (MA)
Goucher Coll (MD)
Grace Coll (IN)
Grand Valley State U (MI)
Greensboro Coll (NC)
Greenville Coll (IL)
Grinnell Coll (IA)
Grove City Coll (PA)
Guilford Coll (NC)
Gustavus Adolphus Coll (MN)
Hamilton Coll (NY)
Hamline U (MN)
Hampden-Sydney Coll (VA)
Hanover Coll (IN)
Harding U (AR)
Hardin-Simmons U (TX)
Hartwick Coll (NY)
Harvard U (MA)
Haverford Coll (PA)
Hendrix Coll (AR)
High Point U (NC)
Hillsdale Coll (MI)
Hiram Coll (OH)
Hobart and William Smith Colls (NY)
Hofstra U (NY)
Hollins U (VA)
Holy Family Coll (PA)
Hood Coll (MD)
Hope Coll (MI)
Houghton Coll (NY)
Houston Baptist U (TX)
Howard U (DC)
Humboldt State U (CA)
Hunter Coll of the City U of NY (NY)
Idaho State U (ID)
Illinois Coll (IL)
Illinois State U (IL)
Illinois Wesleyan U (IL)
Immaculata Coll (PA)
Indiana State U (IN)
Indiana U Bloomington (IN)
Indiana U Northwest (IN)
Indiana U of Pennsylvania (PA)
Indiana U–Purdue U Fort Wayne (IN)
Indiana U–Purdue U Indianapolis (IN)
Indiana U South Bend (IN)
Indiana U Southeast (IN)
Iona Coll (NY)
Iowa State U of Science and Technology (IA)
Ithaca Coll (NY)
Jacksonville State U (AL)
Jacksonville U (FL)
James Madison U (VA)
John Carroll U (OH)
Johns Hopkins U (MD)
Juniata Coll (PA)
Kalamazoo Coll (MI)
Kean U (NJ)
Keene State Coll (NH)
Kent State U (OH)
Kenyon Coll (OH)
King Coll (TN)
King's Coll (PA)
Knox Coll (IL)
Kutztown U of Pennsylvania (PA)
Lafayette Coll (PA)
Lake Erie Coll (OH)
Lake Forest Coll (IL)
Lakehead U (ON, Canada)
Lamar U (TX)
Lane Coll (TN)

La Salle U (PA)
Lawrence U (WI)
Lebanon Valley Coll (PA)
Lehigh U (PA)
Lehman Coll of the City U of NY (NY)
Le Moyne Coll (NY)
Lenoir-Rhyne Coll (NC)
Lewis & Clark Coll (OR)
Lincoln U (MO)
Lincoln U (PA)
Lindenwood U (MO)
Linfield Coll (OR)
Lock Haven U of Pennsylvania (PA)
Long Island U, C.W. Post Campus (NY)
Long Island U, Southampton Coll, Friends World Program (NY)
Longwood Coll (VA)
Loras Coll (IA)
Louisiana Coll (LA)
Louisiana State U and A&M Coll (LA)
Louisiana State U in Shreveport (LA)
Louisiana Tech U (LA)
Loyola Coll in Maryland (MD)
Loyola Marymount U (CA)
Loyola U Chicago (IL)
Loyola U New Orleans (LA)
Luther Coll (IA)
Lycoming Coll (PA)
Lynchburg Coll (VA)
Macalester Coll (MN)
MacMurray Coll (IL)
Madonna U (MI)
Manchester Coll (IN)
Manhattan Coll (NY)
Manhattanville Coll (NY)
Mansfield U of Pennsylvania (PA)
Marian Coll (IN)
Marietta Coll (OH)
Marist Coll (NY)
Marlboro Coll (VT)
Marquette U (WI)
Marshall U (WV)
Mary Baldwin Coll (VA)
Marymount Coll (NY)
Mary Washington Coll (VA)
Marywood U (PA)
McGill U (PQ, Canada)
McNeese State U (LA)
Memorial U of Newfoundland (NF, Canada)
Mercer U (GA)
Mercy Coll (NY)
Mercyhurst Coll (PA)
Meredith Coll (NC)
Merrimack Coll (MA)
Messiah Coll (PA)
Methodist Coll (NC)
Miami U (OH)
Michigan State U (MI)
Middlebury Coll (VT)
Millersville U of Pennsylvania (PA)
Millikin U (IL)
Millsaps Coll (MS)
Mills Coll (CA)
Minnesota State U, Mankato (MN)
Minot State U (ND)
Mississippi Coll (MS)
Missouri Western State Coll (MO)
Molloy Coll (NY)
Monmouth Coll (IL)
Moravian Coll (PA)
Morehead State U (KY)
Morehouse Coll (GA)
Morningside Coll (IA)
Mount Allison U (NB, Canada)
Mount Holyoke Coll (MA)
Mount Mary Coll (WI)
Mount St. Mary's Coll (CA)
Mount Saint Mary's Coll and Seminary (MD)
Mount Saint Vincent U (NS, Canada)
Mount Union Coll (OH)
Muhlenberg Coll (PA)
Murray State U (KY)
Muskingum Coll (OH)
Nazareth Coll of Rochester (NY)
Nebraska Wesleyan U (NE)
Newberry Coll (SC)
New Coll of the U of South Florida (FL)
New York U (NY)

Majors Index
French–French Language Education

Niagara U (NY)
Nicholls State U (LA)
Norfolk State U (VA)
North Carolina Ag and Tech State U (NC)
North Carolina Central U (NC)
North Carolina State U (NC)
North Central Coll (IL)
North Dakota State U (ND)
Northeastern Illinois U (IL)
Northeastern State U (OK)
Northeastern U (MA)
Northern Arizona U (AZ)
Northern Illinois U (IL)
Northern Kentucky U (KY)
Northern Michigan U (MI)
Northern State U (SD)
North Georgia Coll & State U (GA)
North Park U (IL)
Northwestern U (IL)
Northwest Missouri State U (MO)
Oakland U (MI)
Oakwood Coll (AL)
Oberlin Coll (OH)
Occidental Coll (CA)
Ohio Northern U (OH)
The Ohio State U (OH)
Ohio U (OH)
Ohio Wesleyan U (OH)
Oklahoma Baptist U (OK)
Oklahoma City U (OK)
Oklahoma State U (OK)
Olivet Nazarene U (IL)
Oregon State U (OR)
Otterbein Coll (OH)
Ouachita Baptist U (AR)
Pace U, Pleasantville/Briarcliff Campus (NY)
Pacific Lutheran U (WA)
Pacific Union Coll (CA)
Pacific U (OR)
Penn State U Univ Park Campus (PA)
Pepperdine U, Malibu (CA)
Pittsburg State U (KS)
Pitzer Coll (CA)
Plattsburgh State U of NY (NY)
Plymouth State Coll (NH)
Pomona Coll (CA)
Pontifical Catholic U of Puerto Rico (PR)
Portland State U (OR)
Presbyterian Coll (SC)
Principia Coll (IL)
Providence Coll (RI)
Purchase Coll, State U of NY (NY)
Purdue U Calumet (IN)
Queens Coll (NC)
Queens Coll of the City U of NY (NY)
Queen's U at Kingston (ON, Canada)
Randolph-Macon Coll (VA)
Randolph-Macon Woman's Coll (VA)
Redeemer Coll (ON, Canada)
Reed Coll (OR)
Regis Coll (MA)
Regis U (CO)
Rhodes Coll (TN)
Rice U (TX)
Rider U (NJ)
Ripon Coll (WI)
Rivier Coll (NH)
Roanoke Coll (VA)
Rockford Coll (IL)
Rockhurst U (MO)
Rocky Mountain Coll (MT)
Rollins Coll (FL)
Rosemont Coll (PA)
Rutgers, State U of NJ, Camden Coll of Arts & Scis (NJ)
Rutgers, State U of NJ, Douglass Coll (NJ)
Rutgers, State U of NJ, Livingston Coll (NJ)
Rutgers, State U of NJ, Newark Coll of Arts & Scis (NJ)
Rutgers, State U of NJ, Rutgers Coll (NJ)
Rutgers, State U of NJ, U Coll–Camden (NJ)
Rutgers, State U of NJ, U Coll–New Brunswick (NJ)
Saginaw Valley State U (MI)
St. Ambrose U (IA)
Saint Anselm Coll (NH)

Saint Augustine's Coll (NC)
St. Bonaventure U (NY)
St. Cloud State U (MN)
Saint Francis Coll (PA)
St. Francis Xavier U (NS, Canada)
St. John Fisher Coll (NY)
Saint John's U (MN)
St. John's U (NY)
Saint Joseph Coll (CT)
St. Joseph's Coll, New York (NY)
Saint Joseph's U (PA)
St. Lawrence U (NY)
Saint Louis U (MO)
Saint Mary-of-the-Woods Coll (IN)
Saint Mary's Coll (IN)
Saint Mary's Coll of California (CA)
Saint Mary's U (NS, Canada)
Saint Mary's U of Minnesota (MN)
St. Mary's U of San Antonio (TX)
Saint Michael's Coll (VT)
St. Norbert Coll (WI)
St. Olaf Coll (MN)
Saint Xavier U (IL)
Salem Coll (NC)
Salisbury State U (MD)
Salve Regina U (RI)
Samford U (AL)
Sam Houston State U (TX)
San Diego State U (CA)
San Francisco State U (CA)
San Jose State U (CA)
Santa Clara U (CA)
Sarah Lawrence Coll (NY)
Scripps Coll (CA)
Seattle Pacific U (WA)
Seattle U (WA)
Seton Hall U (NJ)
Shippensburg U of Pennsylvania (PA)
Shorter Coll (GA)
Siena Coll (NY)
Simmons Coll (MA)
Simon Fraser U (BC, Canada)
Simon's Rock Coll of Bard (MA)
Simpson Coll (IA)
Skidmore Coll (NY)
Slippery Rock U of Pennsylvania (PA)
Smith Coll (MA)
Sonoma State U (CA)
South Dakota State U (SD)
Southeastern Louisiana U (LA)
Southeast Missouri State U (MO)
Southern Illinois U Carbondale (IL)
Southern Methodist U (TX)
Southern Utah U (UT)
Southwestern U (TX)
Southwest Missouri State U (MO)
Southwest Texas State U (TX)
Spelman Coll (GA)
Spring Arbor Coll (MI)
Stanford U (CA)
State U of NY at Albany (NY)
State U of NY at Binghamton (NY)
State U of NY at Buffalo (NY)
State U of NY at New Paltz (NY)
State U of NY at Oswego (NY)
State U of NY at Stony Brook (NY)
State U of NY Coll at Brockport (NY)
State U of NY Coll at Buffalo (NY)
State U of NY Coll at Cortland (NY)
State U of NY Coll at Fredonia (NY)
State U of NY Coll at Geneseo (NY)
State U of NY Coll at Oneonta (NY)
State U of NY Coll at Potsdam (NY)
State U of West Georgia (GA)
Stephen F. Austin State U (TX)
Stetson U (FL)
Suffolk U (MA)
Susquehanna U (PA)
Swarthmore Coll (PA)
Sweet Briar Coll (VA)
Syracuse U (NY)
Taylor U (IN)
Temple U (PA)
Tennessee State U (TN)
Tennessee Technological U (TN)
Texas A&M U (TX)
Texas A&M U–Commerce (TX)
Texas Christian U (TX)
Texas Southern U (TX)
Texas Tech U (TX)

Thiel Coll (PA)
Towson U (MD)
Transylvania U (KY)
Trent U (ON, Canada)
Trinity Coll (CT)
Trinity U (TX)
Truman State U (MO)
Tufts U (MA)
Tulane U (LA)
Union Coll (NE)
Union U (TN)
United States Military Academy (NY)
Université de Montréal (PQ, Canada)
Université de Sherbrooke (PQ, Canada)
U du Québec à Chicoutimi (PQ, Canada)
U du Québec à Trois-Rivières (PQ, Canada)
Université Laval (PQ, Canada)
U Coll of Cape Breton (NS, Canada)
The U of Akron (OH)
The U of Alabama (AL)
The U of Alabama at Birmingham (AL)
The U of Alabama in Huntsville (AL)
U of Alaska Fairbanks (AK)
U of Alberta (AB, Canada)
The U of Arizona (AZ)
U of Arkansas (AR)
U of Arkansas at Little Rock (AR)
U of British Columbia (BC, Canada)
U of Calgary (AB, Canada)
U of Calif, Berkeley (CA)
U of Calif, Davis (CA)
U of Calif, Irvine (CA)
U of Calif, Los Angeles (CA)
U of Calif, Riverside (CA)
U of Calif, San Diego (CA)
U of Calif, Santa Barbara (CA)
U of Calif, Santa Cruz (CA)
U of Central Arkansas (AR)
U of Central Florida (FL)
U of Central Oklahoma (OK)
U of Chicago (IL)
U of Cincinnati (OH)
U of Colorado at Boulder (CO)
U of Colorado at Denver (CO)
U of Connecticut (CT)
U of Dallas (TX)
U of Dayton (OH)
U of Delaware (DE)
U of Denver (CO)
U of Evansville (IN)
U of Florida (FL)
U of Georgia (GA)
U of Guelph (ON, Canada)
U of Hawaii at Manoa (HI)
U of Houston (TX)
U of Idaho (ID)
U of Illinois at Chicago (IL)
U of Illinois at Urbana–Champaign (IL)
U of Indianapolis (IN)
The U of Iowa (IA)
U of Kansas (KS)
U of Kentucky (KY)
U of King's Coll (NS, Canada)
U of La Verne (CA)
The U of Lethbridge (AB, Canada)
U of Louisiana at Monroe (LA)
U of Louisville (KY)
U of Maine (ME)
U of Maine at Fort Kent (ME)
U of Maine at Presque Isle (ME)
U of Manitoba (MB, Canada)
U of Maryland, Baltimore County (MD)
U of Maryland, Coll Park (MD)
U of Massachusetts Amherst (MA)
U of Massachusetts Boston (MA)
U of Massachusetts Dartmouth (MA)
U of Miami (FL)
U of Michigan (MI)
U of Michigan–Dearborn (MI)
U of Michigan–Flint (MI)
U of Minnesota, Morris (MN)
U of Minnesota, Twin Cities Campus (MN)
U of Mississippi (MS)
U of Missouri–Columbia (MO)

U of Missouri–Kansas City (MO)
U of Missouri–St. Louis (MO)
The U of Montana–Missoula (MT)
U of Montevallo (AL)
U of Nebraska at Kearney (NE)
U of Nebraska at Omaha (NE)
U of Nebraska–Lincoln (NE)
U of Nevada, Las Vegas (NV)
U of Nevada, Reno (NV)
U of New Brunswick, Fredericton (NB, Canada)
U of New Brunswick, Saint John (NB, Canada)
U of New Hampshire (NH)
U of New Mexico (NM)
U of New Orleans (LA)
The U of North Carolina at Asheville (NC)
The U of North Carolina at Charlotte (NC)
The U of North Carolina at Greensboro (NC)
The U of North Carolina at Wilmington (NC)
U of North Dakota (ND)
U of Northern Colorado (CO)
U of Northern Iowa (IA)
U of North Texas (TX)
U of Notre Dame (IN)
U of Oklahoma (OK)
U of Oregon (OR)
U of Pennsylvania (PA)
U of Pittsburgh (PA)
U of Prince Edward Island (PE, Canada)
U of Puerto Rico, Mayagüez Campus (PR)
U of Puerto Rico, Río Piedras (PR)
U of Puget Sound (WA)
U of Redlands (CA)
U of Regina (SK, Canada)
U of Rhode Island (RI)
U of Richmond (VA)
U of Rochester (NY)
U of St. Thomas (MN)
U of St. Thomas (TX)
U of San Diego (CA)
U of San Francisco (CA)
The U of Scranton (PA)
U of South Alabama (AL)
U of South Carolina (SC)
U of South Carolina Spartanburg (SC)
U of South Dakota (SD)
U of Southern California (CA)
U of Southern Indiana (IN)
U of Southern Maine (ME)
U of South Florida (FL)
The U of Tennessee at Chattanooga (TN)
The U of Tennessee at Martin (TN)
The U of Tennessee Knoxville (TN)
The U of Texas at Arlington (TX)
The U of Texas at Austin (TX)
The U of Texas at San Antonio (TX)
The U of Texas–Pan American (TX)
The U of the District of Columbia (DC)
U of the Pacific (CA)
U of the Sacred Heart (PR)
U of the South (TN)
U of Toronto (ON, Canada)
U of Tulsa (OK)
U of Utah (UT)
U of Vermont (VT)
U of Victoria (BC, Canada)
U of Virginia (VA)
U of Virginia's Coll at Wise (VA)
U of Washington (WA)
U of Waterloo (ON, Canada)
The U of Western Ontario (ON, Canada)
U of Windsor (ON, Canada)
The U of Winnipeg (MB, Canada)
U of Wisconsin–Eau Claire (WI)
U of Wisconsin–Green Bay (WI)
U of Wisconsin–La Crosse (WI)
U of Wisconsin–Madison (WI)
U of Wisconsin–Milwaukee (WI)
U of Wisconsin–Parkside (WI)
U of Wisconsin–Platteville (WI)
U of Wisconsin–River Falls (WI)
U of Wisconsin–Stevens Point (WI)
U of Wisconsin–Whitewater (WI)
U of Wyoming (WY)
Ursinus Coll (PA)
Utah State U (UT)

Valdosta State U (GA)
Valparaiso U (IN)
Vanderbilt U (TN)
Vassar Coll (NY)
Villanova U (PA)
Virginia Commonwealth U (VA)
Virginia Polytechnic Inst and State U (VA)
Virginia Wesleyan Coll (VA)
Wabash Coll (IN)
Wake Forest U (NC)
Walla Walla Coll (WA)
Walsh U (OH)
Wartburg Coll (IA)
Washington & Jefferson Coll (PA)
Washington and Lee U (VA)
Washington Coll (MD)
Washington State U (WA)
Washington U in St. Louis (MO)
Wayne State Coll (NE)
Wayne State U (MI)
Weber State U (UT)
Webster U (MO)
Wellesley Coll (MA)
Wells Coll (NY)
Wesleyan U (CT)
West Chester U of Pennsylvania (PA)
Western Carolina U (NC)
Western Illinois U (IL)
Western Kentucky U (KY)
Western Maryland Coll (MD)
Western Michigan U (MI)
Western State Coll of Colorado (CO)
Western Washington U (WA)
Westminster Coll (MO)
Westminster Coll (PA)
Westmont Coll (CA)
Wheaton Coll (IL)
Wheaton Coll (MA)
Wheeling Jesuit U (WV)
Whitman Coll (WA)
Whittier Coll (CA)
Whitworth Coll (WA)
Wichita State U (KS)
Widener U (PA)
Wilfrid Laurier U (ON, Canada)
Wilkes U (PA)
Willamette U (OR)
William Jewell Coll (MO)
Williams Coll (MA)
Winona State U (MN)
Wittenberg U (OH)
Wofford Coll (SC)
Wright State U (OH)
Xavier U (OH)
Xavier U of Louisiana (LA)
Yale U (CT)
Yeshiva U (NY)
York Coll of the City U of New York (NY)
York U (ON, Canada)
Youngstown State U (OH)

FRENCH LANGUAGE EDUCATION

Abilene Christian U (TX)
Anderson U (IN)
Arkansas State U (AR)
Baylor U (TX)
Berea Coll (KY)
Berry Coll (GA)
Blue Mountain Coll (MS)
Bowling Green State U (OH)
Bridgewater Coll (VA)
Brigham Young U (UT)
Canisius Coll (NY)
The Catholic U of America (DC)
Central Michigan U (MI)
Central Missouri State U (MO)
Coll of St. Catherine (MN)
Colorado State U (CO)
Concordia Coll (MN)
Daemen Coll (NY)
David Lipscomb U (TN)
Duquesne U (PA)
East Carolina U (NC)
Eastern Michigan U (MI)
Elmhurst Coll (IL)
Elmira Coll (NY)
Framingham State Coll (MA)
Georgia Southern U (GA)
Grace Coll (IN)
Hardin-Simmons U (TX)
Indiana U Bloomington (IN)
Indiana U Northwest (IN)

Majors Index
French Language Education–Geography

Indiana U–Purdue U Indianapolis (IN)
Indiana U South Bend (IN)
Ithaca Coll (NY)
Juniata Coll (PA)
King Coll (TN)
Louisiana Tech U (LA)
Luther Coll (IA)
Manhattanville Coll (NY)
Mansfield U of Pennsylvania (PA)
Marymount Coll (NY)
McGill U (PQ, Canada)
Messiah Coll (PA)
Missouri Western State Coll (MO)
Molloy Coll (NY)
New York U (NY)
Niagara U (NY)
North Carolina Central U (NC)
North Carolina State U (NC)
North Dakota State U (ND)
Ohio U (OH)
Oklahoma Baptist U (OK)
Plymouth State Coll (NH)
St. Ambrose U (IA)
St. John's U (NY)
St. Olaf Coll (MN)
Salve Regina U (RI)
Seton Hill Coll (PA)
Southeastern Louisiana U (LA)
Southwest Missouri State U (MO)
The U of Arizona (AZ)
U of Central Arkansas (AR)
U of Illinois at Chicago (IL)
U of Illinois at Urbana–Champaign (IL)
U of Indianapolis (IN)
The U of Iowa (IA)
U of Minnesota, Duluth (MN)
U of Nebraska–Lincoln (NE)
The U of North Carolina at Chapel Hill (NC)
The U of North Carolina at Charlotte (NC)
U of North Texas (TX)
The U of Tennessee at Martin (TN)
U of Waterloo (ON, Canada)
U of Wisconsin–River Falls (WI)
Washington U in St. Louis (MO)
Weber State U (UT)
Western Carolina U (NC)
Wheeling Jesuit U (WV)
Youngstown State U (OH)

GENERAL RETAILING/WHOLESALING
U of New Haven (CT)
U of South Carolina (SC)

GENERAL STUDIES
Alfred U (NY)
Antioch Southern California/Santa Barbara (CA)
Arkansas State U (AR)
Arkansas Tech U (AR)
Bluefield State Coll (WV)
Brandon U (MB, Canada)
Bridgewater Coll (VA)
Calumet Coll of Saint Joseph (IN)
Carroll Coll (MT)
The Catholic U of America (DC)
Central Coll (IA)
City U (WA)
Coll of Mount St. Joseph (OH)
Columbia International U (SC)
Crown Coll (MN)
Cumberland Coll (KY)
East Tennessee State U (TN)
Emporia State U (KS)
Fairleigh Dickinson U, Teaneck-Hackensack Campus (NJ)
Ferrum Coll (VA)
Fitchburg State Coll (MA)
Georgia Southern U (GA)
Harding U (AR)
Howard Payne U (TX)
Idaho State U (ID)
Indiana U Bloomington (IN)
Indiana U East (IN)
Indiana U Kokomo (IN)
Indiana U Northwest (IN)
Indiana U of Pennsylvania (PA)
Indiana U–Purdue U Fort Wayne (IN)
Indiana U–Purdue U Indianapolis (IN)
Indiana U South Bend (IN)
Indiana U Southeast (IN)

Indiana Wesleyan U (IN)
Kent State U (OH)
Lambuth U (TN)
La Roche Coll (PA)
Liberty U (VA)
Louisiana State U and A&M Coll (LA)
Louisiana Tech U (LA)
Loyola U New Orleans (LA)
Michigan Technological U (MI)
Missouri Western State Coll (MO)
Morehead State U (KY)
Mount Marty Coll (SD)
Mount St. Clare Coll (IA)
Mount Saint Mary's Coll and Seminary (MD)
Nicholls State U (LA)
Northwestern State U of Louisiana (LA)
Ohio U (OH)
Okanagan U Coll (BC, Canada)
Open Learning Agency (BC, Canada)
Our Lady of Holy Cross Coll (LA)
Penn State U at Erie, The Behrend Coll (PA)
Rochester Inst of Technology (NY)
Saginaw Valley State U (MI)
Seattle Pacific U (WA)
Seton Hill Coll (PA)
Shenandoah U (VA)
Siena Heights U (MI)
Simon Fraser U (BC, Canada)
Southeastern Louisiana U (LA)
Southeastern U (DC)
Southwestern Assemblies of God U (TX)
Southwestern Coll (KS)
Spring Hill Coll (AL)
Texas A&M U–Texarkana (TX)
Texas Christian U (TX)
Texas Tech U (TX)
Trinity Western U (BC, Canada)
Troy State U Montgomery (AL)
U of Calgary (AB, Canada)
U of Dayton (OH)
U of Louisiana at Lafayette (LA)
U of Louisiana at Monroe (LA)
U of Maine at Machias (ME)
U of Massachusetts Amherst (MA)
U of Miami (FL)
U of Michigan (MI)
U of Missouri–St. Louis (MO)
U of Mobile (AL)
U of Nebraska at Kearney (NE)
U of Nebraska at Omaha (NE)
U of Nevada, Reno (NV)
U of New Mexico (NM)
U of New Orleans (LA)
U of North Alabama (AL)
U of North Texas (TX)
U of Puerto Rico, Río Piedras (PR)
U of St. Thomas (TX)
U of South Florida (FL)
U of Washington (WA)
U of Wisconsin–Green Bay (WI)
U of Wisconsin–Stevens Point (WI)
U System Coll for Lifelong Learning (NH)
Western Kentucky U (KY)
Western Washington U (WA)
West Texas A&M U (TX)

GENETICS
Ball State U (IN)
California State U, Fullerton (CA)
Cedar Crest Coll (PA)
Cornell U (NY)
Dartmouth Coll (NH)
The Evergreen State Coll (WA)
Florida State U (FL)
Hampshire Coll (MA)
Harvard U (MA)
Iowa State U of Science and Technology (IA)
Jacksonville State U (AL)
McGill U (PQ, Canada)
Missouri Southern State Coll (MO)
North Dakota State U (ND)
The Ohio State U (OH)
Ohio Wesleyan U (OH)
Rochester Inst of Technology (NY)
Rutgers, State U of NJ, Camden Coll of Arts & Scis (NJ)
Rutgers, State U of NJ, Douglass Coll (NJ)

Rutgers, State U of NJ, Livingston Coll (NJ)
Rutgers, State U of NJ, Rutgers Coll (NJ)
Rutgers, State U of NJ, U Coll–Camden (NJ)
Rutgers, State U of NJ, U Coll–New Brunswick (NJ)
St. Cloud State U (MN)
Sarah Lawrence Coll (NY)
Texas A&M U (TX)
U of Alberta (AB, Canada)
U of British Columbia (BC, Canada)
U of Calif, Berkeley (CA)
U of Calif, Davis (CA)
U of Georgia (GA)
U of Kansas (KS)
U of Manitoba (MB, Canada)
U of Minnesota, Twin Cities Campus (MN)
U of Rochester (NY)
U of Toronto (ON, Canada)
The U of Western Ontario (ON, Canada)
U of Wisconsin–Madison (WI)
Washington State U (WA)
Western Kentucky U (KY)
Worcester Polytechnic Inst (MA)

GEOCHEMISTRY
Bridgewater State Coll (MA)
Brown U (RI)
California Inst of Technology (CA)
Columbia Coll (NY)
Hampshire Coll (MA)
Harvard U (MA)
Millersville U of Pennsylvania (PA)
New Mexico Inst of Mining and Technology (NM)
Northern Arizona U (AZ)
Pomona Coll (CA)
State U of NY at Oswego (NY)
State U of NY Coll at Cortland (NY)
State U of NY Coll at Fredonia (NY)
State U of NY Coll at Geneseo (NY)
U of Calif, Los Angeles (CA)
U of New Brunswick, Fredericton (NB, Canada)
U of Waterloo (ON, Canada)
West Chester U of Pennsylvania (PA)

GEOGRAPHY
Appalachian State U (NC)
Aquinas Coll (MI)
Arizona State U (AZ)
Arkansas State U (AR)
Auburn U (AL)
Augustana Coll (IL)
Austin Peay State U (TN)
Ball State U (IN)
Bellevue U (NE)
Bemidji State U (MN)
Bishop's U (PQ, Canada)
Bloomsburg U of Pennsylvania (PA)
Boston U (MA)
Bowie State U (MD)
Bowling Green State U (OH)
Brandon U (MB, Canada)
Bridgewater State Coll (MA)
Brigham Young U (UT)
Brock U (ON, Canada)
Bucknell U (PA)
California State Polytechnic U, Pomona (CA)
California State U, Chico (CA)
California State U, Dominguez Hills (CA)
California State U, Fresno (CA)
California State U, Fullerton (CA)
California State U, Hayward (CA)
California State U, Long Beach (CA)
California State U, Los Angeles (CA)
California State U, Northridge (CA)
California State U, Sacramento (CA)
California State U, San Bernardino (CA)
California State U, Stanislaus (CA)
California U of Pennsylvania (PA)
Calvin Coll (MI)

Carleton U (ON, Canada)
Carroll Coll (WI)
Carthage Coll (WI)
Central Connecticut State U (CT)
Central Michigan U (MI)
Central Missouri State U (MO)
Cheyney U of Pennsylvania (PA)
Chicago State U (IL)
City Coll of the City U of NY (NY)
Clarion U of Pennsylvania (PA)
Clark U (MA)
Colgate U (NY)
Concord Coll (WV)
Concordia U (IL)
Concordia U (NE)
Concordia U (PQ, Canada)
Dartmouth Coll (NH)
DePaul U (IL)
DePauw U (IN)
Dickinson State U (ND)
East Carolina U (NC)
Eastern Illinois U (IL)
Eastern Kentucky U (KY)
Eastern Michigan U (MI)
Eastern Washington U (WA)
East Stroudsburg U of Pennsylvania (PA)
East Tennessee State U (TN)
Edinboro U of Pennsylvania (PA)
Elmhurst Coll (IL)
Emory & Henry Coll (VA)
Fitchburg State Coll (MA)
Florida Atlantic U (FL)
Florida State U (FL)
Framingham State Coll (MA)
Francis Marion U (SC)
Frostburg State U (MD)
George Mason U (VA)
The George Washington U (DC)
Georgia Southern U (GA)
Georgia State U (GA)
Gustavus Adolphus Coll (MN)
Hampshire Coll (MA)
Hofstra U (NY)
Humboldt State U (CA)
Hunter Coll of the City U of NY (NY)
Illinois State U (IL)
Indiana State U (IN)
Indiana U Bloomington (IN)
Indiana U of Pennsylvania (PA)
Indiana U–Purdue U Indianapolis (IN)
Indiana U Southeast (IN)
Jacksonville State U (AL)
Jacksonville U (FL)
James Madison U (VA)
Johns Hopkins U (MD)
Kansas State U (KS)
Keene State Coll (NH)
Kent State U (OH)
Kutztown U of Pennsylvania (PA)
Lakehead U (ON, Canada)
Lehman Coll of the City U of NY (NY)
Lock Haven U of Pennsylvania (PA)
Long Island U, C.W. Post Campus (NY)
Long Island U, Southampton Coll, Friends World Program (NY)
Longwood Coll (VA)
Louisiana State U and A&M Coll (LA)
Louisiana State U in Shreveport (LA)
Louisiana Tech U (LA)
Macalester Coll (MN)
Mansfield U of Pennsylvania (PA)
Marshall U (WV)
Mary Washington Coll (VA)
McGill U (PQ, Canada)
Memorial U of Newfoundland (NF, Canada)
Miami U (OH)
Michigan State U (MI)
Middlebury Coll (VT)
Millersville U of Pennsylvania (PA)
Minnesota State U, Mankato (MN)
Morehead State U (KY)
Mount Allison U (NB, Canada)
Mount Holyoke Coll (MA)
Murray State U (KY)
New Mexico State U (NM)
Nipissing U (ON, Canada)
Norfolk State U (VA)
North Carolina Central U (NC)

Northeastern Illinois U (IL)
Northeastern State U (OK)
Northern Arizona U (AZ)
Northern Illinois U (IL)
Northern Kentucky U (KY)
Northern Michigan U (MI)
Northwest Missouri State U (MO)
The Ohio State U (OH)
Ohio U (OH)
Ohio Wesleyan U (OH)
Oklahoma State U (OK)
Old Dominion U (VA)
Open Learning Agency (BC, Canada)
Oregon State U (OR)
Penn State U Univ Park Campus (PA)
Pittsburg State U (KS)
Plattsburgh State U of NY (NY)
Plymouth State Coll (NH)
Portland State U (OR)
Queens Coll of the City U of NY (NY)
Queen's U at Kingston (ON, Canada)
Radford U (VA)
Regents Coll (NY)
Rowan U (NJ)
Rutgers, State U of NJ, Cook Coll (NJ)
Rutgers, State U of NJ, Douglass Coll (NJ)
Rutgers, State U of NJ, Livingston Coll (NJ)
Rutgers, State U of NJ, Rutgers Coll (NJ)
Rutgers, State U of NJ, U Coll–New Brunswick (NJ)
Ryerson Polytechnic U (ON, Canada)
St. Cloud State U (MN)
Saint Mary's U (NS, Canada)
Salem State Coll (MA)
Salisbury State U (MD)
Samford U (AL)
Sam Houston State U (TX)
San Diego State U (CA)
San Francisco State U (CA)
San Jose State U (CA)
Shippensburg U of Pennsylvania (PA)
Simon Fraser U (BC, Canada)
Simon's Rock Coll of Bard (MA)
Slippery Rock U of Pennsylvania (PA)
Sonoma State U (CA)
South Dakota State U (SD)
Southeast Missouri State U (MO)
Southern Illinois U Carbondale (IL)
Southern Illinois U Edwardsville (IL)
Southern Oregon U (OR)
Southwest Missouri State U (MO)
Southwest Texas State U (TX)
State U of NY at Albany (NY)
State U of NY at Binghamton (NY)
State U of NY at Buffalo (NY)
State U of NY at New Paltz (NY)
State U of NY Coll at Buffalo (NY)
State U of NY Coll at Cortland (NY)
State U of NY Coll at Geneseo (NY)
State U of NY Coll at Oneonta (NY)
State U of West Georgia (GA)
Stephen F. Austin State U (TX)
Stetson U (FL)
Syracuse U (NY)
Temple U (PA)
Texas A&M U (TX)
Texas A&M U–Commerce (TX)
Texas A&M U–Kingsville (TX)
Texas Tech U (TX)
Towson U (MD)
Trent U (ON, Canada)
Trinity Western U (BC, Canada)
United States Air Force Academy (CO)
United States Military Academy (NY)
Université de Montréal (PQ, Canada)
Université de Sherbrooke (PQ, Canada)
U du Québec à Chicoutimi (PQ, Canada)
U du Québec à Trois-Rivières (PQ, Canada)

Majors Index
Geography–Geology

Université Laval (PQ, Canada)
U Coll of the Fraser Valley (BC, Canada)
The U of Akron (OH)
The U of Alabama (AL)
U of Alaska Fairbanks (AK)
U of Alberta (AB, Canada)
The U of Arizona (AZ)
U of Arkansas (AR)
U of British Columbia (BC, Canada)
U of Calgary (AB, Canada)
U of Calif, Berkeley (CA)
U of Calif, Irvine (CA)
U of Calif, Los Angeles (CA)
U of Calif, Riverside (CA)
U of Calif, Santa Barbara (CA)
U of Central Arkansas (AR)
U of Chicago (IL)
U of Cincinnati (OH)
U of Colorado at Boulder (CO)
U of Colorado at Colorado Springs (CO)
U of Colorado at Denver (CO)
U of Connecticut (CT)
U of Delaware (DE)
U of Denver (CO)
U of Florida (FL)
U of Georgia (GA)
U of Guelph (ON, Canada)
U of Hawaii at Manoa (HI)
U of Idaho (ID)
U of Illinois at Chicago (IL)
U of Illinois at Urbana–Champaign (IL)
The U of Iowa (IA)
U of Kansas (KS)
U of Kentucky (KY)
The U of Lethbridge (AB, Canada)
U of Louisiana at Monroe (LA)
U of Louisville (KY)
U of Maine at Farmington (ME)
U of Manitoba (MB, Canada)
U of Maryland, Baltimore County (MD)
U of Maryland, Coll Park (MD)
U of Massachusetts Amherst (MA)
U of Massachusetts Boston (MA)
The U of Memphis (TN)
U of Miami (FL)
U of Michigan (MI)
U of Michigan–Flint (MI)
U of Minnesota, Duluth (MN)
U of Minnesota, Twin Cities Campus (MN)
U of Missouri–Columbia (MO)
U of Missouri–Kansas City (MO)
The U of Montana–Missoula (MT)
U of Nebraska at Kearney (NE)
U of Nebraska at Omaha (NE)
U of Nebraska–Lincoln (NE)
U of Nevada, Reno (NV)
U of New Hampshire (NH)
U of New Mexico (NM)
U of New Orleans (LA)
U of North Alabama (AL)
The U of North Carolina at Chapel Hill (NC)
The U of North Carolina at Charlotte (NC)
The U of North Carolina at Greensboro (NC)
The U of North Carolina at Wilmington (NC)
U of North Dakota (ND)
U of Northern Colorado (CO)
U of Northern Iowa (IA)
U of North Texas (TX)
U of Oklahoma (OK)
U of Oregon (OR)
U of Pittsburgh at Johnstown (PA)
U of Puerto Rico, Río Piedras (PR)
U of Regina (SK, Canada)
U of St. Thomas (MN)
U of South Alabama (AL)
U of South Carolina (SC)
U of Southern California (CA)
U of Southern Maine (ME)
U of Southern Mississippi (MS)
U of South Florida (FL)
The U of Tennessee at Martin (TN)
The U of Tennessee Knoxville (TN)
The U of Texas at Austin (TX)
The U of Texas at Dallas (TX)
The U of Texas at San Antonio (TX)
U of the District of Columbia (DC)
U of the Pacific (CA)
U of Toronto (ON, Canada)
U of Utah (UT)
U of Vermont (VT)
U of Victoria (BC, Canada)
U of Washington (WA)
U of Waterloo (ON, Canada)
The U of Western Ontario (ON, Canada)
U of Windsor (ON, Canada)
The U of Winnipeg (MB, Canada)
U of Wisconsin–Eau Claire (WI)
U of Wisconsin–La Crosse (WI)
U of Wisconsin–Madison (WI)
U of Wisconsin–Milwaukee (WI)
U of Wisconsin–Parkside (WI)
U of Wisconsin–Platteville (WI)
U of Wisconsin–River Falls (WI)
U of Wisconsin–Stevens Point (WI)
U of Wisconsin–Whitewater (WI)
U of Wyoming (WY)
Utah State U (UT)
Valparaiso U (IN)
Vassar Coll (NY)
Villanova U (PA)
Virginia Polytechnic Inst and State U (VA)
Wayne State Coll (NE)
Wayne State U (MI)
Weber State U (UT)
West Chester U of Pennsylvania (PA)
Western Carolina U (NC)
Western Illinois U (IL)
Western Kentucky U (KY)
Western Michigan U (MI)
Western Oregon U (OR)
Western Washington U (WA)
Westfield State Coll (MA)
West Texas A&M U (TX)
West Virginia U (WV)
Wilfrid Laurier U (ON, Canada)
William Paterson U of New Jersey (NJ)
Wittenberg U (OH)
Worcester State Coll (MA)
Wright State U (OH)
York U (ON, Canada)
Youngstown State U (OH)

GEOLOGICAL ENGINEERING
Auburn U (AL)
Colorado School of Mines (CO)
Cornell U (NY)
Harvard U (MA)
Memorial U of Newfoundland (NF, Canada)
Michigan Technological U (MI)
Millersville U of Pennsylvania (PA)
Montana Tech of The U of Montana (MT)
New Mexico State U (NM)
Oregon State U (OR)
Queen's U at Kingston (ON, Canada)
Rutgers, State U of NJ, Newark Coll of Arts & Scis (NJ)
South Dakota School of Mines and Technology (SD)
U du Québec à Chicoutimi (PQ, Canada)
Université Laval (PQ, Canada)
The U of Akron (OH)
U of Alaska Fairbanks (AK)
The U of Arizona (AZ)
U of British Columbia (BC, Canada)
U of Calgary (AB, Canada)
U of Calif, Los Angeles (CA)
U of Idaho (ID)
U of Manitoba (MB, Canada)
U of Minnesota, Twin Cities Campus (MN)
U of Mississippi (MS)
U of Missouri–Rolla (MO)
U of Nevada, Reno (NV)
U of New Brunswick, Fredericton (NB, Canada)
U of New Brunswick, Saint John (NB, Canada)
U of North Dakota (ND)
U of Oklahoma (OK)
U of Toronto (ON, Canada)
U of Utah (UT)
U of Waterloo (ON, Canada)
Wright State U (OH)

GEOLOGY
Abilene Christian U (TX)
Acadia U (NS, Canada)
Adams State Coll (CO)
Albion Coll (MI)
Alfred U (NY)
Allegheny Coll (PA)
Amherst Coll (MA)
Antioch Coll (OH)
Appalachian State U (NC)
Arizona State U (AZ)
Arkansas Tech U (AR)
Ashland U (OH)
Auburn U (AL)
Augustana Coll (IL)
Austin Peay State U (TN)
Baldwin-Wallace Coll (OH)
Ball State U (IN)
Bates Coll (ME)
Baylor U (TX)
Beloit Coll (WI)
Bemidji State U (MN)
Bloomsburg U of Pennsylvania (PA)
Boise State U (ID)
Boston Coll (MA)
Boston U (MA)
Bowdoin Coll (ME)
Bowling Green State U (OH)
Bradley U (IL)
Brandon U (MB, Canada)
Bridgewater State Coll (MA)
Brigham Young U (UT)
Brock U (ON, Canada)
Brooklyn Coll of the City U of NY (NY)
Brown U (RI)
Bryn Mawr Coll (PA)
Bucknell U (PA)
California Inst of Technology (CA)
California Lutheran U (CA)
California State Polytechnic U, Pomona (CA)
California State U, Chico (CA)
California State U, Dominguez Hills (CA)
California State U, Fresno (CA)
California State U, Fullerton (CA)
California State U, Hayward (CA)
California State U, Long Beach (CA)
California State U, Los Angeles (CA)
California State U, Northridge (CA)
California State U, Sacramento (CA)
California State U, San Bernardino (CA)
California State U, Stanislaus (CA)
California U of Pennsylvania (PA)
Calvin Coll (MI)
Carleton Coll (MN)
Carleton U (ON, Canada)
Case Western Reserve U (OH)
Castleton State Coll (VT)
Centenary Coll of Louisiana (LA)
Central Michigan U (MI)
Central Missouri State U (MO)
City Coll of the City U of NY (NY)
Clarion U of Pennsylvania (PA)
Clemson U (SC)
Cleveland State U (OH)
Colby Coll (ME)
Colgate U (NY)
Coll of Charleston (SC)
The Coll of William and Mary (VA)
The Coll of Wooster (OH)
The Colorado Coll (CO)
Colorado State U (CO)
Columbia Coll (MO)
Columbia Coll (NY)
Columbia U, School of General Studies (NY)
Columbus State U (GA)
Cornell Coll (IA)
Cornell U (NY)
Denison U (OH)
DePauw U (IN)
Dickinson Coll (PA)
Duke U (NC)
Earlham Coll (IN)
East Carolina U (NC)
Eastern Illinois U (IL)
Eastern Kentucky U (KY)
Eastern Michigan U (MI)
Eastern New Mexico U (NM)
Eastern Washington U (WA)
Edinboro U of Pennsylvania (PA)
Elizabeth City State U (NC)
The Evergreen State Coll (WA)
Florida Atlantic U (FL)
Florida International U (FL)
Florida State U (FL)
Fort Hays State U (KS)
Fort Lewis Coll (CO)
Franklin and Marshall Coll (PA)
George Mason U (VA)
The George Washington U (DC)
Georgia Southern U (GA)
Georgia Southwestern State U (GA)
Georgia State U (GA)
Grand Valley State U (MI)
Guilford Coll (NC)
Gustavus Adolphus Coll (MN)
Hamilton Coll (NY)
Hampshire Coll (MA)
Hanover Coll (IN)
Hardin-Simmons U (TX)
Hartwick Coll (NY)
Harvard U (MA)
Haverford Coll (PA)
Hobart and William Smith Colls (NY)
Hofstra U (NY)
Hope Coll (MI)
Howard U (DC)
Humboldt State U (CA)
Idaho State U (ID)
Illinois State U (IL)
Indiana State U (IN)
Indiana U Bloomington (IN)
Indiana U Northwest (IN)
Indiana U of Pennsylvania (PA)
Indiana U–Purdue U Fort Wayne (IN)
Indiana U–Purdue U Indianapolis (IN)
Iowa State U of Science and Technology (IA)
Jacksonville State U (AL)
James Madison U (VA)
Juniata Coll (PA)
Kansas State U (KS)
Keene State Coll (NH)
Kent State U (OH)
Kutztown U of Pennsylvania (PA)
Lafayette Coll (PA)
Lakehead U (ON, Canada)
Lake Superior State U (MI)
Lamar U (TX)
La Salle U (PA)
Lawrence U (WI)
Lehman Coll of the City U of NY (NY)
Lewis-Clark State Coll (ID)
Lock Haven U of Pennsylvania (PA)
Long Island U, C.W. Post Campus (NY)
Long Island U, Southampton Coll, Friends World Program (NY)
Louisiana State U and A&M Coll (LA)
Louisiana Tech U (LA)
Macalester Coll (MN)
Marietta Coll (OH)
Marshall U (WV)
Mary Washington Coll (VA)
McGill U (PQ, Canada)
Memorial U of Newfoundland (NF, Canada)
Mercyhurst Coll (PA)
Mesa State Coll (CO)
Miami U (OH)
Michigan State U (MI)
Michigan Technological U (MI)
Middlebury Coll (VT)
Middle Tennessee State U (TN)
Midwestern State U (TX)
Millersville U of Pennsylvania (PA)
Millsaps Coll (MS)
Mississippi State U (MS)
Moravian Coll (PA)
Morehead State U (KY)
Mount Allison U (NB, Canada)
Mount Holyoke Coll (MA)
Mount Union Coll (OH)
Murray State U (KY)
Muskingum Coll (OH)
New Jersey City U (NJ)
New Mexico Inst of Mining and Technology (NM)
New Mexico State U (NM)
North Carolina State U (NC)
Northeastern U (MA)
Northern Arizona U (AZ)
Northern Illinois U (IL)
Northern Kentucky U (KY)
Northland Coll (WI)
Northwestern U (IL)
Northwest Missouri State U (MO)
Norwich U (VT)
Oberlin Coll (OH)
Occidental Coll (CA)
The Ohio State U (OH)
Ohio U (OH)
Ohio Wesleyan U (OH)
Oklahoma State U (OK)
Old Dominion U (VA)
Olivet Nazarene U (IL)
Oregon State U (OR)
Pacific Lutheran U (WA)
Penn State U Univ Park Campus (PA)
Plattsburgh State U of NY (NY)
Pomona Coll (CA)
Portland State U (OR)
Princeton U (NJ)
Purdue U (IN)
Queens Coll of the City U of NY (NY)
Queen's U at Kingston (ON, Canada)
Radford U (VA)
Regents Coll (NY)
Rensselaer Polytechnic Inst (NY)
Rice U (TX)
The Richard Stockton Coll of New Jersey (NJ)
Rider U (NJ)
Rocky Mountain Coll (MT)
Rutgers, State U of NJ, Cook Coll (NJ)
Rutgers, State U of NJ, Douglass Coll (NJ)
Rutgers, State U of NJ, Livingston Coll (NJ)
Rutgers, State U of NJ, Newark Coll of Arts & Scis (NJ)
Rutgers, State U of NJ, Rutgers Coll (NJ)
Rutgers, State U of NJ, U Coll–New Brunswick (NJ)
St. Francis Xavier U (NS, Canada)
St. Lawrence U (NY)
Saint Louis U (MO)
Saint Mary's U (NS, Canada)
St. Mary's U of San Antonio (TX)
St. Norbert Coll (WI)
Salem State Coll (MA)
Sam Houston State U (TX)
San Diego State U (CA)
San Francisco State U (CA)
San Jose State U (CA)
Sarah Lawrence Coll (NY)
Scripps Coll (CA)
Simon's Rock Coll of Bard (MA)
Skidmore Coll (NY)
Slippery Rock U of Pennsylvania (PA)
Smith Coll (MA)
Sonoma State U (CA)
South Dakota School of Mines and Technology (SD)
Southeast Missouri State U (MO)
Southern Illinois U Carbondale (IL)
Southern Methodist U (TX)
Southern Oregon U (OR)
Southern Utah U (UT)
Southwest Missouri State U (MO)
Stanford U (CA)
State U of NY at Albany (NY)
State U of NY at Binghamton (NY)
State U of NY at Buffalo (NY)
State U of NY at New Paltz (NY)
State U of NY at Oswego (NY)
State U of NY at Stony Brook (NY)
State U of NY Coll at Brockport (NY)
State U of NY Coll at Buffalo (NY)
State U of NY Coll at Cortland (NY)
State U of NY Coll at Fredonia (NY)
State U of NY Coll at Geneseo (NY)
State U of NY Coll at Oneonta (NY)
State U of NY Coll at Potsdam (NY)
State U of West Georgia (GA)

Majors Index
Geology–German

Stephen F. Austin State U (TX)
Sul Ross State U (TX)
Syracuse U (NY)
Temple U (PA)
Tennessee Technological U (TN)
Texas A&M U (TX)
Texas A&M U–Commerce (TX)
Texas A&M U–Kingsville (TX)
Texas Christian U (TX)
Texas Tech U (TX)
Trinity U (TX)
Tufts U (MA)
Tulane U (LA)
Union Coll (NY)
Université de Montréal (PQ, Canada)
U du Québec à Chicoutimi (PQ, Canada)
Université Laval (PQ, Canada)
The U of Akron (OH)
The U of Alabama (AL)
U of Alaska Fairbanks (AK)
U of Alberta (AB, Canada)
The U of Arizona (AZ)
U of Arkansas (AR)
U of Arkansas at Little Rock (AR)
U of British Columbia (BC, Canada)
U of Calgary (AB, Canada)
U of Calif, Berkeley (CA)
U of Calif, Davis (CA)
U of Calif, Los Angeles (CA)
U of Calif, Riverside (CA)
U of Calif, Santa Barbara (CA)
U of Calif, Santa Cruz (CA)
U of Cincinnati (OH)
U of Colorado at Boulder (CO)
U of Colorado at Denver (CO)
U of Connecticut (CT)
U of Dayton (OH)
U of Delaware (DE)
U of Florida (FL)
U of Georgia (GA)
U of Hawaii at Manoa (HI)
U of Houston (TX)
U of Idaho (ID)
U of Illinois at Chicago (IL)
U of Illinois at Urbana–Champaign (IL)
The U of Iowa (IA)
U of Kansas (KS)
U of Kentucky (KY)
U of Louisiana at Lafayette (LA)
U of Louisiana at Monroe (LA)
U of Maine (ME)
U of Maine at Farmington (ME)
U of Maine at Presque Isle (ME)
U of Manitoba (MB, Canada)
U of Maryland, Coll Park (MD)
U of Massachusetts Amherst (MA)
The U of Memphis (TN)
U of Miami (FL)
U of Michigan (MI)
U of Minnesota, Duluth (MN)
U of Minnesota, Morris (MN)
U of Minnesota, Twin Cities Campus (MN)
U of Mississippi (MS)
U of Missouri–Columbia (MO)
U of Missouri–Kansas City (MO)
U of Missouri–Rolla (MO)
The U of Montana–Missoula (MT)
U of Nebraska at Omaha (NE)
U of Nebraska–Lincoln (NE)
U of Nevada, Las Vegas (NV)
U of Nevada, Reno (NV)
U of New Brunswick, Fredericton (NB, Canada)
U of New Hampshire (NH)
U of New Mexico (NM)
U of New Orleans (LA)
U of North Alabama (AL)
The U of North Carolina at Chapel Hill (NC)
The U of North Carolina at Charlotte (NC)
The U of North Carolina at Wilmington (NC)
U of North Dakota (ND)
U of Northern Iowa (IA)
U of Notre Dame (IN)
U of Oklahoma (OK)
U of Oregon (OR)
U of Pennsylvania (PA)
U of Pittsburgh (PA)
U of Pittsburgh at Bradford (PA)
U of Pittsburgh at Johnstown (PA)

U of Puerto Rico, Mayagüez Campus (PR)
U of Puget Sound (WA)
U of Regina (SK, Canada)
U of Rhode Island (RI)
U of Rochester (NY)
U of St. Thomas (MN)
U of South Alabama (AL)
U of South Carolina (SC)
U of Southern California (CA)
U of Southern Indiana (IN)
U of Southern Maine (ME)
U of Southern Mississippi (MS)
U of South Florida (FL)
The U of Tennessee at Chattanooga (TN)
The U of Tennessee at Martin (TN)
The U of Tennessee Knoxville (TN)
The U of Texas at Arlington (TX)
The U of Texas at Austin (TX)
The U of Texas at Dallas (TX)
The U of Texas at San Antonio (TX)
U of the Pacific (CA)
U of the South (TN)
U of Toronto (ON, Canada)
U of Tulsa (OK)
U of Utah (UT)
U of Vermont (VT)
U of Victoria (BC, Canada)
U of Washington (WA)
U of Waterloo (ON, Canada)
The U of Western Ontario (ON, Canada)
U of Windsor (ON, Canada)
U of Wisconsin–Eau Claire (WI)
U of Wisconsin–Madison (WI)
U of Wisconsin–Milwaukee (WI)
U of Wisconsin–Parkside (WI)
U of Wisconsin–Platteville (WI)
U of Wisconsin–River Falls (WI)
U of Wyoming (WY)
Utah State U (UT)
Valparaiso U (IN)
Vanderbilt U (TN)
Vassar Coll (NY)
Virginia Polytechnic Inst and State U (VA)
Washington and Lee U (VA)
Washington State U (WA)
Wayne State U (MI)
Weber State U (UT)
Wellesley Coll (MA)
West Chester U of Pennsylvania (PA)
Western Carolina U (NC)
Western Illinois U (IL)
Western Kentucky U (KY)
Western Michigan U (MI)
Western Montana Coll of The U of Montana (MT)
Western State Coll of Colorado (CO)
Western Washington U (WA)
West Texas A&M U (TX)
West Virginia U (WV)
Wheaton Coll (IL)
Whitman Coll (WA)
Wichita State U (KS)
Williams Coll (MA)
Winona State U (MN)
Wittenberg U (OH)
Wright State U (OH)
York Coll of the City U of New York (NY)
Youngstown State U (OH)

GEOPHYSICAL ENGINEERING
Colorado School of Mines (CO)
Harvard U (MA)
Montana Tech of The U of Montana (MT)
Tufts U (MA)
U of Calif, Los Angeles (CA)
U of Toronto (ON, Canada)
Worcester Polytechnic Inst (MA)

GEOPHYSICS AND SEISMOLOGY
Baylor U (TX)
Boise State U (ID)
Boston Coll (MA)
Bowling Green State U (OH)
Brown U (RI)
California Inst of Technology (CA)
California State U, Northridge (CA)
Columbia Coll (NY)

Eastern Michigan U (MI)
Hampshire Coll (MA)
Harvard U (MA)
Hope Coll (MI)
Kansas State U (KS)
McGill U (PQ, Canada)
Memorial U of Newfoundland (NF, Canada)
Michigan Technological U (MI)
New Mexico Inst of Mining and Technology (NM)
Northern Arizona U (AZ)
Oregon State U (OR)
Rice U (TX)
St. Lawrence U (NY)
Saint Louis U (MO)
San Jose State U (CA)
Southern Methodist U (TX)
Stanford U (CA)
State U of NY Coll at Fredonia (NY)
State U of NY Coll at Geneseo (NY)
Texas A&M U (TX)
Texas Tech U (TX)
Université de Sherbrooke (PQ, Canada)
The U of Akron (OH)
U of Alaska Fairbanks (AK)
U of Alberta (AB, Canada)
U of British Columbia (BC, Canada)
U of Calgary (AB, Canada)
U of Calif, Berkeley (CA)
U of Calif, Riverside (CA)
U of Calif, Santa Barbara (CA)
U of Calif, Santa Cruz (CA)
U of Chicago (IL)
U of Delaware (DE)
U of Hawaii at Manoa (HI)
U of Houston (TX)
U of Minnesota, Twin Cities Campus (MN)
U of Missouri–Rolla (MO)
U of Nevada, Reno (NV)
U of New Brunswick, Fredericton (NB, Canada)
U of New Orleans (LA)
U of Oklahoma (OK)
U of Regina (SK, Canada)
U of South Carolina (SC)
The U of Texas at Austin (TX)
The U of Texas at Dallas (TX)
U of the Pacific (CA)
U of Toronto (ON, Canada)
U of Tulsa (OK)
U of Utah (UT)
U of Victoria (BC, Canada)
U of Washington (WA)
The U of Western Ontario (ON, Canada)
U of Wisconsin–Madison (WI)
Western Michigan U (MI)
Western Washington U (WA)
Wright State U (OH)

GEOTECHNICAL ENGINEERING
Montana Tech of The U of Montana (MT)
The Ohio State U (OH)

GERMAN
Adrian Coll (MI)
Agnes Scott Coll (GA)
Albion Coll (MI)
Alfred U (NY)
Allegheny Coll (PA)
Alma Coll (MI)
Amherst Coll (MA)
Anderson U (IN)
Antioch Coll (OH)
Aquinas Coll (MI)
Arizona State U (AZ)
Arkansas Tech U (AR)
Auburn U (AL)
Augsburg Coll (MN)
Augustana Coll (IL)
Augustana Coll (SD)
Austin Coll (TX)
Baker U (KS)
Baldwin-Wallace Coll (OH)
Ball State U (IN)
Bard Coll (NY)
Barnard Coll (NY)
Bates Coll (ME)
Baylor U (TX)
Bellarmine Coll (KY)

Beloit Coll (WI)
Bemidji State U (MN)
Bennington Coll (VT)
Berea Coll (KY)
Berry Coll (GA)
Bethany Coll (WV)
Bethel Coll (KS)
Birmingham-Southern Coll (AL)
Bishop's U (PQ, Canada)
Bloomsburg U of Pennsylvania (PA)
Boise State U (ID)
Boston Coll (MA)
Boston U (MA)
Bowdoin Coll (ME)
Bowling Green State U (OH)
Bradley U (IL)
Brandeis U (MA)
Bridgewater Coll (VA)
Brigham Young U (UT)
Brock U (ON, Canada)
Brooklyn Coll of the City U of NY (NY)
Brown U (RI)
Bryn Mawr Coll (PA)
Bucknell U (PA)
Butler U (IN)
California Lutheran U (CA)
California State U, Chico (CA)
California State U, Fullerton (CA)
California State U, Long Beach (CA)
California State U, Northridge (CA)
California State U, Sacramento (CA)
California U of Pennsylvania (PA)
Calvin Coll (MI)
Canisius Coll (NY)
Carleton Coll (MN)
Carleton U (ON, Canada)
Carnegie Mellon U (PA)
Carthage Coll (WI)
Case Western Reserve U (OH)
The Catholic U of America (DC)
Centenary Coll of Louisiana (LA)
Central Coll (IA)
Central Connecticut State U (CT)
Central Methodist Coll (MO)
Central Michigan U (MI)
Central Missouri State U (MO)
Centre Coll (KY)
Chestnut Hill Coll (PA)
Christopher Newport U (VA)
Citadel, The Military Coll of South Carolina (SC)
Claremont McKenna Coll (CA)
Clark Atlanta U (GA)
Clemson U (SC)
Cleveland State U (OH)
Coe Coll (IA)
Colby Coll (ME)
Colgate U (NY)
Coll of Charleston (SC)
Coll of Saint Benedict (MN)
Coll of the Holy Cross (MA)
Coll of the Ozarks (MO)
The Coll of William and Mary (VA)
The Coll of Wooster (OH)
The Colorado Coll (CO)
Colorado State U (CO)
Columbia Coll (NY)
Columbia U, School of General Studies (NY)
Concordia Coll (MN)
Concordia U (NE)
Concordia U (PQ, Canada)
Concordia U Wisconsin (WI)
Connecticut Coll (CT)
Cornell Coll (IA)
Cornell U (NY)
Creighton U (NE)
Dalhousie U (NS, Canada)
Dana Coll (NE)
Dartmouth Coll (NH)
David Lipscomb U (TN)
Davidson Coll (NC)
Denison U (OH)
DePaul U (IL)
DePauw U (IN)
Dickinson Coll (PA)
Doane Coll (NE)
Dordt Coll (IA)
Drake U (IA)
Drew U (NJ)
Drury U (MO)
Duke U (NC)
Duquesne U (PA)

Earlham Coll (IN)
East Carolina U (NC)
Eastern Kentucky U (KY)
Eastern Mennonite U (VA)
Eastern Michigan U (MI)
East Tennessee State U (TN)
Eckerd Coll (FL)
Edinboro U of Pennsylvania (PA)
Elizabethtown Coll (PA)
Elmhurst Coll (IL)
Emory U (GA)
Fairfield U (CT)
Florida Atlantic U (FL)
Florida International U (FL)
Florida State U (FL)
Fordham U (NY)
Fort Hays State U (KS)
Franklin and Marshall Coll (PA)
Furman U (SC)
George Mason U (VA)
Georgetown Coll (KY)
Georgetown U (DC)
The George Washington U (DC)
Georgia Southern U (GA)
Georgia State U (GA)
Gettysburg Coll (PA)
Gonzaga U (WA)
Gordon Coll (MA)
Goshen Coll (IN)
Grace Coll (IN)
Graceland Coll (IA)
Grand Valley State U (MI)
Grinnell Coll (IA)
Guilford Coll (NC)
Gustavus Adolphus Coll (MN)
Hamilton Coll (NY)
Hamline U (MN)
Hampden-Sydney Coll (VA)
Hanover Coll (IN)
Hardin-Simmons U (TX)
Hartwick Coll (NY)
Harvard U (MA)
Hastings Coll (NE)
Haverford Coll (PA)
Heidelberg Coll (OH)
Hendrix Coll (AR)
Hillsdale Coll (MI)
Hiram Coll (OH)
Hofstra U (NY)
Hollins U (VA)
Hope Coll (MI)
Howard U (DC)
Humboldt State U (CA)
Hunter Coll of the City U of NY (NY)
Idaho State U (ID)
Illinois Coll (IL)
Illinois State U (IL)
Illinois Wesleyan U (IL)
Immaculata Coll (PA)
Indiana State U (IN)
Indiana U Bloomington (IN)
Indiana U of Pennsylvania (PA)
Indiana U–Purdue U Fort Wayne (IN)
Indiana U–Purdue U Indianapolis (IN)
Indiana U South Bend (IN)
Indiana U Southeast (IN)
Iowa State U of Science and Technology (IA)
Ithaca Coll (NY)
Jacksonville State U (AL)
James Madison U (VA)
John Carroll U (OH)
Johns Hopkins U (MD)
Juniata Coll (PA)
Kalamazoo Coll (MI)
Kent State U (OH)
Kenyon Coll (OH)
Knox Coll (IL)
Kutztown U of Pennsylvania (PA)
Lafayette Coll (PA)
Lake Erie Coll (OH)
Lake Forest Coll (IL)
Lakeland Coll (WI)
La Salle U (PA)
Lawrence U (WI)
Lebanon Valley Coll (PA)
Lehigh U (PA)
Lenoir-Rhyne Coll (NC)
Lewis & Clark Coll (OR)
Linfield Coll (OR)
Lock Haven U of Pennsylvania (PA)
Long Island U, C.W. Post Campus (NY)

Majors Index
German–Gerontology

Long Island U, Southampton Coll, Friends World Program (NY)
Longwood Coll (VA)
Loras Coll (IA)
Louisiana State U and A&M Coll (LA)
Loyola Coll in Maryland (MD)
Loyola U Chicago (IL)
Loyola U New Orleans (LA)
Luther Coll (IA)
Lycoming Coll (PA)
Manchester Coll (IN)
Mansfield U of Pennsylvania (PA)
Marian Coll (IN)
Marlboro Coll (VT)
Marquette U (WI)
Marshall U (WV)
Mary Baldwin Coll (VA)
Mary Washington Coll (VA)
Massachusetts Inst of Technology (MA)
McGill U (PQ, Canada)
Memorial U of Newfoundland (NF, Canada)
Mercer U (GA)
Mercyhurst Coll (PA)
Messiah Coll (PA)
Miami U (OH)
Michigan State U (MI)
Middlebury Coll (VT)
Midland Lutheran Coll (NE)
Millersville U of Pennsylvania (PA)
Millikin U (IL)
Millsaps Coll (MS)
Mills Coll (CA)
Minnesota State U, Mankato (MN)
Minot State U (ND)
Moravian Coll (PA)
Morehouse Coll (GA)
Mount Allison U (NB, Canada)
Mount Holyoke Coll (MA)
Mount Saint Mary's Coll and Seminary (MD)
Mount Saint Vincent U (NS, Canada)
Mount Union Coll (OH)
Muhlenberg Coll (PA)
Murray State U (KY)
Muskingum Coll (OH)
Nazareth Coll of Rochester (NY)
Nebraska Wesleyan U (NE)
Newberry Coll (SC)
New Coll of the U of South Florida (FL)
New York U (NY)
North Carolina State U (NC)
North Central Coll (IL)
North Dakota State U (ND)
Northeastern State U (OK)
Northeastern U (MA)
Northern Arizona U (AZ)
Northern Illinois U (IL)
Northern State U (SD)
Northwestern U (IL)
Oakland U (MI)
Oberlin Coll (OH)
The Ohio State U (OH)
Ohio U (OH)
Ohio Wesleyan U (OH)
Oklahoma Baptist U (OK)
Oklahoma City U (OK)
Oklahoma State U (OK)
Oregon State U (OR)
Pacific Lutheran U (WA)
Pacific U (OR)
Penn State U Univ Park Campus (PA)
Pepperdine U, Malibu (CA)
Pitzer Coll (CA)
Pomona Coll (CA)
Portland State U (OR)
Presbyterian Coll (SC)
Princeton U (NJ)
Principia Coll (IL)
Purdue U Calumet (IN)
Queens Coll of the City U of NY (NY)
Queen's U at Kingston (ON, Canada)
Randolph-Macon Coll (VA)
Randolph-Macon Woman's Coll (VA)
Reed Coll (OR)
Regis Coll (MA)
Rensselaer Polytechnic Inst (NY)
Rhodes Coll (TN)
Rice U (TX)

Rider U (NJ)
Ripon Coll (WI)
Rockford Coll (IL)
Rollins Coll (FL)
Rosemont Coll (PA)
Rutgers, State U of NJ, Camden Coll of Arts & Scis (NJ)
Rutgers, State U of NJ, Douglass Coll (NJ)
Rutgers, State U of NJ, Livingston Coll (NJ)
Rutgers, State U of NJ, Newark Coll of Arts & Scis (NJ)
Rutgers, State U of NJ, Rutgers Coll (NJ)
Rutgers, State U of NJ, U Coll–Camden (NJ)
Rutgers, State U of NJ, U Coll–New Brunswick (NJ)
St. Ambrose U (IA)
St. Cloud State U (MN)
St. John Fisher Coll (NY)
Saint John's U (MN)
Saint Joseph's U (PA)
St. Lawrence U (NY)
Saint Louis U (MO)
Saint Mary's Coll of California (CA)
Saint Mary's U (NS, Canada)
St. Norbert Coll (WI)
St. Olaf Coll (MN)
Salem Coll (NC)
Samford U (AL)
Sam Houston State U (TX)
San Diego State U (CA)
San Francisco State U (CA)
San Jose State U (CA)
Sarah Lawrence Coll (NY)
Scripps Coll (CA)
Seattle Pacific U (WA)
Seattle U (WA)
Simon's Rock Coll of Bard (MA)
Simpson Coll (IA)
Skidmore Coll (NY)
Smith Coll (MA)
Sonoma State U (CA)
South Dakota State U (SD)
Southeast Missouri State U (MO)
Southern Illinois U Carbondale (IL)
Southern Methodist U (TX)
Southern Utah U (UT)
Southwestern U (TX)
Southwest Missouri State U (MO)
Southwest Texas State U (TX)
Stanford U (CA)
State U of NY at Binghamton (NY)
State U of NY at Buffalo (NY)
State U of NY at New Paltz (NY)
State U of NY at Oswego (NY)
State U of NY at Stony Brook (NY)
State U of NY Coll at Cortland (NY)
Stetson U (FL)
Susquehanna U (PA)
Swarthmore Coll (PA)
Sweet Briar Coll (VA)
Syracuse U (NY)
Temple U (PA)
Tennessee Technological U (TN)
Texas A&M U (TX)
Texas Lutheran U (TX)
Texas Southern U (TX)
Texas Tech U (TX)
Towson U (MD)
Trent U (ON, Canada)
Trinity Coll (CT)
Trinity U (TX)
Truman State U (MO)
Tufts U (MA)
Tulane U (LA)
Union Coll (NE)
United States Military Academy (NY)
Université de Montréal (PQ, Canada)
The U of Akron (OH)
The U of Alabama (AL)
The U of Alabama at Birmingham (AL)
The U of Alabama in Huntsville (AL)
U of Alaska Fairbanks (AK)
U of Alberta (AB, Canada)
The U of Arizona (AZ)
U of Arkansas (AR)
U of British Columbia (BC, Canada)
U of Calgary (AB, Canada)
U of Calif, Berkeley (CA)

U of Calif, Davis (CA)
U of Calif, Irvine (CA)
U of Calif, Los Angeles (CA)
U of Calif, Riverside (CA)
U of Calif, San Diego (CA)
U of Calif, Santa Barbara (CA)
U of Calif, Santa Cruz (CA)
U of Central Oklahoma (OK)
U of Chicago (IL)
U of Cincinnati (OH)
U of Colorado at Boulder (CO)
U of Colorado at Denver (CO)
U of Connecticut (CT)
U of Dallas (TX)
U of Dayton (OH)
U of Delaware (DE)
U of Denver (CO)
U of Evansville (IN)
U of Florida (FL)
U of Georgia (GA)
U of Hawaii at Manoa (HI)
U of Houston (TX)
U of Idaho (ID)
U of Illinois at Chicago (IL)
U of Illinois at Urbana–Champaign (IL)
U of Indianapolis (IN)
The U of Iowa (IA)
U of Kansas (KS)
U of Kentucky (KY)
U of King's Coll (NS, Canada)
U of La Verne (CA)
The U of Lethbridge (AB, Canada)
U of Louisville (KY)
U of Maine (ME)
U of Manitoba (MB, Canada)
U of Maryland, Baltimore County (MD)
U of Maryland, Coll Park (MD)
U of Massachusetts Amherst (MA)
U of Massachusetts Boston (MA)
U of Miami (FL)
U of Michigan (MI)
U of Michigan–Dearborn (MI)
U of Michigan–Flint (MI)
U of Minnesota, Morris (MN)
U of Minnesota, Twin Cities Campus (MN)
U of Mississippi (MS)
U of Missouri–Columbia (MO)
U of Missouri–Kansas City (MO)
U of Missouri–St. Louis (MO)
The U of Montana–Missoula (MT)
U of Nebraska at Kearney (NE)
U of Nebraska at Omaha (NE)
U of Nebraska–Lincoln (NE)
U of Nevada, Las Vegas (NV)
U of Nevada, Reno (NV)
U of New Brunswick, Fredericton (NB, Canada)
U of New Hampshire (NH)
U of New Mexico (NM)
The U of North Carolina at Asheville (NC)
The U of North Carolina at Chapel Hill (NC)
The U of North Carolina at Charlotte (NC)
The U of North Carolina at Greensboro (NC)
U of North Dakota (ND)
U of Northern Colorado (CO)
U of Northern Iowa (IA)
U of North Texas (TX)
U of Notre Dame (IN)
U of Oklahoma (OK)
U of Oregon (OR)
U of Pennsylvania (PA)
U of Pittsburgh (PA)
U of Prince Edward Island (PE, Canada)
U of Puget Sound (WA)
U of Redlands (CA)
U of Regina (SK, Canada)
U of Rhode Island (RI)
U of Richmond (VA)
U of Rochester (NY)
U of St. Thomas (MN)
The U of Scranton (PA)
U of South Alabama (AL)
U of South Carolina (SC)
U of South Dakota (SD)
U of Southern California (CA)
U of Southern Indiana (IN)
U of South Florida (FL)
The U of Tennessee Knoxville (TN)
The U of Texas at Arlington (TX)

The U of Texas at Austin (TX)
The U of Texas at San Antonio (TX)
U of the District of Columbia (DC)
U of the Pacific (CA)
U of the South (TN)
U of Toronto (ON, Canada)
U of Tulsa (OK)
U of Utah (UT)
U of Vermont (VT)
U of Victoria (BC, Canada)
U of Virginia (VA)
U of Washington (WA)
U of Waterloo (ON, Canada)
The U of Western Ontario (ON, Canada)
U of Windsor (ON, Canada)
The U of Winnipeg (MB, Canada)
U of Wisconsin–Eau Claire (WI)
U of Wisconsin–Green Bay (WI)
U of Wisconsin–La Crosse (WI)
U of Wisconsin–Madison (WI)
U of Wisconsin–Milwaukee (WI)
U of Wisconsin–Parkside (WI)
U of Wisconsin–Platteville (WI)
U of Wisconsin–River Falls (WI)
U of Wisconsin–Stevens Point (WI)
U of Wisconsin–Whitewater (WI)
U of Wyoming (WY)
Ursinus Coll (PA)
Utah State U (UT)
Valparaiso U (IN)
Vanderbilt U (TN)
Vassar Coll (NY)
Villanova U (PA)
Virginia Commonwealth U (VA)
Virginia Polytechnic Inst and State U (VA)
Virginia Wesleyan Coll (VA)
Wabash Coll (IN)
Wake Forest U (NC)
Walla Walla Coll (WA)
Wartburg Coll (IA)
Washington & Jefferson Coll (PA)
Washington and Lee U (VA)
Washington Coll (MD)
Washington State U (WA)
Washington U in St. Louis (MO)
Wayne State Coll (NE)
Wayne State U (MI)
Weber State U (UT)
Webster U (MO)
Wellesley Coll (MA)
Wells Coll (NY)
Wesleyan U (CT)
West Chester U of Pennsylvania (PA)
Western Carolina U (NC)
Western Kentucky U (KY)
Western Maryland Coll (MD)
Western Michigan U (MI)
Western Washington U (WA)
Westminster Coll (PA)
Wheaton Coll (IL)
Wheaton Coll (MA)
Whitman Coll (WA)
Wilfrid Laurier U (ON, Canada)
Willamette U (OR)
Williams Coll (MA)
Winona State U (MN)
Wittenberg U (OH)
Wofford Coll (SC)
Wright State U (OH)
Xavier U (OH)
Yale U (CT)
York U (ON, Canada)
Youngstown State U (OH)

GERMAN LANGUAGE EDUCATION
Anderson U (IN)
Baylor U (TX)
Berea Coll (KY)
Berry Coll (GA)
Bridgewater Coll (VA)
Brigham Young U (UT)
Canisius Coll (NY)
The Catholic U of America (DC)
Central Missouri State U (MO)
Colorado State U (CO)
Concordia Coll (MN)
Duquesne U (PA)
East Carolina U (NC)
Eastern Michigan U (MI)
Elmhurst Coll (IL)
Georgia Southern U (GA)
Grace Coll (IN)

Hardin-Simmons U (TX)
Indiana U Bloomington (IN)
Indiana U–Purdue U Indianapolis (IN)
Indiana U South Bend (IN)
Ithaca Coll (NY)
Juniata Coll (PA)
Luther Coll (IA)
Mansfield U of Pennsylvania (PA)
Messiah Coll (PA)
North Dakota State U (ND)
Ohio U (OH)
Oklahoma Baptist U (OK)
St. Ambrose U (IA)
St. Olaf Coll (MN)
Southwest Missouri State U (MO)
The U of Arizona (AZ)
U of Illinois at Chicago (IL)
U of Illinois at Urbana–Champaign (IL)
The U of Iowa (IA)
U of Minnesota, Duluth (MN)
U of Nebraska–Lincoln (NE)
The U of North Carolina at Chapel Hill (NC)
The U of North Carolina at Charlotte (NC)
U of North Texas (TX)
The U of Tennessee at Martin (TN)
U of Wisconsin–River Falls (WI)
Washington U in St. Louis (MO)
Weber State U (UT)
Western Carolina U (NC)
Youngstown State U (OH)

GERONTOLOGICAL SERVICES
Bowling Green State U (OH)
Cazenovia Coll (NY)
Mount Saint Vincent U (NS, Canada)
Saint Mary-of-the-Woods Coll (IN)
U of Northern Colorado (CO)

GERONTOLOGY
Alfred U (NY)
Alma Coll (MI)
Bethune-Cookman Coll (FL)
Bishop's U (PQ, Canada)
Bowling Green State U (OH)
California State U, Dominguez Hills (CA)
California State U, Hayward (CA)
California State U, Los Angeles (CA)
California State U, Northridge (CA)
California State U, Sacramento (CA)
California U of Pennsylvania (PA)
Case Western Reserve U (OH)
Cedar Crest Coll (PA)
Chestnut Hill Coll (PA)
Coll of Mount St. Joseph (OH)
Coll of the Holy Cross (MA)
Coll of the Ozarks (MO)
Dominican U (IL)
Felician Coll (NJ)
Framingham State Coll (MA)
Gwynedd-Mercy Coll (PA)
Iona Coll (NY)
John Carroll U (OH)
Kent State U (OH)
King's Coll (PA)
Langston U (OK)
Lindenwood U (MO)
Long Island U, Southampton Coll, Friends World Program (NY)
Lourdes Coll (OH)
Lynn U (FL)
Madonna U (MI)
Mars Hill Coll (NC)
McKendree Coll (IL)
Mercy Coll (NY)
Mount St. Mary's Coll (CA)
Mount Saint Vincent U (NS, Canada)
National-Louis U (IL)
Nazareth Coll of Rochester (NY)
The Ohio State U (OH)
Plymouth State Coll (NH)
Pontifical Catholic U of Puerto Rico (PR)
Quinnipiac U (CT)
St. Cloud State U (MN)
Saint Mary-of-the-Woods Coll (IN)
San Diego State U (CA)
Shaw U (NC)

Southeastern Oklahoma State U (OK)
Southwest Missouri State U (MO)
State U of NY Coll at Brockport (NY)
State U of NY Coll at Fredonia (NY)
State U of NY Coll at Oneonta (NY)
Stephen F. Austin State U (TX)
Thomas Edison State Coll (NJ)
Towson U (MD)
The U of Akron (OH)
U of Arkansas at Pine Bluff (AR)
U of Evansville (IN)
U of Guelph (ON, Canada)
U of Maryland University Coll (MD)
U of Massachusetts Boston (MA)
U of Missouri–St. Louis (MO)
U of Nebraska at Omaha (NE)
The U of North Carolina at Greensboro (NC)
U of North Texas (TX)
U of Southern California (CA)
U of South Florida (FL)
U of Windsor (ON, Canada)
Utica Coll of Syracuse U (NY)
Wagner Coll (NY)
Weber State U (UT)
Western Michigan U (MI)
Wichita State U (KS)
York Coll of the City U of New York (NY)
York U (ON, Canada)

GRAPHIC DESIGN/COMMERCIAL ART/ILLUSTRATION
Abilene Christian U (TX)
Academy of Art Coll (CA)
The Advertising Arts Coll (CA)
Alberta Coll of Art and Design (AB, Canada)
Alfred U (NY)
American Academy of Art (IL)
American InterContinental U (CA)
American InterContinental U, Atlanta (GA)
American InterContinental U, Atlanta (GA)
American InterContinental U (United Kingdom)
American U (DC)
Anderson Coll (SC)
Anderson U (IN)
Andrews U (MI)
Appalachian State U (NC)
Arizona State U (AZ)
Art Academy of Cincinnati (OH)
Art Center Coll of Design (CA)
The Art Inst of Atlanta (GA)
The Art Inst of Boston at Lesley (MA)
The Art Inst of Colorado (CO)
The Art Inst of Philadelphia (PA)
The Art Inst of Phoenix (AZ)
The Art Inst of Portland (OR)
Art Inst of Southern California (CA)
Art Insts International at San Francisco (CA)
Ashland U (OH)
Atlanta Coll of Art (GA)
Auburn U (AL)
Avila Coll (MO)
Baker Coll of Flint (MI)
Baker Coll of Owosso (MI)
Ball State U (IN)
Barton Coll (NC)
Beaver Coll (PA)
Bellevue U (NE)
Bemidji State U (MN)
Biola U (CA)
Black Hills State U (SD)
Bluffton Coll (OH)
Boston U (MA)
Bradley U (IL)
Brenau U (GA)
Brescia U (KY)
Bridgewater State Coll (MA)
Brigham Young U (UT)
Buena Vista U (IA)
Cabrini Coll (PA)
California Coll of Arts and Crafts (CA)
California Inst of the Arts (CA)
California Polytechnic State U, San Luis Obispo (CA)

California State Polytechnic U, Pomona (CA)
California State U, Dominguez Hills (CA)
California State U, Fresno (CA)
California State U, Fullerton (CA)
California State U, Hayward (CA)
California State U, Long Beach (CA)
California State U, Los Angeles (CA)
California State U, Northridge (CA)
California State U, San Bernardino (CA)
Campbell U (NC)
Cardinal Stritch U (WI)
Carnegie Mellon U (PA)
Carroll Coll (WI)
Carson-Newman Coll (TN)
Carthage Coll (WI)
Cazenovia Coll (NY)
Centenary Coll (NJ)
Ctr for Creative Studies—Coll of Art and Design (MI)
Central Michigan U (MI)
Central Missouri State U (MO)
Champlain Coll (VT)
Chapman U (CA)
Chatham Coll (PA)
Chicago State U (IL)
Chowan Coll (NC)
Clark U (MA)
Clemson U (SC)
Cleveland Inst of Art (OH)
Cogswell Polytechnical Coll (CA)
Coker Coll (SC)
Colby-Sawyer Coll (NH)
Coll of Mount St. Joseph (OH)
The Coll of New Jersey (NJ)
Coll of Notre Dame (CA)
Coll of Our Lady of the Elms (MA)
The Coll of Saint Rose (NY)
The Coll of Southeastern Europe, The American U of Athens (Greece)
Coll of Visual Arts (MN)
Colorado State U (CO)
Columbia Coll (MO)
Columbia Coll (SC)
Columbia Coll Chicago (IL)
Columbus Coll of Art and Design (OH)
Concord Coll (WV)
Concordia U (IL)
Concordia U (NE)
Concordia U (PQ, Canada)
Concordia U Wisconsin (WI)
Cooper Union for the Advancement of Science & Art (NY)
The Corcoran Coll of Art and Design (DC)
Cornish Coll of the Arts (WA)
Creighton U (NE)
Curry Coll (MA)
Daemen Coll (NY)
David Lipscomb U (TN)
DePaul U (IL)
Dominican U (IL)
Dordt Coll (IA)
Drake U (IA)
Drexel U (PA)
Eastern Kentucky U (KY)
Eastern New Mexico U (NM)
Edgewood Coll (WI)
Emmanuel Coll (MA)
Endicott Coll (MA)
Escuela de Artes Plasticas de Puerto Rico (PR)
Fairleigh Dickinson U, Florham-Madison Campus (NJ)
Fairleigh Dickinson U, Teaneck-Hackensack Campus (NJ)
Fairmont State Coll (WV)
Fashion Inst of Technology (NY)
Felician Coll (NJ)
Fitchburg State Coll (MA)
Flagler Coll (FL)
Florida A&M U (FL)
Florida Southern Coll (FL)
Fontbonne Coll (MO)
Fordham U (NY)
Fort Hays State U (KS)
Franklin Pierce Coll (NH)
Freed-Hardeman U (TN)
Gallaudet U (DC)
Georgian Court Coll (NJ)

Georgia Southwestern State U (GA)
Grace Coll (IN)
Graceland Coll (IA)
Grand Canyon U (AZ)
Grand Valley State U (MI)
Grand View Coll (IA)
Hampshire Coll (MA)
Hampton U (VA)
Harding U (AR)
Howard U (DC)
Huntington Coll (IN)
Illinois Wesleyan U (IL)
Indiana State U (IN)
Indiana U Bloomington (IN)
Inter American U of PR, Metropolitan Campus (PR)
International Academy of Design (FL)
Iowa State U of Science and Technology (IA)
Iowa Wesleyan Coll (IA)
John Brown U (AR)
Judson Coll (IL)
Kansas City Art Inst (MO)
Keene State Coll (NH)
Kendall Coll of Art and Design (MI)
Kent State U (OH)
Kutztown U of Pennsylvania (PA)
Lamar U (TX)
Lambuth U (TN)
La Roche Coll (PA)
La Salle U (PA)
La Sierra U (CA)
Lewis U (IL)
Limestone Coll (SC)
Long Island U, C.W. Post Campus (NY)
Long Island U, Southampton Coll (NY)
Longwood Coll (VA)
Louisiana Coll (LA)
Louisiana Tech U (LA)
Loyola U New Orleans (LA)
Lubbock Christian U (TX)
Lycoming Coll (PA)
Lyndon State Coll (VT)
Lynn U (FL)
Madonna U (MI)
Maharishi U of Management (IA)
Maine Coll of Art (ME)
Marietta Coll (OH)
Marshall U (WV)
Mary Baldwin Coll (VA)
Maryland Inst, Coll of Art (MD)
Maryville U of Saint Louis (MO)
Massachusetts Coll of Art (MA)
McKendree Coll (IL)
Memphis Coll of Art (TN)
Mercy Coll (NY)
Meredith Coll (NC)
Millersville U of Pennsylvania (PA)
Millikin U (IL)
Milwaukee Inst of Art and Design (WI)
Minneapolis Coll of Art and Design (MN)
Minnesota State U, Mankato (MN)
Minnesota State U Moorhead (MN)
Mississippi Coll (MS)
Missouri Southern State Coll (MO)
Missouri Western State Coll (MO)
Monmouth U (NJ)
Montana State U–Northern (MT)
Montserrat Coll of Art (MA)
Moore Coll of Art and Design (PA)
Moravian Coll (PA)
Morningside Coll (IA)
Mount Ida Coll (MA)
Mount Mary Coll (WI)
Mount Olive Coll (NC)
Mount Senario Coll (WI)
Nazareth Coll of Rochester (NY)
New Mexico Highlands U (NM)
New World School of the Arts (FL)
New York City Tech Coll of the City U of NY (NY)
New York Inst of Technology (NY)
New York U (NY)
North Carolina State U (NC)
Northeastern State U (OK)
Northeastern U (MA)
Northern Arizona U (AZ)
Northern Kentucky U (KY)
Northern Michigan U (MI)
Northwestern Coll (MN)
Northwest Missouri State U (MO)

Northwest Nazarene U (ID)
Notre Dame Coll (NH)
Nova Scotia Coll of Art and Design (NS, Canada)
Ohio Northern U (OH)
The Ohio State U (OH)
Oklahoma Christian U of Science and Arts (OK)
Oklahoma City U (OK)
Oklahoma State U (OK)
Olivet Nazarene U (IL)
O'More Coll of Design (TN)
Otis Coll of Art and Design (CA)
Pacific Northwest Coll of Art (OR)
Paier Coll of Art, Inc. (CT)
Park U (MO)
Parsons School of Design, New School U (NY)
Pennsylvania Coll of Technology (PA)
Pennsylvania School of Art & Design (PA)
Penn State U Univ Park Campus (PA)
Philadelphia U (PA)
Pittsburg State U (KS)
Plymouth State Coll (NH)
Point Loma Nazarene U (CA)
Portland State U (OR)
Pratt Inst (NY)
Rhode Island School of Design (RI)
Ringling School of Art and Design (FL)
Rivier Coll (NH)
Robert Morris Coll (IL)
Roberts Wesleyan Coll (NY)
Rochester Inst of Technology (NY)
Rocky Mountain Coll of Art & Design (CO)
Rowan U (NJ)
Rutgers, State U of NJ, Mason Gross School of Arts (NJ)
Ryerson Polytechnic U (ON, Canada)
Sacred Heart U (CT)
St. Cloud State U (MN)
St. John's U (NY)
Saint Mary's U of Minnesota (MN)
St. Norbert Coll (WI)
Salem State Coll (MA)
Samford U (AL)
Sam Houston State U (TX)
San Diego State U (CA)
San Jose State U (CA)
Savannah Coll of Art and Design (GA)
School of the Art Inst of Chicago (IL)
School of the Museum of Fine Arts (MA)
School of Visual Arts (NY)
Schreiner Coll (TX)
Seton Hall U (NJ)
Seton Hill Coll (PA)
Simmons Coll (MA)
Simpson Coll (IA)
Southeast Missouri State U (MO)
Southwest Baptist U (MO)
Southwestern Oklahoma State U (OK)
Southwest Texas State U (TX)
State U of NY at Farmingdale (NY)
State U of NY at New Paltz (NY)
State U of NY at Oswego (NY)
State U of NY Coll at Buffalo (NY)
State U of NY Coll at Fredonia (NY)
Suffolk U (MA)
Syracuse U (NY)
Taylor U (IN)
Temple U (PA)
Texas A&M U–Commerce (TX)
Texas Christian U (TX)
Texas Tech U (TX)
Thomas More Coll (KY)
Trinity Christian Coll (IL)
Truman State U (MO)
Union Coll (NE)
Université Laval (PQ, Canada)
The U of Akron (OH)
U of Bridgeport (CT)
U of Central Oklahoma (OK)
U of Cincinnati (OH)
U of Dayton (OH)
U of Delaware (DE)
U of Denver (CO)
U of Evansville (IN)

U of Florida (FL)
U of Hartford (CT)
U of Illinois at Chicago (IL)
U of Illinois at Urbana–Champaign (IL)
U of Indianapolis (IN)
U of Massachusetts Dartmouth (MA)
U of Miami (FL)
U of Michigan (MI)
U of Minnesota, Duluth (MN)
U of Minnesota, Twin Cities Campus (MN)
U of Missouri–St. Louis (MO)
U of Montevallo (AL)
U of Oregon (OR)
U of Saint Francis (IN)
U of San Francisco (CA)
U of Sioux Falls (SD)
U of South Alabama (AL)
U of South Dakota (SD)
The U of Tennessee at Martin (TN)
The U of Tennessee Knoxville (TN)
The U of Texas at Arlington (TX)
The U of the Arts (PA)
U of the Pacific (CA)
U of Tulsa (OK)
U of Washington (WA)
U of Wisconsin–Parkside (WI)
U of Wisconsin–Platteville (WI)
U of Wisconsin–Stevens Point (WI)
Upper Iowa U (IA)
Utah State U (UT)
Villa Julie Coll (MD)
Virginia Commonwealth U (VA)
Walla Walla Coll (WA)
Wartburg Coll (IA)
Washington U in St. Louis (MO)
Waynesburg Coll (PA)
Wayne State Coll (NE)
Weber State U (UT)
Webster U (MO)
Western Connecticut State U (CT)
Western Kentucky U (KY)
Western Maryland Coll (MD)
Western Michigan U (MI)
Western State Coll of Colorado (CO)
Western Washington U (WA)
Westfield State Coll (MA)
West Liberty State Coll (WV)
West Texas A&M U (TX)
West Virginia Wesleyan Coll (WV)
Westwood Coll of Technology (CO)
White Pines Coll (NH)
Wichita State U (KS)
William Paterson U of New Jersey (NJ)
William Woods U (MO)
Winona State U (MN)
Wittenberg U (OH)
Woodbury U (CA)
York Coll of Pennsylvania (PA)
York U (ON, Canada)
Youngstown State U (OH)

GRAPHIC/PRINTING EQUIPMENT
Andrews U (MI)
Appalachian State U (NC)
Arkansas State U (AR)
California Polytechnic State U, San Luis Obispo (CA)
California State U, Los Angeles (CA)
Central Missouri State U (MO)
Chowan Coll (NC)
Drexel U (PA)
Fairmont State Coll (WV)
Ferris State U (MI)
Florida A&M U (FL)
Georgia Southern U (GA)
Indiana State U (IN)
Kean U (NJ)
Murray State U (KY)
Pennsylvania Coll of Technology (PA)
Pittsburg State U (KS)
Rochester Inst of Technology (NY)
Southwest Texas State U (TX)
Texas A&M U–Commerce (TX)
U of the District of Columbia (DC)
West Virginia U Inst of Technology (WV)

Majors Index
Greek (Ancient and Medieval)–Health/Physical Education

GREEK (ANCIENT AND MEDIEVAL)
Amherst Coll (MA)
Asbury Coll (KY)
Bard Coll (NY)
Barnard Coll (NY)
Baylor U (TX)
Boston U (MA)
Brandeis U (MA)
Brock U (ON, Canada)
Brown U (RI)
Bryn Mawr Coll (PA)
Calvary Bible Coll and Theological Seminary (MO)
Carleton Coll (MN)
Dartmouth Coll (NH)
Duke U (NC)
Duquesne U (PA)
Elmira Coll (NY)
Franklin and Marshall Coll (PA)
Hobart and William Smith Colls (NY)
Hunter Coll of the City U of NY (NY)
Indiana U Bloomington (IN)
Loyola U Chicago (IL)
McGill U (PQ, Canada)
Miami U (OH)
Mount Allison U (NB, Canada)
Multnomah Bible Coll and Biblical Seminary (OR)
New Coll of the U of South Florida (FL)
The Ohio State U (OH)
Randolph-Macon Woman's Coll (VA)
Rutgers, State U of NJ, Douglass Coll (NJ)
Rutgers, State U of NJ, Livingston Coll (NJ)
Rutgers, State U of NJ, Rutgers Coll (NJ)
Rutgers, State U of NJ, U Coll–New Brunswick (NJ)
Samford U (AL)
Santa Clara U (CA)
Smith Coll (MA)
Swarthmore Coll (PA)
Sweet Briar Coll (VA)
The U of Akron (OH)
U of Calif, Berkeley (CA)
U of Chicago (IL)
U of Georgia (GA)
U of Guelph (ON, Canada)
U of Nebraska–Lincoln (NE)
U of Notre Dame (IN)
U of St. Thomas (MN)
The U of Scranton (PA)
U of Southern California (CA)
The U of Texas at Austin (TX)
U of Vermont (VT)
U of Victoria (BC, Canada)
U of Washington (WA)
The U of Western Ontario (ON, Canada)
Wake Forest U (NC)
Washington U in St. Louis (MO)
Wellesley Coll (MA)
Wheaton Coll (IL)

GREEK (MODERN)
Ball State U (IN)
Bard Coll (NY)
Belmont U (TN)
Boise Bible Coll (ID)
Boston U (MA)
Brooklyn Coll of the City U of NY (NY)
Brown U (RI)
Butler U (IN)
Calvin Coll (MI)
Carleton U (ON, Canada)
Claremont McKenna Coll (CA)
Colgate U (NY)
The Coll of William and Mary (VA)
The Coll of Wooster (OH)
Concordia U Wisconsin (WI)
Cornell Coll (IA)
Cornell U (NY)
Creighton U (NE)
DePauw U (IN)
Dickinson Coll (PA)
Emory U (GA)
Florida State U (FL)
Fordham U (NY)
Furman U (SC)
Gettysburg Coll (PA)
Hamilton Coll (NY)
Hampden-Sydney Coll (VA)
Harvard U (MA)
Haverford Coll (PA)
John Carroll U (OH)
Kenyon Coll (OH)
La Salle U (PA)
Lehman Coll of the City U of NY (NY)
Long Island U, Southampton Coll, Friends World Program (NY)
Loyola Marymount U (CA)
Luther Coll (IA)
Macalester Coll (MN)
Marlboro Coll (VT)
McGill U (PQ, Canada)
Memorial U of Newfoundland (NF, Canada)
Monmouth Coll (IL)
Mount Holyoke Coll (MA)
Muhlenberg Coll (PA)
New York U (NY)
Oberlin Coll (OH)
The Ohio State U (OH)
Ohio U (OH)
Queens Coll of the City U of NY (NY)
Queen's U at Kingston (ON, Canada)
Randolph-Macon Coll (VA)
Rhodes Coll (TN)
Rockford Coll (IL)
Saint Louis U (MO)
Saint Mary's Coll of California (CA)
St. Olaf Coll (MN)
Southern Wesleyan U (SC)
Syracuse U (NY)
Trent U (ON, Canada)
Tufts U (MA)
Tulane U (LA)
U of Alberta (AB, Canada)
U of British Columbia (BC, Canada)
U of Calif, Los Angeles (CA)
The U of Iowa (IA)
U of Manitoba (MB, Canada)
U of Michigan (MI)
U of Minnesota, Twin Cities Campus (MN)
U of New Brunswick, Fredericton (NB, Canada)
U of New Hampshire (NH)
U of Oregon (OR)
U of Regina (SK, Canada)
U of Richmond (VA)
The U of Tennessee at Chattanooga (TN)
U of the South (TN)
U of Toronto (ON, Canada)
U of Utah (UT)
U of Windsor (ON, Canada)
The U of Winnipeg (MB, Canada)
U of Wisconsin–Madison (WI)
U of Wisconsin–Milwaukee (WI)
Ursinus Coll (PA)
Wabash Coll (IN)
Wilfrid Laurier U (ON, Canada)
Wright State U (OH)
York U (ON, Canada)

HEALTH AIDE
Campbell U (NC)

HEALTH EDUCATION
Abilene Christian U (TX)
Anderson U (IN)
Appalachian State U (NC)
Aquinas Coll (MI)
Arkansas State U (AR)
Armstrong Atlantic State U (GA)
Ashland U (OH)
Athens State U (AL)
Auburn U (AL)
Augsburg Coll (MN)
Austin Peay State U (TN)
Baldwin-Wallace Coll (OH)
Ball State U (IN)
Baylor U (TX)
Belmont U (TN)
Bemidji State U (MN)
Berry Coll (GA)
Bethel Coll (MN)
Bluffton Coll (OH)
Bowling Green State U (OH)
Briar Cliff Coll (IA)
Bridgewater State Coll (MA)
California State U, Chico (CA)
California State U, Northridge (CA)
California State U, San Bernardino (CA)
Campbellsville U (KY)
Capital U (OH)
Carroll Coll (WI)
Cedarville Coll (OH)
Centenary Coll of Louisiana (LA)
Central Michigan U (MI)
Chicago State U (IL)
Christopher Newport U (VA)
Clark Atlanta U (GA)
Coll of Mount Saint Vincent (NY)
Concord Coll (WV)
Concordia Coll (MN)
Concordia U (NE)
Concordia U at St. Paul (MN)
Cumberland Coll (KY)
Curry Coll (MA)
Dakota Wesleyan U (SD)
Dalhousie U (NS, Canada)
David Lipscomb U (TN)
Defiance Coll (OH)
Delaware State U (DE)
East Carolina U (NC)
Eastern Illinois U (IL)
Eastern Kentucky U (KY)
Eastern Mennonite U (VA)
Eastern Washington U (WA)
East Stroudsburg U of Pennsylvania (PA)
Elon Coll (NC)
Emporia State U (KS)
Florida A&M U (FL)
Florida International U (FL)
Florida State U (FL)
Fort Valley State U (GA)
Freed-Hardeman U (TN)
Friends U (KS)
Gardner-Webb U (NC)
George Fox U (OR)
George Mason U (VA)
Georgia Coll and State U (GA)
Graceland Coll (IA)
Gustavus Adolphus Coll (MN)
Gwynedd-Mercy Coll (PA)
Hamline U (MN)
Hampton U (VA)
Heidelberg Coll (OH)
Hunter Coll of the City U of NY (NY)
Idaho State U (ID)
Illinois State U (IL)
Indiana State U (IN)
Indiana U of Pennsylvania (PA)
Indiana U–Purdue U Indianapolis (IN)
Inter American U of PR, Metropolitan Campus (PR)
Iowa State U of Science and Technology (IA)
Ithaca Coll (NY)
Jacksonville State U (AL)
John Brown U (AR)
Johnson C. Smith U (NC)
Keene State Coll (NH)
Kent State U (OH)
Lamar U (TX)
Lee U (TN)
Lehman Coll of the City U of NY (NY)
Liberty U (VA)
Lincoln Memorial U (TN)
Lincoln U (PA)
Linfield Coll (OR)
Lock Haven U of Pennsylvania (PA)
Long Island U, C.W. Post Campus (NY)
Longwood Coll (VA)
Louisiana Coll (LA)
Luther Coll (IA)
Lynchburg Coll (VA)
Malone Coll (OH)
Manchester Coll (IN)
Manhattan Coll (NY)
Marshall U (WV)
Marywood U (PA)
Mayville State U (ND)
Miami U (OH)
MidAmerica Nazarene U (KS)
Middle Tennessee State U (TN)
Milligan Coll (TN)
Minnesota State U, Mankato (MN)
Minnesota State U Moorhead (MN)
Missouri Baptist Coll (MO)
Missouri Valley Coll (MO)
Montana State U–Billings (MT)
Morehead State U (KY)
Morgan State U (MD)
Murray State U (KY)
Muskingum Coll (OH)
New Mexico Highlands U (NM)
Nicholls State U (LA)
Norfolk State U (VA)
North Carolina Ag and Tech State U (NC)
North Carolina Central U (NC)
North Central Coll (IL)
Northeastern State U (OK)
Northern Arizona U (AZ)
Northern Illinois U (IL)
Northern Michigan U (MI)
Northern State U (SD)
Northwestern Oklahoma State U (OK)
Northwest Missouri State U (MO)
Ohio Northern U (OH)
Ohio U (OH)
Ohio Wesleyan U (OH)
Oklahoma State U (OK)
Otterbein Coll (OH)
Peru State Coll (NE)
Philander Smith Coll (AR)
Pittsburg State U (KS)
Plymouth State Coll (NH)
Portland State U (OR)
Queen's U at Kingston (ON, Canada)
Radford U (VA)
Rocky Mountain Coll (MT)
St. Ambrose U (IA)
St. Cloud State U (MN)
Saint Mary's Coll of California (CA)
Salem State Coll (MA)
San Francisco State U (CA)
Slippery Rock U of Pennsylvania (PA)
Southeastern Oklahoma State U (OK)
Southern Illinois U Carbondale (IL)
Southern Illinois U Edwardsville (IL)
Southern Oregon U (OR)
Southwest State U (MN)
State U of NY Coll at Brockport (NY)
State U of NY Coll at Cortland (NY)
Syracuse U (NY)
Tabor Coll (KS)
Temple U (PA)
Tennessee State U (TN)
Tennessee Technological U (TN)
Texas A&M U (TX)
Texas A&M U–Commerce (TX)
Texas A&M U–Kingsville (TX)
Texas Southern U (TX)
Troy State U (AL)
Union Coll (KY)
The U of Akron (OH)
The U of Alabama (AL)
The U of Alabama at Birmingham (AL)
The U of Arizona (AZ)
U of Arkansas at Little Rock (AR)
U of Central Arkansas (AR)
U of Central Oklahoma (OK)
U of Cincinnati (OH)
U of Dayton (OH)
U of Delaware (DE)
U of Detroit Mercy (MI)
U of Florida (FL)
U of Georgia (GA)
The U of Iowa (IA)
U of Kansas (KS)
U of Kentucky (KY)
The U of Lethbridge (AB, Canada)
U of Maine (ME)
U of Maine at Farmington (ME)
U of Maine at Presque Isle (ME)
U of Maryland, Coll Park (MD)
U of Minnesota, Duluth (MN)
The U of Montana–Missoula (MT)
U of Nebraska at Omaha (NE)
U of Nebraska–Lincoln (NE)
U of Nevada, Las Vegas (NV)
U of Nevada, Reno (NV)
U of New Brunswick, Fredericton (NB, Canada)
U of New Mexico (NM)
The U of North Carolina at Greensboro (NC)
The U of North Carolina at Pembroke (NC)
U of Northern Iowa (IA)
U of North Texas (TX)
U of Regina (SK, Canada)
U of Richmond (VA)
U of Rio Grande (OH)
U of Saint Francis (IN)
U of St. Thomas (MN)
U of Sioux Falls (SD)
U of South Alabama (AL)
The U of Tennessee Knoxville (TN)
The U of Texas–Pan American (TX)
U of the District of Columbia (DC)
U of Toronto (ON, Canada)
U of Utah (UT)
U of Wisconsin–La Crosse (WI)
U of Wyoming (WY)
Upper Iowa U (IA)
Urbana U (OH)
Ursinus Coll (PA)
Utah State U (UT)
Valley City State U (ND)
Virginia Commonwealth U (VA)
Virginia Polytechnic Inst and State U (VA)
Washington State U (WA)
West Chester U of Pennsylvania (PA)
Western Connecticut State U (CT)
Western Illinois U (IL)
Western Kentucky U (KY)
Western Michigan U (MI)
Western Montana Coll of The U of Montana (MT)
Western Washington U (WA)
West Liberty State Coll (WV)
West Virginia State Coll (WV)
West Virginia U Inst of Technology (WV)
West Virginia Wesleyan Coll (WV)
William Paterson U of New Jersey (NJ)
William Penn U (IA)
Wilmington Coll (OH)
Winona State U (MN)
Wright State U (OH)
Xavier U of Louisiana (LA)
York Coll of the City U of New York (NY)
Youngstown State U (OH)

HEALTH FACILITIES ADMINISTRATION
Carson-Newman Coll (TN)
Coll of Mount Saint Vincent (NY)
Eastern Coll (PA)
Ithaca Coll (NY)
Ohio U (OH)
St. John's U (NY)
Southern Illinois U Carbondale (IL)
Southwest Texas State U (TX)
The U of Alabama (AL)
U of Pennsylvania (PA)
Worcester State Coll (MA)
Youngstown State U (OH)

HEALTH/MEDICAL BIOSTATISTICS
Insto Tecno Estudios Sups Monterrey (Mexico)

HEALTH OCCUPATIONS EDUCATION
New York Inst of Technology (NY)
North Carolina State U (NC)
The U of Iowa (IA)
U of Louisville (KY)
U of Maine at Farmington (ME)

HEALTH/PHYSICAL EDUCATION
Abilene Christian U (TX)
Anderson U (IN)
Arkansas State U (AR)
Asbury Coll (KY)
Austin Peay State U (TN)
Baylor U (TX)
Bethel Coll (KS)
Bethel Coll (TN)
Black Hills State U (SD)
Brevard Coll (NC)
Bridgewater Coll (VA)
Bridgewater State Coll (MA)
Brigham Young U (UT)
Brigham Young U–Hawaii Campus (HI)
California State U, Sacramento (CA)
Cameron U (OK)

Majors Index
Health/Physical Education–Hearing Sciences

Campbell U (NC)
Castleton State Coll (VT)
Cedarville Coll (OH)
Central Michigan U (MI)
Christopher Newport U (VA)
Coll of St. Catherine (MN)
Coll of the Ozarks (MO)
Concordia Coll (MN)
Concordia U (NE)
Dana Coll (NE)
Doane Coll (NE)
Eastern Coll (PA)
Eastern Michigan U (MI)
East Tennessee State U (TN)
East Texas Baptist U (TX)
Elmhurst Coll (IL)
Emory & Henry Coll (VA)
Freed-Hardeman U (TN)
Georgia Southern U (GA)
Hastings Coll (NE)
Indiana U of Pennsylvania (PA)
Iowa State U of Science and Technology (IA)
Ithaca Coll (NY)
Jacksonville State U (AL)
James Madison U (VA)
Johnson State Coll (VT)
La Sierra U (CA)
Liberty U (VA)
Louisiana Tech U (LA)
Luther Coll (IA)
Lyndon State Coll (VT)
Malone Coll (OH)
Marywood U (PA)
Miami U (OH)
Middle Tennessee State U (TN)
Minnesota State U Moorhead (MN)
Montana State U–Bozeman (MT)
New England Coll (NH)
Northwest Nazarene U (ID)
Oklahoma Baptist U (OK)
Oklahoma State U (OK)
Plymouth State Coll (NH)
Point Loma Nazarene U (CA)
Queen's U at Kingston (ON, Canada)
Redeemer Coll (ON, Canada)
Roanoke Coll (VA)
St. Mary's U of San Antonio (TX)
Salisbury State U (MD)
Samford U (AL)
San Jose State U (CA)
Schreiner Coll (TX)
South Dakota State U (SD)
Southern Illinois U Edwardsville (IL)
Southwestern Adventist U (TX)
Southwestern Coll (KS)
Southwest State U (MN)
Southwest Texas State U (TX)
Stephen F. Austin State U (TX)
Tennessee Wesleyan Coll (TN)
Texas A&M International U (TX)
Texas Southern U (TX)
Texas Tech U (TX)
Texas Woman's U (TX)
Trinity Western U (BC, Canada)
U du Québec à Trois-Rivières (PQ, Canada)
U of Delaware (DE)
U of Houston (TX)
U of Illinois at Chicago (IL)
U of Illinois at Urbana–Champaign (IL)
U of Kansas (KS)
U of Louisiana at Monroe (LA)
U of Louisville (KY)
U of Missouri–Kansas City (MO)
U of Montevallo (AL)
U of North Alabama (AL)
The U of North Carolina at Charlotte (NC)
U of Oklahoma (OK)
U of Rio Grande (OH)
U of St. Thomas (MN)
U of San Francisco (CA)
U of Science and Arts of Oklahoma (OK)
U of Southern Mississippi (MS)
The U of Tennessee at Martin (TN)
The U of Texas at Arlington (TX)
The U of Texas at Austin (TX)
The U of Texas at San Antonio (TX)
The U of Texas–Pan American (TX)
U of West Florida (FL)
U of Wisconsin–Stevens Point (WI)
Walla Walla Coll (WA)

Weber State U (UT)
West Texas A&M U (TX)
William Penn U (IA)
York U (ON, Canada)
Youngstown State U (OH)

HEALTH PHYSICS/RADIOLOGIC HEALTH
Bloomsburg U of Pennsylvania (PA)
Thomas Edison State Coll (NJ)
U of Nevada, Las Vegas (NV)

HEALTH PRODUCTS/SERVICES MARKETING
Carlow Coll (PA)

HEALTH SCIENCE
Albany State U (GA)
Alma Coll (MI)
American U (DC)
Armstrong Atlantic State U (GA)
Athens State U (AL)
Azusa Pacific U (CA)
Ball State U (IN)
Barat Coll (IL)
Bastyr U (WA)
Benedictine U (IL)
Boise State U (ID)
Boston U (MA)
Bradley U (IL)
Brigham Young U (UT)
Brock U (ON, Canada)
Brooklyn Coll of the City U of NY (NY)
California State U, Chico (CA)
California State U, Dominguez Hills (CA)
California State U, Fresno (CA)
California State U, Hayward (CA)
California State U, Long Beach (CA)
California State U, Los Angeles (CA)
California State U, Northridge (CA)
California State U, San Bernardino (CA)
Campbell U (NC)
Carlow Coll (PA)
Castleton State Coll (VT)
Cedar Crest Coll (PA)
Centenary Coll of Louisiana (LA)
Chadron State Coll (NE)
Chapman U (CA)
Clemson U (SC)
Coll of Mount Saint Vincent (NY)
The Coll of St. Scholastica (MN)
Coll of the Ozarks (MO)
Colorado Tech U (CO)
Columbus State U (GA)
Dalhousie U (NS, Canada)
Delaware State U (DE)
Eastern Nazarene Coll (MA)
East Tennessee State U (TN)
Erskine Coll (SC)
Fairmont State Coll (WV)
Florida Atlantic U (FL)
Florida Gulf Coast U (FL)
Florida International U (FL)
Gannon U (PA)
Gettysburg Coll (PA)
Graceland Coll (IA)
Grand Valley State U (MI)
Gwynedd-Mercy Coll (PA)
Hampshire Coll (MA)
Hiram Coll (OH)
Inter American U of PR, San Germán Campus (PR)
Johnson State Coll (VT)
Kalamazoo Coll (MI)
Kansas State U (KS)
Lamar U (TX)
Lock Haven U of Pennsylvania (PA)
Long Island U, Brooklyn Campus (NY)
Longwood Coll (VA)
Manchester Coll (IN)
Maryville U of Saint Louis (MO)
MCP Hahnemann U (PA)
Medical U of South Carolina (SC)
Merrimack Coll (MA)
Milligan Coll (TN)
Minnesota State U, Mankato (MN)
Missouri Southern State Coll (MO)
Montana Tech of The U of Montana (MT)

Morris Coll (SC)
Mount Olive Coll (NC)
New Jersey City U (NJ)
Newman U (KS)
Northeastern U (MA)
Northwest Missouri State U (MO)
Oakland U (MI)
Oklahoma State U (OK)
Open Learning Agency (BC, Canada)
Oregon State U (OR)
Otterbein Coll (OH)
Our Lady of Holy Cross Coll (LA)
Pacific U (OR)
Pennsylvania Coll of Technology (PA)
Queen's U at Kingston (ON, Canada)
St. Olaf Coll (MN)
San Diego State U (CA)
San Francisco State U (CA)
San Jose State U (CA)
Sonoma State U (CA)
State U of NY Coll at Brockport (NY)
State U of NY Coll at Cortland (NY)
State U of NY Coll at Potsdam (NY)
Syracuse U (NY)
Texas Southern U (TX)
Touro Coll (NY)
Towson U (MD)
Truman State U (MO)
The Union Inst (OH)
U du Québec à Trois-Rivières (PQ, Canada)
U of Arkansas (AR)
U of Arkansas at Little Rock (AR)
U of Central Florida (FL)
U of Colorado at Colorado Springs (CO)
U of Florida (FL)
U of Hartford (CT)
U of Maryland, Baltimore County (MD)
U of Missouri–St. Louis (MO)
U of Nevada, Las Vegas (NV)
U of New Brunswick, Saint John (NB, Canada)
U of North Florida (FL)
U of Rochester (NY)
U of St. Francis (IL)
U of Saint Francis (IN)
U of St. Thomas (MN)
U of Southern California (CA)
U of Southern Maine (ME)
The U of Texas at San Antonio (TX)
The U of Texas at Tyler (TX)
U of Waterloo (ON, Canada)
The U of Western Ontario (ON, Canada)
U of Wisconsin–Milwaukee (WI)
Ursinus Coll (PA)
Valdosta State U (GA)
Walla Walla Coll (WA)
Warner Pacific Coll (OR)
Wayne State U (MI)
West Chester U of Pennsylvania (PA)
Western Baptist Coll (OR)
West Liberty State Coll (WV)
William Paterson U of New Jersey (NJ)
Winona State U (MN)
York U (ON, Canada)
Youngstown State U (OH)

HEALTH SERVICES ADMINISTRATION
Albertus Magnus Coll (CT)
Alfred U (NY)
Alvernia Coll (PA)
Appalachian State U (NC)
Auburn U (AL)
Augustana Coll (SD)
Baker Coll of Auburn Hills (MI)
Baker Coll of Flint (MI)
Baker Coll of Muskegon (MI)
Baker Coll of Owosso (MI)
Baker Coll of Port Huron (MI)
Beaver Coll (PA)
Bellevue U (NE)
Belmont U (TN)
Benedictine U (IL)
Black Hills State U (SD)
Bowling Green State U (OH)

Brock U (ON, Canada)
California Coll for Health Sciences (CA)
California State U, Chico (CA)
California State U, Dominguez Hills (CA)
California State U, Long Beach (CA)
California State U, Northridge (CA)
California State U, San Bernardino (CA)
Calumet Coll of Saint Joseph (IN)
Cedar Crest Coll (PA)
Clayton Coll & State U (GA)
Cleary Coll (MI)
Coll of Mount St. Joseph (OH)
The Coll of St. Scholastica (MN)
The Coll of West Virginia (WV)
Concordia Coll (MI)
Concordia Coll (MN)
Concordia U (NE)
Concordia U (OR)
Concordia U Wisconsin (WI)
Creighton U (NE)
Dallas Baptist U (TX)
Davenport Coll of Business (MI)
Davenport Coll of Business, Kalamazoo Campus (MI)
David N. Myers Coll (OH)
Detroit Coll of Business (MI)
Dominican Coll of Blauvelt (NY)
Duquesne U (PA)
Eastern Kentucky U (KY)
Eastern Michigan U (MI)
Eastern Washington U (WA)
Ferris State U (MI)
Fisk U (TN)
Florida A&M U (FL)
Florida Atlantic U (FL)
Florida International U (FL)
Franklin U (OH)
Friends U (KS)
Governors State U (IL)
Gwynedd-Mercy Coll (PA)
Harding U (AR)
Harris-Stowe State Coll (MO)
Hastings Coll (NE)
Heidelberg Coll (OH)
Howard Payne U (TX)
Idaho State U (ID)
Indiana U Northwest (IN)
Indiana U–Purdue U Fort Wayne (IN)
Indiana U–Purdue U Indianapolis (IN)
Indiana U South Bend (IN)
Inst of Public Administration (Ireland)
Iona Coll (NY)
Ithaca Coll (NY)
John Brown U (AR)
Johnson & Wales U (RI)
King's Coll (PA)
Lander U (SC)
Langston U (OK)
Lasell Coll (MA)
Lehman Coll of the City U of NY (NY)
Lindenwood U (MO)
Long Island U, C.W. Post Campus (NY)
Lynn U (FL)
Macon State Coll (GA)
Marshall U (WV)
Martin Methodist Coll (TN)
Mary Baldwin Coll (VA)
Maryville U of Saint Louis (MO)
Marywood U (PA)
McMurry U (TX)
Mercy Coll (NY)
Methodist Coll (NC)
Metropolitan State Coll of Denver (CO)
Milligan Coll (TN)
Minnesota State U Moorhead (MN)
Montana State U–Billings (MT)
Montana State U–Bozeman (MT)
Mount St. Clare Coll (IA)
Mount St. Mary's Coll (CA)
National-Louis U (IL)
National U (CA)
Newbury Coll (MA)
New Mexico Highlands U (NM)
Norfolk State U (VA)
Northeastern State U (OK)
Northeastern U (MA)
Ohio Dominican Coll (OH)

Ohio U (OH)
Oregon State U (OR)
Peirce Coll (PA)
Penn State U Univ Park Campus (PA)
Point Park Coll (PA)
Presentation Coll (SD)
Providence Coll (RI)
Quinnipiac U (CT)
Robert Morris Coll (PA)
Ryerson Polytechnic U (ON, Canada)
St. Francis Coll (NY)
St. Joseph's Coll, New York (NY)
St. Joseph's Coll, Suffolk Campus (NY)
Saint Joseph's U (PA)
Saint Leo U (FL)
Saint Mary's U of Minnesota (MN)
Saint Peter's Coll (NJ)
San Jose State U (CA)
Seton Hill Coll (PA)
Slippery Rock U of Pennsylvania (PA)
Southeastern U (DC)
Southern Adventist U (TN)
Southwestern Adventist U (TX)
Southwestern Oklahoma State U (OK)
Southwest Texas State U (TX)
State U of NY Coll at Fredonia (NY)
State U of NY Inst of Tech at Utica/Rome (NY)
Stonehill Coll (MA)
Tennessee State U (TN)
Texas Southern U (TX)
Thomas Edison State Coll (NJ)
Towson U (MD)
The U of Arizona (AZ)
U of Central Arkansas (AR)
U of Central Florida (FL)
U of Cincinnati (OH)
U of Connecticut (CT)
U of Detroit Mercy (MI)
U of Evansville (IN)
U of Great Falls (MT)
U of Houston–Clear Lake (TX)
U of Illinois at Springfield (IL)
U of Kentucky (KY)
U of La Verne (CA)
The U of Lethbridge (AB, Canada)
U of Maryland, Baltimore County (MD)
U of Maryland University Coll (MD)
U of Miami (FL)
U of Michigan–Dearborn (MI)
U of Michigan–Flint (MI)
U of Nevada, Las Vegas (NV)
U of New England (ME)
U of New Hampshire (NH)
The U of North Carolina at Chapel Hill (NC)
U of Pittsburgh (PA)
U of Rhode Island (RI)
The U of Scranton (PA)
U of South Dakota (SD)
U of Southern Indiana (IN)
U of Victoria (BC, Canada)
U of Wisconsin–Eau Claire (WI)
U of Wisconsin–Milwaukee (WI)
U System Coll for Lifelong Learning (NH)
Ursuline Coll (OH)
Waynesburg Coll (PA)
Weber State U (UT)
Webster U (MO)
Western Carolina U (NC)
Western Kentucky U (KY)
West Virginia U Inst of Technology (WV)
Wheeling Jesuit U (WV)
Wichita State U (KS)
Winona State U (MN)
Worcester State Coll (MA)
York Coll (NE)
York Coll of Pennsylvania (PA)

HEARING SCIENCES
Arizona State U (AZ)
Brigham Young U (UT)
Indiana U Bloomington (IN)
Stephen F. Austin State U (TX)
Texas Tech U (TX)
U of Northern Colorado (CO)
The U of Tennessee Knoxville (TN)

Majors Index
Heating/Air Conditioning/Refrigeration–History

HEATING/AIR CONDITIONING/ REFRIGERATION
Ferris State U (MI)
Pennsylvania Coll of Technology (PA)

HEAVY EQUIPMENT MAINTENANCE
Ferris State U (MI)
Pittsburg State U (KS)

HEBREW
Bard Coll (NY)
Brandeis U (MA)
Calvary Bible Coll and Theological Seminary (MO)
Cleveland Coll of Jewish Studies (OH)
Concordia U (PQ, Canada)
Concordia U Wisconsin (WI)
Cornell U (NY)
Harvard U (MA)
Hebrew Theological Coll (IL)
Hofstra U (NY)
Hunter Coll of the City U of NY (NY)
Lehman Coll of the City U of NY (NY)
Long Island U, Southampton Coll, Friends World Program (NY)
Luther Coll (IA)
Machzikei Hadath Rabbinical Coll (NY)
New York U (NY)
The Ohio State U (OH)
Queens Coll of the City U of NY (NY)
State U of NY at Binghamton (NY)
Temple U (PA)
Touro Coll (NY)
U of Alberta (AB, Canada)
U of Calif, Los Angeles (CA)
U of Michigan (MI)
U of Minnesota, Twin Cities Campus (MN)
U of Oregon (OR)
U of Regina (SK, Canada)
The U of Texas at Austin (TX)
U of Toronto (ON, Canada)
U of Wisconsin–Madison (WI)
U of Wisconsin–Milwaukee (WI)
Washington U in St. Louis (MO)
Wheaton Coll (IL)
Yeshiva U (NY)
York U (ON, Canada)

HIGHER EDUCATION ADMINISTRATION
Bowling Green State U (OH)

HISPANIC-AMERICAN STUDIES
Arizona State U (AZ)
Barton Coll (NC)
Boston Coll (MA)
Brown U (RI)
California State U, Northridge (CA)
Columbia Coll (NY)
Columbia U, School of General Studies (NY)
Connecticut Coll (CT)
Cornell U (NY)
The Evergreen State Coll (WA)
Fordham U (NY)
Goshen Coll (IN)
Hampshire Coll (MA)
Harvard U (MA)
Hofstra U (NY)
Hunter Coll of the City U of NY (NY)
Inter American U of PR, San Germán Campus (PR)
Johns Hopkins U (MD)
Lewis & Clark Coll (OR)
Long Island U, Southampton Coll, Friends World Program (NY)
McGill U (PQ, Canada)
Mills Coll (CA)
Mount Saint Mary Coll (NY)
New York U (NY)
Pomona Coll (CA)
Queen's U at Kingston (ON, Canada)
Rutgers, State U of NJ, Douglass Coll (NJ)
Rutgers, State U of NJ, Livingston Coll (NJ)
Rutgers, State U of NJ, Newark Coll of Arts & Scis (NJ)
Rutgers, State U of NJ, Rutgers Coll (NJ)
Rutgers, State U of NJ, U Coll–New Brunswick (NJ)
St. Francis Coll (NY)
St. Olaf Coll (MN)
Scripps Coll (CA)
State U of NY at Albany (NY)
State U of NY Coll at Oneonta (NY)
Trent U (ON, Canada)
Tulane U (LA)
Université de Montréal (PQ, Canada)
The U of Arizona (AZ)
U of Calif, Berkeley (CA)
U of Calif, Davis (CA)
U of Michigan (MI)
U of Michigan–Dearborn (MI)
U of Northern Colorado (CO)
U of Puerto Rico, Mayagüez Campus (PR)
U of San Diego (CA)
U of Southern California (CA)
U of Southern Maine (ME)
The U of Texas at San Antonio (TX)
U of Toronto (ON, Canada)
U of Windsor (ON, Canada)
U of Wisconsin–Madison (WI)
Vassar Coll (NY)
Wheaton Coll (MA)
Willamette U (OR)
York U (ON, Canada)

HISTORY
Abilene Christian U (TX)
Acadia U (NS, Canada)
Adams State Coll (CO)
Adelphi U (NY)
Adrian Coll (MI)
Agnes Scott Coll (GA)
Alabama State U (AL)
Albany State U (GA)
Albertson Coll of Idaho (ID)
Albertus Magnus Coll (CT)
Albion Coll (MI)
Albright Coll (PA)
Alderson-Broaddus Coll (WV)
Alfred U (NY)
Alice Lloyd Coll (KY)
Allegheny Coll (PA)
Allentown Coll of St. Francis de Sales (PA)
Alma Coll (MI)
Alvernia Coll (PA)
Alverno Coll (WI)
American Coll of Thessaloníki (Greece)
American International Coll (MA)
American Military U (VA)
American U (DC)
American U in Cairo (Egypt)
The American U of Paris (France)
Amherst Coll (MA)
Anderson Coll (SC)
Anderson U (IN)
Andrews U (MI)
Anna Maria Coll (MA)
Antioch Coll (OH)
Appalachian State U (NC)
Aquinas Coll (MI)
Arizona State U (AZ)
Arizona State U West (AZ)
Arkansas State U (AR)
Arkansas Tech U (AR)
Armstrong Atlantic State U (GA)
Asbury Coll (KY)
Ashland U (OH)
Assumption Coll (MA)
Athabasca U (AB, Canada)
Athens State U (AL)
Atlantic Baptist U (NB, Canada)
Atlantic Union Coll (MA)
Auburn U (AL)
Auburn U Montgomery (AL)
Augsburg Coll (MN)
Augustana Coll (IL)
Augustana Coll (SD)
Augusta State U (GA)
Austin Coll (TX)
Austin Peay State U (TN)
Averett Coll (VA)
Avila Coll (MO)
Azusa Pacific U (CA)
Baker U (KS)
Baldwin-Wallace Coll (OH)
Ball State U (IN)
Barat Coll (IL)
Bard Coll (NY)
Barnard Coll (NY)
Barry U (FL)
Bartlesville Wesleyan Coll (OK)
Barton Coll (NC)
Bates Coll (ME)
Baylor U (TX)
Bay Path Coll (MA)
Beaver Coll (PA)
Belhaven Coll (MS)
Bellarmine Coll (KY)
Bellevue U (NE)
Belmont Abbey Coll (NC)
Belmont U (TN)
Beloit Coll (WI)
Bemidji State U (MN)
Benedictine Coll (KS)
Benedictine U (IL)
Bennington Coll (VT)
Bentley Coll (MA)
Berea Coll (KY)
Baruch Coll of the City U of NY (NY)
Berry Coll (GA)
Bethany Coll (KS)
Bethany Coll (WV)
Bethel Coll (IN)
Bethel Coll (KS)
Bethel Coll (MN)
Bethel Coll (TN)
Bethune-Cookman Coll (FL)
Biola U (CA)
Birmingham-Southern Coll (AL)
Bishop's U (PQ, Canada)
Blackburn Coll (IL)
Black Hills State U (SD)
Bloomfield Coll (NJ)
Bloomsburg U of Pennsylvania (PA)
Blue Mountain Coll (MS)
Bluffton Coll (OH)
Boise State U (ID)
Boston Coll (MA)
Boston U (MA)
Bowdoin Coll (ME)
Bowie State U (MD)
Bowling Green State U (OH)
Bradley U (IL)
Brandeis U (MA)
Brandon U (MB, Canada)
Brenau U (GA)
Brescia U (KY)
Brevard Coll (NC)
Briar Cliff Coll (IA)
Bridgewater Coll (VA)
Bridgewater State Coll (MA)
Brigham Young U (UT)
Brigham Young U–Hawaii Campus (HI)
Brock U (ON, Canada)
Brooklyn Coll of the City U of NY (NY)
Brown U (RI)
Bryan Coll (TN)
Bryant Coll (RI)
Bryn Athyn Coll of the New Church (PA)
Bryn Mawr Coll (PA)
Bucknell U (PA)
Buena Vista U (IA)
Butler U (IN)
Cabrini Coll (PA)
Caldwell Coll (NJ)
California Baptist U (CA)
California Inst of Technology (CA)
California Lutheran U (CA)
California Polytechnic State U, San Luis Obispo (CA)
California State Polytechnic U, Pomona (CA)
California State U, Chico (CA)
California State U, Dominguez Hills (CA)
California State U, Fresno (CA)
California State U, Fullerton (CA)
California State U, Hayward (CA)
California State U, Long Beach (CA)
California State U, Los Angeles (CA)
California State U, Northridge (CA)
California State U, Sacramento (CA)
California State U, San Bernardino (CA)
California State U, San Marcos (CA)
California State U, Stanislaus (CA)
California U of Pennsylvania (PA)
Calvin Coll (MI)
Cameron U (OK)
Campbellsville U (KY)
Campbell U (NC)
Canisius Coll (NY)
Capital U (OH)
Cardinal Stritch U (WI)
Carleton Coll (MN)
Carleton U (ON, Canada)
Carlow Coll (PA)
Carnegie Mellon U (PA)
Carroll Coll (MT)
Carroll Coll (WI)
Carson-Newman Coll (TN)
Carthage Coll (WI)
Case Western Reserve U (OH)
Castleton State Coll (VT)
Catawba Coll (NC)
The Catholic U of America (DC)
Cedar Crest Coll (PA)
Cedarville Coll (OH)
Centenary Coll (NJ)
Centenary Coll of Louisiana (LA)
Central Coll (IA)
Central Connecticut State U (CT)
Central Methodist Coll (MO)
Central Michigan U (MI)
Central Missouri State U (MO)
Centre Coll (KY)
Chadron State Coll (NE)
Chaminade U of Honolulu (HI)
Chapman U (CA)
Charleston Southern U (SC)
Chatham Coll (PA)
Chestnut Hill Coll (PA)
Chicago State U (IL)
Chowan Coll (NC)
Christendom Coll (VA)
Christian Brothers U (TN)
Christopher Newport U (VA)
Citadel, The Military Coll of South Carolina (SC)
City Coll of the City U of NY (NY)
Claflin U (SC)
Claremont McKenna Coll (CA)
Clarion U of Pennsylvania (PA)
Clark Atlanta U (GA)
Clarke Coll (IA)
Clarkson U (NY)
Clark U (MA)
Clemson U (SC)
Cleveland Coll of Jewish Studies (OH)
Cleveland State U (OH)
Coastal Carolina U (SC)
Coe Coll (IA)
Coker Coll (SC)
Colby Coll (ME)
Colgate U (NY)
Coll Misericordia (PA)
Coll of Charleston (SC)
Coll of Mount St. Joseph (OH)
Coll of Mount Saint Vincent (NY)
The Coll of New Jersey (NJ)
The Coll of New Rochelle (NY)
Coll of Notre Dame (CA)
Coll of Notre Dame of Maryland (MD)
Coll of Our Lady of the Elms (MA)
Coll of Saint Benedict (MN)
Coll of St. Catherine (MN)
Coll of Saint Elizabeth (NJ)
Coll of St. Joseph (VT)
Coll of Saint Mary (NE)
The Coll of Saint Rose (NY)
The Coll of St. Scholastica (MN)
The Coll of Southeastern Europe, The American U of Athens (Greece)
Coll of Staten Island of the City U of NY (NY)
Coll of the Holy Cross (MA)
Coll of the Ozarks (MO)
Coll of the Southwest (NM)
The Coll of William and Mary (VA)
The Coll of Wooster (OH)
Colorado Christian U (CO)
The Colorado Coll (CO)
Colorado State U (CO)
Columbia Coll (MO)
Columbia Coll (NY)
Columbia Coll (SC)
Columbia Union Coll (MD)
Columbia U, School of General Studies (NY)
Columbus State U (GA)
Concord Coll (WV)
Concordia Coll (MN)
Concordia Coll (NY)
Concordia U (CA)
Concordia U (IL)
Concordia U (NE)
Concordia U (PQ, Canada)
Concordia U at Austin (TX)
Concordia U at St. Paul (MN)
Concordia U Coll of Alberta (AB, Canada)
Concordia U Wisconsin (WI)
Connecticut Coll (CT)
Converse Coll (SC)
Coppin State Coll (MD)
Cornell Coll (IA)
Cornell U (NY)
Cornerstone U (MI)
Covenant Coll (GA)
Creighton U (NE)
Crichton Coll (TN)
Crown Coll (MN)
Culver-Stockton Coll (MO)
Cumberland Coll (KY)
Curry Coll (MA)
Daemen Coll (NY)
Dakota Wesleyan U (SD)
Dalhousie U (NS, Canada)
Dallas Baptist U (TX)
Dana Coll (NE)
Dartmouth Coll (NH)
David Lipscomb U (TN)
Davidson Coll (NC)
Defiance Coll (OH)
Delaware State U (DE)
Delta State U (MS)
Denison U (OH)
DePaul U (IL)
DePauw U (IN)
Deree Coll (Greece)
Dickinson Coll (PA)
Dickinson State U (ND)
Doane Coll (NE)
Dominican Coll of Blauvelt (NY)
Dominican U (IL)
Dominican U of California (CA)
Dordt Coll (IA)
Dowling Coll (NY)
Drake U (IA)
Drew U (NJ)
Drexel U (PA)
Drury U (MO)
Duke U (NC)
Duquesne U (PA)
D'Youville Coll (NY)
Earlham Coll (IN)
East Carolina U (NC)
East Central U (OK)
Eastern Coll (PA)
Eastern Connecticut State U (CT)
Eastern Illinois U (IL)
Eastern Kentucky U (KY)
Eastern Mennonite U (VA)
Eastern Michigan U (MI)
Eastern Nazarene Coll (MA)
Eastern New Mexico U (NM)
Eastern Oregon U (OR)
Eastern Washington U (WA)
East Stroudsburg U of Pennsylvania (PA)
East Tennessee State U (TN)
East Texas Baptist U (TX)
Eckerd Coll (FL)
Edgewood Coll (WI)
Edinboro U of Pennsylvania (PA)
Elizabeth City State U (NC)
Elizabethtown Coll (PA)
Elmhurst Coll (IL)
Elmira Coll (NY)
Elon Coll (NC)
Emmanuel Coll (GA)
Emmanuel Coll (MA)
Emory & Henry Coll (VA)
Emory U (GA)
Emporia State U (KS)
Erskine Coll (SC)
Eugene Lang Coll, New School U (NY)
Evangel U (MO)
The Evergreen State Coll (WA)
Fairfield U (CT)

Majors Index
History

Fairleigh Dickinson U, Florham-Madison Campus (NJ)
Fairleigh Dickinson U, Teaneck-Hackensack Campus (NJ)
Fairmont State Coll (WV)
Faulkner U (AL)
Felician Coll (NJ)
Ferrum Coll (VA)
Fisk U (TN)
Fitchburg State Coll (MA)
Flagler Coll (FL)
Florida A&M U (FL)
Florida Atlantic U (FL)
Florida Gulf Coast U (FL)
Florida International U (FL)
Florida Southern Coll (FL)
Florida State U (FL)
Fontbonne Coll (MO)
Fordham U (NY)
Fort Hays State U (KS)
Fort Lewis Coll (CO)
Framingham State Coll (MA)
Franciscan U of Steubenville (OH)
Francis Marion U (SC)
Franklin and Marshall Coll (PA)
Franklin Coll of Indiana (IN)
Franklin Coll Switzerland (Switzerland)
Franklin Pierce Coll (NH)
Freed-Hardeman U (TN)
Fresno Pacific U (CA)
Friends U (KS)
Frostburg State U (MD)
Furman U (SC)
Gallaudet U (DC)
Gannon U (PA)
Gardner-Webb U (NC)
Geneva Coll (PA)
George Fox U (OR)
George Mason U (VA)
Georgetown Coll (KY)
Georgetown U (DC)
The George Washington U (DC)
Georgia Coll and State U (GA)
Georgian Court Coll (NJ)
Georgia Southern U (GA)
Georgia Southwestern State U (GA)
Georgia State U (GA)
Gettysburg Coll (PA)
Glenville State Coll (WV)
Goddard Coll (VT)
Gonzaga U (WA)
Gordon Coll (MA)
Goshen Coll (IN)
Goucher Coll (MD)
Graceland Coll (IA)
Grand Canyon U (AZ)
Grand Valley State U (MI)
Grand View Coll (IA)
Green Mountain Coll (VT)
Greensboro Coll (NC)
Greenville Coll (IL)
Grinnell Coll (IA)
Grove City Coll (PA)
Guilford Coll (NC)
Gustavus Adolphus Coll (MN)
Gwynedd-Mercy Coll (PA)
Hamilton Coll (NY)
Hamline U (MN)
Hampden-Sydney Coll (VA)
Hampshire Coll (MA)
Hampton U (VA)
Hannibal-LaGrange Coll (MO)
Hanover Coll (IN)
Harding U (AR)
Hardin-Simmons U (TX)
Hartwick Coll (NY)
Harvard U (MA)
Hastings Coll (NE)
Haverford Coll (PA)
Hawaii Pacific U (HI)
Heidelberg Coll (OH)
Henderson State U (AR)
Hendrix Coll (AR)
Heritage Coll (WA)
High Point U (NC)
Hillsdale Coll (MI)
Hiram Coll (OH)
Hobart and William Smith Colls (NY)
Hofstra U (NY)
Hollins U (VA)
Holy Family Coll (PA)
Holy Names Coll (CA)
Hood Coll (MD)
Hope Coll (MI)

Houghton Coll (NY)
Houston Baptist U (TX)
Howard Payne U (TX)
Howard U (DC)
Humboldt State U (CA)
Hunter Coll of the City U of NY (NY)
Huntingdon Coll (AL)
Huntington Coll (IN)
Idaho State U (ID)
Illinois Coll (IL)
Illinois State U (IL)
Illinois Wesleyan U (IL)
Immaculata Coll (PA)
Indiana State U (IN)
Indiana U Bloomington (IN)
Indiana U Northwest (IN)
Indiana U of Pennsylvania (PA)
Indiana U–Purdue U Fort Wayne (IN)
Indiana U–Purdue U Indianapolis (IN)
Indiana U South Bend (IN)
Indiana U Southeast (IN)
Indiana Wesleyan U (IN)
Inter American U of PR, Fajardo Campus (PR)
Inter American U of PR, Metropolitan Campus (PR)
Inter American U of PR, San Germán Campus (PR)
Iona Coll (NY)
Iowa State U of Science and Technology (IA)
Iowa Wesleyan Coll (IA)
Ithaca Coll (NY)
Jacksonville State U (AL)
Jacksonville U (FL)
James Madison U (VA)
Jamestown Coll (ND)
Jarvis Christian Coll (TX)
Jewish Theological Seminary of America (NY)
John Brown U (AR)
John Carroll U (OH)
Johns Hopkins U (MD)
Johnson C. Smith U (NC)
Johnson State Coll (VT)
Judson Coll (AL)
Judson Coll (IL)
Juniata Coll (PA)
Kalamazoo Coll (MI)
Kansas State U (KS)
Kean U (NJ)
Keene State Coll (NH)
Kent State U (OH)
Kentucky Christian Coll (KY)
Kentucky State U (KY)
Kentucky Wesleyan Coll (KY)
Kenyon Coll (OH)
Keuka Coll (NY)
King Coll (TN)
King's Coll (PA)
The King's U Coll (AB, Canada)
Knox Coll (IL)
Kutztown U of Pennsylvania (PA)
Lafayette Coll (PA)
LaGrange Coll (GA)
Lake Forest Coll (IL)
Lakehead U (ON, Canada)
Lakeland Coll (WI)
Lake Superior State U (MI)
Lamar U (TX)
Lambuth U (TN)
Lander U (SC)
Lane Coll (TN)
Langston U (OK)
La Roche Coll (PA)
La Salle U (PA)
La Sierra U (CA)
Lawrence U (WI)
Lebanon Valley Coll (PA)
Lees-McRae Coll (NC)
Lee U (TN)
Lehigh U (PA)
Lehman Coll of the City U of NY (NY)
Le Moyne Coll (NY)
LeMoyne-Owen Coll (TN)
Lenoir-Rhyne Coll (NC)
LeTourneau U (TX)
Lewis & Clark Coll (OR)
Lewis-Clark State Coll (ID)
Lewis U (IL)
Liberty U (VA)
Limestone Coll (SC)
Lincoln Memorial U (TN)

Lincoln U (MO)
Lincoln U (PA)
Lindenwood U (MO)
Lindsey Wilson Coll (KY)
Linfield Coll (OR)
Lock Haven U of Pennsylvania (PA)
Long Island U, Brooklyn Campus (NY)
Long Island U, C.W. Post Campus (NY)
Long Island U, Southampton Coll (NY)
Long Island U, Southampton Coll, Friends World Program (NY)
Longwood Coll (VA)
Loras Coll (IA)
Louisiana Coll (LA)
Louisiana State U and A&M Coll (LA)
Louisiana State U in Shreveport (LA)
Louisiana Tech U (LA)
Lourdes Coll (OH)
Loyola Coll in Maryland (MD)
Loyola Marymount U (CA)
Loyola U Chicago (IL)
Loyola U New Orleans (LA)
Lubbock Christian U (TX)
Luther Coll (IA)
Lycoming Coll (PA)
Lynchburg Coll (VA)
Lynn U (FL)
Lyon Coll (AR)
Macalester Coll (MN)
MacMurray Coll (IL)
Madonna U (MI)
Malone Coll (OH)
Manchester Coll (IN)
Manhattan Coll (NY)
Manhattanville Coll (NY)
Mansfield U of Pennsylvania (PA)
Marian Coll (IN)
Marian Coll of Fond du Lac (WI)
Marietta Coll (OH)
Marist Coll (NY)
Marlboro Coll (VT)
Marquette U (WI)
Marshall U (WV)
Mars Hill Coll (NC)
Mary Baldwin Coll (VA)
Marycrest International U (IA)
Marygrove Coll (MI)
Marymount Coll (NY)
Marymount Manhattan Coll (NY)
Maryville Coll (TN)
Maryville U of Saint Louis (MO)
Mary Washington Coll (VA)
Massachusetts Coll of Liberal Arts (MA)
Massachusetts Inst of Technology (MA)
McGill U (PQ, Canada)
McKendree Coll (IL)
McMurry U (TX)
McNeese State U (LA)
McPherson Coll (KS)
Memorial U of Newfoundland (NF, Canada)
Mercer U (GA)
Mercy Coll (NY)
Mercyhurst Coll (PA)
Meredith Coll (NC)
Merrimack Coll (MA)
Mesa State Coll (CO)
Messiah Coll (PA)
Methodist Coll (NC)
Metropolitan State Coll of Denver (CO)
Metropolitan State U (MN)
Miami U (OH)
Michigan State U (MI)
Michigan Technological U (MI)
MidAmerica Nazarene U (KS)
Middlebury Coll (VT)
Middle Tennessee State U (TN)
Midland Lutheran Coll (NE)
Midwestern State U (TX)
Millersville U of Pennsylvania (PA)
Milligan Coll (TN)
Millikin U (IL)
Millsaps Coll (MS)
Mills Coll (CA)
Minnesota State U, Mankato (MN)
Minnesota State U Moorhead (MN)
Minot State U (ND)
Mississippi Coll (MS)

Mississippi State U (MS)
Mississippi U for Women (MS)
Mississippi Valley State U (MS)
Missouri Baptist Coll (MO)
Missouri Southern State Coll (MO)
Missouri Valley Coll (MO)
Missouri Western State Coll (MO)
Molloy Coll (NY)
Monmouth Coll (IL)
Monmouth U (NJ)
Montana State U–Billings (MT)
Montana State U–Bozeman (MT)
Montreat Coll (NC)
Moravian Coll (PA)
Morehead State U (KY)
Morehouse Coll (GA)
Morgan State U (MD)
Morningside Coll (IA)
Morris Coll (SC)
Mount Allison U (NB, Canada)
Mount Holyoke Coll (MA)
Mount Marty Coll (SD)
Mount Mary Coll (WI)
Mount Mercy Coll (IA)
Mount Olive Coll (NC)
Mount Saint Mary Coll (NY)
Mount St. Mary's Coll (CA)
Mount Saint Mary's Coll and Seminary (MD)
Mount Saint Vincent U (NS, Canada)
Mount Senario Coll (WI)
Mount Union Coll (OH)
Mount Vernon Nazarene Coll (OH)
Muhlenberg Coll (PA)
Multnomah Bible Coll and Biblical Seminary (OR)
Murray State U (KY)
Muskingum Coll (OH)
Nazareth Coll of Rochester (NY)
Nebraska Wesleyan U (NE)
Newberry Coll (SC)
New Coll of the U of South Florida (FL)
New England Coll (NH)
New Jersey City U (NJ)
New Jersey Inst of Technology (NJ)
Newman U (KS)
New Mexico Highlands U (NM)
New Mexico State U (NM)
New York U (NY)
Niagara U (NY)
Nicholls State U (LA)
Nichols Coll (MA)
Nipissing U (ON, Canada)
Norfolk State U (VA)
North Carolina Ag and Tech State U (NC)
North Carolina Central U (NC)
North Carolina State U (NC)
North Carolina Wesleyan Coll (NC)
North Central Coll (IL)
North Dakota State U (ND)
Northeastern Illinois U (IL)
Northeastern State U (OK)
Northeastern U (MA)
Northern Arizona U (AZ)
Northern Illinois U (IL)
Northern Kentucky U (KY)
Northern Michigan U (MI)
Northern State U (SD)
North Georgia Coll & State U (GA)
Northland Coll (WI)
North Park U (IL)
Northwest Coll (WA)
Northwestern Coll (IA)
Northwestern Coll (MN)
Northwestern Oklahoma State U (OK)
Northwestern State U of Louisiana (LA)
Northwestern U (IL)
Northwest Missouri State U (MO)
Northwest Nazarene U (ID)
Norwich U (VT)
Notre Dame Coll (NH)
Notre Dame Coll of Ohio (OH)
Nyack Coll (NY)
Oakland U (MI)
Oakwood Coll (AL)
Oberlin Coll (OH)
Occidental Coll (CA)
Oglethorpe U (GA)
Ohio Dominican Coll (OH)
Ohio Northern U (OH)
The Ohio State U (OH)
Ohio U (OH)

Ohio Wesleyan U (OH)
Okanagan U Coll (BC, Canada)
Oklahoma Baptist U (OK)
Oklahoma Christian U of Science and Arts (OK)
Oklahoma City U (OK)
Oklahoma Panhandle State U (OK)
Oklahoma State U (OK)
Old Dominion U (VA)
Olivet Nazarene U (IL)
Open Learning Agency (BC, Canada)
Oregon State U (OR)
Ottawa U (KS)
Otterbein Coll (OH)
Ouachita Baptist U (AR)
Our Lady of Holy Cross Coll (LA)
Our Lady of the Lake U of San Antonio (TX)
Pace U, New York City Campus (NY)
Pace U, Pleasantville/Briarcliff Campus (NY)
Pacific Lutheran U (WA)
Pacific Union Coll (CA)
Pacific U (OR)
Paine Coll (GA)
Palm Beach Atlantic Coll (FL)
Park U (MO)
Penn State U Abington Coll (PA)
Penn State U at Erie, The Behrend Coll (PA)
Penn State U Univ Park Campus (PA)
Pepperdine U, Malibu (CA)
Peru State Coll (NE)
Pfeiffer U (NC)
Piedmont Coll (GA)
Pikeville Coll (KY)
Pine Manor Coll (MA)
Pittsburg State U (KS)
Pitzer Coll (CA)
Plattsburgh State U of NY (NY)
Plymouth State Coll (NH)
Point Loma Nazarene U (CA)
Point Park Coll (PA)
Pomona Coll (CA)
Pontifical Catholic U of Puerto Rico (PR)
Portland State U (OR)
Prairie View A&M U (TX)
Presbyterian Coll (SC)
Princeton U (NJ)
Principia Coll (IL)
Providence Coll (RI)
Providence Coll and Theological Seminary (MB, Canada)
Purchase Coll, State U of NY (NY)
Purdue U (IN)
Purdue U Calumet (IN)
Queens Coll (NC)
Queens Coll of the City U of NY (NY)
Queen's U at Kingston (ON, Canada)
Quincy U (IL)
Quinnipiac U (CT)
Radford U (VA)
Ramapo Coll of New Jersey (NJ)
Randolph-Macon Coll (VA)
Randolph-Macon Woman's Coll (VA)
Redeemer Coll (ON, Canada)
Reed Coll (OR)
Regents Coll (NY)
Regis Coll (MA)
Regis U (CO)
Rhodes Coll (TN)
Rice U (TX)
The Richard Stockton Coll of New Jersey (NJ)
Richmond, The American International U in London (United Kingdom)
Rider U (NJ)
Ripon Coll (WI)
Rivier Coll (NH)
Roanoke Coll (VA)
Roberts Wesleyan Coll (NY)
Rochester Coll (MI)
Rockford Coll (IL)
Rockhurst U (MO)
Rocky Mountain Coll (MT)
Roger Williams U (RI)
Rollins Coll (FL)
Rosemont Coll (PA)
Rowan U (NJ)

Majors Index
History

Russell Sage Coll (NY)
Rust Coll (MS)
Rutgers, State U of NJ, Camden Coll of Arts & Scis (NJ)
Rutgers, State U of NJ, Douglass Coll (NJ)
Rutgers, State U of NJ, Livingston Coll (NJ)
Rutgers, State U of NJ, Newark Coll of Arts & Scis (NJ)
Rutgers, State U of NJ, Rutgers Coll (NJ)
Rutgers, State U of NJ, U Coll–Camden (NJ)
Rutgers, State U of NJ, U Coll–Newark (NJ)
Rutgers, State U of NJ, U Coll–New Brunswick (NJ)
Sacred Heart U (CT)
Saginaw Valley State U (MI)
St. Ambrose U (IA)
St. Andrews Presbyterian Coll (NC)
Saint Anselm Coll (NH)
Saint Augustine's Coll (NC)
St. Bonaventure U (NY)
St. Cloud State U (MN)
St. Edward's U (TX)
St. Francis Coll (NY)
Saint Francis Coll (PA)
St. Francis Xavier U (NS, Canada)
St. John Fisher Coll (NY)
Saint John's U (MN)
St. John's U (NY)
Saint Joseph Coll (CT)
Saint Joseph's Coll (IN)
Saint Joseph's Coll (ME)
St. Joseph's Coll, New York (NY)
St. Joseph's Coll, Suffolk Campus (NY)
Saint Joseph's U (PA)
St. Lawrence U (NY)
Saint Leo U (FL)
Saint Louis U (MO)
Saint Martin's Coll (WA)
Saint Mary Coll (KS)
Saint Mary-of-the-Woods Coll (IN)
Saint Mary's Coll (IN)
Saint Mary's Coll of California (CA)
St. Mary's Coll of Maryland (MD)
Saint Mary's U (NS, Canada)
Saint Mary's U of Minnesota (MN)
St. Mary's U of San Antonio (TX)
Saint Michael's Coll (VT)
St. Norbert Coll (WI)
St. Olaf Coll (MN)
Saint Peter's Coll (NJ)
St. Thomas U (FL)
Saint Vincent Coll (PA)
Saint Xavier U (IL)
Salem Coll (NC)
Salem State Coll (MA)
Salisbury State U (MD)
Salve Regina U (RI)
Samford U (AL)
Sam Houston State U (TX)
San Diego State U (CA)
San Francisco State U (CA)
San Jose State U (CA)
Santa Clara U (CA)
Sarah Lawrence Coll (NY)
Savannah State U (GA)
Schreiner Coll (TX)
Scripps Coll (CA)
Seattle Pacific U (WA)
Seattle U (WA)
Seton Hall U (NJ)
Seton Hill Coll (PA)
Shawnee State U (OH)
Shenandoah U (VA)
Shepherd Coll (WV)
Shippensburg U of Pennsylvania (PA)
Shorter Coll (GA)
Siena Coll (NY)
Siena Heights U (MI)
Silver Lake Coll (WI)
Simmons Coll (MA)
Simon Fraser U (BC, Canada)
Simpson Coll (IA)
Simpson Coll and Graduate School (CA)
Skidmore Coll (NY)
Slippery Rock U of Pennsylvania (PA)
Smith Coll (MA)
Sonoma State U (CA)
South Dakota State U (SD)

Southeastern Louisiana U (LA)
Southeastern Oklahoma State U (OK)
Southeast Missouri State U (MO)
Southern Adventist U (TN)
Southern Arkansas U–Magnolia (AR)
Southern Illinois U Carbondale (IL)
Southern Illinois U Edwardsville (IL)
Southern Methodist U (TX)
Southern Oregon U (OR)
Southern Utah U (UT)
Southern Wesleyan U (SC)
Southwest Baptist U (MO)
Southwestern Adventist U (TX)
Southwestern Coll (KS)
Southwestern Oklahoma State U (OK)
Southwestern U (TX)
Southwest Missouri State U (MO)
Southwest State U (MN)
Southwest Texas State U (TX)
Spalding U (KY)
Spelman Coll (GA)
Spring Arbor Coll (MI)
Spring Hill Coll (AL)
Stanford U (CA)
State U of NY at Albany (NY)
State U of NY at Binghamton (NY)
State U of NY at Buffalo (NY)
State U of NY at New Paltz (NY)
State U of NY at Oswego (NY)
State U of NY at Stony Brook (NY)
State U of NY Coll at Brockport (NY)
State U of NY Coll at Buffalo (NY)
State U of NY Coll at Cortland (NY)
State U of NY Coll at Fredonia (NY)
State U of NY Coll at Geneseo (NY)
State U of NY Coll at Oneonta (NY)
State U of NY Coll at Potsdam (NY)
State U of West Georgia (GA)
Stephen F. Austin State U (TX)
Stephens Coll (MO)
Sterling Coll (KS)
Stetson U (FL)
Stevens Inst of Technology (NJ)
Stillman Coll (AL)
Stonehill Coll (MA)
Suffolk U (MA)
Sul Ross State U (TX)
Susquehanna U (PA)
Swarthmore Coll (PA)
Sweet Briar Coll (VA)
Syracuse U (NY)
Tabor Coll (KS)
Talladega Coll (AL)
Taylor U (IN)
Teikyo Post U (CT)
Temple U (PA)
Tennessee State U (TN)
Tennessee Technological U (TN)
Tennessee Wesleyan Coll (TN)
Texas A&M International U (TX)
Texas A&M U (TX)
Texas A&M U–Commerce (TX)
Texas A&M U–Kingsville (TX)
Texas A&M U–Texarkana (TX)
Texas Christian U (TX)
Texas Lutheran U (TX)
Texas Southern U (TX)
Texas Tech U (TX)
Texas Wesleyan U (TX)
Texas Woman's U (TX)
Thiel Coll (PA)
Thomas Edison State Coll (NJ)
Thomas More Coll (KY)
Thomas U (GA)
Toccoa Falls Coll (GA)
Tougaloo Coll (MS)
Touro Coll (NY)
Towson U (MD)
Transylvania U (KY)
Trent U (ON, Canada)
Trevecca Nazarene U (TN)
Trinity Christian Coll (IL)
Trinity Coll (CT)
Trinity U (TX)
Trinity Western U (BC, Canada)
Troy State U (AL)
Troy State U Dothan (AL)
Troy State U Montgomery (AL)
Truman State U (MO)

Tufts U (MA)
Tulane U (LA)
Tusculum Coll (TN)
Tuskegee U (AL)
Union Coll (KY)
Union Coll (NE)
Union Coll (NY)
The Union Inst (OH)
Union U (TN)
United States Air Force Academy (CO)
United States Military Academy (NY)
United States Naval Academy (MD)
Universidad Adventista de las Antillas (PR)
Universidad del Turabo (PR)
Université de Montréal (PQ, Canada)
Université de Sherbrooke (PQ, Canada)
U du Québec à Chicoutimi (PQ, Canada)
U du Québec à Trois-Rivières (PQ, Canada)
Université Laval (PQ, Canada)
U Coll of Cape Breton (NS, Canada)
U Coll of the Fraser Valley (BC, Canada)
The U of Akron (OH)
The U of Alabama (AL)
The U of Alabama at Birmingham (AL)
The U of Alabama in Huntsville (AL)
U of Alaska Fairbanks (AK)
U of Alberta (AB, Canada)
The U of Arizona (AZ)
U of Arkansas (AR)
U of Arkansas at Little Rock (AR)
U of Arkansas at Monticello (AR)
U of Arkansas at Pine Bluff (AR)
U of Baltimore (MD)
U of British Columbia (BC, Canada)
U of Calgary (AB, Canada)
U of Calif, Berkeley (CA)
U of Calif, Davis (CA)
U of Calif, Irvine (CA)
U of Calif, Los Angeles (CA)
U of Calif, Riverside (CA)
U of Calif, San Diego (CA)
U of Calif, Santa Barbara (CA)
U of Calif, Santa Cruz (CA)
U of Central Arkansas (AR)
U of Central Florida (FL)
U of Central Oklahoma (OK)
U of Charleston (WV)
U of Chicago (IL)
U of Cincinnati (OH)
U of Colorado at Boulder (CO)
U of Colorado at Colorado Springs (CO)
U of Colorado at Denver (CO)
U of Connecticut (CT)
U of Dallas (TX)
U of Dayton (OH)
U of Delaware (DE)
U of Denver (CO)
U of Detroit Mercy (MI)
U of Evansville (IN)
The U of Findlay (OH)
U of Florida (FL)
U of Georgia (GA)
U of Great Falls (MT)
U of Guelph (ON, Canada)
U of Hartford (CT)
U of Hawaii at Manoa (HI)
U of Houston (TX)
U of Houston–Clear Lake (TX)
U of Idaho (ID)
U of Illinois at Chicago (IL)
U of Illinois at Springfield (IL)
U of Illinois at Urbana–Champaign (IL)
U of Indianapolis (IN)
The U of Iowa (IA)
U of Kansas (KS)
U of Kentucky (KY)
U of King's Coll (NS, Canada)
U of La Verne (CA)
The U of Lethbridge (AB, Canada)
U of Louisiana at Lafayette (LA)
U of Louisiana at Monroe (LA)
U of Louisville (KY)
U of Maine (ME)

U of Maine at Farmington (ME)
U of Maine at Machias (ME)
U of Maine at Presque Isle (ME)
U of Manitoba (MB, Canada)
U of Mary Hardin-Baylor (TX)
U of Maryland, Baltimore County (MD)
U of Maryland, Coll Park (MD)
U of Maryland University Coll (MD)
U of Massachusetts Amherst (MA)
U of Massachusetts Boston (MA)
U of Massachusetts Dartmouth (MA)
U of Massachusetts Lowell (MA)
The U of Memphis (TN)
U of Miami (FL)
U of Michigan (MI)
U of Michigan–Dearborn (MI)
U of Michigan–Flint (MI)
U of Minnesota, Duluth (MN)
U of Minnesota, Morris (MN)
U of Minnesota, Twin Cities Campus (MN)
U of Mississippi (MS)
U of Missouri–Columbia (MO)
U of Missouri–Kansas City (MO)
U of Missouri–Rolla (MO)
U of Missouri–St. Louis (MO)
U of Mobile (AL)
The U of Montana–Missoula (MT)
U of Montevallo (AL)
U of Nebraska at Kearney (NE)
U of Nebraska at Omaha (NE)
U of Nebraska–Lincoln (NE)
U of Nevada, Las Vegas (NV)
U of Nevada, Reno (NV)
U of New Brunswick, Fredericton (NB, Canada)
U of New Brunswick, Saint John (NB, Canada)
U of New Hampshire (NH)
U of New Hampshire at Manchester (NH)
U of New Haven (CT)
U of New Mexico (NM)
U of North Alabama (AL)
The U of North Carolina at Asheville (NC)
The U of North Carolina at Chapel Hill (NC)
The U of North Carolina at Charlotte (NC)
The U of North Carolina at Greensboro (NC)
The U of North Carolina at Pembroke (NC)
The U of North Carolina at Wilmington (NC)
U of North Dakota (ND)
U of Northern Colorado (CO)
U of Northern Iowa (IA)
U of North Florida (FL)
U of North Texas (TX)
U of Notre Dame (IN)
U of Oklahoma (OK)
U of Oregon (OR)
U of Pennsylvania (PA)
U of Pittsburgh (PA)
U of Pittsburgh at Bradford (PA)
U of Pittsburgh at Johnstown (PA)
U of Portland (OR)
U of Prince Edward Island (PE, Canada)
U of Puerto Rico, Mayagüez Campus (PR)
U of Puget Sound (WA)
U of Redlands (CA)
U of Regina (SK, Canada)
U of Rhode Island (RI)
U of Richmond (VA)
U of Rio Grande (OH)
U of Rochester (NY)
U of St. Francis (IL)
U of Saint Francis (IN)
U of St. Thomas (MN)
U of St. Thomas (TX)
U of San Diego (CA)
U of San Francisco (CA)
U of Science and Arts of Oklahoma (OK)
The U of Scranton (PA)
U of Sioux Falls (SD)
U of South Alabama (AL)
U of South Carolina (SC)
U of South Carolina Spartanburg (SC)

U of South Dakota (SD)
U of Southern California (CA)
U of Southern Colorado (CO)
U of Southern Indiana (IN)
U of Southern Maine (ME)
U of Southern Mississippi (MS)
U of South Florida (FL)
The U of Tampa (FL)
The U of Tennessee at Chattanooga (TN)
The U of Tennessee at Martin (TN)
The U of Tennessee Knoxville (TN)
The U of Texas at Arlington (TX)
The U of Texas at Austin (TX)
The U of Texas at Dallas (TX)
The U of Texas at San Antonio (TX)
The U of Texas at Tyler (TX)
The U of Texas–Pan American (TX)
U of the District of Columbia (DC)
U of the Ozarks (AR)
U of the Pacific (CA)
U of the Sacred Heart (PR)
U of the South (TN)
U of Toronto (ON, Canada)
U of Tulsa (OK)
U of Utah (UT)
U of Vermont (VT)
U of Victoria (BC, Canada)
U of Virginia (VA)
U of Virginia's Coll at Wise (VA)
U of Washington (WA)
U of Waterloo (ON, Canada)
The U of West Alabama (AL)
The U of Western Ontario (ON, Canada)
U of West Florida (FL)
U of Windsor (ON, Canada)
The U of Winnipeg (MB, Canada)
U of Wisconsin–Eau Claire (WI)
U of Wisconsin–Green Bay (WI)
U of Wisconsin–La Crosse (WI)
U of Wisconsin–Madison (WI)
U of Wisconsin–Milwaukee (WI)
U of Wisconsin–Parkside (WI)
U of Wisconsin–Platteville (WI)
U of Wisconsin–River Falls (WI)
U of Wisconsin–Stevens Point (WI)
U of Wisconsin–Superior (WI)
U of Wisconsin–Whitewater (WI)
U of Wyoming (WY)
Urbana U (OH)
Ursinus Coll (PA)
Ursuline Coll (OH)
Utah State U (UT)
Utica Coll of Syracuse U (NY)
Valdosta State U (GA)
Valley City State U (ND)
Valparaiso U (IN)
Vanderbilt U (TN)
Vanguard U of Southern California (CA)
Vassar Coll (NY)
Villanova U (PA)
Virginia Commonwealth U (VA)
Virginia Intermont Coll (VA)
Virginia Military Inst (VA)
Virginia Polytechnic Inst and State U (VA)
Virginia Union U (VA)
Virginia Wesleyan Coll (VA)
Wabash Coll (IN)
Wagner Coll (NY)
Wake Forest U (NC)
Walla Walla Coll (WA)
Walsh U (OH)
Warner Pacific Coll (OR)
Warner Southern Coll (FL)
Warren Wilson Coll (NC)
Wartburg Coll (IA)
Washington & Jefferson Coll (PA)
Washington and Lee U (VA)
Washington Coll (MD)
Washington State U (WA)
Washington U in St. Louis (MO)
Wayland Baptist U (TX)
Waynesburg Coll (PA)
Wayne State Coll (NE)
Wayne State U (MI)
Weber State U (UT)
Webster U (MO)
Wellesley Coll (MA)
Wells Coll (NY)
Wesleyan Coll (GA)
Wesleyan U (CT)
Wesley Coll (DE)

Majors Index
History–Horticulture Science

West Chester U of Pennsylvania (PA)
Western Carolina U (NC)
Western Connecticut State U (CT)
Western Illinois U (IL)
Western Kentucky U (KY)
Western Maryland Coll (MD)
Western Michigan U (MI)
Western New England Coll (MA)
Western Oregon U (OR)
Western State Coll of Colorado (CO)
Western Washington U (WA)
Westfield State Coll (MA)
West Liberty State Coll (WV)
Westminster Coll (MO)
Westminster Coll (PA)
Westminster Coll (UT)
Westmont Coll (CA)
West Texas A&M U (TX)
West Virginia State Coll (WV)
West Virginia U (WV)
West Virginia U Inst of Technology (WV)
West Virginia Wesleyan Coll (WV)
Wheaton Coll (IL)
Wheaton Coll (MA)
Wheeling Jesuit U (WV)
Whitman Coll (WA)
Whittier Coll (CA)
Whitworth Coll (WA)
Wichita State U (KS)
Widener U (PA)
Wilfrid Laurier U (ON, Canada)
Wilkes U (PA)
Willamette U (OR)
William Jewell Coll (MO)
William Paterson U of New Jersey (NJ)
William Penn U (IA)
Williams Baptist Coll (AR)
Williams Coll (MA)
William Tyndale Coll (MI)
William Woods U (MO)
Wilmington Coll (OH)
Wingate U (NC)
Winona State U (MN)
Winston-Salem State U (NC)
Winthrop U (SC)
Wisconsin Lutheran Coll (WI)
Wittenberg U (OH)
Wofford Coll (SC)
Woodbury U (CA)
Worcester Polytechnic Inst (MA)
Worcester State Coll (MA)
Wright State U (OH)
Xavier U (OH)
Xavier U of Louisiana (LA)
Yale U (CT)
Yeshiva U (NY)
York Coll (NE)
York Coll of Pennsylvania (PA)
York Coll of the City U of New York (NY)
York U (ON, Canada)
Youngstown State U (OH)

HISTORY EDUCATION
Abilene Christian U (TX)
Adams State Coll (CO)
Appalachian State U (NC)
Baylor U (TX)
Berry Coll (GA)
Bethel Coll (TN)
Bowling Green State U (OH)
Bridgewater Coll (VA)
Brigham Young U (UT)
Carroll Coll (MT)
The Catholic U of America (DC)
Central Michigan U (MI)
Christian Brothers U (TN)
Citadel, The Military Coll of South Carolina (SC)
The Coll of New Jersey (NJ)
Coll of the Ozarks (MO)
Concordia Coll (MN)
Concordia Coll (IL)
Concordia U (NE)
Crown Coll (MN)
Culver-Stockton Coll (MO)
Dana Coll (NE)
Dominican Coll of Blauvelt (NY)
Eastern Michigan U (MI)
East Texas Baptist U (TX)
Elmhurst Coll (IL)
Elmira Coll (NY)
Framingham State Coll (MA)
Hardin-Simmons U (TX)
Hastings Coll (NE)
Huntingdon Coll (AL)
Huron U (SD)
Johnson State Coll (VT)
King Coll (TN)
Liberty U (VA)
Luther Coll (IA)
Maryville Coll (TN)
McGill U (PQ, Canada)
McKendree Coll (IL)
Mercer U (GA)
Mount Marty Coll (SD)
Nazareth Coll of Rochester (NY)
North Carolina Central U (NC)
North Dakota State U (ND)
Northwest Coll (WA)
Northwest Nazarene U (ID)
Oklahoma Baptist U (OK)
Rocky Mountain Coll (MT)
St. Ambrose U (IA)
Salve Regina U (RI)
Seton Hill Coll (PA)
Southwestern Oklahoma State U (OK)
Southwest Missouri State U (MO)
Talladega Coll (AL)
Tennessee Wesleyan Coll (TN)
Texas A&M International U (TX)
Texas Wesleyan U (TX)
Trevecca Nazarene U (TN)
Trinity Christian Coll (IL)
Union Coll (NE)
The U of Arizona (AZ)
U of Delaware (DE)
U of Illinois at Chicago (IL)
The U of Iowa (IA)
U of Maryland, Coll Park (MD)
U of Nebraska–Lincoln (NE)
The U of North Carolina at Charlotte (NC)
U of North Texas (TX)
U of Rio Grande (OH)
The U of Tennessee at Martin (TN)
U of Wisconsin–River Falls (WI)
U of Wisconsin–Superior (WI)
Wartburg Coll (IA)
Washington U in St. Louis (MO)
Weber State U (UT)
Western Montana Coll of The U of Montana (MT)
Wheeling Jesuit U (WV)
York Coll (NE)
York U (ON, Canada)
Youngstown State U (OH)

HISTORY OF PHILOSOPHY
Bard Coll (NY)
Bennington Coll (VT)
Brandeis U (MA)
The Evergreen State Coll (WA)
Hampshire Coll (MA)
Harvard U (MA)
Marlboro Coll (VT)
Marquette U (WI)
St. John's Coll (NM)
U of Regina (SK, Canada)
U of Southern California (CA)
U of Toronto (ON, Canada)

HISTORY OF SCIENCE AND TECHNOLOGY
Bard Coll (NY)
Brevard Coll (NC)
Case Western Reserve U (OH)
Cornell U (NY)
Georgia Inst of Technology (GA)
Hampshire Coll (MA)
Harvard U (MA)
Johns Hopkins U (MD)
Massachusetts Inst of Technology (MA)
Oregon State U (OR)
U of Chicago (IL)
U of Pennsylvania (PA)
U of Pittsburgh (PA)
U of Toronto (ON, Canada)
U of Washington (WA)
U of Wisconsin–Madison (WI)
Worcester Polytechnic Inst (MA)

HOME ECONOMICS
Abilene Christian U (TX)
Appalachian State U (NC)
Ashland U (OH)
Auburn U (AL)
Baldwin-Wallace Coll (OH)
Ball State U (IN)
Baylor U (TX)
Bennett Coll (NC)
Bluffton Coll (OH)
Bridgewater Coll (VA)
California State Polytechnic U, Pomona (CA)
California State U, Long Beach (CA)
California State U, Los Angeles (CA)
California State U, Northridge (CA)
Campbell U (NC)
Carson-Newman Coll (TN)
Central Michigan U (MI)
Central Missouri State U (MO)
Coll of St. Catherine (MN)
Coll of the Ozarks (MO)
Colorado State U (CO)
Concordia U (NE)
David Lipscomb U (TN)
Delaware State U (DE)
Delta State U (MS)
East Central U (OK)
Eastern Illinois U (IL)
Eastern Kentucky U (KY)
Eastern New Mexico U (NM)
East Tennessee State U (TN)
Fairmont State Coll (WV)
Florida State U (FL)
Fontbonne Coll (MO)
Framingham State Coll (MA)
Freed-Hardeman U (TN)
George Fox U (OR)
Hampton U (VA)
Henderson State U (AR)
Idaho State U (ID)
Immaculata Coll (PA)
Indiana State U (IN)
Inter American U of PR, Metropolitan Campus (PR)
Iowa State U of Science and Technology (IA)
Jacksonville State U (AL)
Keene State Coll (NH)
Kent State U (OH)
Lamar U (TX)
Langston U (OK)
Madonna U (MI)
Marshall U (WV)
Marymount Coll (NY)
McNeese State U (LA)
Mercyhurst Coll (PA)
Meredith Coll (NC)
Miami U (OH)
Michigan State U (MI)
Minnesota State U, Mankato (MN)
Mississippi State U (MS)
Montana State U–Bozeman (MT)
Morehead State U (KY)
Morgan State U (MD)
Mount Saint Vincent U (NS, Canada)
Mount Vernon Nazarene Coll (OH)
Nicholls State U (LA)
Norfolk State U (VA)
North Carolina Ag and Tech State U (NC)
North Carolina Central U (NC)
Northeastern State U (OK)
Northwestern State U of Louisiana (LA)
Northwest Missouri State U (MO)
Oakwood Coll (AL)
Ohio U (OH)
Oklahoma State U (OK)
Olivet Nazarene U (IL)
Oregon State U (OR)
Ouachita Baptist U (AR)
Pacific Union Coll (CA)
Pittsburg State U (KS)
Point Loma Nazarene U (CA)
Pontifical Catholic U of Puerto Rico (PR)
Purdue U (IN)
Queens Coll of the City U of NY (NY)
Saint Joseph Coll (CT)
Sam Houston State U (TX)
San Francisco State U (CA)
Seton Hill Coll (PA)
Southeast Missouri State U (MO)
Southern Utah U (UT)
Southwest Texas State U (TX)
State U of NY Coll at Oneonta (NY)
Stephen F. Austin State U (TX)
Tennessee Technological U (TN)
Texas A&M U–Kingsville (TX)
Texas Southern U (TX)
Texas Tech U (TX)
Texas Woman's U (TX)
The U of Akron (OH)
The U of Alabama (AL)
U of Alberta (AB, Canada)
U of Arkansas at Pine Bluff (AR)
U of British Columbia (BC, Canada)
U of Central Arkansas (AR)
U of Central Oklahoma (OK)
U of Houston (TX)
U of Idaho (ID)
U of Illinois at Urbana–Champaign (IL)
U of Louisiana at Monroe (LA)
U of Manitoba (MB, Canada)
U of Mississippi (MS)
U of Montevallo (AL)
U of Nebraska at Omaha (NE)
U of New Hampshire (NH)
U of New Mexico (NM)
U of North Alabama (AL)
The U of North Carolina at Greensboro (NC)
U of Puerto Rico, Río Piedras (PR)
U of Southern Mississippi (MS)
The U of Tennessee at Chattanooga (TN)
The U of Tennessee at Martin (TN)
The U of Texas at Austin (TX)
U of the District of Columbia (DC)
The U of Western Ontario (ON, Canada)
U of Wisconsin–Madison (WI)
Utah State U (UT)
Washington State U (WA)
Wayne State Coll (NE)
Western Illinois U (IL)
West Virginia U (WV)
Youngstown State U (OH)

HOME ECONOMICS EDUCATION
Abilene Christian U (TX)
Appalachian State U (NC)
Ashland U (OH)
Auburn U (AL)
Baldwin-Wallace Coll (OH)
Ball State U (IN)
Berea Coll (KY)
Bluffton Coll (OH)
Bowling Green State U (OH)
Bridgewater Coll (VA)
California State U, Northridge (CA)
Campbell U (NC)
Carson-Newman Coll (TN)
Central Michigan U (MI)
Central Missouri State U (MO)
Cheyney U of Pennsylvania (PA)
Coll of St. Catherine (MN)
Coll of the Ozarks (MO)
Colorado State U (CO)
Concordia Coll (MN)
Concordia U (NE)
Cornell U (NY)
Delta State U (MS)
East Carolina U (NC)
Eastern Illinois U (IL)
Eastern Kentucky U (KY)
Eastern Michigan U (MI)
Fairmont State Coll (WV)
Ferris State U (MI)
Florida International U (FL)
Florida State U (FL)
Fontbonne Coll (MO)
Fort Valley State U (GA)
Framingham State Coll (MA)
George Fox U (OR)
Georgia Southern U (GA)
Hampton U (VA)
Immaculata Coll (PA)
Indiana State U (IN)
Indiana U of Pennsylvania (PA)
Inter American U of PR, Metropolitan Campus (PR)
Iowa State U of Science and Technology (IA)
Jacksonville State U (AL)
Keene State Coll (NH)
Kent State U (OH)
Lamar U (TX)
Langston U (OK)
Madonna U (MI)
Marshall U (WV)
Marymount Coll (NY)
Marywood U (PA)
McNeese State U (LA)
Mercyhurst Coll (PA)
Miami U (OH)
Michigan State U (MI)
Minnesota State U, Mankato (MN)
Mississippi Coll (MS)
Morehead State U (KY)
Mount Mary Coll (WI)
Mount Saint Vincent U (NS, Canada)
Mount Vernon Nazarene Coll (OH)
Murray State U (KY)
New Mexico State U (NM)
North Carolina Ag and Tech State U (NC)
North Carolina Central U (NC)
North Dakota State U (ND)
Northeastern State U (OK)
Northern Arizona U (AZ)
Northern Illinois U (IL)
Northwestern State U of Louisiana (LA)
Northwest Missouri State U (MO)
Oakwood Coll (AL)
Olivet Nazarene U (IL)
Ouachita Baptist U (AR)
Pacific Union Coll (CA)
Pittsburg State U (KS)
Pontifical Catholic U of Puerto Rico (PR)
Queens Coll of the City U of NY (NY)
Saint Joseph Coll (CT)
Sam Houston State U (TX)
Seattle Pacific U (WA)
Seton Hill Coll (PA)
South Dakota State U (SD)
Southeast Missouri State U (MO)
Southern Utah U (UT)
Southwest Missouri State U (MO)
State U of NY Coll at Oneonta (NY)
Tennessee Technological U (TN)
Texas A&M U–Kingsville (TX)
The U of Akron (OH)
The U of Alabama (AL)
U of Alberta (AB, Canada)
The U of Arizona (AZ)
U of Arkansas (AR)
U of Arkansas at Pine Bluff (AR)
U of British Columbia (BC, Canada)
U of Central Arkansas (AR)
U of Central Oklahoma (OK)
U of Georgia (GA)
U of Idaho (ID)
U of Illinois at Springfield (IL)
U of Minnesota, Twin Cities Campus (MN)
U of Montevallo (AL)
U of Nevada, Reno (NV)
U of New Brunswick, Fredericton (NB, Canada)
U of New Mexico (NM)
U of North Texas (TX)
The U of Tennessee at Martin (TN)
The U of Tennessee Knoxville (TN)
U of the District of Columbia (DC)
U of Utah (UT)
U of Wisconsin–Madison (WI)
U of Wisconsin–Stevens Point (WI)
U of Wisconsin–Stout (WI)
U of Wyoming (WY)
Utah State U (UT)
Washington State U (WA)
Wayne State Coll (NE)
Western Carolina U (NC)
Western Kentucky U (KY)
Western Michigan U (MI)
Winthrop U (SC)
Youngstown State U (OH)

HORTICULTURE SCIENCE
Auburn U (AL)
Berry Coll (GA)
Brigham Young U (UT)
California Polytechnic State U, San Luis Obispo (CA)
California State Polytechnic U, Pomona (CA)
Cameron U (OK)
Christopher Newport U (VA)
Clemson U (SC)
Coll of the Ozarks (MO)
Colorado State U (CO)
Cornell U (NY)

Majors Index
Horticulture Science–Humanities

Delaware Valley Coll (PA)
Eastern Kentucky U (KY)
Florida A&M U (FL)
Florida Southern Coll (FL)
Iowa State U of Science and Technology (IA)
Kansas State U (KS)
McGill U (PQ, Canada)
Michigan State U (MI)
Mississippi State U (MS)
Montana State U–Bozeman (MT)
Murray State U (KY)
Naropa U (CO)
New Mexico State U (NM)
North Carolina State U (NC)
North Dakota State U (ND)
Northwest Missouri State U (MO)
The Ohio State U (OH)
Oklahoma State U (OK)
Oregon State U (OR)
Penn State U Univ Park Campus (PA)
Purdue U (IN)
Rutgers, State U of NJ, Cook Coll (NJ)
Sam Houston State U (TX)
Southeastern Louisiana U (LA)
Southeast Missouri State U (MO)
Southwest Missouri State U (MO)
Southwest Texas State U (TX)
State U of NY Coll of A&T at Cobleskill (NY)
Stephen F. Austin State U (TX)
Tennessee Technological U (TN)
Texas A&M U (TX)
Texas A&M U–Kingsville (TX)
Texas Tech U (TX)
Thomas Edison State Coll (NJ)
U of Arkansas (AR)
U of Calif, Davis (CA)
U of Connecticut (CT)
U of Delaware (DE)
U of Florida (FL)
U of Guelph (ON, Canada)
U of Hawaii at Manoa (HI)
U of Idaho (ID)
U of Illinois at Urbana–Champaign (IL)
U of Maryland, Coll Park (MD)
U of Minnesota, Crookston (MN)
U of Nebraska–Lincoln (NE)
U of New Hampshire (NH)
U of Puerto Rico, Mayagüez Campus (PR)
U of Vermont (VT)
U of Wisconsin–Madison (WI)
U of Wisconsin–River Falls (WI)
Utah State U (UT)
Virginia Polytechnic Inst and State U (VA)
Washington State U (WA)
West Virginia U (WV)

HORTICULTURE SERVICES
Iowa State U of Science and Technology (IA)
McGill U (PQ, Canada)
Nova Scotia Ag Coll (NS, Canada)
South Dakota State U (SD)
Stephen F. Austin State U (TX)
Texas Tech U (TX)
U of Georgia (GA)
U of Guelph (ON, Canada)
U of Vermont (VT)

HOSPITALITY MANAGEMENT
American InterContinental U, Atlanta (GA)
Arkansas Tech U (AR)
Becker Coll (MA)
Belmont U (TN)
Boston U (MA)
Bowling Green State U (OH)
Central Michigan U (MI)
Concord Coll (WV)
Delta State U (MS)
Eastern Illinois U (IL)
Eastern Michigan U (MI)
Endicott Coll (MA)
Ferris State U (MI)
Florida International U (FL)
Florida State U (FL)
Husson Coll (ME)
Indiana Inst of Technology (IN)
Indiana U–Purdue U Fort Wayne (IN)
Johnson & Wales U (RI)

Johnson State Coll (VT)
Kendall Coll (IL)
Lakeland Coll (WI)
Madonna U (MI)
Mercyhurst Coll (PA)
Metropolitan State Coll of Denver (CO)
Morgan State U (MD)
Mount Saint Vincent U (NS, Canada)
National American U–St. Paul Campus (MN)
New Hampshire Coll (NH)
New York City Tech Coll of the City U of NY (NY)
North Carolina Central U (NC)
Nova Southeastern U (FL)
The Ohio State U (OH)
The Ohio State U at Lima (OH)
Penn State U Univ Park Campus (PA)
Robert Morris Coll (PA)
Rochester Inst of Technology (NY)
Ryerson Polytechnic U (ON, Canada)
Saint Louis U (MO)
San Francisco State U (CA)
San Jose State U (CA)
Siena Heights U (MI)
Southern Vermont Coll (VT)
Stephen F. Austin State U (TX)
Syracuse U (NY)
Tiffin U (OH)
Tuskegee U (AL)
U Coll of Cape Breton (NS, Canada)
U of Central Florida (FL)
U of Denver (CO)
U of Hawaii at Manoa (HI)
U of Kentucky (KY)
U of Massachusetts Amherst (MA)
U of Nevada, Las Vegas (NV)
U of Nevada, Reno (NV)
U of New Brunswick, Saint John (NB, Canada)
U of New Haven (CT)
U of New Orleans (LA)
U of Prince Edward Island (PE, Canada)
U of South Carolina (SC)
Western Carolina U (NC)
Youngstown State U (OH)

HOSPITALITY/RECREATION MARKETING
Rochester Inst of Technology (NY)

HOTEL AND RESTAURANT MANAGEMENT
Appalachian State U (NC)
Ashland U (OH)
Auburn U (AL)
Baltimore International Coll (MD)
Barber-Scotia Coll (NC)
Becker Coll (MA)
Belmont U (TN)
Berea Coll (KY)
Bethune-Cookman Coll (FL)
Boston U (MA)
Brigham Young U–Hawaii Campus (HI)
California State Polytechnic U, Pomona (CA)
Canisius Coll (NY)
Central Michigan U (MI)
Central Missouri State U (MO)
Champlain Coll (VT)
Cheyney U of Pennsylvania (PA)
Chicago State U (IL)
The Coll of Southeastern Europe, The American U of Athens (Greece)
Coll of the Ozarks (MO)
Colorado State U (CO)
Concord Coll (WV)
Cornell U (NY)
Davenport Coll of Business (MI)
Delaware State U (DE)
Drexel U (PA)
East Carolina U (NC)
East Stroudsburg U of Pennsylvania (PA)
Fairleigh Dickinson U, Florham-Madison Campus (NJ)
Fairleigh Dickinson U, Teaneck-Hackensack Campus (NJ)
Florida Southern Coll (FL)

Georgia Southern U (GA)
Georgia State U (GA)
Golden Gate U (CA)
Grand Valley State U (MI)
Hampton U (VA)
Howard U (DC)
Huston-Tillotson Coll (TX)
Indiana U of Pennsylvania (PA)
Inter American U of PR, Aguadilla Campus (PR)
Iowa State U of Science and Technology (IA)
James Madison U (VA)
Johnson & Wales U (RI)
Kansas State U (KS)
Kendall Coll (IL)
Keuka Coll (NY)
Lakeland Coll (WI)
Langston U (OK)
Lasell Coll (MA)
Lebanon Valley Coll (PA)
Lynn U (FL)
Marywood U (PA)
Mercyhurst Coll (PA)
Michigan State U (MI)
Morgan State U (MD)
Mount Ida Coll (MA)
Mount Mary Coll (WI)
Mount Saint Vincent U (NS, Canada)
Newbury Coll (MA)
New England Culinary Inst (VT)
New Hampshire Coll (NH)
New Mexico State U (NM)
New York Inst of Technology (NY)
New York U (NY)
Niagara U (NY)
Norfolk State U (VA)
North Carolina Wesleyan Coll (NC)
North Dakota State U (ND)
Northern Arizona U (AZ)
Northwood U (MI)
Oklahoma State U (OK)
Peirce Coll (PA)
Plattsburgh State U of NY (NY)
Purdue U (IN)
Purdue U Calumet (IN)
Rochester Inst of Technology (NY)
Ryerson Polytechnic U (ON, Canada)
St. John's U (NY)
Saint Leo U (FL)
St. Thomas U (FL)
Sierra Nevada Coll (NV)
South Dakota State U (SD)
Southern Oregon U (OR)
Southern Vermont Coll (VT)
Southwest Missouri State U (MO)
State U of NY Coll at Buffalo (NY)
State U of NY Coll at Oneonta (NY)
Texas A&M U–Kingsville (TX)
Texas Tech U (TX)
Thomas Coll (ME)
Thomas Edison State Coll (NJ)
Tiffin U (OH)
United States International U (CA)
The U of Alabama (AL)
U of Arkansas at Pine Bluff (AR)
U of Calgary (AB, Canada)
U of Central Oklahoma (OK)
U of Delaware (DE)
U of Denver (CO)
The U of Findlay (OH)
U of Guelph (ON, Canada)
U of Houston (TX)
U of Illinois at Urbana–Champaign (IL)
U of Louisiana at Lafayette (LA)
U of Maine at Machias (ME)
U of Maryland University Coll (MD)
U of Minnesota, Crookston (MN)
U of Missouri–Columbia (MO)
U of New Hampshire (NH)
U of New Haven (CT)
U of North Texas (TX)
U of San Francisco (CA)
U of Southern Mississippi (MS)
The U of Tennessee Knoxville (TN)
U of Victoria (BC, Canada)
U of Wisconsin–Stout (WI)
Washington State U (WA)
Webber Coll (FL)
Western Kentucky U (KY)
Widener U (PA)
Youngstown State U (OH)

HOUSING STUDIES
Auburn U (AL)
Florida State U (FL)
Iowa State U of Science and Technology (IA)
Ohio U (OH)
Southwest Missouri State U (MO)
U of Arkansas (AR)
U of Georgia (GA)
U of Missouri–Columbia (MO)
U of Northern Iowa (IA)
Western Kentucky U (KY)

HUMAN ECOLOGY
California State U, Hayward (CA)
Cameron U (OK)
Chadron State Coll (NE)
Coll of the Atlantic (ME)
Concordia U (PQ, Canada)
Cornell U (NY)
Emory U (GA)
The Evergreen State Coll (WA)
Goddard Coll (VT)
Hampton U (VA)
Kansas State U (KS)
Lambuth U (TN)
Long Island U, Southampton Coll, Friends World Program (NY)
Marlboro Coll (VT)
Marshall U (WV)
Marymount U (NY)
Mercyhurst Coll (PA)
Morgan State U (MD)
Mount Saint Vincent U (NS, Canada)
Regis U (CO)
Rutgers, State U of NJ, Douglass Coll (NJ)
Seton Hill Coll (PA)
State U of NY Coll at Oneonta (NY)
Sterling Coll (VT)
U of Alberta (AB, Canada)
U of Calif, Irvine (CA)
U of Manitoba (MB, Canada)

HUMANITIES
Albertus Magnus Coll (CT)
Alma Coll (MI)
Antioch Coll (OH)
Arizona State U (AZ)
Athens State U (AL)
Atlanta Christian Coll (GA)
Augsburg Coll (MN)
Barat Coll (IL)
Bard Coll (NY)
Becker Coll (MA)
Belhaven Coll (MS)
Bemidji State U (MN)
Bennington Coll (VT)
Biola U (CA)
Bishop's U (PQ, Canada)
Bloomsburg U of Pennsylvania (PA)
Bluefield State Coll (WV)
Bluffton Coll (OH)
Bowling Green State U (OH)
Brevard Coll (NC)
Brigham Young U (UT)
Brock U (ON, Canada)
Bryn Athyn Coll of the New Church (PA)
Burlington Coll (VT)
California State Polytechnic U, Pomona (CA)
California State U, Chico (CA)
California State U, Dominguez Hills (CA)
California State U, Monterey Bay (CA)
California State U, Northridge (CA)
California State U, Sacramento (CA)
California State U, San Bernardino (CA)
Canisius Coll (NY)
Carleton U (ON, Canada)
Carnegie Mellon U (PA)
Catawba Coll (NC)
Chaminade U of Honolulu (HI)
Charleston Southern U (SC)
Clarion U of Pennsylvania (PA)
Clarkson U (NY)
Colgate U (NY)
Coll of Mount St. Joseph (OH)
Coll of Notre Dame (CA)
Coll of Saint Benedict (MN)

Coll of Saint Mary (NE)
The Coll of St. Scholastica (MN)
Coll of Santa Fe (NM)
Colorado Christian U (CO)
Colorado State U (CO)
Columbia Coll (MO)
Columbia International U (SC)
Concordia Coll (MN)
Concordia U (CA)
Concordia U (OR)
Concordia U Wisconsin (WI)
Daemen Coll (NY)
Dominican Coll of Blauvelt (NY)
Dominican U of California (CA)
Dowling Coll (NY)
Drexel U (PA)
Eastern Washington U (WA)
Eckerd Coll (FL)
Edinboro U of Pennsylvania (PA)
Elmira Coll (NY)
Eugene Lang Coll, New School U (NY)
The Evergreen State Coll (WA)
Fairleigh Dickinson U, Florham-Madison Campus (NJ)
Fairleigh Dickinson U, Teaneck-Hackensack Campus (NJ)
Faulkner U (AL)
Felician Coll (NJ)
Florida Atlantic U (FL)
Florida Inst of Technology (FL)
Florida International U (FL)
Florida Southern Coll (FL)
Florida State U (FL)
Fort Lewis Coll (CO)
Framingham State Coll (MA)
Franciscan U of Steubenville (OH)
Freed-Hardeman U (TN)
Fresno Pacific U (CA)
Gannon U (PA)
The George Washington U (DC)
Georgian Court Coll (NJ)
Goddard Coll (VT)
Golden Gate U (CA)
Grand Valley State U (MI)
Guilford Coll (NC)
Hampden-Sydney Coll (VA)
Hampshire Coll (MA)
Harding U (AR)
Harvard U (MA)
Hawaii Pacific U (HI)
Hofstra U (NY)
Holy Family Coll (PA)
Holy Names Coll (CA)
Hope Coll (MI)
Houghton Coll (NY)
Indiana State U (IN)
Indiana U Kokomo (IN)
Jacksonville U (FL)
John Carroll U (OH)
John F. Kennedy U (CA)
Johns Hopkins U (MD)
Johnson State Coll (VT)
Juniata Coll (PA)
Kansas State U (KS)
Kenyon Coll (OH)
Lambuth U (TN)
Lawrence Technological U (MI)
Lees-McRae Coll (NC)
LeMoyne-Owen Coll (TN)
Lesley Coll (MA)
Lincoln Memorial U (TN)
Lock Haven U of Pennsylvania (PA)
Long Island U, Brooklyn Campus (NY)
Long Island U, Southampton Coll, Friends World Program (NY)
Loyola Marymount U (CA)
Loyola U New Orleans (LA)
Lubbock Christian U (TX)
Lynn U (FL)
Macalester Coll (MN)
Maranatha Baptist Bible Coll (WI)
Marist Coll (NY)
Marlboro Coll (VT)
Marylhurst U (OR)
Maryville U of Saint Louis (MO)
Massachusetts Inst of Technology (MA)
McGill U (PQ, Canada)
Medaille Coll (NY)
Memorial U of Newfoundland (NF, Canada)
Mercyhurst Coll (PA)
Mesa State Coll (CO)
Messiah Coll (PA)

Majors Index
Humanities–Human Services

Michigan State U (MI)
Middlebury Coll (VT)
Midland Lutheran Coll (NE)
Midwestern State U (TX)
Milligan Coll (TN)
Minnesota State U, Mankato (MN)
Missouri Southern State Coll (MO)
Monmouth Coll (IL)
Montana State U–Northern (MT)
Mount Allison U (NB, Canada)
Mount Aloysius Coll (PA)
Mount St. Clare Coll (IA)
Mount Saint Vincent U (NS, Canada)
Muskingum Coll (OH)
New Hampshire Coll (NH)
New York U (NY)
North Central Coll (IL)
North Dakota State U (ND)
Northern Arizona U (AZ)
North Greenville Coll (SC)
Northwestern Coll (IA)
Northwestern U (IL)
Northwest Missouri State U (MO)
Oakland City U (IN)
The Ohio State U (OH)
Ohio Wesleyan U (OH)
Oklahoma Baptist U (OK)
Oklahoma City U (OK)
Oklahoma Panhandle State U (OK)
Our Lady of the Lake Coll (LA)
Pacific U (OR)
Penn State U Harrisburg Campus of the Capital Coll (PA)
Pepperdine U, Malibu (CA)
Pfeiffer U (NC)
Plymouth State Coll (NH)
Polytechnic U, Brooklyn Campus (NY)
Pomona Coll (CA)
Portland State U (OR)
Principia Coll (IL)
Providence Coll (RI)
Providence Coll and Theological Seminary (MB, Canada)
Purdue U (IN)
Purdue U Calumet (IN)
Queens Coll of the City U of NY (NY)
Quincy U (IL)
Redeemer Coll (ON, Canada)
Regis U (CO)
Roberts Wesleyan Coll (NY)
Rockford Coll (IL)
Rosemont Coll (PA)
St. Gregory's U (OK)
Saint John's U (MN)
Saint Joseph Coll (CT)
Saint Joseph's U (PA)
Saint Louis U (MO)
Saint Martin's Coll (WA)
Saint Mary-of-the-Woods Coll (IN)
Saint Mary's Coll (IN)
St. Norbert Coll (WI)
Saint Peter's Coll (NJ)
Sam Houston State U (TX)
San Diego State U (CA)
San Francisco State U (CA)
San Jose State U (CA)
Sarah Lawrence Coll (NY)
Seattle U (WA)
Seton Hall U (NJ)
Seton Hill Coll (PA)
Shawnee State U (OH)
Sheldon Jackson Coll (AK)
Shimer Coll (IL)
Shorter Coll (GA)
Siena Heights U (MI)
Sierra Nevada Coll (NV)
Simon Fraser U (BC, Canada)
Southeastern Louisiana U (LA)
Southern Methodist U (TX)
Southwest Missouri State U (MO)
Spring Hill Coll (AL)
Stanford U (CA)
State U of NY at Stony Brook (NY)
State U of NY Coll at Buffalo (NY)
State U of NY Coll at Old Westbury (NY)
State U of NY Maritime Coll (NY)
Stephen F. Austin State U (TX)
Stetson U (FL)
Stevens Inst of Technology (NJ)
Suffolk U (MA)
Tabor Coll (KS)
Tennessee State U (TN)
Texas Wesleyan U (TX)

Thomas Edison State Coll (NJ)
Thomas U (GA)
Tiffin U (OH)
Toccoa Falls Coll (GA)
Touro Coll (NY)
Trent U (ON, Canada)
Trinity U (TX)
Trinity Western U (BC, Canada)
Union Coll (NY)
The Union Inst (OH)
United States Air Force Academy (CO)
United States Military Academy (NY)
Universidad del Turabo (PR)
The U of Akron (OH)
U of Alberta (AB, Canada)
The U of Arizona (AZ)
U of Bridgeport (CT)
U of Calgary (AB, Canada)
U of Calif, Irvine (CA)
U of Calif, Riverside (CA)
U of Central Florida (FL)
U of Charleston (WV)
U of Chicago (IL)
U of Cincinnati (OH)
U of Colorado at Boulder (CO)
U of Detroit Mercy (MI)
U of Houston–Clear Lake (TX)
U of Houston–Downtown (TX)
U of Houston–Victoria (TX)
U of Illinois at Urbana–Champaign (IL)
U of Kansas (KS)
The U of Lethbridge (AB, Canada)
U of Louisville (KY)
U of Maryland University Coll (MD)
U of Massachusetts Amherst (MA)
U of Michigan (MI)
U of Michigan–Dearborn (MI)
U of Missouri–St. Louis (MO)
U of New England (ME)
U of New Hampshire (NH)
U of New Hampshire at Manchester (NH)
U of New Mexico (NM)
U of North Dakota (ND)
U of Northern Iowa (IA)
U of Oklahoma (OK)
U of Pennsylvania (PA)
U of Pittsburgh (PA)
U of Pittsburgh at Johnstown (PA)
U of Puerto Rico, Mayagüez Campus (PR)
U of Puerto Rico, Río Piedras (PR)
U of Regina (SK, Canada)
U of Rio Grande (OH)
U of San Diego (CA)
U of South Florida (FL)
The U of Tennessee at Chattanooga (TN)
The U of Texas at Austin (TX)
The U of Texas at Dallas (TX)
The U of Texas at San Antonio (TX)
U of the Pacific (CA)
U of the Sacred Heart (PR)
U of the Sciences in Philadelphia (PA)
U of the Virgin Islands (VI)
U of Toronto (ON, Canada)
U of Washington (WA)
U of West Florida (FL)
U of Windsor (ON, Canada)
U of Wisconsin–Green Bay (WI)
U of Wisconsin–Parkside (WI)
U of Wyoming (WY)
Ursuline Coll (OH)
Villa Julie Coll (MD)
Virginia Wesleyan Coll (VA)
Waldorf Coll (IA)
Walla Walla Coll (WA)
Warren Wilson Coll (NC)
Washington Coll (MD)
Washington State U (WA)
Wesleyan U (CT)
Western Baptist Coll (OR)
Western Oregon U (OR)
Western Washington U (WA)
Widener U (PA)
Willamette U (OR)
William Paterson U of New Jersey (NJ)
Wittenberg U (OH)
Wofford Coll (SC)
Woodbury U (CA)
Worcester Polytechnic Inst (MA)

Xavier U (OH)
Yale U (CT)
York Coll (NE)
York Coll of Pennsylvania (PA)
York U (ON, Canada)

HUMAN RESOURCES MANAGEMENT

Abilene Christian U (TX)
Amber U (TX)
American International Coll (MA)
Anderson Coll (SC)
Athens State U (AL)
Auburn U (AL)
Auburn U Montgomery (AL)
Baker Coll of Owosso (MI)
Ball State U (IN)
Barat Coll (IL)
Barton Coll (NC)
Bayamón Central U (PR)
Baylor U (TX)
Bay Path Coll (MA)
Beaver Coll (PA)
Becker Coll (MA)
Bellarmine Coll (KY)
Baruch Coll of the City U of NY (NY)
Birmingham-Southern Coll (AL)
Bishop's U (PQ, Canada)
Black Hills State U (SD)
Boise State U (ID)
Boston Coll (MA)
Bowling Green State U (OH)
Brescia U (KY)
Briar Cliff Coll (IA)
Brock U (ON, Canada)
Cabrini Coll (PA)
California Polytechnic State U, San Luis Obispo (CA)
California State Polytechnic U, Pomona (CA)
California State U, Chico (CA)
California State U, Dominguez Hills (CA)
California State U, Fresno (CA)
California State U, Hayward (CA)
California State U, Long Beach (CA)
California State U, Los Angeles (CA)
Calvary Bible Coll and Theological Seminary (MO)
Carleton U (ON, Canada)
The Catholic U of America (DC)
Central Michigan U (MI)
Central Missouri State U (MO)
Chestnut Hill Coll (PA)
Clarkson U (NY)
Cleary Coll (MI)
Coll of Saint Elizabeth (NJ)
The Coll of Southeastern Europe, The American U of Athens (Greece)
Colorado Christian U (CO)
Colorado Tech U (CO)
Concordia Coll (MI)
Concordia U (PQ, Canada)
Davenport Coll of Business, Lansing Campus (MI)
DePaul U (IL)
Dominican Coll of Blauvelt (NY)
Dominican U of California (CA)
Drexel U (PA)
East Central U (OK)
Eastern Michigan U (MI)
Eastern New Mexico U (NM)
Eastern Washington U (WA)
East Tennessee State U (TN)
Eckerd Coll (FL)
École des Hautes Études Commerciales (PQ, Canada)
Faulkner U (AL)
Florida Atlantic U (FL)
Florida International U (FL)
Florida Southern Coll (FL)
Florida State U (FL)
Framingham State Coll (MA)
Franklin U (OH)
Freed-Hardeman U (TN)
Friends U (KS)
George Fox U (OR)
The George Washington U (DC)
Georgia Southwestern State U (GA)
Georgia State U (GA)
Golden Gate U (CA)
Governors State U (IL)

Grand Canyon U (AZ)
Grand Valley State U (MI)
Gwynedd-Mercy Coll (PA)
Harding U (AR)
Hastings Coll (NE)
Hawaii Pacific U (HI)
Holy Names Coll (CA)
Huston-Tillotson Coll (TX)
Idaho State U (ID)
Indiana Inst of Technology (IN)
Indiana State U (IN)
Inter American U of PR, San Germán Campus (PR)
Ithaca Coll (NY)
Judson Coll (IL)
Juniata Coll (PA)
Kent State U (OH)
King's Coll (PA)
Lakehead U (ON, Canada)
La Salle U (PA)
Lewis U (IL)
Lincoln U (PA)
Lindenwood U (MO)
Loras Coll (IA)
Louisiana Tech U (LA)
Loyola U Chicago (IL)
Mansfield U of Pennsylvania (PA)
Marietta Coll (OH)
Marquette U (WI)
McGill U (PQ, Canada)
Medaille Coll (NY)
Mercyhurst Coll (PA)
Meredith Coll (NC)
Mesa State Coll (CO)
Messiah Coll (PA)
Metropolitan State U (MN)
Miami U (OH)
Michigan State U (MI)
MidAmerica Nazarene U (KS)
Millikin U (IL)
Muhlenberg Coll (PA)
National U (CA)
Nazareth Coll of Rochester (NY)
Newbury Coll (MA)
Niagara U (NY)
Nichols Coll (MA)
North Carolina State U (NC)
Northeastern Illinois U (IL)
Northeastern State U (OK)
Northeastern U (MA)
Notre Dame Coll of Ohio (OH)
Oakland City U (IN)
Oakland U (MI)
The Ohio State U (OH)
Ohio U (OH)
Oklahoma Baptist U (OK)
Oklahoma State U (OK)
Olivet Nazarene U (IL)
Our Lady of the Lake U of San Antonio (TX)
Pace U, New York City Campus (NY)
Palm Beach Atlantic Coll (FL)
Peace Coll (NC)
Philadelphia U (PA)
Plymouth State Coll (NH)
Point Park Coll (PA)
Portland State U (OR)
Purdue U Calumet (IN)
Quinnipiac U (CT)
Redeemer Coll (ON, Canada)
Regents Coll (NY)
Rider U (NJ)
Robert Morris Coll (PA)
Roberts Wesleyan Coll (NY)
Rockhurst U (MO)
Ryerson Polytechnic U (ON, Canada)
St. Cloud State U (MN)
Saint Francis Coll (PA)
St. John Fisher Coll (NY)
St. Joseph's Coll, New York (NY)
St. Joseph's Coll, Suffolk Campus (NY)
Saint Leo U (FL)
Saint Louis U (MO)
Saint Mary-of-the-Woods Coll (IN)
Saint Mary's U (NS, Canada)
St. Mary's U of San Antonio (TX)
Samford U (AL)
Sam Houston State U (TX)
San Jose State U (CA)
Seton Hill Coll (PA)
Silver Lake Coll (WI)
Simpson Coll and Graduate School (CA)
Southwestern Coll (KS)

State U of NY at Oswego (NY)
Susquehanna U (PA)
Temple U (PA)
Texas A&M U–Commerce (TX)
Texas A&M U–Texarkana (TX)
Thomas Coll (ME)
Thomas Edison State Coll (NJ)
Tiffin U (OH)
Trinity Christian Coll (IL)
Troy State U Montgomery (AL)
Universidad Metropolitana (PR)
Université de Montréal (PQ, Canada)
U du Québec à Trois-Rivières (PQ, Canada)
The U of Akron (OH)
U of Alaska Fairbanks (AK)
U of Alberta (AB, Canada)
The U of Arizona (AZ)
U of Baltimore (MD)
U of Detroit Mercy (MI)
The U of Findlay (OH)
U of Florida (FL)
U of Guelph (ON, Canada)
U of Hawaii at Manoa (HI)
U of Idaho (ID)
U of Indianapolis (IN)
The U of Iowa (IA)
The U of Lethbridge (AB, Canada)
U of Maryland, Coll Park (MD)
U of Miami (FL)
U of Michigan–Flint (MI)
U of Minnesota, Duluth (MN)
U of Nebraska at Omaha (NE)
U of Nevada, Las Vegas (NV)
U of Nevada, Reno (NV)
U of New Brunswick, Fredericton (NB, Canada)
U of New Brunswick, Saint John (NB, Canada)
U of New Haven (CT)
U of Pennsylvania (PA)
U of Puerto Rico, Humacao U Coll (PR)
U of Puerto Rico, Mayagüez Campus (PR)
U of Puerto Rico, Río Piedras (PR)
U of Saint Francis (IN)
U of St. Thomas (MN)
U of South Dakota (SD)
The U of Texas at San Antonio (TX)
U of Waterloo (ON, Canada)
U of Wisconsin–Milwaukee (WI)
U of Wisconsin–Whitewater (WI)
U System Coll for Lifelong Learning (NH)
Urbana U (OH)
Ursuline Coll (OH)
Utah State U (UT)
Valley City State U (ND)
Vanderbilt U (TN)
Virginia Polytechnic Inst and State U (VA)
Washington U in St. Louis (MO)
Weber State U (UT)
Webster U (MO)
Western Illinois U (IL)
Western Michigan U (MI)
Western State Coll of Colorado (CO)
Western Washington U (WA)
Westminster Coll (UT)
Wichita State U (KS)
Wilmington Coll (DE)
Winona State U (MN)
Worcester State Coll (MA)
Xavier U (OH)
York Coll (NE)
York U (ON, Canada)

HUMAN SERVICES

Adrian Coll (MI)
Alaska Pacific U (AK)
Albertus Magnus Coll (CT)
Albion Coll (MI)
American International Coll (MA)
Anderson Coll (SC)
Assumption Coll (MA)
Audrey Cohen Coll (NY)
Baldwin-Wallace Coll (OH)
Barat Coll (IL)
Beaver Coll (PA)
Becker Coll (MA)
Bethel Coll (TN)
Black Hills State U (SD)
Burlington Coll (VT)

Majors Index
Human Services–Industrial Engineering

California State U, Dominguez Hills (CA)
California State U, Fullerton (CA)
California State U, Monterey Bay (CA)
California State U, San Bernardino (CA)
Calumet Coll of Saint Joseph (IN)
Carson-Newman Coll (TN)
Cazenovia Coll (NY)
Champlain Coll (VT)
Coll of Notre Dame (CA)
Coll of Notre Dame of Maryland (MD)
Coll of St. Joseph (VT)
Coll of Saint Mary (NE)
Connecticut Coll (CT)
Cornell U (NY)
Dakota Wesleyan U (SD)
Delaware State U (DE)
Doane Coll (NE)
Elmira Coll (NY)
Elon Coll (NC)
The Evergreen State Coll (WA)
Fairmont State Coll (WV)
Fitchburg State Coll (MA)
Florida Gulf Coast U (FL)
Fontbonne Coll (MO)
Framingham State Coll (MA)
Friends U (KS)
Geneva Coll (PA)
The George Washington U (DC)
Grace Bible Coll (MI)
Grand View Coll (IA)
Hannibal-LaGrange Coll (MO)
Hastings Coll (NE)
Hawaii Pacific U (HI)
High Point U (NC)
Hilbert Coll (NY)
Holy Names Coll (CA)
Indiana Inst of Technology (IN)
Judson Coll (IL)
Kendall Coll (IL)
Kentucky Wesleyan Coll (KY)
LaGrange Coll (GA)
Lake Superior State U (MI)
La Roche Coll (PA)
Lasell Coll (MA)
Lenoir-Rhyne Coll (NC)
Lesley Coll (MA)
Lincoln U (PA)
Lindenwood U (MO)
Lindsey Wilson Coll (KY)
Manhattan Coll (NY)
Mansfield U of Pennsylvania (PA)
Marian Coll of Fond du Lac (WI)
Martin Methodist Coll (TN)
McMurry U (TX)
Medaille Coll (NY)
Mercer U (GA)
Merrimack Coll (MA)
Mesa State Coll (CO)
Metropolitan State Coll of Denver (CO)
Metropolitan State U (MN)
Milligan Coll (TN)
Millikin U (IL)
Missouri Valley Coll (MO)
Montana State U–Billings (MT)
Montreat Coll (NC)
Mount Olive Coll (NC)
Mount St. Clare Coll (IA)
Mount Saint Mary Coll (NY)
National-Louis U (IL)
New York City Tech Coll of the City U of NY (NY)
Northeastern U (MA)
Northern Kentucky U (KY)
Ottawa U (KS)
Our Lady of the Lake U of San Antonio (TX)
Pace U, New York City Campus (NY)
Pace U, Pleasantville/Briarcliff Campus (NY)
Park U (MO)
Pennsylvania Coll of Technology (PA)
Pikeville Coll (KY)
Pine Manor Coll (MA)
Quinnipiac U (CT)
Saint Joseph's U (PA)
Saint Leo U (FL)
Saint Mary-of-the-Woods Coll (IN)
Saint Mary's U of Minnesota (MN)
Salish Kootenai Coll (MT)
Siena Heights U (MI)

Simmons Coll (MA)
Southwest Baptist U (MO)
State U of NY Coll at Potsdam (NY)
Suffolk U (MA)
Tennessee Wesleyan Coll (TN)
Texas A&M U–Kingsville (TX)
Touro Coll (NY)
Trinity Coll of Vermont (VT)
Trinity Western U (BC, Canada)
Tyndale Coll & Seminary (ON, Canada)
U Coll of the Fraser Valley (BC, Canada)
U of Alaska Fairbanks (AK)
U of Baltimore (MD)
U of Bridgeport (CT)
U of Detroit Mercy (MI)
U of Great Falls (MT)
U of Maine at Machias (ME)
U of Massachusetts Boston (MA)
U of Minnesota, Morris (MN)
U of Nebraska at Omaha (NE)
U of New England (ME)
U of Regina (SK, Canada)
U of Rhode Island (RI)
U of Saint Francis (IN)
The U of Tennessee at Chattanooga (TN)
The U of Tennessee Knoxville (TN)
The U of Texas–Pan American (TX)
U of the Pacific (CA)
Upper Iowa U (IA)
Villanova U (PA)
Virginia Polytechnic Inst and State U (VA)
Virginia Wesleyan Coll (VA)
Walsh U (OH)
Western Michigan U (MI)
Western Washington U (WA)
William Penn U (IA)
Wingate U (NC)
York Coll (NE)

HYDRAULIC TECHNOLOGY
The Ohio State U (OH)

INDIVIDUAL/FAMILY DEVELOPMENT
Abilene Christian U (TX)
Amber U (TX)
Antioch Coll (OH)
Ashland U (OH)
Auburn U (AL)
Baylor U (TX)
Boston Coll (MA)
Bowling Green State U (OH)
California State U, Hayward (CA)
California State U, Long Beach (CA)
California State U, San Bernardino (CA)
Cameron U (OK)
Central Michigan U (MI)
Colorado State U (CO)
Concordia Coll (MI)
Cornell U (NY)
Crown Coll (MN)
DePaul U (IL)
East Carolina U (NC)
Eastern Michigan U (MI)
East Tennessee State U (TN)
Eckerd Coll (FL)
Geneva Coll (PA)
Georgia Southern U (GA)
Goddard Coll (VT)
Hampshire Coll (MA)
Harvard U (MA)
Hawaii Pacific U (HI)
Hellenic Coll (MA)
Hope International U (CA)
Indiana U Bloomington (IN)
Indiana U of Pennsylvania (PA)
Kansas State U (KS)
Kent State U (OH)
Kentucky State U (KY)
Lee U (TN)
Louisiana State U and A&M Coll (LA)
Miami U (OH)
Mississippi U for Women (MS)
Mitchell Coll (CT)
Murray State U (KY)
National-Louis U (IL)
Northern Illinois U (IL)
Ohio U (OH)
Oregon State U (OR)

Pacific Oaks Coll (CA)
Penn State U Altoona Coll (PA)
Penn State U Shenango Campus of the Commonwealth Coll (PA)
Penn State U Univ Park Campus (PA)
Purdue U (IN)
Radford U (VA)
Saint Xavier U (IL)
Samford U (AL)
Sarah Lawrence Coll (NY)
Seton Hill Coll (PA)
South Dakota State U (SD)
Southwest Missouri State U (MO)
Southwest Texas State U (TX)
State U of NY at Oswego (NY)
Stephen F. Austin State U (TX)
Syracuse U (NY)
Texas Tech U (TX)
Texas Woman's U (TX)
The U of Alabama (AL)
The U of Arizona (AZ)
U of Arkansas (AR)
U of Calif, Davis (CA)
U of Connecticut (CT)
U of Delaware (DE)
U of Georgia (GA)
U of Houston (TX)
U of Illinois at Urbana–Champaign (IL)
U of Kentucky (KY)
U of Louisiana at Lafayette (LA)
U of Maine (ME)
U of Missouri–Columbia (MO)
U of Nevada, Reno (NV)
U of New England (ME)
The U of North Carolina at Charlotte (NC)
The U of North Carolina at Greensboro (NC)
U of Rhode Island (RI)
The U of Texas at Austin (TX)
U of Utah (UT)
U of Vermont (VT)
U of Wisconsin–Stout (WI)
U of Wyoming (WY)
Utah State U (UT)
Utica Coll of Syracuse U (NY)
Vanderbilt U (TN)
Warner Pacific Coll (OR)
Washington State U (WA)
Wayne State U (MI)
Western Carolina U (NC)
Wheelock Coll (MA)

INDUSTRIAL ARTS
Andrews U (MI)
Appalachian State U (NC)
Ball State U (IN)
Bemidji State U (MN)
Berea Coll (KY)
California State U, Fresno (CA)
California State U, Los Angeles (CA)
Chadron State Coll (NE)
Chicago State U (IL)
Clemson U (SC)
Coll of the Ozarks (MO)
Colorado State U (CO)
Eastern Kentucky U (KY)
Elizabeth City State U (NC)
Fairmont State Coll (WV)
Fitchburg State Coll (MA)
Florida A&M U (FL)
Fort Hays State U (KS)
Humboldt State U (CA)
Indiana State U (IN)
Keene State Coll (NH)
Langston U (OK)
Lincoln U (MO)
McPherson Coll (KS)
Millersville U of Pennsylvania (PA)
Minnesota State U, Mankato (MN)
Murray State U (KY)
New Mexico Highlands U (NM)
Norfolk State U (VA)
North Carolina Ag and Tech State U (NC)
Northeastern State U (OK)
Northern Arizona U (AZ)
Northern State U (SD)
Northwestern State U of Louisiana (LA)
Ohio Northern U (OH)
Oklahoma Panhandle State U (OK)
Oklahoma State U (OK)
Pacific Union Coll (CA)

Peru State Coll (NE)
Pittsburg State U (KS)
St. Cloud State U (MN)
St. John Fisher Coll (NY)
San Diego State U (CA)
San Francisco State U (CA)
Southern Utah U (UT)
Southwestern Oklahoma State U (OK)
State U of NY at Oswego (NY)
State U of NY Coll at Buffalo (NY)
Sul Ross State U (TX)
Tennessee State U (TN)
Texas A&M U–Commerce (TX)
U of Alberta (AB, Canada)
U of Arkansas at Pine Bluff (AR)
U of British Columbia (BC, Canada)
U of Central Oklahoma (OK)
U of Southern Colorado (CO)
U of Southern Maine (ME)
U of the District of Columbia (DC)
U of Wisconsin–Platteville (WI)
Valley City State U (ND)
Walla Walla Coll (WA)
Western Michigan U (MI)
Western Montana Coll of The U of Montana (MT)
Western State Coll of Colorado (CO)
William Penn U (IA)

INDUSTRIAL ARTS EDUCATION
Abilene Christian U (TX)
Black Hills State U (SD)
Brigham Young U (UT)
California State U, Chico (CA)
Central Michigan U (MI)
Central Missouri State U (MO)
The Coll of New Jersey (NJ)
Coll of the Ozarks (MO)
Concordia U (NE)
Eastern Michigan U (MI)
Georgia Southern U (GA)
Kean U (NJ)
Kent State U (OH)
Middle Tennessee State U (TN)
Mississippi State U (MS)
Montana State U–Bozeman (MT)
Morehead State U (KY)
New York Inst of Technology (NY)
Northern Illinois U (IL)
The Ohio State U (OH)
Oklahoma Panhandle State U (OK)
Purdue U (IN)
Southwest Missouri State U (MO)
Texas A&M U (TX)
Texas Southern U (TX)
Texas Wesleyan U (TX)
U of Central Arkansas (AR)
U of Georgia (GA)
U of Idaho (ID)
U of Nebraska–Lincoln (NE)
U of Nevada, Reno (NV)
U of New Mexico (NM)
U of Northern Iowa (IA)
U of Southern Mississippi (MS)
U of Wisconsin–Stout (WI)
U of Wyoming (WY)
Utah State U (UT)
Virginia Polytechnic Inst and State U (VA)

INDUSTRIAL ENGINEERING
Arizona State U (AZ)
Auburn U (AL)
Boston U (MA)
Bradley U (IL)
California Polytechnic State U, San Luis Obispo (CA)
California State Polytechnic U, Pomona (CA)
California State U, Fresno (CA)
California State U, Hayward (CA)
California State U, Northridge (CA)
Central Michigan U (MI)
Clarkson U (NY)
Clemson U (SC)
Cleveland State U (OH)
The Coll of Southeastern Europe, The American U of Athens (Greece)
Columbia U, School of Engineering & Applied Sci (NY)
Concordia U (PQ, Canada)
Cornell U (NY)
Dalhousie U (NS, Canada)

Drexel U (PA)
Eastern Nazarene Coll (MA)
Elizabethtown Coll (PA)
Ferris State U (MI)
Florida A&M U (FL)
Florida State U (FL)
Georgia Inst of Technology (GA)
Grand Valley State U (MI)
Hofstra U (NY)
Insto Tecno Estudios Sups Monterrey, León (Mexico)
Insto Tecno Estudios Sups Monterrey (Mexico)
Insto Tecno Estudios Sups Monterrey, Querétaro (Mexico)
Insto Tecno Estudios Sups Monterrey, Tampico (Mexico)
Iowa State U of Science and Technology (IA)
Kansas State U (KS)
Kent State U (OH)
Kettering U (MI)
Lamar U (TX)
Lawrence Technological U (MI)
Lehigh U (PA)
Louisiana State U and A&M Coll (LA)
Louisiana Tech U (LA)
Marquette U (WI)
Memorial U of Newfoundland (NF, Canada)
Mercer U (GA)
Miami U (OH)
Michigan State U (MI)
Michigan Technological U (MI)
Midwestern State U (TX)
Milwaukee School of Engineering (WI)
Mississippi State U (MS)
Montana State U–Bozeman (MT)
Morgan State U (MD)
New Jersey Inst of Technology (NJ)
New Mexico State U (NM)
New York Inst of Technology (NY)
North Carolina Ag and Tech State U (NC)
North Carolina State U (NC)
North Dakota State U (ND)
Northeastern U (MA)
Northern Illinois U (IL)
Northern Kentucky U (KY)
Northwestern U (IL)
The Ohio State U (OH)
Oklahoma State U (OK)
Oregon State U (OR)
Penn State U Univ Park Campus (PA)
Polytechnic U of Puerto Rico (PR)
Purdue U (IN)
Purdue U Calumet (IN)
Rensselaer Polytechnic Inst (NY)
Rochester Inst of Technology (NY)
Rutgers, State U of NJ, Coll of Engineering (NJ)
Ryerson Polytechnic U (ON, Canada)
St. Ambrose U (IA)
Saint Augustine's Coll (NC)
St. Cloud State U (MN)
St. Mary's U of San Antonio (TX)
San Jose State U (CA)
Seattle U (WA)
South Dakota School of Mines and Technology (SD)
Southern Illinois U Edwardsville (IL)
Stanford U (CA)
State U of NY at Binghamton (NY)
State U of NY at Buffalo (NY)
State U of NY at Farmingdale (NY)
Tennessee State U (TN)
Tennessee Technological U (TN)
Texas A&M U (TX)
Texas A&M U–Commerce (TX)
Texas A&M U–Kingsville (TX)
Texas Tech U (TX)
Tufts U (MA)
Universidad del Turabo (PR)
U du Québec à Trois-Rivières (PQ, Canada)
The U of Alabama (AL)
The U of Alabama in Huntsville (AL)
The U of Arizona (AZ)
U of Arkansas (AR)
U of Calgary (AB, Canada)
U of Calif, Berkeley (CA)
U of Central Florida (FL)

Majors Index
Industrial Engineering–Information Sciences/Systems

U of Cincinnati (OH)
U of Connecticut (CT)
U of Florida (FL)
U of Hartford (CT)
U of Houston (TX)
U of Idaho (ID)
U of Illinois at Chicago (IL)
The U of Iowa (IA)
U of Louisville (KY)
U of Manitoba (MB, Canada)
U of Massachusetts Amherst (MA)
The U of Memphis (TN)
U of Miami (FL)
U of Michigan (MI)
U of Michigan–Dearborn (MI)
U of Minnesota, Duluth (MN)
U of Minnesota, Twin Cities Campus (MN)
U of Missouri–Columbia (MO)
U of Nebraska–Lincoln (NE)
U of New Haven (CT)
U of New Mexico (NM)
U of Oklahoma (OK)
U of Pittsburgh (PA)
U of Pittsburgh at Bradford (PA)
U of Puerto Rico, Mayagüez Campus (PR)
U of Regina (SK, Canada)
U of Rhode Island (RI)
U of San Diego (CA)
U of Southern California (CA)
U of Southern Colorado (CO)
U of South Florida (FL)
The U of Tennessee at Chattanooga (TN)
The U of Tennessee Knoxville (TN)
The U of Texas at Arlington (TX)
The U of Texas–Pan American (TX)
U of Toronto (ON, Canada)
U of Washington (WA)
U of Windsor (ON, Canada)
U of Wisconsin–Madison (WI)
U of Wisconsin–Milwaukee (WI)
U of Wisconsin–Platteville (WI)
U of Wisconsin–Stout (WI)
Virginia Polytechnic Inst and State U (VA)
Washington State U (WA)
Wayne State U (MI)
Western Michigan U (MI)
Western New England Coll (MA)
West Virginia U (WV)
Wichita State U (KS)
Worcester Polytechnic Inst (MA)
Youngstown State U (OH)

INDUSTRIAL RADIOLOGIC TECHNOLOGY
Alderson-Broaddus Coll (WV)
Andrews U (MI)
Armstrong Atlantic State U (GA)
Baker Coll of Owosso (MI)
Barat Coll (IL)
Boise State U (ID)
Briar Cliff Coll (IA)
California State U, Northridge (CA)
Coll Misericordia (PA)
Columbus State U (GA)
Concordia U Wisconsin (WI)
Fairleigh Dickinson U, Florham-Madison Campus (NJ)
Francis Marion U (SC)
Friends U (KS)
Howard U (DC)
Jamestown Coll (ND)
Madonna U (MI)
Marian Coll of Fond du Lac (WI)
Mars Hill Coll (NC)
Minot State U (ND)
National-Louis U (IL)
Newman U (KS)
Oregon Health Sciences U (OR)
Oregon Inst of Technology (OR)
Saint Joseph's Coll (ME)
Saint Mary's Coll (MI)
Thomas Jefferson U (PA)
U of Arkansas for Medical Sciences (AR)
U of Oklahoma Health Sciences Center (OK)
U of St. Francis (IL)
U of Sioux Falls (SD)

INDUSTRIAL TECHNOLOGY
Abilene Christian U (TX)
Andrews U (MI)
Arizona State U East (AZ)

Baker Coll of Flint (MI)
Ball State U (IN)
Bemidji State U (MN)
Berea Coll (KY)
Black Hills State U (SD)
Boise State U (ID)
Bowling Green State U (OH)
Bradley U (IL)
California Polytechnic State U, San Luis Obispo (CA)
California State U, Chico (CA)
California State U, Fresno (CA)
California State U, Long Beach (CA)
California State U, Los Angeles (CA)
California U of Pennsylvania (PA)
Central Connecticut State U (CT)
Central Missouri State U (MO)
Cheyney U of Pennsylvania (PA)
Colorado State U (CO)
East Carolina U (NC)
Eastern Illinois U (IL)
Eastern Kentucky U (KY)
Eastern Michigan U (MI)
Eastern New Mexico U (NM)
Eastern Washington U (WA)
East Tennessee State U (TN)
Elizabeth City State U (NC)
Fairmont State Coll (WV)
Fashion Inst of Technology (NY)
Ferris State U (MI)
Fitchburg State Coll (MA)
Georgia Southern U (GA)
Illinois Inst of Technology (IL)
Illinois State U (IL)
Indiana State U (IN)
Indiana U–Purdue U Fort Wayne (IN)
Insto Tecno Estudios Sups Monterrey (Mexico)
Iowa State U of Science and Technology (IA)
Jacksonville State U (AL)
Kean U (NJ)
Keene State Coll (NH)
Kent State U (OH)
Lake Superior State U (MI)
Lamar U (TX)
Langston U (OK)
Metropolitan State Coll of Denver (CO)
Middle Tennessee State U (TN)
Millersville U of Pennsylvania (PA)
Minnesota State U, Mankato (MN)
Minnesota State U Moorhead (MN)
Mississippi State U (MS)
Mississippi Valley State U (MS)
Montana State U–Northern (MT)
Morehead State U (KY)
Murray State U (KY)
New Jersey Inst of Technology (NJ)
New York Inst of Technology (NY)
North Carolina Ag and Tech State U (NC)
Northeastern State U (OK)
Northeastern U (MA)
Northern Illinois U (IL)
Northern Kentucky U (KY)
Northern Michigan U (MI)
Northwestern State U of Louisiana (LA)
Ohio Northern U (OH)
Oklahoma Panhandle State U (OK)
Oklahoma State U (OK)
Oregon Inst of Technology (OR)
Pacific Union Coll (CA)
Pittsburg State U (KS)
Prairie View A&M U (TX)
Purdue U (IN)
Purdue U Calumet (IN)
Regents Coll (NY)
Rochester Inst of Technology (NY)
Roger Williams U (RI)
Rowan U (NJ)
Saginaw Valley State U (MI)
Sam Houston State U (TX)
San Jose State U (CA)
South Dakota State U (SD)
Southeastern Louisiana U (LA)
Southeastern Oklahoma State U (OK)
Southeast Missouri State U (MO)
Southern Arkansas U–Magnolia (AR)
Southern Illinois U Carbondale (IL)
Southern Polytechnic State U (GA)

Southwestern Coll (KS)
Southwestern Oklahoma State U (OK)
State U of NY at Farmingdale (NY)
State U of NY Coll at Buffalo (NY)
State U of NY Inst of Tech at Utica/Rome (NY)
Tennessee State U (TN)
Tennessee Technological U (TN)
Texas A&M U–Kingsville (TX)
Texas Southern U (TX)
Thomas Edison State Coll (NJ)
U of Arkansas at Pine Bluff (AR)
U of Dayton (OH)
U of Houston (TX)
U of Idaho (ID)
U of Louisiana at Lafayette (LA)
The U of Memphis (TN)
U of Nebraska at Omaha (NE)
U of Nebraska–Lincoln (NE)
U of New Haven (CT)
The U of North Carolina at Charlotte (NC)
U of North Dakota (ND)
U of North Iowa (IA)
U of North Texas (TX)
U of Rio Grande (OH)
U of Southern Mississippi (MS)
The U of West Alabama (AL)
U of West Florida (FL)
U of Wisconsin–Platteville (WI)
U of Wisconsin–Stout (WI)
Wayne State U (MI)
Weber State U (UT)
Western Carolina U (NC)
Western Illinois U (IL)
Western Kentucky U (KY)
Western Michigan U (MI)
Western Washington U (WA)
William Penn U (IA)

INFORMATION SCIENCES/SYSTEMS
Alabama State U (AL)
Albertus Magnus Coll (CT)
Alfred U (NY)
Alma Coll (MI)
Alvernia Coll (PA)
American International Coll (MA)
American U (DC)
The American U in Dubai (United Arab Emirates)
Andrews U (MI)
Aquinas Coll (MI)
Ashland U (OH)
Athabasca U (AB, Canada)
Athens State U (AL)
Atlantic Union Coll (MA)
Baker Coll of Flint (MI)
Baker Coll of Jackson (MI)
Baker Coll of Muskegon (MI)
Baker Coll of Owosso (MI)
Baker Coll of Port Huron (MI)
Baker U (KS)
Baldwin-Wallace Coll (OH)
Ball State U (IN)
Barat Coll (IL)
Barry U (FL)
Bartlesville Wesleyan Coll (OK)
Belhaven Coll (MS)
Belmont Abbey Coll (NC)
Belmont U (TN)
Bemidji State U (MN)
Baruch Coll of the City U of NY (NY)
Berry Coll (GA)
Bethany Coll (KS)
Bethune-Cookman Coll (FL)
Bloomfield Coll (NJ)
Boise State U (ID)
Boston U (MA)
Bradley U (IL)
Brigham Young U–Hawaii Campus (HI)
Brock U (ON, Canada)
Buena Vista U (IA)
California Baptist U (CA)
California Lutheran U (CA)
California State Polytechnic U, Pomona (CA)
California State U, Chico (CA)
California State U, Dominguez Hills (CA)
California State U, Hayward (CA)
California State U, Northridge (CA)
Calumet Coll of Saint Joseph (IN)
Cameron U (OK)

Campbellsville U (KY)
Carleton U (ON, Canada)
Carlow Coll (PA)
Carnegie Mellon U (PA)
Carroll Coll (WI)
Carson-Newman Coll (TN)
Catawba Coll (NC)
Cedar Crest Coll (PA)
Cedarville Coll (OH)
Centenary Coll (NJ)
Central Coll (IA)
Champlain Coll (VT)
Chapman U (CA)
Chicago State U (IL)
Chowan Coll (NC)
Christopher Newport U (VA)
Claflin U (SC)
Clarion U of Pennsylvania (PA)
Clark Atlanta U (GA)
Clarke Coll (IA)
Clayton Coll & State U (GA)
Cleary Coll (MI)
Clemson U (SC)
Cleveland State U (OH)
Coll Misericordia (PA)
Coll of Charleston (SC)
Coll of Mount St. Joseph (OH)
Coll of Notre Dame of Maryland (MD)
Coll of Saint Elizabeth (NJ)
Coll of St. Joseph (VT)
Coll of Saint Mary (NE)
The Coll of Saint Rose (NY)
The Coll of West Virginia (WV)
Colorado Christian U (CO)
Colorado State U (CO)
Colorado Tech U (CO)
Colorado Tech U Denver Campus (CO)
Columbia Coll (MO)
Columbus State U (GA)
Concord Coll (WV)
Concordia U (IL)
Cornell U (NY)
Cornerstone U (MI)
Culver-Stockton Coll (MO)
Dakota State U (SD)
Daniel Webster Coll (NH)
Davenport Coll of Business (MI)
Davenport Coll of Business, Lansing Campus (MI)
David Lipscomb U (TN)
Delaware State U (DE)
Delaware Valley Coll (PA)
DePaul U (IL)
DeVry Inst of Technology (AZ)
DeVry Inst of Technology, Fremont (CA)
DeVry Inst of Technology, Long Beach (CA)
DeVry Inst of Technology, Pomona (CA)
DeVry Inst of Technology, Alpharetta (GA)
DeVry Inst of Technology, Decatur (GA)
DeVry Inst of Technology, Addison (IL)
DeVry Inst of Technology, Chicago (IL)
DeVry Inst of Technology (MO)
DeVry Inst of Technology (NY)
DeVry Inst of Technology (OH)
DeVry Inst of Technology (TX)
Dominican Coll of Blauvelt (NY)
Dominican U (IL)
Dowling Coll (NY)
Drake U (IA)
Drexel U (PA)
Eastern Kentucky U (KY)
Eastern Mennonite U (VA)
Eastern Michigan U (MI)
Eastern Washington U (WA)
École des Hautes Études Commerciales (PQ, Canada)
Edgewood Coll (WI)
Elizabeth City State U (NC)
Elmira Coll (NY)
Emporia State U (KS)
Fairfield U (CT)
Fairleigh Dickinson U, Florham-Madison Campus (NJ)
Fairleigh Dickinson U, Teaneck-Hackensack Campus (NJ)
Faulkner U (AL)
Ferris State U (MI)
Ferrum Coll (VA)

Fitchburg State Coll (MA)
Florida A&M U (FL)
Florida Inst of Technology (FL)
Florida International U (FL)
Florida Metropolitan U-Tampa Coll, Brandon (FL)
Fontbonne Coll (MO)
Fordham U (NY)
Fort Hays State U (KS)
Fort Lewis Coll (CO)
Francis Marion U (SC)
Freed-Hardeman U (TN)
Gallaudet U (DC)
George Mason U (VA)
Georgetown Coll (KY)
Georgia Coll and State U (GA)
Georgia Southwestern State U (GA)
Glenville State Coll (WV)
Golden Gate U (CA)
Goldey-Beacom Coll (DE)
Gonzaga U (WA)
Goshen Coll (IN)
Grand Valley State U (MI)
Grand View Coll (IA)
Gwynedd-Mercy Coll (PA)
Hampton U (VA)
Hannibal-LaGrange Coll (MO)
Harris-Stowe State Coll (MO)
Harvard U (MA)
Hawaii Pacific U (HI)
Heidelberg Coll (OH)
Herzing Coll (GA)
High Point U (NC)
Hofstra U (NY)
Hollins U (VA)
Houston Baptist U (TX)
Howard Payne U (TX)
Howard U (DC)
Humboldt State U (CA)
Humphreys Coll (CA)
Huron U (SD)
Husson Coll (ME)
Idaho State U (ID)
Illinois Coll (IL)
Illinois Inst of Technology (IL)
Indiana Inst of Technology (IN)
Indiana State U (IN)
Indiana U–Purdue U Fort Wayne (IN)
Insto Tecno Estudios Sups Monterrey, León (Mexico)
Insto Tecno Estudios Sups Monterrey (Mexico)
Inter American U of PR, Metropolitan Campus (PR)
Inter American U of PR, San Germán Campus (PR)
Iona Coll (NY)
Iowa Wesleyan Coll (IA)
James Madison U (VA)
John Jay Coll of Criminal Justice, the City U of NY (NY)
Johnson & Wales U (RI)
Johnson C. Smith U (NC)
Johnson State Coll (VT)
Jones Coll (FL)
Judson Coll (AL)
Judson Coll (IL)
Kansas State U (KS)
Kendall Coll (IL)
Kettering U (MI)
King Coll (TN)
Lakehead U (ON, Canada)
Lamar U (TX)
Lambuth U (TN)
La Salle U (PA)
Lasell Coll (MA)
La Sierra U (CA)
Lawrence Technological U (MI)
Lees-McRae Coll (NC)
Lee U (TN)
Lehigh U (PA)
LeTourneau U (TX)
Limestone Coll (SC)
Lincoln U (MO)
Lock Haven U of Pennsylvania (PA)
Long Island U, Brooklyn Campus (NY)
Long Island U, C.W. Post Campus (NY)
Loras Coll (IA)
Loyola U Chicago (IL)
Loyola U New Orleans (LA)
MacMurray Coll (IL)
Macon State Coll (GA)

Majors Index
Information Sciences/Systems–Interdisciplinary Studies

Madonna U (MI)
Manhattan Coll (NY)
Mansfield U of Pennsylvania (PA)
Marietta Coll (OH)
Marist Coll (NY)
Marquette U (WI)
Marshall U (WV)
Marymount Coll (NY)
Mayville State U (ND)
McGill U (PQ, Canada)
McKendree Coll (IL)
McMurry U (TX)
Medaille Coll (NY)
Memorial U of Newfoundland (NF, Canada)
Mercer U (GA)
Mercy Coll (NY)
Mercyhurst Coll (PA)
Meredith Coll (NC)
Mesa State Coll (CO)
Messiah Coll (PA)
Metropolitan State U (MN)
Michigan Technological U (MI)
Midwestern State U (TX)
Minnesota State U, Mankato (MN)
Mississippi U for Women (MS)
Missouri Southern State Coll (MO)
Missouri Western State Coll (MO)
Monroe Coll, Bronx (NY)
Monroe Coll, New Rochelle (NY)
Montana State U–Northern (MT)
Montana Tech of The U of Montana (MT)
Morgan State U (MD)
Mount Aloysius Coll (PA)
Mount Olive Coll (NC)
Mount Saint Vincent U (NS, Canada)
Mount Union Coll (OH)
National American U (MO)
National American U–St. Paul Campus (MN)
National-Louis U (IL)
National U (CA)
Nazareth Coll of Rochester (NY)
Nebraska Wesleyan U (NE)
New Hampshire Coll (NH)
New Jersey Inst of Technology (NJ)
Newman U (KS)
New Mexico Highlands U (NM)
New Mexico State U (NM)
New York Inst of Technology (NY)
New York U (NY)
Niagara U (NY)
North Carolina Central U (NC)
North Carolina Wesleyan Coll (NC)
Northeastern U (MA)
Northern Arizona U (AZ)
Northern Kentucky U (KY)
Northern Michigan U (MI)
Northland Coll (WI)
Northwestern Oklahoma State U (OK)
Northwestern State U of Louisiana (LA)
Northwest Missouri State U (MO)
Norwich U (VT)
Notre Dame Coll of Ohio (OH)
Nova Southeastern U (FL)
Oakland City U (IN)
Oakwood Coll (AL)
Ohio Dominican Coll (OH)
The Ohio State U (OH)
Ohio U (OH)
Oklahoma Baptist U (OK)
Oklahoma Christian U of Science and Arts (OK)
Oklahoma Panhandle State U (OK)
Oklahoma State U (OK)
Olivet Nazarene U (IL)
Open Learning Agency (BC, Canada)
Oregon State U (OR)
Ottawa U (KS)
Pace U, New York City Campus (NY)
Pace U, Pleasantville/Briarcliff Campus (NY)
Pacific Union Coll (CA)
Palm Beach Atlantic Coll (FL)
Penn State U Abington Coll (PA)
Penn State U Berks Cmps of Berks-Lehigh Valley Coll (PA)
Penn State U Lehigh Valley Cmps of Berks-Lehigh Valley Coll (PA)
Penn State U Univ Park Campus (PA)

Pfeiffer U (NC)
Philadelphia U (PA)
Piedmont Coll (GA)
Pittsburg State U (KS)
Plymouth State Coll (NH)
Polytechnic U, Brooklyn Campus (NY)
Polytechnic U, Farmingdale Campus (NY)
Purdue U Calumet (IN)
Queens Coll (NC)
Quincy U (IL)
Quinnipiac U (CT)
Ramapo Coll of New Jersey (NJ)
Regents Coll (NY)
Rensselaer Polytechnic Inst (NY)
The Richard Stockton Coll of New Jersey (NJ)
Richmond, The American International U in London (United Kingdom)
Rider U (NJ)
Rivier Coll (NH)
Roanoke Coll (VA)
Rochester Inst of Technology (NY)
Rockhurst U (MO)
Roger Williams U (RI)
Rowan U (NJ)
Russell Sage Coll (NY)
Rutgers, State U of NJ, Camden Coll of Arts & Scis (NJ)
Rutgers, State U of NJ, Newark Coll of Arts & Scis (NJ)
Rutgers, State U of NJ, U Coll–Camden (NJ)
Rutgers, State U of NJ, U Coll–Newark (NJ)
Ryerson Polytechnic U (ON, Canada)
St. Ambrose U (IA)
St. Cloud State U (MN)
St. Francis Xavier U (NS, Canada)
St. John's U (NY)
Saint Leo U (FL)
Saint Martin's Coll (WA)
Saint Mary Coll (KS)
Saint Mary-of-the-Woods Coll (IN)
Saint Mary's Coll (MI)
St. Mary's U of San Antonio (TX)
Saint Peter's Coll (NJ)
St. Thomas U (FL)
Salve Regina U (RI)
San Francisco State U (CA)
Seton Hill Coll (PA)
Shippensburg U of Pennsylvania (PA)
Siena Heights U (MI)
Simpson Coll (IA)
Slippery Rock U of Pennsylvania (PA)
Southeastern Oklahoma State U (OK)
Southeastern U (DC)
Southwest Baptist U (MO)
Southwestern Adventist U (TX)
Southwestern Coll (KS)
State U of NY at Albany (NY)
State U of NY at Binghamton (NY)
State U of NY at Oswego (NY)
State U of NY at Stony Brook (NY)
State U of NY Coll at Buffalo (NY)
State U of NY Coll at Fredonia (NY)
State U of NY Coll at Old Westbury (NY)
State U of NY Inst of Tech at Utica/Rome (NY)
Stetson U (FL)
Suffolk U (MA)
Susquehanna U (PA)
Syracuse U (NY)
Taylor U (IN)
Temple U (PA)
Tennessee Technological U (TN)
Tennessee Wesleyan Coll (TN)
Texas A&M International U (TX)
Texas A&M U–Commerce (TX)
Texas A&M U–Kingsville (TX)
Texas Lutheran U (TX)
Texas Wesleyan U (TX)
Thiel Coll (PA)
Thomas More Coll (KY)
Tiffin U (OH)
Towson U (MD)
Trevecca Nazarene U (TN)
Trinity Christian Coll (IL)
Troy State U Dothan (AL)

Tulane U (LA)
Tusculum Coll (TN)
Union Coll (KY)
Union Coll (NE)
Union U (TN)
United States Military Academy (NY)
Universidad Metropolitana (PR)
Université de Sherbrooke (PQ, Canada)
U du Québec à Chicoutimi (PQ, Canada)
U du Québec à Trois-Rivières (PQ, Canada)
U Coll of Cape Breton (NS, Canada)
The U of Akron (OH)
U of Alberta (AB, Canada)
U of Arkansas at Little Rock (AR)
U of Baltimore (MD)
U of Bridgeport (CT)
U of Calif, Davis (CA)
U of Calif, Santa Cruz (CA)
U of Charleston (WV)
U of Cincinnati (OH)
U of Dayton (OH)
U of Detroit Mercy (MI)
U of Great Falls (MT)
U of Guelph (ON, Canada)
U of Hartford (CT)
U of Houston (TX)
U of Houston–Clear Lake (TX)
U of Indianapolis (IN)
The U of Iowa (IA)
U of Mary Hardin-Baylor (TX)
U of Maryland, Baltimore County (MD)
U of Maryland, Coll Park (MD)
U of Maryland University Coll (MD)
U of Massachusetts Lowell (MA)
U of Miami (FL)
U of Michigan–Dearborn (MI)
U of Minnesota, Crookston (MN)
U of Missouri–Kansas City (MO)
U of Mobile (AL)
The U of Montana–Missoula (MT)
U of Nebraska at Omaha (NE)
U of New Brunswick, Fredericton (NB, Canada)
U of New Mexico (NM)
U of Northern Iowa (IA)
U of North Texas (TX)
U of Pittsburgh at Bradford (PA)
U of Puerto Rico, Mayagüez Campus (PR)
U of San Francisco (CA)
The U of Scranton (PA)
U of Sioux Falls (SD)
U of South Alabama (AL)
U of South Dakota (SD)
U of Southern Colorado (CO)
U of South Florida (FL)
The U of Tampa (FL)
The U of Tennessee at Chattanooga (TN)
The U of Texas at San Antonio (TX)
The U of Texas–Pan American (TX)
U of the District of Columbia (DC)
U of the Pacific (CA)
U of the Sacred Heart (PR)
U of Tulsa (OK)
U of Vermont (VT)
U of Washington (WA)
U of Windsor (ON, Canada)
The U of Winnipeg (MB, Canada)
U of Wisconsin–Green Bay (WI)
U of Wisconsin–Parkside (WI)
U of Wisconsin–River Falls (WI)
U of Wisconsin–Superior (WI)
U of Wyoming (WY)
Utah State U (UT)
Valdosta State U (GA)
Valley City State U (ND)
Villa Julie Coll (MD)
Villanova U (PA)
Virginia Commonwealth U (VA)
Virginia Polytechnic Inst and State U (VA)
Waldorf Coll (IA)
Wartburg Coll (IA)
Washington U in St. Louis (MO)
Wayne State Coll (NE)
Wayne State U (MI)
Weber State U (UT)
Webster U (MO)

West Chester U of Pennsylvania (PA)
Western Michigan U (MI)
Western New England Coll (MA)
Westfield State Coll (MA)
West Liberty State Coll (WV)
Westminster Coll (PA)
West Texas A&M U (TX)
West Virginia Wesleyan Coll (WV)
Westwood Coll of Technology (CO)
Wilkes U (PA)
William Jewell Coll (MO)
William Woods U (MO)
Wingate U (NC)
Winona State U (MN)
Woodbury U (CA)
Worcester Polytechnic Inst (MA)
Xavier U (OH)
Xavier U of Louisiana (LA)
York Coll of Pennsylvania (PA)
York Coll of the City U of New York (NY)
Youngstown State U (OH)

INORGANIC CHEMISTRY
Florida State U (FL)
McGill U (PQ, Canada)

INSTITUTIONAL FOOD SERVICES
Johnson & Wales U (RI)

INSTITUTIONAL FOOD WORKERS
Indiana U of Pennsylvania (PA)
Murray State U (KY)

INSTRUMENTATION TECHNOLOGY
Athens State U (AL)
Indiana State U (IN)
Providence Coll (RI)
U of Southern Colorado (CO)

INSURANCE AND RISK MANAGEMENT
Appalachian State U (NC)
Ball State U (IN)
Baylor U (TX)
Bradley U (IL)
California State Polytechnic U, Pomona (CA)
Coll of Insurance (NY)
The Coll of Southeastern Europe, The American U of Athens (Greece)
Delta State U (MS)
Drake U (IA)
Eastern Kentucky U (KY)
Ferris State U (MI)
Florida International U (FL)
Florida State U (FL)
Georgia State U (GA)
Howard U (DC)
Illinois State U (IL)
Illinois Wesleyan U (IL)
Indiana State U (IN)
Mercyhurst Coll (PA)
Minnesota State U, Mankato (MN)
Mississippi State U (MS)
Northeastern U (MA)
The Ohio State U (OH)
Penn State U Univ Park Campus (PA)
St. Cloud State U (MN)
Seattle U (WA)
Southwest Missouri State U (MO)
Temple U (PA)
Texas Southern U (TX)
Thomas Edison State Coll (NJ)
U of Calgary (AB, Canada)
U of Central Oklahoma (OK)
U of Cincinnati (OH)
U of Connecticut (CT)
U of Florida (FL)
U of Georgia (GA)
U of Hartford (CT)
U of Louisiana at Lafayette (LA)
U of Louisiana at Monroe (LA)
The U of Memphis (TN)
U of Minnesota, Twin Cities Campus (MN)
U of Mississippi (MS)
U of North Texas (TX)
U of Pennsylvania (PA)
U of South Carolina (SC)

U of Wisconsin–Madison (WI)
Washington State U (WA)

INTERDISCIPLINARY STUDIES
Abilene Christian U (TX)
Agnes Scott Coll (GA)
Alaska Bible Coll (AK)
Albertus Magnus Coll (CT)
Albright Coll (PA)
Alfred U (NY)
Alice Lloyd Coll (KY)
Amber U (TX)
American U (DC)
American U of Rome (Italy)
Amherst Coll (MA)
Anna Maria Coll (MA)
Antioch Coll (OH)
Arizona State U (AZ)
Arizona State U East (AZ)
Arizona State U West (AZ)
Atlantic Baptist U (NB, Canada)
Augsburg Coll (MN)
Austin Coll (TX)
Austin Peay State U (TN)
Averett U (VA)
Baldwin-Wallace Coll (OH)
Barat Coll (IL)
Bard Coll (NY)
Bates Coll (ME)
Baylor U (TX)
Beloit Coll (WI)
Bennett Coll (NC)
Bennington Coll (VT)
Bentley Coll (MA)
Baruch Coll of the City U of NY (NY)
Berry Coll (GA)
Bethany Coll (WV)
Bethany Coll of the Assemblies of God (CA)
Bethel Coll (TN)
Birmingham-Southern Coll (AL)
Blackburn Coll (IL)
Bloomfield Coll (NJ)
Bloomsburg U of Pennsylvania (PA)
Boise State U (ID)
Boston Coll (MA)
Boston U (MA)
Bowdoin Coll (ME)
Brevard Coll (NC)
Briar Cliff Coll (IA)
Brigham Young U–Hawaii Campus (HI)
Brock U (ON, Canada)
Brooklyn Coll of the City U of NY (NY)
Bryn Athyn Coll of the New Church (PA)
Burlington Coll (VT)
California Lutheran U (CA)
California State U, Chico (CA)
California State U, Dominguez Hills (CA)
California State U, Fullerton (CA)
California State U, Hayward (CA)
California State U, Long Beach (CA)
California State U, Los Angeles (CA)
California State U, Monterey Bay (CA)
California State U, San Bernardino (CA)
Calvin Coll (MI)
Cameron U (OK)
Capital U (OH)
Carleton Coll (MN)
Carleton U (ON, Canada)
Carnegie Mellon U (PA)
Carroll Coll (WI)
Carson-Newman Coll (TN)
Catawba Coll (NC)
The Catholic U of America (DC)
Centenary Coll of Louisiana (LA)
Central Coll (IA)
Central Methodist Coll (MO)
Central Michigan U (MI)
Chadron State Coll (NE)
Chatham Coll (PA)
Christopher Newport U (VA)
Clark Atlanta U (GA)
Clarkson U (NY)
Clark U (MA)
Cleveland State U (OH)
Coastal Carolina U (SC)
Coe Coll (IA)

Majors Index
Interdisciplinary Studies–Interior Architecture

Coll of Mount Saint Vincent (NY)
The Coll of New Rochelle (NY)
Coll of Notre Dame of Maryland (MD)
Coll of Our Lady of the Elms (MA)
The Coll of Saint Rose (NY)
Coll of Staten Island of the City U of NY (NY)
Coll of the Atlantic (ME)
Coll of the Ozarks (MO)
The Coll of West Virginia (WV)
The Coll of William and Mary (VA)
The Coll of Wooster (OH)
The Colorado Coll (CO)
Columbia Coll Chicago (IL)
Concordia U (OR)
Concordia U (PQ, Canada)
Concordia U at St. Paul (MN)
Connecticut Coll (CT)
Cornell Coll (IA)
Cornell U (NY)
Cornerstone U (MI)
Covenant Coll (GA)
Dallas Baptist U (TX)
Dana Coll (NE)
DePaul U (IL)
DePauw U (IN)
Dominican U of California (CA)
Dowling Coll (NY)
Drew U (NJ)
Drexel U (PA)
Earlham Coll (IN)
Eastern Kentucky U (KY)
Eastern Michigan U (MI)
Eastern Washington U (WA)
East Tennessee State U (TN)
Eckerd Coll (FL)
Elmhurst Coll (IL)
Elmira Coll (NY)
Emerson Coll (MA)
Emmanuel Coll (MA)
Emory & Henry Coll (VA)
Eugene Lang Coll, New School U (NY)
The Evergreen State Coll (WA)
Felician Coll (NJ)
Florida Inst of Technology (FL)
Fordham U (NY)
Framingham State Coll (MA)
Franklin U (OH)
Freed-Hardeman U (TN)
Friends U (KS)
George Fox U (OR)
George Mason U (VA)
Georgetown U (DC)
The George Washington U (DC)
Georgia State U (GA)
Gettysburg Coll (PA)
Goddard Coll (VT)
Goucher Coll (MD)
Grand Valley State U (MI)
Grand View Coll (IA)
Greensboro Coll (NC)
Grinnell Coll (IA)
Gustavus Adolphus Coll (MN)
Hampshire Coll (MA)
Hardin-Simmons U (TX)
Harris-Stowe State Coll (MO)
Harvard U (MA)
Hastings Coll (NE)
Hawaii Pacific U (HI)
Hendrix Coll (AR)
Heritage Coll (WA)
Hillsdale Coll (MI)
Hillsdale Free Will Baptist Coll (OK)
Hobart and William Smith Colls (NY)
Hofstra U (NY)
Hollins U (VA)
Hope Coll (MI)
Hope International U (CA)
Houston Baptist U (TX)
Howard Payne U (TX)
Huntingdon Coll (AL)
Idaho State U (ID)
Illinois Coll (IL)
Illinois Wesleyan U (IL)
Indiana State U (IN)
Indiana U–Purdue U Fort Wayne (IN)
Iona Coll (NY)
Iowa State U of Science and Technology (IA)
Ithaca Coll (NY)
Jacksonville U (FL)
John Brown U (AR)
John Carroll U (OH)

Johnson & Wales U (RI)
Jones Coll (FL)
Judson Coll (AL)
Juniata Coll (PA)
Kalamazoo Coll (MI)
Keene State Coll (NH)
Kendall Coll (IL)
Kent State U, Stark Campus (OH)
Kentucky Christian Coll (KY)
Kentucky Wesleyan Coll (KY)
Kenyon Coll (OH)
Keuka Coll (NY)
Lake Superior State U (MI)
Lamar U (TX)
Lambuth U (TN)
Lander U (SC)
Lane Coll (TN)
Lasell Coll (MA)
Lees-McRae Coll (NC)
Lehman Coll of the City U of NY (NY)
LeTourneau U (TX)
Lewis-Clark State Coll (ID)
Liberty U (VA)
Long Island U, Brooklyn Campus (NY)
Long Island U, C.W. Post Campus (NY)
Long Island U, Southampton Coll, Friends World Program (NY)
Louisiana Coll (LA)
Loyola Coll in Maryland (MD)
Luther Coll (IA)
Lycoming Coll (PA)
Macalester Coll (MN)
Maharishi U of Management (IA)
Manchester Coll (IN)
Marlboro Coll (VT)
Marquette U (WI)
Mars Hill Coll (NC)
Martin Luther Coll (MN)
Mary Baldwin Coll (VA)
Marylhurst U (OR)
Marymount Coll (NY)
Mary Washington Coll (VA)
Marywood U (PA)
Massachusetts Coll of Liberal Arts (MA)
Massachusetts Inst of Technology (MA)
McPherson Coll (KS)
Mercy Coll (NY)
Merrimack Coll (MA)
Miami U (OH)
Michigan State U (MI)
Middle Tennessee State U (TN)
Midwestern State U (TX)
Millikin U (IL)
Mills Coll (CA)
Minneapolis Coll of Art and Design (MN)
Minnesota State U Moorhead (MN)
Mississippi State U (MS)
Missouri Baptist Coll (MO)
Molloy Coll (NY)
Monmouth U (NJ)
Montana State U–Northern (MT)
Morehouse Coll (GA)
Morningside Coll (IA)
Mount Allison U (NB, Canada)
Mount Holyoke Coll (MA)
Mount Saint Mary Coll (NY)
Mount Saint Mary's Coll and Seminary (MD)
Mount Saint Vincent U (NS, Canada)
Mount Union Coll (OH)
Muskingum Coll (OH)
Naropa U (CO)
National U (CA)
Nazareth Coll of Rochester (NY)
Nebraska Wesleyan U (NE)
New Mexico Inst of Mining and Technology (NM)
New Mexico State U (NM)
New York Inst of Technology (NY)
New York U (NY)
Norfolk State U (VA)
North Central U (MN)
North Dakota State U (ND)
Northern Arizona U (AZ)
North Greenville Coll (SC)
Northland Coll (WI)
Northwest Coll (WA)
Northwestern U (IL)
Notre Dame Coll (NH)
Nova Southeastern U (FL)

Nyack Coll (NY)
Oakland City U (IN)
Oakland U (MI)
Oakwood Coll (AL)
Oberlin Coll (OH)
Oglethorpe U (GA)
Ohio Dominican Coll (OH)
Oklahoma Baptist U (OK)
Olivet Nazarene U (IL)
Oregon State U (OR)
Pace U, New York City Campus (NY)
Pace U, Pleasantville/Briarcliff Campus (NY)
Pacific Union Coll (CA)
Penn State U Univ Park Campus (PA)
Pepperdine U, Malibu (CA)
Piedmont Coll (GA)
Plattsburgh State U of NY (NY)
Plymouth State Coll (NH)
Pomona Coll (CA)
Prairie View A&M U (TX)
Purdue U (IN)
Queens Coll of the City U of NY (NY)
Queen's U at Kingston (ON, Canada)
Quincy U (IL)
Radford U (VA)
Ramapo Coll of New Jersey (NJ)
Reformed Bible Coll (MI)
Regis Coll (MA)
Rensselaer Polytechnic Inst (NY)
Rhodes Coll (TN)
The Richard Stockton Coll of New Jersey (NJ)
Ripon Coll (WI)
Rochester Coll (MI)
Rochester Inst of Technology (NY)
Rocky Mountain Coll (MT)
Rollins Coll (FL)
Russell Sage Coll (NY)
Rutgers, State U of NJ, Camden Coll of Arts & Scis (NJ)
Rutgers, State U of NJ, Cook Coll (NJ)
Rutgers, State U of NJ, Douglass Coll (NJ)
Rutgers, State U of NJ, Livingston Coll (NJ)
Rutgers, State U of NJ, Newark Coll of Arts & Scis (NJ)
Rutgers, State U of NJ, Rutgers Coll (NJ)
Rutgers, State U of NJ, U Coll–Camden (NJ)
Rutgers, State U of NJ, U Coll–Newark (NJ)
Rutgers, State U of NJ, U Coll–New Brunswick (NJ)
Saginaw Valley State U (MI)
St. Andrews Presbyterian Coll (NC)
St. Bonaventure U (NY)
St. Cloud State U (MN)
St. Francis Coll (NY)
St. John Fisher Coll (NY)
St. John's Coll (MD)
Saint Joseph's U (PA)
Saint Mary Coll (KS)
Saint Mary's Coll (IN)
Saint Mary's Coll of California (CA)
St. Mary's Coll of Maryland (MD)
Saint Mary's U (NS, Canada)
Saint Mary's U of Minnesota (MN)
St. Norbert Coll (WI)
Salem Coll (NC)
San Diego State U (CA)
Santa Clara U (CA)
Sarah Lawrence Coll (NY)
Schiller International U (Germany)
Seton Hill Coll (PA)
Sheldon Jackson Coll (AK)
Shippensburg U of Pennsylvania (PA)
Silver Lake Coll (WI)
Simon's Rock Coll of Bard (MA)
Smith Coll (MA)
Sonoma State U (CA)
South Dakota School of Mines and Technology (SD)
Southeastern Coll of the Assemblies of God (FL)
Southeast Missouri State U (MO)
Southern Oregon U (OR)
Southwest State U (MN)
Stanford U (CA)

State U of NY at Albany (NY)
State U of NY at Binghamton (NY)
State U of NY at Stony Brook (NY)
State U of NY Coll at Brockport (NY)
State U of NY Coll at Fredonia (NY)
State U of NY Coll at Oneonta (NY)
State U of NY Coll at Potsdam (NY)
Stephen F. Austin State U (TX)
Stephens Coll (MO)
Sterling Coll (KS)
Stillman Coll (AL)
Stonehill Coll (MA)
Suffolk U (MA)
Sweet Briar Coll (VA)
Syracuse U (NY)
Tabor Coll (KS)
Taylor U, Fort Wayne Campus (IN)
Temple U (PA)
Tennessee Wesleyan Coll (TN)
Texas A&M U (TX)
Texas A&M U–Commerce (TX)
Texas A&M U–Texarkana (TX)
Texas Southern U (TX)
Texas Tech U (TX)
Texas Woman's U (TX)
Thomas Aquinas Coll (CA)
Tougaloo Coll (MS)
Touro Coll (NY)
Towson U (MD)
Trent U (ON, Canada)
Trinity Coll (CT)
Troy State U Montgomery (AL)
United States Air Force Academy (CO)
United States Military Academy (NY)
Unity Coll (ME)
Université de Montréal (PQ, Canada)
Université de Sherbrooke (PQ, Canada)
Université Laval (PQ, Canada)
The U of Akron (OH)
The U of Alabama (AL)
U of Alaska Fairbanks (AK)
The U of Arizona (AZ)
U of Baltimore (MD)
U of Bridgeport (CT)
U of British Columbia (BC, Canada)
U of Calif, Berkeley (CA)
U of Calif, San Diego (CA)
U of Calif, Santa Barbara (CA)
U of Chicago (IL)
U of Connecticut (CT)
U of Florida (FL)
U of Hartford (CT)
U of Houston (TX)
U of Houston–Clear Lake (TX)
U of Houston–Downtown (TX)
U of Idaho (ID)
U of Illinois at Springfield (IL)
The U of Iowa (IA)
U of Judaism (CA)
U of Kentucky (KY)
U of Maine at Farmington (ME)
U of Maryland, Baltimore County (MD)
U of Maryland, Coll Park (MD)
U of Massachusetts Amherst (MA)
U of Massachusetts Boston (MA)
U of Massachusetts Dartmouth (MA)
The U of Memphis (TN)
U of Michigan (MI)
U of Michigan–Dearborn (MI)
U of Minnesota, Crookston (MN)
U of Minnesota, Duluth (MN)
U of Missouri–Columbia (MO)
U of Missouri–Kansas City (MO)
U of Missouri–St. Louis (MO)
The U of Montana–Missoula (MT)
U of Nebraska at Omaha (NE)
U of Nebraska–Lincoln (NE)
U of New Hampshire (NH)
The U of North Carolina at Chapel Hill (NC)
The U of North Carolina at Greensboro (NC)
U of Northern Colorado (CO)
U of North Texas (TX)
U of Pennsylvania (PA)
U of Pittsburgh (PA)

U of Portland (OR)
U of Puerto Rico, Río Piedras (PR)
U of Puget Sound (WA)
U of Redlands (CA)
U of Regina (SK, Canada)
U of Rhode Island (RI)
U of Richmond (VA)
U of Rochester (NY)
U of St. Thomas (MN)
U of San Francisco (CA)
U of Sioux Falls (SD)
U of South Carolina Spartanburg (SC)
U of Southern California (CA)
U of Southern Mississippi (MS)
The U of Tennessee at Chattanooga (TN)
The U of Tennessee at Martin (TN)
The U of Texas at Arlington (TX)
The U of Texas at Dallas (TX)
The U of Texas at San Antonio (TX)
The U of Texas at Tyler (TX)
The U of Texas–Pan American (TX)
U of the Pacific (CA)
U of the Sacred Heart (PR)
U of Vermont (VT)
U of Virginia's Coll at Wise (VA)
U of Washington (WA)
U of Waterloo (ON, Canada)
The U of Winnipeg (MB, Canada)
U of Wisconsin–Green Bay (WI)
U of Wisconsin–Milwaukee (WI)
U of Wisconsin–Parkside (WI)
Valparaiso U (IN)
Vanderbilt U (TN)
Vanguard U of Southern California (CA)
Vassar Coll (NY)
Villa Julie Coll (MD)
Virginia Commonwealth U (VA)
Virginia Intermont Coll (VA)
Virginia Polytechnic Inst and State U (VA)
Virginia Wesleyan Coll (VA)
Warren Wilson Coll (NC)
Washington and Lee U (VA)
Washington U in St. Louis (MO)
Wayne State Coll (NE)
Wayne State U (MI)
Webster U (MO)
Wesleyan Coll (GA)
Wesleyan U (CT)
Western Baptist Coll (OR)
Western Kentucky U (KY)
Western Oregon U (OR)
Western Washington U (WA)
West Liberty State Coll (WV)
Westminster Coll (PA)
Westminster Coll (UT)
West Texas A&M U (TX)
West Virginia U (WV)
Wheaton Coll (IL)
Wheaton Coll (MA)
William Jewell Coll (MO)
William Woods U (MO)
Wingate U (NC)
Wisconsin Lutheran Coll (WI)
Wittenberg U (OH)
Worcester Polytechnic Inst (MA)
Yale U (CT)
Yeshiva U (NY)
York Coll (NE)
York U (ON, Canada)

INTERIOR ARCHITECTURE
Arizona State U (AZ)
Auburn U (AL)
California Coll of Arts and Crafts (CA)
Central Michigan U (MI)
Central Missouri State U (MO)
Cornell U (NY)
Kansas State U (KS)
Lawrence Technological U (MI)
Louisiana State U and A&M Coll (LA)
Louisiana Tech U (LA)
Michigan State U (MI)
Minneapolis Coll of Art and Design (MN)
Southwest Texas State U (TX)
Stephen F. Austin State U (TX)
Texas Tech U (TX)
U of Bridgeport (CT)
U of Houston (TX)
U of Idaho (ID)

Majors Index
Interior Architecture–International Business

U of Louisiana at Lafayette (LA)
U of Nevada, Las Vegas (NV)
U of New Haven (CT)
U of Oklahoma (OK)
The U of Texas at Arlington (TX)
The U of Texas at San Antonio (TX)
U of Washington (WA)
Washington State U (WA)
Woodbury U (CA)

INTERMEDIA
The Art Inst of Portland (OR)
Augusta State U (GA)
Calumet Coll of Saint Joseph (IN)
Columbia Coll Chicago (IL)
Columbus Coll of Art and Design (OH)
Eastern Coll (PA)
Emerson Coll (MA)
Indiana U of Pennsylvania (PA)
Maharishi U of Management (IA)
Maryland Inst, Coll of Art (MD)
Massachusetts Coll of Art (MA)
Minneapolis Coll of Art and Design (MN)
Ramapo Coll of New Jersey (NJ)
State U of NY Coll at Fredonia (NY)
U of Calif, San Diego (CA)
U of Massachusetts Dartmouth (MA)
U of Michigan (MI)
U of Puerto Rico, Río Piedras (PR)

INTERNATIONAL AGRICULTURE
Arizona State U East (AZ)
Cornell U (NY)
Eastern Mennonite U (VA)
Insto Tecno Estudios Sups Monterrey (Mexico)
Iowa State U of Science and Technology (IA)
MidAmerica Nazarene U (KS)
U of Calif, Davis (CA)
U of Wyoming (WY)
Utah State U (UT)

INTERNATIONAL BUSINESS
Adams State Coll (CO)
Adrian Coll (MI)
Albertus Magnus Coll (CT)
Albright Coll (PA)
Alfred U (NY)
Alma Coll (MI)
Alverno Coll (WI)
American InterContinental U, Atlanta (GA)
American International Coll (MA)
American U (DC)
The American U of Paris (France)
American U of Rome (Italy)
Appalachian State U (NC)
Aquinas Coll (MI)
Arizona State U West (AZ)
Arkansas State U (AR)
Assumption Coll (MA)
Auburn U (AL)
Augsburg Coll (MN)
Avila Coll (MO)
Babson Coll (MA)
Baker U (KS)
Barat Coll (IL)
Barry U (FL)
Baylor U (TX)
Bay Path Coll (MA)
Beaver Coll (PA)
Bellarmine Coll (KY)
Belmont U (TN)
Benedictine U (IL)
Berkeley Coll, New York (NY)
Berkeley Coll, White Plains (NY)
Baruch Coll of the City U of NY (NY)
Bethany Coll (KS)
Bethune-Cookman Coll (FL)
Birmingham-Southern Coll (AL)
Bishop's U (PQ, Canada)
Boise State U (ID)
Boston U (MA)
Bowling Green State U (OH)
Bradley U (IL)
Bridgewater Coll (VA)
Bridgewater State Coll (MA)
Brigham Young U–Hawaii Campus (HI)
Brock U (ON, Canada)

Buena Vista U (IA)
Butler U (IN)
Caldwell Coll (NJ)
California Lutheran U (CA)
California State Polytechnic U, Pomona (CA)
California State U, Dominguez Hills (CA)
California State U, Fresno (CA)
California State U, Fullerton (CA)
California State U, Long Beach (CA)
California State U, Los Angeles (CA)
California State U, Monterey Bay (CA)
California State U, Northridge (CA)
Campbell U (NC)
Cardinal Stritch U (WI)
Carleton U (ON, Canada)
Cedarville Coll (OH)
Central Coll (IA)
Central Connecticut State U (CT)
Central Michigan U (MI)
Chapman U (CA)
Chatham Coll (PA)
Christian Brothers U (TN)
Christopher Newport U (VA)
Claremont McKenna Coll (CA)
Clarion U of Pennsylvania (PA)
Clarke Coll (IA)
Coll of Charleston (SC)
The Coll of New Jersey (NJ)
Coll of Notre Dame (CA)
Coll of Notre Dame of Maryland (MD)
Coll of St. Catherine (MN)
The Coll of St. Scholastica (MN)
Coll of Santa Fe (NM)
The Coll of Southeastern Europe, The American U of Athens (Greece)
Coll of Staten Island of the City U of NY (NY)
Columbia Coll (MO)
Concordia Coll (MN)
Concordia U (PQ, Canada)
Converse Coll (SC)
Cornell Coll (IA)
Creighton U (NE)
Davenport Coll of Business (MI)
DePaul U (IL)
Detroit Coll of Business (MI)
Detroit Coll of Business, Warren Campus (MI)
Dickinson Coll (PA)
Dickinson State U (ND)
Dominican Coll of Blauvelt (NY)
Dominican U (IL)
Dowling Coll (NY)
Drake U (IA)
Drexel U (PA)
Duquesne U (PA)
D'Youville Coll (NY)
Eastern Mennonite U (VA)
Eastern Michigan U (MI)
Eckerd Coll (FL)
École des Hautes Études Commerciales (PQ, Canada)
Elizabethtown Coll (PA)
Elmhurst Coll (IL)
Elmira Coll (NY)
Emporia State U (KS)
Fairleigh Dickinson U, Florham-Madison Campus (NJ)
Fairleigh Dickinson U, Teaneck-Hackensack Campus (NJ)
Ferris State U (MI)
Ferrum Coll (VA)
Finlandia U (MI)
Florida Atlantic U (FL)
Florida International U (FL)
Florida Southern Coll (FL)
Florida State U (FL)
Fordham U (NY)
Fort Lewis Coll (CO)
Framingham State Coll (MA)
Franklin Coll of Indiana (IN)
Franklin Coll Switzerland (Switzerland)
Franklin Pierce Coll (NH)
Fresno Pacific U (CA)
Friends U (KS)
Gannon U (PA)
Georgetown Coll (KY)
Georgetown U (DC)
The George Washington U (DC)

Georgia Southern U (GA)
Gettysburg Coll (PA)
Golden Gate U (CA)
Goldey-Beacom Coll (DE)
Gonzaga U (WA)
Grace Coll (IN)
Graceland Coll (IA)
Grand Canyon U (AZ)
Grand Valley State U (MI)
Green Mountain Coll (VT)
Grove City Coll (PA)
Gustavus Adolphus Coll (MN)
Hamline U (MN)
Hampshire Coll (MA)
Harding U (AR)
Hawaii Pacific U (HI)
High Point U (NC)
Hiram Coll (OH)
Hofstra U (NY)
Holy Family Coll (PA)
Howard U (DC)
Huntingdon Coll (AL)
Husson Coll (ME)
Illinois State U (IL)
Illinois Wesleyan U (IL)
Immaculata Coll (PA)
Indiana U of Pennsylvania (PA)
Insto Tecno Estudios Sups Monterrey, León (Mexico)
Insto Tecno Estudios Sups Monterrey (Mexico)
Insto Tecno Estudios Sups Monterrey, Querétaro (Mexico)
Insto Tecno Estudios Sups Monterrey, Tampico (Mexico)
Iona Coll (NY)
Iowa State U of Science and Technology (IA)
Iowa Wesleyan Coll (IA)
Ithaca Coll (NY)
Jacksonville U (FL)
James Madison U (VA)
John Brown U (AR)
Johnson & Wales U (RI)
Judson Coll (IL)
Juniata Coll (PA)
King's Coll (PA)
Kutztown U of Pennsylvania (PA)
LaGrange Coll (GA)
Lake Erie Coll (OH)
Lakeland Coll (WI)
La Roche Coll (PA)
Lasell Coll (MA)
Lebanon Valley Coll (PA)
Lehigh U (PA)
Lenoir-Rhyne Coll (NC)
Lincoln U (CA)
Linfield Coll (OR)
Long Island U, Southampton Coll, Friends World Program (NY)
Loras Coll (IA)
Louisiana State U and A&M Coll (LA)
Loyola Coll in Maryland (MD)
Loyola U New Orleans (LA)
Luther Coll (IA)
Lycoming Coll (PA)
Lynn U (FL)
Madonna U (MI)
Maine Maritime Academy (ME)
Manhattan Coll (NY)
Manhattanville Coll (NY)
Mansfield U of Pennsylvania (PA)
Marietta Coll (OH)
Marquette U (WI)
Mars Hill Coll (NC)
Marycrest International U (IA)
Marygrove Coll (MI)
Marymount Coll (NY)
Marymount Manhattan Coll (NY)
Maryville Coll (TN)
Massachusetts Maritime Academy (MA)
McGill U (PQ, Canada)
McPherson Coll (KS)
Mercer U (GA)
Meredith Coll (NC)
Merrimack Coll (MA)
Messiah Coll (PA)
Metropolitan State U (MN)
Millersville U of Pennsylvania (PA)
Millikin U (IL)
Minnesota State U, Mankato (MN)
Minnesota State U Moorhead (MN)
Moravian Coll (PA)
Mount Allison U (NB, Canada)
Mount Saint Mary Coll (NY)

Mount St. Mary's Coll (CA)
Mount Union Coll (OH)
Muskingum Coll (OH)
National-Louis U (IL)
Nebraska Wesleyan U (NE)
Neumann Coll (PA)
Newbury Coll (MA)
New Hampshire Coll (NH)
New Mexico State U (NM)
New York U (NY)
Niagara U (NY)
North Central Coll (IL)
Northeastern U (MA)
Northern State U (SD)
North Park U (IL)
Northwestern Coll (MN)
Northwest Missouri State U (MO)
Northwest Nazarene U (ID)
Northwood U (MI)
Northwood U, Florida Campus (FL)
Northwood U, Texas Campus (TX)
Notre Dame Coll of Ohio (OH)
Ohio Dominican Coll (OH)
Ohio Northern U (OH)
The Ohio State U (OH)
Ohio U (OH)
Ohio Wesleyan U (OH)
Oklahoma Baptist U (OK)
Oklahoma City U (OK)
Oklahoma State U (OK)
Oregon State U (OR)
Otterbein Coll (OH)
Pace U, New York City Campus (NY)
Pace U, Pleasantville/Briarcliff Campus (NY)
Pacific Lutheran U (WA)
Pacific Union Coll (CA)
Palm Beach Atlantic Coll (FL)
Penn State U Univ Park Campus (PA)
Pepperdine U, Malibu (CA)
Philadelphia U (PA)
Pine Manor Coll (MA)
Plattsburgh State U of NY (NY)
Quinnipiac U (CT)
Ramapo Coll of New Jersey (NJ)
Regents Coll (NY)
Rhodes Coll (TN)
Richmond, The American International U in London (United Kingdom)
Rider U (NJ)
Rochester Inst of Technology (NY)
Roger Williams U (RI)
Rollins Coll (FL)
Ryerson Polytechnic U (ON, Canada)
Sacred Heart U (CT)
St. Ambrose U (IA)
St. Andrews Presbyterian Coll (NC)
St. Bonaventure U (NY)
St. Cloud State U (MN)
St. Edward's U (TX)
Saint Francis Coll (PA)
St. John Fisher Coll (NY)
Saint Joseph's Coll (IN)
Saint Joseph's Coll (ME)
Saint Leo U (FL)
Saint Louis U (MO)
Saint Mary's Coll (IN)
Saint Mary's Coll of California (CA)
Saint Mary's U of Minnesota (MN)
St. Mary's U of San Antonio (TX)
St. Norbert Coll (WI)
Saint Peter's Coll (NJ)
St. Thomas U (FL)
Saint Xavier U (IL)
Salem Coll (NC)
Sam Houston State U (TX)
San Diego State U (CA)
San Francisco State U (CA)
San Jose State U (CA)
Savannah State U (GA)
Schiller International U (Germany)
Seattle U (WA)
Seton Hill Coll (PA)
Shenandoah U (VA)
Simpson Coll (IA)
Slippery Rock U of Pennsylvania (PA)
Southern Adventist U (TN)
Southwestern Adventist U (TX)
Spring Hill Coll (AL)
State U of NY at New Paltz (NY)
State U of NY Coll at Brockport (NY)

Stephen F. Austin State U (TX)
Stetson U (FL)
Taylor U (IN)
Teikyo Post U (CT)
Temple U (PA)
Tennessee Technological U (TN)
Texas A&M U–Kingsville (TX)
Texas A&M U–Texarkana (TX)
Texas Christian U (TX)
Texas Tech U (TX)
Texas Wesleyan U (TX)
Thiel Coll (PA)
Thomas Coll (ME)
Thomas Edison State Coll (NJ)
Tiffin U (OH)
Touro Coll (NY)
Trinity U (TX)
United States International U (CA)
The U of Akron (OH)
U of Alaska Fairbanks (AK)
U of Alberta (AB, Canada)
U of Arkansas at Little Rock (AR)
U of Baltimore (MD)
U of Bridgeport (CT)
U of British Columbia (BC, Canada)
U of Dayton (OH)
U of Denver (CO)
U of Detroit Mercy (MI)
U of Evansville (IN)
The U of Findlay (OH)
U of Georgia (GA)
U of Hawaii at Manoa (HI)
U of Indianapolis (IN)
The U of Iowa (IA)
U of La Verne (CA)
The U of Lethbridge (AB, Canada)
U of Maryland, Coll Park (MD)
The U of Memphis (TN)
U of Miami (FL)
U of Minnesota, Twin Cities Campus (MN)
U of Mississippi (MS)
U of Missouri–Columbia (MO)
The U of Montana–Missoula (MT)
U of Nebraska–Lincoln (NE)
U of Nevada, Las Vegas (NV)
U of Nevada, Reno (NV)
U of New Brunswick, Fredericton (NB, Canada)
U of New Haven (CT)
The U of North Carolina at Charlotte (NC)
U of North Florida (FL)
U of Oklahoma (OK)
U of Oregon (OR)
U of Pittsburgh at Bradford (PA)
U of Portland (OR)
U of Puget Sound (WA)
U of Rhode Island (RI)
U of Richmond (VA)
U of Rio Grande (OH)
U of Saint Francis (IN)
U of St. Thomas (MN)
U of San Francisco (CA)
The U of Scranton (PA)
U of Southern California (CA)
U of Southern Mississippi (MS)
The U of Tampa (FL)
The U of Tennessee at Martin (TN)
The U of Texas at Arlington (TX)
The U of Texas–Pan American (TX)
U of the Pacific (CA)
U of Tulsa (OK)
U of Victoria (BC, Canada)
U of Washington (WA)
U of Wisconsin–La Crosse (WI)
Utica Coll of Syracuse U (NY)
Valparaiso U (IN)
Vanguard U of Southern California (CA)
Villanova U (PA)
Warren Wilson Coll (NC)
Wartburg Coll (IA)
Washington State U (WA)
Washington U in St. Louis (MO)
Wayne State Coll (NE)
Webber Coll (FL)
Webster U (MO)
Wesleyan Coll (GA)
Western Carolina U (NC)
Western New England Coll (MA)
Western State Coll of Colorado (CO)
Western Washington U (WA)
Westminster Coll (MO)
Westminster Coll (PA)

Majors Index
International Business–Judaic Studies

Westminster Coll (UT)
Wheeling Jesuit U (WV)
Whitworth Coll (WA)
Wichita State U (KS)
Widener U (PA)
William Jewell Coll (MO)
William Paterson U of New Jersey (NJ)
Wittenberg U (OH)
Wofford Coll (SC)
Woodbury U (CA)
York Coll of Pennsylvania (PA)
York U (ON, Canada)

INTERNATIONAL BUSINESS MARKETING
American U (DC)
Central Michigan U (MI)
Eastern Michigan U (MI)
Oklahoma Baptist U (OK)
York U (ON, Canada)

INTERNATIONAL ECONOMICS
Albertus Magnus Coll (CT)
American U (DC)
The American U of Paris (France)
Assumption Coll (MA)
Austin Coll (TX)
Bard Coll (NY)
Benedictine U (IL)
Bentley Coll (MA)
Brandeis U (MA)
Brock U (ON, Canada)
California State U, Los Angeles (CA)
Carson-Newman Coll (TN)
Carthage Coll (WI)
The Catholic U of America (DC)
Claremont McKenna Coll (CA)
Coll of St. Catherine (MN)
École des Hautes Études Commerciales (PQ, Canada)
Fairleigh Dickinson U, Florham-Madison Campus (NJ)
Framingham State Coll (MA)
Franklin Coll Switzerland (Switzerland)
Georgetown U (DC)
Gettysburg Coll (PA)
Hamline U (MN)
Hampshire Coll (MA)
Harvard U (MA)
Hastings Coll (NE)
Hiram Coll (OH)
Howard U (DC)
John Carroll U (OH)
Lawrence U (WI)
Long Island U, Southampton Coll, Friends World Program (NY)
Longwood Coll (VA)
Marlboro Coll (VT)
Middlebury Coll (VT)
Muhlenberg Coll (PA)
Rhodes Coll (TN)
Rockford Coll (IL)
Ryerson Polytechnic U (ON, Canada)
Seattle U (WA)
State U of NY at New Paltz (NY)
State U of West Georgia (GA)
Suffolk U (MA)
Taylor U (IN)
U of Calif, Los Angeles (CA)
U of Calif, Santa Cruz (CA)
U of Central Arkansas (AR)
U of Puget Sound (WA)
U of Richmond (VA)
U of the Pacific (CA)
Valparaiso U (IN)
Washington U in St. Louis (MO)
Westminster Coll (PA)
Youngstown State U (OH)

INTERNATIONAL FINANCE
Boston U (MA)
The Catholic U of America (DC)
École des Hautes Études Commerciales (PQ, Canada)
Franklin Coll Switzerland (Switzerland)
International Coll of the Cayman Islands (Cayman Islands)
Rochester Inst of Technology (NY)
Ryerson Polytechnic U (ON, Canada)
U of Southern California (CA)

Washington U in St. Louis (MO)
York U (ON, Canada)

INVESTMENTS AND SECURITIES
Babson Coll (MA)
Duquesne U (PA)

ISLAMIC STUDIES
Brandeis U (MA)
Hampshire Coll (MA)
Harvard U (MA)
Long Island U, Southampton Coll, Friends World Program (NY)
The Ohio State U (OH)
U of Calif, Santa Barbara (CA)
U of Michigan (MI)
The U of Texas at Austin (TX)
U of Toronto (ON, Canada)
Washington U in St. Louis (MO)

ITALIAN
Albertus Magnus Coll (CT)
American U of Rome (Italy)
Arizona State U (AZ)
Bard Coll (NY)
Barnard Coll (NY)
Bishop's U (PQ, Canada)
Boston Coll (MA)
Boston U (MA)
Brandeis U (MA)
Brigham Young U (UT)
Brock U (ON, Canada)
Brooklyn Coll of the City U of NY (NY)
Brown U (RI)
Bryn Mawr Coll (PA)
California State U, Northridge (CA)
Carleton U (ON, Canada)
Central Connecticut State U (CT)
City Coll of the City U of NY (NY)
Claremont McKenna Coll (CA)
Columbia Coll (NY)
Columbia U, School of General Studies (NY)
Concordia U (PQ, Canada)
Connecticut Coll (CT)
Cornell U (NY)
Dartmouth Coll (NH)
DePaul U (IL)
Dickinson Coll (PA)
Dominican U (IL)
Drew U (NJ)
Duke U (NC)
Emory U (GA)
Florida International U (FL)
Florida State U (FL)
Fordham U (NY)
Georgetown U (DC)
Gonzaga U (WA)
Harvard U (MA)
Haverford Coll (PA)
Hofstra U (NY)
Hunter Coll of the City U of NY (NY)
Indiana U Bloomington (IN)
Iona Coll (NY)
Johns Hopkins U (MD)
Lake Erie Coll (OH)
La Salle U (PA)
Lehman Coll of the City U of NY (NY)
Long Island U, C.W. Post Campus (NY)
Long Island U, Southampton Coll, Friends World Program (NY)
Loyola U Chicago (IL)
Marlboro Coll (VT)
McGill U (PQ, Canada)
Mercy Coll (NY)
Middlebury Coll (VT)
Mount Holyoke Coll (MA)
Nazareth Coll of Rochester (NY)
New York U (NY)
Northeastern U (MA)
Northwestern U (IL)
The Ohio State U (OH)
Penn State U Univ Park Campus (PA)
Providence Coll (RI)
Queens Coll of the City U of NY (NY)
Queen's U at Kingston (ON, Canada)
Rosemont Coll (PA)
Rutgers, State U of NJ, Douglass Coll (NJ)

Rutgers, State U of NJ, Livingston Coll (NJ)
Rutgers, State U of NJ, Newark Coll of Arts & Scis (NJ)
Rutgers, State U of NJ, Rutgers Coll (NJ)
Rutgers, State U of NJ, U Coll–New Brunswick (NJ)
St. John Fisher Coll (NY)
St. John's U (NY)
San Francisco State U (CA)
Santa Clara U (CA)
Sarah Lawrence Coll (NY)
Scripps Coll (CA)
Seton Hall U (NJ)
Smith Coll (MA)
Stanford U (CA)
State U of NY at Albany (NY)
State U of NY at Binghamton (NY)
State U of NY at Buffalo (NY)
State U of NY at Stony Brook (NY)
Sweet Briar Coll (VA)
Syracuse U (NY)
Temple U (PA)
Trinity Coll (CT)
Tulane U (LA)
The U of Akron (OH)
U of Alberta (AB, Canada)
The U of Arizona (AZ)
U of British Columbia (BC, Canada)
U of Calif, Berkeley (CA)
U of Calif, Davis (CA)
U of Calif, Los Angeles (CA)
U of Calif, San Diego (CA)
U of Calif, Santa Barbara (CA)
U of Calif, Santa Cruz (CA)
U of Chicago (IL)
U of Colorado at Boulder (CO)
U of Connecticut (CT)
U of Delaware (DE)
U of Denver (CO)
U of Georgia (GA)
U of Houston (TX)
U of Illinois at Chicago (IL)
U of Illinois at Urbana–Champaign (IL)
The U of Iowa (IA)
U of Kentucky (KY)
U of Maryland, Coll Park (MD)
U of Massachusetts Amherst (MA)
U of Massachusetts Boston (MA)
U of Michigan (MI)
U of Minnesota, Twin Cities Campus (MN)
U of Notre Dame (IN)
U of Oregon (OR)
U of Pennsylvania (PA)
U of Pittsburgh (PA)
U of Rhode Island (RI)
The U of Scranton (PA)
U of South Carolina (SC)
U of Southern California (CA)
U of South Florida (FL)
The U of Tennessee Knoxville (TN)
The U of Texas at Austin (TX)
U of Toronto (ON, Canada)
U of Victoria (BC, Canada)
U of Virginia (VA)
U of Washington (WA)
U of Windsor (ON, Canada)
U of Wisconsin–Madison (WI)
U of Wisconsin–Milwaukee (WI)
Vassar Coll (NY)
Washington U in St. Louis (MO)
Wayne State U (MI)
Wellesley Coll (MA)
Wesleyan U (CT)
Yale U (CT)
York Coll of the City U of New York (NY)
York U (ON, Canada)
Youngstown State U (OH)

JAPANESE
Antioch Coll (OH)
Arizona State U (AZ)
Ball State U (IN)
Bates Coll (ME)
Bennington Coll (VT)
Brigham Young U (UT)
California State U, Fullerton (CA)
California State U, Long Beach (CA)
California State U, Los Angeles (CA)
Carnegie Mellon U (PA)

Claremont McKenna Coll (CA)
Colgate U (NY)
Connecticut Coll (CT)
Cornell U (NY)
DePaul U (IL)
Eastern Michigan U (MI)
The Evergreen State Coll (WA)
Georgetown U (DC)
Gustavus Adolphus Coll (MN)
Harvard U (MA)
Hobart and William Smith Colls (NY)
Indiana U Bloomington (IN)
Long Island U, Southampton Coll, Friends World Program (NY)
Middlebury Coll (VT)
Mount Union Coll (OH)
North Central Coll (IL)
The Ohio State U (OH)
Pacific U (OR)
Penn State U Univ Park Campus (PA)
Pomona Coll (CA)
Portland State U (OR)
San Diego State U (CA)
San Francisco State U (CA)
San Jose State U (CA)
Scripps Coll (CA)
Stanford U (CA)
State U of NY at Albany (NY)
U of Alaska Fairbanks (AK)
U of Alberta (AB, Canada)
U of British Columbia (BC, Canada)
U of Calif, Berkeley (CA)
U of Calif, Davis (CA)
U of Calif, Los Angeles (CA)
U of Calif, San Diego (CA)
U of Calif, Santa Barbara (CA)
U of Calif, Santa Cruz (CA)
U of Chicago (IL)
U of Colorado at Boulder (CO)
The U of Findlay (OH)
U of Georgia (GA)
U of Hawaii at Manoa (HI)
The U of Iowa (IA)
U of Kansas (KS)
U of Maryland, Coll Park (MD)
U of Massachusetts Amherst (MA)
U of Michigan (MI)
U of Minnesota, Twin Cities Campus (MN)
The U of Montana–Missoula (MT)
U of Notre Dame (IN)
U of Oregon (OR)
U of Pittsburgh (PA)
U of Regina (SK, Canada)
U of Rochester (NY)
U of Southern California (CA)
U of the Pacific (CA)
U of Toronto (ON, Canada)
U of Utah (UT)
U of Victoria (BC, Canada)
U of Washington (WA)
U of Windsor (ON, Canada)
U of Wisconsin–Madison (WI)
Ursinus Coll (PA)
Washington U in St. Louis (MO)
Wellesley Coll (MA)
Williams Coll (MA)
York U (ON, Canada)

JAZZ
Aquinas Coll (MI)
Augustana Coll (IL)
Bard Coll (NY)
Benedictine U (IL)
Bennington Coll (VT)
Berklee Coll of Music (MA)
Bowling Green State U (OH)
Brevard Coll (NC)
California Inst of the Arts (CA)
Capital U (OH)
Chicago State U (IL)
Concordia U (PQ, Canada)
DePaul U (IL)
Eastern Illinois U (IL)
Five Towns Coll (NY)
Goddard Coll (VT)
Hampshire Coll (MA)
Hampton U (VA)
Indiana U Bloomington (IN)
Ithaca Coll (NY)
Johnson State Coll (VT)
Lamar U (TX)

Long Island U, Brooklyn Campus (NY)
Long Island U, Southampton Coll, Friends World Program (NY)
Loyola U New Orleans (LA)
Manhattan School of Music (NY)
McGill U (PQ, Canada)
New England Conservatory of Music (MA)
New York U (NY)
North Carolina Central U (NC)
North Central Coll (IL)
Oberlin Coll (OH)
The Ohio State U (OH)
Open Learning Agency (BC, Canada)
Rowan U (NJ)
Rutgers, State U of NJ, Mason Gross School of Arts (NJ)
St. Francis Xavier U (NS, Canada)
Simon's Rock Coll of Bard (MA)
State U of NY at New Paltz (NY)
Temple U (PA)
Texas Southern U (TX)
Université de Montréal (PQ, Canada)
U of Cincinnati (OH)
U of Hartford (CT)
The U of Iowa (IA)
The U of Maine at Augusta (ME)
U of Miami (FL)
U of Michigan (MI)
U of Minnesota, Duluth (MN)
U of North Florida (FL)
U of North Texas (TX)
U of Rochester (NY)
U of Southern California (CA)
The U of the Arts (PA)
Virginia Union U (VA)
Webster U (MO)
Western Washington U (WA)
Westfield State Coll (MA)
William Paterson U of New Jersey (NJ)
York U (ON, Canada)

JUDAIC STUDIES
American U (DC)
Bard Coll (NY)
Brandeis U (MA)
Brooklyn Coll of the City U of NY (NY)
Brown U (RI)
City Coll of the City U of NY (NY)
Clark U (MA)
Cleveland Coll of Jewish Studies (OH)
Cornell U (NY)
Dartmouth Coll (NH)
DePaul U (IL)
Dickinson Coll (PA)
Emory U (GA)
Florida Atlantic U (FL)
The George Washington U (DC)
Gratz Coll (PA)
Hamline U (MN)
Hampshire Coll (MA)
Harvard U (MA)
Hebrew Theological Coll (IL)
Hofstra U (NY)
Hunter Coll of the City U of NY (NY)
Indiana U Bloomington (IN)
Jewish Theological Seminary of America (NY)
Kol Yaakov Torah Center (NY)
Lehman Coll of the City U of NY (NY)
Machzikei Hadath Rabbinical Coll (NY)
McGill U (PQ, Canada)
Mesivta Torah Vodaath Rabbinical Seminary (NY)
Mount Holyoke Coll (MA)
New York U (NY)
Oberlin Coll (OH)
The Ohio State U (OH)
Penn State U Univ Park Campus (PA)
Queens Coll of the City U of NY (NY)
Queen's U at Kingston (ON, Canada)
Rutgers, State U of NJ, Douglass Coll (NJ)
Rutgers, State U of NJ, Livingston Coll (NJ)

Majors Index
Judaic Studies–Latin (Ancient and Medieval)

Rutgers, State U of NJ, Rutgers Coll (NJ)
Rutgers, State U of NJ, U Coll–New Brunswick (NJ)
Scripps Coll (CA)
State U of NY at Albany (NY)
State U of NY at Binghamton (NY)
State U of NY at New Paltz (NY)
State U of NY Coll at Brockport (NY)
Temple U (PA)
Touro Coll (NY)
Trinity Coll (CT)
Tufts U (MA)
Tulane U (LA)
Université Laval (PQ, Canada)
The U of Arizona (AZ)
U of Calif, Los Angeles (CA)
U of Calif, San Diego (CA)
U of Chicago (IL)
U of Cincinnati (OH)
U of Florida (FL)
U of Hartford (CT)
U of Judaism (CA)
U of Manitoba (MB, Canada)
U of Maryland, Coll Park (MD)
U of Massachusetts Amherst (MA)
U of Miami (FL)
U of Michigan (MI)
U of Minnesota, Twin Cities Campus (MN)
U of Missouri–Kansas City (MO)
U of Oregon (OR)
U of Pennsylvania (PA)
U of Southern California (CA)
U of Toronto (ON, Canada)
U of Washington (WA)
Washington U in St. Louis (MO)
Wellesley Coll (MA)
Yale U (CT)
Yeshiva Ohr Elchonon Chabad/W Coast Talmudical Sem (CA)
Yeshiva U (NY)
York U (ON, Canada)

LABORATORY ANIMAL MEDICINE
Mount Ida Coll (MA)
North Carolina Ag and Tech State U (NC)
Quinnipiac U (CT)
Thomas Edison State Coll (NJ)

LABOR/PERSONNEL RELATIONS
Athabasca U (AB, Canada)
Bowling Green State U (OH)
Brock U (ON, Canada)
California State U, Dominguez Hills (CA)
California State U, Los Angeles (CA)
Carleton U (ON, Canada)
Clarion U of Pennsylvania (PA)
Cleveland State U (OH)
Cornell U (NY)
Ferris State U (MI)
Governors State U (IL)
Grand Valley State U (MI)
Hampshire Coll (MA)
Indiana U Bloomington (IN)
Indiana U Kokomo (IN)
Indiana U Northwest (IN)
Indiana U–Purdue U Fort Wayne (IN)
Indiana U–Purdue U Indianapolis (IN)
Indiana U South Bend (IN)
Indiana U Southeast (IN)
Ithaca Coll (NY)
Lakehead U (ON, Canada)
Le Moyne Coll (NY)
McGill U (PQ, Canada)
Memorial U of Newfoundland (NF, Canada)
Northern Kentucky U (KY)
Ohio U (OH)
Pace U, New York City Campus (NY)
Penn State U Univ Park Campus (PA)
Queens Coll of the City U of NY (NY)
Rockhurst U (MO)
Rowan U (NJ)
Rutgers, State U of NJ, Douglass Coll (NJ)

Rutgers, State U of NJ, Livingston Coll (NJ)
Rutgers, State U of NJ, Rutgers Coll (NJ)
Rutgers, State U of NJ, U Coll–New Brunswick (NJ)
Saint Francis Coll (PA)
Saint Joseph's U (PA)
San Francisco State U (CA)
Seton Hall U (NJ)
State U of NY Coll at Fredonia (NY)
State U of NY Coll at Old Westbury (NY)
State U of NY Coll at Potsdam (NY)
Tennessee Technological U (TN)
Texas A&M U–Commerce (TX)
Thomas Edison State Coll (NJ)
Université de Montréal (PQ, Canada)
U du Québec à Hull (PQ, Canada)
U Coll of Cape Breton (NS, Canada)
U of Alberta (AB, Canada)
U of British Columbia (BC, Canada)
U of Detroit Mercy (MI)
The U of Iowa (IA)
The U of Lethbridge (AB, Canada)
U of Manitoba (MB, Canada)
U of Maryland, Coll Park (MD)
U of Massachusetts Boston (MA)
U of Nevada, Las Vegas (NV)
The U of North Carolina at Chapel Hill (NC)
U of Puerto Rico, Río Piedras (PR)
U of the Pacific (CA)
U of Toronto (ON, Canada)
U of Windsor (ON, Canada)
U of Wisconsin–Madison (WI)
U of Wisconsin–Milwaukee (WI)
U of Wisconsin–Parkside (WI)
Wayne State U (MI)
Westminster Coll (PA)
West Virginia U Inst of Technology (WV)
Winona State U (MN)
York U (ON, Canada)
Youngstown State U (OH)

LANDSCAPE ARCHITECTURE
Arizona State U (AZ)
Auburn U (AL)
Ball State U (IN)
California Polytechnic State U, San Luis Obispo (CA)
California State Polytechnic U, Pomona (CA)
City Coll of the City U of NY (NY)
Clemson U (SC)
Coll of the Atlantic (ME)
Colorado State U (CO)
Cornell U (NY)
Delaware Valley Coll (PA)
Eastern Kentucky U (KY)
Florida A&M U (FL)
Iowa State U of Science and Technology (IA)
Kansas State U (KS)
Louisiana State U and A&M Coll (LA)
Michigan State U (MI)
Mississippi State U (MS)
North Carolina Ag and Tech State U (NC)
North Carolina State U (NC)
North Dakota State U (ND)
Northwest Missouri State U (MO)
The Ohio State U (OH)
Oklahoma State U (OK)
Penn State U Univ Park Campus (PA)
Purdue U (IN)
Rhode Island School of Design (RI)
Rutgers, State U of NJ, Cook Coll (NJ)
Ryerson Polytechnic U (ON, Canada)
State U of NY Coll of Environ Sci and Forestry (NY)
Temple U (PA)
Texas A&M U (TX)
Texas Tech U (TX)
Université de Montréal (PQ, Canada)
The U of Arizona (AZ)

U of Arkansas (AR)
U of British Columbia (BC, Canada)
U of Calif, Berkeley (CA)
U of Calif, Davis (CA)
U of Connecticut (CT)
U of Florida (FL)
U of Georgia (GA)
U of Guelph (ON, Canada)
U of Idaho (ID)
U of Illinois at Urbana–Champaign (IL)
U of Kentucky (KY)
U of Maryland, Coll Park (MD)
U of Massachusetts Amherst (MA)
U of Michigan (MI)
U of Minnesota, Twin Cities Campus (MN)
U of Nevada, Las Vegas (NV)
U of Oregon (OR)
U of Rhode Island (RI)
U of Southern California (CA)
The U of Texas at Arlington (TX)
U of Toronto (ON, Canada)
U of Washington (WA)
U of Wisconsin–Madison (WI)
Utah State U (UT)
Virginia Polytechnic Inst and State U (VA)
West Virginia U (WV)

LANDSCAPING MANAGEMENT
Andrews U (MI)
Colorado State U (CO)
Eastern Kentucky U (KY)
Mississippi State U (MS)
The Ohio State U (OH)
Oregon State U (OR)
Penn State U Univ Park Campus (PA)
South Dakota State U (SD)
Tennessee Technological U (TN)
U of Georgia (GA)
U of Maryland, Coll Park (MD)
The U of Tennessee at Martin (TN)
U of Vermont (VT)

LAND USE MANAGEMENT
The Evergreen State Coll (WA)
Frostburg State U (MD)
Grand Valley State U (MI)
Metropolitan State Coll of Denver (CO)
Northern Arizona U (AZ)
Northern Michigan U (MI)
Northland Coll (WI)
State U of NY Coll of Environ Sci and Forestry (NY)
U of Alberta (AB, Canada)
U of Maryland, Coll Park (MD)
U of Wisconsin–Platteville (WI)
U of Wisconsin–River Falls (WI)

LASER/OPTICAL TECHNOLOGY
Oregon Inst of Technology (OR)
Regents Coll (NY)
State U of NY Inst of Tech at Utica/Rome (NY)

LATIN AMERICAN STUDIES
Adelphi U (NY)
American U (DC)
Austin Coll (TX)
Ball State U (IN)
Bard Coll (NY)
Barnard Coll (NY)
Baylor U (TX)
Beloit Coll (WI)
Boston U (MA)
Bowdoin Coll (ME)
Brandeis U (MA)
Brigham Young U (UT)
Brown U (RI)
Bucknell U (PA)
California State U, Chico (CA)
California State U, Fullerton (CA)
California State U, Hayward (CA)
California State U, Los Angeles (CA)
Carleton Coll (MN)
Carleton U (ON, Canada)
Central Coll (IA)
Chapman U (CA)
City Coll of the City U of NY (NY)
Claremont McKenna Coll (CA)
Colby Coll (ME)
Colgate U (NY)

Coll of Notre Dame (CA)
Coll of the Holy Cross (MA)
The Coll of William and Mary (VA)
The Coll of Wooster (OH)
Colorado State U (CO)
Columbia Coll (NY)
Cornell Coll (IA)
Cornell U (NY)
Dartmouth Coll (NH)
Denison U (OH)
DePaul U (IL)
Earlham Coll (IN)
Emory U (GA)
The Evergreen State Coll (WA)
Flagler Coll (FL)
Florida State U (FL)
Fordham U (NY)
Fort Lewis Coll (CO)
George Mason U (VA)
The George Washington U (DC)
Gettysburg Coll (PA)
Grinnell Coll (IA)
Gustavus Adolphus Coll (MN)
Hamline U (MN)
Hampshire Coll (MA)
Hanover Coll (IN)
Harvard U (MA)
Haverford Coll (PA)
Hobart and William Smith Colls (NY)
Hood Coll (MD)
Hunter Coll of the City U of NY (NY)
Illinois Wesleyan U (IL)
Indiana State U (IN)
Indiana U Bloomington (IN)
Johns Hopkins U (MD)
Kent State U (OH)
Lake Forest Coll (IL)
Lehman Coll of the City U of NY (NY)
Lock Haven U of Pennsylvania (PA)
Long Island U, Southampton Coll, Friends World Program (NY)
Luther Coll (IA)
Macalester Coll (MN)
Marlboro Coll (VT)
Massachusetts Inst of Technology (MA)
McGill U (PQ, Canada)
Mount Holyoke Coll (MA)
New York U (NY)
Northwestern U (IL)
Oakland U (MI)
Oberlin Coll (OH)
The Ohio State U (OH)
Ohio U (OH)
Penn State U Univ Park Campus (PA)
Pitzer Coll (CA)
Plattsburgh State U of NY (NY)
Portland State U (OR)
Queens Coll of the City U of NY (NY)
Queen's U at Kingston (ON, Canada)
Ripon Coll (WI)
Rollins Coll (FL)
Rutgers, State U of NJ, Douglass Coll (NJ)
Rutgers, State U of NJ, Livingston Coll (NJ)
Rutgers, State U of NJ, Rutgers Coll (NJ)
Rutgers, State U of NJ, U Coll–New Brunswick (NJ)
St. Cloud State U (MN)
Samford U (AL)
San Diego State U (CA)
Sarah Lawrence Coll (NY)
Scripps Coll (CA)
Seattle Pacific U (WA)
Simon Fraser U (BC, Canada)
Simon's Rock Coll of Bard (MA)
Smith Coll (MA)
Southern Methodist U (TX)
Stanford U (CA)
State U of NY at Albany (NY)
State U of NY at Binghamton (NY)
State U of NY at New Paltz (NY)
State U of NY Coll at Brockport (NY)
Stetson U (FL)
Syracuse U (NY)
Temple U (PA)
Texas Christian U (TX)

Texas Tech U (TX)
Trinity U (TX)
Tulane U (LA)
United States Military Academy (NY)
U Coll of the Fraser Valley (BC, Canada)
The U of Alabama (AL)
U of Alberta (AB, Canada)
The U of Arizona (AZ)
U of British Columbia (BC, Canada)
U of Calgary (AB, Canada)
U of Calif, Berkeley (CA)
U of Calif, Los Angeles (CA)
U of Calif, Riverside (CA)
U of Calif, San Diego (CA)
U of Calif, Santa Barbara (CA)
U of Calif, Santa Cruz (CA)
U of Chicago (IL)
U of Cincinnati (OH)
U of Colorado at Boulder (CO)
U of Connecticut (CT)
U of Delaware (DE)
U of Denver (CO)
U of Idaho (ID)
U of Illinois at Chicago (IL)
U of Illinois at Urbana–Champaign (IL)
The U of Iowa (IA)
U of Kansas (KS)
U of Kentucky (KY)
U of Miami (FL)
U of Michigan (MI)
U of Minnesota, Morris (MN)
U of Minnesota, Twin Cities Campus (MN)
U of Nebraska–Lincoln (NE)
U of Nevada, Las Vegas (NV)
U of New Mexico (NM)
The U of North Carolina at Chapel Hill (NC)
The U of North Carolina at Greensboro (NC)
U of Northern Iowa (IA)
U of Pennsylvania (PA)
U of Puerto Rico, Mayagüez Campus (PR)
U of Rhode Island (RI)
U of Richmond (VA)
U of South Carolina (SC)
The U of Texas at Austin (TX)
U of the Pacific (CA)
U of Toronto (ON, Canada)
U of Vermont (VT)
U of Washington (WA)
U of Wisconsin–Eau Claire (WI)
U of Wisconsin–Madison (WI)
U of Wisconsin–Milwaukee (WI)
Vanderbilt U (TN)
Vassar Coll (NY)
Walsh U (OH)
Warren Wilson Coll (NC)
Washington Coll (MD)
Washington U in St. Louis (MO)
Wesleyan U (CT)
Western Michigan U (MI)
Western Washington U (WA)
Yale U (CT)
York U (ON, Canada)

LATIN (ANCIENT AND MEDIEVAL)
Acadia U (NS, Canada)
Amherst Coll (MA)
Asbury Coll (KY)
Augustana Coll (IL)
Austin Coll (TX)
Ball State U (IN)
Bard Coll (NY)
Barnard Coll (NY)
Baylor U (TX)
Boston U (MA)
Bowling Green State U (OH)
Brandeis U (MA)
Brigham Young U (UT)
Brooklyn Coll of the City U of NY (NY)
Brown U (RI)
Bryn Mawr Coll (PA)
Butler U (IN)
Calvin Coll (MI)
Carleton Coll (MN)
Carleton U (ON, Canada)
Carroll Coll (MT)
The Catholic U of America (DC)
Centenary Coll of Louisiana (LA)

Majors Index
Latin (Ancient and Medieval)–(Pre)Law

Claremont McKenna Coll (CA)
Colgate U (NY)
The Coll of New Rochelle (NY)
The Coll of William and Mary (VA)
The Coll of Wooster (OH)
Concordia Coll (MN)
Concordia U (PQ, Canada)
Cornell Coll (IA)
Cornell U (NY)
Creighton U (NE)
Dartmouth Coll (NH)
DePauw U (IN)
Dickinson Coll (PA)
Duke U (NC)
Duquesne U (PA)
Elmira Coll (NY)
Emory U (GA)
Florida State U (FL)
Fordham U (NY)
Franklin and Marshall Coll (PA)
Furman U (SC)
Gettysburg Coll (PA)
Hamilton Coll (NY)
Hampden-Sydney Coll (VA)
Harvard U (MA)
Haverford Coll (PA)
Hobart and William Smith Colls (NY)
Hope Coll (MI)
Hunter Coll of the City U of NY (NY)
Indiana State U (IN)
Indiana U Bloomington (IN)
John Carroll U (OH)
Kent State U (OH)
Kenyon Coll (OH)
La Salle U (PA)
Lehman Coll of the City U of NY (NY)
Lenoir-Rhyne Coll (NC)
Louisiana State U and A&M Coll (LA)
Loyola Marymount U (CA)
Loyola U Chicago (IL)
Luther Coll (IA)
Macalester Coll (MN)
Marlboro Coll (VT)
Marshall U (WV)
Mary Washington Coll (VA)
McGill U (PQ, Canada)
Memorial U of Newfoundland (NF, Canada)
Mercer U (GA)
Miami U (OH)
Michigan State U (MI)
Monmouth Coll (IL)
Mount Allison U (NB, Canada)
Mount Holyoke Coll (MA)
Muhlenberg Coll (PA)
New Coll of the U of South Florida (FL)
New York U (NY)
Oberlin Coll (OH)
The Ohio State U (OH)
Ohio U (OH)
Queens Coll of the City U of NY (NY)
Queen's U at Kingston (ON, Canada)
Randolph-Macon Coll (VA)
Randolph-Macon Woman's Coll (VA)
Rhodes Coll (TN)
Rockford Coll (IL)
Rutgers, State U of NJ, Douglass Coll (NJ)
Rutgers, State U of NJ, Livingston Coll (NJ)
Rutgers, State U of NJ, Rutgers Coll (NJ)
Rutgers, State U of NJ, U Coll–New Brunswick (NJ)
Saint Anselm Coll (NH)
St. Bonaventure U (NY)
Saint Louis U (MO)
Saint Mary's Coll of California (CA)
St. Olaf Coll (MN)
Samford U (AL)
Santa Clara U (CA)
Sarah Lawrence Coll (NY)
Scripps Coll (CA)
Seattle Pacific U (WA)
Smith Coll (MA)
Southwest Missouri State U (MO)
State U of NY at Albany (NY)
Swarthmore Coll (PA)
Sweet Briar Coll (VA)

Syracuse U (NY)
Texas Tech U (TX)
Trent U (ON, Canada)
Tufts U (MA)
Tulane U (LA)
The U of Akron (OH)
U of Alberta (AB, Canada)
U of British Columbia (BC, Canada)
U of Calif, Berkeley (CA)
U of Calif, Los Angeles (CA)
U of Chicago (IL)
U of Delaware (DE)
U of Georgia (GA)
U of Guelph (ON, Canada)
U of Houston (TX)
U of Idaho (ID)
The U of Iowa (IA)
U of Maine (ME)
U of Manitoba (MB, Canada)
U of Massachusetts Boston (MA)
U of Michigan (MI)
U of Minnesota, Twin Cities Campus (MN)
The U of Montana–Missoula (MT)
U of Nebraska–Lincoln (NE)
U of New Brunswick, Fredericton (NB, Canada)
U of New Hampshire (NH)
The U of North Carolina at Greensboro (NC)
U of Notre Dame (IN)
U of Oregon (OR)
U of Regina (SK, Canada)
U of Richmond (VA)
U of St. Thomas (MN)
The U of Scranton (PA)
U of South Dakota (SD)
U of Southern California (CA)
The U of Tennessee at Chattanooga (TN)
The U of Texas at Austin (TX)
U of the Pacific (CA)
U of the South (TN)
U of Toronto (ON, Canada)
U of Vermont (VT)
U of Victoria (BC, Canada)
U of Washington (WA)
The U of Western Ontario (ON, Canada)
U of Windsor (ON, Canada)
The U of Winnipeg (MB, Canada)
U of Wisconsin–Madison (WI)
U of Wisconsin–Milwaukee (WI)
Ursinus Coll (PA)
Valparaiso U (IN)
Vassar Coll (NY)
Wabash Coll (IN)
Wake Forest U (NC)
Washington U in St. Louis (MO)
Wellesley Coll (MA)
West Chester U of Pennsylvania (PA)
Western Michigan U (MI)
Westminster Coll (PA)
Wheaton Coll (IL)
Wichita State U (KS)
Wilfrid Laurier U (ON, Canada)
Wright State U (OH)
Yale U (CT)
York U (ON, Canada)
Youngstown State U (OH)

(PRE)LAW

Abilene Christian U (TX)
Acadia U (NS, Canada)
Adams State Coll (CO)
Albertson Coll of Idaho (ID)
Albertus Magnus Coll (CT)
Albion Coll (MI)
Albright Coll (PA)
Alderson-Broaddus Coll (WV)
Alfred U (NY)
Alice Lloyd Coll (KY)
Alma Coll (MI)
Alvernia Coll (PA)
American International Coll (MA)
American U (DC)
Anderson U (IN)
Andrews U (MI)
Antioch Coll (OH)
Aquinas Coll (MI)
Arizona State U (AZ)
Ashland U (OH)
Atlantic Union Coll (MA)
Auburn U (AL)
Augsburg Coll (MN)

Augustana Coll (IL)
Augustana Coll (SD)
Austin Coll (TX)
Averett Coll (VA)
Avila Coll (MO)
Azusa Pacific U (CA)
Baker U (KS)
Baldwin-Wallace Coll (OH)
Ball State U (IN)
Barber-Scotia Coll (NC)
Bard Coll (NY)
Barry U (FL)
Bartlesville Wesleyan Coll (OK)
Barton Coll (NC)
Baylor U (TX)
Beaver Coll (PA)
Bellarmine Coll (KY)
Belmont Abbey Coll (NC)
Belmont U (TN)
Beloit Coll (WI)
Bemidji State U (MN)
Benedictine Coll (KS)
Benedictine U (IL)
Berry Coll (GA)
Bethany Coll (WV)
Bethel Coll (IN)
Bethel Coll (MN)
Biola U (CA)
Birmingham-Southern Coll (AL)
Blackburn Coll (IL)
Blue Mountain Coll (MS)
Bluffton Coll (OH)
Bowling Green State U (OH)
Brandeis U (MA)
Brandon U (MB, Canada)
Brevard Coll (NC)
Briar Cliff Coll (IA)
Bridgewater State Coll (MA)
Buena Vista U (IA)
California Lutheran U (CA)
California State Polytechnic U, Pomona (CA)
California State U, Dominguez Hills (CA)
California State U, Fresno (CA)
California State U, Fullerton (CA)
California State U, Northridge (CA)
Calumet Coll of Saint Joseph (IN)
Calvin Coll (MI)
Campbellsville U (KY)
Campbell U (NC)
Capital U (OH)
Cardinal Stritch U (WI)
Carleton U (ON, Canada)
Carroll Coll (MT)
Carthage Coll (WI)
Catawba Coll (NC)
Cedar Crest Coll (PA)
Cedarville Coll (OH)
Centenary Coll of Louisiana (LA)
Central Christian Coll of Kansas (KS)
Centre Coll (KY)
Chadron State Coll (NE)
Chapman U (CA)
Charleston Southern U (SC)
Chicago State U (IL)
Chowan Coll (NC)
Christian Brothers U (TN)
Christopher Newport U (VA)
City Coll of the City U of NY (NY)
Claremont McKenna Coll (CA)
Clarkson U (NY)
Clark U (MA)
Clemson U (SC)
Coe Coll (IA)
Coker Coll (SC)
Coll Misericordia (PA)
Coll of Mount Saint Vincent (NY)
The Coll of New Jersey (NJ)
The Coll of New Rochelle (NY)
Coll of Notre Dame (CA)
Coll of Notre Dame of Maryland (MD)
Coll of Our Lady of the Elms (MA)
Coll of Saint Benedict (MN)
Coll of St. Catherine (MN)
Coll of Saint Elizabeth (NJ)
Coll of St. Joseph (VT)
Coll of Saint Mary (NE)
Coll of Santa Fe (NM)
Coll of Staten Island of the City U of NY (NY)
Coll of the Holy Cross (MA)
The Coll of Wooster (OH)
Colorado State U (CO)
Columbia Coll (MO)

Columbia Coll (SC)
Columbia Union Coll (MD)
Columbus State U (GA)
Concordia Coll (MI)
Concordia Coll (MN)
Concordia Coll (NY)
Concordia U (CA)
Concordia U (IL)
Concordia U at Austin (TX)
Concordia U Wisconsin (WI)
Converse Coll (SC)
Coppin State Coll (MD)
Cornell U (NY)
Cornerstone U (MI)
Covenant Coll (GA)
Crichton Coll (TN)
Cumberland Coll (KY)
Curry Coll (MA)
Dakota State U (SD)
Dakota Wesleyan U (SD)
Dalhousie U (NS, Canada)
David Lipscomb U (TN)
Defiance Coll (OH)
DePaul U (IL)
Dickinson Coll (PA)
Dickinson State U (ND)
Dominican Coll of Blauvelt (NY)
Dominican U (IL)
Drake U (IA)
Drury U (MO)
D'Youville Coll (NY)
Earlham Coll (IN)
East Central U (OK)
Eastern Illinois U (IL)
Eastern Kentucky U (KY)
Eastern Nazarene Coll (MA)
Eastern Oregon U (OR)
Eastern Washington U (WA)
Eckerd Coll (FL)
Edgewood Coll (WI)
Elizabethtown Coll (PA)
Elmhurst Coll (IL)
Elmira Coll (NY)
Elon Coll (NC)
Emerson Coll (MA)
Emmanuel Coll (GA)
Emmanuel Coll (MA)
Emory & Henry Coll (VA)
Evangel U (MO)
The Evergreen State Coll (WA)
Fairleigh Dickinson U, Teaneck-Hackensack Campus (NJ)
Faulkner U (AL)
Felician Coll (NJ)
Florida State U (FL)
Fontbonne Coll (MO)
Fordham U (NY)
Fort Hays State U (KS)
Fort Lewis Coll (CO)
Framingham State Coll (MA)
Franciscan U of Steubenville (OH)
Francis Marion U (SC)
Franklin Pierce Coll (NH)
Freed-Hardeman U (TN)
Fresno Pacific U (CA)
Frostburg State U (MD)
Furman U (SC)
Gannon U (PA)
Gardner-Webb U (NC)
George Mason U (VA)
Georgetown Coll (KY)
The George Washington U (DC)
Georgian Court Coll (NJ)
Georgia Southwestern State U (GA)
Gettysburg Coll (PA)
Glenville State Coll (WV)
Goshen Coll (IN)
Graceland Coll (IA)
Grand Canyon U (AZ)
Grand Valley State U (MI)
Grand View Coll (IA)
Greenville Coll (IL)
Grove City Coll (PA)
Guilford Coll (NC)
Gustavus Adolphus Coll (MN)
Gwynedd-Mercy Coll (PA)
Hamline U (MN)
Hampton U (VA)
Harding U (AR)
Hardin-Simmons U (TX)
Hartwick Coll (NY)
Harvard U (MA)
Hastings Coll (NE)
Haverford Coll (PA)
Heidelberg Coll (OH)
High Point U (NC)

Hiram Coll (OH)
Hobart and William Smith Colls (NY)
Holy Family Coll (PA)
Hood Coll (MD)
Houghton Coll (NY)
Houston Baptist U (TX)
Howard Payne U (TX)
Humboldt State U (CA)
Huntingdon Coll (AL)
Huntington Coll (IN)
Illinois Coll (IL)
Illinois Wesleyan U (IL)
Immaculata Coll (PA)
Indiana State U (IN)
Indiana U Bloomington (IN)
Indiana U–Purdue U Indianapolis (IN)
Indiana Wesleyan U (IN)
Iowa State U of Science and Technology (IA)
Iowa Wesleyan Coll (IA)
Ithaca Coll (NY)
Jacksonville U (FL)
John Brown U (AR)
John Carroll U (OH)
John Jay Coll of Criminal Justice, the City U of NY (NY)
Johnson C. Smith U (NC)
Judson Coll (IL)
Juniata Coll (PA)
Kent State U (OH)
Kentucky Wesleyan Coll (KY)
King Coll (TN)
King's Coll (PA)
LaGrange Coll (GA)
Lake Erie Coll (OH)
Lake Forest Coll (IL)
Lakeland Coll (WI)
Lake Superior State U (MI)
Lambuth U (TN)
Lander U (SC)
Langston U (OK)
La Sierra U (CA)
Lawrence U (WI)
Lebanon Valley Coll (PA)
Lees-McRae Coll (NC)
Le Moyne Coll (NY)
Lenoir-Rhyne Coll (NC)
LeTourneau U (TX)
Lewis & Clark Coll (OR)
Lewis-Clark State Coll (ID)
Lewis U (IL)
Limestone Coll (SC)
Lincoln Memorial U (TN)
Lindenwood U (MO)
Lindsey Wilson Coll (KY)
Lock Haven U of Pennsylvania (PA)
Long Island U, Brooklyn Campus (NY)
Long Island U, C.W. Post Campus (NY)
Long Island U, Southampton Coll (NY)
Longwood Coll (VA)
Louisiana Coll (LA)
Lourdes Coll (OH)
Loyola U Chicago (IL)
Lubbock Christian U (TX)
Luther Coll (IA)
Lycoming Coll (PA)
Lynchburg Coll (VA)
Lynn U (FL)
MacMurray Coll (IL)
Madonna U (MI)
Maharishi U of Management (IA)
Malone Coll (OH)
Manchester Coll (IN)
Manhattan Coll (NY)
Manhattanville Coll (NY)
Mansfield U of Pennsylvania (PA)
Marian Coll (IN)
Marian Coll of Fond du Lac (WI)
Marietta Coll (OH)
Marist Coll (NY)
Marlboro Coll (VT)
Marquette U (WI)
Marshall U (WV)
Mars Hill Coll (NC)
Marycrest International U (IA)
Marymount Coll (NY)
Maryville Coll (TN)
Maryville U of Saint Louis (MO)
Mary Washington Coll (VA)
Marywood U (PA)

Majors Index
(Pre)Law–Law Enforcement/Police Science

Massachusetts Coll of Liberal Arts (MA)
Massachusetts Inst of Technology (MA)
Mayville State U (ND)
McKendree Coll (IL)
McMurry U (TX)
Medaille Coll (NY)
Mercy Coll (NY)
Mercyhurst Coll (PA)
Merrimack Coll (MA)
Methodist Coll (NC)
Miami U (OH)
Michigan State U (MI)
Middlebury Coll (VT)
Midland Lutheran Coll (NE)
Midwestern State U (TX)
Millikin U (IL)
Minnesota State U, Mankato (MN)
Minnesota State U Moorhead (MN)
Minot State U (ND)
Mississippi Coll (MS)
Missouri Valley Coll (MO)
Molloy Coll (NY)
Montreat Coll (NC)
Morgan State U (MD)
Morningside Coll (IA)
Mount Allison U (NB, Canada)
Mount Aloysius Coll (PA)
Mount Mary Coll (WI)
Mount Mercy Coll (IA)
Mount St. Clare Coll (IA)
Mount Saint Mary Coll (NY)
Mount St. Mary's Coll (CA)
Mount Saint Mary's Coll and Seminary (MD)
Mount Senario Coll (WI)
Mount Vernon Nazarene Coll (OH)
Muhlenberg Coll (PA)
Muskingum Coll (OH)
Nazareth Coll of Rochester (NY)
Newberry Coll (SC)
Newbury Coll (MA)
New England Coll (NH)
New Jersey Inst of Technology (NJ)
Newman U (KS)
New Mexico Highlands U (NM)
New Mexico State U (NM)
New York U (NY)
Niagara U (NY)
North Central Coll (IL)
North Dakota State U (ND)
Northeastern State U (OK)
Northeastern U (MA)
Northern Arizona U (AZ)
Northern Kentucky U (KY)
Northern Michigan U (MI)
Northern State U (SD)
Northland Coll (WI)
North Park U (IL)
Northwest Coll (WA)
Northwestern Oklahoma State U (OK)
Northwest Missouri State U (MO)
Northwest Nazarene U (ID)
Notre Dame Coll (NH)
Notre Dame Coll of Ohio (OH)
Nova Southeastern U (FL)
Oakland City U (IN)
Oakland U (MI)
Oglethorpe U (GA)
The Ohio State U (OH)
Ohio U (OH)
Ohio Wesleyan U (OH)
Oklahoma Baptist U (OK)
Oklahoma Christian U of Science and Arts (OK)
Oklahoma City U (OK)
Oklahoma State U (OK)
Olivet Nazarene U (IL)
Otterbein Coll (OH)
Pacific Union Coll (CA)
Palm Beach Atlantic Coll (FL)
Pepperdine U, Malibu (CA)
Peru State Coll (NE)
Pfeiffer U (NC)
Piedmont Coll (GA)
Pittsburg State U (KS)
Point Park Coll (PA)
Polytechnic U, Brooklyn Campus (NY)
Polytechnic U, Farmingdale Campus (NY)
Pontifical Catholic U of Puerto Rico (PR)
Presbyterian Coll (SC)
Purdue U Calumet (IN)

Queens Coll (NC)
Queens Coll of the City U of NY (NY)
Quinnipiac U (CT)
Redeemer Coll (ON, Canada)
Regis U (CO)
Rensselaer Polytechnic Inst (NY)
Ripon Coll (WI)
Rivier Coll (NH)
Roberts Wesleyan Coll (NY)
Rochester Inst of Technology (NY)
Rockford Coll (IL)
Rocky Mountain Coll (MT)
Rollins Coll (FL)
Rowan U (NJ)
Rust Coll (MS)
Rutgers, State U of NJ, Camden Coll of Arts & Scis (NJ)
Rutgers, State U of NJ, Cook Coll (NJ)
Rutgers, State U of NJ, Douglass Coll (NJ)
Rutgers, State U of NJ, Livingston Coll (NJ)
Rutgers, State U of NJ, Newark Coll of Arts & Scis (NJ)
Rutgers, State U of NJ, Rutgers Coll (NJ)
Rutgers, State U of NJ, U Coll–Camden (NJ)
St. Andrews Presbyterian Coll (NC)
Saint Anselm Coll (NH)
St. Bonaventure U (NY)
St. Cloud State U (MN)
St. Francis Coll (NY)
Saint Francis Coll (PA)
St. Francis Xavier U (NS, Canada)
Saint John's U (MN)
Saint Joseph Coll (CT)
Saint Joseph's Coll (ME)
St. Joseph's Coll, New York (NY)
St. Joseph's Coll, Suffolk Campus (NY)
Saint Leo U (FL)
Saint Louis U (MO)
Saint Martin's Coll (WA)
Saint Mary-of-the-Woods Coll (IN)
Saint Mary's Coll (MI)
Saint Mary's Coll of California (CA)
Saint Mary's Coll (NS, Canada)
Saint Mary's U of Minnesota (MN)
Saint Michael's Coll (VT)
St. Norbert Coll (WI)
St. Olaf Coll (MN)
St. Thomas U (FL)
Saint Xavier U (IL)
Salem State Coll (MA)
Salve Regina U (RI)
Samford U (AL)
San Diego State U (CA)
Sarah Lawrence Coll (NY)
Schreiner Coll (TX)
Seattle Pacific U (WA)
Seton Hill Coll (PA)
Shawnee State U (OH)
Siena Coll (NY)
Siena Heights U (MI)
Simmons Coll (MA)
Simon's Rock Coll of Bard (MA)
Simpson Coll (IA)
Sonoma State U (CA)
South Dakota State U (SD)
Southeast Missouri State U (MO)
Southern Oregon U (OR)
Southwestern Oklahoma State U (OK)
Southwest State U (MN)
Spalding U (KY)
State U of NY at Binghamton (NY)
State U of NY at New Paltz (NY)
State U of NY at Oswego (NY)
State U of NY Coll at Brockport (NY)
State U of NY Coll at Buffalo (NY)
State U of NY Coll at Cortland (NY)
State U of NY Coll at Fredonia (NY)
State U of NY Coll at Geneseo (NY)
State U of NY Coll at Oneonta (NY)
State U of NY Coll of Environ Sci and Forestry (NY)
State U of West Georgia (GA)
Stephen F. Austin State U (TX)
Stephens Coll (MO)
Stetson U (FL)

Stevens Inst of Technology (NJ)
Stonehill Coll (MA)
Suffolk U (MA)
Sul Ross State U (TX)
Susquehanna U (PA)
Syracuse U (NY)
Tabor Coll (KS)
Talladega Coll (AL)
Taylor U (IN)
Taylor U, Fort Wayne Campus (IN)
Tennessee Technological U (TN)
Tennessee Wesleyan Coll (TN)
Texas A&M U–Kingsville (TX)
Texas Lutheran U (TX)
Texas Wesleyan U (TX)
Thiel Coll (PA)
Thomas More Coll (KY)
Touro Coll (NY)
Trinity U (TX)
Trinity Western U (BC, Canada)
Tri-State U (IN)
Truman State U (MO)
Tusculum Coll (TN)
Union Coll (KY)
Union U (TN)
United States Military Academy (NY)
U Coll of Cape Breton (NS, Canada)
The U of Akron (OH)
U of Alaska Fairbanks (AK)
U of Alberta (AB, Canada)
U of Arkansas at Monticello (AR)
U of Bridgeport (CT)
U of British Columbia (BC, Canada)
U of Calif, Riverside (CA)
U of Charleston (WV)
U of Cincinnati (OH)
U of Colorado at Colorado Springs (CO)
U of Dallas (TX)
U of Dayton (OH)
U of Detroit Mercy (MI)
U of Evansville (IN)
U of Great Falls (MT)
U of Houston (TX)
U of Illinois at Chicago (IL)
U of Indianapolis (IN)
The U of Iowa (IA)
U of La Verne (CA)
The U of Lethbridge (AB, Canada)
U of Louisiana at Lafayette (LA)
U of Louisiana at Monroe (LA)
U of Manitoba (MB, Canada)
U of Mary Hardin-Baylor (TX)
U of Maryland, Baltimore County (MD)
U of Minnesota, Duluth (MN)
U of Minnesota, Morris (MN)
U of Minnesota, Twin Cities Campus (MN)
U of Missouri–Rolla (MO)
U of Missouri–St. Louis (MO)
The U of Montana–Missoula (MT)
U of Montevallo (AL)
U of Nebraska at Omaha (NE)
U of Nebraska–Lincoln (NE)
U of New Brunswick, Fredericton (NB, Canada)
U of New England (ME)
The U of North Carolina at Greensboro (NC)
The U of North Carolina at Pembroke (NC)
U of Pennsylvania (PA)
U of Pittsburgh at Bradford (PA)
U of Pittsburgh at Johnstown (PA)
U of Portland (OR)
U of Puget Sound (WA)
U of Regina (SK, Canada)
U of Rio Grande (OH)
U of Saint Francis (IN)
U of St. Thomas (TX)
U of San Diego (CA)
U of San Francisco (CA)
U of Sioux Falls (SD)
U of South Alabama (AL)
U of South Dakota (SD)
U of Southern Colorado (CO)
The U of Tampa (FL)
U of the Pacific (CA)
U of Toronto (ON, Canada)
U of Tulsa (OK)
U of Victoria (BC, Canada)
U of Windsor (ON, Canada)
The U of Winnipeg (MB, Canada)

U of Wisconsin–La Crosse (WI)
U of Wisconsin–Milwaukee (WI)
U of Wisconsin–Parkside (WI)
U of Wisconsin–River Falls (WI)
U of Wisconsin–Superior (WI)
U of Wisconsin–Whitewater (WI)
Urbana U (OH)
Ursinus Coll (PA)
Ursuline Coll (OH)
Utah State U (UT)
Utica Coll of Syracuse U (NY)
Valdosta State U (GA)
Valley City State U (ND)
Vanguard U of Southern California (CA)
Villa Julie Coll (MD)
Villanova U (PA)
Virginia Commonwealth U (VA)
Virginia Intermont Coll (VA)
Virginia Wesleyan Coll (VA)
Wabash Coll (IN)
Wagner Coll (NY)
Walla Walla Coll (WA)
Walsh U (OH)
Warner Pacific Coll (OR)
Warner Southern Coll (FL)
Washington Coll (MD)
Washington State U (WA)
Washington U in St. Louis (MO)
Wayland Baptist U (TX)
Waynesburg Coll (PA)
Webber Coll (FL)
Wells Coll (NY)
West Chester U of Pennsylvania (PA)
Western Baptist Coll (OR)
Western Maryland Coll (MD)
Western Montana Coll of The U of Montana (MT)
Western State Coll of Colorado (CO)
Western Washington U (WA)
Westfield State Coll (MA)
West Liberty State Coll (WV)
Westminster Coll (MO)
Westminster Coll (PA)
Westmont Coll (CA)
West Virginia Wesleyan Coll (WV)
Whitworth Coll (WA)
Wilkes U (PA)
Willamette U (OR)
William Jewell Coll (MO)
William Paterson U of New Jersey (NJ)
William Penn U (IA)
Williams Baptist Coll (AR)
William Tyndale Coll (MI)
William Woods U (MO)
Wilmington Coll (OH)
Wingate U (NC)
Winona State U (MN)
Wittenberg U (OH)
Wofford Coll (SC)
Worcester Polytechnic Inst (MA)
Xavier U of Louisiana (LA)
Yeshiva U (NY)
York Coll (NE)
York Coll of Pennsylvania (PA)
York U (ON, Canada)
Youngstown State U (OH)

LAW AND LEGAL STUDIES
American U (DC)
Amherst Coll (MA)
Avila Coll (MO)
Bay Path Coll (MA)
Becker Coll (MA)
California State U, Chico (CA)
Chapman U (CA)
Christopher Newport U (VA)
Claremont McKenna Coll (CA)
Coll of Our Lady of the Elms (MA)
Coll of the Atlantic (ME)
The Coll of West Virginia (WV)
Concordia U (IL)
DePaul U (IL)
East Central U (OK)
Gannon U (PA)
Grand Valley State U (MI)
Hamline U (MN)
Hampshire Coll (MA)
Hilbert Coll (NY)
Hood Coll (MD)
Inst of Public Administration (Ireland)
Insto Tecno Estudios Sups Monterrey (Mexico)

John Jay Coll of Criminal Justice, the City U of NY (NY)
Lake Superior State U (MI)
Manhattanville Coll (NY)
Marshall U (WV)
Marymount Coll (NY)
Marywood U (PA)
McGill U (PQ, Canada)
Methodist Coll (NC)
Mount Ida Coll (MA)
National U (CA)
Newbury Coll (MA)
New England Coll (NH)
North Carolina Wesleyan Coll (NC)
Northeastern U (MA)
Nova Southeastern U (FL)
Oberlin Coll (OH)
Park U (MO)
Pennsylvania Coll of Technology (PA)
Point Park Coll (PA)
Quinnipiac U (CT)
Ramapo Coll of New Jersey (NJ)
Rivier Coll (NH)
Schreiner Coll (TX)
Scripps Coll (CA)
South Coll (FL)
State U of NY Coll at Fredonia (NY)
Suffolk U (MA)
Texas Wesleyan U (TX)
Towson U (MD)
United States Air Force Academy (CO)
Université de Montréal (PQ, Canada)
Université de Sherbrooke (PQ, Canada)
Université Laval (PQ, Canada)
U of Alberta (AB, Canada)
U of Baltimore (MD)
U of Calgary (AB, Canada)
U of Calif, Berkeley (CA)
U of Calif, Santa Barbara (CA)
U of Calif, Santa Cruz (CA)
U of Detroit Mercy (MI)
U of Evansville (IN)
U of Hartford (CT)
U of Houston–Clear Lake (TX)
U of Illinois at Springfield (IL)
U of Massachusetts Amherst (MA)
U of Massachusetts Boston (MA)
U of Miami (FL)
The U of Montana–Missoula (MT)
U of New Brunswick, Fredericton (NB, Canada)
U of Pennsylvania (PA)
U of Pittsburgh (PA)
The U of Tennessee at Chattanooga (TN)
U of Windsor (ON, Canada)
U of Wisconsin–Superior (WI)
Valdosta State U (GA)
Villa Julie Coll (MD)
Webster U (MO)
William Woods U (MO)
Wilson Coll (PA)
Winona State U (MN)
York U (ON, Canada)

LAW ENFORCEMENT/POLICE SCIENCE
American International Coll (MA)
Becker Coll (MA)
Bemidji State U (MN)
Boise State U (ID)
California State U, Hayward (CA)
Carleton U (ON, Canada)
Champlain Coll (VT)
Chicago State U (IL)
Coll of the Ozarks (MO)
Dakota Wesleyan U (SD)
Defiance Coll (OH)
East Central U (OK)
Eastern Kentucky U (KY)
Fairmont State Coll (WV)
Ferris State U (MI)
George Mason U (VA)
Grand Valley State U (MI)
Hannibal-LaGrange Coll (MO)
Hardin-Simmons U (TX)
Howard U (DC)
Indiana State U (IN)
Jacksonville State U (AL)
John Jay Coll of Criminal Justice, the City U of NY (NY)
Lake Superior State U (MI)

Majors Index
Law Enforcement/Police Science–Literature

Lamar U (TX)
Langston U (OK)
Lewis-Clark State Coll (ID)
Louisiana Coll (LA)
MacMurray Coll (IL)
Madonna U (MI)
Mansfield U of Pennsylvania (PA)
Marshall U (WV)
Memorial U of Newfoundland (NF, Canada)
Mercyhurst Coll (PA)
Metropolitan State U (MN)
Minnesota State U, Mankato (MN)
Mississippi Coll (MS)
Missouri Southern State Coll (MO)
Mount Senario Coll (WI)
Northeastern State U (OK)
Northeastern U (MA)
Northern Michigan U (MI)
Northern State U (SD)
Northwestern Oklahoma State U (OK)
Oklahoma City U (OK)
Purdue U Calumet (IN)
Rowan U (NJ)
Saint Louis U (MO)
Sam Houston State U (TX)
Southeast Missouri State U (MO)
Southwest Texas State U (TX)
State U of NY Coll of Technology at Canton (NY)
Stephen F. Austin State U (TX)
Texas A&M U–Commerce (TX)
Texas Southern U (TX)
Tiffin U (OH)
Truman State U (MO)
U of Cincinnati (OH)
The U of Tennessee at Chattanooga (TN)
The U of Texas–Pan American (TX)
U of Toronto (ON, Canada)
The U of Winnipeg (MB, Canada)
U of Wisconsin–Milwaukee (WI)
Utica Coll of Syracuse U (NY)
Virginia Commonwealth U (VA)
Wartburg Coll (IA)
Wayne State Coll (NE)
Weber State U (UT)
West Chester U of Pennsylvania (PA)
Western Connecticut State U (CT)
Western Oregon U (OR)
Western State Coll of Colorado (CO)
Winona State U (MN)
York Coll of Pennsylvania (PA)
Youngstown State U (OH)

LEGAL ADMINISTRATIVE ASSISTANT
Ball State U (IN)
Davenport Coll of Business, Kalamazoo Campus (MI)
Eastern Michigan U (MI)
Northwest Missouri State U (MO)
Peirce Coll (PA)
Robert Morris Coll (IL)
South Coll (FL)
Tabor Coll (KS)
Texas A&M U–Commerce (TX)

LIBRARY SCIENCE
Appalachian State U (NC)
Clarion U of Pennsylvania (PA)
Concord Coll (WV)
Florida State U (FL)
Indiana State U (IN)
Inter American U of PR, Metropolitan Campus (PR)
Kutztown U of Pennsylvania (PA)
Lakehead U (ON, Canada)
Longwood Coll (VA)
Murray State U (KY)
Northeastern State U (OK)
Ohio Dominican Coll (OH)
St. Cloud State U (MN)
Spalding U (KY)
Texas Woman's U (TX)
U of Central Oklahoma (OK)
U of Nebraska at Omaha (NE)
U of Southern Mississippi (MS)
U of the District of Columbia (DC)
Western Kentucky U (KY)

LINGUISTICS
Bartlesville Wesleyan Coll (OK)
Baylor U (TX)
Boston U (MA)
Brandeis U (MA)
Brigham Young U (UT)
Brock U (ON, Canada)
Brooklyn Coll of the City U of NY (NY)
Brown U (RI)
California State U, Dominguez Hills (CA)
California State U, Fresno (CA)
California State U, Fullerton (CA)
California State U, Northridge (CA)
Carleton U (ON, Canada)
Central Coll (IA)
City Coll of the City U of NY (NY)
Cleveland State U (OH)
The Coll of William and Mary (VA)
Concordia U (PQ, Canada)
Cornell U (NY)
Crown Coll (MN)
Dalhousie U (NS, Canada)
Dartmouth Coll (NH)
DePaul U (IL)
Duke U (NC)
Eastern Michigan U (MI)
Florida Atlantic U (FL)
Florida State U (FL)
Georgetown U (DC)
Grinnell Coll (IA)
Hampshire Coll (MA)
Harvard U (MA)
Indiana State U (IN)
Indiana U Bloomington (IN)
Inter American U of PR, San Germán Campus (PR)
Iowa State U of Science and Technology (IA)
Judson Coll (IL)
Lawrence U (WI)
Lehman Coll of the City U of NY (NY)
Long Island U, Southampton Coll, Friends World Program (NY)
Macalester Coll (MN)
Marlboro Coll (VT)
Massachusetts Inst of Technology (MA)
McGill U (PQ, Canada)
Memorial U of Newfoundland (NF, Canada)
Miami U (OH)
Michigan State U (MI)
Millersville U of Pennsylvania (PA)
Moody Bible Inst (IL)
New York U (NY)
Northeastern Illinois U (IL)
Northeastern U (MA)
Northwestern U (IL)
Oakland U (MI)
The Ohio State U (OH)
Ohio U (OH)
Pitzer Coll (CA)
Pomona Coll (CA)
Portland State U (OR)
Queens Coll of the City U of NY (NY)
Queen's U at Kingston (ON, Canada)
Reed Coll (OR)
Rice U (TX)
Rutgers, State U of NJ, Douglass Coll (NJ)
Rutgers, State U of NJ, Livingston Coll (NJ)
Rutgers, State U of NJ, Rutgers Coll (NJ)
Rutgers, State U of NJ, U Coll–New Brunswick (NJ)
St. Cloud State U (MN)
San Diego State U (CA)
San Jose State U (CA)
Scripps Coll (CA)
Simon Fraser U (BC, Canada)
Southern Illinois U Carbondale (IL)
Stanford U (CA)
State U of NY at Albany (NY)
State U of NY at Binghamton (NY)
State U of NY at Buffalo (NY)
State U of NY at Oswego (NY)
State U of NY at Stony Brook (NY)
Swarthmore Coll (PA)
Syracuse U (NY)
Temple U (PA)
Trinity Western U (BC, Canada)
Tulane U (LA)
Université de Montréal (PQ, Canada)
U du Québec à Chicoutimi (PQ, Canada)
U of Alaska Fairbanks (AK)
U of Alberta (AB, Canada)
The U of Arizona (AZ)
U of British Columbia (BC, Canada)
U of Calgary (AB, Canada)
U of Calif, Berkeley (CA)
U of Calif, Davis (CA)
U of Calif, Irvine (CA)
U of Calif, Los Angeles (CA)
U of Calif, Riverside (CA)
U of Calif, San Diego (CA)
U of Calif, Santa Barbara (CA)
U of Calif, Santa Cruz (CA)
U of Chicago (IL)
U of Cincinnati (OH)
U of Colorado at Boulder (CO)
U of Connecticut (CT)
U of Delaware (DE)
U of Florida (FL)
U of Georgia (GA)
U of Illinois at Urbana–Champaign (IL)
The U of Iowa (IA)
U of Kansas (KS)
U of Kentucky (KY)
U of King's Coll (NS, Canada)
U of Maryland, Baltimore County (MD)
U of Maryland, Coll Park (MD)
U of Massachusetts Amherst (MA)
U of Michigan (MI)
U of Minnesota, Twin Cities Campus (MN)
U of Mississippi (MS)
U of Missouri–Columbia (MO)
U of Missouri–St. Louis (MO)
The U of Montana–Missoula (MT)
U of Nevada, Las Vegas (NV)
U of New Brunswick, Fredericton (NB, Canada)
U of New Hampshire (NH)
U of New Mexico (NM)
The U of North Carolina at Chapel Hill (NC)
The U of North Carolina at Greensboro (NC)
U of Northern Iowa (IA)
U of Oklahoma (OK)
U of Oregon (OR)
U of Pennsylvania (PA)
U of Pittsburgh (PA)
U of Regina (SK, Canada)
U of Rochester (NY)
U of Southern California (CA)
U of Southern Maine (ME)
The U of Texas at Austin (TX)
U of Toronto (ON, Canada)
U of Utah (UT)
U of Victoria (BC, Canada)
U of Washington (WA)
The U of Western Ontario (ON, Canada)
U of Windsor (ON, Canada)
U of Wisconsin–Madison (WI)
U of Wisconsin–Milwaukee (WI)
Washington State U (WA)
Wayne State U (MI)
Wellesley Coll (MA)
Western Washington U (WA)
Yale U (CT)
York U (ON, Canada)

LITERATURE
Agnes Scott Coll (GA)
Alderson-Broaddus Coll (WV)
Alfred U (NY)
Alma Coll (MI)
American U (DC)
Anderson Coll (SC)
Antioch Coll (OH)
Augustana Coll (IL)
Barat Coll (IL)
Bard Coll (NY)
Barry U (FL)
Beaver Coll (PA)
Beloit Coll (WI)
Bennington Coll (VT)
Baruch Coll of the City U of NY (NY)
Bethel Coll (MN)
Bishop's U (PQ, Canada)
Blackburn Coll (IL)
Boise State U (ID)
Brandeis U (MA)
Brevard Coll (NC)
Brock U (ON, Canada)
Brown U (RI)
Bryan Coll (TN)
Burlington Coll (VT)
California Inst of Technology (CA)
California State U, Dominguez Hills (CA)
California State U, Long Beach (CA)
California State U, Northridge (CA)
Capital U (OH)
Carnegie Mellon U (PA)
Carroll Coll (WI)
Carson-Newman Coll (TN)
Castleton State Coll (VT)
Cazenovia Coll (NY)
Centenary Coll of Louisiana (LA)
Chapman U (CA)
Chicago State U (IL)
Christendom Coll (VA)
Christopher Newport U (VA)
City Coll of the City U of NY (NY)
Claremont McKenna Coll (CA)
Clark U (MA)
Coe Coll (IA)
The Coll of New Rochelle (NY)
Coll of St. Catherine (MN)
Coll of Staten Island of the City U of NY (NY)
Coll of the Atlantic (ME)
Coll of the Holy Cross (MA)
Columbia Coll (SC)
Columbia U, School of General Studies (NY)
Columbus State U (GA)
Concordia U (NE)
Concordia U (PQ, Canada)
Concordia U at St. Paul (MN)
Dalhousie U (NS, Canada)
Defiance Coll (OH)
DePaul U (IL)
Drexel U (PA)
Duke U (NC)
East Central U (OK)
Eastern Kentucky U (KY)
Eastern Nazarene Coll (MA)
Eastern Washington U (WA)
Eckerd Coll (FL)
Elmira Coll (NY)
Emmanuel Coll (MA)
Emory U (GA)
Eugene Lang Coll, New School U (NY)
The Evergreen State Coll (WA)
Fairleigh Dickinson U, Florham-Madison Campus (NJ)
Fitchburg State Coll (MA)
Florida State U (FL)
Fordham U (NY)
Fort Lewis Coll (CO)
Framingham State Coll (MA)
Franklin Coll Switzerland (Switzerland)
Franklin Pierce Coll (NH)
Fresno Pacific U (CA)
Friends U (KS)
George Mason U (VA)
Gettysburg Coll (PA)
Goddard Coll (VT)
Gonzaga U (WA)
Graceland Coll (IA)
Grand Canyon U (AZ)
Grand Valley State U (MI)
Grove City Coll (PA)
Hamilton Coll (NY)
Hampshire Coll (MA)
Harvard U (MA)
Hastings Coll (NE)
Hawaii Pacific U (HI)
High Point U (NC)
Holy Family Coll (PA)
Houghton Coll (NY)
Hunter Coll of the City U of NY (NY)
Immaculata Coll (PA)
Indiana U Bloomington (IN)
Insto Tecno Estudios Sups Monterrey (Mexico)
Inter American U of PR, Metropolitan Campus (PR)
Inter American U of PR, San Germán Campus (PR)
Jewish Theological Seminary of America (NY)
John Carroll U (OH)
Johnson State Coll (VT)
Judson Coll (IL)
Kenyon Coll (OH)
Lakeland Coll (WI)
Lake Superior State U (MI)
La Salle U (PA)
Long Island U, Southampton Coll (NY)
Long Island U, Southampton Coll, Friends World Program (NY)
Loras Coll (IA)
Lycoming Coll (PA)
Maharishi U of Management (IA)
Manhattan Coll (NY)
Marist Coll (NY)
Marlboro Coll (VT)
Marymount Coll (NY)
Massachusetts Coll of Liberal Arts (MA)
Massachusetts Inst of Technology (MA)
McGill U (PQ, Canada)
Memorial U of Newfoundland (NF, Canada)
Middlebury Coll (VT)
Millersville U of Pennsylvania (PA)
Minnesota State U, Mankato (MN)
Missouri Southern State Coll (MO)
Montreat Coll (NC)
Morningside Coll (IA)
Mount Allison U (NB, Canada)
Mount Saint Vincent U (NS, Canada)
Mount Vernon Nazarene Coll (OH)
Naropa U (CO)
Nazareth Coll of Rochester (NY)
New Coll of the U of South Florida (FL)
New York U (NY)
North Central Coll (IL)
Northern Arizona U (AZ)
North Park U (IL)
Northwest Missouri State U (MO)
The Ohio State U (OH)
Ohio Wesleyan U (OH)
Olivet Nazarene U (IL)
Oregon State U (OR)
Otterbein Coll (OH)
Pace U, New York City Campus (NY)
Pace U, Pleasantville/Briarcliff Campus (NY)
Pacific Lutheran U (WA)
Pacific U (OR)
Penn State U Harrisburg Campus of the Capital Coll (PA)
Pitzer Coll (CA)
Purchase Coll, State U of NY (NY)
Purdue U Calumet (IN)
Queens Coll of the City U of NY (NY)
Quinnipiac U (CT)
Ramapo Coll of New Jersey (NJ)
Reed Coll (OR)
Regents Coll (NY)
Richmond, The American International U in London (United Kingdom)
Rochester Coll (MI)
Rockford Coll (IL)
Sacred Heart U (CT)
St. Andrews Presbyterian Coll (NC)
St. Edward's U (TX)
Saint Francis Coll (PA)
St. John's Coll (NM)
St. Joseph's Coll, New York (NY)
Saint Leo U (FL)
Saint Mary's Coll (IN)
Saint Mary's Coll of California (CA)
Salem State Coll (MA)
San Diego State U (CA)
San Francisco State U (CA)
Sarah Lawrence Coll (NY)
Schreiner Coll (TX)
Seton Hill Coll (PA)
Shimer Coll (IL)
Simon's Rock Coll of Bard (MA)
Skidmore Coll (NY)
Sonoma State U (CA)
Southeast Missouri State U (MO)
Southern Vermont Coll (VT)
Southwestern U (TX)
Southwest State U (MN)
State U of NY at Binghamton (NY)
State U of NY Coll at Brockport (NY)
State U of NY Coll at Old Westbury (NY)

Majors Index
Literature–Management Science

State U of NY Coll at Potsdam (NY)
Syracuse U (NY)
Taylor U (IN)
Thomas More Coll of Liberal Arts (NH)
Touro Coll (NY)
Trent U (ON, Canada)
United States Military Academy (NY)
Université de Montréal (PQ, Canada)
U du Québec à Chicoutimi (PQ, Canada)
The U of Akron (OH)
U of Alberta (AB, Canada)
U of Baltimore (MD)
U of Calif, Irvine (CA)
U of Calif, San Diego (CA)
U of Calif, Santa Cruz (CA)
U of Cincinnati (OH)
U of Evansville (IN)
U of Houston–Clear Lake (TX)
The U of Iowa (IA)
U of Judaism (CA)
U of Michigan (MI)
U of Missouri–St. Louis (MO)
U of New Brunswick, Fredericton (NB, Canada)
U of New Hampshire (NH)
The U of North Carolina at Pembroke (NC)
U of North Texas (TX)
U of Pittsburgh at Bradford (PA)
U of Pittsburgh at Johnstown (PA)
U of Redlands (CA)
The U of Texas at Dallas (TX)
U of the Sacred Heart (PR)
U of the South (TN)
U of Toronto (ON, Canada)
U of Victoria (BC, Canada)
U of Windsor (ON, Canada)
U of Wisconsin–Milwaukee (WI)
Washington U in St. Louis (MO)
Wayne State Coll (NE)
Webster U (MO)
West Chester U of Pennsylvania (PA)
Western Montana Coll of The U of Montana (MT)
Western Washington U (WA)
Westfield State Coll (MA)
Westminster Coll (MO)
West Virginia Wesleyan Coll (WV)
Wheaton Coll (MA)
Wilkes U (PA)
William Paterson U of New Jersey (NJ)
Williams Coll (MA)
Wittenberg U (OH)
Yale U (CT)
York U (ON, Canada)

LOGISTICS AND MATERIALS MANAGEMENT
Auburn U (AL)
Bowling Green State U (OH)
Central Michigan U (MI)
Duquesne U (PA)
Elmhurst Coll (IL)
Georgia Coll and State U (GA)
Georgia Southern U (GA)
Iowa State U of Science and Technology (IA)
Maine Maritime Academy (ME)
Northeastern U (MA)
The Ohio State U (OH)
Penn State U Univ Park Campus (PA)
Portland State U (OR)
St. John's U (NY)
State U of NY at Oswego (NY)
Thomas Edison State Coll (NJ)
U of Arkansas (AR)
U of Maryland, Coll Park (MD)
U of Nevada, Reno (NV)
U of North Texas (TX)
The U of Tennessee Knoxville (TN)
Wayne State U (MI)
Weber State U (UT)
Western Michigan U (MI)

MACHINE TECHNOLOGY
Indiana State U (IN)

MANAGEMENT INFORMATION SYSTEMS/BUSINESS DATA PROCESSING
Adrian Coll (MI)
Alderson-Broaddus Coll (WV)
Allentown Coll of St. Francis de Sales (PA)
Amber U (TX)
American Coll of Thessaloniki (Greece)
American InterContinental U (CA)
American InterContinental U, Atlanta (GA)
American InterContinental U (United Kingdom)
American International Coll (MA)
American U (DC)
Anderson U (IN)
Arizona State U (AZ)
Auburn U (AL)
Auburn U Montgomery (AL)
Augsburg Coll (MN)
Augustana Coll (SD)
Azusa Pacific U (CA)
Babson Coll (MA)
Baker Coll of Flint (MI)
Ball State U (IN)
Barry U (FL)
Bayamón Central U (PR)
Baylor U (TX)
Bay Path Coll (MA)
Beaver Coll (PA)
Bellevue U (NE)
Baruch Coll of the City U of NY (NY)
Bethel Coll (MN)
Bishop's U (PQ, Canada)
Boston Coll (MA)
Boston U (MA)
Bowling Green State U (OH)
Bridgewater Coll (VA)
Bridgewater State Coll (MA)
Buena Vista U (IA)
Cabrini Coll (PA)
California Polytechnic State U, San Luis Obispo (CA)
California State U, Chico (CA)
California State U, Dominguez Hills (CA)
California State U, Fresno (CA)
California State U, Fullerton (CA)
California State U, Hayward (CA)
California State U, Northridge (CA)
California State U, San Bernardino (CA)
Canisius Coll (NY)
Capitol Coll (MD)
Carleton U (ON, Canada)
Carson-Newman Coll (TN)
Central Connecticut State U (CT)
Central Michigan U (MI)
Central Missouri State U (MO)
Charleston Southern U (SC)
Chatham Coll (PA)
Chicago State U (IL)
Christian Brothers U (TN)
Clarke Coll (IA)
Clarkson U (NY)
Clayton Coll & State U (GA)
Cleary Coll (MI)
Coll Misericordia (PA)
The Coll of New Jersey (NJ)
Coll of St. Catherine (MN)
Coll of Santa Fe (NM)
Colorado Christian U (CO)
Colorado Tech U (CO)
Concordia U (NE)
Concordia U (PQ, Canada)
Concordia U at St. Paul (MN)
Creighton U (NE)
Dallas Baptist U (TX)
Dalton State Coll (GA)
Daniel Webster Coll (NH)
Delta State U (MS)
DePaul U (IL)
Detroit Coll of Business (MI)
Detroit Coll of Business–Flint (MI)
Dominican Coll of Blauvelt (NY)
Dordt Coll (IA)
Drexel U (PA)
Duquesne U (PA)
East Carolina U (NC)
Eastern Coll (PA)
Eastern Illinois U (IL)
Eastern Michigan U (MI)
Eastern New Mexico U (NM)
Eastern Washington U (WA)
École des Hautes Études Commerciales (PQ, Canada)
Elmhurst Coll (IL)
Fairfield U (CT)
Ferris State U (MI)
Florida Gulf Coast U (FL)
Florida Southern Coll (FL)
Florida State U (FL)
Fontbonne Coll (MO)
Fordham U (NY)
Gannon U (PA)
Gardner-Webb U (NC)
George Fox U (OR)
Georgetown Coll (KY)
Georgia Southern U (GA)
Goldey-Beacom Coll (DE)
Governors State U (IL)
Grace Coll (IN)
Graceland Coll (IA)
Grand Valley State U (MI)
Greenville Coll (IL)
Hawaii Pacific U (HI)
Henderson State U (AR)
Husson Coll (ME)
Illinois Coll (IL)
Indiana State U (IN)
Indiana U Bloomington (IN)
Indiana U of Pennsylvania (PA)
Insto Tecno Estudios Sups Monterrey, León (Mexico)
Insto Tecno Estudios Sups Monterrey (Mexico)
Inter American U of PR, Metropolitan Campus (PR)
Iona Coll (NY)
Iowa State U of Science and Technology (IA)
Jacksonville U (FL)
Jamestown Coll (ND)
Johnson State Coll (VT)
Judson Coll (IL)
Juniata Coll (PA)
Lakehead U (ON, Canada)
La Salle U (PA)
LeTourneau U (TX)
Lewis U (IL)
Lincoln U (CA)
Lindenwood U (MO)
Longwood Coll (VA)
Loras Coll (IA)
Louisiana Tech U (LA)
Loyola U Chicago (IL)
Luther Coll (IA)
MacMurray Coll (IL)
Marquette U (WI)
Maryville U of Saint Louis (MO)
Metropolitan State U (MN)
Miami U (OH)
Michigan Technological U (MI)
Middle Tennessee State U (TN)
Midland Lutheran Coll (NE)
Millikin U (IL)
Minnesota State U Moorhead (MN)
Minot State U (ND)
Mississippi State U (MS)
Missouri Southern State Coll (MO)
Montana State U–Billings (MT)
Montreat Coll (NC)
Morgan State U (MD)
Morningside Coll (IA)
Mount Saint Vincent U (NS, Canada)
Murray State U (KY)
National American U (MO)
National American U–St. Paul Campus (MN)
Nazareth Coll of Rochester (NY)
New Hampshire Coll (NH)
New Mexico Highlands U (NM)
New York Inst of Technology (NY)
New York U (NY)
Nicholls State U (LA)
Nichols Coll (MA)
North Central Coll (IL)
North Dakota State U (ND)
Northeastern U (MA)
Northern Arizona U (AZ)
Northern Kentucky U (KY)
Northern Michigan U (MI)
Northern State U (SD)
Northwestern Coll (MN)
Northwest Missouri State U (MO)
Northwood U, Florida Campus (FL)
Northwood U, Texas Campus (TX)
Oakland U (MI)
Ohio U (OH)
Oklahoma Baptist U (OK)
Oklahoma City U (OK)
Oklahoma State U (OK)
Old Dominion U (VA)
Oregon Inst of Technology (OR)
Oregon State U (OR)
Pace U, New York City Campus (NY)
Pacific Lutheran U (WA)
Pacific Union Coll (CA)
Penn State U at Erie, The Behrend Coll (PA)
Penn State U Univ Park Campus (PA)
Peru State Coll (NE)
Philadelphia U (PA)
Point Loma Nazarene U (CA)
Radford U (VA)
Regents Coll (NY)
Rensselaer Polytechnic Inst (NY)
Robert Morris Coll (IL)
Robert Morris Coll (PA)
Rochester Inst of Technology (NY)
Rockford Coll (IL)
Rocky Mountain Coll (MT)
Rowan U (NJ)
Saint Francis Coll (PA)
St. Francis Xavier U (NS, Canada)
St. John Fisher Coll (NY)
Saint Joseph's Coll (IN)
Saint Joseph's U (PA)
Saint Louis U (MO)
Saint Martin's Coll (WA)
Saint Mary's Coll (IN)
St. Norbert Coll (WI)
Salem State Coll (MA)
Salisbury State U (MD)
San Jose State U (CA)
Santa Clara U (CA)
Savannah State U (GA)
Seattle U (WA)
Seton Hall U (NJ)
Seton Hill Coll (PA)
Shawnee State U (OH)
Simmons Coll (MA)
Southeastern U (DC)
Southeast Missouri State U (MO)
Southern Adventist U (TN)
Southern Illinois U Edwardsville (IL)
Southern Methodist U (TX)
Southwestern Coll (KS)
Southwest Missouri State U (MO)
Southwest Texas State U (TX)
Spring Hill Coll (AL)
State U of West Georgia (GA)
Suffolk U (MA)
Taylor U, Fort Wayne Campus (IN)
Teikyo Post U (CT)
Texas A&M U (TX)
Texas A&M U–Commerce (TX)
Texas A&M U–Texarkana (TX)
Texas Tech U (TX)
Texas Wesleyan U (TX)
Thiel Coll (PA)
Thomas Coll (ME)
Tiffin U (OH)
Trinity Christian Coll (IL)
Tri-State U (IN)
United States International U (CA)
Université de Sherbrooke (PQ, Canada)
U du Québec à Chicoutimi (PQ, Canada)
U du Québec à Hull (PQ, Canada)
U Coll of Cape Breton (NS, Canada)
The U of Alabama (AL)
The U of Alabama in Huntsville (AL)
U of Alberta (AB, Canada)
The U of Arizona (AZ)
U of Arkansas at Monticello (AR)
U of British Columbia (BC, Canada)
U of Calgary (AB, Canada)
U of Central Arkansas (AR)
U of Central Florida (FL)
U of Cincinnati (OH)
U of Colorado at Boulder (CO)
U of Connecticut (CT)
U of Dayton (OH)
U of Detroit Mercy (MI)
U of Georgia (GA)
U of Hartford (CT)
U of Hawaii at Manoa (HI)
U of Houston (TX)
U of Houston–Downtown (TX)
U of Idaho (ID)
U of Illinois at Chicago (IL)
The U of Iowa (IA)
The U of Lethbridge (AB, Canada)
U of Louisville (KY)
U of Massachusetts Dartmouth (MA)
The U of Memphis (TN)
U of Minnesota, Twin Cities Campus (MN)
U of Mississippi (MS)
U of Missouri–Rolla (MO)
U of Missouri–St. Louis (MO)
U of Nebraska at Omaha (NE)
U of Nevada, Las Vegas (NV)
U of New Orleans (LA)
U of North Alabama (AL)
The U of North Carolina at Charlotte (NC)
The U of North Carolina at Greensboro (NC)
U of Northern Iowa (IA)
U of Notre Dame (IN)
U of Oklahoma (OK)
U of Pennsylvania (PA)
U of Phoenix (AZ)
U of Redlands (CA)
U of Rhode Island (RI)
U of Richmond (VA)
U of St. Francis (IL)
U of St. Thomas (TX)
U of San Francisco (CA)
U of Sioux Falls (SD)
U of Southern Mississippi (MS)
U of South Florida (FL)
The U of Tennessee at Martin (TN)
The U of Texas at Arlington (TX)
The U of Texas at Austin (TX)
The U of Texas at San Antonio (TX)
The U of Texas–Pan American (TX)
U of Tulsa (OK)
U of Washington (WA)
The U of West Alabama (AL)
U of West Florida (FL)
U of Wisconsin–Eau Claire (WI)
U of Wisconsin–La Crosse (WI)
U of Wisconsin–Milwaukee (WI)
U of Wisconsin–River Falls (WI)
U of Wisconsin–Whitewater (WI)
Upper Iowa U (IA)
Utah State U (UT)
Vanguard U of Southern California (CA)
Villa Julie Coll (MD)
Villanova U (PA)
Virginia Polytechnic Inst and State U (VA)
Virginia Union U (VA)
Walla Walla Coll (WA)
Washington State U (WA)
Wayne State U (MI)
Weber State U (UT)
Webster U (MO)
Western Carolina U (NC)
Western Connecticut State U (CT)
Western Illinois U (IL)
Western Kentucky U (KY)
Western Michigan U (MI)
Western Washington U (WA)
Westfield State Coll (MA)
Westminster Coll (MO)
Wichita State U (KS)
Wingate U (NC)
Winona State U (MN)
Winston-Salem State U (NC)
Worcester Polytechnic Inst (MA)
Wright State U (OH)
Yeshiva U (NY)
York U (ON, Canada)
Youngstown State U (OH)

MANAGEMENT SCIENCE
Abilene Christian U (TX)
American Military U (VA)
Arkansas Tech U (AR)
Averett Coll (VA)
Barat Coll (IL)
Caldwell Coll (NJ)
Central Methodist Coll (MO)
Clarion U of Pennsylvania (PA)
The Coll of St. Scholastica (MN)
The Coll of Southeastern Europe, The American U of Athens (Greece)
Dalhousie U (NS, Canada)
Duquesne U (PA)

Majors Index
Management Science–Mass Communications

Eastern Coll (PA)
École des Hautes Études Commerciales (PQ, Canada)
Franklin U (OH)
Georgia Inst of Technology (GA)
Goucher Coll (MD)
Inst of Public Administration (Ireland)
Kean U (NJ)
Louisiana State U and A&M Coll (LA)
Louisiana Tech U (LA)
Maharishi U of Management (IA)
Massachusetts Inst of Technology (MA)
McGill U (PQ, Canada)
Metropolitan State Coll of Denver (CO)
Miami U (OH)
Millersville U of Pennsylvania (PA)
Minnesota State U, Mankato (MN)
Northeastern U (MA)
Northwest Coll (WA)
Oakland City U (IN)
Oklahoma State U (OK)
Plymouth State Coll (NH)
Rider U (NJ)
Rockhurst U (MO)
Rutgers, State U of NJ, Douglass Coll (NJ)
Rutgers, State U of NJ, Livingston Coll (NJ)
Rutgers, State U of NJ, Rutgers Coll (NJ)
Rutgers, State U of NJ, U Coll–New Brunswick (NJ)
Saint Louis U (MO)
Shippensburg U of Pennsylvania (PA)
Simon Fraser U (BC, Canada)
Southeastern Oklahoma State U (OK)
Southern Adventist U (TN)
Southern Methodist U (TX)
Southwestern Coll (KS)
State U of NY at Binghamton (NY)
State U of NY at Oswego (NY)
Trinity U (TX)
Tuskegee U (AL)
United States Coast Guard Academy (CT)
The U of Alabama (AL)
U of Calif, San Diego (CA)
U of Florida (FL)
The U of Iowa (IA)
U of Kentucky (KY)
U of Maryland, Coll Park (MD)
U of Minnesota, Morris (MN)
U of Nebraska–Lincoln (NE)
U of North Dakota (ND)
U of Pennsylvania (PA)
The U of Scranton (PA)
U of South Carolina (SC)
U of Southern California (CA)
U of South Florida (FL)
U of Washington (WA)
U of Wyoming (WY)
Wake Forest U (NC)
Wheeling Jesuit U (WV)
York U (ON, Canada)

MARINE BIOLOGY
Alabama State U (AL)
Auburn U (AL)
Ball State U (IN)
Barry U (FL)
Bemidji State U (MN)
Boston U (MA)
Brown U (RI)
California State U, Fullerton (CA)
California State U, Long Beach (CA)
Coastal Carolina U (SC)
Coll of Charleston (SC)
Coll of the Atlantic (ME)
Dalhousie U (NS, Canada)
East Stroudsburg U of Pennsylvania (PA)
Eckerd Coll (FL)
The Evergreen State Coll (WA)
Fairleigh Dickinson U, Florham-Madison Campus (NJ)
Fairleigh Dickinson U, Teaneck-Hackensack Campus (NJ)
Florida Inst of Technology (FL)
Florida State U (FL)
Gettysburg Coll (PA)

Hampshire Coll (MA)
Hampton U (VA)
Harvard U (MA)
Hawaii Pacific U (HI)
Hofstra U (NY)
Humboldt State U (CA)
Huntingdon Coll (AL)
Jacksonville State U (AL)
Juniata Coll (PA)
Long Island U, Southampton Coll (NY)
Maine Maritime Academy (ME)
Marlboro Coll (VT)
McGill U (PQ, Canada)
Memorial U of Newfoundland (NF, Canada)
Millersville U of Pennsylvania (PA)
Mississippi State U (MS)
Missouri Southern State Coll (MO)
Nicholls State U (LA)
Northeastern U (MA)
The Ohio State U (OH)
Ohio U (OH)
Pine Manor Coll (MA)
The Richard Stockton Coll of New Jersey (NJ)
Roger Williams U (RI)
Rutgers, State U of NJ, Cook Coll (NJ)
Rutgers, State U of NJ, Douglass Coll (NJ)
Rutgers, State U of NJ, Livingston Coll (NJ)
Rutgers, State U of NJ, Rutgers Coll (NJ)
Rutgers, State U of NJ, U Coll–New Brunswick (NJ)
Saint Francis Coll (PA)
Salem State Coll (MA)
Samford U (AL)
San Francisco State U (CA)
San Jose State U (CA)
Sarah Lawrence Coll (NY)
Savannah State U (GA)
Sheldon Jackson Coll (AK)
Sonoma State U (CA)
Southwestern Coll (KS)
Southwest Texas State U (TX)
Spring Hill Coll (AL)
Stetson U (FL)
Suffolk U (MA)
Texas A&M U (TX)
Texas A&M U at Galveston (TX)
Troy State U (AL)
Unity Coll (ME)
The U of Alabama (AL)
U of British Columbia (BC, Canada)
U of Calif, Los Angeles (CA)
U of Calif, Santa Barbara (CA)
U of Calif, Santa Cruz (CA)
U of Guelph (ON, Canada)
U of King's Coll (NS, Canada)
U of Maine (ME)
U of Maine at Machias (ME)
U of Maryland, Coll Park (MD)
U of Miami (FL)
U of New Brunswick, Saint John (NB, Canada)
U of New England (ME)
U of New Hampshire (NH)
U of New Haven (CT)
U of North Alabama (AL)
The U of North Carolina at Wilmington (NC)
U of Puerto Rico, Humacao U Coll (PR)
U of Rhode Island (RI)
U of South Alabama (AL)
U of South Carolina (SC)
U of Southern California (CA)
U of Southern Mississippi (MS)
U of the Virgin Islands (VI)
U of Victoria (BC, Canada)
The U of West Alabama (AL)
U of West Florida (FL)
U of Wisconsin–Superior (WI)
Waynesburg Coll (PA)
Western Washington U (WA)
Wittenberg U (OH)

MARINE SCIENCE
Cornell U (NY)
Dowling Coll (NY)
The Evergreen State Coll (WA)
Hampton U (VA)
Jacksonville U (FL)

Kutztown U of Pennsylvania (PA)
Maine Maritime Academy (ME)
Massachusetts Maritime Academy (MA)
Memorial U of Newfoundland (NF, Canada)
Oregon State U (OR)
Rider U (NJ)
Saint Paul's Coll (VA)
Salem State Coll (MA)
State U of NY Maritime Coll (NY)
Suffolk U (MA)
Texas A&M U (TX)
Texas A&M U at Galveston (TX)
United States Coast Guard Academy (CT)
U of Alberta (AB, Canada)
U of New Hampshire (NH)
U of San Diego (CA)
The U of Tampa (FL)

MARINE TECHNOLOGY
Lamar U (TX)
Texas A&M U (TX)
Thomas Edison State Coll (NJ)

MARITIME SCIENCE
Coll of the Atlantic (ME)
Maine Maritime Academy (ME)
Massachusetts Maritime Academy (MA)
State U of NY Maritime Coll (NY)
Texas A&M U (TX)
Texas A&M U at Galveston (TX)
United States Merchant Marine Academy (NY)

MARKETING/DISTRIBUTION EDUCATION
Appalachian State U (NC)
Bowling Green State U (OH)
Central Michigan U (MI)
Colorado State U (CO)
East Carolina U (NC)
Eastern Michigan U (MI)
Eastern New Mexico U (NM)
Kent State U (OH)
Middle Tennessee State U (TN)
New Hampshire Coll (NH)
North Carolina State U (NC)
U of Central Arkansas (AR)
U of Georgia (GA)
U of Nebraska–Lincoln (NE)
U of North Dakota (ND)
U of Pittsburgh (PA)
U of Wisconsin–Stout (WI)
Utah State U (UT)
Virginia Polytechnic Inst and State U (VA)
Western Michigan U (MI)

MARKETING RESEARCH
Ashland U (OH)
Baker Coll of Jackson (MI)
Boston U (MA)
Bowling Green State U (OH)
Carthage Coll (WI)
Concordia U (PQ, Canada)
Ithaca Coll (NY)
Louisiana Coll (LA)
McGill U (PQ, Canada)
Methodist Coll (NC)
Metropolitan State Coll of Denver (CO)
Mount Saint Vincent U (NS, Canada)
Newbury Coll (MA)
New Hampshire Coll (NH)
Rochester Inst of Technology (NY)
Saginaw Valley State U (MI)
Troy State U Montgomery (AL)
U of Houston–Clear Lake (TX)
U of Nebraska at Omaha (NE)
York U (ON, Canada)

MARRIAGE AND FAMILY COUNSELING
Friends U (KS)
Oklahoma Baptist U (OK)
Oklahoma State U (OK)
Saint Paul U (ON, Canada)
The U of North Carolina at Greensboro (NC)

MASS COMMUNICATIONS
Adelphi U (NY)
Adrian Coll (MI)

Alabama State U (AL)
Albertus Magnus Coll (CT)
Albion Coll (MI)
Alderson-Broaddus Coll (WV)
Alfred U (NY)
Allentown Coll of St. Francis de Sales (PA)
Alma Coll (MI)
American International Coll (MA)
American U (DC)
American U in Cairo (Egypt)
The American U of Paris (France)
Anderson Coll (SC)
Anderson U (IN)
Andrews U (MI)
Antioch Coll (OH)
Ashland U (OH)
Atlantic Baptist U (NB, Canada)
Auburn U (AL)
Augsburg Coll (MN)
Augustana Coll (IL)
Augustana Coll (SD)
Austin Coll (TX)
Austin Peay State U (TN)
Avila Coll (MO)
Baker U (KS)
Baldwin-Wallace Coll (OH)
Barber-Scotia Coll (NC)
Barry U (FL)
Bartlesville Wesleyan Coll (OK)
Barton Coll (NC)
Beaver Coll (PA)
Belmont U (TN)
Beloit Coll (WI)
Bemidji State U (MN)
Bennett Coll (NC)
Berry Coll (GA)
Bethel Coll (MN)
Bethune-Cookman Coll (FL)
Black Hills State U (SD)
Bloomfield Coll (NJ)
Bloomsburg U of Pennsylvania (PA)
Bluffton Coll (OH)
Boise State U (ID)
Boston Coll (MA)
Boston U (MA)
Bowie State U (MD)
Bowling Green State U (OH)
Brenau U (GA)
Briar Cliff Coll (IA)
Brock U (ON, Canada)
Bryan Coll (TN)
Buena Vista U (IA)
California Lutheran U (CA)
California State Polytechnic U, Pomona (CA)
California State U, Dominguez Hills (CA)
California State U, Fresno (CA)
California State U, Fullerton (CA)
California State U, Hayward (CA)
California State U, Long Beach (CA)
California State U, Sacramento (CA)
California State U, San Bernardino (CA)
Calvary Bible Coll and Theological Seminary (MO)
Calvin Coll (MI)
Cameron U (OK)
Campbellsville U (KY)
Canisius Coll (NY)
Capital U (OH)
Carleton U (ON, Canada)
Carnegie Mellon U (PA)
Carroll Coll (WI)
Carson-Newman Coll (TN)
Catawba Coll (NC)
Centenary Coll (NJ)
Centenary Coll of Louisiana (LA)
Central Missouri State U (MO)
Chaminade U of Honolulu (HI)
Champlain Coll (VT)
Chapman U (CA)
Cheyney U of Pennsylvania (PA)
City Coll of the City U of NY (NY)
City U (WA)
Claflin U (SC)
Clark Atlanta U (GA)
Clarke Coll (IA)
Clark U (MA)
Cleveland State U (OH)
Coker Coll (SC)
Coll of Mount Saint Vincent (NY)
The Coll of New Rochelle (NY)

Coll of Notre Dame (CA)
Coll of Notre Dame of Maryland (MD)
Coll of Saint Benedict (MN)
Coll of St. Catherine (MN)
Coll of Saint Mary (NE)
Coll of Staten Island of the City U of NY (NY)
Coll of the Ozarks (MO)
The Coll of Wooster (OH)
Colorado Christian U (CO)
Columbia Union Coll (MD)
Columbus State U (GA)
Concord Coll (WV)
Concordia Coll (MN)
Concordia U (NE)
Concordia U (PQ, Canada)
Concordia U at Austin (TX)
Concordia U at St. Paul (MN)
Concordia U Wisconsin (WI)
Cornell U (NY)
Cornerstone U (MI)
Creighton U (NE)
Culver-Stockton Coll (MO)
Curry Coll (MA)
Dallas Baptist U (TX)
David Lipscomb U (TN)
Defiance Coll (OH)
Delaware State U (DE)
Denison U (OH)
DePaul U (IL)
DePauw U (IN)
Dickinson State U (ND)
Doane Coll (NE)
Dominican U (IL)
Dordt Coll (IA)
Drake U (IA)
Drexel U (PA)
Drury U (MO)
East Central U (OK)
Eastern Kentucky U (KY)
Eastern Nazarene Coll (MA)
Eastern New Mexico U (NM)
Eastern Washington U (WA)
East Tennessee State U (TN)
Edgewood Coll (WI)
Emerson Coll (MA)
Emmanuel Coll (MA)
Emory & Henry Coll (VA)
Evangel U (MO)
The Evergreen State Coll (WA)
Fairfield U (CT)
Felician Coll (NJ)
Ferris State U (MI)
Florida A&M U (FL)
Florida State U (FL)
Fordham U (NY)
Fort Hays State U (KS)
Fort Lewis Coll (CO)
Fort Valley State U (GA)
Framingham State Coll (MA)
Francis Marion U (SC)
Franklin Pierce Coll (NH)
Freed-Hardeman U (TN)
Fresno Pacific U (CA)
Frostburg State U (MD)
Gallaudet U (DC)
Gardner-Webb U (NC)
George Mason U (VA)
Georgetown Coll (KY)
The George Washington U (DC)
Georgia Coll and State U (GA)
Gonzaga U (WA)
Gordon Coll (MA)
Goshen Coll (IN)
Goucher Coll (MD)
Governors State U (IL)
Grace Coll (IN)
Grand Canyon U (AZ)
Grand Valley State U (MI)
Grand View Coll (IA)
Greenville Coll (IL)
Grove City Coll (PA)
Guilford Coll (NC)
Gustavus Adolphus Coll (MN)
Hamilton Coll (NY)
Hamline U (MN)
Hampshire Coll (MA)
Hampton U (VA)
Hannibal-LaGrange Coll (MO)
Hanover Coll (IN)
Harding U (AR)
Hardin-Simmons U (TX)
Hastings Coll (NE)
Hawaii Pacific U (HI)
Heidelberg Coll (OH)
High Point U (NC)

Majors Index
Mass Communications–Materials Engineering

Hiram Coll (OH)
Hofstra U (NY)
Hood Coll (MD)
Houghton Coll (NY)
Houston Baptist U (TX)
Howard U (DC)
Huntington Coll (IN)
Huston-Tillotson Coll (TX)
Idaho State U (ID)
Illinois Coll (IL)
Illinois State U (IL)
Indiana State U (IN)
Indiana U Bloomington (IN)
Indiana U Northwest (IN)
Indiana U South Bend (IN)
Insto Tecno Estudios Sups Monterrey (Mexico)
Insto Tecno Estudios Sups Monterrey, Querétaro (Mexico)
Iona Coll (NY)
Iowa State U of Science and Technology (IA)
Iowa Wesleyan Coll (IA)
Ithaca Coll (NY)
John Brown U (AR)
John Carroll U (OH)
Johnson & Wales U (RI)
Johnson C. Smith U (NC)
Judson Coll (IL)
Keene State Coll (NH)
Kent State U (OH)
Kentucky Mountain Bible Coll (KY)
Lake Erie Coll (OH)
Lamar U (TX)
Lambuth U (TN)
Lander U (SC)
Lane Coll (TN)
Langston U (OK)
La Salle U (PA)
Lees-McRae Coll (NC)
Lee U (TN)
Lehman Coll of the City U of NY (NY)
Lenoir-Rhyne Coll (NC)
Lewis & Clark Coll (OR)
Lewis-Clark State Coll (ID)
Lewis U (IL)
Lincoln Memorial U (TN)
Lindenwood U (MO)
Lindsey Wilson Coll (KY)
Lock Haven U of Pennsylvania (PA)
Long Island U, Brooklyn Campus (NY)
Long Island U, Southampton Coll (NY)
Long Island U, Southampton Coll, Friends World Program (NY)
Loras Coll (IA)
Louisiana Coll (LA)
Louisiana State U and A&M Coll (LA)
Louisiana State U in Shreveport (LA)
Loyola Marymount U (CA)
Lubbock Christian U (TX)
Luther Coll (IA)
Lycoming Coll (PA)
Lynchburg Coll (VA)
Lynn U (FL)
Madonna U (MI)
Manchester Coll (IN)
Mansfield U of Pennsylvania (PA)
Marian Coll (IN)
Marian Coll of Fond du Lac (WI)
Marietta Coll (OH)
Marist Coll (NY)
Marquette U (WI)
Marshall U (WV)
Mars Hill Coll (NC)
Mary Baldwin Coll (VA)
Marycrest International U (IA)
Marylhurst U (OR)
Marymount Coll (NY)
Marymount Manhattan Coll (NY)
Massachusetts Coll of Liberal Arts (MA)
McKendree Coll (IL)
McMurry U (TX)
McNeese State U (LA)
Medaille Coll (NY)
Menlo Coll (CA)
Mercyhurst Coll (PA)
Meredith Coll (NC)
Mesa State Coll (CO)
Methodist Coll (NC)
Metropolitan State U (MN)

Miami U (OH)
Michigan State U (MI)
MidAmerica Nazarene U (KS)
Middle Tennessee State U (TN)
Midland Lutheran Coll (NE)
Midwestern State U (TX)
Milligan Coll (TN)
Mills Coll (CA)
Minnesota State U, Mankato (MN)
Minnesota State U Moorhead (MN)
Mississippi Valley State U (MS)
Missouri Southern State Coll (MO)
Missouri Valley Coll (MO)
Monmouth Coll (IL)
Montana State U–Billings (MT)
Montana State U–Northern (MT)
Montreat Coll (NC)
Morgan State U (MD)
Morningside Coll (IA)
Mount Ida Coll (MA)
Mount Saint Mary Coll (NY)
Mount Union Coll (OH)
Mount Vernon Nazarene Coll (OH)
Muhlenberg Coll (PA)
Muskingum Coll (OH)
Nebraska Wesleyan U (NE)
Newberry Coll (SC)
New England Coll (NH)
Newman U (KS)
New Mexico Highlands U (NM)
New Mexico State U (NM)
New York Inst of Technology (NY)
New York U (NY)
Niagara U (NY)
Nicholls State U (LA)
Norfolk State U (VA)
North Carolina Ag and Tech State U (NC)
North Central Coll (IL)
North Central U (MN)
North Dakota State U (ND)
Northeastern U (MA)
Northern Arizona U (AZ)
Northern Michigan U (MI)
North Greenville Coll (SC)
North Park U (IL)
Northwestern Coll (IA)
Northwestern Oklahoma State U (OK)
Northwest Missouri State U (MO)
Oakwood Coll (AL)
Oglethorpe U (GA)
Ohio Northern U (OH)
Ohio U (OH)
Oklahoma Baptist U (OK)
Oklahoma Christian U of Science and Arts (OK)
Oklahoma City U (OK)
Olivet Nazarene U (IL)
Oregon State U (OR)
Ottawa U (KS)
Otterbein Coll (OH)
Ouachita Baptist U (AR)
Pacific Lutheran U (WA)
Pacific Union Coll (CA)
Pacific U (OR)
Paine Coll (GA)
Pfeiffer U (NC)
Piedmont Coll (GA)
Pine Manor Coll (MA)
Pittsburg State U (KS)
Pitzer Coll (CA)
Plattsburgh State U of NY (NY)
Point Loma Nazarene U (CA)
Point Park Coll (PA)
Pontifical Catholic U of Puerto Rico (PR)
Presentation Coll (SD)
Principia Coll (IL)
Purdue U Calumet (IN)
Queens Coll (NC)
Queens Coll of the City U of NY (NY)
Quinnipiac U (CT)
Randolph-Macon Woman's Coll (VA)
Regents Coll (NY)
Reinhardt Coll (GA)
Rensselaer Polytechnic Inst (NY)
Richmond, The American International U in London (United Kingdom)
Robert Morris Coll (PA)
Rockhurst U (MO)
Rowan U (NJ)
Russell Sage Coll (NY)
Rust Coll (MS)

Rutgers, State U of NJ, Cook Coll (NJ)
Rutgers, State U of NJ, Douglass Coll (NJ)
Rutgers, State U of NJ, Livingston Coll (NJ)
Rutgers, State U of NJ, Rutgers Coll (NJ)
Rutgers, State U of NJ, U Coll–New Brunswick (NJ)
Sacred Heart U (CT)
St. Ambrose U (IA)
St. Andrews Presbyterian Coll (NC)
St. Bonaventure U (NY)
St. Cloud State U (MN)
Saint Francis Coll (PA)
St. John Fisher Coll (NY)
Saint John's U (MN)
Saint Joseph's Coll (IN)
Saint Joseph's Coll (ME)
Saint Mary Coll (KS)
Saint Mary-of-the-Woods Coll (IN)
Saint Mary's Coll (MI)
Saint Mary's Coll of California (CA)
St. Mary's U of San Antonio (TX)
St. Thomas U (FL)
Salem Coll (NC)
Salem State Coll (MA)
San Diego State U (CA)
Savannah State U (GA)
Seattle U (WA)
Seton Hill Coll (PA)
Shaw U (NC)
Shepherd Coll (WV)
Simmons Coll (MA)
Simpson Coll (IA)
Slippery Rock U of Pennsylvania (PA)
Sonoma State U (CA)
South Dakota State U (SD)
Southeastern Louisiana U (LA)
Southeast Missouri State U (MO)
Southern Adventist U (TN)
Southern Arkansas U–Magnolia (AR)
Southern Illinois U Edwardsville (IL)
Southern Utah U (UT)
Southern Vermont Coll (VT)
Southwestern Adventist U (TX)
Southwestern Oklahoma State U (OK)
Southwestern U (TX)
Southwest Missouri State U (MO)
Southwest Texas State U (TX)
Spalding U (KY)
Spring Arbor Coll (MI)
State U of NY at Albany (NY)
State U of NY at Buffalo (NY)
State U of NY at New Paltz (NY)
State U of NY at Oswego (NY)
State U of NY Coll at Brockport (NY)
State U of NY Coll at Buffalo (NY)
State U of NY Coll at Fredonia (NY)
State U of NY Coll at Oneonta (NY)
State U of NY Coll at Potsdam (NY)
State U of West Georgia (GA)
Stephens Coll (MO)
Stetson U (FL)
Stillman Coll (AL)
Sul Ross State U (TX)
Susquehanna U (PA)
Tabor Coll (KS)
Taylor U (IN)
Temple U (PA)
Tennessee State U (TN)
Texas A&M U–Kingsville (TX)
Texas Christian U (TX)
Texas Lutheran U (TX)
Texas Southern U (TX)
Texas Wesleyan U (TX)
Texas Woman's U (TX)
Thomas More Coll (KY)
Toccoa Falls Coll (GA)
Towson U (MD)
Trevecca Nazarene U (TN)
Truman State U (MO)
Tulane U (LA)
Union U (TN)
Universidad del Turabo (PR)
Université de Montréal (PQ, Canada)

Université de Sherbrooke (PQ, Canada)
U du Québec à Trois-Rivières (PQ, Canada)
Université Laval (PQ, Canada)
The U of Akron (OH)
U of Alaska Fairbanks (AK)
U of Arkansas (AR)
U of Baltimore (MD)
U of Bridgeport (CT)
U of Calif, Berkeley (CA)
U of Calif, San Diego (CA)
U of Central Oklahoma (OK)
U of Charleston (WV)
U of Cincinnati (OH)
U of Colorado at Boulder (CO)
U of Dayton (OH)
U of Delaware (DE)
U of Detroit Mercy (MI)
U of Dubuque (IA)
U of Evansville (IN)
U of Georgia (GA)
U of Great Falls (MT)
U of Illinois at Springfield (IL)
U of Illinois at Urbana–Champaign (IL)
The U of Iowa (IA)
U of Louisiana at Lafayette (LA)
U of Maine (ME)
U of Mary Hardin-Baylor (TX)
U of Maryland, Coll Park (MD)
The U of Memphis (TN)
U of Michigan (MI)
U of Michigan–Flint (MI)
U of Minnesota, Morris (MN)
U of Minnesota, Twin Cities Campus (MN)
U of Missouri–Columbia (MO)
U of Missouri–Kansas City (MO)
U of Missouri–St. Louis (MO)
U of Mobile (AL)
U of Montevallo (AL)
U of Nebraska at Kearney (NE)
U of Nebraska at Omaha (NE)
U of New Hampshire (NH)
U of New Hampshire at Manchester (NH)
U of New Mexico (NM)
The U of North Carolina at Asheville (NC)
The U of North Carolina at Greensboro (NC)
The U of North Carolina at Pembroke (NC)
U of North Texas (TX)
U of Oregon (OR)
U of Pittsburgh at Bradford (PA)
U of Pittsburgh at Johnstown (PA)
U of Portland (OR)
U of Puerto Rico, Río Piedras (PR)
U of Regina (SK, Canada)
U of Rio Grande (OH)
U of St. Francis (IL)
U of Saint Francis (IN)
U of St. Thomas (MN)
U of San Diego (CA)
U of San Francisco (CA)
U of Sioux Falls (SD)
U of South Alabama (AL)
U of South Dakota (SD)
U of Southern California (CA)
U of Southern Colorado (CO)
The U of Tampa (FL)
The U of Tennessee at Chattanooga (TN)
The U of Texas at San Antonio (TX)
The U of Texas–Pan American (TX)
U of the Arts (PA)
U of the Pacific (CA)
U of the Sacred Heart (PR)
U of Toronto (ON, Canada)
U of Tulsa (OK)
U of Utah (UT)
U of Windsor (ON, Canada)
U of Wisconsin–Madison (WI)
U of Wisconsin–Milwaukee (WI)
U of Wisconsin–Platteville (WI)
U of Wisconsin–Superior (WI)
U of Wisconsin–Whitewater (WI)
Upper Iowa U (IA)
Urbana U (OH)
Ursinus Coll (PA)
Utica Coll of Syracuse U (NY)
Valdosta State U (GA)
Vanderbilt U (TN)

Vanguard U of Southern California (CA)
Villa Julie Coll (MD)
Villanova U (PA)
Virginia Commonwealth U (VA)
Waldorf Coll (IA)
Walla Walla Coll (WA)
Walsh U (OH)
Wartburg Coll (IA)
Washington State U (WA)
Wayland Baptist U (TX)
Wayne State Coll (NE)
Wesley Coll (DE)
West Chester U of Pennsylvania (PA)
Western Connecticut State U (CT)
Western State Coll of Colorado (CO)
Western Washington U (WA)
Westfield State Coll (MA)
West Liberty State Coll (WV)
Westminster Coll (PA)
West Texas A&M U (TX)
West Virginia State Coll (WV)
West Virginia U (WV)
Whitworth Coll (WA)
Widener U (PA)
Wilfrid Laurier U (ON, Canada)
Wilkes U (PA)
William Paterson U of New Jersey (NJ)
Wilmington Coll (OH)
Wilson Coll (PA)
Wingate U (NC)
Winona State U (MN)
Winston-Salem State U (NC)
Winthrop U (SC)
Worcester State Coll (MA)
Wright State U (OH)
Xavier U of Louisiana (LA)
Yeshiva U (NY)
York Coll of Pennsylvania (PA)
York U (ON, Canada)
Youngstown State U (OH)

MATERIALS ENGINEERING
Arizona State U (AZ)
Auburn U (AL)
Brown U (RI)
California Polytechnic State U, San Luis Obispo (CA)
California State Polytechnic U, Pomona (CA)
California State U, Long Beach (CA)
California State U, Northridge (CA)
Carnegie Mellon U (PA)
Case Western Reserve U (OH)
Clarkson U (NY)
Cornell U (NY)
Drexel U (PA)
Florida State U (FL)
Georgia Inst of Technology (GA)
Harvard U (MA)
Illinois Inst of Technology (IL)
Johns Hopkins U (MD)
Lehigh U (PA)
Massachusetts Inst of Technology (MA)
Mercyhurst Coll (PA)
Michigan State U (MI)
Michigan Technological U (MI)
Montana Tech of The U of Montana (MT)
New Jersey Inst of Technology (NJ)
New Mexico Inst of Mining and Technology (NM)
New York U (NY)
North Carolina State U (NC)
Northwestern U (IL)
The Ohio State U (OH)
Purdue U (IN)
Rensselaer Polytechnic Inst (NY)
Saint Augustine's Coll (NC)
San Jose State U (CA)
Stanford U (CA)
The U of Alabama at Birmingham (AL)
U of British Columbia (BC, Canada)
U of Calif, Berkeley (CA)
U of Calif, Davis (CA)
U of Calif, Los Angeles (CA)
U of Connecticut (CT)
U of Florida (FL)
The U of Iowa (IA)
U of Kentucky (KY)

Majors Index
Materials Engineering–Mathematics

U of Maryland, Coll Park (MD)
U of Michigan (MI)
U of Minnesota, Twin Cities Campus (MN)
U of New Haven (CT)
U of Pennsylvania (PA)
U of Pittsburgh (PA)
The U of Tennessee Knoxville (TN)
U of Toronto (ON, Canada)
U of Utah (UT)
U of Washington (WA)
The U of Western Ontario (ON, Canada)
U of Windsor (ON, Canada)
U of Wisconsin–Milwaukee (WI)
Virginia Polytechnic Inst and State U (VA)
Washington State U (WA)
Wayne State U (MI)
Western Michigan U (MI)
Winona State U (MN)
Worcester Polytechnic Inst (MA)
Wright State U (OH)
Youngstown State U (OH)

MATERIALS SCIENCE
Alfred U (NY)
Athens State U (AL)
California Inst of Technology (CA)
Carnegie Mellon U (PA)
Case Western Reserve U (OH)
Clarkson U (NY)
Columbia U, School of Engineering & Applied Sci (NY)
Cornell U (NY)
Duke U (NC)
Harvard U (MA)
Johns Hopkins U (MD)
Massachusetts Inst of Technology (MA)
Michigan State U (MI)
Montana Tech of The U of Montana (MT)
New Jersey Inst of Technology (NJ)
Northwestern U (IL)
The Ohio State U (OH)
Oregon State U (OR)
Rice U (TX)
Stanford U (CA)
United States Air Force Academy (CO)
The U of Arizona (AZ)
U of Calif, Los Angeles (CA)
U of Illinois at Urbana–Champaign (IL)
U of Maryland, Coll Park (MD)
U of Michigan (MI)
U of Minnesota, Twin Cities Campus (MN)
U of Toronto (ON, Canada)
U of Utah (UT)
Worcester Polytechnic Inst (MA)

MATHEMATICAL STATISTICS
American U (DC)
Appalachian State U (NC)
Barnard Coll (NY)
Baruch Coll of the City U of NY (NY)
Bowling Green State U (OH)
Brigham Young U (UT)
Brock U (ON, Canada)
California Polytechnic State U, San Luis Obispo (CA)
California State Polytechnic U, Pomona (CA)
California State U, Chico (CA)
California State U, Hayward (CA)
California State U, Long Beach (CA)
California State U, Northridge (CA)
Carleton U (ON, Canada)
Carnegie Mellon U (PA)
Case Western Reserve U (OH)
Central Michigan U (MI)
Cleveland State U (OH)
The Coll of New Jersey (NJ)
Colorado State U (CO)
Columbia Coll (NY)
Columbia U, School of General Studies (NY)
Concordia U (PQ, Canada)
Cornell U (NY)
Dalhousie U (NS, Canada)
DePaul U (IL)
Eastern Kentucky U (KY)
Eastern Michigan U (MI)

Eastern New Mexico U (NM)
Florida International U (FL)
Florida State U (FL)
Fort Lewis Coll (CO)
Framingham State Coll (MA)
The George Washington U (DC)
Grand Valley State U (MI)
Hampshire Coll (MA)
Harvard U (MA)
Hunter Coll of the City U of NY (NY)
Iowa State U of Science and Technology (IA)
Kansas State U (KS)
Kettering U (MI)
Lehigh U (PA)
Loyola U Chicago (IL)
Luther Coll (IA)
Marquette U (WI)
McGill U (PQ, Canada)
Memorial U of Newfoundland (NF, Canada)
Mercyhurst Coll (PA)
Mesa State Coll (CO)
Miami U (OH)
Michigan State U (MI)
Michigan Technological U (MI)
Millersville U of Pennsylvania (PA)
Mills Coll (CA)
Mount Holyoke Coll (MA)
Mount Saint Vincent U (NS, Canada)
New Jersey Inst of Technology (NJ)
New York U (NY)
North Carolina State U (NC)
Northern Arizona U (AZ)
Northwestern U (IL)
Oakland U (MI)
Ohio Northern U (OH)
The Ohio State U (OH)
Ohio Wesleyan U (OH)
Penn State U Univ Park Campus (PA)
Plymouth State Coll (NH)
Purdue U (IN)
Queens Coll of the City U of NY (NY)
Queen's U at Kingston (ON, Canada)
Rice U (TX)
Rochester Inst of Technology (NY)
Rutgers, State U of NJ, Douglass Coll (NJ)
Rutgers, State U of NJ, Livingston Coll (NJ)
Rutgers, State U of NJ, Rutgers Coll (NJ)
Rutgers, State U of NJ, U Coll–New Brunswick (NJ)
St. Cloud State U (MN)
St. Mary's U of San Antonio (TX)
San Diego State U (CA)
San Francisco State U (CA)
San Jose State U (CA)
Sonoma State U (CA)
Southern Methodist U (TX)
State U of NY at Stony Brook (NY)
State U of NY Coll at Oneonta (NY)
Stevens Inst of Technology (NJ)
Temple U (PA)
Université de Montréal (PQ, Canada)
Université de Sherbrooke (PQ, Canada)
Université Laval (PQ, Canada)
U Coll of the Fraser Valley (BC, Canada)
The U of Akron (OH)
U of Alaska Fairbanks (AK)
U of Alberta (AB, Canada)
U of British Columbia (BC, Canada)
U of Calgary (AB, Canada)
U of Calif, Berkeley (CA)
U of Calif, Davis (CA)
U of Calif, Riverside (CA)
U of Calif, Santa Barbara (CA)
U of Central Florida (FL)
U of Chicago (IL)
U of Connecticut (CT)
U of Denver (CO)
U of Florida (FL)
U of Georgia (GA)
U of Guelph (ON, Canada)
U of Houston (TX)
U of Illinois at Chicago (IL)

U of Illinois at Urbana–Champaign (IL)
The U of Iowa (IA)
U of King's Coll (NS, Canada)
U of Manitoba (MB, Canada)
U of Maryland, Coll Park (MD)
U of Michigan (MI)
U of Missouri–Columbia (MO)
U of Missouri–Kansas City (MO)
The U of Montana–Missoula (MT)
U of Nebraska at Kearney (NE)
U of Nevada, Las Vegas (NV)
U of New Brunswick, Fredericton (NB, Canada)
U of New Brunswick, Saint John (NB, Canada)
U of New Hampshire (NH)
The U of North Carolina at Greensboro (NC)
U of North Florida (FL)
U of Oregon (OR)
U of Pennsylvania (PA)
U of Pittsburgh (PA)
U of Regina (SK, Canada)
U of Rochester (NY)
U of South Alabama (AL)
U of South Carolina (SC)
U of South Dakota (SD)
The U of Tennessee Knoxville (TN)
The U of Texas at Dallas (TX)
The U of Texas at San Antonio (TX)
U of Toronto (ON, Canada)
U of Vermont (VT)
U of Victoria (BC, Canada)
U of Washington (WA)
U of Waterloo (ON, Canada)
The U of Western Ontario (ON, Canada)
U of Windsor (ON, Canada)
The U of Winnipeg (MB, Canada)
U of Wisconsin–Madison (WI)
U of Wisconsin–Milwaukee (WI)
U of Wyoming (WY)
Utah State U (UT)
Virginia Commonwealth U (VA)
Virginia Polytechnic Inst and State U (VA)
Washington U in St. Louis (MO)
Western Michigan U (MI)
West Virginia U (WV)
Wilfrid Laurier U (ON, Canada)
Winona State U (MN)
Worcester Polytechnic Inst (MA)
Wright State U (OH)
Xavier U of Louisiana (LA)
York U (ON, Canada)

MATHEMATICS
Abilene Christian U (TX)
Acadia U (NS, Canada)
Adams State Coll (CO)
Adelphi U (NY)
Adrian Coll (MI)
Agnes Scott Coll (GA)
Alabama A&M U (AL)
Alabama State U (AL)
Albany State U (GA)
Albertson Coll of Idaho (ID)
Albertus Magnus Coll (CT)
Albion Coll (MI)
Albright Coll (PA)
Alderson-Broaddus Coll (WV)
Alfred U (NY)
Allegheny Coll (PA)
Allentown Coll of St. Francis de Sales (PA)
Allen U (SC)
Alma Coll (MI)
Alvernia Coll (PA)
Alverno Coll (WI)
American International Coll (MA)
American U (DC)
American U in Cairo (Egypt)
Amherst Coll (MA)
Anderson U (IN)
Andrews U (MI)
Antioch Coll (OH)
Appalachian State U (NC)
Aquinas Coll (MI)
Arizona State U (AZ)
Arkansas State U (AR)
Arkansas Tech U (AR)
Armstrong Atlantic State U (GA)
Asbury Coll (KY)
Ashland U (OH)
Assumption Coll (MA)

Athens State U (AL)
Atlantic Union Coll (MA)
Auburn U (AL)
Auburn U Montgomery (AL)
Augsburg Coll (MN)
Augustana Coll (IL)
Augustana Coll (SD)
Augusta State U (GA)
Austin Coll (TX)
Austin Peay State U (TN)
Averett Coll (VA)
Avila Coll (MO)
Azusa Pacific U (CA)
Baker U (KS)
Baldwin-Wallace Coll (OH)
Ball State U (IN)
Barat Coll (IL)
Barber-Scotia Coll (NC)
Bard Coll (NY)
Barnard Coll (NY)
Barry U (FL)
Bartlesville Wesleyan Coll (OK)
Barton Coll (NC)
Bates Coll (ME)
Baylor U (TX)
Beaver Coll (PA)
Belhaven Coll (MS)
Bellarmine Coll (KY)
Bellevue U (NE)
Belmont U (TN)
Beloit Coll (WI)
Bemidji State U (MN)
Benedictine Coll (KS)
Benedictine U (IL)
Bennett Coll (NC)
Bennington Coll (VT)
Bentley Coll (MA)
Berea Coll (KY)
Baruch Coll of the City U of NY (NY)
Berry Coll (GA)
Bethany Coll (KS)
Bethany Coll (WV)
Bethel Coll (IN)
Bethel Coll (KS)
Bethel Coll (MN)
Bethel Coll (TN)
Bethune-Cookman Coll (FL)
Biola U (CA)
Birmingham-Southern Coll (AL)
Bishop's U (PQ, Canada)
Blackburn Coll (IL)
Black Hills State U (SD)
Bloomsburg U of Pennsylvania (PA)
Blue Mountain Coll (MS)
Bluffton Coll (OH)
Boise State U (ID)
Boston Coll (MA)
Boston U (MA)
Bowdoin Coll (ME)
Bowie State U (MD)
Bowling Green State U (OH)
Bradley U (IL)
Brandeis U (MA)
Brandon U (MB, Canada)
Brevard Coll (NC)
Briar Cliff Coll (IA)
Bridgewater Coll (VA)
Bridgewater State Coll (MA)
Brigham Young U (UT)
Brigham Young U–Hawaii Campus (HI)
Brock U (ON, Canada)
Brooklyn Coll of the City U of NY (NY)
Brown U (RI)
Bryan Coll (TN)
Bryn Mawr Coll (PA)
Bucknell U (PA)
Buena Vista U (IA)
Butler U (IN)
Cabrini Coll (PA)
Caldwell Coll (NJ)
California Baptist U (CA)
California Inst of Technology (CA)
California Lutheran U (CA)
California Polytechnic State U, San Luis Obispo (CA)
California State Polytechnic U, Pomona (CA)
California State U, Chico (CA)
California State U, Dominguez Hills (CA)
California State U, Fresno (CA)
California State U, Fullerton (CA)
California State U, Hayward (CA)

California State U, Long Beach (CA)
California State U, Los Angeles (CA)
California State U, Northridge (CA)
California State U, Sacramento (CA)
California State U, San Bernardino (CA)
California State U, San Marcos (CA)
California State U, Stanislaus (CA)
California U of Pennsylvania (PA)
Calvin Coll (MI)
Cameron U (OK)
Campbellsville U (KY)
Campbell U (NC)
Canisius Coll (NY)
Capital U (OH)
Cardinal Stritch U (WI)
Carleton Coll (MN)
Carleton U (ON, Canada)
Carlow Coll (PA)
Carnegie Mellon U (PA)
Carroll Coll (MT)
Carroll Coll (WI)
Carson-Newman Coll (TN)
Carthage Coll (WI)
Case Western Reserve U (OH)
Castleton State Coll (VT)
Catawba Coll (NC)
The Catholic U of America (DC)
Cedar Crest Coll (PA)
Cedarville Coll (OH)
Centenary Coll (NJ)
Centenary Coll of Louisiana (LA)
Central Coll (IA)
Central Connecticut State U (CT)
Central Methodist Coll (MO)
Central Michigan U (MI)
Central Missouri State U (MO)
Centre Coll (KY)
Chadron State Coll (NE)
Charleston Southern U (SC)
Chatham Coll (PA)
Chestnut Hill Coll (PA)
Cheyney U of Pennsylvania (PA)
Chicago State U (IL)
Chowan Coll (NC)
Christian Brothers U (TN)
Christopher Newport U (VA)
Citadel, The Military Coll of South Carolina (SC)
City Coll of the City U of NY (NY)
Claflin U (SC)
Claremont McKenna Coll (CA)
Clarion U of Pennsylvania (PA)
Clark Atlanta U (GA)
Clarke Coll (IA)
Clarkson U (NY)
Clark U (MA)
Clemson U (SC)
Cleveland State U (OH)
Coe Coll (IA)
Coker Coll (SC)
Colby Coll (ME)
Colgate U (NY)
Coll Misericordia (PA)
Coll of Charleston (SC)
Coll of Mount St. Joseph (OH)
Coll of Mount Saint Vincent (NY)
The Coll of New Jersey (NJ)
The Coll of New Rochelle (NY)
Coll of Notre Dame of Maryland (MD)
Coll of Our Lady of the Elms (MA)
Coll of Saint Benedict (MN)
Coll of St. Catherine (MN)
Coll of Saint Elizabeth (NJ)
Coll of Saint Mary (NE)
The Coll of Saint Rose (NY)
The Coll of St. Scholastica (MN)
Coll of Santa Fe (NM)
The Coll of Southeastern Europe, The American U of Athens (Greece)
Coll of Staten Island of the City U of NY (NY)
Coll of the Holy Cross (MA)
Coll of the Ozarks (MO)
Coll of the Southwest (NM)
The Coll of William and Mary (VA)
The Coll of Wooster (OH)
Colorado Christian U (CO)
The Colorado Coll (CO)
Colorado School of Mines (CO)
Colorado State U (CO)

Majors Index
Mathematics

Columbia Coll (MO)
Columbia Coll (NY)
Columbia Coll (SC)
Columbia Union Coll (MD)
Columbia U, School of General Studies (NY)
Columbus State U (GA)
Concord Coll (WV)
Concordia Coll (MI)
Concordia Coll (MN)
Concordia Coll (NY)
Concordia U (CA)
Concordia U (IL)
Concordia U (NE)
Concordia U (PQ, Canada)
Concordia U Coll of Alberta (AB, Canada)
Concordia U Wisconsin (WI)
Connecticut Coll (CT)
Converse Coll (SC)
Coppin State Coll (MD)
Cornell Coll (IA)
Cornell U (NY)
Cornerstone U (MI)
Creighton U (NE)
Culver-Stockton Coll (MO)
Cumberland Coll (KY)
Daemen Coll (NY)
Dakota State U (SD)
Dakota Wesleyan U (SD)
Dalhousie U (NS, Canada)
Dallas Baptist U (TX)
Dana Coll (NE)
Dartmouth Coll (NH)
David Lipscomb U (TN)
Davidson Coll (NC)
Defiance Coll (OH)
Delaware State U (DE)
Delaware Valley Coll (PA)
Delta State U (MS)
Denison U (OH)
DePaul U (IL)
DePauw U (IN)
Dickinson Coll (PA)
Dickinson State U (ND)
Doane Coll (NE)
Dominican Coll of Blauvelt (NY)
Dominican U (IL)
Dominican U of California (CA)
Dordt Coll (IA)
Dowling Coll (NY)
Drake U (IA)
Drew U (NJ)
Drexel U (PA)
Drury U (MO)
Duke U (NC)
Duquesne U (PA)
Earlham Coll (IN)
East Carolina U (NC)
East Central U (OK)
Eastern Coll (PA)
Eastern Connecticut State U (CT)
Eastern Illinois U (IL)
Eastern Kentucky U (KY)
Eastern Mennonite U (VA)
Eastern Michigan U (MI)
Eastern Nazarene Coll (MA)
Eastern Oregon U (OR)
Eastern Washington U (WA)
East Stroudsburg U of Pennsylvania (PA)
East Tennessee State U (TN)
East Texas Baptist U (TX)
Eckerd Coll (FL)
Edgewood Coll (WI)
Edinboro U of Pennsylvania (PA)
Elizabeth City State U (NC)
Elizabethtown Coll (PA)
Elmhurst Coll (IL)
Elmira Coll (NY)
Elon Coll (NC)
Emmanuel Coll (MA)
Emory & Henry Coll (VA)
Emory U (GA)
Emporia State U (KS)
Erskine Coll (SC)
Evangel U (MO)
The Evergreen State Coll (WA)
Fairfield U (CT)
Fairleigh Dickinson U, Florham-Madison Campus (NJ)
Fairleigh Dickinson U, Teaneck-Hackensack Campus (NJ)
Fairmont State Coll (WV)
Felician Coll (NJ)
Ferris State U (MI)
Ferrum Coll (VA)

Fisk U (TN)
Fitchburg State Coll (MA)
Florida A&M U (FL)
Florida Atlantic U (FL)
Florida Gulf Coast U (FL)
Florida International U (FL)
Florida Southern Coll (FL)
Florida State U (FL)
Fontbonne Coll (MO)
Fordham U (NY)
Fort Hays State U (KS)
Fort Lewis Coll (CO)
Fort Valley State U (GA)
Framingham State Coll (MA)
Franciscan U of Steubenville (OH)
Francis Marion U (SC)
Franklin and Marshall Coll (PA)
Franklin Coll of Indiana (IN)
Franklin Pierce Coll (NH)
Freed-Hardeman U (TN)
Fresno Pacific U (CA)
Friends U (KS)
Frostburg State U (MD)
Furman U (SC)
Gallaudet U (DC)
Gannon U (PA)
Gardner-Webb U (NC)
George Fox U (OR)
George Mason U (VA)
Georgetown Coll (KY)
Georgetown U (DC)
The George Washington U (DC)
Georgia Coll and State U (GA)
Georgia Inst of Technology (GA)
Georgian Court Coll (NJ)
Georgia Southern U (GA)
Georgia Southwestern State U (GA)
Georgia State U (GA)
Gettysburg Coll (PA)
Gonzaga U (WA)
Gordon Coll (MA)
Goshen Coll (IN)
Goucher Coll (MD)
Grace Coll (IN)
Graceland Coll (IA)
Grand Canyon U (AZ)
Grand Valley State U (MI)
Greensboro Coll (NC)
Greenville Coll (IL)
Grinnell Coll (IA)
Grove City Coll (PA)
Guilford Coll (NC)
Gustavus Adolphus Coll (MN)
Gwynedd-Mercy Coll (PA)
Hamilton Coll (NY)
Hamline U (MN)
Hampden-Sydney Coll (VA)
Hampshire Coll (MA)
Hampton U (VA)
Hannibal-LaGrange Coll (MO)
Hanover Coll (IN)
Harding U (AR)
Hardin-Simmons U (TX)
Hartwick Coll (NY)
Harvard U (MA)
Harvey Mudd Coll (CA)
Hastings Coll (NE)
Haverford Coll (PA)
Heidelberg Coll (OH)
Henderson State U (AR)
Hendrix Coll (AR)
Heritage Coll (WA)
High Point U (NC)
Hillsdale Coll (MI)
Hiram Coll (OH)
Hobart and William Smith Colls (NY)
Hofstra U (NY)
Hollins U (VA)
Holy Family Coll (PA)
Hood Coll (MD)
Hope Coll (MI)
Houghton Coll (NY)
Houston Baptist U (TX)
Howard Payne U (TX)
Howard U (DC)
Humboldt State U (CA)
Hunter Coll of the City U of NY (NY)
Huntingdon Coll (AL)
Huntington Coll (IN)
Huston-Tillotson Coll (TX)
Idaho State U (ID)
Illinois Coll (IL)
Illinois State U (IL)
Illinois Wesleyan U (IL)

Immaculata Coll (PA)
Indiana State U (IN)
Indiana U Bloomington (IN)
Indiana U Kokomo (IN)
Indiana U Northwest (IN)
Indiana U of Pennsylvania (PA)
Indiana U–Purdue U Fort Wayne (IN)
Indiana U–Purdue U Indianapolis (IN)
Indiana U South Bend (IN)
Indiana U Southeast (IN)
Indiana Wesleyan U (IN)
Inter American U of PR, Metropolitan Campus (PR)
Inter American U of PR, San Germán Campus (PR)
Iona Coll (NY)
Iowa State U of Science and Technology (IA)
Iowa Wesleyan Coll (IA)
Ithaca Coll (NY)
Jacksonville State U (AL)
Jacksonville U (FL)
James Madison U (VA)
Jamestown Coll (ND)
Jarvis Christian Coll (TX)
John Brown U (AR)
John Carroll U (OH)
Johns Hopkins U (MD)
Johnson C. Smith U (NC)
Johnson State Coll (VT)
Judson Coll (AL)
Judson Coll (IL)
Juniata Coll (PA)
Kalamazoo Coll (MI)
Kansas State U (KS)
Kean U (NJ)
Keene State Coll (NH)
Kent State U (OH)
Kentucky State U (KY)
Kentucky Wesleyan Coll (KY)
Kenyon Coll (OH)
Keuka Coll (NY)
King Coll (TN)
King's Coll (PA)
Knox Coll (IL)
Kutztown U of Pennsylvania (PA)
Lafayette Coll (PA)
LaGrange Coll (GA)
Lake Erie Coll (OH)
Lake Forest Coll (IL)
Lakehead U (ON, Canada)
Lakeland Coll (WI)
Lake Superior State U (MI)
Lamar U (TX)
Lambuth U (TN)
Lander U (SC)
Lane Coll (TN)
Langston U (OK)
La Salle U (PA)
La Sierra U (CA)
Lawrence Technological U (MI)
Lawrence U (WI)
Lebanon Valley Coll (PA)
Lees-McRae Coll (NC)
Lee U (TN)
Lehigh U (PA)
Lehman Coll of the City U of NY (NY)
Le Moyne Coll (NY)
LeMoyne-Owen Coll (TN)
Lenoir-Rhyne Coll (NC)
LeTourneau U (TX)
Lewis & Clark Coll (OR)
Lewis-Clark State Coll (ID)
Lewis U (IL)
Liberty U (VA)
Lincoln Memorial U (TN)
Lincoln U (MO)
Lincoln U (PA)
Lindenwood U (MO)
Linfield Coll (OR)
Lock Haven U of Pennsylvania (PA)
Long Island U, Brooklyn Campus (NY)
Long Island U, C.W. Post Campus (NY)
Longwood Coll (VA)
Loras Coll (IA)
Louisiana Coll (LA)
Louisiana State U and A&M Coll (LA)
Louisiana State U in Shreveport (LA)
Louisiana Tech U (LA)

Loyola Coll in Maryland (MD)
Loyola Marymount U (CA)
Loyola U Chicago (IL)
Loyola U New Orleans (LA)
Lubbock Christian U (TX)
Luther Coll (IA)
Lycoming Coll (PA)
Lynchburg Coll (VA)
Lyndon State Coll (VT)
Lyon Coll (AR)
Macalester Coll (MN)
MacMurray Coll (IL)
Madonna U (MI)
Maharishi U of Management (IA)
Malone Coll (OH)
Manchester Coll (IN)
Manhattan Coll (NY)
Manhattanville Coll (NY)
Mansfield U of Pennsylvania (PA)
Marian Coll (IN)
Marian Coll of Fond du Lac (WI)
Marietta Coll (OH)
Marist Coll (NY)
Marlboro Coll (VT)
Marquette U (WI)
Marshall U (WV)
Mars Hill Coll (NC)
Mary Baldwin Coll (VA)
Marycrest International U (IA)
Marygrove Coll (MI)
Marymount U (NY)
Maryville Coll (TN)
Maryville U of Saint Louis (MO)
Mary Washington Coll (VA)
Marywood U (PA)
Massachusetts Coll of Liberal Arts (MA)
Massachusetts Inst of Technology (MA)
Mayville State U (ND)
McGill U (PQ, Canada)
McKendree Coll (IL)
McMurry U (TX)
McNeese State U (LA)
McPherson Coll (KS)
Memorial U of Newfoundland (NF, Canada)
Mercer U (GA)
Mercy Coll (NY)
Mercyhurst Coll (PA)
Meredith Coll (NC)
Merrimack Coll (MA)
Mesa State Coll (CO)
Messiah Coll (PA)
Methodist Coll (NC)
Metropolitan State Coll of Denver (CO)
Miami U (OH)
Michigan State U (MI)
Michigan Technological U (MI)
MidAmerica Nazarene U (KS)
Middlebury Coll (VT)
Middle Tennessee State U (TN)
Midland Lutheran Coll (NE)
Midwestern State U (TX)
Millersville U of Pennsylvania (PA)
Milligan Coll (TN)
Millikin U (IL)
Millsaps Coll (MS)
Mills Coll (CA)
Minnesota State U, Mankato (MN)
Minnesota State U Moorhead (MN)
Minot State U (ND)
Mississippi Coll (MS)
Mississippi State U (MS)
Mississippi U for Women (MS)
Mississippi Valley State U (MS)
Missouri Baptist Coll (MO)
Missouri Southern State Coll (MO)
Missouri Valley Coll (MO)
Missouri Western State Coll (MO)
Molloy Coll (NY)
Monmouth Coll (IL)
Monmouth U (NJ)
Montana State U–Billings (MT)
Montana State U–Bozeman (MT)
Montana Tech of The U of Montana (MT)
Montreat Coll (NC)
Moravian Coll (PA)
Morehead State U (KY)
Morehouse Coll (GA)
Morgan State U (MD)
Morningside Coll (IA)
Morris Coll (SC)
Mount Allison U (NB, Canada)
Mount Holyoke Coll (MA)

Mount Marty Coll (SD)
Mount Mary Coll (WI)
Mount Mercy Coll (IA)
Mount Saint Mary Coll (NY)
Mount St. Mary's Coll (CA)
Mount Saint Mary's Coll and Seminary (MD)
Mount Saint Vincent U (NS, Canada)
Mount Senario Coll (WI)
Mount Union Coll (OH)
Mount Vernon Nazarene Coll (OH)
Muhlenberg Coll (PA)
Murray State U (KY)
Muskingum Coll (OH)
National-Louis U (IL)
National U (CA)
Nazareth Coll of Rochester (NY)
Nebraska Wesleyan U (NE)
Newberry Coll (SC)
New Coll of the U of South Florida (FL)
New Jersey City U (NJ)
New Jersey Inst of Technology (NJ)
Newman U (KS)
New Mexico Highlands U (NM)
New Mexico Inst of Mining and Technology (NM)
New Mexico State U (NM)
New York Inst of Technology (NY)
New York U (NY)
Niagara U (NY)
Nicholls State U (LA)
Nichols Coll (MA)
Nipissing U (ON, Canada)
Norfolk State U (VA)
North Carolina Ag and Tech State U (NC)
North Carolina Central U (NC)
North Carolina State U (NC)
North Carolina Wesleyan Coll (NC)
North Central Coll (IL)
North Dakota State U (ND)
Northeastern Illinois U (IL)
Northeastern State U (OK)
Northeastern U (MA)
Northern Arizona U (AZ)
Northern Illinois U (IL)
Northern Kentucky U (KY)
Northern Michigan U (MI)
Northern State U (SD)
North Georgia Coll & State U (GA)
Northland Coll (WI)
North Park U (IL)
Northwestern Coll (IA)
Northwestern Coll (MN)
Northwestern Oklahoma State U (OK)
Northwestern State U of Louisiana (LA)
Northwestern U (IL)
Northwest Missouri State U (MO)
Northwest Nazarene U (ID)
Norwich U (VT)
Notre Dame Coll of Ohio (OH)
Nyack Coll (NY)
Oakland City U (IN)
Oakland U (MI)
Oakwood Coll (AL)
Oberlin Coll (OH)
Occidental Coll (CA)
Oglethorpe U (GA)
Ohio Dominican Coll (OH)
Ohio Northern U (OH)
The Ohio State U (OH)
Ohio U (OH)
Ohio Wesleyan U (OH)
Okanagan U Coll (BC, Canada)
Oklahoma Baptist U (OK)
Oklahoma Christian U of Science and Arts (OK)
Oklahoma City U (OK)
Oklahoma Panhandle State U (OK)
Oklahoma State U (OK)
Old Dominion U (VA)
Olivet Nazarene U (IL)
Open Learning Agency (BC, Canada)
Oregon State U (OR)
Ottawa U (KS)
Otterbein Coll (OH)
Ouachita Baptist U (AR)
Our Lady of Holy Cross Coll (LA)
Our Lady of the Lake U of San Antonio (TX)
Pace U, New York City Campus (NY)

Majors Index
Mathematics

Pace U, Pleasantville/Briarcliff Campus (NY)
Pacific Lutheran U (WA)
Pacific Union Coll (CA)
Pacific U (OR)
Paine Coll (GA)
Palm Beach Atlantic Coll (FL)
Park U (MO)
Penn State U at Erie, The Behrend Coll (PA)
Penn State U Univ Park Campus (PA)
Pepperdine U, Malibu (CA)
Peru State Coll (NE)
Pfeiffer U (NC)
Philander Smith Coll (AR)
Piedmont Coll (GA)
Pikeville Coll (KY)
Pittsburg State U (KS)
Pitzer Coll (CA)
Plattsburgh State U of NY (NY)
Plymouth State Coll (NH)
Point Loma Nazarene U (CA)
Polytechnic U, Brooklyn Campus (NY)
Pomona Coll (CA)
Pontifical Catholic U of Puerto Rico (PR)
Portland State U (OR)
Prairie View A&M U (TX)
Presbyterian Coll (SC)
Princeton U (NJ)
Principia Coll (IL)
Providence Coll (RI)
Purchase Coll, State U of NY (NY)
Purdue U (IN)
Purdue U Calumet (IN)
Queens Coll (NC)
Queens Coll of the City U of NY (NY)
Queen's U at Kingston (ON, Canada)
Quincy U (IL)
Quinnipiac U (CT)
Radford U (VA)
Ramapo Coll of New Jersey (NJ)
Randolph-Macon Coll (VA)
Randolph-Macon Woman's Coll (VA)
Redeemer Coll (ON, Canada)
Reed Coll (OR)
Regents Coll (NY)
Regis Coll (MA)
Regis U (CO)
Rensselaer Polytechnic Inst (NY)
Rhodes Coll (TN)
Rice U (TX)
The Richard Stockton Coll of New Jersey (NJ)
Richmond, The American International U in London (United Kingdom)
Rider U (NJ)
Ripon Coll (WI)
Rivier Coll (NH)
Roanoke Coll (VA)
Roberts Wesleyan Coll (NY)
Rochester Coll (MI)
Rochester Inst of Technology (NY)
Rockford Coll (IL)
Rockhurst U (MO)
Rocky Mountain Coll (MT)
Roger Williams U (RI)
Rollins Coll (FL)
Rose-Hulman Inst of Technology (IN)
Rosemont Coll (PA)
Rowan U (NJ)
Russell Sage Coll (NY)
Rust Coll (MS)
Rutgers, State U of NJ, Camden Coll of Arts & Scis (NJ)
Rutgers, State U of NJ, Douglass Coll (NJ)
Rutgers, State U of NJ, Livingston Coll (NJ)
Rutgers, State U of NJ, Newark Coll of Arts & Scis (NJ)
Rutgers, State U of NJ, Rutgers Coll (NJ)
Rutgers, State U of NJ, U Coll–Camden (NJ)
Rutgers, State U of NJ, U Coll–New Brunswick (NJ)
Sacred Heart U (CT)
Saginaw Valley State U (MI)
St. Ambrose U (IA)

St. Andrews Presbyterian Coll (NC)
Saint Anselm Coll (NH)
Saint Augustine's Coll (NC)
St. Bonaventure U (NY)
St. Cloud State U (MN)
St. Edward's U (TX)
St. Francis Coll (NY)
Saint Francis Coll (PA)
St. Francis Xavier U (NS, Canada)
St. John Fisher Coll (NY)
Saint John's U (MN)
St. John's U (NY)
Saint Joseph Coll (CT)
Saint Joseph's Coll (IN)
Saint Joseph's Coll (ME)
St. Joseph's Coll, New York (NY)
St. Joseph's Coll, Suffolk Campus (NY)
Saint Joseph's U (PA)
St. Lawrence U (NY)
Saint Louis U (MO)
Saint Martin's Coll (WA)
Saint Mary Coll (KS)
Saint Mary-of-the-Woods Coll (IN)
Saint Mary's Coll (IN)
Saint Mary's Coll of California (CA)
St. Mary's Coll of Maryland (MD)
Saint Mary's U (NS, Canada)
Saint Mary's U of Minnesota (MN)
St. Mary's U of San Antonio (TX)
Saint Michael's Coll (VT)
St. Norbert Coll (WI)
St. Olaf Coll (MN)
Saint Paul's Coll (VA)
Saint Peter's Coll (NJ)
Saint Vincent Coll (PA)
Saint Xavier U (IL)
Salem Coll (NC)
Salem State Coll (MA)
Salisbury State U (MD)
Salve Regina U (RI)
Samford U (AL)
Sam Houston State U (TX)
San Diego State U (CA)
San Francisco State U (CA)
San Jose State U (CA)
Santa Clara U (CA)
Sarah Lawrence Coll (NY)
Savannah State U (GA)
Schreiner Coll (TX)
Scripps Coll (CA)
Seattle Pacific U (WA)
Seattle U (WA)
Seton Hall U (NJ)
Seton Hill Coll (PA)
Shawnee State U (OH)
Shaw U (NC)
Shenandoah U (VA)
Shepherd Coll (WV)
Shippensburg U of Pennsylvania (PA)
Shorter Coll (GA)
Siena Coll (NY)
Siena Heights U (MI)
Silver Lake Coll (WI)
Simmons Coll (MA)
Simon Fraser U (BC, Canada)
Simon's Rock Coll of Bard (MA)
Simpson Coll (IA)
Simpson Coll and Graduate School (CA)
Skidmore Coll (NY)
Slippery Rock U of Pennsylvania (PA)
Smith Coll (MA)
Sonoma State U (CA)
South Dakota School of Mines and Technology (SD)
South Dakota State U (SD)
Southeastern Louisiana U (LA)
Southeastern Oklahoma State U (OK)
Southeast Missouri State U (MO)
Southern Adventist U (TN)
Southern Arkansas U–Magnolia (AR)
Southern Illinois U Carbondale (IL)
Southern Illinois U Edwardsville (IL)
Southern Methodist U (TX)
Southern Oregon U (OR)
Southern Polytechnic State U (GA)
Southern Utah U (UT)
Southern Wesleyan U (SC)
Southwest Baptist U (MO)
Southwestern Adventist U (TX)
Southwestern Coll (KS)

Southwestern Oklahoma State U (OK)
Southwestern U (TX)
Southwest Missouri State U (MO)
Southwest State U (MN)
Southwest Texas State U (TX)
Spalding U (KY)
Spelman Coll (GA)
Spring Arbor Coll (MI)
Spring Hill Coll (AL)
Stanford U (CA)
State U of NY at Albany (NY)
State U of NY at Binghamton (NY)
State U of NY at Buffalo (NY)
State U of NY at New Paltz (NY)
State U of NY at Oswego (NY)
State U of NY at Stony Brook (NY)
State U of NY Coll at Brockport (NY)
State U of NY Coll at Buffalo (NY)
State U of NY Coll at Cortland (NY)
State U of NY Coll at Fredonia (NY)
State U of NY Coll at Geneseo (NY)
State U of NY Coll at Old Westbury (NY)
State U of NY Coll at Oneonta (NY)
State U of NY Coll at Potsdam (NY)
State U of NY Inst of Tech at Utica/Rome (NY)
State U of West Georgia (GA)
Stephen F. Austin State U (TX)
Stephens Coll (MO)
Sterling Coll (KS)
Stetson U (FL)
Stillman Coll (AL)
Stonehill Coll (MA)
Suffolk U (MA)
Sul Ross State U (TX)
Susquehanna U (PA)
Swarthmore Coll (PA)
Sweet Briar Coll (VA)
Syracuse U (NY)
Tabor Coll (KS)
Talladega Coll (AL)
Taylor U (IN)
Temple U (PA)
Tennessee State U (TN)
Tennessee Technological U (TN)
Tennessee Wesleyan Coll (TN)
Texas A&M International U (TX)
Texas A&M U (TX)
Texas A&M U–Commerce (TX)
Texas A&M U–Kingsville (TX)
Texas A&M U–Texarkana (TX)
Texas Christian U (TX)
Texas Lutheran U (TX)
Texas Southern U (TX)
Texas Tech U (TX)
Texas Wesleyan U (TX)
Texas Woman's U (TX)
Thiel Coll (PA)
Thomas Edison State Coll (NJ)
Thomas More Coll (KY)
Tougaloo Coll (MS)
Touro Coll (NY)
Towson U (MD)
Transylvania U (KY)
Trent U (ON, Canada)
Trevecca Nazarene U (TN)
Trinity Christian Coll (IL)
Trinity Coll (CT)
Trinity U (TX)
Trinity Western U (BC, Canada)
Tri-State U (IN)
Troy State U (AL)
Troy State U Dothan (AL)
Troy State U Montgomery (AL)
Truman State U (MO)
Tufts U (MA)
Tulane U (LA)
Tusculum Coll (TN)
Tuskegee U (AL)
Union Coll (KY)
Union Coll (NE)
Union Coll (NY)
Union U (TN)
United States Air Force Academy (CO)
United States Military Academy (NY)
United States Naval Academy (MD)
Universidad del Turabo (PR)

Université de Montréal (PQ, Canada)
Université de Sherbrooke (PQ, Canada)
U du Québec à Chicoutimi (PQ, Canada)
U du Québec à Trois-Rivières (PQ, Canada)
Université Laval (PQ, Canada)
U Coll of Cape Breton (NS, Canada)
U Coll of the Fraser Valley (BC, Canada)
The U of Akron (OH)
The U of Alabama (AL)
The U of Alabama at Birmingham (AL)
The U of Alabama in Huntsville (AL)
U of Alaska Fairbanks (AK)
U of Alberta (AB, Canada)
The U of Arizona (AZ)
U of Arkansas (AR)
U of Arkansas at Little Rock (AR)
U of Arkansas at Monticello (AR)
U of Arkansas at Pine Bluff (AR)
U of Bridgeport (CT)
U of British Columbia (BC, Canada)
U of Calgary (AB, Canada)
U of Calif, Berkeley (CA)
U of Calif, Davis (CA)
U of Calif, Irvine (CA)
U of Calif, Los Angeles (CA)
U of Calif, Riverside (CA)
U of Calif, San Diego (CA)
U of Calif, Santa Barbara (CA)
U of Calif, Santa Cruz (CA)
U of Central Arkansas (AR)
U of Central Florida (FL)
U of Central Oklahoma (OK)
U of Chicago (IL)
U of Cincinnati (OH)
U of Colorado at Boulder (CO)
U of Colorado at Colorado Springs (CO)
U of Colorado at Denver (CO)
U of Connecticut (CT)
U of Dallas (TX)
U of Dayton (OH)
U of Delaware (DE)
U of Denver (CO)
U of Detroit Mercy (MI)
U of Evansville (IN)
The U of Findlay (OH)
U of Florida (FL)
U of Georgia (GA)
U of Great Falls (MT)
U of Guelph (ON, Canada)
U of Hartford (CT)
U of Hawaii at Manoa (HI)
U of Houston (TX)
U of Houston–Victoria (TX)
U of Idaho (ID)
U of Illinois at Chicago (IL)
U of Illinois at Springfield (IL)
U of Illinois at Urbana–Champaign (IL)
U of Indianapolis (IN)
The U of Iowa (IA)
U of Kansas (KS)
U of Kentucky (KY)
U of King's Coll (NS, Canada)
U of La Verne (CA)
The U of Lethbridge (AB, Canada)
U of Louisiana at Lafayette (LA)
U of Louisiana at Monroe (LA)
U of Louisville (KY)
U of Maine (ME)
The U of Maine at Augusta (ME)
U of Maine at Farmington (ME)
U of Maine at Presque Isle (ME)
U of Manitoba (MB, Canada)
U of Mary Hardin-Baylor (TX)
U of Maryland, Baltimore County (MD)
U of Maryland, Coll Park (MD)
U of Maryland University Coll (MD)
U of Massachusetts Amherst (MA)
U of Massachusetts Boston (MA)
U of Massachusetts Dartmouth (MA)
U of Massachusetts Lowell (MA)
The U of Memphis (TN)
U of Miami (FL)
U of Michigan (MI)
U of Michigan–Dearborn (MI)

U of Michigan–Flint (MI)
U of Minnesota, Duluth (MN)
U of Minnesota, Morris (MN)
U of Minnesota, Twin Cities Campus (MN)
U of Mississippi (MS)
U of Missouri–Columbia (MO)
U of Missouri–Kansas City (MO)
U of Missouri–St. Louis (MO)
U of Mobile (AL)
The U of Montana–Missoula (MT)
U of Montevallo (AL)
U of Nebraska at Kearney (NE)
U of Nebraska at Omaha (NE)
U of Nebraska–Lincoln (NE)
U of Nevada, Las Vegas (NV)
U of Nevada, Reno (NV)
U of New Brunswick, Fredericton (NB, Canada)
U of New Hampshire (NH)
U of New Haven (CT)
U of New Mexico (NM)
U of New Orleans (LA)
U of North Alabama (AL)
The U of North Carolina at Asheville (NC)
The U of North Carolina at Chapel Hill (NC)
The U of North Carolina at Charlotte (NC)
The U of North Carolina at Greensboro (NC)
The U of North Carolina at Pembroke (NC)
The U of North Carolina at Wilmington (NC)
U of North Dakota (ND)
U of Northern Colorado (CO)
U of Northern Iowa (IA)
U of North Florida (FL)
U of North Texas (TX)
U of Notre Dame (IN)
U of Oklahoma (OK)
U of Oregon (OR)
U of Pennsylvania (PA)
U of Pittsburgh (PA)
U of Pittsburgh at Bradford (PA)
U of Pittsburgh at Johnstown (PA)
U of Portland (OR)
U of Prince Edward Island (PE, Canada)
U of Puerto Rico, Mayagüez Campus (PR)
U of Puerto Rico, Río Piedras (PR)
U of Puget Sound (WA)
U of Redlands (CA)
U of Regina (SK, Canada)
U of Rhode Island (RI)
U of Richmond (VA)
U of Rio Grande (OH)
U of Rochester (NY)
U of St. Francis (IL)
U of St. Thomas (MN)
U of St. Thomas (TX)
U of San Diego (CA)
U of San Francisco (CA)
U of Science and Arts of Oklahoma (OK)
The U of Scranton (PA)
U of Sioux Falls (SD)
U of South Alabama (AL)
U of South Carolina (SC)
U of South Carolina Spartanburg (SC)
U of South Dakota (SD)
U of Southern California (CA)
U of Southern Colorado (CO)
U of Southern Indiana (IN)
U of Southern Maine (ME)
U of Southern Mississippi (MS)
U of South Florida (FL)
The U of Tampa (FL)
The U of Tennessee at Chattanooga (TN)
The U of Tennessee at Martin (TN)
The U of Tennessee Knoxville (TN)
The U of Texas at Arlington (TX)
The U of Texas at Austin (TX)
The U of Texas at Dallas (TX)
The U of Texas at San Antonio (TX)
The U of Texas at Tyler (TX)
The U of Texas–Pan American (TX)
U of the District of Columbia (DC)
U of the Ozarks (AR)
U of the Pacific (CA)
U of the Sacred Heart (PR)

Majors Index
Mathematics–Mechanical Engineering

U of the South (TN)
U of the Virgin Islands (VI)
U of Toronto (ON, Canada)
U of Tulsa (OK)
U of Utah (UT)
U of Vermont (VT)
U of Victoria (BC, Canada)
U of Virginia (VA)
U of Virginia's Coll at Wise (VA)
U of Washington (WA)
U of Waterloo (ON, Canada)
The U of West Alabama (AL)
The U of Western Ontario (ON, Canada)
U of West Florida (FL)
U of Windsor (ON, Canada)
The U of Winnipeg (MB, Canada)
U of Wisconsin–Eau Claire (WI)
U of Wisconsin–Green Bay (WI)
U of Wisconsin–La Crosse (WI)
U of Wisconsin–Madison (WI)
U of Wisconsin–Milwaukee (WI)
U of Wisconsin–Parkside (WI)
U of Wisconsin–Platteville (WI)
U of Wisconsin–River Falls (WI)
U of Wisconsin–Stevens Point (WI)
U of Wisconsin–Superior (WI)
U of Wisconsin–Whitewater (WI)
U of Wyoming (WY)
Upper Iowa U (IA)
Ursinus Coll (PA)
Ursuline Coll (OH)
Utah State U (UT)
Utica Coll of Syracuse U (NY)
Valdosta State U (GA)
Valley City State U (ND)
Valparaiso U (IN)
Vanderbilt U (TN)
Vanguard U of Southern California (CA)
Vassar Coll (NY)
Villanova U (PA)
Virginia Commonwealth U (VA)
Virginia Intermont Coll (VA)
Virginia Military Inst (VA)
Virginia Polytechnic Inst and State U (VA)
Virginia Union U (VA)
Virginia Wesleyan Coll (VA)
Voorhees Coll (SC)
Wabash Coll (IN)
Wagner Coll (NY)
Wake Forest U (NC)
Walla Walla Coll (WA)
Walsh U (OH)
Warren Wilson Coll (NC)
Wartburg Coll (IA)
Washington & Jefferson Coll (PA)
Washington and Lee U (VA)
Washington Coll (MD)
Washington State U (WA)
Washington U in St. Louis (MO)
Wayland Baptist U (TX)
Waynesburg Coll (PA)
Wayne State Coll (NE)
Wayne State U (MI)
Weber State U (UT)
Webster U (MO)
Wellesley Coll (MA)
Wells Coll (NY)
Wesleyan Coll (GA)
Wesleyan U (CT)
West Chester U of Pennsylvania (PA)
Western Baptist Coll (OR)
Western Carolina U (NC)
Western Connecticut State U (CT)
Western Illinois U (IL)
Western Kentucky U (KY)
Western Maryland Coll (MD)
Western Michigan U (MI)
Western Montana Coll of The U of Montana (MT)
Western New England Coll (MA)
Western Oregon U (OR)
Western State Coll of Colorado (CO)
Western Washington U (WA)
Westfield State Coll (MA)
West Liberty State Coll (WV)
Westminster Coll (MO)
Westminster Coll (PA)
Westminster Coll (UT)
Westmont Coll (CA)
West Texas A&M U (TX)
West Virginia State Coll (WV)
West Virginia U (WV)

West Virginia U Inst of Technology (WV)
West Virginia Wesleyan Coll (WV)
Wheaton Coll (IL)
Wheaton Coll (MA)
Wheeling Jesuit U (WV)
Whitman Coll (WA)
Whittier Coll (CA)
Whitworth Coll (WA)
Wichita State U (KS)
Widener U (PA)
Wilfrid Laurier U (ON, Canada)
Wilkes U (PA)
Willamette U (OR)
William Jewell Coll (MO)
William Paterson U of New Jersey (NJ)
Williams Coll (MA)
William Tyndale Coll (MI)
William Woods U (MO)
Wilmington Coll (OH)
Wilson Coll (PA)
Wingate U (NC)
Winona State U (MN)
Winston-Salem State U (NC)
Winthrop U (SC)
Wisconsin Lutheran Coll (WI)
Wittenberg U (OH)
Wofford Coll (SC)
Worcester Polytechnic Inst (MA)
Worcester State Coll (MA)
Wright State U (OH)
Xavier U (OH)
Xavier U of Louisiana (LA)
Yale U (CT)
Yeshiva U (NY)
York Coll (NE)
York Coll of Pennsylvania (PA)
York Coll of the City U of New York (NY)
York U (ON, Canada)
Youngstown State U (OH)

MATHEMATICS/COMPUTER SCIENCE
Alfred U (NY)
Anderson U (IN)
Averett Coll (VA)
Avila Coll (MO)
Boston U (MA)
Brandon U (MB, Canada)
Brescia U (KY)
Brevard Coll (NC)
Brown U (RI)
Carlow Coll (PA)
Central Coll (IA)
Chestnut Hill Coll (PA)
Coll of Saint Benedict (MN)
Coll of Santa Fe (NM)
Drew U (NJ)
Ithaca Coll (NY)
King Coll (TN)
Lake Superior State U (MI)
Maryville Coll (TN)
McGill U (PQ, Canada)
McMurry U (TX)
Morehead State U (KY)
Mount Allison U (NB, Canada)
Mount Saint Vincent U (NS, Canada)
Rochester Inst of Technology (NY)
Saginaw Valley State U (MI)
Saint John's U (MN)
Saint Joseph's Coll (IN)
Saint Mary's Coll (IN)
St. Norbert Coll (WI)
Southern Oregon U (OR)
Stanford U (CA)
State U of NY at Binghamton (NY)
Stonehill Coll (MA)
Swarthmore Coll (PA)
Trinity Western U (BC, Canada)
U of Houston–Clear Lake (TX)
U of Illinois at Chicago (IL)
U of Illinois at Urbana–Champaign (IL)
U of Oregon (OR)
U of Puerto Rico, Humacao U Coll (PR)
U of Waterloo (ON, Canada)
Washington State U (WA)
Washington U in St. Louis (MO)
York U (ON, Canada)

MATHEMATICS EDUCATION
Abilene Christian U (TX)
Adams State Coll (CO)

Alvernia Coll (PA)
Anderson U (IN)
Appalachian State U (NC)
Arkansas State U (AR)
Arkansas Tech U (AR)
Bayamón Central U (PR)
Baylor U (TX)
Berea Coll (KY)
Berry Coll (GA)
Bethany Coll (KS)
Bethel Coll (IN)
Bethune-Cookman Coll (FL)
Blue Mountain Coll (MS)
Boston U (MA)
Bridgewater Coll (VA)
Brigham Young U (UT)
Brigham Young U–Hawaii Campus (HI)
Brock U (ON, Canada)
Cabrini Coll (PA)
California State U, Chico (CA)
Canisius Coll (NY)
Carroll Coll (MT)
Castleton State Coll (VT)
The Catholic U of America (DC)
Cedarville Coll (OH)
Central Michigan U (MI)
Central Missouri State U (MO)
Chowan Coll (NC)
Christian Brothers U (TN)
Citadel, The Military Coll of South Carolina (SC)
Clemson U (SC)
The Coll of New Jersey (NJ)
Coll of Our Lady of the Elms (MA)
Coll of St. Catherine (MN)
Coll of the Ozarks (MO)
Colorado Christian U (CO)
Colorado State U (CO)
Concordia Coll (MN)
Concordia U (IL)
Concordia U (NE)
Concordia U (OR)
Culver-Stockton Coll (MO)
Cumberland Coll (KY)
Daemen Coll (NY)
Dana Coll (NE)
Delta State U (MS)
Dominican Coll of Blauvelt (NY)
Duquesne U (PA)
East Carolina U (NC)
Eastern Michigan U (MI)
East Texas Baptist U (TX)
Elmhurst Coll (IL)
Elmira Coll (NY)
Felician Coll (NJ)
Florida Atlantic U (FL)
Florida Inst of Technology (FL)
Florida International U (FL)
Florida State U (FL)
Freed-Hardeman U (TN)
Geneva Coll (PA)
George Fox U (OR)
Georgia Southern U (GA)
Grace Coll (IN)
Greensboro Coll (NC)
Greenville Coll (IL)
Gustavus Adolphus Coll (MN)
Harding U (AR)
Hardin-Simmons U (TX)
Hastings Coll (NE)
Huntingdon Coll (AL)
Indiana U Bloomington (IN)
Indiana U Northwest (IN)
Indiana U of Pennsylvania (PA)
Indiana U–Purdue U Fort Wayne (IN)
Indiana U South Bend (IN)
Indiana U Southeast (IN)
Indiana Wesleyan U (IN)
Ithaca Coll (NY)
Johnson State Coll (VT)
Judson Coll (AL)
Juniata Coll (PA)
Keuka Coll (NY)
King Coll (TN)
La Roche Coll (PA)
Le Moyne Coll (NY)
Liberty U (VA)
Limestone Coll (SC)
Lincoln U (PA)
Long Island U, C.W. Post Campus (NY)
Luther Coll (IA)
Lyndon State Coll (VT)
Manhattanville Coll (NY)
Mansfield U of Pennsylvania (PA)

Marymount Coll (NY)
Maryville Coll (TN)
Mayville State U (ND)
McGill U (PQ, Canada)
McKendree Coll (IL)
Mercer U (GA)
Messiah Coll (PA)
MidAmerica Nazarene U (KS)
Minnesota State U Moorhead (MN)
Mississippi Valley State U (MS)
Molloy Coll (NY)
Morehead State U (KY)
Mount Marty Coll (SD)
Nazareth Coll of Rochester (NY)
New York Inst of Technology (NY)
New York U (NY)
Niagara U (NY)
North Carolina Central U (NC)
North Carolina State U (NC)
North Dakota State U (ND)
Northern Kentucky U (KY)
Northwestern Coll (MN)
Northwest Nazarene U (ID)
Oakland City U (IN)
Ohio U (OH)
Oklahoma Baptist U (OK)
Penn State U Harrisburg Campus of the Capital Coll (PA)
Philadelphia Coll of Bible (PA)
Pikeville Coll (KY)
Plymouth State Coll (NH)
Queens Coll (NC)
Rivier Coll (NH)
Rocky Mountain Coll (MT)
St. Ambrose U (IA)
Saint Augustine's Coll (NC)
St. John Fisher Coll (NY)
St. John's U (NY)
St. Olaf Coll (MN)
Saint Xavier U (IL)
Salve Regina U (RI)
Seattle Pacific U (WA)
Seton Hill Coll (PA)
Shaw U (NC)
Southeastern Coll of the Assemblies of God (FL)
Southeastern Louisiana U (LA)
Southeastern Oklahoma State U (OK)
Southern Arkansas U–Magnolia (AR)
Southwestern Coll (KS)
Southwest Missouri State U (MO)
Southwest State U (MN)
Syracuse U (NY)
Talladega Coll (AL)
Tennessee Wesleyan Coll (TN)
Texas A&M International U (TX)
Texas Wesleyan U (TX)
Thomas Coll (ME)
Trevecca Nazarene U (TN)
Trinity Christian Coll (IL)
Tri-State U (IN)
Union Coll (NE)
U du Québec à Trois-Rivières (PQ, Canada)
The U of Arizona (AZ)
U of Arkansas (AR)
U of Calif, San Diego (CA)
U of Central Arkansas (AR)
U of Central Florida (FL)
U of Delaware (DE)
U of Georgia (GA)
U of Illinois at Chicago (IL)
U of Illinois at Urbana–Champaign (IL)
U of Indianapolis (IN)
The U of Iowa (IA)
U of Louisiana at Monroe (LA)
U of Maine at Farmington (ME)
U of Maryland, Coll Park (MD)
U of Minnesota, Duluth (MN)
U of Minnesota, Twin Cities Campus (MN)
U of Mississippi (MS)
The U of Montana–Missoula (MT)
U of Nebraska–Lincoln (NE)
U of Nevada, Reno (NV)
The U of North Carolina at Chapel Hill (NC)
The U of North Carolina at Charlotte (NC)
U of Northern Iowa (IA)
U of North Florida (FL)
U of North Texas (TX)
U of Oklahoma (OK)
U of Rio Grande (OH)

U of Southern Colorado (CO)
U of South Florida (FL)
The U of Tennessee at Martin (TN)
U of Vermont (VT)
U of Waterloo (ON, Canada)
U of West Florida (FL)
U of Wisconsin–River Falls (WI)
U of Wisconsin–Superior (WI)
Utah State U (UT)
Wartburg Coll (IA)
Washington U in St. Louis (MO)
Wayne State U (MI)
Western Carolina U (NC)
Western Montana Coll of The U of Montana (MT)
Westmont Coll (CA)
Wheeling Jesuit U (WV)
William Penn U (IA)
York Coll (NE)
York U (ON, Canada)
Youngstown State U (OH)

MECHANICAL DESIGN TECHNOLOGY
Bowling Green State U (OH)
Indiana State U (IN)
Lincoln U (MO)
Pittsburg State U (KS)

MECHANICAL DRAFTING
Pennsylvania Coll of Technology (PA)
Purdue U (IN)
U of Advancing Computer Technology (AZ)

MECHANICAL ENGINEERING
Alabama A&M U (AL)
Alfred U (NY)
American U in Cairo (Egypt)
Andrews U (MI)
Arizona State U (AZ)
Arkansas Tech U (AR)
Auburn U (AL)
Baker Coll of Flint (MI)
Bethel Coll (IN)
Boston U (MA)
Bradley U (IL)
Brigham Young U (UT)
Brown U (RI)
Bucknell U (PA)
California Inst of Technology (CA)
California Maritime Academy (CA)
California Polytechnic State U, San Luis Obispo (CA)
California State Polytechnic U, Pomona (CA)
California State U, Chico (CA)
California State U, Fresno (CA)
California State U, Fullerton (CA)
California State U, Long Beach (CA)
California State U, Los Angeles (CA)
California State U, Northridge (CA)
California State U, Sacramento (CA)
Calvin Coll (MI)
Carleton U (ON, Canada)
Carnegie Mellon U (PA)
Case Western Reserve U (OH)
The Catholic U of America (DC)
Cedarville Coll (OH)
Christian Brothers U (TN)
City Coll of the City U of NY (NY)
Clarkson U (NY)
Clemson U (SC)
Cleveland State U (OH)
The Coll of Southeastern Europe, The American U of Athens (Greece)
Colorado School of Mines (CO)
Colorado State U (CO)
Columbia U, School of Engineering & Applied Sci (NY)
Concordia U (PQ, Canada)
Cooper Union for the Advancement of Science & Art (NY)
Cornell U (NY)
Dalhousie U (NS, Canada)
Delaware State U (DE)
Drexel U (PA)
Duke U (NC)
Eastern Nazarene Coll (MA)
Florida A&M U (FL)
Florida Atlantic U (FL)
Florida Inst of Technology (FL)

Majors Index
Mechanical Engineering–Medical Laboratory Technician

Florida International U (FL)
Florida State U (FL)
Frostburg State U (MD)
Gallaudet U (DC)
Gannon U (PA)
The George Washington U (DC)
Georgia Inst of Technology (GA)
Gonzaga U (WA)
Grand Valley State U (MI)
Grove City Coll (PA)
Harvard U (MA)
Henry Cogswell Coll (WA)
Hofstra U (NY)
Howard U (DC)
Illinois Inst of Technology (IL)
Indiana Inst of Technology (IN)
Indiana U–Purdue U Fort Wayne (IN)
Indiana U–Purdue U Indianapolis (IN)
Insto Tecno Estudios Sups Monterrey (Mexico)
Insto Tecno Estudios Sups Monterrey, Querétaro (Mexico)
Iowa State U of Science and Technology (IA)
Jacksonville U (FL)
John Brown U (AR)
Johns Hopkins U (MD)
Johnson & Wales U (RI)
Kansas State U (KS)
Kettering U (MI)
Lafayette Coll (PA)
Lakehead U (ON, Canada)
Lake Superior State U (MI)
Lamar U (TX)
Lawrence Technological U (MI)
Lehigh U (PA)
LeTourneau U (TX)
Louisiana State U and A&M Coll (LA)
Louisiana Tech U (LA)
Loyola Marymount U (CA)
Manhattan Coll (NY)
Marquette U (WI)
Massachusetts Inst of Technology (MA)
McGill U (PQ, Canada)
Memorial U of Newfoundland (NF, Canada)
Mercer U (GA)
Michigan State U (MI)
Michigan Technological U (MI)
Milwaukee School of Engineering (WI)
Minnesota State U, Mankato (MN)
Mississippi State U (MS)
Montana State U–Bozeman (MT)
Montana Tech of The U of Montana (MT)
New Jersey Inst of Technology (NJ)
New Mexico State U (NM)
New York Inst of Technology (NY)
New York U (NY)
North Carolina Ag and Tech State U (NC)
North Carolina State U (NC)
North Dakota State U (ND)
Northeastern U (MA)
Northern Arizona U (AZ)
Northern Illinois U (IL)
Northwestern U (IL)
Norwich U (VT)
Oakland U (MI)
Ohio Northern U (OH)
The Ohio State U (OH)
Ohio U (OH)
Oklahoma Christian U of Science and Arts (OK)
Oklahoma State U (OK)
Old Dominion U (VA)
Oregon State U (OR)
Penn State U at Erie, The Behrend Coll (PA)
Penn State U Univ Park Campus (PA)
Polytechnic U, Brooklyn Campus (NY)
Polytechnic U, Farmingdale Campus (NY)
Polytechnic U of Puerto Rico (PR)
Portland State U (OR)
Prairie View A&M U (TX)
Princeton U (NJ)
Purdue U (IN)
Purdue U Calumet (IN)

Queen's U at Kingston (ON, Canada)
Rensselaer Polytechnic Inst (NY)
Rice U (TX)
Rochester Inst of Technology (NY)
Rose-Hulman Inst of Technology (IN)
Rowan U (NJ)
Rutgers, State U of NJ, Coll of Engineering (NJ)
Ryerson Polytechnic U (ON, Canada)
Saginaw Valley State U (MI)
Saint Augustine's Coll (NC)
Saint Louis U (MO)
Saint Martin's Coll (WA)
San Diego State U (CA)
San Francisco State U (CA)
San Jose State U (CA)
Santa Clara U (CA)
Seattle U (WA)
South Dakota School of Mines and Technology (SD)
South Dakota State U (SD)
Southern Illinois U Carbondale (IL)
Southern Illinois U Edwardsville (IL)
Southern Methodist U (TX)
Stanford U (CA)
State U of NY at Binghamton (NY)
State U of NY at Buffalo (NY)
State U of NY at Stony Brook (NY)
State U of NY Maritime Coll (NY)
Stevens Inst of Technology (NJ)
Syracuse U (NY)
Temple U (PA)
Tennessee State U (TN)
Tennessee Technological U (TN)
Texas A&M U (TX)
Texas A&M U–Kingsville (TX)
Texas Tech U (TX)
Trinity Coll (CT)
Tri-State U (IN)
Tufts U (MA)
Tulane U (LA)
Tuskegee U (AL)
Union Coll (NY)
United States Air Force Academy (CO)
United States Coast Guard Academy (CT)
United States Military Academy (NY)
United States Naval Academy (MD)
Universidad del Turabo (PR)
Université de Sherbrooke (PQ, Canada)
U du Québec à Trois-Rivières (PQ, Canada)
U du Québec en Abitibi-Témiscamingue (PQ, Canada)
Université Laval (PQ, Canada)
The U of Akron (OH)
The U of Alabama (AL)
The U of Alabama at Birmingham (AL)
The U of Alabama in Huntsville (AL)
U of Alaska Fairbanks (AK)
U of Alberta (AB, Canada)
The U of Arizona (AZ)
U of Arkansas (AR)
U of British Columbia (BC, Canada)
U of Calgary (AB, Canada)
U of Calif, Berkeley (CA)
U of Calif, Davis (CA)
U of Calif, Irvine (CA)
U of Calif, Los Angeles (CA)
U of Calif, Riverside (CA)
U of Calif, San Diego (CA)
U of Calif, Santa Barbara (CA)
U of Central Florida (FL)
U of Cincinnati (OH)
U of Colorado at Boulder (CO)
U of Colorado at Colorado Springs (CO)
U of Colorado at Denver (CO)
U of Connecticut (CT)
U of Dayton (OH)
U of Delaware (DE)
U of Denver (CO)
U of Detroit Mercy (MI)
U of Evansville (IN)
U of Florida (FL)
U of Hartford (CT)
U of Hawaii at Manoa (HI)
U of Houston (TX)

U of Idaho (ID)
U of Illinois at Chicago (IL)
U of Illinois at Urbana–Champaign (IL)
The U of Iowa (IA)
U of Kansas (KS)
U of Kentucky (KY)
U of Louisiana at Lafayette (LA)
U of Louisville (KY)
U of Maine (ME)
U of Manitoba (MB, Canada)
U of Maryland, Baltimore County (MD)
U of Maryland, Coll Park (MD)
U of Massachusetts Amherst (MA)
U of Massachusetts Dartmouth (MA)
U of Massachusetts Lowell (MA)
The U of Memphis (TN)
U of Miami (FL)
U of Michigan (MI)
U of Michigan–Dearborn (MI)
U of Minnesota, Twin Cities Campus (MN)
U of Mississippi (MS)
U of Missouri–Columbia (MO)
U of Missouri–Kansas City (MO)
U of Missouri–Rolla (MO)
U of Missouri–St. Louis (MO)
U of Nebraska–Lincoln (NE)
U of Nevada, Las Vegas (NV)
U of Nevada, Reno (NV)
U of New Brunswick, Fredericton (NB, Canada)
U of New Brunswick, Saint John (NB, Canada)
U of New Hampshire (NH)
U of New Haven (CT)
U of New Mexico (NM)
U of New Orleans (LA)
The U of North Carolina at Charlotte (NC)
U of North Dakota (ND)
U of Notre Dame (IN)
U of Oklahoma (OK)
U of Pennsylvania (PA)
U of Pittsburgh (PA)
U of Pittsburgh at Bradford (PA)
U of Portland (OR)
U of Puerto Rico, Mayagüez Campus (PR)
U of Regina (SK, Canada)
U of Rhode Island (RI)
U of Rochester (NY)
U of St. Thomas (MN)
U of South Alabama (AL)
U of South Carolina (SC)
U of Southern California (CA)
U of South Florida (FL)
The U of Tennessee at Chattanooga (TN)
The U of Tennessee Knoxville (TN)
The U of Texas at Arlington (TX)
The U of Texas at Austin (TX)
The U of Texas at San Antonio (TX)
The U of Texas at Tyler (TX)
The U of Texas–Pan American (TX)
U of the District of Columbia (DC)
U of the Pacific (CA)
U of Toronto (ON, Canada)
U of Tulsa (OK)
U of Utah (UT)
U of Vermont (VT)
U of Victoria (BC, Canada)
U of Virginia (VA)
U of Washington (WA)
U of Waterloo (ON, Canada)
The U of Western Ontario (ON, Canada)
U of Windsor (ON, Canada)
U of Wisconsin–Madison (WI)
U of Wisconsin–Milwaukee (WI)
U of Wisconsin–Platteville (WI)
U of Wyoming (WY)
Utah State U (UT)
Valparaiso U (IN)
Vanderbilt U (TN)
Villanova U (PA)
Virginia Commonwealth U (VA)
Virginia Military Inst (VA)
Virginia Polytechnic Inst and State U (VA)
Walla Walla Coll (WA)
Washington State U (WA)
Washington U in St. Louis (MO)
Wayne State U (MI)

Western Michigan U (MI)
Western New England Coll (MA)
West Virginia U (WV)
West Virginia U Inst of Technology (WV)
Wichita State U (KS)
Widener U (PA)
Wilkes U (PA)
William Penn U (IA)
Winona State U (MN)
Worcester Polytechnic Inst (MA)
Wright State U (OH)
Yale U (CT)
York Coll of Pennsylvania (PA)
Youngstown State U (OH)

MECHANICAL ENGINEERING TECHNOLOGY
Alabama A&M U (AL)
Andrews U (MI)
Arizona State U East (AZ)
Bluefield State Coll (WV)
Boise State U (ID)
California Polytechnic State U, San Luis Obispo (CA)
California State Polytechnic U, Pomona (CA)
California State U, Sacramento (CA)
Central Connecticut State U (CT)
Central Michigan U (MI)
Cleveland State U (OH)
Delaware State U (DE)
Eastern Washington U (WA)
Fairleigh Dickinson U, Teaneck-Hackensack Campus (NJ)
Fairmont State Coll (WV)
Georgia Southern U (GA)
Indiana State U (IN)
Indiana U–Purdue U Fort Wayne (IN)
Indiana U–Purdue U Indianapolis (IN)
Johnson & Wales U (RI)
Kansas State U (KS)
Kent State U (OH)
Lakehead U (ON, Canada)
Lake Superior State U (MI)
LeTourneau U (TX)
Metropolitan State Coll of Denver (CO)
Michigan Technological U (MI)
Millersville U of Pennsylvania (PA)
Milwaukee School of Engineering (WI)
Montana State U–Bozeman (MT)
Murray State U (KY)
New Jersey Inst of Technology (NJ)
New York Inst of Technology (NY)
Northeastern U (MA)
Oklahoma State U (OK)
Oregon Inst of Technology (OR)
Penn State U at Erie, The Behrend Coll (PA)
Penn State U Harrisburg Campus of the Capital Coll (PA)
Pittsburg State U (KS)
Point Park Coll (PA)
Purdue U Calumet (IN)
Purdue U North Central (IN)
Regents Coll (NY)
Rochester Inst of Technology (NY)
Savannah State U (GA)
Southern Polytechnic State U (GA)
Southwest Missouri State U (MO)
State U of NY Coll at Buffalo (NY)
State U of NY Coll of Technology at Alfred (NY)
State U of NY Inst of Tech at Utica/Rome (NY)
Temple U (PA)
Texas Tech U (TX)
Thomas Edison State Coll (NJ)
U du Québec en Abitibi-Témiscamingue (PQ, Canada)
The U of Akron (OH)
U of Arkansas at Little Rock (AR)
U of Cincinnati (OH)
U of Dayton (OH)
U of Hartford (CT)
U of Houston–Downtown (TX)
U of Maine (ME)
U of Massachusetts Dartmouth (MA)
U of New Hampshire (NH)
U of New Hampshire at Manchester (NH)

The U of North Carolina at Charlotte (NC)
U of North Texas (TX)
U of Pittsburgh at Johnstown (PA)
U of Rio Grande (OH)
U of Southern Colorado (CO)
U of Southern Mississippi (MS)
Wayne State U (MI)
Weber State U (UT)
Wentworth Inst of Technology (MA)
Western Kentucky U (KY)
Youngstown State U (OH)

MEDICAL ADMINISTRATIVE ASSISTANT
Baker Coll of Auburn Hills (MI)
Peirce Coll (PA)
Tabor Coll (KS)

MEDICAL ASSISTANT
California State U, Dominguez Hills (CA)
Jones Coll (FL)
Robert Morris Coll (IL)
U of New England (ME)

MEDICAL DIETICIAN
The Ohio State U (OH)
U of Illinois at Chicago (IL)

MEDICAL ILLUSTRATING
Alma Coll (MI)
Beaver Coll (PA)
Clark Atlanta U (GA)
Cleveland Inst of Art (OH)
Iowa State U of Science and Technology (IA)
Rochester Inst of Technology (NY)
Texas Woman's U (TX)
Tulane U (LA)
U of Toronto (ON, Canada)

MEDICAL LABORATORY ASSISTANT
California State U, Chico (CA)
U of Vermont (VT)

MEDICAL LABORATORY TECHNICIAN
Alabama State U (AL)
Alfred U (NY)
Andrews U (MI)
Auburn U (AL)
Barry U (FL)
Bloomsburg U of Pennsylvania (PA)
California State U, Dominguez Hills (CA)
California State U, Hayward (CA)
California State U, Northridge (CA)
California U of Pennsylvania (PA)
Columbus State U (GA)
Concordia U (NE)
Cumberland Coll (KY)
DePaul U (IL)
East Central U (OK)
East Stroudsburg U of Pennsylvania (PA)
Edinboro U of Pennsylvania (PA)
Ferris State U (MI)
Gardner-Webb U (NC)
Holy Family Coll (PA)
Hunter Coll of the City U of NY (NY)
Indiana State U (IN)
Iowa Wesleyan Coll (IA)
Longwood Coll (VA)
Louisiana Coll (LA)
Marquette U (WI)
Massachusetts Coll of Liberal Arts (MA)
Milligan Coll (TN)
Morgan State U (MD)
Mount Saint Mary Coll (NY)
Northeastern U (MA)
Northern Michigan U (MI)
Northern State U (SD)
Northwestern Oklahoma State U (OK)
Northwest Missouri State U (MO)
Pace U, New York City Campus (NY)
Purdue U Calumet (IN)
Quinnipiac U (CT)
Shawnee State U (OH)
Sonoma State U (CA)

Majors Index
Medical Laboratory Technician–Medical Technology

Thomas Edison State Coll (NJ)
U of Alberta (AB, Canada)
U of British Columbia (BC, Canada)
U of Missouri–Kansas City (MO)
The U of Montana–Missoula (MT)
U of New England (ME)
U of New Hampshire (NH)
The U of North Carolina at Pembroke (NC)
U of Utah (UT)
Weber State U (UT)
Winona State U (MN)

MEDICAL LABORATORY TECHNOLOGIES
Auburn U (AL)
Averett Coll (VA)
The Coll of St. Scholastica (MN)
Columbus State U (GA)
Fairleigh Dickinson U, Teaneck-Hackensack Campus (NJ)
Felician Coll (NJ)
The George Washington U (DC)
Marshall U (WV)
Michigan State U (MI)
Oakland U (MI)
Quinnipiac U (CT)
Rutgers, State U of NJ, Newark Coll of Arts & Scis (NJ)
Southeastern Oklahoma State U (OK)
U of Cincinnati (OH)
U of Illinois at Springfield (IL)
U of Nevada, Las Vegas (NV)
U of New England (ME)
U of Oklahoma (OK)
U of Regina (SK, Canada)

MEDICAL MICROBIOLOGY
U of Wisconsin–La Crosse (WI)

MEDICAL NUTRITION
Elmhurst Coll (IL)

MEDICAL OFFICE MANAGEMENT
U of Phoenix (AZ)

MEDICAL PHARMACOLOGY AND PHARMACEUTICAL SCIENCES
Campbell U (NC)
The U of Montana–Missoula (MT)

MEDICAL RADIOLOGIC TECHNOLOGY
Arkansas State U (AR)
Bloomsburg U of Pennsylvania (PA)
Gannon U (PA)
Idaho State U (ID)
Indiana U Northwest (IN)
Indiana U–Purdue U Indianapolis (IN)
La Roche Coll (PA)
Loma Linda U (CA)
McNeese State U (LA)
Mount Marty Coll (SD)
Northwestern State U of Louisiana (LA)
Presentation Coll (SD)
Southern Illinois U Carbondale (IL)
Southwest Missouri State U (MO)
Southwest Texas State U (TX)
State U of New York Upstate Medical University (NY)
Thomas Edison State Coll (NJ)
The U of Alabama at Birmingham (AL)
U of Central Arkansas (AR)
U of Central Florida (FL)
U of Hartford (CT)
U of Louisiana at Monroe (LA)
U of Nebraska Medical Center (NE)
U of Nevada, Las Vegas (NV)
U of Prince Edward Island (PE, Canada)
U of Vermont (VT)
Wayne State U (MI)
Weber State U (UT)

MEDICAL RECORDS ADMINISTRATION
Arkansas Tech U (AR)
Baker Coll of Auburn Hills (MI)
Baker Coll of Flint (MI)

Carroll Coll (MT)
Chicago State U (IL)
Clark Atlanta U (GA)
Coll of Saint Mary (NE)
Dakota State U (SD)
Duquesne U (PA)
East Carolina U (NC)
East Central U (OK)
Eastern Kentucky U (KY)
Ferris State U (MI)
Florida A&M U (FL)
Florida International U (FL)
Georgia State U (GA)
Gwynedd-Mercy Coll (PA)
Illinois State U (IL)
Indiana U Northwest (IN)
Indiana U–Purdue U Indianapolis (IN)
Kean U (NJ)
Loma Linda U (CA)
Long Island U, C.W. Post Campus (NY)
Louisiana Tech U (LA)
Macon State Coll (GA)
Medical Coll of Georgia (GA)
Norfolk State U (VA)
The Ohio State U (OH)
Pace U, New York City Campus (NY)
Regis U (CO)
Southwestern Oklahoma State U (OK)
Southwest Texas State U (TX)
State U of NY Inst of Tech at Utica/Rome (NY)
Temple U (PA)
Tennessee State U (TN)
Texas Southern U (TX)
The U of Alabama at Birmingham (AL)
U of Central Florida (FL)
U of Illinois at Chicago (IL)
U of Kansas (KS)
U of Louisiana at Lafayette (LA)
U of Mississippi Medical Center (MS)
U of Pittsburgh (PA)
U of Wisconsin–Milwaukee (WI)
Western Carolina U (NC)

MEDICAL RECORDS TECHNOLOGY
Robert Morris Coll (IL)

MEDICAL TECHNOLOGY
Adams State Coll (CO)
Albright Coll (PA)
Alderson-Broaddus Coll (WV)
Allentown Coll of St. Francis de Sales (PA)
Alvernia Coll (PA)
American International Coll (MA)
Anderson Coll (SC)
Anderson U (IN)
Andrews U (MI)
Appalachian State U (NC)
Aquinas Coll (MI)
Arizona State U (AZ)
Arkansas State U (AR)
Arkansas Tech U (AR)
Armstrong Atlantic State U (GA)
Assumption Coll (MA)
Atlantic Union Coll (MA)
Auburn U (AL)
Augustana Coll (SD)
Augusta State U (GA)
Austin Peay State U (TN)
Averett Coll (VA)
Avila Coll (MO)
Baldwin-Wallace Coll (OH)
Ball State U (IN)
Barry U (FL)
Belmont Abbey Coll (NC)
Belmont U (TN)
Bemidji State U (MN)
Benedictine U (IL)
Bethune-Cookman Coll (FL)
Blackburn Coll (IL)
Bloomfield Coll (NJ)
Bloomsburg U of Pennsylvania (PA)
Blue Mountain Coll (MS)
Bluffton Coll (OH)
Boise State U (ID)
Boston U (MA)
Bowling Green State U (OH)
Bradley U (IL)

Brescia U (KY)
Briar Cliff Coll (IA)
Bridgewater Coll (VA)
Cabrini Coll (PA)
Caldwell Coll (NJ)
California State U, Dominguez Hills (CA)
California State U, Northridge (CA)
Calvin Coll (MI)
Cameron U (OK)
Campbellsville U (KY)
Canisius Coll (NY)
Carroll Coll (MT)
Carroll Coll (WI)
Carson-Newman Coll (TN)
Catawba Coll (NC)
The Catholic U of America (DC)
Cedar Crest Coll (PA)
Cedarville Coll (OH)
Central Michigan U (MI)
Central Missouri State U (MO)
Cheyney U of Pennsylvania (PA)
Clarion U of Pennsylvania (PA)
Coe Coll (IA)
Coker Coll (SC)
Coll Misericordia (PA)
Coll of Mount St. Joseph (OH)
Coll of Our Lady of the Elms (MA)
Coll of Saint Benedict (MN)
Coll of St. Catherine (MN)
Coll of Saint Elizabeth (NJ)
Coll of Saint Mary (NE)
The Coll of Saint Rose (NY)
Coll of Staten Island of the City U of NY (NY)
Coll of the Ozarks (MO)
Columbia Coll (SC)
Columbia Union Coll (MD)
Concord Coll (WV)
Concordia Coll (MN)
Culver-Stockton Coll (MO)
Daemen Coll (NY)
Defiance Coll (OH)
Delta State U (MS)
DePauw U (IN)
Dominican U (IL)
Dordt Coll (IA)
East Carolina U (NC)
Eastern Illinois U (IL)
Eastern Kentucky U (KY)
Eastern Mennonite U (VA)
Eastern Michigan U (MI)
Eastern New Mexico U (NM)
Eastern Washington U (WA)
East Tennessee State U (TN)
East Texas Baptist U (TX)
Eckerd Coll (FL)
Edgewood Coll (WI)
Elmhurst Coll (IL)
Elmira Coll (NY)
Elon Coll (NC)
Emory & Henry Coll (VA)
Erskine Coll (SC)
Evangel U (MO)
Fairleigh Dickinson U, Teaneck-Hackensack Campus (NJ)
Felician Coll (NJ)
Ferris State U (MI)
Ferrum Coll (VA)
Finch U of Health Sciences/Chicago Medical School (IL)
Fitchburg State Coll (MA)
Florida Atlantic U (FL)
Florida Gulf Coast U (FL)
Fort Hays State U (KS)
Framingham State Coll (MA)
Francis Marion U (SC)
Gannon U (PA)
Gardner-Webb U (NC)
George Mason U (VA)
Georgetown Coll (KY)
The George Washington U (DC)
Georgia Southern U (GA)
Georgia State U (GA)
Graceland Coll (IA)
Grand Valley State U (MI)
Greensboro Coll (NC)
Gwynedd-Mercy Coll (PA)
Hamline U (MN)
Harding U (AR)
Hardin-Simmons U (TX)
Hartwick Coll (NY)
Henderson State U (AR)
High Point U (NC)
Houghton Coll (NY)
Houston Baptist U (TX)
Howard Payne U (TX)

Howard U (DC)
Humboldt State U (CA)
Idaho State U (ID)
Illinois Coll (IL)
Illinois State U (IL)
Illinois Wesleyan U (IL)
Indiana State U (IN)
Indiana U East (IN)
Indiana U Kokomo (IN)
Indiana U of Pennsylvania (PA)
Indiana U–Purdue U Fort Wayne (IN)
Indiana U–Purdue U Indianapolis (IN)
Indiana U Southeast (IN)
Indiana Wesleyan U (IN)
Inter American U of PR, Fajardo Campus (PR)
Inter American U of PR, Metropolitan Campus (PR)
Inter American U of PR, San Germán Campus (PR)
Iona Coll (NY)
Jacksonville U (FL)
Jamestown Coll (ND)
Jewish Hospital Coll of Nursing and Allied Health (MO)
John Brown U (AR)
Kansas State U (KS)
Kean U (NJ)
Kent State U (OH)
Kentucky State U (KY)
Kentucky Wesleyan Coll (KY)
Keuka Coll (NY)
King Coll (TN)
King's Coll (PA)
Kutztown U of Pennsylvania (PA)
Lake Superior State U (MI)
Lamar U (TX)
Lander U (SC)
Langston U (OK)
La Roche Coll (PA)
Lebanon Valley Coll (PA)
Lees-McRae Coll (NC)
Lee U (TN)
Lenoir-Rhyne Coll (NC)
Lewis U (IL)
Lincoln Memorial U (TN)
Lincoln U (MO)
Lindenwood U (MO)
Lock Haven U of Pennsylvania (PA)
Loma Linda U (CA)
Long Island U, Brooklyn Campus (NY)
Long Island U, C.W. Post Campus (NY)
Longwood Coll (VA)
Loras Coll (IA)
Louisiana Coll (LA)
Louisiana State U Health Sciences Center (LA)
Louisiana Tech U (LA)
Luther Coll (IA)
Lycoming Coll (PA)
Madonna U (MI)
Malone Coll (OH)
Manchester Coll (IN)
Mansfield U of Pennsylvania (PA)
Marian Coll of Fond du Lac (WI)
Marist Coll (NY)
Marshall U (WV)
Mary Baldwin Coll (VA)
Marymount Coll (NY)
Maryville U of Saint Louis (MO)
Marywood U (PA)
Massachusetts Coll of Liberal Arts (MA)
McKendree Coll (IL)
McMurry U (TX)
McNeese State U (LA)
MCP Hahnemann U (PA)
Medical Coll of Georgia (GA)
Mercy Coll (NY)
Mercyhurst Coll (PA)
Miami U (OH)
Michigan State U (MI)
Michigan Technological U (MI)
Midwestern State U (TX)
Millersville U of Pennsylvania (PA)
Minnesota State U, Mankato (MN)
Minnesota State U Moorhead (MN)
Minot State U (ND)
Mississippi State U (MS)
Missouri Southern State Coll (MO)
Missouri Western State Coll (MO)
Monmouth U (NJ)

Moravian Coll (PA)
Morehead State U (KY)
Morgan State U (MD)
Morningside Coll (IA)
Mount Marty Coll (SD)
Mount Mercy Coll (IA)
Mount Saint Mary Coll (NY)
Mount Vernon Nazarene Coll (OH)
Murray State U (KY)
Muskingum Coll (OH)
National-Louis U (IL)
New Mexico Inst of Mining and Technology (NM)
New York Inst of Technology (NY)
Norfolk State U (VA)
North Dakota State U (ND)
Northeastern State U (OK)
Northern Illinois U (IL)
Northern Michigan U (MI)
Northern State U (SD)
North Park U (IL)
Northwestern Coll (IA)
Northwestern State U of Louisiana (LA)
Northwest Missouri State U (MO)
Norwich U (VT)
Notre Dame Coll of Ohio (OH)
Oakland U (MI)
Oakwood Coll (AL)
Ohio Northern U (OH)
The Ohio State U (OH)
Oklahoma Christian U of Science and Arts (OK)
Oklahoma Panhandle State U (OK)
Oklahoma State U (OK)
Old Dominion U (VA)
Olivet Nazarene U (IL)
Oregon Health Sciences U (OR)
Oregon State U (OR)
Our Lady of Holy Cross Coll (LA)
Our Lady of the Lake U of San Antonio (TX)
Pace U, New York City Campus (NY)
Pace U, Pleasantville/Briarcliff Campus (NY)
Pacific Union Coll (CA)
Peru State Coll (NE)
Pikeville Coll (KY)
Pittsburg State U (KS)
Plattsburgh State U of NY (NY)
Pontifical Catholic U of Puerto Rico (PR)
Prairie View A&M U (TX)
Purdue U (IN)
Purdue U Calumet (IN)
Quincy U (IL)
Quinnipiac U (CT)
Radford U (VA)
Roanoke Coll (VA)
Roberts Wesleyan Coll (NY)
Rochester Inst of Technology (NY)
Rockhurst U (MO)
Rush U (IL)
Rutgers, State U of NJ, Camden Coll of Arts & Scis (NJ)
Rutgers, State U of NJ, Douglass Coll (NJ)
Rutgers, State U of NJ, Livingston Coll (NJ)
Rutgers, State U of NJ, Newark Coll of Arts & Scis (NJ)
Rutgers, State U of NJ, U Coll–Camden (NJ)
Rutgers, State U of NJ, U Coll–New Brunswick (NJ)
Saginaw Valley State U (MI)
Saint Augustine's Coll (NC)
St. Bonaventure U (NY)
St. Cloud State U (MN)
St. Francis Coll (NY)
Saint Francis Coll (PA)
St. John's U (NY)
Saint Joseph Coll (CT)
Saint Joseph's Coll (IN)
Saint Leo U (FL)
Saint Louis U (MO)
Saint Mary-of-the-Woods Coll (IN)
Saint Mary's Coll (IN)
Saint Mary's U of Minnesota (MN)
St. Norbert Coll (WI)
Salem Coll (NC)
Salem State Coll (MA)
Salisbury State U (MD)
Salve Regina U (RI)
Sam Houston State U (TX)
Seattle U (WA)

Majors Index
Medical Technology–(Pre)Medicine

Seton Hill Coll (PA)
Shippensburg U of Pennsylvania (PA)
Simpson Coll (IA)
Slippery Rock U of Pennsylvania (PA)
South Dakota State U (SD)
Southeastern Oklahoma State U (OK)
Southeast Missouri State U (MO)
Southern Adventist U (TN)
Southern Arkansas U–Magnolia (AR)
Southern Wesleyan U (SC)
Southwest Baptist U (MO)
Southwestern Adventist U (TX)
Southwestern Oklahoma State U (OK)
Southwest Missouri State U (MO)
Southwest Texas State U (TX)
Spalding U (KY)
State U of NY at Albany (NY)
State U of NY at Buffalo (NY)
State U of NY at Stony Brook (NY)
State U of NY Coll at Brockport (NY)
State U of NY Coll at Fredonia (NY)
State U of New York Upstate Medical University (NY)
Stephen F. Austin State U (TX)
Stetson U (FL)
Stonehill Coll (MA)
Suffolk U (MA)
Tabor Coll (KS)
Taylor U (IN)
Tennessee State U (TN)
Texas Southern U (TX)
Texas Woman's U (TX)
Thiel Coll (PA)
Thomas Jefferson U (PA)
Thomas More Coll (KY)
Trevecca Nazarene U (TN)
Tusculum Coll (TN)
Tuskegee U (AL)
Union Coll (KY)
Union Coll (NE)
Union U (TN)
The U of Akron (OH)
The U of Alabama (AL)
The U of Alabama at Birmingham (AL)
The U of Arizona (AZ)
U of Arkansas for Medical Sciences (AR)
U of Bridgeport (CT)
U of Central Florida (FL)
U of Central Oklahoma (OK)
U of Cincinnati (OH)
U of Connecticut (CT)
U of Delaware (DE)
U of Evansville (IN)
The U of Findlay (OH)
U of Hartford (CT)
U of Hawaii at Manoa (HI)
U of Houston (TX)
U of Idaho (ID)
U of Illinois at Chicago (IL)
U of Indianapolis (IN)
The U of Iowa (IA)
U of Kansas (KS)
U of Kentucky (KY)
U of Louisiana at Monroe (LA)
U of Louisville (KY)
U of Maine (ME)
U of Mary Hardin-Baylor (TX)
U of Massachusetts Amherst (MA)
U of Massachusetts Boston (MA)
U of Massachusetts Dartmouth (MA)
U of Massachusetts Lowell (MA)
U of Michigan (MI)
U of Michigan–Flint (MI)
U of Minnesota, Twin Cities Campus (MN)
U of Mississippi (MS)
U of Mississippi Medical Center (MS)
U of Missouri–St. Louis (MO)
The U of Montana–Missoula (MT)
U of Nebraska Medical Center (NE)
U of Nevada, Reno (NV)
U of New England (ME)
U of New Haven (CT)
U of New Orleans (LA)
The U of North Carolina at Charlotte (NC)

The U of North Carolina at Greensboro (NC)
The U of North Carolina at Pembroke (NC)
The U of North Carolina at Wilmington (NC)
U of North Dakota (ND)
U of Northern Colorado (CO)
U of North Texas (TX)
U of Pittsburgh (PA)
U of Pittsburgh at Bradford (PA)
U of Pittsburgh at Johnstown (PA)
U of Puerto Rico, Mayagüez Campus (PR)
U of Rhode Island (RI)
U of Rio Grande (OH)
U of St. Francis (IL)
U of Saint Francis (IN)
U of Science and Arts of Oklahoma (OK)
The U of Scranton (PA)
U of Sioux Falls (SD)
U of South Alabama (AL)
U of South Carolina (SC)
U of South Dakota (SD)
U of Southern Mississippi (MS)
U of South Florida (FL)
The U of Tennessee at Chattanooga (TN)
The U of Tennessee Knoxville (TN)
The U of Texas at Arlington (TX)
The U of Texas at Austin (TX)
The U of Texas at Tyler (TX)
The U of Texas–Pan American (TX)
U of the District of Columbia (DC)
U of the Sciences in Philadelphia (PA)
U of Vermont (VT)
U of Virginia's Coll at Wise (VA)
U of Washington (WA)
U of West Florida (FL)
U of Wisconsin–La Crosse (WI)
U of Wisconsin–Madison (WI)
U of Wisconsin–Milwaukee (WI)
U of Wisconsin–Stevens Point (WI)
U of Wyoming (WY)
Utah State U (UT)
Virginia Commonwealth U (VA)
Wagner Coll (NY)
Walla Walla Coll (WA)
Wartburg Coll (IA)
Waynesburg Coll (PA)
Wayne State Coll (NE)
Wayne State U (MI)
Weber State U (UT)
Wesley Coll (DE)
Western Carolina U (NC)
Western Connecticut State U (CT)
Western Illinois U (IL)
Western Kentucky U (KY)
Westfield State Coll (MA)
West Liberty State Coll (WV)
West Texas A&M U (TX)
West Virginia U (WV)
Wichita State U (KS)
Wilkes U (PA)
William Jewell Coll (MO)
Winona State U (MN)
Winston-Salem State U (NC)
Winthrop U (SC)
Wright State U (OH)
Xavier U (OH)
York Coll of Pennsylvania (PA)
York Coll of the City U of New York (NY)
Youngstown State U (OH)

MEDICINAL/PHARMACEUTICAL CHEMISTRY
Butler U (IN)
Ohio Northern U (OH)
State U of NY at Buffalo (NY)
U of Calif, San Diego (CA)

(PRE)MEDICINE
Abilene Christian U (TX)
Acadia U (NS, Canada)
Adams State Coll (CO)
Adrian Coll (MI)
Alabama State U (AL)
Albertson Coll of Idaho (ID)
Albertus Magnus Coll (CT)
Albion Coll (MI)
Albright Coll (PA)
Alderson-Broaddus Coll (WV)
Alfred U (NY)
Alice Lloyd Coll (KY)

Allentown Coll of St. Francis de Sales (PA)
Alma Coll (MI)
Alvernia Coll (PA)
American International Coll (MA)
American U (DC)
Anderson U (IN)
Andrews U (MI)
Antioch Coll (OH)
Appalachian State U (NC)
Aquinas Coll (MI)
Arizona State U (AZ)
Ashland U (OH)
Athens State U (AL)
Atlantic Union Coll (MA)
Auburn U (AL)
Augsburg Coll (MN)
Augustana Coll (IL)
Augustana Coll (SD)
Averett Coll (VA)
Avila Coll (MO)
Baker U (KS)
Baldwin-Wallace Coll (OH)
Ball State U (IN)
Bard Coll (NY)
Barnard Coll (NY)
Barry U (FL)
Bartlesville Wesleyan Coll (OK)
Barton Coll (NC)
Baylor U (TX)
Beaver Coll (PA)
Bellarmine Coll (KY)
Belmont Abbey Coll (NC)
Belmont U (TN)
Beloit Coll (WI)
Bemidji State U (MN)
Benedictine U (IL)
Bennington Coll (VT)
Berea Coll (KY)
Berry Coll (GA)
Bethany Coll (WV)
Bethel Coll (IN)
Bethel Coll (MN)
Bethel Coll (TN)
Birmingham-Southern Coll (AL)
Blackburn Coll (IL)
Bloomfield Coll (NJ)
Blue Mountain Coll (MS)
Bluffton Coll (OH)
Boise State U (ID)
Boston Coll (MA)
Boston U (MA)
Bowdoin Coll (ME)
Brandeis U (MA)
Brandon U (MB, Canada)
Brevard Coll (NC)
Briar Cliff Coll (IA)
Bryan Coll (TN)
Buena Vista U (IA)
California Lutheran U (CA)
California Polytechnic State U, San Luis Obispo (CA)
California State Polytechnic U, Pomona (CA)
California State U, Chico (CA)
California State U, Dominguez Hills (CA)
California State U, Fullerton (CA)
California State U, Hayward (CA)
California State U, Northridge (CA)
Calvin Coll (MI)
Campbellsville U (KY)
Campbell U (NC)
Capital U (OH)
Cardinal Stritch U (WI)
Carroll Coll (MT)
Carroll Coll (WI)
Carthage Coll (WI)
Catawba Coll (NC)
Cedar Crest Coll (PA)
Cedarville Coll (OH)
Centenary Coll of Louisiana (LA)
Central Missouri State U (MO)
Centre Coll (KY)
Chadron State Coll (NE)
Chapman U (CA)
Charleston Southern U (SC)
Chicago State U (IL)
Chowan Coll (NC)
Christian Brothers U (TN)
City Coll of the City U of NY (NY)
Claflin U (SC)
Claremont McKenna Coll (CA)
Clarkson U (NY)
Clark U (MA)
Clemson U (SC)
Cleveland State U (OH)

Coe Coll (IA)
Coker Coll (SC)
Coll Misericordia (PA)
Coll of Charleston (SC)
Coll of Mount Saint Vincent (NY)
The Coll of New Jersey (NJ)
The Coll of New Rochelle (NY)
Coll of Notre Dame (CA)
Coll of Notre Dame of Maryland (MD)
Coll of Our Lady of the Elms (MA)
Coll of Saint Benedict (MN)
Coll of St. Catherine (MN)
Coll of Saint Elizabeth (NJ)
Coll of Saint Mary (NE)
Coll of Santa Fe (NM)
Coll of Staten Island of the City U of NY (NY)
Coll of the Holy Cross (MA)
Coll of the Ozarks (MO)
The Coll of Wooster (OH)
Colorado State U (CO)
Columbia Coll (MO)
Columbia Coll (SC)
Columbia Union Coll (MD)
Columbus State U (GA)
Concord Coll (WV)
Concordia Coll (MI)
Concordia Coll (MN)
Concordia U (CA)
Concordia U (IL)
Concordia U (OR)
Concordia U at Austin (TX)
Concordia U Wisconsin (WI)
Converse Coll (SC)
Coppin State Coll (MD)
Cornell U (NY)
Cornerstone U (MI)
Covenant Coll (GA)
Cumberland Coll (KY)
Dakota State U (SD)
Dakota Wesleyan U (SD)
Dalhousie U (NS, Canada)
David Lipscomb U (TN)
Defiance Coll (OH)
DePaul U (IL)
Dickinson Coll (PA)
Dickinson State U (ND)
Dominican U (IL)
Dordt Coll (IA)
Drake U (IA)
Drexel U (PA)
Drury U (MO)
D'Youville Coll (NY)
Earlham Coll (IN)
East Central U (OK)
Eastern Illinois U (IL)
Eastern Kentucky U (KY)
Eastern Mennonite U (VA)
Eastern Michigan U (MI)
Eastern Nazarene Coll (MA)
Eastern New Mexico U (NM)
Eastern Oregon U (OR)
Eastern Washington U (WA)
Eckerd Coll (FL)
Edgewood Coll (WI)
Elizabethtown Coll (PA)
Elmhurst Coll (IL)
Elmira Coll (NY)
Elon Coll (NC)
Emmanuel Coll (MA)
Emory & Henry Coll (VA)
Evangel U (MO)
The Evergreen State Coll (WA)
Fairleigh Dickinson U, Teaneck-Hackensack Campus (NJ)
Felician Coll (NJ)
Florida Southern Coll (FL)
Florida State U (FL)
Fontbonne Coll (MO)
Fordham U (NY)
Fort Lewis Coll (CO)
Framingham State Coll (MA)
Franciscan U of Steubenville (OH)
Francis Marion U (SC)
Franklin Pierce Coll (NH)
Freed-Hardeman U (TN)
Fresno Pacific U (CA)
Friends U (KS)
Furman U (SC)
Gannon U (PA)
Gardner-Webb U (NC)
Georgetown Coll (KY)
The George Washington U (DC)
Georgian Court Coll (NJ)
Georgia Southwestern State U (GA)

Gettysburg Coll (PA)
Glenville State Coll (WV)
Goshen Coll (IN)
Graceland Coll (IA)
Grand Canyon U (AZ)
Grand Valley State U (MI)
Greenville Coll (IL)
Grove City Coll (PA)
Guilford Coll (NC)
Gustavus Adolphus Coll (MN)
Gwynedd-Mercy Coll (PA)
Hamline U (MN)
Hampshire Coll (MA)
Hampton U (VA)
Harding U (AR)
Hardin-Simmons U (TX)
Hartwick Coll (NY)
Harvard U (MA)
Hastings Coll (NE)
Haverford Coll (PA)
Hawaii Pacific U (HI)
Heidelberg Coll (OH)
High Point U (NC)
Hillsdale Coll (MI)
Hiram Coll (OH)
Hobart and William Smith Colls (NY)
Holy Family Coll (PA)
Hood Coll (MD)
Houghton Coll (NY)
Houston Baptist U (TX)
Howard Payne U (TX)
Humboldt State U (CA)
Huntingdon Coll (AL)
Huntington Coll (IN)
Huston-Tillotson Coll (TX)
Illinois Coll (IL)
Illinois Wesleyan U (IL)
Immaculata Coll (PA)
Indiana State U (IN)
Indiana U Bloomington (IN)
Indiana U–Purdue U Fort Wayne (IN)
Indiana U–Purdue U Indianapolis (IN)
Indiana Wesleyan U (IN)
Inter American U of PR, Metropolitan Campus (PR)
Iowa State U of Science and Technology (IA)
Iowa Wesleyan Coll (IA)
Ithaca Coll (NY)
Jacksonville U (FL)
John Brown U (AR)
John Carroll U (OH)
Johnson C. Smith U (NC)
Johnson State Coll (VT)
Judson Coll (IL)
Juniata Coll (PA)
Kansas State U (KS)
Kent State U (OH)
Kentucky Wesleyan Coll (KY)
King Coll (TN)
King's Coll (PA)
LaGrange Coll (GA)
Lake Erie Coll (OH)
Lake Forest Coll (IL)
Lakeland Coll (WI)
Lake Superior State U (MI)
Lambuth U (TN)
Lander U (SC)
Langston U (OK)
La Salle U (PA)
La Sierra U (CA)
Lawrence U (WI)
Lebanon Valley Coll (PA)
Lees-McRae Coll (NC)
Lehigh U (PA)
Le Moyne Coll (NY)
LeMoyne-Owen Coll (TN)
Lenoir-Rhyne Coll (NC)
LeTourneau U (TX)
Lewis & Clark Coll (OR)
Lewis U (IL)
Lincoln Memorial U (TN)
Lindenwood U (MO)
Lindsey Wilson Coll (KY)
Lock Haven U of Pennsylvania (PA)
Long Island U, Brooklyn Campus (NY)
Long Island U, C.W. Post Campus (NY)
Longwood Coll (VA)
Lourdes Coll (OH)
Loyola U Chicago (IL)
Luther Coll (IA)

Majors Index
(Pre)Medicine–Medieval/Renaissance Studies

Lycoming Coll (PA)
Lynchburg Coll (VA)
Lynn U (FL)
MacMurray Coll (IL)
Madonna U (MI)
Maharishi U of Management (IA)
Manchester Coll (IN)
Manhattan Coll (NY)
Manhattanville Coll (NY)
Mansfield U of Pennsylvania (PA)
Marian Coll (IN)
Marian Coll of Fond du Lac (WI)
Marietta Coll (OH)
Marist Coll (NY)
Marlboro Coll (VT)
Marquette U (WI)
Marshall U (WV)
Mars Hill Coll (NC)
Marycrest International U (IA)
Marymount Coll (NY)
Maryville Coll (TN)
Maryville U of Saint Louis (MO)
Mary Washington Coll (VA)
Mass Coll of Pharmacy and Allied Health Sciences (MA)
Massachusetts Inst of Technology (MA)
Mayville State U (ND)
McKendree Coll (IL)
McMurry U (TX)
McPherson Coll (KS)
Medgar Evers Coll of the City U of NY (NY)
Memorial U of Newfoundland (NF, Canada)
Mercy Coll (NY)
Mercyhurst Coll (PA)
Meredith Coll (NC)
Merrimack Coll (MA)
Methodist Coll (NC)
Miami U (OH)
Michigan State U (MI)
Michigan Technological U (MI)
Middlebury Coll (VT)
Midland Lutheran Coll (NE)
Midwestern State U (TX)
Milligan Coll (TN)
Millikin U (IL)
Mills Coll (CA)
Minnesota State U, Mankato (MN)
Minnesota State U Moorhead (MN)
Minot State U (ND)
Mississippi Coll (MS)
Missouri Southern State Coll (MO)
Missouri Valley Coll (MO)
Molloy Coll (NY)
Montreat Coll (NC)
Morgan State U (MD)
Morningside Coll (IA)
Mount Allison U (NB, Canada)
Mount Mary Coll (WI)
Mount Mercy Coll (IA)
Mount St. Clare Coll (IA)
Mount Saint Mary Coll (NY)
Mount St. Mary's Coll (CA)
Mount Saint Mary's Coll and Seminary (MD)
Mount Vernon Nazarene Coll (OH)
Muhlenberg Coll (PA)
Muskingum Coll (OH)
Nazareth Coll of Rochester (NY)
Newberry Coll (SC)
New Jersey Inst of Technology (NJ)
Newman U (KS)
New Mexico Highlands U (NM)
New Mexico Inst of Mining and Technology (NM)
New Mexico State U (NM)
New York Inst of Technology (NY)
New York U (NY)
Niagara U (NY)
Nicholls State U (LA)
North Carolina Wesleyan Coll (NC)
North Central Coll (IL)
North Dakota State U (ND)
Northeastern State U (OK)
Northern Arizona U (AZ)
Northern Kentucky U (KY)
Northern Michigan U (MI)
Northern State U (SD)
North Georgia Coll & State U (GA)
Northland Coll (WI)
North Park U (IL)
Northwestern Oklahoma State U (OK)
Northwest Missouri State U (MO)
Northwest Nazarene U (ID)

Notre Dame Coll of Ohio (OH)
Nova Southeastern U (FL)
Oakland City U (IN)
Oakland U (MI)
Oglethorpe U (GA)
The Ohio State U (OH)
Ohio U (OH)
Ohio Wesleyan U (OH)
Oklahoma Baptist U (OK)
Oklahoma Christian U of Science and Arts (OK)
Oklahoma City U (OK)
Oklahoma State U (OK)
Olivet Nazarene U (IL)
Oregon Inst of Technology (OR)
Oregon State U (OR)
Otterbein Coll (OH)
Our Lady of the Lake U of San Antonio (TX)
Pace U, New York City Campus (NY)
Pacific Union Coll (CA)
Pacific U (OR)
Paine Coll (GA)
Palm Beach Atlantic Coll (FL)
Penn State U Univ Park Campus (PA)
Pepperdine U, Malibu (CA)
Peru State Coll (NE)
Pfeiffer U (NC)
Philadelphia U (PA)
Piedmont Coll (GA)
Pittsburg State U (KS)
Pitzer Coll (CA)
Polytechnic U, Brooklyn Campus (NY)
Polytechnic U, Farmingdale Campus (NY)
Pomona Coll (CA)
Pontifical Catholic U of Puerto Rico (PR)
Presbyterian Coll (SC)
Purdue U (IN)
Purdue U Calumet (IN)
Queens Coll (NC)
Queens Coll of the City U of NY (NY)
Quincy U (IL)
Quinnipiac U (CT)
Redeemer Coll (ON, Canada)
Regis U (CO)
Rensselaer Polytechnic Inst (NY)
Ripon Coll (WI)
Rivier Coll (NH)
Roberts Wesleyan Coll (NY)
Rochester Inst of Technology (NY)
Rockford Coll (IL)
Rocky Mountain Coll (MT)
Roger Williams U (RI)
Rollins Coll (FL)
Rowan U (NJ)
Rutgers, State U of NJ, Camden Coll of Arts & Scis (NJ)
Rutgers, State U of NJ, Cook Coll (NJ)
Rutgers, State U of NJ, Douglass Coll (NJ)
Rutgers, State U of NJ, Livingston Coll (NJ)
Rutgers, State U of NJ, Newark Coll of Arts & Scis (NJ)
Rutgers, State U of NJ, Rutgers Coll (NJ)
Rutgers, State U of NJ, U Coll–Camden (NJ)
Sacred Heart U (CT)
St. Andrews Presbyterian Coll (NC)
Saint Anselm Coll (NH)
Saint Augustine's Coll (NC)
St. Bonaventure U (NY)
St. Cloud State U (MN)
St. Francis Coll (NY)
Saint Francis Coll (PA)
St. Francis Xavier U (NS, Canada)
Saint John's U (MN)
Saint Joseph Coll (CT)
Saint Joseph's Coll (ME)
St. Joseph's Coll, New York (NY)
St. Joseph's Coll, Suffolk Campus (NY)
Saint Leo U (FL)
Saint Louis U (MO)
Saint Martin's Coll (WA)
Saint Mary-of-the-Woods Coll (IN)
Saint Mary's Coll (MI)
Saint Mary's Coll of California (CA)
Saint Mary's U (NS, Canada)

Saint Mary's U of Minnesota (MN)
Saint Michael's Coll (VT)
St. Norbert Coll (WI)
St. Olaf Coll (MN)
St. Thomas U (FL)
Saint Xavier U (IL)
Salem State Coll (MA)
Salve Regina U (RI)
Samford U (AL)
San Diego State U (CA)
Sarah Lawrence Coll (NY)
Schreiner Coll (TX)
Seattle Pacific U (WA)
Seton Hill Coll (PA)
Shawnee State U (OH)
Siena Coll (NY)
Simmons Coll (MA)
Simon's Rock Coll of Bard (MA)
Simpson Coll (IA)
Skidmore Coll (NY)
Slippery Rock U of Pennsylvania (PA)
Sonoma State U (CA)
South Dakota State U (SD)
Southeast Missouri State U (MO)
Southern Oregon U (OR)
Southwestern Oklahoma State U (OK)
Southwest State U (MN)
Spalding U (KY)
Spring Hill Coll (AL)
State U of NY at New Paltz (NY)
State U of NY at Oswego (NY)
State U of NY Coll at Brockport (NY)
State U of NY Coll at Buffalo (NY)
State U of NY Coll at Cortland (NY)
State U of NY Coll at Fredonia (NY)
State U of NY Coll at Geneseo (NY)
State U of NY Coll at Oneonta (NY)
State U of NY Coll of Environ Sci and Forestry (NY)
State U of West Georgia (GA)
Stephens Coll (MO)
Stetson U (FL)
Stevens Inst of Technology (NJ)
Stonehill Coll (MA)
Suffolk U (MA)
Sul Ross State U (TX)
Susquehanna U (PA)
Syracuse U (NY)
Tabor Coll (KS)
Talladega Coll (AL)
Taylor U (IN)
Tennessee Technological U (TN)
Tennessee Wesleyan Coll (TN)
Texas A&M U–Kingsville (TX)
Texas Lutheran U (TX)
Texas Southern U (TX)
Texas Wesleyan U (TX)
Thiel Coll (PA)
Thomas More Coll (KY)
Touro Coll (NY)
Trinity Christian Coll (IL)
Trinity U (TX)
Trinity Western U (BC, Canada)
Tri-State U (IN)
Troy State U (AL)
Truman State U (MO)
Tusculum Coll (TN)
Union Coll (KY)
Union U (TN)
United States Military Academy (NY)
Universidad Metropolitana (PR)
Université de Montréal (PQ, Canada)
Université de Sherbrooke (PQ, Canada)
Université Laval (PQ, Canada)
U Coll of Cape Breton (NS, Canada)
The U of Akron (OH)
The U of Alabama (AL)
U of Alaska Fairbanks (AK)
U of Alberta (AB, Canada)
U of Arkansas at Monticello (AR)
U of Arkansas at Pine Bluff (AR)
U of Bridgeport (CT)
U of British Columbia (BC, Canada)
U of Charleston (WV)
U of Cincinnati (OH)

U of Colorado at Colorado Springs (CO)
U of Dallas (TX)
U of Dayton (OH)
U of Detroit Mercy (MI)
U of Evansville (IN)
The U of Findlay (OH)
U of Great Falls (MT)
U of Guelph (ON, Canada)
U of Houston (TX)
U of Idaho (ID)
U of Indianapolis (IN)
The U of Iowa (IA)
U of Judaism (CA)
U of La Verne (CA)
U of Maine (ME)
U of Manitoba (MB, Canada)
U of Mary Hardin-Baylor (TX)
U of Maryland, Baltimore County (MD)
U of Massachusetts Amherst (MA)
U of Minnesota, Duluth (MN)
U of Minnesota, Morris (MN)
U of Minnesota, Twin Cities Campus (MN)
U of Missouri–Rolla (MO)
U of Missouri–St. Louis (MO)
The U of Montana–Missoula (MT)
U of Montevallo (AL)
U of Nebraska at Omaha (NE)
U of Nebraska–Lincoln (NE)
U of Nevada, Reno (NV)
U of New Brunswick, Fredericton (NB, Canada)
U of New England (ME)
U of New Hampshire (NH)
U of New Orleans (LA)
The U of North Carolina at Greensboro (NC)
U of North Texas (TX)
U of Notre Dame (IN)
U of Oklahoma (OK)
U of Oregon (OR)
U of Pennsylvania (PA)
U of Pittsburgh at Bradford (PA)
U of Pittsburgh at Johnstown (PA)
U of Portland (OR)
U of Prince Edward Island (PE, Canada)
U of Puerto Rico, Mayagüez Campus (PR)
U of Puget Sound (WA)
U of Regina (SK, Canada)
U of Rio Grande (OH)
U of St. Francis (IL)
U of Saint Francis (IN)
U of St. Thomas (TX)
U of San Diego (CA)
U of San Francisco (CA)
U of Sioux Falls (SD)
U of South Alabama (AL)
U of South Dakota (SD)
U of Southern Colorado (CO)
The U of Tampa (FL)
The U of Tennessee at Chattanooga (TN)
The U of Tennessee at Martin (TN)
The U of Texas–Pan American (TX)
U of the Ozarks (AR)
U of the Pacific (CA)
U of the Sciences in Philadelphia (PA)
U of Toronto (ON, Canada)
U of Tulsa (OK)
U of Victoria (BC, Canada)
U of Windsor (ON, Canada)
The U of Winnipeg (MB, Canada)
U of Wisconsin–La Crosse (WI)
U of Wisconsin–Milwaukee (WI)
U of Wisconsin–Parkside (WI)
U of Wisconsin–River Falls (WI)
U of Wisconsin–Whitewater (WI)
Upper Iowa U (IA)
Urbana U (OH)
Ursinus Coll (PA)
Ursuline Coll (OH)
Utah State U (UT)
Utica Coll of Syracuse U (NY)
Valdosta State U (GA)
Valley City State U (ND)
Villa Julie Coll (MD)
Villanova U (PA)
Virginia Commonwealth U (VA)
Virginia Intermont Coll (VA)
Virginia Wesleyan Coll (VA)
Wabash Coll (IN)
Wagner Coll (NY)

Walla Walla Coll (WA)
Walsh U (OH)
Warner Pacific Coll (OR)
Warren Wilson Coll (NC)
Washington Coll (MD)
Washington State U (WA)
Washington U in St. Louis (MO)
Wayland Baptist U (TX)
Waynesburg Coll (PA)
Wayne State Coll (NE)
Wells Coll (NY)
West Chester U of Pennsylvania (PA)
Western Connecticut State U (CT)
Western Maryland Coll (MD)
Western Montana Coll of The U of Montana (MT)
Western State Coll of Colorado (CO)
Western Washington U (WA)
Westfield State Coll (MA)
West Liberty State Coll (WV)
Westminster Coll (MO)
Westminster Coll (PA)
Westmont Coll (CA)
West Virginia State Coll (WV)
West Virginia Wesleyan Coll (WV)
Wheaton Coll (MA)
Whitworth Coll (WA)
Widener U (PA)
Wilkes U (PA)
Willamette U (OR)
William Jewell Coll (MO)
William Paterson U of New Jersey (NJ)
William Penn U (IA)
Williams Baptist Coll (AR)
William Woods U (MO)
Wilmington Coll (OH)
Wingate U (NC)
Winona State U (MN)
Wittenberg U (OH)
Wofford Coll (SC)
Worcester Polytechnic Inst (MA)
Xavier U of Louisiana (LA)
Yeshiva U (NY)
York Coll (NE)
York Coll of Pennsylvania (PA)
York U (ON, Canada)
Youngstown State U (OH)

MEDIEVAL/RENAISSANCE STUDIES

Bard Coll (NY)
Barnard Coll (NY)
Bates Coll (ME)
Brown U (RI)
Carleton U (ON, Canada)
Cleveland State U (OH)
The Coll of William and Mary (VA)
Columbia Coll (NY)
Connecticut Coll (CT)
Cornell Coll (IA)
Cornell U (NY)
Dickinson Coll (PA)
Duke U (NC)
Emory U (GA)
Fordham U (NY)
Goddard Coll (VT)
Guilford Coll (NC)
Hampshire Coll (MA)
Hanover Coll (IN)
Harvard U (MA)
Hobart and William Smith Colls (NY)
Long Island U, Southampton Coll, Friends World Program (NY)
Marlboro Coll (VT)
Memorial U of Newfoundland (NF, Canada)
Mount Allison U (NB, Canada)
Mount Holyoke Coll (MA)
New Coll of the U of South Florida (FL)
New York U (NY)
The Ohio State U (OH)
Ohio Wesleyan U (OH)
Penn State U Univ Park Campus (PA)
Plymouth State Coll (NH)
Queen's U at Kingston (ON, Canada)
Rutgers, State U of NJ, Douglass Coll (NJ)
Rutgers, State U of NJ, Livingston Coll (NJ)

Majors Index
Medieval/Renaissance Studies–Middle School Education

Rutgers, State U of NJ, Rutgers Coll (NJ)
Rutgers, State U of NJ, U Coll–New Brunswick (NJ)
St. Olaf Coll (MN)
Smith Coll (MA)
Southern Methodist U (TX)
State U of NY at Albany (NY)
State U of NY at Binghamton (NY)
Swarthmore Coll (PA)
Syracuse U (NY)
Tulane U (LA)
U of British Columbia (BC, Canada)
U of Calgary (AB, Canada)
U of Calif, Santa Barbara (CA)
U of Chicago (IL)
The U of Iowa (IA)
U of Manitoba (MB, Canada)
U of Michigan (MI)
U of Michigan–Dearborn (MI)
U of Nebraska–Lincoln (NE)
U of Notre Dame (IN)
U of the South (TN)
U of Toronto (ON, Canada)
U of Victoria (BC, Canada)
U of Waterloo (ON, Canada)
Vassar Coll (NY)
Washington and Lee U (VA)
Washington U in St. Louis (MO)
Wellesley Coll (MA)
Wesleyan U (CT)

MENTAL HEALTH/REHABILITATION
Brandon U (MB, Canada)
Elmira Coll (NY)
Evangel U (MO)
Franklin U (OH)
Governors State U (IL)
Louisiana State U Health Sciences Center (LA)
Marshall U (WV)
MCP Hahnemann U (PA)
Morgan State U (MD)
Newman U (KS)
New York Inst of Technology (NY)
Northern Kentucky U (KY)
Pittsburg State U (KS)
Plymouth State Coll (NH)
St. Cloud State U (MN)
Thomas Edison State Coll (NJ)
Tufts U (MA)
U of Maine at Farmington (ME)
U of New England (ME)
Wright State U (OH)

METAL/JEWELRY ARTS
Adams State Coll (CO)
Alberta Coll of Art and Design (AB, Canada)
Arizona State U (AZ)
Beaver Coll (PA)
Bowling Green State U (OH)
California Coll of Arts and Crafts (CA)
California State U, Long Beach (CA)
Ctr for Creative Studies—Coll of Art and Design (MI)
Cleveland Inst of Art (OH)
Colorado State U (CO)
Eastern Kentucky U (KY)
Grand Valley State U (MI)
Indiana U Bloomington (IN)
Kent State U (OH)
Long Island U, Southampton Coll, Friends World Program (NY)
Maine Coll of Art (ME)
Massachusetts Coll of Art (MA)
Memphis Coll of Art (TN)
Moore Coll of Art and Design (PA)
Northern Arizona U (AZ)
Northern Michigan U (MI)
Northwest Missouri State U (MO)
Nova Scotia Coll of Art and Design (NS, Canada)
Pratt Inst (NY)
Rhode Island School of Design (RI)
Rochester Inst of Technology (NY)
Savannah Coll of Art and Design (GA)
School of the Museum of Fine Arts (MA)
Seton Hill Coll (PA)
Simon's Rock Coll of Bard (MA)
State U of NY at New Paltz (NY)

State U of NY Coll at Brockport (NY)
Syracuse U (NY)
Temple U (PA)
Texas Woman's U (TX)
The U of Akron (OH)
The U of Iowa (IA)
U of Massachusetts Dartmouth (MA)
U of Michigan (MI)
U of North Texas (TX)
U of Oregon (OR)
The U of Texas at Arlington (TX)
The U of the Arts (PA)
U of Washington (WA)
U of Wisconsin–Milwaukee (WI)
Virginia Commonwealth U (VA)

METALLURGICAL ENGINEERING
Bethel Coll (IN)
Colorado School of Mines (CO)
Dalhousie U (NS, Canada)
Harvard U (MA)
Illinois Inst of Technology (IL)
Iowa State U of Science and Technology (IA)
McGill U (PQ, Canada)
Michigan Technological U (MI)
Montana Tech of The U of Montana (MT)
New Mexico Inst of Mining and Technology (NM)
The Ohio State U (OH)
Oregon State U (OR)
Penn State U Univ Park Campus (PA)
South Dakota School of Mines and Technology (SD)
Université Laval (PQ, Canada)
The U of Alabama (AL)
U of Alberta (AB, Canada)
U of British Columbia (BC, Canada)
U of Cincinnati (OH)
U of Idaho (ID)
U of Illinois at Urbana–Champaign (IL)
U of Michigan (MI)
U of Missouri–Rolla (MO)
U of Nevada, Reno (NV)
U of Pittsburgh (PA)
U of Pittsburgh at Bradford (PA)
The U of Tennessee Knoxville (TN)
U of Toronto (ON, Canada)
U of Utah (UT)
U of Washington (WA)
U of Wisconsin–Madison (WI)
Worcester Polytechnic Inst (MA)

METALLURGICAL TECHNOLOGY
U of Cincinnati (OH)

METALLURGY
Eastern Michigan U (MI)
U of Toronto (ON, Canada)
Worcester Polytechnic Inst (MA)

MEXICAN-AMERICAN STUDIES
California State U, Dominguez Hills (CA)
California State U, Fresno (CA)
California State U, Fullerton (CA)
California State U, Hayward (CA)
California State U, Long Beach (CA)
California State U, Los Angeles (CA)
California State U, Northridge (CA)
California State U, San Bernardino (CA)
Claremont McKenna Coll (CA)
Concordia U at Austin (TX)
The Evergreen State Coll (WA)
Hampshire Coll (MA)
Long Island U, Southampton Coll, Friends World Program (NY)
Loyola Marymount U (CA)
Metropolitan State Coll of Denver (CO)
Pitzer Coll (CA)
Pomona Coll (CA)
San Diego State U (CA)
San Francisco State U (CA)
Scripps Coll (CA)
Sonoma State U (CA)
Southern Methodist U (TX)
Stanford U (CA)

Sul Ross State U (TX)
U of Calif, Davis (CA)
U of Calif, Los Angeles (CA)
U of Calif, Riverside (CA)
U of Calif, Santa Barbara (CA)
U of Michigan (MI)
U of Minnesota, Twin Cities Campus (MN)
U of Southern California (CA)
The U of Texas–Pan American (TX)
U of Washington (WA)

MICROBIOLOGY/BACTERIOLOGY
Arizona State U (AZ)
Auburn U (AL)
Ball State U (IN)
Bowling Green State U (OH)
Brigham Young U (UT)
California Polytechnic State U, San Luis Obispo (CA)
California State Polytechnic U, Pomona (CA)
California State U, Chico (CA)
California State U, Dominguez Hills (CA)
California State U, Fresno (CA)
California State U, Fullerton (CA)
California State U, Long Beach (CA)
California State U, Los Angeles (CA)
California State U, Northridge (CA)
Clemson U (SC)
Colorado State U (CO)
Cornell U (NY)
Dalhousie U (NS, Canada)
Duquesne U (PA)
Eastern Kentucky U (KY)
Eastern Washington U (WA)
The Evergreen State Coll (WA)
Framingham State Coll (MA)
Hampshire Coll (MA)
Harvard U (MA)
Humboldt State U (CA)
Idaho State U (ID)
Indiana U Bloomington (IN)
Inter American U of PR, Arecibo Campus (PR)
Inter American U of PR, San Germán Campus (PR)
Iowa State U of Science and Technology (IA)
Juniata Coll (PA)
Kansas State U (KS)
Louisiana State U and A&M Coll (LA)
Maharishi U of Management (IA)
McGill U (PQ, Canada)
Memorial U of Newfoundland (NF, Canada)
Miami U (OH)
Michigan State U (MI)
Michigan Technological U (MI)
Minnesota State U, Mankato (MN)
Mississippi State U (MS)
Mississippi U for Women (MS)
Missouri Southern State Coll (MO)
Montana State U–Bozeman (MT)
New Mexico State U (NM)
North Carolina State U (NC)
North Dakota State U (ND)
Northeastern State U (OK)
Northern Arizona U (AZ)
Northern Michigan U (MI)
Notre Dame Coll (NH)
The Ohio State U (OH)
Ohio Wesleyan U (OH)
Oklahoma State U (OK)
Oregon State U (OR)
Penn State U Univ Park Campus (PA)
Pomona Coll (CA)
Purdue U Calumet (IN)
Quinnipiac U (CT)
Rutgers, State U of NJ, Camden Coll of Arts & Scis (NJ)
Rutgers, State U of NJ, Douglass Coll (NJ)
Rutgers, State U of NJ, Livingston Coll (NJ)
Rutgers, State U of NJ, Rutgers Coll (NJ)
Rutgers, State U of NJ, U Coll–Camden (NJ)

Rutgers, State U of NJ, U Coll–New Brunswick (NJ)
St. Cloud State U (MN)
Salve Regina U (RI)
San Diego State U (CA)
San Francisco State U (CA)
San Jose State U (CA)
Sonoma State U (CA)
South Dakota State U (SD)
Southern Illinois U Carbondale (IL)
Southwest Texas State U (TX)
Texas A&M U (TX)
Texas Tech U (TX)
Université de Montréal (PQ, Canada)
Université de Sherbrooke (PQ, Canada)
Université Laval (PQ, Canada)
The U of Akron (OH)
The U of Alabama (AL)
U of Alberta (AB, Canada)
The U of Arizona (AZ)
U of Arkansas (AR)
U of British Columbia (BC, Canada)
U of Calif, Davis (CA)
U of Calif, Los Angeles (CA)
U of Calif, San Diego (CA)
U of Calif, Santa Barbara (CA)
U of Central Florida (FL)
U of Cincinnati (OH)
U of Florida (FL)
U of Georgia (GA)
U of Guelph (ON, Canada)
U of Hawaii at Manoa (HI)
U of Houston–Downtown (TX)
U of Idaho (ID)
U of Illinois at Urbana–Champaign (IL)
The U of Iowa (IA)
U of Kansas (KS)
U of King's Coll (NS, Canada)
U of Louisiana at Lafayette (LA)
U of Maine (ME)
U of Manitoba (MB, Canada)
U of Maryland, Coll Park (MD)
U of Maryland University Coll (MD)
U of Massachusetts Amherst (MA)
U of Miami (FL)
U of Michigan (MI)
U of Michigan–Dearborn (MI)
U of Minnesota, Twin Cities Campus (MN)
U of Missouri–Columbia (MO)
The U of Montana–Missoula (MT)
U of New Brunswick, Fredericton (NB, Canada)
U of New Hampshire (NH)
U of Oklahoma (OK)
U of Pittsburgh (PA)
U of Puerto Rico, Humacao U Coll (PR)
U of Puerto Rico, Mayagüez Campus (PR)
U of Rhode Island (RI)
U of Rochester (NY)
U of South Florida (FL)
The U of Tennessee Knoxville (TN)
The U of Texas at Arlington (TX)
The U of Texas at Austin (TX)
U of the Sciences in Philadelphia (PA)
U of Toronto (ON, Canada)
U of Vermont (VT)
U of Victoria (BC, Canada)
U of Washington (WA)
The U of Western Ontario (ON, Canada)
U of Windsor (ON, Canada)
U of Wisconsin–Madison (WI)
Wagner Coll (NY)
Washington State U (WA)
Weber State U (UT)
West Chester U of Pennsylvania (PA)
Wittenberg U (OH)
Worcester Polytechnic Inst (MA)
Xavier U of Louisiana (LA)

MIDDLE EASTERN STUDIES
American U (DC)
American U in Cairo (Egypt)
Barnard Coll (NY)
Brandeis U (MA)
Brigham Young U (UT)
Brown U (RI)
Carleton U (ON, Canada)

Coll of the Holy Cross (MA)
Columbia Coll (NY)
Columbia International U (SC)
Columbia U, School of General Studies (NY)
Cornell U (NY)
Emory & Henry Coll (VA)
Fordham U (NY)
The George Washington U (DC)
Hampshire Coll (MA)
Harvard U (MA)
Indiana State U (IN)
Indiana U Bloomington (IN)
Johns Hopkins U (MD)
Long Island U, Southampton Coll, Friends World Program (NY)
McGill U (PQ, Canada)
New York U (NY)
Oberlin Coll (OH)
The Ohio State U (OH)
Portland State U (OR)
Princeton U (NJ)
Queens Coll of the City U of NY (NY)
Rutgers, State U of NJ, Douglass Coll (NJ)
Rutgers, State U of NJ, Livingston Coll (NJ)
Rutgers, State U of NJ, Rutgers Coll (NJ)
Rutgers, State U of NJ, U Coll–New Brunswick (NJ)
Smith Coll (MA)
Southwest Texas State U (TX)
United States Military Academy (NY)
The U of Arizona (AZ)
U of Arkansas (AR)
U of Calif, Berkeley (CA)
U of Calif, Los Angeles (CA)
U of Calif, Santa Barbara (CA)
U of Chicago (IL)
U of Connecticut (CT)
U of Massachusetts Amherst (MA)
U of Michigan (MI)
U of Minnesota, Twin Cities Campus (MN)
U of Pennsylvania (PA)
The U of Texas at Austin (TX)
U of Toronto (ON, Canada)
U of Utah (UT)
U of Washington (WA)
Washington U in St. Louis (MO)
William Tyndale Coll (MI)

MIDDLE SCHOOL EDUCATION
Albany State U (GA)
Alverno Coll (WI)
American International Coll (MA)
Antioch Coll (OH)
Appalachian State U (NC)
Arkansas Tech U (AR)
Asbury Coll (KY)
Ashland U (OH)
Augusta State U (GA)
Avila Coll (MO)
Baldwin-Wallace Coll (OH)
Barton Coll (NC)
Bellarmine Coll (KY)
Bennett Coll (NC)
Berea Coll (KY)
Berry Coll (GA)
Black Hills State U (SD)
Bowling Green State U (OH)
Brandon U (MB, Canada)
Brenau U (GA)
Brescia U (KY)
Bridgewater State Coll (MA)
Bryan Coll (TN)
Campbell U (NC)
Canisius Coll (NY)
Carthage Coll (WI)
Catawba Coll (NC)
Cedar Crest Coll (PA)
Centenary Coll of Louisiana (LA)
Central Methodist Coll (MO)
Central Missouri State U (MO)
Christopher Newport U (VA)
Clark Atlanta U (GA)
Clarke Coll (IA)
Clark U (MA)
Clayton Coll & State U (GA)
Coker Coll (SC)
Coll of Mount St. Joseph (OH)
Coll of Mount Saint Vincent (NY)
Coll of the Atlantic (ME)
Coll of the Ozarks (MO)

Majors Index
Middle School Education–Modern Languages

Coll of the Southwest (NM)
Columbia Coll (MO)
Columbus State U (GA)
Concordia Coll (NY)
Concordia U (NE)
Concordia U at St. Paul (MN)
Concordia U Wisconsin (WI)
Cumberland Coll (KY)
Dakota Wesleyan U (SD)
David Lipscomb U (TN)
East Carolina U (NC)
Eastern Illinois U (IL)
Eastern Kentucky U (KY)
Eastern Mennonite U (VA)
Eastern Nazarene Coll (MA)
Elmira Coll (NY)
Elon Coll (NC)
Emmanuel Coll (GA)
The Evergreen State Coll (WA)
Fitchburg State Coll (MA)
Fontbonne Coll (MO)
Georgia Coll and State U (GA)
Georgia Southern U (GA)
Georgia Southwestern State U (GA)
Georgia State U (GA)
Goddard Coll (VT)
Gordon Coll (MA)
Governors State U (IL)
Grand View Coll (IA)
Greensboro Coll (NC)
Hampton U (VA)
Harris-Stowe State Coll (MO)
High Point U (NC)
Idaho State U (ID)
Illinois State U (IL)
Indiana State U (IN)
Indiana Wesleyan U (IN)
Ithaca Coll (NY)
Jacksonville State U (AL)
John Brown U (AR)
Johnson Bible Coll (TN)
Johnson State Coll (VT)
Judson Coll (AL)
Kentucky Christian Coll (KY)
Kentucky Wesleyan Coll (KY)
King Coll (TN)
LaGrange Coll (GA)
Lakeland Coll (WI)
Lake Superior State U (MI)
Lambuth U (TN)
Lesley Coll (MA)
Lindenwood U (MO)
Long Island U, Southampton Coll, Friends World Program (NY)
Lourdes Coll (OH)
Luther Coll (IA)
Lynn U (FL)
Malone Coll (OH)
Manhattan Coll (NY)
Marian Coll of Fond du Lac (WI)
Marquette U (WI)
Marymount Coll (NY)
Maryville U of Saint Louis (MO)
Massachusetts Coll of Liberal Arts (MA)
Memorial U of Newfoundland (NF, Canada)
Mercer U (GA)
Merrimack Coll (MA)
Mesa State Coll (CO)
Miami U (OH)
MidAmerica Nazarene U (KS)
Midland Lutheran Coll (NE)
Midway Coll (KY)
Minnesota State U Moorhead (MN)
Missouri Baptist Coll (MO)
Morehead State U (KY)
Morehouse Coll (GA)
Mount Mercy Coll (IA)
Mount Olive Coll (NC)
Mount St. Clare Coll (IA)
Mount Union Coll (OH)
Murray State U (KY)
Nebraska Wesleyan U (NE)
New York U (NY)
Nicholls State U (LA)
North Carolina Wesleyan Coll (NC)
Northern Kentucky U (KY)
North Georgia Coll & State U (GA)
Northland Coll (WI)
Northwest Coll (WA)
Northwest Missouri State U (MO)
Oakland City U (IN)
Oglethorpe U (GA)
Ohio Northern U (OH)
Ohio U (OH)

Oklahoma State U (OK)
Otterbein Coll (OH)
Ouachita Baptist U (AR)
Peru State Coll (NE)
Piedmont Coll (GA)
Pikeville Coll (KY)
Plymouth State Coll (NH)
Reinhardt Coll (GA)
Sacred Heart U (CT)
Saint Anselm Coll (NH)
St. Cloud State U (MN)
St. Joseph's Coll, New York (NY)
Saint Louis U (MO)
Saint Mary's U of Minnesota (MN)
San Diego State U (CA)
Southeast Missouri State U (MO)
Southwest Baptist U (MO)
Southwest Missouri State U (MO)
State U of NY Coll at Cortland (NY)
State U of NY Coll at Old Westbury (NY)
State U of NY Coll at Potsdam (NY)
Syracuse U (NY)
Taylor U (IN)
Thomas More Coll (KY)
Thomas U (GA)
Toccoa Falls Coll (GA)
Transylvania U (KY)
Trinity Christian Coll (IL)
Tusculum Coll (TN)
Union Coll (KY)
U of Delaware (DE)
U of Georgia (GA)
U of Kansas (KS)
U of Kentucky (KY)
U of Maine at Machias (ME)
U of Michigan–Dearborn (MI)
U of Minnesota, Duluth (MN)
U of Missouri–Columbia (MO)
U of Missouri–St. Louis (MO)
U of Nebraska–Lincoln (NE)
The U of North Carolina at Chapel Hill (NC)
The U of North Carolina at Charlotte (NC)
The U of North Carolina at Greensboro (NC)
The U of North Carolina at Wilmington (NC)
U of North Dakota (ND)
U of Northern Iowa (IA)
U of North Florida (FL)
U of Pittsburgh at Bradford (PA)
U of Regina (SK, Canada)
U of Richmond (VA)
U of Sioux Falls (SD)
U of South Dakota (SD)
U of Southern Colorado (CO)
U of the Ozarks (AR)
U of West Florida (FL)
U of Wisconsin–Platteville (WI)
Upper Iowa U (IA)
Urbana U (OH)
Valdosta State U (GA)
Villa Julie Coll (MD)
Virginia Commonwealth U (VA)
Virginia Wesleyan Coll (VA)
Wagner Coll (NY)
Warner Pacific Coll (OR)
Washington U in St. Louis (MO)
Webster U (MO)
Wesleyan Coll (GA)
Western Carolina U (NC)
Western Kentucky U (KY)
Westminster Coll (MO)
West Virginia Wesleyan Coll (WV)
Wheeling Jesuit U (WV)
William Woods U (MO)
Wingate U (NC)
Winona State U (MN)
Winston-Salem State U (NC)
Wittenberg U (OH)
Xavier U (OH)
Xavier U of Louisiana (LA)
York Coll (NE)
York U (ON, Canada)
Youngstown State U (OH)

MILITARY SCIENCE
American Military U (VA)
Centenary Coll of Louisiana (LA)
DePaul U (IL)
Drake U (IA)
Eastern Washington U (WA)
Hampton U (VA)
Indiana State U (IN)

Jacksonville State U (AL)
La Salle U (PA)
Longwood Coll (VA)
Minnesota State U, Mankato (MN)
Monmouth Coll (IL)
Northwest Missouri State U (MO)
Purdue U Calumet (IN)
Rensselaer Polytechnic Inst (NY)
United States Military Academy (NY)
U of Connecticut (CT)
The U of Iowa (IA)
The U of Texas–Pan American (TX)
U of Washington (WA)
York Coll (NE)

MINING/MINERAL ENGINEERING
Colorado School of Mines (CO)
Dalhousie U (NS, Canada)
McGill U (PQ, Canada)
Michigan Technological U (MI)
Montana Tech of The U of Montana (MT)
New Mexico Inst of Mining and Technology (NM)
Oregon State U (OR)
Penn State U Univ Park Campus (PA)
Queen's U at Kingston (ON, Canada)
South Dakota School of Mines and Technology (SD)
Southern Illinois U Carbondale (IL)
U du Québec en Abitibi-Témiscamingue (PQ, Canada)
Université Laval (PQ, Canada)
U of Alaska Fairbanks (AK)
U of Alberta (AB, Canada)
The U of Arizona (AZ)
U of British Columbia (BC, Canada)
U of Idaho (ID)
U of Kentucky (KY)
U of Missouri–Rolla (MO)
U of Nevada, Reno (NV)
U of Pittsburgh at Bradford (PA)
U of Utah (UT)
U of Wisconsin–Madison (WI)
Virginia Polytechnic Inst and State U (VA)
West Virginia U (WV)

MINING TECHNOLOGY
Bluefield State Coll (WV)

MISSIONARY STUDIES
Abilene Christian U (TX)
Alaska Bible Coll (AK)
Asbury Coll (KY)
Bethesda Christian U (CA)
Biola U (CA)
Briercrest Bible Coll (SK, Canada)
Canadian Bible Coll (SK, Canada)
Cascade Coll (OR)
Cedarville Coll (OH)
Central Christian Coll of Kansas (KS)
Circleville Bible Coll (OH)
Crown Coll (MN)
Eastern Coll (PA)
Eastern Pentecostal Bible Coll (ON, Canada)
Emmaus Bible Coll (IA)
Eugene Bible Coll (OR)
Faith Baptist Bible Coll and Theological Seminary (IA)
Freed-Hardeman U (TN)
George Fox U (OR)
Global U of the Assemblies of God (MO)
God's Bible School and Coll (OH)
Harding U (AR)
Hillsdale Free Will Baptist Coll (OK)
Hobe Sound Bible Coll (FL)
Hope International U (CA)
John Brown U (AR)
Kentucky Mountain Bible Coll (KY)
Manhattan Christian Coll (KS)
Mid-Continent Coll (KY)
Moody Bible Inst (IL)
Multnomah Bible Coll and Biblical Seminary (OR)
Northwestern Coll (MN)
Northwest Nazarene U (ID)
Nyack Coll (NY)
Oak Hills Christian Coll (MN)
Oklahoma Baptist U (OK)

Reformed Bible Coll (MI)
Simpson Coll and Graduate School (CA)
Southeastern Coll of the Assemblies of God (FL)
Southwestern Assemblies of God U (TX)
Trinity Baptist Coll (FL)
Trinity Western U (BC, Canada)

MODERN LANGUAGES
Albion Coll (MI)
Alfred U (NY)
Alma Coll (MI)
American U (DC)
Atlantic Union Coll (MA)
Ball State U (IN)
Bard Coll (NY)
Beloit Coll (WI)
Bemidji State U (MN)
Benedictine Coll (KS)
Bennington Coll (VT)
Bishop's U (PQ, Canada)
Blue Mountain Coll (MS)
Brooklyn Coll of the City U of NY (NY)
Brown U (RI)
Buena Vista U (IA)
Capital U (OH)
Carleton U (ON, Canada)
Carnegie Mellon U (PA)
Carthage Coll (WI)
Chicago State U (IL)
Claremont McKenna Coll (CA)
Clark U (MA)
Clemson U (SC)
Coll of Mount Saint Vincent (NY)
The Coll of New Rochelle (NY)
Coll of Notre Dame of Maryland (MD)
The Coll of St. Scholastica (MN)
Coll of the Holy Cross (MA)
The Coll of William and Mary (VA)
Concordia U (PQ, Canada)
Converse Coll (SC)
Cornell Coll (IA)
Cornell U (NY)
Creighton U (NE)
DePaul U (IL)
Eastern Washington U (WA)
Eckerd Coll (FL)
Elizabethtown Coll (PA)
Elmira Coll (NY)
Fairfield U (CT)
Fordham U (NY)
Fort Lewis Coll (CO)
Framingham State Coll (MA)
Franklin Coll Switzerland (Switzerland)
Gannon U (PA)
Gettysburg Coll (PA)
Gordon Coll (MA)
Greenville Coll (IL)
Grove City Coll (PA)
Hamilton Coll (NY)
Harvard U (MA)
Hastings Coll (NE)
Hobart and William Smith Colls (NY)
Howard Payne U (TX)
Immaculata Coll (PA)
Iona Coll (NY)
Judson Coll (AL)
Kentucky Wesleyan Coll (KY)
Kenyon Coll (OH)
King Coll (TN)
Lake Erie Coll (OH)
Lambuth U (TN)
La Salle U (PA)
Lee U (TN)
Lenoir-Rhyne Coll (NC)
Lewis & Clark Coll (OR)
Long Island U, Brooklyn Campus (NY)
Long Island U, Southampton Coll, Friends World Program (NY)
Longwood Coll (VA)
Loras Coll (IA)
Louisiana Coll (LA)
Luther Coll (IA)
Manhattan Coll (NY)
Marian Coll of Fond du Lac (WI)
Marietta Coll (OH)
Marlboro Coll (VT)
Marshall U (WV)
Marymount Coll (NY)
Mary Washington Coll (VA)

Merrimack Coll (MA)
MidAmerica Nazarene U (KS)
Middlebury Coll (VT)
Minnesota State U, Mankato (MN)
Mississippi Coll (MS)
Monmouth Coll (IL)
Mount Allison U (NB, Canada)
Mount Saint Vincent U (NS, Canada)
Mount Vernon Nazarene Coll (OH)
Nazareth Coll of Rochester (NY)
New York U (NY)
North Central Coll (IL)
Northeastern U (MA)
Northern Arizona U (AZ)
North Park U (IL)
Oakland U (MI)
Olivet Nazarene U (IL)
Pace U, New York City Campus (NY)
Pace U, Pleasantville/Briarcliff Campus (NY)
Pacific Lutheran U (WA)
Pacific U (OR)
Pomona Coll (CA)
Presbyterian Coll (SC)
Purchase Coll, State U of NY (NY)
Queens Coll of the City U of NY (NY)
Redeemer Coll (ON, Canada)
Rivier Coll (NH)
Saint Anselm Coll (NH)
St. Bonaventure U (NY)
Saint Francis Coll (PA)
St. Francis Xavier U (NS, Canada)
Saint Joseph Coll (CT)
St. Joseph's Coll, New York (NY)
St. Lawrence U (NY)
Saint Louis U (MO)
Saint Mary's Coll (IN)
Saint Mary's Coll of California (CA)
St. Mary's Coll of Maryland (MD)
Saint Mary's U (NS, Canada)
Saint Michael's Coll (VT)
Sarah Lawrence Coll (NY)
Scripps Coll (CA)
Seton Hill Coll (PA)
Slippery Rock U of Pennsylvania (PA)
Southwestern U (TX)
State U of NY Coll at Potsdam (NY)
Stephens Coll (MO)
Suffolk U (MA)
Sweet Briar Coll (VA)
Syracuse U (NY)
Trent U (ON, Canada)
Trinity Coll (CT)
United States Military Academy (NY)
Université de Montréal (PQ, Canada)
U du Québec à Chicoutimi (PQ, Canada)
The U of Akron (OH)
U of Alberta (AB, Canada)
U of Central Oklahoma (OK)
U of Chicago (IL)
The U of Lethbridge (AB, Canada)
U of Louisiana at Lafayette (LA)
U of Maine (ME)
U of Maryland, Baltimore County (MD)
U of Missouri–St. Louis (MO)
U of Mobile (AL)
U of New Brunswick, Fredericton (NB, Canada)
U of New Hampshire (NH)
U of St. Thomas (TX)
U of Southern Maine (ME)
U of South Florida (FL)
U of the Pacific (CA)
U of Toronto (ON, Canada)
U of Victoria (BC, Canada)
U of Windsor (ON, Canada)
U of Wisconsin–Parkside (WI)
Ursinus Coll (PA)
Virginia Commonwealth U (VA)
Virginia Military Inst (VA)
Walla Walla Coll (WA)
Walsh U (OH)
Washington U in St. Louis (MO)
Wayne State Coll (NE)
West Chester U of Pennsylvania (PA)
Westminster Coll (PA)
Westmont Coll (CA)

Majors Index
Modern Languages-Music

Widener U (PA)
Wilmington Coll (OH)
Winthrop U (SC)
Wittenberg U (OH)
Wright State U (OH)
York U (ON, Canada)

MOLECULAR BIOLOGY
Arizona State U (AZ)
Assumption Coll (MA)
Auburn U (AL)
Ball State U (IN)
Bard Coll (NY)
Beloit Coll (WI)
Benedictine U (IL)
Bethel Coll (MN)
Boston U (MA)
Bradley U (IL)
Bridgewater State Coll (MA)
Brigham Young U (UT)
Brown U (RI)
California Inst of Technology (CA)
California Lutheran U (CA)
California State U, Fresno (CA)
California State U, Fullerton (CA)
California State U, Northridge (CA)
California State U, San Marcos (CA)
Cedar Crest Coll (PA)
Centre Coll (KY)
Chestnut Hill Coll (PA)
Clarion U of Pennsylvania (PA)
Clarkson U (NY)
Clark U (MA)
Coe Coll (IA)
Colby Coll (ME)
Colgate U (NY)
Coll of Our Lady of the Elms (MA)
Concordia U (PQ, Canada)
Cornell U (NY)
Dartmouth Coll (NH)
Dickinson Coll (PA)
The Evergreen State Coll (WA)
Florida A&M U (FL)
Florida Inst of Technology (FL)
Florida State U (FL)
Fort Lewis Coll (CO)
Grove City Coll (PA)
Hamilton Coll (NY)
Hampshire Coll (MA)
Hampton U (VA)
Harvard U (MA)
Humboldt State U (CA)
Juniata Coll (PA)
Kenyon Coll (OH)
Lehigh U (PA)
Long Island U, Brooklyn Campus (NY)
Long Island U, C.W. Post Campus (NY)
Marlboro Coll (VT)
Marquette U (WI)
McGill U (PQ, Canada)
Meredith Coll (NC)
Middlebury Coll (VT)
Millersville U of Pennsylvania (PA)
Muskingum Coll (OH)
Northwestern U (IL)
Ohio Northern U (OH)
The Ohio State U (OH)
Oklahoma State U (OK)
Otterbein Coll (OH)
Pomona Coll (CA)
Princeton U (NJ)
Rutgers, State U of NJ, Camden Coll of Arts & Scis (NJ)
Rutgers, State U of NJ, Douglass Coll (NJ)
Rutgers, State U of NJ, Livingston Coll (NJ)
Rutgers, State U of NJ, Rutgers Coll (NJ)
Rutgers, State U of NJ, U Coll–Camden (NJ)
Rutgers, State U of NJ, U Coll–New Brunswick (NJ)
San Francisco State U (CA)
San Jose State U (CA)
Scripps Coll (CA)
Southwest Missouri State U (MO)
State U of NY at Albany (NY)
State U of NY Coll at Brockport (NY)
Stetson U (FL)
Texas A&M U (TX)
Texas Tech U (TX)
Tulane U (LA)

U of Alberta (AB, Canada)
U of Calgary (AB, Canada)
U of Calif, Berkeley (CA)
U of Calif, Los Angeles (CA)
U of Calif, San Diego (CA)
U of Calif, Santa Barbara (CA)
U of Calif, Santa Cruz (CA)
U of Colorado at Boulder (CO)
U of Connecticut (CT)
U of Denver (CO)
U of Great Falls (MT)
U of Guelph (ON, Canada)
U of Idaho (ID)
U of Maine (ME)
U of Maryland, Coll Park (MD)
The U of Memphis (TN)
U of Michigan (MI)
U of Minnesota, Duluth (MN)
U of New Brunswick, Fredericton (NB, Canada)
U of New Hampshire (NH)
U of Pittsburgh (PA)
U of Southern California (CA)
The U of Texas at Austin (TX)
U of Toronto (ON, Canada)
U of Vermont (VT)
U of Washington (WA)
The U of Winnipeg (MB, Canada)
U of Wisconsin–Madison (WI)
U of Wisconsin–Parkside (WI)
U of Wisconsin–Superior (WI)
U of Wyoming (WY)
Vanderbilt U (TN)
Wells Coll (NY)
Wesleyan U (CT)
West Chester U of Pennsylvania (PA)
Western State Coll of Colorado (CO)
Western Washington U (WA)
Westminster Coll (PA)
William Jewell Coll (MO)
Winston-Salem State U (NC)
Worcester Polytechnic Inst (MA)
Yale U (CT)
York U (ON, Canada)

MORTUARY SCIENCE
Cincinnati Coll of Mortuary Science (OH)
Gannon U (PA)
Milligan Coll (TN)
Mount Ida Coll (MA)
Point Park Coll (PA)
St. John's U (NY)
Southern Illinois U Carbondale (IL)
Thiel Coll (PA)
U of Central Oklahoma (OK)
U of Minnesota, Twin Cities Campus (MN)
U of the District of Columbia (DC)
Wayne State U (MI)

MOVEMENT THERAPY
Brock U (ON, Canada)

MUSEUM STUDIES
Baylor U (TX)
Beloit Coll (WI)
Coll of the Atlantic (ME)
Framingham State Coll (MA)
Jewish Theological Seminary of America (NY)
Juniata Coll (PA)
Long Island U, Southampton Coll, Friends World Program (NY)
Luther Coll (IA)
Oklahoma Baptist U (OK)
Pine Manor Coll (MA)
Randolph-Macon Woman's Coll (VA)
Tusculum Coll (TN)
The U of Iowa (IA)
The U of North Carolina at Greensboro (NC)
Virginia Commonwealth U (VA)
Western Maryland Coll (MD)

MUSIC
Abilene Christian U (TX)
Acadia U (NS, Canada)
Adams State Coll (CO)
Adelphi U (NY)
Adrian Coll (MI)
Agnes Scott Coll (GA)
Alabama State U (AL)
Albany State U (GA)

Albertson Coll of Idaho (ID)
Albion Coll (MI)
Alderson-Broaddus Coll (WV)
Allegheny Coll (PA)
Allen U (SC)
Alma Coll (MI)
Alverno Coll (WI)
American U (DC)
Amherst Coll (MA)
Anderson Coll (SC)
Andrews U (MI)
Anna Maria Coll (MA)
Antioch Coll (OH)
Appalachian State U (NC)
Aquinas Coll (MI)
Arizona State U (AZ)
Arkansas State U (AR)
Arkansas Tech U (AR)
Arlington Baptist Coll (TX)
Armstrong Atlantic State U (GA)
Asbury Coll (KY)
Ashland U (OH)
Assumption Coll (MA)
Atlanta Christian Coll (GA)
Atlantic Union Coll (MA)
Augsburg Coll (MN)
Augustana Coll (IL)
Augustana Coll (SD)
Augusta State U (GA)
Austin Coll (TX)
Austin Peay State U (TN)
Averett Coll (VA)
Avila Coll (MO)
Azusa Pacific U (CA)
Baker U (KS)
Baldwin-Wallace Coll (OH)
Ball State U (IN)
Barat Coll (IL)
Bard Coll (NY)
Barnard Coll (NY)
Bartlesville Wesleyan Coll (OK)
Bates Coll (ME)
Baylor U (TX)
Belhaven Coll (MS)
Bellarmine Coll (KY)
Belmont U (TN)
Beloit Coll (WI)
Bemidji State U (MN)
Benedictine Coll (KS)
Benedictine U (IL)
Bennett Coll (NC)
Bennington Coll (VT)
Berea Coll (KY)
Berklee Coll of Music (MA)
Baruch Coll of the City U of NY (NY)
Berry Coll (GA)
Bethany Bible Coll (NB, Canada)
Bethany Coll (KS)
Bethany Coll (WV)
Bethel Coll (IN)
Bethel Coll (KS)
Bethel Coll (MN)
Bethune-Cookman Coll (FL)
Biola U (CA)
Birmingham-Southern Coll (AL)
Bishop's U (PQ, Canada)
Blackburn Coll (IL)
Black Hills State U (SD)
Bloomsburg U of Pennsylvania (PA)
Blue Mountain Coll (MS)
Bluffton Coll (OH)
Boise State U (ID)
Boston Coll (MA)
Bowdoin Coll (ME)
Bowling Green State U (OH)
Bradley U (IL)
Brandeis U (MA)
Brandon U (MB, Canada)
Brenau U (GA)
Brevard Coll (NC)
Briar Cliff Coll (IA)
Bridgewater Coll (VA)
Bridgewater State Coll (MA)
Briercrest Bible Coll (SK, Canada)
Brigham Young U (UT)
Brigham Young U–Hawaii Campus (HI)
Brock U (ON, Canada)
Brooklyn Coll of the City U of NY (NY)
Brown U (RI)
Bryan Coll (TN)
Bryn Mawr Coll (PA)
Bucknell U (PA)
Buena Vista U (IA)

Butler U (IN)
Caldwell Coll (NJ)
California Baptist U (CA)
California Inst of the Arts (CA)
California Lutheran U (CA)
California Polytechnic State U, San Luis Obispo (CA)
California State Polytechnic U, Pomona (CA)
California State U, Chico (CA)
California State U, Dominguez Hills (CA)
California State U, Fresno (CA)
California State U, Fullerton (CA)
California State U, Hayward (CA)
California State U, Long Beach (CA)
California State U, Los Angeles (CA)
California State U, Northridge (CA)
California State U, Sacramento (CA)
California State U, San Bernardino (CA)
California State U, Stanislaus (CA)
Calvary Bible Coll and Theological Seminary (MO)
Calvin Coll (MI)
Cameron U (OK)
Campbellsville U (KY)
Campbell U (NC)
Capital U (OH)
Cardinal Stritch U (WI)
Carleton Coll (MN)
Carleton U (ON, Canada)
Carnegie Mellon U (PA)
Carroll Coll (WI)
Carson-Newman Coll (TN)
Carthage Coll (WI)
Case Western Reserve U (OH)
Castleton State Coll (VT)
Catawba Coll (NC)
The Catholic U of America (DC)
Cedar Crest Coll (PA)
Cedarville Coll (OH)
Centenary Coll of Louisiana (LA)
Central Coll (IA)
Central Connecticut State U (CT)
Central Methodist Coll (MO)
Central Michigan U (MI)
Central Missouri State U (MO)
Centre Coll (KY)
Chadron State Coll (NE)
Chapman U (CA)
Charleston Southern U (SC)
Chatham Coll (PA)
Chestnut Hill Coll (PA)
Cheyney U of Pennsylvania (PA)
Chicago State U (IL)
Chowan Coll (NC)
Christopher Newport U (VA)
City Coll of the City U of NY (NY)
Claflin U (SC)
Claremont McKenna Coll (CA)
Clark Atlanta U (GA)
Clarke Coll (IA)
Clark U (MA)
Clayton Coll & State U (GA)
Cleveland Inst of Music (OH)
Cleveland State U (OH)
Coe Coll (IA)
Coker Coll (SC)
Colby Coll (ME)
Colgate U (NY)
Coll of Charleston (SC)
Coll of Mount St. Joseph (OH)
The Coll of New Jersey (NJ)
Coll of Notre Dame (CA)
Coll of Notre Dame of Maryland (MD)
Coll of Saint Benedict (MN)
Coll of St. Catherine (MN)
Coll of Saint Elizabeth (NJ)
The Coll of Saint Rose (NY)
The Coll of St. Scholastica (MN)
Coll of Santa Fe (NM)
Coll of Staten Island of the City U of NY (NY)
Coll of the Atlantic (ME)
Coll of the Holy Cross (MA)
Coll of the Ozarks (MO)
The Coll of William and Mary (VA)
The Coll of Wooster (OH)
Colorado Christian U (CO)
The Colorado Coll (CO)
Colorado State U (CO)
Columbia Coll (NY)

Columbia Coll (SC)
Columbia Coll Chicago (IL)
Columbia International U (SC)
Columbia Union Coll (MD)
Columbia U, School of General Studies (NY)
Columbus State U (GA)
Concordia Coll (MI)
Concordia Coll (MN)
Concordia Coll (NY)
Concordia U (CA)
Concordia U (IL)
Concordia U (NE)
Concordia U (PQ, Canada)
Concordia U at Austin (TX)
Concordia U at St. Paul (MN)
Concordia U Coll of Alberta (AB, Canada)
Concordia U Wisconsin (WI)
Connecticut Coll (CT)
Converse Coll (SC)
Cornell Coll (IA)
Cornell U (NY)
Cornerstone U (MI)
Cornish Coll of the Arts (WA)
Covenant Coll (GA)
Creighton U (NE)
Crown Coll (MN)
Culver-Stockton Coll (MO)
Cumberland Coll (KY)
The Curtis Inst of Music (PA)
Dalhousie U (NS, Canada)
Dallas Baptist U (TX)
Dana Coll (NE)
Dartmouth Coll (NH)
David Lipscomb U (TN)
Davidson Coll (NC)
Delaware State U (DE)
Delta State U (MS)
Denison U (OH)
DePaul U (IL)
DePauw U (IN)
Deree Coll (Greece)
Dickinson Coll (PA)
Dickinson State U (ND)
Doane Coll (NE)
Dominican U of California (CA)
Dordt Coll (IA)
Dowling Coll (NY)
Drake U (IA)
Drew U (NJ)
Drexel U (PA)
Drury U (MO)
Duke U (NC)
Duquesne U (PA)
Earlham Coll (IN)
East Central U (OK)
Eastern Coll (PA)
Eastern Illinois U (IL)
Eastern Kentucky U (KY)
Eastern Mennonite U (VA)
Eastern Michigan U (MI)
Eastern Nazarene Coll (MA)
Eastern New Mexico U (NM)
Eastern Oregon U (OR)
Eastern Washington U (WA)
East Tennessee State U (TN)
East Texas Baptist U (TX)
Eckerd Coll (FL)
Edgewood Coll (WI)
Edinboro U of Pennsylvania (PA)
Elizabeth City State U (NC)
Elizabethtown Coll (PA)
Elmhurst Coll (IL)
Elmira Coll (NY)
Elon Coll (NC)
Emmanuel Coll (GA)
Emory & Henry Coll (VA)
Emory U (GA)
Emporia State U (KS)
Erskine Coll (SC)
Evangel U (MO)
The Evergreen State Coll (WA)
Fisk U (TN)
Five Towns Coll (NY)
Florida A&M U (FL)
Florida Atlantic U (FL)
Florida International U (FL)
Florida Southern Coll (FL)
Florida State U (FL)
Fordham U (NY)
Fort Hays State U (KS)
Fort Lewis Coll (CO)
Franklin and Marshall Coll (PA)
Franklin Pierce Coll (NH)
Freed-Hardeman U (TN)
Free Will Baptist Bible Coll (TN)

Majors Index
Music

Fresno Pacific U (CA)
Friends U (KS)
Frostburg State U (MD)
Furman U (SC)
Gardner-Webb U (NC)
Geneva Coll (PA)
George Fox U (OR)
George Mason U (VA)
Georgetown Coll (KY)
The George Washington U (DC)
Georgia Coll and State U (GA)
Georgian Court Coll (NJ)
Georgia Southern U (GA)
Georgia Southwestern State U (GA)
Gettysburg Coll (PA)
Goddard Coll (VT)
Gonzaga U (WA)
Gordon Coll (MA)
Goshen Coll (IN)
Goucher Coll (MD)
Grace Bible Coll (MI)
Graceland Coll (IA)
Grand Canyon U (AZ)
Grand Valley State U (MI)
Greensboro Coll (NC)
Greenville Coll (IL)
Grinnell Coll (IA)
Guilford Coll (NC)
Gustavus Adolphus Coll (MN)
Hamilton Coll (NY)
Hamline U (MN)
Hampshire Coll (MA)
Hampton U (VA)
Hannibal-LaGrange Coll (MO)
Hanover Coll (IN)
Harding U (AR)
Hardin-Simmons U (TX)
Hartwick Coll (NY)
Harvard U (MA)
Hastings Coll (NE)
Haverford Coll (PA)
Heidelberg Coll (OH)
Henderson State U (AR)
Hendrix Coll (AR)
Hillsdale Coll (MI)
Hiram Coll (OH)
Hobart and William Smith Colls (NY)
Hofstra U (NY)
Hollins U (VA)
Holy Names Coll (CA)
Hope Coll (MI)
Houghton Coll (NY)
Houston Baptist U (TX)
Howard Payne U (TX)
Howard U (DC)
Humboldt State U (CA)
Hunter Coll of the City U of NY (NY)
Huntingdon Coll (AL)
Huntington Coll (IN)
Huston-Tillotson Coll (TX)
Idaho State U (ID)
Illinois Coll (IL)
Illinois State U (IL)
Illinois Wesleyan U (IL)
Immaculata Coll (PA)
Indiana State U (IN)
Indiana U Bloomington (IN)
Indiana U of Pennsylvania (PA)
Indiana U–Purdue U Fort Wayne (IN)
Indiana U Southeast (IN)
Indiana Wesleyan U (IN)
Inter American U of PR, Fajardo Campus (PR)
Inter American U of PR, Metropolitan Campus (PR)
Inter American U of PR, San Germán Campus (PR)
Iowa State U of Science and Technology (IA)
Iowa Wesleyan Coll (IA)
Ithaca Coll (NY)
Jacksonville State U (AL)
Jacksonville U (FL)
Jamestown Coll (ND)
Jarvis Christian Coll (TX)
Jewish Theological Seminary of America (NY)
John Brown U (AR)
Johns Hopkins U (MD)
Johnson State Coll (VT)
Judson Coll (AL)
Judson Coll (IL)
The Juilliard School (NY)

Kalamazoo Coll (MI)
Kansas State U (KS)
Kean U (NJ)
Keene State Coll (NH)
Kent State U (OH)
Kentucky Christian Coll (KY)
Kentucky Mountain Bible Coll (KY)
Kentucky State U (KY)
Kentucky Wesleyan Coll (KY)
Kenyon Coll (OH)
King Coll (TN)
The King's U Coll (AB, Canada)
Knox Coll (IL)
Kutztown U of Pennsylvania (PA)
Lafayette Coll (PA)
LaGrange Coll (GA)
Lake Erie Coll (OH)
Lake Forest Coll (IL)
Lakehead U (ON, Canada)
Lakeland Coll (WI)
Lamar U (TX)
Lambuth U (TN)
Lander U (SC)
Lane Coll (TN)
Langston U (OK)
La Salle U (PA)
La Sierra U (CA)
Lawrence U (WI)
Lebanon Valley Coll (PA)
Lee U (TN)
Lehigh U (PA)
Lehman Coll of the City U of NY (NY)
Lenoir-Rhyne Coll (NC)
Lewis & Clark Coll (OR)
Lewis U (IL)
Liberty U (VA)
Limestone Coll (SC)
Lincoln U (PA)
Lindenwood U (MO)
Linfield Coll (OR)
Lock Haven U of Pennsylvania (PA)
Long Island U, Brooklyn Campus (NY)
Long Island U, C.W. Post Campus (NY)
Long Island U, Southampton Coll, Friends World Program (NY)
Longwood Coll (VA)
Loras Coll (IA)
Louisiana Coll (LA)
Louisiana State U and A&M Coll (LA)
Louisiana Tech U (LA)
Loyola Marymount U (CA)
Loyola U Chicago (IL)
Loyola U New Orleans (LA)
Lubbock Christian U (TX)
Luther Coll (IA)
Lycoming Coll (PA)
Lynchburg Coll (VA)
Lynn U (FL)
Lyon Coll (AR)
Macalester Coll (MN)
MacMurray Coll (IL)
Madonna U (MI)
Malone Coll (OH)
Manchester Coll (IN)
Manhattan School of Music (NY)
Manhattanville Coll (NY)
Mannes Coll of Music, New School U (NY)
Mansfield U of Pennsylvania (PA)
Maranatha Baptist Bible Coll (WI)
Marian Coll (IN)
Marian Coll of Fond du Lac (WI)
Marietta Coll (OH)
Marlboro Coll (VT)
Marshall U (WV)
Mars Hill Coll (NC)
Mary Baldwin Coll (VA)
Marygrove Coll (MI)
Marylhurst U (OR)
Maryville Coll (TN)
Maryville U of Saint Louis (MO)
Mary Washington Coll (VA)
Marywood U (PA)
Massachusetts Coll of Liberal Arts (MA)
Massachusetts Inst of Technology (MA)
McGill U (PQ, Canada)
McKendree Coll (IL)
McMurry U (TX)
McNeese State U (LA)
McPherson Coll (KS)

Memorial U of Newfoundland (NF, Canada)
Mercer U (GA)
Mercy Coll (NY)
Mercyhurst Coll (PA)
Meredith Coll (NC)
Mesa State Coll (CO)
Messenger Coll (MO)
Messiah Coll (PA)
Methodist Coll (NC)
Miami U (OH)
Michigan State U (MI)
Mid-America Bible Coll (OK)
MidAmerica Nazarene U (KS)
Middlebury Coll (VT)
Middle Tennessee State U (TN)
Midland Lutheran Coll (NE)
Midwestern State U (TX)
Millersville U of Pennsylvania (PA)
Milligan Coll (TN)
Millikin U (IL)
Millsaps Coll (MS)
Mills Coll (CA)
Minnesota State U, Mankato (MN)
Minnesota State U Moorhead (MN)
Minot State U (ND)
Mississippi Coll (MS)
Mississippi Valley State U (MS)
Missouri Southern State Coll (MO)
Missouri Western State Coll (MO)
Molloy Coll (NY)
Monmouth Coll (IL)
Monmouth U (NJ)
Montana State U–Billings (MT)
Montreat Coll (NC)
Moravian Coll (PA)
Morehead State U (KY)
Morehouse Coll (GA)
Morgan State U (MD)
Morningside Coll (IA)
Mount Allison U (NB, Canada)
Mount Holyoke Coll (MA)
Mount Marty Coll (SD)
Mount Mary Coll (WI)
Mount Mercy Coll (IA)
Mount St. Clare Coll (IA)
Mount St. Mary's Coll (CA)
Mount Union Coll (OH)
Mount Vernon Nazarene Coll (OH)
Muhlenberg Coll (PA)
Multnomah Bible Coll and Biblical Seminary (OR)
Murray State U (KY)
Muskingum Coll (OH)
Naropa U (CO)
Nazareth Coll of Rochester (NY)
Nebraska Wesleyan U (NE)
Newberry Coll (SC)
New Coll of the U of South Florida (FL)
New Jersey City U (NJ)
New Mexico Highlands U (NM)
New Mexico State U (NM)
New World School of the Arts (FL)
Nicholls State U (LA)
Norfolk State U (VA)
North American Baptist Coll & Edmonton Baptist Sem (AB, Canada)
North Carolina Central U (NC)
North Carolina School of the Arts (NC)
North Central Coll (IL)
North Central U (MN)
North Dakota State U (ND)
Northeastern Illinois U (IL)
Northeastern State U (OK)
Northeastern U (MA)
Northern Arizona U (AZ)
Northern Illinois U (IL)
Northern Kentucky U (KY)
Northern Michigan U (MI)
Northern State U (SD)
North Georgia Coll & State U (GA)
North Greenville Coll (SC)
Northland Coll (WI)
North Park U (IL)
Northwest Coll (WA)
Northwestern Coll (IA)
Northwestern Coll (MN)
Northwestern Oklahoma State U (OK)
Northwestern State U of Louisiana (LA)
Northwestern U (IL)
Northwest Missouri State U (MO)
Northwest Nazarene U (ID)

Nyack Coll (NY)
Oak Hills Christian Coll (MN)
Oakland City U (IN)
Oakland U (MI)
Oakwood Coll (AL)
Oberlin Coll (OH)
Occidental Coll (CA)
Ohio Northern U (OH)
The Ohio State U (OH)
Ohio U (OH)
Ohio Wesleyan U (OH)
Oklahoma Baptist U (OK)
Oklahoma Christian U of Science and Arts (OK)
Oklahoma City U (OK)
Oklahoma State U (OK)
Olivet Nazarene U (IL)
Open Learning Agency (BC, Canada)
Oregon State U (OR)
Ottawa U (KS)
Otterbein Coll (OH)
Ouachita Baptist U (AR)
Our Lady of the Lake U of San Antonio (TX)
Pacific Lutheran U (WA)
Pacific Union Coll (CA)
Pacific U (OR)
Palm Beach Atlantic Coll (FL)
Peabody Conserv of Music of Johns Hopkins U (MD)
Penn State U Univ Park Campus (PA)
Pepperdine U, Malibu (CA)
Peru State Coll (NE)
Pfeiffer U (NC)
Philadelphia Coll of Bible (PA)
Philander Smith Coll (AR)
Piedmont Baptist Coll (NC)
Piedmont Coll (GA)
Pittsburg State U (KS)
Plymouth State Coll (NH)
Point Loma Nazarene U (CA)
Pomona Coll (CA)
Portland State U (OR)
Prairie Bible Coll (AB, Canada)
Prairie View A&M U (TX)
Presbyterian Coll (SC)
Princeton U (NJ)
Principia Coll (IL)
Providence Coll (RI)
Providence Coll and Theological Seminary (MB, Canada)
Purchase Coll, State U of NY (NY)
Queens Coll (NC)
Queens Coll of the City U of NY (NY)
Queen's U at Kingston (ON, Canada)
Quincy U (IL)
Radford U (VA)
Randolph-Macon Coll (VA)
Randolph-Macon Woman's Coll (VA)
Redeemer Coll (ON, Canada)
Reed Coll (OR)
Regents Coll (NY)
Rhodes Coll (TN)
Rice U (TX)
Rider U (NJ)
Ripon Coll (WI)
Roanoke Coll (VA)
Roberts Wesleyan Coll (NY)
Rochester Coll (MI)
Rocky Mountain Coll (MT)
Rocky Mountain Coll (AB, Canada)
Rollins Coll (FL)
Rowan U (NJ)
Rust Coll (MS)
Rutgers, State U of NJ, Camden Coll of Arts & Scis (NJ)
Rutgers, State U of NJ, Douglass Coll (NJ)
Rutgers, State U of NJ, Livingston Coll (NJ)
Rutgers, State U of NJ, Mason Gross School of Arts (NJ)
Rutgers, State U of NJ, Newark Coll of Arts & Scis (NJ)
Rutgers, State U of NJ, Rutgers Coll (NJ)
Rutgers, State U of NJ, U Coll–Camden (NJ)
Rutgers, State U of NJ, U Coll–New Brunswick (NJ)
Saginaw Valley State U (MI)
St. Ambrose U (IA)

St. Cloud State U (MN)
St. Francis Xavier U (NS, Canada)
Saint John's U (MN)
Saint Joseph's Coll (IN)
St. Lawrence U (NY)
Saint Louis U (MO)
Saint Mary-of-the-Woods Coll (IN)
Saint Mary's Coll (IN)
Saint Mary's Coll of California (CA)
St. Mary's Coll of Maryland (MD)
St. Mary's U of San Antonio (TX)
Saint Michael's Coll (VT)
St. Norbert Coll (WI)
St. Olaf Coll (MN)
Saint Vincent Coll (PA)
Saint Xavier U (IL)
Salem Coll (NC)
Salisbury State U (MD)
Salve Regina U (RI)
Sam Houston State U (TX)
San Diego State U (CA)
San Francisco Conservatory of Music (CA)
San Francisco State U (CA)
San Jose Christian Coll (CA)
San Jose State U (CA)
Santa Clara U (CA)
Sarah Lawrence Coll (NY)
Savannah State U (GA)
Scripps Coll (CA)
Seattle Pacific U (WA)
Seton Hall U (NJ)
Seton Hill Coll (PA)
Shaw U (NC)
Shenandoah U (VA)
Shepherd Coll (WV)
Shorter Coll (GA)
Siena Heights U (MI)
Sierra Nevada Coll (NV)
Silver Lake Coll (WI)
Simmons Coll (MA)
Simon Fraser U (BC, Canada)
Simon's Rock Coll of Bard (MA)
Simpson Coll (IA)
Simpson Coll and Graduate School (CA)
Skidmore Coll (NY)
Slippery Rock U of Pennsylvania (PA)
Smith Coll (MA)
Sonoma State U (CA)
South Dakota State U (SD)
Southeastern Coll of the Assemblies of God (FL)
Southeastern Oklahoma State U (OK)
Southeast Missouri State U (MO)
Southern Adventist U (TN)
Southern Illinois U Carbondale (IL)
Southern Illinois U Edwardsville (IL)
Southern Methodist U (TX)
Southern Oregon U (OR)
Southern Utah U (UT)
Southern Wesleyan U (SC)
Southwest Baptist U (MO)
Southwestern Adventist U (TX)
Southwestern Assemblies of God U (TX)
Southwestern Coll (KS)
Southwestern Oklahoma State U (OK)
Southwestern U (TX)
Southwest Missouri State U (MO)
Southwest State U (MN)
Southwest Texas State U (TX)
Spelman Coll (GA)
Spring Arbor Coll (MI)
Stanford U (CA)
State U of NY at Albany (NY)
State U of NY at Binghamton (NY)
State U of NY at Buffalo (NY)
State U of NY at New Paltz (NY)
State U of NY at Oswego (NY)
State U of NY at Stony Brook (NY)
State U of NY Coll at Buffalo (NY)
State U of NY Coll at Fredonia (NY)
State U of NY Coll at Geneseo (NY)
State U of NY Coll at Oneonta (NY)
State U of NY Coll at Potsdam (NY)
State U of West Georgia (GA)
Steinbach Bible Coll (MB, Canada)
Stephen F. Austin State U (TX)
Sterling Coll (KS)

Majors Index
Music–Music Education

Stetson U (FL)
Stillman Coll (AL)
Sul Ross State U (TX)
Susquehanna U (PA)
Swarthmore Coll (PA)
Sweet Briar Coll (VA)
Syracuse U (NY)
Tabor Coll (KS)
Talladega Coll (AL)
Taylor U (IN)
Taylor U, Fort Wayne Campus (IN)
Temple U (PA)
Tennessee State U (TN)
Tennessee Technological U (TN)
Tennessee Wesleyan Coll (TN)
Texas A&M U–Commerce (TX)
Texas A&M U–Kingsville (TX)
Texas Christian U (TX)
Texas Lutheran U (TX)
Texas Southern U (TX)
Texas Tech U (TX)
Texas Wesleyan U (TX)
Texas Woman's U (TX)
Thomas Edison State Coll (NJ)
Thomas U (GA)
Toccoa Falls Coll (GA)
Tougaloo Coll (MS)
Towson U (MD)
Trevecca Nazarene U (TN)
Trinity Bible Coll (ND)
Trinity Christian Coll (IL)
Trinity Coll (CT)
Trinity Coll of Florida (FL)
Trinity U (TX)
Trinity Western U (BC, Canada)
Truman State U (MO)
Tufts U (MA)
Tulane U (LA)
Tyndale Coll & Seminary (ON, Canada)
Union Coll (KY)
Union Coll (NE)
Union U (TN)
Universidad Adventista de las Antillas (PR)
Université de Montréal (PQ, Canada)
Université de Sherbrooke (PQ, Canada)
Université Laval (PQ, Canada)
The U of Akron (OH)
The U of Alabama (AL)
The U of Alabama at Birmingham (AL)
The U of Alabama in Huntsville (AL)
U of Alaska Fairbanks (AK)
U of Alberta (AB, Canada)
The U of Arizona (AZ)
U of Arkansas (AR)
U of Arkansas at Little Rock (AR)
U of Arkansas at Monticello (AR)
U of Arkansas at Pine Bluff (AR)
U of Bridgeport (CT)
U of British Columbia (BC, Canada)
U of Calgary (AB, Canada)
U of Calif, Berkeley (CA)
U of Calif, Davis (CA)
U of Calif, Irvine (CA)
U of Calif, Los Angeles (CA)
U of Calif, Riverside (CA)
U of Calif, San Diego (CA)
U of Calif, Santa Barbara (CA)
U of Calif, Santa Cruz (CA)
U of Central Oklahoma (OK)
U of Charleston (WV)
U of Chicago (IL)
U of Cincinnati (OH)
U of Colorado at Boulder (CO)
U of Colorado at Denver (CO)
U of Connecticut (CT)
U of Dayton (OH)
U of Delaware (DE)
U of Denver (CO)
U of Evansville (IN)
U of Florida (FL)
U of Georgia (GA)
U of Guelph (ON, Canada)
U of Hartford (CT)
U of Hawaii at Manoa (HI)
U of Houston (TX)
U of Idaho (ID)
U of Illinois at Chicago (IL)
U of Illinois at Urbana–Champaign (IL)
U of Indianapolis (IN)

The U of Iowa (IA)
U of Kansas (KS)
U of La Verne (CA)
The U of Lethbridge (AB, Canada)
U of Louisiana at Monroe (LA)
U of Louisville (KY)
U of Maine (ME)
U of Maine at Farmington (ME)
U of Manitoba (MB, Canada)
U of Maryland, Baltimore County (MD)
U of Maryland, Coll Park (MD)
U of Massachusetts Amherst (MA)
U of Massachusetts Boston (MA)
U of Massachusetts Dartmouth (MA)
The U of Memphis (TN)
U of Miami (FL)
U of Michigan (MI)
U of Michigan–Dearborn (MI)
U of Michigan–Flint (MI)
U of Minnesota, Duluth (MN)
U of Minnesota, Morris (MN)
U of Minnesota, Twin Cities Campus (MN)
U of Mississippi (MS)
U of Missouri–Columbia (MO)
U of Missouri–Kansas City (MO)
U of Missouri–St. Louis (MO)
U of Mobile (AL)
The U of Montana–Missoula (MT)
U of Montevallo (AL)
U of Nebraska at Kearney (NE)
U of Nebraska at Omaha (NE)
U of Nebraska–Lincoln (NE)
U of Nevada, Las Vegas (NV)
U of Nevada, Reno (NV)
U of New Hampshire (NH)
U of New Haven (CT)
U of New Orleans (LA)
U of North Alabama (AL)
The U of North Carolina at Asheville (NC)
The U of North Carolina at Chapel Hill (NC)
The U of North Carolina at Pembroke (NC)
The U of North Carolina at Wilmington (NC)
U of North Dakota (ND)
U of Northern Colorado (CO)
U of Northern Iowa (IA)
U of North Florida (FL)
U of North Texas (TX)
U of Notre Dame (IN)
U of Oklahoma (OK)
U of Oregon (OR)
U of Pennsylvania (PA)
U of Pittsburgh (PA)
U of Portland (OR)
U of Prince Edward Island (PE, Canada)
U of Puerto Rico, Río Piedras (PR)
U of Puget Sound (WA)
U of Redlands (CA)
U of Regina (SK, Canada)
U of Rhode Island (RI)
U of Richmond (VA)
U of Rio Grande (OH)
U of Rochester (NY)
U of St. Thomas (MN)
U of St. Thomas (TX)
U of San Diego (CA)
U of Science and Arts of Oklahoma (OK)
U of Sioux Falls (SD)
U of South Alabama (AL)
U of South Carolina (SC)
U of South Dakota (SD)
U of Southern California (CA)
U of Southern Colorado (CO)
U of Southern Maine (ME)
U of Southern Mississippi (MS)
The U of Tampa (FL)
The U of Tennessee at Chattanooga (TN)
The U of Tennessee at Martin (TN)
The U of Tennessee Knoxville (TN)
The U of Texas at Arlington (TX)
The U of Texas at Austin (TX)
The U of Texas at San Antonio (TX)
The U of Texas at Tyler (TX)
The U of Texas–Pan American (TX)
The U of the Arts (PA)
U of the District of Columbia (DC)
U of the Ozarks (AR)

U of the Pacific (CA)
U of the South (TN)
U of Toronto (ON, Canada)
U of Tulsa (OK)
U of Utah (UT)
U of Vermont (VT)
U of Victoria (BC, Canada)
U of Virginia (VA)
U of Washington (WA)
U of Waterloo (ON, Canada)
The U of Western Ontario (ON, Canada)
U of Windsor (ON, Canada)
The U of Winnipeg (MB, Canada)
U of Wisconsin–Eau Claire (WI)
U of Wisconsin–Green Bay (WI)
U of Wisconsin–La Crosse (WI)
U of Wisconsin–Madison (WI)
U of Wisconsin–Milwaukee (WI)
U of Wisconsin–Parkside (WI)
U of Wisconsin–Platteville (WI)
U of Wisconsin–River Falls (WI)
U of Wisconsin–Stevens Point (WI)
U of Wisconsin–Superior (WI)
U of Wisconsin–Whitewater (WI)
U of Wyoming (WY)
Upper Iowa U (IA)
Ursinus Coll (PA)
Utah State U (UT)
Valdosta State U (GA)
Valley City State U (ND)
Valparaiso U (IN)
Vanderbilt U (TN)
Vanguard U of Southern California (CA)
Vassar Coll (NY)
Virginia Commonwealth U (VA)
Virginia Polytechnic Inst and State U (VA)
Virginia Union U (VA)
Virginia Wesleyan Coll (VA)
Wabash Coll (IN)
Wagner Coll (NY)
Wake Forest U (NC)
Walla Walla Coll (WA)
Warner Pacific Coll (OR)
Wartburg Coll (IA)
Washington and Lee U (VA)
Washington Bible Coll (MD)
Washington Coll (MD)
Washington State U (WA)
Washington U in St. Louis (MO)
Wayland Baptist U (TX)
Wayne State Coll (NE)
Wayne State U (MI)
Weber State U (UT)
Webster U (MO)
Wellesley Coll (MA)
Wells Coll (NY)
Wesleyan Coll (GA)
Wesleyan U (CT)
West Chester U of Pennsylvania (PA)
Western Baptist Coll (OR)
Western Carolina U (NC)
Western Connecticut State U (CT)
Western Illinois U (IL)
Western Kentucky U (KY)
Western Maryland Coll (MD)
Western Michigan U (MI)
Western Montana Coll of The U of Montana (MT)
Western Oregon U (OR)
Western State Coll of Colorado (CO)
Western Washington U (WA)
Westfield State Coll (MA)
Westminster Choir Coll of Rider U (NJ)
Westminster Coll (PA)
Westmont Coll (CA)
West Texas A&M U (TX)
West Virginia U (WV)
West Virginia Wesleyan Coll (WV)
Wheaton Coll (IL)
Wheaton Coll (MA)
Whitman Coll (WA)
Whittier Coll (CA)
Whitworth Coll (WA)
Wichita State U (KS)
Wilfrid Laurier U (ON, Canada)
Wilkes U (PA)
Willamette U (OR)
William Jewell Coll (MO)
William Paterson U of New Jersey (NJ)
Williams Baptist Coll (AR)

Williams Coll (MA)
William Tyndale Coll (MI)
Wingate U (NC)
Winona State U (MN)
Winthrop U (SC)
Wisconsin Lutheran Coll (WI)
Wittenberg U (OH)
Worcester Polytechnic Inst (MA)
Wright State U (OH)
Xavier U (OH)
Xavier U of Louisiana (LA)
Yale U (CT)
Yeshiva U (NY)
York Coll (NE)
York Coll of Pennsylvania (PA)
York Coll of the City U of New York (NY)
York U (ON, Canada)
Youngstown State U (OH)

MUSICAL INSTRUMENT TECHNOLOGY
Ball State U (IN)
Barton Coll (NC)
Bellarmine Coll (KY)
Connecticut Coll (CT)
LaGrange Coll (GA)
Malone Coll (OH)
New York U (NY)
Plymouth State Coll (NH)
Susquehanna U (PA)
The U of Texas at San Antonio (TX)
U of Washington (WA)

MUSIC BUSINESS MANAGEMENT AND MERCHANDISING
Anderson U (IN)
Appalachian State U (NC)
Baldwin-Wallace Coll (OH)
Bellarmine Coll (KY)
Belmont U (TN)
Benedictine Coll (KS)
Berklee Coll of Music (MA)
Berry Coll (GA)
Boise State U (ID)
Bryan Coll (TN)
Butler U (IN)
Capital U (OH)
Clarion U of Pennsylvania (PA)
Coker Coll (SC)
Coll of the Ozarks (MO)
Columbia Coll Chicago (IL)
Columbia Union Coll (MD)
DePaul U (IL)
DePauw U (IN)
Drake U (IA)
Elizabeth City State U (NC)
Elmhurst Coll (IL)
Erskine Coll (SC)
Ferris State U (MI)
Five Towns Coll (NY)
Florida Southern Coll (FL)
Friends U (KS)
Geneva Coll (PA)
Grace Bible Coll (MI)
Grand Canyon U (AZ)
Grove City Coll (PA)
Hardin-Simmons U (TX)
Heidelberg Coll (OH)
Illinois Wesleyan U (IL)
Indiana State U (IN)
Jacksonville U (FL)
Johnson State Coll (VT)
Lewis U (IL)
Luther Coll (IA)
Madonna U (MI)
Manhattanville Coll (NY)
Mansfield U of Pennsylvania (PA)
Marian Coll of Fond du Lac (WI)
Methodist Coll (NC)
Middle Tennessee State U (TN)
Millersville U of Pennsylvania (PA)
Millikin U (IL)
Minnesota State U, Mankato (MN)
Minnesota State U Moorhead (MN)
Mississippi U for Women (MS)
Monmouth U (NJ)
Montreat Coll (NC)
New York U (NY)
Northeastern U (MA)
North Park U (IL)
Northwest Missouri State U (MO)
Ohio Northern U (OH)
Oklahoma City U (OK)

Oklahoma State U (OK)
Otterbein Coll (OH)
Peru State Coll (NE)
Point Loma Nazarene U (CA)
Quincy U (IL)
Saint Augustine's Coll (NC)
Saint Mary's U of Minnesota (MN)
Saint Xavier U (IL)
South Dakota State U (SD)
Southern Oregon U (OR)
Southwestern Oklahoma State U (OK)
State U of NY Coll at Fredonia (NY)
State U of NY Coll at Oneonta (NY)
State U of NY Coll at Potsdam (NY)
Susquehanna U (PA)
Syracuse U (NY)
Tabor Coll (KS)
Taylor U (IN)
Trevecca Nazarene U (TN)
Union Coll (KY)
Union U (TN)
U of Charleston (WV)
U of Evansville (IN)
U of Hartford (CT)
U of Idaho (ID)
The U of Memphis (TN)
U of Miami (FL)
U of New Haven (CT)
U of Puget Sound (WA)
U of Sioux Falls (SD)
U of Southern California (CA)
The U of Texas at Arlington (TX)
U of the Pacific (CA)
Valparaiso U (IN)
Warner Pacific Coll (OR)
Westfield State Coll (MA)
Wheaton Coll (IL)
William Paterson U of New Jersey (NJ)
Wingate U (NC)
Winona State U (MN)

MUSIC CONDUCTING
Bowling Green State U (OH)
Brevard Coll (NC)
Calvin Coll (MI)
Luther Coll (IA)
Mannes Coll of Music, New School U (NY)

MUSIC EDUCATION
Abilene Christian U (TX)
Acadia U (NS, Canada)
Adams State Coll (CO)
Adelphi U (NY)
Adrian Coll (MI)
Alabama A&M U (AL)
Alabama State U (AL)
Alderson-Broaddus Coll (WV)
Allen U (SC)
Alma Coll (MI)
Alverno Coll (WI)
Anderson Coll (SC)
Anderson U (IN)
Andrews U (MI)
Anna Maria Coll (MA)
Appalachian State U (NC)
Aquinas Coll (MI)
Arizona State U (AZ)
Arkansas State U (AR)
Arkansas Tech U (AR)
Arlington Baptist Coll (TX)
Armstrong Atlantic State U (GA)
Asbury Coll (KY)
Ashland U (OH)
Atlantic Union Coll (MA)
Auburn U (AL)
Augsburg Coll (MN)
Augustana Coll (IL)
Augustana Coll (SD)
Augusta State U (GA)
Baker U (KS)
Baldwin-Wallace Coll (OH)
Ball State U (IN)
Baylor U (TX)
Belmont U (TN)
Beloit Coll (WI)
Bemidji State U (MN)
Benedictine Coll (KS)
Benedictine U (IL)
Bennett Coll (NC)
Berea Coll (KY)
Berklee Coll of Music (MA)

Majors Index
Music Education

Berry Coll (GA)
Bethany Coll (KS)
Bethany Coll of the Assemblies of God (CA)
Bethel Coll (IN)
Bethel Coll (MN)
Bethune-Cookman Coll (FL)
Birmingham-Southern Coll (AL)
Blue Mountain Coll (MS)
Bluffton Coll (OH)
Boise State U (ID)
Boston U (MA)
Bowie State U (MD)
Bowling Green State U (OH)
Bradley U (IL)
Brandon U (MB, Canada)
Brenau U (GA)
Brevard Coll (NC)
Bridgewater Coll (VA)
Brigham Young U (UT)
Brock U (ON, Canada)
Brooklyn Coll of the City U of NY (NY)
Bryan Coll (TN)
Bucknell U (PA)
Buena Vista U (IA)
Butler U (IN)
California Lutheran U (CA)
California State U, Chico (CA)
California State U, Dominguez Hills (CA)
California State U, Fresno (CA)
California State U, Fullerton (CA)
California State U, Northridge (CA)
Calvary Bible Coll and Theological Seminary (MO)
Calvin Coll (MI)
Cameron U (OK)
Campbellsville U (KY)
Campbell U (NC)
Capital U (OH)
Carroll Coll (WI)
Carson-Newman Coll (TN)
Carthage Coll (WI)
Case Western Reserve U (OH)
Castleton State Coll (VT)
Catawba Coll (NC)
The Catholic U of America (DC)
Cedarville Coll (OH)
Centenary Coll of Louisiana (LA)
Central Coll (IA)
Central Connecticut State U (CT)
Central Methodist Coll (MO)
Central Michigan U (MI)
Central Missouri State U (MO)
Chapman U (CA)
Charleston Southern U (SC)
Chestnut Hill Coll (PA)
Chicago State U (IL)
Chowan Coll (NC)
Christopher Newport U (VA)
City Coll of the City U of NY (NY)
Claflin U (SC)
Clarion U of Pennsylvania (PA)
Clark Atlanta U (GA)
Clarke Coll (IA)
Cleveland Inst of Music (OH)
Coastal Carolina U (SC)
Coe Coll (IA)
Coker Coll (SC)
The Coll of New Jersey (NJ)
Coll of Saint Benedict (MN)
Coll of St. Catherine (MN)
The Coll of Saint Rose (NY)
Coll of the Ozarks (MO)
The Coll of Wooster (OH)
Colorado Christian U (CO)
Colorado State U (CO)
Columbia Coll (SC)
Columbus State U (GA)
Concord Coll (WV)
Concordia Coll (MN)
Concordia Coll (NY)
Concordia U (IL)
Concordia U (NE)
Concordia U at St. Paul (MN)
Concordia U Wisconsin (WI)
Converse Coll (SC)
Cornell Coll (IA)
Cornerstone U (MI)
Crown Coll (MN)
Culver-Stockton Coll (MO)
Cumberland Coll (KY)
Dakota State U (SD)
Dallas Baptist U (TX)
Dana Coll (NE)
David Lipscomb U (TN)

Delaware State U (DE)
Delta State U (MS)
DePaul U (IL)
DePauw U (IN)
Dickinson State U (ND)
Dordt Coll (IA)
Dowling Coll (NY)
Drake U (IA)
Drury U (MO)
Duquesne U (PA)
East Carolina U (NC)
East Central U (OK)
Eastern Illinois U (IL)
Eastern Kentucky U (KY)
Eastern Mennonite U (VA)
Eastern Michigan U (MI)
Eastern Nazarene Coll (MA)
Eastern New Mexico U (NM)
Eastern Washington U (WA)
East Texas Baptist U (TX)
Elizabeth City State U (NC)
Elizabethtown Coll (PA)
Elmhurst Coll (IL)
Elon Coll (NC)
Emporia State U (KS)
Erskine Coll (SC)
Evangel U (MO)
Fairmont State Coll (WV)
Fisk U (TN)
Five Towns Coll (NY)
Florida A&M U (FL)
Florida Atlantic U (FL)
Florida International U (FL)
Florida Southern Coll (FL)
Florida State U (FL)
Fort Hays State U (KS)
Fort Lewis Coll (CO)
Freed-Hardeman U (TN)
Free Will Baptist Bible Coll (TN)
Fresno Pacific U (CA)
Friends U (KS)
Furman U (SC)
Gardner-Webb U (NC)
Geneva Coll (PA)
George Fox U (OR)
Georgetown Coll (KY)
Georgia Coll and State U (GA)
Georgian Court Coll (NJ)
Georgia Southern U (GA)
Georgia Southwestern State U (GA)
Gettysburg Coll (PA)
Glenville State Coll (WV)
God's Bible School and Coll (OH)
Gonzaga U (WA)
Gordon Coll (MA)
Goshen Coll (IN)
Grace Bible Coll (MI)
Grace Coll (IN)
Graceland Coll (IA)
Grand Canyon U (AZ)
Grand Valley State U (MI)
Greensboro Coll (NC)
Greenville Coll (IL)
Grove City Coll (PA)
Gustavus Adolphus Coll (MN)
Hamline U (MN)
Hampton U (VA)
Hannibal-LaGrange Coll (MO)
Harding U (AR)
Hardin-Simmons U (TX)
Hartwick Coll (NY)
Hastings Coll (NE)
Heidelberg Coll (OH)
Hobe Sound Bible Coll (FL)
Hofstra U (NY)
Hope Coll (MI)
Hope International U (CA)
Houghton Coll (NY)
Houston Baptist U (TX)
Howard Payne U (TX)
Humboldt State U (CA)
Huntingdon Coll (AL)
Huntington Coll (IN)
Idaho State U (ID)
Illinois State U (IL)
Illinois Wesleyan U (IL)
Immaculata Coll (PA)
Indiana State U (IN)
Indiana U Bloomington (IN)
Indiana U of Pennsylvania (PA)
Indiana U–Purdue U Fort Wayne (IN)
Indiana U South Bend (IN)
Indiana Wesleyan U (IN)
Inter American U of PR, Metropolitan Campus (PR)

Inter American U of PR, San Germán Campus (PR)
Iowa State U of Science and Technology (IA)
Iowa Wesleyan Coll (IA)
Ithaca Coll (NY)
Jacksonville State U (AL)
Jacksonville U (FL)
Jarvis Christian Coll (TX)
John Brown U (AR)
Johnson State Coll (VT)
Judson Coll (AL)
Judson Coll (IL)
Kansas State U (KS)
Kean U (NJ)
Keene State Coll (NH)
Kent State U (OH)
Kentucky Christian Coll (KY)
Kentucky State U (KY)
Kentucky Wesleyan Coll (KY)
Lakeland Coll (WI)
Lamar U (TX)
Lambuth U (TN)
Lander U (SC)
Langston U (OK)
La Sierra U (CA)
Lawrence U (WI)
Lebanon Valley Coll (PA)
Lee U (TN)
Lenoir-Rhyne Coll (NC)
Liberty U (VA)
Limestone Coll (SC)
Lincoln U (MO)
Lindenwood U (MO)
Long Island U, C.W. Post Campus (NY)
Long Island U, Southampton Coll, Friends World Program (NY)
Longwood Coll (VA)
Loras Coll (IA)
Louisiana Coll (LA)
Louisiana State U and A&M Coll (LA)
Louisiana Tech U (LA)
Loyola U New Orleans (LA)
Lubbock Christian U (TX)
Luther Coll (IA)
Lycoming Coll (PA)
MacMurray Coll (IL)
Madonna U (MI)
Malone Coll (OH)
Manchester Coll (IN)
Manhattanville Coll (NY)
Mansfield U of Pennsylvania (PA)
Maranatha Baptist Bible Coll (WI)
Marian Coll (IN)
Marian Coll of Fond du Lac (WI)
Marshall U (WV)
Mars Hill Coll (NC)
Maryville Coll (TN)
Mary Washington Coll (VA)
Marywood U (PA)
McGill U (PQ, Canada)
McMurry U (TX)
McNeese State U (LA)
McPherson Coll (KS)
Memorial U of Newfoundland (NF, Canada)
Mercer U (GA)
Mercy Coll (NY)
Mercyhurst Coll (PA)
Meredith Coll (NC)
Mesa State Coll (CO)
Messiah Coll (PA)
Methodist Coll (NC)
Metropolitan State Coll of Denver (CO)
Miami U (OH)
Michigan State U (MI)
Mid-America Bible Coll (OK)
MidAmerica Nazarene U (KS)
Midland Lutheran Coll (NE)
Midwestern State U (TX)
Millersville U of Pennsylvania (PA)
Milligan Coll (TN)
Millikin U (IL)
Minnesota State U, Mankato (MN)
Minnesota State U Moorhead (MN)
Minot State U (ND)
Mississippi Coll (MS)
Mississippi State U (MS)
Mississippi U for Women (MS)
Mississippi Valley State U (MS)
Missouri Baptist Coll (MO)
Missouri Southern State Coll (MO)
Missouri Western State Coll (MO)
Montana State U–Billings (MT)

Montana State U–Bozeman (MT)
Moravian Coll (PA)
Morehead State U (KY)
Morningside Coll (IA)
Mount Marty Coll (SD)
Mount Mary Coll (WI)
Mount Mercy Coll (IA)
Mount St. Clare Coll (IA)
Mount St. Mary's Coll (CA)
Mount Senario Coll (WI)
Mount Union Coll (OH)
Mount Vernon Nazarene Coll (OH)
Murray State U (KY)
Muskingum Coll (OH)
Nazareth Coll of Rochester (NY)
Nebraska Wesleyan U (NE)
Newberry Coll (SC)
New Jersey City U (NJ)
New Mexico Highlands U (NM)
New Mexico State U (NM)
New York U (NY)
Nicholls State U (LA)
Norfolk State U (VA)
North Carolina Ag and Tech State U (NC)
North Carolina Central U (NC)
North Dakota State U (ND)
Northeastern State U (OK)
Northern Arizona U (AZ)
Northern Illinois U (IL)
Northern Michigan U (MI)
Northern State U (SD)
North Georgia Coll & State U (GA)
North Greenville Coll (SC)
Northland Coll (WI)
North Park U (IL)
Northwest Coll (WA)
Northwestern Coll (IA)
Northwestern Coll (MN)
Northwestern Oklahoma State U (OK)
Northwestern State U of Louisiana (LA)
Northwestern U (IL)
Northwest Missouri State U (MO)
Northwest Nazarene U (ID)
Nyack Coll (NY)
Oakland City U (IN)
Oakland U (MI)
Oakwood Coll (AL)
Oberlin Coll (OH)
Ohio Northern U (OH)
The Ohio State U (OH)
Ohio U (OH)
Ohio Wesleyan U (OH)
Oklahoma Baptist U (OK)
Oklahoma Christian U of Science and Arts (OK)
Oklahoma City U (OK)
Oklahoma State U (OK)
Olivet Nazarene U (IL)
Ottawa U (KS)
Otterbein Coll (OH)
Ouachita Baptist U (AR)
Pacific Lutheran U (WA)
Pacific Union Coll (CA)
Pacific U (OR)
Paine Coll (GA)
Palm Beach Atlantic Coll (FL)
Peabody Conserv of Music of Johns Hopkins U (MD)
Penn State U Univ Park Campus (PA)
Pepperdine U, Malibu (CA)
Peru State Coll (NE)
Pfeiffer U (NC)
Piedmont Baptist Coll (NC)
Piedmont Coll (GA)
Pittsburg State U (KS)
Plymouth State Coll (NH)
Pontifical Catholic U of Puerto Rico (PR)
Presbyterian Coll (SC)
Queens Coll of the City U of NY (NY)
Queen's U at Kingston (ON, Canada)
Quincy U (IL)
Reformed Bible Coll (MI)
Reinhardt Coll (GA)
Rider U (NJ)
Ripon Coll (WI)
Roberts Wesleyan Coll (NY)
Rochester Coll (MI)
Rocky Mountain Coll (MT)
Rowan U (NJ)
Rust Coll (MS)

Rutgers, State U of NJ, Mason Gross School of Arts (NJ)
St. Ambrose U (IA)
Saint Augustine's Coll (NC)
St. Cloud State U (MN)
Saint John's U (MN)
Saint Joseph Coll (CT)
Saint Joseph's Coll (IN)
Saint Mary-of-the-Woods Coll (IN)
Saint Mary's Coll (IN)
Saint Mary's U of Minnesota (MN)
Saint Michael's Coll (VT)
St. Norbert Coll (WI)
St. Olaf Coll (MN)
Saint Vincent Coll (PA)
Saint Xavier U (IL)
Samford U (AL)
Sam Houston State U (TX)
San Jose State U (CA)
Seattle Pacific U (WA)
Seton Hill Coll (PA)
Shenandoah U (VA)
Shorter Coll (GA)
Siena Heights U (MI)
Silver Lake Coll (WI)
Simpson Coll (IA)
Simpson Coll and Graduate School (CA)
Slippery Rock U of Pennsylvania (PA)
Sonoma State U (CA)
South Dakota State U (SD)
Southeastern Coll of the Assemblies of God (FL)
Southeastern Louisiana U (LA)
Southeastern Oklahoma State U (OK)
Southeast Missouri State U (MO)
Southern Adventist U (TN)
Southern Arkansas U–Magnolia (AR)
Southern Methodist U (TX)
Southern Utah U (UT)
Southern Wesleyan U (SC)
Southwest Baptist U (MO)
Southwestern Coll (KS)
Southwestern Oklahoma State U (OK)
Southwestern U (TX)
Southwest Missouri State U (MO)
Southwest State U (MN)
Southwest Texas State U (TX)
State U of NY at Buffalo (NY)
State U of NY Coll at Fredonia (NY)
State U of NY Coll at Potsdam (NY)
State U of West Georgia (GA)
Stephen F. Austin State U (TX)
Sterling Coll (KS)
Stetson U (FL)
Susquehanna U (PA)
Syracuse U (NY)
Tabor Coll (KS)
Talladega Coll (AL)
Taylor U (IN)
Temple U (PA)
Tennessee Technological U (TN)
Tennessee Wesleyan Coll (TN)
Texas A&M U–Commerce (TX)
Texas A&M U–Kingsville (TX)
Texas Christian U (TX)
Texas Southern U (TX)
Texas Wesleyan U (TX)
Thomas U (GA)
Toccoa Falls Coll (GA)
Towson U (MD)
Transylvania U (KY)
Trevecca Nazarene U (TN)
Trinity Christian Coll (IL)
Troy State U (AL)
Union Coll (KY)
Union Coll (NE)
Union U (TN)
Universidad Adventista de las Antillas (PR)
Université Laval (PQ, Canada)
The U of Akron (OH)
The U of Alabama (AL)
The U of Alabama at Birmingham (AL)
U of Alaska Fairbanks (AK)
U of Alberta (AB, Canada)
The U of Arizona (AZ)
U of Arkansas (AR)
U of Arkansas at Monticello (AR)
U of Arkansas at Pine Bluff (AR)

Majors Index
Music Education–Musicology

U of British Columbia (BC, Canada)
U of Central Arkansas (AR)
U of Central Florida (FL)
U of Central Oklahoma (OK)
U of Charleston (WV)
U of Cincinnati (OH)
U of Colorado at Boulder (CO)
U of Connecticut (CT)
U of Dayton (OH)
U of Delaware (DE)
U of Evansville (IN)
U of Florida (FL)
U of Georgia (GA)
U of Hartford (CT)
U of Idaho (ID)
U of Illinois at Urbana–Champaign (IL)
U of Indianapolis (IN)
The U of Iowa (IA)
U of Kansas (KS)
U of Kentucky (KY)
U of La Verne (CA)
The U of Lethbridge (AB, Canada)
U of Louisiana at Lafayette (LA)
U of Louisiana at Monroe (LA)
U of Maine (ME)
U of Mary Hardin-Baylor (TX)
U of Maryland, Coll Park (MD)
U of Miami (FL)
U of Michigan (MI)
U of Michigan–Flint (MI)
U of Minnesota, Duluth (MN)
U of Minnesota, Twin Cities Campus (MN)
U of Missouri–Columbia (MO)
U of Missouri–Kansas City (MO)
U of Missouri–St. Louis (MO)
The U of Montana–Missoula (MT)
U of Montevallo (AL)
U of Nebraska at Omaha (NE)
U of Nebraska–Lincoln (NE)
U of Nevada, Reno (NV)
U of New Brunswick, Fredericton (NB, Canada)
U of New Hampshire (NH)
U of New Mexico (NM)
U of New Orleans (LA)
The U of North Carolina at Chapel Hill (NC)
The U of North Carolina at Charlotte (NC)
The U of North Carolina at Greensboro (NC)
The U of North Carolina at Pembroke (NC)
U of North Dakota (ND)
U of Northern Colorado (CO)
U of Northern Iowa (IA)
U of North Florida (FL)
U of North Texas (TX)
U of Oklahoma (OK)
U of Oregon (OR)
U of Portland (OR)
U of Prince Edward Island (PE, Canada)
U of Puget Sound (WA)
U of Redlands (CA)
U of Regina (SK, Canada)
U of Rhode Island (RI)
U of Rio Grande (OH)
U of Rochester (NY)
U of St. Thomas (MN)
U of St. Thomas (TX)
U of Sioux Falls (SD)
U of South Alabama (AL)
U of South Carolina (SC)
U of South Dakota (SD)
U of Southern California (CA)
U of Southern Colorado (CO)
U of Southern Maine (ME)
U of Southern Mississippi (MS)
U of South Florida (FL)
The U of Tennessee at Chattanooga (TN)
The U of Tennessee at Martin (TN)
The U of Tennessee Knoxville (TN)
The U of Texas at San Antonio (TX)
U of the District of Columbia (DC)
U of the Ozarks (AR)
U of the Pacific (CA)
U of the Virgin Islands (VI)
U of Toronto (ON, Canada)
U of Tulsa (OK)
U of Utah (UT)
U of Vermont (VT)

U of Victoria (BC, Canada)
U of Washington (WA)
The U of Western Ontario (ON, Canada)
U of Windsor (ON, Canada)
U of Wisconsin–La Crosse (WI)
U of Wisconsin–Madison (WI)
U of Wisconsin–Milwaukee (WI)
U of Wisconsin–Parkside (WI)
U of Wisconsin–River Falls (WI)
U of Wisconsin–Stevens Point (WI)
U of Wisconsin–Superior (WI)
U of Wisconsin–Whitewater (WI)
U of Wyoming (WY)
Upper Iowa U (IA)
Utah State U (UT)
Valdosta State U (GA)
Valley City State U (ND)
Valparaiso U (IN)
VanderCook Coll of Music (IL)
Virginia Commonwealth U (VA)
Virginia Wesleyan Coll (VA)
Wagner Coll (NY)
Walla Walla Coll (WA)
Warner Pacific Coll (OR)
Warner Southern Coll (FL)
Wartburg Coll (IA)
Washington Bible Coll (MD)
Wayland Baptist U (TX)
Wayne State Coll (NE)
Weber State U (UT)
Webster U (MO)
West Chester U of Pennsylvania (PA)
Western Baptist Coll (OR)
Western Carolina U (NC)
Western Connecticut State U (CT)
Western Kentucky U (KY)
Western Maryland Coll (MD)
Western Michigan U (MI)
Western Montana Coll of The U of Montana (MT)
Western State Coll of Colorado (CO)
Western Washington U (WA)
Westfield State Coll (MA)
West Liberty State Coll (WV)
Westminster Choir Coll of Rider U (NJ)
Westminster Coll (PA)
West Virginia State Coll (WV)
West Virginia Wesleyan Coll (WV)
Wheaton Coll (IL)
Whitworth Coll (WA)
Wichita State U (KS)
Wilkes U (PA)
Willamette U (OR)
William Jewell Coll (MO)
William Paterson U of New Jersey (NJ)
Williams Baptist Coll (AR)
Wilmington Coll (OH)
Wingate U (NC)
Winona State U (MN)
Winston-Salem State U (NC)
Winthrop U (SC)
Wittenberg U (OH)
Wright State U (OH)
Xavier U (OH)
Xavier U of Louisiana (LA)
York Coll (NE)
York Coll of Pennsylvania (PA)
York U (ON, Canada)
Youngstown State U (OH)

MUSIC (GENERAL PERFORMANCE)
Adams State Coll (CO)
American U (DC)
Anderson U (IN)
Appalachian State U (NC)
Arizona State U (AZ)
Arkansas State U (AR)
Augusta State U (GA)
Bard Coll (NY)
Bartlesville Wesleyan Coll (OK)
Baylor U (TX)
Berklee Coll of Music (MA)
Black Hills State U (SD)
Boston U (MA)
Bowling Green State U (OH)
Bradley U (IL)
Brandon U (MB, Canada)
Brevard Coll (NC)
Brigham Young U (UT)
Brigham Young U–Hawaii Campus (HI)
California State U, Chico (CA)
Calvin Coll (MI)
Cameron U (OK)
Capital U (OH)
Carnegie Mellon U (PA)
The Catholic U of America (DC)
Central Methodist Coll (MO)
Clarion U of Pennsylvania (PA)
Colorado Christian U (CO)
Colorado State U (CO)
Columbia Coll Chicago (IL)
Concordia Coll (MN)
Concordia U (PQ, Canada)
DePauw U (IN)
Duquesne U (PA)
East Carolina U (NC)
Eastern Michigan U (MI)
Eastern Nazarene Coll (MA)
Elon Coll (NC)
Florida State U (FL)
Geneva Coll (PA)
Georgia Southern U (GA)
Georgia State U (GA)
Gordon Coll (MA)
Hamline U (MN)
Henderson State U (AR)
Idaho State U (ID)
Illinois State U (IL)
Indiana U of Pennsylvania (PA)
Indiana U South Bend (IN)
Ithaca Coll (NY)
Jacksonville U (FL)
James Madison U (VA)
Johnson State Coll (VT)
Kent State U (OH)
Louisiana State U and A&M Coll (LA)
Louisiana Tech U (LA)
Loyola U New Orleans (LA)
Luther Coll (IA)
Mansfield U of Pennsylvania (PA)
Marygrove Coll (MI)
McGill U (PQ, Canada)
Mercer U (GA)
Metropolitan State Coll of Denver (CO)
Miami U (OH)
Millikin U (IL)
Mississippi Coll (MS)
Missouri Baptist Coll (MO)
Mount Allison U (NB, Canada)
Mount Union Coll (OH)
New York U (NY)
Northwestern Coll (MN)
Northwest Nazarene U (ID)
The Ohio State U (OH)
Old Dominion U (VA)
Open Learning Agency (BC, Canada)
Peace Coll (NC)
Penn State U Univ Park Campus (PA)
Piedmont Coll (GA)
Saint Augustine's Coll (NC)
Saint Mary's U of Minnesota (MN)
Saint Vincent Coll (PA)
Salem Coll (NC)
Samford U (AL)
San Francisco Conservatory of Music (CA)
San Jose State U (CA)
Seton Hall U (NJ)
Seton Hill Coll (PA)
Shenandoah U (VA)
Simpson Coll (IA)
Slippery Rock U of Pennsylvania (PA)
Southeastern Louisiana U (LA)
Southeastern Oklahoma State U (OK)
Southern Adventist U (TN)
Southern Methodist U (TX)
Southwest Missouri State U (MO)
Southwest Texas State U (TX)
State U of NY at Binghamton (NY)
State U of NY at Buffalo (NY)
Stephen F. Austin State U (TX)
Stetson U (FL)
Syracuse U (NY)
Texas Tech U (TX)
Texas Woman's U (TX)
Transylvania U (KY)
Trinity Christian Coll (IL)
Trinity U (TX)
Union Coll (NE)
The U of Arizona (AZ)
U of Central Arkansas (AR)

U of Central Florida (FL)
U of Denver (CO)
U of Georgia (GA)
U of Hartford (CT)
U of Hawaii at Manoa (HI)
U of Houston (TX)
U of Idaho (ID)
U of Illinois at Urbana–Champaign (IL)
U of Indianapolis (IN)
U of Kentucky (KY)
U of Louisiana at Lafayette (LA)
U of Louisiana at Monroe (LA)
U of Louisville (KY)
U of Mary Hardin-Baylor (TX)
U of Maryland, Coll Park (MD)
U of Massachusetts Amherst (MA)
U of Massachusetts Lowell (MA)
U of Miami (FL)
The U of Montana–Missoula (MT)
U of Nevada, Reno (NV)
U of New Mexico (NM)
U of North Carolina at Chapel Hill (NC)
The U of North Carolina at Charlotte (NC)
U of North Dakota (ND)
U of Northern Iowa (IA)
U of North Florida (FL)
U of North Texas (TX)
U of Puget Sound (WA)
U of Redlands (CA)
U of Rhode Island (RI)
U of St. Thomas (MN)
U of Southern California (CA)
U of Southern Maine (ME)
U of South Florida (FL)
The U of Texas at Arlington (TX)
The U of Texas at Austin (TX)
U of Vermont (VT)
U of Washington (WA)
U of West Florida (FL)
U of Wyoming (WY)
Valparaiso U (IN)
Wartburg Coll (IA)
Washington State U (WA)
Weber State U (UT)
Webster U (MO)
Western Michigan U (MI)
West Texas A&M U (TX)
Wheeling Jesuit U (WV)
William Jewell Coll (MO)
William Tyndale Coll (MI)
York U (ON, Canada)
Youngstown State U (OH)

MUSIC HISTORY
Appalachian State U (NC)
Aquinas Coll (MI)
Baldwin-Wallace Coll (OH)
Bard Coll (NY)
Baylor U (TX)
Belmont U (TN)
Bennington Coll (VT)
Birmingham-Southern Coll (AL)
Boston U (MA)
Bowling Green State U (OH)
Brandeis U (MA)
Brandon U (MB, Canada)
Brevard Coll (NC)
Bucknell U (PA)
Butler U (IN)
California State U, Fresno (CA)
California State U, Fullerton (CA)
California State U, Long Beach (CA)
California State U, Northridge (CA)
Calvin Coll (MI)
The Catholic U of America (DC)
Central Michigan U (MI)
Christopher Newport U (VA)
The Coll of Wooster (OH)
Converse Coll (SC)
Eugene Lang Coll, New School U (NY)
Fairfield U (CT)
Florida State U (FL)
Fordham U (NY)
Goddard Coll (VT)
Hampshire Coll (MA)
Harvard U (MA)
Hastings Coll (NE)
Indiana U Bloomington (IN)
Keene State Coll (NH)
Lafayette Coll (PA)
La Salle U (PA)

Long Island U, Southampton Coll, Friends World Program (NY)
Luther Coll (IA)
Marlboro Coll (VT)
McGill U (PQ, Canada)
Memorial U of Newfoundland (NF, Canada)
Mount Allison U (NB, Canada)
Nazareth Coll of Rochester (NY)
New England Conservatory of Music (MA)
New York U (NY)
Northeastern U (MA)
Northern Arizona U (AZ)
North Greenville Coll (SC)
Northwestern U (IL)
Oberlin Coll (OH)
The Ohio State U (OH)
Ohio U (OH)
Otterbein Coll (OH)
Queens Coll of the City U of NY (NY)
Randolph-Macon Woman's Coll (VA)
Rockford Coll (IL)
Rollins Coll (FL)
St. Cloud State U (MN)
Saint Joseph's Coll (IN)
Sarah Lawrence Coll (NY)
Seton Hall U (NJ)
Simmons Coll (MA)
Southwestern U (TX)
State U of NY at New Paltz (NY)
State U of NY Coll at Fredonia (NY)
State U of NY Coll at Potsdam (NY)
Temple U (PA)
Texas Christian U (TX)
The U of Akron (OH)
U of Alberta (AB, Canada)
U of British Columbia (BC, Canada)
U of Calif, San Diego (CA)
U of Chicago (IL)
U of Cincinnati (OH)
U of Hartford (CT)
U of Idaho (ID)
U of Illinois at Urbana–Champaign (IL)
The U of Iowa (IA)
U of Kansas (KS)
U of Kentucky (KY)
U of Louisville (KY)
U of Michigan (MI)
U of Michigan–Dearborn (MI)
U of Missouri–St. Louis (MO)
U of New Hampshire (NH)
The U of North Carolina at Greensboro (NC)
U of North Texas (TX)
U of Redlands (CA)
U of Richmond (VA)
U of Rochester (NY)
The U of Texas at Austin (TX)
U of the Pacific (CA)
U of the South (TN)
U of Toronto (ON, Canada)
U of Vermont (VT)
U of Victoria (BC, Canada)
U of Washington (WA)
The U of Western Ontario (ON, Canada)
U of Windsor (ON, Canada)
U of Wisconsin–La Crosse (WI)
U of Wisconsin–Milwaukee (WI)
Virginia Commonwealth U (VA)
Washington U in St. Louis (MO)
West Chester U of Pennsylvania (PA)
Western Connecticut State U (CT)
Western Maryland Coll (MD)
Western Michigan U (MI)
Western Washington U (WA)
Westfield State Coll (MA)
Wheaton Coll (IL)
Wright State U (OH)
York U (ON, Canada)
Youngstown State U (OH)

MUSICOLOGY
Brown U (RI)
Texas Christian U (TX)
U of Calif, Los Angeles (CA)
U of Denver (CO)
U of Oregon (OR)

Majors Index
Musicology–Music (Voice and Choral/Opera Performance)

U of Washington (WA)
York U (ON, Canada)

MUSIC (PIANO AND ORGAN PERFORMANCE)
Abilene Christian U (TX)
Acadia U (NS, Canada)
Andrews U (MI)
Anna Maria Coll (MA)
Appalachian State U (NC)
Aquinas Coll (MI)
Auburn U (AL)
Augustana Coll (IL)
Baldwin-Wallace Coll (OH)
Ball State U (IN)
Barry U (FL)
Belmont U (TN)
Benedictine Coll (KS)
Bennington Coll (VT)
Berklee Coll of Music (MA)
Berry Coll (GA)
Bethel Coll (IN)
Birmingham-Southern Coll (AL)
Blue Mountain Coll (MS)
Boston U (MA)
Bowling Green State U (OH)
Brandon U (MB, Canada)
Brenau U (GA)
Brevard Coll (NC)
Brigham Young U–Hawaii Campus (HI)
Bryan Coll (TN)
Bucknell U (PA)
Butler U (IN)
California Inst of the Arts (CA)
California State U, Fullerton (CA)
California State U, Northridge (CA)
Calvary Bible Coll and Theological Seminary (MO)
Calvin Coll (MI)
Cameron U (OK)
Campbellsville U (KY)
Campbell U (NC)
Capital U (OH)
Carson-Newman Coll (TN)
Catawba Coll (NC)
The Catholic U of America (DC)
Cedarville Coll (OH)
Centenary Coll of Louisiana (LA)
Chapman U (CA)
Cleveland Inst of Music (OH)
Coker Coll (SC)
Coll of Notre Dame (CA)
Columbia Coll (SC)
Columbus State U (GA)
Concordia Coll (MI)
Concordia Coll (MN)
Concordia U (IL)
Concordia U (NE)
Converse Coll (SC)
Cornish Coll of the Arts (WA)
The Curtis Inst of Music (PA)
Dallas Baptist U (TX)
David Lipscomb U (TN)
DePaul U (IL)
Drake U (IA)
Eastern Illinois U (IL)
Eastern Washington U (WA)
East Texas Baptist U (TX)
Erskine Coll (SC)
Five Towns Coll (NY)
Florida Baptist Theological Coll (FL)
Florida State U (FL)
Friends U (KS)
Furman U (SC)
Georgetown Coll (KY)
Grace Coll (IN)
Grand Canyon U (AZ)
Grand Valley State U (MI)
Hannibal-LaGrange Coll (MO)
Harding U (AR)
Hardin-Simmons U (TX)
Hastings Coll (NE)
Heidelberg Coll (OH)
Houghton Coll (NY)
Howard Payne U (TX)
Huntingdon Coll (AL)
Huntington Coll (IN)
Illinois Wesleyan U (IL)
Indiana State U (IN)
Indiana U Bloomington (IN)
Indiana U–Purdue U Fort Wayne (IN)
Inter American U of PR, San Germán Campus (PR)
Ithaca Coll (NY)

The Juilliard School (NY)
Lamar U (TX)
Lambuth U (TN)
Lawrence U (WI)
Lee U (TN)
Lincoln Christian Coll (IL)
Louisiana Coll (LA)
Loyola U New Orleans (LA)
Luther Coll (IA)
Manhattan School of Music (NY)
Mannes Coll of Music, New School U (NY)
Mansfield U of Pennsylvania (PA)
Marshall U (WV)
Maryville Coll (TN)
McGill U (PQ, Canada)
McMurry U (TX)
Memorial U of Newfoundland (NF, Canada)
Meredith Coll (NC)
Mid-America Bible Coll (OK)
Milligan Coll (TN)
Minnesota State U, Mankato (MN)
Minnesota State U Moorhead (MN)
Mississippi Coll (MS)
Missouri Southern State Coll (MO)
Montreat Coll (NC)
Mount Allison U (NB, Canada)
Mount Vernon Nazarene Coll (OH)
Newberry Coll (SC)
New England Conservatory of Music (MA)
New World School of the Arts (FL)
New York U (NY)
North Carolina School of the Arts (NC)
North Central Coll (IL)
Northeastern State U (OK)
Northern Arizona U (AZ)
Northern Michigan U (MI)
North Greenville Coll (SC)
Northwest Coll (WA)
Northwestern Coll (MN)
Northwestern U (IL)
Northwest Missouri State U (MO)
Nyack Coll (NY)
Oberlin Coll (OH)
The Ohio State U (OH)
Ohio U (OH)
Oklahoma Baptist U (OK)
Oklahoma City U (OK)
Olivet Nazarene U (IL)
Otterbein Coll (OH)
Ouachita Baptist U (AR)
Pacific Lutheran U (WA)
Pacific Union Coll (CA)
Peabody Conserv of Music of Johns Hopkins U (MD)
Pittsburg State U (KS)
Plymouth State Coll (NH)
Prairie View A&M U (TX)
Queens Coll (NC)
Queens Coll of the City U of NY (NY)
Rider U (NJ)
Roberts Wesleyan Coll (NY)
Saint Mary-of-the-Woods Coll (IN)
Saint Mary's Coll (IN)
St. Olaf Coll (MN)
Samford U (AL)
San Francisco Conservatory of Music (CA)
Sarah Lawrence Coll (NY)
Seton Hill Coll (PA)
Shenandoah U (VA)
Shorter Coll (GA)
Southeast Missouri State U (MO)
Southern Methodist U (TX)
Southwestern Oklahoma State U (OK)
Southwestern U (TX)
State U of NY Coll at Fredonia (NY)
State U of NY Coll at Potsdam (NY)
Stetson U (FL)
Susquehanna U (PA)
Syracuse U (NY)
Tabor Coll (KS)
Taylor U (IN)
Temple U (PA)
Texas A&M U–Commerce (TX)
Texas Christian U (TX)
Texas Southern U (TX)
Toccoa Falls Coll (GA)
Trinity Christian Coll (IL)
Truman State U (MO)

Union U (TN)
The U of Akron (OH)
U of Alberta (AB, Canada)
U of British Columbia (BC, Canada)
U of Central Oklahoma (OK)
U of Cincinnati (OH)
U of Delaware (DE)
The U of Iowa (IA)
U of Kansas (KS)
U of Miami (FL)
U of Michigan (MI)
U of Minnesota, Duluth (MN)
U of Missouri–Kansas City (MO)
U of Montevallo (AL)
U of New Hampshire (NH)
The U of North Carolina at Greensboro (NC)
U of North Texas (TX)
U of Oklahoma (OK)
U of Redlands (CA)
U of Sioux Falls (SD)
U of South Dakota (SD)
U of Southern California (CA)
The U of Tennessee at Chattanooga (TN)
The U of Tennessee at Martin (TN)
The U of Texas at Arlington (TX)
The U of the Arts (PA)
U of the Pacific (CA)
U of Tulsa (OK)
U of Victoria (BC, Canada)
U of Washington (WA)
The U of Western Ontario (ON, Canada)
Valdosta State U (GA)
Vanderbilt U (TN)
Virginia Commonwealth U (VA)
Walla Walla Coll (WA)
Weber State U (UT)
Webster U (MO)
Wesleyan Coll (GA)
West Chester U of Pennsylvania (PA)
Westminster Choir Coll of Rider U (NJ)
Wheaton Coll (IL)
Whitworth Coll (WA)
William Tyndale Coll (MI)
Wingate U (NC)
Wittenberg U (OH)
Xavier U of Louisiana (LA)
York U (ON, Canada)
Youngstown State U (OH)

MUSIC THEORY AND COMPOSITION
Appalachian State U (NC)
Arizona State U (AZ)
Bard Coll (NY)
Baylor U (TX)
Berklee Coll of Music (MA)
Boston U (MA)
Bowling Green State U (OH)
Bradley U (IL)
Brandon U (MB, Canada)
Brevard Coll (NC)
Brigham Young U (UT)
Brown U (RI)
Bucknell U (PA)
Calvin Coll (MI)
Cameron U (OK)
Campbell U (NC)
Carnegie Mellon U (PA)
Carson-Newman Coll (TN)
The Catholic U of America (DC)
Central Michigan U (MI)
Central Missouri State U (MO)
Christopher Newport U (VA)
Concordia Coll (MN)
Dallas Baptist U (TX)
DePauw U (IN)
East Carolina U (NC)
Florida State U (FL)
Georgia Southern U (GA)
Indiana Wesleyan U (IN)
Ithaca Coll (NY)
Jacksonville U (FL)
Loyola U New Orleans (LA)
Luther Coll (IA)
Mannes Coll of Music, New School U (NY)
McGill U (PQ, Canada)
Memorial U of Newfoundland (NF, Canada)
Meredith Coll (NC)
Minnesota State U Moorhead (MN)

New England Conservatory of Music (MA)
New York U (NY)
Northwest Nazarene U (ID)
Nyack Coll (NY)
The Ohio State U (OH)
Ohio U (OH)
Oklahoma Baptist U (OK)
Oklahoma City U (OK)
Ouachita Baptist U (AR)
Rider U (NJ)
Samford U (AL)
San Jose State U (CA)
Seton Hill Coll (PA)
Shenandoah U (VA)
Simon's Rock Coll of Bard (MA)
Southern Adventist U (TN)
Southern Methodist U (TX)
Stetson U (FL)
Susquehanna U (PA)
Syracuse U (NY)
Texas Christian U (TX)
Texas Tech U (TX)
Trinity U (TX)
U of Delaware (DE)
U of Georgia (GA)
U of Hartford (CT)
U of Houston (TX)
U of Idaho (ID)
U of Illinois at Urbana–Champaign (IL)
U of Kansas (KS)
U of Louisville (KY)
U of Miami (FL)
U of Michigan (MI)
U of Nevada, Las Vegas (NV)
U of Northern Iowa (IA)
U of North Texas (TX)
U of Redlands (CA)
U of Rhode Island (RI)
U of Rochester (NY)
U of Southern California (CA)
The U of Texas at Arlington (TX)
The U of Texas at Austin (TX)
U of Victoria (BC, Canada)
U of Washington (WA)
U of Wyoming (WY)
Valparaiso U (IN)
Wartburg Coll (IA)
Washington State U (WA)
Washington U in St. Louis (MO)
Webster U (MO)
Western Michigan U (MI)
Westminster Choir Coll of Rider U (NJ)
West Texas A&M U (TX)
William Jewell Coll (MO)
York U (ON, Canada)
Youngstown State U (OH)

MUSIC THERAPY
Alverno Coll (WI)
Anna Maria Coll (MA)
Appalachian State U (NC)
Arizona State U (AZ)
Augsburg Coll (MN)
Baldwin-Wallace Coll (OH)
Berklee Coll of Music (MA)
Chapman U (CA)
Charleston Southern U (SC)
Cleveland State U (OH)
The Coll of Wooster (OH)
Colorado State U (CO)
Duquesne U (PA)
East Carolina U (NC)
Eastern Michigan U (MI)
Elizabethtown Coll (PA)
Florida State U (FL)
Georgia Coll and State U (GA)
Immaculata Coll (PA)
Indiana U–Purdue U Fort Wayne (IN)
Long Island U, Southampton Coll, Friends World Program (NY)
Loyola U New Orleans (LA)
Mansfield U of Pennsylvania (PA)
Maryville U of Saint Louis (MO)
Marywood U (PA)
Mercyhurst Coll (PA)
Michigan State U (MI)
Molloy Coll (NY)
Nazareth Coll of Rochester (NY)
Ohio U (OH)
Open Learning Agency (BC, Canada)
Queens Coll (NC)
Radford U (VA)

Saint Mary-of-the-Woods Coll (IN)
Sam Houston State U (TX)
Shenandoah U (VA)
Slippery Rock U of Pennsylvania (PA)
Southern Methodist U (TX)
Southwestern Oklahoma State U (OK)
State U of NY at New Paltz (NY)
State U of NY Coll at Fredonia (NY)
Temple U (PA)
Tennessee Technological U (TN)
Texas Woman's U (TX)
U of Dayton (OH)
U of Evansville (IN)
U of Georgia (GA)
The U of Iowa (IA)
U of Kansas (KS)
U of Louisville (KY)
U of Miami (FL)
U of Minnesota, Twin Cities Campus (MN)
U of Missouri–Kansas City (MO)
U of the Pacific (CA)
U of Windsor (ON, Canada)
U of Wisconsin–Eau Claire (WI)
U of Wisconsin–Milwaukee (WI)
Utah State U (UT)
Wartburg Coll (IA)
Western Michigan U (MI)
West Texas A&M U (TX)
Wilfrid Laurier U (ON, Canada)
Willamette U (OR)

MUSIC (VOICE AND CHORAL/ OPERA PERFORMANCE)
Abilene Christian U (TX)
Acadia U (NS, Canada)
Adams State Coll (CO)
Alma Coll (MI)
American U (DC)
Andrews U (MI)
Anna Maria Coll (MA)
Appalachian State U (NC)
Aquinas Coll (MI)
Augustana Coll (IL)
Baldwin-Wallace Coll (OH)
Ball State U (IN)
Bard Coll (NY)
Barry U (FL)
Bellarmine Coll (KY)
Belmont U (TN)
Benedictine Coll (KS)
Bennington Coll (VT)
Berklee Coll of Music (MA)
Berry Coll (GA)
Bethel Coll (IN)
Birmingham-Southern Coll (AL)
Black Hills State U (SD)
Blue Mountain Coll (MS)
Boston U (MA)
Bowling Green State U (OH)
Brandon U (MB, Canada)
Brenau U (GA)
Brevard Coll (NC)
Brigham Young U–Hawaii Campus (HI)
Bryan Coll (TN)
Bucknell U (PA)
Butler U (IN)
California Inst of the Arts (CA)
California State U, Fullerton (CA)
California State U, Long Beach (CA)
California State U, Northridge (CA)
Calvary Bible Coll and Theological Seminary (MO)
Calvin Coll (MI)
Cameron U (OK)
Campbellsville U (KY)
Capital U (OH)
Carroll Coll (WI)
Carson-Newman Coll (TN)
Catawba Coll (NC)
The Catholic U of America (DC)
Cedarville Coll (OH)
Centenary Coll of Louisiana (LA)
Chapman U (CA)
Charleston Southern U (SC)
Clarke Coll (IA)
Cleveland Inst of Music (OH)
Coker Coll (SC)
Coll of Notre Dame (CA)
The Coll of Wooster (OH)
Colorado Christian U (CO)
Columbia Coll (SC)

1060 www.petersons.com Peterson's Guide to Four-Year Colleges 2001

Columbus State U (GA)
Concordia Coll (MN)
Concordia U (IL)
Concordia U (NE)
Converse Coll (SC)
Cornish Coll of the Arts (WA)
The Curtis Inst of Music (PA)
Dallas Baptist U (TX)
David Lipscomb U (TN)
DePaul U (IL)
Drake U (IA)
Eastern New Mexico U (NM)
Eastern Washington U (WA)
East Texas Baptist U (TX)
Erskine Coll (SC)
Five Towns Coll (NY)
Florida Baptist Theological Coll (FL)
Florida State U (FL)
Friends U (KS)
Furman U (SC)
Georgetown Coll (KY)
Georgia Coll and State U (GA)
God's Bible School and Coll (OH)
Grand Canyon U (AZ)
Grand Valley State U (MI)
Hannibal-LaGrange Coll (MO)
Harding U (AR)
Hardin-Simmons U (TX)
Hastings Coll (NE)
Heidelberg Coll (OH)
Houghton Coll (NY)
Howard Payne U (TX)
Huntingdon Coll (AL)
Huntington Coll (IN)
Illinois Wesleyan U (IL)
Immaculata Coll (PA)
Indiana State U (IN)
Indiana U Bloomington (IN)
Indiana U–Purdue U Fort Wayne (IN)
Inter American U of PR, San Germán Campus (PR)
Ithaca Coll (NY)
Jacksonville U (FL)
John Brown U (AR)
Judson Coll (IL)
The Juilliard School (NY)
Lamar U (TX)
Lambuth U (TN)
Langston U (OK)
Lawrence U (WI)
Lee U (TN)
Lincoln Christian Coll (IL)
Lindenwood U (MO)
Louisiana Coll (LA)
Luther Coll (IA)
Manhattan School of Music (NY)
Mannes Coll of Music, New School U (NY)
Mansfield U of Pennsylvania (PA)
Marshall U (WV)
Mars Hill Coll (NC)
Maryville Coll (TN)
McGill U (PQ, Canada)
McMurry U (TX)
Memorial U of Newfoundland (NF, Canada)
Mercyhurst Coll (PA)
Meredith Coll (NC)
Michigan State U (MI)
Mid-America Bible Coll (OK)
MidAmerica Nazarene U (KS)
Milligan Coll (TN)
Millikin U (IL)
Minnesota State U, Mankato (MN)
Minnesota State U Moorhead (MN)
Mississippi Coll (MS)
Missouri Southern State Coll (MO)
Montreat Coll (NC)
Mount Allison U (NB, Canada)
Mount Mercy Coll (IA)
Mount St. Mary's Coll (CA)
Mount Vernon Nazarene Coll (OH)
Newberry Coll (SC)
New England Conservatory of Music (MA)
New World School of the Arts (FL)
New York U (NY)
North Carolina School of the Arts (NC)
North Central Coll (IL)
Northeastern State U (OK)
Northern Arizona U (AZ)
Northern Michigan U (MI)
Northern State U (SD)
North Greenville Coll (SC)

North Park U (IL)
Northwest Coll (WA)
Northwestern Coll (MN)
Northwestern U (IL)
Northwest Missouri State U (MO)
Nyack Coll (NY)
Oakland U (MI)
Oberlin Coll (OH)
The Ohio State U (OH)
Ohio U (OH)
Oklahoma Baptist U (OK)
Oklahoma Christian U of Science and Arts (OK)
Oklahoma City U (OK)
Olivet Nazarene U (IL)
Otterbein Coll (OH)
Ouachita Baptist U (AR)
Pacific Lutheran U (WA)
Palm Beach Atlantic Coll (FL)
Peabody Conserv of Music of Johns Hopkins U (MD)
Peru State Coll (NE)
Pittsburg State U (KS)
Plymouth State Coll (NH)
Prairie View A&M U (TX)
Queens Coll (NC)
Queens Coll of the City U of NY (NY)
Randolph-Macon Woman's Coll (VA)
Rider U (NJ)
Roberts Wesleyan Coll (NY)
Rochester Coll (MI)
Rowan U (NJ)
St. Cloud State U (MN)
Saint Mary-of-the-Woods Coll (IN)
Saint Mary's Coll (IN)
St. Olaf Coll (MN)
Saint Xavier U (IL)
Samford U (AL)
San Francisco Conservatory of Music (CA)
San Jose State U (CA)
Sarah Lawrence Coll (NY)
Seton Hill Coll (PA)
Shorter Coll (GA)
Southeast Missouri State U (MO)
Southwestern Oklahoma State U (OK)
State U of NY Coll at Fredonia (NY)
State U of NY Coll at Potsdam (NY)
Stetson U (FL)
Susquehanna U (PA)
Syracuse U (NY)
Tabor Coll (KS)
Talladega Coll (AL)
Taylor U (IN)
Temple U (PA)
Texas A&M U–Commerce (TX)
Texas Christian U (TX)
Texas Southern U (TX)
Texas Wesleyan U (TX)
Toccoa Falls Coll (GA)
Trinity Christian Coll (IL)
Trinity U (TX)
Truman State U (MO)
Union Coll (KY)
Union U (TN)
The U of Akron (OH)
U of Alberta (AB, Canada)
U of British Columbia (BC, Canada)
U of Central Oklahoma (OK)
U of Charleston (WV)
U of Cincinnati (OH)
U of Delaware (DE)
U of Idaho (ID)
U of Illinois at Urbana–Champaign (IL)
The U of Iowa (IA)
U of Kansas (KS)
U of Miami (FL)
U of Michigan (MI)
U of Missouri–Kansas City (MO)
U of Montevallo (AL)
U of Nebraska at Omaha (NE)
U of New Hampshire (NH)
The U of North Carolina at Greensboro (NC)
U of North Texas (TX)
U of Oklahoma (OK)
U of Oregon (OR)
U of Redlands (CA)
U of Sioux Falls (SD)
U of South Alabama (AL)

U of South Dakota (SD)
U of Southern California (CA)
The U of Tennessee at Chattanooga (TN)
The U of Tennessee at Martin (TN)
The U of Texas at Arlington (TX)
The U of the Arts (PA)
U of the Pacific (CA)
U of Tulsa (OK)
U of Victoria (BC, Canada)
U of Washington (WA)
The U of Western Ontario (ON, Canada)
U of Wisconsin–Milwaukee (WI)
Valdosta State U (GA)
Vanderbilt U (TN)
Virginia Commonwealth U (VA)
Walla Walla Coll (WA)
Washington U in St. Louis (MO)
Webster U (MO)
Wesleyan Coll (GA)
West Chester U of Pennsylvania (PA)
Western Michigan U (MI)
Westfield State Coll (MA)
Westminster Choir Coll of Rider U (NJ)
Westminster Coll (PA)
Wheaton Coll (IL)
Whitworth Coll (WA)
William Paterson U of New Jersey (NJ)
William Tyndale Coll (MI)
Wingate U (NC)
Winona State U (MN)
Wittenberg U (OH)
York U (ON, Canada)
Youngstown State U (OH)

NATIVE AMERICAN STUDIES
Bemidji State U (MN)
Black Hills State U (SD)
Brandon U (MB, Canada)
California State U, Hayward (CA)
Colgate U (NY)
Cornell U (NY)
Dartmouth Coll (NH)
The Evergreen State Coll (WA)
Hampshire Coll (MA)
Humboldt State U (CA)
Lake Superior State U (MI)
Long Island U, Southampton Coll, Friends World Program (NY)
Morningside Coll (IA)
Naropa U (CO)
Northeastern State U (OK)
Northland Coll (WI)
San Diego State U (CA)
Sonoma State U (CA)
Stanford U (CA)
State U of NY at Buffalo (NY)
State U of NY Coll at Potsdam (NY)
Trent U (ON, Canada)
U Coll of Cape Breton (NS, Canada)
U of Alaska Fairbanks (AK)
U of Alberta (AB, Canada)
U of Calif, Berkeley (CA)
U of Calif, Davis (CA)
U of Calif, Riverside (CA)
The U of Iowa (IA)
The U of Lethbridge (AB, Canada)
U of Minnesota, Duluth (MN)
U of Minnesota, Twin Cities Campus (MN)
The U of Montana–Missoula (MT)
The U of North Carolina at Pembroke (NC)
U of North Dakota (ND)
U of Oklahoma (OK)
U of Regina (SK, Canada)
U of Science and Arts of Oklahoma (OK)
U of Toronto (ON, Canada)
U of Washington (WA)
U of Wisconsin–Eau Claire (WI)
U of Wisconsin–Milwaukee (WI)

NATURAL RESOURCES CONSERVATION
Coll of Santa Fe (NM)
The Evergreen State Coll (WA)
Harvard U (MA)
Humboldt State U (CA)
Indiana State U (IN)
Iowa Wesleyan Coll (IA)

Kent State U (OH)
Long Island U, C.W. Post Campus (NY)
Long Island U, Southampton Coll, Friends World Program (NY)
Louisiana Tech U (LA)
Marlboro Coll (VT)
McGill U (PQ, Canada)
Michigan State U (MI)
Montana State U–Bozeman (MT)
Muskingum Coll (OH)
North Carolina State U (NC)
Northern Michigan U (MI)
Northland Coll (WI)
Northwest Missouri State U (MO)
Penn State U Univ Park Campus (PA)
Peru State Coll (NE)
Purdue U (IN)
Rutgers, State U of NJ, Cook Coll (NJ)
Southeastern Oklahoma State U (OK)
State U of NY Coll of Environ Sci and Forestry (NY)
Sterling Coll (VT)
Texas Tech U (TX)
Unity Coll (ME)
U of Alberta (AB, Canada)
U of British Columbia (BC, Canada)
U of Calif, Berkeley (CA)
U of Calif, Davis (CA)
U of Connecticut (CT)
U of Kentucky (KY)
U of Maryland, Coll Park (MD)
The U of Montana–Missoula (MT)
U of Nebraska–Lincoln (NE)
U of Nevada, Reno (NV)
U of New Hampshire (NH)
U of Rhode Island (RI)
U of Vermont (VT)
U of Wisconsin–Milwaukee (WI)
U of Wisconsin–River Falls (WI)
U of Wisconsin–Stevens Point (WI)
Upper Iowa U (IA)
Washington State U (WA)
Winona State U (MN)

NATURAL RESOURCES MANAGEMENT
Alaska Pacific U (AK)
Albright Coll (PA)
Arizona State U East (AZ)
Ball State U (IN)
Bowling Green State U (OH)
California State U, Chico (CA)
Clark U (MA)
Colorado State U (CO)
Cornell U (NY)
Delaware State U (DE)
Eastern Oregon U (OR)
The Evergreen State Coll (WA)
Fort Hays State U (KS)
Grand Valley State U (MI)
Humboldt State U (CA)
Huntington Coll (IN)
Iowa State U of Science and Technology (IA)
Johnson State Coll (VT)
Long Island U, Southampton Coll, Friends World Program (NY)
Michigan State U (MI)
North Carolina State U (NC)
North Dakota State U (ND)
Northern Arizona U (AZ)
Northland Coll (WI)
The Ohio State U (OH)
Oregon State U (OR)
Rochester Inst of Technology (NY)
Rutgers, State U of NJ, Cook Coll (NJ)
Sheldon Jackson Coll (AK)
State U of NY Coll of Environ Sci and Forestry (NY)
Sterling Coll (VT)
Texas A&M U (TX)
Tuskegee U (AL)
Unity Coll (ME)
U of Alaska Fairbanks (AK)
U of Alberta (AB, Canada)
U of British Columbia (BC, Canada)
U of Calif, Berkeley (CA)
U of Calif, Davis (CA)
U of Calif, San Diego (CA)
U of Connecticut (CT)

U of Delaware (DE)
U of Guelph (ON, Canada)
U of Houston–Clear Lake (TX)
U of Idaho (ID)
U of La Verne (CA)
U of Louisiana at Lafayette (LA)
U of Maine (ME)
U of Massachusetts Amherst (MA)
U of Miami (FL)
U of Michigan (MI)
U of Michigan–Flint (MI)
U of Minnesota, Crookston (MN)
U of Minnesota, Twin Cities Campus (MN)
The U of Montana–Missoula (MT)
U of Nebraska–Lincoln (NE)
U of Nevada, Reno (NV)
U of New Hampshire (NH)
U of Rhode Island (RI)
U of Southern California (CA)
U of the South (TN)
U of Vermont (VT)
U of Washington (WA)
The U of Western Ontario (ON, Canada)
U of Windsor (ON, Canada)
U of Wisconsin–Madison (WI)
U of Wisconsin–Stevens Point (WI)
Utah State U (UT)
Warren Wilson Coll (NC)
Washington State U (WA)
Western Carolina U (NC)
Western Washington U (WA)
West Virginia U (WV)

NATURAL RESOURCES PROTECTIVE SERVICES
The Ohio State U (OH)
Unity Coll (ME)

NAVAL ARCHITECTURE/MARINE ENGINEERING
Maine Maritime Academy (ME)
Massachusetts Inst of Technology (MA)
Massachusetts Maritime Academy (MA)
Memorial U of Newfoundland (NF, Canada)
State U of NY Maritime Coll (NY)
Texas A&M U (TX)
Texas A&M U at Galveston (TX)
United States Coast Guard Academy (CT)
United States Merchant Marine Academy (NY)
United States Naval Academy (MD)
U of Michigan (MI)
U of New Brunswick, Saint John (NB, Canada)
U of New Orleans (LA)
Webb Inst (NY)

NAVAL SCIENCE
Hampton U (VA)
Massachusetts Inst of Technology (MA)
Rensselaer Polytechnic Inst (NY)
State U of NY Maritime Coll (NY)
U of Idaho (ID)
U of Pennsylvania (PA)
U of Washington (WA)
York Coll (NE)

NEUROSCIENCE
Allegheny Coll (PA)
Amherst Coll (MA)
Baldwin-Wallace Coll (OH)
Bates Coll (ME)
Bishop's U (PQ, Canada)
Boston U (MA)
Bowdoin Coll (ME)
Bowling Green State U (OH)
Brandeis U (MA)
Brock U (ON, Canada)
Brown U (RI)
California Inst of Technology (CA)
Cedar Crest Coll (PA)
Chatham Coll (PA)
Clark U (MA)
Colgate U (NY)
The Colorado Coll (CO)
Columbia Coll (NY)
Concordia U (PQ, Canada)
Connecticut Coll (CT)
Cornell U (NY)
Dalhousie U (NS, Canada)

Majors Index
Neuroscience–Nutrition Studies

Drew U (NJ)
Emory U (GA)
Fairfield U (CT)
Franklin and Marshall Coll (PA)
Hamilton Coll (NY)
Hampshire Coll (MA)
Harvard U (MA)
Haverford Coll (PA)
John Carroll U (OH)
Johns Hopkins U (MD)
Kenyon Coll (OH)
King's Coll (PA)
Lawrence U (WI)
Lehigh U (PA)
Macalester Coll (MN)
Manhattanville Coll (NY)
Memorial U of Newfoundland (NF, Canada)
Muskingum Coll (OH)
New York U (NY)
Northwestern U (IL)
Oberlin Coll (OH)
Ohio Wesleyan U (OH)
Pomona Coll (CA)
Regis U (CO)
Rice U (TX)
Scripps Coll (CA)
Smith Coll (MA)
Texas Christian U (TX)
Trinity Coll (CT)
U of Calif, Los Angeles (CA)
U of Calif, Riverside (CA)
U of Delaware (DE)
U of King's Coll (NS, Canada)
The U of Lethbridge (AB, Canada)
U of Maryland, Coll Park (MD)
U of Minnesota, Twin Cities Campus (MN)
U of Pittsburgh (PA)
U of Rochester (NY)
The U of Scranton (PA)
U of Southern California (CA)
The U of Texas at Dallas (TX)
U of Toronto (ON, Canada)
Washington and Lee U (VA)
Washington State U (WA)
Washington U in St. Louis (MO)
Wellesley Coll (MA)
Wesleyan U (CT)
Westmont Coll (CA)

NONPROFIT/PUBLIC MANAGEMENT
Austin Peay State U (TN)
Brevard Coll (NC)
Detroit Coll of Business (MI)
Detroit Coll of Business–Flint (MI)
Detroit Coll of Business, Warren Campus (MI)
Fresno Pacific U (CA)
Manchester Coll (IN)
Southern Adventist U (TN)
Warren Wilson Coll (NC)
Worcester State Coll (MA)

NUCLEAR ENGINEERING
California State U, Northridge (CA)
Georgia Inst of Technology (GA)
Kansas State U (KS)
Massachusetts Inst of Technology (MA)
North Carolina State U (NC)
Oregon State U (OR)
Penn State U Univ Park Campus (PA)
Purdue U (IN)
Rensselaer Polytechnic Inst (NY)
Texas A&M U (TX)
United States Military Academy (NY)
The U of Arizona (AZ)
U of Calif, Berkeley (CA)
U of Cincinnati (OH)
U of Florida (FL)
U of Illinois at Urbana–Champaign (IL)
U of Maryland, Coll Park (MD)
U of Michigan (MI)
U of Missouri–Rolla (MO)
U of New Mexico (NM)
The U of Tennessee Knoxville (TN)
U of Toronto (ON, Canada)
U of Wisconsin–Madison (WI)
Worcester Polytechnic Inst (MA)

NUCLEAR MEDICAL TECHNOLOGY
Aquinas Coll (MI)
Barry U (FL)
Benedictine U (IL)
California State U, Dominguez Hills (CA)
Cedar Crest Coll (PA)
Coll of Staten Island of the City U of NY (NY)
Ferris State U (MI)
Houston Baptist U (TX)
Indiana U of Pennsylvania (PA)
Indiana U–Purdue U Indianapolis (IN)
Lebanon Valley Coll (PA)
Long Island U, Brooklyn Campus (NY)
Long Island U, C.W. Post Campus (NY)
Manhattan Coll (NY)
Mass Coll of Pharmacy and Allied Health Sciences (MA)
Medical Coll of Georgia (GA)
Millersville U of Pennsylvania (PA)
Oakland U (MI)
Old Dominion U (VA)
Peru State Coll (NE)
Rochester Inst of Technology (NY)
St. Cloud State U (MN)
Saint Louis U (MO)
Saint Mary's U of Minnesota (MN)
Salem State Coll (MA)
State U of NY at Buffalo (NY)
Thomas Edison State Coll (NJ)
The U of Alabama at Birmingham (AL)
U of Arkansas for Medical Sciences (AR)
U of Central Arkansas (AR)
U of Cincinnati (OH)
The U of Findlay (OH)
The U of Iowa (IA)
U of Louisville (KY)
U of Missouri–Columbia (MO)
U of Nebraska Medical Center (NE)
U of Nevada, Las Vegas (NV)
U of Oklahoma Health Sciences Center (OK)
U of St. Francis (IL)
U of Vermont (VT)
U of Wisconsin–La Crosse (WI)
Virginia Commonwealth U (VA)
Weber State U (UT)
Wheeling Jesuit U (WV)
York Coll of Pennsylvania (PA)

NUCLEAR PHYSICS
California Inst of Technology (CA)
Harvard U (MA)
Worcester Polytechnic Inst (MA)

NUCLEAR TECHNOLOGY
Regents Coll (NY)
San Jose State U (CA)
Thomas Edison State Coll (NJ)

NURSERY MANAGEMENT
Colorado State U (CO)

NURSING ADMINISTRATION
Central Methodist Coll (MO)
Clarkson Coll (NE)
Emmanuel Coll (MA)
Framingham State Coll (MA)
Nazareth Coll of Rochester (NY)
Ryerson Polytechnic U (ON, Canada)
U of San Francisco (CA)
The U of Western Ontario (ON, Canada)
Wheeling Jesuit U (WV)

NURSING (ADULT HEALTH)
Franklin U (OH)
Northern Kentucky U (KY)
Okanagan U Coll (BC, Canada)
Pennsylvania Coll of Technology (PA)
U du Québec à Trois-Rivières (PQ, Canada)

NURSING (ANESTHETIST)
Webster U (MO)

NURSING (FAMILY PRACTICE)
Mass Coll of Pharmacy and Allied Health Sciences (MA)
U du Québec à Trois-Rivières (PQ, Canada)
U of Virginia's Coll at Wise (VA)

NURSING (MATERNAL/CHILD HEALTH)
U of Washington (WA)

NURSING (MIDWIFERY)
Marquette U (WI)
Ryerson Polytechnic U (ON, Canada)
U du Québec à Trois-Rivières (PQ, Canada)

NURSING (PSYCHIATRIC/MENTAL HEALTH)
Brandon U (MB, Canada)
Open Learning Agency (BC, Canada)

NURSING (PUBLIC HEALTH)
Malone Coll (OH)
Ryerson Polytechnic U (ON, Canada)
U du Québec à Trois-Rivières (PQ, Canada)
U of San Francisco (CA)
U of Washington (WA)

NURSING SCIENCE
Brandon U (MB, Canada)
Brock U (ON, Canada)
Cedar Crest Coll (PA)
Clarke Coll (IA)
Clarkson Coll (NE)
Coll of Saint Elizabeth (NJ)
Daemen Coll (NY)
Dominican Coll of Blauvelt (NY)
Elmira Coll (NY)
Emporia State U (KS)
Georgetown Coll (KY)
Holy Family Coll (PA)
Holy Names Coll (CA)
Immaculata Coll (PA)
Inter American U of PR, Aguadilla Campus (PR)
Kean U (NJ)
La Roche Coll (PA)
Long Island U, C.W. Post Campus (NY)
Millersville U of Pennsylvania (PA)
Missouri Baptist Coll (MO)
Monmouth U (NJ)
Mount Aloysius Coll (PA)
National U (CA)
Nebraska Wesleyan U (NE)
New Jersey City U (NJ)
The Ohio State U (OH)
Pace U, New York City Campus (NY)
Pace U, Pleasantville/Briarcliff Campus (NY)
Penn State U Harrisburg Campus of the Capital Coll (PA)
Penn State U Schuylkill Campus of the Capital Coll (PA)
Queens Coll (NC)
The Richard Stockton Coll of New Jersey (NJ)
St. Francis Xavier U (NS, Canada)
Saint Joseph's Coll (IN)
Saint Peter's Coll (NJ)
Southern Adventist U (TN)
Thomas Edison State Coll (NJ)
U of Delaware (DE)
U of Kansas (KS)
U of New Hampshire at Manchester (NH)
U of Victoria (BC, Canada)
U of Wisconsin–Green Bay (WI)
Western Kentucky U (KY)
Wichita State U (KS)
York U (ON, Canada)

NURSING (SURGICAL)
Texas A&M International U (TX)
Wheeling Jesuit U (WV)

NUTRITIONAL SCIENCES
Benedictine U (IL)
Boston U (MA)
Brigham Young U (UT)
California State U, Los Angeles (CA)
Cornell U (NY)
La Salle U (PA)
McGill U (PQ, Canada)
Mount Saint Vincent U (NS, Canada)
New York Inst of Technology (NY)
The Ohio State U (OH)
Russell Sage Coll (NY)
Rutgers, State U of NJ, Cook Coll (NJ)
Rutgers, State U of NJ, Douglass Coll (NJ)
Rutgers, State U of NJ, U Coll–New Brunswick (NJ)
Texas A&M U (TX)
Texas Woman's U (TX)
Université Laval (PQ, Canada)
The U of Arizona (AZ)
U of Calif, Berkeley (CA)
U of Connecticut (CT)
U of Delaware (DE)
U of Guelph (ON, Canada)
U of Hawaii at Manoa (HI)
The U of North Carolina at Chapel Hill (NC)
U of Vermont (VT)
U of Wisconsin–Green Bay (WI)

NUTRITION SCIENCE
Acadia U (NS, Canada)
Andrews U (MI)
Appalachian State U (NC)
Ashland U (OH)
Bastyr U (WA)
Bluffton Coll (OH)
Bowling Green State U (OH)
Brooklyn Coll of the City U of NY (NY)
California Polytechnic State U, San Luis Obispo (CA)
California State Polytechnic U, Pomona (CA)
California State U, Fresno (CA)
California State U, Northridge (CA)
California State U, San Bernardino (CA)
Carson-Newman Coll (TN)
Case Western Reserve U (OH)
Cedar Crest Coll (PA)
Coll of Saint Benedict (MN)
Coll of St. Catherine (MN)
Coll of the Ozarks (MO)
Colorado State U (CO)
Concordia Coll (MN)
Cornell U (NY)
Delaware State U (DE)
Dominican U (IL)
Drexel U (PA)
Florida State U (FL)
Fort Valley State U (GA)
Framingham State Coll (MA)
Gallaudet U (DC)
Hampshire Coll (MA)
Hampton U (VA)
Howard U (DC)
Hunter Coll of the City U of NY (NY)
Immaculata Coll (PA)
Indiana State U (IN)
Indiana U Bloomington (IN)
Iowa State U of Science and Technology (IA)
Ithaca Coll (NY)
Jacksonville State U (AL)
Keene State Coll (NH)
Langston U (OK)
Lehman Coll of the City U of NY (NY)
Long Island U, C.W. Post Campus (NY)
Long Island U, Southampton Coll, Friends World Program (NY)
Madonna U (MI)
Mansfield U of Pennsylvania (PA)
Marymount Coll (NY)
McGill U (PQ, Canada)
McNeese State U (LA)
Memorial U of Newfoundland (NF, Canada)
Michigan State U (MI)
Middle Tennessee State U (TN)
Minnesota State U, Mankato (MN)
Morgan State U (MD)
Mount Marty Coll (SD)
Mount Saint Vincent U (NS, Canada)
New Mexico State U (NM)
New York U (NY)
North Carolina Ag and Tech State U (NC)
North Carolina Central U (NC)
North Dakota State U (ND)
Northeastern State U (OK)
Northwest Missouri State U (MO)
Notre Dame Coll of Ohio (OH)
Ohio U (OH)
Oklahoma State U (OK)
Oregon State U (OR)
Pacific Union Coll (CA)
Pepperdine U, Malibu (CA)
Plattsburgh State U of NY (NY)
Prairie View A&M U (TX)
Queens Coll of the City U of NY (NY)
Ryerson Polytechnic U (ON, Canada)
St. Francis Xavier U (NS, Canada)
Saint John's U (MN)
Saint Joseph Coll (CT)
Sam Houston State U (TX)
San Diego State U (CA)
San Jose State U (CA)
Seattle Pacific U (WA)
Seton Hill Coll (PA)
Simmons Coll (MA)
South Dakota State U (SD)
Southeast Missouri State U (MO)
Syracuse U (NY)
Tennessee Technological U (TN)
Texas A&M U (TX)
Texas A&M U–Kingsville (TX)
Tuskegee U (AL)
Université de Montréal (PQ, Canada)
Université Laval (PQ, Canada)
The U of Akron (OH)
U of Alberta (AB, Canada)
U of British Columbia (BC, Canada)
U of Calif, Davis (CA)
U of Central Oklahoma (OK)
U of Cincinnati (OH)
U of Dayton (OH)
U of Delaware (DE)
U of Guelph (ON, Canada)
U of Illinois at Urbana–Champaign (IL)
U of Kentucky (KY)
U of Maine (ME)
U of Manitoba (MB, Canada)
U of Maryland, Coll Park (MD)
U of Michigan (MI)
U of Minnesota, Twin Cities Campus (MN)
U of Missouri–Columbia (MO)
U of New Hampshire (NH)
U of Northern Iowa (IA)
U of Oklahoma Health Sciences Center (OK)
U of Prince Edward Island (PE, Canada)
The U of Tennessee Knoxville (TN)
U of Toronto (ON, Canada)
U of Vermont (VT)
The U of Western Ontario (ON, Canada)
U of Wisconsin–Madison (WI)
Utah State U (UT)
Virginia Polytechnic Inst and State U (VA)
Winthrop U (SC)

NUTRITION STUDIES
Appalachian State U (NC)
Auburn U (AL)
Bradley U (IL)
California State U, Chico (CA)
Coll of Saint Elizabeth (NJ)
Edinboro U of Pennsylvania (PA)
Eastern Michigan U (MI)
Florida State U (FL)
Framingham State Coll (MA)
Georgia Southern U (GA)
Idaho State U (ID)
Indiana U of Pennsylvania (PA)
Ithaca Coll (NY)
James Madison U (VA)
Kansas State U (KS)
Kent State U (OH)
Lambuth U (TN)
Loyola U Chicago (IL)

Majors Index
Nutrition Studies–Painting

Mansfield U of Pennsylvania (PA)
Marygrove Coll (MI)
Murray State U (KY)
Northern Illinois U (IL)
Penn State U Univ Park Campus (PA)
Purdue U (IN)
Saint Louis U (MO)
Southern Illinois U Carbondale (IL)
Southwest Texas State U (TX)
Stephen F. Austin State U (TX)
Syracuse U (NY)
Texas Christian U (TX)
Texas Southern U (TX)
Texas Tech U (TX)
Texas Woman's U (TX)
The U of Alabama (AL)
U of Arkansas (AR)
U of Delaware (DE)
U of Georgia (GA)
U of Houston (TX)
U of Idaho (ID)
U of Illinois at Urbana–Champaign (IL)
U of Kentucky (KY)
U of Massachusetts Amherst (MA)
U of Nebraska–Lincoln (NE)
U of Nevada, Reno (NV)
U of New Mexico (NM)
The U of North Carolina at Greensboro (NC)
U of Northern Iowa (IA)
U of Puerto Rico, Río Piedras (PR)
U of Rhode Island (RI)
The U of Texas at Austin (TX)
U of Vermont (VT)
U of Wisconsin–Stout (WI)
U of Wyoming (WY)
Washington State U (WA)
Wayne State U (MI)
Western Kentucky U (KY)
Western Michigan U (MI)

OCCUPATIONAL HEALTH AND INDUSTRIAL HYGIENE
California State U, Fresno (CA)
Illinois State U (IL)
Montana Tech of The U of Montana (MT)
Oakland U (MI)
Ohio U (OH)
Ryerson Polytechnic U (ON, Canada)
Saint Augustine's Coll (NC)

OCCUPATIONAL SAFETY/HEALTH TECHNOLOGY
Ball State U (IN)
Bayamón Central U (PR)
California State U, Fresno (CA)
California State U, Northridge (CA)
Central Missouri State U (MO)
Fairmont State Coll (WV)
Ferris State U (MI)
Grand Valley State U (MI)
Indiana State U (IN)
Indiana U of Pennsylvania (PA)
Jacksonville State U (AL)
Keene State Coll (NH)
Madonna U (MI)
MCP Hahnemann U (PA)
Mercy Coll (NY)
Millersville U of Pennsylvania (PA)
Montana Tech of The U of Montana (MT)
Murray State U (KY)
National U (CA)
North Carolina Ag and Tech State U (NC)
Oregon State U (OR)
Penn State U Univ Park Campus (PA)
Rochester Inst of Technology (NY)
Saint Augustine's Coll (NC)
Southeastern Oklahoma State U (OK)
Southwest Baptist U (MO)
Texas Southern U (TX)
U of New Haven (CT)
U of North Dakota (ND)

OCCUPATIONAL THERAPY ASSISTANT
Grand Valley State U (MI)

OCEAN ENGINEERING
California State U, Long Beach (CA)
Florida Atlantic U (FL)
Florida Inst of Technology (FL)
Massachusetts Inst of Technology (MA)
Memorial U of Newfoundland (NF, Canada)
Texas A&M U (TX)
Texas A&M U at Galveston (TX)
United States Naval Academy (MD)
U of New Hampshire (NH)
U of Rhode Island (RI)
Virginia Polytechnic Inst and State U (VA)

OCEANOGRAPHY
Central Michigan U (MI)
Florida Inst of Technology (FL)
Florida State U (FL)
Hampshire Coll (MA)
Hawaii Pacific U (HI)
Humboldt State U (CA)
Lamar U (TX)
Maine Maritime Academy (ME)
Memorial U of Newfoundland (NF, Canada)
Millersville U of Pennsylvania (PA)
North Carolina State U (NC)
Nova Southeastern U (FL)
Rider U (NJ)
Rutgers, State U of NJ, Cook Coll (NJ)
San Jose State U (CA)
Sheldon Jackson Coll (AK)
State U of NY Maritime Coll (NY)
Texas A&M U at Galveston (TX)
United States Naval Academy (MD)
U of British Columbia (BC, Canada)
U of Miami (FL)
U of Michigan (MI)
U of New England (ME)
U of New Hampshire (NH)
U of San Diego (CA)
U of Victoria (BC, Canada)
U of Washington (WA)

OFFICE MANAGEMENT
Arkansas Tech U (AR)
Baker Coll of Flint (MI)
Berkeley Coll, White Plains (NY)
Bowling Green State U (OH)
Central Michigan U (MI)
Central Missouri State U (MO)
Concordia Coll (MN)
Delta State U (MS)
Detroit Coll of Business (MI)
Emporia State U (KS)
Georgia Coll and State U (GA)
Indiana U of Pennsylvania (PA)
International Coll of the Cayman Islands (Cayman Islands)
Mayville State U (ND)
Middle Tennessee State U (TN)
Mississippi Valley State U (MS)
Northwestern Coll (MN)
Peirce Coll (PA)
Radford U (VA)
Southeastern Oklahoma State U (OK)
Stephen F. Austin State U (TX)
Texas Southern U (TX)
Texas Woman's U (TX)
U of Houston–Downtown (TX)
U of Nebraska–Lincoln (NE)
U of North Dakota (ND)
U of South Carolina (SC)
U of the Sacred Heart (PR)
Weber State U (UT)
West Texas A&M U (TX)
Youngstown State U (OH)

OPERATING ROOM TECHNICIAN
State U of New York Upstate Medical University

OPERATIONS MANAGEMENT
Appalachian State U (NC)
Auburn U (AL)
Baker Coll of Flint (MI)
Baylor U (TX)
Boston U (MA)
Bowling Green State U (OH)
California State U, Chico (CA)
California State U, Stanislaus (CA)
Central Michigan U (MI)
Clarkson U (NY)
Concordia U (NE)
Dalton State Coll (GA)
DeVry Inst of Technology (AZ)
DeVry Inst of Technology, Fremont (CA)
DeVry Inst of Technology, Long Beach (CA)
DeVry Inst of Technology, Pomona (CA)
DeVry Inst of Technology, West Hills (CA)
DeVry Inst of Technology, Alpharetta (GA)
DeVry Inst of Technology, Decatur (GA)
DeVry Inst of Technology, Addison (IL)
DeVry Inst of Technology, Chicago (IL)
DeVry Inst of Technology (MO)
DeVry Inst of Technology (OH)
DeVry Inst of Technology (TX)
Florida Southern Coll (FL)
Florida State U (FL)
Franklin U (OH)
Golden Gate U (CA)
Indiana U–Purdue U Fort Wayne (IN)
Indiana U–Purdue U Indianapolis (IN)
Kent State U (OH)
Kettering U (MI)
Louisiana Tech U (LA)
Loyola U Chicago (IL)
Miami U (OH)
Michigan State U (MI)
Michigan Technological U (MI)
Millikin U (IL)
Missouri Baptist Coll (MO)
National U (CA)
Northern Illinois U (IL)
The Ohio State U (OH)
Ohio U (OH)
Penn State U Univ Park Campus (PA)
Purdue U (IN)
Regents Coll (NY)
Saginaw Valley State U (MI)
Sam Houston State U (TX)
San Jose State U (CA)
Seattle U (WA)
Tennessee Technological U (TN)
Texas Southern U (TX)
Thomas Edison State Coll (NJ)
Tri-State U (IN)
The U of Arizona (AZ)
U of Arkansas (AR)
U of Delaware (DE)
U of Houston (TX)
U of Idaho (ID)
U of Indianapolis (IN)
U of Maryland, Coll Park (MD)
U of Nebraska at Kearney (NE)
U of Nebraska at Omaha (NE)
The U of North Carolina at Asheville (NC)
The U of North Carolina at Charlotte (NC)
U of North Texas (TX)
U of Pennsylvania (PA)
U of St. Francis (IL)
U of St. Thomas (MN)
Utah State U (UT)
Washington U in St. Louis (MO)
Western Washington U (WA)
Worcester State Coll (MA)
Youngstown State U (OH)

OPERATIONS RESEARCH
Babson Coll (MA)
Baruch Coll of the City U of NY (NY)
Boston Coll (MA)
California State U, Northridge (CA)
Carleton U (ON, Canada)
Columbia U, School of Engineering & Applied Sci (NY)
Concordia U (PQ, Canada)
Cornell U (NY)
DePaul U (IL)
Georgia State U (GA)
Iona Coll (NY)
Mercy Coll (NY)
Miami U (OH)
New York U (NY)
United States Air Force Academy (CO)
United States Coast Guard Academy (CT)
United States Military Academy (NY)
Université de Montréal (PQ, Canada)
Université de Sherbrooke (PQ, Canada)
U du Québec à Trois-Rivières (PQ, Canada)
U of Cincinnati (OH)
U of Denver (CO)
U of Michigan–Flint (MI)
U of New Brunswick, Fredericton (NB, Canada)
U of New Haven (CT)
U of Waterloo (ON, Canada)
Virginia Commonwealth U (VA)
Worcester Polytechnic Inst (MA)
York U (ON, Canada)

OPHTHALMIC MEDICAL ASSISTANT
Alderson-Broaddus Coll (WV)

OPHTHALMIC/OPTOMETRIC SERVICES
Ferris State U (MI)
Gannon U (PA)
Indiana U Bloomington (IN)
Inter American U of PR, Metropolitan Campus (PR)
Northeastern State U (OK)
State U of NY at New Paltz (NY)
State U of NY Coll at Oneonta (NY)
Université de Montréal (PQ, Canada)
U of Waterloo (ON, Canada)

OPTICS
The Ohio State U (OH)
Rose-Hulman Inst of Technology (IN)
Saginaw Valley State U (MI)
The U of Alabama in Huntsville (AL)
U of Rochester (NY)
Worcester Polytechnic Inst (MA)

OPTOMETRIC/OPHTHALMIC LABORATORY TECHNICIAN
Louisiana State U Health Sciences Center (LA)

ORGANIC CHEMISTRY
Florida State U (FL)
McGill U (PQ, Canada)
The U of Scranton (PA)

ORGANIZATIONAL BEHAVIOR
Boston U (MA)
Bridgewater Coll (VA)
Brown U (RI)
Denison U (OH)
Loyola U New Orleans (LA)
Memorial U of Newfoundland (NF, Canada)
Miami U (OH)
Mid-Continent Coll (KY)
Missouri Baptist Coll (MO)
Northern Kentucky U (KY)
Northwestern Coll (MN)
Oakland City U (IN)
Philander Smith Coll (AR)
St. Ambrose U (IA)
Saint Louis U (MO)
Southern Methodist U (TX)
Thomas Edison State Coll (NJ)
U Coll of Cape Breton (NS, Canada)
U of Houston (TX)
U of La Verne (CA)
U of North Texas (TX)
U of Pennsylvania (PA)
Wayne State U (MI)
York U (ON, Canada)

ORGANIZATIONAL PSYCHOLOGY
Abilene Christian U (TX)
Averett Coll (VA)
Bridgewater State Coll (MA)
California State U, Hayward (CA)
Clarkson U (NY)
Fitchburg State Coll (MA)
Georgia Inst of Technology (GA)
Husson Coll (ME)
Ithaca Coll (NY)
Lincoln U (PA)
Maryville U of Saint Louis (MO)
Middle Tennessee State U (TN)
Moravian Coll (PA)
Pine Manor Coll (MA)
Point Loma Nazarene U (CA)
Saint Louis U (MO)
Saint Xavier U (IL)
U of Wisconsin–Parkside (WI)

ORNAMENTAL HORTICULTURE
Auburn U (AL)
California Polytechnic State U, San Luis Obispo (CA)
California State Polytechnic U, Pomona (CA)
California State U, Fresno (CA)
Cornell U (NY)
Delaware Valley Coll (PA)
Eastern Kentucky U (KY)
Florida A&M U (FL)
Florida Southern Coll (FL)
Fort Valley State U (GA)
Iowa State U of Science and Technology (IA)
Long Island U, Southampton Coll, Friends World Program (NY)
The Ohio State U (OH)
U of Arkansas (AR)
U of Delaware (DE)
U of Illinois at Urbana–Champaign (IL)
The U of Tennessee Knoxville (TN)
U of the District of Columbia (DC)

ORTHOTICS/PROSTHETICS
Florida International U (FL)
U of Washington (WA)

PACIFIC AREA STUDIES
Brigham Young U–Hawaii Campus (HI)

PAINTING
Adams State Coll (CO)
American Academy of Art (IL)
The Art Inst of Boston at Lesley (MA)
Atlanta Coll of Art (GA)
Barat Coll (IL)
Bard Coll (NY)
Barton Coll (NC)
Bellarmine Coll (KY)
Bethany Coll (KS)
Birmingham-Southern Coll (AL)
Boston U (MA)
Bowling Green State U (OH)
Brevard Coll (NC)
California Coll of Arts and Crafts (CA)
California State U, Hayward (CA)
California State U, Stanislaus (CA)
The Catholic U of America (DC)
Cleveland Inst of Art (OH)
Coll of Santa Fe (NM)
The Coll of Southeastern Europe, The American U of Athens (Greece)
Colorado State U (CO)
Columbus Coll of Art and Design (OH)
Concordia U (PQ, Canada)
Escuela de Artes Plasticas de Puerto Rico (PR)
Grace Coll (IN)
Harding U (AR)
Indiana Wesleyan U (IN)
Kansas City Art Inst (MO)
Kent State U (OH)
Lyme Academy of Fine Arts (CT)
Maharishi U of Management (IA)
Maine Coll of Art (ME)
Maryland Inst, Coll of Art (MD)
Massachusetts Coll of Art (MA)
McMurry U (TX)
Memorial U of Newfoundland (NF, Canada)
Memphis Coll of Art (TN)
Milwaukee Inst of Art and Design (WI)
Minneapolis Coll of Art and Design (MN)

Majors Index
Painting–Philosophy

Minnesota State U Moorhead (MN)
Nova Scotia Coll of Art and Design (NS, Canada)
The Ohio State U (OH)
Ohio U (OH)
Pacific Northwest Coll of Art (OR)
Paier Coll of Art, Inc. (CT)
Pine Manor Coll (MA)
Plymouth State Coll (NH)
Rivier Coll (NH)
Rocky Mountain Coll of Art & Design (CO)
Rutgers, State U of NJ, Mason Gross School of Arts (NJ)
Sam Houston State U (TX)
San Francisco Art Inst (CA)
Savannah Coll of Art and Design (GA)
School of Visual Arts (NY)
Seton Hill Coll (PA)
Shawnee State U (OH)
Simon's Rock Coll of Bard (MA)
State U of NY Coll at Brockport (NY)
Syracuse U (NY)
Texas Woman's U (TX)
Trinity Christian Coll (IL)
U of Connecticut (CT)
U of Dallas (TX)
U of Great Falls (MT)
U of Hartford (CT)
U of Houston (TX)
U of Illinois at Urbana–Champaign (IL)
The U of Iowa (IA)
U of Kansas (KS)
U of Massachusetts Dartmouth (MA)
U of Miami (FL)
U of Michigan (MI)
U of North Texas (TX)
U of Puerto Rico, Río Piedras (PR)
U of San Francisco (CA)
The U of Texas at Arlington (TX)
U of Washington (WA)
Virginia Commonwealth U (VA)
Washington U in St. Louis (MO)
Webster U (MO)
York U (ON, Canada)

PALEONTOLOGY
Bowling Green State U (OH)
Long Island U, Southampton Coll, Friends World Program (NY)
Mercyhurst Coll (PA)
South Dakota School of Mines and Technology (SD)
U of Alberta (AB, Canada)
U of Delaware (DE)
U of Toronto (ON, Canada)

PARALEGAL/LEGAL ASSISTANT
Anna Maria Coll (MA)
Avila Coll (MO)
Ball State U (IN)
Boston U (MA)
Brenau U (GA)
Calumet Coll of Saint Joseph (IN)
Calvary Bible Coll and Theological Seminary (MO)
Cedar Crest Coll (PA)
Champlain Coll (VT)
Coll of Mount St. Joseph (OH)
Coll of Our Lady of the Elms (MA)
Coll of Saint Mary (NE)
Concordia U Wisconsin (WI)
Davenport Coll of Business (MI)
Davenport Coll of Business, Kalamazoo Campus (MI)
David N. Myers Coll (OH)
Eastern Kentucky U (KY)
Gannon U (PA)
Georgia Coll and State U (GA)
Grand Valley State U (MI)
Hamline U (MN)
Hampton U (VA)
Hilbert Coll (NY)
Howard Payne U (TX)
Humphreys Coll (CA)
Husson Coll (ME)
International Coll (FL)
Johnson & Wales U (RI)
Jones Coll (FL)
Lake Erie Coll (OH)
Lake Superior State U (MI)
Lasell Coll (MA)
Madonna U (MI)
Marist Coll (NY)

Maryville U of Saint Louis (MO)
McMurry U (TX)
Mercy Coll (NY)
Midway Coll (KY)
Minnesota State U Moorhead (MN)
Mississippi Coll (MS)
Mississippi U for Women (MS)
Morehead State U (KY)
Nebraska Wesleyan U (NE)
New York City Tech Coll of the City U of NY (NY)
Notre Dame Coll (NH)
Notre Dame Coll of Ohio (OH)
Peirce Coll (PA)
Quinnipiac U (CT)
Rivier Coll (NH)
Robert Morris Coll (IL)
Roger Williams U (RI)
St. John's U (NY)
Saint Mary-of-the-Woods Coll (IN)
Southern Illinois U Carbondale (IL)
Stephen F. Austin State U (TX)
Suffolk U (MA)
Teikyo Post U (CT)
Texas Woman's U (TX)
Thomas Edison State Coll (NJ)
U of Central Florida (FL)
U of Great Falls (MT)
U of La Verne (CA)
U of Maryland University Coll (MD)
U of Nebraska at Omaha (NE)
U of St. Thomas (MN)
U of San Diego (CA)
U of Southern Mississippi (MS)
The U of Tennessee at Chattanooga (TN)
U of West Florida (FL)
U of West Los Angeles (CA)
U of Wisconsin–Superior (WI)
Valdosta State U (GA)
Villa Julie Coll (MD)
Virginia Intermont Coll (VA)
Wesley Coll (DE)
William Woods U (MO)
Winona State U (MN)

PASTORAL COUNSELING
Abilene Christian U (TX)
Alaska Bible Coll (AK)
American Indian Coll of the Assemblies of God, Inc (AZ)
Barclay Coll (KS)
Belhaven Coll (MS)
Bellarmine Coll (KY)
Belmont U (TN)
Bethany Coll of the Assemblies of God (CA)
Bethesda Christian U (CA)
Biola U (CA)
Boise Bible Coll (ID)
Brescia U (KY)
Briercrest Bible Coll (SK, Canada)
Calvary Bible Coll and Theological Seminary (MO)
Campbellsville U (KY)
Cedarville Coll (OH)
Central Bible Coll (MO)
Central Christian Coll of Kansas (KS)
Coll Dominicain de Philosophie et de Théologie (ON, Canada)
Coll of Mount St. Joseph (OH)
Colorado Christian U (CO)
Columbia International U (SC)
Concordia U (IL)
Concordia U (NE)
Concordia U at St. Paul (MN)
Concordia U Wisconsin (WI)
Cornerstone U (MI)
Crown Coll (MN)
Dallas Baptist U (TX)
Dordt Coll (IA)
Eastern Mennonite U (VA)
Eastern Nazarene Coll (MA)
East Texas Baptist U (TX)
Emmanuel Coll (GA)
Eugene Bible Coll (OR)
Faith Baptist Bible Coll and Theological Seminary (IA)
Faulkner U (AL)
Florida Baptist Theological Coll (FL)
Fresno Pacific U (CA)
George Fox U (OR)
Global U of the Assemblies of God (MO)
God's Bible School and Coll (OH)

Grace Bible Coll (MI)
Grace Coll (IN)
Greenville Coll (IL)
Hannibal-LaGrange Coll (MO)
Hardin-Simmons U (TX)
Hebrew Theological Coll (IL)
Houghton Coll (NY)
Huntington Coll (AL)
Indiana Wesleyan U (IN)
John Brown U (AR)
John Wesley Coll (NC)
Kentucky Christian Coll (KY)
LaGrange Coll (GA)
Lee U (TN)
Lenoir-Rhyne Coll (NC)
LIFE Bible Coll (CA)
Loras Coll (IA)
Madonna U (MI)
Malone Coll (OH)
Manhattan Christian Coll (KS)
Marylhurst U (OR)
Mercyhurst Coll (PA)
Milligan Coll (TN)
Morris Coll (SC)
Multnomah Bible Coll and Biblical Seminary (OR)
Nazarene Bible Coll (CO)
Nebraska Christian Coll (NE)
Newman U (KS)
North Central U (MN)
North Greenville Coll (SC)
Northwest Coll (WA)
Northwestern Coll (MN)
Northwest Nazarene U (ID)
Notre Dame Coll of Ohio (OH)
Nyack Coll (NY)
Oklahoma Baptist U (OK)
Oklahoma Christian U of Science and Arts (OK)
Ouachita Baptist U (AR)
Pacific Union Coll (CA)
Patten Coll (CA)
Providence Coll (RI)
Providence Coll and Theological Seminary (MB, Canada)
Redeemer Coll (ON, Canada)
Reformed Bible Coll (MI)
Roberts Wesleyan Coll (NY)
Rochester Coll (MI)
Rocky Mountain Coll (AB, Canada)
Saint Francis Coll (PA)
Saint Mary-of-the-Woods Coll (IN)
Saint Mary's Coll (MI)
Saint Mary's U of Minnesota (MN)
St. Thomas U (FL)
San Jose Christian Coll (CA)
Simpson Coll and Graduate School (CA)
Southeastern Coll of the Assemblies of God (FL)
Southwestern Assemblies of God U (TX)
Southwestern Coll of Christian Ministries (OK)
Spalding U (KY)
Tabor Coll (KS)
Taylor U, Fort Wayne Campus (IN)
Toccoa Falls Coll (GA)
Trinity Baptist Coll (FL)
Trinity Bible Coll (ND)
Trinity Coll of Florida (FL)
Trinity Lutheran Coll (WA)
Tyndale Coll & Seminary (ON, Canada)
Union Coll (KY)
Union Coll (NE)
Universidad Adventista de las Antillas (PR)
U of St. Thomas (TX)
U of Sioux Falls (SD)
Vanguard U of Southern California (CA)
Walsh U (OH)
Warner Pacific Coll (OR)
Western Baptist Coll (OR)
Williams Baptist Coll (AR)
William Tyndale Coll (MI)

PATHOLOGY
U of Connecticut (CT)

PEACE AND CONFLICT STUDIES
American U (DC)
Antioch Coll (OH)
Bluffton Coll (OH)
Briar Cliff Coll (IA)
Chapman U (CA)

Clark U (MA)
Colgate U (NY)
Coll of Saint Benedict (MN)
Coll of the Holy Cross (MA)
DePauw U (IN)
Earlham Coll (IN)
Eastern Mennonite U (VA)
Elizabethtown Coll (PA)
Fordham U (NY)
Goddard Coll (VT)
Goshen Coll (IN)
Guilford Coll (NC)
Hampshire Coll (MA)
Haverford Coll (PA)
Juniata Coll (PA)
Kent State U (OH)
Long Island U, Southampton Coll, Friends World Program (NY)
Manchester Coll (IN)
Manhattan Coll (NY)
Molloy Coll (NY)
Mount Saint Vincent U (NS, Canada)
Northland Coll (WI)
The Ohio State U (OH)
Rocky Mountain Coll (MT)
Saint John's U (MN)
U of Calif, Berkeley (CA)
The U of North Carolina at Chapel Hill (NC)
U of Pennsylvania (PA)
U of St. Thomas (MN)
The U of Winnipeg (MB, Canada)
U of Wisconsin–Milwaukee (WI)
Wayne State U (MI)
Wellesley Coll (MA)
Whitworth Coll (WA)

PERFUSION TECHNOLOGY
Duquesne U (PA)
MCP Hahnemann U (PA)
Medical U of South Carolina (SC)
Rush U (IL)
State U of New York Upstate Medical University (NY)
Thomas Edison State Coll (NJ)

PETROLEUM ENGINEERING
California State Polytechnic U, Pomona (CA)
Colorado School of Mines (CO)
Louisiana State U and A&M Coll (LA)
Marietta Coll (OH)
Montana Tech of The U of Montana (MT)
New Mexico Inst of Mining and Technology (NM)
Penn State U Univ Park Campus (PA)
Stanford U (CA)
Texas A&M U (TX)
Texas A&M U–Kingsville (TX)
Texas Tech U (TX)
U of Alaska Fairbanks (AK)
U of Alberta (AB, Canada)
U of Calif, Berkeley (CA)
U of Kansas (KS)
U of Louisiana at Lafayette (LA)
U of Missouri–Rolla (MO)
U of Oklahoma (OK)
U of Pittsburgh at Bradford (PA)
U of Regina (SK, Canada)
U of Southern California (CA)
The U of Texas at Austin (TX)
U of Toronto (ON, Canada)
U of Tulsa (OK)
West Virginia U (WV)

PETROLEUM TECHNOLOGY
Mercyhurst Coll (PA)
Nicholls State U (LA)
Texas Tech U (TX)
U Coll of Cape Breton (NS, Canada)

PHARMACOLOGY
Belmont U (TN)
State U of NY at Stony Brook (NY)
U of Alberta (AB, Canada)
U of British Columbia (BC, Canada)
U of Calif, Santa Barbara (CA)
U of Cincinnati (OH)
U of the Sciences in Philadelphia (PA)
U of Toronto (ON, Canada)

The U of Western Ontario (ON, Canada)
U of Wisconsin–Madison (WI)

(PRE)PHARMACY STUDIES
Abilene Christian U (TX)
Adams State Coll (CO)
Ashland U (OH)
Barry U (FL)
Barton Coll (NC)
Bellarmine Coll (KY)
Belmont Abbey Coll (NC)
Blue Mountain Coll (MS)
Brevard Coll (NC)
Carroll Coll (MT)
Central Missouri State U (MO)
Christian Brothers U (TN)
Coll of Saint Benedict (MN)
Coll of the Ozarks (MO)
Cumberland Coll (KY)
Elmhurst Coll (IL)
Florida State U (FL)
Freed-Hardeman U (TN)
Holy Family Coll (PA)
Juniata Coll (PA)
Kent State U (OH)
King Coll (TN)
King's Coll (PA)
Le Moyne Coll (NY)
Long Island U, C.W. Post Campus (NY)
Mayville State U (ND)
McPherson Coll (KS)
Meredith Coll (NC)
Missouri Southern State Coll (MO)
Mount Allison U (NB, Canada)
The Ohio State U (OH)
Oklahoma Baptist U (OK)
Roberts Wesleyan Coll (NY)
Saint John's U (MN)
Saint Martin's Coll (WA)
Saint Mary-of-the-Woods Coll (IN)
Saint Xavier U (IL)
Samford U (AL)
Tennessee Wesleyan Coll (TN)
Union U (TN)
The U of Akron (OH)
The U of Iowa (IA)
U of Kansas (KS)
U of Mary Hardin-Baylor (TX)
U of Miami (FL)
U of Minnesota, Duluth (MN)
U of Minnesota, Morris (MN)
The U of Montana–Missoula (MT)
U of Nebraska–Lincoln (NE)
U of Nevada, Reno (NV)
The U of Tennessee at Martin (TN)
U of Wisconsin–Parkside (WI)
U of Wisconsin–River Falls (WI)
Valley City State U (ND)
Washington U in St. Louis (MO)
Westmont Coll (CA)
York U (ON, Canada)

PHARMACY ADMINISTRATION AND PHARMACEUTICS
Drake U (IA)
State U of NY at Buffalo (NY)

PHARMACY TECHNICIAN/ASSISTANT
The U of Montana–Missoula (MT)

PHILOSOPHY
Acadia U (NS, Canada)
Adelphi U (NY)
Agnes Scott Coll (GA)
Albertson Coll of Idaho (ID)
Albion Coll (MI)
Albright Coll (PA)
Alfred U (NY)
Allegheny Coll (PA)
Alma Coll (MI)
Alvernia Coll (PA)
Alverno Coll (WI)
American International Coll (MA)
American U (DC)
American U in Cairo (Egypt)
Amherst Coll (MA)
Anderson U (IN)
Antioch Coll (OH)
Aquinas Coll (MI)
Arizona State U (AZ)
Arkansas State U (AR)
Asbury Coll (KY)
Ashland U (OH)
Assumption Coll (MA)

Majors Index
Philosophy

Athens State U (AL)
Auburn U (AL)
Augsburg Coll (MN)
Augustana Coll (IL)
Augustana Coll (SD)
Austin Coll (TX)
Austin Peay State U (TN)
Azusa Pacific U (CA)
Baker U (KS)
Baldwin-Wallace Coll (OH)
Ball State U (IN)
Bard Coll (NY)
Barnard Coll (NY)
Barry U (FL)
Barton Coll (NC)
Bates Coll (ME)
Bayamón Central U (PR)
Baylor U (TX)
Beaver Coll (PA)
Belhaven Coll (MS)
Bellarmine Coll (KY)
Bellevue U (NE)
Belmont Abbey Coll (NC)
Belmont U (TN)
Beloit Coll (WI)
Bemidji State U (MN)
Benedictine Coll (KS)
Benedictine U (IL)
Bennington Coll (VT)
Bentley Coll (MA)
Berea Coll (KY)
Baruch Coll of the City U of NY (NY)
Berry Coll (GA)
Bethany Coll (KS)
Bethany Coll (WV)
Bethel Coll (IN)
Bethel Coll (MN)
Biola U (CA)
Birmingham-Southern Coll (AL)
Bishop's U (PQ, Canada)
Bloomfield Coll (NJ)
Bloomsburg U of Pennsylvania (PA)
Bluffton Coll (OH)
Boise State U (ID)
Boston Coll (MA)
Boston U (MA)
Bowdoin Coll (ME)
Bowie State U (MD)
Bowling Green State U (OH)
Bradley U (IL)
Brandeis U (MA)
Brandon U (MB, Canada)
Brevard Coll (NC)
Bridgewater Coll (VA)
Bridgewater State Coll (MA)
Brigham Young U (UT)
Brock U (ON, Canada)
Brooklyn Coll of the City U of NY (NY)
Brown U (RI)
Bryn Mawr Coll (PA)
Bucknell U (PA)
Buena Vista U (IA)
Butler U (IN)
Cabrini Coll (PA)
California Baptist U (CA)
California Lutheran U (CA)
California Polytechnic State U, San Luis Obispo (CA)
California State Polytechnic U, Pomona (CA)
California State U, Chico (CA)
California State U, Dominguez Hills (CA)
California State U, Fresno (CA)
California State U, Fullerton (CA)
California State U, Hayward (CA)
California State U, Long Beach (CA)
California State U, Los Angeles (CA)
California State U, Northridge (CA)
California State U, Sacramento (CA)
California State U, San Bernardino (CA)
California State U, Stanislaus (CA)
California U of Pennsylvania (PA)
Calvin Coll (MI)
Canisius Coll (NY)
Capital U (OH)
Carleton Coll (MN)
Carleton U (ON, Canada)
Carlow Coll (PA)
Carnegie Mellon U (PA)

Carroll Coll (MT)
Carson-Newman Coll (TN)
Carthage Coll (WI)
Case Western Reserve U (OH)
Catawba Coll (NC)
The Catholic U of America (DC)
Cedar Crest Coll (PA)
Cedarville Coll (OH)
Centenary Coll of Louisiana (LA)
Central Coll (IA)
Central Connecticut State U (CT)
Central Methodist Coll (MO)
Central Michigan U (MI)
Centre Coll (KY)
Chaminade U of Honolulu (HI)
Chapman U (CA)
Chatham Coll (PA)
Christendom Coll (VA)
Christopher Newport U (VA)
City Coll of the City U of NY (NY)
City U (WA)
Claremont McKenna Coll (CA)
Clarion U of Pennsylvania (PA)
Clark Atlanta U (GA)
Clarke Coll (IA)
Clark U (MA)
Clemson U (SC)
Cleveland State U (OH)
Coe Coll (IA)
Colby Coll (ME)
Colgate U (NY)
Coll Dominicain de Philosophie et de Théologie (ON, Canada)
Coll Misericordia (PA)
Coll of Charleston (SC)
Coll of Mount Saint Vincent (NY)
The Coll of New Jersey (NJ)
The Coll of New Rochelle (NY)
Coll of Notre Dame (CA)
Coll of Saint Benedict (MN)
Coll of St. Catherine (MN)
Coll of Saint Elizabeth (NJ)
The Coll of Southeastern Europe, The American U of Athens (Greece)
Coll of Staten Island of the City U of NY (NY)
Coll of the Atlantic (ME)
Coll of the Holy Cross (MA)
Coll of the Ozarks (MO)
The Coll of William and Mary (VA)
The Coll of Wooster (OH)
The Colorado Coll (CO)
Colorado State U (CO)
Columbia Coll (NY)
Columbia U, School of General Studies (NY)
Concordia Coll (MN)
Concordia U (IL)
Concordia U (PQ, Canada)
Concordia U Coll of Alberta (AB, Canada)
Connecticut Coll (CT)
Coppin State Coll (MD)
Cornell Coll (IA)
Cornell U (NY)
Covenant Coll (GA)
Creighton U (NE)
Curry Coll (MA)
Dakota Wesleyan U (SD)
Dalhousie U (NS, Canada)
Dallas Baptist U (TX)
Dartmouth Coll (NH)
David Lipscomb U (TN)
Davidson Coll (NC)
Denison U (OH)
DePaul U (IL)
DePauw U (IN)
Deree Coll (Greece)
Dickinson Coll (PA)
Doane Coll (NE)
Dominican U (IL)
Dordt Coll (IA)
Drake U (IA)
Drew U (NJ)
Drexel U (PA)
Drury U (MO)
Duke U (NC)
Duquesne U (PA)
D'Youville Coll (NY)
Earlham Coll (IN)
East Carolina U (NC)
Eastern Coll (PA)
Eastern Illinois U (IL)
Eastern Kentucky U (KY)
Eastern Michigan U (MI)
Eastern Washington U (WA)

East Stroudsburg U of Pennsylvania (PA)
East Tennessee State U (TN)
Eckerd Coll (FL)
Edinboro U of Pennsylvania (PA)
Elizabethtown Coll (PA)
Elmhurst Coll (IL)
Elmira Coll (NY)
Elon Coll (NC)
Emory & Henry Coll (VA)
Emory U (GA)
Eugene Lang Coll, New School U (NY)
The Evergreen State Coll (WA)
Fairfield U (CT)
Fairleigh Dickinson U, Florham-Madison Campus (NJ)
Fairleigh Dickinson U, Teaneck-Hackensack Campus (NJ)
Felician Coll (NJ)
Ferrum Coll (VA)
Fisk U (TN)
Flagler Coll (FL)
Florida A&M U (FL)
Florida Atlantic U (FL)
Florida International U (FL)
Florida State U (FL)
Fordham U (NY)
Fort Hays State U (KS)
Fort Lewis Coll (CO)
Franciscan U of Steubenville (OH)
Franklin and Marshall Coll (PA)
Franklin Coll of Indiana (IN)
Freed-Hardeman U (TN)
Friends U (KS)
Frostburg State U (MD)
Furman U (SC)
Gallaudet U (DC)
Gannon U (PA)
Geneva Coll (PA)
George Mason U (VA)
Georgetown Coll (KY)
Georgetown U (DC)
The George Washington U (DC)
Georgia Southern U (GA)
Georgia State U (GA)
Gettysburg Coll (PA)
Goddard Coll (VT)
Gonzaga U (WA)
Gordon Coll (MA)
Goucher Coll (MD)
Grand Valley State U (MI)
Greenville Coll (IL)
Grinnell Coll (IA)
Grove City Coll (PA)
Guilford Coll (NC)
Gustavus Adolphus Coll (MN)
Hamilton Coll (NY)
Hamline U (MN)
Hampden-Sydney Coll (VA)
Hampshire Coll (MA)
Hanover Coll (IN)
Hardin-Simmons U (TX)
Hartwick Coll (NY)
Harvard U (MA)
Hastings Coll (NE)
Haverford Coll (PA)
Heidelberg Coll (OH)
Hendrix Coll (AR)
High Point U (NC)
Hillsdale Coll (MI)
Hiram Coll (OH)
Hobart and William Smith Colls (NY)
Hofstra U (NY)
Hollins U (VA)
Hood Coll (MD)
Hope Coll (MI)
Houghton Coll (NY)
Howard Payne U (TX)
Howard U (DC)
Humboldt State U (CA)
Hunter Coll of the City U of NY (NY)
Huntingdon Coll (AL)
Huntington Coll (IN)
Idaho State U (ID)
Illinois Coll (IL)
Illinois State U (IL)
Illinois Wesleyan U (IL)
Indiana U Bloomington (IN)
Indiana U Northwest (IN)
Indiana U of Pennsylvania (PA)
Indiana U–Purdue U Fort Wayne (IN)

Indiana U–Purdue U Indianapolis (IN)
Indiana U South Bend (IN)
Indiana U Southeast (IN)
Indiana Wesleyan U (IN)
Iona Coll (NY)
Iowa State U of Science and Technology (IA)
Ithaca Coll (NY)
Jacksonville U (FL)
James Madison U (VA)
Jamestown Coll (ND)
Jewish Theological Seminary of America (NY)
John Carroll U (OH)
Johns Hopkins U (MD)
Judson Coll (IL)
Kalamazoo Coll (MI)
Kansas State U (KS)
Kean U (NJ)
Kent State U (OH)
Kentucky Wesleyan Coll (KY)
Kenyon Coll (OH)
King's Coll (PA)
The King's U Coll (AB, Canada)
Knox Coll (IL)
Kutztown U of Pennsylvania (PA)
Lafayette Coll (PA)
Lake Forest Coll (IL)
Lakehead U (ON, Canada)
Lakeland Coll (WI)
La Salle U (PA)
Lawrence U (WI)
Lebanon Valley Coll (PA)
Lehigh U (PA)
Lehman Coll of the City U of NY (NY)
Le Moyne Coll (NY)
Lenoir-Rhyne Coll (NC)
Lewis & Clark Coll (OR)
Lewis U (IL)
Lincoln U (MO)
Lincoln U (PA)
Linfield Coll (OR)
Lock Haven U of Pennsylvania (PA)
Long Island U, Brooklyn Campus (NY)
Long Island U, C.W. Post Campus (NY)
Long Island U, Southampton Coll, Friends World Program (NY)
Longwood Coll (VA)
Loras Coll (IA)
Louisiana Coll (LA)
Louisiana State U and A&M Coll (LA)
Loyola Coll in Maryland (MD)
Loyola Marymount U (CA)
Loyola U Chicago (IL)
Loyola U New Orleans (LA)
Luther Coll (IA)
Lycoming Coll (PA)
Lynchburg Coll (VA)
Lyon Coll (AR)
Macalester Coll (MN)
MacMurray Coll (IL)
Manchester Coll (IN)
Manhattan Coll (NY)
Manhattanville Coll (NY)
Mansfield U of Pennsylvania (PA)
Marian Coll (IN)
Marietta Coll (OH)
Marlboro Coll (VT)
Marquette U (WI)
Mary Baldwin Coll (VA)
Maryville U of Saint Louis (MO)
Mary Washington Coll (VA)
Massachusetts Coll of Liberal Arts (MA)
Massachusetts Inst of Technology (MA)
McGill U (PQ, Canada)
McKendree Coll (IL)
McMurry U (TX)
McPherson Coll (KS)
Memorial U of Newfoundland (NF, Canada)
Mercer U (GA)
Mercyhurst Coll (PA)
Merrimack Coll (MA)
Messiah Coll (PA)
Metropolitan State Coll of Denver (CO)
Metropolitan State U (MN)
Miami U (OH)
Michigan State U (MI)

Middlebury Coll (VT)
Middle Tennessee State U (TN)
Millersville U of Pennsylvania (PA)
Millikin U (IL)
Millsaps Coll (MS)
Mills Coll (CA)
Minnesota State U, Mankato (MN)
Minnesota State U Moorhead (MN)
Mississippi State U (MS)
Missouri Valley Coll (MO)
Molloy Coll (NY)
Monmouth Coll (IL)
Montana State U–Bozeman (MT)
Moravian Coll (PA)
Morehead State U (KY)
Morehouse Coll (GA)
Morgan State U (MD)
Morningside Coll (IA)
Mount Allison U (NB, Canada)
Mount Holyoke Coll (MA)
Mount Mary Coll (WI)
Mount St. Mary's Coll (CA)
Mount Saint Mary's Coll and Seminary (MD)
Mount Saint Vincent U (NS, Canada)
Mount Union Coll (OH)
Mount Vernon Nazarene Coll (OH)
Muhlenberg Coll (PA)
Murray State U (KY)
Muskingum Coll (OH)
Nazareth Coll of Rochester (NY)
Nebraska Wesleyan U (NE)
Newberry Coll (SC)
New Coll of the U of South Florida (FL)
New England Coll (NH)
New Jersey City U (NJ)
New Mexico State U (NM)
New York U (NY)
Niagara U (NY)
Nipissing U (ON, Canada)
North Carolina State U (NC)
North Carolina Wesleyan Coll (NC)
North Central Coll (IL)
Northeastern Illinois U (IL)
Northeastern U (MA)
Northern Arizona U (AZ)
Northern Illinois U (IL)
Northern Kentucky U (KY)
Northern Michigan U (MI)
Northland Coll (WI)
North Park U (IL)
Northwest Coll (WA)
Northwestern Coll (IA)
Northwestern U (IL)
Northwest Missouri State U (MO)
Northwest Nazarene U (ID)
Nyack Coll (NY)
Oakland U (MI)
Oberlin Coll (OH)
Occidental Coll (CA)
Oglethorpe U (GA)
Ohio Dominican Coll (OH)
Ohio Northern U (OH)
The Ohio State U (OH)
Ohio U (OH)
Ohio Wesleyan U (OH)
Okanagan U Coll (BC, Canada)
Oklahoma Baptist U (OK)
Oklahoma City U (OK)
Oklahoma State U (OK)
Old Dominion U (VA)
Olivet Nazarene U (IL)
Open Learning Agency (BC, Canada)
Oregon State U (OR)
Otterbein Coll (OH)
Ouachita Baptist U (AR)
Our Lady of the Lake U of San Antonio (TX)
Pacific Lutheran U (WA)
Pacific U (OR)
Paine Coll (GA)
Palm Beach Atlantic Coll (FL)
Penn State U Univ Park Campus (PA)
Pepperdine U, Malibu (CA)
Piedmont Coll (GA)
Pitzer Coll (CA)
Plattsburgh State U of NY (NY)
Plymouth State Coll (NH)
Point Loma Nazarene U (CA)
Pomona Coll (CA)
Pontifical Catholic U of Puerto Rico (PR)
Portland State U (OR)

Majors Index
Philosophy–Photography

Presbyterian Coll (SC)
Princeton U (NJ)
Principia Coll (IL)
Providence Coll (RI)
Purchase Coll, State U of NY (NY)
Purdue U (IN)
Purdue U Calumet (IN)
Queens Coll (NC)
Queens Coll of the City U of NY (NY)
Queen's U at Kingston (ON, Canada)
Quincy U (IL)
Radford U (VA)
Randolph-Macon Coll (VA)
Randolph-Macon Woman's Coll (VA)
Redeemer Coll (ON, Canada)
Reed Coll (OR)
Regents Coll (NY)
Regis U (CO)
Rensselaer Polytechnic Inst (NY)
Rhodes Coll (TN)
Rice U (TX)
The Richard Stockton Coll of New Jersey (NJ)
Rider U (NJ)
Ripon Coll (WI)
Roanoke Coll (VA)
Roberts Wesleyan Coll (NY)
Rockford Coll (IL)
Rockhurst U (MO)
Rocky Mountain Coll (MT)
Roger Williams U (RI)
Rollins Coll (FL)
Rosemont Coll (PA)
Rutgers, State U of NJ, Camden Coll of Arts & Scis (NJ)
Rutgers, State U of NJ, Douglass Coll (NJ)
Rutgers, State U of NJ, Livingston Coll (NJ)
Rutgers, State U of NJ, Newark Coll of Arts & Scis (NJ)
Rutgers, State U of NJ, Rutgers Coll (NJ)
Rutgers, State U of NJ, U Coll–Camden (NJ)
Rutgers, State U of NJ, U Coll–Newark (NJ)
Rutgers, State U of NJ, U Coll–New Brunswick (NJ)
Sacred Heart Major Seminary (MI)
Sacred Heart U (CT)
St. Ambrose U (IA)
St. Andrews Presbyterian Coll (NC)
Saint Anselm Coll (NH)
St. Bonaventure U (NY)
St. Charles Borromeo Seminary, Overbrook (PA)
St. Cloud State U (MN)
St. Edward's U (TX)
St. Francis Coll (NY)
Saint Francis Coll (PA)
St. Francis Xavier U (NS, Canada)
St. John Fisher Coll (NY)
St. John's Seminary Coll (CA)
Saint John's Seminary Coll of Liberal Arts (MA)
Saint John's U (MN)
St. John's U (NY)
Saint Joseph Coll (CT)
Saint Joseph's Coll (IN)
Saint Joseph's Coll (ME)
Saint Joseph's U (PA)
St. Lawrence U (NY)
Saint Louis U (MO)
Saint Mary's Coll (IN)
Saint Mary's Coll (MI)
Saint Mary's Coll of California (CA)
St. Mary's Coll of Maryland (MD)
Saint Mary's U (NS, Canada)
Saint Mary's U of Minnesota (MN)
St. Mary's U of San Antonio (TX)
Saint Michael's Coll (VT)
St. Norbert Coll (WI)
St. Olaf Coll (MN)
Saint Paul U (ON, Canada)
Saint Peter's Coll (NJ)
Saint Vincent Coll (PA)
Saint Xavier U (IL)
Salem Coll (NC)
Salisbury State U (MD)
Salve Regina U (RI)
Samford U (AL)
Sam Houston State U (TX)
San Diego State U (CA)

San Francisco State U (CA)
San Jose State U (CA)
Santa Clara U (CA)
Sarah Lawrence Coll (NY)
Schreiner Coll (TX)
Scripps Coll (CA)
Seattle Pacific U (WA)
Seattle U (WA)
Seton Hall U (NJ)
Seton Hill Coll (PA)
Shaw U (NC)
Siena Coll (NY)
Siena Heights U (MI)
Simmons Coll (MA)
Simon Fraser U (BC, Canada)
Simon's Rock Coll of Bard (MA)
Simpson Coll (IA)
Skidmore Coll (NY)
Slippery Rock U of Pennsylvania (PA)
Smith Coll (MA)
Sonoma State U (CA)
Southeast Missouri State U (MO)
Southern Illinois U Carbondale (IL)
Southern Illinois U Edwardsville (IL)
Southern Methodist U (TX)
Southwestern U (TX)
Southwest Missouri State U (MO)
Southwest State U (MN)
Southwest Texas State U (TX)
Spalding U (KY)
Spelman Coll (GA)
Spring Arbor Coll (MI)
Spring Hill Coll (AL)
Stanford U (CA)
State U of NY at Albany (NY)
State U of NY at Binghamton (NY)
State U of NY at Buffalo (NY)
State U of NY at New Paltz (NY)
State U of NY at Oswego (NY)
State U of NY at Stony Brook (NY)
State U of NY Coll at Brockport (NY)
State U of NY Coll at Buffalo (NY)
State U of NY Coll at Cortland (NY)
State U of NY Coll at Fredonia (NY)
State U of NY Coll at Geneseo (NY)
State U of NY Coll at Old Westbury (NY)
State U of NY Coll at Oneonta (NY)
State U of NY Coll at Potsdam (NY)
State U of West Georgia (GA)
Stephens Coll (MO)
Sterling Coll (KS)
Stetson U (FL)
Stevens Inst of Technology (NJ)
Stillman Coll (AL)
Stonehill Coll (MA)
Suffolk U (MA)
Susquehanna U (PA)
Swarthmore Coll (PA)
Sweet Briar Coll (VA)
Syracuse U (NY)
Tabor Coll (KS)
Taylor U (IN)
Temple U (PA)
Texas A&M U (TX)
Texas Christian U (TX)
Texas Lutheran U (TX)
Texas Tech U (TX)
Thiel Coll (PA)
Thomas Edison State Coll (NJ)
Thomas More Coll (KY)
Thomas More Coll of Liberal Arts (NH)
Toccoa Falls Coll (GA)
Touro Coll (NY)
Towson U (MD)
Transylvania U (KY)
Trent U (ON, Canada)
Trinity Christian Coll (IL)
Trinity Coll (CT)
Trinity U (TX)
Trinity Western U (BC, Canada)
Truman State U (MO)
Tufts U (MA)
Tulane U (LA)
Union Coll (NY)
Union U (TN)
United States Military Academy (NY)
Université de Montréal (PQ, Canada)

Université de Sherbrooke (PQ, Canada)
U du Québec à Trois-Rivières (PQ, Canada)
Université Laval (PQ, Canada)
U Coll of Cape Breton (NS, Canada)
The U of Akron (OH)
The U of Alabama (AL)
The U of Alabama at Birmingham (AL)
The U of Alabama in Huntsville (AL)
U of Alaska Fairbanks (AK)
U of Alberta (AB, Canada)
The U of Arizona (AZ)
U of Arkansas (AR)
U of Arkansas at Little Rock (AR)
U of British Columbia (BC, Canada)
U of Calgary (AB, Canada)
U of Calif, Berkeley (CA)
U of Calif, Davis (CA)
U of Calif, Irvine (CA)
U of Calif, Los Angeles (CA)
U of Calif, Riverside (CA)
U of Calif, San Diego (CA)
U of Calif, Santa Barbara (CA)
U of Calif, Santa Cruz (CA)
U of Central Arkansas (AR)
U of Central Florida (FL)
U of Central Oklahoma (OK)
U of Charleston (WV)
U of Chicago (IL)
U of Cincinnati (OH)
U of Colorado at Boulder (CO)
U of Colorado at Colorado Springs (CO)
U of Colorado at Denver (CO)
U of Connecticut (CT)
U of Dallas (TX)
U of Dayton (OH)
U of Delaware (DE)
U of Denver (CO)
U of Detroit Mercy (MI)
U of Dubuque (IA)
U of Evansville (IN)
The U of Findlay (OH)
U of Florida (FL)
U of Georgia (GA)
U of Guelph (ON, Canada)
U of Hartford (CT)
U of Hawaii at Manoa (HI)
U of Houston (TX)
U of Idaho (ID)
U of Illinois at Chicago (IL)
U of Illinois at Urbana–Champaign (IL)
U of Indianapolis (IN)
The U of Iowa (IA)
U of Kansas (KS)
U of Kentucky (KY)
U of King's Coll (NS, Canada)
U of La Verne (CA)
The U of Lethbridge (AB, Canada)
U of Louisiana at Lafayette (LA)
U of Louisville (KY)
U of Maine (ME)
U of Maine at Farmington (ME)
U of Manitoba (MB, Canada)
U of Maryland, Baltimore County (MD)
U of Maryland, Coll Park (MD)
U of Massachusetts Amherst (MA)
U of Massachusetts Boston (MA)
U of Massachusetts Dartmouth (MA)
U of Massachusetts Lowell (MA)
The U of Memphis (TN)
U of Miami (FL)
U of Michigan (MI)
U of Michigan–Dearborn (MI)
U of Michigan–Flint (MI)
U of Minnesota, Duluth (MN)
U of Minnesota, Morris (MN)
U of Minnesota, Twin Cities Campus (MN)
U of Mississippi (MS)
U of Missouri–Columbia (MO)
U of Missouri–Kansas City (MO)
U of Missouri–Rolla (MO)
U of Missouri–St. Louis (MO)
The U of Montana–Missoula (MT)
U of Nebraska at Omaha (NE)
U of Nebraska–Lincoln (NE)
U of Nevada, Las Vegas (NV)
U of Nevada, Reno (NV)

U of New Brunswick, Fredericton (NB, Canada)
U of New Brunswick, Saint John (NB, Canada)
U of New Hampshire (NH)
U of New Haven (CT)
U of New Mexico (NM)
U of New Orleans (LA)
The U of North Carolina at Asheville (NC)
The U of North Carolina at Chapel Hill (NC)
The U of North Carolina at Charlotte (NC)
The U of North Carolina at Greensboro (NC)
The U of North Carolina at Pembroke (NC)
The U of North Carolina at Wilmington (NC)
U of North Dakota (ND)
U of Northern Colorado (CO)
U of Northern Iowa (IA)
U of North Florida (FL)
U of North Texas (TX)
U of Notre Dame (IN)
U of Oklahoma (OK)
U of Oregon (OR)
U of Pennsylvania (PA)
U of Pittsburgh (PA)
U of Portland (OR)
U of Prince Edward Island (PE, Canada)
U of Puerto Rico, Mayagüez Campus (PR)
U of Puerto Rico, Rio Piedras (PR)
U of Puget Sound (WA)
U of Redlands (CA)
U of Regina (SK, Canada)
U of Rhode Island (RI)
U of Richmond (VA)
U of Rochester (NY)
U of St. Thomas (MN)
U of St. Thomas (TX)
U of San Diego (CA)
U of San Francisco (CA)
The U of Scranton (PA)
U of Sioux Falls (SD)
U of South Alabama (AL)
U of South Carolina (SC)
U of South Dakota (SD)
U of Southern California (CA)
U of Southern Indiana (IN)
U of Southern Maine (ME)
U of Southern Mississippi (MS)
U of South Florida (FL)
The U of Tennessee at Chattanooga (TN)
The U of Tennessee at Martin (TN)
The U of Tennessee Knoxville (TN)
The U of Texas at Arlington (TX)
The U of Texas at Austin (TX)
The U of Texas at San Antonio (TX)
The U of Texas–Pan American (TX)
U of the District of Columbia (DC)
U of the Pacific (CA)
U of the South (TN)
U of Toronto (ON, Canada)
U of Tulsa (OK)
U of Utah (UT)
U of Vermont (VT)
U of Victoria (BC, Canada)
U of Virginia (VA)
U of Washington (WA)
U of Waterloo (ON, Canada)
The U of Western Ontario (ON, Canada)
U of West Florida (FL)
U of Windsor (ON, Canada)
The U of Winnipeg (MB, Canada)
U of Wisconsin–Eau Claire (WI)
U of Wisconsin–Green Bay (WI)
U of Wisconsin–La Crosse (WI)
U of Wisconsin–Madison (WI)
U of Wisconsin–Milwaukee (WI)
U of Wisconsin–Parkside (WI)
U of Wisconsin–Platteville (WI)
U of Wisconsin–Stevens Point (WI)
U of Wyoming (WY)
Urbana U (OH)
Ursinus Coll (PA)
Ursuline Coll (OH)
Utah State U (UT)
Utica Coll of Syracuse U (NY)
Valdosta State U (GA)
Valparaiso U (IN)

Vanderbilt U (TN)
Vassar Coll (NY)
Villanova U (PA)
Virginia Commonwealth U (VA)
Virginia Polytechnic Inst and State U (VA)
Virginia Wesleyan Coll (VA)
Wabash Coll (IN)
Wadhams Hall Seminary-Coll (NY)
Wake Forest U (NC)
Walla Walla Coll (WA)
Walsh U (OH)
Wartburg Coll (IA)
Washington & Jefferson Coll (PA)
Washington and Lee U (VA)
Washington Coll (MD)
Washington State U (WA)
Washington U in St. Louis (MO)
Wayne State U (MI)
Webster U (MO)
Wellesley Coll (MA)
Wells Coll (NY)
Wesleyan Coll (GA)
Wesleyan U (CT)
West Chester U of Pennsylvania (PA)
Western Carolina U (NC)
Western Illinois U (IL)
Western Kentucky U (KY)
Western Maryland Coll (MD)
Western Michigan U (MI)
Western Oregon U (OR)
Western Washington U (WA)
Westminster Coll (MO)
Westminster Coll (PA)
Westminster Coll (UT)
Westmont Coll (CA)
West Virginia U (WV)
West Virginia Wesleyan Coll (WV)
Wheaton Coll (IL)
Wheaton Coll (MA)
Wheeling Jesuit U (WV)
Whitman Coll (WA)
Whittier Coll (CA)
Whitworth Coll (WA)
Wichita State U (KS)
Wilfrid Laurier U (ON, Canada)
Wilkes U (PA)
Willamette U (OR)
William Jewell Coll (MO)
William Paterson U of New Jersey (NJ)
Williams Coll (MA)
Wilmington Coll (OH)
Wilson Coll (PA)
Wingate U (NC)
Winthrop U (SC)
Wittenberg U (OH)
Wofford Coll (SC)
Worcester Polytechnic Inst (MA)
Wright State U (OH)
Xavier U (OH)
Xavier U of Louisiana (LA)
Yale U (CT)
Yeshiva U (NY)
York Coll of the City U of New York (NY)
York U (ON, Canada)
Youngstown State U (OH)

PHOTOGRAPHIC TECHNOLOGY

Kent State U (OH)
Rochester Inst of Technology (NY)
Ryerson Polytechnic U (ON, Canada)

PHOTOGRAPHY

Academy of Art Coll (CA)
Adams State Coll (CO)
Alberta Coll of Art and Design (AB, Canada)
Alfred U (NY)
American InterContinental U (CA)
American InterContinental U, Atlanta (GA)
American InterContinental U, Atlanta (GA)
American InterContinental U (United Kingdom)
Andrews U (MI)
Arizona State U (AZ)
Art Academy of Cincinnati (OH)
Art Center Coll of Design (CA)
The Art Inst of Boston at Lesley (MA)
Atlanta Coll of Art (GA)
Ball State U (IN)

Majors Index
Photography–Physical Education

Barat Coll (IL)
Bard Coll (NY)
Barry U (FL)
Barton Coll (NC)
Beaver Coll (PA)
Bennington Coll (VT)
Bowling Green State U (OH)
Bradley U (IL)
Briar Cliff Coll (IA)
Brigham Young U (UT)
Brooks Inst of Photography (CA)
California Coll of Arts and Crafts (CA)
California Inst of the Arts (CA)
California State U, Fullerton (CA)
California State U, Hayward (CA)
California State U, Long Beach (CA)
California State U, Northridge (CA)
Carson-Newman Coll (TN)
Cazenovia Coll (NY)
Ctr for Creative Studies—Coll of Art and Design (MI)
Central Missouri State U (MO)
Cleveland Inst of Art (OH)
Coker Coll (SC)
Coll of Santa Fe (NM)
The Coll of Southeastern Europe, The American U of Athens (Greece)
Coll of Staten Island of the City U of NY (NY)
Coll of Visual Arts (MN)
Colorado State U (CO)
Columbia Coll (MO)
Columbia Coll Chicago (IL)
Columbus Coll of Art and Design (OH)
Concordia U (PQ, Canada)
The Corcoran Coll of Art and Design (DC)
Cornell U (NY)
Dominican U (IL)
Drexel U (PA)
The Evergreen State Coll (WA)
Fitchburg State Coll (MA)
Fordham U (NY)
Gallaudet U (DC)
Goddard Coll (VT)
Governors State U (IL)
Grand Valley State U (MI)
Hampshire Coll (MA)
Hampton U (VA)
Indiana U Bloomington (IN)
Indiana Wesleyan U (IN)
Inter American U of PR, San Germán Campus (PR)
Ithaca Coll (NY)
Kansas City Art Inst (MO)
Kent State U (OH)
Long Island U, C.W. Post Campus (NY)
Long Island U, Southampton Coll, Friends World Program (NY)
Louisiana Tech U (LA)
Maine Coll of Art (ME)
Marlboro Coll (VT)
Marshall U (WV)
Maryland Inst, Coll of Art (MD)
Massachusetts Coll of Art (MA)
McNeese State U (LA)
Memorial U of Newfoundland (NF, Canada)
Memphis Coll of Art (TN)
Milwaukee Inst of Art and Design (WI)
Minneapolis Coll of Art and Design (MN)
Montserrat Coll of Art (MA)
Moore Coll of Art and Design (PA)
Morningside Coll (IA)
Mount Allison U (NB, Canada)
Nazareth Coll of Rochester (NY)
New England Coll (NH)
New World School of the Arts (FL)
New York U (NY)
Northeastern U (MA)
Northern Michigan U (MI)
Nova Scotia Coll of Art and Design (NS, Canada)
The Ohio State U (OH)
Ohio U (OH)
Otis Coll of Art and Design (CA)
Pacific Northwest Coll of Art (OR)
Parsons School of Design, New School U (NY)
Pine Manor Coll (MA)

Pratt Inst (NY)
Rhode Island School of Design (RI)
Ringling School of Art and Design (FL)
Rivier Coll (NH)
Rochester Inst of Technology (NY)
Rutgers, State U of NJ, Mason Gross School of Arts (NJ)
Ryerson Polytechnic U (ON, Canada)
St. Edward's U (TX)
St. John's U (NY)
Salem State Coll (MA)
Sam Houston State U (TX)
San Francisco Art Inst (CA)
San Jose State U (CA)
Sarah Lawrence Coll (NY)
Savannah Coll of Art and Design (GA)
School of the Museum of Fine Arts (MA)
School of Visual Arts (NY)
Seattle U (WA)
Simon's Rock Coll of Bard (MA)
State U of NY at New Paltz (NY)
State U of NY Coll at Buffalo (NY)
State U of NY Coll at Potsdam (NY)
Syracuse U (NY)
Temple U (PA)
Texas A&M U–Commerce (TX)
Texas Southern U (TX)
Texas Woman's U (TX)
Thomas Edison State Coll (NJ)
Trinity Christian Coll (IL)
The U of Akron (OH)
U of Calif, Santa Cruz (CA)
U of Central Oklahoma (OK)
U of Dayton (OH)
U of Hartford (CT)
U of Houston (TX)
U of Idaho (ID)
U of Illinois at Chicago (IL)
U of Illinois at Urbana–Champaign (IL)
The U of Iowa (IA)
U of Maryland, Baltimore County (MD)
U of Massachusetts Dartmouth (MA)
U of Miami (FL)
U of Michigan (MI)
U of Missouri–St. Louis (MO)
U of Montevallo (AL)
U of North Texas (TX)
U of San Francisco (CA)
U of South Alabama (AL)
U of South Dakota (SD)
The U of Texas at Arlington (TX)
The U of the Arts (PA)
U of Washington (WA)
Virginia Intermont Coll (VA)
Washington U in St. Louis (MO)
Weber State U (UT)
Webster U (MO)
White Pines Coll (NH)
Wright State U (OH)
York U (ON, Canada)
Youngstown State U (OH)

PHYSICAL AND THEORETICAL CHEMISTRY
Florida State U (FL)

PHYSICAL EDUCATION
Abilene Christian U (TX)
Adams State Coll (CO)
Adelphi U (NY)
Adrian Coll (MI)
Alabama A&M U (AL)
Alabama State U (AL)
Albany State U (GA)
Albertson Coll of Idaho (ID)
Albion Coll (MI)
Alderson-Broaddus Coll (WV)
Alice Lloyd Coll (KY)
Allen U (SC)
American U of Puerto Rico (PR)
Anderson Coll (SC)
Anderson U (IN)
Andrews U (MI)
Appalachian State U (NC)
Aquinas Coll (MI)
Arkansas State U (AR)
Arkansas Tech U (AR)
Armstrong Atlantic State U (GA)
Asbury Coll (KY)

Ashland U (OH)
Athens State U (AL)
Atlantic Union Coll (MA)
Auburn U (AL)
Augsburg Coll (MN)
Augustana Coll (IL)
Augustana Coll (SD)
Augusta State U (GA)
Austin Coll (TX)
Averett Coll (VA)
Azusa Pacific U (CA)
Baker U (KS)
Baldwin-Wallace Coll (OH)
Ball State U (IN)
Barry U (FL)
Bartlesville Wesleyan Coll (OK)
Barton Coll (NC)
Bayamón Central U (PR)
Baylor U (TX)
Bellevue U (NE)
Belmont U (TN)
Bemidji State U (MN)
Benedictine Coll (KS)
Berea Coll (KY)
Berry Coll (GA)
Bethany Coll (KS)
Bethany Coll (WV)
Bethel Coll (IN)
Bethel Coll (MN)
Bethel Coll (TN)
Bethune-Cookman Coll (FL)
Biola U (CA)
Blackburn Coll (IL)
Blue Mountain Coll (MS)
Bluffton Coll (OH)
Boise State U (ID)
Boston U (MA)
Bowling Green State U (OH)
Brevard Coll (NC)
Briar Cliff Coll (IA)
Bridgewater State Coll (MA)
Brigham Young U (UT)
Brigham Young U–Hawaii Campus (HI)
Brock U (ON, Canada)
Brooklyn Coll of the City U of NY (NY)
Bryan Coll (TN)
Buena Vista U (IA)
California Baptist U (CA)
California Lutheran U (CA)
California Polytechnic State U, San Luis Obispo (CA)
California State Polytechnic U, Pomona (CA)
California State U, Chico (CA)
California State U, Dominguez Hills (CA)
California State U, Fresno (CA)
California State U, Fullerton (CA)
California State U, Hayward (CA)
California State U, Long Beach (CA)
California State U, Los Angeles (CA)
California State U, Northridge (CA)
California State U, San Bernardino (CA)
California State U, Stanislaus (CA)
Calvin Coll (MI)
Cameron U (OK)
Campbellsville U (KY)
Campbell U (NC)
Canisius Coll (NY)
Capital U (OH)
Carroll Coll (MT)
Carroll Coll (WI)
Carson-Newman Coll (TN)
Carthage Coll (WI)
Castleton State Coll (VT)
Catawba Coll (NC)
Cedarville Coll (OH)
Centenary Coll of Louisiana (LA)
Central Connecticut State U (CT)
Central Methodist Coll (MO)
Central Michigan U (MI)
Central Missouri State U (MO)
Chadron State Coll (NE)
Chapman U (CA)
Charleston Southern U (SC)
Chicago State U (IL)
Chowan Coll (NC)
Christopher Newport U (VA)
Citadel, The Military Coll of South Carolina (SC)
Claflin U (SC)
Clark Atlanta U (GA)

Clarke Coll (IA)
Cleveland State U (OH)
Coastal Carolina U (SC)
Coe Coll (IA)
Coker Coll (SC)
Coll of Charleston (SC)
Coll of Mount St. Joseph (OH)
Coll of Mount Saint Vincent (NY)
The Coll of New Jersey (NJ)
Coll of St. Catherine (MN)
Coll of the Ozarks (MO)
Coll of the Southwest (NM)
The Coll of William and Mary (VA)
Colorado State U (CO)
Columbus State U (GA)
Concord Coll (WV)
Concordia Coll (MI)
Concordia Coll (MN)
Concordia U (IL)
Concordia U (NE)
Concordia U (OR)
Concordia U at St. Paul (MN)
Concordia U Wisconsin (WI)
Coppin State Coll (MD)
Cornell Coll (IA)
Cornerstone U (MI)
Crown Coll (MN)
Culver-Stockton Coll (MO)
Cumberland Coll (KY)
Dakota State U (SD)
Dakota Wesleyan U (SD)
Dallas Baptist U (TX)
Dana Coll (NE)
David Lipscomb U (TN)
Defiance Coll (OH)
Delaware State U (DE)
Delta State U (MS)
Denison U (OH)
DePaul U (IL)
Dickinson State U (ND)
Doane Coll (NE)
Dordt Coll (IA)
Drury U (MO)
East Carolina U (NC)
East Central U (OK)
Eastern Connecticut State U (CT)
Eastern Illinois U (IL)
Eastern Kentucky U (KY)
Eastern Mennonite U (VA)
Eastern Michigan U (MI)
Eastern Nazarene Coll (MA)
Eastern New Mexico U (NM)
Eastern Oregon U (OR)
Eastern Washington U (WA)
East Stroudsburg U of Pennsylvania (PA)
East Texas Baptist U (TX)
Edinboro U of Pennsylvania (PA)
Elizabeth City State U (NC)
Elmhurst Coll (IL)
Elon Coll (NC)
Emporia State U (KS)
Erskine Coll (SC)
Evangel U (MO)
Fairmont State Coll (WV)
Faulkner U (AL)
Ferrum Coll (VA)
Florida A&M U (FL)
Florida International U (FL)
Florida Southern Coll (FL)
Florida State U (FL)
Fort Hays State U (KS)
Fort Lewis Coll (CO)
Fort Valley State U (GA)
Franklin Coll of Indiana (IN)
Freed-Hardeman U (TN)
Free Will Baptist Bible Coll (TN)
Fresno Pacific U (CA)
Friends U (KS)
Frostburg State U (MD)
Gallaudet U (DC)
Gardner-Webb U (NC)
George Fox U (OR)
George Mason U (VA)
Georgetown Coll (KY)
Georgia Coll and State U (GA)
Georgia Southern U (GA)
Georgia Southwestern State U (GA)
Georgia State U (GA)
Gettysburg Coll (PA)
Glenville State Coll (WV)
Gonzaga U (WA)
Goshen Coll (IN)
Grace Coll (IN)
Graceland Coll (IA)
Grand Canyon U (AZ)

Grand Valley State U (MI)
Greensboro Coll (NC)
Greenville Coll (IL)
Guilford Coll (NC)
Gustavus Adolphus Coll (MN)
Hamline U (MN)
Hampton U (VA)
Hannibal-LaGrange Coll (MO)
Hanover Coll (IN)
Harding U (AR)
Hardin-Simmons U (TX)
Hastings Coll (NE)
Heidelberg Coll (OH)
Henderson State U (AR)
Hendrix Coll (AR)
High Point U (NC)
Hillsdale Coll (MI)
Hofstra U (NY)
Hope Coll (MI)
Houghton Coll (NY)
Howard Payne U (TX)
Howard U (DC)
Humboldt State U (CA)
Hunter Coll of the City U of NY (NY)
Huntingdon Coll (AL)
Huntington Coll (IN)
Huron U (SD)
Husson Coll (ME)
Huston-Tillotson Coll (TX)
Idaho State U (ID)
Illinois Coll (IL)
Illinois State U (IL)
Indiana State U (IN)
Indiana U Bloomington (IN)
Indiana U of Pennsylvania (PA)
Indiana U–Purdue U Indianapolis (IN)
Indiana Wesleyan U (IN)
Inter American U of PR, Fajardo Campus (PR)
Inter American U of PR, Metropolitan Campus (PR)
Inter American U of PR, San Germán Campus (PR)
Iowa Wesleyan Coll (IA)
Ithaca Coll (NY)
Jacksonville State U (AL)
Jacksonville U (FL)
Jamestown Coll (ND)
Jarvis Christian Coll (TX)
John Brown U (AR)
John Carroll U (OH)
Johnson C. Smith U (NC)
Johnson State Coll (VT)
Judson Coll (IL)
Kean U (NJ)
Keene State Coll (NH)
Kent State U (OH)
Kentucky State U (KY)
Kentucky Wesleyan Coll (KY)
Lakehead U (ON, Canada)
Lamar U (TX)
Lambuth U (TN)
Lander U (SC)
Lane Coll (TN)
Langston U (OK)
Lees-McRae Coll (NC)
Lee U (TN)
LeMoyne-Owen Coll (TN)
Lenoir-Rhyne Coll (NC)
LeTourneau U (TX)
Lewis-Clark State Coll (ID)
Lewis U (IL)
Liberty U (VA)
Limestone Coll (SC)
Lincoln Memorial U (TN)
Lincoln U (MO)
Lincoln U (PA)
Lindenwood U (MO)
Lindsey Wilson Coll (KY)
Linfield Coll (OR)
Lock Haven U of Pennsylvania (PA)
Long Island U, Brooklyn Campus (NY)
Long Island U, C.W. Post Campus (NY)
Longwood Coll (VA)
Loras Coll (IA)
Louisiana Coll (LA)
Louisiana State U and A&M Coll (LA)
Louisiana State U in Shreveport (LA)
Louisiana Tech U (LA)
Lubbock Christian U (TX)

Majors Index
Physical Education–Physical Sciences

Luther Coll (IA)
Lynchburg Coll (VA)
Lyndon State Coll (VT)
MacMurray Coll (IL)
Malone Coll (OH)
Manchester Coll (IN)
Manhattan Coll (NY)
Maranatha Baptist Bible Coll (WI)
Marian Coll (IN)
Marshall U (WV)
Mars Hill Coll (NC)
Maryville Coll (TN)
Marywood U (PA)
Mayville State U (ND)
McGill U (PQ, Canada)
McKendree Coll (IL)
McMurry U (TX)
McNeese State U (LA)
McPherson Coll (KS)
Memorial U of Newfoundland (NF, Canada)
Meredith Coll (NC)
Mesa State Coll (CO)
Messiah Coll (PA)
Methodist Coll (NC)
Miami U (OH)
Michigan State U (MI)
MidAmerica Nazarene U (KS)
Midland Lutheran Coll (NE)
Milligan Coll (TN)
Millikin U (IL)
Minnesota State U, Mankato (MN)
Minnesota State U Moorhead (MN)
Minot State U (ND)
Mississippi State U (MS)
Mississippi U for Women (MS)
Mississippi Valley State U (MS)
Missouri Baptist Coll (MO)
Missouri Southern State Coll (MO)
Missouri Valley Coll (MO)
Monmouth Coll (IL)
Montana State U–Billings (MT)
Montana State U–Northern (MT)
Morehead State U (KY)
Morehouse Coll (GA)
Morgan State U (MD)
Morningside Coll (IA)
Mount Marty Coll (SD)
Mount Union Coll (OH)
Mount Vernon Nazarene Coll (OH)
Murray State U (KY)
Muskingum Coll (OH)
Nebraska Wesleyan U (NE)
Newberry Coll (SC)
New England Coll (NH)
New Mexico Highlands U (NM)
New Mexico State U (NM)
Nicholls State U (LA)
Norfolk State U (VA)
North Carolina Ag and Tech State U (NC)
North Carolina Central U (NC)
North Carolina Wesleyan Coll (NC)
North Central Coll (IL)
North Dakota State U (ND)
Northeastern Illinois U (IL)
Northeastern State U (OK)
Northeastern U (MA)
Northern Arizona U (AZ)
Northern Illinois U (IL)
Northern Kentucky U (KY)
Northern Michigan U (MI)
Northern State U (SD)
North Georgia Coll & State U (GA)
North Park U (IL)
Northwest Coll (WA)
Northwestern Coll (IA)
Northwestern Coll (MN)
Northwestern Oklahoma State U (OK)
Northwestern State U of Louisiana (LA)
Northwest Missouri State U (MO)
Northwest Nazarene U (ID)
Norwich U (VT)
Oakland City U (IN)
Oakwood Coll (AL)
Ohio Northern U (OH)
The Ohio State U (OH)
Ohio U (OH)
Ohio Wesleyan U (OH)
Oklahoma Baptist U (OK)
Oklahoma Christian U of Science and Arts (OK)
Oklahoma City U (OK)
Oklahoma Panhandle State U (OK)
Oklahoma State U (OK)

Old Dominion U (VA)
Olivet Nazarene U (IL)
Oregon State U (OR)
Ottawa U (KS)
Otterbein Coll (OH)
Ouachita Baptist U (AR)
Pacific Lutheran U (WA)
Pacific Union Coll (CA)
Palm Beach Atlantic Coll (FL)
Pepperdine U, Malibu (CA)
Peru State Coll (NE)
Pfeiffer U (NC)
Philadelphia Coll of Bible (PA)
Philander Smith Coll (AR)
Piedmont Baptist Coll (NC)
Pittsburg State U (KS)
Plymouth State Coll (NH)
Pontifical Catholic U of Puerto Rico (PR)
Purdue U (IN)
Queens Coll of the City U of NY (NY)
Queen's U at Kingston (ON, Canada)
Quincy U (IL)
Radford U (VA)
Reinhardt Coll (GA)
Rice U (TX)
Ripon Coll (WI)
Rockford Coll (IL)
Rocky Mountain Coll (MT)
Rowan U (NJ)
Rust Coll (MS)
Saginaw Valley State U (MI)
St. Ambrose U (IA)
St. Andrews Presbyterian Coll (NC)
Saint Augustine's Coll (NC)
St. Bonaventure U (NY)
St. Cloud State U (MN)
St. Edward's U (TX)
St. Francis Coll (NY)
St. Francis Xavier U (NS, Canada)
Saint Joseph's Coll (IN)
Saint Joseph's Coll (ME)
Saint Leo U (FL)
Saint Mary's Coll of California (CA)
St. Olaf Coll (MN)
Salem State Coll (MA)
Salisbury State U (MD)
Samford U (AL)
San Diego State U (CA)
San Francisco State U (CA)
San Jose State U (CA)
Seattle Pacific U (WA)
Shenandoah U (VA)
Simpson Coll (IA)
Slippery Rock U of Pennsylvania (PA)
Sonoma State U (CA)
South Dakota State U (SD)
Southeastern Louisiana U (LA)
Southeastern Oklahoma State U (OK)
Southeast Missouri State U (MO)
Southern Adventist U (TN)
Southern Arkansas U–Magnolia (AR)
Southern Illinois U Carbondale (IL)
Southern Oregon U (OR)
Southern Utah U (UT)
Southern Wesleyan U (SC)
Southwest Baptist U (MO)
Southwestern Coll (KS)
Southwestern Oklahoma State U (OK)
Southwestern U (TX)
Southwest Missouri State U (MO)
Southwest State U (MN)
Spring Arbor Coll (MI)
State U of NY Coll at Brockport (NY)
State U of NY Coll at Cortland (NY)
State U of West Georgia (GA)
Sterling Coll (KS)
Stillman Coll (AL)
Sul Ross State U (TX)
Syracuse U (NY)
Tabor Coll (KS)
Taylor U (IN)
Temple U (PA)
Tennessee State U (TN)
Tennessee Technological U (TN)
Tennessee Wesleyan Coll (TN)
Texas A&M International U (TX)
Texas A&M U (TX)
Texas A&M U–Commerce (TX)
Texas A&M U–Kingsville (TX)

Texas Christian U (TX)
Texas Lutheran U (TX)
Texas Southern U (TX)
Texas Wesleyan U (TX)
Towson U (MD)
Transylvania U (KY)
Trevecca Nazarene U (TN)
Trinity Christian Coll (IL)
Trinity Western U (BC, Canada)
Tri-State U (IN)
Troy State U (AL)
Tusculum Coll (TN)
Union Coll (KY)
Union Coll (NE)
Union U (TN)
Universidad del Turabo (PR)
Université de Montréal (PQ, Canada)
Université de Sherbrooke (PQ, Canada)
U du Québec à Chicoutimi (PQ, Canada)
Université Laval (PQ, Canada)
The U of Akron (OH)
The U of Alabama (AL)
The U of Alabama at Birmingham (AL)
U of Alaska Fairbanks (AK)
U of Alberta (AB, Canada)
The U of Arizona (AZ)
U of Arkansas (AR)
U of Arkansas at Monticello (AR)
U of Arkansas at Pine Bluff (AR)
U of Calif, Davis (CA)
U of Central Arkansas (AR)
U of Central Florida (FL)
U of Central Oklahoma (OK)
U of Cincinnati (OH)
U of Connecticut (CT)
U of Dayton (OH)
U of Delaware (DE)
U of Evansville (IN)
The U of Findlay (OH)
U of Florida (FL)
U of Georgia (GA)
U of Great Falls (MT)
U of Idaho (ID)
U of Indianapolis (IN)
U of Kansas (KS)
U of Kentucky (KY)
U of La Verne (CA)
The U of Lethbridge (AB, Canada)
U of Louisiana at Lafayette (LA)
U of Louisiana at Monroe (LA)
U of Maine (ME)
U of Maine at Presque Isle (ME)
U of Manitoba (MB, Canada)
U of Mary Hardin-Baylor (TX)
U of Maryland, Coll Park (MD)
U of Massachusetts Boston (MA)
U of Michigan (MI)
U of Minnesota, Duluth (MN)
U of Minnesota, Twin Cities Campus (MN)
U of Missouri–Kansas City (MO)
U of Missouri–St. Louis (MO)
U of Mobile (AL)
The U of Montana–Missoula (MT)
U of Nebraska at Kearney (NE)
U of Nebraska at Omaha (NE)
U of Nebraska–Lincoln (NE)
U of Nevada, Las Vegas (NV)
U of Nevada, Reno (NV)
U of New Brunswick, Fredericton (NB, Canada)
U of New Hampshire (NH)
U of New Mexico (NM)
U of New Orleans (LA)
The U of North Carolina at Chapel Hill (NC)
The U of North Carolina at Greensboro (NC)
The U of North Carolina at Pembroke (NC)
The U of North Carolina at Wilmington (NC)
U of North Dakota (ND)
U of Northern Iowa (IA)
U of North Florida (FL)
U of North Texas (TX)
U of Pittsburgh (PA)
U of Puerto Rico, Mayagüez Campus (PR)
U of Regina (SK, Canada)
U of Rhode Island (RI)
U of Richmond (VA)
U of Rio Grande (OH)

U of St. Thomas (MN)
U of San Francisco (CA)
U of Sioux Falls (SD)
U of South Alabama (AL)
U of South Carolina (SC)
U of South Carolina Spartanburg (SC)
U of South Dakota (SD)
U of Southern Colorado (CO)
U of Southern Indiana (IN)
U of Southern Mississippi (MS)
U of South Florida (FL)
The U of Tampa (FL)
The U of Tennessee at Chattanooga (TN)
The U of Texas at Arlington (TX)
The U of Texas–Pan American (TX)
U of the District of Columbia (DC)
U of the Ozarks (AR)
U of the Pacific (CA)
U of Toronto (ON, Canada)
U of Utah (UT)
U of Vermont (VT)
U of Victoria (BC, Canada)
U of Virginia (VA)
The U of West Alabama (AL)
The U of Western Ontario (ON, Canada)
U of West Florida (FL)
U of Windsor (ON, Canada)
U of Wisconsin–La Crosse (WI)
U of Wisconsin–Madison (WI)
U of Wisconsin–River Falls (WI)
U of Wisconsin–Stevens Point (WI)
U of Wisconsin–Superior (WI)
U of Wisconsin–Whitewater (WI)
U of Wyoming (WY)
Upper Iowa U (IA)
Ursinus Coll (PA)
Utah State U (UT)
Valdosta State U (GA)
Valley City State U (ND)
Valparaiso U (IN)
Vanguard U of Southern California (CA)
Virginia Commonwealth U (VA)
Virginia Intermont Coll (VA)
Voorhees Coll (SC)
Walla Walla Coll (WA)
Walsh U (OH)
Warner Pacific Coll (OR)
Warner Southern Coll (FL)
Wartburg Coll (IA)
Washington State U (WA)
Wayland Baptist U (TX)
Wayne State Coll (NE)
Wayne State U (MI)
Weber State U (UT)
Wesley Coll (DE)
West Chester U of Pennsylvania (PA)
Western Carolina U (NC)
Western Illinois U (IL)
Western Kentucky U (KY)
Western Maryland Coll (MD)
Western Michigan U (MI)
Western Montana Coll of The U of Montana (MT)
Western State Coll of Colorado (CO)
Western Washington U (WA)
Westfield State Coll (MA)
West Liberty State Coll (WV)
Westminster Coll (MO)
Westmont Coll (CA)
West Virginia State Coll (WV)
West Virginia U (WV)
West Virginia Wesleyan Coll (WV)
Wheaton Coll (IL)
Whittier Coll (CA)
Whitworth Coll (WA)
Wichita State U (KS)
Wilfrid Laurier U (ON, Canada)
Willamette U (OR)
William Paterson U of New Jersey (NJ)
William Penn U (IA)
Williams Baptist Coll (AR)
William Woods U (MO)
Wilmington Coll (OH)
Wingate U (NC)
Winona State U (MN)
Winston-Salem State U (NC)
Winthrop U (SC)
Wright State U (OH)
Xavier U of Louisiana (LA)
York Coll (NE)

York Coll of the City U of New York (NY)
York U (ON, Canada)
Youngstown State U (OH)

PHYSICAL SCIENCES

Albertus Magnus Coll (CT)
Allegheny Coll (PA)
Antioch Coll (OH)
Arkansas Tech U (AR)
Armstrong Atlantic State U (GA)
Asbury Coll (KY)
Auburn U Montgomery (AL)
Augusta State U (GA)
Bard Coll (NY)
Bemidji State U (MN)
Biola U (CA)
Black Hills State U (SD)
Brevard Coll (NC)
Bridgewater Coll (VA)
Brigham Young U–Hawaii Campus (HI)
Brock U (ON, Canada)
California Baptist U (CA)
California Inst of Technology (CA)
California Polytechnic State U, San Luis Obispo (CA)
California State U, Chico (CA)
California State U, Hayward (CA)
California State U, Sacramento (CA)
California State U, Stanislaus (CA)
Calvin Coll (MI)
Centenary Coll of Louisiana (LA)
Central Connecticut State U (CT)
Central Michigan U (MI)
Chowan Coll (NC)
Coe Coll (IA)
Colgate U (NY)
Coll of Notre Dame (CA)
Colorado State U (CO)
Columbia Coll (SC)
Concordia U (IL)
Concordia U (NE)
Concordia U (OR)
Concordia U at St. Paul (MN)
Defiance Coll (OH)
Doane Coll (NE)
Drexel U (PA)
Eastern Michigan U (MI)
Eastern Washington U (WA)
East Stroudsburg U of Pennsylvania (PA)
Emporia State U (KS)
The Evergreen State Coll (WA)
Florida State U (FL)
Fordham U (NY)
Fort Hays State U (KS)
Framingham State Coll (MA)
Freed-Hardeman U (TN)
Georgia Southwestern State U (GA)
Goddard Coll (VT)
Goshen Coll (IN)
Graceland Coll (IA)
Grand Canyon U (AZ)
Grand Valley State U (MI)
Hampshire Coll (MA)
Hampton U (VA)
Hardin-Simmons U (TX)
Harvard U (MA)
Houghton Coll (NY)
Humboldt State U (CA)
Indiana State U (IN)
Judson Coll (IL)
Kansas State U (KS)
Kutztown U of Pennsylvania (PA)
La Sierra U (CA)
Lenoir-Rhyne Coll (NC)
Lincoln U (PA)
Lock Haven U of Pennsylvania (PA)
Lyndon State Coll (VT)
Manhattan Coll (NY)
Mansfield U of Pennsylvania (PA)
Maryville Coll (TN)
Massachusetts Inst of Technology (MA)
Mayville State U (ND)
McMurry U (TX)
McPherson Coll (KS)
Mesa State Coll (CO)
Michigan State U (MI)
Michigan Technological U (MI)
Middlebury Coll (VT)
Midland Lutheran Coll (NE)
Midwestern State U (TX)

Majors Index
Physical Sciences–Physics

Minnesota State U, Mankato (MN)
Minot State U (ND)
Mississippi U for Women (MS)
Muhlenberg Coll (PA)
Northern Arizona U (AZ)
Northwest Missouri State U (MO)
Oklahoma Baptist U (OK)
Olivet Nazarene U (IL)
Oregon State U (OR)
Pacific Union Coll (CA)
Peru State Coll (NE)
Pittsburg State U (KS)
Radford U (VA)
Rensselaer Polytechnic Inst (NY)
Rowan U (NJ)
St. Cloud State U (MN)
St. Francis Xavier U (NS, Canada)
St. John's U (NY)
Saint Michael's Coll (VT)
San Diego State U (CA)
San Francisco State U (CA)
San Jose State U (CA)
Shawnee State U (OH)
Slippery Rock U of Pennsylvania (PA)
Southern Utah U (UT)
Southwest State U (MN)
Texas A&M International U (TX)
Trent U (ON, Canada)
Tri-State U (IN)
Troy State U (AL)
Troy State U Dothan (AL)
U du Québec à Chicoutimi (PQ, Canada)
U of Alberta (AB, Canada)
U of Arkansas at Monticello (AR)
U of Calif, Berkeley (CA)
U of Calif, Riverside (CA)
U of Central Arkansas (AR)
U of Dayton (OH)
U of Guelph (ON, Canada)
U of Houston–Clear Lake (TX)
U of Maryland, Coll Park (MD)
U of Michigan–Dearborn (MI)
U of Michigan–Flint (MI)
U of Missouri–St. Louis (MO)
U of Pittsburgh (PA)
U of Pittsburgh at Bradford (PA)
U of Puerto Rico, Mayagüez Campus (PR)
U of Rio Grande (OH)
U of Southern California (CA)
U of the Pacific (CA)
U of Wisconsin–River Falls (WI)
U of Wisconsin–Superior (WI)
Walsh U (OH)
Warner Pacific Coll (OR)
Washington U in St. Louis (MO)
Wayland Baptist U (TX)
Wayne State Coll (NE)
Western Montana Coll of The U of Montana (MT)
Westfield State Coll (MA)
Wheaton Coll (IL)
William Paterson U of New Jersey (NJ)
Winona State U (MN)
Wittenberg U (OH)
York Coll of Pennsylvania (PA)
York U (ON, Canada)

PHYSICIAN ASSISTANT
Alderson-Broaddus Coll (WV)
Augsburg Coll (MN)
Bethel Coll (TN)
Boise State U (ID)
Butler U (IN)
California State U, Dominguez Hills (CA)
Catawba Coll (NC)
City Coll of the City U of NY (NY)
Coll of Staten Island of the City U of NY (NY)
The Coll of West Virginia (WV)
Daemen Coll (NY)
U of Osteopathic Medicine and Health Sciences (IA)
Duquesne U (PA)
D'Youville Coll (NY)
East Carolina U (NC)
Elmhurst Coll (IL)
Gannon U (PA)
Gardner-Webb U (NC)
The George Washington U (DC)
Grand Valley State U (MI)
Guilford Coll (NC)
High Point U (NC)

Howard U (DC)
Idaho State U (ID)
King's Coll (PA)
Le Moyne Coll (NY)
Lenoir-Rhyne Coll (NC)
Long Island U, Brooklyn Campus (NY)
Louisiana Coll (LA)
Louisiana State U Health Sciences Center (LA)
Marquette U (WI)
Mars Hill Coll (NC)
Marywood U (PA)
MCP Hahnemann U (PA)
Medical Coll of Georgia (GA)
Medical U of South Carolina (SC)
Methodist Coll (NC)
New York Inst of Technology (NY)
Nova Southeastern U (FL)
Oregon Health Sciences U (OR)
Pace U, New York City Campus (NY)
Pace U, Pleasantville/Briarcliff Campus (NY)
Peru State Coll (NE)
Philadelphia U (PA)
Rochester Inst of Technology (NY)
Rocky Mountain Coll (MT)
Saint Francis Coll (PA)
St. John's U (NY)
Saint Louis U (MO)
Salem Coll (NC)
Seton Hill Coll (PA)
Southern Illinois U Carbondale (IL)
State U of NY at Stony Brook (NY)
Touro Coll (NY)
Union Coll (NE)
The U of Alabama at Birmingham (AL)
The U of Findlay (OH)
U of Kentucky (KY)
U of New England (ME)
U of New Mexico (NM)
U of South Dakota (SD)
U of Texas Medical Branch at Galveston (TX)
U of the Sciences in Philadelphia (PA)
U of Washington (WA)
U of Wisconsin–La Crosse (WI)
U of Wisconsin–Madison (WI)
Wagner Coll (NY)
Wake Forest U (NC)
Wichita State U (KS)

PHYSICS
Abilene Christian U (TX)
Acadia U (NS, Canada)
Adams State Coll (CO)
Adelphi U (NY)
Adrian Coll (MI)
Agnes Scott Coll (GA)
Alabama A&M U (AL)
Albertson Coll of Idaho (ID)
Albion Coll (MI)
Alfred U (NY)
Allegheny Coll (PA)
Alma Coll (MI)
American U (DC)
American U in Cairo (Egypt)
Amherst Coll (MA)
Anderson U (IN)
Andrews U (MI)
Antioch Coll (OH)
Appalachian State U (NC)
Arizona State U (AZ)
Arkansas State U (AR)
Ashland U (OH)
Athens State U (AL)
Auburn U (AL)
Augsburg Coll (MN)
Augustana Coll (IL)
Augustana Coll (SD)
Augusta State U (GA)
Austin Coll (TX)
Austin Peay State U (TN)
Azusa Pacific U (CA)
Baker U (KS)
Baldwin-Wallace Coll (OH)
Ball State U (IN)
Bard Coll (NY)
Barnard Coll (NY)
Bates Coll (ME)
Baylor U (TX)
Belmont U (TN)
Beloit Coll (WI)
Bemidji State U (MN)

Benedictine Coll (KS)
Benedictine U (IL)
Bennington Coll (VT)
Berea Coll (KY)
Berry Coll (GA)
Bethany Coll (WV)
Bethel Coll (KS)
Bethel Coll (MN)
Bethune-Cookman Coll (FL)
Birmingham-Southern Coll (AL)
Bishop's U (PQ, Canada)
Bloomsburg U of Pennsylvania (PA)
Bluffton Coll (OH)
Boise State U (ID)
Boston Coll (MA)
Boston U (MA)
Bowdoin Coll (ME)
Bowling Green State U (OH)
Bradley U (IL)
Brandeis U (MA)
Brandon U (MB, Canada)
Brevard Coll (NC)
Bridgewater Coll (VA)
Bridgewater State Coll (MA)
Brigham Young U (UT)
Brock U (ON, Canada)
Brooklyn Coll of the City U of NY (NY)
Brown U (RI)
Bryn Mawr Coll (PA)
Bucknell U (PA)
Buena Vista U (IA)
Butler U (IN)
California Inst of Technology (CA)
California Lutheran U (CA)
California Polytechnic State U, San Luis Obispo (CA)
California State Polytechnic U, Pomona (CA)
California State U, Chico (CA)
California State U, Dominguez Hills (CA)
California State U, Fresno (CA)
California State U, Fullerton (CA)
California State U, Hayward (CA)
California State U, Long Beach (CA)
California State U, Los Angeles (CA)
California State U, Northridge (CA)
California State U, Sacramento (CA)
California State U, San Bernardino (CA)
California State U, Stanislaus (CA)
California U of Pennsylvania (PA)
Calvin Coll (MI)
Cameron U (OK)
Campbellsville U (KY)
Canisius Coll (NY)
Carleton Coll (MN)
Carleton U (ON, Canada)
Carnegie Mellon U (PA)
Carthage Coll (WI)
Case Western Reserve U (OH)
The Catholic U of America (DC)
Centenary Coll of Louisiana (LA)
Central Coll (IA)
Central Connecticut State U (CT)
Central Methodist Coll (MO)
Central Missouri State U (MO)
Centre Coll (KY)
Chadron State Coll (NE)
Chatham Coll (PA)
Christian Brothers U (TN)
Christopher Newport U (VA)
Citadel, The Military Coll of South Carolina (SC)
City Coll of the City U of NY (NY)
Claremont McKenna Coll (CA)
Clarion U of Pennsylvania (PA)
Clark Atlanta U (GA)
Clarkson U (NY)
Clark U (MA)
Clemson U (SC)
Cleveland State U (OH)
Coe Coll (IA)
Colby Coll (ME)
Colgate U (NY)
Coll of Charleston (SC)
Coll of Mount Saint Vincent (NY)
The Coll of New Jersey (NJ)
The Coll of New Rochelle (NY)
Coll of Notre Dame of Maryland (MD)
Coll of Saint Benedict (MN)

Coll of St. Catherine (MN)
The Coll of Southeastern Europe, The American U of Athens (Greece)
Coll of Staten Island of the City U of NY (NY)
Coll of the Holy Cross (MA)
The Coll of William and Mary (VA)
The Coll of Wooster (OH)
The Colorado Coll (CO)
Colorado State U (CO)
Columbia Coll (MO)
Columbia Coll (NY)
Columbia U, School of General Studies (NY)
Columbia U, School of Engineering & Applied Sci (NY)
Concordia Coll (MN)
Concordia U (PQ, Canada)
Connecticut Coll (CT)
Cornell Coll (IA)
Cornell U (NY)
Creighton U (NE)
Cumberland Coll (KY)
Curry Coll (MA)
Dakota State U (SD)
Dalhousie U (NS, Canada)
Dartmouth Coll (NH)
David Lipscomb U (TN)
Davidson Coll (NC)
Delaware State U (DE)
Denison U (OH)
DePaul U (IL)
DePauw U (IN)
Dickinson Coll (PA)
Doane Coll (NE)
Dordt Coll (IA)
Drake U (IA)
Drew U (NJ)
Drexel U (PA)
Drury U (MO)
Duke U (NC)
Duquesne U (PA)
Earlham Coll (IN)
East Carolina U (NC)
East Central U (OK)
Eastern Illinois U (IL)
Eastern Kentucky U (KY)
Eastern Michigan U (MI)
Eastern Nazarene Coll (MA)
Eastern New Mexico U (NM)
Eastern Oregon U (OR)
Eastern Washington U (WA)
East Stroudsburg U of Pennsylvania (PA)
East Tennessee State U (TN)
Eckerd Coll (FL)
Edinboro U of Pennsylvania (PA)
Elizabeth City State U (NC)
Elizabethtown Coll (PA)
Elmhurst Coll (IL)
Elon Coll (NC)
Emmanuel Coll (MA)
Emory & Henry Coll (VA)
Emory U (GA)
Emporia State U (KS)
Erskine Coll (SC)
The Evergreen State Coll (WA)
Fairfield U (CT)
Fisk U (TN)
Florida A&M U (FL)
Florida Atlantic U (FL)
Florida Inst of Technology (FL)
Florida International U (FL)
Florida Southern Coll (FL)
Florida State U (FL)
Fordham U (NY)
Fort Hays State U (KS)
Fort Lewis Coll (CO)
Francis Marion U (SC)
Franklin and Marshall Coll (PA)
Franklin Coll of Indiana (IN)
Frostburg State U (MD)
Furman U (SC)
Gallaudet U (DC)
Geneva Coll (PA)
George Mason U (VA)
Georgetown Coll (KY)
Georgetown U (DC)
The George Washington U (DC)
Georgia Inst of Technology (GA)
Georgian Court Coll (NJ)
Georgia Southern U (GA)
Georgia State U (GA)
Gettysburg Coll (PA)
Gonzaga U (WA)
Gordon Coll (MA)

Goshen Coll (IN)
Grand Valley State U (MI)
Greenville Coll (IL)
Grinnell Coll (IA)
Grove City Coll (PA)
Guilford Coll (NC)
Gustavus Adolphus Coll (MN)
Hamilton Coll (NY)
Hamline U (MN)
Hampden-Sydney Coll (VA)
Hampshire Coll (MA)
Hampton U (VA)
Hanover Coll (IN)
Harding U (AR)
Hardin-Simmons U (TX)
Hartwick Coll (NY)
Harvard U (MA)
Harvey Mudd Coll (CA)
Hastings Coll (NE)
Haverford Coll (PA)
Heidelberg Coll (OH)
Henderson State U (AR)
Hendrix Coll (AR)
Hillsdale Coll (MI)
Hiram Coll (OH)
Hobart and William Smith Colls (NY)
Hofstra U (NY)
Hollins U (VA)
Hope Coll (MI)
Houghton Coll (NY)
Houston Baptist U (TX)
Howard U (DC)
Humboldt State U (CA)
Hunter Coll of the City U of NY (NY)
Idaho State U (ID)
Illinois Coll (IL)
Illinois Inst of Technology (IL)
Illinois State U (IL)
Illinois Wesleyan U (IL)
Immaculata Coll (PA)
Indiana State U (IN)
Indiana U Bloomington (IN)
Indiana U of Pennsylvania (PA)
Indiana U–Purdue U Fort Wayne (IN)
Indiana U–Purdue U Indianapolis (IN)
Indiana U South Bend (IN)
Insto Tecno Estudios Sups Monterrey (Mexico)
Iona Coll (NY)
Iowa State U of Science and Technology (IA)
Ithaca Coll (NY)
Jacksonville State U (AL)
Jacksonville U (FL)
James Madison U (VA)
Jarvis Christian Coll (TX)
John Carroll U (OH)
Johns Hopkins U (MD)
Juniata Coll (PA)
Kalamazoo Coll (MI)
Kansas State U (KS)
Keene State Coll (NH)
Kent State U (OH)
Kentucky Wesleyan Coll (KY)
Kenyon Coll (OH)
Kettering U (MI)
King Coll (TN)
Knox Coll (IL)
Kutztown U of Pennsylvania (PA)
Lafayette Coll (PA)
Lake Forest Coll (IL)
Lakehead U (ON, Canada)
Lamar U (TX)
Lane Coll (TN)
Lawrence Technological U (MI)
Lawrence U (WI)
Lebanon Valley Coll (PA)
Lehigh U (PA)
Lehman Coll of the City U of NY (NY)
Le Moyne Coll (NY)
Lenoir-Rhyne Coll (NC)
Lewis & Clark Coll (OR)
Lewis U (IL)
Lincoln U (MO)
Lincoln U (PA)
Linfield Coll (OR)
Lock Haven U of Pennsylvania (PA)
Long Island U, Brooklyn Campus (NY)
Long Island U, C.W. Post Campus (NY)

Majors Index
Physics

Longwood Coll (VA)
Loras Coll (IA)
Louisiana Coll (LA)
Louisiana State U and A&M Coll (LA)
Louisiana State U in Shreveport (LA)
Louisiana Tech U (LA)
Loyola Coll in Maryland (MD)
Loyola Marymount U (CA)
Loyola U Chicago (IL)
Loyola U New Orleans (LA)
Luther Coll (IA)
Lycoming Coll (PA)
Lynchburg Coll (VA)
Macalester Coll (MN)
MacMurray Coll (IL)
Maharishi U of Management (IA)
Manchester Coll (IN)
Manhattan Coll (NY)
Mansfield U of Pennsylvania (PA)
Marietta Coll (OH)
Marlboro Coll (VT)
Marquette U (WI)
Marshall U (WV)
Mary Baldwin Coll (VA)
Mary Washington Coll (VA)
Massachusetts Coll of Liberal Arts (MA)
Massachusetts Inst of Technology (MA)
McGill U (PQ, Canada)
McMurry U (TX)
McNeese State U (LA)
Memorial U of Newfoundland (NF, Canada)
Mercer U (GA)
Mercyhurst Coll (PA)
Merrimack Coll (MA)
Mesa State Coll (CO)
Messiah Coll (PA)
Metropolitan State Coll of Denver (CO)
Miami U (OH)
Michigan State U (MI)
Michigan Technological U (MI)
MidAmerica Nazarene U (KS)
Middlebury Coll (VT)
Middle Tennessee State U (TN)
Midwestern State U (TX)
Millersville U of Pennsylvania (PA)
Millikin U (IL)
Millsaps Coll (MS)
Minnesota State U, Mankato (MN)
Minnesota State U Moorhead (MN)
Minot State U (ND)
Mississippi Coll (MS)
Mississippi State U (MS)
Missouri Southern State Coll (MO)
Monmouth Coll (IL)
Montana State U–Bozeman (MT)
Moravian Coll (PA)
Morehead State U (KY)
Morehouse Coll (GA)
Morgan State U (MD)
Morningside Coll (IA)
Mount Allison U (NB, Canada)
Mount Holyoke Coll (MA)
Mount Union Coll (OH)
Muhlenberg Coll (PA)
Murray State U (KY)
Muskingum Coll (OH)
Nebraska Wesleyan U (NE)
New Coll of the U of South Florida (FL)
New Jersey City U (NJ)
New Jersey Inst of Technology (NJ)
New Mexico Inst of Mining and Technology (NM)
New Mexico State U (NM)
New York Inst of Technology (NY)
New York U (NY)
Norfolk State U (VA)
North Carolina Ag and Tech State U (NC)
North Carolina Central U (NC)
North Carolina State U (NC)
North Central Coll (IL)
North Dakota State U (ND)
Northeastern Illinois U (IL)
Northeastern State U (OK)
Northeastern U (MA)
Northern Arizona U (AZ)
Northern Illinois U (IL)
Northern Kentucky U (KY)
Northern Michigan U (MI)
North Georgia Coll & State U (GA)

North Park U (IL)
Northwestern State U of Louisiana (LA)
Northwestern U (IL)
Northwest Missouri State U (MO)
Northwest Nazarene U (ID)
Norwich U (VT)
Oakland U (MI)
Oberlin Coll (OH)
Occidental Coll (CA)
Oglethorpe U (GA)
Ohio Northern U (OH)
The Ohio State U (OH)
Ohio U (OH)
Ohio Wesleyan U (OH)
Okanagan U Coll (BC, Canada)
Oklahoma Baptist U (OK)
Oklahoma City U (OK)
Oklahoma State U (OK)
Old Dominion U (VA)
Open Learning Agency (BC, Canada)
Oregon State U (OR)
Otterbein Coll (OH)
Ouachita Baptist U (AR)
Pace U, New York City Campus (NY)
Pace U, Pleasantville/Briarcliff Campus (NY)
Pacific Lutheran U (WA)
Pacific Union Coll (CA)
Pacific U (OR)
Penn State U at Erie, The Behrend Coll (PA)
Penn State U Univ Park Campus (PA)
Pittsburg State U (KS)
Pitzer Coll (CA)
Plattsburgh State U of NY (NY)
Point Loma Nazarene U (CA)
Polytechnic U, Brooklyn Campus (NY)
Pomona Coll (CA)
Pontifical Catholic U of Puerto Rico (PR)
Portland State U (OR)
Prairie View A&M U (TX)
Presbyterian Coll (SC)
Princeton U (NJ)
Principia Coll (IL)
Purdue U (IN)
Purdue U Calumet (IN)
Queens Coll of the City U of NY (NY)
Queen's U at Kingston (ON, Canada)
Ramapo Coll of New Jersey (NJ)
Randolph-Macon Coll (VA)
Randolph-Macon Woman's Coll (VA)
Reed Coll (OR)
Regents Coll (NY)
Rensselaer Polytechnic Inst (NY)
Rhodes Coll (TN)
Rice U (TX)
The Richard Stockton Coll of New Jersey (NJ)
Rider U (NJ)
Ripon Coll (WI)
Roanoke Coll (VA)
Roberts Wesleyan Coll (NY)
Rochester Inst of Technology (NY)
Rockhurst U (MO)
Rocky Mountain Coll (MT)
Rollins Coll (FL)
Rose-Hulman Inst of Technology (IN)
Rust Coll (MS)
Rutgers, State U of NJ, Camden Coll of Arts & Scis (NJ)
Rutgers, State U of NJ, Douglass Coll (NJ)
Rutgers, State U of NJ, Livingston Coll (NJ)
Rutgers, State U of NJ, Newark Coll of Arts & Scis (NJ)
Rutgers, State U of NJ, Rutgers Coll (NJ)
Rutgers, State U of NJ, U Coll–Camden (NJ)
Rutgers, State U of NJ, U Coll–New Brunswick (NJ)
Saginaw Valley State U (MI)
St. Ambrose U (IA)
St. Bonaventure U (NY)
St. Cloud State U (MN)
St. Francis Xavier U (NS, Canada)

St. John Fisher Coll (NY)
Saint John's U (MN)
St. John's U (NY)
Saint Joseph's U (PA)
St. Lawrence U (NY)
Saint Louis U (MO)
Saint Mary's Coll of California (CA)
St. Mary's Coll of Maryland (MD)
Saint Mary's U (NS, Canada)
Saint Mary's U of Minnesota (MN)
St. Mary's U of San Antonio (TX)
Saint Michael's Coll (VT)
St. Norbert Coll (WI)
St. Olaf Coll (MN)
Saint Peter's Coll (NJ)
Saint Vincent Coll (PA)
Salisbury State U (MD)
Samford U (AL)
Sam Houston State U (TX)
San Diego State U (CA)
San Francisco State U (CA)
San Jose State U (CA)
Santa Clara U (CA)
Sarah Lawrence Coll (NY)
Scripps Coll (CA)
Seattle Pacific U (WA)
Seattle U (WA)
Seton Hall U (NJ)
Seton Hill Coll (PA)
Shaw U (NC)
Shippensburg U of Pennsylvania (PA)
Siena Coll (NY)
Simon Fraser U (BC, Canada)
Simon's Rock Coll of Bard (MA)
Skidmore Coll (NY)
Slippery Rock U of Pennsylvania (PA)
Smith Coll (MA)
Sonoma State U (CA)
South Dakota School of Mines and Technology (SD)
South Dakota State U (SD)
Southeastern Louisiana U (LA)
Southeastern Oklahoma State U (OK)
Southeast Missouri State U (MO)
Southern Adventist U (TN)
Southern Illinois U Carbondale (IL)
Southern Illinois U Edwardsville (IL)
Southern Methodist U (TX)
Southern Oregon U (OR)
Southern Polytechnic State U (GA)
Southwestern Adventist U (TX)
Southwestern Coll (KS)
Southwestern Oklahoma State U (OK)
Southwestern U (TX)
Southwest Missouri State U (MO)
Southwest Texas State U (TX)
Spelman Coll (GA)
Spring Arbor Coll (MI)
Stanford U (CA)
State U of NY at Albany (NY)
State U of NY at Binghamton (NY)
State U of NY at Buffalo (NY)
State U of NY at New Paltz (NY)
State U of NY at Oswego (NY)
State U of NY at Stony Brook (NY)
State U of NY Coll at Brockport (NY)
State U of NY Coll at Buffalo (NY)
State U of NY Coll at Cortland (NY)
State U of NY Coll at Fredonia (NY)
State U of NY Coll at Geneseo (NY)
State U of NY Coll at Oneonta (NY)
State U of NY Coll at Potsdam (NY)
State U of West Georgia (GA)
Stephen F. Austin State U (TX)
Stetson U (FL)
Stevens Inst of Technology (NJ)
Stillman Coll (AL)
Suffolk U (MA)
Susquehanna U (PA)
Swarthmore Coll (PA)
Sweet Briar Coll (VA)
Syracuse U (NY)
Talladega Coll (AL)
Taylor U (IN)
Temple U (PA)
Tennessee State U (TN)
Tennessee Technological U (TN)
Texas A&M U (TX)

Texas A&M U–Commerce (TX)
Texas A&M U–Kingsville (TX)
Texas Christian U (TX)
Texas Lutheran U (TX)
Texas Southern U (TX)
Texas Tech U (TX)
Thiel Coll (PA)
Thomas Edison State Coll (NJ)
Thomas More Coll (KY)
Tougaloo Coll (MS)
Towson U (MD)
Transylvania U (KY)
Trent U (ON, Canada)
Trevecca Nazarene U (TN)
Trinity Coll (CT)
Trinity U (TX)
Truman State U (MO)
Tufts U (MA)
Tulane U (LA)
Tuskegee U (AL)
Union Coll (KY)
Union Coll (NE)
Union Coll (NY)
Union U (TN)
United States Air Force Academy (CO)
United States Military Academy (NY)
United States Naval Academy (MD)
Université de Montréal (PQ, Canada)
Université de Sherbrooke (PQ, Canada)
U du Québec à Chicoutimi (PQ, Canada)
U du Québec à Trois-Rivières (PQ, Canada)
Université Laval (PQ, Canada)
U Coll of the Fraser Valley (BC, Canada)
The U of Akron (OH)
The U of Alabama (AL)
The U of Alabama at Birmingham (AL)
The U of Alabama in Huntsville (AL)
U of Alaska Fairbanks (AK)
U of Alberta (AB, Canada)
The U of Arizona (AZ)
U of Arkansas (AR)
U of Arkansas at Little Rock (AR)
U of Arkansas at Pine Bluff (AR)
U of British Columbia (BC, Canada)
U of Calgary (AB, Canada)
U of Calif, Berkeley (CA)
U of Calif, Davis (CA)
U of Calif, Irvine (CA)
U of Calif, Los Angeles (CA)
U of Calif, Riverside (CA)
U of Calif, San Diego (CA)
U of Calif, Santa Barbara (CA)
U of Calif, Santa Cruz (CA)
U of Central Arkansas (AR)
U of Central Florida (FL)
U of Central Oklahoma (OK)
U of Chicago (IL)
U of Cincinnati (OH)
U of Colorado at Boulder (CO)
U of Colorado at Colorado Springs (CO)
U of Colorado at Denver (CO)
U of Connecticut (CT)
U of Dallas (TX)
U of Dayton (OH)
U of Delaware (DE)
U of Denver (CO)
U of Evansville (IN)
U of Florida (FL)
U of Georgia (GA)
U of Guelph (ON, Canada)
U of Hartford (CT)
U of Hawaii at Manoa (HI)
U of Houston (TX)
U of Houston–Downtown (TX)
U of Idaho (ID)
U of Illinois at Chicago (IL)
U of Illinois at Urbana–Champaign (IL)
U of Indianapolis (IN)
The U of Iowa (IA)
U of Kansas (KS)
U of Kentucky (KY)
U of King's Coll (NS, Canada)
U of La Verne (CA)
The U of Lethbridge (AB, Canada)
U of Louisiana at Lafayette (LA)

U of Louisiana at Monroe (LA)
U of Louisville (KY)
U of Maine (ME)
U of Manitoba (MB, Canada)
U of Maryland, Baltimore County (MD)
U of Maryland, Coll Park (MD)
U of Massachusetts Amherst (MA)
U of Massachusetts Boston (MA)
U of Massachusetts Dartmouth (MA)
U of Massachusetts Lowell (MA)
The U of Memphis (TN)
U of Miami (FL)
U of Michigan (MI)
U of Michigan–Dearborn (MI)
U of Michigan–Flint (MI)
U of Minnesota, Duluth (MN)
U of Minnesota, Morris (MN)
U of Minnesota, Twin Cities Campus (MN)
U of Mississippi (MS)
U of Missouri–Columbia (MO)
U of Missouri–Kansas City (MO)
U of Missouri–Rolla (MO)
U of Missouri–St. Louis (MO)
The U of Montana–Missoula (MT)
U of Nebraska at Kearney (NE)
U of Nebraska at Omaha (NE)
U of Nebraska–Lincoln (NE)
U of Nevada, Las Vegas (NV)
U of Nevada, Reno (NV)
U of New Brunswick, Fredericton (NB, Canada)
U of New Hampshire (NH)
U of New Haven (CT)
U of New Mexico (NM)
U of New Orleans (LA)
U of North Alabama (AL)
The U of North Carolina at Asheville (NC)
The U of North Carolina at Chapel Hill (NC)
The U of North Carolina at Charlotte (NC)
The U of North Carolina at Greensboro (NC)
The U of North Carolina at Wilmington (NC)
U of North Dakota (ND)
U of Northern Colorado (CO)
U of Northern Iowa (IA)
U of North Florida (FL)
U of North Texas (TX)
U of Notre Dame (IN)
U of Oklahoma (OK)
U of Oregon (OR)
U of Pennsylvania (PA)
U of Pittsburgh (PA)
U of Portland (OR)
U of Prince Edward Island (PE, Canada)
U of Puerto Rico, Humacao U Coll (PR)
U of Puerto Rico, Mayagüez Campus (PR)
U of Puget Sound (WA)
U of Redlands (CA)
U of Regina (SK, Canada)
U of Rhode Island (RI)
U of Richmond (VA)
U of Rochester (NY)
U of St. Thomas (MN)
U of San Diego (CA)
U of San Francisco (CA)
U of Science and Arts of Oklahoma (OK)
The U of Scranton (PA)
U of South Alabama (AL)
U of South Carolina (SC)
U of South Dakota (SD)
U of Southern California (CA)
U of Southern Colorado (CO)
U of Southern Maine (ME)
U of Southern Mississippi (MS)
U of South Florida (FL)
The U of Tennessee at Chattanooga (TN)
The U of Tennessee Knoxville (TN)
The U of Texas at Arlington (TX)
The U of Texas at Austin (TX)
The U of Texas at Dallas (TX)
The U of Texas at San Antonio (TX)
The U of Texas–Pan American (TX)
U of the District of Columbia (DC)
U of the Ozarks (AR)

Majors Index
Physics–Political Science

U of the Pacific (CA)
U of the South (TN)
U of Toronto (ON, Canada)
U of Tulsa (OK)
U of Utah (UT)
U of Vermont (VT)
U of Victoria (BC, Canada)
U of Virginia (VA)
U of Washington (WA)
U of Waterloo (ON, Canada)
The U of Western Ontario (ON, Canada)
U of West Florida (FL)
U of Windsor (ON, Canada)
The U of Winnipeg (MB, Canada)
U of Wisconsin–Eau Claire (WI)
U of Wisconsin–La Crosse (WI)
U of Wisconsin–Madison (WI)
U of Wisconsin–Milwaukee (WI)
U of Wisconsin–Parkside (WI)
U of Wisconsin–River Falls (WI)
U of Wisconsin–Stevens Point (WI)
U of Wisconsin–Whitewater (WI)
U of Wyoming (WY)
Ursinus Coll (PA)
Utah State U (UT)
Utica Coll of Syracuse U (NY)
Valdosta State U (GA)
Valparaiso U (IN)
Vanderbilt U (TN)
Vassar Coll (NY)
Villanova U (PA)
Virginia Commonwealth U (VA)
Virginia Military Inst (VA)
Virginia Polytechnic Inst and State U (VA)
Wabash Coll (IN)
Wagner Coll (NY)
Wake Forest U (NC)
Walla Walla Coll (WA)
Wartburg Coll (IA)
Washington & Jefferson Coll (PA)
Washington and Lee U (VA)
Washington Coll (MD)
Washington State U (WA)
Washington U in St. Louis (MO)
Wayne State U (MI)
Weber State U (UT)
Wellesley Coll (MA)
Wells Coll (NY)
Wesleyan U (CT)
West Chester U of Pennsylvania (PA)
Western Carolina U (NC)
Western Illinois U (IL)
Western Kentucky U (KY)
Western Maryland Coll (MD)
Western Michigan U (MI)
Western State Coll of Colorado (CO)
Western Washington U (WA)
Westminster Coll (MO)
Westminster Coll (PA)
Westminster Coll (UT)
Westmont Coll (CA)
West Texas A&M U (TX)
West Virginia U (WV)
West Virginia Wesleyan Coll (WV)
Wheaton Coll (IL)
Wheaton Coll (MA)
Wheeling Jesuit U (WV)
Whitman Coll (WA)
Whittier Coll (CA)
Whitworth Coll (WA)
Wichita State U (KS)
Widener U (PA)
Wilfrid Laurier U (ON, Canada)
Wilkes U (PA)
Willamette U (OR)
William Jewell Coll (MO)
Williams Coll (MA)
Winona State U (MN)
Wittenberg U (OH)
Wofford Coll (SC)
Worcester Polytechnic Inst (MA)
Wright State U (OH)
Xavier U (OH)
Xavier U of Louisiana (LA)
Yale U (CT)
Yeshiva U (NY)
York Coll of the City U of New York (NY)
York U (ON, Canada)
Youngstown State U (OH)

PHYSICS EDUCATION
Abilene Christian U (TX)
Appalachian State U (NC)
Arkansas State U (AR)
Baylor U (TX)
Berry Coll (GA)
Bethel Coll (IN)
Bethune-Cookman Coll (FL)
Bowling Green State U (OH)
Bridgewater Coll (VA)
Brigham Young U (UT)
Canisius Coll (NY)
Central Michigan U (MI)
Central Missouri State U (MO)
Christian Brothers U (TN)
The Coll of New Jersey (NJ)
Colorado State U (CO)
Concordia Coll (MN)
Concordia U (NE)
Duquesne U (PA)
Eastern Michigan U (MI)
Elmhurst Coll (IL)
Florida Inst of Technology (FL)
Greenville Coll (IL)
Gustavus Adolphus Coll (MN)
Hardin-Simmons U (TX)
Hastings Coll (NE)
Indiana U Bloomington (IN)
Indiana U–Purdue U Fort Wayne (IN)
Indiana U South Bend (IN)
Ithaca Coll (NY)
Juniata Coll (PA)
King Coll (TN)
Luther Coll (IA)
Malone Coll (OH)
Mansfield U of Pennsylvania (PA)
Maryville Coll (TN)
McGill U (PQ, Canada)
New York Inst of Technology (NY)
New York U (NY)
North Carolina Central U (NC)
North Dakota State U (ND)
Rocky Mountain Coll (MT)
St. Ambrose U (IA)
St. John's U (NY)
Saint Vincent Coll (PA)
Seton Hill Coll (PA)
Southern Arkansas U–Magnolia (AR)
Southwest Missouri State U (MO)
Union Coll (NE)
Universidad Metropolitana (PR)
The U of Arizona (AZ)
U of Calif, San Diego (CA)
U of Central Arkansas (AR)
U of Delaware (DE)
U of Illinois at Chicago (IL)
U of Illinois at Urbana–Champaign (IL)
U of Nebraska–Lincoln (NE)
U of North Texas (TX)
U of Rio Grande (OH)
U of Waterloo (ON, Canada)
U of Wisconsin–River Falls (WI)
Utah State U (UT)
Washington U in St. Louis (MO)
Weber State U (UT)
Wheeling Jesuit U (WV)
York U (ON, Canada)
Youngstown State U (OH)

PHYSIOLOGICAL PSYCHOLOGY/ PSYCHOBIOLOGY
Albright Coll (PA)
Averett Coll (VA)
Barnard Coll (NY)
Baylor U (TX)
Beaver Coll (PA)
Bowdoin Coll (ME)
Centre Coll (KY)
Chatham Coll (PA)
Claremont McKenna Coll (CA)
Coll of Notre Dame of Maryland (MD)
Drew U (NJ)
Florida Atlantic U (FL)
Grand Valley State U (MI)
Hamilton Coll (NY)
Hampshire Coll (MA)
Harvard U (MA)
Hiram Coll (OH)
Holy Family Coll (PA)
Hope International U (CA)
Johns Hopkins U (MD)
La Roche Coll (PA)
La Sierra U (CA)
Lebanon Valley Coll (PA)
Lincoln U (PA)
Long Island U, Southampton Coll (NY)
Long Island U, Southampton Coll, Friends World Program (NY)
Luther Coll (IA)
Lynchburg Coll (VA)
McGill U (PQ, Canada)
Mount Allison U (NB, Canada)
Nebraska Wesleyan U (NE)
Oberlin Coll (OH)
Occidental Coll (CA)
Pitzer Coll (CA)
Quinnipiac U (CT)
Ripon Coll (WI)
Scripps Coll (CA)
Simmons Coll (MA)
State U of NY at Binghamton (NY)
State U of NY at New Paltz (NY)
Swarthmore Coll (PA)
U of Calif, Los Angeles (CA)
U of Calif, Riverside (CA)
U of Calif, Santa Cruz (CA)
U of Evansville (IN)
The U of Lethbridge (AB, Canada)
U of Miami (FL)
U of New Brunswick, Fredericton (NB, Canada)
U of Pennsylvania (PA)
U of Southern California (CA)
Vassar Coll (NY)
Washington Coll (MD)
Westminster Coll (PA)
Wheaton Coll (MA)
Wilson Coll (PA)
Wittenberg U (OH)
York Coll (NE)

PHYSIOLOGY
Boston U (MA)
California State U, Fresno (CA)
California State U, Long Beach (CA)
Cornell U (NY)
Florida State U (FL)
Hampshire Coll (MA)
McGill U (PQ, Canada)
Michigan State U (MI)
Minnesota State U, Mankato (MN)
Northern Michigan U (MI)
Okanagan U Coll (BC, Canada)
Queen's U at Kingston (ON, Canada)
Rutgers, State U of NJ, Camden Coll of Arts & Scis (NJ)
Rutgers, State U of NJ, Cook Coll (NJ)
Rutgers, State U of NJ, Douglass Coll (NJ)
Rutgers, State U of NJ, Livingston Coll (NJ)
Rutgers, State U of NJ, Rutgers Coll (NJ)
Rutgers, State U of NJ, U Coll–Camden (NJ)
Rutgers, State U of NJ, U Coll–New Brunswick (NJ)
St. Cloud State U (MN)
San Francisco State U (CA)
San Jose State U (CA)
Sonoma State U (CA)
Southern Illinois U Carbondale (IL)
Southwest Texas State U (TX)
The U of Akron (OH)
U of Alberta (AB, Canada)
The U of Arizona (AZ)
U of British Columbia (BC, Canada)
U of Calif, Davis (CA)
U of Calif, San Diego (CA)
U of Calif, Santa Barbara (CA)
U of Connecticut (CT)
U of Illinois at Urbana–Champaign (IL)
U of Kansas (KS)
U of Minnesota, Twin Cities Campus (MN)
U of New Brunswick, Fredericton (NB, Canada)
U of Toronto (ON, Canada)
The U of Western Ontario (ON, Canada)

PLANT BREEDING
Brigham Young U (UT)
Cornell U (NY)
North Dakota State U (ND)

PLANT PATHOLOGY
Cornell U (NY)
The Ohio State U (OH)
State U of NY Coll of Environ Sci and Forestry (NY)
U of Florida (FL)

PLANT PHYSIOLOGY
The Ohio State U (OH)
State U of NY Coll of Environ Sci and Forestry (NY)

PLANT PROTECTION
California State Polytechnic U, Pomona (CA)
Colorado State U (CO)
Florida A&M U (FL)
Iowa State U of Science and Technology (IA)
Mississippi State U (MS)
North Dakota State U (ND)
The Ohio State U (OH)
State U of NY Coll of Environ Sci and Forestry (NY)
Texas Tech U (TX)
U of Arkansas (AR)
U of Delaware (DE)
U of Georgia (GA)
U of Nebraska–Lincoln (NE)
The U of Tennessee Knoxville (TN)

PLANT SCIENCES
Arkansas State U (AR)
California State U, Fresno (CA)
Cornell U (NY)
Florida State U (FL)
Louisiana State U and A&M Coll (LA)
Louisiana Tech U (LA)
McGill U (PQ, Canada)
Middle Tennessee State U (TN)
Montana State U–Bozeman (MT)
Nova Scotia Ag Coll (NS, Canada)
The Ohio State U (OH)
Oklahoma State U (OK)
Rutgers, State U of NJ, Cook Coll (NJ)
Southern Illinois U Carbondale (IL)
Southwest Texas State U (TX)
State U of NY Coll of Environ Sci and Forestry (NY)
Texas A&M U (TX)
Tuskegee U (AL)
The U of Arizona (AZ)
U of British Columbia (BC, Canada)
U of Calif, Los Angeles (CA)
U of Florida (FL)
U of Idaho (ID)
U of Maryland, Coll Park (MD)
U of Massachusetts Amherst (MA)
U of Minnesota, Twin Cities Campus (MN)
U of Missouri–Columbia (MO)
The U of Tennessee Knoxville (TN)
U of Vermont (VT)
The U of Western Ontario (ON, Canada)
Utah State U (UT)
Washington State U (WA)
West Virginia U (WV)

PLASTICS ENGINEERING
Ball State U (IN)
Case Western Reserve U (OH)
Eastern Michigan U (MI)
Ferris State U (MI)
Kettering U (MI)
U of Massachusetts Lowell (MA)
U of Toronto (ON, Canada)
Winona State U (MN)

PLASTICS TECHNOLOGY
Ball State U (IN)
Eastern Michigan U (MI)
Ferris State U (MI)
Pennsylvania Coll of Technology (PA)
Penn State U at Erie, The Behrend Coll (PA)
Pittsburg State U (KS)

Shawnee State U (OH)
Western Washington U (WA)

PLAY/SCREENWRITING
Bard Coll (NY)
Columbia Coll Chicago (IL)
Concordia U (PQ, Canada)
Emerson Coll (MA)
New York U (NY)
Simon's Rock Coll of Bard (MA)
U of Michigan (MI)
U of Southern California (CA)
York U (ON, Canada)

POLITICAL SCIENCE
Abilene Christian U (TX)
Acadia U (NS, Canada)
Adams State Coll (CO)
Adelphi U (NY)
Adrian Coll (MI)
Agnes Scott Coll (GA)
Alabama A&M U (AL)
Alabama State U (AL)
Albany State U (GA)
Albertson Coll of Idaho (ID)
Albertus Magnus Coll (CT)
Albion Coll (MI)
Albright Coll (PA)
Alderson-Broaddus Coll (WV)
Alfred U (NY)
Allegheny Coll (PA)
Allentown Coll of St. Francis de Sales (PA)
Alma Coll (MI)
Alvernia Coll (PA)
American International Coll (MA)
American U (DC)
American U in Cairo (Egypt)
Amherst Coll (MA)
Anderson U (IN)
Andrews U (MI)
Anna Maria Coll (MA)
Antioch Coll (OH)
Appalachian State U (NC)
Aquinas Coll (MI)
Arizona State U (AZ)
Arizona State U West (AZ)
Arkansas State U (AR)
Armstrong Atlantic State U (GA)
Ashland U (OH)
Assumption Coll (MA)
Athens State U (AL)
Auburn U (AL)
Auburn U Montgomery (AL)
Augsburg Coll (MN)
Augustana Coll (IL)
Augustana Coll (SD)
Augusta State U (GA)
Austin Coll (TX)
Austin Peay State U (TN)
Averett Coll (VA)
Avila Coll (MO)
Azusa Pacific U (CA)
Baker U (KS)
Baldwin-Wallace Coll (OH)
Ball State U (IN)
Barat Coll (IL)
Barber-Scotia Coll (NC)
Bard Coll (NY)
Barnard Coll (NY)
Barry U (FL)
Bartlesville Wesleyan Coll (OK)
Barton Coll (NC)
Bates Coll (ME)
Baylor U (TX)
Beaver Coll (PA)
Bellarmine Coll (KY)
Bellevue U (NE)
Belmont Abbey Coll (NC)
Belmont U (TN)
Beloit Coll (WI)
Bemidji State U (MN)
Benedictine Coll (KS)
Benedictine U (IL)
Bennett Coll (NC)
Berea Coll (KY)
Baruch Coll of the City U of NY (NY)
Berry Coll (GA)
Bethany Coll (KS)
Bethany Coll (WV)
Bethel Coll (MN)
Bethune-Cookman Coll (FL)
Birmingham-Southern Coll (AL)
Bishop's U (PQ, Canada)
Blackburn Coll (IL)
Black Hills State U (SD)

Majors Index
Political Science

Bloomfield Coll (NJ)
Bloomsburg U of Pennsylvania (PA)
Bluffton Coll (OH)
Boise State U (ID)
Boston Coll (MA)
Boston U (MA)
Bowdoin Coll (ME)
Bowie State U (MD)
Bowling Green State U (OH)
Bradley U (IL)
Brandeis U (MA)
Brandon U (MB, Canada)
Brenau U (GA)
Bridgewater Coll (VA)
Bridgewater State Coll (MA)
Brigham Young U (UT)
Brigham Young U–Hawaii Campus (HI)
Brock U (ON, Canada)
Brooklyn Coll of the City U of NY (NY)
Brown U (RI)
Bryn Mawr Coll (PA)
Bucknell U (PA)
Buena Vista U (IA)
Butler U (IN)
Cabrini Coll (PA)
Caldwell Coll (NJ)
California Baptist U (CA)
California Lutheran U (CA)
California Polytechnic State U, San Luis Obispo (CA)
California State Polytechnic U, Pomona (CA)
California State U, Chico (CA)
California State U, Dominguez Hills (CA)
California State U, Fresno (CA)
California State U, Fullerton (CA)
California State U, Hayward (CA)
California State U, Long Beach (CA)
California State U, Los Angeles (CA)
California State U, Northridge (CA)
California State U, Sacramento (CA)
California State U, San Bernardino (CA)
California State U, San Marcos (CA)
California State U, Stanislaus (CA)
California U of Pennsylvania (PA)
Calumet Coll of Saint Joseph (IN)
Calvin Coll (MI)
Cameron U (OK)
Campbellsville U (KY)
Campbell U (NC)
Canisius Coll (NY)
Capital U (OH)
Carleton Coll (MN)
Carleton U (ON, Canada)
Carnegie Mellon U (PA)
Carroll Coll (MT)
Carroll Coll (WI)
Carson-Newman Coll (TN)
Carthage Coll (WI)
Case Western Reserve U (OH)
Catawba Coll (NC)
The Catholic U of America (DC)
Cedar Crest Coll (PA)
Cedarville Coll (OH)
Centenary Coll (NJ)
Centenary Coll of Louisiana (LA)
Central Coll (IA)
Central Connecticut State U (CT)
Central Methodist Coll (MO)
Central Michigan U (MI)
Central Missouri State U (MO)
Centre Coll (KY)
Chaminade U of Honolulu (HI)
Chapman U (CA)
Charleston Southern U (SC)
Chatham Coll (PA)
Chestnut Hill Coll (PA)
Cheyney U of Pennsylvania (PA)
Chicago State U (IL)
Christendom Coll (VA)
Christopher Newport U (VA)
Citadel, The Military Coll of South Carolina (SC)
City Coll of the City U of NY (NY)
City U (WA)
Claremont McKenna Coll (CA)
Clarion U of Pennsylvania (PA)
Clark Atlanta U (GA)

Clarkson U (NY)
Clark U (MA)
Clemson U (SC)
Cleveland State U (OH)
Coastal Carolina U (SC)
Coe Coll (IA)
Coker Coll (SC)
Colby Coll (ME)
Colgate U (NY)
Coll of Charleston (SC)
The Coll of New Jersey (NJ)
The Coll of New Rochelle (NY)
Coll of Notre Dame (CA)
Coll of Notre Dame of Maryland (MD)
Coll of Saint Benedict (MN)
Coll of St. Catherine (MN)
Coll of St. Joseph (VT)
Coll of Santa Fe (NM)
The Coll of Southeastern Europe, The American U of Athens (Greece)
Coll of Staten Island of the City U of NY (NY)
Coll of the Holy Cross (MA)
Coll of the Ozarks (MO)
The Coll of William and Mary (VA)
The Coll of Wooster (OH)
Colorado Christian U (CO)
The Colorado Coll (CO)
Colorado State U (CO)
Columbia Coll (MO)
Columbia Coll (NY)
Columbia Coll (SC)
Columbia U, School of General Studies (NY)
Columbus State U (GA)
Concord Coll (WV)
Concordia Coll (MN)
Concordia U (CA)
Concordia U (IL)
Concordia U (PQ, Canada)
Concordia U Coll of Alberta (AB, Canada)
Connecticut Coll (CT)
Converse Coll (SC)
Cornell Coll (IA)
Cornell U (NY)
Creighton U (NE)
Cumberland Coll (KY)
Curry Coll (MA)
Dalhousie U (NS, Canada)
Dallas Baptist U (TX)
David Lipscomb U (TN)
Davidson Coll (NC)
Delaware State U (DE)
Delta State U (MS)
Denison U (OH)
DePaul U (IL)
DePauw U (IN)
Dickinson Coll (PA)
Dickinson State U (ND)
Doane Coll (NE)
Dominican Coll of Blauvelt (NY)
Dominican U (IL)
Dominican U of California (CA)
Dordt Coll (IA)
Dowling Coll (NY)
Drake U (IA)
Drew U (NJ)
Drexel U (PA)
Drury U (MO)
Duke U (NC)
Duquesne U (PA)
Earlham Coll (IN)
East Carolina U (NC)
East Central U (OK)
Eastern Coll (PA)
Eastern Connecticut State U (CT)
Eastern Illinois U (IL)
Eastern Kentucky U (KY)
Eastern Michigan U (MI)
Eastern New Mexico U (NM)
Eastern Washington U (WA)
East Stroudsburg U of Pennsylvania (PA)
East Tennessee State U (TN)
Eckerd Coll (FL)
Edgewood Coll (WI)
Edinboro U of Pennsylvania (PA)
Elizabeth City State U (NC)
Elizabethtown Coll (PA)
Elmhurst Coll (IL)
Elmira Coll (NY)
Elon Coll (NC)
Emmanuel Coll (MA)
Emory & Henry Coll (VA)

Emory U (GA)
Emporia State U (KS)
Eugene Lang Coll, New School U (NY)
Evangel U (MO)
The Evergreen State Coll (WA)
Fairfield U (CT)
Fairleigh Dickinson U, Florham-Madison Campus (NJ)
Fairleigh Dickinson U, Teaneck-Hackensack Campus (NJ)
Fairmont State Coll (WV)
Faulkner U (AL)
Felician Coll (NJ)
Ferrum Coll (VA)
Fisk U (TN)
Fitchburg State Coll (MA)
Florida A&M U (FL)
Florida Atlantic U (FL)
Florida International U (FL)
Florida Southern Coll (FL)
Florida State U (FL)
Fordham U (NY)
Fort Hays State U (KS)
Fort Lewis Coll (CO)
Fort Valley State U (GA)
Framingham State Coll (MA)
Franciscan U of Steubenville (OH)
Francis Marion U (SC)
Franklin and Marshall Coll (PA)
Franklin Coll of Indiana (IN)
Franklin Pierce Coll (NH)
Fresno Pacific U (CA)
Friends U (KS)
Frostburg State U (MD)
Furman U (SC)
Gannon U (PA)
Gardner-Webb U (NC)
Geneva Coll (PA)
George Mason U (VA)
Georgetown Coll (KY)
Georgetown U (DC)
The George Washington U (DC)
Georgia Coll and State U (GA)
Georgia Southern U (GA)
Georgia Southwestern State U (GA)
Georgia State U (GA)
Gettysburg Coll (PA)
Goddard Coll (VT)
Golden Gate U (CA)
Gonzaga U (WA)
Gordon Coll (MA)
Goshen Coll (IN)
Goucher Coll (MD)
Grand Canyon U (AZ)
Grand Valley State U (MI)
Grand View Coll (IA)
Greensboro Coll (NC)
Greenville Coll (IL)
Grinnell Coll (IA)
Grove City Coll (PA)
Guilford Coll (NC)
Gustavus Adolphus Coll (MN)
Hamilton Coll (NY)
Hamline U (MN)
Hampden-Sydney Coll (VA)
Hampshire Coll (MA)
Hampton U (VA)
Hanover Coll (IN)
Harding U (AR)
Hardin-Simmons U (TX)
Hartwick Coll (NY)
Harvard U (MA)
Hastings Coll (NE)
Haverford Coll (PA)
Hawaii Pacific U (HI)
Heidelberg Coll (OH)
Henderson State U (AR)
Hendrix Coll (AR)
Heritage Coll (WA)
High Point U (NC)
Hillsdale Coll (MI)
Hiram Coll (OH)
Hobart and William Smith Colls (NY)
Hofstra U (NY)
Hollins U (VA)
Hood Coll (MD)
Hope Coll (MI)
Houghton Coll (NY)
Houston Baptist U (TX)
Howard Payne U (TX)
Howard U (DC)
Humboldt State U (CA)
Hunter Coll of the City U of NY (NY)

Huntingdon Coll (AL)
Huston-Tillotson Coll (TX)
Idaho State U (ID)
Illinois Coll (IL)
Illinois Inst of Technology (IL)
Illinois State U (IL)
Illinois Wesleyan U (IL)
Indiana State U (IN)
Indiana U Bloomington (IN)
Indiana U Northwest (IN)
Indiana U of Pennsylvania (PA)
Indiana U–Purdue U Fort Wayne (IN)
Indiana U–Purdue U Indianapolis (IN)
Indiana U South Bend (IN)
Indiana U Southeast (IN)
Indiana Wesleyan U (IN)
Inter American U of PR, Metropolitan Campus (PR)
Inter American U of PR, San Germán Campus (PR)
Iona Coll (NY)
Iowa State U of Science and Technology (IA)
Ithaca Coll (NY)
Jacksonville State U (AL)
Jacksonville U (FL)
James Madison U (VA)
Jamestown Coll (ND)
Jarvis Christian Coll (TX)
John Carroll U (OH)
Johns Hopkins U (MD)
Johnson C. Smith U (NC)
Johnson State Coll (VT)
Juniata Coll (PA)
Kalamazoo Coll (MI)
Kansas State U (KS)
Kean U (NJ)
Keene State Coll (NH)
Kent State U (OH)
Kentucky State U (KY)
Kentucky Wesleyan Coll (KY)
Kenyon Coll (OH)
King Coll (TN)
King's Coll (PA)
Knox Coll (IL)
Kutztown U of Pennsylvania (PA)
Lafayette Coll (PA)
LaGrange Coll (GA)
Lake Forest Coll (IL)
Lakehead U (ON, Canada)
Lake Superior State U (MI)
Lamar U (TX)
Lambuth U (TN)
Lander U (SC)
La Salle U (PA)
La Sierra U (CA)
Lawrence U (WI)
Lebanon Valley Coll (PA)
Lehigh U (PA)
Lehman Coll of the City U of NY (NY)
Le Moyne Coll (NY)
LeMoyne-Owen Coll (TN)
Lenoir-Rhyne Coll (NC)
Lewis & Clark Coll (OR)
Lewis U (IL)
Liberty U (VA)
Lincoln U (MO)
Lincoln U (PA)
Lindenwood U (MO)
Linfield Coll (OR)
Lock Haven U of Pennsylvania (PA)
Long Island U, Brooklyn Campus (NY)
Long Island U, C.W. Post Campus (NY)
Long Island U, Southampton Coll (NY)
Long Island U, Southampton Coll, Friends World Program (NY)
Longwood Coll (VA)
Loras Coll (IA)
Louisiana State U and A&M Coll (LA)
Louisiana State U in Shreveport (LA)
Louisiana Tech U (LA)
Loyola Coll in Maryland (MD)
Loyola Marymount U (CA)
Loyola U Chicago (IL)
Loyola U New Orleans (LA)
Luther Coll (IA)
Lycoming Coll (PA)
Lynchburg Coll (VA)

Lynn U (FL)
Lyon Coll (AR)
Macalester Coll (MN)
MacMurray Coll (IL)
Manchester Coll (IN)
Manhattan Coll (NY)
Manhattanville Coll (NY)
Mansfield U of Pennsylvania (PA)
Marian Coll of Fond du Lac (WI)
Marietta Coll (OH)
Marist Coll (NY)
Marlboro Coll (VT)
Marquette U (WI)
Marshall U (WV)
Mars Hill Coll (NC)
Mary Baldwin Coll (VA)
Marygrove Coll (MI)
Marymount Coll (NY)
Marymount Manhattan Coll (NY)
Maryville Coll (TN)
Maryville U of Saint Louis (MO)
Mary Washington Coll (VA)
Massachusetts Inst of Technology (MA)
McGill U (PQ, Canada)
McKendree Coll (IL)
McMurry U (TX)
McNeese State U (LA)
Medaille Coll (NY)
Memorial U of Newfoundland (NF, Canada)
Mercer U (GA)
Mercy Coll (NY)
Mercyhurst Coll (PA)
Meredith Coll (NC)
Merrimack Coll (MA)
Mesa State Coll (CO)
Messiah Coll (PA)
Methodist Coll (NC)
Metropolitan State Coll of Denver (CO)
Miami U (OH)
Michigan State U (MI)
Middlebury Coll (VT)
Middle Tennessee State U (TN)
Midwestern State U (TX)
Millersville U of Pennsylvania (PA)
Millikin U (IL)
Millsaps Coll (MS)
Minnesota State U, Mankato (MN)
Minnesota State U Moorhead (MN)
Mississippi Coll (MS)
Mississippi State U (MS)
Mississippi U for Women (MS)
Mississippi Valley State U (MS)
Missouri Southern State Coll (MO)
Missouri Valley Coll (MO)
Missouri Western State Coll (MO)
Molloy Coll (NY)
Monmouth Coll (IL)
Monmouth U (NJ)
Montana State U–Bozeman (MT)
Moravian Coll (PA)
Morehead State U (KY)
Morehouse Coll (GA)
Morgan State U (MD)
Morningside Coll (IA)
Morris Coll (SC)
Mount Allison U (NB, Canada)
Mount Holyoke Coll (MA)
Mount Mercy Coll (IA)
Mount Saint Mary Coll (NY)
Mount St. Mary's Coll (CA)
Mount Saint Mary's Coll and Seminary (MD)
Mount Saint Vincent U (NS, Canada)
Mount Union Coll (OH)
Muhlenberg Coll (PA)
Murray State U (KY)
Muskingum Coll (OH)
Nazareth Coll of Rochester (NY)
Nebraska Wesleyan U (NE)
Neumann Coll (PA)
Newberry Coll (SC)
New Coll of the U of South Florida (FL)
New England Coll (NH)
New Hampshire Coll (NH)
New Jersey City U (NJ)
New Mexico Highlands U (NM)
New Mexico State U (NM)
New York Inst of Technology (NY)
New York U (NY)
Niagara U (NY)
Nicholls State U (LA)
Norfolk State U (VA)

Majors Index
Political Science

North Carolina Ag and Tech State U (NC)
North Carolina Central U (NC)
North Carolina State U (NC)
North Carolina Wesleyan Coll (NC)
North Central Coll (IL)
North Dakota State U (ND)
Northeastern Illinois U (IL)
Northeastern State U (OK)
Northeastern U (MA)
Northern Arizona U (AZ)
Northern Illinois U (IL)
Northern Kentucky U (KY)
Northern Michigan U (MI)
Northern State U (SD)
North Georgia Coll & State U (GA)
North Park U (IL)
Northwestern Coll (IA)
Northwestern Oklahoma State U (OK)
Northwestern State U of Louisiana (LA)
Northwestern U (IL)
Northwest Missouri State U (MO)
Northwest Nazarene U (ID)
Norwich U (VT)
Notre Dame Coll of Ohio (OH)
Oakland U (MI)
Oberlin Coll (OH)
Occidental Coll (CA)
Oglethorpe U (GA)
Ohio Dominican Coll (OH)
Ohio Northern U (OH)
The Ohio State U (OH)
Ohio U (OH)
Ohio Wesleyan U (OH)
Okanagan U Coll (BC, Canada)
Oklahoma Baptist U (OK)
Oklahoma City U (OK)
Oklahoma State U (OK)
Old Dominion U (VA)
Oregon State U (OR)
Ottawa U (KS)
Otterbein Coll (OH)
Ouachita Baptist U (AR)
Our Lady of the Lake U of San Antonio (TX)
Pace U, New York City Campus (NY)
Pace U, Pleasantville/Briarcliff Campus (NY)
Pacific Lutheran U (WA)
Pacific Union Coll (CA)
Pacific U (OR)
Palm Beach Atlantic Coll (FL)
Park U (MO)
Penn State U at Erie, The Behrend Coll (PA)
Penn State U Univ Park Campus (PA)
Pepperdine U, Malibu (CA)
Pfeiffer U (NC)
Philander Smith Coll (AR)
Pine Manor Coll (MA)
Pittsburg State U (KS)
Pitzer Coll (CA)
Plattsburgh State U of NY (NY)
Plymouth State Coll (NH)
Point Loma Nazarene U (CA)
Point Park Coll (PA)
Pomona Coll (CA)
Pontifical Catholic U of Puerto Rico (PR)
Portland State U (OR)
Prairie View A&M U (TX)
Presbyterian Coll (SC)
Princeton U (NJ)
Principia Coll (IL)
Providence Coll (RI)
Purchase Coll, State U of NY (NY)
Purdue U (IN)
Purdue U Calumet (IN)
Queens Coll (NC)
Queens Coll of the City U of NY (NY)
Queen's U at Kingston (ON, Canada)
Quincy U (IL)
Quinnipiac U (CT)
Radford U (VA)
Ramapo Coll of New Jersey (NJ)
Randolph-Macon Coll (VA)
Randolph-Macon Woman's Coll (VA)
Redeemer Coll (ON, Canada)
Reed Coll (OR)
Regents Coll (NY)

Regis Coll (MA)
Regis U (CO)
Rhodes Coll (TN)
Rice U (TX)
The Richard Stockton Coll of New Jersey (NJ)
Richmond, The American International U in London (United Kingdom)
Rider U (NJ)
Ripon Coll (WI)
Roanoke Coll (VA)
Rockford Coll (IL)
Rockhurst U (MO)
Rocky Mountain Coll (MT)
Roger Williams U (RI)
Rollins Coll (FL)
Rosemont Coll (PA)
Rowan U (NJ)
Russell Sage Coll (NY)
Rust Coll (MS)
Rutgers, State U of NJ, Camden Coll of Arts & Scis (NJ)
Rutgers, State U of NJ, Douglass Coll (NJ)
Rutgers, State U of NJ, Livingston Coll (NJ)
Rutgers, State U of NJ, Newark Coll of Arts & Scis (NJ)
Rutgers, State U of NJ, Rutgers Coll (NJ)
Rutgers, State U of NJ, U Coll–Camden (NJ)
Rutgers, State U of NJ, U Coll–Newark (NJ)
Rutgers, State U of NJ, U Coll–New Brunswick (NJ)
Sacred Heart U (CT)
Saginaw Valley State U (MI)
St. Ambrose U (IA)
St. Andrews Presbyterian Coll (NC)
Saint Anselm Coll (NH)
Saint Augustine's Coll (NC)
St. Bonaventure U (NY)
St. Cloud State U (MN)
St. Edward's U (TX)
St. Francis Coll (NY)
Saint Francis Coll (PA)
St. Francis Xavier U (NS, Canada)
St. John Fisher Coll (NY)
Saint John's U (MN)
St. John's U (NY)
Saint Joseph Coll (CT)
Saint Joseph's Coll (IN)
St. Joseph's Coll, New York (NY)
Saint Joseph's U (PA)
St. Lawrence U (NY)
Saint Leo U (FL)
Saint Louis U (MO)
Saint Martin's Coll (WA)
Saint Mary Coll (KS)
Saint Mary's Coll (IN)
Saint Mary's Coll of California (CA)
St. Mary's Coll of Maryland (MD)
Saint Mary's U (NS, Canada)
Saint Mary's U of Minnesota (MN)
St. Mary's U of San Antonio (TX)
Saint Michael's Coll (VT)
St. Norbert Coll (WI)
St. Olaf Coll (MN)
Saint Paul's Coll (VA)
Saint Peter's Coll (NJ)
St. Thomas U (FL)
Saint Vincent Coll (PA)
Saint Xavier U (IL)
Salem State Coll (MA)
Salisbury State U (MD)
Salve Regina U (RI)
Samford U (AL)
Sam Houston State U (TX)
San Diego State U (CA)
San Francisco State U (CA)
San Jose State U (CA)
Santa Clara U (CA)
Sarah Lawrence Coll (NY)
Savannah State U (GA)
Scripps Coll (CA)
Seattle Pacific U (WA)
Seattle U (WA)
Seton Hall U (NJ)
Seton Hill Coll (PA)
Shepherd Coll (WV)
Shippensburg U of Pennsylvania (PA)
Siena Coll (NY)
Simmons Coll (MA)
Simon Fraser U (BC, Canada)

Simon's Rock Coll of Bard (MA)
Simpson Coll (IA)
Skidmore Coll (NY)
Slippery Rock U of Pennsylvania (PA)
Smith Coll (MA)
Sonoma State U (CA)
South Dakota State U (SD)
Southeastern Louisiana U (LA)
Southeastern Oklahoma State U (OK)
Southeast Missouri State U (MO)
Southern Arkansas U–Magnolia (AR)
Southern Illinois U Carbondale (IL)
Southern Illinois U Edwardsville (IL)
Southern Methodist U (TX)
Southern Oregon U (OR)
Southern Utah U (UT)
Southwest Baptist U (MO)
Southwestern Oklahoma State U (OK)
Southwestern U (TX)
Southwest Missouri State U (MO)
Southwest State U (MN)
Southwest Texas State U (TX)
Spelman Coll (GA)
Spring Hill Coll (AL)
Stanford U (CA)
State U of NY at Albany (NY)
State U of NY at Binghamton (NY)
State U of NY at Buffalo (NY)
State U of NY at New Paltz (NY)
State U of NY at Oswego (NY)
State U of NY at Stony Brook (NY)
State U of NY Coll at Brockport (NY)
State U of NY Coll at Buffalo (NY)
State U of NY Coll at Cortland (NY)
State U of NY Coll at Fredonia (NY)
State U of NY Coll at Geneseo (NY)
State U of NY Coll at Oneonta (NY)
State U of NY Coll at Potsdam (NY)
State U of West Georgia (GA)
Stephen F. Austin State U (TX)
Stephens Coll (MO)
Stetson U (FL)
Stonehill Coll (MA)
Suffolk U (MA)
Sul Ross State U (TX)
Susquehanna U (PA)
Swarthmore Coll (PA)
Sweet Briar Coll (VA)
Syracuse U (NY)
Taylor U (IN)
Temple U (PA)
Tennessee State U (TN)
Tennessee Technological U (TN)
Texas A&M International U (TX)
Texas A&M U (TX)
Texas A&M U–Commerce (TX)
Texas A&M U–Kingsville (TX)
Texas Christian U (TX)
Texas Lutheran U (TX)
Texas Southern U (TX)
Texas Tech U (TX)
Texas Wesleyan U (TX)
Texas Woman's U (TX)
Thiel Coll (PA)
Thomas Edison State Coll (NJ)
Thomas More Coll of Liberal Arts (NH)
Thomas U (GA)
Tougaloo Coll (MS)
Touro Coll (NY)
Towson U (MD)
Transylvania U (KY)
Trent U (ON, Canada)
Trinity Coll (CT)
Trinity U (TX)
Trinity Western U (BC, Canada)
Troy State U (AL)
Troy State U Montgomery (AL)
Truman State U (MO)
Tufts U (MA)
Tulane U (LA)
Tuskegee U (AL)
Union Coll (KY)
Union Coll (NE)
Union U (TN)
United States Air Force Academy (CO)

United States Coast Guard Academy (CT)
United States International U (CA)
United States Military Academy (NY)
United States Naval Academy (MD)
Université de Montréal (PQ, Canada)
U du Québec à Chicoutimi (PQ, Canada)
Université Laval (PQ, Canada)
U Coll of Cape Breton (NS, Canada)
The U of Akron (OH)
The U of Alabama (AL)
The U of Alabama at Birmingham (AL)
The U of Alabama in Huntsville (AL)
U of Alaska Fairbanks (AK)
U of Alberta (AB, Canada)
The U of Arizona (AZ)
U of Arkansas (AR)
U of Arkansas at Little Rock (AR)
U of Arkansas at Monticello (AR)
U of Arkansas at Pine Bluff (AR)
U of Baltimore (MD)
U of British Columbia (BC, Canada)
U of Calgary (AB, Canada)
U of Calif, Berkeley (CA)
U of Calif, Davis (CA)
U of Calif, Irvine (CA)
U of Calif, Los Angeles (CA)
U of Calif, Riverside (CA)
U of Calif, Santa Barbara (CA)
U of Calif, Santa Cruz (CA)
U of Central Arkansas (AR)
U of Central Florida (FL)
U of Central Oklahoma (OK)
U of Charleston (WV)
U of Chicago (IL)
U of Cincinnati (OH)
U of Colorado at Boulder (CO)
U of Colorado at Colorado Springs (CO)
U of Colorado at Denver (CO)
U of Connecticut (CT)
U of Dallas (TX)
U of Dayton (OH)
U of Delaware (DE)
U of Denver (CO)
U of Detroit Mercy (MI)
U of Evansville (IN)
The U of Findlay (OH)
U of Florida (FL)
U of Georgia (GA)
U of Guelph (ON, Canada)
U of Hartford (CT)
U of Hawaii at Manoa (HI)
U of Houston (TX)
U of Idaho (ID)
U of Illinois at Chicago (IL)
U of Illinois at Springfield (IL)
U of Illinois at Urbana–Champaign (IL)
U of Indianapolis (IN)
The U of Iowa (IA)
U of Judaism (CA)
U of Kansas (KS)
U of Kentucky (KY)
U of King's Coll (NS, Canada)
U of La Verne (CA)
The U of Lethbridge (AB, Canada)
U of Louisiana at Lafayette (LA)
U of Louisiana at Monroe (LA)
U of Louisville (KY)
U of Maine (ME)
U of Maine at Farmington (ME)
U of Maine at Presque Isle (ME)
U of Manitoba (MB, Canada)
U of Mary Hardin-Baylor (TX)
U of Maryland, Baltimore County (MD)
U of Maryland, Coll Park (MD)
U of Massachusetts Amherst (MA)
U of Massachusetts Boston (MA)
U of Massachusetts Dartmouth (MA)
U of Massachusetts Lowell (MA)
The U of Memphis (TN)
U of Miami (FL)
U of Michigan (MI)
U of Michigan–Dearborn (MI)
U of Michigan–Flint (MI)
U of Minnesota, Duluth (MN)
U of Minnesota, Morris (MN)

U of Minnesota, Twin Cities Campus (MN)
U of Mississippi (MS)
U of Missouri–Columbia (MO)
U of Missouri–Kansas City (MO)
U of Missouri–St. Louis (MO)
U of Mobile (AL)
U of Montevallo (AL)
U of Nebraska at Kearney (NE)
U of Nebraska at Omaha (NE)
U of Nebraska–Lincoln (NE)
U of Nevada, Las Vegas (NV)
U of Nevada, Reno (NV)
U of New Brunswick, Fredericton (NB, Canada)
U of New Brunswick, Saint John (NB, Canada)
U of New Hampshire (NH)
U of New Haven (CT)
U of New Mexico (NM)
U of New Orleans (LA)
U of North Alabama (AL)
The U of North Carolina at Asheville (NC)
The U of North Carolina at Chapel Hill (NC)
The U of North Carolina at Charlotte (NC)
The U of North Carolina at Greensboro (NC)
The U of North Carolina at Pembroke (NC)
The U of North Carolina at Wilmington (NC)
U of North Dakota (ND)
U of Northern Colorado (CO)
U of Northern Iowa (IA)
U of North Florida (FL)
U of North Texas (TX)
U of Notre Dame (IN)
U of Oklahoma (OK)
U of Oregon (OR)
U of Pennsylvania (PA)
U of Pittsburgh (PA)
U of Pittsburgh at Bradford (PA)
U of Pittsburgh at Johnstown (PA)
U of Portland (OR)
U of Prince Edward Island (PE, Canada)
U of Puerto Rico, Mayagüez Campus (PR)
U of Puerto Rico, Río Piedras (PR)
U of Puget Sound (WA)
U of Redlands (CA)
U of Regina (SK, Canada)
U of Rhode Island (RI)
U of Richmond (VA)
U of Rio Grande (OH)
U of Rochester (NY)
U of St. Francis (IL)
U of St. Thomas (MN)
U of St. Thomas (TX)
U of San Diego (CA)
U of San Francisco (CA)
U of Science and Arts of Oklahoma (OK)
The U of Scranton (PA)
U of Sioux Falls (SD)
U of South Alabama (AL)
U of South Carolina (SC)
U of South Carolina Spartanburg (SC)
U of South Dakota (SD)
U of Southern California (CA)
U of Southern Colorado (CO)
U of Southern Indiana (IN)
U of Southern Maine (ME)
U of Southern Mississippi (MS)
U of South Florida (FL)
The U of Tampa (FL)
The U of Tennessee at Chattanooga (TN)
The U of Tennessee at Martin (TN)
The U of Tennessee Knoxville (TN)
The U of Texas at Arlington (TX)
The U of Texas at Austin (TX)
The U of Texas at Dallas (TX)
The U of Texas at San Antonio (TX)
The U of Texas at Tyler (TX)
The U of Texas–Pan American (TX)
U of the District of Columbia (DC)
U of the Ozarks (AR)
U of the Pacific (CA)
U of the South (TN)
U of Toronto (ON, Canada)
U of Tulsa (OK)

Majors Index
Political Science–Psychology

U of Utah (UT)
U of Vermont (VT)
U of Victoria (BC, Canada)
U of Virginia (VA)
U of Virginia's Coll at Wise (VA)
U of Washington (WA)
U of Waterloo (ON, Canada)
The U of Western Ontario (ON, Canada)
U of West Florida (FL)
U of Windsor (ON, Canada)
The U of Winnipeg (MB, Canada)
U of Wisconsin–Eau Claire (WI)
U of Wisconsin–Green Bay (WI)
U of Wisconsin–La Crosse (WI)
U of Wisconsin–Madison (WI)
U of Wisconsin–Milwaukee (WI)
U of Wisconsin–Parkside (WI)
U of Wisconsin–Platteville (WI)
U of Wisconsin–River Falls (WI)
U of Wisconsin–Stevens Point (WI)
U of Wisconsin–Superior (WI)
U of Wisconsin–Whitewater (WI)
U of Wyoming (WY)
Ursinus Coll (PA)
Utah State U (UT)
Utica Coll of Syracuse U (NY)
Valdosta State U (GA)
Valparaiso U (IN)
Vanderbilt U (TN)
Vanguard U of Southern California (CA)
Vassar Coll (NY)
Villanova U (PA)
Virginia Commonwealth U (VA)
Virginia Intermont Coll (VA)
Virginia Polytechnic Inst and State U (VA)
Virginia Union U (VA)
Virginia Wesleyan Coll (VA)
Voorhees Coll (SC)
Wabash Coll (IN)
Wagner Coll (NY)
Wake Forest U (NC)
Walsh U (OH)
Warren Wilson Coll (NC)
Wartburg Coll (IA)
Washington & Jefferson Coll (PA)
Washington and Lee U (VA)
Washington Coll (MD)
Washington State U (WA)
Washington U in St. Louis (MO)
Wayland Baptist U (TX)
Waynesburg Coll (PA)
Wayne State Coll (NE)
Wayne State U (MI)
Weber State U (UT)
Webster U (MO)
Wellesley Coll (MA)
Wells Coll (NY)
Wesleyan Coll (GA)
Wesleyan U (CT)
Wesley Coll (DE)
West Chester U of Pennsylvania (PA)
Western Carolina U (NC)
Western Connecticut State U (CT)
Western Illinois U (IL)
Western Kentucky U (KY)
Western Maryland Coll (MD)
Western Michigan U (MI)
Western New England Coll (MA)
Western Oregon U (OR)
Western State Coll of Colorado (CO)
Western Washington U (WA)
Westfield State Coll (MA)
West Liberty State Coll (WV)
Westminster Coll (MO)
Westminster Coll (PA)
Westminster Coll (UT)
Westmont Coll (CA)
West Texas A&M U (TX)
West Virginia State Coll (WV)
West Virginia U (WV)
West Virginia Wesleyan Coll (WV)
Wheaton Coll (IL)
Wheaton Coll (MA)
Wheeling Jesuit U (WV)
Whitman Coll (WA)
Whittier Coll (CA)
Whitworth Coll (WA)
Wichita State U (KS)
Widener U (PA)
Wilfrid Laurier U (ON, Canada)
Wilkes U (PA)
Willamette U (OR)

William Jewell Coll (MO)
William Paterson U of New Jersey (NJ)
William Penn U (IA)
Williams Coll (MA)
William Woods U (MO)
Wilmington Coll (OH)
Winona State U (MN)
Winston-Salem State U (NC)
Winthrop U (SC)
Wittenberg U (OH)
Wofford Coll (SC)
Woodbury U (CA)
Worcester Polytechnic Inst (MA)
Wright State U (OH)
Xavier U (OH)
Xavier U of Louisiana (LA)
Yale U (CT)
Yeshiva U (NY)
York Coll of Pennsylvania (PA)
York Coll of the City U of New York (NY)
York U (ON, Canada)
Youngstown State U (OH)

POLYMER CHEMISTRY
Carnegie Mellon U (PA)
Georgia Inst of Technology (GA)
Harvard U (MA)
Millersville U of Pennsylvania (PA)
North Dakota State U (ND)
Rochester Inst of Technology (NY)
State U of NY Coll of Environ Sci and Forestry (NY)
U of Southern Mississippi (MS)
U of Wisconsin–Stevens Point (WI)
Winona State U (MN)

PORTUGUESE
Brigham Young U (UT)
Brown U (RI)
Florida International U (FL)
Georgetown U (DC)
Harvard U (MA)
Indiana U Bloomington (IN)
Long Island U, Southampton Coll, Friends World Program (NY)
Marlboro Coll (VT)
New York U (NY)
The Ohio State U (OH)
Rutgers, State U of NJ, Douglass Coll (NJ)
Rutgers, State U of NJ, Livingston Coll (NJ)
Rutgers, State U of NJ, Rutgers Coll (NJ)
Rutgers, State U of NJ, U Coll–New Brunswick (NJ)
Saint Louis U (MO)
Smith Coll (MA)
Tulane U (LA)
United States Military Academy (NY)
U of Calif, Los Angeles (CA)
U of Calif, Santa Barbara (CA)
U of Connecticut (CT)
U of Florida (FL)
U of Illinois at Urbana–Champaign (IL)
The U of Iowa (IA)
U of Massachusetts Amherst (MA)
U of Massachusetts Dartmouth (MA)
U of Minnesota, Twin Cities Campus (MN)
U of New Mexico (NM)
The U of Scranton (PA)
The U of Texas at Austin (TX)
U of Toronto (ON, Canada)
U of Wisconsin–Madison (WI)
Vanderbilt U (TN)
Yale U (CT)

POULTRY SCIENCE
Auburn U (AL)
Clemson U (SC)
Coll of the Ozarks (MO)
Cornell U (NY)
Louisiana State U and A&M Coll (LA)
Mississippi State U (MS)
North Carolina State U (NC)
Stephen F. Austin State U (TX)
Texas A&M U (TX)
Tuskegee U (AL)
U of Arkansas (AR)

U of British Columbia (BC, Canada)
U of Calif, Davis (CA)
U of Florida (FL)
U of Georgia (GA)
U of Wisconsin–Madison (WI)
Virginia Polytechnic Inst and State U (VA)

PRINTMAKING
Academy of Art Coll (CA)
Adams State Coll (CO)
Alberta Coll of Art and Design (AB, Canada)
Alfred U (NY)
Arizona State U (AZ)
The Art Inst of Boston at Lesley (MA)
Atlanta Coll of Art (GA)
Ball State U (IN)
Bennington Coll (VT)
Birmingham-Southern Coll (AL)
Bowling Green State U (OH)
California Coll of Arts and Crafts (CA)
California State U, Fullerton (CA)
California State U, Hayward (CA)
California State U, Long Beach (CA)
California State U, Stanislaus (CA)
Cleveland Inst of Art (OH)
Coll of Santa Fe (NM)
Coll of Visual Arts (MN)
Colorado State U (CO)
Columbus Coll of Art and Design (OH)
Concordia U (PQ, Canada)
The Corcoran Coll of Art and Design (DC)
Emmanuel Coll (MA)
Escuela de Artes Plasticas de Puerto Rico (PR)
Framingham State Coll (MA)
Grand Valley State U (MI)
Indiana Wesleyan U (IN)
Kansas City Art Inst (MO)
Kent State U (OH)
Long Island U, Southampton Coll, Friends World Program (NY)
Longwood Coll (VA)
Maine Coll of Art (ME)
Marshall U (WV)
Maryland Inst, Coll of Art (MD)
Massachusetts Coll of Art (MA)
McNeese State U (LA)
Memorial U of Newfoundland (NF, Canada)
Memphis Coll of Art (TN)
Milwaukee Inst of Art and Design (WI)
Minneapolis Coll of Art and Design (MN)
Minnesota State U Moorhead (MN)
Mississippi U for Women (MS)
Montserrat Coll of Art (MA)
Mount Allison U (NB, Canada)
New World School of the Arts (FL)
Northern Arizona U (AZ)
Northern Michigan U (MI)
Nova Scotia Coll of Art and Design (NS, Canada)
The Ohio State U (OH)
Ohio U (OH)
Pacific Northwest Coll of Art (OR)
Plymouth State Coll (NH)
Pratt Inst (NY)
Rhode Island School of Design (RI)
Rutgers, State U of NJ, Mason Gross School of Arts (NJ)
School of the Art Inst of Chicago (IL)
School of the Museum of Fine Arts (MA)
Seton Hill Coll (PA)
Simon's Rock Coll of Bard (MA)
Sonoma State U (CA)
State U of NY Coll at Buffalo (NY)
Syracuse U (NY)
Trinity Christian Coll (IL)
U of Alberta (AB, Canada)
U of Calif, Santa Cruz (CA)
U of Connecticut (CT)
U of Dallas (TX)
U of Houston (TX)
The U of Iowa (IA)
U of Kansas (KS)

U of Massachusetts Dartmouth (MA)
U of Miami (FL)
U of Michigan (MI)
U of Missouri–St. Louis (MO)
U of Montevallo (AL)
U of North Texas (TX)
U of Oklahoma (OK)
U of Oregon (OR)
U of San Francisco (CA)
U of South Alabama (AL)
U of South Dakota (SD)
The U of Texas at Arlington (TX)
The U of the Arts (PA)
U of Washington (WA)
Virginia Commonwealth U (VA)
Washington U in St. Louis (MO)
Webster U (MO)
York U (ON, Canada)
Youngstown State U (OH)

PSYCHIATRIC/MENTAL HEALTH SERVICES
Edinboro U of Pennsylvania (PA)
Franciscan U of Steubenville (OH)
MCP Hahnemann U (PA)
Pennsylvania Coll of Technology (PA)

PSYCHOLOGY
Abilene Christian U (TX)
Acadia U (NS, Canada)
Adams State Coll (CO)
Adelphi U (NY)
Adrian Coll (MI)
Agnes Scott Coll (GA)
Alabama A&M U (AL)
Alabama State U (AL)
Alaska Pacific U (AK)
Albany State U (GA)
Albertson Coll of Idaho (ID)
Albertus Magnus Coll (CT)
Albion Coll (MI)
Albright Coll (PA)
Alderson-Broaddus Coll (WV)
Alfred U (NY)
Allegheny Coll (PA)
Allentown Coll of St. Francis de Sales (PA)
Alma Coll (MI)
Alvernia Coll (PA)
Alverno Coll (WI)
American Coll of Thessaloniki (Greece)
American International Coll (MA)
American U (DC)
American U in Cairo (Egypt)
Amherst Coll (MA)
Anderson Coll (SC)
Anderson U (IN)
Andrews U (MI)
Anna Maria Coll (MA)
Antioch Coll (OH)
Appalachian State U (NC)
Aquinas Coll (MI)
Arizona State U (AZ)
Arizona State U East (AZ)
Arizona State U West (AZ)
Arkansas State U (AR)
Arkansas Tech U (AR)
Armstrong Atlantic State U (GA)
Asbury Coll (KY)
Ashland U (OH)
Assumption Coll (MA)
Athabasca U (AB, Canada)
Athens State U (AL)
Atlantic Baptist U (NB, Canada)
Atlantic Union Coll (MA)
Auburn U (AL)
Auburn U Montgomery (AL)
Augsburg Coll (MN)
Augustana Coll (IL)
Augustana Coll (SD)
Augusta State U (GA)
Austin Coll (TX)
Austin Peay State U (TN)
Avila Coll (MO)
Azusa Pacific U (CA)
Baker U (KS)
Baldwin-Wallace Coll (OH)
Ball State U (IN)
Barat Coll (IL)
Bard Coll (NY)
Barnard Coll (NY)
Barry U (FL)
Barton Coll (NC)
Bastyr U (WA)

Bates Coll (ME)
Bayamón Central U (PR)
Baylor U (TX)
Bay Path Coll (MA)
Beaver Coll (PA)
Becker Coll (MA)
Belhaven Coll (MS)
Bellarmine Coll (KY)
Bellevue U (NE)
Belmont Abbey Coll (NC)
Belmont U (TN)
Beloit Coll (WI)
Bemidji State U (MN)
Benedictine Coll (KS)
Benedictine U (IL)
Bennett Coll (NC)
Bennington Coll (VT)
Berea Coll (KY)
Berry Coll (GA)
Bethany Coll (KS)
Bethany Coll (WV)
Bethany Coll of the Assemblies of God (CA)
Bethel Coll (IN)
Bethel Coll (KS)
Bethel Coll (MN)
Bethel Coll (TN)
Bethune-Cookman Coll (FL)
Biola U (CA)
Birmingham-Southern Coll (AL)
Bishop's U (PQ, Canada)
Blackburn Coll (IL)
Black Hills State U (SD)
Bloomfield Coll (NJ)
Bloomsburg U of Pennsylvania (PA)
Blue Mountain Coll (MS)
Bluffton Coll (OH)
Boise State U (ID)
Boston Coll (MA)
Boston U (MA)
Bowdoin Coll (ME)
Bowie State U (MD)
Bowling Green State U (OH)
Bradley U (IL)
Brandeis U (MA)
Brandon U (MB, Canada)
Brenau U (GA)
Brescia U (KY)
Briar Cliff Coll (IA)
Bridgewater Coll (VA)
Bridgewater State Coll (MA)
Brigham Young U (UT)
Brigham Young U–Hawaii Campus (HI)
Brock U (ON, Canada)
Brooklyn Coll of the City U of NY (NY)
Brown U (RI)
Bryan Coll (TN)
Bryn Mawr Coll (PA)
Bucknell U (PA)
Buena Vista U (IA)
Burlington Coll (VT)
Butler U (IN)
Cabrini Coll (PA)
Caldwell Coll (NJ)
California Baptist U (CA)
California Lutheran U (CA)
California Polytechnic State U, San Luis Obispo (CA)
California State Polytechnic U, Pomona (CA)
California State U, Chico (CA)
California State U, Dominguez Hills (CA)
California State U, Fresno (CA)
California State U, Fullerton (CA)
California State U, Hayward (CA)
California State U, Long Beach (CA)
California State U, Los Angeles (CA)
California State U, Northridge (CA)
California State U, Sacramento (CA)
California State U, San Bernardino (CA)
California State U, San Marcos (CA)
California State U, Stanislaus (CA)
California U of Pennsylvania (PA)
Calumet Coll of Saint Joseph (IN)
Calvin Coll (MI)
Cambridge Coll (MA)

Majors Index
Psychology

Cameron U (OK)
Campbellsville U (KY)
Campbell U (NC)
Canisius Coll (NY)
Capital U (OH)
Cardinal Stritch U (WI)
Carleton Coll (MN)
Carleton U (ON, Canada)
Carlos Albizu U (FL)
Carlow Coll (PA)
Carnegie Mellon U (PA)
Carroll Coll (MT)
Carroll Coll (WI)
Carson-Newman Coll (TN)
Carthage Coll (WI)
Cascade Coll (OR)
Case Western Reserve U (OH)
Castleton State Coll (VT)
Catawba Coll (NC)
The Catholic U of America (DC)
Cedar Crest Coll (PA)
Cedarville Coll (OH)
Centenary Coll (NJ)
Centenary Coll of Louisiana (LA)
Central Coll (IA)
Central Connecticut State U (CT)
Central Methodist Coll (MO)
Central Michigan U (MI)
Central Missouri State U (MO)
Centre Coll (KY)
Chadron State Coll (NE)
Chaminade U of Honolulu (HI)
Chapman U (CA)
Charleston Southern U (SC)
Chatham Coll (PA)
Chestnut Hill Coll (PA)
Cheyney U of Pennsylvania (PA)
Chicago State U (IL)
Chowan Coll (NC)
Christian Brothers U (TN)
Christopher Newport U (VA)
Citadel, The Military Coll of South Carolina (SC)
City Coll of the City U of NY (NY)
City U (WA)
Claremont McKenna Coll (CA)
Clarion U of Pennsylvania (PA)
Clark Atlanta U (GA)
Clarke Coll (IA)
Clarkson U (NY)
Clark U (MA)
Clemson U (SC)
Cleveland State U (OH)
Coastal Carolina U (SC)
Coe Coll (IA)
Coker Coll (SC)
Colby Coll (ME)
Colby-Sawyer Coll (NH)
Colgate U (NY)
Coll Misericordia (PA)
Coll of Charleston (SC)
Coll of Mount St. Joseph (OH)
Coll of Mount Saint Vincent (NY)
The Coll of New Jersey (NJ)
The Coll of New Rochelle (NY)
Coll of Notre Dame (CA)
Coll of Notre Dame of Maryland (MD)
Coll of Our Lady of the Elms (MA)
Coll of Saint Benedict (MN)
Coll of St. Catherine (MN)
Coll of Saint Elizabeth (NJ)
Coll of St. Joseph (VT)
Coll of Saint Mary (NE)
The Coll of Saint Rose (NY)
The Coll of St. Scholastica (MN)
Coll of Santa Fe (NM)
The Coll of Southeastern Europe, The American U of Athens (Greece)
Coll of Staten Island of the City U of NY (NY)
Coll of the Atlantic (ME)
Coll of the Holy Cross (MA)
Coll of the Ozarks (MO)
Coll of the Southwest (NM)
The Coll of William and Mary (VA)
The Coll of Wooster (OH)
Colorado Christian U (CO)
The Colorado Coll (CO)
Colorado State U (CO)
Columbia Coll (MO)
Columbia Coll (NY)
Columbia Coll (SC)
Columbia International U (SC)
Columbia Union Coll (MD)

Columbia U, School of General Studies (NY)
Columbus State U (GA)
Concord Coll (WV)
Concordia Coll (MI)
Concordia Coll (MN)
Concordia U (CA)
Concordia U (IL)
Concordia U (NE)
Concordia U (OR)
Concordia U (PQ, Canada)
Concordia U at St. Paul (MN)
Concordia U Coll of Alberta (AB, Canada)
Concordia U Wisconsin (WI)
Connecticut Coll (CT)
Converse Coll (SC)
Coppin State Coll (MD)
Cornell Coll (IA)
Cornell U (NY)
Cornerstone U (MI)
Covenant Coll (GA)
Creighton U (NE)
Crichton Coll (TN)
Crown Coll (MN)
Culver-Stockton Coll (MO)
Cumberland Coll (KY)
Curry Coll (MA)
Daemen Coll (NY)
Dakota Wesleyan U (SD)
Dalhousie U (NS, Canada)
Dallas Baptist U (TX)
Dana Coll (NE)
Dartmouth Coll (NH)
David Lipscomb U (TN)
Davidson Coll (NC)
Defiance Coll (OH)
Delaware State U (DE)
Delta State U (MS)
Denison U (OH)
DePaul U (IL)
DePauw U (IN)
Deree Coll (Greece)
Dickinson Coll (PA)
Dickinson State U (ND)
Doane Coll (NE)
Dominican Coll of Blauvelt (NY)
Dominican U (IL)
Dominican U of California (CA)
Dordt Coll (IA)
Dowling Coll (NY)
Drake U (IA)
Drew U (NJ)
Drexel U (PA)
Drury U (MO)
Duke U (NC)
Duquesne U (PA)
Earlham Coll (IN)
East Carolina U (NC)
East Central U (OK)
Eastern Coll (PA)
Eastern Connecticut State U (CT)
Eastern Illinois U (IL)
Eastern Kentucky U (KY)
Eastern Mennonite U (VA)
Eastern Michigan U (MI)
Eastern Nazarene Coll (MA)
Eastern New Mexico U (NM)
Eastern Oregon U (OR)
Eastern Washington U (WA)
East Stroudsburg U of Pennsylvania (PA)
East Tennessee State U (TN)
East Texas Baptist U (TX)
Eckerd Coll (FL)
Edgewood Coll (WI)
Edinboro U of Pennsylvania (PA)
Elizabeth City State U (NC)
Elizabethtown Coll (PA)
Elmhurst Coll (IL)
Elmira Coll (NY)
Elon Coll (NC)
Emmanuel Coll (GA)
Emmanuel Coll (MA)
Emory & Henry Coll (VA)
Emory U (GA)
Emporia State U (KS)
Endicott Coll (MA)
Erskine Coll (SC)
Eugene Lang Coll, New School U (NY)
Evangel U (MO)
The Evergreen State Coll (WA)
Fairfield U (CT)
Fairleigh Dickinson U, Florham-Madison Campus (NJ)

Fairleigh Dickinson U, Teaneck-Hackensack Campus (NJ)
Fairmont State Coll (WV)
Faulkner U (AL)
Felician Coll (NJ)
Ferrum Coll (VA)
Fisk U (TN)
Fitchburg State Coll (MA)
Flagler Coll (FL)
Florida A&M U (FL)
Florida Atlantic U (FL)
Florida Gulf Coast U (FL)
Florida Inst of Technology (FL)
Florida International U (FL)
Florida Southern Coll (FL)
Florida State U (FL)
Fontbonne Coll (MO)
Fordham U (NY)
Fort Hays State U (KS)
Fort Lewis Coll (CO)
Fort Valley State U (GA)
Framingham State Coll (MA)
Franciscan U of Steubenville (OH)
Francis Marion U (SC)
Franklin and Marshall Coll (PA)
Franklin Coll of Indiana (IN)
Franklin Pierce Coll (NH)
Freed-Hardeman U (TN)
Fresno Pacific U (CA)
Friends U (KS)
Frostburg State U (MD)
Furman U (SC)
Gallaudet U (DC)
Gannon U (PA)
Gardner-Webb U (NC)
Geneva Coll (PA)
George Fox U (OR)
George Mason U (VA)
Georgetown Coll (KY)
Georgetown U (DC)
The George Washington U (DC)
Georgia Coll and State U (GA)
Georgian Court Coll (NJ)
Georgia Southern U (GA)
Georgia Southwestern State U (GA)
Georgia State U (GA)
Gettysburg Coll (PA)
Goddard Coll (VT)
Golden Gate U (CA)
Gonzaga U (WA)
Gordon Coll (MA)
Goshen Coll (IN)
Goucher Coll (MD)
Governors State U (IL)
Grace Coll (IN)
Graceland Coll (IA)
Grand Canyon U (AZ)
Grand Valley State U (MI)
Grand View Coll (IA)
Greensboro Coll (NC)
Greenville Coll (IL)
Grinnell Coll (IA)
Grove City Coll (PA)
Guilford Coll (NC)
Gustavus Adolphus Coll (MN)
Gwynedd-Mercy Coll (PA)
Hamilton Coll (NY)
Hamline U (MN)
Hampden-Sydney Coll (VA)
Hampshire Coll (MA)
Hampton U (VA)
Hannibal-LaGrange Coll (MO)
Hanover Coll (IN)
Harding U (AR)
Hardin-Simmons U (TX)
Hartwick Coll (NY)
Harvard U (MA)
Hastings Coll (NE)
Haverford Coll (PA)
Hawaii Pacific U (HI)
Heidelberg Coll (OH)
Henderson State U (AR)
Hendrix Coll (AR)
Heritage Coll (WA)
High Point U (NC)
Hilbert Coll (NY)
Hillsdale Coll (MI)
Hiram Coll (OH)
Hobart and William Smith Colls (NY)
Hofstra U (NY)
Hollins U (VA)
Holy Family Coll (PA)
Holy Names Coll (CA)
Hood Coll (MD)
Hope Coll (MI)

Hope International U (CA)
Houghton Coll (NY)
Houston Baptist U (TX)
Howard Payne U (TX)
Howard U (DC)
Humboldt State U (CA)
Hunter Coll of the City U of NY (NY)
Huntingdon Coll (AL)
Huntington Coll (IN)
Huston-Tillotson Coll (TX)
Idaho State U (ID)
Illinois Coll (IL)
Illinois Inst of Technology (IL)
Illinois State U (IL)
Illinois Wesleyan U (IL)
Immaculata Coll (PA)
Indiana State U (IN)
Indiana U Bloomington (IN)
Indiana U East (IN)
Indiana U Kokomo (IN)
Indiana U Northwest (IN)
Indiana U of Pennsylvania (PA)
Indiana U–Purdue U Fort Wayne (IN)
Indiana U–Purdue U Indianapolis (IN)
Indiana U South Bend (IN)
Indiana U Southeast (IN)
Indiana Wesleyan U (IN)
Inter American U of PR, Metropolitan Campus (PR)
Inter American U of PR, San Germán Campus (PR)
Iona Coll (NY)
Iowa State U of Science and Technology (IA)
Iowa Wesleyan Coll (IA)
Ithaca Coll (NY)
Jacksonville State U (AL)
Jacksonville U (FL)
James Madison U (VA)
Jamestown Coll (ND)
John Brown U (AR)
John Carroll U (OH)
John F. Kennedy U (CA)
John Jay Coll of Criminal Justice, the City U of NY (NY)
Johns Hopkins U (MD)
Johnson C. Smith U (NC)
Johnson State Coll (VT)
John Wesley Coll (NC)
Judson Coll (AL)
Judson Coll (IL)
Juniata Coll (PA)
Kalamazoo Coll (MI)
Kansas State U (KS)
Kean U (NJ)
Keene State Coll (NH)
Kendall Coll (IL)
Kent State U (OH)
Kentucky Christian Coll (KY)
Kentucky State U (KY)
Kentucky Wesleyan Coll (KY)
Kenyon Coll (OH)
Keuka Coll (NY)
King Coll (TN)
King's Coll (PA)
The King's U Coll (AB, Canada)
Knox Coll (IL)
Kutztown U of Pennsylvania (PA)
Lafayette Coll (PA)
LaGrange Coll (GA)
Lake Erie Coll (OH)
Lake Forest Coll (IL)
Lakehead U (ON, Canada)
Lakeland Coll (WI)
Lake Superior State U (MI)
Lamar U (TX)
Lambuth U (TN)
Lander U (SC)
Langston U (OK)
La Roche Coll (PA)
La Salle U (PA)
Lasell Coll (MA)
La Sierra U (CA)
Lawrence U (WI)
Lebanon Valley Coll (PA)
Lees-McRae Coll (NC)
Lee U (TN)
Lehigh U (PA)
Lehman Coll of the City U of NY (NY)
Le Moyne Coll (NY)
Lenoir-Rhyne Coll (NC)
LeTourneau U (TX)
Lewis & Clark Coll (OR)

Lewis-Clark State Coll (ID)
Lewis U (IL)
Liberty U (VA)
Limestone Coll (SC)
Lincoln Memorial U (TN)
Lincoln U (MO)
Lincoln U (PA)
Lindenwood U (MO)
Linfield Coll (OR)
Lock Haven U of Pennsylvania (PA)
Long Island U, Brooklyn Campus (NY)
Long Island U, C.W. Post Campus (NY)
Long Island U, Southampton Coll (NY)
Long Island U, Southampton Coll, Friends World Program (NY)
Longwood Coll (VA)
Loras Coll (IA)
Louisiana Coll (LA)
Louisiana State U and A&M Coll (LA)
Louisiana State U in Shreveport (LA)
Louisiana Tech U (LA)
Lourdes Coll (OH)
Loyola Coll in Maryland (MD)
Loyola Marymount U (CA)
Loyola U Chicago (IL)
Loyola U New Orleans (LA)
Lubbock Christian U (TX)
Luther Coll (IA)
Lycoming Coll (PA)
Lynchburg Coll (VA)
Lyndon State Coll (VT)
Lynn U (FL)
Lyon Coll (AR)
Macalester Coll (MN)
MacMurray Coll (IL)
Madonna U (MI)
Maharishi U of Management (IA)
Malone Coll (OH)
Manchester Coll (IN)
Manhattan Coll (NY)
Manhattanville Coll (NY)
Mansfield U of Pennsylvania (PA)
Marian Coll (IN)
Marian Coll of Fond du Lac (WI)
Marietta Coll (OH)
Marist Coll (NY)
Marlboro Coll (VT)
Marquette U (WI)
Marshall U (WV)
Mars Hill Coll (NC)
Mary Baldwin Coll (VA)
Marycrest International U (IA)
Marygrove Coll (MI)
Marymount Coll (NY)
Marymount Manhattan Coll (NY)
Maryville Coll (TN)
Maryville U of Saint Louis (MO)
Mary Washington Coll (VA)
Marywood U (PA)
Massachusetts Coll of Liberal Arts (MA)
McGill U (PQ, Canada)
McKendree Coll (IL)
McMurry U (TX)
McNeese State U (LA)
McPherson Coll (KS)
Medaille Coll (NY)
Medgar Evers Coll of the City U of NY (NY)
Memorial U of Newfoundland (NF, Canada)
Mercer U (GA)
Mercy Coll (NY)
Mercyhurst Coll (PA)
Meredith Coll (NC)
Merrimack Coll (MA)
Mesa State Coll (CO)
Messiah Coll (PA)
Methodist Coll (NC)
Metropolitan State Coll of Denver (CO)
Metropolitan State U (MN)
Miami U (OH)
Michigan State U (MI)
MidAmerica Nazarene U (KS)
Middlebury Coll (VT)
Middle Tennessee State U (TN)
Midland Lutheran Coll (NE)
Midway Coll (KY)
Midwestern State U (TX)
Millersville U of Pennsylvania (PA)

Majors Index
Psychology

Milligan Coll (TN)
Millikin U (IL)
Millsaps Coll (MS)
Mills Coll (CA)
Minnesota State U, Mankato (MN)
Minnesota State U Moorhead (MN)
Minot State U (ND)
Mississippi Coll (MS)
Mississippi State U (MS)
Mississippi U for Women (MS)
Missouri Baptist Coll (MO)
Missouri Southern State Coll (MO)
Missouri Valley Coll (MO)
Missouri Western State Coll (MO)
Molloy Coll (NY)
Monmouth Coll (IL)
Monmouth U (NJ)
Montana State U–Billings (MT)
Montana State U–Bozeman (MT)
Moravian Coll (PA)
Morehead State U (KY)
Morehouse Coll (GA)
Morgan State U (MD)
Morningside Coll (IA)
Mount Allison U (NB, Canada)
Mount Aloysius Coll (PA)
Mount Holyoke Coll (MA)
Mount Mercy Coll (IA)
Mount Olive Coll (NC)
Mount St. Clare Coll (IA)
Mount Saint Mary Coll (NY)
Mount St. Mary's Coll (CA)
Mount Saint Mary's Coll and Seminary (MD)
Mount Saint Vincent U (NS, Canada)
Mount Union Coll (OH)
Mount Vernon Nazarene Coll (OH)
Muhlenberg Coll (PA)
Murray State U (KY)
Muskingum Coll (OH)
Naropa U (CO)
National-Louis U (IL)
National U (CA)
Nazareth Coll of Rochester (NY)
Nebraska Wesleyan U (NE)
Neumann Coll (PA)
Newberry Coll (SC)
New Coll of the U of South Florida (FL)
New England Coll (NH)
New Hampshire Coll (NH)
New Jersey City U (NJ)
Newman U (KS)
New Mexico Highlands U (NM)
New Mexico Inst of Mining and Technology (NM)
New Mexico State U (NM)
New York Inst of Technology (NY)
New York U (NY)
Niagara U (NY)
Nicholls State U (LA)
Nichols Coll (MA)
Nipissing U (ON, Canada)
Norfolk State U (VA)
North Carolina Ag and Tech State U (NC)
North Carolina Central U (NC)
North Carolina State U (NC)
North Carolina Wesleyan Coll (NC)
North Central Coll (IL)
North Central U (MN)
North Dakota State U (ND)
Northeastern Illinois U (IL)
Northeastern State U (OK)
Northeastern U (MA)
Northern Arizona U (AZ)
Northern Illinois U (IL)
Northern Kentucky U (KY)
Northern Michigan U (MI)
Northern State U (SD)
North Georgia Coll & State U (GA)
Northland Coll (WI)
North Park U (IL)
Northwest Coll (WA)
Northwestern Coll (IA)
Northwestern Coll (MN)
Northwestern Oklahoma State U (OK)
Northwestern State U of Louisiana (LA)
Northwestern U (IL)
Northwest Missouri State U (MO)
Northwest Nazarene U (ID)
Norwich U (VT)
Notre Dame Coll of Ohio (OH)
Nova Southeastern U (FL)
Nyack Coll (NY)
Oak Hills Christian Coll (MN)
Oakland U (MI)
Oakwood Coll (AL)
Oberlin Coll (OH)
Occidental Coll (CA)
Oglethorpe U (GA)
Ohio Dominican Coll (OH)
Ohio Northern U (OH)
The Ohio State U (OH)
The Ohio State U at Lima (OH)
Ohio U (OH)
Ohio Valley Coll (WV)
Ohio Wesleyan U (OH)
Okanagan U Coll (BC, Canada)
Oklahoma Baptist U (OK)
Oklahoma Christian U of Science and Arts (OK)
Oklahoma City U (OK)
Oklahoma Panhandle State U (OK)
Oklahoma State U (OK)
Old Dominion U (VA)
Olivet Nazarene U (IL)
Open Learning Agency (BC, Canada)
Oregon State U (OR)
Ottawa U (KS)
Otterbein Coll (OH)
Ouachita Baptist U (AR)
Our Lady of the Lake U of San Antonio (TX)
Pace U, New York City Campus (NY)
Pace U, Pleasantville/Briarcliff Campus (NY)
Pacific Lutheran U (WA)
Pacific Union Coll (CA)
Pacific U (OR)
Paine Coll (GA)
Palm Beach Atlantic Coll (FL)
Park U (MO)
Peace Coll (NC)
Penn State U at Erie, The Behrend Coll (PA)
Penn State U Harrisburg Campus of the Capital Coll (PA)
Penn State U Schuylkill Campus of the Capital Coll (PA)
Penn State U Univ Park Campus (PA)
Pepperdine U, Malibu (CA)
Peru State Coll (NE)
Pfeiffer U (NC)
Philadelphia U (PA)
Philander Smith Coll (AR)
Piedmont Coll (GA)
Pikeville Coll (KY)
Pine Manor Coll (MA)
Pittsburg State U (KS)
Pitzer Coll (CA)
Plattsburgh State U of NY (NY)
Plymouth State Coll (NH)
Point Loma Nazarene U (CA)
Point Park Coll (PA)
Pomona Coll (CA)
Pontifical Catholic U of Puerto Rico (PR)
Portland State U (OR)
Prairie View A&M U (TX)
Presbyterian Coll (SC)
Princeton U (NJ)
Providence Coll (RI)
Purchase Coll, State U of NY (NY)
Purdue U (IN)
Purdue U Calumet (IN)
Queens Coll (NC)
Queens Coll of the City U of NY (NY)
Queen's U at Kingston (ON, Canada)
Quincy U (IL)
Quinnipiac U (CT)
Radford U (VA)
Randolph-Macon Coll (VA)
Randolph-Macon Woman's Coll (VA)
Redeemer Coll (ON, Canada)
Reed Coll (OR)
Regents Coll (NY)
Regis Coll (MA)
Regis U (CO)
Rensselaer Polytechnic Inst (NY)
Rhodes Coll (TN)
Rice U (TX)
The Richard Stockton Coll of New Jersey (NJ)
Richmond, The American International U in London (United Kingdom)
Rider U (NJ)
Ripon Coll (WI)
Rivier Coll (NH)
Roanoke Coll (VA)
Roberts Wesleyan Coll (NY)
Rochester Coll (MI)
Rochester Inst of Technology (NY)
Rockford Coll (IL)
Rockhurst U (MO)
Rocky Mountain Coll (MT)
Roger Williams U (RI)
Rollins Coll (FL)
Rosemont Coll (PA)
Rowan U (NJ)
Russell Sage Coll (NY)
Rutgers, State U of NJ, Camden Coll of Arts & Scis (NJ)
Rutgers, State U of NJ, Douglass Coll (NJ)
Rutgers, State U of NJ, Livingston Coll (NJ)
Rutgers, State U of NJ, Newark Coll of Arts & Scis (NJ)
Rutgers, State U of NJ, Rutgers Coll (NJ)
Rutgers, State U of NJ, U Coll–Camden (NJ)
Rutgers, State U of NJ, U Coll–Newark (NJ)
Rutgers, State U of NJ, U Coll–New Brunswick (NJ)
Sacred Heart U (CT)
Saginaw Valley State U (MI)
St. Ambrose U (IA)
St. Andrews Presbyterian Coll (NC)
Saint Anselm Coll (NH)
Saint Augustine's Coll (NC)
St. Bonaventure U (NY)
St. Cloud State U (MN)
St. Edward's U (TX)
St. Francis Coll (NY)
Saint Francis Coll (IN)
St. Francis Xavier U (NS, Canada)
St. John Fisher Coll (NY)
Saint John's U (MN)
St. John's U (NY)
Saint Joseph Coll (CT)
Saint Joseph's Coll (IN)
Saint Joseph's Coll (ME)
St. Joseph's Coll, New York (NY)
St. Joseph's Coll, Suffolk Campus (NY)
Saint Joseph's U (PA)
St. Lawrence U (NY)
Saint Leo U (FL)
Saint Louis U (MO)
Saint Martin's Coll (WA)
Saint Mary Coll (KS)
Saint Mary-of-the-Woods Coll (IN)
Saint Mary's Coll (IN)
Saint Mary's Coll (MI)
Saint Mary's Coll of California (CA)
St. Mary's Coll of Maryland (MD)
Saint Mary's U (NS, Canada)
Saint Mary's U of Minnesota (MN)
St. Mary's U of San Antonio (TX)
Saint Michael's Coll (VT)
St. Norbert Coll (WI)
St. Olaf Coll (MN)
Saint Peter's Coll (NJ)
St. Thomas U (FL)
Saint Vincent Coll (PA)
Saint Xavier U (IL)
Salem Coll (NC)
Salem State Coll (MA)
Salisbury State U (MD)
Salve Regina U (RI)
Samford U (AL)
Sam Houston State U (TX)
San Diego State U (CA)
San Francisco State U (CA)
San Jose State U (CA)
Santa Clara U (CA)
Sarah Lawrence Coll (NY)
Schreiner Coll (TX)
Scripps Coll (CA)
Seattle Pacific U (WA)
Seattle U (WA)
Seton Hall U (NJ)
Seton Hill Coll (PA)
Shaw U (NC)
Shenandoah U (VA)
Shepherd Coll (WV)
Shippensburg U of Pennsylvania (PA)
Shorter Coll (GA)
Siena Coll (NY)
Siena Heights U (MI)
Silver Lake Coll (WI)
Simmons Coll (MA)
Simon Fraser U (BC, Canada)
Simon's Rock Coll of Bard (MA)
Simpson Coll (IA)
Simpson Coll and Graduate School (CA)
Skidmore Coll (NY)
Slippery Rock U of Pennsylvania (PA)
Smith Coll (MA)
Sonoma State U (CA)
South Dakota State U (SD)
Southeastern Coll of the Assemblies of God (FL)
Southeastern Louisiana U (LA)
Southeastern Oklahoma State U (OK)
Southeast Missouri State U (MO)
Southern Adventist U (TN)
Southern Arkansas U–Magnolia (AR)
Southern Illinois U Carbondale (IL)
Southern Illinois U Edwardsville (IL)
Southern Methodist U (TX)
Southern Oregon U (OR)
Southern Utah U (UT)
Southern Vermont Coll (VT)
Southern Wesleyan U (SC)
Southwest Baptist U (MO)
Southwestern Adventist U (TX)
Southwestern Coll (KS)
Southwestern Oklahoma State U (OK)
Southwestern U (TX)
Southwest Missouri State U (MO)
Southwest State U (MN)
Southwest Texas State U (TX)
Spalding U (KY)
Spelman Coll (GA)
Spring Arbor Coll (MI)
Spring Hill Coll (AL)
Stanford U (CA)
State U of NY at Albany (NY)
State U of NY at Binghamton (NY)
State U of NY at Buffalo (NY)
State U of NY at New Paltz (NY)
State U of NY at Oswego (NY)
State U of NY at Stony Brook (NY)
State U of NY Coll at Brockport (NY)
State U of NY Coll at Buffalo (NY)
State U of NY Coll at Cortland (NY)
State U of NY Coll at Fredonia (NY)
State U of NY Coll at Geneseo (NY)
State U of NY Coll at Old Westbury (NY)
State U of NY Coll at Oneonta (NY)
State U of NY Coll at Potsdam (NY)
State U of NY Inst of Tech at Utica/Rome (NY)
State U of West Georgia (GA)
Stephen F. Austin State U (TX)
Stephens Coll (MO)
Stetson U (FL)
Stonehill Coll (MA)
Suffolk U (MA)
Sul Ross State U (TX)
Susquehanna U (PA)
Swarthmore Coll (PA)
Sweet Briar Coll (VA)
Syracuse U (NY)
Tabor Coll (KS)
Talladega Coll (AL)
Taylor U (IN)
Taylor U, Fort Wayne Campus (IN)
Teikyo Post U (CT)
Temple U (PA)
Tennessee State U (TN)
Tennessee Technological U (TN)
Tennessee Wesleyan Coll (TN)
Texas A&M International U (TX)
Texas A&M U (TX)
Texas A&M U–Commerce (TX)
Texas A&M U–Kingsville (TX)
Texas A&M U–Texarkana (TX)
Texas Christian U (TX)
Texas Lutheran U (TX)
Texas Southern U (TX)
Texas Tech U (TX)
Texas Wesleyan U (TX)
Texas Woman's U (TX)
Thiel Coll (PA)
Thomas Edison State Coll (NJ)
Thomas More Coll (KY)
Thomas U (GA)
Tiffin U (OH)
Toccoa Falls Coll (GA)
Tougaloo Coll (MS)
Touro Coll (NY)
Towson U (MD)
Transylvania U (KY)
Trent U (ON, Canada)
Trevecca Nazarene U (TN)
Trinity Bible Coll (ND)
Trinity Christian Coll (IL)
Trinity Coll (CT)
Trinity Coll of Vermont (VT)
Trinity U (TX)
Trinity Western U (BC, Canada)
Tri-State U (IN)
Troy State U (AL)
Troy State U Dothan (AL)
Troy State U Montgomery (AL)
Truman State U (MO)
Tufts U (MA)
Tulane U (LA)
Tusculum Coll (TN)
Tuskegee U (AL)
Union Coll (KY)
Union Coll (NE)
Union Coll (NY)
The Union Inst (OH)
Union U (TN)
United States International U (CA)
United States Military Academy (NY)
Universidad del Turabo (PR)
Universidad Metropolitana (PR)
Université de Montréal (PQ, Canada)
Université de Sherbrooke (PQ, Canada)
U du Québec à Chicoutimi (PQ, Canada)
U du Québec à Trois-Rivières (PQ, Canada)
U du Québec en Abitibi-Témiscamingue (PQ, Canada)
Université Laval (PQ, Canada)
U Coll of Cape Breton (NS, Canada)
U Coll of the Fraser Valley (BC, Canada)
The U of Akron (OH)
The U of Alabama (AL)
The U of Alabama at Birmingham (AL)
The U of Alabama in Huntsville (AL)
U of Alaska Fairbanks (AK)
U of Alberta (AB, Canada)
The U of Arizona (AZ)
U of Arkansas (AR)
U of Arkansas at Little Rock (AR)
U of Arkansas at Monticello (AR)
U of Arkansas at Pine Bluff (AR)
U of Baltimore (MD)
U of British Columbia (BC, Canada)
U of Calgary (AB, Canada)
U of Calif, Berkeley (CA)
U of Calif, Davis (CA)
U of Calif, Irvine (CA)
U of Calif, Los Angeles (CA)
U of Calif, Riverside (CA)
U of Calif, San Diego (CA)
U of Calif, Santa Barbara (CA)
U of Calif, Santa Cruz (CA)
U of Central Arkansas (AR)
U of Central Florida (FL)
U of Central Oklahoma (OK)
U of Charleston (WV)
U of Chicago (IL)
U of Cincinnati (OH)
U of Colorado at Boulder (CO)
U of Colorado at Colorado Springs (CO)
U of Colorado at Denver (CO)
U of Connecticut (CT)
U of Dallas (TX)
U of Dayton (OH)
U of Delaware (DE)
U of Denver (CO)
U of Detroit Mercy (MI)

Majors Index
Psychology–Public Administration

U of Dubuque (IA)
U of Evansville (IN)
The U of Findlay (OH)
U of Florida (FL)
U of Georgia (GA)
U of Great Falls (MT)
U of Guelph (ON, Canada)
U of Hartford (CT)
U of Hawaii at Manoa (HI)
U of Houston (TX)
U of Houston–Clear Lake (TX)
U of Houston–Downtown (TX)
U of Idaho (ID)
U of Illinois at Chicago (IL)
U of Illinois at Springfield (IL)
U of Illinois at Urbana–Champaign (IL)
U of Indianapolis (IN)
The U of Iowa (IA)
U of Judaism (CA)
U of Kansas (KS)
U of Kentucky (KY)
U of King's Coll (NS, Canada)
U of La Verne (CA)
The U of Lethbridge (AB, Canada)
U of Louisiana at Lafayette (LA)
U of Louisiana at Monroe (LA)
U of Louisville (KY)
U of Maine (ME)
U of Maine at Farmington (ME)
U of Maine at Machias (ME)
U of Manitoba (MB, Canada)
U of Mary Hardin-Baylor (TX)
U of Maryland, Baltimore County (MD)
U of Maryland, Coll Park (MD)
U of Maryland University Coll (MD)
U of Massachusetts Amherst (MA)
U of Massachusetts Boston (MA)
U of Massachusetts Dartmouth (MA)
U of Massachusetts Lowell (MA)
The U of Memphis (TN)
U of Miami (FL)
U of Michigan (MI)
U of Michigan–Dearborn (MI)
U of Michigan–Flint (MI)
U of Minnesota, Duluth (MN)
U of Minnesota, Morris (MN)
U of Minnesota, Twin Cities Campus (MN)
U of Mississippi (MS)
U of Missouri–Columbia (MO)
U of Missouri–Kansas City (MO)
U of Missouri–Rolla (MO)
U of Missouri–St. Louis (MO)
U of Mobile (AL)
The U of Montana–Missoula (MT)
U of Montevallo (AL)
U of Nebraska at Kearney (NE)
U of Nebraska at Omaha (NE)
U of Nebraska–Lincoln (NE)
U of Nevada, Las Vegas (NV)
U of Nevada, Reno (NV)
U of New Brunswick, Fredericton (NB, Canada)
U of New Brunswick, Saint John (NB, Canada)
U of New England (ME)
U of New Hampshire (NH)
U of New Hampshire at Manchester (NH)
U of New Haven (CT)
U of New Mexico (NM)
U of New Orleans (LA)
U of North Alabama (AL)
The U of North Carolina at Asheville (NC)
The U of North Carolina at Chapel Hill (NC)
The U of North Carolina at Charlotte (NC)
The U of North Carolina at Greensboro (NC)
The U of North Carolina at Pembroke (NC)
The U of North Carolina at Wilmington (NC)
U of North Dakota (ND)
U of Northern Colorado (CO)
U of Northern Iowa (IA)
U of North Florida (FL)
U of North Texas (TX)
U of Notre Dame (IN)
U of Oklahoma (OK)
U of Oregon (OR)
U of Pennsylvania (PA)

U of Phoenix (AZ)
U of Pittsburgh (PA)
U of Pittsburgh at Bradford (PA)
U of Pittsburgh at Johnstown (PA)
U of Portland (OR)
U of Prince Edward Island (PE, Canada)
U of Puerto Rico, Mayagüez Campus (PR)
U of Puerto Rico, Río Piedras (PR)
U of Puget Sound (WA)
U of Redlands (CA)
U of Regina (SK, Canada)
U of Rhode Island (RI)
U of Richmond (VA)
U of Rochester (NY)
U of St. Francis (IL)
U of Saint Francis (IN)
U of St. Thomas (MN)
U of St. Thomas (TX)
U of San Diego (CA)
U of San Francisco (CA)
U of Science and Arts of Oklahoma (OK)
The U of Scranton (PA)
U of Sioux Falls (SD)
U of South Alabama (AL)
U of South Carolina Spartanburg (SC)
U of South Dakota (SD)
U of Southern California (CA)
U of Southern Colorado (CO)
U of Southern Indiana (IN)
U of Southern Maine (ME)
U of Southern Mississippi (MS)
U of South Florida (FL)
The U of Tampa (FL)
The U of Tennessee at Chattanooga (TN)
The U of Tennessee at Martin (TN)
The U of Tennessee Knoxville (TN)
The U of Texas at Arlington (TX)
The U of Texas at Austin (TX)
The U of Texas at Dallas (TX)
The U of Texas at San Antonio (TX)
The U of Texas at Tyler (TX)
The U of Texas–Pan American (TX)
U of the District of Columbia (DC)
U of the Ozarks (AR)
U of the Pacific (CA)
U of the Sacred Heart (PR)
U of the Sciences in Philadelphia (PA)
U of the South (TN)
U of the Virgin Islands (VI)
U of Toronto (ON, Canada)
U of Tulsa (OK)
U of Utah (UT)
U of Vermont (VT)
U of Victoria (BC, Canada)
U of Virginia (VA)
U of Virginia's Coll at Wise (VA)
U of Washington (WA)
U of Waterloo (ON, Canada)
The U of West Alabama (AL)
The U of Western Ontario (ON, Canada)
U of West Florida (FL)
U of Windsor (ON, Canada)
The U of Winnipeg (MB, Canada)
U of Wisconsin–Eau Claire (WI)
U of Wisconsin–Green Bay (WI)
U of Wisconsin–La Crosse (WI)
U of Wisconsin–Madison (WI)
U of Wisconsin–Milwaukee (WI)
U of Wisconsin–Parkside (WI)
U of Wisconsin–Platteville (WI)
U of Wisconsin–River Falls (WI)
U of Wisconsin–Stevens Point (WI)
U of Wisconsin–Stout (WI)
U of Wisconsin–Superior (WI)
U of Wisconsin–Whitewater (WI)
U of Wyoming (WY)
Upper Iowa U (IA)
Urbana U (OH)
Ursinus Coll (PA)
Ursuline Coll (OH)
Utah State U (UT)
Utica Coll of Syracuse U (NY)
Valdosta State U (GA)
Valparaiso U (IN)
Vanderbilt U (TN)
Vanguard U of Southern California (CA)
Vassar Coll (NY)
Villa Julie Coll (MD)

Villanova U (PA)
Virginia Commonwealth U (VA)
Virginia Intermont Coll (VA)
Virginia Military Inst (VA)
Virginia Polytechnic Inst and State U (VA)
Virginia Union U (VA)
Virginia Wesleyan Coll (VA)
Wabash Coll (IN)
Wagner Coll (NY)
Wake Forest U (NC)
Walla Walla Coll (WA)
Walsh U (OH)
Warner Pacific Coll (OR)
Warner Southern Coll (FL)
Warren Wilson Coll (NC)
Wartburg Coll (IA)
Washington & Jefferson Coll (PA)
Washington and Lee U (VA)
Washington Coll (MD)
Washington State U (WA)
Washington U in St. Louis (MO)
Wayland Baptist U (TX)
Waynesburg Coll (PA)
Wayne State Coll (NE)
Wayne State U (MI)
Weber State U (UT)
Webster U (MO)
Wellesley Coll (MA)
Wells Coll (NY)
Wesleyan Coll (GA)
Wesleyan U (CT)
Wesley Coll (DE)
West Chester U of Pennsylvania (PA)
Western Baptist Coll (OR)
Western Carolina U (NC)
Western Connecticut State U (CT)
Western Illinois U (IL)
Western Kentucky U (KY)
Western Maryland Coll (MD)
Western Michigan U (MI)
Western New England Coll (MA)
Western Oregon U (OR)
Western State Coll of Colorado (CO)
Western Washington U (WA)
Westfield State Coll (MA)
West Liberty State Coll (WV)
Westminster Coll (MO)
Westminster Coll (PA)
Westminster Coll (UT)
Westmont Coll (CA)
West Texas A&M U (TX)
West Virginia State Coll (WV)
West Virginia U (WV)
West Virginia Wesleyan Coll (WV)
Wheaton Coll (IL)
Wheaton Coll (MA)
Wheeling Jesuit U (WV)
Whitman Coll (WA)
Whittier Coll (CA)
Whitworth Coll (WA)
Wichita State U (KS)
Widener U (PA)
Wilfrid Laurier U (ON, Canada)
Wilkes U (PA)
Willamette U (OR)
William Jewell Coll (MO)
William Paterson U of New Jersey (NJ)
William Penn U (IA)
Williams Baptist Coll (AR)
Williams Coll (MA)
William Tyndale Coll (MI)
William Woods U (MO)
Wilmington Coll (OH)
Wingate U (NC)
Winona State U (MN)
Winston-Salem State U (NC)
Winthrop U (SC)
Wisconsin Lutheran Coll (WI)
Wittenberg U (OH)
Wofford Coll (SC)
Woodbury U (CA)
Worcester State Coll (MA)
Wright State U (OH)
Xavier U (OH)
Xavier U of Louisiana (LA)
Yale U (CT)
Yeshiva U (NY)
York Coll (NE)
York Coll of Pennsylvania (PA)
York Coll of the City U of New York (NY)
York U (ON, Canada)
Youngstown State U (OH)

PUBLIC ADMINISTRATION

Abilene Christian U (TX)
Alfred U (NY)
American International Coll (MA)
American U (DC)
Athabasca U (AB, Canada)
Athens State U (AL)
Auburn U (AL)
Augustana Coll (IL)
Bayamón Central U (PR)
Baylor U (TX)
Baruch Coll of the City U of NY (NY)
Blackburn Coll (IL)
Boise State U (ID)
Bowie State U (MD)
Bowling Green State U (OH)
Brevard Coll (NC)
Brock U (ON, Canada)
Buena Vista U (IA)
California State Polytechnic U, Pomona (CA)
California State U, Chico (CA)
California State U, Dominguez Hills (CA)
California State U, Fresno (CA)
California State U, Fullerton (CA)
California State U, Hayward (CA)
California State U, Los Angeles (CA)
California State U, Sacramento (CA)
California State U, San Bernardino (CA)
Calvin Coll (MI)
Campbell U (NC)
Canisius Coll (NY)
Carleton U (ON, Canada)
Carroll Coll (MT)
Carroll Coll (WI)
Catawba Coll (NC)
Cedarville Coll (OH)
Central Methodist Coll (MO)
Christopher Newport U (VA)
Coll of Staten Island of the City U of NY (NY)
Concordia U (PQ, Canada)
Crown Coll (WA)
David Lipscomb U (TN)
David N. Myers Coll (OH)
Doane Coll (NE)
Dominican Coll of Blauvelt (NY)
Eastern Michigan U (MI)
Eastern Washington U (WA)
Edgewood Coll (WI)
Elon Coll (NC)
Evangel U (MO)
The Evergreen State Coll (WA)
Ferris State U (MI)
Fisk U (TN)
Florida A&M U (FL)
Florida Atlantic U (FL)
Florida International U (FL)
Fordham U (NY)
Framingham State Coll (MA)
George Mason U (VA)
Georgia Coll and State U (GA)
Golden Gate U (CA)
Governors State U (IL)
Grand Valley State U (MI)
Hamline U (MN)
Harding U (AR)
Hawaii Pacific U (HI)
Heidelberg Coll (OH)
Henderson State U (AR)
Heritage Coll (WA)
Huntingdon Coll (AL)
Indiana State U (IN)
Indiana U Bloomington (IN)
Indiana U Northwest (IN)
Indiana U–Purdue U Fort Wayne (IN)
Indiana U–Purdue U Indianapolis (IN)
Indiana U South Bend (IN)
Inst of Public Administration (Ireland)
Inter American U of PR, San Germán Campus (PR)
Iowa State U of Science and Technology (IA)
James Madison U (VA)
John Carroll U (OH)
John Jay Coll of Criminal Justice, the City U of NY (NY)
Juniata Coll (PA)
Kean U (NJ)

Kentucky State U (KY)
Kutztown U of Pennsylvania (PA)
Lakeland Coll (WI)
La Salle U (PA)
Lewis U (IL)
Lincoln U (MO)
Lindenwood U (MO)
Long Island U, Brooklyn Campus (NY)
Long Island U, C.W. Post Campus (NY)
Louisiana Coll (LA)
Madonna U (MI)
Marist Coll (NY)
Medgar Evers Coll of the City U of NY (NY)
Mercyhurst Coll (PA)
Metropolitan State U (MN)
Miami U (OH)
Michigan State U (MI)
Minnesota State U, Mankato (MN)
Mississippi Valley State U (MS)
Missouri Valley Coll (MO)
Mount Aloysius Coll (PA)
Northeastern U (MA)
Northern Arizona U (AZ)
Northern Kentucky U (KY)
Northern Michigan U (MI)
Northern State U (SD)
Northwest Missouri State U (MO)
Oakland U (MI)
Ohio Wesleyan U (OH)
Open Learning Agency (BC, Canada)
Our Lady of the Lake U of San Antonio (TX)
Park U (MO)
Penn State U Univ Park Campus (PA)
Piedmont Coll (GA)
Plymouth State Coll (NH)
Point Park Coll (PA)
Pontifical Catholic U of Puerto Rico (PR)
Roger Williams U (RI)
Ryerson Polytechnic U (ON, Canada)
Saginaw Valley State U (MI)
St. Ambrose U (IA)
St. Cloud State U (MN)
Saint Francis Coll (PA)
St. John's U (NY)
Saint Joseph's U (PA)
Saint Leo U (FL)
Saint Mary's U of Minnesota (MN)
St. Thomas U (FL)
Samford U (AL)
San Diego State U (CA)
San Jose State U (CA)
Seattle U (WA)
Seton Hill Coll (PA)
Shaw U (NC)
Shenandoah U (VA)
Shippensburg U of Pennsylvania (PA)
Siena Heights U (MI)
Slippery Rock U of Pennsylvania (PA)
Southeastern U (DC)
Southwest Missouri State U (MO)
Southwest State U (MN)
Southwest Texas State U (TX)
Stephen F. Austin State U (TX)
Stonehill Coll (PA)
Suffolk U (MA)
Talladega Coll (AL)
Tennessee State U (TN)
Texas A&M U–Kingsville (TX)
Texas Southern U (TX)
Texas Woman's U (TX)
Thomas Edison State Coll (NJ)
The Union Inst (OH)
Universidad del Turabo (PR)
The U of Arizona (AZ)
U of Arkansas (AR)
U of Calif, Riverside (CA)
U of Central Arkansas (AR)
U of Central Florida (FL)
U of Central Oklahoma (OK)
U of Denver (CO)
U of Hartford (CT)
U of La Verne (CA)
The U of Lethbridge (AB, Canada)
U of Maine (ME)
The U of Maine at Augusta (ME)
U of Manitoba (MB, Canada)
U of Massachusetts Boston (MA)

Majors Index
Public Administration–Radio/Television Broadcasting

U of Michigan–Dearborn (MI)
U of Michigan–Flint (MI)
U of Mississippi (MS)
U of Missouri–St. Louis (MO)
U of Nebraska at Omaha (NE)
U of New Haven (CT)
The U of North Carolina at Pembroke (NC)
U of North Dakota (ND)
U of Northern Iowa (IA)
U of Oklahoma (OK)
U of Oregon (OR)
U of Pittsburgh (PA)
U of Regina (SK, Canada)
U of San Francisco (CA)
The U of Scranton (PA)
U of Southern California (CA)
The U of Tennessee at Martin (TN)
The U of Tennessee Knoxville (TN)
The U of Texas at Dallas (TX)
The U of Texas–Pan American (TX)
U of the District of Columbia (DC)
U of Toronto (ON, Canada)
U of Victoria (BC, Canada)
U of Washington (WA)
The U of Western Ontario (ON, Canada)
U of Windsor (ON, Canada)
U of Wisconsin–Green Bay (WI)
U of Wisconsin–La Crosse (WI)
U of Wisconsin–Stevens Point (WI)
U of Wisconsin–Whitewater (WI)
Upper Iowa U (IA)
Wagner Coll (NY)
Washington State U (WA)
Waynesburg Coll (PA)
Wayne State Coll (NE)
Wayne State U (MI)
West Chester U of Pennsylvania (PA)
Western Michigan U (MI)
Western Oregon U (OR)
Westminster Coll (MO)
West Texas A&M U (TX)
West Virginia U Inst of Technology (WV)
Winona State U (MN)
Winston-Salem State U (NC)
York Coll of Pennsylvania (PA)
York U (ON, Canada)
Youngstown State U (OH)

PUBLIC HEALTH
Alma Coll (MI)
Boise State U (ID)
Brock U (ON, Canada)
California State U, Dominguez Hills (CA)
California State U, Long Beach (CA)
Central Michigan U (MI)
Cumberland Coll (KY)
Eastern Kentucky U (KY)
Eastern Washington U (WA)
East Tennessee State U (TN)
Grand Valley State U (MI)
Hampshire Coll (MA)
Hunter Coll of the City U of NY (NY)
Indiana State U (IN)
Indiana U Bloomington (IN)
Indiana U–Purdue U Indianapolis (IN)
Minnesota State U, Mankato (MN)
New Mexico State U (NM)
Ohio U (OH)
Oregon State U (OR)
The Richard Stockton Coll of New Jersey (NJ)
Rutgers, State U of NJ, Cook Coll (NJ)
Rutgers, State U of NJ, Douglass Coll (NJ)
Rutgers, State U of NJ, Livingston Coll (NJ)
Rutgers, State U of NJ, Rutgers Coll (NJ)
Rutgers, State U of NJ, U Coll–New Brunswick (NJ)
Ryerson Polytechnic U (ON, Canada)
St. Joseph's Coll, New York (NY)
San Diego State U (CA)
Slippery Rock U of Pennsylvania (PA)
Truman State U (MO)
Tufts U (MA)

U of Cincinnati (OH)
The U of Lethbridge (AB, Canada)
U of Minnesota, Twin Cities Campus (MN)
The U of Tennessee Knoxville (TN)
U of Washington (WA)
U of Wisconsin–Eau Claire (WI)
West Chester U of Pennsylvania (PA)
William Paterson U of New Jersey (NJ)
Winona State U (MN)
York U (ON, Canada)

PUBLIC HEALTH EDUCATION/PROMOTION
Appalachian State U (NC)
Coastal Carolina U (SC)
East Carolina U (NC)
Georgia Southern U (GA)
Ithaca Coll (NY)
Plymouth State Coll (NH)
St. Francis Coll (NY)
Thomas Edison State Coll (NJ)
The U of North Carolina at Chapel Hill (NC)
U of Northern Colorado (CO)
U of North Texas (TX)
U of St. Thomas (MN)
Walla Walla Coll (WA)
Western Washington U (WA)
Worcester State Coll (MA)

PUBLIC POLICY ANALYSIS
Albion Coll (MI)
Baruch Coll of the City U of NY (NY)
Coll of the Atlantic (ME)
The Coll of William and Mary (VA)
Columbia Coll (SC)
Concordia U (PQ, Canada)
Cornell U (NY)
DePaul U (IL)
Dickinson Coll (PA)
Duke U (NC)
Eastern Washington U (WA)
Edgewood Coll (WI)
The Evergreen State Coll (WA)
The George Washington U (DC)
Georgia Inst of Technology (GA)
Grand Valley State U (MI)
Hamilton Coll (NY)
Hampden-Sydney Coll (VA)
Hampshire Coll (MA)
Harvard U (MA)
Indiana U Bloomington (IN)
Lincoln U (PA)
Long Island U, Southampton Coll, Friends World Program (NY)
Michigan State U (MI)
Muskingum Coll (OH)
New Coll of the U of South Florida (FL)
North Carolina State U (NC)
Oakland U (MI)
Occidental Coll (CA)
Penn State U Harrisburg Campus of the Capital Coll (PA)
Pomona Coll (CA)
Princeton U (NJ)
Rice U (TX)
St. Cloud State U (MN)
St. Mary's Coll of Maryland (MD)
Saint Peter's Coll (NJ)
Saint Vincent Coll (PA)
San Jose State U (CA)
Sarah Lawrence Coll (NY)
Simmons Coll (MA)
Southern Methodist U (TX)
Stanford U (CA)
State U of NY at Albany (NY)
Suffolk U (MA)
Syracuse U (NY)
Texas Southern U (TX)
Trinity Coll (CT)
United States Military Academy (NY)
U of Chicago (IL)
U of Cincinnati (OH)
U of Massachusetts Boston (MA)
U of Missouri–St. Louis (MO)
The U of North Carolina at Chapel Hill (NC)
U of Oregon (OR)
U of Pennsylvania (PA)
U of Rhode Island (RI)
U of Southern California (CA)

U of Wisconsin–Whitewater (WI)
Washington and Lee U (VA)
Wells Coll (NY)
Western Michigan U (MI)
Western State Coll of Colorado (CO)
York U (ON, Canada)

PUBLISHING
Benedictine U (IL)
Emerson Coll (MA)
Graceland Coll (IA)
Rochester Inst of Technology (NY)
Saint Mary's U of Minnesota (MN)
U of Missouri–Columbia (MO)

PURCHASING/CONTRACTS MANAGEMENT
American U of Puerto Rico (PR)
Arizona State U (AZ)
Bloomfield Coll (NJ)
California State U, Hayward (CA)
Eastern Michigan U (MI)
Miami U (OH)
Michigan State U (MI)
The Ohio State U (OH)
Thomas Edison State Coll (NJ)
The U of Alabama in Huntsville (AL)
U of Houston–Downtown (TX)
U of the District of Columbia (DC)

QUALITY CONTROL TECHNOLOGY
California State U, Long Beach (CA)
Ferris State U (MI)
Winona State U (MN)

QUANTITATIVE ECONOMICS
Haverford Coll (PA)
Southern Methodist U (TX)
United States Naval Academy (MD)
U of Calif, San Diego (CA)
U of Dayton (OH)
U of Northern Iowa (IA)
U of Rhode Island (RI)

RABBINICAL/TALMUDIC STUDIES
Kol Yaakov Torah Center (NY)
Rabbinical Seminary of America (NY)
Talmudical Yeshiva of Philadelphia (PA)
Yeshiva Karlin Stolin Rabbinical Inst (NY)

RADIOLOGICAL SCIENCE
Austin Peay State U (TN)
Avila Coll (MO)
Champlain Coll (VT)
Clarion U of Pennsylvania (PA)
Clarkson Coll (NE)
The George Washington U (DC)
Holy Family Coll (PA)
Indiana U Northwest (IN)
Loyola U New Orleans (LA)
Manhattan Coll (NY)
Mass Coll of Pharmacy and Allied Health Sciences (MA)
Medical Coll of Georgia (GA)
Midwestern State U (TX)
Mount Aloysius Coll (PA)
The Ohio State U (OH)
Oregon Inst of Technology (OR)
Quinnipiac U (CT)
Rutgers, State U of NJ, Cook Coll (NJ)
St. Francis Coll (NY)
San Diego State U (CA)
State U of New York Upstate Medical University (NY)
Suffolk U (MA)
U of Charleston (WV)
The U of Findlay (OH)
U of Michigan (MI)
U of Missouri–Columbia (MO)
The U of North Carolina at Chapel Hill (NC)
U of St. Francis (IL)
U of South Alabama (AL)
Virginia Commonwealth U (VA)

RADIO/TELEVISION BROADCASTING
Alabama State U (AL)
American U (DC)
Appalachian State U (NC)
Arizona State U (AZ)
Arkansas State U (AR)
Ashland U (OH)
Auburn U (AL)
Barry U (FL)
Belmont U (TN)
Bemidji State U (MN)
Biola U (CA)
Boston U (MA)
Bowling Green State U (OH)
Brooklyn Coll of the City U of NY (NY)
Buena Vista U (IA)
California State U, Chico (CA)
California State U, Fresno (CA)
California State U, Fullerton (CA)
California State U, Long Beach (CA)
California State U, Los Angeles (CA)
California State U, Northridge (CA)
Cameron U (OK)
Campbell U (NC)
Capital U (OH)
Castleton State Coll (VT)
Cedarville Coll (OH)
Central Michigan U (MI)
Central Missouri State U (MO)
Chicago State U (IL)
Colorado State U (CO)
Columbia Coll Chicago (IL)
Columbia Coll–Hollywood (CA)
Concordia Coll (MN)
Curry Coll (MA)
Drake U (IA)
East Central U (OK)
Eastern Illinois U (IL)
Eastern Kentucky U (KY)
Eastern Nazarene Coll (MA)
Eastern New Mexico U (NM)
Eastern Washington U (WA)
Emerson Coll (MA)
Evangel U (MO)
Florida State U (FL)
Fordham U (NY)
Fort Hays State U (KS)
Franklin Pierce Coll (NH)
Freed-Hardeman U (TN)
Gallaudet U (DC)
Gannon U (PA)
Geneva Coll (PA)
George Fox U (OR)
The George Washington U (DC)
Georgia Southern U (GA)
Grand Valley State U (MI)
Grand View Coll (IA)
Hampshire Coll (MA)
Harding U (AR)
Hastings Coll (NE)
Howard U (DC)
Indiana State U (IN)
Indiana U Bloomington (IN)
Ithaca Coll (NY)
John Brown U (AR)
Kent State U (OH)
Kutztown U of Pennsylvania (PA)
Lamar U (TX)
Langston U (OK)
La Salle U (PA)
Lindenwood U (MO)
Lock Haven U of Pennsylvania (PA)
Long Island U, Brooklyn Campus (NY)
Long Island U, C.W. Post Campus (NY)
Loras Coll (IA)
Lyndon State Coll (VT)
Mansfield U of Pennsylvania (PA)
Marietta Coll (OH)
Marist Coll (NY)
Marshall U (WV)
Marywood U (PA)
Mercy Coll (NY)
Mercyhurst Coll (PA)
Mesa State Coll (CO)
Messiah Coll (PA)
Milligan Coll (TN)
Murray State U (KY)
Muskingum Coll (OH)
New York Inst of Technology (NY)
New York U (NY)

Northeastern U (MA)
Northern Arizona U (AZ)
Northern Kentucky U (KY)
Northwestern Coll (MN)
Northwestern U (IL)
Northwest Missouri State U (MO)
Ohio U (OH)
Oklahoma Baptist U (OK)
Oklahoma Christian U of Science and Arts (OK)
Oklahoma City U (OK)
Olivet Nazarene U (IL)
Otterbein Coll (OH)
Pacific Lutheran U (WA)
Pacific U (OR)
Pittsburg State U (KS)
Point Park Coll (PA)
Purdue U Calumet (IN)
Queens Coll of the City U of NY (NY)
Quincy U (IL)
Rider U (NJ)
Rowan U (NJ)
Rust Coll (MS)
Ryerson Polytechnic U (ON, Canada)
Sacred Heart U (CT)
St. Ambrose U (IA)
St. Cloud State U (MN)
Saint Joseph's Coll (ME)
Sam Houston State U (TX)
San Diego State U (CA)
San Francisco State U (CA)
San Jose State U (CA)
Southeast Missouri State U (MO)
Southern Illinois U Carbondale (IL)
Southern Methodist U (TX)
Southwest State U (MN)
Spring Hill Coll (AL)
State U of NY at New Paltz (NY)
State U of NY Coll at Brockport (NY)
State U of NY Coll at Buffalo (NY)
State U of NY Coll at Fredonia (NY)
Stephen F. Austin State U (TX)
Stephens Coll (MO)
Syracuse U (NY)
Temple U (PA)
Texas A&M U–Commerce (TX)
Texas Christian U (TX)
Texas Southern U (TX)
Texas Tech U (TX)
Texas Wesleyan U (TX)
Toccoa Falls Coll (GA)
Union U (TN)
The U of Alabama (AL)
U of Alaska Fairbanks (AK)
The U of Arizona (AZ)
U of Arkansas at Little Rock (AR)
U of Calif, Los Angeles (CA)
U of Central Florida (FL)
U of Central Oklahoma (OK)
U of Cincinnati (OH)
U of Dayton (OH)
U of Detroit Mercy (MI)
U of Florida (FL)
U of Houston (TX)
U of Idaho (ID)
The U of Iowa (IA)
U of Kansas (KS)
U of Kentucky (KY)
U of La Verne (CA)
U of Louisiana at Monroe (LA)
U of Miami (FL)
U of Mississippi (MS)
U of Missouri–Columbia (MO)
The U of Montana–Missoula (MT)
U of Montevallo (AL)
U of Nebraska at Omaha (NE)
The U of North Carolina at Greensboro (NC)
U of Northern Iowa (IA)
U of North Texas (TX)
U of Oklahoma (OK)
U of Oregon (OR)
U of Pittsburgh at Bradford (PA)
U of San Francisco (CA)
U of Sioux Falls (SD)
U of South Alabama (AL)
U of South Dakota (SD)
U of Southern California (CA)
U of Southern Colorado (CO)
U of Southern Mississippi (MS)
The U of Tennessee Knoxville (TN)
The U of Texas at Arlington (TX)
The U of Texas at Austin (TX)

Majors Index
Radio/Television Broadcasting–Recreation and Leisure Studies

U of the Pacific (CA)
U of Utah (UT)
U of Windsor (ON, Canada)
U of Wisconsin–Madison (WI)
U of Wisconsin–River Falls (WI)
U of Wisconsin–Superior (WI)
Valdosta State U (GA)
Vanguard U of Southern California (CA)
Virginia Commonwealth U (VA)
Walla Walla Coll (WA)
Washington State U (WA)
Waynesburg Coll (PA)
Wayne State U (MI)
Weber State U (UT)
Webster U (MO)
Western Kentucky U (KY)
Western Michigan U (MI)
Western State Coll of Colorado (CO)
Westfield State Coll (MA)
Westminster Coll (PA)
William Woods U (MO)
Winona State U (MN)
York Coll of Pennsylvania (PA)
Youngstown State U (OH)

RADIO/TELEVISION BROADCASTING TECHNOLOGY
Alabama A&M U (AL)
Asbury Coll (KY)
Eastern Michigan U (MI)
East Stroudsburg U of Pennsylvania (PA)
Emerson Coll (MA)
Hofstra U (NY)
Lewis U (IL)
Southwest Texas State U (TX)
Texas Tech U (TX)
Trevecca Nazarene U (TN)
U of Georgia (GA)
U of Southern California (CA)

RANGE MANAGEMENT
Abilene Christian U (TX)
Brigham Young U (UT)
California State U, Chico (CA)
Chadron State Coll (NE)
Colorado State U (CO)
Fort Hays State U (KS)
Humboldt State U (CA)
Montana State U–Bozeman (MT)
New Mexico State U (NM)
North Dakota State U (ND)
Oklahoma State U (OK)
Oregon State U (OR)
South Dakota State U (SD)
Southwest Texas State U (TX)
Stephen F. Austin State U (TX)
Sul Ross State U (TX)
Texas A&M U (TX)
Texas A&M U–Kingsville (TX)
Texas Tech U (TX)
U of Alberta (AB, Canada)
The U of Arizona (AZ)
U of British Columbia (BC, Canada)
U of Calif, Davis (CA)
U of Idaho (ID)
U of Nebraska–Lincoln (NE)
U of Nevada, Reno (NV)
U of Wyoming (WY)
Utah State U (UT)
Washington State U (WA)

READING EDUCATION
Abilene Christian U (TX)
Aquinas Coll (MI)
Averett Coll (VA)
Baylor U (TX)
Belmont U (TN)
Boise State U (ID)
Bowling Green State U (OH)
Catawba Coll (NC)
Central Missouri State U (MO)
Chicago State U (IL)
City Coll of the City U of NY (NY)
Clarion U of Pennsylvania (PA)
Clemson U (SC)
Eastern Washington U (WA)
Grand Valley State U (MI)
Hardin-Simmons U (TX)
Indiana State U (IN)
Jarvis Christian Coll (TX)
Longwood Coll (VA)
Luther Coll (IA)
Lyndon State Coll (VT)

Marycrest International U (IA)
McMurry U (TX)
Millersville U of Pennsylvania (PA)
Mount Saint Vincent U (NS, Canada)
Norfolk State U (VA)
Northeastern State U (OK)
Northwest Missouri State U (MO)
Ohio U (OH)
Our Lady of Holy Cross Coll (LA)
Pacific Lutheran U (WA)
Plymouth State Coll (NH)
St. Cloud State U (MN)
Saint Joseph's Coll (ME)
St. Mary's U of San Antonio (TX)
State U of NY Coll at Cortland (NY)
Tennessee State U (TN)
Texas A&M International U (TX)
Texas A&M U–Commerce (TX)
Texas Southern U (TX)
Texas Wesleyan U (TX)
The U of Akron (OH)
U of Alberta (AB, Canada)
U of British Columbia (BC, Canada)
U of Central Arkansas (AR)
U of Central Oklahoma (OK)
U of Georgia (GA)
U of Mary Hardin-Baylor (TX)
U of Missouri–St. Louis (MO)
The U of Montana–Missoula (MT)
U of New Orleans (LA)
U of Northern Iowa (IA)
U of North Texas (TX)
U of Regina (SK, Canada)
The U of Texas–Pan American (TX)
U of Vermont (VT)
U of Wisconsin–Superior (WI)
Upper Iowa U (IA)
Walsh U (OH)
Westfield State Coll (MA)
Wingate U (NC)
Winona State U (MN)
Wright State U (OH)
York Coll (NE)

REAL ESTATE
Appalachian State U (NC)
Arizona State U (AZ)
Ball State U (IN)
Baylor U (TX)
California State Polytechnic U, Pomona (CA)
California State U, Dominguez Hills (CA)
California State U, Fresno (CA)
California State U, Hayward (CA)
California State U, Los Angeles (CA)
California State U, Northridge (CA)
Christopher Newport U (VA)
Clarion U of Pennsylvania (PA)
Colorado State U (CO)
David N. Myers Coll (OH)
Eastern Kentucky U (KY)
Eastern Michigan U (MI)
East Tennessee State U (TN)
Florida Atlantic U (FL)
Florida International U (FL)
Florida State U (FL)
Georgia State U (GA)
Indiana U Bloomington (IN)
Minnesota State U, Mankato (MN)
Mississippi State U (MS)
Morehead State U (KY)
New York U (NY)
The Ohio State U (OH)
Penn State U Univ Park Campus (PA)
St. Cloud State U (MN)
St. John's U (NY)
San Diego State U (CA)
San Francisco State U (CA)
Schreiner Coll (TX)
Shippensburg U of Pennsylvania (PA)
Southern Methodist U (TX)
State U of West Georgia (GA)
Temple U (PA)
Texas A&M U–Kingsville (TX)
Texas Christian U (TX)
Thomas Edison State Coll (NJ)
U of Central Oklahoma (OK)
U of Cincinnati (OH)
U of Connecticut (CT)
U of Denver (CO)
U of Florida (FL)

U of Georgia (GA)
U of Hawaii at Manoa (HI)
U of Houston–Downtown (TX)
The U of Memphis (TN)
U of Miami (FL)
U of Mississippi (MS)
U of Missouri–Columbia (MO)
U of Nebraska at Omaha (NE)
U of Nevada, Las Vegas (NV)
U of New Orleans (LA)
U of Northern Iowa (IA)
U of North Texas (TX)
U of Oklahoma (OK)
U of Pennsylvania (PA)
U of St. Thomas (MN)
U of South Carolina (SC)
U of Southern California (CA)
The U of Texas at Arlington (TX)
U of Tulsa (OK)
U of Wisconsin–Madison (WI)
U of Wisconsin–Milwaukee (WI)
Virginia Commonwealth U (VA)
Washington State U (WA)
Webster U (MO)

RECREATIONAL THERAPY
Alderson-Broaddus Coll (WV)
Ashland U (OH)
Belmont Abbey Coll (NC)
California State U, Hayward (CA)
California State U, Northridge (CA)
Catawba Coll (NC)
Coll of Mount St. Joseph (OH)
Columbus State U (GA)
Concordia U (PQ, Canada)
East Carolina U (NC)
Eastern Illinois U (IL)
Eastern Kentucky U (KY)
Eastern Washington U (WA)
Gallaudet U (DC)
Grand Valley State U (MI)
Green Mountain Coll (VT)
Hampton U (VA)
Indiana Inst of Technology (IN)
Indiana State U (IN)
Indiana U Bloomington (IN)
Ithaca Coll (NY)
Kent State U (OH)
Lake Superior State U (MI)
Lock Haven U of Pennsylvania (PA)
Long Island U, Southampton Coll, Friends World Program (NY)
Longwood Coll (VA)
Mars Hill Coll (NC)
Minnesota State U, Mankato (MN)
Northland Coll (WI)
Northwest Missouri State U (MO)
Ohio U (OH)
Pacific Lutheran U (WA)
Pittsburg State U (KS)
St. Andrews Presbyterian Coll (NC)
St. Joseph's Coll, Suffolk Campus (NY)
San Jose State U (CA)
Shorter Coll (GA)
Slippery Rock U of Pennsylvania (PA)
Southwestern Oklahoma State U (OK)
State U of NY Coll at Cortland (NY)
The U of Findlay (OH)
The U of Iowa (IA)
U of New Hampshire (NH)
U of St. Francis (IL)
U of Southern Maine (ME)
U of the Pacific (CA)
U of Wisconsin–La Crosse (WI)
U of Wisconsin–Milwaukee (WI)
Utica Coll of Syracuse U (NY)
Voorhees Coll (SC)
Western Carolina U (NC)
West Virginia State Coll (WV)
Winona State U (MN)
Winston-Salem State U (NC)
York Coll of Pennsylvania (PA)

RECREATION AND LEISURE STUDIES
Alabama State U (AL)
Alaska Pacific U (AK)
Alderson-Broaddus Coll (WV)
Appalachian State U (NC)
Arizona State U (AZ)
Arizona State U West (AZ)
Armstrong Atlantic State U (GA)
Ashland U (OH)

Auburn U (AL)
Belmont U (TN)
Bemidji State U (MN)
Bethany Coll (KS)
Black Hills State U (SD)
Bluffton Coll (OH)
Boston U (MA)
Bowling Green State U (OH)
Brevard Coll (NC)
Bridgewater State Coll (MA)
Brock U (ON, Canada)
California Polytechnic State U, San Luis Obispo (CA)
California State U, Chico (CA)
California State U, Dominguez Hills (CA)
California State U, Fresno (CA)
California State U, Hayward (CA)
California State U, Long Beach (CA)
California State U, Northridge (CA)
California State U, Sacramento (CA)
Calvin Coll (MI)
Campbellsville U (KY)
Carson-Newman Coll (TN)
Carthage Coll (WI)
Catawba Coll (NC)
Central Christian Coll of Kansas (KS)
Central Michigan U (MI)
Central Missouri State U (MO)
Chadron State Coll (NE)
Cheyney U of Pennsylvania (PA)
Chicago State U (IL)
Christopher Newport U (VA)
Concordia U (PQ, Canada)
Dalhousie U (NS, Canada)
Delaware State U (DE)
Dordt Coll (IA)
Eastern Illinois U (IL)
Eastern Kentucky U (KY)
Eastern Mennonite U (VA)
Eastern Washington U (WA)
East Stroudsburg U of Pennsylvania (PA)
Elon Coll (NC)
Emporia State U (KS)
Evangel U (MO)
Ferris State U (MI)
Ferrum Coll (VA)
Franklin Coll of Indiana (IN)
Frostburg State U (MD)
George Mason U (VA)
Georgetown Coll (KY)
Georgia Coll and State U (GA)
Georgia Southern U (GA)
Georgia Southwestern State U (GA)
Gordon Coll (MA)
Graceland Coll (IA)
Green Mountain Coll (VT)
Greenville Coll (IL)
Hannibal-LaGrange Coll (MO)
High Point U (NC)
Houghton Coll (NY)
Houston Baptist U (TX)
Howard Payne U (TX)
Humboldt State U (CA)
Huntingdon Coll (AL)
Huntington Coll (IN)
Indiana State U (IN)
Indiana U Bloomington (IN)
Ithaca Coll (NY)
Jacksonville State U (AL)
Johnson State Coll (VT)
Kansas State U (KS)
Lakehead U (ON, Canada)
Lake Superior State U (MI)
Lehman Coll of the City U of NY (NY)
Lincoln U (PA)
Lock Haven U of Pennsylvania (PA)
Long Island U, Southampton Coll, Friends World Program (NY)
Lynchburg Coll (VA)
Lyndon State Coll (VT)
Marshall U (WV)
Mars Hill Coll (NC)
Maryville Coll (TN)
Memorial U of Newfoundland (NF, Canada)
Mercyhurst Coll (PA)
Messiah Coll (PA)
Metropolitan State Coll of Denver (CO)

Midland Lutheran Coll (NE)
Minnesota State U, Mankato (MN)
Mississippi U for Women (MS)
Missouri Valley Coll (MO)
Morgan State U (MD)
Morningside Coll (IA)
Morris Coll (SC)
Mount Olive Coll (NC)
New England Coll (NH)
New York U (NY)
Norfolk State U (VA)
North Carolina Ag and Tech State U (NC)
North Dakota State U (ND)
Northern Arizona U (AZ)
Northern Michigan U (MI)
Northland Coll (WI)
Northwest Missouri State U (MO)
Northwest Nazarene U (ID)
Ohio U (OH)
Oklahoma Baptist U (OK)
Oklahoma Panhandle State U (OK)
Oklahoma State U (OK)
Oregon State U (OR)
Pacific Union Coll (CA)
Pittsburg State U (KS)
Plymouth State Coll (NH)
Radford U (VA)
Redeemer Coll (ON, Canada)
St. Joseph's Coll, Suffolk Campus (NY)
Salem State Coll (MA)
San Diego State U (CA)
San Francisco State U (CA)
San Jose State U (CA)
Shaw U (NC)
Sheldon Jackson Coll (AK)
Shepherd Coll (WV)
Shorter Coll (GA)
Slippery Rock U of Pennsylvania (PA)
South Dakota State U (SD)
Southeastern Oklahoma State U (OK)
Southeast Missouri State U (MO)
Southern Illinois U Carbondale (IL)
Southern Wesleyan U (SC)
Southwest Baptist U (MO)
Southwestern Oklahoma State U (OK)
Southwest Missouri State U (MO)
State U of NY Coll at Brockport (NY)
State U of NY Coll at Cortland (NY)
State U of NY Coll of Environ Sci and Forestry (NY)
State U of West Georgia (GA)
Sterling Coll (VT)
Taylor U (IN)
Temple U (PA)
Tennessee State U (TN)
Tennessee Wesleyan Coll (TN)
Texas Tech U (TX)
Thomas Edison State Coll (NJ)
Troy State U (AL)
Tyndale Coll & Seminary (ON, Canada)
Universidad Metropolitana (PR)
U du Québec à Trois-Rivières (PQ, Canada)
U Coll of Cape Breton (NS, Canada)
U of Alberta (AB, Canada)
U of Arkansas (AR)
U of Arkansas at Pine Bluff (AR)
U of Calgary (AB, Canada)
U of Hawaii at Manoa (HI)
U of Idaho (ID)
U of Illinois at Urbana–Champaign (IL)
The U of Iowa (IA)
The U of Lethbridge (AB, Canada)
U of Maine at Machias (ME)
U of Maine at Presque Isle (ME)
U of Mary Hardin-Baylor (TX)
The U of Memphis (TN)
U of Michigan (MI)
U of Minnesota, Duluth (MN)
U of Mississippi (MS)
U of Missouri–Columbia (MO)
U of Mobile (AL)
The U of Montana–Missoula (MT)
U of Nebraska at Kearney (NE)
U of Nebraska at Omaha (NE)
U of Nevada, Las Vegas (NV)
U of Nevada, Reno (NV)

Majors Index
Recreation and Leisure Studies–Retail Management

U of New Brunswick, Fredericton (NB, Canada)
U of New Hampshire (NH)
U of New Mexico (NM)
The U of North Carolina at Chapel Hill (NC)
The U of North Carolina at Pembroke (NC)
U of North Dakota (ND)
U of Northern Iowa (IA)
U of North Texas (TX)
U of St. Francis (IL)
U of South Alabama (AL)
U of South Dakota (SD)
U of Southern Colorado (CO)
U of Southern Mississippi (MS)
The U of Tennessee at Chattanooga (TN)
The U of Texas–Pan American (TX)
U of the District of Columbia (DC)
U of Utah (UT)
U of Vermont (VT)
U of Waterloo (ON, Canada)
U of Wisconsin–La Crosse (WI)
U of Wisconsin–Madison (WI)
U of Wisconsin–Milwaukee (WI)
Upper Iowa U (IA)
Virginia Commonwealth U (VA)
Virginia Wesleyan Coll (VA)
Warner Southern Coll (FL)
Warren Wilson Coll (NC)
Washington State U (WA)
Wayne State Coll (NE)
Wayne State U (MI)
Western Michigan U (MI)
Western State Coll of Colorado (CO)
Western Washington U (WA)
Westfield State Coll (MA)
West Texas A&M U (TX)
West Virginia State Coll (WV)
West Virginia U (WV)
William Paterson U of New Jersey (NJ)
William Penn U (IA)
Wingate U (NC)
Winona State U (MN)
York Coll of Pennsylvania (PA)

RECREATION/LEISURE FACILITIES MANAGEMENT
Appalachian State U (NC)
Arkansas Tech U (AR)
Asbury Coll (KY)
Ball State U (IN)
Brigham Young U (UT)
California State U, Chico (CA)
California State U, Sacramento (CA)
California U of Pennsylvania (PA)
Central Michigan U (MI)
Clemson U (SC)
Coll of St. Joseph (VT)
Coll of the Ozarks (MO)
Colorado State U (CO)
Columbus State U (GA)
Concord Coll (WV)
Culver-Stockton Coll (MO)
Delaware State U (DE)
East Carolina U (NC)
Eastern Illinois U (IL)
Eastern Kentucky U (KY)
Eastern Michigan U (MI)
Eastern Washington U (WA)
Florida International U (FL)
Florida State U (FL)
Franklin Pierce Coll (NH)
George Mason U (VA)
Georgia State U (GA)
Grand Valley State U (MI)
Green Mountain Coll (VT)
Hannibal-LaGrange Coll (MO)
Henderson State U (AR)
High Point U (NC)
Humboldt State U (CA)
Huntingdon Coll (AL)
Illinois State U (IL)
Indiana Inst of Technology (IN)
Indiana State U (IN)
Indiana U Bloomington (IN)
Indiana U Southeast (IN)
Indiana Wesleyan U (IN)
John Brown U (AR)
Johnson & Wales U (RI)
Kansas State U (KS)
Kean U (NJ)
Kent State U (OH)

Lake Superior State U (MI)
Lock Haven U of Pennsylvania (PA)
Long Island U, Southampton Coll, Friends World Program (NY)
Lyndon State Coll (VT)
Lynn U (FL)
Marshall U (WV)
Mercyhurst Coll (PA)
Methodist Coll (NC)
Michigan State U (MI)
Middle Tennessee State U (TN)
Minnesota State U, Mankato (MN)
Missouri Valley Coll (MO)
Missouri Western State Coll (MO)
Morehead State U (KY)
Mount Marty Coll (SD)
New England Coll (NH)
New Mexico State U (NM)
North Carolina State U (NC)
Northland Coll (WI)
Oak Hills Christian Coll (MN)
The Ohio State U (OH)
Ohio U (OH)
Old Dominion U (VA)
Oregon State U (OR)
Penn State U Univ Park Campus (PA)
San Jose State U (CA)
Savannah State U (GA)
Sheldon Jackson Coll (AK)
Slippery Rock U of Pennsylvania (PA)
South Dakota State U (SD)
Southern Illinois U Edwardsville (IL)
Southwest Texas State U (TX)
State U of NY Coll at Cortland (NY)
Sterling Coll (VT)
Stillman Coll (AL)
Texas A&M U (TX)
Texas Christian U (TX)
Thomas U (GA)
Tri-State U (IN)
Union U (TN)
Unity Coll (ME)
U of Alberta (AB, Canada)
U of Connecticut (CT)
U of Delaware (DE)
U of Florida (FL)
U of Maine (ME)
U of Maine at Machias (ME)
U of Maryland, Coll Park (MD)
U of Minnesota, Twin Cities Campus (MN)
U of New England (ME)
U of New Hampshire (NH)
The U of North Carolina at Greensboro (NC)
The U of North Carolina at Wilmington (NC)
U of Northern Colorado (CO)
The U of Tennessee at Martin (TN)
The U of Tennessee Knoxville (TN)
U of Vermont (VT)
U of Wisconsin–La Crosse (WI)
U of Wyoming (WY)
Virginia Commonwealth U (VA)
Washington State U (WA)
Webber Coll (FL)
Western Carolina U (NC)
Western Illinois U (IL)
Western Kentucky U (KY)
Western State Coll of Colorado (CO)
West Virginia U (WV)
Wingate U (NC)
Winona State U (MN)

REHABILITATION THERAPY
Arkansas Tech U (AR)
Baker Coll of Muskegon (MI)
Boston U (MA)
California State U, Los Angeles (CA)
East Stroudsburg U of Pennsylvania (PA)
Florida State U (FL)
Ithaca Coll (NY)
Montana State U–Billings (MT)
Northeastern U (MA)
Queen's U at Kingston (ON, Canada)
San Diego State U (CA)
Stephen F. Austin State U (TX)
Thomas U (GA)
Université de Montréal (PQ, Canada)

U of British Columbia (BC, Canada)
U of Calgary (AB, Canada)
U of Florida (FL)
U of Maine at Farmington (ME)
U of Manitoba (MB, Canada)
U of North Texas (TX)
The U of Texas–Pan American (TX)
U of Toronto (ON, Canada)
York U (ON, Canada)

RELIGIOUS EDUCATION
Alaska Bible Coll (AK)
Andrews U (MI)
Aquinas Coll (MI)
Asbury Coll (KY)
Ashland U (OH)
Barclay Coll (KS)
Bethany Bible Coll (NB, Canada)
Biola U (CA)
Boise Bible Coll (ID)
Bryan Coll (TN)
California Lutheran U (CA)
Calvary Bible Coll and Theological Seminary (MO)
Campbellsville U (KY)
Canadian Bible Coll (SK, Canada)
Cardinal Stritch U (WI)
Carroll Coll (MT)
The Catholic U of America (DC)
Centenary Coll of Louisiana (LA)
Central Bible Coll (MO)
Circleville Bible Coll (OH)
Cleveland Coll of Jewish Studies (OH)
Coll of Mount St. Joseph (OH)
Coll of Saint Benedict (MN)
Columbia Coll (SC)
Concordia U (CA)
Concordia U (IL)
Concordia U (NE)
Concordia U (OR)
Concordia U at St. Paul (MN)
Cornerstone U (MI)
Crown Coll (MN)
Dallas Baptist U (TX)
Defiance Coll (OH)
DePaul U (IL)
Eastern Nazarene Coll (MA)
Eastern Pentecostal Bible Coll (ON, Canada)
East Texas Baptist U (TX)
Erskine Coll (SC)
Eugene Bible Coll (OR)
Faith Baptist Bible Coll and Theological Seminary (IA)
Faulkner U (AL)
Florida Baptist Theological Coll (FL)
Florida Southern Coll (FL)
Free Will Baptist Bible Coll (TN)
Gardner-Webb U (NC)
George Fox U (OR)
Global U of the Assemblies of God (MO)
God's Bible School and Coll (OH)
Gordon Coll (MA)
Grace Bible Coll (MI)
Griggs U (MD)
Hannibal-LaGrange Coll (MO)
Harding U (AR)
Heritage Baptist Coll & Heritage Theological Sem (ON, Canada)
Hillsdale Free Will Baptist Coll (OK)
Holy Family Coll (PA)
Houghton Coll (NY)
Howard Payne U (TX)
Huntingdon Coll (AL)
Indiana Wesleyan U (IN)
John Brown U (AR)
John Carroll U (OH)
John Wesley Coll (NC)
Kentucky Christian Coll (KY)
Kentucky Mountain Bible Coll (KY)
LaGrange Coll (GA)
La Roche Coll (PA)
La Salle U (PA)
Lee U (TN)
Lenoir-Rhyne Coll (NC)
Lincoln Christian Coll (IL)
Louisiana Coll (LA)
Loyola U New Orleans (LA)
Manhattan Christian Coll (KS)
Maranatha Baptist Bible Coll (WI)
Marian Coll (IN)
Mars Hill Coll (NC)
Marywood U (PA)

McGill U (PQ, Canada)
McMurry U (TX)
Mercyhurst Coll (PA)
Messiah Coll (PA)
MidAmerica Nazarene U (KS)
Mid-Continent Coll (KY)
Milligan Coll (TN)
Minnesota Bible Coll (MN)
Missouri Baptist Coll (MO)
Moody Bible Inst (IL)
Morris Coll (SC)
Mount Mary Coll (WI)
Mount Vernon Nazarene Coll (OH)
Multnomah Bible Coll and Biblical Seminary (OR)
Nazarene Bible Coll (CO)
Nazarene Indian Bible Coll (NM)
Nebraska Christian Coll (NE)
North Central U (MN)
North Greenville Coll (SC)
Northwest Coll (WA)
Northwestern Coll (IA)
Northwestern Coll (MN)
Northwest Nazarene U (ID)
Nyack Coll (NY)
Oakland City U (IN)
Oakwood Coll (AL)
Oklahoma Baptist U (OK)
Oklahoma Christian U of Science and Arts (OK)
Oklahoma City U (OK)
Olivet Nazarene U (IL)
Ozark Christian Coll (MO)
Pepperdine U, Malibu (CA)
Pfeiffer U (NC)
Prairie Bible Coll (AB, Canada)
Providence Coll and Theological Seminary (MB, Canada)
Reformed Bible Coll (MI)
St. Bonaventure U (NY)
Saint John's U (MN)
St. Louis Christian Coll (MO)
Saint Mary-of-the-Woods Coll (IN)
Saint Mary's Coll (IN)
Saint Mary's U of Minnesota (MN)
Saint Vincent Coll (PA)
Samford U (AL)
Seattle Pacific U (WA)
Seton Hall U (NJ)
Seton Hill Coll (PA)
Simpson Coll and Graduate School (CA)
Southeastern Coll of the Assemblies of God (FL)
Southern Adventist U (TN)
Southwestern Assemblies of God U (TX)
Southwestern Coll of Christian Ministries (OK)
Sterling Coll (KS)
Taylor U (IN)
Taylor U, Fort Wayne Campus (IN)
Texas Wesleyan U (TX)
Thiel Coll (PA)
Toccoa Falls Coll (GA)
Trinity Baptist Coll (FL)
Trinity Bible Coll (ND)
Trinity Christian Coll (IL)
Trinity Lutheran Coll (WA)
Tyndale Coll & Seminary (ON, Canada)
Union Coll (KY)
Union Coll (NE)
Universidad Adventista de las Antillas (PR)
U du Québec à Chicoutimi (PQ, Canada)
U of Dayton (OH)
U of Mobile (AL)
U of the Ozarks (AR)
Vanguard U of Southern California (CA)
Warner Pacific Coll (OR)
Washington Bible Coll (MD)
Wayland Baptist U (TX)
Wesley Coll (MS)
Western Baptist Coll (OR)
Westminster Coll (PA)
West Virginia Wesleyan Coll (WV)
Wheaton Coll (IL)
Williams Baptist Coll (AR)
William Tyndale Coll (MI)
York Coll (NE)

RESPIRATORY THERAPY
Armstrong Atlantic State U (GA)
Boise State U (ID)

California Coll for Health Sciences (CA)
Champlain Coll (VT)
The Coll of West Virginia (WV)
Columbia Union Coll (MD)
Columbus State U (GA)
Dakota State U (SD)
Florida A&M U (FL)
Gannon U (PA)
Georgia State U (GA)
Indiana U of Pennsylvania (PA)
Indiana U–Purdue U Indianapolis (IN)
La Roche Coll (PA)
Lee U (TN)
Loma Linda U (CA)
Long Island U, Brooklyn Campus (NY)
Louisiana State U Health Sciences Center (LA)
Medical Coll of Georgia (GA)
Midland Lutheran Coll (NE)
Midwestern State U (TX)
Millersville U of Pennsylvania (PA)
National-Louis U (IL)
Nebraska Methodist Coll of Nursing & Allied Health (NE)
North Dakota State U (ND)
Northeastern U (MA)
The Ohio State U (OH)
Our Lady of Holy Cross Coll (LA)
Pace U, New York City Campus (NY)
Point Park Coll (PA)
Quinnipiac U (CT)
Salisbury State U (MD)
Shenandoah U (VA)
Southwest Missouri State U (MO)
Southwest Texas State U (TX)
State U of NY at Stony Brook (NY)
State U of New York Upstate Medical University (NY)
Tennessee State U (TN)
Texas Southern U (TX)
Thomas Edison State Coll (NJ)
Universidad Metropolitana (PR)
The U of Alabama at Birmingham (AL)
U of Bridgeport (CT)
U of Central Arkansas (AR)
U of Central Florida (FL)
U of Charleston (WV)
U of Hartford (CT)
U of Kansas (KS)
U of Louisville (KY)
U of Missouri–Columbia (MO)
U of South Alabama (AL)
U of Texas Medical Branch at Galveston (TX)
U of the Ozarks (AR)
Weber State U (UT)
Wheeling Jesuit U (WV)
York Coll of Pennsylvania (PA)
Youngstown State U (OH)

RETAILING OPERATIONS
Johnson & Wales U (RI)

RETAIL MANAGEMENT
Belmont U (TN)
Bluffton Coll (OH)
California State U, Northridge (CA)
Champlain Coll (VT)
Chicago State U (IL)
David N. Myers Coll (OH)
Drexel U (PA)
Eastern Kentucky U (KY)
École des Hautes Études Commerciales (PQ, Canada)
Ferris State U (MI)
Fontbonne Coll (MO)
Governors State U (IL)
Indiana U Bloomington (IN)
John F. Kennedy U (CA)
Johnson & Wales U (RI)
Lasell Coll (MA)
Lewis-Clark State Coll (ID)
Lindenwood U (MO)
Marshall U (WV)
Marywood U (PA)
Mount Ida Coll (MA)
Newbury Coll (MA)
New Hampshire Coll (NH)
Northern Michigan U (MI)
Northwest Missouri State U (MO)
Ohio U (OH)
Philadelphia U (PA)

Majors Index
Retail Management–Russian/Slavic Area Studies

Rowan U (NJ)
Ryerson Polytechnic U (ON, Canada)
Salem State Coll (MA)
San Francisco State U (CA)
Simmons Coll (MA)
Syracuse U (NY)
Thomas Coll (ME)
Thomas Edison State Coll (NJ)
U of Central Oklahoma (OK)
U of Montevallo (AL)
U of Nebraska at Omaha (NE)
Winona State U (MN)
Youngstown State U (OH)

ROBOTICS
Harvard U (MA)
Montana Tech of The U of Montana (MT)
The Ohio State U (OH)
Pacific Union Coll (CA)
Peru State Coll (NE)
U du Québec à Trois-Rivières (PQ, Canada)
U of New Mexico (NM)
Worcester Polytechnic Inst (MA)

ROBOTICS TECHNOLOGY
Indiana U–Purdue U Indianapolis (IN)
Lake Superior State U (MI)
Purdue U (IN)
U of Rio Grande (OH)

ROMANCE LANGUAGES
Albertus Magnus Coll (CT)
Bard Coll (NY)
Beloit Coll (WI)
Baruch Coll of the City U of NY (NY)
Bowdoin Coll (ME)
Bryn Mawr Coll (PA)
Cameron U (OK)
Carleton Coll (MN)
The Catholic U of America (DC)
City Coll of the City U of NY (NY)
Colgate U (NY)
The Colorado Coll (CO)
Cornell U (NY)
Dartmouth Coll (NH)
DePauw U (IN)
Dowling Coll (NY)
Elmira Coll (NY)
Fordham U (NY)
Franklin Coll Switzerland (Switzerland)
Gettysburg Coll (PA)
Harvard U (MA)
Haverford Coll (PA)
Hunter Coll of the City U of NY (NY)
Kenyon Coll (OH)
Long Island U, Southampton Coll, Friends World Program (NY)
Manhattanville Coll (NY)
Marlboro Coll (VT)
Middlebury Coll (VT)
Mount Allison U (NB, Canada)
Mount Holyoke Coll (MA)
New York U (NY)
Northwest Missouri State U (MO)
Oberlin Coll (OH)
Olivet Nazarene U (IL)
Pitzer Coll (CA)
Point Loma Nazarene U (CA)
Pomona Coll (CA)
Princeton U (NJ)
Queens Coll of the City U of NY (NY)
Redeemer Coll (ON, Canada)
Ripon Coll (WI)
St. Joseph's Coll, New York (NY)
Sarah Lawrence Coll (NY)
State U of NY at Albany (NY)
Tufts U (MA)
U of Alberta (AB, Canada)
U of British Columbia (BC, Canada)
U of Chicago (IL)
U of Cincinnati (OH)
U of Maine (ME)
U of Maryland, Coll Park (MD)
U of Michigan (MI)
U of Nevada, Las Vegas (NV)
U of New Brunswick, Fredericton (NB, Canada)
U of New Hampshire (NH)

The U of North Carolina at Chapel Hill (NC)
U of Oregon (OR)
U of Pennsylvania (PA)
U of Toronto (ON, Canada)
U of Vermont (VT)
U of Victoria (BC, Canada)
U of Washington (WA)
U of Windsor (ON, Canada)
Ursinus Coll (OH)
Walsh U (OH)
Washington U in St. Louis (MO)
Wesleyan U (CT)
West Chester U of Pennsylvania (PA)
Wheeling Jesuit U (WV)
York U (ON, Canada)

RUSSIAN
American U (DC)
Amherst Coll (MA)
Arizona State U (AZ)
Bard Coll (NY)
Barnard Coll (NY)
Bates Coll (ME)
Baylor U (TX)
Beloit Coll (WI)
Boston Coll (MA)
Boston U (MA)
Bowdoin Coll (ME)
Bowling Green State U (OH)
Brandeis U (MA)
Brigham Young U (UT)
Brooklyn Coll of the City U of NY (NY)
Brown U (RI)
Bryn Mawr Coll (PA)
Bucknell U (PA)
California State U, Northridge (CA)
Carleton Coll (MN)
Carleton U (ON, Canada)
Carnegie Mellon U (PA)
Claremont McKenna Coll (CA)
Colgate U (NY)
Coll of the Holy Cross (MA)
The Coll of Wooster (OH)
The Colorado Coll (CO)
Columbia Coll (NY)
Columbia U, School of General Studies (NY)
Connecticut Coll (CT)
Cornell Coll (IA)
Cornell U (NY)
Dalhousie U (NS, Canada)
Dartmouth Coll (NH)
Dickinson Coll (PA)
Drew U (NJ)
Duke U (NC)
Eckerd Coll (FL)
Emory U (GA)
The Evergreen State Coll (WA)
Ferrum Coll (VA)
Florida State U (FL)
Fordham U (NY)
Georgetown U (DC)
The George Washington U (DC)
Goucher Coll (MD)
Grinnell Coll (IA)
Gustavus Adolphus Coll (MN)
Harvard U (MA)
Haverford Coll (PA)
Hobart and William Smith Colls (NY)
Hofstra U (NY)
Howard U (DC)
Hunter Coll of the City U of NY (NY)
Indiana State U (IN)
Indiana U Bloomington (IN)
Indiana U of Pennsylvania (PA)
Iowa State U of Science and Technology (IA)
James Madison U (VA)
Johns Hopkins U (MD)
Juniata Coll (PA)
Kent State U (OH)
Knox Coll (IL)
Kutztown U of Pennsylvania (PA)
La Salle U (PA)
Lawrence U (WI)
Lehman Coll of the City U of NY (NY)
Lincoln U (PA)
Long Island U, Southampton Coll, Friends World Program (NY)
Loyola U New Orleans (LA)
Macalester Coll (MN)

Marist Coll (NY)
Massachusetts Inst of Technology (MA)
McGill U (PQ, Canada)
Memorial U of Newfoundland (NF, Canada)
Miami U (OH)
Michigan State U (MI)
Middlebury Coll (VT)
Mount Holyoke Coll (MA)
New Coll of the U of South Florida (FL)
New York U (NY)
Northeastern U (MA)
Northern Illinois U (IL)
Norwich U (VT)
Oakland U (MI)
Oberlin Coll (OH)
The Ohio State U (OH)
Ohio U (OH)
Oklahoma State U (OK)
Ouachita Baptist U (AR)
Penn State U Univ Park Campus (PA)
Pitzer Coll (CA)
Pomona Coll (CA)
Portland State U (OR)
Principia Coll (IL)
Queens Coll of the City U of NY (NY)
Reed Coll (OR)
Rider U (NJ)
Rutgers, State U of NJ, Douglass Coll (NJ)
Rutgers, State U of NJ, Livingston Coll (NJ)
Rutgers, State U of NJ, Rutgers Coll (NJ)
Rutgers, State U of NJ, U Coll–New Brunswick (NJ)
Saint Louis U (MO)
St. Olaf Coll (MN)
San Diego State U (CA)
San Francisco State U (CA)
Sarah Lawrence Coll (NY)
Scripps Coll (CA)
Seattle Pacific U (WA)
Smith Coll (MA)
Southern Illinois U Carbondale (IL)
Southern Methodist U (TX)
State U of NY at Albany (NY)
State U of NY at Stony Brook (NY)
Swarthmore Coll (PA)
Syracuse U (NY)
Temple U (PA)
Texas A&M U (TX)
Trinity Coll (CT)
Trinity U (TX)
Truman State U (MO)
Tufts U (MA)
Tulane U (LA)
United States Military Academy (NY)
The U of Akron (OH)
U of Alaska Fairbanks (AK)
U of Alberta (AB, Canada)
The U of Arizona (AZ)
U of British Columbia (BC, Canada)
U of Calgary (AB, Canada)
U of Calif, Davis (CA)
U of Calif, Irvine (CA)
U of Calif, Los Angeles (CA)
U of Calif, Riverside (CA)
U of Calif, San Diego (CA)
U of Calif, Santa Cruz (CA)
U of Chicago (IL)
U of Delaware (DE)
U of Denver (CO)
U of Florida (FL)
U of Georgia (GA)
U of Hawaii at Manoa (HI)
U of Illinois at Chicago (IL)
U of Illinois at Urbana–Champaign (IL)
The U of Iowa (IA)
U of Kansas (KS)
U of Kentucky (KY)
U of King's Coll (NS, Canada)
U of Louisville (KY)
U of Manitoba (MB, Canada)
U of Maryland, Baltimore County (MD)
U of Maryland, Coll Park (MD)
U of Massachusetts Boston (MA)
U of Michigan (MI)

U of Minnesota, Twin Cities Campus (MN)
U of Missouri–Columbia (MO)
The U of Montana–Missoula (MT)
U of Nebraska–Lincoln (NE)
U of New Brunswick, Fredericton (NB, Canada)
U of New Hampshire (NH)
U of New Mexico (NM)
The U of North Carolina at Chapel Hill (NC)
The U of North Carolina at Greensboro (NC)
U of Northern Iowa (IA)
U of Notre Dame (IN)
U of Oklahoma (OK)
U of Oregon (OR)
U of Pennsylvania (PA)
U of Pittsburgh (PA)
U of Regina (SK, Canada)
U of Rochester (NY)
The U of Scranton (PA)
U of South Alabama (AL)
U of Southern California (CA)
U of South Florida (FL)
The U of Tennessee Knoxville (TN)
The U of Texas at Arlington (TX)
The U of Texas at Austin (TX)
U of the South (TN)
U of Toronto (ON, Canada)
U of Utah (UT)
U of Vermont (VT)
U of Victoria (BC, Canada)
U of Washington (WA)
U of Waterloo (ON, Canada)
The U of Western Ontario (ON, Canada)
U of Windsor (ON, Canada)
U of Wisconsin–Madison (WI)
U of Wisconsin–Milwaukee (WI)
U of Wyoming (WY)
Vanderbilt U (TN)
Vassar Coll (NY)
Wake Forest U (NC)
Washington State U (WA)
Washington U in St. Louis (MO)
Wayne State U (MI)
Wellesley Coll (MA)
Wesleyan U (CT)
West Chester U of Pennsylvania (PA)
Wheaton Coll (MA)
Williams Coll (MA)
Yale U (CT)
York U (ON, Canada)
Youngstown State U (OH)

RUSSIAN/SLAVIC AREA STUDIES
American U (DC)
Bard Coll (NY)
Barnard Coll (NY)
Baylor U (TX)
Beloit Coll (WI)
Boston Coll (MA)
Brandeis U (MA)
Brock U (ON, Canada)
Brown U (RI)
California State U, Fullerton (CA)
Carleton U (ON, Canada)
Colby Coll (ME)
Colgate U (NY)
The Coll of William and Mary (VA)
Columbia Coll (NY)
Concordia Coll (MN)
Cornell Coll (IA)
Cornell U (NY)
Dartmouth Coll (NH)
DePauw U (IN)
Dickinson Coll (PA)
Drew U (NJ)
Duke U (NC)
The Evergreen State Coll (WA)
Florida State U (FL)
Fordham U (NY)
Franklin and Marshall Coll (PA)
George Mason U (VA)
The George Washington U (DC)
Grand Valley State U (MI)
Gustavus Adolphus Coll (MN)
Hamilton Coll (NY)
Hamline U (MN)
Hampshire Coll (MA)
Harvard U (MA)
Hobart and William Smith Colls (NY)
Indiana U Bloomington (IN)

Kent State U (OH)
Knox Coll (IL)
Lafayette Coll (PA)
La Salle U (PA)
Lawrence U (WI)
Lehigh U (PA)
Long Island U, Southampton Coll, Friends World Program (NY)
Louisiana State U and A&M Coll (LA)
Macalester Coll (MN)
Marlboro Coll (VT)
Massachusetts Inst of Technology (MA)
McGill U (PQ, Canada)
Middlebury Coll (VT)
Mount Holyoke Coll (MA)
Muhlenberg Coll (PA)
New York U (NY)
Oakland U (MI)
Oberlin Coll (OH)
The Ohio State U (OH)
Randolph-Macon Woman's Coll (VA)
Rhodes Coll (TN)
Rice U (TX)
Rutgers, State U of NJ, Douglass Coll (NJ)
Rutgers, State U of NJ, Livingston Coll (NJ)
Rutgers, State U of NJ, Rutgers Coll (NJ)
Rutgers, State U of NJ, U Coll–New Brunswick (NJ)
St. Olaf Coll (MN)
San Diego State U (CA)
Smith Coll (MA)
Southern Methodist U (TX)
Southwest Texas State U (TX)
State U of NY at Albany (NY)
Stetson U (FL)
Syracuse U (NY)
Texas Tech U (TX)
Tufts U (MA)
Tulane U (LA)
The U of Alabama (AL)
The U of Alabama in Huntsville (AL)
U of Alaska Fairbanks (AK)
U of Alberta (AB, Canada)
U of British Columbia (BC, Canada)
U of Calif, Los Angeles (CA)
U of Calif, Riverside (CA)
U of Calif, Santa Cruz (CA)
U of Chicago (IL)
U of Colorado at Boulder (CO)
U of Connecticut (CT)
U of Houston (TX)
U of Illinois at Urbana–Champaign (IL)
U of Kansas (KS)
U of Louisville (KY)
U of Manitoba (MB, Canada)
U of Maryland, Coll Park (MD)
U of Massachusetts Amherst (MA)
U of Michigan (MI)
U of Minnesota, Twin Cities Campus (MN)
U of Missouri–Columbia (MO)
The U of Montana–Missoula (MT)
U of New Mexico (NM)
The U of North Carolina at Chapel Hill (NC)
U of Northern Iowa (IA)
U of Regina (SK, Canada)
U of Rochester (NY)
U of Southern Maine (ME)
The U of Texas at Austin (TX)
U of the South (TN)
U of Toronto (ON, Canada)
U of Vermont (VT)
U of Victoria (BC, Canada)
U of Washington (WA)
U of Waterloo (ON, Canada)
U of Wisconsin–Milwaukee (WI)
Washington and Lee U (VA)
Washington U in St. Louis (MO)
Wellesley Coll (MA)
Wesleyan U (CT)
Western Michigan U (MI)
Wheaton Coll (MA)
Wittenberg U (OH)
Yale U (CT)
York U (ON, Canada)

Majors Index
Sacred Music–Science Education

SACRED MUSIC
Alderson-Broaddus Coll (WV)
Anderson U (IN)
Appalachian State U (NC)
Aquinas Coll (MI)
Atlantic Union Coll (MA)
Augustana Coll (IL)
Barclay Coll (KS)
Baylor U (TX)
Belmont U (TN)
Bethany Coll of the Assemblies of God (CA)
Bethel Coll (IN)
Bethel Coll (MN)
Bethesda Christian U (CA)
Bethune-Cookman Coll (FL)
Boise Bible Coll (ID)
Brevard Coll (NC)
Briercrest Bible Coll (SK, Canada)
Bryan Coll (TN)
Calvary Bible Coll and Theological Seminary (MO)
Calvin Coll (MI)
Campbellsville U (KY)
Canadian Bible Coll (SK, Canada)
Cedarville Coll (OH)
Centenary Coll of Louisiana (LA)
Central Baptist Coll (AR)
Central Bible Coll (MO)
Charleston Southern U (SC)
Circleville Bible Coll (OH)
Coll of the Ozarks (MO)
Colorado Christian U (CO)
Columbia Coll (SC)
Concordia Coll (MI)
Concordia Coll (NY)
Concordia U (IL)
Concordia U (NE)
Concordia U at St. Paul (MN)
Cumberland Coll (KY)
Dallas Baptist U (TX)
Drake U (IA)
Eastern Nazarene Coll (MA)
East Texas Baptist U (TX)
Erskine Coll (SC)
Eugene Bible Coll (OR)
Evangel U (MO)
Faith Baptist Bible Coll and Theological Seminary (IA)
Florida Baptist Theological Coll (FL)
Florida Southern Coll (FL)
Free Will Baptist Bible Coll (TN)
Fresno Pacific U (CA)
Friends U (KS)
Furman U (SC)
Gardner-Webb U (NC)
God's Bible School and Coll (OH)
Grand Canyon U (AZ)
Greenville Coll (IL)
Gustavus Adolphus Coll (MN)
Hannibal-LaGrange Coll (MO)
Hardin-Simmons U (TX)
Heritage Baptist Coll & Heritage Theological Sem (ON, Canada)
Hillsdale Free Will Baptist Coll (OK)
Hope International U (CA)
Houghton Coll (NY)
Houston Baptist U (TX)
Howard Payne U (TX)
Indiana Wesleyan U (IN)
Johnson Bible Coll (TN)
Lambuth U (TN)
Lenoir-Rhyne Coll (NC)
Lincoln Christian Coll (IL)
Louisiana Coll (LA)
Loyola U New Orleans (LA)
Malone Coll (OH)
Manhattan Christian Coll (KS)
Maranatha Baptist Bible Coll (WI)
Mars Hill Coll (NC)
Marywood U (PA)
McMurry U (TX)
Mid-America Bible Coll (OK)
MidAmerica Nazarene U (KS)
Milligan Coll (TN)
Millikin U (IL)
Minnesota Bible Coll (MN)
Mississippi Coll (MS)
Missouri Baptist Coll (MO)
Moody Bible Inst (IL)
Mount Vernon Nazarene Coll (OH)
Nazarene Bible Coll (CO)
Nebraska Christian Coll (NE)
Newberry Coll (SC)
North Carolina Central U (NC)
North Central U (MN)
Northeastern State U (OK)
North Greenville Coll (SC)
North Park U (IL)
Northwest Bible Coll (AB, Canada)
Northwest Coll (WA)
Northwest Nazarene U (ID)
Nyack Coll (NY)
Oak Hills Christian Coll (MN)
Oklahoma Baptist U (OK)
Oklahoma City U (OK)
Olivet Nazarene U (IL)
Ouachita Baptist U (AR)
Ozark Christian Coll (MO)
Pacific Lutheran U (WA)
Palm Beach Atlantic Coll (FL)
Patten Coll (CA)
Pfeiffer U (NC)
Piedmont Coll (GA)
Point Loma Nazarene U (CA)
Rider U (NJ)
Saint Joseph's Coll (IN)
St. Louis Christian Coll (MO)
St. Olaf Coll (MN)
Saint Xavier U (IL)
Samford U (AL)
Seton Hill Coll (PA)
Shorter Coll (GA)
Simpson Coll and Graduate School (CA)
Southeastern Coll of the Assemblies of God (FL)
Southwestern Assemblies of God U (TX)
Southwestern Coll of Christian Ministries (OK)
Southwestern Oklahoma State U (OK)
Southwestern U (TX)
Stetson U (FL)
Susquehanna U (PA)
Taylor U (IN)
Toccoa Falls Coll (GA)
Trevecca Nazarene U (TN)
Union Coll (KY)
Union U (TN)
U of Mary Hardin-Baylor (TX)
Valparaiso U (IN)
Warner Southern Coll (FL)
Wartburg Coll (IA)
Wayland Baptist U (TX)
Westminster Choir Coll of Rider U (NJ)
Westminster Coll (PA)
William Jewell Coll (MO)
Williams Baptist Coll (AR)
William Tyndale Coll (MI)
York Coll (NE)

SAFETY AND SECURITY TECHNOLOGY
Eastern Kentucky U (KY)
Indiana State U (IN)
Indiana U of Pennsylvania (PA)
John Jay Coll of Criminal Justice, the City U of NY (NY)
Keene State Coll (NH)
Madonna U (MI)
Marshall U (WV)
Mercy Coll (NY)
Southeast Missouri State U (MO)
State U of NY at Farmingdale (NY)
U of Central Oklahoma (OK)
U of Southern California (CA)
U of Wisconsin–Whitewater (WI)
York Coll of Pennsylvania (PA)

SANITATION TECHNOLOGY
Grand Valley State U (MI)

SCANDINAVIAN AREA STUDIES
Luther Coll (IA)
U of Michigan (MI)
U of Washington (WA)

SCANDINAVIAN LANGUAGES
Augsburg Coll (MN)
Augustana Coll (IL)
Concordia Coll (MN)
Gustavus Adolphus Coll (MN)
Harvard U (MA)
Long Island U, Southampton Coll, Friends World Program (NY)
Luther Coll (IA)
North Park U (IL)
Pacific Lutheran U (WA)
St. Olaf Coll (MN)
U of Alberta (AB, Canada)
U of Calif, Berkeley (CA)
U of Calif, Los Angeles (CA)
U of Minnesota, Twin Cities Campus (MN)
U of North Dakota (ND)
The U of Texas at Austin (TX)
U of Washington (WA)
U of Wisconsin–Madison (WI)

SCHOOL PSYCHOLOGY
Bowling Green State U (OH)
Crichton Coll (TN)
Fort Hays State U (KS)
Texas Wesleyan U (TX)

SCIENCE EDUCATION
Abilene Christian U (TX)
Adams State Coll (CO)
Adrian Coll (MI)
Alabama State U (AL)
Albany State U (GA)
Albertson Coll of Idaho (ID)
Alderson-Broaddus Coll (WV)
Alfred U (NY)
Alice Lloyd Coll (KY)
Alvernia Coll (PA)
Alverno Coll (WI)
Anderson U (IN)
Andrews U (MI)
Antioch Coll (OH)
Appalachian State U (NC)
Armstrong Atlantic State U (GA)
Ashland U (AL)
Auburn U (AL)
Averett Coll (VA)
Baldwin-Wallace Coll (OH)
Ball State U (IN)
Bartlesville Wesleyan Coll (OK)
Barton Coll (NC)
Bayamón Central U (PR)
Baylor U (TX)
Beloit Coll (WI)
Bemidji State U (MN)
Benedictine Coll (KS)
Benedictine U (IL)
Bennett Coll (NC)
Berry Coll (GA)
Bethel Coll (IN)
Bethel Coll (MN)
Bloomsburg U of Pennsylvania (PA)
Blue Mountain Coll (MS)
Boise State U (ID)
Boston U (MA)
Bowling Green State U (OH)
Brigham Young U–Hawaii Campus (HI)
Brock U (ON, Canada)
Bryan Coll (TN)
Buena Vista U (IA)
California Lutheran U (CA)
California State U, Chico (CA)
California State U, San Marcos (CA)
Calvin Coll (MI)
Campbellsville U (KY)
Canisius Coll (NY)
Capital U (OH)
Cardinal Stritch U (WI)
Carroll Coll (WI)
Carthage Coll (WI)
Castleton State Coll (VT)
Cedar Crest Coll (PA)
Cedarville Coll (OH)
Centenary Coll of Louisiana (LA)
Central Methodist Coll (MO)
Central Michigan U (MI)
Central Missouri State U (MO)
Charleston Southern U (SC)
Chicago State U (IL)
Christopher Newport U (VA)
Citadel, The Military Coll of South Carolina (SC)
Clarion U of Pennsylvania (PA)
Clark Atlanta U (GA)
Clemson U (SC)
Coe Coll (IA)
Coll of Mount Saint Vincent (NY)
Coll of Our Lady of the Elms (MA)
Coll of Saint Mary (NE)
Coll of Santa Fe (NM)
Coll of the Atlantic (ME)
Coll of the Ozarks (MO)
Coll of the Southwest (NM)
Colorado Christian U (CO)
Colorado State U (CO)
Columbia Coll (MO)
Columbia Coll (SC)
Columbus State U (GA)
Concordia Coll (MN)
Concordia Coll (NY)
Concordia U (IL)
Concordia U (NE)
Concordia U (OR)
Concordia U at St. Paul (MN)
Concordia U Wisconsin (WI)
Coppin State Coll (MD)
Cornerstone U (MI)
Culver-Stockton Coll (MO)
Cumberland Coll (KY)
Daemen Coll (NY)
Dallas Baptist U (TX)
Dana Coll (NE)
Defiance Coll (OH)
Delaware State U (DE)
Delta State U (MS)
Dickinson State U (ND)
Dominican Coll of Blauvelt (NY)
Drake U (IA)
Drexel U (PA)
Duquesne U (PA)
D'Youville Coll (NY)
East Carolina U (NC)
Eastern Kentucky U (KY)
Eastern Mennonite U (VA)
Eastern Michigan U (MI)
Eastern Washington U (WA)
East Texas Baptist U (TX)
Elizabethtown Coll (PA)
Elmira Coll (NY)
Elon Coll (NC)
Emporia State U (KS)
Evangel U (MO)
Fairmont State Coll (WV)
Ferris State U (MI)
Florida Atlantic U (FL)
Florida Inst of Technology (FL)
Florida International U (FL)
Florida State U (FL)
Fort Hays State U (KS)
Framingham State Coll (MA)
Franklin Coll of Indiana (IN)
Freed-Hardeman U (TN)
Fresno Pacific U (CA)
Friends U (KS)
Georgia Southern U (GA)
Georgia Southwestern State U (GA)
Gettysburg Coll (PA)
Glenville State Coll (WV)
Goshen Coll (IN)
Governors State U (IL)
Grace Coll (IN)
Graceland Coll (IA)
Grand Canyon U (AZ)
Grand Valley State U (MI)
Grand View Coll (IA)
Greensboro Coll (NC)
Greenville Coll (IL)
Grove City Coll (PA)
Gwynedd-Mercy Coll (PA)
Hamline U (MN)
Harding U (AR)
Hardin-Simmons U (TX)
Hastings Coll (NE)
Heidelberg Coll (OH)
Heritage Coll (WA)
Houghton Coll (NY)
Howard Payne U (TX)
Huntingdon Coll (AL)
Huntington Coll (IN)
Huron U (SD)
Illinois Wesleyan U (IL)
Indiana State U (IN)
Indiana U Bloomington (IN)
Indiana U of Pennsylvania (PA)
Indiana U–Purdue U Fort Wayne (IN)
Indiana U South Bend (IN)
Indiana U Southeast (IN)
Indiana Wesleyan U (IN)
Inter American U of PR, San Germán Campus (PR)
Iona Coll (NY)
Ithaca Coll (NY)
Johnson C. Smith U (NC)
Judson Coll (AL)
Judson Coll (IL)
Juniata Coll (PA)
Kent State U (OH)
LaGrange Coll (GA)
Lakehead U (ON, Canada)
Lakeland Coll (WI)
La Salle U (PA)
Lees-McRae Coll (NC)
Le Moyne Coll (NY)
Lenoir-Rhyne Coll (NC)
Lewis-Clark State Coll (ID)
Liberty U (VA)
Lincoln Memorial U (TN)
Lincoln U (MO)
Lincoln U (PA)
Lock Haven U of Pennsylvania (PA)
Long Island U, Southampton Coll (NY)
Longwood Coll (VA)
Loras Coll (IA)
Louisiana Coll (LA)
Louisiana State U in Shreveport (LA)
Luther Coll (IA)
Lyndon State Coll (VT)
Malone Coll (OH)
Manchester Coll (IN)
Manhattan Coll (NY)
Mansfield U of Pennsylvania (PA)
Maranatha Baptist Bible Coll (WI)
Marian Coll of Fond du Lac (WI)
Marshall U (WV)
Mars Hill Coll (NC)
Marycrest International U (IA)
Marymount Coll (NY)
Marywood U (PA)
Mayville State U (ND)
McGill U (PQ, Canada)
McMurry U (TX)
Memorial U of Newfoundland (NF, Canada)
Mercer U (GA)
Mercyhurst Coll (PA)
Mesa State Coll (CO)
Methodist Coll (NC)
Miami U (OH)
Michigan State U (MI)
Michigan Technological U (MI)
MidAmerica Nazarene U (KS)
Midland Lutheran Coll (NE)
Millersville U of Pennsylvania (PA)
Milligan Coll (TN)
Minnesota State U, Mankato (MN)
Minnesota State U Moorhead (MN)
Minot State U (ND)
Mississippi Coll (MS)
Mississippi U for Women (MS)
Mississippi Valley State U (MS)
Missouri Valley Coll (MO)
Montana State U–Billings (MT)
Montana State U–Northern (MT)
Moravian Coll (PA)
Morehead State U (KY)
Morningside Coll (IA)
Mount Mercy Coll (IA)
Mount Vernon Nazarene Coll (OH)
Muskingum Coll (OH)
Nazareth Coll of Rochester (NY)
Nebraska Wesleyan U (NE)
New Mexico Highlands U (NM)
New Mexico Inst of Mining and Technology (NM)
New York U (NY)
Niagara U (NY)
Nicholls State U (LA)
North Carolina State U (NC)
North Central Coll (IL)
North Dakota State U (ND)
Northern Arizona U (AZ)
Northern Kentucky U (KY)
Northern Michigan U (MI)
Northland Coll (WI)
Northwestern Oklahoma State U (OK)
Northwestern State U of Louisiana (LA)
Northwest Missouri State U (MO)
Oakland City U (IN)
Oakwood Coll (AL)
Ohio Dominican Coll (OH)
Ohio U (OH)
Oklahoma Baptist U (OK)
Oklahoma Christian U of Science and Arts (OK)
Oklahoma City U (OK)
Oklahoma Panhandle State U (OK)
Oklahoma State U (OK)
Olivet Nazarene U (IL)
Otterbein Coll (OH)
Ouachita Baptist U (AR)
Our Lady of Holy Cross Coll (LA)
Pacific Lutheran U (WA)

Peru State Coll (NE)
Pikeville Coll (KY)
Pittsburg State U (KS)
Plymouth State Coll (NH)
Pontifical Catholic U of Puerto Rico (PR)
Purdue U Calumet (IN)
Queens Coll of the City U of NY (NY)
Queen's U at Kingston (ON, Canada)
Rensselaer Polytechnic Inst (NY)
Rider U (NJ)
Rockford Coll (IL)
Rocky Mountain Coll (MT)
Rowan U (NJ)
Rust Coll (MS)
Saginaw Valley State U (MI)
St. Ambrose U (IA)
St. Cloud State U (MN)
Saint Francis Coll (PA)
St. John Fisher Coll (NY)
St. John's U (NY)
St. Joseph's Coll, New York (NY)
Saint Mary's U of Minnesota (MN)
St. Olaf Coll (MN)
Samford U (AL)
San Diego State U (CA)
Seattle Pacific U (WA)
Seton Hill Coll (PA)
Shawnee State U (OH)
Shorter Coll (GA)
Slippery Rock U of Pennsylvania (PA)
Southeastern Coll of the Assemblies of God (FL)
Southeastern Louisiana U (LA)
Southeastern Oklahoma State U (OK)
Southeast Missouri State U (MO)
Southern Arkansas U–Magnolia (AR)
Southern Illinois U Edwardsville (IL)
Southwestern Coll (KS)
Southwestern Oklahoma State U (OK)
Southwest Missouri State U (MO)
State U of NY at Buffalo (NY)
State U of NY at New Paltz (NY)
State U of NY at Oswego (NY)
State U of NY Coll at Buffalo (NY)
State U of NY Coll at Cortland (NY)
State U of NY Coll at Fredonia (NY)
State U of NY Coll at Old Westbury (NY)
State U of NY Coll at Oneonta (NY)
State U of NY Coll at Potsdam (NY)
State U of NY Coll of Environ Sci and Forestry (NY)
State U of West Georgia (GA)
Syracuse U (NY)
Tabor Coll (KS)
Talladega Coll (AL)
Taylor U (IN)
Temple U (PA)
Texas A&M International U (TX)
Texas Wesleyan U (TX)
Towson U (MD)
Trinity Christian Coll (IL)
Tri-State U (IN)
Troy State U (AL)
Troy State U Dothan (AL)
Union Coll (KY)
Union U (TN)
Universidad Metropolitana (PR)
U du Québec à Chicoutimi (PQ, Canada)
The U of Akron (OH)
U of Alberta (AB, Canada)
The U of Arizona (AZ)
U of Arkansas (AR)
U of British Columbia (BC, Canada)
U of Central Arkansas (AR)
U of Central Florida (FL)
U of Central Oklahoma (OK)
U of Charleston (WV)
U of Dayton (OH)
U of Delaware (DE)
U of Detroit Mercy (MI)
U of Evansville (IN)
The U of Findlay (OH)
U of Georgia (GA)
U of Illinois at Chicago (IL)
U of Illinois at Urbana–Champaign (IL)
U of Indianapolis (IN)
The U of Iowa (IA)
U of Kentucky (KY)
The U of Lethbridge (AB, Canada)
U of Louisiana at Monroe (LA)
U of Maine at Farmington (ME)
U of Maine at Presque Isle (ME)
U of Manitoba (MB, Canada)
U of Maryland, Coll Park (MD)
U of Michigan–Dearborn (MI)
U of Minnesota, Duluth (MN)
U of Minnesota, Twin Cities Campus (MN)
U of Mississippi (MS)
U of Missouri–Columbia (MO)
U of Missouri–St. Louis (MO)
The U of Montana–Missoula (MT)
U of Nebraska–Lincoln (NE)
U of Nevada, Reno (NV)
U of New Brunswick, Fredericton (NB, Canada)
U of New England (ME)
U of New Hampshire (NH)
U of New Orleans (LA)
The U of North Carolina at Pembroke (NC)
U of North Dakota (ND)
U of Northern Iowa (IA)
U of North Florida (FL)
U of North Texas (TX)
U of Notre Dame (IN)
U of Oklahoma (OK)
U of Pittsburgh at Johnstown (PA)
U of Regina (SK, Canada)
U of Rio Grande (OH)
U of Saint Francis (IN)
U of St. Thomas (MN)
U of Sioux Falls (SD)
U of South Alabama (AL)
U of South Dakota (SD)
U of Southern California (CA)
U of Southern Colorado (CO)
U of South Florida (FL)
The U of Tennessee at Chattanooga (TN)
The U of Tennessee at Martin (TN)
The U of Texas at San Antonio (TX)
U of the Ozarks (AR)
U of the Pacific (CA)
U of the Sciences in Philadelphia (PA)
U of Tulsa (OK)
U of Utah (UT)
U of Vermont (VT)
U of Washington (WA)
U of Waterloo (ON, Canada)
U of West Florida (FL)
U of Windsor (ON, Canada)
U of Wisconsin–Eau Claire (WI)
U of Wisconsin–La Crosse (WI)
U of Wisconsin–Madison (WI)
U of Wisconsin–Platteville (WI)
U of Wisconsin–River Falls (WI)
U of Wisconsin–Superior (WI)
Upper Iowa U (IA)
Urbana U (OH)
Utah State U (UT)
Valley City State U (ND)
Villa Julie Coll (MD)
Virginia Wesleyan Coll (VA)
Walsh U (OH)
Warner Pacific Coll (OR)
Warner Southern Coll (FL)
Washington U in St. Louis (MO)
Wayne State Coll (NE)
Wayne State U (MI)
Weber State U (UT)
West Chester U of Pennsylvania (PA)
Western Carolina U (NC)
Western Kentucky U (KY)
Western Montana Coll of The U of Montana (MT)
Western State Coll of Colorado (CO)
Western Washington U (WA)
Westfield State Coll (MA)
West Virginia State Coll (WV)
Wheeling Jesuit U (WV)
Wichita State U (KS)
Widener U (PA)
William Penn U (IA)
William Woods U (MO)
Wilmington Coll (OH)
Wingate U (NC)
Winona State U (MN)
Wittenberg U (OH)
Wright State U (OH)
Xavier U (OH)
Xavier U of Louisiana (LA)
York Coll (NE)
York Coll of Pennsylvania (PA)
York U (ON, Canada)
Youngstown State U (OH)

SCIENCE/TECHNOLOGY AND SOCIETY
Brevard Coll (NC)
Cazenovia Coll (NY)
Columbia Coll (SC)
Cornell U (NY)
Drexel U (PA)
Georgia Inst of Technology (GA)
Grinnell Coll (IA)
James Madison U (VA)
Lehigh U (PA)
Massachusetts Inst of Technology (MA)
New Jersey Inst of Technology (NJ)
The Ohio State U (OH)
Pitzer Coll (CA)
Rensselaer Polytechnic Inst (NY)
Rutgers, State U of NJ, Newark Coll of Arts & Scis (NJ)
Scripps Coll (CA)
Slippery Rock U of Pennsylvania (PA)
Stanford U (CA)
Texas Southern U (TX)
U of Maryland University Coll (MD)
U of Nevada, Reno (NV)
Vassar Coll (NY)
Virginia Wesleyan Coll (VA)
Washington U in St. Louis (MO)
Wesleyan U (CT)
Worcester Polytechnic Inst (MA)
York U (ON, Canada)

SCULPTURE
Academy of Art Coll (CA)
Adams State Coll (CO)
Alberta Coll of Art and Design (AB, Canada)
Alfred U (NY)
Antioch Coll (OH)
Aquinas Coll (MI)
Arizona State U (AZ)
Art Academy of Cincinnati (OH)
The Art Inst of Boston at Lesley (MA)
Atlanta Coll of Art (GA)
Ball State U (IN)
Barat Coll (IL)
Bard Coll (NY)
Bellarmine Coll (KY)
Bennington Coll (VT)
Bethany Coll (KS)
Birmingham-Southern Coll (AL)
Boston U (MA)
Bowling Green State U (OH)
Brevard Coll (NC)
California Coll of Arts and Crafts (CA)
California Inst of the Arts (CA)
California State U, Fullerton (CA)
California State U, Hayward (CA)
California State U, Long Beach (CA)
California State U, Northridge (CA)
California State U, Stanislaus (CA)
Carnegie Mellon U (PA)
The Catholic U of America (DC)
Ctr for Creative Studies—Coll of Art and Design (MI)
Cleveland Inst of Art (OH)
Coll of Santa Fe (NM)
The Coll of Southeastern Europe, The American U of Athens (Greece)
Coll of Visual Arts (MN)
Colorado State U (CO)
Columbus Coll of Art and Design (OH)
Concordia U (PQ, Canada)
The Corcoran Coll of Art and Design (DC)
Cornell U (NY)
DePaul U (IL)
Drake U (IA)
Eastern Kentucky U (KY)
Escuela de Artes Plasticas de Puerto Rico (PR)
Framingham State Coll (MA)
Goddard Coll (VT)
Grand Valley State U (MI)
Hampshire Coll (MA)
Indiana U Bloomington (IN)
Inter American U of PR, San Germán Campus (PR)
Kansas City Art Inst (MO)
Kent State U (OH)
Long Island U, Southampton Coll, Friends World Program (NY)
Longwood Coll (VA)
Lyme Academy of Fine Arts (CT)
Maharishi U of Management (IA)
Maine Coll of Art (ME)
Marlboro Coll (VT)
Marshall U (WV)
Maryland Inst, Coll of Art (MD)
Massachusetts Coll of Art (MA)
Memorial U of Newfoundland (NF, Canada)
Memphis Coll of Art (TN)
Mercyhurst Coll (PA)
Milwaukee Inst of Art and Design (WI)
Minneapolis Coll of Art and Design (MN)
Minnesota State U, Mankato (MN)
Minnesota State U Moorhead (MN)
Montserrat Coll of Art (MA)
Moore Coll of Art and Design (PA)
Mount Allison U (NB, Canada)
New World School of the Arts (FL)
New York U (NY)
Northern Arizona U (AZ)
Northern Michigan U (MI)
Northwest Missouri State U (MO)
Nova Scotia Coll of Art and Design (NS, Canada)
The Ohio State U (OH)
Ohio U (OH)
Otis Coll of Art and Design (CA)
Pacific Northwest Coll of Art (OR)
Parsons School of Design, New School U (NY)
Plymouth State Coll (NH)
Portland State U (OR)
Pratt Inst (NY)
Queens Coll of the City U of NY (NY)
Rhode Island School of Design (RI)
Rochester Inst of Technology (NY)
Rocky Mountain Coll of Art & Design (CO)
Rutgers, State U of NJ, Mason Gross School of Arts (NJ)
San Francisco Art Inst (CA)
Sarah Lawrence Coll (NY)
School of the Art Inst of Chicago (IL)
School of the Museum of Fine Arts (MA)
School of Visual Arts (NY)
Seton Hill Coll (PA)
Simon's Rock Coll of Bard (MA)
Sonoma State U (CA)
State U of NY at New Paltz (NY)
State U of NY Coll at Brockport (NY)
State U of NY Coll at Buffalo (NY)
State U of NY Coll at Potsdam (NY)
Syracuse U (NY)
Temple U (PA)
Texas A&M U—Commerce (TX)
Texas Woman's U (TX)
Trinity Christian Coll (IL)
The U of Akron (OH)
U of Alberta (AB, Canada)
U of Calif, Santa Cruz (CA)
U of Central Oklahoma (OK)
U of Dallas (TX)
U of Evansville (IN)
U of Hartford (CT)
U of Houston (TX)
U of Illinois at Urbana–Champaign (IL)
The U of Iowa (IA)
U of Kansas (KS)
U of Massachusetts Dartmouth (MA)
U of Miami (FL)
U of Michigan (MI)
U of Montevallo (AL)
U of North Carolina at Greensboro (NC)
U of North Texas (TX)
U of Oregon (OR)
U of Puerto Rico, Río Piedras (PR)
U of South Alabama (AL)
U of South Dakota (SD)
The U of Tennessee at Chattanooga (TN)
The U of Texas at Arlington (TX)
The U of the Arts (PA)
U of the Pacific (CA)
U of Washington (WA)
U of Windsor (ON, Canada)
U of Wisconsin–Milwaukee (WI)
Virginia Commonwealth U (VA)
Washington U in St. Louis (MO)
Webster U (MO)
Western Michigan U (MI)
Wittenberg U (OH)
York U (ON, Canada)

SECONDARY EDUCATION
Abilene Christian U (TX)
Acadia U (NS, Canada)
Adams State Coll (CO)
Adrian Coll (MI)
Alabama A&M U (AL)
Alabama State U (AL)
Albany State U (GA)
Albertson Coll of Idaho (ID)
Albertus Magnus Coll (CT)
Albion Coll (MI)
Albright Coll (PA)
Alderson-Broaddus Coll (WV)
Alfred U (NY)
Alice Lloyd Coll (KY)
Allentown Coll of St. Francis de Sales (PA)
Alma Coll (MI)
Alverno Coll (WI)
American International Coll (MA)
Anderson Coll (SC)
Andrews U (MI)
Antioch Coll (OH)
Aquinas Coll (MI)
Arizona State U (AZ)
Arizona State U West (AZ)
Arkansas Baptist Coll (AR)
Armstrong Atlantic State U (GA)
Ashland U (OH)
Assumption Coll (MA)
Athens State U (AL)
Atlantic Union Coll (MA)
Auburn U (AL)
Auburn U Montgomery (AL)
Augsburg Coll (MN)
Augustana Coll (IL)
Augustana Coll (SD)
Averett Coll (VA)
Baldwin-Wallace Coll (OH)
Ball State U (IN)
Barat Coll (IL)
Bartlesville Wesleyan Coll (OK)
Barton Coll (NC)
Baylor U (TX)
Beaver Coll (PA)
Bellarmine Coll (KY)
Belmont Abbey Coll (NC)
Beloit Coll (WI)
Bemidji State U (MN)
Benedictine Coll (KS)
Benedictine U (IL)
Berea Coll (KY)
Berry Coll (GA)
Bethel Coll (IN)
Bethel Coll (MN)
Biola U (CA)
Birmingham-Southern Coll (AL)
Blackburn Coll (IL)
Bloomsburg U of Pennsylvania (PA)
Bluffton Coll (OH)
Boise State U (ID)
Boston Coll (MA)
Bowie State U (MD)
Bowling Green State U (OH)
Brandon U (MB, Canada)
Brescia U (KY)
Brevard Coll (NC)
Briar Cliff Coll (IA)
Bridgewater Coll (VA)
Brigham Young U–Hawaii Campus (HI)
Brock U (ON, Canada)
Brooklyn Coll of the City U of NY (NY)

Majors Index
Secondary Education

Bryan Coll (TN)
Bucknell U (PA)
Buena Vista U (IA)
Butler U (IN)
California Lutheran U (CA)
Calumet Coll of Saint Joseph (IN)
Calvary Bible Coll and Theological Seminary (MO)
Calvin Coll (MI)
Campbellsville U (KY)
Campbell U (NC)
Canisius Coll (NY)
Capital U (OH)
Cardinal Stritch U (WI)
Carroll Coll (MT)
Carson-Newman Coll (TN)
Carthage Coll (WI)
Catawba Coll (NC)
The Catholic U of America (DC)
Cedar Crest Coll (PA)
Cedarville Coll (OH)
Centenary Coll (NJ)
Centenary Coll of Louisiana (LA)
Central Coll (IA)
Central Missouri State U (MO)
Centre Coll (KY)
Chadron State Coll (NE)
Charleston Southern U (SC)
Cheyney U of Pennsylvania (PA)
Chicago State U (IL)
Christopher Newport U (VA)
City Coll of the City U of NY (NY)
Clark Atlanta U (GA)
Clarke Coll (IA)
Clark U (MA)
Clemson U (SC)
Coastal Carolina U (SC)
Coe Coll (IA)
Coker Coll (SC)
Coll Misericordia (PA)
Coll of Mount Saint Vincent (NY)
The Coll of New Jersey (NJ)
The Coll of New Rochelle (NY)
Coll of Notre Dame (CA)
Coll of Our Lady of the Elms (MA)
Coll of Saint Benedict (MN)
Coll of St. Catherine (MN)
Coll of St. Joseph (VT)
Coll of Saint Mary (NE)
Coll of Santa Fe (NM)
Coll of the Atlantic (ME)
Coll of the Ozarks (MO)
Coll of the Southwest (NM)
Colorado Christian U (CO)
Columbia Coll (MO)
Columbia Coll (SC)
Columbus State U (GA)
Concord Coll (WV)
Concordia Coll (MI)
Concordia Coll (MN)
Concordia Coll (NY)
Concordia U (CA)
Concordia U (IL)
Concordia U (NE)
Concordia U (OR)
Concordia U at Austin (TX)
Concordia U at St. Paul (MN)
Concordia U Wisconsin (WI)
Converse Coll (SC)
Coppin State Coll (MD)
Cornell Coll (IA)
Cornerstone U (MI)
Crichton Coll (TN)
Cumberland Coll (KY)
Dakota State U (SD)
Dakota Wesleyan U (SD)
Dallas Baptist U (TX)
Dana Coll (NE)
David Lipscomb U (TN)
Defiance Coll (OH)
Delaware Valley Coll (PA)
Delta State U (MS)
DePaul U (IL)
Dickinson State U (ND)
Doane Coll (NE)
Dominican Coll of Blauvelt (NY)
Dordt Coll (IA)
Dowling Coll (NY)
Drake U (IA)
Drexel U (PA)
Drury U (MO)
Duquesne U (PA)
D'Youville Coll (NY)
East Central U (OK)
Eastern Coll (PA)
Eastern Illinois U (IL)
Eastern Kentucky U (KY)

Eastern Mennonite U (VA)
Eastern Michigan U (MI)
Eastern Nazarene Coll (MA)
Eastern Washington U (WA)
East Stroudsburg U of Pennsylvania (PA)
East Texas Baptist U (TX)
Elizabeth City State U (NC)
Elizabethtown Coll (PA)
Elmhurst Coll (IL)
Elmira Coll (NY)
Elon Coll (NC)
Emmanuel Coll (MA)
Emory U (GA)
Emporia State U (KS)
Evangel U (MO)
The Evergreen State Coll (WA)
Fairfield U (CT)
Fairmont State Coll (WV)
Faulkner U (AL)
Ferris State U (MI)
Fitchburg State Coll (MA)
Flagler Coll (FL)
Florida Gulf Coast U (FL)
Florida Southern Coll (FL)
Florida State U (FL)
Fontbonne Coll (MO)
Fordham U (NY)
Fort Lewis Coll (CO)
Framingham State Coll (MA)
Franklin Coll of Indiana (IN)
Franklin Pierce Coll (NH)
Freed-Hardeman U (TN)
Free Will Baptist Bible Coll (TN)
Fresno Pacific U (CA)
Friends U (KS)
Frostburg State U (MD)
Furman U (SC)
Gallaudet U (DC)
Gannon U (PA)
Gardner-Webb U (NC)
Geneva Coll (PA)
Georgetown Coll (KY)
Georgia Southwestern State U (GA)
Gettysburg Coll (PA)
Glenville State Coll (WV)
Goddard Coll (VT)
Gonzaga U (WA)
Goshen Coll (IN)
Grace Bible Coll (MI)
Graceland Coll (IA)
Grand Canyon U (AZ)
Grand Valley State U (MI)
Grand View Coll (IA)
Green Mountain Coll (VT)
Greensboro Coll (NC)
Greenville Coll (IL)
Grove City Coll (PA)
Guilford Coll (NC)
Gustavus Adolphus Coll (MN)
Gwynedd-Mercy Coll (PA)
Hamline U (MN)
Hampshire Coll (MA)
Hampton U (VA)
Hannibal-LaGrange Coll (MO)
Hardin-Simmons U (TX)
Harris-Stowe State Coll (MO)
Hastings Coll (NE)
Heidelberg Coll (OH)
Heritage Coll (WA)
High Point U (NC)
Hillsdale Coll (MI)
Hiram Coll (OH)
Hobe Sound Bible Coll (FL)
Hofstra U (NY)
Holy Family Coll (PA)
Hope Coll (MI)
Houghton Coll (NY)
Houston Baptist U (TX)
Howard Payne U (TX)
Humboldt State U (CA)
Hunter Coll of the City U of NY (NY)
Huntingdon Coll (AL)
Huntington Coll (IN)
Huron U (SD)
Huston-Tillotson Coll (TX)
Idaho State U (ID)
Illinois Coll (IL)
Illinois Wesleyan U (IL)
Immaculata Coll (PA)
Indiana State U (IN)
Indiana U Bloomington (IN)
Indiana U East (IN)
Indiana U Northwest (IN)
Indiana U of Pennsylvania (PA)

Indiana U–Purdue U Fort Wayne (IN)
Indiana U–Purdue U Indianapolis (IN)
Indiana U South Bend (IN)
Indiana U Southeast (IN)
Indiana Wesleyan U (IN)
Inter American U of PR, Arecibo Campus (PR)
Inter American U of PR, Metropolitan Campus (PR)
Inter American U of PR, San Germán Campus (PR)
Iona Coll (NY)
Iowa State U of Science and Technology (IA)
Iowa Wesleyan Coll (IA)
Ithaca Coll (NY)
Jacksonville State U (AL)
Jacksonville U (FL)
Jarvis Christian Coll (TX)
John Brown U (AR)
John Carroll U (OH)
Johnson C. Smith U (NC)
Johnson State Coll (VT)
Judson Coll (AL)
Judson Coll (IL)
Juniata Coll (PA)
Kansas State U (KS)
Keene State Coll (NH)
Kent State U (OH)
Kentucky Wesleyan Coll (KY)
King Coll (TN)
King's Coll (PA)
Kutztown U of Pennsylvania (PA)
LaGrange Coll (GA)
Lake Forest Coll (IL)
Lakehead U (ON, Canada)
Lakeland Coll (WI)
Lake Superior State U (MI)
Lamar U (TX)
Lambuth U (TN)
Langston U (OK)
La Salle U (PA)
La Sierra U (CA)
Lawrence U (WI)
Lebanon Valley Coll (PA)
Lees-McRae Coll (NC)
Lee U (TN)
Le Moyne Coll (NY)
LeMoyne-Owen Coll (TN)
Lenoir-Rhyne Coll (NC)
LeTourneau U (TX)
Lewis U (IL)
Liberty U (VA)
Lincoln Christian Coll (IL)
Lincoln Memorial U (TN)
Lindenwood U (MO)
Lock Haven U of Pennsylvania (PA)
Long Island U, Brooklyn Campus (NY)
Long Island U, C.W. Post Campus (NY)
Long Island U, Southampton Coll (NY)
Long Island U, Southampton Coll, Friends World Program (NY)
Longwood Coll (VA)
Loras Coll (IA)
Louisiana Coll (LA)
Louisiana State U and A&M Coll (LA)
Louisiana State U in Shreveport (LA)
Louisiana Tech U (LA)
Lubbock Christian U (TX)
Luther Coll (IA)
Lycoming Coll (PA)
Lynchburg Coll (VA)
Lynn U (FL)
MacMurray Coll (IL)
Madonna U (MI)
Manchester Coll (IN)
Manhattan Coll (NY)
Manhattanville Coll (NY)
Mansfield U of Pennsylvania (PA)
Maranatha Baptist Bible Coll (WI)
Marian Coll (IN)
Marian Coll of Fond du Lac (WI)
Marietta Coll (OH)
Marist Coll (NY)
Marquette U (WI)
Marshall U (WV)
Mars Hill Coll (NC)
Marymount Coll (NY)
Maryville U of Saint Louis (MO)

Mary Washington Coll (VA)
Marywood U (PA)
Massachusetts Coll of Liberal Arts (MA)
McGill U (PQ, Canada)
McKendree Coll (IL)
McMurry U (TX)
McNeese State U (LA)
McPherson Coll (KS)
Memorial U of Newfoundland (NF, Canada)
Mercy Coll (NY)
Mercyhurst Coll (PA)
Merrimack Coll (MA)
Mesa State Coll (CO)
Methodist Coll (NC)
Miami U (OH)
Michigan State U (MI)
Michigan Technological U (MI)
Mid-America Bible Coll (OK)
MidAmerica Nazarene U (KS)
Middlebury Coll (VT)
Midland Lutheran Coll (NE)
Midwestern State U (TX)
Millersville U of Pennsylvania (PA)
Milligan Coll (TN)
Minnesota State U, Mankato (MN)
Minnesota State U Moorhead (MN)
Minot State U (ND)
Mississippi State U (MS)
Mississippi U for Women (MS)
Missouri Southern State Coll (MO)
Missouri Valley Coll (MO)
Molloy Coll (NY)
Monmouth Coll (IL)
Monmouth U (NJ)
Montana State U–Billings (MT)
Montana State U–Bozeman (MT)
Montana State U–Northern (MT)
Montreat Coll (NC)
Moravian Coll (PA)
Morehouse Coll (GA)
Morgan State U (MD)
Morningside Coll (IA)
Morris Coll (SC)
Mount Marty Coll (SD)
Mount Mary Coll (WI)
Mount Mercy Coll (IA)
Mount St. Clare Coll (IA)
Mount Saint Mary Coll (NY)
Mount St. Mary's Coll (CA)
Mount Saint Mary's Coll and Seminary (MD)
Mount Saint Vincent U (NS, Canada)
Mount Senario Coll (WI)
Mount Vernon Nazarene Coll (OH)
Muhlenberg Coll (PA)
Muskingum Coll (OH)
Nazareth Coll of Rochester (NY)
Nebraska Christian Coll (NE)
Newberry Coll (SC)
New England Coll (NH)
New Hampshire Coll (NH)
Newman U (KS)
New Mexico Highlands U (NM)
New Mexico State U (NM)
New York U (NY)
Niagara U (NY)
Nicholls State U (LA)
Nichols Coll (MA)
North Carolina State U (NC)
North Carolina Wesleyan Coll (NC)
North Central Coll (IL)
North Central U (MN)
North Dakota State U (ND)
Northeastern State U (OK)
Northern Arizona U (AZ)
Northern Michigan U (MI)
Northern State U (SD)
North Georgia Coll & State U (GA)
Northland Coll (WI)
North Park U (IL)
Northwest Coll (WA)
Northwestern Coll (IA)
Northwestern Oklahoma State U (OK)
Northwestern State U of Louisiana (LA)
Northwestern U (IL)
Northwest Missouri State U (MO)
Northwest Nazarene U (ID)
Notre Dame Coll (NH)
Notre Dame Coll of Ohio (OH)
Nova Southeastern U (FL)
Nyack Coll (NY)
Oakland City U (IN)

Oakland U (MI)
Oglethorpe U (GA)
Ohio Dominican Coll (OH)
Ohio U (OH)
Ohio Wesleyan U (OH)
Oklahoma Baptist U (OK)
Oklahoma Christian U of Science and Arts (OK)
Oklahoma City U (OK)
Oklahoma Panhandle State U (OK)
Oklahoma State U (OK)
Olivet Nazarene U (IL)
Otterbein Coll (OH)
Ouachita Baptist U (AR)
Our Lady of Holy Cross Coll (LA)
Pace U, New York City Campus (NY)
Pace U, Pleasantville/Briarcliff Campus (NY)
Pacific Lutheran U (WA)
Pacific U (OR)
Paine Coll (GA)
Palm Beach Atlantic Coll (FL)
Penn State U Harrisburg Campus of the Capital Coll (PA)
Penn State U Univ Park Campus (PA)
Pepperdine U, Malibu (CA)
Peru State Coll (NE)
Piedmont Baptist Coll (NC)
Piedmont Coll (GA)
Pikeville Coll (KY)
Pine Manor Coll (MA)
Pittsburg State U (KS)
Plattsburgh State U of NY (NY)
Plymouth State Coll (NH)
Point Park Coll (PA)
Pontifical Catholic U of Puerto Rico (PR)
Principia Coll (IL)
Providence Coll (RI)
Purdue U Calumet (IN)
Queens Coll (NC)
Queens Coll of the City U of NY (NY)
Queen's U at Kingston (ON, Canada)
Redeemer Coll (ON, Canada)
Reformed Bible Coll (MI)
Rider U (NJ)
Ripon Coll (WI)
Rivier Coll (NH)
Roberts Wesleyan Coll (NY)
Rockhurst U (MO)
Rocky Mountain Coll (MT)
Roger Williams U (RI)
Rowan U (NJ)
Sacred Heart U (CT)
St. Ambrose U (IA)
Saint Anselm Coll (NH)
St. Bonaventure U (NY)
St. Cloud State U (MN)
Saint Francis Coll (NY)
Saint Francis Coll (PA)
St. Francis Xavier U (NS, Canada)
Saint John's U (MN)
St. John's U (NY)
Saint Joseph Coll (CT)
Saint Joseph's Coll (IN)
Saint Joseph's Coll (ME)
St. Joseph's Coll, New York (NY)
St. Joseph's Coll, Suffolk Campus (NY)
Saint Joseph's U (PA)
Saint Leo U (FL)
Saint Louis U (MO)
Saint Martin's Coll (WA)
Saint Mary-of-the-Woods Coll (IN)
Saint Mary's Coll of California (CA)
Saint Mary's U (NS, Canada)
Saint Michael's Coll (VT)
St. Olaf Coll (MN)
St. Thomas U (FL)
Salisbury State U (MD)
Salve Regina U (RI)
San Diego State U (CA)
Seton Hall U (NJ)
Seton Hill Coll (PA)
Shawnee State U (OH)
Sheldon Jackson Coll (AK)
Shepherd Coll (WV)
Shorter Coll (GA)
Siena Coll (NY)
Siena Heights U (MI)
Simmons Coll (MA)
Simpson Coll (IA)

Majors Index
Secondary Education–Social Science Education

Simpson Coll and Graduate School (CA)
Slippery Rock U of Pennsylvania (PA)
South Dakota State U (SD)
Southeastern Oklahoma State U (OK)
Southeast Missouri State U (MO)
Southern Utah U (UT)
Southwest Baptist U (MO)
Southwestern Assemblies of God U (TX)
Southwestern Oklahoma State U (OK)
Southwest State U (MN)
Spalding U (KY)
Spring Arbor Coll (MI)
Spring Hill Coll (AL)
State U of NY at Albany (NY)
State U of NY at New Paltz (NY)
State U of NY at Oswego (NY)
State U of NY at Stony Brook (NY)
State U of NY Coll at Brockport (NY)
State U of NY Coll at Buffalo (NY)
State U of NY Coll at Cortland (NY)
State U of NY Coll at Fredonia (NY)
State U of NY Coll at Old Westbury (NY)
State U of NY Coll at Oneonta (NY)
State U of NY Coll at Potsdam (NY)
State U of West Georgia (GA)
Suffolk U (MA)
Susquehanna U (PA)
Syracuse U (NY)
Tabor Coll (KS)
Taylor U (IN)
Temple U (PA)
Tennessee Technological U (TN)
Tennessee Wesleyan Coll (TN)
Texas A&M U–Commerce (TX)
Texas A&M U–Kingsville (TX)
Texas Christian U (TX)
Texas Southern U (TX)
Texas Wesleyan U (TX)
Thiel Coll (PA)
Thomas More Coll (KY)
Toccoa Falls Coll (GA)
Tougaloo Coll (MS)
Transylvania U (KY)
Trent U (ON, Canada)
Trevecca Nazarene U (TN)
Trinity Baptist Coll (FL)
Trinity Christian Coll (IL)
Trinity Coll of Vermont (VT)
Trinity Western U (BC, Canada)
Tri-State U (IN)
Troy State U (AL)
Troy State U Dothan (AL)
Tufts U (MA)
Tusculum Coll (TN)
Union Coll (KY)
Union Coll (NE)
Union U (TN)
Universidad Adventista de las Antillas (PR)
Universidad Metropolitana (PR)
Université de Montréal (PQ, Canada)
Université de Sherbrooke (PQ, Canada)
U du Québec à Chicoutimi (PQ, Canada)
U du Québec à Hull (PQ, Canada)
U du Québec à Trois-Rivières (PQ, Canada)
U du Québec en Abitibi-Témiscamingue (PQ, Canada)
Université Laval (PQ, Canada)
The U of Akron (OH)
The U of Alabama (AL)
The U of Alabama at Birmingham (AL)
U of Alberta (AB, Canada)
The U of Arizona (AZ)
U of Arkansas at Pine Bluff (AR)
U of British Columbia (BC, Canada)
U of Calgary (AB, Canada)
U of Central Oklahoma (OK)
U of Cincinnati (OH)
U of Dallas (TX)
U of Dayton (OH)
U of Delaware (DE)
U of Detroit Mercy (MI)
U of Evansville (IN)
The U of Findlay (OH)
U of Hartford (CT)
U of Hawaii at Manoa (HI)
U of Idaho (ID)
U of Illinois at Chicago (IL)
U of Illinois at Springfield (IL)
U of Indianapolis (IN)
The U of Iowa (IA)
U of Kansas (KS)
U of La Verne (CA)
U of Louisiana at Lafayette (LA)
U of Maine (ME)
U of Maine at Farmington (ME)
U of Maine at Presque Isle (ME)
U of Manitoba (MB, Canada)
U of Mary Hardin-Baylor (TX)
U of Maryland, Coll Park (MD)
U of Miami (FL)
U of Michigan (MI)
U of Michigan–Dearborn (MI)
U of Michigan–Flint (MI)
U of Minnesota, Morris (MN)
U of Mississippi (MS)
U of Missouri–Kansas City (MO)
U of Missouri–St. Louis (MO)
U of Mobile (AL)
The U of Montana–Missoula (MT)
U of Nebraska at Omaha (NE)
U of Nevada, Las Vegas (NV)
U of New Brunswick, Fredericton (NB, Canada)
U of New England (ME)
U of New Mexico (NM)
U of New Orleans (LA)
U of North Alabama (AL)
The U of North Carolina at Chapel Hill (NC)
The U of North Carolina at Pembroke (NC)
U of North Florida (FL)
U of North Texas (TX)
U of Oklahoma (OK)
U of Pittsburgh at Bradford (PA)
U of Pittsburgh at Johnstown (PA)
U of Portland (OR)
U of Prince Edward Island (PE, Canada)
U of Puerto Rico, Río Piedras (PR)
U of Redlands (CA)
U of Regina (SK, Canada)
U of Rhode Island (RI)
U of Richmond (VA)
U of Rio Grande (OH)
U of Saint Francis (IN)
U of St. Thomas (TX)
U of San Francisco (CA)
The U of Scranton (PA)
U of Sioux Falls (SD)
U of South Alabama (AL)
U of South Carolina Spartanburg (SC)
U of South Dakota (SD)
U of Southern Colorado (CO)
U of Southern Indiana (IN)
The U of Tampa (FL)
The U of Tennessee at Chattanooga (TN)
The U of Texas–Pan American (TX)
U of the Pacific (CA)
U of the Sacred Heart (PR)
U of Tulsa (OK)
U of Utah (UT)
U of Vermont (VT)
U of Victoria (BC, Canada)
U of Washington (WA)
The U of Western Ontario (ON, Canada)
U of Windsor (ON, Canada)
The U of Winnipeg (MB, Canada)
U of Wisconsin–La Crosse (WI)
U of Wisconsin–Madison (WI)
U of Wisconsin–Milwaukee (WI)
U of Wisconsin–Parkside (WI)
U of Wisconsin–Platteville (WI)
U of Wisconsin–River Falls (WI)
U of Wisconsin–Stevens Point (WI)
U of Wisconsin–Whitewater (WI)
U of Wyoming (WY)
Upper Iowa U (IA)
Urbana U (OH)
Ursinus Coll (PA)
Ursuline Coll (OH)
Utah State U (UT)
Utica Coll of Syracuse U (NY)
Valdosta State U (GA)
Valley City State U (ND)
Valparaiso U (IN)
Vanderbilt U (TN)
Vanguard U of Southern California (CA)
Villanova U (PA)
Virginia Commonwealth U (VA)
Virginia Intermont Coll (VA)
Virginia Wesleyan Coll (VA)
Wagner Coll (NY)
Walsh U (OH)
Warner Pacific Coll (OR)
Warren Wilson Coll (NC)
Wartburg Coll (IA)
Washington State U (WA)
Washington U in St. Louis (MO)
Waynesburg Coll (PA)
Weber State U (UT)
Webster U (MO)
Wells Coll (NY)
Wesley Coll (DE)
West Chester U of Pennsylvania (PA)
Western Baptist Coll (OR)
Western Connecticut State U (CT)
Western Montana Coll of The U of Montana (MT)
Western Oregon U (OR)
Western State Coll of Colorado (CO)
Western Washington U (WA)
Westfield State Coll (MA)
West Liberty State Coll (WV)
Westminster Coll (MO)
Westmont Coll (CA)
West Virginia State Coll (WV)
West Virginia U (WV)
West Virginia Wesleyan Coll (WV)
Wheeling Jesuit U (WV)
Whitworth Coll (WA)
Wichita State U (KS)
Wilkes U (PA)
William Jewell Coll (MO)
William Paterson U of New Jersey (NJ)
William Penn U (IA)
William Woods U (MO)
Wilmington Coll (OH)
Wingate U (NC)
Winona State U (MN)
Wittenberg U (OH)
Wright State U (OH)
Xavier U of Louisiana (LA)
York Coll (NE)
York Coll of Pennsylvania (PA)
York U (ON, Canada)
Youngstown State U (OH)

SECRETARIAL SCIENCE
Alabama State U (AL)
Albany State U (GA)
Allen U (SC)
American U of Puerto Rico (PR)
Appalachian State U (NC)
Arkansas State U (AR)
Baker Coll of Flint (MI)
Baker Coll of Muskegon (MI)
Baker Coll of Owosso (MI)
Baker Coll of Port Huron (MI)
Bayamón Central U (PR)
Belmont U (TN)
Bluefield State Coll (WV)
California State U, Northridge (CA)
Campbellsville U (KY)
Cedarville Coll (OH)
Coleman Coll (CA)
Cumberland Coll (KY)
Davenport Coll of Business, Kalamazoo Campus (MI)
Davenport Coll of Business, Lansing Campus (MI)
David N. Myers Coll (OH)
East Central U (OK)
Eastern Illinois U (IL)
Eastern Kentucky U (KY)
Elizabeth City State U (NC)
Evangel U (MO)
Florida A&M U (FL)
Fort Hays State U (KS)
Fort Valley State U (GA)
Hofstra U (NY)
Humphreys Coll (CA)
Husson Coll (ME)
Inter American U of PR, Aguadilla Campus (PR)
Inter American U of PR, Arecibo Campus (PR)
Inter American U of PR, Fajardo Campus (PR)
Inter American U of PR, Metropolitan Campus (PR)
Inter American U of PR, San Germán Campus (PR)
Jones Coll (FL)
Lake Superior State U (MI)
Lamar U (TX)
Langston U (OK)
Lee U (TN)
Lincoln Christian Coll (IL)
Lincoln U (MO)
Louisiana Coll (LA)
Maranatha Baptist Bible Coll (WI)
Mayville State U (ND)
Mercyhurst Coll (PA)
Mesa State Coll (CO)
Midland Lutheran Coll (NE)
Morehead State U (KY)
Mount Vernon Nazarene Coll (OH)
Murray State U (KY)
North Carolina Ag and Tech State U (NC)
Northern State U (SD)
Northwest Missouri State U (MO)
Oakwood Coll (AL)
Pace U, New York City Campus (NY)
Pacific Union Coll (CA)
Peirce Coll (PA)
Pontifical Catholic U of Puerto Rico (PR)
Robert Morris Coll (IL)
Robert Morris Coll (PA)
Rust Coll (MS)
Ryerson Polytechnic U (ON, Canada)
Salem State Coll (MA)
Southeast Missouri State U (MO)
Southern Adventist U (TN)
Southwestern Adventist U (TX)
State U of West Georgia (GA)
Suffolk U (MA)
Sul Ross State U (TX)
Tabor Coll (KS)
Tennessee State U (TN)
Texas A&M U–Commerce (TX)
Texas Woman's U (TX)
Trinity Bible Coll (ND)
Union Coll (KY)
Universidad Adventista de las Antillas (PR)
Universidad del Turabo (PR)
Universidad Metropolitana (PR)
U of Idaho (ID)
U of Maine at Machias (ME)
The U of Montana–Missoula (MT)
The U of North Carolina at Pembroke (NC)
U of Puerto Rico at Ponce (PR)
U of Puerto Rico, Humacao U Coll (PR)
U of Puerto Rico, Mayagüez Campus (PR)
U of Puerto Rico, Río Piedras (PR)
U of Sioux Falls (SD)
The U of Texas–Pan American (TX)
U of the Sacred Heart (PR)
U of Wisconsin–Superior (WI)
Valdosta State U (GA)
Valley City State U (ND)
Weber State U (UT)
Winona State U (MN)
Youngstown State U (OH)

SIGN LANGUAGE INTERPRETATION
Bethel Coll (IN)
Bloomsburg U of Pennsylvania (PA)
California State U, Northridge (CA)
Coll of St. Catherine–Minneapolis (MN)
Columbia Coll Chicago (IL)
Converse Coll (SC)
Gallaudet U (DC)
Gardner-Webb U (NC)
Indiana U–Purdue U Indianapolis (IN)
Long Island U, Southampton Coll, Friends World Program (NY)
Madonna U (MI)
Maryville Coll (TN)
Mount Aloysius Coll (PA)
North Central U (MN)
Northeastern U (MA)
Ozark Christian Coll (MO)
U of Arkansas at Little Rock (AR)
U of New Hampshire at Manchester (NH)
U of New Mexico (NM)
The U of North Carolina at Greensboro (NC)
U of Rochester (NY)
Western Oregon U (OR)
William Woods U (MO)
York U (ON, Canada)

SLAVIC LANGUAGES
Barnard Coll (NY)
Boston Coll (MA)
Brown U (RI)
Columbia U, School of General Studies (NY)
Cornell U (NY)
Duke U (NC)
Harvard U (MA)
Indiana U Bloomington (IN)
Long Island U, Southampton Coll, Friends World Program (NY)
Northwestern U (IL)
Queens Coll of the City U of NY (NY)
Rutgers, State U of NJ, Newark Coll of Arts & Scis (NJ)
Saint Mary's Coll (MI)
Stanford U (CA)
State U of NY at Albany (NY)
U of Alberta (AB, Canada)
U of British Columbia (BC, Canada)
U of Calif, Berkeley (CA)
U of Calif, Los Angeles (CA)
U of Calif, Santa Barbara (CA)
U of Chicago (IL)
U of Georgia (GA)
U of Illinois at Chicago (IL)
U of Manitoba (MB, Canada)
U of Pittsburgh (PA)
U of Regina (SK, Canada)
The U of Scranton (PA)
The U of Texas at Austin (TX)
U of Toronto (ON, Canada)
U of Victoria (BC, Canada)
U of Virginia (VA)
U of Washington (WA)
U of Windsor (ON, Canada)
U of Wisconsin–Madison (WI)
U of Wisconsin–Milwaukee (WI)
Wayne State U (MI)

SOCIAL/PHILOSOPHICAL FOUNDATIONS OF EDUCATION
Texas Southern U (TX)
Washington U in St. Louis (MO)

SOCIAL PSYCHOLOGY
Clarion U of Pennsylvania (PA)
Florida Atlantic U (FL)
Maryville U of Saint Louis (MO)
U of Nevada, Reno (NV)
U of Wisconsin–Superior (WI)

SOCIAL SCIENCE EDUCATION
Abilene Christian U (TX)
Arkansas State U (AR)
Baylor U (TX)
Blue Mountain Coll (MS)
Bowling Green State U (OH)
Bridgewater Coll (VA)
California State U, Chico (CA)
Carroll Coll (MT)
Central Michigan U (MI)
The Coll of St. Scholastica (MN)
Coll of Santa Fe (NM)
Concordia U (IL)
Concordia U (NE)
Dana Coll (NE)
Delta State U (MS)
Eastern Michigan U (MI)
East Stroudsburg U of Pennsylvania (PA)
Elmira Coll (NY)
Elon Coll (NC)
Florida Atlantic U (FL)
Florida International U (FL)
Florida State U (FL)
Georgia Southern U (GA)
Hastings Coll (NE)
Henderson State U (AR)
Hope International U (CA)
Johnson State Coll (VT)
Judson Coll (AL)

Majors Index
Social Science Education–Social Sciences

Liberty U (VA)
Luther Coll (IA)
Lyndon State Coll (VT)
Mansfield U of Pennsylvania (PA)
Maryville Coll (TN)
Mayville State U (ND)
McGill U (PQ, Canada)
McKendree Coll (IL)
Millikin U (IL)
Mississippi Coll (MS)
Mississippi Valley State U (MS)
North Dakota State U (ND)
Northwest Nazarene U (ID)
Oklahoma Baptist U (OK)
Rivier Coll (NH)
Rocky Mountain Coll (MT)
St. Ambrose U (IA)
Samford U (AL)
Seattle Pacific U (WA)
Simpson Coll and Graduate School (CA)
Southwestern Oklahoma State U (OK)
Union Coll (NE)
The U of Arizona (AZ)
U of Central Florida (FL)
U of Georgia (GA)
U of Illinois at Chicago (IL)
U of Maine at Farmington (ME)
U of Minnesota, Twin Cities Campus (MN)
The U of Montana–Missoula (MT)
U of Nebraska–Lincoln (NE)
U of Nevada, Reno (NV)
U of Northern Iowa (IA)
U of Rio Grande (OH)
U of Southern California (CA)
U of South Florida (FL)
U of Vermont (VT)
U of West Florida (FL)
U of Wisconsin–River Falls (WI)
U of Wisconsin–Superior (WI)
Warner Southern Coll (FL)
Wartburg Coll (IA)
Washington U in St. Louis (MO)
Weber State U (UT)
Westminster Coll (UT)
Westmont Coll (CA)
William Penn U (IA)
York U (ON, Canada)
Youngstown State U (OH)

SOCIAL SCIENCES
Adams State Coll (CO)
Adrian Coll (MI)
Alabama State U (AL)
Albertus Magnus Coll (CT)
Alma Coll (MI)
Alvernia Coll (PA)
Alverno Coll (WI)
American International Coll (MA)
American U (DC)
Andrews U (MI)
Antioch Coll (OH)
Appalachian State U (NC)
Aquinas Coll (MI)
Arizona State U West (AZ)
Asbury Coll (KY)
Ashland U (OH)
Augsburg Coll (MN)
Averett Coll (VA)
Azusa Pacific U (CA)
Ball State U (IN)
Barat Coll (IL)
Bard Coll (NY)
Bartlesville Wesleyan Coll (OK)
Barton Coll (NC)
Bellevue U (NE)
Bemidji State U (MN)
Benedictine Coll (KS)
Benedictine U (IL)
Bennington Coll (VT)
Berry Coll (GA)
Bethany Coll of the Assemblies of God (CA)
Bethel Coll (IN)
Bethel Coll (KS)
Biola U (CA)
Bishop's U (PQ, Canada)
Black Hills State U (SD)
Bloomsburg U of Pennsylvania (PA)
Bluefield State Coll (WV)
Blue Mountain Coll (MS)
Bluffton Coll (OH)
Boise State U (ID)
Bowling Green State U (OH)

Brescia U (KY)
Brock U (ON, Canada)
Buena Vista U (IA)
Caldwell Coll (NJ)
California Baptist U (CA)
California Inst of Technology (CA)
California Lutheran U (CA)
California Polytechnic State U, San Luis Obispo (CA)
California State Polytechnic U, Pomona (CA)
California State U, Chico (CA)
California State U, Los Angeles (CA)
California State U, Sacramento (CA)
California State U, San Bernardino (CA)
California State U, San Marcos (CA)
California State U, Stanislaus (CA)
California U of Pennsylvania (PA)
Calvin Coll (MI)
Campbellsville U (KY)
Campbell U (NC)
Cardinal Stritch U (WI)
Carnegie Mellon U (PA)
Carroll Coll (MT)
Carthage Coll (WI)
Castleton State Coll (VT)
Cazenovia Coll (NY)
Cedarville Coll (OH)
Centenary Coll of Louisiana (LA)
Central Coll (IA)
Central Connecticut State U (CT)
Central Michigan U (MI)
Chaminade U of Honolulu (HI)
Chapman U (CA)
Charleston Southern U (SC)
Cheyney U of Pennsylvania (PA)
Clarion U of Pennsylvania (PA)
Clark Atlanta U (GA)
Clarkson U (NY)
Cleveland State U (OH)
Colgate U (NY)
Coll of Notre Dame (CA)
Coll of Saint Benedict (MN)
Coll of St. Catherine (MN)
Coll of Saint Mary (NE)
Coll of the Southwest (NM)
Colorado State U (CO)
Concordia Coll (MI)
Concordia Coll (NY)
Concordia U (NE)
Concordia U (OR)
Concordia U (PQ, Canada)
Concordia U at St. Paul (MN)
Connecticut Coll (CT)
Coppin State Coll (MD)
Dana Coll (NE)
David N. Myers Coll (OH)
Defiance Coll (OH)
Delta State U (MS)
DePaul U (IL)
Dickinson State U (ND)
Doane Coll (NE)
Dominican Coll of Blauvelt (NY)
Dominican U (IL)
Dordt Coll (IA)
Dowling Coll (NY)
Drexel U (PA)
Eastern Illinois U (IL)
Eastern Michigan U (MI)
Eastern Nazarene Coll (MA)
Eastern New Mexico U (NM)
Eastern Washington U (WA)
Edgewood Coll (WI)
Edinboro U of Pennsylvania (PA)
Elizabeth City State U (NC)
Elizabethtown Coll (PA)
Elmira Coll (NY)
Emporia State U (KS)
Eugene Lang Coll, New School U (NY)
Evangel U (MO)
The Evergreen State Coll (WA)
Faulkner U (AL)
Felician Coll (NJ)
Ferrum Coll (VA)
Flagler Coll (FL)
Florida A&M U (FL)
Florida Atlantic U (FL)
Florida Gulf Coast U (FL)
Florida Southern Coll (FL)
Florida State U (FL)
Fontbonne Coll (MO)
Fordham U (NY)

Fort Valley State U (GA)
Framingham State Coll (MA)
Freed-Hardeman U (TN)
Fresno Pacific U (CA)
Friends U (KS)
Frostburg State U (MD)
Gardner-Webb U (NC)
Georgia Southwestern State U (GA)
Gettysburg Coll (PA)
Goddard Coll (VT)
Governors State U (IL)
Graceland Coll (IA)
Grand Canyon U (AZ)
Grand Valley State U (MI)
Gustavus Adolphus Coll (MN)
Hamline U (MN)
Hampshire Coll (MA)
Hampton U (VA)
Harding U (AR)
Harvard U (MA)
Hawaii Pacific U (HI)
Heritage Coll (WA)
Hofstra U (NY)
Holy Family Coll (PA)
Hope International U (CA)
Houghton Coll (NY)
Howard Payne U (TX)
Humboldt State U (CA)
Illinois State U (IL)
Indiana State U (IN)
Indiana Wesleyan U (IN)
Inter American U of PR, San Germán Campus (PR)
Iona Coll (NY)
Ithaca Coll (NY)
James Madison U (VA)
John Brown U (AR)
Johns Hopkins U (MD)
Johnson C. Smith U (NC)
Judson Coll (IL)
Juniata Coll (PA)
Kansas State U (KS)
Keene State Coll (NH)
Kendall Coll (IL)
Kent State U (OH)
Kentucky State U (KY)
Keuka Coll (NY)
The King's U Coll (AB, Canada)
Lake Erie Coll (OH)
Lakeland Coll (WI)
Lake Superior State U (MI)
Lane Coll (TN)
La Salle U (PA)
Lebanon Valley Coll (PA)
Lees-McRae Coll (NC)
Lee U (TN)
LeMoyne-Owen Coll (TN)
Lesley Coll (MA)
Lewis-Clark State Coll (ID)
Liberty U (VA)
Lincoln U (MO)
Lock Haven U of Pennsylvania (PA)
Long Island U, Brooklyn Campus (NY)
Long Island U, Southampton Coll (NY)
Long Island U, Southampton Coll, Friends World Program (NY)
Loras Coll (IA)
Loyola U New Orleans (LA)
Lynchburg Coll (VA)
Lyndon State Coll (VT)
Lynn U (FL)
Macalester Coll (MN)
Madonna U (MI)
Malone Coll (OH)
Manhattan Coll (NY)
Mansfield U of Pennsylvania (PA)
Marlboro Coll (VT)
Marshall U (WV)
Mars Hill Coll (NC)
Marycrest International U (IA)
Marygrove Coll (MI)
Marylhurst U (OR)
Marywood U (PA)
Mayville State U (ND)
McKendree Coll (IL)
McPherson Coll (KS)
Medaille Coll (NY)
Memorial U of Newfoundland (NF, Canada)
Mercer U (GA)
Mercyhurst Coll (PA)
Mesa State Coll (CO)
Metropolitan State U (MN)

Michigan State U (MI)
Michigan Technological U (MI)
Middlebury Coll (VT)
Middle Tennessee State U (TN)
Midland Lutheran Coll (NE)
Mills Coll (CA)
Minnesota State U, Mankato (MN)
Minot State U (ND)
Mississippi Coll (MS)
Mississippi U for Women (MS)
Missouri Baptist Coll (MO)
Missouri Southern State Coll (MO)
Montana State U–Northern (MT)
Montreat Coll (NC)
Moravian Coll (PA)
Morehead State U (KY)
Morris Coll (SC)
Mount Holyoke Coll (MA)
Mount St. Clare Coll (IA)
Mount Saint Mary Coll (NY)
Mount St. Mary's Coll (CA)
Mount Saint Vincent U (NS, Canada)
Mount Senario Coll (WI)
Mount Vernon Nazarene Coll (OH)
Muhlenberg Coll (PA)
Muskingum Coll (OH)
National-Louis U (IL)
Nazareth Coll of Rochester (NY)
New Coll of the U of South Florida (FL)
New Hampshire Coll (NH)
New York Inst of Technology (NY)
New York U (NY)
Niagara U (NY)
North Carolina Ag and Tech State U (NC)
North Central Coll (IL)
North Dakota State U (ND)
Northern Arizona U (AZ)
Northern Illinois U (IL)
Northern Kentucky U (KY)
Northern Michigan U (MI)
North Georgia Coll & State U (GA)
Northland Coll (WI)
North Park U (IL)
Northwest Coll (WA)
Northwestern Coll (MN)
Northwestern Oklahoma State U (OK)
Northwestern State U of Louisiana (LA)
Northwest Missouri State U (MO)
Northwest Nazarene U (ID)
Nyack Coll (NY)
Oakland City U (IN)
Oakwood Coll (AL)
Ohio Dominican Coll (OH)
The Ohio State U (OH)
Ohio U (OH)
Oklahoma Baptist U (OK)
Oklahoma Panhandle State U (OK)
Olivet Nazarene U (IL)
Ouachita Baptist U (AR)
Our Lady of Holy Cross Coll (LA)
Our Lady of the Lake U of San Antonio (TX)
Pace U, New York City Campus (NY)
Pace U, Pleasantville/Briarcliff Campus (NY)
Pacific Union Coll (CA)
Penn State U Abington Coll (PA)
Peru State Coll (NE)
Pfeiffer U (NC)
Piedmont Coll (GA)
Pikeville Coll (KY)
Pittsburg State U (KS)
Point Loma Nazarene U (CA)
Point Park Coll (PA)
Polytechnic U, Brooklyn Campus (NY)
Portland State U (OR)
Presbyterian Coll (SC)
Providence Coll (RI)
Providence Coll and Theological Seminary (MB, Canada)
Purdue U (IN)
Quinnipiac U (CT)
Radford U (VA)
Ramapo Coll of New Jersey (NJ)
Richmond, The American International U in London (United Kingdom)
Robert Morris Coll (PA)
Roberts Wesleyan Coll (NY)
Rockford Coll (IL)

Rocky Mountain Coll (AB, Canada)
Roger Williams U (RI)
Rosemont Coll (PA)
St. Bonaventure U (NY)
St. Cloud State U (MN)
St. Edward's U (TX)
St. Francis Coll (NY)
St. Gregory's U (OK)
Saint John's U (MN)
St. John's U (NY)
Saint Joseph Coll (CT)
Saint Joseph's Coll (IN)
St. Joseph's Coll, New York (NY)
St. Joseph's Coll, Suffolk Campus (NY)
Saint Joseph's U (PA)
Saint Mary-of-the-Woods Coll (IN)
Saint Mary's Coll (MI)
Saint Mary's U of Minnesota (MN)
Saint Paul's Coll (VA)
Saint Peter's Coll (NJ)
Saint Xavier U (IL)
Salem State Coll (MA)
San Diego State U (CA)
San Francisco State U (CA)
San Jose State U (CA)
Sarah Lawrence Coll (NY)
Shawnee State U (OH)
Sheldon Jackson Coll (AK)
Shimer Coll (IL)
Shorter Coll (GA)
Siena Heights U (MI)
Silver Lake Coll (WI)
Simpson Coll (IA)
Simpson Coll and Graduate School (CA)
Southern Illinois U Carbondale (IL)
Southern Methodist U (TX)
Southern Oregon U (OR)
Southern Utah U (UT)
Southern Wesleyan U (SC)
Southwest Baptist U (MO)
Southwestern Adventist U (TX)
Southwestern U (TX)
Spalding U (KY)
Spring Arbor Coll (MI)
Spring Hill Coll (AL)
State U of NY at Buffalo (NY)
State U of NY at Stony Brook (NY)
State U of NY Coll at Old Westbury (NY)
State U of West Georgia (GA)
Stephen F. Austin State U (TX)
Stephens Coll (MO)
Stetson U (FL)
Suffolk U (MA)
Sul Ross State U (TX)
Syracuse U (NY)
Tabor Coll (KS)
Taylor U (IN)
Texas A&M International U (TX)
Texas A&M U–Commerce (TX)
Texas Wesleyan U (TX)
Thomas Edison State Coll (NJ)
Thomas U (GA)
Tiffin U (OH)
Toccoa Falls Coll (GA)
Towson U (MD)
Trent U (ON, Canada)
Trevecca Nazarene U (TN)
Trinity Western U (BC, Canada)
Tri-State U (IN)
Troy State U (AL)
Troy State U Dothan (AL)
Troy State U Montgomery (AL)
Union Coll (NE)
Union Coll (NY)
The Union Inst (OH)
United States Air Force Academy (CO)
Universidad del Turabo (PR)
Universidad Metropolitana (PR)
Université de Montréal (PQ, Canada)
U du Québec à Chicoutimi (PQ, Canada)
U du Québec à Hull (PQ, Canada)
U du Québec en Abitibi-Témiscamingue (PQ, Canada)
The U of Arizona (AZ)
U of Arkansas at Pine Bluff (AR)
U of Bridgeport (CT)
U of British Columbia (BC, Canada)
U of Calif, Berkeley (CA)
U of Calif, Irvine (CA)
U of Calif, Riverside (CA)

Majors Index
Social Sciences–Social Work

U of Central Florida (FL)
U of Chicago (IL)
U of Cincinnati (OH)
U of Denver (CO)
The U of Findlay (OH)
U of Great Falls (MT)
U of Houston–Downtown (TX)
U of Houston–Victoria (TX)
The U of Iowa (IA)
U of La Verne (CA)
The U of Lethbridge (AB, Canada)
The U of Maine at Augusta (ME)
U of Maine at Fort Kent (ME)
U of Maryland University Coll (MD)
U of Michigan (MI)
U of Michigan–Dearborn (MI)
U of Michigan–Flint (MI)
U of Minnesota, Morris (MN)
U of Missouri–St. Louis (MO)
U of Mobile (AL)
The U of Montana–Missoula (MT)
U of Montevallo (AL)
U of Nevada, Las Vegas (NV)
U of New England (ME)
The U of North Carolina at Chapel Hill (NC)
U of North Dakota (ND)
U of Northern Colorado (CO)
U of North Texas (TX)
U of Pennsylvania (PA)
U of Pittsburgh (PA)
U of Pittsburgh at Bradford (PA)
U of Pittsburgh at Johnstown (PA)
U of Puerto Rico, Mayagüez Campus (PR)
U of Puerto Rico, Río Piedras (PR)
U of Regina (SK, Canada)
U of Rio Grande (OH)
U of St. Thomas (MN)
U of Sioux Falls (SD)
U of Southern Colorado (CO)
U of Southern Indiana (IN)
U of Southern Maine (ME)
U of South Florida (FL)
The U of Tampa (FL)
U of the Ozarks (AR)
U of the Pacific (CA)
U of the Sacred Heart (PR)
U of the South (TN)
U of the Virgin Islands (VI)
U of Utah (UT)
U of Washington (WA)
U of West Florida (FL)
U of Windsor (ON, Canada)
U of Wisconsin–Madison (WI)
U of Wisconsin–Platteville (WI)
U of Wisconsin–River Falls (WI)
U of Wisconsin–Stevens Point (WI)
U of Wisconsin–Superior (WI)
U of Wyoming (WY)
Upper Iowa U (IA)
Utica Coll of Syracuse U (NY)
Valley City State U (ND)
Valparaiso U (IN)
Vanguard U of Southern California (CA)
Virginia Wesleyan Coll (VA)
Warner Pacific Coll (OR)
Warner Southern Coll (FL)
Washington State U (WA)
Washington U in St. Louis (MO)
Wayland Baptist U (TX)
Waynesburg Coll (PA)
Wayne State Coll (NE)
Webster U (MO)
Wesleyan U (CT)
West Chester U of Pennsylvania (PA)
Western Baptist Coll (OR)
Western Carolina U (NC)
Western Connecticut State U (CT)
Western Kentucky U (KY)
Western Montana Coll of The U of Montana (MT)
Western Oregon U (OR)
Western State Coll of Colorado (CO)
Westfield State Coll (MA)
Westminster Coll (UT)
Westmont Coll (CA)
West Texas A&M U (TX)
Widener U (PA)
William Paterson U of New Jersey (NJ)
William Tyndale Coll (MI)
Wilmington Coll (OH)
Wilson Coll (PA)

Wingate U (NC)
Winona State U (MN)
Winston-Salem State U (NC)
Wisconsin Lutheran Coll (WI)
Wittenberg U (OH)
Worcester Polytechnic Inst (MA)
York U (ON, Canada)
Youngstown State U (OH)

SOCIAL STUDIES EDUCATION

Abilene Christian U (TX)
Adams State Coll (CO)
Alverno Coll (WI)
Anderson U (IN)
Appalachian State U (NC)
Arkansas Tech U (AR)
Augustana Coll (SD)
Baylor U (TX)
Bethany Coll (KS)
Bethel Coll (IN)
Bethune-Cookman Coll (FL)
Bloomsburg U of Pennsylvania (PA)
Boston U (MA)
Bowling Green State U (OH)
Brescia U (KY)
Bridgewater Coll (VA)
Brigham Young U (UT)
Cabrini Coll (PA)
Canisius Coll (NY)
Carlow Coll (PA)
Castleton State Coll (VT)
Cedarville Coll (OH)
Central Methodist Coll (MO)
Central Michigan U (MI)
Central Missouri State U (MO)
Citadel, The Military Coll of South Carolina (SC)
Clarion U of Pennsylvania (PA)
Colby-Sawyer Coll (NH)
Coll of St. Catherine (MN)
Colorado Christian U (CO)
Colorado State U (CO)
Concordia Coll (MN)
Concordia U (OR)
Crown Coll (MN)
Cumberland Coll (KY)
Daemen Coll (NY)
Duquesne U (PA)
East Carolina U (NC)
Eastern Michigan U (MI)
East Texas Baptist U (TX)
Edinboro U of Pennsylvania (PA)
Elmira Coll (NY)
Elon Coll (NC)
Erskine Coll (SC)
George Fox U (OR)
Greensboro Coll (NC)
Greenville Coll (IL)
Gustavus Adolphus Coll (MN)
Hardin-Simmons U (TX)
Hastings Coll (NE)
Huston-Tillotson Coll (TX)
Indiana U Bloomington (IN)
Indiana U Northwest (IN)
Indiana U of Pennsylvania (PA)
Indiana U–Purdue U Indianapolis (IN)
Indiana U South Bend (IN)
Indiana U Southeast (IN)
Indiana Wesleyan U (IN)
Ithaca Coll (NY)
Johnson State Coll (VT)
Juniata Coll (PA)
Kent State U (OH)
Keuka Coll (NY)
Le Moyne Coll (NY)
Limestone Coll (SC)
Lincoln U (PA)
Long Island U, C.W. Post Campus (NY)
Malone Coll (OH)
Manhattanville Coll (NY)
Mansfield U of Pennsylvania (PA)
Marymount Coll (NY)
McGill U (PQ, Canada)
Mercer U (GA)
Messiah Coll (PA)
Miami U (OH)
MidAmerica Nazarene U (KS)
Millersville U of Pennsylvania (PA)
Minnesota State U, Mankato (MN)
Minnesota State U Moorhead (MN)
Mississippi Coll (MS)
Molloy Coll (NY)
Nazareth Coll of Rochester (NY)
New York Inst of Technology (NY)

New York U (NY)
Niagara U (NY)
North Carolina State U (NC)
Northwestern Coll (MN)
Oakland City U (IN)
Ohio U (OH)
Oklahoma Baptist U (OK)
Penn State U Harrisburg Campus of the Capital Coll (PA)
Philadelphia Coll of Bible (PA)
Pikeville Coll (KY)
Plymouth State Coll (NH)
Rocky Mountain Coll (MT)
Saint Augustine's Coll (NC)
St. John's U (NY)
Saint Mary's U of Minnesota (MN)
St. Mary's U of San Antonio (TX)
St. Olaf Coll (MN)
Seton Hill Coll (PA)
Shaw U (NC)
Southeastern Coll of the Assemblies of God (FL)
Southeastern Louisiana U (LA)
Southeastern Oklahoma State U (OK)
Southern Arkansas U–Magnolia (AR)
Syracuse U (NY)
Texas A&M International U (TX)
Texas Wesleyan U (TX)
The U of Arizona (AZ)
U of Arkansas (AR)
U of Central Arkansas (AR)
U of Charleston (WV)
U of Illinois at Urbana–Champaign (IL)
U of Indianapolis (IN)
The U of Iowa (IA)
U of Kentucky (KY)
U of Louisiana at Monroe (LA)
U of Maryland, Coll Park (MD)
U of Minnesota, Duluth (MN)
U of Mississippi (MS)
U of Nevada, Reno (NV)
U of New Orleans (LA)
The U of North Carolina at Chapel Hill (NC)
U of Oklahoma (OK)
U of Pittsburgh at Johnstown (PA)
U of St. Thomas (MN)
U of Southern Colorado (CO)
U of Wisconsin–Eau Claire (WI)
U of Wisconsin–La Crosse (WI)
U of Wisconsin–River Falls (WI)
U of Wisconsin–Superior (WI)
Virginia Intermont Coll (VA)
Washington U in St. Louis (MO)
Wayne State U (MI)
Weber State U (UT)
Western Carolina U (NC)
Wheaton Coll (IL)
Wheeling Jesuit U (WV)
York Coll (NE)
York U (ON, Canada)
Youngstown State U (OH)

SOCIAL WORK

Abilene Christian U (TX)
Adams State Coll (CO)
Adelphi U (NY)
Adrian Coll (MI)
Alabama A&M U (AL)
Alabama State U (AL)
Albany State U (GA)
Allentown Coll of St. Francis de Sales (PA)
Allen U (SC)
Alvernia Coll (PA)
Anderson U (IN)
Andrews U (MI)
Anna Maria Coll (MA)
Appalachian State U (NC)
Arizona State U (AZ)
Arizona State U West (AZ)
Arkansas Baptist Coll (AR)
Arkansas State U (AR)
Asbury Coll (KY)
Ashland U (OH)
Atlantic Union Coll (MA)
Auburn U (AL)
Augsburg Coll (MN)
Augustana Coll (SD)
Austin Peay State U (TN)
Avila Coll (MO)
Azusa Pacific U (CA)
Baldwin-Wallace Coll (OH)
Ball State U (IN)

Barton Coll (NC)
Bayamón Central U (PR)
Baylor U (TX)
Belmont U (TN)
Bemidji State U (MN)
Bennett Coll (NC)
Bethany Coll (KS)
Bethany Coll (WV)
Bethel Coll (KS)
Bethel Coll (MN)
Bloomfield Coll (NJ)
Bloomsburg U of Pennsylvania (PA)
Bluffton Coll (OH)
Boise State U (ID)
Bowie State U (MD)
Bowling Green State U (OH)
Bradley U (IL)
Brescia U (KY)
Briar Cliff Coll (IA)
Bridgewater State Coll (MA)
Brigham Young U (UT)
Brigham Young U–Hawaii Campus (HI)
Buena Vista U (IA)
Cabrini Coll (PA)
California State U, Chico (CA)
California State U, Fresno (CA)
California State U, Hayward (CA)
California State U, Long Beach (CA)
California State U, Los Angeles (CA)
California State U, Northridge (CA)
California State U, Sacramento (CA)
California State U, San Bernardino (CA)
California U of Pennsylvania (PA)
Calvin Coll (MI)
Campbellsville U (KY)
Campbell U (NC)
Capital U (OH)
Carleton U (ON, Canada)
Carlow Coll (PA)
Carroll Coll (MT)
Carroll Coll (WI)
Carthage Coll (WI)
Castleton State Coll (VT)
The Catholic U of America (DC)
Cedar Crest Coll (PA)
Cedarville Coll (OH)
Central Connecticut State U (CT)
Central Michigan U (MI)
Central Missouri State U (MO)
Chadron State Coll (NE)
Champlain Coll (VT)
Chapman U (CA)
Chatham Coll (PA)
Christopher Newport U (VA)
Clark Atlanta U (GA)
Clarke Coll (IA)
Cleveland State U (OH)
Coker Coll (SC)
Coll Misericordia (PA)
Coll of Mount St. Joseph (OH)
The Coll of New Rochelle (NY)
Coll of Our Lady of the Elms (MA)
Coll of Saint Benedict (MN)
Coll of St. Catherine (MN)
The Coll of Saint Rose (NY)
The Coll of St. Scholastica (MN)
Coll of Staten Island of the City U of NY (NY)
Coll of the Ozarks (MO)
The Coll of West Virginia (WV)
Colorado State U (CO)
Columbia Coll (MO)
Columbia Coll (SC)
Concord Coll (WV)
Concordia Coll (MN)
Concordia Coll (NY)
Concordia U (CA)
Concordia U (IL)
Concordia U (OR)
Concordia U Wisconsin (WI)
Coppin State Coll (MD)
Cornerstone U (MI)
Creighton U (NE)
Cumberland Coll (KY)
Daemen Coll (NY)
Dalhousie U (NS, Canada)
Dana Coll (NE)
David Lipscomb U (TN)
Defiance Coll (OH)
Delaware State U (DE)
Delta State U (MS)

Dickinson State U (ND)
Dominican Coll of Blauvelt (NY)
Dordt Coll (IA)
D'Youville Coll (NY)
East Carolina U (NC)
East Central U (OK)
Eastern Coll (PA)
Eastern Connecticut State U (CT)
Eastern Kentucky U (KY)
Eastern Mennonite U (VA)
Eastern Michigan U (MI)
Eastern Nazarene Coll (MA)
Eastern Washington U (WA)
East Tennessee State U (TN)
Edinboro U of Pennsylvania (PA)
Elizabeth City State U (NC)
Elizabethtown Coll (PA)
Elmira Coll (NY)
Endicott Coll (MA)
Evangel U (MO)
Ferris State U (MI)
Ferrum Coll (VA)
Florida A&M U (FL)
Florida Atlantic U (FL)
Florida International U (FL)
Florida State U (FL)
Fordham U (NY)
Fort Hays State U (KS)
Fort Valley State U (GA)
Franciscan U of Steubenville (OH)
Franklin Pierce Coll (NH)
Freed-Hardeman U (TN)
Fresno Pacific U (CA)
Frostburg State U (MD)
Gallaudet U (DC)
Gannon U (PA)
George Fox U (OR)
George Mason U (VA)
Georgian Court Coll (NJ)
Georgia State U (GA)
Gordon Coll (MA)
Goshen Coll (IN)
Governors State U (IL)
Grace Coll (IN)
Grand Valley State U (MI)
Greenville Coll (IL)
Gwynedd-Mercy Coll (PA)
Hampton U (VA)
Harding U (AR)
Hardin-Simmons U (TX)
Hawaii Pacific U (HI)
Henderson State U (AR)
Heritage Coll (WA)
Holy Family Coll (PA)
Hood Coll (MD)
Hope Coll (MI)
Hope International U (CA)
Howard Payne U (TX)
Howard U (DC)
Humboldt State U (CA)
Idaho State U (ID)
Illinois State U (IL)
Immaculata Coll (PA)
Indiana State U (IN)
Indiana U Bloomington (IN)
Indiana U East (IN)
Indiana U–Purdue U Indianapolis (IN)
Indiana Wesleyan U (IN)
Inter American U of PR, Arecibo Campus (PR)
Inter American U of PR, Fajardo Campus (PR)
Inter American U of PR, Metropolitan Campus (PR)
Iona Coll (NY)
Iowa Wesleyan Coll (IA)
Jacksonville State U (AL)
James Madison U (VA)
Johnson C. Smith U (NC)
Juniata Coll (PA)
Kansas State U (KS)
Kean U (NJ)
Kentucky Christian Coll (KY)
Kentucky State U (KY)
Keuka Coll (NY)
Kutztown U of Pennsylvania (PA)
LaGrange Coll (GA)
Lakehead U (ON, Canada)
Lamar U (TX)
La Salle U (PA)
La Sierra U (CA)
Lehman Coll of the City U of NY (NY)
LeMoyne-Owen Coll (TN)
Lewis-Clark State Coll (ID)
Lewis U (IL)

Majors Index
Social Work–Sociology

Limestone Coll (SC)
Lincoln Memorial U (TN)
Lincoln U (PA)
Lindenwood U (MO)
Lindsey Wilson Coll (KY)
Lock Haven U of Pennsylvania (PA)
Long Island U, Brooklyn Campus (NY)
Long Island U, C.W. Post Campus (NY)
Long Island U, Southampton Coll, Friends World Program (NY)
Longwood Coll (VA)
Loras Coll (IA)
Louisiana Coll (LA)
Lourdes Coll (OH)
Loyola U Chicago (IL)
Lubbock Christian U (TX)
Luther Coll (IA)
MacMurray Coll (IL)
Madonna U (MI)
Malone Coll (OH)
Manchester Coll (IN)
Manhattan Coll (NY)
Mansfield U of Pennsylvania (PA)
Marian Coll of Fond du Lac (WI)
Marist Coll (NY)
Marquette U (WI)
Marshall U (WV)
Mars Hill Coll (NC)
Mary Baldwin Coll (VA)
Marycrest International U (IA)
Marygrove Coll (MI)
Marymount Coll (NY)
Marywood U (PA)
Massachusetts Coll of Liberal Arts (MA)
McGill U (PQ, Canada)
McKendree Coll (IL)
Memorial U of Newfoundland (NF, Canada)
Mercy Coll (NY)
Mercyhurst Coll (PA)
Meredith Coll (NC)
Messiah Coll (PA)
Methodist Coll (NC)
Metropolitan State Coll of Denver (CO)
Metropolitan State U (MN)
Miami U (OH)
Michigan State U (MI)
Middle Tennessee State U (TN)
Midwestern State U (TX)
Millersville U of Pennsylvania (PA)
Minnesota State U, Mankato (MN)
Minnesota State U Moorhead (MN)
Minot State U (ND)
Mississippi Coll (MS)
Mississippi State U (MS)
Mississippi Valley State U (MS)
Missouri Western State Coll (MO)
Molloy Coll (NY)
Monmouth U (NJ)
Morehead State U (KY)
Morgan State U (MD)
Mount Mary Coll (WI)
Mount Mercy Coll (IA)
Mount Senario Coll (WI)
Mount Vernon Nazarene Coll (OH)
Muhlenberg Coll (PA)
Murray State U (KY)
Nazareth Coll of Rochester (NY)
Nebraska Wesleyan U (NE)
New Mexico Highlands U (NM)
New Mexico State U (NM)
New York U (NY)
Niagara U (NY)
Norfolk State U (VA)
North Carolina Ag and Tech State U (NC)
North Carolina Central U (NC)
North Carolina State U (NC)
Northeastern Illinois U (IL)
Northeastern State U (OK)
Northern Arizona U (AZ)
Northern Kentucky U (KY)
Northern Michigan U (MI)
Northwestern Coll (IA)
Northwestern Oklahoma State U (OK)
Northwestern State U of Louisiana (LA)
Northwest Nazarene U (ID)
Oakwood Coll (AL)
Oglethorpe U (GA)
Ohio Dominican Coll (OH)

The Ohio State U (OH)
Ohio U (OH)
Okanagan U Coll (BC, Canada)
Oklahoma Baptist U (OK)
Our Lady of the Lake U of San Antonio (TX)
Pacific Lutheran U (WA)
Pacific Union Coll (CA)
Pacific U (OR)
Philadelphia Coll of Bible (PA)
Philander Smith Coll (AR)
Pittsburg State U (KS)
Plattsburgh State U of NY (NY)
Plymouth State Coll (NH)
Point Loma Nazarene U (CA)
Pontifical Catholic U of Puerto Rico (PR)
Prairie View A&M U (TX)
Presentation Coll (SD)
Providence Coll (RI)
Purdue U Calumet (IN)
Quincy U (IL)
Radford U (VA)
Ramapo Coll of New Jersey (NJ)
Redeemer Coll (ON, Canada)
Reformed Bible Coll (MI)
Regis Coll (MA)
The Richard Stockton Coll of New Jersey (NJ)
Roberts Wesleyan Coll (NY)
Rochester Coll (MI)
Rochester Inst of Technology (NY)
Rockford Coll (IL)
Rust Coll (MS)
Rutgers, State U of NJ, Camden Coll of Arts & Scis (NJ)
Rutgers, State U of NJ, Livingston Coll (NJ)
Rutgers, State U of NJ, Newark Coll of Arts & Scis (NJ)
Rutgers, State U of NJ, U Coll–Camden (NJ)
Rutgers, State U of NJ, U Coll–Newark (NJ)
Ryerson Polytechnic U (ON, Canada)
Sacred Heart U (CT)
Saginaw Valley State U (MI)
Saint Anselm Coll (NH)
St. Augustine Coll (IL)
St. Cloud State U (MN)
St. Edward's U (TX)
St. Francis Coll (NY)
Saint Francis Coll (PA)
Saint John's U (MN)
Saint Joseph Coll (CT)
Saint Joseph's Coll (ME)
Saint Leo U (FL)
Saint Louis U (MO)
Saint Mary's Coll (IN)
St. Olaf Coll (MN)
Salem State Coll (MA)
Salisbury State U (MD)
Salve Regina U (RI)
San Diego State U (CA)
San Francisco State U (CA)
San Jose State U (CA)
Savannah State U (GA)
Seattle U (WA)
Seton Hall U (NJ)
Seton Hill Coll (PA)
Shaw U (NC)
Shepherd Coll (WV)
Shippensburg U of Pennsylvania (PA)
Siena Coll (NY)
Siena Heights U (MI)
Skidmore Coll (NY)
Slippery Rock U of Pennsylvania (PA)
Southeastern Coll of the Assemblies of God (FL)
Southeastern Louisiana U (LA)
Southeast Missouri State U (MO)
Southern Adventist U (TN)
Southern Arkansas U–Magnolia (AR)
Southern Illinois U Carbondale (IL)
Southern Illinois U Edwardsville (IL)
Southern Vermont Coll (VT)
Southwestern Adventist U (TX)
Southwestern Coll of Christian Ministries (OK)
Southwestern Oklahoma State U (OK)
Southwest Missouri State U (MO)
Southwest State U (MN)

Southwest Texas State U (TX)
Spalding U (KY)
Spring Arbor Coll (MI)
State U of NY at Albany (NY)
State U of NY at New Paltz (NY)
State U of NY at Stony Brook (NY)
State U of NY Coll at Brockport (NY)
State U of NY Coll at Buffalo (NY)
State U of NY Coll at Cortland (NY)
State U of NY Coll at Fredonia (NY)
Stephen F. Austin State U (TX)
Suffolk U (MA)
Syracuse U (NY)
Talladega Coll (AL)
Taylor U (IN)
Taylor U, Fort Wayne Campus (IN)
Temple U (PA)
Tennessee State U (TN)
Tennessee Technological U (TN)
Texas A&M U–Commerce (TX)
Texas A&M U–Kingsville (TX)
Texas Christian U (TX)
Texas Lutheran U (TX)
Texas Southern U (TX)
Texas Tech U (TX)
Thomas U (GA)
Trinity Coll of Vermont (VT)
Troy State U (AL)
Tuskegee U (AL)
Union Coll (NE)
Union U (TN)
The Union Inst (OH)
Universidad del Turabo (PR)
Université de Montréal (PQ, Canada)
Université de Sherbrooke (PQ, Canada)
U du Québec à Chicoutimi (PQ, Canada)
U du Québec à Hull (PQ, Canada)
U du Québec en Abitibi-Témiscamingue (PQ, Canada)
Université Laval (PQ, Canada)
U Coll of the Fraser Valley (BC, Canada)
The U of Akron (OH)
The U of Alabama (AL)
The U of Alabama at Birmingham (AL)
U of Alaska Fairbanks (AK)
U of Arkansas (AR)
U of Arkansas at Little Rock (AR)
U of Arkansas at Monticello (AR)
U of Arkansas at Pine Bluff (AR)
U of British Columbia (BC, Canada)
U of Calgary (AB, Canada)
U of Calif, Berkeley (CA)
U of Central Florida (FL)
U of Cincinnati (OH)
U of Detroit Mercy (MI)
The U of Findlay (OH)
U of Georgia (GA)
U of Hawaii at Manoa (HI)
U of Illinois at Chicago (IL)
U of Illinois at Springfield (IL)
U of Illinois at Urbana–Champaign (IL)
U of Indianapolis (IN)
The U of Iowa (IA)
U of Kansas (KS)
U of Kentucky (KY)
U of Lethbridge (AB, Canada)
U of Louisiana at Monroe (LA)
U of Maine (ME)
U of Maine at Presque Isle (ME)
U of Manitoba (MB, Canada)
U of Mary Hardin-Baylor (TX)
U of Maryland, Baltimore County (MD)
U of Massachusetts Boston (MA)
The U of Memphis (TN)
U of Michigan–Flint (MI)
U of Mississippi (MS)
U of Missouri–Columbia (MO)
U of Missouri–St. Louis (MO)
The U of Montana–Missoula (MT)
U of Montevallo (AL)
U of Nebraska at Kearney (NE)
U of Nebraska at Omaha (NE)
U of Nevada, Las Vegas (NV)
U of Nevada, Reno (NV)
U of New Hampshire (NH)
U of New Haven (CT)
U of North Alabama (AL)

The U of North Carolina at Charlotte (NC)
The U of North Carolina at Greensboro (NC)
The U of North Carolina at Pembroke (NC)
The U of North Carolina at Wilmington (NC)
U of North Dakota (ND)
U of Northern Iowa (IA)
U of North Texas (TX)
U of Oklahoma (OK)
U of Pittsburgh (PA)
U of Pittsburgh at Bradford (PA)
U of Portland (OR)
U of Puerto Rico, Humacao U Coll (PR)
U of Puerto Rico, Río Piedras (PR)
U of Regina (SK, Canada)
U of Rio Grande (OH)
U of St. Francis (IL)
U of Saint Francis (IN)
U of St. Thomas (MN)
U of Sioux Falls (SD)
U of South Dakota (SD)
U of Southern Colorado (CO)
U of Southern Indiana (IN)
U of Southern Maine (ME)
U of Southern Mississippi (MS)
U of South Florida (FL)
The U of Tennessee at Chattanooga (TN)
The U of Tennessee at Martin (TN)
The U of Tennessee Knoxville (TN)
The U of Texas at Arlington (TX)
The U of Texas at Austin (TX)
The U of Texas–Pan American (TX)
U of the District of Columbia (DC)
U of the Sacred Heart (PR)
U of the Virgin Islands (VI)
U of Vermont (VT)
U of Victoria (BC, Canada)
U of Washington (WA)
U of Waterloo (ON, Canada)
The U of Western Ontario (ON, Canada)
U of West Florida (FL)
U of Windsor (ON, Canada)
U of Wisconsin–Eau Claire (WI)
U of Wisconsin–Green Bay (WI)
U of Wisconsin–Madison (WI)
U of Wisconsin–Milwaukee (WI)
U of Wisconsin–River Falls (WI)
U of Wisconsin–Superior (WI)
U of Wisconsin–Whitewater (WI)
U of Wyoming (WY)
Ursuline Coll (OH)
Utah State U (UT)
Valparaiso U (IN)
Virginia Commonwealth U (VA)
Virginia Intermont Coll (VA)
Virginia Union U (VA)
Walla Walla Coll (WA)
Warner Pacific Coll (OR)
Warner Southern Coll (FL)
Warren Wilson Coll (NC)
Wartburg Coll (IA)
Washington State U (WA)
Wayne State U (MI)
Weber State U (UT)
West Chester U of Pennsylvania (PA)
Western Carolina U (NC)
Western Connecticut State U (CT)
Western Illinois U (IL)
Western Kentucky U (KY)
Western Maryland Coll (MD)
Western Michigan U (MI)
Western New England Coll (MA)
West Texas A&M U (TX)
West Virginia State Coll (WV)
West Virginia U (WV)
Wheelock Coll (MA)
Whittier Coll (CA)
Wichita State U (KS)
Widener U (PA)
William Woods U (MO)
Wilmington Coll (OH)
Winona State U (MN)
Winthrop U (SC)
Wright State U (OH)
Xavier U (OH)
York Coll of the City U of New York (NY)
York U (ON, Canada)
Youngstown State U (OH)

SOCIOBIOLOGY
Beloit Coll (WI)
Cornell U (NY)
Hampshire Coll (MA)
Harvard U (MA)
Long Island U, Southampton Coll, Friends World Program (NY)
Tufts U (MA)

SOCIOLOGY
Abilene Christian U (TX)
Acadia U (NS, Canada)
Adams State Coll (CO)
Adelphi U (NY)
Adrian Coll (MI)
Agnes Scott Coll (GA)
Alabama A&M U (AL)
Alabama State U (AL)
Albany State U (GA)
Albertson Coll of Idaho (ID)
Albertus Magnus Coll (CT)
Albion Coll (MI)
Alderson-Broaddus Coll (WV)
Alfred U (NY)
Allen U (SC)
Alma Coll (MI)
American International Coll (MA)
American U (DC)
American U in Cairo (Egypt)
Amherst Coll (MA)
Anderson U (IN)
Andrews U (MI)
Antioch Coll (OH)
Appalachian State U (NC)
Aquinas Coll (MI)
Arizona State U (AZ)
Arizona State U West (AZ)
Arkansas State U (AR)
Arkansas Tech U (AR)
Asbury Coll (KY)
Ashland U (OH)
Assumption Coll (MA)
Athabasca U (AB, Canada)
Athens State U (AL)
Atlantic Baptist U (NB, Canada)
Atlantic Union Coll (MA)
Auburn U (AL)
Auburn U Montgomery (AL)
Augsburg Coll (MN)
Augustana Coll (IL)
Augustana Coll (SD)
Augusta State U (GA)
Austin Coll (TX)
Austin Peay State U (TN)
Averett Coll (VA)
Avila Coll (MO)
Azusa Pacific U (CA)
Baker U (KS)
Baldwin-Wallace Coll (OH)
Ball State U (IN)
Barat Coll (IL)
Barber-Scotia Coll (NC)
Bard Coll (NY)
Barnard Coll (NY)
Barry U (FL)
Bates Coll (ME)
Baylor U (TX)
Beaver Coll (PA)
Bellarmine Coll (KY)
Bellevue U (NE)
Belmont Abbey Coll (NC)
Belmont U (TN)
Beloit Coll (WI)
Bemidji State U (MN)
Benedictine Coll (KS)
Benedictine U (IL)
Bennett Coll (NC)
Bennington Coll (VT)
Berea Coll (KY)
Baruch Coll of the City U of NY (NY)
Berry Coll (GA)
Bethany Coll (KS)
Bethel Coll (IN)
Bethune-Cookman Coll (FL)
Biola U (CA)
Birmingham-Southern Coll (AL)
Bishop's U (PQ, Canada)
Black Hills State U (SD)
Bloomfield Coll (NJ)
Bloomsburg U of Pennsylvania (PA)
Bluffton Coll (OH)
Boise State U (ID)
Boston Coll (MA)
Boston U (MA)
Bowdoin Coll (ME)

Majors Index
Sociology

Bowie State U (MD)
Bowling Green State U (OH)
Bradley U (IL)
Brandeis U (MA)
Brandon U (MB, Canada)
Briar Cliff Coll (IA)
Bridgewater Coll (VA)
Bridgewater State Coll (MA)
Brigham Young U (UT)
Brock U (ON, Canada)
Brooklyn Coll of the City U of NY (NY)
Brown U (RI)
Bryn Mawr Coll (PA)
Bucknell U (PA)
Butler U (IN)
Cabrini Coll (PA)
Caldwell Coll (NJ)
California Lutheran U (CA)
California State Polytechnic U, Pomona (CA)
California State U, Chico (CA)
California State U, Dominguez Hills (CA)
California State U, Fresno (CA)
California State U, Fullerton (CA)
California State U, Hayward (CA)
California State U, Long Beach (CA)
California State U, Los Angeles (CA)
California State U, Northridge (CA)
California State U, Sacramento (CA)
California State U, San Bernardino (CA)
California State U, San Marcos (CA)
California State U, Stanislaus (CA)
California U of Pennsylvania (PA)
Calumet Coll of Saint Joseph (IN)
Calvin Coll (MI)
Cameron U (OK)
Campbellsville U (KY)
Canisius Coll (NY)
Capital U (OH)
Cardinal Stritch U (WI)
Carleton Coll (MN)
Carleton U (ON, Canada)
Carlow Coll (PA)
Carroll Coll (MT)
Carroll Coll (WI)
Carson-Newman Coll (TN)
Carthage Coll (WI)
Case Western Reserve U (OH)
Castleton State Coll (VT)
Catawba Coll (NC)
The Catholic U of America (DC)
Cedar Crest Coll (PA)
Cedarville Coll (OH)
Centenary Coll (NJ)
Centenary Coll of Louisiana (LA)
Central Coll (IA)
Central Connecticut State U (CT)
Central Methodist Coll (MO)
Central Michigan U (MI)
Central Missouri State U (MO)
Centre Coll (KY)
Chadron State Coll (NE)
Chapman U (CA)
Charleston Southern U (SC)
Chestnut Hill Coll (PA)
Cheyney U of Pennsylvania (PA)
Chicago State U (IL)
Christopher Newport U (VA)
City Coll of the City U of NY (NY)
City U (WA)
Claflin U (SC)
Clarion U of Pennsylvania (PA)
Clark Atlanta U (GA)
Clarke Coll (IA)
Clarkson U (NY)
Clark U (MA)
Clemson U (SC)
Cleveland State U (OH)
Coastal Carolina U (SC)
Coe Coll (IA)
Coker Coll (SC)
Colby Coll (ME)
Colgate U (NY)
Coll of Charleston (SC)
Coll of Mount St. Joseph (OH)
Coll of Mount Saint Vincent (NY)
The Coll of New Jersey (NJ)
The Coll of New Rochelle (NY)
Coll of Notre Dame (CA)
Coll of Our Lady of the Elms (MA)

Coll of Saint Benedict (MN)
Coll of St. Catherine (MN)
Coll of Saint Elizabeth (NJ)
The Coll of Saint Rose (NY)
The Coll of Southeastern Europe, The American U of Athens (Greece)
Coll of Staten Island of the City U of NY (NY)
Coll of the Holy Cross (MA)
Coll of the Ozarks (MO)
The Coll of William and Mary (VA)
The Coll of Wooster (OH)
The Colorado Coll (CO)
Colorado State U (CO)
Columbia Coll (MO)
Columbia Coll (NY)
Columbia Coll (SC)
Columbia U, School of General Studies (NY)
Columbus State U (GA)
Concord Coll (WV)
Concordia Coll (MI)
Concordia Coll (MN)
Concordia U (IL)
Concordia U (NE)
Concordia U (PQ, Canada)
Concordia U at St. Paul (MN)
Concordia U Coll of Alberta (AB, Canada)
Connecticut Coll (CT)
Converse Coll (SC)
Cornell Coll (IA)
Cornell U (NY)
Cornerstone U (MI)
Covenant Coll (GA)
Creighton U (NE)
Culver-Stockton Coll (MO)
Curry Coll (MA)
Dakota Wesleyan U (SD)
Dalhousie U (NS, Canada)
Dallas Baptist U (TX)
Dana Coll (NE)
Dartmouth Coll (NH)
Davidson Coll (NC)
Delaware State U (DE)
Denison U (OH)
DePaul U (IL)
DePauw U (IN)
Deree Coll (Greece)
Dickinson Coll (PA)
Doane Coll (NE)
Dominican U (IL)
Dordt Coll (IA)
Dowling Coll (NY)
Drake U (IA)
Drew U (NJ)
Drexel U (PA)
Drury U (MO)
Duke U (NC)
Duquesne U (PA)
D'Youville Coll (NY)
Earlham Coll (IN)
East Carolina U (NC)
East Central U (OK)
Eastern Coll (PA)
Eastern Connecticut State U (CT)
Eastern Illinois U (IL)
Eastern Kentucky U (KY)
Eastern Mennonite U (VA)
Eastern Michigan U (MI)
Eastern Nazarene Coll (MA)
Eastern New Mexico U (NM)
Eastern Oregon U (OR)
Eastern Washington U (WA)
East Stroudsburg U of Pennsylvania (PA)
East Tennessee State U (TN)
East Texas Baptist U (TX)
Eckerd Coll (FL)
Edgewood Coll (WI)
Edinboro U of Pennsylvania (PA)
Elizabeth City State U (NC)
Elizabethtown Coll (PA)
Elmhurst Coll (IL)
Elmira Coll (NY)
Elon Coll (NC)
Emmanuel Coll (MA)
Emory & Henry Coll (VA)
Emory U (GA)
Emporia State U (KS)
Eugene Lang Coll, New School U (NY)
Evangel U (MO)
The Evergreen State Coll (WA)
Fairfield U (CT)

Fairleigh Dickinson U, Florham-Madison Campus (NJ)
Fairleigh Dickinson U, Teaneck-Hackensack Campus (NJ)
Fairmont State Coll (WV)
Felician Coll (NJ)
Fisk U (TN)
Fitchburg State Coll (MA)
Florida A&M U (FL)
Florida Atlantic U (FL)
Florida International U (FL)
Florida Southern Coll (FL)
Florida State U (FL)
Fordham U (NY)
Fort Hays State U (KS)
Fort Lewis Coll (CO)
Fort Valley State U (GA)
Framingham State Coll (MA)
Franciscan U of Steubenville (OH)
Francis Marion U (SC)
Franklin and Marshall Coll (PA)
Franklin Coll of Indiana (IN)
Franklin Pierce Coll (NH)
Friends U (KS)
Frostburg State U (MD)
Furman U (SC)
Gallaudet U (DC)
Gardner-Webb U (NC)
Geneva Coll (PA)
George Fox U (OR)
George Mason U (VA)
Georgetown Coll (KY)
Georgetown U (DC)
The George Washington U (DC)
Georgia Coll and State U (GA)
Georgian Court Coll (NJ)
Georgia Southern U (GA)
Georgia Southwestern State U (GA)
Georgia State U (GA)
Gettysburg Coll (PA)
Goddard Coll (VT)
Gonzaga U (WA)
Gordon Coll (MA)
Goshen Coll (IN)
Goucher Coll (MD)
Grace Coll (IN)
Graceland Coll (IA)
Grand Canyon U (AZ)
Grand Valley State U (MI)
Greensboro Coll (NC)
Greenville Coll (IL)
Grinnell Coll (IA)
Grove City Coll (PA)
Guilford Coll (NC)
Gustavus Adolphus Coll (MN)
Gwynedd-Mercy Coll (PA)
Hamilton Coll (NY)
Hamline U (MN)
Hampshire Coll (MA)
Hampton U (VA)
Hanover Coll (IN)
Harding U (AR)
Hardin-Simmons U (TX)
Hartwick Coll (NY)
Harvard U (MA)
Hastings Coll (NE)
Haverford Coll (PA)
Hawaii Pacific U (HI)
Henderson State U (AR)
Hendrix Coll (AR)
Heritage Coll (WA)
High Point U (NC)
Hillsdale Coll (MI)
Hiram Coll (OH)
Hobart and William Smith Colls (NY)
Hofstra U (NY)
Hollins U (VA)
Holy Family Coll (PA)
Holy Names Coll (CA)
Hood Coll (MD)
Hope Coll (MI)
Houghton Coll (NY)
Houston Baptist U (TX)
Howard Payne U (TX)
Howard U (DC)
Humboldt State U (CA)
Hunter Coll of the City U of NY (NY)
Huntington Coll (IN)
Huston-Tillotson Coll (TX)
Idaho State U (ID)
Illinois Coll (IL)
Illinois State U (IL)
Illinois Wesleyan U (IL)
Immaculata Coll (PA)

Indiana State U (IN)
Indiana U Bloomington (IN)
Indiana U East (IN)
Indiana U Kokomo (IN)
Indiana U Northwest (IN)
Indiana U of Pennsylvania (PA)
Indiana U–Purdue U Fort Wayne (IN)
Indiana U–Purdue U Indianapolis (IN)
Indiana U South Bend (IN)
Indiana U Southeast (IN)
Indiana Wesleyan U (IN)
Inter American U of PR, Fajardo Campus (PR)
Inter American U of PR, Metropolitan Campus (PR)
Inter American U of PR, San Germán Campus (PR)
Iona Coll (NY)
Iowa State U of Science and Technology (IA)
Iowa Wesleyan Coll (IA)
Ithaca Coll (NY)
Jacksonville State U (AL)
Jacksonville U (FL)
James Madison U (VA)
Jarvis Christian Coll (TX)
John Carroll U (OH)
Johns Hopkins U (MD)
Johnson C. Smith U (NC)
Johnson State Coll (VT)
Judson Coll (IL)
Juniata Coll (PA)
Kalamazoo Coll (MI)
Kansas State U (KS)
Kean U (NJ)
Keene State Coll (NH)
Kent State U (OH)
Kentucky State U (KY)
Kentucky Wesleyan Coll (KY)
Kenyon Coll (OH)
Keuka Coll (NY)
King's Coll (PA)
The King's U Coll (AB, Canada)
Knox Coll (IL)
Kutztown U of Pennsylvania (PA)
Lafayette Coll (PA)
Lake Erie Coll (OH)
Lake Forest Coll (IL)
Lakehead U (ON, Canada)
Lakeland Coll (WI)
Lake Superior State U (MI)
Lamar U (TX)
Lambuth U (TN)
Lander U (SC)
Lane Coll (TN)
Langston U (OK)
La Roche Coll (PA)
La Salle U (PA)
Lasell Coll (MA)
La Sierra U (CA)
Lees-McRae Coll (NC)
Lee U (TN)
Lehigh U (PA)
Lehman Coll of the City U of NY (NY)
Le Moyne Coll (NY)
LeMoyne-Owen Coll (TN)
Lenoir-Rhyne Coll (NC)
Lewis & Clark Coll (OR)
Lewis U (IL)
Lincoln U (MO)
Lincoln U (PA)
Lindenwood U (MO)
Linfield Coll (OR)
Lock Haven U of Pennsylvania (PA)
Long Island U, Brooklyn Campus (NY)
Long Island U, C.W. Post Campus (NY)
Long Island U, Southampton Coll (NY)
Long Island U, Southampton Coll, Friends World Program (NY)
Longwood Coll (VA)
Loras Coll (IA)
Louisiana Coll (LA)
Louisiana State U and A&M Coll (LA)
Louisiana State U in Shreveport (LA)
Louisiana Tech U (LA)
Lourdes Coll (OH)
Loyola Coll in Maryland (MD)
Loyola Marymount U (CA)

Loyola U Chicago (IL)
Loyola U New Orleans (LA)
Luther Coll (IA)
Lycoming Coll (PA)
Lynchburg Coll (VA)
Macalester Coll (MN)
Madonna U (MI)
Manchester Coll (IN)
Manhattan Coll (NY)
Manhattanville Coll (NY)
Mansfield U of Pennsylvania (PA)
Marian Coll (IN)
Marlboro Coll (VT)
Marquette U (WI)
Marshall U (WV)
Mars Hill Coll (NC)
Mary Baldwin Coll (VA)
Marymount Coll (NY)
Marymount Manhattan Coll (NY)
Maryville Coll (TN)
Maryville U of Saint Louis (MO)
Mary Washington Coll (VA)
Massachusetts Coll of Liberal Arts (MA)
McGill U (PQ, Canada)
McKendree Coll (IL)
McMurry U (TX)
McNeese State U (LA)
McPherson Coll (PA)
Memorial U of Newfoundland (NF, Canada)
Mercer U (GA)
Mercy Coll (NY)
Mercyhurst Coll (PA)
Meredith Coll (NC)
Merrimack Coll (MA)
Mesa State Coll (CO)
Messiah Coll (PA)
Methodist Coll (NC)
Metropolitan State Coll of Denver (CO)
Miami U (OH)
Michigan State U (MI)
MidAmerica Nazarene U (KS)
Middlebury Coll (VT)
Middle Tennessee State U (TN)
Midland Lutheran Coll (NE)
Midwestern State U (TX)
Millersville U of Pennsylvania (PA)
Milligan Coll (TN)
Millikin U (IL)
Millsaps Coll (MS)
Mills Coll (CA)
Minnesota State U, Mankato (MN)
Minnesota State U Moorhead (MN)
Minot State U (ND)
Mississippi Coll (MS)
Mississippi State U (MS)
Mississippi Valley State U (MS)
Missouri Southern State Coll (MO)
Missouri Valley Coll (MO)
Molloy Coll (NY)
Monmouth Coll (IL)
Montana State U–Billings (MT)
Montana State U–Bozeman (MT)
Moravian Coll (PA)
Morehead State U (KY)
Morehouse Coll (GA)
Morgan State U (MD)
Morningside Coll (IA)
Morris Coll (SC)
Mount Allison U (NB, Canada)
Mount Holyoke Coll (MA)
Mount Mercy Coll (IA)
Mount Saint Mary Coll (NY)
Mount St. Mary's Coll (CA)
Mount Saint Mary's Coll and Seminary (MD)
Mount Saint Vincent U (NS, Canada)
Mount Union Coll (OH)
Mount Vernon Nazarene Coll (OH)
Muhlenberg Coll (PA)
Murray State U (KY)
Muskingum Coll (OH)
Nazareth Coll of Rochester (NY)
Nebraska Wesleyan U (NE)
Newberry Coll (SC)
New Coll of the U of South Florida (FL)
New England Coll (NH)
New Jersey City U (NJ)
Newman U (KS)
New Mexico Highlands U (NM)
New Mexico State U (NM)
New York Inst of Technology (NY)
New York U (NY)

Majors Index
Sociology

Niagara U (NY)
Nicholls State U (LA)
Nipissing U (ON, Canada)
Norfolk State U (VA)
North Carolina Ag and Tech State U (NC)
North Carolina Central U (NC)
North Carolina State U (NC)
North Carolina Wesleyan Coll (NC)
North Central Coll (IL)
North Dakota State U (ND)
Northeastern Illinois U (IL)
Northeastern State U (OK)
Northeastern U (MA)
Northern Arizona U (AZ)
Northern Illinois U (IL)
Northern Kentucky U (KY)
Northern Michigan U (MI)
Northern State U (SD)
North Georgia Coll & State U (GA)
Northland Coll (WI)
North Park U (IL)
Northwestern Coll (IA)
Northwestern Oklahoma State U (OK)
Northwestern State U of Louisiana (LA)
Northwestern U (IL)
Northwest Missouri State U (MO)
Oakland U (MI)
Oberlin Coll (OH)
Occidental Coll (CA)
Oglethorpe U (GA)
Ohio Dominican Coll (OH)
Ohio Northern U (OH)
The Ohio State U (OH)
Ohio U (OH)
Ohio Wesleyan U (OH)
Oklahoma Baptist U (OK)
Oklahoma City U (OK)
Oklahoma State U (OK)
Old Dominion U (VA)
Open Learning Agency (BC, Canada)
Oregon State U (OR)
Ottawa U (KS)
Otterbein Coll (OH)
Ouachita Baptist U (AR)
Our Lady of the Lake U of San Antonio (TX)
Pace U, New York City Campus (NY)
Pace U, Pleasantville/Briarcliff Campus (NY)
Pacific Lutheran U (WA)
Pacific Union Coll (CA)
Pacific U (OR)
Paine Coll (GA)
Park U (MO)
Penn State U Harrisburg Campus of the Capital Coll (PA)
Penn State U Univ Park Campus (PA)
Pepperdine U, Malibu (CA)
Peru State Coll (NE)
Pfeiffer U (NC)
Philander Smith Coll (AR)
Piedmont Coll (GA)
Pikeville Coll (KY)
Pine Manor Coll (MA)
Pittsburg State U (KS)
Pitzer Coll (CA)
Plattsburgh State U of NY (NY)
Plymouth State Coll (NH)
Point Loma Nazarene U (CA)
Pomona Coll (CA)
Pontifical Catholic U of Puerto Rico (PR)
Portland State U (OR)
Prairie View A&M U (TX)
Presbyterian Coll (SC)
Princeton U (NJ)
Principia Coll (IL)
Providence Coll (RI)
Purchase Coll, State U of NY (NY)
Purdue U (IN)
Purdue U Calumet (IN)
Queens Coll of the City U of NY (NY)
Queen's U at Kingston (ON, Canada)
Quincy U (IL)
Quinnipiac U (CT)
Radford U (VA)
Ramapo Coll of New Jersey (NJ)
Randolph-Macon Coll (VA)

Randolph-Macon Woman's Coll (VA)
Redeemer Coll (ON, Canada)
Reed Coll (OR)
Regents Coll (NY)
Regis Coll (MA)
Regis U (CO)
Rhodes Coll (TN)
Rice U (TX)
The Richard Stockton Coll of New Jersey (NJ)
Richmond, The American International U in London (United Kingdom)
Rider U (NJ)
Ripon Coll (WI)
Rivier Coll (NH)
Roanoke Coll (VA)
Roberts Wesleyan Coll (NY)
Rockford Coll (IL)
Rockhurst U (MO)
Rocky Mountain Coll (MT)
Rollins Coll (FL)
Rosemont Coll (PA)
Rowan U (NJ)
Russell Sage Coll (NY)
Rust Coll (MS)
Rutgers, State U of NJ, Camden Coll of Arts & Scis (NJ)
Rutgers, State U of NJ, Douglass Coll (NJ)
Rutgers, State U of NJ, Livingston Coll (NJ)
Rutgers, State U of NJ, Newark Coll of Arts & Scis (NJ)
Rutgers, State U of NJ, Rutgers Coll (NJ)
Rutgers, State U of NJ, U Coll–Camden (NJ)
Rutgers, State U of NJ, U Coll–Newark (NJ)
Rutgers, State U of NJ, U Coll–New Brunswick (NJ)
Sacred Heart U (CT)
Saginaw Valley State U (MI)
St. Ambrose U (IA)
Saint Anselm Coll (NH)
Saint Augustine's Coll (NC)
St. Bonaventure U (NY)
St. Cloud State U (MN)
St. Edward's U (TX)
St. Francis Coll (NY)
Saint Francis Coll (PA)
St. Francis Xavier U (NS, Canada)
St. John Fisher Coll (NY)
Saint John's U (MN)
St. John's U (NY)
Saint Joseph Coll (CT)
Saint Joseph's Coll (IN)
Saint Joseph's Coll (ME)
St. Joseph's Coll, New York (NY)
St. Joseph's Coll, Suffolk Campus (NY)
Saint Joseph's U (PA)
St. Lawrence U (NY)
Saint Leo U (FL)
Saint Louis U (MO)
Saint Mary Coll (KS)
Saint Mary's Coll (IN)
Saint Mary's Coll (MI)
Saint Mary's Coll of California (CA)
St. Mary's Coll of Maryland (MD)
Saint Mary's Coll (NS, Canada)
Saint Mary's U of Minnesota (MN)
St. Mary's U of San Antonio (TX)
Saint Michael's Coll (VT)
St. Norbert Coll (WI)
St. Olaf Coll (MN)
Saint Paul's Coll (VA)
Saint Peter's Coll (NJ)
St. Thomas U (FL)
Saint Vincent Coll (PA)
Saint Xavier U (IL)
Salem Coll (NC)
Salem State Coll (MA)
Salisbury State U (MD)
Salve Regina U (RI)
Samford U (AL)
Sam Houston State U (TX)
San Diego State U (CA)
San Francisco State U (CA)
San Jose State U (CA)
Santa Clara U (CA)
Sarah Lawrence Coll (NY)
Savannah State U (GA)
Scripps Coll (CA)
Seattle Pacific U (WA)

Seattle U (WA)
Seton Hall U (NJ)
Seton Hill Coll (PA)
Shaw U (NC)
Shenandoah U (VA)
Shepherd Coll (WV)
Shippensburg U of Pennsylvania (PA)
Shorter Coll (GA)
Siena Coll (NY)
Simmons Coll (MA)
Simon Fraser U (BC, Canada)
Simpson Coll (IA)
Skidmore Coll (NY)
Slippery Rock U of Pennsylvania (PA)
Smith Coll (MA)
Sonoma State U (CA)
South Dakota State U (SD)
Southeastern Louisiana U (LA)
Southeastern Oklahoma State U (OK)
Southeast Missouri State U (MO)
Southern Arkansas U–Magnolia (AR)
Southern Illinois U Carbondale (IL)
Southern Illinois U Edwardsville (IL)
Southern Methodist U (TX)
Southern Oregon U (OR)
Southern Utah U (UT)
Southwest Baptist U (MO)
Southwestern U (TX)
Southwest Missouri State U (MO)
Southwest State U (MN)
Southwest Texas State U (TX)
Spalding U (KY)
Spelman Coll (GA)
Spring Arbor Coll (MI)
Stanford U (CA)
State U of NY at Albany (NY)
State U of NY at Binghamton (NY)
State U of NY at Buffalo (NY)
State U of NY at New Paltz (NY)
State U of NY at Oswego (NY)
State U of NY at Stony Brook (NY)
State U of NY Coll at Brockport (NY)
State U of NY Coll at Buffalo (NY)
State U of NY Coll at Cortland (NY)
State U of NY Coll at Fredonia (NY)
State U of NY Coll at Geneseo (NY)
State U of NY Coll at Old Westbury (NY)
State U of NY Coll at Oneonta (NY)
State U of NY Coll at Potsdam (NY)
State U of NY Inst of Tech at Utica/Rome (NY)
State U of West Georgia (GA)
Stephen F. Austin State U (TX)
Stetson U (FL)
Stillman Coll (AL)
Stonehill Coll (MA)
Suffolk U (MA)
Susquehanna U (PA)
Sweet Briar Coll (VA)
Syracuse U (NY)
Tabor Coll (KS)
Talladega Coll (AL)
Taylor U (IN)
Teikyo Post U (CT)
Temple U (PA)
Tennessee State U (TN)
Tennessee Technological U (TN)
Texas A&M International U (TX)
Texas A&M U (TX)
Texas A&M U–Commerce (TX)
Texas A&M U–Kingsville (TX)
Texas Christian U (TX)
Texas Southern U (TX)
Texas Tech U (TX)
Texas Wesleyan U (TX)
Texas Woman's U (TX)
Thiel Coll (PA)
Thomas Edison State Coll (NJ)
Thomas More Coll (KY)
Thomas U (GA)
Tougaloo Coll (MS)
Touro Coll (NY)
Towson U (MD)
Transylvania U (KY)
Trent U (ON, Canada)
Trinity Christian Coll (IL)
Trinity Coll (CT)

Trinity U (TX)
Troy State U (AL)
Troy State U Dothan (AL)
Truman State U (MO)
Tufts U (MA)
Tulane U (LA)
Tuskegee U (AL)
Union Coll (KY)
Union Coll (NY)
Union U (TN)
United States International U (CA)
Université de Montréal (PQ, Canada)
Université Laval (PQ, Canada)
U Coll of Cape Breton (NS, Canada)
U Coll of the Fraser Valley (BC, Canada)
The U of Akron (OH)
The U of Alabama (AL)
The U of Alabama at Birmingham (AL)
The U of Alabama in Huntsville (AL)
U of Alaska Fairbanks (AK)
U of Alberta (AB, Canada)
The U of Arizona (AZ)
U of Arkansas (AR)
U of Arkansas at Little Rock (AR)
U of Arkansas at Pine Bluff (AR)
U of British Columbia (BC, Canada)
U of Calgary (AB, Canada)
U of Calif, Berkeley (CA)
U of Calif, Davis (CA)
U of Calif, Irvine (CA)
U of Calif, Los Angeles (CA)
U of Calif, Riverside (CA)
U of Calif, San Diego (CA)
U of Calif, Santa Barbara (CA)
U of Calif, Santa Cruz (CA)
U of Central Arkansas (AR)
U of Central Florida (FL)
U of Central Oklahoma (OK)
U of Chicago (IL)
U of Cincinnati (OH)
U of Colorado at Boulder (CO)
U of Colorado at Colorado Springs (CO)
U of Colorado at Denver (CO)
U of Connecticut (CT)
U of Dayton (OH)
U of Delaware (DE)
U of Denver (CO)
U of Detroit Mercy (MI)
U of Dubuque (IA)
U of Evansville (IN)
The U of Findlay (OH)
U of Florida (FL)
U of Georgia (GA)
U of Great Falls (MT)
U of Guelph (ON, Canada)
U of Hartford (CT)
U of Hawaii at Manoa (HI)
U of Houston (TX)
U of Houston–Clear Lake (TX)
U of Idaho (ID)
U of Illinois at Chicago (IL)
U of Illinois at Springfield (IL)
U of Illinois at Urbana–Champaign (IL)
U of Indianapolis (IN)
The U of Iowa (IA)
U of Kansas (KS)
U of Kentucky (KY)
U of King's Coll (NS, Canada)
U of La Verne (CA)
The U of Lethbridge (AB, Canada)
U of Louisiana at Lafayette (LA)
U of Louisiana at Monroe (LA)
U of Louisville (KY)
U of Maine (ME)
U of Maine at Farmington (ME)
U of Maine at Presque Isle (ME)
U of Manitoba (MB, Canada)
U of Mary Hardin-Baylor (TX)
U of Maryland, Baltimore County (MD)
U of Maryland, Coll Park (MD)
U of Maryland University Coll (MD)
U of Massachusetts Amherst (MA)
U of Massachusetts Boston (MA)
U of Massachusetts Dartmouth (MA)
U of Massachusetts Lowell (MA)
The U of Memphis (TN)
U of Miami (FL)

U of Michigan (MI)
U of Michigan–Dearborn (MI)
U of Michigan–Flint (MI)
U of Minnesota, Duluth (MN)
U of Minnesota, Morris (MN)
U of Minnesota, Twin Cities Campus (MN)
U of Mississippi (MS)
U of Missouri–Columbia (MO)
U of Missouri–Kansas City (MO)
U of Missouri–St. Louis (MO)
U of Mobile (AL)
The U of Montana–Missoula (MT)
U of Montevallo (AL)
U of Nebraska at Kearney (NE)
U of Nebraska at Omaha (NE)
U of Nebraska–Lincoln (NE)
U of Nevada, Las Vegas (NV)
U of Nevada, Reno (NV)
U of New Brunswick, Fredericton (NB, Canada)
U of New Brunswick, Saint John (NB, Canada)
U of New Hampshire (NH)
U of New Haven (CT)
U of New Mexico (NM)
U of New Orleans (LA)
U of North Alabama (AL)
The U of North Carolina at Asheville (NC)
The U of North Carolina at Chapel Hill (NC)
The U of North Carolina at Charlotte (NC)
The U of North Carolina at Greensboro (NC)
The U of North Carolina at Pembroke (NC)
The U of North Carolina at Wilmington (NC)
U of North Dakota (ND)
U of Northern Colorado (CO)
U of Northern Iowa (IA)
U of North Florida (FL)
U of North Texas (TX)
U of Notre Dame (IN)
U of Oklahoma (OK)
U of Oregon (OR)
U of Pennsylvania (PA)
U of Pittsburgh (PA)
U of Pittsburgh at Bradford (PA)
U of Pittsburgh at Johnstown (PA)
U of Portland (OR)
U of Prince Edward Island (PE, Canada)
U of Puerto Rico, Mayagüez Campus (PR)
U of Puerto Rico, Río Piedras (PR)
U of Puget Sound (WA)
U of Redlands (CA)
U of Regina (SK, Canada)
U of Rhode Island (RI)
U of Richmond (VA)
U of Rio Grande (OH)
U of St. Thomas (MN)
U of San Diego (CA)
U of San Francisco (CA)
U of Science and Arts of Oklahoma (OK)
The U of Scranton (PA)
U of Sioux Falls (SD)
U of South Alabama (AL)
U of South Carolina (SC)
U of South Carolina Spartanburg (SC)
U of South Dakota (SD)
U of Southern California (CA)
U of Southern Colorado (CO)
U of Southern Indiana (IN)
U of Southern Maine (ME)
U of South Florida (FL)
The U of Tampa (FL)
The U of Tennessee at Chattanooga (TN)
The U of Tennessee at Martin (TN)
The U of Tennessee Knoxville (TN)
The U of Texas at Arlington (TX)
The U of Texas at Austin (TX)
The U of Texas at Dallas (TX)
The U of Texas at San Antonio (TX)
The U of Texas at Tyler (TX)
The U of Texas–Pan American (TX)
U of the District of Columbia (DC)
U of the Ozarks (AR)
U of the Pacific (CA)
U of Toronto (ON, Canada)

Majors Index
Sociology–Spanish

U of Tulsa (OK)
U of Utah (UT)
U of Vermont (VT)
U of Victoria (BC, Canada)
U of Virginia (VA)
U of Washington (WA)
U of Waterloo (ON, Canada)
The U of West Alabama (AL)
The U of Western Ontario (ON, Canada)
U of West Florida (FL)
U of Windsor (ON, Canada)
The U of Winnipeg (MB, Canada)
U of Wisconsin–Eau Claire (WI)
U of Wisconsin–La Crosse (WI)
U of Wisconsin–Madison (WI)
U of Wisconsin–Milwaukee (WI)
U of Wisconsin–Parkside (WI)
U of Wisconsin–River Falls (WI)
U of Wisconsin–Stevens Point (WI)
U of Wisconsin–Superior (WI)
U of Wisconsin–Whitewater (WI)
U of Wyoming (WY)
Upper Iowa U (IA)
Urbana U (OH)
Ursinus Coll (PA)
Ursuline Coll (OH)
Utah State U (UT)
Utica Coll of Syracuse U (NY)
Valdosta State U (GA)
Valparaiso U (IN)
Vanderbilt U (TN)
Vanguard U of Southern California (CA)
Vassar Coll (NY)
Villanova U (PA)
Virginia Commonwealth U (VA)
Virginia Polytechnic Inst and State U (VA)
Virginia Union U (VA)
Virginia Wesleyan Coll (VA)
Voorhees Coll (SC)
Wagner Coll (NY)
Wake Forest U (NC)
Walla Walla Coll (WA)
Walsh U (OH)
Warren Wilson Coll (NC)
Wartburg Coll (IA)
Washington & Jefferson Coll (PA)
Washington and Lee U (VA)
Washington Coll (MD)
Washington State U (WA)
Waynesburg Coll (PA)
Wayne State Coll (NE)
Wayne State U (MI)
Weber State U (UT)
Webster U (MO)
Wellesley Coll (MA)
Wells Coll (NY)
Wesleyan U (CT)
West Chester U of Pennsylvania (PA)
Western Carolina U (NC)
Western Connecticut State U (CT)
Western Illinois U (IL)
Western Kentucky U (KY)
Western Maryland Coll (MD)
Western Michigan U (MI)
Western New England Coll (MA)
Western Oregon U (OR)
Western State Coll of Colorado (CO)
Western Washington U (WA)
Westfield State Coll (MA)
West Liberty State Coll (WV)
Westminster Coll (MO)
Westminster Coll (PA)
Westminster Coll (UT)
Westmont Coll (CA)
West Texas A&M U (TX)
West Virginia State Coll (WV)
West Virginia U (WV)
West Virginia Wesleyan Coll (WV)
Wheaton Coll (IL)
Wheaton Coll (MA)
Whitman Coll (WA)
Whittier Coll (CA)
Whitworth Coll (WA)
Wichita State U (KS)
Widener U (PA)
Wilfrid Laurier U (ON, Canada)
Wilkes U (PA)
Willamette U (OR)
William Paterson U of New Jersey (NJ)
William Penn U (IA)
Williams Coll (MA)

Wingate U (NC)
Winona State U (MN)
Winston-Salem State U (NC)
Winthrop U (SC)
Wittenberg U (OH)
Wofford Coll (SC)
Worcester State Coll (MA)
Wright State U (OH)
Xavier U (OH)
Xavier U of Louisiana (LA)
Yale U (CT)
Yeshiva U (NY)
York Coll of Pennsylvania (PA)
York Coll of the City U of New York (NY)
York U (ON, Canada)
Youngstown State U (OH)

SOCIO-PSYCHOLOGICAL SPORTS STUDIES
Greensboro Coll (NC)
Ithaca Coll (NY)
U of Minnesota, Twin Cities Campus (MN)

SOIL CONSERVATION
Ball State U (IN)
California State Polytechnic U, Pomona (CA)
Colorado State U (CO)
The Ohio State U (OH)
U of Delaware (DE)
U of Maryland, Coll Park (MD)
U of New Hampshire (NH)
The U of Tennessee at Martin (TN)
U of Wisconsin–Stevens Point (WI)
Utah State U (UT)

SOIL SCIENCES
Colorado State U (CO)
Cornell U (NY)
McGill U (PQ, Canada)
New Mexico State U (NM)
The Ohio State U (OH)
Penn State U Univ Park Campus (PA)
The U of Arizona (AZ)
U of British Columbia (BC, Canada)
U of Delaware (DE)
U of Florida (FL)
U of Georgia (GA)
U of Hawaii at Manoa (HI)
U of Idaho (ID)
U of Illinois at Urbana–Champaign (IL)
U of Minnesota, Twin Cities Campus (MN)
U of Nebraska–Lincoln (NE)
U of Vermont (VT)
U of Wisconsin–River Falls (WI)
Utah State U (UT)
Washington State U (WA)

SOLAR TECHNOLOGY
Hampshire Coll (MA)

SOUTH ASIAN LANGUAGES
Yale U (CT)

SOUTH ASIAN STUDIES
Barnard Coll (NY)
Brown U (RI)
The Coll of Wooster (OH)
Concordia U (PQ, Canada)
Gettysburg Coll (PA)
Hampshire Coll (MA)
Harvard U (MA)
Long Island U, Southampton Coll, Friends World Program (NY)
Oakland U (MI)
U of Calif, Santa Cruz (CA)
U of Chicago (IL)
U of Manitoba (MB, Canada)
U of Michigan (MI)
U of Minnesota, Twin Cities Campus (MN)
U of Missouri–Columbia (MO)
U of Pennsylvania (PA)
U of Toronto (ON, Canada)
U of Washington (WA)
Ursinus Coll (PA)

SOUTHEAST ASIAN STUDIES
Cornell U (NY)
Hampshire Coll (MA)
Harvard U (MA)

Long Island U, Southampton Coll, Friends World Program (NY)
Middlebury Coll (VT)
Tufts U (MA)
U of Calif, Berkeley (CA)
U of Calif, Los Angeles (CA)
U of Calif, Santa Cruz (CA)
U of Chicago (IL)
U of Michigan (MI)
U of Washington (WA)
U of Wisconsin–Madison (WI)

SPANISH
Abilene Christian U (TX)
Adams State Coll (CO)
Adelphi U (NY)
Adrian Coll (MI)
Agnes Scott Coll (GA)
Alabama State U (AL)
Albany State U (GA)
Albertson Coll of Idaho (ID)
Albertus Magnus Coll (CT)
Albion Coll (MI)
Albright Coll (PA)
Alfred U (NY)
Allegheny Coll (PA)
Allentown Coll of St. Francis de Sales (PA)
Alma Coll (MI)
American International Coll (MA)
American U (DC)
Amherst Coll (MA)
Anderson Coll (SC)
Anderson U (IN)
Andrews U (MI)
Antioch Coll (OH)
Appalachian State U (NC)
Aquinas Coll (MI)
Arizona State U (AZ)
Arizona State U West (AZ)
Arkansas State U (AR)
Arkansas Tech U (AR)
Asbury Coll (KY)
Ashland U (OH)
Assumption Coll (MA)
Atlantic Union Coll (MA)
Auburn U (AL)
Augsburg Coll (MN)
Augustana Coll (IL)
Augustana Coll (SD)
Augusta State U (GA)
Austin Coll (TX)
Austin Peay State U (TN)
Azusa Pacific U (CA)
Baker U (KS)
Baldwin-Wallace Coll (OH)
Ball State U (IN)
Barat Coll (IL)
Bard Coll (NY)
Barnard Coll (NY)
Barry U (FL)
Bates Coll (ME)
Baylor U (TX)
Beaver Coll (PA)
Bellarmine Coll (KY)
Bellevue U (NE)
Belmont U (TN)
Beloit Coll (WI)
Bemidji State U (MN)
Benedictine Coll (KS)
Benedictine U (IL)
Bennington Coll (VT)
Berea Coll (KY)
Berry Coll (GA)
Bethany Coll (WV)
Bethel Coll (KS)
Bethel Coll (MN)
Biola U (CA)
Birmingham-Southern Coll (AL)
Bishop's U (PQ, Canada)
Blackburn Coll (IL)
Black Hills State U (SD)
Bloomfield Coll (NJ)
Bloomsburg U of Pennsylvania (PA)
Blue Mountain Coll (MS)
Bluffton Coll (OH)
Boise State U (ID)
Boston U (MA)
Bowdoin Coll (ME)
Bowling Green State U (OH)
Bradley U (IL)
Brandeis U (MA)
Brescia U (KY)
Briar Cliff Coll (IA)

Bridgewater Coll (VA)
Bridgewater State Coll (MA)
Brigham Young U (UT)
Brock U (ON, Canada)
Brooklyn Coll of the City U of NY (NY)
Brown U (RI)
Bryn Mawr Coll (PA)
Bucknell U (PA)
Buena Vista U (IA)
Butler U (IN)
Cabrini Coll (PA)
Caldwell Coll (NJ)
California Lutheran U (CA)
California State Polytechnic U, Pomona (CA)
California State U, Chico (CA)
California State U, Dominguez Hills (CA)
California State U, Fresno (CA)
California State U, Fullerton (CA)
California State U, Hayward (CA)
California State U, Long Beach (CA)
California State U, Los Angeles (CA)
California State U, Northridge (CA)
California State U, Sacramento (CA)
California State U, San Bernardino (CA)
California State U, San Marcos (CA)
California State U, Stanislaus (CA)
California U of Pennsylvania (PA)
Calvin Coll (MI)
Campbell U (NC)
Canisius Coll (NY)
Capital U (OH)
Cardinal Stritch U (WI)
Carleton Coll (MN)
Carleton U (ON, Canada)
Carnegie Mellon U (PA)
Carroll Coll (MT)
Carroll Coll (WI)
Carson-Newman Coll (TN)
Carthage Coll (WI)
Case Western Reserve U (OH)
Castleton State Coll (VT)
Catawba Coll (NC)
The Catholic U of America (DC)
Cedar Crest Coll (PA)
Cedarville Coll (OH)
Centenary Coll of Louisiana (LA)
Central Coll (IA)
Central Connecticut State U (CT)
Central Methodist Coll (MO)
Central Michigan U (MI)
Central Missouri State U (MO)
Centre Coll (KY)
Chapman U (CA)
Charleston Southern U (SC)
Chatham Coll (PA)
Chestnut Hill Coll (PA)
Cheyney U of Pennsylvania (PA)
Chicago State U (IL)
Christopher Newport U (VA)
Citadel, The Military Coll of South Carolina (SC)
City Coll of the City U of NY (NY)
Claremont McKenna Coll (CA)
Clarion U of Pennsylvania (PA)
Clark Atlanta U (GA)
Clarke Coll (IA)
Clark U (MA)
Clemson U (SC)
Cleveland State U (OH)
Coe Coll (IA)
Coker Coll (SC)
Colby Coll (ME)
Colgate U (NY)
Coll of Charleston (SC)
Coll of Mount Saint Vincent (NY)
The Coll of New Jersey (NJ)
The Coll of New Rochelle (NY)
Coll of Our Lady of the Elms (MA)
Coll of Saint Benedict (MN)
Coll of St. Catherine (MN)
Coll of Saint Elizabeth (NJ)
The Coll of Saint Rose (NY)
Coll of Staten Island of the City U of NY (NY)
Coll of the Holy Cross (MA)
Coll of the Ozarks (MO)
The Coll of William and Mary (VA)
The Coll of Wooster (OH)
The Colorado Coll (CO)

Colorado State U (CO)
Columbia Coll (NY)
Columbia Coll (SC)
Columbia U, School of General Studies (NY)
Concordia Coll (MN)
Concordia Coll (NE)
Concordia U (PQ, Canada)
Concordia U at Austin (TX)
Concordia U Wisconsin (WI)
Converse Coll (SC)
Cornell Coll (IA)
Cornell U (NY)
Cornerstone U (MI)
Creighton U (NE)
Daemen Coll (NY)
Dalhousie U (NS, Canada)
Dana Coll (NE)
Dartmouth Coll (NH)
David Lipscomb U (TN)
Davidson Coll (NC)
Delaware State U (DE)
Denison U (OH)
DePaul U (IL)
DePauw U (IN)
Dickinson Coll (PA)
Dickinson State U (ND)
Doane Coll (NE)
Dominican Coll of Blauvelt (NY)
Dominican U (IL)
Dordt Coll (IA)
Drake U (IA)
Drew U (NJ)
Drury U (MO)
Duke U (NC)
Duquesne U (PA)
Earlham Coll (IN)
East Carolina U (NC)
Eastern Coll (PA)
Eastern Connecticut State U (CT)
Eastern Kentucky U (KY)
Eastern Mennonite U (VA)
Eastern Michigan U (MI)
Eastern Nazarene Coll (MA)
Eastern New Mexico U (NM)
Eastern Washington U (WA)
East Stroudsburg U of Pennsylvania (PA)
East Tennessee State U (TN)
East Texas Baptist U (TX)
Eckerd Coll (FL)
Edgewood Coll (WI)
Edinboro U of Pennsylvania (PA)
Elizabethtown Coll (PA)
Elmhurst Coll (IL)
Elmira Coll (NY)
Elon Coll (NC)
Emmanuel Coll (MA)
Emory & Henry Coll (VA)
Emory U (GA)
Erskine Coll (SC)
Evangel U (MO)
The Evergreen State Coll (WA)
Fairfield U (CT)
Fairleigh Dickinson U, Florham-Madison Campus (NJ)
Fairleigh Dickinson U, Teaneck-Hackensack Campus (NJ)
Ferrum Coll (VA)
Fisk U (TN)
Flagler Coll (FL)
Florida A&M U (FL)
Florida Atlantic U (FL)
Florida Gulf Coast U (FL)
Florida International U (FL)
Florida Southern Coll (FL)
Florida State U (FL)
Fordham U (NY)
Fort Hays State U (KS)
Fort Lewis Coll (CO)
Framingham State Coll (MA)
Franciscan U of Steubenville (OH)
Francis Marion U (SC)
Franklin and Marshall Coll (PA)
Franklin Coll of Indiana (IN)
Fresno Pacific U (CA)
Friends U (KS)
Furman U (SC)
Gallaudet U (DC)
Gardner-Webb U (NC)
Geneva Coll (PA)
George Fox U (OR)
George Mason U (VA)
Georgetown Coll (KY)
Georgetown U (DC)
The George Washington U (DC)
Georgia Coll and State U (GA)

Majors Index
Spanish

Georgian Court Coll (NJ)
Georgia Southern U (GA)
Georgia Southwestern State U (GA)
Georgia State U (GA)
Gettysburg Coll (PA)
Gonzaga U (WA)
Gordon Coll (MA)
Goshen Coll (IN)
Goucher Coll (MD)
Grace Coll (IN)
Graceland Coll (IA)
Grand Valley State U (MI)
Greensboro Coll (NC)
Greenville Coll (IL)
Grinnell Coll (IA)
Grove City Coll (PA)
Guilford Coll (NC)
Gustavus Adolphus Coll (MN)
Hamilton Coll (NY)
Hamline U (MN)
Hampden-Sydney Coll (VA)
Hanover Coll (IN)
Harding U (AR)
Hardin-Simmons U (TX)
Hartwick Coll (NY)
Harvard U (MA)
Hastings Coll (NE)
Haverford Coll (PA)
Heidelberg Coll (OH)
Henderson State U (AR)
Hendrix Coll (AR)
Heritage Coll (WA)
High Point U (NC)
Hillsdale Coll (MI)
Hiram Coll (OH)
Hobart and William Smith Colls (NY)
Hofstra U (NY)
Hollins U (VA)
Holy Family Coll (PA)
Hood Coll (MD)
Hope Coll (MI)
Houghton Coll (NY)
Houston Baptist U (TX)
Howard Payne U (TX)
Howard U (DC)
Humboldt State U (CA)
Hunter Coll of the City U of NY (NY)
Idaho State U (ID)
Illinois Coll (IL)
Illinois State U (IL)
Illinois Wesleyan U (IL)
Immaculata Coll (PA)
Indiana State U (IN)
Indiana U Bloomington (IN)
Indiana U Northwest (IN)
Indiana U of Pennsylvania (PA)
Indiana U–Purdue U Fort Wayne (IN)
Indiana U–Purdue U Indianapolis (IN)
Indiana U South Bend (IN)
Indiana U Southeast (IN)
Indiana Wesleyan U (IN)
Inter American U of PR, Metropolitan Campus (PR)
Inter American U of PR, San Germán Campus (PR)
Iona Coll (NY)
Iowa State U of Science and Technology (IA)
Ithaca Coll (NY)
Jacksonville State U (AL)
Jacksonville U (FL)
James Madison U (VA)
John Carroll U (OH)
Johns Hopkins U (MD)
Juniata Coll (PA)
Kalamazoo Coll (MI)
Kean U (NJ)
Keene State Coll (NH)
Kent State U (OH)
Kenyon Coll (OH)
King Coll (TN)
King's Coll (PA)
Knox Coll (IL)
Kutztown U of Pennsylvania (PA)
Lafayette Coll (PA)
Lake Erie Coll (OH)
Lake Forest Coll (IL)
Lakeland Coll (WI)
Lamar U (TX)
Lander U (SC)
La Salle U (PA)
La Sierra U (CA)

Lawrence U (WI)
Lebanon Valley Coll (PA)
Lehigh U (PA)
Lehman Coll of the City U of NY (NY)
Le Moyne Coll (NY)
Lenoir-Rhyne Coll (NC)
Lewis & Clark Coll (OR)
Lincoln U (PA)
Lindenwood U (MO)
Linfield Coll (OR)
Lock Haven U of Pennsylvania (PA)
Long Island U, C.W. Post Campus (NY)
Long Island U, Southampton Coll, Friends World Program (NY)
Longwood Coll (VA)
Loras Coll (IA)
Louisiana Coll (LA)
Louisiana State U and A&M Coll (LA)
Louisiana State U in Shreveport (LA)
Louisiana Tech U (LA)
Loyola Coll in Maryland (MD)
Loyola Marymount U (CA)
Loyola U Chicago (IL)
Loyola U New Orleans (LA)
Lubbock Christian U (TX)
Luther Coll (IA)
Lycoming Coll (PA)
Lynchburg Coll (VA)
Lyon Coll (AR)
Macalester Coll (MN)
MacMurray Coll (IL)
Madonna U (MI)
Malone Coll (OH)
Manchester Coll (IN)
Manhattan Coll (NY)
Manhattanville Coll (NY)
Mansfield U of Pennsylvania (PA)
Marian Coll (IN)
Marian Coll of Fond du Lac (WI)
Marietta Coll (OH)
Marist Coll (NY)
Marlboro Coll (VT)
Marquette U (WI)
Marshall U (WV)
Mars Hill Coll (NC)
Mary Baldwin Coll (VA)
Marymount Coll (NY)
Maryville Coll (TN)
Mary Washington Coll (VA)
Marywood U (PA)
Massachusetts Inst of Technology (MA)
McGill U (PQ, Canada)
McMurry U (TX)
McNeese State U (LA)
McPherson Coll (KS)
Memorial U of Newfoundland (NF, Canada)
Mercer U (GA)
Mercy Coll (NY)
Mercyhurst Coll (PA)
Meredith Coll (NC)
Merrimack Coll (MA)
Messiah Coll (PA)
Methodist Coll (NC)
Metropolitan State Coll of Denver (CO)
Miami U (OH)
Michigan State U (MI)
MidAmerica Nazarene U (KS)
Middlebury Coll (VT)
Midland Lutheran Coll (NE)
Midwestern State U (TX)
Millersville U of Pennsylvania (PA)
Millikin U (IL)
Millsaps Coll (MS)
Minnesota State U, Mankato (MN)
Minnesota State U Moorhead (MN)
Minot State U (ND)
Mississippi Coll (MS)
Mississippi U for Women (MS)
Missouri Southern State Coll (MO)
Missouri Western State Coll (MO)
Molloy Coll (NY)
Monmouth Coll (IL)
Montana State U–Billings (MT)
Moravian Coll (PA)
Morehead State U (KY)
Morehouse Coll (GA)
Morningside Coll (IA)
Mount Allison U (NB, Canada)
Mount Holyoke Coll (MA)

Mount Mary Coll (WI)
Mount St. Mary's Coll (CA)
Mount Saint Mary's Coll and Seminary (MD)
Mount Saint Vincent U (NS, Canada)
Mount Union Coll (OH)
Mount Vernon Nazarene Coll (OH)
Muhlenberg Coll (PA)
Murray State U (KY)
Muskingum Coll (OH)
Nazareth Coll of Rochester (NY)
Nebraska Wesleyan U (NE)
Newberry Coll (SC)
New Coll of the U of South Florida (FL)
New Jersey City U (NJ)
New Mexico Highlands U (NM)
New York U (NY)
Niagara U (NY)
Norfolk State U (VA)
North Carolina Central U (NC)
North Carolina State U (NC)
North Central Coll (IL)
North Dakota State U (ND)
Northeastern Illinois U (IL)
Northeastern State U (OK)
Northeastern U (MA)
Northern Arizona U (AZ)
Northern Illinois U (IL)
Northern Kentucky U (KY)
Northern Michigan U (MI)
Northern State U (SD)
North Georgia Coll & State U (GA)
North Park U (IL)
Northwestern Coll (IA)
Northwestern Coll (MN)
Northwestern Oklahoma State U (OK)
Northwestern U (IL)
Northwest Missouri State U (MO)
Notre Dame Coll of Ohio (OH)
Oakland U (MI)
Oakwood Coll (AL)
Oberlin Coll (OH)
Occidental Coll (CA)
Ohio Dominican Coll (OH)
Ohio Northern U (OH)
The Ohio State U (OH)
Ohio U (OH)
Ohio Wesleyan U (OH)
Oklahoma Baptist U (OK)
Oklahoma Christian U of Science and Arts (OK)
Oklahoma City U (OK)
Oklahoma State U (OK)
Olivet Nazarene U (IL)
Oregon State U (OR)
Otterbein Coll (OH)
Ouachita Baptist U (AR)
Our Lady of the Lake U of San Antonio (TX)
Pace U, Pleasantville/Briarcliff Campus (NY)
Pacific Lutheran U (WA)
Pacific Union Coll (CA)
Pacific U (OR)
Peace Coll (NC)
Penn State U Univ Park Campus (PA)
Pepperdine U, Malibu (CA)
Piedmont Coll (GA)
Pittsburg State U (KS)
Pitzer Coll (CA)
Plattsburgh State U of NY (NY)
Plymouth State Coll (NH)
Point Loma Nazarene U (CA)
Pomona Coll (CA)
Pontifical Catholic U of Puerto Rico (PR)
Portland State U (OR)
Prairie View A&M U (TX)
Presbyterian Coll (SC)
Principia Coll (IL)
Providence Coll (RI)
Purchase Coll, State U of NY (NY)
Purdue U Calumet (IN)
Queens Coll (NC)
Queens Coll of the City U of NY (NY)
Queen's U at Kingston (ON, Canada)
Quinnipiac U (CT)
Randolph-Macon Coll (VA)
Randolph-Macon Woman's Coll (VA)
Reed Coll (OR)

Regis Coll (MA)
Regis U (CO)
Rhodes Coll (TN)
Rice U (TX)
Rider U (NJ)
Ripon Coll (WI)
Rivier Coll (NH)
Roanoke Coll (VA)
Rockford Coll (IL)
Rockhurst U (MO)
Rocky Mountain Coll (MT)
Rollins Coll (FL)
Rosemont Coll (PA)
Rowan U (NJ)
Russell Sage Coll (NY)
Rutgers, State U of NJ, Camden Coll of Arts & Scis (NJ)
Rutgers, State U of NJ, Douglass Coll (NJ)
Rutgers, State U of NJ, Livingston Coll (NJ)
Rutgers, State U of NJ, Newark Coll of Arts & Scis (NJ)
Rutgers, State U of NJ, Rutgers Coll (NJ)
Rutgers, State U of NJ, U Coll–Camden (NJ)
Rutgers, State U of NJ, U Coll–New Brunswick (NJ)
Sacred Heart U (CT)
Saginaw Valley State U (MI)
St. Ambrose U (IA)
Saint Anselm Coll (NH)
Saint Augustine's Coll (NC)
St. Bonaventure U (NY)
St. Cloud State U (MN)
St. Edward's U (TX)
Saint Francis Coll (PA)
St. John Fisher Coll (NY)
St. John's Seminary Coll (CA)
Saint John's U (MN)
St. John's U (NY)
Saint Joseph Coll (CT)
St. Joseph's Coll, New York (NY)
Saint Joseph's U (PA)
St. Lawrence U (NY)
Saint Louis U (MO)
Saint Mary Coll (KS)
Saint Mary-of-the-Woods Coll (IN)
Saint Mary's Coll (IN)
Saint Mary's Coll of California (CA)
Saint Mary's U of Minnesota (MN)
St. Mary's U of San Antonio (TX)
Saint Michael's Coll (VT)
St. Norbert Coll (WI)
St. Olaf Coll (MN)
Saint Peter's Coll (NJ)
Saint Vincent Coll (PA)
Saint Xavier U (IL)
Salem Coll (NC)
Salisbury State U (MD)
Salve Regina U (RI)
Samford U (AL)
Sam Houston State U (TX)
San Diego State U (CA)
San Francisco State U (CA)
San Jose State U (CA)
Santa Clara U (CA)
Sarah Lawrence Coll (NY)
Scripps Coll (CA)
Seattle Pacific U (WA)
Seattle U (WA)
Seton Hall U (NJ)
Seton Hill Coll (PA)
Shippensburg U of Pennsylvania (PA)
Shorter Coll (GA)
Siena Coll (NY)
Siena Heights U (MI)
Simmons Coll (MA)
Simon Fraser U (BC, Canada)
Simon's Rock Coll of Bard (MA)
Simpson Coll (IA)
Skidmore Coll (NY)
Slippery Rock U of Pennsylvania (PA)
Smith Coll (MA)
Sonoma State U (CA)
South Dakota State U (SD)
Southeastern Louisiana U (LA)
Southeast Missouri State U (MO)
Southern Arkansas U–Magnolia (AR)
Southern Illinois U Carbondale (IL)
Southern Methodist U (TX)
Southern Oregon U (OR)
Southern Utah U (UT)

Southwest Baptist U (MO)
Southwestern U (TX)
Southwest Missouri State U (MO)
Southwest State U (MN)
Southwest Texas State U (TX)
Spelman Coll (GA)
Spring Arbor Coll (MI)
Spring Hill Coll (AL)
Stanford U (CA)
State U of NY at Albany (NY)
State U of NY at Binghamton (NY)
State U of NY at Buffalo (NY)
State U of NY at New Paltz (NY)
State U of NY at Oswego (NY)
State U of NY at Stony Brook (NY)
State U of NY Coll at Brockport (NY)
State U of NY Coll at Buffalo (NY)
State U of NY Coll at Cortland (NY)
State U of NY Coll at Fredonia (NY)
State U of NY Coll at Geneseo (NY)
State U of NY Coll at Old Westbury (NY)
State U of NY Coll at Oneonta (NY)
State U of NY Coll at Potsdam (NY)
State U of West Georgia (GA)
Stephen F. Austin State U (TX)
Stetson U (FL)
Suffolk U (MA)
Sul Ross State U (TX)
Susquehanna U (PA)
Swarthmore Coll (PA)
Sweet Briar Coll (VA)
Syracuse U (NY)
Taylor U (IN)
Temple U (PA)
Tennessee State U (TN)
Tennessee Technological U (TN)
Texas A&M International U (TX)
Texas A&M U (TX)
Texas A&M U–Commerce (TX)
Texas A&M U–Kingsville (TX)
Texas Christian U (TX)
Texas Lutheran U (TX)
Texas Southern U (TX)
Texas Tech U (TX)
Texas Wesleyan U (TX)
Texas Woman's U (TX)
Thiel Coll (PA)
Towson U (MD)
Transylvania U (KY)
Trent U (ON, Canada)
Trinity Christian Coll (IL)
Trinity Coll (CT)
Trinity U (TX)
Truman State U (MO)
Tufts U (MA)
Tulane U (LA)
Union Coll (NE)
Union U (TN)
United States Military Academy (NY)
Universidad Adventista de las Antillas (PR)
Universidad del Turabo (PR)
Université de Montréal (PQ, Canada)
Université Laval (PQ, Canada)
The U of Akron (OH)
The U of Alabama (AL)
The U of Alabama at Birmingham (AL)
The U of Alabama in Huntsville (AL)
U of Alaska Fairbanks (AK)
U of Alberta (AB, Canada)
The U of Arizona (AZ)
U of Arkansas (AR)
U of Arkansas at Little Rock (AR)
U of British Columbia (BC, Canada)
U of Calgary (AB, Canada)
U of Calif, Berkeley (CA)
U of Calif, Davis (CA)
U of Calif, Irvine (CA)
U of Calif, Los Angeles (CA)
U of Calif, Riverside (CA)
U of Calif, San Diego (CA)
U of Calif, Santa Barbara (CA)
U of Calif, Santa Cruz (CA)
U of Central Arkansas (AR)
U of Central Florida (FL)
U of Central Oklahoma (OK)

Majors Index
Spanish–Special Education

U of Chicago (IL)
U of Cincinnati (OH)
U of Colorado at Boulder (CO)
U of Colorado at Colorado Springs (CO)
U of Colorado at Denver (CO)
U of Connecticut (CT)
U of Dallas (TX)
U of Dayton (OH)
U of Delaware (DE)
U of Denver (CO)
U of Evansville (IN)
The U of Findlay (OH)
U of Florida (FL)
U of Georgia (GA)
U of Guelph (ON, Canada)
U of Hawaii at Manoa (HI)
U of Houston (TX)
U of Idaho (ID)
U of Illinois at Chicago (IL)
U of Illinois at Urbana–Champaign (IL)
U of Indianapolis (IN)
The U of Iowa (IA)
U of Kansas (KS)
U of Kentucky (KY)
U of King's Coll (NS, Canada)
U of La Verne (CA)
U of Louisiana at Monroe (LA)
U of Louisville (KY)
U of Maine (ME)
U of Manitoba (MB, Canada)
U of Mary Hardin-Baylor (TX)
U of Maryland, Baltimore County (MD)
U of Maryland, Coll Park (MD)
U of Massachusetts Amherst (MA)
U of Massachusetts Boston (MA)
U of Massachusetts Dartmouth (MA)
U of Miami (FL)
U of Michigan (MI)
U of Michigan–Dearborn (MI)
U of Michigan–Flint (MI)
U of Minnesota, Duluth (MN)
U of Minnesota, Morris (MN)
U of Minnesota, Twin Cities Campus (MN)
U of Mississippi (MS)
U of Missouri–Columbia (MO)
U of Missouri–Kansas City (MO)
U of Missouri–St. Louis (MO)
U of Mobile (AL)
The U of Montana–Missoula (MT)
U of Montevallo (AL)
U of Nebraska at Kearney (NE)
U of Nebraska at Omaha (NE)
U of Nebraska–Lincoln (NE)
U of Nevada, Las Vegas (NV)
U of Nevada, Reno (NV)
U of New Brunswick, Fredericton (NB, Canada)
U of New Hampshire (NH)
U of New Mexico (NM)
U of New Orleans (LA)
The U of North Carolina at Asheville (NC)
The U of North Carolina at Charlotte (NC)
The U of North Carolina at Greensboro (NC)
The U of North Carolina at Wilmington (NC)
U of North Dakota (ND)
U of Northern Colorado (CO)
U of Northern Iowa (IA)
U of North Florida (FL)
U of North Texas (TX)
U of Notre Dame (IN)
U of Oklahoma (OK)
U of Oregon (OR)
U of Pennsylvania (PA)
U of Pittsburgh (PA)
U of Portland (OR)
U of Prince Edward Island (PE, Canada)
U of Puerto Rico, Río Piedras (PR)
U of Puget Sound (WA)
U of Redlands (CA)
U of Rhode Island (RI)
U of Richmond (VA)
U of Rochester (NY)
U of St. Thomas (MN)
U of St. Thomas (TX)
U of San Diego (CA)
U of San Francisco (CA)
The U of Scranton (PA)

U of South Alabama (AL)
U of South Carolina (SC)
U of South Carolina Spartanburg (SC)
U of South Dakota (SD)
U of Southern California (CA)
U of Southern Colorado (CO)
U of Southern Indiana (IN)
U of South Florida (FL)
The U of Tampa (FL)
The U of Tennessee at Chattanooga (TN)
The U of Tennessee at Martin (TN)
The U of Tennessee Knoxville (TN)
The U of Texas at Arlington (TX)
The U of Texas at Austin (TX)
The U of Texas at San Antonio (TX)
The U of Texas at Tyler (TX)
The U of Texas–Pan American (TX)
U of the District of Columbia (DC)
U of the Pacific (CA)
U of the Sacred Heart (PR)
U of the South (TN)
U of Toronto (ON, Canada)
U of Tulsa (OK)
U of Utah (UT)
U of Vermont (VT)
U of Victoria (BC, Canada)
U of Virginia (VA)
U of Virginia's Coll at Wise (VA)
U of Washington (WA)
U of Waterloo (ON, Canada)
The U of Western Ontario (ON, Canada)
U of Windsor (ON, Canada)
U of Wisconsin–Eau Claire (WI)
U of Wisconsin–Green Bay (WI)
U of Wisconsin–La Crosse (WI)
U of Wisconsin–Madison (WI)
U of Wisconsin–Milwaukee (WI)
U of Wisconsin–Parkside (WI)
U of Wisconsin–Platteville (WI)
U of Wisconsin–River Falls (WI)
U of Wisconsin–Stevens Point (WI)
U of Wisconsin–Whitewater (WI)
U of Wyoming (WY)
Ursinus Coll (PA)
Utah State U (UT)
Valdosta State U (GA)
Valley City State U (ND)
Valparaiso U (IN)
Vanderbilt U (TN)
Vanguard U of Southern California (CA)
Villanova U (PA)
Virginia Commonwealth U (VA)
Virginia Polytechnic Inst and State U (VA)
Virginia Wesleyan Coll (VA)
Wabash Coll (IN)
Wagner Coll (NY)
Wake Forest U (NC)
Walla Walla Coll (WA)
Walsh U (OH)
Wartburg Coll (IA)
Washington & Jefferson Coll (PA)
Washington and Lee U (VA)
Washington Coll (MD)
Washington State U (WA)
Washington U in St. Louis (MO)
Wayland Baptist U (TX)
Wayne State Coll (NE)
Wayne State U (MI)
Weber State U (UT)
Webster U (MO)
Wellesley Coll (MA)
Wells Coll (NY)
Wesleyan Coll (GA)
Wesleyan U (CT)
West Chester U of Pennsylvania (PA)
Western Carolina U (NC)
Western Connecticut State U (CT)
Western Illinois U (IL)
Western Kentucky U (KY)
Western Maryland Coll (MD)
Western Michigan U (MI)
Western Oregon U (OR)
Western State Coll of Colorado (CO)
Western Washington U (WA)
Westminster Coll (MO)
Westminster Coll (PA)
Westmont Coll (CA)
West Texas A&M U (TX)
Wheaton Coll (IL)

Wheeling Jesuit U (WV)
Whitman Coll (WA)
Whittier Coll (CA)
Whitworth Coll (WA)
Wichita State U (KS)
Widener U (PA)
Wilfrid Laurier U (ON, Canada)
Wilkes U (PA)
Willamette U (OR)
William Jewell Coll (MO)
William Paterson U of New Jersey (NJ)
Williams Coll (MA)
William Woods U (MO)
Wilmington Coll (OH)
Wingate U (NC)
Winona State U (MN)
Winston-Salem State U (NC)
Wisconsin Lutheran Coll (WI)
Wittenberg U (OH)
Wofford Coll (SC)
Worcester State Coll (MA)
Wright State U (OH)
Xavier U (OH)
Xavier U of Louisiana (LA)
Yale U (CT)
York Coll of Pennsylvania (PA)
York Coll of the City U of New York (NY)
York U (ON, Canada)
Youngstown State U (OH)

SPANISH LANGUAGE EDUCATION

Abilene Christian U (TX)
Adams State Coll (CO)
Anderson U (IN)
Arkansas State U (AR)
Bayamón Central U (PR)
Baylor U (TX)
Berea Coll (KY)
Berry Coll (GA)
Blue Mountain Coll (MS)
Bowling Green State U (OH)
Bridgewater Coll (VA)
Brigham Young U (UT)
Canisius Coll (NY)
Carroll Coll (MT)
The Catholic U of America (DC)
Cedarville Coll (OH)
Central Michigan U (MI)
Central Missouri State U (MO)
The Coll of New Jersey (NJ)
Coll of St. Catherine (MN)
Colorado State U (CO)
Concordia Coll (MN)
Concordia U (NE)
Daemen Coll (NY)
Duquesne U (PA)
East Carolina U (NC)
Eastern Michigan U (MI)
East Texas Baptist U (TX)
Elmhurst Coll (IL)
Elmira Coll (NY)
Flagler Coll (FL)
Framingham State Coll (MA)
Georgia Southern U (GA)
Grace Coll (IN)
Greensboro Coll (NC)
Greenville Coll (IL)
Hardin-Simmons U (TX)
Indiana U Bloomington (IN)
Indiana U Northwest (IN)
Indiana U–Purdue U Indianapolis (IN)
Indiana U South Bend (IN)
Inter American U of PR, Aguadilla Campus (PR)
Ithaca Coll (NY)
King Coll (TN)
La Roche Coll (PA)
Luther Coll (IA)
Malone Coll (OH)
Manhattanville Coll (NY)
Mansfield U of Pennsylvania (PA)
Marymount Coll (NY)
Maryville Coll (TN)
Messiah Coll (PA)
MidAmerica Nazarene U (KS)
Minnesota State U Moorhead (MN)
Missouri Western State Coll (MO)
Molloy Coll (NY)
Niagara U (NY)
North Carolina Central U (NC)
North Carolina State U (NC)
North Dakota State U (ND)
Ohio U (OH)

Oklahoma Baptist U (OK)
Piedmont Coll (GA)
Plymouth State Coll (NH)
St. Ambrose U (IA)
St. John's U (NY)
St. Olaf Coll (MN)
Salve Regina U (RI)
Seton Hill Coll (PA)
Southeastern Louisiana U (LA)
Southeastern Oklahoma State U (OK)
Southern Arkansas U–Magnolia (AR)
Southwest Missouri State U (MO)
Texas A&M International U (TX)
The U of Arizona (AZ)
U of Central Arkansas (AR)
U of Illinois at Chicago (IL)
U of Illinois at Urbana–Champaign (IL)
U of Indianapolis (IN)
The U of Iowa (IA)
U of Minnesota, Duluth (MN)
U of Nebraska–Lincoln (NE)
The U of North Carolina at Chapel Hill (NC)
The U of North Carolina at Charlotte (NC)
U of North Texas (TX)
U of Southern Colorado (CO)
The U of Tennessee at Martin (TN)
U of Wisconsin–River Falls (WI)
Washington U in St. Louis (MO)
Weber State U (UT)
Western Carolina U (NC)
Wheeling Jesuit U (WV)
Youngstown State U (OH)

SPECIAL EDUCATION

Abilene Christian U (TX)
Alabama A&M U (AL)
Alabama State U (AL)
Albany State U (GA)
Alderson-Broaddus Coll (WV)
American International Coll (MA)
American U (DC)
American U of Puerto Rico (PR)
Aquinas Coll (MI)
Arizona State U (AZ)
Arizona State U West (AZ)
Arkansas State U (AR)
Armstrong Atlantic State U (GA)
Ashland U (OH)
Athens State U (AL)
Augustana Coll (SD)
Augusta State U (GA)
Austin Peay State U (TN)
Avila Coll (MO)
Baldwin-Wallace Coll (OH)
Ball State U (IN)
Barat Coll (IL)
Barry U (FL)
Barton Coll (NC)
Bayamón Central U (PR)
Baylor U (TX)
Beaver Coll (PA)
Bellarmine Coll (KY)
Belmont Abbey Coll (NC)
Belmont U (TN)
Benedictine Coll (KS)
Benedictine U (IL)
Bennett Coll (NC)
Bethel Coll (TN)
Bethune-Cookman Coll (FL)
Black Hills State U (SD)
Bloomsburg U of Pennsylvania (PA)
Bluffton Coll (OH)
Boise State U (ID)
Boston Coll (MA)
Boston U (MA)
Bowie State U (MD)
Bowling Green State U (OH)
Brenau U (GA)
Brescia U (KY)
Bridgewater Coll (VA)
Bridgewater State Coll (MA)
Brigham Young U–Hawaii Campus (HI)
Buena Vista U (IA)
Cabrini Coll (PA)
California State U, Northridge (CA)
California U of Pennsylvania (PA)
Calvin Coll (MI)
Canisius Coll (NY)
Cardinal Stritch U (WI)
Carlow Coll (PA)

Carson-Newman Coll (TN)
Carthage Coll (WI)
Cedarville Coll (OH)
Centenary Coll (NJ)
Central Connecticut State U (CT)
Central Missouri State U (MO)
Cheyney U of Pennsylvania (PA)
Chicago State U (IL)
City Coll of the City U of NY (NY)
Clarion U of Pennsylvania (PA)
Clarke Coll (IA)
Clemson U (SC)
Cleveland State U (OH)
Coll Misericordia (PA)
Coll of Charleston (SC)
Coll of Mount St. Joseph (OH)
Coll of Mount Saint Vincent (NY)
The Coll of New Jersey (NJ)
The Coll of New Rochelle (NY)
Coll of Notre Dame of Maryland (MD)
Coll of Our Lady of the Elms (MA)
Coll of Saint Elizabeth (NJ)
Coll of St. Joseph (VT)
Coll of Saint Mary (NE)
The Coll of Saint Rose (NY)
Coll of the Southwest (NM)
Columbia Coll (SC)
Columbus State U (GA)
Concord Coll (WV)
Concordia U (NE)
Converse Coll (SC)
Coppin State Coll (MD)
Creighton U (NE)
Culver-Stockton Coll (MO)
Cumberland Coll (KY)
Curry Coll (MA)
Daemen Coll (NY)
Dakota State U (SD)
Dakota Wesleyan U (SD)
Dana Coll (NE)
Defiance Coll (OH)
Delaware State U (DE)
Delta State U (MS)
Doane Coll (NE)
Dominican Coll of Blauvelt (NY)
Dowling Coll (NY)
Duquesne U (PA)
D'Youville Coll (NY)
East Central U (OK)
Eastern Illinois U (IL)
Eastern Kentucky U (KY)
Eastern Mennonite U (VA)
Eastern Michigan U (MI)
Eastern Nazarene Coll (MA)
Eastern New Mexico U (NM)
Eastern Oregon U (OR)
Eastern Washington U (WA)
East Stroudsburg U of Pennsylvania (PA)
East Tennessee State U (TN)
Edinboro U of Pennsylvania (PA)
Elizabeth City State U (NC)
Elmhurst Coll (IL)
Elon Coll (NC)
Erskine Coll (SC)
Evangel U (MO)
Fairmont State Coll (WV)
Felician Coll (NJ)
Fitchburg State Coll (MA)
Florida Atlantic U (FL)
Florida Gulf Coast U (FL)
Fontbonne Coll (MO)
Freed-Hardeman U (TN)
Furman U (SC)
Gannon U (PA)
Geneva Coll (PA)
Georgia Coll and State U (GA)
Georgian Court Coll (NJ)
Georgia Southern U (GA)
Georgia Southwestern State U (GA)
Glenville State Coll (WV)
Gonzaga U (WA)
Gordon Coll (MA)
Grand Canyon U (AZ)
Grand Valley State U (MI)
Grand View Coll (IA)
Green Mountain Coll (VT)
Greensboro Coll (NC)
Greenville Coll (IL)
Gwynedd-Mercy Coll (PA)
Hampton U (VA)
Hastings Coll (NE)
Heidelberg Coll (OH)
High Point U (NC)
Holy Family Coll (PA)

Peterson's Guide to Four-Year Colleges 2001

Majors Index
Special Education–Speech-Language Pathology/Audiology

Hood Coll (MD)
Houston Baptist U (TX)
Huntington Coll (IN)
Idaho State U (ID)
Illinois State U (IL)
Indiana State U (IN)
Indiana U Bloomington (IN)
Indiana U of Pennsylvania (PA)
Indiana U South Bend (IN)
Indiana U Southeast (IN)
Indiana Wesleyan U (IN)
Inter American U of PR, Arecibo Campus (PR)
Inter American U of PR, Fajardo Campus (PR)
Inter American U of PR, Metropolitan Campus (PR)
Inter American U of PR, San Germán Campus (PR)
Iona Coll (NY)
Jacksonville State U (AL)
Jacksonville U (FL)
James Madison U (VA)
Jarvis Christian Coll (TX)
John Brown U (AR)
John Carroll U (OH)
Johnson Bible Coll (TN)
Juniata Coll (PA)
Kean U (NJ)
Keene State Coll (NH)
Kent State U (OH)
Keuka Coll (NY)
King's Coll (PA)
Kutztown U of Pennsylvania (PA)
Lamar U (TX)
Lambuth (TN)
Lander U (SC)
Langston U (OK)
La Salle U (PA)
Lasell Coll (MA)
La Sierra U (CA)
Lee U (TN)
Lesley Coll (MA)
Lewis-Clark State Coll (ID)
Liberty U (VA)
Lincoln U (MO)
Lindenwood U (MO)
Lock Haven U of Pennsylvania (PA)
Long Island U, Brooklyn Campus (NY)
Long Island U, C.W. Post Campus (NY)
Long Island U, Southampton Coll, Friends World Program (NY)
Longwood Coll (VA)
Loras Coll (IA)
Louisiana Coll (LA)
Louisiana State U in Shreveport (LA)
Louisiana Tech U (LA)
Loyola Coll in Maryland (MD)
Loyola U Chicago (IL)
Luther Coll (IA)
Lynchburg Coll (VA)
Lyndon State Coll (VT)
MacMurray Coll (IL)
Madonna U (MI)
Manchester Coll (IN)
Manhattan Coll (NY)
Mansfield U of Pennsylvania (PA)
Marian Coll (IN)
Marist Coll (NY)
Marymount Coll (NY)
Marywood U (PA)
McNeese State U (LA)
McPherson Coll (KS)
Medgar Evers Coll of the City U of NY (NY)
Memorial U of Newfoundland (NF, Canada)
Mercy Coll (NY)
Mercyhurst Coll (PA)
Methodist Coll (NC)
Miami (OH)
Michigan State U (MI)
Middle Tennessee State U (TN)
Millersville U of Pennsylvania (PA)
Milligan Coll (TN)
Minnesota State U Moorhead (MN)
Minot State U (ND)
Mississippi Coll (MS)
Mississippi State U (MS)
Mississippi U for Women (MS)
Missouri Southern State Coll (MO)
Missouri Valley Coll (MO)
Molloy Coll (NY)

Monmouth Coll (IL)
Monmouth U (NJ)
Montana State U–Billings (MT)
Morehead State U (KY)
Morningside Coll (IA)
Mount Marty Coll (SD)
Mount Saint Mary Coll (NY)
Mount Vernon Nazarene Coll (OH)
Murray State U (KY)
Muskingum Coll (OH)
Nazareth Coll of Rochester (NY)
Nebraska Wesleyan U (NE)
Newberry Coll (SC)
New England Coll (NH)
New Jersey City U (NJ)
New Mexico Highlands U (NM)
New Mexico State U (NM)
New York U (NY)
Niagara U (NY)
Nicholls State U (LA)
Norfolk State U (VA)
North Carolina Ag and Tech State U (NC)
Northeastern Illinois U (IL)
Northeastern State U (OK)
Northern Arizona U (AZ)
Northern Illinois U (IL)
Northern Kentucky U (KY)
Northern Michigan U (MI)
Northern State U (SD)
North Georgia Coll & State U (GA)
Northwest Coll (WA)
Northwestern Oklahoma State U (OK)
Northwestern State U of Louisiana (LA)
Northwest Missouri State U (MO)
Notre Dame Coll (NH)
Nova Southeastern U (FL)
Ohio Dominican Coll (OH)
The Ohio State U (OH)
Oklahoma Baptist U (OK)
Oklahoma Christian U of Science and Arts (OK)
Ouachita Baptist U (AR)
Our Lady of the Lake U of San Antonio (TX)
Pacific Lutheran U (WA)
Pacific Oaks Coll (CA)
Penn State U Univ Park Campus (PA)
Peru State Coll (NE)
Pfeiffer U (NC)
Philander Smith Coll (AR)
Piedmont Coll (GA)
Plattsburgh State U of NY (NY)
Plymouth State Coll (NH)
Pontifical Catholic U of Puerto Rico (PR)
Presbyterian Coll (SC)
Providence Coll (RI)
Purdue U Calumet (IN)
Quincy U (IL)
Rivier Coll (NH)
Rowan U (NJ)
Russell Sage Coll (NY)
Saginaw Valley State U (MI)
Saint Augustine's Coll (NC)
St. Cloud State U (MN)
St. John's U (NY)
Saint Joseph Coll (CT)
St. Joseph's Coll, New York (NY)
St. Joseph's Coll, Suffolk Campus (NY)
Saint Leo U (FL)
Saint Louis U (MO)
Saint Martin's Coll (WA)
Saint Mary-of-the-Woods Coll (IN)
Salve Regina U (RI)
Seattle Pacific U (WA)
Seton Hall U (NJ)
Seton Hill Coll (PA)
Simmons Coll (MA)
Slippery Rock U of Pennsylvania (PA)
Southeastern Coll of the Assemblies of God (FL)
Southeastern Louisiana U (LA)
Southeastern Oklahoma State U (OK)
Southeast Missouri State U (MO)
Southern Illinois U Carbondale (IL)
Southern Illinois U Edwardsville (IL)
Southern Utah U (UT)
Southern Wesleyan U (SC)
Southwestern Oklahoma State U (OK)

Southwest Missouri State U (MO)
Spalding U (KY)
State U of NY at New Paltz (NY)
State U of NY Coll at Buffalo (NY)
State U of NY Coll at Geneseo (NY)
State U of NY Coll at Old Westbury (NY)
State U of West Georgia (GA)
Syracuse U (NY)
Tabor Coll (KS)
Temple U (PA)
Tennessee State U (TN)
Tennessee Technological U (TN)
Texas A&M International U (TX)
Texas A&M U–Commerce (TX)
Texas Christian U (TX)
Texas Southern U (TX)
Touro Coll (NY)
Towson U (MD)
Trinity Christian Coll (IL)
Trinity Coll of Vermont (VT)
Troy State U (AL)
Troy State U Dothan (AL)
Tufts U (MA)
Tusculum Coll (TN)
Union Coll (KY)
Union U (TN)
Universidad del Turabo (PR)
Universidad Metropolitana (PR)
Université de Montréal (PQ, Canada)
Université de Sherbrooke (PQ, Canada)
U du Québec à Chicoutimi (PQ, Canada)
U du Québec à Hull (PQ, Canada)
U du Québec en Abitibi-Témiscamingue (PQ, Canada)
The U of Akron (OH)
The U of Alabama (AL)
The U of Alabama at Birmingham (AL)
The U of Arizona (AZ)
U of Arkansas (AR)
U of Arkansas at Monticello (AR)
U of Arkansas at Pine Bluff (AR)
U of British Columbia (BC, Canada)
U of Central Arkansas (AR)
U of Central Florida (FL)
U of Central Oklahoma (OK)
U of Cincinnati (OH)
U of Connecticut (CT)
U of Dayton (OH)
U of Delaware (DE)
U of Detroit Mercy (MI)
U of Evansville (IN)
The U of Findlay (OH)
U of Florida (FL)
U of Georgia (GA)
U of Hartford (CT)
U of Idaho (ID)
U of Illinois at Urbana–Champaign (IL)
U of Kentucky (KY)
The U of Lethbridge (AB, Canada)
U of Louisiana at Lafayette (LA)
U of Louisiana at Monroe (LA)
U of Maine at Farmington (ME)
U of Mary Hardin-Baylor (TX)
U of Maryland, Coll Park (MD)
The U of Memphis (TN)
U of Miami (FL)
U of Minnesota, Duluth (MN)
U of Mississippi (MS)
U of Missouri–St. Louis (MO)
U of Nebraska at Kearney (NE)
U of Nebraska at Omaha (NE)
U of Nebraska–Lincoln (NE)
U of Nevada, Las Vegas (NV)
U of Nevada, Reno (NV)
U of New Brunswick, Fredericton (NB, Canada)
U of New Mexico (NM)
U of North Alabama (AL)
The U of North Carolina at Pembroke (NC)
The U of North Carolina at Wilmington (NC)
U of Northern Iowa (IA)
U of North Florida (FL)
U of North Texas (TX)
U of Oklahoma (OK)
U of Regina (SK, Canada)
U of St. Francis (IL)

U of Saint Francis (IN)
The U of Scranton (PA)
U of South Alabama (AL)
U of South Dakota (SD)
U of Southern Mississippi (MS)
U of South Florida (FL)
The U of Tennessee at Chattanooga (TN)
The U of Tennessee at Martin (TN)
The U of Tennessee Knoxville (TN)
The U of Texas–Pan American (TX)
U of the District of Columbia (DC)
U of the Pacific (CA)
U of Victoria (BC, Canada)
The U of West Alabama (AL)
The U of Western Ontario (ON, Canada)
U of West Florida (FL)
U of Windsor (ON, Canada)
U of Wisconsin–Eau Claire (WI)
U of Wisconsin–Madison (WI)
U of Wisconsin–Milwaukee (WI)
U of Wisconsin–Superior (WI)
U of Wisconsin–Whitewater (WI)
U of Wyoming (WY)
Upper Iowa U (IA)
Utah State U (UT)
Valdosta State U (GA)
Vanderbilt U (TN)
Virginia Commonwealth U (VA)
Virginia Union U (VA)
Walsh U (OH)
Warner Southern Coll (FL)
Washington State U (WA)
Wayne State Coll (NE)
Wayne State U (MI)
Webster U (MO)
West Chester U of Pennsylvania (PA)
Western Carolina U (NC)
Western Illinois U (IL)
Western Kentucky U (KY)
Western State Coll of Colorado (CO)
Western Washington U (WA)
Westfield State Coll (MA)
Westminster Coll (UT)
Wheelock Coll (MA)
Whitworth Coll (WA)
William Paterson U of New Jersey (NJ)
William Penn U (IA)
William Woods U (MO)
Winona State U (MN)
Winston-Salem State U (NC)
Winthrop U (SC)
Wittenberg U (OH)
Wright State U (OH)
Xavier U (OH)
Xavier U of Louisiana (LA)
York U (ON, Canada)
Youngstown State U (OH)

SPEECH EDUCATION
Abilene Christian U (TX)
Anderson U (IN)
Arkansas Tech U (AR)
Baylor U (TX)
Bowling Green State U (OH)
Cedarville Coll (OH)
Central Michigan U (MI)
Central Missouri State U (MO)
Coll of St. Catherine (MN)
Colorado State U (CO)
Concordia Coll (MN)
Concordia U (IL)
Concordia U (NE)
Dana Coll (NE)
East Texas Baptist U (TX)
Elmira Coll (NY)
Emporia State U (KS)
Greenville Coll (IL)
Hastings Coll (NE)
Howard Payne U (TX)
Indiana U Bloomington (IN)
Indiana U–Purdue U Fort Wayne (IN)
Indiana U–Purdue U Indianapolis (IN)
Ithaca Coll (NY)
Louisiana Tech U (LA)
Malone Coll (OH)
Minnesota State U Moorhead (MN)
Northwest Nazarene U (ID)
Ohio U (OH)
Oklahoma Baptist U (OK)
Saint Mary's U of Minnesota (MN)

St. Olaf Coll (MN)
Samford U (AL)
Southeastern Louisiana U (LA)
Southeastern Oklahoma State U (OK)
Southwest Missouri State U (MO)
Southwest State U (MN)
Texas Wesleyan U (TX)
The U of Arizona (AZ)
U of Arkansas (AR)
U of Central Arkansas (AR)
U of Illinois at Urbana–Champaign (IL)
U of Indianapolis (IN)
The U of Iowa (IA)
U of Louisiana at Monroe (LA)
U of Maryland, Coll Park (MD)
U of Nebraska–Lincoln (NE)
U of North Carolina at Chapel Hill (NC)
U of North Texas (TX)
U of Rio Grande (OH)
William Jewell Coll (MO)
Youngstown State U (OH)

SPEECH-LANGUAGE PATHOLOGY
Brigham Young U (UT)
Central Missouri State U (MO)
Duquesne U (PA)
Emerson U (MA)
James Madison U (VA)
Louisiana Coll (LA)
Loyola Coll in Maryland (MD)
Miami U (OH)
Rockhurst U (MO)
Saint Louis U (MO)
Saint Xavier U (IL)
U of Maryland, Coll Park (MD)
U of Nebraska at Omaha (NE)
U of Nebraska–Lincoln (NE)
U of Nevada, Reno (NV)
U of Northern Colorado (CO)
U of Northern Iowa (IA)
U of Science and Arts of Oklahoma (OK)
The U of Tennessee Knoxville (TN)
Wayne State U (MI)

SPEECH-LANGUAGE PATHOLOGY/AUDIOLOGY
Abilene Christian U (TX)
Adelphi U (NY)
Andrews U (MI)
Appalachian State U (NC)
Arkansas State U (AR)
Auburn U (AL)
Augustana Coll (IL)
Augustana Coll (SD)
Baldwin-Wallace Coll (OH)
Ball State U (IN)
Brescia U (KY)
Brooklyn Coll of the City U of NY (NY)
Butler U (IN)
California State U, Fresno (CA)
California State U, Fullerton (CA)
California State U, Hayward (CA)
California State U, Long Beach (CA)
California State U, Northridge (CA)
California State U, Sacramento (CA)
Calvin Coll (MI)
Centenary Coll of Louisiana (LA)
Central Michigan U (MI)
Clarion U of Pennsylvania (PA)
Cleveland State U (OH)
Coll of Our Lady of the Elms (MA)
The Coll of Wooster (OH)
Columbia Coll (SC)
Delta State U (MS)
East Carolina U (NC)
Eastern Illinois U (IL)
Eastern Kentucky U (KY)
Eastern New Mexico U (NM)
Eastern Washington U (WA)
East Stroudsburg U of Pennsylvania (PA)
Elmhurst Coll (IL)
Elmira Coll (NY)
Emerson Coll (MA)
Florida Atlantic U (FL)
Florida State U (FL)
Fontbonne Coll (MO)
Fort Hays State U (KS)
Geneva Coll (PA)

Majors Index
Speech-Language Pathology/Audiology–Speech/Rhetorical Studies

The George Washington U (DC)
Governors State U (IL)
Hampton U (VA)
Hardin-Simmons U (TX)
Hofstra U (NY)
Idaho State U (ID)
Illinois State U (IL)
Indiana State U (IN)
Indiana U Bloomington (IN)
Indiana U–Purdue U Fort Wayne (IN)
Iona Coll (NY)
Ithaca Coll (NY)
Kent State U (OH)
Kutztown U of Pennsylvania (PA)
Lamar U (TX)
Lambuth U (TN)
La Salle U (PA)
Lehman Coll of the City U of NY (NY)
Loma Linda U (CA)
Long Island U, C.W. Post Campus (NY)
Louisiana State U and A&M Coll (LA)
Louisiana State U in Shreveport (LA)
Louisiana Tech U (LA)
Marquette U (WI)
Marshall U (WV)
Marymount Manhattan Coll (NY)
Marywood U (PA)
Mercy Coll (NY)
Miami U (OH)
Michigan State U (MI)
Minnesota State U, Mankato (MN)
Minnesota State U Moorhead (MN)
Minot State U (ND)
Mississippi U for Women (MS)
Molloy Coll (NY)
Murray State U (KY)
Nazareth Coll of Rochester (NY)
New Mexico State U (NM)
New York U (NY)
Norfolk State U (VA)
Northeastern State U (OK)
Northeastern U (MA)
Northern Michigan U (MI)
Northern State U (SD)
Northwestern U (IL)
Northwest Nazarene U (ID)
The Ohio State U (OH)
Ohio U (OH)
Oklahoma State U (OK)
Old Dominion U (VA)
Ouachita Baptist U (AR)
Our Lady of the Lake U of San Antonio (TX)
Pace U, New York City Campus (NY)
Pace U, Pleasantville/Briarcliff Campus (NY)
Pacific Union Coll (CA)
Penn State U Univ Park Campus (PA)
Plattsburgh State U of NY (NY)
Purdue U (IN)
Queens Coll of the City U of NY (NY)
The Richard Stockton Coll of New Jersey (NJ)
St. Cloud State U (MN)
St. John's U (NY)
Saint Louis U (MO)
San Diego State U (CA)
San Francisco State U (CA)
San Jose State U (CA)
Shaw U (NC)
Southeast Missouri State U (MO)
Southern Illinois U Edwardsville (IL)
Southwest Missouri State U (MO)
Southwest Texas State U (TX)
State U of NY at Buffalo (NY)
State U of NY at New Paltz (NY)
State U of NY Coll at Buffalo (NY)
State U of NY Coll at Cortland (NY)
State U of NY Coll at Fredonia (NY)
State U of NY Coll at Geneseo (NY)
Stephen F. Austin State U (TX)
Syracuse U (NY)
Temple U (PA)
Tennessee State U (TN)
Texas Christian U (TX)
Texas Woman's U (TX)
Thiel Coll (PA)

Towson U (MD)
Université de Montréal (PQ, Canada)
The U of Akron (OH)
The U of Alabama (AL)
U of Arkansas at Little Rock (AR)
U of Central Arkansas (AR)
U of Central Florida (FL)
U of Central Oklahoma (OK)
U of Cincinnati (OH)
U of Florida (FL)
U of Hawaii at Manoa (HI)
U of Houston (TX)
U of Illinois at Urbana–Champaign (IL)
The U of Iowa (IA)
U of Kentucky (KY)
U of Louisiana at Lafayette (LA)
U of Louisiana at Monroe (LA)
U of Maryland, Coll Park (MD)
U of Minnesota, Duluth (MN)
U of Minnesota, Twin Cities Campus (MN)
U of Mississippi (MS)
The U of Montana–Missoula (MT)
U of Montevallo (AL)
U of Nebraska at Omaha (NE)
U of Nevada, Reno (NV)
U of New Hampshire (NH)
U of New Mexico (NM)
The U of North Carolina at Greensboro (NC)
U of North Dakota (ND)
U of North Texas (TX)
U of Oklahoma Health Sciences Center (OK)
U of Oregon (OR)
U of Redlands (CA)
U of South Alabama (AL)
U of South Dakota (SD)
U of Southern Mississippi (MS)
The U of Tennessee Knoxville (TN)
The U of Texas at Dallas (TX)
The U of Texas–Pan American (TX)
U of the District of Columbia (DC)
U of the Pacific (CA)
U of Tulsa (OK)
U of Utah (UT)
U of Vermont (VT)
U of Virginia (VA)
U of Washington (WA)
U of Wisconsin–Milwaukee (WI)
U of Wisconsin–Stevens Point (WI)
U of Wyoming (WY)
Utah State U (UT)
Valdosta State U (GA)
Washington State U (WA)
West Chester U of Pennsylvania (PA)
Western Kentucky U (KY)
Western Michigan U (MI)
Western Washington U (WA)
West Virginia U (WV)
Wichita State U (KS)
Worcester State Coll (MA)
Xavier U of Louisiana (LA)
Yeshiva U (NY)

SPEECH/RHETORICAL STUDIES

Abilene Christian U (TX)
Adams State Coll (CO)
Alabama State U (AL)
Albany State U (GA)
Alderson-Broaddus Coll (WV)
Anderson Coll (SC)
Appalachian State U (NC)
Arkansas State U (AR)
Arkansas Tech U (AR)
Asbury Coll (KY)
Ashland U (OH)
Auburn U (AL)
Augsburg Coll (MN)
Augustana Coll (IL)
Austin Coll (TX)
Baker U (KS)
Ball State U (IN)
Bates Coll (ME)
Baylor U (TX)
Belmont U (TN)
Bemidji State U (MN)
Berry Coll (GA)
Bethel Coll (MN)
Blackburn Coll (IL)
Black Hills State U (SD)
Bloomsburg U of Pennsylvania (PA)
Blue Mountain Coll (MS)

Bluffton Coll (OH)
Bowling Green State U (OH)
Brooklyn Coll of the City U of NY (NY)
Buena Vista U (IA)
Butler U (IN)
California Lutheran U (CA)
California Polytechnic State U, San Luis Obispo (CA)
California State U, Chico (CA)
California State U, Fresno (CA)
California State U, Fullerton (CA)
California State U, Hayward (CA)
California State U, Long Beach (CA)
California State U, Los Angeles (CA)
California State U, Northridge (CA)
Calvin Coll (MI)
Cameron U (OK)
Capital U (OH)
Carson-Newman Coll (TN)
Carthage Coll (WI)
Cedarville Coll (OH)
Centenary Coll of Louisiana (LA)
Central Michigan U (MI)
Central Missouri State U (MO)
Chadron State Coll (NE)
Chapman U (CA)
Charleston Southern U (SC)
Clarion U of Pennsylvania (PA)
Clark Atlanta U (GA)
Coe Coll (IA)
The Coll of New Jersey (NJ)
Coll of St. Catherine (MN)
Coll of the Ozarks (MO)
The Coll of Wooster (OH)
Colorado State U (CO)
Concordia Coll (MN)
Concordia U (NE)
Cornell Coll (IA)
Cornerstone U (MI)
Creighton U (NE)
Cumberland Coll (KY)
David Lipscomb U (TN)
Defiance Coll (OH)
Denison U (OH)
Dickinson State U (ND)
Doane Coll (NE)
Dowling Coll (NY)
Drake U (IA)
East Central U (OK)
Eastern Illinois U (IL)
Eastern Kentucky U (KY)
Eastern Michigan U (MI)
Eastern New Mexico U (NM)
Eastern Washington U (WA)
East Stroudsburg U of Pennsylvania (PA)
East Tennessee State U (TN)
East Texas Baptist U (TX)
Emerson Coll (MA)
Evangel U (MO)
Fairmont State Coll (WV)
Fisk U (TN)
Florida Atlantic U (FL)
Friends U (KS)
Frostburg State U (MD)
Geneva Coll (PA)
Georgetown Coll (KY)
The George Washington U (DC)
Georgia Southern U (GA)
Georgia State U (GA)
Gonzaga U (WA)
Graceland Coll (IA)
Grand Canyon U (AZ)
Greenville Coll (IL)
Gustavus Adolphus Coll (MN)
Hannibal-LaGrange Coll (MO)
Harding U (AR)
Hardin-Simmons U (TX)
Hastings Coll (NE)
Henderson State U (AR)
Hillsdale Coll (MI)
Hofstra U (NY)
Houston Baptist U (TX)
Howard Payne U (TX)
Humboldt State U (CA)
Huntingdon Coll (AL)
Illinois Coll (IL)
Illinois State U (IL)
Indiana State U (IN)
Indiana U Bloomington (IN)
Indiana U South Bend (IN)
Iona Coll (NY)

Iowa State U of Science and Technology (IA)
Ithaca Coll (NY)
Judson Coll (IL)
Kent State U (OH)
Kutztown U of Pennsylvania (PA)
La Salle U (PA)
Lehman Coll of the City U of NY (NY)
Lewis-Clark State Coll (ID)
Lewis U (IL)
Lock Haven U of Pennsylvania (PA)
Long Island U, Brooklyn Campus (NY)
Longwood Coll (VA)
Loras Coll (IA)
Louisiana Coll (LA)
Louisiana State U and A&M Coll (LA)
Louisiana State U in Shreveport (LA)
Louisiana Tech U (LA)
Lynchburg Coll (VA)
Manchester Coll (IN)
Mansfield U of Pennsylvania (PA)
Maranatha Baptist Bible Coll (WI)
Marietta Coll (OH)
Marquette U (WI)
Marshall U (WV)
Marymount Coll (NY)
McKendree Coll (IL)
McNeese State U (LA)
Mercy Coll (NY)
Metropolitan State Coll of Denver (CO)
Miami U (OH)
Minnesota State U, Mankato (MN)
Minnesota State U Moorhead (MN)
Mississippi Valley State U (MS)
Missouri Valley Coll (MO)
Missouri Western State Coll (MO)
Monmouth Coll (IL)
Morehead State U (KY)
Morgan State U (MD)
Mount Mercy Coll (IA)
Mount Saint Mary's Coll and Seminary (MD)
Murray State U (KY)
Newberry Coll (SC)
New Mexico State U (NM)
North Carolina Ag and Tech State U (NC)
North Central Coll (IL)
North Dakota State U (ND)
Northeastern Illinois U (IL)
Northern Arizona U (AZ)
Northern Kentucky U (KY)
Northern Michigan U (MI)
Northern State U (SD)
North Park U (IL)
Northwestern Coll (IA)
Northwestern Oklahoma State U (OK)
Northwestern U (IL)
Northwest Missouri State U (MO)
Northwest Nazarene U (ID)
Ohio Northern U (OH)
Ohio U (OH)
Oklahoma Baptist U (OK)
Oklahoma Christian U of Science and Arts (OK)
Oklahoma City U (OK)
Oklahoma State U (OK)
Old Dominion U (VA)
Olivet Nazarene U (IL)
Oregon State U (OR)
Otterbein Coll (OH)
Ouachita Baptist U (AR)
Our Lady of the Lake U of San Antonio (TX)
Pace U, New York City Campus (NY)
Pace U, Pleasantville/Briarcliff Campus (NY)
Penn State U Univ Park Campus (PA)
Pepperdine U, Malibu (CA)
Peru State Coll (NE)
Pittsburg State U (KS)
Point Loma Nazarene U (CA)
Portland State U (OR)
Rensselaer Polytechnic Inst (NY)
Rider U (NJ)
Ripon Coll (WI)
Rowan U (NJ)
St. Cloud State U (MN)

St. John's U (NY)
St. Joseph's Coll, New York (NY)
St. Joseph's Coll, Suffolk Campus (NY)
St. Mary's U of San Antonio (TX)
St. Olaf Coll (MN)
Samford U (AL)
Sam Houston State U (TX)
San Diego State U (CA)
San Francisco State U (CA)
San Jose State U (CA)
Shippensburg U of Pennsylvania (PA)
Simpson Coll (IA)
South Dakota State U (SD)
Southeast Missouri State U (MO)
Southern Illinois U Carbondale (IL)
Southern Illinois U Edwardsville (IL)
Southern Utah U (UT)
Southwest Texas State U (TX)
Spring Arbor Coll (MI)
State U of NY at Albany (NY)
State U of NY at New Paltz (NY)
State U of NY Coll at Brockport (NY)
State U of NY Coll at Cortland (NY)
State U of NY Coll at Oneonta (NY)
State U of NY Coll at Potsdam (NY)
State U of West Georgia (GA)
Stephen F. Austin State U (TX)
Stetson U (FL)
Suffolk U (MA)
Susquehanna U (PA)
Syracuse U (NY)
Temple U (PA)
Texas A&M U (TX)
Texas A&M U–Kingsville (TX)
Texas Christian U (TX)
Texas Southern U (TX)
Texas Tech U (TX)
Texas Wesleyan U (TX)
Trevecca Nazarene U (TN)
Trinity U (TX)
Troy State U (AL)
Truman State U (MO)
Union U (TN)
U Coll of Cape Breton (NS, Canada)
The U of Akron (OH)
The U of Alabama (AL)
The U of Alabama in Huntsville (AL)
U of Alaska Fairbanks (AK)
U of Arkansas at Little Rock (AR)
U of Arkansas at Monticello (AR)
U of Arkansas at Pine Bluff (AR)
U of Calif, Berkeley (CA)
U of Calif, Davis (CA)
U of Central Arkansas (AR)
U of Central Florida (FL)
U of Central Oklahoma (OK)
U of Dubuque (IA)
U of Georgia (GA)
U of Hawaii at Manoa (HI)
U of Houston (TX)
U of Illinois at Chicago (IL)
U of Illinois at Urbana–Champaign (IL)
The U of Iowa (IA)
U of Kansas (KS)
U of Kentucky (KY)
U of Louisiana at Monroe (LA)
U of Maine (ME)
U of Michigan–Dearborn (MI)
U of Minnesota, Morris (MN)
The U of Montana–Missoula (MT)
U of Montevallo (AL)
U of Nebraska at Kearney (NE)
U of Nebraska at Omaha (NE)
U of New Mexico (NM)
U of North Alabama (AL)
The U of North Carolina at Greensboro (NC)
The U of North Carolina at Wilmington (NC)
U of Pittsburgh (PA)
U of Richmond (VA)
U of Sioux Falls (SD)
U of South Dakota (SD)
U of Southern Colorado (CO)
U of South Florida (FL)
The U of Tennessee Knoxville (TN)
The U of Texas at Arlington (TX)
The U of Texas at Austin (TX)
The U of Texas at Tyler (TX)

Majors Index
Speech/Rhetorical Studies–Systems Engineering

The U of Texas–Pan American (TX)
U of the Pacific (CA)
U of the Virgin Islands (VI)
U of Utah (UT)
U of Washington (WA)
U of Waterloo (ON, Canada)
U of Wisconsin–La Crosse (WI)
U of Wisconsin–Platteville (WI)
U of Wisconsin–River Falls (WI)
U of Wisconsin–Superior (WI)
U of Wisconsin–Whitewater (WI)
Utah State U (UT)
Utica Coll of Syracuse U (NY)
Valdosta State U (GA)
Vanguard U of Southern California (CA)
Wabash Coll (IN)
Walla Walla Coll (WA)
Wayne State Coll (NE)
West Chester U of Pennsylvania (PA)
Western Kentucky U (KY)
West Texas A&M U (TX)
West Virginia Wesleyan Coll (WV)
Wheaton Coll (IL)
Whitworth Coll (WA)
Willamette U (OR)
William Jewell Coll (MO)
Wingate U (NC)
Winona State U (MN)
Yeshiva U (NY)
York Coll of Pennsylvania (PA)
York Coll of the City U of New York (NY)
Youngstown State U (OH)

SPEECH THERAPY
Adelphi U (NY)
Auburn U (AL)
Augustana Coll (IL)
Coll of Our Lady of the Elms (MA)
Columbia Coll (SC)
Eastern Kentucky U (KY)
Eastern Washington U (WA)
Emerson Coll (MA)
Fontbonne Coll (MO)
Hampton U (VA)
Indiana State U (IN)
Indiana U Bloomington (IN)
Iona Coll (NY)
Lamar U (TX)
Lambuth U (TN)
Murray State U (KY)
Nicholls State U (LA)
Northeastern State U (OK)
Northwestern U (IL)
Ohio U (OH)
Queens Coll of the City U of NY (NY)
St. Cloud State U (MN)
Southeast Missouri State U (MO)
State U of NY at New Paltz (NY)
State U of NY Coll at Fredonia (NY)
State U of NY Coll at Geneseo (NY)
Temple U (PA)
Texas A&M U–Kingsville (TX)
Texas Southern U (TX)
U of British Columbia (BC, Canada)
U of Central Oklahoma (OK)
The U of Iowa (IA)
U of New Hampshire (NH)
U of Oklahoma Health Sciences Center (OK)
U of Redlands (CA)
The U of Texas–Pan American (TX)
U of the Pacific (CA)
U of Wisconsin–Madison (WI)
U of Wisconsin–River Falls (WI)
West Chester U of Pennsylvania (PA)
Xavier U of Louisiana (LA)

SPORT/FITNESS ADMINISTRATION
Albertson Coll of Idaho (ID)
Allentown Coll of St. Francis de Sales (PA)
Alvernia Coll (PA)
Anderson Coll (SC)
Arkansas Tech U (AR)
Augustana Coll (SD)
Averett Coll (VA)
Baldwin-Wallace Coll (OH)
Ball State U (IN)

Barber-Scotia Coll (NC)
Barry U (FL)
Barton Coll (NC)
Baylor U (TX)
Becker Coll (MA)
Belhaven Coll (MS)
Belmont Abbey Coll (NC)
Bemidji State U (MN)
Benedictine Coll (KS)
Bethany Coll (WV)
Black Hills State U (SD)
Bluffton Coll (OH)
Bowling Green State U (OH)
Brock U (ON, Canada)
Campbell U (NC)
Carroll Coll (MT)
Cazenovia Coll (NY)
Centenary Coll (NJ)
Central Methodist Coll (MO)
Champlain Coll (VT)
Chowan Coll (NC)
Christopher Newport U (VA)
Colby-Sawyer Coll (NH)
Concordia Coll (MI)
Concordia U (CA)
Concordia U (NE)
Concordia U (OR)
Cornerstone U (MI)
Crown Coll (MN)
Daniel Webster Coll (NH)
Defiance Coll (OH)
Delaware State U (DE)
Delaware Valley Coll (PA)
Eastern Connecticut State U (CT)
Eastern Mennonite U (VA)
Elmhurst Coll (IL)
Elon Coll (NC)
Endicott Coll (MA)
Erskine Coll (SC)
Faulkner U (AL)
Flagler Coll (FL)
Franklin Pierce Coll (NH)
Fresno Pacific U (CA)
Gardner-Webb U (NC)
George Fox U (OR)
Georgia Southern U (GA)
Glenville State Coll (WV)
Gonzaga U (WA)
Graceland Coll (IA)
Greensboro Coll (NC)
Guilford Coll (NC)
Harding U (AR)
Hastings Coll (NE)
High Point U (NC)
Holy Family Coll (PA)
Huntingdon Coll (AL)
Husson Coll (ME)
Indiana State U (IN)
Indiana U Bloomington (IN)
Indiana Wesleyan U (IN)
Iowa Wesleyan Coll (IA)
Ithaca Coll (NY)
Johnson State Coll (VT)
Judson Coll (IL)
Keene State Coll (NH)
Kentucky Wesleyan Coll (KY)
LeTourneau U (TX)
Liberty U (VA)
Limestone Coll (SC)
Lock Haven U of Pennsylvania (PA)
Longwood Coll (VA)
Loras Coll (IA)
Luther Coll (IA)
Lynchburg Coll (VA)
Lyndon State Coll (VT)
Lynn U (FL)
MacMurray Coll (IL)
Marian Coll of Fond du Lac (WI)
Marshall U (WV)
Mars Hill Coll (NC)
McGill U (PQ, Canada)
Medaille Coll (NY)
Mercyhurst Coll (PA)
Meredith Coll (NC)
Methodist Coll (NC)
Miami U (OH)
Minnesota State U, Mankato (MN)
Minnesota State U Moorhead (MN)
Mississippi U for Women (MS)
Missouri Baptist Coll (MO)
Montana State U–Billings (MT)
Montana State U–Bozeman (MT)
Montreat Coll (NC)
Morgan State U (MD)
Mount Union Coll (OH)
Mount Vernon Nazarene Coll (OH)

Nebraska Wesleyan U (NE)
Neumann Coll (PA)
New England Coll (NH)
New Hampshire Coll (NH)
New York U (NY)
Nichols Coll (MA)
North Greenville Coll (SC)
Northwestern Coll (MN)
Northwestern State U of Louisiana (LA)
Northwest Missouri State U (MO)
Ohio Northern U (OH)
Ohio U (OH)
Otterbein Coll (OH)
Pfeiffer U (NC)
Plymouth State Coll (NH)
Principia Coll (IL)
Quincy U (IL)
Robert Morris Coll (PA)
Rochester Coll (MI)
Sacred Heart U (CT)
St. Ambrose U (IA)
St. Andrews Presbyterian Coll (NC)
St. John's U (NY)
Saint Leo U (FL)
St. Thomas U (FL)
Salem State Coll (MA)
Seton Hall U (NJ)
Shawnee State U (OH)
Simpson Coll (IA)
Slippery Rock U of Pennsylvania (PA)
Southern Adventist U (TN)
Southwest Baptist U (MO)
Southwestern Coll (KS)
State U of NY Coll at Brockport (NY)
Stetson U (FL)
Taylor U (IN)
Temple U (PA)
Tennessee Wesleyan Coll (TN)
Texas Wesleyan U (TX)
Thomas Coll (ME)
Tiffin U (OH)
Towson U (MD)
Tri-State U (IN)
Tulane U (LA)
Tusculum Coll (TN)
Union Coll (KY)
Union Coll (NE)
Union U (TN)
U Coll of Cape Breton (NS, Canada)
U of Alberta (AB, Canada)
U of Dayton (OH)
U of Georgia (GA)
The U of Iowa (IA)
U of Louisville (KY)
U of Massachusetts Amherst (MA)
U of Miami (FL)
U of Michigan (MI)
U of Nebraska at Kearney (NE)
U of Nevada, Las Vegas (NV)
U of New England (ME)
U of New Haven (CT)
U of Pittsburgh at Bradford (PA)
U of Regina (SK, Canada)
U of San Francisco (CA)
U of South Carolina (SC)
The U of Tennessee at Martin (TN)
The U of Tennessee Knoxville (TN)
U of the Pacific (CA)
U of Tulsa (OK)
U of Victoria (BC, Canada)
U of Windsor (ON, Canada)
U of Wisconsin–La Crosse (WI)
Valparaiso U (IN)
Virginia Intermont Coll (VA)
Warner Southern Coll (FL)
Wartburg Coll (IA)
Washington State U (WA)
Wayne State Coll (NE)
Webber Coll (FL)
Western Baptist Coll (OR)
Western Carolina U (NC)
Western New England Coll (MA)
West Virginia U (WV)
Wheeling Jesuit U (WV)
Widener U (PA)
William Penn U (IA)
Wilmington Coll (DE)
Wilmington Coll (OH)
Wingate U (NC)
Winona State U (MN)
Winthrop U (SC)
Xavier U (OH)
York Coll of Pennsylvania (PA)

York U (ON, Canada)
Youngstown State U (OH)

STRINGED INSTRUMENTS
Acadia U (NS, Canada)
Alma Coll (MI)
Appalachian State U (NC)
Aquinas Coll (MI)
Augustana Coll (IL)
Baldwin-Wallace Coll (OH)
Ball State U (IN)
Benedictine Coll (KS)
Bennington Coll (VT)
Berklee Coll of Music (MA)
Brevard Coll (NC)
Butler U (IN)
California Inst of the Arts (CA)
California State U, Fullerton (CA)
California State U, Northridge (CA)
Capital U (OH)
Centenary Coll of Louisiana (LA)
Chapman U (CA)
Cleveland Inst of Music (OH)
Coll of Notre Dame (CA)
Columbus State U (GA)
Converse Coll (SC)
Cornish Coll of the Arts (WA)
The Curtis Inst of Music (PA)
David Lipscomb U (TN)
DePaul U (IL)
Eastern Washington U (WA)
Five Towns Coll (NY)
Florida State U (FL)
Friends U (KS)
Grand Valley State U (MI)
Harding U (AR)
Hardin-Simmons U (TX)
Hastings Coll (NE)
Heidelberg Coll (OH)
Houghton Coll (NY)
Howard Payne U (TX)
Illinois Wesleyan U (IL)
Indiana U–Purdue U Fort Wayne (IN)
Inter American U of PR, San Germán Campus (PR)
The Juilliard School (NY)
Lamar U (TX)
Lawrence U (WI)
Lindenwood U (MO)
Luther Coll (IA)
Manhattan School of Music (NY)
Mannes Coll of Music, New School U (NY)
Marshall U (WV)
Mars Hill Coll (NC)
Memorial U of Newfoundland (NF, Canada)
Meredith Coll (NC)
Michigan State U (MI)
Mount Allison U (NB, Canada)
New England Conservatory of Music (MA)
New World School of the Arts (FL)
New York U (NY)
Northern Arizona U (AZ)
Northern Michigan U (MI)
Northwest Missouri State U (MO)
Oberlin Coll (OH)
Oklahoma City U (OK)
Olivet Nazarene U (IL)
Otterbein Coll (OH)
Palm Beach Atlantic Coll (FL)
Peabody Conserv of Music of Johns Hopkins U (MD)
Pittsburg State U (KS)
Queens Coll of the City U of NY (NY)
Queen's U at Kingston (ON, Canada)
St. Olaf Coll (MN)
San Francisco Conservatory of Music (CA)
Sarah Lawrence Coll (NY)
Seton Hill Coll (PA)
State U of NY Coll at Fredonia (NY)
State U of NY Coll at Potsdam (NY)
Susquehanna U (PA)
Syracuse U (NY)
Temple U (PA)
The U of Akron (OH)
U of Alberta (AB, Canada)
U of British Columbia (BC, Canada)
U of Central Oklahoma (OK)

U of Cincinnati (OH)
The U of Iowa (IA)
U of Kansas (KS)
U of Miami (FL)
U of Michigan (MI)
U of Missouri–Kansas City (MO)
U of New Hampshire (NH)
U of North Texas (TX)
U of Oklahoma (OK)
U of South Dakota (SD)
U of Southern California (CA)
The U of Tennessee at Martin (TN)
The U of the Arts (PA)
U of the Pacific (CA)
U of Washington (WA)
The U of Western Ontario (ON, Canada)
U of Wisconsin–Milwaukee (WI)
Vanderbilt U (TN)
Virginia Commonwealth U (VA)
West Chester U of Pennsylvania (PA)
Wheaton Coll (IL)
Xavier U of Louisiana (LA)
Youngstown State U (OH)

STRUCTURAL ENGINEERING
Clarkson U (NY)
Johnson & Wales U (RI)
The Ohio State U (OH)
U of Calif, San Diego (CA)
U of Southern California (CA)

SURVEYING
California State Polytechnic U, Pomona (CA)
California State U, Fresno (CA)
East Tennessee State U (TN)
Ferris State U (MI)
Metropolitan State Coll of Denver (CO)
Michigan Technological U (MI)
New Jersey Inst of Technology (NJ)
New Mexico State U (NM)
Oregon Inst of Technology (OR)
Polytechnic U of Puerto Rico (PR)
Purdue U (IN)
Southern Polytechnic State U (GA)
Southwest Texas State U (TX)
State U of NY Coll of Technology at Alfred (NY)
Thomas Edison State Coll (NJ)
U of Arkansas at Little Rock (AR)
U of Florida (FL)
U of Maine (ME)
U of New Brunswick, Fredericton (NB, Canada)
U of New Brunswick, Saint John (NB, Canada)
U of Puerto Rico, Mayagüez Campus (PR)
U of Toronto (ON, Canada)
U of Wisconsin–Madison (WI)

SYSTEMS ENGINEERING
Boston U (MA)
California State U, Northridge (CA)
Carleton U (ON, Canada)
Case Western Reserve U (OH)
Eastern Nazarene Coll (MA)
Florida International U (FL)
George Mason U (VA)
The George Washington U (DC)
Harvard U (MA)
Insto Tecno Estudios Sups Monterrey, León (Mexico)
Insto Tecno Estudios Sups Monterrey (Mexico)
Insto Tecno Estudios Sups Monterrey, Querétaro (Mexico)
Insto Tecno Estudios Sups Monterrey, Tampico (Mexico)
Kettering U (MI)
Maine Maritime Academy (ME)
Montana Tech of The U of Montana (MT)
New Jersey Inst of Technology (NJ)
Oakland U (MI)
The Ohio State U (OH)
Point Park Coll (PA)
Rensselaer Polytechnic Inst (NY)
Richmond, The American International U in London (United Kingdom)
United States Military Academy (NY)
United States Naval Academy (MD)

Majors Index
Systems Engineering–Theater Arts/Drama

The U of Arizona (AZ)
U of Calif, San Diego (CA)
U of Detroit Mercy (MI)
U of Florida (FL)
U of Pennsylvania (PA)
U of Regina (SK, Canada)
U of St. Thomas (MN)
U of Southern California (CA)
U of Virginia (VA)
U of Waterloo (ON, Canada)
Washington U in St. Louis (MO)
Worcester Polytechnic Inst (MA)

SYSTEMS SCIENCE AND THEORY
Indiana U Bloomington (IN)
Miami U (OH)
Providence Coll (RI)
Stanford U (CA)
U of Kansas (KS)
Washington U in St. Louis (MO)
Yale U (CT)

TEACHER ASSISTANT/AIDE
Long Island U, Southampton Coll, Friends World Program (NY)

TEACHING ENGLISH AS A SECOND LANGUAGE
Alaska Bible Coll (AK)
Alma Coll (MI)
Bartlesville Wesleyan Coll (OK)
Brigham Young U–Hawaii Campus (HI)
California State U, Northridge (CA)
Calvin Coll (MI)
Carleton U (ON, Canada)
Carroll Coll (MT)
Coll of Our Lady of the Elms (MA)
Concordia U (PQ, Canada)
Concordia U Wisconsin (WI)
Doane Coll (NE)
Eastern Nazarene Coll (MA)
Goshen Coll (IN)
Hawaii Pacific U (HI)
Hobe Sound Bible Coll (FL)
Inter American U of PR, Aguadilla Campus (PR)
Inter American U of PR, Arecibo Campus (PR)
Inter American U of PR, Fajardo Campus (PR)
Inter American U of PR, Metropolitan Campus (PR)
Inter American U of PR, San Germán Campus (PR)
John Brown U (AR)
Johnson Bible Coll (TN)
Langston U (OK)
Liberty U (VA)
Long Island U, Southampton Coll, Friends World Program (NY)
Maryville Coll (TN)
McGill U (PQ, Canada)
Mercy Coll (NY)
Millersville U of Pennsylvania (PA)
Moody Bible Inst (IL)
Northwest Coll (WA)
Northwestern Coll (MN)
Nyack Coll (NY)
Ohio Dominican Coll (OH)
Oklahoma Christian U of Science and Arts (OK)
Providence Coll and Theological Seminary (MB, Canada)
Queens Coll of the City U of NY (NY)
Saint Mary's U (NS, Canada)
Simmons Coll (MA)
State U of NY at Stony Brook (NY)
Texas Wesleyan U (TX)
Toccoa Falls Coll (GA)
Union U (TN)
United States International U (CA)
U du Québec à Chicoutimi (PQ, Canada)
U of Alberta (AB, Canada)
U of British Columbia (BC, Canada)
U of Delaware (DE)
The U of Findlay (OH)
The U of Montana–Missoula (MT)
U of New Brunswick, Fredericton (NB, Canada)
U of Northern Iowa (IA)
U of Puerto Rico, Humacao U Coll (PR)

U of the Pacific (CA)
U of Victoria (BC, Canada)
U of Washington (WA)
U of Wisconsin–River Falls (WI)
York U (ON, Canada)

TECHNICAL EDUCATION
Bowling Green State U (OH)
Colorado State U (CO)
Idaho State U (ID)
Mississippi State U (MS)
New York City Tech Coll of the City U of NY (NY)
New York Inst of Technology (NY)
The Ohio State U (OH)
U of Illinois at Urbana–Champaign (IL)
U of Nebraska at Kearney (NE)
U of Nebraska–Lincoln (NE)
The U of Tennessee Knoxville (TN)
U of Wisconsin–Stout (WI)
Utah State U (UT)
Wayne State U (MI)

TECHNICAL WRITING
Alderson-Broaddus Coll (WV)
Boise State U (ID)
Bowling Green State U (OH)
Carlow Coll (PA)
Carnegie Mellon U (PA)
Carroll Coll (MT)
Cedarville Coll (OH)
Chicago State U (IL)
Christian Brothers U (TN)
Clarkson U (NY)
Coll of Santa Fe (NM)
Drexel U (PA)
Ferris State U (MI)
Fitchburg State Coll (MA)
Gannon U (PA)
Grand Valley State U (MI)
Indiana State U (IN)
James Madison U (VA)
La Roche Coll (PA)
Lawrence Technological U (MI)
Madonna U (MI)
Maryville Coll (TN)
Mercyhurst Coll (PA)
Metropolitan State U (MN)
Miami U (OH)
Michigan Technological U (MI)
Milwaukee School of Engineering (WI)
Montana Tech of The U of Montana (MT)
Mount Mary Coll (WI)
New Jersey Inst of Technology (NJ)
New Mexico Inst of Mining and Technology (NM)
New York Inst of Technology (NY)
Northern Arizona U (AZ)
Northwestern Coll (MN)
Oklahoma State U (OK)
Oregon State U (OR)
Pennsylvania Coll of Technology (PA)
Plymouth State Coll (NH)
Polytechnic U, Brooklyn Campus (NY)
Rensselaer Polytechnic Inst (NY)
San Francisco State U (CA)
San Jose State U (CA)
Southern Polytechnic State U (GA)
Southwest Missouri State U (MO)
Spring Hill Coll (AL)
State U of NY Inst of Tech at Utica/Rome (NY)
Tennessee Technological U (TN)
U of Arkansas at Little Rock (AR)
U of Baltimore (MD)
U of Delaware (DE)
U of Hartford (CT)
U of Houston–Downtown (TX)
The U of Montana–Missoula (MT)
U of Pittsburgh at Bradford (PA)
U of Victoria (BC, Canada)
U of Washington (WA)
Weber State U (UT)
Winthrop U (SC)
Worcester Polytechnic Inst (MA)
York U (ON, Canada)
Youngstown State U (OH)

TELECOMMUNICATIONS
Ball State U (IN)
Baylor U (TX)
Bowling Green State U (OH)

Butler U (IN)
California State Polytechnic U, Pomona (CA)
California State U, Hayward (CA)
California State U, Monterey Bay (CA)
Cameron U (OK)
Capitol Coll (MD)
Champlain Coll (VT)
Colorado Tech U (CO)
Columbia Coll–Hollywood (CA)
Eastern New Mexico U (NM)
Ferris State U (MI)
Golden Gate U (CA)
Grand Valley State U (MI)
Hampshire Coll (MA)
Howard Payne U (TX)
Indiana State U (IN)
Indiana U Bloomington (IN)
Ithaca Coll (NY)
Kutztown U of Pennsylvania (PA)
Marylhurst U (OR)
Marywood U (PA)
Michigan State U (MI)
Morgan State U (MD)
Murray State U (KY)
New York City Tech Coll of the City U of NY (NY)
New York Inst of Technology (NY)
Northern Arizona U (AZ)
The Ohio State U (OH)
Ohio U (OH)
Oklahoma Baptist U (OK)
Pacific U (OR)
Pepperdine U, Malibu (CA)
Queens Coll of the City U of NY (NY)
Rochester Inst of Technology (NY)
St. John's U (NY)
Saint Mary's U of Minnesota (MN)
San Diego State U (CA)
Southern Polytechnic State U (GA)
State U of NY Inst of Tech at Utica/Rome (NY)
Syracuse U (NY)
Texas Southern U (TX)
Tusculum Coll (TN)
U of Florida (FL)
U of St. Thomas (MN)
U of Southern Colorado (CO)
The U of Texas at Dallas (TX)
U of the Sacred Heart (PR)
U of Wisconsin–Platteville (WI)
Western Michigan U (MI)
Westminster Coll (PA)
Wingate U (NC)
Winona State U (MN)
Youngstown State U (OH)

TEXTILE ARTS
Academy of Art Coll (CA)
Adams State Coll (CO)
Alberta Coll of Art and Design (AB, Canada)
Bowling Green State U (OH)
California Coll of Arts and Crafts (CA)
California State U, Long Beach (CA)
California State U, Northridge (CA)
Ctr for Creative Studies—Coll of Art and Design (MI)
Cleveland Inst of Art (OH)
Colorado State U (CO)
Concordia U (PQ, Canada)
Cornell U (NY)
Fashion Inst of Technology (NY)
Finlandia U (MI)
Kansas City Art Inst (MO)
Kent State U (OH)
Long Island U, Southampton Coll, Friends World Program (NY)
Maryland Inst, Coll of Art (MD)
Massachusetts Coll of Art (MA)
Memphis Coll of Art (TN)
Mercyhurst Coll (PA)
Moore Coll of Art and Design (PA)
Northern Michigan U (MI)
Northwest Missouri State U (MO)
Nova Scotia Coll of Art and Design (NS, Canada)
Oregon State U (OR)
Philadelphia U (PA)
Rhode Island School of Design (RI)
Savannah Coll of Art and Design (GA)

School of the Art Inst of Chicago (IL)
Syracuse U (NY)
Texas Woman's U (TX)
U of Massachusetts Dartmouth (MA)
U of Michigan (MI)
U of North Texas (TX)
U of Oregon (OR)
The U of the Arts (PA)
U of Washington (WA)
U of Wisconsin–Milwaukee (WI)

TEXTILE SCIENCES/ ENGINEERING
Auburn U (AL)
Clemson U (SC)
Georgia Inst of Technology (GA)
North Carolina Central U (NC)
North Carolina State U (NC)
Philadelphia U (PA)
Texas Tech U (TX)
Université de Sherbrooke (PQ, Canada)
U of Massachusetts Dartmouth (MA)

THEATER ARTS/DRAMA
Abilene Christian U (TX)
Acadia U (NS, Canada)
Adams State Coll (CO)
Adelphi U (NY)
Adrian Coll (MI)
Agnes Scott Coll (GA)
Alabama State U (AL)
Albertson Coll of Idaho (ID)
Albertus Magnus Coll (CT)
Albion Coll (MI)
Albright Coll (PA)
Alderson-Broaddus Coll (WV)
Alfred U (NY)
Allegheny Coll (PA)
Allentown Coll of St. Francis de Sales (PA)
Alma Coll (MI)
American U (DC)
American U in Cairo (Egypt)
Amherst Coll (MA)
Anderson Coll (SC)
Anderson U (IN)
Antioch Coll (OH)
Appalachian State U (NC)
Arizona State U (AZ)
Arkansas State U (AR)
Armstrong Atlantic State U (GA)
Ashland U (OH)
Auburn U (AL)
Augsburg Coll (MN)
Augustana Coll (IL)
Augustana Coll (SD)
Averett Coll (VA)
Avila Coll (MO)
Baker U (KS)
Baldwin-Wallace Coll (OH)
Ball State U (IN)
Barat Coll (IL)
Bard Coll (NY)
Barnard Coll (NY)
Barry U (FL)
Barton Coll (NC)
Bates Coll (ME)
Baylor U (TX)
Beaver Coll (PA)
Belhaven Coll (MS)
Belmont U (TN)
Beloit Coll (WI)
Bemidji State U (MN)
Benedictine Coll (KS)
Bennington Coll (VT)
Berea Coll (KY)
Berry Coll (GA)
Bethany Coll (WV)
Bethany Coll of the Assemblies of God (CA)
Bethel Coll (IN)
Bethel Coll (MN)
Bethel Coll (TN)
Birmingham-Southern Coll (AL)
Bishop's U (PQ, Canada)
Bloomsburg U of Pennsylvania (PA)
Blue Mountain Coll (MS)
Boise State U (ID)
Boston Coll (MA)
Bowie State U (MD)
Bowling Green State U (OH)
Bradley U (IL)

Brandeis U (MA)
Brenau U (GA)
Brevard Coll (NC)
Briar Cliff Coll (IA)
Bridgewater State Coll (MA)
Brigham Young U (UT)
Brock U (ON, Canada)
Brooklyn Coll of the City U of NY (NY)
Brown U (RI)
Bucknell U (PA)
Buena Vista U (IA)
Butler U (IN)
California Baptist U (CA)
California Inst of the Arts (CA)
California Lutheran U (CA)
California State Polytechnic U, Pomona (CA)
California State U, Chico (CA)
California State U, Dominguez Hills (CA)
California State U, Fresno (CA)
California State U, Fullerton (CA)
California State U, Hayward (CA)
California State U, Long Beach (CA)
California State U, Monterey Bay (CA)
California State U, Northridge (CA)
California State U, Sacramento (CA)
California State U, San Bernardino (CA)
California State U, Stanislaus (CA)
California U of Pennsylvania (PA)
Calvin Coll (MI)
Cameron U (OK)
Campbell U (NC)
Cardinal Stritch U (WI)
Carleton U (ON, Canada)
Carnegie Mellon U (PA)
Carroll Coll (MT)
Carroll Coll (WI)
Carson-Newman Coll (TN)
Carthage Coll (WI)
Case Western Reserve U (OH)
Castleton State Coll (VT)
Catawba Coll (NC)
The Catholic U of America (DC)
Cedar Crest Coll (PA)
Cedarville Coll (OH)
Centenary Coll of Louisiana (LA)
Central Coll (IA)
Central Connecticut State U (CT)
Central Methodist Coll (MO)
Central Michigan U (MI)
Central Missouri State U (MO)
Centre Coll (KY)
Chadron State Coll (NE)
Chapman U (CA)
Chatham Coll (PA)
Cheyney U of Pennsylvania (PA)
Christopher Newport U (VA)
City Coll of the City U of NY (NY)
Claremont McKenna Coll (CA)
Clarion U of Pennsylvania (PA)
Clark Atlanta U (GA)
Clarke Coll (IA)
Clark U (MA)
Cleveland State U (OH)
Coastal Carolina U (SC)
Coe Coll (IA)
Coker Coll (SC)
Colby Coll (ME)
Colgate U (NY)
Coll of Charleston (SC)
Coll of Notre Dame (CA)
Coll of Saint Benedict (MN)
Coll of St. Catherine (MN)
Coll of Santa Fe (NM)
Coll of Staten Island of the City U of NY (NY)
Coll of the Holy Cross (MA)
Coll of the Ozarks (MO)
The Coll of William and Mary (VA)
The Coll of Wooster (OH)
Colorado Christian U (CO)
The Colorado Coll (CO)
Colorado State U (CO)
Columbia Coll (NY)
Columbia Coll Chicago (IL)
Columbia Coll, School of General Studies (NY)
Columbus State U (GA)
Concordia Coll (MN)
Concordia U (CA)
Concordia U (IL)

Majors Index
Theater Arts/Drama

Concordia U (NE)
Concordia U (OR)
Concordia U (PQ, Canada)
Concordia U at St. Paul (MN)
Concordia U Wisconsin (WI)
Connecticut Coll (CT)
Converse Coll (SC)
Cornell Coll (IA)
Cornell U (NY)
Cornish Coll of the Arts (WA)
Creighton U (NE)
Culver-Stockton Coll (MO)
Cumberland Coll (KY)
Dakota Wesleyan U (SD)
Dalhousie U (NS, Canada)
Dartmouth Coll (NH)
Davidson Coll (NC)
Delaware State U (DE)
Denison U (OH)
DePaul U (IL)
Dickinson Coll (PA)
Dickinson State U (ND)
Doane Coll (NE)
Dominican U (IL)
Dordt Coll (IA)
Dowling Coll (NY)
Drake U (IA)
Drew U (NJ)
Drury U (MO)
Duke U (NC)
Duquesne U (PA)
Earlham Coll (IN)
East Carolina U (NC)
Eastern Illinois U (IL)
Eastern Kentucky U (KY)
Eastern Mennonite U (VA)
Eastern Michigan U (MI)
Eastern Nazarene Coll (MA)
Eastern New Mexico U (NM)
Eastern Oregon U (OR)
Eastern Washington U (WA)
East Stroudsburg U of Pennsylvania (PA)
East Texas Baptist U (TX)
Eckerd Coll (FL)
Edgewood Coll (WI)
Edinboro U of Pennsylvania (PA)
Elmhurst Coll (IL)
Elmira Coll (NY)
Elon Coll (NC)
Emerson Coll (MA)
Emory & Henry Coll (VA)
Emory U (GA)
Emporia State U (KS)
Eugene Lang Coll, New School U (NY)
The Evergreen State Coll (WA)
Fairleigh Dickinson U, Florham-Madison Campus (NJ)
Fairleigh Dickinson U, Teaneck-Hackensack Campus (NJ)
Fairmont State Coll (WV)
Ferrum Coll (VA)
Fisk U (TN)
Fitchburg State Coll (MA)
Five Towns Coll (NY)
Flagler Coll (FL)
Florida A&M U (FL)
Florida Atlantic U (FL)
Florida Gulf Coast U (FL)
Florida International U (FL)
Florida Southern Coll (FL)
Florida State U (FL)
Fontbonne Coll (MO)
Fordham U (NY)
Fort Lewis Coll (CO)
Francis Marion U (SC)
Franklin and Marshall Coll (PA)
Franklin Coll of Indiana (IN)
Franklin Pierce Coll (NH)
Freed-Hardeman U (TN)
Frostburg State U (MD)
Furman U (SC)
Gallaudet U (DC)
Gannon U (PA)
George Mason U (VA)
Georgetown Coll (KY)
The George Washington U (DC)
Georgia Coll and State U (GA)
Georgia Southern U (GA)
Georgia State U (GA)
Gettysburg Coll (PA)
Goddard Coll (VT)
Gonzaga U (WA)
Goshen Coll (IN)
Goucher Coll (MD)
Graceland Coll (IA)

Grand Canyon U (AZ)
Grand Valley State U (MI)
Grand View Coll (IA)
Green Mountain Coll (VT)
Greensboro Coll (NC)
Greenville Coll (IL)
Grinnell Coll (IA)
Guilford Coll (NC)
Gustavus Adolphus Coll (MN)
Hamilton Coll (NY)
Hamline U (MN)
Hampshire Coll (MA)
Hampton U (VA)
Hannibal-LaGrange Coll (MO)
Hanover Coll (IN)
Harding U (AR)
Hardin-Simmons U (TX)
Hartwick Coll (NY)
Harvard U (MA)
Hastings Coll (NE)
Heidelberg Coll (OH)
Henderson State U (AR)
Hendrix Coll (AR)
High Point U (NC)
Hillsdale Coll (MI)
Hiram Coll (OH)
Hobart and William Smith Colls (NY)
Hofstra U (NY)
Hollins U (VA)
Hope Coll (MI)
Howard Payne U (TX)
Howard U (DC)
Humboldt State U (CA)
Hunter Coll of the City U of NY (NY)
Huntingdon Coll (AL)
Huntington Coll (IN)
Idaho State U (ID)
Illinois Coll (IL)
Illinois State U (IL)
Illinois Wesleyan U (IL)
Indiana State U (IN)
Indiana U Bloomington (IN)
Indiana U Northwest (IN)
Indiana U of Pennsylvania (PA)
Indiana U–Purdue U Fort Wayne (IN)
Indiana U South Bend (IN)
Iona Coll (NY)
Iowa State U of Science and Technology (IA)
Ithaca Coll (NY)
Jacksonville State U (AL)
Jacksonville U (FL)
James Madison U (VA)
Jamestown Coll (ND)
Johnson State Coll (VT)
Judson Coll (IL)
The Juilliard School (NY)
Kalamazoo Coll (MI)
Kansas State U (KS)
Kean U (NJ)
Keene State Coll (NH)
Kent State U (OH)
Kenyon Coll (OH)
King's Coll (PA)
Knox Coll (IL)
Kutztown U of Pennsylvania (PA)
LaGrange Coll (GA)
Lake Erie Coll (OH)
Lakeland Coll (WI)
Lamar U (TX)
Lambuth U (TN)
Lander U (SC)
Langston U (OK)
Lawrence U (WI)
Lees-McRae Coll (NC)
Lehigh U (PA)
Lehman Coll of the City U of NY (NY)
Le Moyne Coll (NY)
Lenoir-Rhyne Coll (NC)
Lewis & Clark Coll (OR)
Lewis-Clark State Coll (ID)
Lewis U (IL)
Lindenwood U (MO)
Linfield Coll (OR)
Lock Haven U of Pennsylvania (PA)
Long Island U, C.W. Post Campus (NY)
Long Island U, Southampton Coll, Friends World Program (NY)
Longwood Coll (VA)
Louisiana Coll (LA)

Louisiana State U and A&M Coll (LA)
Loyola Marymount U (CA)
Loyola U Chicago (IL)
Loyola U New Orleans (LA)
Luther Coll (IA)
Lycoming Coll (PA)
Lynchburg Coll (VA)
Lyon Coll (AR)
Macalester Coll (MN)
MacMurray Coll (IL)
Maharishi U of Management (IA)
Malone Coll (OH)
Manchester Coll (IN)
Manhattanville Coll (NY)
Mansfield U of Pennsylvania (PA)
Marian Coll (IN)
Marietta Coll (OH)
Marist Coll (NY)
Marlboro Coll (VT)
Marquette U (WI)
Marshall U (WV)
Mars Hill Coll (NC)
Mary Baldwin Coll (VA)
Marymount Coll (NY)
Marymount Manhattan Coll (NY)
Maryville Coll (TN)
Mary Washington Coll (VA)
Marywood U (PA)
Massachusetts Coll of Liberal Arts (MA)
Massachusetts Inst of Technology (MA)
McMurry U (TX)
McNeese State U (LA)
McPherson Coll (KS)
Memorial U of Newfoundland (NF, Canada)
Mercer U (GA)
Meredith Coll (NC)
Mesa State Coll (CO)
Messiah Coll (PA)
Methodist Coll (NC)
Miami U (OH)
Michigan State U (MI)
Middlebury Coll (VT)
Middle Tennessee State U (TN)
Midland Lutheran Coll (NE)
Midwestern State U (TX)
Millersville U of Pennsylvania (PA)
Milligan Coll (TN)
Millikin U (IL)
Millsaps Coll (MS)
Mills Coll (CA)
Minnesota State U, Mankato (MN)
Minnesota State U Moorhead (MN)
Minot State U (ND)
Mississippi U for Women (MS)
Missouri Southern State Coll (MO)
Missouri Valley Coll (MO)
Monmouth Coll (IL)
Montana State U–Billings (MT)
Morehead State U (KY)
Morehouse Coll (GA)
Morgan State U (MD)
Morningside Coll (IA)
Mount Allison U (NB, Canada)
Mount Holyoke Coll (MA)
Mount Mercy Coll (IA)
Mount Union Coll (OH)
Mount Vernon Nazarene Coll (OH)
Muhlenberg Coll (PA)
Murray State U (KY)
Muskingum Coll (OH)
Naropa U (CO)
National-Louis U (IL)
Nazareth Coll of Rochester (NY)
Nebraska Wesleyan U (NE)
Newberry Coll (SC)
New England Coll (NH)
New Mexico State U (NM)
New World School of the Arts (FL)
New York U (NY)
Niagara U (NY)
North Carolina Ag and Tech State U (NC)
North Carolina Central U (NC)
North Carolina School of the Arts (NC)
North Carolina Wesleyan Coll (NC)
North Central Coll (IL)
North Dakota State U (ND)
Northeastern Coll (OK)
Northeastern U (MA)
Northern Arizona U (AZ)
Northern Illinois U (IL)
Northern Kentucky U (KY)

Northern Michigan U (MI)
Northern State U (SD)
North Park U (IL)
Northwest Coll (WA)
Northwestern Coll (IA)
Northwestern Coll (MN)
Northwestern Oklahoma State U (OK)
Northwestern State U of Louisiana (LA)
Northwestern U (IL)
Northwest Missouri State U (MO)
Oakland U (MI)
Oberlin Coll (OH)
Occidental Coll (CA)
Ohio Northern U (OH)
The Ohio State U (OH)
Ohio U (OH)
Ohio Wesleyan U (OH)
Oklahoma Baptist U (OK)
Oklahoma Christian U of Science and Arts (OK)
Oklahoma City U (OK)
Oklahoma State U (OK)
Old Dominion U (VA)
Oregon State U (OR)
Ottawa U (KS)
Otterbein Coll (OH)
Ouachita Baptist U (AR)
Our Lady of the Lake U of San Antonio (TX)
Pace U, New York City Campus (NY)
Pace U, Pleasantville/Briarcliff Campus (NY)
Pacific Lutheran U (WA)
Pacific U (OR)
Palm Beach Atlantic Coll (FL)
Pepperdine U, Malibu (CA)
Peru State Coll (NE)
Pfeiffer U (NC)
Piedmont Coll (GA)
Pine Manor Coll (MA)
Pitzer Coll (CA)
Plattsburgh State U of NY (NY)
Plymouth State Coll (NH)
Point Loma Nazarene U (CA)
Point Park Coll (PA)
Pomona Coll (CA)
Portland State U (OR)
Prairie View A&M U (TX)
Presbyterian Coll (SC)
Principia Coll (IL)
Providence Coll and Theological Seminary (MB, Canada)
Purchase Coll, State U of NY (NY)
Purdue U (IN)
Queens Coll (NC)
Queens Coll of the City U of NY (NY)
Queen's U at Kingston (ON, Canada)
Radford U (VA)
Randolph-Macon Coll (VA)
Randolph-Macon Woman's Coll (VA)
Redeemer Coll (ON, Canada)
Reed Coll (OR)
Regis Coll (MA)
Rhodes Coll (TN)
Richmond, The American International U in London (United Kingdom)
Ripon Coll (WI)
Roanoke Coll (VA)
Rockford Coll (IL)
Rockhurst U (MO)
Rocky Mountain Coll (MT)
Roger Williams U (RI)
Rollins Coll (FL)
Rowan U (NJ)
Russell Sage Coll (NY)
Rutgers, State U of NJ, Camden Coll of Arts & Scis (NJ)
Rutgers, State U of NJ, Douglass Coll (NJ)
Rutgers, State U of NJ, Livingston Coll (NJ)
Rutgers, State U of NJ, Mason Gross School of Arts (NJ)
Rutgers, State U of NJ, Newark Coll of Arts & Scis (NJ)
Rutgers, State U of NJ, Rutgers Coll (NJ)
Rutgers, State U of NJ, U Coll–Camden (NJ)

Rutgers, State U of NJ, U Coll–New Brunswick (NJ)
Ryerson Polytechnic U (ON, Canada)
Sacred Heart U (CT)
Saginaw Valley State U (MI)
St. Ambrose U (IA)
St. Cloud State U (MN)
St. Edward's U (TX)
Saint John's U (MN)
St. Lawrence U (NY)
Saint Louis U (MO)
Saint Martin's Coll (WA)
Saint Mary Coll (KS)
Saint Mary-of-the-Woods Coll (IN)
Saint Mary's Coll (IN)
Saint Mary's Coll of California (CA)
St. Mary's Coll of Maryland (MD)
Saint Mary's U of Minnesota (MN)
Saint Michael's Coll (VT)
St. Olaf Coll (MN)
Saint Vincent Coll (PA)
Salem State Coll (MA)
Salve Regina U (RI)
Samford U (AL)
Sam Houston State U (TX)
San Diego State U (CA)
San Francisco State U (CA)
San Jose State U (CA)
Santa Clara U (CA)
Sarah Lawrence Coll (NY)
Scripps Coll (CA)
Seattle Pacific U (WA)
Seattle U (WA)
Seton Hill Coll (PA)
Shaw U (NC)
Shenandoah U (VA)
Shorter Coll (GA)
Siena Heights U (MI)
Simon Fraser U (BC, Canada)
Simon's Rock Coll of Bard (MA)
Simpson Coll (IA)
Skidmore Coll (NY)
Slippery Rock U of Pennsylvania (PA)
Smith Coll (MA)
Sonoma State U (CA)
South Dakota State U (SD)
Southeastern Oklahoma State U (OK)
Southeast Missouri State U (MO)
Southern Arkansas U–Magnolia (AR)
Southern Illinois U Carbondale (IL)
Southern Illinois U Edwardsville (IL)
Southern Methodist U (TX)
Southern Oregon U (OR)
Southern Utah U (UT)
Southwest Baptist U (MO)
Southwestern Coll (KS)
Southwestern U (TX)
Southwest Missouri State U (MO)
Southwest State U (MN)
Southwest Texas State U (TX)
Spalding U (KY)
Spelman Coll (GA)
Spring Hill Coll (AL)
Stanford U (CA)
State U of NY at Albany (NY)
State U of NY at Binghamton (NY)
State U of NY at Buffalo (NY)
State U of NY at New Paltz (NY)
State U of NY at Stony Brook (NY)
State U of NY Coll at Brockport (NY)
State U of NY Coll at Buffalo (NY)
State U of NY Coll at Fredonia (NY)
State U of NY Coll at Geneseo (NY)
State U of NY Coll at Oneonta (NY)
State U of NY Coll at Potsdam (NY)
State U of West Georgia (GA)
Stephen F. Austin State U (TX)
Stephens Coll (MO)
Sterling Coll (KS)
Stetson U (FL)
Suffolk U (MA)
Sul Ross State U (TX)
Susquehanna U (PA)
Swarthmore Coll (PA)
Sweet Briar Coll (VA)
Syracuse U (NY)
Taylor U (IN)
Temple U (PA)

Majors Index
Theater Arts/Drama–Theology

Texas A&M U (TX)
Texas A&M U–Commerce (TX)
Texas A&M U–Kingsville (TX)
Texas Christian U (TX)
Texas Lutheran U (TX)
Texas Southern U (TX)
Texas Tech U (TX)
Texas Wesleyan U (TX)
Texas Woman's U (TX)
Thomas Edison State Coll (NJ)
Thomas More Coll (KY)
Towson U (MD)
Transylvania U (KY)
Trevecca Nazarene U (TN)
Trinity Bible Coll (ND)
Trinity Coll (CT)
Trinity U (TX)
Trinity Western U (BC, Canada)
Troy State U (AL)
Truman State U (MO)
Tufts U (MA)
Tulane U (LA)
Union Coll (KY)
Union U (TN)
U Coll of the Fraser Valley (BC, Canada)
The U of Akron (OH)
The U of Alabama (AL)
U of Alaska Fairbanks (AK)
U of Alberta (AB, Canada)
The U of Arizona (AZ)
U of Arkansas (AR)
U of Arkansas at Little Rock (AR)
U of Arkansas at Pine Bluff (AR)
U of British Columbia (BC, Canada)
U of Calgary (AB, Canada)
U of Calif, Berkeley (CA)
U of Calif, Davis (CA)
U of Calif, Irvine (CA)
U of Calif, Los Angeles (CA)
U of Calif, Riverside (CA)
U of Calif, San Diego (CA)
U of Calif, Santa Barbara (CA)
U of Calif, Santa Cruz (CA)
U of Central Florida (FL)
U of Central Oklahoma (OK)
U of Cincinnati (OH)
U of Colorado at Boulder (CO)
U of Colorado at Denver (CO)
U of Connecticut (CT)
U of Dallas (TX)
U of Dayton (OH)
U of Denver (CO)
U of Detroit Mercy (MI)
U of Evansville (IN)
The U of Findlay (OH)
U of Florida (FL)
U of Georgia (GA)
U of Guelph (ON, Canada)
U of Hartford (CT)
U of Hawaii at Manoa (HI)
U of Houston (TX)
U of Idaho (ID)
U of Illinois at Chicago (IL)
U of Illinois at Urbana–Champaign (IL)
U of Indianapolis (IN)
The U of Iowa (IA)
U of Kansas (KS)
U of Kentucky (KY)
U of King's Coll (NS, Canada)
U of La Verne (CA)
The U of Lethbridge (AB, Canada)
U of Louisville (KY)
U of Maine (ME)
U of Maine at Farmington (ME)
U of Manitoba (MB, Canada)
U of Maryland, Baltimore County (MD)
U of Maryland, Coll Park (MD)
U of Massachusetts Amherst (MA)
U of Massachusetts Boston (MA)
The U of Memphis (TN)
U of Miami (FL)
U of Michigan (MI)
U of Michigan–Flint (MI)
U of Minnesota, Duluth (MN)
U of Minnesota, Morris (MN)
U of Minnesota, Twin Cities Campus (MN)
U of Mississippi (MS)
U of Missouri–Columbia (MO)
U of Missouri–Kansas City (MO)
U of Mobile (AL)
The U of Montana–Missoula (MT)
U of Montevallo (AL)

U of Nebraska at Kearney (NE)
U of Nebraska at Omaha (NE)
U of Nebraska–Lincoln (NE)
U of Nevada, Las Vegas (NV)
U of Nevada, Reno (NV)
U of New Brunswick, Fredericton (NB, Canada)
U of New Hampshire (NH)
U of New Mexico (NM)
U of New Orleans (LA)
The U of North Carolina at Asheville (NC)
The U of North Carolina at Chapel Hill (NC)
The U of North Carolina at Charlotte (NC)
The U of North Carolina at Greensboro (NC)
The U of North Carolina at Pembroke (NC)
U of North Dakota (ND)
U of Northern Colorado (CO)
U of Northern Iowa (IA)
U of North Texas (TX)
U of Notre Dame (IN)
U of Oklahoma (OK)
U of Oregon (OR)
U of Pennsylvania (PA)
U of Pittsburgh (PA)
U of Pittsburgh at Johnstown (PA)
U of Portland (OR)
U of Puerto Rico, Río Piedras (PR)
U of Puget Sound (WA)
U of Regina (SK, Canada)
U of Richmond (VA)
U of St. Thomas (MN)
U of St. Thomas (TX)
U of Science and Arts of Oklahoma (OK)
The U of Scranton (PA)
U of Sioux Falls (SD)
U of South Alabama (AL)
U of South Carolina (SC)
U of South Dakota (SD)
U of Southern California (CA)
U of Southern Maine (ME)
U of Southern Mississippi (MS)
U of South Florida (FL)
The U of Tampa (FL)
The U of Tennessee at Chattanooga (TN)
The U of Tennessee Knoxville (TN)
The U of Texas at Arlington (TX)
The U of Texas at Austin (TX)
The U of Texas at Tyler (TX)
The U of Texas–Pan American (TX)
The U of the Arts (PA)
U of the District of Columbia (DC)
U of the Ozarks (AR)
U of the Pacific (CA)
U of the Sacred Heart (PR)
U of the South (TN)
U of the Virgin Islands (VI)
U of Toronto (ON, Canada)
U of Tulsa (OK)
U of Utah (UT)
U of Vermont (VT)
U of Victoria (BC, Canada)
U of Virginia (VA)
U of Virginia's Coll at Wise (VA)
U of Washington (WA)
U of Waterloo (ON, Canada)
The U of Western Ontario (ON, Canada)
U of West Florida (FL)
U of Windsor (ON, Canada)
The U of Winnipeg (MB, Canada)
U of Wisconsin–Eau Claire (WI)
U of Wisconsin–Green Bay (WI)
U of Wisconsin–La Crosse (WI)
U of Wisconsin–Madison (WI)
U of Wisconsin–Milwaukee (WI)
U of Wisconsin–Parkside (WI)
U of Wisconsin–River Falls (WI)
U of Wisconsin–Stevens Point (WI)
U of Wisconsin–Superior (WI)
U of Wisconsin–Whitewater (WI)
U of Wyoming (WY)
Utah State U (UT)
Utica Coll of Syracuse U (NY)
Valdosta State U (GA)
Valparaiso U (IN)
Vanderbilt U (TN)
Vanguard U of Southern California (CA)
Vassar Coll (NY)
Virginia Commonwealth U (VA)

Virginia Intermont Coll (VA)
Virginia Polytechnic Inst and State U (VA)
Virginia Wesleyan Coll (VA)
Wabash Coll (IN)
Wagner Coll (NY)
Wake Forest U (NC)
Warren Wilson Coll (NC)
Washington and Lee U (VA)
Washington Coll (MD)
Washington State U (WA)
Washington U in St. Louis (MO)
Wayland Baptist U (TX)
Wayne State Coll (NE)
Wayne State U (MI)
Weber State U (UT)
Webster U (MO)
Wellesley Coll (MA)
Wells Coll (NY)
Wesleyan U (CT)
West Chester U of Pennsylvania (PA)
Western Carolina U (NC)
Western Connecticut State U (CT)
Western Illinois U (IL)
Western Kentucky U (KY)
Western Maryland Coll (MD)
Western Michigan U (MI)
Western Montana Coll of The U of Montana (MT)
Western Oregon U (OR)
Western State Coll of Colorado (CO)
Western Washington U (WA)
Westminster Coll (PA)
Westmont Coll (CA)
West Texas A&M U (TX)
West Virginia U (WV)
West Virginia Wesleyan Coll (WV)
Wheaton Coll (MA)
Whitman Coll (WA)
Whittier Coll (CA)
Whitworth Coll (WA)
Wichita State U (KS)
Wilfrid Laurier U (ON, Canada)
Wilkes U (PA)
Willamette U (OR)
William Jewell Coll (MO)
William Paterson U of New Jersey (NJ)
Williams Coll (MA)
William Woods U (MO)
Wilmington Coll (OH)
Winona State U (MN)
Winthrop U (SC)
Wittenberg U (OH)
Wright State U (OH)
Yeshiva U (NY)
York Coll of the City U of New York (NY)
York U (ON, Canada)
Youngstown State U (OH)

THEATER DESIGN
Baylor U (TX)
Boston U (MA)
Carroll Coll (MT)
Centenary Coll (NJ)
Coll of Santa Fe (NM)
Columbia Coll Chicago (IL)
Concordia U (PQ, Canada)
Dickinson Coll (PA)
Emerson Coll (MA)
Florida State U (FL)
Greensboro Coll (NC)
Ithaca Coll (NY)
Kent State U (OH)
Louisiana Coll (LA)
Maharishi U of Management (IA)
Memorial U of Newfoundland (NF, Canada)
New York City Tech Coll of the City U of NY (NY)
New York U (NY)
Ohio U (OH)
Oklahoma City U (OK)
Penn State U Univ Park Campus (PA)
Plymouth State Coll (NH)
Ryerson Polytechnic U (ON, Canada)
Seton Hill Coll (PA)
Syracuse U (NY)
Tabor Coll (KS)
Texas Tech U (TX)
Trinity U (TX)
The U of Arizona (AZ)

U of Connecticut (CT)
U of Delaware (DE)
U of Kansas (KS)
U of Michigan (MI)
U of Northern Iowa (IA)
U of Southern California (CA)
Webster U (MO)
Western Michigan U (MI)
York U (ON, Canada)

THEOLOGY
Alaska Bible Coll (AK)
Allentown Coll of St. Francis de Sales (PA)
Alvernia Coll (PA)
Anderson U (IN)
Andrews U (MI)
Appalachian Bible Coll (WV)
Assumption Coll (MA)
Atlanta Christian Coll (GA)
Atlantic Union Coll (MA)
Augsburg Coll (MN)
Avila Coll (MO)
Azusa Pacific U (CA)
Baker U (KS)
Baptist Missionary Assoc Theol Sem (TX)
Barry U (FL)
Bartlesville Wesleyan Coll (OK)
Bellarmine Coll (KY)
Belmont Abbey Coll (NC)
Benedictine Coll (KS)
Bethany Coll of the Assemblies of God (CA)
Biola U (CA)
Boston Coll (MA)
Briar Cliff Coll (IA)
Briercrest Bible Coll (SK, Canada)
California State U, Sacramento (CA)
Calumet Coll of Saint Joseph (IN)
Calvary Bible Coll and Theological Seminary (MO)
Calvin Coll (MI)
Canadian Bible Coll (SK, Canada)
Carlow Coll (PA)
Carroll Coll (MT)
Cedarville U (OH)
Central Bible Coll (MO)
Central Christian Coll of Kansas (KS)
Christendom Coll (VA)
Circleville Bible Coll (OH)
Cleveland Coll of Jewish Studies (OH)
Coll Dominicain de Philosophie et de Théologie (ON, Canada)
Coll of Saint Benedict (MN)
Coll of St. Catherine (MN)
Colorado Christian U (CO)
Columbia Union Coll (MD)
Concordia U (IL)
Concordia U (NE)
Concordia U (OR)
Concordia U (PQ, Canada)
Concordia U at St. Paul (MN)
Concordia U Wisconsin (WI)
Creighton U (NE)
Crown Coll (MN)
Dakota Wesleyan U (SD)
David Lipscomb U (TN)
Dordt Coll (IA)
Duquesne U (PA)
Eastern Coll (PA)
Eastern Mennonite U (VA)
Eastern Pentecostal Bible Coll (ON, Canada)
East Texas Baptist U (TX)
Elmhurst Coll (IL)
Faulkner U (AL)
Florida Baptist Theological Coll (FL)
Florida Christian Coll (FL)
Fordham U (NY)
Franciscan U of Steubenville (OH)
Friends U (KS)
Gannon U (PA)
George Fox U (OR)
Global U of the Assemblies of God (MO)
Grace Bible Coll (MI)
Grand Canyon U (AZ)
Greenville Coll (IL)
Griggs U (MD)
Hannibal-LaGrange Coll (MO)
Hanover Coll (IN)
Hardin-Simmons U (TX)

Hebrew Theological Coll (IL)
Hellenic Coll (MA)
Heritage Baptist Coll & Heritage Theological Sem (ON, Canada)
Heritage Bible Coll (NC)
Hillsdale Free Will Baptist Coll (OK)
Hobe Sound Bible Coll (FL)
Holy Trinity Orthodox Seminary (NY)
Howard Payne U (TX)
Huntington Coll (IN)
Immaculata Coll (PA)
Indiana Wesleyan U (IN)
John Brown U (AR)
John Wesley Coll (NC)
King's Coll (PA)
Lee U (TN)
Lenoir-Rhyne Coll (NC)
LIFE Bible Coll (CA)
Lincoln Christian Coll (IL)
Loras Coll (IA)
Louisiana Coll (LA)
Loyola Marymount U (CA)
Luther Coll (IA)
Manhattan Christian Coll (KS)
Marian Coll (IN)
Marquette U (WI)
Martin Luther Coll (MN)
Merrimack Coll (MA)
Mid-America Bible Coll (OK)
Minnesota Bible Coll (MN)
Mount Saint Mary's Coll and Seminary (MD)
Mount Vernon Nazarene Coll (OH)
Multnomah Bible Coll and Biblical Seminary (OR)
Nebraska Christian Coll (NE)
Newman U (KS)
North Greenville Coll (SC)
North Park U (IL)
Northwest Bible Coll (AB, Canada)
Northwest Coll (WA)
Northwestern Coll (IA)
Northwest Nazarene U (ID)
Notre Dame Coll of Ohio (OH)
Nyack Coll (NY)
Oakland City U (IN)
Oakwood Coll (AL)
Ohio Dominican Coll (OH)
Oklahoma Baptist U (OK)
Olivet Nazarene U (IL)
Ouachita Baptist U (AR)
Ozark Christian Coll (MO)
Pacific Union Coll (CA)
Piedmont Baptist Coll (NC)
Point Loma Nazarene U (CA)
Pontifical Catholic U of Puerto Rico (PR)
Prairie Bible Coll (AB, Canada)
Providence Coll (RI)
Providence Coll and Theological Seminary (MB, Canada)
Quincy U (IL)
Rabbinical Seminary of America (NY)
Redeemer Coll (ON, Canada)
Reformed Bible Coll (MI)
Rockhurst U (MO)
St. Ambrose U (IA)
Saint Anselm Coll (NH)
St. Gregory's U (OK)
St. John's Seminary Coll (CA)
Saint John's U (MN)
St. John's U (NY)
Saint Joseph's U (PA)
St. Louis Christian Coll (MO)
Saint Louis U (MO)
Saint Mary Coll (KS)
Saint Mary's Coll (IN)
Saint Mary-of-the-Woods Coll (IN)
Saint Mary's Coll (IN)
Saint Mary's Coll of California (CA)
Saint Mary's U of Minnesota (MN)
St. Mary's U of San Antonio (TX)
Saint Paul U (ON, Canada)
San Jose Christian Coll (CA)
Seton Hill Coll (PA)
Silver Lake Coll (WI)
Southeastern Coll of the Assemblies of God (FL)
Southern Adventist U (TN)
Southern Christian U (AL)
Southwestern Adventist U (TX)
Southwestern Coll of Christian Ministries (OK)
Spring Hill Coll (AL)
Talmudical Yeshiva of Philadelphia (PA)

Majors Index
Theology–Urban Studies

Taylor U (IN)
Texas Lutheran U (TX)
Thomas More Coll (KY)
Toccoa Falls Coll (GA)
Trinity Bible Coll (ND)
Trinity Christian Coll (IL)
Union Coll (NE)
Union U (TN)
Universidad Adventista de las Antillas (PR)
Université de Montréal (PQ, Canada)
Université de Sherbrooke (PQ, Canada)
U du Québec à Chicoutimi (PQ, Canada)
U du Québec à Trois-Rivières (PQ, Canada)
Université Laval (PQ, Canada)
U of Dallas (TX)
U of Dubuque (IA)
U of Notre Dame (IN)
U of Portland (OR)
U of St. Francis (IL)
U of St. Thomas (MN)
U of St. Thomas (TX)
U of San Francisco (CA)
U of Toronto (ON, Canada)
Valparaiso U (IN)
Walla Walla Coll (WA)
Walsh U (OH)
Warner Pacific Coll (OR)
Washington Bible Coll (MD)
Western Baptist Coll (OR)
Williams Baptist Coll (AR)
William Tyndale Coll (MI)
Wisconsin Lutheran Coll (WI)
Wittenberg U (OH)
Xavier U (OH)
Xavier U of Louisiana (LA)
Yeshiva Karlin Stolin Rabbinical Inst (NY)
Yeshiva Ohr Elchonon Chabad/W Coast Talmudical Sem (CA)
York Coll (NE)

(PRE)THEOLOGY
Alma Coll (MI)
Ashland U (OH)
Atlanta Christian Coll (GA)
Blue Mountain Coll (MS)
California Christian Coll (CA)
Central Christian Coll of Kansas (KS)
Christian Brothers U (TN)
Circleville Bible Coll (OH)
Coll of Saint Benedict (MN)
Coll of Santa Fe (NM)
Columbia International U (SC)
Concordia U (IL)
Concordia U (OR)
Emmaus Bible Coll (IA)
Geneva Coll (PA)
Kentucky Mountain Bible Coll (KY)
Loyola U Chicago (IL)
Luther Coll (IA)
Martin Luther Coll (MN)
Minnesota State U, Mankato (MN)
Moody Bible Inst (IL)
Mount Allison U (NB, Canada)
Northwestern Coll (MN)
Ohio Wesleyan U (OH)
Redeemer Coll (ON, Canada)
Reformed Bible Coll (MI)
Saint John's U (MN)
Saint Xavier U (IL)
Southeastern Coll of the Assemblies of God (FL)
Southwestern Coll (KS)
Tennessee Wesleyan Coll (TN)
Trinity Christian Coll (IL)
U of Dallas (TX)
U of Indianapolis (IN)
U of North Texas (TX)
U of Rio Grande (OH)
Valparaiso U (IN)
Warner Southern Coll (FL)
Westmont Coll (CA)

THEORETICAL AND MATHEMATICAL PHYSICS
Bridgewater Coll (VA)
U of Guelph (ON, Canada)

TOOL AND DIE MAKING
Utah State U (UT)

TOURISM/TRAVEL MARKETING
Central Missouri State U (MO)
Eastern Michigan U (MI)
Johnson & Wales U (RI)
Mount Saint Vincent U (NS, Canada)
Plymouth State Coll (NH)
Rochester Inst of Technology (NY)
U of Guelph (ON, Canada)
U of the Sacred Heart (PR)

TOXICOLOGY
Ashland U (OH)
Bloomfield Coll (NJ)
Clarkson U (NY)
Coll of Saint Elizabeth (NJ)
Eastern Michigan U (MI)
Fairleigh Dickinson U, Teaneck-Hackensack Campus (NJ)
Felician Coll (NJ)
Humboldt State U (CA)
Minnesota State U, Mankato (MN)
Monmouth U (NJ)
Northeastern U (MA)
St. John's U (NY)
Texas Southern U (TX)
U of Guelph (ON, Canada)
U of Louisiana at Monroe (LA)
U of the Sciences in Philadelphia (PA)
U of Toronto (ON, Canada)
The U of Western Ontario (ON, Canada)
U of Wisconsin–Madison (WI)

TRADE AND INDUSTRIAL EDUCATION
Athens State U (AL)
Auburn U (AL)
Ball State U (IN)
Bemidji State U (MN)
California Polytechnic State U, San Luis Obispo (CA)
California State U, Fresno (CA)
California State U, Long Beach (CA)
California State U, San Bernardino (CA)
Central Connecticut State U (CT)
Clemson U (SC)
Colorado State U (CO)
Dakota State U (SD)
Delaware State U (DE)
Eastern Kentucky U (KY)
Florida A&M U (FL)
Florida International U (FL)
Georgia Southern U (GA)
Gustavus Adolphus Coll (MN)
Indiana State U (IN)
Indiana U of Pennsylvania (PA)
Iowa State U of Science and Technology (IA)
Keene State Coll (NH)
Kent State U (OH)
Louisiana State U and A&M Coll (LA)
Madonna U (MI)
McGill U (PQ, Canada)
Memorial U of Newfoundland (NF, Canada)
Morehead State U (KY)
Murray State U (KY)
New York City Tech Coll of the City U of NY (NY)
New York Inst of Technology (NY)
New York U (NY)
North Carolina Ag and Tech State U (NC)
Northeastern State U (OK)
Northern Arizona U (AZ)
Northern Kentucky U (KY)
Oklahoma State U (OK)
Pittsburg State U (KS)
Prairie View A&M U (TX)
San Diego State U (CA)
San Francisco State U (CA)
Southeast Missouri State U (MO)
Southern Illinois U Carbondale (IL)
State U of NY at Oswego (NY)
State U of NY Coll at Buffalo (NY)
Temple U (PA)
Texas A&M U–Commerce (TX)
U du Québec à Chicoutimi (PQ, Canada)
The U of Akron (OH)
U of Alberta (AB, Canada)
U of Arkansas (AR)

U of Arkansas at Pine Bluff (AR)
U of Central Florida (FL)
U of Central Oklahoma (OK)
U of Idaho (ID)
U of Louisville (KY)
U of Nebraska at Omaha (NE)
U of Nebraska–Lincoln (NE)
U of Nevada, Reno (NV)
U of New Hampshire (NH)
U of North Dakota (ND)
U of Northern Iowa (IA)
U of North Florida (FL)
U of Pittsburgh (PA)
U of Regina (SK, Canada)
U of Southern Maine (ME)
U of South Florida (FL)
U of the District of Columbia (DC)
U of the Virgin Islands (VI)
U of West Florida (FL)
U of Wyoming (WY)
Valdosta State U (GA)
Virginia Polytechnic Inst and State U (VA)
Wayland Baptist U (TX)
Western Illinois U (IL)
Western Kentucky U (KY)
Western Michigan U (MI)

TRANSPORTATION ENGINEERING
Dowling Coll (NY)
The Ohio State U (OH)
Rensselaer Polytechnic Inst (NY)
U of Pennsylvania (PA)
Worcester Polytechnic Inst (MA)

TRANSPORTATION TECHNOLOGIES
Auburn U (AL)
California State U, Los Angeles (CA)
Dowling Coll (NY)
Eastern Kentucky U (KY)
Iowa State U of Science and Technology (IA)
Maine Maritime Academy (ME)
Niagara U (NY)
North Carolina Ag and Tech State U (NC)
Pacific Union Coll (CA)
Peru State Coll (NE)
Robert Morris Coll (PA)
Saint Louis U (MO)
San Francisco State U (CA)
State U of NY at Farmingdale (NY)
Tennessee State U (TN)
Texas A&M U at Galveston (TX)
Texas Southern U (TX)
U of Cincinnati (OH)
U of Maryland, Coll Park (MD)
U of North Florida (FL)

TRAVEL-TOURISM MANAGEMENT
Alaska Pacific U (AK)
American InterContinental U (CA)
American InterContinental U, Atlanta (GA)
American InterContinental U, Atlanta (GA)
Arkansas State U (AR)
Ball State U (IN)
Black Hills State U (SD)
Brigham Young U–Hawaii Campus (HI)
Brock U (ON, Canada)
Champlain Coll (VT)
Coastal Carolina U (SC)
The Coll of Southeastern Europe, The American U of Athens (Greece)
Concord Coll (WV)
Daemen Coll (NY)
DePaul U (IL)
Dowling Coll (NY)
Eastern Kentucky U (KY)
Fairleigh Dickinson U, Teaneck-Hackensack Campus (NJ)
Fort Lewis Coll (CO)
Grand Valley State U (MI)
Hawaii Pacific U (HI)
Inter American U of PR, Fajardo Campus (PR)
Johnson & Wales U (RI)
Johnson State Coll (VT)
Kent State U (OH)

Lasell Coll (MA)
Long Island U, Southampton Coll, Friends World Program (NY)
Lynn U (FL)
Mansfield U of Pennsylvania (PA)
Mount Saint Vincent U (NS, Canada)
New Hampshire Coll (NH)
New Mexico Highlands U (NM)
New Mexico State U (NM)
New York U (NY)
Niagara U (NY)
North Carolina State U (NC)
Northeastern State U (OK)
Northwestern State U of Louisiana (LA)
Open Learning Agency (BC, Canada)
Our Lady of Holy Cross Coll (LA)
Robert Morris Coll (IL)
Robert Morris Coll (PA)
Rochester Inst of Technology (NY)
Ryerson Polytechnic U (ON, Canada)
St. Thomas U (FL)
Salem State Coll (MA)
Slippery Rock U of Pennsylvania (PA)
Southeast Missouri State U (MO)
Texas A&M U (TX)
Tiffin U (OH)
United States International U (CA)
U Coll of Cape Breton (NS, Canada)
U of Alaska Fairbanks (AK)
U of Calgary (AB, Canada)
U of Maine at Machias (ME)
U of Nevada, Las Vegas (NV)
U of New Hampshire (NH)
U of New Haven (CT)
The U of Texas at San Antonio (TX)
U of the Sacred Heart (PR)
Virginia Commonwealth U (VA)
Virginia Polytechnic Inst and State U (VA)
Webber Coll (FL)
Western Michigan U (MI)

TURF MANAGEMENT
Colorado State U (CO)
The Ohio State U (OH)
Penn State U Univ Park Campus (PA)
U of Georgia (GA)
U of Maryland, Coll Park (MD)
U of Rhode Island (RI)

URBAN STUDIES
Albertus Magnus Coll (CT)
Aquinas Coll (MI)
Augsburg Coll (MN)
Barnard Coll (NY)
Baylor U (TX)
Bellevue U (NE)
Beulah Heights Bible Coll (GA)
Boston U (MA)
Brown U (RI)
California State Polytechnic U, Pomona (CA)
California State U, Northridge (CA)
Canisius Coll (NY)
Carleton U (ON, Canada)
Cleveland State U (OH)
Coll of Charleston (SC)
Coll of Mount Saint Vincent (NY)
The Coll of Wooster (OH)
Columbia Coll (NY)
Columbia U, School of General Studies (NY)
Concordia U (PQ, Canada)
Connecticut Coll (CT)
Cornell U (NY)
David Lipscomb U (TN)
DePaul U (IL)
Eastern Coll (PA)
Eastern Washington U (WA)
Elmhurst Coll (IL)
Eugene Lang Coll, New School U (NY)
The Evergreen State Coll (WA)
Fordham U (NY)
Framingham State Coll (MA)
Furman U (SC)
George Mason U (VA)
Georgia State U (GA)
Hamline U (MN)

Hampshire Coll (MA)
Harris-Stowe State Coll (MO)
Harvard U (MA)
Haverford Coll (PA)
Hobart and William Smith Colls (NY)
Hunter Coll of the City U of NY (NY)
Indiana State U (IN)
Indiana U Bloomington (IN)
Iona Coll (NY)
Langston U (OK)
Lehigh U (PA)
Long Island U, Southampton Coll, Friends World Program (NY)
Loyola Marymount U (CA)
Macalester Coll (MN)
Malone Coll (OH)
Manhattan Coll (NY)
Marquette U (WI)
Massachusetts Inst of Technology (MA)
McGill U (PQ, Canada)
Metropolitan State Coll of Denver (CO)
Minnesota State U, Mankato (MN)
Morehouse Coll (GA)
Mount Mercy Coll (IA)
New Coll of the U of South Florida (FL)
New Jersey City U (NJ)
New York U (NY)
Norfolk State U (VA)
Northeastern Illinois U (IL)
North Park U (IL)
Northwestern U (IL)
Oglethorpe U (GA)
The Ohio State U (OH)
Ohio U (OH)
Ohio Wesleyan U (OH)
Portland State U (OR)
Queens Coll of the City U of NY (NY)
Rhodes Coll (TN)
Rockford Coll (IL)
Rutgers, State U of NJ, Camden Coll of Arts & Scis (NJ)
Rutgers, State U of NJ, Douglass Coll (NJ)
Rutgers, State U of NJ, Livingston Coll (NJ)
Rutgers, State U of NJ, Rutgers Coll (NJ)
Rutgers, State U of NJ, U Coll–Camden (NJ)
Rutgers, State U of NJ, U Coll–New Brunswick (NJ)
Ryerson Polytechnic U (ON, Canada)
St. Cloud State U (MN)
Saint Louis U (MO)
St. Olaf Coll (MN)
Saint Peter's Coll (NJ)
San Diego State U (CA)
San Francisco State U (CA)
Sarah Lawrence Coll (NY)
Shippensburg U of Pennsylvania (PA)
Stanford U (CA)
State U of NY at Albany (NY)
State U of NY Coll at Buffalo (NY)
Taylor U, Fort Wayne Campus (IN)
Temple U (PA)
Trinity U (TX)
Tufts U (MA)
Université de Montréal (PQ, Canada)
U of Alberta (AB, Canada)
U of British Columbia (BC, Canada)
U of Calgary (AB, Canada)
U of Calif, San Diego (CA)
U of Cincinnati (OH)
U of Connecticut (CT)
The U of Lethbridge (AB, Canada)
U of Michigan–Flint (MI)
U of Minnesota, Duluth (MN)
U of Minnesota, Twin Cities Campus (MN)
U of Missouri–Kansas City (MO)
U of Missouri–St. Louis (MO)
U of Nebraska at Omaha (NE)
The U of North Carolina at Greensboro (NC)
U of Pennsylvania (PA)
U of Pittsburgh (PA)
U of Richmond (VA)

Majors Index
Urban Studies–Women's Studies

U of San Diego (CA)
U of Southern California (CA)
The U of Tampa (FL)
The U of Tennessee at Chattanooga (TN)
U of the District of Columbia (DC)
U of the Sacred Heart (PR)
U of Toronto (ON, Canada)
U of Utah (UT)
The U of Western Ontario (ON, Canada)
The U of Winnipeg (MB, Canada)
U of Wisconsin–Green Bay (WI)
U of Wisconsin–Madison (WI)
U of Wisconsin–Milwaukee (WI)
Vanderbilt U (TN)
Vassar Coll (NY)
Virginia Commonwealth U (VA)
Virginia Polytechnic Inst and State U (VA)
Washington U in St. Louis (MO)
Wayne State U (MI)
Wittenberg U (OH)
Worcester State Coll (MA)
Wright State U (OH)
York U (ON, Canada)
Youngstown State U (OH)

VETERINARIAN ASSISTANT
Michigan State U (MI)
Morehead State U (KY)
Murray State U (KY)
U of Nebraska–Lincoln (NE)

VETERINARY SCIENCES
Becker Coll (MA)
Lincoln Memorial U (TN)
Mercy Coll (NY)
Pontifical Catholic U of Puerto Rico (PR)
Texas A&M U (TX)
Université de Montréal (PQ, Canada)
The U of Arizona (AZ)
U of Guelph (ON, Canada)
U of Idaho (ID)
U of Maryland, Coll Park (MD)
U of Wyoming (WY)
Wagner Coll (NY)
Washington State U (WA)

VETERINARY TECHNOLOGY
Mercy Coll (NY)
Michigan State U (MI)
Mount Ida Coll (MA)
Newberry Coll (SC)
North Dakota State U (ND)
Quinnipiac U (CT)

VISUAL/PERFORMING ARTS
American Academy of Art (IL)
Antioch Coll (OH)
Arizona State U West (AZ)
Art Center Coll of Design (CA)
Bard Coll (NY)
Bennington Coll (VT)
Brevard Coll (NC)
Brigham Young U (UT)
Brown U (RI)
California State U, San Marcos (CA)
Cazenovia Coll (NY)
Christopher Newport U (VA)
Concordia Coll (MI)
Delta State U (MS)
East Stroudsburg U of Pennsylvania (PA)
Emerson Coll (MA)
Flagler Coll (FL)
Frostburg State U (MD)
Green Mountain Coll (VT)
International Fine Arts Coll (FL)
Iowa State U of Science and Technology (IA)
Ithaca Coll (NY)
Jacksonville U (FL)
Johnson State Coll (VT)
Kutztown U of Pennsylvania (PA)
Loyola U New Orleans (LA)
Maharishi U of Management (IA)
Maryland Inst, Coll of Art (MD)
Marywood U (PA)
Mount Saint Mary's Coll and Seminary (MD)
Ohio U (OH)
Penn State U Abington Coll (PA)
Penn State U Altoona Coll (PA)
Penn State U Univ Park Campus (PA)
Providence Coll (RI)
Regis U (CO)
The Richard Stockton Coll of New Jersey (NJ)
Roger Williams U (RI)
Saint Augustine's Coll (NC)
St. Bonaventure U (NY)
Saint Mary Coll (KS)
Saint Peter's Coll (NJ)
San Jose State U (CA)
Savannah Coll of Art and Design (GA)
Seton Hill Coll (PA)
Shenandoah U (VA)
Simon's Rock Coll of Bard (MA)
South Dakota State U (SD)
Southwest Missouri State U (MO)
The U of Alabama at Birmingham (AL)
The U of Arizona (AZ)
U of Louisiana at Lafayette (LA)
U of Maine at Machias (ME)
U of Maryland, Baltimore County (MD)
U of Michigan (MI)
The U of North Carolina at Wilmington (NC)
U of North Texas (TX)
U of Rio Grande (OH)
U of St. Francis (IL)
U of San Francisco (CA)
The U of Tampa (FL)
The U of Tennessee at Martin (TN)
The U of Texas at Austin (TX)
Western Kentucky U (KY)
West Virginia U (WV)
Wichita State U (KS)
York U (ON, Canada)

VOCATIONAL REHABILITATION COUNSELING
East Carolina U (NC)
Emporia State U (KS)
U of Wisconsin–Stout (WI)

WATER RESOURCES
Colorado State U (CO)
East Central U (OK)
The Evergreen State Coll (WA)
Grand Valley State U (MI)
Heidelberg Coll (OH)
Humboldt State U (CA)
Montana State U–Northern (MT)
Northern Michigan U (MI)
Northland Coll (WI)
Ohio U (OH)
Rensselaer Polytechnic Inst (NY)
Rutgers, State U of NJ, Cook Coll (NJ)
St. Francis Xavier U (NS, Canada)
State U of NY Coll at Brockport (NY)
State U of NY Coll at Oneonta (NY)
State U of NY Coll of Environ Sci and Forestry (NY)
U of Maryland, Coll Park (MD)
U of New Hampshire (NH)
U of Regina (SK, Canada)
U of Southern California (CA)
U of Vermont (VT)
U of Wisconsin–Madison (WI)
U of Wisconsin–Stevens Point (WI)
Utah State U (UT)
Wright State U (OH)

WATER RESOURCES ENGINEERING
State U of NY Coll of Environ Sci and Forestry (NY)
U of Guelph (ON, Canada)
U of Nevada, Reno (NV)
U of Southern California (CA)

WATER TREATMENT TECHNOLOGY
Mississippi Valley State U (MS)
Murray State U (KY)

WELDING TECHNOLOGY
Ferris State U (MI)
LeTourneau U (TX)
Montana Tech of The U of Montana (MT)
Pennsylvania Coll of Technology (PA)
Regents Coll (NY)

WESTERN CIVILIZATION
Bard Coll (NY)
Belmont U (TN)
Carnegie Mellon U (PA)
Concordia U (PQ, Canada)
The Evergreen State Coll (WA)
Gettysburg Coll (PA)
Grand Valley State U (MI)
Harvard U (MA)
Long Island U, Southampton Coll, Friends World Program (NY)
Saint Anselm Coll (NH)
St. John's Coll (MD)
St. John's Coll (NM)
Sarah Lawrence Coll (NY)
Thomas Aquinas Coll (CA)
U of King's Coll (NS, Canada)
The U of Western Ontario (ON, Canada)
Western Washington U (WA)

WESTERN EUROPEAN STUDIES
Central Coll (IA)
Grinnell Coll (IA)
Knox Coll (IL)
The Ohio State U (OH)
St. Francis Coll (NY)
Seattle U (WA)
U of Houston (TX)
U of Nebraska–Lincoln (NE)

WILDLIFE BIOLOGY
Adams State Coll (CO)
Arizona State U (AZ)
Arkansas Tech U (AR)
Baker U (KS)
Ball State U (IN)
Brigham Young U (UT)
Clemson U (SC)
Coll of the Atlantic (ME)
The Evergreen State Coll (WA)
Framingham State Coll (MA)
Grand Canyon U (AZ)
Grand Valley State U (MI)
Iowa State U of Science and Technology (IA)
Kansas State U (KS)
McGill U (PQ, Canada)
Midwestern State U (TX)
New Mexico State U (NM)
Northeastern State U (OK)
Northern Michigan U (MI)
Northland Coll (WI)
Northwest Missouri State U (MO)
Ohio U (OH)
St. Cloud State U (MN)
State U of NY Coll of Environ Sci and Forestry (NY)
Unity Coll (ME)
U of Alaska Fairbanks (AK)
U of Guelph (ON, Canada)
U of Michigan (MI)
U of New Brunswick, Fredericton (NB, Canada)
U of New Hampshire (NH)
U of Vermont (VT)
Washington State U (WA)
West Texas A&M U (TX)
Winona State U (MN)

WILDLIFE MANAGEMENT
Arkansas State U (AR)
Auburn U (AL)
Brigham Young U (UT)
Colorado State U (CO)
Delaware State U (DE)
Eastern Kentucky U (KY)
Eastern New Mexico U (NM)
Fort Hays State U (KS)
Framingham State Coll (MA)
Frostburg State U (MD)
Grand Valley State U (MI)
Humboldt State U (CA)
Lake Superior State U (MI)
Lincoln Memorial U (TN)
Long Island U, Southampton Coll, Friends World Program (NY)
Louisiana State U and A&M Coll (LA)
McGill U (PQ, Canada)
McNeese State U (LA)
Michigan State U (MI)
Mississippi State U (MS)
Murray State U (KY)
New Mexico State U (NM)
Northern Arizona U (AZ)
Northland Coll (WI)
Northwestern Oklahoma State U (OK)
Northwest Missouri State U (MO)
The Ohio State U (OH)
Oklahoma State U (OK)
Oregon State U (OR)
Peru State Coll (NE)
Pittsburg State U (KS)
Purdue U (IN)
Purdue U Calumet (IN)
Rutgers, State U of NJ, Cook Coll (NJ)
South Dakota State U (SD)
Southeastern Oklahoma State U (OK)
Southwest Missouri State U (MO)
Southwest Texas State U (TX)
State U of NY Coll of Environ Sci and Forestry (NY)
Stephen F. Austin State U (TX)
Sterling Coll (VT)
Sul Ross State U (TX)
Tennessee Technological U (TN)
Texas A&M U (TX)
Texas A&M U–Kingsville (TX)
Texas Tech U (TX)
U of Alberta (AB, Canada)
The U of Arizona (AZ)
U of Arkansas at Monticello (AR)
U of British Columbia (BC, Canada)
U of Delaware (DE)
U of Georgia (GA)
U of Idaho (ID)
U of Maine (ME)
U of Maryland, Coll Park (MD)
U of Massachusetts Amherst (MA)
The U of Montana–Missoula (MT)
U of Nebraska–Lincoln (NE)
U of Nevada, Reno (NV)
U of New Brunswick, Fredericton (NB, Canada)
U of New Hampshire (NH)
U of Puerto Rico, Humacao U Coll (PR)
U of Rhode Island (RI)
The U of Tennessee at Martin (TN)
The U of Tennessee Knoxville (TN)
U of Vermont (VT)
U of Washington (WA)
U of Wisconsin–Madison (WI)
U of Wisconsin–Stevens Point (WI)
U of Wyoming (WY)
Utah State U (UT)
Warren Wilson Coll (NC)
Washington State U (WA)
West Virginia U (WV)
Winona State U (MN)

WIND AND PERCUSSION INSTRUMENTS
Acadia U (NS, Canada)
Alma Coll (MI)
Appalachian State U (NC)
Augustana Coll (IL)
Baldwin-Wallace Coll (OH)
Ball State U (IN)
Berklee Coll of Music (MA)
Bowling Green State U (OH)
Brevard Coll (NC)
Bryan Coll (TN)
Butler U (IN)
California State U, Fullerton (CA)
California State U, Northridge (CA)
Capital U (OH)
Centenary Coll of Louisiana (LA)
Chapman U (CA)
Chicago State U (IL)
Cleveland Inst of Music (OH)
Columbus State U (GA)
Concordia Coll (MN)
Concordia U (IL)
The Curtis Inst of Music (PA)
David Lipscomb U (TN)
DePaul U (IL)
Eastern Washington U (WA)
Five Towns Coll (NY)
Florida State U (FL)
Georgia Southwestern State U (GA)
Grand Canyon U (AZ)
Grand Valley State U (MI)
Hardin-Simmons U (TX)
Houghton Coll (NY)
Howard Payne U (TX)
Illinois Wesleyan U (IL)
Indiana U Bloomington (IN)
Indiana U–Purdue U Fort Wayne (IN)
Inter American U of PR, San Germán Campus (PR)
The Juilliard School (NY)
Lambuth U (TN)
Lawrence U (WI)
Luther Coll (IA)
Manhattan School of Music (NY)
Mannes Coll of Music, New School U (NY)
Marshall U (WV)
Mars Hill Coll (NC)
Maryville Coll (TN)
Memorial U of Newfoundland (NF, Canada)
Mercyhurst Coll (PA)
Meredith Coll (NC)
Minnesota State U, Mankato (MN)
Minnesota State U Moorhead (MN)
Missouri Southern State Coll (MO)
Mount Allison U (NB, Canada)
Mount Vernon Nazarene Coll (OH)
New England Conservatory of Music (MA)
New World School of the Arts (FL)
New York U (NY)
Northern Arizona U (AZ)
Northern Michigan U (MI)
Northwestern U (IL)
Northwest Missouri State U (MO)
Oberlin Coll (OH)
Oklahoma Baptist U (OK)
Oklahoma Christian U of Science and Arts (OK)
Oklahoma City U (OK)
Olivet Nazarene U (IL)
Otterbein Coll (OH)
Palm Beach Atlantic Coll (FL)
Peabody Conserv of Music of Johns Hopkins U (MD)
Peru State Coll (NE)
Pittsburg State U (KS)
Prairie View A&M U (TX)
Queens Coll of the City U of NY (NY)
St. Olaf Coll (MN)
San Francisco Conservatory of Music (CA)
Sarah Lawrence Coll (NY)
Seton Hill Coll (PA)
Southeast Missouri State U (MO)
Southwestern Oklahoma State U (OK)
State U of NY Coll at Fredonia (NY)
State U of NY Coll at Potsdam (NY)
Susquehanna U (PA)
Syracuse U (NY)
Temple U (PA)
Texas Southern U (TX)
Texas Wesleyan U (TX)
The U of Akron (OH)
U of Alberta (AB, Canada)
U of Central Oklahoma (OK)
U of Cincinnati (OH)
The U of Iowa (IA)
U of Kansas (KS)
U of Miami (FL)
U of Michigan (MI)
U of Missouri–Kansas City (MO)
U of New Hampshire (NH)
U of North Texas (TX)
U of Oklahoma (OK)
U of Sioux Falls (SD)
U of South Dakota (SD)
U of Southern California (CA)
The U of Tennessee at Martin (TN)
The U of the Arts (PA)
U of the Pacific (CA)
The U of Western Ontario (ON, Canada)
U of Wisconsin–Milwaukee (WI)
Vanderbilt U (TN)
Virginia Commonwealth U (VA)
Wheaton Coll (IL)
Xavier U of Louisiana (LA)

WOMEN'S STUDIES
Agnes Scott Coll (GA)
Albion Coll (MI)
Allegheny Coll (PA)

Majors Index
Women's Studies–Zoology

American U (DC)
Amherst Coll (MA)
Antioch Coll (OH)
Arizona State U (AZ)
Arizona State U West (AZ)
Athabasca U (AB, Canada)
Augsburg Coll (MN)
Augustana Coll (IL)
Barnard Coll (NY)
Bates Coll (ME)
Beloit Coll (WI)
Bishop's U (PQ, Canada)
Bowdoin Coll (ME)
Bowling Green State U (OH)
Brock U (ON, Canada)
Brooklyn Coll of the City U of NY (NY)
Brown U (RI)
Bucknell U (PA)
Burlington Coll (VT)
California State U, Fresno (CA)
California State U, Long Beach (CA)
California State U, Northridge (CA)
California State U, Sacramento (CA)
California State U, San Marcos (CA)
Carleton Coll (MN)
Carleton U (ON, Canada)
Case Western Reserve U (OH)
Chapman U (CA)
Chatham Coll (PA)
City Coll of the City U of NY (NY)
Claremont McKenna Coll (CA)
Colby Coll (ME)
Colgate U (NY)
The Coll of New Rochelle (NY)
Coll of St. Catherine (MN)
Coll of Staten Island of the City U of NY (NY)
Coll of the Holy Cross (MA)
The Coll of William and Mary (VA)
The Coll of Wooster (OH)
The Colorado Coll (CO)
Columbia Coll (NY)
Columbia U, School of General Studies (NY)
Concordia U (PQ, Canada)
Connecticut Coll (CT)
Cornell Coll (IA)
Cornell U (NY)
Curry Coll (MA)
Dalhousie U (NS, Canada)
Dartmouth Coll (NH)
Denison U (OH)
DePaul U (IL)
DePauw U (IN)
Drew U (NJ)
Duke U (NC)
Earlham Coll (IN)
East Carolina U (NC)
Eastern Michigan U (MI)
Eckerd Coll (FL)
Emory U (GA)
Eugene Lang Coll, New School U (NY)
The Evergreen State Coll (WA)
Florida International U (FL)
Florida State U (FL)
Fordham U (NY)
Franklin and Marshall Coll (PA)
Gettysburg Coll (PA)
Goddard Coll (VT)
Goucher Coll (MD)
Grand Valley State U (MI)
Grinnell Coll (IA)
Guilford Coll (NC)
Hamilton Coll (NY)
Hamline U (MN)
Hampshire Coll (MA)
Harvard U (MA)
Haverford Coll (PA)
Hobart and William Smith Colls (NY)
Hollins U (VA)
Hunter Coll of the City U of NY (NY)
Indiana State U (IN)
Indiana U Bloomington (IN)
Indiana U–Purdue U Fort Wayne (IN)
Indiana U South Bend (IN)
Iowa State U of Science and Technology (IA)
Kansas State U (KS)
Kenyon Coll (OH)
Knox Coll (IL)
Lake Forest Coll (IL)
Long Island U, Southampton Coll, Friends World Program (NY)
Longwood Coll (VA)
Macalester Coll (MN)
Marlboro Coll (VT)
Marquette U (WI)
Massachusetts Inst of Technology (MA)
McGill U (PQ, Canada)
Memorial U of Newfoundland (NF, Canada)
Metropolitan State U (MN)
Michigan State U (MI)
Middlebury Coll (VT)
Mills Coll (CA)
Minnesota State U, Mankato (MN)
Mount Holyoke Coll (MA)
Mount Saint Vincent U (NS, Canada)
Nazareth Coll of Rochester (NY)
Nebraska Wesleyan U (NE)
New England Coll (NH)
New York U (NY)
Nipissing U (ON, Canada)
Oakland U (MI)
Oberlin Coll (OH)
Occidental Coll (CA)
The Ohio State U (OH)
Ohio Wesleyan U (OH)
Old Dominion U (VA)
Pacific Lutheran U (WA)
Penn State U Univ Park Campus (PA)
Pitzer Coll (CA)
Pomona Coll (CA)
Portland State U (OR)
Purchase Coll, State U of NY (NY)
Purdue U Calumet (IN)
Queen's U at Kingston (ON, Canada)
Randolph-Macon Coll (VA)
Rosemont Coll (PA)
Rutgers, State U of NJ, Douglass Coll (NJ)
Rutgers, State U of NJ, Livingston Coll (NJ)
Rutgers, State U of NJ, Newark Coll of Arts & Scis (NJ)
Rutgers, State U of NJ, Rutgers Coll (NJ)
Rutgers, State U of NJ, U Coll–New Brunswick (NJ)
Sacred Heart U (CT)
St. Francis Xavier U (NS, Canada)
Saint Mary's Coll of California (CA)
Saint Mary's U (NS, Canada)
St. Olaf Coll (MN)
San Diego State U (CA)
San Francisco State U (CA)
Sarah Lawrence Coll (NY)
Scripps Coll (CA)
Simmons Coll (MA)
Simon Fraser U (BC, Canada)
Simon's Rock Coll of Bard (MA)
Skidmore Coll (NY)
Smith Coll (MA)
Sonoma State U (CA)
Southwestern U (TX)
Spelman Coll (GA)
Stanford U (CA)
State U of NY at Albany (NY)
State U of NY at Buffalo (NY)
State U of NY at New Paltz (NY)
State U of NY at Oswego (NY)
State U of NY at Stony Brook (NY)
State U of NY Coll at Brockport (NY)
State U of NY Coll at Fredonia (NY)
State U of NY Coll at Potsdam (NY)
Suffolk U (MA)
Syracuse U (NY)
Temple U (PA)
Towson U (MD)
Trent U (ON, Canada)
Trinity Coll (CT)
Tufts U (MA)
Tulane U (LA)
U of Alberta (AB, Canada)
The U of Arizona (AZ)
U of British Columbia (BC, Canada)
U of Calgary (AB, Canada)
U of Calif, Berkeley (CA)
U of Calif, Davis (CA)
U of Calif, Irvine (CA)
U of Calif, Los Angeles (CA)
U of Calif, Riverside (CA)
U of Calif, San Diego (CA)
U of Calif, Santa Barbara (CA)
U of Calif, Santa Cruz (CA)
U of Colorado at Boulder (CO)
U of Connecticut (CT)
U of Delaware (DE)
U of Denver (CO)
U of Georgia (GA)
U of Guelph (ON, Canada)
U of Hartford (CT)
The U of Iowa (IA)
U of Kansas (KS)
U of King's Coll (NS, Canada)
The U of Lethbridge (AB, Canada)
U of Louisville (KY)
U of Maine (ME)
U of Manitoba (MB, Canada)
U of Maryland, Coll Park (MD)
U of Massachusetts Amherst (MA)
U of Massachusetts Boston (MA)
U of Miami (FL)
U of Michigan (MI)
U of Michigan–Dearborn (MI)
U of Minnesota, Duluth (MN)
U of Minnesota, Twin Cities Campus (MN)
The U of Montana–Missoula (MT)
U of Nebraska–Lincoln (NE)
U of Nevada, Las Vegas (NV)
U of Nevada, Reno (NV)
U of New Hampshire (NH)
The U of North Carolina at Chapel Hill (NC)
The U of North Carolina at Greensboro (NC)
U of Oklahoma (OK)
U of Oregon (OR)
U of Pennsylvania (PA)
U of Regina (SK, Canada)
U of Rhode Island (RI)
U of Richmond (VA)
U of Rochester (NY)
U of St. Thomas (MN)
U of South Carolina (SC)
U of Southern California (CA)
U of Southern Maine (ME)
U of South Florida (FL)
U of Toronto (ON, Canada)
U of Utah (UT)
U of Vermont (VT)
U of Victoria (BC, Canada)
U of Washington (WA)
U of Waterloo (ON, Canada)
The U of Western Ontario (ON, Canada)
U of Windsor (ON, Canada)
The U of Winnipeg (MB, Canada)
U of Wisconsin–Madison (WI)
U of Wisconsin–Milwaukee (WI)
U of Wisconsin–Whitewater (WI)
U of Wyoming (WY)
Vassar Coll (NY)
Warren Wilson Coll (NC)
Washington State U (WA)
Washington U in St. Louis (MO)
Wayne State U (MI)
Wellesley Coll (MA)
Wells Coll (NY)
Wesleyan U (CT)
Western Michigan U (MI)
Western Washington U (WA)
Wheaton Coll (MA)
Wichita State U (KS)
Wilfrid Laurier U (ON, Canada)
Yale U (CT)
York U (ON, Canada)

WOOD SCIENCE/PAPER TECHNOLOGY

Memphis Coll of Art (TN)
Miami U (OH)
Mississippi State U (MS)
North Carolina State U (NC)
Oregon State U (OR)
Pittsburg State U (KS)
State U of NY Coll of Environ Sci and Forestry (NY)
Université Laval (PQ, Canada)
U of British Columbia (BC, Canada)
U of Idaho (ID)
U of Maine (ME)
U of Massachusetts Amherst (MA)
U of Minnesota, Twin Cities Campus (MN)
U of Toronto (ON, Canada)
U of Washington (WA)
U of Wisconsin–Stevens Point (WI)
Western Michigan U (MI)
West Virginia U (WV)

ZOOLOGY

Andrews U (MI)
Arizona State U (AZ)
Arkansas State U (AR)
Auburn U (AL)
Ball State U (IN)
Brandon U (MB, Canada)
Brigham Young U (UT)
California State Polytechnic U, Pomona (CA)
California State U, Fresno (CA)
California State U, Fullerton (CA)
California State U, Long Beach (CA)
Coll of the Atlantic (ME)
Colorado State U (CO)
Concordia U (PQ, Canada)
Connecticut Coll (CT)
Cornell U (NY)
Eastern Washington U (WA)
The Evergreen State Coll (WA)
Florida State U (FL)
Fort Valley State U (GA)
Howard U (DC)
Humboldt State U (CA)
Idaho State U (ID)
Iowa State U of Sciences and Technology (IA)
Juniata Coll (PA)
Kent State U (OH)
Mars Hill Coll (NC)
McGill U (PQ, Canada)
Memorial U of Newfoundland (NF, Canada)
Miami U (OH)
Michigan State U (MI)
North Carolina State U (NC)
North Dakota State U (ND)
Northeastern State U (OK)
Northern Arizona U (AZ)
Northern Michigan U (MI)
Northland Coll (WI)
Northwest Missouri State U (MO)
The Ohio State U (OH)
Ohio Wesleyan U (OH)
Oklahoma State U (OK)
Olivet Nazarene U (IL)
Oregon State U (OR)
Quinnipiac U (CT)
Rutgers, State U of NJ, Camden Coll of Arts & Scis (NJ)
Rutgers, State U of NJ, Newark Coll of Arts & Scis (NJ)
Rutgers, State U of NJ, U Coll–Camden (NJ)
St. Cloud State U (MN)
San Francisco State U (CA)
Sonoma State U (CA)
Southeastern Oklahoma State U (OK)
Southern Illinois U Carbondale (IL)
Southern Utah U (UT)
Southwest Texas State U (TX)
State U of NY at Oswego (NY)
State U of NY Coll of Environ Sci and Forestry (NY)
Tabor Coll (KS)
Texas A&M U (TX)
Texas Tech U (TX)
The U of Akron (OH)
U of Alberta (AB, Canada)
U of Arkansas (AR)
U of Calgary (AB, Canada)
U of Calif, Davis (CA)
U of Calif, Santa Barbara (CA)
U of Florida (FL)
U of Guelph (ON, Canada)
U of Hawaii at Manoa (HI)
U of Idaho (ID)
The U of Iowa (IA)
U of Maine (ME)
U of Manitoba (MB, Canada)
U of Maryland, Coll Park (MD)
U of Michigan (MI)
The U of Montana–Missoula (MT)
U of Nevada, Reno (NV)
U of New Brunswick, Fredericton (NB, Canada)
U of New Hampshire (NH)
U of Oklahoma (OK)
U of Rhode Island (RI)
U of South Dakota (SD)
The U of Tennessee Knoxville (TN)
The U of Texas at Austin (TX)
U of Toronto (ON, Canada)
U of Vermont (VT)
U of Victoria (BC, Canada)
U of Washington (WA)
The U of Western Ontario (ON, Canada)
U of Wisconsin–Madison (WI)
U of Wisconsin–Milwaukee (WI)
Utah State U (UT)
Washington State U (WA)
Weber State U (UT)
Winona State U (MN)

1999–2000 CHANGES IN INSTITUTIONS

The following is an alphabetical listing of institutions that have recently closed, merged with other institutions, or changed their name or status. For name changes, the former name appears first, followed by the new name.

American Conservatory of Music, Chicago, IL; no longer eligible for inclusion.

American InterContinental University, Dubai, United Arab Emirates; name changed to The American University in Dubai.

The Art Institute of Boston at Lesley College, Boston, MA; name changed to The Art Institute of Boston at Lesley.

The Art Institutes International at Portland, Portland, OR; name changed to The Art Institute of Portland.

Baruch College of the City University of New York, New York, NY; name changed to Bernard M. Baruch College of the City University of New York.

Berean University of the Assemblies of God, Springfield, MO; name changed to Global University of the Assemblies of God.

Bradford College, Haverhill, MA, closed.

Caribbean Center for Advanced Studies/Miami Institute of Psychology, Miami, FL; name changed to Carlos Albizu University.

Claflin College, Orangeburg, SC; name changed to Claflin University.

Clinch Valley College of the University of Virginia, Wise, VA; name changed to University of Virginia's College at Wise.

The Colorado Institute of Art, Denver, CO; name changed to The Art Institute of Colorado.

Columbia College, Chicago, IL; name changed to Columbia College Chicago.

Commonwealth International University, Billings, MT; name changed to Education America–Billings Campus.

Commonwealth International University, Billings, MT, closed.

The Corcoran School of Art, Washington, DC; name changed to The Corcoran College of Art and Design.

Dominican College of San Rafael, San Rafael, CA; name changed to Dominican University of California.

Dominion College, Seattle, WA; no longer eligible for inclusion.

Drury College, Springfield, MO; name changed to Drury University.

Huron International University, San Diego, San Diego, CA, closed.

ICI University, Irving, TX; merged with, Berean University to form Global University of the Assemblies of God.

John Jay College of Criminal Justice, the City University of New York, New York, NY; name changed to John Jay College of Criminal Justice of the City University of New York.

Logan College of Chiropractic, Chesterfield, MO; name changed to Logan University of Chiropractic.

Louisiana State University Medical Center, New Orleans, LA; name changed to Louisiana State University Health Sciences Center.

Lutheran Bible Institute of Seattle, Issaquah, WA; name changed to Trinity Lutheran College.

Mesivta Torah Vodaath Seminary, Brooklyn, NY; name changed to Mesivta Torah Vodaath Rabbinical Seminary.

Missouri Technical School, St. Louis, MO; name changed to Missouri Tech.

Moorhead State University, Moorhead, MN; name changed to Minnesota State University Moorhead.

Morrison College, Reno, NV; name changed to Morrison University.

Northeast Louisiana University, Monroe, LA; name changed to University of Louisiana at Monroe.

Northwest Baptist Theological College, Langley, BC, closed.

Pace University, New York, NY; name changed to Pace University, New York City Campus.

Park College, Parkville, MO; name changed to Park University.

Philadelphia College of Textiles and Science, Philadelphia, PA; name changed to Philadelphia University.

Quinnipiac College, Hamden, CT; name changed to Quinnipiac University.

Rutgers, The State University of New Jersey, College of Engineering, Piscataway, NJ; name changed to Rutgers, The State University of New Jersey, School of Engineering.

St. John's College, Winnipeg, MB; no longer eligible for inclusion.

State University of New York Health Science Center at Syracuse, Syracuse, NY; name changed to State University of New York Upstate Medical University.

Suomi College, Hancock, MI; name changed to Finlandia University.

Thomas College, Thomasville, GA; name changed to Thomas University.

1999-2000 Changes in Institutions

University of Central Texas, Killeen, TX, closed.

University of Osteopathic Medicine and Health Sciences, Des Moines, IA; name changed to Des Moines University Osteopathic Medical Center.

University of Southwestern Louisiana, Lafayette, LA; name changed to University of Louisiana at Lafayette.

Viterbo College, La Crosse, WI; name changed to Viterbo University.

Washington and Jefferson College, Washington, PA; name changed to Washington & Jefferson College.

William Penn College, Oskaloosa, IA; name changed to William Penn University.

INDEX OF COLLEGES AND UNIVERSITIES

This index gives the page locations of various entries for all the colleges and universities in this book. The page numbers for the college profiles are printed in regular type, those for profiles with special announcements in italic type, and those for in-depth descriptions in boldface type. When there is more than one number in boldface type, it indicates that the institution has more than one in-depth message; in most such cases, the first of the series is a general institutional description.

Abilene Christian University (TX)	777, **1124**
Academy of Art College (CA)	89, **1126**
Acadia University (NS, Canada)	892, **1128**
Adams State College (CO)	141, **1130**
Adelphi University (NY)	*518*, **1132**
Adrian College (MI)	*391*, **1134**
The Advertising Arts College (CA)	89
Agnes Scott College (GA)	199, **1136**
Alabama Agricultural and Mechanical University (AL)	55
Alabama State University (AL)	55
Alaska Bible College (AK)	69
Alaska Pacific University (AK)	70
Albany College of Pharmacy of Union University (NY)	519
Albany State University (GA)	199, **1138**
Alberta College of Art and Design (AB, Canada)	893
Albert A. List College of Jewish Studies (NY)	519
Albertson College of Idaho (ID)	224, **1140**
Albertus Magnus College (CT)	*154*, **1142**
Albion College (MI)	*392*, **1144**
Albright College (PA)	*676*, **1146**
Al Collins Graphic Design School (AZ)	72
Alcorn State University (MS)	435
Alderson-Broaddus College (WV)	854, **1148**
Alfred University (NY)	*519*, **1150**
Alice Lloyd College (KY)	310
Allegheny College (PA)	*677*, **1152**
Allegheny University of the Health Sciences (PA)	677
Allen College (IA)	283
Allentown College of St. Francis de Sales (PA)	677
Allen University (SC)	736
Alma College (MI)	*392*, **1154**
Alvernia College (PA)	*678*, **1156**
Alverno College (WI)	864, **1158**
Amber University (TX)	778
American Academy of Art (IL)	228
American Baptist College of American Baptist Theological Seminary (TN)	756
American Bible College and Seminary (OK)	653
The American College (United Kingdom)	938
The American College (CA)	89
The American College (GA)	200
American College of Prehospital Medicine (FL)	173
American College of Thessaloniki (Greece)	925
American Indian College of the Assemblies of God, Inc. (AZ)	72
The American Institute for Computer Sciences (AL)	56
American InterContinental University (CA)	89
American InterContinental University (DC)	167
American InterContinental University (FL)	173
American InterContinental University, Atlanta (GA)	200, **1160**
American InterContinental University, Atlanta (GA)	200
American InterContinental University (United Kingdom)	938
American International College (MA)	357, **1162**
American Military University (VA)	823
American University (DC)	167, **1164**
American University in Cairo (Egypt)	923
The American University in Dubai (United Arab Emirates)	937
The American University of Paris (France)	924
American University of Puerto Rico (PR)	882
American University of Rome (Italy)	927, **1166**
Amherst College (MA)	357
Anderson College (SC)	736, **1168**
Anderson University (IN)	*261*, **1170**
Andrew Jackson University (AL)	56
Andrews University (MI)	393, **1172**
Angelo State University (TX)	778, **1174**
Anna Maria College (MA)	358, **1176**
Antioch College (OH)	620, **1178**
Antioch Southern California/Los Angeles (CA)	90
Antioch Southern California/Santa Barbara (CA)	90
Antioch University Seattle (WA)	843
Appalachian Bible College (WV)	855
Appalachian State University (NC)	590
Aquinas College (MI)	393, **1180**
Aquinas College (TN)	756
Arizona State University (AZ)	72, **1182**
Arizona State University East (AZ)	73
Arizona State University West (AZ)	73
Arkansas Baptist College (AR)	79
Arkansas State University (AR)	79, **1184**
Arkansas Tech University (AR)	79
Arlington Baptist College (TX)	778
Armstrong Atlantic State University (GA)	201
Armstrong University (CA)	90, **1186**
Arnold & Marie Schwartz College of Pharmacy and Health Sciences (NY)	520
Art Academy of Cincinnati (OH)	620, **1188**
Art Center College of Design (CA)	90
The Art Institute of Atlanta (GA)	201
The Art Institute of Boston at Lesley (MA)	358, **1190**
The Art Institute of Colorado (CO)	141
The Art Institute of Fort Lauderdale (FL)	173
The Art Institute of Philadelphia (PA)	678
The Art Institute of Phoenix (AZ)	74
The Art Institute of Portland (OR)	664, **1192**
Art Institute of Southern California (CA)	91, **1194**
The Art Institute of Washington (VA)	823
Art Institutes International at San Francisco (CA)	91
Asbury College (KY)	311, **1196**
Ashland University (OH)	621, **1198**
Assumption College (MA)	359, **1200**
Athabasca University (AB, Canada)	893
Athens State University (AL)	56
Atlanta Christian College (GA)	201
Atlanta College of Art (GA)	202, **1202**
Atlantic Baptist University (NB, Canada)	893
Atlantic College (PR)	882
Atlantic Union College (MA)	359
Auburn University (AL)	56, **1204**
Auburn University Montgomery (AL)	57
Audrey Cohen College (NY)	520, **1206**
Augsburg College (MN)	*418*
Augustana College (IL)	228
Augustana College (SD)	750, **1208**
Augustana University College (AB, Canada)	894
Augusta State University (GA)	202, **1210**
Aurora University (IL)	*229*, **1212**
Austin College (TX)	779, **1214**
Austin Peay State University (TN)	757
Averett College (VA)	823
Avila College (MO)	443
Azusa Pacific University (CA)	*91*, **1216**
Babson College (MA)	359, **1218**
Baker College of Auburn Hills (MI)	394
Baker College of Cadillac (MI)	394
Baker College of Flint (MI)	394
Baker College of Jackson (MI)	395
Baker College of Mount Clemens (MI)	395
Baker College of Muskegon (MI)	395
Baker College of Owosso (MI)	396
Baker College of Port Huron (MI)	396
Baker University (KS)	300, **1220**
Baldwin-Wallace College (OH)	621
Ball State University (IN)	*261*, **1222**
Baltimore Hebrew University (MD)	342
Baltimore International College (MD)	342, **1224**
Baptist Bible College (MO)	443
Baptist Bible College of Indianapolis (IN)	262
Baptist Bible College of Pennsylvania (PA)	679
Baptist Memorial College of Health Sciences (TN)	757
Baptist Missionary Association Theological Seminary (TX)	779
Barat College (IL)	229, **1226**
Barber-Scotia College (NC)	591
Barclay College (KS)	*300*
Bard College (NY)	520
Barnard College (NY)	520, **1228**
Barry University (FL)	*173*, **1230**
Bartlesville Wesleyan College (OK)	653
Barton College (NC)	591, **1232**
Bassist College (OR)	664
Bastyr University (WA)	843
Bates College (ME)	333, **1234**
Bayamón Central University (PR)	882
Bayamón Technological University College (PR)	883
Baylor College of Dentistry (TX)	779
Baylor University (TX)	*779*, **1236**
Bay Path College (MA)	360, **1238**
Beacon College (GA)	202
Beaver College (PA)	679, **1240**
Becker College (MA)	*360*, **1242**
Belhaven College (MS)	*436*
Bellarmine College (KY)	311
Bellevue University (NE)	472
Bellin College of Nursing (WI)	864
Belmont Abbey College (NC)	592, **1244**
Belmont University (TN)	757, **1246**
Beloit College (WI)	*865*, **1248**
Bemidji State University (MN)	418
Benedict College (SC)	737
Benedictine College (KS)	*301*, **1250**
Benedictine University (IL)	229, **1252**
Bennett College (NC)	592
Bennington College (VT)	814, **1254**
Bentley College (MA)	361, **1256**
Berea College (KY)	*312*, **1258**
Berkeley College, New York (NY)	521, **1260**
Berkeley College, White Plains (NY)	521
Berklee College of Music (MA)	361, **1262**
Bernard M. Baruch College of the City University of New York (NY)	521, **1264**
Berry College (GA)	203
Bethany Bible College (NB, Canada)	894
Bethany Bible Institute (SK, Canada)	894
Bethany College (KS)	301
Bethany College (WV)	855, **1266**
Bethany College of the Assemblies of God (CA)	92

Peterson's Guide to Four-Year Colleges 2001   www.petersons.com   1105

Index of Colleges and Universities

Beth Benjamin Academy of Connecticut (CT)	154
Bethel College (IN)	262
Bethel College (KS)	302, **1268**
Bethel College (MN)	*419*, **1270**
Bethel College (TN)	758
Bethesda Christian University (CA)	92, **1272**
Beth HaMedrash Shaarei Yosher Institute (NY)	522
Beth Hatalmud Rabbinical College (NY)	522
Beth Medrash Govoha (NJ)	492
Bethune-Cookman College (FL)	174, **1274**
Beulah Heights Bible College (GA)	203
Biola University (CA)	93, **1276**
Birmingham-Southern College (AL)	*57*, **1278**
Bishop's University (PQ, Canada)	894, **1280**
Blackburn College (IL)	230, **1282**
Black Hills State University (SD)	750
Blessing-Rieman College of Nursing (IL)	230
Bloomfield College (NJ)	492, **1284**
Bloomsburg University of Pennsylvania (PA)	679
Bluefield College (VA)	823
Bluefield State College (WV)	856
Blue Mountain College (MS)	436
Bluffton College (OH)	622, **1286**
Boise Bible College (ID)	225
Boise State University (ID)	225
Boricua College (NY)	522
Boston Architectural Center (MA)	362, **1288**
Boston College (MA)	*362*, **1290**
Boston Conservatory (MA)	363
Boston University (MA)	*363*, **1292**
Bowdoin College (ME)	334, **1294**
Bowie State University (MD)	343, **1296**
Bowling Green State University (OH)	622, **1298**
Bradley University (IL)	231
Brandeis University (MA)	364, **1300**
Brandon University (MB, Canada)	894
Brenau University (GA)	203, **1302**
Brescia University (KY)	*312*, **1304**
Brevard College (NC)	592, **1306**
Brewton-Parker College (GA)	204
Briar Cliff College (IA)	*283*, **1308**
Briarcliffe College (NY)	522, **1310**
Bridgewater College (VA)	*824*, **1312**
Bridgewater State College (MA)	364, **1314**
Briercrest Bible College (SK, Canada)	895
Brigham Young University (UT)	811
Brigham Young University–Hawaii Campus (HI)	222
Brock University (ON, Canada)	895, **1316**
Brooklyn College of the City University of New York (NY)	522, **1318**
Brooks Institute of Photography (CA)	93
Brown University (RI)	731, **1320**
Bryan College (TN)	758
Bryant and Stratton College, Cleveland (OH)	623
Bryant and Stratton College, Virginia Beach (VA)	824
Bryant College (RI)	732, **1322**
Bryn Athyn College of the New Church (PA)	680
Bryn Mawr College (PA)	*680*, **1324**
Bucknell University (PA)	*681*, **1326**
Buena Vista University (IA)	284
Burlington College (VT)	*815*
Butler University (IN)	*262*, **1328**
Cabrini College (PA)	*681*, **1330**
Caldwell College (NJ)	*493*, **1332**
California Baptist University (CA)	93
California Christian College (CA)	94
California College for Health Sciences (CA)	94
California College of Arts and Crafts (CA)	94, **1334**
California Institute of Integral Studies (CA)	95
California Institute of Technology (CA)	*95*, **1336**
California Institute of the Arts (CA)	*96*, **1338**
California Lutheran University (CA)	*96*, **1340**
California Maritime Academy (CA)	97
California National University for Advanced Studies (CA)	97
California Polytechnic State University, San Luis Obispo (CA)	97
California State Polytechnic University, Pomona (CA)	97, **1342**
California State University, Bakersfield (CA)	98
California State University, Chico (CA)	98
California State University, Dominguez Hills (CA)	99
California State University, Fresno (CA)	99
California State University, Fullerton (CA)	99
California State University, Hayward (CA)	100
California State University, Long Beach (CA)	100
California State University, Los Angeles (CA)	101
California State University, Monterey Bay (CA)	101
California State University, Northridge (CA)	101
California State University, Sacramento (CA)	102
California State University, San Bernardino (CA)	102
California State University, San Marcos (CA)	103
California State University, Stanislaus (CA)	103
California University of Pennsylvania (PA)	*682*, **1344**
Calumet College of Saint Joseph (IN)	263
Calvary Bible College and Theological Seminary (MO)	443
Calvin College (MI)	396, **1346**
Cambridge College (MA)	365, **1348**
Camden College of Arts and Sciences (NJ)	493
Cameron University (OK)	654
Campbellsville University (KY)	313
Campbell University (NC)	593, **1350**
Canadian Bible College (SK, Canada)	896
Canisius College (NY)	523, **1352**
Capital University (OH)	*623*, **1354**
Capitol College (MD)	*343*, **1356**
Cardinal Stritch University (WI)	*865*, **1358**
Caribbean Center for Advanced Studies/ Miami Institute of Psychology (FL)	174
Caribbean University (PR)	883
Carleton College (MN)	419, **1360**
Carleton University (ON, Canada)	896, **1362**
Carlos Albizu University (FL)	174
Carlow College (PA)	682, **1364**
Carnegie Mellon University (PA)	683, **1366**
Carroll College (MT)	467, **1368**
Carroll College (WI)	*866*, **1370**
Carson-Newman College (TN)	759, **1372**
Carthage College (WI)	*866*, **1374**
Cascade College (OR)	664
Case Western Reserve University (OH)	*623*, **1376**
Castleton State College (VT)	*815*, **1378**
Catawba College (NC)	593, **1380**
Catherine Booth Bible College (MB, Canada)	897
The Catholic University of America (DC)	168, **1382**
Cazenovia College (NY)	*523*, **1384**
Cedar Crest College (PA)	*683*, **1386**
Cedarville College (OH)	624
Centenary College (NJ)	*493*, **1388**
Centenary College of Louisiana (LA)	324
Center for Creative Studies—College of Art and Design (MI)	397, **1390**
Central Baptist College (AR)	80
Central Bible College (MO)	444
Central Christian College of Kansas (KS)	302
Central Christian College of the Bible (MO)	444
Central College (IA)	284, **1392**
Central Connecticut State University (CT)	154, **1394**
Central Methodist College (MO)	444
Central Michigan University (MI)	397
Central Missouri State University (MO)	445, **1396**
Central Pentecostal College (SK, Canada)	897
Central State University (OH)	624
Central Washington University (WA)	844
Central Yeshiva Tomchei Tmimim-Lubavitch (NY)	524
Centre College (KY)	313
Chadron State College (NE)	472, **1398**
Chaminade University of Honolulu (HI)	222, **1400**
Champlain College (VT)	*816*, **1402**
Chaparral College (AZ)	74
Chapman University (CA)	103, **1404**
Charles R. Drew University of Medicine and Science (CA)	104
Charleston Southern University (SC)	*737*, **1406**
Charter Oak State College (CT)	155
Chatham College (PA)	*684*, **1408**
Chestnut Hill College (PA)	*684*, **1410**
Cheyney University of Pennsylvania (PA)	*685*, **1412**
Chicago State University (IL)	231
Chowan College (NC)	*594*, **1414**
Christendom College (VA)	824
Christian Brothers University (TN)	759
Christian Heritage College (CA)	104
Christian Life College (IL)	232
Christopher Newport University (VA)	825, **1416**
Cincinnati Bible College and Seminary (OH)	625
Cincinnati College of Mortuary Science (OH)	625
Circleville Bible College (OH)	625
The Citadel, The Military College of South Carolina (SC)	*737*, **1418**
City College of the City University of New York (NY)	*524*, **1420**
City University (WA)	*844*, **1422**
Claflin University (SC)	738
Claremont McKenna College (CA)	*104*, **1424**
Clarion University of Pennsylvania (PA)	*685*, **1426**
Clark Atlanta University (GA)	*204*, **1428**
Clarke College (IA)	285
Clarkson College (NE)	472, **1430**
Clarkson University (NY)	*524*, **1432**
Clark University (MA)	365
Clayton College & State University (GA)	205
Clear Creek Baptist Bible College (KY)	313
Clearwater Christian College (FL)	175
Cleary College (MI)	398, **1434**
Clemson University (SC)	*738*, **1436**
Cleveland Chiropractic College of Kansas City (MO)	445
Cleveland Chiropractic College of Los Angeles (CA)	105
Cleveland College of Jewish Studies (OH)	625
Cleveland Institute of Art (OH)	*626*, **1438**
Cleveland Institute of Music (OH)	*626*, **1440**
Cleveland State University (OH)	627
Clinch Valley College of the University of Virginia (VA)	825
Coastal Carolina University (SC)	739
Coe College (IA)	*285*, **1442**
Cogswell Polytechnical College (CA)	*105*, **1444**
Coker College (SC)	*739*, **1446**
Colby College (ME)	*334*, **1448**
Colby-Sawyer College (NH)	484, **1450**
Colegio Biblico Pentecostal (PR)	883
Colegio Pentecostal Mizpa (PR)	883
Colegio Universitario del Este (PR)	883
Coleman College (CA)	105
Colgate University (NY)	525
Collège Dominicain de Philosophie et de Théologie (ON, Canada)	897
College for Lifelong Learning of the University System of New Hampshire (NH)	484

Index of Colleges and Universities

College Misericordia (PA)	686, **1452**
College of Aeronautics (NY)	525, **1454**
College of Charleston (SC)	*739*
College of Emmanuel and St. Chad (SK, Canada)	897
College of Insurance (NY)	526, **1456**
College of Mount St. Joseph (OH)	627, **1458**
College of Mount Saint Vincent (NY)	526, **1460**
The College of New Jersey (NJ)	*494*, **1462**
The College of New Rochelle (NY)	526, **1464**
College of Notre Dame (CA)	106, **1466**
College of Notre Dame of Maryland (MD)	344, **1468**
College of Our Lady of the Elms (MA)	365, **1470**
College of Saint Benedict (MN)	420, **1472**
College of St. Catherine (MN)	420, **1474**
College of St. Catherine–Minneapolis (MN)	421
College of Saint Elizabeth (NJ)	*494*, **1476**
College of St. Francis (IL)	232
College of St. Joseph (VT)	816, **1478**
College of Saint Mary (NE)	473
The College of Saint Rose (NY)	527, **1480**
The College of St. Scholastica (MN)	421, **1482**
College of Santa Fe (NM)	512, **1484**
The College of Southeastern Europe, The American University of Athens (Greece)	925
College of Staten Island of the City University of New York (NY)	527, **1486**
College of the Atlantic (ME)	335, **1488**
College of the Holy Cross (MA)	366
College of the Ozarks (MO)	445
College of the Southwest (NM)	513, **1490**
College of Visual Arts (MN)	421
The College of West Virginia (WV)	856, **1492**
The College of William and Mary (VA)	825
The College of Wooster (OH)	628, **1494**
Collége universitaire de Saint-Boniface (MB, Canada)	897
Colorado Christian University (CO)	142, **1496**
The Colorado College (CO)	*142*, **1498**
The Colorado Institute of Art (CO)	143
Colorado School of Mines (CO)	143
Colorado State University (CO)	143, **1500**
Colorado Technical University (CO)	144
Colorado Technical University Denver Campus (CO)	144
Colorado Technical University Sioux Falls Campus (SD)	751
Columbia Bible College (BC, Canada)	897
Columbia College (MO)	446, **1502**
Columbia College (PR)	883
Columbia College (SC)	740, **1504**
Columbia College Chicago (IL)	232, **1506**
Columbia College–Hollywood (CA)	106, **1508**
Columbia College of Nursing (WI)	867
Columbia International University (SC)	740, **1510**
Columbia Union College (MD)	344, **1512**
Columbia University, Barnard College (NY)	528
Columbia University, Columbia College (NY)	528, **1514**
Columbia University, School of General Studies (NY)	528, **1516**
Columbia University, The Fu Foundation School of Engineering and Applied Science (NY)	529
Columbus College of Art and Design (OH)	628, **1518**
Columbus State University (GA)	205
Commonwealth College, Virginia Beach (VA)	826
Commonwealth International University (CO)	144
Community Hospital of Roanoke Valley–College of Health Sciences (VA)	826
Conception Seminary College (MO)	446
Concord College (WV)	857, **1520**
Concord College (MB, Canada)	897
Concordia College (AL)	58
Concordia College (MI)	398

Concordia College (MN)	*422*
Concordia College (NY)	529, **1522**
Concordia University (CA)	106
Concordia University (IL)	232
Concordia University (NE)	473
Concordia University (OR)	664, **1524**
Concordia University (PQ, Canada)	898, **1526**
Concordia University at Austin (TX)	780
Concordia University at St. Paul (MN)	422
Concordia University College of Alberta (AB, Canada)	898
Concordia University Wisconsin (WI)	867, **1528**
Connecticut College (CT)	155, **1530**
Conservatory of Music of Puerto Rico (PR)	883
Converse College (SC)	741, **1532**
Cook College (NJ)	495
Cooper Union for the Advancement of Science and Art (NY)	530, **1534**
Coppin State College (MD)	345
The Corcoran College of Art and Design (DC)	169
Cornell College (IA)	286
Cornell University (NY)	530, **1536**
Cornerstone University (MI)	398
Cornish College of the Arts (WA)	844
Covenant College (GA)	205
Creighton University (NE)	474, **1538**
Crichton College (TN)	760
The Criswell College (TX)	780
Crown College (MN)	423, **1540**
Crown College (WA)	845
The Culinary Institute of America (NY)	531, **1542**
Culver-Stockton College (MO)	447, **1544**
Cumberland College (KY)	*314*, **1546**
Cumberland University (TN)	760
Curry College (MA)	366, **1548**
The Curtis Institute of Music (PA)	686
C.W. Post Campus of Long Island University (NY)	531
Daemen College (NY)	531, **1550**
Dakota State University (SD)	751
Dakota Wesleyan University (SD)	751
Dalhousie University (NS, Canada)	898, **1552**
Dallas Baptist University (TX)	781
Dallas Christian College (TX)	781, **1554**
Dalton State College (GA)	206
Dana College (NE)	474
Daniel Webster College (NH)	484, **1556**
Darkei Noam Rabbinical College (NY)	532
Dartmouth College (NH)	485, **1558**
Davenport College of Business (MI)	399
Davenport College of Business, Kalamazoo Campus (MI)	399
Davenport College of Business, Lansing Campus (MI)	400
David Lipscomb University (TN)	760, **1560**
David N. Myers College (OH)	629
Davidson College (NC)	594, **1562**
Davis & Elkins College (WV)	857, **1564**
Deaconess College of Nursing (MO)	447
Defiance College (OH)	629, **1566**
Delaware State University (DE)	165
Delaware Valley College (PA)	687, **1568**
Delta State University (MS)	436
Denison University (OH)	630, **1570**
Denver Institute of Technology (CO)	144
Denver Technical College (CO)	144
Denver Technical College at Colorado Springs (CO)	145
DePaul University (IL)	233, **1572**
DePauw University (IN)	*263*, **1574**
Deree College (Greece)	925
Design Institute of San Diego (CA)	107, **1576**
Des Moines University Osteopathic Medical Center (IA)	286
Detroit College of Business (MI)	400
Detroit College of Business–Flint (MI)	400
Detroit College of Business, Warren Campus (MI)	401

DeVry Institute (NJ)	495
DeVry Institute of Technology (AZ)	74
DeVry Institute of Technology, Fremont (CA)	107
DeVry Institute of Technology, Long Beach (CA)	108
DeVry Institute of Technology, Pomona (CA)	108
DeVry Institute of Technology, West Hills (CA)	108
DeVry Institute of Technology, Alpharetta (GA)	206
DeVry Institute of Technology, Decatur (GA)	207
DeVry Institute of Technology, Addison (IL)	233
DeVry Institute of Technology, Chicago (IL)	233
DeVry Institute of Technology (MO)	448
DeVry Institute of Technology (NY)	532
DeVry Institute of Technology (OH)	630
DeVry Institute of Technology (TX)	781
Dickinson College (PA)	687
Dickinson State University (ND)	615, **1578**
Dillard University (LA)	324
Divine Word College (IA)	286
Dixie State College of Utah (UT)	811
Doane College (NE)	475
Dr. William M. Scholl College of Podiatric Medicine (IL)	234
Dominican College of Blauvelt (NY)	532, **1580**
Dominican School of Philosophy and Theology (CA)	109
Dominican University (IL)	234, **1582**
Dominican University of California (CA)	109, **1584**
Dordt College (IA)	286, **1586**
Douglass College (NJ)	495
Dowling College (NY)	532
Drake University (IA)	287, **1588**
Draughons Junior College (AL)	58
Drew University (NJ)	*495*, **1590**
Drexel University (PA)	688, **1592**
Drury University (MO)	448
Duke University (NC)	595, **1594**
Duquesne University (PA)	688
D'Youville College (NY)	533, **1596**
Earlham College (IN)	264, **1598**
East Carolina University (NC)	595
East Central University (OK)	654
Eastern College (PA)	689, **1600**
Eastern Connecticut State University (CT)	155, **1602**
Eastern Illinois University (IL)	235
Eastern Kentucky University (KY)	314
Eastern Mennonite University (VA)	826, **1604**
Eastern Michigan University (MI)	401
Eastern Nazarene College (MA)	367, **1606**
Eastern New Mexico University (NM)	513, **1608**
Eastern Oregon University (OR)	*665*
Eastern Pentecostal Bible College (ON, Canada)	899
Eastern Washington University (WA)	845, **1610**
Eastman School of Music (NY)	533
East Stroudsburg University of Pennsylvania (PA)	689
East Tennessee State University (TN)	*761*
East Texas Baptist University (TX)	782
East-West University (IL)	235
Eckerd College (FL)	175, **1612**
École des Hautes Études Commerciales (PQ, Canada)	899
Ecole Hôtelière de Lausanne (Switzerland)	936
Edgewood College (WI)	868, **1614**
Edinboro University of Pennsylvania (PA)	690, **1616**
Education America–Denver Campus (CO)	145
Education America–Tampa Technical Institute Campus (FL)	175
Edward Waters College (FL)	175
Electronic Data Processing College of Puerto Rico (PR)	884

Index of Colleges and Universities

Elizabeth City State University (NC)	596, **1618**
Elizabethtown College (PA)	*690*, **1620**
Elmhurst College (IL)	235, **1622**
Elmira College (NY)	533, **1624**
Elms College (MA)	367
Elon College (NC)	*596*, **1626**
Embry-Riddle Aeronautical University (AZ)	75, **1628**
Embry-Riddle Aeronautical University (FL)	*175*, **1630**
Embry-Riddle Aeronautical University, Extended Campus (FL)	176
Emerson College (MA)	*367*, **1632**
Emmanuel Bible College (CA)	109
Emmanuel Bible College (ON, Canada)	899
Emmanuel College (GA)	207
Emmanuel College (MA)	368, **1634**
Emmaus Bible College (IA)	287
Emory & Henry College (VA)	*827*, **1636**
Emory University (GA)	*207*, **1638**
Emporia State University (KS)	302
Endicott College (MA)	368, **1640**
Erskine College (SC)	741, **1642**
Escuela de Artes Plasticas de Puerto Rico (PR)	884
Eugene Bible College (OR)	*666*
Eugene Lang College, New School University (NY)	*534*, **1644**
Eureka College (IL)	236
Evangel University (MO)	*448*
The Evergreen State College (WA)	845, **1646**
Fairfield University (CT)	156
Fairleigh Dickinson University, Florham-Madison Campus (NJ)	496
Fairleigh Dickinson University (NJ)	*496*, **1648**
Fairmont State College (WV)	857, **1650**
Faith Baptist Bible College and Theological Seminary (IA)	288
Fashion Institute of Technology (NY)	534, **1652**
Faulkner University (AL)	58
Fayetteville State University (NC)	597
Felician College (NJ)	497, **1654**
Ferris State University (MI)	402, **1656**
Ferrum College (VA)	827, **1658**
Finch University of Health Sciences/The Chicago Medical School (IL)	236
Finlandia University (MI)	402, **1660**
Fisher College (MA)	369, **1662**
Fisk University (TN)	*761*, **1664**
Fitchburg State College (MA)	369, **1666**
Five Towns College (NY)	*535*, **1668**
Flagler College (FL)	*176*, **1670**
Florida Agricultural and Mechanical University (FL)	177, **1672**
Florida Atlantic University (FL)	177, **1674**
Florida Baptist Theological College (FL)	178
Florida Christian College (FL)	178
Florida College (FL)	179
Florida Gulf Coast University (FL)	179
Florida Institute of Technology (FL)	179, **1676**
Florida International University (FL)	180, **1678**
Florida Memorial College (FL)	180
Florida Metropolitan University–Fort Lauderdale College (FL)	181
Florida Metropolitan University–Orlando College, Melbourne (FL)	181
Florida Metropolitan University–Orlando College, North (FL)	181
Florida Metropolitan University–Orlando College, South (FL)	181
Florida Metropolitan University–Tampa College (FL)	181
Florida Metropolitan University–Tampa College, Brandon (FL)	182
Florida Metropolitan University–Tampa College, Lakeland (FL)	182
Florida Metropolitan University–Tampa College, Pinellas (FL)	182
Florida Southern College (FL)	182, **1680**
Florida State University (FL)	183, **1682**
Fontbonne College (MO)	449
Fordham University (NY)	535, **1684**
Fort Hays State University (KS)	303
Fort Lewis College (CO)	145
Fort Valley State University (GA)	208, **1686**
Framingham State College (MA)	369, **1688**
Franciscan University of Steubenville (OH)	630, **1690**
Francis Marion University (SC)	742, **1692**
Franklin and Marshall College (PA)	691
Franklin College of Indiana (IN)	265, **1694**
Franklin College Switzerland (Switzerland)	936, **1696**
Franklin Institute of Boston (MA)	370
Franklin Pierce College (NH)	485
Franklin University (OH)	631
Freed-Hardeman University (TN)	762
Free Will Baptist Bible College (TN)	762
Fresno Pacific University (CA)	110, **1698**
Friends University (KS)	303
Friends World College (NY)	536
Frostburg State University (MD)	345, **1700**
Furman University (SC)	742
Gallaudet University (DC)	169
Gannon University (PA)	691, **1702**
Gardner-Webb University (NC)	597, **1704**
Geneva College (PA)	692, **1706**
George Fox University (OR)	*666*, **1708**
George Mason University (VA)	828, **1710**
Georgetown College (KY)	315, **1712**
Georgetown University (DC)	*169*, **1714**
The George Washington University (DC)	170
Georgia Baptist College of Nursing (GA)	208
Georgia College and State University (GA)	209
Georgia Institute of Technology (GA)	209
Georgian Court College (NJ)	497, **1716**
Georgia Southern University (GA)	210
Georgia Southwestern State University (GA)	210, **1718**
Georgia State University (GA)	211, **1720**
Gettysburg College (PA)	692
Glenville State College (WV)	858
Global University of the Assemblies of God (MO)	449
GMI Engineering & Management Institute (MI)	402
Goddard College (VT)	817, **1722**
God's Bible School and College (OH)	631
Golden Gate University (CA)	110
Goldey-Beacom College (DE)	165
Gonzaga University (WA)	846, **1724**
Gordon College (MA)	370, **1726**
Goshen College (IN)	265, **1728**
Goucher College (MD)	346, **1730**
Governors State University (IL)	236
Grace Bible College (MI)	402
Grace College (IN)	266, **1732**
Graceland College (IA)	288, **1734**
Grace University (NE)	475
Grambling State University (LA)	324
Grand Canyon University (AZ)	75, **1736**
Grand Valley State University (MI)	403
Grand View College (IA)	289, **1738**
Grantham College of Engineering (LA)	325
Gratz College (PA)	693
Great Lakes Christian College (MI)	403
Green Mountain College (VT)	817
Greensboro College (NC)	597, **1740**
Greenville College (IL)	236, **1742**
Griggs University (MD)	346
Grinnell College (IA)	289, **1744**
Grove City College (PA)	693, **1746**
Guilford College (NC)	598, **1748**
Gustavus Adolphus College (MN)	423, **1750**
Gwynedd-Mercy College (PA)	694, **1752**
Hamilton College (NY)	536, **1754**
Hamilton Technical College (IA)	290
Hamline University (MN)	424
Hampden-Sydney College (VA)	828, **1756**
Hampshire College (MA)	371, **1758**
Hampton University (VA)	829, **1760**
Hannibal-LaGrange College (MO)	450
Hanover College (IN)	266, **1762**
Harding University (AR)	80, **1764**
Hardin-Simmons University (TX)	782
Harrington Institute of Interior Design (IL)	237, **1766**
Harris-Stowe State College (MO)	450
Hartford College for Women (CT)	156, **1768**
Hartwick College (NY)	536, **1770**
Harvard University (MA)	371, **1772**
Harvey Mudd College (CA)	110, **1774**
Haskell Indian Nations University (KS)	303
Hastings College (NE)	475
Haverford College (PA)	694, **1776**
Hawaii Pacific University (HI)	223, **1778**
Hebrew College (MA)	371
Hebrew Theological College (IL)	237
Heidelberg College (OH)	632, **1780**
Hellenic College (MA)	372
Henderson State University (AR)	81
Hendrix College (AR)	81, **1782**
Henry Cogswell College (WA)	846
Heritage Baptist College and Heritage Theological Seminary (ON, Canada)	900
Heritage Bible College (NC)	598
Heritage College (WA)	847
Herzing College (AL)	58
Herzing College (GA)	211
Herzing College (WI)	868
Hesser College (NH)	486, **1784**
High Point University (NC)	599, **1786**
Hilbert College (NY)	*537*, **1788**
Hillsdale College (MI)	404, **1790**
Hillsdale Free Will Baptist College (OK)	655
Hiram College (OH)	632, **1792**
Hobart and William Smith Colleges (NY)	*537*, **1794**
Hobe Sound Bible College (FL)	183
Hofstra University (NY)	538, **1796**
Hollins University (VA)	829, **1798**
Holy Apostles College and Seminary (CT)	157
Holy Family College (PA)	695
Holy Names College (CA)	111
Holy Trinity Orthodox Seminary (NY)	539
Hood College (MD)	346, **1800**
Hope College (MI)	404, **1802**
Hope International University (CA)	111
Hotel Management School, "Les Roches" (Switzerland)	937
Houghton College (NY)	539, **1804**
Houston Baptist University (TX)	783
Howard Payne University (TX)	783
Howard University (DC)	170, **1806**
Humboldt State University (CA)	112
Humphreys College (CA)	112
Hunter College of the City University of New York (NY)	539, **1808**
Huntingdon College (AL)	59, **1810**
Huntington College (IN)	*267*
Huron University (SD)	752, **1812**
Huron University USA in London (United Kingdom)	938
Husson College (ME)	335, **1814**
Huston-Tillotson College (TX)	784
Idaho State University (ID)	226, **1816**
Illinois College (IL)	238
The Illinois Institute of Art (IL)	238
The Illinois Institute of Art at Schaumburg (IL)	238
Illinois Institute of Technology (IL)	238, **1818**
Illinois State University (IL)	239
Illinois Wesleyan University (IL)	239
Immaculata College (PA)	695, **1820**
Indiana Institute of Technology (IN)	267
Indiana State University (IN)	268, **1822**
Indiana University Bloomington (IN)	268
Indiana University East (IN)	269
Indiana University Kokomo (IN)	269
Indiana University Northwest (IN)	269
Indiana University of Pennsylvania (PA)	696, **1824**

Index of Colleges and Universities

Indiana University–Purdue University Fort Wayne (IN)	270
Indiana University–Purdue University Indianapolis (IN)	270
Indiana University South Bend (IN)	271
Indiana University Southeast (IN)	271
Indiana Wesleyan University (IN)	271, **1826**
Institute for Christian Studies (TX)	784
Institute of Computer Technology (CA)	113
Institute of Public Administration (Ireland)	926
Instituto Tecnológico y de Estudios Superiores de Monterrey, Campus Central de Veracruz (Mexico)	929
Instituto Tecnológico y de Estudios Superiores de Monterrey, Campus Chiapas (Mexico)	929
Instituto Tecnológico y de Estudios Superiores de Monterrey, Campus Chihuahua (Mexico)	930
Instituto Tecnológico y de Estudios Superiores de Monterrey, Campus Ciudad de México (Mexico)	930
Instituto Tecnológico y de Estudios Superiores de Monterrey, Campus Ciudad Juárez (Mexico)	930
Instituto Tecnológico y de Estudios Superiores de Monterrey, Campus Ciudad Obregón (Mexico)	930
Instituto Tecnológico y de Estudios Superiores de Monterrey, Campus Colima (Mexico)	930
Instituto Tecnológico y de Estudios Superiores de Monterrey, Campus Estado de México (Mexico)	931
Instituto Tecnológico y de Estudios Superiores de Monterrey, Campus Guadalajara (Mexico)	931
Instituto Tecnológico y de Estudios Superiores de Monterrey, Campus Hidalgo (Mexico)	931
Instituto Tecnológico y de Estudios Superiores de Monterrey, Campus Irapuato (Mexico)	931
Instituto Tecnológico y de Estudios Superiores de Monterrey, Campus Laguna (Mexico)	931
Instituto Tecnológico y de Estudios Superiores de Monterrey, Campus León (Mexico)	932
Instituto Tecnológico y de Estudios Superiores de Monterrey, Campus Mazatlán (Mexico)	932
Instituto Tecnológico y de Estudios Superiores de Monterrey, Campus Monterrey (Mexico)	932
Instituto Tecnológico y de Estudios Superiores de Monterrey, Campus Morelos (Mexico)	933
Instituto Tecnológico y de Estudios Superiores de Monterrey, Campus Querétaro (Mexico)	933
Instituto Tecnológico y de Estudios Superiores de Monterrey, Campus Saltillo (Mexico)	933
Instituto Tecnológico y de Estudios Superiores de Monterrey, Campus San Luis Potosí (Mexico)	933
Instituto Tecnológico y de Estudios Superiores de Monterrey, Campus Sinaloa (Mexico)	934
Instituto Tecnológico y de Estudios Superiores de Monterrey, Campus Sonora Norte (Mexico)	934
Instituto Tecnológico y de Estudios Superiores de Monterrey, Campus Tampico (Mexico)	934
Instituto Tecnológico y de Estudios Superiores de Monterrey, Campus Toluca (Mexico)	934
Instituto Tecnológico y de Estudios Superiores de Monterrey, Campus Zacatecas (Mexico)	934
Inter American University of Puerto Rico, Aguadilla Campus (PR)	884
Inter American University of Puerto Rico, Arecibo Campus (PR)	884
Inter American University of Puerto Rico, Barranquitas Campus (PR)	885
Inter American University of Puerto Rico, Bayamón Campus (PR)	885
Inter American University of Puerto Rico, Fajardo Campus (PR)	885
Inter American University of Puerto Rico, Guayama Campus (PR)	885
Inter American University of Puerto Rico, Metropolitan Campus (PR)	885
Inter American University of Puerto Rico, Ponce Campus (PR)	886
Inter American University of Puerto Rico, San Germán Campus (PR)	886
Interior Designers Institute (CA)	113
International Academy of Design (FL)	184
International Academy of Merchandising & Design, Ltd. (IL)	240
International Baptist College (AZ)	76
International Bible College (AL)	59
International Business College, Fort Wayne (IN)	272
International College (FL)	184
International College and Graduate School (HI)	223
International College of the Cayman Islands (Cayman Islands)	923, **1828**
International Fine Arts College (FL)	185
International University (CO)	145
Iona College (NY)	540, **1830**
Iowa State University of Science and Technology (IA)	290, **1832**
Iowa Wesleyan College (IA)	290
Ithaca College (NY)	540, **1834**
ITT Technical Institute, Phoenix (AZ)	76
ITT Technical Institute, Anaheim (CA)	113
ITT Technical Institute, Hayward (CA)	113
ITT Technical Institute, Oxnard (CA)	113
ITT Technical Institute, Rancho Cordova (CA)	113
ITT Technical Institute, San Bernardino (CA)	113
ITT Technical Institute, San Diego (CA)	113
ITT Technical Institute, Sylmar (CA)	114
ITT Technical Institute, West Covina (CA)	114
ITT Technical Institute (CO)	145
ITT Technical Institute, Fort Lauderdale (FL)	185
ITT Technical Institute, Jacksonville (FL)	185
ITT Technical Institute, Maitland (FL)	185
ITT Technical Institute, Tampa (FL)	185
ITT Technical Institute (ID)	226
ITT Technical Institute, Hoffman Estates (IL)	240
ITT Technical Institute, Fort Wayne (IN)	272
ITT Technical Institute, Indianapolis (IN)	272
ITT Technical Institute, Newburgh (IN)	272
ITT Technical Institute (MO)	451
ITT Technical Institute (NM)	514
ITT Technical Institute (OR)	666
ITT Technical Institute, Knoxville (TN)	763
ITT Technical Institute, Nashville (TN)	763
ITT Technical Institute (UT)	811
ITT Technical Institute (VA)	830
ITT Technical Institute, Seattle (WA)	847
ITT Technical Institute (WI)	868
Jackson State University (MS)	437
Jacksonville State University (AL)	59
Jacksonville University (FL)	185, **1836**
Michigan State University (MI)	408, **1838**
James Madison University (VA)	830
Jamestown College (ND)	616
Jarvis Christian College (TX)	784
Jersey City State College (NJ)	498
Jewish Hospital College of Nursing and Allied Health (MO)	451
Jewish Theological Seminary of America (NY)	541, **1840**
John Brown University (AR)	82, **1842**
John Cabot University (Italy)	927
John Carroll University (OH)	633, **1844**
John F. Kennedy University (CA)	114
John Jay College of Criminal Justice of the City University of New York (NY)	541, **1846**
Johns Hopkins University (MD)	347, **1848, 1850**
Johnson & Wales University (FL)	186
Johnson & Wales University (RI)	732, **1852**
Johnson & Wales University (SC)	743
Johnson Bible College (TN)	763
Johnson C. Smith University (NC)	599, **1854**
Johnson State College (VT)	817, **1856**
John Wesley College (NC)	600
Jones College (FL)	186
Jones International University (CO)	145
Judson College (AL)	60
Judson College (IL)	240, **1858**
The Juilliard School (NY)	542
Juniata College (PA)	696, **1860**
Kalamazoo College (MI)	405
Kansas City Art Institute (MO)	451
Kansas Newman College (KS)	304
Kansas State University (KS)	304, **1862**
Kansas Wesleyan University (KS)	304
Kean University (NJ)	498, **1864**
Keene State College (NH)	486, **1866**
Kehilath Yakov Rabbinical Seminary (NY)	542
Kendall College (IL)	241
Kendall College of Art and Design (MI)	405, **1868**
Kennesaw State University (GA)	211
Kent State University (OH)	633, **1870**
Kent State University, Geauga Campus (OH)	634
Kent State University, Stark Campus (OH)	634
Kentucky Christian College (KY)	315
Kentucky Mountain Bible College (KY)	316
Kentucky State University (KY)	316, **1872**
Kentucky Wesleyan College (KY)	316, **1874**
Kenyon College (OH)	634
Kettering College of Medical Arts (OH)	635
Kettering University (MI)	406, **1876**
Keuka College (NY)	542
Keystone College (PA)	697
King College (TN)	763
King's College (PA)	697, **1878**
The King's University College (AB, Canada)	900
Knox College (IL)	241, **1880**
Kol Yaakov Torah Center (NY)	543
Kutztown University of Pennsylvania (PA)	697, **1882**
Laboratory Institute of Merchandising (NY)	543, **1884**
Lafayette College (PA)	698, **1886**
LaGrange College (GA)	211, **1888**
Lake Erie College (OH)	635, **1890**
Lake Forest College (IL)	242, **1892**
Lakehead University (ON, Canada)	900, **1894**
Lakeland College (WI)	868
Lake Superior State University (MI)	406, **1896**
Lakeview College of Nursing (IL)	242
Lamar University (TX)	785
Lambuth University (TN)	764, **1898**
Lancaster Bible College (PA)	698
Lander University (SC)	743
Lane College (TN)	764
Langston University (OK)	655
La Roche College (PA)	699, **1900**
La Salle University (PA)	699
Lasell College (MA)	372, **1902**
La Sierra University (CA)	114
Laurentian University (ON, Canada)	901
Laval University (PQ, Canada)	901
Lawrence Technological University (MI)	407, **1904**

Index of Colleges and Universities

Lawrence University (WI)	869, **1906**
The Leadership Institute of Seattle (WA)	847
Lebanese American University (Lebanon)	928
Lebanon Valley College (PA)	700, **1908**
Lee College at the University of Judaism (CA)	115
Lees-McRae College (NC)	600
Lee University (TN)	765
Lehigh University (PA)	700, **1910**
Lehman College of the City University of New York (NY)	543, **1912**
Le Moyne College (NY)	544, **1914**
LeMoyne-Owen College (TN)	765
Lenoir-Rhyne College (NC)	600, **1916**
Lesley College (MA)	373, **1918**
Lester L. Cox College of Nursing and Health Sciences (MO)	452
LeTourneau University (TX)	785
Lewis & Clark College (OR)	667, **1920**
Lewis-Clark State College (ID)	226
Lewis University (IL)	243, **1922**
Liberty University (VA)	830, **1924**
LIFE Bible College (CA)	115
Life University (GA)	212
Limestone College (SC)	743, **1926**
Lincoln Christian College (IL)	243
Lincoln Memorial University (TN)	766
Lincoln University (CA)	115
Lincoln University (MO)	452
Lincoln University (PA)	701, **1928**
Lindenwood University (MO)	452, **1930**
Lindsey Wilson College (KY)	317
Linfield College (OR)	667, **1932**
Lipscomb University (TN)	766
List College of Jewish Studies (NY)	544
Livingston College (NJ)	498
Livingstone College (NC)	601
Lock Haven University of Pennsylvania (PA)	701, **1934**
Logan University of Chiropractic (MO)	453
Loma Linda University (CA)	115
Long Island University, Brentwood Campus (NY)	544
Long Island University, Brooklyn Campus (NY)	544, **1936**
Long Island University, C.W. Post Campus (NY)	545, **1938**
Long Island University, Friends World Program (NY)	546, **1940**
Long Island University, Southampton College (NY)	545, **1942**
Longwood College (VA)	831
Loras College (IA)	291, **1944**
Louise Salinger Academy of Fashion (CA)	116
Louisiana College (LA)	325
Louisiana Scholars' College at Northwestern State University of Louisiana (LA)	329, **1946**
Louisiana State University and Agricultural and Mechanical College (LA)	325, **1948**
Louisiana State University Health Sciences Center (LA)	326
Louisiana State University in Shreveport (LA)	326
Louisiana Tech University (LA)	327, **1950**
Lourdes College (OH)	635
Loyola College in Maryland (MD)	347, **1952**
Loyola Marymount University (CA)	116, **1954**
Loyola University Chicago (IL)	243, **1956**
Loyola University New Orleans (LA)	327, **1958**
Lubbock Christian University (TX)	786
Lutheran Bible Institue of Seattle (WA)	847
Lutheran College of Health Professions (IN)	273
Luther College (IA)	291, **1960**
Luther Rice Bible College and Seminary (GA)	212
Lycoming College (PA)	702
Lyme Academy of Fine Arts (CT)	157
Lynchburg College (VA)	831, **1962**
Lyndon State College (VT)	818, **1964**
Lynn University (FL)	186, **1966**
Lyon College (AR)	82
Macalester College (MN)	424
Machzikei Hadath Rabbinical College (NY)	546
MacMurray College (IL)	244
Macon State College (GA)	212
Madonna University (MI)	407
Magdalen College (NH)	486
Magnolia Bible College (MS)	437
Maharishi University of Management (IA)	292, **1968**
Maine College of Art (ME)	336, **1970**
Maine Maritime Academy (ME)	336
Malone College (OH)	635, **1972**
Manchester College (IN)	273, **1974**
Manhattan Christian College (KS)	304
Manhattan College (NY)	547, **1976**
Manhattan School of Music (NY)	547, **1978**
Manhattanville College (NY)	548, **1980**
Mankato State University (MN)	425
Mannes College of Music, New School University (NY)	548, **1982**
Mansfield University of Pennsylvania (PA)	702, **1984**
Maple Springs Baptist Bible College and Seminary (MD)	348
Maranatha Baptist Bible College (WI)	870
Marian College (IN)	273, **1986**
Marian College of Fond du Lac (WI)	870, **1988**
Marietta College (OH)	636
Marist College (NY)	548, **1990**
Marlboro College (VT)	818, **1992**
Marquette University (WI)	870
Marshall University (WV)	858, **1994**
Mars Hill College (NC)	601, **1996**
Martin Luther College (MN)	425
Martin Methodist College (TN)	766
Martin University (IN)	274
Mary Baldwin College (VA)	832
Marycrest International University (IA)	292, **1998**
Marygrove College (MI)	407, **2000**
Maryland Institute, College of Art (MD)	348, **2002**
Marylhurst University (OR)	668, **2004**
Marymount College (NY)	549, **2006**
Marymount Manhattan College (NY)	550, **2008**
Marymount University (VA)	832, **2010**
Maryville College (TN)	767, **2012**
Maryville University of Saint Louis (MO)	453, **2014**
Mary Washington College (VA)	832, **2016**
Marywood University (PA)	703, **2018**
Mason Gross School of the Arts (NJ)	498
Massachusetts College of Art (MA)	373
Massachusetts College of Liberal Arts (MA)	374, **2020**
Massachusetts College of Pharmacy and Health Sciences (MA)	374, **2022**
Massachusetts Institute of Technology (MA)	375, **2024**
Massachusetts Maritime Academy (MA)	375, **2026**
The Master's College and Seminary (CA)	116
Mayo School of Health-Related Sciences (MN)	425
Mayville State University (ND)	616
McGill University (PQ, Canada)	901, **2028**
The McGregor School of Antioch University (OH)	637
McKendree College (IL)	244, **2030**
McMaster University (ON, Canada)	901
McMurry University (TX)	786, **2032**
McNeese State University (LA)	328
MCP Hahnemann University (PA)	703, **2034**
McPherson College (KS)	305
Medaille College (NY)	550
Medcenter One College of Nursing (ND)	617
Medgar Evers College of the City University of New York (NY)	551
Medical College of Georgia (GA)	213
Medical University of South Carolina (SC)	744
Memorial University of Newfoundland (NF, Canada)	901, **2036**
Memphis College of Art (TN)	767
Menlo College (CA)	116, **2038**
Mennonite College of Nursing (IL)	245
Mercer University (GA)	213, **2040**
Mercy College (NY)	551, **2042**
Mercy College of Health Sciences (IA)	293
Mercyhurst College (PA)	704, **2044**
Meredith College (NC)	602, **2046**
Merrimack College (MA)	376, **2048**
Mesa State College (CO)	146
Mesivta of Eastern Parkway Rabbinical Seminary (NY)	551
Mesivta Tifereth Jerusalem of America (NY)	551
Mesivta Torah Vodaath Rabbinical Seminary (NY)	551
Messenger College (MO)	454
Messiah College (PA)	704, **2050**
Methodist College (NC)	602
Metropolitan College of Court Reporting (AZ)	76
Metropolitan College of Court Reporting (NM)	514
Metropolitan State College of Denver (CO)	146
Metropolitan State University (MN)	425
Miami University (OH)	637
Miami University–Hamilton Campus (OH)	637
Miami University–Middletown Campus (OH)	637
Michigan Christian College (MI)	408
Michigan State University (MI)	408, **1838**
Michigan Technological University (MI)	408
Mid-America Bible College (OK)	655
MidAmerica Nazarene University (KS)	305
Mid-Continent College (KY)	317
Middlebury College (VT)	819, **2052**
Middle Tennessee State University (TN)	767
Midland Lutheran College (NE)	476, **2054**
Midway College (KY)	318, **2056**
Midwestern State University (TX)	787
Miles College (AL)	60
Millersville University of Pennsylvania (PA)	705, **2058**
Milligan College (TN)	768, **2060**
Millikin University (IL)	245
Millsaps College (MS)	437
Mills College (CA)	117, **2062**
Milwaukee Institute of Art and Design (WI)	871
Milwaukee School of Engineering (WI)	871, **2064**
Minneapolis College of Art and Design (MN)	426, **2066**
Minnesota Bible College (MN)	426
Minnesota State University, Mankato (MN)	427
Minnesota State University Moorhead (MN)	427
Minot State University (ND)	617
Mirrer Yeshiva (NY)	552
Mississippi College (MS)	438
Mississippi State University (MS)	438
Mississippi University for Women (MS)	439
Mississippi Valley State University (MS)	439
Missouri Baptist College (MO)	454
Missouri Southern State College (MO)	454, **2068**
Missouri Tech (MO)	455
Missouri Valley College (MO)	455, **2070**
Missouri Western State College (MO)	455
Mitchell College (CT)	157, **2072**
Molloy College (NY)	552, **2074**
Monmouth College (IL)	245
Monmouth University (NJ)	498, **2076**
Monroe College, Bronx (NY)	552, **2078**
Monroe College, New Rochelle (NY)	552
Montana State University–Billings (MT)	468, **2080**
Montana State University–Bozeman (MT)	468, **2082**
Montana State University–Northern (MT)	469

Index of Colleges and Universities

Montana Tech of The University of Montana (MT)	469, **2084**
Montclair State University (NJ)	499, **2086**
Monterey Institute of International Studies (CA)	117
Montreat College (NC)	602, **2088**
Montserrat College of Art (MA)	376, **2090**
Moody Bible Institute (IL)	246
Moore College of Art and Design (PA)	705, **2092**
Moorhead State University (MN)	428
Moravian College (PA)	706, **2094**
Morehead State University (KY)	318, **2096**
Morehouse College (GA)	213
Morgan State University (MD)	348, **2098**
Morningside College (IA)	*293*, **2100**
Morris Brown College (GA)	214
Morris College (SC)	744
Morrison University (NV)	482
Mount Allison University (NB, Canada)	902
Mount Aloysius College (PA)	706, **2102**
Mount Angel Seminary (OR)	668
Mount Carmel College of Nursing (OH)	637
Mount Holyoke College (MA)	377, **2104**
Mount Ida College (MA)	377, **2106**
Mount Marty College (SD)	752, **2108**
Mount Mary College (WI)	872, **2110**
Mount Mercy College (IA)	293, **2112**
Mount Olive College (NC)	603, **2114**
Mount St. Clare College (IA)	*294*, **2116**
Mount Saint Mary College (NY)	552, **2118**
Mount St. Mary's College (CA)	118, **2120**
Mount Saint Mary's College and Seminary (MD)	*349*, **2122**
Mount Saint Vincent University (NS, Canada)	902, **2124**
Mount Senario College (WI)	872
Mt. Sierra College (CA)	118
Mount Union College (OH)	*638*, **2126**
Mount Vernon College (DC)	171
Mount Vernon Nazarene College (OH)	638
Muhlenberg College (PA)	707, **2128**
Multnomah Bible College and Biblical Seminary (OR)	668
Murray State University (KY)	318
Musicians Institute (CA)	118
Muskingum College (OH)	639
NAES College (IL)	246
Naropa University (CO)	147, **2130**
National American University, Colorado Springs (CO)	147
National American University, Denver (CO)	147
National American University (MO)	456
National American University (NM)	514
National American University (SD)	753, **2132**
National American University–St. Paul Campus (MN)	428
National American University–Sioux Falls Branch (SD)	753
National Business College, Salem (VA)	833
The National College of Chiropractic (IL)	247
The National Hispanic University (CA)	118
National-Louis University (IL)	247, **2134**
National University (CA)	118
Nazarene Bible College (CO)	147
Nazarene Indian Bible College (NM)	514
Nazareth College of Rochester (NY)	553, **2136**
Nebraska Christian College (NE)	476
Nebraska Methodist College of Nursing and Allied Health (NE)	477
Nebraska Wesleyan University (NE)	477
Ner Israel Rabbinical College (MD)	349
Ner Israel Yeshiva College of Toronto (ON, Canada)	903
Neumann College (PA)	707, **2138**
Newark College of Arts and Sciences (NJ)	499
Newberry College (SC)	745, **2140**
Newbury College (MA)	*378*, **2142**
New College of California (CA)	119, **2144**
New College of the University of South Florida (FL)	*187*, **2146**
New England College (NH)	487, **2148**
New England College of Finance (MA)	378
New England College of Optometry (MA)	378
New England Conservatory of Music (MA)	378
New England Culinary Institute (VT)	819
New England Institute of Applied Arts and Sciences (MA)	378
New England Institute of Technology (RI)	733
The New England School of Art and Design at Suffolk University (MA)	378
New Hampshire College (NH)	*487*, **2150**
New Jersey City University (NJ)	499, **2152**
New Jersey Institute of Technology (NJ)	500, **2154**
Newman University (KS)	306
New Mexico Highlands University (NM)	514
New Mexico Institute of Mining and Technology (NM)	515, **2156**
New Mexico State University (NM)	515, **2158**
New Orleans Baptist Theological Seminary (LA)	328
New School Bachelor of Arts, New School University (NY)	553, **2160**
Newschool of Architecture (CA)	119
New School University, Eugene Lang College (NY)	554
New School University, Mannes College of Music (NY)	554
New School University, Parsons School of Design (NY)	554
New World School of the Arts (FL)	187
New York City Technical College of the City University of New York (NY)	554
The New York College for Wholistic Health Education & Research (NY)	*554*
New York Institute of Technology (NY)	554, **2162**
New York School of Interior Design (NY)	*555*, **2164**
New York State College of Ceramics (NY)	555
New York University (NY)	555, **2166**
Niagara University (NY)	*556*, **2168**
Nicholls State University (LA)	328
Nichols College (MA)	378, **2170**
The Nigerian Baptist Theological Seminary (Nigeria)	936
Nipissing University (ON, Canada)	903
Norfolk State University (VA)	833
North Adams State College (MA)	379
North American Baptist College and Edmonton Baptist Seminary (AB, Canada)	903
North Carolina Agricultural and Technical State University (NC)	603, **2172**
North Carolina Central University (NC)	604, **2174**
North Carolina School of the Arts (NC)	604
North Carolina State University (NC)	605
North Carolina Wesleyan College (NC)	605, **2176**
North Central College (IL)	247, **2178**
North Central University (MN)	428
North Dakota State University (ND)	617
Northeastern Illinois University (IL)	248
Northeastern State University (OK)	656
Northeastern University (MA)	379, **2180**
Northeast Louisiana University (LA)	329
Northern Arizona University (AZ)	76, **2182**
Northern Illinois University (IL)	248
Northern Kentucky University (KY)	319, **2184**
Northern Michigan University (MI)	409
Northern State University (SD)	753
North Georgia College & State University (GA)	214, **2186**
North Greenville College (SC)	745
Northland College (WI)	873
North Park University (IL)	249, **2188**
Northwest Bible College (AB, Canada)	904
Northwest Christian College (OR)	669
Northwest College (WA)	847
Northwest College of Art (WA)	848
Northwestern College (IA)	*294*, **2190**
Northwestern College (MN)	*428*
Northwestern College (OH)	639
Northwestern Health Sciences University (MN)	429
Northwestern Oklahoma State University (OK)	656
Northwestern Polytechnic University (CA)	119
Northwestern University (IL)	249
Northwest Missouri State University (MO)	456
Northwest Nazarene University (ID)	*227*, **2192**
Northwood University (MI)	*409*, **2194**
Northwood University, Florida Campus (FL)	188
Northwood University, Texas Campus (TX)	787
Norwich University (VT)	819, **2196**
Notre Dame College (NH)	488, **2198**
Notre Dame College of Ohio (OH)	*639*, **2200**
Nova Scotia Agricultural College (NS, Canada)	904
Nova Scotia College of Art and Design (NS, Canada)	904, **2202**
Nova Southeastern University (FL)	*188*, **2204**
Nyack College (NY)	556
Oak Hills Christian College (MN)	429
Oakland City University (IN)	274
Oakland University (MI)	410, **2206**
Oakwood College (AL)	60
Oberlin College (OH)	*640*, **2208**
Occidental College (CA)	119
Oglala Lakota College (SD)	753
Oglethorpe University (GA)	214, **2210**
Ohio Dominican College (OH)	*640*, **2212**
Ohio Northern University (OH)	641, **2214**
The Ohio State University (OH)	641
The Ohio State University at Lima (OH)	642
The Ohio State University at Marion (OH)	642
The Ohio State University–Mansfield Campus (OH)	642
The Ohio State University–Newark Campus (OH)	642
Ohio University (OH)	642, **2216**
Ohio University–Chillicothe (OH)	643
Ohio University–Eastern (OH)	643
Ohio University–Lancaster (OH)	643
Ohio University–Southern Campus (OH)	643
Ohio University–Zanesville (OH)	643
Ohio Valley College (WV)	859
Ohio Wesleyan University (OH)	644, **2218**
Ohr Hameir Theological Seminary (NY)	557
Ohr Somayach/Joseph Tanenbaum Educational Center (NY)	557
Okanagan University College (BC, Canada)	904
Oklahoma Baptist University (OK)	657, **2220**
Oklahoma Christian University of Science and Arts (OK)	657
Oklahoma City University (OK)	657, **2222**
Oklahoma Panhandle State University (OK)	658
Oklahoma State University (OK)	658
Old Dominion University (VA)	834
Olivet College (MI)	410
Olivet Nazarene University (IL)	250, **2224**
O'More College of Design (TN)	768
Ontario Bible College (ON, Canada)	905
Open Learning Agency (BC, Canada)	905
Oral Roberts University (OK)	659
Oregon College of Art and Craft (OR)	669
Oregon Health Sciences University (OR)	669
Oregon Institute of Technology (OR)	669
Oregon State University (OR)	670, **2226**
Otis College of Art and Design (CA)	120, **2228**
Ottawa University (KS)	306
Otterbein College (OH)	644, **2230**
Ouachita Baptist University (AR)	83
Our Lady of Holy Cross College (LA)	*329*
Our Lady of the Lake College (LA)	330
Our Lady of the Lake University of San Antonio (TX)	788, **2232**

Index of Colleges and Universities

Ozark Christian College (MO) 457
Pace University, New York City Campus (NY) 557, **2234**
Pace University, Pleasantville/Briarcliff Campus (NY) 557
Pacific Lutheran University (WA) 848, **2236**
Pacific Northwest College of Art (OR) 670
Pacific Oaks College (CA) 120
Pacific States University (CA) 121
Pacific Union College (CA) 121
Pacific University (OR) 671, **2238**
Paier College of Art, Inc. (CT) 157, **2240**
Paine College (GA) 215, **2242**
Palm Beach Atlantic College (FL) *189*, **2244**
Palmer College of Chiropractic (IA) 295
Park University (MO) 457
Parsons School of Design, New School University (NY) 558
Patten College (CA) 121
Paul Quinn College (TX) 788
Paul Smith's College of Arts and Sciences (NY) 558, **2246**
Peabody Conservatory of Music of The Johns Hopkins University (MD) 349
Peace College (NC) 606, **2248**
Peirce College (PA) *708*, **2250**
Pennsylvania College of Optometry (PA) 708
Pennsylvania College of Technology (PA) 708, **2252**
Pennsylvania School of Art & Design (PA) 709
Pennsylvania State University Abington College (PA) 709, **2254**
Pennsylvania State University Altoona College (PA) 709, **2256**
Pennsylvania State University at Erie, The Behrend College (PA) *710*, **2258**
Pennsylvania State University Berks Campus of the Berks–Lehigh Valley College (PA) 710
Pennsylvania State University Delaware County Campus of the Commonwealth College (PA) 711
Pennsylvania State University Harrisburg Campus of the Capital College (PA) *711*
Pennsylvania State University Lehigh Valley Campus of the Berks-Lehigh Valley College (PA) 711
Pennsylvania State University Schuylkill Campus of the Capital College (PA) 712
Pennsylvania State University Shenango Campus of the Commonwealth College (PA) 712
Pennsylvania State University University Park Campus (PA) 712
Pepperdine University, Malibu (CA) 122, **2260**
Peru State College (NE) 478, **2262**
Pfeiffer University (NC) 606, **2264**
Philadelphia College of Bible (PA) 713
Philadelphia College of Pharmacy and Science (PA) 713
Philadelphia College of Textiles and Science (PA) 713
Philadelphia University (PA) 713, **2266**
Philander Smith College (AR) 83
Piedmont Baptist College (NC) 607
Piedmont College (GA) 215, **2268**
Pikeville College (KY) 319
Pine Manor College (MA) 379, **2270**
Pittsburg State University (KS) 307
Pitzer College (CA) 122, **2272**
Platt College (CO) 148
Plattsburgh State University of New York (NY) 558, **2274**
Plymouth State College (NH) 488, **2276**
Point Loma Nazarene University (CA) 123
Point Park College (PA) 714, **2278**
Polytechnic University, Brooklyn Campus (NY) 559, **2280**
Polytechnic University, Farmingdale Campus (NY) 559

Polytechnic University of Puerto Rico (PR) 886
Pomona College (CA) 123, **2282**
Pontifical Catholic University of Puerto Rico (PR) 887
Pontifical College Josephinum (OH) 645
Portland State University (OR) 671
Potomac College (DC) 171
Practical Bible College (NY) 560
Prairie Bible College (AB, Canada) 905
Prairie View A&M University (TX) 788, **2284**
Pratt Institute (NY) *560*, **2286**
Presbyterian College (SC) 746, **2288**
Prescott College (AZ) 77, **2290**
Presentation College (SD) 754
Princeton University (NJ) 500, **2292**
Principia College (IL) 250
Providence College (RI) 733, **2294**
Providence College and Theological Seminary (MB, Canada) 905
Puget Sound Christian College (WA) 849
Purchase College, State University of New York (NY) 561, **2296**
Purdue University (IN) 274
Purdue University Calumet (IN) 275
Purdue University North Central (IN) 275
Queens College (NC) 607
Queens College of the City University of New York (NY) 561, **2298**
Queen's University at Kingston (ON, Canada) 906, **2300**
Quincy University (IL) 251, **2302**
Quinnipiac University (CT) *158*, **2304**
Rabbinical Academy Mesivta Rabbi Chaim Berlin (NY) 562
Rabbinical College Beth Shraga (NY) 562
Rabbinical College Bobover Yeshiva B'nei Zion (NY) 562
Rabbinical College Ch'san Sofer (NY) 562
Rabbinical College of America (NJ) 501
Rabbinical College of Long Island (NY) 562
Rabbinical Seminary Adas Yereim (NY) 562
Rabbinical Seminary M'kor Chaim (NY) 562
Rabbinical Seminary of America (NY) 562
Radford University (VA) 834, **2306**
Ramapo College of New Jersey (NJ) 501, **2308**
Randolph-Macon College (VA) 835, **2310**
Randolph-Macon Woman's College (VA) 835, **2312**
Redeemer College (ON, Canada) 906
Reed College (OR) 672, **2314**
Reformed Bible College (MI) *411*
Regents College (NY) 562, **2316**
Regis College (MA) 380, **2318**
Regis University (CO) *148*, **2320**
Reinhardt College (GA) 216
Rensselaer Polytechnic Institute (NY) 563, **2322**
Research College of Nursing (MO) 457
Rhode Island College (RI) 733
Rhode Island School of Design (RI) 734
Rhodes College (TN) 769, **2324**
Rice University (TX) 789, **2326**
The Richard Stockton College of New Jersey (NJ) 501, **2328**
Richmond, The American International University in London (United Kingdom) 938, **2330**
Rider University (NJ) 502, **2332**
Ringling School of Art and Design (FL) 189
Ripon College (WI) 873, **2334**
Rivier College (NH) *489*, **2336**
Roanoke Bible College (NC) 607
Roanoke College (VA) 836
Robert Morris College (IL) 251, **2338**
Robert Morris College (PA) *714*, **2340**
Roberts Wesleyan College (NY) 563, **2342**
Rochester College (MI) 411
Rochester Institute of Technology (NY) 564, **2344**
Rockford College (IL) 251, **2346**
Rockhurst University (MO) 458, **2348**
Rocky Mountain College (MT) 469, **2350**
Rocky Mountain College (AB, Canada) 906

Rocky Mountain College of Art & Design (CO) 148
Roger Williams University (RI) 734, **2352**
Rollins College (FL) *190*, **2354**
Roosevelt University (IL) 252, **2356**
Rose-Hulman Institute of Technology (IN) 275
Rosemont College (PA) 715, **2358**
Rowan University (NJ) 502, **2360**
Royal Military College of Canada (ON, Canada) 907
Royal Roads University (BC, Canada) 907
Rush University (IL) 252
Russell Sage College (NY) 564, **2362**
Rust College (MS) 440
Rutgers, The State University of New Jersey, Camden College of Arts and Sciences (NJ) 503
Rutgers, The State University of New Jersey, College of Nursing (NJ) 503
Rutgers, The State University of New Jersey, College of Pharmacy (NJ) 504
Rutgers, The State University of New Jersey, Cook College (NJ) 504
Rutgers, The State University of New Jersey, Douglass College (NJ) 505
Rutgers, The State University of New Jersey, Livingston College (NJ) 505
Rutgers, The State University of New Jersey, Mason Gross School of the Arts (NJ) 506
Rutgers, The State University of New Jersey, Newark College of Arts and Sciences (NJ) 507
Rutgers, The State University of New Jersey, Rutgers College (NJ) 507
Rutgers, The State University of New Jersey, School of Engineering (NJ) 508
Rutgers, The State University of New Jersey, University College–Camden (NJ) 508
Rutgers, The State University of New Jersey, University College–Newark (NJ) 508
Rutgers, The State University of New Jersey, University College–New Brunswick (NJ) 509
Ryerson Polytechnic University (ON, Canada) 907
Sacred Heart Major Seminary (MI) 411
Sacred Heart University (CT) *158*, **2364**
Saginaw Valley State University (MI) 412
St. Ambrose University (IA) 295, **2366**
St. Andrews Presbyterian College (NC) 608, **2368**
Saint Anselm College (NH) 489, **2370**
Saint Anthony College of Nursing (IL) 253
St. Augustine College (IL) 253
Saint Augustine's College (NC) 608
St. Bonaventure University (NY) 565, **2372**
St. Charles Borromeo Seminary, Overbrook (PA) 715
St. Cloud State University (MN) 429
St. Edward's University (TX) 789, **2374**
Saint Francis College (IN) 276
St. Francis College (NY) 566, **2376**
Saint Francis College (PA) 716, **2378**
Saint Francis Medical Center College of Nursing (IL) 253
St. Francis Xavier University (NS, Canada) 908, **2380**
St. Gregory's University (OK) 659
St. John Fisher College (NY) 566, **2382**
St. John's College (IL) 253
St. John's College (MD) 350, **2384**
St. John's College (NM) 516
St. John's Seminary College (CA) 124
Saint John's Seminary College of Liberal Arts (MA) 380
Saint John's University (MN) 430
St. John's University (NY) 567, **2386**
St. John Vianney College Seminary (FL) 190
Saint Joseph College (CT) 159, **2388**
Saint Joseph College of Nursing (IL) 254

Index of Colleges and Universities

Saint Joseph's College (IN)	276, **2390**
Saint Joseph's College (ME)	*337*, **2392**
St. Joseph's College, New York (NY)	*567*, **2394**
St. Joseph's College, Suffolk Campus (NY)	568
Saint Joseph Seminary College (LA)	330
Saint Joseph's University (PA)	716, **2396**
St. Lawrence University (NY)	568, **2398**
Saint Leo University (FL)	190, **2400**
St. Louis Christian College (MO)	458
St. Louis College of Pharmacy (MO)	459, **2402**
Saint Louis University (MO)	459
Saint Luke's College (MO)	460
Saint Martin's College (WA)	849, **2404**
Saint Mary College (KS)	307
Saint Mary-of-the-Woods College (IN)	276, **2406**
Saint Mary's College (IN)	277, **2408**
Saint Mary's College (MI)	412, **2410**
Saint Mary's College of California (CA)	124, **2412**
St. Mary's College of Maryland (MD)	*350*, **2414**
Saint Mary's University (NS, Canada)	908, **2416**
Saint Mary's University of Minnesota (MN)	430, **2418**
St. Mary's University of San Antonio (TX)	789, **2420**
Saint Michael's College (VT)	820, **2422**
St. Norbert College (WI)	*874*, **2424**
St. Olaf College (MN)	431
Saint Paul's College (VA)	836
Saint Paul University (ON, Canada)	908
Saint Peter's College (NJ)	*509*, **2426**
St. Thomas Aquinas College (NY)	569, **2428**
St. Thomas University (FL)	*191*, **2430**
St. Thomas University (NB, Canada)	909
Saint Vincent College (PA)	717
Saint Xavier University (IL)	254, **2432**
Salem College (NC)	*609*, **2434**
Salem State College (MA)	381
Salem-Teikyo University (WV)	859, **2436**
Salisbury State University (MD)	*351*, **2438**
Salish Kootenai College (MT)	470
Salve Regina University (RI)	735, **2440**
Samford University (AL)	*61*, **2442**
Sam Houston State University (TX)	790
Samuel Merritt College (CA)	124
San Diego State University (CA)	125
San Francisco Art Institute (CA)	*125*, **2444**
San Francisco Conservatory of Music (CA)	126
San Francisco State University (CA)	126
San Jose Christian College (CA)	126
San Jose State University (CA)	127
Santa Clara University (CA)	127, **2446**
Sarah Lawrence College (NY)	*569*, **2448**
Savannah College of Art and Design (GA)	216, **2450**
Savannah State University (GA)	217, **2452**
Schiller International University (FL)	*191*, **2454**
Schiller International University (France)	924
Schiller International University (Germany)	924
Schiller International University (Spain)	936
Schiller International University (United Kingdom)	939
Schiller International University, American College of Switzerland (Switzerland)	937
School of the Art Institute of Chicago (IL)	254, **2456**
School of the Museum of Fine Arts (MA)	381, **2458**
School of Visual Arts (NY)	569, **2460**
Schreiner College (TX)	790, **2462**
Scripps College (CA)	128, **2464**
Seattle Pacific University (WA)	*849*, **2466**
Seattle University (WA)	850, **2468**
Seton Hall University (NJ)	510, **2470**
Seton Hill College (PA)	*717*, **2472**
Shasta Bible College (CA)	128
Shawnee State University (OH)	645, **2474**
Shaw University (NC)	609
Sheldon Jackson College (AK)	70
Shenandoah University (VA)	836, **2476**
Shepherd College (WV)	*859*, **2478**
Shimer College (IL)	255, **2480**
Shippensburg University of Pennsylvania (PA)	718, **2482**
Shorter College (GA)	217, **2484**
Sh'or Yoshuv Rabbinical College (NY)	570
Siena College (NY)	*570*, **2486**
Siena Heights University (MI)	*413*, **2488**
Sierra Nevada College (NV)	482, **2490**
Silver Lake College (WI)	*874*
Simmons College (MA)	381, **2492**
Simon Fraser University (BC, Canada)	909
Simon's Rock College of Bard (MA)	382, **2494**
Simpson College (IA)	296, **2496**
Simpson College and Graduate School (CA)	128
Sinte Gleska University (SD)	754
Skidmore College (NY)	570, **2498**
Slippery Rock University of Pennsylvania (PA)	718, **2500**
Smith College (MA)	382, **2502**
Sojourner-Douglass College (MD)	351
Sonoma State University (CA)	129
Southampton College of Long Island University (NY)	571
South Carolina State University (SC)	746
South College (AL)	61
South College (FL)	192
South College (GA)	218
South Dakota School of Mines and Technology (SD)	754
South Dakota State University (SD)	*755*
Southeast College of Technology (AL)	62
Southeastern Baptist College (MS)	440
Southeastern Bible College (AL)	62
Southeastern College of the Assemblies of God (FL)	192
Southeastern Louisiana University (LA)	330
Southeastern Oklahoma State University (OK)	660
Southeastern University (DC)	171, **2504**
Southeast Missouri State University (MO)	460
Southern Adventist University (TN)	769
Southern Arkansas University–Magnolia (AR)	84
Southern Baptist Theological Seminary (KY)	320
Southern California Bible College & Seminary (CA)	129
Southern California College (CA)	129
Southern California Institute of Architecture (CA)	129, **2506**
Southern Christian University (AL)	62
Southern Connecticut State University (CT)	159, **2508**
Southern Illinois University Carbondale (IL)	255, **2510**
Southern Illinois University Edwardsville (IL)	256
Southern Methodist College (SC)	746
Southern Methodist University (TX)	791, **2512**
Southern Nazarene University (OK)	660
Southern Oregon University (OR)	672, **2514**
Southern Polytechnic State University (GA)	218, **2516**
Southern University and Agricultural and Mechanical College (LA)	330
Southern University at New Orleans (LA)	330
Southern Utah University (UT)	811
Southern Vermont College (VT)	820, **2518**
Southern Wesleyan University (SC)	746
Southwest Baptist University (MO)	*460*
Southwestern Adventist University (TX)	791
Southwestern Assemblies of God University (TX)	792
Southwestern Christian College (TX)	792
Southwestern College (AZ)	77
Southwestern College (KS)	307
Southwestern College of Christian Ministries (OK)	660
Southwestern Oklahoma State University (OK)	661
Southwestern University (TX)	792
Southwest Missouri State University (MO)	461, **2520**
Southwest State University (MN)	431
Southwest Texas State University (TX)	793, **2522**
Spalding University (KY)	320
Spelman College (GA)	*218*, **2524**
Spring Arbor College (MI)	413, **2526**
Springfield College (MA)	*383*, **2528**
Spring Hill College (AL)	62
Stanford University (CA)	130, **2530**
State University of New York at Albany (NY)	571, **2532**
State University of New York at Binghamton (NY)	571, **2534**
State University of New York at Buffalo (NY)	*572*, **2536, 2538**
State University of New York at Farmingdale (NY)	*573*, **2540**
State University of New York at New Paltz (NY)	573
State University of New York at Oswego (NY)	574, **2542**
State University of New York at Stony Brook (NY)	*574*, **2544**
State University of New York College at Brockport (NY)	575, **2546**
State University of New York College at Buffalo (NY)	*575*, **2548**
State University of New York College at Cortland (NY)	576
State University of New York College at Fredonia (NY)	576, **2550**
State University of New York College at Geneseo (NY)	577, **2552**
State University of New York College at Old Westbury (NY)	*577*, **2554**
State University of New York College at Oneonta (NY)	578, **2556**
State University of New York College at Plattsburgh (NY)	578
State University of New York College at Potsdam (NY)	*578*, **2558**
State University of New York College at Purchase (NY)	579
State University of New York College of Agriculture and Technology at Cobleskill (NY)	579, **2560**
State University of New York College of Agriculture and Technology at Morrisville (NY)	579
State University of New York College of Environmental Science and Forestry (NY)	579, **2562**
State University of New York College of Technology at Alfred (NY)	580
State University of New York College of Technology at Canton (NY)	580
State University of New York College of Technology at Delhi (NY)	580
State University of New York Empire State College (NY)	*580*
State University of New York Health Science Center at Brooklyn (NY)	581
State University of New York Institute of Technology at Utica/Rome (NY)	*581*, **2564**
State University of New York Maritime College (NY)	*581*, **2566**
State University of New York Upstate Medical University (NY)	582
State University of West Georgia (GA)	219, **2568**
Steinbach Bible College (MB, Canada)	909
Stephen F. Austin State University (TX)	793
Stephens College (MO)	461, **2570**
Sterling College (KS)	308
Sterling College (VT)	821, **2572**
Stern College for Women (NY)	582
Stetson University (FL)	*192*, **2574**
Stevens Institute of Technology (NJ)	510, **2576**
Stillman College (AL)	63
Stonehill College (MA)	*383*, **2578**

Index of Colleges and Universities

Strayer University (DC)	171
Suffolk University (MA)	384
Sullivan College (KY)	320, **2580**
Sul Ross State University (TX)	794
Suomi College (MI)	414, **1660**
Susquehanna University (PA)	719, **2582**
Swarthmore College (PA)	*719*, **2584**
Sweet Briar College (VA)	837, **2586**
Syracuse University (NY)	582, **2588**
Syracuse University, Utica College (NY)	583
Tabor College (KS)	308
Talladega College (AL)	63, **2590**
Talmudical Academy of New Jersey (NJ)	511
Talmudical Institute of Upstate New York (NY)	583
Talmudical Seminary Oholei Torah (NY)	583
Talmudical Yeshiva of Philadelphia (PA)	720
Talmudic College of Florida (FL)	193
Tarleton State University (TX)	794
Taylor University (IN)	*277*, **2592**
Taylor University, Fort Wayne Campus (IN)	278
Technical University of British Columbia (BC, Canada)	909
Technical University of Nova Scotia (NS, Canada)	910
Teikyo Loretto Heights University (CO)	149
Teikyo Post University (CT)	*160*, **2594**
Télé-université (PQ, Canada)	910
Telshe Yeshiva–Chicago (IL)	256
Temple University (PA)	*720*, **2596**
Tennessee State University (TN)	770, **2598**
Tennessee Technological University (TN)	770, **2600, 2602**
Tennessee Temple University (TN)	771
Tennessee Wesleyan College (TN)	771
Texas A&M International University (TX)	794
Texas A&M University (TX)	795
Texas A&M University at Galveston (TX)	795, **2604**
Texas A&M University–Commerce (TX)	796
Texas A&M University–Corpus Christi (TX)	796
Texas A&M University–Kingsville (TX)	797
Texas A&M University System Health Science Center (TX)	797
Texas A&M University–Texarkana (TX)	797
Texas Chiropractic College (TX)	798
Texas Christian University (TX)	*798*, **2606**
Texas College (TX)	798
Texas Lutheran University (TX)	*798*, **2608**
Texas Southern University (TX)	799
Texas Tech University (TX)	799, **2610**
Texas Wesleyan University (TX)	800
Texas Woman's University (TX)	800, **2612**
Thiel College (PA)	721, **2614**
Thomas Aquinas College (CA)	130
Thomas College (ME)	337
Thomas Edison State College (NJ)	511, **2616**
Thomas Jefferson University (PA)	721, **2618**
Thomas More College (KY)	321, **2620**
Thomas More College of Liberal Arts (NH)	490, **2622**
Thomas University (GA)	219
Tiffin University (OH)	645, **2624**
Toccoa Falls College (GA)	220, **2626**
Torah Temimah Talmudical Seminary (NY)	583
Tougaloo College (MS)	440
Touro College (NY)	583, **2628**
Towson University (MD)	351, **2630**
Transylvania University (KY)	321, **2632**
Trent University (ON, Canada)	910, **2634**
Trevecca Nazarene University (TN)	771, **2636**
Trinity Baptist College (FL)	193
Trinity Bible College (ND)	618
Trinity Christian College (IL)	256, **2638**
Trinity College (CT)	160, **2640**
Trinity College (DC)	*172*, **2642**
Trinity College of Florida (FL)	193
Trinity College of Nursing (IL)	256
Trinity College of Vermont (VT)	*821*, **2644**
Trinity International University (IL)	257
Trinity International University, South Florida Campus (FL)	194
Trinity Lutheran College (WA)	850
Trinity University (TX)	801, **2646**
Trinity Western University (BC, Canada)	910
Tri-State University (IN)	*278*, **2648**
Troy State University (AL)	63, **2650**
Troy State University Dothan (AL)	64
Troy State University Montgomery (AL)	64
Truman State University (MO)	462
Tufts University (MA)	384
Tulane University (LA)	331, **2652**
Tusculum College (TN)	*772*, **2654**
Tuskegee University (AL)	65, **2656**
Tyndale College & Seminary (ON, Canada)	911
Union College (KY)	322, **2658**
Union College (NE)	478, **2660**
Union College (NY)	*583*, **2662**
The Union Institute (OH)	646
Union University (TN)	772
United States Air Force Academy (CO)	149, **2664**
United States Coast Guard Academy (CT)	161, **2666**
United States International University (CA)	131
United States International University–Africa (Kenya)	928
United States International University–Mexico (Mexico)	935
United States Merchant Marine Academy (NY)	584, **2668**
United States Military Academy (NY)	584, **2670**
United States Naval Academy (MD)	352
United States Open University (DE)	166
United Talmudical Seminary (NY)	585
Unity College (ME)	*338*, **2672**
Universidad Adventista de las Antillas (PR)	887
Universidad de las Americas, A.C. (Mexico)	935
Universidad de las Américas–Puebla (Mexico)	935
Universidad del Turabo (PR)	887
Universidad Metropolitana (PR)	888
Universidad Politécnica de Puerto Rico (PR)	888
Université de Moncton (NB, Canada)	911
Université de Montréal (PQ, Canada)	911
Université de Sherbrooke (PQ, Canada)	912
Université du Québec à Chicoutimi (PQ, Canada)	912
Université du Québec à Hull (PQ, Canada)	912
Université du Québec à Montréal (PQ, Canada)	912
Université du Québec à Rimouski (PQ, Canada)	912
Université du Québec à Trois-Rivières (PQ, Canada)	912
Université du Québec, École de technologie supérieure (PQ, Canada)	913
Université du Québec en Abitibi-Témiscamingue (PQ, Canada)	913
Université du Québec, Télé-université (PQ, Canada)	913
Université Laval (PQ, Canada)	913, **2674**
Université Sainte-Anne (NS, Canada)	914, **2676**
University at Albany, State University of New York (NY)	585
University College of Cape Breton (NS, Canada)	914, **2678**
University College of the Cariboo (BC, Canada)	914
University College of the Fraser Valley (BC, Canada)	914
University of Advancing Computer Technology (AZ)	77, **2680**
The University of Akron (OH)	*646*, **2682**
The University of Alabama (AL)	65
The University of Alabama at Birmingham (AL)	65, **2684**
The University of Alabama in Huntsville (AL)	66, **2686**
University of Alaska Anchorage (AK)	70, **2688**
University of Alaska Fairbanks (AK)	70, **2690**
University of Alaska Southeast (AK)	71, **2692**
University of Alberta (AB, Canada)	915
The University of Arizona (AZ)	77
University of Arkansas (AR)	84, **2694**
University of Arkansas at Little Rock (AR)	85
University of Arkansas at Monticello (AR)	85
University of Arkansas at Pine Bluff (AR)	85
University of Arkansas for Medical Sciences (AR)	86
University of Baltimore (MD)	352, **2696**
University of Biblical Studies and Seminary (OK)	661
University of Bridgeport (CT)	*161*, **2698**
University of British Columbia (BC, Canada)	915, **2700**
University of Calgary (AB, Canada)	915
University of California, Berkeley (CA)	131
University of California, Davis (CA)	131
University of California, Irvine (CA)	132
University of California, Los Angeles (CA)	132
University of California, Riverside (CA)	*133*, **2702**
University of California, San Diego (CA)	133
University of California, Santa Barbara (CA)	134
University of California, Santa Cruz (CA)	134
University of Central Arkansas (AR)	*86*, **2704**
University of Central Florida (FL)	194, **2706**
University of Central Oklahoma (OK)	661
University of Charleston (WV)	860, **2708**
University of Chicago (IL)	257, **2710**
University of Cincinnati (OH)	647, **2712**
University of Colorado at Boulder (CO)	149, **2714**
University of Colorado at Colorado Springs (CO)	150
University of Colorado at Denver (CO)	150
University of Colorado Health Sciences Center (CO)	151
University of Connecticut (CT)	*162*, **2716**
University of Dallas (TX)	801
University of Dayton (OH)	647, **2718, 2720**
University of Delaware (DE)	166
University of Denver (CO)	151
University of Detroit Mercy (MI)	*414*, **2722**
University of Dubuque (IA)	297
University of Evansville (IN)	*279*, **2724**
The University of Findlay (OH)	*648*, **2726**
University of Florida (FL)	194
University of Georgia (GA)	220
University of Great Falls (MT)	470, **2728**
University of Guam (GU)	882
University of Guelph (ON, Canada)	916, **2730**
University of Hartford (CT)	162, **2732**
University of Hawaii at Hilo (HI)	223
University of Hawaii at Manoa (HI)	223
University of Hawaii–West Oahu (HI)	224
University of Houston (TX)	802, **2734**
University of Houston–Clear Lake (TX)	802
University of Houston–Downtown (TX)	803
University of Houston–Victoria (TX)	803
University of Idaho (ID)	227
University of Illinois at Chicago (IL)	257, **2736**
University of Illinois at Springfield (IL)	258
University of Illinois at Urbana–Champaign (IL)	258
University of Indianapolis (IN)	279, **2738**
The University of Iowa (IA)	297
University of Judaism (CA)	135, **2740**
University of Kansas (KS)	309
University of Kentucky (KY)	322
University of King's College (NS, Canada)	916
University of La Verne (CA)	*135*, **2742**
The University of Lethbridge (AB, Canada)	917

1114

Index of Colleges and Universities

University of Louisiana at Lafayette (LA)	331, **2744**
University of Louisiana at Monroe (LA)	331
University of Louisville (KY)	323
University of Maine (ME)	338, **2746**
The University of Maine at Augusta (ME)	339
University of Maine at Farmington (ME)	339
University of Maine at Fort Kent (ME)	339, **2748**
University of Maine at Machias (ME)	340, **2750**
University of Maine at Presque Isle (ME)	340
University of Manitoba (MB, Canada)	917
University of Mary (ND)	618
University of Mary Hardin-Baylor (TX)	803, **2752**
University of Maryland, Baltimore County (MD)	353, **2754**
University of Maryland, College Park (MD)	353, **2756**
University of Maryland Eastern Shore (MD)	354, **2758**
University of Maryland University College (MD)	354, **2760**
University of Massachusetts Amherst (MA)	385, **2762**
University of Massachusetts Boston (MA)	385, **2764**
University of Massachusetts Dartmouth (MA)	386, **2766**
University of Massachusetts Lowell (MA)	386, **2768**
University of Medicine and Dentistry of New Jersey (NJ)	511
The University of Memphis (TN)	773, **2770**
University of Miami (FL)	195
University of Michigan (MI)	414
University of Michigan–Dearborn (MI)	415
University of Michigan–Flint (MI)	415
University of Minnesota, Crookston (MN)	432, **2772**
University of Minnesota, Duluth (MN)	432
University of Minnesota, Morris (MN)	433
University of Minnesota, Twin Cities Campus (MN)	433
University of Mississippi (MS)	441
University of Mississippi Medical Center (MS)	441
University of Missouri–Columbia (MO)	462
University of Missouri–Kansas City (MO)	463, **2774**
University of Missouri–Rolla (MO)	463, **2776**
University of Missouri–St. Louis (MO)	464, **2778**
University of Mobile (AL)	67
University of Mobile–Latin American Branch Campus (Nicaragua)	935
The University of Montana–Missoula (MT)	471
University of Montevallo (AL)	67, **2780**
University of Nebraska at Kearney (NE)	479
University of Nebraska at Omaha (NE)	479
University of Nebraska–Lincoln (NE)	480, **2782**
University of Nebraska Medical Center (NE)	480
University of Nevada, Las Vegas (NV)	482, **2784**
University of Nevada, Reno (NV)	483, **2786**
University of New Brunswick, Fredericton (NB, Canada)	917
University of New Brunswick, Saint John (NB, Canada)	918
University of New England (ME)	341, **2788**
University of New Hampshire (NH)	490
University of New Hampshire at Manchester (NH)	491
University of New Haven (CT)	163, **2790**
University of New Mexico (NM)	516
University of New Mexico–Gallup (NM)	517
University of New Orleans (LA)	332, **2792**
University of North Alabama (AL)	67
The University of North Carolina at Asheville (NC)	610
The University of North Carolina at Chapel Hill (NC)	610
The University of North Carolina at Charlotte (NC)	611
The University of North Carolina at Greensboro (NC)	611
The University of North Carolina at Pembroke (NC)	612, **2794**
The University of North Carolina at Wilmington (NC)	612
University of North Dakota (ND)	618
University of Northern British Columbia (BC, Canada)	918
University of Northern Colorado (CO)	151
University of Northern Iowa (IA)	297
University of North Florida (FL)	195
University of North Texas (TX)	804
University of Notre Dame (IN)	280, **2796**
University of Oklahoma (OK)	662
University of Oklahoma Health Sciences Center (OK)	662
University of Oregon (OR)	673, **2798**
University of Ottawa (ON, Canada)	918, **2800**
University of Pennsylvania (PA)	722
University of Phoenix (AZ)	78
University of Pittsburgh (PA)	722, **2802**
University of Pittsburgh at Bradford (PA)	723, **2804**
University of Pittsburgh at Greensburg (PA)	723, **2806**
University of Pittsburgh at Johnstown (PA)	724
University of Portland (OR)	673
University of Prince Edward Island (PE, Canada)	918
University of Puerto Rico, Aguadilla University College (PR)	888
University of Puerto Rico at Arecibo (PR)	888
University of Puerto Rico at Ponce (PR)	888
University of Puerto Rico, Carolina Regional College (PR)	889
University of Puerto Rico, Cayey University College (PR)	889
University of Puerto Rico, Colegio Regional de la Montaña (PR)	889
University of Puerto Rico, Humacao University College (PR)	889
University of Puerto Rico, Mayagüez Campus (PR)	890
University of Puerto Rico, Medical Sciences Campus (PR)	890
University of Puerto Rico, Río Piedras (PR)	890
University of Puget Sound (WA)	851, **2808**
University of Redlands (CA)	136, **2810**
University of Regina (SK, Canada)	919
University of Rhode Island (RI)	735, **2812**
University of Richmond (VA)	837
University of Rio Grande (OH)	648, **2814**
University of Rochester (NY)	585, **2816**
University of St. Francis (IL)	259, **2818**
University of Saint Francis (IN)	280
University of St. Thomas (MN)	434, **2820**
University of St. Thomas (TX)	804, **2822**
University of San Diego (CA)	136, **2824**
University of San Francisco (CA)	137, **2826**
University of Sarasota (FL)	196
University of Saskatchewan (SK, Canada)	919
University of Science and Arts of Oklahoma (OK)	662
The University of Scranton (PA)	724, **2828**
University of Sioux Falls (SD)	755
University of South Alabama (AL)	68
University of South Carolina (SC)	747, **2830**
University of South Carolina Aiken (SC)	747
University of South Carolina Spartanburg (SC)	748
University of South Dakota (SD)	756
University of Southern California (CA)	137, **2832**
University of Southern Colorado (CO)	152
University of Southern Indiana (IN)	281
University of Southern Maine (ME)	341, **2834**
University of Southern Mississippi (MS)	442
University of South Florida (FL)	196
University of South Florida, New College (FL)	196
University of Southwestern Louisiana (LA)	332
The University of Tampa (FL)	196, **2836**
The University of Tennessee at Chattanooga (TN)	773
The University of Tennessee at Martin (TN)	774, **2838**
The University of Tennessee Knoxville (TN)	774
The University of Tennessee Memphis (TN)	775
The University of Texas at Arlington (TX)	805
The University of Texas at Austin (TX)	805
The University of Texas at Brownsville (TX)	806
The University of Texas at Dallas (TX)	806, **2840**
The University of Texas at El Paso (TX)	806
The University of Texas at San Antonio (TX)	807
The University of Texas at Tyler (TX)	807
The University of Texas Health Science Center at San Antonio (TX)	808
The University of Texas–Houston Health Science Center (TX)	808
The University of Texas Medical Branch at Galveston (TX)	808
The University of Texas of the Permian Basin (TX)	808
The University of Texas–Pan American (TX)	808
The University of Texas Southwestern Medical Center at Dallas (TX)	809
The University of the Arts (PA)	725, **2842**
University of the District of Columbia (DC)	172, **2844**
University of the Incarnate Word (TX)	809, **2846**
University of the Ozarks (AR)	87
University of the Pacific (CA)	138, **2848**
University of the Sacred Heart (PR)	890
University of the Sciences in Philadelphia (PA)	725, **2850**
University of the South (TN)	775
University of the State of New York, Regents College (NY)	586
University of the Virgin Islands (VI)	891, **2852**
University of Toledo (OH)	649
University of Toronto (ON, Canada)	919
University of Tulsa (OK)	663, **2854**
University of Utah (UT)	812
University of Vermont (VT)	822, **2856**
University of Victoria (BC, Canada)	919
University of Virginia (VA)	838
University of Virginia's College at Wise (VA)	838
University of Washington (WA)	851
University of Waterloo (ON, Canada)	920
The University of West Alabama (AL)	68
The University of Western Ontario (ON, Canada)	920
University of West Florida (FL)	197, **2858**
University of West Los Angeles (CA)	138, **2860**
University of Windsor (ON, Canada)	921, **2862**
The University of Winnipeg (MB, Canada)	921
University of Wisconsin–Eau Claire (WI)	875
University of Wisconsin–Green Bay (WI)	875, **2864**
University of Wisconsin–La Crosse (WI)	876
University of Wisconsin–Madison (WI)	876
University of Wisconsin–Milwaukee (WI)	877
University of Wisconsin–Oshkosh (WI)	877
University of Wisconsin–Parkside (WI)	877
University of Wisconsin–Platteville (WI)	877
University of Wisconsin–River Falls (WI)	878
University of Wisconsin–Stevens Point (WI)	878
University of Wisconsin–Stout (WI)	879
University of Wisconsin–Superior (WI)	879
University of Wisconsin–Whitewater (WI)	880
University of Wyoming (WY)	881, **2866**
University System College for Lifelong Learning (NH)	491
Upper Iowa University (IA)	298
Urbana University (OH)	649, **2868**
Ursinus College (PA)	726, **2870**
Ursuline College (OH)	649

Index of Colleges and Universities

Utah State University (UT)	812
Utah Valley State College (UT)	813
Utica College of Syracuse University (NY)	586, 2872
Valdosta State University (GA)	220
Valley City State University (ND)	619
Valley Forge Christian College (PA)	726
Valparaiso University (IN)	281, 2874
Vanderbilt University (TN)	775, 2876
VanderCook College of Music (IL)	259, 2878
Vanguard University of Southern California (CA)	138, 2880
Vassar College (NY)	586, 2882
Vermont Technical College (VT)	822, 2884
Villa Julie College (MD)	355, 2886
Villanova University (PA)	726, 2888
Virginia College at Birmingham (AL)	69
Virginia Commonwealth University (VA)	839, 2890
Virginia Intermont College (VA)	839, 2892
Virginia Military Institute (VA)	840, 2894
Virginia Polytechnic Institute and State University (VA)	840
Virginia State University (VA)	841
Virginia Union University (VA)	841, 2896
Virginia Wesleyan College (VA)	842, 2898
Viterbo University (WI)	880, 2900
Voorhees College (SC)	748, 2902
Wabash College (IN)	282
Wadhams Hall Seminary-College (NY)	587
Wagner College (NY)	587, 2904
Wake Forest University (NC)	613
Waldorf College (IA)	298
Walla Walla College (WA)	852
Walsh College of Accountancy and Business Administration (MI)	416
Walsh University (OH)	650, 2906
Warner Pacific College (OR)	674, 2908
Warner Southern College (FL)	197
Warren Wilson College (NC)	613, 2910
Wartburg College (IA)	298, 2912
Washburn University of Topeka (KS)	309
Washington & Jefferson College (PA)	727, 2914
Washington and Lee University (VA)	842, 2916
Washington Bible College (MD)	355
Washington College (MD)	356, 2918
Washington State University (WA)	852
Washington University in St. Louis (MO)	464, 2920
Wayland Baptist University (TX)	809
Waynesburg College (PA)	728, 2922
Wayne State College (NE)	480
Wayne State University (MI)	416
Webber College (FL)	198, 2924
Webb Institute (NY)	588, 2926
Weber State University (UT)	813
Webster University (MO)	465, 2928
Wellesley College (MA)	387, 2930
Wells College (NY)	588, 2932
Wentworth Institute of Technology (MA)	387, 2934
Wesleyan College (GA)	221, 2936
Wesleyan University (CT)	163, 2938
Wesley College (DE)	166, 2940
Wesley College (MS)	442
Westbrook College (ME)	342
West Chester University of Pennsylvania (PA)	728, 2942
Western Baptist College (OR)	674
Western Carolina University (NC)	614, 2944
Western Connecticut State University (CT)	164
Western Illinois University (IL)	260, 2946
Western International University (AZ)	78
Western Kentucky University (KY)	323
Western Maryland College (MD)	356, 2948
Western Michigan University (MI)	417, 2950
Western Montana College of The University of Montana (MT)	471, 2952
Western New England College (MA)	388, 2954
Western New Mexico University (NM)	517
Western Oregon University (OR)	675, 2956
Western Pentecostal Bible College (BC, Canada)	921
Western State College of Colorado (CO)	152, 2958
Western States Chiropractic College (OR)	675
Western Washington University (WA)	853
Westfield State College (MA)	388
West Liberty State College (WV)	860
Westminster Choir College of Rider University (NJ)	511, 2960
Westminster College (MO)	465, 2962
Westminster College (PA)	729, 2964
Westminster College (UT)	813, 2966
Westmont College (CA)	139, 2968
West Suburban College of Nursing (IL)	260
West Texas A&M University (TX)	810
West Virginia State College (WV)	861
West Virginia University (WV)	861
West Virginia University at Parkersburg (WV)	862
West Virginia University Institute of Technology (WV)	862, 2970
West Virginia Wesleyan College (WV)	862, 2972
Westwood College of Technology (CO)	153
Wheaton College (IL)	260, 2974
Wheaton College (MA)	389, 2976
Wheeling Jesuit University (WV)	863, 2978
Wheelock College (MA)	389, 2980
White Pines College (NH)	491, 2982
Whitman College (WA)	853, 2984
Whittier College (CA)	139, 2986
Whitworth College (WA)	854, 2988
Wichita State University (KS)	310
Widener University (PA)	729, 2990
Wilberforce University (OH)	650, 2992
Wiley College (TX)	810
Wilfrid Laurier University (ON, Canada)	921, 2994
Wilkes University (PA)	730, 2996
Willamette University (OR)	675
William and Catherine Booth College (MB, Canada)	922
William Carey College (MS)	442
William Jewell College (MO)	466, 2998
William Paterson University of New Jersey (NJ)	512, 3000
William Penn University (IA)	299, 3002
Williams Baptist College (AR)	87
Williams College (MA)	390
William Smith College (NY)	589
William Tyndale College (MI)	417
William Woods University (MO)	466, 3004
Wilmington College (DE)	167, 3006
Wilmington College (OH)	651
Wilson College (PA)	730, 3008
Wingate University (NC)	614, 3010
Winona State University (MN)	434
Winston-Salem State University (NC)	615
Winthrop University (SC)	749, 3012
Wisconsin Lutheran College (WI)	880
Wittenberg University (OH)	651
Wofford College (SC)	749, 3014
Woodbury University (CA)	140, 3016
Worcester Polytechnic Institute (MA)	390
Worcester State College (MA)	391, 3018
World College (VA)	843
Wright State University (OH)	652, 3020
Xavier University (OH)	652, 3022
Xavier University of Louisiana (LA)	332
Yale University (CT)	164
Yeshiva Beth Moshe (PA)	731
Yeshiva College (NY)	589
Yeshiva Derech Chaim (NY)	589
Yeshiva Geddolah of Greater Detroit Rabbinical College (MI)	417
Yeshiva Karlin Stolin Rabbinical Institute (NY)	589
Yeshiva of Nitra Rabbinical College (NY)	589
Yeshiva Ohr Elchonon Chabad/West Coast Talmudical Seminary (CA)	140
Yeshiva Shaar Hatorah Talmudic Research Institute (NY)	589
Yeshivath Viznitz (NY)	589
Yeshivath Zichron Moshe (NY)	589
Yeshivat Mikdash Melech (NY)	589
Yeshiva Toras Chaim Talmudical Seminary (CO)	153
Yeshiva University (NY)	589
York College (NE)	481
York College of Pennsylvania (PA)	731
York College of the City University of New York (NY)	590, 3024
York University (ON, Canada)	922, 3026
Youngstown State University (OH)	653, 3028

GEOGRAPHICAL INDEX OF IN-DEPTH DESCRIPTIONS

UNITED STATES AND TERRITORIES

Alabama
Auburn University	1204
Birmingham-Southern College	1278
Huntingdon College	1810
Samford University	2442
Talladega College	2590
Troy State University	2650
Tuskegee University	2656
The University of Alabama at Birmingham	2684
The University of Alabama in Huntsville	2686
University of Montevallo	2780

Alaska
University of Alaska Anchorage	2688
University of Alaska Fairbanks	2690
University of Alaska Southeast	2692

Arizona
Arizona State University	1182
Embry-Riddle Aeronautical University	1628
Grand Canyon University	1736
Northern Arizona University	2182
Prescott College	2290
University of Advancing Computer Technology	2680

Arkansas
Arkansas State University	1184
Harding University	1764
Hendrix College	1782
John Brown University	1842
University of Arkansas	2694
University of Central Arkansas	2704

California
Academy of Art College	1126
Armstrong University	1186
Art Institute of Southern California	1194
Azusa Pacific University	1216
Bethesda Christian University	1272
Biola University	1276
California College of Arts and Crafts	1334
California Institute of Technology	1336
California Institute of the Arts	1338
California Lutheran University	1340
California State Polytechnic University, Pomona	1342
Chapman University	1404
Claremont McKenna College	1424
Cogswell Polytechnical College	1444
College of Notre Dame	1466
Columbia College–Hollywood	1508
Design Institute of San Diego	1576
Dominican University of California	1584
Fresno Pacific University	1698
Harvey Mudd College	1774
Loyola Marymount University	1954
Menlo College	2038
Mills College	2062
Mount St. Mary's College	2120
New College of California	2144
Otis College of Art and Design	2228
Pepperdine University	2260
Pitzer College	2272
Pomona College	2282
Saint Mary's College of California	2412
San Francisco Art Institute	2444
Santa Clara University	2446
Scripps College	2464
Southern California Institute of Architecture	2506
Stanford University	2530
University of California, Riverside	2702
University of Judaism	2740
University of La Verne	2742
University of Redlands	2810
University of San Diego	2824
University of San Francisco	2826
University of Southern California	2832
University of the Pacific	2848
University of West Los Angeles	2860
Vanguard University of Southern California	2880
Westmont College	2968
Whittier College	2986
Woodbury University	3016

Colorado
Adams State College	1130
Colorado Christian University	1496
The Colorado College	1498
Colorado State University	1500
Naropa University	2130
Regis University	2320
United States Air Force Academy	2664
University of Colorado at Boulder	2714
Western State College of Colorado	2958

Connecticut
Albertus Magnus College	1142
Central Connecticut State University	1394
Connecticut College	1530
Eastern Connecticut State University	1602
Hartford College for Women	1768
Mitchell College	2072
Paier College of Art, Inc.	2240
Quinnipiac University	2304
Sacred Heart University	2364
Saint Joseph College	2388
Southern Connecticut State University	2508
Teikyo Post University	2594
Trinity College	2640
United States Coast Guard Academy	2666
University of Bridgeport	2698
University of Connecticut	2716
University of Hartford	2732
University of New Haven	2790
Wesleyan University	2938

Delaware
Wesley College	2940
Wilmington College	3006

District of Columbia
American University	1164
The Catholic University of America	1382
Georgetown University	1714
Howard University	1806
Southeastern University	2504
Trinity College	2642
University of the District of Columbia	2844

Florida
Barry University	1230
Bethune-Cookman College	1274
Eckerd College	1612
Embry-Riddle Aeronautical University	1630
Flagler College	1670
Florida Agricultural and Mechanical University	1672
Florida Atlantic University	1674
Florida Institute of Technology	1676
Florida International University	1678
Florida Southern College	1680
Florida State University	1682
Jacksonville University	1836
Lynn University	1966
New College of the University of South Florida	2146
Nova Southeastern University	2204
Palm Beach Atlantic College	2244
Rollins College	2354
Saint Leo University	2400
St. Thomas University	2430
Schiller International University	2454
Stetson University	2574
University of Central Florida	2706
The University of Tampa	2836
University of West Florida	2858
Webber College	2924

Georgia
Agnes Scott College	1136
Albany State University	1138
American InterContinental University	1160
Atlanta College of Art	1202
Augusta State University	1210
Brenau University	1302
Clark Atlanta University	1428
Emory University	1638
Fort Valley State University	1686
Georgia Southwestern State University	1718
Georgia State University	1720
LaGrange College	1888
Mercer University	2040
North Georgia College & State University	2186
Oglethorpe University	2210
Paine College	2242
Piedmont College	2268
Savannah College of Art and Design	2450
Savannah State University	2452
Shorter College	2484
Southern Polytechnic State University	2516
Spelman College	2524
State University of West Georgia	2568
Toccoa Falls College	2626
Wesleyan College	2936

Hawaii
Chaminade University of Honolulu	1400
Hawaii Pacific University	1778

Idaho
Albertson College of Idaho	1140
Idaho State University	1816
Northwest Nazarene University	2192

Illinois
Aurora University	1212
Barat College	1226
Benedictine University	1252
Blackburn College	1282
Columbia College Chicago	1506
DePaul University	1572
Dominican University	1582
Elmhurst College	1622
Greenville College	1742
Harrington Institute of Interior Design	1766
Illinois Institute of Technology	1818
Judson College	1858
Knox College	1880
Lake Forest College	1892
Lewis University	1922
Loyola University Chicago	1956
McKendree College	2030
National-Louis University	2134
North Central College	2178
North Park University	2188
Olivet Nazarene University	2224
Quincy University	2302
Robert Morris College	2338
Rockford College	2346
Roosevelt University	2356
Saint Xavier University	2432
School of the Art Institute of Chicago	2456
Shimer College	2480
Southern Illinois University Carbondale	2510
Trinity Christian College	2638
University of Chicago	2710
University of Illinois at Chicago	2736
University of St. Francis	2818
VanderCook College of Music	2878
Western Illinois University	2946
Wheaton College	2974

Indiana
Anderson University	1170
Ball State University	1222
Butler University	1328
DePauw University	1574
Earlham College	1598
Franklin College of Indiana	1694
Goshen College	1728
Grace College	1732
Hanover College	1762
Indiana State University	1822
Indiana Wesleyan University	1826
Manchester College	1974
Marian College	1986
Saint Joseph's College	2390
Saint Mary-of-the-Woods College	2406
Saint Mary's College	2408
Taylor University	2592
Tri-State University	2648
University of Evansville	2724
University of Indianapolis	2738
University of Notre Dame	2796
Valparaiso University	2874

Peterson's Guide to Four-Year Colleges 2001   www.petersons.com

Geographical Index of In-Depth Descriptions
Iowa–New Jersey

Iowa
Briar Cliff College	1308
Central College	1392
Coe College	1442
Dordt College	1586
Drake University	1588
Graceland College	1734
Grand View College	1738
Grinnell College	1744
Iowa State University of Science and Technology	1832
Loras College	1944
Luther College	1960
Maharishi University of Management	1968
Marycrest International University	1998
Morningside College	2100
Mount Mercy College	2112
Mount St. Clare College	2116
Northwestern College	2190
St. Ambrose University	2366
Simpson College	2496
Wartburg College	2912
William Penn University	3002

Kansas
Baker University	1220
Benedictine College	1250
Bethel College	1268
Kansas State University	1862

Kentucky
Asbury College	1196
Berea College	1258
Brescia University	1304
Cumberland College	1546
Georgetown College	1712
Kentucky State University	1872
Kentucky Wesleyan College	1874
Midway College	2056
Morehead State University	2096
Northern Kentucky University	2184
Sullivan College	2580
Thomas More College	2620
Transylvania University	2632
Union College	2658

Louisiana
Louisiana State University and Agricultural and Mechanical College	1948
Louisiana Tech University	1950
Loyola University New Orleans	1958
Northwestern State University of Louisiana	1946
Tulane University	2652
University of Louisiana at Lafayette	2744
University of New Orleans	2792

Maine
Bates College	1234
Bowdoin College	1294
Colby College	1448
College of the Atlantic	1488
Husson College	1814
Maine College of Art	1970
Saint Joseph's College	2392
Unity College	2672
University of Maine	2746
University of Maine at Fort Kent	2748
University of Maine at Machias	2750
University of New England	2788
University of Southern Maine	2834

Maryland
Baltimore International College	1224
Bowie State University	1296
Capitol College	1356
College of Notre Dame of Maryland	1468
Columbia Union College	1512
Frostburg State University	1700
Goucher College	1730
Hood College	1800
Johns Hopkins University	1848, 1850
Loyola College in Maryland	1952
Maryland Institute, College of Art	2002
Morgan State University	2098
Mount Saint Mary's College and Seminary	2122
St. John's College	2384
St. Mary's College of Maryland	2414
Salisbury State University	2438
Towson University	2630
University of Baltimore	2696
University of Maryland, Baltimore County	2754
University of Maryland, College Park	2756
University of Maryland Eastern Shore	2758
University of Maryland University College	2760
Villa Julie College	2886
Washington College	2918
Western Maryland College	2948

Massachusetts
American International College	1162
Anna Maria College	1176
The Art Institute of Boston at Lesley	1190
Assumption College	1200
Babson College	1218
Bay Path College	1238
Becker College	1242
Bentley College	1256
Berklee College of Music	1262
Boston Architectural Center	1288
Boston College	1290
Boston University	1292
Brandeis University	1300
Bridgewater State College	1314
Cambridge College	1348
College of Our Lady of the Elms	1470
Curry College	1548
Eastern Nazarene College	1606
Emerson College	1632
Emmanuel College	1634
Endicott College	1640
Fisher College	1662
Fitchburg State College	1666
Framingham State College	1688
Gordon College	1726
Hampshire College	1758
Harvard University	1772
Lasell College	1902
Lesley College	1918
Massachusetts College of Liberal Arts	2020
Massachusetts College of Pharmacy and Health Sciences	2022
Massachusetts Institute of Technology	2024
Massachusetts Maritime Academy	2026
Merrimack College	2048
Montserrat College of Art	2090
Mount Holyoke College	2104
Mount Ida College	2106
Newbury College	2142
Nichols College	2170
Northeastern University	2180
Pine Manor College	2270
Regis College	2318
School of the Museum of Fine Arts	2458
Simmons College	2492
Simon's Rock College of Bard	2494
Smith College	2502
Springfield College	2528
Stonehill College	2578
University of Massachusetts Amherst	2762
University of Massachusetts Boston	2764
University of Massachusetts Dartmouth	2766
University of Massachusetts Lowell	2768
Wellesley College	2930
Wentworth Institute of Technology	2934
Western New England College	2954
Wheaton College	2976
Wheelock College	2980
Worcester State College	3018

Michigan
Adrian College	1134
Albion College	1144
Alma College	1154
Andrews University	1172
Aquinas College	1180
Calvin College	1346
Center for Creative Studies—College of Art and Design	1390
Cleary College	1434
Ferris State University	1656
Finlandia University	1660
Hillsdale College	1790
Hope College	1802
Kendall College of Art and Design	1868
Kettering University	1876
Lake Superior State University	1896
Lawrence Technological University	1904
Marygrove College	2000
Michigan State University	1838
Northwood University	2194
Oakland University	2206
Saint Mary's College	2410
Siena Heights University	2488
Spring Arbor College	2526
University of Detroit Mercy	2722
Western Michigan University	2950

Minnesota
Bethel College	1270
Carleton College	1360
College of Saint Benedict	1472
College of St. Catherine	1474
The College of St. Scholastica	1482
Crown College	1540
Gustavus Adolphus College	1750
Minneapolis College of Art and Design	2066
Saint Mary's University of Minnesota	2418
University of Minnesota, Crookston	2772
University of St. Thomas	2820

Missouri
Central Missouri State University	1396
Columbia College	1502
Culver-Stockton College	1544
Lindenwood University	1930
Maryville University of Saint Louis	2014
Missouri Southern State College	2068
Missouri Valley College	2070
Rockhurst University	2348
St. Louis College of Pharmacy	2402
Southwest Missouri State University	2520
Stephens College	2570
University of Missouri–Kansas City	2774
University of Missouri–Rolla	2776
University of Missouri–St. Louis	2778
Washington University in St. Louis	2920
Webster University	2928
Westminster College	2962
William Jewell College	2998
William Woods University	3004

Montana
Carroll College	1368
Montana State University–Billings	2080
Montana State University–Bozeman	2082
Montana Tech of The University of Montana	2084
Rocky Mountain College	2350
University of Great Falls	2728
Western Montana College of The University of Montana	2952

Nebraska
Chadron State College	1398
Clarkson College	1430
Creighton University	1538
Midland Lutheran College	2054
Peru State College	2262
Union College	2660
University of Nebraska–Lincoln	2782

Nevada
Sierra Nevada College	2490
University of Nevada, Las Vegas	2784
University of Nevada, Reno	2786

New Hampshire
Colby-Sawyer College	1450
Daniel Webster College	1556
Dartmouth College	1558
Hesser College	1784
Keene State College	1866
New England College	2148
New Hampshire College	2150
Notre Dame College	2198
Plymouth State College	2276
Rivier College	2336
Saint Anselm College	2370
Thomas More College of Liberal Arts	2622
White Pines College	2982

New Jersey
Bloomfield College	1284
Caldwell College	1332
Centenary College	1388
The College of New Jersey	1462
College of Saint Elizabeth	1476
Drew University	1590
Fairleigh Dickinson University	1648
Felician College	1654
Georgian Court College	1716
Kean University	1864
Monmouth University	2076
Montclair State University	2086
New Jersey City University	2152
New Jersey Institute of Technology	2154
Princeton University	2292
Ramapo College of New Jersey	2308
The Richard Stockton College of New Jersey	2328

Geographical Index of In-Depth Descriptions
New Jersey–Pennsylvania

Rider University	2332
Rowan University	2360
Saint Peter's College	2426
Seton Hall University	2470
Stevens Institute of Technology	2576
Thomas Edison State College	2616
Westminster Choir College of Rider University	2960
William Paterson University of New Jersey	3000

New Mexico
College of Santa Fe	1484
College of the Southwest	1490
Eastern New Mexico University	1608
New Mexico Institute of Mining and Technology	2156
New Mexico State University	2158

New York
Adelphi University	1132
Alfred University	1150
Audrey Cohen College	1206
Barnard College	1228
Berkeley College	1260
Bernard M. Baruch College of the City University of New York	1264
Briarcliffe College	1310
Brooklyn College of the City University of New York	1318
Canisius College	1352
Cazenovia College	1384
City College of the City University of New York	1420
Clarkson University	1432
College of Aeronautics	1454
College of Insurance	1456
College of Mount Saint Vincent	1460
The College of New Rochelle	1464
The College of Saint Rose	1480
College of Staten Island of the City University of New York	1486
Columbia College	1514
Columbia University, School of General Studies	1516
Concordia College	1522
Cooper Union for the Advancement of Science and Art	1534
Cornell University	1536
The Culinary Institute of America	1542
Daemen College	1550
Dominican College of Blauvelt	1580
D'Youville College	1596
Elmira College	1624
Eugene Lang College, New School University	1644
Fashion Institute of Technology	1652
Five Towns College	1668
Fordham University	1684
Hamilton College	1754
Hartwick College	1770
Hilbert College	1788
Hobart and William Smith Colleges	1794
Hofstra University	1796
Houghton College	1804
Hunter College of the City University of New York	1808
Iona College	1830
Ithaca College	1834
Jewish Theological Seminary of America	1840
John Jay College of Criminal Justice of the City University of New York	1846
Laboratory Institute of Merchandising	1884
Lehman College of the City University of New York	1912
Le Moyne College	1914
Long Island University, Brooklyn Campus	1936
Long Island University, C.W. Post Campus	1938
Long Island University, Friends World Program	1940
Long Island University, Southampton College	1942
Manhattan College	1976
Manhattan School of Music	1978
Manhattanville College	1980
Mannes College of Music, New School University	1982
Marist College	1990
Marymount College	2006
Marymount Manhattan College	2008
Mercy College	2042
Molloy College	2074
Monroe College	2078
Mount Saint Mary College	2118
Nazareth College of Rochester	2136
New School Bachelor of Arts, New School University	2160
New York Institute of Technology	2162
New York School of Interior Design	2164
New York University	2166
Niagara University	2168
Pace University, New York City Campus	2234
Paul Smith's College of Arts and Sciences	2246
Plattsburgh State University of New York	2274
Polytechnic University, Brooklyn Campus	2280
Pratt Institute	2286
Purchase College, State University of New York	2296
Queens College of the City University of New York	2298
Regents College	2316
Rensselaer Polytechnic Institute	2322
Roberts Wesleyan College	2342
Rochester Institute of Technology	2344
Russell Sage College	2362
St. Bonaventure University	2372
St. Francis College	2376
St. John Fisher College	2382
St. John's University	2386
St. Joseph's College, New York	2394
St. Lawrence University	2398
St. Thomas Aquinas College	2428
Sarah Lawrence College	2448
School of Visual Arts	2460
Siena College	2486
Skidmore College	2498
State University of New York at Albany	2532
State University of New York at Binghamton	2534
State University of New York at Buffalo	2536, 2538
State University of New York at Buffalo	2536, 2538
State University of New York at Farmingdale	2540
State University of New York at Oswego	2542
State University of New York at Stony Brook	2544
State University of New York College at Brockport	2546
State University of New York College at Buffalo	2548
State University of New York College at Fredonia	2550
State University of New York College at Geneseo	2552
State University of New York College at Old Westbury	2554
State University of New York College at Oneonta	2556
State University of New York College at Potsdam	2558
State University of New York College of Agriculture and Technology at Cobleskill	2560
State University of New York College of Environmental Science and Forestry	2562
State University of New York Institute of Technology at Utica/Rome	2564
State University of New York Maritime College	2566
Syracuse University	2588
Touro College	2628
Union College	2662
United States Merchant Marine Academy	2668
United States Military Academy	2670
University of Rochester	2816
Utica College of Syracuse University	2872
Vassar College	2882
Wagner College	2904
Webb Institute	2926
Wells College	2932
York College of the City University of New York	3024

North Carolina
Barton College	1232
Belmont Abbey College	1244
Brevard College	1306
Campbell University	1350
Catawba College	1380
Chowan College	1414
Davidson College	1562
Duke University	1594
Elizabeth City State University	1618
Elon College	1626
Gardner-Webb University	1704
Greensboro College	1740
Guilford College	1748
High Point University	1786
Johnson C. Smith University	1854
Lenoir-Rhyne College	1916
Mars Hill College	1996
Meredith College	2046
Montreat College	2088
Mount Olive College	2114
North Carolina Agricultural and Technical State University	2172
North Carolina Central University	2174
North Carolina Wesleyan College	2176
Peace College	2248
Pfeiffer University	2264
St. Andrews Presbyterian College	2368
Salem College	2434
The University of North Carolina at Pembroke	2794
Warren Wilson College	2910
Western Carolina University	2944
Wingate University	3010

North Dakota
Dickinson State University	1578

Ohio
Antioch College	1178
Art Academy of Cincinnati	1188
Ashland University	1198
Bluffton College	1286
Bowling Green State University	1298
Capital University	1354
Case Western Reserve University	1376
Cleveland Institute of Art	1438
Cleveland Institute of Music	1440
College of Mount St. Joseph	1458
The College of Wooster	1494
Columbus College of Art and Design	1518
Defiance College	1566
Denison University	1570
Franciscan University of Steubenville	1690
Heidelberg College	1780
Hiram College	1792
John Carroll University	1844
Kent State University	1870
Lake Erie College	1890
Malone College	1972
Mount Union College	2126
Notre Dame College of Ohio	2200
Oberlin College	2208
Ohio Dominican College	2212
Ohio Northern University	2214
Ohio University	2216
Ohio Wesleyan University	2218
Otterbein College	2230
Shawnee State University	2474
Tiffin University	2624
The University of Akron	2682
University of Cincinnati	2712
University of Dayton	2718, 2720
The University of Findlay	2726
University of Rio Grande	2814
Urbana University	2868
Walsh University	2906
Wilberforce University	2992
Wright State University	3020
Xavier University	3022
Youngstown State University	3028

Oklahoma
Oklahoma Baptist University	2220
Oklahoma City University	2222
University of Tulsa	2854

Oregon
The Art Institute of Portland	1192
Concordia University	1524
George Fox University	1708
Lewis & Clark College	1920
Linfield College	1932
Marylhurst University	2004
Oregon State University	2226
Pacific University	2238
Reed College	2314
Southern Oregon University	2514
University of Oregon	2798
Warner Pacific College	2908
Western Oregon University	2956

Pennsylvania
Albright College	1146
Allegheny College	1152
Alvernia College	1156
Beaver College	1240
Bryn Mawr College	1324
Bucknell University	1326
Cabrini College	1330
California University of Pennsylvania	1344
Carlow College	1364
Carnegie Mellon University	1366
Cedar Crest College	1386
Chatham College	1408
Chestnut Hill College	1410
Cheyney University of Pennsylvania	1412
Clarion University of Pennsylvania	1426
College Misericordia	1452
Delaware Valley College	1568
Drexel University	1592
Eastern College	1600
Edinboro University of Pennsylvania	1616
Elizabethtown College	1620
Gannon University	1702
Geneva College	1706
Grove City College	1746
Gwynedd-Mercy College	1752
Haverford College	1776
Immaculata College	1820
Indiana University of Pennsylvania	1824
Juniata College	1860
King's College	1878

Geographical Index of In-Depth Descriptions
Pennsylvania–Virgin Islands

Kutztown University of Pennsylvania	1882
Lafayette College	1886
La Roche College	1900
Lebanon Valley College	1908
Lehigh University	1910
Lincoln University	1928
Lock Haven University of Pennsylvania	1934
Mansfield University of Pennsylvania	1984
Marywood University	2018
MCP Hahnemann University	2034
Mercyhurst College	2044
Messiah College	2050
Millersville University of Pennsylvania	2058
Moore College of Art and Design	2092
Moravian College	2094
Mount Aloysius College	2102
Muhlenberg College	2128
Neumann College	2138
Peirce College	2250
Pennsylvania College of Technology	2252
Pennsylvania State University Abington College	2254
Pennsylvania State University Altoona College	2256
Pennsylvania State University at Erie, The Behrend College	2258
Philadelphia University	2266
Point Park College	2278
Robert Morris College	2340
Rosemont College	2358
Saint Francis College	2378
Saint Joseph's University	2396
Seton Hill College	2472
Shippensburg University of Pennsylvania	2482
Slippery Rock University of Pennsylvania	2500
Susquehanna University	2582
Swarthmore College	2584
Temple University	2596
Thiel College	2614
Thomas Jefferson University	2618
University of Pittsburgh	2802
University of Pittsburgh at Bradford	2804
University of Pittsburgh at Greensburg	2806
The University of Scranton	2828
The University of the Arts	2842
University of the Sciences in Philadelphia	2850
Ursinus College	2870
Villanova University	2888
Washington & Jefferson College	2914
Waynesburg College	2922
West Chester University of Pennsylvania	2942
Westminster College	2964
Widener University	2990
Wilkes University	2996
Wilson College	3008

Rhode Island

Brown University	1320
Bryant College	1322
Johnson & Wales University	1852
Providence College	2294
Roger Williams University	2352
Salve Regina University	2440
University of Rhode Island	2812

South Carolina

Anderson College	1168
Charleston Southern University	1406
The Citadel, The Military College of South Carolina	1418
Clemson University	1436
Coker College	1446
Columbia College	1504
Columbia International University	1510
Converse College	1532
Erskine College	1642
Francis Marion University	1692
Limestone College	1926
Newberry College	2140
Presbyterian College	2288
University of South Carolina	2830
Voorhees College	2902
Winthrop University	3012
Wofford College	3014

South Dakota

Augustana College	1208
Huron University	1812
Mount Marty College	2108
National American University	2132

Tennessee

Belmont University	1246
Carson-Newman College	1372
David Lipscomb University	1560
Fisk University	1664
Lambuth University	1898
Maryville College	2012
Milligan College	2060
Rhodes College	2324
Tennessee State University	2598
Tennessee Technological University	2600, 2602
Tennessee Technological University	2600, 2602
Trevecca Nazarene University	2636
Tusculum College	2654
The University of Memphis	2770
The University of Tennessee at Martin	2838
Vanderbilt University	2876

Texas

Abilene Christian University	1124
Angelo State University	1174
Austin College	1214
Baylor University	1236
Dallas Christian College	1554
McMurry University	2032
Our Lady of the Lake University of San Antonio	2232
Prairie View A&M University	2284
Rice University	2326
St. Edward's University	2374
St. Mary's University of San Antonio	2420
Schreiner College	2462
Southern Methodist University	2512
Southwest Texas State University	2522
Texas A&M University at Galveston	2604
Texas Christian University	2606
Texas Lutheran University	2608
Texas Tech University	2610
Texas Woman's University	2612
Trinity University	2646
University of Houston	2734
University of Mary Hardin-Baylor	2752
University of St. Thomas	2822
The University of Texas at Dallas	2840
University of the Incarnate Word	2846

Utah

Westminster College	2966

Vermont

Bennington College	1254
Castleton State College	1378
Champlain College	1402
College of St. Joseph	1478
Goddard College	1722
Johnson State College	1856
Lyndon State College	1964
Marlboro College	1992
Middlebury College	2052
Norwich University	2196
Saint Michael's College	2422
Southern Vermont College	2518
Sterling College	2572
Trinity College of Vermont	2644
University of Vermont	2856
Vermont Technical College	2884

Virginia

Bridgewater College	1312
Christopher Newport University	1416
Eastern Mennonite University	1604
Emory & Henry College	1636
Ferrum College	1658
George Mason University	1710
Hampden-Sydney College	1756
Hampton University	1760
Hollins University	1798
Liberty University	1924
Lynchburg College	1962
Marymount University	2010
Mary Washington College	2016
Radford University	2306
Randolph-Macon College	2310
Randolph-Macon Woman's College	2312
Shenandoah University	2476
Sweet Briar College	2586
Virginia Commonwealth University	2890
Virginia Intermont College	2892
Virginia Military Institute	2894
Virginia Union University	2896
Virginia Wesleyan College	2898
Washington and Lee University	2916

Washington

City University	1422
Eastern Washington University	1610
The Evergreen State College	1646
Gonzaga University	1724
Pacific Lutheran University	2236
Saint Martin's College	2404
Seattle Pacific University	2466
Seattle University	2468
University of Puget Sound	2808
Whitman College	2984
Whitworth College	2988

West Virginia

Alderson-Broaddus College	1148
Bethany College	1266
The College of West Virginia	1492
Concord College	1520
Davis & Elkins College	1564
Fairmont State College	1650
Marshall University	1994
Salem-Teikyo University	2436
Shepherd College	2478
University of Charleston	2708
West Virginia University Institute of Technology	2970
West Virginia Wesleyan College	2972
Wheeling Jesuit University	2978

Wisconsin

Alverno College	1158
Beloit College	1248
Cardinal Stritch University	1358
Carroll College	1370
Carthage College	1374
Concordia University Wisconsin	1528
Edgewood College	1614
Lawrence University	1906
Marian College of Fond du Lac	1988
Milwaukee School of Engineering	2064
Mount Mary College	2110
Ripon College	2334
St. Norbert College	2424
University of Wisconsin–Green Bay	2864
Viterbo University	2900

Wyoming

University of Wyoming	2866

Virgin Islands

University of the Virgin Islands	2852

Geographical Index of In-Depth Descriptions
Canada–United Kingdom

CANADA

British Columbia
University of British Columbia 2700

Newfoundland
Memorial University of Newfoundland 2036

Nova Scotia
Acadia University 1128
Dalhousie University 1552
Mount Saint Vincent University 2124
Nova Scotia College of Art and Design 2202
St. Francis Xavier University 2380
Saint Mary's University 2416
Université Sainte-Anne 2676
University College of Cape Breton 2678

Ontario
Brock University 1316
Carleton University 1362
Lakehead University 1894
Queen's University at Kingston 2300
Trent University 2634
University of Guelph 2730
University of Ottawa 2800
University of Windsor 2862
Wilfrid Laurier University 2994
York University 3026

Quebec
Bishop's University 1280
Concordia University 1526
McGill University 2028
Université Laval 2674

CAYMAN ISLANDS
International College of the Cayman Islands 1828

ITALY
American University of Rome 1166

SWITZERLAND
Franklin College Switzerland 1696

UNITED KINGDOM
Richmond, The American International University in London 2330

FEE BASED IN-DEPTH INFORMATION

In-Depth Descriptions
Of the Colleges:

An Inside Look at Nearly 1,000 Colleges and Universities

The descriptions presented in this section provide a wealth of statistics that are crucial components in the college decision-making equation—components such as tuition, financial aid, and major fields of study. This section shifts the focus to a variety of other factors, some of them intangible, that should also be considered. The following two-page descriptions are offered to provide a greater overview of nearly 1,000 of the 2,004 colleges and universities previously profiled in this book. Prepared exclusively by college officials, they are designed to help give students a better sense of the individuality of each institution, in terms that include campus environment, student activities, and lifestyle. Such quality-of-life intangibles can be the deciding factors in the college selection process. The absence from this section of any college or university does not constitute an editorial decision on the part of Peterson's. In essence, this section is an open forum for colleges and universities, on a voluntary basis, to communicate their particular messages to prospective college students. The colleges included have paid a fee to Peterson's to provide this information to you. The descriptions are arranged alphabetically by the official name of the institution.

ABILENE CHRISTIAN UNIVERSITY
ABILENE, TEXAS

The University

Abilene Christian University (ACU) offers an exceptional education in a distinctive Christian environment at an affordable price. ACU believes strongly in the dignity and worth of the individual and in academic integrity, achieving success, and enjoying life. Christian education at ACU integrates faith and hands-on learning, represented in every facet of campus life.

Founded in 1906, ACU is an independent comprehensive university with an enrollment of approximately 4,600 students and is one of the largest private universities in the Southwest. The school is affiliated with the Churches of Christ and is governed by its own Board of Trustees.

The University offers 117 bachelor's programs, more than thirty master's programs, and one doctoral program. Work completed at ACU is accepted by all colleges and universities in the United States. The University is accredited by the Commission on Colleges of the Southern Association of Colleges and Schools, and the College of Business Administration is accredited by the Association of Collegiate Business Schools and Programs (ACBSP).

As a teaching institution, ACU emphasizes a dynamic personal relationship between professors and their students. Qualified faculty members, not graduate assistants, teach underclass students, and when professors do research, undergraduates work with them. Each year, some of the nation's top companies come to campus to interview because they hold ACU graduates in high regard for their blend of creativity, technical skills, thorough training, and moral integrity. ACU students have an acceptance rate of more than 80 percent to medical and other professional schools, well above the national average. The *Optimist*, the ACU student newspaper, has been rated All-American every year since 1975.

ACU supports an environment of honesty, Christian care, and relationships that start even before classes begin. Each fall during Welcome Week, upperclass students help freshmen adjust to the social side of college life through diverse activities, including heart-to-heart discussions and possibly the world's largest game of Twister. The student body is enriched by people from forty-seven states and sixty-one countries. More than 200 international students are enrolled at ACU.

The University is a member of the National Collegiate Athletic Association (NCAA) and the Lone Star Conference. ACU competes in NCAA Division II athletics, including men's baseball, football, and golf; women's softball and volleyball; and basketball, cross-country, tennis, and outdoor and indoor track and field for both men and women. The University also offers an intramural sports program for its students, and the ACU soccer club competes against other college and university soccer clubs.

Active campus organizations, including men's and women's social clubs, offer students a variety of interests and opportunities for involvement. Movie nights, devotionals, big-name concerts, intercollegiate sports, and student productions ensure that students can find great entertainment without leaving campus.

Location

Abilene, Texas, has the reputation of being a friendly city and was named an All-America City. It is located 180 miles west of Dallas and has a population of about 110,000. Its climate is relatively warm, although it occasionally snows during the winter. Residents of Abilene are served by shopping malls, major restaurant chains, specialty shops, and a regional airport. The city is second only to Houston in cultural events per capita in Texas, and it has one of the lowest crime rates in the state.

Majors and Degrees

The Bachelor of Arts degree is awarded in art, art for all-level teacher certification, art history, art/marketing, biblical text, biochemistry, biology, business administration and international studies, chemistry, Christian ministry, communication disorders, computer science, English, French, graphic design/advertising, Greek, history, human communication, international studies, life/earth science, mathematics, missions, music, political science, sociology, Spanish, theater, and youth and family ministry.

The Bachelor of Science degree is available in agricultural business; animal science; biochemistry; biology; broadcast journalism; chemistry; Christian ministry/preaching; computer science; criminal justice; electronic media; engineering physics; environmental science; exercise science; fashion merchandising; food, nutrition, and dietetics; general family and consumer sciences; human development and family studies; industrial technology; interior design; journalism; mathematics; medical technology; microelectronics; missions; photojournalism; physics; predentistry; pre-engineering; premedicine; preoptometry; preveterinary medicine; psychology; public administration; range and agronomy; religious journalism; social work; sociology; and youth and family ministry. Also, the Bachelor of Science degree is offered in elementary and secondary education, with specialization in numerous areas. A Bachelor of Science in Nursing degree is also available.

The Bachelor of Business Administration degree is offered in accounting, financial management, human resource management, management, and marketing. The Bachelor of Fine Arts degree is available in art and theater, and the Bachelor of Music degree (with teacher certification) is offered in instrumental, piano, and vocal (all levels).

The Associate of Science degree is offered in family and consumer sciences (child development) and industrial technology (construction technology, general drafting technology, and prearchitecture). The Bachelor of Applied Studies offers adults the opportunity to combine previous college experience, on-the-job training, and courses at ACU to complete their degrees. Areas of emphasis include biblical and related sciences, corporate training, family studies, general business, human services, industrial technology, liberal arts, psychology, and teacher preparation.

The preprofessional programs offered by ACU are of special interest. In general, students attend ACU for one to four years and then transfer to a professional school to complete their degree. During the past decade, more than 80 percent of ACU graduates who applied to medical and dental schools were accepted, putting ACU among the top preprofessional schools in the state.

Academic Program

A minimum of 128 semester hours is required for most baccalaureate degrees, with 30 of these hours in a major and a total of 33 hours in upper-division work. All degrees require 15 hours of Bible studies, and most require courses in communication/speech, English, exercise science, fine arts, mathematics, science, and social and behavioral science.

ACU serves a broad spectrum of students. To help challenge the exceptionally bright student, CLEP and a comprehensive honors program are available. For the underprepared, developmental programs are offered by a well-equipped learning center. The University also offers various enriching seminars and lectures by internationally known guests such as Max Lucado, James Dobson, Marilyn Quayle, George Bush, William Bennett, and Ray Bradbury.

Off-Campus Arrangements

In the World Class program, students may study in countries such as China, England, and Mexico. All courses completed during this cultural and educational experience are counted toward the student's degree.

Academic Facilities

Resources of the Abilene Christian University library include books, microforms, audiovisual materials, government documents, and periodicals that total more than 1.7 million items. Online research and access to a local library consortium greatly expand student access to worldwide resources. The 15,000-square-foot Learning Enhancement Center (LEC) offers free tutoring at all levels, numerous audiovisual materials, and a thirty-workstation Macintosh computer lab. More than 700 computers across campus are available to students during days and evenings.

Exercise science and athletic activities are centered in the huge exercise science complex, which contains several gymnasiums, training rooms, racquetball courts, an Olympic-size swimming pool, a recently refurbished coliseum, and a state-of-the-art fitness center for student athletes. The 43,500-square-foot Teague Special Events Center is used for a variety of special events that occur in both the ACU and Abilene communities. The renovated four-story science facility contains laboratories, an outstanding collection of experimental equipment, an observatory, and computer labs. A three-story communications complex houses art studios and classrooms, newspaper and yearbook workshops, a low-power VHF TV station that broadcasts on a local station and on cable, an FM National Public Radio station, and a complete family and consumer sciences division.

In addition to 100-acre and 400-acre farms, the University has access to 2,500 acres of land for observation, research, and study projects. Students enrolled in agriculture, environment, biology, and ecology courses are able to study basic and applied science in an integrated setting.

Classrooms in the Mabee Business Building and Biblical Studies Building are equipped with the latest in audiovisual and computer equipment. Business students work in a lab equipped with state-of-the-art Apple Power Macs and Pentium processors.

Costs

The typical expenses for 1999–2000 for two semesters included tuition and fees (30 semester hours), $9810; room, $1750; board, $2270; books, $530; and miscellaneous course fees, $480, for a total of $14,840. Personal expenses vary according to an individual's needs. All fees are subject to change.

Financial Aid

Eighty-five percent of ACU students are assisted through loans, grants, scholarships, and/or employment. In 1998–99, more than $39 million in financial aid was awarded to ACU students. The number of students employed on campus was 1,265. Academic scholarships are awarded according to scores on standardized tests such as the SAT I and ACT examinations, class rank, and leadership activities. Full tuition scholarships are offered to National Merit Finalists. All financial aid forms may be obtained through the ACU Student Financial Services Office. It is suggested, and even required for some financial aid programs, that applicants for aid complete a need analysis form, preferably the Free Application for Federal Student Aid (FAFSA).

Faculty

ACU has a faculty of outstanding teachers, scholars, and specialists. Seventy-one percent of full-time faculty members hold a doctorate or the highest degree in their field. There are 207 full-time and 102 part-time faculty members committed to educating the whole student, academically, socially, and spiritually. A student-teacher ratio of 18:1 allows students ready access to their teachers for counseling on careers, academics, and personal issues.

Student Government

Abilene Christian University has an active, progressive Students' Association, of which every full-time student is a member. Officers of the association and the Student Senate carry out various social and community service programs. The Student Foundation promotes awareness of the purposes of ACU and maintains communication among the administration, students, and alumni.

Admission Requirements

To qualify for admission, a student must have graduated from high school and must submit information concerning SAT I or ACT scores, high school class rank, and reference letters. Generally, transfer students are required to have a 2.0 grade point average or better. Abilene Christian University does not discriminate on the basis of race, color, age, or national or ethnic origin in its admissions, employment opportunities, educational programs, or activities that it sponsors.

Application and Information

Prospective students should write or call the office below for application forms and financial aid information, indicating their academic and social areas of interest. Applicants should submit the necessary forms with a nonrefundable $25 processing fee ($45 for international applicants) and have their academic records (SAT I or ACT scores, transcript, and class rank) sent to the University. Residence hall room reservations, accompanied by a $100 deposit, should be made early to ensure choice of a dorm. Students are encouraged to visit the campus at any time.

Office of Admissions
Abilene Christian University
ACU Station, Box 29000
Abilene, Texas 79699-9000

Telephone: 915-674-2650
            800-460-6228 (toll-free)
E-mail: info@admissions.acu.edu
World Wide Web: http://www.acu.edu

ACU's Biblical Studies Building features a magnificent chapel, a huge amphitheater, and the latest in instructional technology.

ACADEMY OF ART COLLEGE
SAN FRANCISCO, CALIFORNIA

The College

In 1929, Academy of Art College founder Richard S. Stephens, who was the advertising creative director of *Sunset* magazine, acted on his belief that "aspiring artists and designers, given proper instruction, hard work, and dedication, can learn the skills needed to become successful professionals." His new school of advertising art consisted of 46 students meeting in one room on San Francisco's Kearny Street. The instructors, who were professional artists, brought "real-world" problems, situations, solutions, and practical experience to the students. Thus was born the school's unofficial philosophy by the founder: Hire today's best practicing professionals to teach the art and design professionals of tomorrow. At that time, advertising consisted primarily of illustrations, photos, and copy. Consequently, it became necessary to teach beginning students the fundamentals of drawing, painting, color, light, and photography as well as layout and typography.

When Richard A. Stephens succeeded his father as president in 1951, he added a Foundations Department to ensure that all students comprehended the basic principles of traditional art and design. Illustration soon expanded to include fine arts (drawing, painting, sculpture, and printmaking), and advertising design spawned the Graphic Design Department. Fashion (design, textiles, and merchandising) and Interior Design Departments were also added. In 1966 the Academy officially became a college, with approval from the California Department of Education to issue a Bachelor of Fine Arts degree. In another decade, the Master of Fine Arts degree was offered. Five more buildings were purchased, and by 1992, there were more than 2,500 Academy students. In that year, the leadership of the Academy was turned over to the third generation in the family, Elisa Stephens, granddaughter of the school's founder. She quickly determined that the school's small support department, computer arts, had enormous potential for preparing people for multimedia careers when allied with such companies as Silicon Graphics, Pixar, Adobe, and Walt Disney Productions. It is now the fastest-growing department at the Academy.

Today, the Academy of Art College is the largest private art and design school in the nation and has an enrollment of more than 5,000 students from nearly every country in the world. One third of the student body is made up of international students. The Academy has nineteen facilities that house classrooms, studios, galleries, and dormitories. The students, who are admitted through an open enrollment policy (there is no portfolio requirement since the severe cutback in high school art classes), aspire to earn either an A.A., B.F.A., or M.F.A. degree or a Certificate in one of ten art and design majors. The school maintains a fleet of buses to connect the different points of the campus, all of which are in the city limits of San Francisco, one of the world's most vibrant and beautiful cities. The faculty, which is 90 percent part-time and made up of working art and design professionals, is recruited from all across the nation, drawn to the creative and intellectual center that is the Bay Area. Extensive senior-year internship programs allow students to gain valuable experience and develop strong portfolios in their chosen field before graduation.

Location

The city of San Francisco is one of the great cultural centers of the world, a melting pot of diversity, ethnicity, and creativity that has spawned major museums and galleries, world-class opera and theaters, dance companies, film production and recording studios, technological innovation, performing artists ranging from classical to popular music, and numerous other cultural opportunities. The city's status as a tourist mecca located on the Pacific Rim ensures that one encounters people from all corners of the world. The climate is moderate and offers kaleidoscopic blends of sunshine and fog nine months of the year. The Northpoint campus is located at world-famous Pier 39; one can view Alcatraz Island from classroom windows. Four other buildings are two blocks from historic Union Square in the commercial heart of the city. Three other buildings are located near the Financial District. The city offers myriad locations for field trips and studio visits. World-renowned artists display their creations in the Academy's large Bush Street gallery. The Academy of Art College is an urban institution that both draws upon and contributes to the cultural wealth of the community in which it resides.

Majors and Degrees

The Academy of Art College offers A.A. and B.F.A. degrees and Certificates in the following majors: advertising (account planning, art direction, copywriting, and television commercials); computer arts (animation, digital imaging, graphic design, multimedia, special effects, 2-D and 3-D modeling, video games, and Web design); fashion (fashion design, knitwear design, fashion illustration, merchandising, and textiles for fashion); fine art (drawing and painting, printmaking, and sculpture); graphic design (branding and print, corporate identity, and packaging design); illustration (cartooning, children's books, editorial, and feature film animation); industrial design studios (automotive design and product design); interior architecture and design (commercial and residential interior architecture and furniture design); motion pictures, television, and video (acting, cinematography, editing, music videos, production/direction, and screenwriting), and photography (advertising, documentary, fashion, fine art, photo illustration, and portraiture).

Academic Program

A total of 132 credit units must be completed to earn a Bachelor of Fine Arts degree, consisting of 18 units of foundations courses, 60 units in the major, 12 units of art electives, and 42 units of liberal arts/art history courses. First-year students must complete six foundations courses, English, art history, and introduction to the computer before the end of the year. Fundamental courses are related specifically to the student's major to prepare the student to begin intense focus courses in his or her field by the sophomore year. All major courses of study are structured so that the student builds upon skills learned the previous semester and advances to the next level of technical or creative proficiency. Some related major courses may be taken concurrently. Each course is worth 3 credits. Liberal arts courses teach practical applications for forging a professional career in art and design. International students who come from countries where English is not the primary language may take additional ESL classes, as determined by English language proficiency testing. Students are advised to meet with departmental directors at least once during the academic year to have their progress assessed. Portfolios are reviewed before the junior year to determine whether or not a student has progressed sufficiently to continue study at the Academy.

Academic Facilities

The Academy's facilities reflect its commitment to training students for careers in art and design; not only do students have access to some of the most advanced facilities in the nation, but the Academy continually invests in new equipment to ensure that the college remains on the cutting edge of technology. By learning on industry-standard equipment, students gain valuable professional techniques that make them highly employable.

The Academy's eight-story Digital Arts Center offers students from the Computer Arts, Motion Pictures and Video, Advertising, and Fashion Departments access to an incredible array of technology. The center has more than 700 computer workstations, including 100 Silicon Graphics workstations, 300 Adobe premiere workstations, and 200 autoCAD workstations. Students also have the use of fourteen Avid digital editing suites, seven multitrack sound editing studios, one dedicated blue screen studio, and various other video equipment.

The photography department occupies its own building and shares half of another Academy building with the fine arts, painting, and printmaking department. Photography students can utilize a wide range of equipment, including full-length shooting studios; Hasselblad, Canon, and Sinar cameras; Broncolor, Norman, and Speedotron strobe systems; seven black-and-white darkrooms; a color lab facility with fifteen single print stations; and the latest technology available for digital imaging and output. In addition, the Academy's modern, professional studio is one of the largest of any photography school in the nation and is ideal for shooting automobiles, motorcycles, and large sets.

The Academy's Fine Art Sculpture Center is a 58,000-square-foot facility that houses state-of-the-art studios for figure, ceramic, neon/illumination, bronze, metal fabrication, and mold-making sculpture. Students also have use of an off-site bronze-casting facility.

When students graduate from the Academy, they have the opportunity to exhibit in one of three nonprofit galleries in the heart of downtown San Francisco's premier gallery district. These street-level facilities are an excellent way for students to promote and sell their work and to gain networking experience.

The Academy's nineteen facilities allow students to pursue their studies in an environment that is geared toward an outstanding career preparation. The college's emphasis on upgrading equipment and facilities means that students benefit from the latest technology and enter the job market with a valuable set of skills.

The Academy Library houses more than 28,000 books and magazines, as well as 375 CD-ROM titles, 100,000 slides, and 1,200 videos. Computers with Internet access are available to students as well as an online catalog, color scanners, and color and black-and-white copiers. Workshops and electronic study guides are also available.

The Academy Resource Center offers all students free learning support services that include study hall, tutoring, mentoring, midpoint review and study skills workshops, a writing lab, a state-of-the-art multimedia language lab, an English for Art Program, and a Conversation Partner Program.

Costs

Tuition for 2000 is $500 per credit unit for undergraduates. A full-time student carries either 12 or 15 units per semester. There is a nonrefundable $120 registration fee—$100 is applicable toward tuition. Lab fees run from $25 to $400 per semester, depending on the class. Tuition and fees are subject to change at any time. Art supplies can run from $250 to $500 per semester, depending on the major. The Academy operates an artists' supply store with substantial discounts for registered students. The Academy has most of the expensive technical equipment available for students to borrow or available for use in a lab.

The Academy of Art College operates eight campus housing facilities within the city. Several housing options are offered, and costs vary from $6600 to $10,000 per academic year (fall and spring semesters). For further information, students may contact the Academy Housing Office directly at 415-263-7727 or by e-mail at housing@academyart.edu.

Financial Aid

The Academy offers financial aid packages consisting of grants, loans, and work-study to eligible students with a demonstrated need. Low-interest loans are available to all eligible students, regardless of need. As financial aid programs, procedures, and eligibility requirements change frequently, applicants should contact the Financial Aid Office for current requirements at 79 New Montgomery Street, 3rd Floor, San Francisco, California 94105, or by telephone at the toll-free number listed below.

Faculty

The Academy averages 500 instructors each semester, most of whom are full-time art and design professionals and part-time teachers. The student-to-teacher ratio for undergraduate classes averages 20:1.

Student Government

Although there is no formal student government, each department has between 2 and 3 student representatives who meet with the president as needed throughout the semester to discuss any student issues.

Admission Requirements

Applicants for the B.F.A. program must have a high school diploma or GED equivalent. International students take a written and speech test to determine which ESL classes may have to be completed. Most ESL classes can be taken in conjunction with art and design classes. All foundations classes offer specialized ESL sections with instructors trained for language assistance. The application fee is $100 for undergraduates.

Application and Information

Students may apply to enter the Academy at the beginning of the spring, fall, or summer semesters. Information in this profile is subject to change. Students should contact the Academy of Art College for current information or visit its Web site, which is listed below.

Further information and a catalog may be obtained by contacting:

Academy of Art College Admissions Department
79 New Montgomery Street
San Francisco, California 94105

Telephone: 415-274-2222
          800-544-ARTS (toll-free)
Fax: 415-263-4130
E-mail: info@academyart.edu
World Wide Web: http://www.academyart.edu

The city of San Francisco is a dynamic setting for campus life at the Academy.

ACADIA UNIVERSITY
WOLFVILLE, NOVA SCOTIA, CANADA

The University

Acadia University has been providing students with a leading undergraduate education for more than 160 years. The 250-acre campus welcomes more than 3,600 students from more than forty countries around the globe and has the highest percentage of international students at the undergraduate level in Canada. Along with rich library resources and a modern art gallery, Acadia's residence rooms and classrooms are equipped with state-of-the-art computing capabilities, which is part of a philosophy that places a strong emphasis on learning and living in a supportive environment. Students play a wide range of varsity and club sports and participate in a variety of student clubs and organizations. The University is nationally renowned for its school spirit.

This year, for the sixth year in a row, a reputational survey by *Maclean's* magazine ranked Acadia as the best overall primarily undergraduate university in Canada. The survey of high school guidance counselors, university officials, and corporate leaders also placed Acadia at the top in quality and innovation and second in producing the leaders of tomorrow. In 1998, *U.S. News & World Report* cited Acadia as a "first-rate liberal arts college."

Acadia University has embarked on the next evolution in learning through The Acadia Advantage, an academic initiative that integrates the use of notebook computers into the undergraduate curriculum. This unique undertaking enhances the University's teaching and learning environment. Acadia's students receive IBM ThinkPad computers for their use as an integral part of their learning experience during the academic year. Acadia Advantage students learn in classrooms without walls, use their computers to download class notes, participate in chat groups, e-mail their professors, and explore the world via the Internet. Students apply the information they find there to their studies in class. Through The Acadia Advantage, students use today's technology to develop the advanced analytical skills they need to adapt to ever-changing study and work environments.

Research opportunities are abundant at Acadia. The University's small faculties and low student-teacher ratio (13:1) enable students to work closely with faculty members on research projects to gain valuable experience in their field of choice. Acadia's research specialties include wildlife and environmental biology, estuarine research, biotechnology, and various facets of instructional technology, as well as a wide range of research in the humanities and social sciences. All science programs, as well as the business administration program, offer co-op education and internship options, which combine classroom study and paid work experience.

The Environmental Sciences Research Centre, the Botanical Gardens, and the Campus Meeting Place are proposed to sit on approximately 8 acres on the west side of the Acadia campus. The complex will consist of a botanical garden and glasshouse that feature the representative plants, habitat, and rocks of northeastern North America. The large, informal facility will serve as a gathering place for students, faculty and staff members, and community members.

Acadia also offers several graduate degrees and is affiliated with Acadia Divinity College.

Location

Acadia is located in the historic town of Wolfville, situated on the shores of the Minas Basin in the heart of Nova Scotia's Annapolis Valley. Acadia combines the best of rural life with the rich resources of a university community. A town of 3,800 (not including the student population), Wolfville is an hour outside of Halifax, Nova Scotia's provincial capital. It is also home to Canada's acclaimed Atlantic Theatre Festival and is the site of the world's highest tides.

Acadia and Wolfville are inextricably linked in virtually everything that goes on. Many students volunteer their time to help out in the community, while Wolfville citizens participate in the University's choral and dramatic presentations, attend lectures and services on campus, and participate in sporting events by cheering for the Acadia Axemen and Axettes.

Majors and Degrees

The Faculty of Arts offers the Bachelor of Arts degree (major, honors) in Canadian studies, classics, economics, English, French, German, history, music, philosophy, political science, sociology, theatre studies, and women's studies. Students in the Faculty of Arts may also complete an environmental arts option within their program.

The Faculty of Pure and Applied Science offers the Bachelor of Science degree (major, honors) in biology, chemistry, environmental science, geology, mathematics and statistics, physics, and psychology; the Bachelor of Computer Science (honors specialization); the Bachelor of Science in nutrition; and the Certificate of Applied Science, which is a two-year program that leads to entry into a third-year Bachelor of Engineering degree at Dalhousie University, Halifax, Nova Scotia. Students in the Faculty of Science may complete a health-care option within their program.

The Faculty of Professional Studies offers the Bachelor of Business Administration, the Bachelor of Education, the Bachelor of Kinesiology, and the Bachelor of Recreation Management degrees.

Academic Program

All programs require 120 credit hours (four years) to complete except for the Certificate in Applied Science, which requires 66 credit hours (two years), and the postbaccalaureate Bachelor of Education degree, which requires 63 credit hours (two years). The academic year has two sessions: fall and winter (September–April), as well as an intersession (May–August).

Off-Campus Arrangements

To encourage students to develop a global perspective, Acadia allows students to study abroad in their third year. Students can participate in direct exchanges with universities in the U.K., France, and the U.S. Exchanges can also be arranged with institutions in New England through the Nova Scotia–New England Student Exchange Program.

Academic Facilities

Acadia University's Vaughan Memorial Library is a research and teaching centre that houses more than 1 million items, including books, magazines, scholarly journals, newspapers, government publications, electronic databases, audiovisual material, microform, special collections, and archival materials.

The library contains data connections for students' laptop computers at its study carrels and is home to Acadia's User Support Centre (USC). The USC, which is open for more than 80 hours per week, answers students' questions about their computers and any software they are using. It also runs a free help line and functions as a service centre for any computer hardware problems that arise. It provides free classes to help familiarize students with their computers and software.

Costs

Tuition for the 1999–2000 school year for international students was $9700. All students pay a student organization fee, which was $147 for the academic year. Although the cost of books and supplies varies by program, the average cost was approximately $700 per year. The cost of room and board on campus was approximately $550 per month; however, this cost can vary based on the meal plan students choose. (All fees are in Canadian dollars.)

Tuition at Acadia University includes not only the cost of courses but also the use of an IBM ThinkPad laptop computer, complete with software and accessories for the school year, as well as access to Acadia's fully wired campus.

Financial Aid

Acadia offers scholarships in many areas. American students are automatically considered for entrance scholarships when they present an A average, an exceptional extracurricular record, and letter(s) of recommendation. Renewable scholarships, valued up to $7000 per academic year, are available and are generally awarded on the basis of academic merit. Emergency short-term loans or bursaries are available as well. Students are also eligible for on-campus employment, including student assistantships and approximately 1,200 hourly paid jobs.

Faculty

Acadia University has 253 full-time and 58 part-time faculty members, all of whom teach at both the graduate and undergraduate levels and hold graduate degrees. The faculty-student ratio is 1:13.

Student Government

Every part-time and full-time student at Acadia University is a member of the Acadia Students' Union (ASU). The ASU is a student-managed organization that operates its own students' centre. The ASU addresses many of the social, legal, political, cultural, and educational needs of the students at Acadia. It is a self-governing body committed to student development through the provision of services and representation of its members.

Admission Requirements

Students are required to meet the following minimum academic requirements: graduate from an American high school with a combined score of 1100 on the SAT I, the International Baccalaureate (I.B.) Diploma, or two General Certificate of Education (GCE) A-level examinations or equivalent at the C level or above. Applicants who have one year of study beyond GCE O- levels are considered on an individual basis. Requirements specific to other education systems can be obtained by contacting the admissions office. Students who are not native speakers of English must have a minimum TOEFL score of 550.

Application and Information

Prospective students can obtain application forms from the admissions office or on line at http://www.acadiau.ca/reg/application.html. There is a Can$25 application fee, and applications are not complete without copies of all high school transcripts and other records of academic work.

It is recommended that students apply as soon as possible to receive first consideration for competitive, limited-enrollment programs, biology, chemistry, environmental science, kinesiology, and recreation management.

For more information or to request application information, students should contact:

Liason and Recruitment Office
Acadia University
Wolfville, Nova Scotia B0P 1X0
Canada
Telephone: 902-585-1222
Fax: 902-585-1081
E-mail: ask.acadia@acadiau.ca
World Wide Web: http://www.acadiau.ca

Acadia students plug into the University network at the Students' Centre.

ADAMS STATE COLLEGE
ALAMOSA, COLORADO

The College

Adams State College is dedicated to offering a high-quality education with a personal touch. The academic and social atmosphere of the campus allows each student to feel at home. The College has excellent physical facilities. Attractive academic buildings are complemented by a complete and comfortable College Center. The student body is composed of individuals from various ethnic and racial backgrounds. The 1999–2000 enrollment was 2,230, including 274 graduate students. Forty-four percent of the undergraduate students are men. The dignity of each person as an individual is paramount, and equal consideration is extended to all. The close working relationship between students and the members of the faculty and administration is indicative of the importance of the individual at Adams State. At the graduate level, Adams State offers programs leading to the Master of Arts degree in elementary education, guidance and counseling, secondary education, special education/moderate needs (level one), art, and physical education.

Adams State College is accredited by the North Central Association of Colleges and Schools, the National Council for Accreditation of Teacher Education, the Council for Accreditation of Counseling and Related Educational Programs, and the National Association of Schools of Music. The College is an institutional member of the American Council on Education and the American Association of Colleges for Teacher Education. It is approved by the American Association of University Women. Adams State is also a member of the North Central Conference on Summer Schools, the Midwestern Association of Graduate Schools, the Association of Collegiate Business Schools and Programs, and the American Assembly of Collegiate Schools of Business.

Location

The College is located in the city of Alamosa, which has a population of approximately 9,000. Alamosa is in the center of the San Luis Valley, about 220 miles south and slightly west of Denver. The city is located at the junction of U.S. Highways 160 and 285 on the route of the Old Navajo Trail. Both bus and airline services are available to and from Alamosa. The College is located close to the art centers at Taos and Santa Fe and near excellent recreational opportunities for hiking, mountain climbing, rafting, fishing, and hunting. The Wolf Creek ski area is within an hour's drive of the campus. The San Luis Valley is almost level and is larger than the state of Connecticut. It is surrounded by ranges of mountains that rise more than 6,500 feet above the elevation of Alamosa, which is 7,500 feet above sea level. In the beautiful Sangre de Cristo range to the east, majestic Mount Blanca towers 14,363 feet above sea level. This mountain is nearly equaled in height and is rivaled in beauty by the rugged Crestone Peak and Crestone needles in the same range. The Continental Divide, winding through the San Juan mountain range, is the western boundary of the valley. The floor of the valley is occupied by fertile grain and vegetable farms and extensive grazing lands. Through the center of the valley flows the Rio Grande del Norte.

Majors and Degrees

Bachelor of Arts or Bachelor of Science degrees are awarded in art (emphasis in art education, art history, ceramics, design, drawing, fiber, metalsmithing, painting, photography, printmaking, sculpture, or water media), biology (emphasis required in allied health, botany, science education, wildlife, or zoology), business administration (emphasis required in accounting, advertising, business computer systems, business education, economics, finance, general business, management, marketing, office management, pre–international business, or small business), chemistry (emphasis in allied health or science education), elementary education licensure, English (emphasis required in communications: print/radio, liberal arts, or secondary teacher licensure), exercise physiology and leisure science (emphasis in athletic training, coaching, sport and exercise management, or teacher licensure), geology (emphasis in earth science or environmental science), Hispanic/Southwest studies, history/government (emphasis in history, government, or social studies education), mathematics (emphasis in computer science or math education), medical technology, music (emphasis in music education, K–12 or secondary, or performance), physics (emphasis in science education), psychology, selected studies (emphasis in liberal arts), sociology (emphasis in criminology, general sociology, and social welfare), Spanish (emphasis in foreign language for secondary teacher licensure), and speech/theater. Associate of Arts degree programs are also available. Preprofessional studies are offered in architectural engineering, dentistry, engineering, law, medicine, nursing, optometry, osteopathy, pharmacy, physical therapy, and veterinary medicine.

Academic Program

The academic year is divided into fall and spring semesters. Normally, the baccalaureate degree is earned in eight semesters, while the Associate of Arts degree is earned in four. The associate degree is conferred upon completion of an approved curriculum with a total of 60 hours of academic credit and, in some A.A. programs, 2 additional hours of credit in physical education activities. The Bachelor of Arts or Bachelor of Science degree is conferred upon completion of an approved curriculum with a total of 120 hours of academic credit plus 2 to 4 semester hours of credit in physical education activities. A minimum cumulative scholastic average of 2.0 must be earned in all courses taken at Adams State College for the A.A., B.S., and B.A. degrees in all areas except teacher education, for which a minimum cumulative grade point average of 2.75 must be earned in all work attempted. All requirements of the general education courses and the major must be satisfied. Students transferring from a two-year college must earn at least 60 additional semester hours to graduate from Adams State College with a bachelor's degree. Opportunities are available for independent study, special-topics courses, and discussion groups on current issues.

Off-Campus Arrangements

A number of low-cost tours to nearby points of historical, archaeological, and ethnological interest are arranged by the College, usually in the spring and summer months.

Academic Facilities

The library, which serves as a government depository, has 154,603 books, 35,368 bound periodicals, 373,460 government documents, 637,258 ERIC microfiche, and 3,265 other nonbook items.

A state-of-the-art science and mathematics building opened in 1998. A new art building is under construction and is expected to be complete by fall 2000.

Costs

For the 2000–01 academic year, the approximate comprehensive cost of tuition, fees, room, and board for residence hall students who are Colorado residents is $7800. For nonresident students, the approximate cost is $11,800. Married student housing units, with utilities furnished, are available at about $375 per month.

Financial Aid

Opportunities for financial aid are provided through scholarships, grants, loan funds, and part-time employment. Entering freshmen may gain consideration for all types of financial aid by completing the Free Application for Federal Student Aid and submitting it by March 1 of the year of expected fall enrollment. All undergraduate students are also encouraged to apply for a Federal Pell Grant. Scholarships (entitled National Scholarships) are available for nonresidents of Colorado who reside in Adams State residence halls. The value of each of these scholarships is one half the cost of nonresident tuition for one year (approximately $2800). To be eligible for one of these scholarships, an entering freshman must have ranked in the top third of his or her high school graduating class or ranked in the top third on the ACT or SAT I (national norms for ACT composite or SAT I combined scores). Transfer students may qualify for the scholarship if they have maintained a GPA of 2.5 or higher for 12 or more semester hours of academic credit.

Faculty

Adams State College has 101 full-time faculty members. Of these, 90 hold a doctorate and 11, a master's degree. Faculty members have received degrees from more than 100 colleges and universities. In addition to carrying out their teaching assignments, faculty members serve as counselors and advisers and as members of many committees.

Student Government

Each student at Adams State College becomes a member of the Associated Students and Faculty organization upon registration. The organization was founded to promote cooperation between students and faculty members of the College. The general social life, social programs, and other student activities are directed by this organization. Elected officers and representatives of the student body and elected faculty members form the Associated Students and Faculty Senate, which regulates matters pertaining to student life.

Admission Requirements

Applicants to a bachelor's degree program should meet the following criteria: a class rank in the upper two thirds of their high school graduating class or a grade point average of at least 2.0 and a composite ACT score of at least 21 or a combined 970 on SAT I scores. Students ranking in the lower third of their high school graduating class and who have less than a 2.0 average may be considered for admission to the A.A. degree program under the condition that they may be required to register for remedial classes. Upon successful completion of at least one semester of academic work at Adams State College with a minimum 2.0 grade point average, an A.A. student may transfer to the baccalaureate degree program. Prospective transfer students must have at least a C (2.0) average to be unconditionally accepted for admission to Adams State College. Those not meeting this criterion are considered individually. In the case of repeated courses, honor points for grade point averages are compiled on the basis of performance in the repeat.

Application and Information

Applications for admission to Adams State should be completed well in advance of the beginning of the semester to which admission is sought. Applications received less than thirty days prior to the beginning of a semester may cause a delay in registration. Freshman applicants must submit the application for undergraduate admission to Colorado collegiate institutions, which is available from most Colorado high school counselors or from the Adams State College Admissions Office. The freshman applicant should submit this completed application along with a nonrefundable $20 application fee and have his or her high school mail a copy of the high school transcript directly to the Admissions Office at Adams State. The student should also submit ACT or SAT I scores to the Admissions Office. Transfer applicants must also submit the application for undergraduate admission to Colorado collegiate institutions and a nonrefundable $20 application fee. In addition, the student must request that all colleges previously attended forward transcripts to support the student's request for admission. If the student has completed fewer than 12 semester hours of credit, he or she must also submit an official high school transcript and ACT or SAT I scores. Application forms, financial aid forms, and other information are mailed upon request. Inquiries should be made to:

Admissions Office
Adams State College
Alamosa, Colorado 81102
Telephone: 719-587-7712
           800-824-6494 (toll-free)
Fax: 719-587-7522
E-mail: ascadmit@adams.edu
World Wide Web: http://www.adams.edu

The Rex Activity Center on the campus of Adams State College.

ADELPHI UNIVERSITY
GARDEN CITY, NEW YORK

The University

Adelphi University, founded in 1896, was Long Island's first private institution of higher learning. Adelphi is chartered by the Board of Regents of the University of the State of New York. It is fully accredited by the Middle States Association of Colleges and Schools and by the New York State Education Department, the National League for Nursing Accrediting Commission, the American Psychological Association, the American Speech-Language and Hearing Association, and the Council on Social Work Education. It is a member of the College Board and the Association of American Colleges/Universities.

A nonsectarian, independent university, Adelphi welcomes men and women of all backgrounds who display intellectual inquisitiveness, academic commitment, and a desire for achievement and purpose in life. The University offers education to approximately 6,000 students. Thirty-six states and forty countries are represented in its diverse student body. The campus is located on 75 greenbelt acres in Garden City, New York, 20 miles east of New York City and easily accessible by public transportation. The University also has two modern extension centers, one in Manhattan and one in Huntington.

Adelphi University is composed of eight schools: the College of Arts and Sciences, the Honors College, the School of Management and Business, the School of Education, the School of Nursing, the School of Social Work, the Gordon F. Derner Institute of Advanced Psychological Studies, and University College.

The Graduate School of Arts and Sciences offers programs leading to the M.A. and M.S. degrees. The Graduate School of Management and Business offers the M.S. in accounting and in finance, the M.B.A., and the M.B.A./CPA programs. Graduate degrees in the School of Social Work are the M.S.W. and D.S.W., and the School of Nursing offers the M.S. degree. The School of Education offers a variety of programs leading to the M.A., M.S., and D.A. degrees. The Derner Institute of Advanced Psychological Studies offers an M.A. in general psychology, the Ph.D., and postdoctoral programs. Certificate programs are offered in several of these graduate areas.

Five University residence halls accommodate approximately 1,000 students. The Residential Life staff at Adelphi is committed to bringing education to the residence halls. A lecture and discussion series brings faculty members together with students to examine events of the day and issues related to the classroom. In addition, about 200 seminars, workshops, and events are offered each year. Faculty and guest lecturers lead discussions on such topics as American politics, ethnic diversity, legal affairs, job interviewing, sexual conduct, and AIDS.

Opportunities for enhancing life beyond the classroom abound at Adelphi. Students participate in intramural and intercollegiate athletics (including nationally ranked men's and women's soccer, women's softball, and men's baseball, basketball, and lacrosse), drama productions, community-service groups, and clubs. The University gymnasium houses a swimming pool; basketball, racquetball, and squash courts; weight-training and exercise rooms; and dance studios. Other physical education facilities include tennis courts, a large indoor running track, and separate fields for baseball, lacrosse, soccer, and softball. In addition, a vast array of activities such as movies, exhibits, cabarets, symposia, and field trips are scheduled every semester.

The Adelphi student newspapers (*Delphian* and *Afrika Unbound*), the yearbook (*Oracle*), and *Ascent*, the student literary magazine, welcome writers and photographers.

In the Ruth S. Harley University Center—the central meeting place on campus—Adelphi students browse in the recently renovated bookstore, sip a cappuccino and go on line in the Cyber-Cafe, and enjoy a vast array of activities including movies, comedy shows, lectures, dance parties, and musical events. Cultural trips are also offered. The University Center also houses Adelphi's sixty student organizations.

Location

Adelphi's main campus is located in the picturesque and architecturally distinctive suburban community of Garden City, New York, a village of stately homes, historic buildings, and parks. The cultural and commercial resources of New York City and the recreation and entertainment of Long Island are only a short distance away.

Majors and Degrees

Studies leading to the degrees of Bachelor of Arts, Bachelor of Fine Arts, Bachelor of Science, Bachelor of Business Administration, and Bachelor of Science in Education are offered at Adelphi University.

Majors offered lead to the B.A. in anthropology, art, art education, biology, chemistry, communications, computer science, dance, economics, English, environmental studies, history, international studies, Latin American studies, mathematics, philosophy, physical education, physics, political science, psychology, sociology, and speech arts/communicative disorders.

The B.S. is offered in art, biochemistry, biology, chemistry, computer science, finance, mathematics, music, music education, nursing, physical education, and social welfare. The B.B.A. is conferred in accounting and management. The B.F.A. is granted in theater. The B.S.Ed. is granted in elementary education.

Teacher-training programs lead to provisional state certification in the fields of elementary and secondary education at the end of four calendar years. Students who wish to obtain certification in secondary education major in art, English, foreign languages (French and Spanish), mathematics, music, physical education, the sciences (biology, chemistry, and physics), or social studies (anthropology, economics, history, political science, and sociology).

Combined graduate and undergraduate programs are offered in business, education, nursing, physics, and social work.

Adelphi also offers a seven-year optometry program leading to the B.S. and O.D. degrees in cooperation with the State University of New York's College of Optometry and a seven-year dental program leading to the B.S. and D.M.D. degrees in cooperation with the Tufts University School of Dental Medicine.

University College provides degree programs for adult students who attend classes in the evening and on weekends. It offers the Bachelor of Arts in humanistic studies, fine arts, and the social sciences and the Bachelor of Science in management and communications. University College houses the General Studies Program.

Academic Program

The goal of the academic program at Adelphi is to provide higher education that cultivates the intellect and prepares students for the future. Consistent with the University's approach to liberal learning, students take part in the University's general education requirements.

A minimum of 120 credits is required for a baccalaureate degree, with a specified number in the chosen major. Double majors and various minors may be elected. Seniors of superior academic ability may be admitted to graduate courses in their major field.

Off-Campus Arrangements

Adelphi University offers study-abroad programs in Europe, Asia, Latin America, and Africa. Qualified Adelphi students may also apply for admission to overseas programs sponsored by other accredited universities.

Academic Facilities

The University libraries are composed of the Swirbul Library, the Science Library, and the libraries at the Manhattan and Huntington centers. These libraries contain 632,000 volumes and 767,000 items in microformat, plus 43,000 audiovisual items and 1,000 periodical subscriptions. The University libraries are fully automated. Total holdings are accessible through ALICAT (the Adelphi Libraries Catalog Online). As an enhancement of the traditional reference services, computerized information retrieval services are available for accessing some 300 extensive national databases.

The Swirbul Library is also the center of information technology on campus. Its amenities include a battery of personal computers that are fully networked for student use, a faculty development lab, and a technology infrastructure that reaches into every classroom and every part of the curriculum to provide Web-based learning and other applications of communication and information media.

The University recently completed the $1.7-million renovation of the Olmsted Theatre, including a new storage area for props and scenery, a new lobby, a concession stand and box office, handicapped accessibility, and an additional 90 seats bringing the new seating capacity to 314.

Costs

In 1999–2000, the annual tuition cost for full-time undergraduates was $14,750. Additional charges included room and board costs of $6500. Adelphi recently announced its intention to hold tuition increases to the level of inflation or below for the next three years.

Financial Aid

The Office of Student Financial Services administers federal and New York State programs that provide funds to assist students in pursuing their academic goals. In addition to grants based on need, Adelphi annually offers almost 1,000 of its own scholarships based on merit, talent, and extracurricular excellence.

Faculty

At Adelphi, the quality of education is entrusted to its distinguished faculty members, who are noted for their serious commitment to students, as well as for their research and professional contributions. Here, professors, not graduate assistants, teach undergraduate courses, and students do not encounter large, impersonal lecture halls. Outside the classroom, students find faculty members from the newly developed Society of Mentors in their offices at regular hours or at any of a number of other sites on campus, ready to explore ideas.

Student Government

The Student Government Association is the elected student group that represents the opinions of the full-time undergraduate body to the administration and other groups. The Student Government Association hosts speakers, sponsors awareness days, and serves as a voice for student concerns and interests.

Admission Requirements

Recommended admission qualifications include graduation from a four-year public or private high school or equivalent credentials, 4 years of English, 3 years of science, 3 years of mathematics, 2–3 years of a foreign language or languages, and 4 additional units chosen from the fields mentioned or from history and social studies. Official test results from the SAT I or ACT are required.

Personal interviews and campus tours are strongly recommended for all applicants. Arrangements can be made by contacting the Office of Admissions.

Application and Information

The following admission credentials should be submitted by applicants: a completed application for admission, the application fee, an official high school transcript or graduate equivalency diploma, official results of the SAT I or ACT, and a personal essay. Transfer students must submit official transcripts from all colleges previously attended.

Applications are reviewed on a rolling basis. Candidates who wish to be given priority consideration for financial aid and housing, however, should apply by February 15 for the fall semester and November 1 for the spring.

For more information, students should contact:

University Admissions
Adelphi University
Garden City, New York 11530

Telephone: 800-ADELPHI (toll-free)
E-mail: admissions@adelphi.edu
World Wide Web: http://www.adelphi.edu

ADRIAN COLLEGE
ADRIAN, MICHIGAN

The College

Adrian College, chartered in 1859, is a private liberal arts college affiliated with the United Methodist Church. Recognized for providing high-quality education by the *College Board Review* and *U.S. News & World Report*, Adrian is characterized by teaching excellence and individual treatment of students. The College's mission is to maintain a learning environment that stimulates individual growth and academic excellence. To fulfill this mission, the College is committed to fostering creativity, encouraging ethical values and the pursuit of truth, and helping students develop the necessary skills to lead satisfying lives and careers within a global society.

In fall 1999, Adrian College enrolled 1,060 students (509 men and 551 women), of whom 993 were full-time. Approximately 90 percent of the student body is of traditional college age. Currently, students come from sixteen states, but most come from the surrounding Midwest states of Michigan, Ohio, and Indiana. The international student population represents Ghana, India, Ireland, Japan, Kenya, Russia, South Africa, and Zambia.

Adrian College students enjoy a lifestyle that combines residential life with academic challenges and social opportunities. Nearly all of Adrian's students live on campus in one of nine residence halls that provide unique living and learning environments for residents. With more than sixty-five organizations to choose from, students can apply their talents, interests, and skills in extracurricular activities ranging from academic honoraries and religious, cultural, and social organizations to intercollegiate and intramural athletic teams. Adrian College is a member of the NCAA Division III and the Michigan Intercollegiate Athletics Association. The Merillat Sport and Fitness Center is an 80,000-square-foot multisport forum that includes basketball, volleyball, and tennis courts surrounded by a 1/10-mile indoor track as well as two racquetball courts, an athletic training room, a weight-training and conditioning room, classrooms, a physiology laboratory, and a dance studio. The performance gymnasium, which seats 1,300 people, is host to numerous intercollegiate basketball and volleyball matches.

Location

Adrian College is located in Adrian, Michigan, the county seat of Lenawee County in the southeastern part of the state. Adrian is a city of approximately 22,000 people, situated in the center of an agricultural, industrial, and recreational area. State and U.S. highways and nearby expressways provide convenient access to the metropolitan areas of Detroit, Toledo, Chicago, Indianapolis, Cleveland, and Pittsburgh. Both the Detroit and Toledo airports are within an hour's drive of the College.

Majors and Degrees

Adrian College is authorized by its Board of Trustees to grant the following degrees: Associate of Arts, Bachelor of Science, Bachelor of Arts, Bachelor of Fine Arts, Bachelor of Music, Bachelor of Music Education, and Bachelor of Business Administration. Majors include accountancy; art; arts management; biology; business administration (management or marketing); chemistry; communication arts and sciences; criminal justice; earth science; economics; English (journalism, literature, or writing); environmental science; environmental studies; exercise science; fashion merchandising; French; German; health, physical education, and recreation; history; human services; interior design; international business; international studies; mathematics; music; philosophy/religion; physics; political science; psychology; religion; sociology; Spanish; teacher education; and theater. Students may also choose to design their own major, in consultation with the appropriate department chairpersons, or even major in two or more areas of study. Professional certification areas include elementary and secondary education. Preprofessional programs are offered in architecture, art therapy, dentistry, engineering, law, medicine, optometry, pharmacy, physical therapy, podiatry, seminary, and veterinary studies.

Academic Program

Distribution requirements are designed to emphasize liberal education through a broad understanding of the liberal arts and have been established in several liberal arts areas (arts, humanities, social sciences, natural and physical sciences, and cross-cultural perspective) and in basic skill areas that indicate education proficiency (communication, linguistics, and physical development). All students must complete at least one course in religion or philosophy and at least one 4-hour laboratory science course. Students must also declare their major during their sophomore year. Successful completion of a minimum of 124 semester hours, with at least 30 hours at the most advanced level, is needed to obtain a baccalaureate degree. Up to 60 semester hours may be earned through nontraditional credit programs such as CLEP, PEP, LLE, Advanced Placement, and others. An honors program is open to highly motivated students of proven ability. Successful completion of the honors program is noted on the student's transcript and diploma.

Adrian maintains a two-semester calendar. The first semester runs from late August to mid-December; the second semester from early January to the end of April. A May term and summer session are offered for students who wish to intensify or accelerate their studies.

Off-Campus Arrangements

Participation in approved off-campus and cooperative programs can help students earn academic credit. Adrian offers a variety of ways to visit and study other cultures through established formal arrangements, as well as gain professional experience via cooperative arrangements with a variety of off-campus sites. Formal arrangements for study abroad are available in Australia, Austria, Britain, China, France, Germany, Hong Kong, Italy, Japan, Mexico, the Netherlands, Russia, and Spain, although students may arrange opportunities to study in other countries through the departments of foreign languages, history, business administration, or political science. Opportunities for domestic study and living experience are available through the Appalachian Semester, the Philadelphia Urban Semester, American University's Washington Semester, and programs offered by the Urban Life Center in Chicago and the Washington Center.

Career internships, available in all academic disciplines, provide all students with opportunities to test their career interests and develop job-related skills through College-approved work experiences. Students may earn up to 12 semester hours working for domestic or international employers.

Academic Facilities

Shipman Library includes a complete line of academic library services. The collection numbers more than 82,000 volumes, plus substantial holdings of microforms, art prints, sound recordings, and subscriptions to more than 750 periodicals. The College completed a $6-million library expansion and renovation project in summer 2000.

Computer terminals and printers for student use are located in Jones Hall, Mahan Hall, North Hall, Peele Hall, and Shipman Library. Access to IBM and IBM-compatible personal computers, printers, scanners, and Internet services is available to students at no charge. Many classrooms and all residence hall rooms are networked for Internet access.

General chemistry and biology laboratories equipped with sophisticated chemical and biochemical instrumentation are provided by the College. Labs for psychology, language study, physics, acoustical studies, and tissue culture provide students with access to a variety of research opportunities. Special facilities include art studios, music practice rooms, greenhouses, and a planetarium.

Downs Hall, the only remaining building from Adrian College's original campus, houses the Stubnitz Gallery of Art and the Downs Studio Theater, a 199-seat facility with a thrust-style stage, where most student theater productions take place. Dawson Auditorium, with its traditional proscenium stage, is used for College musical and theatrical productions, Adrian Symphony concerts, and guest artist appearances.

Costs

Full-time tuition for 1999–2000 was $13,650, and room and board were approximately $4460. The required activity fee of $100 covered the cost of student participation in a variety of campuswide social activities and attendance at Adrian College sports events. The average cost of books and supplies was about $400 per year. No additional costs for laboratory or computer use are assessed.

Financial Aid

Adrian College strives to make a high-quality private liberal arts education affordable to its students through various forms of financial assistance. Approximately 85 percent of the student body receives some form of financial aid through scholarships, grants, loans, and campus employment. The College also participates in all applicable Michigan aid programs, as well as the Federal Work-Study, Federal Pell Grant, and Federal Supplemental Educational Opportunity Grant (FSEOG) programs. The Federal Perkins Loan, Federal Stafford Student Loan, TERI Supplemental Loan, and Federal Parent Loan (PLUS) programs are also available. A number of part-time positions are available for those who wish to work on campus while earning applicable financial assistance. For those with a demonstrated record of high academic ability, merit-based scholarship assistance is available.

To be considered for any financial assistance, a student must complete the Free Application for Federal Student Aid (FAFSA) form, which is used to conduct a need analysis for the student. The FAFSA may be obtained from most high school counselors or directly from the Adrian College Office of Financial Aid.

Faculty

Teaching with a personal approach is a top priority at Adrian College. Classes at Adrian are not conducted by teaching assistants. Instead, classes are taught by dedicated faculty members—most of whom hold the terminal degree in their field. With a student-faculty ratio of 13:1 and an average class size of 14, students are assured of a high-quality education that unites challenge and opportunity within a framework of personal and institutional support.

Student Government

Adrian College Student Government is the student organization charged with representing student views on matters of institutional policy and operation at all levels of College organization. As a student organization, it also provides students with a common forum where their individual ideas may be heard, debated, and perhaps adopted. Appropriations and other major decisions are made in full-senate sessions. Other work is carried out through the Cooperative Activities Board or through the College governance system. Any student who wishes to run for student-elected office may do so.

Admission Requirements

Adrian College enrolls qualified students regardless of gender, race, color, creed, physical disability, sexual orientation, or national or ethnic origin. Applicants should present at least 15 units of secondary school preparation, including 4 units of English, 3 units of mathematics, 3 units in sciences, 2 units in social sciences, and 2 units in foreign language.

Students applying for freshman admission must also perform satisfactorily on either the ACT or the SAT I and must request that their scores be sent directly to Adrian College. The average high school GPA of entering Adrian College students who have taken college-preparatory courses during their four years of high school is 3.2. The mean ACT composite score is 22. Transfer students must be eligible to return immediately to the last attended college and must have an above-average cumulative GPA. Prospective transfer students must request an official transcript from each college attended to be sent directly to the Office of Admissions at Adrian College. Nontraditional students must complete a different application for admission but are evaluated on the same basis as traditional freshmen. A GED equivalency certificate may be substituted for a full high school transcript.

Students from other countries are always welcome at Adrian College and are encouraged to apply. International applicants must file an international application for admission and must submit complete secondary school records, transcripts of any university credit, and TOEFL test scores demonstrating sufficient fluency in English to participate in the regular instructional program of the College. A minimum TOEFL score of 500 is required for admission. A full program of services for international students includes English as a second language (ESL) classes for further assistance in English, housing and food service, and pick-up service from the airport. International students are eligible for grants that cover the cost of room and board for the academic year.

Application and Information

A nonrefundable fee of $20 must be submitted with an application for admission. Application can be made anytime following the completion of the junior year of high school. Students are usually notified of the admissions decision within two weeks after the application file is complete. Campus visits are strongly encouraged but not required.

For more information about Adrian College or to schedule a campus visit, students should contact:

Office of Admissions
Adrian College
110 South Madison Street
Adrian, Michigan 49221-2575

Telephone: 517-265-5161 Ext. 4326
                800-877-2246 (toll-free)
E-mail: admissions@adrian.edu
World Wide Web: http://www.adrian.edu

AGNES SCOTT COLLEGE
ATLANTA, GEORGIA

The College
For more than a century, minds have sparked minds at Agnes Scott College, a highly selective, independent, national liberal arts college for women, located in metropolitan Atlanta. In offering the world for women, Agnes Scott's curriculum encourages students to become fluent across disciplines, across continents, and across centuries. Founded in 1889 by Presbyterians, Agnes Scott is a diverse and growing residential community of scholars, with one of the largest endowments per student of any college or university in the country.

Agnes Scott was the first accredited college or university in Georgia, and the College's Phi Beta Kappa chapter is the second oldest in the state. Agnes Scott's tradition of academic excellence continues today with a student body numbering 900. Students come from thirty-six states, the District of Columbia, the U.S. Virgin Islands, and twenty-nine countries, and 90 percent of traditional-age students live on campus in residence halls and apartments. More than 25 percent represent diverse ethnic or cultural backgrounds.

Students may pursue special interests in the arts (music, dance, and theater); with clubs for international cultures, politics, cultural awareness, religious affiliations, and foreign languages; and through student publications, sports, and volunteer community service. Social Council plans dances, mixers, and parties with neighboring colleges. Traditional annual highlights are Black Cat (the culmination of first-year student orientation), Senior Investiture, and Sophomore Family Weekend. The College sponsors a variety of events, from lectures by noted authorities to concerts by world-famous artists; each spring, the Writers' Festival brings well-known authors and poets to the campus for readings and informal meetings with students.

The College is a member of the NCAA Division III and sponsors seven varsity sports: basketball, cross-country, soccer, softball, swimming, tennis, and volleyball. Club and intramural sports are also available. The Woodruff Physical Activities Building features an eight-lane swimming pool, a large weight and aerobic exercise room, a gymnasium, and an athletic training room. The Gellerstedt track is an all-weather, six-lane running track circling varsity soccer's game field.

In addition to undergraduate study, Agnes Scott offers a Master of Arts in Teaching secondary English that prepares students to teach high school English, with a focus on gender equity and diversity as well as on the art of teaching writing.

Location
The 100-acre wooded campus is located in metropolitan Atlanta and the historic residential community of Decatur. Six miles away is downtown Atlanta, accessible by a rapid-transit rail station two blocks from campus and weekend shuttle service to popular destinations. An international city, Atlanta offers a multitude of opportunities for personal contact with most of the world's cultures and for study, through internships and volunteer work, with art, business, educational, and political organizations. Atlanta is the cultural center of the South, with entertainment and cultural events and facilities ranging from rock concerts to performances by the Atlanta Symphony Orchestra, from local theater to touring Broadway shows, and from recreational parks to major-league sports.

Majors and Degrees
Agnes Scott College confers the Bachelor of Arts degree with majors in art, astrophysics, biochemistry and molecular biology, biology, chemistry, classical languages and literatures, classical civilization, economics, economics and business, English, English literature–creative writing, French, German studies, history, international relations, mathematics, mathematics-economics, mathematics-physics, music, philosophy, physics, political science, psychology, religious studies, sociology-anthropology, Spanish, theater, and women's studies. Students may design their own interdisciplinary majors. Through a dual-degree program, a student may combine three years of liberal arts studies at Agnes Scott with two years of specialized engineering studies at Georgia Tech, receiving a bachelor's degree from each institution. Also available is a 3-4 Master of Architecture program offered with Washington University in St. Louis, resulting in a bachelor's degree from Agnes Scott and a master's degree from Washington University. Certificates are awarded in postbaccalaureate premedical and postbaccalaureate teacher certification programs.

Academic Program
Agnes Scott's curriculum is designed to help students gain an understanding of the humanities and fine arts, natural sciences and mathematics, and social sciences, with particular competence in one or two disciplines. The graduation requirement of 122 semester hours includes specific standards in English composition, physical education, and foreign language. The Language Across the Curriculum Program links foreign languages with other disciplines. Students prepare for world citizenship through a curriculum with international perspectives. Five Agnes Scott seniors in the past seven years have been awarded Fulbright scholarships, and 2 students were 1998 Goldwater Scholars.

The Atlanta Semester: in Women, Leadership, and Social Change provides an opportunity for Agnes Scott students and women from colleges and universities across the country to combine internships with independent research projects, interdisciplinary academic course work, and a weekly speakers' forum. The Preparatory Program for Business is designed to facilitate a student's entry into the business world. The state-approved teacher education program leads to the Georgia professional certificate, which is recognized and accepted by most states. The Return-to-College Program provides women beyond traditional college age with the opportunity to complete the Bachelor of Arts degree.

Off-Campus Arrangements
Study abroad enriches classroom learning experiences and expands world views. Agnes Scott offers two faculty-led programs—Global Awareness and Global Connections. Recent destinations have included England, France, Ghana, Greece, Ireland, Japan, Jordan, and Mexico. Agnes Scott has a scholarly exchange agreement with Japan's Kinjo Gakuin University and is the only women's college admitted to the International Student Exchange Program (ISEP), which provides study-abroad opportunities with more than 110 institutions in thirty-five countries.

With opportunities to cross-register at member institutions of the Atlanta Regional Consortium for Higher Education (ARCHE),

Agnes Scott students enjoy the advantages of a small-college environment while benefiting from a variety of programs at neighboring schools, including Emory University, Spelman College, and Georgia Institute of Technology. ARCHE shares courses of instruction, library services, visiting scholars, faculty research, and departmental conferences. Air Force and Navy ROTC programs are available through cross-registration. An exchange program with Mills College in Oakland, California, enables students to study for a semester or year in the San Francisco Bay area. Students may participate in the Washington Semester program, coordinated by American University, or the PLEN Public Policy Semester, both in Washington, D.C.

Academic Facilities

Agnes Scott College has embarked on a $130-million building program to enhance academic and student life facilities. A renovated and expanded Evans Dining Hall, with a marketplace servery, and a new 500-car parking structure and public safety facility opened for the 1999–2000 academic year. A new Alston Campus Center and a renovated and expanded Bradley Observatory will open fall 2000. McCain Library, renovated and doubled in size, will be fully operational in early 2001. A landscape master plan and tree management program are being implemented, and construction on a new science building is scheduled to begin during the 2000–01 academic year..

McCain Library contains 208,283 volumes, 9,800 audiovisual items, and 30,900 microforms and receives 896 periodicals. It holds several noteworthy collections of rare books and manuscripts, including one of the leading Robert Frost collections and the papers of alumna Catherine Marshall. Agnes Scott's reciprocal library service gives students direct access to thirty additional libraries in the Atlanta-Athens area. Extensive electronic resources are available through the GALILEO project of the University System of Georgia.

Personal computers are available to students in the Academic Computing Center, the Center for Writing and Speaking, the Science Resource Center, the Macintosh lab, and residence halls. An interactive learning center, a multimedia classroom, and a computer network with one port per student in residence hall rooms are part of Agnes Scott's commitment to keeping pace with current technologies.

The Dana Fine Arts Building houses the departments of theater and art; its facilities include a thrust-stage theater, two floors of balcony art studios, pottery and sculpture studios with kilns, and a darkroom. The Dalton Galleries exhibit the College's permanent and traveling collections and student and faculty member exhibitions. Presser Hall contains soundproof recording studios and practice rooms for music students. Gaines Chapel, with a 3,000-pipe Austin organ, has a large stage for dance, music, and theatrical performances. Maclean Auditorium, which houses a Schlicker organ, is used for chamber music concerts and student recitals.

Campbell Science Building has laboratories and computer facilities for experimentation and research in biology, chemistry, physics, and psychology. The College's 30-inch Beck telescope, one of the largest in the Southeast, resides in Bradley Observatory and is available for student research.

Costs

Tuition for 2000–01 is $16,600. Residence costs, including room, board, and health services, are $6900, and the student activity and College events fee is $145. Personal expenses, including books and supplies, are estimated at $1600.

Financial Aid

Agnes Scott admits students without regard to financial need, and the College makes every effort to meet the need of qualified students whose resources are insufficient to meet expenses. Approximately 60 percent of students receive need-based financial assistance through grants, loans, and campus employment. Outstanding first-year students are offered renewable merit-based Honor Scholarships, and music scholarships are available for new students intending to major in music. Achievement Awards, Community Service Awards, Middle Income Assistance Awards, and Transfer Scholarships are also offered.

Faculty

A 10:1 student-faculty ratio allows for small classes with lively participation and individual attention. One hundred percent of Agnes Scott's regular full-time faculty members hold the highest degree in their field. Senior faculty members teach first-year students as well as upperclass students. Every student is assigned a faculty adviser to assist in course selection and academic counseling.

Student Government

Agnes Scott is a self-governing community, and each student is a member of the Student Government Association. A strong honor system places responsibility for integrity, honesty, and judgment in self-government on the individual and allows unproctored tests and self-scheduled final examinations. Regulations governing student life are made by the students with approval of the Judicial Review Committee, on which the Student Government Association, Student Senate, Honor Court, and Residence Hall Association presidents serve as voting members. Policies are formulated with the goal of maintaining an individual's maximum freedom within the framework of community responsibility.

Admission Requirements

Agnes Scott admits, without regard to race, color, creed, national or ethnic origin, or physical handicap, students whose academic and personal qualities give promise of success. Transfer and international students are welcome. Each applicant's school record, SAT I or ACT scores, recommendations, and essay are reviewed carefully, and interviews are recommended but not required. Arrangements for an interview at the College, a campus tour with a student guide, and visits to classes may be made through the Office of Admission.

Application and Information

An application for admission and supporting credentials should be filed with the Office of Admission by the following dates: November 15 for early decision, with notification by December 15; January 15 for scholarship candidates; March 1 for regular decision; and November 1 for the spring semester.

Associate Vice President for
    Enrollment and Director of Admission
Agnes Scott College
141 East College Avenue
Atlanta/Decatur, Georgia 30030-3797
Telephone: 404-471-6285
    800-868-8602 (toll-free)
Fax: 404-471-6414
E-mail: admission@agnesscott.edu
World Wide Web: http://www.agnesscott.edu

ALBANY STATE UNIVERSITY
ALBANY, GEORGIA

The University

Founded in 1903, Albany State University, a unit of the University System of Georgia, is accredited by the Southern Association of Colleges and Schools and holds membership in more than fifty professional organizations. The mission of Albany State University includes teaching, research, and community service. Albany State University has taken its place as a regional institution of higher learning, serving more than twenty-four counties in southwest Georgia with graduate and undergraduate courses in more than forty fields.

The total enrollment of the University is 3,226; 2,817 are undergraduates. More than two thirds of the students live off campus, but residence halls are maintained on campus for men and women.

An aggressive $140-million rebuilding plan is completed at the University, which was damaged extensively during the flooding of the Flint River in 1994. All new state-of-the-art facilities include new dormitories, classrooms and laboratories, a dining hall, an athletic complex, and an administration/academic building.

Continuing education and community service are emphasized in programs that foster strong links with the community through lectures, classes, facility sharing, concerts, and an active industry cluster. Students can choose from more than fifty special interest clubs on campus, including fraternities, sororities, and student government organizations. University athletics include baseball, basketball, cross-country, football, tennis, track and field, and volleyball.

In addition to its undergraduate degree programs, Albany State University grants master's degrees in business administration, criminal justice, education, nursing, public administration, school counseling, and the education specialist degree in educational administration and supervision through the Graduate School. Collaborative programs with the Medical College of Georgia and Valdosta State University offer the Master of Physical Therapy and the Doctor of Education degrees, respectively.

In a past edition of *U.S. News & World Report*'s "America's Best Colleges," Albany State University was ranked among the top sixty-five Southern colleges and universities. ASU was ranked in the second of four tiers, and its 61 percent graduation rate was the highest of the thirty-two schools in the tier.

At ASU, extracurricular and cocurricular opportunities abound. Whether students prefer athletics, politics, religious organizations, fraternities or sororities, student government, performing arts, or ROTC, there is something for everyone. The strong religious traditions that are a foundation of the lives of many ASU students are nurtured in the regular Sunday school classes held on campus and through attendance at many of the community's churches. With spacious new dorms and a 22,432-square-foot dining hall that is easily accessed from the University's Pedestrian Mall, students find that ASU has its own distinctive character, style, and ambiance.

Location

Albany is one of the most progressive cities in the South, with a population exceeding 100,000. It is a major center for education, recreation, health services, commerce, and industry. Albany is 32 miles south of Plains, Georgia, home of former president Jimmy Carter, and just a 3-hour drive from the Gulf Coast beaches and Atlanta.

Majors and Degrees

Albany State University provides innovative instructional and professional programs through its four academic colleges (Arts and Sciences, Business, Education, and Health Professions) and the Graduate School.

The College of Arts and Sciences grants the Bachelor of Arts degree in art, biology, chemistry, computer science, criminal justice, English, history, mathematics, modern languages, music, political science, psychology, sociology, and speech and theater. The College of Arts and Sciences also grants the Bachelor of Science degree in biology, English, mathematics, and music; the Bachelor of Social Work degree in social work; and the Associate of Arts degree in forensic science and security management.

The College of Business, accredited by the Association of Collegiate Business Schools and Programs, offers programs leading to the Bachelor of Science degree in accounting, administrative systems, management, and marketing.

The College of Education grants Bachelor of Science degrees in early childhood education; health, physical education, and recreation; middle grades education; science education; and special education.

The College of Nursing and Allied Health Sciences, which is accredited by the National League for Nursing Accrediting Commission, offers the Bachelor of Science in Nursing and the Bachelor of Science in Allied Health.

Preprofessional programs in dentistry, medicine, and pharmacy may be developed within a major in either biology or chemistry. A transfer program in engineering is offered in cooperation with the Georgia Institute of Technology, as is a 3-2 dual-degree program.

Academic Program

The core curriculum of the University System of Georgia is the general educational foundation upon which all degree programs are built. Candidates for the baccalaureate degree must satisfactorily complete a basic general education program during their freshman and sophomore years that consists of 60 hours in the following areas: essential skills, 9 hours; institutional options, 5 hours; humanities/fine arts, 6 hours; mathematics and technology, 10 hours; social science, 12 hours; and courses specifically appropriate to the student's major, 18 hours. A student generally chooses a major during the sophomore year and upon completion of the core program takes major courses and electives necessary to fulfill the hours required for graduation.

The University operates on the semester system, with each semester in the regular session extending over a period of approximately fifteen weeks. The summer session is eight weeks. Students who register for a full academic load may take 12–16 hours. Most courses are offered on a 3-semester-hour basis.

Albany State grants advanced placement and up to 3 semester hours of credit for satisfactory scores on examinations of the College Board's Advanced Placement Program. Credit may also be obtained through College-Level Examination Program (CLEP) subject examinations and examinations completed through the Defense Activity for Non-Traditional Education Support (DANTES). Albany State accepts credit earned by examination at other accredited institutions of higher learning.

The Post-Secondary Option at Albany State offers academically superior high school juniors and seniors an opportunity to enroll for college credit prior to the completion of their high school program of study, provided they live close enough to Albany State to attend classes at the University while still in high school.

Off-Campus Arrangements

Students enrolled in cooperative education at Albany State may be employed for specific periods in off-campus work.

Study-abroad programs sponsored by the University System of Georgia are open to all majors.

Academic Facilities

The resources of the James Pendergrast Memorial Library include more than 200,000 books and bound volumes, 9,580 books in microform, 13,480 documents in microform, 1,066 current serial subscriptions, and three CD-ROM electronic indexes. There are more than 640,540 physical units of microform of all types. The library subscribes to Dialog Information Retrieval Service and uses telefacsimile service. In addition, it networks with the Georgia Library Information Network, SOLINET, OCLC, and GOLD. Many pamphlets, maps, and manuscripts are available. Among the book collections are many sets of volumes and complete works. Materials are constantly being added in support of current teaching and research. Coin-operated copying machines and microform reader-printers are located on the first, second, and third floors of the three-story structure. The University's computer center is designed to provide the most modern time-sharing capabilities possible for both the instructional and the administrative services components. A computer is available for every 7 students.

Costs

Estimated fees per semester for Georgia residents for 2000–01 are $2800, including the matriculation fee; health, activity, and athletics fees; board; room; and laundry. Out-of-state students pay an estimated additional fee of $2800 per semester. Off-campus students may purchase meal cards for $25 or $50. Books and supplies cost approximately $375 per semester, and all students pay a graduation fee of $30. (Fees are subject to change.)

Financial Aid

Albany State University provides financial assistance through scholarships, loans, and employment. Some major sources of aid are the Federal Pell Grant, Federal Supplemental Educational Opportunity Grant, Federal Perkins Loan, and Federal Direct Student Loan Program. The HOPE Scholarship Program provides financial assistance to students who graduated from a Georgia high school in 1993 or later with a B average. Student employment is offered through the Federal Work-Study Program. Students receiving aid are given priority in subsequent years provided that they still need assistance and apply before the deadline. Additional information may be obtained by contacting the financial aid officer at the University.

Faculty

The University's teaching faculty consists of 160 highly qualified members, 71 percent of whom hold doctoral degrees in their respective disciplines. Faculty members are recruited from broad areas. Albany State University professors are expected to do research in addition to regular teaching duties. The faculty-student ratio of 1:20 and the relatively small size of the student body support excellent communication and rapport among students and faculty members.

Student Government

Student Government provides students with a powerful voice and active involvement in academic and administrative policy-making through the Student Leaders, Student Government Association, Board of Managers, and ASU's *Student Voice* newspaper.

Admission Requirements

An applicant is generally declared eligible for admission if he or she meets one of the following criteria: graduation from an accredited high school, satisfactory completion of the General Educational Development (GED) test, or possession of a State Department of Education High School Equivalency Certificate. The SAT I or the ACT is required of all applicants for admission.

Albany State welcomes graduates of accredited junior colleges and students from other senior colleges who present evidence that they have left the college last attended in good standing and satisfy all admission requirements for transfer students, as outlined in the Albany State University catalog.

The early admission program at Albany State University offers the academically superior high school senior an opportunity to be admitted as a beginning freshman after his or her junior year of high school.

Application and Information

Applications are processed upon receipt of the completed application form, official high school transcript, and SAT I or ACT scores. An application fee of $20 is required.

To arrange an interview or obtain more detailed information about the academic program, students should contact:

Director of Recruitment Admissions
Albany State University
504 College Drive
Albany, Georgia 31705-2797
Telephone: 912-430-4646
           800-822-RAMS (toll-free in Georgia)

James Pendergrast Memorial Library is the largest facility of its kind in southwest Georgia, with more than 200,000 volumes and seating for more than 900 users. It also houses ASU's state-of-the-art Student Technology Lab, which is open seven days a week, five days until midnight, to provide computer and lab assistance.

ALBERTSON COLLEGE OF IDAHO
CALDWELL, IDAHO

The College

Students come to Albertson College of Idaho because they are looking for a personalized education and a place where they can feel at home. A private, liberal arts college founded in 1891 as the College of Idaho, Albertson is nationally recognized today as one of the best liberal arts colleges in the West. At Albertson College, students find that the focus is on them. Small classes and caring faculty members nurture and challenge academic growth. Students can expect an education focused on the liberal arts—arts, humanities, and sciences—an education designed to prepare them for the future by emphasizing the values and standards of judgment required for lifelong learning, personal development, and community leadership.

Because it is a small residential college (approximately 750 undergraduates, with nearly 50 percent living on campus), students are involved in the campus community. Through classroom participation, volunteer activities, and more than 100 leadership roles, students play a significant role in campus life. The average age of an Albertson student is 20. Five percent of Albertson students describe themselves as minority students. The majority of students come from the Pacific Northwest, but about twenty states are represented overall. Student life at Albertson College includes special interest groups and athletics, as well as sororities, fraternities, and other social organizations. The McCain Center, the new student union, opened in fall 1999 and features a game room, student government offices, a movie theater, and a café.

One factor that sets Albertson College apart from other institutions is friendliness. Students say they immediately feel they belong when they step on campus. Most students are already known by some faculty members, admission counselors, and upperclassmen through the recruiting process; the relationships continue once the student is enrolled at the College.

In July 1999, Dr. Kevin Learned became the College's tenth president. A former CPA, entrepreneur, and business professor who was educated at liberal arts institutions, Learned brings a new energy and charisma to the campus. Helping students to be successful in college and beyond is a priority for the new president.

Location

Albertson College is located just 25 miles from Boise, Idaho's vibrant capital city and center of government and industry. Southwest Idaho has earned a national reputation for its dynamic economy, relaxed quality of life, and world-class recreational activities that include skiing, white-water boating, fly-fishing, and mountain biking. Boise has museums, concerts, plays, nightclubs, and coffee shops centered in the heart of the downtown area.

In Caldwell, Albertson College has become the heart of the arts community, with a world-class string trio, performing arts series, and outstanding programs in music, art, and theater.

The diverse mix of companies operating in southwest Idaho provides outstanding opportunities for students to learn outside the classroom. Local businesses offer internships, summer employment, and mentoring experiences along with scholarships and other financial support. Several Fortune 500 companies and hundreds of innovative high-tech businesses call the area home, giving students the option of getting a taste of their career interests long before they graduate.

Majors and Degrees

Albertson College offers bachelor's degrees in twenty-seven majors, including accounting, anthropology/sociology, art, biology, business administration, chemistry, computer science/mathematics, creative writing, economics, English, English teaching, history, international business, mathematics, mathematics teaching, music, philosophy, physical education teaching, physics, political science, pre-engineering, psychology, religion, social studies teaching, Spanish, sports and fitness center management, and theater.

Albertson offers preprofessional programs in health sciences and law. Both programs have an enviable record of producing graduates who are accepted into medical and law schools. Cooperative programs in accounting, economics, engineering, law, management, and natural resources enable students to complete a course of study in the liberal arts at the College and then transfer to take upper-level course work at universities, including Columbia and Washington University in St. Louis. Albertson also offers a five-year M.B.A. degree program in cooperation with Boise State University, Gonzaga University, Willamette University, and the University of Idaho.

Academic Program

The study of the liberal arts and sciences is the core of Albertson College's curriculum. Students examine the history of human thought and develop reasoning and thinking skills through scholarly research, scientific analysis, and creative expression.

In order to graduate, a student must complete at least 124 semester units, including specific general graduation requirements, a major field of study, at least 30 units in residence courses, and independent work at the upper-division level.

The Gipson Scholar Program allows students with superior high school records to design individual courses of study without meeting general graduation requirements. The Albertson Leadership Program is offered to freshmen who demonstrate leadership potential. Students exhibiting outstanding intellectual and scholarly achievement may be eligible for the Honors Program. The College actively encourages and supports student candidates for Rhodes, Marshall, Goldwater, Fulbright, Danforth, Mellon, Rotary, and other scholarly awards.

The academic calendar is divided into a thirteen-week fall semester, a six-week winter term, and a thirteen-week spring semester.

Off-Campus Arrangements

Students can study abroad for a semester, summer, or academic year and receive academic credit. Programs are sponsored by either the overseas institution or other U.S. colleges or universities. In each case, students receive academic credit from Albertson College of Idaho. During each six-week winter and some summer sessions, Albertson professors lead study programs to overseas destinations. These programs have recently taken students to Australia, Costa Rica, England, France, Greece, Israel, Italy, and Mexico. Faculty members will accompany students to Cuba in winter 2001.

Academic Facilities

The College's Terteling and Shannon Libraries contain 178,885 bound volumes, 27,850 microform items, 820 periodical subscriptions, 75,000 government documents, and 1,476 records/tapes/CDs. In 1996, each residence hall room was wired to accommodate students' personal computers and allow free access to the Internet, e-mail, and other College computer services. In addition, each residence hall has its own computer lab. Students also have Internet access in eight additional campus computer labs.

The College has constructed four new facilities since 1991. The J. A. Albertson Activities Center, a 75,000-square-foot facility, has a full-service exercise center, basketball arena, Olympic-size swimming pool, classrooms, and offices. The Kathryn Albertson International Center is 35,000 square feet of modern language and economics classrooms, faculty offices, the Shannon Library, and a computer lab. The Langroise Center for the Performing and Fine Arts is a 54,000-square-foot facility that houses a 188-seat recital hall, a studio theater, art studios, music classrooms, and practice rooms. The College has an 800-seat auditorium, an art gallery, a museum of natural history, a planetarium, a gem and mineral collection, and athletic fields.

Costs

Tuition for the 1999–2000 academic year was $16,000. A double room was $2000; board was $2200. Additional costs for fees, books, supplies, personal expenses, and travel were estimated at $1800.

Financial Aid

Albertson College requires the ACI Application for Financial Aid and Scholarships and the Free Application for Federal Student Aid (FAFSA) for consideration for all federal, state, and institutional program funding. The College participates in the Federal Pell Grant program, Federal Perkins Loan program, Federal Supplemental Educational Opportunity Grant program, Federal Work-Study Program, Federal Stafford Student Loans (both subsidized and unsubsidized), and the Federal Parent Loan for Undergraduate Students (PLUS) Program. In addition to these federal programs, Idaho and several programs from other states have approved Albertson students to receive their funding. The College has an extensive Honors Scholarship Program, ACI Grant Program, and ACI Scholarship Program, for which 97 percent of students qualify for consideration for scholarships and grant aid. Albertson has approximately 125 endowed scholarship funds, generating nearly 500 individual scholarships for students. On-campus employment is also available. The College participates in the Federal Work-Study Program and the Idaho Work-Study program. The College also has its own work-study program. Aid is awarded on a rolling basis, with a February 15 priority consideration date. The College awards aid on both a merit and a need basis.

Faculty

Professors choose Albertson College because they want to teach. All classes are taught by professors, not graduate assistants. Ninety-four percent of the 60 full-time faculty members hold the highest degree in their field. The College maintains a 12:1 student/faculty ratio. Professors are assigned as academic advisers to each entering student, and upper-division students may choose advisers from their major departments. Through periodic meetings, advisers assist students in planning programs and in maintaining progress toward graduation. Students interact with their professors on a personal level. Together, they participate in service projects, intramural basketball and volleyball teams, backpacking weekend excursions, social gatherings, and frequent meals.

Student Government

The Associated Students of Albertson College of Idaho (ASACI) is served by an Executive Council and the ASACI Senate. They oversee all student organizations, the campus newspaper, the yearbook, intramurals, Greek life, residence hall councils, student fees, and student activities. ASACI is actively involved in Board of Trustee committees and campus task forces. Students also participate in campus decision making. Residence hall governments have input in residence hall policies, common area damage assessments, and educational program funding.

Admission Requirements

Freshman applicants may begin the application process anytime after their junior year in high school. In order to be considered for admission, students should submit the application for admission, a $25 nonrefundable application fee, ACT or SAT I test scores, a guidance counselor and/or teacher evaluation, a personal statement, a transcript of any college work completed, and an official high school transcript. The high school transcript must include all work from the ninth grade to the date of application. Upon graduation, a final transcript must be submitted. GED test scores may be presented in lieu of official high school records provided the average score is at least 50 with no subscore below 45.

Transfer applicants who have already completed at least 28 semester units or 35 quarter units of continuous enrollment at accredited colleges or universities are considered for admission on the basis of their academic record (rather than the secondary school record) provided they have a cumulative GPA of 2.0 or better. Students who have completed fewer than 28 semester or 35 quarter units should apply as freshman applicants but may be granted advanced credit for that work. Transfer applicants should submit the application, a $25 nonrefundable application fee, official ACT/SAT or GED scores, a personal statement, and official transcripts from all postsecondary institutions attended. A teacher evaluation and clearance report from the last institution attended full-time are also required.

Application and Information

The first application deadline for priority consideration is February 15. Applications received by this date are given priority in admission and financial aid. Applicants who complete the application process by February 15 receive notification of the decision on or before March 1. Notification becomes rolling and based on availability for applications completed after February 15. Admitted students responding with their tuition deposit of $250 on or before May 1 are guaranteed a place in the class. The final deadline for freshman applications is June 1 and, for transfer applications, August 1. Any application submitted after these dates is considered by petition only. For more information, students should contact the Albertson College Admission Office at the address listed below.

Dennis P. Bergvall, Dean of Admission
Albertson College of Idaho
2112 Cleveland Boulevard
Caldwell, Idaho 83605

Telephone: 208-459-5305
           800-224-3246 or 800-AC-Idaho (toll-free)
Fax: 208-459-5757
E-mail: admission@acofi.edu
World Wide Web: http://www.acofi.edu

The McCain Center is the hub of campus activity; it houses a café, movie theater, game room, bookstore, and offices for student organizations.

ALBERTUS MAGNUS COLLEGE
NEW HAVEN, CONNECTICUT

The College

Founded in 1925 by the Dominican Sisters of St. Mary of the Springs, Albertus Magnus College educates men and women to become leaders in all walks of life. The College is committed to providing a liberal arts education rooted in the Dominican tradition of scholarship. Professors at Albertus strive to help their students develop in all areas; as much attention is paid to the nurturing of a student's aesthetic, physical, and moral capacities as to his or her intellectual capabilities. In 1992, the College began offering its first graduate-level course of study through the Master of Arts in Liberal Studies program. Most recently, the College has expanded its capacities on the graduate level by offering the Master of Science in Management program and the Master of Arts in Art Therapy program.

The 1,400 students who attend Albertus come from various parts of the United States, Europe, Africa, Asia, and South and Central America. The highest percentage come from Connecticut, Massachusetts, New York, and New Jersey. About 70 percent of the students live on campus in student housing that has been converted from large former estate homes. Rooms are assigned to freshmen on the basis of a questionnaire sent to the incoming class. Upperclass students choose rooms according to a lottery system. The housing program fosters a strong sense of community spirit, and students often plan parties and other social events in their residence halls. The Campus Center is a hub of student activities such as comedians, live music, contests, and other unique functions.

There are dozens of on-campus organizations. They include the intramural athletic association, a Future Business Leaders of America chapter, and numerous journalistic and creative writing options, such as *Breakwater* (literary magazine), *Prospect* (yearbook), and *Silverhorn* (newspaper). The Multicultural Student Union, a student organization composed of members of minority groups, provides compelling, diverse points of view.

The College has recently introduced Arts in Action, which offers students an opportunity to participate in the performing arts. Students may also share in the excitement of live drama through the College's professionally managed ACT 2 Theatre, providing a number of artistic, academic, and recreational possibilities. In addition, students are encouraged to become part of the New Haven community through extracurricular and volunteer activities.

The Cosgrove, Marcus, Messer Athletic Center houses an Olympic-size pool, a Jacuzzi, three racquetball courts, a weight room, dance studio, and gymnasium. In addition to this facility, there are soccer and softball fields, an outdoor track, and several tennis courts. Albertus fields intercollegiate athletic teams in baseball, basketball, cross-country, soccer, and tennis for men and basketball, cross-country, soccer, softball, tennis, and volleyball for women. Albertus's teams compete in NCAA Division III/Great Northeast Athletic Conference (GNAC).

Location

New Haven is a college town, and many activities are planned for the benefit of the students from all seven area colleges and universities. Lectures and musical performances presented by renowned figures as well as a variety of sports events draw large audiences. The city has some of the finest theaters in the country, including Long Wharf and the Yale Repertory Theater. The Yale Art Gallery, the Yale Center for British Arts and British Studies (which houses the largest collection of British materials outside England), museums, and movie theaters are equally accessible. Large shopping facilities, excellent restaurants, and several recreational areas are only a short distance from the Albertus Magnus College campus.

Through the College's system of internships for juniors and seniors, Albertus students have become increasingly involved in New Haven community life and gain valuable practical professional training. Often, internships lead to permanent positions with local area companies and corporations.

Majors and Degrees

Albertus Magnus College confers the Bachelor of Arts, Bachelor of Science, Bachelor of Fine Arts, and Associate of Arts degrees. The areas of study include accounting, art (education, history, and studio), art therapy, biology, biology-chemistry, business administration, chemistry, child care and community psychology, classical languages and literature, communications, computer science, criminal justice, drama, economics, English, finance, foreign language, general studies, graphic design, health-care management, history, humanities, human services, industrial and organizational psychology, international business, mathematics, performance arts theater, philosophy/religion, physical sciences, political science, predentistry, prelaw, premedicine, preoptometry, pre–veterinary studies, psychology, social gerontology, social science, social work, sociology, teacher preparation (K–12), urban studies, and visual and performing arts.

Academic Program

The B.A. and B.S. degrees require 120 credits for graduation, the B.F.A. requires 129 credits, and the A.A. requires 60 credits. Within these credit hours, students take core courses to fulfill broad distributional requirements and courses for the major. Students may relate academic study to work experience through a system of academically credited internships. The College's Office of Career Services, which aids students with internship placement, also helps graduating students prepare for career direction and job placement. The Academic Development Center provides personal instruction to students who need extra help with their school work. The center also caters to those students with learning disabilities. Students who show a strong academic potential may pursue a course of study through the College's honors program.

Off-Campus Arrangements

Cross-registration is available with the University of New Haven, Yale University, and Quinnipiac College. Students may take internships for college credit at various Yale University facilities or at area industries, psychological institutes, hospitals, law firms, banks, laboratories, and public and private agencies. Through a study-abroad program, students may also spend a semester or a year abroad.

Academic Facilities

Rosary Hall, the original College building, now houses a library collection of 110,000 volumes, 600 periodicals, 4,400 pieces of microfilm, and full access to the Internet. The Media Center has equipment that students may use to produce new materials as well as review older materials. Interlibrary services with the University of New Haven and Quinnipiac College are also available. Walsh Hall Science Building provides the most modern scientific equipment available for students majoring in biological and physical sciences. Aquinas Hall, the main academic building, houses the academic computer labs, which are equipped with personal computers, digital scanners, laser printers, and full Internet access. Every classroom in Aquinas Hall is laptop compatible.

Costs

The costs for the 2000-01 school year are $14,343 for tuition, $6512 for room and board, and $400 for student fees. Expenses for books, travel, and personal supplies vary.

Financial Aid

Albertus Magnus College offers a variety of merit-based scholarships to students who have achieved high academic standing in high school. The College offers the Mohun Scholarships, which award $5000 per year toward tuition, to students who attended Catholic high schools. In addition, all students may compete for the Presidential Scholarships, which award a one-third tuition reduction annually. The Valedictorian/Salutatorian scholarships award full tuition annually. Students from the New Haven area public schools may compete for the New Haven Area Scholarships, which award up to 75 percent tuition reduction annually. Transfer students of superior academic ability are eligible for a $3500 transfer scholarship. Interested students should contact the Office of Admission for the specifics of these and other scholarship awards.

Approximately 85 percent of the College's students receive financial aid in some form. The College requires that students file the Albertus Magnus College financial aid application form and the Free Application for Federal Student Aid (FAFSA) to be considered for Albertus scholarships and grants, Federal Perkins Loans, Federal Supplemental Educational Opportunity Grants, and Federal Work-Study awards. There is no specific deadline to apply for financial aid, which is awarded on a rolling basis; however, it is recommended that applicants file for aid by February 15 for priority consideration.

Faculty

Faculty members at Albertus come from leading universities of the United States and abroad and are one of the College's greatest assets. Ninety percent of the 75 full- and part-time faculty members hold a Ph.D. or the equivalent. Their primary concern is teaching, although the work of many faculty members has been published. Students find faculty members accessible for academic or personal counseling and for campus sports and activities.

Student Government

Through the Student Government Association (SGA), Albertus students have the primary responsibility for governing their own residential and social life. All full-time matriculated students are members of the SGA and, through its committees and officers, manage student government and social affairs and participate in the campus judicial system. Students serve on faculty committees, the Academic Policy Committee, and the Library Committee.

Admission Requirements

Albertus Magnus College welcomes applications from men and women of all ages, nationalities, and ethnic, cultural, racial, and religious groups. Applicants may be admitted as freshmen or as transfer, provisional, or special students.

In evaluating freshman candidates, the Office of Admission considers a student's application, counselor recommendation, high school transcript, extracurricular activities, and scores on the SAT I or ACT. Emphasis is placed on the student's record of performance rather than on the results of standardized tests. Sixteen high school units in academic subjects are required for entrance.

Transfer students are welcome at the College. They must submit high school and college records (if necessary) for evaluation in addition to the application and the recommendation.

Interviews are recommended for freshman and transfer applicants.

Application and Information

The College accepts students on a rolling admission basis for entrance. As soon as all of a candidate's admission material has been received, his or her application is considered, and notification is made as soon as a decision has been reached.

Application forms, recommendation forms, and information may be obtained by contacting:

Office of Admission
Albertus Magnus College
700 Prospect Street
New Haven, Connecticut 06511-1189
Telephone: 203-773-8501
           800-578-9160 (toll-free)
Fax: 203-773-5248
E-mail: admissions@albertus.edu
World Wide Web: http://www.albertus.edu

Beautiful Rosary Hall.

ALBION COLLEGE
ALBION, MICHIGAN

The College
"The liberal arts at work" is the theme adopted by Albion College to demonstrate the relationship between a liberal arts education in college and success in the professions after graduation. At Albion, the liberal arts will work for students who aspire to successful careers in medicine, law, teaching, business, the arts, and many other areas.

Albion College is a national liberal arts college founded in 1835 and is related to the United Methodist Church. Surveys show that Albion students enroll not only for the excellence of the academic programs but also for the high level of personal attention received from faculty members at the College. The College is accredited by the North Central Association of Colleges and Schools and was the first private college in Michigan with a Phi Beta Kappa chapter to recognize the outstanding scholarship of its students. Six academic institutes are available: the Gerald R. Ford Institute for Public Service, the Carl A. Gerstacker Liberal Arts Program in Professional Management, the Pre-Med/Allied Health Institute, the Honors Institute, the Fritz Shurmur Education Institute, and the Institute for the Study of the Environment.

Albion's 1999–2000 enrollment was 1,529 (684 men and 845 women). Approximately 90 percent of Albion's students are from Michigan; the rest come from thirty-three states and seventeen countries. Albion is a residential college and campus life is important for every student. Numerous concerts, theater productions, and art exhibits take place throughout the year. A student-run Union Board selects first-run movies, concerts, and other entertainment, and nationally known speakers and entertainers are sponsored by the Albion Performing Arts and Lecture Series. The Kellogg Center, completed in 1996, provides space for concerts and dances, meeting rooms and offices for student organizations, the college bookstore, and a snack bar. More than 100 student organizations include clubs in academic departments, student publications, a campus radio station, religious fellowship groups, the Black Student Alliance, intercollegiate and intramural athletics, and national fraternities and sororities.

Ninety-six percent of students live on campus. Residence halls, located within walking distance of other campus buildings, are coed, with separate sections for men and women. A comprehensive student services program includes a career development office that assists students in exploring career options and arranges on-campus interviews with employers and graduate schools. More than 40 percent of Albion graduates go directly to graduate or professional school each year; virtually everyone seeking immediate employment has found a position six months after graduation. Within five years of graduation, more than 75 percent of Albion alumni have enrolled for graduate work.

Location
A 1½-hour drive west of Detroit and a 3-hour drive east of Chicago, the College is located on I-94 in the small city of Albion (population 10,000). Eight other colleges and universities, including Michigan State and the University of Michigan, are located within an hour's drive. The 90-acre main campus is a few blocks from the downtown business section. Students and faculty members are very involved in community activities such as volunteer efforts and internships. The College's Student Volunteer Bureau organizes involvement with programs serving children and adults. Albion faculty members founded the all-volunteer Albion Area Ambulance Service.

Majors and Degrees
Albion College awards the Bachelor of Arts and Bachelor of Fine Arts degrees. Majors include American studies, anthropology and sociology, biology, chemistry, computer science, economics and management, English, French, geological sciences, German, history, international studies, mathematics, mathematics/economics, philosophy, physics, political science, psychology, public policy, religious studies, Spanish, speech communication and theater, and visual arts. Individually designed majors, created with faculty approval, are also offered.

Students may be certified in secondary education and for grades K–12 in art, music, and physical education. Elementary certification is offered through a four-year, on-campus program leading to a bachelor's degree and through a five-year B.A./M.S. program with Bank Street College of Education in New York City.

Preprofessional programs include business management, dentistry, law, medicine, and the ministry. Combined three-year preprofessional programs, involving three years of study at Albion and additional work at other institutions, are available in engineering, health services and nursing, natural resources management, and public policy. Students in these programs are awarded the bachelor's degree from Albion after completing one additional year of study at the participating institutions.

Academic Program
Albion expects its students to gain a broad knowledge in the arts and sciences while also developing an area of specialization. To graduate with the Bachelor of Arts degree, students must complete 31 units (124 semester hours); to earn the Bachelor of Fine Arts degree, visual arts majors must complete 34 units (136 semester hours). All students must pass a writing examination.

To introduce students to important areas of knowledge, Albion has a core curriculum requirement for study in the natural sciences and mathematics, the social sciences, the humanities, interdisciplinary studies, and the fine arts, together with additional studies in gender and ethnicity studies. The core curriculum and the requirements for a major total about one half to two thirds of a student's program at Albion. The remainder can be used for electives, to complete a second major, or for a six- to eight-course sequence in business management, computer science, human services, mass communication, public service, or women's studies. Independent study and on-the-job internships for academic credit are also available.

College credit can be obtained through Advanced Placement examinations, College-Level Examination Program (CLEP) tests, or Albion departmental examinations.

Off-Campus Arrangements
Albion College, together with the Great Lakes Colleges Association, offers off-campus study in Australia, Costa Rica, the Dominican Republic, France, Germany, Great Britain, India, Israel, Japan, Mexico, Russia, Spain, and several African countries. Semester-long programs are available in the United States through the Washington (D.C.) Center for Learning Alternatives, the New York City Arts Program, the Philadelphia Center, the Chicago Urban Life Center, the Newberry Library Program in the Humanities (Chicago), and the Oak Ridge National Laboratory (Tennessee). All arrangements are supervised by the director of off-campus programs.

Academic Facilities

Olin Hall, the $4.5-million home of the biology and psychology departments, features excellent laboratory equipment, including scanning and transmission electron microscopes. In the Stockwell/Mudd Libraries, researchers are helped by a computerized catalog of the College's book and periodical collections and by access to national databases in many different academic areas.

Other prominent campus facilities include the Herrick Center for Speech and Theatre and the 135-acre Whitehouse Nature Center, a preserve used for both science instruction and recreation. The Dow Recreation and Wellness Center offers a 1/9-mile indoor track, multipurpose court space, a swimming pool, weight-training facilities for physical education courses, intramural sports, individual conditioning, and wellness programs.

Albion students also have access to Digital Equipment Corporation VAX 4000-200 computers and to the Internet through PCs located throughout the campus. More than 500 microcomputers are available for various research activities.

Costs

Costs for the 1999–2000 academic year were $17,984 for tuition and $5220 for room and board; there were a $176 student activity fee and a $74 health fee. Laboratory fees and music lessons are additional, as are personal expenses and travel. Costs are the same for both in-state and out-of-state students.

Financial Aid

Every student admitted to Albion College will receive financial assistance if need is determined from the Free Application for Federal Student Aid (FAFSA). Families should file the FAFSA as soon as possible after January 1 so that the College receives the analysis from the federal government by February 15. For each student, Albion will build a financial aid package using federal grants and loans and College aid funds. Many Michigan residents are eligible for state scholarships and grants of more than $2000 that are reserved for people attending private colleges and universities in the state. More than 50 percent of Albion students also have jobs on campus. Students must apply for admission and be accepted before a financial aid package is prepared. Students with strong academic records are also eligible for academic scholarships. These range from a few thousand dollars to full tuition. The scholarship application deadline is February 1. Students with special talent in art, music, and theater may qualify for scholarships in these areas of up to $3000.

Faculty

Eighty-nine percent of Albion's faculty hold the doctorate or terminal degree in their field. There are 110 full-time faculty members. Courses and laboratories are taught by regular faculty members and not by graduate teaching assistants. The average class size is 19. First- and second-year courses have average enrollments of 24 students, with the exception of special First Year Experience courses, which limit enrollment to 16 students. Upper-level courses average 15 students.

Albion's faculty members are dedicated to teaching at a liberal arts college. Faculty members know their students personally and are available outside class hours for discussion and counseling. They are also active scholars and researchers, as shown by the grants that they receive from the National Science Foundation, the National Endowment for the Humanities, and many other sources.

Student Government

An elected Student Senate oversees the operation of campus organizations and disburses student activity fee funds to these groups. The Board of Trustees invites Student Senate members to sit on its committees for academic and student affairs, institutional advancement, and buildings and grounds. Student representatives also sit on the faculty's Educational Policies Committee, which reviews the College curriculum.

Admission Requirements

Albion is a selective national liberal arts college, and admission is mainly based on the applicant's academic record in high school with special attention to the college-preparatory courses completed. Standard test scores from either the ACT or SAT are also an important factor, as are personal qualifications and accomplishments outside the classroom. The College seeks a diverse enrollment without regard to race, religion, or national origin. In 1999, entering freshmen had an average GPA of 3.6, and 69 percent ranked in the top 25 percent of their high school class. The middle 50 percent of enrolled freshmen have ACT scores between 22 and 28. Prospective freshmen can take either the SAT I or ACT. These exams are not required of transfer students who have earned at least a semester of college credit. Candidates for admission are expected to be graduates of an accredited high school or preparatory school and have at least 15 acceptable credit units. Applicants should have a strong background in English, mathematics, and the laboratory and social sciences. Home-schooled applicants are reviewed on an individual basis and need to complete either the SAT I or ACT. International applicants are welcome and must have a minimum TOEFL score of 550 and submit a Declaration of Finances form to show adequate financial resources. An interview may be required. Arrangements for a personal campus visit should be made in advance in writing, by phone, or by e-mail.

Application and Information

Applicants for admission are accepted at any time, but most students apply after September 1 of their senior year in high school. Before a decision is made, applicants must submit an application form and $20 application fee (there is no fee for Web applications), high school transcripts, test score results, and recommendations. Students should submit all materials by April 1. Albion has a rolling admissions policy and responds to applicants approximately four weeks after an admissions file is complete. Albion is also a member of the Common Application and will accept applications completed on its Web site. Students who have decided that Albion College is their first choice can apply by December 1 under the Early Decision Program and will receive an admissions decision by December 15. Financial aid applicants will also receive a preliminary financial aid award. For further information, students should contact:

Albion College
611 East Porter Street
Albion, Michigan 49224

Telephone: 800-858-6770 (toll-free)
Fax: 517-629-0569
E-mail: admissions@albion.edu
World Wide Web: http://www.albion.edu

Robinson Hall.

ALBRIGHT COLLEGE
READING, PENNSYLVANIA

The College

Albright College is renowned for its openness and warmth. As one professor noted, the College's motto ought to be "excellence without attitude." For all the accomplishments of its students and faculty members, Albright is not a pretentious place. The College is an easy place for students to be heard, have an impact, and achieve their dreams.

With Albright's 1,350 students coming from twenty-six states and twenty-one foreign countries, they learn to interact with people representing a wide array of social, ethnic, cultural, and economic backgrounds. The Albright community is characterized by mutual respect, and this sense of community is evident in the diverse activities that enrich the lives of students and faculty and staff members.

More than eighty clubs and organizations enhance the life of the College, including performing arts groups, religious organizations, student government, volunteer service organizations, student publications, and political action groups. In addition, approximately 25 percent of Albright students belong to one of Albright's nationally affiliated fraternities and sororities.

Intercollegiate, intramural, and club sports are a major part of the extracurricular life at Albright. Three quarters of all students participate in some form of athletic competition. At the intercollegiate level, Albright is a member of the Middle Atlantic Conference, one of the strongest conferences in NCAA's Division III.

Albright's athletic facilities are excellent. They include the LifeSport Center, an indoor recreational gym that features four indoor basketball courts; four racquetball courts; a $1/10$-mile track; accommodations for indoor tennis, badminton, and volleyball; and baseball and softball batting cages. The 2,000-seat Bollman Center recently underwent a $400,000 renovation and is now among the finest indoor events facilities at the Division III level. The completely remodeled fitness center houses equipment to satisfy the needs of both the serious year-round athlete and the casual user. The 25-yard Albright Natatorium is one of the best swimming facilities in the conference.

Location

The College is located on a 110-acre suburban campus in Reading, Pennsylvania, a city of 80,000 in a metropolitan area of 250,000. Albright's location provides the perfect balance between the excitement of the city of Reading, with its numerous cultural opportunities, active nightlife, and renowned outlet stores, and the recreational and sporting opportunities of southeastern Pennsylvania.

Things to do in and around Reading include Ambush Paintball, shopping the "Outlet Capital of the World", the Blue Marsh Ski Area, Joe's Bistro 614, the Reading Phillies, Dorney Park and Wildwater Kingdom, the Reading Comedy Outlet, Appalachian Trail, and Maplegrove Raceway.

Albright is an hour from Philadelphia and the Pocono Mountains ski resorts, 2 hours from Baltimore, and 3 hours from New York and Washington, D.C.

Majors and Degrees

Albright offers the Bachelor of Arts (B.A.) or Bachelor of Science (B.S.) in the following majors: accounting; American civilization; art; biochemistry; biology; business administration (finance, international business, management, and marketing); chemistry; child and family studies; communications; computer science; crime and justice; economics; education (early childhood, elementary, secondary, and special); environmental science; European studies; French; history; Latin American studies; mathematics; philosophy; political science; psychobiology; psychology; religious studies; sociology (anthropology, general, applied, and family studies); Spanish; textiles and design; theater; and visual and apparel merchandising.

Combinable majors (must be combined with a major above) include anthropology, cognitive science and artificial intelligence, criminology, digital media, environmental policy, journalism, optics, physics, and women's studies.

Preprofessional programs are available in dentistry, law, medicine, and veterinary medicine.

Academic Program

Albright offers fifty programs of study, including excellent preprofessional programs, a strong honors program, special offerings such as marine science (in which students study at the Bermuda Research Station), and unique interdisciplinary majors such as psychobiology and digital media.

Albright's flexible curriculum expands students' vistas by allowing them to combine majors and design their own individual programs of study. Albright's classrooms are interactive. Students perform research side by side with Albright's faculty members. For example, classes analyze whether the Fourth Amendment has been truly put into practice in state legal cases. Students have also presented their findings at national and international symposiums.

Academic advising is a vital part of the support system provided to Albright students. Whether a student is strongly committed to a specific field of study or is unsure of a career and academic direction, the College's counseling network is designed to meet his or her needs.

Off-Campus Arrangements

Off-campus study options for Albright students include study abroad (Tel Aviv University in Israel, University of Guadalajara in Mexico, American University in France, Studio Art Centers International in Italy, and American Soviet Theatre Initiative in Russia); domestic programs (the Washington, D.C., Center; the National Theatre Institute in Connecticut; Duke University's Marine Science Lab in Beaufort, North Carolina, and Bermuda Station for Research; Fashion Institute of Technology in New York; and Humpback Whale Migration Research in Hawaii); internships at Internal Revenue Service (accounting), Bayer Corporation (chemistry), Caron Foundation (psychology), Reading Hospital and Medical Center (premed), and Macy's (apparel merchandising); and independent study programs.

Academic Facilities

Albright students and faculty members have access to outstanding teaching, research, social, and athletic facilities. The

College's newest buildings include the Center for the Arts, the LifeSports Center and Natatorium, and the Center for Computing and Mathematics, which houses the College's central computers and IBM/Macintosh computer labs. Additional computer labs are available in every academic building, and all student residence hall rooms are wired for computers for every student.

The Center for the Arts, considered a work of art, is home to the Freedman Art Gallery, Roop Recital Hall, and Meridian Theatre, as well as studios and modern facilities for instruction and exhibition of the arts.

The Gingrich Library is central to the intellectual life of the College. It contains more than 210,000 volumes and receives approximately 800 magazine and newspaper subscriptions. In addition to providing an automated catalog system and Internet access, the library is a member of a number of consortiums and online services that connect students to more than 4 million volumes. The library also houses the Holocaust Library and Resource Center.

The Merner-Pfeiffer Hall of Science contains fourteen comprehensive biology and chemistry laboratories, which include a full range of spectrophotometers, centrifuges, and chromatographs, as well as two electron microscopes.

Other academic facilities include foreign language laboratories, a satellite dish for language instruction, a greenhouse, a child-development center, and laboratories for psychological and physiological testing and research.

Costs

The comprehensive cost for the 2000–01 academic year is $26,350. This includes $19,760 for tuition, $6,040 for room and board, and $550 for fees.

Financial Aid

Albright offers numerous merit scholarships and awards in addition to generous need-based financial aid awards. The College has pledged to help families make Albright affordable.

Albright believes that high school students who have excelled academically and demonstrated leadership skills add to the quality of life at the College. For this reason, Albright offers a variety of scholarships, ranging in value from $20,000 to $50,000 for four years.

In addition, the College gives a variety of awards, ranging from $2000 to $12,000 ($500 to $3000 per year). Often, recipients of scholarships also earn one or more awards that go to members of the National Honor Society; students with special talent (art, music, theater, computer science, history, and others); class valedictorians and salutatorians; National Merit Finalists, Semifinalists, and Commended Students; outstanding students of color; HOBY alumni; and Eagle Scouts and Girl Scout Gold Award winners.

Financial aid is also awarded on the basis of demonstrated family financial need. Students who receive scholarships are also eligible for financial aid; in fact, most scholarship and award recipients also receive need-based financial aid.

Students applying for financial aid must submit the Free Application for Federal Student Aid (FAFSA) no later than March 1.

Faculty

The key factor in Albright's successful counseling services is its faculty. The College's distinguished full-time faculty numbers 77; 96 percent of the faculty members hold either the Ph.D. or terminal degree in their field of specialization. The faculty members are legendary for being available to students and for keeping their doors open.

Admission Requirements

Albright looks for students who will thrive in a close-knit, academically challenging, and extracurricularly active community of learners. Admission is primarily based on a student's academic preparation and extracurricular activities.

Applicants must submit an application, high school transcript, counselor and teacher recommendations, and SAT I or ACT scores. Freshmen applications should be received by March 1. Albright welcomes transfer and international student applicants.

Application and Information

An application and information may be obtained by contacting the College by mail, telephone, or e-mail.

Admission Office
Albright College
13th and Bern Streets
P.O. Box 15234
Reading, Pennsylvania 19612-5234
Telephone: 610-921-7512
          800-252-1856 (toll-free)
E-mail: albright@alb.edu
World Wide Web: http://www.albright.edu

Albright values each student's unique qualities.

ALDERSON–BROADDUS COLLEGE
PHILIPPI, WEST VIRGINIA

The College

Located on a mountaintop overlooking the Tygart River valley in Philippi, West Virginia, Alderson-Broaddus College is a four-year, coeducational, independent liberal arts college with a history of educational excellence and innovation. Affiliated with the American Baptist Churches, U.S.A., the College has been preparing men and women for leadership for more than 125 years. Today, more than 725 men and women from thirty-eight states and eight countries study at Alderson-Broaddus, preparing for the future with quality programs in a variety of fields.

Alderson-Broaddus emphasizes an innovative approach to quality liberal arts education. For example, the College pioneered the first undergraduate physician assistant program in the nation. With a state-of-the-art computer network in advance of most universities, the College also makes extensive computer resources available to all students and programs of study. Close student-faculty relationships and an average class size of 15 encourage involvement. Hands-on experience begins in the freshman year in all fields—from nursing to broadcasting, education to political science, biology to music. Alderson-Broaddus is accredited by the North Central Association of Colleges and Schools. The baccalaureate program in nursing is accredited by the National League for Nursing. The Physician Assistant Program is accredited by the Commission on Accreditation of Allied Health Programs (CAAHEP). The teacher education programs are accredited by the National Council for Accreditation of Teacher Education (NCATE).

More than fifty student organizations and hundreds of activities provide opportunities for recreation, personal development, and service. The A-B Battlers have a championship tradition in intercollegiate athletics that includes baseball, basketball, cross-country, and soccer for men and basketball, cross-country, softball, and volleyball for women. A wide range of intramural sports involves most of the student body. The attractions of West Virginia's unspoiled state and national parks are nearby.

The wooded 170-acre campus offers outstanding facilities, including modern academic facilities, a 7,200-watt FM radio station, an on-campus cafe, an art gallery, a bookstore, a post office, student lounges, and a sports coliseum with a pool, two gyms, a racquetball court, and a fitness center.

The College provides varied, comfortable residential options and a flexible, high-quality meal plan. There are excellent medical facilities on campus and in the surrounding area.

In addition to undergraduate degrees in various programs, Alderson-Broaddus also offers the M.S. degree for physician assistants.

Location

Located in the historic town of Philippi, West Virginia, Alderson-Broaddus enjoys a safe and secure environment and the friendly atmosphere of a college town but has easy access to wider resources. Clarksburg is 25 minutes away, Morgantown and West Virginia University, 1 hour, and Pittsburgh and Charleston, 2 hours. Alderson-Broaddus is 17 miles from I-79's Exit 115 and is accessible by nearby bus and airline service.

Majors and Degrees

The College offers programs leading to the B.A. and B.S. degrees in accounting, applied mathematics, applied music, biology, business administration, Christian studies, church music, communications, communications (mass communications track, speech track, and theater track), computer science, cytotechnology, elementary education, environmental science—biology track and chemistry track, history, literature, management information systems, marketing, medical science/physician assistant studies, medical technology, music education, nursing, ophthalmic medical technology, political science, psychology, radiography, recreation leadership, recreation leadership—therapeutic recreation track, secondary education, sociology, special education/elementary, sports medicine, and writing. Associate degrees may be obtained in business, general studies, and natural sciences.

Alderson-Broaddus also offers a diversified major in liberal arts for students who prefer not to specialize at the undergraduate level.

Preprofessional courses are available in such areas as dentistry, law, medicine, the ministry, and physical therapy.

Academic Program

The academic year consists of two 15-week semesters. Students generally take 15 to 18 semester hours each semester. In addition, the College offers a 10-week summer term.

Completion of 128 hours of study is required for graduation. Most of the degree requirements are fulfilled through on-campus study, but some majors require off-campus field work and internships for which credit is awarded. With the help of their academic advisers, students select courses to fulfill requirements for liberal studies and a major. Students may choose elective minors in such areas as business, computer science, education, recreation, and technical writing. An honors program offers academically talented students opportunities for independent scholarship and research.

Off-Campus Arrangements

In years when there is sufficient student demand, the College offers an International Studies program. Also with the proper clearance, Alderson-Broaddus students may enroll in any one of a number of overseas experiences administered by other cooperating institutions or agencies.

Certain majors require specific field or clinical internship experiences; other majors make such internships optional. Students may elect to do independent or guided, individualized study for credit in a pre-approved subject area while off campus.

Academic Facilities

The College offers modern, well-equipped facilities to support academic programs, including labs with up-to-date advanced instrumentation, a television and radio broadcast studio with public access channeling and a 7,200-watt FM station, a campuswide computer network with individual accounts for all students, a 725-seat theater, and separate facilities for the natural sciences, nursing and allied health, the humanities, the social sciences, education, athletics, and administration. The library houses more than 107,000 volumes and subscribes to more than 800 periodicals. The Hazel Ruby McQuain Research Center provides computerized, international access to current information in many fields. Wilcox Chapel is a meaningful addition to the religious life on campus and also houses the music department.

Costs

The cost of attending Alderson-Broaddus is low compared with that of most private colleges in the East. Room, board, tuition, and fees for 2000–01 are $18,990. Costs are subject to change, and the Admissions Office can provide up-to-date information.

Financial Aid

Alderson-Broaddus College has an excellent program of financial aid that includes merit, performance, and need-based grants and scholarships, loans, and college work-study. Applicants requesting financial aid are required to submit the Free Application for Federal Student Aid (FAFSA). Nearly 99 percent of all students receive some form of financial assistance.

Faculty

Alderson-Broaddus has a faculty of approximately 62 full-time members, 45 percent of whom hold terminal degrees in their fields. The student-faculty ratio is 13:1.

Student Government

A number of avenues are provided for student participation in decision making at Alderson-Broaddus. The Student Government Association consists of student officials elected by the entire student body. Students also serve on the President's Staff and in other groups responsible for determining College policy.

Admission Requirements

Alderson-Broaddus College admits qualified students of any race, color, or national or ethnic origin. There are no geographic or other quotas, although certain programs are limited to specific numbers of enrollees.

Applicants to the nursing and physician assistant programs are expected to have strong college-preparatory backgrounds with above-average grades in science, particularly in biology and chemistry. Other programs are more flexible.

Applicants are required to submit ACT or SAT I scores for admission purposes. Consequently, it is advisable to take these tests prior to enrollment, but students may take the test on campus during new-student orientation. Advanced Placement (AP) and College-Level Examination Program (CLEP) scores are accepted as additional indicators of an applicant's ability. Advanced standing may be awarded for satisfactory scores on AP or CLEP tests.

Applicants are encouraged to visit the campus and have a personal interview. Applicants to the physician assistant program are required to have a personal interview.

Alderson-Broaddus welcomes transfers from other colleges. Transfer students must submit high school and college transcripts for evaluation in addition to ACT or SAT results. Credit will be granted for all courses successfully completed at another accredited institution if the student has maintained at least a 2.0 cumulative GPA and the course work is applicable to the College's curriculum. Students with 29 or more transferable semester credit hours may not be required to submit ACT or SAT results.

Application and Information

General admission to the College is on a rolling basis. Students seeking freshman admission must submit a completed application form, a $10 nonrefundable application fee, results of the ACT or SAT, and official copies of secondary school transcripts. In addition to these materials, transfer students must submit a transfer clearance form, provided by Alderson-Broaddus College, and official transcripts from all colleges attended. Separate application requirements apply to the physician assistant program. Specific information and applicable deadlines are forwarded with application materials.

When requesting information, applicants should specify a major interest area or note that they are undecided. For additional information, students should contact:

Admissions Office
Alderson-Broaddus College
P.O. Box 2003
Philippi, West Virginia 26416
Telephone: 800-263-1549 (toll-free)
E-mail: admissions@ab.edu

Students outside of Withers-Brandon Hall on the Alderson-Broaddus campus.

ALFRED UNIVERSITY
ALFRED, NEW YORK

The University

Alfred University is a residential institution of 2,500 graduate and undergraduate students, located 70 miles south of Rochester, between the Finger Lakes region and the Allegheny Mountains in western New York State. Alfred is composed of the privately endowed Colleges of Business, Liberal Arts and Sciences, and Engineering and Professional Studies, as well as the publicly supported New York State College of Ceramics, which is composed of the School of Art and Design and the School of Ceramic Engineering and Materials Science. Alfred is noted for its superior academic quality, outstanding faculty, and commitment to student development. While privately endowed, Alfred University is host to the internationally renowned New York State College of Ceramics, which is regarded as the world leader in the field of ceramic engineering. The state of New York has identified Alfred University as one of its ten centers for advanced technology research.

The following graduate degrees are offered: Master of Arts and Doctor of Psychology in school psychology; Master of Business Administration; Master of Professional Studies in community services administration; Master of Science in Education, with concentrations in twelve different areas; Master of Science in electrical and mechanical engineering; Master of Fine Arts in ceramics, electronic integrated arts, glass, and sculpture; Master of Science in ceramic engineering, glass science, and materials science and engineering; and Doctor of Philosophy in ceramics and glass science.

One distinctive characteristic of Alfred University is the diversity of its student body. With men and women nearly equal in number, the University's 2,000 undergraduates include representatives from forty-three U.S. states and territories as well as from twenty different nations. Those from the United States come from rural, urban, and suburban neighborhoods, as well as public, parochial, and private secondary schools.

Alfred has a strong commitment to student development through residential life. Students are required to live on campus their first two years, and about 75 percent of all students reside on campus. Housing options include traditional residence halls, suites, and on-campus apartments. Alternative options such as off-campus specialty housing and fraternity or sorority houses are also available for upperclass students.

Alfred University students come from various social, cultural, and economic backgrounds, which are reflected by campus organizations such as Hillel, Women's Issues Coalition (WIC), and the African, Latino, Asian, Native American (ALANA) Team. Students participate in and support AU athletic events, which are held on Merrill Field or in McLane Center. The University schedules a variety of nationally acclaimed performers who attract students and area residents alike. Students participate in nearly 100 campus clubs and organizations, such as the American Ceramic Society, Forest People, Jazz Ensemble, Karate Club, and Ski Club.

Location

The village of Alfred is a classic college community. Local businesses cater to student and faculty needs, and the cities of Hornell and Wellsville, within 12 miles of the campus, offer additional restaurants, theaters, and recreational facilities.

Majors and Degrees

The bachelor's degree is offered in a variety of majors, and double majors, interdisciplinary majors, and dual degrees are available as well. There are also more than forty minors, ranging from astronomy to women's studies. (Programs marked * are offered through the New York State College of Ceramics.)

The College of Business offers the B.S. in accounting, health planning and management, and business administration with career emphases in business economics, entrepreneurial studies, family business, finance, international business, management, management information systems, and marketing. The College of Business is accredited by the AACSB–The International Association for Management Education.

The College of Liberal Arts and Sciences offers the B.A. in biology, chemistry, communications studies, comparative cultures, computer science, criminal justice studies, economics, elementary education, English, environmental studies, fine arts, general science, geology, gerontology, history, mathematics, modern languages (French, German, and Spanish), performing arts, philosophy, physics, political science, psychology, public administration, and sociology. Preprofessional programs are available in dentistry, law, medicine, and veterinary medicine. The Track II option permits the student, in cooperation with a team of faculty advisers, to design an individual academic program tailored to meet his or her needs.

The College of Engineering and Professional Studies offers the B.S. in athletic training, electrical engineering, and mechanical engineering.

The School of Ceramic Engineering and Materials Science awards the B.S. in ceramic engineering;* glass engineering science,* with concentrations in photonic and optical materials, electronic ceramics, bioceramics, composites and structural materials, and manufacturing; and materials science and engineering.*

The School of Art and Design confers the B.F.A. in art education,* ceramics,* electronic arts,* glass,* graphic design,* painting,* photography,* printmaking,* sculpture,* video,* and wood design.*

Academic Program

All academic programs require courses in the liberal arts and sciences; however, specific graduation requirements differ for each college and school within the University. All candidates are required to satisfy a physical education requirement through courses or proficiency examinations. To encourage students with strong ability and initiative, the University recognizes the Advanced Placement and International Baccalaureate programs. In addition, the University offers its own challenge examination program for currently enrolled students. The University Honors Program is open to all majors and requires an additional essay application for admission to the program. Army ROTC is also available.

Off-Campus Arrangements

A significant number of Alfred University students study abroad in countries such as France, Germany, Great Britain, and Switzerland through University programs or programs maintained by other universities. Additional off-campus programs include the Washington Semester with American University and the United Nations Semester with Drew University. Students also participate in numerous cooperative education and internship experiences.

Academic Facilities

Herrick Memorial Library and Scholes Library of Ceramics house 330,000 volumes, 60,000 government documents, 154,000 slides, and 1,000 journal subscriptions, with access to an additional 3,000 journals through Internet workstations. Three campus buildings are devoted to engineering and contain some of the most complete facilities in the world, including a radioisotope lab, petrographic and metallographic labs, five electron microscopes, and a glass drawing tower. The Science Center features a genetic engineering laboratory, and the Stull Observatory houses seven principle telescopes and is considered one of the finest teaching facilities in the country.

Harder Hall is a multimillion-dollar fine arts facility that features studio space for all media, the most extensive kiln facility in the nation (thirty-eight indoor and outdoor kilns), two galleries, and Holmes auditorium. The Miller Performing Arts Center houses a flexible theater with state-of-the-art sound and lighting equipment, individual and group rehearsal rooms, and acting and dance studios.

The campus is fully wired with switched 100-mbit Ethernet network access in every residence hall room, classroom, and office. The student-computer ratio is 7:1, with a wide range of computer access options, including open computer labs in residence halls, libraries, and academic buildings and a laptop-lending program. Connection to the Internet is through a T-1 line, and all Internet services (including e-mail) are provided at no additional charge. The Helpdesk facility provides service-oriented support for technology needs.

Costs

Private-sector (Colleges of Business, Engineering and Professional Studies, and Liberal Arts and Sciences) tuition and fees for freshmen entering in fall 1999 were $19,074. For the 1999–2000 academic year, tuition and fees for the New York State College of Ceramics (Schools of Art and Design and Ceramic Engineering and Materials Science) were $9448 for in-state students and $12,808 for out-of-state students. Room and board for all students in 1999–2000 were $7174.

Financial Aid

During the 1999–2000 academic year, University-funded aid sources provided more than $16 million to undergraduate students. For private-sector programs, 95 percent of freshmen received some form of financial assistance. In the New York State College of Ceramics, 88 percent of freshmen received some form of aid. Aid administered by the University usually consists of a combination of scholarships or grants-in-aid, loans, and part-time work. Students may be eligible for financial assistance under the Federal Pell Grant, Federal Supplemental Educational Opportunity Grant, Federal Perkins Loan, and Federal Work-Study programs. New York State residents may be eligible for aid under the Tuition Assistance Program. The University sponsors National Merit Scholarships, departmental talent awards, Presidential, Southern Tier, transfer scholarships, and the Johnathan Allen Award for Leadership.

Faculty

There are 164 full-time faculty members; 88 percent of the teaching faculty hold the doctorate or highest degree in their field. While the faculty are actively involved in research or other scholarly activities, the education at Alfred is classroom oriented. The average class size is 18, and the ratio of faculty to students is 1:12. Courses are taught by faculty members, not teaching assistants. All faculty members serve as academic advisers, and students who need special help find their instructors accessible and responsive.

Student Government

The Student Senate has elected officials, receives an annual appropriation, and disburses funds to other campus organizations to finance their activities. It also elects student representatives to various University and college committees and sponsors a leadership seminar.

Admission Requirements

Candidates for admission are required to complete a college-preparatory program of 16 academic units or provide evidence of an equivalent education. The 16 units should include 4 in English, 2–3 in social studies and history, 2–3 in mathematics, and 2–3 in laboratory science. The remaining units are usually completed in a foreign language or in any of the aforementioned fields. Specific requirements of the colleges within the University vary. Admissions criteria include secondary school record, cumulative average, class rank, recommendations from guidance counselors or teachers, and SAT I or ACT scores. The SAT II: Writing Test is recommended for placement purposes. Personal accomplishments and extracurricular activities are also reviewed before a final decision is made regarding each candidate. An on-campus interview is highly recommended.

The Opportunity Programs at Alfred are a blend between the privately endowed colleges of Alfred (through the HEOP program) and the New York State College of Ceramics (through the EOP program). These programs enable students whose economic and educational circumstances have placed limitations on their opportunities to further their education.

Application and Information

Candidates must submit a completed Alfred University application form or the Common Application form, SAT I or ACT results, a letter of recommendation, and a $40 application fee. Students who visit campus receive an application fee waiver certificate that may be used on that day or at a later time. They must also have their high school guidance office send a copy of their transcript. Applicants to the School of Art and Design must submit a portfolio of their work, normally fifteen to twenty slides. The application and portfolio deadline under the early decision plan is December 1, with notification by December 15. The application and portfolio deadline for regular admission is February 1, with notification by mid-March. Transfer applicants should file an application by August 1 for September admission or December 1 for January admission. The School of Art and Design has different application and portfolio deadlines for transfer students, dependent upon the student's previous course work in art. Students should contact the Office of Admissions for further information regarding these deadlines.

Applications and inquiries should be addressed to:

Katherine McCarthy
Director of Admissions
Alumni Hall
Alfred University
Saxon Drive
Alfred, New York 14802
Telephone: 607-871-2115
           800-541-9229 (toll-free)
Fax: 607-871-2198
E-mail: admwww@alfred.edu
World Wide Web: http://www.alfred.edu

ALLEGHENY COLLEGE
MEADVILLE, PENNSYLVANIA

The College

Founded on America's western frontier in 1815, Allegheny is a classical, selective college of the liberal arts and sciences. Although highly regarded as a preprofessional school, its impact on students goes well beyond preparation for careers. Allegheny not only develops in its students such essential skills as writing, critical thinking, and problem solving, but also fosters a capacity for lifelong learning, the ability to manage everyday affairs, responsible citizenship, social skills, and values. While nonsectarian in outlook and practice, Allegheny has been affiliated with the United Methodist Church since 1833.

The 1,800 students come from forty states and fifteen other countries. Eight percent are members of minority groups and three fourths reside on campus. On-campus residence is required of freshmen and sophomores and optional for other students, but it is guaranteed for all four years for all who seek it. Faculty members describe Allegheny students as active and hardworking. Approximately 70 percent come from the highest fifth of their high school class, 1 in 3 was president of a student organization, and 70 percent were active in volunteer service groups. At Allegheny, students sustain more than 100 clubs, committees, and organizations in drama, dance, vocal and instrumental music, publications, radio, religious life, politics, social service, professional and multicultural interest areas, and the governance of student life. Intramural athletics involve three fourths of the students, and the varsity program is one of the best in NCAA Division III. Of the twenty teams for men and women, about half are nationally ranked each year.

Location

Located in Meadville, Pennsylvania (population 14,000), in the picturesque rolling foothills of the Allegheny Mountains, the College takes advantage of the enormous variety of recreational opportunities in the area. The students use the shopping, entertainment, and restaurant facilities in the city, and most are actively involved in volunteer work with community service organizations such as Habitat for Humanity.

Students also enjoy the many advantages of Pittsburgh and Cleveland, both 90 miles from Meadville. These and other cities are easily accessible by several interstate highways. Erie International Airport is 40 miles away by interstate highway, and Meadville is served by bus.

Majors and Degrees

Departmental majors leading to Bachelor of Arts or Bachelor of Science degrees are offered in applied computing, art (studio or history), art and technology, biology, chemistry, communication arts, computer science, economics, English, environmental geology, environmental science, environmental studies, French, geology, German, history, international studies, mathematics, music, neuroscience, philosophy, physics, political science, psychology, religious studies, Spanish, theater, and women's studies. Preprofessional programs are offered in dentistry, law, medicine, and veterinary medicine.

Students also may design their own majors, combining various departmental and divisional courses into a variety of comprehensive, coherent programs. In recent years, such majors have included American and Asian studies, arts administration, and communication design.

The College offers cooperative 3-2 liberal arts/professional programs in engineering with Case Western Reserve University, Columbia University, Duke University, the University of Pittsburgh, and Washington University. There is a 3-1 program with the University of Rochester that leads to a bachelor's degree from Allegheny and certification in medical technology, while a 3-4 program in nursing leads to a doctorate from Case Western Reserve. Teachers are certified at the elementary and secondary levels through a summer cooperative program with Chatham College.

Academic Program

Allegheny ensures that students develop wholeness across the divisions of knowledge (arts and humanities, social sciences, and natural sciences) as well as expertise in one or more fields. Each student must complete 131 semester credit hours; the major may require 32 to 48 semester credit hours, including a junior seminar and the distinctive Senior Project, while the remainder are electives and Liberal Studies Program courses. The innovative Liberal Studies Program includes two freshman seminars, with strong advising and writing components; a sophomore writing and speaking course; and some in-depth study in a subject outside the division of the major. Writing proficiency is emphasized throughout the Allegheny years—it is a central objective of the seminars. It is developed further in the sophomore writing course, after students have mastered some college-level material, and it must be demonstrated in all other courses.

The independent study option allows students to pursue an interest not included in the formal College curriculum. Through this option, each student designs a course program, with the agreement of a faculty adviser, to be completed on or off campus.

Every freshman is assigned both a student adviser and a faculty adviser (the latter teaches the first freshman seminar); students may choose a different adviser in later years. Entering students who have no commitment to a major field are encouraged to use the first two years to investigate the offerings of various departments. They also are offered special advising to help them identify a major by the start of the junior year.

Off-Campus Arrangements

In cooperation with other colleges and universities, the College offers a number of credit-carrying study opportunities to augment the Allegheny student's educational experience. Among these are the Washington Semester with American University in Washington, D.C.; Boston University's programs in Australia, Ecuador, France, and Niger; study in sustainable development in Costa Rica; and the marine sciences semester at Duke University. Allegheny sponsors the Seville Program in Spain, the Allegheny in Cologne program in Germany, and student exchanges with the University of Natal in South Africa, the University of Sheffield in England, and a number of institutions in the Commonwealth of Independent States. Study abroad is also individually arranged and has recently taken students to Austria, Colombia, Greece, New Zealand, Sweden, and Switzerland.

An extensive array of undergraduate internships enables students to relate their academic preparation to associated career areas, often while earning college credit. The Allegheny

College Center for Experiential Learning (ACCEL), established in 1998, uniquely coordinates student access to "real life" opportunities, including internships, off-campus study, service-learning, and leadership development programs.

Academic Facilities

The library currently has a collection of 420,000 bound volumes, 227,000 titles on microform, 1,000 periodicals, and 261,000 U.S. government and Pennsylvania state documents. The library also houses noteworthy Americana and Ida Tarbell collections. A computer laboratory, an audiovisual center, and a forty-eight-station music listening system are in the main library as well.

In academic computing, for which there are no charges, more than 200 PCs are networked and available for students' use in all disciplines 24 hours a day. All residence hall rooms provide direct access to the Internet and the campus network for students with their own computers. College facilities also include a 283-acre environmental research reserve, an observatory and planetarium, a state-of-the-art television studio, and the Bowman, Penelec & Megahan Art Galleries. Two science buildings serve as national models, and a $13-million sport and fitness center opened in 1997.

Costs

For 2000–01, tuition at Allegheny is $21,290, an inclusive fee that covers health service, activities and laboratory charges, and all extra charges except those for private instruction in music. The annual fee for room and board is $5100. Several payment plans are available.

Financial Aid

A large number of merit-based scholarships are awarded annually, making the College more affordable even to families who do not qualify for need-based financial aid. Also, scholarships, grants, loans, and campus employment are awarded to students who need assistance to meet College expenses. The Free Application for Federal Student Aid (FAFSA), which establishes an applicant's eligibility for virtually all institutional, state, and federal assistance, must be submitted by February 15. Notices about the receipt of financial aid are sent to students shortly after their acceptance by the College. Nine out of ten students receive some form of financial aid.

Faculty

Allegheny's faculty is deeply committed to teaching, advising, and working closely with students. Ninety-four percent of the 140 full-time members hold terminal degrees in their respective fields, and there is a balance between highly experienced teachers and younger faculty members. All are active and highly regarded in their disciplines. The faculty includes authors of scholarly books (such as *Congressional Women* and *Comedy from Shakespeare to Sheridan*), research scientists, and performing artists.

Student Government

Through Allegheny Student Government (ASG), undergraduates assume an active role in formulating College policy, developing curricular changes and improvements, governing their personal conduct, organizing and promoting cultural programs, and implementing the social calendar. Through its administration of the student activity fee, ASG serves as coordinator of most campus activities. Nearly all committees of the faculty include students, so that the student point of view can be represented in the governance of the College.

Admission Requirements

The College actively seeks an academically able, geographically diverse, and ethnically varied student body that possesses a broad distribution of special talents and individual experiences. This heterogeneous mix of freshmen and transfer students enriches the learning process for all students, both in and out of the classroom setting.

In the selection process, all information available on each applicant is carefully considered, and the College places more importance on performance in school than on standardized test scores or other criteria. Candidates for admission should follow a college-preparatory program in high school that includes four solid or major subjects, such as English, social studies, math, science, and foreign language, each year. Either the SAT I or ACT must be taken by December of the final year of high school.

Early decision, early admission, deferred entrance, and advanced standing programs are offered. Personal interviews are strongly encouraged. Transfer students are admitted both semesters.

Application and Information

The application for admission should be submitted by February 15 (January 15 for early decision), and the SAT I or ACT results should be forwarded to the College by each candidate. Applicants for early decision are notified on a rolling basis through January 31. Regular applicants are informed of the admission decision by April 1.

Office of Admissions
Allegheny College
Meadville, Pennsylvania 16335-3902
Telephone: 814-332-4351
              800-521-5293 (toll-free)
E-mail: admiss@admin.alleg.edu
World Wide Web: http://www.alleg.edu

Bentley Hall, completed in 1820 and still the main administration building.

ALMA COLLEGE
ALMA, MICHIGAN

The College

Regarded as one of the nation's best liberal arts colleges, Alma College is in its second century of superior education and professional distinction. Founded by Presbyterians in 1886, Alma remains a private liberal arts institution committed to a values-oriented style of education. In a time when many professionals find that their technical training is already out of date, Alma's graduates are entering the job market with an education that will always serve them. Alma's academic philosophy, rooted in the liberal arts tradition and providing a broad educational base with flexible, innovative course work, has earned Alma a Phi Beta Kappa chapter. Classes are small—the average size is 20—enabling students to do more than just listen. Students enjoy the rigorous academic atmosphere; 81 percent of the faculty members hold the highest degree in their field.

In fall 1999, Alma College enrolled a total of 1,383 students (589 men and 794 women), of whom 1,337 were full-time. Alma's students are high achievers from the upper ranks of some of the best high schools in Michigan and its surrounding states. Current students come from nineteen states and twelve countries. Entering freshmen have an average high school GPA of 3.60; their mean ACT composite score of 24.9 is approximately equivalent to a combined SAT I score of 1140. More than three fourths of the freshmen enrolled in 1999 ranked in the top 25 percent of their high school class; 37 percent ranked in the top 10 percent. Nearly all of Alma's students live on campus. Housing units vary in size, accommodating from 10 to 200 students each. Single rooms, double-occupancy rooms, and 4-person suites are available. There are no all-freshman dormitories because the College believes that the interaction between freshmen and upperclass students is important. Each housing unit is supervised by a full-time director, who is assisted by student staff members.

The lifestyle that Alma students enjoy combines residential life with academic challenges. Flexible academic programs enable students to get involved in their favorite activities and to develop new interests. With more than 100 student organizations to choose from, students have the chance to put their talents to work. Organizations and activities include eighteen varsity athletic teams for men and women, the Student Congress, vocal and instrumental performing groups, symphony orchestra, national fraternities and sororities, theater and dance groups, intramural sports, the yearbook, the newspaper, and many more. Students enjoy Alma's outdoor athletic complex, which features a multipurpose playing field of artificial turf, baseball and softball fields, tennis courts, an eight-lane track, and soccer fields. Even as students have fun, they develop valuable skills for their future. The Hamilton Dining Commons and downtown shops are a short walk from the main academic area on campus.

Location

Easily reached from Chicago, Detroit, Indianapolis, Milwaukee, Cleveland, and Cincinnati, Alma College is located in the heart of Michigan's lower peninsula. The city of Alma (population of about 10,000) is well-known as Scotland, USA, for its annual Highland Festival. Alma's relaxed, safe, small-town atmosphere enables students to concentrate on educational priorities, while both the metropolitan and recreational areas of Michigan are readily accessible. Tri Cities and Lansing airports are nearby.

Majors and Degrees

Alma offers four degrees: Bachelor of Arts, Bachelor of Fine Arts, Bachelor of Music, and Bachelor of Science. Departmental and interdepartmental majors are possible. Majors include art and design, biochemistry, biology, business administration, chemistry, communication, computer and information systems management, computer science, economics, education, English, exercise and health science, foreign service, French, German, history, international business, mathematics, music, philosophy, physics, political science, psychology, public service, religious studies, sociology, Spanish, and theater and dance. Interdisciplinary majors may be designed in such fields as environmental studies, foreign service, gerontology, medical illustration, public health, and women's studies. Preprofessional programs prepare students for further study and careers in dentistry, engineering, law, medicine, the ministry, and occupational therapy. Academic minors are available in American studies, art history, Christian education, cognitive science, environmental studies, gerontology, public health, women's studies, and many other fields.

Alma College offers cooperative 3-2 and 4-2 pre-engineering programs with the University of Michigan School of Engineering, Michigan Technological University, and Washington University in St. Louis. A 3-2 program in occupational therapy is offered in conjunction with Washington University in St. Louis.

Academic Program

The College operates on a 4-4-1 calendar—two 4-month terms in the fall and winter and one 1-month term in the spring. During the spring term, there are opportunities for international study as well as for on-campus instruction and research. In keeping with Alma's philosophy of educating the whole person, the College requires that all students complete liberal arts courses spanning the humanities, the natural sciences, and the social sciences. The B.A. and B.S. degree programs require the completion of 136 credits; the B.F.A. and B.M. degree programs, 148 credits.

Highly qualified students are challenged by Alma's honors program, featuring a specially designed freshman course that explores the methods of communication used in the liberal arts disciplines. The honors concept extends throughout the four years at Alma.

Alma accepts credits earned through the Advanced Placement (AP) Program, the College-Level Examination Program (CLEP), the International Baccalaureate Diploma (I.B.) program, and examinations designed by Alma's academic departments.

Off-Campus Arrangements

Numerous opportunities for international study are available through the College, including offerings in Australia, Austria, England, France, Germany, India, Japan, Mexico, Scotland, and Spain. A wide variety of options for housing, including placements in private homes, are featured. Alma's Program of Studies in France, a cooperative venture with the prestigious Alliance Française in Paris, can accommodate any student from beginner to advanced for periods of time from one month to one year. This program currently attracts students from more than 100 U.S. colleges and universities (including Cornell, Duke, Harvard, and Stanford) and is the largest American program for undergraduates in Paris. Students considering careers in international business may enroll in an international marketing or multinational business administration seminar held in Wollongong, Australia. Here, along with an Alma faculty member, students visit Pacific Rim corporations while investigating financial, management, and marketing techniques. During the spring term, more than 400 courses are available through Alma's membership in the May Term Consortium. Internships provide Alma students with experience related to their educational or career goals. On-the-job experience may be arranged in many fields through work in businesses, industries, and government and community agencies.

Academic Facilities

Twenty-four main buildings with up-to-date facilities and an outdoor sports complex are arranged around a scenic central mall on Alma's 100-acre campus. It is a short walk to the fully automated library, which houses more than 230,400 volumes. The Dow and Kapp Science Centers provide research and instructional facilities for biology, biochemistry, chemistry, and physics. Swanson Academic Center houses classrooms and faculty offices. The Eddy Music Building, Clack Art Center, and Heritage Center for the Performing Arts offer rehearsal, exhibition, and performance space for art and design, music, theater, and dance. The Colina Library Wing opened in 1996, and the McIntyre Center for Exercise and Health Science opened in 1998.

Instruction at Alma is supported by computer technology. In 1998, Alma launched a three-year technology emphasis to enhance the College's infrastructure, equipment, and faculty/student training. Students are encouraged to bring their own computers to campus to best utilize available services. Access to the Internet, the campus network, the library, e-mail, and a variety of printers is available in all of Alma's eight residence halls. A user fee is charged for residence hall room hookups. Student computer labs in academic departments throughout the campus provide access to Macintosh and IBM-compatible PC systems as well as Sun SPARCstations and Silicon Graphics UNIX systems. Computer classrooms in the library and Swanson Academic Center are staffed by student assistants.

Costs

Tuition for 2000–01 is $15,734. Room and board costs for the fall and winter terms total $5726. Students who attend during the spring term pay a $141 tuition charge and a $393 board charge but no room charge. A student activity fee of $144 is charged each year, and a charge of $218 for the Preterm is added to freshman-year costs. Books, supplies, and personal expenses (including travel, clothing, and entertainment) are estimated at $2100 a year.

Financial Aid

At Alma, students can achieve scholarship recognition regardless of need on the basis of outstanding scholastic achievement. Several academically competitive scholarship programs provide awards for eligible students, including a full tuition scholarship for National Merit Finalists. The College also offers performance scholarships in recognition of individual talent, as well as grants, loans, and deferred-payment plans. Up to 400 campus and community jobs are filled by Alma students yearly. To apply for aid, students are required only to file the Free Application for Federal Student Aid (FAFSA) in January of the year of prospective enrollment at Alma.

Faculty

A look at Alma's faculty shows a diversity of backgrounds; 81 percent of the 90 full-time faculty members hold the highest degree in their field. Superior undergraduate teaching is the first priority of Alma's faculty members; no graduate students teach classes, nor are there television lecture courses at Alma. Classes at Alma are small; the faculty-student ratio is 1:14.6. Faculty members are accessible and willing to assist students. They are also recognized as scholars in their fields; their research has been supported by such organizations as the Michigan Council for the Arts, the National Science Foundation, the Council for the International Exchange of Scholars (Fulbright scholarships), and the National Endowment for the Humanities.

Student Government

Alma encourages students to build leadership skills through involvement in student government and campus organizations. Members of the Alma College Student Congress represent all major student organizations as well as individual students. This group works as a liaison with the administration to implement or revise campus policies, develop a budget and coordinate the expenditure of student activity fees, manage the campus radio station and student publications, and resolve problems. Alma's Union Board, composed of students representing each residence hall, oversees most of the regular entertainment scheduled on campus. As a residential campus, Alma is governed by rules prohibiting academic dishonesty, gambling, cohabitation, infringements on others' rights, illegal use of alcoholic beverages and drugs, and damage to personal property.

Admission Requirements

To be considered for admission, applicants should have an average of B or higher in high school and a composite score of 22 or higher on the ACT or a combined score of 1030 or higher on the SAT I. All applicants are encouraged to schedule an admission interview on campus. Transfer students must have earned an average of B or higher at their previous college. No more than 62 semester hours or 90 quarter hours of course work completed with a grade of C or better may be transferred to Alma. International students are asked to submit records of previous schooling and must show competence in English through the Test of English as a Foreign Language (TOEFL).

Application and Information

Students may apply at any time after completing their junior year of high school. Freshman applicants should send the completed application for admission along with a $20 nonrefundable application fee, high school transcripts, and ACT or SAT I scores. Students are required to submit a recommendation from their high school guidance counselor. Early decision applications are due by November 1. Transfer students should submit transcripts from all colleges and high schools attended, the completed application for admission, a $20 nonrefundable application fee, a financial aid transcript, and a Transfer Recommendation Form from the last college attended. Applications are handled on a rolling basis; students should hear about admission decisions within three weeks after sending an application and records. Alma College's nondiscrimination policy includes age, color, creed, gender, national origin, physical ability, race, religion, and sexual orientation.

All records and forms should be mailed to:
Admissions Office
Alma College
614 West Superior Street
Alma, Michigan 48801-1599

Telephone: 800-321-ALMA (toll-free)
E-mail: admissions@alma.edu
World Wide Web: http://www.alma.edu
   http://www.alma.edu/admissions/application.htm (to apply)

ALVERNIA COLLEGE
READING, PENNSYLVANIA

The College

Alvernia College is a Catholic liberal arts college of 1,500 men and women that stresses the development of the whole person—academically, emotionally, and spiritually. With a student-faculty ratio of 14:1, Alvernia offers a personalized environment where the faculty knows and cares about each student. Located on a beautiful 80-acre campus on the outskirts of Reading, Alvernia offers a setting conducive to learning and is conveniently accessible. It is chartered by the commonwealth of Pennsylvania, fully accredited by the Middle States Association of Colleges and Schools, and sponsored by the Bernardine Franciscan Sisters.

Alvernia participates in a full range of intercollegiate sports, including baseball, basketball, cross-country, field hockey, golf, lacrosse, soccer, softball, tennis, and volleyball. The College is a member of the NCAA Division III, the ECAC, and the Pennsylvania Athletic Conference.

Student organizations include the American Chemistry Society, Athletic Association, Campus Ministry, Chorale, Foreign Language Club, Intercultural Club, Journalism Club, Math Club, Phi Beta Lambda, Science Club, Sigma Tau Delta, and Student Government Association. Formal and informal dances, formal and buffet dinners, informal club socials, picnics, parties, coffeehouses, and student entertainment all provide occasions for social development and friendly relationships. Resident students live in a coed dorm that has spacious rooms and several student lounges or in town houses for upperclassmen. A student center, used by both resident and commuting students, provides excellent study and recreational facilities. A new campus center and a new residence hall opened in fall 1999.

Alvernia College's student body consists of people of all ages and walks of life. Alvernia offers both a traditional course schedule and a year-round continuing education program designed to give working adults the opportunity to earn a degree in fewer than four years. In addition, courses are offered on Saturday, in the summer, and in the evening under the traditional semester schedule. Alvernia College also offers graduate programs leading to the Master in Education and the Master in Business Administration.

Location

Alvernia College is located 3 miles from the center of the city of Reading, in the scenic Blue Mountain area of eastern Pennsylvania. Its campus overlooks Angelica Lake, noted for its rustic beauty. The College has easy access to the metropolitan areas of New York, Philadelphia, and Harrisburg, where students can take advantage of the cultural, historical, and educational attractions these cities have to offer.

Majors and Degrees

Alvernia College offers the Bachelor of Arts, Bachelor of Science, Bachelor of Science in Nursing, and Associate in Science degrees. Bachelor of Arts or Bachelor of Science candidates can major in the following baccalaureate degree areas: accounting, addiction studies, athletic training, biochemistry, biology, biology/medical technology, chemistry, chemistry/medical technology, communication, computer information systems, criminal justice administration, education (early childhood, elementary, and secondary, with major areas in biology, chemistry, English, general science, mathematics, and social studies), English, forensic science, general science, health services management, history, liberal studies, management, mathematics, nursing, occupational therapy, philosophy/theology, political science, psychology, social work, and sports management. Students can take double majors in areas that are closely related.

Associate degree programs are available in accounting, nursing, personnel management, and physical therapist assistant studies.

Academic Program

The academic program is designed to help students to think logically and critically, to comprehend accurately, and to communicate effectively. The College concentrates on the personal development of its students by fostering academic integrity, social responsibility, and moral values. The educational program is based on a commitment to develop the whole person into a responsible individual. Therefore, students not only are required to demonstrate proficiency in those skills demanded by their chosen professional concentration but also are expected to take advantage of the opportunity to grow intellectually and spiritually and to be responsible to themselves and to society.

Alvernia offers an honors program designed to prepare students for graduate school. The course focuses on a current topic for study and discussion. During their junior year, students will choose a topic for their thesis, which they will present and defend.

To earn a bachelor's degree, students must complete a minimum of 124 credits, with 54 credits in the liberal arts, 40 in the major, and 30 in electives, although these requirements may vary according to the major program. Students must earn 68 credits in nursing or 68 credits in the physical therapist assistant program to be awarded the Associate in Science degree.

Academic Facilities

Alvernia opened a library facility in 1991 that can hold more than 100,000 volumes, including reference works, books for general circulation, and bound periodicals. The library currently subscribes to 850 periodicals covering all areas of study taught at the College, and more than 1,440 volumes of back issues are in the microfilm collection. The library also houses the Audio-Visual Center, which has 23,000 pieces of audiovisual material, including more than 4,750 music records and scores. The science building houses several modern laboratories for science majors and research facilities for psychology majors. Alvernia also has an art studio.

Costs

For 2000–01, the basic tuition fee is $12,950; room and board are $5800.

Financial Aid

More than 85 percent of the students attending Alvernia receive some type of financial aid. The types of aid most commonly received are Pennsylvania Higher Education Assistance Agency grants for Pennsylvania residents, Federal Pell Grants, and numerous scholarships from private sources, as well as grants and scholarships from the College itself. This aid is awarded on the basis of academic performance and financial need. The deadline for application for Alvernia College aid is April 1. In addition, Alvernia participates in the federally funded Federal Work-Study Program. Student loans are also available.

Faculty

The faculty consists of 58 full-time and 78 part-time members, each dedicated to teaching and serving the needs of every student. The faculty is as diversified as the many fields of interest that its members represent. For example, the criminal justice administration program and the addiction studies program employ adjunct faculty members who possess expertise in their professional areas in addition to excellent educational credentials. The use of such faculty members is intended to enhance the theoretical portions of professional training with practical professional knowledge.

Student Government

The Student Government strives to promote responsible student action and to serve as a link between students, administration, and faculty. It is composed of a president, vice president, secretary, treasurer, and chief justice elected by the student body and is augmented by 2 representatives from each class.

Admission Requirements

Admission requirements normally include a high school diploma with 16 Carnegie units in the following subjects: English, 4 units; mathematics, 2 units; science, 2 units; social studies, 2 units; and modern languages, 2 units. The remaining units may be made up of academic electives. The College is willing to consider good students whose preparation does not include all of these subjects. Nursing students must fulfill the admission requirements established by the Pennsylvania State Board of Nurse Examiners. The State High School Equivalency Diploma is generally recognized as fulfilling the minimum entrance requirements. Applicants to the freshman class are required to take the SAT I; the ACT is also acceptable. Outstanding candidates will be considered for entrance to Alvernia at the end of their junior year of high school on the basis of requests made by the candidate and the high school. With the approval of their school officials, students may also be admitted to certain courses during their senior year in high school, simultaneously earning credit toward the high school diploma and a college degree.

Application and Information

Applicants should submit an application for admission and enclose the nonrefundable $25 processing fee. The application form may be obtained from the Admissions Office. Applicants should have an official copy of their high school record sent to the Admissions Office, along with the results of the SAT I or ACT.

A personal interview, while not required, is often desirable for the prospective student. All interested students and their families are invited to visit the College for a tour of the campus and a personal interview with a member of the Admissions Office staff. It is advisable to make an appointment by mail or phone at least one week in advance. The College reserves the right to request an interview if certain aspects of an application need clarification.

Because the College has a rolling admission policy, an applicant is notified of acceptance by the director of admissions shortly after the necessary credentials are on file and have been reviewed, generally within one month of the time an application has been completed. To reserve a place in the freshman class, all students must make a $100 deposit by May 1. An additional $200 deposit is required of all resident students to reserve housing. These deposits are credited to the student's account for the first semester but are not refunded if the student fails to attend the College. All full-time students are required to return a medical history/health form to the health center. Residents need to submit this form before moving into the residence hall. Transfer students should have a grade point average of 2.0 or higher on a 4.0 scale and should be aware that only grades of C or better are eligible for credit transfer. Alvernia will accept a maximum of 70 transfer credits; the remaining 30 required for graduation must be earned at Alvernia and must satisfy all graduation requirements. A detailed analysis of credits to be transferred is done only after students have been accepted by the College. For more information or to schedule a visit, students should contact:

Director of Admissions
Alvernia College
Reading, Pennsylvania 19607
Telephone: 610-796-8220
          888-ALVERNIA (toll-free)
Fax: 610-796-8336
World Wide Web: http://www.alvernia.edu

Friends gather near the Franco Library on the beautiful campus of Alvernia College.

ALVERNO COLLEGE
MILWAUKEE, WISCONSIN

The College

Alverno is a fully accredited four-year liberal arts college with a century-old tradition of enabling women to assume leadership in professional fields. Founded by the School Sisters of St. Francis, the College seeks a diverse student body and welcomes students of all religious, racial, ethnic, and cultural backgrounds from all geographic areas. There are currently 1,878 students enrolled.

Alverno's primary aim is the individual development of each student. Education must not only acquaint a person with the history and wisdom of the past but must also develop her ability to operate effectively in a changing world. The capacity to see and think from a variety of perspectives, to weigh evidence and to formulate sound conclusions, to apply creative solutions to complex problems—these are the abilities that today's woman needs for effective management of her personal and professional life.

Career development is fully integrated into the Alverno curriculum. Beginning with required freshman seminars and continuing with credit-bearing courses in the majors, students develop career-planning skills for their lifetime. They participate in informational interviews, internships, resume workshops, and personal career exploration using the resources of Alverno's Career Lab. This approach to career development accounts for the fact that within one year of graduation, 94 percent of Alverno alumnae are employed in jobs directly related to their course of study.

Students take advantage of social and athletic activities on and off campus. Intercollegiate sports include basketball and volleyball. Club soccer and a fitness center are also available on campus. Alverno's student activities center, the Pipeline, is a gathering place with food, entertainment, and a variety of activities. Instrumental, theatrical, and choral groups provide creative outlets for students with interest and talents in these areas. There are more than two dozen student organizations and interest groups, including award-winning chapters of the Association of Women in Communication and Students in Free Enterprise (SIFE).

Location

Alverno's 40-acre campus is located in a residential area on the south side of Milwaukee, with easy access to recreational opportunities and entertainment. The College is 15 minutes from downtown Milwaukee, which has outstanding facilities, including the Marcus Center for the Performing Arts, museums, theaters, galleries, shopping malls, and some of the country's finest ethnic restaurants. The city sponsors major cultural, athletic, and civic events that provide an additional educational and recreational dimension for students.

Cooperative programs with business, industry, and special interest groups within the community give each student a variety of learning experiences off campus and enable her to make a contribution through service projects in her areas of interest.

Majors and Degrees

Alverno College confers the Bachelor of Arts degree with major areas of concentration in art, art education, art therapy, biology, business and management, chemistry, English, environmental science, history, international business, management accounting, mathematics, philosophy, professional communication, psychology, religious studies, and social science; the Bachelor of Music degree with major areas of concentration in music, music education, music performance/pedagogy, and music therapy; and the Bachelor of Science degree with major areas of concentration in elementary education and nursing. Alverno also offers programs designed for students planning additional professional study in dentistry, law, medicine, and veterinary science.

Alverno Weekend College grants baccalaureate degrees in communication, management, and technology; community leadership and development; management; management accounting; nursing (open only to registered nurses); and professional communication. Students attend classes every other weekend between late August and May.

Academic Program

Alverno's learning process prepares students to succeed and to contribute to society. The curriculum includes academic course work that supplies knowledge in a student's chosen field. It also develops her abilities in communication, analysis, problem solving, value judgments, and social interaction, as well as in dealing with the environment, the contemporary world, and the arts and humanities. Each Alverno student acquires necessary knowledge and also gains the abilities to make use of what she knows in her personal and professional life.

Off-Campus Arrangements

The student's learning experience is enhanced through the internship, or Off-Campus Experiential Learning (OCEL), program. OCEL provides internship opportunities for students to work from one to three semesters in business, industry, and social and government agencies. Through OCEL, the student gains a working knowledge of her field and insights that cannot be attained through course work alone.

Opportunities to study abroad include short-term travel courses and semester-abroad programs in a variety of countries.

Academic Facilities

The Teaching, Learning and Technology Center opened in January 1999. This 73,000-square-foot building houses state-of-the-art science labs, multimedia production facilities, computing facilities, and a conference center.

The computer facilities house 100 networked IBM-compatible and Mac computers as well as laser printers, scanners, CD-ROMs, and zip drives. Computers are set up for e-mail, Internet access, and a variety of office and course-related software applications.

The multimedia facilities are located in the Center for Instructional Communication (CIC), which houses twelve computers equipped with the latest software, digital cameras, scanners, and a color printer. Nonlinear digital editing software is installed on the computers to allow students to produce multimedia presentations. The CIC also offers soundproof editing suites, fully equipped video production studios, and a videoconferencing center.

The Nursing Education Building provides facilities specifically designed to meet the needs of nursing students, including a library and a clinical nursing resource center. The resource center allows students to practice their nursing therapeutic skills and to participate in simulated clinical experiences. Computers are equipped with interactive nursing software. RNs and senior students who serve as mentors staff the resource center.

The Alverno College Library provides online access to its print, microform, and electronic collections of more than 350,000 items as well as to worldwide resources available through the Internet. The library is part of an automated catalog network and delivery system with other colleges. The staff offers course-integrated library research instruction.

Costs

For 2000–01, tuition is $5700 per semester (tuition for nursing is $6072), and room and board are $2305 per semester. Books cost approximately $250 per semester. Personal expenses vary, depending on a student's needs.

Financial Aid

Financial aid is available in the form of scholarships, grants, loans, and campus work-study programs. Nearly 91 percent of the students enrolled full-time receive some form of financial assistance. The average award per recipient is $7530.

Faculty

Consisting of men and women, Alverno's full-time faculty numbers 100. Faculty members also serve as academic advisers to students in their major areas of concentration.

Student Government

In addition to membership in Alverno's Student Association, students can join one of more than twenty-five student organizations and interest groups or the Student Activities Planning Team. This gives students an active voice and leadership role in what happens on campus. Programming opportunities include events such as the Metro Milwaukee Leadership Conference and National Collegiate Alcohol Awareness Week. Some groups or activities, such as food and clothing drives, are student-initiated and supported by the professional staff.

Admission Requirements

Candidates applying for admission to Alverno directly after completing high school should have received credit for seventeen academic subjects. This credit should include at least 4 units in English, with the rest distributed among foreign languages, history and the social sciences, mathematics, and natural sciences.

All students must complete an evaluation of their abilities through the Communication Placement Assessment before beginning classes.

Application and Information

Students who wish to apply for admission can apply on line or can write, call, or e-mail the Admissions Office for the necessary forms. An application is considered complete on receipt of the application form with the application fee, a high school transcript, and ACT scores. Students may submit any additional evidence they believe will help the College judge their capacity to benefit from an Alverno education.

Alverno's admission policy permits notification of acceptance within three weeks of receipt of all credentials. Acceptance is contingent upon satisfactory completion of the secondary school courses.

For more information about Alverno College, interested students should contact:

Admissions Office
Alverno College
3400 South 43rd Street
P.O. Box 343922
Milwaukee, Wisconsin 53234-3922
Telephone: 414-382-6100
           800-933-3401 (toll-free)
E-mail: admissions@alverno.edu
World Wide Web: http://www.alverno.edu

Students are offered unparalleled leadership opportunities at Alverno College.

AMERICAN INTERCONTINENTAL UNIVERSITY

ATLANTA, GEORGIA; DUBAI, UNITED ARAB EMIRATES; DULLES, VIRGINIA; FORT LAUDERDALE, FLORIDA; LONDON, ENGLAND; LOS ANGELES, CALIFORNIA; AND WASHINGTON, D.C.

The University

American InterContinental University (formerly the American College) is a private, coeducational, nondenominational institution with a reputation of academic excellence that offers global career-oriented education to a diverse student body. The University was established in 1970 and has since grown to an international network of seven campuses. This international campus network gives students the opportunity to transfer between the campuses and provides them with the intercontinental experience that is important for their personal development and professional achievement.

American InterContinental University (AIU) is accredited by the Commission on Colleges of the Southern Association of Colleges and Schools (SACS). The baccalaureate programs in interior design at the Atlanta and Los Angeles campuses are accredited by the Foundation for Interior Design Education Research (FIDER), and the advertising program at the Dubai campus is accredited by the International Advertising Association (IAA).

The University is recognized worldwide as a top educator in business administration (computer systems management, management, marketing, and advertising), international business, fashion design and marketing, interior design, visual communication (graphic design, illustration, and photography), media production (audio production), and information technology. The student body is composed of students from all fifty states and more than 120 countries. Atlanta, Los Angeles, London, and Dubai offer an English as a second language (ESL) program. Associate, bachelor's, and master's degrees are conferred by the University.

AIU offers comprehensive career counseling to students. The University has an active placement office that seeks to provide students with part-time employment opportunities during their studies at the University, as well as placement services to assist students who have graduated.

Students have the option of residing in modern, attractively furnished apartments with a variety of amenities, which may include swimming pools, tennis courts, and a clubhouse on-site. Living in college housing is encouraged, although not required, for nonresident students.

Locations

AIU's campuses are in seven of the most dynamic cities in the world—Atlanta, Dubai, Dulles, Fort Lauderdale, London, Los Angeles, and Washington, D.C.

Atlanta is the home of many major corporations and is rapidly increasing its international profile as a result of the 1996 Summer Olympic Games and the success of its professional sporting teams. The Atlanta–Buckhead campus is located on Peachtree Road, only minutes away from a number of the city's internationally recognized institutions, including the High Museum of Art, CNN studios, and the Atlanta Apparel Mart. The Dunwoody campus is located in the growing business community just north of Atlanta.

The Los Angeles campus is located close to Marina del Rey. It is convenient to metropolitan Los Angeles attractions and destinations, including the city's downtown area and the beaches.

AIU's Washington, D.C., campus is located in the heart of the capital of the U.S. Only two blocks from the White House and adjacent to the World Bank, the campus is close to a wide array of shops and restaurants.

AIU is planning to open a new campus in Dulles, Virginia. The campus will be conveniently located in the high-tech corridor near an interstate highway and Dulles International Airport.

Interested students should call AIU's toll-free number for more details about the Dulles campus.

The metropolitan area of Miami-Fort Lauderdale has long been noted for its international flavor, global business activities, transportation and tourism, and aquatic sports activities. The campus is located in the community of Sunrise, perfectly situated near beaches, interstate highways and air transportation, a quaint shopping district, and the cafés and galleries of Las Olas Boulevard.

As an international center of business and culture, London is one of the world's most important capital cities. Its vast resources offer students an exciting academic, cultural, and social environment in which to study and develop. Located between Hyde and Regent's Park in central London, the AIU campus is only three blocks from the shopping district of Oxford Street. The attractive urban campus provides quick and easy access to places such as Buckingham Palace, Piccadilly Circus, and the West End, London's central theater district.

On the shores of the Arabian Gulf, Dubai is a leading center for business and tourism in the Middle East. Students experience a fascinating blend of modern amenities and colorful traditions. The campus is located in Jameira near beautiful beach and park facilities and is only a short drive from the city's thriving business center.

Majors and Degrees

AIU offers undergraduate bachelor's degree programs in business administration (B.B.A.) at the Atlanta–Buckhead, London, and Dubai campuses and associate and bachelor's degree programs in fine arts (A.A. and B.F.A.), with concentrations in interior design, fashion design, fashion marketing, and multimedia and communication, at the Atlanta–Buckhead, Los Angeles, London, and Dubai campuses and in information technology (B.I.T.) and international business administration (B.B.A.) at the Atlanta–Dunwoody; Washington, D.C.; Fort Lauderdale; and Los Angeles campuses.

Academic Program

The academic year is divided into four to seven academic quarters of varying lengths. The University operates on a 12-month scheduling plan as well as traditional quarters. Depending on the campus, two complete academic quarters are offered during the summer months (May through September). Students can attend one or both summer quarters and earn full credit for an academic quarter in each summer session. In addition, the London campus offers two 4-week summer sessions during June and July that focus on European business, culture, and the arts as a part of the Study Abroad Program and regular academic schedule.

To qualify for the associate degree, a student must complete 120–130 credit hours with a cumulative grade point average of 2.0 or higher. To qualify for the bachelor's degree, a student must complete 190–200 credit hours with a cumulative grade point average of 2.0 or higher. For both degree programs, a minimum of the four final terms must be in residence at the University.

The normal academic load in the Undergraduate Program is 15 credit hours per quarter. Certain programs (B.I.T. and B.B.A. at the Atlanta–Dunwoody, Fort Lauderdale, Los Angeles, and Washington, D.C., campuses) are accelerated, allowing qualified students to complete their degrees in less time than through traditional institutions.

Off-Campus Arrangements

AIU offers students the opportunity to participate in a number of University-sponsored internship programs. Eligible students who have completed 100 credit hours and have maintained a minimum overall GPA of 2.5 (3.0 for business majors) may, through practical experience, earn up to 20 credit hours toward their degree in an approved off-campus program. In the past, students have participated in internship programs at companies such as Brunschwig & Fils, Laura Ashley, Paramount Studios, and Merrill Lynch.

Students may also travel on University-sponsored study tours, earning up to 5 academic credit hours toward their degrees. They are required to complete sketchbooks, journals, and projects in order to receive credit. In the past, study tours have included Barcelona, China, Florence, Hong Kong, Milan, New York, and Paris. The program is available through the Atlanta–Buckhead, Dubai, London, and Los Angeles campuses.

Academic Facilities

AIU's campuses in London, Atlanta–Buckhead, and Dubai maintain modern, well-planned, and well-equipped facilities. Each classroom provides a comfortable and aesthetically pleasing environment to facilitate students' educational growth. Fashion design and interior design studios contain sophisticated industry equipment. The visual communication facilities include professionally equipped darkroom and photographic studios as well as classrooms with modern drafting tables and other studio supplies. Video production studios house state-of-the-art sound and video equipment. The Macintosh and PC labs house the latest computers and printers as well as the most technically advanced software available commercially. The Library Resource Center includes more than 70,000 volumes to support the major programs of study, a large number of subscriptions to international journals and periodicals, slides, tapes, films, audiovisual equipment, and a vast collection of fabric swatches, carpet samples, and other materials related to the students' studies.

The Atlanta–Dunwoody, Fort Lauderdale, Los Angeles, and Washington, D.C., campuses feature more than 1,000 ports to deliver data, voice, and video throughout the building. Seats in classrooms and team rooms are wired, allowing students to connect their laptop computers to the Internet and AIU's network. Smaller team rooms provide space for collaborative learning, allowing students to work together to solve real business problems. Each campus houses a multimedia and learning resource center, including a library complete with the latest technology and media equipment.

The London campus is composed of eight buildings that house lecture rooms, Mac and PC computer labs, and art, design, photography, and video production studios. The Interior Design Resource Center contains a comprehensive collection of materials and catalogs of the interior design industry.

The new and expanded Dubai campus provides students with exceptional academic resources and state-of-the-art facilities, such as design labs, art studios, Mac and PC labs, a photographic studio and darkroom, an interior design resource room, a student union with food service, a campus bookstore, and the largest English library in the United Arab Emirates.

Costs

The 1999–2000 undergraduate tuition and fees per term (based on a 15-credit-hour academic load) were $3810 for Atlanta and $4140 for Los Angeles. The cost included the use of reference and library facilities, lab and studio fees, student activities, guest lectures, and incidental services. Undergraduate classes taken during the academic term that exceeded the 15-credit-hour load carried an additional charge of $1270 per 5-credit-hour class in Atlanta and $1380 per 5-credit-hour class in Los Angeles. Students are responsible for providing materials and supplies required for class, such as basic art, design, and drafting supplies. Advanced classes require additional supplies, and costs are determined by each student's choice of items. A student taking fewer than 15 credit hours per term is considered part-time. The fee for a single undergraduate class was $1270 in Atlanta and $1380 in Los Angeles. Dormitory accommodations are provided by the term for those students who request them. The fee per term was $1450 in Atlanta and $1500 in Los Angeles.

Financial Aid

American InterContinental University offers a variety of scholarships, grants, loans, and part-time employment to help defray the cost of education. University-administered federal funding includes Federal Supplemental Educational Opportunity Grants and Federal Work-Study Program awards. Additional federal funding includes Federal Pell Grants, Federal Subsidized and Unsubsidized Stafford Student Loans, and Federal PLUS loans. University-administered state funding includes the HOPE scholarship (for Georgia residents only) and Cal Grants (for California residents only). The University also directly administers its own scholarship programs, which include the Founders Scholarship Award, the Travilla Scholarship, the Emilio Pucci Scholarship, the George Thomas (Lord Tonypandy) Scholarship, the Terry O'Neill/Douglas Hayward Scholarship, the Paul Anderson Youth Home Scholarship, the Guy Milner Scholarship, and the International Baccalaureate Scholarship. The University also holds an annual high school/secondary school scholarship competition. Other sources of aid available to students may include vocational rehabilitation funds, Social Security and veterans' benefits, and private scholarships. For further information on financial aid, students should contact the Student Financial Aid Office on either campus.

Faculty

The faculty at the University includes qualified educators and distinguished leaders in their fields, such as award-winning interior and fashion designers, exhibiting artists and photographers, authors, illustrators, lawyers, accountants, and business professionals.

Student Government

Students have a voice in the governance of the campuses through participation in the Student Government Association (SGA). SGA officers are elected by and represent the student body.

Admission Requirements

AIU welcomes candidates for admission who can profit from its programs and who present strong evidence of purpose and qualities of good character. The prospective student must have graduated from high school, must be pursuing high school graduation, or must have earned an equivalency diploma.

Application and Information

Candidates must complete and submit an application for admission, an official transcript of their high school record to date or proof of high school graduation, and two letters of recommendation supporting the applicant's suitability for attending the University. For additional information, students should contact:

Director of Admissions
American InterContinental University
Global Communications Center
6600 Peachtree-Dunwoody Road
500 Embassy Row
Atlanta, Georgia 30328

Telephone: 888-999-4248 (toll-free)
World Wide Web: http://www.aiuniv.edu

AMERICAN INTERNATIONAL COLLEGE
SPRINGFIELD, MASSACHUSETTS

The College
American International College opened in 1885. Today, the College has a wide geographic representation, and the 1,200 students come from thirty states and several countries; the ratio of men to women is even. The majority are graduates of public high schools. About 48 percent are commuting students; all others live in the five residence halls. Students participate in a wide variety of activities that reflect their interests, ranging from volunteer work in the surrounding community to singing in the Chorale to sports. Varsity athletics include men's baseball, basketball, football, golf, hockey, lacrosse, soccer, tennis, and wrestling and women's basketball, field hockey, lacrosse, soccer, softball, tennis, and volleyball. There are forty separate student clubs and organizations.

Location
American International College is located in Springfield, Massachusetts, a city of 165,000 people, which is the seat of Hampden County and the metropolitan center for half a million people. Springfield is also the transportation center of western New England, easily reached by automobile on Interstate 91 and the Massachusetts Turnpike, by rail via major north-south and east-west lines, and by plane via Bradley International Airport. There are a number of cultural offerings in the area, including the Springfield Symphony, Civic Center, and Stage West Theatre Company.

Majors and Degrees
The Bachelor of Arts degree is offered in the School of Arts and Sciences. Students may select majors in the areas of biology, chemistry, communications, economics, English, history, interdepartmental science, liberal studies, mathematics, medical technology, philosophy, political science, public administration, sociology, and Spanish. Preprofessional programs in dentistry, law, medicine, optometry, physical therapy, podiatry, and veterinary science are also available. Minors are available in these disciplines as well as in the fields of journalism and athletic coaching.

The School of Business Administration awards the degree of Bachelor of Science in Business Administration. Majors include accounting, economics, entrepreneurship, finance, general business, human resource management, information systems, international business, management, marketing, and marketing communications.

The School of Psychology and Education offers the Bachelor of Arts degree with a major in psychology. The Bachelor of Science degree is offered in criminal justice, early childhood education, elementary education, human services, secondary education, and special education. Due to changing teacher certification requirements, students seeking certification must also complete the requirements of a second major from the School of Arts and Sciences.

The Division of Nursing awards a Bachelor of Science in Nursing degree through a four-year undergraduate program as well as through an upper-division program for registered nurses. The Division of Nursing is accredited by the National League for Nursing Accrediting Commission.

The Division of Occupational Therapy offers an accredited 4½-year program leading to a Bachelor of Science degree in occupational therapy.

The Division of Physical Therapy offers an accredited 5½-year program leading to a master's degree in physical therapy.

Academic Program
General requirements are virtually the same for all majors. A basic English course and two years of physical education are required. Other requirements are 12 semester hours in the social sciences, 3 in literature, 6 in humanities, and 8 in a science area (courses without laboratories carry 3 semester hours of credit). To graduate, students are required to complete a minimum total of 120 hours of academic credit with a C average or better.

A special four-year program, the Supportive Service Program, assists students with learning disabilities to function in a regular college curriculum.

Off-Campus Arrangements
Opportunities for international study are available. Individually designed courses of study can be arranged at international universities for a summer, a single semester, or a full year of residence. It is possible to transfer up to one full year of credit for such study.

Qualified students are allowed to participate in off-campus internships under the supervision and guidance of experienced personnel. The type of work and the amount of supervision a student receives are left to the discretion of the faculty member to whom the student is assigned. This program is designed to provide all students with an opportunity to gain practical experience in their field of study and is required of the students in the business disciplines and in communications, criminal justice, education, human services, nursing, and physical therapy.

Academic Facilities
James J. Shea Sr. Memorial Library (1980) houses 125,000 volumes, 519 current periodicals, 14,800 bound periodicals, 12,759 units of microfilm, and 3,423 sound recordings and tapes. An area for group study, a media center, and individual study carrels are provided for students.

Amaron Hall is the primary facility for liberal arts and business classrooms. It also houses a microcomputer laboratory and the computer center, which consists of a cluster of Digital VAXstations, Digital VT 320 terminals, and AT-class personal computers on an Ethernet network. Old Science and the newer Breck Hall of Science buildings provide up-to-date classrooms and laboratories for science, mathematics, preprofessional studies, and nursing. The Curtis Blake Child Development Center serves as a diagnostic center for children with learning difficulties and offers graduate-level courses in special education. The center also provides services for specially selected college-age students with learning disabilities.

A new Health Science Center opened in 1996 and is the academic center for the physical therapy, occupational therapy, and nursing programs. The 30,000-square-foot facility includes an amphitheater, several laboratories, classrooms, and faculty and administrative offices.

Costs
The comprehensive 1999–2000 fee for tuition, room, board, and miscellaneous expenses was approximately $19,500. Books and supplies are approximately $500. Personal expenses average $1000 per year.

Financial Aid
American International College provides aid from institutional and external sources to assist 67 percent of the student body. The average financial aid package for the 1999–2000 school year was $9900. Scholarships and loans are available to those who demonstrate financial need and maintain an acceptable record of aca-

demic work and campus citizenship. Campus employment is available, and about 55 percent of the students earn a portion of their expenses. The College participates in the Federal Perkins Loan, Federal Supplemental Educational Opportunity Grant, Federal Pell Grant, and Federal Work-Study programs. Academic scholarships are available for eligible freshmen, and additional College grants are awarded on a need basis. Applications for scholarships and loans should be made to the Office of Financial Aid by April 15 for the following academic year, but they are accepted as long as funds are available. Applications for aid from early decision plan applicants must be received by October 15. Both the Free Application for Federal Student Aid (FAFSA) and the American International College financial aid form are required. Students should write to the director of financial aid for additional information about financial aid or to the Admissions Office for information about academic scholarships.

Faculty

The emphasis of the faculty is on teaching. The full-time faculty numbers 86, of whom 46 have doctorates. All teach freshman courses, and all faculty members, including department chairmen, serve as advisers to undergraduate students. The faculty-student ratio is 1:15.

Student Government

All students are members of the Student Government Association, and the elected officers play an important role in the administration of the College. Serious disciplinary problems are adjudicated by the various levels of the Student Judicial System, as well as by the academic dean and the director of student affairs. In addition, students are largely responsible for social activities at the College.

Admission Requirements

Students applying for admission must be graduates of an approved secondary school and must have successfully completed 16 units of study or show evidence of equivalent education. Among subjects that should be a part of a student's secondary program are English (4 units) and a selection from mathematics, science, social studies, and foreign languages. Applicants should take the SAT I. The Committee on Admission also considers the applicant's class rank and a letter of recommendation in making its decision. Attention is given to the total course program and school attended by each applicant. American International College has no geographic or other quotas. Transfer applications are welcomed.

An interview at the College is recommended but not required of applicants to most of the programs; however, an on-campus interview is required of applicants to the Supportive Service Program. Guides offer campus tours to all guests; class attendance or an overnight stay may be arranged through the Admissions Office. Admission staff members also visit schools throughout the Northeast each year, and candidates who are unable to visit the campus are urged to meet with staff members or talk with alumni in their home area.

Application and Information

A completed application includes a transcript of the candidate's school work, scores on the SAT I, and a letter of recommendation. Everything should be sent to the address given below; a catalog or other information booklets may be requested from the same office. Decision letters are sent on a rolling basis.

The dean of admissions is glad to advise prospective students who wish to write or telephone for additional information.

    Dean of Admissions
    American International College
    1000 State Street
    Springfield, Massachusetts 01109
    Telephone: 413-747-6201
               800-242-3142 (toll-free)
    E-mail: pmiller@acad.aic.edu
    World Wide Web: http://www.aic.edu

Adams Hall is the administration building.

AMERICAN UNIVERSITY
WASHINGTON, D.C.

The University

American University (AU) is for students who want to understand—and influence—how the world works. AU's academically rigorous curriculum enables students to combine serious theoretical study with meaningful real-world learning experiences. Whatever major students choose, they acquire a solid foundation in the liberal arts and pursue in-depth study in their chosen fields.

American's unique core curriculum, its Washington, D.C., location, and its emphasis on the practical application of knowledge prepare students to be major contributors in their fields. Many AU students choose to study more than one field in order to prepare for their professional futures. For example, premed students can major in international studies in order to prepare for a career in international health. Or students can major in CLEG, which combines courses in communication, legal institutions, economics, and government. The University understands that tomorrow's careers will require an understanding of a wide variety of fields, and it encourages students to transcend the traditional boundaries of academic disciplines.

AU's more than 5,000 undergraduates are a microcosm of the world's diversity. From across the United States and from more than 150 countries, they share a desire to shape tomorrow's world. AU actively promotes international understanding, and this is reflected in its curricula offerings, faculty research, and the regular presence of world leaders on campus.

Location

At the top of Embassy Row in prestigious northwest Washington, D.C., American University's campus is a safe, liveable 84-acre home base. Students have easy access to the University shuttle, the subway, and taxis to all the incomparable resources of the nation's capital. AU is convenient to Ronald Reagan Washington National Airport, Dulles International Airport, and Baltimore Washington International Airport and to Union Station and interstate highways.

Majors and Degrees

The College of Arts and Sciences awards B.A., B.F.A., and B.S. degrees in the arts, humanities, sciences, and social sciences through its twenty academic units.

The School of International Service offers the B.A. in international studies and in language and area studies.

The School of Public Affairs offers the B.A. degree in justice, law and society, and political science. The school also offers CLEG, a unique interdisciplinary program that combines courses in communication, law, economics, and government.

The School of Communication is a professional school that offers training in broadcast journalism, print journalism, public communication, and visual media.

The Kogod School of Business offers the B.S. in accountancy and the Bachelor of Science in Business Administration (B.S.B.A.) with specializations in accountancy, computer information systems, economics, enterprise management, finance, human resource management, international business, marketing, and fields related to international service, including communications, development, and regional area studies.

Academic Program

The General Education Program, AU's core curriculum, teaches students to balance different perspectives, communicate convincingly, and gather knowledge from a wide variety of fields. These are skills that will be necessary for students planning on making an impact in their profession and contributing to society. Students choose ten classes from more than 150 specially designed courses. Two classes must be taken in each of the five following areas: social institutions and behavior, traditions that shape the Western world, international and intercultural experience, the creative arts, and the natural sciences. The first class in each area serves as the foundation course and must be followed by a second, more specialized course in an approved sequence.

These innovative courses are a vital part of students' intellectual and professional preparation: they improve writing and critical thinking skills; offer new and balanced scholarship on ethical principles, gender, race, class, and culture; and incorporate quantitative and computing skills as appropriate for that field. In addition, all students are required to complete two courses in English composition and one in college-level mathematics.

The educational goals of the College of Arts and Sciences include teaching students to examine Western and non-Western cultures, appreciate scientific inquiry, master written and oral expression, develop the ability to analyze and synthesize information, and build an understanding of the moral and ethical dimensions that underlie decision making. Working with faculty members, peer mentors, and professional academic counselors, students select courses and majors, plan cooperative employment and internships, and determine programs of study to achieve these goals. The strong liberal arts curriculum of the college is enhanced by the educational, social, cultural, artistic, and scientific resources of Washington, D.C. The individual strengths of each department are heightened by students' ability to cross the lines between disciplines—expanding their educational horizons while acquiring the skills and knowledge required to be successful in their chosen careers.

American's School of International Service has the largest faculty of its kind in the United States and, as such, is able to offer serious students a breadth of study in international relations. The international studies program begins with foundation courses and core courses to provide students with the tools to explore specific areas of study in greater depth. Students select an area specialization from among these regions: Africa, the Americas, Asia, Europe, the Middle East, or Russia and Central Eurasia. These studies are augmented with a functional field of concentration in international politics, U.S. foreign policy, Islamic studies, international environmental politics, international communication, international development, international economic policy, or peace and conflict resolution. The language and area studies program provides a strong foundation in language and culture courses, complemented by a special concentration in related social science courses. Students choose to focus in one of four areas: French/West Europe, German/West Europe, Spanish/Latin America, Russian/East Europe.

Students in the School of Public Affairs are engaged in learning about local, national, and international politics; public institutions; public policy; crime; justice; and law. These areas frame a comprehensive program that incorporates classroom learning, individualized research projects, relevant field studies, and professional training. Washington's facilities for scholarly research in public affairs and resources for work opportunities and personal enrichment are limitless. Students can observe and participate directly in virtually every aspect of government, politics, and justice.

The goal of the School of Communication is to develop liberally educated, professionally trained communicators who are equipped intellectually and ethically to convey the issues of contemporary society. The curriculum is carried out in the environment of Washington, D.C., the communications center of the world. The school draws heavily on the resources of the federal city for its adjunct faculty, for the material in its curriculum, and for involving students with Washington's communicators and communication facilities. A strong liberal arts curriculum is emphasized to ensure students' abilities to interpret the world around them.

The Kogod School of Business prepares students to become business leaders by combining business theory from the classroom with practical experience gained through working in Washington's dynamic business community. The school offers a business curriculum that emphasizes critical skills and topics such as communication, teamwork, computers, ethics, and global business. Nearly every major U.S. corporation and many multinational firms have a presence in the Washington, D.C., area, providing Kogod students with limitless opportunities to enhance classroom theory through internships and cooperative education experiences.

Off-Campus Arrangements

The University's Career Center provides more than 500 students each year with direct field experience in jobs related to their educational and career goals. Such professional training may be with private business, industry, community and social service organizations, or local, state, or federal governments. Full-time faculty members from nearly all University departments serve as program coordinators.

American University administers its own exciting study-abroad program, called the World Capitals Program. Students can study in Beijing, Berlin, Brussels, Buenos Aires, Copenhagen, Jerusalem, London, Madrid, Moscow, Paris, Perugia (Italy), Prague, Rome, Santiago, and Zimbabwe/South Africa. Built into most of these programs are opportunities to tour the country, meet and talk with national leaders and academicians, and participate in internships.

Academic Facilities

The University's facilities include a state-of-the-art language resource center and science laboratories; well-equipped buildings for art, chemistry, and music; and a sports center with indoor and outdoor tracks, soccer and intramural fields, an Olympic-size pool, and a state-of-the-art fitness center. There are fourteen classroom buildings, a 50,000-watt broadcast center, and an interdenominational religious center. The library is a member of the OCLC network, which gives students online access to 2,000 other member libraries. The University's computer is one of the largest IBM mainframe models and is supplemented with many remote terminals and personal computer labs for undergraduate use 24 hours a day.

Costs

Undergraduate tuition and fees for the 1999–2000 academic year were $20,118. Room and board costs averaged $7655 for the year. The University offers several installment payment plans.

Financial Aid

American University recognizes academic achievement and potential and offers merit scholarships to approximately 20 percent of each freshman class. These scholarships are not based upon financial need, and no separate application forms are required. The scholarships include awards of up to full tuition.

The University also supports a multimillion-dollar financial assistance program. Families must apply by March 1 for priority consideration.

Faculty

The faculty represents a rich mix of academic and professional training. Its 463 full-time members are nationally and internationally recognized in their fields.

An important part of American's academic program is the integration of practicing professionals into the faculty. The talent pool available in Washington, D.C., is enormous. Students have the opportunity to learn from professionals from such organizations as the World Bank, National Institutes of Health, Associated Press, the National Endowment for the Arts, the John F. Kennedy Center for the Performing Arts, the National Aeronautics and Space Administration, and private industry. These faculty members bring a real-world perspective to the classroom experience. The student-faculty ratio is 14:1.

Student Government

The Student Confederation is the representative student government for all full-time undergraduates. There are also school and college councils.

Admission Requirements

Admission to AU is selective and competitive. The University seeks accomplished, well-prepared students. Each freshman applicant is reviewed individually, with careful consideration given to the high school record, SAT I or ACT scores, the essay, extracurricular activities, and letters of recommendation. Special emphasis is given to leadership qualities, volunteerism, and entrepreneurship. The middle 50 percent of incoming students have grade point averages between 2.9 and 3.3 (on a 4.0 scale) and combined SAT I scores between 1100 and 1300. Approximately 20 National Merit Finalists and Semifinalists enroll each year.

Transfer applicants are welcome. A minimum GPA of 2.5 (on a 4.0 scale) on all university-level work completed is necessary for admission consideration.

Application and Information

The deadline for early decision freshmen is November 15, and notification is made by December 30. The regular decision deadline is February 1. While most freshmen are admitted for the fall semester, students may also apply for summer or spring semester entry. Transfer applicants apply for all three terms. Students should call for application dates.

For further information and application forms for admission, interested students should contact:

Undergraduate Admissions
American University
4400 Massachusetts Avenue, NW
Washington, D.C. 20016-8001
Telephone: 202-885-6000
Fax: 202-885-1025
E-mail: afa@american.edu
World Wide Web: http://www.american.edu

THE AMERICAN UNIVERSITY OF ROME
ROME, ITALY

The University

The American University of Rome is a private, independent American institution of higher education in Rome that was founded in 1969 by a distinguished group of American and Italian educators in order to promote cross-cultural understanding. The University offers American degree programs to undergraduate students pursuing degrees at other universities.

The American University of Rome is the oldest independent, four-year, degree-granting, American institution of higher learning in Rome, Italy. The University seeks to fortify students with knowledge and ideas through general education in the liberal arts, while providing solid training in professional disciplines, especially business administration, communication, international relations, and Italian studies. The University also offers cinema and opera courses as well as courses in architecture and archaeology. The American University of Rome attempts to prepare students for a global community by encouraging civil discussion and respectful dialogue in the classroom, in public forums, and in social activities. The University also enables students from the United States and other universities to participate in a semester or yearlong learning and living experience in Italy that enriches their knowledge and appreciation of ancient, past, and modern cultures.

Approximately half of the students are in a degree program and half are in the study-abroad program. The majority of the students are American. Approximately 10 to 15 percent are Italian, and 20 percent are other nationalities. The typical student is between 18 and 23 years of age. The male-female ratio is 28 percent male to 72 percent female.

Location

The University is located in a prestigious area on the crest of Rome's highest hill, the Janiculum, just a few minutes' walk from the historic Trastevere district. A lovely four-story villa contains offices; student lounges; classrooms; art, design and architecture studios; and the George A. Tesoro Auditorium. The auditorium is used for public lectures and concerts in addition to academic activities. Adjacent to the villa is a newly renovated building that houses the library, computer laboratories, faculty offices, and classrooms. With its own garden of historic Roman pines, the campus is located in close proximity to the major parks of Villa Sciarra and Villa Pamphili and the renowned American Academy of Rome. The neighborhood offers a full range of amenities, including restaurants, shops, cafes, and an outdoor market. Located just off the ancient route of Via Aurelia, the University is easily reached by car, and parking is ample. It is connected to the center of Rome by several bus lines.

Majors and Degrees

The American University of Rome offers a strong undergraduate curriculum with an international perspective. Associate degrees are offered in business administration and liberal arts. The Bachelor of Arts degree is awarded in communications, interdisciplinary studies, international relations, and Italian studies. The Bachelor of Science degree is awarded in business administration.

Academic Program

All new and transfer students applying directly to the American University of Rome must take the City University of New York (CUNY) proficiency test in reading, writing, and mathematics, which is given at the beginning of each semester. These scores are used for English and mathematics placement.

All students are required to satisfy general education requirements by completing courses in three major academic areas: humanities, social sciences, and mathematics–natural sciences. Some degree programs also require students to complete general education electives, which are courses outside the student's major area of study. All degree-seeking students must complete one year of English composition and conversation, although this requirement may be waived if a student has achieved a high score in advanced placement English. During the freshman year, students are expected to be enrolled in either Developmental English or English Composition and Reading.

A student normally takes five courses (15 semester hours) each semester. A student is considered a sophomore after having completed 30 hours of credit; a junior, once he or she has completed 60 hours of credit and officially declares a major field of study or enrolls in a degree program; a senior after having completed 90 hours of course work.

One semester credit hour equals, at a minimum, 15 classroom contact hours of lectures, 30 hours of laboratory, and 45 hours of practicum. Internships also carry 3 semester credits and require 135 hours of work experience.

Off-Campus Arrangements

Freshman and sophomore students in Rome are enrolled for the first 60 credits in the American University of Rome–College of Staten Island Articulation Program so that students in Italy may embark on a course of study that leads to a degree offered in the United States by one of CUNY's most innovative and technologically advanced campuses, the College of Staten Island. The College offers more than sixty different degree programs, from accounting to computer science, from economics to psychology, and many more. Students in the program complete general education requirements in Rome and then spend a period of residence at the College of Staten Island to complete their degree.

Academic Facilities

The American University of Rome has a specialized library of course-related books and periodicals. The American University of Rome also provides electronic library services to its students and faculty members. These holdings are supplemented by a number of sizeable libraries in the city, which are available to all students, including the Library of the British Council, the Library of the Church of Santa Susanna, and the Centro Studi Americani. The University library can access a central catalogue of the Italian National Library System and also participates in interlibrary loan programs.

There are two computer laboratories on campus that are available to students at scheduled times. All computers are IBM-compatible and have access to e-mail, the Internet, and network printers. One laboratory is located in the library and is principally devoted to student research and term paper requirements. The other is open to student use when not occupied by computer science and other classes.

In addition to overhead and slide projectors, an extensive slide collection, and various stereo systems, the American University of Rome possesses trisystem videotape televisions for projecting films for cinema classes and other purposes. The videotape collection includes films that are essential to courses in Italian cinema and Italian opera as well as general cultural programs. Students also have access to a television that is linked to a satellite system.

Although the University does not possess its own residence halls, it makes arrangements through a designated local agent for students to rent apartments in the vicinity of the University. Apartments have quadruple or quintuple occupancy. The school also makes housing arrangements with pensioni (lodging houses). Students may also make their own housing arrangements and thus assume full responsibility for securing their own housing. Those who choose to work with University-designated agents receive the benefits of a global housing agreement but, in turn, are subject to regulations that govern conduct in the apartments and are required to sign a pledge to this effect.

Costs

The comprehensive tuition fee at the American University of Rome for the current academic year for full-time undergraduates is $9768. A nonrefundable tuition deposit of $100 is required from all new students, payable by the deadline indicated on the acceptance letter. The tuition deposit is then deducted from the final tuition payment, prior to the commencement of the semester. Some courses require travel or attendance at cultural events as required by the course instructor. The cost of these events and travel are not included in tuition and must be paid by the student. Housing costs range from $2420 to $3400.

Financial Aid

The American University of Rome is authorized by the United States Department of Education to participate in Title IV student financial assistance programs. Students who qualify may participate in the Federal Family Education Loan (FFEL) program. Financial aid available through FFEL includes subsidized and unsubsidized Federal Stafford loans and PLUS loans.

Faculty

The American University of Rome has 36 faculty members. Many of the faculty members have Ph.D.s, and the majority are bilingual. All faculty members are readily accessible to act as teachers as well as advisers. The University also invites visiting professors from other American universities.

Student Government

Students are encouraged to take an active role in the student government as a way of contributing to the continued growth and development of the University. Elected officers of the student government meet regularly with the University administration to discuss matters of administrative and academic relevance. They also take responsibility for directing a variety of student social activities, athletic tournaments, club activities, and cultural events. The government maintains funds for these activities, and the student officers enjoy a wide degree of autonomy in managing these financial resources.

Admission Requirements

The fundamental requirement for admission is a high school diploma or its equivalent. Students with a certain number of O levels may be admitted, as well as students who have earned an Italian maturità, French baccalauréat, German abitur, or any other lyceum-equivalent diploma. Applicants for admission from high schools are required to submit an official transcript (including proof of high school completion); the application form, completed and accompanied by a nonrefundable application fee; a personal recommendation from the principal, a guidance counselor, a professor, or a teacher; SAT I scores; and a 200 to 500 word personal statement in which the candidate indicates how a study experience in Rome will help further his or her career and life aims.

All supporting documentation, transcripts, and letters of recommendation must be submitted prior to registration. Students who have completed their high school studies with the equivalent of a 2.5 grade point average on a 4.0 scale are generally admitted. However, students with a lower level of academic performance may also be accepted if letters of recommendation, personal interviews, and SAT I or other standard test scores indicate that the student has the aptitude required to pursue studies at the University. The SAT I requirement may be waived for non-U.S. nationals and for applicants who attend high schools outside the United States. If accepted, these candidates generally are admitted as probationary students. Transfer students with an equivalent of 60 semester credit hours of university study may seek a waiver for SAT I and high school transcript requirements. The American University of Rome's SAT I institutional code for reporting purposes is 0262.

Application and Information

Applicants are notified of the admission decision four to six weeks after the application, supporting credentials, recommendation, and $55 application fee are received.

Prospective students are encouraged to visit the campus. An application for admission and further information may be obtained by contracting the American University of Rome at either its U.S. address or its Rome address.

Director of Administration–Registrar
The American University of Rome
Via Pietro Roselli, 4
Rome, Italy 00153
Telephone: 011-39-0658330919 (direct dial from U.S.)
Fax: 011-39-0658330992 (direct fax from U.S.)
E-mail: aurinfo@aur.edu

The American University of Rome
1025 Connecticut Avenue, Northwest, Suite 601
Washington, DC 20036
Telephone: 202-331-8327
          888-791-8327 (toll-free)
Fax: 202-296-9577
E-mail: aur.homeoffice@dc.aur.edu
World Wide Web: http://www.aur.edu

ANDERSON COLLEGE
ANDERSON, SOUTH CAROLINA

The College

Anderson College, founded in 1911, is a private, coeducational, four-year liberal arts college sponsored by the South Carolina Baptist Convention. The College offers a Christian educational program whereby students are provided opportunities to develop intellectually, physically, spiritually, socially, and morally.

Anderson College enrolls approximately 1,100 students, 75 percent of whom attend full-time. In addition, about one half of the student population lives in campus housing. In the typical academic year, the College enrolls students from more than twenty states and fifteen or more countries. The student body consists primarily of traditional-age students and of students from upstate South Carolina; however, many are nontraditional-age students and come from other geographic areas. Campus housing is available to international students.

A comprehensive program of student activities is provided, including varsity and intramural athletics, Christian ministry opportunities, theater, clubs and organizations, student government, and student-sponsored social activities. Intercollegiate sports programs for men include baseball, basketball, cross-country, track, golf, soccer, tennis, and wrestling. Intercollegiate sports programs for women include basketball, cross-country, track, equestrian, golf, soccer, softball, tennis, and volleyball. Anderson College is a member of NCAA Division II and of the CVAC (Carolinas-Virginia) conference.

The central campus of the College, which includes a small wooded park, athletic facilities, and student housing, occupies a 32-acre tract in an attractive, quiet neighborhood in the city of Anderson. In addition to the central campus, some buildings and parking areas are located on adjacent land.

Location

The city of Anderson is located in the northwestern section of South Carolina, halfway between Atlanta, Georgia, and Charlotte, North Carolina. The city serves as a shopping hub for a large area of northwestern South Carolina and northeastern Georgia. Anderson is served by Interstate Highway 85 and the Greenville/Spartanburg Airport.

Majors and Degrees

Anderson College offers the Bachelor of Arts degree with majors in art (general studio, graphic design, interior design, and painting/drawing), Christian ministry, communications (writing, journalism, and speech/theater), English, history, liberal studies, music, psychology, religion, and Spanish. The Bachelor of Science degree is awarded in biology, business (accounting, computer information services, finance and economics, management, and marketing), elementary/early childhood education, mathematics, middle school education, physical education (sport science), and special education. The Bachelor of Science in Medical Technology and the Bachelor of Science in Human Services and Resources are also offered. Two other degrees, Bachelor of Music Education and Bachelor of Business Administration, are also offered, the latter being a degree program designed for adult students. Teacher certification programs are offered in elementary/early childhood education (PK–8); K–12 programs in art, music, and physical education; and secondary programs (7–12) in biology, English, mathematics, social studies, and Spanish. The two-year Associate in Arts degree is also offered.

Academic Program

The College follows the semester calendar and offers three summer sessions. A minimum of 64 credit hours is required for the associate degree and a minimum of 128 credit hours for the bachelor's degree.

In order to graduate from any degree program of the College, a student must complete a general education component and a major studies component and must satisfy competence requirements in reading, writing, mathematics, and speaking. The ethical dimension of life is emphasized in all programs. Students have the opportunity to participate in internship experiences, study-travel, and overseas study.

Academic Facilities

Anderson College's Callie Stringer Rainey Fine Arts Center provides the finest facility in upstate South Carolina for art, theatrical, musical, and community functions and houses chapel services and other campus events. The Watkins Teaching Center contains most of the classrooms, the computer laboratory, conference rooms, and faculty offices. Other academic facilities on campus include the 60,000-volume Johnston Memorial Library, Merritt Administration Building, Merritt Auditorium, Vandiver Hall, and Journalism Building.

Costs

Charges for 2000–01 are $7850 per semester, including tuition, fees, room, and board. For commuting students, the cost is $5447 per semester for tuition and fees. Books and supplies cost approximately $400 per semester. Charges for international students are the same as for regular boarding students. Personal expenses for transportation, recreation, and miscellaneous needs vary with the individual student. Students may keep cars on campus; there is a $12 fee for a parking permit.

Financial Aid

It is the intent of Anderson College to provide financial assistance to all accepted students who, without such aid, would be unable to attend. More than 90 percent of the College's students receive an average award of $4500 per year, and there are different sources of financial aid available to qualified students. It is best to complete and mail all required forms as soon as possible, since most aid is awarded on a first-come, first-served basis for qualified applicants. The first-award deadline is March 15. The Financial Aid Office awards aid regardless of race, creed, place of national origin, or ethnic group.

Faculty

A faculty of 94 full-time and part-time professors brings the student-faculty ratio to 15:1, allowing for small classes and easy accessibility to professors and instructors. Sixty-three percent of the College's faculty members have a Ph.D. or other equivalent terminal degree.

Student Government

The entire student body is represented in the Student Government Association by 3 elected officers who form the executive branch of the association. Senators from each class are also elected and help plan student activities for social and educational enrichment.

Admission Requirements

Anderson College seeks to admit those who show promise of academic and social success at the College. Each applicant's record is examined for evidence reflecting potential for intellectual and social maturity, strength of character, and seriousness of purpose. The major factors considered in admission include graduation from high school, high school grades in college-preparatory courses, high school curriculum, and SAT I or ACT scores. In addition, the College may choose to examine further any applicant by use of personal interviews or tests administered by the College.

TOEFL scores are required of international applicants; this requirement may be waived if English is the student's native language. A score of 550 is recommended. The SAT I is not required of nonnative English-speaking students. An I-20 (student visa) can normally be issued within two weeks of receipt of all required admission materials.

Anderson College admits students without regard to race, age, creed, color, gender, physical handicap, or national or ethnic origin.

Application and Information

Qualified students are encouraged to apply as early as possible during their final year of high school. The Admissions Office processes applications on a rolling basis, which enables the College to notify a candidate of the admission decision within two weeks after all credentials have been received. Interested students are encouraged to visit the campus.

For further information and application materials, students should contact:

Director of Admissions
Anderson College
316 Boulevard
Anderson, South Carolina 29621
Telephone: 864-231-2030
          800-542-3594 (toll-free)
Fax: 864-231-2033

The Merritt Administration Building, built in 1912, is the centerpiece of Anderson College's 32-acre campus.

ANDERSON UNIVERSITY
ANDERSON, INDIANA

The University

Anderson University is a private, liberal arts community established in 1917 and dedicated to the scholarly and spiritual growth of its students. Today, approximately 2,300 students from forty-five states and fifteen countries compose this learning community. The University is accredited by the North Central Association of Colleges and Schools and has specific program accreditations from the National Council for Accreditation of Teacher Education, the National League for Nursing, the National Association of Schools of Music, the Council on Social Work Education, the National Athletic Training Association, and the Association of Collegiate Business Schools and Programs.

The University consists of the Colleges of Professional Studies, Science and Humanities, and Arts. The University also operates a division of adult and continuing education and a graduate School of Theology. The School of Theology, which opened in 1950, enrolls approximately 100 students and offers five different degrees in the area of professional ministry.

The University is located on 99 rolling acres on the suburban northeastern side of the city of Anderson, Indiana. The physical plant consists of twenty-two main campus buildings, including seven academic buildings and eight residence halls. Separate residence halls are maintained for men and women. Students who do not live at home are required to live on campus unless permitted to live elsewhere by the Dean of Students. All students may keep cars on campus.

Artists, musicians, lecturers, and various public figures appear on campus each year, often in conjunction with the University's Chapel-Convocation Program, which is held twice each week in the 2,200-seat Robert H. Reardon Auditorium. The entire campus convenes for Chapel-Convocation, and student attendance is required.

Concerts, plays, films, variety shows, retreats, special trips, intramural sports, and other special events are a part of the University activities calendar. Varsity sports are another important campus activity for both spectators and players. Anderson University is a member of the National Collegiate Athletic Association and the Heartland Collegiate Athletic Conference. Women's sports include basketball, cross-country, golf, soccer, softball, tennis, track and field, and volleyball. Men compete in intercollegiate baseball, basketball, cross-country, football, golf, soccer, tennis, and track and field. An outdoor athletics complex provides fields for softball, baseball, football, and soccer and includes an all-weather track for track and field. A bowling alley and an outstanding game room are a part of the recreational facilities. Students can participate in a number of extracurricular activities such as the campus newspaper, the yearbook, the 6,000-watt commercial FM radio station, special interest clubs, and religious fellowships.

As part of its commitment to maintain a distinctive life-style as a Christian university, the school prohibits the use of tobacco in any form and the use of alcoholic beverages and illegal drugs. High moral and ethical standards of behavior are expected of members of the campus community.

Location

Anderson University is located in a residential area of Anderson, Indiana, a city of 60,000 people. Community and University relationships are strong, and many alumni have settled in the Anderson area. While Anderson offers its own cultural and recreational opportunities, the city of Indianapolis, located approximately 35 miles southwest of Anderson, provides additional concert and entertainment opportunities. Indianapolis is the home of the Indianapolis Symphony Orchestra, the Museum of Art, the Indiana Pacers, the Indianapolis Colts, the Market Square Arena, the Convention Center, and the Hoosier Dome. The Greater Anderson area is served by highway, bus, train, and air transportation.

Majors and Degrees

Anderson University offers the Bachelor of Arts degree in accounting, American studies, athletic training, Bible, biology, business administration, chemistry, Christian ministries, church music, computer science, computer science–business, computer science–mathematics, criminal justice, drama, economics, English, family science, finance, fine arts, French, German, graphic design, history, management, marketing, mass communications, mathematics, music business, music performance, philosophy, physical education, physics, political science, psychology, religion, social work, sociology, Spanish, and visual arts. The Bachelor of Science is offered in nursing. Individualized majors may also be arranged.

Students may major in teaching in the following subject areas: elementary education, English, French, German, health and safety, mathematics, music education, physical education, science, social studies, Spanish, speech communication and theater, and visual arts.

Also offered are preprofessional programs in allopathic medicine, chiropractic, dentistry, engineering, law, medical technology, medicine, occupational therapy, optometry, osteopathic medicine, pharmacy, physical therapy, podiatry, seminary studies, and veterinary medicine.

A two-year Associate of Arts degree is offered in criminal justice.

Academic Program

A specific set of requirements must be satisfied for each major. Students in the bachelor's degree programs must complete a minimum of 124 semester hours and earn 248 credit points to graduate. All students must also complete a specified number of hours in courses from the core curriculum. The core curriculum, which offers students a great degree of flexibility in class selection, assures the student that he or she will be exposed to several key knowledge areas, including arts and humanities, the contemporary world, the environment, individual behavior, and problem solving. Before graduation, all students must demonstrate competence in three skill areas: English (reading, writing, and oral expression), foreign language, and mathematics.

Students may qualify for advanced standing in various subjects through examination and may earn credit through the College Board's Advanced Placement Program and College-Level Examination Program. Departmental honors programs allow selected students to do intensive work in their chosen field.

The University follows a traditional semester calendar. A two-week international term offered over the Christmas break gives students the opportunity to travel and study abroad or participate in a nontraditional learning experience.

Off-Campus Arrangements

The University's Study, Serve and Share (Tri-S) program takes approximately 500 student travelers to thirty different countries each year. Through this Peace Corps–type program, students sample international settings while learning, serving, working, and observing the host culture. Academic credit may be earned for the Tri-S experience.

Academic Facilities

The Robert A. Nicholson Library contains 246,817 volumes, 8,847 units of audiovisual material, 38,788 volumes of microfiche, 4,263 reels of microfilm, 2,626 units of ultrafiche, and 2,823 volumes of music sound recordings. The library also maintains subscriptions to 1,074 periodicals. Facilities include typing booths, listening rooms, housing for U.S. government documents, and seating for more than 500 students. The Nicholson Library also houses the Charles E. Wilson Archives, which contain the personal papers of the former president of General Motors and U.S. Secretary of Defense.

The Krannert Fine Arts Center offers the music and art departments more than 70,000 square feet of practice and performance space. Music facilities include performance halls for both instrumental and choral performance, thirty individual practice rooms and workrooms, control-recording facilities, classrooms, and faculty offices. In addition to classroom space, the building's art modules contain facilities for work in ceramics, hot glass, sculpture, woodworking, welding/brazing, metalworking, graphic design, photography, painting, and drawing. The art and music modules are linked by the Wilson Galleries, a modern showcase for student and professional exhibits.

Hartung Hall, the University's recently renovated science center, provides excellent laboratory and classroom facilities for the study of the Bible and religion, biology, chemistry, nursing, physics, and psychology. A radio station/mass communications center, Byrum (performance) Hall, Bennett Natatorium, the athletics complex, and Decker Hall, the 80,000-square-foot administration-classroom building, are also a part of the well-equipped campus.

Costs

In 2000–01, tuition for the academic year is $14,680, a room is $2750, and board is $2000, for a total of $19,430. Most students budget about $1600 each year for books and other incidental expenses above tuition, room, and board.

Financial Aid

More than 90 percent of Anderson University students receive financial aid through scholarships, grants, loans, and employment. The University participates in the Federal Work-Study Program and assists students in applying for aid through the Federal Pell and Federal Supplemental Educational Opportunity Grant programs, the Federal Perkins Loan Program, and the Federal Stafford Student Loan Program. A variety of scholarship programs are also available. These include the Matching Church Scholarship; Presidential, Academic Honors, and Distinguished Student (academic) Scholarships; and music and departmental scholarship programs. Students applying for aid must submit the Free Application for Federal Student Aid. A financial aid transcript from each school previously attended is required of all transfer applicants. Aid is awarded on the basis of financial eligibility or outstanding academic achievement.

Faculty

In its attempt to provide a distinctively Christian environment where Christian values are emphasized, the University strives to attract personnel who have not only the highest credentials but also a Christian commitment. Sixty-six percent of faculty members hold the terminal degree in their field of study. The faculty consists of 160 full-time and 70 part-time members.

Student Government

The Student Government consists of elected officers and representatives. Members of the Student Government, faculty, staff, and administration compose a board that addresses campus issues raised by members of the student body.

Admission Requirements

Each applicant is evaluated individually on the basis of the total application packet, which must include academic records from the applicant's high school (and college, if any), SAT I or ACT scores, references, and a personal essay. Also helpful are recommendations from pastors and guidance counselors. To qualify for admission, applicants should carry a grade average of C or higher and should rank in the upper half of their class. The University recommends that students have the following units in their high school background: 4 units of English, 3 units of mathematics, 2 units of a foreign language, 3 units of science, and 3 units of social studies. Also considered in the evaluation of each application is the student's seriousness of purpose, personality and character, expressed willingness to live within the standards of the Anderson University community, and service to school, church, and community.

Anderson University does not discriminate on the basis of faith, race, color, national or ethnic origin, sex, or handicap in the administration of its admission policies, educational policies, scholarship and loan programs, athletics or other school-administered programs, or employment.

Application and Information

Anderson University requires each student to submit an application form and a $20 nonrefundable fee, an official high school transcript, SAT I or ACT scores, two references, and a medical form. Transcripts of all college work and a Transfer Student Information form, completed by an official from each college previously attended, are required of all transfer students. The University also requires a personal essay.

Applications are accepted throughout the year. New students, including transfers, may enter in either the fall or spring semester. The University follows a rolling admission format, notifying students of the admission decision as soon as their application file is complete. For applications and financial aid forms or for more information, students should contact:

Jim King
Director of Admissions
Anderson University
Anderson, Indiana 46012
Telephone: 765-641-4080
           800-428-6414 (toll-free)
Fax: 765-641-4091
E-mail: info@anderson.edu
World Wide Web: http://www.anderson.edu

ANDREWS UNIVERSITY
BERRIEN SPRINGS, MICHIGAN

The University

Established in 1874, Andrews University continues to grow as a world-class institution of higher learning. *U.S. News & World Report* has placed Andrews on its list of the top 200 colleges and universities in America for the past six years. The University maintains affiliations with colleges on every continent except Antarctica. Many of its faculty members have international teaching and research experience. More than 25 percent of the 3,000 students at Andrews each year are international and come from more than 100 countries, making campus life an international experience that strengthens the academic and social programs.

The University is divided into six schools: College of Arts and Sciences, College of Technology, Division of Architecture, School of Business, School of Education, and the Seventh-day Adventist Theological Seminary. The University is accredited by the North Central Association of Colleges and Schools. In addition, ten individual programs have accreditation from professional associations: allied health, architecture, chemistry, dietetics, music, nursing, physical therapy, social work, speech-language pathology and audiology, and teacher education, as well as all of the degree programs offered by the Theological Seminary.

Andrews University is operated by the Seventh-day Adventist Church, and most students are members of that church. However, the University has an open admissions policy that encourages students from all religious backgrounds to apply, and almost 20 percent of the student body are not members of the church.

Location

The neatly manicured campus sprawls over 1,600 acres of former farm land in rural southwestern Michigan. The campus is a designated arboretum, with more than 260 varieties of shrubs and trees. All buildings on the campus are within walking distance. Shopping and service centers are within an easy 1-mile walk of campus and include barber and beauty shops, a post office, banks, a grocery store, a variety store, a hardware store, a florist, bookstores, restaurants, and a medical center.

Chicago is less than 2 hours away. The shopping centers and cultural activities in South Bend, Indiana, and St. Joseph/Benton Harbor, Michigan, are just 30 minutes away. Lake Michigan, with its 200-foot-high sand dunes and water activities, is less than 30 minutes away.

Majors and Degrees

Andrews University offers degrees at every level, from the associate and bachelor's through master's and doctoral degrees. There are more than 150 different degree possibilities, including accounting, agriculture, allied health administration, architecture, art, automotive technology, aviation, behavioral science, biochemistry, biology, biophysics, botany, business, chemistry, communication, computer engineering technology, computer science, dietetics, economics, electronics engineering technology, elementary education, English, family studies, finance, French, German, graphic arts, health psychology, health and wellness, history, horticulture, industrial and operations engineering, journalism and mass media, language for international trade, management, marketing, mathematics, mechanical engineering technology, media technology, music, nursing, nutrition science, physical education, physics, political economy, psychology, public relations, religion, secondary education, sociology, Spanish, speech-language pathology and audiology, technology education, theology, and zoology.

Academic Program

First-time freshmen are assigned an academic adviser to help them plan class schedules and choose career options. A typical class load is 16 academic credits per semester. Each academic credit generally requires 1 hour of class attendance per week, plus an additional 2 hours of study and preparation each week. Even with this busy academic schedule, Andrews students typically work 10 to 15 hours each week.

Andrews Scholars is an honors organization that allows members to take honors classes and promotes student research. Students who qualify may graduate with honors. The Counseling and Testing Center offers diagnostic testing for learning difficulties as well as personal counseling. The Career Planning and Placement Office creates job fairs each year and helps with career placement in other ways.

Off-Campus Arrangements

Students can enhance their academic experience in several ways through study and service abroad. Language study programs are available in Argentina, Austria, France, Greece, Italy, Kenya, Singapore, and Spain. Andrews University also has affiliation and extension agreements with schools in Australia, England, India, Nigeria, Russia, South Africa, Trinidad, and Zimbabwe.

Many students choose to spend a summer or a year in service to humanity through the Student Missionary program or the Taskforce Volunteer program. Service learning is a required component of degrees at Andrews University.

Academic Facilities

The James White Library has collections totaling nearly 1 million volumes and subscribes to 2,800 periodicals. Its holdings include maps, microfilm, videotapes and audiotapes, and rare Seventh-day Adventist historical documents. The electronic JeWeL system provides online access to the library's catalogs as well as to several important periodical indexes. JeWeL includes access to global information resources through the World Wide Web.

Andrews' facilities also include a fiber-optic network throughout the campus that links computers and other telecommunications equipment. All students have access to the Internet through the Andrews computing center. The University maintains modern laboratories in science, allied health, computing, graphic arts, photography, and other areas. Its twenty-seven buildings include Chan Shun Hall and Harrigan Hall as recent additions.

Costs

Tuition for the 2000–01 school year is $12,600. Room and board are approximately $5576 for the year.

Financial Aid

Andrews University provides aid to all students who have financial need. The University participates in the Federal Pell Grant, Federal Supplemental Educational Opportunity Grant, Michigan Grant, Federal Perkins Loan, and Federal Direct Student Loan programs. In addition, the University awards almost $6 million in financial aid from its own funds each year. In 1999–2000, aid totaled $24 million. About 90 percent of undergraduate students received some form of financial aid. The average yearly student aid package was about $8000.

Freshmen are eligible for academic scholarships that range from $1500 to $10,000. In order to qualify for need-based financial aid, students must file the Free Application for Federal Student Aid (FAFSA) and a short Andrews Aid Application. To ensure that all financial aid is in place for the new school year, all papers should be filed by March 31, although Michigan residents should file by February 15 for a priority award that includes the Michigan Grant.

Faculty

Student surveys indicate that the best thing about Andrews University is the faculty. Almost all classes have fewer than 25 students, and the student/faculty ratio is 13:1. Even in large classes, teachers know the students by name.

Faculty members are not only personable, but many are highly recognized scholars in their respective disciplines. They have received awards from national and international societies. Every year they present papers at national conventions. They publish articles in respected journals of research. More than 70 percent of the faculty members hold earned doctorates or have the highest degree in their field.

Student Government

The purposes of the Andrews University Student Association (AUSA) are to serve the University community and contribute to the fuller unfolding of the Adventist program of education, to serve as a channel for organizing student activities, to provide a vehicle for the expression of student opinion, and to provide opportunity for leadership experience and the development of skills in organization and administration.

Admission Requirements

Student admissions counselors assist with the admission process. Undergraduate applicants must submit an application, two recommendations, official transcripts from high school and any colleges attended, and an ACT or SAT I score. Low academic achievement or poor recommendations may result in a student's failure to be accepted.

Freshman applicants should have 4 years of English, 2 years of math, 2 years of history, and 2 years of science, including one lab science class.

Campus visits are beneficial to students as they make their decision for college. Students should make arrangements for a free campus visit by calling the number below. Applicants are accepted on a rolling basis.

Application and Information

Inquiries and correspondence may be directed to:
Enrollment Services
Andrews University
Berrien Springs, Michigan 49104-0740
Telephone: 800-253-2874 (toll-free)

ANGELO STATE UNIVERSITY
SAN ANGELO, TEXAS

The University
Founded in 1928, Angelo State University (ASU) is recognized as one of the United States' most outstanding regional public universities. A proud member of the Texas State University System, ASU subscribes to a proven traditional approach of undergraduate education while encouraging modern instructional techniques in intimate classroom settings. One of the University's major goals is to provide a stimulating educational climate that offers students maximum opportunities for academic achievement and personal growth. To achieve this goal, ASU maintains a distinguished student body and a superb faculty. Of the approximately 6,300 students enrolled, 6,000 are undergraduates. This diverse student population is drawn from throughout Texas, forty-seven other states, and twenty-five countries.

Location
The 268-acre campus of Angelo State University is in San Angelo, an attractive and progressive city of 100,000 in the heart of Texas at the gateway to the scenic hill country. The attractively landscaped campus is located near the downtown business district in one of the city's finest residential areas. The cultural and entertainment offerings of the campus are complemented by those of the community, including a symphony orchestra, art museums, popular concerts, and a host of special events. Three recreational lakes and lakefront areas are available in and around San Angelo, providing a wide variety of facilities for picnicking, swimming, fishing, and many water sports.

Majors and Degrees
Angelo State University provides forty-five undergraduate programs in thirty-one disciplines leading to six baccalaureate degrees and one associate degree.

The Bachelor of Arts degree is offered in art, communication, drama, English, French, German, government, government with criminal justice option, history, journalism, mathematics, music, psychology, sociology, and Spanish. Programs for teacher certification at the elementary level are available as interdisciplinary programs in fine arts, language arts, and social studies.

The Bachelor of Business Administration degree may be earned in accounting, business, business with international option, computer science, finance, finance with a real estate option, management, and marketing. The University's undergraduate and graduate business programs are accredited by the Association of Collegiate Business Schools and Programs. A five-year integrated undergraduate/graduate program in accounting is designed to fulfill state requirements for eligibility for the Certified Public Accountancy (CPA) examination.

The Bachelor of Music degree is offered in music.

The Bachelor of Science degree is offered in animal science, applied physics, biology, chemistry, computer science, economics, kinesiology, mathematics, medical technology, physics, and psychology. Programs for teacher certification at the elementary level are available as interdisciplinary programs in early childhood, math/science, and special learning and development.

The University also offers a Bachelor of General Studies degree, Bachelor of Science in Nursing degree, and an Associate in Applied Science in Nursing degree.

In addition, students may pursue courses and advising designed to help them meet entrance requirements to various professional schools, including dentistry, engineering, law, medicine, occupational therapy, pharmacy, physical therapy, and veterinary medicine.

Academic Program
The academic requirements at ASU are designed to give the student a broad background in the liberal arts and to enhance that foundation with discipline-specific courses. Curricula are continually evaluated to ensure the best and most current educational experience possible. Baccalaureate-seeking students must file a degree plan prior to the first semester of their junior year or the completion of 70 semester hours. Faculty advisers monitor students' progress from the beginning of the academic program until completion.

Two-year and four-year aerospace studies programs for men and women are also available. Completion of these programs leads to a commission in the U.S. Air Force.

The college year consists of a long session and a summer session. The long session is divided into fall and spring semesters, each approximately 16 weeks long. The summer session is divided into two 6-week terms.

Off-Campus Arrangements
The International Studies Program provides academic study and travel opportunities in Mexico and in European and Central American countries. These arrangements carry college credit. Other off-campus programs include professional internships in education, government, journalism, and public administration and cooperative education programs in nursing and medical technology offered in conjunction with numerous local medical centers.

ASU operates a 4,643-acre multiple-purpose agricultural production and wildlife management area called the Management, Instruction, and Research (MIR) Center. Located at O. C. Fisher Lake near San Angelo, the MIR Center is one of the most complete domestic livestock and range and wildlife management facilities in the Southwest.

Academic Facilities
Attractive and well-maintained academic buildings enable ASU students to study in some of the most pleasant and modern facilities to be found. Classrooms range from the intimacy of seminar-oriented size to a small number of lecture halls. Specialized and general research laboratories serve many of the University's programs, including the applied sciences, nursing, communication, journalism, kinesiology, education, business, and computer science, among others. The Porter Henderson Library is the focal point of academic life at ASU. Containing more than 1 million holdings in bound volumes, government documents, and microforms accessible by an online cataloging system, the Henderson Library ranks among the finest libraries in Texas. The West Texas Collection of archival material

admirably meets the genealogical and historical interests of students and faculty members desiring to learn more about the distinct West Texas heritage.

A radio/television studio, modular and proscenium theaters, a planetarium, musical rehearsal and recital halls, art studios, recreational facilities, and a Language Learning Center provide ASU students with exceptional opportunities for learning and fun outside the classroom. An extensive network of student-accessible microcomputer laboratories further complements the academic mission of the computer-intensive campus.

Costs

In 1999–2000, state residents registered for a normal course load of 15 semester hours (full-time study) paid approximately $1121 per semester for required tuition and fees. Room and board charges ranged from $1350 to $2161 per semester, depending upon the meal plans and residence hall selected. Tuition and required fees for out-of-state students were around $4316 per semester. Books and supplies were estimated to cost from $200 to $400 per semester.

Financial Aid

To assist students toward meeting their financial responsibilities, the Office of Student Financial Aid administers a wide variety of programs from funds provided by the federal government and the state of Texas, including funds from the Federal Work-Study, Federal Pell Grant, Federal Supplemental Educational Opportunity Grant, Federal Perkins Loan, Federal Family Education Loan, Texas Public Educational Grant, and State Student Incentive Grant programs. In addition, numerous scholarships are awarded annually through the financial aid office in recognition of academic achievement, outstanding leadership, and exceptional promise or potential.

One of the most distinctive features of the University is the Robert G. Carr and Nona K. Carr Academic Scholarship Program. One of the largest privately endowed academic scholarship programs in the nation, this program provides scholarships ranging in value from $1500 to $6000 annually. More than 900 students enrolled at Angelo State University receive these awards. To compete favorably for one of these renewable scholarships, a student must normally rank in the top 15 percent of his or her class and present a composite score of 25 or higher on the ACT Assessment or a combined math and verbal score of 1140 or higher on the SAT I.

Students interested in the University's Air Force ROTC program may also apply for scholarships awarded through the Air Force ROTC detachment. These awards are funded by an endowment established by the late Mr. and Mrs. Robert G. Carr. This unique program provides scholarships ranging in value from $500 to $1500 annually to qualified cadets enrolled in the University's ROTC program.

Faculty

Angelo State University retains a distinguished faculty. In terms of academic preparation, the faculty ranks near the top of all colleges and universities in the South. Approximately 60 percent of the faculty hold earned doctorates in their teaching field. Faculty members are selected with great care; the University seeks to obtain the services of individuals who are prominent scholars and dedicated teachers who will merit the confidence of the students. Faculty members are associated with many of the nation's leading research universities, conduct special assignments in numerous countries, have acquired professional experience with some of the nation's leading business firms, conduct extensive applied and theoretical research, and travel internationally.

Student Government

The Student Senate is the official representative organization of the Angelo State University student body. As the primary forum for student opinion, the Student Senate provides a mutually beneficial communication link between the student body and administrative officials.

Admission Requirements

High school graduates are admitted to Angelo State University on a competitive basis. Applicants from accredited U.S. high schools must meet one of the following requirements: (1) they must satisfactorily complete the Texas Scholars Program or the Texas advanced high school program; (2) they must rank in the top half of their senior class at the time of application or graduate in the top half of their graduating class; (3) they must present a minimum composite score of 23 on the ACT Assessment or a minimum combined verbal and math score of 1030 on the SAT I if ranked in the third quarter or of 30 or 1270 if ranked in the fourth quarter; or (4) they must have a 50 percent or greater probability of earning an overall C average (2.0 GPA) during the freshman year at the University as computed from their high school grades and ACT or SAT I scores. Students who do not qualify for regular admission may qualify for provisional admission. Transfer students who have completed 18 or more hours of college-level work will be admitted providing they have maintained at least a 2.0 cumulative GPA. Students with less than 18 college-level hours must also meet the criteria established for high school students. The University welcomes applications from international students, who are considered on the basis of their secondary school record, their ACT or SAT I scores, and their Test of English as a Foreign Language (TOEFL) scores (550 minimum).

Application and Information

High school applicants are required to submit an application for admission, results of the ACT or SAT I, and appropriate academic transcripts. Requests for information and admission application forms should be made to:

Office of Admissions
Angelo State University
Box 11014, ASU Station
San Angelo, Texas 76909
Telephone: 915-942-2041
          800-946-8627 (toll-free)

The Angelo State University Robert and Nona Carr Education–Fine Arts Building.

ANNA MARIA COLLEGE
PAXTON, MASSACHUSETTS

The College

Anna Maria College, a private, comprehensive, four-year, coeducational Catholic college, was founded in 1946 by the Sisters of Saint Anne in Marlboro, Massachusetts. In 1952, the College moved to its current 180-acre campus in Paxton, Massachusetts. Originally a women's college, the College has been coeducational since 1973. The 500 full-time undergraduate students come from thirteen states and 14 other countries.

The College is an unusually close-knit community. Small class sizes allow for mentor relationships to develop between faculty members and students. Freshman and sophomore classes generally have between 16 and 20 students; some upper-level classes have as few as 5 students. Faculty members teach and advise students based on their knowledge of each person as an individual, and classes are never taught by graduate assistants.

Criminal justice is the most popular program on campus, followed by education (early childhood, elementary, art, and music), business administration, social work, and psychology. The College also offers special majors such as music therapy and art therapy. Five-year programs are available in business administration (B.B.A./M.B.A.), psychology (B.A./M.A.), and criminal justice (B.S./M.A.).

The College is accredited by the New England Association of Schools and Colleges, the Council on Social Work Education, and the National Agency for Clinical Laboratory Sciences. The College is also approved by the American Bar Association, Massachusetts Department of Education, and the National Association for Music Therapy.

More than 70 percent of Anna Maria College's undergraduates reside on campus in the residence halls. Students enjoy a full social life both on campus and within the college town atmosphere of nearby Worcester. A professional theater group, the New England Theatre Company, is in residence at the College. Annual events enjoyed by all students include the Variety Show, and Winterfest, Harvest, and Spring Weekends.

The College's NCAA Division III athletic program offers intercollegiate competition for men (baseball, basketball, cross-country, golf, and soccer) and women (basketball, cross-country, field hockey, soccer, softball, and volleyball). Intramural athletics and the coed club sport of cheerleading are also available to students who do not wish to participate on varsity teams.

The College is linked to the Internet. More than 500 computer hookups link classrooms, offices, the Academic Computing Center, computer labs, the library, and all residence hall rooms.

Location

Anna Maria College is located on a 180-acre wooded campus in Paxton, Massachusetts, 8 miles from downtown Worcester. The city offers numerous professional and cultural opportunities; Boston, Providence, and Hartford are only an hour away.

Local attractions include big-name entertainment and minor league hockey at the Worcester Centrum; art, history, and science museums; classical music performances at Mechanics Hall; the Worcester Common Fashion Outlets; theater; and day and night skiing at Wachusett Mountain.

Majors and Degrees

Anna Maria College offers a four-year curriculum of undergraduate instruction leading to the following degrees: Bachelor of Arts in art, art and business, art education and art therapy, biology, early childhood education, elementary education, English, English teaching (grades 5–9), history/political science, human growth and development, liberal studies, middle school teaching (grades 5–9), music, paralegal studies, psychology, social relations, social studies teaching (grades 5–9), social work, and Spanish teaching (grades PK–9 or 5–12); Bachelor of Business Administration with concentrations in accounting, finance, management, management information systems, and marketing; Bachelor of Fine Arts in art; Bachelor of Music in music education, music education and music therapy, music therapy, and performance (voice, piano); Bachelor of Science in criminal justice; Associate in Arts in paralegal studies; and Associate in Science in business administration. Special programs include 3-2 engineering (B.A./B.S.) with Worcester Polytechnic Institute, secondary education and gerontology studies with the colleges of Worcester Consortium, prelaw, and premedicine.

Academic Program

Successful career planning today must take into account that all professions are evolving. A career chosen today may be very different ten years from now. Given this reality, the College has committed itself to a program of study that forms a partnership between academics and career development: the Universal Curriculum. The Universal Curriculum is designed to allow students maximum preparation in their career choice by combining practical experience through internships with classroom learning. The College's mission is to give students the best preparation possible for entry into the professional setting through career-oriented liberal arts.

A typical plan of study at the College covers the following areas (credits in parentheses): religious studies (6), philosophy (6), English (6), history (3), literature (3), language or culture (3), fine arts (3), social/behavioral science (3), analytical skills (9), and liberal arts electives (18). These requirements vary from major to major. In addition, students take courses within their chosen fields. In total, 120 credits and a minimum 2.0 cumulative grade point average are required for graduation, as well as participation in the elements of the Universal Curriculum.

As part of the Universal Curriculum, the College offers Encounter Days four times a year, which focus on professional development, spiritual enhancement, cultural appreciation, and wellness. On- and off-campus experiences are designed to broaden students' understanding in these areas.

Students may also develop a Career Assessment Portfolio to document their personal and professional growth during their four years at the College. Upon graduation, the portfolio serves as proof of their accomplishments and abilities.

Off-Campus Arrangements

Anna Maria College is a member of the Colleges of Worcester Consortium. Through this group of fifteen area colleges (Anna Maria College, Assumption College, Atlantic Union College, Becker College, Clark University, College of the Holy Cross, Fitchburg State College, Massachusetts College of Pharmacy and Applied Health, Mount Wachusett Community College, Nichols College, Quinsigamond Community College, Tufts University School of Veterinary Medicine, University of Massachusetts Medical School, Worcester Polytechnic Institute, and Worcester State College), students may enroll in nonmajor courses at any of the member institutions and have credits transferred at no additional cost. The College offers several other off-campus opportunities for which academic credits are awarded. There is an exchange program with Holy Names College in California, where students may elect to study for one semester. The College participates, along with sixteen other New England colleges, in the New England–Quebec student exchange program. Through this program, students (especially those studying French language and literature) may choose to spend a year at one of a number of schools in Quebec. The College also provides opportunities for study abroad with additional programs in Rome, Latin America, and Nova Scotia. Students are also eligible to apply for Army and Air Force ROTC programs, available through the Colleges of Worcester Consortium.

Academic Facilities

The Mondor-Eagan Library houses the College's volumes, stacks, periodicals, study rooms, computer center, resource centers, and language laboratory. The library also houses the main computer terminal, which links the combined material resources of central and western Massachusetts libraries, making more than 4 million books and periodicals accessible to students. Classrooms are located in Trinity Hall, Cardinal Cushing Hall, and Foundress Hall. Foundress Hall houses the Zecco Performing Arts Center. Trinity Hall also houses the learning center. Among the other buildings are St. Joseph's Hall for sciences, Miriam Hall for music and performance, and the Moll Art Center, which has studios, classrooms, and an exhibit hall.

Costs

Tuition for the 2000–01 academic year is $14,645. Room and board expenses are $6200. For music students, tuition is $16,645 in lieu of fees for private lessons. A tuition freeze is in effect for all students, subject to yearly approval by the Anna Maria College Board of Trustees for each upcoming first-year class.

Financial Aid

More than 85 percent of the freshmen at the College receive financial aid in the form of scholarships, grants, loans, and work-study program awards. Some available sources of funds are the Federal Pell Grant, Federal Supplemental Educational Opportunity Grant, and Federal Perkins Loan programs. To apply for aid, students should submit the Free Application for Federal Student Aid (FAFSA) to Federal Student Aid Programs. Aid is awarded on the basis of need. Non-need-based scholarships are also available. For further information, students should call 508-849-3366.

Faculty

The College has 84 full- and part-time faculty members, 98 percent of whom are lay and 2 percent of whom are religious personnel. Faculty members have a deep respect for scholarship and research and are dedicated to teaching and to the success of the student. Graduate assistants do not teach classes at Anna Maria College.

Student Government

The Student Government Association (SGA) is the official representative of the student body, serving as the link between it and the administration. More than twenty clubs and organizations under the SGA offer many activities and opportunities to students, who are encouraged to participate in the government of student life at the College.

Admission Requirements

At Anna Maria College, every application is considered individually and weighed on its own merits. Emphasis is placed on the applicant's transcript, recommendations, and SAT I or ACT scores. Extracurricular activities and leadership positions are also important. Successful completion of a four-year college-preparatory program is required. Application for admission to the College is encouraged for all academically qualified candidates regardless of race, religion, age, gender, or creed.

Application and Information

To apply, students should submit a completed application form and an essay with the required $30 fee, request that an official high school transcript be sent to the Admission Office, forward the results of the SAT I or ACT, submit two letters of recommendation (one must be from a guidance counselor), and, if they wish, schedule a personal interview. The application priority deadline is March 1. To apply as a transfer student, the applicant must submit official transcripts of all postsecondary courses completed and a course-description catalog from each college or university attended in addition to following the steps given above.

Anna Maria College invites students to learn more about the College by visiting the campus. Students should call the Undergraduate Admission Office to schedule an appointment. For detailed information about the College's distinctive programs and campus community, prospective students should contact:

Jane Patricia Fidler
Associate Director of Admission
Anna Maria College
50 Sunset Lane
Paxton, Massachusetts 01612-1198
Telephone: 508-849-3360
           800-344-4586 (toll-free)
Fax: 508-849-3362
E-mail: admission@annamaria.edu
World Wide Web: http://www.annamaria.edu

Socquet House, built in 1750, is currently used as the residence for the Sisters of St. Anne.

ANTIOCH COLLEGE
YELLOW SPRINGS, OHIO

The College

Antioch College is a private, independent liberal arts college that blends practical work experience with classroom learning and participatory community governance.

Antioch's mission is to empower its students through an understanding of the force of knowledge and its use in action. The College's curriculum encourages both respect for established wisdom and also the courage to challenge it. Its cooperative education program provides essential life and work experience. Active participation in community governance offers actual responsibility for policy decisions that affect college life.

Antioch students experiment. With the faculty members, they develop plans for their own education. Antioch students are intelligent decision makers and informed risk takers who become creative thinkers and courageous practitioners. An Antioch education provides a framework for self-motivated learners to express themselves and their creative talents within and beyond standard parameters—and succeed.

Antioch College inspires a respect for all of life: self, others, and the earth. With respect to its own history and values, Antioch reaffirms its commitment to the education of women and ethnic minority groups.

College policy focuses on standards of moderation, sensitivity to the rights and needs of others, integrity, and honesty. Dress on campus is casual. Many students own bicycles, and students are permitted to have cars. Possession of firearms is forbidden. While on campus, students are expected to live in residence halls; limited housing is available for married students. Support services include medical attention provided by the infirmary, health insurance coverage on and off campus, and psychological counseling.

Antioch draws students from across the United States and around the world for its enrollment of approximately 650 students. Of the 1998 entering class, 80 percent were out-of-state students.

Location

Yellow Springs (population 4,600) is 18 miles from Dayton and 60 miles from both Cincinnati and the state capital of Columbus. The village of Yellow Springs is not a typical small country town; it is a vital intellectual and cultural community that provides diverse activities, participatory arts organizations, and political and social groups. Yellow Springs residents include professionals and artists who are socially concerned, politically active, and immensely interested in the arts.

Majors and Degrees

Antioch College awards the Bachelor of Arts (B.A.) and the Bachelor of Science (B.S.) degrees. The academic program offers eight interdisciplinary majors, with the flexibility for students to create their own major across areas from among these majors. The majors offered are history, philosophy, and religious studies, supported by faculty in history, philosophy, and religious studies; cultural and interdisciplinary studies, supported by faculty in African/African-American studies, communications, education studies (including teacher certification), environmental studies, peace studies, and women's studies; literature, languages, and culture, supported by faculty in creative writing, languages and cultures, and literature; biological and environmental sciences, supported by faculty in biological and environmental science; physical sciences, supported by faculty in chemistry, computer science, environmental sciences, mathematics, and physics; self, society, and culture, supported by faculty in anthropology, psychology, and sociology; social and global studies, supported by faculty in economics, international relations, management, and political science; and visual and performing arts, supported by faculty in dance, music, theater, and visual arts (ceramics, painting, sculpture).

Degrees for self-designed majors are offered. A preparatory program in professional medicine is also available. The College offers a dual-degree option for engineering majors in cooperation with Washington University in St. Louis, Missouri.

Academic Program

An Antioch education incorporates three principal elements: classroom learning, required work experience (co-op), and student participation in campus governance. This academic program provides opportunities to apply the theories of the classroom to the realities of the work world. Plus, active campus self-governance gives Antioch students the opportunity to realize themselves as effective and forceful decision makers.

Antioch encourages students to understand their roles as members of a vast and complex world. The College's curriculum reflects a commitment to representing the contributions of women, various ethnic groups, and other countries and cultures. This commitment is achieved, in part, through the "cross-cultural experience" requirement, during which students immerse themselves in a culture different from their own for a period of three to twelve months. This requirement may be fulfilled through co-op. Study abroad is optional, but approximately 40 percent of students study abroad at some point.

Each academic year is composed of three trimesters. During the fall and spring trimesters, students enroll in three to four courses per study term. The summer trimester consists of three 4-week blocks in which students participate in a single intensive course each month. Students are in one of two divisions that alternate use of the college campus and off-campus work experiences. One division begins in the summer trimester. All students study full-time on campus for a total of seven 15-week trimesters. Students work full-time off campus, usually in paying jobs located throughout the country and the world, for a total of five 16-week trimesters. B.A. or B.S. degree requirements include a minimum of 107 classroom academic credits divided among general education, the major, and electives. Five trimesters of off-campus co-op work are also required to earn the bachelor's degree. Students may initiate courses and independent study programs to meet degree requirements.

Placement and credit are awarded for scores of 4 and 5 on the College Board Advanced Placement tests and for appropriate scores on CLEP general examinations. Transfer students must earn at least half of their academic credits and must complete three or more co-op work trimesters while in residence at Antioch.

Off-Campus Arrangements

Antioch College is dedicated to new ways of learning. The College offers formal arrangements for students to study in off-campus settings. These include environmental study in the Florida Everglades, Appalachian, Northwest, and Southwest regions; study abroad through Antioch Education Abroad; and co-op assignments in both urban and rural environments. Additional off-campus opportunities, both in the United States and abroad, are available through the twelve-member Great Lakes Colleges Association and the Southwestern Ohio Council for Higher Education.

Academic Facilities

The Olive Kettering Memorial Library houses 330,000 volumes and continues to expand its collection. A full range of online library services is available. Interlibrary loans are available from other universities and colleges through Antioch's membership in the twelve-institution Southwestern Ohio Council for Higher Education. The College's Instructional Systems Department provides audiovisual facilities and services, which include a foreign language material collection; a video section, which contains a library of videotapes produced by students and faculty members; equipment for loan to Antioch community members; and a learning laboratory. The Computer Center is used in academic and co-op programs as well as for administrative data processing. The Outdoor Education Center, located adjacent to campus in the 1,000-acre Glen Helen nature preserve, furnishes sites for environmental programs. The Charles F. Kettering Laboratory, a science research facility, currently houses a variety of scientific projects.

Costs

Tuition, room and board, and fees for the 1999–2000 academic year totaled $24,397. In addition, an estimated $600–$1000 was needed for incidental expenses, books, and travel. Co-op job salaries vary. Most salaries are sufficient to cover travel and living expenses; some include only room and board, while others offer a salary that may assist students with future college expenses. Stipends are provided to relieve co-op transition costs.

Financial Aid

Approximately 80 percent of all Antioch students receive financial assistance. Types of aid include scholarships, loans, Federal Work-Study (FWS) Program jobs, tuition grants, and Federal Pell and Federal Supplemental Educational Opportunity grants. Loans and FWS part-time jobs are included in all financial aid combination packages. Antioch uses the Free Application for Federal Student Aid (FAFSA) for analysis of need. Transfer students are eligible for the same aid consideration as first-year students.

Faculty

Antioch strives to arrange individually tailored learning to meet each student's needs, interests, and abilities. The College's able faculty are dedicated to academic and career counseling as well as teaching, and students actively participate in the process of designing their own education. There are 60 full-time faculty members, and another 27 serve part-time. Six faculty members supervise the co-op work program. Four full-time professionals staff the library. The usual student-faculty ratio is 10:1, and the average class size is 12. The co-op plan assigns half of all students to campus during any given trimester, allowing for personalized advising and instruction and student interaction. Faculty members write narrative summary evaluations of students' work for all courses.

Student Government

Antioch's long tradition of student and faculty member participation is evident in its regulating structures. Two major councils constitute the governing bodies of the campus: the Community Council and the Administrative Council. Community Council, the legislative body of Community Government (CG), is composed of elected students and nonstudents (faculty members and college employees). It assumes responsibility for the quality of life on campus. The Council maintains a newspaper; a student union building (containing office space for CG staff and student-interest groups); weekly films; music concerts; and diverse social and cultural activities. The community manager, an elected student, administers CG policies. Student and faculty representatives also serve on the Administrative Council, an advisory body to the president. This board counsels budget, curriculum, personnel, faculty hiring, planning, and financial aid matters.

Admission Requirements

Antioch seeks students from diverse social, religious, socioeconomic, geographic, and philosophical backgrounds. In evaluating a candidate's qualifications, Antioch emphasizes qualities of openness to change, ability to work independently, and self-direction. Personal qualities are as important as academic abilities in admission consideration.

Scores on either the ACT or the SAT I are highly recommended but not required. A college-preparatory program is strongly recommended. Antioch recognizes and respects variations in standard programs, such as independent study projects, pass/fail courses, and enrollment in alternative school programs.

Transfer students are welcome and are encouraged to apply; each year roughly one third of entering students are transfers. Admissions notification is on a rolling basis. The recommended application deadline for early action or January entrance is November 15 with notification by December 15. The recommended deadline for summer or fall admission is February 1. Applications received after February 1 are considered on a case-by-case basis. The Candidates Reply Date, in either case, is May 1.

Application and Information

Descriptive materials, application papers, and financial aid and scholarship forms are available from the Office of Admissions. Completed applications should be returned with a nonrefundable $35 fee. This fee can be waived in cases of extreme hardship when endorsed by the candidate's secondary school counselor. An enrollment deposit of $150, not refundable until graduation, is required before entrance.

Requests for additional information should be sent to:

Office of Admissions
Antioch College
795 Livermore Street
Yellow Springs, Ohio 45387
Telephone: 937-767-6400
        800-543-9436 (toll-free)
Fax: 937-767-6473
E-mail: admissions@antioch-college.edu
World Wide Web: http://www.antioch-college.edu

AQUINAS COLLEGE
GRAND RAPIDS, MICHIGAN

The College
Located on the eastern edge of the city of Grand Rapids, Aquinas enjoys all of the advantages of Michigan's second-largest city and is just a 3-hour drive from Detroit or Chicago. The Aquinas College campus is an interesting blend of early-nineteenth-century architecture coupled with modern-day structures. The campus abounds with natural beauty; it has been called the most beautiful small campus in Michigan. Its ninety species of trees, winding woodland paths, and inviting creeks and ponds create a peaceful 107-acre environment that students of all ages find welcoming. Founded by the Dominican Sisters of Grand Rapids in 1886, Aquinas has a Catholic heritage and a Christian tradition. The Dominican tradition of working and serving remains alive at Aquinas. It is lived out by Aquinas students who volunteer their time and talents in the Grand Rapids community and by those who travel to places such as Oaxaca, Mexico; Appalachia, Kentucky; or any of a dozen other service learning project sites. An ability to see the world from different perspectives is the hallmark of an Aquinas-educated student. Aquinas, a coeducational liberal arts college, offers an approach to learning and living that teaches students unlimited ways of seeing the world. That is why every Aquinas student enrolls in the humanities program, a two-semester exploration of the best that has been thought, written, composed, and painted. And as students find their way in the world of thought, the core curriculum in natural science ensures that they discover the workings of the physical world as well. An Aquinas education makes graduates more employable. Each year, almost 200 Aquinas students find businesses, government agencies, and other organizations eager to offer field experience and internship opportunities. Students can participate in a molecular genetics research project at a government facility in the state of Washington, work on historic preservation projects with the Michigan Bureau of History in Lansing, or learn about politics from the inside as a congressional intern in Washington, D.C. Nine out of 10 applicants recommended by the Aquinas premedical advisory committee are admitted to medical school, and 19 of 20 are accepted into other graduate programs. In all, more than 90 percent of Aquinas seniors find jobs or enroll in graduate school soon after graduation. Aquinas sees a liberal arts education as career preparation. The Aquinas general education plan exposes students to the necessary skills that enable them to become critical thinkers, articulate speakers, strong writers, and effective problem solvers. Aquinas faculty members insist that students carry values as well as skills into the workplace. The College's curriculum, with its more than forty majors and cognates, is designed to provide students with both breadth and depth and to foster a thirst for knowledge and truth and a spirit of intellectual dialogue and inquiry. Coupled with nationally recognized co-op and internship programs, it prepares students to both live and work in the rapidly changing world of today and tomorrow.

Arriving from places as near as Grand Rapids, Chicago, and Detroit and as far as India and China, the 2,559 students include 1,368 full-time, 626 part-time, and 565 graduate students. The Insignis program at Aquinas encourages students of exceptional academic ability to participate in social and intellectual activities such as lectures and receptions for visiting scholars and trips to places of cultural interest. Aquinas offers more than thirty student organizations, ranging from intramural teams and departmental clubs to a wide variety of musical groups, student publications, and service organizations.

In addition to its undergraduate degrees, Aquinas also offers Master in the Art of Teaching, Master in Education, Master in Science Education, and Master of Management (with concentrations in marketing, organizational development, health-care management, and international business) degrees.

Location
Aquinas' location in Grand Rapids allows students to reap the benefits of west Michigan's economic, educational, and cultural center. The city is one of the fastest-growing areas in the Great Lakes region. Grand Rapids combines big-city excitement and small-town charm. There are cosmopolitan amenities ranging from four-star hotels and restaurants to top-notch cultural facilities and entertainment venues. In addition to established attractions such as the Gerald R. Ford Presidential Museum, the Van Andel Public Museum, an expanded zoo, the 5,500-seat Old Kent Park stadium for Whitecaps minor-league baseball, and the 70-acre Fredrik Meijer Gardens, recent attractions include the more than 12,000-seat Van Andel Arena, home to the Grand Rapids Griffins IHL hockey team and a venue for nationally known music concerts and performances. These major facilities add to the list of popular points of interest, festivals, and special events. With nearly half a million residents, there are abundant recreation, arts, and cultural opportunities available.

Majors and Degrees
Aquinas College offers the following undergraduate degree programs: Bachelor of Arts, Bachelor of Fine Arts, Bachelor of Arts in general education, Bachelor of Music Education, Bachelor of Science, Bachelor of Science in Business Administration, Bachelor of Science in environmental science, and Bachelor of Science in international business. Beginning in fall 2000, a Bachelor of Science in Nursing degree program will be offered in collaboration with the University of Detroit Mercy and St. Mary's Mercy Medical Center. Majors and programs of study are offered in accounting, accounting/business administration, art, art/business administration, art history, biology, business administration, business administration/communication arts, business administration/sports management, chemistry, communication arts, community leadership, computer information systems, conductive education, drawing, economics, education, English, environmental science, environmental studies, foreign language, French, geography, German, gerontology, health, history, international studies, Japanese, journalism/publications, Latin, learning disabilities, mathematics, medical technology, music, not-for-profit management, nuclear medicine technology, organizational communication, painting, philosophy, photography, physical education and recreation, physics, political science, pre-engineering, printmaking, psychology, religious studies, sculpture, social science, sociology, Spanish, studio art, urban studies, and women's studies. Preprofessional courses are available in dentistry, law, and medicine.

Associate degrees are also available, including the Associate of Arts in liturgical music and ministry and the Associate of Science.

Academic Program
In addition to their major and minor fields of study, students take an integrated skills course called Inquiry and Expression. This course spans the entire freshman year and has an emphasis on writing integrated with reading critically, oral communication skills, critical thinking, library/electronic research methods, computer utilization, and basic quantitative reasoning. The thematic content is American Pluralism: The Individual in a Diverse America. Sophomores take a yearlong course in the humanities. As juniors they are required to take 3 hours in Religious Dimensions of Human Existence, with a choice among three categories: Scripture, Catholic/Christian

Thought, or Contemporary Religious Experience. The senior year includes a capstone course called Global Perspective. Students are also required to be proficient in a second language through the 201 level. There also is a distribution plan in the general education plan covering The Individual in a Global Community; Myth, Mind, Body, and Spirit; Natural World; Artistic and Creative Studies; and Quantitative Reasoning and Technology. A required career/professional development component begins in summer orientation and is apportioned over four years; topics include assessment of students' strengths, skills, and interests; development of goals, a learning plan, and setting a direction; focus on the individual—wellness, personal finances, and leadership/team skills; awareness of careers, professions, and graduate study; information on making and maintaining a professional portfolio and resume; participating in a professional/career mentor program; career fairs and networking; and experiential learning (choices include co-op, internship, service learning, service trips, and study abroad). The College follows a two-semester calendar with a summer session. Aquinas also accepts credit through CLEP and Advanced Placement.

Off-Campus Arrangements

Students have the option of participating in the Dominican College Campus Interchange Program. Cooperating colleges are Barry University in Miami, Florida; Dominican College in San Rafael, California; and St. Thomas Aquinas College in Spark Hill, New York. Students can increase their foreign language skills through cultural-immersion programs in Costa Rica, France, Spain, Germany, or Peru. Two Aquinas faculty members accompany 25 students to Aquinas' study center in Tully Cross, Ireland. Students have the opportunity to earn a full semester of credit, travel abroad, and live in a rural Irish community. The curriculum is centered on several aspects of Irish studies. A semester in Montana on a Native American reservation is a new off-campus learning opportunity. An exchange program in Japan will also be available in fall 2000.

Academic Facilities

The Woodhouse Library resources include a public access catalog, audiovisual materials, circulation and course reserve materials, reference services, and interlibrary loan services (free access to more than 27 million books and documents from libraries across the country). Two main computer labs and several remote labs are available for student use. The graphics lab contains equipment that is largely image-oriented and has Apple IIe's for those using Apple software, VAX terminals for statistics and programming, and the College's Macintosh SE terminals. The text lab has print-oriented computers with IBM-compatible applications. Labs are open seven days a week and are staffed by trained assistants/tutors. Albertus Magnus Hall of Science features the handicapped-accessible Baldwin Observatory and a greenhouse. Other facilities include the Cook Carriage House; a student center; and the modern Art and Music Center, featuring a dark room, a 200-seat recital hall, an art gallery, and a sculpture studio. The Jarecki Center for Advanced Learning opened in fall 1999, as did three new apartment buildings, providing another housing option.

Costs

For 2000–01, tuition is $14,034, and room and board are $4884, for a total of $18,918. Other expenses, including books, travel, and personal supplies, average $2000.

Financial Aid

Aquinas College awards both merit-based financial assistance and traditional need-based assistance to qualified students. The Spectrum Scholarship Program was developed to recognize students' achievements in academics, leadership, and service. More than 50 percent of entering freshmen receive some form of financial assistance. The College administers the traditional grant and loan programs, including Federal Stafford Student Loans and Federal PLUS loans. Athletic grants are also available. The College participates in the Facts Tuition Management Plan. This plan assists students in paying costs over a period of time. To apply for financial assistance, students must complete the Free Application for Federal Student Aid (FAFSA).

Faculty

Aquinas faculty members are teachers first: while research plays an important part in the Aquinas faculty development, teaching remains the number one priority. In addition to teaching, faculty members serve as academic advisers, mentors, and advisers to various clubs and organizations on campus. With a student-professor ratio of 13:1, faculty members give individual attention and assistance to students. All classes and labs are taught by faculty members, not graduate assistants. Approximately 70 percent of Aquinas faculty members have doctoral or terminal degrees.

Student Government

The Student Senate is the governing body of Aquinas students. Senators are chosen by securing twenty-five signatures of students in support of their involvement. These students have both voice and vote on issues facing the College's Academic Assembly. The senate is responsible for many of the academic, social, recreational, and cultural activities brought to campus.

Admission Requirements

Freshman and transfer applications are received on a rolling basis. A candidate for admission to Aquinas is considered on the basis of academic preparation, scholarship, and character. Admission depends on a number of factors, including high school academic record and ACT or SAT I test scores. Transfer students must present a minimum 2.0 grade point average on a 4.0 scale. All applicants need to remit a $25 application fee. Online applications do not require an application fee. The admissions office reserves the right to review applications on a case-by-case basis. Curriculum, extracurricular activities, and any extenuating circumstances are considered in the decision. Letters of recommendation are encouraged but not required.

Application and Information

For further information, interested students should contact:
Paula Meehan
Dean of Admissions
Aquinas College
1607 Robinson Road, SE
Grand Rapids, Michigan 49506
Telephone: 616-732-4460
        800-678-9593 (toll-free)
E-mail: admissions@aquinas.edu
World Wide Web: http://www.aquinas.edu

Classes are sometimes held outside on Aquinas' beautiful campus.

ARIZONA STATE UNIVERSITY
TEMPE, ARIZONA

The University

Founded in 1885, Arizona State University (ASU) is among the largest universities in the United States. The University has three campuses: ASU Main in Tempe, ASU East in Mesa, and ASU West in Phoenix. Undergraduates, numbering 33,948, constitute about 75 percent of the total enrollment. While 72 percent of ASU students are Arizona residents, all states and more than 125 countries are represented. More than 7,000 students are African American, Hispanic, Asian American, or Native American. ASU's modern buildings and facilities are set on an 814-acre campus in a landscaped oasis of palm trees, desert vegetation, and fountains, warmed by the year-round Arizona sunshine. ASU has twenty-six fraternities and nineteen sororities, a counseling center, health service, academic tutorial help for students through the Learning Resource Center, career services, academic advising centers, a campus newspaper, a television and radio station, and more than 400 clubs and organizations. On-campus residence halls house more than 4,500 students, and a variety of off-campus apartments and rentals are available nearby. A comprehensive Freshman Year Experience program offers freshmen the opportunity to develop success skills in academics and extracurricular activities. Excellent men's and women's intercollegiate athletic teams compete in one of the most comprehensive facilities of any university in the country. In addition, there is an intramural program that provides more than thirty sports opportunities. Entertainment and cultural series bring to the campus popular artists, films, speakers, and performing arts presentations. Orientation programs for new students and their parents are offered throughout the year, including special programs in New York, Chicago, Seattle, and Los Angeles. The University Honors College gives students an opportunity to live and learn in a community devoted to academic excellence and personal achievement. Several outstanding ASU students have received such prestigious awards as the Rhodes, Marshall, and Truman Scholarships, and membership on the USA Today All-USA Academic First Team. The Graduate College offers eighty-seven master's degrees and forty-nine doctoral or terminal degrees, including the Juris Doctor.

Location

ASU is located in Tempe, a city of 158,000 people, which adjoins Phoenix, Scottsdale, and Mesa. This metropolitan area, with a population of almost 3 million, incorporates the values of an urban environment with the beauty of the Sonoran desert, nearby lakes and mountains (three skiing areas), and the Grand Canyon.

Majors and Degrees

The College of Architecture and Environmental Design awards the Bachelor of Science in Design (B.S.D.) degree in architectural studies, graphic design, housing and urban development, industrial design, and interior design; the Bachelor of Science in Landscape Architecture (B.S.L.A.) in landscape architecture; and the Bachelor of Science in Planning (B.S.P.) in urban planning. The College of Business awards the B.S. degree in accountancy, computer information systems, economics, finance, management, marketing, real estate, and supply chain management. The College of Education awards the Bachelor of Arts in Education (B.A.E.) degree in early childhood, elementary (bilingual education and English as a second language), secondary (biological sciences, business education, chemistry, Chinese, communication, economics, English, family resources and human development, French, geography, German, history, Japanese, journalism, mathematics, mathematics/chemistry, mathematics/physics, physical education, physics, physics/chemistry, political science, Russian, social studies, and Spanish), and special education. The College of Engineering and Applied Sciences awards the Bachelor of Science (B.S.) degree in computer science and construction (general building, heavy, residential, and specialty construction) and the Bachelor of Science in Engineering (B.S.E.) degree in aerospace, chemical, civil (environmental engineering), computer systems, electrical, industrial, and mechanical engineering; bioengineering; engineering special studies (manufacturing engineering and premedical engineering), and materials science and engineering. The College of Fine Arts awards the Bachelor of Arts (B.A.) degree in art (art history, photographic studies, and studio art), music, and theater; the Bachelor of Fine Arts (B.F.A.) in art (art education, ceramics, drawing, fibers, intermedia, metals, painting, photography, printmaking, and sculpture), dance (choreography, dance education, dance studies, and performance), and theater (theater education); and the Bachelor of Music (B.M.) degree in music education (choral–general, instrumental, and string), music therapy, performance (guitar, jazz, keyboard, music theater, orchestral instrument, piano accompanying, and voice), and theory and composition (composition and theory). The College of Liberal Arts and Sciences awards the B.A. and/or B.S. degree in African American studies, anthropology, Asian languages (Chinese and Japanese), biochemistry, biology (biology and society and chemistry), chemistry, Chicana and Chicano studies, clinical laboratory sciences, computer science, conservation biology, economics, English, exercise science/physical education (exercise and wellness, exercise science, and physical education), family resources and human development (in business, family studies/child development, and human nutrition–dietetics), French, geography, geology, German, history, humanities (architecture; architecture, culture, and society; business; design; film studies; humanities/liberal arts; justice studies; and planning), interdisciplinary studies, Italian, mathematics (applied, computational, general, and pure mathematics and statistics and probability), microbiology, molecular biosciences/biotechnology, philosophy, physics, plant biology (environmental science and ecology, molecular biosciences/biotechnology, and urban horticulture), political science, psychology, religious studies, Russian, sociology, Spanish, speech and hearing science, and women's studies. The College of Nursing awards the Bachelor of Science in Nursing (B.S.N.) degree. The College of Public Programs awards the B.A. degree in broadcasting, communication, and journalism; the B.S. in communication, justice studies, and recreation (recreation management and tourism); and the Bachelor of Social Work (B.S.W.) degree. The Division of Undergraduate Academic Services offers a Bachelor of Interdisciplinary Studies (B.I.S.) degree.

The following degree programs are offered at the ASU East campus. The Morrison School of Agribusiness and Resource Management awards the Bachelor of Science (B.S.) degree in agribusiness (general agribusiness, food science, international agribusiness, pre-veterinary medicine, and professional golf management) and environmental resources (natural resource management) and the Bachelor of Applied Sciences (B.A.S.) degree in applied science (consumer products technology, food retailing, and resource team specialist). The College of Technology and Applied Sciences awards the Bachelor of Science (B.S.) degree in aeronautical engineering technology, aeronautical management technology (airway science flight management and airway science management), electronics engineering technology (computer systems, electronic systems, microelectronics, and telecommunications), industrial technology (environmental technology management, industrial technology management, and information technology), and manufacturing engineering technology and the Bachelor of Applied Science (B.A.S.) degree in applied science (aviation maintenance technology, aviation management technology, computer systems administration, digital media management, digital publishing, emergency management, fire service management, instrumentation, microcomputer systems, operations management technology, production technology, semiconductor technology, software technology applications, and technical graphics). East College awards the Bachelor of Science (B.S.) degree in applied psychology and business administration.

Academic Program

ASU is on a semester system with three summer sessions (one 8-week session and two 5-week sessions) and one winter session. Students plan an individual program of study that includes general studies, core courses, and degree requirements. Undergraduates must complete a minimum of 35 hours in the General Studies Program, which consists of five core areas and three awareness areas. The core areas are literacy and critical inquiry, numeracy, humanities and fine arts, social and behavioral sciences, and natural sciences. The three awareness areas are global awareness, historical awareness, and cultural diversity in the United States. Several of the colleges require completion of specific core courses before enrollment in major or upper-division courses. Each degree program has individual requirements related to courses in the major, specialty options or emphases, and, in some cases, GPA. Overall requirements for graduation with a bachelor's degree include completion of a minimum of 120 semester hours, 50 of which are in the upper division; demonstration of proficiency in written English; maintenance of a minimum cumulative GPA of 2.0 (on a scale in which 4.0 is equivalent to A); and completion of a minimum of 30 hours of credit, including the final 12, in residence. Most of the colleges and degree programs stipulate additional requirements; are selective in admitting students to a major, upper-division, or professional program; and may have additional graduation requirements. Most degree programs can be completed in four years. ASU's academic programs are fully accredited by the principal educational and professional accrediting organizations. Students may pursue interdisciplinary programs that lead to a bachelor's degree or program emphasis in a variety of areas including Asian and Southeast Asian studies, health physics, the humanities, Jewish studies, Latin American studies, museum studies, Russian and Eastern European studies, and women's studies. Qualified students may work with individual faculty members toward the development of a degree program designed around a special interest. The University Honors College is available for students of exceptional academic merit. Four-year Army and Air Force ROTC programs are also offered. Special opportunities for advanced placement and credit are available for students who earn scores of 4 or 5 (or, in some cases, 3) on the Advanced Placement (AP) tests of the College Board; scores of 500 or higher on the general examinations and 50 or higher on subject examinations of the College-Level Examination Program (CLEP); or acceptable scores on comprehensive examinations by course and on proficiency examinations. Various restrictions and limitations may apply, as noted in the *University Catalog*.

Off-Campus Arrangements

During the academic year, student exchange and study-abroad programs exist at many universities in a number of countries.

Academic Facilities

Seven libraries provide a combined total of 8 million bound and microformed volumes and more than 32,000 periodical subscriptions. Other specialized academic resources include the Deer Valley Rock Art Center, Geology Museum, Anthropology Museum, Planetarium, Meteorite Collection, Architecture Gallery of Design, Herbarium, Solar Energy Research Laboratory, University Art Collections, KAET (University Public Broadcasting Service television station), Music Recital Theater, Lyceum Theater, Louise Lincoln Kerr Cultural Center, and Nelson Fine Arts Center. The Grady Gammage Memorial Auditorium, designed by Frank Lloyd Wright, is among the finest facilities of its kind in the Southwest.

Costs

For 1999–2000, costs for full-time (12 hours or more) in-state students for the academic year (two semesters) were as follows: registration fee, $2261; room and board, $5010; and books and supplies, $700. Out-of-state students paid an additional annual tuition fee of $7152. (Fees for 2000–01 are subject to change.) Personal and travel expenses are extra.

Financial Aid

ASU helps approximately 37,000 students each year to finance their higher educations. Financial aid from federal, state, local, institutional, and private sources is awarded in the form of scholarships, loans, grants, and work-study employment. An applicant for federal financial aid should apply for admission and complete the Free Application for Federal Student Aid (FAFSA). For priority consideration, applicants should mail the completed FAFSA form by February 15.

Faculty

ASU has 1,747 faculty members engaged in research, teaching, and service; many have national and international recognition and prestige. More than 82 percent hold doctorates or professional terminal degrees. The student-faculty ratio is 19:1.

Student Government

The Associated Students of Arizona State University (ASASU) is the official representative student organization on campus. Elected and appointed positions provide outstanding opportunities for students to experience leadership, responsibility, and involvement.

Admission Requirements

Nonresident freshmen must rank in the upper quarter of their graduating class or have a minimum 3.0 GPA or have a minimum ACT composite score of 24 or a minimum combined SAT score of 1110. Nonresident freshmen who have a GPA of 2.57–2.99 are encouraged to apply and are considered on a case-by-case basis. Resident freshmen must rank in the upper quarter of their graduating class or have a minimum 3.0 GPA or have a minimum ACT composite score of 22 or a minimum combined SAT score of 1040. Resident freshmen who rank in the second quarter of their graduating class or have a cumulative GPA of 2.5–2.99 may be admitted with conditions. All freshmen must meet competency requirements in English, mathematics, laboratory sciences, social sciences, foreign language, and fine arts; the requirements may be fulfilled by appropriate high school course work or SAT or ACT scores. Resident transfer students with up to 23 transferable credits must meet the same entrance requirements as freshman resident applicants, as listed above. Nonresident transfer students with up to 23 transferable credits must meet the same entrance requirements as nonresident freshmen, as listed above. Nonresident transfer students with 24 or more transferable credits must have a minimum GPA of 2.5. All transfer students under 22 years of age who have not completed an AGEC or associate's or higher degree must also meet competency requirements in English, mathematics, laboratory sciences, foreign language, fine arts, and social sciences; these requirements may be fulfilled through appropriate high school course work, SAT or ACT scores, transferable community college course work, or a combination of these. Many colleges or departments require a higher minimum GPA for transfer students.

Application and Information

The fall application priority date is April 15. The application for admission, transcripts, and test scores should be submitted no later than thirty days prior to the beginning of the semester for which entrance is desired. High school applicants are encouraged to apply during the fall of their senior year. Upon request, an ASU viewbook may be obtained, which includes an application for admission and information about academic programs, admission, housing, and financial aid. Prospective students and parents who would like to receive a viewbook or visit the University, meet with an admissions representative, and go on a campus tour on any weekday, or on selected Saturdays, should contact:

Undergraduate Admissions
Arizona State University
P.O. Box 870112
Tempe, Arizona 85287-0112
Telephone: 480-965-7788
E-mail: ugradinq@asu.edu
World Wide Web: http://www.asu.edu

ARKANSAS STATE UNIVERSITY
JONESBORO, ARKANSAS

The University

Founded in 1909, Arkansas State University (ASU) is one of the premier institutions of higher education in the state. With technologically advanced facilities and a population of more than 14,000 students (including those at the branch campuses), the University is a major educational force in the state. The main campus, which is located on 900 acres in Jonesboro, has a student population of more than 10,000. Students come from forty-two states and territories and fifty-three countries.

Currently, campus activities are centered at the Carl R. Reng Center. The building serves students with a bookstore, food service, a game room, a lounge, meeting rooms, and a ballroom. In fall 2001, the University will open a new student union with a recreation center. The union will house a post office, retail shops, a food court, lounges, and a fitness center.

The University's athletic teams compete in NCAA Division I as part of the Sun Belt Conference. Men's sports include baseball, basketball, cross-country, golf, indoor and outdoor track, tennis, and football (Big West Conference). Women's sports include basketball, golf, indoor and outdoor track, tennis, and volleyball. A comprehensive intramural program gives all students an opportunity to participate in organized sports. ASU has thirteen fraternities, eight sororities, and more than 160 clubs that serve religious, ethnic, departmental, and other special interests.

Location

As the largest city in northeastern Arkansas, Jonesboro offers a number of attractive alternatives to campus activities. The city, with a population of 51,000, has many shopping areas and hospitals and is the economic hub of northeastern Arkansas and southeastern Missouri. Caraway Road, which runs through the University, is one of the main business streets in the city. Community activities, which range from the Jonesboro Fine Arts Council to the Jonesboro Saddle Club, welcome participation by ASU students. The area also offers many places of worship for students.

The area surrounding Jonesboro offers many forms of activity. Craighead Forest Park provides facilities for fishing and boating and has an attractive picnic area where many ASU groups hold outdoor parties. A few miles north of Jonesboro is Crowley's Ridge State Park, which has two lakes, picnic pavilions, and campgrounds. Jonesboro is within easy driving distance of Lake Norfork, Lake Charles, and Greers Ferry Lake, all ideal for fishing, boating, and camping. The city is an hour's drive from Memphis and a little more than 2 hours from Little Rock.

Majors and Degrees

Arkansas State University offers eighty-eight associate and baccalaureate degrees in addition to sixty-five postbaccalaureate degrees. These degrees are offered in eight colleges and one independent department. The University also has a distinguished honors program for exceptionally qualified students. Preprofessional programs are available in chiropractic, dental hygiene, dentistry, forestry, law, medicine, occupational therapy, optometry, pharmacy, respiratory therapy, and veterinary medicine. Some degrees are offered off campus.

Academic Program

The academic year at ASU consists of two semesters in the fall and spring and two 5-week summer terms. General requirements for all bachelor's degrees include completing a minimum of 124 semester hours and meeting the requirements for a degree as outlined by the respective colleges. An average of C or better must be maintained on all courses completed, as well as an average of C or better in the major field. At least 32 semester hours (including 18 of the last 24 hours earned in a degree program) must be completed in residence at ASU; some programs require additional residency hours. Credits may be earned through the College-Level Examination Program (CLEP) and/or Advanced Placement.

Academic courses are offered through twenty-five departments in eight colleges and one independent department. Classes are offered from 8 a.m. to 9:50 p.m. The Center for Regional Programs also schedules credit courses at various locations off campus at times convenient for working students.

Academic Facilities

The Dean B. Ellis Library, a highlight of the campus tour, subscribes to more than 2,322 periodicals. The library contains a total of 1,550,000 holdings, comprising 536,900 books and bound volumes, 531,307 federal and state documents, and 482,122 units of microtext. It features automated shelving, a computerized checkout system, and a wide range of microfilm materials and is joined with libraries across the nation through the Online Computer Library Center (OCLC) system. The library also houses the Learning Resources Center and the museum. The museum provides resource materials for teaching and research and is nationally known for its art and historical collections. ASU's Laboratory Sciences Center is a sophisticated complex serving students in the fields of biology, chemistry, physics, and the physical sciences. Its 140,000 square feet contain twenty-five laboratory areas, photographic facilities, environmental chambers, and a greenhouse, as well as a full range of modern scientific equipment. The physical education complex has four full-length basketball courts, conditioning and weight rooms, a gymnastics area, racquetball courts, game rooms, and a 25-yard, six-lane indoor pool. The Communications Building features the latest radio-television and photojournalism equipment in the professionally equipped studios, control rooms, darkrooms, and newsroom.

Costs

For 1999–2000, tuition for 12 to 18 credits was assessed at a flat rate of $1176 (plus fees) for Arkansas residents and $3012 (plus fees) for nonresidents. The cost for a residence hall room and board averaged approximately $1460 per semester. The average cost of books was $250 per semester. Students 60 years of age and older may attend ASU tuition-free, space permitting. Costs are subject to change.

Financial Aid

Scholarships are awarded to Arkansas residents who have graduated from accredited Arkansas high schools. High school–age students who earn the GED may also be eligible for scholarships. Awards are based on various criteria, such as ACT/SAT test scores, rank in class, and high school GPA. The deadline date is April 1. A limited number of privately funded scholarships are available to freshmen as well as transfer students. Awards are based on criteria set by individual scholarship donors. The deadline date for these scholarships is

March 1. Need-based assistance comes in the form of grants, loans, and employment. It is provided through federal and state sources. ASU recommends that all students apply for financial aid by February 15 for the upcoming fall semester. To apply for aid, students should use the Free Application for Federal Student Aid (FAFSA). Sixty-six percent of all full-time students receive some sort of aid.

Faculty

ASU has 422 full-time and 56 part-time faculty members, and 87 percent hold the terminal degree in their field. There are approximately 247 members on the graduate faculty, most of whom teach at the undergraduate level as well. The student-faculty ratio is 19:1. Faculty members provide students with instruction and counseling and also participate in professional organizations and community affairs.

Student Government

The Student Government Association (SGA) provides an official voice through which students may express their opinions and interests. Student participation is encouraged in the overall policymaking and decision-making processes of the University. All ASU students are members of the SGA, with the Student Senate, composed of SGA officers and senators, serving as the governing body. The SGA sponsors a committee to hear student grievances, provides assistance with voter registration, participates in campus planning sessions, produces an off-campus-housing directory, and sponsors Homecoming Week activities.

Admission Requirements

High school students applying for early admission are required to have a minimum GPA of 2.75 on a seven-semester transcript and have English, math, reading, and composite scores of 19 or better on the ACT. For regular admission, students need a GPA of 2.5 or better for eight semesters and have English, math, reading, and composite scores of 19 or better on the ACT. Applicants for the College of Nursing and Health Professions must meet a minimum ACT score requirement. Midyear admission is permitted at ASU. Conditional admission is possible for students with a GPA of 2.0 or above but who have English, math, reading, and composite scores below 19 on the ACT. Transfer students who have completed fewer than 14 acceptable semester hours with a cumulative GPA of 2.0 or higher at a regionally accredited college or university are admitted on the same basis as that of entering freshmen. Transfer students who have completed more than 13 acceptable hours with a cumulative GPA of 2.0 or higher at a regionally accredited college or university may be admitted to the University. Transfer students with fewer than 24 acceptable hours must either show evidence of compliance with state laws governing remediation or present ACT/SAT I scores. Proof of immunization against measles and rubella is required of all entering students who were born after January 1, 1957. Male students between the ages of 18 and 25 must show proof of registration with the Selective Service System.

Application and Information

Each candidate for admission is required to submit a formal application on a form provided by the University and to pay a $15 nonrefundable processing fee, along with sending official transcripts of all high school and college work completed. New freshmen and transfer students with fewer than 24 acceptable hours must also submit scores from either the SAT I or ACT to the University. Applicants are strongly urged to take either the SAT I or ACT at an area test center as early as possible, preferably during October, December, or February of their senior year in high school. Individuals who wish to pursue courses of special interest without submitting academic credentials may accumulate up to 12 semester hours of undergraduate nondegree credit. Thereafter, nondegree students must comply with University admission requirements.

For more information concerning the University's programs, students should contact:

Admissions Office
Arkansas State University
P.O. Box 1630
State University, Arkansas 72467
Telephone: 870-972-3024
              800-382-3030 (toll-free)
E-mail: admissions@chickasaw.astate.edu
World Wide Web: http://www.astate.edu

Students on the campus of Arkansas State University.

ARMSTRONG UNIVERSITY
Undergraduate School of Business Administration
OAKLAND, CALIFORNIA

The University
Founded in 1918, Armstrong is a small, independent university. The institution's urban setting in the San Francisco Bay Area, a major business center, and its faculty members, many of whom are involved in developing and demonstrating their expertise in today's business world, reflect Armstrong University's practical approach to education for a career in business. Education at Armstrong is a very personal matter. A seasoned faculty combined with the multicultural student body create a diverse and stimulating learning environment and give the student an opportunity to develop the international perspective vital to success in today's business world. Learning is also enhanced by giving students the experience of interacting with a worldwide network of students and alumni involved in international business.

Students at the University have varied backgrounds. Some were accepted directly from high school, while many others had gained professional experience prior to their admission to the undergraduate programs. Armstrong recognizes that there are a variety of approaches to achieving educational objectives. Requirements for degree programs can be fulfilled through Armstrong's courses, transfer credit, and credit by examination.

Armstrong operates on the semester system. Two semesters equal one academic year. There are also two summer sessions, each lasting four weeks.

Armstrong University is accredited by the Accrediting Council for Independent Colleges and Schools and offers classes in the day and evening.

Location
Armstrong is located in the San Francisco Bay Area. The area is noted for its cosmopolitan atmosphere, its fine educational institutions, and its proximity to Silicon Valley, the high-technology center of the United States.

Majors and Degrees
Armstrong's undergraduate programs are offered through the School of Business Administration and lead to the Bachelor of Business Administration (B.B.A.). The B.B.A. degree is awarded in accounting, finance, international business, management, management information systems (MIS), and marketing. This degree program is ideal for students who desire in-depth business education with a concentration.

Academic Program
The undergraduate program leading to the B.B.A. degree consists of three components: a general education, which provides students with a solid background in the arts and sciences; a business core, which includes a sharpening of skills specifically required of people in the business world; and a field of concentration, which allows the student to develop a deeper knowledge and understanding of one particular area of business. Candidates for the B.B.A. must complete a minimum of 120 credits and have a grade point average of at least 2.0.

Most of the courses make use of state-of-the-art computer equipment and the latest business software.

Academic Facilities
The library is fully automated and offers access to a variety of electronic information sources, including CD-ROMs, online databases, and the Internet, in addition to a large print collection of 10,000 volumes, 170 periodicals, and 800 corporate annual reports. Armstrong is equipped with a fully networked state-of-the-art computer learning center. Microcomputers give every student easy access to a broad range of software. This configuration allows students to operate the equipment as a local area network (LAN).

Costs
Undergraduate tuition in 2000–01 is $198 per credit; the minimum full-time course load is 12 units per term. Books and instructional supplies cost approximately $350 per year for full-time students. Although Armstrong has no University-owned residence facilities, adequate housing is available in the many residential areas within commuting distance. The Dean of Students and the Armstrong University Student Association (AUSA) provide students with current information on local housing and an updated listing of what is available. The average cost for students sharing an apartment and cooking their own meals was $7500 per student per academic year.

Financial Aid
Financial aid is available. Students should contact the University for financial aid information.

Faculty
The professors at Armstrong University are distinguished academics who have significant experience in business practice and education. Each possesses a doctoral degree or other terminal degree, such as Master of Business Administration. Classes are small in order to give students high-quality contact with instructors. Instructors are experienced in working with students from diverse backgrounds. Faculty members are available outside of class to give students additional academic counseling. The undergraduate program director works closely with students throughout their academic career to ensure that students get the assistance they need in a timely and effective manner.

Student Government
The Armstrong University Student Association (AUSA) is the student organization. Each registered student is a member and is eligible to vote in student elections and participate in AUSA activities. The Student Council, the governing body of AUSA, has both elected and appointed members. The Student Council plans and organizes activities for AUSA.

Student government officers gain experience in organizational and administrative skills important for success in business. All students are encouraged to take part in student activities and student government. Communication among students and between students and the University administration is fostered by student publications.

Admission Requirements
Armstrong believes that all individuals who are interested in education for business and who are willing and able to progress

toward the educational goals they have set for themselves should have the opportunity to develop their knowledge and abilities. The University seeks to achieve diversity in its student body and welcomes applications from international students, transfer students, students resuming their education, and older women and men who have delayed entrance to college. It is the responsibility of the applicant to present evidence that he or she is capable of pursuing higher education and that the experience will be beneficial for all concerned. Applicants for admission may apply to enter at the start of the fall or spring semester or at the start of the summer sessions.

Applicants for admission to the undergraduate programs must present evidence of high school graduation or the equivalent. Many students may transfer credits earned at other colleges and universities. An official evaluation of transferable credit is prepared for the applicant by the Registrar's Office as part of the admission process and is sent to the transfer applicant.

Application and Information

Each applicant must submit an application for admission; official transcripts from all high schools, colleges, and universities attended; and a nonrefundable application-processing fee. TOEFL scores are required of all applicants whose native language is not English and who graduated from an institution where English was not used as the only language of instruction. International applicants must also submit a statement of financial support. Applicants whose scholastic record may not accurately reflect their academic abilities may choose to submit such supplemental materials as letters of recommendation, standardized test scores, a personal statement of educational objectives, and a summary of work experience.

Applications are processed when all materials have been received by the admissions office. The applicant is informed of the decision as soon as the application is acted upon by the Board of Admissions.

For further information and an application form, candidates should write to or call:

Office of Admissions
Armstrong University
1608 Webster Street
Oakland, California 94612
Telephone: 510-835-7900
              800-222-9297 (toll-free)
Fax: 510-835-8935
E-mail: info@armstrong-u.edu
World Wide Web: http://www.armstrong-u.edu

ART ACADEMY OF CINCINNATI
CINCINNATI, OHIO

The Academy
The Art Academy of Cincinnati is a small, independent college of art for students seeking a superior education in the creation and understanding of art. It is accredited by the National Association of Schools of Art and Design and the Commission on Institutions of Higher Education of the North Central Association of Colleges and Schools.

The Academy's origins reach back to the early nineteenth century, when individual artists offered classes in Cincinnati. In 1869 the school was established as the McMicken School of Art and Design. When the Cincinnati Museum Association was established in 1885, the school's founder suggested affiliating the art school with the museum. On November 26, 1887, the Art Academy was officially dedicated in its present location.

Students are attracted to the Academy for several reasons, particularly the closeness of the community of 225 full-time students. Faculty members are familiar with each individual's talents and needs, and there is a focus on the visual arts that only a professional art college can offer. Another outstanding advantage is the close relationship between the Academy and its neighbor, the Cincinnati Art Museum.

Location
The Art Academy of Cincinnati is located in Cincinnati, Ohio, a major metropolitan area. It is set in Eden Park, a 184-acre metropolitan park that also features an outdoor amphitheater, Mirror Lake, the Krohn Conservatory, the Playhouse in the Park theater, and the Cincinnati Art Museum. Like Rome, the city of Cincinnati is built on seven hills. As the Art Academy is located on one of the hills, it affords a spectacular view of the city, the Ohio River and its valley, and northern Kentucky. This scenery has inspired the images and styles of noted artists for the last century.

Greater Cincinnati is a center for social, cultural, and educational activities; there is something for everyone. The city is the home of the Reds (baseball), the Bengals (football), and the up-and-coming Cyclones (hockey). Kings Island, Coney Island, the Beach, Americana, and Surf Cincinnati are all amusement parks located near the city. The Academy itself is located minutes from downtown, where the nationally acclaimed Symphony Orchestra, Cincinnati Ballet Company, Cincinnati Opera, and May Festival Chorus perform. The Contemporary Arts Center, Taft Museum, Historical Society, Cincinnati Zoo, and Museum of Natural History are all a quick ride from the campus. Since the Academy is on the Metro bus line, students have easy access to Greater Cincinnati and northern Kentucky events.

Majors and Degrees
The Art Academy offers four-year programs leading to the Bachelor of Fine Arts degree in three areas: Fine Arts, with painting, printmaking, photography, and sculpture; Communication Arts, with digital multimedia, graphic design, and illustration; and Art History.

A five-semester Associate of Science degree in graphic design is available through an intensive, career-focused, accelerated program of study that enables students to enter the professional design market at an earlier date.

Academic Program
In completing the Bachelor of Fine Arts degree, a student is exposed to an integration of studio work, liberal studies, and art history, supporting the Academy's philosophy that the artist's strongest imagery and most effective visual statements come from a broad and rich mind.

Fine Arts students select a major area of emphasis and supplement their education with electives. The curriculum supports the understanding and benefits of the interrelationships of the various media, broadens students' visual concerns, and expands their self-expression. The Fine Arts Program is augmented by guest lecture series, seminars, workshops, visits to private collections, and field trips to museums and galleries in Cincinnati as well as to institutions in Chicago, Cleveland, Columbus, Detroit, Indianapolis, New York, and Washington, D.C.

The Communication Arts Program offers professional career-oriented instruction in studio skills and seminars that integrate conceptual processes, media skills, technical methods, problem-solving theory, and social/historical references to applied design. The Academy is an educational leader in the integration of computer technology and the creative process of art and design. Students are introduced during their first year to the use of computers for solving problems and creating ideas. The Communication Arts Program gives students practical experience that will help them to move easily into business opportunities after graduation. Students in this program encounter the problems faced by the professional designer, illustrator, and photographer in today's business world.

Graduation requirements for the Bachelor of Fine Arts degree in Fine Arts and Communication Arts are 84 studio credit hours, 33 credits of liberal studies, and 15 art history credits, for a total of 132 credits. Graduation requirements for the Bachelor of Fine Arts in Art History are 66 studio credit hours, 33 hours of liberal studies, and 33 hours of art history for a total of 132 credit hours. Graduation requirements for the Associate of Science degree are 47 studio hours, 9 liberal studies hours, and 9 art history hours, for a total of 65 hours.

Academic Facilities
The Academy has three buildings. The first was designed specifically to be an art school. The second is a school building that has been renovated to allow for the light and space needed for art classes. The Chidlaw Gallery is used for the professional display of students' works. In addition, there are exhibition areas in the lobbies of both Academy buildings, and students often show in other Cincinnati galleries and businesses. The third is a 6,000-square-foot sculpture facility with a hot glass shop.

Every student at the Academy is automatically a member of the Cincinnati Art Museum, which is one of the fifteen largest museums in the United States. As members, students are invited to exhibit openings, lectures, film series, special exhibits, and other museum-sponsored events. The resources of the museum's library are also available to students. The library has 53,000 volumes for circulation and reference, as well as an outstanding collection of clippings, monographs, and documents related to the visual arts.

Two computer labs are available to students. The computers have word processing, graphic design, and illustration capabilities.

Costs

Full-time instructional fees are $12,200 for 2000–2001.

Financial Aid

Currently, 95 percent of Academy students receive financial aid. The Art Academy of Cincinnati participates in federal and state programs, including grants, loans, and scholarships. Institutional merit scholarships and institutional loans are also available.

Full-time freshmen or transfer students may apply for an Entrance Scholarship. The applicant's portfolio must be submitted by March 15 for judging. Those applying for financial aid through the federal government or the Art Academy must submit the Free Application for Federal Student Aid (FAFSA) by March 15 for priority consideration.

Faculty

There are 18 full-time faculty members; 16 have received a master's degree or its equivalent as their highest earned degree, and 1 has a doctorate. The Academy has 30 part-time faculty members. The student-faculty ratio is 12:1.

Student Government

Although the Art Academy of Cincinnati does not have a formal student government, its students have a strong voice in the arena of student issues and rights.

Admission Requirements

Applicants must have taken the SAT or ACT tests and should have a GPA of 2.5 or above. A portfolio review will be arranged unless the applicant lives more than 150 miles away (in which case slides may be sent).

The Art Academy seeks talented students dedicated to pursuing a degree in visual art. Applicants should demonstrate observational keenness, a strong sense of design, inventiveness, and technical ability. International and transfer students are welcome. The Office of Admissions accepts calls on specific questions regarding admission to the Academy. It is the policy of the Art Academy that no person shall be subject to discrimination as a student or employee because of race, color, sex, or national origin.

Application and Information

SAT I or ACT scores, transcripts from high school, and a $25 fee must be sent to the Office of Admissions by June 30 of the year prior to registration (March 1 for scholarship consideration).

For further information regarding admission, financial assistance, academic programs, and student/parent visits, students may contact:

Office of Admissions
Art Academy of Cincinnati
1125 St. Gregory Street
Cincinnati, Ohio 45202
Telephone: 513-721-5205
               800-323-5692 (toll-free)

The Art Academy's Eden Park Building, which adjoins the Cincinnati Art Museum, dates back to 1887.

ART INSTITUTE OF BOSTON AT LESLEY COLLEGE
BOSTON, MASSACHUSETTS

The Institute

Founded in 1912, The Art Institute of Boston (AIB) is a professional college of visual arts that offers program and course work designed to prepare students for successful careers as illustrators, animators, graphic designers, Web designers, photographers, and exhibiting fine artists. AIB provides students with an intimate, challenging, and supportive environment that balances personal artistic expression with practical career goals.

The student body of 500 students comes from 33 states and 27 other countries, creating a global community of young artists with a stimulating variety of backgrounds and viewpoints. The nature of the College allows students to form close ties with other students and with faculty and staff members, most of whom are practicing professional artists. Studio classes are small and intimate—with an average of 13 students per instructor—which allows for personal attention and an emphasis on self-exploration and the development of an individual style. Students are prepared for careers by exposure to the most current trends and technology in their fields and internships and freelance opportunities that provide them with professional connections for career opportunities after graduation.

The College also offers activities such as major exhibitions, student exhibits, lectures, art auctions, special event–related parties, as well as a visiting artist program that brings prominent artists to campus for lectures and workshops.

In 1998 the Art Institute of Boston merged with Lesley College. AIB's strengths as a professional college of the visual arts are now combined with the resources of a university, providing students with expanded educational opportunities that are not usually found at most independent colleges of art, yet preserving the character of a small, private art college.

The College provides a variety of dormitory housing options for students: Garden Hall Residences located near the AIB campus in Back Bay, lodging in a Victorian house on the Cambridge campus of Lesley College (shuttle service provided), and a traditional residence hall at Hostelling-International located in the Fenway area.

Artist's Resources at the Art Institute of Boston maintains current job listings and provides information on competitions, fellowships and grants, exhibition opportunities, and other resources for artists. Career counseling with faculty members occurs within each department. A close student-faculty relationship is instrumental in helping students finding work in their chosen fields.

Masters' programs in expressive therapies and art education are offered in conjunction with Lesley College.

Location

Boston is an extraordinary college town. Just under 225,000 students live and study here every year at seventy institutions of higher learning. The city offers all the human and institutional resources expected in a major cultural, educational, and commercial center. World-class art exhibitions, concerts, lectures, theater, sports, and popular entertainment are among its riches. The spirit is cosmopolitan, but the setting is distinctive of Boston, with its historic neighborhoods, parks, and nearby New England rural and coastal areas.

The Art Institute of Boston students use the city's extensive resources as a part of their learning environment in many ways—for artistic and academic research, for internships and job opportunities, and for personal recreation. Full-time students receive free admission to the Museum of Fine Arts, Boston.

Majors and Degree

The Art Institute of Boston awards the Bachelor of Fine Arts degree in design, fine arts, illustration/animation, and photography as well as combined degrees in fine arts/illustration and illustration/design. A three-year diploma program is available in each of the degree areas. A two-year professional certificate program is offered in illustration and design.

Candidates for the graphic design program can study advertising and corporate communications, publishing and book design, and Web design. The illustration program offers specializations in advertising, book, editorial, and animation illustration. Fine arts students choose from drawing, painting, printmaking, and sculpture as concentrations, with courses available in ceramics, installation, and electronic arts. Photography students specialize in either commercial, documentary, fine arts, or media photography. An intensive precollege program is available for high school students throughout the academic year and the summer.

Academic Programs

AIB's challenging curriculum is structured to provide students with an understanding of the process of visual communication and expression, along with the social, historical, and cultural influences that shape the world and inform their imaginations.

AIB's rigorous first-year foundation includes intensive study in drawing and visual perception. Photography students take a unique foundation, with a direct immersion in the conceptual, technical, and historic aspects of photography. The foundation supplies students with the skills, insights, and fluency of expression that are necessary to meet the challenges of further study in art.

After the foundation year, students choose a major that can include unique specializations, combined majors, and a wide variety of interdisciplinary courses and workshops. Student take core courses in their major and continue with more individualized instruction, working closely with the faculty of working professional artists, toward their personal and professional goals. Students prepare for careers in the visual arts with real world studio assignments and professional internships, giving them valuable first hand experience in their intended fields. AIB's artist's resources center keeps student current with information about job listings, competitions, fellowships and grants, and exhibition opportunities.

As an integral part of their study, all degree and diploma students take a blend of required and elective liberal arts courses. These courses are designed to develop effective communication skills, give a firm academic grounding in the history of their major area of study, and to allow students to pursue individual interests that stimulate their imaginations and interests.

AIB offers both day and evening degree credit courses during the fall, spring, and summer semesters. In addition, the continuing and professional education program offers evening and weekend courses, workshops, and intensive seminars in the areas of visual arts, liberal arts, and career development to be taken by artists, educators, and professionals.

Off-Campus Arrangements

The Art Institute of Boston at Lesley College offers a merit-based, semester-long illustration program in Rotterdam, Holland. Students also have the option to study visual arts and Italian language at The Art Institute of Florence or visual art at Burren College of Art in Ireland; photography students can participate in an exchange program in Paris, France. Students may take an intensive year-long course of study and studio work in New York City or spend their junior year at one of thirty schools in the Association of Independent Colleges of Art and Design (AICAD) located across the country. AIB also offers students the opportunity to take classes at the Boston Architectural Center and the Maine Photographic Workshop.

Academic Facilities

The Art Institute of Boston's facilities include three Macintosh computer laboratories, an Oxberry master animation stand, video animation stands, a photography lab with color and black-and-white printers, a printmaking lab with etching and lithography presses, a wood shop, a metals studio with welding facilities, and a clay lab with kilns. Senior fine arts students have their own individual studios in which to create.

The Art Institute of Boston was selected to join the New Media Centers Program, a consortium of higher education institutions and digital technology companies dedicated to advancing learning through new media. Plans for the AIB Center include expanded multimedia programs using state-of-the-art technology and equipment.

The AIB library collection is devoted principally to the visual arts and contains more than 9,000 books, 70 serial titles, 26,000 slides, a video viewing room, more than 250 art-related videos, and a picture reference file of 10,000 photographs and illustrations. The library has the National Gallery of Art's American Art Collection on videodisc, a visual reference of more than 26,000 images spanning three centuries.

In addition, the Eleanor De Wolfe Ludcke Library at Lesley provides a state-of-the-art multimedia resource center and a collection of 62,000 books, 700 current periodicals, 2,200 computer software and CD-ROM titles, 650 film and video titles, media material, and circulating media equipment. Students have borrowing privileges at six additional libraries through the Fenway Library Consortium.

The Art Institute of Boston sponsors a full program of exhibitions and lectures by visiting artists. The gallery presents major exhibitions of contemporary and historical work by established and emerging artists, including the alumni of the Art Institute of Boston. Students have the opportunity to assist in mounting exhibitions and to personally meet visiting artists. There are a student gallery and areas reserved for showing student work year-round. Gallery South exhibits the work of student photographers throughout the year, including group and senior exhibitions.

Costs

Tuition for the 2000–01 academic year is $12,500. Dormitory costs are approximately $7600 per year. Material and supply costs vary according to individual and departmental requirements. In general, foundation, fine arts, illustration, and design students spend approximately $1500 per year for supplies, while photography students can expect to spend about $2300 per year, with further expenses dependent upon the equipment chosen by the individual student. Students in areas other than photography and design are charged a $670 fee, while photography and design students are charged a $770 fee.

Financial Aid

More than 70 percent of students receive aid each year through AIB's active financial aid program. Awards are made on the basis of need as determined by the United States Department of Education, which analyzes all the financial resources of the student. The Financial Aid Office's goal is to help students meet established needs through a combination of Federal Pell Grants, Federal Stafford Student Loans, Federal Work-Study, other federal grants, scholarships, and state programs.

Various merit-based and need-based scholarships are available. The Art Institute of Boston administers more than $3.5 million in scholarships, financial aid, and loans for students each year. The application deadline for merit scholarships is February 16, 2001; the deadline is March 17 for need-based awards.

Faculty

The Art Institute of Boston at Lesley College has 73 full- and part-time faculty members, 95 percent of whom have advanced degrees in their field; 89 percent are practicing artists, designers, illustrators, and photographers. The student-faculty ratio is 10:1.

Student Government

Each year, the student government, whose adviser is a member of the Student Services Office staff, is responsible for a full program of social events, lecture and film series, and out-of-town visits to important exhibitions. In addition, students can share their thoughts with the president in monthly informal round table discussions.

Admission Requirements

In considering applications for admission, the Art Institute of Boston looks for artistic potential and personal commitment. A portfolio of original work is an important part of the application; academic grades, test scores, letters of recommendation, and extracurricular activities are also strongly evaluated. A school visit gives applicants the opportunity to present their portfolios, discuss their goals and interests with an admissions counselor, and determine how they may benefit from AIB's programs. SAT I or ACT scores are required of applicants who have graduated from high school since 1995.

Application and Information

Admission decisions are made on a rolling basis. Applications are reviewed as they are received, and the applicant can expect a decision within three weeks of having completed the application. To ensure a place in the desired program and in order to meet application deadlines for financial aid, students are encouraged to apply by the priority deadline of February 16, 2001. The complete application consists of an application form with essay and fee, transcript(s) of grades, SAT I scores, an interview, and a portfolio. Transfer and international students are encouraged to apply.

For further information, students should contact:
 Brad White
 Director of Admissions
 Art Institute of Boston at Lesley College
 700 Beacon Street
 Boston, Massachusetts 02215-2598
 Telephone: 617-585-6600
          800-773-0494 (toll-free)
 E-mail: admissions@aiboston.edu
 World Wide Web: http://www.aiboston.edu

Visiting artist Richard Yarde instructs a fine arts student in the AIB studios.

THE ART INSTITUTE OF PORTLAND
PORTLAND, OREGON

The Institute

The Art Institute of Portland is a leader in preparing students for creative careers. The Institute's reputation is built on focused programs taught by an outstanding faculty of experienced professionals. Founded in 1963 as Bassist College, the Institute benefits from thirty-five years of education excellence combined with the strength that comes from being a member of the Art Institute's family. The Art Institute's system of colleges prepares students for careers in the creative and visual arts.

The Art Institute of Portland continues to develop its programs to keep pace with changes in the design fields and in world commerce. The Institute maintains close relationships with working professionals locally and around the world and ensures its students receive an education that is both professionally current and academically sound.

The Institute is an independent, private, nondenominational, coeducational, proprietary college, the governance of which is vested in its Board of Trustees.

The Art Institute of Portland is accredited by the Commission on Colleges of the Northwest Association of Schools and Colleges. The Institute also meets all requirements of the State of Oregon Office of Degree Authorization.

Services such as housing, part-time student employment, and graduate employment services are available. The college has instituted a career services department that offers instruction in job search skills, resume writing, and interviewing and networking; individual job search assistance for students seeking full-time employment in their field of interest and for students seeking part-time employment while completing their program of study; and access to a national job search network.

Location

The campus is located in downtown Portland, offering easy access to museums, galleries, parks, shops, and the Willamette River. Students enjoy spectacular views of Mount Saint Helens, Mount Hood, and the cityscape from the campus's rooftop deck. The Columbia Gorge (30 minutes away), Mount Hood (45 minutes away), and the Pacific Ocean (2 hours away) offer a variety of recreational opportunities.

Portland, nicknamed the "Rose City," is famous for Forest Park, where miles of hiking trails connect to Washington Park, the Japanese Gardens, Pittock Mansion, and the Portland City Zoo.

Portland is home to an active performing and visual arts community. Because the college is located downtown, students are able to be part of the community every day. Bustling coffeehouses and microbreweries; Powell's City of Books, the largest bookstore west of the Rockies; and events that draw visitors from around the world, such as the Portland Rose Festival, all make Portland a great place to live. Buses and MAX, Portland's light-rail system, provide students with convenient and inexpensive access to much that the city has to offer.

Majors and Degrees

The Art Institute of Portland offers associate and baccalaureate degrees in apparel design, computer animation, graphic design, interior design, multimedia and web design.

Apparel designers and developers combine imagination with technical know-how and problem-solving skills to produce the latest in fashion and technical apparel within a highly competitive environment. Students at the Institute develop their skills in design, sketching and illustration, draping and patternmaking, garment construction and critical analysis, and computer-aided design while honing their creative problem-solving skills through a variety of design challenges. The student's development is guided by professionals from the apparel industry, including instructors, guest presenters, and internship employers with diverse backgrounds and experience. Students have the opportunity to exhibit their work in annual fashion shows. The process of apparel design and development is completed by studies in marketing, merchandising, presentation, and entrepreneurship.

Advertising, television, film and video, entertainment, game design, architecture, education, and businesses, including legal and insurance companies, are among the industries that make use of the design, illustration, and modeling skills developed by computer animation graduates. Careers such as animator, compositor, storyboard artist, character designer, special effects artist, broadcast graphics designer, background painter, clean-up artist, and video postproduction artist are at the forefront of a field that is repackaging information in creative new ways. The computer animator is a skilled and specialized visual communicator who combines individual artistic talent with technological expertise to create impressions in a moving-image format.

Some of today's most dynamic industries are based on graphic design. The fields of advertising, publishing, television, and graphic design offer great opportunities for trained visual communicators, especially designers and artists. Advertising agencies require the talents of many professionals. Art directors work with writers to develop original concepts, supervising a creative process that relies on the expertise of layout artists, production artists, illustrators, photographers, and printers. In the field of publishing, art directors and designers work with editors and journalists to design and produce magazines, books, and newspapers. Graphic designers create a vast range of visual communication, including corporate identity programs, consumer package designs, annual reports, exhibit materials, direct mail, brochures, and multimedia presentations.

An interior designer's expertise includes the ability to create a variety of spaces, components, and elements within environments designed for human needs and the human spirit. The education of interior design students stresses development of creativity, technical skill, and critical thinking. A foundation in cultural, art, and design history; written, graphic, and computer-aided design communication skills; construction principles and techniques; and business principles provide students with a broad and comprehensive resource base as a designer. The Art Institute of Portland supports the transition from academic to professional worlds with contacts in the industry and assistance in determining and reaching career goals.

Multimedia and web design is an exciting new field of integrated electronic communications that is becoming an essential part of the business, education, and entertainment industries. The advent of multimedia has established a regeneration of energy in business that has led to the creation of employment opportunities that require an individual who can combine sound, graphic arts, text, and video/film to enhance the dissemination of information. By working in classrooms and computer labs, students develop a foundation in drawing and design, image manipulation, multimedia system design, script writing, sound, video, and animation. More complex course work involves combining multimedia tools to integrate text, sound, images, animation, and video to complete a project. Students also learn about the structure of electronic games, information design, interactive authoring, computers in animation, and video/teleconferencing.

Academic Program

The Art Institute of Portland faculty members and administrators strive to provide a relevant education to prepare students for real-world careers in design. Department chairs work closely with professionals in the field to determine the needs of specific professions and form curricula around those needs. Regardless of their major, students are required to complete an internship and acquire a liberal arts background. Internships themselves often lead to professional contacts and mentors to assist in the shaping of the student's career. The broad backgrounds of faculty members and students encourage interaction on student work and progress. The design curricula are embedded in a liberal arts background.

Academic Facilities

Consisting of over 20,000 carefully selected volumes, the library is a good special-collection library, with holdings in apparel, design, interior design, graphic design, home furnishings, and emerging new fields in media arts.

The library is a subscriber to most of the current magazines and scholarly journals in the Institute's fields of specialization. Most significant of the library's specific resources are extensive collections of nineteenth-century publications, such as *Godey's Lady Book*, *Peterson's Magazine*, Racinet's encyclopedic *Le Costume Historique*, and *Costume of the Russian Empire*.

In addition, the library houses state and federal documents related to the Institute's fields of concentration and a substantial collection of audiovisual resources, including films, slides, audiocassettes, videotape recordings, and CDs. During orientation to the Art Institutes International at Portland, all students receive specialized training in using the library to full advantage. This innovative, short instructional program relates the library directly to the student and teaches a quick, effective, and easy way to research topics in their specialized fields. Computers are available in the library for student word processing and research on the Internet.

The Art Institute of Portland has three well-equipped multistation computer labs to facilitate instruction in computer applications, including CAD software packages for interior design, apparel design, computer animation, graphic design, and multimedia and web design. The computer lab is open during the day, evening, and weekends to facilitate student progress. Laboratory technical assistants are available during lab hours.

The Art Institute of Portland has dedicated computers resident in the library for access to the Internet. All students have free e-mail accounts assigned to them in the fall for use throughout the year. Free Internet access is available any time the library is open. Courses are available to students who do not have experience on the Internet. Additional Internet access sites will be added during the 1999–2000 academic year.

Costs

Tuition for full-time students (15 credits) is $4260 per quarter or $12,780 per year. Students can expect books and supplies to range between $1200 and $2100 per year. Payment plans are welcome and encouraged; arrangements are made with the Planning Office.

Financial Aid

Financial aid is available in the form of a variety of grant, loan, and scholarship programs. High school seniors should consult their guidance office for scholarship applications.

The Art Institute of Portland participates in the major student financial aid programs offered by the U.S. Department of Education. Eligibility for all federal financial aid programs may be determined using one application form, the Free Application for Federal Student Aid (FAFSA). This form is available from the Financial Aid Office at the Art Institute of Portland or from a high school counselor.

The Art Institute of Portland recognizes that the student and the student's parents (if the student is a dependent) have the primary responsibility in meeting the student's college-related expenses. Financial aid is meant to help bridge the gap between the estimated family contribution (from information submitted on the FAFSA) and the cost of education. Financial aid is not meant to cover all of the student's expenses, nor is it implied that all of the student's need will be met by financial aid. The Financial Aid Office works with students and parents to discuss ways to meet college-related expenses.

Student employment positions are located on campus. A listing of potential jobs is located on campus bulletin boards. Scholarship applications are available in the Financial Aid Office. The Potential for Excellence Scholarship, Alumni Scholarship, Fashion Group Scholarship, Merit Scholarship, and other outside/private scholarships are offered.

Faculty

With a student-faculty ratio of 15:1, the Institute offers individualized instruction and practical learning experiences. The Art Institute of Portland employs 10 full-time faculty members and as many as 75 adjunct faculty members. In addition to teaching course work, many faculty members are working artists and designers. Department chairs serve as academic advisers.

Student Government

The primary function of the student association is to act as a liaison between the student body and the administration and faculty. The student association works with the staff and faculty in coordinating student activities and in benefitting the college community. Students elect their officers from the entire student body and select a representative from each major to sit on the association board. Student association members play a strong role in graduation planning and preparation, as well as special events and college promotion. In 1996–97, members of the student association worked with alumni and administration to create a mentoring program for the purpose of enhancing the college experience and encouraging outside relationships for career purposes.

Admission Requirements

The Art Institute of Portland seeks students who are diverse, dedicated, creative, and ambitious. The curriculum at the Institute is both challenging and demanding. Students desiring to be successful should seek out information about the rigors, realities, and rewards of careers in design before completing their applications for admission. Admissions staff members and faculty members of the Institute advise applicants further about design.

Admission is based on a personal interview followed by a review of high school transcripts and a personal written statement. Letters of recommendation, a portfolio (if available), and SAT I or ACT scores are optional, though encouraged. Prospective students should start the application process as early as possible in the senior year of high school. The Art Institute of Portland enrolls students at any time.

Application and Information

For further information about admission and the Art Institutes International at Portland, students should contact:

Admissions Office
Art Institute of Portland
2000 SW 5th Avenue
Portland, Oregon 97201
Telephone: 503-228-6528
         888-228-6528 (toll-free)
Fax: 503-228-4227
World Wide Web: http://www.aii.edu

ART INSTITUTE OF SOUTHERN CALIFORNIA
LAGUNA BEACH, CALIFORNIA

The Institute

The mission of the Art Institute of Southern California is to prepare women and men for careers as creative artists and designers in a culturally and ethnically diverse world through a curriculum that emphasizes the acquisition of skills based on observation, representation, and concept development. The Institute is committed to offering its curriculum through accredited degree programs that imaginatively combine studio work with academic studies and to sharing its resources with the broader community through continuing education and exhibition programs.

The spectacular seacoast of Laguna Beach has been a magnet for artists since the nineteenth century, and the city's famed beach, canyon, and luminous natural light still attract the attention of artists and visitors from all over the world, lending the area a truly cosmopolitan air.

The Art Institute was founded as the Laguna Beach School of Art in 1961 under the auspices of the Laguna Beach Festival of Arts and the Laguna Beach Art Association (Laguna Art Museum) and was financed by a grant from the Festival of Arts and private contributions. The school opened on the festival's grounds in 1962 with the mission of providing the region with art education of the highest quality. In 1977, the school relocated to its present site in Laguna Canyon and was accredited by the National Association of Schools of Art and Design in 1981. In 1997, the Art Institute was accredited by the Western Association of Schools and Colleges (WASC), bringing to it an even higher level of national recognition and respect. It is the only four-year, fully accredited professional college of art and design in Orange County, and one of only four in southern California.

Location

The Art Institute of Southern California occupies several acres in Laguna Canyon, approximately 1 mile from the Pacific Ocean. The contemporary wood architecture of the campus buildings blends with a mature grove of sycamore trees and the rugged hillsides. The temperate climate encourages swimming, surfing, and other year-round water activities, and there is a full range of outdoor recreation within an easy distance, including mountain skiing, desert and canyon hiking, biking, and more. Orange County, one of California's fastest-growing areas, offers a remarkable array of arts and entertainment activities.

The charming city of Laguna Beach itself is noted for its fine restaurants, its scores of artist's galleries and shops, the acclaimed Laguna Playhouse, and the Laguna Art Museum. Each summer, the famous Laguna Beach Festival of Arts and Pageant of the Masters draw people from across the nation and around the world, celebrating the unique artistic history of the city.

Within an easy drive are the Orange County Art Museum, the Bowers Museum of Cultural Art, and many other museums. The Orange County Performing Arts Center presents the world's finest ballet companies, touring Broadway shows, jazz, classical music, opera, and more, and South Coast Repertory presents award-winning plays. There are opportunities to attend numerous professional sports events in the area and many opportunities to participate in amateur sports. Libraries and bookstores abound in nearly every community and Orange County boasts the largest population of home computer enthusiasts in the nation.

Within an hour's drive to the north is the excitement of Los Angeles, with the countless resources this cultural capital has to offer, such as the J. Paul Getty Center for the Arts, the Los Angeles County Museum, the Museum of Contemporary Art, the Norton Simon Museum, the Huntington Library and Gallery, the Los Angeles Music Center, and many more. Approximately an hour to the south is the beautiful city of San Diego and the San Diego Museum of Art, the La Jolla Museum of Contemporary Art, La Jolla Playhouse, and more—and just further south is Mexico, with its rich cultural and artistic tradition.

Majors and Degrees

The Art Institute of Southern California offers the Bachelor of Fine Arts (B.F.A.) degree in fine arts (drawing and painting) and in visual communication (classical animation, graphic design, and illustration) with disciplines in photography, printmaking, and sculpture.

Academic Program

The Art Institute gives the student the training and background necessary to develop the skills, knowledge, techniques, and critical thinking required of an artist or designer. Although studio work is the core of the curriculum, the Art Institute believes that studies in the liberal arts are essential to the development of each artist and seeks to provide a program that offers new fields and challenges to the creative mind.

The Institute realizes that proper training and experience in art should include knowledge of contemporary theory, criticism, and the twentieth-century tradition. In order to further broaden students' knowledge, the college sponsors visits and lectures by artists, art historians, scholars, and art critics. These lectures and critiques are scheduled throughout the year and are also open to the public. A visiting artist residency program offers students an opportunity to work with an artist in a particular field, while the visiting art teacher lectures and exhibits his or her work in the galleries.

Academic Facilities

The Art Institute's campus includes eleven studios and an administration building. The studios are equipped for drawing, painting, illustration, graphic design, sculpture, computer art, and printmaking. The M. Paul Stiker Administration Building houses all staff offices, the Salyer Library, the Ettinger Gallery, and the Reynolds (Student) Gallery. The Art Institute represents the work of accomplished artists and scholars in exhibitions in the Ettinger and Reynolds Galleries. Throughout the year, the Institute also sponsors public receptions and artist slide lectures to broaden knowledge of current developments in the arts. A full schedule of exhibitions is available at the Administration Building.

Costs

The Art Institute is proud to offer the most affordable tuition of any of the four-year art and design schools in southern California. Tuition for the academic year 2000–01 is $13,200. This includes all texts and fees. Art supplies average $1800 annually. Room and board cost approximately $5800. The college does not offer dormitory facilities, but the student housing coordinator will assist students in locating housing. Students should allow $575 for transportation and $1400 for personal expenses.

Financial Aid

The Art Institute offers a wide range of financial aid to its students. Federal aid to eligible students includes Federal Pell Grants, Federal Supplemental Educational Opportunity Grants, Federal Work-Study, Federal Stafford Loans (subsidized and unsubsidized), and Federal PLUS Loans. California state grants, which consist of Cal Grant A and Cal Grant B, have a deadline of March 2 each year for the following fall semester. Students must be residents of California to receive a Cal Grant. The Institute offers merit and competitive scholarships that are privately funded. For current information on financial aid, students should contact the Financial Aid Office at 949-376-6000, ext. 223.

Faculty

The faculty is composed of professional artists and designers, art historians, scholars, and educators with distinguished professional and teaching experience. Classes are small, with an average student-faculty ratio of 10:1. These small classes enable students to receive personal attention from their instructors and to work actively with them. The majority of the members of the fine arts faculty have their own studios and exhibit their works regionally, nationally, and internationally. The classical animation, graphic design, and illustration faculty is composed of professionals, each working in his or her area of expertise.

Student Government

Students have an informal organization for the purpose of promoting social activities, student exhibitions, and art sales. Students meet, as necessary, to plan events, coordinate field trips, and relay concerns to the faculty and staff. Students may request to speak at faculty meetings by submitting a written request to the Faculty Senate. One student is selected each year to serve as the student representative to the Board of Trustees.

Admission Requirements

Students who are interested in applying must complete and submit an application to the office of admissions, attaching a nonrefundable $35 application fee. Those seeking admission to the B.F.A. program must be high school graduates or the equivalent. Applicants must also present official sealed transcripts from their high school of graduation and colleges attended, plus one letter of recommendation and a two-page personal statement of intent (typed essay). Applicants are also required to submit a ten-piece portfolio that must include a minimum of four observational drawings.

Transfer students who wish to apply credits to the B.F.A. program must request each institution formerly attended to forward an official transcript to the Admissions Office. A transfer credit evaluation is carried out to determine which credits will be accepted. Liberal arts course work completed with a grade of C or better may be accepted; a portfolio must be presented for transfer of studio credits.

The Admissions Committee reviews the qualifications of each student on the basis of a balanced picture that includes academic achievements, creative ability, and artistic and professional goals for the purpose of evaluating advising and placement. Based on the committee's decision, a written notification of acceptance or nonacceptance will be mailed by the Director of Admissions within three weeks of application. Students admitted to the program will experience regular faculty review and evaluation of work completed in class as the measure of their progress.

The Art Institute of Southern California administers its programs without discrimination on the basis of race, creed, color, gender, national origin, or handicap.

Application and Information

A videotape and CD-ROM introducing the Art Institute and its programs are available upon request. For more information and an application form, students should contact:

Admissions Office
Art Institute of Southern California
2222 Laguna Canyon Road
Laguna Canyon, California 92651
Telephone: 949-376-6000
              800-255-0762 (toll-free)
Fax: 949-376-6009
World Wide Web: http://www.aisc.edu

The Art Institute is located in the historic seashore artist colony of Laguna Beach.

ASBURY COLLEGE
WILMORE, KENTUCKY

The College

Founded in 1890, Asbury College is a Christian, independent, coeducational institution founded in the Wesleyan-Holiness tradition. The College's mission is to provide a high-quality, Christ-centered, residential liberal arts education that equips men and women, through a commitment to academic excellence and spiritual vitality, for a lifetime of learning, leadership, and service to their professions, society, and family and the church.

A distinguishing mark of Asbury's Christian community is that the members are committed to a set of basic principles that are considered essential to maintain the spirit and health of the community. At Asbury College, the basic tenet of the community is found in Jesus's two great commandments in Matthew 22:37–40: "You shall love the Lord your God with all your heart, and with all your soul, and with all your mind…And…you shall love your neighbor as yourself." Thus, members of the Asbury community seek to love God and practice self-sacrificial love in relationship to others. Such disciplined community living is inherent preparation for servant-leaders who give their lives to fulfill a cause greater than themselves.

Citing the Christian and academic reputation of the College as their primary reason for selecting Asbury, a record of 360 freshmen were enrolled this year. The current enrollment is 1,317 students from forty-two states and twenty countries. Kentucky, Ohio, Indiana, Florida, and Pennsylvania are the five states that are represented most. Asbury offers more than forty-five majors and programs of study within the liberal arts curriculum and confers the degrees of Bachelor of Arts and Bachelor of Science in education. The most popular majors are in the Departments of Education, Communication Arts, Business and Economics, Christian Ministries and Missions, and Psychology.

Organizations and clubs are an important part of student life at Asbury. Positions on the *Collegian* (student newspaper) and the *Asburian* (yearbook) are open to all students. Students can become involved in the Ministerial Association, Christian Service Association, Fellowship of Christian Athletes, and Community Involvement, Art, Speech, English, Foreign Student, French, and Spanish clubs. Students may also participate in the Women's Vocal Ensemble, Men's Glee Club, Jazz Ensemble, Concert Choir, and Concert Band. Student honor societies include Alpha Psi Omega (drama), Phi Alpha Theta (history), Phi Sigma Tau (philosophy), Sigma Zeta (science and mathematics), Sigma Tau Delta (English), and Sigma Delta Pi (Spanish). Among the professional organizations that students may join are the American Guild of Organists, the Music Educators National Conference, the Kentucky Intercollegiate Press Association, the Student National Education Association, and the Student Association for Health, Physical Education and Recreation.

Asbury recognizes the value of athletics and maintains a program of intramural and intercollegiate sports. Intercollegiate sports for men are baseball, basketball, cross-country, soccer, swimming, and tennis. For women, basketball, cross-country, softball, swimming, tennis, and volleyball are offered. Intramural activities include basketball, flag football, golf, soccer, softball, tennis, volleyball, and walleyball. Asbury also sponsors a Christian Witness gymnastics team that tours each spring semester.

Eighty-five percent of Asbury students reside in College residence halls. Duplexes for married students are available. Counseling and health services are available to all students. Asbury maintains a well-equipped clinic with a competent, experienced staff consisting of registered nurses and a physician.

Location

Wilmore, a small, quiet town, is located in the heart of the famous Bluegrass region, 15 miles southwest of Lexington, Kentucky, the second-largest city in the commonwealth. Surrounding Wilmore are reminders of the state's pioneer history, including Fort Harrod, Boonesborough, and Shakertown, a restored religious community dating from the 1800s. Near Lexington is the Kentucky Horse Park. Camping, rock-climbing, boating, and fishing are available at nearby Red River Gorge and Natural Bridge, and Mammoth Cave National Park is less than 2 hours from Wilmore.

Lexington has theaters, an opera house, a symphony orchestra, and Rupp Arena, where programs ranging from basketball games to performances by well-known musicians are presented. In addition to the majors listed below, a master's degree in economics is offered in conjunction with the London School of Economics, England.

Majors and Degrees

Asbury College confers the degrees of Bachelor of Arts and Bachelor of Science in Education. Majors are available in accounting, applied communication, art, Bible, biblical languages, biology, biology health science, business management, chemistry, chemistry-biology, Christian ministries, classical languages, early elementary education (K–4), engineering (with the University of Kentucky), English, French, Greek, history, journalism, Latin, mathematics, media communications, medical technology, middle school education (5–8), missions, music, nursing (with the University of Kentucky), philosophy, physical education, psychology, recreation, secondary education (art, biology, chemistry, English, French, mathematics, music, physical education, social studies, and Spanish), social work, sociology, and Spanish.

Academic Program

Asbury operates on a sixteen-week semester system with two 4-week summer sessions. To qualify for graduation, students must complete a minimum of 124 semester hours with an overall grade point average of at least 2.0 (2.5 in teacher education programs).

The liberal arts core requirements are as follows: foreign language (9), English literature (6), laboratory science (6), Western civilization (6), computer science/mathematics (3), English composition (3), music and art appreciation (3), New Testament (3) Old Testament (3), philosophy (3), Christian theology (3), physical education (3), psychology/sociology/anthropology (3), speech (3), and theology (3).

Students may be granted college credit for satisfactory performance on AP tests in certain subjects. Advanced standing in foreign language is also available to qualifying students. Further detailed information is available from the College.

Off-Campus Arrangements

Qualified students may participate in the American Studies Program in Washington, D.C.; the Holy Land Studies Program in Israel; and the Wesleyan Urban Coalition Program in Chicago, as well as in the Latin American Studies Program.

Academic Facilities

College facilities that are available to students include a computer center and several well-equipped chemistry, biology, physics, computer, and language laboratories. The College also has a radio station and an outstanding TV studio with a 24-hour cable station. The Morrison-Kenyon Library has approximately 168,000 volumes, 620 periodicals, 1,024 units of microfilm and microfiche, and 7,902 records and tapes.

Costs

For 2000–01, annual expenses are $13,644 for tuition, $412 for fees, and $3566 for room and board.

Financial Aid

Approximately 85 percent of the College's students receive some type of financial assistance. The various aid programs include academic scholarships, Federal Pell Grants, Federal Supplemental Educational Opportunity Grants, Kentucky Higher Education Assistance Authority Grants, Federal Perkins Loans, Federal Stafford Student Loans, state loans, United Methodist Student Loans, institutional grants and loans, institutional employment, and Federal Work-Study awards. Asbury offers honor scholarships, including a few full tuition grants. Merit Finalists receive 60 percent tuition scholarships.

To apply for aid, students should complete the Free Application for Federal Student Aid (FAFSA). Priority consideration is given to those who file before March 1. Financial need is defined as the difference between the amount a family can pay and the total expenses for the academic year. If there is a deficit, the student is considered to have financial need. The awards are made on the basis of financial need. Notification of awards begins early in April. For more information, students may contact the financial aid office (telephone: 606-858-3511 or 2195; 800-823-4502 (toll-free)).

Faculty

Asbury has a full-time faculty of more than 80 members. The part-time faculty usually numbers about 50. Each student has a faculty member as an adviser. Faculty members are personally interested in each student and are willing to assist advisees in any way possible. Many faculty members offer hospitality by opening their homes to students. Asbury's faculty-student ratio is 1:14. Approximately 70 percent of the full-time faculty members hold an earned doctorate.

Student Government

The objectives of the student government organization are to act as a unifying force, bringing the institution as a whole into vital contact with current issues in college life; to help students find opportunities in college life in a mature Christian spirit, through recommendation and administration; and to promote an atmosphere for intellectual, spiritual, and cultural development. Regulations for student life are explained in the student handbook. The use of tobacco, alcoholic beverages, and illegal drugs is strictly prohibited.

Admission Requirements

The Asbury College faculty strongly recommends that applicants should have completed the following requirements in grades 9 through 12: 4 years of English, including 1 year of composition; 3 or 4 years of mathematics (algebra, geometry, advanced algebra, and other advanced math); 2 years of social studies, of which 1 year should be history; 2 or 3 years of laboratory science; and 2 years of the same foreign language. Applicants should have a grade point average of at least 2.5. Students should take the ACT examination or the SAT I and have a minimum ACT composite score of 22 or a combined SAT I score of 1030. Freshmen entering Asbury have had an average ACT composite score of 24, an SAT I combined score of 1105, and a high school grade point average of 3.4. Transfer students must have maintained an average of C or better at the college or university last attended.

Application and Information

Students may apply for freshman admission during the spring of their junior year or during their senior year in high school. Notification of admission decisions is given within 24 hours after the following have been received: the application and $25 application fee, transcripts, a pastor's recommendation, a high school counselor's recommendation (for high school students only), and a personal recommendation. Enrollment is cut off at resident capacity. Admission decisions are made and financial assistance is awarded by Asbury College without regard to race, color, sex, national origin, or handicap.

Further information may be obtained by contacting:

Stan F. Wiggam
Dean of Admissions
Asbury College
Wilmore, Kentucky 40390
Telephone: 606-858-3511 or 2142
              800-888-1818 (toll-free)
Fax: 606-858-3921
World Wide Web: http://www.asbury.edu

Dr. Alan Moulton teaches a psychology class on Asbury's picturesque semicircle.

ASHLAND UNIVERSITY
ASHLAND, OHIO

The University

Education at Ashland University (AU) goes beyond small classes, low student-faculty ratios, and personal attention. The campus-wide philosophy of "Accent on the Individual" means that students are challenged to grow and change in a community of respect where they can discover their true potential.

Ashland University is a mid-sized regional teaching university, historically related to the Brethren Church. Its mission is to serve the educational needs of all students—undergraduate and graduate, traditional and nontraditional, full- and part-time—by providing educational programs of high quality in an environment that is both challenging and supportive.

The educational and social environment is built upon a long-standing commitment to Judeo-Christian values and a tradition that stresses the importance of each individual. In this environment, the members of the Ashland University community continually seek ways to challenge and support each other to develop intellectually, spiritually, socially, culturally, and physically.

Ashland University is home to 1,950 full-time undergraduate students, 85 percent of whom are from Ohio. Students also come from twenty-seven other states and twenty-three other countries. The University's total enrollment of 5,800 students includes students in graduate programs in business, education, and theology; a professional program in nursing; and thirteen off-campus degree-granting program centers throughout Ohio. Students of minority groups account for 6 percent of the student population. Twenty-five percent of the incoming class are transfer students.

Ashland is a residential campus, with men's and women's residence halls and options for coed divided housing, three-room suites, sorority suites, residential fraternity houses, and Scholar Floors.

AU is a six-time recipient of an award for having the best student programming in the nation. More than 100 student organizations are available on campus. Ten men's teams and eight women's teams compete at the NCAA Division II level, several of which are in contention for national titles each year.

In 1997, AU completed a $5-million campus technology enhancement project that included the installation of a campuswide fiber optic computer network, which allows students and faculty members to have Internet access, including e-mail and World Wide Web capabilities, from their rooms, homes, and offices, respectively. Also, the Patterson Instructional Technology Center opened and features the latest in technology, including teleconferencing, a distance-learning classroom, multimedia classrooms, and an instructional media resource center in addition to AU's computer lab.

Also new to the campus is a beautiful 55,000-square-foot student center with several student lounges, a unique bookstore, a grill and snack bar, a game room, a health and aerobic center with locker rooms and showers, and many meeting rooms.

Location

Ashland is an attractive community of 22,000, midway between Cleveland and Columbus. The most recent FBI statistics show Ashland as having the lowest violent crime in the state for cities with populations between 10,000 and 24,999. *The Rating Guide to Life in America's Small Cities* lists the Ashland, Ohio, area as having the lowest crime rate of micropolitan areas in the U.S.

Majors and Degrees

Ashland University confers seven baccalaureate degrees: the Bachelor of Arts, Bachelor of Music, Bachelor of Science, and Bachelor of Science in Business Administration, Education, Nursing (completion degree for RNs), and Social Work. Majors are offered in accounting, adapted physical education, American studies, art*, athletic training, biology*, broadcast sales and station management, business administration, business management, business management with health specialization, chemistry*, child and family studies, Christian school education, commercial art, computer science*, creative writing*, criminal justice, dietetics, economics*, education, education of the handicapped, electronic media production, elementary education, English*, environmental science, fashion merchandising, finance, fine art, foods and nutrition, French*, geology, health*, health administration management, history*, home economics*, hotel/restaurant management, international studies, journalism*, K-12 education specialist, kindergarten-primary education, management information systems, marketing, mathematics*, middle grades education, music*, musical theater, philosophy, physical education, physics*, political science, predentistry, pre-engineering, prekindergarten education, prelaw, premedical technology, premedicine, pre-optometry, prepharmacy, pre–physical therapy, preseminary, pre-veterinary medicine, psychology*, public communication, radio-television, recreation, religion, school business manager, school treasurer, science*, secondary education, social studies*, social work, sociology*, Spanish*, special education, speech*, sports communication, theater*, therapeutic recreation, and toxicology. (Majors marked with * are education certification areas.) The University also awards the Associate in Arts degree in art, criminal justice, office administration, and radio-TV and in a two-year curriculum in general education.

Academic Program

At Ashland, learning is about understanding new ideas, solving problems, and pushing limits. Through small classes, which allow individual instruction, field experiences in every academic area, academic support services, and an honor's program for students with minimum GPAs of 3.5, AU's goal of helping students excel is achieved.

Institutional requirements are designed to allow for interdisciplinary opportunities in the students' programs. Basic degree requirements include English composition (6 hours), contemporary issues (4 hours), communications (3 hours), religion (3 hours), and physical education (2 hours). Distribution requirements in humanities (6 hours), social science (6 hours), science/mathematics (6 hours), fine/performing arts (6 hours), and business/economics (3 hours), or interdisciplinary seminars substituted for distribution requirements, complete the degree requirements.

There are two semesters in the University's academic year. Classification of students is based on progress toward meeting degree requirements in terms of semester hours earned, as follows: freshman, 1–29 semester hours; sophomore, 30–59; junior, 60–89; senior, 90 or more. A total of 128 semester hours of credit is needed for graduation.

Off-Campus Arrangements

Study semesters are available at both foreign and domestic universities. Commercial art and fashion merchandising students have the option of spending their junior year at one of the art institutes in Pittsburgh, Atlanta, Dallas, Fort Lauderdale, Houston, Philadelphia, Seattle, or Denver. Some art majors spend a semester in New York City through an affiliate program with Hunter College or Drew University. In cooperation with the Ohio Agricultural Research Center in Wooster, Ohio, selected science majors may spend one semester or more participating in the agriscience program. Ashland's classrooms extend around the world, with overseas student teaching opportunities, summer language classes, faculty-sponsored student tours, mission trips, and other special programs. Numerous study abroad opportunities are available.

Academic Facilities

Ashland's facilities include nine computer labs, modern science laboratories, fully-equipped radio/TV studios, music studios and practice rooms, art studios and a gallery, a 750-seat theater, and a nursery and Montessori school. Physical education facilities include a natatorium, three basketball courts, a sauna, a training room, a fitness center, and a field house with an indoor banked track. The Gill Center for Business and Economic Education is the only resource and clearing house for business intelligence to be operated by a small liberal arts school. The Ashbrook Center, a nationally known institute for the study of public affairs, publishes scholarly books, hosts academic forums, and sponsors lectures by famous political speakers. The new technology center includes state-of-the-art computer equipment, multimedia technology, and distance learning classrooms.

Costs

Tuition for the 2000–01 school year is $15,134, fees total $400, room is $2958, and board is $2652. The total cost of tuition, fees, room, and board is $21,144.

Financial Aid

Approximately 98 percent of Ashland University's students receive financial assistance, enabling them to receive the benefits of a private college education. Each year AU makes available more than $25 million in scholarships, grants, loans, and employment. Awards are based on outstanding scholarship, accomplishment, talent, and/or financial need.

To apply for financial assistance, students must file the Free Application for Federal Student Aid (FAFSA) with the federal government and submit the Ashland University Financial Aid Application to the AU Financial Aid Office.

Faculty

Ashland's teaching faculty includes 200 full-time members, 80 percent of whom hold doctorate degrees. The faculty's first priority is teaching, placing emphasis on individual instruction and helping students achieve. They listen, advise, coordinate internship and research opportunities, write letters of recommendation, and introduce professional perspectives into every class.

Student Government

Ashland University allows its students a role of major importance and responsibility in the conduct of all affairs relating to their lives as members of the University community. The Student Senate acts as the principal governing body and serves as a liaison between students and the faculty and administration. More than 100 other student organizations exist, ranging from Orientation Team to intramurals, from Campus Activities Board to community service. HOPE Christian Fellowship and the Fellowship of Christian Athletes are among the largest on campus. Thirty percent of AU students are involved in sororities and fraternities.

Admission Requirements

Ashland strongly recommends that applicants have 16 units of college-preparatory high school credit to ensure that they have sufficient background for college work. Freshman applicants must present an official transcript of courses and grades from secondary school and scores on either the SAT I or ACT examination. Each applicant is encouraged to visit the campus for an interview with an admission counselor. A visit provides the applicant with an opportunity to see the campus and ask questions of students and faculty members.

Transfer students from accredited institutions are considered for admission to Ashland provided that they are in good standing socially and academically (having at least a C average or a 2.0 GPA) at any institutions attended previously.

Applicants who complete their secondary education through an alternative program (e.g., home schooling) must present evidence that they have been adequately prepared for university work to be considered for admission to AU. Such evidence may include appropriate scores on ACT or SAT tests, a high school equivalency diploma (GED test), satisfactory achievement on state or nationally normed tests that evaluate achievement level in high school academic subjects, and adequate performance on AU placement tests.

Application and Information

Freshman applicants are encouraged to submit applications early in the senior year of high school. To be considered for admission, a student must submit a completed and signed application form; a secondary school transcript listing rank in class and all courses and grades, beginning with the ninth grade; scores on the SAT I or ACT; and a nonrefundable $25 application fee. Transfer students will be considered for admission after they have submitted the application form, an official college transcript from all colleges previously attended, and the nonrefundable $25 application fee. An enrollment deposit of $100, which ensures accepted students a place in their class, is due thirty days after acceptance and is nonrefundable after May 1.

Additional information may be obtained by contacting:

Director of Admission
Ashland University
Ashland, Ohio 44805
Telephone: 419-289-5052
           800-882-1548 (toll-free)
Fax: 419-289-5999
E-mail: auadmsn@ashland.edu
World Wide Web: http://www.ashland.edu

In 1997, the 55,000-square-foot Hawkins-Conard Student Center opened, featuring several student lounges, a fitness center, a grill and a snack bar, an auditorium, and numerous meeting rooms.

ASSUMPTION COLLEGE
WORCESTER, MASSACHUSETTS

The College

In the rich tradition of St. Augustine and Catholic higher education, Assumption College was founded in 1904. Today, it is a thriving, independent, private, coeducational institution offering undergraduate and graduate programs in liberal arts and preprofessional majors.

Location

Assumption College occupies a beautifully landscaped 145-acre campus in the residential Westwood Hills section of Worcester, Massachusetts. Its location in a city with nine other colleges and universities affords the student many academic and social advantages. In addition, Worcester has many fine cultural facilities, including the Worcester Art Museum, a nationally known music festival, a symphony orchestra, and the New England Science Center. Facilities for winter and summer sports and for all sorts of recreational activities abound in Worcester and its vicinity. Boston, Massachusetts, and Providence, Rhode Island, are in proximity (45 minutes), and the Worcester Regional Airport extends opportunities to and from many other metropolitan centers.

Majors and Degrees

The College offers Bachelor of Arts degrees in accounting, art history, biology/biological sciences, chemistry, classics, communication, computer science, economics, English, environmental sciences, foreign languages, French, global studies, history, international business, international economics, management, marketing, mathematics, music, philosophy, political science, psychology, social and rehabilitation services, sociology, Spanish, studio art, and theology.

Special programs are offered in elementary education, middle school education, secondary education, medical technology, premedical/predental/prelaw, and engineering (3-2 program with Worcester Polytechnic Institute).

Academic Program

Father Emmanuel d'Alzon, founder of the Assumptionists, dedicated Assumption College to the "pursuit of truth, wherever it may be found." The College continues that pursuit of truth through the liberal education program. The students and faculty come together to contemplate the books, ideas, people, and events that have shaped civilization, so that the students might be better prepared to make their own contributions in the future.

Finding the truth about oneself and the nature of the surrounding world means learning not only how to ask questions but how to find the answers. That is why so many of the classes at Assumption are discussions, not lectures, and why the faculty assigns cooperative projects, frequent writing, and hands-on assignments designed to teach the student how to think, not memorize.

Assumption College follows a traditional two-semester calendar, running from late August to mid-May. The Continuing Education and Graduate School offers two summer sessions for its students. Army and Air Force ROTC programs are also available.

Students must complete a core curriculum of two courses of English, one of which is composition; two courses of philosophy; two courses of theology; two of the following three courses: mathematics, a laboratory science, and a third year of a foreign language; and one each of literature, history, social science, and either art, music, or theater. A total of 120 semester credit hours must be completed, with 9 to 12 semester credit hours in the upper division of the major.

Off-Campus Arrangements

In 1967, Assumption College joined with the other institutions of higher learning in the Worcester area to organize the Colleges of Worcester Consortium. Through the cooperation of fourteen Worcester area colleges, Assumption students may cross-register for academic credit at any of the participating colleges and may enjoy cultural events through those colleges.

Assumption College encourages qualified students to spend a semester or year abroad as an integral part of their undergraduate education. In the past five years, Assumption College students have studied abroad in Australia, Austria, the Czech Republic, England, France, Germany, Greece, Ireland, Italy, the Netherlands, and Spain.

Students at Assumption practice classroom theories through internships designed to help them explore their professional choices and broaden their workplace skills. For example, local, national, and international sites where current Assumption students have recently completed internships include the Department of Commerce, Central America Bureau; the Department of State, NAFTA Agreement; Smith Barney; Fidelity; Dean Witter Reynolds; AT&T; and the Alliance Française in Paris.

Academic Facilities

The Emmanuel d'Alzon Library has a seating capacity of 350 readers in a variety of arrangements conducive to study, research, and relaxation. In addition to its collection of 180,000 volumes, the library subscribes to 1,198 journal titles that support the concentrations of study offered at the College. Access to other resources is obtained through participation in local, regional, and national library networks and the World Wide Web.

Founders Hall houses the College's computer center. More than 100 computers are accessible to students, with applications ranging from word processing and e-mail to multimedia production, Web authoring, advanced nonlinear editing, and CD production. All offices, classrooms, and labs are connected to the World Wide Web. A technology-based classroom opened in the Fuller Building in fall 1996. During the summer 1997, all residence hall rooms were connected to the campus network. Resident students with Windows 95 or Macintosh Ethernet computers have unlimited access to the campus network and the World Wide Web.

Responding to continued enrollment growth and interest in the sciences, Assumption College is also moving forward on plans for a new state-of-the-art science and technology center. This building is scheduled for completion in fall 2002.

Costs

For 2000–01, tuition is $17,950 and room and board charges are $6980. The board plan is required for all freshmen and for all residents without cooking facilities. A student government fee costs $170. The total for tuition, room and board charges, and the fee is $25,100.

Financial Aid

Assumption College offers financial aid based on demonstrated need and scholastic promise. The College requires the Free Application for Federal Student Aid (FAFSA). This form should be filed by February 1 so that Assumption receives the processed application by the March 1 deadline.

The College offers merit awards to qualified students. Monies given through this program reflect the College's commitment to upholding a campus culture that champions academic excellence and student leadership.

Faculty

Assumption College faculty members—93 percent of whom hold doctoral or terminal degrees in their field—represent diverse fields of specialization and a wide range of professional experience. They are distinguished by an unusually deep dedication to their students, putting in far more than the minimum requirement of 10 office hours a week.

Student Government

As a very active organization, the Student Government Association (S.G.A.) attempts to move closer to the fulfillment of the ideals of self-government. The elected representatives of the student body constitute the Student Senate of S.G.A. This group is responsible for the recognition and financing of student clubs and activities and for serving as the official means of communication and coordination with the Assumption College student community.

Admission Requirements

Admission to Assumption College is limited to men and women of character, intelligence, and motivation who are selected from applicants who have completed the prescribed secondary school requirements. Assumption College supports the efforts of secondary school officials and governing bodies to have their schools achieve regional accredited status to provide reliable assurance of quality of the education preparation of its applicants for admission.

Application and Information

Interviews are not required but are strongly recommended, as is a campus visit. Appointments can be scheduled Monday–Friday. Group Information Sessions are held most Saturdays in the fall.

Applicants must submit a completed application, a $40 application fee, official transcripts, SAT I or ACT scores, a recommendation, and an essay. All applications for the freshman class, as well as all supporting credentials, must be filed in the Office of Admissions by March 1. Applications for early decision must be received by November 15.

For more information, students should contact:

Office of Admissions
Assumption College
500 Salisbury Street
P.O. Box 15005
Worcester, Massachusetts 01615-0005
Telephone: 508-767-7285
              888-882-7786 (toll-free)
E-mail: ugradadm@assumption.edu
World Wide Web: http://www.assumption.edu

The Plourde Recreation Center provides students with one of the most fully equipped facilities in the region.

ATLANTA COLLEGE OF ART
ATLANTA, GEORGIA

The College

The Atlanta College of Art provides an educational environment for the career-minded student with a talent and passion for art or design. Founded in 1928, the College is an accredited institutional member of the National Association of Schools of Art and Design and the Commission on Colleges of the Southern Association of Colleges and Schools. Approximately 430 students from across the U.S. and from abroad compose a highly charged, creative community that nurtures the development of educated, effective, and successful professionals in the visual arts.

The Atlanta College of Art is a founding member of the Woodruff Arts Center, the focus of the cultural life of the region. As the only art college in the United States that shares its campus with three other arts organizations—the High Museum of Art, the Alliance Theater, and the Atlanta Symphony Orchestra—the College is able to offer students access to a variety of art forms and resources on a working and thriving campus.

Lombardy Hall provides on-campus housing for 120 students. The double-occupancy apartments are furnished, and each is equipped with an efficiency kitchen. The Student Affairs Office provides information about convenient apartment rentals to students who choose not to live in the residence hall. In addition, the Student Affairs Office provides career planning services and coordinates an internship program for students wishing to gain professional work experience to complement their academic and studio training. Recent internship sponsors have included American Museum of Papermaking, CNN Headline News, Coca-Cola, Georgia Pacific Corporation, IBM, Museum of Modern Art, Turner Publishing, and Zoo Atlanta.

Students are encouraged to become involved in the extracurricular life of the College. A variety of clubs and organizations are recognized and funded by the College to give students opportunities for enrichment beyond the classroom.

Location

Atlanta offers students the best of the Sun Belt: long, bright, crisp fall and spring seasons with short, mild winters in the largest cosmopolitan center in the Southeast. With one of the fastest-growing economies in the nation, Atlanta is a city bursting with newness and enormous energy while still retaining its traditions and flavor. The city has a flourishing grassroots art scene—an optimal environment for the emerging artist or designer. Atlanta has scores of galleries and alternative spaces that exhibit a broad variety of artwork; a ballet and opera; numerous movie houses showing new releases and foreign and classic films; a growing number of theater companies, large and small; many opportunities for rock, jazz, and avant-garde music; outdoor performances; and the annual Piedmont Park Arts Festival. In addition, Atlanta has a myriad of natural areas and parks, restaurants and coffee houses of every description, and four professional sports teams.

The Atlanta College of Art is located in Midtown, the cultural heart of the city, a neighborhood where skyscrapers soar above tree-lined streets filled with restored older residences, some dating from the Victorian era. The Arts Center Station of MARTA, Atlanta's clean, safe, and efficient rapid transit system, is located just across the street from the College residence hall and offers easy access to many points of interest.

Majors and Degrees

The Atlanta College of Art offers a four-year program leading to the Bachelor of Fine Arts degree in communication design (advertising design, graphic design, and illustration), drawing, electronic arts (computer animation, digital art, digital multimedia, and video), interior design, painting, photography, printmaking, and sculpture. With faculty guidance, students may also develop their own individualized major.

Academic Program

The College's first-year Foundation Program combines visual studies courses, which emphasize visual thinking and problem solving, with courses in drawing and liberal arts as well as work in a studio area of choice. In the sophomore year, students develop their own course of study with a faculty adviser, either electing an established major or designing their own individualized major program. During the course of study, studio work is combined with courses in art history and criticism, English, literature, philosophy, psychology, anthropology, sociology, science, and math in a ratio of 2:1. These liberal arts courses reflect the notion that the making of art and the making of the artist are imaginative and reflective tasks and not simply technical ones, and they embody the conviction that the best artists and designers are those who can appreciate how tradition influences their work and is affected by it.

Operating on a two-semester academic year with an optional concentrated summer session, the College requires that students complete 120 credit hours for the B.F.A. degree: 78 in studio (12 credits in visual studies, 12 credits in drawing, 30–36 credits in the major, and 18–24 credits in studio electives) and 42 in liberal arts (12 credits in art history, 18 credits in the humanities, 3 credits in natural science, 6 credits in social science, and 3 credits in math).

Off-Campus Arrangements

The Atlanta College of Art is a member of the Association of Independent Colleges of Art and Design. The College's membership in this group allows students to study at other member schools for a semester or a year under a student mobility program. Because the College is also a member of the Atlanta Regional Consortium for Higher Education, students are able to take courses and attend lectures and events at other area colleges and universities, such as Emory University and Georgia Institute of Technology. Students may also study abroad in a variety of programs. Faculty members, the Student Affairs Office, and the Office of the Vice President of Academic Affairs assist in the choice of an appropriate program.

Academic Facilities

Along with an on-campus sculpture building and residence hall, the Atlanta College of Art occupies space on all four floors of the Woodruff Arts Center. College facilities include visual studies studios; drawing studios; a photo shooting studio and darkrooms; silkscreen, lithography, and intaglio and relief printmaking studios; papermaking and bookbinding facilities; painting studios; design studios; video and computer studios; a sculpture building, which includes a complete woodshop, a foundry, and working studios; and academic classrooms. Advanced-level students in painting, design, and sculpture are allotted individual work spaces.

The two-story library, with its expanse of windows overlooking Peachtree Street, offers a view of the Atlanta College of Art. The library has approximately 30,000 volumes and 70,000 slides and houses the Georgia Artists Registry, which has 1,500 files on Georgia artists. The library subscribes to more than 200 periodicals and houses the second-largest collection of artists' books (more than 1,000) in the country.

The Rich Auditorium, which seats more than 400, is the scene of many events, including visiting artists' lectures, performances, film series, and other College gatherings.

The stunning Atlanta College of Art Gallery, a museum-quality space of 3,850 square feet, shows eight to ten exhibitions a year, including the annual faculty show, juried student and graduating senior shows, contemporary exhibitions organized by the gallery, and traveling exhibitions featuring works by internationally recognized artists such as Antonio Muntadas, Thomas Woodruff, Deborah Bright, and Hannah Wilke. Gallery 100 offers exhibits of student work that are changed weekly and is maintained by the students themselves. The High Museum of Art is an integral part of the College's academic life; faculty members often take classes to the museum, and visiting artists, critics, and curators give lectures and gallery talks there, often in conjunction with studio demonstrations, critiques of student work, and workshops at the College.

Costs

Tuition for the 2000–2001 academic year is $13,800 for full-time students. The cost of a double-occupancy apartment in the residence hall is $4250. General fees total $384, and the housing activity fee totals $50.

Financial Aid

The Atlanta College of Art offers extensive financial assistance to students, combining institutional funds with funds from federal and state grant and loan programs. Each year, need-based grants, loans, and work-study jobs are awarded to students who apply for financial assistance using the Free Application of Federal Student Aid and the College's own financial aid form. While the priority deadline for applying for financial aid is March 15, awards are made on a first-come, first-served basis. The College also offers Merit Scholarships to both entering students and returning students. The Presidential Scholarship is awarded on the basis of the excellence of the portfolio and scholastic achievement. The School of Excellence award is given in recognition of the high quality of the student's high school or two-year college art program and the students' achievement in that program. The Dean's Scholarship is awarded on the basis of ACT or SAT I scores. Georgia residents are eligible for the Georgia Tuition Equalization Grant and the Hope Scholarship program.

Faculty

The 430 degree-seeking, full-time students at the College find that the 12:1 student-faculty ratio facilitates the personal attention and encouragement that are crucial to the development and nurturing of creative talent. The 24 full-time and approximately 65 adjunct professors at the College are dedicated professionals who combine active careers as artists and designers with a primary commitment to teaching. Faculty influence is expanded by an extensive schedule of national and international visiting artists and designers, who lecture and critique student work.

Student Government

Representatives of the student body are organized in the Student Alliance for the purpose of governance. This group oversees the funding of other student organizations, acts as a liaison between students and the administration, and plans activities for the entire student body. The College is committed to student involvement throughout the campus.

Admission Requirements

The Atlanta College of Art welcomes applications from high school graduates, recipients of high school equivalency certificates, and college transfer students. Applicants to the College must submit the following materials for evaluation: a completed application for admissions, a $30 nonrefundable application fee, an essay, official transcripts from high school and all colleges attended, SAT I or ACT scores, two letters of recommendation, and a portfolio of twelve to fifteen pieces of work, including a minimum of five drawings from direct observation.

Application and Information

Students are admitted to the College on a rolling basis, and an admission decision is made as soon as the applicant file is complete. While there is no official deadline for submission of an application, students are encouraged to apply by March 1 for priority consideration for admission, financial aid, and scholarships.

For an application and more information, students should contact:

Director of Enrollment Management
Atlanta College of Art
Woodruff Arts Center
1280 Peachtree Street, NE
Atlanta, Georgia 30309
Telephone: 404-733-5100
         800-832-2104 (toll-free)
E-mail: acainfo@woodruffcenter.org
World Wide Web: http://www.aca.edu

Students and faculty members at a gallery opening.

AUBURN UNIVERSITY
AUBURN, ALABAMA

The University

Auburn University was chartered in 1856 as East Alabama Male College. In 1872, the University was designated as a land-grant institution and has since evolved into a major comprehensive university, the largest in the state of Alabama. The campus consists of more than 1,800 beautiful acres, surrounded by farms and woodlands. The student body is composed of students from all fifty states, the District of Columbia, Puerto Rico, the Virgin Islands, and ninety countries. Auburn freshmen score well above the national averages; in 1999, Auburn averages were 23.1 on the ACT (composite score) and 1109 on the SAT I (combined score). About 16 percent of all undergraduates live on campus, and a wide variety of off-campus housing is available in the form of apartments, condominiums, and trailer parks. The campus offers numerous extracurricular activities, including nineteen sororities, twenty-eight fraternities, and more than 300 chartered and officially recognized organizations. Most are open to any interested student. Auburn offers an extremely active intramural sports and recreational services program in both team and individual activities. For students interested in musical organizations, Auburn offers a University Concert Choir, the University Singers, Gospel Choir, Men's Chorus, Women's Chorus, various ensembles, the University Orchestra, an Opera Workshop, and Marching and Concert bands. In addition, eight or nine theatrical productions are presented each year by the Auburn University Theatre. All students are welcome to audition for these productions, although casting priority is given to theater majors and minors. The Auburn Studio of the Alabama Public Television Network regularly produces programs for the Alabama Educational Television network, and a campus radio station, WEGL-FM, is operated by Auburn students.

Nationally recognized ROTC programs are available in three branches of service: Air Force, Army, and Navy/Marine Corps. Each of the three units is ranked among the top ten in the nation. Auburn is one of only seven schools in the Nuclear Enlisted Commissioning Program. It owns and operates the 334-acre Robert E. Pitts Auburn-Opelika Airport, providing flight education and fuel, maintenance, and airplane storage. The Auburn University Aviation Department is fully certified by the FAA as an Air Agency with examining authority for private, commercial, instrument, and multiengine courses.

Auburn University has been accredited by the Southern Association of Colleges and Schools since 1922, with specific programs accredited by the AACSB–The International Association for Management Education, the National Architectural Accrediting Board, the National Association of Schools of Art and Design, the National Association of Schools of Music, the Foundation for Interior Design Education Research, the American Council on Pharmaceutical Education, the Accreditation Board for Engineering and Technology, the Society of American Foresters, the National League for Nursing, the American Psychological Association, the National Council for Accreditation of Teacher Education, and many others. Auburn University offers, in addition to the undergraduate degree programs, more than 130 graduate-level programs. The Doctor of Pharmacy from the School of Pharmacy and the Doctor of Veterinary Medicine from the College of Veterinary Medicine are offered as first professional degrees.

Location

The city of Auburn (population about 30,000) is located in the east central part of Alabama, 60 miles northeast of Montgomery, 120 miles southeast of Birmingham, and 110 miles southwest of Atlanta, Georgia. Interstate 85 provides easy access to both Montgomery and Atlanta. Auburn is a small residential area and is often referred to as the "loveliest village of the plains." The University and the local community offer that rare blend of mutual support and cooperation evident only in a true university community.

Majors and Degrees

Auburn University offers 140 baccalaureate degree programs. The College of Agriculture confers the Bachelor of Science (B.S.) in agricultural business and economics, agricultural journalism, agricultural science, agronomy and soils, animal and dairy science, entomology, fisheries management, horticulture, poultry science, rural sociology, and several pre–veterinary medicine options. The College of Architecture, Design, and Construction offers Bachelor of Architecture (five-year) degrees in architecture and landscape architecture, the dual degree in architecture and interior design, the Bachelor of Science in environmental design, as well as a Bachelor of Industrial Design, Bachelor of Interior Design, and Bachelor of Science in Building Science. The College of Business and School of Accountancy grant a B.S. in business administration with professional option programs in accounting, business economics, finance, human resources management, international business, management, management information systems, marketing, operations management, and transportation and physical distribution. The College of Education provides teacher preparation programs leading to a B.S. in early childhood education, elementary education, English/language arts, foreign language (French, German, and Spanish), health, mathematics, music, physical education, science (biology, chemistry, general science, and physics), social science (economics, general social science, geography, history, political science, psychology, and sociology), special education, and vocational education. In addition, Bachelor of Science programs that are not teacher preparatory are available in adult education, exercise science, health promotion, recreation and sports management, and rehabilitation services. The College of Engineering offers curricula leading to the degrees of Bachelor of Aerospace Engineering, Aviation Management, Chemical Engineering, Civil Engineering, Computer Engineering, Computer Science, Electrical Engineering, Geological Engineering, Industrial and Systems Engineering, Textile Chemistry, Textile Engineering, and Textile Management and Technology. In addition, the B.S. is offered in agricultural engineering, environmental science, and forest engineering. The School of Forestry grants the B.S. in forestry. The School of Human Sciences offers the B.S. in apparel merchandising, design and production, human development and family studies, hotel and restaurant management, interior environments, and nutrition and food science. The College of Liberal Arts and School of Fine Arts award the Bachelor of Arts, Bachelor of Science, or Bachelor of Fine Arts in the following areas: anthropology, art, communication, communication disorders, corporate journalism, criminal justice, criminology, English, foreign languages–international trade, French, geography, German, health services administration, history, journalism, mass communication, philosophy, political science, psychology, public administration, public relations, social work, sociology, Spanish, theater, and visual arts. The School of Nursing provides study leading to the Bachelor of Science in Nursing. The College of Sciences and Mathematics offers the B.S. in applied discrete mathematics, applied mathematics, biochemistry, botany, chemistry, earth sciences, geology, laboratory technology, marine biology, mathematics, medical technology, microbiology, molecular biology, physics, wildlife science, and zoology. Preprofessional programs are offered in dentistry, medicine, occupational therapy, optometry, pharmacy, physical therapy, and veterinary medicine.

Academic Program

The academic year consists of three 10-week quarters (late September to early June). An additional summer quarter is in session from mid-June to late August. A common core curriculum is required. Undergraduate degree programs require from 180 to 270 credit hours. The average requirement is 192. Entering freshmen with extraordinarily high academic aptitude, an ACT composite score of at least 29 or an SAT I combined score of 1280 or more, and a minimum high school grade point average of 3.5 are eligible for consideration for admission into the honors program. The honors program provides individualized intellectual opportunities, smaller classes, and possible accelerated entry into graduate work. Advanced credit may be awarded on the basis of proficiency examinations, the Advanced Placement Program of the College Board, or the College-Level Examination Program (CLEP). A strong Co-op Education Program is available in agriculture, architecture, biological sciences, business, education, engineering, fine arts, forestry, human sciences, liberal arts, and science and mathematics in undergraduate as well as graduate programs.

Academic Facilities

The Ralph Brown Draughon Library is the main library on campus, with branch libraries located in the School of Architecture and the College of Veterinary Medicine. Computerized catalogs provide quick access to catalog records for most library items. Recently completed major projects include a $21-million expansion of the main library and the construction of a $10-million chemistry building, the $7.5-million Harbert Engineering Center for aerospace engineering, a $3.6-million biological research facility, a $15-million building for the College of Business, a 19,000-square-foot greenhouse complex costing $1.35 million, a 12,000-square-foot expansion of the Hoerlein Small Animal Clinic costing $1.5 million, an $875,000 veterinary research facility, a $20.8-million renovation of residence halls, the $10.5-million Martin Swim Center, an $8.9-million athletics center, a $1-million Satellite Uplink, a $550,000 educational television facility, the $1-million Ware Diagnostic Imaging Center in the Veterinary Medicine Complex, two residence halls costing $9.5 million, and the $12.5-million Rouse Life Sciences Building.

Costs

Undergraduate Alabama residents paid $9802 for the 1999–2000 academic year (three quarters). This figure included approximately $2976 for tuition, $600 for books and supplies, $4011 for room and board, $729 for transportation, and $1486 for miscellaneous personal expenses. Out-of-state students paid an additional fee of $5790.

Financial Aid

Financial Aid: During 1998–99, more than 10,000 students received more than $52 million in student aid funds through the University and through Federal Stafford Student Loans from commercial lenders. Financial assistance includes University loans, scholarships, part-time employment, and federal programs, such as the Federal Pell Grant, Federal Supplemental Educational Opportunity Grant, Federal Work-Study, Federal Perkins Loan, Health Professions student loans, and William D. Ford Direct Loans.

Financial aid application packets are available in January for the following academic year from the Office of Student Financial Aid, 203 Martin Hall, Auburn University, Alabama 36849. Applications received by April 15 are given priority consideration.

Scholarships: Prospective freshmen with superior ACT or SAT I scores and a 3.0 high school GPA who are on file with the University's Office of Admissions by December 1 are given automatic consideration for academic scholarships. The University's most prestigious scholarships include the Vulcan Presidential Honors Scholarship ($4000 per year), the Blount Presidential Scholarship ($5000 per year), and the McWane Foundation Scholarship ($6000 per year). These scholarships are awarded in late January. The University also offers general and departmental scholarships ranging from partial to full tuition. These scholarships are open to all class levels and are typically awarded in February. For entering freshmen, these scholarships are awarded primarily based on test scores, high school GPA, and need (in some cases). Auburn University actively participates in the National Merit Scholarship Program and National Achievement Scholarship Program. In-state National Merit Semifinalists and National Merit Finalists who name Auburn as their first choice receive a four-year scholarship in the amount of in-state tuition. In fall 1998, 122 National Merit Finalists were enrolled at Auburn University. Excellent scholarship opportunities are also available in the Air Force, Army, and Naval/Marine ROTC programs.

Faculty

Approximately 83 percent of the 1,145 full-time faculty members hold terminal degrees in their field. The Auburn University faculty generates almost one fifth of the entire student credit hour production of the state of Alabama. Auburn's standing as a research university and the quality of its faculty are documented by the growth in research funds provided by contracts and grants—a 33 percent increase in the last five years. Auburn's Space Power Institute is the leading institute in a five-university consortium researching the large amounts of electrical power needed to operate space stations.

Student Government

The Student Government Association (SGA) is the controlling body of all student projects and organizations. All students become members of SGA after paying their tuition and fees. Active participation is encouraged, as all student activities are governed by the SGA. The SGA is the voice of the students, promoting cooperation and communication with the faculty, administration, the Auburn City Council, and the state legislature.

Admission Requirements

Freshman admission to Auburn University is based on either ACT or SAT I scores and high school academic grade point average. Transfer students with fewer than 48 quarter hours or 32 semester hours must also meet freshman requirements.

Application and Information

Applications are accepted with a nonrefundable $25 application fee ($50 international application fee). There is no provision for a fee waiver. The closing date is determined by the number of applicants accepted; admission is on a rolling basis. Students must be accepted before they can apply for their choice of campus housing.

For more information about Auburn University, interested students should contact:

Director of Admissions
202 Martin Hall
Auburn University
Auburn University, Alabama 36849-5145
Telephone: 334-844-4080
        800-AUBURN9 (toll-free in Alabama)
E-mail: admissions@mail.auburn.edu
World Wide Web: http://www.auburn.edu/admissions

AUDREY COHEN COLLEGE
NEW YORK, NEW YORK

The College

Founded in 1964, Audrey Cohen College offers the student a unique Purpose-Centered System of Education, a design developed by the College. (The curriculum and its components are registered with the U.S. Patent Office.) This system examines the global, information- and service-centered economy, which employs more than 80 percent of the American work force, and responds to the questions: What must professionals be able to do, and how can they prepare for demanding and changing roles?

Audrey Cohen College alone has reinvented higher education to reflect the needs of this economy. Its graduates pursue careers in such diverse areas as banking, child welfare, community affairs, corrections, counseling, early childhood education, finance, gerontology, government, health administration, human resources, law, management, marketing, personnel administration, psychology, public administration, public health, social work, and student services.

Over a three-semester-long calendar year, the College enrolls approximately 2,230 students (about 870 men and 1,360 women). The College is approved for the training of veterans and other eligible people by the New York State Education Department and is fully accredited by the Middle States Association of Colleges and Schools.

If they choose, students are able to work full-time while pursuing their studies full-time, the latter being a College requirement. This becomes possible because of the strong educational relationships the College develops with students' employers. These enable students to use the workplace to complete a required component of the curriculum. For students who are not employed, the College's Field Placement Office develops a challenging internship site.

In addition to its undergraduate programs, the College offers two 3-semester-long master's programs: the M.S. in administration and the M.B.A. in media management.

The College has adapted its Purpose-Centered System of Education to the elementary/secondary experience, and this system is being used by schools around the country.

Location

The College's main location is in lower Manhattan, New York City, adjacent to Greenwich Village, the financial district, and SoHo and TriBeCa's flourishing media and artistic communities. It is convenient to all public transportation and easily accessible to major thoroughfares. Extension centers and sites are located in the Bronx, northeastern Queens, and Staten Island.

Majors and Degrees

Audrey Cohen College offers the Bachelor of Professional Studies degree in business and in human services. An Associate of Arts in human services degree program is also featured.

Academic Program

In both the School for Business and the School for Human Services, each semester of study is organized around a major Purpose, which research has shown to be critical for professionals in a global, information- and service-centered economy. There are eight Purposes in each of the programs. One is "Developing Professional Relationships," another is "Effective Supervision," a third is "Managing Human Resources," and so on.

Five courses (whose names remain constant) called Dimensions of Learning, Action and Assessment define how each Purpose is viewed holistically. These courses are Values and Ethics, Self and Others, Systems, Skills, and Purpose. Theory presented in each of these classes is specific to the Purpose of the semester and has incorporated the social and behavioral sciences, the humanities, and professional studies. They are all fused into a transdisciplinary model.

At the College, knowledge becomes the basis for taking action to improve the world. Thus, simultaneous to attending classes, students must show each semester, at their work site or at an internship, how they have taken theory from all five courses and used it to address an organizational need related to their Purpose. The College terms this taking Constructive Action and awards credit upon its successful completion. In each class, the professor incorporates material covered in other classes within that specific Purpose, thus ensuring the holistic, action-centered education that exemplifies the College. Education at Audrey Cohen College is always a vital experience.

While the College offers three full semesters of study each calendar year, there is no requirement that a student continue without interruption. However, the majority of students do, enabling them to complete their bachelor's degree in $2\frac{2}{3}$ years. (Students who transfer or who are accepted into the Advanced Standing Option can further reduce the time.)

An Associate of Arts degree program in human services can be completed in one year and four months. The program is designed for students who wish to enter into the human services field and explore up to three different internship opportunities. The degree features a four-semester sequence and comprises both classwork and fieldwork.

Academic Facilities

The College offers a variety of support services and maintains a state-of-the-art library of human services and business literature. This technologically sophisticated library provides storage, retrieval, and dissemination from both in-house library materials and outside online information sources, including the Internet. The collection is cataloged using the Library of Congress system. The Learning Center provides the College with expanded applications that support undergraduate and graduate education. These applications include Windows 97 and Microsoft Office Professional. In addition, an innovative video network provides instructors with a sophisticated means of distributing problems and complete flexibility in involving students with the solution process. Computer technology is built into the curriculum, which is designed to promote computer literacy. The Student Services Office provides an array of curricular and cocurricular support services to assist students with their academic programs.

Through the Advanced Standing Option, School for Human Services students with significant work experience and/or related educational courses may be able to apply their demonstrated past experience to the College degree requirements. These students may be granted exemption from up to three performance areas. Application for this option is made in either the first or second semester of study; acceptance requires the approval of the Director of Advanced Standing.

Transfer applicants to undergraduate programs may be able to receive transfer credit for related individual courses. For evaluation of transfer credit, students should arrange a special interview with the dean of the program to which they are applying.

Within the School for Human Services, formal credit-bearing field placements may also receive transfer credit. Transfer students who have earned an associate degree from an accredited institution in a human services specialization may be eligible for up to 64 transfer credits. Official transcripts are evaluated by the dean of that school. Such students can then complete their baccalaureate degree requirements within 1⅓ years of study.

Transfer applicants to the School for Business should be employed or in an approved internship site in order to be eligible for continued registration into the second semester.

Costs

For 1999–2000, charges per semester were $4720 for the School for Human Services and $4960 for the School for Business. The College charged $1380 for participation in the Advanced Standing Program. Students who stay enrolled are ensured that their tuition will not increase. Audrey Cohen College does not maintain dormitories since many students commute from their homes; however, New York City is home to many student residences not assigned to any particular institution of higher education.

Financial Aid

Audrey Cohen College participates in the federally administered Federal Pell Grant, Federal Stafford Student Loan, and Federal PLUS loan programs and in the Tuition Assistance Program (TAP) sponsored and administered by New York State for its state residents. The College also has limited resources under two other federal financial aid programs: the Federal Supplemental Educational Opportunity Grant Program and the Federal Work-Study Program. In addition, the College has its own scholarship program. Applicants may file through the College Scholarship Service or apply for federal funds directly at the College following their admission. State TAP applications are sent directly to the student once the federal applications have been processed.

Faculty

The School for Human Services has 14 full-time faculty members and 53 adjunct members. Five full-time faculty members and 30 adjuncts currently make up the School for Business faculty. More than 80 percent of the faculty have earned a doctoral degree. Many of the business faculty members have corporate affiliations as well as academic experience. Full-time faculty members serve as mentors and advisers to students, monitor student performance in the field, and work closely with students in the planning and execution of all phases of their program.

Student Government

Students are represented on most institutional committees, and 2 students are on the College's Board of Trustees. The Student Government Association seeks the active involvement of all students. A special Student Activities Committee also plays a key role in student life, scheduling special events throughout the year.

Admission Requirements

The College programs are rigorous and require sufficiently developed skills in English usage, vocabulary, reading comprehension, spelling, and mathematics as evidenced by the Test of Adult Basic Education (TABE). Students recently graduated from high school may substitute scores on the SAT I and the high school record for scores on the TABE. Individual counseling on requirements and qualifications is available from the admission staff.

Application and Information

All applicants must complete and return the application with a $20 application fee, take the Test of Adult Basic Education (TABE) at the College, have a personal interview with an admissions counselor, submit two letters of reference, provide official transcripts from each educational institution previously attended, and submit proof of immunization against measles, mumps, and rubella. Each applicant is also required to write an essay during the admission testing process. Applicants are informed of decisions as soon as all application materials have been received and evaluated. Electronic applications are featured on the College's Web site.

For additional information, students should contact:

Admissions Office
Audrey Cohen College
75 Varick Street
New York, New York 10013

Telephone: 212-343-1234 Ext. 5001
Fax: 212-343-8470
World Wide Web: http://www.audrey-cohen.edu

AUGUSTANA COLLEGE
SIOUX FALLS, SOUTH DAKOTA

The College

Augustana College was founded in Chicago in 1860 by Norwegian immigrants and moved westward with the pioneers, finally settling in Sioux Falls in 1918. Today, the College enrolls approximately 1,750 men and women; seventeen states and more than a dozen other countries are represented in the student body. A selective, residential liberal arts college of the Evangelical Lutheran Church in America, Augustana is a community dedicated to five shared fundamental values: Christianity, liberal arts, excellence, community, and service.

The College offers a Bachelor of Arts degree and is accredited by the North Central Association of Colleges and Schools. Selected programs are accredited by the National Council for the Accreditation of Teacher Education, South Dakota Division of Education, Council on Education of the Deaf, National League for Nursing, South Dakota Board of Nursing, the American Medical Association for Medical Technology and X-Ray Technology, Committee on Professional Training of the American Chemical Society, the National Association of Schools of Music, and the Council on Social Work Education (undergraduate).

Sixty-five percent of Augustana's students live in one of six on-campus residence halls. Involvement in the life of the campus is a vital part of the College's student life mission. More than sixty organizations invite student participation and leadership in student government, an extensive music program, theater, debate, KAUR-FM radio, and special interest clubs and activities. The College is a member of the North Central Conference, recognized as the finest NCAA Division II conference in the nation.

Morrison Commons serves as the student union, which contains student association and student services offices, a dining room, a bookstore, Back Alley, the Huddle snack bar, and meeting rooms. The College's athletic and recreation facility, the Elmen Center, is a modern fitness center that houses a pool, training facilities, an indoor track, racquetball/handball courts, a weight room, and the 4,000-seat Hall Forum for intercollegiate and intramural athletics. Opened in February 2000, the Mortenson Center and Student Street contains a 270-seat theater with thrust stage and offices for the Division of Student Services.

The Chapel of Reconciliation serves as the focal point of Christian worship and outreach on campus. Students from all faith traditions are welcome.

Location

The city of Sioux Falls (population 120,000) is the largest city in the state of South Dakota and lies in a fertile, gently rolling area within 15 miles of both the Minnesota and Iowa borders. Sioux Falls is recognized as one of the leading medical, retail, and industrial cities in the Upper Midwest and provides numerous opportunities for internships, part-time employment, postgraduate employment, student teaching, and other social and educational benefits. Sioux Falls is the home of the EROS Data Center, Raven Industries, several national trucking firms, the nation's largest stockyards, and Citibank's credit-card operations. The city is located at the intersection of transcontinental Interstates 90 and 29, is served by five commercial airlines, and has extensive bus service.

Majors and Degrees

Augustana College awards the Bachelor of Arts degree in the following major areas: accounting, art, athletic training, biology, business administration, chemistry, communication/business, communication, communicative disorders, computer science, economics, education (elementary, middle school, and secondary), education of the deaf and hard of hearing, engineering management, engineering physics, English, exercise and sports studies, exercise science, fitness management, French, German, government and international affairs, health services administration, health/physical education/recreation, history, interdepartmental studies, international studies, journalism, management information systems, mathematics, medical technology, modern foreign languages, music, nursing, philosophy, physics, psychology, religion, social work, sociology, Spanish, special education (endorsements available in communicative disorders, teaching of the learning disabled, teaching of the mentally retarded, teaching of the physically handicapped), and theater.

Preprofessional programs and special concentrations are available in biological chemistry, biophysics, chemical engineering, dentistry, gender studies, gerontology and geriatrics, engineering studies, environmental studies, law, medicine, mortuary science, Native American studies, Norwegian, occupational therapy, optometry, parish ministries, pharmacy, physical therapy, Russian and post-Soviet area studies, theology, and veterinary science.

Academic Program

Candidates for the baccalaureate degree are required to complete 130 semester hours, a major, and the general education requirements. The 59-credit-hour general education requirements are distributed among four areas: Exploring Self and Relationships (6 hours), Strengthening Skills for Living and Working in a Changing World (10 hours), Developing Knowledge for a Changing World (34 hours), and Developing Values, Perspectives and Commitment (9 hours). Augustana will grant credit to students who achieve acceptable scores on the Advanced Placement, CLEP, and International Baccalaureate examinations.

The academic year is divided into two semesters of fourteen weeks each, a January Interim of four weeks, and a summer term of eight weeks.

Off-Campus Arrangements

Augustana offers an educational program that is both international and intercultural in scope. Believing that interpersonal, intercultural, and international relations are a vital aspect of a student's education, the College sees the whole world as its classroom. Many international educational opportunities exist, including those offered through Augustana in the Centre for Medieval and Renaissance Studies, England; the Institute of European Studies; the American Institute of Foreign Study; the Scandinavian Urban Studies Term; and others. Students may also participate in overseas study and travel during the January interim.

Other off-campus arrangements are made through the Higher Education Consortium for Urban Affairs (HECUA), the Upper Midwest Association for Intercultural Exchange (UMAIE), the

Lutheran College Semester in Washington, D.C., the Washington Semester Program of American University, and reciprocal arrangements with other colleges.

Academic Facilities

The College has nineteen academic and housing units on a 100-acre campus. The Mikkelsen Library contains a computer lab, 230,000 bound volumes, and 1,000 journal subscriptions and is a member of the South Dakota Library Network, providing access to 3 million records. The library provides information resources in a wide variety of formats, from books to the Internet. The Center for Western Studies is also located in this facility. Gilbert Science Center ranks among the finest facilities for natural science instruction in the Midwest and houses a Foucault pendulum, a three-environment greenhouse, a scanning electron microscope, an isotope ratio mass spectrometer, nuclear magnetic resonance instruments, a Newtonian reflecting telescope, computer lab, and equipment for field research. The Humanities Center contains music practice and performance rooms, including Kresge Recital Hall, as well as classrooms for the Humanities Division. The centerpiece of the $35-million Augustana Renewal Campaign is the new 61,000-square-foot social science facility, the Madsen Center, which opened fall 1999. Every academic building contains a computer lab, as does each residence hall, and every room is wired for full Internet and cable access. The computer-student ratio is 1:5.

Costs

Educational fees for the 2000–01 academic year total $14,592, and room and board cost $4260. The student activity fee is $162. Expenses for books, travel, and personal supplies are estimated at $1300.

Financial Aid

For 1999–2000, 93 percent of Augustana's students received financial assistance totaling more than $16 million. Application for federal, state, or institutional aid is made by completing the Free Application for Federal Student Aid (FAFSA).

Sources of aid include the Federal Pell Grant and other federally funded programs. In addition, the College funds a variety of scholarships and grants. The Regents, Pro Musica, English, Debate, Theatre, Science, National Merit, and Augustana scholarships are available to students who have demonstrated outstanding achievement in academics or special talents. Applicants interested in further details should contact the Office of Admission.

Faculty

The Augustana faculty comprises 105 full-time tenured and tenure-track teaching professors, of whom 90 percent hold a doctoral or terminal degree. No courses are taught by graduate assistants. The student-faculty ratio of 13:1 provides the basis for an active faculty advising system. Professors have office hours and are also available for counseling and assistance at other times.

Student Government

The Augustana Student Senate nominates and elects students from each class to serve as representatives to the governing council. The council is involved in the allocation and distribution of funds to all student organizations and in the making of policy recommendations to the College administration. Students serve on faculty and support committees, are elected to judicial committees and dorm councils, and have a voice in all major College projects.

Admission Requirements

Each applicant to Augustana is considered on the basis of a thorough evaluation of his or her achievements, qualifications, and desire to meet the academic standards set by the faculty members. The Admissions Committee reviews the high school transcript, class rank, ACT or SAT I scores, personal recommendations, and extracurricular activities of each applicant. While not required, a personal interview is strongly recommended. Each applicant is considered on the basis of his or her probable success at Augustana, and admission is offered without regard to a student's gender, physical handicap, race, color, creed, national origin, or ethnic group.

Transfer students who have attended another four-year regionally accredited institution of collegiate rank will generally be admitted with a grade point average of 2.0 or above. Transfer students from an accredited community or junior college can normally have a maximum of 16 semester hours of credit applied toward their baccalaureate degree for each semester of satisfactory work. A maximum of 65 semester hours can be granted toward the degree.

Application and Information

The application for admission and the transcripts covering previous academic work may be submitted to the Office of Admission anytime after the second semester of the applicant's junior year in high school. Admission is offered on a rolling basis; however, students seeking financial aid should have applied and been offered admission prior to June 1.

To obtain catalogs, application forms, and additional information on admission, academic programs, and financial aid, prospective students should contact:

Office of Admission
Augustana College
2001 South Summit
Sioux Falls, South Dakota 57197
Telephone: 800-727-2844 (toll-free)
E-mail: info@inst.augie.edu
World Wide Web: http://www.augie.edu

Former Soviet Union President Mikhail Gorbachev was the third annual Boe Forum lecturer. Other speakers have been Colin Powell, George Bush, John Major, Barbara Bush, and Desmond Tutu.

AUGUSTA STATE UNIVERSITY
AUGUSTA, GEORGIA

The University

Augusta State University (ASU) is the premiere nonresidential university in the thirty-four–institution University System of Georgia. Tracing its roots back to 1783 when college-level classes were offered at a local academy, the college was officially founded in 1925 when it became the first public junior college in the state. In the 1960s it became a senior college, and in 1996 it became a state university. This long tradition of academe makes the learning experience at Augusta State unique. Students are educated for society; it not only makes for better world citizens, it instills the skills that are crucial for success in any major and in any career—an ability to speak well, write clearly, and approach problems reasonably.

A strong emphasis is placed on the liberal arts and sciences in subjects that make for a well-rounded person. These courses are successfully blended with innovative, specialized career preparation by faculty members who are experts in their fields.

Diverse backgrounds, experiences, and ages of ASU students supplement classroom education, as students from thirty-five states and more than fifty countries enrich the campus environment. A vast majority of students have full- or part-time jobs, and their professional experiences provide another element to the educational experience. To accommodate working students, the University maintains an hourly child-care service on campus.

An active campus life offers students and their families a wide range of cultural opportunities through concerts, theatrical productions, lectures, films, art exhibitions, and special programming. More than forty-eight organizations are chartered, giving leadership opportunities in fraternities, sororities, honor societies, professional organizations, social groups, student government, activities, and publications (literary magazine and newspaper). Intramural sports offer competitive athletic events such as rowing and six-time national championship table tennis.

In intercollegiate athletics, Augusta State is a member of the Peach Belt Athletic Conference and NCAA Division II in ten sports as well as Division I in golf. Women compete in basketball, cross-country, softball, tennis, and volleyball; men compete in baseball, basketball, cross-country, golf, soccer, and tennis. Intercollegiate sports take place at the Forest Hills campus, where playing fields, an 18-hole golf course, an indoor walking track, and fitness equipment also provide noncompetitive opportunities. A swimming pool is located on the main campus.

The main 72-acre campus on Walton Way, which houses most of the administrative and academic facilities, is undergoing a major physical redesign. Recently constructed is a $19.4-million science building. The 122,000-square-foot building is the first of three planned buildings. Currently under construction is an $18.2-million classroom complex; the third planned building will be a classroom complex of similar size.

Washington Hall is the center of student life. It houses a bookstore, a cafeteria, game rooms, a billiard room, television rooms, and offices for student activities and meetings. The University's START-UP Center is also located there. The center is a beginning point for new students to familiarize themselves with the campus and to assist them in their academic pursuits.

Augusta State is the largest feeder school to the Medical College of Georgia, which is also located in Augusta. Biology is the largest major on campus.

In addition to undergraduate degrees, ASU offers the Master of Business Administration, Master of Education, Master of Public Administration, Master of Science in psychology, and a Specialist degree in education. The Master of Business Administration and Master of Public Administration degrees are earned entirely through evening classes.

Augusta State is accredited by the Commission on Colleges of the Southern Association of Colleges and Schools (1866 Southern Lane, Decatur, Georgia 30033-4097; telephone: 404-679-4501) to award associate, bachelor's, master's, and specialist degrees. All teacher education degree programs for elementary, special, secondary, and P–12 teachers, administrators, counselors, and supervisors are approved by the Georgia Professional Standards Commission and are accredited by the National Council for Accreditation of Teacher Education. The nursing program is accredited by the National League for Nursing Accrediting Commission and approved by the Georgia Board of Nursing. The music programs are accredited by the National Association of Schools of Music. The College of Business is accredited by AACSB–The International Association for Management Education.

Location

Augusta State is located in Augusta, Georgia, the second-largest city in Georgia and home to the internationally famous Masters Golf Tournament. Its location on the Savannah River, the border between the states of South Carolina and Georgia, offers abundant recreational opportunities. Its proximity to two state capitals, the beaches, and the mountains makes its location ideal for enjoying a wide variety of cultural and leisure activities. The city of Augusta offers ballet, theater, opera, and a symphony. Art galleries, museums, a national science center, minor league baseball and hockey, and a host of other entertainment facilities provide outlets for nearly every taste. Adjacent to the city is Fort Gordon, headquarters of the U.S. Army Signal Corps, the largest training center in the world for electronic communications.

Majors and Degrees

More than fifty majors are offered that lead to degrees at the associate, bachelor's, master's, and specialist levels as well as to a corporate doctoral degree. Augusta State University offers the Associate of Arts; the Associate of Applied Science in criminal justice; the Associate of Science; the Associate of Science in nursing; the Bachelor of Arts in art, communications (broadcast/film, drama, journalism, public relations/advertising, and speech), criminal justice, elementary education (early childhood and middle grades), English (creative writing, English, and professional writing), French, history, music, political science (international studies, legal studies, political science, and public administration), psychology, secondary teacher education (art, English, French, history, music, political science, and Spanish), sociology, and Spanish; the Bachelor of Business Administration in accounting, finance, management, and marketing; the Bachelor of Fine Arts in studio art; the Bachelor of Music in music education and performance; the Bachelor of Science in biology, chemistry (preprofessional and professional), computer science, mathematics, physical science, and physics; and the Bachelor of Science in Education in health and physical education, secondary teacher education (biology, chemistry, mathematics, and physics), and special education.

Academic Program

The core curriculum (about the first two years of study) is the same for all students, offering a broad foundation in the liberal arts and sciences. Those courses are fully transferable to any other institution in the University System of Georgia and to most other institutions, should the need arise. ASU students work closely with advisers who assist in the planning and scheduling of courses required in their major fields of study.

Flexible class scheduling is offered throughout the day and evening. The academic offerings at Augusta State are organized into three colleges: the Pamplin College of Arts and Sciences, the College of Business Administration, and the College of Education. Classes are organized on a semester system, and most majors require about 120 hours to complete.

Academic support services are provided through a writing center, tutors, and a Counseling and Testing Center. Students with special needs are assisted through a Disability Services Office to ensure that all students have equal access to programs and activities offered at Augusta State.

Undergraduate students are encouraged to participate in research with each other and with faculty members and to present their findings at area conferences. Because of close associations with area businesses and industries, students have opportunities for internships and co-ops in the community. They may also study abroad or take part in exchange programs with other universities. An interdisciplinary Honors Program offers students of superior scholarship additional opportunities for research and provides both challenge and reward to those who want a broader, more comprehensive curriculum.

Academic Facilities

Reese Library offers academic support to ASU students through more than 469,000 volumes and 2,000 periodicals. Electronically, Augusta State is linked with every library at every public college and university in the state, as well as with many public libraries. This and interlibrary loans make statewide academic resources available to all students.

Students have access to about 280 computers on campus, with two computer labs being open 24 hours a day. From all sites, the Internet and its resources, which include free student e-mail accounts, may be accessed.

Student performances in theater and music are held at the Grover C. Maxwell Performing Arts Theatre, a 750-seat auditorium that is frequently used by community groups. It also is an exhibition site for art displays, as is the Fine Arts Hall.

Costs

For residents of Georgia, undergraduate tuition for 1999–2000 was approximately $2025. Expenses for books and supplies were estimated to be around $600 a year. Residents of Edgefield and Aiken Counties in South Carolina pay the same tuition rate as Georgia residents. Tuition for nonresidents of Georgia was approximately $7025 for undergraduate studies.

Financial Aid

Serious students should not let financial need keep them from an education. The University makes every effort to award financial assistance to deserving students whose resources do not meet expenses. Federal, state, and private aid is available through scholarships, loans, and grants. Campus employment may also be available. More than 65 percent of ASU students receive some type of financial aid.

Faculty

The University owes much of its success to faculty members, whose dedication is to teaching. Classes are taught by faculty members, not graduate assistants, and senior faculty members teach courses at all levels. Close contact exists between faculty members and students, with a student-faculty ratio of 27:1. Faculty members serve as advisers to students for assistance in course selection and academic counseling. Of the 192 full-time faculty members, 134 have doctorates.

Although faculty members continue to consult with business and industry, to research, and to publish, their primary dedication is to teaching. Close interaction with faculty members provides opportunities for students to learn through the minds, experiences, and imaginations of others. It offers opportunities to explore new interests and to see the world from different perspectives.

Student Government

The Student Government Association (SGA) is divided into four branches: the Student Senate, the Jaguar Activities Board, the Student Judicial Cabinet, and the Executive Branch, which is composed of the 3 SGA officers and the branch chairs. The SGA president represents the student body to the University administration in matters that students feel are pertinent to their interests. The SGA and its president appoint 54 students to 16 student-faculty committees to make or recommend most University policy. The executive officers and student senators, who are elected by the students to represent each department, are available to any student with a difficulty, suggestion, or grievance.

The Student Senate is the recognized legislative body responsible for any matters related to the students or student interest. The senate meets weekly each semester. The senate has four standing committees that investigate student concerns and make appropriate recommendations to faculty and administration. The Jaguar Activities Board is responsible for providing social as well as educational entertainment for the campus community. The board meets weekly each quarter. The Judicial Cabinet hears cases referred by the Dean of Students and interprets the Constitution. The cabinet meets as needed. Funds for equipment, supplies, travel expenses, and campus free phones are received from the student activity budget. Students are encouraged to take leadership roles in SGA.

Admission Requirements

Augusta State University is an equal opportunity institution. It admits students whose academic qualities give promise of success without regard to race, age, creed, national or ethnic origin, or physical handicap.

An application for admission and supporting credentials should be filed with the Office of Admissions. Campus tours are encouraged and are provided by the Office of Admissions.

Application and Information

For more information, students should contact:
Office of Admissions
Augusta State University
2500 Walton Way
Augusta, Georgia 30904-2200
Telephone: 706-737-1632
          800-341-4373 (toll-free)
E-mail: admissio@aug.edu
World Wide Web: http://www.aug.edu

AURORA UNIVERSITY
AURORA, ILLINOIS

The University

Aurora University was founded in 1893. The school has grown substantially over the years and has taken on many new challenges. In 1938, it was one of the first small colleges to achieve regional accreditation. In 1947, the college's evening program was instituted—one of the nation's first adult education programs at a liberal arts college. In 1985, Aurora College was reorganized as Aurora University, reflecting both the increased size of the institution and the needs associated with its many new programs. In addition to the University College of Arts and Sciences, the University comprises the John and Judy Dunham School of Business and Professional Studies, the School of Nursing, George Williams College of Aurora University, and New College (adult and continuing education). Today, the University enrolls 4,000 students in more than forty undergraduate programs and six graduate programs in business, recreation administration, social work, and teaching. Courses are offered at other sites in Illinois, Iowa, and Wisconsin, in addition to the Aurora campus.

The University's student body includes 360 on-campus, traditional-age students; 1,000 undergraduate commuters; 1,000 graduate students; and more than 1,600 students at off-campus sites. The majority of Aurora's students come from the upper-Midwest region, but twenty states and five countries are also represented.

Social life is based on campus, and most activities are campuswide. Aurora has more than thirty musical, literary, religious, social, and service clubs and organizations. There are also nine fraternities and sororities for students interested in Greek life. Aurora University has a long history of excellence in both intercollegiate and intramural athletics. A member of the NCAA Division III, Aurora fields intercollegiate teams in baseball, basketball, football, golf, soccer, softball, tennis, and volleyball, often with championship results.

Aurora University is accredited at the bachelor's and master's degree levels by the Commission on Institutions of Higher Education of the North Central Association of Colleges and Schools, and its programs are accredited by the National League for Nursing Accrediting Commission, Illinois Department of Professional Regulation, Council on Social Work Education, and National Recreation and Park Association/American Association of Leisure and Recreation.

Location

Aurora University is located in an attractive residential neighborhood on the southwest side of Aurora, Illinois, which has a population of more than 122,000 and is the state's third-largest city. The 27-acre main campus is located only minutes from the Illinois Research and Development Corridor, the site of dozens of nationally and internationally based businesses and industries. Located within an hour's drive or train ride away is Chicago, one of the most vibrant cities in the world.

Majors and Degrees

The Bachelor of Arts degree is awarded in accounting, biology, business administration, communication (corporate and professional, interdisciplinary, and mass communication/TV production), computer science, computer science/business information systems, computer science/electronics, criminal justice, elementary education, English, finance, history, management, marketing, mathematics, physical education (K–12 teacher certification), political science, psychology and sociology. The Bachelor of Science degree is awarded in biology, biology–environmental science, business administration, computer science, finance, health science (predentistry, premedicine, pre–physical therapy, and pre–veterinary studies), management, marketing, nursing, physical education (athletic training and fitness leadership), recreation administration (commercial recreation management, outdoor leadership, program management, and therapeutic recreation), and social work. The Bachelor of Science in professional studies is awarded in organizational management, group work–youth development, programming and management, and criminal justice management. The University also offers supplemental majors in prelaw and secondary education, as well as the YMCA Senior Director Certificate Program.

Academic Program

Aurora University offers academic programs combining a liberal arts foundation with majors emphasizing career preparation and selected concentrations. Graduates are educated to be purposeful, ethical, and proficient—equipped for worthwhile careers and productive lives and for venturing out into a changing world.

To earn a bachelor's degree, students are required to fulfill the general degree requirements of the University and the major requirements for an approved major; complete at least 120 semester hours with a GPA of at least 2.0 on a 4.0 scale, including at least 60 semester hours at a senior college; and complete at least 30 semester hours, including the last twenty-four for the degree and at least eighteen semester hours in the major, at Aurora University.

Aurora University accepts credits earned through the CLEP, DANTES, ACT-PREP, and NLN Mobility testing programs. In addition, the Life Experience Assessment Program (LEAP) is available to students who have significant prior learning from career experience or individual study.

The University observes a trimester calendar year (one 11-week term and two 10-week terms), with classes beginning in early September and concluding in late May.

Off-Campus Arrangements

There is a three-week travel-study program in the American West as well as travel-study programs to Mexico and England. The University also has off-campus sites in Chicago (nursing and group work programs) and at the University's Lake Geneva campus in Williams Bay, Wisconsin.

Academic Facilities

The major buildings at Aurora are marked by the distinctive, red-tiled roofs specified by Charles Eckhart in his donation for the original campus. Dunham Hall houses state-of-the-art computer facilities as well as the Schingoethe Center for Native American Cultures. A state-of-the-art television studio, serving both the University's communication program and the local cable system, is located in Stephens Hall; other facilities include the fully equipped Perry Theatre, science labs, flora-fauna complex, and the College Commons. Music practice rooms, piano labs, and a spacious art studio are also available. Charles B. Phillips Library has more than 107,000 volumes, 190,000 microform units, and approximately 700 current periodical subscriptions. In addition, the library provides access to approximately 3,700 journals in electronic full-text.

Costs

Tuition for the 2000–01 school year is $12,918 for full-time students (24 to 33 semester hours per year), while yearly room and board costs are $4914.

Financial Aid

Aurora University's financial aid program has been designed to make it possible for any academically qualified student to afford the benefits of a private education. The University works with students to determine the amount of their costs and to identify all available resources so that students can meet these expenses. There are many criteria for awarding financial aid, including financial need, academic performance or potential, leadership skills, and involvement in extracurricular activities. In addition to need-based financial aid, Aurora University offers several academic scholarships, including the Board of Trustees Scholarship, Crimi Scholarship, Solon B. Cousins Scholarship, Aurora University Achievement Grant, and Dean's Grant.

Faculty

Members of the faculty develop special relationships with students. The favorable student-faculty ratio of 15:1 ensures that students receive plenty of individual attention in class. Instructors also make time for students outside of class, acting as mentors, advisers, and friends who are eager to answer questions, to join students in sports and social activities, and even to invite students to their homes for occasional dinners.

Student Government

The student body is represented by the AUSA (Aurora University Student Association), which provides funding for various student groups on campus. Students are also active members of committees ranging from faculty searches to academic standards and are provided with certain voting privileges.

Admission Requirements

The Aurora University Committee on Admissions considers the complete record of a candidate for admission. The University seeks qualified students from varied geographical, cultural, economic, racial, and religious backgrounds. No single or inflexible set of admission standards is applied. Two general qualities are considered in each candidate: academic ability, enabling the student to benefit from a high-quality academic program, and a diversity of talents and interests that can contribute to making the campus community a better and more interesting place for learning. An application for admission to Aurora University is considered on the basis of the academic ability, achievements, activities, and motivation of the student. Transfer students with fewer than 30 semester hours of credit should apply in the same manner as freshman applicants. Transfer students with more than 15 semester hours may be admitted to Aurora University if they have a transferable overall GPA of 2.0 or higher. Aurora accepts a maximum of 90 semester hours of transfer credits from a combination of two- and four-year schools. A maximum of 60 semester hours may be transferred from two-year schools. For further information, students should contact a transfer counselor in the Admissions and Financial Aid Office.

Application and Information

To apply for admission to Aurora University, the following items should be sent to the Admissions and Financial Aid Office: a completed application form, an official transcript from the guidance counselor, and official ACT or SAT I scores. Transfer students should submit official transcripts from each college or university attended, along with the completed application.

Applications and further information may be obtained by contacting:

Admissions and Financial Aid Office
Aurora University
347 South Gladstone
Aurora, Illinois 60506
Telephone: 630-844-5533
        800-PICKAU-1 (toll-free)
E-mail: admissions@aurora.edu
World Wide Web: http://www.aurora.edu

An aerial view of Aurora University in Aurora, Illinois.

AUSTIN COLLEGE
SHERMAN, TEXAS

The College

Austin College is considered among the nation's finest four-year coeducational liberal arts colleges. Founded in 1849, Austin College is affiliated, through a covenant relationship, with the Presbyterian Church (U.S.A.). The College prepares students to pursue challenging career goals and provides a framework within which each student may mature academically, socially, and personally. Approximately two thirds of students pursue an advanced degree within five years of graduation.

The current undergraduate enrollment is limited to 1,200 students. The majority of the College's students live on campus. A choice of living styles is offered in the various residence halls and in the Bryan Apartments, which house upperclass students who prefer apartment living to the regular residence halls. German, French, Japanese, and Spanish majors may live in a language residence on campus, in which the target language is spoken in common areas. Students from ten countries, as well as from all minority groups, are included in the student population. All students are allowed to have cars on campus.

Intercollegiate athletics include eight sports for men and six for women. Students can also participate in intramural and other recreational activities. Opportunities are available to attend cultural events and to participate in an a cappella choir, a jazz ensemble, the Sherman Symphony, theatrical performances, art exhibits, campus publications, local sororities and fraternities, and student government. Many leadership opportunities are provided in areas outside the classroom.

Austin College's office of career planning and placement helps students develop future goals and strategies to meet those goals. A computerized career network system provides specific information on hundreds of occupational fields as well as the steps students should consider in order to enter those fields. In addition, students may find summer or part-time employment in the Sherman-Denison area, home to major corporate operations such as those of Johnson & Johnson, Folgers, Texas Instruments, MEMC Southwest, and Nabisco.

The College has an outstanding theater and conference center, an indoor swimming pool, a tennis stadium, handball courts, football and soccer fields, and other modern recreational facilities. The College also maintains a 28-acre recreational area on Lake Texoma, about 20 miles from the main campus.

Location

The Austin College campus is in Sherman, Texas, 60 miles north of Dallas, in a metropolitan area of 90,000 people, which includes Denison, a city of similar size located just north of Sherman near Lake Texoma. Austin College students may participate in civic, cultural, religious, and social activities in the Sherman community. The growing Dallas–Fort Worth metroplex provides students with numerous cultural and social opportunities.

Majors and Degrees

The Bachelor of Arts degree is offered in American studies, art, biology, business administration, chemistry, classics, communication arts, economics, English, exercise and sport science, French, German, history, international economics and finance, international studies, Latin American studies, mathematics/computer science, music, philosophy, physics, political science, psychology, religion, sociology, and Spanish.

Through the Austin Teacher Program, a special five-year teacher education program, a student earns both the Bachelor of Arts degree and the Master of Arts in Teaching degree.

Austin College also has excellent preprofessional programs in engineering, law, medicine, and theology.

Academic Program

The emphasis of Austin College's academic program is on a student's individual development throughout his or her college career. Considerable importance is placed on a special freshman-year program and close student-faculty relationships. Flexible degree-planning options include a regular liberal arts program, a special degree plan, and a departmental honors program. One course is taken in the four-week January term, and four courses are taken in each of the other terms—fall and spring. Two courses may be taken in the optional summer term, which is seven weeks in length. Students can pursue individualized study or field studies and internships.

In 1995, the College began a four-year program for a limited number of freshmen called the Leadership Institute at Austin College. Each student selected for the program receives a $10,000 renewable scholarship and participates in the institute's programs, which include the opportunity for students to be involved in community service as well as internships in national and international settings; a combination of academic and practical experiences; a required course on at least one culture other than the student's own; participation in an international experience; and a mentor relationship with a local, state, or national leader.

Off-Campus Arrangements

Students have opportunities for study in England, France, Germany, Spain, Japan, and other countries through the Institute of European and Asian Studies, and they can participate in the Washington Summer Symposium or Austin College in Mexico programs as well. Students can also become involved in field study through the social sciences laboratory or individually arranged programs.

Academic Facilities

The College's excellent facilities include the new Robert J. and Mary Wright Campus Center, well-equipped science classrooms and laboratories, a computer center, complete fine arts facilities including two theaters, and modern athletic facilities. A state-of-the-art library with more than 300,000 volumes and 900 periodicals maximizes research and learning opportunities. A campuswide fiber-optic computer network provides access to on-campus resources and the Internet. Three environmental research areas are all within a short drive of the main campus.

Costs

The basic charge for students entering in 2000–2001 (including tuition, fees, room, and board) is approximately $21,343 for boarding students and $15,452 for nonboarding students.

Financial Aid

Assistance is given in three forms: grants and/or scholarships, loans, and on-campus jobs. Students applying for need-based financial aid should request a financial aid application from Austin College and should also submit the Free Application for Federal Student Aid (FAFSA). Competitive awards, based on merit rather than on financial need, are also available. The application for admission serves as the application for most of these awards, which range in value from $2000 to $12,000. Separate applications are necessary for full-tuition scholarships, Leadership Institute Scholarships, and Junior/Community College Full-Tuition Scholarships. About 85 percent of all students received aid in 1999–2000.

Faculty

Of the full-time faculty members, 98 percent hold terminal degrees. Faculty members holding earned doctorates teach at all levels. In addition to carrying out their academic and professional responsibilities, faculty members participate in the governance of the College and serve as students' mentors. With a student-faculty ratio of 13:1 and an average class size of 23, the emphasis at Austin College is on classroom excellence.

Student Government

Under a community-government partnership plan, in which students and members of the faculty and administration are all participants, student involvement and leadership are important aspects of College governance. The College is committed to high principles in scholarship and general behavior.

Admission Requirements

Admission is competitive, with four times the number of applicants as places in the freshman class. Transfer students are subject to the same type of rigorous standards required of freshman applicants. Students who cannot fulfill these requirements will be considered on an individual basis. Two admission deadlines have been established for freshman applicants for fall 2000. December 1 is the early decision and early action I deadline and January 15 is the early action II deadline. Students are notified of an admission decision approximately four weeks after each deadline. After January 15, applications are considered on a rolling basis and are given consideration on a space-available basis. May 1 is the candidate's reply deadline for all admitted students. To reserve a place in the entering class, a $300 deposit is required by May 1. The College's early admission program allows qualified students to enroll after their junior year of high school. Admission to Austin College is on an equal basis, regardless of color, race, sex, religion, national origin, or handicap.

Application and Information

A completed application form, including a $35 nonrefundable application fee, SAT I or ACT scores, two letters of reference, and a transcript from each high school and college attended must be submitted to Austin College. Application forms for admission and financial aid should be requested from the College's Admission Office. Students may request a complimentary loan copy of the *Austin College Video Visit* by calling Videc, Inc., at 800-255-0384 (toll-free).

For more information, students should contact:
Admission Office
Austin College
900 North Grand Avenue, Suite 6N
Sherman, Texas 75090
Telephone: 903-813-3000
          800-442-5363 (toll-free)
Fax: 903-813-3198
E-mail: admission@austinc.edu
World Wide Web: http://www.austinc.edu

Austin College students enjoy a quiet moment between classes.

AZUSA PACIFIC UNIVERSITY
AZUSA, CALIFORNIA

The University
Celebrating 100 years of excellence in Christian higher education, Azusa Pacific University (APU) is a coeducational, independent, interdenominational university founded in 1899. Azusa Pacific earned university status in 1981. Committed to the goal of each student's personal, spiritual, and academic growth, APU provides extensive opportunities for student development with academic emphases in liberal arts and professional studies.

The University is divided into one college and five schools: the College of Liberal Arts and Sciences and the Schools of Music, Nursing, Education and Behavioral Studies, Business and Management, and Theology.

On-campus residential living is a distinctive feature of student life at APU, with several areas from which to choose. Each differs in size, location, structure, type, and activities. Each area sponsors individual and large-group events, academic and social experiences, spiritual and cultural encounters, indoor and outdoor recreational opportunities, and highly structured and spontaneous activities.

The University's 5,400 students (2,795 of whom are undergraduates) come from twenty-four states and thirty-two nations and represent more than thirty religious denominations. APU students are strong academically, entering with an average GPA of 3.4. They are often leaders in their high schools, churches, and communities. Azusa Pacific offers excellent leadership development programs that teach students how to be positive contributors to their communities, jobs, and society.

Nineteen master's degree programs and three doctorates are offered in addition to the undergraduate programs listed below.

Location
Azusa Pacific University is located in the foothills of the San Gabriel Valley communities of Azusa and Glendora, 26 miles northeast of Los Angeles. APU is only an hour's drive from beaches, amusement parks, mountains, ski resorts, and cultural centers. The climate is moderate, mostly warm and dry throughout the school year.

Majors and Degrees
Azusa Pacific University grants the Bachelor of Arts degree in the fields of art, biblical studies, biology, business administration, chemistry, Christian ministries, communication, English, global studies, history, liberal studies, mathematics, mathematics/physics, music, philosophy, physical education, political science, psychology, social science, social work, sociology, Spanish, and theology. The Bachelor of Science degree is awarded in the fields of accounting, applied health, biochemistry, biology, chemistry, computer science, life science, management information systems, marketing, mathematics, nursing, and physics.

Preprofessional programs are available in dentistry, law, and medicine. Pre-engineering degree programs (3-2 and 2-2) are also offered.

The Department of Religion and Philosophy offers a ministry credential program that combines academic study with practicum and leads to the Bachelor of Arts degree.

Academic Program
Azusa Pacific University operates on the semester system and offers two summer sessions.

The minimum number of credits required for a bachelor's degree is 126. About half of these units must be completed in general studies requirements as follows: skills and University requirements, 21–33 units; aesthetics and the creative arts, 3 units; heritage and institutions, 3 units; identity and relationships, 3 units; language and literature, 3 units; nature, 4 units; God's Word and the Christian response, 18 units; and integrative electives, 6–8 units. Areas of concentration vary in their requirements, and many offer several emphases within the major.

The University grants credit for certain scores on Advanced Placement tests and College-Level Examination Program tests, college courses taken while in high school, and the International Baccalaureate.

Academic Facilities
The newly renovated William V. Marshburn Library at Azusa Pacific University houses more than 750,000 items, including 1,593 periodicals and 149,288 books. It offers enhanced traditional services as well as state-of-the-art features that facilitate undergraduate research. APOLIS, the library's automated system, includes the library catalog and several bibliographic databases to periodical literature. CD-ROM workstations and online services offer electronic access to materials from around the world. Special collections house many rare and valuable items. The Media Center has an extensive collection of scores, videocassettes, and compact discs as well as graphic art materials and equipment. Ten professional librarians are available for assistance.

Opened in January 1998, the $8-million Hugh and Hazel Darling Library offers students a vast collection of printed books, reference materials, serials, and microfilm as well as 180 computer carrels and 220 workstations with access to more than 100 licensed databases and Web resources globally. There are also five classrooms equipped with video projectors, computers, and ISDN lines for distance learning; an auditorium with tiered seating; and a TV studio. The design of the building is meant to meet the needs of the twenty-first-century learner.

The Academic Computer Center serves all APU students. It is equipped with PC and Macintosh computers and laser printers, connected by a Novell-based local area network. A wide variety of software is available to fulfill students' needs.

Outstanding features of the Carl E. Wynn Science Center include an electron microscope facility with both scanning and transmission instrumentation for use in cellular and molecular biology, physiology, and ecology courses and practical facilities, such as a greenhouse to support botany. The Departments of Biology and Chemistry and Mathematics and Physics offer vigorous programs with the support of the science center.

APU enjoys state-of-the-art School of Theology, School of Music, and chapel complexes. The C. P. Haggard School of Theology includes a research library, seminar and conference rooms, six classrooms, and faculty and administrative offices. The two-story School of Music contains three large rehearsal rooms, twenty-two instrumental and voice practice rooms, classrooms, and faculty offices. The Munson Chapel seats 300 and is used for intimate group gatherings, choir and orchestra performances, and special chapel programs.

APU's attractive, landscaped, 73-acre campus houses many contemporary facilities, including Engstrom Hall, a 300-bed residence hall; the $5-million Wilden Hall of Business and Management, the University's signature building; and a modern, lighted athletic complex. All facilities are barrier-free.

A 3,500-seat event center, designed to meet the University's and community's needs, is scheduled for completion in 2000.

Costs

Expenses per year for 2000–01 are estimated as follows: tuition, $14,860; room, $2470 to $3600; board, $850 to $2550; and books and supplies, $800.

Financial Aid

Azusa Pacific University offers financial aid in the form of employment, loans, grants, and scholarships. More than 82 percent of the student body receives some form of aid. Each year, approximately $4 million in institutional aid is awarded. Students must reapply for aid yearly. Financial aid for international students may be more limited due to government restrictions and differences in educational systems.

Faculty

The student-faculty ratio is 15:1. There are 216 full-time faculty members and 400 part-time faculty members. The faculty is primarily a teaching staff; the graduate and undergraduate faculty are in essence the same group. No graduate students serve as undergraduate instructors. Faculty members are highly supportive of and involved in many student activities; they also provide academic advising.

Student Government

Elections for student-body officers are held annually. Officers of the student government are elected by the student body at large. The student government includes a model senate. It is responsible for overseeing the snack bar, student activities, student publications, and student union.

Students are asked to use personal discretion in activities that may be spiritually or morally destructive. In particular, students are expected to refrain from smoking, drinking, and using or possessing illegal drugs while in residence at the University.

Admission Requirements

Azusa Pacific seeks students who are committed to their own personal, intellectual, and spiritual growth. Consequently, these areas are considered in the admission evaluation. Applicants are required to have earned a minimum GPA of 2.5 in high school or a minimum GPA of 2.0 in previous college work. Both transfer students and international students who graduated from non-English-speaking schools also need a GPA of at least 2.5. Transfer, international, and older students are encouraged to apply.

Application and Information

Applicants must submit official transcripts of high school and/or previous college work, two references, a signed statement of agreement, and scores on either the ACT or SAT I. A nonrefundable $45 application fee must be submitted with the application. International students do not need ACT or SAT I scores, but a TOEFL score is required. A $65 application fee applies, and specific application deadlines are enforced. APU follows a rolling admission policy each semester. Notification of the Admissions Committee's decision can be expected approximately two weeks after receipt of all completed application materials.

For further information, prospective
students should contact:

Deana Porterfield, Dean of Admissions
Office of Undergraduate Admissions
Azusa Pacific University
901 E. Alosta Avenue
P. O. Box 7000
Azusa, California 91702-7000

Telephone: 626-812-3016
　　　　　 800-TALK-APU (information requests)
Fax: 626-812-3096

For further information, international
students should contact:

Mary Grams, Director
Office of International Student Services
Azusa Pacific University
901 E. Alosta Avenue
P. O. Box 7000
Azusa, California 91702-7000
Telephone: 626-812-3055
Fax: 626-969-7180

The $8-million Hugh and Hazel Darling Library offers a spectacular array of resources in an environment that is conducive to learning.

BABSON COLLEGE
WELLESLEY, MASSACHUSETTS

The College

Babson College has long been recognized for its leadership role in providing management education. It is located on a 450-acre wooded campus in Wellesley, Massachusetts, 14 miles west of Boston. The current undergraduate enrollment is 605 women and 1,096 men. An independent, coeducational institution, Babson is accredited by the AACSB–The International Association for Management Education and the New England Association of Schools and Colleges. It was the first college of business administration not affiliated with a university system to receive AACSB accreditation. Today, Babson is a comprehensive college of management that offers an undergraduate program leading to the B.S. degree, a graduate program leading to the M.B.A. degree, and continuing education seminars and programs for management professionals. In educating students for leadership, Babson works closely with the business community, nonprofit organizations, and alumni. Students are encouraged to be innovative, to experiment with business ventures, and to participate in campus activities—in essence, to emulate managers. Babson faculty members frequently ask executives from Boston and the nearby Route 128 industrial belt to address classes. In their course work, students often analyze case study data furnished by local companies. Babson's interest in entrepreneurship and leadership is also reflected in the curriculum. The undergraduate program offers a concentration in entrepreneurial studies, and the graduate program offers elective courses in entrepreneurship. Undergraduate and graduate students can gain hands-on experience through a specialized elective, Management Consulting Field Experience (MCFE).

Approximately 90 percent of the undergraduate student body lives on campus in one of fourteen residence halls. Housing options include coed residence halls with single-sex floors and wings for women, fraternity and sorority housing, and substance-free and multicultural housing.

Babson's Recreation and Special Events Center houses a 220-meter, six-lane track; a field house; a gymnasium with three basketball courts; five squash and two racquetball courts; a fitness center; a dance/aerobics studio; saunas; and a sports medicine facility.

Location

Wellesley is 30 minutes by car from Boston, a city renowned for its cultural and recreational facilities. Boston offers theaters, museums, libraries, art galleries, sports, and music. There are more than sixty colleges and universities in the area, providing further opportunities for cultural exchange and research.

Majors and Degrees

The College offers the Bachelor of Science degree. The undergraduate curriculum is three-tiered, including a foundation, intermediate, and advanced program. Students design their own learning plans for the advanced part of the program. The learning plan consists of upper-level elective courses, both liberal arts and management; field-based experiences; and cocurricular activities. Students work with a faculty mentor to design a unique advanced program. Advanced electives may include accounting, economics, entrepreneurship, finance/investments, information systems, international areas, law, management, marketing, and quantitative methods.

Academic Program

Babson College offers a course of study that prepares men and women for managerial careers in business, industry, and nonprofit organizations. The College focuses on educating innovative leaders capable of initiating, managing, and implementing change. The structure of undergraduate study, leading to the Bachelor of Science degree, provides knowledge of the primary disciplines of business as well as the liberal arts, a concentration in one of several divisions of management, and a variety of electives in the liberal arts and business management. To earn the B.S., students are required to complete a minimum of 128 semester hours with a C average or better. Transfer students must complete a minimum of 64 semester hours at Babson. Students are required to take their last 32 semester hours (eight courses) at Babson or in Babson-approved cross-registration programs.

Babson's curriculum is divided into a Foundation Program, an Intermediate Program, and an Advanced Program through which students progress during their time at Babson. Required Foundation and Intermediate Program courses include quantitative methods, statistics and regression analysis, rhetoric, arts and humanities, history and society, law economics, the Freshman Management Experience, and science. The Advanced Program is essentially a self-designed individual course of study that incorporates some minimal structural elements. A crucial aspect of the curriculum is the Integrated Management Core (IMC), which presents the management core in a three-semester integrated sequence.

Students may be granted credit or advanced course placement for successful scores on either the College-Level Examination Program (CLEP) or Advanced Placement examinations administered by the College Board.

The College operates on a two-semester academic calendar; semesters run from September to December and from late January through May. An optional credit-bearing three-week winter session is offered in January, and two 6-week summer sessions are offered mid-May to mid-August.

Off-Campus Arrangements

Babson has a cooperative cross-registration program with Regis College in Weston, Pine Manor College in Brookline, and Brandeis University in Waltham and a course-exchange program with Wellesley College in Wellesley. The programs offer access to liberal arts courses, including a wide range of foreign languages. A Babson student may take one course each semester at one of the other colleges for full academic credit.

Babson's study-abroad program enables students to spend one or both semesters of their junior year or a summer at a college or university overseas. Full academic credit is given for approved management and nonmanagement courses. Babson offers study abroad through exchanges with Babson's anchor schools in a number of countries. Students also have participated in programs offered by other institutions, such as Semester at Sea.

Academic Facilities

Horn Library contains more than 130,000 volumes serving all areas of curricular study at Babson, with room for growth to 170,000 volumes. The catalog of this collection is stored on microfilm, and ten readers and a printer attachment are available for students' use. More than 346,000 titles are available in microform. There are also 1,545 periodical titles as well as a collection on investment services that includes microfiche copies of the annual 10K reports of more than 11,000 companies. The library houses a fully equipped media services department with a production room, ten group-study rooms and two seminar rooms, 350 microcomputers, a reading room that is open 24 hours a day, a soundproof typing room with typewriters, and the Study Skills Resource Center for writing, speech, and math. The third floor houses the Sir Isaac Newton Room, the Babson Archives, and the Roger Babson Museum. Computers are a vital part of the Babson educational program. All students are given individual password-protected accounts. Information resources and network services are now delivered to fifty-six different buildings and more than 4,500 individual serving locations. Points of access include forty-five classrooms, science labs, group-study rooms, and public access labs across campus. Three of the five labs in the Horn Computer Center are available to faculty members for hands-on classes. One lab is open 24 hours, seven days a week. The 24-hour lab has Windows-based computers. Direct laser printing is available from each workstation at a ratio of ten systems for each printer. Access to the network is also available directly from residence hall rooms for people with IBM-compatible computers and PowerMacs capable of running Microsoft Windows. Respective faculty members now use the network as a teaching tool in the classroom or for self-paced instruction outside the classroom. Many of the software programs and information resources are also used by faculty members as a productivity tool to create syllabi, calculate grades, and do research. Students gain practical skills in how to become more efficient by using the network regularly and by being immersed in an environment where the appropriate use of information technology is demonstrated by faculty and staff alike. Many statistical and practical applications, such as financial modeling packages, are available on the network.

Among the College's other facilities are a new campus center, which houses the bookstore, mailroom, Crossroads Café, and credit union. Other additions include a new center for performing arts, an interfaith chapel, a center for entrepreneurial studies, and newly renovated classrooms.

Costs

For 2000–01, tuition and fees are $21,952, and room and board costs with the full dining plan are $8746. Books, supplies, and personal expenses are estimated at $1830.

Financial Aid

Financial assistance is awarded on the basis of demonstrated financial need. Applications for financial aid are considered apart from the admission decision, so no student should be discouraged from applying for admission simply because he or she has financial need. Nearly half of all Babson students receive some form of financial aid. Employment and loans are also available. Financial aid is only available to citizens, permanent residents, and resident immigrants of the United States. Application for aid is made by submitting the Free Application for Federal Student Aid (FAFSA) and the Financial Aid PROFILE of the College Scholarship Service. The application deadline for the September term is February 15; for the January term, November 15.

Faculty

Babson is a college in which students form close relationships with the faculty. There are 206 faculty members. Of the 155 full-time members, 90 percent hold doctoral degrees or the equivalent. Many professors have had extensive experience in business, education, and government. Others bring firsthand knowledge of management problems to the classroom through their corporate consulting. Faculty members maintain a realistic balance between the theoretical and the practical.

Student Government

Student Government, an elected body of students, promotes students' interests; allocates funds to campus organizations for academic, social, and recreational activities; licenses student-run businesses; and works with the administration and faculty to formulate and maintain student regulations.

Admission Requirements

In selecting new students, the admission office collects biographical data, evidence of academic achievement, test scores, personal statements, and references for each candidate. The College believes that the best admission decisions are made only after a thorough review of all applicants and their credentials. Evaluation is based upon comparisons of the qualifications of those who apply. There are no minimums, no cutoffs, and no absolute criteria. To a large extent, the degree of competition is set by the caliber of the applicants themselves. Consideration is given to the depth and rigor of each candidate's academic program, consistency of achievement, and progress from one year to the next. The profile of the previous school or college an applicant attended, including the postgraduate plans of members of recent graduating classes, is also examined. Special attention is focused on the candidate's foundation in mathematics and English. The admission committee carefully reviews courses taken, math aptitude, and standardized test scores. Reading and writing skills, as well as verbal expression, are measured using English grades, essays, and standardized test scores. Also important are intangible personal qualities—responsibility, initiative, and productivity. There is no standard format for the submission of this information, so Babson relies on letters of recommendation, references, personal statements, and observations during personal interviews. Interviews are strongly recommended. The College also evaluates extracurricular activities and work experience, seeking candidates who have exceptional leadership qualities and have participated in activities that have potential carryover to college. Efforts are made to enroll students with diverse backgrounds and experiences. Applicants are encouraged, therefore, to submit as much information as might be warranted in presenting a case to the Admission Committee.

Application and Information

The deadline for regular decision freshman applicants for the September term is February 1; applicants are notified of a decision by April 1. All accepted regular decision freshman applicants must notify Babson of their enrollment intention by the Candidates Reply Date of May 1. The early decision I deadline is December 1; applicants are notified by January 1 and should reply to the offer of admission by January 20. The early decision II deadline is January 1; applicants are notified by February 1 and should reply to the offer of admission by February 20. The early action I deadline is December 1; applicants are notified by January 1 and have until May 1 to notify Babson of their enrollment intention. The early action II deadline is January 1; applicants are notified by February 1 and have until May 1 to notify Babson of their enrollment intention. The deadline for applications for the January term is November 1. Transfer students must submit their applications for the September term by April 1, though March 1 is recommended; applicants are notified by May 1 and have until June 1 to notify Babson of their enrollment intention. Campus visits and interviews with the admission staff members are strongly recommended. For further information or application forms, students should contact:

Office of Undergraduate Admission
Mustard Hall
Babson College
Babson Park, Massachusetts 02457-0310
Telephone: 781-239-5522
              800-488-3696 (toll-free)
Fax: 781-239-4006
E-mail: ugradadmission@babson.edu

BAKER UNIVERSITY
BALDWIN CITY, KANSAS

The University

Baker University was established in 1858 as the first four-year college in the state of Kansas. With 142 years of tradition, Baker embodies an unusual blend of innovation and tradition, quality, and community. Affiliated with the United Methodist Church, the University is dedicated to excellence in liberal and professional education, to the integration of learning with faith and values, and to the personal development of each community member.

Twenty-one buildings on a 26-acre tract make up the campus in Baldwin City. The buildings stand around the perimeter of the campus, leaving the interior for rolling lawns, winding walks, and traditional lamps under a canopy of towering trees. The beauty of the campus has been enhanced by the renovation of the campus's earliest buildings. The stained-glass windows and proud tower of Parmenter Hall, the stately neo-Gothic architecture of Mulvane Hall, and the early pioneer architecture of the Pulliam Center remind one of Baker's rich heritage. The George F. Collins Jr. Sports and Convention Center is an outstanding facility for student and community athletics.

There are 2,600 men and women enrolled in the University, with more than 800 undergraduates on the Baldwin campus in the College of Arts and Sciences. The University attracts the serious student who expects to encounter challenge in the classroom but also enjoys participating in the multitude of extracurricular activities—sports, debate, radio, the newspaper, theater, music, and departmental and special interest organizations. Five residence halls, including new student apartments, provide comfortable housing for all freshmen and upperclass students. After the freshman year residence hall experience, students may choose to live either in a residence hall or in one of Baker's eight fraternity and sorority houses.

Baker University is a pioneer in the development of accelerated degree programs tailored to meet the needs of the working adult. More than 1,800 men and women from the greater Kansas City area, Lawrence, and Topeka choose Baker's School of Professional and Graduate Studies for its blend of quality, efficiency, and convenience. Students have the opportunity to earn a Bachelor of Business Administration, a Bachelor of Science in Management, a Master of Science in Management, a Master of Business Administration, a Master of Liberal Arts, or a Master of Arts in Education degree.

The Baker University School of Nursing opened in 1991 and offers the Bachelor of Science in Nursing.

Baker University is accredited at the bachelor's and master's degree levels by the North Central Association and is affiliated with the United Methodist Church. The B.S.N. program is accredited by the National League for Nursing Accrediting Commission; the Teacher Education Program by the Kansas State Board of Education; music programs by the National Association of Schools of Music; and business programs by the Association of Collegiate Business Schools and Programs.

Location

The main campus is in Baldwin City, a community of 3,000 people located 35 miles southwest of Kansas City. Baker students enjoy its college-town atmosphere but also take full advantage of nearby metropolitan areas. Kansas City offers many cultural and social attractions. Lawrence, Kansas, is only 15 minutes to the north, and Topeka, the state capital, is a 45-minute drive to the northwest. The School of Professional and Graduate Studies has its center in Overland Park, a suburb of Kansas City, and offers its programs in a number of locations. The School of Nursing is located at the Stormont-Vail Regional Health Center in Topeka.

Majors and Degrees

Baker's College of Arts and Sciences confers the Bachelor of Arts, Bachelor of Science, Bachelor of Music, and Bachelor of Music Education degrees. Majors offered include accounting, art education, art history, biology, business management, chemistry, computer information systems, computer science, economics, education, elementary education, engineering (in conjunction with Washington University and the University of Kansas), English, environmental chemistry, forestry (in conjunction with Duke University), French, German, history, international business, mass communication, mathematics, music, music education, nursing, philosophy, physical education, physics, political science, psychology, religion, sociology, Spanish, speech communication, studio art, theater, and wildlife biology.

Academic Program

The College of Arts and Sciences operates on a 4-1-4 academic calendar with two 5-week sessions of summer school. The month of January is set aside for Interterm, a period when students enroll in only one class. Interterm classes may be taken on campus or abroad, and internships are numerous. Baker emphasizes the liberal arts tradition through a recently restructured general education program that develops fundamental intellectual skills and provides experiences and ideas that will assist the student in making informed decisions as a member of society. Baker graduates include four Rhodes scholars (more than any private school in the state) and two recipients of the Pulitzer Prize in Journalism. Two recent graduates have been awarded the prestigious Goldwater Scholarship for their excellence in the area of science.

To complete a bachelor's degree at Baker, a student must successfully complete 132 semester hours with a Baker GPA of at least 2.0 (on a 4.0 scale).

The Baker honors program provides an opportunity for highly qualified students to complete advanced work in regular classes for honors credit and take special honors sections of courses. Honors participants are required to have a minimum 3.5 high school GPA and a minimum composite score of 27 on the ACT.

Off-Campus Arrangements

Students may study off campus during Interterm. Some study within the United States, while others participate in one of several Baker-sponsored Interterms abroad. The Harlaxton Semester program allows students to spend a semester studying in England, enjoying many travel and learning opportunities. The Career Development Center assists students in exploring a variety of professional career options, either off campus for a semester or combined with regular course work, while academic credit is earned. The center also sponsors the Alumni Mentoring Program.

Academic Facilities

The College of Arts and Sciences in Baldwin City offers excellent academic facilities in a traditional campus setting. Three of its classroom buildings are on the National Historic Register. Parmenter Hall, built in 1865 and renovated in 1990, houses an art studio in the loft. Case Hall, built in 1904 and renovated in 1992, serves the humanities and social sciences. Pulliam Center for Journalism and Communications was constructed in 1868. Other classroom buildings include Mulvane Science Hall, Owens Musical Arts Building, Rice Auditorium, George F. Collins Jr. Sports and Convention Center, and Mabee Memorial Hall, which houses the Departments of Business and Economics, Physical Education and Recreation, Psychology, and Sociology. Mabee Hall was completely renovated in 1995, adding considerable computer lab space and a state-of-the-art fitness center. Collins Library, which will soon undergo a complete redesign, has a computerized catalog with access beyond its own 65,000-volume collection to more than 2.5 million items in fourteen regional libraries. It provides more than 600 periodicals and makes more than 300 computerized databases available through membership in Dialog information retrieval service. The library houses several special collections, including the Quayle Rare Bible Collection and the Methodist Historical Library. On the lower level, the library houses Baker's continually growing computer laboratories and the Academic Skills Center. Computers in the library and in residence hall computer labs offer Internet and e-mail access.

Costs

Tuition for the 2000–01 academic year for undergraduates in the College of Arts and Sciences is $12,300. Double-occupancy room and board for the year are $4750. Full-time undergraduates should plan to spend up to $400 per semester for books and supplies.

Financial Aid

Ninety-two percent of the College's full-time students receive financial assistance. Special four-year academic scholarships, not based on need, are available for students with outstanding academic, leadership, and test records. These scholarships, up to $5000 in value, are renewable each year if the recipient performs in accordance with scholarship regulations. Baker leads the state in the amount of Kansas State Scholar funds awarded to its students.

Financial assistance is available on both a need and no-need basis to full-time students in the University. Aid based on need is given to students who demonstrate genuine need, as determined by an approved need analysis form, a Baker financial aid application, and transcripts, which must be submitted to Baker's Financial Aid Office. Applications for financial aid should be submitted as early as possible, since aid is awarded on a rolling basis and may be exhausted by the summer months.

The University participates in all federally supported student aid programs, including the Federal Perkins Loan, Federal Pell Grant, Federal Supplemental Educational Opportunity Grant, and Federal Work-Study Programs. Approximately 42 percent of the students secure jobs through the Federal Work-Study Program. Special financial assistance is available for students who are residents of Kansas through the Kansas Tuition Grant Program and the Kansas State Scholar Program.

Faculty

The College's student-faculty ratio is 13:1. The average class size is about 20 students. Baker's faculty is dedicated primarily to teaching, and no graduate students serve as instructors. More than two thirds of the faculty have terminal degrees in their field, and all faculty have advanced degrees. Professors are readily available outside of class for assisting students. As a residential community, faculty and student participation in extracurricular activities is extensive.

Student Government

The College's official student governing organization is the Student Senate. Members of the senate are elected from organizations on campus, and the president of the senate is invited to attend faculty meetings and general sessions of the Board of Trustees. The Student Senate allocates an ample student activity fund for campus events and student projects and plays a major role in ensuring that student opinion is heard within the University community. Faculty search committees also regularly involve students in the search for new faculty members.

Admission Requirements

Applications for admission are reviewed by an admission committee. In most cases, applicants with an ACT composite score of at least 21 (combined SAT I of at least 990) or a minimum 3.0 high school grade point average are admitted. Other applicants are evaluated on an individual basis. Transfers must have a minimum 2.7 transfer grade point average for admission. International students must also submit TOEFL scores (minimum score of 525 required) and a statement of financial support but are not required to submit ACT or SAT I scores.

Application and Information

Applications are considered in the order in which they are received, and an announcement of the admission decision is made immediately upon receipt of transcripts, ACT or SAT I results, and recommendations. When submitting the application for admission, the student must include a $20 fee or the application cannot be processed. After admission is granted, the student is asked to submit his or her residence hall contract and a $100 deposit. The deposit is nonrefundable after June 1.

Director of Admission
P.O. Box 65
Baker University
Baldwin City, Kansas 66006
Telephone: 913-594-6451 Ext. 307
        800-873-4282 (toll-free)
E-mail: admission@george.bakeru.edu
World Wide Web: http://www.bakeru.edu

Baker's campus consists of twenty-one buildings on 26 acres.

BALL STATE UNIVERSITY
MUNCIE, INDIANA

The University

Ball State University was founded as a state institution in 1918, but its antecedents date from the late nineteenth century when the Ball family, prominent industrialists, purchased and donated to the state of Indiana the campus and buildings of the Muncie Normal Institute. In 1922 the Board of Trustees gave the school the name of Ball Teachers College, and in 1929 the school became Ball State Teachers College. In 1965 the Indiana General Assembly renamed the institution Ball State University in recognition of its phenomenal growth in enrollment, in physical facilities, and in the variety and quality of its educational programs and services. The fifty-eight buildings on the 955-acre campus reflect the changing architectural styles of the twentieth century.

The total University enrollment stands at 17,459. In fall 1999, undergraduate enrollment was 6,921 men and 8,421 women. The majority of entering freshmen were 18 to 19 years old and single; they had come from families with 2 or more children and from cities of moderate to large size; 7 percent belonged to a minority group. About 8 percent of Ball State freshmen came from outside the state of Indiana. There were 350 students from eighty-six countries other than the United States.

There are more than 300 student organizations that provide extracurricular activities. These include leadership programs, departmental organizations, honorary societies, music groups, religious organizations, fraternities, sororities, governing groups, special interest organizations, and service groups. The University Health Service staff members offer health education, provide care in cases of acute illness and injury while a student is in attendance, and serve as medical advisers for the University.

Location

The Ball State campus is in a pleasant, residential area of Muncie, an industrial city of 78,000 people in east-central Indiana, 56 miles northeast of Indianapolis. The city's cultural features include the Muncie Symphony Orchestra, the Civic Theater, and the Artists Series and Concert Series presented in the John R. Emens University-Community Auditorium located on the Ball State campus.

Majors and Degrees

Ball State's academic programs are offered through the University's seven colleges, which are the College of Applied Sciences and Technology; College of Architecture and Planning; College of Business; College of Communication, Information, and Media; College of Fine Arts; College of Sciences and Humanities; and Teachers College. The degrees awarded are associate degrees in arts and science, bachelor's degrees in arts, fine arts, music, and science, and bachelor's degrees in architecture (five-year program), landscape architecture (five-year program), and urban planning and development (five-year program). The fields of study include accounting, actuarial science, administrative information technology (two years), advertising, anthropology, apparel design, architecture (five years), art, athletic training, biology, business administration (two or four years), business education and office administration, chemical technology (two years), chemistry, classical culture, classical languages (Latin and Greek), communication studies, computer science, criminal justice and criminology (two or four years), dance, dietetics, dietetic technology (two years), early childhood education, economics, elementary education, English, exercise science and wellness, family and consumer sciences (general), family and consumer sciences (vocational education), fashion merchandising, finance, food management (two years), general studies (two or four years), geography, geology, graphic arts management, graphic design, health and safety education, health science, hearing impairments, history (American, United States, world, and world civilization), home economics, home economics (vocational), industrial supervision (two years), industrial technology, interior design/housing, international business, Japanese, journalism (two or four years), journalism education, junior high/middle school education, kindergarten/primary education, landscape architecture (five years), Latin American studies, legal assistance (two or four years), management, manufacturing engineering technology, manufacturing technology (two years), marketing, marketing education, mathematical economics, mathematics, medical technology, merchandising, modern languages (French, German, Japanese, and Spanish), music (composition, guitar, music education, music engineering technology, natural resources and environmental management, organ, piano, symphonic instruments, and voice), natural resources, nuclear medicine technology (two years), nursing, office systems administration, philosophy, physical education, physics, political science, printing technology (two years), psychology, public service (two years), radiation therapy (two years), radiography (two years), religious studies, residential property management, school media services, science teaching, social studies teaching, social work, sociology, Spanish, special education (mentally and physically handicapped and hearing impairments), speech communication and theater, speech pathology and audiology, sport administration, technology education, telecommunications, theater, urban planning (five years), visual arts education, and vocational trade. Preprofessional programs are offered in audiology, dental hygiene, dentistry, engineering (chemical, general, and metallurgical), law, medicine, optometry, pharmacy, and veterinary medicine.

Academic Program

Undergraduate programs combine general studies with majors and minors. Most degrees require 126 semester hours, at least a 2.0 grade point average, and the last year in residence. The academic calendar consists of fall and spring semesters and two summer terms.

The Honors College, a four-year University-wide program featuring special course offerings, colloquia, seminars, and independent study, is especially designed to challenge the talented student. University College is organized to provide support services to students undecided about their majors. The Learning Center is structured to meet the needs of certain recent Indiana high school graduates, GED awardees, veterans, and students whose past academic records indicate underpreparedness in basic skills.

The University, recognizing that there are other ways to obtain an education than through regular enrollment in a class, grants a maximum of 63 credit hours through any combination of credit for successful scores on Advanced Placement tests or College-Level Examination Program tests, credit for military service, credit by departmental examination, and credit by departmental authorization.

Off-Campus Arrangements

Numerous opportunities for study abroad are available to students who have completed at least one semester of their studies. The London Centre offers students a living and learning experience in Regent's Park of central London. The Honors College offers study at Westminster College in Oxford, England. Departments offering University-sponsored programs in Great Britain and optional continental tours are elementary education at Middlesex Polytechnic, architecture in London, and nursing in London. Anthropology students have the opportunity to study in Jamaica. Foreign language students are encouraged to polish their skills through summer programs in Canada, Latin America, and Europe.

Academic Facilities

The library collections total 1.1 million volumes, 343,104 microforms, 551,770 units of audiovisual materials, and 3,568 current periodicals. Professional collections are housed in the Architecture Library and the Science–Health Science Library. A K–12 school library is maintained at the Burris Laboratory School. Separate materials in the main library are the music collection, special collections, archives, government publications, maps, and educational resources.

Facilities on campus also include an art gallery, an observatory and planetarium, outdoor laboratories, a solar-energy research center, fully equipped science laboratories, a human-performance laboratory, state-of-the-art teaching classrooms, and music laboratories. University Computing Services provides a full range of computing and systems services for students, faculty members, and the administration.

Costs

Expenses for 1999–2000 are $3576 for general fees for Indiana residents or $9736 for general fees for nonresident (out-of-state) students, $4520 for room and board, and $800 (average) for books and supplies. Between $1800 and $2500 is considered reasonable for personal expenses and transportation.

Financial Aid

Through a program of scholarships, grants, loans, and employment, Ball State's Office of Scholarships and Financial Aid provides aid for deserving students. The Free Application for Federal Student Aid, obtainable from a high school guidance counselor, should be filed no later than March 1.

Faculty

Ball State's instructional programs are carried out by 893 full-time faculty members, approximately 67 percent of whom hold earned doctoral degrees. Faculty members serve on the University Senate and on numerous senate and campus committees. Full-time academic advisers work with freshmen. Six advising centers around campus work with departments and their faculty advisers.

Student Government

The all-campus student governing group is the Ball State University Student Association, composed of executive, legislative, and judicial branches. All students are encouraged to participate in such activities as proposing changes in University policy, working for expanded and improved educational programs at Ball State, and lobbying at the city and state levels. One student is appointed to serve on the University's Board of Trustees. In addition, representatives from the Student Association are appointed to serve on numerous boards, committees, and councils on campus, including the University Senate and its committees.

Admission Requirements

Undergraduate applicants are considered for admission to Ball State University after the Office of Admissions has received the application for admission, the $25 nonrefundable application fee, the secondary school record (official transcript) or GED high school equivalency scores and certificate, and scores on either the SAT I or ACT.

Transfer students must, in addition, submit a transcript from each vocational or advanced educational institution attended beyond high school. The transcripts must be forwarded to Ball State directly from the institutions attended.

It is suggested that prospective applicants visit the campus and talk with a member of the admission staff.

Application and Information

High school students should complete an application in the fall of their senior year. Application materials must be submitted by March 1 for priority consideration for the autumn semester and by December 1 for the spring semester. Requests for appointments and information should be addressed to:

Dean of Admissions and Financial Aid
Ball State University
Muncie, Indiana 47306

Telephone: 765-285-8300
               800-482-4BSU (toll-free)
               765-285-2205 (TDD users only)
E-mail: askus@bsu.edu
        visitus@bsu.edu
World Wide Web: http://www.bsu.edu

BALTIMORE INTERNATIONAL COLLEGE

SCHOOL OF CULINARY ARTS
SCHOOL OF BUSINESS AND MANAGEMENT
BALTIMORE, MARYLAND; VIRGINIA, COUNTY CAVAN, IRELAND

The College

The Baltimore International College, a regionally accredited independent college, was founded in 1972 to provide theoretical and technical skills education for individuals seeking careers as hospitality professionals. The College is committed to providing students with the knowledge and ability necessary for employment and success in the hospitality industry.

In 1985, the College was authorized by the state of Maryland to grant associate degrees. As part of the College's continued growth, restaurant and food service management and innkeeping management were added to its curriculum. In 1987, the Virginia Park Campus in Ireland was founded, enabling students to study under European chefs and hoteliers in a European environment. In 1996, the College was granted accreditation by the Commission on Institutions of Higher Education of the Middle States Association of Colleges and Schools. In 1998, the College was authorized by the state of Maryland to grant four-year baccalaureate degrees. In addition to classrooms, offices, dorms, and student apartments, the College's nineteen-building campus in Baltimore includes a campus bookstore, a student union, a hotel, an inn, a restaurant, parking, student dining facilities, student housing facilities, a Career Development Center, and a Learning Resources Center, which includes a library, two academic computer labs, and an art gallery.

Location

The College's main campus, located in downtown Baltimore, is just two blocks from the city's famous Inner Harbor, a location that puts the College in the midst of numerous hotels and restaurants. The city offers year-round cultural and entertainment opportunities, such as theater, opera, the Baltimore Symphony Orchestra, museums, sporting events, and festivals. Other attractions in Baltimore that are within walking distance of the College are the National Aquarium, Harborplace, Oriole Park at Camden Yards, PSINet Stadium, Maryland Science Center, and many historic sites, including Fort McHenry, the neighborhood of Mount Vernon, and the Walters Art Gallery. Baltimore also has parks and miles of waterfront for those who enjoy outdoor recreation. Washington, D.C., the nation's capital, is just 30 miles from downtown Baltimore. The city of Baltimore is easily accessed by major highways and bus, rail, and air service. Baltimore/Washington International Airport is a short drive from the campus.

Majors and Degrees

Baltimore International College offers baccalaureate degrees in culinary management and hotel, restaurant, and catering management. The College also offers associate degrees in food and beverage management, hotel/motel/innkeeping management, professional baking and pastry, professional cooking, and professional cooking and baking. In addition, students can receive professional certificates in culinary arts, professional baking and pastry, professional cooking, and professional cooking and baking.

Academic Program

The College provides a comprehensive curriculum, which includes an honors study-abroad program at the Baltimore International College, Virginia Park Campus, near Dublin, Ireland.

The College's professional cooking program and the combined program in professional cooking and baking operate throughout the calendar year; new classes begin in the spring, summer, and fall. The professional baking and pastry program begins in the fall and summer semesters. The College's business and management programs accept freshmen in the fall semester. The culinary arts certificate, which combines cooking and baking, is available through evening classes and begins in the fall and spring semesters.

To earn an associate degree in professional cooking, professional baking and pastry, or professional cooking and baking, the student must complete 62 to 63 credits. To earn an associate degree in food and beverage management or hotel/motel/innkeeping management, the student must complete fifty-four courses; this program is intended for students who already have a strong academic background. The associate degree program combines technical, hands-on courses with general education courses (such as nutrition, psychology, English, and mathematics) as well as an internship or externship.

The associate degree is offered separately and is part of the 2+2 program at Baltimore International College. In the 2+2 program, students receive their two-year degree and then continue to complete a four-year bachelor's degree in culinary management or hotel, restaurant, and catering management.

Off-Campus Arrangements

The honors program has been developed for qualified culinary arts and business and management majors. The honors program is taught at the College's historic 100-acre Virginia Park Campus in County Cavan, Ireland. Culinary students who are selected for the honors program further enhance their skills in and knowledge of European cuisine, baking, pastry, and à la carte service. Business and management students selected for the honors program have the opportunity to learn the day-to-day operation of a hotel and restaurant, from reception to housekeeping and from restaurant management to accounting. Students fully enjoy the cross-cultural experience of living in an English-speaking foreign country.

Academic Facilities

The nineteen-building campus in Baltimore includes kitchens, storerooms, cooking demonstration theaters, academic classrooms, multipurpose rooms, a library, two computer labs, a student union, and auxiliary services. Public operations that function as in-house training for students include the Mount Vernon Hotel and Bay Atlantic Seafood, the Hopkins Inn, and the College Club.

The Virginia Park Campus is located on 100 acres, 50 miles from Dublin, and offers student housing, with laboratory kitchens and lecture facilities. The complex also includes the Park Hotel, with public operations that function as in-house training for students, including the Marquis Dining Room and the Marchioness Ballroom. The Park Hotel has thirty-six guest rooms. All students enjoy unlimited golf and fishing as well as hiking trails.

The College's Career Development Center offers students access to information about careers in food service and hospitality management. The College's Career Development Services are located in the Career Information Center, where coordinators organize on-campus recruiting and offer workshops and assistance in resume writing and interviewing skills.

The College's Learning Resources Center is a member of an interlibrary loan network that enables users to borrow from public, academic, and private libraries throughout Maryland. The library's current core collection has approximately 11,500 volumes, 200 periodicals, and almost 700 audiovisual selections. The library offers students access to the Internet, a worldwide network of electronic information. In-house services include two computer labs, electronic databases for research, and a photocopier.

The College's art gallery is part of the Learning Resources Center and features a permanent display of edible art. Student participation in all exhibits is encouraged. Culinary competitions are held in the gallery.

The Office of Student Services offers general advisement for all students, peer tutoring on request, and a variety of referrals for support services. In addition, Student Services provides many recreation and leisure activities, including the student union, a series of activities sponsored by the College, and information about cultural programs around the city. Student Services also provides ongoing support to the College's alumni through surveys, mailings about the College's growth, and involvement in College-sponsored events such as open houses, resume referrals, and career fairs. A new semiannual publication, *Alumni News*, is also sent to all alumni and is provided to all students.

Costs

Tuition for 2000–01 is $5779. Fees range from $150 to $2361, depending on a student's major. Student housing costs range from $2550 to $4275 per semester for dormitory-style housing (includes meal plan) and from $1659 to $2730 per semester for apartment-style housing.

Financial Aid

Students receive financial aid from federal, state, institutional, and private sources and may be employed during their attendance as full-time students. The forms of financial aid available at the College through federal sources include the Federal Pell Grant, the Federal Supplemental Educational Opportunity Grant, the Federal Work-Study Program, the Federal Perkins Loan, the Federal Subsidized and Unsubsidized Stafford Student Loans, PLUS loans, and veterans' educational benefits. Students are encouraged to investigate the scholarship programs in their home state and apply for state scholarships if the grants can be used in Maryland. The College also offers its own series of scholarships and payment options. In 1999–2000, College-funded scholarships averaged $4000 per academic year for in-state students and $4600 per academic year for out-of-state students. Students can request a financial aid application from the Student Financial Planning Office. The College employs the Federal Methodology of Need Analysis, approved by the U.S. Department of Education, as a fair and equitable means of determining the family's ability to contribute to the student's educational expenses, as well as eligibility for other financial programs.

Faculty

Baltimore International College faculty members include 29 chefs and academic instructors of high academic distinction. The student-faculty ratio averages 15:1 in culinary labs and 25:1 in academic classes. Each student is assigned to a faculty adviser who oversees the student's progress and answers questions about academic and career concerns. Students are encouraged to discuss program-related issues with and seek career advice from their faculty adviser.

Student Government

Many students become junior members of the Greater Baltimore Chapter of the American Culinary Federation. Membership is open to all students in good standing. Meetings, which are held monthly, are announced at the College.

Admission Requirements

Creativity and skill of students must be matched by dedication. The College seeks candidates who desire a professional career in the hospitality industry.

Individuals seeking admission to the College must have earned a high school diploma or have passed the GED. Applicants must either pass the College's Admissions Test, take developmental courses during their first semester, or have one of the following: a minimum SAT score of 430 verbal and 420 math, a minimum composite ACT score of 16, minimum CLEP scores in the 50th percentile in math and English composition with essay, a secondary degree, or 16 credit hours at the postsecondary level with a minimum average of C in math and English. Transfer students must submit an official college transcript as well as catalog course descriptions for credits they wish to transfer.

The College affords equally to all students the rights, privileges, programs, activities, scholarships and loan programs, and other programs administered by the College without regard to race, color, creed, sex, age, handicap, or national or ethnic origin.

Application and Information

Applicants are required to submit an application form along with a $35 nonrefundable fee. Requests by the College for additional information must be handled in a timely manner. An admission decision is made as soon as a file is complete. Upon acceptance, applicants are asked to submit a $65 tuition deposit.

For additional information, students should contact:
Office of Admissions
Commerce Exchange
Baltimore International College
17 Commerce Street
Baltimore, Maryland 21202-3230
Telephone: 410-752-4710 Ext. 120
            800-624-9926 Ext. 120 (toll-free)
E-mail: admissions@bic.edu
World Wide Web: http://www.bic.edu

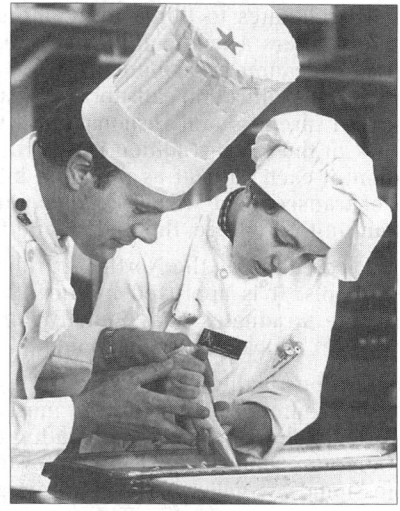

Small classes at Baltimore International College enable students to receive individual instruction that helps them perfect their skills.

BARAT COLLEGE
LAKE FOREST, ILLINOIS

The College

Barat College is an independent, coeducational liberal arts institution in a Catholic tradition that offers baccalaureate and select professional and graduate degrees. Governed by an independent Board of Trustees, the College integrates a vigorous curriculum with a distinctive educational philosophy founded by the Society of the Sacred Heart. Students, faculty members, administrators, alumni, and trustees represent a wide range of religious, socioeconomic, and ethnic backgrounds. Barat traces its origin to nineteenth-century France and Saint Madeleine Sophie Barat, who founded the Society of the Sacred Heart in 1800. The model of Sacred Heart education was unique in its time because of its commitment to a rigorous, value-based, formal education of women—with the expectation that these women would assume responsibility for influence and leadership in the world. Since then, the society has established a large number of schools and colleges in many countries. Philippine Duchesne brought this endeavor to the United States in 1818. Barat College began as an academy for young women in Chicago in 1858 and subsequently moved to Lake Forest, Illinois (30 miles north of Chicago), in 1904. In 1918, the state of Illinois chartered Barat as a four-year college. Governance of the College passed from the Society of the Sacred Heart to an independent Board of Trustees in 1969. In the early 1970s, Barat became a leader in the college adult reentry movement, and in 1982, it became coeducational.

Barat makes a fundamental commitment to help each student seek the full development of her or his analytical and synthesizing intellectual abilities and to foster critical appreciation of moral, cultural, and artistic values. Barat believes that the study of the arts, humanities, and social sciences is essential to a complete education. The College affirms freedom of thought and expression and respect for the sacredness of personal belief. It works to create an atmosphere of open inquiry, confidence, and mutual support for the pursuit of truth. Barat expects its graduates to think and communicate effectively. The College offers a curriculum that integrates liberal and professional education as a foundation for personal and career fulfillment. This education calls forth and is enlivened by a sense of social awareness and responsibility. Above all, the abiding hallmark of the Barat tradition is a particular concern for the education of each student as a unique intellectual and moral person of transcendent worth, an individual who is an active participant in the College, the nation, and the world.

Barat College is accredited by the North Central Association of Colleges and Schools. It is approved by the Illinois Office of Education. Eligible graduates may qualify for elementary, secondary, or special education certification.

The hub of the campus is the Main Administration Building. It houses faculty and administrative offices, most of the classrooms, all music and art studios, the Math and Computer Center, the Communication Skills Program and Center, a chapel, a professional art gallery, a student art gallery, and a student lounge and recreation room. This building is interconnected by corridor walkways to the Merrill and Stuart Residence Halls, the O'Shaughnessy Dining Hall, the Hilton Complex (which includes a gym, a fitness center, and a 235-seat theater), and the 635-seat, thrust-stage Drake Theatre. Apart from this main complex stand Dougherty Residence Hall, Cuneo Science Hall (lecture halls; chemistry, biology, and psychology labs; and some faculty offices), and the Sr. Madeleine Sophie Cooney Library, a state-of-the-art library resource center.

Location

Barat's campus site is magnificent—30 acres of lawn, woods, and ravines six blocks from Lake Michigan. Students enjoy its special beauties in all seasons. Located in suburban Lake Forest, 30 scenic miles north of Chicago's superb cultural life, Barat offers students easy access to O'Hare International Airport by car or bus and to the city of Chicago by commuter railroad. For students in search of day or weekend outings, Barat has easy access to the lakes and ski trails of southern Wisconsin.

Majors and Degrees

Barat College offers the Bachelor of Arts degree in business (with concentrations in accounting, marketing, entrepreneurial studies, and leadership), chemistry/biology (with concentrations in biology, chemistry, science/math/computer studies, and health studies [RNs only]), economics (with concentrations in economics, banking and finance, and international trade and finance), education (with concentrations in elementary education, secondary education, special education, and certification only), English (with concentrations in English and communication arts), humanities (with concentrations in art history, history, music, and philosophy), math/computer studies (with concentrations in mathematics, math/computer studies, and computing and information systems), political science (with concentrations in political science, international relations/foreign policy, and American government/public policy), psychology (with concentrations in psychology, art therapy, dance therapy, and business psychology/human resources emphasis), sociology (with concentrations in sociology and community service), studio arts (with concentrations in studio arts, computer graphics, photography, sculpture, drawing, mixed media, ceramics, printmaking, fiber, painting, and art therapy), and theater (with concentrations in acting/directing and design/technical theater). Barat College also has a dance conservatory, which offers Bachelor of Arts and Bachelor of Fine Arts degrees in dance and dance therapy, a Bachelor of Fine Arts in art, and joint-venture programs in medical radiation physics, medical imaging sciences, and engineering.

Academic Program

The College operates on a semester plan. The first term extends from early September to mid-December. The second term extends from mid-January to early May. Summer sessions are offered from mid-May through August. (The Business Leadership Program operates on an accelerated seven-week schedule). A student must complete 120 semester hours of academic credit with a cumulative GPA of at least 2.0, along with completing competency requirements in writing skills and mathematics, to be eligible for graduation. Of the 120 credits, a minimum of 12 semester hours must be completed in each of the four categories of the Barat general education experience: The Natural, Physical and Mathematical Worlds; Human Society—Past and Present; Creative Expression and Critics; and Inquiry into the Human Experience—Textual Analysis. At least 5 hours must be completed in writing (W), speech (S), and international/multicultural (I/MC) courses.

Off-Campus Arrangements

International study programs are open to students who have been enrolled full-time at Barat for at least two semesters. Financial aid awards are applicable to these programs. Through affiliations with a variety of institutes, the College makes possible broad international study options that supplement most curricular programs. International study sites include Africa, the British Isles, continental Europe, Latin America, and South Asia. In addition, Barat students may enroll or take classes through a cooperative agreement with Lake Forest College at its campus, which is located less than 1 mile from the Barat campus.

Academic Facilities

The Madeleine Sophie Cooney Library is a state-of-the-art, technologically advanced library. The library's collections total some 115,000 volumes, including approximately 350 current periodical subscriptions. Its collection development policies are designed to purchase for local use the most important works for the undergraduate disciplines taught at the College. Increasingly, newer technologies are being employed to provide online access to information sources held both internally and externally. To augment local collections, the library belongs to several consortia that provide for resource sharing. These include the Illinois Library Computer System Organization (ILCSO), consisting of forty-five academic and research libraries throughout Illinois; the LIBRAS consortium of eighteen northeastern Illinois private college libraries; and the North Suburban Library System, consisting of nearly 300 local libraries. It also uses OCLC, the world's largest bibliographic utility, to enter local catalog holdings and to expand interlibrary borrowing privileges for its patrons beyond state and national boundaries.

Costs

For the 2000–01 academic year, tuition for full-time students is $13,950, with room and board costs of $5500 per year. Expenses such as books, supplies, laboratory or special fees and transportation are not included in these costs.

Financial Aid

Barat College administers several scholarship and financial aid programs for students in need of financial assistance to meet educational costs. Approximately 80 percent of the students enrolled at the College are eligible for some type of assistance through federal, state, and institutional programs. Financial aid is based on financial need, which is determined by an analysis of family and student resources. All scholarships and awards at Barat College are designed to be combined in a flexible way to help cover the recipient's cost of education. Financial need is not a requirement for the academic and talent awards; however, those recipients whose processed Free Application for Federal Student Aid (FAFSA) indicates additional need are offered a financial aid package, combining scholarships and awards with federal and state funds. The FAFSA and the Barat College Application for Financial Aid are available from the Office of Admissions or Student Financial Planning.

Faculty

Doctoral or terminal degrees are held by 81 percent of the faculty members, with a student-teacher ratio of 13:1. Small, informal classes encourage students to express themselves, and faculty members are willing to meet individually with students.

Student Government

All students may participate in Student Government. The Student Governing Board is responsible for addressing issues that are relevant to student life and government through its committees and in coordination with the Dean of Students Office. It coordinates campus activities and serves as a liaison between the administration and the student body. Student opinions and viewpoints on both academic and nonacademic issues are encouraged.

Admission Requirements

Barat College welcomes inquiries and applications from qualified students interested in pursuing a high-quality education and provides significant support during the admission process. The selection of students is based on each applicant's complete academic record. Barat College admission decisions are made on a rolling basis and are contingent upon the applicant's successful completion of a college-preparatory program in an accredited high school or the General Educational Development (GED) examination. A freshman applicant should submit a completed application form with the $20 application fee, an official transcript, ACT or SAT scores, a teacher recommendation, a secondary school report, and a personal statement. Students may also apply to Barat College via the Internet at the address listed below.

Application and Information

Applicants for admission for the fall and spring semesters are accepted on a rolling basis. Applicants are strongly encouraged to complete and submit the application package two weeks prior to the beginning of each semester; however, to ensure a position in the incoming class, applications should be completed as early as possible. The student's completed application, recommendations, application fee, and supporting credentials (transcripts, recommendations, test scores) should be send to:

Mary Kay Farrell
Assistant Vice President for Admissions
Barat College
700 East Westleigh Road
Lake Forest, Illinois 60045
Telephone: 847-295-4260
Fax: 847-604-6300
E-mail: admissions@barat.edu
World Wide Web: http://www.barat.edu

Students form lasting friendships at Barat.

BARNARD COLLEGE
NEW YORK, NEW YORK

The College

Barnard College was among the pioneers in the late nineteenth-century crusade to make higher education available to young women. Founded in 1889, it became part of the Columbia University system in 1900 and today serves 2,300 students who come from nearly every state and more than thirty-five countries. It remains an independent affiliate of the university, and students at the two schools may cross-register for courses at either institution. Barnard students have access to Columbia University libraries and receive their degree from the University. Barnard College, however, has remained a small, independent liberal arts college, devoted solely to the undergraduate education of women. The College has its own Board of Trustees, faculty, and administrative staff, its own endowment, and sole ownership of its property and physical plant. It offers the intimacy of a small college with all the added advantages of access to a major university.

The self-contained Barnard campus occupies 4 acres of urban property along Broadway between 116th and 120th streets. Barnard Hall, with its newly renovated Ethel S. LeFrak '41 and Samuel J. LeFrak Gymnasium and Julius S. Held Lecture Hall, stands opposite the main gates of the College, while the south end of the campus contains the Brooks, Reid, Hewitt, and Sulzberger Hall dormitory complex. Additional housing is located nearby, and some options for coed housing are available. Millicent McIntosh Center, the focus of student activities, has a cafeteria, a lounge, and bowling alleys, as well as other facilities.

Location

Barnard is located in New York City. In so cosmopolitan a setting, cultural, educational, and internship opportunities abound. New York is the College's laboratory and museum, its most constant and energizing resource.

Majors and Degrees

Barnard College confers a Bachelor of Arts (A.B.) degree in the following subjects: American studies, ancient studies, anthropology, architecture, art history, Asian and Middle Eastern cultures, biochemistry, biological sciences, biopsychology, chemistry, classics (Greek and Latin), comparative literature, computer science, dance, economic history, economics, education, English, environmental science, foreign area studies, French, German, history, Italian, linguistics, mathematics, medieval and Renaissance studies, music, Pan-African studies, philosophy, physics and astronomy, political science, psychology, religion, Russian, sociology, Spanish, statistics, theater, urban affairs, and women's studies.

Barnard College also offers double- and joint-degree programs in cooperation with other schools within the Columbia University community. These include a five-year (4-1) program offered in conjunction with the School of International Affairs, in which a student earns both an A.B. degree and a Master in International Affairs (M.I.A.) degree, and a five-year (4-1) program combining undergraduate studies with the graduate program in public affairs and administration, in which a student earns both an A.B. degree and a Master of Public Administration (M.P.A.) degree. In cooperation with the School of Law, Barnard offers an accelerated program in interdisciplinary legal education, in which selected students can begin their legal studies after three years of undergraduate course work. The School of Engineering and Applied Science and Barnard College offer a five-year (3-2) program in all branches of engineering, including aerospace, civil, and electrical engineering, in which candidates receive both an A.B. and a B.S. degree. In a five-year (3-2) program with the Juilliard School, a student can earn both an A.B. degree and an M.M. degree. In cooperation with the Jewish Theological Seminary, students may earn an A.B. degree from Barnard and another undergraduate degree from the seminary.

Academic Program

Students are recommended by the faculty members of Barnard College to the Trustees of Columbia University for the degree of Bachelor of Arts. The degree requires the satisfactory completion of 120 points of academic work and two terms of physical education. Basic requirements include one semester of first-year English, one semester of a first-year seminar in liberal studies, two semesters of laboratory science, and the equivalent of two years of college-level study in a foreign language. In keeping with Barnard College's mission as a liberal arts college with a broad-based educational philosophy, students must also take two semesters outside the major in the social sciences and in the humanities and one semester in quantitative reasoning. This last requirement can be fulfilled through courses in quantitative reasoning, computer science, mathematics, and logic or through other courses in the sciences and social sciences that emphasize statistical analysis.

Advanced placement credit is available, as are opportunities for independent or honors work. Barnard operates on a two-semester calendar, with classes beginning in early September. The fall semester ends in mid-December; classes resume for the spring semester in mid-January and end in mid-May.

Off-Campus Arrangements

Barnard College is an independent affiliate of Columbia University. As such, its students have open access to the courses, libraries, and other facilities of Columbia. With special permission, students may also register for classes in the graduate and professional schools. A program offered in cooperation with the Jewish Theological Seminary, located two blocks from Barnard, allows students to take courses for credit. In similar arrangements with the Juilliard School and the nearby Manhattan School of Music, qualified Barnard students may take music lessons in a conservatory setting.

Under the auspices of Reid Hall in Paris, a Barnard-Columbia facility, several semester-long and full-year programs are offered. Students of classics are eligible to study at the Intercollegiate Center for Classical Studies in Rome. Qualified students may also study at Oxford (Somerville College), Cambridge (Newnham College), the University of London (University College, London School of Economics, King's College, or Queen Mary College), or the University of Warwick. Qualified students are also eligible to study in Germany, Italy, and Japan. Students may also participate in an exchange program with Spelman College in Atlanta.

Because of its location in New York City, Barnard offers its students a wide variety of work experiences through its extensive internship program.

Academic Facilities

Milbank Hall, the oldest building on campus, houses administrative and faculty offices, classrooms, the Arthur Ross Greenhouse, and the Minor Latham Playhouse. Millicent McIntosh Center includes music practice rooms. Fourteen-story Altschul Hall, devoted mainly to the sciences, has classrooms, department offices, and the most modern laboratory equipment.

Wollman Library offers three floors of reading areas and more than 170,000 volumes in open stacks. Students also have access to the 6 million volumes of Columbia's Butler Library.

Costs

Tuition and fees for 2000–01 are $23,056. Housing costs are $5802 for room and $3556 for board.

Financial Aid

All financial aid supplied or administered by Barnard is awarded on the basis of demonstrated need, as determined by federal regulations and the College's Office of Financial Aid. Barnard gives no merit scholarships. College aid is supplementary to family resources. Once need has been established, it is Barnard's policy to cover 100 percent of that need through grants and self-help awards (work and/or loans). A student who is admitted to Barnard with a Barnard College Grant may expect grants in future years, provided that she continues to meet economic and academic eligibility. Approximately 58 percent of the students at Barnard receive financial aid.

Barnard College has a need-blind admission policy in which all applications are judged on merit without reference to the applicant's financial circumstances.

Faculty

Barnard College has 178 full-time teaching faculty members and 105 part-time members. The student-faculty ratio is 11:1. Although actively engaged in research and publication in their respective fields, Barnard faculty members regard teaching as their primary commitment. All students have faculty advisers who assist them in selecting courses and designing individual academic programs.

Student Government

Every Barnard student is a member of the Student Government Association, which sponsors numerous extracurricular activities. These include the College newspaper, the literary magazine, dramatic groups, political and religious organizations, and preprofessional and departmental clubs. Cooperation between Barnard and Columbia groups is common. Students, faculty members, and administrators serve on tripartite committees and share responsibility for policy recommendations on curriculum, housing, financial aid, orientation, and the library.

Admission Requirements

The Committee on Admissions selects young women of proven academic strength who exhibit the potential for further intellectual growth. Careful consideration is given to candidates' high school records, recommendations, standardized test scores, and special abilities and interests. While admission is highly selective, no one criterion determines acceptance. Each applicant is considered in terms of her individual qualities of mind and spirit and her potential for successfully completing her program of study at Barnard.

Candidates for admission to the first-year class must have taken a college-preparatory program at an approved secondary school or have an equivalent level of education. A recommended program comprises 4 years of work in English, 3 years in mathematics, 3 or 4 years in a foreign language, 2 years in science (with laboratory), and 1 year in history. Barnard also requires candidates to submit scores on the SAT I and on three SAT II Subject Tests, including the SAT II: Writing Test or SAT II: Literature, or the ACT. An interview is recommended.

Application and Information

Applicants for first-year admission should apply to Barnard in the fall of their senior year of high school. Applications must be received by January 15 and should be accompanied by a nonrefundable fee of $45. Students will be notified of the admission decision in early April. Well-qualified high school seniors who have selected Barnard as their first-choice college may apply under the Early Decision Plan. Applications must be submitted by November 15. Barnard accepts transfer students to the sophomore and junior classes. Applications can be submitted beginning March 1 for admission in September and by November 15 for admission in January.

For more information about Barnard College, students should contact:

Dean of Admissions
Barnard College
Columbia University
New York, New York 10027

Telephone: 212-854-2014
Fax: 212-854-6220
E-mail: admissions@barnard.edu
World Wide Web: http://www.barnard.edu

A view of Milbank Hall from McIntosh Plaza at Barnard College.

BARRY UNIVERSITY
MIAMI SHORES, FLORIDA

The University

Founded as Barry College in 1940 by the Dominican Sisters of Adrian, Michigan, Barry has grown significantly, yet it remains true to its mission of providing high-quality academics, a caring environment, a religious dimension, and community service. Originally a Catholic college for women, Barry College became Barry University, a Catholic, coeducational, international university, in 1981. In 1940, enrollment totaled 30 students; enrollment in 1999 was 7,909 (2,539 full-time undergraduates). Drawing its first classes from seven states, Barry now enrolls students from forty-nine states and territories and more than eighty countries. The University is accredited by the Southern Association of Colleges and Schools. Barry awards bachelor's, master's, specialist, and doctoral degrees.

Barry's beautifully landscaped campus and Spanish-style architecture offer an outstanding environment for quiet reflection and study. Seven residence halls accommodate 700 undergraduate students. Freshmen are required to live on campus if they are not living at home with parents or relatives. All students may keep cars on campus. Student services available on campus include counseling, career development and placement, campus ministry, and health services. The University has a snack bar, a cafeteria, a post office, a student center, a performing arts center, a television studio, a radio station, an athletic training room, a human performance lab, a biomechanics lab, a health and sports center (complete with a strength and conditioning room), and an outdoor recreation center.

Intercollegiate sports (NCAA Division II) for men include baseball, basketball, golf, soccer, and tennis; women's teams include basketball, crew, golf, soccer, softball, tennis, and volleyball. Intramural sports include basketball, flag football, 4-on-4 flag football, golf, sand volleyball, soccer, street hockey, tennis, 3-on-3 basketball, volleyball, and Wiffle ball.

Location

Miami Shores is located between the cities of Miami and Fort Lauderdale, giving students access to all the recreational facilities and cultural opportunities of South Florida. Golf, tennis, swimming, soccer, scuba and skin diving, waterskiing, and sailing are available all year long. Miami also offers football's Miami Dolphins; its NBA team, the Miami Heat; its National League baseball team, the Florida Marlins; its NHL team, the Florida Panthers; and Major League Soccer's Miami Fusion. The New World Symphony, the Opera Guild of Greater Miami, the Miami Film Festival, and the Miami City Ballet provide a full season of highly acclaimed performances, as do the Coconut Grove Playhouse and the Broward Center for the Performing Arts. Well-known personalities entertain regularly in the area. Also easily accessible are the Florida Keys, the Everglades, national parks, and marine and state parks.

Majors and Degrees

Barry University offers the Bachelor of Arts degree in advertising, art (ceramics and painting and drawing), broadcast communication, communication studies, English (literature, professional writing, and secondary education), French, general studies, history (secondary education), international studies, liberal studies, philosophy, photography (biomedical/forensic, computer imaging, creative, and photo/communication), prelaw, public relations, Spanish, theater (musical theater), and theology.

The Bachelor of Science degree is offered in accounting, athletic training (premedicine option and pre–physical therapy), biology (biotechnology, ecological studies track, major for the medical laboratory technician, histotechnology track, marine biology track, predentistry, premedicine, preoptometry, prepharmacy, pre–physical therapy, pre–physician assistant studies, prepodiatry, preveterinary medicine, and three-year accelerated option), cardiovascular perfusion, chemistry (environmental track, predentistry, premedicine, and prepharmacy), computer science, criminology, cytotechnology, diagnostic medical ultrasound technology, economics/finance, elementary education, engineering (dual degree and pre-engineering), exceptional student education, exercise science (premedicine option and pre–physical therapy), international business, management, management information systems, marketing, mathematical sciences (secondary education), medical technology, nuclear medicine technology, physical education (grades K–8 and 6–12), political science (secondary education), pre–K through primary education (Montessori), psychology, sociology, and sport management (diving industry and golf industry tracks).

The University also offers the Bachelor of Science in Nursing (accelerated option, basic option, LPN to B.S.N. option, RN to B.S.N. option, RN to B.S.N./M.S.N. option, three-year option, and two-year option). The Bachelor of Fine Arts and the Bachelor of Music are also offered.

Minor concentrations are available in specific subject areas as well as in the interdisciplinary areas of Africana studies, peace studies, and women's studies.

Students may obtain teaching certification in secondary education for specific areas. Teaching certification is also available for pre-K through primary education, elementary education, and exceptional student education. A certificate program in the translation and interpretation of Spanish is offered.

Seven undergraduate degree programs are also offered to adult students through the School of Adult and Continuing Education. These include the Bachelor of Professional Studies, the Bachelor of Liberal Studies, the Bachelor of Public Administration, and the Bachelor of Science in legal studies, health services administration, information technology, and professional administration.

Academic Program

The University operates on a semester plan. The first semester extends from the end of August to mid-December, and the second semester extends from mid-January to early May. Two 6-week sessions are offered during the summer. A student must maintain a minimum cumulative grade point average of 2.0 (or C) and earn a minimum of 120 credits for a degree. Of these 120 credits, 9 must be in philosophy and theology, 9 in communication—oral and written, 9 in humanities and arts, 9 in physical or natural sciences and mathematics, and 9 in social and behavioral sciences. The traditional full-time academic load is 12 to 18 credits each semester and 6 credits each summer term. Candidates for degree programs may elect either a major area of specialization or a broad liberal arts program and must satisfy all requirements of the program that they choose to follow, including all professional preparation requirements. Exceptionally well qualified seniors may earn up to 6 hours of graduate credit with the recommendation of the department chairperson and the dean. Internships are required for many majors.

An ELS Language Centers program is available to international students needing to increase language proficiency. The Clinical Center for Advanced Learning offers a program designed to assist students with learning disabilities who have the intellectual potential and motivation to complete a four-year degree.

The University also offers an active honors program designed to add breadth and depth to the educational experience. The approach is interdisciplinary.

Off-Campus Arrangements

Barry University offers summer programs in Europe. In addition, Barry is a member of the College Consortium for International

Studies, enabling students to participate in programs in twenty-five countries offered by member colleges and universities.

Barry University students may enroll in Air Force ROTC courses through cross-registration at a nearby university.

Academic Facilities

The D. Inez Andreas School of Business Building houses faculty and administrative offices, four traditional classrooms, two classrooms that have been specifically designed for accounting classes, four classrooms that are multimedia equipped, and two large executive training classrooms.

The Fine Arts Quadrangle contains art and music studios; photography dark rooms, labs, and computer imaging lab; theater dressing rooms; the Pelican theater; and the Broad Performing Arts Center, with 1,000-seat capacity.

The Garner Building houses the Academic Computing Center (main lab open to current students, faculty, and staff), the Department of Communication (David Brinkley Television Studio), the Clinical Center for Advanced Learning, a language lab, and a number of computer-equipped classrooms.

The Health and Sports Center accommodates classrooms, administrative and faculty offices, a strength and conditioning room, a 1,500-seat capacity gymnasium, a human performance lab, an athletic training room, and locker rooms. The sports complex includes baseball, racquetball, softball, soccer, and tennis facilities.

The Lehman Building houses the administrative offices of the School of Arts and Sciences, classrooms, and archives, including the Congressman William Lehman papers.

The Monsignor William Barry Memorial Library houses a collection of 806,375 items and 1,851 periodical titles. The University library also participates in a number of library networks, including the Southeast Florida Library Information Network, the Florida Library Information Network, and the Southeastern Library Network, making texts and other materials easily accessible through library exchange.

The Powers Building houses the Adrian Dominican School of Education and the Ellen Whiteside McDonnell School of Social Work. The facility contains administrative offices, classrooms, seminar rooms, and student lounges.

The Weigand Center contains science labs, classrooms, and an auditorium used by nursing, podiatric, and the physical and natural sciences. The Natural and Health Sciences building expands the laboratory facilities available for student instruction and research. This facility includes classrooms, seminar rooms, and offices.

Costs

For 1999–2000, tuition for full-time undergraduate students for the academic year was $15,530. Student services fees are included in tuition. Room and board costs averaged $6220, depending on the choice of room. Expenses such as books, supplies, laboratory or other special fees, and transportation are not included in these costs.

Financial Aid

Barry University offers an excellent scholarship and grant program, awarding scholarships each year to students who have demonstrated academic success and promise. These scholarships and grants may be renewed for up to four years as long as the students meet the renewal criteria. Barry need-based grants and athletic scholarships are also available.

The University also participates in the Federal Pell and Federal Supplemental Educational Opportunity Grant programs, the Federal Perkins Loan Program, the Federal Work-Study Program, the Florida Resident Access Grant Program, the Florida Student Assistance Grant, Florida Bright Futures Scholarships, and the Federal Family Educational Loan Program. Barry awards financial assistance on the basis of financial need and academic excellence. Applicants must submit the Free Application for Federal Student Aid (FAFSA) in order to be considered for aid. More than 85 percent of undergraduate full-time students receive assistance from the University. Additional information may be obtained by calling the Office of Financial Aid at 305-899-3673 or 800-695-2279 (toll-free).

Faculty

Faculty members are easily accessible to students and are committed to providing individualized attention. The undergraduate faculty of the Schools of Adult and Continuing Education, Arts and Sciences, Business, Education, Human Performance and Leisure Sciences, Natural and Health Sciences, and Nursing participates in a dynamic academic advisement program. Doctorates are held by 80 percent of the faculty members, and the student-faculty ratio is 13:1.

Student Government

The Student Government Association serves as a liaison between the student body and the administration and faculty. All undergraduate students are members of the association, which is governed by an Executive Board that consists of 4 members and the Senate, which consists of 16 elected representatives. Twelve members are elected during the spring semester, and the remaining four places are filled early in the fall semester. Unless otherwise specified, meetings of the Senate are open, and students are invited and encouraged to attend the weekly sessions.

Admission Requirements

In reviewing the credentials of students seeking admission to Barry University, the Admissions Committee considers an applicant's composite efforts. Candidates must present the following credentials: the completed application form, official high school or college transcripts, and the results of the SAT I or of the ACT.

Application and Information

The University reviews applications as they are completed. Students are advised of their acceptance once the Admissions Committee has reviewed all required documents. Students may apply any time after completion of the junior year in high school. It is advisable to apply early.

The student's completed application form, including a $30 non-refundable application fee and supporting credentials (listed above), should be sent to:

Ms. Marcia Nance
Dean of Enrollment Services
Barry University
11300 Northeast Second Avenue
Miami Shores, Florida 33161-6695
Telephone: 305-899-3100
           800-695-2279 (toll-free)
Fax: 305-899-2971
E-mail: admissions@mail.barry.edu
World Wide Web: http://www.barry.edu

Barry offers an outstanding environment for quiet reflection and study.

BARTON COLLEGE
WILSON, NORTH CAROLINA

The College

Founded in 1902 as the first degree-granting institution in eastern North Carolina, Barton College opened its doors to 107 students with one building on 5 acres of campus. Today, Barton welcomes approximately 1,300 students from twenty-six states and eleven countries to a campus of twenty-two buildings on 62 acres.

The College offers several avenues of assistance for students, especially during the freshman year. Barton College Seminar is an innovative freshman advising program designed to assist students in making the transition from home and high school to college and residence hall life. All freshmen meet with their adviser once each week in a classroom seminar setting. Outside the classroom experience, the Barton College Seminar also offers exposure to a variety of cultural and social events, including concerts, lectures, art exhibits, drama productions, and sports events. Inside the classroom, Barton's student-centered core curriculum enhances academic success through a concentrated seven-week delivery system. With this approach, Barton freshmen fulfill at least two general college requirements during each of 4 seven-week periods comprising the first academic year, then complete the remaining basic requirements during the sophomore year. This innovative approach to the core, taken in concert with electives and major courses, provides students with an outstanding foundation from which the total liberal arts experience is achieved.

Barton's Student Development Program includes residence life programs, special activities, and counseling services that provide for the students' cultural, social, and emotional development. In addition, Barton has approximately thirty clubs and organizations in which students can be involved, including academic organizations, specialty clubs, fraternities, and sororities. Another vital component of student life is the Career Services Center. The center provides a vigorous on-campus recruiting program that brings approximately 130 recruiters to Barton's campus annually, representing corporations, government, and educational areas. In addition, several hundred other employers seek to hire Barton students each year. Barton's graduates rank exceptionally well in obtaining employment in their chosen field of study, and their salaries are competitive with those of students from other North Carolina colleges and universities.

On-campus housing is provided in four residence halls: Hilley, Hackney, Waters, and Wenger. All four facilities feature cable television and information technology access in each room.

Offering a strong, competitive sports program, Barton College's Bulldogs compete in the NCAA Division II and the Carolinas-Virginia Athletic Conference. The intercollegiate sports program includes women's basketball, cross-country, fast-pitch softball, soccer, tennis, and volleyball and men's baseball, basketball, cross-country, golf, soccer, and tennis. A wide variety of intramural sports are offered to the entire campus community. All students and especially those involved in Barton's intramural, physical education, and athletic programs benefit from the new Kennedy Recreation and Intramural Center that features an indoor swimming pool, walking/jogging areas, an auxiliary gym, and a weight/fitness room. Barton also has a twelve-court tennis complex to add to its outstanding facilities package.

Location

Wilson is in the coastal plain region of eastern North Carolina. The city provides an excellent home for the College and is within easy driving distance of several metropolitan areas and scenic attractions. The state capital of Raleigh is a 45-minute drive to the west; to the north, Richmond is 2 hours away and Washington, D.C., is 4 hours away. The beautiful Atlantic coast of North Carolina is 100 miles from the campus, and the scenic Blue Ridge Mountains are easily accessible. Located on Interstate 95, Wilson is also accessible by U.S. Routes 264, 117, and 301 and North Carolina Routes 42 and 58. Wilson is 15 minutes from the Rocky Mount/Wilson Airport and 1 hour from Raleigh/Durham International Airport. Amtrak has daily service with one northbound and one southbound departure.

The College's historic neighborhood is just a few minutes from busy downtown Wilson. Banks, theaters, the shopping mall, and restaurants are close by. Many of Wilson's arts and cultural events take place on the College campus. The Wilson community (population 42,000) enjoys a mild climate that has an average annual temperature of 65 degrees.

Majors and Degrees

Barton College offers six baccalaureate degrees: Bachelor of Arts, Bachelor of Science, Bachelor of Fine Arts, Bachelor of Nursing, Bachelor of Social Work, and Bachelor of Liberal Studies. These degrees are administered by five schools. The School of Arts and Sciences offers programs in art education (K–12), art studio (with concentrations in ceramics, graphic design, painting, and photography), biology* (preprofessional programs in dentistry, medical technology, medicine, physical therapy, and veterinary medicine), chemistry (preprofessional program in pharmacy), English*, environmental science, Hispanic studies*, history, mass communications (concentrations include audio recording technology, broadcast/video production, print and electronic journalism), mathematics* (preprofessional program in engineering), philosophy, physical education (with teacher licensure), political science (concentrations include business and pre-law), religion, social studies (with teacher licensure), sports management, and theater (concentrations include design, management, and performance). The School of Behavioral Sciences offers programs in criminal justice, psychology, and social work. The School of Business offers programs in accounting, business administration (concentrations include finance, general business, management, marketing), computer information systems, and management of human resources. The School of Education offers programs in education of the deaf and hard of hearing (K–12), elementary education (K–6), middle school education (6–9), and special education: specific learning disabilities (K–12). The School of Nursing offers a program in nursing. (Programs indicated with a * are available with or without a teacher licensure program.

Minors can be earned in accounting, American studies, art (studio), biology, business administration, chemistry, communications, computer information systems, criminal justice, economics, English, French, geography, gerontology, Hispanic studies, history, mathematics, physical education, political science, psychology, religion and philosophy, theater, and writing.

Academic Program

The major areas of study have a global focus, so students are assured of a high-quality academic program. Expanded travel opportunities and concentrated study are enhanced by Barton's 4-1-4 semester system featuring the January Term. Barton College offers a strong liberal arts tradition, and students follow a core curriculum during their freshman and sophomore years. In so doing, students are exposed to a variety of disciplines. Through a carefully guided advising program they declare a major area of study at the end of their freshman year or at the beginning of their sophomore year. At that point, they begin an intense and challenging program of study in their chosen field while completing general college requirements.

Barton College's nursing and education programs are ranked among the best in North Carolina. The School of Business majors (accounting, business administration, and management of human resources) continue to be popular areas of study. Barton is one of the few colleges on the East Coast to offer a program for the education of the deaf and the hard of hearing. Also unique is the recording technology program, which features a 32-track digital recording studio. The School of Behavioral Sciences offers a fully accredited social work degree as well as a psychology major and a new criminal justice major with law enforcement certification available to students choosing that track.

Off-Campus Arrangements

Each year students participate in faculty-led trips to different areas of the world. Students recognize this travel as an excellent opportunity to enrich their college experience. Depending on the nature and destination of the travel, students may obtain college credit for their participation. Barton also has exchange agreements with colleges in Europe and Asia for extended overseas study offered in conjunction with the Global Focus international emphasis.

Academic Facilities

Barton College has a fiber-optic underground network that includes an infrastructure of data, voice and video wiring to selective classrooms, all faculty member offices, a majority of administrative offices, and two data connections in each residence hall room. The Willis N. Hackney Library is open 86.5 hours per week to serve the College community. BARTON LINC, the College's library information network center, offers a variety of services for users, including library information (hours, services, etc.), library online catalog, connection to other databases, connection to other libraries, and connection to subject-related Internet sites. The library's collection includes 150,701 volumes and U.S. government documents, as well as a substantial collection of microfilm, maps, filmstrips, and pamphlets. It also subscribes to 389 periodicals and newspapers. The Media Center, located on the first floor of the library, provides checkout service for audiovisual equipment. There are facilities for overhead transparency production and audiotape and videotape duplication as well as other production services.

Located on the first floor of the newly renovated and refurbished J. W. Hines Hall are two computer labs for classes and individual student use. Mini computer labs are also available for student use in the Nursing Education Building and Moye Science Hall. The Nursing Education Building also has a new multimedia center with a state-of-the-art projection system, installed for a broad range of lecture and teaching purposes. The new Sam and Marjorie Ragan Writing Center supplements Barton's commitment to language and writing as vital components of the liberal arts curriculum. Students have access to more than 125 computer terminals on campus.

WEDT-TV, a local cable television station operated by Barton College and staffed by Barton students, is located in the Roma Hackney Music Building. The TV studio offers up-to-date equipment and facilities for study and use in television, videotape, and audiotape production. The Hackney Music Building also houses classrooms, the College's library for recordings and musical scores, and the Sarah Lynn Kennedy Recording Studio. Moye Science Hall provides classrooms, laboratories, a greenhouse, and research-related study areas for students. The Nursing Education Building houses classrooms and a laboratory for the nursing program. Case Art Building provides classrooms, private and class studios, and a museum with two art galleries for Barton's permanent art collection and for visiting exhibits. It also houses state-of-the-art computer graphics and darkroom labs.

Costs

Expenses for the 2000–01 year include tuition, $10,812; room, $2044; seven-day board plan, $2226; technology fee, $400; and general fee, $250. These total $15,732 for the year. The estimated cost of books per semester is $600.

Financial Aid

The objective of the financial aid program at Barton College is to provide financial assistance to qualified students who would not otherwise be able to begin or continue their college education. Financial aid is awarded on the basis of need. (Financial need exists when the total cost of education exceeds the amount of money a student and family can reasonably make available from income and assets.) Barton College requires that all applicants for financial aid complete the Free Application for Federal Student Aid (FAFSA) as a means of determining financial need. Approximately 84 percent of Barton students receive financial aid. Aid comes from federal, state, and institutional resources and may be awarded as scholarships, grants, loans, or work-study. In addition, many students apply for part-time jobs on campus or in the community through the Career Services Center.

Students are encouraged to apply early for financial aid and should have their completed application in the Financial Aid Office by June 1 in order to ensure receipt of awards by the beginning of the fall semester. Every effort is made to process completed applications received after this date; however, earlier applications receive top priority in the awards process.

Faculty

Faculty members at Barton College recognize the importance of personalized attention for the students' learning experience. Because of the 12:1 student-faculty ratio, professors at Barton are able to teach small classes and have the opportunity to meet and to get to know their students as individuals. Faculty members make every effort to be accessible to students between classes and during regularly scheduled office hours. Professors at Barton are committed to the success of their students. Barton has 92 faculty members, of whom 66 are full-time. More than 73 percent of the full-time faculty members have obtained the highest degree available in their field.

Student Government

The Student Government Association (SGA) of Barton College provides students with opportunities to express themselves on issues of concern. Student government also provides a setting for studying the democratic process. The officers of the SGA are elected by the members of the student body, and the president of the SGA serves as an ex officio member of the College Board of Trustees.

Admission Requirements

To be considered for admission to Barton College, a student must have a high school diploma or its equivalent with a minimum total of 12 college-preparatory units. The following courses are recommended: English, 4 units; mathematics, 3 or more units (algebra I and one additional upper-level mathematics course such as geometry or algebra II are required); natural sciences, 2 or more units (one lab science is required); social sciences, 2 or more units; and foreign language, 2 or more units (encouraged, but not required). A student applying for admission must also take the SAT I and achieve a score that, when considered along with the high school record, predicts probable success in college. ACT scores are also accepted.

Application and Information

To apply for admission to the College, a student must submit a completed application, a nonrefundable $25 application fee, and an official transcript of high school credits. A copy of SAT I or ACT scores should be sent to the Department of Admissions by the testing agency. International applicants whose native language is not English must also submit the results of the Test of English as a Foreign Language (TOEFL). Students are encouraged to apply early and are usually notified of a decision within two weeks of the admission office's receipt of the completed application and information.

For further information, students may contact:

Department of Admissions
Barton College
Box 5000
Wilson, North Carolina 27893-7000
Telephone: 252-399-6318
          800-345-4973 (toll-free)
Fax: 252-399-6572
E-mail: enroll@barton.edu
World Wide Web: http://www.barton.edu

BATES COLLEGE
LEWISTON, MAINE

The College

Bates is recognized as one of the nation's finest colleges of the liberal arts and sciences. Founded in 1855, Bates was the first coeducational college in the East and is among the oldest in the nation. The College's tradition of attracting students from varied racial, ethnic, socioeconomic, geographic, and religious backgrounds has long influenced campus life. On principle, Bates insists that all organizations on campus be open to everyone; there are no fraternities or sororities at Bates. Nearly all students live on campus in College-owned residence halls and Victorian houses. One dining hall is centrally located on campus to accommodate all students.

While Bates graduates are expected to make significant contributions to their occupational fields, Bates's educational vision goes beyond preparing students for the challenges they will face in their working lives. That vision recognizes that the role of the College is to develop, encourage, and direct its students in the discovery of their own intellectual and moral potential.

The 1,650 students enrolled at Bates represent forty-eight states and forty-six countries. Faculty members teach all classes. The student-faculty ratio of about 11:1 provides students many opportunities to work closely with members of the faculty. Students are able to choose their own faculty advisers after their first year, and some students decide to create interdisciplinary majors with the help of these advisers.

One of the attractions of Bates for students is the opportunity to live in Maine, a state that offers beautiful landscape, an interesting diversity of people, and a strong sense of living history. Students enjoy their interaction with members of the Lewiston-Auburn community, as they often take part in community service activities and career internships. More than seventy campus clubs and organizations attract students and faculty. Some of the most popular include the outing club, the International Club, debate, dance, theater, and music. The Bates Multicultural Center sponsors exhibits, theater, lectures, workshops, meetings, forums, and parties. The coordinator of multicultural affairs organizes the center and assists with programs that stimulate discussions relevant to multiculturalism throughout the campus.

Bates encourages men and women to pursue and develop athletic interests at their chosen level of participation. About 60 percent of the students play on one of the many intramural sports teams. The College sponsors a full program of club sports. Fencing, ice hockey, rugby, and water polo and men's volleyball compete with other colleges. There are thirty varsity teams (fifteen men's and fifteen women's) that participate at the Division III level (except skiing, which is Division I) and are members of the New England Small College Athletic Conference. Men's intercollegiate competition is offered in baseball, basketball, crew, cross-country, football, golf, indoor track, lacrosse, nordic skiing, outdoor track, skiing, soccer, squash, swimming, and tennis. Women's teams include basketball, crew, cross-country, field hockey, indoor track, lacrosse, nordic skiing, outdoor track, skiing, soccer, softball, squash, swimming, tennis, and volleyball. The gymnasium, field house, and arena house a 200-meter, six-lane indoor track; a 25-meter, eight-lane swimming pool; four indoor tennis courts; six squash courts; two racquetball courts; weight and fitness equipment; an ice rink and fitness center; a new tennis complex that features eight outdoor tennis courts with lighting; an outdoor track; basketball courts; a new lighted astroturf field for field hockey and lacrosse; and playing fields for baseball, football, soccer, and softball.

One of the most distinguishing characteristics of Bates is its 4-4-1 academic calendar. Most Bates students enroll in four courses during each of the two semesters of the traditional school year, which runs from September through mid-April. The Short Term, a five-week period of intensive study in one subject of interest, is held from late April through the month of May. Two Short Term credits are required for graduation. Some students choose to enroll in courses offered both on and off campus, but many others take advantage of this time to do independent research, job-shadowing, and internships.

Location

Bates is located in Lewiston, about 35 miles north of Portland and 140 miles north of Boston. Less than an hour's drive from both the western mountains and the ocean, the twin cities of Lewiston and Auburn on the Androscoggin River have a combined population of 60,000. Students are able to take advantage of opportunities for community service and career internships in hospitals and schools and with law firms, businesses, and social-service agencies.

Majors and Degrees

Bates offers the Bachelor of Arts and Bachelor of Science degrees in thirty-two fields: African American studies, American cultural studies, anthropology, art, Asian studies, biological chemistry, biology, chemistry, Chinese, classical and medieval studies, East Asian studies, economics, English, environmental studies, French, geology, German, history, Japanese, mathematics, music, neuroscience, philosophy, physics and astronomy, political science, psychology, religion, rhetoric, Russian, sociology, Spanish, theater, and women's studies. Other fields of study include computer studies and education. An increasing number of students design their own interdisciplinary majors.

Through the College's Dual-Degree Program, students interested in both engineering and the liberal arts and sciences may receive both a B.A. or B.S. from Bates and a B.S. from an affiliated school of engineering. The first three years are spent at Bates in an arts and science curriculum and the following two years at Columbia University School of Engineering, Rensselaer Polytechnic Institute, Case Western Reserve University, Washington University in St. Louis, Dartmouth College, or another approved school for engineering.

Academic Program

Students are expected to explore a wide variety of academic areas and common patterns of study, as well as to complete a major or concentrated focus of study. The General Education requirements at Bates reflect the faculty's belief that all graduating students should have a critical appreciation of scientific and social scientific knowledge and understanding, as well as a disciplined study in the humanities and history. First-Year Seminars (limited to 15 first-year students) serve as elective courses that offer both close instruction in reason and writing and an informal setting. This allows students to become well acquainted with their professor and each other.

Bates is one of the few colleges and universities in the country with a senior thesis requirement. The thesis takes the place of one course during either the fall or winter semester of the senior year. The opportunity to do extensive research and critical analysis in one specific area proves to be an invaluable experience for students.

Bates features a Center for Service-Learning, which goes beyond traditional volunteerism by incorporating community service into academic course work. The center has aided hundreds of Bates students and professors in the formation of tight bonds within the local community. More than half of the student body has engaged in a service-learning project, while a third of the faculty has included a service component in their courses.

Off-Campus Arrangements

Bates offers its students a number of opportunities to study at other colleges and universities across the country and abroad. Almost one half of the junior class spends either a semester or the year away from Bates. In addition to the Junior Semester and Junior Year Abroad programs, Bates has offered fall semester programs in Chile, China, Croatia, France, Japan, Spain, Germany, and Ecuador. These programs are open to first-year and upperclass students. Bates is a member of both the ISLE and SITA consortia, which give students the opportunity to study in Sri Lanka and in India. Students have also chosen to participate in off-campus programs in the U.S., including American University in Washington, D.C.; the Williams College–Mystic Seaport Program in American Maritime Studies; and exchanges with McGill University in Montreal, Washington and Lee University in Virginia, and Morehouse and Spelman colleges in Georgia. The Colby-Bates-Bowdoin Study Abroad Consortium, recently funded by the Andrew W. Mellon Foundation, hosts semester programs in Cape Town, London, and Quito, Equador.

Academic Facilities

Pettengill Hall, a new five-level academic building featuring classrooms, labs, offices, and an expansive common area for community events, opened in fall 1999. The 91,000-square-foot building brings together seven social science departments and four related interdisciplinary programs.

The George and Helen Ladd Library is one of the most central facilities of the College, housing books, periodicals, government publications, music scores, maps, microforms, sound recordings, video recordings, access to online databases, and material on CD-ROM. In all, the library owns more than 490,000 volumes in print, 280,000 units of microform, and 25,000 recordings and provides access to more than 1,000 sources of information on line. A collection of online resources from Bates, Bowdoin, Colby, and the University of Maine provides information about the periodical holdings of other libraries.

The Edmund S. Muskie Archives provides students and faculty with sources of primary documentation on local, state, and national politics; the workings of the U.S. Senate; and major issues concerning U.S. foreign relations following World War II. Edmund S. Muskie graduated from Bates in 1936.

The Olin Arts Center houses the Museum of Art, which features the College's permanent collection and works by exhibiting artists. This facility also includes art, music, and recording studios, as well as individual and group rehearsal rooms. A 300-seat concert hall provides for the College Concert Series and weekly Noonday Concerts.

Newly renovated Carnegie Science and Dana Chemistry halls house the laboratory facilities for the natural sciences. Astronomy students and faculty members use the Stephens Observatory with its 0.32-meter reflecting telescope and the Spitz A-3 planetarium projector.

Costs

For the 2000–01 academic year, the comprehensive fee is $32,650. This includes tuition, room, and twenty meals per week.

Financial Aid

Financial aid is awarded to students on the basis of need. About 45 percent of the students receive some form of aid. Forty percent receive grant aid from the College. The average award includes a grant, loans, and work-study employment on campus. Financial aid, based on documented need, is available for highly qualified international students.

Faculty

Bates has 196 full- and part-time faculty members. Ninety-nine percent hold doctoral or terminal degrees in their field. The student-faculty ratio is about 11:1. Faculty members serve as both academic and thesis advisers to students. The Bates faculty not only is accessible to students but also is visible on campus. Faculty members participate in student-run organizations and support students in all aspects of extracurricular life on campus.

Student Government

Bates students play an active role in developing programs and implementing changes on campus. The Representative Assembly, composed of a number of committees and subcommittees, is committed to maintaining a strong academic, social, and cultural environment. The RA represents the entire student body and proposes a yearly budget for more than seventy organizations on campus.

Admission Requirements

Admission to Bates is highly selective. The College seeks promising individuals from a diverse range of backgrounds. Academic, extracurricular, and personal achievements are carefully considered in the evaluation of a candidate's preparation, ability, and character. The College does not require standardized testing for admission, but students may choose to have their scores considered as part of the application. An interview is highly recommended for admission. Students are encouraged to visit campus for a tour and a personal meeting with an admissions officer. If students are unable to visit the campus, the Admissions Office will arrange alumni interviews for students in the U.S. and abroad. Bates uses the Common Application and a required supplement.

Application and Information

Applications for regular admission must be submitted to the Admissions Office by January 15; candidates are notified by mid-April. Students who have decided that Bates is their first-choice college are invited to apply under the early decision plan. Students who apply by November 15 (Round 1) will be notified of their decision by December 15. Applicants filing after December 1 but before January 1 (Round 2) will be notified by January 24. For more information, students should contact:

Dean of Admissions
Bates College
23 Campus Avenue
Lewiston, Maine 04240
Telephone: 207-786-6000
Fax: 207-786-6025
TDD: 207-786-6024
E-mail: admissions@bates.edu
      finaid@bates.edu
World Wide Web: http://www.bates.edu

BAYLOR UNIVERSITY
WACO, TEXAS

The University

Baylor University was chartered by the Republic of Texas in 1845 and is the state's oldest institution of higher education. The world's largest Baptist university, Baylor is affiliated with the Baptist General Convention of Texas. As one of the nation's major academic church-related universities providing liberal arts and professional education in a Christian environment, Baylor emphasizes high academic and personal standards. Excellence is a tradition, a practice, and a promise. Students come to Baylor from all states and a number of other countries. Baylor has 11,472 undergraduates and a total of 13,334 men and women in attendance. More than 250 social, service, professional, religious, and honorary student organizations, including national fraternities and sororities, provide opportunities for recreation, the development of social skills, spiritual and intellectual stimulation, and pursuit of individual interests. Special University activities include numerous cultural events, including films, talks by prominent lecturers, and performances by musicians and entertainers. In addition to offering varsity sports as a member of NCAA Division I and of the Big 12 Athletic Conference, Baylor provides an extensive, balanced program of intramurals. A recreation center provides special facilities for boating, canoeing, sailing, swimming, and tennis. On-campus housing is provided in eleven residence halls. About 2,300 of the 3,606 spaces are reserved for freshmen. Housing applications will not be accepted prior to admission to the University. Priority for housing is based on the date the housing application is received in the Residence Life Office. For late applicants, priority is based on the date the housing deposit is received.

The Baylor School of Law offers the Juris Doctor degree. Graduate work is offered in the College of Arts and Sciences and the Schools of Business, Education, Engineering and Computer Science, and Music; in Institutes and Special Studies; in the School of Nursing at Dallas; and in the U.S. Army Academy of Health Sciences at San Antonio. The George W. Truett Seminary, in Waco, offers the Master of Divinity degree.

Location

Located on the banks of the Brazos River in central Texas, Waco is a thriving city of 110,000 people. The city is very near the population and geographical core of the state; within 100 miles of Dallas, Fort Worth, and Austin; and within easy driving distance of Houston, San Antonio, and the Gulf Coast. Recreational and entertainment facilities, restaurants, and cultural activities of all kinds are numerous. Baylor University's 432-acre campus adjoins the historic Brazos River near downtown Waco.

Majors and Degrees

Baylor University's undergraduate programs are available in the College of Arts and Sciences; the Schools of Business, Education, Engineering and Computer Science, Music, and Nursing; and in Institutes and Special Studies. There are 155 baccalaureate degree programs and more than 100 major areas of study.

The College of Arts and Sciences, the Schools of Business and Education, and the Institutes and Special Studies offer departmental and intra-university programs leading to the Bachelor of Arts (B.A.), Bachelor of Science (B.S.), Bachelor of Science in Aviation Sciences (B.S.A.S.), Bachelor of Science in Education (B.S.Ed.), Bachelor of Science in Family and Consumer Sciences (B.S.F.C.S.), Bachelor of Fine Arts (B.F.A.), or Bachelor of Business Administration (B.B.A.) degrees. Undergraduate majors in these schools and colleges include accounting, acting, administrative information systems, American studies, anthropology, applied mathematics, archaeology, architecture (with Washington University), art, art history, Asian studies, aviation sciences, basic business, biblical and related languages, biochemistry, biology, business administration, business-broadcasting, business-journalism, chemistry, child and family studies, church recreation, classics, communication sciences and disorders, communication specialist studies, computer information systems, computer science, dentistry (combination program with an accredited dental school), design, dietetics, earth sciences, economics, elementary education, English, entrepreneurship, environmental studies, fashion design, fashion merchandising, finance, financial services/planning, foreign service, forestry (final year at Duke University), French, general family and consumer science, geology, geophysics, German, Greek, health, health/fitness studies, health science studies, history, human performance, human resources management, information systems, insurance, interdisciplinary studies, interior design, international business, journalism, Latin, Latin American studies, law, life-earth science, management, marketing, mathematics, medical technology and biology, medicine (combination program with an accredited medical school), museum studies, music, neuroscience, operations management, optometry (combination program with an accredited optometry school), performance, philosophy, physical education, physical science, physics, political science, professional writing, psychology, public administration, quantitative business analysis, reading, real estate, recreation, regional/urban studies, religion, Russian (9 hours required with another Russian program), science, secondary education, Slavic studies, social studies, social work, sociology, Spanish, special education, speech and language therapy, speech communication, studio art, telecommunication, theater arts, and university scholars. In addition, programs are available in prebusiness, predentistry, pre-dental hygiene, pre-education, prelaw, premedicine, prenursing, pre-occupational therapy, pre-optometry, pre-physical therapy, prepharmacy, and pre-veterinary medicine.

The School of Engineering and Computer Science offers programs of study leading to the Bachelor of Science in Engineering (B.S.E.) degree with electrical and mechanical options or Bachelor of Science in Computer Science (B.S.C.S.).

The School of Music offers programs of study leading to the Bachelor of Music (B.M.) degree in applied music, church music, composition, history and literature, pedagogy, and theory. The Bachelor of Music Education (B.M.E.) degree is designed for prospective teachers in public schools and offers concentrations in choral and instrumental instruction.

The School of Nursing combines a liberal arts curriculum and professional preparation in a four-year program leading to the Bachelor of Science in Nursing (B.S.N.) degree. Nursing majors complete their first two years on the Waco campus and then move to Dallas for two years in the professional component of the curriculum.

Academic Program

Baylor, a Phi Beta Kappa university ranking in the top 1 percent in numbers of National Merit Scholars enrolled, operates on a two-semester academic year plus two 6-week summer sessions. In the first two years, students select courses that provide a broadly based liberal arts education. All students who are admitted to Baylor University as freshmen enter either the College of Arts and Sciences, the School of Music, or a preprofessional program in the School of Business, the School of Education, School of Engineering and Computer Science, or the School of Nursing. Students pursuing degrees in one of the other professional schools may apply for admission to a specific degree program during the second year. Those students admitted to the University who intend to major in music should also qualify for admission to the School of Music at the time they enter the University in order to avoid undue delay in the completion of their degree program. Many of Baylor's students enter with credit hours earned through credit by examination. A number of these superior students elect to participate in the honors program, an enrichment course of study. As an alternative to the traditional general education requirements, the Baylor Interdisciplinary Core offers a set of comprehensive and cohesive interdisciplinary courses organized around three sequences of courses (world cultures, the natural world, and the social world).

Off-Campus Arrangements

Students may enroll in summer study-abroad programs in Cyprus, Egypt, England, France, Germany, Greece, Israel, Italy, Scotland, Spain, Switzerland, Thailand, Turkey, and Wales. One-year exchange programs are available with universities in Argentina, Australia, Azerbaijan, Canada, China, England, Finland, France, Hong Kong, Indonesia, Japan, Korea, Mexico, the Netherlands, Slovakia, South Africa, Thailand, and Uzbekistan.

Academic Facilities

Learning resource materials, housed in the six libraries on campus, total more than 1.5 million bound volumes. Modern scientific laboratories and equipment, computer science facilities, a speech and hearing clinic, the Castellaw Communications Center, and the Glasscock Energy Research Center offer students practical experience. The Hooper-Schaefer Fine Arts Center is available for work in the visual and performing arts.

Costs

The estimated direct total cost for 2000–01 is $17,176. Tuition is $10,650 (30 hours at $355 per semester hour), residence hall rooms are $2248, board (twenty meals per week) is $2990, and required fees are $1288. The total figure does not include the cost of books, travel, or personal expenditures. Books and supplies are estimated at $716 per year. Travel costs and personal expenditures vary with the individual. Costs are subject to change.

Financial Aid

Four basic forms of financial aid are available and are based on merit (as shown by achievement, National Merit status, and SAT I or ACT scores) and need (as determined by the FAFSA). These programs include scholarships, grants, loans, and on-campus jobs. About 75 percent of the students receive assistance. Students will be considered for scholarships by virtue of the application for admission. Students may obtain a FAFSA from their high school counselor or local college or university.

Faculty

Baylor's faculty numbers 655, and most have doctoral or other terminal degrees. Ninety-three percent of all classes are taught by faculty members. Most faculty members are actively engaged in research, several hold special chairs in their respective fields, and all are dedicated to challenging and teaching students. All faculty members work with undergraduates and serve as academic advisers to the students. The student-faculty ratio is 18:1, and a typical class numbers 30 students.

Student Government

Baylor University Student Government, whose members are elected by popular vote, is a vital and influential force in campus activities. With more than 250 active student organizations, numerous traditional events, special involvement programs, entertainment programs, and leadership laboratories, there are plenty of opportunities for students to get involved in campus life.

Admission Requirements

Priority admission is given to applicants who have earned a top 10 percent class rank, with no minimum ACT or SAT I score required, and to applicants who have earned a top 50 percent class rank, with at least a 24 on the ACT or an 1100 on the SAT I. Other applicants who do not qualify for priority admission may be considered for regular or conditional admission at the discretion of the Admissions Committee. Conditional admission may require attendance in summer school and entrance with special requirements. Required high school units are English, 4; college-preparatory mathematics, 3; laboratory science, 2; foreign language, 2; and social science, 2 (1 in history). Prospective freshmen should take the SAT I or ACT examination not later than the second semester of their junior year in high school and have the results sent to Baylor by the testing company. Freshman applications should be made at the end of the junior year or early in the senior year.

Students who wish to transfer to Baylor and who have completed at least 30 semester hours must present official transcripts from each college attended verifying a minimum overall grade point average of 2.5 (on a 4.0 scale) and must be eligible to return to the last school attended. Transfer students who seek admission with fewer than 30 semester hours must meet all the admission requirements for beginning freshmen. In addition, all transfer students must meet the same minimum course requirements for admission that are required for beginning freshmen. A student may present a high school transcript or a college transcript to verify that the course requirements have been fulfilled. Transfer students should plan to apply no later than the end of their sophomore year in order to meet the Baylor residence requirement of 60 semester hours.

Baylor offers admission to a limited number of superior high school students who have completed their junior year through an Advanced Studies/Early Admission Program. Applicants must rank in the top 10 percent of their class, score at least 1300 on the SAT I or 30 on the ACT, and have recommendations from both the high school counselor and principal. Interviews and campus visits are recommended.

Application and Information

Notifications of acceptance are based on a review of an applicant's complete file and begin by mid-September on a rolling admission basis. The complete file includes a general application for admission with a $35 application fee, an official high school transcript giving the applicant's rank in class, and official scores on the SAT I or ACT. To receive early consideration for admission, students are urged to apply by September, when the process begins. Requests for application forms and inquiries should be addressed to:

Office of Admission Services
Baylor University
P.O. Box 97056
Waco, Texas 76798-7056
Telephone: 254-710-3435
        800-BAYLOR-U (toll-free)
World Wide Web: http://www.baylor.edu

BAY PATH COLLEGE
LONGMEADOW, MASSACHUSETTS

The College

Founded in 1897, Bay Path College today offers baccalaureate and associate degrees. As a pioneer in innovative programs for women, the College educates women to become confident and resourceful contributors to an increasingly interdependent world through its focus on leadership, communication, and technology. Students are challenged to accept the responsibilities and to experience the rewards of leadership throughout their college career. The College thoroughly integrates opportunities to build and strengthen technological, analytical, and oral and written communication skills into the curriculum so that students may interact successfully with others, both professionally and personally.

The core of the 44-acre campus is the site of the former Wallace estate, and the Georgian architecture of the buildings reflects that of the estate's mansion, Deepwood Hall, which is now the College's administration building. Attractive residence halls provide comfortable accommodations for students and are wired for voice mail, video, and data. The S. Prestley Blake Student Center houses a spacious dining room, student lounges, television room, game room, the College store, and a snack bar. A tennis court and the Fitness and Wellness Center, fully equipped with exercise equipment, provide both formal and informal fitness opportunities. Playing fields, a running track, and an athletic club house accommodate varsity sports.

Through the College's comprehensive extracurricular program, students have a choice of a wide variety of on-campus clubs, organizations, and athletic activities. Bay Path also sponsors an annual "Capitals of the World" trip; weekend or day trips to New York City, Boston, Montreal, and Cape Cod; and ski trips to nearby slopes and major New England resorts. Two full-scale musical productions are presented by students each year. The Bay Path Chorale, the Keynotes (a select singing group), and the Bay Path Dance Company appear both on campus and for clubs and other organizations throughout New England. Social events and other collaborative activities are scheduled with neighboring colleges and with such institutions as West Point and the Coast Guard Academy. Although 50 percent of the 656 women enrolled reside on campus, commuting students are fully involved in College life.

The College's Career Services Center assists graduates who seek immediate employment; this service is available to them throughout their lives at no cost. In recent years, 95 to 98 percent of Bay Path's students have obtained jobs upon graduation.

Bay Path is a member of the College Entrance Examination Board, the Association of Independent Colleges and Universities in Massachusetts, the College Board, the National Association of College Admission Counselors, the National Association of Independent Colleges and Universities, and the Women's College Coalition.

Location

Longmeadow, Massachusetts, is a residential town just south of Springfield, Massachusetts, and 23 miles north of Hartford, Connecticut. Located in the city of Springfield are the Basketball Hall of Fame, a flourishing repertory theater, an excellent symphony orchestra, fine museums, and a civic center that is the site of numerous cultural and sporting events.

Transportation by air, bus, or rail is convenient. Bay Path is 20 minutes from Bradley International Airport in Windsor Locks, Connecticut; 1½ hours from Boston; and 2½ hours from New York City.

Majors and Degrees

Bay Path offers bachelor's degrees, associate degrees, concentrations, and certificates in accounting, business, communications, computer information technology, criminal justice, dispute resolution, early childhood education, elementary education, English, fine and performing arts, gerontology, history, human resource management, interior design, international business, legal studies, liberal studies, occupational therapy, occupational therapy assistant studies, paralegal studies, psychology, science, and travel and hospitality.

The College is accredited by the New England Association of Schools and Colleges. The paralegal programs at associate, baccalaureate, and certificate levels are approved by the American Bar Association. The occupational therapy assistant program is accredited by the Accreditation Council for Occupational Therapy Education of AOTA. The occupational therapy program has developing program status with ACOTE.

Academic Program

Bay Path's programs prepare women either for entry into careers or for continued studies. A minimum of 60 credits must be completed successfully to earn an associate degree, and a minimum of 120 credits are required for a baccalaureate. The general education requirements are intended to provide students with a foundation for learning in the humanities and fine arts, mathematics, and the natural and social sciences, regardless of their choice of major. The courses are all directed toward fulfilling the College's mission. All of the course offerings incorporate one or more of the three themes of the College's vision statement, Bay Path 2001: leadership, communication, and technology.

Internships are an integral part of many programs, and students are placed with professionals in local, regional, and national businesses for on-the-job experience. Bay Path interns work in law firms, hotels, retail stores, travel agencies, decorating firms, insurance companies, airline offices, cruise lines, social service agencies, correctional facilities, schools, and hospitals.

The Career Development Summit for seniors, held prior to the spring semester, gives them the opportunity to individually appraise their career potential. It includes interactive workshops, networking opportunities, and keynote addresses by leaders from the business community. The Career Exploration Semester is offered to those who are undecided about career plans. This special program allows students to assess their interests and abilities before selecting a Bay Path career program while also earning credits toward their degree.

English as a second language is offered as a course and a program to help international students gain the necessary language skills to complete a degree program.

Off-Campus Arrangements

Through Bay Path's membership in the Cooperating Colleges of Greater Springfield, a consortium of eight colleges, interested Bay Path students may take courses at these neighboring colleges and can share networked library resources.

Academic Facilities

Carr Hall houses a fully equipped theater, science laboratories, and faculty offices. Glen Hall features classrooms with modern business technology, an interior design studio, and four microcomputer laboratories. A preschool on campus provides opportunities for laboratory training for education majors. The

Catok Art Center is specifically designed for the study and practice of art and music and also serves as an art gallery, which contains only a portion of an extensive art collection on display throughout the campus. The Frank and Marion Hatch Library has an automated library system, cataloging, and extensive book, periodical, tape, and record collections. Elliott House contains the occupational therapy laboratory and faculty offices.

Costs

Costs for 1999–2000 were $13,010 for tuition and $6864 for room and board.

Financial Aid

Bay Path is keenly interested in admitting talented women who are serious about their education, and it encourages such students to apply regardless of their financial means. Scholarships, grants, loans, and employment opportunities are available. The Bay Path Scholar's Program for high-ability students provides almost full tuition assistance that is renewable for four years, based on meeting established criteria. Bay Path has a commitment to continue to aid qualified students who receive aid in their freshman year; every effort is made to maintain or increase the funding level to enable these students to graduate. Approximately 85 percent of current Bay Path students receive some form of financial aid. Financial aid applicants are reviewed beginning on December 15.

Faculty

The small size of the student population encourages the development of close, professional interactions among students and Bay Path faculty. Faculty members, all experts in their field, have teaching as their primary concern, but they devote many additional hours to participation with students in academic, social, and cultural activities. Sixty percent of the faculty members have a doctoral degree or a terminal degree.

Student Government

The Student Government, composed of 3 officers and 21 student representatives, assists the administration in deciding a number of matters, leads the way in the observance of regulations, and helps to create a spirit of mutual understanding and cooperation between the student body and the College administration.

Admission Requirements

The satisfactory completion of a recognized high school program or equivalent is required for admission. The Admissions Committee evaluates a student's academic record, class rank, recommendations, and test scores. Official transcripts are required, and an interview is strongly encouraged. Transfer students are welcome and should submit transcripts of all previously attended colleges. Students are selected who are best qualified in ability, scholarship, and motivation to complete the College's program of study.

In accordance with state and federal laws, Bay Path College does not discriminate against any student who applies for admission or is enrolled at the College.

Application and Information

The College follows a rolling admissions policy and encourages students to apply early. Notification of decision is generally within two weeks of receiving the completed application and accompanying materials. The candidate reply is due by May 1. For September enrollment, December 1 is the application deadline recommended for early decision consideration, with notification by December 15. The candidate reply is due by May 1. The application, application fee, and all credentials must be received before the admission process can begin.

The completed application should be sent to the Office of Admissions, together with a $25 nonrefundable application fee or fee-waiver request.

For application forms and additional information, students should contact:

Dean of Enrollment Services
Bay Path College
588 Longmeadow Street
Longmeadow, Massachusetts 01106
Telephone: 413-565-1331
        800-782-7284 (toll-free outside 413 area code)
Fax: 413-565-1105
E-mail: admiss@baypath.edu
World Wide Web: http://www.baypath.edu

Deepwood Hall, the administration building.

BEAVER COLLEGE
GLENSIDE, PENNSYLVANIA

The College

A coeducational college founded in 1853, Beaver College has many of the characteristics of a university yet retains a small-college atmosphere. Its diverse student population represents a cross section of cultural and socioeconomic backgrounds. Enrollment includes 1,264 full-time and 381 part-time undergraduates and 1,140 graduate students. At present, Beaver students come from twenty-three states and twenty-five other countries, and 70 percent of the full-time undergraduate population reside on campus. The diversity of the resident student body is further enhanced by students from many countries who attend the American Language Academy, which is based at the College. Adult students attend classes through the Continuing Education Program, take noncredit courses through the Community Scholars Program, or pursue bachelor's degrees in business administration through the Weekend College or corporate programs.

Campus life, including clubs, athletics, and cultural and social events, is rich and varied. Community service is part of the Beaver College experience. Students volunteer on neighborhood improvement projects, work at literacy or gerontology centers, and assist disadvantaged or disabled children. NCAA Division III intercollegiate competition is offered in field hockey, lacrosse, softball, and volleyball for women; in baseball for men; and in basketball, cross-country, golf, equestrian sports, soccer, swimming, tennis, and track for both men and women. Intramural sports offer many other athletic opportunities.

Master's programs are offered in the fields of counseling, education, English, environmental education, genetic counseling, health administration, health education, humanities, international peace and conflict resolution, physical therapy, and physician assistant studies. A Doctorate in Physical Therapy (D.P.T.) program is offered.

In spring 1999, two additional sports fields and extra tennis courts were added to the campus.

Location

Set on a beautiful former private estate in Glenside, a suburb of Philadelphia, Beaver College offers urban resources in a countrylike setting. The focal point of the campus is the unique Grey Towers Castle, a National Historic Landmark. The $6.5-million athletic and recreation center opened its doors in 1993. In 1995, the College completed a state-of-the-art Health Sciences Center. Knight Hall, a contemporary residence hall featuring suite-style accommodations, opened in 1997. The College completed expansion of the dining complex and student center and refurbished Murphy Hall, one of Beaver's most historic buildings, at roughly the same time. Construction has already begun on a new Physician Assistant facility. Because the College is only 25 minutes from the center of Philadelphia, Beaver students have ready access to the dozens of museums, galleries, performing arts centers, night spots, and historic, government, and commercial sites in this vital metropolitan area. New York City and Washington, D.C., are just a few hours away by car or train, as are recreation areas such as the New Jersey shore and the Pocono Mountains.

Majors and Degrees

The Bachelor of Arts is offered in art, art history, biology, business administration, chemistry, communications, computer science, education (early childhood, elementary, and secondary), English, health administration, history, interdisciplinary science, international business and culture, mathematics, philosophy, political science, psychobiology, psychology, science illustration, sociology, Spanish, and theater/theater art/English. The Bachelor of Science is offered in accounting, business administration, chemistry, chemistry and business, computer science, finance, health administration, management, management information systems, marketing, mathematics, and personnel/human resources administration. The Bachelor of Fine Arts degree is awarded to students majoring in studio arts with concentrations in ceramics, graphic design and illustration, interior design, metals and jewelry, painting, photography, and printmaking. Preparation for certification in art education is offered in conjunction with the B.F.A. program, as is preparation for graduate study in art therapy. A five-year program combines the Bachelor of Arts in education with a Master of Education in special education. Preparation for actuarial examinations comes through the Actuarial Science Program.

The physician assistant studies 4+2 program provides a four-year undergraduate degree in a related field and is followed by two years of study in the Master of Science in Physician Assistant Studies (M.S.P.A.S.) degree program at Beaver. Qualified candidates are assured admission to the Master of Science in Physician Assistant Studies program. The College offers a combined undergraduate and graduate (4+3) program leading to the Doctorate in Physical Therapy (D.P.T.). Beaver College undergraduates who meet established criteria are assured admission to the graduate track. The International Peace and Conflict Resolution Program provides a four-year undergraduate degree followed by two years of study in the Master of Arts in international peace and conflict resolution.

A dual-degree (3+2) program in engineering is offered in conjunction with Columbia University. An accelerated program with Pennsylvania College of Optometry leads to the Bachelor of Arts/Doctor of Optometry degrees. Preprofessional preparation is offered for dentistry, law, medicine, optometry, physical therapy, and theology as well as in other areas.

The evening program offers part-time study leading to the Bachelor of Science and postbaccalaureate certificates in business administration and in computer science as well as the Bachelor of Arts in communications and in English. The Weekend College offers bachelor's degrees in business administration and corporate communication.

Academic Program

The academic program provides students with a solid background of liberal arts and sciences integrated with courses in their chosen areas of interest. Students explore a variety of interests and can engage in research, internships, or cooperative education placements. Such experiences enable students to gain relevant work experience while putting their academic training to use. The Cooperative Education Program, for instance, provides students with the opportunity to combine on-campus study with off-campus employment in a program that helps them earn both credit and income.

Highly qualified freshmen, sophomores, and juniors may enhance their education through the Honors Program, which includes special seminars, independent study, and cultural events.

Credit toward graduation is granted for scores of 3 or better on the Advanced Placement examinations of the College Board. Exemption from or credit for courses may also be earned through the College-Level Examination Program (CLEP) and locally administered examinations at the discretion of the department concerned.

The academic year is divided into two semesters. Summer sessions begin in May and continue through early August. Most students carry four academic courses in each regular semester; 128 semester hours are required for graduation.

Off-Campus Arrangements

Beaver College operates one of the largest campus-based study-abroad programs in the country. Through this program, students may participate in any of more than 100 programs at locations in

Australia, Britain (including the Universities of Aberdeen, Bristol, Edinburgh, London, and York), Greece, Ireland, Italy, Korea, Mexico, Northern Ireland, and Spain and at the Austro-American Institute of Education in Vienna. London Preview is an opportunity available to freshmen in good standing to spend a week in London during spring break. The cost is $245 and includes round-trip airfare, housing, and programming. Off-campus study in the Philadelphia area includes internships and fieldwork in most majors. The College offers the Washington (D.C.) Semester at American University. Juniors and seniors may enroll for one advanced course each semester at the University of Pennsylvania.

Academic Facilities

Boyer Hall of Science houses the biology, chemistry and physics, genetic counseling, mathematics and computer science, physician assistant studies, psychology, and sociology departments. Individual laboratories are available for both faculty and student research.

The Health Sciences Center houses the Department of Physical Therapy. Taylor Hall is home to the business administration, economics, education, English, health administration, history, philosophy and religion, and political science departments. Murphy Hall houses the communications, music, and theater departments as well as video production and digital imaging studios. Students have easy access to campus computer facilities and to the Internet. Internet services include the World Wide Web, Telnet, ftp, and e-mail. Students are also provided with the ability to put up a personal Web page. The campus network extends to each room in the residence halls. Computer facilities include an Alpha mainframe with Ethernet connections to more than thirty on-site and dial-up workstations. There are also four microcomputer labs and a Mac lab. The fine arts department offers a state-of-the-art computer graphics system to allow students to work with and master this technique of graphic design as well as desktop publishing and computer-aided design systems. A prime academic resource on campus is the Atwood Library, which not only offers an extensive collection of books, journals, periodicals, microforms, and audio materials but also provides links to college and community library resources throughout the metropolitan area.

Costs

The charge for tuition in 2000–01 is $17,550. Student fees are $280 per year. Room and board charges are $7740 per year. Books and supplies average about $300 per semester.

Financial Aid

Every effort is made to see that students requiring financial assistance are able to attend Beaver. Aid is awarded on the basis of need, as determined by the Free Application for Federal Student Aid (FAFSA) and the Beaver College Financial Aid Application, and is available in the form of grants, loans, and part-time employment or some combination of the three. In 1999, 94 percent of the enrolled students received some form of financial aid, including need-based aid and merit awards. Scholarships are presented annually to students who have achieved academic distinction or have been recognized for outstanding extracurricular accomplishments. Distinguished Scholarships, ranging from $8000 to $70,200 over four years, and the Beaver College Achievement Awards, ranging from $4000 to $24,000 over four years, recognize academic excellence, leadership, and extracurricular accomplishments. Candidates have outstanding records of achievement, pursue competitive programs of study, and often excel in leadership, community service, and extracurricular activities. Transfer students are given special consideration. Financial Analysis Service Today (FAST) enables families to find out what the expected family contribution toward college costs and the estimated Beaver College financial aid package will be. This service is available from September through January of the senior year of high school. To receive full consideration for financial aid, students should complete their applications and submit the FAFSA and the Beaver College Financial Aid Application by March 1.

Faculty

Beaver College has a faculty with a primary commitment to teaching. Most classes range in size from 15 to 20 people, and the ratio of students to faculty is 13:1, so professors come to know and care about their students. This fosters an environment in which students and faculty collaborate on research and writing and engage in informal discussions, field trips, and other special activities outside the classroom. Eighty-five percent of the Beaver faculty hold doctorates or terminal degrees, and all courses are taught by faculty members rather than graduate assistants.

Student Government

Student life is largely self-regulated by the Student Government Organization (SGO) through the Student Senate. Most students feel that the SGO has proved effective in working with the faculty and administration on matters of student concern, as well as in developing the social climate of the College. Students serve on most major faculty committees, and student leaders attend Board of Trustees meetings.

Admission Requirements

Students are carefully selected on the basis of educational preparation, intellectual promise, and potential. Each candidate's credentials are reviewed individually by members of the enrollment management staff. Particular emphasis is placed on the candidate's academic record, including the type of program followed and the grades and class rank earned. Standardized test scores, counselor and teacher recommendations, participation in school and community activities, and other supporting credentials are also considered.

Freshman applicants must submit an official high school transcript, standardized test scores (SAT I or ACT), and counselor and teacher recommendations. Applicants should pursue a college-preparatory program, usually consisting of 16 academic units. Early admission, early decision, deferred admission, and advanced placement are available. Students may be admitted through the Gateway To Success or Act 101 Program. Students are encouraged to visit the campus for a student-guided tour and an admission interview.

Transfer applicants may apply for the fall term or at midyear and must submit official college transcripts. In some cases, transfer applicants will be required to submit high school transcripts and SAT I or ACT scores.

Application and Information

Students are encouraged to submit their applications as early as possible in the senior year. Admission decisions are made on a rolling basis, and applicants are usually notified within a month of the date of completion of the application.

Requests for further information should be directed to:
Office of Enrollment Management
Beaver College
450 South Easton Road
Glenside, Pennsylvania 19038-3295
Telephone: 215-572-2910
          888-BEAVER-3 (888-232-8373) (toll-free)
E-mail: admiss@beaver.edu
World Wide Web: http://www.beaver.edu

Grey Towers Castle, Beaver College.

BECKER COLLEGE
WORCESTER AND LEICESTER, MASSACHUSETTS

The College

Located in the heart of Massachusetts, Becker is a distinctive New England college. Becker College encompasses two individual campuses that are located 6 miles apart, each with its own residence halls, library, and academic facilities. The Worcester campus was founded in 1887 by E. C. A. Becker. The Leicester campus began as an academy in 1784 and is the nineteenth-oldest campus in the country. Both schools have sustained a long-standing tradition of high-quality education. In 1974, Becker and Leicester began working together to expand academic offerings and provide broader social and recreational opportunities for their students. As a result of their close cooperation, the two were formally consolidated in 1977 as the Worcester campus and Leicester campus of Becker College.

Today, with an enrollment of about 1,100 men and women from twenty states and fifteen countries, Becker College continues the tradition of excellence. The small classes and supportive academic environment offer students the individual attention and recognition they deserve. On the Worcester campus, gracious older homes have been restored and serve as residence halls. In Leicester, students may choose to live in restored homes or contemporary residence halls. Whether they live on or off campus, students share in the strong sense of community spirit that prevails at Becker.

Extracurricular activities offered through student organizations and the campus activities office provide a rich and varied college experience. Becker strongly encourages student involvement and participation for enhanced learning, personal development, and enjoyment. Student clubs and organizations include the Black Student Union, Community Service Club, *Hawk's Eye* student newspaper, Multicultural Club, Outdoors Club, Ski Club, Travel Club, and yearbook as well as a number of others. As a small college responsive to student needs, Becker makes every effort to support new clubs and student organizations. Since student interests vary from year to year, new ideas and suggestions are always welcome.

Athletics are an important part of extracurricular activities for Becker students. More than 50 percent participate in intramural or recreational sports. Becker College is a member of the NCAA Division III. Varsity athletics for men include baseball, basketball, cross-country, soccer, and tennis. Women's varsity sports are basketball, cross-country, field hockey, soccer, softball, tennis, and volleyball. Equestrian riding is offered as a coed sport.

Location

With campuses in Worcester and Leicester, Massachusetts, Becker College enjoys an ideal location and easy access. Becker's Worcester campus is situated in the Elm Park section of Worcester, a quiet area of tree-lined streets and lovely old homes that is a short walk from the downtown business district. With a population of 165,000, the city of Worcester is New England's second-largest urban center. The city is 1 hour from Boston, Massachusetts; Hartford, Connecticut; and Providence, Rhode Island and 3 hours from New York City. Air, rail, and bus transportation connect Worcester to all major points. The Worcester Regional Transit Authority provides regular bus service throughout the city.

Becker's Leicester campus surrounds the historic village green at the junction of Routes 9 and 56 in Leicester center. The town of Leicester is located 6 miles from the Worcester campus. Students on the Leicester campus have the opportunity to participate in the cultural, social, and recreational activities of the metropolitan area while living in a small New England town, rich in history that predates the American Revolution.

Becker's two campuses are linked via campus shuttle and Worcester Regional Transit Authority bus service.

Majors and Degrees

Becker College awards Bachelor of Science degrees in business administration, with concentrations in accounting and financial information systems, hospitality and tourism management, human resources management, management, marketing management, and sports management; criminal justice, with concentrations in criminal justice administration and policing; kinesiology, with concentrations in exercise science and health and fitness; legal studies; and veterinary science, with concentrations in clinical medicine and laboratory animal medicine. Bachelor of Arts degrees are awarded in psychology, with concentrations in child studies, early childhood education (Pre-K to grade 3), elementary education (grades 1–6), and human services, and liberal arts (planned for fall 2000). Associate in Science degrees are awarded in accounting, animal care, business administration, communications, computer information systems, criminal justice administration, early childhood education, graphic design, human services, interior design, liberal arts, liberal studies, nursing (RN), occupational therapy assistant studies, paralegal studies, physical therapist assistant studies, special education paraeducator studies, speech-language pathology assistant studies, sports management, and veterinary technology.

Academic Program

To graduate with a Bachelor of Arts or Bachelor of Science degree, students must complete a minimum of 122 credits with a cumulative GPA of 2.0 or higher. For an Associate in Science degree, a minimum of 60 credits with a GPA of 2.0 or higher is required. Thirty percent of the total credits must be in the area of general studies. Many programs require clinical fieldwork or internships for graduation.

Becker College operates on a two-semester academic calendar. Classes begin in September and end in May.

Off-Campus Arrangements

Becker is a member of the Colleges of Worcester Consortium, an association of ten Worcester-area colleges and universities that sponsors interlibrary loan services, social events, and a course cross-registration system to broaden course offerings. Full-time students may take one course per semester free of charge at any other consortium institution with permission of their faculty advisers. Member institutions include Anna Maria College, Assumption College, Clark University, College of the Holy Cross, Quinsigamond Community College, Tufts University School of Veterinary Medicine, the University of Massachusetts Medical School, Worcester Polytechnic Institute, and Worcester State College.

Academic Facilities

The newly renovated Academic Center on the Worcester campus contains the Ruska Library, state-of-the-art computer labs, science labs, classrooms, conference facilities, and a modern lecture hall. A new Health Sciences Education Center opened in January 2000.

The Leicester campus academic center contains classrooms, lecture halls, science labs, computer labs, and a campus radio station (WBKR). Other facilities include an animal health center, a preschool, and a video production center.

Academic Support Centers are located on both campuses. The centers are dedicated to helping Becker students achieve academic success. Services include one-on-one and group content tutoring, study skills instruction and workshops, and writing seminars. The purpose of the Academic Support Centers is to provide appropriate academic assistance to all students. Professional staff members, peer tutors, and faculty members work together to foster a supportive learning environment. The staff engages in a partnership with students to help them achieve their goals. Academic support is available to all students at no additional cost.

Costs

Tuition and fees for 1999–2000 were $11,710; room and board costs were $5830. Books and personal expenses are estimated at $1500.

Financial Aid

Financial aid is available for all eligible students through federal, state, and Becker College programs. Approximately 85 percent of all Becker students receive some form of financial assistance. Financial aid comes in the form of grants and scholarships, student loans, and work-study. Most types of financial assistance require that a student demonstrate financial need. All students who wish to apply for aid must complete the Free Application for Federal Student Aid (FAFSA) and the Becker College Application for Financial Aid. The application deadline is rolling; however, students are encouraged to apply as soon as possible after January 1. Incoming freshmen receive financial aid award announcements beginning in March.

Faculty

Becker College has a faculty of 126 members. Becker faculty members are committed to personalized teaching and are one of the College's greatest resources. The student-faculty ratio of 15:1 allows students to get the individual attention and recognition they deserve.

Student Government

The Student Government Association (SGA) is charged with overseeing all clubs and organizations and any activities funded by the student activity fee. SGA officers and members hold regular meetings to maintain and improve the quality of campus life, focusing on student needs and expectations. Membership may include elected representatives from each residence hall and the commuter population, as well as student leaders from many organizations.

Admission Requirements

To be considered for admission, students must submit a completed application, a $25 application fee, an official secondary school transcript, and SAT I or ACT scores. Letters of recommendation are recommended. Becker requires a minimum 2.0 cumulative GPA for admission. Students applying to health science majors are required to demonstrate proficiency in math and science. Becker College recognizes that all students are individuals and considers each applicant's personal strengths and achievements.

Application and Information

Applications are accepted on a rolling basis and reviewed upon receipt of all required materials. Most applicants are notified of admission decisions within two to three weeks of completion of their application. For more information, prospective students should contact:

Office of Admissions
Becker College
61 Sever Street
Worcester, Massachusetts 01609
Telephone: 508-791-9241 Ext. 245
          877-5BECKER (523-2537) (toll-free)
Fax: 508-890-1500
E-mail: admissions@beckercollege.edu
World Wide Web: http://www.beckercollege.edu

Originally built in 1719, the historic Reuben Swan Tavern houses the admissions and financial aid offices on the Leicester campus.

BELMONT ABBEY COLLEGE
BELMONT, NORTH CAROLINA

The College
The most notable characteristics of Belmont Abbey College are its warmth and friendliness. Its origins in Christian tradition are exemplified in the lives of the monks and staff members who belong to the community of Belmont Abbey. The strong family nature of the community directly influences the campus and classroom atmosphere. Because the College is small, students know the faculty and administration, and the development of lifelong friendships is common.

Residence life gives the student opportunities to develop both social and academic ideals. The sense of community is featured in both the academic and social aspects of the College.

The student body of approximately 1,000 men and women represents thirty-five states and sixteen countries. This diversity adds a valuable dimension to the student's educational experience. The College is coeducational, and approximately 50 percent of the students live on campus. Cars are permitted for all.

There are many extracurricular activities for students. The College Union offers a full program of social events and entertainment, and the active intramural sports program involves more than 80 percent of the students. Intercollegiate sports for men include baseball, basketball, cross-country, golf, soccer, and tennis. Intercollegiate sports for women include basketball, cross-country, soccer, softball, and tennis. Other campus activities include fraternities, sororities, the campus ministry, the student newspaper, the literary magazine, the Outdoor Leadership Program, the Abbey Players theater group, and student government.

Location
The College is situated in rolling, wooded country on a 650-acre campus just on the fringe of Belmont, a small town of 6,000 people. Belmont is 10 miles west of Charlotte, a community of about 450,000 people, which offers many opportunities for entertainment and cultural and recreational activity. Ten miles west of Belmont is Gastonia (population 50,000). Lakes abound in the immediate area, and it is only a 2-hour drive to the mountains and winter sports areas. Charlotte International Airport is a 15-minute drive away, and I-85 is adjacent to the campus.

Majors and Degrees
The degrees of Bachelor of Arts and Bachelor of Science are offered with fields of concentration in the following areas: accounting, biology, business management, computer information systems, economics, elementary education, English, history, middle grades education, philosophy/theology, political science, psychology, secondary education, sociology, and therapeutic recreation.

Preprofessional training in law, medicine, optometry, pharmacy, and veterinary medicine are available.

Degrees awarded through the Adult Degree Program and Weekend College (described in the Academic Program section) are in accounting, business administration, computer information systems, economics, elementary education, and liberal studies.

Academic Program
The academic program is built on a distinctive core curriculum that responds to the diverse nature and needs of the traditional-age student. The core reflects more than 100 years of commitment to liberal arts, Catholic, and Benedictine values and emphasizes faith, truth, social justice, the place of the individual in community, international studies, and the use of primary sources in the pursuit of knowledge.

A cumulative average of at least C (2.0 on a 4.0 scale) is required for graduation.

The Adult Degree Program and Weekend College serve students who need to attend college in a program outside the traditional day school program. Students in the Adult Degree Program attend classes three nights each week. Students can earn up to 12 semester hours of credit (this is considered full-time), making them eligible to apply for federal, state, and institutional financial aid. Students in the Weekend College attend classes Friday night and Saturday and can earn up to 12 semester hours of credit.

Off-Campus Arrangements
Through the Charlotte Area Educational Consortium, a cooperative group of twelve colleges and universities, students have free access to all course offerings not available on the home campus and to library holdings of other colleges. Study abroad may be arranged on an individual basis with a departmental chairman and the academic dean. Internship programs with credit, especially in the social sciences and professional studies, are available.

Academic Facilities
The age of the College (founded 1876) is reflected in some of its stately old buildings, all of which have been renovated. The library, science building, physical education center, and Student Commons Center are newer additions.

Costs
Tuition, room and board (nineteen meals), and required fees for 2000–01 are $19,838 per year. This cost is reduced by $1600 annually for North Carolina residents through the North Carolina Legislative Tuition Grant program. Books and supplies average $250 per semester.

Financial Aid
College-administered aid comes from the full range of federal programs—Federal Pell Grants and Federal Supplemental Educational Opportunity Grants, Federal Work-Study awards, Federal Perkins Loans, and Federal Stafford Student Loans. North Carolina students have access to state grant funds administered by the College. Tuition is reduced by $3000 per year for all siblings after the first one is enrolled full-time and paying full tuition. Scholarships based on academic promise as well as Hintemeyer Scholarships for Leaders are granted each year. About 80 percent of all students receive College aid in some form. All applicants for aid must file the Free Application for Federal Student Aid (FAFSA) of the College Scholarship Service with the Financial Aid Office at Belmont Abbey College by March 15. The two criteria for receiving aid are financial need and academic promise.

Numerous companies throughout the region have employees in Belmont Abbey College's Adult Degree Program. Many of these companies provide some form of tuition reimbursement. Belmont Abbey offers a tuition deferment program for students eligible for employer reimbursement.

Faculty

The faculty-student ratio is 1:15. Approximately 15 percent of the teaching faculty are members of the religious community of Belmont Abbey and reside on campus. All faculty members engage both formally and informally in student advising and counseling. A professional counselor is also available. Faculty members teach all class levels without regard to academic rank or length of service.

Student Government

There is a student government elected by the student body. This organization, set up with executive, legislative, and judicial branches, is very influential in campus affairs. In addition, students have voting positions on most standing committees of the College.

Admission Requirements

An applicant's high school preparation should include 4 units in English, 3 in mathematics, 2 in social sciences, 2 in science, and 2 in foreign language. For science and math majors, 4 units in mathematics, 1 in chemistry, and 1 in physics are also recommended. The College requires each applicant to submit a completed application, high school transcripts, and SAT I or ACT scores. For transfer students, a completed application and college transcripts are required. The combined SAT I scores of entering freshmen average 990. Acceptance to Belmont Abbey is based on the high school record, grade point average, and SAT I or ACT scores. A written recommendation relating to academic abilities and participation in extracurricular activities is helpful but not required. Advanced placement and credit are granted on the basis of the CLEP and AP tests of the College Board. A physician's statement of good health is required as well as documentation of all immunizations. An interview is preferred but not mandatory.

Belmont Abbey College does not discriminate against persons on the basis of sex, age, race, color, mental or physical challenge, religion, national or ethnic origin, or status as a disabled or Vietnam Era veteran in the recruitment and admission of students, the recruitment and employment of staff and faculty, or the administration of its educational programs and activities as defined by federal laws and regulations.

Application and Information

An application, together with a $25 nonrefundable application fee, may be submitted for either the fall or spring semester; the deadlines are August 15 and December 31, respectively, but early application is advised. Notification of acceptance is given November 15 and January 15, then on a rolling basis upon completion of application data. A $400 tuition and room-reservation deposit for boarding students or a $200 tuition deposit for commuting students is due thirty days after the notice of acceptance is received.

For further information, prospective students should contact:

Office of Admissions
Belmont Abbey College
Belmont, North Carolina 28012
Telephone: 704-825-6665
　　　　　　888-BAC-0110 (toll-free)
Fax: 704-825-6220
E-mail: belmontabbeycollege.edu
World Wide Web: www.msn.com

Two Belmont Abbey students return to their dorms from the Haid, home of the longstanding Abbey Players theater group and the Haid Ballroom, the site of many weekend dances, open-mike night, and karaoke.

BELMONT UNIVERSITY
NASHVILLE, TENNESSEE

The University

Nationally recognized programs thrive on the Belmont University campus, which is located in the heart of the state capital, known both as Music City, U.S.A., and the Athens of the South (for its many educational institutions). Nashville offers big-city advantages with small-town charm.

Belmont's vision is to be a premier teaching university, bringing together the best of liberal arts and professional education in a consistently caring Christian environment. Central to the fulfillment of that vision are faculty members who have a passion for teaching and the belief that premier teaching is interactive, technology-supported, motivational, creative, and exciting.

With an enrollment of more than 3,000 students, Belmont is the second-largest private college or university in Tennessee. Affiliated with the Tennessee Baptist Convention, it is the state's largest private college or university with a religious affiliation.

In addition to the many international countries represented in the student body, Belmont University attracts students from almost every state in the United States. The culturally diverse institution is committed to listening and learning from everyone. Students of today are helping shape the way students of tomorrow will be educated.

Belmont's beautiful, antebellum campus reflects a long, rich history that dates back to the nineteenth century, when the grounds were Adelicia Acklen's Belle Monte estate. University buildings that were erected over the past 110 years flank the Italianate mansion, which is still used by the campus. On the way to classes that prepare them for the twenty-first century, students enjoy Victorian gardens, statuary, and gazebos that recall a treasured past.

Two prestigious women's schools preceded the comprehensive liberal arts institution: the original Belmont College (1890–1913) and Ward-Belmont (1913–1951). In 1951, the Tennessee Baptist Convention founded the second Belmont College (1951–1991), with an initial coeducational enrollment of 136 students. Soon after celebrating 100 years of education on the same campus, the institution became a university in 1991, culminating a decade of dramatic growth and progress.

In addition to six baccalaureate degrees, Belmont University offers nine graduate degrees: the Master of Business Administration, the Master of Accountancy, the Master of English, the Master of Music, the Master of Music Education, the Master of Education, the Master of Science in Nursing, the Master of Science in Occupational Therapy, and the Master of Science in Physical Therapy.

Location

Belmont University occupies a 62-acre campus in southeast Nashville. With more than 500,000 residents, Nashville is a cultural, educational, health-care, commercial, and financial center in the mid-South. Practical educational opportunities, offered through diverse curriculums, provide students with the hands-on experience they need in preparation for a meaningful career. The city's location halfway between the northern and southern boundaries of the United States, with three intersecting interstate highways and an international airport, makes it accessible to students from across the country.

Majors and Degrees

Belmont University is accredited by the Commission on Colleges of the Southern Association of Colleges and Schools to award associate, baccalaureate, and master's degrees. Belmont grants six undergraduate degrees: the Bachelor of Arts, the Bachelor of Business Administration, the Bachelor of Music, the Bachelor of Science, the Bachelor of Science in Nursing, and the Bachelor of Fine Arts. Majors or concentrations are offered in accounting, accounting/information systems management, art (art education, design communications, and studio art), audio and video production, biology, broadcasting, business, chemistry, child care administration, classics, communication studies, computer science, economics, education licensure (elementary and secondary), engineering physics, English, exercise science, finance, French, general business, German, health, health care management, history, hospitality travel and tourism, information systems management, journalism, management, management science, marketing, marketing/hospitality travel and tourism, mathematics, medical imaging technology, medical technology, music (church music, commercial music, composition, music education, music with an outside minor, musical theater, performance, piano pedagogy, theory), music business, nursing, ophthalmic medical technology, philosophy, physical education, physics, political economy, political science, preprofessional, psychology, religion, science and engineering management, social work, sociology, Spanish, and theater and drama.

Academic Program

Uniquely positioned to provide the best of liberal arts and professional education, Belmont University offers celebrated professional programs structured to provide an academically well-rounded education. Belmont University operates on a two-semester schedule with classes beginning in late August and ending in early May. Two summer sessions are also offered. The academic program is arranged by school: the College of Arts and Sciences, the College of Business Administration, the College of Health Sciences, the College of Visual and Performing Arts, and the School of Religion.

In addition to the degrees offered through the schools, Belmont University offers an honors program, which was created to provide an enrichment opportunity for students who have potential for superior academic performance and who seek added challenge and breadth to their studies. Students enrolled in the honors program are led in designing and working through a flexible, individual curriculum by a private tutor who is an honors faculty member.

The University's advancements in undergraduate research are credited to a faculty committed to helping students practice their disciplines. The annual Belmont Undergraduate Research Symposium puts Belmont at the forefront of this national movement by providing a public forum for in-depth research at the undergraduate level.

Off-Campus Arrangements

Belmont University has contracts for dual-degree programs with Auburn University and University of Tennessee, Knoxville. These programs require three years of study at Belmont University followed by approximately two years of study at one of the above institutions. The course of study at Belmont must be mathematics, physics, or chemistry. Following completion of the academic requirements at both institutions, a student is awarded a Bachelor of Science degree from Belmont University and the appropriate degree from the second institution.

Several programs at Belmont have agreements with area organizations to provide students practical training. Nursing students gain clinical experience at Centennial Medical Center, St. Thomas Hospital, and Summit Hospital. Education students gain classroom experience in Metro-Davidson County Schools. Music business students gain real-world experience through internships in the Nashville music industry and in the Los Angeles, California, area through the Belmont West program of study and internships.

Through a wide variety of international study programs, Belmont offers students the opportunity to broaden and deepen their education while earning credit hours toward their degrees. These programs, which range in duration from two weeks to a year, are available in Australia, the Bahamas, China, Costa Rica, England, France, Germany, Ireland, Italy, Mexico, New Zealand, Nicaragua, Russia, Scotland, South Africa, and Spain.

Academic Facilities

Belmont offers a quiet, secluded environment, and classes are held in nine buildings with the library and other facilities located in proximity to those classrooms.

The renovated and expanded Lila D. Bunch Library includes a microcomputer center and has approximately 212,000 volumes. Adjacent to it is the 300,000-square-foot Leu Art Gallery. Located next to the library is the newly constructed Leu Center for the Visual Arts, featuring state-of-the-art studios with natural lighting and spacious work areas.

The Sam A. Wilson School of Music Building houses classrooms, a resource room, seminar rooms, studio/offices, music practice rooms, a piano lab, and a music technology lab.

The Jack C. Massey Business Center, encompassing 115,000 square feet, provides classrooms, office space, study lounges, seminar and conference rooms, a copy center, a post office, and a convenience store. A state-of-the-art learning center includes five computer labs. In addition, Massey Business Center houses the 9,000-square-foot Center for Music Business, which provides classrooms, an academic resource center, two state-of-the-art recording studios and control rooms, four isolation booths, a MIDI pre–postproduction room, and an engineering repair shop.

Costs

Belmont's tuition and fees are $12,330 per academic year in 2000–01. Room and board in campus residence halls are $5280. Other expenses, including books, travel, and supplies, average $1500.

Financial Aid

The financial aid program at Belmont combines merit-based assistance with need-based assistance to make the University program affordable. Institutional merit awards range from full tuition Presidential Scholarships to performance scholarships. Also included are many levels of academic merit awards. Belmont University also administers traditional state and federal programs, including the Federal Pell Grant, Federal Stafford Student Loan, Federal Perkins Loan, Federal PLUS loan, and Tennessee Student Assistance Grants and Scholarships. Campus employment is available. Parents may arrange monthly tuition payments through an outside vendor. To apply for assistance, the student must complete the Free Application for Federal Student Aid (FAFSA).

Faculty

A highly competent faculty is the paramount attribute of a strong institution of higher education. Belmont University has faculty members who are dedicated to their profession and to the University. Of the more than 195 full-time faculty members, 65 percent hold terminal degrees and another 10 percent actively pursue that degree. Another 30 percent of faculty members have completed formal studies beyond the master's degree.

The influence of the Belmont University faculty is felt beyond the campus. Faculty members are active in church, civic, professional, and academic associations; frequently speak to various groups; and often write for denominational and secular publications. Most faculty members have traveled extensively and many have experienced life in other regions of the United States and abroad.

Student Government

A liaison between the University and student body, the Student Government Association seeks to address educational, social, and spiritual needs of students. As a service organization for the student body, it offers opportunity for campus involvement, acts as the coordinating body for all student organizations, serves as a resource for the campus community, and represents student interests to the faculty and administration.

Admission Requirements

Applicants are considered based on the total picture of a student's present credentials. High school students are considered competitive for admission if they present a rigorous course of college-preparatory academic studies. Students should have an above-average academic and cumulative grade point average and rank in the top half of their graduating class. Any college-level work is also expected to be at the above-average level. A strong correlation between high school grades and entrance examination scores is expected. The personal supplement information, a resume of activities, and recommendations are also strongly considered as positive indicators of success at Belmont. Additional requirements, such as interviews or auditions, are considered in conjunction with the academic credentials for those programs that require them. Each application is considered on an individual basis. No two applicants present the same credentials or the same degree of "fit" with the University. The University desires to work with each student to determine the likelihood for that student to enroll, graduate, and benefit from the Belmont educational experience.

Application and Information

Further information and application materials may be obtained by contacting:

Office of Admissions
Belmont University
1900 Belmont Boulevard
Nashville, Tennessee 37212
Telephone: 615-460-6785
        800-56ENROLL (toll-free)
World Wide Web: http://www.belmont.edu

Belmont University students enjoy a beautiful antebellum campus located in thriving metropolitan Nashville.

BELOIT COLLEGE
BELOIT, WISCONSIN

The College

Beloit College is a four-year, independent, national college of liberal arts and sciences whose focus is great teaching with an emphasis on internationalism, an interdisciplinary approach to study, and experiential learning opportunities. The College attracts students who are actively engaged in learning, who thrive in an atmosphere of discussion, and who are ready to make their mark. Beloit is a residential college, and its 1,150 students come to the campus from forty-nine states and fifty-five countries. The student body is 11 percent international, 1 in 5 students is non-Caucasian, and various religious orientations, socioeconomic backgrounds, and learning styles are represented on campus. Beloit is a dynamic and uncommonly diverse community where cliques, stereotypes, and exclusivity are left behind as students celebrate and thrive on the diversity in their classrooms, in their residence halls, and on their playing fields. Beloit students come from many different places and are varied in their academic interests—not one of the more than fifty majors commands more than 10 percent of the senior class. Founded in 1846 to serve a frontier society, Beloit is Wisconsin's first college.

Beloit students are informed and experienced in political and social issues, and they place a premium on individual expression. The range of student extracurricular activities reflects a spectrum of their interests and involvement. Beloit students serve on the College governance committees, establish their own organizations, oversee the weekly Café Series, and have their own radio and cable TV shows. In a given week, students may have the choice of attending (or organizing) a lecture series, a movie, music performances, a poetry reading, or an environmental debate. Seventy percent of Beloit's students participate in club, intramural, or varsity athletics and use the College's $6-million athletic complex adjacent to the residential side of campus. Those who live on campus—93 percent—may choose to live in residence halls, on quiet floors, on substance-free floors, on the anthropology floor, or in one of the special interest houses, which include four foreign language houses, the Alliance house, the arts co-op, the music house, the outdoor/environmental house, the science fiction and fantasy house, the Voces Latinas house, and the Womyn's Center. Meals, served in two dining halls on campus, are offered on a twenty-meal weekly plan and include vegetarian and vegan meal options.

New students quickly become part of this active and diverse environment through First-Year Initiatives (FYI), an innovative program that places first-year students in an interdisciplinary seminar taught by an experienced professor or staff member. These seminars begin the first day new students arrive on campus and provide an academic class, a social base, and a two-year faculty adviser to assist students in their adjustment to Beloit and to bolster their campus involvement. FYI leads students into a curriculum that is open and collaborative.

Location

Beloit's 40-acre campus is located on the Wisconsin-Illinois state line 90 miles northwest of Chicago, 50 miles south of Madison, and 70 miles southwest of Milwaukee, in a small city that noted anthropologist Margaret Mead once called "American society in a microcosm." Students take advantage of the varied resources offered by the three major metropolitan areas, as well as those offered by the city of Beloit itself. Beloit's hospital, clinics, manufacturers, and various civic and service organizations provide numerous internship, job shadowing, enrichment, and community outreach opportunities. The academic buildings of Beloit College cluster around lawns dotted with pre-Columbian effigy mounds, while across campus, residence halls form a community of their own. A 25-acre athletic field and newly renovated Strong Memorial Stadium are located a few blocks east of the main campus.

Majors and Degrees

Beloit awards Bachelor of Arts and Bachelor of Science degrees in twenty departments and more than fifty fields of study. In the natural sciences and mathematics division, students may choose majors from the Departments of Biology, Chemistry, Geology, Mathematics and Computer Science, and Physics and Astronomy. In the social sciences division, students may choose majors from the Departments of Anthropology, Economics and Management, Education, Political Science and International Relations, Psychology, and Sociology. In the arts and humanities division, majors are offered in the Departments of Art and Art History, Classics, English, History, Modern Languages and Literatures, Music, Philosophy and Religion, Theatre Arts, and Women's Studies. Students are also able to create their own interdisciplinary major. The College offers departmental minors in biology and society, computer science, environmental geology, integrative biology, international economics, management, mathematics, music, philosophy, philosophy and religion, physics, political economy, and religion. Permanent interdisciplinary minors include American studies, Ancient Mediterranean studies, Asian studies, environmental studies, European studies, health-care studies, journalism, Latin American studies, legal studies, linguistics, museum studies, performing arts, Russian studies, and women's studies.

Beloit offers three 3-2 cooperative programs for students interested in engineering and forestry and environmental management and two 2-2 cooperative programs for students in medical technology and nursing. In addition, Beloit offers preprofessional programs in dentistry, medicine, and law. These programs, which have strong advisory and internship bases, complement a major in an appropriate discipline. Beloit students may also earn their teaching certification.

Academic Program

Beloit's academic calendar consists of two 14-week semesters with one-week midterm breaks. Students are required to complete either a major or a major with teaching certification. In addition, Beloit's open curriculum requires two classes from each of the three academic divisions plus an interdisciplinary course, a writing-intensive course, and significant contact with a culture not one's own. Thirty-one units are required for graduation, each unit representing the equivalent of a course of study involving 4 hours of class time a week per semester. Sophomore students work with their faculty advisers to define academic and personal goals, including completion of graduation requirements and declaration of major, and develop a plan for accomplishing them. A comprehensive academic plan (CAP) allows students to shape their time at Beloit and ensure they will reach their goals.

Off-Campus Arrangements

Beloit has a century-old tradition of domestic and international study opportunities, and more than half of Beloit graduates will have studied and/or conducted research in an off-campus program. Domestic programs include the Oak Ridge National Laboratory, Wilderness Field Station, Chicago Semester in the Arts, Urban Education, Urban Studies, Newberry Library, and the Washington Semester. Internships, field terms, and summer employment opportunities are arranged through the office of Field and Career Services. Anthropology field training programs and geology field expeditions take students to domestic and international locations, and further experiential opportunities exist through Beloit's membership in the Keck Consortium in Geology and the Pew Midstates Science and Mathematics Consortium.

At Beloit College study abroad is more of an expectation than a luxury. Whether through Beloit's own extensive World Outlook Program or the Associated Colleges of the Midwest (ACM) and independent programs, Beloit students have studied in more than thirty countries worldwide, including Australia, Brazil, Cameroon, China, Costa Rica, the Czech Republic, Denmark, Ecuador, England, France, Germany, Greece, Hong Kong, Hungary, India, Indonesia, Ireland, Israel, Italy, Jamaica, Japan, Morocco, Nepal, the Netherlands, Poland, Russia, Scotland, Senegal, South Africa, Tahiti, Tanzania, Thailand, Turkey, and Zimbabwe.

Academic Facilities

Beloit's library collection is in excess of a quarter of a million holdings, which include books, periodicals, government documents, an international center, a science library, and other special collections. There are individual and group study areas, a computer lab, and an extensive listening and viewing area for use of audiovisual materials. The library is connected to a statewide interlibrary loan system, and Beloit students have access to the University of Wisconsin-Madison library. The Logan Museum of Anthropology and the Wright Museum of Art give students unparalleled resources for research and work experience in one of just three museum studies programs in the nation offered to undergraduates. The 110,000-square-foot Science Center houses extensive laboratory facilities and equipment, student office space, and an observatory. Science students also perform research on the College's 25-acre woodland prairie. The Neese Performing Arts Theatre complex features a large thrust stage theater, a black box theater, a scenic design studio, a complete costume shop, and Beloit's cable access television studio. The recently renovated World Affairs Center Language Lab includes eighteen student stations equipped with a multimedia PC and tape deck. An enclosed area is used for viewing international videotapes and TV programs and newscasts taken from the lab's satellite antenna. Nearly 900 student-accessible microcomputers and workstations are located throughout the campus, and every residence hall room, classroom, and office has access to the Internet through the campuswide fiber-optic network.

Costs

Tuition and fees for 2000–01 are $21,550, and room (double) and board are $4882 for the academic year. While the cost of books and incidental expenses varies among students, it is estimated at $1300, which brings the total for the 2000–01 academic year to $27,732.

Financial Aid

Beloit College has a need-blind admissions policy and is committed to making the Beloit experience affordable to all qualified students. The financial aid program recognizes two criteria—scholastic ability and financial need—that may qualify students for awards. During the 1999–2000 academic year, about three quarters of Beloit College students received financial assistance through grants, loans, or work-study. The College also awards merit scholarships. The average need-based financial aid award for the members of the 1999 entering class was $17,433, with an average grant component of $12,977. Beloit's attention to providing students high value has won the College recognition. *U.S. News & World Report* and the *Fiske Guide to Colleges* have rated Beloit as among the nation's "best buys" in top colleges.

Faculty

The focus of Beloit's faculty is great teaching. Beloit professors are drawn to work in a setting that emphasizes discussion and collaborative learning in small classes. Of the 91 full-time faculty members, 97 percent hold the highest academic degree in their field. All classes are taught by professors. In classrooms, students and faculty members become immersed in their work—challenging, examining, and discussing. This is easy to do, as the student-faculty ratio is 11:1, and the average class size is 15 students. All Beloit professors are also academic advisers involved in students' academic concerns as well as their adjustment to life at the College. Discussions begun in the classroom are often continued in the dining hall, in the stands at a basketball game, or over dinner at a professor's house.

Student Government

Students at Beloit are actively involved in the governance of the College. The Beloit Students Advocacy Consortium (BelSAC) is the College's student government. Its committees (Governance Committee, Publicity Committee, Food Committee, Organization Task Force, and Programming Board) allow BelSAC to focus on representing the student body and implementing its goals. In addition to this entirely student-run governing body, students are elected to the College's Academic Senate and serve as voting members of major College committees. Students also sit on all academic search committees.

Admission Requirements

Admission to Beloit is selective. Beloit seeks applicants with special qualities and talents as well as those from diverse ethnic, geographic, and economic backgrounds. When reviewing applications, the transcript is the most important element. Beloit has no absolute secondary school requirements, but recommends a strong college-preparatory program. This includes 4 years of English, 4 years of college-preparatory mathematics, 4 years of laboratory science, 4 years of history or social science, and 4 years of a foreign language. Seventh-semester grades may be required. A counselor recommendation is a required part of the application. Teacher recommendations are optional. The essay component of Beloit's application is critical. There is no required topic, so students should write about a topic they believe will represent them well. Either SAT or ACT test scores are required, but they are the least important part of the application. Interviews are not required for admission but are encouraged. Off-campus alumni interviews can be arranged if a student would like to interview but cannot travel to campus. Transfer applications are considered for August or January entrance. Applicants must hold at least a B-average at an accredited college or university.

Application and Information

Beloit has modified rolling admissions, so students may apply at any time. For priority consideration, both in admissions and in financial aid, however, students should file their applications by February 1. Students who do apply by this date will be mailed notification by early March. Early decision applications are due December 1, with notification December 15. Transfer applications for the fall term are due by May 1, for the spring term by December 1. Notification for transfer applications is rolling. For further information, students should contact:

Admissions Office
Beloit College
700 College Street
Beloit, Wisconsin 53511
Telephone: 608-363-2500
            800-356-0751 (toll-free)
Fax: 608-363-2075
E-mail: admiss@beloit.edu
World Wide Web: http://www.beloit.edu

Middle College, which houses the Admissions Office, is at the center of Beloit's New England–style campus.

BENEDICTINE COLLEGE
ATCHISON, KANSAS

The College

Benedictine College (BC) is a four-year, Catholic, residential, coeducational college that provides an outstanding liberal arts education for students of all backgrounds and faiths. Benedictine is distinguished by its unique Discovery College program that offers students exceptional opportunities for research and personal growth.

The College was established as the result of the 1971 merger of Mount St. Scholastica College (founded in 1924) and St. Benedict's College (founded in 1858). The sponsoring monastic communities of Mount St. Scholastica and St. Benedict's Abbey set the tone for the campus, where the dignity of all individuals is respected. Benedictine College fosters scholarship, independent research, and performance in its students and faculty members as a means of participating in and contributing to the broader world of learning.

Benedictine College is unique in that it offers students—even freshmen and sophomores—the opportunity to collaborate with their professors on significant research projects. Faculty members are strongly encouraged to engage students as partners in collaborative learning projects. With a curriculum that emphasizes exploration, collaboration, problem solving, decision making, and investigative methods, students work one-on-one with instructors to publish and present findings at local, regional, and, in some cases, national academic meetings. This is the nature of America's Discovery College.

Every major offers unique, challenging opportunities to pursue careers outside of the classroom. Biology students may participate in Benedictine's nationally respected Wetlands and Wildlife Restoration Project, where they conduct field studies in a restoration area along the nearby Missouri River. History, business, chemistry, education, political science, and sociology faculty members, as well as others, have authored numerous books and articles, and many faculty members have received major grant funding for their research. The business administration program offers students a rare opportunity to learn to manage and take ownership of small businesses. These and other experiences lead students to become the next generation of managers, teachers, scientists, artists, and caregivers.

Benedictine College is fully accredited by the North Central Association of Colleges and Schools.

The College's ethnically diverse student population exceeds 1,000 students, including students from thirty states and thirteen other countries. Benedictine College does not discriminate on the basis of sex, race, color, religion, or national origin.

At Benedictine College, 3 out of 4 students live on campus. Students find the inviting, spacious residence halls offer convenient on-campus living with friendly, supportive staff members in a secure environment. Benedictine offers many different clubs and student organizations—more than thirty-five—to meet just about every interest, including student government, Students in Free Enterprise (SIFE), departmental clubs, Pax Christi, Amnesty International, Hunger Coalition, Knights of Columbus, Chamber Singers, Hispanic Club, African-American Club, *Loomings* literary magazine, *The Raven* yearbook, and *The Circuit* student newspaper.

The Ravens compete in sixteen varsity intercollegiate sports (NAIA and Heart of America Athletic Conference), with men's teams in baseball, basketball, cross-country, football, golf, soccer, tennis, and track and women's teams in basketball, cross-country, golf, soccer, softball, tennis, track, and volleyball. Benedictine's cheerleading and spirit squads have been recognized nationally. In 1996, the College opened a varsity gymnasium and four tennis courts. A football stadium and outdoor track opened in fall 1998.

Both varsity and nonvarsity athletes can benefit by participating in fifteen intramural activities, including competition in men's and women's corecreational basketball, flag football, soccer, softball, and volleyball. All students are welcome to exercise their bodies and minds at the Student Union, with a gymnasium, athletic training rooms, and plenty of fitness-oriented equipment.

The Student Union features a comfortable 500-seat auditorium for concerts, plays, and lectures and also houses a gymnasium, coffee shop, snack and pizza bar, training and exercise rooms, TV room, student government and campus life offices, a Career Development Center, and plenty of space to relax and meet friends. Benedictine's Career Development Center offers students a variety of information and services to assist them in career preparation. Services include individual counseling, career testing, workshops, and seminars, as well as assistance with graduate and professional school applications, resume writing, interviewing skills, cover-letter writing, and job search strategies. In the natural sciences, 75 percent of graduates continue their education in graduate or professional schools, which is nearly double the national average for liberal arts college graduates. The College's record of acceptance into medical colleges is among the best in the Midwest. The Raven network of Benedictine alumni is a valuable resource for current BC students and new graduates. BC alumni can be found working in such prestigious places as the Federal Reserve Bank, Hallmark Cards, and the Mayo Clinic.

Location

Benedictine College is located on a peaceful, wooded campus in Atchison, Kansas, a picturesque town of 12,000 overlooking the Missouri River. The College is less than 1 hour's drive northwest of Kansas City and only 35 minutes from the Kansas City International Airport. Atchison offers shopping, beautiful parks, and a modern regional hospital across the street from the campus.

Majors and Degrees

Benedictine currently offers the following accredited degrees: Associate of Arts (business administration), Bachelor of Arts, Bachelor of Science, and Bachelor of Music Education. Every field of study at Benedictine College includes the opportunity for collaborative, hands-on training, a dynamic curriculum, internships, and a supportive faculty. The College offers four-year majors in accounting, astronomy, biochemistry, biology, business administration, chemistry, computer science, economics, education (certification, elementary, secondary, special education), English, French, history, mass communications, mathematics, music, music education, music marketing, natural science, philosophy, physical education, physics, political science, psychology, religious studies, sociology, social science, Spanish, theater arts, theater arts management, and youth ministry. In addition, the College offers preprofessional study programs in dentistry, 3-2 engineering, law, medical technology, medicine, nursing, occupational therapy, optometry, pharmacy, physical therapy, and veterinary studies. The College also offers certifications in athletic training and coaching. For those students who want or need the freedom to design a major to their unique interests, the College offers a liberal studies major.

Academic Program

Benedictine College divides its academic year into two semesters and one summer session. The semesters are approximately sixteen weeks long. To earn a bachelor's degree from Benedictine College, a student is required to successfully complete 128 semester credit hours of courses numbered above 100. These courses must include courses specified by the student's major department, a total of 40 credit hours numbered 300 or above, the general education requirements of the College, no more than four independent study courses, and no more than 4 credit hours awarded for internship toward the 128 credit hours.

Students must also achieve a minimum final grade point average of 2.0 in both the major and overall course work at Benedictine, successfully complete a comprehensive or standardized examination in his or her major at a level designated by the faculty, and finish the last two semesters of work in residence. The general education requirements for a bachelor's degree are divided into three categories: core requirements, disciplinary requirements, and proficiency requirements. Benedictine College offers opportunities for advanced placement, the College-Level Examination Program (CLEP), and credit for experiential learning to nontraditional students at least 23 years of age. The College also has a cross-enrollment agreement with Missouri Western State College and its Reserve Officers' Training Corps (ROTC).

Off-Campus Arrangements

Benedictine College sponsors a study-abroad program for students of Spanish in Cuernavaca, Mexico. For French students, the affiliation is with the Catholic University of the West at Angers, France. Benedictine students also can study at the Sorbonne in Paris and at the University of Granada in Spain. Students also may opt to study in China, England, Germany, Ireland, the Netherlands, and Wales.

Academic Facilities

The College enhances every student's educational experience with comprehensive facilities, including modern classrooms, nine science laboratories, and a modern computer network with Internet and e-mail access. The BC library is the designated federal depository for the area's congressional district and houses many rare books, including works on monastic history dating from the fifteenth century. The College also is a member of several library consortia, providing students with access to academic and public libraries locally and around the world. The College's Kansas area network (KANRAN) is one of the most sophisticated in America.

Costs

For 2000–01, tuition and fees are $12,500, room is $2040, and board (twenty meals) is $2750. Other estimated expenses are books, $550; personal expenses, $1200; and travel, $800.

Financial Aid

More than 90 percent of Benedictine students receive some form of financial assistance. Benedictine College annually awards more than $4.5 million in institutional aid and offers a generous number of scholarships based on academic achievement, athletic ability, and other achievements and merits. The College participates in the federal grant, work-study, and loan programs, as well as ROTC and state of Kansas financial aid programs. Benedictine's priority deadline for financial aid consideration is April 1.

Faculty

More than 75 percent of Benedictine College faculty members hold terminal degrees, the highest degree in their fields. With a student-faculty ratio of 14:1, students have greater access to professors, who go out of their way to serve students on a personal level. Students are supported by instructors who are not only respected for their professional achievement but also for their commitment to student development. All Benedictine courses are taught by professors, not graduate or teaching assistants.

Student Government

The Student Government is designed to promote the general welfare of the student body in its academic, social, cultural, and religious needs. The executive officers of the student government and class officers are responsible for formulating and executing student government administrative policy.

Admission Requirements

Applicants must submit scores on the SAT I or ACT and all official high school and/or college transcripts. Sixteen units of college-preparatory work are recommended, including 4 units of English, 3 to 4 units of math, 2 to 4 units of foreign language, 2 to 4 units of natural science, 2 units of social science, and 1 unit of history.

Application and Information

The College employs a rolling admission policy. There is a $25 application fee. For further information or to request an application, students should contact:

Kelly J. Vowels
Dean of Enrollment Management
Benedictine College
1020 North Second Street
Atchison, Kansas 66002
Telephone: 913-367-5340
         800-467-5340 (toll-free)
E-mail: bcadmiss@benedictine.edu
World Wide Web: http://www.benedictine.edu

Benedictine College faculty members understand the importance of a personalized education and are committed to lifelong learning. They prove their concern for students by relating to them on a personal level and collaborating with students in research and curriculum design.

BENEDICTINE UNIVERSITY
LISLE, ILLINOIS

The University
Benedictine University was founded in 1887 as St. Procopius College. One hundred thirteen years later, the University remains committed to providing a high-quality, Catholic, liberal education for men and women. The undergraduate enrollment is 1,750 students. The student body comprises students of diverse ages, religions, races, and national origins. Forty-seven percent of the full-time students reside on campus.

Benedictine University is situated on a rolling, tree-covered 108-acre campus of ten major buildings with air-conditioned classrooms and modern, well-equipped laboratories. A student athletic center features three full-size basketball courts, a competition-size swimming pool, three tennis courts, and training facilities. All of the residence halls are comfortable and spacious, and have access to the Internet. Other features include a scenic campus pond, spacious and well-kept athletic fields, and a student center with dining halls, a game room, lounges, bookstore, and meeting rooms.

At Benedictine University, the environment is strengthened by success, not size. Renowned faculty members know students by name and care as much about each student's progress as they do about their own research. Those personal relationships have produced superb results. Acceptance of Benedictine University graduates to medical, dental, and professional schools is significantly above regional and national averages, and the liberal arts curriculum has helped place the University among some of the finest small private schools in the nation.

Benedictine University is highly competitive in varsity sports. Men's varsity sports are baseball, basketball, cross-country, football, golf, soccer, swimming, tennis, and track. Women's varsity sports are basketball, cross-country, golf, soccer, softball, swimming, tennis, track, and volleyball. Student athletes have been selected as all-Americans in baseball, basketball, football, soccer, softball, swimming, track, and volleyball in recent years. Aside from varsity and intramural athletic programs, a variety of organizations exist, including a newspaper, an orchestra, jazz groups, an African-American Student Union, an Indian Student Union, the Coalition of Latin American Students, campus ministry, a drama club, and various other extracurricular and academic organizations.

The graduate division offers the following graduate degrees in the business, education, and health-care areas: the Doctor of Philosophy degree in organization development; the Master of Business Administration; the Master of Arts in education; the Master of Arts in liberal studies; the Master of Education; the Master of Science in counseling psychology, exercise physiology, fitness management, management and organizational behavior, and management information systems; and the Master of Public Health. Students may register for the "Four Plus One" program, which permits the completion of the master's degree in five years in the following areas: B.S. in health sciences or nutrition and the M.S. in exercise physiology and a B.A. in business with the M.B.A. or the M.S. in management/organizational behavior. The University offers a certificate program through the Institute for Management and a variety of graduate level courses in education offered in cooperation with the Office of the Regional Superintendent of TIDE Schools.

Adult undergraduate accelerated programs, taught by distinguished faculty members, are available in the following areas: accounting (B.B.A.), business and economics (B.A.), computer science (B.S.), health administration (B.B.A.), management and organizational behavior (B.B.A.), nursing and health (degree completion for B.S.N.), organizational leadership (B.A.), and psychology (B.A.).

Location
Benedictine University is 25 miles west of Chicago, in suburban Lisle near Naperville, and is easily accessible from the city and suburbs via the interstate highway system. The Burlington Northern train stops in Lisle, and O'Hare International Airport is only a 30-minute drive away. In addition to the many social and cultural offerings of the Chicago metropolitan area, the University enjoys the proximity and use of Argonne National Laboratory, Fermi National Accelerator Laboratory, the Morton Arboretum, a ski hill, riding stables, and several golf courses. The University's location in the high-tech East-West Tollway corridor gives students opportunities for internships and employment.

Majors and Degrees
Benedictine University offers programs leading to the Bachelor of Arts, Bachelor of Business Administration, and Bachelor of Science degrees. Programs are offered in accounting, arts administration, biochemistry, biology, business and economics, chemistry (concentrations in chemical business and marketing, chemistry, and forensic chemistry), clinical laboratory science, communications (concentrations in advertising, broadcasting, journalism, and publishing), computer science, economics, elementary education, engineering science, English language and literature, environmental science, finance, health science, health administration, history, international business and economics, international studies, management and organizational behavior, marketing, mathematics, molecular biology, music (concentrations in jazz studies and music education), nuclear medicine technology, nursing (completion), nutrition, organizational leadership, philosophy, physics (concentrations in engineering physics and physics), political science, prenursing, psychology, social science, sociology (concentrations in criminal justice, social service, and social work), Spanish, special education (concentration in learning disabilities/social-emotional disorders), and writing and publishing.

In many areas of study, students may opt for a double major. Preprofessional programs include dentistry, engineering, law, medical records administration, medicine, optometry, pharmacy, podiatry, and veterinary medicine. Combined professional programs are available with cooperating institutions in clinical lab science, nuclear medicine technology, engineering, occupational therapy, and physical therapy. A joint engineering program is offered with the Illinois Institute of Technology. A 2-2 nursing program is offered in cooperation with Rush University in Chicago; registered nurses may earn a Bachelor of Science degree in nursing. Secondary education certification is available in the following majors: biology, chemistry, economics and business, English, mathematics, music education, physics, and social science.

Academic Program
For graduation, a student must earn at least 120 semester hours, at least half of which must be completed at a four-year regionally accredited college and at least the final 45 semester hours must be completed at Benedictine University. The University makes selective exceptions to the normal academic residency requirement of 45 semester hours for adults who are eligible for the Degree Completion Program. Eligibility is limited to those who have nearly completed their undergraduate studies, but who, for reasons of employment, career change, or family situation, found it necessary to interrupt their studies.

The Second Major Program is designed for people who already have a degree in one area and would like to gain expertise in another. This program allows the student to concentrate on courses that will fulfill the requirements of a second major. The student receives a certificate upon completion.

Each year, a select number of talented and motivated prospective students are invited to participate in the Scholars Program. The program is designed to enhance the college experience by developing students' international awareness and strengthening their leadership ability.

Off-Campus Arrangements

Benedictine University is a member of a three-school consortium in the west suburban Chicago area through which students are able to take classes at the other member colleges. Study abroad and internships abroad are encouraged to complement a liberal education.

Academic Facilities

The Theodore F. Lownik Library houses 180,000 processed volumes. The library is a member of LIBRAS, a cooperative organization of eighteen college libraries in the Chicago area that makes available more than 2 million volumes and 4,500 periodical titles. Through ILCSO (Illinois Library Computer Systems Organization), Lownik Library has access to approximately 20 million items from other Illinois libraries.

Benedictine University has a distance education classroom that provides students with the capability to interact, globally, with other colleges and universities in a classroom setting.

The Academic Computer Center is equipped with a Sequent Symmetry parallel processing computer, which features forty-eight terminals, four printers, and eight dial-up lines for remote access. Four state-of-the-art DOS-based microcomputer labs are available for private student use. Student residence hall rooms are wired for access to the Sequent computer. Internet access is available from all computer labs.

Costs

The cost of tuition for the 2000–01 academic year is $14,500. The average cost of room and board is $5230. Mandatory fees include the health fee, which is $70, and the student activity fee, which is $130.

Financial Aid

In 1999–2000, Benedictine University freshmen received assistance totaling $3.3 million from sources that included loans, scholarships/grants, tuition remission, and employment opportunities. Almost 93 percent of the freshman class participated, receiving an average package of $11,565. Benedictine University has dedicated more than $5 million of the annual budget to providing grants and scholarships to students, including scholarships for study in the humanities and a separate scholarship program designed to attract and serve minority students. Students who wish to apply for aid must complete the Free Application for Federal Student Aid (FAFSA), the Benedictine University application for financial aid, and the Benedictine University application for admission.

Faculty

An important element of the college experience is the opportunity students have for interaction with faculty members. The 14:1 student-faculty ratio allows for this interaction. Of the 86 full-time faculty members, 92 percent hold the Ph.D. or the terminal professional degree in their respective fields. All students are assigned a faculty member as an adviser to help plan programs of study. Small classes and experienced professionals combine to provide an interactive environment in which students know their professors and true learning can take place.

Student Government

All full-time enrolled students are automatically members of the student government. The Student Government Association (SGA) is a representative body elected annually by the students to represent their interests. The SGA is responsible for the annual allocation of the student activity fee.

Admission Requirements

The Benedictine University admission philosophy is to select students who will perform successfully in the University's academic programs and become active members of the University community. Typically, Benedictine University's freshman students are in the top third of their high school graduating class, with about 50 percent in the top quarter, and report better-than-average ACT or SAT I scores. A minimum of 16 units in academic subjects is required, including 4 units of English, 1 unit of algebra, 1 unit of geometry, 1 unit of history, 1 unit of laboratory science, and 2 units of foreign language. Benedictine University does admit some students who fall below these standards. These applicants receive individual consideration by the Committee on Admission. When appropriate, the committee will place conditions and/or restrictions upon students to help them reach their academic potential.

Students interested in transferring to Benedictine University must have a minimum cumulative average of C (2.0 on a 4.0 scale) from all colleges previously attended. Official transcripts from high school and all colleges attended must be submitted directly to the Office of Admissions for evaluation. If fewer than 20 semester hours of transfer credit are submitted, SAT I or ACT scores are required, and the general admission requirements previously described for incoming freshmen with regard to high school curriculum must also be satisfied. High school information is not required with A.A. or A.S. degrees. Credits to be transferred from other institutions are evaluated on the basis of their equivalent at Benedictine University. Grades of D are accepted as transfer credit but do not satisfy Benedictine University requirements, which demand a minimum grade of C.

Requests for admission are considered without regard to the applicant's race, religion, gender, age, or disability.

Application and Information

Applications are reviewed on a rolling basis. Students are encouraged to apply for admission at any time after completing their junior year of high school. Transfer students may apply for admission during their last semester or quarter before anticipated transfer to Benedictine University. Earlier applications are encouraged.

For further information, students should contact:

Office of Admissions
Benedictine University
5700 College Road
Lisle, Illinois 60532-0900

Telephone: 630-829-6300
Fax: 630-829-6301
E-mail: admissions@ben.edu
World Wide Web: http://www.ben.edu

Benedictine Hall, the administration building, is more than 100 years old.

BENNINGTON COLLEGE
BENNINGTON, VERMONT

The College

Bennington College, a liberal arts college founded in 1932, began as and remains an invitation to learn. Bennington is committed to the belief that teachers should do what they teach and should bring their experience to the classroom. This same spirit continues to animate a faculty of working scientists, writers, scholars, and artists eager to teach, in the words of one, "what keeps them awake at night." Students study literature from published poets, design their own experiments alongside chemists engaged in research, study music with composers recording their own work, and explore international relations with a former diplomat. Faculty members teach both the disciplines they practice, such as science, dance, or architecture, and join together to create courses that study subjects from a combination of different disciplinary perspectives.

Because both students and teachers are actively engaged in the work at hand, the relationship between teacher and student is richly collaborative, more like coach to athlete, mentor to apprentice, and ultimately colleague to colleague than expert to nonexpert. Collaboration between faculty members and students works in both directions: faculty members participating in student work and vice versa.

Each academic year consists of three terms: two intensive fourteen-week on-campus terms during the fall and spring and a six-week winter term of off-campus field work. During the winter term, students take their academic interests to the world beyond the college campus, where they pursue jobs and internships in fields that complement their studies, clarify their interests, and prepare them for their future. Students' written reflections on their work experience, as well as reports written by their employers, become part of their academic profile. The campus career center helps students find meaningful work experiences in areas ranging from publishing to politics and from arts administration to teaching. Students graduate from Bennington with a *curriculum vitae* as well as a diploma.

There are 550 undergraduate and more than 100 graduate students currently enrolled at Bennington. Virtually all undergraduates live in College housing.

On the graduate level, Bennington awards the Master of Arts in Teaching (M.A.T.), Master of Fine Arts (M.F.A.), and Master of Arts in Liberal Studies (M.A.L.S.) degrees. There is a one-year postbaccalaureate program in premedical and allied health sciences for students preparing to apply to medical or allied health sciences graduate schools. Students may enter the M.A.T. program in teaching as undergraduate, transfer, or graduate students.

Location

Bennington's 550-acre campus is nestled among the Green Mountains of southwestern Vermont, less than an hour from Albany and 3½ hours from both New York City and Boston. The central dining room looks out over the "edge of the world," a wide commons stretching toward distant mountains, bordered by the whitewashed colonial houses that serve as dormitories. Wooded walking paths link the buildings on campus and lead to a pond, clay tennis courts, soccer fields, and a College-run organic farm.

The region surrounding the College is renowned for its outdoor activities, including hiking, rock climbing, downhill and cross-country skiing, and canoeing.

Majors and Degrees

Students can pursue interests in all of the traditional academic disciplines within the liberal arts (e.g., history, literature, mathematics, philosophy, science, social science) and in the visual and performing arts (architecture, ceramics, classical and jazz music, computer graphics, dance, drama, painting, and sculpture). In addition, Bennington now offers a five-year bachelor's/master's degree in teaching. Graduates of this program are certified in early childhood, elementary, or secondary education and earn a license to teach in the state of Vermont. The degree is recognized in thirty-seven other states, including New York, California, and Massachusetts. Students may apply to this program after their freshman year.

Bennington's faculty members are more committed to providing students with resources for a life of independent thought and self-education than they are with designing majors. From their perspective, a genuine education is actively created rather than passively received. Throughout their education at Bennington, students are challenged to pursue questions and interests that matter to them and are taught the ability to pursue those questions wherever they may lead. It is not presumed that a student's progress need be the progressive elimination of all but one interest called the major; on the contrary, it is presumed that a student may well choose to explore a diverse range of disciplines in depth. Over the four-year period, students continually discuss with their faculty adviser and in writing what courses they intend to take and the reasons why. In these evolving statements of purpose, students design, chart, and argue their course of study. This individualized statement, called the "plan," replaces the traditional major. Student plans are presented at regular intervals to panels of faculty members for further discussion and review.

By taking an active role in crafting their own education, students learn what it takes to discover an intellectual identity and to pursue it. They learn to replace imposed discipline with self-discipline and to deal with a world where the requirements are imposed from within rather than from without. In the process of their education, every Bennington student must individually confront the question, "What is a real education?"

Academic Programs

The programs of study that students design with their advisers are conceived more in the shape of an hourglass (starting broad, then focusing, then broadening again) than in the traditional pyramid structure with its progressive narrowing of focus. During their first year, students explore a wide range of possibilities, investigating the diverse forms of intellectual and imaginative life. In their second and third years, they increasingly immerse themselves in particular subjects, whether in the form of a craft, a discipline, or a question. In their final year, students look outward, extending and deepening the relevance of their own work through connecting it to the work of others and to the world at large. In this final year, students are also encouraged, once again, to explore new, emerging interests.

Faculty members regularly evaluate student performances through written reports that assess academic strengths and weakness, identify areas needing further work, and analyze overall progress.

Bennington also sponsors the July Program, an intensive precollege experience for high school students that offers more than forty liberal arts courses. College credit is available.

Off-Campus Arrangements

The winter term at Bennington requires students to spend seven weeks each year working off-campus in jobs or internships relating to their academic and career interests.

Bennington is a charter member of a consortium associated with The School for Field Studies (SFS). This program offers access to courses in field biology on five continents, providing hands-on education that addresses the world's most critical environmental issues. Bennington's affiliation gives students the opportunity to incorporate SFS courses into the fulfillment of degree requirements.

Through collaborations with a number of other institutions, Bennington offers students a range of options for study abroad. These programs carry academic credit.

Academic Facilities

Most of the classrooms at Bennington are arranged for seminar-style discussions and typically seat 15 to 20 students around a central table. In addition, classes are sometimes held in the campus café or in dormitory common rooms. Faculty members have offices throughout the campus where they meet regularly with students to discuss their work outside of class. The Dickinson Science Building includes fully equipped science labs, a computer center with audio/video digitizing and processing capabilities, and a language lab. The 120,000-square-foot Visual and Performing Arts Center (VAPA) contains three "black box" theaters with state-of-the-art technical support, the Usdan Art Gallery, and studios for music, dance, video, painting, architecture, ceramics, sculpture, printmaking, and photography. Bennington also houses one of the largest sprung wood floors in the world, especially designed for dance performance. Most facilities in VAPA are available for student use 24 hours a day.

New technologies play a central role in facilitating the dynamic relationships between diverse disciplines and between faculty members and student that define the College. Bennington's Center for Audio Technologies consolidates all campus music/audio technology; facilities include an electronic music studio, a computer instructional studio, a language laboratory that uses both existing technologies and creates new ones for the study of foreign language and culture, a digital audio studio, and a lab equipped for the production of graphics, computer art, and multimedia projects. Architecture and design programs are enhanced by computer-aided design (CAD). All dorm rooms are wired for Internet access. Notwithstanding the range of such resources, students and faculty members at Bennington are continually reminded that technologies, new and old, are designed to enhance the creative imagination, as opposed to replacing it.

A College-run farm provides a laboratory for exploring the science, economics, and community development dimensions of organic farming.

Costs

For 1999–2000, total charges were $28,150 (including the health service charge). Bennington estimates that students will need an additional $2000 to cover personal expenses, excluding travel.

Financial Aid

Approximately 80 percent of Bennington students receive financial assistance in some form: need- and merit-based awards, College and federal grant funds, work-study programs, and student and parental loans.

Faculty

Because of its tradition of having a faculty of teacher-practitioners, Bennington faculty members are active artists, writers, and scholars. The student-faculty ratio is currently 7:1. All faculty members teach first-year as well as advanced students.

Student Government

The responsibility students assume in planning a course of study extends to life outside the classroom. Bennington treats the idea and the ideals of self-governance very seriously. Students are expected to discover the balance between freedom and responsibility and to do so by meeting the challenges of self-governance in their academic and nonacademic lives.

Admission Requirements

Bennington looks for students who are alive to the possibilities of what a college education might be and whose passionate curiosity is matched by a capacity for self-discipline. While all parts of each student's application are considered with great care—essays, recommendations, transcripts, class rankings, test scores—the admissions interview is treated with particular seriousness. There are no formulas by which admissions decisions are calculated.

SAT I and ACT scores are required.

Students interested in early admission may apply for admission prior to the completion of high school. Transfer students are accepted for enrollment in the fall and spring terms.

Application and Information

The deadline for freshman applications is January 1; for transfer applications, the deadlines are January 1 (for the spring term) and March 1 (for the fall term). The early decision deadline is November 15, with notifications by December 1. Financial aid applicants should file appropriate financial statements as soon as possible and no later than March 1.

For more information about Bennington College, students should contact:

Office of Admissions and the First Year
Bennington College
Bennington, Vermont 05201
Telephone: 802-440-4312
          800-833-6845 (toll free)
Fax: 802-440-4320
E-mail: admissions@bennington.edu
World Wide Web: http://www.bennington.edu

A student sits behind a state-of-the-art sound board in Jennings Hall mixing down one of his latest compositions.

Peterson's Guide to Four-Year Colleges 2001   www.petersons.com

BENTLEY COLLEGE
WALTHAM, MASSACHUSETTS

The College

Bentley College is committed to providing the most advanced business education possible. Delivered in a stimulating and close-knit campus environment, programs address the evolving needs of business, with an emphasis on theory and practice. Students gain the knowledge, skills, and experience necessary to make meaningful contributions to their careers and community. Concepts and theories that students learn in the classroom come alive in several hands-on, high-tech learning laboratories—each among the first of its kind in higher education.

Students at Bentley study all business disciplines and gain a solid understanding of the latest computer technologies and the ways that businesses use these tools. Students develop the critical ability to manage and analyze the nearly limitless amount of information that drives the business world. Through course work, internships, jobs, campus activities, and study-abroad opportunities, students acquire the communication, teamwork, and leadership skills necessary for career success in today's global economy.

The largest business school in New England, Bentley has an undergraduate population of approximately 4,200 students; nearly half come from communities outside Massachusetts. About 10 percent are international students representing close to seventy countries. Seven out of 10 students live on campus. On-campus housing includes nine residence halls and thirteen apartment-style buildings, all located close to campus activities. Students choose from single-, double-, or triple-occupancy dorm rooms; apartments; or suites.

On-campus activities include a wide range of athletic events, music and theater programs, and more than ninety clubs and student organizations. The Dana Athletic Center features an indoor track, volleyball and racquetball courts, a competition-size indoor pool and diving tank, a weight room, and other facilities. College athletic facilities also include lighted tennis courts and four athletic fields.

An NCAA Division II institution, Bentley is a member of the Northeast-10 Conference, the Eastern Football Conference, and the Division I Metro Atlantic Athletic Conference Hockey League. The College fields eleven varsity teams for men and eleven for women, with teams and individual players routinely qualifying for postseason competition. Students may also take part in intramural sports such as floor hockey and flag football and in recreational activities that include aerobics and fitness training.

Location

With its beautiful landscaping and attractive buildings, the College represents the best of New England college campuses and provides an inviting atmosphere for study and socializing. Located in Waltham, Massachusetts, just 10 miles west of Boston, Bentley's 163-acre suburban campus puts the city's many resources within easy reach. Boston is the country's ultimate college town. From theater to art exhibits, dance clubs to alternative rock concerts, championship sports to championship shopping, Boston has the proverbial "something for everyone." Students do not need a car to get around. The Bentley shuttle makes regular trips to Harvard Square in Cambridge—a great location that is just a short subway ride from Boston.

Majors and Degrees

A strong curriculum focusing on business, people, and technology provides students with many options for shaping an academic program that fits their skills, interests, and career goals. Bachelor of Science degree programs enable students to specialize in a specific business discipline: accountancy, accounting information systems, business communication, computer information systems, economics-finance, finance, management, managerial economics, marketing, and mathematical sciences. Bentley also offers Bachelor of Arts (B.A.) degree programs, with majors in English, history, international culture and economy, liberal arts, and philosophy. Students may also receive a B.A. in mathematics or design their own arts and sciences concentration in areas such as behavioral sciences, communication, or environmental studies.

Minors and concentration programs give students the opportunity to develop expertise in an area outside their major. A marketing major interested in public relations might choose a minor in English, for example, while an accountancy major thinking about a legal or public service career could minor in law. Bentley also has a number of special programs, including those through which students can earn a bachelor's degree and a master's degree in five years.

Academic Program

Known for its distinctive programs at the intersection of business and technology, Bentley offers more than impressive computer resources alone. Here, students learn to use information technology the way business does, as an important tool for planning, producing, marketing, and managing.

The integration of technology into the academic program stretches back more than fifteen years, when Bentley, which was established in 1917, became one of the first colleges in the U.S. to require students to have personal computers. Today, laptops are required for many Bentley courses, with most offering online access to syllabi, discussion groups, course assignments, and other materials. A growing communication network gives students access to the library catalog, centralized computing facilities, e-mail, and the Internet from their campus residences. E-Campus, Bentley's internal computer network, offers an online directory of students and faculty and staff members, the latest word on Bentley news and events, and other useful information for the campus community.

Hands-on experience is another key element of Bentley's academic program. Internships, group consulting projects, service-learning assignments, and other opportunities allow students to apply classroom theory in the real worlds of workplace and community.

Each year, through the Bentley Service-Learning Center, hundreds of students develop their business skills while taking part in projects as diverse as offering tax assistance to area residents and helping immigrants apply for citizenship. The service-learning program has been recognized for leadership in the field of student character development in *The Templeton Guide*, which states, "Bentley's strong commitment to character development and the strength of its program make it a model for colleges and universities nationwide."

Bentley offers an internship program through which students earn course credit toward their degrees and gain valuable work experience in their field of study. There are many internship and career resources in Boston, which makes the city a valuable learning lab for Bentley students. Students have held internship positions in organizations such as IBM, Reebok International, Big Five accounting firms, and Hewlett-Packard.

Close to 96 percent of Bentley students find employment within six months of graduation. The Office of Career Services offers comprehensive programs to help students explore careers, develop contacts, and find employment. Resources include an on-campus recruiting program involving some 250 national and international companies, an online job-listing service available to Bentley students and alumni, an online database of student and alumni resumes, career fairs, and workshops on topics such as effective resume writing, interviewing, and job search strategies.

Off-Campus Arrangements

Through the Joseph M. Cronin International Center, Bentley offers study-abroad programs in various countries, including Australia, Belgium, England, Estonia, France, Japan, Mexico, and Spain. Students may study abroad during the fall, spring, or summer term or for an entire year. Through a cross-registration program, students may enroll at nearby Brandeis University, Regis College, or the Wentworth Institute of Technology to take courses not currently offered at Bentley.

Academic Facilities

Bentley College prepares students to meet the new demands of an information-rich, technology-driven workplace through a business curriculum that integrates technology at every level. Supporting this curriculum is an array of academic resources, including classrooms equipped with multimedia computers and display technology, student computer laboratories with both IBM-compatible and Macintosh computers, and a Virtual Lab that offers online access to specialized software for courses.

Combining state-of-the-art technology and real-time data, the financial Trading Room is a virtual laboratory of world financial markets. The Trading Room offers firsthand exposure to financial concepts such as risk management and asset valuation. Students gain skills and expertise through Trading Room resources that include Reuters 2000 and 3000 products, Market Guide, Bridge, First Call, and Bloomberg.

The Marketing Technologies Showcase is a "best practices" center for studying the forces that drive buying and selling in an increasingly global, electronic economy. A range of high-end applications exposes students to the latest innovations in marketing. Equipped with powerful, networked desktop PCs and an array of specialized software, the showcase is an integral part of information-age marketing programs at Bentley.

The Accounting Center for Electronic Learning and Business Measurement (ACELAB) introduces students to the cutting-edge tools and technologies that have reshaped the profession of accounting. ACELAB resources foster the knowledge and skills needed for tasks such as developing an accounting system and analyzing operational data for management decision making.

Information design programs at Bentley College center on creating IT products and processes that users can intuitively understand and easily employ. The technological hub of these programs is the Design and Usability Testing Center, which offers outstanding up-close exposure to the field. The Design and Usability Testing Center puts into students' hands the same applications employed by technical communicators, Web developers, user interface designers, and usability specialists.

The Solomon R. Baker Library supports Bentley's curriculum with resources that include approximately 200,000 books and journals, 8,000 periodical subscriptions, an extensive collection of annual and 10K reports, and access to electronic databases such as LEXIS-NEXIS, WESTLAW, OCLC, Dialog, and Infotrac 2000. Videoconference equipment is also available in the library.

Costs

Tuition for both resident and nonresident students for the 2000–01 academic year is $18,795. Room and board costs are approximately $8600 (double room, thirteen-meal plan). Additional costs include books, supplies, a laptop computer, and personal and travel expenses.

Financial Aid

Bentley administers more than $36 million in undergraduate financial assistance every year, on the premise that no academically qualified student should have educational choices restricted by lack of financial resources. Bentley offers financial assistance in the form of scholarships, grants, loans, employment, and payment plans. Currently, 7 out of 10 Bentley undergraduates receive some form of financial assistance.

Faculty

Bentley has about 380 full- and part-time faculty members; 82 percent of full-time professors hold doctoral degrees. Following the teacher-scholar model, classes are not taught by teaching assistants or graduate assistants. The average class size is 25 to 30 students. A number of Bentley faculty members are consultants to leading local, national, and international corporations, ensuring students' perspectives on current practices and future directions in key business fields. The student-faculty ratio is 16:1.

Student Government

Bentley has a number of student governing organizations, including the Student Government Association, Senior Class Cabinet, Greek Council, Hall Council Advisory Board, Media Board, Panhellenic Council, and the Graduate Student Association.

Admission Requirements

Students applying for admission to the College are encouraged to complete a solid college-preparatory program. Bentley suggests that this program include 4 years of English, 4 years of mathematics (preferably algebra I and II, geometry, and a senior-year math course), and 3 to 4 years each of history, laboratory science, and foreign language.

Along with the application, students must submit a secondary school transcript, letters of recommendation from a teacher and a counselor, and official results of either the SAT or ACT test. All international students must file an international student application. Applicants who are nonnative speakers of English must also have official results of the Test of English as a Foreign Language (TOEFL) forwarded to the Office of Undergraduate Admission.

Application and Information

The application deadline for students planning to enter in September is February 1. For students planning to enter in January, the deadline is November 15. Candidates for the fall semester are notified by April 1; spring semester candidates are notified by December 5.

Students who have selected Bentley College as their first choice may apply as candidates for early decision. The Early Decision Program is for freshmen who have shown excellent academic achievement and would like to find out early about admission and financial aid. Candidates participating in this program agree that if an offer of admission into Bentley is extended, they will withdraw any applications that have been made to other colleges. Students may also participate in the Early Action Program. This program is for students who would like an early answer about admission but would prefer to keep their options open. The application deadline for both programs is December 1. Bentley College also accepts the Common Application.

For additional information, students should contact:

Office of Undergraduate Admission
Bentley College
175 Forest Street
Waltham, Massachusetts 02452-4705
Telephone: 781-891-2244
                800-523-2354 (toll-free)
Fax: 781-891-3414
E-mail: ugadmission@bentley.edu
World Wide Web: http://www.bentley.edu

BEREA COLLEGE
BEREA, KENTUCKY

The College

Berea College dates its founding to 1855 when a group of abolitionists established a racially integrated one-room school that was based on the biblical maxim "God has made of one blood all peoples of the earth." For the next fifty years, Berea was a monument to racial harmony and equality. Although Kentucky law prevented integration of the student body from 1904–1950, Berea College has a long and distinguished history of interracial education. Among the African-American students who attended Berea during its early days were Dr. Carter G. Woodson, founder of Black History Month, and Julia Britton Hooks, a musician who taught W. C. Handy and whose grandson, Dr. Benjamin Hooks, was the Executive Director of the NAACP for many years. Currently, 25 percent of Berea's 1,500 students are minorities. African American, international, and dual national students make up a large percentage of those students.

Always at the top of its category in national rankings of colleges, Berea was ranked the number one liberal arts college in the South in 1999 by *U.S. News & World Report*. Among the special programs that contribute to the strength of Berea's academic program are the summer research opportunities available in biology, chemistry, and physics; the Term Abroad for language majors; the ceramics apprenticeship program; the January Short Term; and the field study opportunities available in all departments. In recent years, Berea students have received national scholarship awards, including several Watson scholarships, a Truman scholarship, and a Fulbright scholarship. One of the most unusual features of the College is a student work program, which requires all students to work on campus a minimum of 10 hours per week. The work program not only provides a way for students to earn part of their college expenses, but also provides excellent work-learning experiences that enable them to gain valuable on-the-job training.

Berea students find ample opportunities for physical, cultural, and spiritual growth as well. Men and women participate in eight intercollegiate sports each: both participate in basketball, cross-country, soccer, swimming, tennis, and track; men in baseball and golf; and women in softball and volleyball. Berea has produced several All-Americans in basketball, cross-country, and track and field, most recently crowning a national champion in track. Berea has also visited the the NCAA Division II men's basketball tournament, placing in the "Final Four" in 1999. About 75 percent of the men and 50 percent of the women at Berea participate in one or more intramural sports. The Seabury Center, opened in 1995, is a physical education, athletic, recreation, and convocation facility housing two basketball courts, an indoor pool, racquetball courts, an indoor track, weight room, wellness center, and a multipurpose events forum.

The Berea College Concert Choir, the Black Music Ensemble, and the concert, stage, and brass bands provide many performance opportunities for students with an interest in music. The Berea College Country Dancers is a popular performance group that specializes in traditional Appalachian dance and folklore. The Theatre Laboratory presents three or four major productions each year and features a theater artist-in-residence for at least one term each year. The art department has excellent gallery space for the exhibition of work by students, faculty members, and guest artists. Worship opportunities and Christian outreach programs are coordinated by the Campus Christian Center, and Berea students take an active role in the congregations of many local churches. Service is an important dimension of the program at Berea, and many students participate in the organization Students for Appalachia, which provides a variety of services for surrounding communities, including tutoring and adult education. In recent years, several Berea students have received national recognition for their work with SFA.

Nontraditional students make up about 15 percent of Berea's student body. The majority of Berea's students live on campus in sixteen residence halls and a variety of theme houses. Berea also offers many family housing units including several units that accommodate single parents and their children.

Location

Berea is a small city of approximately 10,000 located about 35 miles south of Lexington, Kentucky, the second-largest city in the commonwealth, with a population of more than a quarter of a million. Berea is located on the edge of the Cumberland Mountains and has been described as "where the mountains meet the bluegrass."

Majors and Degrees

Berea College confers the degrees of Bachelor of Arts and Bachelor of Science. Majors are available in agriculture and natural resources, art, biology, business administration, chemistry, child and family studies, classical languages, economics, elementary education, English, French, German, history, mathematics, music, nursing, philosophy, physical education, physics, political science, psychology, religion, sociology, Spanish, technology and industrial arts, and theater. Berea also provides preprofessional preparation for programs of medicine, dentistry, physical therapy, veterinary medicine, law, and engineering.

The College offers dual-degree programs in engineering with the University of Kentucky and Washington University in St. Louis, Missouri. This program of study leads to a Bachelor of Arts degree from Berea College and a Bachelor of Science degree in engineering from either the University of Kentucky or Washington University.

Academic Program

Berea operates on a 4-1-4 calendar. Students normally take four courses in the four-month fall term, one course in the January term, and four courses in the spring term. In all degree programs except nursing, a minimum of thirty-three courses is needed to graduate; nursing requires thirty-five courses. The courses taken must satisfy all general education, major, and major-related requirements.

Most courses in the General Education Program have a strong emphasis on cross-disciplinary learning. Some courses are arranged in sequences, with one course establishing a foundation for the next one. Such courses are taken in the prescribed order; others may be taken at a time of the student's choosing. Courses in the General Education Program include Stories: Encountering Others through Literature; U.S. Traditions: Texts of Freedom and Justice; Introduction to Lifetime Wellness; Introduction to the Arts; Western Traditions I and II; Seminar in

World Issues Since 1945; Seminar in Christianity and Contemporary Culture; an introductory course in the natural sciences; an introductory course in the social sciences; The Arts in Context; Natural Science; and the cultural area requirement. The cultural area requirement may be met by taking two courses in a foreign language or by taking two courses from Appalachian studies, Black studies, or world cultures.

Students may be granted college credit for achieving a score of 4 or 5 on AP tests. Advanced standing in foreign language is also available to qualifying students. Further detailed information is available from the College.

Off-Campus Arrangements

Berea encourages all students to take advantage of study abroad opportunities by providing substantial financial aid to qualifying students. The Berea Term Abroad Program grants up to $8000 for associated costs. Recently, students have traveled to El Salvador, Mexico, France, Denmark, Greece, Austria, Iceland, Germany, Spain, Australia, India, the United Kingdom, Nicaragua, Bolivia, the Czech Republic, Guatemala and other interesting places.

Academic Facilities

The Hutchins Library houses both the library's collections and services as well as the Computer Center. The library has more than 300,000 volumes and subscribes to approximately 1,300 current periodicals. The Charles Martin Hall Science Building, totally renovated in 1986, provides up-to-date classrooms, state-of-the-art laboratory space, and a planetarium. The Jelkyl Drama Center offers excellent facilities for the active theater program. The Draper Building, built in 1938, is the largest classroom facility on campus.

Costs

The College awards a full tuition scholarship, currently worth $16,600 per year, to every admitted student. Fees for 1998–99 are $200. Room and board cost $3871. Most students are eligible for additional financial aid, which brings the average first-year cost to about $1000. Many freshmen can pay all room and board costs from participation in the College's work program.

Financial Aid

All students accepted to attend Berea College are awarded financial aid based on need. The College assures that each student's need, as determined through a needs analysis process, is met. This is accomplished through a combination of the student's and family's resources, the College's work program, public and private grants and scholarships, and a College grant or loan for any remaining need.

Faculty

Berea has 118 full-time faculty members, 91 percent of whom hold doctorates or appropriate terminal degrees, and 37 part-time faculty members. The student-faculty ratio is 11:1.

While professors consider teaching to be their first priority, they also find time to pursue their own scholarly work. Students are often involved in research. This sometimes leads to joint publications or presentations at professional meetings.

Student Government

The Student Government Association (SGA) oversees campus elections, provides student services, and maintains a loan fund and accident fund. The SGA also works closely with clubs and organizations on campus and helps select representatives to serve on various committees, including College faculty committees, which help govern the student community.

Admission Requirements

Admission is limited to students whose families would have a difficult time financing a college education without assistance. Eligibility for admission from a need standpoint is determined by Berea's Family Resource Questionnaire or the expected parental contribution computed from the Free Application for Federal Student Aid.

Since Berea's academic program is a challenging one, most successful applicants to the College in recent years have scored between 20 and 30 on the ACT and between 930 and 1350 on the SAT I tests and have ranked in the top 20 percent of their high school class. Preference in admission is given to students living in the Appalachian region of the United States, but 30 percent come from other parts of the United States and the rest of the world.

Application and Information

The College operates on a rolling admissions basis, and decisions are made as files become complete. Berea has a limited number of spaces for new students each year. Qualified early applicants for the fall term are more likely to gain admission if they complete the application process prior to November 30. The freshman and transfer class is usually filled by May 1. A limited number of spaces are available for students who wish to enter in the spring term beginning in February. Applications for the spring term should be submitted by November 15. International students may apply for the fall semester only. International applications are due March 1.

The Admissions Office is open from 8 a.m. to 5 p.m. on weekdays and from 8 a.m. until noon on Saturdays. For further information, a campus tour and interview, or an application form, prospective students should contact:

Office of Admissions
Berea College
CPO 2220
Berea, Kentucky 40404
Telephone: 606-985-3500
          800-326-5948 (toll-free)
E-mail: admissions@berea.edu
World Wide Web: http://www.berea.edu

A laboratory class at the Hall Science Building.

BERKELEY COLLEGE

NEW YORK CITY AND WHITE PLAINS, NEW YORK

The College

Established in 1931, Berkeley College's emphasis on providing students of all generations with a high-quality education has never changed. Berkeley draws its strength from balancing academic preparation, professional training, and hands-on experience. Since its inception, the College has evolved and expanded to be recognized as a premier educator in preparing men and women for careers in business.

The Commission on Higher Education of the Middle States Association of Colleges and Schools accredits all campuses. The New York City and Westchester campuses are authorized by the New York State Board of Regents to confer the degrees of Bachelor of Business Administration, Associate in Science, and Associate in Applied Science, and their programs are registered by the New York State Education Department. The American Bar Association (ABA) approves the paralegal studies programs at all campuses.

Berkeley's total enrollment of nearly 4,200 students at all five campuses includes day and evening and full- and part-time students who represent fifty other countries. Berkeley's commitment to excellence constitutes the primary objective of the College. Small classes, individualized advisement and counseling, and the development of the students' creative and analytical skills support this commitment. Because Berkeley believes that teaching should encompass both conceptual and practical perspectives, faculty members are selected for their academic credentials and professional experience. Their experience in business brings an added intellectual reality to the classroom, resulting in a challenging and stimulating learning environment.

Berkeley also offers a number of organizations, clubs, and activities that are designed to meet the educational, cultural, and social needs and interests of students. There are a number of on-campus clubs that plan special events for social as well as personal growth. The Westchester campus provides residence facilities. In New York City, housing is available in nearby student residences or in apartments throughout the city.

Berkeley's full-service placement division has 25 placement advisers who specialize in each major field of study. Berkeley's placement professionals work with students to identify career options, set up and place students in internship positions, develop and refine resume and interviewing skills, and schedule interviews. Berkeley's placement specialists continue to be available to Berkeley graduates throughout their careers.

Location

Berkeley College is comprised of five diverse locations, giving students the choices and opportunities of both urban and suburban campuses. The two New York locations range from the ultimate urban to the suburban/country setting. The New York City campus, in the heart of Manhattan's East Side next to Grand Central Station, is for students who want to take advantage of the total metropolitan experience. Many international students attend the Westchester campus because they enjoy the intimacy of residential living in a country setting. Located on 10 acres of wooded serenity on the border of White Plains, the campus allows students to enjoy the complete college experience.

Majors and Degrees

Bachelor of Business Administration degree programs are offered in accounting, e-business, general business, international business, management, marketing, and office systems management. Associate degree programs are offered in business administration, with specializations in accounting, management, marketing, and office systems management. Associate degree programs also include e-business, fashion marketing and management, interior design, international business, and paralegal studies.

Academic Program

Berkeley College specializes in offering a superior value in higher education, with programs that balance traditional academic preparation with professional training and hands-on experience. These programs are designed to deliver the type of knowledge and skills that employers are looking for and include working experience in the area of the student's interest. The programs are flexible yet concentrated, supplying an essential foundation for moving to a higher level in a current job or for launching a successful new career. Last year, 95 percent of all graduates available for placement were employed in positions related to their studies at Berkeley College.

Ongoing academic advisement, as well as peer and faculty tutoring, are also provided. Instructors are available for tutoring on a schedule that the Academic Resource Center and Learning Labs make available at the beginning of each quarter.

Academic advisers can explore the following options with students: credit for acceptable scores on national standardized examinations, including Advanced Placement exams (sponsored by the College Board), the College-Level Examination Program (CLEP), and the ACT Proficiency Examination Program, and professional certification exams in the American Council on Education (ACE) exam guide.

Berkeley grants credit as recommended by standard assessment guides, including the national Program on Non-Collegiate Sponsored Instruction (PONSI), the ACE, and the Defense Activity for Non-Traditional Education Support (DANTES). Berkeley also assesses possible credit awards for portfolios. This procedure requires the submission of a well-written and fully documented experiential learning portfolio for faculty evaluation.

Off-Campus Arrangements

Berkeley's study-abroad offerings overseas provide exciting opportunities for students to experience an internationalized program of study. Since the College is validated (accredited) in the United Kingdom, Berkeley students have the unique opportunity to complete a British B.A. (Honours) degree at the prestigious Regent's Business School in London or to spend a quarter studying overseas in a study-abroad program in one of the affiliated campuses in Geneva, Leiden (the Netherlands), London, or Vienna, including the well-known European Business School in London.

Berkeley's degree programs provide the best balance of academics and important application of this learning directly in the students' chosen fields via an internship experience. By enhancing their education with a professional internship,

Berkeley students gain valuable work experience and a network of important business contacts before they graduate.

Academic Facilities

Berkeley College's extensive and powerful technology infrastructure supports academic study at the undergraduate level. Each campus has its own library, with an online public access catalog that provides local and remote access to 58,400 electronic databases, Internet access, 700 periodical subscriptions, and an audiovisual collection of 6,940 items. Each library provides a variety of services, including reference materials, group instruction, and orientations.

Costs

In 2000–01, day students pay $12,585 per year for tuition. Berkeley also makes the unusual promise to students of protecting them from any tuition increase as long as they maintain continuous full-time enrollment. Boarding students pay an additional residence fee of $4500 and a meal plan fee of $3600 (seventeen meals weekly) or $3300 (fifteen meals weekly). Students at Berkeley's New York City campus are housed at Sussex House, a newly renovated eight-story building located on the edge of Times Square. It is only five blocks from the College's Academic Center. A wide variety of residence options are available at Sussex House.

Financial Aid

Because the College administration believes that no one should be denied a Berkeley education for lack of funds and that students may need to supplement their own resources to meet college costs, a wide variety of financial assistance programs and financing options are offered.

Faculty

Largely, the character and competence of the faculty members determine the success of any educational program. Berkeley's instructors are chosen for their professional experience as well as for their academic credentials. Several of Berkeley's administrators are nationally recognized leaders in business education, authors, lecturers, and consultants.

Student Government

All students are members of the Student Government Association (SGA). Elected SGA officers meet regularly and act as a liaison between students and administration concerning social and academic matters. Students often take advantage of the open-door policy.

Students also participate in the College's governance by serving on the Faculty Association's Learning Resources and Student Affairs Committees. Participation provides students with both experience and training in responsible leadership. The SGA serves in an advisory capacity in the planning of campus activities and events. Activities include, but are not limited to, picnics, ski weekends, theater parties, charity drives, and dude ranch weekends.

Admission Requirements

Basic requirements for admission to Berkeley College include graduation from an accredited high school or equivalent and an entrance exam or SAT I/ACT scores. A personal interview is strongly recommended. The following credentials must be submitted as part of the application process: a completed application form, a nonrefundable $35 application fee, and an unofficial transcript (for currently enrolled high school students) or a high school diploma or its equivalent (for high school graduates). Students who graduated from an accredited high school or its equivalent and then attended a college or university are considered transfer students. To be considered for admission, transfer students must submit an application for admission and the nonrefundable $35 application fee, a transcript from each college or university attended, and a high school transcript or GED. For all students, applications are accepted after credentials are received.

To be admitted directly to the upper division, students must have completed either a relevant associate degree or at least 60 semester/90 quarter credits in appropriate course work with a grade of C or better at Berkeley or another regionally accredited institution.

Application and Information

Applications are accepted on an ongoing basis. All prospective students should contact the Director of Admissions at the Berkeley College campus most convenient to them.

Director of Admissions
New York City Campus
Berkeley College
3 East 43rd Street
New York, New York 10017
Telephone: 212-986-4343
        800-446-5400 (toll-free)
Fax: 212-697-3371
E-mail: info@berkeleycollege.edu
World Wide Web: http://www.berkeleycollege.edu

Director of Admissions
Westchester Campus
Berkeley College
40 West Red Oak Lane
White Plains, New York 10604
Telephone: 914-694-1122
        800-446-5400 (toll-free)
Fax: 914-694-5832

BERKLEE COLLEGE OF MUSIC
BOSTON, MASSACHUSETTS

The College
Founded in 1945, Berklee College of Music is the world's largest independent music college and the premier institution for the study of contemporary music. The College's nearly 3,000 students and more than 350 faculty members interact in an environment designed to provide the most complete learning experience possible, including all of the opportunities and challenges presented by a career in the contemporary music industry. Using Berklee's extensive facilities, students develop musical competencies in such areas as composition, performance, and recording/production and also learn to make the informed business decisions necessary to career success.

Since the College's inception, one of its primary goals has been to foster international understanding through the medium of contemporary music. Young musicians come to Berklee from every corner of the earth to study popular music, and, as a result, Berklee is a uniquely international college.

At the graduate level, Berklee collaborates with the Boston Conservatory to offer the Master of Music in jazz studies degree. Students may concentrate on composition, pedagogy, or performance.

In addition to the curriculum, a student will find a complete schedule of student events and organizations. The Student Organizations and Activities Program (SOAP) sponsors more than sixty groups and clubs in which students can debate politics, take part in community service, explore spirituality, or join an international club or an intramural sports team. Throughout the year, SOAP sponsors special events such as movies, parties, dances, and special interest workshops.

Location
Berklee College of Music is located in Boston's historic Back Bay. An international hub of intellectual and creative exploration, the neighborhood includes treasure-filled museums and galleries and world-class performing arts centers such as Symphony Hall, the Wang Center, and the Berklee Performance Center. Boston is also home to many of the world's other great colleges and universities. In addition to the music made at Berklee, there is a lively club and concert scene in the area with coffee houses featuring folk and bluegrass music; neighborhood clubs offering jazz, reggae, and world music; and clubs specializing in alternative rock, blues, dance, and country-western music.

Berklee students participate in intramural sports and fitness programs at nearby institutions; watch Boston's professional sports teams play in the Fleet Center or at Fenway Park or other area sports venues; attend theater, club, and concert hall events year-round throughout the city; and walk, skate, or bike through the city's many scenic parks and public gardens. The College is located within walking distance of Boston's public transportation system, allowing students to take advantage of all that Boston has to offer.

Majors and Degrees
Berklee offers a Bachelor of Music (B.M.) degree program and a four-year program leading to the professional diploma. Students may choose to major in composition, contemporary writing and production, film scoring, jazz composition, music business/management, music education, music production and engineering, music synthesis, music therapy, performance, professional music, and songwriting. The College offers a five-year, dual-major option in which students graduate with an even more marketable education that expands their career options in the music industry.

Academic Program
The Bachelor of Music program offers a complete music curriculum combined with general education courses such as English, history, languages, mathematics, philosophy, and physical or social science. Intensive concentration in music subjects provides students with the necessary tools for developing their musical talents to the fullest and preparing for the multifaceted and ever-changing demands of today's professional music. The degree program is especially appropriate for students who wish to earn a formal degree, are interested in pursuing a career in music education, music therapy, or business/management or want to continue their studies at the graduate level.

The diploma is designed for students who want to focus exclusively on contemporary music studies and still get the benefits of a Berklee experience.

All students must complete the Core Music Curriculum, which consists of harmony, arranging, ear training/solfège, and introduction to music technology; instrumental studies; ensembles and instrumental labs; and the concentrate courses designated for each major. All degree candidates must complete the general education curriculum and traditional studies courses.

Off-Campus Arrangements
Through the Professional Arts Consortium (ProArts), an association of six area institutions of higher education dedicated to the performing and visual arts, Berklee students can take courses at leading Boston area arts institutions in such areas as communications, modern dance, visual arts, ballet, architectural and graphic design, theater arts, and liberal arts. The other members of the consortium are Boston Architectural Center, the Boston Conservatory, Emerson College, Massachusetts College of Art, and the School of the Museum of Fine Arts.

Students who major in music business/management may be eligible to receive credit for their Berklee course work toward an M.B.A. from Suffolk University.

The Berklee International Network is a shared endeavor designed to promote the effectiveness of contemporary music education among members and to advance the value of contemporary music education internationally. Berklee faculty and staff members visit network member schools annually to conduct workshops and clinics and to audition students for scholarships for full-time study at Berklee. There are currently thirteen members of the network: Conservatorio Souza Lima in São Paulo, Brazil; Fundacio L'Aula de Musica Moderna i Jazz in Barcelona, Spain; Rimon School of Jazz and Contemporary Music in Tel Aviv, Israel; Phillipos Nakas Conservatory in Athens, Greece; American School of Modern Music in Paris, France; Pop and Jazz Conservatory in Helsinki, Finland; Koyo Conservatoire in Kobe, Japan; PAN School of Music in Tokyo, Japan; Jazz and Rock Schule in Freiburg, Germany; Escuela de Música del Buenos Aires Art Center Loft in Buenos Aires, Argentina; International College of Music–Malaysia in Kuala Lumpur, Malaysia; Seaoul Jazz Academy in Seoul, Korea; and Academia de Musica Fermatta in Mexico City, Mexico.

Academic Facilities
Berklee students have the chance to work in the College's state-of-the-art music technology facilities, using some of the most sophisticated recording and synthesis equipment currently available, in addition to facilities specifically designed for the areas of composition, arranging, and film scoring. The facilities at Berklee are furnished with the instruments and

equipment that are being used in the world beyond the classroom. Berklee's performance facilities include the Berklee Performance Center, a 1,200-seat concert hall hosting more than 250 student, faculty, and other concerts each year; four recital halls equipped with a variety of sound reinforcement systems; more than forty ensemble rooms; seventy-five private instruction studios; 250 private practice rooms; and an outdoor concert pavilion.

Technological facilities include the Recording Studio Complex, consisting of ten studio facilities that include 8-, 16-, and 24-track digital and analog recording capability; synthesis labs, featuring more than 250 MIDI digitally equipped synthesizers, drum machines, sequencers, and computers, including hard-disk recording; Learning Center, equipped with forty computer-based MIDI workstations; Professional Writing Division MIDI Lab; and film scoring labs, providing professional training in the areas of film music composition, editing, sequencing, and computer applications.

Costs

Tuition and fees for the 2000–01 year are $16,880. Room and board fees are $8890. While the cost of books tends to vary among students, it is estimated at about $500 per year.

Financial Aid

A very large percentage of the student body receives some form of financial aid, so no student should allow financial barriers to stop him or her from applying to the College. Funds are available from many different sources, including Berklee and federal and state programs. Students are eligible for merit-based scholarships and, in cases of demonstrated need, federal assistance is provided. Subsidized loans, a tuition-installment plan, and campus employment are also available. Financial aid counselors are available to students and their families to discuss the various options available to them. Students should be aware that there are specific deadlines for federal and state fund applications and for scholarships.

Faculty

The personal attention students receive from teachers at Berklee guides them beyond the theoretical so that they can apply what they've learned in their next ensemble rehearsal, evening jam session, or gig. All instruction is administered by Berklee's approximately 350 faculty members. Teachers are talented artists who demonstrate their commitment to music education in the classroom—and beyond. Most faculty members also write and arrange music, perform in concert halls and clubs, make recordings, or perform on television and radio—some do it all. All faculty members bring to the classroom a knowledge of music and the wisdom that comes from professional music experience.

Student Government

In recent years, student leaders have become more involved in the decision making of the College, and the Council of Students was created in response to the students' need for a student-run forum to discuss issues of importance to them as well as to prioritize their needs for presentation to the faculty and administration. The council provides adequate channels for expression of student viewpoints in areas of College life at Berklee and promotes the general welfare, interests, opinions, and activities of Berklee students.

Admission Requirements

To make sure that students are prepared for Berklee's exciting and challenging educational experience, all students must have a minimum of 2 years of formal music study on their principal instrument, covering standard methods and materials in preparation for college-level music study and/or significant practical experience in musical performance; knowledge of written music fundamentals (including rhythmic notation, melodic notation in treble and bass clefs, key signatures, major and minor scales, intervals, and construction of triads and seventh chords); a diploma from an accredited secondary school with satisfactory marks in college-preparatory courses; and, for degree candidates only, satisfactory scores on either the SAT I, ACT, or TOEFL (for international students).

Application and Information

Students intending to begin studies in September should submit their applications by March 1. This preferred filing date allows applicants to take full advantage of housing, financial aid, and scholarship opportunities at the College. Applications are permitted after March; however, the Office of Admissions (and other offices that serve students) can provide the best service to those who apply earliest. Applications are considered in the order in which they are completed.

Applicants considering the January or May semester should apply at least three months in advance. International students should apply at least six months in advance. All applicants are encouraged to visit the College and take part in a campus tour and information session. Together they will provide an overview of the College and the admission process. Hours of operation are 9 a.m. to 5 p.m., Monday through Friday. Student-led tours take visitors through administrative buildings, the Berklee Performance Center, the Career Resource Center, and the Learning Center. Information sessions offer insight into Berklee's admission requirements and life at the College. The sessions are presented by admissions representatives. Open Houses are offered on selected Saturdays throughout the year. These include a campus tour, an information session, and, when possible, special student ensemble performances.

For further information, students should contact:

Office of Admissions
Berklee College of Music
1140 Boylston Street
Boston, Massachusetts 02215
Telephone: 617-266-1400 Ext. 2222 (worldwide)
           800-421-0084 (toll-free inside the United States and Canada)
Fax: 617-747-2047
E-mail: admissions@berklee.edu
World Wide Web: http://www.berklee.edu

Students performing at Berklee College of Music.

BERNARD M. BARUCH COLLEGE OF THE CITY UNIVERSITY OF NEW YORK
NEW YORK, NEW YORK

The College

Baruch College, one of the best academic resources in the New York City area, has earned a reputation for excellence that extends to all parts of the world, attracting students from New York State, neighboring states, and abroad. A senior institution of The City University of New York (CUNY), Baruch offers students a broad array of majors through its three schools: the Zicklin School of Business, the Weissman School of Arts and Sciences, and the School of Public Affairs.

Baruch is accredited by the Middle States Association of Colleges and Schools. All baccalaureate and master's programs in business offered by the Zicklin School of Business are accredited by the AACSB–The International Association for Management Education. In addition to the business accreditation, both the undergraduate and graduate accountancy curriculums have been awarded the accounting accreditation from the AACSB.

The student body is remarkably diverse, reflecting the extraordinary ethnic spectrum of the city. Baruch currently enrolls more than 15,000 students, of whom more than 13,000 attend the Zicklin School of Business. Eighty-three percent of those enrolled are undergraduates. There are more than 100 student clubs and organizations representing a wide range of interests: academic, artistic, cultural, ethnic, professional, and athletic. Intercollegiate sports include, among others, basketball, tennis, and volleyball. The Sidney Mishkin Gallery mounts notable exhibitions of photographs, drawings, prints, and paintings. The Jean Cocteau Repertory Theatre Company, the Alexander String Quartet, and the Milt Hinton Jazz Workshop are in residence at the College.

In addition to its extensive array of undergraduate majors, Baruch offers graduate programs leading to the M.B.A., M.P.A., M.S., M.S.Ed., M.S.I.L.R., and Ph.D. An M.B.A. in health care administration and an M.P.A. in health policy and administration are offered jointly with the Mount Sinai School of Medicine; a J.D./M.B.A. is offered jointly with Brooklyn Law School.

The National Association of State Boards of Accountancy rated Baruch one of the top schools in the country for the number of candidates with advanced degrees who successfully take the CPA examination. Recent graduate business school surveys cited Baruch's M.B.A. program among the nation's top graduate programs in business for both quality and value.

Location

Baruch is located in the Gramercy Park/Flatiron section of Manhattan, which is easily accessible by public transportation from other boroughs, surrounding counties, and New Jersey and Connecticut. The College's central location in one of the most dynamic cultural centers of the world gives students an unequaled learning environment and access to innumerable facilities.

Majors and Degrees

The Zicklin School of Business, the largest collegiate business school in the country, awards the Bachelor of Business Administration (B.B.A.) degree with majors in accountancy, computer information systems, economics, finance and investments, industrial/organizational psychology, management, marketing, operations research, public administration, and statistics.

The Weissman School of Arts and Sciences awards the Bachelor of Arts (B.A.) degree in thirteen major fields: actuarial science, business communication, economics, English, history, mathematics, music, philosophy, political science, psychology, sociology, Spanish, and statistics. It also offers interdisciplinary specializations in arts administration, business journalism, and management of musical enterprises. In addition, ad hoc majors allow students to design programs that combine two or more areas of interest.

The School of Public Affairs offers programs in both public affairs and real estate/metropolitan development, leading to a Bachelor of Science (B.S.) degree.

Academic Program

Baruch College requires that all students take general liberal arts courses as the necessary preparation and framework within which specialized knowledge can be most effectively used.

Baruch's degree programs in business require 124 credits. Candidates for the B.B.A. are required to take at least half of their credits in the liberal arts and sciences. The business base is made up of 29 required credits, and students must take a minimum of 24 credits in the major field. The degree programs in the arts and sciences and public affairs require 120 credits. Candidates for the B.A. degree are expected to complete the base curriculum (at least 54 credits) in their freshman and sophomore years, select a major field of study by their junior year, and complete at least 90 credits in the arts and sciences. All students must maintain an overall C average or better and a C average or better in their major. Students can design a minor by using their free electives to take 12 credits in a specific discipline or 12 credits of intermediate and advanced courses outside their area of specialization. At least 60 percent of the credits in the major must be taken at Baruch.

College credits may be obtained through the University of the State of New York's Regents College Examinations and the College-Level Examination Program. Business students may obtain up to 6 credits for current business experience related to their major during their senior year.

Entering freshmen may receive a maximum of 16 credits for Advanced Placement (AP) examinations on which appropriate grades have been earned and for work completed in recognized prefreshman programs.

Off-Campus Arrangements

Students may study abroad for credit for a semester or a year through exchange programs with the University of Paris, Ecole Supérieure de Commerce of Rouen (France), Middlesex University (England), Tel-Aviv University (Israel), Mannheim University (Germany), and Universidad Iberoamericana (Mexico).

Academic Facilities

Baruch's Information and Technology Building houses The William and Anita Newman Library, one of the most technologically advanced facilities in New York. In addition to traditional holdings, the 1,400-seat library provides access to several hundred online databases through the Dow Jones News/Retrieval, LEXIS-NEXIS, and Dialog services and to information resources in CD-ROM format. Students and faculty have access to the 4.5 million volumes in the CUNY library system. The Baruch Computing and Technology Center, which has 500 computer workstations in an open-access lab, offers hardware ranging from microcomputers to mainframes, various software packages, and access to the global Internet.

Baruch's award-winning Computer Center for Visually Impaired People provides access to specialized computer equipment and to data in such forms as Braille, large print, and synthetic speech. Staff members are available to translate class material to Braille. In addition, the center has a Kurzweil Reading Machine.

Costs

For a New York State resident, the 2000–01 undergraduate tuition for full-time attendance (a minimum of 12 credits or the equivalent) is $1600 per semester; for part-time study, tuition is $135 per credit. For nonresidents, tuition for full-time study is $3400 per semester; for part-time study, $285 per credit. In addition, full-time day students pay a $60 activity fee; part-time day students pay a $30.85 activity fee. Tuition and fees are subject to change without notice.

Financial Aid

Financial aid is available for eligible students through various state and federal programs, which include the New York State Tuition Assistance Program (TAP), Federal Pell Grant Program, Federal Supplemental Educational Opportunity Grant Program, Federal Perkins Loan Program, and Federal Work-Study Program. To apply for aid, students must complete the Free Application for Federal Student Aid. Applications are processed as long as funds are available.

Baruch rewards academic excellence with generous scholarships to entering freshmen each year. The Henry and Lucy Moses and the Abraham Rosenberg Excellence Scholarships are the most selective and provide $5000 a year. Students must have a combined SAT I score of at least 1360 and a minimum grade point average (GPA) of 90 to be considered. The Presidential Scholarships award $4000 a year. To be considered, students must have a combined SAT I score of 1200 or above and a minimum GPA of 87. The Baruch Incentive Grant offers awards ranging from $500 to $1000 a year to students with a minimum GPA of 85 and an SAT I score of 1100.

Faculty

Baruch's faculty is recognized for leadership, academic honor, and distinction. Members include Yoshihiro Tsurumi, an expert on cultural and economic relations between the United States and Japan; Distinguished Professor David Reynolds, award-winning biographer of Walt Whitman; and E. S. Savas, an expert on privatization of public enterprises.

The faculty is made up of approximately 415 full-time and 350 part-time members. Eighty-seven percent hold doctorates. Full-time faculty members teach undergraduate introductory courses as well as advanced undergraduate and graduate courses. Faculty members also serve as advisers to student organizations and preprofessional programs.

Student Government

The two student government organizations, which represent the undergraduate and graduate students, oversee the granting of club charters and the allocation of student activity fees and participate in campus educational and community affairs.

Admission Requirements

Freshman applicants are screened initially to select those with a minimum of 3 units of both high school English and math and a minimum of two lab sciences. Students who meet these criteria will be admitted based on their overall high school performance and their performance on these index subjects. Alternately, the College will admit students with a minimum combined SAT I score of 1100. Students with a GED score of at least 300 will be considered, provided that they have satisfactorily completed the required high school units of English and math. Freshmen are required to submit SAT scores.

The best preparation for success at Baruch College is a full program of college-preparatory courses in high school completed with high grades. The College strongly recommends a minimum of 4 years of English, 4 years of social studies, 3 years of mathematics, 2 years of a foreign language, 2 years of lab sciences, and 1 year of performing or visual arts. Mathematics courses are especially important for Baruch's degree programs, and elementary algebra and geometry should be completed prior to enrollment. For students interested in majoring in business, mathematics, or science, 4 units of mathematics, including trigonometry and precalculus, are recommended.

Students who have attended a college or postsecondary institution must meet admission requirements based on the number of credits they have completed. Prospective transfer students with fewer than 24 credits must have a minimum cumulative GPA of 2.5 and an acceptable academic course of study as outlined above. Applicants with between 25 and 34.9 earned credits must have a GPA of 2.5 or above; those with 35 to 59.9 credits must have a GPA of at least 2.25; and those with 60 or more credits must have a GPA of at least 2.0.

Application and Information

All freshman applications that are received complete with all official documentation and fees on or before October 15 for spring admission or December 15 for fall admission will be processed first. Complete transfer applications received on or before October 15 for February admission or March 1 for September admission will be processed first. Any freshman or transfer applications received after the dates indicated above will be processed on a space-available basis.

Requests to schedule an appointment with an admissions counselor, to join a campus tour, or for application materials and additional information should be made to:

Office of Undergraduate Admissions
Bernard M. Baruch College of The City University of New York
17 Lexington Avenue, Box H-0720
New York, New York 10010-5585
Telephone: 212-802-2300
Fax: 212-802-2310
E-mail: admissions@baruch.cuny.edu
World Wide Web: http://www.baruch.cuny.edu

BETHANY COLLEGE
BETHANY, WEST VIRGINIA

The College
Bethany is a National Liberal Arts I College. It is the oldest degree-granting institution in West Virginia and was founded in 1840 by Alexander Campbell, an innovative nineteenth-century educator, religious leader, author, agriculturist, and businessman. The College has actively maintained its affiliation with the Christian Church (Disciples of Christ) since its inception.

The student body represents a broad spectrum of economic, social, and religious backgrounds. Students from thirty-one states and twenty-four countries are represented. Students live in the College's nineteen residence halls, ten of which provide quarters for Bethany's six national fraternities and four national sororities. The student union houses the College bookstore, a darkroom, music listening rooms, a spacious lounge, and an art exhibit area. Intercollegiate athletics involve a third of the men on campus and more than 20 percent of the women; approximately 70 percent of the students participate in intramural sports. There are thirty-eight clubs and organizations, and Bethany's concert-lecture series brings an array of nationally known speakers and entertainers to the campus. Student drama, chorus, choir, jazz, and chamber music groups offer numerous concerts. Other activities include first-run movies and in-depth conferences on current issues.

The College is a member of the Academic Common Market, a venture of institutions in southern states with an interstate agreement for the sharing of academic programs. This allows Bethany graduates to apply for enrollment in eighty graduate degree programs in other common market states at in-state tuition rates.

Townspeople, consisting almost entirely of faculty and staff families, are closely involved with the 750 students. Faculty-student interaction is natural in this environment. Student-administration relations are friendly and informal, and student input is sought in both academic and extracurricular matters.

Location
The 1,600-acre campus is located in the Allegheny foothills in the northern panhandle of West Virginia, 2 miles from Pennsylvania and 5 miles from Ohio. The center of the Wheeling metropolitan area is 15 miles away, and Pittsburgh is 39 miles to the northeast. The community has a rich history, and the College has gained national recognition by having five sites placed on the National Register of Historic Places. Two sites are National Historic Landmarks. The cultural activities and attractions of Pittsburgh and Wheeling are readily available, as are professional sporting events. Famous parks and museums, as well as a zoo, are just a few miles away. Bethany's location combines the advantages of a rural campus with proximity to a metropolitan community.

Majors and Degrees
Bethany College confers Bachelor of Science and Bachelor of Arts degrees. Major work is offered in accounting, biochemistry, biology, chemistry, communications (advertising, journalism, public relations, and radio-TV), computer science, economics and business, elementary and secondary education, English, environmental science, environmental studies, fine arts, foreign languages, French, German, history, interdisciplinary studies, international relations, mathematics, music, philosophy, physical education, physics, political communication, political science, psychology, religious studies, social work, Spanish, special education, theater, and visual arts.

Preprofessional education is available in engineering, law, medical and health professions, ministry, and pre–physical therapy.

Academic Program
The College provides a four-year liberal arts education that combines freedom in designing individual programs with sufficient structure to ensure depth, breadth, and integration of knowledge. This plan involves a first-year seminar program, a writing proficiency requirement, a senior project, a senior comprehensive examination (with oral and written parts), a seminar in biblical literature, a wellness course, and a foreign language requirement.

The academic calendar consists of two 15-week semesters and a 2-week interim session in January. The fall semester begins in late August and ends before Christmas; the spring semester runs from mid-January to early May. Students may elect to use the January term for intensive study on campus or for working off campus. Some courses are offered for the full 15 weeks; others, for the first or second half of the semester. This division provides additional flexibility for students involved in off-campus study and internships. The College's Office of Career and Professional Development offers placement, interviewing, and counseling services.

Off-Campus Arrangements
Special arrangements with Case Western Reserve University, Columbia University, and Washington University provide opportunities for students interested in becoming engineers. Students in history, political science, or economics can participate in a West Virginia legislative program. Other opportunities include the University of Quebec; the Inter-American University of Puerto Rico; Universidad Blas Pascal of Argentina; Kansai Gaidai University of Osaka, Japan; and the University of Karlstad in Sweden.

Bethany-sponsored semester offerings include the Pamplona Study Program (Spain), Oxford Semester (England), Paris Sorbonne Program (France), Heidelberg Study Program (Germany), Regent's Program (London), and the Seigakuin Program (Japan). Tuition and airfare allowance are included as part of the student's regular charges for these programs.

Academic Facilities
Special facilities include the T. W. Phillips Memorial Library; a student-operated FM radio station and television station; Kirkpatrick Hall, which houses laboratories and classrooms for the biology and psychology departments; a modern recreation center; and Richardson Hall, which houses the computer center and facilities for the chemistry, physics, and mathematics departments. The campus is linked to the Internet system. Steinman Fine Arts Center provides facilities for education, music, and theater. It includes a fully equipped theater, teaching studios, studio-classrooms, a rehearsal room for choral and instrumental groups, and individual practice rooms. The Bethany Conference Center houses offices, seminar rooms, exhibition areas, and a circular conference room for continuing education activities.

Costs

Tuition and general fees for 2000–01 are $19,141, room and board are $6909, Student Board of Governors fees are $354, and the technology fee is $200. Total costs are $26,604. Studio fees for art and music are extra.

Financial Aid

The College maintains an extensive scholarship and financial aid program. Approximately 65 percent of the College's students receive financial aid in the form of a package, which may include scholarships, grants, loans, and campus employment. Awards are made on the basis of need as determined by the Free Application for Federal Student Aid (FAFSA). The College attempts to provide adequate aid to enable all qualified students to attend Bethany.

Faculty

The College has a dedicated faculty of 56 members, who encourage free discussion and independent thought. Seventy-five percent of the faculty members have terminal degrees, and many have published widely. The College's relationship with the town allows an easy interaction between students and faculty members. Often what is started in the classroom is finished outside it, and insight often comes in the informal, after-class meetings between professor and student that are an integral part of a Bethany education.

Student Government

The Student Government Association, with representatives from all residence groups, manages a substantial budget and appropriates funds for diverse student activities. Representatives are appointed to many faculty committees, including those concerned with curricula, cultural programs, schedules, athletics, religious life, international education, and the library.

Admission Requirements

Admission to Bethany is competitive and is based on a careful review of all credentials presented by the candidates, and the Committee on Admission accepts those it considers best qualified. The College seeks students who have prepared themselves for a liberal arts curriculum by taking at least 15 units of college-preparatory work. Students who have developed individual programs will be given special evaluation by the Committee on Admission. Prospective freshman students must take the SAT I or the ACT examination.

Transfer and international students are welcome. Students who have received or will receive an Associate of Arts or Associate of Science degree are especially encouraged to apply.

An interview with an admission officer is strongly recommended but not required. Appointments for an on-campus interview, a tour of the College, and/or classroom visitations may be arranged through the Admission Office. Students who are not able to visit the campus may be able to arrange for an interview with an admission officer near their home.

Application and Information

Application for admission to the freshman class should be made during the final year of high school. Students are notified of the decisions of the Committee on Admission by mail, beginning in October and continuing throughout the year as completed applications are received.

To be considered for admission, students must submit an application for admission, an application fee ($25), an official secondary school transcript, a personal profile, one recommendation, and SAT I or ACT scores. Supporting documents that might be of help in the admission process (e.g., poetry, plays, music, artwork, photography, and journalistic writings) may also be submitted.

Requests for further information should be sent to:

Admission Office
Bethany College
Bethany, West Virginia 26032
Telephone: 304-829-7611
         800-922-7611 (toll-free)
Fax: 304-829-7142
E-mail: b.ralph@mail.bethanywv.edu
World Wide Web: http://www.bethanywv.edu

"Old Main," a symbol of Bethany College since 1858, is designated a National Historic Landmark.

BETHEL COLLEGE
NORTH NEWTON, KANSAS

The College

Founded in 1887, Bethel College is a liberal arts and sciences undergraduate college affiliated with the General Conference Mennonite Church. By tradition and by choice, it continues to base its mission on its academic and theological identity. Bethel seeks to be a community of learners, committed to the search for authentic faith and empirical understanding, and providing intellectual, cultural, and spiritual leadership for society and the church. To those ends, the College maintains a residential environment designed to foster integrative learning experiences, including student organizations, campus worship services, public lectures, symposia, and cultural events. At Bethel, 85 percent of the freshmen and two thirds of the entire student body of more than 500 students live on campus. The sense of community afforded by the residential nature of the campus is invigorating.

Bethel's curriculum is founded on a general education program in the liberal arts and sciences and is geared toward students of moderate to high academic ability. Distinctive elements include requirements in the study of religion and global issues. The College offers twenty-four majors and fourteen specialized programs in traditional liberal arts and selected career areas. Bethel has a diverse community of learners, with students from twenty-five states, thirteen countries, and more than thirty religious denominations.

Bethel's programs are informed by four central values of the mission statement: an ethic of discipleship that recognizes Jesus Christ as Messiah and model for the Christian life and prizes a high level of commitment and free conviction; an ethic of scholarship that believes academic achievement to be a logical outcome of intellectual stewardship and esteems both discipline and creativity; an ethic of service that deems concern for the powerless to be intrinsic to the Christian gospel and stresses peacemaking and voluntary service; and an ethic of integrity that celebrates the fundamental connections between spirit and mind, faith and learning, and individual and community and fosters personal development through participation in a range of activities.

The Bethel campus includes the historic Administration Building, two libraries, a performing arts center, a science hall, a student center, two gymnasiums, a natural history museum, athletic fields, and three residence halls.

The Administration Building is the dominating landmark of the College. Home to the campus Chapel and its Dobson pipe organ, the Administration Building was built in 1888 and is listed in the National Register of Historic Places. Thresher Gymnasium (seating capacity of 2,000) is home to varsity women's volleyball and men's and women's basketball. The Schultz Student Center is a hub of student activity, with a cafeteria, snack bar, game room, bookstore, and meeting rooms. The campus facilities are clustered around an open, grassy area referred to as The Green. The Green, with its benches and fountain, is a gathering place for students.

More than two thirds of Bethel students live on campus in one of three residence halls: Goering Hall, Haury Hall, and Warkentin Court. Each residence hall is supervised by an on-site staff and offers recreational and lounge areas and laundry and vending facilities. A new residence facility is under construction.

Location

The 90-acre, tree-lined Bethel College campus is in North Newton, which is adjacent to the city of Newton (population 20,000). Located in the rich agricultural and industrial region of south-central Kansas, Bethel borders Interstate 135 and Kansas Highway 15. Wichita, the largest city in Kansas, lies 30 minutes to the south, and Hutchinson is 30 minutes west of the campus. Between Newton, Wichita, and Hutchinson, a wide variety of services and attractions are available to students. These include the Kansas Cosmosphere and Space Center, a world-renowned space museum; several art museums; music theater; opera; symphonies; professional baseball, hockey, and soccer; an ice sports center; and multiple malls and shopping centers. Wichita is served by eight major airlines, and Amtrak train service is available in Newton.

Majors and Degrees

Bethel College grants Bachelor of Arts and Bachelor of Science degrees. Majors include accounting, art, Bible and religion, biology, business administration, chemistry, communication arts, elementary education, English, fine arts, German, global peace and justice, health management, history, history and social sciences, mathematical sciences, music, natural science, nursing, physics, psychology, social sciences, social work, and Spanish. Within these majors, students may concentrate in the following specialized areas: computer science, economics, environmental studies, international development, mass media, peace studies, political science, sociology, speech, and theater arts. Preprofessional programs are offered in engineering, law, medicine, and ministry.

Academic Program

Bethel operates on a 4-1-4 academic calendar. Four-month semesters in the spring and fall are supported by the one-month Interterm in January. Interterm allows for a time of focused study in one selected class, either on campus or through several off-campus options. Interterm study-travel options have included an English literature class in London, a biology class in the jungle of Belize in Central America, a theater class in New York, and an art class in a snowbound cabin in the Colorado Rockies. Through this multifaceted learning environment, Bethel is committed to the diverse educational goals of its students. The many forms and fields of knowledge facilitate intellectual, cultural, and spiritual learning in the Bethel community. The general education requirement of 55 credit hours ensures development of academic skills and disciplines and of integrative learning. Graduation from Bethel requires at least 124 credit hours with a minimum grade point average of 2.0.

Off-Campus Arrangements

Bethel offers a wide variety of formal study-abroad programs. Students enrolled in these programs are considered to be enrolled as full-time Bethel students living off campus. Academic progress and financial aid are generally the same as for on-campus programs. Bethel students may participate in study-abroad programs at seventeen colleges and universities in twelve countries.

Academic Facilities

The Mantz Library has a collection of more than 105,000 volumes and 250 periodical subscriptions. The library also houses the Career Development Office and the Center for Academic Development, which provides academic support in the form of tutoring and supplemental instruction. Additional support is available for postbaccalaureate placement exams, including the GRE, MCAT, and LSAT. Adjacent to the Mantz Library is the Mennonite Library and Archives, which houses 45,000 volumes of Mennonite historical and genealogical information.

The Fine Arts Center includes Krehbiel Auditorium, which is used for theater, concerts, and lectures. The Fine Arts Center also houses an art gallery; music rehearsal areas; a computerized music composition lab; studios of KBCU, the campus radio station; and offices of the *Collegian*, the student newspaper.

The Science Hall provides classrooms and laboratories for biology, chemistry, mathematics, physics, and psychology. Two networked computer laboratories are available in this facility. A new science center is under construction.

Memorial Hall houses the nursing department (classrooms, labs, and research computers), the Wellness Center (exercise and weight rooms), the Academic Health Center (student clinic), Harms Sports Medicine Center (athletic training), and an auditorium and intramural gymnasium (seating capacity of 2,800).

The Franz Art Center has multiple art studios for painting, drawing, ceramics, and photography.

Costs

Costs for a full-time student for the 2000–01 academic year include tuition and fees, $11,800, and room and board, $4700. Interterm is included in these costs if a student is enrolled full-time for either the spring or fall term.

Financial Aid

Bethel College administers a broad spectrum of financial aid intended to make the educational experience affordable for qualified students. Through merit-based financial aid (academic and performance), students may receive assistance ranging from $2340 to $7020 per year. For qualified students, need-based aid is available in the form of Bethel, state, and federal grant and loan programs. Most Bethel students receive some type of financial assistance.

Faculty

Bethel has 39 full-time and 15 part-time faculty members. Of the full-time faculty members, 69 percent have terminal degrees. Faculty members of all ranks teach first-year students in addition to upperclassmen. Bethel faculty members are active in scholarly research and regularly enlist students as collaborators in their research. No classes at Bethel are taught by teaching assistants or graduate assistants. The student-faculty ratio is 10:1. As is consistent with the emphasis Bethel places on global awareness and service, 67 percent of Bethel faculty members have been engaged in overseas service and travel.

Student Government

Student government at Bethel is based on the federal model and consists of twenty-seven elected offices and several appointed positions. The executive branch comprises the Student Body President and Vice-President. The Senate has 5 senators from each class, 3 commuter senators, one senator from the International Club, and one from the multicultural organization. Student government provides an opportunity for student advocacy and leadership development.

Admission Requirements

Bethel seeks to enroll a broad range of students with a demonstrated desire and ability to learn. Admission is competitive, and applicants must provide school transcripts and standardized test scores. Freshman applicants should present a minimum GPA of 2.5 and a minimum ACT score of 19 or SAT I score of 890. Transfer applicants should present a minimum college GPA of 2.0. International applicants are required to present a minimum TOEFL score of 540 on the paper-based version or 207 on the computer-based version. All prospective students are encouraged to visit campus, either during a group-visit event or an individual campus visit. The College admits students without regard to race, color, sex, handicap, or national or ethnic origin.

Application and Information

Interested students are invited to request an application for admission from the Admissions Office and return it with the required documents and a $20 application fee. Although admission is granted on a rolling basis through the beginning of each semester, early application is encouraged for priority consideration for financial aid, class selection, and housing.

For more information, students should contact:

Office of Admissions
Bethel College
300 East 27th Street
North Newton, Kansas 67117
Telephone: 316-283-2500
          800-522-1887 (toll-free)
Fax: 316-284-5870
E-mail: admissions@bethelks.edu
World Wide Web: http://www.bethelks.edu

Bethel College students and faculty members visit on the steps of one of the two libraries on the campus.

BETHEL COLLEGE
ST. PAUL, MINNESOTA

The College

Bethel College began its four-year Christian liberal arts program in 1945 but traces its roots to Bethel Theological Seminary, founded in 1871. Bethel is a ministry of the churches of the Baptist General Conference. The College encourages growth and learning in a distinctly Christian environment, continually striving to help students discover and develop the skills God has given them. Campus lifestyle expectations have been designed to build unity within diversity. All Bethel students, faculty, and staff members are expected to follow those expectations during their time as members of the Bethel community. Bethel's 3,000 students represent a wide range of national and international cultures and more than thirty denominations. Most of Bethel's students are between 18 and 22 years of age, but older and younger students bring a welcome diversity to campus life. Bethel students are involved in a wealth of cocurricular activities, from music to ministry, Bible study to broadcasting, theater to tennis, and art to athletics. Bethel sports teams compete in NCAA Division III and the Minnesota Intercollegiate Athletic Conference. The Sports and Recreation Center is used almost continuously for intercollegiate and intramural sports events and personal recreation, and a newly completed Community Life Center provides a 1700-seat performance hall and chapel.

The campus, built in the 1970s, is the newest among Minnesota colleges. Versatile buildings are centers for the sciences, humanities, physical education, learning resources, and fine arts. A series of skyways and breezeways connects the facilities and makes getting to and from class a pleasure—even in the heart of winter. Residence life at Bethel takes many forms. Traditional college dorm rooms, spacious suites, town houses—whatever their preference, Bethel students find a warm, family atmosphere in their living areas. All freshman and sophomore students, except those who are married or living with their parents while in attendance, are required to live in College housing.

In addition to the undergraduate degree programs described below, Bethel offers Master of Arts degrees in communication, counseling psychology, nursing, and organizational studies and a Master of Education degree with programs in curriculum and instruction, educational leadership, middle school licensure, and special education. Classes meet one evening a week for 4 hours, and course work is integrated with students' professional responsibilities.

Location

The Bethel campus borders Lake Valentine in Arden Hills and comprises 231 acres of beauty and tranquility, conducive to study and leisure. Just 15 minutes from downtown St. Paul or Minneapolis, Bethel enjoys the benefits of both cities, noted nationally for their high quality of life. The Twin Cities are home for the headquarters of most of Minnesota's twenty-four billion-dollar corporations, as well as thirty-three major shopping malls and the world's largest shopping mall, the Mall of America. Here culture thrives with an international array of music, theater, and art. At the all-weather Metrodome and the Target Center, sports fans cheer their favorite pro teams—the Minnesota Vikings, Twins, and Timberwolves. Abundant recreation exists year-round in this busy metropolis, which has more than 900 lakes and 500 parks.

Majors and Degrees

The Bachelor of Arts (B.A.) degree is offered with major concentrations in art, art education, athletic training, biblical and theological studies, biology, business, business and political science, business management, chemistry, communication, community health, computer science, economics, economics and finance, education, English literature, English literature and writing, environmental studies, history, international relations, mathematics, media communication, music, philosophy, physical education, physics, political science, pre-engineering, psychology, social work, sociocultural studies, Spanish, theater arts, Third World studies, writing, and youth ministry.

The Bachelor of Science (B.S.) degree is offered with major concentrations in biochemistry/molecular biology, biology, chemistry, computer science, nursing, and physics. The Bachelor of Music (B.Mus.) is offered in applied performance. The Bachelor of Music Education (B.Mus.Ed.) is offered with an emphasis in instrumental K–12 and vocal K–12. A dual-degree program, granting both the B.A. and the B.S., is offered in engineering through a formal agreement between Bethel and a number of accredited universities in the Midwest.

Academic minors are available in most of the major disciplines listed above and in the following areas: Asian studies, athletic coaching, biblical languages (Hebrew and Greek), cross-cultural missions, family studies, French, German, health, management information systems, modern world languages, sacred music, and social welfare studies.

Bethel's Program in Adult College Education (PACE) is a college degree completion program offering bachelor's degrees in business management, nursing, and organizational studies. PACE is designed for adults who have completed at least two years of college and seek to apply learning to professional interests. Students attend a 4-hour class one night a week and move through the program with the same group of 20 or fewer adults. PACE courses are taught by Bethel College faculty members.

Academic Program

Bethel was named among the top ten liberal arts colleges in the Midwest by *U.S. News & World Report* in 1999. Bethel's general education curriculum has become a model for many other liberal arts colleges nationwide. Students are required to take classes that will give them a broad view of the world and their role as Christians. General education classes are grouped around the following themes: Bible and theology, Western heritage, world citizenship, self-understanding, science and technology, and health and wholeness. In addition, in order to graduate, all Bethel students must demonstrate competence in mathematics, writing, speaking, and computing.

Bethel College follows a 4-1-4 academic calendar, consisting of two 15-week semesters and a 3-week Interim in January. A full-time academic load for each semester is 12 to 18 credits. To graduate, a student must complete a minimum of 122 credits with a cumulative grade point average of at least 2.0 and a minimum 2.25 grade point average in his or her major. Also required are 50 credits of general education. Bethel awards advanced placement in recognition of learning that has been achieved apart from a college classroom situation. A maximum of 30 advanced placement credits can be applied toward a degree program. Students may also individualize their academic program through directed studies with faculty members and through academic internships with off-campus institutions.

Off-Campus Arrangements

Bethel students may participate in a number of off-campus extension programs. The American Studies Program of the Christian College Coalition provides work-study opportunities in Washington, D.C. The coalition also sponsors a Latin American Studies Program, which offers students an opportunity to study in Costa Rica. The Hollywood Film Studies Program gives students of any major a semester learning and working experience in Los Angeles, the world's film capital. The Christian College Consortium Visitor Program is designed to give students an opportunity to take advantage of course offerings and varied experiences on other

Christian college campuses throughout the United States. In cooperation with Westmont College of Santa Barbara, California, Bethel students have the opportunity to attend an urban studies program in San Francisco. The AuSable Trails Institute in Michigan offers intensive courses in environmental studies. Through the Upper Midwest Association for Intercultural Education, Bethel students study abroad during Interim. In the spring semester of alternate years, Bethel students can study and travel in Great Britain under the direction of a faculty member from the Bethel Department of English Literature and Language. Bethel is also associated with the Institute of Holy Land Studies in Jerusalem, which offers undergraduate and graduate courses in biblical archaeology, geography, history, languages, and literature.

Academic Facilities

Bethel's Community Life Center offers a beautiful auditorium with outstanding acoustical design that makes it one of the best performance halls in the upper Midwest. The Bethel Learning Resource Center offers books, slides, magazines, microfilm, pamphlets, filmstrips, tapes, films, maps, records, film loops, and videotapes—320,000 items in all. Bethel participates in a library consortium program, which offers access to a combined 1.3 million volumes through computer search and interlibrary loan systems. Bethel students are assigned computer accounts, allowing them access to a wealth of academic computing services, including word processors and word processing software. The Bethel science labs and music practice rooms are modern and well equipped. At least four plays are performed each year in the Bethel Theatre.

Costs

For 1999–2000, tuition was $15,300, and room and board costs were $5410. Bethel College tuition costs are lower than average for Minnesota private colleges. Bethel College housing costs are set each spring for incoming freshmen and transfer students and housing rates are then frozen and do not increase during a student's stay at Bethel. Freshmen living on campus must purchase the three-meal-per-day basic meal plan; upperclass students have a variety of meal plans from which to choose. The actual cost of attending Bethel depends on the amount of financial aid a student receives.

Financial Aid

Bethel College strives to make it financially possible for every qualified student to attend. Each year, nearly 90 percent of the students receive some kind of financial aid, including scholarships, grants, loans, and assistance in the form of on-campus employment. Students who wish to be considered for financial aid must first be admitted to the College and then submit a Family Financial Statement (FFS). Bethel's priority deadline is April 15 of each year. Students who have completed and mailed all necessary forms by this date receive first consideration.

Faculty

Nothing determines the quality of a college more than the people who teach there. Bethel professors combine strong academic credentials with commitment to Jesus Christ. Bethel faculty members are known for their warmth and caring. It's not hard to receive personal attention, since there are only 17 students to every faculty member. Professors are very accessible to students during regular office hours as well as at other times. Of Bethel's 131 full-time faculty members, the majority have earned doctorates. The Bethel faculty is complemented by 47 part-time instructors.

Student Government

As active and integral parts of the Bethel community, the Student Association and Senate function in a variety of strategic campus areas. In addition to representing student needs to the administration, they oversee student publications and campus social activities and provide a forum for influential student-faculty committees. Guiding the affairs of the Student Association, the Executive Board is composed of the president, chair of the Senate, and 5 vice presidents. With 4 senators representing each academic class, a total of 16 senators are elected by their respective constituencies.

Admission Requirements

Bethel College seeks students who desire an education based on strong academics in a Christian environment. To be considered for admission, the student must graduate from an accredited high school, rank in the top 50 percent of his or her high school class, and meet minimum test score requirements (92 on the PSAT, 920 on the SAT I, or 21 on the ACT). Transcripts, two references, and commitment to Bethel's Christian lifestyle standards are also required. Bethel recommends that students take 4 years of English, 3 years of mathematics, 3 years of science, and 2 years of social studies while in high school. Transfer students are welcome. On-campus interviews are not required but are strongly recommended.

Application and Information

Students wishing to apply for admission to Bethel must send the following: a completed Bethel application form with a $25 nonrefundable application fee; test scores from the PSAT, SAT I, or ACT; transcripts of all course work completed at the high school and college levels; and references from a pastor and an adult friend or employer. Admission decisions are made on a rolling basis. Although there is no deadline, applicants for fall admission are encouraged to complete their files before May 1.

For further information about specific Bethel programs and campus visit opportunities, students should contact:

Office of Admissions
Bethel College
3900 Bethel Drive
St. Paul, Minnesota 55112
Telephone: 651-638-6242
        800-255-8706 Ext. 6242 (toll-free)
Fax: 651-635-1490
E-mail: bcoll-admit@bethel.edu
World Wide Web: http://www.bethel.edu
AOL Keyword: Bethel

Bethel's Community Life Center.

BETHESDA CHRISTIAN UNIVERSITY
ANAHEIM, CALIFORNIA

The University
Because of a great vision held by Dr. David Yonggi Cho, senior pastor of the Yoido Full Gospel Church, to train leadership for the worldwide church, a school came into being. Bethesda Christian (BCU) started in fall 1976 in Pasadena, California. The mission of BCU is to equip Korean- and English-speaking students with professional competence, academic excellence, and spiritual integrity so that they will perform more effectively in their careers and be prepared to make meaningful contributions to their churches and the kingdom of God at large as Christian ministers or lay leaders.

BCU plans to add a Los Angeles campus and a dormitory at the present campus in the near future. At this time, there is no on-campus housing provided by BCU, but there is ample and affordable housing available in the surrounding areas of BCU.

The total number of students enrolled in BCU is 186. Currently, almost all students are first- or second-generation Koreans. Approximately 53 percent of the students at BCU are men. BCU is seeking students with dedication and commitment to serving God's kingdom.

There are 46 students enrolled in BCU's graduate program. BCU offers a Master's degree in religion and the Master of Divinity. (M.Div.).

The University is a candidate member of the Accrediting Association of Bible Colleges (AABC).

ESL classes are provided for the many international students who attend BCU. BCU is approved by the INS to grant the I-20 to international students. Approval for the I-20 is granted after a student has met all the necessary requirements.

Location
BCU is located in sunny, central Anaheim, only 25 minutes from Los Angeles and the beach. Anaheim is the home of numerous recreational attractions, including Disneyland and Knott's Berry Farm. There is a shopping plaza adjacent to the University, and several parks surround the area. A beautiful mountain ski resort is only 2 hours away. BCU is conveniently located near two major airports, LAX and Orange County (John Wayne) Airport.

Major and Degrees
BCU offers three undergraduate programs: church music, early childhood education, and religion. Minors are offered in Biblical studies, missionary ministries, and pastoral ministries. Also, ESL certificate programs and the E.C.E. certification program are offered.

Academic Program
The B.A. program is a four-year program (with a total of 125 semester units/12 units per semester is required for a full-time course load). All B.A. programs require 30 to 34 units of Bible/theology.

The B.A. in religion is a broad-based program designed to give the student in-depth academic training in the liberal arts and knowledge about the Christian faith. This program offers 3 major concentrations in Biblical studies, missionary ministries, and pastoral ministries (13 units of ministry and 26 units of the chosen concentration).

The B.A. in church music is designed to prepare students for a career in music ministry and performance. It provides the student with the necessary skills to use music to impact God's kingdom (requirement of 61 units of music).

The B.A. in early childhood education and ministry is designed to equip students with age-appropriate evangelistic and Christian education skills so that students are able to operate a preschool in a church (requirement of 46 units of E.C.).

Academic Facilities
BCU is located in an attractive facility that includes an administrative area, a chapel, a conference room, a student center, a computer lab, a 26,000-volume library with online research services, and faculty offices. There is a common dining area, although specific meal plans are not offered.

Costs
Tuition For the 2000–01 academic year is $120 per unit. There is a registration fee of $20 and a library fee of $20 each semester. The one-time application fee is $25. The audit fee for B.A. classes is $50.

Financial Aid
Federal student financial aid includes Federal Pell Grants, which provide up to $3000 a year, and Direct Loans, which have low interest rates and which are payable after graduation. The deadline for loan applications is at the beginning of each semester. Scholarships are also available for honor students achieving a 4.0 grade point average during any semester or for any member of a pastor's family, excluding married children.

Faculty
It is the goal of BCU that faculty members possess not only the highest academic credentials but also show evidence in their own life that they are committed to ministry and spiritual growth. Faculty members must be able to show continuing involvement in the ministry of the Christian church outside of their ministry at BCU. Faculty members are encouraged to participate as much as possible in student relationships outside of the classroom as well as in the formal arena of classroom instruction. The 7 full-time and 35 part-time faculty members are committed to their students. Most of the faculty members at BCU have earned the highest degree in their field. The student-faculty ratio is 8:1.

Student Government

Each year, the student body selects officers to provide leadership in both undergraduate and graduate programs. Student body officers are responsible for planning student activities and integrating new students into the community of BCU. Student leaders also arrange student chapel services and provide advice on the development of student handbooks.

Admission Requirements

BCU encourages applications from anyone who desires an education based on Christian principles. Generally, entering students must have earned a high school diploma or its equivalent. Students must prove that they are committed Christians. Students must have official notification of admission before they will be allowed to register for classes.

In addition to the application form, the applicant should submit three letters of reference (from a pastor, academic reference, and a lay leader) and an essay describing his or her Christian experience. Admissions deadlines are January 1 for the spring semester and July 1 for the fall semester.

Application and Information

Office of Admission
Bethesda Christian University
730 North Euclid Street
Anaheim, California 92801

Telephone: 714-517-1945
Fax: 714-517-1948
E-mail: admin@bcu.edu
World Wide Web: http://www.bcu.edu

BETHUNE-COOKMAN COLLEGE
DAYTONA BEACH, FLORIDA

The College
Bethune-Cookman College is a private, liberal arts, career-oriented, coeducational, residential institution, which operates on a semester calendar and is affiliated with the United Methodist Church. The College is a result of a merger between the Daytona Educational and Industrial Training School for Negro Girls (founded by Mary McLeod Bethune in 1904) and the Darnell Cookman Institute for Men (founded in 1872). It is accredited by the Commission on Colleges of the Southern Association of Colleges and Schools to award the bachelor's degree, and by the Florida State Department of Education, the University Senate of the United Methodist Church, the AMA Committee on Allied Health Education and Accreditation, the National Council for Accreditation of Teacher Education, and the National League for Nursing Accrediting Commission. The College is approved by the Florida State Board of Nursing Licensure.

High academic standards, curriculum flexibility, concern for the individual student, and an emphasis on a broad Christian way of life are trademarks of the institution. The 2,600 students at Bethune-Cookman College come from forty-three states and twenty-three international countries. The campus' cultural and social activities include choirs, band, drama, student publications, radio broadcasting, clubs, and Greek letter organizations, as well as intramural and NCAA division I-AA intercollegiate athletics.

Location
Bethune-Cookman College is located in the Atlantic coast city of Daytona Beach, Florida, amid a metropolitan area that has a population of more than 160,000. Its location on Doctor Mary McLeod Bethune Boulevard provides easy access to local business centers, churches, theaters, museums, beaches, recreational facilities, and bus and air terminals. The College is within 100 miles of the Kennedy Space Center, Walt Disney World/EPCOT Center, Sea World, Universal Studios, Marineland, and other such attractions.

Majors and Degrees
The Bachelor of Science degree is awarded in accounting, biology, business administration, business education, chemistry, computer information systems, computer science, criminal justice, elementary education, gerontology, hospitality management, international business, mathematics, medical technology, nursing, physical education, physics, psychology, specific learning disabilities, and varying exceptionalities. The Bachelor of Arts degree is awarded in church music, English, history, international studies, liberal studies, mass communications, modern languages, music, political science, religion and philosophy, social science education, and sociology. The majors in biology, chemistry, English, mathematics, modern languages, music, and physics can carry teacher certification. A dual-degree program in engineering is offered in cooperation with University of Florida, University of Central Florida, Florida Atlantic University, Florida A & M University, and Tuskegee University. Army and Air Force ROTC programs are offered in cooperation with Embry Riddle Aeronautical University in Daytona Beach.

Academic Program
The academic program follows an educational core-concept approach. Student progress is monitored by the Division of General Studies. Sequences are required in biology, English, general psychology, mathematics, modern languages, physical education, physical science, religion, and social science. A developmental program seeks to provide courses and growth experiences that develop student competence in communications and mathematics skills for those needing remedial assistance. Academic support and reinforcement activities include individual conferences, periodic academic evaluation, and access to five laboratories for tutoring in reading, writing, speech, mathematics, science, and study skills. The Bethune-Cookman College Honors Program is designed to broaden intellectual horizons and to integrate various areas of knowledge, individualized learning, and independent research. Student Support Service programs are designed to improve student retention as well as academic and personal development. These programs, designed to increase successful matriculation in major fields of study, enrich the curriculum by reinforcing academic skills and course content necessary for success. A cooperative education program and other career-related field experiences are major components in several fields of study.

To receive a degree from Bethune-Cookman College, a student must complete a major in an academic field of study with a minimum of 124 semester hours of work with a minimum cumulative grade point average of 2.0. Upon recommendation of the instructor, a student exhibiting outstanding competence in a given course may receive credit by examination in lieu of taking the course.

Off-Campus Arrangements
The College operates Continuing Education Program sites in Florida in Belle Glade, Bradenton, Fort Pierce, Gainesville, Lake Wales, Sanford, and West Palm Beach. A branch campus is located in Spuds, Florida.

Academic Facilities
Facilities on the 60-acre campus include twelve classroom buildings, a student union building, an infirmary, nine dormitories, a gymnasium, an athletic weightroom, a library resource center, and five administrative buildings. The library resource center houses an open-stack collection of more than 156,861 volumes, 41,914 microforms, 5,355 films and slides, 1,792 audiocassettes and videocassettes, 800 journals and magazine subscriptions, and a special collection of African-American and Methodist historical materials. The campus Learning Resource Center includes a nonprint media center, a graphics studio, and an ITV studio. The College operates an academic computer center system, with outlets in all classroom buildings. There is also a telecommunications satellite network for mass communications majors.

Costs
For the 2000-01 academic year, the basic cost for tuition and fees is $8988, and room and board are $5686. The approximate cost of books and supplies is $600 per year. Other expenditures for travel, amusement, and incidentals vary according to individual needs.

Financial Aid

The financial aid program includes competitive academic, athletic, band, and choir scholarships; work study awards; and federal and state grants and loans. Applications should be filed by March 1. Notification of awards is generally made in the spring. Applicants for federal and state loans, a grant-in-aid, or a work-study award must file the Free Application for Federal Student Aid (FAFSA).

Faculty

There are 132 full-time teaching faculty members, 53 percent of whom hold the doctorate degree. The student-faculty ratio is 17:1. The faculty members participate actively in all phases of college life.

Student Government

The Student Government Association (SGA) is the representative body for students. The SGA president is the student representative on the College Board of Trustees. There are student representatives on virtually every college committee.

Admission Requirements

There is a ten-year restriction on accepting previously earned credits. Students accepted with an A.A. degree and passing scores on the College Level Academic Skills Test (CLAST) will be admitted to the upper level, but they must have earned a C or higher in English, mathematics, reading, and speech. A.A. degree holders without a CLAST score must take the CLAST examination on the next available date. If the student takes the examination and does not pass one or more of the subtests, he or she must enroll in the course which corresponds with the failed subtest. Passing scores on the CLAST are a graduation requirement for all students

Application and Information

The college operates on a two-semester plan with an additional seven-week summer session. Qualified applicants may register at the beginning of any term.

The closing date for students applying for admission for the fall semester is July 30 and November 30 for the spring semester. Students interested in attending Bethune-Cookman College should write to the Assistant Vice President for Enrollment Management for information and application forms:

Assistant Vice President for Enrollment Management
Bethune-Cookman College
640 Doctor Mary McLeod Bethune Boulevard
Daytona Beach, Florida 32114
Telephone: 904-255-1401
                800-448-0228 (toll-free)
E-mail: admissions@cookman.edu
World Wide Web: http://www.bethune.cookman.edu

BIOLA UNIVERSITY
LA MIRADA, CALIFORNIA

The University
Biola is a private Christian university established in 1908 in Los Angeles with a mission of biblically-centered education, scholarship, and service to equip men and women in mind and character to impact the world for the Lord Jesus Christ. More than 3,800 students, who are among the most ethnically diverse body of any Christian college in the U.S., are challenged yearly by faculty members and staff to integrate their faith and learning pursuant to their academic and vocational goals. Biola is a member of the Council for Christian Colleges and Universities (CCCU), an organization consisting of ninety-four Christian institutions across the U.S.

Location
Biola University's 95-acre campus is located in La Mirada, 22 miles southeast of Los Angeles on the border of Orange County. Centrally located in southern California, Biola is just a short drive to both the beaches and the mountains. Hollywood, the entertainment capital of the world, is just 30 minutes away, and unlimited cultural experiences are available in Orange County and Los Angeles. Los Angeles is the home of the Natural History Museum, the Hollywood Bowl, the Great Western Forum, and Dodger Stadium. Disneyland, Anaheim Stadium, and the Arrowhead Pond Arena are a short drive south of Biola. Five major airports, including LAX and John Wayne, are within an hour's drive of campus. For internships and career opportunities, there are numerous choices.

Majors and Degrees
The Bachelor of Arts and Bachelor of Science degrees are offered with majors in anthropology, art, Bible, biochemistry, biological sciences, business administration, Christian education, communication, communication disorders, computer science, education/liberal studies, English, history, humanities, intercultural studies, mathematics, music, nursing, philosophy, physical education, physical science, prechiropractic, prelaw, pre–physical therapy, psychology, radio-television-film, social science, sociology, and Spanish. A 3-2 engineering program is offered cooperatively with the University of Southern California.

In all, Biola offers 145 programs ranging from the B.A. to the Ph.D. at six schools that include the School of Arts and Sciences, Talbot School of Theology, Rosemead School of Psychology, the School of Business, the School of Continuing Studies, and the School of Intercultural Studies. All are regionally and professionally accredited and based on evangelical Christianity.

Academic Program
The academic year consists of two fifteen-week semesters. There are also two summer sessions for three and five weeks each plus a three-week interterm each January. As a fully accredited national university, Biola University seeks to instruct Christian men and women in order to produce graduates who are competent in their field of study, knowledgeable in biblical studies, and equipped to serve the Christian community and society at large.

Religious and convocation requirements include 30 hours of biblical studies, attendance at chapel three times a week, and participation in student ministry.

Off-Campus Arrangements
Biola offers study-abroad programs in Israel, China, Korea, and Baja, California. The University also participates in the CCCU programs in Central America (Honduras, Costa Rica), England, Russia, Egypt, Washington D.C. and the Middle East and at the Au Sable Institute, the Los Angeles Film Institute, and the Colorado Springs Focus on the Family Institute. Each program has unique requirements for admission.

Biola's BOLD (Biola Organizational Leadership Degree) program, in which students who are 25 years or older can complete their college degree in eighteen months, has extension campuses in Aliso Viejo, Vista, Chino, Newberry, and Inglewood, California. Admission requirements are unique to the program and include completion of a minimum of 60 transferable semester units from an accredited college.

Biola offers courses to teachers in Hong Kong as part of the Biola-RICE (Research Institute for Christian Education) agreement.

Academic Facilities
The Rose Memorial Library has more than 252,000 books and currently subscribes to more than 1,200 periodical titles. The library provides access to its holdings by SCROLL, the online public access catalog and circulation system and an increasing number of CD-ROM index databases available for patron searching. Construction of a new library resource center should be completed in summer 2001.

Additional facilities include a media center, an on-campus radio station, a TV/film studio, an art studio, an art gallery, and an outdoor pool. Access to the Internet may be found by way of computers in the residence halls as well as throughout the campus. E-mail, Internet research, World Wide Web browsing, word processing, desktop publishing, multimedia presentation, graphic arts design, and application programming may all be accomplished at the computer center and in Biola's computerized classroom. Resources include two computerized classrooms equipped with Windows NT and Macintosh computers, plus a fully equipped computer lab with more than fifty computers (Mac and PC). Scanners and high-speed black-and-white and color laser printers are also available in the lab. Students can connect to the Internet via Ethernet (in most residence halls) or AppleTalk (in all residence halls) or by using the computer lab equipment. Connection to the Internet is via a high-speed T1 line.

Costs
Biola University holds the belief that every student, regardless of financial status, should have the opportunity to make an investment in his or her tomorrow. Therefore, the University strives to keep the cost of a Biola education within the financial reach of students and their families. For 2000–01, Biola tuition is $16,630, room averages $2778, and board averages $2494. For on-campus students, the total cost represents a 4.3 percent increase over 1999–2000.

Financial Aid
Biola offers a generous financial aid program, with $8 million in institutional funds devoted to undergraduates alone. In addition, hundreds of University students receive state and federal

grants and scholarships. Eighty percent of Biola students receive some level of financial aid, with the average award being $8000.

Institutional scholarships include the Academic Scholarship ($500 to $6500), the Community Service Scholarships ($2500), and Scholarships for Underrepresented Students of Ethnicity (SURGE; $4000 to $6000), all of which are renewable. Other aid options include departmental scholarships (for athletics, music, and forensics, among others), international scholarships, dependent scholarships (for families where the primary income is in Christian ministry), and church-matching scholarships. Excellent loan programs and on-campus work opportunities round out the aid packages of most Biola students.

All students are urged to apply for financial aid by March 2, which coincides with the California aid deadline. Applicants should complete the Free Application for Federal Student Aid (FAFSA) and Biola's one-page form, the University Aid Application. In addition, California residents should complete the state GPA verification form.

Faculty

The University's faculty members are mentors and role models in addition to professors. Two-thirds of all faculty members have earned doctorates. There are 157 full-time and 132 part-time faculty members. Some have won awards as Fulbright and National Endowment for the Humanities scholars. The student-faculty ratio is 18:1.

Faculty members remain on the cutting edge of their fields by continuing their education as they teach students. Research grants provide professors the time and resources not only to publish in their discipline but also to participate in seminars with topics such as Christianity and science and postmodernism. At these seminars, they consider how to integrate their faith within their fields and broaden their knowledge of other areas. This experience is brought back to their classrooms for their students' benefit.

Student Government

The purpose of the Associated Student Government of Biola University is to develop a community that is seeking the person of God and is committed to glorifying God in all its thoughts and actions. There are two student government bodies. The Executive Council (elected by the students) is the legislative body that represents the student body, which includes the nine residential halls. The Services Council plans and executes student activities. The Associated Student Government operates on a budget of more than $200,000 a year to produce student chapels, social events, intramurals and missions opportunities, club activities, and community events.

Admission Requirements

Biola seeks students who want to make a difference with their lives and impact the world for Jesus Christ. Candidate selection is based on SAT I and ACT scores, high school transcripts, and school recommendations. In addition, each applicant must be an evangelical believer in the Christian faith, must submit a reference letter from a pastor, and must go through an interview process. Freshmen who entered Biola in fall 1999 had an average combined SAT I score of 1092 and an average GPA of 3.52.

Application and Information

The Office of Admissions is open from 8 a.m. to 5 p.m. on weekdays. To visit the campus or to request information, students can call or write:

Director of Admissions
Biola University
13800 Biola Avenue
La Mirada, California 90639-0001
Telephone: 800-OK-BIOLA (toll-free)
E-mail: admissions@biola.edu
World Wide Web: http://www.biola.edu

Two students discuss classes near one of the nine residence halls as the sun goes down on another day at Biola University.

BIRMINGHAM–SOUTHERN COLLEGE
BIRMINGHAM, ALABAMA

The College

Birmingham-Southern College was created through a merger of Southern University (established in 1856) and Birmingham College (established in 1898). Since 1959, when *Harper's* called it "one of the leading small colleges in the South," Birmingham-Southern continues to be recognized as one of the nation's outstanding liberal arts institutions. In 1996 alone: *U.S. News & World Report* ranked Birmingham-Southern College as one of the top "National Liberal Arts Colleges," one of the "best values" in higher education, and one of the "Most Efficient Schools"; *Money* ranked Birmingham-Southern as one of the 100 best college buys; *The Insiders Guide to the Colleges*, compiled and edited by the *Yale Daily News*, ranked Birmingham-Southern "among the best and most noteworthy in North America"; and *The National Review College Guide, The Fiske Guide to Colleges,* and *The Princeton Review 1995 Edition of the Student Access Guide to the Best 286 Colleges* recognized Birmingham-Southern as one of the top liberal arts colleges in America. In 1992–93, medical and law schools accepted Birmingham-Southern graduates at a rate considerably above the national average. In *The Right College 1992,* Birmingham-Southern ranked fifth nationally in the percentage of male graduates going on to medical school. The only universities ahead of Birmingham-Southern in admission of male graduates to medical schools were Emory, Johns Hopkins, Harvard, and Stanford. The College is also known for its music, fine arts, computer science, and business programs as well as its liberal arts emphasis. Birmingham-Southern is one of only two Alabama institutions with a Phi Beta Kappa chapter. It has nationally ranked baseball, basketball, soccer, and tennis programs. Birmingham-Southern has a number of social fraternities and sororities, several service organizations, and intramural sports programs. Enrollment averages 650 men and 880 women.

At the graduate level, Birmingham-Southern offers a Master of Arts program in public and private management.

Location

Located in rolling country on a 197-acre campus in western Birmingham, the College is just 3 miles via I-59 from the downtown business district. Birmingham, Alabama's largest city, was recently honored by the U.S. Conference of Mayors as the "Most Livable City in America," and offers fine restaurants, museums, city and state parks, and theater. Its offerings are supplemented by the activities of four other Birmingham colleges. Birmingham's 17,000-seat Civic Center Coliseum is the setting for many outstanding cultural and athletic events.

Majors and Degrees

Birmingham-Southern offers the undergraduate degrees of Bachelor of Arts, Bachelor of Science, Bachelor of Music, Bachelor of Music Education, and Bachelor of Fine Arts. Departmental majors include accounting, art, biology, business administration, chemistry, computer science, dance, economics, education, English, French, German, history, international studies, mathematics, music, music education, philosophy, physics, political science, psychology, religion, sociology, Spanish, and theater arts. Individualized and interdisciplinary majors are also available.

Academic Program

The College operates on a 4-1-4 calendar. Thirty-six units are required for the bachelor's degree; these comprise 32 regular term units and 4 Interim Term units. The minimum residence requirement is two years. In addition to its traditional liberal arts programs, Birmingham-Southern offers a number of individualized learning opportunities to meet students' special needs and career goals. These are the Honors Program, the Americas Project, the Mentor Program, independent study, the student internship program, individualized majors, and the Interim Term. The College emphasizes international opportunities for students through course offerings, visitors to campus, and international travel/study programs. Through the Associated Colleges of the South, the College offers international programs in England, Brazil, and Central Europe.

Credit is available through CLEP and Advanced Placement tests. Credit may also be earned through a College-approved internship program.

Birmingham-Southern offers several special programs, including a six-week Summer Scholars Term for high school juniors and a dual-enrollment program that enables high school seniors to take college-credit courses. The College also offers a degree-granting Adult Studies Program.

Off-Campus Arrangements

The College sponsors an internship program through which students may earn credit for actual work experience. Depending on their major, students may be assigned positions in business, government, industry, human services, or other preprofessional areas of interest. Students may also take part in a cooperative exchange program that enables them to take courses at the University of Alabama at Birmingham, Miles College, or Samford University. They may also participate in Army ROTC at the University of Alabama at Birmingham or Air Force ROTC at Samford University.

Academic Facilities

Birmingham-Southern's highly unusual facilities include the Robert R. Meyer Planetarium, the first public planetarium in Alabama, and the College Theatre, which has three revolve-lift stages and is the only one of its kind in the nation. The N. E. Miles Library currently holds 270,296 bound volumes and 51,554 microform volumes. Recent academic additions include the Olin Computer Science/Mathematics Center, built in 1985; the $6.5-million Marguerite Jones Harbert Building, containing classrooms, laboratories, seminar rooms, and computer facilities, completed in 1988; and the Elton Bryson Stephens Science Laboratory Center, which houses chemistry and physics laboratory space, completed in 1990. Also completed in 1990 was the Lee and Nancy Bruno Residence Hall for women.

Costs

For 1999–2000, the total expense for the academic year was $22,973 for students living on campus and $15,998 for commuters. Additional fees are charged for individual music instruction. The figures quoted include fees for automobile registration, student insurance, student activity fee, tuition, dormitory accommodations and meals (for campus residents), books, and supplies.

Financial Aid

Birmingham-Southern feels strongly that well-qualified students should have an opportunity for a college education regardless of economic circumstances. Approximately 85 percent of the College's students receive financial aid of some kind. Scholarships and grants range from $500 to full tuition and may be renewed annually. Each student requesting financial assistance must submit the Free Application for Federal Student Aid (FAFSA). With the exception of the College's competitive scholarship programs and the Alabama Student Grant, all financial assistance awarded through the Office of Student Financial Aid is based on a demonstrated need determined from the required forms. Preference is given to those students who file by the March 1 priority deadline. The average award for those students who demonstrated need for the 1999–2000 academic year was approximately $11,500. In addition to the need-based programs, Birmingham-Southern awards more than $1.5 million in merit-based scholarships through a scholarship competition held in February.

Faculty

The faculty is composed of 101 full-time and 47 part-time teaching members; approximately 90 percent hold a Ph.D. degree or the terminal degree in their field. In addition to teaching, the faculty's major responsibility is advising students. Faculty members are actively involved in cocurricular activities planned primarily for students, and all are assigned a limited number of student advisees. They work closely with these students in planning and developing individual programs to fulfill the students' career interests. The student-faculty ratio is 12:1, and no freshman English class has more than 16 students.

Student Government

The Student Government Association of the College is chartered to operate under a constitution developed by the students, faculty, and administration. Through a large measure of self-government, this organization helps provide a well-balanced intellectual, educational, and social cocurricular program for all students. The Honor Code makes each student responsible for upholding the social and academic standards of the College. Students serve on numerous College committees, including recruitment, curriculum, fund-raising, and governance task forces.

Admission Requirements

Approximately 325 freshmen are selected for admission on the basis of high school record, ACT or SAT I scores, academic courses attempted, an admission essay, an interview, and recommendations of school officials. Applicants are expected to have completed at least 16 units of course work, 12 of which must be in academic subjects. Four units of English and at least two units each of mathematics, history, science, and social sciences are required, and two units of a foreign language are recommended. Students are encouraged to take more than the minimum units required in academic subjects.

Early admission, deferred entrance, and advanced standing are available. Although an interview is not required except in the case of early admission, each applicant is encouraged to visit the campus and talk with an admissions counselor or the vice president for admissions services.

Transfer applicants must have at least a C average (2.0 on a 4.0 scale) on a full schedule of courses acceptable to Birmingham-Southern and a status of good standing with a clear academic and social record from the last college attended. If the applicant has attended more than one college, his or her overall average at these schools must meet the minimum academic-year grade point average required at Birmingham-Southern. Transfer students may enroll at the beginning of any term.

Application and Information

The College has an admission priority date of January 15. After January 15, the College continues to consider applications on a rolling admission basis.

Preview Days are held in October and November.

Inquiries concerning admission should be addressed to:

DeeDee Barnes Bruns
Dean of Admission and Financial Aid
Birmingham-Southern College
900 Arkadelphia Road
Birmingham, Alabama 35254
Telephone: 205-226-4696
          800-523-5793 (toll-free)
E-mail: admission@bsc.edu
World Wide Web: http://www.bsc.edu

A Birmingham-Southern professor and student enjoy a conversation.

BISHOP'S UNIVERSITY
LENNOXVILLE, QUEBEC, CANADA

The University

Bishop's is a predominately residential university whose primary concern is offering undergraduate students a quality education in arts, education, sciences, and business administration. Its academic programmes are broadly based and stress the interrelationships of disciplines rather than their specializations. The residential aspect and small size of the University encourage an informal atmosphere in academic and social situations. Emphasis is placed on personal contact between faculty members and students through small classes and frequent use of seminars, laboratories, and tutorials. Self-directed study is encouraged through student research projects and special independent study programmes. Approximately 1,900 full-time and 500 part-time students were enrolled in Bishop's courses in 1999–2000.

Bishop's was founded as Bishop's College in 1843 under the sponsorship of the Right Reverend G. J. Mountain, third Anglican Bishop of Quebec, with the assistance of a group of clergy and laymen of the Eastern Townships. According to the intention of its founders, Bishop's was to have two functions: to offer the country at large the blessing of a sound and liberal education and to provide training for the clergy. Ten years later, in 1853, the college received a royal charter granting it the right to confer degrees.

The administration of Bishop's remained under the aegis of the Church of England until 1947 when the Corporation of the University was reconstituted as a nondenominational body. Theology was taught at the University until 1970, when the Faculty of Divinity was replaced with the Department of Religious Studies.

Bishop's offers undergraduate students the opportunity to pursue degrees at the Bachelor of Arts, Bachelor of Science, Bachelor of Business Administration, and Bachelor of Education levels in five divisions: business, education, humanities, natural sciences, and social sciences. Students are encouraged to study on as broad a front as they are capable of handling. Bishop's believes that a liberal arts education is the most practical preparation for career options in the twenty-first century, and the University is sure that it will enable its graduates to live richer and more satisfying lives. Students are encouraged to combine honours, majors, or minors not only within their given division, but also outside the division.

Bishop's University is a public university with a full-time student body of 1,900 students: 40 percent from Quebec, 50 percent from other Canadian provinces, and 10 percent from the United States and some forty other countries. Approximately 18 percent of students list French as their mother tongue. The language of instruction at Bishop's is English.

The Bishop's residence community consists of six buildings and is home to more than 500 men and women, 400 of whom are first-year students. All six buildings contain designated quiet areas offering students minimum noise tolerance 24 hours a day/seven days a week. Common areas within each residence are designated smoke free, as are certain individual rooms. All residence rooms are wired for Internet access. Twenty resident assistants are in place to make the transition to residence life and university life a smooth one. Residence spaces are allocated on a first-come, first-served basis once a student has been admitted to the University.

Students have access to a wide range of extracurricular activities. The student government oversees and funds more than fifty clubs and organizations on campus, including a campus radio station, newspaper, and yearbook. There are numerous academic, political, and general interest clubs available to all students. Athletics play a major role in the lives of Bishop's students. Full-time students may participate in intercollegiate sports including basketball, football, golf, rugby, skiing, and soccer. More than twenty intramural sports are available to all students, along with a wide variety of noncredit recreational programmes.

Location

Bishop's University is located in Lennoxville, Quebec, in the heart of the Eastern Townships of Quebec. Blessed with some of the finest outdoor opportunities in Canada, the area is less than a day's drive from Ottawa, Toronto, Boston, and New York City. Lennoxville is within a 2-hour drive of Montreal, Quebec City, Vermont, New Hampshire, and Maine. The city of Sherbrooke (population 150,000) is 5 minutes from campus.

Lennoxville (population 5,000) is a community that revolves around education; in addition to Bishop's University, it is home to Bishop's College School and Champlain Regional College, as well as the local elementary and high school. While it is primarily an English-speaking town, the French language is commonly heard. Lennoxville is a place where people can use their language of choice without concern. For those of all backgrounds, the bilingual environment offers a truly enriching opportunity.

Majors and Degrees

Bishop's undergraduate programmes lead to bachelor's degrees in arts, education, science, and business administration. Subjects offered for major or minor specialization in arts include art administration, anthropology, biology, business administration, Canadian studies, classical studies, communication and cultural studies, drama, economics, educational studies, English, English as a second language, Études françaises et québécoises, fine arts, geography, gerontology (clinical/medical or sociological/community), history, international studies, mathematics, modern languages (German, Italian, Japanese, and Spanish), music, philosophy, political economy, political studies, psychology, psychology and human resource management, public administration, public policy, Quebec studies, religion, sociology, and women's studies. In science, the major and minor subjects are biochemistry, biology, chemistry, computer science, environmental studies, information and decision science, mathematics, neuroscience, physics, and science teaching. In business, the concentration subjects are accounting, finance, general business management, human resources, information systems, international business, management science, and marketing. In education, students may concentrate in primary- or secondary-level education.

Students may design their programmes within a broad framework of options; a student may opt to major in a single subject (e.g., English, psychology, or chemistry), in a group of subjects represented by a division of the University (e.g., humanities, natural sciences, or social sciences), or in some combination of subjects from more than one division (e.g., geography and history). Honours programmes are offered in many subjects. Majors or honours and minor specializations may be combined in a programme.

Academic Programme

The academic year has two regular semesters: fall term (September to December) and winter term (January to May). Two summer sessions are also offered: early May to mid-June and mid-June to late July.

1280   www.petersons.com   *Peterson's Guide to Four-Year Colleges 2001*

Applicants who have completed an appropriate level of education outside the province of Quebec may be considered for entrance to a University programme generally requiring 120 credits—normally a minimum of eight semesters or four years. Adjustments in programme length may be made for students with International Baccalaureate or Advanced Placement courses. Applicants who have completed a Quebec Diploma of Collegial Studies are admitted to a 90-credit, three-year programme.

Off-Campus Arrangements

Bishop's University participates in a number of exchange programmes whereby students can spend a semester or an academic year at a designated university in more than twenty countries worldwide. Students on exchange programmes will pay tuition and related expenses at Bishop's, not at the host institution. Credits earned on an exchange programme are counted toward a student's Bishop's degree, but do not count in the student's cumulative average.

Academic Facilities

Within the last ten years, more than $33 million has been invested in improvements to the Bishop's campus, including many of the academic facilities.

The John Bassett Memorial Library has a seating capacity of more than 500 and houses a collection of more than 475,000 items, including books, microforms, maps, and audiovisual materials. The library also subscribes to more than 2,000 periodical titles.

There are more than 150 computers available on campus for student use, with the majority found in the Cole Computer Centre, giving students access to numerous applications as well as to the Internet. All residence rooms are wired for Internet use.

A three-hectare wetland conservation area on Bishop's campus serves as a field laboratory and observation area of the biology and geology students, as well as the focus for local birdwatchers and naturalists.

Centennial Theatre houses a charming and efficient main theatre with seating for 600 to 700. Superbly equipped, it provides an excellent learning facility as well as a splendid focus for finished products. The Studio Theatre functions as a dynamic multipurpose environment for traditional and experimental presentations. It seats 175 people in a technically sophisticated yet intimate space that can adapt to the special needs of theatre and music.

The majority of the classrooms and laboratories have been renovated within the last five years, including a number of "smart" classrooms.

Costs

For the 1999–2000 academic year, tuition fees for a normal full-time course load of 30 credits were $1668 for Quebec students, $3468 for students from the rest of Canada, and between $8268 and $9168 for visa students, depending on their program. Student service and association fees were $650 for the academic year. Residence fees (including meal plan) ranged from $4400 to $5400. Personal expenses such as transportation, clothing, and amusement are extra. (All figures are in Canadian dollars.)

Financial Aid

Scholarship awards range in value from $1000 to $5500 and are renewable annually. They are based on outstanding academic achievement or a combination of outstanding academic achievement and leadership qualities without reference to financial need. A second/third-year programme offers scholarships each year to students who did not receive Entrance Scholarships.

Faculty

All classes and laboratories at Bishop's are taught by professors. Bishop's professors devote their full attention to teaching; research is also encouraged and many faculty members have active programs. The student-faculty ratio is 16:1, with first-year class size averaging 35 students; in upper-year classes the average drops to 17. There are 105 full-time professors and 34 part-time professors at Bishop's.

Student Government

The Student Representative Council (S.R.C.) consists of an Executive Caucus, a General Council, and 12 student representatives forming a 17-member Executive Committee. The council serves the students' association on a broad scale. It selects students to serve on various University governing bodies and committees. The S.R.C. is also responsible for coordination and funding of the more than fifty clubs and organizations on campus.

Admission Requirements

Admission is based on a review of the whole academic dossier, including academic performance in the past year, rank in graduating class, and scores on standardized tests (if applicable). Students are expected to have a 75 percent average or equivalent, depending on where they have completed their studies. Admission is moderately difficult. Transfer applicants are evaluated on the basis of their university/college record and the criteria listed above.

Application and Information

The application deadline for September admission is March 1. Students may also enter Bishop's in January; the deadline for application to the winter semester is October 15. Students who apply before the deadline will normally be notified within one month as to their status at Bishop's. There is a $55 nonrefundable application fee that must accompany the application.

For information on admission or to schedule a visit to Bishop's, students should contact:

Tom Peterson
The Liaison Office
Bishop's University
Lennoxville, Quebec J1M 1Z7
Canada
Telephone: 819–822–9600 Ext. 2681
           800–567–2792 Ext. 2681 (toll-free)
Fax: 819-822-9661
E-mail: liaison@ubishops.ca
World Wide Web: http://www.ubishops.ca

Students relaxing in front of historic McGreer Hall.

BLACKBURN COLLEGE
CARLINVILLE, ILLINOIS

The College

Blackburn College is a small, independent, coeducational college with an academic emphasis on liberal arts, science, and teacher preparation. Blackburn was founded in 1837 and is affiliated with Presbyterian U.S.A. The 80-acre campus is home to 500 students and 100 faculty and staff members. There are sixteen major buildings, including six residence halls, a library, an art center, a dining hall, academic buildings, a music conservatory complex, a science building, a gymnasium with an indoor pool, a student center, a physical plant facility, and an administration building.

An important feature of Blackburn College is the Work Program, which has won wide recognition in American education. Blackburn is one of only seven colleges in the country to offer such a program, which is the only student-managed program of its kind. It enables the school to have the lowest tuition among any private four-year college in Illinois, and the tuition is among the lowest in the country.

Established in 1913, the Work Program relies on all resident students to work 160 hours per semester (10 hours per week) in a college-assigned job. Some students may have the opportunity to earn extra money by working up to 10 hours a week on campus. Commuter students may participate in the Work Program if their petition is approved. The Work Program helps to keep college overhead expenses down. Everyone—students, faculty members, and staff members—is involved in the success of the program. Work may be assigned according to a student's interests or experience in any of the following areas: academic, administrative, athletic services, dining services, library, bookstore, campus maintenance, security, student center, janitorial, or in community service. A Work Committee of twelve students makes all of the basic managerial decisions necessary and oversees the entire program. Work managers gain valuable experience in the tasks of scheduling, supervision, and management, as well as daily details. Students who participate in the program grasp lifelong principles—work together, accept responsibility, and function effectively in a variety of work experiences. The Work Program generates a true sense of community on campus. The partnership between work and a liberal education offers every student a chance to apply their growing knowledge to everyday tasks.

As an academic complement to the Work Program, Blackburn offers an innovative Leadership Program that allows students to graduate with the degree of their choice plus a Leadership Certificate. The Leadership Program was nationally recognize by the Templeton Guide: *Colleges of Character* in fall 1999. The program helps students develop practical leadership competencies as well as conceptual understanding, gives them an opportunity for guided reflection of their campus work experience, and instills in them a sense of appreciation for the contributions of all workers.

Location

Blackburn College is located in Carlinville, Illinois, a quiet community of nearly 6,000 people. Although it is not principally a college town, Blackburn is the business and professional center for the area. The campus is on the edge of town, adjacent to the low, rolling Midwestern countryside. The largest urban areas nearby are Springfield, the capital of Illinois, 45 miles to the north, and St. Louis, Missouri, 60 miles south. Carlinville is serviced by Amtrak, which operates between Chicago (220 miles north) and St. Louis. The closest major airports are in Springfield and St. Louis.

Majors and Degrees

Blackburn College offers the following majors leading to the B.A. degree: accounting, art, art with K-12 certification, biology, biology with secondary certification, business administration (management and leadership), chemistry, computer science, criminal justice, elementary education, English, British and American literature, English with secondary certification, history, history with secondary certification, international business and economics, mathematics, mathematics with secondary certification, medical technology, music, music with K-12 certification, physical education (education or management option), physical education with K-12 certification, political science, psychology, public administration, social science with secondary certification, Spanish, and Spanish with secondary certification. Students may also devise a double or interdisciplinary major to meet their individual interests and goals.

A 3-2 degree program in engineering is offered through Washington University in St. Louis, Missouri. The program leads to a Bachelor of Science degree in engineering and applied sciences from Washington State University and a Bachelor of Arts in another field from Blackburn College. Preprofessional preparation is offered in dentistry, law, medicine, nursing, physical therapy, and veterinary science.

COMPASS is Blackburn College's degree completion program for adult learners. COMPASS enables working adults to complete a bachelor's degree in Organizational Management while they pursue their career. The COMPASS program meets the educational needs of people who are past traditional college age who want to complete their undergraduate education.

Academic Program

The academic program at Blackburn College provides a broad-based liberal arts education, enabling students to study a wide variety of subjects in detail and depth. The strong liberal arts education offers students an effective knowledge base. Students must complete divisional requirements to earn a B.A. degree. Blackburn operates on a semester calendar. Credit is granted to students to receiving scores of 3, 4, and 5 on the Advanced Placement tests of the College Board and who successfully pass specific CLEP subject-area examinations.

Through its nationally acclaimed Work Program and the efforts of the Career Development Center, Blackburn has created a useful and practical program to help students choose a career and prepare for them effectively. Career planning begins during the freshman and sophomore years and culminates in workshops and seminars in the senior year. The Career Development Center offers placement services to graduating seniors and alumni.

The elementary and secondary education programs are recognized by the Illinois Certification Board and the State Superintendent of Public Instruction. Blackburn College is accredited by the North Central Association of Colleges and Schools.

Off-Campus Arrangements

The college offers a variety of opportunities for off-campus study. Each fall, through the Mexico program, between 5 and 10 Blackburn students enroll for a semester at the National Autonomous University of Mexico, located in the heart of Mexico City.

The Washington Semester program offers students a practical learning experience in all areas of government. Classes are conducted at the American University in Washington, D.C. The college also participates in an internship and study program under the auspices of the Washington Center for Learning Alternatives. Students work in government and political offices for 35 hours a week, attending seminars and undertaking study projects.

The British Study Program provides students with a semester at the University of Wales, Swansea, beginning in January. Participation is open to qualified students from any academic department, with emphasis on those applying during their junior year.

Internship Programs, in conjunction with any of the major disciplines, involve working and learning experience off campus. Many exciting opportunities are available for students in business, government, and service agencies.

Academic Facilities

Blackburn's academic facilities include an 80,000-volume library with spacious areas for individual study. A specially constructed wing provides for audiovisual presentations to classes. The library also has access to an additional 600,000 volumes through an interlibrary system. The Bothwell Conservatory of Music houses a 450-seat theater with a proscenium stage and set-construction workshops. Extensive laboratory facilities are provided in Olin Science Building and Alumni Hall of Biology. Renner, the art building, contains studios for painting, ceramics, and graphics. Hudson Hall, the main academic building, has been renovated with state-of-the-art technology to bring Blackburn into the 21st century. Each classroom is now equipped with video and data technology to assist in educating today's student.

Costs

The total cost for tuition, fees, and room and board for 2000–01 is $11,965. This figure does not include the cost of books (approximately $500 per year) and personal expenses. Tuition alone is only $8190.

Financial Aid

Approximately 90 percent of Blackburn College students receive some form of financial aid; the average aid package is about $6900 per year. Students may receive aid from the Illinois State Scholarship Commission, the Federal Pell Grant Program, Blackburn grants, and variety of loan programs. The application deadline for priority awards is April 1. Applications received after that date are considered as long as funds remain available.

Faculty

The primary concern of the college's highly professional faculty is the development of each student. Blackburn is a small college; therefore, students and professors know each other as individuals. Eighty-five percent of the faculty members hold the highest degree in their field. Classes are small, averaging 18 students, and the faculty-student ratio is 1:14. Professors participate actively in all phases of College life.

Student Government

The opinions and experiences of students are taken seriously. Students can participate fully in College activities through the Student Senate and the Board of Student Activities.

Admission Requirements

Blackburn needs and attracts young people who have confidence in themselves and are willing to make a direct working contribution to their own college life. Applicants should have a minimum grade point average of 2.8, should rank in the top 50 percent of their high school class, and should have a minimum combined score of 990 on the SAT I or a minimum composite score of 20 on the ACT.

Some highly qualified students may enter after their junior year in high school. No distinction is made between them and regular applicants after they arrive on campus.

Transfer applicants are considered on the basis of their high school and college records. Credit is accepted for liberal arts courses; credits earned at nonaccredited institutions may be accepted provisionally.

All applicants must submit scores on either the SAT I or the ACT.

Application and Information

Blackburn has a rolling admission plan, considering applications on the basis of six semesters of high school work. Application forms can be obtained from the Office of Admissions. Applicants should see that all their academic records are sent to the College, including the high school transcript, ACT or SAT I scores, and college transcripts if an applicant is transferring from another institution. Each application is evaluated by 4 faculty members and 2 students. Applicants are notified within three weeks, however, the committee may ask to delay its final decision until it has additional academic or related information. Blackburn does not charge a fee for applying.

For more information about Blackburn and its distinctive educational program, students should contact:

Director of Admissions
Blackburn College
Carlinville, IL 62626
Telephone: 800-233-3550 (toll-free)
E-mail: admit@mail.blackburn.edu
World Wide Web: http://www.blackburn.edu

One of the buildings at Blackburn College.

BLOOMFIELD COLLEGE
BLOOMFIELD, NEW JERSEY

The College
Founded in 1868, Bloomfield College (BC) is an independent four-year coeducational college that offers programs in the liberal arts and sciences, creative arts and technology, and professional studies, which include accounting, business administration, computer information systems, criminal justice, materials management, nursing, prechiropractic, and the sciences. Bloomfield is accredited by the Middle States Association of Colleges and Schools, and the nursing program is accredited by the National League for Nursing Accrediting Commission. The College is chartered by the state of New Jersey, and its academic programs are approved by the New Jersey Commission on Higher Education. The accounting program is a Registered Accounting Curriculum for Public Accountancy in the State of New Jersey and meets the state's educational requirements for candidates applying to sit for the CPA examination. The College is affiliated with the Presbyterian Church (U.S.A.) through the Synod of the Northeast and is a member of the Association of Presbyterian Colleges and Universities.

With more than thirty organizations to choose from, students have many opportunities to engage in cocurricular programs that will enrich their educational experience. In addition to an active student government, activities include the Nursing Student Association, the Association of Latin American Students, the International Student Association, and a variety of departmental clubs and social organizations. Campus publications include *In Print*, the College yearbook, and *Common Ground*, the honors literary magazine. The College Center is the social and recreational focus of the College community. Meeting rooms, a snack bar, lounges, a game room, and the Office of Student Activities are all located there. Centrally located in the College Center, the Golden Eagle Bookstore is a convenient place to buy textbooks, school supplies, magazines, gifts, clothes, snacks, and personal items. Bloomfield College has a full program of intercollegiate and intramural sports and recreational activities. Men's intercollegiate sports are baseball, basketball, and soccer. Women's intercollegiate sports are basketball, soccer, softball, and volleyball. The College is a member of the National Association of Intercollegiate Athletics, the Central Atlantic College Conference, and the New Jersey Association of Intercollegiate Athletics for Women. In addition to general on-campus housing, the College provides a residence hall for first-year students, as well as for seniors and honors students. "Theme" houses are also available on campus. Housing priority is given to first-year students and students who live beyond a reasonable commuting distance. A complete residence life program provides academic, social, and recreational programs for resident students. The Center for Academic Development offers individual tutoring and group workshops to all students. Academic advising is ongoing, and students meet with their adviser before registering each semester. Other support services include the Enhanced Counseling Program, the Educational Opportunity Fund Program, personal counseling, career counseling and placement, women's services, and the College Health Service.

Location
Located in Bloomfield, New Jersey, a suburban, residential community just 15 miles from New York City, the College attracts resident students from many geographic areas, as well as commuter students from the New Jersey/New York metropolitan area. Bloomfield is easily accessible by bus, train, or car from northern New Jersey and from the boroughs of Manhattan, the Bronx, Staten Island, and Brooklyn as well as Rockland and Westchester counties in New York.

Majors and Degrees
Bloomfield College offers the Bachelor of Arts and Bachelor of Science degrees. Majors and their concentrations include accounting (professional accounting and general accounting), biology (biomedical laboratory science, environmental studies, general biology, prechiropractic studies, prepodiatric studies, and preprofessional studies), business administration (business management, with specializations in computer information systems and materials management), chemistry (biochemistry and general chemistry), clinical laboratory sciences (cytotechnology, medical technology, and toxicology), computer information systems, creative arts and technology, education, English (communications and literature), history, mathematics, nursing, philosophy, political science (general and public policy), psychology, religion, and sociology (criminal justice and general sociology).

Bloomfield College maintains a joint Bachelor of Science/Doctor of Chiropractic degree program with the following accredited chiropractic colleges: New York Chiropractic College, New York; University of Bridgeport College of Chiropractic, Connecticut; Palmer College of Chiropractic, Iowa; Los Angeles College of Chiropractic, California; Life Chiropractic College, Georgia; Life Chiropractic College West, California; Cleveland Chiropractic College, Missouri; Cleveland Chiropractic College, California; Northwestern College of Chiropractic, Minnesota; Logan College of Chiropractic, Missouri; and Parker College of Chiropractic, Texas. Bloomfield College offers three versions of the prechiropractic program, each preparing students for admission to chiropractic colleges offering the Doctor of Chiropractic (D.C.) degree. (See Academic Program section below.) Bloomfield offers certificate programs in industrial/organizational psychology and materials management. BC also offers a Microsoft Certified System Engineer (MCSE) program, one of the software industry's leading certification programs.

Academic Program
Degree candidacy requires the successful completion of at least 33 course units; a full course unit is equivalent to 4 semester hours. A minimum of 16 course units must be completed at an advanced level. Four categories of courses are offered at the College: general education courses, distribution courses, specific major and major required courses, and elective courses. Course requirements for the degree vary among majors. The prechiropractic program is a sequence of courses preparing the student for study for the Doctor of Chiropractic (D.C.) degree. The student may either complete graduation requirements for a bachelor's degree or transfer from Bloomfield College directly into a D.C. program after three years. Other special programs available at Bloomfield College include an RN/B.S.N. Transfer Program for nursing students who already have a two-year degree; the Educational Opportunity Fund Program, a state-funded program of educational and special services for

disadvantaged students; English as a second language; an honors program; a circus program, under the auspices of the division of creative arts and technology, in which students join a performing troupe; Weekend College, a complete degree program for adults that is offered on alternate weekends; and various internship programs.

The Bloomfield College academic calendar consists of 15-week fall and spring semesters and an optional summer session consisting of a 14-week term or two 7-week terms.

Off-Campus Arrangements

Through an arrangement with Fairleigh Dickinson University, Bloomfield students may spend a semester of study at Wroxton College in England during their sophomore, junior, or senior year. Unlike study-abroad programs at many colleges, the Wroxton experience is affordable because financial aid is available to qualified students. Opportunities available through the Wroxton program include studying Shakespeare at the Shakespeare Institute in Stratford-upon-Avon, exploring world politics with scholars from Oxford University, and planned trips to London, Paris, and Edinburgh. Travel to other parts of Europe during a ten-day midterm break is also available. Through Bloomfield's membership in the Consortium for International Studies, students may study in eighteen European, African, Asian, and South American countries.

Academic Facilities

The Bloomfield College library houses a collection of more than 64,000 titles, including subscriptions to more than 400 periodicals and 1,000 electronic journals, an up-to-date reference collection, and thousands of reels of microfilm and microfiche, as well as musical recordings and scores, films, and videotapes. The library is particularly proud of its extensive audiovisual collection. The library has an online, automated card catalog, offers access to four databases on the Internet, and holds a variety of CD-ROMs in the humanities, nursing, and social sciences. Library instruction and research assistance make the library a complete learning center. The academic computing facilities consist of four laboratories. The three main computer labs, located in the Science Building, are networked. They offer students the use of sixty computers and fifteen printers. Widely used software, such as Windows, WordPerfect, Microsoft Word for Windows, Excel, and Lotus 1-2-3, is available, as are popular database and statistics packages and programming languages and packages used by specific disciplines such as biology, mathematics, and nursing. Graphics packages and desktop publishing packages are also available. The fourth lab, located in the College library, has fifteen computers and five printers that are used primarily for writing and research. Training in word processing is available through the computer labs. They are open for student use Monday through Thursday from 8 a.m. to 10 p.m., Friday from 8 a.m. to 9:30 p.m., and Saturday from 9 a.m. to 5 p.m. The library computer lab is also open on Sunday from 4 p.m. to 10 p.m. A new, state-of-the-art library will be completed in spring 2000.

Costs

Tuition in 1999–2000 for full-time students was $10,300 per year. Tuition for part-time students was $260 per credit. Room and board for resident students were $5150 per year. Fees totaled $150.

Financial Aid

In 1999–2000, Bloomfield College students received more than $13.5 million in scholarships and financial aid, with more than 90 percent of the full-time day student population receiving some form of financial assistance. Academic scholarships are administered by the Office of Admission; athletic scholarships are administered by the athletics department. College, state, and federal programs, such as grants, loans, and work-study, are administered by the Financial Aid Office.

Faculty

A highly qualified and diverse faculty instructs more than 2,000 students of all ages in day, evening, and weekend sessions, with a student-faculty ratio of 17:1. Approximately 65 percent of the full-time faculty members have earned doctorates or terminal degrees.

Student Government

The Bloomfield College Day Student Government represents registered day students, all organized student groups and clubs, and the College's academic divisions. It also serves as a vehicle of communication for student concerns and interests. The Bloomfield College Evening Student Council provides a means of communication among evening students, faculty, and administration and assists the College in meeting the educational needs of the evening student. The administrative staff and the College faculty serve as advisers to all student government activities and enterprises.

Admission Requirements

Bloomfield College admits qualified applicants who demonstrate motivation, desire, and the potential to benefit from and contribute to programs of study in the liberal arts and sciences, creative arts and technology, and professional studies. Applicants are accepted throughout the year on a rolling basis and are notified within one week of the College's receipt of required materials. Once admitted, students are placed according to their academic preparation and achievement. The College's mission is to prepare students to meet a standard of excellence in a multiracial, multicultural society, and admission is open to all qualified students without regard to race, color, creed, religion, national or ethnic origin, sex, age, or physical disability. The College welcomes applications from high school seniors, transfer students, and adult students returning to school.

Application and Information

All applicants are encouraged to visit the College to discuss their academic and career plans with an admission counselor. Applicants may also spend a day on campus attending classes and talking with students, faculty members, and administrators about academic programs and student activities as well as the issues of admission and financial assistance. Recommended application deadlines are May 15 for the fall semester, December 15 for the spring semester, and May 15 for the summer session. Applications received after these dates are considered on a space-available basis. For further information, students may contact:

Lourdes Mangual de Delgado
Vice President for Enrollment Management
   and Dean of Admission
Bloomfield College
1 Park Place
Bloomfield, New Jersey 07003
Telephone: 973-748-9000 Ext. 230
          800-848-4555 (toll-free)
Fax: 973-748-0916
E-mail: admission@bloomfield.edu
World Wide Web: http://www.bloomfield.edu

BLUFFTON COLLEGE
BLUFFTON, OHIO

The College

Bluffton College is a fully accredited, four-year Christian liberal arts college in northwestern Ohio. Founded in 1899 by regional leaders of the General Conference Mennonite Church, it is today affiliated with the Central and Eastern districts of the General Conference. Shaped by this historic peace church tradition and coupled with its desire for excellence in all programs, Bluffton College seeks to prepare students of all backgrounds for life as well as vocation, for responsible citizenship, for service to all peoples, and ultimately for the purposes of God's universal kingdom.

More than 1,000 students from several states and many other countries study at Bluffton College, which is accredited by the North Central Association of Colleges and Schools (30 North LaSalle Street, Suite 2400, Chicago, Illinois 60602; 800-621-7440, toll-free). The College continues to receive national recognition in *Barron's Best Buys in College Education* for providing outstanding quality at a reasonable price. Bluffton is one of only a handful of Ohio colleges to be included in the prestigious *John Templeton Foundation Honor Roll of Character-Building Colleges*.

The student life program is rich with opportunities for personal and spiritual growth. Weekly chapel services and biweekly Sunday morning worship services provide a community context for joint worship. Examples of the many groups in which students participate include BASIC (Brothers And Sisters In Christ), Diakonia (Christian service/outreach groups), Habitat for Humanity, and PALS Drug Awareness programs. The Honor System, practiced in all classes and throughout campus life, promotes honest, open communication between all members of the campus community.

Students participate in many organizations and activities, including vocal and instrumental music, departmental and preprofessional clubs, student newspaper, student government, and many others. As a member of the NCAA Division III and the Heartland Collegiate Athletic Conference, Bluffton fields varsity athletic teams for both men and women. Men's sports include baseball, basketball, cross-country, football, golf, soccer, tennis, and track. Varsity teams for women include basketball, cross-country, golf, soccer, softball, tennis, track, and volleyball. Bluffton is the first NCAA Division III college in Ohio and the nation to be selected for the NCAA Life Skills program, which helps prepare student athletes for life after college.

Residence life is integral to the campus community. All students are required to live in campus housing unless they are married or commuting from home. No self-selective fraternities or sororities are permitted, and students are expected to adhere to campus standards of conduct, which prohibit the use of tobacco, alcohol, and drugs. A satisfaction guarantee is offered to new residential students.

In addition to its undergraduate degrees, Bluffton offers a Master of Arts in Education and a Master of Organizational Management.

Location

Bluffton College is located just off Interstate 75, midway between Lima and Findlay, Ohio, in the Allen County village of Bluffton (population 3,400). Several restaurants and a movie theater are within walking distance of campus, and easy access to I-75 provides many additional opportunities in Findlay, Lima, Toledo, Dayton, and Columbus.

The campus is situated on 60 beautifully wooded acres and is adjacent to the 130-acre Bluffton College Nature Preserve.

Majors and Degrees

Bluffton College offers Bachelor of Arts degrees. Bachelor's degrees are available in accounting; adolescent/young adult, multi-age, and vocational education; apparel/textiles merchandising and design; art; biology; business administration; chemistry; child development; communication; computer science; criminal justice; dietetics; early childhood education; economics; English; family and consumer sciences; food and nutrition–dietetics; food and nutrition–wellness, health, physical education, and recreation (HPER); history; information systems; intervention specialist studies (special education); mathematics; middle childhood education; music; music education; physics; premedicine; psychology; recreation management; religion; social studies; social work; sociology; Spanish; Spanish/economics; sport management; and youth ministries and recreation. In addition, a number of minors, preprofessional programs, and special programs are available, including prelaw, peace and conflict studies, TESOL studies, women's studies, and self-designed majors.

Academic Program

The Bluffton College curriculum is centered on a new liberal arts and sciences general education program. The strength of this program lies in the many integrated courses in social science, humanities, fine arts, and natural sciences that build upon one another as students advance toward earning their degree. Courses in Bible and theology, an integrated cross-cultural course, and a capstone course titled Christian Values in a Global Community complete the general education program. Key components of the general education curriculum include the First Year Seminar for new students and the cross-cultural requirement. Students seeking a bachelor's degree must complete a minimum of 122 semester hours of academic work and maintain a minimum overall grade point average of 2.0.

Off-Campus Arrangements

Bluffton College offers several semester-long international and cross-cultural opportunities. Current programs include study in Northern Ireland, Poland, Central America, and Mexico. Bluffton is also a member of the Council of Christian Colleges and Universities, which offers study programs at various U.S. locations, including Washington, D.C., as well as international programs in the Middle East, Russia, and Central America. Many Bluffton students participate in short-term off-campus projects with organizations such as Habitat for Humanity, Witness for Peace, and the Urban Life Center in Chicago. In addition, Bluffton students may complete up to four supervised independent study courses, which may be used for off-campus study.

Academic Facilities

The Musselman Library, a 1930 building of Georgian colonial architecture, was the gift of Mr. and Mrs. C. H. Musselman. It holds approximately 148,000 volumes, 116,000 microfilm units, approximately 4,000 current periodicals, and more than 350 CD-ROMs. The library has about 4,500 maps and receives many important U.S. government publications as a selective depository library. The library is a member of both the OPAL (Ohio Private Academic Libraries) and the OhioLINK consortia. Through OhioLINK, Bluffton College students and faculty and staff members have access to more than 24 million library items held at more than seventy college and university libraries throughout the state, to more than 60 separate databases, and to hundreds of full-text periodicals.

The newest facility on campus is the Al and Marie Yoder Recital Hall. Connected to Mosiman Hall, the music building, Yoder Hall provides a state-of-the-art performance facility for student recitals and guest artists. Weekly chapel services are also held in Yoder Hall.

Completed in 1991, the Sauder Visual Arts Center contains an art gallery and classroom and offers studio facilities for printing, painting, drawing, sculpture, ceramics, woodworking, welding, and photography. Shoker Science Center is a unique underground science facility that houses integrated laboratories for all the sciences, a science library, and instructional computers. College Hall serves as the main administrative building and includes the Education Department, several classrooms, and the Educational Media Center. The Mara Alva Family and Consumer Sciences House is a nine-room Cape Cod–style house that serves as a home-management residence for students in the department.

Founders Hall is a complete physical education facility, containing a main gymnasium, a newly renovated auxiliary gymnasium, and a weight room. Other recent additions to campus include the Salzman Stadium and Ramseyer Hall, a new residence hall for 111 students.

A new academic center, Centennial Hall, is under construction that will bring together many of the academic disciplines. The academic center will be a multilevel building at the center of campus and will contain state-of-the-art computing facilities, a new media center, technologically enhanced classrooms, and faculty offices. The academic center is scheduled to open in summer 2000.

Primary student computer access is provided through the microcomputer center located in Centennial Hall. All students may have e-mail addresses, and Internet access is provided in the lab. In addition, computers are located in residence halls, academic departments, and other locations on campus. All residence halls are equipped for students who wish to bring their own computer.

Costs

Tuition for the 2000–01 school year (based on 24 to 34 semester hours per year) is $14,076. Board is $3046 and room is $2076, for a total of $19,198. There is also a $250 technology fee. Books and personal expenses are additional.

Financial Aid

Nearly 100 percent of Bluffton College students receive some form of financial aid. Some awards are based solely on financial need, such as the Bluffton College Grant, while others are tied to academic achievement or demonstrated leadership and service to others. Scholarships and grants unique to Bluffton include the Presidential Scholarship Competition; the Academic Honors Scholarship; the Tuition Equalization Scholarship Program, for students scoring at least 23 on the ACT or 1050 on the SAT I and ranking in the top 25 percent of their class or achieving at least a 3.0 grade point average; Leadership/Service Grants, which are available to students who demonstrate significant contributions outside the classroom in school, church, and community activities; and Church Matching Scholarships, which award up to $2000 to students whose church has awarded them a scholarship to attend Bluffton. Additional College awards include scholarships for music and art and need-based grants to dependents of ministers and those serving in foreign missions. The Learn and Earn program provides an opportunity for many students to work on campus to help with expenses and gain valuable work experience.

Faculty

A high-quality program depends on a superior faculty. Students at Bluffton are taught by 65 full-time faculty members and more than 33 part-time faculty members. Nearly 80 percent of the full-time faculty members have earned the doctorate or appropriate terminal degree, and all faculty members teach on a regular basis. Many faculty members continue to research and write yet remain committed to teaching. The faculty members are very approachable and work together with students to create a unique learning environment based on mutual trust and respect.

Student Government

A democratic atmosphere prevails in the Bluffton College campus community. The Student Senate is a very important part of the campus community and actively represents the interests of the student body to the administration. Composed of students elected from each of the four classes, the Senate has primary responsibility in the areas of cocurricular activities. Hall associations are organized for the purpose of self-government and social activities.

Admission Requirements

Requirements for admission to the first-year class include graduation from a secondary school or a GED certificate; satisfactory secondary school work, with preference given to students ranking in the top half of their class and who have taken the recommended secondary preparation of 4 units of English, 3 units of mathematics, and 3 units each of social sciences, science, and a foreign language; and satisfactory performance on either the ACT or SAT I. Also considered are participation in cocurricular activities, moral character, purpose for college study, and recommendations.

Application and Information

Application for admission should be made at the end of the junior year or early in the senior year of high school. The deadline for submitting the application for the fall term is May 31. For all other terms the deadline is fifteen days prior to the intended date of enrollment.

Applicants must complete and return the application with a $20 fee along with recommendations from the school guidance counselor and a teacher, a high school transcript, and scores from either the ACT or the SAT I. A personal campus visit and interview are strongly encouraged.

The Office of Admissions operates on a rolling basis and makes its decision and notifies the applicant soon after receiving the required items. Students wishing to receive additional information may contact:

Office of Admissions
Bluffton College
280 West College Avenue
Bluffton, Ohio 45817-1196
Telephone: 419-358-3257
           800-488-3257 (toll-free)
Fax: 419-358-3232
E-mail: admissions@bluffton.edu
World Wide Web: http://www.bluffton.edu

Students enjoy Bluffton College's wooded campus.

Peterson's Guide to Four-Year Colleges 2001   www.petersons.com

THE BOSTON ARCHITECTURAL CENTER
School of Architecture
School of Interior Design
BOSTON, MASSACHUSETTS

The School

The Boston Architectural Center (BAC) has roots that can be traced to 1889, when the Boston Architectural Club established a formal school of architecture fashioned after the atelier teaching method. The atelier idea was practical: students would learn their profession by working for and being mentored by an architect.

Today, the architecture and interior design programs at the BAC still offer this unique learning mode that integrates both academic study and professional experience. All degree students work in the design profession during the day and attend classes at night. This manner of learning allows students to gain professional training in their field while attending school. The BAC faculty is comprised of respected professionals from design firms in the Boston area, many of whom are at the Center on a volunteer basis. This special relationship between the Center and the profession allows the BAC to offer an exceptional education and maintain an affordable tuition. The fusion of education and practice provides BAC graduates with a solid preparation for a career in design, a professional network, and the most direct route to a professional license. Prior to graduation, architecture students can complete the intern requirements for NCARB (National Council of Architectural Registration Boards) licensing. Interior design students can fulfill a majority of the intern requirements for NCIDQ (National Council for Interior Design Qualification) certification.

The BAC is a private institution that awards bachelor's and master's degrees in both architecture and interior design. The school is accredited by the New England Association of Schools and Colleges and the National Architectural Accreditation Board. The average age of a BAC student is 26; 85 percent have previous college experience.

Location

Located in Boston's historic Back Bay, the BAC is close to many cultural and educational institutions and is easily accessible by public transportation. The Center occupies two adjoining buildings on Newbury Street, known for its abundance of fine restaurants, shops, and art galleries. Within walking distance of the BAC are Symphony Hall, Fenway Park, The Museum of Fine Arts, the Isabella Stewart Gardner Museum, and Boston's Public Gardens. Boston is a livable community that is rich in diversity and offers entertainment suitable to a variety of tastes.

Majors and Degrees

The BAC awards bachelor's and master's degrees in architecture and interior design. Although there are not specified majors within the degree programs, students have the opportunity to enroll in electives that explore the diversity of the design profession; they include preservation architecture, interior architecture, CAD, and facilities management.

Academic Program

Like the careers of architecture and interior design, the BAC degree programs are demanding, rewarding, and multidisciplinary. Both programs combine classroom and professional learning to unite theory and practice. To graduate a student must earn 122 academic credits and 54 practice credits. It is possible to complete the program in approximately seven years. The BAC follows the traditional semester calendar, and a range of classes is offered in the eight-week summer session.

During the day, students are employed in paid professional positions to fulfill the practice component of the degree requirement. BAC students enlist their supervisors as mentors and together they endorse a statement of professional goals and objectives. Practice skill levels range from entry-level clerical support to design and project management. The 54 practice credits, which are earned through contract learning as approved by the American Council on Education, may be completed in approximately three years of full-time work. After completion of the practice curriculum degree requirement, work credit may be applied to the NCARB intern requirement and the NCIDQ intern requirement. During the evening, students participate in the academic curriculum, which consists of courses in history and theory, visual studies, technology and management, the arts and sciences, and design studios. At the heart of these studies is the design studio sequence. Instead of using terms such as freshman and sophomore, BAC students' grade levels are defined by their studio levels.

The academic curriculum is divided into three segments. In Segment I, or Foundation, architecture and interior design students participate in similar course work. Foundation studios focus on basic design principles and are supported by visual studies and CAD courses. Other Foundation classes focus on architectural history, construction technology, ethical issues in design practice, computer use, and structural systems. About half of the general education classes are completed in Segment I; they include humanities, mathematics, physics, and writing. Rounding off the Foundation studies, students participate in a sketch problem, which is a twelve-hour design charette. Segment I concludes with a portfolio review, which a student must pass before progressing to the next level of design studios.

The two degree programs separate to focus on their respective disciplines via Segment II. Architecture design studios emphasize building design but also cover a wide range of topics, including urban design and the theoretical issues of form-making and design study. Interior design studios focus on the creation of meaningful interior space through layout and form, color, light, and finish and explore the challenges associated with institutional, commercial, retail, and residential environments. Segment II studios for both programs are complemented by advanced courses in technology and management, history and theory, arts and sciences, and visual studies. Segment II includes three sketch problems and concludes with a portfolio review.

Segment III begins with advanced design studios and professional electives related to the student's area of concentration. The final phase of Segment III is Thesis, a two-semester project conducted with the counsel of a thesis adviser and a panel of experts. Students conceptualize and frame their own Thesis design project, which not only highlights each student's personal design style but also unites the skills, education, and experience gained through both academic and practical learning. The final presentation of this rigorous exploration of design issues is an actual structure or interior.

Progression through the BAC programs is measured by educational progress standards of the academic and practice curriculum, minimum credit requirements, and quantitative grade point average requirements. Students' work is qualitatively evaluated through a series of portfolio and progress reviews. Portfolios are evaluated on the basis of demonstrated growth and progress as well as the ability to synthesize learning from all educational settings and integrate that learning into design work.

Off-Campus Arrangements

Through the Pro-Arts Consortium, BAC students have the opportunity to register for one course per semester at one of the five nearby art and design schools, including the Berklee School of Music, the Boston Conservatory, Emerson College, Massachusetts College of Art, and The School of the Museum of Fine Arts. Students also have borrowing privileges at the libraries of all Pro-Arts institutions. The BAC and the Art Institute of Boston have a cross-registration agreement that includes a large selection of course offerings. The cost of both arrangements is covered by BAC tuition.

The Tours committee of the BAC sponsors an annual study-abroad program that students may participate in either for credit or for pleasure. The tours are ten days to two weeks in duration and are usually preceded by an accompanying elective course instructed by the tour guide. Recent destinations have included India, Japan, Hungary, Austria, Mexico, Italy, and Egypt.

Academic Facilities

The BAC Library houses an impressive collection of 25,000 books and 120 periodicals. Resources focus on architecture, interior design, urban planning, energy conservation, and architectural history. In addition, the BAC maintains a slide library, which contains approximately 40,000 architecture and interior design images that survey historical and contemporary designs.

The Interior Design Materials Library houses a collection of reference materials that pertain to interior products and current samples of finishes, furniture, lighting equipment, and construction materials. Students make use of the Materials Library for research, specification, and actual samples.

Fully equipped computer facilities that house Macintosh, 486, and Pentium-based computer systems are available for student use. Word processing, spreadsheet, desktop publishing, and CAD applications are supported. A variety of two- and three-dimensional–design, modeling, rendering, and animation applications are available on the Macintosh systems. Additional equipment includes a pen dot graphics plotter, a color/black and white scanner, a high-resolution laser printer, and a dye-sublimation printer.

Media Services offers a wide range of audiovisual support for BAC students. Equipment such as slide, overhead, and opaque projectors; video playback decks; and a videotape library are available. Students may also utilize the BAC's photography studio, copy stand, and complete black and white darkroom.

The BAC Woodstudio contains hand and power tools, work benches, and a supply of wood stock suitable for small projects. Classes related to woodworking design are offered in this 700-square-foot facility.

Costs

For the 2000–01 academic year, BAC tuition is $3341 per semester. Additional administrative fees may apply. All students must pay a $10 student government fee. Massachusetts state law requires that all full-time students be covered by a qualifying health plan. In the case that a student does not already have coverage, a comprehensive health insurance package is available through the BAC at an additional cost.

Financial Aid

The BAC provides both institutional and federal or state-funded assistance to qualified students who demonstrate financial need. Sources of aid include federally funded subsidized loans and federal, state, and institutional grants and scholarships. Tuition, fees, food, housing, books, supplies, transportation, and personal costs are taken into account to determine need. Institutional aid is available to qualified students who have completed one semester. Numerous design scholarships and awards are also available.

Faculty

The academic faculty of the BAC consists of 275 dedicated practitioners of the design industries. Approximately 90 percent of the faculty members hold advanced or professional degrees. Students benefit from a tutorial relationship with instructors because of small class size. The overall student-faculty ratio is 8:1 in lecture classes and 6:1 in design studios.

Also unique to the BAC is the Practice Curriculum Faculty, a group of dedicated architects and interior designers who counsel students on a one-to-one basis. Their function is to review students' progress through the practice component and assess their professional development. This personal advising nurtures the mentoring relationship that exists between BAC students and the profession.

Student Government

All full-time degree students are members of Atelier, the BAC student organization. Atelier's primary purposes are to expand students' educational opportunities through student-initiated activities, advocate concerns and interests of students to the administration of the school, and assist students in achieving their professional goals. Atelier operates a student lounge, publishes the student newspaper (*Noumenon*), sponsors the student journal (*Theory/Praxis*), holds the charter for the Boston region AIAS (American Institute of Architecture Students), and organizes social events and exhibits of art and student work. Officers of Atelier are voting members of the BAC Board of Directors and are represented on each of its committees.

All interior design students participate in the Interior Design Student Organization (IDSO). The IDSO develops and coordinates special events such as lectures and exhibits and focuses on issues that explore the students' interests in the design field.

Admission Requirements

The BAC remains dedicated to its founders' goal of allowing all who are interested to pursue a design education. Students may enter the BAC upon completion of high school or the equivalent. An official high school transcript or certificate of a GED, a complete application, and an application fee are the only admission requirements. Standardized test scores are not required. The BAC is restricted in its ability to admit international students and is only admitting master's students at this time. Therefore, international applicants to the bachelor's program must supply the BAC with evidence of legal immigrant or nonimmigrant status.

Applicants interested in transferring academic credit from other institutions must submit official transcripts, copies of course descriptions, and a BAC Transfer of Academic Credit application. Although a portfolio is not required, one that demonstrates fine arts and design ability can be submitted for possible advanced standing in the design studio sequence.

Application and Information

Applications are reviewed and letters of admission are issued on a rolling basis. Students are admitted to the entering class of their choice on a space availability basis. It is strongly suggested that students submit their applications to the BAC at least six months prior to the desired entering semester.

Admissions Office
Boston Architectural Center
320 Newbury Street
Boston, Massachusetts 02115

Telephone: 617-585-0123
Fax: 617-585-0121
E-mail: admissions@the-bac.edu
World Wide Web: http://www.the-bac.edu

BOSTON COLLEGE
CHESTNUT HILL, MASSACHUSETTS

The College

Boston College (BC) was founded in 1863 by the Jesuits to serve the sons of Boston's Irish immigrants. Today a coeducational university on more than 200 acres in Chestnut Hill, BC may seem a world apart from the small school in the crowded heart of Boston that was its first home. Through more than thirteen decades of growth and change, however, BC has held fast to the Jesuit ideals that inspired its founders. A Jesuit education today, as a century ago, is grounded in the liberal arts and in a commitment to the service of others.

As the needs of its student body have grown, so have the university's offerings: twelve schools, colleges, and institutes now offer eleven degree programs and two certificate programs. Undergraduates may enroll in the College of Arts and Sciences, the Wallace E. Carroll School of Management, the School of Nursing, or the School of Education.

BC's 8,900 undergraduates come from many backgrounds. The university draws from all fifty states and more than ninety countries. Students' religious and cultural backgrounds are similarly diverse. Today, the university's AHANA (African-American, Hispanic, Asian, and Native American) and international students comprise more than 20 percent of the undergraduate student body.

In today's complex and increasingly diverse world, the university believes that the best education is one that broadens a student's capacity to reason, to think, and to make critical judgments in a wide range of areas. Thus, each BC student fulfills a core of liberal arts courses from which he or she can pursue degrees in more than fifty areas of study and choose from more than 1,400 class sections throughout the university.

According to several recent national publications, BC is in the top tier of the nation's colleges and universities. The foundation for that achievement is the university's scholars and researchers—more than 650 full-time professionals who make up the faculty. The kinship between teachers and students is one of the hallmarks of a BC education; that relationship is nurtured by a student-teacher ratio of 13:1. The median class size at the university is 25 students.

At BC, learning continues beyond the classroom in more than 170 student-run organizations. These include student government, honor societies, language and cultural organizations, performance ensembles, political groups, preprofessional clubs, publications, and service organizations. BC also sponsors seventeen varsity teams for men and sixteen for women, all of which compete at the NCAA Division I level. The university also supports twenty club and twenty-one intramural sports.

Location

Located in the Chestnut Hill section of Newton, BC sits on the doorstep of one of America's great cities, a center of culture and education for more than three centuries. It is an energetic, cosmopolitan city that draws life and enthusiasm from the more than 200,000 college students in residence during the academic year. Located just 6 miles from downtown Boston and with easy access to the city via the trolley system that stops at the foot of the campus, BC offers the best of both worlds: a scenic suburban setting neighboring an exciting metropolitan center.

Majors and Degrees

The College of Arts and Sciences (A&S) is the oldest and largest of the four undergraduate schools at BC. A&S students must complete thirty-eight 1-semester courses, thirty-two of them in A&S departments. The normal course load is five courses per semester for the first three years and four courses per semester during the senior year. The undergraduate curriculum includes the University Core Curriculum and ten to twelve courses in the major field, with the remainder of courses chosen as electives. A&S offers degrees in the following areas: art history, biochemistry, biology, chemistry, classical studies, communication, computer science, economics, English, environmental geosciences, film studies, French, geology and geophysics, Germanic studies, Hispanic studies, history, Italian, linguistics, mathematics, music, philosophy, physics, political science, psychology, Romance languages and literatures, Slavic and Eastern languages, sociology, studio art, theater, and theology. Preprofessional advisement is also available in medical, dental, and legal programs. Students can also select from more than twenty interdisciplinary programs.

The Carroll School of Management (CSOM) educates students to be leaders in business and industry and in public agencies, educational institutions, and service organizations. The School offers concentrations in accounting, computer science, economics, finance, general management, human resource management, management information systems, marketing, and operations and strategic management and places special emphasis on ethical management and international management.

The Lynch School of Education (LSOE) prepares students for education and human services professions. Programs provide a general education, professional preparation, and specialized education in the major field. Fieldwork in area schools is closely linked to course work in each specialization. LSOE awards degrees upon completion of thirty-eight courses, including the University Core, a major field of study in education, and a second major in a subject field or an interdisciplinary area in A&S that complements the student's program. Areas of specialization include early childhood education, elementary education, human development, secondary education, and special needs education.

The School of Nursing (SON) offers a four-year program of study leading to a Bachelor of Science degree. The three major components to the curriculum are nursing major courses, electives, and the required University Core. In all courses, principles of wellness, illness, rehabilitation, and health maintenance serve as a theoretical basis in preparing students for professional nursing practice. Nursing courses include traditional classes, simulated and audiovisual laboratory activities on campus, and clinical learning activities in health-care settings.

Academic Program

Every BC education is centered on a core curriculum—a set of required courses. BC offers a core curriculum because it believes in the unity of knowledge. While the core, which is continually reviewed by a committee of faculty members, varies somewhat by school, its common elements include literature, natural science, writing, philosophy, theology, social science, mathematics, art, and the study of a non-European culture.

There are a wide variety of extraordinary academic programs that BC students can participate in to enhance their educational experience. They include, among others, honors programs within each of the university's four undergraduate schools, Undergraduate Faculty Research Fellows, the Scholar of the College, PULSE, and Perspectives on Western Culture.

Off-Campus Arrangements

BC encourages all students to take part in internship programs. More than 70 percent of BC undergraduates participate in at least one internship over their college years. Internships can be paid or unpaid and may take place during the academic year or the summer; some carry academic credit.

BC students may take on the challenge of international study in programs administered by BC at universities in more than twenty countries. BC students who study abroad typically do so in their junior year, but there is also a range of summer-abroad opportunities. The Office of International Programs helps students with program selection and applications and maintains a library of reference books and professional evaluations of international study programs.

Academic Facilities

BC's eight libraries contain 1.7 million printed volumes, more than 3.2 million items in microform, 171,000 government documents, 12 million manuscripts and archival items, and a wide collection of films. The resources of the library system range from some of Europe's earliest printed books to hundreds of computerized databases. Students with personal computers have dorm-room access to these databases as well as to Quest and other library information sources through InfoEagle, the campus information network.

Research laboratories in the state-of-the-art science facilities have been specially designed to accommodate the advanced instrumentation required for modern science and to provide flexibility for accommodating new equipment. The Merkert Chemistry Center was carefully designed to place classrooms, laboratories, computer facilities, and office space in proximity and to facilitate interaction among faculty members, researchers, and students. In addition to the Center's 109,000-square-foot undergraduate teaching laboratories, special labs are designed and outfitted for research and teaching in physical, theoretical, organic, and inorganic chemistry and in biochemistry.

Costs

Tuition for the 2000–01 academic year is $22,680. The freshman room rate is $4810. The board plan, which is required for all resident freshmen, is $3700. Freshman mandatory fees, which include a charge for on-campus orientation, total $840.

Financial Aid

BC maintains a financial aid program to assist deserving and qualified students who might otherwise not be able to attend the university. Due to the limited availability of funds, BC may not be able to meet the demonstrated need of every student applying for financial aid. Overall, 47 percent of students receive some form of need-based financial aid. The average need-based award in 1999–2000 was more than $19,000. This assistance included more than $10 million in need-based grants. The university offers financial aid to students based on need as demonstrated by completion of the College Scholarship Service's Financial Aid PROFILE and the Free Application for Federal Student Aid (FAFSA). All requirements and deadlines and complete instructions are available in BC admission literature. An application for financial aid in no way affects a decision on admission.

Each year, BC chooses 15 incoming freshmen as Presidential Scholars to receive merit-based half-tuition scholarships. Students are selected from all candidates who apply through the early action program.

Faculty

BC has 650 full-time faculty members. Of these faculty members, 97 percent hold doctoral degrees. The 130 Jesuits living on the BC campus make up the largest Jesuit community in the world. About half are active in the university's administration and teaching.

Student Government

The Undergraduate Government of Boston College (UGBC), formed in 1968, is divided into three branches: the Executive, the Senate, and the Judiciary. The Executive is led by the president and vice president, who are elected in the spring of each year by the entire student body. UGBC's goal is to serve the students by providing services and opportunities and by representing them in the best manner possible to the university community. To accomplish this goal, UGBC provides many educational, social, and cultural programs, such as concerts, lectures, roundtables, and other programs.

Admission Requirements

The undergraduate admission staff pays particular attention to students who have done well in a demanding college-preparatory curriculum, including Advanced Placement and honors courses when available. For the class of 2004, there were nearly 21,000 applications for 2,100 places. The majority of incoming freshmen ranked in the top 10 percent of their class. The SAT I scores of the middle half of enrolling freshmen were 1210–1360. On the ACT, scores of the middle half were between 27 and 30.

Application and Information

Students applying to Boston College for a place in the freshman class must complete both the Common Application and the Boston College Supplemental Application. Both forms are available at any of the following Web sites: www.commonapp.org, www.embark.com, and www.collegeboard.org.

Students applying through the regular admission program must submit both forms, along with the $55 application fee, by January 15. Candidates are notified of action taken on their application between April 1 and April 15. Admitted students intending to matriculate are required to forward an acceptance fee to be received by the admission office by May 1.

Students with superior academic credentials who view Boston College as a top choice may apply through the nonbinding early action program. These applicants must submit both application forms, along with the $55 application fee, by November 1. Candidates learn of their admission decision before December 25 but have the standard deadline (May 1) to reserve their places as freshmen.

BC accepts transfer applicants each semester. Transfer candidates should request applications for transfer admission from the Office of Undergraduate Admission. In addition to the high school records and standardized test results, transfer applicants must furnish transcripts from all postsecondary institutions they have attended.

For more information, students should contact:

Office of Undergraduate Admission
Devlin Hall 208
Boston College
Chestnut Hill, Massachusetts 02467
Telephone: 617-552-3100
              800-360-2522 (toll-free)
Fax: 617-552-0798
E-mail: ugadmis@bc.edu
World Wide Web: http://www.bc.edu

Located just 6 miles from downtown Boston, Boston College offers the best of both worlds: a scenic suburban setting neighboring an exciting metropolitan center.

BOSTON UNIVERSITY
BOSTON, MASSACHUSETTS

The University
A private, nonsectarian, coeducational university located on the banks of the Charles River, Boston University is an energizing community. As a major research institution, the University fosters creativity and innovation. As an undergraduate institution, its faculty comprises some of the world's foremost experts who are dedicated to the art of teaching. Of the classes held in the freshman and sophomore years, the vast majority contain fewer than 30 students. Together, the ten undergraduate schools and colleges offer more than 130 programs of study in areas as diverse as music, international relations, education, physical therapy, biomedical engineering, broadcast journalism, and management. With students from all fifty states and more than 100 countries, Boston University has one of the most culturally diverse student bodies in the United States. The campus community supports more than 350 different student organizations, ranging from ice broomball teams to performing arts groups, community service activities to student government, and clubs with cultural and professional as well as academic affiliations.

Location
Boston is an international center of cultural and intellectual activity, with a concentration of facilities for higher education unrivaled throughout the world. Home to many fine museums, baseball's Fenway Park, an active theater district, and the Boston Symphony Orchestra, the city has a vibrant energy all its own. Because 1 in 5 residents is a college student, Boston is also the ultimate college town.

Majors and Degrees
Boston University grants the B.A., B.S., B.S.B.A., B.S.Ed., B.A.S., B.L.S., B.A.A., Mus.B., and B.F.A. undergraduate degrees. Of the University's sixteen schools and colleges, ten offer opportunities for undergraduate study. The following information indicates the range of undergraduate programs available.

Students in the College of Arts and Sciences may concentrate in American studies, ancient Greek, ancient Greek and Latin, anthropology, archaeology, art history, astronomy, astronomy/physics, biochemistry, biochemistry/molecular biology, biology, biology with a specialization in ecology and conservation biology, biology with a specialization in marine science, biology with a specialization in neuroscience, chemistry, classical civilization, classics/philosophy, classics/religion, computer science, earth sciences, East Asian studies, economics, economics/mathematics, English, environmental analysis and policy, environmental earth science, environmental science, French/continental European literatures, French language and literature, geography, geology, German/continental European literatures, German language and literature, Hispanic/continental European literatures, Hispanic language and literature, history, independent concentration, international relations, Italian/continental European literatures, Italian studies, Latin, Latin American studies, linguistics, mathematics, mathematics/computer science, mathematics/mathematics education, mathematics/philosophy, modern Greek studies, music (nonperformance), philosophy, philosophy/anthropology, philosophy/physics, philosophy/political science, philosophy/psychology, philosophy/religion, physics, planetary/space science, political science, psychology, religion, Russian/continental European literatures, Russian language and literature, Russian/Eastern European studies, sociology, and urban studies/public policy. Special curricula include seven-year programs in liberal arts and dentistry and liberal arts and medicine; the Modular Medical Integrated Curriculum; a dual-degree program; and various combined B.A./M.A. degree programs.

The College of Communication offers major programs of undergraduate study in film and television, journalism (including broadcast journalism, magazine journalism, news-editorial print journalism, and photojournalism), and advertising, mass communications, and public relations.

Majors in the College of Engineering include aerospace, biomedical, computer systems, electrical, interdisciplinary, manufacturing, and mechanical engineering.

Areas of concentration in the School of Education include bilingual education, early childhood education, deaf studies, elementary education, English education, history and social science education, human movement (including physical education), mathematics education, modern foreign language education, science education, and special education.

The School of Hospitality Administration offers a rigorous program in the management of hotels, restaurants, food and beverage service, travel and tourism, and entertainment.

Concentrations in the School of Management include accounting, finance, general management, international management, management information systems, marketing, operations management, and organizational behavior.

The School for the Arts offers programs in music (history and literature of music, music education, performance, and theory and composition), theater arts (acting; directing; scenic, costume, and lighting design; stage management; production; technical production; and theater studies), and visual arts (art education, graphic design, painting, and sculpture).

Sargent College of Health and Rehabilitation Sciences offers programs in athletic training, clinical exercise physiology, communication disorders, human physiology, nutritional sciences, and rehabilitation and human services, as well as five-year combined B.S./M.S. degree programs in physical therapy and occupational therapy.

The College of General Studies offers a two-year liberal-arts-based program that features a core curriculum and intensive team teaching It is designed for those students who wish to sharpen their learning skills in preparation for entry at the junior level into select schools and colleges of the University.

The University Professors allow exceptionally able students to seek degrees in areas that combine, bridge, or fall between established University disciplines. Students follow a core curriculum for two years, then design their own course of study for the remaining two years.

The Metropolitan College Science and Engineering Program offers a five-semester program for those students who need additional preparation for studying the sciences or engineering.

Academic Program
A Boston University education combines the elements of a traditional liberal arts education with training for the professions. In addition, highly qualified freshmen and sophomores may be invited to participate in honors programs in the College of Arts and Sciences or the School of Management.

Boston University has programs that take students around the world. Internships, fieldwork, and study-abroad opportunities are offered on six continents in twenty-one cities within sixteen countries. The University has a series of internships in Beijing,

1292   www.petersons.com   *Peterson's Guide to Four-Year Colleges 2001*

Dublin, London, Madrid, Moscow, Paris, and Sydney in art/architecture, business/economics, human health services, journalism/communications, and visual/performing arts. Fieldwork programs may be found in Belize and Ecuador, with study-abroad options in Dresden, Grenoble, Haifa, Madrid, Niamey, Oxford, Padova, and Venice. Summer study programs exist in Australia, China, England, France, Italy, Scotland, and Spain.

Boston University operates on a calendar of two semesters and two summer terms. Students generally take four courses each semester; thirty-two courses are required for graduation. Most degree programs are built around a core of humanities and social and natural sciences. Concentrations require eight to thirteen courses. Electives generally total 30–40 percent of the courses taken, allowing for interdisciplinary study.

Academic Facilities

Two of the newest facilities on campus include the Photonics Center and the School of Management building. The Photonics Center features research labs designed to support industry partners who seek to develop new photonics-based products in addition to College of Engineering classroom and laboratory space. The School of Management building represents one of the most technologically advanced educational facilities in the country, with more than 2,000 data and communication ports as well as a dedicated career center and management library.

The Office of Information Technology provides a cluster of large multiuser IBM RS/6000 computers supporting a wide range of applications such as e-mail, World Wide Web browsing, word processing, programming, and research; public computing facilities equipped with workstations, terminals, and laser printers; and a high-speed campus network interconnecting these resources and linking them to the Internet. The Center for Computational Science hosts the SGI Power Challenge Array and the SGI Origin2000 supercomputer, the first two of three generations of supercomputers being acquired by the University from Silicon Graphics. Additional computing resources are available through the various colleges and departments. An 850-seat proscenium theater, studio space for visual arts students, more than 100 practice rooms for music, and a 575-seat music performance center are indicative of the academic support provided by facilities. More than 2 million library volumes and 3.6 million microform units are contained in Mugar Memorial Library, where the Twentieth-Century Archives are held, including the papers of Martin Luther King Jr., Theodore Roosevelt, Robert Frost, and Bette Davis.

Costs

Tuition for 2000–01 is $24,700; room and board are $8450. University and college fees come to $344. These costs are exclusive of books, supplies, travel, and personal expenses.

Financial Aid

The Office of Financial Assistance offers both financial and advisory resources to students and their families who request help in meeting the expenses of attending Boston University. Information, counseling, and referrals are available to all families, regardless of income level or financial circumstances. In addition to providing both need-based and merit awards to many students, the office serves a much larger constituency of students and parents. Financial assistance officers review with students and their families the available means of financing an education, whether through the University or through external funding sources.

Financial aid can take several forms and may be awarded in a variety of combinations. Types of aid include scholarships and grants, state and federal grants and loans, and federal Work-Study and other part-time employment. When applying for financial aid, students should understand that University and federal student aid funds are limited. The University is unable to meet the full calculated need of every student offered admission. Those students with the strongest academic records are given priority for receiving available funds. In addition, as part of Boston University's commitment to excellence, the University recognizes academic achievement through a number of merit award programs.

Faculty

Students are taught by faculty members who distinguish themselves by their ability, experience, research, and publications. In addition to fulfilling their classroom responsibilities, faculty members are accessible as academic and career advisers who assist students in obtaining internships as well research opportunities.

Student Government

Each school and college has its own student government, which regulates student affairs within the school or college. The University-wide student governing body, the Student Union, has representation from all University schools and colleges. Each residence hall also has its own student government, composed of elected representatives from each floor.

Admission Requirements

The Board of Admissions considers each candidate individually. Primary emphasis is placed on the strength of the secondary school record, but required test scores (SAT I or ACT), character, breadth of interest, school recommendations, and other personal qualifications are also carefully evaluated. Secondary school graduation or an equivalency diploma is required of all candidates; for the School for the Arts, an audition or a portfolio is required. For certain programs, interviews and SAT II Subject Test scores are required. The *Undergraduate Bulletin* or the *Boston University Application for Admission* should be consulted for specific information.

Students with earned credit from other colleges may be admitted. Applicants are considered for September or January entrance. Transfer students are not eligible for admission to the Accelerated Liberal Arts Medical or Dental Programs, the College of General Studies, the Metropolitan College Science and Engineering Program, or Sargent College's physical therapy program. January admission to the School for the Arts (Divisions of Theatre and Visual Arts) and Sargent College's occupational therapy and nutritional sciences programs are also not available to transfer students. Boston University does maintain programs of early decision (binding agreement), early admission, and deferred admission.

Boston University admits qualified students regardless of their race, color, national origin, religion, sex, age, or disability to all its programs and activities.

Application and Information

Application forms and information are available by writing to the address below. The deadline for applications is January 1 (accelerated-program applicants must file by December 1). Candidates for financial aid should complete the College Scholarship Service (CSS) Financial Aid PROFILE and the Free Application for Federal Student Aid (FAFSA) in time for the evaluation to reach the University by February 15. Transfer students applying for September admission should submit their applications, CSS/Financial Aid PROFILE forms, and Free Application for Federal Student Aid (FAFSA) forms by April 1.

Office of Admissions
Boston University
121 Bay State Road
Boston, Massachusetts 02215
Telephone: 617-353-2300
E-mail: admissions@bu.edu
World Wide Web: http://www.bu.edu/admissions

BOWDOIN COLLEGE
BRUNSWICK, MAINE

The College

Bowdoin is an independent, nonsectarian, coeducational, residential undergraduate college of 1,550 students. It was chartered in 1794. Its first president declared in 1802 that Bowdoin's mission was to serve "the Common Good," a declaration of essential purpose that has endured.

Bowdoin provides students with a liberal arts education of the highest quality in a distinctive atmosphere that allows them to pursue their own intellectual interests and develop their talents. Bowdoin students work hard, but the environment at the College is one of collaboration, not competition. Bowdoin students are independent, and many pursue a personal academic interest by designing an independent study course. This allows them to explore topics that might not be covered in an existing course and to work closely with a faculty mentor. Bowdoin students come from forty-seven states and thirty countries. To enhance the educational scope and stimulation of the Bowdoin community, the College encourages applications from students who represent cultures, regions, or backgrounds that will contribute to the diversity of the campus community.

Maine is a region of great variety, with cities, large and small towns, rural areas, beaches, and a rocky coastline. Most Bowdoin students enjoy their interaction with the state; they often take part in recreational, cultural, political, or social service activities available in the Brunswick area, in Portland (25 miles from campus), and at other locations around the state.

A campus union, constructed in the former Hyde Athletic Cage, provides a central gathering place for the Bowdoin community. The vibrant, multilevel Smith Union contains a pub and grill, café, bookstore, convenience store, mailroom, and meeting areas and provides varied spaces for relaxation and entertainment.

Students are largely responsible for numerous extracurricular activities. Among the more than eighty active organizations are a weekly newspaper, FM radio station, cable television station, film society, student environmental group, and outing club. Musical organizations abound, including a chamber choir, orchestra, chorus, concert band, wind ensemble, and men's, women's, and coed double quartets. The Department of Theater and Dance provides opportunities in theater and in ballet, modern, and jazz dance, supplemented by student productions through Masque and Gown and the dance group VAGUE. A major renovation and construction project completed in the spring of 2000 resulted in a new 600-seat theater, a laboratory theater, and new rehearsal and design space for Bowdoin's expanding program in theater arts.

Student organizations include an African-American Society, Latin American Student Organization, Asian Student Association, Korean-American Student Association, Bowdoin Women's Association, a gay/lesbian organization, and a variety of political and special interest groups. Religious interests are served by several organizations, and more than 300 students are involved in voluntary service programs. In addition, the College encourages and supports a wide range of lectures, performances, and events. The Student Union Committee and other student organizations plan community service projects, concerts, parties, and weekend social events.

Bowdoin fields thirty-two varsity teams (thirteen men's, fourteen women's, and two coed) in seventeen intercollegiate sports. Men's intercollegiate competition is offered in baseball, basketball, cross-country, football, hockey, lacrosse, skiing, soccer, squash, swimming, tennis, and track (winter and spring). Women's teams are fielded in basketball, cross-country, field hockey, ice hockey, lacrosse, skiing, soccer, softball, squash, swimming, tennis, track (winter and spring), and volleyball. Bowdoin fields coed sailing and golf teams. College-supported club sports include men's and women's crew, coed water polo, men's and women's Ultimate Frisbee, men's volleyball, and men's and women's rugby. Intramural programs involve hundreds of men and women in ten different sports. Facilities include two gymnasiums; a field house with an indoor track, four tennis courts, and a sixteen-lane swimming pool; sixteen squash courts; an ice arena; an all-weather outdoor track; eight tennis hard courts; and 35 acres of playing fields. An all-purpose artificial-surface field will be completed in spring 2000. The 4,800-square-foot Watson Fitness Center features up-to-date cardiovascular and strength-training equipment.

College housing is provided for all first-year and sophomore students and is available for most upperclass students. In 1997, the College began a new residential housing system that links each of five upperclass houses and residence halls with a first-year dormitory. Students who live off campus may arrange partial board bills in the College dining rooms. Two new residences, each housing about 50 students, feature suites and lounges. Another new residence, accommodating 120 students, opened in September 1999.

Location

Bowdoin is located in Brunswick, a coastal New England town of 22,000. Like most of the towns around it, Brunswick has a long history and strong traditions. Colonial and Federal in architecture, and largely residential, Brunswick features bookstores, record shops, coffeehouses, and restaurants. The town center is a very short walk from campus.

Majors and Degrees

Bowdoin offers the Bachelor of Arts degree in the following areas: Africana studies, anthropology, art history and criticism, Asian studies, biochemistry, biology, chemistry, classics, classics/archaeology, computer science, economics, English, French, geology, German, government and legal studies, history, mathematics, music, neuroscience, philosophy, physics and astronomy, psychology, religion, Romance languages, Russian, sociology, Spanish, visual arts, and women's studies. A coordinate major in environmental studies is also offered. Additional interdisciplinary majors are offered in related fields, and students may choose a self-designed major. Programs are offered in arctic studies, film studies, Latin American studies, and theater and dance. Courses in education are offered to supplement majors in teaching fields. Courses are also offered in architecture and gay and lesbian studies.

Bowdoin participates in joint liberal arts–engineering programs with California Institute of Technology and Columbia University and in a liberal arts–law program with the latter.

Academic Program

The liberal arts are the center of a Bowdoin education. Academic advisers work with students in their selection of courses, majors, optional off-campus study, and full academic programs.

In the first two years, students explore the liberal arts through their choice of at least two courses in each of the three divisions of the curriculum: natural sciences and mathematics, social and behavioral sciences, and humanities. Students also take two courses that focus on non-Eurocentric cultures or societies to learn about the ways in which different people perceive, express, and cope with the challenges of life. Small classes, including numerous first-year seminars, and independent study directly with professors are important features of a Bowdoin education.

1294   www.petersons.com   Peterson's Guide to Four-Year Colleges 2001

To be awarded the Bachelor of Arts degree, a student must complete a total of thirty-two courses; spend four semesters in residence, at least two of them during the junior and senior years; and fulfill the requirements of a major program. Students may elect a single major, a double major, or an interdisciplinary or self-designed major, and may also choose a minor program in most areas of the curriculum.

Bowdoin operates on a two-semester calendar. First-semester classes begin near Labor Day, and examinations take place prior to the winter break. The second semester begins in mid-January and ends with examinations in mid-May.

Off-Campus Arrangements

Bowdoin offers its students many opportunities to participate in a variety of domestic and international programs. All study away from campus must be approved by the Office of Off-Campus Study and the student's major department. Students may apply to study in virtually any country; the Office of Off-Campus Study has a list of approved programs. The College charges a per-semester or annual administrative fee for participation in non-Bowdoin study abroad programs. Bowdoin co-sponsors intercollegiate study abroad programs in Sri Lanka, South India, Rome, and Stockholm. Three new study-away programs, sponsored jointly with Bates and Colby Colleges, have been developed. Two opened in fall 1999, in London, England, and in Quito, Ecuador, and the third opens in summer 2000 in Cape Town, South Africa. Defined domestic exchange programs include the Williams College–Mystic Seaport program, the National Theater Institute program, and the Twelve College Exchange program. Approximately one in three juniors takes advantage of these opportunities for off-campus study. There are also opportunities for off-campus fieldwork in biology, biochemistry, arctic studies, and coastal studies.

Academic Facilities

Bowdoin covers a tract of about 110 acres and includes more than eighty buildings on the central campus and surrounding streets. The nucleus of academic life is the Hawthorne-Longfellow Library, which contains approximately 900,000 volumes and provides access to extensive electronic resources. The Hatch Science Library and an online catalog linking Bowdoin, Bates, Colby, and the University of Maine provide unusual resources for an undergraduate liberal arts college. The Bowdoin College Museum of Art and the Peary-MacMillan Arctic Museum contain collections that are among the nation's finest college collections, while the Visual Arts Center provides an auditorium, galleries, and studios for the use of Bowdoin students. For musicians, Gibson Hall provides classrooms, practice rooms, recital halls, a music library, a recording studio, an electronic music studio, and lounges. Academic Computing Services, a department of Bowdoin's Computing Center, manages seven widely accessible microcomputer laboratories for student, faculty, and staff use; provides computer assistance services and supports faculty instructional and research activities; and manages the College's central computers and network. A new $20-million building for the sciences, housing the departments of geology, biology, environmental studies, and chemistry, opened in 1997, and renovation of Searles Hall for physics, math, and computer science was completed in fall 1999. Bowdoin's off-campus facilities include the Breckinridge Public Affairs Center in York, Maine; a Coastal Studies Center, which includes a terrestrial lab, a marine lab, and a renovated farmhouse for seminar and studio space; and additional stations for marine and ornithological research located near the campus and at Kent Island in the Bay of Fundy, Canada.

Costs

Tuition for 2000–01 is $25,345, fees are $545 (this includes the student activities fee of $270 and the health services fee of $275), and room and board total $6760—for a total fee of $32,650. Travel costs vary. Books and personal expenses are estimated at $1825.

Financial Aid

Bowdoin does not want cost to be an obstacle to anyone who wants to attend the College. Financial aid at Bowdoin is need-based, and Bowdoin meets the full, demonstrated need of all admitted U.S. applicants for all four years. Aid may include grants, loans, and campus jobs. In 1998–99, about 40 percent of Bowdoin students received approximately $12.3 million in need-based aid. Awards to entering students ranged from $500 to $32,000. The average aid award last year was $19,647.

Faculty

Bowdoin is a wholly undergraduate institution, and all of its students are taught by professors rather than graduate teaching assistants. There are 151 full-time teaching faculty members; the student-faculty ratio is about 10:1. Faculty members serve as academic advisers, and many also serve as advisers to student organizations. The Bowdoin faculty is both accessible and involved, and students and students and teachers gather informally frequently throughout the year.

Student Government

Bowdoin's student government was reformed in 1997 to create a large two-part structure composed of the Student Assembly and the Executive Committee. The Assembly consists of class presidents, house officers, and open positions. The Executive Committee consists of 9 students elected at large. Students are also elected to serve as representatives to committees of the Board of Trustees and of the faculty.

Admission Requirements

Bowdoin is highly selective. Academic accomplishments and talents are given the greatest weight in the admission process. Extracurricular activities and written recommendations are also very important. Added consideration is given to those with demonstrated skills in leadership, communication, social service, the arts, athletics, and other areas in which the College has programs. The College does not require SAT I, SAT II: Subject Test, or ACT scores for admission, but scores will be considered if a student chooses to submit them. About 20 percent of Bowdoin's accepted applicants in 1999 decided not to submit standardized test scores. Beyond requiring evidence of intellectual commitment, the College seeks diversity in the selection of each new class. About a third of each entering class is accepted under the College's early decision program.

Application and Information

Application materials include the Common Application and the Bowdoin Supplement. Both are included in the Bowdoin Viewbook or are sent by the Bowdoin College Admissions Office upon request. Materials required with the application include a School Report, two teacher recommendations, a supplementary essay, a mid-year School Report, and $55 application fee or an application fee waiver. An interview with either a staff member in the Bowdoin Admissions Office on campus or with a Bowdoin alumni interviewer in a student's area is strongly recommended but not required. Candidates should make appointments in advance by letter or phone. Campus tours are available weekdays and most Saturday mornings throughout the year. Group information sessions are held several times per week throughout the spring, summer, and fall. Students should call the Admissions Office to confirm schedules. There are two early decision options. Students who apply by November 15 under the Early Decision I option are notified by late December. Early Decision II applications are due by January 1, and applicants are notified in mid-February. Regular applications are also due by January 1; candidates are notified by mid-April.

Admissions
Bowdoin College
5000 College Station
Brunswick, Maine 04011-8441
Telephone: 207-725-3100
Fax: 207-725-3101
World Wide Web: http://www.bowdoin.edu

BOWIE STATE UNIVERSITY
BOWIE, MARYLAND

The University

Bowie State University began as a normal school in the city of Baltimore in 1865, and it has evolved over the years into a four-year, coeducational, liberal arts institution. It is currently situated on a beautiful 337-acre campus in Prince Georges County, Maryland, and offers both graduate and undergraduate programs of study. Teacher education programs were established in 1925; in 1935, with state authorization, a four-year program for the training of elementary school teachers was begun and the school became the Maryland State Teachers College at Bowie. In 1951, with the approval of the State Board of Education, its governing body at the time, the college established a teacher-preparation curriculum for the training of teachers for the core program in the junior high schools. Ten years later, permission was granted to institute a teacher-training program for secondary education. A liberal arts program was established in 1963, and the institution's name was changed to Bowie State College. In 1988, Bowie State achieved university status.

Bowie State University received its first state funding of $5000 in 1908. Its physical plant is valued at more than $37 million, and its current enrollment is 5,024 students, 1,870 of whom are in the Graduate School. The University has twenty-one buildings on campus with the addition of the new $21-million state-of-the-art Center for Learning and Technology (opens in fall 2000). Two of the buildings (the Communication Arts Center and the physical education complex) were completed in 1973, and an administration building opened in 1977. Five residence halls, including Goodloe Hall, the honors students' residence, and Alex Haley Hall, the new (completed in 1994) state-of-the-art residence hall, house approximately 800 students. The $2.6-million physical education complex houses a 3,000-seat basketball arena, an Olympic-size swimming pool with underwater viewing windows and facilities for 200 spectators, an apparatus gymnasium, a dance studio, a wrestling room, a weight-training room, eight handball/squash courts, a therapy room, and offices for instructors and coaches. The $5.5-million University Activities Center includes a cafeteria.

Bowie State University considers the student activities program a vital part of the total educational program. Students have access to more than forty different activities. These include student government, the student union, intercollegiate athletics, eight fraternities and sororities, numerous departmental clubs and preprofessional organizations, and music and drama organizations.

The Graduate School grants the Master of Education in six areas of concentration; the Master of Arts in administrative management, counseling psychology, English, human resource development, organizational communications, and teaching; and the Master of Science in applied computational math, computer science, management information systems, and nursing. The Adler-Dreikurs Institute of Human Relations at Bowie State University is the first fully accredited master's-degree-granting Adlerian institute in the United States.

A Doctorate of Education in education leadership begins in spring 2000.

Bowie State University admits students without regard to sex, religion, or nationality, and the University does not discriminate on the basis of race, creed, color, national or ethnic origin, age, sex, or handicap. The University is accredited by the Middle States Association of Colleges and Schools and approved by the Maryland State Department of Education. Its programs in teacher education, social work education, nursing (for RNs only), business, and computer science are accredited by the National Council for Accreditation of Teacher Education, the National Council on Social Work Education, the National League for Nursing Accrediting Commission, the Maryland Board of Nursing, the Association of Collegiate Business Schools and Programs, and the Computer Science Accreditation Commission of the Computing Sciences Accreditation Board, respectively.

Location

Bowie, Maryland, is in a triangle formed by Annapolis (20 miles east), Baltimore (25 miles north), and Washington, D.C. (17 miles southwest). The suburban setting provides an ideal, safe environment for students and scholars, with access to all of the important cultural, governmental, and business activities in any of the three metropolitan areas.

Majors and Degrees

Bowie State University offers the Bachelor of Arts or Bachelor of Science degree with majors in biology, business administration, communications media, computer science, computer technology, early childhood education, elementary education, English, English education, fine art, government, history, mathematics, nursing, pedology, psychology, science education, social work, sociology/criminal justice, and technology. Dual-degree programs are offered in engineering and dentistry. The nursing program is designed for nurses who currently hold RN licensure but wish to complete the B.S. degree.

Academic Program

The University operates on a semester calendar. Academic offerings can be divided into four main areas: humanities, science and mathematics, social sciences, and education. To receive a bachelor's degree, a student must earn a minimum of 120 semester hours with a cumulative grade point average of 2.0 or better. Students who enter through the University College of Excellence (UCE) are provided the opportunity to complete the General Education Program, acquire lifelong learning skills for a competitive world, and make a successful transition into their junior year. General studies requirements include communication skills, 9 hours; humanities, 9 hours; social sciences, 18 hours; science and mathematics, 9 hours; and physical education, 2 hours. The remaining credit hours can be electives or from major and minor areas of interest. Students must also pass the test of Proficiency in the English Language and must take the national standardized test in their major area.

The Honors Program is designed for students with outstanding academic records and potential and provides a special educational opportunity for young adults with exceptional talent. The program is comprehensive and multidisciplinary in structure and interdisciplinary in application. It has been designed to provide a creative approach to the teaching/learning process and to present activities that will encourage the shaping of students' own experiences.

The Special Services Project is a federally funded program designed to retain and graduate first-generation, low-income, and disabled students who have been admitted to Bowie State University. The purpose of the project is to help students overcome academic and nonacademic barriers to academic success, through participation in specially designed activities, including counseling, tutoring, and workshops on test taking and study skills.

Through the Cooperative Education Program, a student may choose either the alternate or parallel programs of study and work in business, industry, government, or a social-service agency. This program is open to Bowie State students who have completed at least one academic year with a minimum cumulative grade point average of 2.0.

The University participates in the College-Level Examination Program (CLEP), administered by the Educational Testing Service for the College Board, and in the Defense Activity for Non-Traditional Education Support (DANTES) program. The University also has a program for awarding students credit for learning acquired through life and work experience. Under this program, students document their backgrounds in a portfolio, which is reviewed by the faculty. Through all of these programs, qualified students may receive up to 30 credit hours toward their degree.

Bowie State University offers an Army ROTC program. Two-year and three-year scholarships are available.

Academic Facilities

The Communication Arts Center, a $6.5-million building that houses the humanities division, contains classrooms, offices, conference rooms, and studio-laboratories and seats 450 patrons. The $8.8-million, 290,000-volume Thurgood Marshall Library is centrally located on campus and provides excellent equipment and reference departments for the student body. The microfilm file contains 389,000 items; periodicals number 1,376. Campus research facilities include science laboratories, television and radio studios, language laboratories, and the Adler-Dreikurs Institute. Access to the library collection is provided through Victor Web, the electronic catalog that also links users to millions of University System of Maryland (USM) volumes.

Costs

In 2000–01, the estimated annual cost of tuition, fees, board, and room for a freshman who is a Maryland resident is $9000; for a non-Maryland resident, the cost is $14,600. The annual cost for a commuting student who is a Maryland resident is $3778; the cost for a commuting student who is not a Maryland resident is $9349.

Financial Aid

Federal Pell Grants, Supplemental Grants, Work-Study, Perkins Loans, and Direct Loans are available. University scholarships, tuition waivers, and diversity grants are awarded. Most awards are based on need. Merit scholarships could be offered to students with cumulative grade point averages of at least 3.2 and minimum SAT I scores of 1150. Full-tuition awards are possible for out-of-state students who have a minimum cumulative grade point average of 3.4 and a minimum SAT I score of 1250. More than 65 percent of all undergraduate students receive some form of financial aid. Scholarships and assistantships are offered through the Model Institutions for Excellence Program for Science, Engineering, and Mathematics. Deadlines are April 1 for the fall semester and November 15 for the spring semester.

Faculty

More than 75 percent of the 160 full-time faculty members have earned doctoral degrees. The faculty-student ratio is 1:18.

Student Government

All students are members of the Student Government Association, which, in cooperation with the administration, sets the standards for student life. Students are encouraged to assume leadership roles and to participate in the various programs and activities of the University. The Residence Hall Council provides opportunities for students to participate in the administration of residence life and in the cultural growth of the campus community.

Admission Requirements

Maryland residents applying for admission should have a minimum cumulative grade point average in their core high school courses of 2.2 (on a 4.0 scale) and a minimum SAT I score of 900 (or a minimum ACT score of 19). Out-of-state residents should have a minimum cumulative grade point average of 2.6 and a minimum SAT I score of 950 (or a minimum ACT score of 20). A sliding scale is used for students who have higher grade point averages or SAT I scores. Conditional admission may be offered to in-state students with minimum cumulative grade point averages that range from 2.0 to 2.19 and minimum SAT I scores of 830 to 899 (or a minimum ACT score of 17). Conditional admission may be offered to out-of-state students with minimum cumulative grade point averages of 2.2 to 2.59 and minimum SAT I scores of 860 to 949 (or a minimum score of 18 on the ACT). The SAT II: Writing Test is required for all freshman applicants. Applicants must have earned a high school diploma or a GED. The following courses are required: English, 4 credits; social science/history, 3 credits; mathematics (algebra I, algebra II, and geometry), 3 credits; laboratory sciences, 2 credits; foreign language, 2 credits; and electives, 6 credits. A $40 application fee is charged, and a health certificate must be submitted before entering the University.

Transfer students must have a minimum 2.0 cumulative grade point average for a minimum of 24 transferable credits, or SAT I scores will be required. International students and mature adults are encouraged to apply.

Application and Information

The application deadline is April 1 for the fall semester and November 1 for spring. For an application form, students should contact:

Office of Enrollment, Recruitment and Registration
Bowie State University
Bowie, Maryland 20715-9465
Telephone: 301-464-6566
        410-880-4100 Ext. 6566(from the Baltimore-Columbia area)
World Wide Web: http://www.bowiestate.edu

Flags representing the international student population of Bowie State University frame the entrance to the 337-acre campus.

BOWLING GREEN STATE UNIVERSITY
BOWLING GREEN, OHIO

The University

Bowling Green State University (BGSU) offers the personal attention and opportunities for involvement characteristic of a smaller school, combined with the expert faculty, premier facilities, and modern resources of a large, sophisticated university. A residential campus, BGSU offers round-the-clock education that extends beyond the classroom. Student activities and organizations add balance to a BGSU education.

About 6,900 of BGSU's 19,000 students live on campus, which is known for its friendly atmosphere. That warmth, combined with several other distinctive characteristics, makes BGSU a learning community where students are challenged, nourished, and encouraged to be creative while achieving their full potential. The Bowling Green experience centers around five core values: respect for one another, cooperation, intellectual and spiritual growth, creative imaginings, and pride in a job well done.

BGSU also offers thirteen master's degrees in sixty-five fields, two specialist degree programs, and fourteen doctoral programs in more than sixty areas of specialization.

BGSU's friendly atmosphere is enhanced by its physically compact campus. The Bowling Green community is a typical college town with most businesses within walking or biking distance of residence halls. Bicycles are a popular means of transportation, but all students are permitted to have cars.

Of the 19,000 students enrolled at BGSU, 16,000 are undergraduate students, 10 percent come from outside the state of Ohio (including 509 from other countries), and 1,401 are African American, Native American, Hispanic, or Asian American. Students are actively involved outside of class, participating in more than 200 student organizations or attending one of the 300 or more special events offered each month. Residence halls are learning communities. In fall 1999, there was one computer laboratory for each residence complex and one personal computer available for every 20 resident students. Every residence hall room has high-speed Ethernet connections to the University's computing backbone.

Location

The city of Bowling Green, Ohio, population 28,500 (including students), is located in northwest Ohio about 20 miles south of Toledo. A typical college town, it is within a comfortable driving distance of all major cities in Ohio and is within an easy commute from nearby towns.

Majors and Degrees

Fully accredited by the North Central Association of Colleges and Secondary Schools, Bowling Green State University offers 165 undergraduate majors in seven undergraduate colleges: Arts and Sciences, Business Administration, Education and Human Development, Health and Human Services, Musical Arts, Technology, and the regional Firelands College in Huron, Ohio. Numerous programs within these colleges are accredited by their respective national accrediting agencies.

Four-year undergraduate programs are available and lead to the following degrees: Bachelor of Applied Health Sciences, Bachelor of Arts, Bachelor of Arts in Communication, Bachelor of Fine Arts, Bachelor of Liberal Studies, Bachelor of Music, Bachelor of Science, Bachelor of Science in Business Administration, Bachelor of Science in apparel merchandising and product development, Bachelor of Science in applied microbiology, Bachelor of Science in child and family community services, Bachelor of Science in communication disorders, Bachelor of Science in consumer and family resource management, Bachelor of Science in criminal justice, Bachelor of Science in dietetics, Bachelor of Science in economics, Bachelor of Science in education, Bachelor of Science in environmental health, Bachelor of Science in food science and nutrition, Bachelor of Science in gerontology, Bachelor of Science in interior design, Bachelor of Science in journalism, Bachelor of Science in medical technology, Bachelor of Science in nursing, Bachelor of Science in social work, and Bachelor of Science in technology. The physical therapy curriculum has undergone a major revision from a baccalaureate to a master's degree. BGSU–Firelands College offers seventeen programs that lead to associate degrees in applied business, applied sciences, nursing, science, and technical study.

Every entering student has the option of enrolling in an undergraduate college with a declared major or of enrolling as an undecided student. Students who are undecided about a college begin their studies in premajor advising, where approximately 500 new students enroll each year.

Academic Program

The academic program at BGSU is designed to help all students achieve their full potential. The University is committed to graduating culturally literate, self-assured, technologically sophisticated, productive citizens who are prepared to be leaders in the twenty-first century. All students, regardless of their major, take a core group of general education courses.

Classroom work is closely integrated with out-of-class experiences in the residence halls and off campus. A number of special-interest housing options are available, including the Chapman Learning Community, where students live, learn, and interact with faculty members and one another as part of a living/learning residential environment. A Health Sciences Residential Community is available to students interested in a health science–related field. The College of Musical Arts offers a similar housing option.

Bowling Green also offers a challenging honors program, special honors housing, and the opportunity to complete a senior honors project for graduation with University or departmental honors. Academic advising and tutoring services are also available. Bowling Green has Army and Air Force ROTC programs.

Off-Campus Arrangements

BGSU emphasizes education with a global perspective. About 275 BGSU students go abroad each year. Study-abroad programs range from a full academic year to a few weeks and are available at twenty-seven sites in nineteen countries.

BGSU also participates in the National Student Exchange Program with 122 other colleges and universities in the U.S., and the University is a "learning partner" in the Washington Center internship program, which provides full-time internships and short-term academic seminars for college students in the nation's capital.

In all undergraduate colleges, BGSU students are given the opportunity for hands-on experiences that bring what they learn in the classroom to life. Every Bowling Green student can take advantage of at least one opportunity to gain practical experience related to his or her major.

Cooperative education, an "earn-while-you-learn" program, places about 1,000 students annually who earn an average of $10 per hour. The University's co-op program ranks in the top 10 percent in the country for numbers of placements and is open to all students regardless of their major.

Academic Facilities

Extensive state-of-the-art facilities support the work of faculty members and students at Bowling Green. The Jerome Library, with more than 6 million books, journals, periodicals, and other materials, is equipped with computerized searching networks that can locate materials from almost anywhere in the world. Individual libraries and collections offer additional specialized resources.

Comprehensive computing resources are also available on the Bowling Green campus. The University has thirty instructional computing lab facilities across campus, with twenty to ninety systems per lab. Several labs have highly specialized hardware and software for individual disciplines. Every residence complex has its own computer lab, and all residence hall rooms are wired for high-speed connection to the University's computing network (e-mail, the Internet, and library resources).

Olscamp Hall, a classroom building with seating for 2,000, is equipped for "teleteaching"/distance learning, with capabilities for sending and receiving classroom activity to and from all parts of the world. BGSU also has a modern Physical Sciences Laboratory Building and planetarium, a recently renovated Fine Arts Center, and outstanding music facilities.

Costs

A full-time undergraduate student living on campus in standard housing and with the minimum meal plan paid $9502 in 1999–2000. Out-of-state students paid a surcharge of $5548, for a total of $15,050. Students are encouraged to budget about $700 a year for books and supplies and an additional $1950 for other expenses (entertainment, clothing, transportation, laundry, etc.).

Financial Aid

About 60 percent of BGSU students receive some kind of financial aid. In 1999–2000, the University awarded 2,000 academic scholarships that totaled $5.8 million. Bowling Green offers a renewable scholarship equivalent to 100 percent of the total cost of fees, room, and meals to National Merit Finalists, National Achievement Finalists, and National Hispanic Scholars with a minimum 3.3 grade point average. National Merit Semifinalists, National Achievement Semifinalists, and National Hispanic Honorable Mention Recipients with the minimum 3.3 GPA are offered renewable scholarships that cover fees only. Student employment, grants, and loans are other options available. BGSU employs about 4,500 students annually. Students apply for aid by completing the Free Application for Federal Student Aid (FAFSA). Students who are eligible for academic scholarships are automatically considered if their credentials are submitted to the Office of Admissions by January 15. Contact the Office of Admissions for additional information.

Faculty

At the heart of Bowling Green State University are 723 full-time faculty members who devote their energies to teaching, research, and working closely with students. Many are national and international experts in their field; others are authors; still others have won awards for both teaching and research. Their reputations as scholars, authors, and teachers complement the faculty's role as people who care about students and the future of the University. The personal attention students receive from the faculty and support staff accounts for Bowling Green's distinction as a friendly campus.

Student Government

The Undergraduate Student Government (USG) is the representative body for Bowling Green's undergraduate students. Leaders and delegates are elected by the entire student body and carry the students' voice to both the University Board of Trustees and the Faculty Senate. Both an undergraduate and a graduate student are appointed each year by the governor to the University Board of Trustees.

Admission Requirements

High school seniors can apply to BGSU beginning August 1 before their senior year. Admission to the fall semester is competitive. Nonresidents of Ohio are considered for admission on the same basis as in-state students. To be admitted, a freshman applicant must be a graduate of a high school approved or accredited by the state or have earned a high school equivalency diploma. Results of either the ACT or SAT I are required (ACT preferred). An applicant is considered on the basis of high school course work, cumulative GPA, official ACT or SAT I results, and class rank. The University also considers the diversity of the student body and applicants' special abilities, talents, and achievements in making admission decisions.

Admission to the University for transfer students is determined by their college academic credentials. Several academic majors and programs have specific requirements for transfer students, but, in general, a minimum 2.0 GPA is required for students who have earned at least 60 semester hours; a minimum 2.5 GPA is required for students who have earned fewer than 60 semester (90 quarter) hours.

Application and Information

Prospective students are encouraged to apply to Bowling Green and have all admission credentials complete before February 1 of the year they intend to enroll. Notification of admission decisions begins on October 15 for those who have submitted all credentials and continues on a rolling basis. Bowling Green does not discriminate in admission on the basis of race, sex, color, national origin, religion, creed, age, marital status, mental or physical disability, or veteran status. To obtain an application for admission, students should contact:

Office of Admissions
110 McFall Center
Bowling Green State University
Bowling Green, Ohio 43403
Telephone: 419-372-BGSU
Fax: 419-372-6955
E-mail: admissions@bgnet.bgsu.edu
World Wide Web: http://choose.bgsu.edu

BRANDEIS UNIVERSITY
WALTHAM, MASSACHUSETTS

The University

Brandeis combines two important traditions in higher education: the dedication to teaching that is characteristic of a small, selective college and the facilities and renowned faculty usually associated with a large research university.

Brandeis is a national and international, nonsectarian institution. From its founding in 1948 by the American Jewish community, the University has endorsed a religious pluralism that attracts bright and highly motivated students from culturally diverse backgrounds. The current student body consists of about 3,100 undergraduates, including men and women from nearly every state and fifty countries. Seventy-four percent of the students come from out of state. The Graduate School of Arts and Sciences offers programs in twenty-six fields and certificates in two postbaccalaureate programs and attracts an international group of graduate students. Brandeis's two graduate schools, the Florence Heller Graduate School for Advanced Studies in Social Welfare and the Graduate School of International Economics and Finance, offer graduate degrees at the master's and doctoral levels.

Students participate in a wide range of activities, from sports to theater and government. The University's more than 210 student clubs and organizations provide unlimited opportunities for a varied and extensive extracurricular life.

Brandeis competes at the NCAA Division III level and is one of nine top private universities that make up the University Athletic Association (UAA). Men compete in varsity baseball, basketball, cross-country, fencing, golf, indoor and outdoor track and field, soccer, swimming and diving, and tennis. Women compete in basketball, cross-country, fencing, indoor and outdoor track and field, soccer, softball, swimming and diving, tennis, and volleyball. There is a coed varsity sailing team. Club sports include bicycling, crew, lacrosse, martial arts, rugby, skiing, soccer, squash, tae kwon do, ultimate Frisbee, volleyball, water polo, and weight lifting. Students also play intramural sports and enjoy recreational activities that range from football to Frisbee. The Joseph S. and Clara Ford Athletic and Recreation Complex provides facilities for all of the above, including indoor and outdoor tracks and tennis courts, weight-training facilities, squash courts, a dance/aerobics room, and the largest field house on any New England campus.

More than 85 percent of the students live on campus. Freshmen and sophomores are guaranteed on-campus housing in eight of the nine residential quads. Every quad has a live-in professional staff person and upperclass peer advisers. Each year, some faculty members live on campus as part of the Resident Scholar Program, through which they plan dorm activities relating to their fields of interest. Three dining halls serve the student body; these include a variety of alternate dining options, from kosher meals to deli-style, Mexican, and Middle Eastern fare.

Location

Brandeis is in Waltham, Massachusetts, a community of 58,000 just 10 miles west of Boston. The University's location combines the benefits of urban life with those of an active campus. The MBTA train line gives easy access to cultural, social, and athletic events in Cambridge and downtown Boston. The campus is also convenient to neighboring beach and mountain resorts. Perhaps the greatest advantage of the location is the social and intellectual interaction afforded by proximity to other Boston-area colleges and universities.

Majors and Degrees

Brandeis University offers the Bachelor of Arts degree in thirty-two fields of concentration: African and Afro-American studies, American studies, anthropology, biochemistry, biology, chemistry, classical studies, comparative literature, computer science, economics, English and American literature, European cultural studies, fine arts, French, general science, German, history, Islamic and Middle Eastern studies, Latin American studies, linguistics and cognitive science, mathematics, music, Near Eastern and Judaic studies, neuroscience, philosophy, physics, politics, psychology, Russian, sociology, Spanish, and theater arts. The Bachelor of Science degree is offered in biology, chemistry, neuroscience, and physics. Students may pursue a double concentration or design independent concentrations. In addition to choosing a concentration, undergraduates may follow interdisciplinary programs in several fields: East Asian studies; education; environmental studies; film studies; health, law, and society; humanities; international business; international studies; Islamic and Middle Eastern studies; Italian studies; journalism; Latin American studies; legal studies; medieval studies; peace and conflict studies; Russian and Eastern European studies; and women's studies. Students may also complete a minor in the following fields: African and Afro-American studies, anthropology, art history, chemistry, classical studies, computer science, economics, English and American literature, French, linguistics, mathematics, modern German literature, music, Near Eastern and Judaic studies, philosophy (language, logic, and the philosophy of science; metaphysics and the philosophy of mind; philosophy; or value theory), physics, Russian literature, Spanish, and theater arts. A creative writing track is available in the English department. A combined-degree program is offered with the Columbia University School of Engineering. Preprofessional advising in architecture, business and management, dentistry, law, and medicine prepares students for admission to professional schools after college.

Exceptional undergraduates may enroll in four-year combined B.A./M.A. programs in the Departments of Anthropology, Biochemistry, Biology, Chemistry, Classical Studies, History, Mathematics, Neuroscience, and Physics. Five-year combined B.A./M.A. programs are available in computer science, international economics and finance, and Near Eastern and Judaic studies.

Academic Program

Brandeis seeks to reaffirm and refresh its strong commitment to liberal education through curricular innovation. A core curriculum is in place to maintain flexibility while ensuring exposure to course work in each of the four major schools: Creative Arts, Humanities, Sciences, and Social Sciences.

Students generally consult with a faculty adviser in the department of major interest to choose a concentration before the end of their sophomore year. To earn a bachelor's degree, undergraduates complete thirty-two semester courses, including the requirements of a field of concentration. Advanced placement credit, credit for the International Baccalaureate and other international exams, and transfer credit are available upon approval of the registrar.

Brandeis offers numerous opportunities for independent research and fieldwork at the undergraduate level. Most departments offer honors and freshman seminar programs, and students engaged in approved research work may apply for funding from the University. The Hiatt Career Development Center, a leader in the field of career placement, arranges internships in all areas of concentration.

Brandeis operates on a two-semester calendar. Classes for the fall term generally begin in early September, and examinations take place before the winter break. Classes for the spring term begin in late January and end in mid-May.

Off-Campus Arrangements

Opportunities exist for study abroad in forty-three countries under the auspices of a variety of programs sponsored by international and American universities. Brandeis also has a special arrangement for a full-year study program at University College in London.

Through a cross-registration agreement, courses not offered at Brandeis may be taken at Tufts University, Boston University, Boston College, and Wellesley College. Students may also take business courses at Babson College and Bentley College.

Academic Facilities

The Goldfarb and Farber Libraries and the Gerstenzang Science Library together contain more than 1 million bound volumes, 870,000 microforms, 16,000 current serial subscriptions, and forty CD-ROM databases. Brandeis participates in the Boston Library Consortium, which allows undergraduates access to most major university libraries in the Boston area.

Forty-one academic facilities offer undergraduates substantial resources in the arts and sciences. The Berlin Premedical Center contains extensive laboratories devoted to preparing students for careers as physicians. The Volen National Center for Complex Systems hosts research in large, complex systems, with the brain and intelligence as the system of greatest interest. The Computer Science Department has a network of workstations from Silicon Graphics, Hewlett-Packard, Sun, and Apple; its facilities also include a sixteen-processor SGT Onyx and a 4096-processor Maspar MP. Many laboratories and departments throughout the campus maintain specialized computing facilities. For general student use, the University maintains four computing facilities that house a combination of Macintosh and IBM-PC computers and a variety of printers and external peripherals. For specific information, students should contact the Office of Admissions.

The Spingold Theater Arts Center provides three theaters, as well as dance and rehearsal rooms. Nathan Seifer Auditorium, an undergraduate facility, provides opportunities for students to become involved in all aspects of theater production. The Slosberg Music Center hosts more than sixty performances by undergraduate musicians and visiting professionals each year. The permanent collection of American art of the post–World War II era at the Rose Art Museum is considered the finest at any university in the New England area.

Costs

Tuition costs, including fees, were $25,174 for the 1999–2000 academic year, and the cost of room and board averaged $7040.

Financial Aid

Financial aid at Brandeis is based on need, as determined by information provided on the Free Application for Federal Student Aid (FAFSA) and the College Scholarship Service's Financial Aid PROFILE. However, a significant number of grants up to $19,000 annually are available on the basis of academic merit. Need-based aid packages generally include scholarship, loan, and work-study components. Last year, 68 percent of the student body received some form of aid. The University realizes that need is not necessarily determined strictly by income and designs each aid package individually.

Faculty

The faculty at Brandeis consists of men and women united by their commitment to undergraduate education. Ninety-seven percent of the 316 full-time and 145 part-time professors hold doctoral degrees. The student-faculty ratio of approximately 9:1 allows for a rigorous but personal academic environment. Graduate teaching assistants conduct a limited number of entry-level classes. The median class size is 16.

Student Government

The undergraduate student government, the Student Senate, consists of 8 elected class senators, 10 elected residential senators, and an executive board, who represent their constituents' interests to the University administration through the Dean of Student Affairs. The undergraduate student activity fee generates approximately $750,000 for distribution to more than 200 recognized organizations. Ninety undergraduates serve on thirty-four University committees. Two undergraduates and 1 graduate student serve as student representatives to the Board of Trustees.

Admission Requirements

Brandeis places the most emphasis on the applicant's secondary school record. Teacher recommendations, the personal statement, and standardized test scores contribute to the evaluation as well. Prospective students should have followed a strong academic preparatory course while in high school, generally having completed 4 years of English; 3 years of a foreign language, including senior study when possible; at least 3 years of college-preparatory mathematics; and a minimum of 1 year each of history and laboratory science. Brandeis expects its applicants to present scores on the College Board's SAT I and on three SAT II Subject Tests. The Writing Subject Test is required. Applicants may submit scores from the ACT in lieu of the SAT I and SAT II Subject Tests. Students whose native language is not English must submit scores from both the Test of English as a Foreign Language (TOEFL) and the SAT I.

Transfer students, while not required to submit Subject Test scores, are expected to send copies of their SAT I scores as well as transcripts of any credit-granting courses taken. High school transcripts are required.

All candidates for admission are reviewed individually. The Office of Admissions strongly encourages each applicant to arrange for an interview on campus or through an Alumni Admissions Council member in the student's home area.

Application and Information

Individuals interested in applying as early decision candidates should submit application materials before January 1. Regular applicants should submit part I of the application by January 1 and part II by January 31. Transfer students should submit their applications before April 1. The Office of Admissions notifies early decision candidates within four weeks after receiving completed applications. Regular admission candidates receive notification by April 1, and transfer candidates by June 10.

Requests for information and application materials may be directed to:

Office of Admissions
Brandeis University
Waltham, Massachusetts 02454-9110
Telephone: 781-736-3500
        800-622-0622 (toll-free outside Massachusetts)
E-mail: sendinfo@brandeis.edu
World Wide Web: http://www.brandeis.edu

BRENAU UNIVERSITY
The Women's College of Brenau University
GAINESVILLE, GEORGIA

The University and The College

The Women's College of Brenau University is a four-year, private, nondenominational liberal arts college for women. The name *Brenau*, derived from German and Latin, means "refined gold." A constantly evolving educational program combines a broad base in the liberal arts with career-oriented majors for women of all ages. A student-teacher ratio of 13:1, a rich heritage of well over 100 years, and nationally recognized excellence attract more than 600 women from throughout the United States, Europe, Latin America, and Asia.

The University's Evening and Weekend College offers undergraduate and graduate instruction, both on and off campus. Approximately 1,700 students enroll in this program, which adds diversity in faculty expertise and library resources to the Women's College program. Qualified Women's College students may enroll in selected evening and weekend courses with the permission of the academic vice president.

The Women's College student is provided with opportunities to learn through participation. Many degree plans emphasize hands-on activities, laboratory experiences, and internships. Leadership experiences are plentiful in campus organizations, including eight national sororities (Alpha Chi Omega, Alpha Delta Pi, Alpha Gamma Delta, Alpha Kappa Alpha, Chi Omega, Delta Delta Delta, Phi Mu, and Zeta Tau Alpha), special interest groups, and professional and honorary societies. Recreation activities abound in a geographic area rich in natural resources. There are intramural and intercollegiate competitions and outdoor activities such as hiking on the Appalachian Trail, camping, horseback riding, boating, swimming, scuba diving, waterskiing and snow skiing, golf, and tennis. Gainesville is a cultural and economic center of northeast Georgia, and Brenau is the center of much of this activity. A few examples of this are a version of "Meet the Press" called the Brenau News Forum, a weekly feature on the College's own WBCX-FM and area cable TV; nationally recognized artists and performers, showcased in Pearce Auditorium (a lovely European-style opera theater); and a wide variety of events featuring award-winning students and faculty members. Special guests include current newsmakers, national leaders, writers, and scholars. These people bring a real-life perspective and in-depth knowledge to augment the academic preparation and extensive practical experience of the faculty.

Location

Brenau is located 50 miles northeast of Atlanta at the foothills of the Blue Ridge Mountains in Gainesville, Georgia. The metropolitan area, with a population of 100,000, has a wide variety of recreational opportunities. Gainesville is bordered by Lake Sidney Lanier, the largest freshwater lake in Georgia. Sky Valley, a modern snow-skiing resort, is only an hour's drive from the campus. There are seven colleges and universities within an hour's drive.

Majors and Degrees

The School of Business and Mass Communication offers programs leading to the Bachelor of Business Administration degree with majors in accounting, corporate communications, management, and marketing. In addition, it offers the Bachelor of Science in public administration and the Bachelor of Arts and the Bachelor of Science in mass communications, with concentrations in broadcasting, corporate communications, journalism, and public relations.

The School of Education and Human Development offers programs leading to the Bachelor of Arts and Bachelor of Science degrees in early childhood education, human resources management, middle grades education, psychology, and special education.

The School of Fine Arts and Humanities offers programs leading to the Bachelor of Arts degree in conflict resolution/legal studies and international studies. Programs are also offered leading to the Bachelor of Arts or Bachelor of Science degrees in English, fashion merchandising (a B.F.A. is also available), history/political science, and theater. The Bachelor of Arts and Bachelor of Fine Arts degrees in art and design (commercial, education, studio), arts management, dance (education, pedagogy, performance), interior design (B.F.A. only), music theater, and theater are offered, as is the Bachelor of Music degree in music education, accompanying, and performance (piano or vocal).

The School of Health and Science offers programs that lead to the Bachelor of Arts or the Bachelor of Science degrees in biology, environmental science, and environmental studies. The Bachelor of Science in Nursing degree is offered by the Department of Nursing. The Department of Occupational Therapy offers a combination Bachelor of Science/Master of Science degree in occupational therapy. Students completing prerequisite courses at Brenau are given preference in selection for the clinical portion of the program.

Academic Program

To receive a degree, students must complete a minimum of 120 semester hours of college work, maintain an overall quality point average of at least 2.0 in all academic work not related to the area of concentration, maintain a minimum quality point average of 2.5 in all academic work related to the area of concentration, spend a minimum of three semesters in attendance at Brenau University and complete a minimum of 45 semester hours of academic work during that period, and complete the requirements in general education, the degree program, and the upper-division concentration. Excellent laboratory experiences are offered in both lower- and upper-division courses, and internships are either offered or required in most academic areas.

Nursing students must have a minimum 2.5 cumulative average to enter clinical courses, which begin in the fall of their junior year. At least a 2.5 average must be maintained to graduate.

Pre–occupational therapy students are selected for the program during the senior year of high school, based upon GPA, SAT I scores, and a personal interview. Interested students should contact the Admissions Office for details of the selection process.

Two summer sessions, special summer institutes, and continuing education programs provide additional opportunities for study.

Brenau's English as a second language program (ESL) provides concentrated instruction in English in a culturally enriching environment.

Qualified entering freshmen may receive advanced placement and academic credit through the Advanced Placement Program, the College-Level Examination Program (CLEP), or an appropriate college achievement test. Credit may also be granted for work or extracollegiate experience.

Brenau's Learning Disability Program, designed for above-average students with a diagnosed learning disability, provides assistance and tutors where appropriate.

Brenau offers a Leadership Development Program, which provides students with essential leadership skills. Field projects, leadership retreats, internships, and courses in leadership are offered during the year.

Off-Campus Arrangements

The Women's College coordinates and sponsors various travel programs, which may be combined with a college credit program taken in the period preceding or following travel. Conducted during the regular academic year and during the summer, tours have included Mexico and the People's Republic of China, Africa and Europe, and places of interest within the United States. A junior-year-abroad program in Austria, England, France, the Netherlands, Spain, and the Yucatán peninsula is available.

Academic Facilities

Students have access to the Brenau Trustee Library, the Northeast Georgia Medical Center Library, science laboratories, five computer labs (including the Redwine Technology Center), a TV studio, and a radio station.

Costs

For 1999–2000, the tuition fee for the Women's College is $11,730, and the room and board fee is $6876, for a total of $18,606. The charge per semester hour credit is $391. Students who are not yet 22 years of age or who are not residing with their parents locally are required to live in University housing.

Financial Aid

The University uses the Free Application for Federal Student Aid (FAFSA) to determine eligibility for all need-based financial assistance. Students must also submit the Brenau University Application for Financial Aid. Residents of Georgia enrolled as full-time undergraduate students are eligible to receive state tuition grants. Scholarship aid is offered for academic achievement and for special talent in such areas as art, athletics, communications, dance, music, and theater. Other aid, provided on the basis of need, is available through the Federal Pell Grant, Federal Supplemental Educational Opportunity Grant, Federal Perkins Loan, Federal Work-Study, and Federal Stafford Loan programs as well as through institutional and private grant sources. Veterans' benefits are available also to those who qualify. Applications for institutional scholarships and grants should be submitted by May 1 for the following academic year. Applications for Federal Pell Grants and Federal Stafford Loans must be completed a minimum of six weeks before the student's beginning semester.

Faculty

All members of the faculty teach, and all counsel and advise students. Members of the faculty and professional staff hold degrees from major American and international universities; approximately 90 percent have doctoral or terminal degrees, and all hold membership in various professional organizations.

Student Government

An active student government association is responsible, in conjunction with the University administration, for making and maintaining social regulations concerning students. Brenau has an honor code administered by a student honor court, which is advised and reviewed by a faculty advisory committee. An executive council, composed of presidents of campus organizations, sororities, and dormitories, is responsible for coordinating activities and maintaining the University calendar, and it acts as a liaison between administration, faculty, and students. Student representatives sit on all major committees.

Admission Requirements

Students applying for admission to the Women's College should have completed 16 units within a college-preparatory curriculum or the equivalent at an accredited secondary school. Applicants should submit a transcript of their high school work, an application for admission accompanied by a nonrefundable fee of $30, test results from the ACT or the College Board's SAT I, a recommendation written by the high school guidance counselor, and a health certificate. Admission decisions are made on a rolling basis. The early acceptance plan and early decision plan are designed to ensure the admission of qualified applicants. Candidates for early admission and early decision are advised to complete the entrance examinations in the spring of their junior year in secondary school.

Brenau welcomes applications from prospective transfer students and junior college graduates. In accord with recommendations from the American Council on Education and the American Association of Community and Junior Colleges, Brenau has adopted the following policy: all graduates of an accredited junior college with an A.A. or A.S. degree are admitted to upper-division status as juniors or seniors in the department of their selection, subject to the departmental and degree requirements; grades of C or better are assigned the same credit as those awarded by Brenau.

Application and Information

For additional information, students should contact:

Dean of Admissions
Undergraduate Admissions
Brenau University
One Centennial Circle
Gainesville, Georgia 30501

Telephone: 770-534-6100
              800-252-5119 (toll-free)
E-mail: upchurch@lib.brenau.edu

Students selected for the preprofessional program in occupational therapy are given preference in selection for the clinical portion of the program.

BRESCIA UNIVERSITY
OWENSBORO, KENTUCKY

The University

Brescia University prepares its students for successful careers and for service to others. Brescia was founded by the Ursuline Sisters of Mount Saint Joseph in 1950 as a Catholic liberal arts college. It began as the Mount Saint Joseph College for Women at Maple Mount, Kentucky, in 1925. The school is committed to the concept of values-centered education with a strong emphasis on Christian values. The Southern Association of Colleges and Schools accredits Brescia to award associate and baccalaureate degrees and the Master of Science in Management degree. The University of Louisville offers the Master of Science in Social Work on Brescia's campus. Students pursuing a master's degree may also complete their field-placement work locally. All of Brescia's teacher education programs are accredited by the Kentucky Department of Education.

Currently, 783 students are enrolled at the University. Thirty-three percent are men, and 67 percent are women. The average age of full-time students is 23. Half of the entire student population is under 25. The cosmopolitan student body comes from as far away as Cyprus, Nigeria, the West Indies, and Honduras and from fifteen U.S. states. About 80 percent of students live off campus. Brescia is renovating its campus facilities and anticipates that the number of on-campus residential units will increase. Students can choose from a variety of extracurricular activities, including the *Brescian* (yearbook), the *Brescia Broadcast* (student newspaper), the Brescia Owensboro Student Catholic Organization, the Christian Student Union, the Alpha Chi National Honor Society, the Brescia Student National Education Association, the International Student Organization, the Ichabod Society (students with interests in all forms of literature), the Student Government Association, the National Speech-Language-Hearing Association, the Social Work Club, and the Math/Computer Science Club. The Brescia Little Theater performs dramatic productions in an intimate setting. Brescia formed a women's choir, which has proven to be very popular. Students and faculty members may enjoy lunchtime concerts that feature jazz, blues, and chamber music. Campus facilities include an indoor walking track, a racquetball court, fitness facilities, a weight room, and an attractively furnished Study Pavilion.

Brescia strongly encourages community service. Campus ministry provides numerous ways in which students may interact with the community. These include the Safe Foundation to prevent child abuse, the Council for Exceptional Children, the Special Olympics, and programs for the homeless and needy. Environmental issues are very important at Brescia, and guest speakers are invited to the campus to update the community on these issues. Students have served as mentors for Big Brothers/Big Sisters. University athletic teams have helped provide recreational opportunities and share their facilities with local teens. Awareness activities include breast cancer awareness, rape victims services, and Martin Luther King Jr. Day observances. Brescia highly recommends its Career Development Program. Brescia guarantees that each student who completes the four-year degree program will receive a job offer or be accepted at a graduate school within twelve months after graduation. If not, the student may return to Brescia tuition-free to pursue additional undergraduate course work. The program emphasizes community service, resume writing, interview skills, and portfolio development. Students in the Career Development Program partner with a faculty member and a Brescia graduate. Student Support Services offers counseling and tutoring to low-income or first-generation college students, based on academic need. Tickets to many plays, musicals, and symphony performances are available to participants at no cost. The Brescia Bearcats, members of the NAIA, compete in varsity men's baseball, basketball, golf, and tennis and in women's basketball, golf, soccer, softball, tennis, and volleyball. There are three residence halls for women and five for men. Many students live in a newly constructed student apartment complex on campus.

Location

Brescia University's 6-acre campus is located near downtown Owensboro, Kentucky. Owensboro is just 45 minutes from Evansville, Indiana; 2 hours southwest of Louisville, Kentucky (home of the Kentucky Derby); and 2 hours north of Nashville, Tennessee.

Owensboro is well-known as the "Barbecue Capital of the World." Owensboro has a Barbecue Festival in May and a July Summer Festival. The Riverpark Center in Owensboro offers a multitude of productions. Ice skating, ballet, the David Copperfield Choir, and *Grease* are just a sampling of the entertainment available.

Majors and Degrees

Brescia University offers an Associate of Arts degree in catechetical leadership ministry, human relations, liberal arts, and pastoral ministry. Brescia also offers the Associate of Science degree in business, engineering studies, and engineering technology. The Bachelor of Arts degree is available in a variety of study areas, including art, art education, art therapy: emphasis in art, art therapy: emphasis in psychology, English, English: emphasis in professional writing, general studies, graphic design, history, pastoral ministry, psychology, religious studies, social studies, and Spanish. Minors for the Bachelor of Arts degree may be chosen from the following: English, history, pastoral ministry, political science, psychology, religious studies, sociology, Spanish, and women's studies. Majors for the Bachelor of Science degree are accounting, business, business: economic and finance emphasis, business: health-care administration emphasis, business: marketing and management emphasis, chemistry, communication sciences and disorders, computer and mathematical sciences, early elementary education, general studies, human resource development, mathematics, medical technology, middle grades education, science (with an area of concentration), and special education. Minors for the Bachelor of Science degree are accounting, biology, business, chemistry, computer studies, finance/economics, mathematics, and physics. Brescia also offers the Bachelor of Social Work degree. Brescia offers a dual-degree program in chemistry/chemical engineering through the University of Louisville.

Teacher certification/endorsement is offered in the following areas: art education, early elementary education, middle grades and secondary education (grades 8–12) in English, mathematics, science, social studies, Spanish, and special education in the areas of learning and behavior disorders and moderate and severe disabilities. Candidates graduate with a license to teach in Kentucky schools. The license may be reciprocal in other states.

Preprofessional programs are offered in art therapy, communication sciences and disorders, cytotechnology, dentistry, engineering, law, medicine, optometry, pharmacy, and veterinary medicine. These programs lead to further undergraduate or graduate studies at professional graduate schools. Brescia students enjoy a 97 percent acceptance rate by graduate and professional schools.

Academic Program

There are two semesters at Brescia—fall and spring. Intersession is offered in May. A summer session is offered in June and July. In addition, Brescia has a Weekend College Program that is divided into four modules. Candidates for the associate degree must earn a minimum of 63 credit hours, with a minimum of 27 credit hours of general education requirements. Bachelor's degree candidates must earn a minimum of 128 credit hours, of which at least 42 credit hours are in upper-division courses. They must also complete 57 credit hours of general education courses and complete a major program of study with a 2.5 (C) grade point average or better in all upper-division courses in the selected major and minor. A minimum cumulative grade point average of 2.0 on a 4.0 scale must be achieved. Brescia graduates should be committed to the following values: continued personal, intellectual, and spiritual growth; the welfare of others; respect for the physical environment; and respect for the appreciation of the diversity in cultures. Brescia's Ministry Formation Program is the only accredited undergraduate program of its kind in the nation.

Academic Facilities

The Brescia University campus consists of sixteen buildings within a two-block area near downtown Owensboro. Facilities include the library, the science building, the administration building, the campus center, the graduate center, and residence halls. The library, the campus center, and the classroom buildings are accessible to people with disabilities. The library has more than 151,000 volumes and is fully automated, with access to the Kentucky Library Network (300 libraries). Biology and medical technology students view the human body through computer simulations with the powerful ADAM, while mathematics students graph 3-D space curves and solve large systems of equations with Mathematica. Computer science and physics students learn from state-of-the-art IBM hardware and software packages. There are two computer labs available for students on campus. Every student may receive access to the Internet and e-mail.

Costs

The full-time tuition for 1999–2000 is $8990. Part-time tuition is $300 per credit hour. Room and board costs vary from $3924 to $4200 depending on the student's choice of a single or double room and number of meals. A technology fee of $40 per semester is assessed for each student. Other fees vary according to the student's course work but are typically $50. New books are estimated to cost about $650. A $50 deposit is required for housing.

Financial Aid

Annual financial aid awarded by Brescia exceeds $3 million. More than 85 percent of Brescia students receive scholarships or financial aid. Students receive aid through the many federal and state programs in which the University participates and through the University's deferred payment plan. Brescia also awards scholarships annually to incoming students on the basis of academic excellence and leadership qualities. Students who wish to be considered for financial aid should complete the Free Application for Federal Student Aid (FAFSA). Preference is given to applications received by March 1. Students may obtain the FAFSA by contacting their high school counselor or the University's Web site (address below).

Faculty

Brescia's faculty consists of 67 full- and part-time members. There are almost equal numbers of men and women, and the faculty includes both lay and religious members. More than 70 percent of the full-time faculty members have earned terminal degrees. A 14:1 student-faculty ratio assures students of individualized attention.

Student Government

Brescia students participate in University governance through the Student Government Association. They are represented on the Board of Trustees committees, where their representative has voting rights.

Admission Requirements

Admission to Brescia is personal, like the University itself. Each interested student is assigned an admission counselor who answers questions, arranges campus visits, and makes sure that concerns and needs of the person are addressed.

Applications to Brescia are reviewed on an individual basis. Grades and course work receive strong consideration. College-preparatory and liberal arts courses are recommended. Standardized test scores are taken into consideration. Students are asked to submit a high school transcript or GED score report and an ACT or SAT I score report. Transfer students must submit official transcripts from each college they attended. The Test of English as a Foreign Language (TOEFL) is required for nonnative speakers of English. High school transcripts showing proof of graduation date are also required.

While not required, all prospective students are encouraged to schedule a campus visit. This provides an opportunity for the student to meet with faculty and staff members and students, sit in on a class, ask questions, have lunch, and get a feel for Brescia University.

Application and Information

Applications are considered as they are received. Applications and transcripts should be submitted with a $25 nonrefundable application fee. Admission is on a rolling basis. Applications must be received by March 15 for scholarship consideration. Recommendations are optional. Students may e-mail the admissions staff at the address below. Students may e-mail individual counselors and financial aid staff members through Brescia's Web site at the address below.

For further information, students and parents should contact:

Rick Eber
Director of Admissions
Brescia University
717 Frederica Street
Owensboro, Kentucky 42301
Telephone: 800-264-1234 (toll-free)
E-mail: admissions@brescia.edu
World Wide Web: http://brescia.edu

Students gather in Brescia's comfortable Study Pavilion.

BREVARD COLLEGE
BREVARD, NORTH CAROLINA

The College

Founded in 1853, Brevard is a church-related, coeducational liberal arts college that offers innovative four-year and two-year curriculums, with specialties in music, art, environmental studies, wilderness leadership, and other interdisciplinary majors, on a beautiful mountain campus near Asheville, North Carolina. The College's low student-faculty ratio of 9:1, a covenant that binds faculty members and students in a nurturing community of learning, rich cultural offerings, numerous opportunities for student leadership, nationally competitive athletic programs, and incomparable access to national parks, forest, wilderness areas, and white-water recreational rivers make Brevard distinctive.

Inspired by its setting among the world's oldest mountains and founded upon the principles of the Christian faith, Brevard College has the purpose of educating students in the tradition of the liberal arts and in the spirit of love and service. The College's faculty and staff, academic and cocurricular programs, financial resources, and support services are devoted to providing an educational climate that fosters respect for learning and beauty, creativity and hard work, tolerance and personal integrity, intellect and love of knowledge, and vigorous activity and spiritual reflection. As a result of this commitment, the College has long attracted and welcomed highly motivated students who are already prepared to learn as well as other less-prepared students who need personal help from faculty and staff members in order to adjust to a rigorous academic program. Though the great majority of residential students are of traditional college age, the College offers various continuing education programs for adult learners as well as intensive summer programs for talented high school students in fine arts, English as a second language (ESL), environmental studies, wilderness education, and athletics.

The student body is drawn from twenty-seven states and sixteen other countries. Seventy percent of the students reside on campus. Each year the freshman class of approximately 400 is an energetic mixture of women and men with widespread interests in leadership, science, athletics, music, art, writing, global issues, and wilderness and environmental concerns. Planned musical events, athletic contests, and social activities keep students busy on weekends. Intercollegiate athletic competition in the National Association of Intercollegiate Athletics (NAIA) and the Tennessee Virginia Athletic Conference (TVAC) is available for both women and men. Women compete in basketball, cross-country, soccer, softball, tennis, indoor and outdoor track-and-field, and volleyball. Men compete in baseball, basketball, cross-country, golf, soccer, and indoor and outdoor track-and-field. The College athletic department is ranked fourteenth in the NAIA by *USA Today* and has been awarded the National Association of Collegiate Athletic Directors Sears Cup for athletic excellence in men's and women's athletics. There is also a wide range of intramural activities on campus. The School for Wilderness Education provides opportunities for outdoor activities such as backpacking, mountain biking, rock climbing, and kayaking. Brevard College has a history of excellence in athletics.

Coltrane Commons is the center for student activities and houses several lounges, a television room, snack bar, the College post office, a bookstore, the commuter lounge, a computer center, the game room, and the Underground (coffeehouse). Boshamer Gymnasium has two playing floors, a weight room, and an Olympic-size heated swimming pool.

Other athletic facilities include an all-weather track, two soccer fields, baseball and softball fields, and six all-weather tennis courts. Also on campus are the A. G. Myers Dining Hall, five dormitories, and a new apartment-style residential complex.

The College is accredited by the Southern Association of Colleges and Schools, the University Senate of the United Methodist Church, and the National Association of Schools of Music and is affiliated with the Western North Carolina Conference of the United Methodist Church.

Location

Brevard is located on a 120-acre residential campus in the small city of Brevard, a community of cultural sophistication and natural beauty that is often cited in national surveys as one of the safest and most culturally desirable communities in the nation. Transylvania County contains more than 100 major waterfalls. The Blue Ridge Parkway forms the county's northern boundary, and U.S. 276, which winds through the Pisgah National Forest, is North Carolina's Forest Heritage National Scenic Byway. In proximity are the Great Smoky Mountains National Park and several famed recreational rivers, including the Nantahala, Ocoee, Chattooga, and French Broad, providing opportunities for campers, mountain bikers, and kayakers. Winter offers both downhill and cross-country skiing. Brevard is 20 minutes by four-lane highway from the Asheville Regional Airport, 1½ hours from Greenville-Spartanburg, South Carolina, and less than 3 hours by car from Charlotte, North Carolina, and Atlanta, Georgia.

Majors and Degrees

At Brevard College, students can explore many fields of study, including majors in art, ecology, English, environmental studies, exercise science, history, integrated studies, interdisciplinary studies, mathematics, music, organizational leadership, and wilderness leadership and experiential education. Within the majors, the following emphases are available: allied art, archaeology, art, art history, church music, composition, computer science, conducting, creative writing, environmental history, environmental journalism, exercise gerontology and allied medical fields, fitness leadership, jazz studies, literary studies, modern American history, music history, natural sciences, physics, prelaw, premedicine, Southern history, teaching/coaching, theater arts, theater studies, twentieth-century Europe, and vocal/instrumental performance. North Carolina teaching certificates may be earned in art, English, math, science, and social studies.

The College continues to offer its liberal arts curriculum leading to associate degrees in the arts (A.A.), the sciences (A.S.), and the fine arts (A.F.A.). In addition, a two-year terminal diploma track, designed to lead to employment upon completion of the program, is available in wilderness education with certification in outdoor leadership.

Academic Program

The core liberal arts curriculum of the College requires each student to build a strong base in languages and literature, religion, humanities, mathematics and analytical reasoning, history, natural and social sciences, fine arts, and environmental studies. Students are exposed to other cultures and have significant opportunities for volunteer work in the community.

The curriculum utilizes classroom studies in the Pisgah National Forest, Davidson and French Broad River ecosystems,

Great Smoky Mountain National Park, and the Cradle of Forestry in America, which is designated as a National Historic Site. Through the "Voice of the Rivers," Brevard College offers select students the opportunity to make the world their classroom in an experiential program that combines wilderness leadership and environmental studies. Programs in music and art afford talented students excellent educational and performance opportunities at the College and in off-campus settings, such as the Asheville Art Museum, the famed Brevard Music Center, and the Brevard Chamber Orchestra.

Consistent with the philosophy of the College, various courses at Brevard College use service as a learning component to enhance the classroom environment. Coordination of the student's service experience is performed by the Center for Service Learning, which works with students to prepare transcripts detailing their cocurricular accomplishments.

Off-Campus Arrangements

The College sponsors a variety of academic and service learning opportunities in the surrounding community and overseas, including Westminster College in Oxford, England, and Tbilisi State University in the former Republic of Georgia. Through the College's School of Wilderness Studies, numerous opportunities exist for internships or employment with recreational camps and mountain or white-water outfitters in the region. The College also has developed a relationship with the Georgian State School for Mountain Guides in the high Caucasus Mountains of Europe. Through the service learning program, students may join a volunteer team working abroad in such locations as Bolivia, Mexico, Zimbabwe, or Korea.

Academic Facilities

The 103-year-old campus reflects the beauty of its mountain setting, the balance of tradition, and the energy of change. Particularly significant are the College's diverse facilities for the fine arts that offer opportunities for students and interested community residents to experience the insight of distinguished lecturers; the talent of musicians, dancers, and actors; and the creativity of artists. Sims Art Center and Dunham Music Hall will be linked across King's Creek with the Porter Center for Performing Arts. This cultural triad will offer two large music halls, an experimental theater, a sacred music center, practice rooms, an amphitheater, well-equipped labs for computer-aided design (CAD) and electronic music, two art galleries, a sculpture garden, a dance studio, and many teaching and rehearsal spaces. Further downstream is the College's Old Barn Theater. The proximity of these facilities reinforces the College's philosophy of teaching the arts in relation to one another.

The James A. Jones Library is an integral part of the intellectual life at Brevard College. Students have access to a variety of information resources that support and promote the instructional programs and educational goals of Brevard College, including 50,000 books, 220 periodical subscriptions, 2,700 microforms, and 1,800 audiovisual materials including compact discs and videos. Valuable electronic resources are available on CD-ROM, campus LAN, or World Wide Web, including the library catalog of the Mountain College Library Network for materials owned by Brevard College and nearby colleges. A separate listening library for music, which has both tape and disc facilities, is housed in the music building. Other major buildings on campus include the McLarty-Goodson Classroom Building for the humanities and social sciences, the Bryan Moore Classroom Building for the natural sciences, and the Beam Administration Building.

Costs

For 2000–01, estimated annual costs for students residing on campus are tuition, $10,660; room, $1920; board, $2900; and fees, $1510, for a total cost of $16,990. There is an international student fee of $1250. All students who are permanent North Carolina residents receive a Legislative Tuition Grant of $1750 per year.

Financial Aid

Opportunities for student financial aid are available to every student who can show financial need, superior academic achievement, or talent in athletics, art, drama, or music. All students desiring financial aid must submit the Free Application for Federal Student Aid (FAFSA). The College annually awards more than $200,000 in merit scholarships to select students who display academic excellence, unselfish character, and leadership potential as Brevard Scholars. These students participate in a variety of enriched intellectual, cultural, and leadership programs and work closely with distinguished professors who serve both as advisers and program directors. The Angier B. Duke Scholarships, awarded only by Brevard College and Duke University, are the premier scholarships among more than eighty Brevard Scholars Awards made each year.

Faculty

Brevard College has gathered a faculty and staff notable for the quality of their academic preparation, their character, and their love of teaching. Approximately 60 full-time and 30 part-time faculty members create a low 1:9 ratio between faculty members and students, allowing for small classes and the development of close student-teacher relationships. The College's faculty members pride themselves on being as devoted to the teaching of freshmen and sophomores as to the mentoring of juniors and seniors.

Student Government

Vigorous student leadership is expressed through the Student Government Association (SGA), the Social Board, the Judicial Board, and numerous other student organizations. SGA leaders meet regularly with administration, faculty members, and trustees.

Admission Requirements

Admission to Brevard College is based on motivation, academic achievement, unselfish character, and leadership potential. The College is interested in enrolling not only students who give proof of academic curiosity and ability but also those who add to the diversity of the student body. It seeks students who will contribute to the campus community and display a willingness to place themselves in situations that call for personal initiative and leadership. The record of past achievement is considered in conjunction with ability, as measured by the SAT I or ACT. Standardized tests are usually used as supportive contributive factors rather than as determinative factors in admission decisions.

Application and Information

Students must submit an application for admission, a recommendation from the guidance counselor on the form provided by the Office of Admissions, official SAT I or ACT scores, and an official high school transcript. Students are advised of the admission decision as soon as all required application materials are received. In addition, Brevard College requires a medical history and a physical examination of each applicant prior to enrollment to the College.

For more information, students should contact:

Vice President and Dean for Admissions and Financial Aid
Brevard College
400 North Broad Street
Brevard, North Carolina 28712
Telephone: 828-884-8300
        800-527-9090 (toll-free)
Fax: 828-884-3790
E-mail: admissions@brevard.edu
World Wide Web: http://www.brevard.edu

BRIAR CLIFF COLLEGE
SIOUX CITY, IOWA

The College

Briar Cliff College (BCC) is a close-knit community of learners—approximately 1,000 students and faculty members—committed to higher education within a liberal arts and Catholic perspective. Following in the Franciscan tradition of service, caring, and respect for all, Briar Cliff offers its students a quality education that combines a broad-based intellectual foundation with career development, hands-on experiential learning, and cutting-edge technology.

Founded in 1930 and accredited by the North Central Association of Colleges and Schools, Briar Cliff is a coeducational institution that takes advantage of the services and opportunities of a thriving metropolitan area and the small-town warmth for which the Midwest is known. The College includes students from twenty-four states and nine other countries who come from varied socioeconomic groups and ethnic and religious heritages and who add vitality and richness to the intellectual and social life of the community. Briar Cliff follows a three-term calendar (three 10-week terms) and also offers two 5-week summer sessions and Fast Forward, an accelerated one-week summer program.

Briar Cliff College encourages cocurricular and sports participation as meaningful complements to classroom and laboratory learning. Ninety-five percent of students participate in at least one cocurricular activity. Nearly thirty student organizations and nine NAIA intercollegiate sports options (men's baseball and wrestling, women's softball and volleyball, and men's and women's basketball, golf, soccer, and track and cross-country) contribute to campus life and student development. In addition to on-campus involvement, BCC students volunteer time and energy to local charities and social service organizations, including food banks, community centers, soup kitchens, and Habitat for Humanity. Each year, students take a leadership role, providing Siouxland with nearly 10,000 hours of volunteer service.

Four residence halls serve men and women. Students may choose traditional single and double rooms or suite-style small-group options. Two food service locations, a traditional dining hall and a pub-style restaurant, provide a change of setting and menu selections for diners.

Briar Cliff offers an extensive system of career and personal counseling, academic assessment and developmental course work, tutoring, English as a second language instruction, multicultural student services, and campus ministries. Of the BCC alumni who returned a recent survey, 95 percent had found jobs or were accepted into graduate school within six months of graduation from Briar Cliff.

Location

Briar Cliff's scenic campus is located on the western edge of the city and overlooks the metropolitan area. While in a primarily residential area, the College is only minutes from downtown and the city's major shopping and recreational districts. Sioux City is in the midst of an economic renaissance that provides many cultural and internship possibilities for students. In addition, the tri-state area provides exciting outdoor recreational options.

Majors and Degrees

Briar Cliff awards the Bachelor of Arts, the Bachelor of Science, the Bachelor of Science in Nursing, and the Associate of Arts degrees. Four-year degrees are offered in accounting; art; biology; business administration; chemistry; computer information systems; criminal justice; education (elementary, secondary, and special education); English; environmental science; health, physical education, and recreation; history; human resource management; mass communications; mathematics; medical technology; music (voice, piano, and organ); nursing; political science; psychology; radiologic technology; social work; sociology; Spanish; sports science; theater; theology; and writing. Preprofessional courses of study include chiropractic, church ministry, dentistry, engineering, law, medicine, occupational therapy, pharmacy, physical therapy, physician's assistant studies, and veterinary medicine. Minors include coaching endorsements, management information systems, peace studies, philosophy, physics, political science, recreation and leisure, sociology, and writing/linguistics. Two-year programs are offered in liberal arts and theology.

Briar Cliff participates in a 3-2 program in engineering with Iowa State University. Students spend three years at Briar Cliff taking liberal arts and basic engineering courses and finish the program at Iowa State. At the completion of the program, the student earns a Bachelor of Arts from Briar Cliff and a Bachelor of Science in Engineering from Iowa State. The College also offers a 1-2-1 cooperative program with Marian Health Center for the Bachelor of Science in radiologic technology.

Academic Program

Briar Cliff degree programs include general education courses, courses within the major field of study, and electives. There are thirty-four targeted courses of study. Students must complete thirty-six term courses and twelve 1-hour courses. Before graduation, students must complete the three components of the general education program: Intellectual Foundations, Competencies, and Service. In addition, each senior normally completes the Senior Liberal Arts Colloquium, an interdisciplinary course, which explores issues that affect the contemporary world and yet are of timeless universal importance.

Off-Campus Arrangements

Briar Cliff students are encouraged to see the world as a classroom. Students intern with top organizations in Iowa and throughout the United States. Students may participate in an internship/seminar program through the Chicago Metropolitan Center. Another option is the Washington Center, which is a learning laboratory/internship center for students who would like to learn more about the workings of the federal government and the institutions that are headquartered in the nation's capital. Other formal internship programs are available with local firms (Gateway, MCI, and IBP, for example) and industries, in education, or with government agencies.

Students who are interested in study abroad may choose any country that suits their educational or career goals. Special opportunities are available for study in England, Wales, Austria, France, Spain, the Netherlands, Mexico, and the People's Republic of China.

Academic Facilities

Mueller Library houses almost 110,000 books, 35,000 microform titles, and 10,000 records, tapes, and CDs and receives nearly 2,000 periodicals. An on-campus computer network is available 24 hours a day for student use.

Of special note to biology, premed, and health career students is a cadaver laboratory.

Meis Recital Hall is an acoustically intimate setting for musical performances and the distinguished lecture series. The College Theatre is a state-of-the-art structure that hosts theater department productions, including dramas, children's theater, and musicals, each year.

Costs

Tuition at Briar Cliff is comparable to that of similar private colleges. Tuition for 2000–01 is $13,560, and room and board are $4767 for the academic year. The cost of books and personal expenses varies with each student but is estimated to be $1650. Total cost for the academic year is $19,977.

Financial Aid

Briar Cliff's aid programs bring out-of-pocket costs in line with those of a state institution for many students. Briar Cliff maintains a need-blind admission policy and works with each family to secure financial aid and scholarships for which they are eligible. This strong commitment to families is demonstrated by the fact that the average freshman financial aid package in 1999–2000 was more than $12,690. Approximately 96 percent of Briar Cliff students receive some form of financial aid, including scholarships, grants, loans, and work-study. Merit-based scholarships are awarded in amounts up to full tuition. Total aid awarded in 1999–2000 was just over $8.8 million.

The Free Application for Federal Student Aid (FAFSA) is the institutional application used to determine need-based financial aid and scholarships. Students interested in merit-based, talent, leadership, or athletic scholarships should contact the Office of Admissions for more details.

Faculty

Briar Cliff's faculty members hold teaching as their first priority. Classes are kept small (the average class size is 15 and the student-faculty ratio is 12:1) to encourage classroom interaction, to promote intellectual development and creativity, and to challenge students to examine new ideas. All classes are taught by professors (71 percent of whom have earned the Ph.D. or similar terminal degree in their disciplines). In addition to classroom instruction and seeing students during regular office hours, nearly all of the 73 full-time faculty members engage in academic advising, supervise internships, and act as mentors.

Student Government

The Student Government Association (SGA) is the main voice and political force for the student body and works to develop and maintain free and open communication among students, faculty members, and the administration. Student representation on College committees ensures vital input regarding academics, student life, and College-wide policies. In addition, the SGA coordinates campus programming, organizations, and activities with the Office of Student Activities.

The Residence Life Staff and the Vision Program serve the unique needs of their constituencies and provide additional educational, social, and programming opportunities of a specialized nature.

Admission Requirements

Briar Cliff looks for students who will make a contribution to the intellectual and cocurricular life of the community and who are the best match for its services and programs. The majority of students are in the top two fifths of their graduating class, have earned at least a 3.2 GPA, and have an ACT score of at least 22. There is no cutoff, however, as each application is weighed on individual merit, academic promise, cocurricular involvement, and personal characteristics.

The College expects a minimum preparation of 16 units of academic course work, including English, foreign language, mathematics, natural sciences, and social studies. Honors, Advanced Placement, and Postsecondary Enrollment Options Act classes are highly encouraged when offered. On-campus interviews are highly recommended but are not required.

Briar Cliff welcomes transfer and international students. Official transcripts from each institution attended are required. Non-English-speaking international students must submit TOEFL scores.

Applications for admission are accepted and reviewed on a rolling basis.

Application and Information

Students can visit Briar Cliff's home page on the Internet. General information, as well as admission-specific data, is available at the Web address listed below.

Briar Cliff's Office of Admissions is open weekdays from 8 a.m. until 4:30 p.m. and on selected Saturdays throughout the year. Tours and interviews should be scheduled in advance, if possible. To ask questions or request information, schedule a campus tour, or arrange for an interview, students should contact:

Office of Admissions
Briar Cliff College
3303 Rebecca Street
Sioux City, Iowa 51104
Telephone: 712-279-5200
            800-662-3303 (toll-free)
E-mail: admissions@briar-cliff.edu
World Wide Web: http://www.briar-cliff.edu

Small classes and a low student-faculty ratio guarantee personalized attention.

BRIARCLIFFE COLLEGE
BETHPAGE, NEW YORK

The College
Briarcliffe College was established in 1966 to serve the educational needs of Long Island residents. A suburb of New York City, Long Island experienced a rapid growth in population that resulted in a potential labor force that attracted many top corporations. The College has grown from an original enrollment of 18 women to the current coeducational enrollment of more than 2,000 students per year. Day, evening, weekend, and summer classes are offered.

A wide range of student activities is coordinated through the College's division of student affairs. Briarcliffe students have many opportunities to participate in college life through academic, social, service, and athletic programs. Typical events include theater trips, guest speakers, community service and charitable activities, concerts, and dances. Special interest clubs for law, broadcasting, computers, and other academic areas are active on campus. The athletic department sponsors intercollegiate and intramural sports. Scholarships are awarded for men's baseball, women's softball, women's soccer, and men's and women's bowling. The cheerleading squad promotes school spirit and is also actively involved in community and fundraising activities.

A high-technology, small-business incubator is located on the main campus. The incubator provides up to twenty young companies with a supportive environment in which to grow. The companies are able to share resources, access the research and intellectual strengths of Briarcliffe College, and provide internship experiences for students.

Location
Briarcliffe College is located in Bethpage, New York, a suburban Long Island community approximately 20 miles east of New York City. A branch campus in Patchogue serves residents on the eastern portion of the island. Both the main campus and the branch are in communities thriving with educational, cultural, and recreational opportunities.

Most students commute by car to Briarcliffe College; however, the campuses are easily reached by public transportation. John F. Kennedy International Airport and LaGuardia Airport are less than a ½-hour drive from the main campus. Long Island's Islip-MacArthur Airport is just 10 minutes from the branch campus in Patchogue.

Majors and Degrees
Briarcliffe College confers the Bachelor of Business Administration (B.B.A.), Associate in Applied Science (A.A.S.), and Associate in Occupational Studies (A.O.S.) degrees. Program proposals are currently under development for the Bachelor of Science and Bachelor of Fine Arts degrees.

Program majors are offered in business administration, computer-aided design and drafting, computer applications specialist studies, computer information systems, graphic design, networking and computer technology, office technologies, and telecommunications. Within the office technologies major, a concentration is offered in legal assisting (paralegal).

The Bachelor of Business Administration degree offers concentrations in information technology, management, and marketing.

Academic Program
The multilevel structure of the academic program enables students to enroll immediately in four-year programs or to earn a credential by completing short-term diploma or associate degree programs. Briarcliffe College provides a rich, career-oriented curriculum that prepares students to initiate or advance in their careers.

A minimum of 120 credits is required to earn a bachelor's degree, and 60 credits are required for an associate degree. Diploma programs may be completed in two semesters of full-time study by successfully finishing prescribed course work.

In addition to courses directly related to the major field of study, there is a general education requirement for each degree program. A minimum of 42 general education credits is required for the B.B.A. degree, and a minimum of 21 credits in general education are required for the A.A.S. degree.

The College operates on a traditional two-semester calendar for day classes and an innovative evening schedule that enables students to begin classes at four points during the year to earn semester-hour credits.

Academic Facilities
The main campus building is a 240,000-square-foot facility that was purchased by the College in 1996. The size of the building makes it possible for Briarcliffe College to house lecture halls, computer labs, an electronics lab, conference rooms, faculty offices, counseling offices, and the College library all under one roof. The main campus is wired with fiber-optic cables and connected to the Internet through cable modems and T-1 lines. The branch campus is also served with a T-1 line that connects it to the main network. Computers throughout the College are connected using sophisticated network technology. Briarcliffe College has computer labs that operate on DOS/Windows, Macintosh, and UNIX platforms.

The Briarcliffe College Library supports the academic program with electronic and traditional bibliographic resources. The library is a member of the Long Island Library Resource Council and serves a New York State Electronic Gateway, enabling students and faculty members to access information and materials from libraries throughout the world. Software used throughout the curriculum is installed in computers available for student use in the library.

Specialized programs in networking technology and telecommunications are supported by an electronics laboratory. Student members of the Briarcliffe Amateur Radio Club (BARC) operate a short-wave radio station.

An art studio provides a setting for students to draw still-life and live models. Design software that students are likely to encounter when they enter the workforce is installed on Mac and PC platforms for use by graphic design and architectural design students.

Costs
The tuition for full-time students during the 2000–01 academic year is $4950 per semester. Full-time tuition charges apply to students enrolled in 12 to 18 credits. Tuition for part-time students is $290 per credit.

Financial Aid
Briarcliffe College offers a wide variety of financial aid programs, including scholarships, grants, loans, and work-study. Need-based and achievement-based awards are available. All applicants for financial aid are expected to complete

the Briarcliffe College Financial Aid Application and the Free Application for Federal Student Aid (FAFSA). New York State residents receive an Express Tuition Assistance Program Application (ETA), which must also be completed.

Briarcliffe College directly funds several scholarship programs. The Presidential Scholarship is awarded to first-time college students who have earned at least an 80 high school average and have cumulative math and verbal SAT I scores of at least 1075. Daniel Turan Memorial Scholarships are competitive awards for students who have completed a sequence of business courses in high school. An Alumni Scholarship exam is administered twice each year for high school seniors. Alumni Scholarships may award as much as $9000 for a bachelor's degree program. Program-Specific Scholarships are competitive awards valued up to $6000 in each major program offered at Briarcliffe College. Athletic scholarships are awarded to outstanding athletes in baseball, bowling, soccer, and softball.

Transfer Scholarships are available to students who have earned associate degrees at accredited community or junior colleges.

Faculty

The primary responsibility of all faculty members at Briarcliffe College is to provide effective learning experiences for their students. There are 49 full-time and 48 part-time faculty members. Faculty members set aside weekly office hours to meet with students and to provide academic advisement and program guidance.

Student Government

The Student Government Association (SGA), through its elected officers, is the official voice of the student body in campus governance. All matriculated students are voting members of the SGA. The SGA sponsors social, cultural, and athletic activities both on and off campus. The College views extracurricular activities as an important component of each student's education and relies heavily on the SGA to identify and support programs that inspire active participation by a broad cross-section of the College community.

Admission Requirements

Briarcliffe College has established admissions criteria that recognize the diversity of the college-going population. Regular admission as a matriculating student (one who is taking courses with the intention of earning a degree) requires a high school diploma or the equivalent.

Each applicant to the College is encouraged to meet with one of Briarcliffe's admissions counselors. Previous academic records, scores on standardized testing, and recommendations submitted by the applicant are all considered by the Admissions Office in making a determination of acceptance.

Transfer students are welcome at Briarcliffe College. Course work in which the student has earned at least a C grade at an accredited college is considered for transfer. International students should contact the Admissions Office or check the College Web site (listed below) for information on admission and obtaining an I-20A/B form.

Application and Information

Students who are applying for fall semester admission are encouraged to submit their applications before January 1. The College has a rolling admissions policy that permits admissions decisions to be made as applications and supporting documentation are reviewed, beginning in December. Applications for the spring and summer terms should be submitted at least sixty days before classes are scheduled to begin. Late applications are considered on a space-available basis.

Additional information and application materials are available by contacting Briarcliffe College at the following address:

Admissions Office
Briarcliffe College
1055 Stewart Avenue
Bethpage, New York 11714-3545
Telephone: 516-470-6000
Fax: 516-470-6020
E-mail: info@bcl.edu
World Wide Web: http://www.bcl.edu

The picnic area near the main campus building is a popular spot to get together with friends.

BRIDGEWATER COLLEGE
BRIDGEWATER, VIRGINIA

The College

Bridgewater is a fully accredited liberal arts college. It was founded in 1880 in Virginia's Shenandoah Valley. The College is affiliated with the Church of the Brethren but has no denominational quotas. Enrollment is slightly more than 1,100, facilitating the exchange of ideas and interaction with the faculty. Great importance is placed on maintaining academic rigor and quality.

The student body is composed of men and women from a variety of backgrounds and experiences. Students come mainly from Virginia and the mid-Atlantic states; seventeen states and ten countries are represented in the student body.

A large variety of clubs, societies, and organizations exist on campus to meet students' needs and interests. A complete schedule of intercollegiate sports for men and women is offered during each session, and an extensive intramural sports program for men and women promotes sportsmanship, leadership, physical health, and team play.

Seven residence halls are located on campus, three for men and four for women. New students are assigned to a dormitory room with another new student of compatible interests through a nonautomated housing selection process.

Located in a scenic and historic setting in the beautiful Shenandoah Valley, the 190-acre campus has a complex of buildings of different periods and styles of architecture, surrounded by lawns and many beautiful trees. The campus has a friendly atmosphere and distinctive charm and personality. The Kline Campus Center has dining rooms, a snack shop, a post office, a bookstore, a billiards room, lounges, and offices for student publications and organizations.

Location

The town of Bridgewater, with a population of 3,900, is situated along the North River in the heart of Virginia's Shenandoah Valley, 7 miles south of the city of Harrisonburg. Students can enjoy skiing, hiking, canoeing, bicycling, and other seasonal outdoor sports in the area. Bridgewater is convenient to the urban areas of Washington, D.C.; Richmond; and Roanoke. Air transportation is available at Shenandoah Valley Regional Airport, 13 miles from campus. The valley area is rich in the history of the early United States and the Civil War.

Majors and Degrees

Bridgewater College awards the Bachelor of Arts degree in allied health science, art, biology, business administration, chemistry, computer science, economics, English, family and consumer sciences, French, German, health and exercise science, history, history and political science, information systems management, international studies, liberal studies (available only to students in the elementary and special education programs), mathematics, medical technology, music, nutrition and wellness, philosophy and religion, physical science, physics, physics and mathematics, political science, psychology, sociology, and Spanish. The College offers the Bachelor of Science degree in allied health science, biology, business administration, chemistry, computer science, economics, family and consumer sciences, health and exercise science, information systems management, managerial economics, mathematics, medical technology, nutrition and wellness, physical science, physics, physics and mathematics, political science, psychology, sociology, and sports medicine.

In addition, the College offers four-year curricula leading to the bachelor's degree and a state-approved program of teacher preparation at the PK–6 and 6–12 levels. Art education, music education, physical education, and special education certification is offered for grades PK–12. In addition, through reciprocity agreements, students who complete Bridgewater's teacher education program may be certified to teach in many states.

Minors may be pursued in art, athletic coaching, biology, business administration, chemistry, church music, communications, computer information systems, computer science, economics, English, family and consumer sciences, French, German, history, mathematics, music, nutrition and wellness, peace studies, philosophy and religion, physics, political science, psychology, social work, sociology, Spanish, and theater and speech.

A dual-degree program in forestry is offered in cooperation with the School of Forestry and Environmental Studies at Duke University. A dual-degree program in veterinary medicine is offered in cooperation with the Virginia-Maryland Regional College of Veterinary Medicine at Virginia Tech.

Academic Program

The curriculum at Bridgewater is divided into four major parts, each with its own requirements and objectives: general education, field of major, field of minor (optional), and elective courses. The general education courses are designed to ensure that students acquire an understanding of people and their cultural, social, and natural environments. Field-of-major courses provide depth and breadth of study in a major area. Students may add to their curriculum by completing minor field requirements that are related to their major field of study. Elective studies increase skills and understanding in a major field, meet vocational interests, or fulfill requirements for graduate or professional schools.

A minimum of 123 credits must be earned to graduate; at least 48 credits must be chosen from courses at the junior and senior levels. A quality point average of at least 2.0 must be earned in all work attempted and in the major. Candidates for graduation must pass a written comprehensive examination in their major field(s) of concentration. Flexibility is added to the academic program through an internship program, honors projects, independent study, and an honors program.

In the Personal Development Portfolio (PDP) program, each student is paired with a faculty mentor who aids the student's development in each of eight personal dimensions: academics, citizenship, cultural awareness, esthetics, ethical development, leadership, social skills, and wellness. The program culminates in an enhanced resume, documenting achievement in these dimensions and supplementing the academic transcript. A new general education curriculum for first-year students and sophomores focuses on effective writing, oral communication, quantitative reasoning, critical thinking, and wellness.

Students may be exempted from certain requirements by demonstrating proficiency in written expression, quantitative reasoning, or foreign languages. Credit and advanced placement are awarded to students on the basis of scores on Advanced Placement tests of the College Board. In order to be considered for exemption from certain requirements, students must earn scores of 3 or higher on Advanced Placement tests.

Bridgewater has an academic calendar that provides a January interterm experience.

Off-Campus Arrangements

The Brethren Colleges Abroad program gives students the opportunity to study for a year or a semester at the Philipps Universität, Marburg, Germany; the University of Strasbourg and the University of Nancy, France; the University of

Barcelona, Spain; the Dalian University of Foreign Languages, People's Republic of China; Cheltenham and Gloucester College of Higher Education, Cheltenham, England; Hokusei Gakuen University, Sapporo, Japan; the University of LaVerne, Athens, Greece; Universidad San Francisco de Quito, Quito, Ecuador; Universidad Veracruzana, Xalapa, Mexico; or Cochin University of Science and Technology, Cochin, Kerala, India.

Academic Facilities

The Alexander Mack Memorial Library houses 170,988 volumes, 615 current subscriptions, and 6,931 microform units. Cole Hall, which has seating for 650, is equipped with a stage, dressing rooms, a lighting system, motion picture and sound equipment, two concert grand pianos, and a fifty-one-rank Möller pipe organ. The College is equipped with numerous microcomputers and UNIX minicomputers. These machines are fully networked and connected to the Internet. Also available are soundproof practice rooms for music students or groups. Health and physical education facilities include a large gymnasium, a 25-meter indoor pool, playing fields, and an all-weather track.

The McKinney Center for Science and Mathematics opened in 1995 and includes modern science and computer laboratories, numerous classrooms, and faculty offices. Bowman Hall has recently been renovated to house humanities departments and the C. E. Shull Information Technology Center.

Costs

The basic cost for 2000–01 is $21,940, including tuition, fees, and room and board. The estimated cost for books and supplies is $760. Additional fees are charged for private instrumental or voice instruction. Accounts are payable by the semester or through a monthly payment plan arranged off campus.

Financial Aid

Scholarships, grants, loans, and on-campus jobs are available for qualified students and are awarded in individualized financial aid packages. All applicants for any kind of financial aid must submit the Free Application for Federal Student Aid (FAFSA) by March 1. A number of outstanding academic scholarships are available, ranging from one quarter to full tuition. A work-study program provides jobs for more than 360 students. In 1999–2000, 75 percent of the students received need-based aid. Awards are made for one year only; students must demonstrate satisfactory academic progress for renewal. Early application is advised.

McKinney Achievement in a Community of Excellence (ACE) scholarships are awarded based solely on high school class rank. Applicants meeting all admissions requirements and ranking in the top 30th percentile of their high school class are eligible for ACE awards ranging from 25 percent to 60 percent of tuition. Selected incoming freshmen who rank in the top 5 percent of their high school graduating class may receive a President's Merit ACE Award based on academic achievement and standardized test scores. This award provides full tuition.

Faculty

The faculty consists of 74 full-time members, 73 percent of whom hold the terminal degree. Several part-time faculty members bring unique skills to various departments. The student-faculty ratio is 14:1, which facilitates the exchange of ideas and the development of close relationships between faculty members and students. Faculty members also serve as faculty advisers, major professors, and sponsors of student organizations and activities.

Student Government

The Student Senate, by appointing members to faculty committees and through its own structure, involves students in many aspects of the operation of the College. It acts as a liaison to the faculty and administration by advocating the opinions of the student body and by interpreting the ideals and standards of the College to the students. The student body president, vice president, and senators are elected by the students.

Admission Requirements

Bridgewater College seeks students with above-average preparation who demonstrate a serious attitude toward studies. The faculty expects excellence in student performance. Although a majority of the students are from Virginia, College policy does not demand that Virginia applicants be accepted first. International students are welcomed at Bridgewater. The admissions policy for transfers is much the same as that for freshman applicants; a high school transcript is required, and students must have maintained a grade point average of 2.0 or better on previous college work. Decisions are made after a careful study of academic background (including rank in class, GPA, and course selection), SAT I scores, and letters of recommendation. An on-campus interview is strongly recommended. Rank in the upper half of the high school graduating class and strong SAT I scores are required. Scores on SAT II Subject Tests are not required but are strongly recommended. ACT scores are accepted in lieu of SAT I scores. The College seeks to enroll qualified students regardless of sex, race, color, creed, handicap, or national or ethnic origin.

Application and Information

Information relating to Bridgewater College, including the College *Catalog,* electronic requests for information, and electronic application, can be accessed through the College's World Wide Web site.

Application may be made between completion of the junior year of high school and June 1 of the year of enrollment. Under the College's rolling admissions policy, students can expect notification of the admission decision within thirty days of the College's receipt of all records and credentials. Arrangements can be made for deferred entrance.

Students who wish to request information by mail may write to:
Brian C. Hildebrand
Dean for Enrollment Management
Bridgewater College
402 East College Street
Bridgewater, Virginia 22812
Telephone: 540-828-5375
         800-759-8328 (toll-free)
E-mail: admissions@bridgewater.edu
World Wide Web: http://www.bridgewater.edu

The Writing Center, which opened in 1998, helps students from all courses of study improve their writing skills.

BRIDGEWATER STATE COLLEGE
BRIDGEWATER, MASSACHUSETTS

The College

Bridgewater State College was founded in 1840 and has grown from a teacher-preparation school of 21 students to a comprehensive, liberal arts institution that enrolls more than 9,000 students each year (7,300 undergraduates) in day, evening, and summer programs.

The College offers students a lively cultural, social, and recreational life to enhance the learning experience. The Rondileau Campus Center is the location of many of the student-life activities. Cultural, educational, and entertainment programs, including lectures by guest speakers, concerts, exhibits, and movies, are regularly featured. There are also more than 100 student clubs and organizations in a variety of interest areas. The intercollegiate varsity athletic teams compete under NCAA Division III. Men's teams include baseball, basketball, cross-country, football, soccer, swimming, tennis, track and field, and wrestling. Teams for women include basketball, cross-country, field hockey, lacrosse, soccer, softball, swimming, tennis, track and field, and volleyball. A number of club sports are open to students; these include men's lacrosse, Ultimate Frisbee, karate, cheerleading, men's ice hockey, and men's and women's rugby.

The Bridgewater State College campus has eight residence halls and twenty academic/administrative buildings spread over 235 acres. The atmosphere at Bridgewater is friendly and informal, based on the concept that the College is a community of people with shared interests and goals. A number of important student services (including career, academic, and personal counseling; disability and health services; and housing assistance) are available.

The College offers twenty-eight graduate programs leading to master's degrees or to Certificates of Advanced Graduate Studies.

Location

Bridgewater State College is located in Bridgewater, Massachusetts, a community of more than 20,000 people, approximately 30 miles south of Boston and 25 miles north of Cape Cod. The area is near many cultural, recreational, and historic sites. Train service is available several times daily to Boston from the MBTA Commuter Rail station located in the center of campus.

Majors and Degrees

Bridgewater State College confers the Bachelor of Arts, Bachelor of Science, and Bachelor of Science in Education degrees.

Undergraduate majors are offered in anthropology, art, aviation science (aviation management and flight training), biology, business (see "management science"), chemistry, communication arts and sciences (dance education, speech communication, speech education, theater arts, and theater education), computer science, early childhood education, earth sciences, economics, elementary education, English, geography, history, management science (accounting, energy and environmental resources management, finance, general management, global management, information systems management, marketing, and transportation), mathematics, music, philosophy, physical education, physics, political science, psychology, social work, sociology, Spanish, and special education (communication disorders).

Academic Program

Bridgewater State College offers a full range of study in twenty-eight degree areas. The goal of the academic program is to prepare broadly educated individuals in the liberal arts and the professions. The Academic Achievement Center provides academic counseling and assistance to all freshmen. All students must complete the core program of general education courses to earn a bachelor's degree. Students must complete 120 semester hours of credit, of which at least 30–36 hours must be taken in the major field. Selected students may enroll in departmental or College-wide honors programs.

The College operates on a traditional two-semester calendar and offers two optional summer sessions.

Off-Campus Arrangements

Bridgewater State College participates in three programs that allow students to take courses for credit at other institutions of higher education. College Academic Program Sharing (CAPS) provides full-time students with the opportunity to take courses offered at any of the other Massachusetts state colleges. The College is also a member of the Southeastern Association for Cooperation of Higher Education in Massachusetts (SACHEM), a consortium of public and private colleges that includes Bristol Community, Cape Cod Community, Dean, Massasoit Community, Stonehill, and Wheaton colleges; Massachusetts Maritime Academy; and the University of Massachusetts at Dartmouth. This past year Bridgewater also joined National Student Exchange Program, which allows students to spend a term at other public colleges and universities in the United States.

Students are also encouraged to pursue internships within their major field that provide opportunities to earn college credit while gaining practical experience. Faculty advisers assist students in securing internships in which they work with professionals in business, industry, education, and government.

Academic Facilities

The John Joseph Moakley Center for Technological Applications is named in honor of the distinguished congressman from Massachusetts. The Moakley Center opened in 1995. Technological resources in the building include four technology-integrated classrooms, the primary campus open-access computer lab, a TV studio/control room, a teleconference facility, and a large lecture hall with integrated, computer-based display technology. The entire building is connected to the comprehensive campuswide voice, data, and video network.

Among the many special resources at Bridgewater State College is the Clement C. Maxwell Library, a four-story structure that currently houses 300,000 volumes, receives 1,500 periodicals, and accommodates 2,500 people. College facilities also include an astronomy observatory, radio and television production facilities, a Zeiss electron microscope, a sophisticated electronic learning laboratory, the Burnell Campus Laboratory School, a Human Performance Laboratory, and the Teacher Technology Center.

Costs

For 1999–2000, tuition for full-time study was $1090 per year for Massachusetts residents and $7050 per year for out-of-state students. Fees averaged $1860 per year, books averaged $600, a room averaged $2500, and board averaged $1800. These costs are subject to change.

Financial Aid

Many sources of financial aid are available to Bridgewater students, including Federal Pell Grants, Federal Supplemental Educational Opportunity Grants, Federal Perkins Loans, Federal Stafford Student Loans, HELP loans, alumni scholarships, and Federal Work-Study awards. The Financial Aid Office has prepared an informative brochure detailing methods of application and guidelines for qualification. For a copy, prospective applicants should write to the Financial Aid Office or telephone 508-531-1341. Students are required to submit the Free Application for Federal Student Aid (FAFSA). Applications for financial aid for the fall semester must be received by the preceding March 1.

Faculty

Currently, the College faculty has 262 full-time members and 229 part-time members, 81 percent of whom hold earned doctorates. There are many opportunities for personal contact and interaction between faculty members and students at Bridgewater, since the student-faculty ratio is 18:1 and the emphasis of the faculty is on classroom instruction. Students discover that faculty members are interested in them as individuals and are eager to help them succeed. Graduate students do not teach any courses.

Student Government

Every Bridgewater student is automatically a member of the Student Government Association. Bridgewater's special philosophy of maintaining a College community means that all the people who are part of it—students, faculty, administrators, staff, and alumni—are partners in an educational program whose goal is academic excellence. The Student Government Association is the official representative of the students' point of view, and its officers, elected by the students themselves, organize activities and projects that benefit the student body and the College as a whole.

Admission Requirements

The basic aim of the admission requirements is to ensure the selection of students who have demonstrated intellectual capacity, motivation, and character and who have a record of scholastic achievement. Consideration is given to applicants regardless of their race, religion, national origin, sex, age, color, ethnic origin, or handicap. Three important factors are considered in the freshman admission process: secondary school preparation, College Board or ACT test scores, and personal qualifications. Students may provide a written essay with their application. Neither personal interviews nor recommendations from teachers or counselors are required. Transfer students must submit an official transcript from each college previously attended.

Early admission may be offered to outstanding students when they have completed their junior year of high school. An early action plan is also available.

The College also encourages qualified international students to apply for admission. The application procedures should be completed at least nine months before the desired date of enrollment. Scores on the Test of English as a Foreign Language (TOEFL) must be submitted.

Application and Information

Applications for freshman admission should be filed on or before March 1. Freshmen seeking on-campus housing should apply before March 1. Students who wish to transfer to Bridgewater from another college should apply by December 1 for January admission or by April 1 for September admission.

Students interested in the early admission option should take the SAT I or ACT exams early in the second semester of their junior year. Students choosing the early action option should submit an application and all supporting materials no later than November 15. Early action candidates will be sent a decision letter by December 15.

An application form and further information may be obtained by contacting:

Steve King
Director of Admissions
Bridgewater State College
Bridgewater, Massachusetts 02325

Telephone: 508-531-1237
Fax: 508-531-1746
E-mail: admission@bridgew.edu
World Wide Web: http://www.bridgew.edu

BROCK UNIVERSITY
ST. CATHARINES, ONTARIO, CANADA

The University

Brock University, recent recipient of the Small School of the Year Award, is recognized worldwide for its strong sense of community and dedication to excellent academic programming. Brock prides itself on its commitment to the seminar system and to small-group learning and on its strong career focus, offering many alternatives to combine hands-on practical training and work experience with academic studies. Brock's 10,453 students (6,509 full-time) have the opportunity to work closely with professors and to become directly involved in research projects, many of which have won international acclaim. In addition to excelling in academic pursuits, the majority of Brock students are active in residence, recreation, and club activities, as well as in Brock varsity athletics.

Brock's six faculties include more than forty departments and interdepartmental programs that offer more than 100 undergraduate major programs (most of which can be combined) and nine graduate programs. Although Brock is considered a midsize university by Canadian standards, it has retained the qualities associated with a small university: a friendly atmosphere and close personal attention.

Location

Brock is located in St. Catharines, Ontario, Canada, a beautiful city in the Niagara region on the edge of Lake Ontario. Brock is only 1 hour from the exciting city of Toronto, the provincial capital, and only 15 minutes from Niagara Falls, a premiere tourist attraction. It is also close to the United States border. St. Catharines offers students the best of both worlds: the opportunity to study in a safe, friendly atmosphere, while also providing easy access to large urban centres. The Niagara region offers countless forms of entertainment and recreational and cultural activities as well as a rich history and one of the mildest climates in Canada. Brock's campus is located in the south end of St. Catharines, where the Niagara Escarpment rises to rich farmlands and overlooks the city below. Modern buildings are nestled in a parklike setting with outdoor appeal in every season.

Majors and Degrees

A Bachelor of Arts (humanities) is offered in applied language studies, Canadian and European union studies, Canadian studies, classics, contemporary cultural studies, dramatic literature, English, French, general linguistics, German, great books/liberal studies, history, international studies, Italian, music (also offered as a Bachelor of Music), philosophy, Spanish, theatre, and visual arts. A Bachelor of Arts (social sciences) is offered in child and youth studies, communications studies (business*, information technology, media and culture, and social policy), economics, environmental economics, environmental policy, film studies, geography, international political economy, labor studies, politics, popular culture, psychology, sociology, and women's studies. Also offered in the Faculty of Social Sciences is a Bachelor of Business Economics*. A Bachelor of Business Administration* is offered with concentrations in accounting, entrepreneurship, finance, general management, human resource management, international business, marketing, and public administration. The Faculty of Business also offers a highly acclaimed Bachelor of Accounting*. A Bachelor of Science is offered in biochemistry, biological sciences, biotechnology, chemistry, computer science*, computing and business*, computing and solid-state device technology, earth sciences, environmental science, mathematics, neuroscience, oenology and viticulture* (grape growing and wine making), physical geography, and physics. In the Faculty of Applied Health Sciences, the following degrees may be obtained: Bachelor of Physical Education (with majors in disability studies, kinesiology, and movement studies); Bachelor of Recreation and Leisure Studies; Bachelor of Tourism Studies; Bachelor of Sport Management*; Bachelor of Arts in community health*, community health/child studies, and workplace health*; and a Bachelor of Science in health sciences*. A Bachelor of Education (consecutive) is offered in preservice, continuing studies, and technological studies. A Bachelor of Education (concurrent) is offered in physical education (primary/junior: grades JK–6), child studies (primary/junior: grades JK–6), French (intermediate/senior: grades 7–OAC), and science (junior/intermediate: grades 4–10). (An asterisk (*) indicates a co-op is available in the program.)

Academic Program

Brock University operates on an academic year that runs from September until May. Students interested in the Faculty of Business can also apply for entrance in January. Spring and summer sessions are offered May through August for students who wish to continue their studies throughout the year or for those who may be working on a degree elsewhere.

Students may also take part in the unique Experience Plus and Next Experience Plus programs, which include computer-based training, employability skills training, and volunteer and paid employment opportunities designed to improve career planning and practical employability skills.

Off-Campus Arrangements

The Office of International Services offers a number of exchange programs with institutions in Germany, Wales, England, Korea, Japan, France, and the Unites States. Summer courses are available in Italy. The classics department offers archeological training at work excavations, usually in Cypress. Study tours in Europe are also offered. Most exchange programs are available to all Brock students.

Academic Facilities

Students at Brock have the opportunity to experience top-notch academic, recreational, and spiritual facilities. The James A. Gibson Library holds more than 1 million acquisitions. Brock also houses a unique map library. Students take advantage of Brock's eight computer labs to research articles, write papers, and chat with friends. Every student receives an e-mail address at registration, and all residence rooms are fully wired for computer use. Brock's Building of Applied Health Sciences features the Leo LeBlanc Rowing Center and the Eleanor Misener Aquatic Center. Three theatres on campus host a variety of talent for Brock students and the community at large. Other services include campus ministries, health services, the housing office, and the athletic injury clinic.

Costs

Tuition for visa students for the 2000–01 academic year is Can$9525. On-campus housing and a meal plan are approximately Can$5000. Book costs vary depending on the program but average Can$800. Health insurance is approximately $580. Miscellaneous items (e.g., clothing, transportation, and entertainment) are extra. Tuition does not vary from program to program.

Financial Aid

Visa students can apply for in-course scholarships and bursaries. Brock offers limited scholarship opportunities for incoming visa students. Athletic scholarships are not offered at Ontario universities.

Faculty

The total number of Brock faculty members is 322, 84 percent of whom are tenured. Faculty members at Brock believe a strong link between teaching and research provides the best environment for education. Their research success is reflected in the many research grants and contracts that are awarded to Brock each year. Quality of education is important; Brock employs more Ph.D.'s than most Ontario universities. Faculty members have received many teaching awards because Brock professors are known to care about their students and the progress they are making in and outside of the classroom.

Student Government

All undergraduate registered students are members of the Brock University Student's Union (BUSU). Each spring, union members elect a president; vice president, finance; vice president, University Affairs; and 2 vice presidents of student services to preside over BUSU and the students' administrative council (BUSAC). BUSAC is composed of student representatives from each faculty in the University and the residences, including a representative for off-campus and part-time students. BUSAC acts as a political lobby and social organizer, and it is responsible for managing the affairs of the union and implementing policies for the students of the University. BUSU sponsors and supports programs such as Orientation Week, the General Store, the Social Awareness Resource Centre, the Ombuds Officer, the Brock Press, a food bank, and many others. BUSU also sponsors more than fifty clubs a year. Students also participate in the setting of University policy by electing representatives to sit on the senate and on the Board of Trustees.

Admission Requirements

International students are welcome at Brock. U.S. residents must have completed grade 12 with high grades at an accredited school. SAT I scores are taken into consideration if marks are lower. All applicants must also meet faculty-specific prerequisites. In addition, programs may request a personal profile, audition, or interview.

All international student applicants whose first language is not English must provide results of TOEFL (minimum score: 550), MELAB (minimum score: 85), IELTS (minimum score: 6.5), or the successful completion of Level 5 of Brock's English language programs. Remedial English courses may be required under certain conditions.

Application and Information

Application for fall entry for all applicants must be received by June 1. International applicants should contact the admissions office for an application or visit the Web site.

To find out more about becoming a Brock student, applicants can contact:

Recruitment and Liaison Services
Brock University
500 Glenridge Avenue
St. Catharines, Ontario L2S 3A1
Canada
Telephone: 905-688-5550 Ext. 4293
Fax: 905-988-4283
E-mail: liaison@spartan.ac.brocku.ca
World Wide Web: http://www.brocku.ca

Personal attention, high academic quality, and comfortable living style are what Brock is all about.

BROOKLYN COLLEGE OF THE CITY UNIVERSITY OF NEW YORK
BROOKLYN, NEW YORK

The College

Brooklyn College, since its founding in 1930, has fostered a tradition of academic excellence and achievement. Among its more than 120,000 graduates are many of the nation's outstanding men and women in the fields of education, the humanities, the performing arts, science and medicine, the social sciences, government and public service, law and justice, accounting, business and industry, athletics, and communications. Brooklyn College is the third-oldest senior college of the City University of New York (CUNY). It is housed in eleven main buildings on a 26-acre tree-lined campus. The current undergraduate enrollment is about 11,000 men and women.

The Student Union Building Organization (SUBO) is the focal point of social activity on campus. It contains lounges, conference and meeting rooms, a computer lab, game rooms, art displays, study rooms, music rooms, a television room, and a penthouse with a domed skylight. Brooklyn College's students participate in more than 130 chartered campus groups, including academic clubs, honor societies, athletics groups, special interest groups, and performing arts organizations. Special lectures, concerts, and events are scheduled throughout the year. Fraternities and sororities provide social and community service activities. The Hillel Foundation, Intervarsity Christian Fellowship, and Newman Center are among the many special interest clubs on campus. Student publications include newspapers, magazines, and journals. Students also operate WBCR, the Brooklyn College radio station. Recreation and sports facilities consist of a swimming pool, seven outdoor tennis courts, a recently Astroturf-surfaced athletics field, six gymnasiums, an outdoor track, a fitness center, weight-lifting equipment, outdoor handball courts, and indoor racquetball and squash courts.

The Student Center/Library Cafe is one of Brooklyn College's newest facilities for undergraduate students. It was funded by a $1.6-million grant from the City Council. The Student Center is available to assist students with their academic needs 24 hours a day. It is conveniently located on campus and provides a safe and friendly atmosphere. Equipped with state-of-the-art computers, laptops, Internet access, and data management programs, the Library Cafe provides a quaint atmosphere in which students can enjoy a coffee break while attending to their studies.

The Office of Services for Students with Disabilities provides counseling and other assistance to students with disabilities to ensure that they have complete access to College programs and facilities. College and departmental counseling programs provide all students with academic and personal counseling. Career, preprofessional, veterans', and psychological counseling services are also available, and job referral services are offered.

Location

Brooklyn College is located in the residential Midwood section of Brooklyn. The campus is near the Brooklyn Museum, the Brooklyn Botanic Garden, and Prospect Park. Within a short distance are all the cultural, recreational, and entertainment facilities of New York City. All major IND and IRT trains are easily accessible from the college.

Majors and Degrees

Brooklyn College awards the Bachelor of Arts (B.A.), Bachelor of Science (B.S.), Bachelor of Music (B.M.), and Bachelor of Fine Arts (B.F.A.) degrees. Majors are available in the following areas: accounting; Africana studies; American studies; anthropology; art; biology; broadcast journalism; business, management, and finance; Caribbean studies; chemistry; classics; comparative literature; computer and information science; creative writing; economics; education (bilingual/bicultural education, early childhood education, elementary education, education of the speech and hearing handicapped, and secondary education with certification in sixteen subject areas); English; film; French; geology; health and nutrition sciences; history; Italian; journalism; Judaic studies; linguistics; mathematics; mathematics-computational; music; music composition; music performance; philosophy; physical education; physics; political science; psychology; Puerto Rican and Latino studies; religious studies; Russian; sociology; Spanish; speech (audiology, speech and hearing science, speech-language pathology, and teaching of the speech and hearing handicapped); studio art; television and radio; theater; and women's studies. Certificate programs are offered in accounting, computers and programming, and film production; credits earned in these programs are applicable toward a baccalaureate degree.

Students interested in economics and computer applications may apply to enter a 4½-year program that leads to both the Bachelor of Science and the Master of Professional Studies (M.P.S.) degrees.

Brooklyn College and the State University of New York Health Science Center at Brooklyn offer a coordinated eight-year honors program that leads to B.A. and M.D. degrees. The program is limited each year to 20 qualified students who are admitted only in the fall term following their graduation from high school.

Professional options include the opportunity for qualified students to earn a B.A. or B.S. degree from Brooklyn College by satisfactorily completing all requirements for graduation and by also satisfactorily completing at least one year's work in an accredited dental, engineering, law, medical, or veterinary school. Students interested in pursuing an engineering degree may participate in Brooklyn College's approved two-year pre-engineering program. Students attend Brooklyn College for two years of pre-engineering studies and then transfer to Polytechnic University, City College, or the College of Staten Island for an additional two years of study to fulfill the Bachelor of Science degree requirements in a specific engineering field.

Academic Program

The liberal arts education at Brooklyn College consists of three kinds of study: the College-wide CORE curriculum, which provides a diverse educational experience in the liberal arts for all students; major studies, which comprise specialized, intensive study in one discipline; and elective courses, selected from more than seventy-five areas of study. The undergraduate curriculum aims to prepare students to make rational career and personal choices by developing their intellect in critical and independent thinking, their ability to acquire and organize large amounts of knowledge, and their ability to communicate in writing and speech with precision and force. Students pursuing a bachelor's degree must successfully complete a minimum of 120 credits.

The Scholars Program offers students who combine academic excellence with initiative and inquisitiveness the opportunity to take classes and special courses that are open only to members of the program. Students who qualify based on intellectual ability are also offered a variety of opportunities for honors work in their regular courses through the Honors Program.

The Honors Academy comprises four units: the Scholars Program; the B.A./M.D. Program; the Ford Colloquium, which prepares undergraduates for graduate school and careers in research and college teaching; and the Mellon Minority

Undergraduate Fellowship, a two-year program for members of minority groups who are considering scholarly study in the humanities. Applications for all four programs may be obtained in the Honors Academy Office or the Office of Admissions.

Students who have completed college-level courses in high school may be considered for exemption, with or without credit, from equivalent college courses on the basis of Advanced Placement tests given by the College Board. Brooklyn College gives exemption examinations in subjects not offered by the College Board. Students completing 3 years of foreign language in high school are exempt from the College's language requirement.

Brooklyn College offers two unique programs—the High School Enrichment Program and the Summer High School/College Bridge Program. These programs provide high school juniors and seniors with the opportunity to earn transferable college credits. Academically strong high school students are introduced to college-level instruction and may enroll in regular college credit courses for which they qualify. Participation includes an evaluation of the student's high school transcript and SAT or PSAT scores. Help is provided in selecting courses to meet the student's needs and interests.

The academic calendar consists of a fall and a spring semester. Two summer sessions are available. Classes are offered in day, evening, and weekend sessions.

Academic Facilities

The Gideonse Library began major reconstruction in spring 1999 with a $54 million grant from city and state of New York funds for renovations at Brooklyn College. The grant funds a complete external expansion and internal renovation of LaGuardia Hall, Gideonse Library, and LaGuardia Reading Room. Currently, Gideonse Library includes more than 1.25 million bound volumes, nearly 4,900 periodical subscriptions, and 19,000 records and tapes. Specialized libraries are the Gerboth Music Library, which houses scores, recordings, and technical/specialized books; the Costas Memorial Library, which provides books, journals, and periodicals in the classics; and an Investment Library that electronically provides access to data on publicly held corporations, stock markets, commodities exchanges, and economic forecasting indexes. The Brooklyn Center for the Performing Arts at Brooklyn College, which presents music, dance, and theater productions, contains a 2,500-seat auditorium, a theater, a recital hall, and a workshop theater. The College Computer Center is a state-of-the-art facility that supports student course requirements as well as research. Other special facilities include microcomputer learning centers, a language laboratory, art studios, an advanced color-television studio, an early childhood education center, a speech and hearing center, psychology laboratories, laser laboratories, an astronomical observatory, an optical mineralogy laboratory, a greenhouse, an aquatic research center, and a nuclear physics laboratory.

Costs

In 2000–01, New York State residents pay tuition of $1600 per semester for full-time attendance (12 or more credits or the equivalent) or $135 per credit for part-time programs. Non–New York residents and international students pay tuition of $3400 per semester for full-time attendance or $285 per credit for part-time programs. Tuition for the summer session is $135 per credit for New York State residents and $285 per credit for out-of-state and international students. The College is a commuter institution and does not have on-campus housing.

Financial Aid

Admission decisions and financial aid and scholarship decisions are made independently of each other, and an application for aid does not hinder a student's opportunity for admission. Financial assistance is available for eligible students through state and federal grant, loan, and work-study programs.

New students with strong SAT scores and strong high school or college academic records are encouraged to apply for annual scholarships. Continuing students may qualify for one of more than 400 scholarships, prizes, and awards that are given each year to Brooklyn College students. The requirements vary for each, but recipients are chosen based on academic performance, financial need, and other criteria stipulated by the donors. Scholarships range from $100 to $3200 per year. Awards and prizes are one-time gifts of cash; the amounts vary from $50 to $1200. For information about scholarships and awards, students should contact the Office of Admissions, 1203 Plaza (telephone: 718-951-4796).

Faculty

The College has an outstanding faculty (490 full-time and 394 part-time) whose members have demonstrated excellence in teaching and scholarly research. More than 90 percent hold a doctoral degree or the equivalent in their field of study. Faculty members assist in the academic advisement of entering students and provide counseling to students majoring in their department. They also hold regular office hours and are generally available to support undergraduate as well as graduate student activities.

Student Government

Student governments are active in both the day and evening divisions. Students are elected to positions on the associations by the entire student body. Students also serve on the Policy Council, the major College-wide governing body.

Admission Requirements

High school students, students who want to transfer from other institutions, and adults returning to school are encouraged to apply. Admission criteria are set by the City University of New York and involve a combination of a student's GPA, academic units, and/or a minimum SAT I score of 1100. Students must meet two out of the three requirements. Minimum requirements include a high school average of 81, with successful completion of 12 or more high school academic units (of which at least 5 units must include 2 or more years of English and 2 or more years of math). The recommended high school preparation for the College's curriculum is 4 years of English, 4 years of social studies, 3 years of mathematics, 3 years of science, and 3 years of a foreign language. Students seeking admission to the Scholars Program or the B.A./M.D. Program must present a high school average of 90 or better, exceptional SAT I or ACT scores, letters of recommendation, and an autobiographical essay and have a personal interview. Qualified high school juniors may apply for early admission.

Students with special educational needs may qualify for admission into the Search for Education, Elevation, Knowledge (SEEK) program.

Application and Information

Application for admission to the undergraduate program for the fall or spring semester should be made on a standard CUNY application form, available from the Office of Admissions at any CUNY college. Application forms for the Honors Academy, the Scholars Program, the B.A./M.D. Program, the Mellon Minority Undergraduate Fellowship, and the summer session are available only through Brooklyn College. Although applications for admission are processed by the City University on a rolling basis, applicants who apply before January 15 for fall admission and before October 15 for spring admission receive prompt notification of their admission status and have the best opportunity for comprehensive advisement and course registration.

For an application form, additional financial aid information, scholarship information, and brochures, students should contact:

Office of Admissions
1203 Plaza
Brooklyn College of the City University of New York
Brooklyn, New York 11210
Telephone: 718-951-5001
E-mail: adminqry@brooklyn.cuny.edu

BROWN UNIVERSITY
PROVIDENCE, RHODE ISLAND

The University

The history of Brown University reaches back over more than two centuries and tells of a university constantly undergoing change. Brown was established with a charter from the Colony's General Assembly in 1764, and the first men registered at the college in 1765. The first women were admitted in 1891, when the establishment of the Women's College in Brown University marked the beginning of eighty years of a coordinate structure for educating women within the University. Brown is now a coeducational institution, drawing men and women from all over the United States and many other countries to participate in the academic and extracurricular life of an Ivy League university. There are more than 7,000 students at Brown, of whom more than 5,500 are undergraduates.

A profile of the average Brown student is practically impossible to create. Here, the typical student is atypical and happy to be so. The diversity of Brown's student body is, in fact, one of the characteristics in which the University takes most pride. Given this diversity, however, there are still some generalizations that might apply to the Brown student body as a whole. One of them is that students have a deep concern for both the process and the quality of education. Another is the students' willingness, even eagerness, to become involved. Finally, it can be said that Brown students are highly motivated to seek advanced study after their undergraduate years.

Brown students feel a commitment to learn—and live—outside of the classroom. More than 200 clubs and activities thrive on the Brown campus. These range from athletic and recreational programs to community-service organizations and environmental-action groups; music, drama, and theater groups; literary publications; political organizations; clubs for vocational interests; and the nation's first college radio station. Specific activities vary from year to year according to student interest.

Brown's Graduate School offers courses leading to the degrees of Master of Arts, Master of Science, Master of Arts in Teaching, Master of Medical Science, Master of Fine Arts, and Doctor of Philosophy.

Location

Providence, by virtue of its size, location, and diversity, offers many advantages to the college student. A city large enough to support a convention center and a large, active Civic Center that draws top entertainment and sports events, Providence is still small enough to offer involvement in local politics, community service, and cultural activities. Providence also offers an excellent repertory company and a major performing arts center as well as museums, concert halls, and a good commercial transportation system. It does not overwhelm the newcomer.

Majors and Degrees

Brown University offers the following degree programs for undergraduates: the Bachelor of Arts (A.B.), the Bachelor of Science (Sc.B.), a five-year program leading to the combined Bachelor of Science and Bachelor of Arts (Sc.B. and A.B.), and the Program in Liberal Medical Education, leading to a Bachelor of Arts or Bachelor of Science at the end of four years and an M.D. degree four years later (from the Brown Medical School).

Within a degree program, Brown students elect a concentration that is the focus of their undergraduate work. Standardized concentrations are available in the following areas: Afro-American studies, American civilization, ancient studies, anthropology (anthropology-linguistics), applied mathematics (applied mathematics–biology, applied mathematics–computer science, and applied mathematics–economics), architectural history and studies, art (applied art and art history), art-semiotics, biological and medical sciences (aquatic biology, biochemistry, biology, biomedical ethics, biophysics, computational biology, human biology, molecular biology, and neuroscience), chemistry (biochemistry, chemistry, and geology–chemistry), Chinese language, classics (ancient history, classical archaeology, classics, Greek, Latin, and Sanskrit), cognitive neuroscience, cognitive science, community health, comparative literature, computational biology, computer science, computer technology (engineering), development studies, East Asian studies, economics (economics-engineering, economics-mathematics, and economics–operations research), educational studies, Egyptology, engineering (biomedical, chemical, civil, computer, electrical, materials, and mechanical engineering), English and American literature, environmental studies, ethics and political philosophy, ethnic studies, French studies, geological sciences (geology-biology, geology-chemistry, and geology-physics/mathematics), German studies, Hispanic studies, history, history and Chinese language, international relations, Italian studies, Judaic studies, late antique cultures, Latin American studies, linguistics, literatures (combination of any two literatures offered), mathematics (mathematical economics, mathematics-computer science, and mathematics-physics), media/culture, medieval cultures, music, neuroscience, old-world art/archaeology, philosophy (ethics and political philosophy, logic, and the philosophy of science), physics, political science, Portuguese and Brazilian language and studies, psychology, public- and private-sector organizations, public policy/American institutions, religious studies, Renaissance studies, Russian language and literature, Russian studies, sexuality and society, sociology, South Asian studies, statistics, theater arts and dramatic literature, urban studies, visual art, and women's studies. In addition, each student at Brown may pursue study in any academic area through either independent study or an independent concentration program of the student's design.

Academic Program

Brown's philosophy of education, promoted by students and endorsed by the faculty, can be simply stated: students will get more out of their education, and it will serve them better, if it is tailored to their individual needs and goals. Because Brown's curriculum has no distribution requirements, students have both the latitude and the responsibility to create an academic program that will reflect genuine and enduring personal accomplishment.

A student may register for and complete a maximum of forty semester courses; a minimum of thirty semester courses must be completed satisfactorily to earn a diploma. Course work can be evaluated by one of two grading systems at Brown: the ABC/No Credit option or the Satisfactory/No Credit option. Work that is judged by the instructor to be unsatisfactory receives no credit, and the student's registration in the class never appears on a formal transcript. A written analysis of the student's work, in the form of a Course Performance Report, may be requested. The student must complete a concentration in order to graduate. This ensures an in-depth study that is centered on the unit provided by a discipline or disciplines, a problem, a theme, or a broad question.

Advanced Placement credit is available, as are opportunities for independent or honors work. Brown operates on a two-semester calendar. The first term begins in early September and continues through mid-December, while the second term runs from late January until mid-May.

Off-Campus Arrangements

Brown students can enroll in as many as four courses at the Rhode Island School of Design (Brown's neighbor on College Hill). Many students choose to study abroad for a semester or a year; Brown directly sponsors fifty-seven programs in eighteen countries.

Academic Facilities

The main campus of Brown University occupies an area of approximately 140 acres. More than fifty buildings are devoted to classroom, laboratory, research, library, office, and conference use by departments of instruction. The University Library, containing more than 5 million items, includes the John D. Rockefeller Jr. Library, the John Hay Library, the Sciences Library, the Orwig Music Library, the John Carter Brown Library, and the Ann Mary Brown Library. The University provides extensive modern laboratory and computer facilities designed for undergraduate and graduate instruction as well as research. The Performing Arts Complex, the Catherine Bryan Dill Center for the Performing Arts, includes the Leeds Theater, the Stuart Theater, and the Ashamu Dance Studio.

Costs

Tuition for the 2000–01 year is $25,600. The cost of room and board is $7346. Fees total $774. Books and personal expenses are estimated at $2080.

Financial Aid

The Financial Aid Office makes all awards on the basis of the candidate's need, as determined from the Financial Aid PROFILE analysis of the College Scholarship Service. A three-part package of aid is awarded, consisting of a scholarship, a loan, and a campus job. The University also participates in the federally funded Federal Work-Study, Federal Supplemental Educational Opportunity Grant (FSEOG), and Federal Perkins Loan programs. Candidates should file the PROFILE application and the Free Application for Federal Student Aid (FAFSA) by February 1 and are notified of their award in April. Approximately 38 percent of students in each entering class receive University scholarship aid.

Faculty

Brown's faculty consists of 547 full-time and 168 visiting and adjunct teaching professors. Faculty members teach both graduate and undergraduate students, and each professor must teach an undergraduate class every year. The student-faculty ratio is 8:1, allowing for extensive counseling of students by the faculty. All professors have weekly office hours during which they are available to students. Faculty and students serve jointly on approximately a dozen University committees concerning student affairs. While faculty members usually do not live in student dormitories, some members serve as dormitory liaisons, and the majority live close to the campus.

Student Government

The Brown Undergraduate Council of Students, a group of elected representatives, has primary responsibility for the disbursement of more than $500,000 in student moneys. These funds are distributed among the more than 200 clubs, organizations, and activities that form the basis of extracurricular life at Brown. In addition, Brown undergraduates participate actively with faculty and administration on a host of campus committees concerned with University policies.

Admission Requirements

Individuals are considered for admission to Brown on the basis of academic and personal qualities. A strong scholastic background and the intellectual ability to meet the demands of a rigorous academic program are required. Secondary school records, teacher and counselor evaluations, and the results of standardized tests are all important factors in a decision. To obtain a diverse student body, Brown also reviews each candidate's credentials in light of the individual's strengths. Special interests, talents, and qualities are important; the Board of Admission is concerned with the extent to which each applicant might contribute in his or her own way to the total life of the University.

Application and Information

Students may apply to Brown by submitting an application for admission (Forms 1 and 1A) and the subsequent Forms 2 through 4, which include a personal statement, secondary school reports, and teacher references. The SAT I and any three SAT II: Subject Tests of the College Board or the ACT of the American College Testing Service must be taken. No interview is necessary. The application deadline for all forms is January 1. Notification is in early April. A fall notification plan, called early action, offers candidates the opportunity to apply in November (with a deadline of November 1 for all forms) and receive an admission notification in mid-December.

Information and application materials may be obtained by contacting:

Dorothy H. Testa
Associate Director of Admission
Brown University
45 Prospect Street
Providence, Rhode Island 02912
Telephone: 401-863-7924
E-mail: admission_undergraduate@brown.edu
World Wide Web: http://www.brown.edu

BRYANT COLLEGE
SMITHFIELD, RHODE ISLAND

The College

Bryant College has a 137-year-old tradition of excellence in business education. Bryant is internationally recognized and accredited by AACSB–The International Association for Management Education and the New England Association of Schools and Colleges. Through challenging academic programs, Bryant students develop critical-thinking and problem-solving skills. Courses are designed to prepare students for the competitive global market, providing technological, cultural, and international business knowledge. By complementing the strong business curriculum with liberal arts courses, Bryant prepares its graduates to succeed throughout their careers.

College programs focus on the intellectual and professional development of each student, preparing him or her for leadership positions in a wide range of careers. Bryant graduates are successful businesspeople in corporate, nonprofit, and entrepreneurial organizations throughout the country and the world. Career exploration, direction, and planning begin as early as the freshman year.

The undergraduate enrollment of 2,487 students comprises 61 percent men and 39 percent women. Students come from thirty-two states and forty-three countries. Bryant has all the advantages of a small community, including the development of close relationships and understanding among students, faculty, and College administrators. Opportunities for the exchange of ideas and a flow of dialogue between students and faculty members are readily available. Students build awareness of the impact that business decisions have on society and understand the relationship between business functions and the larger spectrum of human need and well-being.

Bryant's modern campus includes the Unistructure, which houses most faculty and administrative offices, classrooms, the Edith M. Hodgson Memorial Library, Janikies Auditorium, and dining facilities. Other buildings include the Bryant Student Center, which contains many meeting and eating places, and the Koffler Technology Center. Residential housing is guaranteed for all interested students, and 79 percent of students live on campus. Students may progress from the family-like freshman complex to suite-style dormitories and finally to town-house apartments. The Multipurpose Activities Center houses a gymnasium and various athletic courts as well as a Nautilus room.

Through the Graduate School, Bryant College offers the Master of Business Administration (M.B.A.) degree with concentrations in accounting, computer information systems, finance, general business, international business, management, marketing, and operations management. Master of Science in Taxation (M.S.T.) and Master of Science in Accounting (M.S.A.) degrees as well as Certificate of Advanced Graduate Studies (C.A.G.S.) programs are also offered.

Students have many opportunities to participate in a wide variety of intellectual, practical activities, such as internships and student-faculty research. The John H. Chafee Center for International Business is made up of outreach programs that link Bryant directly to New England businesses. Students can utilize the Center's resources for research and reference and as an opportunity for internships and assistantships.

Location

The College relocated in 1971 from Providence to a 387-acre campus of typical New England countryside. Bryant's central location is only 15 minutes from the state capital of Providence, which offers a variety of ethnic restaurants, professional sports events, music concerts, and a nationally acclaimed theater. Rhode Island's geographic, historic, and cultural attractions include Newport's world-class sailing, jazz festivals, and stunning mansions. Bryant is only 1 hour from Boston and 3 hours from New York City, providing easy access to the cultural and social amenities of these two major metropolitan areas.

Majors and Degrees

Bryant College offers programs leading to the Bachelor of Science in Business Administration (B.S.B.A.) degree with eight concentrations: accounting, accounting information systems, applied actuarial mathematics, computer information systems, finance, financial services, management, and marketing. The College also offers programs leading to the Bachelor of Arts in Liberal Studies (B.A.L.S.) degree with five concentrations: communication, economics, English, history, and international studies. Business students pursue a minor in one of fifteen liberal arts disciplines.

Students can pursue a Bachelor of Science in business administration or a Bachelor of Arts in liberal studies on a part-time basis.

Academic Program

Students pursuing a four-year baccalaureate degree must complete a core curriculum upon which they can build an academic program directed toward a career in business or related areas. The liberal arts are blended with professional business courses. Graduation requirements in the four-year programs include a minimum of 122 semester hours. Bryant College operates on a semester plan.

Entering students may receive credit through the Advanced Placement (AP) Program or the College-Level Examination Program (CLEP) administered by the College Board. Credit is also awarded for International Baccalaureate (IB) Higher Level exams. Bryant participates in the Army ROTC Program.

Off-Campus Arrangements

Bryant College offers students a wide variety of opportunities to expand their learning beyond the confines of the classroom. When studying abroad for a semester, students gain cultural exposure as well as intellectual knowledge. Bryant students may choose to study in Eastern Europe, Western Europe, Asia, Mexico, Canada, Australia, or a variety of other areas.

Students may gain practical experience in their field of study through the College internship program. Each year, nearly 300 students get started on their careers through internships or practicums at such firms as Walt Disney World, Fidelity Investments, PricewaterhouseCoopers, and New England Patriots and at a variety of nonprofit organizations.

Academic Facilities

The Edith M. Hodgson Memorial Library houses one of the region's most comprehensive collection of business materials in the state. Library holdings include more than 126,000 items in a variety of formats, including books, bound journals, microfilm, videos, audiocassettes, and CD-ROMs. Subject specialties include finance, management, taxation, small business, and corporate histories. Current subscriptions to more than 3,000 journals and newspapers are available in traditional hard-copy format or electronically via the on-site Power Pages CD-ROM network or via Proquest Direct on the Web. Bryant's own International Trade Data Network is also available for student use. The reference department is further enhanced by online access to the LEXIS-NEXIS service, Dialog, Bridge Information Systems, and the World Wide Web. Online access to ISI's Emerging Markets database, Proquest Direct, and *Encyclopedia Britannica* is available campuswide via the Internet. The latest news is available to students in the CNN/CNBC lounge. Membership in the Consortium of Rhode Island Academic and Research Libraries grants students access to other major research libraries in the state. Through an electronic interlibrary loan system, students can obtain special items from regional, national, and international libraries. Copy machines, microfilm readers and printers, and study rooms are also available for student use.

Bryant's Koffler Technology Center houses approximately 145 terminals, microcomputers, and networked workstations for student use. It also provides a software library, an applied actuarial mathematics laboratory, advanced workstations, access to e-mail and the Internet, and desktop publishing applications. In addition, every room in the residence halls is wired to connect students to the College's computer network.

Costs

For 2000–01, the tuition is $17,330 and the residence hall room and board fee is $7250. The town-house room fee is $5500 for a single-occupancy room and $5200 for a double-occupancy room. There are special fees for the summer sessions.

Financial Aid

Bryant has a comprehensive program of merit- and need-based financial aid. Approximately 90 percent of freshmen receive financial aid through a combination of scholarships, loans, grants, and part-time jobs. Bryant uses the Free Application for Federal Student Aid (FAFSA) and the CSS Financial Aid PROFILE. The FAFSA must be filed after January 1. Both forms must be filed before February 15. For further information, students should contact the Director of Financial Aid.

Faculty

Teaching is considered the prime responsibility of Bryant's full-time faculty. Emphasis is placed on imparting knowledge of each discipline directly to the students. Bryant faculty members are also active in original research projects, publishing, consulting, and community service. Seventy-nine percent of Bryant's faculty members have doctoral degrees or the highest degree possible in their field.

Student Government

The Student Senate is the student governing body. It serves as a channel of communication between the students and the faculty and administrators. The Student Senate has approved sixty professional, religious, and social organizations on campus and works closely with the Student Programming Board to organize cultural and social programs for the Bryant community.

Admission Requirements

Bryant College seeks students who are motivated learners and have a history of academic achievement. Candidates are considered individually by the Admissions Committee. Acceptances are based upon the quality of scholastic achievement shown by the applicant. Scores earned on the SAT I or on the ACT must be submitted. The committee places great weight on recommendations from the secondary school guidance office and faculty members concerning character and personal qualifications not shown in the academic record. Interviews, though not required, are highly recommended.

Application and Information

As early as possible in the senior year of high school, the applicant should complete an official application form and send it to the Office of Admission, together with a nonrefundable fee of $50 ($80 for students submitting non-U.S. education credentials). It is also the responsibility of the applicant to request that the secondary school guidance office send a copy of the student's school record directly to Bryant and to have SAT I or ACT scores sent to the College. International applicants must also submit TOEFL scores and a completed Certificate of Finance form.

Bryant offers a modified rolling admissions calendar. Application review begins November 1. Notification is sent as decisions are reached. Students must submit commitment deposits by May 1. Students who wish to be considered for all scholarships should apply by January 15.

For further information, students should contact:

Dean of Admission and Financial Aid
Bryant College
1150 Douglas Pike
Smithfield, Rhode Island 02917-1285

For admission information:
Telephone: 401-232-6100
           800-622-7001 (toll-free)
Fax: 401-232-6741
E-mail: admissions@bryant.edu

For financial aid information:
Telephone: 401-232-6020
           800-248-4036 (toll-free)
E-mail: finaid@bryant.edu

Bryant's striking, modern campus is ideally located 15 minutes from Providence and 1 hour from Boston.

BRYN MAWR COLLEGE
BRYN MAWR, PENNSYLVANIA

The College
Bryn Mawr College was founded in 1885 by the Quakers to provide for women the same rigorous and stimulating university-level education as was then available only to men. Bryn Mawr was the first college in the country to grant a Ph.D. to a woman, and it remains today the only predominantly women's institution with an extensive graduate program.

Bryn Mawr's 1,242 undergraduate students currently represent forty-nine states, several American possessions, and more than fifty countries. Twenty-seven percent of the undergraduates are members of minority groups in the United States, and another 11 percent are citizens of other countries. Graduate students and special students bring even greater diversity to the campus. The total enrollment of the College is 1,779.

Nearly all Bryn Mawr undergraduates live on either the Bryn Mawr or nearby Haverford College campus. One of Bryn Mawr's eleven residence halls and all of Haverford's are coeducational through the student-run residence exchange. At Bryn Mawr, members of all four classes live in each of the halls, which accommodate from 60 to 145 students each and range in style from collegiate Gothic to Louis Kahn–designed modern. Other choices of residence on campus include an African-American Cultural Center and language houses, which have Chinese-, French-, German-, Hebrew-, Italian-, Russian-, or Spanish-speaking students.

A wide variety of student-run extracurricular groups, many of them shared with Haverford College, provide opportunities for those interested in musical, political, literary, service-oriented, dramatic, religious, or other activities. The College sponsors various programs to bring leaders from the fields of scholarship, business, politics, the arts, and religion to the campus for public lectures and informal meetings with students.

Sports activities are offered for competition and recreation. The College's athletics facilities include a modern athletics complex, tennis courts, two playing fields, an archery range, and a dance studio. Bryn Mawr students also use Haverford's athletics facilities and, in some cases, join its classes or practice with its teams. Intercollegiate sports include badminton, basketball, cross-country, field hockey, lacrosse, soccer, swimming, tennis, and volleyball.

Location
Bryn Mawr's 135-acre suburban campus is 11 miles and 17 minutes by train from the center of Philadelphia, the nation's fifth-largest city, and all its cultural, commercial, historical, entertainment, and transportation facilities. A few of the city's resources are the Philadelphia Museum of Art, the Philadelphia Academy of Music, numerous theaters, professional and collegiate athletics, some of the nation's most important historic areas, and many intriguing neighborhoods within the metropolitan area, including a thriving Chinatown and an open-air Italian market.

Majors and Degrees
Bryn Mawr College grants the Bachelor of Arts (A.B.) degree with majors and concentrations in more than forty areas: Africana studies, anthropology, astronomy, biology, chemistry, classical and Near Eastern archaeology, classical languages, classical studies, comparative literature, computer science, East Asian studies, economics, English, feminist and gender studies, fine arts, French and French studies, geology, German and German studies, Greek, growth and structure of cities, Hebrew and Judaic studies, Hispanic and Hispanic American studies, history, history of art, international economic relations, Italian, Latin, mathematics, music, neural and behavioral sciences, peace and conflict studies, philosophy, physics, political science, psychology, religion, Romance languages, Russian, sociology, and Spanish. Students also develop independent majors.

Through an unusually broad cooperative arrangement with Haverford College, Bryn Mawr students may major in any of Haverford's nineteen coordinate departments or in astronomy, classics, music, or religion while earning a Bachelor of Arts degree from Bryn Mawr.

Also offered are 3-2 programs in engineering and in city and regional planning in cooperation with the University of Pennsylvania.

Academic Program
Bryn Mawr's curriculum is designed to encourage breadth of learning and training in the fundamentals of scholarship in the first two years and mature and sophisticated study in depth in a major program during the last two years. Its main purpose is to prepare the student for the lifelong pleasure of educating herself. A rigorous but flexible framework of divisional requirements and majors encourages each student's academic independence.

To earn the A.B. degree, a student must complete a two-semester interdisciplinary course in critical thinking and writing, the College Seminars. The first College Seminar must be taken in the student's first semester at Bryn Mawr, and the second must be completed within the first two years. A total of 32 units of work are required for graduation that also include one course to meet the quantitative requirement, work to demonstrate proficiency in a foreign language, 6 units to meet divisional requirements (two each in the humanities, social sciences, and natural and physical sciences), a major subject sequence, and elective units to complete an undergraduate program.

Major requirements vary among the departmental and interdepartmental programs available at Bryn Mawr and Haverford; each student chooses and plans her major in consultation with her dean and faculty adviser. Honors projects and independent study are options offered to outstanding students. The sequence of courses required by medical schools or those sequences giving good preparation for law school or leading to secondary school teaching certification can be combined with most of the major programs.

Bryn Mawr's academic calendar is coordinated with Haverford's and is divided into two semesters, the first beginning early in September and ending before Christmas and the second running from mid-January to mid-May.

Off-Campus Arrangements
In addition to offering the extensive cooperative arrangements with Haverford College that enable students at both colleges to major in any department on either campus, Bryn Mawr gives students the opportunity to take courses for credit and without additional fees at Swarthmore College and the University of Pennsylvania. Exchange programs with other U.S. institutions include a semester or year exchange with Spelman College in Atlanta.

Students may take the junior year abroad in Paris, Geneva, Munich, Florence, Rome, London, or any of many other cities through one of the plans of study in which Bryn Mawr participates. The College's own international ventures include five summer language-study centers—the Institut d'Études Françaises d'Avignon; the Centro de Estudios Hispánicos en Madrid; the Bryn Mawr College/University of Pennsylvania Italian Studies Summer Institute in Florence; and a program at the Pushkin Institute of Russian Language in Moscow—and two archaeological excavations—a prehistoric site in the Nemea Valley, Greece, and a Neolithic site in eastern Turkey. Students may attend the Intercollegiate Center for Classical Studies in Rome, of which Bryn Mawr is a sponsoring member; the American School of Classical Studies in Athens; or the American Academy at Rome. Anthropology students may apply to study in Kenya under the auspices of research programs directed by Dr. Richard Leakey. Other countries in which Bryn Mawr students have recently worked and studied include Canada, Israel, Japan, Mexico, Peru, Scotland, and Zimbabwe. Academic credit for all work done abroad is arranged within the student's department.

Academic Facilities

More than 1 million volumes in a network of open-stack libraries at Bryn Mawr and an additional 400,000 volumes at Haverford are available through cross-listed catalogs. Other facilities include a language laboratory, computer facilities, and the Science Center, which has a new $22-million science library and chemistry wing. An art and archaeology addition to Thomas Library opened in 1997 and houses seminar rooms, research facilities, and a state-of-the-art Visual Resources Center. Special departmental research collections include American and European anthropological and archaeological artifacts; recordings of the music of native peoples from all parts of the world; an extensive and important geologic collection of minerals and maps; a study collection of Greek and Roman minor arts, especially vases and coins; Medieval manuscripts and late Medieval printed books (the third-largest collection of incunabula in the nation); and distinguished library holdings of American, Asian, and African books.

Costs

For 2000–01, tuition is $23,520, and room and board are $8340. College activities fees and the student government association fee total $640. For students taking laboratory sciences, laboratory fees are $35. The average cost for books and supplies is $650, and personal expenses are about $750.

Financial Aid

More than 52 percent of Bryn Mawr's undergraduates are receiving grant assistance, usually in combination with loans and campus employment. All aid is awarded on the basis of demonstrated need. The College meets 100 percent of institutional eligibility and continues to do so throughout a student's four years if the student continues to qualify. The average financial aid award in 1998–99 was $20,802, and more than $10 million was distributed in grant support. Students must submit the FAFSA (Free Application for Federal Student Aid) and the Financial Aid PROFILE from the College Scholarship Service, both available in high school guidance offices. In addition, the College requires a copy of the family's most recent tax return and W-2 forms. Applicants who are not citizens of the U.S. must instead file the Foreign Student Financial Aid Application. Prospective freshmen are notified of the admission and financial aid decisions at the same time.

Faculty

The members of Bryn Mawr's faculty of 90 men and 139 women teach all the College's students, from freshmen through Ph.D. candidates, and find teaching and research complementary and equally rewarding. Classes are small, and individual conferences and informal meetings are frequent. The student-faculty ratio is about 9:1, but the numerical figure is not as important as the common ideal of scholarship that brings the two groups together.

Student Government

Undergraduates take complete responsibility for self-governance, for extracurricular activities, and for the social honor system. The Self-Government Association, established in 1892, was the first student-run system in the country. Today, it coordinates many activities with Haverford's Student Council and cosponsors many others.

Students at Bryn Mawr share with the faculty the supervision of the Academic Honor System, under which they take full responsibility for the integrity of all their scholarly efforts—from original research papers to self-scheduled exams. A student curriculum committee works actively with its faculty counterpart; student representatives participate in all admission decisions with faculty members of the Admissions Committee, help to formulate the policies of the College's Investment Responsibility Committee, and sit in on meetings of the Board of Trustees of the College. Students are always encouraged to take a responsible role in the governance of the College community.

Admission Requirements

Bryn Mawr's freshman class of about 350 is selected from applicants from all parts of the United States and many countries; no geographical, economic, ethnic, or other discriminatory guidelines are used. The Admissions Committee looks for an excellent school and test record and asks the applicant's counselor and teachers for an estimate of her character and readiness for college. Such qualities as integrity, vitality, a sense of humor, independence, and sensitivity to others are important, as are any special talents or interests. Early decision, early admission, deferred entrance, and advanced placement options are available to qualified students.

Basic high school academic requirements include 4 years of English, 3 years of mathematics, at least 1 year each of a laboratory science and history, and a solid foundation in at least one foreign language. The SAT I and SAT II Subject Tests in Writing and two other areas must be taken by November of the senior year for early decision applicants and January for regular decision applicants. The ACT may be substituted. An interview, either at the College or with a local alumnae representative, is strongly recommended. Application forms should be submitted by November 15 for fall early decision applicants, by January 1 for winter early decision applicants, and by January 15 for regular decision applicants.

Transfer students must complete a minimum of two years' work at Bryn Mawr to qualify for the A.B. degree.

Application and Information

The Admissions Office is open from 9 to 5 on weekdays and, during the fall, from 9 to 1 on Saturdays. For further information, an application form, or the name of a local alumnae representative, prospective students should contact:

Director of Admissions
Bryn Mawr College
Bryn Mawr, Pennsylvania 19010-2899
Telephone: 610-526-5152
Fax: 610-526-7471

BUCKNELL UNIVERSITY
LEWISBURG, PENNSYLVANIA

The University
As one of the top private liberal arts colleges in the nation, Bucknell University offers its students a solid foundation in the arts and sciences. Unlike many other liberal arts schools, however, Bucknell provides an unusual array of choices for its students. From traditional majors such as history, economics, and anthropology to programs in animal behavior, environmental studies, Japanese and East Asian studies, and international relations and from studies in the humanities, social sciences, and sciences to professionally oriented programs in engineering, education, business, and music, Bucknell students have many more options than are usually found in a school of 3,350 students. At the same time, Bucknell students enjoy the special attention usually associated with small, private colleges. Professors take time to know their students personally, both in and out of the classroom.

Bucknell attracts students from throughout the United States and abroad. Most live on campus in the residence halls and in special interest houses, such as the African-American Studies House. There are several recently completed residence halls on campus. Students spend time outside the classroom in a wide variety of activities, choosing from more than 120 clubs and organizations. A large number of students participate in intramural and intercollegiate (Division I) athletics; work on one of the several student newspapers or the radio station; are active in student government; help with community volunteer projects; perform with one of the music, drama, and dance groups; or join a fraternity or sorority. There are fourteen fraternities and eight sororities on campus. Students are also able to enjoy the recently renovated social/entertainment pub.

Location
Students and faculty members study together in what has been described as one of the most beautiful campuses in the East. Located in central Pennsylvania in the scenic Susquehanna River valley, Bucknell is within 3 to 4 hours of most of the major Eastern cities, including New York City, Baltimore, Philadelphia, and Washington, D.C.

Majors and Degrees
Bucknell offers the Bachelor of Arts degree in animal behavior, anthropology, art, biology, chemistry, classics (Greek and Latin), comparative humanities, computer science, East Asian studies (China or Japan), economics, education, English, environmental studies, French, geography, geology, German, history, international relations, Latin American studies, mathematics, music (music education, music history, music theory and composition, and performance), philosophy, physics, political science, psychology, religion, Russian, sociology (general, human services, and legal studies), Spanish, theater, and women's studies; the Bachelor of Music degree; the Bachelor of Science degree in animal behavior, biology, cell biology and biochemistry, chemistry, computer science, engineering (chemical, civil, computer science, electrical, and mechanical), environmental studies, geology, mathematics, and physics; the Bachelor of Science in Business Administration degree in accounting and management; and Bachelor of Science in Education degrees in early childhood development, educational research, elementary education, and secondary education. A five-year combined curriculum leads to the B.S. in an engineering field and a B.A. in another discipline.

Academic Program
Although requirements for each degree vary, all students are required to successfully complete three writing courses. Special programs are offered to encourage each student's personal and intellectual development. Examples are the freshman foundation seminars, an introductory engineering course open to students in the College of Arts and Sciences, an honors program, and the Residential Colleges. The Residential Colleges combine classroom and out-of-class activities, with each college centered on a theme, such as the arts, humanities, global affairs, environmental issues, or social justice.

Bucknell prepares students for the challenges of the twenty-first century. Whether students plan to begin their careers immediately after graduating or go on to professional or graduate schools, professors strive to help them to use their skills and talents, to reason and comprehend, and to interact and communicate with global citizens in an increasingly complex society.

Off-Campus Arrangements
Nearly 40 percent of each graduating class has spent one or two semesters studying on approved programs in Europe, Asia, the Middle East, Africa, Australia, New Zealand, and Central or South America. Bucknell sponsors three of its own programs in England, France, and Barbados and is affiliated with programs worldwide. About 10 percent of those studying off campus attend internship programs in Philadelphia or Washington, D.C. All institutional financial aid is portable for off-campus study.

Academic Facilities
Bucknell provides unusually fine facilities to students, including a recently completed science center, an outstanding library, a performing arts center with a 1,200-seat concert hall, a large field house, and computer labs throughout the campus. Multiple microcomputer "electronic classrooms" are in use throughout the campus. All academic, administrative, and residential buildings are connected to the campus Ethernet network, which was upgraded to high-speed ATM technology during the summer of 1996. The University is served by a dedicated, high-speed connection to the Internet.

Costs
The cost of tuition and fees for 2000–01 is $29,435, including $23,698 for tuition, $5596 for room and board, and $141 for student fees.

Financial Aid
More than $20 million in financial aid was awarded to freshman applicants in the fall of 1999, with an average award of $19,000. Financial aid applicants must file the Financial Aid PROFILE with the College Scholarship Service before January 1.

Faculty

Bucknell has 270 full-time and 26 part-time members on the teaching faculty; 98 percent hold doctorates or appropriate terminal degrees. The student-faculty ratio is 12:1. The most celebrated professors teach freshmen as well as advanced students; no classes are taught by graduate students.

Although professors consider teaching to be their first priority, they also find time to pursue their own scholarly work. Students are often involved in faculty members' research and special projects, which sometimes leads to joint publications or presentations at professional meetings.

Student Government

The Bucknell Student Government represents the student body, working with the faculty and administration to achieve student goals. It also dispenses funds for most student clubs and organizations. Its representatives serve on standing committees of the Board of Trustees and other University governance groups.

Admission Requirements

Admission decisions focus on the quality of preparation as demonstrated by achievement in rigorous high school courses, SAT I or ACT scores, talent and contribution to school or community, and evidence of strong character and integrity. The University actively seeks qualified students from throughout the United States and abroad.

Application and Information

Applications should be filed before January 1 of the senior year in high school for notification by March 25. SAT I or ACT results must be submitted before March 1. Early decision candidates may apply for Early Decision-Round One consideration by November 15 or Early Decision-Round Two consideration by January 1. Applications for transfer students should be submitted by April 1 for studies beginning in the following fall and by December 1 for the spring semester.

Mark Davies
Dean of Admissions
Bucknell University
Lewisburg, Pennsylvania 17837
Telephone: 570-577-1101
Fax: 570-577-3538
E-mail: admissions@bucknell.edu
World Wide Web: http://www.bucknell.edu

Bucknell students often say that they fell in love with the campus when they saw it for the first time. The Academic Quad, shown here, is one of their favorite spots on campus.

BUTLER UNIVERSITY
INDIANAPOLIS, INDIANA

The University

Butler University is an independent, coeducational, nonsectarian university with a total undergraduate enrollment of approximately 3,500 students. Butler students are exposed to both breadth and depth in academic programs. Butler offers a comprehensive set of programs to help improve the educational success of students as part of a project called the Learning Initiative. These programs are designed to help students negotiate the transitions from high school to college, from liberal education to a specific academic discipline, and from college to career.

The Butler Summer Academy—Transition I—assists students who are considering enrolling at Butler. The Academy consists of a residential college-preparatory session, a creative writing camp, and a residential emerging leaders camp that focuses on leadership, team building, and community service. Transition II—from liberal education to a specific discipline—is designed to assist students in choosing a major, selecting the right courses, developing a portfolio of achievements throughout the college career, and succeeding in college life. The heart of this phase is the Learning Resource Center, which takes a holistic approach to the needs of students. In the final transition, Transition III—from college to career and community—Butler helps students manage the move from the campus environment to the greater community to begin work or graduate preparation and careers. Some of the more innovative elements include Liberal Arts Works, an integrated program of internships and networking opportunities designed for liberal arts majors, and the Center for Citizenship and Community, which supports student and faculty member research in active citizenship while encouraging the development of courses that foster student involvement in community building.

A core curriculum encourages students to gain a broad knowledge in humanities, the arts, social sciences, natural sciences, and mathematics while considering an area for specialized study. The core courses, usually completed during the first four semesters, are designed to prepare students to read and write critically, speak articulately, think independently, and work effectively. Students may choose to major in one of, or any combination of, more than sixty major academic fields of study offered in five degree-granting colleges. Graduate programs are also available within these colleges.

Butler has a scenic college campus set within a major metropolitan city, an advantage distinguishing Butler from many other colleges. Located in a historic Northside neighborhood, the campus is home to 80 percent of the University's full-time students. On-campus housing includes residence halls, the houses of thirteen national fraternities and sororities, and the national award-winning Hampton House, a servant leadership residence community. Butler's students represent almost every state in the nation and more than thirty countries, reflecting a diversity of cultures, interests, aspirations, personalities, and experiences. Butler students can take advantage of nearly 100 different activities and student organizations, which include, but are not limited to, social groups, various religious groups, service clubs, honorary societies, performance groups, fraternities and sororities, intramural teams, and varsity athletics. Butler is NCAA Division I in all sports except for football (NCAA Division IAA). Fitness and training facilities are located throughout the campus. Students can take advantage of an indoor fitness facility in Atherton Union, featuring weight machines and aerobics classes, and of the Outdoor Fitness Trail. Butler students can take advantage of a variety of campus and professional programs, including Broadway shows at the 2,200-seat Clowes Memorial Hall, the city's premier performing arts and education center; Hinkle Fieldhouse, an 11,000-seat fieldhouse, home of Butler basketball; the Butler Bowl, a 20,000-seat football stadium; and the Hilton U. Brown Theatre, a 4,000-seat outdoor theater.

Butler University is accredited by the North Central Association of Colleges and Schools.

Location

Located just 5 miles from the heart of the thriving city of Indianapolis and surrounded by well-established residential communities, Butler's 290-acre campus remains a serenely beautiful area with its playing fields, a formal botanical garden, and a nature preserve. Its urban location enables Butler to offer students a wide range of internship opportunities in positions providing excellent preparation both for graduate professional schools and for careers. Indianapolis, Indiana's state capital and the twelfth-largest city in the nation, offers Butler students a wide range of recreational and cultural activities. Cultural advantages include the Indianapolis Symphony Orchestra, the Indiana Repertory Theatre and several community theaters, the Indianapolis Museum of Art (just two blocks from campus), the Eiteljorg Museum, and the world's largest children's museum. Indianapolis also hosts numerous ethnic and cultural citywide celebrations, including the Greek Festival, Broad Ripple Art Fair, Talbot Art Fair, Penrod Art Fair, the International Festival, and Indy Festivals. The Indianapolis Motor Speedway is the hub of a circle of professional sports in the city: basketball, football, hockey, and baseball have homes in three major sports arenas. Indianapolis is referred to as "the amateur sports capital," and is the host of more than 360 national and international amateur sporting events. Butler has been the proud cohost of the NCAA Final Four Championship in 1991, 1997, and 2000 and will cohost again in 2006; Indianapolis is home to the NCAA national headquarters and Hall of Champions. Butler students enjoy sporting events, restaurants, shopping, concerts, and movies throughout the community.

Majors and Degrees

Baccalaureate degrees are offered through Butler University's five colleges. The College of Liberal Arts and Sciences provides majors in the following fields: actuarial science, actuarial sciences/management (five-year B.S./M.B.A.), anthropology, biology, chemistry, computer science, economics, English, French, French business studies, German, German business studies, Greek, history, international studies, journalism, Latin, mathematics, philosophy, physics, political science, psychology, public and corporate communications, religious studies, sociology, sociology and criminal justice, Spanish, Spanish business studies, speech, speech and language pathology, undecided-humanities, undecided-natural sciences, and undecided-social sciences.

The College of Business Administration offers majors in accounting, economics, finance, international management, marketing, and undecided-business.

The Jordan College of Fine Arts offers majors in arts administration, dance, dance performance, music, music education, music performance, music theory and composition, piano pedagogy, telecommunication arts, theater, and undecided-fine arts.

The College of Education offers degrees in both elementary education and secondary education. Early childhood/elementary education majors may concentrate in early childhood education, reading, special education, or undecided-education. Middle/secondary education majors may concentrate in any academic area (English, history, math, etc.) and in athletic training, physical education, reading, special education, or undecided-education.

The College of Pharmacy and Health Sciences offers two majors. A major in pharmacy (Pharm.D. degree) is available, as is a major in physician assistant studies (B.S.P.A.). An undecided–health sciences program is also available.

Butler also offers preprofessional programs in dentistry, engineering, forestry, law, medicine, seminary, and veterinary medicine.

Special programs include the engineering dual-degree program, offered by Butler University, the Purdue School of Engineering and Technology, and Indiana University Purdue University Indianapolis. Students receive a Bachelor of Science degree in a selected liberal arts and sciences major (biology, chemistry, computer science, mathematics, and physics)(Butler) and a Bachelor of Science degree in computer science or electrical and mechanical engineering (Purdue). For students who are undecided about their major field of study, Butler offers the Exploratory Major Program, where students develop a personalized academic plan to help choose the major that best meets their interests and abilities.

Academic Program

All candidates for the baccalaureate degree must complete the University core requirement and at least 45 semester hours of work at Butler University. At least 30 of the 45 hours must be in the college granting the degree. An Honors Program is available to all eligible students. The opportunities for honors students include honors courses, honors thesis, and graduation honors. Butler is a sponsoring institution for the National Merit Scholarship Program. Students have a unique opportunity to become involved in undergraduate research with the annual Undergraduate Research Conference hosted on campus. Butler offers advanced placement, with appropriate academic credit, in most subjects covered by either the Advanced Placement (AP) examinations or the College-Level Examination Program (CLEP) tests. Students may enroll in Air Force and Army ROTC programs.

Off-Campus Arrangements

One of the largest study-abroad programs in the United States is hosted by Butler University's Institute for Study Abroad (ISA), which sends students from American colleges and universities to Australia, Ireland, Scotland, New Zealand, and England. In addition, Butler offers the Butler Directed Study Abroad Program, which is a flexible program tailored to the needs and interests of the students. These programs are available to students primarily during their junior year. Butler is also a member of the International Student Exchange Program (ISEP). Through ISEP, students can study at any one of more than 100 member universities in more than forty countries.

Academic Facilities

Butler has incorporated state-of-the-art technologies throughout the campus. These include MS-DOS and Macintosh microcomputers; seventeen Ethernet-networked computer labs; electronic and multimedia classrooms; VAX, Internet, and e-mail; World Wide Web student home pages; a fiber-optic infrastructure in residence halls for cable and Internet access; an electronic language laboratory; an international studies center; telephone systems with free voice mail; and a 24-hour computer lab in the Atherton Student Union and in each residence hall. Butler began operation of its public television station, WTBU, Channel 69, in 1992. At WTBU, which is affiliated with the Corporation for Public Broadcasting, telecommunication arts students are active in program production. A new communications building is currently under construction and will house WTBU and the telecommunication arts, journalism, and speech communication departments. Butler's library system contains more than 286,000 volumes and a computer database where students can search holdings in all library locations. Irwin Library System also houses a rare books collection, the archives, the National Track and Field Hall of Fame Library, online library catalog access, and basic research tools. Holcomb Observatory and Planetarium features a 38-inch telescope, the largest in the state.

Costs

For the 2000–01 academic year, tuition is $18,040 for full-time undergraduate students. Room and board are $6140 per year. Books are estimated at $300 per semester. The tuition for the professional pharmacy program/physician assistant studies program is $19,410.

Financial Aid

Butler University offers a variety of financial assistance programs based on the demonstration of academic excellence, performance talent, or financial need. The University awards academic scholarships based on merit to students who have displayed outstanding high school achievement and have excelled in leadership and community service. Performance awards are available in areas such as music, dance, theater, and athletics. Academic departments offer scholarships for students in certain majors. On-campus employment and work-study programs are also available. All students who are seeking need-based financial assistance are required to file the Free Application for Federal Student Aid (FAFSA) and the Butler University Application for Financial Assistance.

Faculty

Teaching has top priority for Butler's 247 full-time faculty members; 81 percent of them hold the highest degree in their fields. Many of them are active in national research programs, write for publication, consult in government and business, and participate in the arts. With a comfortable teaching load, Butler's faculty members have time to work with students individually. The student-faculty ratio is 13:1. All classes are taught by professors; there are no teaching assistants.

Student Government

The Student Government Association (SGA) is the official student government of Butler University. SGA sponsors numerous campus events, including concerts, live entertainment, movies, sporting events, and lectures by world-renowned political and social leaders such as Mikhail Gorbachev, Myrlie Evans-Williams, Dr. Jane Goodall, and Toni Morrison.

Admission Requirements

Applicants are expected to complete a minimum of 17 academic units in high school, including 4 years of English, 3 years each of laboratory sciences and mathematics, and 2 years each of history or social studies and of foreign language. A candidate for admission typically ranks in the upper third of his or her high school class and should submit satisfactory results of the SAT I or the ACT. The program in the Jordan College of Fine Arts requires an audition by the applicant. Besides these factors, the Admission Committee considers the applicant's leadership skills, motivation, and a writing sample. Students who wish to transfer from another regionally accredited college or university are considered if they are in good standing and have a grade point average of 2.0 (C) or better in their previous academic work. Transfer students must submit official transcripts of all college work.

Application and Information

Although regular admission is on a rolling basis, students may choose to apply for early admission. Butler offers two nonbinding early admission programs (not early decision) with specific benefits associated with each program. The application priority date for Early Admission I is December 1 of the senior year. The benefits of the Early Admission I program are 1) early course registration, 2) early consideration for academic scholarships, 3) priority housing, and 4) optional living learning center participation. The application priority date for Early Admission II is February 1. The Early Admission II program carries the first three benefits of Early Admission I. The priority date to be considered for merit scholarships is February 1. Scholarship notification is on a rolling basis and begins December 15. Campus visits and interviews are strongly recommended, though not required, and are arranged on a daily basis. Several open house programs are also scheduled throughout the year. Interested students and their families are encouraged to call the Office of Admission to make arrangements for campus visits. For further information, students may contact:

Office of Admission
Butler University
4600 Sunset Avenue
Indianapolis, Indiana 46208-3485
Telephone: 317-940-8100
          888-940-8100 (toll-free)
Fax: 317-940-8150
E-mail: admission@butler.edu
World Wide Web: http://admission.butler.edu
                http://www.butler.edu

CABRINI COLLEGE
RADNOR, PENNSYLVANIA

The College
Cabrini College, a Catholic institution for men and women, is concerned with the full intellectual, personal, and social development of each student. The College's programs are organized to help students welcome the changes in their lives with vigor, initiative, and confidence. While academic excellence is the priority at Cabrini, students are encouraged to participate in activities that will help them develop socially, culturally, and spiritually. Although founded as a private Catholic college, the institution is proud of its diverse student body and accepts students of all denominations. Cabrini enrolls approximately 2,100 men and women. The student community is a friendly one, characterized by close and long-standing ties to the faculty. Cabrini College is sponsored by the Missionary Sisters of the Sacred Heart of Jesus and is named for that institution's founder, St. Frances Xavier Cabrini, the first U.S. citizen to be canonized. Mother Cabrini's commitment to service to others and education of the heart are key parts of the College's programs.

More than 57 percent of Cabrini's full-time students live on campus in a variety of housing accommodations, including traditional residence halls for men and women, single-family homes, and a 120- bed, apartment-style complex. The College provides a full range of services to students, including placement, career, and personal counseling; a tutoring program; and health services. Students can participate in seventeen intercollegiate sports for men and women as well as an intramural sports program. Other popular extracurricular activities are the theater program, the College chorus, the ethnic student alliance, departmental clubs, and campus ministry. Students are encouraged to join the College's award-winning newspaper, the literary journal, and the yearbook. The campus radio station, WYBF-FM, and television studio are available to all students.

Cabrini also provides a Master of Education degree and a new Master of Science in organization leadership.

Location
Cabrini offers students the best of both worlds—a wooded, spacious, 112-acre suburban campus near King of Prussia and a half hour away from Philadelphia. The College is close enough for students to take advantage of the many cultural, social, and educational opportunities of the city. Students may visit Philadelphia's art museums or historic sites or travel to the First Union Center to see national sporting events or performances by professional musicians. Cabrini also is close to many other Philadelphia-area colleges, which sponsor activities of interest to students.

Majors and Degrees
Cabrini offers the Bachelor of Arts degree with major programs in American studies, arts administration, communication, English, French, graphic design, history, liberal arts, organizational management (accelerated), philosophy, political science, professional communications (accelerated), psychology, religious studies, sociology, Spanish, and studio art. The Bachelor of Science degree is offered with major programs in accounting, biology/premedicine, business administration, chemistry, clinical laboratory sciences/medical technology, computer information science, environmental science, finance, human resource management, Internet computing, management information systems, marketing, mathematics, and sports science. An individualized major, designed by the student using existing courses, can lead to a B.A. or B.S. degree. The Bachelor of Social Work degree, which is accredited by the Council on Social Work, is awarded to graduates completing the social work major. The Bachelor of Science in Education degree is available with majors in early childhood, elementary, and special education; these programs also lead to teacher certification in each of the three fields. Education majors are certified to teach in Pennsylvania and reciprocating states. Teacher certification for secondary education is offered in biology, chemistry, communications, English, mathematics, and social studies (concentration in history). Preprofessional programs in biotechnology, law, nursing, occupational therapy, pharmacy, and physical therapy are designed by faculty advisers to meet the needs of individual students. Academic concentrations include advertising, chemical technical management, computer-mediated communication, criminal justice, economics, human-computer interaction, international business, journalism and writing, management information systems, nonprofit management, professional communication, public administration, systems administration and management, systems training and technical support, theater, video/audio/recording arts/photography/new communication technology, and women's studies.

Academic Program
Cabrini College's academic program gives students a well-rounded educational experience—one that includes a strong liberal arts and science base as well as professional development in a specific career field. All students take core curriculum competency and distribution requirement courses to supplement the in-depth knowledge acquired within each major. The core distribution requirements include courses in the following areas: contemporary issues; cultural diversity; heritage; imagination, creativity, and aesthetic appreciation; natural science; the individual and society; religious studies; and values and commitments. In addition, students take two seminar classes, Self-Understanding and the Common Good, in their freshman and junior years, respectively. The Common Good seminar includes a service learning component. Cabrini's core curriculum has been developed by its faculty to help students understand themselves, their society, and the world around them. Within each major, Cabrini's curriculum is designed to help students develop professional skills in their chosen career field. Classroom instruction in all majors is supplemented by internships, through which juniors and seniors can earn credit and often a salary for working in a job related to their career interest. Cooperative Education at Cabrini College is an optional academic program in which students learn to apply theoretical principles in a professional environment while earning academic credit (based on the number of hours worked and the value of the work experience gained) and income.

All education majors participate in fieldwork beginning in the sophomore year. Social work majors spend 600 hours in direct practice before graduation. Cabrini students can choose a double major, and a free elective system encourages students to broaden their academic backgrounds.

Students may pursue their studies on a full-time or part-time basis during the school year. The College enables students to take courses in the evening, on Saturday, or during the summer and offers accelerated degree programs in organizational management and professional communications.

Off-Campus Arrangements
Cabrini participates with area colleges in a number of cooperative programs that enrich educational opportunities. Through an exchange program with nearby Villanova University, Eastern College, Rosemont College, and Valley Forge College, full-time students may elect courses offered on the other campuses; no

additional tuition fees are charged, and credit is automatically transferred. Cabrini also maintains affiliations with Thomas Jefferson University and Widener University for allied health programs, the Pennsylvania College of Podiatric Medicine for an accelerated medical program, and KAJEM Recording Arts Studio for communication. The clinical laboratory sciences/medical technology program is conducted in cooperation with major hospital schools of medical technology.

Academic Facilities

Cabrini's 175,000-volume library, which includes 8,132 microforms, serves as a comprehensive resource for students. The library has a complete microfilm collection and subscribes to 515 current periodicals. Cabrini is a member of the Tri-State College Library Cooperative and the Online Computer Library Center (OCLC), so additional resources at other libraries in the area are just a keystroke away. The College's computer laboratory, open to all students, and five state-of-the-art computer classroom facilities are equipped with IBM or Macintosh computers. Research facilities include the biology, chemistry, and psychology laboratories. A modern, fully equipped communication center houses the College's television studio, FM radio station, newsroom (with facilities for desktop publishing), graphic design laboratory, and photography darkroom.

A great resource for education majors is The Children's School. Education majors have the opportunity to observe, do fieldwork, and student teach at the school. The College's educational resource center provides students with access to teaching materials, ranging from videos and transparencies to children's literature.

Costs

Tuition for full-time students in 1999–2000 was $15,250; room and board were $7200 for the year. A general fee of $750 covers student registration, health services, activities, library use, testing, and publications. Textbooks and supplies are approximately $700 per year, and fees of $25 to $100 are charged for laboratory and other miscellaneous courses. Students with cars secure a $45 parking permit annually.

Financial Aid

Last year, 88 percent of Cabrini's undergraduates shared more than $11.3 million in financial aid in the form of scholarship, grant, loan, and work-study funds. The College's most prestigious academic scholarship is the Alumni Recognition scholarship, awarded annually to an outstanding student. A special application, due by December 31, is required. Achievement Scholarships are available to applicants with strong credentials. In addition to Cabrini College scholarships and grants, federal funds are available through Federal Pell Grants, Federal Supplemental Educational Opportunity Grants, Federal Work-Study Program awards, and Federal Perkins Loans. State grants are available through students' home states. Veterans are eligible for assistance under the G.I. bill. In addition, the College offers work-study and other employment opportunities through which a student may earn money to pay for college education expenses. Federal Stafford Student Loans are available through most local banks. Students may apply for such loans directly to the lending agency. All financial aid is offered for a one-year period but is renewable upon application as long as the student gives evidence of financial need. Applicants for financial aid must submit the Free Application for Federal Student Aid (FAFSA), ideally before February 15 in order to expedite processing of the request for financial aid and by April 1 at the latest.

Faculty

Cabrini's average class size is 18, and the College's faculty is committed to developing and challenging the individual skills of each student. Faculty members are known for their dedication to teaching and getting to know their students personally. Each full-time student has a faculty adviser who assists in arranging a program designed to meet the student's objectives.

Student Government

The Student Government Association (SGA) of Cabrini College facilitates all communication pertaining to students within the College community. The association exists to make known the views of the student body and to look after its interests with respect to the faculty members, administration, and educational policies of the College.

Admission Requirements

The Admissions Committee considers applicants on the basis of their high school record, SAT I or ACT scores, class rank, and other indicators of potential to succeed in college-level studies, such as recommendations. Applications for admission are reviewed without regard to sex, race, creed, color, national origin, age, or handicap. Applicants should be graduates of an accredited high school (or present equivalent credentials) and have a minimum of 15 units of credit: 4 in English, 2 in a foreign language, 3 in college-preparatory mathematics, 3 in science, and 3 in social studies. Cabrini also conducts an early admission program through which students with superior ability and a sound academic background may begin college studies at the end of the junior year in high school. Applicants may apply for advanced standing at Cabrini through the Advanced Placement (AP) Program and the College-Level Examination Program (CLEP) of the College Board. The College's graduate and continuing studies office administers CLEP and DANTES tests.

Cabrini welcomes transfers from other accredited institutions. Such applicants should have a GPA of 2.2 or better to be considered for transfer. Students transferring from Becker College, Bucks County Community College, Community College of Philadelphia, Manor College, Delaware County Community College, Montgomery County Community College, Harcum College, Harrisburg Area Community College, Peirce College, Reading Community College, or Valley Forge Military College with an A.A. or A.S. degree and a minimum 2.5 GPA receive credit for all previous course work. Two-year-college students are encouraged to follow a course of liberal and general studies during their first two years at another institution if they expect to continue their studies at a four-year college such as Cabrini.

A campus visit, while not required, is recommended for the prospective student. The Admissions Office offers individual interviews and group information sessions on weekdays and select Saturdays. Students conduct campus tours, which may include class visits and informal meetings with faculty members and administrators. Those planning to visit the campus should contact a member of the Admissions Office staff for information. Representatives of the College visit high schools in various cities.

Application and Information

Applicants for freshman admission are requested to have SAT I or ACT scores and official high school transcripts sent to the Admissions Office along with the application for admission. Transfer students must submit an application and high school and college transcripts. A nonrefundable application fee of $25 must accompany the application. The Admissions Committee maintains a rolling admission policy until the class is filled and takes action on an application when all the necessary credentials are on file.

Joanne Mayberry, Director of Admissions
Cabrini College
610 King of Prussia Road
Radnor, Pennsylvania 19087-3698

Telephone: 610-902-8552
          800-848-1003 (toll-free)
E-mail: admit@cabrini.edu
World Wide Web: http://www.cabrini.edu

CALDWELL COLLEGE
CALDWELL, NEW JERSEY

The College

Caldwell College is a Catholic, coeducational, four-year liberal arts institution rooted in a proud 700-year Dominican tradition of rigorous scholarship, committed teaching, and ethical values. Founded in 1939 by the Sisters of St. Dominic, Caldwell's most popular offerings include undergraduate degrees in business, education, and psychology. In addition, the College offers graduate degrees in contemporary management and accounting, counseling psychology, curriculum and instruction, educational administration, liberal studies, and pastoral ministry. Beginning in fall 2000, a concentration in art therapy is available for students in the graduate counseling psychology program. The College also offers an individualized major for students seeking a concentrated major that allows them to design their own course work with administrative approval. Caldwell offers twenty-seven undergraduate degrees, seven graduate programs, and a Caldwell Scholars Program. Also offered are an adult undergraduate program and a uniquely structured distance education external degree program for adult learners. In addition, the College offers graduate-level certificates in supervision and teacher certification. In 1998, the College began offering accelerated options that combine the curricular opportunities of the distance education program with traditional on-campus offerings. Individuals may take off-campus and on-campus offerings as well as seven-week accelerated Saturday classes.

The Caldwell College Web site makes information about the College easily accessible (http://www.caldwell.edu). The common goal of all programs of study is to prepare men and women for rewarding careers and leadership roles in a global marketplace. The College supports its academic programs with a wide variety of student services. The Office of Career Development provides ongoing career counseling, career education, and interest testing for students to clarify personal goals and explore academic and career opportunities. A career planning course and a Career Library offer additional resources for students. Caldwell College sponsors experiential learning programs that encourage students to participate in work-based internship opportunities. Approximately 40 percent of the students who participate in internship and cooperative education programs are offered full-time positions when they graduate. The office also assists students and alumni who are seeking full- and part-time employment.

The College has a strong relationship with the New Jersey business community. The College's Business Advisory Council was formed in 1994 with the belief that business leaders and educators needed to share their resources so both students and the business community could prepare for the challenges of the global marketplace. Through guest lectures by corporate leaders, mentoring programs, and interaction during business conferences, students learn how to be successful in today's workplace. The Business Advisory Council includes about 40 members from companies such as Bell Atlantic, Broad Bank, First Union Bank, Lucent Technologies, Mita, PNC Bank, Prudential, PSE&G, Ricoh, Sovereign Bank, and Summit Bank.

Caldwell enrolls 2,078 full-time, part-time, and graduate students each year. The College enrolled its largest freshman class ever in 1998 and 1999 and continues its tremendous growth while maintaining its liberal arts character. Fully qualified faculty members and a 13:1 student-faculty ratio provide students with close, personal attention. Approximately 91 percent of full-time students are from New Jersey. In addition, Caldwell's rich cultural diversity attracts individuals from northeastern and mid-Atlantic states and from more than eighteen other countries. The cultural mix of full-time, part-time, and graduate students includes white, 68 percent; African-American, 13 percent; Hispanic, 8 percent; Asian-American, 4 percent; and international, approximately 7 percent.

About one third of full-time students live on campus. Single, double, triple, and a few quad rooms are available. All students, both commuters and residents, including incoming freshmen, may have automobiles on campus. A rich program of student activities involves both residents and commuters in campus life. A variety of clubs and organizations, including publications, are available. Guest artists, musicians, authors, and speakers appear on campus regularly. Student social life features dances and other open activities. An on-campus fitness center provides students with health and exercise opportunities. The center is equipped with cardiovascular equipment, including treadmills, stationary bicycles, steppers, and combination weight machines. The College is a provisional member of the National Collegiate Athletic Association (NCAA) Division II and a member of the National Association of Intercollegiate Athletics (NAIA). Caldwell fields intercollegiate teams in men's baseball, basketball, soccer, and tennis; women's basketball, soccer, softball, and tennis; and coed golf. The College also sponsors a variety of intramural sports.

Location

The College is located on a beautiful, secure 70-acre campus, 20 miles west of New York City in suburban Caldwell, New Jersey. Students can enjoy numerous educational, cultural, and social experiences that Caldwell and the region offer and still enjoy a relaxed campus atmosphere. The center of town, with a variety of shops and restaurants, is within walking distance. Area attractions include theaters, museums, parks, ski resorts, malls, the New Jersey Performing Arts Center, the Meadowlands sports complex, and the New Jersey shore. Many corporate headquarters are readily accessible from Caldwell and provide a variety of internship opportunities. The College is convenient to major highways, including Routes 280, 80, and 287 and the Garden State Parkway and the New Jersey Turnpike, and the campus can be reached by public transportation.

Majors and Degrees

Caldwell College offers twenty-seven undergraduate Bachelor of Arts (B.A.), Bachelor of Science (B.S.), and Bachelor of Fine Arts (B.F.A.) degrees. The B.A. is offered in art, biology, chemistry, communication arts, criminal justice, elementary education, English, French, history, an individualized major, mathematics, music, political science, psychology, religious studies, social studies, sociology, and Spanish. The B.S. is offered in accounting, business administration, computer information systems, computer science, international business, management, marketing, and medical technology. The B.F.A. is offered in art. The education department offers teacher certification programs in elementary education (nursery school through grade 8) and for teaching grades K–12 in art, biology, English, French, mathematics, music, social studies, and Spanish. A certification program in school nursing is also available to registered nurses.

Academic Program

Eligibility for a degree requires completion of a minimum of 122 credits and a GPA of at least 2.0 (C). Students must also complete major courses with a minimum grade of C and satisfy all other departmental requirements. All programs require that students successfully pass a form of outcomes assessment in the senior year. To complete the liberal arts requirements, students must select courses from computer literacy, English, fine arts, foreign language, history, mathematics, natural sciences, philosophy, physical education, public speaking, religious studies, and social sciences. In 1997, the Writing Across the Curriculum program was introduced to systematically develop a student's ability to write well regardless of his or her major. Opportunities for independent study, internships, co-ops, double majors, minors, and certificate programs are available. The Caldwell Scholars Program challenges gifted students with both interdisciplinary studies and a directed honors project and is supplemented by guest lectures.

Students must score a 3, 4, or 5 on the College Board's Advanced Placement test to receive advanced placement or credit for completed work. Students may receive credit for knowledge gained through independent study or experience through the College-Level Examination Program (CLEP). All students are encouraged to participate in internships.

The English as a Second Language Program helps students with limited English proficiency master English for academic success. Courses of study include four levels of composition, three levels of grammar and communication, and two levels of reading.

A TOEFL score is required with the application. The adult undergraduate program encourages adults to return to college to finish their degree, earn a new degree, or enjoy learning for pleasure. Through day, evening, and Saturday courses, the College highlights the importance of lifelong learning. Adult students can earn credit through Caldwell's Prior Learning Assessment Policy, provided they can demonstrate acquired knowledge that corresponds with course requirements.

Off-Campus Arrangements

In fall 1998, the College signed an exchange program agreement with the Catholic University of Korea that for the first time provides male students with broad international educational opportunities to better prepare themselves for the global marketplace. The College signed its first exchange program agreement in 1995 with Duksung Women's University in Korea. Since then, 3 female students have attended Duksung, and the College has hosted 6 female students. The latest articulation agreement now makes it possible for both male and female students to earn credits for business, education, music, science, and other courses while learning the Korean culture, economy, and language. In addition, the College has established both undergraduate and graduate affiliation programs for students in health-related majors to help to accelerate their career goal of becoming health professionals.

Academic Facilities

Campus facilities include a library, four classroom and office buildings, and a theater. An academic building, opened in 1997, is equipped with state-of-the-art technology, including an Interactive Television Classroom (ITV) that can provide interactive learning opportunities simultaneously to and from various geographic locations. Wide-screen video and computer graphic capability are also available, as is satellite reception. Jennings Library contains 127,000 volumes and subscribes to more than 800 journals. The library's own home page on the World Wide Web provides links to the New York Public Library, the United States Supreme Court database, the United States Security and Exchange Commission, and the Vatican archives, among others. Dial-up access is available from off-campus sites to both the online public access catalog and a number of online databases, including ERIC and PsychLIT, as well as ABInform Global and the Wilson full-text indexes. The art department contains a gallery studio featuring professional and student work. A curriculum laboratory has texts for K–12, visual aids, films, and other resources. A broadcast studio provides hands-on experience in working with television and radio production equipment. The Communication Arts Department continues to expand with the recent purchase of a state-of-the-art nonlinear videotape editing system that trains students to create, edit, and produce videos. Five computer classrooms and four computer laboratories house Pentium PCs with Internet and e-mail access, Macintosh computers, laser printers, and scanners. All buildings on campus are connected by fiber optics. The language laboratory includes modern audio and computer stations. The media center provides instructional resources that use film, audio, video, and satellite technologies.

Costs

For the 2000–01 academic year, full-time tuition and fees are $13,100 and campus room and board are $6250. Undergraduate tuition for part-time students is $337 per credit hour.

Financial Aid

Seventy-six percent of current students receive financial aid. The Federal Financial Aid Program sources include the Federal Pell Grant, Federal Stafford Student Loan, Federal Work-Study, and Federal Supplemental Educational Opportunity Grant programs. Caldwell College awards full and partial scholarships for academic and athletic excellence. In addition, special interest and privately sponsored scholarships, tuition grants, and campus employment are available. New Jersey offers tuition aid grants for state residents. The New Jersey Educational Opportunity Fund (EOF) makes it possible for all students to pursue higher education, especially the educationally and economically disadvantaged, for whom college might otherwise be an unrealistic goal. All financial aid applicants must file the Free Application for Federal Student Aid (FAFSA). The priority filing deadline is April 15.

Faculty

There are 67 full-time faculty members, with 80 percent having earned their doctoral/terminal degree. There are 4 full-time English as a second language (ESL) and Learning Center instructors and 83 adjunct faculty members. Classes average 15 students, with a student-faculty ratio of 13:1.

Student Government

Caldwell College's students, through the Student Government Association and Resident and Commuter Council, shape many nonacademic policies and regulations. Students also help determine total College policy through representation on several College standing committees.

Admission Requirements

The admission office reviews each applicant's high school record, class rank, and SAT I or ACT scores and determines the student's ability to succeed at Caldwell College. A student must complete at least 16 high school academic units, including 4 years of English, 2 years of foreign language, 2 years of mathematics, 2 years of science, and 1 year of history. Caldwell College does not discriminate against applicants on the basis of race, color, creed, age, national or ethnic origin, or handicap.

Application and Information

Applicants are accepted throughout the school year through a rolling admissions policy; however, applicants are encouraged to apply early. A nonrefundable $40 fee must accompany each application. Applicants are notified of their admission eligibility after their credentials have been received and evaluated.

For further information, students should contact:

Executive Director of Admissions
Caldwell College
9 Ryerson Avenue
Caldwell, New Jersey 07006-6195
Telephone: 973-618-3500
           888-864-9516 (toll-free outside New Jersey)
Fax: 973-618-3600
E-mail: admissions@caldwell.edu
World Wide Web: http://www.caldwell.edu

The Caldwell College athletic program expects to be a full member of the NCAA Division II by fall 2001.

CALIFORNIA COLLEGE OF ARTS AND CRAFTS
OAKLAND AND SAN FRANCISCO, CALIFORNIA

The College

The California College of Arts and Crafts (CCAC) was founded in 1907 with a new approach to art education—to offer training in a wide range of disciplines, creating a spirit of collaboration between artists, craftspeople, and designers. In the ensuing years, the College has expanded its commitment by offering an interdisciplinary curriculum that educates students in the full range of fine arts, architecture, and design studies in the context of a small, private four-year college. Today, CCAC's undergraduate enrollment is about 1,200 men and women.

The College maintains close ties with the professional art community as well as with the community at large. Founded in 1998, the CCAC Institute offers a wide range of leading-edge programs, including exhibitions, lectures, artist residencies, performances, symposia, and publications in the fields of art, architecture, and design. Other programs for the public include extended education classes for adults and students grades 6–12.

The College is comprised of two campuses in Oakland and San Francisco. The schools of architecture design, as well as selected fine arts programs, are based in San Francisco in a beautiful, light-filled structure located in the heart of the city's design district. The Oakland campus features a blend of Victorian and modern structures in a 4-acre garden setting. CCAC's Oakland residence hall primarily serves freshmen; off-campus apartments are also available.

CCAU offers four graduate programs: the M.F.A. degree program in design, the M.F.A. degree program in writing, the M.A. degree program in visual criticism, and the M.F.A. degree program in fine arts. Concentrations in the fine arts program include ceramics, drawing/painting, film/video/performance, glass, jewelry/metal arts, photography, printmaking, sculpture, textiles, and wood/furniture. All inquiries and correspondence about the graduate program should be sent to the Director of Enrollment Services.

CCAC is accredited by the Western Association of Schools and Colleges and the National Association of Schools of Art and Design. The interior design program is accredited by the Foundation for Interior Design Education Research, and the architecture program is accredited by the National Architectural Accrediting Board.

Location

CCAC's San Francisco campus moved to a newly renovated 160,000-square-foot facility in fall 1996. The campus occupies half a city block in the heart of San Francisco's exciting design district. It includes dedicated studio space for 75 graduate students, classrooms and instructional studios, four image shops, the Timken Lecture Hall, academic office space, the Simpson Library, and the Logan Center—encompassing the Logan Galleries, the Pollack/Long Graduate Student Galleries, a cafe, and a service bureau.

The Oakland campus is in a predominantly residential area of homes, apartments, and flats 2 miles north of the center of Metropolitan Oakland and 3 miles south of the University of California at Berkeley. Within view of the campus are the city of San Francisco, the Golden Gate, and the hills of Marin County. The College community has access to the San Francisco Bay Area's wealth of educational, cultural, and recreational facilities. Public transportation—bus or Bay Area Rapid Transit—is readily available, and freeways are close and convenient for travel by car.

Majors and Degrees

CCAC offers four-year programs leading to the Bachelor of Fine Arts (B.F.A.) degree in ceramics, fashion design, film/video/performance, furniture/wood, glass, graphic design, illustration, industrial design, interior architecture, metal arts/jewelry, painting/drawing, photography, printmaking, sculpture, and textiles. In addition, the College offers a five-year program leading to the Bachelor of Architecture (B.Arch.) degree.

Academic Program

The Bachelor of Fine Arts degree requires the completion of a minimum of 126 semester units, of which 75 must be in studio work and 51 must be in humanities and sciences. Most undergraduates at CCAC begin in a foundation—or core—program designed to orient them to a variety of two- and three-dimensional art and design media as well as to strengthen their communication skills and refine and develop their knowledge of history. Students select a major after completing this program.

A diversified program of arts and humanities reflects the philosophy at CCAC that a professional art education occurs in the context of the education of the whole individual. The relative flexibility of CCAC's curriculum enables students to explore a variety of media, to change majors without changing schools, to receive supplementary training in the arts, and to develop programs related to individual interests, abilities, and long-range career goals.

The Bachelor of Architecture, a five-year degree program, requires the completion of a minimum of 162 units, including the one-semester core program with an orientation to two-dimensional and three-dimensional media and a nine-semester major program.

CCAC operates on the semester academic calendar, with the fall and spring terms constituting a full academic year. The summer term consists of a six-week session and a precollege program. Extended Education programs are offered in fall, winter, and spring sessions.

Off-Campus Arrangements

There are many supplementary educational opportunities for CCAC students, including the chance to take courses at Mills College, Holy Names College in Oakland, and the University of San Francisco through cross-registration and to participate in the mobility program through the Association of Independent Colleges of Art and Design.

CCAU is also supportive of students wishing to study abroad. Currently, the College has established study-abroad exchange programs with schools in France, Germany, the Netherlands, and Sweden.

Academic Facilities

Studio facilities occupy most of CCAC's instructional buildings. Special facilities include the two-story Noni Eccles Treadwell Ceramic Arts Center and the Shaklee Building, which houses a foundry and studios for sculpture, metal arts, jewelry, and glass. Founders Hall houses an auditorium, the media center, and the Meyer Library, which has more than 35,000 volumes and periodical subscriptions and 400 audiotapes, videotapes, and CDs. In addition to a variety of informal exhibition spaces, the College operates several galleries. In Oakland, there are three exhibition spaces: the Isabelle Percy West Gallery and the Irwin Student Gallery, both of which show student work, and the Oliver Art Center's Tecoah Bruce Gallery, which is programmed by the CCAC Institute and features the work of international contemporary artists. In San Francisco, the Kent and Vicki Logan Center opened in April 1999, with three state-of-the-art gallery spaces devoted to local, national, and international exhibitions of architecture, design, and fine art presented by the CCAC Institute. The San Francisco campus also features two galleries that focus on student exhibitions: the Graduate Student Gallery and the Tecoah and Thomas Bruce Galleries.

Other facilities include three drawing studios, three painting studios, and a large print shop with three litho presses, three etching presses, two Vandercook proofing presses, and a vertical graphic arts camera.

CCAC has one of the most extensive glass facilities in the United States. It includes a 700-pound continuous-melt furnace, a pot furnace, slumping facilities, and a complete coldworking facility.

Sculpture facilities at CCAC include a metal foundry and shop; studios for wax, plaster, and clay; a machine shop; welding facilities; woodworking equipment; and the Barclay Simpson Sculpture Studio, which supports the making of large-scale metal and glass sculpture.

Photography facilities, available to students 70 hours a week, include two large black-and-white and color darkrooms, ten individual darkrooms for color printing, a mounting and finishing room, an artificial-lighting studio, a copy camera darkroom, printing and film-processing equipment, and large-format cameras.

CCAC's film and video studios have Super-8 and 16-mm equipment for shooting and editing. The studios can accommodate video in all formats and feature Avid, Protocols, and Media 100 digital image and sound editing systems as well as tape-to-tape editing systems.

CCAC's ceramics facility consists of 5,400 square feet of studio space, including two complete pot shops, fully stocked and equipped glaze rooms, sixteen large gas kilns, and several electric kilns for outsized as well as regular firing.

A wide range of textile facilities are available to students. These include weaving studios, a variety of looms, a Macomber computerized loom, printing and silkscreening studios, dye rooms, and workrooms.

The metal arts/jewelry facilities at CCAC include a metal foundry and equipment for metalsmithing, electroforming, photofabrication, and enameling.

Students at CCAC have access to a wide range of digital technologies. CCAC's academic computer labs on both campuses offer the most current hardware and software available for artists, architects, and designers. Digital tools include scanning devices, video and audio sampling and editing capabilities, 3-D rendering and animation, digital cameras, graphic tablets, and CD recording. The library computer facility offers a highly refined research system that allows students to easily search the library catalogs as well as those of other institutions of higher education. Students also use the library computer labs for Internet and e-mail access as well as for word processing. CCAC also assists students with financing the purchase of their own computers and provides students with wireless connections to the campus network.

CCAC's new San Francisco campus is devoted to the architecture, design, and graduate programs, with selected fine arts offerings. Phase One of the facility opened in fall 1996 and features studios, classrooms, student galleries, critique spaces, a 133-seat lecture hall, four computer labs, dedicated studio space for upper-division students, and three large studios for model making and wood/furniture. The 100,000-square-foot Carroll/Weisel Hall opened in April 1999. It includes individual dedicated studios for senior painting students, fashion facilities, classrooms, seminar rooms, offices, and the Logan Center—an extensive public area that features a large entry court, the three Logan Galleries, the Pollack/Long Graduate Student Gallery, a café, and a service bureau.

Costs

Tuition and fees for the fall and spring terms in 2000–01 are $19,279 per year for full-time (12–18 units) undergraduate students. For part-time students, tuition is $803 per unit. California and out-of-state residents pay the same tuition. Residence hall fees (for room only) in 1999–2000 were $3500 by contract for the fall through spring year, $1750 for spring only. Estimated expenses for one academic year (two semesters) for a student living off campus are approximately $27,000. This covers tuition of $18,284, room and board of $5858, books and supplies of $810, and miscellaneous expenses of $1908. The Enrollment Services Office maintains a local housing list to assist students in finding off-campus housing. Meals in the cafe are available on a cash basis to the entire campus community.

Financial Aid

Scholarships, grants, loans, and work-study awards are available for students on the basis of merit and financial need. Students applying for aid in 2000–01 should submit the Free Application for Federal Student Aid (FAFSA) to the Federal Student Aid Processing Agency by March 2. Students should also submit all additional documents required by CCAC by March 1 for priority consideration. CCAC continues to fund students after the priority deadline as long as funds remain available. Applications for Federal Pell Grants and Federal Direct Student Loans may be submitted throughout the school year. CCAC is approved for veterans attending under the Veterans Administration Educational Benefits Program. Approximately 60 percent of students attending CCAC during the 1999–2000 year received some type of financial aid. CCAC also offers an extended interest-free payment plan.

Faculty

The CCAC faculty of 293 practicing professional artists, designers, craftspeople, and scholars (35 full-time and 258 part-time) offers students a strong foundation in basic skills as well as constant exposure to both traditional and contemporary aesthetic values.

Student Government

The CCAC Student Council organizes extracurricular activities and sponsors special events throughout the year. Its president is also the student representative to the Board of Trustees.

Admission Requirements

All students admitted to the undergraduate programs leading to the Bachelor of Fine Arts and Bachelor of Architecture degrees must have a high school diploma or its equivalent. The Admission Review Committee considers the qualifications of each applicant on the basis of a balanced picture that includes an evaluation of academic achievement, the statement of purpose, and supporting documents such as test scores, letters of recommendation, and portfolios of student art.

CCAC admissions policy recognizes the fact that not everyone has had equal access to art education before applying. Some applicants have limited art experience. In every case the total picture each applicant presents—including academic achievement, artistic achievement, and personal goals—is taken into account.

Application and Information

CCAC has a rolling admissions deadline. Applications received by the priority filing dates of March 1 for fall admission and October 1 for spring will be given first consideration for registration, housing, and financial aid opportunities. The application fee is $40. Persons who wish to take one or more individual classes may register as nondegree students on a space-available basis and receive College credit for courses completed.

For undergraduate application forms, current College bulletins, or any additional information, students should contact:

Director of Enrollment Services
California College of Arts and Crafts
1111 Eighth Street
San Francisco, California 94107
Telephone: 800-447-1ART (toll-free)
World Wide Web: http://www.ccac-art.edu

CALIFORNIA INSTITUTE OF TECHNOLOGY
PASADENA, CALIFORNIA

The Institute

Caltech is a small, private research institution located in Pasadena, California. The Caltech community consists of 900 undergraduate and 1,100 graduate students, all sharing a passion for science, mathematics, and engineering. Caltech hosts 432 full-time tenure-track faculty members, which creates an extremely favorable student-faculty ratio across all undergraduate programs.

Housing is guaranteed for all Caltech students, and freshmen live on campus. Institute housing on and off campus is available all four years. Each undergraduate house on campus functions independently through a self-elected executive committee, which allows the house to establish its own rules as well as organize social and interhouse athletic events. All houses and students are represented equally within the student government organization, the Associated Students of the California Institute of Technology (ASCIT).

The Caltech Honor System is a code of behavior that applies to all aspects of campus life. It is an agreement that "no member of the Caltech Community shall take unfair advantage of any other member of the Caltech Community." It works because students believe in preserving the integrity of the scientific process, respecting their peers, and fostering a collaborative learning environment.

There are more than eighty-five extracurricular academic, cultural, musical, professional, religious, and social organizations in which to participate. The athletic program includes NCAA Division III, intramural, physical education, and ASCIT-sponsored athletic events. Last year, 80 percent of the undergraduates participated in at least one intramural sport, and a third played on at least one intercollegiate athletic team.

Location

Caltech is located in Pasadena, California, a city of approximately 135,000 inhabitants about 10 miles northeast of Los Angeles. The Institute is in the center of a residential district but within a few blocks of shopping facilities and "Old Town" Pasadena. Pasadena and Metropolitan Los Angeles provide abundant cultural and recreational opportunities.

Majors and Degrees

Caltech offers a four-year undergraduate program that leads to the Bachelor of Science degree with options in applied mathematics; applied physics; astronomy; biology; chemical engineering; chemistry; economics; electrical engineering; engineering and applied science; geochemistry; geology; geophysics; history; independent studies; literature; mathematics; physics; planetary science; science, ethics, and society; and social science. The program includes thorough instruction in the basic sciences of biology, chemistry, mathematics, and physics and requires a variety of courses in the humanities and social sciences. Near the end of the first year, students select an option; during the second year, they begin to specialize.

Academic Program

The first year of undergraduate study is essentially the same for all students at the Institute. Each student is assigned an individual faculty adviser for the freshman year. When a student selects an option (major), an option adviser is assigned. In conference with his or her adviser, the student then develops a program of study for the next three years. The program includes Institute-wide requirements in physics, mathematics, chemistry, biology, and humanities. Beyond these requirements, the student and adviser choose from a wide range of engineering and science electives to build a solid foundation for the student's prospective field of interest. A student may, with exceptional freedom, petition to change his or her major interest at any time. Many students decide to prepare for graduate study, while others choose to enter professional employment immediately after graduation.

Undergraduate students are encouraged to participate in research. Research activities are an important aspect of the faculty's work, and undergraduate students are given an opportunity to become involved in these activities.

In addition to research opportunities during the academic year, Caltech sponsors the Summer Undergraduate Research Fellowship (SURF) program. Each summer, approximately 300 undergraduate students conduct original research during a ten-week period. At the conclusion of the summer, students present the results of their work by submitting a paper and making an oral presentation. The fellowship carries a stipend.

Academic Facilities

All branches of science and engineering are served by the many superbly equipped laboratories on campus. Included among the many types of equipment available to undergraduate researchers are a high-current, high-stability particle accelerator, scanning electron microscopes, and a nuclear magnetic resonance spectrometer built around one of the world's most stable superconducting magnets that operates at one of the highest possible magnetic fields. Mead Laboratory, used for freshman chemistry, is the most sophisticated in the country. Off-campus installations are the Jet Propulsion Laboratory (JPL), which Caltech operates for NASA, and the Palomar Observatory, which houses the 200-inch Hale telescope. In cooperation with the University of California at Berkeley, Caltech operates the W. M. Keck Observatory in Mauna Kea, Hawaii. The 10-meter Keck Telescope is the world's largest. A modern computer network (Ethernet) has been installed on campus; it links the student houses, the computing center, and all the teaching and research facilities. Undergraduates use both the educational and research computers. The Caltech library system is a network of libraries with services that include electronic access to information sources, literature searching, document delivery, interlibrary loans, and an electronic catalog. The libraries collectively subscribe to 5,100 journals, contain more than 559,595 volumes, and have extensive collections of microfilm, government documents, archives, and maps.

Costs

Tuition, health plan coverage, and other student fees for the 1999–2000 academic year were $19,260, books and supplies were $876, and personal expenses were $1620. Room and board in the student houses, including ten meals per week while the Institute is in session, cost approximately $6000. Meals not covered by board contract cost $1605. The total estimated cost was $29,361.

Financial Aid

Caltech admits students on the basis of academic and personal strengths without regard to their ability to meet the full cost of education. Caltech is strongly committed to meeting the demonstrated financial need of every admitted student. The calculated need, determined by an analysis of the appropriate federal and Caltech supplementary forms, may be met by a combination of grant, loan, and work. The Institute participates in the Cal Grant, the Federal Pell Grant, the Federal Supplemental Educational Opportunity Grant, the Federal Work-Study, the Federal Perkins Loan, and the Federal PLUS loan programs. In addition, the Institute offers several alternative financing options to assist families in paying for a Caltech education. All students who would be unable to attend Caltech without financial assistance are encouraged to apply for financial aid at the time they apply for admission.

Faculty

The faculty consists of 432 full-time professors and 762 members in the positions of emeritus, visiting professor, research associate, visiting associate, senior research fellow, instructor, lecturer, and research fellow. There is no distinction between the undergraduate and graduate faculty. Undergraduate students may enroll in graduate-level courses. Courses are taught by members of the full-time faculty. In some courses, graduate students provide some assistance in grading papers and in laboratory work.

Student Government

Undergraduate students are organized as the Associated Students of the California Institute of Technology, Inc. (ASCIT). This organization functions in relation to all student activities; it organizes social events and funds a variety of clubs and organizations. Its responsibilities include the honor system and board of control. ASCIT also sponsors a coffeehouse and weekly movies and publishes the *Research Opportunities Handbook for Undergraduates* as well as a weekly paper, *California Tech*, and an annual, *The Big T*, both of which are staffed entirely by students. Undergraduate students also sit with most of the faculty committees concerned with the governing of faculty matters.

Admission Requirements

Applicants should have 4 years of mathematics, 3 years of English, 1 year of physics, 1 year of chemistry, 1 year of U.S. history or government, and 5 years of other academic subjects. College Board tests required to be taken not later than the December series of the senior year of high school are the SAT I and the SAT II: Subject Tests in Mathematics (level IIC), Writing, and in Biology, Chemistry, or Physics. Caltech welcomes applications regardless of gender or ethnic or religious background.

California Institute of Technology complies with Title IX (Education Amendments of 1972), Title VII (Civil Rights Act of 1964), and Section 504 of the Rehabilitation Act of 1973 as amended, prohibiting discrimination on the basis of sex, race, creed, color, national origin, or handicaps in its educational programs and activities, including admission and employment.

Application and Information

An application for admission to the freshman class must be postmarked either before November 1 for early action or before January 1 for regular decision. Application forms for financial aid can be obtained from the Office of Financial Aid. Notification of the action of the Admissions Committee is sent by April 1. Students are admitted only once each year for fall matriculation. Requests for application material should be made to:

Office of Admissions
Mail Code 55-63
California Institute of Technology
Pasadena, California 91125
Telephone: 626-395-6341
               800-568-8324 (toll-free)
E-mail: ugadmissions@caltech.edu
World Wide Web: http://www.admissions.caltech.edu

On the lawn in front of one of the seven undergraduate student houses.

CALIFORNIA INSTITUTE OF THE ARTS
VALENCIA, CALIFORNIA

The Institute

California Institute of the Arts is a single complex of six professional schools—Art, Critical Studies, Dance, Film/Video, Music, and Theater—conceived as a community of artists. The Institute is a training ground, a performance center, and a laboratory of the arts.

Interaction among the arts is a fundamental premise of the Institute, and the several schools have developed numerous special programs, such as performance art, electronic art, video art, and world music, that cross traditional disciplinary lines. Whenever possible, the faculty resources of each school are available to all other schools.

The faculty members are all working artists and eminent educators, and the standards in all five schools are professional. Students are accepted as artists on the assumption that they come to the Institute to develop the talents they bring.

California Institute of the Arts was established in 1961 through the merger of Chouinard Art School (founded in 1921) and the Los Angeles Conservatory of Music (founded in 1883). It moved into a 500,000-square-foot facility in 1972; all five schools of the Institute, plus administrative offices, food services, studio spaces, classrooms, and theaters, are housed within this modern, architecturally striking building on the 60-acre campus.

The total enrollment of the Institute is 1,232 men and women, of whom 804 are undergraduates.

At the graduate level, the Institute awards the Master of Fine Arts degree in art, dance, film/video, music, theater, and writing. Advanced certificates are offered in art, dance, film/video, music, and theater.

Location

The campus, just north of Los Angeles, is situated on the crest of one of several gently rolling hills, overlooking the planned community of Valencia. The area traditionally has been devoted to agriculture and cattle ranching. In the last few years, numerous housing developments have been built, and light industry has located there as Los Angeles spreads to the north. Today, the valley's population is 150,000. Interstate Highway 5, the major north-south artery in California, runs alongside the campus. It connects with more than half a dozen major southern California freeways.

Majors and Degrees

California Institute of the Arts offers the Bachelor of Fine Arts degree and certificates in art, dance, film/video, music, and theater.

Academic Program

Students must enroll in a particular school. A modified grading system is in effect, and the curriculum of each school is determined by the special demands of its disciplines. Instruction proceeds according to the student's preparation and need, with the student receiving guidance from a faculty mentor. Continuation in programs depends on demonstrated ability.

The academic calendar consists of two semesters. Programs are designed for maximum flexibility to accommodate special projects, and each school organizes its own schedule to meet its particular needs.

Academic Facilities

The Institute consists of studios, workshops, theaters, galleries, editing rooms, sound stages, electronic music and television studios, and a video research studio. Certain facilities, such as the modular theater, are among the most remarkable anywhere.

The library contains a collection designed especially for the Institute. In addition to holding more than 70,000 volumes, the library includes recordings, films, videotapes, and slides, which, instead of just being audiovisual aids for instructors' use, enable students to progress on their own in obtaining knowledge relevant to their specific studies.

Costs

Tuition for 2000–01 is $19,750 for the academic year. Room charges range from $2850 to $4300 per year, and board costs between $2600 and $3204. The cost of books and supplies varies according to major.

Financial Aid

California Institute of the Arts offers the following financial aid programs: Institute scholarships and work program, Federal Supplemental Educational Opportunity Grants, Federal Work-Study Program awards, and Federal Perkins Loans. The Institute is also eligible to certify Federal Stafford Student Loans from banks. Details of these financial aid programs are available from the Financial Aid Office upon request.

Faculty

The faculty numbers approximately 274, including both full- and part-time members. The student-faculty ratio is about 7:1.

Deans of the six schools comprising the Institute are Tom Lawson, Art; Richard Hebdige, Critical Studies; Cristyne Lawson, Dance; Hartmut Bitomsky, Film/Video; David Rosenboom, Music; and Susan Solt, Theater.

Student Government

Student government is conducted through the Student Council, whose members are elected by the student body. In addition, students are active participants in a variety of Institute-wide standing committees, the composition of which also includes trustees, faculty members, and staff members.

Admission Requirements

Admission to the Institute is based on an applicant's talent and potential. The School of Art requires a portfolio review; the Schools of Dance, Music, and Theater require auditions. Applicants to the School of Film/Video are asked to submit samples of their work.

Admission to California Institute of the Arts and employment by the Institute are based on qualifications and talent, without regard to the individual's race, color, creed, sex, sexual orientation, or age.

Application and Information

For application forms and additional information, prospective students should contact:

Office of Admissions
California Institute of the Arts
24700 McBean Parkway
Valencia, California 91355
Telephone: 661-255-1050
          800-292-ARTS (toll-free in California)
          800-545-ARTS (toll-free outside California)
E-mail: admiss@calarts.edu
World Wide Web: http://www.calarts.edu

CalArts has extensive facilities for all the visual and performing arts.

CALIFORNIA LUTHERAN UNIVERSITY
THOUSAND OAKS, CALIFORNIA

The University

California Lutheran University (CLU) is an institution of liberal arts and sciences founded in 1959. Its growth over the years is attributed to its reputation for high academic standards, its concerned faculty, its Christian commitment and Lutheran tradition, and its beautiful southern California location.

CLU offers personalized learning in a rigorous academic environment, utilizing the latest in technology. CLU is one of the first universities of its size to become fully integrated onto the "information superhighway." A campuswide computer network offers students access to the worlds of science, literature, and global communications from residence hall rooms, classrooms, and on-campus laboratories. The network (called CLUnet) provides access to the Internet, e-mail, and a variety of application software.

A university of the Evangelical Lutheran Church in America, CLU is committed to helping students develop a sense of ethics, values, and good judgment that will lead them to live productively and effectively in society. CLU offers thirty-four majors within the divisions of humanities, creative arts, natural sciences, and social sciences. In addition, undergraduate preprofessional preparation is available in dentistry, law, medicine, and optometry.

CLU is large enough to provide access to a wide variety of organizations, sports, and other activities, but small enough for students to have ample opportunities to develop their leadership skills. CLU's 290-acre campus is home to about 850 of the 1,350 undergraduate students. The student body represents forty countries and twenty-seven states.

At CLU, students are encouraged to participate in the variety of extracurricular activities available, including student publications (yearbook, newspaper, and an award-winning literary magazine), cultural and recreational activities, debate, drama, intercollegiate and intramural athletics, choir, band, and professional, honorary, and academic clubs and societies.

KCLU 88.3 FM, a National Public Radio affiliate based on the CLU campus, provides a valuable service to the community and a valuable resource and opportunity to students who are interested in communication arts and broadcasting.

More than 1,000 students are enrolled in CLU's graduate programs. Master's degrees are awarded in business administration, education, marriage and family counseling, psychology, and public administration.

CLU is accredited by the Western Association of Schools and Colleges.

Location

Poised at the intersection of the Americas on the Pacific Rim, CLU's location helps prepare students for careers in a global society. Thousand Oaks, with a population of about 100,000, offers the conveniences of an urban area with clean, high-tech industries, while maintaining the scenic natural beauty of open space and rolling hills. It is consistently ranked among the safest cities in the nation by the FBI.

Because of its location midway between Santa Barbara and Los Angeles and 15 miles inland from the Pacific Ocean, CLU offers students numerous recreational and cultural opportunities. In addition to the Thousand Oaks Civic Arts Plaza and CLU's on-campus Cultural Events Series, Santa Barbara and Los Angeles offer world-renowned museums, concert halls, and premier productions.

Majors and Degrees

Undergraduate degrees are offered in accounting, administration of justice, art, athletic training, biochemistry and molecular biology, biology, business administration, chemistry, communication arts, computer information systems, computer science, drama, economics, education/liberal arts, English, French, geology, German, history, interdisciplinary studies, international studies, mathematics, mathematics/computer science, multimedia, music, philosophy, physical education, physics/electrooptics, political science, psychology, religion, social science, sociology, and Spanish.

Minors are offered in art, biology, business administration, coaching, communication arts, computer science, drama, economics, English, environmental studies, ethnic studies, French, German, history, interdisciplinary studies, international business, music, philosophy, political science, psychology, religion, sociology, Spanish, and women's studies.

Academic Program

The requirements for the Bachelor of Arts and Bachelor of Science degrees are designed to provide students with a broad program of liberal arts study and an opportunity to concentrate in a chosen field.

At CLU, learning transcends books and lectures as the University's value-based education involves the whole person, enhancing academic and spiritual growth. Based on the liberal arts and sciences, CLU's innovative core curriculum combines perspectives from various disciplines, setting the stage for creative solutions and new approaches to complex modern issues. Students entering as freshmen must participate in the Cluster Program, which integrates two separate courses of study to examine how they affect one another.

Degree requirements include completion of 124 semester credits, 40 of which must be in the upper division. At least the final 30 credits taken prior to graduation must be completed at CLU.

California Lutheran University operates on a semester calendar, with the fall semester beginning in September and the spring semester beginning in late January.

Off-Campus Arrangements

CLU supports students who wish to benefit academically, culturally, and socially from contact with people and environments different from their own. Students may take courses abroad while maintaining their student status at CLU by enrolling in one of the study-abroad programs offered. Among the countries in which students can study are Australia, Austria, Costa Rica, China, England, France, Japan, Mexico, the Netherlands, and Spain.

CLU also offers ROTC opportunities with both the Air Force and the Army in coordination with the University of California, Los Angeles and the University of California, Santa Barbara.

Academic Facilities

Recent campus additions include the 600-seat Samuelson Chapel, with its towering wall of stained glass, mahogany carvings, and handcrafted Steiner-Reck organ, dedicated in 1991; the state-of-the-art Ahmanson Science Center, equipped with an interactive computer simulation laboratory, dedicated in 1988; and the 110,000-volume Pearson Library, which provides access to numerous journals, microforms, audiovisual software, and electronic databases. Through the Online Computer Library Center, the library has access to resources in more than 17,000 libraries in more than forty countries.

The refurbished Preus-Brandt Forum is a 250-seat lecture/performance center equipped with the most modern sound and lighting equipment. It is often used for CLU's popular music and drama productions.

A $4.1-million humanities center opened in January 1998. This new project features state-of-the-art classrooms, a free-standing art gallery, an outdoor music and drama amphitheater, and adjacent music practice facilities.

Costs

Tuition for 2000–01 is $16,800 (12–17 credits per semester). Room and board for the year are $6660.

Financial Aid

Available assistance includes need-based and non-need-based college scholarships; low-interest, long-term loans from external sources; Federal Supplemental Educational Opportunity Grants; Federal Pell Grants; and Federal Work-Study. Part-time jobs are available both on and off campus. Applicants for aid should submit the Free Application for Federal Student Aid (FAFSA). The parents' and/or student's most recent IRS 1040 form must also be submitted. The priority application deadline is March 1.

Faculty

California Lutheran University places a high priority on student-faculty interaction and on maintaining a campus environment that is highly conducive to these interactions. The quality of CLU's faculty is among the University's greatest assets. The 96 full-time and 14 part-time undergraduate faculty members are committed to their students, and the small class size enhances their ability to reach out to students on an individual basis. Eighty-eight percent of CLU's faculty hold the highest degree available in their field. The student-faculty ratio is 15:1.

Student Government

All undergraduate students carrying 9 or more units are automatically members of the Associated Students of California Lutheran University by virtue of their enrollment in the University. Student governance, including allocation of the student activity fee, is conducted by student body–elected officials.

Admission Requirements

Applicants for admission must complete the application form and submit a high school transcript, SAT I or ACT scores, one recommendation, an essay, and a $35 nonrefundable application fee. An interview is strongly recommended. International students must also submit TOEFL scores.

Required preparation includes 4 years of college-preparatory English, 3 years of mathematics, 2 years of a foreign language, 2 years of social studies, and 1 year of laboratory science.

Transfer applicants must also send a transcript of all college work and should have a minimum 2.75 grade point average.

Application and Information

The priority application deadline is March 1. There is a rolling admission system; notification is continuous from December 1 until June 15.

For additional information, interested students should contact:

Office of Admission
California Lutheran University
60 West Olsen Road
Thousand Oaks, California 91360-2787

Telephone: 805-493-3135
Fax: 805-493-3114
E-mail: cluadm@clunet.edu
World Wide Web: http://www.clunet.edu/

With its excellent weather, studying or relaxing outdoors at CLU is a year-round experience.

CALIFORNIA STATE POLYTECHNIC UNIVERSITY, POMONA
POMONA, CALIFORNIA

The University

California State Polytechnic University, Pomona (Cal Poly Pomona) is located on the eastern edge of Southern California's San Gabriel Valley. Its 1400-acre campus, featuring lush rolling hills, was once the winter ranch of cereal magnate W.K. Kellogg. While the land and its contents were donated to the state in 1949, Kellogg's hilltop home and award-winning Arabian horses remain as lasting reminders of the university's heritage.

As one of a few polytechnical universities in the nation, Cal Poly Pomona's mission is to advance learning and knowledge by linking theory and practice and integrating technology, while preparing students for lifelong learning, leadership, and careers. Its learn-by-doing, polytechnic philosophy has created a reputation of producing well-balance individuals who make an immediate impact. This is the reason Cal Poly Pomona graduates are among the most sought-after in today's marketplace.

Cal Poly Pomona is well-known for the quality of its degree programs. The University has more than sixty undergraduate majors in eight colleges and schools: agriculture; business administration; education and integrative studies; engineering; environmental design; hospitality management; letters, arts, and social sciences; and science.

In addition, Cal Poly Pomona offers a Master of Architecture; Master of Arts in education and English; Master of Business Administration; Master of Landscape Architecture; Master of Public Administration; Master of Science in agriculture, biological sciences, business administration, chemistry, computer science, economics, electrical engineering, engineering, kinesiology, mathematics, and psychology; a Master of Urban and Regional Planning; and forty-eight teaching credentials/certificates.

Cal Poly Pomona is accredited by the Western Association of Schools and Colleges and is authorized by the California State Commission for Teacher Preparation and Licensing to recommend candidates for credentials in several areas. In addition, many of the degree programs are accredited by national organizations.

Students attending Cal Poly Pomona don't face overloaded classrooms or throngs of teaching assistants. In the belief that education should be a face-to-face interaction between real faculty and students, the University strives to maintain a 19:1 student-teacher ratio, and most classrooms seat fewer than 50 students.

A wide variety of activities and opportunities abound on campus, with more than 200 organizations bringing students together based on academic and/or other common interests. Since 1949, student-constructed floats have also appeared in the annual Pasadena Tournament of Roses Parade. About 800 students are involved in social Greek organizations, and the forty ethnically based organizations reflect the diverse student body. Students also enrich their educational experience through community service and volunteer opportunities. With twelve intercollegiate sports, Bronco men's and women's teams have won eleven national championships and compete in the nation's premiere NCAA II conference, and the California Collegiate Athletic Association. In addition, club sports and intramurals involve nearly 2,000 students each year.

As part of the 23-campus California State University system, Cal Poly Pomona's 2,200 faculty and staff serve 18,000 students from thirty-three states and 116 countries worldwide. Nearly 33 percent of the students are Asian American, with close to 25 percent Hispanic, about 7 percent Filipino, 4 percent African American, and nearly 1 percent American Indian. The average age is 23, with a 55-45 percent male-female ratio.

Close to 10 percent of the student body live on campus. Residence halls accommodate approximately 1,300 students. The University Village, a residential complex adjacent to the campus, accommodates some 800 students.

Location

Located just 35 miles southeast of downtown Los Angeles, Cal Poly Pomona offers the excitement of one of the world's most diverse metropolitan areas and Southern California's magnificent weather, while still retaining the serenity of a foothill community. The University's proximity to business and industry makes it ideal for internships and employment opportunities. And the campus is only a short drive from natural (beach, mountains, and desert), cultural (theaters, museums, and galleries), and recreational (Disneyland, Raging Waters, and L.A. County Fairgrounds) sites.

Majors and Degrees

Bachelor of Arts degrees include art; behavioral science; English; gender, ethnicity, and multicultural studies; history; liberal studies; music; philosophy; political science; psychology; sociology; Spanish; and theater. The Bachelor of Architecture is also offered.

Bachelor of Science degrees include aerospace engineering, agricultural biology, agricultural science, agronomy, animal science, anthropology, apparel merchandising and management, biology, biotechnology, botany, business administration (options include accounting; computer information systems; finance, real estate, and law; international business; management and human resources; marketing; and operations management), chemical engineering, chemistry, civil engineering, communication, computer science, construction engineering technology, economics, electrical engineering, electronics/computer engineering technology, engineering technology, food marketing and agribusiness management, foods and nutrition, food science and technology, geography, geology, horticulture, hospitality management, industrial engineering, kinesiology, landscape architecture, landscape irrigation science, manufacturing engineering, materials engineering, mathematics, mechanical engineering, microbiology, physics, social sciences, soil science, urban and regional planning, and zoology.

Academic Program

Classes are offered in four 11-week quarters. Candidates for Bachelor of Arts degrees must earn at least 186 quarter units. The Bachelor of Science degree requires at least 198 quarter units. A graduation writing requirement exists for all baccalaureate degrees.

Currently, the Architecture and Computer Information Systems are impacted and open only to California residents.

Cal Poly Pomona offers Air Force and Army Reserve Officers Training Corps, a California Pre-Doctoral Program, an Educational Opportunity Program, a Teacher Aide Path to Teaching, University Equity Programs, and other special programs.

The University features special centers and institutes, such as the innovative Lyle Center for Regenerative Studies, the Apparel Technology and Research Center, the Center for Turf, Irrigation and Landscape Technology, the Equine Research Center, the Ocean Studies Institute, and the Institute for Cellular and Molecular Biology.

Off-Campus Arrangements

Affiliated with thirty-six recognized universities and institutions of higher education in sixteen countries, the International Center and Cal Poly Study Abroad Programs offer opportunities to earn credit while studying abroad. As active members in the National

Student Exchange, students may complete some course work in a new environment at more than 100 participating institutions throughout the United States and its territories.

Academic Facilities

The library has more than 2.7 million resource materials, as well as online databases and services.

There are dozens of computer labs, which are all staffed with trained personnel; some are open 24 hours per day.

Indicative of Cal Poly Pomona's hands-on learning are the Collins School for Hospitality Management and the University Farm. The Collins School houses a student-run restaurant, demonstration kitchens, and laboratories and features annual presentations by world-famous chefs. The University Farm has more than 700 acres devoted to pastures and livestock, crops, groves, and ornamental plantings.

Cal Poly Pomona is in the midst of a multi-million dollar building campaign to provide new facilities such as an agricultural research facility, a biotechnology building, an engineering lab, a housing community, and additions to the existing Union.

Costs

Academic fees for full-time students (6.1 or more units) in 2000–01 are $1772 for the year. Non-California residents pay an additional $164 per unit. Residence hall housing costs vary from $4934 to $5867 for the academic year, depending on choice of accommodations and meal plan.

Financial Aid

The University administers extensive financial aid programs, and each year more than 49 percent of Cal Poly Pomona students receive more than $47 million in financial aid.

Applications for academic and merit scholarships must be completed by February 15. Applications for financial aid should be completed as early as possible after January 1 and no later than March 2 for the following academic year. Applicants should contact the financial aid office for information and application material.

Faculty

About three fourths of the faculty members have earned terminal degrees. Though research is actively conducted, the emphasis is on teaching students how to practically apply knowledge learned in the classroom. With a student-faculty ratio of 19:1, individual contact is common and encouraged. Faculty members serve as academic advisers for majors in their departments, and many advise cocurricular organizations.

Student Government

The Associated Students, Incorporated (ASI) is an active force in the campus community. As the voice for students in University governance, student leaders participate in University-wide committees, as well as manage and operate the University Union facilities. ASI also sponsors concerts, lectures, and films.

Admission Requirements

Admission requirements and criteria are explained in detail in the CSU Application for Admission and the Cal Poly Pomona catalog.

First-time freshmen must be high school graduates and must have completed the following college-preparatory courses with a C or better: 4 years of college-preparatory English; 3 years of mathematics; 1 year of U.S. history and/or government; 1 year of laboratory science; 2 years of a foreign language; 1 year of visual and performing arts; and 3 years of approved college-preparatory electives. In addition, qualification for admission is based on a combination of grades and scores on either the ACT or the SAT I. Students in the top third of their high school class have excellent potential to succeed at Cal Poly Pomona.

Lower-division transfer students must have completed fewer than 56 transferable semester units (84 quarter units) to qualify for admission so long as they have a grade point average of C or better in all transferable units attempted, are in good standing at the last college or university attended, and meet the admission requirements for first-time freshmen. If such students did not complete all subject requirements in high school, appropriate college courses may be used to make up the missing subjects.

Upper-division transfer students must have completed at least 56 transferable semester units (84 quarter units), have a grade point average of C or better in all transferable units attempted, and should be in good standing at the last college or university attended. If all the aforementioned criteria have been met, applicants may become eligible if they have completed at least 30 semester units (45 quarter units) of college courses with a grade of C or better in courses that meet the general education requirements, which include written communication, oral communication, critical thinking, and mathematics.

For international students, Cal Poly Pomona uses additional requirements to admit students who hold F-1 and J-1 student visas. Verification of English proficiency, financial resources, and academic performance are all important considerations.

All applicants, regardless of citizenship, whose preparatory education was principally in a language other than English must demonstrate competence in English. Undergraduate students who are required to take the TOEFL must score a minimum of 525 on the paper-based test or 193 on the computer-based test. Minimum scores for graduates vary by program.

Admission requirements may be subject to change, and students should consult the CSU application or access the Web site at http://www.csumentor.edu.

Application and Information

Cal Poly Pomona begins accepting applications for the following fall on November 1 of the preceding year. Application deadlines for the fall quarter are April 1 for freshmen and lower-division transfer students and May 1 for upper-division transfer students. Students should contact Student Outreach and Recruitment for application deadlines for summer, winter, and spring. The application fee is $55, but waivers may be granted. Applications may be requested from a California high school, community college, or CSU campus; by writing or calling Student Outreach and Recruitment; or by e-mailing inquiries to generalinfo@csupomona.edu. The University encourages students to apply online over the Internet at http://www.csumentor.edu. Students can access Cal Poly Pomona's home page (http://www.csupomona.edu). For further information, students should contact:

Student Outreach and Recruitment
California State Polytechnic University, Pomona
3801 West Temple Avenue
Pomona, California 91768
Telephone: 909-869-3210

More than 250 student organizations reflect the diverse interests and backgrounds of Cal Poly Pomona students.

CALIFORNIA UNIVERSITY OF PENNSYLVANIA
CALIFORNIA, PENNSYLVANIA

The University

California University of Pennsylvania, one of fourteen institutions of higher learning owned and operated by the Pennsylvania State System of Higher Education, traces its origin to the establishment of an academy in 1852, three years after the community of California was established. (The town derives its name from the gold rush of 1849, the year of its founding.) In 1865, the academy was chartered as a Normal School; in 1874, it was named the South Western State Normal College and devoted to teacher training. In 1914, it was purchased by the Commonwealth of Pennsylvania, and in 1928 it became a four-year, degree-granting state teachers college. In 1959, it became a multipurpose state college. In 1983, it became California University of Pennsylvania. In addition to the undergraduate degrees listed below, the University also offers master's degrees.

The campus, which has thirty-eight buildings, consists of 90 acres situated on a bend of the Monongahela River. A student union with recreational and dining facilities is at the center of the campus. A recreation complex of 98 acres, owned by the Student Association, Inc., is located 2 miles from the campus and has tennis courts, running tracks, picnic areas, a baseball field, and a stadium. Depending upon the season, free bus service is provided to this facility.

Activities include theater and musical offerings—rock, jazz, and classical performances, bands, and choral groups; guest speakers; film series; a television and a radio station; thirteen intercollegiate sports for women and men; intramural sports; a weekly newspaper, a yearbook, and an award-winning literary and arts magazine; social fraternities and sororities; a health and fitness center; low-cost outdoor recreation equipment rental; and numerous particular interest clubs and organizations.

The current enrollment is 5,080 undergraduate students. About 2,730 students commute, 1,152 live on campus in six residence halls, and 1,200 live in off-campus fraternity or sorority houses, rental units, or private homes.

A Counseling Center, staffed by professional counselors, is maintained for students. Tutoring services are provided by the Academic Development Services Department, a Mathematics Lab, a Writing Center, and a Reading Clinic, as well as by many academic departments. The Career Center offers career planning, co-op education, resume services, on-campus recruiting, a computerized guidance system, a simulated interview program, an alumni network, a 24-hour job listing service, and a career resource center.

Location

The campus is located in the borough of California, Pennsylvania, a community of 7,000 people. It is approximately 35 miles south of Pittsburgh in the foothills of the Allegheny Mountains, near Pennsylvania's Laurel Highlands recreational area. Professional baseball, football, and hockey, as well as a variety of cultural activities, are available in Pittsburgh. The area in which the University is located has a number of significant historic sites related to the pre–Revolutionary War era. The University also offers students the option of an off-campus site located in Canonsburg at the Southpointe Technology Park. Other outreach programs are being conducted in the Bedford and Somerset areas.

Majors and Degrees

California University of Pennsylvania offers four baccalaureate degrees: the Bachelor of Arts, the Bachelor of Science, the Bachelor of Science in Education, and the Bachelor of Science in Nursing. Associate of Arts, Associate of Sciences, and Associate of Applied Science degrees are also offered.

The liberal arts majors include communication studies (public relations, radio/television, and speech), earth sciences (broadcast meteorology), geology, humanities (art, English, French, philosophy, Spanish, and theater), interdisciplinary studies (humanities, international studies, parks and recreation management, prelaw, and social sciences), professional writing (business and commercial writing, creative writing, journalism, and scientific and technical writing), and social sciences (anthropology, economics, geography, history, industrial-organizational psychology, political science, psychology, sociology, travel and tourism, and urban studies).

The Bachelor of Science in Education includes majors in athletic training, communication disorders, early childhood education, elementary education, secondary education (biology, chemistry, communication, comprehensive social science, earth science, English, French, general science, mathematics, physics, and Spanish), special education, and technology education (formerly industrial arts education). Dual majors (e.g., in elementary and early childhood education, special education and another education field, communication disorders and another area, or in athletic training and another education field) are available in many education programs. The College of Education and Human Services also offers bachelor's degrees in gerontology and social work and, through cooperative programs with other institutions in the region, provides most of the academic work for certification to teach art.

The Eberly College of Science and Technology offers majors in the areas of administration and management, applied computer science, business administration (accounting, business administration, business economics, computer-based systems management, finance, human resources management, management, and marketing), electrical engineering technology, environmental studies (environmental conservation, environmental pollution control, environmental resources, environmental science, and wildlife biology), graphic communication technology (electrographics, flexography, management, offset lithography, and screen printing), manufacturing technology (automation, computer numerical control, drafting and design, electronics, and industrial management), mathematics and computer science, medical technology, natural sciences (biology, chemistry, earth science, geology, mathematics, natural sciences interdisciplinary, and physics), and pre–health professions (pre-chiropractic medicine, predentistry, premedicine, pre–mortuary science, preoptometry, pre–osteopathic medicine, prepharmacy, pre–podiatric medicine, and pre–veterinary medicine). Cooperative nursing programs are offered with the Community College of Allegheny County and Washington (PA) Hospital. The University offers an upper-division bachelor's degree program in nursing for students who have completed an RN program. Cooperative pre–engineering programs are offered with Penn State and the University of Pittsburgh.

The University provides a variety of programs for part-time and specialized students, including noncredit workshops and industrial training programs. The University confers associate degrees in accounting, administration and management, banking, computer science technology, and screen printing and automation technology (numerical control technology and robotics). It also offers an Associate of Applied Science degree in occupational therapy assistant studies and physical therapist assistant studies. The University offers a cooperative on-campus program with the Community College of Beaver County leading to an associate degree in criminal justice.

Academic Program

Each bachelor's degree requires a minimum of 128 semester hours of credit. A general education requirement encompasses approximately 60 of the 128 credit hours, distributed among the humanities, natural sciences, and social sciences. The remaining 68 hours may be devoted to all aspects of specialization, including the major and professional and related courses. Advanced placement credit and honors courses are offered throughout the University. An honors degree program is also offered for advanced students.

Academic Facilities

The University has traditional library holdings of more than 360,000 volumes, more than 1 million microform units, nearly 1,500 periodical titles, and U.S. government documents. It is a member of the Keystone Library Network, which provides access to library holdings, databases, and electronic resources among fourteen State System of Higher Education libraries. This virtual library electronically links users to a variety of information sources and delivers both text and multimedia sources immediately and seamlessly from any location. The new 80,400-square-foot Eberly Science and Technology Center features state-of-the-art science and computer laboratories and is one of the premiere teaching facilities on campus. The Natali Student Center houses a movie theater complete with surround sound, a student-run radio station, and a cable television station, in addition to a food court and a bookstore. Every residence hall room is wired with fiber optics so that students can bring computers, plug them in, and have immediate access to the Internet and all of its resources. For students who do not have computers of their own, there is a computer lab on every floor of the residence halls. Numerous specialized computer facilities are available across the campus, including ones devoted to meteorology, math and computer science, word processing, accounting, CAD-CAM, robotics, teacher education, art, and chemistry.

Costs

The 1999–2000 tuition for a resident of Pennsylvania was $1809 per semester. For out-of-state students, tuition was $4523 per semester. For a semester, room rent was $1123 (double occupancy) and the nineteen-meal-per-week plan was $1140. Other fees (based on a full-time schedule) included a University service fee of $85, a Student Association fee of $140, a student union building fee of $81, a student center operations and maintenance fee of $75, and an academic support fee of $180.90. The cost of books, materials, and supplies varies with each program and is approximately $400 per semester.

Financial Aid

California University of Pennsylvania has available a number of types of financial aid, including student employment, grant and scholarship aid through the Pennsylvania Higher Education Assistance Agency, federal grants, and student loans. A number of non-need-based academic scholarships are available for talented students. All students must complete the Pennsylvania State Grant and federal financial aid application for need-based aid. The director of financial aid at the University administers all student aid.

Faculty

Classes are taught by 272 full-time and 57 part-time faculty members; no classes are taught by graduate assistants. Doctorates are held by more than 65 percent of the full-time faculty members. Faculty advisers are assigned based on the student's major, department, or school.

Student Government

Student government at California University of Pennsylvania regulates cocurricular activities. It furthers the quality of student life by encouraging and funding diverse student activities, providing experiences in the principles and practices of democratic government, supplying a forum for general student interest, and improving and promoting the cultural standards of the University. Students sit on most important University committees and have a voice in most policy decisions.

Admission Requirements

California University of Pennsylvania welcomes applications from all qualified persons regardless of race, religion, or national origin.

Admission standards have been established by California University of Pennsylvania for the purpose of ascertaining which prospective students are most likely to succeed at the University. An applicant for admission should have graduated from an accredited four-year high school or should possess an equivalency diploma issued by a state department of education. All applicants should submit to the University evidence of their ability to do college-level work, as indicated by such tests as the College Board's SAT I. All applicants are required to have a Social Security number.

Application and Information

The prospective student should obtain from the University the appropriate forms, have them completed in detail, and file them with the University's Director of Admissions. The forms required are the Application for Admission, which should be completed by the applicant, and the Secondary School Record, which is to be completed by the high school principal. A nonrefundable application fee of $25 must be attached to the application. (Money orders should be made payable to California University of Pennsylvania.)

A student who seeks to transfer to California University of Pennsylvania should follow these procedures: (1) complete the same forms as are required for students seeking admission to the University for the first time and forward them to the Office of Admissions; (2) submit with the completed application a check or money order to cover the nonrefundable application fee of $25; and (3) arrange to have all other colleges attended send to the Office of Admissions at California University of Pennsylvania copies of transcripts and statements of honorable dismissal, which must indicate that the applicant has been cleared academically, socially, and financially.

For any additional information regarding admission, students should contact:

Director of Admissions
California University of Pennsylvania
California, Pennsylvania 15419

Telephone: 724-938-4404
E-mail: inquiry@cup.edu

Students and faculty members working together.

CALVIN COLLEGE
GRAND RAPIDS, MICHIGAN

The College

Calvin College is dedicated to relating the Christian faith to the whole learning process; this view affects every area of campus life from the content of each course to volunteer service and life in the residence halls. Calvin is one of the nation's largest and most respected evangelical Christian colleges. The 1999 fall enrollment was 4,273. Calvin maintains a strong affiliation with the Christian Reformed Church, and students from more than sixty other church denominations across North America and the world choose Calvin for its extensive curriculum and Christ-centered mission.

Calvin is deeply committed to being a diverse community and is taking deliberate steps to increase opportunities for women, members of minority groups, and the disabled. Students are challenged not only to obtain a fine education and to prepare for a career but also to live lives of commitment and service.

Students come from nearly every state and more than thirty-five countries. Most students are between 18 and 22 years old; however, those pursuing the Master of Education (M.Ed.) add to the age diversity on campus. The Broene Counseling Center offers career counseling and career resource services as well as personal counseling. The Career Services Office assists students in finding internships and in searching for full-time employment upon graduation.

A wide variety of cocurricular opportunities are available, including music, theater, athletic, artistic, cultural, service, and religious activities and events. Calvin's Service Learning Center provides opportunities for academically based service learning in addition to such programs as big brothers/big sisters, services for the elderly, and school tutoring. Calvin is an NCAA Division III school and participates in the Michigan Intercollegiate Athletic Association; Calvin's athletic teams regularly are ranked nationally in Division III. The men's basketball team won the national championship in 1992; the women's cross-country team captured the national championship in 1998 and 1999.

The 400-acre campus is a modern, well-planned community; its oldest academic building was erected in 1960. Fifteen residence halls, fifteen apartment buildings, and two spacious dining halls accommodate 2,500 resident students. Knollcrest Fieldhouse seats 4,500 around its main court for sporting events or can be used as four separate gymnasiums for the school's many intramural events. It is often the site of conference and regional sports tournaments. The field house also includes a racquetball court; a strength and fitness facility; a six-lane, 25-yard swimming pool; and a diving pool with both one- and three-meter boards. Calvin's outdoor athletic sites include baseball and softball diamonds, a premier soccer field with seating for 1,500 and two practice fields, an eight-lane track, a six-court tennis facility, and two sand volleyball courts.

Location

Calvin's beautifully wooded campus is located in the suburbs of Grand Rapids, which has a population of more than 650,000. Hundreds of restaurants, dozens of theaters, seven shopping malls, and a fine selection of museums and parks are within a 10-minute drive. Lake Michigan beaches, ski areas, parks, and trails are within a 40-minute drive. Cultural and community activities take place weekly on the Calvin campus, on the campuses of six other local colleges, and at De Vos Hall and VanAndel Arena in downtown Grand Rapids. City buses regularly pass by the Calvin campus.

Majors and Degrees

The Bachelor of Arts or Bachelor of Science degree is offered with major concentrations in accounting, art, art history, biochemistry, biology, biotechnology, business, chemistry, classical civilization, classical languages, communication arts and sciences, computer science, criminal justice, Dutch, early childhood education, economics, education, engineering, English, environmental science, environmental studies, film studies, French, geology, German, Greek, history, Latin, mathematics, music, nursing, philosophy, physical education, physics, political science, psychology, recreation, religion and theology, social work, sociology, Spanish, special education, telecommunications, and theater. The Bachelor of Fine Arts (B.F.A.) degree in art is offered in addition to the B.A. degree in art.

Professional programs include prearchitecture, engineering (chemical, civil, electrical/computer, mechanical), prelaw, premedicine/predentistry, natural resources, prepharmacy, pre–physical therapy, pre–seminary studies, social work, and elementary, secondary, and special education. Minor concentrations are available in archaeology, dance, English as a second language, environmental studies, gender studies, Japanese, journalism, missions, and Third World development studies.

Academic Program

Calvin College maintains a strong commitment to a liberal arts curriculum as an integral avenue to help students understand God's world and their place in it. The College follows a 4-1-4 academic calendar, consisting of two 4-month semesters separated by a three-week Interim term during January. Typically, students take four or five courses each semester and one course during the Interim. Graduation requires the successful completion of 124 semester hours.

Core curriculum requirements include foreign language, history, literature and arts, mathematics, natural sciences, philosophy, physical education, religion, social sciences, and written and spoken rhetoric. Some requirements can be satisfied by advanced high school work in foreign language, literature, mathematics, and natural sciences. Qualified students can earn course exemption and/or credit by completing college-level work in high school or by examination. Satisfactory scores on Advanced Placement (AP), International Baccalaureate (I.B.), and/or CLEP exams are also accepted.

Students with a cumulative grade point average of 3.3 or higher can apply to join the Honors Program for advanced-level courses, interdisciplinary courses, and cocurricular opportunities. Students can also benefit from services offered by the Office of Student Academic Services, which provides academic counseling, tutoring, training in study skills, and review courses in key subjects.

Off-Campus Arrangements

Study-abroad programs for a semester or a year are offered in Austria, China, Costa Rica, France, Germany, Great Britain, Honduras, Hungary, the Netherlands, and Spain. Students register for courses in various subjects, and the credits earned are applied toward graduation requirements. The Chicago Metropolitan Study Center, in cooperation with Calvin and other colleges, offers a semester's credit for internship experiences in metropolitan Chicago. Students can also participate in the Oregon Extension Program of Houghton College and programs of the Council for Christian Colleges and Universities: the American Studies Program in Washington, D.C.; the Latin American Studies Program in Central America; a Film Studies Program in Hollywood; a Middle East Studies Program in Cairo,

Egypt; and a Russian Studies Program in Moscow. Along with several other liberal arts colleges, Calvin sponsors the Au Sable Institute of Environmental Studies, which offers creational stewardship experiences in a sylvan setting in the northern part of Michigan's lower peninsula. Calvin's Study in Spain Program is one option students may choose to fulfill their foreign language requirement. Many courses offered during the Interim are also taught abroad.

Academic Facilities

The four-floor Science Complex (1968, 1986, and 1998), in which classrooms and offices surround a center core of laboratories, features an electron microscope, an atom trapper, and an observatory with a 16-inch telescope. In fall 1999, Calvin opened two new facilities on campus: the Engineering Building, which features additional space for engineering students and faculty members to do research and design work, and the DeVries Hall of Science, an addition to the existing science complex that includes medical research laboratories and classrooms. The Spoelhof College Center (1973) houses administrative offices, a social research center, an art gallery, six spacious and well-equipped art studios, and an intimate 340-seat auditorium. In the Fine Arts Center (1966), classrooms and offices of the Departments of English, Music, and Communication Arts and Sciences surround a 1,000-seat auditorium noted for its superb acoustics, its unusual lighting, and the Zondervan Memorial Organ.

The Hekman Library-Hiemenga Hall complex (1962, 1970, 1978, and 1994) includes a five-level, computerized library containing more than 700,000 bound volumes, 2,750 periodicals, an extensive collection of microfiche, records and tapes, and government publications; more than 1,500 students can be comfortably seated at study carrels and tables. The complex also houses the Information Technology Center, the Calvin Center for Christian Scholarship, the Meeter Center for Calvinism Studies, and an Instructional Resources Center that includes a distance-learning classroom, a TV studio, a graphics production lab, and a curriculum center for teacher-education students.

Costs

Tuition for 2000–01 is $14,037; tuition for the Interim is free for full-time students enrolled for at least one semester. Room and board charges are $4895 for resident students with a twenty-one-meal-per-week plan (ten- and fifteen-meal-per-week plans are also available). About $500 is needed for fees and textbooks.

Financial Aid

Sixty percent of Calvin students receive need-based financial aid; demonstrated need is the most important criterion in determining eligibility. Students wishing to be considered for financial aid must be admitted to the College and must submit the Free Application for Federal Student Aid (FAFSA) and Calvin's Supplemental Application for Financial Aid. February 15 is the suggested filing deadline for maximum consideration. Financial awards to eligible applicants consist of state and federal grants, loans, Federal Work-Study funds, and institutional grants and scholarships. Part-time employment is available on campus, and placement preference is given to needy students. Calvin also helps students find off-campus employment and runs a job transportation service that drives them to and from their jobs for a minimal fee.

Faculty

Calvin has an outstanding faculty. Many members have distinguished themselves in their respective fields through publication and research yet each is generally available 10–15 hours per week outside of class for academic and personal counseling. More than 81 percent have earned the highest academic degree in their field. Each faculty member is a professing Christian, committed to the integration of his or her personal faith and discipline. There are 282 full-time and 56 part-time faculty members; the faculty-student ratio is 1:16.

Student Government

The 27-member Student Senate supervises most student activities and oversees the budgets for student publications, homecoming, the film arts, the campus radio station, and the Service-Learning Center. Student members serve on most faculty committees governing the College. Each residence hall has its own governing council and judiciary committee, which work in cooperation with the residence hall staff to enhance community life in the halls. Campus rules are designed to build a Christian academic community. Calvin attempts to aid student development and responsible action by clearly expressing its expectations and de-emphasizing regulations.

Admission Requirements

Students who have a desire and capacity to learn and who are interested in Calvin's Christian atmosphere and curricular emphasis are eligible for admission. Applicants should be graduates of an accredited high school program and should have completed satisfactorily at least 15 units of college-preparatory work, including 3 in English and 3 in algebra and geometry. Applicants with high school averages of C+ (2.5) or higher who score above 20 on the ACT composite or above 470 on both the math and verbal sections of the SAT I are normally given regular admission. Applicants with lower grades and scores, or those with deficiencies in their high school preparation, may be admitted under special conditions that require their participation in the ACCESS Program. Candidates for admission from other countries follow the customary entrance procedures. Students who come from a non-English-speaking culture must demonstrate proficiency in English by satisfactory performance on the Test of English as a Foreign Language (TOEFL).

Application and Information

Applicants must submit a completed application form, a high school or college transcript, results of either the ACT or SAT I, and an educational recommendation completed by a teacher or counselor. Admission decisions are made on a rolling basis beginning in mid-October. Applicants for fall admission are urged to complete their file before February 1, although there is no deadline as long as space remains in the entering class. Campus visits are strongly recommended, although not required. Students and parents are welcome to visit at any time that is convenient for them. The "Fridays at Calvin" campus visit program also provides an excellent opportunity to experience life at Calvin firsthand. For more information about Calvin or about visiting the campus, students should contact:

Admissions Office
Calvin College
3201 Burton Street, SE
Grand Rapids, Michigan 49546

Telephone: 800-688-0122 (toll-free in North America)
Fax: 616-957-8551
E-mail: admissions@calvin.edu
World Wide Web: http://www.calvin.edu

Recognized as one of the finest research libraries in western Michigan, the Hekman Library is a hub of student and faculty activity on the Calvin College campus.

CAMBRIDGE COLLEGE
CAMBRIDGE, MASSACHUSETTS

The College

At Cambridge College, an innovative educational model combines peer teaching and learning with creative instruction. Its programs are known for offering academic substance and rigor in a highly supportive environment. The College has nearly 9,000 graduates in the Boston area, across the country, and around the world. Students choose Cambridge College for its distinctive focus on the needs of working adults and for the diverse community of lifelong learners it provides.

Founded in 1971, Cambridge College offers the degrees of Master of Education (in education and in counseling psychology), Master of Management, and Bachelor of Arts (in psychology) to working adults. Sixty-five percent of the College's more than 1,700 students are women, and more than 40 percent are people of color; the average age of the Cambridge College student is 40. Classes take place in the evenings and on weekends and provide motivated adult students with an atmosphere of intellectual challenge, peer support, and respect for their professional and personal attainments.

Location

Cambridge College is located midway between Harvard and Central Squares in Cambridge, Massachusetts. This vital urban environment combines the diversity and richness of a major metropolitan area with the intellectual resources of a nationally known university community.

Majors and Degrees

Cambridge offers the Bachelor of Arts in psychology, with concentrations in educational psychology (with option to prepare for Massachusetts Advanced Provisional Teacher Certification, grades 1–6), family and community systems, and organizational psychology.

Academic Program

The Bachelor of Arts degree program at Cambridge College supports professional development in a wide variety of careers and graduate programs. It is a liberal arts degree program that prepares people for careers in human services, management, administration, education, or community service; for professional advancement in their current work; or for graduate study.

Cambridge College offers the degree of Bachelor of Arts in psychology with three concentrations: educational psychology (with teacher certification option); family and community systems: human services; and organizational psychology and management.

The concentration in educational psychology examines the processes of teaching and learning through an integrated approach to the study of behavior and thought. One-hundred-twenty credit hours are required: 45 credit hours in general education; 42 credit hours in the psychology major; and 33 credit hours in general education electives. Students choosing the teacher certification option must also complete a 5-credit practicum (student-teaching) experience.

The family and community systems: human services concentration offers students a new model for human and community services; it focuses on the connections between families and community institutions, emphasizing their strengths and capacity for change. One-hundred-twenty credit hours are required: 45 credit hours in general education; 42 credit hours in the psychology major; and 33 credit hours in general education electives. Students in this concentration may also participate in for-credit internship and sponsored learning experiences.

Students in the organizational psychology and management concentration gain skills required for success as an outstanding professional, team member, or manager and learn more about the complex systems that constitute businesses, agencies, and other organizations. One-hundred-twenty credit hours are required: 45 credit hours in general education; 42 credit hours in the psychology major; and 33 credit hours in general education electives.

Cambridge College students join an active, diverse learning community of working adults in an environment of trust and shared vision. The Bachelor of Arts program is shaped by an educational model in which advising, learning, teaching, and assessment work together as an integrated process.

Learners in this supportive community are empowered to synthesize academic and experiential learning with personal values and practical relevance. The Cambridge College learning experience transforms students' personal, professional, and social realities and enables them to participate more effectively in their communities.

Cambridge College provides an education for its students that, in addition to offering academic breadth and depth, goes beyond the traditional ways of organizing knowledge and traditional teaching methods that are often inadequate for adult learners in the contemporary world. Since its founding in 1971, Cambridge College has been offering distinctive programs designed especially for working adults. Its Bachelor of Arts program is based on these years of experience about how they learn most effectively.

Cambridge College is committed to outcomes-based learning in all aspects of undergraduate study. Each program and each course have clearly defined, measurable skills and areas of knowledge to gain; understandings and perspectives to develop; processes to use; and projects to complete. Outcomes-based learning is centered on the learner. Clearly stated learning outcomes provide a baseline for learning and thus facilitate educational planning and enhance learners' abilities to achieve personal and career goals.

The College recognizes the importance and validity of prior learning for academic credit, program planning, shortening time spent in the program, and saving students money. Cambridge College assesses and awards appropriate credit to its students for courses completed at regionally accredited institutions, portfolios documenting prior or current learning, successful completion of nationally standardized subject-area and skills tests, and challenge examinations in writing and mathematics. In addition, the College provides many opportunities for faculty-supervised independent and focused study.

Academic Facilities

All Cambridge College students have the opportunity to use the Harvard Graduate School of Education's Monroe C. Gutman Library. Students who wish to borrow books may apply for a Special Borrower's Card for a fee of $15 per term. Cambridge

College maintains a collection of online research resources, which include ProQuest; ERIC, OCLC's FirstSearch, the Electric Library, and other online library catalogs; and online research resources available through the Internet and the World Wide Web. The College has two computer labs for classroom instruction and student use; these labs offer Internet and Web access.

The Christian A. Johnson Center for Learning and Assessment Services (CLAS) at Cambridge College reflects the College's commitment to respecting students' starting points, fostering development of academic and professional skills, and providing access to working adults from a wide range of backgrounds. The College's academic and advising services encourage students to clarify what they have learned in the past, articulate what they know now, and make a commitment to gaining the skills and knowledge they need for academic and career success.

Cambridge College students and graduates have access, through CLAS, to computer programs that allow users to assess their college-level skills in reading, writing, and math and to build skills in a self-directed environment. CLAS staff are available to assist students in using computer-based support.

Staffed by members of the College's writing faculty, the writing lab offers individual conferences to assist with writing projects in any course. Students sign up at their own initiative or are recommended by faculty members. The math lab supports learners who need help with math problems, assignments, or exams. CLAS also offers support services in English as a Second Language (ESL) as well as providing opportunities for supervised peer tutoring.

Costs

Courses in the Bachelor of Arts program are $250 per credit (1999–2000). Students earning credit through portfolio assessment are charged a fee of $100 per credit hour attempted. Students who wish to earn credit by successfully completing nationally standardized examinations and evaluations (for example, CLEP and DANTES exams) are charged a fee of $100 for each examination.

Cambridge College also charges a nonrefundable application fee of $30, a student services fee of $60 per term and a one-time degree confirmation fee of $50.

Financial Aid

Approximately 85 percent of undergraduate students receive some form of financial aid during the course of their work at Cambridge College. The College's Financial Aid Office offers a broad range of financial assistance, including low-interest loans, grants, scholarships, and work-study opportunities. Depending on their financial situation, income, and credit history, students may be eligible to receive federal assistance (including Federal Pell Grants, Federal Supplementary Educational Opportunity Grants, Federal Stafford Student Loans, and College work-study employment), Massachusetts state scholarships, and private scholarship funds.

Faculty

The student-to-faculty ratio of the Cambridge College Bachelor of Arts program is 17:1. The College has a full-time core faculty of 30, with approximately 120 part-time senior and adjunct faculty members; 82 percent hold terminal degrees.

Student Government

Interested students have the opportunity to participate in a Student Advisory Committee, which meets regularly to discuss issues of concern and to make recommendations to the College's faculty and administration.

Admission Requirements

Since its founding, Cambridge College has sought to provide academically excellent higher education to a diverse population of working adults. Students are admitted to the College on the basis of their understanding of their own educational and career goals, of their commitment to a course of study, and of the motivation demonstrated in their personal and professional lives. Three years of work experience are required. Applicants to Cambridge College are not required to submit results from standardized tests; instead, prospective students are asked to complete a set of assessments designed to demonstrate academic ability, commitment to succeeding scholastically and professionally, and capacity for clearly defining academic and career goals. Life and work experience are considered as an integral part of the admissions decision.

Application and Information

Students may enter Cambridge College in the fall, spring, or summer. For further information, students can contact:

Joy King
Associate Director, Enrollment Services
Bachelor of Arts Program
Cambridge College
1000 Massachusetts Avenue
Cambridge, Massachusetts 02138
Telephone: 800-877-4723 (toll-free)
Fax: 617-349-3561
World Wide Web: http://www.cambridge.edu

CAMPBELL UNIVERSITY
BUIES CREEK, NORTH CAROLINA

The University

Founded in 1887, Campbell University has had the distinction of being North Carolina's second-largest private undergraduate institution. Graduate programs were established, and in 1979 the name of the institution was changed from Campbell College to Campbell University. Its current enrollment is more than 7,800 students. In an average year, the student body comes from about ninety North Carolina counties, fifty states, and forty-six countries. Sixty-six percent of the students come from North Carolina.

Campbell University has established a law school and schools of business, pharmacy, education, and divinity and now awards the J.D., Pharm.D., M.Ed., M.A., M.B.A., M.S., and M.Div. degrees. These additions have increased interest in the general program of the undergraduate college. Completed projects include a $1.2-million classroom building, the Keith Hills housing development and golf course, an indoor swimming pool, a welcome center, and a $3.5-million fine arts complex. A $3.5-million addition to the Norman Adrian Wiggins School of Law, an addition to the Campbell University School of Pharmacy, and the 76,000-square-foot, $11-million Lundy Fetterman School of Business are the newest expansion projects that have been completed.

Campbell University is nonsectarian. Approximately 60 percent of its students are Baptist, but young people of twenty-two other faiths complete its student body. It is concerned with maintaining, for living and learning, an environment consistent with Christian ideals. Among the extracurricular activities available at Campbell are band, choir, and drama groups; religious, political, professional, social, and academic groups; and intercollegiate and intramural sports organizations.

In athletics, the University is a member of NCAA Division I (TAAC Conference) for men and for women (with the exception of wrestling, which is in the Colonial Conference). Men's sports include baseball, basketball, cross-country, golf, soccer, tennis, track, and wrestling. Women's sports include basketball, cheerleading, cross-country, golf, soccer, softball, tennis, track, and volleyball.

A number of activities are available on campus during the summer for junior and senior high school students. One is the nation's oldest summer basketball school. In 1999, about 765 boys were trained in two 1-week sessions, and about 224 girls attended a one-week session.

The University also has campuses offering a variety of undergraduate and graduate courses at Fort Bragg, Goldsboro, Pope Air Force Base, Raleigh, Rocky Mount, Jacksonville, and Morrisville, North Carolina, and in Kuala Lumpur, Malaysia.

Location

Buies Creek is a small, well-kept residential community surrounded by woods and farmland in Harnett County, where North Carolina's coastal plain and Piedmont meet just east of the center of the state. The region is one of the most progressive for education and research in the Southeast. Raleigh, the capital, and Fayetteville are 30 miles away from the campus; within about an hour's driving time are the Research Triangle Park and the city of Durham.

Majors and Degrees

Campbell University confers seven undergraduate degrees: Bachelor of Arts, Bachelor of Science, Bachelor of Applied Science, Bachelor of Business Administration, Bachelor of Health Science, and Bachelor of Social Work and an Associate in Arts degree. The major and/or the concentration may be in any one of the following fields: accounting, advertising, art, biochemistry, biological sciences, biology, broadcasting, business administration, chemistry, church drama, church music, church recreation, clinical research, computer information systems, computer science, drama, economics, elementary education, English, family studies, financial advisement, fitness/wellness management, French, general studies, golf management (PGA certified), government, health and physical education, history, home economics education, international business, international studies, mass communication, mathematics, middle grades education, music, music education, pharmaceutical science, print media/journalism, psychology, public administration, public relations, religion, secondary education, social science, social work, Spanish, sport management, and trust management.

Preprofessional programs are offered in dentistry, engineering, law, medicine, pharmacy, physical therapy, and veterinary medicine.

Academic Program

The curriculum of Campbell University is designed to meet individual needs and interests. During the first two years, students follow a general course of study, the General College Curriculum, to broaden their backgrounds in the basic fields of knowledge. By the end of the sophomore year, they should have selected a major subject for specialized study during the final two years. Basic curriculum requirements for the first two years in semester hours are English, 12; social studies, 6; natural science, 8; religion, 6; music, art appreciation, or drama, 3; foreign language, up to 9, depending on high school credits and the program of study; and health and physical education, 3. Candidates for a bachelor's degree must earn a minimum of 128 credits, including the 3 in health and physical education, while maintaining at least a C average in academic course work; must complete a minimum of 32 semester hours in the departmental major at Campbell; and must average C or better in all courses required for the major. Candidates for the Associate in Arts degree must complete 64 semester hours of work and have at least a 2.0 GPA on all work required for graduation and at least a 2.0 GPA on 80 percent of all work attempted. The University calendar enables students to complete first-semester course work and examinations before Christmas vacation and end the spring session by the middle of May.

Campbell offers a complete curriculum of evening courses on its main campus and at its nearby Fort Bragg campus. The Fort Bragg campus is primarily a service for military personnel on active duty, but classes are open to civilian students.

Campbell offers the nation's first undergraduate program in trust management and since 1968 has been training prospective trust officers for the banks and trust companies of the region. Campbell also sponsors the Southeastern Trust School, a summer institute for trust officers.

Academic programs continue to expand at Campbell University. The charter class entered Campbell's School of Pharmacy in 1986. The school helps serve the health-care needs of North Carolina and beyond. Campbell's School of Education was formally established in 1985 in response to the need for fully qualified educators for the educational system of North Carolina and the country. The University licensure passage rate for 1999 was 96.9 percent.

The Military Science Department offers Army ROTC programs for men and women, leading to commissions as officers in the active Army, Army Reserve, or Army National Guard. In 1989 the Campbell ROTC won the Founder's Award and the Governor's Award as the best detachment in ROTC Region I. In 1999, the unit was rated as the "Best ROTC in the Country." In 1995, an Army ROTC Campbell graduate received the Hughes Trophy.

Off-Campus Arrangements

Credit may be earned in off-campus settings through apprenticeships or internships in communications, government, public education, religious education, psychology, social work, and trust management. Campbell's philosophy on internships is departmental based. Departmental inquiries are welcomed. Other study-abroad opportunities allow students to study in France, Mexico, or Spain.

Academic Facilities

The newly opened Lundy Fetterman School of Business provides 76,000 square feet of state-of-the-art technology for educational enhancement. The Leslie H. Campbell Hall of Science provides the individual student with facilities for research projects, which the University encourages in four sciences. Campbell's own computer center (with an IBM System/36 and IBM Personal Computers) is supplemented by twenty departmental computer labs. It is linked with the Triangle Universities Computation Center of the North Carolina Educational Computer Service. Campbell's Carrie Rich Library houses a collection of more than 210,000 volumes. The D. Rich Memorial Building, housing Turner Auditorium, and the four-story Fred L. Taylor Hall of Religion contain classrooms, laboratories, and faculty offices. The Taylor Bott Rogers Fine Arts Complex, containing 48,820 square feet of space, is well equipped for the wide range of events staged by active music, drama, and art groups. The closed-circuit television equipment of the school's audiovisual center enhances teacher training.

Costs

The estimated 2000–01 comprehensive fee for tuition and general fees is $11,000. On-campus students are provided with board and room at a minimum of $4000.

Financial Aid

Campbell University has private and institutional scholarships, federal grants, loans, and Federal Work-Study Program awards. Loans are available through the Federal Stafford Student Loan Program and the Federal Perkins Loan Program. Needs analysis forms (Free Application for Federal Student Aid) are available January 1 and are due in the Financial Aid Office by March 15 if the applicant wishes to be considered for a maximum award. Ninety-one percent of the student body received financial assistance in 1999–2000. All assistance is offered without regard to race, creed, or national origin.

Faculty

The faculty consists of 439 teachers, of whom approximately 91 percent have earned the doctorate or have completed three years beyond the bachelor's degree. The faculty-student ratio is approximately 1:18. Ninety-seven percent of classes have less than 50 students.

Student Government

Through the Student Government Association (SGA), the student body has an opportunity for self-government and a means to channel ideas and wishes to the proper administrative personnel. The SGA is composed of executive, judicial, and legislative branches. The executive officers are the president, vice president, secretary, treasurer, public relations officer, parliamentarian, executive officer of the Disciplinary Committee, and the presidents of the women's campus, the men's campus, and the day students. The legislative branch includes the Student Congress, made up of representatives from each of the four classes elected by popular vote.

Admission Requirements

The minimum requirements for admission to Campbell include graduation from high school, or equivalent credentials, with at least 12 nonvocational units which must include 4 in English, 3 in mathematics, 2 in science, and 2 in history. Two units of a foreign language are highly desirable. Acceptable scores must be earned on the SAT I or on the ACT.

Application and Information

An application for admission, accompanied by a $15 nonrefundable application fee, must be filed. Students may also apply on line at the e-mail address below. When all records are on file, the Admissions Committee notifies the student of its decision. Application forms and further information may be requested from:

Office of Admissions
Campbell University
P.O. Box 546
Buies Creek, North Carolina 27506

Telephone: 910-893-1320
           910-893-1415 (international)
           800-334-4111 (toll-free)
E-mail: adm@mailcenter.campbell.edu
World Wide Web: http://www.campbell.edu/

Students on the Mall in front of D. Rich Memorial Hall on the "Academic Circle".

CANISIUS COLLEGE
BUFFALO, NEW YORK

The College

Established in 1870 as a liberal arts college, Canisius is one of twenty-eight colleges and universities in the United States that carry on the four-centuries-old Jesuit tradition of higher education. Canisius comprises the College of Arts and Sciences, the Richard J. Wehle School of Business, and the School of Education and Human Services. Of the 4,598 students, 2,804 are enrolled as undergraduates. The student body is divided almost equally between men and women.

The College attracts students from thirty-four states, two territories, Washington, D.C., and thirty-two countries. Most students give as their reasons for coming to Canisius both the solid academic reputation and the personal attention for which the College is justifiably well known.

Canisius College welcomes international students and appreciates the cultural diversity they bring to the College. The international students come from Canada, Europe, and places as far away as Japan, India, and nations in the Middle East. The director of international student programs is available to advise international students and assist them with their adjustment to Canisius and to American culture. Services include an extensive orientation for new students, assistance with immigration regulations, and special tutorial help in English. A summer ESL program is currently available.

Students are encouraged to participate in the many academic, cultural, fraternal, social, and service-oriented organizations and activities of the College. Canisius is a member of the Metro Atlantic Athletic Conference and the National Collegiate Athletic Association. Intercollegiate sports offered are baseball, basketball, cross-country, football, golf, hockey, lacrosse, riflery, soccer, softball, swimming, synchronized swimming, tennis, track, and volleyball. Crew, Rugby, and bowling are offered as club sports. Students, faculty members, and staff may also participate in a variety of intramural activities that include basketball, flag football, floor hockey, indoor soccer, racquetball, softball, tennis, volleyball (coed), and many other sports.

Canisius offers a variety of student housing that ranges from residence halls to apartments, town houses, and College-owned homes.

Location

Canisius College is located in Buffalo, New York State's second-largest city. The campus covers more than 26 acres on Main Street. This location, only minutes away from the center of the city, provides easy access to all parts of the metropolitan area. Buffalo's Metro Rail runs adjacent to the campus and, used in conjunction with the Metro Bus transit system, enables students to go anywhere in the city and suburbs.

The metropolitan area of just over 1.4 million people offers varied athletic, cultural, and entertainment facilities. For sports fans, there are the Buffalo Bills of the National Football League ('90, '91, '92, '93, and '95 AFC champions), the Buffalo Sabres of the National Hockey League, and the Buffalo Bisons (AAA baseball) of the American Association. For the downhill skier, some of the finest skiing in the East on more than twenty slopes is just a 45-minute drive away. Cross-country enthusiasts find trails suitable for everyone from novice to expert. Delaware Park, a 350-acre park with a lake and golf course, and the impressive Buffalo Zoo are adjacent to the campus. For those interested in absorbing culture, the internationally known Albright-Knox Art Gallery holds one of the world's finest collections of nineteenth- and twentieth-century American and European works of art. The city is home to the Buffalo Philharmonic Orchestra. Artpark, a 200-acre state park, offers professional visual and performing arts programs in an open-air environment. Studio Arena Theatre makes available a wide variety of theater experiences, from musicals to classics, new plays, and contemporary American works. The central location of the College also provides many opportunities for students interested in community service, internships, and employment.

Majors and Degrees

The College of Arts and Sciences offers programs of study leading to the Bachelor of Arts degree in art history, biochemistry, communication studies, computer science, criminal justice, economics, English, European studies, history, international relations, mathematics and statistics, modern languages (French, German, and Spanish), philosophy, political science, psychology, religious studies, sociology and anthropology, and urban studies/public administration. The Bachelor of Science degree is awarded in biology, chemistry, clinical laboratory science, computer science, environmental science, and physics.

The Richard J. Wehle School of Business offers programs of study leading to the Bachelor of Science degree in accounting, economics, entrepreneurship, finance, hotel management, management, management computer information systems, and marketing.

The School of Education and Human Services offers degrees in athletic training, elementary/early secondary education, physical education, secondary education, and special education.

Canisius also offers programs in fashion merchandising (in conjunction with the Fashion Institute of Technology), fine arts, and military science and certification programs in gerontology, international business, and women's studies. Preprofessional programs are available in dentistry, engineering, environmental science and forestry (in conjunction with the State University of New York (SUNY) College of Environmental Science and Forestry at Syracuse), law, medicine, and veterinary medicine. An early notification of acceptance agreement exists, for state (New York) residents only, between Canisius and the Schools of Medicine and Dental Medicine of SUNY at Buffalo, SUNY Medical School at Syracuse, and SUNY College of Optometry in New York City. Seven-year joint-degree programs exist between Canisius and the SUNY Buffalo School of Dental Medicine, the Ohio College of Podiatric Medicine, the New York College of Podiatric Medicine, and the SUNY College of Optometry. A five-year combined-degree program leads to the B.A. in a major in one of the liberal arts disciplines and a Master of Business Administration degree.

Academic Program

To earn a bachelor's degree from Canisius College, students must complete forty courses and a minimum of 120 credit hours. Within each curriculum, the courses are distributed into three areas: the core curriculum, major field requirements, and free electives. In keeping with its liberal arts ideals and objectives, the College requires that students complete a rounded program of humanistic studies embracing literature, the physical and social sciences, oral and written communication, philosophy, history, religious studies, and language.

An honors program is available for qualified students. The program includes rigorous and intensive exploration of the arts and sciences in an enriched curriculum with close faculty supervision and small classes.

Students may obtain college credit through the Advanced Placement Program of the College Board. Students with scores of 4 or better on Advanced Placement tests are considered for credit and advanced standing.

Off-Campus Arrangements

In cooperation with other U.S. colleges and universities, Canisius arranges, on an individual basis, for students to spend a semester or a year studying in various countries overseas. Popular choices include Australia, England, France, Germany, Italy, and Spain. Canisius College has its own semester-abroad program in Oviedo, Spain, which offers students the option of a nonpaid internship teaching English in a Spanish school or doing a field placement in psychology. Canisius also has its own semester program in London, England, which includes a one-week seminar taught by a Canisius professor who escorts the group to England. There are also programs in Dortmund, Germany; Beijing, China; Galway, Ireland; Lille, France; Tokyo, Japan; and Morelia, Mexico. The Department of Modern Languages also makes provisions for linguistically qualified students to engage in volunteer service or work/internship programs overseas. The Office of International Student Programs assists students in selecting a study-abroad program, organizes a predeparture orientation, and assists students upon their return to the United States.

Students majoring in international relations and political science may participate in programs in Washington, D.C., or Albany, New York, that have been designed to give students practical experience in their field.

Academic Facilities

The stunning 96,000-square-foot Andrew L. Bouwhuis Library was renovated and expanded in 1988. It houses more than 800,000 books, periodicals, microforms, and other materials. The library also provides online database searching and has a number of computerized reference tools on CD-ROMs.

Instructional computing facilities include 154 personal computers located in student computer laboratories. Macintosh and IBM-compatible personal computers are equipped with color monitors, laser printers, and word processing, electronic mail, and spreadsheet software. All students may use the Macintosh and IBM-compatible computers once they have obtained an account. Students with accounts may use electronic mail to communicate with other members of the Canisius community. Computer users may also communicate with others off campus through the Internet. In addition, several departments maintain a substantial complement of computing equipment for their students.

Students housed in the new Village Townhouses and in Bosch and Frisch Hall may use computer network connections that are available in their rooms. These resident students also have access to voice mail and television that includes several Canisius-originated channels. These residence halls also have 24-hour computer labs.

Costs

For the academic year 1999–2000, tuition was $15,160, room and board were $6340, and fees were $388. Books and supplies are estimated to cost $450. An additional $1130 per year is recommended for travel and personal expenses.

Financial Aid

Of the class of 2003, 95 percent receive some form of financial aid and the average award is $12,948. This aid includes Canisius College scholarships and grants, state grants, state and federal loans, federal grants, and Federal Work-Study awards. Application for financial aid should be completed by January 31. The Free Application for Federal Student Aid (FAFSA) and the TAP application (New York State residents only) must be filed before consideration can be given to applicants. Financial aid is not available to international students.

Faculty

The Canisius College faculty numbers 200 full-time teachers, including Jesuits and lay men and women; more than 88 percent hold doctorates or other terminal degrees. The primary emphasis of the faculty members is teaching, and many also serve as academic advisers. The student-faculty ratio is 18:1.

Student Government

The Undergraduate Student Association comprises the entire undergraduate student body and is represented by elected officers who serve on the Student Senate. The purpose of the senate is to assist and supervise the student activities and to represent the views of the student body to the College administration. In addition, students serve on many College committees.

Admission Requirements

Canisius College welcomes applications from all qualified students without regard to race, creed, color, sex, handicap, or national and ethnic origin. Their acceptability as students is judged by the Committee on Admissions and is based on a combination of factors, including a student's academic ability, strength of character, high school record, rank in class, an essay, aptitude tests (SAT I or ACT), extracurricular activities, and recommendations. An applicant to the College is encouraged to pursue a challenging college-preparatory program in high school. This program of studies should include 16 units of credit in the academic subjects of English, foreign language, mathematics, science, and social studies. Recommendations from teachers or guidance counselors are not required but are encouraged, and they are considered in reviewing applications for admission. Campus interviews are strongly recommended and in some cases may be required.

Transfer students are welcome and are admitted to Canisius in the fall and spring semesters. In addition to meeting the academic standards required of all entering students, transfer students are considered for admission if they have a minimum 2.0 cumulative quality point average when transferring from either a two-year or a four-year accredited institution.

Application and Information

Students are encouraged to submit their applications for admission in the fall of their senior year in high school. The completed application form should be presented to the high school guidance counselor, to be forwarded to the director of admissions with an official high school transcript and any letters of recommendation. Applicants must see that SAT I or ACT scores are sent to the College. Arrangements for interviews may be made by contacting the Office of Admissions at least one week in advance of the desired date for a visit.

Canisius considers applications under a rolling admission policy, beginning December 1. Applicants are notified of the admission decision six to eight weeks after their application has been received.

For application forms and additional information, students should contact:

Jaimie L. Taylor
Canisius College
2001 Main Street
Buffalo, New York 14208
Telephone: 716-888-2200
           800-843-1517 (toll-free)
Fax: 716-888-2377
World Wide Web: http://www.canisius.edu
E-mail: inquiry@gort.canisius.edu

Canisius College is the ideal size for each individual to be an important part of campus life.

CAPITAL UNIVERSITY
COLUMBUS, OHIO

The University

Since its founding in 1830 by the Lutheran Church, Capital has earned a reputation for academic excellence and affordability, an accomplishment that has repeatedly garnered the University a place in *Barron's 300: Best Buys in College Education*. The University's undergraduate and graduate programs are preparing students for lifelong learning in the global environment of the twenty-first century. Students of all backgrounds and religions benefit from Capital's quality liberal arts education that is coupled with professional training. Students also benefit from the attention faculty and staff members pay to their moral, social, and ethical development. Students at Capital are part of the "CAP family," a family that cares about the total growth and well-being of each of its members.

Capital University is composed of three undergraduate colleges—the College of Arts and Sciences, Conservatory of Music, and School of Nursing—and two graduate schools—the Law School and Graduate School of Administration (M.B.A. Program). In addition, the School of Nursing offers the Master of Science in Nursing degree. There is also an Adult Degree Program available in Columbus, Cleveland, and Dayton. Capital offers six undergraduate degrees and six graduate degrees, with more than forty majors and thirty-six minors. Of the approximately 4,000 students enrolled at Capital, almost 1,800 are traditional undergraduates. Approximately 65 percent of these students reside on campus in the University's four residence halls and apartment-style housing for upperclass students.

There are more than sixty student organizations, including a number of musical groups that are open to music and nonmusic majors alike. Other opportunities for involvement include student government, theater, the student newspaper and literary magazine, and the debate team. Numerous opportunities for volunteerism and service projects also exist. Approximately 20 percent of Capital's undergraduates are members of the nine social fraternities and sororities on campus.

Varsity and intramural athletics are offered for men and women. The eight varsity sports for men are baseball, basketball, cross-country, football, golf, soccer, tennis, and wrestling. Women's varsity sports are basketball, cross-country, golf, soccer, softball, tennis, and volleyball. Capital's sports teams are sanctioned by the National Collegiate Athletic Association Division III, and the University is a member of the Ohio Athletic Conference. Intramural sports are also a big part of campus life. In addition, Capital's fitness rooms and activities such as aerobics provide options for students who want to develop their own individual fitness programs.

As a university affiliated with the Lutheran Church, Capital believes that the religious, social, racial, and ethnic diversity found on campus enhances each student's development. In this spirit, worship and study opportunities are offered in a cooperative, ecumenical way.

Location

Capital is located in the Columbus suburb of Bexley. Bexley is primarily a residential community with a number of small shops and restaurants. Downtown Columbus is just 4 miles from campus and easily reached by city buses. As part of a major metropolitan area, Columbus offers a wide variety of social and cultural opportunities. Students can enjoy performances by the Columbus Symphony Orchestra, BalletMet, Opera Columbus, or the Columbus Jazz Orchestra, or they may visit the more than fifty art galleries in the area. There is also an expansive network of parks and recreation facilities, bike trails, and the Columbus Zoo. Many of the city's attractions are free or offer substantial student discounts. In addition, as Ohio's capital and largest city, Columbus is the home of many national and international corporations. These companies offer Capital students unlimited opportunities for internships and employment after graduation.

Majors and Degrees

Capital University offers the Bachelor of Arts degree in art, art therapy, biology, business (accounting, economics, and management), chemistry (major approved by the American Chemical Society), communication, computer science, criminology, economics, education, educational theater, English (literature and professional writing), environmental science, health and fitness management, health education, history, international studies, mathematics, modern languages (French and Spanish), organizational communication, philosophy, physical education, political science, psychology, public relations, radio-television, religion, social work, sociology, and sports medicine/athletic training. Students may also design a multidisciplinary major.

Capital also offers the Bachelor of Fine Arts, Bachelor of General Studies, Bachelor of Science in Nursing (approved by the National League for Nursing Accrediting Commission), and Bachelor of Social Work (approved by the Council on Social Work Education). For music students, Capital offers a Bachelor of Music in jazz studies, keyboard pedagogy (church music, organ, and piano), music education (vocal and instrumental), music industry, music media, music merchandising, music theater, performance (instrumental, organ, piano, and vocal) and composition. The Bachelor of Arts in music is also offered.

A program in engineering, which leads to dual degrees, is offered in cooperation with Washington University in St. Louis and Case Western Reserve University in Cleveland. A similar dual-degree program in pre–occupational therapy is also offered in conjunction with Washington University and the University of Indianapolis.

Academic Program

The academic year consists of two semesters, the first of which begins in late August and ends in December. The second semester begins in early January and ends in early May. Summer classes are available.

For graduation, the College of Arts and Sciences requires the completion of a minimum of 124 semester hours; the School of Nursing requires the completion of 134 semester hours; and, depending on the major, the Conservatory of Music requires the completion of between 124 and 136 semester hours.

In addition to taking courses related to their field of study, all undergraduate students take courses that fulfill a set of general education goals and bring together the University's academic, scientific, religious, and artistic disciplines.

Learning is not confined to the classroom at Capital. All undergraduate students, regardless of their major, may participate in an internship that allows them to apply newly learned skills to on-the-job situations.

Faculty advisers help students select a major, choose appropriate classes, and suggest career options. In addition, staff members in Capital's Career Services Office help students plan careers, provide instruction in resume writing and interviewing, and share information about graduate schools. On-campus recruiting sessions and a job referral service also enhance employment opportunities. In recent years, more than 95 percent of Capital's graduates who used the office's resources found employment or entered graduate school within six months of graduation.

Off-Campus Arrangements

At Capital, one way students learn more about other cultures and countries is through international study.

Capital is the only school in the country that offers a semester of undergraduate study at the Zoltán Kodály Pedagogical Institute of Music in Hungary for students in the Conservatory of Music.

In addition, Capital's Office of International Education offers overseas study opportunities in countries around the world, including France, Germany, Israel, Tanzania, Spain, Ecuador, China, and the Netherlands.

Closer to home, students may participate in a semester internship in one of nearly 500 agencies in the nation's capital through an arrangement with the Washington Center. In addition, cross-registration for enrolled students is available with Columbus College of Art and Design, Columbus State Community College, Ohio Dominican College, The Ohio State University, and Otterbein College.

Academic Facilities

Capital's campus consists of twenty-four buildings, including the Conservatory of Music facilities, which underwent a $6.4-million renovation. Through CAPNet, Capital's campus-wide voice, data, and video network, every residence hall room, classroom, and office is connected to the Internet and the World Wide Web. And, through the library's connection to OhioLINK, students have access to more than 10 million items held by fifty libraries throughout the state. Information Technology provides a television studio and computer labs for student use. The Advanced Computational Laboratory includes an extensive array of computer hardware that allows students to access an extensive collection of scientific software and to simulate a parallel computing environment. A newly created state-of-the-art technology classroom enhances teaching and learning. Nursing students may also use the microcomputers and instructional software contained in the School of Nursing's Helene Fuld Health Trust Learning Resources Laboratory. For the art lover, Chagall, Picasso, and Warhol are as close as Capital's library, which houses the University's Schumacher Gallery and its 2,000-piece collection.

Costs

In 1999–2000, tuition and fees were $16,000. Room and board fees were $4900.

Financial Aid

Approximately 95 percent of Capital's undergraduate students receive some form of financial assistance. To apply, a student must file the Free Application for Federal Student Aid (FAFSA).

University Scholarships of up to $9000 and Challenge Grants of up to $4500 are awarded to incoming freshmen and transfer students on the basis of academic achievement (and standardized test scores for freshmen). Full-tuition scholarships (Collegiate Fellowships) are awarded to incoming freshmen based on academic achievement and an on-campus competition. Music scholarships and participation awards are granted based on music ability as demonstrated during an audition.

Faculty

The University has 194 full- and part-time faculty members for its undergraduate programs. Student-faculty ratios are 16:1 in the College of Arts and Sciences, 4:1 in the Conservatory of Music, and 8:1 in the School of Nursing.

Student Government

There is an active and influential student government on the Capital campus. Students are elected in campuswide elections each spring. Through this organization, students have the opportunity to gain leadership experiences.

Admission Requirements

Capital University admits qualified students regardless of race, color, religion, gender, age, disability, or national or ethnic origin to all the rights, privileges, programs, and activities generally accorded or made available to the students at the University.

To be considered for admission to any of the undergraduate programs, students must submit copies of their high school transcript, ACT or SAT I scores, and a counselor recommendation. Applicants to the Conservatory of Music must also arrange for an audition, either in person or by videotape. Scores on Advanced Placement tests and College-Level Examination Program subject examinations are accepted as additional indicators of an applicant's ability, and course credit may be awarded for satisfactory scores on these examinations.

Campus visits are encouraged. Arrangements for a tour of the campus and an interview, class visits, and appointments with professors may be made through the Admission Office. When an admission representative visits high schools, interested students in the area are notified and encouraged to meet with the representative.

Transfer applicants must be in good social and academic standing and have a minimum grade point average of 2.25 at the institutions they attended previously.

International applicants must submit official secondary school transcripts and photocopies of school leaving certificates, TOEFL scores, SAT I scores if available, and recommendation letters from a guidance counselor or headmaster and from a teacher.

Application and Information

Applications for admission may be submitted starting September 1 for the following year. Applicants are notified of their status as soon as their application is complete. The priority application deadline for the fall semester is April 15. Applications received after April 15 are reviewed on a space-available basis.

For additional information, the student should contact:

Director of Admission
Capital University
2199 East Main Street
Columbus, Ohio 43209-2394
Telephone: 614-236-6101
         800-289-6289 (toll-free)
Fax: 614-236-6926
E-mail: admissions@capital.edu
World Wide Web: http://www.capital.edu

Capital's campus, located in a residential neighborhood, provides an excellent atmosphere for students.

CAPITOL COLLEGE
LAUREL, MARYLAND

The College

Capitol is a private coeducational college that provides practical educational experiences that enable graduates to advance, manage, and communicate changes in the information age. Chartered in 1964, Capitol College offers degree programs in engineering, engineering technology, and information technology. The student body is composed of 519 men and 115 women who come from sixteen states and twenty-one countries. Capitol College is accredited by the Middle States Association of Colleges and Schools. The electrical engineering and all engineering technology programs are accredited by the Technology and Engineering Accreditation Commissions of the Accreditation Board for Engineering and Technology, Inc. (TAC/ABET, EAC/ABET).

Capitol sponsors a variety of extracurricular activities based on student participation and demand. Basketball and soccer are offered on an intercollegiate level, while basketball, flag football, soccer, and softball are offered on an intramural level. The Web Design Club and the student branch of the Institute of Electrical and Electronics Engineers (IEEE) provide professional and social development for their members. Student chapters of the Society of Women Engineers (SWE) and the National Society of Black Engineers (NSBE) promote educational and social growth through sponsored trips, guest speakers, and social activities. The Office of Student Development also plans trips and activities throughout the year. Scholarship and academic achievement are recognized through the Alpha Chi, Tau Alpha Pi, and Eta Kappa Nu national honor societies on campus.

Career development is an integral aspect of the College's mission, and graduates are in great demand by business and industry. Capitol is so certain of the quality of its programs and the market trend for high-technology employees that the College guarantees qualified B.S. degree candidates a job in their field at a nationally competitive salary within ninety days of commencement. For the past twenty-five years, 95 percent of Capitol College graduates have been offered full-time jobs in their fields of study or have chosen to continue on to graduate school within ninety days of graduation. The College's Cooperative Education Program arranges for paid work experience in jobs related to the student's major prior to graduation. Once hired, a student may work full- or part-time to supplement their academic program.

Capitol College's apartment-style residence facilities for men and women provide individual- and double-room accommodations. Students who live in the residence halls have access to complete kitchen facilities in each apartment plus Internet access via a T1 line and standard cable included in the room fee.

Location

Capitol College's 52-acre campus is located in Laurel, Maryland, halfway between Baltimore, Maryland, and Washington, D.C. The Baltimore/Washington metropolitan area is one of the fastest-growing technology markets in the United States. The campus is close to many high-technology corporations and a host of educational, cultural, and recreational attractions. The Smithsonian museums, the Library of Congress, the Kennedy Center for Performing Arts, the MCI Center, FedEx Field, Baltimore's Inner Harbor, the Maryland Science Center, and Oriole Park at Camden Yards are just a few of the sites that are a short drive or Metro ride away.

Majors and Degrees

Capitol College awards Bachelor of Science (B.S.) degrees in computer engineering, electrical engineering, software and Internet applications, and management of information technology. Capitol offers both the Associate in Applied Science (A.A.S.) degree and the B.S. degree in computer engineering technology, electronics engineering technology, telecommunications engineering technology, and management of telecommunications. Capitol also offers MCSE and A+ certifications.

Academic Program

Each department has its own sequence requirements for graduation. To earn a bachelor's degree, students must complete between 123 and 137 semester credit hours. To earn an associate degree, students must complete between 64 and 67 credits. Each degree program includes a core of courses in addition to classes within the major. The core curriculum consists of studies in humanities, mathematics, physical sciences, and social sciences. The average course load is 15 credits per semester.

Advanced standing can be earned through Advanced Placement (AP) and College-Level Examination Program (CLEP) tests. Credits can also be earned through institutional validation examinations.

At Capitol College, learning is centered both in and out of the classroom. Professors are available on a one-on-one basis, and tutors and lab aides are available for additional assistance. In the engineering and technology curricula, students reinforce their classroom lectures with assigned laboratory projects.

Academic Facilities

The campus is small in size but big in technological resources. Capitol College's Student Center, administrative offices, and classrooms are located in M/A-COM, MCI, and Telecommunications Halls. Also located in these buildings are Capitol's state-of-the-art laboratories. From electronics and computers to telecommunications and networking, Capitol stays abreast of the ever-changing trends in high technology.

Recently donated and wired by Bell Atlantic–Maryland, the Capitol Video Lab is a multimedia classroom equipped with eight televisions, three video cameras, a touch-screen control panel with a computer, twelve tables with microphones, a VCR, and a SoftBoard Digital blackboard. Courses can be transmitted to other schools that are connected to the Bell Atlantic Video Network.

The John G. and Beverly A. Puente Library provides students with 100 monthly periodicals, nearly 10,000 volumes no older than five years old, more than twenty-five computer workstations, and a multimedia center with scanner and printer available for student use. The library is also home to the William G. McGowan Center for Innovative Teaching, a multimedia classroom with a network of fifteen interactive computer stations.

Alongside Telecommunications Hall is the Avrum Gudelsky Memorial Auditorium where Capitol hosts commencement and convocation. The auditorium is also used for special events such as educational seminars and student activities.

Costs

For the 1999–2000 academic year, tuition for all degree programs was $11,808. Residential costs ranged from $3000 to

$4000. Capitol has implemented a tuition lock for incoming students that guarantees the tuition initially agreed upon for up to five years, provided that the student remains enrolled full-time and keeps all accounts current with the business office.

Financial Aid

Capitol College maintains an extensive program of financial aid to assist students in financing their education. Aid is available in the form of loans, grants, scholarships, and employment programs. Awards are based on financial need and/or academic ability. All students who wish to apply for aid must submit the Free Application for Federal Student Aid (FAFSA). Students are encouraged to contact the Director of Financial Aid at the College for assistance or for information about institutional scholarships.

Faculty

Teaching at Capitol College demands a focus on the student. The major concern is to challenge yet give students every opportunity to succeed in their programs. Capitol currently has 20 full-time and 32 part-time faculty members, who have amassed extensive teaching credentials and industry experience. Full-time faculty members not only teach but also serve as academic advisers to assist students with planning their programs of study and achieving their academic goals.

Capitol College maintains a student-faculty ratio of 18:1. Individual attention and instruction are key elements of the academic program. Students are constantly encouraged to reach for their potential.

Student Government

Capitol Student Council plays an active role in both the academic and the social activities of the College. It is responsible for ensuring that an effective channel of communication remains open between students, the faculty, and the administration. Representatives of the student body are elected annually.

Admission Requirements

Admission to Capitol is based on educational preparation and the personal abilities necessary for academic success. Applicants must present evidence of having completed a high school course of study or its equivalent. Applicants to the technology programs must have 4 years of English, 3 years of mathematics (through at least algebra II), 2 years of a laboratory science, and 2 years of social sciences. Engineering majors must have a fourth year of math to prepare for college calculus and a third year of science. A foreign language is not a requirement for admission. Results of the SAT I or ACT are required of first-time freshmen. International applicants must submit scores on the Test of English as a Foreign Language (TOEFL). Transfer students must present transcripts of all postsecondary work.

Some applicants may be required to meet with the Admissions Committee. An admissions interview is strongly recommended for all applicants.

Application and Information

An application is considered when the student's file is complete, including a $25 application fee, the required test scores, and transcripts from each school attended. Application forms are available from the Office of Admissions or may be completed on line. Capitol College maintains a rolling admission policy, and applicants are notified of the admission decision within one month of the completion of their file. To receive full consideration for financial aid and housing for the fall semester, students are encouraged to apply by March 1.

For more information, students should contact:

Office of Admissions
Capitol College
11301 Springfield Road
Laurel, Maryland 20708
Telephone: 301-953-3200 (from Washington, D.C.)
           410-792-8800 (from Baltimore)
           800-950-1992 (toll-free outside the Baltimore–
              Washington, D.C., area)
E-mail: admissions@capitol-college.edu
World Wide Web: http://www.capitol-college.edu

MCI and M/A-COM Halls.

CARDINAL STRITCH UNIVERSITY
MILWAUKEE, WISCONSIN

The University

Cardinal Stritch University is a comprehensive, coeducational institution rooted in the liberal arts and established in the Catholic tradition. Since its founding in 1937 by the Sisters of St. Francis of Assisi, Stritch has emerged as the largest Franciscan institution of higher education in North America and the second-largest private university in Wisconsin.

With a total population of 5,300 students on three campuses, Stritch's size can be deceiving. While the University provides all of the resources associated with large universities, it still offers the benefits of personal attention and one-on-one instruction associated with smaller institutions. The University is well prepared for the twenty-first century yet committed to maintaining the high-quality, values-centered education that has defined Stritch's history and continues to attract its diverse student body. At Stritch, a student-faculty ratio of 17:1 allows students easy access to faculty members who give students the personal attention needed to realize their full potential. More than thirty undergraduate and sixteen graduate degree programs are offered within the Colleges of Arts and Sciences, Education, Nursing, and Business and Management. Students can major in one area of concentration or can create a double major or minor to fit specific career and educational goals. After graduation, students can continue to develop their expertise in any of Stritch's graduate programs. The University offers master's degrees in reading/language arts, reading learning disability, religious studies, special education, educational computing, English as a second language, ministry, professional development, computer science education, educational leadership, management, business administration, business administration for health-care professionals, clinical psychology, financial services, and nursing. All of the programs offered through the College of Business and Management and many of the programs offered through the College of Education are geared toward working adults, offering evening courses both on and off campus at an accelerated pace. The master's degree program in the College of Nursing provides innovative and accessible educational opportunities for working nursing professionals who wish to advance their careers as nurse educators in a variety of client communities. The University also offers a doctorate in leadership for the advancement of learning and service in an accelerated weekend/evening format.

With more than thirty student clubs and organizations and ten athletic teams, students discover social, cultural, and professional opportunities beyond the classroom. A member of NAIA Division II, Chicagoland Collegiate Athletic Conference, Cardinal Stritch University offers baseball, basketball, cross-country, soccer, and volleyball for men and basketball, cross-country, soccer, softball, and volleyball for women. Stritch athletes have a distinguished reputation for balancing their athletic and academic skills and have represented the University at the district, regional, and national levels. Service to the community and the world is an essential part of a Stritch education. Whether students are helping to build a house for Habitat for Humanity or leading health lessons in Tanzania, they are active in the social solutions that will ensure a better future.

The main campus, built in the early 1960s, houses a three-story residence hall, which is connected to several academic buildings and allows residents easy and climate-controlled access to many of the University's modern facilities. The student union, field house, bookstore, and auditorium are anchored by the Alfred S. Kliebhan Great Hall, where students study, visit with friends, or simply relax. Serra Dining Hall provides buffet-style meals with numerous menu selections. The chapel facilitates group worship at regular services and opportunities for personal reflection and individual prayer.

Location

Cardinal Stritch University's 40-acre, parklike main campus is situated in a quiet suburban neighborhood just north of Milwaukee. Downtown Milwaukee is a short, 15-minute drive from campus, while access to Lake Michigan is available within several blocks. The campus is conveniently accessible from Interstate 43, which offers a direct, easy route to Mitchell International Airport, the downtown Amtrak train station, and the Greyhound bus depot. The Milwaukee County Transit System provides students with a public transportation option when they are involved in off-campus pursuits. Interstate 43 also is a link to the excitement of downtown, which is home to numerous ethnic and American restaurants, specialty retailers, a downtown mall, the Milwaukee Art Museum, the Milwaukee Public Museum, several conference and performance centers, and various professional theater groups. Sports fans have the opportunity to cheer on the Brewers, Bucks, Waves, Admirals, Rampage, and Mustangs. In the summer and fall, Milwaukee becomes the "City of Festivals" and is host to approximately a dozen lakefront festivals, including Summerfest, which is the largest music festival in the world.

Majors and Degrees

Whether enrolled in the College of Arts and Sciences, Education, Nursing, or Business and Management, students find high-quality academic programs rooted in the liberal arts and designed to fully prepare them for the twenty-first century. The College of Arts and Sciences offers Associate of Arts degrees in art, general studies, and women's studies and bachelor's degree programs (majors and minors) in accounting, art, biology, business, chemistry, communication, computer studies, English, French, graphic design, history, international business, management information systems/business, mathematics, music, philosophy, photography, political science, preprofessional programs, psychology, public relations, religious studies, social studies, sociology, Spanish, theater, and writing.

The College of Education offers a Bachelor of Arts in education (secondary) and a Bachelor of Science in elementary education.

The College of Business and Management offers undergraduate degree programs exclusively designed to meet the special needs of working adults at on- and off-campus locations. Certificate programs and associate and bachelor's degrees are available.

The College of Nursing offers certificate programs as well as associate and bachelor's degrees.

Academic Program

The University strives to help students develop skills needed for a successful career as well as a personal code of ethics by which to live. Each degree program is based upon a foundation of liberal arts courses combined with a concentration in a major area of study. Courses in the general areas of communication, humanities, social and behavioral sciences, mathematics, and the natural sciences are common to all of the programs. The Associate of Arts degree is granted upon completion of 64 credits. The Associate of Science degree in nursing is granted upon completion of 70 credits, and the Associate of Science degree in business requires completion of 64 credits. The Bachelor of Arts degree and the Bachelor of Fine Arts degree require 128 credits, as do the Bachelor of Science degrees in business administration and management. The Bachelor of Science in Nursing degree requires 129 credits.

The dual-advising system for the undergraduate degree programs in the College of Arts and Sciences guarantees that students will graduate in four years. Students work closely with a faculty adviser from the start of their Stritch education to determine required courses and electives. Advisers in the Academic Advising Center help students make their liberal arts core and elective course selections.

Off-Campus Arrangements

Opportunities to study abroad are available. Stritch students have studied in or traveled to such countries as England, Italy, India, Mexico, and Spain as well as the continents of Africa and Australia.

Academic Facilities

An exceptional resource, the state-of-the-art library is easily accessible and contains a wealth of information necessary to complete in-depth research. Staffed by professional librarians, the library's holdings increase daily and now include more than 119,000 items in a variety of formats, as well as 715 periodical titles in either paper or microformat. The library offers the resources of seven college libraries through a combined topcat online public access catalog called SWITCH (the Southeast Wisconsin Information Technology Exchange). In combination with other computer systems, including InfoTrac, ERIC, NEWSBANK, FirstSearch, and CINAHL, students access in-depth research material on almost any subject. The library's resources also include 120 laptop computers that are available for checkout for up to twenty-eight days at a time.

The Academic Computing Center gives students a competitive edge in today's computerized society. The three different computer labs house forty-five IBM and Macintosh personal computers. Laser printers and a document scanner are also available for student use.

The Career Services Center provides internship and job-search services to all Stritch students and alumni. Individual counseling and workshops offered throughout the year include career choices, job-search techniques, resume writing, interviewing, and choosing a major.

The newest addition to the campus is the Center for Communications Studies/Fine Arts, which houses a 400-seat teaching theater, a spacious art gallery, photo labs, music practice rooms, a dance studio, metal and woodworking shops, a graphic arts computer laboratory, and more.

Costs

Full-time tuition for 2000–01 is $11,680; room and board are $4720. Various meal plans are also available. Part-time tuition is $365 per credit for all undergraduate programs except nursing, which is $420 per credit.

Financial Aid

A wide range of financial aid options is available at Cardinal Stritch University, including government-subsidized loan and grant programs as well as University scholarships, on-campus employment opportunities, and off-campus internships. About 80 percent of the full-time students receive financial aid, and the average financial aid package is approximately $9000. Eligibility for need-based grant and loan programs is determined after filing the Free Application for Federal Student Aid (FAFSA). Candidates for financial aid should complete and mail the FAFSA by March 1. The University also offers academic scholarships to those who qualify.

Faculty

Cardinal Stritch University faculty members play an active role in every student's life. Faculty members teach their own classes, so students can benefit directly from their knowledge, expertise, and open-door policy. As a result of the small class sizes, students grow from individual faculty member attention, gain opportunities to participate fully in class discussions, and are challenged to interact with and learn from their peers.

More than 60 percent of the faculty hold doctoral or other terminal degrees. Through their research, writing, and presentations, they keep abreast of the most current trends and continually update the subject matter and teaching techniques of the courses.

Student Government

All full-time undergraduate students are members of the Student Government Association (SGA) and are represented by a 30-member governing body. Student representatives, appointed by the SGA, sit on University academic committees and have a voice in issues related to educational policy and campus life.

Admission Requirements

The average student at Cardinal Stritch University graduated from high school with a B average, achieved a composite score of 23 on the ACT, and ranked in the top 40 percent of his or her high school class. The University considers for acceptance those students who achieve an ACT score of 20 or above or a combined SAT score of 950 or above; rank in the top 50 percent of their high school graduating class; graduate from high school with at least a 2.0 cumulative grade point average (on a 4.0 scale); and complete 16 high school academic units, broken down as follows: 4 years of English, 2 years of mathematics, 2 years of science, 2 years of social studies, and 6 units of academic electives. When applying for admission, students should send the completed application form, $20 application fee, high school transcripts, and ACT and/or SAT scores. On-campus interviews are not required but are recommended.

Transfer students who have fewer than 12 credits from another institution of higher education must submit their high school transcript and ACT or SAT scores. International students are welcome to apply. In addition to the application form and $75 fee, international students should also send a copy of their visa, certified copies of all high school and college transcripts, verification of a score of 213 or better on the Test of English as a Foreign Language (TOEFL), a statement of financial support, and verification of health insurance coverage.

Application and Information

The Admission Office at Cardinal Stritch University accepts applications on a rolling admission basis. Applicants are notified of the decision two weeks after all records are complete.

Inquiries and application materials should be directed to:

David Wegener
Director of Admission
Cardinal Stritch University
6801 North Yates Road
Milwaukee, Wisconsin 53217-3985

Telephone: 414-410-4040
              800-347-8822 Ext. 4040 (toll-free)
E-mail: admityou@stritch.edu
World Wide Web: http://www.stritch.edu

The Center for Communication Studies/Fine Arts is a state-of-the-art facility for the performing and visual arts.

CARLETON COLLEGE
NORTHFIELD, MINNESOTA

The College

Since its inception in 1866, Carleton College has been a coeducational, residential, liberal arts college. Sponsored initially by the Congregationalists, Carleton opened its doors in September 1867 as Northfield College. Four years later, William Carleton of Charlestown, Massachusetts, donated $50,000 to the fledgling college, the result of which was the change of name from Northfield to Carleton. Binding church ties were dropped long ago, and the College continues to welcome students from a kaleidoscope of races, religions, and cultures.

Today, first-year classes number about 500, and the student body is approximately 50 percent men and 50 percent women. The on-campus enrollment of about 1,700 includes students from virtually every state and about twenty other countries. About a quarter are from Minnesota, and the next most represented states are Illinois, California, Wisconsin, New York, Massachusetts, Oregon, and Washington. About 17 percent are students of color, and 11 percent are the first generation of their families to attend college.

Most first-year students choose to take a first-year seminar, some of which deal with contemporary problems or concerns, others with more esoteric material. Many upperclass students do at least some independent study in their major, and a significant number of students take advantage of internship and work experience.

Though academic work takes top priority, Carleton students are actively involved in nearly 100 organizations, clubs, and other activities, ranging from the Carleton Singers (who performed at Carnegie Hall in February 1997) and the improvisational comedy troupe Cujokra to Ultimate Frisbee (Carleton's men's team finished fourth and the women's team second in the 1999 national intercollegiate championships) and one of the top Model United Nations teams in the country. Musicians can play in the orchestra or smaller ensembles or sing in the choir, the Carleton Singers, or the a cappella Knights or Knightengales. Athletes can participate in one of thirteen varsity sports for men or thirteen for women, one of fifteen competitive club teams, or any of ten intramural sports.

Normally, 95 percent of Carleton first-year students return for their sophomore year. The most recent figures available show that 82 percent of first-year students graduated in four years or less, and 88 percent graduated within five years.

Recent construction has doubled the amount of art studio and gallery space and expanded the library to twice its original size and capacity. A new $12-million field house/recreation center opens in March 2000.

Location

Northfield is less than 35 miles from the Minneapolis–St. Paul International Airport and 40 miles from the downtown Twin Cites. Once a traditional small agrarian community, Northfield is also the home of St. Olaf College and several multinational businesses, and a number of its residents now commute to the Twin Cities. Most of the buildings lining the main street of downtown Northfield look today much as they did at the turn of the century. A revitalized river bank (the Cannon River flows through town on its way to the Mississippi) and a core of downtown businesses and shops make shopping on foot or just an afternoon or evening stroll pleasant experiences.

Majors and Degrees

Carleton grants only one undergraduate degree, the Bachelor of Arts. Majors offered are African/African-American studies, American studies, art history, biology, chemistry, classical languages, classical studies, computer science, economics, English, French, French and Francophone studies, geology, German, Greek, history, international relations, Latin, Latin American studies, mathematics, music, philosophy, physics, political science, psychology, religion, Romance languages, Russian, sociology and anthropology, Spanish, studio art, and women's studies. Students may also self-design their own majors.

In addition to a major, students may elect to study one of fifteen concentrations, integrated interdisciplinary programs that cut across traditional boundaries of academic disciplines and serve to both strengthen and complement the major: African/African-American studies, archaeology, cognitive studies, cross-cultural studies, East Asian studies, educational studies, environmental and technology studies, French studies, Latin American studies, medieval studies, political economy, Russian studies, social thought, South Asian studies, and women's studies.

Special programs are available in biochemistry, educational studies, environmental and technology studies, Hebrew/Judaic studies, integrated general studies, linguistics, literary studies, media studies, studies in dance, and theater arts. Carleton offers a teacher education program leading to a secondary teaching license in art, English, French, German, mathematics, Russian, science, the social studies, or Spanish. Elementary licensure is available only in art. The joint liberal arts–engineering program, commonly known as the 3-2 program, is offered in conjunction with either Columbia University or Washington University (Missouri).

Academic Program

Carleton's avowed purpose is to provide a liberal arts education of the highest quality. The College teaches the basic skills upon which all higher achievements rest: to read perceptively, to write and speak clearly, and to think analytically. The Carleton education aims to nurture a sense of curiosity and intellectual adventure, an awareness of method and purpose in a variety of fields, and an affinity for quality and integrity wherever they may be found. These values prepare Carleton graduates to lead fully realized lives in a diverse and changing world.

To this end, the Carleton curriculum balances a traditional emphasis upon classic fields of study, or disciplines, with a complementary offering of distribution courses, electives, and interdisciplinary programs. To be awarded the Bachelor of Arts degree, a student must take at least thirty-five courses, two of which must come from arts and literature, two from the humanities, three from the social sciences, and three from mathematics and the natural sciences. In addition, everyone must take at least one course that is centrally concerned with a culture different from his or her own. All students must also satisfy two proficiency requirements: the writing of English and the learning of a second language.

Carleton students normally choose a major during the spring term of their sophomore year. In any given year, 12–15 students graduate with double majors, and about 15 graduate with special majors. All students must complete an integrative exercise, which could include a comprehensive examination, an extensive research project, a major paper, or a public lecture, in their major field, usually in the senior year.

Carleton's academic year is composed of three 10-week-long terms: fall, winter, and spring.

Off-Campus Arrangements

Two thirds of Carleton students spend at least one term completing an off-campus program. During any one academic year, more than 350 students are involved in off-campus study

1360   www.petersons.com   *Peterson's Guide to Four-Year Colleges 2001*

in locations such as Australia, Japan, China, England, India, Mexico, Costa Rica, the Superior National Forest, and Washington, D.C. Each year the College sponsors as many as ten faculty-led off-campus seminars for Carleton students.

Through membership in a number of consortia, Carleton students may participate in more than twenty additional international programs lasting from a semester to a full year. Students may also select from a list of programs sponsored by other institutions, consortia, and agencies that Carleton has evaluated and approved for academic credit, or they can request approval of a program that they and their academic advisers believe will further their educational goals.

Academic Facilities

The Carleton campus consists of more than 900 acres of land, about 450 of which are the Cowling Arboretum, a game and nature preserve used regularly as an outdoor laboratory for biology, chemistry, and geology as well as a recreational area. Sixteen miles of running and skiing trails crisscross the "arb," which *Runner's World* has named the best place to run in the state of Minnesota.

Approximately thirty buildings are found on the College's main campus of nearly 100 acres. Nine are student residence halls ranging in capacity from 110 to 205. The Music and Drama Center offers a concert hall seating 500 and a theater seating 460, joined by a gallery, ensemble rooms, practice rooms, dressing rooms, and scenery and costume storage rooms.

Three buildings are devoted to the sciences: Olin (physics and psychology), Mudd (chemistry and geology), and the newest, Hulings (biology), a $15-million, four-level building completed in 1995. In addition, Goodsell Observatory houses a 16-inch visual refractor telescope and an 8-inch photographic refractor telescope. The four-story Center for Mathematics and Computing (CMC) opened in 1993 and offers microcomputing labs open around the clock, with lab assistants available 16 hours a day. Several DEC supercomputers linked in a VAXcluster network are housed in the CMC, along with a number of other special-purpose machines. In all, the campus has more than 600 advanced workstations and personal computers, most of which are linked to the central VAX system through serial connections and fiber-optic Ethernet. The College's connection to the Internet provides students with free access to electronic mail, news, and a wide range of other information services.

Costs

For 2000–01, tuition is $24,240; fees, $150; and room and board, $4950. Travel costs vary. Books, supplies, and personal expenses are estimated to be about $600.

Financial Aid

Carleton meets the full demonstrated financial need of every student admitted to the College and continues meeting each student's need for four years or until graduation. An on-campus 8–10-hours-per-week job and a loan opportunity are included in nearly every financial aid package. In 1999–2000, about 80 percent of Carleton students received a total of more than $19 million in financial aid or scholarships from all sources. Sixty percent received grant assistance, and the average need-based grant was $12,490. The only non-need scholarships the College offers are 65–75 Carleton-sponsored National Merit, National Achievement, and National Hispanic Scholarships.

Faculty

All Carleton classes are taught by faculty members rather than graduate students or teaching assistants. Of the 198 teaching faculty members, 172 are full-time, resulting in a student-faculty ratio of 10:1. Of those full-time faculty members, 94 percent hold the highest degree in their academic field. The average class size is about 18, and the average lab size is 15. Most faculty members also serve as academic advisers.

Student Government

Students are actively involved in the governance of the College. Directly below the Board of Trustees is the College Council, chaired by the President, which is composed of 5 faculty members, 5 students, 5 staff members, 1 trustee, and 1 alumnus. The three major policy committees, Education and Curriculum, Student Life, and the Budget Committee, are also made up of faculty members, students, and staff members.

Every student is a member of the Carleton Student Association (CSA). Three officers and 16 senators are elected annually to serve as the CSA Senate, which, among other duties, manages the student activities budget.

Admission Requirements

Carleton normally receives about 3,400 applications for the 500 places available in the first-year class. Admission is based on several considerations: superior academic achievement, personal qualities and interests, participation in extracurricular activities, and potential for development as a student and a graduate of the College. The Admissions Committee weighs all factors to ensure that those students offered admission are not only adequately prepared for the academic work but also will benefit from their total experience at Carleton and will add significantly to the College through their individual talents and personal qualities.

Application and Information

Students interested in applying for admission should contact the Office of Admissions to request an application. Interviews, with either a staff member or an alumni admissions representative, are recommended but not required. A visit to the campus is strongly encouraged. During the academic year, overnight stays, interviews, and class visits are usually available but must be scheduled in advance.

Students who decide that Carleton is their first choice college are encouraged to apply for early decision. The application deadline for regular decision is January 15. Regular decision candidates are notified before April 15, and the candidate's reply date is May 1.

For more information, prospective students should contact:

Office of Admissions
Carleton College
100 South College Street
Northfield, Minnesota 55057
Telephone: 507-646-4190
            800-995-2275 (toll-free)
Fax: 507-646-4526
E-mail: admissions@acs.carleton.edu
World Wide Web: http://www.carleton.edu

An aerial view of the Carleton College campus.

CARLETON UNIVERSITY
OTTAWA, ONTARIO, CANADA

The University

Each year, students from every province and territory in Canada and more than 100 countries around the world make Carleton University their first choice for higher education. Many are attracted by Carleton's reputation as one of Canada's foremost institutions for studies in public affairs, management, and high technology. Others choose Carleton for its innovative Bachelor of Arts program—the first in Canada to offer all entering students intensive seminar classes that involve a maximum of 30 students taught by full-time faculty members. Some students come for the opportunity to work alongside internationally recognized scientists on the cutting edge of research in their fields. Many more are drawn to the University because of its friendly, informal atmosphere; high-quality professional programs; accessible campus; and cooperative education programs, where students get on-the-job training at federal government departments and agencies, nongovernmental organizations, research laboratories, and high-technology and private-sector companies throughout Canada's national capital region.

Carleton University offers undergraduate and graduate programs in more than fifty disciplines. Many have a distinctly Canadian focus and capitalize on Carleton's location in Ottawa, the seat of Canada's federal government and home to dozens of major national institutions, scores of diplomatic missions, hundreds of associations, and one of the largest concentrations of research scientists and high-technology companies in the country.

Founded in 1942, Carleton has pioneered innovative interdisciplinary programs in areas such as environmental studies, criminal justice, women's studies, technology management, and cognitive science. That same pioneering spirit led the University to open its highly competitive and widely acclaimed College of the Humanities, with its rich curriculum in history, literature, philosophy, and languages, in 1995. In response to the growth of new technologies and the need for professionals in new fields, Carleton has recently introduced a communications engineering degree, the first of its kind in North America, as well as three new computational science programs.

Carleton is a major research institution, with more than 90 specialized research centres that attract approximately $26 million a year in sponsored funding. The University is also a national leader in undergraduate teaching. In the last four years, Carleton University has had five 3M teaching award winners. Of the forty awarded during this time Carleton has won 12.5 percent of these awards while representing only 2 percent of the total Canadian faculty members.

Helping students make the critical transition to university studies is an institutional priority. Seminars provide students with strategies to deal with time management, campus resources, financial planning, personal relationships, stress management, and essay writing. Meanwhile, the University's Writing Tutorial Service offers free, one-to-one tutoring to all students to help with class assignments.

Provincially funded, nondenominational, and coeducational, Carleton has more than 14,500 undergraduates, nearly 2,400 graduate students, more than 1,000 professors, and some 900 teaching assistants. International students account for about 4.5 percent of the total enrollment.

Carleton guarantees a residence room to every entering student with an average of 75 percent or better. Students with averages below 75 percent are allocated rooms through a lottery in early July. About 1 out of every 10 Carleton students lives on campus. The University's seven residences offer a choice of smoke-free, limited-smoking, men's, women's, and coed living environments. Students have the choice of three meal plans at Carleton, choosing the plan that best suits their needs. They have the option of taking all meals in the Residence dining halls or selecting flexible arrangements of fewer meals in Residence combined with cash options for eight different cafeterias on campus.

Carleton was one of the first universities in Canada to provide 24-hour attendant care services for students with disabilities. Some residence rooms are expressly designed for students with special needs. An extensive underground tunnel system that links all of Carleton's twenty-nine buildings makes the campus fully accessible and more pleasant for everyone, even in winter.

Carleton's recreational facilities and sports and fitness programs provide plenty of opportunities to get fit and stay fit. The University offers a wide range of men's, women's, and coed intramural sports, plus eight varsity teams for women and nine for men. Recreational facilities include a 50-meter indoor pool, a fitness centre, squash courts, tennis courts, a soccer stadium, and a double gymnasium and practice rooms for martial arts, dance, and aerobics. Fitness classes range from ballet and karate to scuba diving, canoeing, tennis, and rock climbing.

Location

The University's 153-acre campus is one of Canada's most beautiful. Bordered by the Rideau Canal and the Rideau River, it is just minutes away from Parliament Hill and downtown Ottawa. Canada's capital city is a lively blend of culturally diverse communities (English, French and new Canadians), historic landmarks, vibrant high-technology companies, quiet residential neighborhoods, and bustling outdoor markets. Carleton has strong ties to many of Ottawa's political, cultural, and research institutions and to the region's burgeoning high-technology community. Part-time faculty members are drawn from the federal public service, government laboratories, news organizations, social service agencies, and local software and engineering companies.

Majors and Degrees

Carleton offers undergraduate programs leading to bachelor's degrees in architectural studies, arts, commerce, computer science, engineering, humanities, industrial design, international business, journalism, mathematics, music, public affairs and policy management, science, and social work.

There are dozens of majors within the Bachelor of Arts degree program. These include anthropology, art history, biology, Canadian studies, , child studies, criminology and criminal justice, cognitive science, and European and Russian studies.

The Bachelor of Commerce degree program offers options in accounting, business operations analysis, finance, information systems, international business, strategic human resource management, and technology and operations management.

The Bachelor of Computer Science degree program offers four streams—management and business systems, network computing, software and computing, and software engineering.

Within the Bachelor of Engineering degree program, students can choose specializations in aerospace, civil, communications, computer systems, electrical, environmental, mechanical, and software engineering or engineering physics.

Majors within the Bachelor of Science degree program range from applied physics, biology, biochemistry, biotechnology, and chemistry to physical geography and statistics. In response to the growth in biotech and pharmaceutical companies, Carleton has recently introduced new computational programs in biochemistry, biology, and chemistry. In addition, Carleton offers undergraduate certificate programs in English language and composition, French language studies, French language translation, law enforcement studies, public service studies, and teaching English as a second language.

Academic Program

Carleton's undergraduate degree programs are designed to help students achieve their personal development and career goals. In a very real sense, they represent an education for life, placing a heavy emphasis on research, writing, communication, and analytical and critical thinking skills that can last a lifetime and be applied to any number of employment settings. Students develop expertise in a particular discipline and also are encouraged to gain an appreciation for the relationships between and among different bodies of knowledge.

For most programs that lead to degrees in arts and science, students have the option of choosing a 15-credit program of study or a more intensive, more demanding 20-credit honours program. The first is normally completed after three years of full-time study; the honours program normally requires an additional year. Degree programs in other disciplines generally require a total of 20 credits and are also completed after four years of full-time study. A prescribed number of core courses is required in most disciplines. Majors in the three-year degree programs normally require at least six courses in the major subject; honours programs can require as many as 10 courses in the honours subject. Students also have the option of choosing either combined majors or combined honours by focusing their studies on two disciplines. The regular academic year includes two semesters—from September to December and from January to April. Courses are also taught over intersession, which runs from May to August. While students can begin their studies in either September, January, or May, most enter in the fall.

Off-Campus Arrangements

Carleton offers co-op and industrial experience programs, work placements, practicums, and internships in more than thirty disciplines. Most of these options are for degree credit, and many offer students an opportunity to earn extra income. The University has more than fifty academic exchange agreements with educational institutions and governments in some thirty countries, which allows students the option of studying abroad in a variety of disciplines. The Bachelor of International Business degree program requires one year of overseas studies in a foreign language.

Academic Facilities

Carleton's MacOdrum Library houses more than 1 million volumes and an extensive collection of microfilms, archival material, documents, and maps. The University's art gallery houses an impressive collection of Canadian art and hosts traveling exhibits throughout the year. The Paul Menton Centre for Persons with Disabilities offers educational support services to students with physical disabilities, visual impairments, hearing impairments, and learning disabilities. Carleton was one of the first universities in Canada to offer free Internet access to all of its students. Its award-winning CHAT program provides discussion groups, news groups, and e-mail access, which allow students to link up with their professors, classmates, and learning resources 24 hours a day.

Costs

Tuition fees in 1999–2000 ranged from $4290 to $5050 per year, depending on the program. Fees for international students range from $9010 to $10,085 in 2000–01. All of these figures are expressed in Canadian dollars. Canadian residents planning to study in the arts and social sciences should budget about $12,500 per year. Students in professional programs, such as engineering or computer science, should plan for an additional $500 to $1000 per year. These amounts include at least $800 to $1700 for books, $5200 for on-campus room and board or $7800 for off-campus living expenses, at least $440 for local transportation and trips home, $1500 for recreation and entertainment, $200 for clothing and laundry, and $1000 for miscellaneous expenses.

Financial Aid

Each year, Carleton University awards more than $3.5 million to approximately 3,000 new and returning students. The University's highest awards are the prestige scholarships—ten Chancellor's Scholarships, five Nortel Networks Scholarships of Excellence, and five Richard Lewar Scholarships. For all prestige scholarships, students need an admission average of 90 percent or better, as well as a wide range of community or secondary school activities. All of these scholarships can be continued each year that a student is enrolled, provided that an A minus standing is maintained. Scholarships lost in one year can be regained in future years.

All students entering Carleton with a high school average of 80 percent or better are automatically considered for an entrance scholarship. Entrance scholarships are renewable provided an A minus average or better is maintained. All entrance scholarship recipients are given priority for registration and guaranteed a space in residence. Students with an A minus standing who have not been awarded one of the continuing entrance scholarships are automatically awarded a $1000 or $750 in-course scholarship for the following year, provided they meet University criteria. In addition to these general in-course scholarships, the University awards specific in-course scholarships up to $2500.

Faculty

There are 592 full-time faculty members, 12 part-time faculty members, and several hundred part-time sessional lecturers. Of the faculty members, 83 percent hold doctoral degrees. Teaching faculty members are also responsible for research projects. The undergraduate student-faculty ratio is 26:1.

Student Government

The University's student association plays a vital role in enhancing the quality of campus life. It supports the nearly 100 clubs and student organizations that focus on everything from physical fitness to politics.

Admission Requirements

For Canadian residents, courses used for admission differ according to program, and admission averages vary by program.

Applicants who have completed grade 12 in the United States or in a U.S. overseas school are considered for first-year admission. The grade-12 program must include at least four academic units, and a minimum of sixteen academic units must have been completed in grades 9 to 12. Applicants who fail to meet the foregoing requirements but otherwise have a good academic record may be considered for admission to an appropriate Qualifying-University year program. An average of B- or better is required for admission. For honours programs, an average of A or better is required. In either case, applicants must be ranked in the first quarter of their class.

International candidates who have completed senior high school are considered for admission. Specific admission requirements may vary by country. Applicants whose native language is not English are required to provide proof of English language proficiency. The following tests have been approved for this purpose: Carleton University's CAEL Assessment and TOEFL (required score of 580 or better).

Application and Information

For more information, students should contact:
Undergraduate Recruitment
315 Robertson Hall
Carleton University
1125 Colonel By Drive
Ottawa, Ontario K1S 5B6
Canada
Telephone: 613-520-3663
            613-520-4455 (TTY/TDD)
            888-354-4414 (toll-free in Canada)
Fax: 613-520-3847
E-mail: liaison@carleton.ca
World Wide Web: http://www.carleton.ca

CARLOW COLLEGE
PITTSBURGH, PENNSYLVANIA

The College

Carlow College was founded in 1929 in response to a local need for a Catholic women's college. The mission of the College (then called Mount Mercy College) was articulated by its founders, the Sisters of Mercy: "... to graduate the true scholar, with knowledge many sided as well as thorough ... the true woman, with a well-developed sense of duty to God, herself and to her fellow creatures, with a strong self-reliant character, and with ability for real service whatever be her destined sphere of life or her chosen field of labor." While Carlow makes explicit its strong continuing commitment to the education of women, it welcomes male students. The College's mission has been confirmed over the years by the growing number of students who come seeking a solid liberal arts education and preparation for careers. In addition to its undergraduate programs, the College offers graduate programs that lead to the Master of Education degree in art education or early childhood education, with an option for Montessori certification; in early childhood supervision; and in educational leadership. A graduate program in professional leadership or management and technology leads to a Master of Science degree. The Carlow Master of Science in Nursing program includes specializations in home health and gerontology and provides preparation for the nurse practitioner program.

The current enrollment is 1,948 women and 169 men. Carlow's students have various backgrounds and come mainly from the Middle Atlantic states; the majority are from western Pennsylvania. About 75 percent are graduates of public high schools, and approximately 70 percent of the freshmen live on campus in the College's modern dormitory. An active Resident Student Association strives to maintain a climate of responsibility and cooperation among the residents. The Commuter Student Association endeavors to serve the needs of commuting students.

Student support services are organized under a leadership model, and the department is named the Leadership Development Center for Living and Learning. Placement and career counseling, free professional and peer tutorial services, the Learning Center, student health and personal counseling programs, and campus ministry are support services available to students. The department has a large group of students involved in community service and volunteerism. Spring break service projects have taken students to Jamaica, the Virgin Islands, Arizona, Arkansas, and many other locations. Cocurricular organizations include the Student Government Association, the Commuter Student Association, the International Student Association, and United Black Students. Academically or career-oriented organizations include Alpha Phi Omega (national service/honor society), Beta Beta Beta (biology club), the Council for Exceptional Children, Delta Epsilon Sigma (national scholastic honor sorority), Kappa Delta Epsilon (for education majors), Loyola Society (for nursing majors), and Phi Chi Theta (business fraternity). Special interest groups include instrumental ensembles, the Gospel choir Blessed, the Forum for the Awareness and Advancement of Human Rights (FAAHR), Student Athlete Association, and WOLF (Women Organizing and Leading for the Future). The College has a bookstore, dining facilities, gymnasium, swimming pool, and a wellness center. The athletic program includes intercollegiate basketball, softball, soccer, tennis, and volleyball; club crew; cross-country; rugby; and a selection of physical education courses, including aerobics, fitness and weight control, martial arts/self-defense, modern dance, water aerobics, weight training, and yoga. Wellness and fitness services include individual health assessment and fitness programming and nutrition counseling.

Popular campus events include celebrity entertainment, film series, carnivals, Homecoming, Founder's Day, the Christmas concert, St. Patrick's Day celebration and parade, the International Festival, Black History Month events, Women's History Month events, Focus on Women lecture series, and drama productions.

The College's central location gives students opportunities for internships in varied businesses and agencies. Students in health-related fields complete their clinical experiences in the many fine teaching hospitals, clinics, and private health-care facilities in the city of Pittsburgh. City buses stop in front of the campus, and campus parking is available for commuting students.

Location

Carlow College is located on a 13-acre campus in the heart of Oakland, the educational, cultural, and medical center of Pittsburgh. Schenley Park, Carnegie Institute and Museum, Phipps Conservatory, Carnegie Music and Lecture halls, the Scaife Galleries, and the Oakland shopping district are all a short walk from the campus. Downtown Pittsburgh—the nation's fifth-largest corporate-headquarters city—is only a 10-minute bus ride away. Greater Pittsburgh International Airport is a 30-minute drive from Carlow, and exits from Interstate 376 are about a quarter of a mile from the campus.

Majors and Degrees

Carlow College grants the undergraduate degrees of Bachelor of Arts, Bachelor of Science, Bachelor of Science in Nursing, and Bachelor of Social Work. Majors are accounting, art, art/art education, art/art history, art with a certificate in art therapy preparation, art/computer animation, art/graphic design, biology, biology/ecology, business management, business management/communication, chemistry, communication studies, comprehensive social studies (for students in education certification programs only), computer science, creative writing, early childhood education, elementary education, English, health science (available to students who have previously earned an associate degree), history, information systems management, liberal studies, mathematics, nursing, philosophy, professional writing, professional writing/business, professional writing/English, psychology, scientific medical marketing, social work, sociology, special education, theology, and theology/psychology. An independent major, designed by the student, may also be arranged. Certification programs are offered in perfusion technology (biology majors only), school nursing, and secondary education (biology, chemistry, communication, English, general sciences, mathematics, and social studies). Preprofessional programs include dentistry, law, medicine, optometry, osteopathy, pharmacy, physical therapy, podiatry, and veterinary medicine. The College offers 3-2 programs in engineering in three areas: biology/environmental engineering, chemistry/chemical engineering, and mathematics/engineering.

Academic Program

Carlow's primary concern is the development of the student as a lifelong learner. To this end, members of the Carlow community—students, faculty, and staff—try to help one another recognize the integrity and value of each person in the daily life and work of the College. The academic programs are broad and flexible, including opportunities for double majors, single majors with certification in education, minors, certificate programs, and changes of major. Transfer students are accepted into all programs. Persons already possessing a degree may be admitted to a second degree or certification program. The Carlow curriculum is based in the liberal arts, with significant emphasis on career preparation.

The College curriculum operates on the two-semester system, August to December and January to May. Summer sessions, a variable number of weeks in length, are offered every year. Most courses carry 3 credits (laboratory courses, among others, carry 4 credits). Students normally take five courses each semester. Each student must demonstrate basic competence in English composition, speech and interpersonal communication, reading comprehension, and mathematics. Required of all students is one course each in a lab science; history; literature; algebra or logic; a behavioral science, such as psychology or sociology; theology; the arts; philosophy; peace and justice; and a course in women's studies and one in non-Western studies. Students are also required to take an interdisciplinary course, which is selected from a variety of subject areas. Students in nursing, education, social work, psychology, management, perfusion technology, and medical technology are required to do fieldwork as part of their program. Field placements and internships are guaranteed and encouraged in all areas of study. An honors program is open to eligible students. After the first semester of the freshman year, one course per semester (outside of the major) may be taken on a pass-fail basis. Any course may be challenged, for credit or exemption, by passing an examination. CLEP general exam credits may be used for this purpose as well.

The College gives women and men the opportunity to return to the classroom at various stages of their lives. Adult learners may enroll in full-time and part-time degree programs, noncredit enrichment courses, seminars, and workshops. Scheduling options include day, evening, and weekend courses.

Off-Campus Arrangements

After the first semester of the freshman year, full-time students may cross-register for one course per semester at any of the nine other area colleges and universities that are members of the Pittsburgh Council on Higher Education. There is no additional cost for cross-registration.

Academic Facilities

Grace Library, a five-level multipurpose learning center in the heart of the campus, currently contains 96,729 volumes and a variety of full-text electronic resources. The library houses the offices of the president and vice president for academic affairs. The Media Center, Learning Center, mail room, bookstore, Academic Affairs, Advising Center, Career Services, Distance Learning Center, Copy Center, College Archives, and computer laboratories are also located here. Kresge Theatre, a 300-seat lecture/demonstration hall, and the Mellon Galleries—where students, faculty members, and local artists display their works—are located on the fifth level. Curran Hall is a facility for the nursing division and includes specially designed demonstration areas and conference and seminar rooms. Frances Warde Hall houses the education and management divisions and the creative and professional writing programs as well as newly renovated classrooms and seminar spaces. Antonian Hall houses the 1,000-seat Sister Rosemary Heyl Theatre, the social sciences and fine arts departments, classrooms, and staff offices. The cafeteria and the Carlow College Campus School (grades nursery through 8) are located in Tiernan Hall. St. Joseph Hall contains the gymnasium, fitness center, and swimming pool; and Aquinas Hall houses classrooms, the humanities department, the International Student Center, faculty and staff offices, and the Carlow Campus Montessori School. Carlow's new A. J. Palumbo Hall for Science and Technology is home to the Dr. Willam A. Urrichio Division of Natural Sciences and Mathematics. This 95,000-square-foot complex contains fourteen state-of-the-art teaching/research laboratories in physics, organic and advanced chemistry, genetics, cell biology, and gross anatomy; an herbarium to store dry plant specimens; a greenhouse; an amphitheater for scientific presentations; and the Bayer Children's Science Learning Laboratory.

Carlow College's campus computer network features Internet accounts and e-mail addresses, network and Internet access from any location on campus, remote e-mail and Internet access for home users, and one network port per pillow in the residence hall.

Costs

Tuition for 1999–2000 was $12,450 for full-time students. Room and board charges for the year were $5076 for double occupancy. Fees totaled $376.

Financial Aid

Financial aid in the form of grants, scholarships, loans, and student employment is available to eligible applicants. Approximately 95 percent of all full-time students receive some type of financial assistance. The College expects that most aid recipients will assume a portion of their expenses through loans and/or part-time employment. Job opportunities are available on campus in a wide variety of positions, and students will be placed, whenever possible, in positions that coincide with their skills and interests. Basketball, volleyball, softball, soccer, and tennis scholarships are also available.

Faculty

The most valuable resource at the disposal of the Carlow student is a faculty whose primary commitment is to the education of undergraduates. The student-faculty ratio is 13:1, and faculty members are readily available to help plan individualized programs of study, to provide assistance relating to field placements and internships, and to assist in career preparation. The student's major adviser is normally a faculty member in the department. There are currently 199 faculty members, of whom 67 are full-time. Approximately 5 percent are Sisters of Mercy. A number of professional persons from the Pittsburgh area are among the part-time faculty members. Of those, 30 have provided specialized expertise for more than five years, 10 for more than ten years.

Student Government

All registered students are members of the Student Government Association (SGA). Through the SGA, students act as equal participants with the administration, faculty, and staff in general governance. The SGA promotes the general welfare of the students and is the advocate to ensure that the academic, social, and religious needs of students are met. SGA is empowered to charter all student organizations.

Admission Requirements

Generally, Carlow seeks applicants who rank in the upper 40 percent of their graduating class, who have attained at least a B average, and who have followed an academic or college-preparatory curriculum. Applicants are evaluated on the basis of their secondary school record, class rank, and scores on the SAT I or ACT. The Committee on Admissions recognizes that school curricula vary greatly and always gives careful consideration to the application of an able student whose preparation differs from the traditional program. A personal interview is strongly recommended but not required. Overnight visits, including dormitory accommodations, a day of classes, campus tours, and meals, are available and are strongly encouraged. Throughout the year, the College sponsors programs that give candidates the opportunity to tour the campus and meet faculty and staff members and Carlow students.

Application and Information

Although Carlow subscribes to the rolling admission plan, high school students are encouraged to submit an application early in the first semester of the senior year. Students interested in early notification should apply by September 30. Notification of the admission decision for early notification candidates is made by October 30.

For an application form, students should contact:

Director of Admissions
Carlow College
3333 Fifth Avenue
Pittsburgh, Pennsylvania 15213
Telephone: 412-578-6059
    800-333-CARLOW (toll-free)
E-mail: admissions@carlow.edu
World Wide Web: http://www.carlow.edu

CARNEGIE MELLON UNIVERSITY
PITTSBURGH, PENNSYLVANIA

Carnegie Mellon

The University

First envisioned in 1900 by steel magnate and philanthropist Andrew Carnegie, Carnegie Mellon University has steadily built upon its foundations of excellence and innovation to become one of America's leading universities. The University's unique approach to education—giving students the opportunity to become experts in their chosen field while studying a broad range of course work across disciplines—creates leaders and problem solvers for the changing marketplace of today and tomorrow.

Students in this private coeducational university come from all fifty states and more than forty countries. Each year, Carnegie Mellon enrolls a diverse freshman class of approximately 1,280 students. The total undergraduate population is 5,047. Students come from a variety of different social and cultural backgrounds and also represent a wide range of academic and artistic interests. Approximately 10 percent of the student body identifies with an ethnic minority population such as African American, Hispanic/Latino American, or Native American.

Carnegie Mellon spans the best of both worlds. Its traditional 103-acre campus is located within the Pittsburgh city limits. Student activities include more than 100 clubs and organizations, varsity and intramural sports, fraternities and sororities, and student government. A new student center features state-of-the-art recreational and entertainment facilities. Off campus, students can take advantage of three culturally active neighborhoods within walking distance, the largest public park in Pittsburgh, urban and suburban shopping and sightseeing, professional sports, museums, art galleries, amusement parks, and much more.

Approximately 75 percent of students live in the University's ten traditional residence halls, fourteen houses, seven apartment buildings, thirteen fraternity houses, and four sorority houses. Freshmen are required to live on campus, and housing is guaranteed for four years, provided students remain in the University housing system.

Carnegie Mellon wants its students to come away from their undergraduate experience poised to be trendsetters, whether in the business world, the art community, or graduate school. Students will gain the knowledge necessary to succeed professionally, but they will also learn how to maximize their creativity, intellectual playfulness, and analytical skills in order to survive in an ever-changing global environment. The University strives to produce graduates who are adaptable, resourceful, and independent—graduates who communicate effectively, strive to be leaders, and understand their professional and social responsibilities.

In addition to bachelor's degrees, Carnegie Mellon offers master's and doctoral degrees.

Location

Carnegie Mellon is located in the Oakland neighborhood of Pittsburgh, 5 miles from the downtown area. As home to several of the city's colleges, universities, museums, and hospitals, Oakland offers many activities and resources to area students. While Carnegie Mellon has the collegiate feel of a country campus, the surrounding Pittsburgh community provides all of the cultural and social advantages of the big city. The University is 1½ hours from the mountains, which have some of the best skiing in the East, and a short plane ride away from many major metropolitan areas, including Boston, New York City, Chicago, Philadelphia, and Washington, D.C.

Majors and Degrees

Undergraduate majors at Carnegie Mellon include business administration, computer science, engineering (chemical engineering, civil and environmental engineering, electrical and computer engineering, engineering and public policy, materials science and engineering, and mechanical engineering), fine and performing arts (architecture, art, design, drama, and music), liberal arts and professional studies (economics, English, history, modern languages, philosophy, political science, psychology, social and decision sciences, and statistics), and the sciences (biological sciences, chemistry, mathematical sciences, and physics). A Bachelor of Humanities and Arts is also available, as are several interdepartmental majors.

Academic Program

There is no core curriculum at Carnegie Mellon; the only required classes are Computer Skills Workshop and a first-year writing course. Each college has its own requirements for graduation.

Students at Carnegie Mellon have the freedom to design courses of study that cross over majors and disciplines. In fact, some students have double majors, minors, or concentrations in areas other than their principal major. It's not unusual to find an engineering student with a double major in music or an English major with a minor in business administration.

The Bachelor of Humanities and Arts degree program is a unique non-performance-based program at Carnegie Mellon that allows students to pursue interdisciplinary programs in the fine arts, the humanities, and the social sciences. Other special programs include Army, Naval, and Air Force ROTC; a self-defined major and interdepartmental major options in the College of Humanities and Social Sciences; prelaw and premedicine advising programs; and five-year combined bachelor's/master's degree programs.

Carnegie Mellon also has nearly unlimited opportunities for students to participate in undergraduate research, sometimes as early as the second semester of the freshman year. Many departments offer research training courses and academic year and summer research programs. Students can work on research in groups, individually with a professor, or independently through Carnegie Mellon's Small Undergraduate Research Grant (SURG) program.

Off-Campus Arrangements

Carnegie Mellon students can take one course per semester at any of the following colleges and universities in Pittsburgh for full credit: the University of Pittsburgh, Carlow College, Chatham College, Duquesne University, La Roche College, Point Park College, Robert Morris College, Pittsburgh Theological Seminary, and the Community College of Allegheny County.

Carnegie Mellon has several study-abroad programs, including university exchange programs in Chile, Singapore, Mexico, Japan, and Switzerland. Students may also take advantage of study-abroad opportunities through their department or through another university.

Academic Facilities

Carnegie Mellon has a 103-acre main campus with a few outlying research buildings. The campus contains more than fifty academic and administrative buildings and three libraries. The Hunt, Engineering and Science, and Mellon Institute Libraries contain more than 906,000 volumes and 3,889 periodicals. An international online resource sharing system and reciprocal borrowing between Carnegie Mellon and other local universities provide students with almost unlimited library resources.

There are thousands of computers on campus, including Macintosh, IBM, and UNIX systems, which are housed in public clusters in almost every academic building and residence hall. In addition, most departments have their own computer clusters for students to use. For students with their own computers, all of the residence hall rooms are wired to the Andrew network, Carnegie Mellon's high-speed computer network linking the campus and providing access to the outside world.

In addition to academic facilities, Carnegie Mellon features a new University Center with food court and recreational facilities, the historic Kresge Theater for Performing Arts, a studio theater, art galleries, abundant studio and rehearsal space, a gymnasium, and numerous research laboratories. The new Purnell Center for the Arts opened in fall 1999. The campus also borders the largest public park in Pittsburgh, Schenley Park.

Costs

Carnegie Mellon's costs for the 2000–01 academic year are tuition, $24,600, and room, board, and fees, $7399. The cost of books, supplies, and personal expenses is estimated at $2050. The total cost is $34,049. International students must also pay an additional $890 for required health insurance.

Financial Aid

Carnegie Mellon is a need-blind institution, which means that students' personal financial information is not considered in admission decisions. More than 70 percent of students receive some form of financial assistance, with an average award of about $16,000.

Carnegie Mellon uses the Federal Methodology to determine financial aid eligibility. The forms required to apply for financial assistance are the Free Application for Federal Student Aid (FAFSA), the Carnegie Mellon Form, parental W-2s, and both parental and student tax returns. Financial aid packages usually include a combination of loans, grants, and work-study allowances.

Four merit-based scholarships are offered, with awards ranging from $1000 to the cost of half tuition. Every student is eligible for merit-based scholarship consideration with no separate application process. Students are also encouraged to apply for outside scholarships as a source of aid.

Faculty

Carnegie Mellon has approximately 1,100 teaching and research faculty members, and a student-teacher ratio of 9:1. Faculty members are practicing professionals at the forefront of their respective fields. More often than not, faculty members teach both undergraduate and graduate courses. Carnegie Mellon's classes are taught by faculty members, not teaching assistants. Professors, instructors, and lecturers are in the classroom, lab, studio, or workplace creating new knowledge on a daily basis and passing that knowledge on to their students. Undergraduates have the opportunity to work on groundbreaking research projects with award-winning faculty members, many times one-on-one, through assistantships, internships, work-study positions, and extracurricular organizations.

Student Government

Carnegie Mellon's Student Senate is composed of representatives from each college at Carnegie Mellon and exists to promote the welfare of the campus community, distribute budget funds to student groups, provide a liaison between students and the administration, and inform the student body of proposals and changes.

Admission Requirements

Carnegie Mellon looks for strong students, both academically and socially, who have a wide range of interests and activities. There are no minimum grade requirements or standardized test scores, although most of Carnegie Mellon's students tend to have strong test scores and be at the top of their classes. The University uses standardized test scores, including the SAT I or ACT and SAT II Subject Tests; high school performance; and extracurricular activities to make admission decisions. Recommendations from a guidance counselor and from a teacher are also required.

Carnegie Mellon strives to build a class of students that is racially, socially, economically, and geographically diverse. Students come from all fifty states and more than forty countries, and the University is committed to recruiting students from traditionally underrepresented backgrounds, including African Americans, Hispanic/Latino Americans, and Native Americans. Transfer students are also welcome.

Application and Information

Carnegie Mellon has three types of decision plans: early admission, early decision, and regular decision.

Early admission is for high school juniors who wish to skip their senior year to go directly to college. In addition to academic strength, early admission candidates must display maturity and have strong teacher and guidance counselor recommendations. The application deadline for early admission is January 1, and candidates are notified of a decision between March 15 and April 15.

Early decision is for students who declare Carnegie Mellon as their first choice. The early decision plan is a binding agreement; if accepted, students are expected to enroll. The deadline for early decision is November 15 (November 1 for fine arts), and candidates are notified of a decision between December 15 and January 15.

Regular decision is the most popular plan. Applications are due by January 1, and notification occurs between March 15 and April 15.

Students interested in learning more about Carnegie Mellon can arrange to visit the campus. The University offers group information sessions, campus tours, and personal interviews (which are recommended for admission) throughout most of the year. High school juniors can participate in Carnegie Mellon's six-week precollege programs.

Group information sessions and interviews are available for students who cannot come to Pittsburgh. University representatives travel across the United States during the fall of every year. The Office of Admission can provide more information on these options.

For more information about Carnegie Mellon, students should contact:

Carnegie Mellon Office of Admission
5000 Forbes Avenue
Pittsburgh, Pennsylvania 15213-3890
Telephone: 412-268-2082
E-mail: undergraduate-admissions@andrew.cmu.edu
WWW: http://www.cmu.edu/enrollment/admission/

Carnegie Mellon University, located in Pittsburgh, Pennsylvania, is one of America's leading universities.

CARROLL COLLEGE
HELENA, MONTANA

The College

Carroll College believes that a high-quality education must go far beyond the walls of the classroom. Carroll's motto, "Not for School but for Life," expresses the College's commitment to the lifelong development of personal, professional, intellectual, and spiritual facets of each person who shares in the experience of Carroll College. Students succeed in classes and in careers. They look forward to fresh insights and new experiences, and they have a reputation for bringing out the best in themselves and the people they meet throughout their lives. Montana's governor, a Carroll graduate, stated, "Carroll gives you a solid base on which to grow, learn, and achieve, to be a success in all parts of your life."

Carroll maintains a strong academic reputation. Small class sizes and dedicated faculty members create a unique environment where students get to know professors personally and instructors take a genuine interest in each person's education and accomplishments. A student expressed it clearly: "I don't know too many colleges where the chemistry professors give directions to good fishing holes or where students address their administrators by their first names. The students care. The faculty cares. The College cares."

Dedication to teaching has won Carroll national recognition as one of the top six regional liberal arts schools of the West for teaching excellence. Eight current faculty members are past recipients of Fulbright scholarships. Maintaining a philosophy of developing the whole person, more than thirty campus clubs and organizations, including a nationally ranked forensics team; the College radio station; music, theater, and dance organizations; campus newspaper and annual staff; academic societies; student government; and much more, are available for the student to join. Intercollegiate and intramural sports offer all students a chance to play a favorite sport or explore a new one. The Physical Education Center is open to students for swimming, racquetball, volleyball, basketball, weight training, and numerous special events.

The true spirit of Carroll becomes apparent through the exchange of ideas and insights from all religious beliefs and backgrounds. Carroll students explore and express spirituality through campus liturgies, retreats, and a strong campus ministry program. Founded in 1909, the College was constructed with the aid of Bishop John Patrick Carroll and William Howard Taft, the twenty-seventh president of the United States, who laid the cornerstone of St. Charles Hall. In September 1910, Mount Saint Charles College opened its doors for classes, and the first college student graduated in 1916. In 1932, the school's name was changed to Carroll College in honor of its founder.

The quality and value of Carroll are ranked among the best for colleges and universities in America and among the best for regional liberal arts schools in the West. Carroll is accredited by the Northwest Association of Schools and Colleges and holds membership in the National Association of Independent Colleges and Universities, the American Council on Education, the Council of Independent Colleges, the Association of Catholic Colleges and Universities, and the Western Independent Colleges fund.

Carroll College is a private, Catholic, residential, coeducational liberal arts college. As Carroll has a residential campus, students are required to live in one of the College's residence halls for their first two years at Carroll.

Location

Students live and learn in the "Big Sky Country" of Montana among its jagged mountains, freshwater streams, golden meadows, and clear blue skies. Between the mysteries of Yellowstone National Park and the majesty of Glacier National Park, Montanans enjoy some of the most awesome, unspoiled landscapes in the world.

Nestled in the heart of the Rocky Mountains, Carroll is located in Helena, the capital city of Montana. Once a rough-hewn mining camp of the 1860s, the city combines the free-moving, friendly feel of a mountain town with the social and cultural opportunities of an urban center.

Students enjoy Carroll's beautiful 64-acre campus, spread across a rolling, tree-covered hilltop overlooking the Helena Valley. St. Charles Hall, the cornerstone of Carroll, stands at the center of the campus, surrounded by a mix of historic and modern architecture. The campus is located below the cliffs of Mount Helena, one of the largest city parks in America. Mount Helena rises high above the city and encompasses 620 acres of wildflowers, ponderosa pines, alpine wildlife, and breathtaking vistas in every direction. For all-season water sports, Canyon Ferry, Holter, Hauser, and Park Lakes are a short and scenic ride from the campus.

Majors and Degrees

Carroll College offers a four-year Bachelor of Arts degree program with majors in the following areas: accounting, biology, business administration, chemistry, civil engineering, classical languages, communication studies, computer science, elementary education, English, English writing, environmental studies, French, history, international relations, mathematics, nursing, performing arts, philosophy, physical education, political science, psychology, public administration, public relations, secondary education, social work, sociology, Spanish, teaching English to speakers of other languages (TESOL), and theology. Carroll also offers an affiliated 3-2 program in engineering at Columbia University, University of Notre Dame, University of Southern California, Gonzaga University, Montana College of Mineral Science and Technology, and Montana State University.

Preprofessional programs include clinical laboratory science, dentistry, law, medicine, optometry, pharmacy, and veterinary medicine. Special programs at Carroll include the Carroll Intensive Language Institute (CILI), cooperative education and internship opportunities, general studies, an honors scholars program, international study, music, occupational therapy, and preseminary.

Carroll also offers two-year Associate of Arts degrees in business, communication studies, computer science, English, English writing, and visual arts.

Academic Program

The academic year consists of fall and spring semesters and a limited summer term. Courses are structured such that students attend classes in the arts, sciences, humanities, and social sciences for at least four of their eight semesters at Carroll.

Practical experience is gained through internship programs at the state capital, the community hospital, the on-campus television studio, and local businesses; independent studies; and cooperative education programs.

Adult continuing education courses are offered throughout the year, and a special summer schedule of courses is open to all students.

Off-Campus Arrangements

For students seeking an international experience, Carroll offers study-abroad programs in more than thirty-five countries around the world. French and Spanish majors are required to study in a country where their major language is spoken. International study programs, normally undertaken during the junior year, are coordinated through the assigned adviser of foreign languages. In recent years, Carroll students have studied for full-year, semester, or summer sessions in Australia, Denmark, France, Ireland, Italy,

Japan, Mexico, Russia, Scotland, Spain, and Taiwan. Carroll continues to establish new relationships and special international programs with institutions around the globe.

Academic Facilities

Carroll's new, state-of-the-art Fortin Science and Technology Center opens in fall 2000, with 27,000 square feet of classrooms and laboratories. An NBC-affiliated television station is located on the campus and includes a multimedia classroom. Carroll's Corette Library houses an extensive collection of volumes and periodicals, plus research and referral systems.

All classrooms, laboratories, and residence halls are networked for access to the campus computer network, Internet, and e-mail. Computer labs are located throughout the campus. The education laboratory supports teaching majors with Macintosh computers and software, an educational library, and other facilities.

Costs

Carroll College has been nationally recognized for providing an outstanding liberal arts education at a reasonable cost. Carroll has been cited among the top ten regional liberal arts colleges in the West for value and teaching excellence by *U.S. News & World Report* for the past five years.

The reasonable cost of attending Carroll reflects the College's commitment to offering a premium education to all qualified students. For the 2000–01 academic year, Carroll's tuition and fees total $12,238; room and board fees are $4964.

Financial Aid

In the 1999–2000 academic year, Carroll awarded $10.6 million to 73 percent of its incoming freshmen and to 56 percent of its other students in the form of College-sponsored scholarships, federal work-study, and student loan programs, including Federal Pell Grants, Federal Perkins Loans, Federal Stafford Student Loans, PLUS loans for parents, State Student Incentive Grants, and Federal Supplemental Educational Opportunity Grants. Carroll's objective is to make available to every student who is qualified to attend Carroll all financial resources for which he or she is eligible.

More information on Carroll scholarships is available through the Office of Admission. To be considered for scholarships, students must submit a complete admission file by March 1. Carroll requires interested students to submit the Free Application for Federal Student Aid (FAFSA), which is available from high school counselors, as early as possible. This ensures that students are awarded all of the aid for which they qualify.

Faculty

At Carroll, 74 full-time and 25 adjunct faculty members help provide students with the resources, personal support, and academic understanding they need to become successful for the rest of their lives. A 13:1 student-faculty ratio allows for close interaction between students and their professors. All classes at Carroll are taught directly by faculty members; there are no graduate teaching assistants. Faculty members at Carroll are energetic about their teaching and their scholarship. Numerous professors have gained national and international recognition for their research, teaching excellence, conference presentations, and publications in their fields.

Student Government

The Associated Students of Carroll College serves as a medium for students to communicate with the administration and to help make important decisions about campus activities and student life. Each class (freshman, sophomore, junior, and senior) elects its own student officers, with each vice president serving as a student senator. Carroll's Student Senate is made up of elected representatives of each floor of the residence halls, off-campus students, and nontraditional students. Students may also serve on a variety of committees that address specific needs and concerns across the campus.

Admission Requirements

Degree candidates are those who have made application through the Office of Admission for a course of study leading to the Bachelor of Arts degree. Degree candidates may be enrolled on a full-time or part-time basis. Admission decisions are based upon a student's performance during high school, verbal and quantitative skills, secondary school report, letters of recommendation, demonstrated commitment to intellectual achievement, and performance on standardized college entrance examinations.

When applying for admission, candidates are required to submit an application form, official transcripts from the high school and all colleges previously attended, a secondary school report and/or a letter of recommendation, ACT or SAT I scores, and a $25 non-refundable application fee. Transfer students who have successfully completed more than 30 college semester credits with at least a C (2.5) grade average are not required to submit high school transcripts or SAT I/ACT scores.

Application and Information

Carroll College has a rolling admission policy with a priority admission deadline of March 1. Within three weeks of submission of all materials, candidates are notified of acceptance, conditional acceptance, or denial by Carroll's Office of Admission. Students should note that late submission of material may jeopardize their financial aid awards and course registration.

For an application form or further information about Carroll College's people and programs, financial aid and scholarships, student activities, or residential life, students should contact:

Director of Admission
Carroll College
1601 North Benton Avenue
Helena, Montana 59625-0002

Telephone: 406-447-4384
          800-992-3648 (toll-free)
E-mail: enroll@carroll.edu
World Wide Web: http://www.carroll.edu

St. Charles Hall, the historic cornerstone of Carroll's campus, is known as "The Rock."

CARROLL COLLEGE
WAUKESHA, WISCONSIN

The College

Carroll College was chartered by the territorial legislature of Wisconsin in 1846. Carroll College is affiliated with the Presbyterian Church (U.S.A.) but is nonsectarian and ecumenical.

The College realizes that personalized education is the special province of a small college and recognizes the variety of students' individual needs and preferences. Carroll's student body is diverse, with representation from thirty states and thirty-six countries. The campus has more than 1,850 full-time men and women as well as more than 800 part-time students. Additionally, there are more than 100 graduate students on the Carroll campus.

Many opportunities exist for cocurricular involvement. Three fraternities and four sororities draw participation from about 13 percent of the students. A broad variety of special interest organizations provide a full program of campus activities in addition to the all-campus social, intellectual, and athletic events that are scheduled throughout the year. The College's facilities for recreation and athletics include the following: the Van Male Fieldhouse has a basketball court; an indoor track; indoor facilities for badminton, tennis, and volleyball; and an Olympic-size pool. The adjacent Ganfield Gymnasium provides additional space for athletics and recreation. A football field, a soccer field, and a softball diamond are also available.

In addition to the bachelor's degrees Carroll offers, the College also grants the master's degree in education and physical therapy.

Location

The College is located in the city of Waukesha, a residential community of 60,000 people, which is 18 miles west of Milwaukee and 100 miles north of Chicago. The College's proximity to these two major urban centers and to the settings associated with Wisconsin's famous outdoor sports and leisure activities provides Carroll students with numerous opportunities for recreation, entertainment, and enrichment.

Majors and Degrees

Carroll College grants the B.A., B.S., B.S.N., and B.S.Med.Tech. degrees. Areas of study include accounting, actuarial sciences, adaptive education, art, athletic training, biology, business administration, chemistry, coaching, communication, computer science, criminal justice, early childhood education, elementary education, English, environmental science, fitness management, geography, graphic communication, health education, history, human services, international relations, journalism, marine biology, mathematics, medical technology, modern languages and literature, music, nursing, photography, physical education, physical therapy, politics, psychology, public administration, religious studies, secondary education, social work, sociology, Spanish, theater arts, and women's studies. Individually designed majors are also available.

The College grants the B.S.N. degree in collaboration with Columbia College of Nursing in Milwaukee.

Academic Program

The College currently operates on a semester calendar. All students must complete 128 credits with a C average or better. A major, generally consisting of 40 credits, must be completed. General education requirements include the First Year Seminar, English, liberal studies distribution courses, and a capstone experience. B.A. students must take two years of a modern language or the equivalent. B.S. students must take mathematics and either a computer science or logic course. Students may also select a second major or they may select a minor, which generally requires 16 to 28 credits. The honors program offers intensive sections of courses in the arts and sciences for academically talented students.

Advanced placement or credit may be granted to students who have completed the appropriate College Board Advanced Placement examinations. Credit may be granted for a score at or above the 75th percentile on the humanities, natural science, or social science general examination of the College-Level Examination Program (CLEP). Scores on CLEP subject examinations may also qualify to be approved for credit. A total of not more than 48 credit hours may be awarded through CLEP general and subject examinations.

Off-Campus Arrangements

The New Cultural Experiences Program gives all Carroll students the opportunity to study in a different cultural setting. Students may plan an individual program or participate in a planned group experience involving other students and Carroll faculty. Group experiences are offered in locations such as Mexico, England, Australia, China, Belize, Bali, Thailand, Israel, and countries in Europe and Africa. Other off-campus programs include the Washington Semester, the United Nations Semester, and the Junior Year Abroad. In addition, career internships are provided in the Milwaukee-Waukesha area for students interested in gaining practical work experience in their proposed career field. All of these programs carry degree credit, the amount depending upon the nature and duration of the experience.

Academic Facilities

The College library houses more than 182,000 volumes, 18,000 microforms, and 600 periodicals. A $3-million renovation of the library was completed in 1999. The Department of Education is in the Barstow Building with the Modern Language and Communication Departments. Rankin Hall houses the Departments of Biology, Psychology, and Religious Studies, as well as the psychology laboratories. Maxon Hall houses the Departments of Geography and Mathematics. It also contains the laboratories for advanced chemistry, the geography laboratory with independent-study booths and audiovisual instruments, a darkroom, a cartography laboratory, a map library, and a National Weather Service observation station. The chemistry and physics laboratories are in Lowry Hall. All science laboratories are provided with up-to-date equipment. Main Hall houses the Departments of Sociology, Social Work, Business Administration, Economics, and Accounting, as well as the Computer Center. The MacAllister Hall is home to the Departments of English, History, Politics, and Philosophy and houses the Norman FitzGerald Civil War Collection.

The Shattuck Music Center houses a recital hall that seats 150, an auditorium that seats 1,350, and a Schantz seventy-two-stop pipe organ. The Department of Music has a large band-practice room, teaching studios, a multisensing room, a computerized music laboratory, and classrooms; additional practice rooms are in the adjacent Theatre Arts Building. The Humphrey Building houses the Art Department and Humphrey Memorial Chapel.

The College's physical therapy program is located in the recently renovated building adjacent to the College's athletic complex.

Costs

For 2000–01, the tuition is $15,250, and room and board are $4740.

Financial Aid

Approximately 95 percent of Carroll's students receive some form of financial aid. Aid is based on need, as determined by the U.S. Department of Education's Free Application for Federal Student Aid (FAFSA), as well as on scholastic ability and achievement. Generally, students receive a package consisting of a scholarship, a grant, a loan, and/or employment.

Various merit scholarships are available to students. Merit scholarships range from $18,000 to $28,000 over four years and are determined by a student's ACT or SAT I scores and class rank. Students who attend high schools that do not rank are not excluded from consideration for any academic scholarships. Additional scholarships are awarded to qualified students who are interested in music, journalism, nursing, theater, politics, international relations, public administration, history, art, math, or the sciences. Students should contact the Office of Admission for details.

Faculty

The student-faculty ratio at Carroll is approximately 20:1. More than 85 percent of faculty members hold a doctorate in their specialized area of study. There are more than 100 full-time faculty members at Carroll.

Student Government

Through election to the Student Senate and College Activities Board, students have responsibility for nonacademic matters affecting their lives at the College. In addition, there is voting student representation on all College committees, and there are student observers on the Board of Trustees.

Admission Requirements

Carroll's admission procedure is intended to ensure academic and personal success for accepted students. Each candidate is evaluated individually; evidence of the interest in and ability to do college-level work is important. The College exercises careful selection, but no candidate is disqualified because of race, color, religion, sex, national origin, age, disability, sexual orientation, or veteran status.

Application and Information

To be considered, each candidate for freshman admission must submit the following materials: a completed application for admission; a transcript from an accredited high school showing progress toward, or completion of, 15 units of work and graduation; a satisfactory personal evaluation from the high school; and scores on the SAT I or ACT. Transfer students must submit a transcript from every college attended previously and a statement of good standing. Admission decisions are made on a rolling basis until the class is filled. There are no deadlines, but early application is recommended.

Admission to the College may be granted following the completion of three years of high school work, provided that the high school indicates that this is in the applicant's best interest. The candidate may or may not have completed the course work required for high school graduation at the time of admission, but he or she must show unusual promise and achievement.

For more information about Carroll College, prospective students should contact:

Admission Office
Carroll College
100 North East Avenue
Waukesha, Wisconsin 53186
Telephone: 262-524-7220
        800-CARROLL (toll-free)
World Wide Web: http://www.cc.edu

CARSON-NEWMAN COLLEGE
JEFFERSON CITY, TENNESSEE

The College
Founded in 1851 by Tennessee Baptists, Carson-Newman is a private, coeducational, Christian liberal arts college. The College has an enrollment of 2,000 undergraduate and 250 graduate students. The average class size is 16 students, and the male-female ratio is 1:1. Each fall Carson-Newman enrolls approximately 450 freshmen and 150 transfers. While Carson-Newman students come primarily from the Southeastern states, forty-one states are represented.

In addition to its outstanding academics, C-N also provides many opportunities for student involvement in various clubs and organizations, nationally recognized varsity athletics, intramural athletics, music and drama groups, an award-winning forensics team, and many other extracurricular activities. The majority of C-N students live on campus in one of the two men's and three women's residence halls.

Graduate programs in education are available leading to the Master of Arts in Teaching, the Master of Arts in Education, the Master of Education in school counseling, and the Master of Arts in Teaching English as a Second Language degrees. A Master of Science in Nursing program is also offered.

Location
C-N is conveniently located in eastern Tennessee, just 30 miles from Knoxville, which has a population of 450,000, and 45 miles from Gatlinburg, a gateway to the Great Smoky Mountains. Students appreciate the diverse opportunities available in the city and the rural outdoor areas. There are also small towns located near the College that offer shopping, dining, and entertainment.

Majors and Degrees
The eight academic divisions of the College are Business, Education, Family and Consumer Sciences, Fine Arts, Humanities, Natural Sciences and Mathematics, Nursing, and Social Sciences. C-N awards the Bachelor of Arts, Bachelor of Music, Bachelor of Science, and Bachelor of Science in Nursing degrees. In addition, an Associate of Arts in Christian Ministries degree is also offered.

Majors are available in art (art and photography), athletic training, business (accounting, business administration, business economics, general business, international economics, long-term health-care management, and management), church recreation, communication arts and mass communication (broadcasting, drama, general communication, journalism, and speech), computer information systems (computer studies and data processing), computer science, education (athletic coaching, elementary education, leisure services, physical education/health, secondary certification, and special education), English (creative writing and film studies), family and consumer sciences (child and family studies, consumer services, foods and nutrition, interior design and retail, and vocational family and consumer sciences education), foreign language (French, German, and Spanish), general studies, history (social studies), human services, individual directions, mathematics, military science/U.S. Army ROTC or U.S. Air Force ROTC, music (church music, music education, music theory, music with an outside field, piano and organ performance, and vocal performance), natural and physical science (biology and chemistry), nursing, philosophy (philosophy and philosophy/religion), political science, psychology, religion, and sociology.

The College offers extremely strong curricula in preprofessional programs and health professions. Preprofessional programs are offered in dentistry, engineering, health information management, law, medicine, occupational therapy, optometry, physical therapy, and veterinary medicine. In cooperation with several other institutions, C-N offers binary degrees (2-3 and 3-2 programs) in engineering, medical technology, pharmacy, and physical therapy.

Academic Program
The College operates on a traditional semester system. Mayterm is a three-week intensive period of study giving students the opportunity to earn 3 credit hours. Summer term is offered as a six-week program of study.

All baccalaureate degrees require completion of 128 semester hours. Students must complete 51 semester hours in general education requirements and a total of 36 semester hours at junior/senior level. Specific course requirements vary depending on major and degree program. Honors courses, independent study, and internships are available to students who qualify.

Advanced credit is available for students who achieve required scores on AP exams, CLEP tests, and C-N departmental examinations.

New students are assigned a faculty adviser who assists with course selection and student concerns. Career planning services are also available.

The College's exceptionally high placement rate in professional programs in medicine, law, business, and theological study is testimony to the excellence of its rigorous academic program.

Off-Campus Arrangements
Students have the opportunity to spend an entire semester abroad by participating in the London Semester and other study-abroad opportunities. C-N, along with International Enrichment, Inc., provides all academic and nonacademic support services.

The Washington Semester is available as an internship program primarily for political science and prelaw majors. Through the program, students earn credit for work in the nation's capital.

Art and foreign language majors may earn credit while studying and traveling throughout Europe during the three-week Mayterm.

Academic Facilities
C-N offers the facilities and resources necessary for the enrichment of each student's education. Facilities include seven computer labs; a word processing lab; a campuswide computer network; a media service center with more than 200,000 volumes; two theaters for drama production; Thomas Recital Hall, which is in one of the finest music facilities in the Southeast; two art galleries and twenty-three individual art studios; the Lakeway Community Network Channel (LCNC)

television station, which is operated by students in the broadcasting field; and an award-winning 96,000-square-foot Student Activities Center.

Costs

The annual cost at Carson-Newman, including room, board, and tuition, is well below the national average for four-year private colleges. Tuition in 2000–01 is $11,240, room is $1590, board is $2390, the student activity fee is $340, and the technology fee is $340. Total direct charges are $15,900. Students should allow approximately $700 for books per year.

Financial Aid

Carson-Newman allocates thousands of dollars each year to help supplement the resources of families. Financial aid awards are tailored to meet students' economic needs. Carson-Newman participates in all state and federal aid programs and awards aid based on demonstrated need as documented by a need analysis form, such as the Free Application for Federal Student Aid (FAFSA). Carson-Newman also awards academic scholarships based on achievement. Deadline for filing financial aid forms is April 1.

Faculty

Carson-Newman has 122 full-time and 65 part-time faculty members. Of these, 68 percent hold the Ph.D. The student-faculty ratio is 13:1. Faculty members are involved in scholarly pursuits such as authoring books, leading national scholastic organizations, and research, but their primary focus is teaching.

Student Government

The Student Government Association (SGA) represents the entire student body by voicing student concerns in campus affairs. The purpose of SGA is to promote the welfare of every student through justice, to protect individual rights and freedoms, to encourage high standards of conduct, and to train students in the general principles of self-government.

Admission Requirements

Carson-Newman College seeks applicants who demonstrate academic preparation and who possess an appreciation of and sensitivity to a Christian education and a liberal arts curriculum. Carson-Newman accepts applications for freshman and transfer admission for each term of enrollment (fall, spring, and summer). Freshman candidates must have a GPA of 2.25 or higher in the core curriculum and a minimum score of 920 on the SAT I or 19 on the ACT; they must also rank in the top half of their high school graduating class. Transfer applicants must have a minimum cumulative GPA of 2.0 in courses that transfer to Carson-Newman.

Application and Information

Applicants must submit an application for admission, official transcripts, and a nonrefundable $25 application fee. Admission decisions are made on a rolling basis, and students are notified within two weeks of receipt of all required documents. Application deadline is May 1 for fall semester, December 1 for spring semester. Applicants who wish to be considered for full-tuition scholarships must apply by December 31.

For additional information, students should contact:

Office of Undergraduate Admissions
Carson-Newman College
Jefferson City, Tennessee 37760
Telephone: 865-471-3223
              800-678-9061 (toll-free)
E-mail: sgray@cncadmnt.cn.edu
World Wide Web: http://www.cn.edu

Students share unique learning relationships with faculty members at Carson-Newman.

CARTHAGE COLLEGE
KENOSHA, WISCONSIN

The College

Carthage is a four-year private college of the arts and sciences, committed to educating students in the liberal arts tradition. Founded in 1847, Carthage is affiliated with the Evangelical Lutheran Church in America. With this heritage, the College provides a values-centered education to prepare its students for the challenges and complexities of life in the modern world.

Though Carthage attracts the majority of its students from the Midwest, the 1,500 full-time students come from all parts of the world, representing twenty-seven states and eleven other countries.

With a student-faculty ratio of 16:1, the College offers a nurturing, personal education in a way that most larger universities cannot. Carthage is primarily a residential campus, and life in the College residence halls is an important part of the Carthage learning experience. All five residence halls have been recently renovated, and all rooms have outside phone lines and cable television and offer access to the campus computer network and the Internet.

Complementing the academic and residence-life programs are a wide range of extracurricular activities. There are more than seventy clubs and organizations on campus, including social sororities and fraternities; theater, choir, publications, and religious groups; departmental clubs; and a campus radio station. In athletics, the College offers twenty intercollegiate teams for men and women. Among the men's sports are baseball, basketball, cross-country, football, golf, soccer, swimming, tennis, and track and field. Women's sports include basketball, cross-country, golf, soccer, softball, swimming, tennis, track and field, and volleyball. Carthage competes in the College Conference of Illinois and Wisconsin (CCIW), one of the top NCAA Division III conferences in the United States. Men's ice hockey is offered as a club sport. A strong intramural program for both men and women is also available. The College's spacious Physical Education Center, the focal point for these programs, also provides a state-of-the-art fitness center. The W. A. Seidemann Natatorium houses an indoor swimming pool for intercollegiate and recreational use throughout the year. The Todd Wehr Center, the hub of campus life, is home to the student union, a game room, two cafeterias, meeting rooms, and WOH's Place, a nonalcoholic pub.

Carthage is accredited by the North Central Association of Colleges and Schools and holds a variety of professional recognitions, including accreditation of its chemistry program by the American Chemical Society and its music program by the National Association of Schools of Music.

In addition to its undergraduate programs, the College offers a Master in Education degree with concentrations in classroom guidance and counseling, creative arts, language arts, natural science, reading, religion, and social science.

Location

Carthage is located on the shore of Lake Michigan, 60 miles north of Chicago and 30 miles south of Milwaukee. The campus enjoys an idyllic setting on 72 parklike acres, including 2,850 feet of scenic shoreline. In addition to its beautiful natural setting, the College benefits from the easily accessible cultural and educational opportunities offered by its two major metropolitan neighbors.

Majors and Degrees

Carthage awards the Bachelor of Arts degree. Areas of study include accounting; art; athletic training; biology; business administration; chemistry; cognitive disabilities; communications and performing arts; computer science; criminal justice; economics; elementary/middle education; engineering (3-2); English; French; geography; German; graphic design; history; international political economy; Japanese; learning disabilities; marketing; mathematics; music; occupational therapy (3-2); philosophy; physical education; physics; political science; predentistry; prelaw; premedicine; prepharmacy; preveterinary; psychology; recreation, sport, and fitness management; religion; social science; social work; sociology; and Spanish. Certifications are offered in coaching, secondary education, and special education. Students may also design their own majors in order to meet their academic needs and career goals and objectives.

Academic Program

Carthage is a liberal arts college that provides a strong foundation in liberal studies as well as career-oriented and preprofessional programs. Two courses in religious studies; one course in fine arts, humanities, mathematics, and social science; two courses in foreign language; and three freshman and sophomore Heritage seminars, which emphasize critical thinking, reasoning, writing, speaking, and listening through cultural and international studies, comprise a portion of the course requirement areas. Each student also participates in a Junior Symposium, which consists of three linked courses from multiple disciplines. A senior thesis is required as part of each major. A dynamic honors program gives outstanding students special opportunities for growth and learning throughout their four years at the College.

Carthage operates on a year-round academic calendar consisting of fall, spring, and summer academic terms separated by a January term. The month-long J-Term provides opportunities for independent study, special course work, internships, travel for credit, and other special activities.

Off-Campus Arrangements

Carthage maintains several cooperative programs with other institutions, including a 3-2 program in engineering with the University of Wisconsin–Madison; Case Western Reserve University, Cleveland, Ohio; and Washington University in St. Louis, Missouri, and a 3-2 program in occupational therapy with Washington University. Air Force ROTC is available to qualified students.

Carthage students are able to secure internships with both large and small companies, government agencies, and nonprofit organizations. In addition, the College has an active study-abroad program, which enables students to travel to various countries for semester- or year-abroad studies.

Academic Facilities

Lentz Hall houses classrooms, the bookstore, administrative offices, and the Computer Center. The David A. Straz, Jr. Center includes Ruthrauff Library, which holds 210,259 books, 1,159 periodicals, and microfiche equipment; the 400-seat Wartburg Auditorium; and classrooms and laboratories for the science departments, as well as the undergraduate research laboratories. The Johnson Art Center provides Carthage with the impressive 1,800-seat Siebert Chapel, additional classrooms, art studios, and rehearsal studios for the music department. Easily accessible to students, academic resources and support services designed to help every student reach his or her academic potential are strategically located in the residence halls. Comprehensive academic counseling services are also provided to all freshmen and sophomores by full-time professionals in the Advising Center. Each freshman is assigned to an adviser who is also available for counseling in all areas of College life.

Costs

For 2000–01, a comprehensive fee of $22,560 per year includes full-time tuition and fees ($17,350) and room and board ($5210). The cost of books is estimated at $250 per semester.

Financial Aid

More than 90 percent of Carthage students receive some type of financial assistance, and, on the average, their total packages cover nearly two thirds of total cost. The College administers more than $20 million in financial aid each year. A wide range of aid is available, including both need-based and non-need-based scholarships and grants. Carthage participates in all federal and state student financial assistance programs and offers non-need-based student employment. In addition, Carthage awards ten major scholarships per year through the Lincoln/Ruud Scholarship competition.

Faculty

Ninety percent of the full-time faculty members hold a Ph.D. or other terminal degree. Their credentials include degrees from a broad range of highly respected graduate schools. Many faculty members serve as academic advisers to upperclass students, enhancing the student-faculty interaction that is so valued at Carthage.

Student Government

The Student Government Association and the Student Activities Board function as the voice of the students in issues pertinent to student life. Students may serve on a variety of committees that deal with specific areas of student life, such as the committees on religious activities and special events.

Admission Requirements

Carthage selects its students on the basis of a variety of factors. The College seeks students who demonstrate a sound ability to follow their program through to graduation. Carthage strongly recommends that an applicant complete at least 16 units through four years of high school work in English, foreign languages, mathematics, science, and social studies. In addition, the College considers the student's academic grade point average, rank in class, and results of the ACT or SAT I. A visit to the campus (by appointment) is recommended.

Application and Information

To request application forms, information, and additional details, students should contact:

Office of Admissions
Carthage College
2001 Alford Park Drive
Kenosha, Wisconsin 53140-1994
Telephone: 262-551-6000
           800-351-4058 (toll-free)
E-mail: admissions@carthage.edu
World Wide Web: http://www.carthage.edu

Carthage is located on the shore of Lake Michigan in Kenosha, Wisconsin.

CASE WESTERN RESERVE UNIVERSITY
CLEVELAND, OHIO

The University

Formed in 1967 by the federation of Case Institute of Technology and Western Reserve University, Case Western Reserve University is today one of the nation's major independent universities. Currently, 3,380 undergraduates (2,027 men, 1,353 women) are enrolled in programs in engineering, science, management, nursing, the arts, humanities, and the social and behavioral sciences. Students have access to the facilities of a comprehensive university, including graduate and professional schools in applied social sciences, dentistry, graduate studies (humanities, the social and natural sciences, and engineering), nursing, medicine, law, and management. Several undergraduate programs and majors combine the resources of the undergraduate colleges and the graduate and professional schools. Examples include biochemistry and biomedical engineering (CWRU School of Medicine) and accounting and management (Weatherhead School of Management). In addition, collaborative arrangements with neighboring cultural and health-care institutions enable the University to provide special opportunities in other fields.

There are numerous college activities, including those of dozens of professional, religious, political, social, and academic organizations. Nearly every type of interest group, from political organizations to a film society, is represented on campus, and sports are offered at both the varsity and intramural levels. There are eighteen national fraternities and five sororities; approximately 25 to 30 percent of the students participate. Residence halls are coeducational, with the exception of one hall for women. Seventy-five percent of the students reside on campus. Automobiles and motorcycles are permitted.

Students at Case Western Reserve enjoy an especially close interaction with the faculty.

Location

The University is located in University Circle, a cultural extension of the campus, which comprises 500 acres of parks, gardens, museums, schools, hospitals, churches, and human service institutions. The Cleveland Museum of Art, the Cleveland Museum of Natural History, and Severance Hall, home of the Cleveland Orchestra, are within walking distance; downtown Cleveland is 10 minutes away by RTA rapid transit. Cooperation in education and research among University Circle institutions enables students to make full use of resources beyond those of the University itself.

Majors and Degrees

Programs of study leading to the Bachelor of Arts degree comprise the following: American studies, anthropology, art history (joint program with the Cleveland Museum of Art), Asian studies, astronomy, biochemistry, biology, chemistry, classics (Greek and Latin), communication sciences (speech pathology and audiology—collaborative program with Cleveland Hearing and Speech Center), comparative literature, computer science, economics, English, environmental geology, environmental studies, French, French studies, geological sciences, German, German studies, gerontological studies, history, history and philosophy of science and technology, international studies, Japanese studies, mathematics, music (joint program with the Cleveland Institute of Music), natural sciences, nutrition, nutritional biochemistry and metabolism, philosophy, physics, political science, prearchitecture, psychology, religion, sociology, Spanish, statistics, theater arts, and women's studies. Minor areas of concentration within the B.A. curriculum include artificial intelligence, art studio, childhood studies, Chinese, electronics, history of science and technology, human development, Japanese, management information and decision systems, public policy, Russian, and sports medicine.

Bachelor of Science degrees are offered in the following fields: accounting; aerospace engineering; applied mathematics; art education (joint program with the Cleveland Institute of Art); astronomy; biochemistry; biology; biomedical engineering; chemical engineering; chemistry; civil engineering; computer engineering; computer science; electrical engineering; engineering physics; fluid and thermal engineering sciences; geological sciences; management (business); materials science and engineering; mathematics; mechanical engineering; music education; nursing; nutrition; nutritional biochemistry and metabolism; physics; polymer science; statistics; systems and control engineering; and an undesignated engineering major. Course sequences emphasizing architecture, energy, environmental/water resources studies, and power are offered in conjunction with some engineering and science fields.

Exceptionally well qualified high school seniors in some fields are eligible for the Pre-Professional Scholars Program offered in association with the Schools of Dentistry, Law, and Medicine. In addition to being accepted as an undergraduate, each student selected is also awarded a conditional acceptance for admission to the appropriate professional school upon completion of the entrance requirements set by each school. A six-year dental program leading to the D.D.S. degree is also available.

Students may work toward a combined B.A./B.S. degree or integrate undergraduate and graduate studies to complete both the bachelor's and master's degrees in five years or less. Combined B.A./B.S. (3-2) programs in astronomy, biochemistry, and engineering are offered in conjunction with a number of four-year liberal arts colleges.

Academic Program

Through a combination of core curricula, major requirements, and minors or approved course sequences, all undergraduates receive a broad educational base as well as specialized knowledge in their chosen fields.

The University offers students opportunities for independent research and internships or professional practicums in business, health-care, government, arts, or service fields. A five-year co-op option providing two 7-month work periods in industry or government is available for majors in engineering, science, management, accounting, and computer science.

The Undergraduate Scholars Program allows a small number of highly motivated and responsible students to pursue individually tailored baccalaureate programs without the normal credit-hour and course requirements. The program, administered by a faculty committee, must be one that cannot be accomplished within the regular curricula.

Candidates for the B.A. who have been accepted at a school of medicine or dentistry other than one of those at CWRU may exercise the Senior Year In Absentia Privilege, which permits them to substitute the first year of professional studies at an approved school for the final year at Case Western Reserve. The Senior Year in Professional Studies option allows B.A. candidates who are admitted during their junior year to CWRU's school of dentistry, management, medicine, nursing, or social work to substitute the first year of professional school for the final undergraduate year.

The Minority Engineers Industrial Opportunity Program offers a special orientation and support to minority students in secondary schools and academic and financial support to minority undergraduates in engineering.

The University has two 4-month semesters and one 8-week summer program.

Off-Campus Arrangements

Selected students may enroll as juniors and seniors in the Washington Semester, which is conducted each spring at the American University. Students with a B average or higher may participate in the Junior Year Abroad program. Up to 36 hours of credit may be granted for study at a foreign university. Students may also cross-register at other Cleveland-area colleges and universities for one course per semester.

Academic Facilities

The $30-million Kelvin Smith Library opened in 1997. Through reciprocal borrowing arrangements, CWRU students have access to the holdings of the Cleveland Public Library, as well as the libraries of five University Circle institutions; the members of OhioLINK, a network that includes state colleges and universities; the State Library of Ohio; and several private institutions. In addition to more traditional departmental research facilities, the University operates two astronomical observatories, a biological field station, and nearly 100 designated research centers and laboratories, many of them interdisciplinary. CWRUnet, the University's high-speed fiber-optic communications network, links every residence hall room with computing centers, libraries, and databases on and off campus. Other computer facilities on campus offer various models of microcomputers and a wide variety of software programs.

Costs

For 2000–01, tuition and compulsory health and laboratory fees total $20,100. The student activity fee is $160. Room and board cost an average of $5815. Books and supplies come to about $680, and incidental expenses are estimated at $1280. The approximate total cost for the year is $28,035.

Financial Aid

Financial aid consisting of grants, loans, and work assistance is awarded on the basis of a student's need. Last year, all students demonstrating need received financial aid. Applicants must file the Free Application for Federal Student Aid (FAFSA) and the Financial Aid PROFILE of the College Scholarship Service by February 1. A signed copy of the most recent federal tax return (Form 1040) is also required. The University also awards merit-based scholarships ranging from $500 to full tuition. These awards are based solely on the student's academic, creative, or leadership ability.

Faculty

The full-time instructional staff of 2,045, of whom 95 percent hold the Ph.D. or equivalent, is shared by all University students: graduate, undergraduate, and professional. The undergraduate student-faculty ratio is 8:1. Each college provides counselors who are always available for both academic and personal advice. Once a major has been chosen, a member of the department in which the student is majoring acts as his or her academic adviser.

Student Government

The Undergraduate Student Government of Case Western Reserve University represents all undergraduate students. The assembly acts as a liaison between undergraduate students and the faculty, administration, and other groups; grants recognition to undergraduate organizations; and has the responsibility and authority to allocate funds from student activity fees to student organizations.

Admission Requirements

The University requires at least 16 units of full-credit high school work in solid academic subjects, including 4 years of English or its equivalent. All applicants are expected to have completed 3 years of high school mathematics, and students interested in mathematics, science, or engineering majors should have 4. At least 2 years of laboratory science are required of all applicants, and prospective mathematics and science majors must present 3 years. For all engineering candidates, physics and chemistry are required. Two years of foreign language study are recommended for students considering majors in the humanities, arts, and social and behavioral sciences. An interview is not a required part of the admission process, but it is strongly recommended as the best way to learn about the University. Applicants should take the ACT or the SAT I not later than January of their senior year in secondary school. For candidates submitting the SAT I, three SAT II Subject Tests are strongly recommended, including the Writing Test for all students, the Level I or II mathematics test and physics or chemistry for engineering candidates, and two tests of their choice for others.

Application and Information

Freshmen may matriculate in January, June, or August. Students for whom Case Western Reserve University is a definite first choice may apply for early decision by January 1. They are notified within two weeks of receipt of a completed application. The final application deadline is February 1 for April 15 notification. Application deadlines for transfer students are June 30 for fall admission and November 15 for spring admission. The application deadline for the Pre-Professional Scholars Program (medicine, dentistry, or law) is December 15. In addition to its own application form, Case Western Reserve University accepts the Common Application, Apply!, Collegeedge, and College Link forms.

To obtain an application form and financial aid information, students should contact:

Office of Undergraduate Admission
Case Western Reserve University
10900 Euclid Avenue
Cleveland, Ohio 44106-7055
Telephone: 216-368-4450
E-mail: admission@po.cwru.edu
World Wide Web: http://www.cwru.edu

Students at Case Western Reserve University in Cleveland, Ohio.

CASTLETON STATE COLLEGE
CASTLETON, VERMONT

The College

Castleton State College was founded in 1787 and was the first institution of higher learning in Vermont and the eighteenth in the United States. The 130-acre campus is located in Castleton, a historic Vermont village. Sixty percent of the 1,500 full-time undergraduate students at the College are Vermonters; the balance of the student population comes from the New England and Middle Atlantic states.

Castleton is committed to providing an undergraduate education in which the liberal arts and career preparation complement each other. Through an innovative program called Soundings, freshmen earn academic credit by attending a series of special events, which include theater, music, dance, film, debate, and opinion from influential people. New students also participate in the First-Year Seminar, giving them the opportunity to develop the skills of a successful college student.

There are six residence halls, which together accommodate 710 students. Each residence hall room is equipped with at least two Internet hook-ups, which gives each student the opportunity to access the World Wide Web and e-mail using their own personal computer. There is no additional charge for this service. Each room is also equipped with cable TV connections and individual telephone lines. Off-campus housing is available in the Castleton, Fair Haven, and Rutland areas. Students who live on campus eat in Huden Dining Hall. All students are allowed to have automobiles on campus.

More than forty clubs and organizations provide a wide variety of student activities that include club sports, an FM radio station, the student newspaper, and an active outing club. Other clubs relate to college majors and future careers; still others serve the College or local community. There are twelve varsity sports. Men compete in baseball, basketball, cross-country running, lacrosse, soccer, and tennis; women compete in basketball, cross-country running, lacrosse, soccer, softball, and tennis. A majority of Castleton's students are involved in the intramural and recreational sports program. Many students are skiers and snowboarders.

Location

The campus is 12 miles west of Rutland, Vermont's second-largest city. Montreal, Boston, Hartford, Albany, and New York City are all within easy driving distance and are accessible by public transportation from Rutland. Killington and Pico ski areas, Lake Bomoseen, and the Green Mountains provide excellent recreational opportunities and an exceptional living and learning environment.

Majors and Degrees

Castleton State College offers B.A. or B.S. degrees in more than thirty areas of study: accounting, American literature, art, biology, children's literature, computer information systems, corporate communication, criminal justice, digital media, e-commerce, elementary education, environmental science, finance, forensic psychology, geology, health science, history, journalism, management, marketing, mass media, mathematics, music, natural science, physical education, psychology, secondary education, social work, sociology, Spanish, special education, sports medicine, theater arts, and world literature.

Associate degrees can be earned in business, communication, computer programming, criminal justice, general studies, or nursing.

Academic Program

The Castleton curriculum is designed to provide the student with a strong liberal arts background plus the opportunity for career preparation in a specific area. All four-year students are required to complete a 42-credit core of liberal arts courses during the four-year degree program. The first year of study can be used by the undecided student to explore various areas of interest. The student with a specific career interest may begin study in the major field as a freshman, although four-year students are not required to formally declare their major until the end of the sophomore year.

Castleton students typically enroll in five courses each semester. The academic calendar consists of two 15-week semesters and three 4-week summer sessions. Grading is traditional, and a pass/no pass option is available. Internships and field experiences complement many of the academic programs at Castleton and are required in the communication, criminal justice, social work, and education programs.

Students may transfer internally from two-year to four-year programs in business, communication, computer information systems, criminal justice, and general studies. Students who transfer to Castleton after graduating from an accredited two-year college are granted full transfer credit for all academic work up to 64 credits or the number required for the associate degree.

Freshmen achieving at least a 3.5 grade point average in their first year at Castleton are recognized by the Castleton Chapter of Phi Eta Sigma, a national honor society that recognizes freshman scholastic achievement in colleges throughout the country. Outstanding junior and senior scholars are recognized by the Castleton Chapter of Alpha Chi. There are honor societies in theater arts, education, psychology, and Spanish. Students who have achieved a 4.0 grade point average are named to the President's List of Outstanding Students, and those with a 3.5 grade point average or better to the Dean's List.

Academic Facilities

The Calvin Coolidge Library houses a collection of more than 500,000 books, periodicals, microforms, and nonprint media. Access to Castleton's library resources and outside scholarly sources is made possible through numerous online and CD databases; a sophisticated, networked electronic library system; the Internet; and strong consortial relationships within the state of Vermont. An audiovisual media facility is integrated with the library and provides a wide range of services, including film and tape production techniques and showings, plus slide transparency and other instructional services.

Castleton's new Stafford Academic Center houses the Computing Center, a high-tech multimedia lecture hall, distance learning classrooms, and the Departments of Education, Mathematics, and Nursing.

Glenbrook Gymnasium houses the athletic training room, the Human Performance Center, the swimming pool, two racquetball courts, a fitness center, and a large indoor activity area.

The Fine Arts Center contains a 500-seat auditorium; facilities for art, drama, dance, and music; and television studios.

The Florence Black Science Center houses general classrooms and laboratories, a 200-seat auditorium, a precision-instrument room, a herbarium, a darkroom, a computing center, and an astronomical observatory.

There are more than 200 personal computers designated for student use located in labs across campus.

Costs

Costs for 1999–2000 were as follows: tuition for Vermont residents, $4092; for nonresidents, $9588; and for students participating in the New England Regional Student Program, $6156. Room and board expenses totaled $5298, and fees totaled $928.

Financial Aid

Seventy-eight percent of Castleton's full-time undergraduate students receive financial assistance from federal, state, College, or other sources. Grants, loans, and work-study jobs are available for qualified students. Applicants for financial aid should file the Free Application for Federal Student Aid form by February 15 of the senior year in high school. All financial aid awards are based on need.

Most Castleton scholarships are awarded as part of the Castleton Fellows Program. Fellowships range from $1000 to $3000 per year. High school students who are in the top quarter of their class, have a combined SAT I score of at least 1000, or have a cumulative GPA of at least 3.0 on a 4.0 scale and transfer students with a 3.0 GPA are eligible to apply. There are also special scholarships for students wishing to study music or Spanish.

Faculty

The full-time faculty at Castleton consists of 88 men and women, 94 percent of whom hold terminal degrees in their field. Adjunct faculty members, many of them local businesspeople and members of the professions, complement the efforts of the full-time faculty. The student-faculty ratio is 16:1. Each student has a faculty member as an adviser.

Student Government

The Student Association is the chief vehicle of student government. All students registered for 8 or more credit hours are members. Elected representatives hold membership on most College committees, including the Curriculum and Cultural Affairs committees. Students are also able to develop leadership qualities by participating in the various clubs and other organizations on campus.

Admission Requirements

Applicants are evaluated on the basis of their secondary school records, standardized test scores, and recommendations. Admission is granted to those applicants who have demonstrated their ability and potential to meet the challenges of a postsecondary learning experience.

Application and Information

Students may apply for admission through the Castleton Web site below. Under Castleton's rolling admission policy, applications are processed throughout the year, and candidates are notified of the admission decision as soon as their folders are complete. Students are admitted in the fall and spring semesters.

For more information about Castleton State College or to arrange a campus visit, students should contact:

Dean of Enrollment
Castleton State College
Castleton, Vermont 05735
Telephone: 802-468-1213
          800-639-8521 (toll-free)
Fax: 802-468-1476
E-mail: info@castleton.edu
World Wide Web: http://www.castleton.edu

Between classes, students gather on the patio near historic Woodruff Hall.

CATAWBA COLLEGE
SALISBURY, NORTH CAROLINA

The College

Catawba College is a senior coeducational liberal arts college that focuses on the whole individual, educating its students for productive and responsible citizenship. Founded in 1851 by German-American immigrants of the Reformed faith, it provides a values-centered liberal arts education marked by academic challenges and personal attention.

The College is situated on 276 wooded acres. Two of the primary buildings—Ketner Hall, the premier classroom facility, and the Cannon Student Center—were completed in 1988.

The student body consists of 1,200 students from thirty-two states and eight countries. Nearly 90 percent of Catawba's students are from the Eastern Seaboard. About two thirds of the students reside on campus in one of the nine residence halls.

Students can choose from a wide variety of campus activities, including theater productions, choral groups, academic clubs, community service organizations, dances, concerts, bands, student government association, literary societies, and intramurals. Students are encouraged to participate in an array of clubs and organizations, beginning in their freshman year.

The Abernethy Physical Education Center houses racquetball courts, three basketball courts, an indoor swimming pool, weight rooms, and other facilities for extracurricular activities as well as the training of seventeen NCAA Division II varsity athletics teams (men's and women's). A 20-acre athletics complex is composed of two soccer fields, a hockey field, a softball field, a football practice field, and a lacrosse field. Six tennis courts, with lighting and spectator seating, are located on campus.

Religious services and organizations are open to all members of the campus community; religious activities are led by the campus minister.

Location

Catawba is located in Salisbury, a historic Southern city of 25,000 people. The city is situated in the Piedmont section of North Carolina on Interstate 85. The Catawba campus is located on the western edge of Salisbury in a residential section within 5 minutes of downtown. The city has movie theaters, shopping areas, restaurants, a mall, and six public golf courses; other entertainment facilities are available in the immediate area.

Salisbury is located 30 minutes from the greater Charlotte area, one of the fastest-growing areas in the country, and approximately 45 minutes from the cities of Greensboro and Winston-Salem. These cities provide Catawba's students with a wealth of cultural experiences and internship opportunities, plus opportunities to attend professional athletic events. Salisbury is a 4-hour drive from the Atlantic Ocean and about a 2-hour drive from the scenic Appalachian Mountains and ski resorts.

Majors and Degrees

Catawba College grants the Bachelor of Arts degree in the following majors: biology, chemistry, chemistry education, communication arts, comprehensive science education, education (elementary (K–6), middle school (6–9), and secondary (9–12)), English (literature and writing), environmental studies, French, history, mathematics, music (academic studies, applied music, church music, music education, and music management), political science (American politics, international relations, prelaw, and public administration), psychology, religion and philosophy (Christian education, outdoor ministries), sociology, Spanish, and theater arts.

Catawba College awards the Bachelor of Science degree in the following majors: athletic training, biology, business administration (accounting, economics, general business, information systems, international business, management, marketing, and small business management), chemistry, environmental science, information systems (accounting and programming), mathematics, medical technology, physical education, recreation, theater arts administration, and therapeutic recreation.

Catawba College grants the Bachelor of Fine Arts degree in the following majors: musical theater and theater arts.

Academic Program

The College operates on the semester calendar and stresses rigorous academic courses, close contact between students and faculty, and a supportive educational environment. The academic program is intended to give the student opportunities to study in a wide range of fields while concentrating in one (the major). Three types of majors are available: a departmental major; a major constructed around two or more disciplines, such as psychology and religion or literature and theater; and a major that focuses on a particular interest that brings together various disciplines, such as "Nineteenth-Century Europe."

Academic Facilities

The Corriher-Linn-Black Library resources include more than 300,000 volume equivalents in a wide array of print and nonprint formats. Library services include individualized reference assistance, online database searching, group library instruction, on-site borrowing, a document delivery system (including interlibrary loan service), and photocopying. The library subscribes to approximately 500 periodicals. Since the 1890s, the library has been a selective depository for U.S. government documents. Since 1995, it has been a selective depository for North Carolina state documents. The library is connected to the Internet and provides access to library and information sources around the world. The library also participates in the North Carolina Information Network (NCIN) for statewide library and information resources and the Online Computer Library Center (OCLC) via the Southeastern Library Network (SOLINET) for international online access to cataloging and reference services. All students have access to a fifty-station PC network in Ketner Hall as well as forty personal computers in the Cannon Academic Computer Center of the library. Science students also have access to a MicroVAX II.

Laboratories in the Shuford Science Building contain state-of-the-art equipment, including a transmission electron microscope. The 189-acre on-campus ecological preserve and a new 300-acre wildlife refuge provide endless opportunities for research and nature education. The Center for the Environment, a 20,000-square-foot facility that will house the Environmental Science Program, is due to be completed in fall 2001. The Robertson College Community Center includes a 1,509-seat auditorium and a 254-seat theater.

Costs

In 2000–01 tuition and fees for the academic year are $13,330, and room rent and boarding costs are $4980. The total fixed costs for attending Catawba as a boarding student are $18,310. The total fixed costs for attending the College as a commuting student are $13,330. (These costs are subject to change.)

Financial Aid

All students applying for financial assistance must be accepted by the Admissions Office and must submit the Free Application for Federal Student Aid (FAFSA). Financial assistance is available in the form of academic scholarships, athletic scholarships, theater arts scholarships, campus employment, federal and state grants, and a variety of loans.

Faculty

The faculty members serve as advisers to students during registration periods and throughout a student's four years at Catawba. Faculty members are readily accessible to students and participate with them in activities on and off campus. More than 70 percent of the faculty members have doctorates.

Admission Requirements

In seeking admission to Catawba, the student must present evidence of satisfactory educational achievement. The student must be a graduate of an accredited public or private secondary school.

Members of the Catawba Admission Committee, composed of administrative personnel and faculty members, select from among the applicants those students whom they consider to be best qualified for success at Catawba. The factors they consider are grades for six or more semesters, class rank, course selection, standardized test results (including SAT I or ACT scores), an essay, and recommendations of school officials.

Transfer students are strongly urged to send their application and college transcript(s) no later than two weeks prior to the term in which they plan to enroll. Official college transcripts must be mailed directly from the office of the registrar of all previously attended institutions. Grade point averages from prior institutions are used for admission and financial aid purposes.

International students who are able to provide evidence of suitable academic preparation and adequate financial resources are encouraged to apply at least three months prior to the term in which they intend to begin their studies. Acceptable test scores are TOEFL (525) and SAT I verbal (450).

Application and Information

Application forms must be filled out by the student and returned to the Admission Office with a $25 processing fee ($50 for international students). The fee, which is nonrefundable, is not applied to any future College costs. An online application is available at the Web site listed below. The student's scholastic record forms should be prepared by the appropriate secondary school official and sent directly to the Catawba Admissions Office. An applicant is also required to take the SAT I of the College Board or the ACT of American College Testing as part of the Catawba admission procedure and to request that his or her test scores be sent to Catawba.

If applicants have successfully completed Advanced Placement courses in high school and received a score of 3, 4, or 5 on Advanced Placement tests administered by the College Board, they will receive both credit and advanced placement at Catawba. Those seeking advanced placement and credit should confer with their high school counselors to make certain that all materials are sent to the Admissions Office at Catawba. Catawba also participates in the College-Level Examination Program (CLEP) and awards credit to students who receive a grade of C or better on the subject-matter examinations.

While Catawba does not have closing dates for the submission of applications, students are urged to apply early in their senior year. The Admissions Office makes every effort to notify each applicant of the committee's decision within thirty days after the completed application has been received.

After an applicant receives notification of acceptance, he or she should send a $400 enrollment deposit to the Admissions Office by May 1. The deposit is credited to the student's account in the business office and is deducted from the first payment of fees, made at the time of registration when the school term begins.

Chief Enrollment Officer
Catawba College
Salisbury, North Carolina 28144
Telephone: 704-637-4402
          800-228-2922 (toll-free)
E-mail: admission@catawba.edu
World Wide Web: http://www.catawba.edu

Ralph W. Ketner Hall.

THE CATHOLIC UNIVERSITY OF AMERICA
WASHINGTON, D.C.

The University

The Catholic University of America (CUA) offers an outstanding collegiate experience, with challenging undergraduate programs based in the liberal arts. CUA is the national university of the Catholic Church and the only higher education institution established by the U.S. Catholic bishops.

Founded as a graduate institution more than a century ago, CUA introduced undergraduate education in 1904. The University today serves 5,600 students, including 2,400 undergraduates, from all fifty states and more than 100 other countries. Students from all religious traditions are welcome.

While the University maintains a small-college atmosphere with a student-faculty ratio of 10:1, CUA is a major research institution. Undergraduates learn from the same professors that conduct research and teach graduate students.

The University's Washington, D.C., location enriches student life. Cultural, scientific, and political resources are minutes away by Metrorail, a modern mass transit system that stops next to campus.

CUA is noted for the traditional architecture found on its 144-acre residential campus. With housing guaranteed for four years, the majority of undergraduates live on campus in thirteen residence halls. Students are involved in more than 100 student organizations. These include honor societies, community service organizations, academic clubs, minority and international student organizations, professional societies, performing organizations, publications and communications groups, and special interest societies.

CUA is committed to providing a high-quality education for student athletes. The University is a member of NCAA Division III, enabling teams to compete with others that share similar standards of academic and athletic excellence. Men's intercollegiate sports include baseball, basketball, cross-country, football, soccer, swimming, tennis, and track (indoor and outdoor). Women's intercollegiate sports are basketball, cross-country, field hockey, lacrosse, soccer, softball, swimming, tennis, track (indoor and outdoor), and volleyball. Club sports include women's and men's crew and men's ice hockey and rugby. A range of intramural athletics programs are offered.

The 40-acre Raymond A. DuFour Center includes a main arena and stadium; swimming facilities; handball, racquetball, and tennis courts; a dance and aerobics studio; a weight room; indoor and outdoor running tracks; and outdoor playing fields.

The Center for Counseling and Personal Development offers individual tutoring and general seminars on research techniques and study skills. Also available are the reading and study skills program and the career services office.

Location

Located three miles north of the Capitol in residential Washington, D.C., CUA is in the same residential neighborhood as several other educational, medical, and research centers.

Majors and Degrees

Undergraduate degrees are offered in seventy-nine major programs in six of CUA's ten schools: arts and sciences, engineering, architecture and planning, nursing, music, and philosophy.

The School of Arts and Sciences offers the Bachelor of Arts or Bachelor of Science degrees in the following areas: accounting, anthropology, art, biochemistry, biology, business, chemical physics, chemistry, communication and media studies, computer science, drama, economics, education (early childhood, elementary, and secondary), English language and literature, environmental science, financial management, French, German, Greek and Latin, history, human resources, management, mathematics, medical technology, medieval and Byzantine studies, music, philosophy, physics, politics, psychology, religion and religious education, social work, sociology, and Spanish. Prelaw and premedical programs are available. Students can also select double majors and minors. Accelerated degree programs are available to students who perform at exceptional levels. Possibilities include a three-year Bachelor of Arts program, a four-year Bachelor/Master joint-degree program, and a six-year joint Bachelor of Arts/Juris Doctor program with the Columbus School of Law.

The School of Engineering offers programs leading to the first professional degree in biomedical, civil, computer science, construction, electrical, or mechanical engineering. Students can also undertake a dual-degree program in civil engineering and architecture or in an interdisciplinary program such as computer science and engineering.

The School of Architecture and Planning offers the Bachelor of Science in Architecture—a four-year program—and the Master of Architecture—a five-year professional degree program. A dual-degree program is available in architecture and civil engineering.

The School of Nursing offers a four-year program leading to the Bachelor of Science in Nursing degree. Also offered is an accelerated B.S.N. program, a twenty-month sequence for students who have a bachelor's degree in another field.

The Benjamin T. Rome School of Music offers four-year programs leading to Bachelor of Music degrees in composition, music education, music history and literature, musical theater, and performance, including orchestral instruments, organ, piano, or voice.

The School of Philosophy offers three programs leading to the Bachelor of Arts degree, including the program of concentration, prelaw, and the honors program.

Academic Program

Engineering, nursing, music, and architecture students follow study courses that provide professional training integrated with a broad range of academic disciplines. Students in the School of Arts and Sciences undertake a major course of study within a liberal arts curriculum that encompasses the humanities, languages and literature, philosophy, the social sciences, mathematics and natural sciences, and religion. Most majors require the satisfactory completion of forty courses that are 3 credits each for graduation. Certain majors under the Bachelor of Science degree may require additional credits. In addition to the major, students may complete a minor course sequence by utilizing the elective courses included in the undergraduate program.

CUA maintains small undergraduate classes, even for introductory courses. Faculty members who teach graduate students also teach undergraduates, enabling freshmen to engage in dialogues with teachers and scholars. CUA offers outstanding academic research and library facilities and exposure to graduate and professional-level programs.

Also provided is a University-wide honors program for outstanding undergraduates who seek intense intellectual challenges. The program draws from traditional liberal arts disciplines and professional curricula to offer comprehensive academic experiences.

Off-Campus Arrangements

CUA belongs to the Consortium of Universities of the Washington Metropolitan Area. Undergraduates, with the approval of their academic advisers, may undertake course work and research at member institutions. Earned credits are applied to the CUA baccalaureate degree.

Washington-area internships are available for students in almost every academic area. In addition to numerous internship and study opportunities in the Washington area, CUA students can take advantage of exciting study-abroad programs. These programs include British and Irish politics and society programs in London and Dublin, which include parliamentary internships. European studies are offered in Leuven, Belgium. Language and humanities programs are offered in Africa, China, France, Germany, Greece, Italy, Spain, and Venezuela. CUA also sponsors study abroad programs in Hungary, Poland, and Japan.

Academic Facilities

More than 1.6 million volumes are available through the CUA library system. This collection is housed in the John K. Mullen of Denver Memorial Library and in six specialized libraries: chemistry; engineering, architecture, and mathematics; library and information science; music; nursing and biology; and physics. Students also have access to the libraries of the Washington Consortium and institutions such as the Library of Congress, the National Library of Medicine, the Folger Shakespeare Library, and the National Archives.

Catholic University's Center for Planning and Information Technology offers service and support for network, administrative, and academic computing. The center helps members of the University community use information technologies to deliver, access, process, communicate, and disseminate information. The center also provides phone service to members of the campus community.

In addition to a central computing cluster for faculty members and students, various labs, networked classrooms, and technology-equipped classrooms are located throughout the campus. VMS is the central operating system. A Compaq computer cluster is available for use by students and faculty and staff members. A high-speed fiber network links the entire campus to the Internet, including all academic buildings and all residence halls.

The Center for Planning and Information Technology issues a VMS and an NT account to all members of the University community. The VMS account can be used for e-mail and storage of files, and the NT account allows users to log on securely to any machine in an office or computer lab. A campus computing Information Center answers users' computing or information technology questions.

CUA is home to research facilities such as the Vitreous State Laboratory and the centers of excellence for biomedical engineering, Catholic education, and other areas.

Costs

Tuition for the 2000–01 academic year is $19,100, except for the Schools of Engineering and Architecture and Planning, which cost $19,250. Room and board total $8073.

Financial Aid

CUA administers two separate and distinct financial assistance programs: merit scholarships and need-based financial aid. A number of scholarships, awarded on the basis of academic achievement in secondary school, are available. The University offers financial aid to students based on need as demonstrated by the Free Application for Federal Student Aid (FAFSA) and the Institutional Aid Form, which can be found in the CUA admissions application. The College Scholarship Service's Financial Aid PROFILE is required. Loans, work-study, and University grants are available. Candidates who complete the admission application process before February 15 of their senior year of secondary school are considered for academic scholarships and receive priority for financial aid.

Candidates apply for financial aid at the same time they apply for admission. CUA has a need-blind admissions policy and makes admission decisions without regard to financial aid status.

Faculty

CUA has 364 full-time and 296 part-time faculty members. More than 97 percent hold doctoral or appropriate professional degrees. Approximately 15 percent of full-time faculty members are in religious orders; 85 percent are laypersons.

Student Government

The Undergraduate Student Government (USG) is composed of the legislative, academic, and judicial branches and the treasury and program board. Through this organization, students serve on standing committees and send representatives to the University's Academic Senate and Board of Trustees. USG also governs and allocates student activities fees to student organizations, sponsors functions and social events, and protects students' rights.

Admission Requirements

CUA welcomes applications from men and women of character, intelligence, and motivation, regardless of race, creed, sex, ethnic background, or physical disability. CUA is most interested in students best qualified to profit from opportunities offered. For that reason, a selective admission policy is practiced. Successful candidates will have demonstrated achievement both in a challenging secondary school curriculum and on the standardized college entrance examinations.

Admitted candidates traditionally present academic credentials that place them in the top 20 percent of college-bound students nationwide.

Application and Information

Admissions decisions are made on a rolling basis. Applicants for the Early Cardinal Program must apply by November 15 and will be notified by December 15. Regular action scholarship awards and financial aid decisions will be made shortly after the February 15 deadline. Candidates for freshman admission must submit CUA's secondary school report, high school transcripts, scores on the SAT I or ACT, and a $55 application fee.

CUA accepts transfer applicants each semester. Transfer candidates should request applications for transfer admission from the Office of Admissions and Financial Aid. In addition to the high school records and SAT I or ACT scores, transfer students must furnish transcripts from the school the students are attending (a minimum 2.8 GPA is recommended). Transfer applicants are notified of their status on a rolling basis and at least one month prior to the opening of the semester for which they are applying for admission. Financial aid is awarded on the same basis as for freshman students.

Director of Admissions
The Catholic University of America
Washington, D.C. 20064

Telephone: 202-319-5305
           800-673-2772 (toll-free)
Fax: 202-319-6533
E-mail: cua-admissions@cua.edu
World Wide Web: http://www.cua.edu

The Catholic University of America's 144-acre residential campus provides an exceptional atmosphere for learning and living.

CAZENOVIA COLLEGE
CAZENOVIA, NEW YORK

The College

Cazenovia College is a private, independent college located in the central New York community of Cazenovia. The College was founded as a seminary school and later transitioned from a two-year women's college into the four-year coeducational institution that it is today. One of the thirty oldest continuously operating colleges in the United States, the College offers innovative baccalaureate degree programs and continues to offer two-year programs leading to an associate degree. Founded in 1824, Cazenovia College is a residential undergraduate institution drawing traditional age, full-time college students. The undergraduate student body is 33 percent men. Most students come directly from high schools in New York State. Of the 10 percent from outside the state, most are from New England. The majority of students live on campus; fewer than 150 students commute or live off campus. Freshmen are assigned housing based on an interest questionnaire; Sophomore housing assignments are selected by lottery. Student dining facilities are open seven days a week, up to 12 hours a day, and continuously provide students with meals or snacks.

The main campus consists of twenty-four buildings in the heart of the village of Cazenovia. Three of the five residence halls are newly renovated, and all are fully wired for fiber-optic communications, including full Internet and e-mail capability. Nearby, the College athletic complex, home to its NCAA Division III teams, features two gymnasiums, an Olympic-sized swimming pool, outdoor playing fields, and tennis courts. Within walking distance, South Campus houses state-of-the-art computer facilities for interior environmental design, commercial illustration, and advertising/graphic design classes. The College recently purchased a 160-acre farm that is the center for its nationally known equestrian program and champion riding teams. Cazenovia students find the advantages of small-town life combined with nearby opportunities for urban recreation, athletic, and cultural activities. Social life focuses on activities within individual residence halls and campus clubs, as well as dances, theme weekends, student performances, sports events, and intramurals.

Cazenovia College has always been committed to helping students prepare for real-life situations. Students have the opportunity to complete major courses during their first year while blending traditional liberal arts courses into their studies. Each student learns the practical side of a career and develops the versatility to adapt to the competitive marketplace. Cazenovia College is fully accredited by the Middle States Association of Colleges and Schools.

Location

Cazenovia College is situated in the picturesque lakeside village of Cazenovia, New York, a quiet, semirural village of 4,000, in central New York. Many structures in the village are listed on the National Register of Historic Places. The village retains much of its nineteenth-century charm with unique specialty shops, fine inns, and restaurants that cater to a variety of tastes. Cazenovia Lake, less than a quarter-mile away, is enjoyed for its beauty and for the opportunities it provides for summer and winter sports. Lush countryside and numerous ski trails surround the village. In Syracuse, 18 miles away, students can take advantage of a symphony orchestra, a widely acclaimed regional theater, museums, fine restaurants, traveling productions at the Civic Center, and major athletic events at Syracuse University's domed stadium, among other social and cultural offerings. Cazenovia offers a wonderful living and learning environment.

Majors and Degrees

The College offers a B.S. in human services (specializations in counseling and mental health, criminal justice studies, generalist, social services for children and youth, and social services for the elderly); a B.S. in inclusive elementary education; a B.F.A. in interior environmental design; a B.A. in liberal studies (specializations in fine and performing arts, interdisciplinary social sciences, literature and culture, and science and society); a B.S. in liberal and professional studies (specializations in fine and performing arts, interdisciplinary social sciences, literature and culture, and science and society); a B.P.S. in management (specializations in accounting, business management, equine business management, and sport management); a B.F.A. in visual communications; a B.S. in early childhood education and program administration; a B.A. and B.S. in English; a B.S. in social science; an A.A.S. in advertising/graphic design; an A.S. and an A.A.S. in art (studio) (specializations in studio art and photography); an A.S. and an A.A.S. in business management; an A.S. in child studies; an A.A.S. in commercial illustration; an A.A.S. in equine studies (specializations in horsemanship and stable and farm management); an A.A.S. in fashion studies; an A.A. and an A.S. in human services (specializations in counseling and mental health, criminal justice studies, social services for children and youth, and social services for the elderly); an A.S. and an A.A.S. in individualized studies; an A.A.S. in interior environmental design; and an A.A. in liberal arts.

Academic Programs

Part of what distinguishes Cazenovia is the diversity and flexibility of its degree programs. Cazenovia offers a wide range of programs in art, business, early childhood education, equine studies, and human services, as well as in interdisciplinary liberal and professional studies. All students complete a common core grounded in traditional liberal competencies. All students select a major field of study and conclude their work by demonstrating the ability to integrate and apply their knowledge to a culminating project. The general education core now includes required course work in literacy and effective communication. The College's two-year programs are true to the traditional career preparation that is the hallmark of associate degree programs nationwide. Its four-year programs either build upon two-year degree preparation with an innovative and interdisciplinary upper-division structure or are designed as entry-level baccalaureate programs.

Cazenovia offers several special services through its Center for Teaching and Learning, whose programs have been cited by the National Directory of Exemplary Programs. The center offers support services to all students; learning acceleration programs include the Higher Education Opportunity Program and the Title IV student-support services. A strong job placement/transfer counseling program is also available on campus. Cazenovia's Counseling Center offers a wide range of services, including individual counseling by a professional counselor.

To earn an associate degree, a student must complete 60 credits of course work (except where otherwise specified) with a grade point average of not less than 2.0 and satisfy all additional program requirements. Arts and sciences credit requirements vary according to the degree sought. Advanced placement and credit by examination are offered to qualified students, and honors courses are available in selected areas. An independent study arrangement is possible for full-time students. To earn a bachelor's degree, a student must complete 120 credits (except where otherwise specified) with a grade point average of at least 2.0 and satisfy all additional program requirements. Sixty credits must be completed prior to the junior year. The academic year is divided into two 14-week terms, with additional opportunities in the summer.

Off-Campus Arrangements

An increasing focus of the College is experiential education, primarily through service learning and internships. Students are able to integrate academic programs and career development into their learning experience. Each student learns the practical side of a career and develops the versatility to adapt to the competitive marketplace. Students gain valuable experience off campus in major corporations, banks, newspapers, hospitals, local businesses, government agencies, and radio and television. Cazenovia College also has affiliations with the American College in London.

Academic Facilities

The main campus consists of twenty-four buildings on 20 acres in the heart of the village. Classrooms, residence halls, the Morgan Student Center, and administrative buildings surround a centrally located quad that is a popular gathering place for students to study, relax, or join in a volleyball match. A few short blocks away is the south campus, home of Cazenovia's art and design programs.

The Witherill Library has holdings totaling 82,540 pieces, including 61,739 book volumes, 5,676 bound periodicals, 12,329 microfilm reels, 1,097 cataloged videocassettes, and 1,263 additional audiovisual format items. The library is also a member of the national/international OCLC Interlibrary Loan Network, which allows loans to and from libraries all over the United States and the world. In addition, the library's Web page includes subscriptions to eleven online databases, which include more than 2,600 full-text journals, indexes, and abstracts that can be called up at a moment's notice. The library's professional staff is available to assist users on a group or individual basis throughout the academic year. The College's computer resources rival the best wired facilities in the nation. Four main campus facilities (two classrooms and two labs) host seventy-six Pentium III–based Windows NT systems. Two facilities dedicated to art and design host twenty-four G4 Macintosh systems and an up-to-date AutoCAD lab. All facilities support laser printers and scanners and (where appropriate) oversized printers and other specialized peripherals. The College also supports other computer resources, including a small satellite facility located within the science faculty suite. The College maintains a fully-equipped Faculty Development Lab to support the integration of technology into instruction.

The Cazenovia College Center for Teaching and Learning staff of 25 professionals provides workshops and individualized tutoring to help students improve their reading, math, writing, and study skills. The College also has chemistry and biology laboratories and extensive art studios. The Gertrude T. Chapman Art Center is an on-campus art gallery exhibiting the work of contemporary artists. The Howard and Bess Chapman Cultural Center houses changing exhibits of regional, historical, and general cultural interest, as well as art exhibits. At the Cazenovia College Theatre, students produce plays and other entertainment. The theater is also used for film showings and large-group lectures. Cazenovia College's nursery school, the Doug Flutie Jr. Early Childhood Education Center, attended by children from the village, enables students in the early childhood and inclusive elementary education programs to learn firsthand about the care and education of children. Students in the equine studies programs have access to the College's 160-acre farm, which is home to one of the premiere equestrian facilities in the nation.

Costs

For academic year 1999–2000, tuition was $11,230 per year, room was $3178, and board was $2750. Miscellaneous fees were $424, and books were about $800. Personal and travel expenses averaged $1000. Athletics and other miscellaneous fees specific to the academic concentration or course selection totaled about $500.

Financial Aid

Financial aid sources exist at Cazenovia College to bridge the gap between the amount the student's family can pay and the cost of attending the College. Ninety-five percent of students receive some form of financial assistance. Need-based federal, state, and institutional sources are available and include grants, loans, and on-campus work-study arrangements. About 50 percent of the students hold work-study jobs. Merit scholarships not based on financial need are also offered in all subject areas. Transfer scholarships are also available.

Faculty

Cazenovia has 88 faculty members: 45 full-time and 43 part-time. All full-time faculty members must possess the Ph.D. or a relevant professional degree, and all faculty members must demonstrate proficiency in the discipline in which they teach. The faculty is more strongly committed to teaching than to research. Many of the part-time faculty members pursue careers outside the College; their professional experiences enrich the College's programs. The faculty is strongly involved in student life, particularly in program-related student clubs. Faculty members also function as student advisors and academic counselors. The student-faculty ratio is 14:1.

Student Government

The Student Government Association (SGA) is elected and empowered to represent the student body in various aspects of their educational experience at the College. While all students are members of this association, voting membership consists of executive officers, class officers, representatives of the residential communities, commuter representatives, and the student chair of the Community Judicial Board. Responsibilities include allocation of funds to student clubs or organizations, representation of students in the campus governance structure, planning and sponsoring of some campus events, and student contribution to the campus disciplinary process.

Admission Requirements

Cazenovia seeks students whose high school and college records, standardized test scores, official recommendations, and qualities of mind and character promise success in college. Prospective students should send in a completed application, a transcript, test scores (where applicable), and a resume of extracurricular activities. A campus interview is strongly recommended. For freshman applicants, the SAT I or ACT is not required but is recommended. Students who have earned an average of 75 percent or above (on a scale of 0 to 100) in high school and who have a combined SAT I score of at least 950 are most successful at Cazenovia. Freshman applicants should have completed a minimum of six semesters in a regular diploma program in an accredited secondary school. Students may be admitted for deferred entrance or to advanced standing. Transfer applicants must have a minimum overall GPA of 2.0.

Application and Information

Students can apply to either an associate degree or a baccalaureate degree program. The College has no application deadlines. Students are accepted on a rolling basis and are notified of a decision within thirty days. However, the College advises candidates to submit all materials before March 1 for admission in September. There is an application fee of $25.

Tim Williams
Dean for Admission and Financial Aid
Cazenovia College
Cazenovia, New York 13035
Telephone: 315-655-7208
         800-654-3210 (toll-free)
Fax: 315-655-4860

Students on the campus of Cazenovia College.

CEDAR CREST COLLEGE
ALLENTOWN, PENNSYLVANIA

The College
Since its founding in 1867 as an independent liberal arts college for women, Cedar Crest has educated women for leadership in a changing world. Of the approximately 1,700 students who come to the College annually from twenty-six states and fourteen other countries, 814 are full-time undergraduates. The 11:1 student-faculty ratio provides for small classes, individual advising, and independent work in an environment that emphasizes interdisciplinary, values-oriented education. The Honor Philosophy is the most compelling statement of each student's rights and responsibilities for her own academic and cocurricular performance.

Cedar Crest's health science programs, including environmental science, genetic engineering, neuroscience, nuclear medicine, nursing, and nutrition, generate the largest student enrollment. Business and psychology generate the next largest enrollments. The genetic engineering major was the first such program at a women's college and the second at an undergraduate institution. The Miller Family Building doubles the space for student research. New fields of study include forensic science, bioinformatics, and gender studies.

Cedar Crest has a comprehensive wellness program for all students that includes a walkers/runners club, personalized sports training, and nutrition counseling through the College's Allen Center for Nutrition.

Student Affairs sponsors workshops and retreats on leadership and service throughout the year. More than fifty campus organizations offer opportunities in the performing arts, preprofessional areas, environmental awareness, cultural diversity, and much more. An active community service program is comprised of student and faculty volunteers with many groups from Habitat for Humanity to the Girls Club. Healthy lifestyle, community building, and innovative quality of life programs are held regularly in the four residence halls.

The Office of Career Planning offers placement opportunities, internships at nearly 350 companies worldwide, and four-year guidance in preparing for applying and interviewing for jobs and graduate schools.

The Cedar Crest Classics compete in seven NCAA Division III intercollegiate sports: basketball, cross-country, field hockey, lacrosse, softball, tennis, and volleyball. Intramural activities include badminton, basketball, soccer, softball, and tennis. The Equestrian Club competes in collegiate horse shows.

Cedar Crest's academic programs are fully accredited by the Middle States Association of Colleges and Schools, and, where appropriate, by the American Medical Association, American Dietetic Association, American Bar Association, National League for Nursing Accrediting Commission (B.S. only), and National Council on Social Work Education and by the Departments of Education of New York, New Jersey, and Pennsylvania.

Location
Cedar Crest's 84-acre campus, a nationally registered arboretum, is situated in a well-established residential section of Allentown, a mid-sized city (105,000) in the Lehigh Valley of eastern Pennsylvania. In Allentown, students enjoy the Allentown Art Museum, the Pennsylvania Stage Company (an Actors' Equity theater), numerous community theater companies, and public parks with jogging paths, riding trails, picnic areas, and other recreational facilities. Sites for skiing, white-water rafting, and hiking are nearby. By car or bus, Cedar Crest is less than 2 hours from New York City; 1 hour from Philadelphia; just under 3 hours from Washington, D.C.; and 2 hours from the Jersey Shore. The Pocono Mountains are less than an hour away. The Lehigh Valley International Airport, only 10 minutes away, is served by major airlines with connecting flights to most major cities in the United States.

Majors and Degrees
Cedar Crest offers B.A. and B.S. degrees in accounting, art, biochemistry, biology, business administration, chemistry, communications studies, comparative literature, computer science, dance, education (elementary and secondary), English, environmental science, gender studies co-major, genetic engineering, history, information systems, interdisciplinary fine arts, international languages (French and Spanish), international studies, mathematics, medical technology, music, neuroscience, nuclear medicine, nursing, nutrition, paralegal studies, philosophy and religion, political science, psychology, social work, sociology, and theater. With committee approval, a student may pursue a self-designed major.

Preprofessional programs include dentistry, law, medicine, and veterinary medicine.

Certificate programs are offered in accounting, computer science, gerontology, human resource management, management leadership, marketing, nuclear medicine (baccalaureate degree required), paralegal studies, and teacher aide studies.

Certification programs include public school nurse studies (postbaccalaureate), elementary/secondary teacher studies, and social work.

Cedar Crest participates with Georgia Institute of Technology and Washington University in St. Louis in 3-2 dual-degree programs in engineering.

Academic Program
Self-designed majors, double majors, minors, independent study programs, and individual and group research projects support serious concentration at the undergraduate level. Working with her adviser, each student designs a program of study that meets the 120-credit College (nursing: 126 credits) and major requirements as well as her personal interests and professional goals. The College's curriculum is structured to provide course work in the areas that define a liberal arts education: a knowledge-based curriculum with Basic Composition and Construction of Knowledge taught in a computer classroom environment, Scientific Knowledge (The Human Agenda, The Environment), a departmentally determined mathematics requirement, and electives constitute the freshman-year program. The Sophomore Ethical Life Course integrates applied ethics and service-learning opportunities. Acquisition of Knowledge courses are selected in four categories: The Study of Humankind, The Study of Written Texts, The Study of Creativity and Creativity in Practice, and Global Issues and Distinct Cultures. Many of these courses also meet the requirements of majors and minors. Science majors begin conducting advanced research at the freshman level, opening opportunities that often lead to internships at major research institutions.

Highly motivated students with records of academic excellence may participate in the four-year Honors Program. The program incorporates seminars not offered in the regular course schedule with off-campus activities and advanced creative and research projects.

Each major has a Capstone experience that reflects on previous learning and experience and explores issues emerging in the present and expected in the future. The academic program emphasizes independent and faculty-supported student research as a paradigm for dealing effectively with the information explosion.

Off-Campus Arrangements
Internship opportunities enable Cedar Crest students to explore career options and gain practical experience at major corpora-

tions, national nonprofit organizations, and health-care facilities. Students have completed internships as a CNN foreign correspondent with the United Nations, as an FBI honors intern working on a database for DNA fingerprinting, and as research assistants at Cold Spring Harbor Laboratory and other nationally recognized cancer research laboratories. Students may also participate in the Washington Semester at American University or study-abroad programs for a summer, semester, or an entire year or do fieldwork at nearby Hawk Mountain Wildlife Sanctuary.

At no added cost, Cedar Crest students may cross-register at Lehigh University and Allentown, Lafayette, Moravian, and Muhlenberg Colleges, all nearby schools.

Academic Facilities

Cressman Library collections include books, periodicals, and electronic and audiovisual resources. Access to the collections is through an online catalog that also provides access to the Library of Congress, OCLC, remote data and indexing sources, and 1.75 million volumes available with daily delivery through the local academic consortium. Campus-wide Internet/World Wide Web connections provide access to full-text reference tools and journals.

Other buildings on campus house theaters, art galleries, sculpture gardens, student exhibit space, computer labs, multimedia classrooms, a multimedia development lab, music practice rooms, a video production studio, dance and art studios and workshops, a ceramics studio, a state-of-the art nutrition laboratory, spectrophotometry equipment, up-to-date genetic engineering laboratories, a greenhouse, dining services, a bookstore, a post office, a gymnasium, a fitness center, and a new computational biology center. The campus also includes tennis courts and regulation fields for field hockey, lacrosse, and softball.

Costs

For 2000–01, the comprehensive resident fee is $24,225, including $17,790 for tuition and $6465 for room and board. Part-time students pay $506 per credit hour; evening/weekend students pay $266 per credit hour.

Financial Aid

Cedar Crest offers a generous program of financial aid based on academic achievement and financial need, including scholarships, grants, loans, and employment. Federal funds available are Federal Pell Grants, Federal Supplemental Educational Opportunity Grants, Federal Perkins Loans, Federal Work-Study Program awards, and Nursing Student Loans. The size of an award varies with need. More than 80 percent of the students at Cedar Crest receive aid. Students applying for financial aid should file the Free Application for Federal Student Aid (FAFSA). Outstanding international students may also qualify for financial aid.

Applicants who rank in the top 20 percent of their class and score 1150 or higher on the SAT I (24 on the ACT) can qualify for a scholarship of up to one-half tuition per year. Sibling grants are awarded to students when 2 siblings are attending Cedar Crest full-time, concurrently.

Recipients of Girl Scout Gold awards, graduates of Governor's School of Excellence programs, and HOBY alumnae are also eligible for scholarship recognition.

Trustee Scholarships of full tuition for senior year are awarded to students with a Dean's List cumulative GPA of 3.55 at the end of their junior year at Cedar Crest. Students must be enrolled full time at Cedar Crest for three years prior to receiving this full tuition scholarship, net federal and state grants.

A 10-percent reduction in tuition is granted to dependents of United Church of Christ (UCC) ministers. Cort Grants of $1000 per year are awarded to new students who are active members of a UCC congregation.

Students can receive an early estimate of aid eligibility by completing a Cedar Crest financial aid application/planner.

Faculty

Of the 67 full-time faculty members, 76 percent have doctorates or other terminal degrees in their field, and 55 percent are women.

Excellence in teaching is the first priority of the Cedar Crest faculty. At Cedar Crest, research grows out of teaching and becomes part of the learning process. In the last six years, Cedar Crest faculty members have published books and many articles; won Fulbright fellowships, fellowships from the National Education Association and the National Endowment for the Arts, and grants from the National Science Foundation, Allen Foundation, Pennsylvania Department of Education, and the United Church of Christ; served as officers in national professional organizations; and presented research at conferences worldwide.

Student Government

Student Government is a strong and vigorous organization at Cedar Crest. Regular meetings are held to discuss policy, plan student activities, and initiate legislation. Students serve as voting members of College and faculty committees and on the Board of Trustees.

Admission Requirements

Cedar Crest seeks students who have shown academic achievement and promise and those with varied interests, talents, and backgrounds. An academic program providing a good foundation usually includes 4 years of English, 3 of mathematics, 3 of social science, 2 of a laboratory science, 2 of a foreign language, and 3 or 4 academic electives. The College considers good students whose preparation does not include all of these subjects. Through the Advanced Placement Program, qualified applicants may apply for advanced study credits at Cedar Crest.

Application and Information

Students need to submit the application form, an official transcript of the secondary school record, examination results from the SAT I or ACT, and a personal essay.

Cedar Crest has a rolling admission policy; applications are reviewed on a continuing basis. Students are encouraged to apply early in their senior year of high school. Admission is awarded for the fall or spring semester.

Transfer students applying to Cedar Crest must fulfill all of the requirements stated above. They must also submit official transcripts and a catalog from each college previously attended.

International students must complete the international student application form; students educated in non-English-speaking countries must also submit TOEFL examination scores.

An application form, the College catalog, financial aid forms, and additional information may be obtained by contacting:

Vice President for Enrollment
Cedar Crest College
100 College Drive
Allentown, Pennsylvania 18104-6196
Telephone: 800-360-1222 (toll-free)
Fax: 610-606-4647
E-mail: cccadmis@cedarcrest.edu
World Wide Web: http://www.cedarcrest.edu

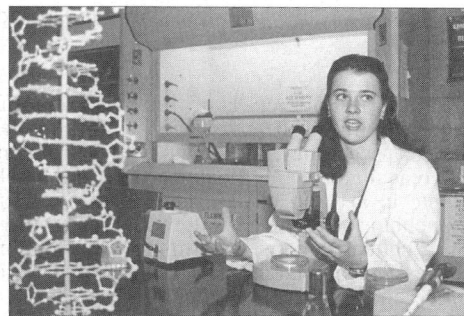

Tracy Litzi, a CCC alumna, talks about the virus she discovered as part of her research at Cedar Crest College.

CENTENARY COLLEGE
HACKETTSTOWN, NEW JERSEY

The College

Founded in 1867, Centenary College blends traditional educational values with a vigorous global vision for the twenty-first century. Located in peaceful Hackettstown in northwest New Jersey, Centenary is four-year, coeducational, independent college with a diverse student body. Distinguished by its caring faculty, small classes, and balanced blend of liberal arts and career studies, Centenary encourages students to stretch beyond their expectations and realize their potential.

Centenary is large enough to offer a variety of academic programs and extracurricular activities and small enough so that students can feel at home. The 42-acre main campus has fourteen principal buildings, a mixture of turn-of-the-century and more modern facilities, in a setting of beautiful trees and shrubs.

Centenary students enjoy a full range of extracurricular activities, including thirteen NCAA Division III intercollegiate varsity athletic teams for both men and women, as well as an assortment of intramural athletic events. Men compete in basketball, cross-country, golf, lacrosse, soccer, and wrestling, while women compete in basketball, cross-country, golf, lacrosse, soccer, softball, and volleyball. Both men and women compete in IHSA equestrian competitions. The High Point Open Rider-Cacchione cup winners attend Centenary, while the women's 1997 basketball team finished as the national runner-up in the NSCAA III national tournament. There are clubs representing many interests, a literary magazine, a newspaper, and choral and dance groups. There are concerts, parties, dances, movie nights, and trips to New York City cultural attractions and to the Poconos for skiing. A fraternity and two sororities sponsor other events. On campus is the Centenary Performing Arts Guild, the only Equity theater in northwest New Jersey. The Centenary Performing Arts Guild sponsors concerts and dance and theater programs.

Centenary's student body is 12 percent international, with students from more than twenty countries. Centenary's International Studies Center provides tutoring and cocurricular support services. A six-week Summer Culture and Language Program offers 6 credits of ESL to college-bound students.

Centenary's athletic facilities include a gymnasium for intercollegiate and intramural sports, varsity team rooms, an aerobic fitness area and wrestling room, an indoor swimming pool, tennis courts, and playing fields for soccer, lacrosse, and softball.

Location

Centenary College is located in Hackettstown, a community of 11,000 people in northwest New Jersey, in the foothills of the Pocono Mountains. The environment is picturesque and safe, while New York City is just an hour's drive away. Hackettstown itself offers a wide variety of convenient stores and services.

Majors and Degrees

The Bachelor of Arts degree is awarded in communication, English, history, individualized studies, international studies, political science, psychology, sociology (with a concentration in criminal justice available), and theater arts. The Bachelor of Fine Arts is available in art and design, fashion design, and interior design. The Bachelor of Science is offered in accounting, business administration (concentrations in computer information systems, global business, management, marketing, and sports management), and equine studies. Elementary education certification is available with a Bachelor of Arts in English, history, or psychology. Secondary certification is available in English, mathematics, and social studies. The Teacher of the Handicapped certificate can be obtained with a Bachelor of Arts degree.

Associate degree programs are offered in art and design, equine studies, fashion, interior design, and liberal arts.

Academic Program

Centenary College's curriculum combines career studies with a solid general education core in the arts, sciences, and humanities. High-quality educational programs meet students' varied interests, needs, and career goals. Each program has its own requirements. However, the following minimum requirements apply to students in all programs: bachelor's degree candidates must complete 128 semester hours with a cumulative grade point average in the total program as well as in their chosen major field of at least 2.0; associate degree candidates must complete 64 semester hours with a minimum 2.0 grade point average. Students in the Education Department must have a minimum 2.75 grade point average. Required and elective courses in the major are complemented by courses in the College core: composition and literature, mathematics, natural science laboratory, fine arts, humanities, international studies, and social and behavioral science. An important part of the core is the distinctive Centenary College Seminars—a sequence continuing through four years that links liberal arts studies with career preparation. Part-time students earn bachelor's or associate degrees through day and evening study. Centenary's Center for Adult and Professional Studies offers the working adult an accelerated Bachelor of Science in Business Administration and an Associate of Arts in Liberal Arts with a business emphasis.

Centenary participates in the Advanced Placement Program and the College-Level Examination Program (CLEP). Up to 15 semester hours of CLEP credit may be applied toward an associate degree and up to 30 hours toward a bachelor's degree. Students age 24 or older may be eligible to apply for Life Learning credits.

Recognizing and challenging the potential of every student is one of Centenary College's most important goals. As an option for college students with mild to moderate learning disabilities, Centenary offers two specially designed assistance programs. Project A.B.L.E. is an intensive learning support program that operates during the fall and spring semesters, and the Step Ahead program is a comprehensive summer residential program designed to strengthen college-level reading and writing and math skills. The FreshStart Program prepares Centenary College freshmen for effective leadership in their professional, personal, and community lives by incorporating academics with campus-life opportunities. The Centenary College Honors Program is an interdisciplinary enrichment program that aims to enhance the academic opportunities for promising and motivated students.

There are two 15-week semesters in the academic year. Classes are also available during the three 6-week summer sessions. The customary program for a full-time student is 15 credit hours per semester. A student in good standing may take up to 18 credit hours.

Academic Facilities

The Seay Building, Ferry Building, Harris & Bettes Smith Learning Center, and Trevorrow Hall are the principal classroom and laboratory buildings. They have a variety of lecture halls, conference rooms, laboratories, art studios, and areas with audiovisual equipment. Whitney Chapel and the Little Theatre are located in the Seay Building.

The Taylor Memorial Learning Resource Center contains approximately 70,000 print materials and more than 20,590 microforms. The audiovisual collection consists of 4,965 items. The learning resource center maintains 211 subscriptions to periodical publications. The electronic resources consist of subscriptions to 9 online databases and eleven CD-ROMs. There are ten multitasking workstations for public use where students can search online resources, utilize Microsoft Office, or search the library's electronic catalog. Computer labs are located inside the Learning Resource Center and in the Seay Building; one is equipped with distance learning facilities. There is also a computer-aided design (CAD) system.

Centenary's telecommunications infrastructure can service more than 1,100 voice/data and video connections. Each resident's room is currently equipped with a telephone line, voice mail, Internet access, and a full multimedia 233 mxx personal computer and HP color printer. Centenary College is certified by Microsoft as an authorized academic training center (ATTP #278789) and offers a help desk to its faculty members and students.

Centenary's 65-acre equestrian center, located about 15 minutes from the main campus, has excellent indoor and outdoor rings, a stadium jumping field, and cross-country facilities. Filly Hill accommodates up to eighty horses. Transportation is provided to students between the main campus and the equestrian center.

The Career Center sponsors a comprehensive four-year program of career development, internships, graduate information, and employment recruiting. Centenary's developmental philosophy fosters awareness, exploration, experience, and choice in concert with personal values. The Career Center offers resources to assist all students and alumni from all majors and at all levels.

WNTI, 91.9 FM, the National Public Radio–affiliated College radio station, operates year-round.

The Northwest New Jersey Regional Women's Center at Centenary College, a resource for women and families in a three-county area, is located in North Hall.

Costs

Costs for the 2000–01 academic year are $14,500 for tuition, $6250 for room and board, and $620 for fees (including a technology fee). Students carrying more than 18 credit hours in a semester are charged the per-credit-hour tuition rate for the additional credit hours. Books and supplies average $666. There is an equine major fee of $1100 per year and an equine skills fee of $580 per year. Participants in the Learning-Disabled Program pay an additional $1900. Personal and travel expenses vary. Fees are subject to change.

Financial Aid

During the 1999–2000 school year, Centenary disbursed more than $5.6 million of financial aid to eligible students. About 82 percent of Centenary's students received some type of assistance in 1999–2000. These funds included Federal Pell Grant, New Jersey Tuition Aid Grant (TAG), New Jersey Edward J. Bloustein Distinguished Scholarship, New Jersey Educational Opportunity Fund Program, Federal Supplemental Educational Opportunity Grant, Federal Perkins Loan, Centenary institutional funds (including grants and scholarships), United Methodist Scholarships, and federal and college work-study funds. Also included were loans from the subsidized and unsubsidized Federal Stafford Student Loan program and Federal PLUS loans.

The philosophy at Centenary is that individuals who are in pursuit of higher education should attain their goals, regardless of financial need. All students, regardless of their financial circumstances, are encouraged to apply for assistance.

The office of financial aid at Centenary is devoted to assisting students in every way to make their education affordable. The staff in the Financial Aid Office guides students and their parents through the process that determines eligibility for financial aid, including grants and loans. A student can receive need-based financial assistance to cover the difference between College costs (tuition and fees, room and board, books, personal expenses, travel costs, etc.) and what the student's family can be expected to contribute based on the information supplied on the Free Application for Federal Student Aid (FAFSA). Merit scholarships are awarded without regard to need.

Students must apply yearly for financial assistance and should submit the FAFSA as soon as possible after January 1. Centenary's college code for the FAFSA is 002599.

Faculty

Centenary's faculty is dedicated to the success of its students. Faculty members are accomplished professionals as well as skilled teachers. Fifty-seven percent have the highest degrees in their field. The student-faculty ratio is a favorable 13:1. Teaching is complemented by a strong advising system that begins as early as the spring of the student's senior year in high school and continues through four years at Centenary.

Student Government

All Centenary students are members of the Student Government Association (SGA) and are encouraged to participate actively in campus life. The SGA executive board includes SGA officers, as well as representatives of the four classes, the Student Activities Board, Judicial Committee, Residence Hall, and Commuters Council. There are student members on several policy-making bodies of the College, including committees of the Board of Trustees.

Admission Requirements

Applicants for admission to Centenary College are individually evaluated. Centenary is interested in a student's overall qualities: academic achievement, cocurricular activities, interests outside of school, and seriousness of purpose. Students must be graduates of an accredited secondary school or the equivalent. Sixteen units of secondary school credit are required. Students must take the SAT I or ACT exam, and scores must be submitted along with official transcripts and the application essay. Transfers with more than 24 transferable credits do not have to submit a SAT I or ACT score. A visit to the campus and an interview are strongly recommended.

Application and Information

Candidates for admission may apply as early as September of their senior year in secondary school. Under Centenary's rolling admission plan, students are notified of the College's decision within two weeks after all credentials have been received. The application fee is $25 for domestic students and $50 for international students.

Students with inquiries are encouraged to contact:

Office of Admissions
Centenary College
400 Jefferson Street
Hackettstown, New Jersey 07840
Telephone: 908-852-1400 Ext. 2217
            800-236-8679 (toll-free)
Fax: 908-852-3454
E-mail: admissions@centenarycollege.edu
World Wide Web: http://www.centenarycollege.edu

The Edward W. Seay Administration Building at Centenary College.

Peterson's Guide to Four-Year Colleges 2001

CENTER FOR CREATIVE STUDIES— COLLEGE OF ART AND DESIGN
DETROIT, MICHIGAN

The College
The Center for Creative Studies—College of Art and Design was established by the Detroit Society of Arts and Crafts. Founded in 1906, the society brought to Detroit exhibits by important artists from around the world. In 1916 it opened its first school, and in 1926 it was formally organized as the Art School of the Detroit Society of Arts and Crafts. The school began by offering course work in the fine arts; courses in crafts, advertising design, industrial design, and photography were added in the 1940s and 1950s. The general studies curriculum was introduced in 1961. The current enrollment is about 975 men and women.

The school was granted membership in the National Association of Schools of Art and Design (NASAD) in 1972. In 1975, the name of the institution was changed to the Center for Creative Studies—College of Art and Design in order to more accurately reflect the broad scope of visual arts offered at the College. Since 1977, the College has been accredited by the North Central Association of Colleges and Schools.

The College is dedicated to providing an educational environment most conducive to the development of outstanding artists and designers. The teaching is directed not only toward developing technical excellence but also toward stimulating intellectual potential. Graduates are well prepared to join the professional world, have the overall ability to carry on their education as desired, are able to communicate effectively, and have a basic understanding of today's artistic, social, and intellectual world and its traditions.

Location
Situated within a 10½-acre complex of award-winning facilities, the College of Art and Design is appropriately located in Detroit's Cultural Center. Twenty-eight major cultural and educational institutions are within easy walking distance. Students have full access to the Detroit Institute of Arts, currently the fifth-largest museum of fine arts in the United States, and to the main branch of the Detroit Public Library, which possesses more than 2 million volumes. Other available facilities include the Institute of Music and Dance, CCS Science Center, Detroit Children's Museum, Detroit Historical Museum, and the Charles H. Wright Museum of African American History.

Majors and Degrees
The Center for Creative Studies—College of Art and Design offers a four-year program leading to the Bachelor of Fine Arts degree. Concentrations are available in animation/digital media: traditional animation, interactive media, and digital animation and video; communication design: art direction, graphic design, and illustration; crafts: ceramics, fiber design, glass, and metalsmithing and jewelry; fine arts: painting, printmaking, and sculpture; industrial design: product design and transportation design; interior design; and photography: applied art, fine art, and biomedical studies. A program in art therapy is available to all students, as is a minor in art history. Concentrations in general crafts and fine arts are available upon departmental recommendation.

Academic Program
The Bachelor of Fine Arts degree requires the completion of 126 credit hours: 84 in studio areas and 42 in general studies courses. All students are required to take core foundation course work in basic drawing, basic design, and figure drawing during their freshman year. They also begin work in their major department during the freshman year or they may begin as an undeclared student. Typical weekly schedules for full-time students comprise 24 studio hours and 6 academic hours.

The Continuing and Community Education Program permits individuals not pursuing a degree to enroll in daytime or evening classes in a broad array of high-quality programming in the visual arts.

Off-Campus Arrangements
Internships and independent study are available. Mobility programs, offered in cooperation with thirty-one other colleges in the Association of Independent Colleges of Art and Design (AICAD), allow students to take advantage of course offerings at other institutions while pursuing a degree at the College. In addition, seniors may study in a studio space in New York City to which CCS has access.

Academic Facilities
The College has more than 130,000 square feet of classroom and studio space. The Kresge-Ford Fine Arts Building provides classrooms, studios, and workshops for painting, sculpture, printmaking, basic design, basic drawing, figure drawing, video, and computer graphics. The Design Arts Building contains classrooms, studios, laboratories, and workshops for communication design, art direction, illustration, industrial design, photography, and woodworking. The Yamasaki Building houses administrative offices and classrooms, studios, and workshops for ceramics, fabric design, glass, and metals and jewelry. Liberal arts courses are conducted in facilities located throughout the campus. The Academic Resource Center houses the library, the center galleries, and all academic technologies. In fall 2001, CCS will open its new 101,000-square-foot Walter B. Ford II Building. This advanced teaching facility will house the departments of animation and digital media, communication design, industrial design, and interior design.

Costs
For 2000–01, tuition and fees are $16,330 for the academic year. Average charges for housing are $3200. The estimated cost of materials and supplies is $1900 in most fields of study.

Financial Aid
The College participates in the Federal Pell Grant, Federal Supplemental Educational Opportunity Grant, Federal Work-Study, and Federal Stafford Student Loan programs. Michigan residents are encouraged to apply for a Michigan Tuition Grant or a Michigan Competitive Scholarship.

The College also awards scholarships, based on artistic ability and academic excellence, to currently enrolled students and prospective students. New students should apply for consideration by March 15. Maximum consideration is given to new students who apply by March 1.

The College attempts to financially assist qualified students who apply, contingent upon the availability of funds.

Faculty
The College has 206 faculty members: 150 in studio areas and 38 in liberal arts. All members of the studio art faculty are

professionals in their individual fields who bring diverse backgrounds and experiences to the classroom.

Student Government

Students participate in the leadership of the school in several ways. The Student Government Association (SGA) is composed of representatives from each department and takes an active role in areas affecting student life. In coordination with the SGA, Student Program Associates organize and sponsor several parties and special events during the year. Associates also sponsor and manage Underground 245, the student gallery.

Admission Requirements

The Admissions Office at the College of Art and Design is dedicated to assisting students in evaluating educational alternatives and career possibilities in the visual arts.

Applicants must have maintained a GPA of at least 2.5 in high school or successfully passed a high school equivalency examination and must submit SAT I or ACT scores and a portfolio of representative work. Applicants who have had previous college experience are required to submit an official transcript from each institution attended. A personal interview is recommended.

Application and Information

Applications for the fall term are accepted through August 15. Qualified candidates are accepted on a space-available basis. Applications for the second semester should be submitted prior to December 1.

For application forms, catalogs, and additional information, students should contact:

Admissions Office
Center for Creative Studies—College of Art and Design
201 East Kirby
Detroit, Michigan 48202
Telephone: 313-664-7425
        800-952-ARTS (toll-free)
World Wide Web: http://www.ccscad.edu

A view of the award-winning Kresge-Ford Fine Arts and Design Arts buildings of the Center for Creative Studies—College of Art and Design.

CENTRAL COLLEGE
PELLA, IOWA

The College

Education with a worldview is one of the exciting dimensions in learning offered at Central College. Established in 1853, Central has a strong liberal arts tradition and during the past three decades has expanded its scope to include study in Europe and Mexico. Almost half of Central's graduates have taken advantage of the College's international programs in Paris, Vienna, the Netherlands, Wales, Spain, Mexico, and London and Colchester, England. Central is a fully accredited liberal arts college affiliated with the Reformed Church in America.

More than 75 percent of those enrolled at Central are Iowans, but the College also attracts students from thirty-seven states and eighteen countries. Some 1,100 students live on campus, either in residence halls or in College-owned houses. Another 200 students are enrolled each year in Central's international studies programs. In addition to following a rigorous academic program, students help plan a variety of social and educational events throughout the year—including weekend entertainment, lectures, guest artist series, and other performances—by serving on the Campus Activities Board. Students produce an annual literary magazine, a yearbook, and a weekly newspaper and operate a campus radio station. There are also numerous active organizations on campus, such as the Fellowship of Christian Athletes, the Mock Trial Team, the speech team, departmental clubs, service groups, and seven local fraternities and sororities. Students may also participate in the music department's A Cappella Choir, Symphonic Wind Ensemble, College-Community Orchestra and Chorus, jazz ensemble, and several other music performance organizations. Many of Central's student activities have been enhanced since the Maytag Student Center opened in 1990.

In intercollegiate athletics, Central offers nine men's sports and eight women's sports. The program has produced more than 90 all-Americans and 25 academic all-Americans in the past ten years. The College is a member of the NCAA Division III and the Iowa Intercollegiate Athletic Conference. For competition and training, the seventeen teams use the Kuyper Athletic Complex, which includes softball, soccer, and baseball fields; a stadium and track; a field house with a 200-meter indoor track and a state-of-the-art training center, added in 1999; and the gymnasium.

Location

Central is located in a town with a legacy from Europe, founded by Dutch immigrants in 1847. Many of Pella's 10,200 residents are of Dutch ancestry. Dutch architecture is apparent throughout the town, and the city's three-day celebration of its heritage each spring attracts more than 100,000 visitors. In addition to its Old World charm, Pella has diversified industries that reach into international markets. The 13,000-acre Red Rock Lake, which offers a full range of recreational activities, and Bos Landen public golf course are just 5 minutes from campus. Des Moines, the state capital, is only 45 minutes away.

Majors and Degrees

Central awards the Bachelor of Arts degree. Majors are available in accounting, art, biology, business management, chemistry, communication, computer science, economics, elementary education, English, environmental studies, exercise science, French, general studies, German, history, information systems, international management, international studies (with emphasis on Latin America or Western Europe), linguistics, mathematics, mathematics/computer science, music, music education, natural science, philosophy, physics, political science, psychology, religion, social science, sociology, sociology/anthropology, Spanish, and theater.

In addition to the undergraduate programs, Central, in cooperation with Washington University in St. Louis, Missouri, offers a 3-4 architecture program that leads to a combined B.A./M.S. degree and 3-2 programs for majors in engineering and occupational therapy.

Academic Program

The academic program at Central College is designed not only to launch careers but also to help students develop their identities, define their values, and discover their special talents. Central is dedicated to the liberal arts tradition and feels it is important to engage students in the broad spectrum of areas that they will encounter in today's world, including science, religion, the humanities, other cultures, and the arts. For Central's top students who would like an additional challenge, the College offers honors courses, beginning in the freshman year. Central is committed to helping students acquire strong communication skills—an ability essential in today's job market. At the heart of Central's liberal arts philosophy is the conviction that the fully educated person must be able to read and listen critically, write clearly, and speak in an articulate manner. Each student must meet a communication skills standard before graduation.

Students may choose either a departmental major or an interdisciplinary major that they have designed to fit their specific interests, including graduate school plans and career goals.

Off-Campus Arrangements

For thirty years, Central has pioneered the development of study-abroad programs in Europe and Mexico. Central has language programs at study centers in Paris, Vienna, and Granada, Spain, and English-language programs in London and Colchester, England; Carmarthen, Wales; Leiden, the Netherlands; and Mérida, Yucatán, Mexico. Each of the programs is staffed by a College resident director, and courses are usually taught by professors from the host country, although in Yucatán some courses are taught by professors from the Iowa campus.

In addition to its international connection, Central offers an urban semester through the Chicago Metropolitan Center and the Washington Center. The course work emphasizes the urban experience, and a wide range of internships are also available. Central's off-campus programs offer full College credit.

Academic Facilities

The Geisler Library houses 210,000 volumes as well as the College archives, media center, and education department. A distance learning classroom provides high-speed voice, video, and data transmission through a connection with the Iowa Communications (fiber-optic) Network. The Vermeer Science Center houses the departments of biology, chemistry, and physics, and a large, multipurpose lab serves all three sciences. There are also smaller labs for advanced research as well as several other specialized workrooms. The Kruidenier Center for Communication and Theatre houses two theaters, a broadcast lab, a scene shop, a costume shop, a makeup room, a seminar room, and a classroom.

Cox-Snow Music Center contains a recital hall, rehearsal spaces, keyboard and computer labs, and a music library. The Mills Gallery provides exhibition space for student, faculty, and visiting art shows adjacent to studio space for ceramics, glassblowing, painting, crafts, and graphic arts.

The Weller Center for Business and International Studies opened in fall 1999 and houses the academic Departments of Accounting, Business Management, Economics, and Modern Languages as well as the Office of International Education. The building is filled with the latest in technology, including multimedia classrooms, a large classroom equipped with a computer at each student's desk, seminar rooms, and a 24-hour computer lab.

Other classroom buildings include Jordan Hall, the International Studies Center, the Arts and Behavioral Sciences Building, and Central Hall. There are also classrooms in the P. H. Kuyper Gymnasium, the H. S. Kuyper Fieldhouse, and the Maytag Student Center.

The computer center is located in Central Hall, with microcomputers and terminals spread throughout the campus. Central's campuswide network provides access to a Digital VAX 3400 time-sharing system, five VAX 3100 graphical workstations, and the online library catalog as well as access to the Internet, the global research and education data network. Students and faculty members have access to 345 microcomputers, used for word processing and spreadsheet applications, as well as discipline-specific software. Each residence hall room is connected to the World Wide Web.

Costs

For 2000–01, costs are $14,638 for tuition, $2578 for room, $2664 for board (twenty-meal plan), and $116 for activity fees, for a total of $19,996.

Financial Aid

Types of assistance include scholarships, grants, loans, and campus employment. More than 95 percent of the student body receives financial assistance, totaling more than $19 million in 1999–2000. To apply for assistance, students must first apply for admission and complete the financial aid section of the application form. In addition, students must file a financial needs analysis form after January 1. (Iowa residents must file before June 1.) Students must name Central (code 001850) in order for the College to receive the needs analysis report.

Students who apply for aid after March 1 are funded on a funds-available basis.

Each year, Central reserves a significant number of Distinguished Scholar Awards, worth up to full tuition, for the most promising freshmen. Eligible students must have a 3.75 cumulative GPA or higher (on a 4.0 scale) and have an ACT composite score of at least 28, or students must be ranked first in their graduating class.

Faculty

More than 85 percent of the faculty members hold doctorates or terminal degrees in their fields. There are 90 full-time and 28 part-time faculty members, and the student-faculty ratio is 13:1. Faculty members serve as academic advisers and make time to take a personal interest in their students.

Student Government

Students plan and schedule social activities and events through the Campus Activities Board. The Student Senate is responsible for a budget of more than $145,000, and assigned senators have voting membership on nearly all College committees. Students also have nonvoting representation on the Board of Trustees.

Admission Requirements

To be considered for admission, a student should be a graduate of an accredited high school or the equivalent, rank in the upper half of the high school graduating class, have at least a 2.5 cumulative grade point average, and achieve test scores on either the ACT or SAT I that are high enough to predict probable success at Central. While specific courses are not required for admission, the College recommends the following preparation: 4 years of English, including literature; 2 or more years of mathematics, including algebra and geometry; 2 or more years of social studies, including American and European history; 2 or more years of lab science; and 2 or more years of foreign languages.

Application and Information

Applications are reviewed and acted upon on a rolling basis beginning October 1. In order to apply for admission to Central, students should submit a completed application with the nonrefundable $25 application fee, have their high school send an official transcript of credits to Central's Office of Admission, have a report of ACT or SAT I scores sent to the Office of Admission, and schedule an interview with a member of the admission staff. The $25 application fee is waived if the applicant brings the completed application when visiting the Central campus or sends the application to Central after completing a campus visit.

Application forms may be obtained by contacting:

Office of Admission
812 University
Campus Box 5100
Central College
Pella, Iowa 50219
Telephone: 515-628-5285
         877-GO-CENTRAL (toll-free)
Fax: 515-628-5316
E-mail: admission@central.edu
World Wide Web: http://www.central.edu

The pond is a favorite gathering place for students.

CENTRAL CONNECTICUT STATE UNIVERSITY
NEW BRITAIN, CONNECTICUT

The University

Central Connecticut State University (CCSU) is a regional, comprehensive public university that is dedicated to learning in the liberal arts and sciences and to education for the professions. Founded in 1849, CCSU is Connecticut's oldest publicly supported institution of higher education. Currently, the University offers bachelor's and master's degrees and sixth-year diplomas in more than fifty areas of study. CCSU is composed of graduate and continuing education areas and four schools: Arts and Sciences, Business, Education and Professional Studies, and Technology. CCSU has earned designation as a statewide Center of Excellence in international education and in technology.

CCSU is the largest of four universities in the Connecticut State University System, enrolling 6,000 full-time and 6,000 part-time students. CCSU's student body represents the spectrum of ethnic and socioeconomic groups. Most students are Connecticut residents, with others coming from more than thirty states and forty other countries. Approximately 1,700 undergraduates live on campus in seven residence halls. Five meal plans are available and include options for different tastes and needs. Memorial Hall is the main dining hall.

The Student Center houses the student newspaper, the radio station, dining areas, a game room, TV lounges, a copy center, and other facilities. Students produce concerts, dances, film series, and other activities. The Student Government Association funds a yearbook, sports clubs, and cultural and special interest groups. More than 100 campus clubs and organizations are available, ranging from academic/career groups to religious, performing, and political clubs as well as fraternities, sororities, and honors and professional societies. Extracurricular activities include movies, intramural sports, lectures, musical and dramatic productions, and art exhibits. CCSU's twenty-one NCAA Division I intercollegiate programs are a major source of excitement. Sports for men include baseball, basketball, cross-country, football, golf, indoor and outdoor track, soccer, swimming and diving, and tennis. Women participate in basketball, cross-country, golf, indoor and outdoor track, lacrosse, soccer, softball, swimming and diving, tennis, and volleyball. Students interested in intramural sports enjoy basketball, flag football, floor hockey, softball, and volleyball. The modern Kaiser Hall Gymnasium offers an Olympic-size swimming pool, modern exercise equipment, a state-of-the-art fitness center, a weight-training room, and an athletic training center. The Kaiser Annex has a running track and tennis and basketball courts.

The Ruthe Boyea Women's Center is a multipurpose program and service center for women in the student body and on the staff and faculty. The University Police Department operates 24 hours per day, 365 days per year. Among the services they provide are day and night escort services, crime prevention and awareness programs, and an emergency phone system throughout campus. The CCSU Fire Marshal's office maintains computerized fire detection/alarm systems.

Location

CCSU is located in New Britain, home to a world-renowned art museum, a minor league baseball team, a 1,200-acre municipal park system, and a wide range of cultural activities. The University, located at the edge of the city, is in the heart of Connecticut, 15 minutes from the state capital of Hartford and its many restaurants, theaters, and sports and concert activities. One of the state's major shopping centers is West Farms Mall, 3 miles from campus. CCSU is 2 hours away from New York and Boston.

Majors and Degrees

CCSU offers the following degrees: Bachelor of Arts, Bachelor of Fine Arts, Bachelor of Science, Bachelor of Science in Engineering Technology, Bachelor of Science in Industrial Technology, and Bachelor of Science in Nursing.

The Bachelor of Arts is awarded in anthropology, art–ceramics, art–graphic design, art–illustration, art–painting, art–printmaking, art–sculpture, communication, criminology, economics, economics–operations research, English, French, geography, geography–planning, German, history, international studies (interdisciplinary), Italian, mathematics, mathematics–actuarial science, mathematics–operations research, mathematics–statistics, music, philosophy, philosophy–applied ethics, political science, political science–public administration, psychology, social work, sociology, Spanish, special studies (interdisciplinary), and theater (B.A./B.F.A.).

Bachelor of Science degree programs include accounting, athletic training, biology, biology–environmental science, chemistry, chemistry–biology, chemistry–business, chemistry–computer science, chemistry–environmental science, civil engineering technology, composites and polymer engineering technology, computer science, earth sciences, education (interdisciplinary), engineering (transfer program with University of Connecticut), entrepreneurship, exercise science and health promotion, finance, general science, graphic design (industrial technology), hospitality and tourism, industrial systems engineering technology, industrial technology, international business, international studies (interdisciplinary), management and organization, management information systems, manufacturing engineering technology, marketing, mechanical engineering technology, medical technology, nursing (B.S.N.), physics, science–environmental interpretation (interdisciplinary), science–physical sciences (interdisciplinary), social science, and special studies (interdisciplinary).

Certifiable programs in education for which a Bachelor of Science is awarded include early childhood education (preK–3), elementary education (1–6), secondary education (7–12), and special subject fields (nursery–12). Subject matter areas for early childhood education are English, general science, and mathematics. Single-subject matter majors for the elementary education program are English, geography, history, mathematics, science–biology, and science–earth sciences. Dual–subject matter programs include English/geography, history/linguistics, history/writing, mathematics/biology, and mathematics/earth sciences. Majors in secondary education include biology, chemistry, earth sciences, English, French, general science, German, history, Italian, mathematics, physics, social sciences, and Spanish. Special subject field majors are art education, music education, physical education, and technology education.

Preprofessional study is offered in prelaw and prehealth/premedical studies.

Academic Program

The graduation requirements for a bachelor's degree are a minimum of 122 to 130 hours of credit. Majors consist of a minimum of 30 to 68 prescribed hours of credit in one specific, approved field. A total of 45 credit hours of general education studies must be completed and include writing, foreign language proficiency, and international requirements. Some of the professional B.S. degree programs enable students to develop a minor or a concentration in addition to the major.

Academically talented students can enroll in the Honors Program, in which interdisciplinary, team-taught courses focus on the themes of Western culture, science and society, and world cultures. Good academic standing and 30 earned academic credits at CCSU make a student eligible for the Cooperative Education Program. Students can earn between $8000 and $13,000 each work term by combining five months of on-campus study with six months of employment.

CCSU operates on a two-semester system. The fall semester usually starts the first week in September and ends in mid-December. The spring semester runs from the third week of January to mid-May. CCSU offers multiple summer sessions from June to August and two 3-week winter sessions in December and January.

The School of Technology's Pathway programs provide a seamless route between other institutions in the Connecticut State University System and Connecticut's community technical colleges without loss of credit or repeated courses.

Off-Campus Arrangements

Internships are available through government offices, newspapers, nonprofit agencies, and many businesses. In addition, off-campus internships are possible through study-abroad and consortium arrangements with the University of Connecticut and other institutions in the Connecticut State University System. The study-abroad program offers students a semester-long or yearlong exchange in which they enroll overseas and study via a cultural immersion program.

Academic Facilities

CCSU's forty buildings on a campus of 300 acres provide students with a full range of learning facilities. The Elihu Burritt Library contains more than 500,000 volumes, more than 3,000 periodical titles, extensive research materials on microfiche and microfilm, and extensive online services and CD-ROM databases. CCSU's online public catalog provides access to the holdings of all four Connecticut State University libraries. The Marcus White Microcomputer Laboratory, a state-of-the-art facility, offers the latest PCs, Macintoshes, printers, scanners, and online capabilities. Other computer facilities are available in the residence halls. The Management Information Systems and Computer Science Departments, as well as the School of Technology, have classroom computers. The Samuel S. T. Chen Art Center's gallery area presents changing exhibits, lectures, and programs.

Costs

Annual tuition and fees for the 2000–01 academic year for Connecticut residents are $3967. Tuition and fees for out-of-state residents are $9720. On-campus room (double occupancy) and board fees for the year are $5792; costs may vary slightly, depending on the meal plan selected. Annual costs for books, travel, and personal expenses vary but are estimated at approximately $2500. All costs are subject to change. Students may contact the Bursar's Office for the most current cost information.

Financial Aid

CCSU's Office of Financial Aid works with students and families to provide assistance to those who are unable to meet educational expenses entirely on their own. Financial aid is provided in three basic forms: grants, work-study employment, and educational loans, which must be repaid. The University offers Connecticut State University Grants, Connecticut Aid for Public Colleges Grants, Federal Pell Grants, Federal Supplemental Educational Opportunity Grants, Federal Direct Stafford Subsidized and Unsubsidized Loans, Federal Direct PLUS Loans (parent loans), and Federal Perkins Loans. Students may also visit Central's Financial Aid Home Page (http://www.ccsu.edu/finaid/) for additional information. Students are required to submit the FAFSA and other basic required documents by deadlines set by the school.

Faculty

Seventy percent of CCSU's faculty members hold doctoral degrees. Others have advanced degrees and are actively involved in research, publishing, and community service. CCSU's faculty members are dedicated to teaching; it is their prime concern and the basis of their students' successes. Due to CCSU's low 17:1 student-faculty ratio, students are better able to take advantage of their professors' expertise and to benefit from personal attention.

Student Government

All of CCSU's full-time undergraduate students are members of the Student Government Association (SGA). The SGA Senate is the representative body of the SGA, and the full-time undergraduates democratically elect its members, the Executive Officers and Senators of the SGA. It promotes student participation in various projects, committees, and organizations at the University and at state and national levels that help shape the University and education in Connecticut. The SGA Senate allocates the SGA portion of the student activity fee to promote and fund student clubs, activities, services, and issues that benefit students and their educational opportunities.

Admission Requirements

CCSU is selective in its admission policy, valuing excellence and achievement in academic scholarship, community and school involvement, and individual achievements. The University welcomes applications from students with a broad range of abilities, interests, and backgrounds and evaluates each student on the merits of his or her readiness to succeed, which is based on past demonstrations of academic and personal success. No applicant is denied admission because of race, color, religious belief, national origin, gender, sexual orientation, age, or disability. A candidate must be a graduate of an accredited high school or preparatory school or hold an equivalency diploma. First-year students' secondary school preparation should include at least 13 units of college-preparatory course work, including English (4 units), mathematics (3 units, including algebra I and II and geometry), science (2 units, including 1 unit of a lab science), social sciences (2 units, including U.S. history), and foreign language (3 units of the same language is recommended). Other factors include the student's academic performance in high school course work, competitive SAT I scores, and rank in class. A personal essay and letters of recommendation are required. Transferring students are encouraged to apply by contacting the Office of Recruitment and Admissions at the address below for details.

Application and Information

Fall semester candidates for admission should apply by May 1 and spring semester candidates by November 1. The Office of Recruitment and Admissions begins notifications by December 1 for fall semester candidates and continues notification on a rolling admission basis. Spring candidates are notified beginning in September. Early admission is recommended for those interested in housing and financial aid. An applicant should submit a completed application with a $40 application fee, an official high school transcript, SAT I scores, rank in class, recommendation letters, and other required documents by stated deadlines.

To request an application, students should contact:

Myrna Garcia-Bowen, Director
Office of Recruitment and Admissions
Central Connecticut State University
1615 Stanley Street
New Britain, Connecticut 06050-4010
Telephone: 860-832-CCSU
          888-733-2278 (toll-free in Connecticut)
E-mail: admissions@ccsu.edu
World Wide Web: http://www.ccsu.edu

CENTRAL MISSOURI STATE UNIVERSITY
WARRENSBURG, MISSOURI

The University

Founded in 1871, Central Missouri State University is a comprehensive public university dedicated to providing personalized education for the 11,000 students representing approximately forty states and sixty other countries. Students live and study in a friendly and inviting environment that embraces skilled faculty members and excellent facilities. Central is proud of its long tradition of preparing students for challenging and rewarding careers, evidenced by the high rate of employment within six months of graduation for the 1997–98 graduates (95.4 percent).

In 1996, the Missouri Coordinating Board for Higher Education designated Central as Missouri's leading institution in professional technology. Central is committed to the comprehensive application of technology throughout the curriculum.

Accredited by North Central Association of Colleges and Schools, Central offers 150 areas of study through four academic colleges. Eighteen programs have achieved professional recognition, which means that Central leads all public regional institutions in Missouri with regard to program-specific accreditations. Sixteen centers and institutes are based at Central.

Central strongly promotes the development of an international perspective among students and faculty members. Exceptional opportunities are available for students to study abroad or participate in internships in universities worldwide.

In addition to instructional buildings, the 1,100-acre campus includes nineteen air-conditioned, suite-style residence halls and a recreational park with lakes for fishing and boating, a heated Olympic-size outdoor pool, and an 18-hole golf course. Central's Multipurpose Building has an Olympic-size indoor pool, a 220-yard indoor track, weight rooms, basketball courts, tennis courts, racquetball and handball courts, and a 12,000-seat arena. Other facilities include an airport and the University Union, which houses cafeterias, a store, and a ten-lane bowling alley and recreation center.

More than 160 student organizations and twenty-four fraternities and sororities provides opportunities for involvement. The University is a member of the Mid-America Intercollegiate Athletic Association, and its teams excel in NCAA Division II baseball, basketball, cross-country, football, golf, indoor and outdoor track, softball, soccer, volleyball, and wrestling.

Location

Central is located in the heart of Warrensburg, a county seat of 15,000 people. Warrensburg is located at the intersection of U.S. Highway 50 and Missouri Highway 13, about 50 miles southeast of Kansas City. Commercial bus services and a main line of Amtrak provide convenient transportation.

Majors and Degrees

Central Missouri State University awards Bachelor of Arts, Bachelor of Science, Bachelor of Science in Education, Bachelor of Science in Business Administration, Bachelor of Music Education, Bachelor of Music, and Bachelor of Fine Arts degrees through the University's thirty-two academic departments. The College of Applied Sciences and Technology has majors in agricultural economics, agricultural technology, agriculture-business, automotive/power technology, aviation technology, construction science management technology, drafting technology, electronics technology, fashion–textiles and clothing in business, graphic arts technology–management, industrial arts and technology, industrial science, industrial technology (management and mechanical), nursing, occupational safety and health, photography, safety management (with options in six areas), secondary education (with options in eight areas), and vocational agriculture education. The College of Arts and Sciences offers majors in actuarial science, art, biology, broadcasting and film, chemistry, commercial art, computer science and mathematics, conservation enforcement, earth science, education (K–12, in five areas), engineering (cooperative 3-2 program), English, French, geography, geology, German, history, instrumental music, interior design, journalism, mass communication, mathematics, medical technology, music (organ, piano, theory-composition, and voice), music education (elementary, instrumental, and vocal), organizational communication, physics, political science, public relations, secondary education (in fourteen areas), social studies, Spanish, speech communication, studio art, and theater. The Harmon College of Business Administration offers majors in accounting, computer information systems, economics, finance, human resource management, management, marketing, office administration, and secondary education in business education. The College of Education and Human Services offers majors in criminal justice administration (with options in three areas), dietetics, education (K–12, in physical education, special education, and speech pathology), elementary education (early childhood education and middle school–junior high school education), general home economics, hotel and restaurant administration, physical education, psychology, psychology (rehabilitation), recreation and tourism, social work, sociology, speech pathology, and vocational home economics.

In addition to the degree programs, Central offers preprofessional programs in dentistry, engineering, law, medicine, optometry, osteopathy, pharmacy, physical therapy, and veterinary medicine.

Career-oriented associate degree programs are offered in the following fields: air-conditioning and refrigeration technology, architectural drafting technology, automotive technology, aviation flight technology, aviation maintenance technology, avionics technology, child development, computer-aided industrial design drafting technology, computer electronics, construction technology, electrical technology, electronics technology, fashion merchandising, graphic arts technology, manufacturing technology, secretarial training, and secretarial training–legal.

Academic Program

Central Missouri State University prepares students to meet challenges in personal growth, as well as in their professional endeavors. To accomplish these goals, the University has established a University Studies Program to complement major course work. A minimum of 124 credit hours is required to earn a bachelor's degree.

The Honors College at Central provides academically talented students with early enrollment privileges, a flexible general studies curriculum, and exceptional international study opportunities. Many of the students choose to reside in Scholars Hall.

Central Missouri's academic year consists of two semesters. Summer school is available in six- and eight-week sessions.

The Office of Extended Campus accommodates part-time students by offering evening and weekend classes at locations on campus and throughout the state.

Academic Facilities

Central's campus contains many exceptional learning facilities to support its varied academic programs. The James C. Kirkpatrick Library, completed in 1999, is one of the most advanced information centers in the Midwest. Containing more than 2.3 million books and documents in a variety of formats, the library offers users a wide range of traditional and electronic services for learning and research.

State-of-the-art facilities are available for speech pathology and audiology. Laboratories are equipped to provide practical preparation for work in the fields of speech and hearing diagnosis and therapy.

Central's KMOS-TV is an educational public television station that broadcasts local and PBS programming to central Missouri. The quality of KMOS-TV equals or exceeds that of the best-equipped middle-market stations in the country. With 100,000 watts of power, KMOS reaches an audience of 1,267,000 people within a 75-mile radius of Warrensburg (including Kansas City). The University's public radio station, KCMW-FM, reaches approximately one fourth of the population of Missouri with its 100,000-watt signal. Students have the opportunity for hands-on experience, and classes in broadcasting are open to all students, regardless of major.

The $5-million Technology Complex consists of a multimedia teaching center, flight simulators, and ground-training facilities. There are specialized shops and laboratories for electricity/electronics, air-conditioning, avionics, aviation, automotive technology, and industrial management and construction, as well as monitoring equipment for solar energy. Max B. Swisher Skyhaven Airport, which is owned and operated by the University, houses thirty University aircraft. A maintenance shop, runways, and a terminal building are used to support the aviation education programs.

Central's facilities include several auditoriums and theaters. The Science Auditorium has a seating capacity of more than 500, a projection room, and a stage. The Education Auditorium can seat 125 students and serves as an educational tool for future teachers. Hendricks Hall, the largest auditorium on campus, can seat 1,473 people. The 500-seat James Highlander Fine Arts Theater features state-of-the-art stage and lighting equipment.

Costs

In 1999–2000, tuition was $99 per credit hour for Missouri residents and $198 per credit hour for nonresidents. For the 1999–2000 academic year, housing cost $1300 per semester, a nineteen-meal-per-week plan cost $752 per semester, and textbook rental cost $15.50 per book.

Financial Aid

Central recognizes students' continuing need for financial assistance. The University extends many opportunities for students to receive as much financial aid as possible through scholarships and awards and participation in federal financial aid programs. Federal Pell Grants, Perkins Loans, Stafford Student Loans, and private organization loans are available to students. There are 1,467 students employed in part-time positions on campus, and many students find employment off campus. About 67 percent of the students at Central currently receive some type of financial assistance. For information, students should write to the Office of Financial Aid, Administration Building 316 at the University or call 660-543-4040. Approximately $3 million is awarded annually in merit-based scholarships and awards. The University honors those it names as Distinguished Scholars with full academic scholarships that pay fees, board and room, and textbook costs. For additional information and applications, students should write to the Scholarships and Awards Officer, Administration 104, Central Missouri State University, or call 660-543-4541.

Faculty

The faculty members at Central exemplify the goals of the institution as they balance personal attention with expertise in their respective fields. Approximately 75 percent of the 425 full-time faculty members hold doctorates. Faculty member-student relationships are excellent at Central, and respect flows both ways to enhance a strong educational bond. Classes tend to be small, and the student-faculty ratio is 17:1. Participation and enthusiasm are key words in describing the degree of interest the faculty members have in student activities and community affairs.

Student Government

Students actively participate in government at Central by becoming members of the Student Government Association, Interfraternity and Panhellenic councils, and Residence Halls Association. Students involved in these organizations represent the voice of the student body, and these prestigious groups are respected by students and faculty members alike.

Admission Requirements

Students considered for admission rank in the upper two thirds of their graduating class, complete the prescribed core curriculum, and achieve a 20–36 ACT score. Scores on the ACT and a final transcript at graduation are required of all first-time freshmen. Students who have successfully met Missouri state requirements on the General Educational Development (GED) test are also considered for admission.

Transfer students from accredited community colleges or other four-year institutions are considered for admission if they have maintained a cumulative grade average of C or better. Students who have obtained an Associate of Arts degree have fulfilled the general studies requirements at Central, unless specific courses are required for major or upper-division University Studies.

Application and Information

A rolling admissions policy at Central makes it possible for students to apply any time during their senior year of high school. Applications should be submitted to the Office of Admissions, preferably during the first semester of the senior year for preferential consideration for housing and financial aid. A $25 fee must accompany applications (international students must submit $50). Central recommends that prospective students visit the campus. Guided tours, question-and-answer sessions with instructors, and campus information are all readily available.

For application forms and additional information about applying, interested students should contact:

Office of Admissions
Administration Building 104
Central Missouri State University
Warrensburg, Missouri 64093

Telephone: 800-956-0177 (toll-free)
Fax: 660-543-8517
E-mail: admit@cmsuvmb.cmsu.edu
World Wide Web: http://www.cmsu.edu

The James C. Kirkpatrick Library.

CHADRON STATE COLLEGE
CHADRON, NEBRASKA

The College
Chadron State College challenges and prepares students to realize academic, personal, and professional success. These successes are developed through experiences in activities on and off campus. Founded in 1911 as Nebraska State Normal School, Chadron State has a proven record of graduates who excel. The professors are approachable and work closely with the students. The total fall 1999 enrollment was 2,768 students. The student body is composed of students from various ethnic and racial backgrounds. The majority of the student population comes from Nebraska, Wyoming, South Dakota, and Colorado; seven other countries are also represented on the campus. Forty percent of the undergraduate students are men.

A combination of academic offerings and faculty expertise enhances the rewards from students' efforts at Chadron State College. Chadron State offers Bachelor of Arts, Bachelor of Science, and Bachelor of Science in Education programs (four-year degrees) as well as the Master of Arts in Education, Master of Business Administration, Master of Science in Education, and Specialist in Education. The College is accredited by the North Central Association of Colleges and Schools, the National Council for Accreditation of Teacher Education, the Council on Social Work Education, and the Nebraska State Department of Education.

A college campus environment in beautiful northwest Nebraska makes the location a great place to live and study. Tall, pine-clad buttes of a national forest extend across the south end of the campus. In addition, two state parks are within driving distance of the College. Chadron State College has seven spacious residence halls, a physical activity center with an indoor track, three versatile basketball/tennis/volleyball courts, a weight-training room, five racquetball courts, and specialized classrooms for dance and gymnastics. Chadron State also has a student center, a beautiful fine arts building with two theaters, an educational technology and distance learning center, a three-story library, and a media center. More than fifty campus clubs and organizations, numerous intramural leagues, and eight intercollegiate NCAA Division II athletic teams offer opportunities for involvement and entertainment.

Location
Chadron is a community of approximately 6,000 people. Located at the junction of U.S. Highways 385 and 20, Chadron has a low crime rate. The national forest and state parks surrounding the city of Chadron provide a beautiful recreational aspect to the College. Students enjoy hiking, mountain biking, hunting, fishing, and camping as favorite pastimes. Fort Robinson, 28 miles west, was once a colorful frontier military post. The Hudson-Meng Bison Kill Site, the Agate Fossil Beds, and the Mammoth Site are nearby. Neighboring Cherry County produces more high-grade beef cattle than any other county in this country. The Black Hills of South Dakota are only an hour's drive to the north.

Major airlines have connections into Rapid City, South Dakota, and Scottsbluff, Nebraska; both are within 2 hours of Chadron. A commuter airline connects Denver, Colorado, and Chadron. Bus service is also available in and out of Chadron. Six major fast food businesses and several fine dining restaurants provide numerous opportunities for eating out. Four theater screens provide movies each night of the week. Many other forms of entertainment can be found in Chadron, as the College brings entertainers and fine arts attractions to the city regularly.

Majors and Degrees
Bachelor of Arts degrees are awarded in art (with an emphasis in two-dimensional, three-dimensional, and commercial graphic design), business administration (with options in accounting, agribusiness, economics, finance, general business, management, management information systems, marketing, office management, and real estate), educational media, English (with an option in journalism), family and consumer sciences (with options in child development, design and merchandising, family and consumer studies, food management, and human services), history, industrial management (with options in agriculture, graphic arts, and manufacturing), justice studies (with an option in criminal justice and legal studies), music (with an option in music performance and commercial music instrumental or vocal emphasis), psychology (with options in general psychology and substance abuse), range management (with options in rangeland business, rangeland livestock production, and range management), recreation, social work, sociology, speech communication, and theater.

Bachelor of Science degrees are awarded in biology (with options in environmental studies, general biology, and human biology), chemistry, clinical laboratory science (medical technology), information systems technology, mathematics (with options in computational mathematics and mathematics), medicinal/pharmaceutical chemistry, and physics.

The Bachelor of Science in Education is offered in art (K–12, with an emphasis in two- or three-dimensional art), basic business education, biology, chemistry, Earth science, economics, educational media, English, English (4–9), family and consumer sciences (4–9 and 7–12), general science, health education, health education (7–12), history, home economics, industrial technology (4–9 and 7–12), language arts (7–12), mathematics, mathematics (4–9), middle grades, music (K–12) and vocal music (K–8), natural science, physical education (K–6, 4–9, and 7–12), physical education and health (K–12), physical science, physics, political science, science (4–9), social science, social science (4–9), sociology, speech communication, speech communication and theater, theater, trade and industrial education (10–12), and vocational business education.

Chadron offers elementary education endorsements in early childhood education (Pre-K–3), elementary education (K–8), and mild/moderate disabilities (K–12 and 7–12). Supplemental endorsements are available in adapted physical education, coaching, computer science, driver education, and family and consumer sciences-related occupations (7–12). Endorsements to teach are offered in diversified occupations (7–12) and vocational special needs/school-to-work (7–12).

Academic Program
Chadron State College has an academic year divided into fall, spring, and summer semesters. Students seeking a baccalaureate degree from Chadron State College must complete the requirements for the program in addition to the general studies requirements. Bachelor of Arts and Bachelor of Science in education degrees are granted upon completion of a minimum total of 125 semester hours—45 of which must be at the 300 or

400 (junior or senior) level. A grade point average of 2.0 (on a 4.0 scale) must be maintained for the Bachelor of Arts programs, and a 2.5 GPA must be maintained for the Bachelor of Science in education programs. No more than 66 credit hours may be transferred or applied toward a baccalaureate degree from a two-year institution.

Chadron State College offers alternative options for earning credit. Course work may be supplemented by internships and a cooperative learning program. Travel opportunities for credit during the school year and the summers are available. Independent studies and the College-Level Examination Program are available as well.

Off-Campus Arrangements

Several low-cost tours and field trips are arranged by the College, usually in the spring and summer months. Internships are encouraged for junior and senior students. Summer travel opportunities are developed for which students may receive credit. In the past, tours have gone to Europe, Japan, Canada, Nassau, and Mexico as well as various parts of the United States, including Alaska and Hawaii.

Academic Facilities

The Reta King Library currently contains 150,402 books, 336,290 microform titles, and 112,500 periodicals. The library provides two computer laboratories, duplicating machines, and microfilm/microfiche readers for student and faculty use. Students also have access to the card catalogs of the two other state colleges in Nebraska and an electronic database with access to 1,000 full-text and 3,000 indexed periodicals. The information highway of the Internet is readily accessible as well. The College has more than 120 terminals, including PCs and Macintosh computers for student use in the computer labs, classrooms, library, and residence halls.

Costs

For the 1999–2000 academic year, the comprehensive cost of tuition, fees, room, and board for Nebraska residents was $5563. For nonresident students the cost was $7438. Other expenses such as books, travel, and supplies cost approximately $1200.

Financial Aid

Students seeking financial aid must complete the application for admission to Chadron State College and submit the $15 required application fee. Undergraduate students should file the Free Application for Federal Student Aid (FAFSA). After receiving the results from the processor, students should forward them to the College Director of Financial Aid. Undergraduate applications for financial assistance provide consideration for the Federal Pell Grant, Federal Work-Study, Federal Perkins Loan, Federal Supplemental Educational Opportunity Grant, Federal PLUS, and Federal Family Education Loan Programs as well as the State Scholarship Award Program and Student Assistance Program. A monthly payment plan is available through the Business Office. CSC provides electronic FAFSA processing.

Faculty

The College currently has a teaching faculty of 151 members (104 full-time, 65 percent of whom have terminal degrees). Ninety-nine percent of the faculty members advise undergraduate students. Each faculty member is involved in student activities. The vast majority of the undergraduate classes are taught by faculty members. The student–undergraduate faculty ratio of 18:1 allows close relationships between faculty members and students.

Student Government

A large number of students are actively involved in the student government. Numerous committees and organizations, including Student Senate, make an impact on the College. Students take part in decisions concerning scholastic, collegiate, intellectual, recreation, social, and cultural activities on and off campus.

Admission Requirements

Chadron State College welcomes inquiries regarding the College's programs and admission requirements. The College has an open admission policy for all students. To ensure a more successful college career, Chadron State recommends that a student pursue the following courses in high school: 4 units of English; 3 units of mathematics; 3 units of social studies, including 1 unit of American history and 1 unit of global studies; 2 units of laboratory science; and other academic courses selected from areas such as foreign language, visual or performing arts, and computer literacy. Applications for admission should be submitted by currently enrolled high school students between the beginning of their last year and one month prior to the beginning of the term for which they seek admission. Individuals who have completed high school should submit their application materials at least one month prior to the beginning of the term for which they wish to be admitted.

Application and Information

The freshman applicant should submit a completed application for admission; a $15 application fee; an official high school transcript reflecting a graduation date, class rank, and overall grade point average; and an official ACT or SAT I score report sent from the testing headquarters. The ACT/SAT I is not required for students who graduated from high school five or more years prior to enrollment at Chadron State. All students must show a physician-validated immunization record.

The transfer applicant should submit a completed application for admission, a $15 application fee, a physician-validated immunization record, and official transcripts from all colleges or universities previously attended. If the student has completed fewer than 12 semester hours of credit, he or she must also submit an official high school transcript and ACT or SAT I scores. Application forms, financial aid forms, and other information are mailed upon request. Campus visits are encouraged. Inquiries should be made to:

Ms. Terie Dawson
Assistant Vice President, Enrollment Management
Chadron State College
1000 Main Street
Chadron, Nebraska 69337-2690
Telephone: 308-432-6263
                800-242-3766 (toll-free)
Fax: 308-432-6229
E-mail: inquire@csc1.edu

CHAMINADE UNIVERSITY OF HONOLULU
HONOLULU, HAWAII

The University

Chaminade University of Honolulu, a private, coeducational institution, was established in 1955 by the Society of Mary (Marianists). Named after Father William Joseph Chaminade, a French Catholic priest who ministered to his people during the late eighteenth and early nineteenth centuries and who founded the Society in 1817, the University today continues the Marianist mission of educating leaders through faith and reason. To achieve this mission, Chaminade forms a community encompassing people from diverse cultural origins, both traditional and nontraditional, who hold a variety of religious beliefs. The University encourages learning through cooperation, self-discipline, caring, and mutual respect while offering individualized attention that promotes personal and intellectual growth. A major goal of the University is to educate and train students for leadership both within Chaminade and in communities beyond the campus. The University advocates a personal concern for social justice, ethics, responsibility, and service to the community and exerts institutional leadership by promoting Chaminade's ideals outside the University community.

At any one time, 2,600 to 2,800 students are enrolled in a range of daytime and evening classes. Of this number, approximately 1,000 are full-time undergraduates, 1,200 are part-time undergraduates, and 500 are graduate students. About 60 percent of the full-time undergraduates are from Hawaii, 24 percent are from the mainland, 13 percent are from U.S. trust territories, and 3 percent are from other countries. Thirty-four states and thirty-one countries are represented in the student body. Approximately one third of the undergraduates do not enter directly after high school; therefore, a sizable segment of the student population is above the age of 22.

Clubs and associations offer all Chaminade students a chance to pursue interests and extend their activities beyond the classroom. Student publications include the *Aulama*, a literary and art magazine; the *Silverword*, the monthly student newspaper; and *Ahinahina*, the Chaminade yearbook. Chaminade also sponsors chapters of Delta Epsilon Sigma, the national scholastic honor society for students at colleges and universities with a Catholic tradition; Phi Alpha Theta, the history national honor society; Delta Mu Delta, a national honor society in business administration; Sigma Tau Delta, the national English honor society; Pi Sigma Alpha, a national honor society in political science, and Alpha Phi Sigma, a national honor society for criminal justice.

Intercollegiate athletic teams are currently sponsored in men's basketball and water polo, women's softball and volleyball, and men's and women's cross-country and tennis. Intramural competitive and noncompetitive sports and recreation programs are open to all students, faculty and staff members, and alumni.

Chaminade University of Honolulu is accredited by the Accrediting Commission for Senior Colleges and Universities of the Western Association of Schools and Colleges. The University also has two sister universities on the mainland: the University of Dayton in Dayton, Ohio, and St. Mary's University in San Antonio, Texas.

Chaminade offers graduate degrees in business administration (M.B.A.), counseling psychology (M.S.C.P.), criminal justice administration (M.S.C.J.A.), education (M.Ed.), pastoral leadership (M.A.P.L.), and public administration (M.P.A.).

Location

Honolulu, a multicultural community, is enriched by a great diversity of ethnic activities and traditions. Chaminade is located on a hillside with a spectacular view sweeping across Waikiki to downtown Honolulu, from Diamond Head to the blue Pacific Ocean. This idyllic site is only minutes from the city, cultural activities, and the beach. The University also operates ten off-campus sites, primarily at military installations on the island of Oahu.

Majors and Degrees

The University offers twenty-four major programs of study at the undergraduate level as well as two associate degree programs. The Bachelor of Arts (B.A.) degree is offered in biology, business administration, chemistry, communication, economics, English, historical and political studies, humanities, international studies, management, philosophy, psychology, religious studies, and social studies; the Bachelor of Fine Arts (B.F.A.) degree is offered in interior design; and the Bachelor of Science (B.S.) degree is offered in accounting, behavioral sciences, biology, computer information science, criminal justice, early childhood education, elementary education, forensic science, and management. The Associate in Arts (A.A.) degree is offered in business administration; the Associate in Science (A.S.) degree is offered in computer science and criminal justice.

Preprofessional programs are offered in law, health sciences, nursing, and engineering. Students can also enroll in a dual-degree program, offered in conjunction with St. Mary's University, that awards a B.A. degree in mathematics from Chaminade and a B.S. degree in engineering from St. Mary's.

Students may elect to pursue a minor program in most major programs as well as in anthropology, history, physics, political science, sociology, and studio art.

Academic Program

The core curriculum at Chaminade is in liberal arts. The University is committed to a broad liberal education for its students and believes that such an education provides a basis for long-term personal growth, a foundation for a career that may encounter job changes, and a background that allows students to rise to leadership positions in their chosen fields and communities. Through undergraduate programs based on the liberal arts tradition, Chaminade seeks to heighten cultural awareness. Coupled with understanding diverse methods of inquiry and participation in Chaminade's multicultural interdependent community, cultural awareness prepares all students for lifelong learning—about themselves, each other, and the world in which they live.

Undergraduate study is structured into four parts: practice in basic skills, liberal arts course work that provides a general education, intensive study in a chosen field of concentration (the major), and elective courses outside the major field to complement general and specialized knowledge. All baccalaureate degrees require a minimum of 124 credit hours of course work with a minimum of 45 hours in upper-division courses. Within these guidelines, the student selects a program of study appropriate to personal needs and interests. All appropriate courses at Chaminade require writing assignments from students. Upper-division courses in most fields train students to write in the style and format appropriate to the discipline.

In all fields of study at Chaminade, students are encouraged to apply their academic experience to on-the-job practice for academic credit. Faculty members may ask students to work with a specific organization, or students may develop internship possibilities on their own. Interns usually have at least junior-level standing, but in special cases sophomores are considered. Depending on the organization with which they work, students may or may not receive a salary for their internship experience.

The Integrated Freshman Program is designed to support the development of students into active learning partners. The curriculum stresses writing as a learning process, focuses on varied kinds of learning experiences outside as well as inside the classroom, and strengthens teamwork among students and teachers.

The First Year Experience Seminar supports students in their transition from high school to college. The program provides an orientation to University functions and resources. This course also helps freshmen adjust to the University, gain a better understanding of the learning process and develop critical-thinking skills and provides a support group for students by examining problems that are common to the freshman experience.

Chaminade cooperates with two major programs that enable students to receive college credit prior to admission. These two programs, Advanced Placement and College-Level Examination Program, are sponsored by the College Board.

Off-Campus Arrangements

In 1990, Chaminade University and its sister universities signed an agreement through which any student at any of the three universities can enroll for their junior year at any of the other campuses. Full credit is given by Chaminade for approved courses taken at either university. Chaminade also encourages students to pursue part of their undergraduate education in another country. A limited number of scholarships are available for qualified students interested in study at Ritsumeikan University or Doshisha University in Kyoto, Japan.

Academic Facilities

Located in Henry Hall, Sullivan Library occupies three floors and houses a collection of approximately 74,000 volumes and 874 periodicals. Special collections include the Oceania Collection, the Catholic Authors Collection, the Julius J. Nodel Judaica Collection, and the David L. Carlson Japan Collection. Services offered include reference consultation, computerized information retrieval, and instruction in library use. Also in Henry Hall, the Computer Center provides students and faculty members with a variety of microcomputers, software programs, and reference materials for instruction, word processing, and programming. The multipurpose Audio Visual Media Resource Center provides instructional media technology support to all divisions of the University, student activities, special programs, and other events. The center is also a resource for films, slides, records, and videotapes.

Costs

Full-time undergraduate tuition for 2000–01 is $6020 per semester. Part-time undergraduate tuition is $400 per semester hour. Housing costs per semester range from $1585 to $2350, depending upon accommodations. Meal plans range from $1270 to $1750 per semester, depending upon the plan chosen. Various other fees for acceptance, independent/individualized directed studies, experiential learning, parking, labs, and studios are also charged. The tuition charged by Chaminade University does not cover the total cost of instruction for each student. The University undertakes to raise the balance through gifts and grants. Tuition and fees must be paid at or prior to the time of registration.

Financial Aid

Those with a high school GPA between 3.5 and 4.0 are eligible for a $5000 yearly scholarship; between 3.0 and 3.49, a $4500 yearly scholarship; between 2.5 and 2.99, a $3500 yearly grant; and between 2.25 to 2.49, a $3000 yearly grant. The Hawaii Grant for new full-time day session students from Hawaii is $1500 per semester. Scholarships and grants, available to regular full-time undergraduate students, are renewable for four years and are awarded without regard to financial need. Students may obtain only one of the Chaminade scholarships or grants. A tuition discount of 20 percent is offered to additional family members when one member of the family is paying full-time tuition.

Faculty

The University is dedicated to teaching and to building the leadership skills of its students, and its major strengths lie in its relatively small size and its talented faculty. Classes are small, allowing faculty members to provide a significant amount of individual and small-group attention. Classes are taught by professors or professionals in their fields, not graduate students.

Student Government

The Chaminade University Student Association is the official representative of the student body. Each full-time student of Chaminade becomes a member upon payment of fees. Membership is open to all students at all instructional sites. The Senate, chaired by the student body president and composed of elected representatives, focuses on improving the quality of undergraduate student life and represents the needs, interests, and concerns of its constituents.

The Dean of Students, through the Director of Residential Life and the Student Council Committee, initiates all disciplinary action. The committee is composed of administrators, faculty and staff members, and students. Chaminade does not condone activities on campus that violate state or federal regulations, including illegal possession of drugs or the illegal consumption of alcoholic beverages. Students found to be in violation of these regulations are subject to immediate disciplinary action.

Admission Requirements

Applications for admission are reviewed for specific majors or, when applicable, for "undecided" status. Chaminade considers several factors when assessing students' preparation for a selected area of study: grades throughout high school, selection of courses in preparation for college, results of either the SAT I or ACT, and an essay that provides information about the applicant's character and record of leadership and service.

Application and Information

Chaminade University has a rolling admission process. As soon as all required information is received by the Admission Office, the application is reviewed by an application committee. Students are notified of the committee's decision usually within three to four weeks. Applications are accepted throughout the year. A $50 fee is payable upon application. Web site applications are also available for a $25 fee. All students desiring housing must file an application along with a $100 deposit applicable to the total cost per semester. Space and placement are not guaranteed without this deposit. A housing damage deposit of $100 is also required. Evidence of health insurance coverage from a U.S. insurer is required of all dormitory residents and international students.

To ensure full consideration for scholarships or grants, students are urged to complete the appropriate application by April 1. Award notices are mailed by April 30. Inquiries and application materials should be sent to:

Admission Office
Chaminade University
3140 Waialae Avenue
Honolulu, Hawaii 96816
Telephone: 808-735-4735
        800-735-3733 (toll-free from the mainland;
           collect from neighboring islands)
Fax: 808-739-4647
E-mail: cuhadm@lava.net
World Wide Web: http://www.chaminade.edu

CHAMPLAIN COLLEGE
BURLINGTON, VERMONT

The College

Champlain College is a coeducational, private, nonprofit college founded in 1878. Its 19-acre campus, home to 1,400 students, is nestled among the stately maple trees of Burlington's historic Hill Section. Many of the College's thirty-three buildings, including most of the dormitories, are restored pre-Victorian- and Victorian-era private homes, which give students a unique atmosphere in which to learn and live.

The two-year and four-year educational programs are designed to provide sound professional training for careers in today's complex world, as well as broadening and enriching experiences in the humanities and general education. Champlain College is recognized as one of the leading career-building colleges in New England, and it has earned the respect of the business, technical, and human services professions for its outstanding skill-building education.

Academic advising is coordinated through the efforts of department chairpeople, academic advisers, personal mentors, and career counselors, who work toward helping students succeed in their academic and professional careers. Confidential health and counseling services are provided on campus as well.

Champlain College's athletic programs are tailored to both the intercollegiate athlete and the intramural athlete. Champlain competes in the National Junior College Athletic Association comprising twenty-one regions and 563 colleges throughout the nation. The women's soccer team won the NJCAA national title in 1998 and 1994, while making it to the finals in five out of the last six seasons. Champlain's men's soccer program also enjoys a national ranking. The men's basketball program has a continuing history of being one of the finest in the country and has tallied four trips to the NJCAA national tournament in the past eight years. Intramural programs include aerobics, basketball, indoor soccer, outing club, skiing, snowboarding, and volleyball.

Location

Burlington is a small city (46,000 people) overlooking majestic Lake Champlain and the Adirondack Mountains of New York to the west. The long and beautiful ridge line of the Green Mountains form the eastern horizon, and, to the north, Montreal, Quebec, is only a 1½-hour drive away. Burlington is one of the nation's most progressive cities, and it is the cultural center of Vermont. Four residential colleges are located in the area, along with one of the leading medical centers on the East Coast. Burlington has an international airport; an Amtrak passenger train route with connections to Montreal, New York City, and Washington; and its own long-distance bus service, Vermont Transit Lines. The Church Street Marketplace, located just a few blocks from campus, attracts people from miles around to its numerous shops and restaurants. Three television stations, fifteen radio stations, and daily newspapers serve the area. The Arts and Entertainment Channel (A&E) has listed Burlington as the nation's "Best Place to Live."

Vermont is known as the ski capital of the East. The challenging slopes of Stowe, Bolton Valley, Mad River Glen, Smuggler's Notch, and Sugarbush are all less than an hour's drive from Champlain College. The nearby mountains, lakes, and streams also provide opportunities for backpacking, hiking, fishing, hunting, canoeing, sailing, and windsurfing. Great in-line skating and bicycling are just 5 minutes from campus on the 7-mile-long recreation path that follows the spectacular shore of Lake Champlain.

Majors and Degrees

Champlain College offers the Associate in Science degree with majors in accounting, business, business management, computer programming, criminal justice, e-business and commerce, early childhood education, hotel-restaurant management, international business, liberal studies, marketing management, media communications/public relations, multimedia and graphic design, networking systems/PC support, occupational therapy assistant studies, paralegal/legal assistant studies, radiography, respiratory therapy, social services, software development, sport management, telecommunications, travel and tourism, and Web design and management. Students may take programs in prelaw.

Champlain College offers the Bachelor of Science degree in accounting, business management, and professional studies. The professional studies program offers eighteen different career concentrations combining practical liberal arts focus in communications, critical thinking, and ethics with career-centered marketable skills to prepare students for the competitive national and international job market.

Academic Program

The curricula offered by the College serve a variety of individual needs. The 2+2 format allows students to earn a two-year associate degree as well as the four-year bachelor's degree. This format gives students the flexibility to enter the workforce after earning their two-year associate degree or to continue their education and earn a four-year bachelor's degree. The College believes that an important part of its mission is preparing its students for success in their chosen careers and as members of the community in which they will live. On-the-job or internship experiences are required for many majors, and a majority of graduates go directly into their chosen career field.

An Army ROTC program is provided in cooperation with the University of Vermont.

Off-Campus Arrangements

Champlain students have a variety of off-campus opportunities that greatly enhance their total educational experience. Eighty-seven percent of the College's majors require an internship experience. These internships give students practical job experience in a professional environment. Many of these internships have led directly to permanent positions after graduation. Educational field trips to Montreal and New York City are required for all students in the hotel restaurant management major. Champlain also offers an International Exchange Program with English-speaking universities in England, France, Sweden, and Switzerland. These programs greatly enhance a student's education by offering a unique life experience while increasing potential employment opportunities.

Academic Facilities

The three-story William R. Hauke Family Campus Center houses an auditorium, a student lounge, a snack bar, a dining room, educational labs for hotel-restaurant management and communications/public relations majors, telecommunications facilities, classrooms, and faculty offices. Freeman Hall houses the microbiology lab and the hotel management/travel and tourism front desk computer teaching classroom for online reservations. Faculty and administrative offices are also located in Freeman.

While incorporating the features of a traditional library, the state-of-the-art Holly D. and Robert E. Miller Information Commons utilizes advanced technologies such as multimedia laboratories, integrated computer networks, specialized electronic classrooms, and online distance learning systems to enhance a student's ability to conduct research. An additional six major academic buildings provide classroom, laboratory, and computer resources. More than 220 computers and terminals are available for students. All campus buildings are linked by fiber-optic cable, enabling students to access the Internet from their dorm rooms and labs. The Student Resource Center offers students individual tutoring in nearly all courses taught at the College and in general study skills. The writing assistance lab is also available to all students, as well as a math/accounting lab.

The Office of Career Planning and Placement offers individual assistance to students before and after graduation. Over the past five years, Champlain graduates have achieved a 97 percent employment/continued education record.

Costs

Tuition for 1999–2000 was $10,485, and room and board totaled $7450. The recreation fee was $100.

Financial Aid

The financial aid program at Champlain College includes loans, grants, scholarships, and work-study awards. Its purpose is to help needy students meet the full cost of their education. The College participates in the Federal Perkins Loan Program, Federal Work-Study, Federal Supplemental Educational Opportunity Grant Program, Federal Pell Grant Program, Federal Stafford Student Loan Program, Vermont Student Assistance Corporation, and state loan and grant programs. The College has committed a substantial sum of institutional money to financial aid. This aid is available primarily on the basis of need.

Qualified students interested in one or more types of financial aid should write to the Office of Financial Aid for an application. To be eligible for financial aid, students are required to complete the Free Application for Federal Student Aid (FAFSA). Vermont students are also required to fill out a Vermont Student Assistance Incentive Grant application.

Champlain also offers a free financial aid estimate program called FAIR (Financial Aid Information Review). FAIR gives prospective students the opportunity to learn at no cost or obligation what their financial contributions to college are likely to be.

Faculty

The College believes its strength lies in its faculty. There are 54 full-time and 117 part-time faculty members whose job it is to teach students, not do research. Most faculty members have completed programs of advanced study, and several have made notable contributions to the business field through lectures, magazine articles, and participation in national and regional conferences.

Student Government

The primary mission of Champlain College Student Government Association is to encourage students to get involved in creating a physical and intellectual environment in which they have a freedom to grow and are challenged to realize their full potential. The Student Government Association's responsibility is to inform and advocate for student's concerns, to promote character and personality development and ethical conduct in students, and to provide creative outlets through supervised extracurricular activities. The Student Government Association is dedicated to listening to the student body, fostering their understanding and appreciation of all people, and creating unity and campus pride.

Admission Requirements

The College requires graduation from a recognized secondary school (or an equivalency certificate) as a condition of acceptance. The College also requires a transcript, an SAT I or ACT test score, and, if possible, a recommendation from the guidance counselor of the last school attended. A personal interview may be required of applicants to certain programs and is recommended for all candidates. Even during the summer months, it may be possible to offer admission to an applicant for the coming fall semester. Students may also start college at midyear.

The baccalaureate programs are part of the 2+2 curriculum format that is a unique feature at Champlain. Students with a 2.5 GPA after two years are automatically eligible for third-year enrollment. Others are encouraged to meet with their adviser before submitting their application for the upper division.

All candidates for transfer admission who have attended another accredited college are required to file an official transcript of all high school and college work with the director of admissions at Champlain College. A student who transfers from an accredited college may be given transfer credit for all courses completed with a grade of C or better.

Admission requirements for the baccalaureate programs are graduation from a recognized high school or achievement of a high school equivalency certificate plus successful completion of at least 45 credit hours (three semesters) of college course work at Champlain College or another college or university.

Champlain College affirms its commitment to providing equal opportunity in education and employment for qualified persons. The College admits students of any race, creed, color, national and ethnic origin, religion, age, sexual orientation, gender, or qualified disability and does not discriminate in the administration of its educational and admission policies, scholarship and loan programs, employment practices, or athletic and other College-administered programs. Implementation of this policy shall be in compliance with federal and state statutes that prohibit discrimination in any form. Champlain College will make reasonable accommodations to the disability of an otherwise-qualified student, applicant, or employee. Those interested should contact Dolly Shaw, Affirmative Action Officer, with any questions or discrimination complaints or if auxiliary aids or services are needed to participate in Champlain College programs or to apply for admission or employment.

Application and Information

Applicants should fill out the application form and forward it with the application fee of $35 to the Admissions Office. Champlain College operates on a rolling admissions basis for its two-year and four-year degree programs, processing applications as soon as they are received; notification of an admission decision is usually made within three to four weeks.

Mailing Address:

    Director of Admissions
    Champlain College
    163 South Willard Street
    P.O. Box 670
    Burlington, Vermont 05402-0670
    Telephone: 802-860-2727
               800-570-5858 (toll-free)
    Fax: 802-860-2775
    E-mail: admission@champlain.edu

Street Address:

    Admissions Office
    Champlain College
    163 South Willard Street
    Burlington, Vermont 05401

The Champlain College campus after a fresh snowfall.

CHAPMAN UNIVERSITY
ORANGE, CALIFORNIA

The University

During its 138-year history, Chapman has evolved from a small, traditional liberal arts college that was founded in 1861 by members of the First Christian Church (Disciples of Christ) into a midsize comprehensive liberal arts and sciences university that is distinguished for its nationally recognized programs in film and television production, business and economics, music, education, communication arts, and the natural and applied sciences. The mission of Chapman University is to provide personalized education of distinction that leads to inquiring, ethical, and productive lives as global citizens.

Chapman's parklike, ivy-covered, and tree-lined campus features a blending of fully refurbished historic structures with the newest in state-of-the-art Internet- and satellite-connected learning environments. Five residence halls and six on-campus apartment buildings are conveniently located on the edge of the campus. Also recently completed have been a five-story parking structure, the 100,000-square-foot School of Law facility, and Liberty Plaza, which features a large section of the Berlin Wall.

Chapman University's academic structure includes the Wilkinson College of Letters and Sciences, the Argyros School of Business and Economics, the School of Communication Arts, the School of Education, the School of Film and Television, the School of Music, and the School of Law. Programs of distinction include the A. Gary Anderson Center for Economic Research, which is internationally recognized for econometric forecasting; the nationally recognized School of Film and Television; and the ABA-accredited School of Law. Other nationally accredited programs include the School of Business and Economics, which is accredited by AACSB–The International Association of Management Education; the IFT-accredited program in food science and nutrition; the NASM-accredited School of Music; and the APTA-accredited graduate program in physical therapy. Chapman was also recently recognized by the Templeton Foundation as one of only 100 colleges nationally to be designated as a Templeton Foundation "Character-Building College."

In addition to approximately 4,000 undergraduate, graduate, and professional school students enrolled on the campus in Orange, Chapman also enrolls more than 5,000 undergraduate and graduate students annually through its College of Lifelong Learning and network of forty Chapman Academic Centers that are located in seven western states.

The University is electric, involving, and outdoor-oriented. In addition to taking advantage of the obvious benefits associated with the southern California climate, Chapman students enjoy a dynamic student activities program. Although predominantly from California, Chapman students come from forty different states; in addition, approximately 10 percent of its students come from thirty-four other countries. Over the past five years, Chapman students have been named Truman Scholars, Coro Fellows, *USA Today* All-USA College Academic Team members, NCAA All-Americans, and NCAA academic all-Americans. Chapman's long and distinguished heritage in intercollegiate sports includes five NCAA national championships in baseball, tennis, and softball. Chapman competes as an independent in the NCAA Division III level and fields teams in baseball, basketball (m/w), crew (m/w), cross-country (m/w), football, golf, lacrosse, soccer (m/w), softball, swimming (w), tennis (m/w), track and field (w), volleyball (w), and water polo (m/w). Approximately 20 percent of Chapman's student body participates in intercollegiate athletics, and last year, 4 student-athletes were honored as all-Americans and 14 as academic all-Americans.

More than seventy clubs and organizations are available, many with commitments to a wide range of community service efforts. Chapman's Greek system includes five nationally chartered fraternities and sororities. A comprehensive intramural sports program involves a myriad of sports activities for all campus community members throughout the school year. On-campus intercollegiate athletic events, music, art, and theater productions provide students with numerous ongoing extracurricular activity options. Chapman's proximity to area recreational and cultural opportunities allows Chapman students to enjoy the essence of what makes Orange County's south coast area an enviable environment in which to live and learn.

Prominent Chapman alumni include the Honorable Loretta Sanchez ('88), member of Congress; the Honorable David Bonior ('85), member of Congress and current House Minority Whip; television and film producer John Copeland ('73); UCLA head basketball coach Steve Lavin ('88); former San Diego Padre stars Tim Flannery ('80) and Randy Jones ('72); and developer/philanthropist George L. Argyros ('65).

Location

Orange County, California, was recently rated by *Places Rated Almanac* as "the #1 place to live in North America," citing superior climate, cultural, recreational, educational, and career-entree opportunities. Los Angeles is 35 miles to the north, and San Diego is 80 miles to the south. Nearby entertainment venues include Disneyland, Knott's Berry Farm, the Orange County Performing Arts Center, major-league baseball, and hockey. Pristine West Coast beaches are less than 10 miles from the campus, and seasonal snow skiing is 90 minutes away. The average year-round temperature on campus is 71 degrees Fahrenheit, and the air is normally smog-free, due to a daily prevailing sea breeze from nearby southwest-facing beaches.

Majors and Degrees

Chapman awards the Bachelor of Arts degree in the fields of art, biology, chemistry, communications, dance, economics, English and comparative literature, film and television, French, health science, history, international studies, liberal studies (elementary education), movement and exercise science, music, peace studies, philosophy, political science, psychology, religion, social science, sociology, Spanish, and theater. The Bachelor of Fine Arts degree is conferred in art, dance, film and television, and theater. The Bachelor of Science degree is offered in accounting, applied mathematics, biology, business administration, chemistry, computer information systems, computer science, environmental science, food science and nutrition, health science, movement and exercise science, and natural science. The Bachelor of Music degree is granted in composition, conducting, music education (vocal and instrumental), music performance (vocal and instrumental), and music therapy.

Preprofessional or prevocational programs are offered in dentistry, law, medicine, physical therapy, social service, teaching, theology, and veterinary medicine.

Academic Program

The requirements for graduation are commensurate with the liberal arts philosophy of education maintained by Chapman. The program of studies is designed to ensure a breadth of subject matter selection in the liberal arts as well as depth of preparation in the student's major field. The minimum graduation requirements include successful completion (C average) of 124 semester credits, of which 36 must be earned in the upper division. Competence in reading, written communication, oral communication, computation, and library usage is required of all students. Chapman's general education sequence provides a broad introduction to the humanities, social sciences, and natural sciences.

Students select general education classes with the guidance of their faculty adviser. A maximum of 32 credits may be gained through Advanced Placement (AP), College-Level Examination Program (CLEP), and departmental examinations.

Chapman's academic year operates on a 4-1-4 modified semester system. January is reserved for an optional Interterm, allowing a period for experimental, short-term course work or individual study.

Ample opportunities are available for alternative learning experiences. Internships and cooperative education programs are recommended. Students may also undertake in-depth individual study or research in their major field in conjunction with a faculty member.

Academic Facilities

The 90,000-square-foot Argyros Forum includes the primary campus dining area, conference and classroom facilities, and associated student offices. Bertea Hall is home to the School of Music. Memorial Auditorium seats 1,000 and is listed on the National Register of Historic Places. The Hutton Sports Center includes a 3,000-seat arena, a 5,000-seat outdoor stadium, four championship tennis courts, and training and fitness facilities for the campus and the surrounding community. Thurmond Clarke Library includes 250,000 hard volumes as well as full Internet services, which include an e-mail account for each student and staff member. Newly completed Beckman Hall for business and information technology houses the Argyros School of Business and Economics, including its endowed centers: the A. Gary Anderson Center for Economic Research, the Ralph W. Leatherby Center for Entrepreneurship and Business Ethics, and the Walter Schmid Center for International Business. The School of Communication Arts includes the Guggenheim Art Gallery and the 250-seat repertory-style Waltmar Theatre. The Hashinger Science Center features laboratories for nuclear science, radiation, crystallography, genetics, food science, and physical therapy.

Costs

For the 2000–01 academic year, full-time tuition and fees (including accident and sickness fee, health center fee, and associated student membership fee) are $20,724. Annual room and board average $7928. Books are estimated at $700 per year.

Financial Aid

More than 85 percent of Chapman students benefit from some form of financial aid or scholarship assistance. Need-based financial awards include a combination of grants, scholarships, loans, and work-study jobs. Awards are renewable, assuming that students complete the annual application process on time. The family contribution component of an award stays mostly the same annually if the family's financial circumstances remain the same. By using a combination of Chapman's internal resources and federal and state funding, an individual financial aid package can be tailored to meet the student's financial need. Merit and talent scholarship awards, regardless of financial need, round out the types of financial assistance that Chapman offers. Chapman offers an Early Aid Estimator service that gives students an up-front picture of what their prospective aid/scholarship eligibility is, rather than waiting for the postadmission, official aid-awarding period. Students asking for information about Chapman automatically receive the Early Estimator form, along with instructions for completion and submission.

Faculty

The University's faculty is composed of 204 full-time and 193 part-time members, more than 80 percent of whom hold doctoral or other terminal degrees. Their primary commitment is to undergraduate teaching, although most are also actively involved in scholarly research and publication. Many faculty members teach both undergraduate and graduate courses. Teaching assistants or graduate assistants are not used for the instruction of undergraduate classes. Chapman's favorable student-faculty ratio of 16:1 allows extensive interaction between the faculty and students.

Student Government

Chapman has an associated student government that actively participates in the administration of the University.

Admission Requirements

Admission to Chapman is selective. In 1999, admission was offered to less than 60 percent of the applicant pool. The University is interested in admitting students whose prior records indicate that they will be successful in a competitive collegiate environment. Freshman applicants are considered for admission based primarily on the nature and sequence of their high school course work, the grade point average achieved, and their results on either the SAT I or ACT examination. Transfer candidates are considered for admission on the basis of their course work and cumulative grade point average earned at other regionally accredited post-secondary institutions.

Application and Information

When applying, candidates are strongly encouraged to visit the campus and meet with a member of the admission staff. Arrangements for an interview and a tour of the campus can be made through the Office of Admission at either of the phone numbers listed below. Freshman applicants can choose between a non-binding November 30 early action application deadline or the January 31 regular application deadline. Transfer applicants must apply before the March 15 transfer deadline. Prospective freshmen who apply after the January 31 deadline are considered on a space-available basis.

For further information, students should contact:

Michael O. Drummy
Associate Dean for Enrollment Services and Chief
   Admission Officer
Chapman University
One University Drive
Orange, California 92866
Telephone: 714-997-6711
         888-CUAPPLY (toll-free)
Fax: 714-997-6713
E-mail: admit@chapman.edu

CHARLESTON SOUTHERN UNIVERSITY
CHARLESTON, SOUTH CAROLINA

The University

Charleston Southern University is a fully accredited four-year liberal arts university. The University's mission is to promote academic excellence in a Christian environment for students of all faiths. The Graduate Studies Program offers Master of Education degrees in elementary and secondary education, a Master of Arts in Teaching, a Master of Criminal Justice, and a Master of Business Administration, with emphases in accounting, finance, global business, health-care administration, and organizational development.

A coeducational university, Charleston Southern University was accepted as an institution by the South Carolina Baptist Convention in 1964. The University has grown from 500 students to more than 2,500 students in its thirty-four years and continues to change to meet the needs of a fast-paced society. Distinctive programs include a computer literacy requirement and an ongoing Personal Values and Ethics Lecture Series.

Charleston Southern University seeks to develop the total person emotionally, intellectually, and spiritually. Programs are designed to prepare students for a successful and fulfilling life. Each major program is combined with a comprehensive liberal arts foundation. Courses in the humanities, the fine arts, natural science, and social science are included in this foundation. These subjects are designed to develop problem-solving skills and the ability to communicate effectively. A special career counseling center is designed to help students plan for the future.

Men's and women's athletic teams compete in the NCAA Division I Big South Conference. The University fields teams in baseball, basketball, cross-country, golf, soccer, softball, tennis, track and field, and volleyball, as well as an NCAA Division I-A football team. For outdoor recreation, there are NCAA-quality tennis courts, putting greens, and athletic fields; nature trails; and a lake for fishing.

Students are informed of campus activities through the University newspaper, *Buc in Print*, published by students under staff supervision. In addition, the University yearbook, *Cutlass;* the *Student Handbook;* and the University literary magazine, *The Sefer,* are published by students under faculty and staff supervision.

Location

Situated on 300 acres, Charleston Southern University is strategically located near Charleston, South Carolina, in the center of the modern growth patterns of North Charleston. Students take advantage of the cultural, historical, and recreational opportunities the city offers. Nearby Interstate 26, with access to I-95, is conveniently located to the campus. Five airlines serve the Charleston area. Mild winters and long summers allow many opportunities for outdoor recreation. Charleston is a city famous for its well-preserved colonial houses, famous gardens and plantations, miles of wide sandy beaches, and major fine arts events, including the Spoleto Festival USA (a kaleidoscope of opera, dance, music, theater, and visual arts).

Majors and Degrees

Charleston Southern University awards the Bachelor of Arts degree with majors in business, English, humanities and fine arts, music (with emphases in vocal performance and church music), music education (with emphases in choral and instrumental), music therapy, religion, Spanish, speech and dramatic arts, and youth ministry. The Bachelor of Science degree is offered with majors in biochemistry, biology, business administration (with emphases in accounting, finance, information systems, management, and marketing), chemistry, computer science/mathematics, criminal justice, early childhood education, economics, elementary education, environmental management, history, mathematics, natural science, nursing, physical education, political science, psychology, social science, and sociology. Minors are offered in most of the above areas, and are also offered in aerospace studies (AFROTC), art, French, philosophy, and physics. The School of Education offers a secondary education minor for several majors to meet teacher certification requirements. The Bachelor of Technology degree is offered to students who have completed an associate degree in a technical field prior to entry.

Preprofessional programs are offered in allied health science, dentistry, engineering, law, medicine, nursing, pharmacy, and seminary. Some of these programs require a four-year degree from CSU while others require two or three years of study at CSU before the student transfers to a professional school.

A nondegree program in athletic training is open to all majors and non-degree-seeking students. This program provides academic and clinical preparation for students pursuing N.A.T.A. (National Athletic Training Association) certification.

Academic Program

The purpose of Charleston Southern University is to help students to develop intellectually, socially, culturally, and spiritually. This is accomplished by ensuring that students receive a well-rounded education. The University requires all students to complete a core of liberal arts courses. The comprehensive course of study is subdivided into general education courses, including courses in English, the fine arts, history, mathematics, computer literacy, foreign language, natural science, religion and philosophy, and the social sciences. In addition, students are offered an opportunity to pursue a field of study in a major and minor area. Elective credits may also be taken to complete the minimum graduation requirements of 125 semester hours.

The academic-year calendar operates on a 4-1-4 system. The fall term begins in early September and ends in December, and the spring term begins in February and ends in May. January is set aside as a one-month Interterm during which students may enroll in one course. Students also have the option of attending two 5-week summer sessions.

An award-winning Air Force ROTC program is available on campus.

Advanced placement credits are given for successful scores on approved tests of the Educational Testing Service. Credit may also be granted for successful scores on the College-Level Examination Program (CLEP) tests.

Academic Facilities

The University has a modern library that contains more than 200,000 volumes, a modern chapel-auditorium with impressive fine arts facilities, and a multipurpose gymnasium. Among the

1406 www.petersons.com *Peterson's Guide to Four-Year Colleges 2001*

other facilities on campus are one of the nation's three Earthquake Centers and a distinctive computer center.

Costs

Tuition for the 1999–2000 academic year was $10,410, and room and board were $4002. Tuition and fees are subject to change.

Financial Aid

A comprehensive financial aid program, consisting of scholarships, grants, loans, and employment, has been established at Charleston Southern. Approximately 90 percent of the student body receives some type of financial assistance. The University participates in the Federal Pell Grant, Federal Supplemental Educational Opportunity Grant (FSEOG), and Federal Work-Study programs. Assistance is also available through Federal Perkins Loans and Federal Stafford Loans. Endowed or donated funds are available for many students; such awards are administered according to the provisions of the contributing agency or person. State tuition grants are available to eligible South Carolina residents.

Students may also be eligible to receive institutional scholarships and grants. Awards are not automatic and are subject to the availability of funds.

At Charleston Southern University, it is understood that financial concerns can often play a major role in the decision on which university to attend. The purpose of the financial aid program is to remove cost from the student's decision and allow the student to decide based on the academic and social environment offered at CSU.

Faculty

Charleston Southern University has a well-qualified and dedicated faculty. Faculty members combine teaching ability and scholarship with a concern for students. The majority hold doctoral degrees. Professors work directly with students in many phases of University life, including academic advising. Once the student selects a major course of study, he or she is assigned a faculty adviser in that major area. The student-teacher ratio is 17:1, which allows for individual attention and facilitates the pursuit of academic excellence.

The University encourages advanced study and research. Excellence in teaching is also recognized through an annual award.

Student Government

All full-time students become members of the Student Government Association upon enrollment. This organization enables students to develop leadership skills while achieving the goals the University has set for them.

Admission Requirements

The enrollment services staff works diligently to maintain a socially, economically, and culturally diverse student body. The University is a private, church-supported educational institution and is committed to a policy of nondiscrimination on the basis of race, sex, color, religion, national origin, or handicap.

Students may be admitted as first-time freshmen or as transfer students with acceptable credit. New freshmen must have official transcripts sent from their high schools and official SAT I and/or ACT scores sent from the appropriate testing service. Transfer students must have official transcripts sent from all colleges previously attended. Interviews are not required, but students are encouraged to visit the campus. Arrangements may be made by calling the Office of Enrollment Services.

Application and Information

Candidates for freshman admission are encouraged to submit applications in the fall of their senior year in secondary school. Transfer students are welcome to apply anytime during the academic year. A $25 nonrefundable application processing fee must be submitted with an application. The University uses a rolling admission system, and students are notified of the admission decision as soon as all application materials have been received and evaluated.

Application forms and other information about Charleston Southern University may be obtained by contacting:

Office of Enrollment Services
Charleston Southern University
9200 University Boulevard
P.O. Box 118087
Charleston, South Carolina 29423-8087
Telephone: 843-863-7050
         800-947-7474 (toll-free)
E-mail: enroll@csuniv.edu
World Wide Web: http://www.csuniv.edu

CHATHAM COLLEGE
PITTSBURGH, PENNSYLVANIA

The College

Chatham College, founded in 1869, is the oldest college for women west of the Alleghenies. Chatham offers a distinctive undergraduate education, preparing students for a lifetime of personal and professional achievement.

The Chatham experience is dedicated to enabling its graduates to have an impact on the world around them. A strong grounding in the liberal arts and sciences, the ability to communicate effectively, an interest in public service, a social consciousness, and an environmental understanding are hallmarks of the Chatham education.

Chatham's outstanding liberal arts base, combined with the capstone experience of the "senior tutorial"—an original research project guided one-on-one by a Chatham professor—provides an excellent bridge to graduate and professional schools. The College offers especially strong preparation for law school, medical school, and science-based graduate programs. Special agreements with other institutions offer early admission to medical school and environmental and occupational health master's degree programs.

Students' personal, professional, and leadership skills are developed to their fullest potential through Chatham's internship program, study abroad, service learning and leadership training opportunities, and personal development seminars. Most students participate in at least two internships in their field; recent examples include the Metropolitan Museum of Art, Delta Waterfowl, the Pennsylvania Senate, the U.S. Department of Justice, the White House, a rural health initiative, and numerous sites in Pittsburgh's corporate, nonprofit, government, health-care, and communications communities. Chatham Abroad, a three-week travel experience with classmates and faculty members during the sophomore year, has taken students to Belize, the Galapagos Islands, Morocco, Egypt, Italy, Spain, France, Ireland, England, and Russia, at no additional tuition.

The student body of 985 represents twenty-eight states and nine other countries. Minority groups represent 23 percent of the Chatham student body. Students live on the 32-acre parklike campus in residence halls that vary from the traditional dormitory and apartment suites to spacious mansions that were formerly private homes. Commuting students participate actively in College life. Health services and personal and career counseling services are available on campus. Students participate in a number of professional, academic, social, and special interest organizations at the College. The College offers NCAA Division III intercollegiate competition in basketball, ice hockey, soccer, softball, tennis, and volleyball and intramural and recreational competition in other sports. There are also several student publications. The College sponsors frequent programs and speakers in the arts, sciences, and public leadership arena. In addition to the more than fifty liberal arts majors and preprofessional programs at the undergraduate level, Chatham offers graduate programs in communication technology, counseling psychology, landscape studies, liberal arts, management, nonfiction writing, occupational therapy, physician assistant studies, physical therapy, and teaching.

Location

Chatham's suburban campus is located 15 minutes from downtown Pittsburgh, one of the most vital and progressive cities in the United States and the location of the headquarters of many of the country's major businesses and industries. The city's cultural, civic, and recreational facilities are easily accessible from the campus. Students use the city as a laboratory for their studies through internships, independent study, and special Interim courses. Students attend performances of the Pittsburgh Symphony, the opera and ballet, readings given by some of the world's most distinguished poets in the International Poetry Forum, and exhibitions at numerous art galleries. The activities of local theater companies are supplemented by frequent performances of national road shows. Nearby ski areas, parks, and the city's three rivers provide opportunities for outdoor recreation. Excellent bus, rail, and plane connections are available to and from most major cities.

Majors and Degrees

Chatham College offers the following departmental majors leading to the Bachelor of Arts or Bachelor of Science degree: accounting, African-American studies, arts management, behavioral neuroscience, biochemistry, biology, chemistry, communication, computing, cultural studies, cybercommunication, economics, English, English and dramatic literature, entrepreneurial management, environmental science, environmental studies, European studies, French, global policy studies, graphic design, history, history of art, international studies, management, management information systems, marketing, mathematics, media arts, media technology, music, philosophy, physics, political science, psychobiology, psychology, social work, Spanish, theater, visual arts, and women's studies. Students may choose a traditional departmental major, an interdepartmental major, a double major, or a self-defined major. Preprofessional programs are offered in dentistry, physical therapy, occupational therapy, physician assistant studies, public health, medicine, law, and veterinary medicine. There is also a 3-2 engineering program. Teacher certification is available through the education program in early childhood, elementary, environmental, and secondary education. Certificates are offered in accounting, conservation ecology, environmental management, gerontology, horticultural landscape studies/design, media technology, and nonfiction writing.

Academic Program

Chatham has a core curriculum that includes seven required interdepartmental courses. Graduation requirements include the core courses, a major, proficiency requirements, and the tutorial—an independent project designed by the student and her adviser.

The College's 4-1-4 academic calendar consists of fall and spring terms, plus a four-week Interim term in January. Interim programs include study abroad, concentrated study, experimental projects, travel and field experiences, internships, interdisciplinary study, and student exchanges with other colleges.

Chatham's Career Services coordinates student internships, placement, workshops, recruitment, and mentor programs as well as health and wellness issues and academic and personal counseling.

The Rachel Carson Institute honors Chatham's 1929 alumna and her commitment to the environment.

Off-Campus Arrangements

All full-time sophomores are eligible to participate in the Chatham Abroad Program. Four trips are sponsored each year to such diverse locations as Russia, Egypt, France, Spain, the Galapagos Islands, and Great Britain. Semester-long study abroad is available through affiliation with programs at other accredited colleges and universities. In addition, juniors may participate in the Washington Semester, offered through American University.

Chatham students may cross-register each term, without payment of additional fees, in one course for credit at any of nine nearby institutions, including Carnegie Mellon University and the University of Pittsburgh. The Internship Program enables students to gain firsthand experience in field placements in a wide variety of agencies, businesses, and professional organizations.

Academic Facilities

The Chatham campus, including residence hall rooms, has been wired with fiber-optic cable to enhance the community's access to the Internet. In addition to the fiber-optic cable, computer equipment includes VAX minicomputers, IBM personal computers, Apple Macintoshes, Macintosh Power PCs, laser printers, scanners, and CD-ROMs. The modern Jennie King Mellon Library has 140,000 volumes and more than 600 current subscriptions, individual study areas, special seminar rooms, and a 285-seat theater. Library facilities at neighboring colleges and universities are also available for Chatham students. Buhl Hall houses state-of-the-art science laboratories and individual laboratory units. Psychology and language laboratories and audiovisual facilities are also available. The Media Center contains equipment used by students to gain experience with some of the sophisticated technology of audio, visual, and video presentations.

Costs

For 1999–2000, tuition was $17,544 per year, and room and board were $5774, for a total of $23,318. The student activities fee is estimated at $150. A one-time deposit of $100 for tuition and $100 for on-campus housing is paid by newly admitted students and is applied to first-semester charges. Regularly enrolled full-time students pay no additional costs for Interim courses except for special supplies or travel. Additional fees are required for art supplies and music lessons. Students are required to have health and accident insurance.

Financial Aid

Financial aid is awarded on the basis of an individual's financial need as determined through the Free Application for Federal Student Aid. The awards combine grants, loans, and employment. The application for aid is usually submitted at the same time as the admission application. Priority financial aid deadline is May 1.

Sources of financial aid include Chatham grants and loans, state grants, Federal Pell Grants, Federal Supplemental Educational Opportunity Grants, federally funded student loans, and jobs provided under the Federal Work-Study Program. Chatham Merit scholarships for entering students are awarded without regard to need on the basis of high academic achievement. They range in value from $1500 to $10,000. Minna Kaufmann Ruud Scholarships are available for students with exceptional ability in vocal music, based on an on-campus audition. Approximately 90 percent of the students at Chatham receive aid administered by the College.

Faculty

Ninety-seven percent of the faculty have earned the doctorate or the highest degree in their field, and all faculty members teach first-year students. The student-faculty ratio is 12:1, ensuring a close student-faculty relationship and individual consideration of students by faculty members. Each student has a faculty adviser.

Student Government

The Chatham Student Government, of which every student is a member, coordinates student involvement in the affairs of the College, gives voice to student concerns, maintains student participation on College committees, and oversees various student boards and organizations. Chatham students serve as voting members on many of the College's planning and policy committees.

Admission Requirements

The prospective student must demonstrate academic strength, motivation, an enthusiasm for learning, and potential for growth. Evaluation is made on the basis of the student's academic record, recommendations, SAT I or ACT scores, involvement in activities, and other submitted material. The College seeks to enroll students representing a variety of cultural, geographical, racial, religious, and socioeconomic backgrounds and with diverse talents in both academic and creative areas.

It is strongly recommended that candidates arrange to visit the College for a personal interview, a tour of the campus with a student guide, observation of one or more classes, and conversations with faculty, staff, and students. Early entrance is available for well-qualified and mature students who wish to begin college at the close of their junior year in high school; early entrance candidates are required to come to the College for interviews. The College also welcomes the opportunity to discuss future educational plans with transfer candidates in good academic standing, including junior college and community college graduates. Chatham grants college course credit for grades of 4 or 5 on the Advanced Placement examinations of the College Board. Certain prerequisite requirements in course offerings may be fulfilled by attaining scores of 3, 4, or 5.

Application and Information

Candidates for admission must file an application with the Admissions Office, together with a nonrefundable $25 processing fee. Applications are accepted on a rolling basis.

Dean of Admissions and Financial Aid
Office of Admissions
Chatham College
Pittsburgh, Pennsylvania 15232
Telephone: 412-365-1290
           800-837-1290 (toll-free)
Fax: 412-365-1609
E-mail: admissions@chatham.edu
World Wide Web: http://www.chatham.edu

View of the Chatham College campus.

CHESTNUT HILL COLLEGE
PHILADELPHIA, PENNSYLVANIA

The College

Chestnut Hill College (CHC) is a four-year Catholic liberal arts college for women. Founded in 1924 by the Sisters of St. Joseph, it is situated on a 45-acre campus overlooking Wissahickon Creek. Conscious of women's roles in society, Chestnut Hill College has chosen to remain a women's college at the traditional-age undergraduate level. It answers a need for well-educated, values-oriented women who can exert a positive influence on the society of the future. Since opportunities for leadership and self-expression are frequent, the Chestnut Hill graduate can enter a competitive world well prepared for success. Students come from fifteen states, thirteen countries, and every imaginable background. There are 372 full-time and 116 part-time undergraduate women in the day programs and 426 women and men enrolled in the accelerated evening and weekend undergraduate program. In addition to its undergraduate degrees, Chestnut Hill awards the M.Ed., M.A., and M.S. in six fields, including elementary education, counseling psychology and human services, holistic spirituality, and technology in education as well as a doctoral degree in clinical psychology (Psy.D.).

When it comes to student activities, students enthusiastically engage in the many clubs and organizations available and participate in everything from aerobics and horseback riding to golf and archery. The College is NCAA Division III and competes in basketball, field hockey, lacrosse, softball, tennis, and volleyball. A swimming pool, a gymnasium, a hockey field, a weight/fitness room, and eight tennis courts provide excellent athletic facilities for Chestnut Hill's students.

Location

Chestnut Hill College is situated in a beautiful historical area at the northwestern edge of Philadelphia. The College is bounded by the wooded hills of Fairmount Park, yet it is only a 30-minute ride by train or car to downtown Philadelphia. There, students can enjoy a wide variety of dining, cultural, and sporting events. Among the many other attractions are the museums that grace Philadelphia, from its landmark Art Museum to the Rodin Museum, the Living History Museum, the Franklin Institute, and numerous others. The city's history is reflected throughout but is most prominent in the areas around Independence Hall, Society Hill, and Penn's Landing. In addition, twenty-five colleges, universities, and medical schools in the area offer opportunities for socialization and an extensive range of activities.

One mile beyond CHC, on Germantown Avenue, is the well-known area of Philadelphia also called Chestnut Hill. Reminiscent of a Colonial village, this section of Philadelphia provides convenient opportunities for shopping, cultural experiences, and transportation to downtown Philadelphia. In all, CHC is a school in a suburban setting with all the advantages of a cosmopolitan experience.

Majors and Degrees

The Bachelor of Arts and Bachelor of Science degrees are offered with majors in accounting, art history, art studio, biochemistry, biology, business administration, chemistry, communications and technology, computer and information science, computer and information technology, computer and mathematical sciences, early childhood education (with an option of Montessori certification), early childhood and elementary education, economics, elementary education, English, environmental science, fine arts and technology, French, history, management, marketing, mathematical sciences, molecular biology, music, music education, political science, psychology, secondary education certification in various disciplines, sociology (with a professional option in criminal justice), and Spanish.

Chestnut Hill College also offers preprofessional programs in allied health fields, dentistry, law, medicine, and veterinary sciences. Cooperative studies are available with La Salle University.

Academic Program

The academic year consists of two 15-week semesters. There are also two 6-week summer sessions.

As a liberal arts college, CHC offers courses of study that provide the student with a broad background in the fine arts and humanities, a knowledge of science, and a keen awareness of the social problems of the day, as well as intensive, in-depth study in a major field.

CHC confers a B.S. or B.A. degree to students who earn 120 semester hours of credit and satisfy specific requirements set by the faculty. Distribution requirements are as follows: 11 semester hours in natural sciences (8 hours of which must be in a laboratory science), 9 semester hours in social sciences, and 21 semester hours in the humanities. In addition to these 41 hours of credit, every student must take 6 semester hours of religious studies, 6 hours beyond the elementary level in a classical or modern foreign language, and 3 hours in a writing course (unless exempted by the English department). As many as 45 of the 120 semester hours may be within the major area.

A student with the ability and proper motivation may be permitted to major in two departments. The student must consult with the chair of each department to determine the feasibility of the proposal and then submit it to the dean of the college for approval. It is understood that she will satisfy the requirements of both departments.

Each year selected freshmen and sophomores are invited into an interdepartmental honors program that challenges intellectual initiative and provides the opportunity for independent study and seminar discussion. The completion of the four honors courses, two elective courses, two laboratory science courses, and an honors paper satisfies all distributional requirements. Students may apply for admission at the beginning of their freshman or sophomore year.

Sophomores of high scholastic standing are invited by their major departments to engage in a program of independent study during their junior and senior years. This opportunity for independent study and original research culminates in an honors thesis, which is a prerequisite for the conferring of honors at graduation.

The art therapy, environmental studies, gerontology, international studies, and women in management certificate programs expose liberal arts students in any major to current principles and practices in business and management.

Off-Campus Arrangements

Students have the advantages of two campuses and two curricula through an agreement with La Salle University, a local coeducational university, that allows students from either school to register for courses at the other institution for full credit without paying extra tuition. Public transportation is available between the two schools.

At CHC, a student may take advantage of the monthlong interim between semesters by coordinating travel and study. A student, with the assistance of one or more of her professors, can use her imagination and interests to develop an off-campus program. Should the program be more lengthy than the interim allows, the student may schedule her travel and study for the summer. Past intersession programs have included studies of French culture in Paris, women in English literature in London, and marine biology in Florida.

Chestnut Hill College participates in a consortium arrangement with ten colleges throughout the nation, founded by the Sisters of St. Joseph. As participants, students can study at any other member institution for a semester or a year, while maintaining status as a full-time Chestnut Hill student.

An average of B or above and approval of the academic dean allow an upperclass student to pursue organized study in another country. The major department must approve the course of study. In recent years, Chestnut Hill College students have enrolled in institutions in London, Rome, Madrid, Vienna, Salzburg, and other European centers.

The growing interest of students in acquiring on-the-job experience while still in college has prompted the development of many departmental internship programs, which provide students with the opportunity to gain professional experience in their major while earning academic credit. Chestnut Hill has also established an office of cooperative education, through which Chestnut Hill College students are assisted in finding salaried jobs that correspond to their career interests and academic pursuits. Co-op students work and attend classes in alternate periods, earning academic credit for their practical experience.

Academic Facilities

CHC's Logue Library houses a collection of 139,585 volumes and 544 current periodicals, a rare book room that contains first editions and special editions, the Gruber Theater, the fine Curriculum Library for elementary education, and an Irish literature collection. Well-equipped science laboratories, a math center, a multimedia technology center, a writing enrichment center, individual practice rooms for music students, a spacious art studio, a planetarium, and an observatory are among the many other outstanding facilities on campus. Opening in fall 2000, Martino Hall, designed to maintain the architectural history of the College, will provide room for a performance center, gymnasium, or convocation center. The second and third floors will house cutting-edge "smart" classrooms.

Costs

General expenses for 1999–2000 were tuition and fees of $16,029 and room and board costs of between $6510 and $7100.

Financial Aid

Financial aid is available in the form of academic scholarships, guaranteed loans, work-study programs, federal grants, and Chestnut Hill College grants. Most of these are based on financial need and are awarded in financial aid packages that combine various forms of aid and are tailored to each student's need. More than 75 percent of CHC students receive financial aid to meet college costs. All applicants for aid should file a copy of the Free Application for Federal Student Aid (FAFSA). Full tuition scholarships are awarded each year strictly on the basis of achievement.

Students should submit a completed application, the application essay, SAT I or ACT scores, a high school transcript, and a letter of recommendation. An interview is recommended and may be required.

Faculty

Evidence of Chestnut Hill's vitality can be seen in its faculty. While their primary interest is teaching, faculty members are also engaged in research, publication, travel, and other professional activities. Of the 109 currently on the faculty, 57 are full-time, with more than 75 percent holding terminal degrees. The men and women who make up this group are deeply interested in both their subject and their students. Their qualifications include degrees from the University of Oxford in England; the University of Paris and the University of Budapest; and the Catholic University of America, Middlebury College, Bryn Mawr College, Columbia University, the University of Notre Dame, the University of Pennsylvania, Duke University, New York University, the New School for Social Research, Purdue University, Temple University, and the University of Minnesota. CHC's faculty-student ratio is 1:12.

Student Government

During a student's four years at CHC, she has the opportunity to think independently and to approach decisions creatively. Judgments concerning all collegiate affairs are made by students in conjunction with the faculty and administration. Several organizations provide structure for the decision-making process. Students join members of the faculty and administration on the Curriculum Committee and the College Council. The Academic, Social-Cultural, and Student Affairs committees of the Student Organization identify, represent, and meet campus needs.

Admission Requirements

CHC welcomes young women whose aptitudes and academic records show a desire to accept a challenge. Applications are judged by the Admissions Committee on the basis of intellectual ability, academic achievement (class rank and performance in high school, including completion of 16 academic units), and SAT I or ACT results. Strong consideration is given to the application essay and counselors' recommendations. CHC has early decision, early admission, and advanced placement programs.

A student wishing to transfer to CHC is asked to submit a transcript from all colleges attended and a letter of recommendation from the dean of students.

Application and Information

Applications are processed on a rolling admission system. To arrange an interview or to obtain more detailed information about the academic program, students should contact:

Elizabeth Becker
Director of Admissions
Chestnut Hill College
9601 Germantown Avenue
Philadelphia, Pennsylvania 19118-2695
Telephone: 215-248-7001
          800-248-0052 (toll-free)
E-mail: chcapply@chc.edu
World Wide Web: http://www.chc.edu

CHEYNEY UNIVERSITY OF PENNSYLVANIA
CHEYNEY, PENNSYLVANIA

The University

Cheyney University was founded in 1837 by Richard Humphreys, a Philadelphia Quaker. Since its inception, Cheyney University has continued to educate American and international students above and beyond the vision of Mr. Humphreys. His dream was a school of higher learning for African-American students "in order to prepare and fit and qualify them to act as teachers...." Cheyney University graduates still become teachers, but students also enter such fields as journalism, medicine, business, science, industrial arts, and communications. Today, Cheyney's students represent a variety of races, cultures, and nationalities.

Students are Cheyney University's highest priority. Above all else, the faculty and staff are in the business of developing human potential and talent. Dedicated faculty members work closely with students and demand from them all that is necessary to prepare them for career success and responsible citizenship.

The 275-acre Cheyney campus is situated on rolling hillsides in southeastern Pennsylvania, an area that is changing from rural to suburban. The surroundings, small classes, and modern facilities provide an ideal atmosphere for learning.

Living on campus is desirable, particularly for first-year students. Off-campus housing is available in nearby communities. Resident students enjoy a rich cultural and social life as well as a sense of community. Facilities include five dormitories, a full-service dining hall, and a student/alumni center. Student interest groups include a drama club (the Cheyney Players), premedical and prelaw societies, the business club, the chess club, the choir, the band, cheerleading, Latino Students in Action, International Students Association, and about twenty other groups. Several honor societies and Greek-letter organizations are also active.

There are numerous opportunities for on-campus recreation. Cheyney has beautifully situated outdoor tennis, volleyball, basketball, and handball courts. The athletic building houses large and small gymnasiums and an Olympic-size swimming pool. The Cheyney Wolves have won national recognition in women's and men's basketball and in wrestling. Other sports include football, men's and women's tennis and track, and women's volleyball. Cheyney's open-tryout policy allows all interested students to try out for any team, provided that they maintain the grade point average required for participation. Students enjoy a full intramural program.

Cheyney is accredited by the Middle States Association of Colleges and Schools, and its programs in education are accredited by the Pennsylvania Department of Education. Graduate programs in education and teacher certification are offered at Cheyney's Urban Center in Center City Philadelphia.

Location

Cheyney is 25 miles west of Philadelphia. SEPTA bus service is available between the campus, Center City Philadelphia, Chester, and several sites in Delaware County. Lancaster is 1½ hours away, and Harrisburg is 2 hours from Cheyney. Wilmington, Delaware, is 15 miles south of Cheyney; New York City and Washington, D.C., are 2 hours away. The campus is easily accessible via the Pennsylvania Turnpike and Interstate 95.

Majors and Degrees

Cheyney grants the Bachelor of Arts degree in biology, chemistry, communication arts, computer and information sciences, economics, English, French, general science, geography, history, mathematics, political science, psychology, social relations (criminal justice and sociology), social science, Spanish, and theater arts. The Bachelor of Science degree is granted in business administration (accounting, management, marketing, office administration, small-business management, and tax accounting); clothing and textiles; hotel, restaurant, and institutional management; and recreation. The Bachelor of Science in Education may be earned in early childhood, elementary, and secondary education (majors in biology, business education, chemistry, English, French, general science, mathematics, social studies, and Spanish); home economics; and special education.

Academic Program

The completion of 128 semester hours is required for a bachelor's degree. Of the 128 hours, 40 percent are in general education; the remainder are required in humanities, social sciences, natural sciences, mathematics, health and physical education, and electives. Army ROTC is available.

Qualified students may undertake independent study projects and internships. A cooperative education program enables students to work and study in alternate semesters. The Department of Sciences and Allied Health arranges summer research projects for science students at nearby medical colleges. The on-campus Head Start site and Academic Achievement Center offer opportunities for education majors to apply classroom concepts in real-life settings. A University internship program coordinator helps students secure internships and places students in accordance with their degree programs or personal interests.

The Academic Skills Center provides support services through tutors and counselors for students who seek academic support. The First-Year Studies Program ensures that each first-year student has the maximum potential to develop his or her academic skills through a series of placement tests in English, math, and reading.

Cheyney's Honors Program is open to all high school graduates, regardless of year of graduation. Students in the Honors Program are enrolled in several classes as a group and have their own special residence halls, complete with computer rooms and reading rooms. Honors students have opportunities to interact and be identified as a group while also participating in the activities of the overall student community.

Academic Facilities

The Leslie Pinckney Hill Library houses approximately 200,000 books plus a periodical collection of more than 23,000 bound volumes and 1,100 current subscriptions. Audiovisual media and CD-ROM full-text/images databases, Internet access, and World Wide Web access are available. The library also houses the famed Schomburg Collection of African-American history and culture on microfilm.

Cheyney's Telecommunications Center consists of a 240-seat auditorium with state-of-the-art satellite television capabilities, a cable television control facility, a television studio, and the

AT&T Distance Learning and Teleconferencing Center. AT&T has installed twenty fully loaded Pentium computers with network access in the Telecommunications Center. Used primarily for instruction of private and public school teachers in Pennsylvania districts in the use of the Internet, the facility is available for use by Cheyney students.

Cheyney has formed a partnership with Navigation Technologies, a company that designs databases for intelligent transportation, travel, and traffic markets. Students use highly sophisticated technology and programs that create economically efficient and environmentally sound transportation systems.

Students in the clothing and textile major have access to computer-aided design software for the creation of patterns for apparel, upholstery, and interior design, among others.

Costs

For the 2000–2001 academic year, estimated tuition for Pennsylvania residents is $4172 and for non-residents is $9046. Estimated room and board costs are $4792. Books and supplies are about $700 per semester. Travel and incidental expenses vary.

Financial Aid

The University makes every possible effort to enable interested and qualified students to take advantage of its educational opportunities. Financial assistance is available in the form of academic scholarships, grants, loans, and the Federal Work-Study Program. Financial aid packages are developed for qualified students based on individual student need. Students wishing to apply for financial aid must complete the Free Application for Federal Student Aid (FAFSA). Students should pay strict attention to all state and federal application deadlines.

Faculty

Cheyney's faculty members have earned degrees at such diverse institutions as Columbia; Fisk; Howard; Juilliard; Temple; Cheyney University of Pennsylvania; the Universities of California, Pennsylvania, and Wisconsin; Nagpur University; Punjabi University; the Universities of Madras and Kerala; and the Sorbonne.

Student Government

All students are members of the Student Government Cooperative Association (SGCA), which sponsors many cultural, educational, and social events and brings speakers and performers to the campus. SGCA and other student representatives sit on all University committees. A student representative is also selected to serve on the University's Council of Trustees.

Admission Requirements

Cheyney University seeks students who have not only academic ability but also talent and diversity. Students are encouraged to provide an overall view of themselves in their application, including extracurricular activities, interests, and academic goals. The Admissions Committee evaluates applicants on the basis of secondary school records, SAT I or ACT scores, and recommendations from teachers and counselors. As part of the State System of Higher Education, the University gives priority to residents of the Commonwealth of Pennsylvania. However, the University welcomes out-of-state and international applicants. The admissions office encourages visits to the campus and arranges tour and information sessions with members of the staff; students should call to make an appointment. Representatives from the admissions office visit many high schools during the year to increase contact with students.

Application and Information

In order to be considered for admission, students must submit a completed admission application, an official copy of the high school transcript, two letters of recommendation, SAT I or ACT scores, and a $20 nonrefundable application fee. Transfer students are required to submit official transcripts from all colleges or universities previously attended. A completed Dean's Recommendation Form is also required for transfer students.

Cheyney encourages all prospective students and parents to visit the campus. For more information and to schedule an individual or group tour, students should contact:

Office of Admissions
Cheyney University of Pennsylvania
Cheyney, Pennsylvania 19319

Telephone: 610-399-2275
　　　　　800-CHEYNEY (toll-free)

CHOWAN COLLEGE
MURFREESBORO, NORTH CAROLINA

The College

Chowan College, a four-year, coeducational liberal arts institution, is founded upon and dedicated to Judeo-Christian principles and values. Originally established in 1848 as a four-year Baptist women's college, Chowan later established itself as one of the leading junior colleges in the South. The second-oldest college of the six institutions affiliated with the North Carolina Baptist State Convention, Chowan returned to four-year status in 1992.

Set amid 300 acres of woodlands embracing beautiful Lake Vann, Chowan's main entrance leads gracefully around a college green to the antebellum mansion known as McDowell Columns. Sixteen other major buildings of contemporary design provide air-conditioned residence, academic, athletic, and recreational facilities. The small-town College campus attracts students from at least twenty-seven states and several countries each year.

Students have many opportunities to become involved and pursue interests outside the classroom. Numerous student activities, intramurals, leadership development programs, and workshops are scheduled throughout the year. Chowan invites students to join more than forty academic, Greek, service, recreational, religious, and social organizations, and forming new organizations is always encouraged.

A member of the NCAA Division III in athletics with a strong winning tradition at the junior college level, Chowan is rapidly establishing a powerful presence in athletics as a four-year school. The College participates in twelve intercollegiate sports: men's baseball, basketball, football, golf, soccer, and tennis; women's basketball, golf, soccer, softball, tennis, and volleyball; and coed cheerleading. Chowan offers a wide variety of intramural sports to all students.

Seventeen principal buildings on campus include facilities for housing and dining; health, counseling, and career services; athletics; and recreation and also include classrooms, a library, computing centers, laboratories, studios, and three major auditoriums for lectures, demonstrations, concerts, and plays.

The Helms Physical Education Center, which seats 3,000 spectators, features a vast six-lane indoor pool and three basketball and racquetball courts. The center is equipped with a weight and fitness center, aerobics gym, and sauna.

Chowan College's Career Center provides students with a personalized, computerized career guidance program to investigate career options, goals, and programs of study. The center maintains graduate school information and credential/placement files for prospective employers.

Location

Chowan College is located in historic Murfreesboro between the Roanoke and Chowan Rivers in northeastern North Carolina. Murfreesboro was designated by Congress in 1790 as an official port of entry, and some of its earliest known inhabitants included members of the Chowanoke Indian tribe. Today, stately old homes and a restored historic district seem to whisper of colonial and antebellum days. Murfreesboro is the location of the boyhood home of Dr. Walter Reed, discoverer of the cure for yellow fever, and the home of Richard Gatling, inventor of the Gatling gun. Local groups offer tours and special events throughout the year.

Majors and Degrees

Chowan College is fully accredited by the Southern Association of Colleges and Schools to offer the Bachelor of Arts, the Bachelor of Science, and the Bachelor of Applied Science degrees. Seventeen majors with varying emphases include art, biology, business administration, criminal justice, elementary education, English, English education, graphic communications, history, liberal studies, mathematics, mathematics education, music, music education, physical education, physical science, psychology, and religion.

The College offers preprofessional programs in dentistry, law, medicine, optometry, pharmacy, physical therapy, and veterinary medicine.

Academic Program

Chowan offers a broad range of undergraduate degrees, all of which carefully integrate effective career preparation with a strong liberal arts education. The integration results in a focus on the knowledge, skills, and qualities necessary for both a successful career and a higher quality of life. Chowan requires at least 120 credit hours for graduation in the College's semester calendar. This requirement includes a 51-credit-hour general education core curriculum in which a student chooses from a selected range of courses, a minimum of 30 credit hours in the student's major field of study, and elective courses. Students may receive college credit for Advanced Placement courses taken in high school and for credits received from the College-Level Examination Program.

Demonstrating a strong commitment to high-quality education in a personal, caring context, Chowan employs 1 professor for every 12 students enrolled. In addition, the College provides each student with a faculty adviser who assists the student in developing an appropriate academic schedule and plan throughout the student's years of study. Tutors and review courses are readily available, as are staffed assistance labs for writing, math, and accounting.

One way in which the College integrates effective career preparation with a strong liberal arts education is through its concern not only for the quantity of students' knowledge but also for the quality and character of students' personal and professional decisions. The Chowan College curricular emphasis on ethics and the Chowan College Center for Ethics provide opportunities for students to participate in discussions and activities that promote ethical inquiry, character formation, and ethical actions in their personal and professional lives. Within this framework, the College is guided by the historic principles of religious and intellectual freedom and is committed to academic excellence, freedom of inquiry and expression, and the search for truth.

Chowan seeks to make intelligent use of technology in the process of learning by taking advantage of technology's ability to facilitate student learning in significant ways and by enhancing student-teacher relationships and communication. This commitment to information technology in a liberal arts setting demonstrates Chowan College's educational mission to integrate effective career preparation with a strong liberal arts education.

Off-Campus Arrangements

Chowan participates in several study-abroad programs. The Washington Semester offers opportunities for internships in the Washington, D.C., area; Salzburg College in Austria integrates a semester of classroom work with field experience and travel; and the East Africa Semester Abroad program offers homestays and travel.

Academic Facilities

Whitaker Library houses more than 101,000 volumes; subscribes to nearly 1,000 journals, magazines, and newspapers;

and offers videos, microfilms, a media center, Internet connections, a reference section, and staff librarians to assist students. An automated library computerization system provides instant campuswide access to an integrated system of cataloging, circulation, acquisitions, serials control, and electronic resources.

Horner Graphics Center offers facilities for imaging technologies, multimedia, offset printing, flexography, and screen printing. Daniel Hall provides music and dance studios and a recital auditorium for drama and concerts. Robert Marks Hall, McSweeney Hall, and Camp Hall offer a variety of classrooms, laboratories, and auditoriums for various humanities, business, science, math, and education departments. Green Hall features studios, a graphics lab, classrooms, ceramic kilns, and an art gallery with rotating exhibits.

Chowan College is a leader among liberal arts colleges in computer and information technology. Through a campuswide fiber-optics network, the College provides access to the Internet, e-mail, and a multitude of other information resources from every office, classroom, and residence hall room on campus. Personal computers may be configured for direct access to the system, or students may utilize fully equipped computer labs around campus.

Costs

Students living on campus during the 2000–01 academic year are charged $11,820 for tuition and fees. A double-occupancy room costs $2240 (private rooms add an additional $800), and a nineteen-meal plan costs $2540. The College reserves the right to change these rates upon making proper notification to the students.

Financial Aid

Financial aid is available to help pay for direct educational costs, including tuition, fees, and books, as well as personal living expenses, such as food, housing, and transportation. Several types of financial aid are available, including grants or scholarships, loans, and work-study. Students must submit the Free Application for Federal Student Aid (FAFSA), which is available on line through the College Web site. Chowan College announces awards in early spring. Qualification for Chowan's incentive grant and scholarship program is determined by SAT I/ACT scores and the cumulative, weighted high school GPA. Awards range from $1000 to $6500 per year for four years. Chowan also offers a $1000 regional incentive grant and a program of grants and scholarships that cover the full cost of tuition for students who have served as president of a high school student council organization. Students should contact the Admissions Office with qualifying information for immediate verification of award status.

Faculty

Chowan employs 53 full-time and 17 adjunct faculty members who provide a warm, friendly atmosphere for learning. The student-faculty ratio of 12:1 ensures a wealth of individual attention to the specific needs of the students and allows professors the opportunity to know students outside of the classroom. Fifty-seven percent of faculty members hold terminal degrees in their field, and each year numerous professors are published in national and professional journals and other publications. Professors are actively involved in students' achievements and lead freshman seminar groups through the first year of College life.

Student Government

All students become members of the Student Government Association upon enrolling at Chowan College. The organization offers opportunities to become involved in College-sponsored activities, to gain experience in democratic procedures, and to participate in the operation of the College. Elected student leaders administer and enforce policies that regulate life within the College community.

Admission Requirements

The admissions committee emphasizes the following factors when considering an applicant: secondary school record (grades 9 through 12), with close examination given to the quality of the academic work performed; standardized test results—SAT I and ACT scores that indicate potential for academic success; and personal characteristics, including involvement in extracurricular activities, leadership qualities, and work experience, which may be addressed in letters of recommendation.

Application and Information

Students should submit an application (available on line through the College Web site) with the $20 application fee and an official high school transcript. The SAT I or ACT results must be mailed to Chowan or be included on the official transcript.

For additional information, students are encouraged to contact:
Admissions Office
Chowan College
Murfreesboro, North Carolina 27855
Telephone: 252-398-6500
          800-488-4101 (toll-free)
Fax: 252-398-1190
E-mail: admissions@chowan.edu
World Wide Web: http://www.chowan.edu

High-tech, high-touch.

CHRISTOPHER NEWPORT UNIVERSITY
NEWPORT NEWS, VIRGINIA

The University

Christopher Newport University (CNU) was founded in 1960 and currently enrolls 5,000 students in ninety areas of study (including six master's degree programs). The University takes pride in its "student-first, teaching-first" community. Small classes taught by full-time faculty members, a beautiful and safe campus, and one of the nation's finest sports programs make CNU a distinctive choice among Virginia's public universities.

Two state-of-the-art residence halls accommodate 1,100 students on campus; a third residence hall will be completed in 2002. The library now offers a gourmet coffee shop called Einstein's. CNU opens its new $16-million Sports and Recreation Center in spring 2000, and work begins next year on a $45-million Center for the Fine and Performing Arts, designed by I.M. Pei.

Location

CNU is located in suburban Newport News, adjacent to Mariner's Park, a pristine 600-acre nature preserve with miles of jogging trails around Lake Maury and along the James River. Newport News is the hub of high-tech industry in Southeastern Virginia and home of the Jefferson Laboratory, the premier physics research facility in the world. CNU students have access to internships there and in many local firms and agencies in areas such as media, health care, education, and social services.

Recently, CNU was rated the sixth-safest campus in the U.S. Its picturesque campus and superb residence facilities receive accolades from students and visitors alike. CNU is the host to the annual Ella Fitzgerald Music Festival.

CNU is 35 miles from the pounding surf and rolling dunes of Virginia Beach, 25 miles from historic Williamsburg, 75 miles from Richmond, and 150 miles from Washington, D.C. Students enjoy the moderate climate year-round and appreciate the easy driving distance to the beach and the region's many recreational opportunities. The newest of these is the Virginia Beach Amphitheater, which attracts major nationally and internationally known musical groups.

Majors and Degrees

The College of Liberal Arts offers the Bachelor of Arts degree in communication studies, English (with concentrations in creative writing, journalism, language arts, literature, and writing); fine and performing arts (with concentrations in fine arts, music, music theater, and theater arts); foreign language (with concentrations in French, German, and Spanish); history (with an interdisciplinary prelaw program available); interdisciplinary studies; leisure studies (with concentrations in fitness management; physical education; and recreation and tourism, with emphases of commercial and entrepreneurial recreation and tourism and public relations and tourism); philosophy (with a concentration available in religious studies); political science (with a concentration available in international relations); psychology (with concentrations in early childhood psychology, general psychology, and industrial/organizational psychology); sociology (with majors available in social work and sociology and a concentration available in culture, socialization, and society for sociology majors). The College of Liberal Arts also offers the Bachelor of Music degree (with concentrations in history/literature, music education, performance, theory/composition, and emphases in instrumental music and choral music for music education concentrators); the Bachelor of Science degree in interdisciplinary studies, leisure studies (with concentrations in fitness management; physical education; and recreation and tourism, with emphases of commercial and entrepreneurial recreation and tourism and public relations and tourism), and psychology (with concentrations in early childhood psychology, general psychology, and industrial/organizational psychology); and the Bachelor of Science in Governmental Administration degree (with concentrations in criminal justice administration, public management, legal studies, and international administration). Minors are available in anthropology, art, English, French, geography, German, government and public affairs, history, music, philosophy, professional writing, psychology, sociology, speech communication, Spanish, and theater arts.

The College of Business, Science and Technology offers the Bachelor of Arts degree in applied physics (with concentrations in science education, and technical writing and editing), biology, economics, interdisciplinary studies, and mathematics (with concentrations in computer science, mathematics education, and physics); the Bachelor of Science degree in applied physics (with concentrations in computation, instrumentation, and solid state/optics), biology (with preprofessional programs in dental, medical, and veterinary studies), computer engineering, computer science, environmental science, interdisciplinary studies, mathematics (with concentrations in computer science, mathematics education, and physics), and ornamental horticulture; the Bachelor of Science in Accounting degree; the Bachelor of Science in Business Administration degree (with concentrations in accounting, economics, finance, international business, management, marketing, and real estate); the Bachelor of Science in Information Science degree (with concentrations in management of information systems, networking and communications, and science of information systems); and the Bachelor of Science in Nursing degree (with concentrations identified as the generic track and the RN-completion track). Minors are available in applied physics, biology, business administration, chemistry, computer science, economics, finance, mathematics, and physics.

A 3-2 cooperative program with the Duke University School of the Environment allows Christopher Newport University students to earn the Bachelor of Science degree from CNU and the Master of Forestry or Master of Environmental Management degree from Duke.

The University offers state-approved teacher education programs in the following areas: art (NK-12); biology (9-12); chemistry (9-12); computer science (9-12); early childhood/elementary education (NK-5); economics (9-12); English (9-12); French (NK-12); German (NK-12); health education (NK-12); history (9-12); mathematics (9-12); middle school education (5-8); physical education (NK-12); physics (9-12); political science (government) (9-12); social studies (9-12); Spanish (NK-12); speech (9-12 and add-on); theater (9-12); and vocal/choral music and instrumental music (NK-12). These state-approved programs require prospective teachers to meet the University's requirements for degrees in the arts or sciences or disciplines appropriate to the endorsements being sought and to complete professional studies courses that meet the requirements for their teaching curriculum.

Academic Program

To be eligible for an undergraduate degree, students must successfully complete 120 academic semester hours and the health/physical education requirement. The last 30 semester hours of credit must be taken in residence.

The first two years of all students' academic programs require successful completion of general education requirements in such areas as English (writing), foreign language, health/physical education, history, humanities, laboratory science, mathematics, and social science. The last two years are devoted to the academic major and electives.

Off-Campus Arrangements

Christopher Newport University administers exchange programs with the following institutions: Autonomous University of Guadalajara (Mexico), Kansai Gaidai University (Japan), and Middlesex Polytechnic (England). CNU offers a $500 stipend for international study to students who participate in the President's Leadership Program. Students may also travel to Europe with the CNU Chamber Singers or worldwide with CNU's award-winning Model U.N. Club.

Academic Facilities

The Captain John Smith Library houses more than 500,000 books, micropieces, and bound periodicals and also offers students access to textual material, periodicals, and information recorded on film, microfilm, records, and tapes. Services include interlibrary loans and extensive computer-assisted bibliographical services.

Academic buildings contain a variety of small classrooms and auditoriums, computer laboratories, specialty laboratories, an art gallery, an instructional technology center, a theater, music recital halls and practice rooms, and a greenhouse/herbarium.

CNU provides one computer for every 10 students and free Internet and e-mail usage for all.

Costs

In-state tuition for full-time students for the 1999–2000 academic year was $3008; nonresident tuition for full-time students was $8776. Books and supplies average $500 per year. The room and board rate for the 2000–01 academic year is $5350.

Financial Aid

The University's financial aid programs serve 40 to 50 percent of the student body. CNU offers every form of federally funded financial aid and a variety of merit scholarships, ranging from $1000 per year to full tuition.

Faculty

Ninety percent of CNU faculty members hold the highest degree in their professional field. In addition to providing high-quality classroom instruction, faculty members work with students to develop academic schedules, supervise independent programs, conduct a wide range of scholarly research, and provide a wealth of services to the community. CNU prides itself on the close, personal relationships between students and professors.

Student Government

The University encourages students to participate in the formulation of rules, regulations, and policies directly affecting student life. Students may get involved with the Student Government Association (SGA) and University committees and councils. SGA awards support monies to many of the eighty active campus clubs and organizations each year.

Admission Requirements

The requirements for a student to be admitted into a degree program are graduation from an accredited secondary school in the upper half of the class (or a GED certificate) and the Virginia Advanced Studies Diploma or its equivalent (4 units in English, 3 units in mathematics to include algebra I and II and geometry, 3 units in science, 3 units in social sciences, and either 3 units in one foreign language or 2 units in each of two foreign languages). Of the students accepted into the freshman class, the midrange SAT I score is 980 to 1150, and the GPA range is 2.8 to 3.4.

Application and Information

Applications, the CNU catalog, and additional information may be obtained through the Internet at the address below or by contacting:

Admissions Office
Christopher Newport University
1 University Place
Newport News, Virginia 23606-2998
Telephone: 757-594-7015
           757-594-7938 (TDD)
           800-333-4CNU (toll-free)
E-mail: admit@cnu.edu
World Wide Web: http://www.cnu.edu

THE CITADEL
CHARLESTON, SOUTH CAROLINA

The College

The Citadel, founded in 1842, has a rich and storied history. Though it has been greatly expanded and modernized, it is basically the same distinctive institution it was when founded. The mission is to graduate leaders who excel in civilian professions and enterprises as well as serve their country in government and the military. The Citadel remains a stronghold of duty, self-discipline, and high ideals in a changing American society.

As a classic military college, The Citadel emphasizes the value of a strict indoctrination for first-year students, who are called knobs. The disciplined lifestyle that begins in the knob year binds cadets into a lifelong, close-knit camaraderie that is one of the strongest forces in their lives after graduation.

Citadel graduates have fought in every American conflict since the Mexican War. Cadets from The Citadel fired the first shots of the Civil War. The Citadel proudly displays on the Corps flag nine battle streamers earned in that war. Citadel graduates continue to serve their country with distinction in all branches of the armed services.

The Corps of Cadets numbers almost 2,000 and represents nearly every state in the union and many other countries. All cadets are required to reside in barracks. An ultramodern physical education center provides splendid facilities for physical education and individual and pickup team sports unrelated to varsity events. An exceptional intramural program includes twenty-eight activities. The student activities building, named for General Mark W. Clark, the late president emeritus, houses the Honor Court room, reception lounge, movie theater, office of the college hostess, photograph darkroom, student publication offices, canteen, dance hall, billiard room, and post office. The beautiful Summerall Chapel, which is a shrine of religion, patriotism, and remembrance, is flexibly designed for use by major denominational groups.

The Citadel, a member of NCAA Division I (football division 1-AA) and the Southern Conference, fields fifteen men's and women's intercollegiate athletic teams. Club sports include bicycling, bowling, boxing, crew, fencing, gymnastics, judo, karate, lacrosse, pistol, rugby, sailing, scuba diving, skydiving, volleyball, and waterskiing. The Citadel has its own boating center and canoes, power boats, and sailboats.

Location

The Citadel is located in one of America's most historic cities, Charleston, South Carolina. The beautiful 100-acre campus is bordered by the Ashley River and historic Hampton Park. The climate is ideal, with an average temperature of 67 degrees. Many excellent ocean beaches are nearby. A Citadel beach club is located just a few minutes away on the lush Isle of Palms. Charleston is famous for its pre-Revolutionary houses and gardens, outstanding restaurants, golf courses, and cultural centers. Entertainment and nightlife abound.

Charleston is served by Amtrak, an international airport, two bus lines, seven taxi companies, a limousine service, and fifteen rental-car firms. The city's transit system stops at The Citadel's main entrance. The campus is readily accessible via Interstate 26 or U.S. Route 17.

Majors and Degrees

Through twenty major and thirteen minor areas of academic concentration, The Citadel provides its students with academic opportunities normally expected only at a university, combined with the personalized attention afforded only by a small liberal arts college. Bachelor of Arts degrees are available in chemistry, English, history, mathematics, modern languages, political science and criminal justice, and psychology. Bachelor of Science degrees are offered in biology, business administration, chemistry, civil engineering, computer science, education, electrical engineering, environmental engineering, mathematics, physical education, and physics.

Academic Program

The Citadel provides a sound education reinforced by the best features of a disciplined environment.

All cadets participate in one of the Reserve Officers' Training Corps programs—Army, Air Force, or Naval/Marine Corps. These programs do not require students to accept a commission or be committed to active duty.

The educational requirements of all majors ensure that the Citadel graduate is conversant with literature, history, and the natural and social sciences. Students learn to evaluate and judge by confronting issues raised in challenging courses.

The Citadel Honors Program is a specially designed educational experience that meets the needs of students with an outstanding record of academic achievement and a sense of intellectual adventure. While pursuing any one of the twenty degree programs offered by The Citadel, Honors students take a series of general education Honors courses concentrated in their first two years and an Honors seminar in their third and fourth years.

The Citadel—a fully accredited, four-year, senior college—is a member of the Southern Association of Colleges and Schools, the American Council on Education, the American Association of Colleges for Teacher Education, and the Association of American Colleges. The civil engineering and electrical engineering departments are accredited by the Accreditation Board for Engineering and Technology. The chemistry department is accredited by the American Chemical Society. The education department is accredited by the National Council for Accreditation of Teacher Education and the National Association of State Directors of Teacher Education and Certification.

Academic Facilities

Twenty-four major buildings are efficiently grouped around a huge parade ground to provide maximum convenience for students. Among the College's academic facilities are the Daniel Library, two engineering buildings, and computer facilities located in all academic areas. The entire campus is linked to a fiber-optic network. Through a consortium arrangement, other local college libraries and facilities are available to cadets. New barracks are under construction and will provide computer connections to the campuswide network and the Internet in every room.

Costs

The Citadel's extremely competitive fee structure includes uniforms, room, board, books, dry cleaning, laundry, athletic events, student publications, infirmary care, and haircuts. The annual fees for 1999–2000 by residence and by class were as follows: for residents of South Carolina, fees for first-year students were $12,898, and for sophomores, juniors, and seniors, $9908. For out-of-state students, fees for first-year students were $18,494, and for sophomores, juniors, and seniors, $15,504.

Financial Aid

The Citadel offers two types of financial assistance: financial aid, which consists of loans and grants that are awarded on the basis of need, and scholarships, which are awarded on the basis of merit. In 1999–2000, more than 65 percent of the Cadet Corps received financial aid and 44 percent received scholarships, ranging from several hundred dollars a year to a student's complete expenses for four years. To be considered for financial aid or scholarships, students must submit an application for enrollment. The deadline for applying for need-based financial aid is March 15 of the senior year in high school.

Faculty

All courses at The Citadel are taught by dedicated faculty members, more than 94 percent of whom hold doctoral degrees. The student-faculty ratio is 18:1. All faculty members are required to set aside time for counseling and assisting cadets with their studies.

Student Government

Cadets form a regiment, composed of a band and bagpipe unit and four battalions of four companies each. Student authority is entrusted to the chain of command and the elected class officials.

A principal aspect of student government is the honor code. Under that code, a cadet does not lie, cheat, or steal or tolerate those who do. An honor committee elected by cadets administers the code.

Admission Requirements

Applicants must be unmarried, between 16 and 21 years of age, physically qualified for enrollment in ROTC, and graduates of an accredited secondary school or have satisfactorily completed the General Educational Development examination. The required high school subjects are 4 units of English; 3 units of mathematics (algebra I, algebra II, and geometry); 3 years of laboratory science; 2 years of the same foreign language; 2 units of social science; 2 units of social studies; 1 unit of U.S. history; and 1 unit of physical education or ROTC. Other considerations include the applicant's rank in class, academic performance, and scores on either the SAT I or ACT. Extracurricular activities are viewed as indications of leadership and desirable character traits. All factors are weighed in the final determination of the applicant's qualifications. The Citadel actively seeks and encourages applications for admission without regard to gender, race, or ability to pay.

Application and Information

Applications may be made at the beginning of the senior year in secondary school. Prospective cadets should arrange to have their SAT I or ACT scores forwarded to The Citadel. While applicants are welcome to visit the campus at any time, special programs are arranged on a designated schedule, during which the prospective applicants reside in barracks.

Inquiries should be addressed to:
Admissions Office
The Citadel
171 Moultrie Street
Charleston, South Carolina 29409
Telephone: 800-868-1842 (toll-free)
E-mail: admissions@citadel.edu
World Wide Web: http://www.citadel.edu

Cadets are offered personalized attention from the faculty and access to the latest technology in a disciplined environment.

CITY COLLEGE OF THE CITY UNIVERSITY OF NEW YORK

NEW YORK, NEW YORK

The College

Since its founding in 1847, the City College of New York (CCNY) has stressed the dual goals of offering access to higher education combined with academic excellence. That policy has had remarkable results, making CCNY one of America's greatest educational success stories. For example, 8 Nobel Prize winners are City College graduates, placing CCNY's graduates among the nation's leaders. The College also ranks ninth among public and private institutions in the number of graduates who have gone on to earn doctorates and ranks among the top dozen in the number of alumni who are members of the prestigious National Academy of Engineering and in producing graduates who have become America's leading business executives. Reflecting the College's commitment to equal educational opportunity, CCNY is also one of the nation's leaders in producing minority engineering graduates and in the number of black graduates who gain admission to medical school. Overall, CCNY graduates exceed the national average in obtaining admission to medical school. The College has more full-time doctoral students in campus-based programs than have all of the other City University of New York (CUNY) colleges combined. City College is internationally known for the research activities of its faculty, which were supported by grants totaling more than $27 million during 1998–99, the largest amount received by a unit of CUNY. The College houses several major centers and institutes, including the Institute for Ultrafast Spectroscopy and Lasers, the CUNY Institute for Transportation Systems, and the new Colin Powell Center for Policy Studies.

The College offers students a wide variety of social activities; more than ninety clubs are organized on campus. Students can also participate in numerous intercollegiate and intramural sports. There are sixteen varsity teams for men and women. The Herman Goldman Center for Sports and Recreation contains outstanding facilities for track and field, baseball, soccer, lacrosse, and softball.

Location

The City College campus occupies 35 acres in Manhattan along Convent Avenue from 131st to 141st Streets in the area known as St. Nicholas Heights. The surrounding neighborhoods are predominantly residential, although there are shopping areas west of the campus along Broadway and south toward 125th Street.

Majors and Degrees

The College of Liberal Arts and Science offers the Bachelor of Arts (B.A.), the Bachelor of Science (B.S.), and the Bachelor of Fine Arts (B.F.A.) degrees in the following majors: American studies; anthropology; art; art history; biochemistry; biology; chemistry; comparative literature; creative writing; earth systems sciences; economics; electronic art and graphic design; English; foreign languages and literature; history; international studies; Jewish studies; management and administration; mathematics; music; philosophy; physics; political science; psychology; public policy and public affairs; sociology; theater; and women's studies. Through the Center for Legal Education, students interested in a career in law may take the six-year B.A./J.D. degree program. The School of Architecture, Urban Design, and Landscape Architecture offers a B.S. in architecture and landscape architecture, and a five-year program leading to the Bachelor of Architecture is available. The Sophie Davis School of Biomedical Education provides a seven-year B.S./M.D. curriculum for highly qualified high school graduates who reside in New York State. The Physician's Assistant Program, also part of the School of Biomedical Education, offers a B.S. degree and is a joint program between City College and Harlem Hospital. This is an upper-division (junior and senior years) program. The School of Education offers programs that lead to the Bachelor of Science in Education (B.S.Ed.) in the following majors: bilingual education, early childhood education, elementary education, and special education for behavioral, emotional, and intellectual handicaps. In addition, students are prepared to teach a wide variety of subjects in secondary schools. The School of Engineering offers the Bachelor of Engineering (B.E.) degree in the fields of chemical, civil, electrical, and mechanical engineering and the B.S. in computer science. The Center for Worker Education is an off-site program that helps adults return to college while continuing their full-time employment. Students can complete a bachelor's degree program in the evening.

Academic Program

City College includes the College of Liberal Arts and Science and the largest complex of professional schools in the City University. These include Schools of Architecture, Education, and Engineering and the Sophie Davis School of Biomedical Education/CUNY Medical School. There are centers in performing arts and legal education, and special programs include four-year bachelor's/master's programs in economics, English, history, mathematics, mathematics education, psychology, and sociology. A Freshman Honors Program is available for qualified students who are interested in advanced research work and independent study. Cooperative education internships are also provided for interested applicants. Such programs as Minority Access to Research Careers (MARC), Minority Biomedical Research Support (MBRS), and City College Research Scholars (CRS) provide paid and volunteer opportunities to do research at various institutions.

City College has a core curriculum that is founded on a strong liberal arts base and is designed to ensure the continued quality and relevance of its academic programs. The core curriculum reflects a global vision of human achievement in an increasingly interdependent world and is designed to provide City College students with superior academic preparation while enhancing their capacity to think critically and creatively. The College has a long history of encouraging independent thought and initiative and continues to foster an educational atmosphere in which students can explore and develop their interests and talents.

For most bachelor's degree programs, the total number of credits necessary to earn a degree is 120; a bachelor's degree in engineering requires up to 136 credits. The College works on a semester calendar and offers a 7½-week summer session.

Off-Campus Arrangements

City College has exchange programs in Austria, China, England, Germany, and Mexico as well as a summer program in the Dominican Republic. Students are able to spend a semester, a full academic year, or a summer term at one of the cooperating schools. Through a cooperative arrangement, students are also able to take courses at the various branches of the City University System.

Academic Facilities

New facilities add a modern tone to the original neo-Gothic buildings, which have been designated state and national landmarks. In addition, a $200-million renovation of the neo-Gothic buildings is nearing completion. The thirteen-story Robert E. Marshak Science Building houses more than 200 teaching and research laboratories, a planetarium, a weather station, an electron microscope, laser research facilities, a science and engineering library, and a major physical education complex. The School of Engineering building recently underwent a $65-million expansion and modernization and has more than forty research laboratories. Aaron Davis Hall contains a 750-seat proscenium theater, a 200-seat experimental theater, and a 75-seat studio workshop for rehearsals. The North Academic Center occupies three full city blocks and has 2,000 classrooms, laboratories, lecture halls, offices, and dining and student activity areas. It includes the Morris Raphael Cohen Library, which houses more than 1 million volumes, the largest collection in the City University.

Computer facilities are extensive at City College. The Computation Center provides services to meet instructional, administrative, and research needs. Numerous computer labs are located throughout the College, utilizing microcomputers and minicomputers to provide research and academic services to students and faculty and staff members.

Costs

In 2000–01, for students who are residents of New York State, the tuition for full-time attendance (12 or more credits or the equivalent) is $1600 per semester, or $3200 per year. Part-time and summer-session students who are residents of New York State pay $135 per credit. Tuition for out-of-state and international students is $3400 per semester, or $6800 per year, for full-time study or $285 per credit for part-time study. Tuition and fees are subject to change. Books, supplies, and commuting and personal expenses average $5300 a year for full-time students who live with their parents and $10,350 for students who live on their own, excluding tuition and moderate activity fees. All students commute to the College, since there are no dormitories.

Financial Aid

Financial assistance is available for eligible City College students through state and federal programs. Students who wish to apply for financial aid must file the Free Application for Federal Student Aid (FAFSA) and the TAP/APTS Application and CUNY Supplement. Among the forms of financial aid available are Federal Supplemental Educational Opportunity Grants, Federal Perkins Loans, and Federal Work-Study Program awards. A large percentage of City College students receive some type of aid. For information, students should contact the Financial Aid Office at City College (telephone: 212-650-5819). City College offers merit scholarships to students who have achieved superior performance in high school or college. The City College Scholars Award, worth a total of $7200 for four years, is available for qualified high school graduates of outstanding ability who reside in New York. Through the Division of the Humanities, the Isaacs Scholarship offers full tuition and expenses for students who plan to major in English. Finally, for students who wish to pursue a career in college teaching, the City College Fellowship, sponsored by the Ford Foundation, offers $2000 per year for undergraduate study, plus additional academic and financial support through graduate study. Although special aid programs have specified application deadlines, students who apply early for assistance have an advantage. For information about deadlines, eligibility, and credentials, students should contact the City College Office of Admissions.

Faculty

City College's outstanding faculty represents a broad range of disciplines, and many members have earned the nation's highest forms of recognition—Guggenheim and Fulbright awards as well as grants that amount to millions of dollars annually in support of their research and scholarship. Eighty-five percent of the faculty members hold Ph.D. degrees. The student-teacher ratio is 15:1.

Student Government

Students have traditionally played an active role in campus government. Each year, two different senates are elected at the undergraduate level: one each for the day and evening divisions. Student government funds pay for the activities of student organizations, which send representatives to a student-faculty administrative committee that advises the College president on matters of an extracurricular nature. Through their representatives, students are given a voice on departmental committees, and they vote on matters of educational policy, budget, and faculty appointments and reappointments.

Admission Requirements

Applicants who wish to be considered for admission to City College as freshmen must have an academic average of 80 or better, have completed a strong Regents-level program in high school, and have minimum scores of 75 percent on the Regents English Language Arts and Math A or Math Sequential I and II exams (New York residents); minimum SAT I scores of 480 on both verbal and math are also required. Qualified high school juniors may apply for early admission. Students with special educational and financial needs may qualify for admission to the Search for Education, Elevation, and Knowledge (SEEK) Program. City College accepts students who wish to transfer from other postsecondary institutions. Requirements for admission vary according to the program and the number of credits completed. Applicants should contact the College for information about admission as a transfer student.

Application and Information

Applications to City College are processed centrally through the City University of New York Processing Center. Although applications are processed on a rolling basis, students who wish a prompt response should adhere to the initial deadline dates of October 16 (spring admission) and January 15 (fall admission). Applications from qualified students that are received after the application deadlines are processed on a space-available basis. Further information and application materials can be obtained from either:

Office of Admissions
The City College of the City University of New York
138th Street and Convent Avenue
New York, New York 10031
Telephone: 212-650-6448 or 6977

Central Admissions Services (O.A.S.)
City University of New York
101 West 31st Street, 6th Floor
New York, New York 10001
Telephone: 212-947-4800
World Wide Web: http://www.ccny.cuny.edu

CITY UNIVERSITY
RENTON, WASHINGTON

The University

City University opened its doors in 1973 with one primary purpose: to provide educational opportunities for those segments of the population not being fully served through traditional means. City University believes that education is a lifelong process, and it is a pioneer in the concept of education unhindered by time, format, or location. City University is a private, nonprofit institution of higher learning, open to anyone with the desire to achieve. Classes are offered in the evening and on weekends in order to meet student needs without interrupting established lifestyles and associations.

City University's students are mainly working adults, drawn from all walks of life. In the 1999–2000 school year, the University enrolled more than 5,500 undergraduate students. Of those, more than 52 percent were women and 17 percent were members of minority groups. Though the majority of students attend classes near their homes in the Pacific Northwest, many live and study at locations around the globe. Often programs are available at the student's workplace through cooperative arrangements with progressive employers or professional associations.

City University is accredited by the Northwest Association of Schools and Colleges. Graduate programs leading to the Master of Arts, the Master of Business Administration, the Master of Education, the Master of Public Administration, the Master of Science, and the Master in Teaching are offered.

Most City University students are already established in either a job or career and have chosen a path they are preparing to follow. As alumni, they are able to realize their career goals in business, in public administration, or in one of several professions.

Location

The University's mission statement specifies a commitment to education that is affordable, accessible, and practical as well as academically sound. Accordingly, the University owns or leases classroom space in metropolitan centers, smaller cities, military installations, or any other space that is convenient for students. Six locations serve the Greater Seattle/Puget Sound area. Classes are also held in Yakima, Spokane, Tri-Cities, and Vancouver in Washington. Other major metropolitan locations include Los Angeles and San Jose, California; Vancouver, British Columbia; Zurich, Switzerland; Frankfurt, Germany; Bratislava and Trencin, Slovakia; and Madrid, Spain.

Majors and Degrees

City University offers a range of programs leading to the Bachelor of Science, the Bachelor of Arts, and the Associate of Science degrees. Students are given a vast array of options and may choose the course of study best suited to their experience, prior learning, and the realization of their personal and professional goals.

City University offers the Bachelor of Science degree with a range of possible majors. These include accounting, business administration, computer systems, e-commerce, general studies, management specialty, and marketing.

Also offered is the Bachelor of Arts degree with concentrations available in international studies, management, marketing, mass communications and journalism, multi-science, philosophy, political science, psychology, and sociology.

The Associate of Science degree is offered in general studies, management, and paralegal studies.

Undergraduate certificate programs—professional credentials for those whose immediate needs do not require the completion of a degree—are offered in accounting, computer programming, internetworking, network/telecommunications, networking technologies, and paralegal studies.

Academic Program

Students who live in other areas may complete a degree program through City University's Distance Learning Program, which serves students worldwide. Distance learning makes completing an education possible anywhere, with communication by mail, telephone, fax, or computer (on line). These courses start the first of every month throughout the year as well as on the traditional quarterly schedule.

Candidates for the bachelor's degree must complete 180 hours of credit by completing regular or distance learning classes or through recognized transfer credits or prior learning experience. Lower-division requirements total 90 credits, including a total of 55 general education credits in the broad areas of basic skills, humanities, natural sciences/mathematics, and social sciences. For most bachelor's degree programs, upper-division course work consists of a series of common core courses that covers the areas of business, ethics, and critical thinking skills. Both B.S. and B.A. students then complete a series of competency courses respective to their degree, followed by major required courses.

All undergraduate programs are designed to allow students to satisfy certain general education requirements through upper-division course work. In addition, B.A. students may be able to satisfy all 55 general education credits through upper-division course work.

For the Associate of Science degree, students complete 90 credit hours, 55 of which are in general education. Each of these programs is wholly compatible with and transferable to baccalaureate degree study. Depending on the particular choice of program, students can complete an undergraduate certificate program with 35 to 45 credits.

The academic year is divided into four quarters. City University offers evening, weekend, and distance learning courses.

Academic Facilities

City University strives to satisfy the informational and research needs of its students at all instructional locations, as well as those enrolled in courses via distance learning. Its library services include extensive reference resources, indexes, and journals. Other services, which may be available by phone, include an online search service and interlibrary loans. Students may access City University's online electronic library via the World Wide Web. City University has entered into cooperative arrangements with libraries in many instructional site communities.

Costs

In 1999–2000, tuition was $165 per undergraduate credit hour.

Additional fees apply for certificate completion, graduation application, and various tests or examinations that the student may request. Textbooks and other instructional materials are additional. All initial applicants to certificate or degree programs pay a nonrefundable application fee of $75.

Financial Aid

To help qualified students achieve their educational and professional goals, City University participates in several financial aid programs. Federal Pell Grants, Federal Supplemental Educational Opportunity Grants, Federal Stafford Student Loans, Federal PLUS loans, and Federal Work-Study are available.

In addition, the University awards scholarships on the basis of financial need, demonstrated academic ability, and other criteria. Employer reimbursement programs and military tuition assistance programs are also available, and all programs are approved for veterans' education benefits.

Students interested in financial aid should contact City University's Financial Aid Office at 425-637-1010 or 800-426-5596 (toll-free) for more information.

Faculty

The University's senior administration and faculty have a University-wide role in quality assurance, academic policies and standards, curricular development, and instructional quality. City University's faculty is composed of distinguished practitioners in the fields of business, education, and government and in civic and research organizations and the legal community. They unite strong academic preparation with active professional careers in the fields in which they teach. Some of the University's approximately 55 core faculty members also serve as senior faculty in charge of various academic disciplines. They oversee more than 1,000 adjunct faculty members instructing in both classroom theory and actual practice at more than a dozen locations around the world. The University draws on this faculty pool to achieve an average class size of 18 students.

Student Government

The philosophy and structure of City University do not lend themselves to the traditional student organization activities revolving around life on a fixed campus. The Student Code of Conduct creates an atmosphere conducive to an uninhibited, scholastically honest learning environment. City University encourages and responds to current and prospective students' comments in an effort to help maintain currency and relevance in its academic offerings.

Admission Requirements

Undergraduate degree programs are generally open to applicants over the age of 18 who hold a high school or GED diploma, who can benefit from postsecondary education, and who are mature enough to manage the responsibilities imposed by university studies. Students who began but did not complete academic careers at other postsecondary institutions are welcome to continue their education at City University. Course work completed at other recognized institutions will be evaluated to determine its applicability to the selected degree and major objective.

To gain admission to the University, students must begin by contacting or meeting with an admissions adviser to select an educational objective and to complete initial enrollment. An application form must be filled out and an application fee submitted. Transcripts and other documentation may be required. International students and veterans will find that additional requirements apply.

A rolling admissions policy governs most City University programs. That is, the University will accept applications and announce admissions decisions continuously throughout the year. Most degree programs may be commenced at the start of the fall, winter, spring, or summer quarters, or at the monthly start of distance learning courses.

Application and Information

Because of City University's rolling admissions policy, applications for admission may be submitted at any time. Response time is usually two to four weeks.

Application forms or other information may be obtained by contacting:

Office of Admissions and Student Affairs
City University
919 Southwest Grady Way
Renton, Washington 98055
Telephone: 425-637-1010
          800-426-5596 (toll-free)
          425-450-4660 (TTY)
Fax: 425-277-2437
E-mail: info@cityu.edu
World Wide Web: http://www.cityu.edu

City University's Academic Center in Renton, Washington.

CLAREMONT McKENNA COLLEGE
CLAREMONT, CALIFORNIA

The College

Founded in 1946 as the third undergraduate college in the cluster of the Claremont Colleges, Claremont McKenna College (CMC) occupies a unique place among American colleges. Through a grounding in the traditional liberal arts, CMC's purpose is to educate future leaders in business, the professions, and public affairs. Economics, government, and international relations are the most popular among twenty-one majors offered at CMC. The College is especially appropriate for students seeking to pursue careers in law, politics, government, international relations, business, management, and finance.

Claremont McKenna College is one of seven institutions—five undergraduate colleges and two graduate schools—that constitute the Claremont Colleges. The others are Harvey Mudd College, Pitzer College, Pomona College, Scripps College, the Claremont Graduate University, and Keck Graduate Institute of Applied Life Sciences.

The current undergraduate enrollment at CMC is 1,020 (576 men and 444 women). Thirty-seven percent of the student body is from out of state and 5 percent is international. Thirty-nine states and twenty-two countries are represented on campus. Thirty-four percent of the students at CMC are members of minority groups.

Because approximately 95 percent of CMC students live on campus in coed residence halls and apartments, campus life is vibrant and active. Dorms provide the foundation for social life at CMC; the student-run dorm government often plans field trips, movie nights, barbecues, dinners, and socials for each dorm or apartment group. Intramural athletic teams are typically formed by each residence hall.

A distinctive aspect of life on the campus is the Athenaeum—a $2-million facility that serves as a social, cultural, and academic center. Faculty members occasionally arrange to meet their classes at the Athenaeum for luncheon, dinner, and coffee hours. The Athenaeum program features guest speakers on a variety of topics four nights a week throughout the academic year. Other special resources at CMC include a center for religious activities, a bookstore that carries more than 40,000 titles, professionally staffed counseling and medical centers, the Office of Black Student Affairs, the Chicano/Latino Student Affairs Center, and an international center.

Claremont supports a wide variety of cultural events—concerts, plays, lectures, conferences, art exhibits, and films—and the Claremont Colleges cooperate to provide organized extracurricular activities. Although each campus is autonomous, many activities include students from several of the colleges. There are intercollegiate athletics programs, a four-college chorus, a five-college theater program, a five-college weekly newspaper, a five-college orchestra, and five-college forensics. Five-college parties are also scheduled throughout the year.

Claremont McKenna College, Harvey Mudd College, and Scripps College are associated in a joint program of intercollegiate and club athletics, physical education, and recreation. Facilities include a football field, a track, a gymnasium (housing two gym floors, a squash court, a Nautilus and weight room, a fitness center, a boxing ring, offices, and locker rooms), a baseball field, a soccer field, a lacrosse field, three swimming pools, eight tennis courts, volleyball courts, intramural fields, and a climbing wall. The sports teams compete in the Southern California Intercollegiate Athletic Conference (SCIAC). The men's teams, known as the Stags, compete in baseball, basketball, cross-country, football, golf, soccer, swimming/diving, tennis, track, and water polo. Women's teams, known as the Athenas, compete in basketball, cross-country, golf, soccer, softball, swimming/diving, tennis, track, volleyball, and water polo. The Claremont-Mudd-Scripps intercollegiate athletics program has been at the top of the SCIAC All-Sports Championship race every year.

Location

Claremont McKenna College is in Claremont, California, a suburban community of 37,000 about 35 miles east of downtown Los Angeles. It is a pleasant town with tree-lined streets and well-tended homes. Other educational resources in Claremont are the School of Theology, the Rancho Santa Ana Botanical Garden, the Blaisdell Institute for Advanced Study in World Cultures and Religions, and the Institute for Antiquity and Christianity.

"The Village," home to attractive restaurants, art galleries, and shops, is only a 10-minute walk from the College. All of the cultural, educational, social, and entertainment centers of greater Los Angeles are nearby, including major art museums, a ranking symphony orchestra, abundant theater productions, and a variety of professional sports teams. Mount Baldy is close by for skiing and hiking, and Pacific Ocean beaches and the Mojave Desert are each only an hour away. The weather throughout the academic year is usually warm, dry, and sunny.

Majors and Degrees

Claremont McKenna College grants the Bachelor of Arts degree in biology; chemistry; economics; economics-accounting, the environment, economics, and politics; French; German; government; history; international relations; literature; management-engineering (a 3-2 program); mathematics; philosophy; physics; politics, philosophy, and economics; psychobiology; psychology; religious studies; science and management; and Spanish. Students often pursue dual and double majors and/or create individualized majors.

In addition to these CMC-based majors, cooperative programs with the other Claremont Colleges allow students to major in American studies, art, Asian studies, Black studies, Chicano studies, film studies, legal studies, music, and theater. Sequences, a series of courses related to a subject and selected from different disciplines, are offered in the areas of Asian-American studies, computer science, ethics, leadership, and women's studies.

Academic Program

Students must satisfactorily complete thirty-two semester courses, including general education and major requirements, in order to graduate. General education requirements include one course in mathematics, one course in English composition and analysis, two courses in the natural sciences, two courses in the humanities, three courses in the social sciences, and a senior thesis. In addition, students must complete a third semester of a foreign language and a Questions of Civilization course.

Depending on the department, credit or advanced placement, or both, may be granted for college courses taken while in high school. Also, CMC may grant credit for scores of 4 or 5 on Advanced Placement (AP) examinations and for scores of 6 or 7 on higher level International Baccalaureate (I.B.) examinations.

CMC sponsors a joint science program with two other Claremont Colleges, Pitzer and Scripps. The Keck Science

Center houses modern laboratories for teaching and research, and a large biological field station is located adjacent to the campus. Virtually all students in the joint science program do independent research, and reports on many student-faculty projects have been published in professional journals.

By intercollegiate agreement, CMC students may take courses not offered at Claremont McKenna at any of the Claremont Colleges. Up to one third of a student's courses may be taken at the other Claremont Colleges.

CMC operates on an early semester calendar, beginning the first week in September and ending in mid-May.

Off-Campus Arrangements

Approximately 40 percent of CMC students elect to study off-campus for a semester or a year. Students may choose from more than seventy-five programs in forty-one countries; CMC's own Washington, D.C. Semester Program; college exchanges with Colby College, Haverford College, Instituto Tecnologico de Mexico, Morehouse College, McGill University (Canada), Spelman College, and The University of Konstanz (Germany); and the Semester in Environmental Science at the Marine Biological Laboratory in Woods Hole, Massachusetts.

Academic Facilities

The Claremont Colleges pool their funds to support impressive central resources: more than 1.9 million volumes in open-stack libraries, sophisticated computers (DEC VAX, IBM 4341, and DECsystem-10), a 2,600-seat concert hall, and a 700-seat theater.

Nine research institutes within Claremont McKenna enrich the curriculum, attract distinguished scholars to the College, and give outstanding students research and internship experience and the opportunity to work closely with faculty scholars. The institutes are the Lowe Institute of Political Economy, the Reed Institute of Applied Mathematics, the Keck Center for International Strategic Studies, the Roberts Environmental Center, the Rose Institute of State and Local Government, the Salvatori Center for the Study of Individual Freedom in the Modern World, the Henry Kravis Leadership Institute, the Gould Center for Humanistic Studies, and the H.N. and Frances C. Berger Institute on Work, Family, and Children.

Costs

Tuition for 2000–01 is $22,580. Room and board cost $7420. Projected expenses for 2000–01, including tuition, fees, room and board, and personal expenses, total $31,750. Travel expenses vary.

Financial Aid

Financial aid is awarded in the form of grants (nonrepayable gift aid), student loans, and part-time employment. Grants range from $1000 to $20,000 per year and average $13,000; loans for entering freshmen average $3000 per year. The total amount of aid a student is awarded is based on need.

The College offers twenty-five McKenna Achievement Awards to members of each entering freshman class. These awards are valued at $5000 each and are renewable for each of the four years, provided the student earns at least a B average. To be considered for one of these awards, a student usually must rank among the top 5 percent in his or her high school class and earn a score of more than 650 on both the mathematical and verbal portions of the SAT I. Candidates must also have excellent school recommendations and strong extracurricular involvement, including leadership, and must have filed a completed application by January 1.

Faculty

CMC's faculty members are teacher-scholars who are dedicated to teaching undergraduates and to making contributions to their disciplines. Except in fields in which the doctorate is not the terminal degree, all tenured faculty members have doctorates. The student-faculty ratio is 9:1, and the average class size is 19.

Student Government

Officers of the Associated Students of Claremont McKenna College are elected each spring and serve a one-year term. Each residence hall is self-governing, and students sit on virtually all faculty, trustee, and staff committees. CMC has a history of active and responsible participation in student government.

Admission Requirements

College admission standards place CMC in the "highly selective" category. Seventy-eight percent of the 1999 freshmen were in the top tenth of their high school graduating class; 94 percent were in the top fifth. The middle 50 percent of the class had SAT I verbal scores ranging from 650 to 740 and SAT I math scores ranging from 650 to 740. CMC strives to enroll a class that is academically strong but also places a strong emphasis on extracurricular involvement, community participation, and leadership potential. Admission to CMC is need blind.

Early decision and deferred entrance are options. Students are encouraged to visit the campus and arrange for a personal conference.

Applicants are expected to furnish transcripts of all academic work in high school and college; a recommendation from a guidance counselor, principal, or headmaster; a recommendation from at least one academic course teacher; two essays; and scores on either the SAT I or ACT (the SAT I is preferred). Students whose native language is not English are strongly encouraged to take the Test of English as a Foreign Language (TOEFL).

Application and Information

Application materials must be received by November 15 from applicants seeking early decision, November 1 for midyear entrance, and January 15 for those seeking entrance in the fall.

Further information is available from:

Richard C. Vos
Dean of Admission and Financial Aid
Claremont McKenna College
890 Columbia Avenue
Claremont, California 91711-6425
Telephone: 909-621-8088
E-mail: admission@mckenna.edu
World Wide Web: http://www.claremontmckenna.edu

View of the Claremont McKenna College campus, with the San Gabriel Mountain Range in the background.

CLARION UNIVERSITY OF PENNSYLVANIA
CLARION, PENNSYLVANIA

The University

Clarion University of Pennsylvania is fully accredited by the Middle States Association of Colleges and Schools. It was founded in 1867 and is one of fourteen state-owned institutions of higher education in Pennsylvania. Its programs in education are accredited by the National Council for Accreditation of Teacher Education and the National Academy of Early Childhood Programs, and its chemistry program is approved by the American Chemical Society. The University is a member of the American Assembly of Collegiate Schools of Business, the American Association of Colleges for Teacher Education, and the American Association of State Colleges and Universities and is an Educational Associate of the Institute of International Education. The Bachelor and Associate of Science in Nursing degree programs have the accreditation of the National League for Nursing. Clarion's graduate program in library science is accredited by the prestigious American Library Association, and its graduate program in speech pathology and audiology is accredited by the Education Standards Board of the American Speech-Language-Hearing Association. The legal business studies program at the Venango campus is approved by the American Bar Association. The occupational therapy assistant program, also at the Venango campus, was recently granted certification by the American Occupational Therapy Association. The Graduate School offers twelve advanced degree programs. Master's degrees are offered in biology (M.S.), business administration (M.B.A.), communication (M.S.), English (M.A.), library science (M.S.L.S.), nursing (M.S.N.), special education (M.S.), and speech pathology and audiology (M.S.). The Master in Education (M.Ed.) degree is awarded in elementary education, mathematics, reading education, and science education.

The University's total enrollment is approximately 5,900 women and men, including students on the main campus at Clarion, on the Venango campus in Oil City, and on the site at West Penn Hospital in Pittsburgh. Seven residence hall facilities are available for students who wish to live on the main campus. The Clarion campus comprises forty buildings on 127 acres. The Venango campus consists of 64 acres with four buildings.

Clarion University's lifestyle of learning is attractive to many people. The educational experience includes not only academics but also social and cultural growth. Personal interaction allows students to become familiar with diverse backgrounds and helps develop understanding and cooperation in community living. The activities on campus include the Autumn Leaf Festival and Homecoming Weekend, coffeehouses, campus movies, rock concerts, intercollegiate and intramural athletics, music and drama performances by Clarion University students and staff members, clubs, Greek organizations, art exhibits, and special performances by noted orchestras, drama groups, and speakers. More than 125 clubs and organizations serve a wide range of student interests. The University recently opened a $6-million student recreation facility. This facility houses a four-lane indoor track, three multisport courts, a climbing wall, and a weight room.

In 1992, the University opened a new student center with recreational, meeting, and fitness areas for students. The center houses the bookstore, a food court, racquetball courts, an aerobic dance studio, a computer lab, a convenience store, a radio station, and offices for various organizations.

Location

Located high on the Allegheny plateau, Clarion University and the Clarion community have much to offer those who seek a place to study undisturbed by the hectic pace of urban life. The rolling wooded countryside, surrounding mountains, and nearby Cook Forest are popular tourist attractions. The spectacular fall foliage makes the annual Autumn Leaf Festival a major attraction, drawing 100,000 visitors or more each year. The scenic Clarion River and its tributaries offer ideal settings for summer boating, fishing, and other water sports. Excellent opportunities for skiing, hiking, camping, and canoeing also exist. The town of Clarion has a growing population of about 7,500 and offers a host of amenities within a few blocks of campus. The town and the University are just off Interstate 80 and are an easy 2-hour drive from urban centers in Erie and Pittsburgh and an hour drive from Youngstown, Ohio.

Majors and Degrees

Clarion University offers more than seventy baccalaureate degree programs, including the Bachelor of Arts (B.A.), the Bachelor of Science (B.S.), the Bachelor of Science in Business Administration (B.S.B.A.), the Bachelor of Music (B.M.), the Bachelor of Fine Arts (B.F.A.), the Bachelor of Science in Nursing (B.S.N.), and the Bachelor of Science in Education (B.S.Ed.). Undergraduate majors in the College of Arts and Sciences include anthropology, art, biology, chemistry, communication, computer application and information systems, computer science, cooperative engineering, earth science, economics, English, environmental geoscience, French, general studies, geography, geology, history, humanities, library science, mathematics, medical technology, molecular biology/biotechnology, music marketing, natural science, philosophy, physics, political science, psychology, social sciences, sociology, sociology/psychology, Spanish, speech communication, speech communication and theater, and theater. Undergraduate majors in the College of Business Administration include accounting, economics, finance, industrial relations, management, management/library science, marketing, real estate, and sports management. Undergraduate majors in the College of Education and Human Services include early childhood education, elementary education, music education, rehabilitative science, secondary education (with certification available in eleven areas), special education, and speech pathology and audiology. Numerous minors, concentrations, and dual certificate programs are available to enhance the student's academic major. A Bachelor of Science degree in athletic training is now offered in conjunction with California University of Pennsylvania.

The School of Nursing at the Venango campus in Oil City offers both the Associate and the Bachelor of Science in Nursing degrees. Clarion now offers a Bachelor of Science degree in the radiological sciences at the Venango campus. The School of Nursing at the Pittsburgh site (West Penn Hospital) offers the bachelor's degree and a nondegree program in general studies. In addition, the Venango campus offers the Associate of Science (A.S.) degree in business administration (with concentrations in accounting, computer processing, general business management, and office management), in the certified occupational therapy assistant program (COTA), in rehabilitative services, and in legal business studies (legal assistant studies and legal secretary studies). The Associate of Arts (A.A.) degree may also be earned at the Venango campus.

Academic Program

A philosophy of liberal education at Clarion allows students to become intellectually well rounded while specializing in one field. The flexibility of the academic program also enables students to have dual majors if they so desire. In most cases, students must complete 128 credits to earn a bachelor's degree and 64 credits to earn an associate degree, but requirements vary according to the specific program.

An honors program for high-achieving students is offered. In addition to this program, scholastic excellence may also be recognized through awards and admission to honorary societies.

The school year is on a semester basis. Entering students may apply for college credit through Advanced Placement programs, by examination, or by courses taught directly in selected high schools by Clarion University faculty members.

Off-Campus Arrangements

Studies abroad, cooperative education, and internship programs with credit are available for students who want to broaden their educational experience. International studies have given students the opportunity to visit Malta, Costa Rica, France, Spain, and many other countries.

Academic Facilities

A farsighted building program has transformed Clarion into one of the most up-to-date campuses in Pennsylvania. However, many of the older, ivy-covered buildings remain to preserve the historical beauty. Campus facilities include a communications center with a color TV studio, a 1,000-watt FM radio station, a photography darkroom, and a large computer center; a science center with forty-two fully equipped laboratories, a planetarium, a greenhouse, and a weather station; a fine arts center, housing a theater, an auditorium, music practice rooms, art studios, and an art gallery; the business administration building, housing case-study classrooms, a computer center, and an auditorium; two libraries, containing more than 380,000 volumes and more than 1 million other resources; and a physical education complex with swimming and diving pools, a gymnasium-auditorium, racquetball courts, and weight-training and fitness rooms.

Costs

Total expenses for full-time students in the 1999–2000 academic year were $8440 for Pennsylvania residents and $10,250 for out-of-state students. These costs included tuition, fees, room, and meals. Books, transportation, entertainment, and personal expenses cost an estimated $1500 for one academic year.

Financial Aid

Clarion University participates in three campus-based federal aid programs: the Federal Perkins Loan, Federal Work-Study, and Federal Supplemental Educational Opportunity Grant programs. The institution also participates in the Federal Pell Grant and Federal Stafford Student Loan programs. Students who are residents of Pennsylvania are potentially eligible for grants and loans through the Pennsylvania Higher Education Assistance Agency (PHEAA) program. In addition, numerous academic scholarships are available to qualified students attending Clarion University.

All aid applicants must file the Free Application for Federal Student Aid (FAFSA). This form is available in all high school guidance offices and the Clarion University Financial Aid Office. It is from this form that a student's financial need is determined. For further information, applicants should contact the University's financial aid director at 814-393-2315.

Faculty

Over the years, the Clarion faculty has included a number of Fulbright lecture appointees. An educational and cultural profile of the faculty indicates a diversity of backgrounds: members have graduated from colleges and universities throughout the United States and from such international institutions as the Universities of Heidelberg, Baghdad, Leningrad, Paris, and Bombay. The 17:1 student-faculty ratio makes it possible to maintain a learning environment in which there is close interaction between students and faculty members. Members of the counseling staff are always available for academic and personal counseling, and all students may take advantage of the career-counseling program. Clarion University counselors are accredited through the International Association of Counseling Services.

Student Government

The Student Senate at Clarion is a vital and active campus organization. Its members allocate all athletic and activity funds, initiate academic and campus policy, and serve on search committees for faculty and administrative positions.

Admission Requirements

Applicants must show evidence of graduation from an approved secondary school or equivalent preparation. Standardized test results from the SAT I or ACT must be submitted with the application. Clarion University does not discriminate on the basis of race, creed, color, sex, or national origin and is an Equal Opportunity/Affirmative Action employer.

Application and Information

Continuous evaluation is the admission policy at Clarion. Students may apply for early admission, regular admission, or admission under the student development and academic support program. Qualified applicants may receive an acceptance offer one year in advance without being required to respond until the spring of their senior year in high school.

Campus visits are welcome, and appointments should be arranged between 9 a.m. and 4 p.m., Monday through Friday, and on some Saturdays. On-campus visitation days, which parents and prospective students are encouraged to attend, are conducted throughout the year.

Application forms and additional information may be obtained by contacting:

Office of Admissions
Clarion University of Pennsylvania
840 Wood Street
Clarion, Pennsylvania 16214

Telephone: 814-393-2306
           800-672-7171 (toll-free in Pennsylvania)
E-mail: admissions@clarion.edu
World Wide Web:
    http://www.clarion.edu/admiss/admiss.htm
    http://www.petersons.com

Students from more than thirty states and thirty-five countries enjoy the tranquil environment of Clarion's scenic campus.

CLARK ATLANTA UNIVERSITY
ATLANTA, GEORGIA

The University
Clark Atlanta University (CAU), incorporated in 1988, is a private, urban, coeducational, predominantly African-American institution of undergraduate, graduate, and professional education. Clark Atlanta University has inherited the historical missions and achievements of its parent institutions, Atlanta University, founded in 1865, and Clark College, founded in 1869.

As one of only two private, comprehensive, historically black universities in the nation that offer degrees from the bachelor's to the doctorate, CAU enrolls approximately 4,026 undergraduate and 1,178 full-time and part-time graduate students from forty states and fifty countries. The University is one of six institutions that make up the Atlanta University Center, the largest consortium of historically black educational institutions in the country.

Members of the faculty are known for their warm and dedicated spirit. They provide the quality of instruction necessary to ensure that their students become productive, creative, and socially responsible citizens. The family spirit at CAU is enhanced by the many traditions that are celebrated each year on campus, including the induction services for freshmen, the United Negro College Fund Drive, Homecoming, Consolidation Day, and the Spring Arts Festival. There are more than sixty chartered student organizations, special interest clubs, and academic honor societies on campus.

The athletic program at Clark Atlanta University receives the support of students, faculty, staff, and alumni. The University is an NCAA Division II school and is a charter member of the Southern Intercollegiate Athletic Conference (SIAC). Sports include baseball, basketball, football, golf, tennis, and track and field for men and basketball, tennis, track and field, and volleyball for women.

Location
One mile east of the campus lie the mirrored skyscrapers and modern expressways of Atlanta. The World Congress Center, the Civic Center, the Arts Alliance Center (home of the Atlanta Symphony Orchestra and the Atlanta Ballet Company), the Martin Luther King, Jr. Center for Nonviolent Social Change, the Atlanta Stadium (home of the Atlanta Braves baseball team), the Dome (home of the Atlanta Falcons football team), the Jimmy Carter Presidential Library, and outstanding entertainment features, such as Underground Atlanta, Stone Mountain Park, and Six Flags Over Georgia amusement park, mark Atlanta as the capital of the Sun Belt.

Majors and Degrees
Clark Atlanta University is made up of the School of Arts and Sciences and the professional Schools of Business Administration, Education, Library and Information Studies, International Affairs and Development, and Social Work. The University offers undergraduate courses that lead to the Bachelor of Arts degree in twenty-seven majors, as follows: accounting, art, business administration, early childhood education, economics, elementary/middle grades education, engineering, English, fashion design and fashion merchandising, French, general science education, German, history, mass media arts, mathematics, music, music education, office administration, philosophy, physical education, political science, political science education, psychology, religion, sociology, Spanish, and speech communication and theater arts. The Bachelor of Science degree is offered with majors in biology, chemistry, community health education, computer science, health information management, mathematics, and physics. The Bachelor of Social Work degree and a dual-degree program in engineering are also offered. In addition, undergraduate students may participate in special programs in child development and hotel restaurant management.

Academic Program
Clark Atlanta University requires that each student become familiar with the technology of the future. Instructional programs in business administration make extensive use of computers, and business education programs are taught in labs equipped with the latest in office automation devices. A model quantitative skills lab has been established to expand the University's pace-setting instructional support system in mathematics, statistics, and computer science. The Mass Media Arts Department houses one of the most complete broadcast training and production facilities in higher education. Clark Atlanta University students are exposed to real-world experiences through internship and cooperative education assignments with some of the leading local and national corporations and agencies.

The minimum number of semester hours that are required for graduation is 122. The normal load for a full-time student is 15 to 18 credit hours. The minimum load that a student may take to be considered full-time is 12 credit hours. A student may take more than 18 hours only if he or she has a grade point average of 3.25 or above or if the department chairperson approves. Every student must take prescribed core courses in English, general mathematics, computer literacy, literature, and social science, as well as other courses that are included under the general education program.

Army, Naval, and Air Force ROTC programs are available.

Academic Facilities
CAU houses one of the most advanced microcomputer-equipped instructional centers of any university its size. This center is used heavily by students for review study in all of the general education courses at the University. The open-stack library that serves CAU is a cooperative venture of the Atlanta University Center; in addition to volumes, it houses audiovisual aids to study, periodicals, microfilm reader facilities, study carrels, and private study areas. Students in the natural sciences have access to modern laboratories operated by the Science Research Center, another facility operated jointly by the Atlanta University Center members.

Costs
For 1999–2000, tuition was $10,250. Room costs ranged from $3534 to $4596 per year. Board was $2440. The student center fee was $200 per year.

Financial Aid
In order to be considered for financial aid, students must complete the Free Application for Federal Student Aid (FAFSA). This application determines eligibility for federal aid and institutional aid. Georgia residents should complete the Georgia Tuition Equalization Grant (GTEG) and Helping Outstanding Pupils Educationally (HOPE) applications. All out-of-state students should complete their state's application(s) for grants or scholarships available for students who will attend out-of-state postsecondary institutions. The FAFSA may be secured from high school guidance offices. All forms and current

information about financial aid may be secured from the CAU financial office. The financial aid application deadline is April 15.

Faculty

The Clark Atlanta University faculty is characterized by its deep and abiding concern for students and their academic well-being. The faculty is composed of 361 full professors, associate and assistant professors, and instructors. The faculty-student ratio is 1:19, which allows for the maximum interaction between faculty members and students. Faculty members serve as advisers to all of the student-organized groups on campus and generally make themselves available for participation in activities beyond their teaching responsibilities.

Student Government

Elected representatives of the student body serve on the University Trustee Board to ensure that students' interests are voiced in the highest governing body of the University. Student government representatives are elected in the spring of each year by vote of the full student body. The Student Government Association (SGA) traditionally assumes leadership in many matters that contribute to the overall effectiveness and quality of life in the University community. A partnership exists between the SGA and the University administration.

Admission Requirements

Admission is based solely on the qualifications of the applicant and is decided without regard to race, creed or any other considerations irrelevant to scholastic aptitude, academic achievement, and desire to achieve in an academic community. The Admissions Committee considers, among other factors, the high school record, college entrance exam scores, letters of recommendation, and a one-page essay.

Application and Information

Clark Atlanta University admits students on a rolling admission basis. However, applications submitted by March 1 for the fall semester and by October 1 for the spring semester receive priority consideration. A processing fee of $35 must accompany the completed application to Clark Atlanta University. This fee is neither refundable nor transferable to another term regardless of the admission decision. It should be paid by cashier's check or money order made payable to Clark Atlanta University. Before action can be taken on an application, the applicant must submit an official copy of the high school transcript, SAT I or ACT scores, an essay, and two recommendations. Transfer applicants must submit official transcripts from all colleges previously attended and two letters of recommendation.

For more information and an application form, students should contact:

Office of Admissions
Clark Atlanta University
223 James P. Brawley Drive, SW
Atlanta, Georgia 30314-4385

Telephone: 404-880-8784
               800-688-3228 (toll-free)
E-mail: pmeadows@cau.edu
World Wide Web: http://www.cau.edu

Harkness Hall, CAU's main administration building.

CLARKSON COLLEGE
OMAHA, NEBRASKA

The College

Clarkson College is a regionally accredited private institution, with exceptional programs for nursing, radiologic technology and medical imaging, occupational therapy assistant and physical therapist assistant studies, and business. The College offers the personal qualities of a small institution and the technological advantages found within a larger educational environment. Founded in 1888, it was the first school of nursing in Nebraska and the thirty-fifth in the nation and was approved to grant academic degrees in 1984. The baccalaureate and master's programs in nursing and the associate allied health programs have professional accreditation.

The current Clarkson enrollment of 406 students consists of individuals of diverse ages and ethnic and cultural backgrounds. The College's Distance Education programs enroll more than 150 students. Student support resources at the College are exceptional. Professional staff members in the offices of admissions, financial aid, student services, and housing are readily available to assist students. Both faculty and staff members are committed to providing the support services needed to ensure that students grow and learn to the maximum of their abilities. The Clarkson Student Nurses' Association, Clarkson Radiography Student Association, Clarkson Physical Therapist Assistant Student Association, and Student Occupational Therapy Association are organizations for students desiring involvement in preprofessional activities.

The main campus building is a modern six-story structure that houses most of the College's classrooms, administrative offices, skills labs, and the College library. Directly southeast of the main facility is a two-story structure that houses classrooms and science labs to support the general education science curriculum. More than 180 hospitals and clinics in the metropolitan area are utilized as clinical practice sites.

Clarkson College has a graduate program leading to the Master of Science in Nursing, with options in administration, education, and family nurse practitioner studies. Continuing education programs provide opportunities for health-care professionals to develop new skills and knowledge and remain current with the changes in the health-care system.

Location

Clarkson College is located just a few minutes from downtown Omaha in a medical center environment shared by Nebraska Health System. With a population of just over 700,000 in the metropolitan area, Omaha offers a variety of cultural experiences normally associated with a city twice its size. Clarkson students have access to Joslyn Art Museum, Omaha Community Playhouse, dinner theaters, the Omaha Symphony, Opera Omaha, and the performing arts series. The city is home to professional baseball, and hockey teams and is the host of the annual College World Series. Omaha's Henry Doorly Zoo offers the Lied Jungle, the largest indoor rain forest, a 50,000-gallon saltwater aquarium, and an IMAX theater.

Majors and Degrees

Clarkson College awards the Bachelor of Science in Nursing degree; the Associate of Science degree in radiologic technology, physical therapist assistant and occupational therapy assistant studies; and the Bachelor of Science degree in business (with an emphasis in health care) and medical imaging. Nursing graduates are eligible to take the NCLEX-RN for professional registered nurse licensure. Graduates of the two-year radiologic technology, physical therapist assistant, and occupational therapy assistant programs take the certification examination appropriate to their specialization.

Academic Program

The goal of Clarkson College is to prepare individuals to be competent in the technical aspects of their profession and broadly educated in the liberal arts and sciences. The curriculum is supported by courses in the liberal arts and sciences and combines knowledge of course content with the development of intellectual and clinical competencies. Each student's curriculum plan reflects the individual's needs and interest. Although degree requirements remain constant, the scheduling of courses within the curriculum may be individualized. The flexibility of the programs permits full-time or part-time enrollment. The academic year begins with the fall semester in August, is followed by the spring semester in January, and ends with the summer semester.

Candidates for the baccalaureate degree must complete 128 semester hours of course work, including 60 hours of general education and support courses. Advanced placement into the curriculum beyond the beginning of the freshman year is accomplished through transfer of credits or credit by examination and other means. The associate degree program requirements also include a general education component.

In addition to the on-campus program, Clarkson provides distance education opportunities. Students are mailed theoretical course materials in audiotape, videotape, and/or printed formats. Faculty follow-up is by telephone conferencing or by use of the Internet, plus library support via mail. Clinical experience is provided through qualified preceptors in each student's community. Distance education programs are expanding. Students interested in this format should contact the College for more information.

Academic Facilities

The library of Clarkson College, with current holdings of more than 13,750 volumes and 285 periodicals, is designed to support both the technical and general education portions of the curriculum, as well as the continuing education programs. It is an important information center for students, faculty, and staff. Computerized databases and reciprocal agreements with area libraries make access to educational resources virtually limitless. Clarkson's Educational Resource Center is designed to enhance the learning process as an extension of both classroom and clinical instruction. An abundance of information is offered on videocassettes, audiocassettes, CD-ROM, filmstrips, motion pictures, and slide programs. Computer-assisted instruction is an important focus in the center. A large computer lab is dedicated for student use. Students learn basic computer skills and have access to a large library of self-paced learning programs. The modern skills laboratories provide realistic settings for practicing clinical skills in each of the health-care professions.

Costs

In 1999–2000, undergraduate students paid $282 per credit hour plus $17 per credit hour for fees (lab fees vary) and an average of $300 for books. Students residing on campus paid $1400 per semester for apartment-style living (board not included). Students are not required to live on campus, and the surrounding neighborhood offers many affordable living options.

Financial Aid

In 1999–2000, the College awarded financial aid to approximately 85 percent of its undergraduate students. Scholarships, grants, loans, and work-study are available to meet the individual financial needs of students who qualify. Scholarships are awarded to outstanding applicants. Students are required to submit the completed Free Application for Federal Student Aid (FAFSA) or the Renewal Application as well as the Clarkson College Financial Aid Information Form for consideration for all forms of aid.

Faculty

Clarkson College has 37 full-time and 4 part-time faculty members, 27 percent of whom hold doctoral degrees. The administration is committed to maintaining a student-faculty ratio of 11:1. Students receive an extraordinary amount of individual contact with faculty members. Thus, faculty members share the academic experience of their students, helping them adjust to academic life and to the life of the health-care professional. Although primarily a teaching faculty, members are noted for their scholarly activity and involve students in various elements of the development and utilization of research as a vital part of professional practice. Faculty members are nationally recognized and active in their professional organizations.

Student Government

Clarkson Student Government Association is the official student organization. Each student is a member. The purposes of SGA are to serve as a communication channel between students and faculty, to sponsor social activities within the College, and to foster the highest standards of honor and integrity among the student population.

Admission Requirements

Clarkson College accepts men and women who have demonstrated the potential to successfully complete the College's educational objectives, who are motivated to succeed, and who are committed to their chosen profession. Qualified applicants are admitted without regard to race, color, national or ethnic origin, handicap, sex, age, marital status, or religion. Performance in high school college-preparatory subjects, scores on the ACT/SAT I examination, and previous postsecondary course work are the primary criteria considered in the admission evaluation.

Application and Information

The enrollment policy of Clarkson College allows potential students to apply anytime during the year. A completed application form, accompanied by the application fee, an official high school transcript or certification of successful completion of the GED, and ACT or SAT I scores should be submitted when seeking admission. Students with previous postsecondary course work should also submit an official transcript from each institution of higher education attended.

For additional information, students should contact:

Enrollment Services
Clarkson College
101 South 42nd Street
Omaha, Nebraska 68131-2739
Telephone: 402-552-3041
800-647-5500 (toll-free)
E-mail: admiss@clrkcol.crhsnet.edu
World Wide Web: http://www.clarksoncollege.edu

Technological resources at Clarkson College promote quality while making learning more exciting.

CLARKSON UNIVERSITY
POTSDAM, NEW YORK

The University

Clarkson University, founded in 1896, offers professional programs in engineering, science, business, liberal arts, and the health sciences. In 1984, it was granted university status by the New York State Board of Regents, and its name was changed from Clarkson College to Clarkson University. Clarkson's students come predominantly from the northeastern United States but also from other states and a number of other countries. About 27 percent of the 2,581 undergraduates enrolled are women. There is a comprehensive Graduate School with eighteen master's degree and eight doctoral programs. The doctorate is offered in chemistry, chemical engineering, civil and environmental engineering, electrical and computer engineering, engineering science, mathematics, mechanical engineering, and physics.

Many extracurricular activities are available to Clarkson students. Organizations include intercollegiate and intramural athletics, student publications (a newspaper and a yearbook), professional and honorary societies, and such organizations as the outing club, pep band, religious clubs, chess club, amateur radio club, automotive association, and photo, drama, railroad, ski, cycle, bridge, rifle, international, outing, and table tennis clubs. The University's recreational facilities include a field house, with racquetball courts, a new 3,000-square-foot fitness center, and a swimming pool, and a $13-million student center, including a 3,000-seat arena. A new outdoor lodge was completed in fall 1999.

Location

Potsdam, New York (population 10,200), a college community, is located in the St. Lawrence River valley of northern New York. The community is the home of both Clarkson University and the State University of New York College at Potsdam. The village of Potsdam, with a combined student population approaching 7,000, is truly a college town. Students from both institutions attend events on either campus, and many combined social and cultural activities are scheduled during the year. Major international cities, such as Montreal, Quebec, and Ottawa, Ontario, are within a 2-hour drive.

Majors and Degrees

The Bachelor of Science degree is offered in accounting, aeronautical engineering, biology, biomolecular science, business administration, chemical engineering, chemistry, civil and environmental engineering, computer engineering, computer science, economics, electrical engineering, finance, history, humanities, industrial engineering (environmental and occupational health), interdisciplinary environmental science and policy, interdisciplinary software engineering, management information systems, manufacturing management, marketing, mathematics, mechanical engineering, political science, physics, Project Aretè (liberal arts/business), psychology, social sciences, and technical communications (telecommunications option). Choices that allow students to begin a general program and choose their major at a later date include engineering studies, science studies, and university studies. An environmental science and policy major is available within the Bachelor of Professional Studies program. Clarkson offers both an honors program and an accelerated three-year bachelor's degree program. Special advising programs are offered in prelaw, premedicine, and pre–physical therapy, a program in which the University offers a master's degree. Preprofessional programs are available in dentistry, law, medicine, physical therapy, and veterinary sciences.

Academic Program

Programs are quite flexible at Clarkson; one third to one half of a program, depending on the department, is open to electives. There are many opportunities for interdisciplinary study, including double majors and minors. Each student must achieve a cumulative GPA of at least 2.0 to qualify for graduation and must earn at least 120 credit hours.

The curriculum in the interdisciplinary engineering and management program, established in 1954, was the first of its kind to be accredited at any college or university in the United States and is designed to provide a balance of courses in engineering, business, science, and liberal arts. Graduates of this program are well prepared for careers in the marketing of industrial and technical products, purchasing, manufacturing, sales, production supervision, technical writing, and entrepreneurial enterprises.

For students who wish to pursue traditional studies in liberal arts combined with professional studies in business, an interdisciplinary program called Project Arete is offered. This program features special interdisciplinary courses that integrate business and liberal arts, personal development modules, individual assessment and advising, cocurricular cultural and recreational activities, and student involvement in program planning.

Students achieving scores of 3 or better on the College Board's Advanced Placement examinations are considered for advanced placement and credit in virtually all academic areas. Advanced standing is most common in English, mathematics, and science.

Off-Campus Arrangements

The Associated Colleges of the St. Lawrence Valley was chartered in 1970 to facilitate cooperative relationships among four distinct institutions: Clarkson University, St. Lawrence University, the State University of New York College at Potsdam, and the State University of New York College of Technology at Canton. Student-oriented objectives include improved coordination of cultural affairs, interlibrary exchange and cross-registration that allows students to pursue two courses per year at other member colleges at no extra cost.

Academic Facilities

The University's 640-acre wooded campus is the site of forty-three buildings, which comprise 1,160,000 square feet of assignable space. Eighty-five percent of these buildings have been built since 1950. Dedicated exclusively to the instructional programs of the University are more than 324,000 square feet, including 66,000 square feet of traditional classrooms and approximately 216,000 square feet assigned as laboratory areas. In the Center for Advanced Materials Processing (a New York State Center for Advanced Technology), there are seventy state-of-the-art research labs. Other labs and research tools include the multidisciplinary engineering and project laboratory for team-based projects, such as Sunrayce competition, mini-Baja, and Formulae SAE racers; a robotics laboratory; a high-voltage lab; electron microscopy; a Class 10 clean room; a polymer fabrication lab; crystal growth labs; and a structural testing lab. In the School of Science there is a virtual reality laboratory, a molecular design laboratory, a human brain electrophysiology laboratory, and other specialized facilities.

Costs

For 2000–01, tuition is $20,600. Room and board (nineteen meals per week) are $4056 and $3725, respectively. Fees are $400 and books, supplies, travel, and personal expenses vary but may come to approximately $2000.

Financial Aid

More than 90 percent of the student body receive some form of financial aid. This aid includes Clarkson University scholarships; state scholarships and awards; state and federal student loans; industrial, endowed, organizational, and individual scholarships; federal grants; and Federal Work-Study awards. More than half the freshmen receive renewable scholarships or grants directly from Clarkson.

Faculty

A full-time faculty of 153 serves both the undergraduate and graduate programs, thus enhancing the opportunities for interchange of knowledge between faculty members and students at all levels. The percentage of earned doctorates is high, and some departments are staffed completely by Ph.D.'s. Courses are taught by faculty members, while graduate students assist in laboratory and recitation situations. The faculty-student ratio is 1:16.

Student Government

The Student Senate and the Interfraternity Council combine to form the student government at Clarkson University. The former supervises all extracurricular activities (except athletics) and has responsibility for the allocation of student activity funds and for other appropriate business. The latter prescribes standards and rules for fraternities. Students are involved in the formation of University policies through membership, with faculty and staff representatives, on all important committees.

Admission Requirements

A thorough preparation in mathematics, science, and English is very important in the academic qualifications of a candidate for admission. Candidates for entrance to the School of Engineering or the School of Science should have successfully completed secondary school courses in physics and chemistry. All candidates for admission are required to take the SAT I or ACT. SAT II Subject Tests are recommended in Writing, Level I or Level II Mathematics, and either Physics or Chemistry (Physics is preferred). The high school record is the most important factor in an admission decision. International students for whom English is a second language must submit a minimum TOEFL score of 550. Clarkson offers an Intensive English Program (CIEP) for those students who require additional language preparation. Conditional admission is available to students enrolling in the CIEP.

An early decision plan is offered on a "first-choice" basis; this plan does not prohibit the student from making other applications, but it does commit the student to withdraw other applications if accepted at Clarkson. Early admission for students who have completed three years of secondary education is encouraged when the academic record, standardized test scores, and recommendations indicate the student has reached a sufficiently high intellectual and emotional level to perform successfully with other college students.

A personal interview is very helpful to the student in formulating his or her college plans. Interviews on campus should be arranged by letter or telephone at least one week prior to the intended visit. The interview is not required but is strongly recommended, especially for early decision candidates. The admission office is open Monday through Friday, from 9 a.m. to 4 p.m., and Saturday by appointment. The University welcomes visitors to the campus and makes arrangements, as requested, for families to tour and meet with academic and other departments on campus.

Application and Information

Office of Undergraduate Admission
Holcroft House
Clarkson University
P.O. Box 5605
Potsdam, New York 13699-5605
Telephone: 315-268-6479 or 6480
           800-527-6577 (toll-free)
Fax: 315-268-7647
E-mail: admission@clarkson.edu
World Wide Web: http://www.clarkson.edu

Clarkson is a leader in project-based learning, providing students with strong communication skills, leadership ability, and technological skill in their fields.

CLEARY COLLEGE
ANN ARBOR AND HOWELL, MICHIGAN

The College
Cleary College is a private college of business with a 117-year history as an institution of higher education. Cleary College operates from two campuses in Michigan. The Washtenaw Campus, located in Ann Arbor, and the Livingston Campus, located in Howell, feature flexible classroom arrangements and meeting rooms as well as the computer, satellite, and telecommunications technology needed by today's students.

Cleary College enrolls approximately 900 commuter students. Cleary students are focused on business careers and most students work while completing their degrees—either on their own or as part of an internship or degree program requirements. Cleary College emphasizes practical application of business theory and enjoys an excellent reputation among area employers for graduating students who succeed in the workplace.

In addition to the on-campus offerings, Cleary College also offers a one-year bachelor's degree completion program at extension sites throughout southeastern Michigan.

Location
Both the Washtenaw and Livingston Campuses of Cleary College are within a short drive from Detroit and Lansing, Michigan. Southeastern Michigan offers a wide variety of educational, employment, and cultural opportunities. The Washtenaw Campus, located within a short distance from two large state universities, provides students with a variety of cultural events as well as additional educational and research opportunities. The Livingston Campus is located in the fastest growing county in Michigan, creating a vibrant community rich in opportunities. Employment levels in both communities support the cooperative and internship employment needs of Cleary students.

Majors and Degrees
Cleary College offers the four-year Bachelor of Business Administration (B.B.A.) degree in the following majors: business management, corporate accounting, e-commerce, finance, health services management, human resource management, management information technology, marketing, and quality management.

Cleary offers the Associate of Business Administration degree in the following majors: accounting, business applications programmer, general studies, and Microsoft Certified Systems Engineer.

Academic Program
Cleary programs are intended for the serious student who has a clear goal—a career in business—and is motivated to apply energy to reach that goal. Emphasis is placed on providing a learning environment that fosters a mastery of current business theory and technology and the application of these skills to real-life business situations. Cleary strives to graduate students who know exactly what to do in their jobs, have the skills to do it well, and as a result are successful and able to make important contributions to their business organizations and communities.

Cleary's B.B.A. programs are offered in two formats: BusinessTrack and Direct Degree. Students can select the format and schedule to suit their specific needs. Candidates for the B.B.A. degree must earn a minimum of 180 quarter credit hours and complete all requisite courses with an average of two honor points for each quarter of credit. Cleary's B.B.A. programs consist of a set of core courses in the major and electives courses. Required core courses are grouped into four areas: communication core (24 quarter credits); critical thinking core (18 quarter credits); civic preparation core (24 quarter credits); and leadership core (18 quarter credits). Cleary offers nine B.B.A. majors that support individual career interests and goals.

The BusinessTrack format is designed for self-motivated, career-focused individuals with little or no college experience. BusinessTrack is an accelerated Bachelor of Business Administration degree program that can be completed in three years. BusinessTrack is designed to prepare individuals for a responsible leadership position in business and industry. BusinessTrack students learn both the practical applications and conceptual skills required by managers in today's rapidly changing business environment. BusinessTrack combines in-class education with instruction over the Internet. BusinessTrack is offered at Cleary's Livingston Campus.

The Direct Degree B.B.A. format is designed specifically for working adults who are interested in advancing their careers and who are capable of bringing significant professional experience to the academic setting. The Direct Degree is a Bachelor of Business Administration completion program students may enroll in regardless of prior college or work experience. The Direct Degree program offers multiple entry levels (levels 2, 3 and 4) to accommodate applicants based on their unique combination of work experience and prior college experience. The program assesses previous academic work, current business knowledge, and professional and technical skills to allow students to use Cleary College academic credits as the capstone education that completes a degree. The Direct Degree includes instruction over the Internet and individual applied research projects—often work-based—with support from faculty members. Direct Degree is offered at Cleary's Washtenaw and Livingston Campuses and at extension sites throughout southeastern Michigan.

Academic Facilities
The Campus Center on each campus houses the library collection and periodicals and offers full online periodical research services and Internet access. The state-of-the-art computer laboratories at each campus provide for a 10:1 student-computer ratio (among the best in southeastern Michigan) and feature Internet access.

Costs
The 1999–2000 tuition rate was $169 per quarter credit hour. Books were approximately $600.

Financial Aid
More than 60 percent of students receive some form of financial assistance. Cleary College participates in state and federal financial aid programs and accepts the Free Application for Federal Student Aid (FAFSA). Some of the financial aid programs Cleary participates in include: the Federal Pell Grant, Federal SEOG, Federal College Work-Study, Federal Stafford

Loan, and Michigan Tuition Grant. In addition, a number of Cleary College scholarships and grants are available to students.

Faculty

Cleary has 85 faculty members, 11 of whom are full-time. Cleary College believes in extensive use of adjunct faculty (people who teach what they do for a living), bringing a real-world focus into the classroom.

Student Government

Cleary College ensures student participation in the governance of the College through the selection of student representatives to the College Senate. The College Senate is the vehicle to augment the role of students in College decision shaping; to establish a means by which the perspective of students, faculty members, and staff members can be articulated; to promote the health and well-being of the College; and to promote the professional and general well-being of the individual constituents of the College.

The Senate consists of 9 members: the College president, 2 students, 2 faculty members, 2 staff members, and 2 administrators. Other than the president, membership is split equally between the two primary campuses of the College. Extension sites may have an independent student representative based on student enrollment and interest. Student Senators serve for one academic year.

The Senate studies problems and questions brought before it by any constituent and makes specific recommendations to the president. Individual members of the Senate are available to the members of the College and fairly represent concerns and issues brought to them. The Senate holds meetings at least once during each of the fall, winter, and spring quarters.

Admission Requirements

Students entering Cleary College must have a minimum 2.5 grade point average and submit official high school transcripts and all postsecondary institution transcripts.

Admission to the BusinessTrack and Direct Degree programs require a completed application and a $25 application fee, a high school or college transcript that documents a 2.5 (minimum) grade point average, and an Internet account. Applicants for the Direct Degree program must also have a minimum of three years of related work experience. Applicants for both programs must own a computer and control software, configuration, and access.

Students entering at Level 4 must transfer a minimum of 90 credit hours (74 with the bridge term) to the College. Students entering at Level 3 must transfer a minimum of 57 credit hours (41 with the bridge term) to the College. Transfer credits may include other college credits, military, CLEP, or directed training.

Application and Information

Applications are accepted all year and must be submitted with a $25 nonrefundable application fee payable to Cleary College.

It is recommended that applications to the BusinessTrack program be submitted at least six weeks prior to the start of the term. BusinessTrack terms begin in September, January, April, and July.

It is recommended that applications to the Direct Degree program be submitted at least eight weeks prior to the start of the term. Direct Degree terms begin in September, October, January, February, April, May, and July.

Additional information and application materials are available from:

Cleary College Admissions Office
3750 Cleary College Drive
Howell, Michigan 48845

Telephone: 888-5-CLEARY (toll-free)
World Wide Web: http://www.cleary.edu

CLEMSON UNIVERSITY
CLEMSON, SOUTH CAROLINA

The University

With a century of service to South Carolina, Clemson University has become one of the nation's leading land-grant institutions. The enrollment of the University has grown from 446 students when it was established in 1889 to more than 16,000 students in 1999–2000. Approximately 66 percent of the students are residents of South Carolina; 34 percent come from all fifty states and ninety-seven countries. The University's diverse curriculum, combined with its 16:1 student-faculty ratio, means that students may enjoy the wide academic selection and special opportunities of a large institution without sacrificing the personal attention of a small one. The campus is conveniently designed for students to walk to and from their classes, and all campus residence halls and apartments are air conditioned.

In addition to seventy-two areas of graduate study, the University offers seventy-five fields of study in five undergraduate colleges: the Colleges of Agriculture, Forestry, and Life Sciences; Architecture, Arts, and Humanities; Business and Public Affairs; Engineering and Science; and Health, Education, and Human Development. Students may participate in military training through Army and Air Force ROTC programs.

Clemson's academic programs are fully accredited by the Southern Association of Colleges and Schools as well as the Accreditation Board for Engineering and Technology, Inc.; AACSB–The International Association for Management Education; the Computing Sciences Accreditation Board; the National Architectural Accrediting Board; the National Council for Accreditation of Teacher Education; the National League for Nursing Accrediting Commission; and the Society of American Foresters.

Clemson's outstanding men's and women's athletic teams compete at the NCAA Division I level and are part of the Atlantic Coast Conference. The University fields teams in baseball, basketball, crew, cross-country, football, golf, indoor and outdoor track, soccer, swimming, tennis, volleyball, and wrestling.

Location

The University is in Clemson, South Carolina (population 12,000), a friendly college town in the northwestern corner of the state. Clemson is less than an hour's drive from larger Anderson and Greenville in South Carolina and about 2½ hours from the major cities of Charlotte and Atlanta in neighboring states. The 1,400-acre campus is nestled in the foothills of the Blue Ridge Mountains and borders the shores of Lake Hartwell.

Majors and Degrees

The College of Agriculture, Forestry, and Life Sciences offers Bachelor of Science degree programs in agricultural and applied economics, with curricula in agricultural economics and community and rural development; agricultural education; agricultural engineering; agricultural mechanization and business; agronomy; animal industries, with curricula in animal, dairy, and veterinary sciences; aquaculture, fisheries, and wildlife biology; biochemistry; biological sciences; food science; forest resource management; horticulture, with a curriculum in turfgrass; microbiology; and packaging science. The Bachelor of Arts degree is also offered in biological sciences. The college also offers prepharmacy, pre–rehabilitation science, and preprofessional studies.

Students in the College of Architecture, Arts, and Humanities may choose from bachelor's degrees in architecture, construction science and management, English, fine arts, history, landscape architecture, language and international trade, modern languages (French, German, and Spanish), philosophy, and speech and communication studies.

The College of Business and Public Affairs offers Bachelor of Arts degrees in economics, political science, psychology, and sociology. Bachelor of Science degrees are offered in accounting, economics, financial management, graphic communications, industrial management, management, marketing, psychology, and sociology.

The College of Engineering and Science offers the Bachelor of Science degree in agricultural engineering, ceramic engineering, chemical engineering, chemistry, civil engineering, computer engineering, computer information systems, computer science, electrical engineering, geology, industrial engineering, mathematical sciences, mechanical engineering, physics, textile chemistry, textile management, and textile science. Bachelor of Arts degrees are offered in chemistry, computer science, geology, mathematical sciences, and physics.

The College of Health, Education, and Human Development offers the Bachelor of Arts degree in early childhood education, elementary education, secondary education, and special education. The secondary education teaching areas are English, history and geography, mathematics, modern languages (French, German, and Spanish), political science and economics, and psychology and sociology. Bachelor of Science degrees are offered in health science; industrial education; mathematics teaching; nursing; parks, recreation, and tourism management; and science teaching. Teaching areas for industrial education are human resource development, industrial technology education, and vocational-technical education. The teaching areas for science are biological sciences, earth science, and physical sciences.

Clemson awards the Bachelor of Arts or Bachelor of Science degree in preprofessional studies to students who have satisfactorily completed three years of undergraduate work in an appropriate curriculum and the first year of an accredited medical, dental, veterinary, law, or other professional graduate program.

Academic Program

The academic year is divided into two semesters. The fall semester begins in mid-August, the spring semester in early January. Two summer sessions are also available. Students average 16 credit hours per semester. Clemson requires all students to complete 38 hours of general education classes specified by the University before graduation. The number of completed credit hours required for graduation ranges from 127 to 146, depending on the major. Army and Air Force ROTC provides 10 hours of military science or aerospace studies that can be counted toward the baccalaureate degree in any program.

Clemson awards credit by examination through the College Board's Advanced Placement (AP) Program. In 1999, 57 percent of the freshmen submitted AP scores, and more than half of them earned college credit. Credit is awarded for a score of 3, 4, or 5 on an AP examination. Placement and credit may also be earned by taking College Board Subject Tests or locally administered examinations.

Calhoun College, Clemson's honors program, is designed for bright students who thrive on achievement. Admission to Calhoun College for incoming freshmen is by invitation, based primarily on SAT I or ACT scores and the high school academic record.

Academic Facilities

Clemson University's modern laboratories and classrooms are well equipped for instruction, research, and lectures. The academic buildings, student housing, service facilities, and equipment are valued at $350 million. Beyond the main campus, stretching into Oconee, Pickens, and Anderson Counties are 24,000 acres of agricultural and forestry research lands that Clemson owns. Throughout the state, an additional 8,300 acres are devoted to its Agricultural Experiment Station research and 4-H Club activities.

A central feature of the campus is the Robert Muldrow Cooper Library with its large reflection pool. This beautiful structure houses more than 1.4 million volumes as well as 1.7 million equivalent pieces on microforms and other materials. Two college and four departmental libraries house additional books and periodicals in their disciplines, and Clemson students have access to even more information through a computer-based bibliographic network that links more than 11,000 libraries nationwide.

The Division of Computing and Information Technology (DCIT) supports the University's computing activities with an extensive network of computers. Facilities include several public-access labs that contain high-end PC, Macintosh, and printing equipment. All students are automatically assigned a computer ID to access a wide range of computing services, including electronic mail, word processing and spreadsheet software, the Internet and the World Wide Web, and student information services such as registration and financial aid.

Costs

Tuition and fees for the 1999–2000 academic year were $3470 for residents of South Carolina and $9456 for out-of-state students. Charges for room and board were $4130 for both groups of students. These figures, which do not include the cost of books and miscellaneous additional expenses, are subject to change for 2000–01.

Financial Aid

The University annually awards approximately $71 million in financial aid to 11,900 students. Financial assistance includes more than 2,500 scholarships that range from $500 to full tuition and fees for scholastic ability and (in some cases) financial need, part-time employment on and off campus, and Federal Pell Grants, Federal Supplemental Educational Opportunity Grants, Federal Perkins Loans, Federal Work-Study, Federal Stafford Student Loans, and state programs. Applications for federal aid are accepted anytime, but those received by April 1 are given priority. All financial aid is awarded on an annual basis; a new application must be filed each year. Application forms for the upcoming academic year are available in January and may be obtained by writing to the Student Financial Aid Office, G01 Sikes Hall, Box 345123, Clemson University, or via electronic mail (finaid@clemson.edu). Clemson uses the Free Application for Federal Student Aid to determine eligibility for need-based scholarships and programs.

Faculty

Clemson's faculty, which is international in composition, has a reputation for excellence in teaching, research, and scholarship. Collectively, they have authored almost 21,000 articles and papers and 460 books. Of 1,025 faculty members, approximately 84 percent hold doctoral or highest terminal degrees. All students are assigned a faculty adviser in their curriculum to assist them with class scheduling and academic planning.

Among the activities of Clemson's professors outside the classroom are editing professional journals, chairing international conferences and symposia, sitting on boards of professional and curriculum registration, and serving actively in national learned societies. Many are licensed, practicing professionals with years of work experience in their fields, sometimes international in scope (some individuals have been advisers to the United Nations and foreign governments). At home, they are consultants to local, state, and national government agencies and to business, industry, and education.

Student Government

Student government provides services for the general benefit of students. It oversees homecoming activities, coordinates athletic spirit and charitable fund-raising drives, recognizes student organizations, allocates funds to organizations, hears cases involving the violation of regulations, reviews traffic violations, provides special minority representation, and periodically improves its constitution.

Student government also represents student opinion in the University committees on which student leaders sit. The power of student government in administrative affairs is primarily through its recommendations.

Admission Requirements

Admission to Clemson, moderately competitive, is based mainly on an applicant's high school record, class rank, and SAT I or ACT scores. The requirements in any given year are related to the number of applications received. There are no set cutoffs for grades, class standing, or SAT I or ACT scores. Clemson does not require an interview but recommends one for those interested in architecture. Transfer applicants must offer 30 semester (45 quarter) hours from an accredited institution, with a minimum grade point average of 2.5 (on a 4.0 scale). International students must submit satisfactory high school credentials as well as TOEFL and SAT I scores.

Application and Information

General information and application forms, released in late September for the next school year, can be requested from the office of undergraduate admissions. Students should call or write:

Undergraduate Admissions
105 Sikes Hall, Box 345124
Clemson University
Clemson, South Carolina 29634-5124
Telephone: 864-656-2287
Fax: 864-656-2464
E-mail: cuadmissions@clemson.edu
World Wide Web: http://www.clemson.edu/

CLEVELAND INSTITUTE OF ART
CLEVELAND, OHIO

The Institute

The Cleveland Institute of Art was established in 1882. Over the years it has earned a reputation for being one of the finest independent, fully accredited professional undergraduate schools of art in the country. CIA attracts students who are serious in their desire to become professional artists and who seek a campus atmosphere that is at once intellectually stimulating and artistically challenging. The fundamental objective of the Cleveland Institute of Art is to provide a superior education for men and women who seek professional art careers. Its goals for students are consistent with the objectives of the National Association of Schools of Art and Design, of which the Institute is a founding and accredited member. These objectives include the ability to think originally and inventively within the creative possibilities of the artist's media and to achieve excellence in the techniques of the visual arts, increased powers of visual awareness and observation, an enthusiastic dedication to the mission of the artist, comprehension of the society and culture that the artist inherits and his or her responsibility to these, and discernment in the judgment of values, both in art and in life.

CIA is committed to education in a way that ensures continued maintenance of such high ideals. The Institute's particular structure and integrity allow for unusual success in its efforts to realize these goals on a day-to-day basis. First, CIA is a small school—the undergraduate enrollment is about 500—which makes possible maximum contact among students, faculty members, and the administration. Students are in daily contact with and guided by a faculty that is made up of some of the nation's most capable artists and craftsmen. Second, it offers a five-year program of sound fundamentals combined with experimentation that develops a logical progression through the five years. The program is a rigorous one, strong in fundamentals, yet sensitive to individual needs and directions. And third, the five-year program is exceptional in that it provides a satisfactory combination of sufficient academic studies and studio time.

In addition to its bachelor's degrees, the Institute offers the studio courses necessary for a student to earn Case Western Reserve University's master's degree in art education.

Location

The Institute's "campus" consists of the 488 acres of parks and buildings known as University Circle, an educational, civic, and cultural complex located 4 miles east of downtown Cleveland. The Cleveland Museum of Art is directly across the street from CIA, Case Western Reserve University is next door, and the world-famous Cleveland Orchestra performs a block away. Within walking distance and offering a variety of cultural and social experiences are the Cleveland Museum of Natural History, the Greater Cleveland Garden Center, the Western Reserve Historical Society, the Cleveland Institute of Music, and twenty-two other institutions.

Majors and Degrees

The Cleveland Institute of Art offers a five-year program leading to a Bachelor of Fine Arts degree. A major may be chosen from one of fifteen studio areas: ceramics, drawing, enameling, fiber, glass, graphic design, illustration, industrial design, interior design, jewelry and metals, medical illustration, painting, photography, printmaking, and sculpture. The medical illustration program is offered in conjunction with the Case Western Reserve University School of Medicine.

Academic Program

A comprehensive liberal arts program, extending over the five years required for the B.F.A., is an integral part of all study at the Institute. The two-year Foundation Program includes art history and world literature along with accompanying studio work in drawing, painting, design, and freshman basics. The other liberal arts requirements are distributed over the remaining three years, with study available in criticism, creative writing, social studies, multicultural studies, aesthetics, and additional history, art history, and literature courses. In the third year, with the beginning of study in a major art field, the student has increasing opportunities to pursue personal artistic objectives. By the fifth year, studio work is essentially independent in nature, under the guidance of a faculty adviser.

The requirements for graduation are 150–153 credits: 95–106 in studio courses and 47–55 in liberal arts courses. Forty-two to 51 hours in a particular studio area constitute a major; optional minors are 9 hours.

Off-Campus Arrangements

CIA is a member of the Association of Independent Colleges of Art and Design (AICAD), a consortium of the principal private colleges of art and design in the country. One of the goals of AICAD is to offer cooperative programs. Among the activities that enhance the educational opportunities available to students are the Student Mobility Program, in which a student can spend a semester or a year at any of the other member schools.

Academic Facilities

CIA is located in two main buildings. One of these buildings is a large factory-loft-like space called McCullough Center, which provides excellent space and light. McCullough Center, a historic landmark, is a former Ford Model T assembly-line factory, which has been renovated and converted into a studio area. The main buildings contain approximately fifty studios, shops, and technical facilities supporting a full industrial-design complex, a sculpture foundry, ceramics and metalworking, fiber study in weaving and textiles, graphic design with accompanying printing equipment, photography, printmaking, drawing, and painting. There are spaces for glassblowing and papermaking. Computer facilities include four separate labs for beginning to advanced studio work supported by the following hardware: sixteen Silicon Graphics Indigo and Indigo2 workstations, one SGI O2 instructor projection station, twenty-two Macintosh PowerPC 7100 and 7200, 13 Macintosh PowerPC 8100 and 8500, twelve Macintosh PowerPC 6500, ten Macintosh ci/cx, six flatbed scanners, one slide scanning station with a Macintosh Quadra 8500 computer, one Macintosh instructor projection station, three Epson Stylus 3000 printers, five LaserWriter output devices, two Tektronix Phaser 300i, one Phaser 240 printer, three Tecktronix Phaser 140 inkjet printers, nine Kingdom Pentium Pro NT workstations, thirty-seven zip drives, twenty-one Bernoulli drives, two Jazz drives, one CD-ROM writer, and one SVGA VCR. The software available within the labs is constantly being updated; currently running programs include Alias/Wavefront Autostudio v8.5, Alias/Wavefront Studio Paint 3D v4.0, Adobe Photoshop 4.0 and

3.0—for Macs and Silicon Graphics, Adobe Illustrator 7.0 and 5.5—for Macs and Silicon Graphics, Adobe PageMaker 6.5, Fractal Design Painter 3.1, Adobe Premier, Vellum, Rhino, 3D Studio Max, Microsoft Word, Microsoft Office 97, Fractal Design Painter, Macromedia Director, QuarkXpress, Netscape Communicator, and T1 Internet capabilities. Computers are used in most majors; a computerized loom is used in the fiber major.

The Jessica Gund Memorial Library is within the main building and houses 42,000 volumes, 260 periodical subscriptions, a visual reference catalog, an artists' books collection, 2,500 sound recordings, more than 300 video tapes, 85,000 slides, and other audiovisual equipment. There are also two galleries for the extensive exhibition schedule, the Reinberger Gallery and a student-run gallery in McCullough Center.

Costs

Tuition and fees for academic year 2000–01 are $15,250; room and board are $5076. The cost of materials was about $1100. (These costs are subject to change.)

Financial Aid

The Institute participates in all of the federal assistance programs, including the Federal Pell Grant, Federal Work-Study, Federal Supplemental Educational Opportunity Grant, and Federal Perkins Loan programs. In addition, the Institute has its own grant program for new and returning students. Financial assistance is offered to students whenever possible. All aid is granted on the basis of financial need, as demonstrated through the Free Application for Federal Student Aid (FAFSA). A certified copy of the most recent federal tax return (Form 1040) and the Cleveland Institute of Art financial aid form are also required.

Merit scholarships, which currently range from $2000 to full tuition, are awarded in a scholarship competition for high school seniors based on outstanding portfolios and strong academic preparation.

Faculty

The Institute has 75 faculty members, of whom 20 teach in liberal arts and 55 in the studio areas. The latter are all practicing professionals in their respective fields who add the dimension of experience to the classroom.

Student Government

The Student Leadership Council is a volunteer organization composed of first- through fifth-year students and representatives from recognized student organizations. The council plans and coordinates student activities and officially presents the views of students to the faculty and administration. It sponsors the annual Student Independent Exhibition in the Reinberger Gallery. Other sponsored activities include managing display cases to exhibit student work and planning holiday parties, a spring picnic, and one or two trips annually to major cities to visit museums and galleries. All interested students may attend council meetings and are encouraged to serve as representatives. Recognized organizations include Student Leadership Council, Students Arts Association, United Nations Club, Nature and Hiking Club, Community Service Association, Queer Alliance, Student Activities Program Board, and the Student Independent Exhibition Committee.

Admission Requirements

At CIA, admission officers counsel prospective students on an individual basis. If a student wants to attend, the Institute wishes to help; it will also help students find alternatives to this college. Any student who wants assistance is encouraged to get in touch with the admissions office.

Applicants must be high school graduates or must pass the high school equivalency examination. A high school transcript and transcripts of any subsequent college study must be filed in the Admissions Office. ACT or SAT scores are also required. No credentials filed for admission will be released after receipt by CIA. A slide portfolio of at least twelve of the applicant's most recent works must also be submitted for review on one of the specified dates. A personal interview is not an admission requirement, although it is recommended.

Application and Information

Applications for the fall term are accepted until July 1. The scholarship application deadline for the fall term is March 1. Applications for entry into the second semester should be submitted prior to November 15.

For applications, catalogs, and any additional information, students should contact:

Admissions Office
Cleveland Institute of Art
University Circle
11141 East Boulevard
Cleveland, Ohio 44106
Telephone: 216-421-7418
           800-223-4700 (toll-free)
World Wide Web: http://www.cia.edu

Student studios in McCullough Center.

CLEVELAND INSTITUTE OF MUSIC
CLEVELAND, OHIO

The Institute
The mission of the Cleveland Institute of Music is to provide its students with a thoroughly professional, world-class education in instrumental and vocal performance, composition, music theory, and audio technology. Moving forward in the twenty-first century, the Institute continues to challenge students to achieve the ultimate within their potential and to provide an outstanding setting to help prepare them for success.

The Cleveland Institute of Music students are viewed as young professionals. They, together with an outstanding faculty of artists, contribute to the climate of excellence within which artistic growth is nurtured. The faculty and administration are pledged to communicating the greatness and importance of music through performance and teaching and are committed to passing along their knowledge of and love for music and to providing the bridge to an exciting and fulfilling career.

Founded in 1920, the Cleveland Institute of Music maintains its current size of approximately 360 undergraduate and graduate students and 90 full- and part-time faculty members by controlling the enrollment through carefully balanced admission policies, thus ensuring personal, individual attention for each student. In admitting the optimum number of students to each performance area rather than an unlimited number, CIM maximizes the performance experiences of its students so that they are well prepared to meet the challenges of professional life. The achievements of the Cleveland Institute of Music's alumni throughout the world are indicative of the Institute's commitment to high quality and professionalism. The distinguished artist faculty includes the principals and other section players of the Cleveland Orchestra, a neighboring institution with which the Institute has a close relationship. Collegiate-level instruction is conducted by members of the CIM faculty and not by teaching assistants.

About 30 percent of CIM's students are in residence at Cutter House, the Institute's residence hall, which is adjacent to the school's main building. In addition to having the usual amenities, each room is connected to the extensive fiber-optic computer network operated by Case Western Reserve University (CWRU), whose campus borders that of CIM. Since all residents are CIM students, practice is permitted in the rooms of Cutter House. Residence hall accommodations are required for freshmen and sophomores.

In addition to the programs of study listed under the Majors and Degrees section, the Cleveland Institute of Music offers programs leading to the following graduate degrees and diplomas: Master of Music, Doctor of Musical Arts, Artist Diploma, and Professional Studies.

Location
CIM is located in University Circle, a cultural, educational, and scientific enclave situated approximately 3 miles east of downtown Cleveland. University Circle comprises more than thirty institutions that together constitute one of the largest diversified cultural complexes in the world. The complex includes museums, libraries, concert halls, colleges and universities, hospitals, gardens, churches, and temples. Occupying 500 acres in one of the most beautiful areas in the city, the facilities of University Circle offer extensive opportunities for serious study in many fields.

Located within easy walking distance of CIM are Case Western Reserve University, with which CIM cooperates in the Joint Music Program, and Severance Hall, home of the Cleveland Orchestra, whose rehearsals are open to CIM students by special arrangement. Students may also visit the Cleveland Museum of Art and enjoy its world-famous collections as well as its annual concert series, featuring world-renowned performers. Easily accessible to Institute students are numerous other University Circle institutions, such as the Cleveland Institute of Art, the Cleveland Playhouse, the Cleveland Museum of Natural History, the Western Reserve Historical Society, and the Cleveland Botanical Garden.

Majors and Degrees
Students may major in accompanying, audio recording, bassoon, bass trombone, cello, clarinet, composition, double bass, eurhythmics, flute, guitar, harp, harpsichord, horn, oboe, orchestral conducting, organ, piano, Suzuki violin pedagogy, theory, timpani and percussion, trombone, trumpet, tuba, viola, violin, and voice.

Through the Joint Music Program with Case Western Reserve University, five-year double-degree programs are available to CIM students. Of the two degrees earned by students in these programs, the Bachelor of Music is one component. Both B.M./B.A. and B.M./B.S. programs may be structured within music or with the CWRU component in a nonmusic field.

Academic Program
CIM programs offer intensive and comprehensive preparation for professional careers in music. All courses at the school revolve around a core of studies in theory, music history, and literature; the core is designed to provide a thorough musical education. At the undergraduate level, additional educational breadth is provided by required liberal arts courses.

An unusually intense performance environment involves students in a wide repertoire, including solo, chamber, orchestral, and operatic literature.

The development of the disciplines and skills required of a solo performer is an integral part of a student's training at CIM. This training, involving access to faculty and visiting artists who are practicing professionals, is augmented by the many master classes, repertoire classes, and recitals offered annually. A concerto competition is held each semester, and approximately 6 to 8 students are selected for either public performances or readings with orchestra.

The orchestral training programs are designed to develop and maintain the disciplines and skills essential in making the smoothest possible transition from school to professional life. Sectional rehearsals and orchestral repertoire classes are conducted by principals of the Cleveland Orchestra. CIM's two symphony orchestras present approximately twenty concerts during the academic year, including multiple performances of two fully staged operas. The orchestras also provide a vehicle by which students in the Composition Department may hear and record readings of their works.

The sequence of opera courses is devoted to the principles of theory and practice of the various arts that combine to create an operatic performance. Emphasis is placed on vocal, musical, stylistic, linguistic, and dramatic techniques. Study stresses the application of these elements to role preparation for operas of different historical periods.

In 1969, the Cleveland Institute of Music and adjacent Case Western Reserve University established the Joint Music Program, offering study at both the undergraduate and graduate levels. This formal, cooperative plan for degree study by music students enrolled at either institution was the result of many years of collaboration between the two schools. While CIM concentrates on the education and training of professionals skilled in the arts of performance, composition, and related musical disciplines, CWRU pursues and develops studies in the fields of music history, musicology, and music education. Each school remains independent while working cooperatively on a mutually shared campus. CIM and CWRU take pride in this endeavor, which makes available to all students the resources of both a professional music school and a large university.

CIM operates on a two-semester calendar, with fall examinations preceding the Christmas holiday recess.

Academic Facilities

The CIM Library contains approximately 48,000 books and scores and 114 periodical subscriptions. The audiovisual facilities contain a sound-recording collection of 19,500 items, including CDs, LPs, audiocassettes and videocassettes, reel-to-reel tapes, laser discs, and CD-ROMs. In addition, the library provides interlibrary loan service, enabling the faculty and students to borrow materials from libraries nationwide.

Through the Joint Music Program with Case Western Reserve University, CIM students have access to the extensive resources of the CWRU libraries, especially those of the Kulas Music Library. The holdings of the CWRU libraries include approximately 1.3 million volumes, 1.9 million microforms, and 7,400 current serial subscriptions. A shared online system with Case Western Reserve University permits the viewing of CWRU library holdings from online public catalogs in the CIM library. Through CIM's relationship with CWRU, there is access to OhioLink, a statewide information network.

The CIM main building, erected in 1961, includes classrooms, teaching studios, practice rooms, the CIM Library, an orchestra library, a specially designed eurhythmics studio, an opera workshop and studio, and a music store. Through connection of the entire CIM facility to Case Western Reserve University's fiber-optic computer network, CWRUnet, CIM provides a Technology Learning Center that enables students to become aware of and accustomed to the ways in which music and technology go hand in hand. In addition, there are two concert and recital halls. Kulas Hall, the concert auditorium, houses three Steinway concert grand pianos and a Holtkamp three-manual tracker organ. Le Pavillon contains a recital hall with two Steinway grand pianos, additional classrooms, the electronic music studios, a meeting room, and a performers' lounge. All studios and practice rooms are equipped with Steinway grand pianos; there are two in every piano teaching studio. There are two Dowd French double harpsichords after Taskin, a Russell double-manual harpsichord after Blanchet, several concert harps, and comprehensive percussion equipment. Adjacent to CIM's main building is the Hazel Road Annex, an additional facility for chamber music, class recitals, individual practice, master classes, and rehearsal and coaching.

Costs

A comprehensive catalog, including information on costs as well as other areas of vital interest, is available upon request.

Financial Aid

The Cleveland Institute of Music offers outstanding professional training for talented musicians. While such training can be costly, CIM provides many forms of financial assistance, including scholarships, fellowships, work-study awards, and loans. Awards are available to full-time students and are based upon both musical capability and financial need. Entrance auditions as well as financial need serve as the basis for determining the eligibility of new students. More than 90 percent of CIM students receive some form of financial assistance.

All applicants must submit a CIM Financial Aid Application, the Free Application for Federal Student Aid (FAFSA), and the Financial Aid PROFILE of the College Scholarship Service (CSS). The CIM code number for the CSS is 1124. Further information is available by contacting the Institute's director of financial aid.

Faculty

The distinguished faculty of performers, composers, and teachers, headed by CIM President David Cerone, includes more than 30 members of the renowned Cleveland Orchestra and many other outstanding musicians. All liberal arts course offerings are taught by members of the faculty of Case Western Reserve University.

Student Government

The Student Forum is the representative government organization of the student body. Members are elected annually by the students. The organization carries on an active dialogue with the administration and addresses the daily and long-term needs of currently enrolled students.

Admission Requirements

Acceptance for study at the Cleveland Institute of Music is determined by musical talent and achievement and academic performance. The Institute expects applicants to have achieved a sufficient musical and academic background demonstrating their potential for successful completion of the intended course of study. Audition appointments are scheduled through the Admission Office upon receipt of the application. Candidates are required to submit two letters of recommendation from appropriate musically qualified individuals as well as all appropriate academic transcripts. Freshman applicants who are U.S. citizens or permanent residents must also submit scores on either the SAT I or American College Testing's ACT Assessment. International applicants for whom English is a second language must submit scores on the Test of English as a Foreign Language (TOEFL) or Michigan English Language Assessment Battery (MELAB).

CIM does not discriminate on the basis of race, color, national or ethnic origin, citizenship, religion, age, sex, sexual orientation, or disability in its admission and scholarship policies, in the educational programs or activities it operates, or in employment.

Application and Information

The application deadline is December 1. Appointments for entrance auditions and required admission examinations are scheduled by the Admission Office upon receipt of the application. There is an application fee of $70.

Director of Admission
Cleveland Institute of Music
11021 East Boulevard
Cleveland, Ohio 44106-1705

Telephone: 216-795-3107
E-mail: cimadmission@po.cwru.edu
World Wide Web: http://www.cim.edu/conserv/admissions

CIM production of Mozart's *Magic Flute*.

COE COLLEGE
CEDAR RAPIDS, IOWA

The College

Coe College is a private, coeducational, liberal arts college that specializes in turning good students into accomplished writers, scientists, musicians, ecologists, artists, bankers, and businesspeople. An unusual sequence of activities, including a required term of practical experience, leads students step-by-step through their four-year program. Ninety-eight percent of Coe graduates are either working or in graduate school within six months of graduation.

The College's 1,200 students enter Coe with an average ACT score of 25 and an average GPA of 3.4; more than 40 percent graduate from Coe with two majors. Students represent thirty-four states and more than eighteen countries; 45 percent come from Iowa, 31 percent from other Midwestern states, 6 percent from abroad, and the remainder from across the U.S.

All students live on campus in one of five residence halls, which offer both single-sex and coed-by-floor options. The halls contain computer labs, vending machines, debit-card laundry facilities, kitchens, and television lounges. Roughly 35 percent of all students, including first-year students, bring cars to campus.

The list of active student clubs at any given time numbers sixty; interests range from literary to activist to social. Twenty-one percent of students belong to one of four national fraternities and three national sororities; nearly three quarters take part in intramural sports.

A member of the Iowa Conference, Coe competes at the NCAA Division III level in men's baseball, basketball, cross-country, diving, football, golf, soccer, swimming, tennis, track, and wrestling and in women's basketball, cross-country, diving, golf, soccer, softball, swimming, tennis, track, and volleyball. Coe's intercollegiate athletes have brought home eleven conference trophies (seven men's trophies, four women's) in the last ten years. Intercollegiate and intramural athletes alike make year-round use of the K. Raymond Clark Racquet Center, which houses four racquetball courts, two squash courts, four indoor and six outdoor tennis courts, a 200-meter indoor track, and weight and exercise rooms. Coe also has an eight-lane, Olympic-size swimming pool with a movable bulkhead and a diving area.

Location

Cedar Rapids, nestled in the rolling hills of eastern Iowa, is a safe and hospitable town of 175,000 people. A relaxed place to live in, the city is within a 5-hour drive of Chicago, Kansas City, Milwaukee, Minneapolis, Omaha, and St. Louis. The Eastern Iowa Airport, a regional airport served by six major airlines, is located in Cedar Rapids. The city offers a major museum of art, a nationally recognized symphony orchestra, and a strong community theater as well as malls, movie theaters, and dance clubs. Iowa City, just 25 minutes by car from campus, is a favorite destination for students in search of shopping, foreign films, and roving poets.

Iowa has the highest literacy rate in the country and attracts more out-of-state college students than all but three other states.

Majors and Degrees

Coe awards the Bachelor of Arts, Bachelor of Science in Nursing, and Bachelor of Music degrees. Majors include accounting, African-American studies, American studies, art, Asian studies, athletic training, biochemistry, biology, business administration, chemistry, classical studies, computer science, economics, education, English, environmental science, French, French studies, gender studies, general science, German, German studies, history, literature, mathematics, molecular biology, music, nursing, philosophy, physical education, physics, political science, pre-architecture, predentistry, pre-engineering, prelaw, premedicine, psychology, public relations, religion, sociology, Spanish, Spanish studies, speech, and theater arts. Students may combine courses from two or more academic areas to create an interdisciplinary concentration.

Student teachers may earn certification in art, elementary, music, physical, and secondary education.

Academic Program

Coe's academic program couples the timelessness of the classics with the immediacy of hands-on learning. In addition to a major, students must complete the first-year seminar, two courses in the natural sciences, two in the social sciences, three courses in Western culture, and three in international culture.

Students must also take part in a series of activities strategically designed to define and focus their career plans. New students begin by building a personal Web page that ultimately serves as an electronic portfolio and includes a resume, writing samples, and a record of their course work that can be accessed by employers and graduate schools worldwide.

Students must also complete 10 hours of community service, attend issue dinners, and take part in career planning seminars. The sequence culminates with a practical experience requirement, which can be satisfied through an internship, research, practicum, or participation in one of Coe's many study-abroad options. An optional Leadership and Service Program, open by application, gives selected students advanced leadership training.

Coe follows a 4-1-4 calendar; students take four courses in the fall, four in the spring, and one course during the month of January.

Off-Campus Arrangements

Coe's location in Cedar Rapids is a big benefit for students who opt to satisfy the practical experience requirement through an internship. Law firms, television stations, marketing agencies, art galleries, accounting firms, and major software and telecommunications companies are all just a few minutes from campus. St. Luke's Medical Laboratories is located across the street from campus. Students may also easily secure internships in Chicago, New York, Washington, D.C., or virtually any other major city in the country.

Those students who choose to study abroad have an equally wide selection. Coe students may earn credit for living and studying in Western and Eastern Europe, Asia, Africa, and Latin America.

Students of the natural and social sciences often satisfy Coe's practical experience requirement through research supervised by a Ph.D. faculty member. Recent topics have included the physical properties of glass compounds (physics), a comparative analysis of trees and grasses in decreasing the fertilizer runoff from farm fields (environmental science), and how EEG patterns differ between highly creative and normal people during problem solving (psychology).

Academic Facilities

Stewart Memorial Library gives students access to two commercial online services and dozens of microcomputers in addition to nearly 200,000 books and bound journals and 883 periodicals, microfilm, and audiovisual materials. The library offers comfortable seating for more than 600, with well-lit group study tables, individual study desks, and conference rooms. The College's $4-million art collection, including works by Grant Wood and Marvin Cone, is displayed in the library galleries.

Coe's $3-million campuswide fiber-optic network connects students and professors with each other and the wider world via the Internet. Residence hall rooms are equipped with one network port for each student, giving students round-the-clock network access. In addition to 150 computers available around campus for general use, Coe offers special computer labs for students of music, teacher education, business, and life and physical sciences. Two general-use labs are open 24 hours a day.

Open 70 hours a week, the Coe Writing Center offers free coffee, computer disks, and advice on everything from grammar to writing style. It is staffed by student tutors who provide help on writing assignments that range from first-year English to senior honors papers.

Dows Fine Arts Center features a 300-seat theater with computerized light boards and a computer-aided design system; spacious fine arts studios for ceramics, painting, drawing, photography, printmaking, sculpture, fabric design, and graphic design; and a well-equipped computer graphics lab with animation capabilities.

In the Peterson Hall of Science, students have hands-on access to a laser with doubling and quadrupling crystals, liquid and gas chromatographs, a UV-visible spectrophotometer, a nuclear quadrupole resonance spectrometer, a Fourier transform infrared spectrometer, and global positioning system (GPS) equipment.

Costs

The costs for 2000–01 are $23,615, including $18,240 for tuition, $5200 for room and board, and $175 for activity fees. Annual miscellaneous costs—books, transportation, and personal expenses—typically range from $1000 to $1500.

Financial Aid

Coe awards renewable merit-based scholarships to students with strong records of accomplishment in academics, fine arts, foreign language, science, writing, and community service.

The average financial aid package offered to incoming students for fall 2000 totals nearly $17,000. To apply for aid, students must submit the Free Application for Federal Student Aid (FAFSA). Iowa residents should submit their forms before March 1 to qualify for the Iowa Tuition Grant. To request an early estimate form, interested students should call 319-399-8540.

Faculty

Coe's 85 full-time and 58 part-time faculty members teach classes with an average size of 16 students. Ninety-two percent hold the highest degree available in their field; all are committed to the students they teach. The student-faculty ratio is 12:1.

Student Government

The student body is governed by the Student Senate, whose members and officers are elected annually by students. In addition to planning campus activities and special events, the Student Senate appoints 2 students to serve as voting members of faculty committees. These committees deal with academic policies, admission and financial aid, athletics, public events, off-campus study, and the library.

Admission Requirements

Coe seeks dynamic students from across the country and around the world who can demonstrate strong academic achievement, intellectual curiosity, extracurricular participation, and community involvement. Coe requires a minimum 3.0 GPA (on a 4.0 scale), either an ACT score of 20 or a combined SAT score of 1000, and a ranking among the top 40 percent of the student's high school class for regular admission. While not required, an on-campus interview is strongly recommended.

Application and Information

In addition to a completed application, interested students should submit official SAT I or ACT results, an official high school transcript, a guidance counselor's recommendation, and a personal essay. For notification by January 6, students should submit all materials by December 15. For notification by March 15, the deadline is March 1. Coe requires a nonrefundable $150 deposit to secure a place in the entering class.

Interested students may attend one of Coe's high school visits, college days, and off-campus receptions or come for one of many visit programs and scholarship competitions. Both students and their parents are invited to contact:

Dennis Trotter
Vice President for Admission and Financial Aid
Office of Admission
Coe College
1220 First Avenue, NE
Cedar Rapids, Iowa 52402
Telephone: 319-399-8500
        877-CALL-COE (toll-free)
Fax: 319-399-8816
E-mail: admission@coe.edu
World Wide Web: http://www.coe.edu

This senior art major satisfied Coe's practical experience requirement with three internships, all in New York City: one at the Leo Castelli Gallery, another with a printmaker, and the third at a senior center on the city's Upper West Side.

COGSWELL POLYTECHNICAL COLLEGE
SUNNYVALE, CALIFORNIA

The College
Cogswell Polytechnical College is dedicated to providing students with a superior education in engineering and the visual arts. Engineering theory combined with practical skills enables graduates to begin work immediately in their chosen areas of engineering and the visual arts.

Established in San Francisco in 1887 as a private, independent institution, Cogswell has developed new programs over the years to meet the emerging needs of technology industries. In 1985, the College moved from San Francisco to Cupertino. In 1994, the College moved to a permanent campus in Sunnyvale to be in proximity to the many technology companies located there. The College operates a day and evening class schedule, enabling students already working to complete their degree requirements. The student body of 400 brings together men and women of diverse ages, nationalities, and backgrounds who share a strong career orientation, a desire to make things function as designed, and a willingness to work together to achieve goals. Faculty members work closely with all students, enabling them to learn both the concepts and skills needed in technology. The independent study program for fire service professionals, Open Learning for the Fire Service, currently has 125 registered students.

Membership is available in clubs that are the student affiliates of the Institute of Electrical and Electronics Engineers (IEEE) and the Audio Engineering Society (AES).

Cogswell College is accredited by the Senior Commission of the Western Association of Schools and Colleges.

Location
Sunnyvale, California, is in the Santa Clara Valley, at the south end of San Francisco Bay. Near the city of San Jose and 40 minutes south of San Francisco, the area offers students many cultural and recreational opportunities. Commonly referred to as Silicon Valley because of the high concentration of technology companies in the area, this location makes it easy for students to be a part of developments in engineering, technology, and digital art.

Majors and Degrees
Cogswell College offers three degree programs with each degree program containing specific concentrations. The Bachelor of Science degree in electrical engineering has concentrations in computer, electrical, mechanical, and music engineering. The Bachelor of Science degree in software engineering has concentrations in computer, electrical, graphics, music, and software engineering. The Bachelor of Arts degree in computer and video imaging offers concentrations in character animation, digital art, digital film, electronic media, entrepreneurship, game design and production, and interactive media.

Cogswell also offers the Open Learning for the Fire Service program to students in California, Arizona, and Nevada. Through correspondence courses administered by the College, fire service personnel may earn a Bachelor of Science degree in fire administration or in fire prevention/technology.

Academic Program
Cogswell College has a trimester system, and the courses of study are carefully designed to provide a student with the theory and practical skills needed in technology industries. Students begin taking courses in their chosen area from the first trimester they enroll. General studies and communication courses round out each year and place technology in its human context.

In keeping with Cogswell's practical approach to education, a senior project is required. Students originate an idea and then design, build, and demonstrate it for faculty members and other students.

The Bachelor of Science in software engineering requires 130 credits. The Bachelor of Science in electrical engineering degree requires 127 credits. The Bachelor of Arts in computer and video imaging requires 124 credits.

Off-Campus Arrangements
The College works with local industries to place students in employment positions appropriate to their major field of study. Many students graduate with actual working experience, and all Cogswell students graduate with the academic preparation necessary for immediate employment and advancement in their careers.

Academic Facilities
Cogswell has four technology laboratories, a UNIX lab, and two computer labs. The College also has a MIDI lab, three audio recording studios, and one sound design lab. The imaging facilities include a PC modeling and animation lab, a PC 2D imaging lab and PC video and integrated media lab, an SGI advanced modeling and animation lab, two illustration labs, an experimental animation lab, a drawing studio, and a PC Internet access and advanced computer applications lab.

Cogswell's library of 12,000 volumes includes the most up-to-date publications in the engineering and imaging fields. The library also subscribes to more than 125 periodicals in the technological sciences as well as in general subject areas.

Costs
Full-time tuition for the 2000–01 academic year is $4200 per trimester for U.S. citizens, residents, and international students. Part-time students pay $350 per credit and may take up to 11 credits. The estimated cost of books and supplies is $600 per year.

Cogswell is a nonresidential campus. Students have a range of housing options around Sunnyvale and in the Greater Bay Area. Cogswell offers dormitory-style housing in commercial apartments under a corporate leasing plan. Students share a two-bedroom, two-bath apartment. Arrangements are made through the College Housing Officer. Costs average $600 per month, including basic furniture and utilities.

Financial Aid
To enable students from diverse economic backgrounds to attend Cogswell, the Financial Aid Office helps students put together an aid package based on their need. In addition to federal and state loans and grants, qualified students may also receive aid from the Cogswell College Scholarship fund and many private scholarships unique to Cogswell. The College has jobs available on campus for work-study students. All programs are approved for veterans' training.

The state of California grants (Cal Grants) have an application deadline of March 2 for the following academic year. All other aid may be requested throughout the year.

For more information or to set up an appointment to discuss particular needs, students should contact the Financial Aid Office.

Faculty

The 16 full-time and 50 part-time faculty members are highly qualified in their fields and continue to be involved with business and industry. The student-faculty ratio of 12:1 fosters a personalized learning experience. Faculty members serve as student advisers and are eager to assist students in achieving their educational goals. The close working relationships among faculty, staff, and students encourage professional preparation in an environment of mutual respect.

Student Government

The Associated Student Body of Cogswell College is the general student membership organization. It gives students the opportunity to plan and direct their own programs, become involved with various aspects of College life, and influence decisions affecting the quality of education and student life at Cogswell.

Admission Requirements

Engineering students may apply for admission at any time during the year. High school students may apply after completion of their junior year. Students applying for the Bachelor of Arts in computer and video imaging have these specific application deadlines: fall trimester, June 1; spring trimester, November 1; and summer trimester, March 1. Final acceptance is given when the official transcript confirms graduation and the completion of final semester grades.

Transfer students are asked to have official transcripts sent directly to the College. These are evaluated individually, on a course-by-course basis. Students from accredited two-year schools may transfer a maximum of 70 semester units; those from four-year schools may transfer a maximum of 94 semester units.

Computer and video imaging students are required to submit a portfolio. Interested students should contact the College for portfolio submission guidelines.

Application and Information

For additional information and an application for admission, students should contact:

Admissions Office
Cogswell Polytechnical College
1175 Bordeaux Drive
Sunnyvale, California 94089-1299
Telephone: 408-541-0100
              800-264-7955 (toll-free)
E-mail: admin@cogswell.edu
World Wide Web: http://www.cogswell.edu

New students...new sign...new campus.

COKER COLLEGE
HARTSVILLE, SOUTH CAROLINA

The College

Founded in 1908, Coker College is a small, private, liberal arts college. Coker enrolled 945 students in 1998–99. The student-faculty ratio is 10:1. Classes are small—no class has more than 20 students. Small class size provides students with opportunities to experience a variety of teaching techniques, although a seminar-style approach, called the Round Table, is the method preferred by the faculty. This instruction is an exchange between students and their senior scholar that takes place at large round tables. The professor's insight, probing questions, and comments guide students on an active journey in the learning process as conclusions are drawn through their powers of reasoning. Throughout its history, Coker College has been a close-knit educational community dedicated to enriching students' lives and expanding their opportunities. The liberal arts curriculum exposes students to the major branches of study and builds their skills of communication, critical thinking, reasoning, and research. Coker is a community in which each person is known and valued and the resulting involvement in academic and campus life creates close and lasting friendships. Personal attention and community spirit have been emphasized since Coker's founding.

The Coker tradition of involvement, individuality, and choice is reflected in the wide variety of extracurricular activities. All Coker students are members of the Student Government Association (SGA), the umbrella organization for all recognized student groups on campus. Student events are scheduled frequently. Among them are dance presentations, theater productions, art shows, musical events, lecture series, student dances, and parties. The intramural program involves nearly every student in traditional and other diverse activities, such as chess, crew, volleyball, and water polo. The College clubhouse, a favorite spot for student canoeing and sunbathing, is located on a 15-acre tract bordering a nearby lake. Intercollegiate athletic teams are fielded in baseball, basketball, cross-country, golf, soccer, and tennis for men and basketball, cross-country, soccer, softball, tennis, and volleyball for women.

The Coker College campus is a traditional, tree-lined Southern campus with stately white-columned residence halls and Georgian brick buildings. All rooms in the residence halls are Internet ready, and in addition to activity lounges, the campus has an after-hours social club.

Coker has recently been recognized as one of the 300 best buys in the nation by *Barron's* and its Round Table teaching style as a model learning experience by *Smart Parents Guide to College*.

Coker has been accredited by the Southern Association of Colleges and Schools since 1922 and its music program by the National Association of Schools of Music since 1942.

Location

Hartsville, an All-American City and a prosperous community of about 28,000, is located in northeastern South Carolina. Air and rail services are available less than 30 minutes away in Florence, where Interstates 95 and 20 intersect. The famous Grand Strand beaches, Columbia (the state capital), and Charlotte, North Carolina, are about 90 minutes away. The mountains are a 3-hour drive.

Majors and Degrees

Coker College offers bachelor's degrees in twenty-nine majors and eighteen minors. The Bachelor of Arts degree is offered in art (with concentrations in fine arts, graphic design, and photography), art education, biology, biology education, chemistry, chemistry education, communication, dance, early childhood education, elementary education, English (concentration in professional writing available), English education, French, history, math education, mathematics, music (with concentrations in organ, piano, and voice), musical theater, political science, psychology (with an option in counseling), religion, sociology (with concentrations in criminology and social work), Spanish, and theater. The Bachelor of Science degree is offered in business administration, medical technology, and physical education (exercise science, physical fitness programming, sports communication, sports management, and teacher education). The Bachelor of Music Education is also awarded.

Multicultural programs are available in African-American and Spanish-American studies.

Preprofessional programs are available in chiropractic, dentistry, divinity, law, medicine, and pharmacy.

Academic Program

Candidates for the bachelor's degree must complete 120 semester hours of study and maintain a minimum 2.0 grade point average. To ensure a broad liberal arts background, the College requires students to complete the following minimum semester-hour requirements: 10 in the natural/physical sciences and mathematics, 9 in the humanities, 6 in nonnative language, 6 in oral and written rhetoric, 6 in the creative and performing arts, 6 in behavioral and social science, and 3 in physical education. In addition, 29–44 semester hours of electives and 30–45 semester hours of major courses are required. Placement exams in English and math are mandatory for all freshmen and recommended for transfer students. The final 30 semester hours must be taken in residence at Coker.

Coker's calendar consists of two 15-week semesters, one 2-week January interim session, and one 5-week summer school session. Coker's program stresses personalized learning. Independent study, special-topics courses, off-campus internships, and career development services are also available. Study abroad is available every semester.

Academic Facilities

Davidson Hall is listed on the National Register of Historic Places. This renovated facility contains faculty offices, classrooms equipped with round tables, and the Charles W. Coker Auditorium. The auditorium is renowned for its design and high-quality acoustics. The Gladys Coker Fort Art Building compares favorably with fine arts facilities at much larger colleges and universities. The state-of-the-art Elizabeth Boatwright Coker Performing Arts Center features two theaters, dance studios, a television studio, audio and video editing suites, and rehearsal and recording studios. The Margaret Coker Lawton Music Building includes a recital hall and practice rooms. The Timberlake-Lawton Physical Education Building includes a heated pool, a weight room, and a gymnasium. The recently renovated William Chambers Coker Science Building houses much equipment rarely available at the undergraduate level, including an NMR. The student computer center is housed here as well. In addition to the 15-acre main campus, Coker has 22 acres of athletic fields, a 30-acre botanical garden and preserve, and a 15-acre park at Prestwood Lake, which includes a boathouse with canoes and sailboats for student use.

Costs

The 1999–2000 comprehensive fee for boarding students was $19,072, which included tuition ($14,352), room ($2670), board ($2050), general fees ($200 for day students only), and the medical fee ($35). The comprehensive fee for nonboarding students was $14,352.

Financial Aid

Coker College endeavors to assist in meeting the financial need of all accepted students through scholarships, grants, loans, work-study opportunities, or a combination of these. Nearly 90 percent of the students receive some financial assistance each year. Forms of financial assistance include competitive academic scholarships, athletic grants, and the College's own need-based financial aid. In addition, a variety of federal and state grants, scholarships, and loans are available. An early estimation service is provided for families whose student has completed the eleventh grade. This service provides the family with an estimate of the financial aid they may expect based upon academic and financial criteria. The Free Application for Federal Student Aid is required of all financial aid applicants. For further information about financial aid, students should contact the Coker Financial Aid Office.

Faculty

Faculty members practice the Coker philosophy of individualized advising and instruction. They are also committed to their particular disciplines. The 10:1 student-faculty ratio enables faculty members to know each student personally. Nearly 85 percent of the faculty hold the highest degree in their field. Only faculty members teach at Coker; there are no teaching assistants.

Student Government

All students are members of the SGA, which offers students leadership opportunities and has a strong voice in all decisions affecting campus life. Students assume responsibilities by serving as residence advisers and directors within the residence halls. Two students serve as members of the Board of Trustees; 1 student is a voting member.

Admission Requirements

Coker College is selective in accepting applicants for admission and seeks students who are well prepared for the demands of college-level work. While several factors are considered in the selection process, success in a challenging college-preparatory curriculum is the primary factor considered. The majority of admitted applicants have completed the following high school courses: four years of college-preparatory English; three years of mathematics that include algebra I, geometry, and algebra II; three years of science that include biology and chemistry with a lab; three years of a foreign language; and three years of social sciences.

Application and Information

An application is reviewed after all required documents have been received. The required documents are as follows: a completed application and the application fee, high school transcripts with end-of-junior-year grades, SAT I or ACT scores, and a recommendation from a high school guidance counselor or principal. Applicants receive an admissions decision approximately three weeks after his or her application is complete.

All prospective students are encouraged to visit the campus and an interview is strongly recommended. Arrangements may be made by calling the Office of Admissions.

Application forms and additional information may be requested from:

Office of Admissions
Coker College
Hartsville, South Carolina 29550
Telephone: 843-383-8050
           800-950-1908 (toll-free)
Fax: 843-383-8056
E-mail: admissions@coker.edu
World Wide Web: http://www.coker.edu

Coker College's size allows students to make and keep lifelong friends.

COLBY COLLEGE
WATERVILLE, MAINE

The College

Colby College is one of America's outstanding liberal arts colleges. Colby expects its students to become knowledgeable across a broad range of subjects, and its educational program also teaches students to learn, preparing them to ask and answer the questions of the future. Students at Colby learn the facts, but they also formulate questions, do research, evaluate ideas, and present and defend their own conclusions. Critical thinking, articulating ideas orally and in writing, developing a capacity for independent work, and exercising the imagination through involvement in the creative process leads the list of Colby's educational precepts. Colby's liberal arts education takes place in a closely knit residential community where the student-faculty ratio is 11:1. Colby enrolls 1,750 students with a diverse range of backgrounds, experiences, and interests. Current students represent forty-six American states and territories, and fifty-two countries. Nearly all students live on campus in College-owned residence halls grouped into three residential commons, each with its own dining hall and student governing board. Cotter Union, with its warm, inviting atmosphere and superb facilities, anchors the social life of the campus and attracts students to an exciting array of exciting and stimulating all-campus events. The Pugh Center, a wing of the Cotter Union, houses a kosher kitchen and meeting rooms for the eleven campus groups that address issues of diversity. Colby is in the fourth year of a $44-million project to renovate all its existing residence hall and dining facilities, and a new apartment complex for members of the senior class opened in fall 1999.

Colby's location in a small Maine city encourages the development of a strong program of activities and events on campus and in the surrounding community. More than ninety campus organizations attract students and faculty members. The most popular include community service organizations, the Outing Club, the drama society, the student newspaper, instrumental and choral music groups, the International Club, and the FM radio station. A lively mixture of cultural opportunities is offered on the campus. On most days, at least two or three events compete for attention, including lectures, films, concerts, poetry readings, dance performances, exhibits, and plays.

The Harold Alfond Athletic Center, one of the largest and most modern facilities in New England, has a field house with an indoor track, an Olympic-size swimming pool, an ice arena, a gymnasium, a fitness center, an aerobics studio, and squash and tennis courts. It is surrounded by 50 acres of playing fields, cross-country skiing and running trails, outdoor tennis courts, and an all-weather outdoor track. There are fifteen varsity teams for men, sixteen for women, one coed team. Besides the varsity teams, there are eleven club sports and many individual and intramural sports opportunities. The winter season invites snowshoeing, tobogganing, skating, cross-country skiing on 8 kilometers of groomed campus trails, and downhill skiing at nearby Sugarloaf/USA.

Location

Colby is located in Waterville, an extended community of more than 40,000 people, which is a service and retail trade center for nearly 20 percent of Maine's population. While the College offers a rich blend of activities on campus, its proximity to wilderness mountains, inland lakes, and the Maine seacoast allows students to enjoy a great variety of outdoor activities. Hiking, skiing, white-water canoeing, and sailing are but a few of the recreational activities available within an hour's drive. The 714-acre campus, ranked as one of the nation's most beautiful, is a state wildlife preserve with a 128-acre arboretum and bird sanctuary, a pond, fields, woods, and meadows. Set on Mayflower Hill, it overlooks Waterville and the Kennebec River valley. The quality of life is enhances by the location, which provides a delightful background for combining serious study, extracurricular activities, and recreation.

Majors and Degrees

Colby offers the Bachelor of Arts degree in anthropology, art, biology, chemistry, classical civilization, classics, computer science, economics, English, French literature, French studies, geology, German studies, government, history, mathematics, music, performing arts, philosophy, physics, psychology, religious studies, sociology, and Spanish. Combined majors of art–art history, art-studio art, biology–cell and molecular biology/biochemistry, biology–environmental science, chemistry-biochemistry, chemistry-cell and molecular biology/biochemistry, chemistry–environmental science, classical civilization–anthropology, classical civilization–English, classics-English, economics–financial markets, economics-mathematics, geology-biology, geology–earth science, geology–environmental science, mathematics–mathematical sciences, and philosophy-mathematics are also offered. Students may also choose from a variety of interdisciplinary majors, such as African-American/American studies, American studies, East Asian studies, environmental studies, international studies, Latin American studies, Russian language and culture, and women's studies. Secondary school teacher certification may be obtained through an interdisciplinary program, and individually designed majors are available. Dual-degree engineering programs exist with Dartmouth College, Case Western Reserve University, and the University of Rochester.

Minors are available in twenty-nine fields of study, including administrative science, Chinese, creative writing, education, human development, indigenous peoples of the Americas, Japanese, and science, technology, society.

Academic Program

The academic program is characterized by a commitment to the liberal arts as the best preparation for both lifelong education and specialized or professional training. Graduation requirements ensure that students are exposed to the breadth of human knowledge through electives and area requirements that include 4 credit hours of English composition and literature, a basic knowledge of one foreign language, 6–8 credit hours in the natural sciences, and a minimum of 5 credit hours in each of the following areas: arts, historical studies, literature, quantitative reasoning, and the social sciences. A wellness requirement must be fulfilled by attending eight wellness lectures.

A minimum of 128 semester credit hours is required for graduation, and at least 113 of these must be earned in conventionally graded academic courses. The remaining 15 may be earned in courses taken pass/fail or through approved noncurricular field experience. Three January Terms, including one during the first year, are also required.

Off-Campus Arrangements

Almost two thirds of Colby's students take advantage of off-campus study opportunities during a January Term, a semester, or an entire academic year. Many choose to participate in one of Colby's own programs in Ireland, France, England, Spain, and Russia. These programs are staffed by Colby faculty members and include intensive language training and social, cultural, historical, and/or theater studies, depending on the program. Others students, advised by the Off-Campus Study Office, select one- or two-semester non-Colby programs or study independently in countries throughout the world. Students may also choose among 3 one-semester programs run cooperatively by Colby, Bates, and Bowdoin in London, Cape Town (South Africa), and Quito (Equador).

Many Colby students opt for off-campus domestic programs such as the Washington Semester, Sea Semester, or the Williams College–Mystic Seaport Program in American Maritime Studies. Others elect exchange programs with Howard University in Washington, D.C., or the Claremont Colleges—Pomona, Pitzer, Claremont McKenna, or Scripps—in California.

Academic Facilities

Miller Library's open-stack system provides direct access to more than 925,000 books, microtexts, and other items; in addition, Colby subscribes to more than 2,400 magazines, journals, and newspapers. As part of the Interlibrary Loan program, students can obtain information from libraries and other sources across the nation and beyond. Facilities include a computerized catalog system, audiovisual center, archives, classrooms and offices, 24-hour computer room, study space for more than half the student body, and several extensive special collections, including the Healy Collection of Irish Literary Renaissance, the Edwin Arlington Robinson writings and memorabilia, and an important collection of Thomas Hardy's works. The library makes a number of resources available through the College's World Wide Web site. An electronic-research classroom, opeing in 2000, will have twenty-six computers for teaching students how to make the best use of electronic information resources for research and how to evaluate the reliability of data.

The Bixler Art and Music Center features Maine's largest art museum with an outstanding permanent collection of American painting and sculpture; studios for painting, printing, design, and wood and metal sculpture; an art and music library; music practice rooms; and a 350-seat auditorium. The library has advanced interactive listening stations where students can do research using thousands of recordings in Colby's collection.

The Center for Performing Arts offers students practical theater experience. The 274-seat Strider Theater has an open stage with orchestra pit, scene and costume shops, and sound and lighting booths. The center includes a fully equipped dance studio and the Cellar Theater for improvisational workshops.

Science facilities, located in four interconnected buildings, include teaching and research laboratories, a suite of environmentally controlled animal rooms, and exhibit space. Colby has sophisticated equipment, including electron microscopes, Silicon Graphics workstations, and nuclear magnetic resonance (NMR) spectrometers—all available to students beginning in the freshman year. Students work on research alongside professors and design research projects of their own to pursue upper-level classes or independently.

Colby's Olin Science Center, completed in 1996, includes a 10,800-square-foot science library; a state-of-the-art case study classroom equipped with audiovisual and electronic technology; computer-equipped classrooms; teaching labs for field biology, environmental science, plant biology, and organismal biology; a research greenhouse; labs for collaborative student-faculty research; and group study areas.

At Colby, computers for student use are found in clusters and specialized teaching labs throughout the campus. The campus network and Internet access are ubiquitous, connecting every classroom, dorm room, office, and laboratory. Residence halls are connected via high-speed Ethernet. An extensive software library is available in the Computer Center, and the Information Technology Services staff members assist students with applications appropriate to each discipline. There are no fees for using any of these services.

Costs

For the 1999–2000 academic year, the comprehensive fee was $31,580. Personal expenses, books, and supplies average $1350 annually.

Financial Aid

Colby awards financial aid on the basis of need. About 70 percent of the students receive some form of financial aid; about 38 percent receive grant aid from the College's own funds. An average award includes a grant, a loan, and on-campus employment.

Faculty

Colby has 164 full- and part-time faculty members whose commitment to teaching is shown through their willingness to work with students beyond the classroom. The student-faculty ratio is 11:1, and the median class size is 17. Ninety-nine percent of the faculty members hold doctorates or final degrees in their fields, and many have national or international reputations in their disciplines. Many students work with faculty members on research projects and write or coauthor papers based on their research. A faculty-in-residence program provides housing for several faculty families in campus residence halls, and there is a faculty-associates program for the other residence halls that fosters involvement in campus life.

Student Government

In the conduct of student affairs, Colby's trustees have delegated extensive autonomy to the students through the Student Government Association (SGA) and the residential Commons system. At the same time, the administration and faculty members are known for being concerned when students individually or collectively need support. The SGA deals with academic, cultural, and residential affairs and receives a grant from the College to support more than ninety clubs and organizations. It sponsors concerts, lectures, movies, dances, and theater performances. The Student Judiciary Board has jurisdiction over most incidents that call for possible disciplinary action against an undergraduate. Students serve on almost all of the College's advisory committees, and 2 students serve as nonvoting representatives to the Board of Trustees.

Admission Requirements

Colby seeks applicants from diverse geographical, racial, and economic backgrounds who have special qualities or talents to contribute to the College. Admission is highly selective, and evaluations are made on the basis of academic achievement and ability and interest and excitement in learning, character, and maturity. The quality of a candidate's preparation is judged by his or her academic record, references from school authorities, and College Board or ACT test scores. A minimum of 16 academic preparatory credits is recommended, including 4 years of English, at least 3 years of a foreign language, 3 years of college-preparatory mathematics, 2 years of a laboratory science, and 2 years of history or social science.

Colby offers the options of early entrance and early decision. Advanced standing may be established by examination, taken either through the department or through the Advanced Placement Program of the College Board, the International Baccalaureate, or other standard tests. Some transfer students with established records are considered for admission each year. Students who do not require financial aid are welcome to apply for admission as visiting students at Colby for one semester only.

All applicants are encouraged to visit the campus for interviews, tours, classes, meals, and, if possible, an overnight stay in the residence halls.

Application and Information

Applications for regular admission must be submitted by January 15. Those wishing to be considered for early decision may choose either the fall or winter option. Fall option applicants must complete the application process by November 15; winter option applicants, by January 1. For applications and admission forms, students should contact:

Admissions and Financial Aid Office
Colby College
Lunder House
4800 Mayflower Hill
Waterville, Maine 04901-8848
Telephone: 207-872-3168
              800-723-3032 (toll-free)
Fax: 207-872-3474
E-mail: admissions@colby.edu
World Wide Web: http://www.colby.edu/

COLBY–SAWYER COLLEGE
NEW LONDON, NEW HAMPSHIRE

The College

Colby-Sawyer College, a coeducational, residential, undergraduate college founded in 1837, evolved from the New England academy tradition and has been engaged in higher education since 1928. The College provides programs of study that innovatively integrate the liberal arts and sciences with professional preparation. Through all of its programs, the College encourages students of varied backgrounds and abilities to realize their full intellectual and personal potential so they may gain understanding about themselves, others, and the major forces shaping our rapidly changing and pluralistic world. At present, students come from all over the United States and seven other countries, with 68 percent of the students coming from outside of New Hampshire. Within the last five years, an apartment-style and a suite-style residence hall have been built to accommodate the College's steady growth in enrollment.

Student athletic involvement occurs at the varsity, club, intramural, and recreational levels. There are eight varsity sports for women (NCAA Division III basketball, lacrosse, soccer, tennis, track and field, and volleyball; ECSC Alpine ski racing; and IHSA riding) and seven for men (NCAA Division III baseball, basketball, soccer, tennis, and track and field; ECSC Alpine ski racing; and IHSA riding). Athletic successes include reserve national champion in riding in 1998; a nationally ranked men's basketball team that competed in the ECAC Championships in three of the last four years, winning in 1998; and conference championships for men's soccer in 1997 and men's baseball in 1998, women's tennis in 1995 and 1996, and women's basketball in 1997, 1998, and 1999. The women's basketball team also made NCAA tournament appearances in 1997, 1998, and 1999. The Alpine ski racing team has participated in USCA National Championships and sent one individual on to NCAA Division I Championships in 1998. The Colby-Sawyer Chargers compete as a member of the Commonwealth Coast Conference.

The College is accredited by the New England Association of Schools and Colleges, and professional programs also carry the appropriate accreditations. Colby-Sawyer has consistently received recognition as one of the top colleges in its category.

Location

Colby-Sawyer's 190-acre campus is located on the crest of a hill in New London, New Hampshire. Its beautifully maintained grounds and stately Georgian architecture create a picturesque and safe environment that is conducive to learning. The College is located in the heart of the Dartmouth–Lake Sunapee region, a four-season recreational and cultural community known for the natural beauty of its lakes and mountains. Boston is only 1½ hours south and Montreal is 3½ hours north. Students have access to major cities by College van or public bus. The nearby seacoast at Portsmouth and the surrounding lakes, mountains, and state parks provide opportunities for biking, camping, canoeing, golf, hiking, ice skating, Nordic and Alpine skiing, swimming, and tennis. Arts and cultural opportunities can be found in New London as well as in nearby Concord, the state capital, and Hanover, the home of Dartmouth College.

Majors and Degrees

Colby-Sawyer offers bachelor's degrees in many fields. The Bachelor of Arts degree is awarded in art; biology; communication studies; English; history, society, and culture; and psychology. The Bachelor of Fine Arts degree is awarded in art and graphic design. The Bachelor of Science degree is awarded in business administration, child development, community and environmental studies, exercise and sport sciences (specializations offered in athletic training, exercise science, and sport management), and nursing. Teacher certification can be earned in art education (K–12), early childhood education (K–3), and biology, English, or social studies secondary education (7–12). Highly motivated, academically strong students may receive approval to design their own interdisciplinary major program of study. An associate degree can be earned in the liberal arts and sciences.

Academic Program

Colby-Sawyer College faculty and staff are excellent at working with students who are undecided on a major and are highly qualified to help students explore their values, talents, and academic and career interests. At Colby-Sawyer College, it is believed that knowledge and experience nurture each other. Therefore, the combination of classroom learning and professional experience is an integral part of each student's education. Through a carefully crafted program offered by the Harrington Center for Career Development, all students are encouraged throughout their four years of study to continue to clarify their interests and goals and to gain practical experiences through student employment, internships, and voluntary service to the community.

Internships are a key element in career development. Colby-Sawyer has an impressive roster of internship opportunities available, and through the internship experience, students often receive their first offer of a permanent position. During the internship, students have an opportunity to work directly with professionals in their field of study while developing valuable contacts who can serve as references and career mentors. Organizations that have recently accepted Colby-Sawyer interns include Merrill Lynch, Continental Cable, Beth Israel Hospital, Blue Cross/Blue Shield, Harvard University Athletic Department, the Buffalo Bisons, the Currier Gallery of Art, the Basketball Hall of Fame, the Olympic Regional Development Authority, Channel 7 (Boston), the Appalachian Mountain Club, and CNN.

Off-Campus Arrangements

Colby-Sawyer encourages students to study abroad for a semester or a year. The study-abroad adviser works closely with students to select an experience and a school best suited to their individual needs and interests. Students have studied in England, Australia, Spain, France, Italy, Ireland, Scotland, and Switzerland.

Colby-Sawyer's membership in the twelve-college New Hampshire College and University Council (NHCUC) allows students to enroll in other NHCUC institutions for a course or for an entire semester.

Academic Facilities

The Susan Colgate Cleveland Library/Learning Center contains 76,295 volumes, 1,023 periodicals, and 189,983 microforms. Access to these materials is provided by a Dynix automated catalog system and by online and CD-ROM databases for periodical research. The library is housed in a unique five-level structure constructed from two pre–Civil War dairy barns masterfully transformed into a warm and inviting facility that has won regional and national architectural awards. The library/learning center also houses a curriculum lab, an audiovisual room, fourteen PC workstations for Internet and library database access, and a networked computer classroom with twenty-five PCs and interactive multimedia teaching equipment with CD-ROM capability. Interlibrary loan service provides access to an extensive array of library holdings throughout New England and the nation.

The magnificent 63,000-square-foot Dan and Kathleen Hogan Sports Center was designed to meet the athletic and recreational needs of Colby-Sawyer College students and members of the local community. This sports center contains a large field house with three multipurpose courts; a suspended walking/jogging track; a six-lane, competition-size swimming pool; and a fitness center furnished with equipment such as StairMasters, Body Master stations, treadmills, rowing ergometers, Nordic cross-country skiing tracks, a Universal gym, stationary bicycles, and a complete selection of free weights. The Hogan Center also houses the Sports Medicine Clinic, which is fully equipped with the latest technology to support the Exercise and Sport Sciences Program.

The Academic Development Center at James House provides comprehensive academic support services for all students, including honors students. The staff consists of faculty members, learning specialists, and student academic counselors who work with students to strengthen their writing, math, and research skills, as well as their study skills, such as time management, note-taking, and exam preparation. Colby-Sawyer's English Language and American Culture Program provides support for international students and others whose first language is not English. Among the services available to students with diagnosed learning differences are classroom modifications, personal counseling, and professional as well as peer tutoring.

The nursing program features a Nursing and Health Laboratory containing resources that simulate clinical practice settings. Students also have access to a computer laboratory with software that helps to prepare them for clinical experiences. The nursing program is enriched by its relationship with Concord, Alice Peck Day, and New London Hospitals, as well as with Dartmouth Hitchcock Medical Center, one of the most well equipped and technologically advanced teaching hospitals in North America.

The Colby-Sawyer campus computing array includes a campus network with Internet access and five computer laboratory/classrooms and six mobile multimedia teaching stations, which provide computer graphics, audio, and video capabilities employing the latest CD-ROM technology. Computing facilities are equipped with the latest Microsoft Windows applications and laser printers for student use. The College now has a 10:1 student-computer ratio.

The Frances Lockwood Bailey Graphic Design Studios are the center of the graphic design facilities. These studios are equipped with computers loaded with the latest versions of graphic design software programs and desktop publishing capability. Students create graphic images while working with digital scanning and optical character recognition, still video photography, and VCR, video camera, and CD-ROM images. Advanced student projects are sent to professional imaging centers to create high-resolution hard copy.

Costs

Tuition, room, and board for 2000–01 are $26,200. In addition to this comprehensive fee, which includes the cost of all student services, there is a $150 technology fee. Approximately $1500 should be allowed for books, supplies, personal expenses, and travel, depending on where students live.

Financial Aid

Through its Financial Aid Program, Colby-Sawyer encourages the attendance of students from a variety of ethnic and cultural backgrounds, economic levels, and geographic regions. Seventy-three percent of the students currently receive some form of financial assistance, and Colby-Sawyer provides more than $4.3 million a year in grant assistance to its students. Both need-based and merit awards are available, including merit awards for outstanding academic achievement or student leadership. Merit awards are also available for students with special talents in art, music, or creative writing and for those students who have been significantly involved in community service. Applicants who wish to be considered for merit awards must be accepted for admission by February 1. Each applicant for need-based aid must submit the Free Application for Federal Student Aid (FAFSA) and the Colby-Sawyer Application for Financial Aid. Priority will be given to students whose completed forms are received before the March 1 deadline. A modest amount of financial assistance is available for international students.

Faculty

Colby-Sawyer has a distinguished faculty and staff dedicated to undergraduate teaching, and a personalized education is ensured by a 12:1 student-faculty ratio and average class size of 18. At Colby-Sawyer, senior faculty members teach first-year students as well as students in the upper classes.

Student Government

The Student Government Association (SGA) is structured to provide considerable interaction among students, faculty members, and staff, and the SGA allocates the resources that fund a multitude of involvement and leadership opportunities outside the classroom. Campus activities include the Campus Activities Board, Dance Club, Alpha Chi Honor Society, yearbook, AIDS/HIV Educators Group, radio station (WSCS 90.9 FM), Drama Club, Admissions Key Association, Art Students League, Student Nurses Association, Environmental Action Committee, *The Courier* (student newspaper), community service, and numerous clubs and intramural teams.

Admission Requirements

The College requires prospective students to present at least 15 units of college-preparatory work. This would usually include 4 years of English, 3 years of mathematics, 2 or more years of social studies, 2 years of a foreign language, and 2 courses in a laboratory science.

While an admissions interview is not required, every applicant is strongly encouraged to visit Colby-Sawyer for a tour and interview. Interviews often play an important part in the final admissions decision.

Application and Information

Colby-Sawyer receives and considers applications throughout the year. Beginning in December, applications are reviewed as soon as they become complete, and candidates are notified as soon as the admissions decision is finalized. A completed application includes a transcript of the candidate's high school work (including first-quarter grades for the senior year), SAT I or ACT scores, two letters of recommendation (one from a teacher and one from a guidance professional), a personal statement, and a $40 nonrefundable application fee. Application forms and additional information may be obtained by contacting:

Office of Admissions
Colby-Sawyer College
100 Main Street
New London, New Hampshire 03257
Telephone: 603-526-3700
        800-272-1015 (toll-free)
Fax: 603-526-3452
E-mail: csadmiss@colby-sawyer.edu
World Wide Web: http://www.colby-sawyer.edu

COLLEGE MISERICORDIA
DALLAS, PENNSYLVANIA

The College

College Misericordia is celebrating its seventy-fifth anniversary as a high-quality liberal arts and professional studies institution. Founded by the Sisters of Mercy of Dallas, Misericordia offers undergraduate and graduate programs to resident and commuter students. Current enrollment is about 1,650 men and women; about half the students range in age from 18 to 22 years old.

Misericordia provides an academic atmosphere designed to stimulate critical thinking, independent judgment, and creativity as well as encouraging the development of curiosity, good study habits, and personal values. The College also cultivates a spirit of community service and a lifelong love of learning in its students through extracurricular activities and challenging academic programs.

The College is fully accredited by the Middle States Association of Colleges and Schools. Its programs in nursing, social work, radiography, occupational therapy, and physical therapy are accredited by the National League for Nursing Accrediting Commission, the Council on Social Work Education, the American Medical Association, the American Occupational Therapy Association, and the American Physical Therapy Association, respectively.

Misericordia operates three residential facilities and eighteen townhouse units with a total capacity for 650 students. Residents have a number of options, including single rooms and wellness housing, and students living in campus housing hold average GPAs of more than 3.2. Each residence hall offers study rooms, laundry facilities, and recreational lounges. The dining hall is located in the Banks Student Center, which also houses the Cougar's Den coffeehouse and snack bar.

There are numerous opportunities for students to become involved in campus activities. Besides Student Government, there are more than twenty-five chartered student clubs and organizations. Cultural events, Campus Ministry, intramural and intercollegiate athletic programs for men and women, performing arts shows, and many other social activities complement and reinforce the academic experience. In keeping with the College's tradition of mercy, justice, service, and hospitality, students also have opportunities to develop leadership potential through a variety of volunteer service projects that benefit the surrounding communities.

Campus Ministry provides opportunities to participate in campus and community programs. These programs are designed to promote social awareness in students. On spring break, students may elect to serve the poor in rural Appalachia or in the South Bronx. A six-week summer Cross-Cultural Ministry Experience in Guyana, South America, awaits selected participants.

Personalized attention is the key to the support available in the Learning Resource Center. A psychologist, counselors, therapists, and peer counselors form a dedicated team of professionals who conduct workshops for students each semester on a variety of topics, including test anxiety, stress management, time management, and goal setting. All services are free of charge to students, and contacts are strictly confidential.

First-year students may join the Guaranteed Placement Program through the Insalaco Center for Career Development. The program includes academic standards; cocurricular activities, such as leadership and service projects; internships; resume development; and interviewing skills. If a student fulfills the requirements of the program and is not employed in his or her field or enrolled in graduate or professional school within six months of graduation, a paid internship is assured. The center also co-presents the Choice Program, offering special guidance for students who have not chosen a major. Opportunities for career exploration, cooperative education, and internships are available for students to develop the knowledge and skills they need to enter the working world.

Student Health Services occupies a state-of-the-art facility. Healthcare staff members provide first aid, assessment and treatment of common illnesses, and referrals for more serious health conditions. Health center activities are directed by a registered nurse with a master's degree in nursing administration under the guidance of a physician. A nurse practitioner is also available. A self-care room offers reference materials and up-to-date information on personal health concerns. All services are confidential.

A rapidly evolving world and development of new technologies have increased the number of adults who seek higher education. Misericordia offers special undergraduate and graduate programs for adults, including the Expressway Program, an accelerated bachelor's degree program that is held at Luzerne County Community College; Women with Children, which provides on-campus housing and support services for single women with children; and evening and weekend formats that work for people with families and full-time jobs.

At College Misericordia, students can earn a master's degree by attending college classes in the evening and/or on weekends. The small-class format enhances critical thinking and decision-making skills and draws out a variety of viewpoints that help broaden the perspectives of the student. Master's degrees are available in education, nursing, and organizational management.

Location

Located on a 100-acre campus in northeastern Pennsylvania, College Misericordia is the oldest institution of higher education in Luzerne County. Expansive lawns and thick stands of trees dominate the campus. It is 9 miles from the city of Wilkes-Barre. The area provides shopping centers, malls, cinemas, sporting events, and a variety of cultural activities. Pennsylvania's largest natural lake and two state parks are nearby, as are Pocono ski resorts. Metropolitan New York and Philadelphia are each within a 3-hour drive. Public transportation is available to and from the campus.

Majors and Degrees

College Misericordia awards the Bachelor of Arts (B.A.) degree in English, history, and liberal studies. The Bachelor of Science (B.S.) degree is awarded in accounting, biochemistry, biology, business administration, chemistry, communications, computer science, elementary education, general studies, liberal studies, management information systems, mathematics, math/computer science, medical imaging, medical technology, philosophy, psychology, secondary education, special education, and sports management. A Bachelor of Science in Nursing (B.S.N.) is awarded to nursing majors, and a Bachelor of Science in Social Work (B.S.W.) is awarded to social work majors. Specializations in accounting, early childhood education and special education, management, marketing, and pre-law and preprofessional occupations are also available. Certification programs include addictions counseling, child welfare services, gerontology, and secondary education and may be taken in support of several degrees offered by Misericordia or as stand-alone programs.

The College offers three 5-year majors in physical therapy, occupational therapy, and speech and language therapy. Students graduate with an entry-level master's degree in physical therapy or occupational therapy and a bachelor's degree in health sciences.

Academic Program

Candidates for the B.A., B.S., B.S.N., or B.S.W. must fulfill a 48-credit liberal arts core curriculum in addition to the requirements of their chosen major to graduate. They must earn at least 36 credit hours in a chosen field. For regularly enrolled students, the average requirement for a baccalaureate degree is a total of 126 credits. Other options open to students include minors, specializations, certifications, and electives.

Courses are offered on a semester basis, beginning in August and January and ending in December and May. Summer, weekend, and accelerated courses are also available.

Academic Facilities

The chemistry, physics, and biology departments all have modern, fully equipped research laboratories available to students in these fields of concentration. State-of-the-art equipment includes high-performance liquid chromatography (HPLC), a rotary evaporator, an infrared spectrophotometer, and gas chromatography. The College also houses an energized radiation laboratory for the medical imaging program. The $5.5-million Anderson Sports and Health Center provides classrooms and laboratories for the occupational therapy, physical therapy, and nursing programs.

College Misericordia maintains one computer for every 22 students. There are four computer laboratories, which offer all students access to e-mail and the World Wide Web. Besides Windows 98 and Microsoft Office Suite, SPSS and programming languages that include Assembler, VISUAL BASIC, C++, Cobol, Java, Proloo, and Pascal are in use; academic departments (including nursing, occupational therapy, physical therapy, biology, chemistry, mathematics, computer science, business, and political science) have software to meet their own specific needs. The Mary Kintz Bevevino Library and the Banks Student Center have more than 150 ports where students can plug in their laptops and access the Internet.

The three-story Mary Kintz Bevevino Library, dedicated in fall 1999, covers 37,500 square feet and houses stacks for 90,000 volumes. Materials include state-of-the-art information and communication technology and a reference section that offers books, serials, and a variety of periodicals as well as reference search tools, CD-ROMs, and an electronic database and microfilm.

Costs

Tuition for 2000–01 is $15,190 per year. The general fee is $760. The instructional technology fee (for full-time students) is $60. Housing options include traditional rooms, suites, town houses, and wellness housing. The average room cost is $3540. All resident students must participate in a meal plan. All freshmen must participate in a nineteen-meal plan. Upperclass residents may choose from a ten-, fourteen-, or nineteen-meal plan. In addition, town-house residents are eligible to choose a five-meal plan. The average board cost is $2930.

Financial Aid

All first-time students applying for financial aid must complete the Free Application for Federal Student Aid (FAFSA) by May 1. This application is used for Federal Pell Grants, Federal Supplemental Educational Opportunity Grants (FSEOG), Subsidized and Unsubsidized Stafford Loans, Perkins Loans, nursing loans, and Work-Study. This application is also used as the basis upon which state and institutional aid is awarded. The College also offers a no-interest monthly payment plan. In addition, many scholarships are available for qualified students, including $400,000 in honors scholarships based on academic abilities and $100,000 in McAuley Awards for freshmen who have experience in leadership roles and volunteer service.

Faculty

There are approximately 161 teaching faculty members, 84 of whom are full-time. A student-faculty ratio of 14:1 results in students receiving a great deal of individual attention from a highly qualified faculty. Fifty-five percent of the faculty members hold doctorates. Besides student academic advising, the faculty members also serve as advisers to clubs.

Student Government

An active student government organization serves as a liaison between the students and the faculty and staff. The administration enables students to become involved by serving as student representatives on various college committees.

Admission Requirements

College Misericordia admits applicants based on their secondary school record, high school recommendation, extracurricular activities, and personal promise. The College requires SAT I or ACT scores. Although a personal interview is highly recommended, it is not necessary for all majors. Misericordia offers both early decision and early admissions programs.

Transfer students with a cumulative average of at least 2.0 (on a 4.0 scale) may be considered for admission and may receive advanced standing. Some majors require a 2.5 or higher cumulative average. Transfer students must submit official high school transcripts. A transcript of work completed at other colleges and universities and proof of honorable dismissal are also required.

Application and Information

Applicants must submit an official application form (available upon request), transcripts, and SAT I or ACT scores. Applicants may also apply for admission on line at the Web address listed below. There is a nonrefundable application fee of $25, which is waived for students who visit the campus.

The College considers applications on a rolling basis, except for the physical therapy program. The deadline for physical therapy applications is February 1. Usually, candidates are notified of the admission decision within three weeks of receipt of all required materials.

Office of Admissions
College Misericordia
301 Lake Street
Dallas, Pennsylvania 18612-1098
Telephone: 570-675-4449
           800-852-7675 (toll free)
Fax: 570-674-6232
E-mail: admiss@miseri.edu
World Wide Web: http://www.miseri.edu

Students at College Misericordia have opportunities in leadership and service and a variety of clubs, sports, and activities to choose from.

COLLEGE OF AERONAUTICS
FLUSHING, NEW YORK

The College

The College of Aeronautics is a private, independent technical college that is chartered by the Board of Regents of the State of New York and is accredited by the Middle States Association of Colleges and Schools. Undergraduate enrollment is approximately 1,300 students. This includes full- and part-time students.

Founded in 1932, the College has enjoyed much success preparing men and women for careers in the aviation and aerospace industries.

Academic and counseling procedures are designed to foster a close relationship between students and faculty members. Instructors are available daily for individual counseling and assistance.

The Student Services Office offers students the opportunity to get involved with various activities within the College. It provides students with college spirit and a sense of unity with others through individual and team growth.

The College, located in the heart of East Coast aviation, air transportation, and electronics industries offers many opportunities for liaison with airlines and private aviation as well as aircraft and electronics manufacturers.

The College of Aeronautics is exceptional in that it emphasizes hands-on technical courses, which are given through a number of laboratory exercises and projects. The practical education provided by the College makes its graduates highly desirable candidates for employment. The Career Development Office offers access to the aviation/aerospace industry. Many of the College's graduates have made important contributions to aeronautical developments through the years, and many hold prestigious positions in the industry today.

Bachelor of Science and Bachelor of Technology graduates may pursue a Master of Business Administration in aviation management through Dowling College.

Off-campus housing for out-of-state applicants can be arranged through the Student Services Office.

Location

Situated directly across from LaGuardia Airport in Flushing, Queens, the College enjoys an atmosphere that is conducive to learning. The College also offers a B.S. degree in airport management at its new off-site location at Stewart International Airport in New Windsor, New York. The cultural, spiritual, and physical needs of the students are met by the outstanding facilities of New York City. Museums include the Metropolitan Museum of Art, the American Museum of Natural History, the Museum of the American Indian, and many smaller collections. The theater district offers up to twenty plays at any given time as well as various concerts, musicals, light opera, and drama. Some of the world's finest restaurants are also to be found in New York. Shea Stadium, home of the New York Mets, is a neighbor of the College. Yankee Stadium, Madison Square Garden, the Nassau Coliseum, and the Meadowlands can be reached easily from the College.

Majors and Degrees

The College offers the Bachelor of Science (B.S.) degree in the areas of airport management, aviation maintenance, avionics (aviation electronics), and computerized design. The Bachelor of Technology (B.T.) degree programs include aviation maintenance and aviation maintenance management. Two different associate degrees are offered at the College: the Associate in Applied Science (A.A.S.) and the Associate in Occupational Studies (A.O.S.). Within the A.A.S. degree there are five program options: aeronautical engineering technology (pre-engineering), aircraft operations (flight), avionics (aviation electronics), computerized design and animated graphics, and aviation maintenance. For the A.O.S. degree, students have one program option, which is airframe and powerplant technology. This program is specially designed for students who wish to concentrate on the mechanical skills involved in airframe and powerplant maintenance operations.

Academic Program

The College has a semester schedule, with starting dates in the fall and spring. Each student has the opportunity to explore the College and the field of aviation technology while also developing the critical, analytical, and communications skills necessary to succeed.

A 60-credit arts and science core is the common thread in all of the Bachelor of Science programs which require the completion of between 128 and 137 credits. The B.T. program in aviation maintenance requires the completion of 134 credits of study; the B.T. in aviation maintenance management requires 136 credits. The A.O.S. degree requires the completion of 90½ credits of study. A.A.S. degree programs require the completion of 64 to 110 credits of study and are easily transferred to the bachelor's degree programs.

The College of Aeronautics offers many different degree options in six primary areas of study: aeronautical engineering technology (pre-engineering), aircraft operations (flight), airport management, avionics (aviation electronics), computerized design, and maintenance.

The newly developed curriculum of the B.S. degree in airport management stresses the fundamentals of business necessary for success in the field of aviation and is offered at both the LaGuardia Airport campus and Stewart International Airport. Students acquire the technical and administrative skills necessary to fulfill the vital role of a manager at today's modern airport. The B.S., B.T., A.A.S., and A.O.S. degree programs in maintenance focus on the technical skills and theoretical knowledge needed to obtain the federal certificates necessary to maintain aircraft. The College's state-of-the-art educational facilities give students the advantage of working with aircraft before entering the professional world.

Students are immersed in a combination of theory and practical applications necessary to begin a career as a commercial pilot in the A.A.S. degree in aircraft operations. Through this program, qualified students may also earn eligibility for the Federal Aviation Administration's private/commercial pilot certificate as well as the required instrument rating.

Designed to bridge the gap between the technician and the engineer, the A.A.S. in aeronautical engineering technology (pre-engineering) gives students the skills necessary to begin their engineering or related careers. This degree program provides ease of transfer to four-year engineering technology programs.

The A.A.S. and B.S. degrees in avionics (aviation electronics) involves the precise study and practice of complex electronics systems, including navigation, communications, surveillance, and flight control.

Understanding technology is no longer a choice in today's computerized world. The College of Aeronautics' A.A.S. and B.S. degrees in computerized design and animated graphics programs teach the latest in animation and 2-D and 3-D graphics imaging techniques. All of these programs utilize the latest hardware and software and allow students to apply their skills to aviation and other career fields as well.

The Air Force ROTC program is designed to develop men and women who will apply their education to initial active duty assignments as Air Force officers. The two major phases of the curriculum are the general military course and the professional officers' course.

Academic Facilities

The College's new building complex features ten state-of-the-art classrooms, a 5,000-square-foot hangar, and an observation tower that overlooks the operations at neighboring LaGuardia Airport. It is designed to combine the hands-on needs of the technician through a variety of laboratory equipment with the general classroom, research, and intellectual requirements of the college student. The new hangar complex provides a realistic aviation setting for students to perform hands-on maintenance and other projects on a variety of aircraft. The present fleet is composed of two twin-engine business jets and several twin- and single-engine general aviation aircraft. In the hangar, the study of turbojet and turboprop aircraft engine theory of operation is further enhanced by the inclusion of four jet engine test cells. The facility is also equipped with composite and corrosion control laboratories that are specifically designed to offer hands-on courses in aircraft composite structures and nondestructive testing procedures. The Prometric Test Center at the College of Aeronautics is authorized by the Federal Aviation Administration (FAA) and provides all written examinations offered by the FAA on computer.

The computer facilities allow a common interface for a number of operating systems, including Novell NetWare 3.12 and 4.1 and Windows NT. The system also supports other operating systems, including Windows 95, Windows for Workgroups, Macintosh, and a UNIX SPARCstation. The College's library offers extensive general, technical, resource, and periodical material totaling more than 62,000 volumes, 137,000 microfiche, and more than 1,000 audiovisual and training materials. The collection contains the latest released findings of the research and development efforts of the aviation and aerospace industries.

Costs

For 1999, tuition, fees, books, and supplies totaled approximately $9350 per academic year (two semesters). In addition to these fees, students seeking the FAA Airframe and Powerplant Certificates are subject to FAA examination fees totaling $180.

Financial Aid

Approximately 80 percent of the students receive financial aid. The maximum amount of financial aid awarded to a freshman is $8148; the average amount awarded is $3300. Financial aid options include the Federal Pell Grant and New York State TAP (Tuition Assistance Program) awards, the FSEOG (Federal Supplemental Educational Opportunity Grant), Federal Stafford Student Loan, and the Federal Perkins Loan.

Faculty

Every faculty member is a professional in the true sense of the word. Faculty members bring to the classroom not only excellent teaching credentials but also many years of invaluable experience in industry. Advising is also an important aspect of the faculty's commitment to the students. The student-faculty ratio is 11:1.

Student Government

The College of Aeronautics Student Government Association serves in an advisory capacity to the president and other administrators of the College in matters related to student affairs.

Admission Requirements

Admission to the College of Aeronautics is open to high school graduates and to holders of a state equivalency certificate (GED). For New York State residents, the minimum score for consideration is 250, and the GED should be taken in the English version. The College has a rolling admissions policy. Applicants who have attended other two- or four-year institutions may be evaluated for acceptance based on their academic records. Transfer credit may also be granted for equivalent courses of study. The required academic and technical aptitudes vary depending on the program. Evaluation of the entering student's educational transcripts might require that the student take remedial courses if that student is lacking certain required subjects for the chosen curriculum. The SAT I is also required for the B.T. and B.S. degrees. In general, success in Bachelor of Science, Bachelor of Technology, and Associate in Applied Science courses depends on academic abilities, while Associate in Occupational Studies courses emphasize technical aptitudes.

Application and Information

The Director of Admissions and the counseling staff are available to advise applicants and their parents and to provide up-to-date information and materials for high school guidance counselors.

For further details, interested persons should contact:

Office of Admissions
College of Aeronautics
LaGuardia Airport
Flushing, New York 11369

Telephone: 718-429-6600 Ext. 118
           800-776-2376 (toll-free)
E-mail: pro@aero.edu
World Wide Web: http://www.aero.edu

The College has recently completed a $16.6-million building complex that features ten state-of-the-art classrooms, a 5,000-square-foot hangar, and an observation tower overlooking the operations at neighboring LaGuardia Airport.

COLLEGE OF INSURANCE
NEW YORK, NEW YORK

The College of Insurance

The College

The College of Insurance was established in 1962 and can trace its genesis back to 1901 when the Insurance Society of New York was founded. The first formal courses were offered by the Insurance Society in 1917, and, in 1947, the School of Insurance was established. In 1962, the Board of Regents of the State of New York amended the society's charter to allow it to establish and maintain the College. This marked the beginning of the only undergraduate baccalaureate-degree-granting institution in the country established and supported by a particular segment of the business world. The College is accredited by the Middle States Association of Colleges and Schools and the New York State Board of Regents.

The College offers carefully designed programs leading to the Associate in Occupational Studies, Bachelor of Business Administration, Bachelor of Science, and Master of Business Administration degrees. In addition, the College sponsors professional development programs, management programs, and technical seminars for industry executives, as well as programs and seminars for members of the state regulatory agencies. The College's Diploma in Risk and Insurance Program is offered to recent college graduates entering the insurance field.

There are more than 2,100 students currently enrolled at the College of Insurance. College activities include annual comedy nights, theme parties, a luncheon series of industry speakers, and community-wide TCI Day. There are also various specialized, national, and regional student organizations. The College has a history of participating in intercollegiate bowling and in intramural leagues in basketball and softball.

Location

The College is located in lower Manhattan, the world's financial center, near Wall Street, the World Trade Center, Greenwich Village, SoHo, Chinatown, and the South Street Seaport. The museums, theaters, sports facilities, restaurants, and parks of the city are all available to the students. New York is one of a handful of cities capable of satisfying almost every interest in art, music, food, theater, sports, and recreation. One of America's most prestigious performing arts facilities, Lincoln Center, and one of the world's premier art museums, the Metropolitan Museum of Art, are a bus or subway ride away from the College.

Majors and Degrees

Undergraduate study leads to either a Bachelor of Business Administration (B.B.A.) degree with a major in insurance or a Bachelor of Science (B.S.) degree with a major in actuarial science.

Academic Program

Bachelor of Business Administration students follow a curriculum that meets the standards of the AACSB–The International Association for Management Education. Course work includes a liberal arts requirement, which ensures a broad-based educational experience. Half of each student's courses are devoted to the study of such traditional areas as communications, history, mathematics, philosophy, and the social sciences. The business core includes accounting, finance, information systems, insurance, law, management, and marketing.

Bachelor of Science students pursue similar courses in the liberal arts and general business subjects. The actuarial science major also requires intensive study in mathematics, probability, and statistics. Electives in actuarial science are designed to prepare students for successful completion of the examinations required for entrance into the Society of Actuaries.

Both the B.B.A. and B.S. degrees require the completion of 126 credit hours for graduation. The College also offers combined B.B.A./M.B.A and B.S./M.B.A. degree programs.

Most full-time students participate in the College's cooperative education program. Co-op students may alternate semesters of full-time study with full-time work in the industry, which provides them with actual on-the-job experience in the office of a sponsoring organization. Cooperative education employers often have work opportunities available in cities other than New York. Thus, students may have the opportunity to attend college in New York and have work terms in locations outside the city. In addition, selected companies with large international operations occasionally send students on overseas assignments for their work term.

Graduates of the cooperative education program not only have a bachelor's degree at the end of their college studies but may also have up to two years of practical business experience. Graduates are employed in many different areas of business, including personnel, administrative, public relations, communications, financial services, and actuarial departments of the companies. They may fill posts as actuaries, managers, supervisors, underwriters, loss and claim adjusters, brokers, agents, and risk managers for many organizations.

Academic Facilities

The world's most comprehensive insurance collection is housed in the Kathryn and Shelby Cullom Davis Library. Including more than 99,000 volumes, periodicals, and files, this collection is a depository of historical material on insurance, as well as a source of current data for the practitioner. The material covers all phases and types of insurance and ranges from a sixteenth-century treatise on marine insurance to the most recent rulings of insurance departments. In addition, the Frederic W. Ecker Liberal Arts Collection is housed at the College. The College's library is a partial depository for federal documents.

The College is in a ten-story building near the World Trade Center. The building houses classroom and office space, dormitory and food-service facilities, the resident life activities program, and a conference center.

Costs

Tuition and fees were $7306 per semester in 1999–2000. The average room and board fee was $8500 per year.

Financial Aid

The College of Insurance seeks to ensure that no qualified student is denied admission for financial reasons, and it awards various College-sponsored scholarships each year, including the Trustees, Presidential, and Leadership scholarships, to eligible students. Cooperative education students usually receive substantial assistance from their corporate sponsor; between 50 and 100 percent of students' tuition charges may be paid for. Students are also eligible for state and federal financial aid in the form of scholarships, grants, and loans. Veterans of the armed forces should consult the Veterans Administration to determine their eligibility for special financial assistance.

Faculty

The College's faculty brings a wealth of diverse academic and business experience to the classroom. Full-time faculty members are also active professionally. Many serve as consultants to industry and provide students with a strong grounding in current business practices. The ratio that exists between full-time students and faculty is 12:1. Part-time instructors are drawn directly from the business world, where many occupy high-level positions.

Student Government

The Student Government Association is the official student governing board of the College. Students sit as members of College administrative committees and work with both faculty members and administrators on College matters.

Admission Requirements

The College seeks, as freshman applicants, highly motivated students who can mature early and accept responsibility. Applicants must graduate from an approved secondary school and have 19 academic units, including four years of English and a minimum of three years of college-preparatory mathematics. A recommendation from the secondary school is also required. Students are required to take the SAT I of the College Board or the ACT examination in their senior year of secondary school. In addition, the College requires applicants to have a personal interview. While class rank, high school achievement, and test scores are all important, consideration is given to other factors, including the student's demonstrated leadership potential.

The College also seeks, as transfer students, highly motivated students from two-year community and junior colleges as well as from four-year public and private institutions.

Application and Information

The College of Insurance employs a rolling admissions policy, and students are permitted to apply throughout the year. The deadline for fall is May 1 for admission and housing. The deadline for transfer students to apply for the fall semester is July 1. Early decision candidates must apply by December 1 and are notified of their acceptance by December 15 for admission in September.

The application for admission must be completed, and a $30 non-refundable application fee is required. Official copies of secondary school and prior college transcripts must be submitted, along with either SAT I or ACT scores. The College's SAT I identification number is 2112.

Materials should be addressed to:
Admissions Office
College of Insurance
101 Murray Street
New York, New York 10007-2165
Telephone: 212-815-9232
          800-356-5146 (toll-free)
Fax: 212-964-3381
E-mail: admissions@tci.edu
World Wide Web: http://www.tci.edu

This ten-story building, near the World Trade Center, is the home of the College of Insurance.

COLLEGE OF MOUNT ST. JOSEPH
CINCINNATI, OHIO

The College

As a private liberal arts college founded in 1920, the College of Mount St. Joseph has a rich history of preparing students for the future. Today, the Mount is a coeducational college with more than 2,200 students, offering an outstanding liberal arts curriculum that emphasizes values, integrity, and social responsibility as well as practical career preparation. Required courses in humanities, science, and the arts are complemented by opportunities for cooperative work experience, a universal computing requirement, specialized professionally oriented courses, and extracurricular opportunities to give students the broad-based background that is in high demand among employers. Students can gain practical experience before graduation through participation in programs such as the Career Exploration Seminar, Career Advising, the Mentoring Council, Professional Development, and on-campus recruiting.

Catholic in tradition, the Mount emphasizes a value-centered education and supports the personal growth of each student. A warm, close-knit campus community encourages students to exercise their talents to their fullest potential in academic, athletic, and leadership activities. Campus organizations include the student government, student newspaper, academic honor societies, international club, departmental clubs, marching and concert band, chamber singers, and intramural athletics. The Mount offers a full intercollegiate athletics program for men and women in the NCAA Division III and is a member of the Heartland Collegiate Athletic Conference (HCAC). Women's programs include basketball, cross-country, soccer, softball, tennis, and volleyball. For men there is baseball, basketball, football, tennis, and wrestling.

Mount students come primarily from the Midwest, but many other regions of the United States and more than twenty-five countries are also represented. Spacious rooms are available in Seton Center Residence Hall. Resident students may keep cars on campus.

The College is accredited by the North Central Association of Colleges and Schools.

Location

Located just 10 minutes from downtown Cincinnati, the College sits on a beautiful 75-acre suburban campus overlooking the Ohio River. The campus is easily accessible from the airport, bus terminal, railway station, and interstate. Well-known for its scenic and rolling hills, greater Cincinnati offers numerous parks, cultural and arts events, professional athletics, shopping areas, and a wide assortment of fine restaurants. In addition to their on-campus activities, Mount students frequently participate in social and service activities with students from other area colleges.

Majors and Degrees

The College of Mount St. Joseph awards bachelor's degrees in accounting, art, art education, athletic training, biological chemistry, biology, business administration, chemistry, chemistry/mathematics, communication arts, computer information systems, computer science with a minor in math, education (inclusive early childhood, middle childhood, adolescent and young adults, physical education, and special education), English, fine arts, general studies, gerontological studies, graphic design, history, humanities, interior design, liberal arts and sciences, mathematics, mathematics/chemistry, medical technology, music, natural history, natural science, nursing, paralegal studies, paralegal studies for nurses, psychology, recreational therapy, religious education, religious pastoral ministry, religious studies, social work, and sociology. Physical therapy majors receive a bachelor's degree in rehabilitation science on their way to obtaining a master's degree.

Associate degrees are offered in accounting, art, business administration, communication arts, computer information systems, general studies, gerontological studies, graphic design, interior design, and paralegal studies. Certificate programs are offered in art education; gerontological studies; graphic design; inclusive early childhood education, middle childhood education, adolescent and young adult education, physical education, and special education; interior design; paralegal studies; paralegal studies for nurses; and parish nurse/health ministries.

Preprofessional programs are available in dentistry, law, medicine, optometry, podiatry, and veterinary medicine.

Academic Program

All majors are backed by a strong liberal arts curriculum that encourages students to develop skills in analytical thinking, problem solving, decision making, and communication. Students must earn 128 credit hours for a bachelor's degree, with 52 of those credits from the liberal arts and science core. For an associate degree, students must earn 64 credit hours, with 27 to 28 of those credits from the liberal arts and science core.

The academic year consists of fall and spring semesters and three summer terms. Day and evening courses are open to traditional students, while adult students may take classes in day, evening, or weekend time frames.

The Mount offers a highly respected Cooperative Education program that makes the benefits of hands-on work experience within their field of study available to students as early as the second semester of their sophomore year. In addition to the financial advantage of being able to work through college, a student can also make the personal contacts that are so important in professional experiences.

Project EXCEL is a special program that offers tutorial services, audiotapes of textbooks, and self-instructional materials to students with learning disabilities. Students learn skills that facilitate success in the college environment. Project EXCEL carries an additional fee for testing and for services while in the program. Interested students must apply for admission through Project EXCEL.

Opportunities are available to study abroad in Heidelberg, Germany, through the Congress/Bundestag program; in London, England, at Thames Valley College and through the Mount's affiliation with Huron University; and in Seville, Spain, through the Spanish American Institute. Art students in the London program may apply for placement in cooperative education positions in London businesses and in institutions such as the BBC, Harrod's, the Taylor Partnership, and Jane Churchill Design, Ltd.

Academic Facilities

The Mount's campus features modern buildings with state-of-the-art learning facilities. The Computer Learning Center offers all students access to IBM and Macintosh systems supporting more than 500 different software packages. Studio San Giuseppe, one of Cincinnati's largest nonprofit galleries, hosts exhibits by local, regional, and national artists as well as by students and faculty members. A beautiful College theater seats more than 1,000 people. Students in the Nursing Department have access to on-campus laboratories and benefit from the department's relationship with nearby hospitals of outstanding quality and reputation.

Costs

For the 2000–01 academic year, tuition is $13,500 and room and board are $5100 (based on a semiprivate room and the thirteen-meals-per-week plan). The College offers private and semiprivate housing accommodations and a variety of meal plans. There is a $45 activities fee per semester and a technology fee of $250 per semester, which provides students with a wireless, hand-held computer to use during their years at the Mount. The cost of books varies depending on course load and major.

Financial Aid

The College of Mount St. Joseph assists as many students as possible who require financial aid. About 80 percent of full-time undergraduate students receive some form of assistance, usually as federal, state, or College grants; work-study awards; and loans. In addition, part-time employment may be available in the metropolitan area for those students with transportation. The Mount offers academic scholarship programs based on merit or on a combination of merit and need in the areas of scholastic achievement and leadership.

Students who wish to apply for financial aid must complete, by April 15, the Free Application for Federal Student Aid (FAFSA). Most scholarships are awarded on a rolling basis. Interested students should inquire as early in their senior year as possible.

Faculty

Because the Mount is a small liberal arts college, the faculty's focus is on teaching. Many faculty members have been recognized regionally and nationally for their research and expertise outside the classroom as well as for their contributions as teachers, particularly in the fields of art, science, math, sociology, and education. The student-faculty ratio of 15:1 encourages personal interaction between students and professors.

Student Government

The Student Government Association (SGA) serves as a vehicle of communication for the student body. The Senate is composed of 14 elected members and serves in an advisory capacity in academic and administrative affairs by its participation in institutional and administrative committees.

There are many opportunities for interested students to participate in SGA-sponsored programs and activities, including Campus Fair, movies, dances, fund-raising events, and community service activities.

Admission Requirements

Admission decisions are based on high school course selection, ACT or SAT I scores, class rank, and grade point average. The College requires 4 units of English, 2 of math (algebra and geometry), 2 of social studies, 2 of science, 2 of foreign language, and 1 of fine arts. Two electives from the areas listed above may be substituted for foreign language. Students are encouraged to submit recommendation letters and personal essays.

Application and Information

Applications are reviewed on a rolling basis. Admission decisions are generally made within two weeks of the date the file is complete. The application fee is $25; the Project EXCEL fee is $60. The physical therapy fee is $50, with an application deadline of January 15. Application fees are nonrefundable and do not apply toward tuition. Students who want to know more about the Mount may arrange a visit by contacting the Office of Admission. In addition to scheduling individual appointments, the College holds Get Acquainted Days throughout the year, giving students the opportunity to visit campus, explore academic programs, and take a tour.

Office of Admission
College of Mount St. Joseph
5701 Delhi Road
Cincinnati, Ohio 45233-1672
Telephone: 513-244-4531
           800-654-9314 (toll-free)
World Wide Web: http://www.msj.edu

The College of Mount St. Joseph provides a liberal arts and professional education for the twenty-first century, integrating life and learning and embracing excellence, respect, diversity, and service.

COLLEGE OF MOUNT SAINT VINCENT
RIVERDALE, NEW YORK

The College

The College of Mount Saint Vincent, a four-year, coeducational, liberal arts college, is a private, independent institution in a public trust. Founded as an academy by the Sisters of Charity of New York in 1847, it introduced postgraduate courses in the late 1800s and in 1910 expanded into a four-year college. It has been coeducational since 1974.

The College currently enrolls students from eleven states and twelve countries. About 50 percent of the students live on campus, although married students are required to live off campus. The current full-time undergraduate enrollment is more than 1,000 men and women.

Career counseling, personal counseling, and health services are available to all students. The Cahill Lounge features live entertainment and numerous student social events. Recognized campus organizations and Student Government committees sponsor a full calendar of events, including formal and informal dances and professional entertainment. Other groups include CAST (Culturally Aware Students of Today), CMSV Chorus, CMSV Players, Circle K, and the Student Nursing Association. Students can gain experience in broadcasting by participating in the work of the campus TV and radio stations, WMSV. Journalists are needed for College publications, such as the *MounTimes* (biweekly), *Fonthill Dial* (semiannual), and *Parapet* (annual). Fifteen academic honor societies have chapters on campus. Cyclists and joggers make good use of the picturesque campus. Facilities for athletics include a gymnasium, a state-of-the-art Fitness Center and Health Lounge, a 60-foot swimming pool, racquetball and tennis courts, a weight room, and a dance studio.

Varsity sports include women's and men's basketball, cross-country, soccer, tennis, and volleyball and women's softball, swimming, and track. There is also an intramural sports program. The College is an active member of the National Collegiate Athletic Association (NCAA) and the Eastern College Athletic Conference (ECAC) on the Division III level.

Mount Saint Vincent students are involved in a wide variety of children's recreation programs and other voluntary community service projects, including tutoring, work in hospitals and senior citizens' homes, and participation in political campaigns. Many cultural programs sponsored by the College are extended to the surrounding community.

The College offers three graduate degree programs: a Master of Science in allied health studies, nursing, and teacher education.

The graduate allied health studies program offers six concentrations: addictions, child and family health, community health education, counseling, health-care management, and health-care systems and policy. This unique major is rooted in health psychology. It allows students with baccalaureates in diverse disciplines to pursue a career-oriented program that enables them to work in health-related settings, including positions in hospitals, clinics, private practices, health maintenance organizations, and pain clinics.

The graduate nursing program offers four programs of study: addictions nursing, nursing administration, adult nurse practitioner, and nursing of the adult and aged. These programs prepare nurses for the complex decision-making process necessary in today's health-care environment by incorporating three graduate business courses into their curriculum. A registered nurse license and baccalaureate degree in nursing are required for application.

The graduate program in teacher education is a Master of Science in urban/multicultural education. It is a values-centered program reflecting the belief that learning and culture are inseparable, as are relationships among learner, teacher, environment, and purpose for learning. A bachelor's degree and a provisional teaching certificate are required for application. Those who are in need of provisional certification can apply for the SPAN program and enter the master's program upon completion.

Location

The campus of Mount Saint Vincent encompasses 70 acres of beautiful rolling lawns, stone walls, wooded fields, and several buildings designated as landmarks of the city of New York. The campus is 11 miles from mid-Manhattan; this proximity offers limitless cultural, social, and academic opportunities to students, all within a short bus or subway ride.

Majors and Degrees

The Bachelor of Arts is granted in biochemistry, biology, business, chemistry, communications, computer science, economics, English, French, health education, history, liberal arts, mathematics, modern foreign languages, psychology, sociology, and Spanish. The Bachelor of Science is conferred in allied health studies, biochemistry, biology, chemistry, computer science, health education, mathematics, nursing, psychology, and special education. Through a cooperative program with Manhattan College, CMSV students may also earn a B.A. in American studies, international studies, philosophy, physical education, religious studies, or urban affairs or a B.S. in physics.

The Department of Teacher Education offers programs for prospective teachers of grades pre-K through 12. In addition to the B.A. and B.S. degrees, these programs lead to provisional New York State certification, which qualifies many out-of-state residents to apply for certification in their home states under the terms of the Interstate Agreement on Qualification of Educational Personnel. Concentrations in learning disabilities and the emotionally handicapped are also offered in addition to the majors in health education, physical education, and special education. Dual certification is available in special education and elementary education with a concentration in English, psychology, or sociology. Dual certification is also available in special education and secondary education, with a concentration in English, history, French, or Spanish.

Certificate programs are offered in addiction studies, adult nurse practitioner studies, nurse case management, and school nurse studies.

Academic Program

The regular academic year is divided into two semesters, with intersessions in January and May. Three summer sessions are held during the months of May, June, and July.

A core curriculum provides a foundation of knowledge for Mount Saint Vincent students, who also benefit from taking the core courses with fellow students all through their four years, regardless of individual majors. The core consists of foundation courses (generally in the freshman and sophomore years), area courses (by the junior year), and enrichment courses (in the junior and senior years).

Candidates for the B.A. must earn 120 credits, and candidates for the B.S. must earn 126 credits, distributed in accordance with the requirements of the curriculum pursued. Of the required credits, 54 are in the core curriculum, and at least 30 must be in the major field. The selection of courses for the remaining credits is planned, with guidance from the student's academic adviser, according to the student's aims and interests. Students who are preparing to teach after graduation follow a program outlined by the Department of Teacher Education.

Special curricular features include the January intersession; an interdisciplinary program in international business and economics; preprofessional programs in dentistry, law, medicine, occupational therapy, and physical therapy; the interdisciplinary liberal arts major, which allows students to tailor an individualized program combining two or three fields of study; and a College honors program as well as one in most academic areas. The College has an extensive internship program that enables students to combine course work with practical, job-related experience. There are more than 500 organizations currently participating in the College's internship program throughout the tristate area.

Off-Campus Arrangements

The College of Mount Saint Vincent has developed a cooperative agreement with nearby Manhattan College that allows both colleges to broaden their educational opportunities through the sharing of facilities, programs of study, and professional faculties. The College of Mount Saint Vincent also participates in the New York State Visiting Student Program and in international study programs in Austria, England, France, Germany, Italy, Spain, and Switzerland.

Academic Facilities

The library contains more than 170,000 volumes, 616 current periodical subscriptions, 9,585 microfilms, and 6,000 audiovisual units (recordings, films, and cassettes). Other facilities include the Audiovisual Center, the Special Collections room, a radio station, a video studio, a television studio, a small theater, a computer graphics center, and the Curriculum Center. The library has access via computer to bibliographic information in libraries across the country. The three-story Science Hall, which houses the joined biology department of Mount Saint Vincent and Manhattan College, contains well-equipped laboratories, a lecture hall, classrooms, darkrooms, and environmental research facilities. In the Administration Building are the Academic Resource Center and the Writing Center, open to all students needing academic assistance; a ceramics studio; photography studio; language lab; snack bar; bookstore; and a computer center, housing two classrooms equipped with full multimedia Pentium computers with access to the Internet and e-mail. These classrooms serve as open labs when classes are not in session. In addition to these computer facilities, there are also satellite computer labs with Internet and e-mail access in the business, nursing, and psychology departments that are available to all students on a limited basis.

Costs

Tuition for the 1999–2000 year was $14,910; room and board were $7020. The motor vehicle registration fee ranges from $55 to $110 per year, depending on the parking lot the student selects. The cost of books, supplies, and personal items is approximately $1000.

Financial Aid

The College awards Academic Scholarships, Citizenship Grants, and federal, state, and institutional financial aid. Academic scholarships range from $1000 to full tuition. To apply for any scholarship or grant, students must have a completed application for admission on file with the Admissions Office by February 1 for freshman applicants. Freshman applicants should submit the Free Application for Federal Student Aid (FAFSA) by March 15; transfer applicants should submit the FAFSA by June 15. Transfer students are required to submit financial aid transcripts from all colleges previously attended. In addition to providing College scholarships, including the Corazón C. Aquino Scholarships, CMSV participates in all available federal and state programs of financial assistance, including Federal Pell Grants, Federal Supplemental Educational Opportunity Grants, Federal Work-Study awards, federal and New York State student loans, and New York State Tuition Assistance Program (TAP) awards. Eligibility for these programs is based on need. More than 85 percent of the students at Mount Saint Vincent receive aid from government or private agencies.

Faculty

The faculty is composed of 74 full-time and 89 part-time members who, in addition to their teaching responsibilities, act as academic advisers and moderate student activities. The student-faculty ratio is approximately 12:1. Of the full-time faculty members, 81 percent hold terminal degrees in their fields.

Student Government

Students participate in College governance through a strong Student Government with elected representatives on most major governing bodies of the College, including the College Senate, the Undergraduate and Graduate Committee, the Policies and Procedures Council, the Orientation Committee, and the Commencement Committee. Student Government leaders meet regularly with members of the Board of Trustees and make most decisions regarding the disbursement of student activities fees and budgeted funds for clubs and organizations. Students also play a central role in discipline through an elected Student Judicial Council. This constitutionally ensured involvement guarantees that students have direct access to information and multiple opportunities to present student views and articulate student needs to both faculty and administrators.

Admission Requirements

Applicants to the College of Mount Saint Vincent must have graduated from an accredited secondary school or possess a high school equivalency diploma, should rank in the upper half of their class, and must achieve satisfactory scores on the SAT I, ACT, or TOEFL. International students who qualify for admission are welcome. Students attending a junior college or another four-year college may apply for admission with advanced standing. Qualified students may enter the College after three years of high school, either as accelerated candidates or as early admission freshmen.

It is strongly recommended that prospective students telephone or write for an interview and tour.

Application and Information

In order to be evaluated for admission, a candidate must present the following: a nonrefundable application fee of $25; a completed application; scores on the SAT I, ACT, or TOEFL; a letter of recommendation; and a high school transcript. Transfer applicants should submit all college transcripts.

The Admissions Committee operates on a modified rolling decision basis. Decisions on regular admission are mailed shortly after December 15. Students applying under the early decision (single-choice) plan should do so before November 15. Recommended transfer application guidelines are June 1 for fall and December 1 for spring.

Information, brochures, and application forms for admission and financial aid may be obtained by contacting:

Lenore M. Mott
Dean of Admission and Financial Aid
College of Mount Saint Vincent
6301 Riverdale Avenue
Riverdale, New York 10471-1093
Telephone: 718-405-3267
         800-665-CMSV (toll-free)
E-mail: admissns@cmsv.edu
World Wide Web: http://www.cmsv.edu

THE COLLEGE OF NEW JERSEY
EWING TOWNSHIP, NEW JERSEY

The College

The College of New Jersey (TCNJ) welcomes talented, well-prepared students who have the motivation to succeed in a rigorous academic environment. It seeks students who get actively involved in their own education and who are serious about preparing for productive and rewarding careers. Founded in 1855, TCNJ is one of the most selective institutions, public or private, in New Jersey and the surrounding states. A state-supported public college, it has an undergraduate enrollment of approximately 5,500 men and women. Formerly Trenton State College, the College changed its name to better reflect its statewide mission.

The College's undergraduate academic programs are accredited by the Commission on Higher Education of the Middle States Association of Colleges and Schools and by professional associations in engineering, nursing, chemistry, music, education, education of the deaf, computer science, and business.

TCNJ is a residential college with nearly two thirds of the undergraduate population living on campus. All full-time freshmen and sophomores are guaranteed on-campus housing, and the College accommodates most juniors and seniors who wish to continue living in residence halls. Living arrangements vary from freshman residence halls to suites and town houses for upperclass students. Special-interest floors are available for the honors program, music program, and others. A nationally recognized residence life program and more than 120 student organizations, ranging from fraternities and sororities to honor societies and special interest clubs, offer students numerous opportunities to grow and develop outside the classroom.

Two theaters and a recital hall offer programs of films, lectures, recitals, concerts, and plays; performers include students, faculty and staff members, internationally known artists, and touring companies of theater, music, and dance. The College has hosted the Flying Karamazov Brothers, novelists Kurt Vonnegut and Maya Angelou, and an international festival of chamber music. TCNJ's theater series has included fully mounted productions of *Carmen, The Mikado,* and *City of Angels.* Many of the events are free; others are presented at a reasonable charge. The College Art Gallery mounts exhibitions of contemporary art; the art department's national competitions in printmaking and drawing have attracted entries from all fifty states and the District of Columbia.

The Student Recreation Center contains eight racquetball courts, four tennis courts that can be converted into basketball or volleyball courts, a weight room, and an indoor track. A new wellness center, offering all the amenities of a state-of-the-art fitness center, opened in 1998. Other modern athletic facilities are a lighted Astroturf field, eight lighted outdoor tennis courts, a 25-meter swimming and diving pool, and an outdoor sand volleyball court.

TCNJ is a member of the National Collegiate Athletic Association (NCAA) and offers twenty-one sports—eleven for men and ten for women. Since 1979, TCNJ athletes have amassed thirty-four national championships in six different sports and twenty-eight runner-up awards, more than any other Division III college or university in the country. Division III, which comprises more institutions of higher learning than either of the other NCAA membership divisions (I and II), represents student-athletes in perhaps their truest form. TCNJ student-athletes have won an impressive share of individual awards as well, ranging from All-Conference to All-American. TCNJ student-athletes meet the same admission and academic standards as other students and, equally important, contribute to a diverse and well-rounded college community. The Office of Intramurals and Recreation Services provides the College community with a wide variety of recreation programs, spirited and competitive intramural programs, and self-governing sports clubs.

Location

The College of New Jersey is located on 289 acres in suburban Ewing Township, New Jersey. Woodlands and lakes surround the academic and residential buildings. Thirty-nine major buildings make up the physical plant; recent additions complement the classic Georgian architecture of the original structures. The campus is 30 miles from Philadelphia and 60 miles from New York's theaters and museums; the nearby towns of Princeton and New Hope offer additional cultural activities.

Majors and Degrees

The College of New Jersey offers programs leading to the Bachelor of Arts, Bachelor of Fine Arts, Bachelor of Music, Bachelor of Science, and Bachelor of Science in Nursing degrees. The B.A. is awarded in art education; communication studies; economics; English, including journalism and professional writing options; history; mathematics and statistics; philosophy; political science; psychology; sociology; and Spanish. The B.F.A. is awarded in fine art and graphic design. The B.M. is awarded in music (performance and education). The B.S. is granted in accountancy; biology; business administration (finance, general business, information systems management, international business, management, and marketing); chemistry; computer science; early childhood education; economics; education for the hearing-impaired; elementary education; engineering science; health and physical education; law and justice; physics, including scientific computer programming; special education; and technological studies. Teacher preparation is available in many arts and science majors.

TCNJ offers a seven-year combined B.S./M.D. degree program with UMDNJ—New Jersey Medical School (Newark) and a seven-year combined B.S./O.D. degree program with the State University of New York College of Optometry. Students may apply to TCNJ for a 4½-year combined B.S./M.A. program in law and justice with Rutgers, The State University of New Jersey (Newark). The College also offers a Medical Careers Advisory Committee for premed students and a Pre-Law Advisement Committee for students planning a career in law.

Academic Program

All baccalaureate degrees require at least 120 credits, including a core curriculum in the traditional arts and sciences.

The thirty-week year is divided into fall and spring semesters; the summer session offers courses in two 5-week sessions and one 6-week session. The average class size for freshman-level lectures is 18 students and for upper-division lectures, 21 students.

All first-year students participate in a program linking residential learning in small classes taught by full-time faculty members with a carefully supervised program of service learning. Seminars, independent studies, and capstone courses give many students the opportunity for challenging advanced study in close collaboration with faculty members. TCNJ students publish the results of these endeavors or present them at national and regional conferences.

The honors program offers gifted students courses that allow normal progress toward the degree yet are broader, more comprehensive, and more challenging than the regular core curriculum. Whenever possible, honors courses are also interdisciplinary, concentrating on central themes within significant periods in the cultural development of civilization. Honors courses in the major consist of either specially designated sections or independent study. All honors classes are small, personal, and stimulating.

Off-Campus Arrangements

TCNJ offers students a variety of full-year and one-semester programs of study abroad as well as study at other state colleges and universities within the United States. Exchange programs are available in Australia, Austria, Canada, Denmark, France, Germany, Greece, Israel, Japan, Mexico, the United Kingdom, and twenty-three other countries. National exchanges are available at 121 participating institutions in forty-three states, the U.S. Virgin Islands, Puerto Rico, and Guam.

Academic Facilities

Supporting the efforts of students and faculty members are the Roscoe L. West Library, housing more than 500,000 volumes and receiving 1,563 periodical subscriptions; the media center; two theaters; a recital hall; the College Art Gallery; and a full range of laboratories to serve scientific, technological, and professional studies. Campuswide networking provides full Internet accessibility from all residence hall rooms and more than twenty student computing laboratories.

Costs

Costs are relatively low because of state funding. For 1999–2000, full-time undergraduate tuition and fees were $5685 for New Jersey residents and $9002 for out-of-state students. Room and board charges for the academic year, with a full meal plan, averaged $6330.

Financial Aid

Approximately half of the full-time undergraduates receive some form of financial aid, such as federal, state, and institutional grants; merit scholarships; student employment; and loan assistance. The Free Application for Federal Student Aid (FAFSA) or Renewal FAFSA is used to apply for all types of aid.

Scholarships and grants include the College of New Jersey Merit Scholars Program, the New Jersey Outstanding Scholars Recruitment Program, the New Jersey Edward J. Bloustein Distinguished Scholars Program, the New Jersey Tuition Aid Grant, Federal Pell Grants, Federal Supplemental Educational Opportunity Grants (FSEOG), Educational Opportunity Fund (EOF), and Army and Air Force ROTC Scholarships, as well as other institutional scholarships. Loans include the Federal Subsidized and Unsubsidized Stafford Loans, the Federal Perkins Loan, the Federal Parent Loan for Undergraduate Students (PLUS), the New Jersey CLASS Loan, nursing loans, and short-term emergency loan funds. Student employment options include the need-based Federal–Work Study Program (on- and off-campus positions) as well as institutionally supported campus jobs.

Faculty

The 328 full-time members of the College of New Jersey faculty are teachers and scholars. While teaching is their primary commitment, they are also active researchers, authors, artists, performers, and regular contributors in their academic disciplines. No classes are taught by TCNJ graduate assistants. The student-faculty ratio is 12:1. From their first day, students study with faculty members who may be researching new ways to use solar energy; writing a new text, play, or novel; or investigating the life cycle of desert ferns. Members of the faculty have attracted many significant grants, fellowships, and awards, including the Bancroft Prize in history and grants from the National Science Foundation, the National Institute for Advanced Study, the Guggenheim Foundation, and the National Endowment for the Humanities. Faculty members mentor their students, preparing them for careers, graduate and professional schools, and prestigious fellowships such as the Truman and Marshall Fellowships recently awarded to TCNJ students.

Student Government

The Student Government Association, comprising all undergraduate students at the College, is governed by elected representatives. The Residence Hall Association provides the mechanism for student input into campus housing policies, and members of the Student Finance Board oversee and administer approximately half a million dollars in student funds. The College Union Board sponsors a wide range of special events, including visits by Fiona Apple, Busta Rhymes, and George Carlin.

Admission Requirements

The College of New Jersey seeks students who can succeed in a highly selective academic program and who show intellectual curiosity, academic talent, and the potential to contribute to the life of the College. The College is committed to attracting students who represent a diversity of economic, racial, social, and geographic backgrounds. A high school record of at least 16 college-preparatory credits, high school class rank, and results of the SAT I are the most important considerations in admission decisions, but special interests, skills, and qualities of all kinds can be influential. Certain departments, such as art, music, and health and physical education, use additional criteria to evaluate candidates seeking admission into their programs. Students are required to take the SAT II: Writing Test for placement purposes only.

Application and Information

Application forms and a prospectus may be obtained by writing to the Office of Admission. The deadline for applications for January admission is November 1 and for September admission, February 15. There is a $50 application fee. Candidates who apply only to the College of New Jersey under the early decision plan may apply before November 15 and will be notified before December 15. For September admission, the College subscribes to the Candidates Reply Date of May 1 for payment of a $100 tuition deposit.

For more information, students should contact:
Director of Admissions
The College of New Jersey
P.O. Box 7718
Ewing, New Jersey 08628-0718
Telephone: 609-771-2131
          800-624-0967 (toll-free)
World Wide Web: http://www.tcnj.edu

The College of New Jersey's tree-lined, 289-acre campus, which provides spectacular fall foliage, offers a beautiful residential setting for students all year long.

THE COLLEGE OF NEW ROCHELLE
NEW ROCHELLE, NEW YORK

The College

The College of New Rochelle (CNR), founded in 1904 by the Ursuline Order, is an independent college that is Catholic in origin and heritage. Its primary purpose is the intellectual development of students through the maintenance of high standards of academic excellence. The College is composed of four separate schools. The School of Arts and Sciences enrolls about 600 young women between the ages of 18 and 22 and offers baccalaureate degree programs in the liberal arts and sciences and a number of professionally oriented fields. The School of Nursing, founded in 1976 and accredited by the National League for Nursing Accrediting Commission, offers baccalaureate and graduate-level professional nursing programs that combine clinical experience with a liberal arts background. About 500 women and men are enrolled in the nursing programs. The School of New Resources, which maintains six branch campuses in New York City, offers a nontraditional baccalaureate program designed specifically for adults. The Graduate School offers professional degree programs in education, art, community/school psychology, gerontology, communication, career development, and counseling.

The main campus includes four residence halls that provide housing for 650 students. Other students live in Westchester County, and some commute from the Greater New York metropolitan area. Students come to CNR from many states and several countries.

Location

The College of New Rochelle is located on a 20-acre campus in New Rochelle, New York, a suburban community in southern Westchester County, half an hour away from New York City and easily accessible by commuter trains and school-sponsored buses. The area contains numerous parks and recreational areas, and the Long Island Sound, with its many beaches, is within walking distance of the campus. Four airports—Kennedy, LaGuardia, Newark, and Westchester—are all within an hour of the College, and Amtrak makes daily stops at New Rochelle. New York City provides countless opportunities, including shopping expeditions, museums, and Broadway plays. Manhattan and the four other boroughs of New York City also contribute immeasurably to the education of the College's students through various internship, honors, and cooperative education programs, which are conducted by CNR in New York City.

Majors and Degrees

The School of Arts and Sciences at the College of New Rochelle confers the Bachelor of Arts (B.A.) degree in art (studio), art history, biology, chemistry, classics, communication arts, economics, English, environmental studies, history, mathematics, modern and classical languages, philosophy, political science, psychology, religious studies, and sociology; the Bachelor of Science (B.S.) degree in art education, biology, business, chemistry, mathematics, and social work; the Bachelor of Fine Arts (B.F.A.) degree in art education, art therapy, and studio art; and a Bachelor of Arts in interdisciplinary studies, which offers the student the viewpoints of several disciplines, including American studies, comparative literature, general science, international studies, and women's studies. A series of field experiences and competency-based learning activities lead to certification in elementary education (PreK–6) and special education (learning disabled and mentally and emotionally handicapped). Preparation for secondary education certification (grades 7–12) is available in art, biology, chemistry, English, French, Latin, mathematics, social studies, and Spanish. Certification is also available in art education (K–12). In addition, CNR offers five-year sequences that lead to both the Bachelor of Arts and Master of Science degrees in community/school psychology or therapeutic education. The School of Nursing offers Bachelor of Science in Nursing (B.S.N.) and Master of Science (M.S.) degree programs. Preprofessional programs are available in art therapy, health professions, law, and medicine.

Academic Program

The College emphasizes the importance of a liberal arts background. Each undergraduate in the Schools of Arts and Sciences and Nursing must complete a variety of courses focusing on philosophy and religious studies, social analysis, literature and the arts, foreign languages, and scientific inquiry. To earn a B.A., B.S., or B.F.A., students must complete 120 credits. Typically, a B.A. degree requires 90 credits in liberal arts and 30 credits in a major area; B.S. and B.F.A. degrees require 60 credits in liberal arts and 60 credits in major and elective courses. To earn a B.S.N. degree, students must complete 120 credits. It is possible to complete graduation requirements in three years. Students who earn successful scores on the College Board's Advanced Placement examinations may qualify for credit and course exemption.

Interdisciplinary studies and dual-degree programs can be designed. Independent study options and seminars play important roles in undergraduate programs as well. The Honors Program, which provides an alternative structure for the liberal arts curriculum, fosters the growth of intellectual independence and initiative, offers the opportunity for independent study and research, and encourages the pursuit of scholarly interests in a broad variety of disciplines. Participation in the Honors Program requires a minimum 3.3 cumulative index. The Learning Support Services staff offers tutoring programs, quiet study areas, and professional tutors and student peer-tutors to help students.

The academic calendar consists of two 15-week semesters; during each semester, students generally take five courses. The fall semester is in session from September through December; the spring semester runs from late January through May. Courses are offered during the January intersession but are not required. Two 5-week summer sessions are also offered.

Off-Campus Arrangements

The College of New Rochelle offers an extensive internship program. Art students assist in the management of SoHo art galleries and the Metropolitan Museum of Art, while continuing to develop their artistic talents. Communication arts majors participate in internships at numerous radio stations, newspapers, film companies, advertising and public relations firms, and national and cable broadcasting networks. Social science majors are offered opportunities with government agencies in Washington, D.C.; Albany; New York City; and New Rochelle. Social work majors complete their fieldwork at a variety of human services agencies, and education majors gain experience through fieldwork and student teaching in local school districts and institutions. Business majors put theory into practice at Merrill Lynch, IBM, and the New York Stock Exchange.

Clinical experiences for School of Nursing students take place in some of the most modern and sophisticated health-care institutions in the world, including Memorial Sloan-Kettering Cancer Center, Columbia-Presbyterian Hospital, and the Albert Einstein College of Medicine.

Students of modern foreign languages are encouraged to study and travel abroad. The College is affiliated with the American Institute of Foreign Study and the Institute of European Studies.

Academic Facilities

The New Rochelle campus contains twenty buildings, including classroom and laboratory facilities, student residences, and centers for academic support services. The Mother Irene Gill Memorial Library holds 200,000 volumes in open stacks. About 3,000 new volumes are purchased each year. Holdings in education, psychology, health services, gerontology, and art are extensive. Gill Library is a member of a consortium of 9,000 libraries around the world. A computer network enables students to search for books or journal articles from any of the member libraries.

The College Center provides technology and programs to assist students in the development of academic, professional, and personal lifetime goals. Facilities include state-of-the-art computer laboratories and classrooms, a computer graphics studio and desktop publishing facilities, photography laboratories, a television studio, the Romita Auditorium, art studios and gallery space, a model classroom for student teachers, and the H. W. Taylor Institute for Entrepreneurial Studies.

More than a dozen laboratories are housed in Rogick Life Science Center and Science Hall. Facilities include a research microscope room, a radiation laboratory and counting room, a plant/animal tissue culture room, a computer room, a darkroom, a greenhouse, and laboratories set aside entirely for student research.

The Learning Center for Nursing is composed of a nursing laboratory, which simulates a hospital setting, and a multimedia laboratory equipped with four mobile television centers and a media library. The computer room in the nursing center contains computers and printers and COMMES, an artificial intelligence system that simulates a professional nursing consultant. The system supports clinical decision-making by students and professional nurses.

The Student Campus Center houses the food service operation, featuring a variety of hot and cold food choices and an attractive, comfortable seating area; a completely renovated bookstore; centralized mailboxes for all students on campus; student activity rooms; and meeting rooms and lounge areas designed to hold large groups of people for lectures and special events.

Costs

Tuition for the 2000–01 academic year is $11,900. Room and board costs are $6250. Total estimated annual costs, including travel, books, and personal expenses, are $20,900.

Financial Aid

Approximately 80 percent of all undergraduate students receive some kind of financial aid through Pell Grants, Supplemental Educational Opportunity Grants, Federal Work-Study Program awards, and student loans. Financial aid awards are based on both need and superior academic performance. New York State residents are encouraged to apply for Tuition Assistance Program (TAP) awards. The College of New Rochelle also has numerous grants and scholarships available. The scholarships are all based on academic achievement and leadership qualities. Amounts vary from $1000 per year to full tuition. All students applying for financial aid are required to fill out a College of New Rochelle financial aid application and to complete the Free Application for Federal Student Aid (FAFSA).

Faculty

In no small measure, the College owes its growth and success to a highly committed faculty and administration. The faculty consists of dedicated scholars and teachers who have been recognized for excellence in teaching. Seventy-five percent of the faculty members hold doctoral degrees or the highest degree available in their field. No graduate students or teaching assistants teach undergraduates. Faculty advisers are available to students for consultation and guidance in academic and career planning. To supplement and complement its faculty, the College invites adjunct professors, artists, business executives, and social workers to teach courses in their areas of expertise. The student-faculty ratio is 11:1.

Student Government

The Office of Campus Activities oversees undergraduate extracurricular activities. The Student Government Association is comprised of elected officials and club and organization leaders.

Admission Requirements

The College is selective in its admission process and evaluates each candidate's secondary school record, class rank, grade point average, extracurricular activities, SAT I or ACT scores, and a counselor's recommendation. The secondary school curriculum should include 16 academic units in English, mathematics, foreign language, social science, and natural science. Applicants to the School of Nursing should complete biology and chemistry lab courses plus one other science course and three years of high school mathematics, including algebra I, algebra II, and geometry. Most applicants rank within the top half of their class and have maintained at least a B average. Students who will have completed 15 high school academic units within three years are invited to apply for early admission. While an admission interview is not required, it is recommended. First time and transfer students may apply for either the September or January term. The high school course of study is carefully considered, and the student must have maintained at least a 2.0 GPA at another institution. Students interested in the School of Nursing must have maintained at least a 2.5 GPA. International students are welcome and must submit scores on the Test of English as a Foreign Language (TOEFL), when necessary. A minimum TOEFL score of 550 is required for admission.

Application and Information

Interested students should begin the admission process early in their senior year. The College accepts applications and renders decisions on a rolling basis. Students particularly interested in the College may apply for early decision; all credentials must arrive in the Office of Admission by November 1. Early decision candidates are notified by December 1. Applications for regular admission are accepted until all class spaces are filled. Housing is assigned according to the date of deposit. Enrollment deferrals are available.

For additional information about the School of Arts & Sciences and the School of Nursing, students should contact:

Sr. Marion Lynch, O.S.U.
Acting Director of Admission
The College of New Rochelle
New Rochelle, New York 10805
Telephone: 800-933-5923 (toll-free)
E-mail: admission@cnr.edu
World Wide Web: http://www.cnr.edu

The College of New Rochelle students catch up on some studying while enjoying the beautiful weather and scenery.

COLLEGE OF NOTRE DAME
BELMONT, CALIFORNIA

The College

College of Notre Dame (CND) has been providing students of all backgrounds and beliefs with an individualized liberal arts education for 149 years. Founded by the Sisters of Notre Dame de Namur in 1851, CND was one of the first four colleges in California chartered to grant the bachelor's degree. It is the mission of the College to help students develop both a broader understanding of the world and the tools required to flourish personally and professionally.

CND's enrollment is approximately 1,750, allowing for closeness among students, faculty, and staff. Classes are kept small; many have only 10–15 students, while the largest classes have 35–40 students.

The College's population is composed of people from diverse ethnic and religious backgrounds, and students come from twenty states and twenty-five countries. CND's small size enables the College to guarantee housing for all new students in either residence halls or apartment complexes. CND is composed of buildings reflecting a variety of architectural styles interspersed with green lawns and trees.

There are many extracurricular opportunities available at CND. Students take part in a wide variety of campus organizations, including the Hawaiian Club, Amnesty International, Alianza Latina, International Club, the *Argonaut* student newspaper, Black Student Union, and *The Bohemian* literary magazine.

There are five main stage theater productions each year for students interested in drama, and musicians perform with an orchestra, a jazz band, a choir, and smaller ensembles. CND competes in the National Association of Intercollegiate Athletics (NAIA) and is a full member of the California Pacific Conference, with five men's and six women's teams. There are also a number of intramural sports programs.

In addition to the undergraduate degrees shown below, the College offers master's degrees in art therapy, business administration, counseling psychology, education, English, music, public administration, and systems management.

Location

College of Notre Dame's campus covers 80 acres of forested hillside in the peaceful community of Belmont, California—only 25 miles south of San Francisco, at the northern edge of Silicon Valley. The San Francisco Bay Area is home to one of the world's most dynamic cities and the technological heart of the nation as well as some of the premier centers of cultural, recreational, and athletic attractions in the country. Students often plan short trips to the beach in Santa Cruz, to the Napa Valley wine country, and to the Sierra Nevada mountains for skiing.

Majors and Degrees

College of Notre Dame offers the Bachelor of Arts degree in art (including a concentration in graphic design), biology, communication, English, French, history, humanities, Latin American studies, liberal studies, music, philosophy, political science, psychology, religious studies, social science, sociology (including concentrations in behavioral science, Christian ministry, and social action), and theater arts.

The Bachelor of Science degree is awarded in biochemistry, biology (including a concentration in environmental studies), biology statistics, business administration (including concentrations in accounting, economics and finance, international business, management, and marketing), computer science, financial statistics, management computer technology, and mathematics.

The Bachelor of Fine Arts is offered in studio art; the Bachelor of Music is offered in music performance.

Students interested in dentistry, law, medicine, teaching (elementary and secondary), pharmacy, physical therapy, and veterinary medicine may enroll in preprofessional programs. Minors are offered in most subjects, and double majors are quite common. Students may enter College of Notre Dame undeclared, but it is necessary to decide on a major by the end of the sophomore year.

In addition to the undergraduate degrees, the College offers elementary and secondary school teaching credentials.

Academic Program

The liberal arts philosophy of the College requires that students complete a core of General Education courses designed to strengthen analytical abilities and develop skills in critical thinking and effective communication. General Education courses range from the arts to English composition to intercultural studies to natural science.

Students also explore career options through an internship in their field of interest or career development classes.

College of Notre Dame operates on a traditional semester system, with two semesters of fifteen weeks each, plus an optional summer session. Students pursuing an undergraduate degree must complete a minimum of 124 semester units. Entering freshmen are granted credit for each Advanced Placement exam passed with a score of 3 or higher.

Off-Campus Arrangements

CND's Study Abroad Program places interested students (preferably as juniors) in colleges and universities in many countries around the world, including Ecuador, England, France, Japan, Mexico, and Russia. Students may also take advantage of exchange programs with the College's sister schools: Emmanuel College in Boston and Trinity College in Washington, D.C.

Academic Facilities

CND's beautiful campus in the wooded hills of Northern California provides an ideal setting in which to study and learn. The College offers modern science laboratories, computer centers, and a fully equipped 600-seat theater. The spacious library holds a collection of more than 100,000 volumes, 550 periodical subscriptions, and 7,500 audio recordings. Special features include the multimedia computer lab and the music technology lab. The Madison Art Center (located in a historic mid-1800s carriage house) is home to modern art studios, a viewing theater, and the Wiegand Art Gallery, which hosts exhibits by students and nationally known professional artists.

Costs

Tuition costs for 1999–2000 were approximately $16,200. The cost of room and board for the academic year ranged from $6400 to $7000, depending on the meal plan chosen by the student, and includes all utilities except for telephone. The total cost of one year (including books and other expenses) was estimated at $22,850.

Financial Aid

College of Notre Dame is committed to making an education affordable for every accepted student. Some form of financial assistance is given to approximately 70 percent of the College's full-time students. Need-based grants, loans, and work-study programs are available through the federal and state governments and the College itself. Merit-based scholarships are offered for students with demonstrated high academic achievement, community service, and leadership experience. Merit Scholarship applications are included in the CND admission application packet.

All students are encouraged to apply for need-based financial assistance. Each applicant for financial aid must submit the Free Application for Federal Student Aid (FAFSA) and the College of Notre Dame Financial Information Form (FIF) by March 2. The FAFSA is available from high school counselors, and the FIF is available from the College's Financial Aid Office at 650-508-3509.

Faculty

College of Notre Dame's distinguished faculty is committed to helping each student reach his or her highest potential. All students are assigned a faculty adviser with whom they meet one-on-one each semester. Advisers and instructors also hold weekly open-office hours. The student-faculty ratio is 14:1, and the average class size is 15. More than 90 percent of the faculty hold doctoral or other terminal degrees.

Student Government

The Associated Students of College of Notre Dame (ASCND) provides many opportunities for participation in student government and the planning of campus activities. Each student is eligible to take part in ASCND as a student representative, and each of the College's governing committees has a student member, thereby ensuring student involvement in the making of administrative decisions.

Admission Requirements

College of Notre Dame welcomes applications from interested students without regard to religious preference, financial need, or ethnic background. The completion of a college-preparatory course pattern, including courses in English, mathematics, natural science, social science, foreign language, and the arts, is required for freshman applicants along with the submission of SAT I or ACT scores. Students for whom English is not their first language must submit a TOEFL score in lieu of the SAT I or ACT. Each applicant is considered individually, taking into account the application essay, a letter of recommendation, and extracurricular achievements in addition to the academic record. Approximately 75 percent of each year's applicants are offered admission.

Transfer students are accepted at all class levels in both fall and spring semesters. Students who have completed more than 30 transferable units are not required to submit high school transcripts or SAT I or ACT scores. Transfer students considering College of Notre Dame may request a preapplication transfer credit evaluation to determine what course work is needed to complete a bachelor's degree.

Application and Information

College of Notre Dame operates on a rolling admission basis. For fall freshman applicants the priority deadline is March 2, while the final deadline is June 1. Transfer students must apply by August 1 for the fall semester and by December 1 for the spring semester.

All interested students are encouraged to visit the College for a campus tour and admission counseling.

For an application packet, to arrange a visit, or for more information, students should contact:

Office of Admission
College of Notre Dame
1500 Ralston Avenue
Belmont, California 94002
Telephone: 650-508-3607
        800-CND-0545 (toll-free)
E-mail: admiss@cnd.edu
World Wide Web: http://www.cnd.edu

Students on the campus of College of Notre Dame.

COLLEGE OF NOTRE DAME OF MARYLAND
BALTIMORE, MARYLAND

The College

Founded in 1873, the College of Notre Dame (CND) of Maryland offers a four-year liberal arts undergraduate program for women. In 1896, it was chartered as the first Catholic college for women in the United States to award the baccalaureate degree.

Notre Dame was chartered by the state of Maryland and is accredited by the Middle States Association of Colleges and Schools and approved by the Maryland Department of Education. Overall enrollment at the College in fall 1999 totaled 3,193. There were 2,091 undergraduate students and 1,102 men and women in the graduate program offering the M.A. in adulthood and aging, liberal arts, management, teaching, and leadership in teaching.

The 58-acre campus has nine major buildings. There are two residence halls: Doyle Hall for freshmen and sophomores and Mary Meletia Hall for juniors and seniors. Each dorm has lounges and study areas, kitchen-dinette areas, laundry facilities, and televisions. Freshmen are assigned roommates on the basis of their response to a questionnaire. Upperclass students choose their own roommates.

Other buildings on the campus house classrooms, labs, study and lounge areas, art and photography studios, music studios, a bookstore, a career planning center, auditoriums, a chapel, a planetarium, a TV studio, a radio station, a dance studio, a fitness center, a computer center, an international center, a state-of-the-art language lab, the Sports and Student Activities Complex, and a new addition to the science center. Campus sports facilities include a field hockey, lacrosse, and soccer playing field; four tennis courts; and basketball, volleyball, and racquetball courts. Notre Dame competes in seven NCAA Division III sports.

Location

Baltimore, one of the largest cities on the East Coast, has come into the national spotlight for its citywide renaissance, including the redeveloped Inner Harbor, which features Harborplace shopping, the National Aquarium, the Science Center, and a busy schedule of concerts and ethnic festivals. The city's fine museums, theaters, and wealth of educational institutions, including the Johns Hopkins University, the Peabody Conservatory of Music, and Maryland Institute, College of Art, are just minutes from campus. Washington, D.C., and colorful Georgetown are easily accessible by Metroliner and are less than an hour's drive from the College. Historic Annapolis and the United States Naval Academy are only 45 minutes away, and Philadelphia and New York City can be easily reached by car, train, or plane.

Majors and Degrees

Notre Dame offers the Bachelor of Arts degree with concentrations in the following fields of study: art, biology, business (emphases in accounting, computer information systems, finance, management, and marketing), chemistry, classical studies, communication arts, computer information systems, computer science, economics, education, English, history, international studies, liberal arts, mathematics, modern foreign languages, music, philosophy, physics, political science, psychology, and religious studies. A dual degree (B.A./B.S.) in nursing is granted in a cooperative program with the Johns Hopkins University. A dual degree (B.A./B.S.) in engineering is granted by Notre Dame in a cooperative program with the University of Maryland or the Johns Hopkins University. A B.A. degree in human services and an RN to B.S.N. program are offered exclusively through the Weekend College.

Four-year preprofessional programs are offered in dentistry, law, medicine, and veterinary medicine, and two-year programs are offered in dental hygiene, medical technology, nursing, pharmacy, and physical therapy. The College also offers a five-year B.A./M.A. program in education.

Academic Program

The curriculum is composed of three parts: general requirements, concentration requirements, and electives. Approximately one third of each student's program of study is made up of general education requirements—courses that Notre Dame considers essential in a liberal arts program. Students select a field of concentration on the basis of their interest and ability and choose one third of their courses in this specialized area. The remaining third of the curriculum enables students to broaden their intellectual and cultural backgrounds by choosing electives in fields of study outside their major. There is an honors program for outstanding students.

Requirements for graduation include the successful completion of general education, concentration, and proficiency requirements and electives totaling 128 credits; a minimum cumulative grade average of C (2.0); and a minimum of two years, normally the last two, of course work at Notre Dame.

The Weekday College for Adult Women is open for full-time and part-time study.

The Weekend College and Center for Graduate Studies are primarily designed for part-time students.

Notre Dame graduates have had a record of success in careers and in admission to graduate study at other institutions. The College's liberal arts program, which includes ample career preparation, works to strengthen that record. A comprehensive program, offered on an individual basis from the freshman year onward, helps students identify career goals and take practical steps toward achieving them. It is administered by professionals in the Career Center.

Off-Campus Arrangements

An internship program enables students to gain experience off campus—in major corporations, banks, newspaper offices, hospitals, local business offices, government agencies, and radio and TV stations, for example—and helps them integrate academic experience and career development. Internships are offered every term and are coordinated through the Career Center. More than 80 percent of the students participate in the highly regarded internship program.

Since 1963, Notre Dame has participated in an exchange program that enables students to take courses at any of the following colleges or universities, with permission of the dean: the Johns Hopkins University, Loyola College, Morgan State University, Towson University, Goucher College, Coppin State College, and Maryland Institute, College of Art. There is also an active social activities exchange program.

Academic Facilities

The award-winning Loyola–Notre Dame Library is the first library in the United States in which the entire collections of two undergraduate colleges have been combined for cooperative use. Constructed on land contiguous to the two colleges, the four-level structure houses more than 375,000 bound volumes and 2,100 periodicals. The library includes an audiovisual center containing 26,000 audiovisual materials and 378,138 microfilm and microfiche units; a reading deck overlooking a pond; study rooms, some of which have computers; and seminar rooms. The recently expanded Knott Science Center houses the biology, chemistry, physics, mathematics, photography, and psychology departments and contains fully equipped laboratories, lecture rooms, an auditorium, three darkrooms, and a planetarium. The Communication Arts Complex in Fourier Hall houses the communication arts department and contains a color television studio, a radio production studio, a soundproof control room, filmmaking equipment, and a graphics lab. The College's Computer Center, open seven days a week, houses four classrooms and separate computer labs. The computer center features fifty Pentium PCs (running Windows 95 with Microsoft Professional Office 97) as a campus standard and twenty networked Power Macs. Students have access to the Internet and the electronic library system and may send e-mail around the world. The complex also includes a VAX cluster for administrative record keeping.

Costs

The cost for the 2000–01 academic year at the College of Notre Dame is $22,675, exclusive of major travel expenses; tuition is $15,600 and room and board are $6800. Student fees are $275. Additional special academic and nonacademic fees, such as parking fees, student activity fees, book fees, and fees for instrumental lessons, are charged as they apply to a particular student. Fees are subject to change.

Financial Aid

Financial aid at Notre Dame is awarded to students who cannot provide the full cost of a Notre Dame education through their own and their families' reasonable efforts. Financial assistance consists of scholarships, grants, loans, and paid part-time employment. Awards are offered to students according to available funds and student eligibility. Eligibility is determined by documented financial need, as demonstrated by the College of Notre Dame Financial Aid Application and the Free Application for Federal Student Aid (FAFSA). Other qualifications considered include the applicant's high school record, scholastic aptitude and achievement as measured by the College Board tests, and special talents, contributions, and achievements. The application deadline for maximum consideration is February 15. For the 1999–2000 academic year, tuition scholarships were available up to full tuition. A new CND financial aid form and FAFSA must be submitted each year to reapply for aid.

Faculty

Notre Dame has 80 full-time and 10 half-time faculty members, all of whom hold as their highest degree a master's or doctoral degree. There are additional associate faculty members at the College. The faculty–undergraduate student ratio is 1:14.

Student Government

All full-time students are members of the Student Association at the College of Notre Dame and are encouraged to help determine College direction. The Student Senate officers and elected representatives from the Student Association have a strong voice in setting College policies. In cooperation with the administration and faculty, these students maintain and encourage those values that are considered important to the school as a whole. In addition, it is the policy of the administration that there always be a student representative at Board of Trustees meetings and on most College-wide standing committees.

Admission Requirements

The Admissions Committee selects students not only on the basis of academic records and test scores but also on the basis of personal character and accomplishments. The College of Notre Dame does not discriminate on the basis of race, color, religion, national or ethnic origin, or handicap in admission to, or treatment in, its educational programs and activities.

Because a strong academic program in high school is the best preparation for successful work at Notre Dame, the Admissions Committee places the greatest emphasis on the candidate's high school record. Applicants must graduate from an accredited high school and offer a minimum of 18 academic units distributed as follows: English, 4 units; foreign language, 3 units; college-preparatory mathematics, 3 units; history, 2 units; science, 2 units; and electives, 4 units. The committee recognizes variation in school curricula and reserves the right to admit students who lack one or more of the above requirements but give promise of doing acceptable college work.

The SAT I is required of all students. Application forms and information about the test are available from high school guidance counselors and from the College Entrance Examination Board, Box 592, Princeton, New Jersey 08541. International students may substitute the Test of English as a Foreign Language (TOEFL) for the SAT I. The TOEFL bulletin and registration form may be obtained by writing to TOEFL, Educational Testing Service, Princeton, New Jersey 08540. International students wishing to improve their English language skills may attend the College's English Language Institute.

Notre Dame admits with advanced standing those transfer applicants who have fulfilled the equivalent of freshman or sophomore class requirements in an accredited college. No credit is granted for a grade of D.

Personal interviews may be required for admission, and all candidates who find it possible to visit the campus are encouraged to do so. The Office of Admissions is open for interviews, by appointment, from 9 a.m. to 4:30 p.m., Monday through Friday, throughout the year. Open house events are held for prospective students and their parents throughout the academic year. Interested students should phone for 2000–01 dates.

Application and Information

For maximum consideration, applications should be received by February 15 for fall semester admission and December 15 for spring semester admission. Applications completed after the deadline are considered on a space-available basis. Students who wish to enter the freshman class should submit the following credentials to the director of admissions: a completed application for admission, including an essay and a student resume, with a nonrefundable $25 application fee; an official transcript of the high school record; scores on the SAT I; a recommendation from the high school guidance director; and a letter of recommendation from an English teacher. International students should also submit TOEFL scores and a completed financial affidavit. Transfer students should submit high school and college transcripts along with a completed application, the $25 nonrefundable fee, and one letter of recommendation.

Additional information and application forms may be obtained from:

Director of Admissions
College of Notre Dame of Maryland
4701 North Charles Street
Baltimore, Maryland 21210
Telephone: 410-532-5330
           800-435-0200 (toll-free in Maryland)
           800-435-0300 (toll-free outside Maryland)
E-mail: admiss@ndm.edu
World Wide Web: http://www.ndm.edu

COLLEGE OF OUR LADY OF THE ELMS
CHICOPEE, MASSACHUSETTS

The College

Elms College is a small, friendly coeducational college in western Massachusetts renowned for its strong academic programs and professional preparation. Known also for its supportive environment, Elms is a place where students get the help they need to reach their career goals. Founded by the Sisters of St. Joseph in 1928, Elms College is the only comprehensive four-year Catholic college in western Massachusetts. Elms has adapted to changing times by developing challenging, innovative programs designed to prepare women and men for professional roles in a wide variety of careers. Elms is proud of graduating students who, by means of a strong internship program, are experienced in their chosen fields. With a 12:1 student-teacher ratio, Elms is small enough to ensure highly personalized instruction, yet large enough to accommodate expanding areas of interest. The curriculum at Elms combines liberal arts with professional disciplines. This perfect balance of focused, marketable career skills and artistic, cultural, and social enrichments broadens the students' breadth of experiences.

Elms offers Bachelor of Arts (B.A.) and Bachelor of Science (B.S.) degrees as well as master's degrees in education (M.A.T. and M.Ed.) and theology (M.A.A.T.). A Master of Social Work (M.S.W.) degree program is offered part-time by Boston College. The student body totals 1,200, of which 550 are full-time undergraduate students.

Students enjoy a wide variety of social and cultural opportunities at Elms. There are movies, outings, and lectures as well as intramural sports, the arts, and an array of campus social and academic clubs. Examples of traditional Elms activities include Homecoming, Midnight Madness, One World Celebration, coffeehouses, Soph Show, Elms Night, 100 Days Party, and champagne breakfast for seniors. Students are encouraged to exercise their leadership skills and get involved in such activities and clubs as the student government, *Elmscript* (the student newspaper), drama club, international club, Umoja (an organization of students of color), and affirmative action committee. The residence halls provide students with comfortable living quarters and are equipped with laundry and kitchen facilities, a computer lab, and lounge areas with televisions.

The Elms College Division III NCAA and ECAC intercollegiate athletics program has four men's athletic teams, basketball, golf, soccer, and swimming. The women's athletic teams at Elms College compete against NCAA Division III colleges in basketball, field hockey, lacrosse, soccer, softball, and swimming. Intramural athletics include aerobics, basketball, floor hockey, swimming, tennis, volleyball, water aerobics, and weight lifting.

Location

Elms College is located minutes from downtown Springfield and Chicopee. The nearby junction of Interstate 90 (the Massachusetts Turnpike) and Interstate 91 provides easy access from all directions. By car, Elms College is approximately 30 minutes from Hartford, Connecticut; 1½ hours from Boston, Massachusetts, and Albany, New York; and 3 hours from the New York City area. Springfield is accessible by Amtrak or by air into Bradley International Airport. The proximity of Elms College to the Berkshire Hills (1 hour), Mount Snow (1½ hours), and Killington, Vermont (2½ hours), ensures easy access to great skiing.

The Greater Springfield/Pioneer Valley region of western Massachusetts is a popular place to attend college. Elms students socialize with students from more than a dozen local colleges, such as the University of Massachusetts, Amherst College, Springfield College, American International College, Western New England College, and Westfield State College. In addition to the variety of events available at nearby colleges, the city of Springfield offers many educational and social activities. The Basketball Hall of Fame, the Museum of Fine Arts, Stage West, the Springfield Symphony Orchestra, and the Springfield Civic Center present a sampling of the excitement generated in this area.

Majors and Degrees

Elms College awards the Bachelor of Arts degree in accounting, American studies, art education, art therapy, biology, business management, chemistry, communication sciences disorders (speech and language pathology/audiology), computer information technology, computer science, early childhood education, elementary education, English, graphic design, health-care management, history, interdepartmental studies (student designed), international studies, legal studies, marketing, mathematics, mathematics and computer science, natural science, paralegal/social services, paralegal studies (ABA approved), psychology, religious studies, secondary education (biology, chemistry, English, French, history, mathematics, and Spanish), sociology, Spanish, special education, teaching English as a second language, and transitional bilingual education. The Bachelor of Science degree is offered in medical technology, nursing (NLNAC accredited), and social work (CSWE accredited).

Minor concentrations are offered in most majors as well as in coaching, computer science, music, philosophy, theater, and women's studies.

Preprofessional programs in dentistry, law, medicine, optometry, and veterinary science are available, as is a program leading to a certificate in advanced paralegal studies. Students can declare double majors with the consent of their advisers.

Academic Program

Elms College offers a student-centered and value-oriented curriculum. The newly designed core program, funded by the prestigious National Endowment for the Humanities, teaches students to communicate effectively and to think critically and creatively. It makes students aware of globalization issues and gives them an understanding of science, art, history, and their own holistic nature. Special options for students include programs in dance (in association with the Dance Conservatory of New England), Army and Air Force ROTC, and Japanese and German language and culture courses.

A minimum of 120 credits is required for graduation. These credits are distributed among core requirements, major requirements, and general electives, which may be used for a minor. Elms offers students the opportunity to qualify for credit and/or advanced placement through several testing programs. Among these are the College Board's Advanced Placement tests and College-Level Examination Program.

Transformational Leadership is an honors program that is designed to challenge students intellectually as well as through the hands-on application of learning. The program involves rigorous honors-level courses and developmental service learning in the local community.

Off-Campus Arrangements

Recognizing that the learning experience comes from outside as well as inside the classroom, Elms has a strong internship program, which offers students in all majors a valuable opportunity for fieldwork and exposure to career possibilities.

Elms is enrolled in a partnership program with the American Institute for Foreign Study, Inc. (AIFS), which is a nationwide organization that provides comprehensive overseas study and travel programs. Through this affiliation, Elms students have the possibility of studying overseas for a semester, year, or summer. Elms has international study programs in France, Ireland, and Spain. A relationship has been formed between Elms College and the University of Ulster in Northern Ireland.

The Sisters of St. Joseph College Consortium student exchange program offers students the opportunity to enrich their educational experience by studying for a semester or year at a member campus throughout the country.

Cooperating Colleges of Greater Springfield (CCGS) is a group of eight private and public colleges that, through the sharing of programs, talents, and facilities, brings to Elms students the educational resources of a university while the initiative and vitality of each independent institution are retained. Elms students may enroll in any undergraduate course offered by the following member colleges: American International College, Bay Path College, Holyoke Community College, Springfield College, Springfield Technical Community College, Western New England College, and Westfield State College.

Academic Facilities

Berchmans Hall, the main classroom and administration building, dominates the front portion of the Elms campus. Included in this magnificent structure are laboratories, the Center for the Arts, and state-of-the-art computer laboratories. Alumnae Library, a contemporary facility, provides an ideal atmosphere for study and research. Its holdings include 143,727 volumes, 2,551 audiovisual items, CD-ROM, government documents, 688 periodicals, and 941 reels of microfilm. The Maguire Center for Health, Fitness, and Athletics features an Olympic-size pool, an aerobics/fitness room, a gymnasium with a suspended indoor track, and the Wellness Center. Other buildings include a modern, highly functional student center, residence halls, and the College chapel.

Costs

For 2000–2001, tuition and fees are $14,720, and room and board costs in College-owned residence halls are $5566 per year.

Financial Aid

With the cost of higher education increasing, the investment by families for a private education becomes more significant. Elms is concerned with these trends and attempts to provide an affordable education of quality. Approximately 87 percent of Elms College students receive financial aid in the form of loans, grants, merit scholarships, or work-study. Catholic school scholarships are available for graduates of Catholic high schools.

In order to receive full consideration for aid, entering students must submit the Free Application for Federal Student Aid (FAFSA), the Elms College institutional form, and additional documents by March 1 of their senior year in secondary school.

Faculty

Elms College has 50 full-time faculty members, of whom 76 percent hold doctoral or terminal degrees, and 45 part-time faculty members, of whom 33 percent hold doctoral or terminal degrees. The members of the Elms faculty are committed to teaching. Many have published articles in scholarly journals, and many serve as academic advisers. They take a personal interest in guiding each student toward his or her academic and career goals.

Student Government

Students are involved in campus governance through the Faculty-Student Senate and the Student Government Association. Major policy decisions related to student life are made by the Faculty-Student Senate, composed of 6 students and 6 faculty members. Other decisions about student life may be made by the Student Government Association, composed of an Executive Board, a Student Council, and a Financial Committee. These forms of governance allow for significant student involvement in all matters related to student life.

Admission Requirements

Elms College is proud of admitting qualified women and men who are eager to experience a value-centered education. In keeping with the College's commitment to a personalized education, the Committee on Admissions carefully reviews the credentials of each applicant. As a competitive college, Elms seeks women and men who have distinguished themselves inside and outside the classroom. Factors considered include the depth and variety of the academic program pursued, the grades achieved in each subject, recommendations from a teacher and/or guidance counselor, scores on the SAT I or ACT, and a personal interview (strongly recommended). Part-time employment, athletics, drama, and participation in student government are but a few of the many fruitful activities that can enhance an application.

Interested students are encouraged to visit the campus and discuss their academic and career aspirations with an admission counselor. Several open house programs are offered during the academic year. Tours and interviews are available year-round.

Application and Information

To apply, students must submit an application with a nonrefundable $30 application fee, scores on the SAT I or ACT, two letters of recommendation, and an official copy of the high school transcript. Transfer applicants should also submit a college transcript from each institution attended and an Elms College transfer application. Students are notified of the admission decision on a rolling basis, beginning in December. Students are admitted to Elms College without regard to race, color, creed, or national origin.

For further information and application materials, students should contact:

Michael Crowley
Director of Admission
Elms College
291 Springfield Street
Chicopee, Massachusetts 01013-2839
Telephone: 413-592-3189
           800-255-ELMS (toll-free)
Fax: 413-594-2781
E-mail: admissions@elm.edu
World Wide Web: http://www.elms.edu

The campus architecture is a pleasing blend of modern and Gothic styles.

COLLEGE OF SAINT BENEDICT
SAINT JOHN'S UNIVERSITY
ST. JOSEPH AND COLLEGEVILLE, MINNESOTA

The College and The University

The College of Saint Benedict (CSB) and Saint John's University (SJU) are private, residential, liberal arts institutions. CSB for women was founded in 1887; SJU for men was founded in 1857. The Carnegie Foundation for the Advancement of Teaching and *U.S. News & World Report* rank CSB and SJU as two of only five Catholic colleges nationwide included in the selective national liberal arts category. The two institutions offer a common curriculum, class schedule, and social and cultural programming. Women and men students attend classes and utilize the services and facilities at both campuses. Each campus, however, addresses the unique needs of the adult development of its students—including gender-specific issues—through residential life programming and activities. Student residence hall options include traditional dormitory rooms, suites, and apartments.

The sponsoring communities of Benedictine women and men continue the centuries-old tradition of a balanced education addressing the developmental needs of mind, body, and spirit. While they are Catholic institutions, CSB and SJU welcome students and faculty members of all faith backgrounds and preferences. The campus ministry staffs provide a wide array of opportunities for spiritual growth.

There are more than sixty clubs and organizations through which students can pursue curricular and cocurricular interests. A campus radio station, student newspapers and literary journals, a debate society, vocal and instrumental music ensembles, political and social action groups, and major-affiliated clubs provide numerous leadership and professional development, as well as social and recreational, opportunities.

Eleven CSB and twelve SJU athletic teams compete in the Minnesota Intercollegiate Athletic Conference and the National Collegiate Athletic Association Division III. Extensive opportunities for intramural and club sports are also available.

Location

The CSB campus is located on 800 acres of forest and ponds in the small residential community of St. Joseph in central Minnesota, just 6 miles west of St. Cloud, a city with a metropolitan population of 185,000. The SJU campus sits in the midst of 2,400 acres of rolling hills, lakes, and forest just 5 miles west of CSB. A college-owned shuttle system provides frequent and convenient transportation between the campuses and into St. Cloud. In addition, because the campuses are located just 70 miles northwest of Minneapolis and St. Paul, students have easy access to the attractions of that major metropolitan area.

Majors and Degrees

Bachelor of Arts degrees are offered in accounting, art, art history, Asian studies, biology, chemistry, classics, communication, computer science, dietetics, economics, education, English, environmental studies, French, gender and women's studies, German, history, humanities, liberal studies, management, mathematics, medieval studies, music, natural science, peace studies, philosophy, physics, political science, psychology, social science, social work, sociology, Spanish, theater, and theology. Bachelor of Science degrees are offered in nursing and nutrition science.

Preprofessional programs are available in dentistry, divinity, forestry, law, medicine, occupational therapy, pharmacy, physical therapy, and veterinary medicine. Certification programs are available in coaching and secondary education. A dual-degree program is offered in engineering.

Academic Program

The faculties of CSB and SJU jointly offer an innovative core curriculum. First-year students participate in a yearlong symposium, limited to 9 men and 9 women, which focuses on the development of oral and written communication skills along with proficiency in a variety of reading styles. Seniors participate in a seminar in which they integrate moral and ethical decision making with contemporary issues. An honors program of challenging interdisciplinary and major course work that approaches topics beyond the general curriculum is available to selected students. The core also requires proficiency in a foreign language, discussion, writing, and mathematics.

Through the service-learning program at CSB and SJU, students are encouraged to apply what they learn in the classroom by including service to the community as a part of the course work.

Academic advising and assistance is available from faculty advisers, professional counselors, peer counselors, tutors, and study groups. Career and employment counseling is also available.

Off-Campus Arrangements

CSB and SJU rank third among bachelor's institutions nationwide in the number of students studying abroad, thanks to an extensive international studies program. Opportunities exist to earn a semester's credits in Australia, Austria, Central America, China, England, France, Greece and Italy, Ireland, South Africa, and Spain. A full-year exchange with Sophia University in Tokyo, Japan, is also available.

Assistance is provided in developing internships in any major. Each year, more than 500 students participate in off-campus experiential learning opportunities.

Academic Facilities

CSB and SJU share a joint library system. The Hill Monastic Manuscript Library is one of the world's foremost resources for medieval study.

CSB's Benedicta Arts Center and SJU's Stephen B. Humphrey Auditorium provide three acoustically excellent performing arenas for college and visiting musical and theater productions. Additional facilities include music rehearsal rooms with pianos, an organ recital hall, a listening library, art studios, an art gallery, a costume and scene shop, a lighting and electrical shop, and a fine arts computer studio. This studio provides state-of-the-art computer access specifically for art, music, and theater students.

The science facilities are up-to-date and complete. SJU's campus provides the ideal field biology setting. Electronic instrumentation is for student use, not just observation. The science center on the CSB campus provides state-of-the-art chemistry and nutrition science classrooms, labs, and computer access. A behavioral science lab and observation room support experimentation by psychology students.

CSB and SJU provide multiple public computer-access areas populated with networked PCs, Power Macintosh computers, Silicon Graphics systems, networked laser and color printers, and the latest versions of the most popular software. Network connections are available for each resident in all residence hall rooms.

Costs

The costs for the 2000–01 academic year are as follows: CSB and SJU tuition, $16,995; average CSB housing and meal contract, $5220; average SJU housing and meal contract, $5129. The cost of books and supplies averages about $600 per year as do personal expenses. Payment plans are available to assist in payment of these costs.

Financial Aid

Assistance for financing an education at CSB and SJU is identified as scholarships for students with excellent academic, service, and leadership records and as grants, employment, and loans for students who demonstrate a need for assistance in paying for college. About 90 percent of the students currently attending the colleges receive financial assistance, many under both (non-need and need) categories.

Renewable scholarships, such as the Regents'/Trustees', which awards $8500 per year; the President's, which ranges from $5500 to $7500 per year; and the Dean's, which ranges from $3000 to $5000 per year, are awarded competitively based on the student's past academic achievement, college entrance test scores, and demonstrated service and leadership. Other scholarships recognize outstanding fine arts students and students with outstanding leadership in diversity.

Students interested in applying for grants, employment, and loans should complete the Free Application for Federal Student Aid (FAFSA). The colleges participate in state and federal financial aid programs such as the Federal Pell Grant, Federal Work-Study, and Federal Stafford Student Loan programs. In addition, the colleges offer generous financial assistance from their own funds to assist students.

Faculty

CSB and SJU students study with 287 full-time and 57 part-time faculty members on the two campuses. More than 80 percent of the full-time faculty members have attained the terminal degree in their field of expertise, and about 15 percent are from the Benedictine communities of women and men. No classes are taught by graduate assistants or in an auditorium setting.

While research and publication are encouraged, they are not pursued at the expense of teaching responsibilities. Entry-level class size averages 22 students. Since class sizes are small, individual attention is the rule. The student-faculty ratio is 13:1.

Student Government

As autonomous governing bodies, the CSB Student Senate (SBS) and the SJU Student Senate (SJS) advance students' interests, involvement, and participation in the institutions. Both the SBS and the SJS oversee elected committees that deal with academic affairs, social affairs, service, and Christian life.

The Joint Events Council, made up of 10 elected students from each campus, is responsible for coordinating cultural and social events for the two campuses.

Admission Requirements

CSB and SJU are moderately selective in their admission standards and seek students who have demonstrated academic achievement and promise as well as those who will bring varied talents and interests to the colleges. A strong academic foundation, including 4 years of English and 3 years of math, science, and social studies, is required; a foreign language is recommended.

Application and Information

Offers of admission are granted on a rolling basis, and applicants should expect to be notified within three weeks of the receipt of their completed application.

CSB and SJU are members of the Common Application and accept Peterson's Universal application. Prospective students can apply on line at the CSB/SJU Web site.

Students are encouraged to visit the campuses for a tour and to meet with an admission counselor. Appointments should be made at least five days in advance.

Application forms and additional information may be obtained by writing or calling:

Admission Office
College of Saint Benedict (for women)
37 South College Avenue
St. Joseph, Minnesota 56374-2099
Telephone: 800-544-1489 (toll-free)
Fax: 320-363-5010
E-mail: admissions@csbsju.edu
World Wide Web: http://www.csbsju.edu

Admission Office
Saint John's University (for men)
P.O. Box 7155
Collegeville, Minnesota 56321-7155
Telephone: 800-245-6467 (toll-free)
Fax: 320-363-3206
E-mail: admissions@csbsju.edu
World Wide Web: http://www.csbsju.edu

The CSB and SJU campuses share 3,200 acres of forested trails, rolling hills, and secluded lakes. Only a few minutes outside of St. Cloud and an hour from Minneapolis and St. Paul, the campuses provide the perfect mix of natural escape and metropolitan access.

COLLEGE OF ST. CATHERINE
ST. PAUL, MINNESOTA

The College

The College of St. Catherine (CSC) is the largest Catholic college for women in the country, enrolling a total of 4,372 students. The undergraduate program offers forty-five majors; master's degrees are awarded in education, library and information science, nursing, occupational therapy, organizational leadership, physical therapy, and theology. A joint master's degree in social work is offered by CSC and the University of St. Thomas. In 1905 when many women's colleges were considered finishing schools, the Sisters of St. Joseph of Carondelet founded the College of St. Catherine and challenged the conventions of women's education. The sisters believed in providing a rigorous education for women and set an unwavering standard of academic excellence. Three basic values have shaped the College since its inception: a devotion to the liberal arts, a belief in the potential of women, and a commitment to the formation of strong personal values. In 1937, CSC became the first Catholic institution to receive a Phi Beta Kappa charter. The College's excellent academic reputation is complemented by its commitment to strengthening students' leadership abilities and to providing a variety of leadership opportunities through student government, clubs, and organizations.

An impressive variety of departments serve the needs of students at CSC. The Career Development Office provides career counseling, information, and resources from the career-preparation stage to the job-hunting process. The O'Neill Center for Academic Development offers programs to sharpen writing, reading, math, and study skills. The Office of Multicultural and International Programs serves as an information and resource center for CSC students of color and international students from thirty countries. The Campus Ministry Office provides a welcoming community for students of all faiths, and the Office of Student Life coordinates a wide variety of social and educational programs each year. The Residence Life Office coordinates residence hall operations, including six residence halls available to all students and two on-campus apartment buildings for upperclass students. Seventy-seven percent of first-year students live on campus. Residence hall rooms are wired for cable television and Internet access.

CSC students may be eligible for membership in twenty-three academic honor societies and can choose from more than thirty different clubs representing academic, social service, recreational, and cultural interests. Students publish an annual literary/arts magazine, yearbook, and biweekly newspaper and are active in NCAA Division III intercollegiate, intramural, and club sports programs. NCAA sports include basketball, cross-country, ice hockey, soccer, softball, swimming/diving, tennis, track, and volleyball.

Location

CSC is conveniently located in a residential area of St. Paul, Minnesota, just 10 minutes from the downtown areas of both St. Paul and Minneapolis. The Twin Cities have innumerable resources for education, entertainment, and culture, including art museums and galleries, concert halls, and theater and dance organizations. St. Paul, which has been called the nation's "Most Liveable City," and Minneapolis, home of the Tyrone Guthrie Theater, Walker Art Center, and Hubert H. Humphrey Metrodome, make up one of the nation's most vital metropolitan areas. The area's 900 lakes, bicycle and ski trails, jogging paths along the Mississippi River (about eight blocks from the campus), beautiful urban parks, and nature centers provide fun and relaxation all year long.

Majors and Degrees

CSC's comprehensive undergraduate program offers the Bachelor of Arts degree in art, biology, chemistry, communication, East Asian studies, English, French, history, music, music education, philosophy, psychology, sociology, Soviet and East European studies, Spanish, theater, theology, and women's studies. Both the Bachelor of Arts degree and the Bachelor of Science degree are offered in accounting, business administration, economics, early childhood education, elementary education, exercise science and nutrition, family and consumer science, fashion merchandising, foods and nutrition, information management, international business and economics, international relations, mathematics, nursing, occupational science, physical education, physics, political science, sales, social work, and speech communication. In addition, CSC students may design their own major. Preprofessional programs are offered in dentistry, engineering, forestry, law, medical technology, medicine, occupational therapy, optometry, pharmacy, physical therapy, and veterinary medicine. Cooperative 3-2 programs in engineering and forestry and environmental studies are offered with Washington University and the University of Minnesota (engineering) and Duke University (forestry and environmental studies). The Minneapolis campus offers a Bachelor of Interpreting (for the deaf and the hard-of-hearing). The Center for Sales Innovation focuses on business-to-business sales. It offers a sales major and minor, continuing education for sales professionals, print and multimedia research resources, and sales internships.

Academic Program

The liberal arts education offered at CSC provides the foundation to meet the challenges of a multicultural, technological society. In addition to courses in their major field of study, CSC students take a core curriculum of liberal arts courses. The core focuses on the increased public involvement and leadership that women will experience in the coming century. It includes two foundation courses, which are required of all students. At least 130 semester credits must be earned for the B.A. or B.S. CSC places emphasis on basic proficiencies, including writing and computer literacy, which are requirements for graduation. The day and evening programs operate on a 4-1-4 academic calendar—two 4-month semesters split by a January term in which students may pursue independent learning experiences, study abroad, or avail themselves of research, internship, or employment opportunities on and off campus.

Off-Campus Arrangements

Thirty additional majors are available through CSC's participation in the Associated Colleges of the Twin Cities, a consortium that enables students from CSC and four neighboring private, coeducational liberal arts colleges to take classes and use the resources of all five campuses without additional cost. Through the Sisters of St. Joseph College Consortium Student Exchange Program, students may spend up to two semesters at another St. Joseph Consortium college.

Global Studies programs enable CSC students to live in other cultures. Semester and academic-year programs, January courses abroad, and summer study programs are available.

Students may apply financial aid received at CSC to international study and may transfer credit received in approved programs at international institutions toward their degree at CSC.

Corporations and agencies in the Twin Cities metropolitan area offer more than 500 internship sites for CSC students. Clinical sites for students in health-care fields are especially numerous in the broad network of hospitals and health-care institutions in the Twin Cities.

Academic Facilities

The Mother Antonia McHugh Fine Arts Complex houses the music, communication, theater, and visual arts departments and the O'Shaughnessy, an 1,800-seat performing arts center. The Theater Arts Building has a studio theater, a dance studio, a scene shop, a dressing room, costume shops, classrooms, and a reception room. The Music Building contains a rehearsal hall, a recital hall with a reception area, twenty practice rooms, classrooms, and the Performing Arts Library. The Visual Arts Building houses the Catherine G. Murphy Art Gallery (in which works by students and by outside artists are exhibited), art studios, seminar rooms, and a lecture hall. The Aimee and Patrick Butler Center for Sports and Fitness offers students opportunities to achieve personal fitness, in addition to providing outstanding training and competition facilities. It houses an eight-lane, 25-yard indoor swimming pool with diving boards and spectator seating, a sauna and spa, a suspended indoor jogging track, a state-of-the-art weight room and cardiovascular workout area, and a 13,000-square-foot gymnasium with courts for volleyball, basketball, and tennis.

The St. Catherine library contains 390,000 bound books and 2,100 journal subscriptions. CSC participates in the Cooperating Libraries in Consortium, making an additional million volumes and 5,000 periodicals available. The library includes the archives and rare book rooms; the Ade Bethune Room, which houses a special collection of this internationally known liturgical artist's artworks and papers; a sizable women's collection; and the Computing Services Center. The College provides students with approximately 250 networked computers in four public labs, academic departments, the learning resource center, residence halls, and other areas. In addition, 200 laptop computers are leased to students. CSC uses Lotus Notes for e-mail, and students have access to the Internet and other online services.

Science laboratories and classrooms, located in Mendel Hall, include an instrument room with humidity and temperature control, chemistry and physics laboratories, up-to-date specialized laboratory equipment, and an astronomy observatory with a research-grade telescope. In addition, the 110-acre campus is an arboretum with hundreds of plant and tree varieties for the study of ecology, horticulture, and botany.

Costs

Basic expenses for 2000–01 include tuition, $15,456; room and board, $4550 (average); and the student activities fee, $122. The cost of books and supplies averages $625 per year.

Financial Aid

CSC is committed to enrolling students of all economic backgrounds, so admission decisions are made without regard to applicants' financial status. The student financial aid program provides more than $20 million a year in the form of grants, scholarships, loans, and employment opportunities from College, federal, and state sources. More than 600 on-campus work-study positions are awarded to students each year. In addition to need-based aid, St. Catherine of Alexandria Merit Scholarships are awarded solely on the basis of academic achievement. In 1999–2000, 94 percent of first-time freshmen and 88 percent of continuing students received aid. The average award for full-time students is $14,754. Several long-term, low-interest, and deferred-payment options are available.

To apply for financial aid, applicants must file the Free Application for Federal Student Aid (FAFSA) and a CSC financial aid questionnaire as soon as possible after January 1. Awards are made on an annual basis, and applicants must reapply each year. Students from other states are awarded the same percentage of grant assistance as students from Minnesota. Financial aid forms should be submitted by April 1 for priority consideration. An early estimate of financial aid is also available.

Faculty

CSC employs 286 faculty members, of whom 137 are full-time. Eighty-two percent of CSC's full-time faculty members have earned the highest degree in their field. Distinguished scholars who are known for their academic and professional achievements, they are also recognized for dedication to teaching— their first priority. The CSC student-faculty ratio is 12:1.

Student Government

The College Association Governing Board (CAGB) serves as a forum for student concerns and as a medium of cooperation and communication between the student body and the faculty and administration. The CAGB recommends College policies, plans social and educational programs for the entire student body, and serves as a gathering organization for many groups of students.

Admission Requirements

To be admitted to the freshman class, a candidate must present a transcript of courses taken through the end of her junior year and test scores that indicate intellectual ability and progress. Admission is based on the applicant's academic record, on the evidence of her ability to do college work and to benefit from it, and on indications of her desire to attend CSC. The 1999–2000 freshman class at CSC had an average ACT composite score of 22.

Application and Information

Applications are processed on a continuous basis. Candidates are informed of the decision of the Admissions Committee within three weeks after submission of the application materials and supporting credentials: a completed application form, accompanied by a $20 application fee; an official high school transcript with all available aptitude and achievement test scores and class rank; a recommendation form; and ACT or SAT I scores.

For further information, students should contact:

Office of Admission
College of St. Catherine
2004 Randolph Avenue
St. Paul, Minnesota 55105
Telephone: 651-690-8850
          800-656-KATE (toll-free)
E-mail: admissions@stkate.edu
World Wide Web: http://www.stkate.edu

COLLEGE OF SAINT ELIZABETH
MORRISTOWN, NEW JERSEY

The College

The College of Saint Elizabeth (CSE), which celebrated its centennial year in 1999–2000, is the first four-year college in New Jersey to grant baccalaureate degrees to women. A Catholic college in the liberal arts tradition, CSE now includes a women's college, coeducational Adult Undergraduate Degree Programs, and a coeducational Graduate Degree Program. An enrollment of approximately 1,800 students encourages considerable student-faculty interaction and fosters a spirit of campuswide friendliness and support. An emphasis is placed on opportunities for individual growth through academic, spiritual, cultural, and civic experiences.

Located on a 200-acre campus, CSE's twelve buildings command a wide view of the surrounding hills. Seventy-two percent of the full-time students live on campus. The majority come from New Jersey, 2 percent from other northeastern states, 1 percent from other states, and 8 percent from other countries. Approximately 56 percent of those who begin as freshmen graduate, and about 47 percent go on to graduate study within five years of leaving college. Two attractive residence halls provide ample private and double rooms. Each residence hall has kitchenettes, laundry facilities, a mail room, lounges, conference rooms, and recreation areas. The student center contains a swimming pool, a gymnasium, a weight room, a drama studio, an art studio, the Rathskeller, a dining room, and the College Store.

Students may belong to extracurricular organizations associated with their academic interests and to such associations as the Leadership Program, Elizabethan Singers, Drama Club, Student Activities Committee, Campus Ministry, Students Take Action Committee, Volunteer Services, Student Government, and varsity athletics. NCAA Division I and Division III team sports include basketball, cross-country, equestrian, soccer, softball, swimming, tennis, and volleyball. Other organizations include a number of Greek-letter honor and professional societies and student affiliates of the American Chemical Society. A broad calendar of cultural and social events is available both on campus and at nearby coeducational Fairleigh Dickinson and Drew Universities. Career Services provides assistance with career preparation and graduate study.

In addition to the majors and degrees listed below, the College offers the M.A. degree in education/human services leadership, educational technology, counseling psychology, and theology and the M.S. degree in nutrition, management, and health-care management.

Location

Morristown is located in the rapidly growing corporate center of Morris County. Neighboring towns and cities, only minutes from campus, offer facilities for shopping and recreation. The College is an hour from the cultural and social opportunities of New York City by car, train, or bus and is near the campuses of Rutgers, Princeton, Fairleigh Dickinson, Seton Hall, Drew, Stevens Institute of Technology, and the County College of Morris. Newark International Airport is approximately 30 minutes and two New York airports are approximately 1 hour from the campus. Local bus routes are easily accessible, and New Jersey Transit, which has a stop at the campus gate, provides excellent rail commuter service from New York City, Hoboken, Newark, the Oranges, Short Hills, Maplewood, Millburn, Summit, Chatham, Madison, and Dover. Routes 287, 80, 280, 46, 78, 24, and 10 are located close by.

Majors and Degrees

The Bachelor of Arts is offered in American studies, art, biochemistry, biology, chemistry, communication, economics, elementary education (N–8 with an option for special education, K–12 coupled with a major leading to either the B.A. or the B.S.), English, French, history, individualized major, international studies, justice studies (criminal justice, legal studies), mathematics, music, philosophy, psychology, religious studies, sociology, and Spanish. The Bachelor of Science is offered in biochemistry, biology (options for cytotechnology, medical technology, and toxicology), business administration (options for accounting, computer information systems, human resource management, management, and marketing), chemistry, computer science, and foods and nutrition. The Bachelor of Science in Nursing degree is offered as an upper-division nursing program.

Academic Program

The requirements for a B.A., B.S., or B.S.N. degree are 128 semester hours of academic credit, competency in writing, First Year Seminar (not required of adult students), 2 credits in fitness/wellness, and successful completion of the comprehensive examination in the major subject. A minimum of 32 credits is required in the major, except for the major in elementary education, which requires 30 credits. The core curriculum requires that students take between 36 and 44 credits distributed among six cluster areas: Literature, Fine Arts, and Language; Foreign Language; Social/Behavioral Sciences; Natural/Physical Sciences and Mathematics/Computer Science; Philosophy/Religion, History; and Perspectives on an Interdependent World. The remaining courses are free electives. With the exception of the sciences, mathematics, and nutrition, the major need not be declared until the end of the sophomore year.

Career preparation includes studies in accounting, business management, communication, computer information systems, computer science, criminal justice and legal studies, foods and nutrition, gerontology, human resource management, management, marketing, premedicine, pre–veterinary studies, secondary education, and social work. Education majors may obtain state certification and/or endorsement in early childhood or special education. The College has a highly successful Leadership Program.

Students interested in becoming registered dietitians may enroll in the dietetic internship program if they hold a baccalaureate degree and meet the current American Dietetic Association course work requirements.

Independent study, field experience, internships, study-abroad opportunities, honors, leadership, and accelerated programs, minors, and double majors are available for qualified students. Successful scores on Advanced Placement tests are honored for placement or credit. Credit is given for successful scores on CLEP subject examinations with essays, on the Thomas Edison College Examination Program (TECEP) examinations, on the Regents College Examination in nursing, DANTES, and ACE College Credit Recommendation, and on portfolio assessment of prior learning.

Courses are offered in the evenings and during the summer. Weekend College programs are offered in accounting, communication, computer information systems, computer science, English, foods and nutrition, human resource management, international studies, management, marketing, and psychology.

Off-Campus Arrangements

A cross-registration policy exists with nearby Fairleigh Dickinson and Drew universities. Qualified students may study abroad during the junior year or in the summer. A January Intersession Program provides opportunities for short-term courses and off-campus experiences. Students have opportunities in Morris County for volunteer service, field experience, and internships in local agencies, institutions, and the corporate headquarters of numerous multinational corporations.

Academic Facilities

Students majoring in biology and chemistry conduct independent research projects under the guidance of highly qualified professors and in conjunction with local research companies. The College has several well-equipped microcomputer laboratories and extensive software. Mahoney Library is a 300-seat air-conditioned facility that provides group and individual study areas. The library's collection includes 140,202 volumes, 3,428 audiovisual titles, 70,351 microforms, 886 periodical subscriptions, and a 4,750-volume curriculum collection for education students. The Phillips Library of Rare Books and Manuscripts houses a variety of special collections. The library is a selective depository for U.S. government documents. Eighteen CD-ROM databases are available for student use, along with three online systems. A TV studio, an editing suite, an ITV classroom, and postproduction facilities are housed in the AV services area.

Costs

Tuition in 2000–01 for incoming full-time freshmen is $14,000, and room and board are $6850. Academic fees are estimated at $530 annually, and other incidental expenses, such as travel, entertainment, clothes, books, and personal expenses, are estimated at about $1900. Part-time students pay $425 per credit.

Financial Aid

Approximately 86 percent of full-time students at the College of Saint Elizabeth receive financial aid. Aid is available from the College itself in the form of scholarships, grants-in-aid, and campus employment and from the federal and state governments in the form of scholarships, grants, loans, and employment. Students who wish to be considered for grants, loans, and campus employment should apply to the College by March 1 for the fall semester and by November 1 for the spring semester. Campus employment is available in the residence halls, laboratories, the library, and College offices, and a limited number of work-study opportunities for qualified students are available both on and off campus. Transfer scholarships and some scholarships for part-time students are also available.

Faculty

The faculty-student ratio is 1:10. The full-time instructional faculty for 1999–2000 included approximately 78 percent with doctorates and 22 percent with master's degrees. Several faculty members hold additional professional credentials. The goals of the faculty are to teach effectively, to be readily available to students, and to pursue research.

Student Government

Students participate in the governance of the College through the Student Organization. The Student Organization elects members to the Student Government, which serves as the student executive branch. Student views on residence life, day-student issues, student activities, and the operations of the student Rathskeller are expressed and acted on through a committee structure. The Academic Life and Student Life committees of the College are composed of both faculty and students, and are engaged in determining methods of implementing institutional goals and increasing student satisfaction with campus life. Students are encouraged to participate fully in the academic community and to exercise considerable influence in social and extracurricular activities. There is an open atmosphere on campus, and students have access to the deans and the president.

Admission Requirements

The College looks for students whose aptitude and academic record demonstrate the ability to meet academic challenges. Normally, a student interested in admission to the College should complete 16 academic units by the end of her senior year, including 3 years of English, 3 years of mathematics and/or science, 2 years of a foreign language, 1 year of U.S. history, and seven upper-level academic electives. Applicants must submit either SAT I or ACT test results. International students must send scores on the Test of English as a Foreign Language (TOEFL). Students applying to the College should submit a secondary school transcript, including courses currently in progress, plus two letters of recommendation from persons who can attest to their academic potential. Students are encouraged to have an on-campus interview and visit the campus. Open Houses are held each spring and fall. Well-qualified students who are recommended by their high school principals may be accepted after three years of high school. Transfers from two- and four-year colleges are accepted for the fall and spring semesters. An applicant who has earned an A.A. degree in a transfer program at an accredited two-year college is eligible for admission with junior-class standing. Through articulation agreements, adult students must admit secondary and previous college transcripts (if any) in addition to the application.

Application and Information

College of Saint Elizabeth
2 Convent Road
Morristown, New Jersey 07960-6989

Telephone: 973-290-4700 (Office of Admission)
973-290-4600 (adult undergraduate degree programs)
800-210-7900 (toll-free) (Office of Admission)

Fax: 973-290-4710 (Office of Admission)
973-290-4676 (adult undergraduate degree programs)

E-mail: apply@liza.st-elizabeth.edu

World Wide Web: http://www.st-elizabeth.edu

Students at the College of Saint Elizabeth.

COLLEGE OF ST. JOSEPH
RUTLAND, VERMONT

The College
The Sisters of St. Joseph founded the College of St. Joseph (CSJ) in 1950. This fully accredited institution allows each student an opportunity to grow intellectually and personally in preparation for the challenges of the "real world." In the Catholic tradition, the entire CSJ community is committed to providing programs and services that promote, support, and enhance the learning process in all aspects of college life.

A personalized experience is the trademark of the College of St. Joseph. The average class size is 16 students, and with a student-faculty ratio of 12:1, all students feel free to ask questions or add their opinion to a hearty classroom dialogue.

The College of St. Joseph recognizes the importance of combining classroom experience with hands-on opportunities. That is why all students seeking a bachelor's degree are provided internship and community service programs related to the student's major.

CSJ students find themselves actively involved in many campus activities, such as intercollegiate sports and diverse clubs and organizations. The College's varsity athletics participate at the NAIA Division II level and are members of the Mayflower Conference. The College currently fields men's and women's basketball and soccer programs. CSJ students also participate in club/intramural programs such as basketball, cross-country skiing, downhill skiing, indoor soccer, softball, and volleyball. Students also enjoy activities such as drama, chorus, student government, academic clubs, the yearbook, and an outing club, to name a few.

Through the Campus Ministry, students can become active in Big Brothers/Big Sisters, local food drives, hunger awareness programs, and other related activities. The Career Planning and Placement Office keeps current listings of job openings for students in all majors. Students can use the DISCOVER, SIGI plus, and GRE–Graduate School Selector computer software to research and identify career choices and graduate school options.

The Graduate Division offers master's degrees in elementary education, general education, reading, school guidance counseling, special education, counseling psychology, and clinical mental health counseling.

Location
Situated in the heart of the Green Mountains, the College of St. Joseph is located on a compact and easily accessible campus nestled within 90 wooded acres of College-owned land on the fringe of Rutland, Vermont's third-largest city. The campus is easily reached via interstate highway as well as by plane, train, and bus. Montreal, Albany, Boston, Hartford, and New York City are all within easy driving distance. In CSJ's own backyard, there is some of the best skiing in the East, with Killington and Pico only a 15-minute drive and five other major ski areas within an hour's drive. Lakes Champlain, Bomoseen, and St. Catherine; the Appalachian Trail and Long Trail; and some of the most beautiful state forests offer exceptional recreational opportunities. The city of Rutland is one of CSJ's greatest classrooms. Many students are involved in internships in various businesses, schools, and social service agencies in the area.

Majors and Degrees
The College of St. Joseph offers the Bachelor of Science degree in accounting, business management, computer information systems, finance, and resort and recreation management. Majors are also available in early childhood education, elementary education, and special education. The teacher-training program leads to teacher certification/licensure. Secondary education certification may be obtained for those majoring in English and selected social studies areas. The College also offers the Bachelor of Arts degree in American studies, communications, English, history, human services, journalism, political science, prelaw, and psychology. In addition, associate degrees in business, human services, and liberal studies are offered.

Academic Program
The College of St. Joseph's academic year consists of two semesters and a three-part summer session. Students complete a core of general education requirements, introducing students to essential knowledge and connecting the various disciplines in a manner that has application to life beyond the campus. General education courses include study in computers, English, fine arts, mathematics, natural science, philosophy and/or religion, the social sciences, and a global awareness component. In addition to these core courses, students must complete the degree requirements of their chosen major.

Project Success, a student support service program, provides personal counseling, mentoring, and tutoring. Career counseling services are available to CSJ students.

Students majoring in the education field must maintain at least a 3.0 grade point average in order to become certified and to be recommended for licensure by the institution to the Vermont Department of Education.

Experiential education is valued, and internship experiences are encouraged for all students enrolled in the four-year bachelor's degree programs. The internship consists of 280 hours of fieldwork and must be completed in the junior or senior year. Internships are commonly fulfilled by working at local businesses, schools, and public service agencies in an area related to the student's major.

Academic Facilities
St. Joseph Hall is the main academic and administrative building of the College. Located in St. Joseph Hall are all classrooms and faculty/administrative offices, the pottery/art studio, the photography lab, the library, and computer labs.

The Athletic Center, completed in 1995, includes a gymnasium, racquetball courts, weight and exercise room, dance and aerobics studio, and ample locker room facilities for athletic teams.

Tuttle Hall, dedicated in 1999, is the College's student activities center. This facility houses the Student Development Office, a 210-seat auditorium/theater, a student lounge/snack bar, and the campus chapel.

Students have virtually unlimited access to computing and word processing facilities. The College's two computer labs are well stocked with Windows-based PCs, including several multimedia CD-ROM computers providing computing, research, word processing, and online accessibility to national computer networks.

The library has 63,000 volumes and subscribes to 251 periodicals. In addition, the library holds an invaluable collection of abstracts in psychology for use by psychology and human services majors. It also houses a special collection of educational tests and curriculum materials to support the College's education division. The library provides PsychLIT and ERIC, CD-ROM bibliographic databases covering the fields of education, psychology, business, and the humanities. CSJ's library also has access to VALS (Vermont Automated Library System), which provides students access to information from other state and regional libraries. Special collections entitled The Kyron Murray McGrath Irish Studies Collection and the Sister St. George Vermont Collection are included in its holdings.

Costs

The tuition for 2000–01 is $11,500; room and board are $6200. There is a student activities fee of $100 and a technology fee of $100, for a total of $17,900. Personal expenses, such as laundry and transportation, vary according to personal needs.

Financial Aid

The College of St. Joseph awards financial aid primarily on the basis of need. St. Joseph also offers merit-based scholarships awarded on the basis of academic performance, leadership qualities, and athletic ability. The deadline for preferential consideration of financial aid requests is March 1. Students are requested to complete and submit the Free Application for Federal Student Aid (FAFSA), which is available at high school guidance offices. Financial aid questions should be directed to the CSJ financial aid office.

Faculty

There are 13 full-time and 51 part-time faculty members at the College. All faculty members are residents of the Rutland area and are available for consultation with students. Undergraduate instruction is the focus of the College, and faculty members are encouraged to keep current with developments in their fields of study. The student-faculty ratio is 12:1.

Student Government

The Student Association is an integral and active element in the governance of the College. Students serve on various faculty committees as well as on the Board of Trustees. The students are responsible for submitting feedback to various departments when policies are made or changed. Students are encouraged to participate in the Student Association. Elections for student offices are held each year.

Admission Requirements

Admission to the College of St. Joseph is not based on one particular academic requirement. Students are evaluated on the basis of their academic potential for success. Each applicant is considered individually, and the College recognizes special capabilities and achievements. CSJ actively seeks students from all ethnic origins and geographic locations. The College requires that students submit SAT I or ACT scores and a high school transcript. Applicants should have pursued a college-preparatory curriculum while in high school. In addition, students need to submit two letters of recommendation, along with a typewritten essay of 200 to 400 words. The admission committee reviews the application only when all of the above are submitted.

Transfer students are considered individually, and a transfer evaluation is prepared by the registrar as part of the admission process. Generally, a grade of C or better is required for credits to be transferred.

While not required for admission, an interview and campus tour are strongly recommended. The College hosts Open House Weekends each year in the fall, which are excellent times to plan a visit. Appointments at other times can also be arranged through the Admissions Office.

Application and Information

The College of St. Joseph adheres to a rolling admission plan for both freshman and transfer students. Applications for the fall semester are reviewed on a regular basis beginning in October. Decisions are typically made within two weeks of receipt of a completed application (including supporting materials). The College adheres to the Candidates Reply Date of May 1 for the fall semester.

For further information, students and parents should contact:

Steven Soba
Dean of Admissions
College of St. Joseph
71 Clement Road
Rutland, Vermont 05701
Telephone: 802-773-5900 Ext. 205
E-mail: admissions@csj.edu
World Wide Web: http://www.csj.edu

Many CSJ students enjoy an afternoon on the slopes at nearby Pico or Killington ski areas after morning classes.

THE COLLEGE OF SAINT ROSE
ALBANY, NEW YORK

The College

The College of Saint Rose is an independent, coeducational institution where academics and career preparation are priorities. The College's progressive liberal education core prepares students to dive into one of the College's thirty-eight undergraduate majors, many of which incorporate a field experience component. The College offers small class sizes, with a student-faculty ratio of 17:1 and an experienced, mentoring faculty. *Money* magazine and *U.S. News & World Report* have ranked Saint Rose as one of the top colleges in the Northeast and the nation, based on such factors as affordability and high academic quality. In addition, in a recent career survey, 94 percent of Saint Rose graduates who responded were either employed or enrolled in a graduate program. With the capital of New York as its convenient location and a distinctly friendly atmosphere on campus, the College of Saint Rose is a place where students realize that they have the ability to change the world.

Saint Rose was founded in 1920 by the Sisters of Saint Joseph of Carondelet and is located in a residential neighborhood. The College encompasses seventy buildings, including a state-of-the-art Science Center, the Hubbard Interfaith Sanctuary, and athletic facilities that include a competition-sized pool, a Fitness Center with state-of-the-art equipment, and a regulation NCAA basketball court.

Saint Rose students comprise a community of leaders. Most of the 2,729 undergraduates at Saint Rose come from New York State and New England, and there are international students on campus who represent many countries. The College of Saint Rose actively seeks to enroll students of all backgrounds who can contribute to and benefit from the experience of shared learning and academic success.

Campus housing includes traditional- and suite-style residence halls as well as thirty-nine historical homes. Each house has its own history, character, and uniqueness and a wrap-around porch and stained-glass windows.

Students participate in organized social activities as well as sixteen associations that are related to academic majors. The College of Saint Rose is a member of the National Collegiate Athletic Association (NCAA) Division II. Intercollegiate teams include men's baseball; men's and women's basketball, cross-country, soccer, and swimming; and women's softball and volleyball.

Location

Saint Rose is nestled in the historic Pine Hills neighborhood of Albany. With more than 61,000 college students in the area, there are always things to do and people to meet. A wide variety of restaurants, shops, museums, and theaters are within walking distance or are easily accessible by buses that stop at Saint Rose.

Majors and Degrees

The College of Saint Rose offers programs of study in the fields of accounting, American studies, applied technology education, art (K–12 education) and studio art, biochemistry, biology, biology-cytotechnology, biology–secondary education, business administration, chemistry, chemistry–secondary education, communication disorders, communications, computer information systems, criminal justice, elementary education, elementary education–special education (SEED), English, English–secondary education, environmental affairs, exploratory, history, history/political science, interdepartmental studies, mathematics, mathematics–secondary education, medical technology, music, music (K–12 education), music/music technology and entertainment arts, prelaw, premed, psychology, religious studies, social studies–secondary education, social work, sociology, sociology/criminal justice, Spanish, Spanish–secondary education, and special education. The College also offers Bachelor of Fine Arts (B.F.A.) degrees in graphic design and studio art.

Academic Program

To earn a bachelor's degree, a student must complete a minimum of 122 credits, including, for most majors, the core curriculum requirement of 42 credits in liberal education, two courses in physical education, and the major requirements as specified. A minimum of 60 credits must be earned on the Saint Rose campus or at one of the colleges in the Hudson-Mohawk Association of Colleges and Universities through cross-registration. A cumulative index of 2.0 and an index of 2.0 in the major field are required for graduation in most majors.

Students are provided with assistance in planning their programs of study by faculty advisers in their major areas and by the Office of Academic Advisement. They may elect double majors or minors or may design their own programs within the guidelines set by the interdepartmental studies major.

The College of Saint Rose offers qualified students the opportunity to pursue an accelerated bachelor's/master's degree program, which can be completed in about five years of study. The College offers these option programs in accounting, business, English, and history. It also offers those who wish to enroll as early matriculation students the option to complete their senior year of high school and freshman year of college simultaneously.

The College's participation in the Hudson-Mohawk Association of Colleges and Universities provides an opportunity for students to enroll in classes at twenty participating colleges and universities in the Capital Region on a space-available basis.

Qualified students also may participate in special transfer programs: a 3+3 option with Albany Law School and a 3+2 engineering option with Union College, Clarkson University, Rensselaer Polytechnic Institute, or Alfred University. Students in these programs complete selected bachelor's degree programs at Saint Rose in three years and transfer to the cooperating institution to finish the professional program.

The College operates on a semester calendar with a fall term extending from August or September to December and a spring term from January to May. Two summer session programs offer undergraduate and graduate evening courses.

Off-Campus Arrangements

The College's most recent affiliation is with the College Consortium for International Studies, which gives students the opportunity to participate in forty study-abroad programs in twenty-eight countries. Saint Rose is also an affiliate of the Center for Cross-Cultural Study, which operates summer, semester, and yearlong study-abroad programs in Seville, Spain. In addition, Saint Rose's partnership with Regent's College in London allows students to study in another country for the same cost as Saint Rose tuition (plus airfare and room and board).

Academic Facilities

The open-stack Neil Hellman Library contains 199,000 bound volumes, 215,000 microforms, 980 professional and academic journal subscriptions, and 1,100 videocassettes. The library provides additional access to information through its online public access catalog (Dynix), a CD-ROM network, and by offering Internet and World Wide Web service. The library is a member of the Capital District Library Council and OCLC. These memberships promote interlibrary cooperation and offer Saint Rose library users access to materials from throughout the country and borrowing privileges at area libraries. A curriculum library and the Educational Media Office provide specialized resources for education majors. Picotte Hall, located about a mile from the main campus, houses the art department classrooms, equipment, and exhibition gallery as well as one of the largest screen printing facilities in the state of New York. The campus also has a Music Center with classrooms, practice rooms, a 16-track professional recording studio, and a music library. Various "smart classrooms" are fully equipped with word processing and presentation software and have World Wide Web and Internet capabilities. Cabrini Hall is the home of the Pauline K. Winkler Speech and Language Center as well as the Career Development Center. Science and mathematics majors will find the latest equipment and research facilities housed within the College's 27,000-square-foot Science Center. The College's campuswide network provides access to all campus computer laboratories and library facilities as well as the Internet, World Wide Web, cable television, and telephones. All PCs on the Saint Rose campus are networked, and network access is available in dormitory rooms and through remote dial-up facilities.

Costs

Tuition for 2000–01 is $12,869. Room and board costs range from $5743 to $6622. Activity fees are $130 per year and are subject to change. The estimated annual costs for books and personal expenses are $850 and $1000, respectively.

Financial Aid

More than 90 percent of the students receive financial aid in the form of scholarships, grants, loans, and part-time employment. The College of Saint Rose participates in the Federal Pell Grant, FSEOG, TAP, and Federal Work-Study programs and in the Federal Perkins Loan and Federal Stafford Student Loan Programs. The College provides ample aid in the form of grants, service awards, and scholarships for need or academic achievement. Candidates for financial assistance must file the Free Application for Federal Student Aid. ISIR and SAR forms should be on file in the Financial Aid Office by March 1.

Faculty

Saint Rose has a full-time faculty of 145 members and a part-time faculty of 186. Eighty-two percent of the College's faculty members hold the degree of Ph.D. or the highest degree available in their field.

Student Government

The Student Association (SA) consists of elected students who want to make life at the College as enjoyable, interesting, and meaningful as possible. It budgets student funds, appoints representatives to College policymaking committees, and assists individual students and clubs in planning and carrying out projects. It also provides an organ of self-government, promotes an exchange of ideas within the College community, fosters opportunities beyond those offered in the formal curriculum, and advances the welfare of the entire College community. SA also oversees the College's thirty-six clubs and organizations.

Admission Requirements

The College wishes to admit students who show evidence of strong academic motivation and the ability to benefit from a challenging liberal and professional education. Admission decisions are made after careful study of all the data available for each candidate. Interviews are strongly recommended but not required. Freshman applicants should submit a high school transcript, a letter of recommendation from a teacher or guidance counselor, and scores on the SAT I or ACT.

Transfer applicants must submit high school and college transcripts, a letter of recommendation from a college instructor, and a written statement of the reasons for transfer.

Application and Information

Students are accepted for admission for the fall and spring semesters on a rolling admissions basis. Interested students should apply by February 1 to be considered for academic scholarships ranging from $1000 to full tuition for each undergraduate year. New students who are accepted for admission are asked to submit a tuition deposit of $100 and a residence deposit (where applicable) of $100. Information on all aspects of the campus and the academic programs can be obtained by contacting the Office of Admissions; this office also can arrange campus tours, classroom visits, and overnight accommodations.

Office of Admissions
The College of Saint Rose
432 Western Avenue
Albany, New York 12203
Telephone: 518-454-5150
           800-637-8556 (toll-free)
Fax: 518-454-2013
E-mail: admit@mail.strose.edu (admissions)
       finaid@mail.strose.edu (financial aid)
World Wide Web: http://www.strose.edu

Located in the historic Pine Hills neighborhood of Albany, New York, the College's classic mix of brick buildings and turn-of-the-century Victorian homes form a small village with a campus green epicenter.

THE COLLEGE OF ST. SCHOLASTICA
DULUTH, MINNESOTA

The College

The College of St. Scholastica provides intellectual and moral preparation for responsible living and meaningful work. An independent comprehensive college, it was founded in the Catholic intellectual tradition and is shaped by Benedictine ideals. The College offers programs in the liberal arts and sciences and professional career fields. The entire St. Scholastica community is committed to an educational process that requires students to meet rigorous academic standards, to broaden the scope of their knowledge, and to be accountable to both self and society.

The College serves 2,080 students. The small, friendly community enables each student to participate in academics, extracurriculars, and recreational activities. A 13:1 student-teacher ratio makes it easy to seek individualized help and encouragement.

St. Scholastica graduates, well known for their academic and professional preparation, enjoy excellent placement opportunities. Last year, 99 percent of graduates either secured employment or enrolled in graduate school within six months of graduation. *U.S. News & World Report* magazine's 2000 "America's Best Colleges" rankings put St. Scholastica in the top tier of Midwestern colleges for academic excellence and affordability.

The College also offers innovative graduate programs, including the Master of Education, Master of Arts in management, Master of Arts in nursing, Master of Arts in occupational therapy, Master of Arts in physical therapy, Master of Arts in exercise physiology, and Master of Arts in health information management.

Today the campus includes the Mitchell Auditorium, an acoustically superb 500-seat music hall; the Science Center, which features a recent $4-million expansion; Our Lady Queen of Peace Chapel; the Myles Reif Recreation Center; the College Library; the St. Scholastica Theatre; majestic Tower Hall; and Somers Residence Hall. Adjoining the campus are St. Scholastica Monastery, the home of the Benedictine Sisters, and the Benedictine Health Center, which serves the needs of the Duluth area and provides many health science and behavioral arts and sciences students with opportunities to obtain practical experience. Somers Residence Hall includes a wing of residence hall suites. Five modular apartment complexes—Grove, Birch, Pine, Maple, and Willow—provide modern and convenient on-campus housing.

Location

The St. Scholastica campus is on a ridge overlooking Lake Superior in a residential area of Duluth, Minnesota. The location offers a safe and tranquil setting for scholarship amid exceptional natural beauty. The cultural and commercial offerings of Duluth, a regional center for shopping, the arts, and tourism, are only 10 minutes away. Duluth is in northeastern Minnesota, a 3-hour drive from Minneapolis–St. Paul. It is well served by Northwest and American Airlines as well as commercial bus lines. An intercity bus line provides efficient local transportation.

Duluth's low crime rate, economic stability, and natural beauty regularly earn it high rankings in national quality of life surveys. The city is an international seaport and a center of development for the health, education, and tourism industries. There are more than 15,000 college students in the Duluth-Superior metropolitan area.

The College's proximity to the Boundary Waters Canoe Area Wilderness, national parks, ski areas, lakes, and rivers allows students to enjoy the outdoors in a way few college students can. A student who values a highly cultured community where extracurricular activities abound will be happy at St. Scholastica. Music students take part in the Duluth-Superior Symphony Orchestra, and theater students feel at home at the Duluth Playhouse, one of the nation's oldest community theaters. Sports enthusiasts can play tennis, racquetball, and golf; use ice boats or snowmobiles; or ice-skate, ski, fish, hunt, and sail in St. Scholastica's backyard. Mont du Lac and Spirit Mountain ski areas are only 20 minutes from campus.

Majors and Degrees

The College of St. Scholastica offers a Bachelor of Arts degree in the following majors: accounting, behavioral arts and sciences, biochemistry, biology, business communication, chemistry, clinical laboratory science, communication and theater arts, computer science/information systems, dietetics/ food and nutrition, economics, education, educational media and technology (licensure), English, exercise physiology, health information management, health sciences, history, humanities, international management, languages and international studies, management, mathematics, music, natural sciences, nursing, occupational therapy (entry master's program), physical therapy (entry master's program), psychology, religious studies, self-designed major, social science/secondary education, and social work.

Minors are available in most of the major fields as well as in American Indian studies, art, French, German, gerontology, medieval and Renaissance studies, philosophy, Russian, self-designed minor, Spanish, theater, and women's studies.

In addition, St. Scholastica offers preprofessional programs in dentistry, engineering, law, medicine, pharmacy, and veterinary medicine. St. Scholastica has a certificate program in gerontology, and the study of aging is a major initiative throughout the College. St. Scholastica offers a licensure program in teacher education.

Academic Program

The curriculum prepares students for their responsibilities as working professionals, as citizens of a democracy, and as individuals who seek to live full lives. The program consists of three parts: general education requirements, a major, and open electives. The major prepares the student for graduate school or for a profession and is normally selected by the end of the sophomore year. Elective courses allow students to pursue particular interests. The general education component seeks to broaden the student's grasp of the accumulated wisdom of the past so that challenges of the present may be met with wisdom, faith, and imagination. At St. Scholastica, 128 semester credits are required for graduation, of which one third are general education credits. The general education program includes a system of area distribution requirements, a First-Year Program, and an upper-division writing course elective. The area distribution requirements cover cultural diversity, social sciences, world languages, literature, analytical reasoning, natural science, history, fine arts, philosophy, religious studies, and electives. The student's last 32 credits before graduation must be earned at St. Scholastica, and a minimum of 16 credits must be earned in a major field at St. Scholastica. The College offers an honors program for students to have enriched learning experiences and to provide a community of support for learners devoted to a vigorous life of the mind. Some majors require an internship that involves work, travel, or study related to a student's academic efforts.

Off-Campus Arrangements

The College offers its programs throughout the region. Several innovative two-plus-two programs bring a St. Scholastica education to students with two years of higher education in northern Minnesota and northern Wisconsin communities. St. Scholastica also has consortium agreements through which students may enroll in courses at other colleges in the region. Clinical experience in the College's health sciences programs is offered at all health-care facilities in Duluth as well as in many other hospitals and health-care centers throughout the United States. The College also offers students the opportunity to study abroad at its study center in Louisburgh, Ireland; in a Russian language exchange program in Petrozavodsk, Karelia, Russia; and in an exchange program in Leipzig, Germany.

Academic Facilities

St. Scholastica's three-story Romanesque library houses more than 120,000 volumes, with special strengths in the health sciences, nursing, Indian studies, and children's materials. Computer workstations link the library to other state and national libraries, the campus network, and the Internet. Library instruction is provided throughout the curriculum. The Science Center has interactive television classroom capabilities. College research facilities include general and physical chemistry laboratories, health sciences laboratories, anatomy laboratories, and two state-of-the-art 24-hour computer labs.

Costs

St. Scholastica's 2000–01 tuition is $16,190. Room and board are $4952.

Financial Aid

The College of St. Scholastica handles a wide variety of financial aid and attempts to meet the needs of any qualified student enrolled. More than 90 percent of full-time students receive some form of aid; the average award is more than $11,000. The College also offers academic scholarships (Benedictine Scholarships). These awards are made on the basis of academic and leadership excellence, not necessarily because of need.

Students desiring to apply for financial aid should file the Free Application for Federal Student Aid (FAFSA) and have the results sent to St. Scholastica. Applications are processed on a first-come, first-served basis only after a student has been accepted by the College.

Faculty

St. Scholastica faculty members are devoted to personalized instruction, and the 13:1 student-teacher ratio is important to them. Faculty members hold advanced degrees from colleges and universities around the world. Three faculty members are recent Fulbright International Scholars.

Student Government

The College trains leaders by encouraging students to hold positions of responsibility. Students manage the Student Senate and are directly involved in policymaking within the College community. They establish policies for the student newspaper and serve on institutional standing committees.

Admission Requirements

The College of St. Scholastica seeks to identify and admit students who have a strong probability of success in a demanding curriculum and rigorous academic major. Historically, the student who successfully demonstrates academic aptitude in high school or in a home school curriculum, has above-average ACT and/or SAT scores, and ranks in the upper half of his or her senior class is admitted to the College. Transfer students must demonstrate similar success in the college-level environment, with a minimum cumulative GPA of 2.0 for admission consideration. The College is an equal opportunity educator and employer.

Application and Information

The College of St. Scholastica requires each applicant to submit an application and a $25 nonrefundable fee, test scores on the SAT or ACT (required prior to enrollment), and an official high school transcript or GED test score. The College admits students on a rolling basis and notifies the applicant of the admission decision as soon as his or her file is complete.

For application and financial aid forms, prospective students should contact:

Brian F. Dalton
Vice President for Enrollment Management
College of St. Scholastica
1200 Kenwood Avenue
Duluth, Minnesota 55811
Telephone: 800-447-5444 (toll-free)
TTY/TDD: 218-723-6790
Fax: 218-723-5991
E-mail: admissions@css.edu

Tower Hall is the center of the College of St. Scholastica campus, which is in one of the most beautiful areas of Minnesota. Nearby are the Boundary Waters Canoe Area Wilderness, national forests and parks, ski areas, and pristine lakes and rivers.

COLLEGE OF SANTA FE
SANTA FE, NEW MEXICO

The College

The College of Santa Fe (CSF) is a culturally dynamic, independent liberal arts institution committed to sound teaching and diligent advising and dedicated to each student's professional, ethical, and individual growth. Academic emphasis is on the arts, business, and education. Located at the base of northern New Mexico's Sangre de Cristo mountains and chartered in 1874 by the territory of New Mexico, it is the oldest educational institution in the state legally authorized to grant degrees. In the 1999 edition of *America's Best Colleges*, published by *U.S. News & World Report*, the College of Santa Fe ranked among the top Western liberal arts colleges.

CSF awards four-year liberal arts and professional degrees in a wide variety of disciplines and also offers graduate programs leading to the degrees of Master of Business Administration and Master of Education in at-risk youth.

Students from forty-two states and five other countries make up the culturally and ethnically diverse student body. The fall 1999 enrollment was 1,774. This figure includes the enrollment both at Santa Fe and at CSF's Albuquerque center. Freshmen who do not live within commuting distance are required to live on campus. Students can take advantage of the Shellaberger Tennis Center, which contains seven outdoor tennis courts and a pro shop that has hundreds of tennis videos and books available to be borrowed by students. The Driscoll Fitness Center offers aerobics and has a weight room, a gym, squash and racquetball courts, and an indoor climbing wall. Winter snow provides excellent skiing at nearby Santa Fe Ski Basin and Taos Ski Valley. The Outdoor Recreation Program provides equipment rental to the students.

Students are encouraged to participate in intramural sports and in a variety of social and cultural organizations and activities, including the *Independent* (the newspaper); *Glyph*, (the College literary annual); the Drama, Science, Social Science, Business, Student Art, Student Writers, International, and Outdoor Clubs; campus ministries; and honor and departmental organizations. CSF's Career Placement Office helps students make career choices; gain hands-on experience through internships, co-op education, and part-time employment in the community; prepare resumes; and begin their job searches.

Location

CSF is located on a 95-acre campus in Santa Fe, the capital city of New Mexico and the oldest capital city in the United States. Sometimes called the "City Different," Santa Fe clings to the rich legacy of its three resident cultures—Indian, Spanish, and Anglo—while welcoming newcomers of many cultures from all over the world. This region of colorful contrasts, which has been called the most interesting 50-mile square in America, offers equal opportunity to hikers and historians, skiers and art lovers, and fishermen and opera buffs. Santa Fe, a city with a population of 65,000, is located 7,000 feet above sea level in a majestic setting at the foot of the Sangre de Cristo mountains. Santa Fe has about 300 days of sunshine a year, but it can snow as early as October and as late as May.

Majors and Degrees

CSF offers the Bachelor of Arts, Bachelor of Science, and Bachelor of Fine Arts degrees in a broad range of majors and concentrations, including accounting applications, acting, applied mathematics/computer science, applied psychology, art, art history, art therapy, arts and entertainment management, biology, computer applications design, conservation science, contemporary music, creative writing, design/theater technology, elementary education (leading to New Mexico state licensure), English, environmental management, environmental science, humanities, mathematics, moving image arts, musical theater, organizational management, pastoral studies, political science, psychology (human services and managerial psychology), religion studies, secondary education, Southwest American studies, technical communication, theater, and theater management. Preprofessional programs are offered in dentistry, engineering, law, medicine, and veterinary science. Students may also elect to design an independent major.

Academic Program

A liberal arts core curriculum is maintained as a degree requirement for all programs. Students must complete 45 semester hours of core courses in the sciences, humanities, philosophy, religion studies, English, speech, social science, and physical education. In the Graduate and External Degree Program, the liberal arts core requirement is 36 semester hours.

CSF offers day, evening, and weekend classes; credit for life experience through the Prior Learning Portfolio; independent study; credit by examination through CLEP; and Advanced Placement examinations. Course challenges may be arranged individually with members of the faculty. The academic calendar consists of two semesters and two optional four-week summer sessions. The fall semester begins in late August and the spring semester in mid-January.

Academic Facilities

CSF offers complete facilities for a wide range of cultural activities, study, worship, and recreation. One of the newest additions is the Visual Arts Center, designed by celebrated Mexican architect Ricardo Legoretta, which houses the Anne and John Marion Center for Photographic Arts, the Thaw Art History Center, Tishman Hall (studio fundamentals), Tipton Hall (lecture hall), and the Santa Fe Art Institute. A printmaking studio, a sculpture area, state-of-the-art darkrooms, and painting and drawing studios provide the setting for learning artistic techniques and realizing creative potential.

The Garson Communications Center is the hub of activity for moving image arts students. The center houses two sound stages and two studios for moving-image productions, complemented by a variety of classrooms and faculty and production offices. Facilities include the New Media Center, a computer lab that contains eleven Macintosh computers for student use. The New Media Center is available to all students but is focused primarily in the moving image and visual arts, with several digital art programs available, including Adobe Photoshop, Adobe Premier, and Macromedia Director 6. The distinctive feature of the Garson Communications Center is that it is utilized by professional filmmakers, and students have the opportunity to gain invaluable on-the-set experience through internships.

Performing arts students spend much of their time in the magnificent Greer Garson Theatre. It offers complete facilities for the Performing Arts Department and for professional theatrical productions. The 500-seat main theater has an orchestra pit and is professionally equipped with sound and lighting facilities. Weckesser Studio Theatre, its smaller counterpart, seats 90. The center also houses a dance studio, a rehearsal room, classrooms, pianos and practice rooms, scenery and costume shops equipped with a computer-aided design system, and a box office. The theater lobby provides gallery exhibition space on two floors.

Near the theater is the Fogelson Library Center, a complex that offers space for study, meetings, classes, and social events. The 53,000-square-foot library has more than 400 subscriptions to periodicals and contains about 10,000 microforms and 150,000 volumes, 8,000 of which make up the library's unrivaled Southwest Collection. The library's automated search services include interactive electronic databases, an online catalog, circulation, interlibrary loan, and CD-ROM indexes and directories. There are also individual and group audio and video facilities. The Institute of American Indian Arts Library is housed on the upper floor of the Fogelson Library.

The Fine Arts Gallery is located in the Southwest Annex, adjacent to the Fogelson Library Center. This 3,500-square-foot gallery features exhibitions year-round; shows are open to students as well as to the community at large.

The Science Building, Brother Luke Hall, is a three-story structure that accommodates ten modern science laboratories, faculty offices, and most science classrooms.

The Campus Computer Center, located on the lower floor of the CSF Forum, features a Pentium Lab with e-mail access and Internet connections to the World Wide Web. There is classroom and office space, and twenty-eight computers, in addition to various word processing, spreadsheet, and data processing programs, are available for student use.

Costs

Tuition for the 2000–01 academic year is $15,750. Room and board are about $4000 per year, depending on the chosen plan. Students should expect to spend $400 to $600 on books and supplies. Personal expenses vary, but they average $1500, depending on travel costs.

Financial Aid

Nearly 75 percent of CSF undergraduates receive some type of financial assistance. Students must file the Free Application for Federal Student Aid (FAFSA). Most aid is awarded on the basis of need, but the College also offers a number of scholarships based on academic achievement and merit. The priority application deadline is March 1. After that date, aid is awarded as funds are available.

Faculty

The faculty-student ratio is 1:14. All classes are taught by faculty members, not by graduate-level teaching assistants. CSF's faculty is dedicated to undergraduate teaching, and its members are easily accessible to students. Nearly 80 percent of the faculty members have earned doctorates or appropriate terminal degrees as well as distinguished professional accomplishments.

Student Government

The College promotes an active student government and encourages all students to participate. Students sit on most College committees and have a nonvoting representative on the Board of Trustees. The members of the Associated Student Government are elected every year; they, along with the Residence Hall Council, coordinate most of the student activities on campus.

Admission Requirements

Admission to the College is based on a student's previous record of academic achievement and scholastic aptitude. All applicants must submit an official copy of their high school transcript or GED scores, copies of either their ACT or SAT I scores (not applicable for students over 21), and official records of any college work previously attempted. All prospective students are strongly encouraged to visit the campus.

Application and Information

The College uses a rolling admission system. Applicants must file an application for admission with a one-time, nonrefundable $25 fee, submit official high school and college transcripts (when applicable), and arrange for ACT or SAT I scores to be sent to the Office of Admissions.

For more information about the College of Santa Fe, students should contact:

Director of Admissions
College of Santa Fe
1600 St. Michael's Drive
Santa Fe, New Mexico 87505-5634
Telephone: 505-473-6133
          800-456-2673 (toll-free outside New Mexico)
Fax: 505-473-6127
World Wide Web: http://www.csf.edu

A view of the campus.

COLLEGE OF STATEN ISLAND OF THE CITY UNIVERSITY OF NEW YORK

STATEN ISLAND, NEW YORK

The College and The University

The College of Staten Island (CSI) is part of the City University of New York, the largest urban university in the country. The College, like the University, is committed to both access and excellence. CSI's superb campus serves the pivotal endeavors of teaching and research that promote discovery and dissemination of knowledge while developing human minds and spirits. CSI was founded in 1976 by the union of two existing colleges within the City University: Staten Island Community College and Richmond College. Staten Island Community College, the first community college in the University system, opened in 1955. Richmond College, the University's first upper-division college, was founded in 1965. CSI's current undergraduate enrollment is slightly more than 11,000 men and women.

A general education is assured through requirements that allow students to explore a range of knowledge and acquire educational breadth in the arts and humanities, mathematics, science, and social sciences. Requirements for the associate degree provide a curriculum based on study in a specific area often directed toward a career. Requirements for the bachelor's degree provide a disciplined and cumulative program of study in a major field of inquiry.

CSI awards the Master of Arts degree in cinema studies, English, environmental science, history, and liberal studies; the Master of Science degree in adult health nursing, biology, and computer science; the Master of Science in Education degree in elementary education, secondary education, and special education; and a sixth-year professional certificate in education supervision and administration. The College offers a combined Bachelor of Science and Master of Science degree in physical therapy. CSI participates with the CUNY Graduate School and University Center and Brooklyn College in a doctoral program in polymer chemistry and with the Graduate School and University Center in doctoral programs in computer science and physics. With the Center for Developmental Neurosciences and Developmental Disabilities, the College participates in CUNY doctoral subprograms in neuroscience (biology) and learning processes (psychology).

Study-abroad opportunities are available through three Culture and Commerce programs emphasizing the study of Italian, French, or Spanish and through the Center for International Service.

The Campus Center incorporates facilities for a complete program of student activities. It contains the main dining facilities, the College health services, a bookstore, offices for student organizations, study lounges, a small performance/cafe space, game rooms, and the studios of WSIA, the student-operated FM radio station. The two-story rotunda space at the heart of the structure contains the dining areas and information services.

Location

The College occupies a 204-acre campus located near the center of Staten Island. The campus is the largest site for a college (public or private) within New York City. Set in a parklike landscape, the grounds and facilities create a rural oasis in an urban setting. In this attractive learning environment, classrooms and academic offices are located in ten buildings that form two quadrangles connected by the campus walk, which extends between the library building and the campus center. Five newly built and equipped buildings—the library building, the campus center, the biological sciences/chemical sciences building, the center for the arts, and the sports and recreation center—provide outstanding facilities for college and community activities.

The College's location offers students the best of two worlds. While Staten Island provides a suburban environment with some of the most interesting landscape in the metropolitan area, Manhattan, the center of cultural and social life of the city, is only 25 minutes from the island by ferry. The Verrazano-Narrows Bridge provides direct access to the island from Brooklyn.

Majors and Degrees

The Associate in Arts degree is offered in liberal arts and sciences. The Associate in Science degree is offered in engineering science, liberal arts and sciences, and liberal arts and sciences with a prearchitecture concentration. The Associate in Applied Science degree is offered in business, civil engineering technology, computer technology, electrical engineering technology, medical laboratory technology, and nursing. A one-year certificate program is offered in medical assistant studies.

The Bachelor of Arts degree is conferred in African-American studies; American studies; art; art with a photography concentration; cinema studies; economics; English; English with a dramatic literature concentration; history; international studies; music; philosophy; political science; psychology; science, letters, and society; sociology/anthropology; social work; Spanish; and women's studies. The Bachelor of Science degree is offered in accounting; art; art with a photography concentration; biochemistry; bioinformatics; biology; business; business with a finance concentration, an international business concentration, a management concentration, or a marketing concentration; chemistry; communications; computer science; computer science/mathematics; dramatic arts; economics; economics with a business specialization or a finance specialization; engineering science; information systems; international studies; mathematics; medical technology; music; music with an electronics concentration; nursing (upper-division program); physical therapy (combined B.S./M.S.); physician assistant studies; and physics.

The teacher education program prepares students for teaching at the early childhood, elementary, and secondary levels. The academic work and field experience meet the requirements for the certification and licensing examinations given by the state and city of New York.

Academic Program

A four-year senior college, CSI offers two-year programs in career areas and in liberal arts and sciences and four-year programs with majors in the traditional fields of study. General education requirements have been established for all degrees. The associate degree programs require 60–64 credits, depending on the field; the bachelor's degree programs require 120 credits, with a few exceptions. Credit may be awarded for experiential learning, internships, and independent study, and credit may be earned by examination. Minors may be taken in several fields, and double majors are permitted. Students may graduate with honors in their field of study in most bachelor's degree majors.

The College follows a semester calendar, with classes scheduled both day and evening; a summer session is also held. The Weekend College, established to provide an opportunity for students with weekday commitments to pursue a college education, offers a variety of course combinations leading to associate and bachelor's degrees.

Off-Campus Arrangements

The College gives a number of courses for credit at off-campus locations throughout the city. These include employee-development programs for major corporations and other programs, supported by grants and by participating employers and unions that provide courses for city and state employees at agency or institutional locations.

Academic Facilities

The academic buildings are designed to house approximately 200 modern laboratories and classrooms. Each also houses a study lounge for students, department and program offices, and offices for faculty members. Academic and research programs are served by a computer network that allows students and faculty members full access to specialized software, the Internet, online library resources, and e-mail. All major computer languages and software packages are supported. The College houses an IBM 4381 computer, and students can access the University's IBM 3090/400 system.

The Center for the Arts complex provides facilities for teaching in the instructional wing and areas of public assembly in the public wing. The complex of public facilities includes a 900-seat auditorium, a 450-seat fully equipped theater, a recital hall, an experimental theater, an art gallery, and a conference center. Classrooms, lecture halls, studios, and offices for faculty members are located in the instructional wing fronting the campus walk.

The library is designed to house approximately 300,000 volumes, computer facilities for database searching, periodical subscriptions, and media services. Small study areas under skylights define a raised central area around a rotunda on the third floor, which provides space for readers within the expanse of the stacks. The collection also includes 1,700 current journal subscriptions, 600,000 titles in microform, and a wide range of audiovisual materials in various formats. The CSI Library is a member of the CUNY-wide integrated library system. Students and faculty members have free access to ERIC as well as various databases on CD-ROM or via the Internet.

The laboratory science building provides facilities for teaching and for two research centers: the Center for Environmental Science and the Center for Developmental Neuroscience and Developmental Disabilities. It consists of a research wing and an instructional wing. State-of-the-art laboratories serve students and faculty members in their teaching and research.

The 77,000 gross-square-foot Sports and Recreation Center is a multipurpose facility providing ball courts, locker rooms, instructional areas, an indoor 25-meter swimming pool, and offices for faculty. Recreational fields occupy the meadows in the northwest quadrant of the campus, providing a green and landscaped open area at the main approach to the campus.

Costs

For 1999–2000, costs for first-time freshmen or non-CUNY transfer students enrolled after June 1, 1992, were $135 per credit (part-time matriculated) or $1600 per semester (full-time matriculated) for New York State residents and $285 per credit (part-time matriculated) or $3400 per semester (full-time matriculated) for out-of-state students.

Financial Aid

Financial aid is available through state and federal programs and includes the New York State Tuition Assistance Program (TAP) awards, Federal Pell Grants, Federal Supplemental Educational Opportunity Grants (FSEOG), Search for Elevation and Education through Knowledge (SEEK) awards, scholarships, Federal Work-Study Program awards, and student loan programs. Information about programs, application procedures, and deadlines is available from the Financial Aid Office.

CSI Presidential Scholarships are awarded annually to full-time students on the basis of academic proficiency and service. In addition, endowments have been established for scholarships in a number of fields. Further information about scholarships is available from the Office of Admissions.

Faculty

The College has a full-time faculty of 300, of whom approximately 80 percent hold a doctoral degree or the equivalent. The faculty members have made significant contributions in many areas of scholarship, creativity, and public service. Numerous faculty members have received prestigious grants and awards, and 30 serve as members of the City University doctoral faculty.

Student Government

The Student Government is composed of 20 elected representatives, and it is through this structure that students are represented in the College's governance.

Admission Requirements

First-year students admitted to four-year programs, the baccalaureate program, are expected to meet one of the following four categories of admission requirements: an SAT I score of 1100 or better, a high school average of at least 80 and at least 13 College Preparatory Initiative (CPI) units (including 5 units in English and mathematics with at least 2 in each), a high school average of at least 78 and at least 15 CPI units (including 5 in English and mathematics with at least two in each), or a GED score of 300 or better. Transfer students with fewer than 25 credits must have a GPA of at least 3.0; with 26 to 39 credits, a GPA of at least 2.5; and with 40 or more credits, a GPA of at least 2.0.

Entering first-year students may be admitted to two-year programs if they have graduated from an accredited high school, have earned an equivalency diploma (GED) with a satisfactory score, or have completed at least six semesters of high school (eleventh grade) and are currently attending high school.

Application and Information

Requests for further information and application materials should be directed to:

Office of Recruitment and Admissions
North Administration Building (2A-404)
College of Staten Island
City University of New York
2800 Victory Boulevard
Staten Island, New York 10314
Telephone: 718-982-2010
E-mail: recruitment@postbox.csi.cuny.edu
World Wide Web: http://www.csi.cuny.edu

COLLEGE OF THE ATLANTIC
BAR HARBOR, MAINE

The College

College of the Atlantic was founded in 1969 to provide an ecological, problem-solving approach to education that combines academic rigor in the arts and sciences with practical application. The College's small size allows students to work closely with the faculty and to design an individualized program suited to their own particular interests. Enrollment during 1999–2000 was 287: 187 women and 100 men. The oceanfront location of the campus allows students to take advantage of the abundant natural resources offered by the Atlantic Ocean and nearby Acadia National Park. The College also sponsors a regular film and speaker series, numerous concerts and dances, informal College parties, musical get-togethers, and recitals. Students, faculty members, and staff form a close-knit College community.

In addition to its undergraduate degrees, the College also offers a Master of Philosophy (M.Phil.) in human ecology.

Location

The College is located in the town of Bar Harbor on Mount Desert Island, Maine, where Acadia National Park is also situated. Connected to the mainland by a causeway, the large, scenic island lies 300 miles north of Boston and 40 miles east of Bangor. In the summer, Bar Harbor teems with tourists. When students return in the fall, the traffic reverses direction and Bar Harbor becomes a quiet coastal Maine village. The Atlantic Ocean and Acadia National Park provide ample opportunities for such outdoor recreational activities as swimming, fishing, canoeing, kayaking, rock climbing, mountain hiking, cross-country skiing, and snowshoeing. Cooperative resource sharing with the Jackson Laboratory, the Mount Desert Island Biological Laboratory, the national park, and the local public school system helps to broaden the scope of COA's educational activities.

Majors and Degrees

College of the Atlantic awards the Bachelor of Arts in Human Ecology. Human ecology emphasizes the understanding of interrelationships between humans and the social, technological, and natural environments. Within the degree focus, students may develop individualized programs in one or more of the following areas: environmental science, humanities, international and regional studies, landscape and building design, marine studies, natural-history-museum studies, public policy, sustainable agriculture and community development, teacher certification, and visual arts.

Academic Program

The academic program is designed to develop an ecological perspective through the understanding of social, biological, and technological interrelationships. With this perspective, students acquire the skills necessary to enter the fields of science, education, business, law, design, the arts, health, or journalism. Forty percent of COA's alumni have pursued graduate or professional education at some of the country's leading institutions. Many different forms of study are available at COA, and small and informal classes are the foundation of the curriculum. Student-initiated workshops, independent studies, internships, and senior projects also provide important learning experiences. Applied learning is the norm, not the exception.

To qualify for graduation, students must complete required interdisciplinary course work, write an essay on human ecology, perform community service, and complete a one-term internship and a one-term senior project.

College of the Atlantic accepts up to two years of transfer credits from accredited colleges if the grades earned were C or better and were earned in courses of an academic nature.

Off-Campus Arrangements

The College's academic program is augmented by exchange agreements with the University of Maine at Orono; the Palacky University in Olomouc, Czech Republic; the Landing School of Boatbuilding in Kennebunk, Maine; and the Multiversidad Franciscana de Americana Latino in Uruguay.

Academic Facilities

Thorndike Library, with more than 35,000 volumes and 410 periodicals, also provides access to libraries throughout the United States, Great Britain, and Canada through OCLC interlibrary loans. COA has zoology, botany, and chemistry laboratories; a herbarium; greenhouses; design and ceramics studios; state-of-the-art computer facilities, including a Geographic Information Systems Lab and a design/graphics computer lab; research boats for marine research and to ferry students and faculty members to College-owned island research stations in the Gulf of Maine; and an 80-acre working organic farm.

Costs

The total cost for the 2000–01 academic year is estimated at $26,724. This includes $20,124 for tuition, $3285 for room, $2238 for board, $480 for books and supplies, a $237 student activities fee, and $360 for personal expenses.

Financial Aid

More than two thirds of the College's students receive some form of financial aid. The Free Application for Federal Student Aid and the College's own form are required by the College to determine a student's eligibility for assistance. Aid is based on established need and academic merit. Financial aid packages generally consist of a combination of scholarships, work-study awards, and loans.

Faculty

With a faculty of 27 full-time and 13 part-time teachers, the student-faculty ratio is 10:1. Eighty-five percent of the full-time faculty members have Ph.D.'s or the equivalent. Courses offered by regular visiting faculty members supplement the curriculum. The primary commitment of the COA faculty is teaching and advising undergraduate students.

Student Government

The College governance system is a combination of pure and representative democracy. Students participate in all facets of decision making and serve on all standing committees. Major policy decisions are brought for review to the All-College Meeting, where members of the faculty, staff, and student body each have one vote.

Admission Requirements

The Admission Committee, composed of students, staff, and faculty members, seeks students who have an enthusiastic and active approach to learning, a strong record of academic achievement, and accompanying intellectual strengths. These qualities should be supplemented with appropriate personal qualities enabling a student to learn in an environment requiring a high degree of self-motivation.

The COA application form contains a series of essay questions that require students to think carefully about College of the Atlantic's educational focus. The application is designed to encourage prospective students to reflect on and express personal reasons for choosing a small college with a focus on human ecology. The answers to these questions, teacher and counselor references, past academic records, and personal interviews are used by the Admission Committee in arriving at its decision. Standardized test scores are optional.

Admission procedures and standards are the same for transfer students as for freshman applicants. Special emphasis is placed on the transfer applicant's college transcript and recommendations. The transfer of credits is determined on an individual basis. All transferring students are required to complete a minimum of two years of study at COA. Applications are also accepted from students at other institutions who wish to spend time at the College as visiting students.

Application and Information

Prospective students are encouraged to visit the College in order to sit in on classes, talk with students and faculty members, and acquire an understanding of the College's individualized educational style. COA employs a deadline date of March 1 for fall admission for first-year students, but offers two early decision options with a December 1 deadline and a January 10 deadline. Transfer students must apply by April 1. Decisions for first-year students are mailed on or about April 1 and on or about April 25 for transfer students. Applicants for winter term should apply by November 15 and for spring term by February 15. Application materials may be obtained by writing to the College or by telephoning the Admission Office at the number below. The application fee is $45. COA endorses the policy set by the National Association of College Admission Counselors, whereby regular admission students have the right to defer accepting any offer of admission until May 1.

Director of Admission
College of the Atlantic
105 Eden Street
Bar Harbor, Maine 04609
Telephone: 207-288-5015
         800-528-0025 (toll-free)
Fax: 207-288-4126
E-mail: inquiry@ecology.coa.edu
World Wide Web: http://www.coa.edu

Mount Desert Rock, 25 miles off Bar Harbor's coast, was recently conveyed to COA through the federal government's Maine Lights acquisition program.

COLLEGE OF THE SOUTHWEST
HOBBS, NEW MEXICO

The College
Established in 1962, College of the Southwest (CSW) is an independent institution offering both bachelor's and master's degrees. CSW dedicates itself to sound academic standards, traditional American values, free enterprise education, and Christian principles. As a result of this dedication, CSW provides exceptional service to students and to the community. In addition to its main campus operation in Hobbs, the College operates a campus in Carlsbad, New Mexico, 70 miles southeast of Hobbs.

Through working together, the Board of Trustees, faculty and staff members, and friends of College of the Southwest are dedicated to building a preeminent educational enterprise—an enterprise designed to prepare students for responsible lives of service, significance, and effectiveness. The CSW educational experience is anchored in Christian principles; free enterprise education; academic distinction; independence of support and governance; debt-free operations; exceptional service to students and to the community; and the relentless pursuit of excellence in each and every endeavor.

College of the Southwest was named in *U.S. News & World Report*'s 1998 "America's Best Colleges" guide as New Mexico's most affordable institution of higher learning and one of America's top 100 most affordable colleges, based on the percentage of financial need met for undergraduates in two 12-credit-hour semesters.

College of the Southwest's faculty and staff members are dedicated to each student's lifelong success. CSW students receive an educational experience available only in an independent, small-college atmosphere and are enabled to achieve their full potential.

CSW's culturally and ethnically diverse student body is currently made up of students from twelve states and three other countries. Fall 1998 saw record enrollment, with 682 students attending.

Students are encouraged to enrich their college experience through participation in campus groups and activities, such as Drama, *Prairie Dog Post* (the campus newspaper), Students in Free Enterprise, Southwest Association of Teachers, Fellowship of Christian Athletes, intramurals, Student Government, Ambassadors Choir, Sigma Tau Delta, and *Southwest Creations* (CSW's literary magazine). In addition to these activities, students participate in weekly inspirational services, campus dances, an annual ski trip, beach volleyball, or golf at beautiful Ocotillo Golf Course. College of the Southwest competes in NAIA men's baseball, women's soccer, and women's volleyball.

Residence halls on the campus provide students with a safe, comfortable, and functional living environment. A prevailing theme that runs throughout the campus is CSW's Christian atmosphere and Southwestern hospitality. Students at College of the Southwest quickly become members of the CSW family. Any single freshman or sophomore under 21 years of age not living with a family member and enrolled for more than 9 hours must live in on-campus housing.

The J. F. Maddox Student Center features a game room, food service, a meeting room, and a bookstore as well as an informal living area suitable for quiet conversation, television viewing, or reading.

The Mabee Physical Fitness Center includes a multipurpose gymnasium for basketball and volleyball, racquetball courts, and a physiology lab. Athletic facilities also include a soccer field and baseball field.

In addition to its undergraduate degrees, College of the Southwest offers a Master of Science in Education degree, with specializations in educational administration, school counseling, and curriculum and instruction.

Location
CSW is located 5 miles north of Hobbs, New Mexico, on the Lovington Highway, New Mexico Highway 18. Hobbs is located in the southeastern corner of New Mexico. Primary industries in the area include oil and gas production, farming, and ranching.

Majors and Degrees
A CSW education is characterized by individual attention and close interaction between students and instructors. Instruction is based on a Christian world view. Degrees offered are the Bachelor of Business Administration, with majors in accounting, finance, general business, management, and marketing; the Bachelor of Science, with majors in athletic training, elementary education, environmental management, K–12 special education, and secondary education; and the Bachelor of Arts and Sciences, with majors in biology, English, history, humanities/fine arts, human relations, mathematics, psychology, and social sciences.

Academic Program
CSW is committed to preparing students for lifelong learning. The purpose of the College is to provide high-quality education with an emphasis on high academic standards, practical application, personal development, and physical well-being. To accomplish this purpose, the College endeavors to create a stimulating academic environment that will help students achieve academically; to practice intellectual inquiry, individual research, and logical reasoning; to help students relate their education to service, practical experience, and leadership in their work, in their homes, and in their communities; and to make available physical education and recreational and athletic activities that will foster physical well-being and enrich the students' leisure activities throughout their lives.

To receive a bachelor's degree from College of the Southwest, a student must complete (or earn) the following: a minimum of 128 to 133 semester hours as specified for the degree sought and 40 or more semester hours at the junior/senior level; a minimum of 62 hours at CSW, of which 60 must be completed after achieving junior standing and 30 after achieving senior standing; a minimum overall grade point average of 2.0 (except where specified by the degree program); and the major (or minor) and electives as allowed for the degree sought.

The main campus academic calendar consists of two semesters and two summer sessions. The fall semester begins in late August and the spring semester in mid-January.

Academic Facilities
Nine major buildings are located on the 162-acre campus, including the J. L. Burke Hall, which houses one classroom and the College's student services and administrative offices, and

the Scarborough Memorial Library, which is the College learning resource center. Special collections include the Raymond F. Waters Collection on Southwestern Literature and History, the J. L. Gardner Collection, the New Mexico Regional Textbook Evaluation Center, and the New Mexico State Textbook Adoption Examination Center for audiovisual software and curriculum aids. The library also provides Internet access to students.

The Science Building offers well-equipped laboratories and related classroom space for effective study.

The Mabee Southwest Heritage Center includes an auditorium, a seminar room, and a formal reception area. Designed to comfortably seat 238 people, the center is available for corporate training, classes, lecture series, multimedia presentations, and musical and dramatic productions.

Costs

Tuition for the 1999–2000 academic year (based on two 12-credit-hour semesters) was estimated at $3600. Room and board were estimated at $3420. The estimated cost for books and fees was $650. The total cost per year at CSW was approximately $7670.

Financial Aid

Nearly 90 percent of CSW undergraduate students receive some type of financial assistance. Financial aid programs at College of the Southwest are funded through a variety of sources. It is intended that the various financial aid programs be used to recognize academic, athletic, or special achievement; to meet financial need; or to provide self-help opportunities through college work-study programs and parent/student loans. While it is not possible to guarantee that funding will be available for every applicant, the aid programs at CSW are designed to help cover the difference between the cost of attending CSW and the student's own resources. Each application is handled on an individual basis in order to determine the type of award that would best serve the student. Financial aid at College of the Southwest includes institutional scholarships and student hourly on-campus work assignments. Students may also apply for named scholarships that are donor funded.

Students may apply for a Federal Pell Grant and a Federal Supplemental Educational Opportunity Grant (FSEOG), which are federally sponsored programs regulated by guidelines and formulas established by the government. Students may apply for a grant from the New Mexico Student Choice Act, which provides scholarship funds for students who attend private institutions within the state. The New Mexico Student Incentive Grant also provides funds for eligible students. These particular programs are for New Mexico residents only. Support from the New Mexico Scholar's Act is available for students who qualify.

Student loans are available to students and parents. A number of lenders exist, and it is the responsibility of the student borrower to choose his or her own lender. CSW students may apply for the Federal Work-Study Program or the New Mexico Work-Study Program. Both programs provide on-campus employment.

Faculty

The student-faculty ratio is 16:1. College of the Southwest's faculty is committed to top-quality instruction, and its members are easily accessible to students. The composition of the CSW faculty is geared to student success. Students are exposed to instruction from faculty members with doctorates or appropriate terminal degrees as well as from distinguished members of the professional community.

Student Government

College of the Southwest promotes an active student government and encourages all students to participate. Members of the Student Government Association are elected annually by the students to represent all students. The SGA plans social activities, serves as a liaison group with the College administration, and functions in other ways to benefit the individual student and the College as a whole.

Admission Requirements

Students may be accepted for admission to College of the Southwest upon graduation from an accredited high school, by transfer from an accredited college or university, by examination, or by individual approval. All applicants must submit an official copy of their high school transcript or GED scores, copies of either their ACT or SAT I scores (not applicable for students over 21), and official records of any college work previously attempted. All prospective students are strongly encouraged to visit the campus.

Application and Information

Applicants to CSW must file an Application for Admission with a one-time, nonrefundable $25 fee for undergraduate work; submit official high school and college transcripts (when applicable); and arrange for ACT or SAT I scores to be sent to the Office of Admissions.

For more information about College of the Southwest, students should contact:

Director of Admissions
College of the Southwest
6610 North Lovington Highway
Hobbs, New Mexico 88240
Telephone: 505-392-6561
           800-530-4400 (toll-free)
Fax: 505-392-6006
World Wide Web: http://www.csw.edu

THE COLLEGE OF WEST VIRGINIA
BECKLEY, WEST VIRGINIA

The College

The College of West Virginia (CWV), founded in 1933 as Beckley College, is a private, not-for-profit college located in southern West Virginia. CWV is dedicated to providing students with a quality, career-oriented education that is firmly rooted in the liberal arts, in a relaxed environment. The mission of The College of West Virginia is to offer educational opportunities in an atmosphere that promotes academic excellence, self-esteem, personal growth, cultural enrichment, and an aesthetic awareness to qualified students who are seeking to maximize their educational investment. The College of West Virginia accomplishes its mission by designing programs that lead to gainful employment through a curriculum that is sensitive to an ever-changing marketplace.

CWV, accredited by the North Central Association of Colleges and Schools, now serves approximately 2,000 students. The diverse student population is a mix of older, nontraditional students seeking to further their education and younger, traditional students seeking initial marketable skills and credentials.

The School of Arts and Sciences at The College of West Virginia offers general studies in the humanities and in the social, natural, and mathematical sciences. These courses provide diverse educational experiences to promote the intellectual development of the individual and to provide the basis for specialized educational development. A degree in interdisciplinary studies offers students concentrations in psychology, communications, ecology, prelaw, and other subjects.

The School of Business prepares students for careers in accounting, aviation, business law, computer information systems, computer science, health-care administration, legal studies, medical informatics, management, office management, and paralegal studies. These programs provide the student with the managerial and technical skills that enable the graduate to identify and respond to complex challenges in business after graduation.

The CWV School of Health Sciences enrolls more than 1,000 students in a wide variety of majors, ranging from nursing to respiratory care, diagnostic medical sonography, medical assisting studies, occupational therapy assistant studies, physical therapist assistant studies, physician assistant studies, and more. These programs are designed to address criteria required for application for certification or licensure in the chosen field as well as for entry into the next level of education in the specific field or a related discipline.

Orientation, academic counseling, tutoring, and job placement are among the services extended to students. Hogan Hall, a 192-bed, coed residence hall, opened in 1997 and offers two-bedroom suites and apartment-style living. The residence hall features lounges, study rooms, and laundry facilities. Four separate meal plans are available.

All CWV students are given a complimentary YMCA membership. The YMCA, located within blocks of the campus, allows students to participate in a variety of sports, including tennis, billiards, swimming, table tennis, bowling, basketball, volleyball, racquetball, and handball.

The College of West Virginia participates in intercollegiate athletic competition in NAIA Division I with men's basketball and women's volleyball and softball.

There are two graduate programs offered at CWV. A Master of Science in Nursing is available with two tracks in which students can enroll (administration/education or family nurse practitioner). The second graduate program allows those possessing an undergraduate degree in one of the allied health sciences to pursue a Master of Health Science degree.

Location

The College of West Virginia is located in the heart of downtown Beckley, West Virginia, a city 50 miles southeast of the state capital of Charleston. Beckley, a city of 20,000, is the county seat of Raleigh County and the population center of southern West Virginia. Within walking distance of campus are banks, churches, restaurants, retail stores, and city and county offices, including the Beckley Municipal Building, the Raleigh County Courthouse, and the Raleigh County Public Library. Soldiers' Memorial Theatre and Arts Center is within one block of the campus. Numerous city, state, and national parks provide students access to breathtaking panoramas as well as hiking, biking, mountain climbing and rappelling, spelunking, picnicking, swimming, and other outdoor recreational activities. In season, the white-water rapids of the Gauley and New Rivers or the slopes of nearby ski areas can provide the adventurous student with thrilling experiences.

Majors and Degrees

Bachelor's and associate degrees are offered in aviation, broadcasting, business administration (with concentrations in accounting, business law, computer information systems, general business, international business, management, and office management), computer science, criminal justice, diagnostic medical sonography, electronics engineering, elementary and secondary education preparation, engineering, environmental studies, general studies, geriatrics, health-care management (with concentrations in health-care administration and medical informatics), interdisciplinary studies (with concentrations in biology, communication studies, ecology, English and literature, prelaw, premedicine, psychology, sociology, and other concentrations under development), legal studies, medical assisting, nursing, occupational therapist assistant studies, paralegal studies, physical therapist assistant studies, physician assistant studies, respiratory care, secretarial science (with concentrations in administrative, legal, and medical), social work, sports medicine, travel, and wellness.

Academic Program

To earn a baccalaureate degree (either a B.S. or B.A.), students must complete a minimum of 128 hours, including 36 hours of general studies, for all programs. During their senior year, most students have the opportunity to work directly in their fields through a practicum, providing hands-on experience and valuable credentials for employment after graduation.

Associate of Science (A.S.) degrees fulfill the requirements of preprofessional studies leading to the four-year baccalaureate degree. An A.S. requires a minimum of 64 hours.

The School of Academic Enrichment and Lifelong Learning provides opportunities for individuals to receive recognition of prior learning and to receive credit for demonstrated college-level learning. College credit may be received through transfer credit, correspondence courses, proficiency examinations, prior experiential learning, and directed independent study. A degree-completion program exists for adult students who already possess 40 college credit hours and who wish to earn their B.S. degree in a compressed amount of time.

Credit may be given to students who earn satisfactory scores through the College-Level Examination Program (CLEP) or a score of 3 or higher on Advanced Placement tests.

Academic Facilities

The rapidly expanding and changing campus of The College of West Virginia currently encompasses nine main buildings as well as four smaller buildings that contain the Erickson Alumni Center, Graduate Studies offices, the Office of the President, and the English Language Institute. Within these halls, learning resources for students include state-of-the-art computer laboratories, computer-assisted instruction, and modern science laboratories. Campus satellite dishes provide distribution of video materials to classrooms.

The Robert C. Byrd Learning Resource Center is a student-centered library and media center. The library houses more than 86,000 titles and provides students with access to more than 1 million books through an automated network that utilizes the databases of various southern West Virginia public libraries. The core collection is supplemented by Pro-Quest CD-ROM databases, Cumulative Index to Nursing and Allied Health Literature (CINAL), Social Issues Resources Index (SIRS), Ebscohost, Westlaw, Wilson Web, Athena, NEWSBANK, and MEDLINE.

The library's Video Lab allows students to check out or watch on premises educational videos on subjects they are studying in which they have an interest. The Learning Resource Center also features a state-of-the-art Media Center and two computer labs that contain sixty multimedia computers, allowing students access to both the Internet and an e-mail service offered by the College.

Costs

The College of West Virginia offers the least expensive tuition of all private institutions in West Virginia. For the 1999–2000 year, tuition and fees for a full-time student were $1920 for 12 credit hours, or $160 per credit hour. In addition to tuition and general registration fees, students enrolling in aviation courses are charged additional fees for all required ground and flight courses, depending on the type of license desired. Students in nursing and health sciences programs must pay additional lab and clinical fees pertaining to their major field of study.

Financial Aid

Eligible students may receive Federal Pell Grants, Federal Supplemental Educational Opportunity Grants, West Virginia Higher Education Grants, and Federal Stafford Student Loans. The Free Application for Federal Student Aid (FAFSA) must be submitted for determination of eligibility. A number of scholarships based on academic merit and/or financial need are available to students in addition to the Federal Work-Study Program.

Faculty

More than 150 full- and part-time instructors are well-qualified to provide students with personalized, high-quality instruction. More than 50 percent of full-time instructors hold the earned doctoral degree. The student-faculty ratio at CWV is 14:1, allowing for a high level of interaction with the students.

Student Government

The Student Government Association (SGA) serves as a vital link in communication between students, administration, and faculty. The SGA is governed by an established constitution, and the student body elects its officers. The primary objectives of the SGA are to enhance the quality of student life through the development of skilled leaders and to provide representation of students' views and opinions on issues related to the College curriculum and extracurricular activities. A Residence Hall Association guides and enhances campus life for students living in Hogan Hall.

Admission Requirements

The College of West Virginia maintains an open-door admission policy with the exception of selective programs. Applicants who are graduates of accredited secondary high schools or who have received a General Educational Development (GED) certificate are eligible to apply. Applications are welcome from all qualified students regardless of age, sex, religion, race, color, creed, national origin, or handicap.

Application and Information

To apply for admission, students must submit to the Office of Admissions a properly completed application, an official current high school transcript or GED certificate, and official ACT scores. Transfer students are welcome and are asked to submit applications and official transcripts from all colleges previously attended. Applicants are notified of their acceptance status as soon as the application process is completed. Applicants for selected curricula or courses may be required to have minimum ACT (or SAT I) scores, take placement tests, or demonstrate other competencies as specified by each degree program.

The College of West Virginia encourages prospective students and their families to arrange a campus visit. The Marketing Department conducts campus tours and advising sessions and is open from 8 a.m. to 5 p.m. Monday through Friday.

For an application form and for more information, students should contact:

Marketing Department
The College of West Virginia
P.O. Box AG
Beckley, West Virginia 25802-2830
Telephone: 304-253-7351
           800-766-6067 (toll-free)
E-mail: gocwv@cwv.edu
World Wide Web: http://www.cwv.edu

THE COLLEGE OF WOOSTER
WOOSTER, OHIO

The College

One of the first coeducational colleges in the country, the College of Wooster was founded in 1866 by Presbyterians who wanted to do "their proper part in the great work of educating those who are to mold society and give shape to all its institutions." Today it is a fully independent, privately endowed liberal arts college with a rich tradition of academic excellence. That tradition defines student life at Wooster, beginning with the First-Year Seminar in Critical Inquiry and culminating in the Independent Study program.

The current enrollment is about 1,700 men and women. Almost all students live on campus, selecting from a variety of housing options. These include Babcock International House for students interested in international studies, Douglass Hall for students with an interest in the humanities and sciences, and Luce Hall, a modern, ninety-six-bed facility arranged in living suites. There are also thirty houses on the edge of campus, many of which serve as living-learning centers for those in community service and volunteer programs.

Wooster's 320-acre campus has thirty-six major buildings, half of them constructed or renovated since 1964. One of the most striking buildings is McGaw Chapel, a multipurpose facility that provides a formal place for worship and also functions as a site for lectures and concerts. The Freedlander Theatre complex provides students, faculty members, and community members with opportunities for academic growth and personal enrichment. Wooster has excellent facilities for physical education, including a nine-hole golf course, an all-weather track, and thirteen hard-surfaced tennis courts. Other facilities include Scheide Music Center; the Flo K. Gault Library for Independent Study, which adjoins the Andrews Library; the Ebert Art Center, which contains an art gallery and substantial facilities for studio art and art history; and the Timken Science Library, which opened in fall 1998. In fall 1999, Wooster completed a renovation and expansion of Severence Chemistry Building, which features new spaces for both student and faculty member research, as well as classrooms, offices, computer rooms, and laboratories for several fields of chemistry.

Most of the social life at Wooster originates from Lowry Center, the student union. The Student Activities Board organizes dances, concerts, films, trips, and many other activities. An arts and crafts program, the music and theater departments, and local social clubs also contribute to the activities on campus. The student entertainment center (The Underground) hosts live bands for dancing, miniconcerts, and folksingers and sometimes serves as a dinner theater.

Location

The College is located in Wooster, Ohio, a city of approximately 23,000. Wooster is 55 miles south of Cleveland and 30 miles west of Akron. An unusually close relationship exists between the College and the community. College-community activities include the Wooster Symphony, a college-community theatrical production, and a variety of volunteer and internship experiences. The community and the College also sponsor an annual performance by the Cleveland Orchestra on campus.

Majors and Degrees

The College of Wooster offers the degrees of Bachelor of Arts, Bachelor of Music, and Bachelor of Music Education. A student may choose from thirty-six possible majors, including seven interdepartmental majors: archaeology, art, art history, biochemistry, biology, black studies, business economics, chemical physics, chemistry, classical studies, communication sciences and disorders, communication studies, comparative literature, computer science, cultural area studies, economics, English, French, geology, German, history, international relations, mathematics, music, philosophy, physics, political science, psychology, religious studies, Russian studies, sociology, Spanish, theater, urban studies, and women's studies. In addition, minors are available in many of the areas above as well as physical education. Students also have the option of designing their own major, contingent upon the approval of the Upperclass Programs Committee. The Department of Education offers all courses necessary for either elementary or secondary teaching licensure.

Wooster offers combined-degree opportunities in cooperation with other institutions; such programs lead to either two bachelor's degrees (one from each institution) or a bachelor's from Wooster and a master's from the cooperating institution. Specific programs are in operation with Columbia University (law), Dartmouth College (business administration), the University of Michigan (economics, engineering, mathematics, and physics), Duke University (forestry and environmental management), Washington University (engineering), and Case Western Reserve University (dentistry, engineering, nursing, and social work).

Academic Program

Wooster's academic program is designed to provide a liberal education that prepares undergraduates for a lifetime of intellectual adventure, allows them to develop harmoniously and independently, and helps them meet new situations as they arise. To be eligible for a Bachelor of Arts degree, a student must successfully complete thirty-two courses, including a First-Year Seminar in Critical Inquiry and three courses of Independent Study. An overall grade point average of at least 2.0 (on a 4.0 scale) is required for graduation. Students may receive credit for work done at other colleges and for scores of 4 or better on the Advanced Placement tests offered by the College Board. Courses are graded A–D or No Credit unless the student exercises an option to take certain courses on a Satisfactory/No Credit basis.

Off-Campus Arrangements

Students who wish to enrich their undergraduate experience by overseas study may choose from a variety of fully accredited programs. Wooster sponsors a number of off-campus programs in the United States and abroad, and, as a member of the Great Lakes Colleges Association, offers off-campus study opportunities in thirteen countries on four continents. There are also programs available through the Institute of European Studies in seven university centers throughout Europe.

A variety of off-campus opportunities within the United States provide both academic and internship experiences. The Washington Semester and the Semester at the United Nations offer extensive possibilities in national and international government. Urban studies centers in Birmingham, Philadelphia, Portland, St. Louis, and San Diego provide many different experiential options. There is also a fine-arts semester in New York City. Other internship possibilities exist in business, the humanities, the natural sciences, and psychology.

Academic Facilities

The College libraries consist of the Andrews Library, the adjacent Flo K. Gault Library for Independent Study, and the nearby Timken Science Library in Frick Hall. Together, the libraries contain more than 1 million books, periodicals, microforms, electronic journals, videotapes, and audio recordings. As a member of CONSORT and OhioLINK, the libraries can provide almost any book from Ohio's academic libraries within two to three days. The libraries subscribe to a wide variety of electronic databases and to some 2,000 periodicals in electronic form, all available campuswide via the computing network. The libraries house more than 300 study carrels, each of which is equipped with electrical and data connections.

Computing is an important part of Wooster's academic environment. All academic buildings and every residence hall room are connected in an interactive computing network. Every residence hall has 24-hour access to a computer room with two to four computers and a laser printer. The fifty systems in the Taylor Hall computer center are available from 8 a.m. to 4 a.m. daily. Computer seminar rooms have recently been built for foreign language and English classes. The College's science facilities contain the most up-to-date laboratory equipment, libraries, computer terminals, and instrumentation, including ultraviolet, visible, and infrared spectrometers; a Raman spectrometer; a scanning electron microscope; a nuclear magnetic resonance spectrometer; a mass spectrometer; an X-ray diffractometer; and various chromatographs.

A well-equipped Reading and Writing Center offers workshops on study skills, the research paper, and critical reading. Through individualized programs, the highly qualified staff helps students develop their skills.

The Freedlander Theater complex contains excellent technical equipment and a separate theater for students' experimental productions. The speech facility itself houses a radio station, TV studios, and a speech and hearing clinic that also serves the community.

The Scheide Music Center, a 35,000-square-foot complex, contains five classrooms, eleven teaching studios, twenty-three soundproof practice rooms, a music library, and a listening lab. The Timken Rehearsal Hall and the acoustically balanced Gault Recital Hall are "tunable" so that the halls can be rendered "live" to greater or lesser degrees.

The Ebert Art Center, which opened in the fall of 1997, has expansive space for studio art and art history. The building is a combination of extensive renovation to Severance Art and the addition of the Sussel Art Gallery. This facility clears the way for the renovation of Frick Hall into a consolidated science library.

Costs

The comprehensive fee (room, board, tuition, and fees) for 2000–01 is $27,200.

Financial Aid

Almost all financial assistance is awarded on the basis of need, as determined by the Free Application for Federal Student Aid (FAFSA). Aid is allocated when students are admitted to the College. Financial assistance information and forms should be requested at the time of application. Applications for aid should be submitted by March 1.

Merit aid is available on a competitive basis. The College Scholar program offers eight awards of $16,000 each per year, based on a competitive examination. Additional awards of $9000 to $11,000 per year are available. Selected entering students receive academic and achievement awards independent of the College Scholars program. Synod of the Covenant Scholarships for Presbyterian communicants are available, as are Scottish Arts awards.

The Clarence B. Allen Scholarship program awards up to five scholarships of $16,000 a year to entering African-American students with a demonstrated record of academic achievement and promise of continued success in college. The Arthur Holly Compton Scholarships are awarded to students who demonstrate unusual aptitude for Wooster's program of Independent Study. Compton Scholarships are awarded for $7000 and $14,000 annually.

Music scholarships of $8000 each are awarded to entering first-year students based on auditions in voice or on an instrument. A 15-minute performance of works representing several styles of music is required.

Theater scholarships of $8000 each are awarded on a competitive basis. An audition is required.

Byron E. Morris Scholarships of up to $6000 are awarded to students who have a demonstrated record of achievement in their school or community in the areas of volunteer/community service or leadership.

Faculty

The faculty members and administration, 95 percent of whom (excluding those in performance areas) hold a doctoral degree, are dedicated to meeting the educational needs of individual students; they strive to help them realize their inherent potential. The student-faculty ratio is less than 12:1.

Student Government

The Campus Council, which consists of representatives from the student body, faculty, and administration, is the main legislative body in the areas of student life and cocurricular affairs. The Student Government Association, the Black Students Association, and the International Student Association also contribute to policymaking at Wooster. Students may attend open meetings of the faculty and are represented on virtually all faculty committees; they may also send representatives to observe meetings of the Board of Trustees.

Each residence hall establishes its own standards within College expectations. The College community feels that the most effective human relationships are based on trust and confidence.

Admission Requirements

A candidate for admission to the College should have earned a minimum of 16 academic units in high school, with emphases in English, foreign language, mathematics, natural science, and social studies. The student must present satisfactory scores on either the SAT I or the ACT. No College Board Subject Test scores are required.

The application deadline to be considered for competitive merit scholarships is January 7. The deadline for regular admission is February 15. Students are notified of the decision by April 1 and must reply by May 1. Early Decision I applicants must apply by December 15 and are notified on January 1. Early Decision II candidates must apply by January 15 and are notified by February 1. Deferred admission is available, as is admission at the end of the junior year of high school. Students are encouraged to visit the campus and have a personal interview.

The College of Wooster does not discriminate on the basis of age, sex, race, creed, national origin, handicap, sexual orientation, or political affiliation in the admission of students or in their participation in College educational programs, activities, financial aid, or employment.

Application and Information

Director of Admissions
The College of Wooster
Wooster, Ohio 44691
Telephone: 330-263-2000 Ext. 2270 or 2322
           800-877-9905 (toll-free)
Fax: 330-263-2621
E-mail: admissions@wooster.edu
World Wide Web: http://www.wooster.edu

COLORADO CHRISTIAN UNIVERSITY
LAKEWOOD, COLORADO

The University

Located in the foothills of the Rocky Mountains, Colorado Christian University (CCU) is the region's leading evangelical university. Graduates of the institution are found in strategic areas around the world in a wide variety of ministries, education, government service, business, management, computer science, private industry, and other professions.

As a Christian university, CCU respects the inherent need of all men and women for personal spiritual development. The University integrates its diverse fields of study with biblical truth: each academic discipline (philosophy, business, drama, education, psychology, music, and the physical, social, and behavioral sciences) is taught by instructors who have clear biblical presuppositions for their disciplines.

Community service and personal development are integral parts of the educational program of the University. Through service to the community, students discover their gifts, develop skills, appreciate the significance and practical application of what they are learning in the classroom, learn to lead and to work with others, and experience the joy and personal rewards of community involvement.

A variety of social, athletic, and cultural opportunities are available at Colorado Christian University. In intercollegiate sports, CCU competes in Division II of the NCAA and is part of the Rocky Mountain Athletic Conference. CCU offers men's and women's basketball, cross-country, soccer, and tennis; men's golf; and women's volleyball. Academic and social clubs, discipleship groups, and University retreats provide informal opportunities for students and faculty members to spend time together in recreation, instruction, and fellowship. Both the band and the choir participate in tours on an annual basis, in Colorado and the nation. All students are invited to audition and participate in the performing and creative arts of the University, regardless of declared major.

Campus housing provides one- and two-bedroom apartment-style living, including kitchens, living rooms, and balconies in the apartment units. In addition, a dining hall and food service are available to all resident students. Meal plans are available to students to accommodate differing schedules.

Colorado Christian University is accredited by the North Central Association of Colleges and Schools. The University is nondenominational and serves individuals and faculty members representing more than thirty Christian denominations. The University enrolls more than 3,000 students from forty-three states and twenty-two other countries in its undergraduate programs. The University offers graduate and adult degree-completion programs, with off-campus centers in Lakewood, Denver, Morrison, Colorado Springs, Fort Collins, and Grand Junction. CCU owns and operates radio stations KWBI in the Front Range, KDRH in Glenwood Springs, and KJOL in Grand Junction. There is also a student-run radio station (KORE) on the Lakewood campus.

Location

Located in the thriving Denver suburb of Lakewood, CCU is about 15 minutes from Denver's popular LoDo area, which is home to coffee houses, international-style shopping, and major professional sports teams, including the MLB Colorado Rockies, the NFL Denver Broncos, the NBA Denver Nuggets, and the NHL Colorado Avalanche.

The Denver Performing Arts Complex is also minutes from campus, where internationally acclaimed symphonies, ballet, theater, and opera productions are performed year-round. Directly west of CCU and less than 2 hours away are many of the world's best skiing, snowboarding, bicycling, hiking, climbing, white-water rafting, and fly-fishing locations. Denver has more than 250 days of sunshine each year, moderate winters, and mild summer days with comfortably low humidity.

Majors and Degrees

Colorado Christian University offers students more than thirty undergraduate majors with numerous concentrations and special emphases. CCU confers bachelor's degrees through five academic schools. Bachelor of Arts degrees are offered through the School of Music, Theatre and Arts in art, music, and theater; through the School of Humanities and Sciences in communication, English, history and political science, liberal arts, psychology, and social science; through the School of Education in teacher education in elementary, middle school, and secondary concentrations (with teacher certification); and through the School of Biblical and Theological Studies in biblical studies and youth ministries.

Bachelor of Science majors are offered through the School of Business in accounting, business administration, and computer information systems. Students may select a minor or concentration in applied technology, management, marketing, nonprofit management, second languages, or other areas. B.S. degrees are also available through the School of Humanities and Sciences in biology, health and physical education, mathematics, and science.

Bachelor's degrees in music education, music ministry, and music performance are also offered. Other programs include Christian leadership, computer applications, language studies, outdoor leadership, and radio broadcasting.

Students may select a minor or a concentration in most major fields and in foreign languages.

Academic Program

Colorado Christian University operates under a semester system offering fall, spring, and summer sessions. To qualify for graduation, students in all majors must complete the required minimum number of credits for their chosen major, including general education and electives. Colorado Christian University recognizes the importance of arts and sciences; therefore, the general education requirements include course work in behavioral and social sciences (12 credit hours), communication (9 credit hours), computer (3 credit hours), humanities (9 credit hours), mathematics (3 credit hours), natural science (6 credit hours), and biblical studies (12 credit hours). The freshman year begins with a semester-long integration course providing information, activities, classes, and programs to assist the student in assimilating to University life.

Colorado Christian University may grant college credit for course work taken at another accredited college through Advanced Placement, International Baccalaureate, College-Level Examination Program, DANTES, or Armed Forces Education, or by examination.

ROTC programs are available to students through cooperation with other colleges in the metropolitan Denver area. Specific ROTC information is available from the Office of Admission.

Off-Campus Arrangements

As a member of the Council of Christian Colleges and Universities, CCU offers students the opportunity to spend a semester abroad in programs designed to integrate Christian commitment in a world context. The American Studies Program places students in federal, public, and private agencies in Washington, D.C., where students can gain insights into government and public policy. Costa Rica is the setting for the Latin American Studies Program, where students can integrate their faith with knowledge and experience in a Third World country. The Middle East Studies Program in Cairo, Egypt, provides students with the opportunity to study cultures, religions, and conflicts within this diverse and strategic region. The Russian Studies Program affords students the opportunity to study Russian language, history, culture, and current events in the cities of Moscow, Nizhni Novgorod, and St. Petersburg. The L.A. Film Institute Program prepares students for the challenges and responsibilities of quality filmmaking.

Other programs offer majors through cooperation with other state universities or institutes. Students complete general requirements at CCU and professional courses at cooperating institutions.

Academic Facilities

The CCU library includes a computer lab, a curriculum lab, audiovisual equipment loan, and book, video, and music collections. Students have access to 1,200 full-text journals via the Internet, which augments 400 print journals in the library. Religion, education, psychology, business, and periodical and newspaper indexes are offered through the CCU library with cooperative programs for borrowing materials from other libraries. Computer searching (Z39.50 software) is performed for and by students to obtain the best resources for their assignments. The Music Facility has a separate music library and also provides power Macintosh computers, multitimbral synthesizers, computer ear-training programs, Finale, Mosaic, Professional Performer, Tap Master rhythm laboratory, and facilities with grand pianos. Athletic facilities, PC and Macintosh computer labs, a student center and bookstore, the Lambotte Theatre, and other facilities all enrich academic life for CCU students.

Costs

The 2000–01 cost for tuition (12–16 credit hours) and fees is $5700 per semester for traditional undergraduate students. Room charges range from $1500 to $1600, and board charges range from $350 to $1135 per semester. All freshmen are required to live on campus and participate in a meal plan unless living at home with parents or a legal guardian in the Denver metro area.

Financial Aid

Colorado Christian University provides a financial aid program to assist students who need additional resources to meet their educational costs. Students who qualify may be eligible for institutional scholarships and grants based on their talent in the areas of academics, music, drama, or athletics or based on their financial need. Students may also qualify for assistance through federal grant, work, or loan programs. Students applying for financial aid must file the Free Application for Federal Student Aid (FAFSA) and submit an institutional financial aid form to the University.

Faculty

CCU faculty members teach primarily undergraduate courses. Small class sizes (most classes have fewer than 25 students), combined with a teaching rather than research faculty, assure students of personal, quality instruction. Faculty members teach all classes without the aid of undergraduate instructors. Forty-three percent of full-time faculty members hold doctoral degrees. An advantage of CCU's faculty is that professors are practitioners in their field—they come with background and experience in the real world, not just from classroom textbooks. This element offers practical, relevant training for students. Faculty members also serve as advisers and mentors to students. They take a sincere and active role in the personal, academic, and spiritual lives of the students.

Student Government

The Associated Students of Colorado Christian University includes all registered students. Officers are chosen annually by election from within the student body and serve through the Student Government Association (SGA). Voicing the concerns and needs of the students to the University administration and providing opportunities for fun and fellowship are at the core of the SGA. SGA serves students through three distinct branches: the Executive Council, Senate, and Program and Activities Crew.

Admission Requirements

Applicants are evaluated on the basis of academic ability, personal and professional goals, character, and Christian commitment. Those applying for all programs are expected to have a high school diploma or the equivalent, with a satisfactory grade point average. Students applying as first-time freshmen or those with fewer than 30 transfer credits should submit the Application for Admission, a high school transcript, SAT I or ACT scores, and two character recommendations. Students applying for transfer admission should submit the Application for Admission, all college transcripts, and two character recommendations.

In order to provide a solid foundation for college-level work, it is recommended that the applicant present the equivalent of 16 academic units from an approved high school. Home school students are welcome to apply for admission by following the application procedures listed above. A GED diploma may be required of a home school student at the discretion of the admission committee if there is evidence of a discrepancy between the high school transcript and the standardized test scores.

Application and Information

For a viewbook and application, CCU video, or catalog, students should contact:

Office of Admission
Colorado Christian University
180 South Garrison Street
Lakewood, Colorado 80226

Telephone: 303-963-3200
           800-44-FAITH (toll-free)
Fax: 303-963-3201
E-mail: admission@ccu.edu
World Wide Web: http://www.ccu.edu

Students enjoy spring retreat.

COLORADO COLLEGE
COLORADO SPRINGS, COLORADO

The College

Founded in 1874, Colorado College is one of the oldest colleges in the American West. Among national liberal arts and science colleges in the U.S., the College is distinct in two ways: it employs a one-course-at-a-time approach (the Block Plan) in structuring its curriculum, and it is located in the Rocky Mountain West. The College's 1,900-member student body includes students from all fifty states and thirty other countries. Seven percent of the students are international, and 14 percent are members of racial or ethnic minority groups. Two thirds of the students live on campus each year, and housing is guaranteed for all four years. There are more than 100 student groups that range from community service organizations to political clubs to spiritual groups. There are eighteen varsity sports (nine women's and nine men's) as well as club and intramural sports. Eighty percent of the students graduate after four years of enrollment, and almost two thirds of the students go on to graduate school within five years of graduation. Colorado College attracts independent, individualistic students, in the tradition of the old American West.

Regardless of the course of study taken at Colorado College, students are educated broadly and prepared for a wide range of careers. Because most people change careers a number of times in their professional lives, a liberal arts education at Colorado College is the most profoundly practical education available. Professors teach their students to read carefully, write effectively, speak authoritatively, and think critically. They emphasize the analysis of a problem more so than any one answer to that problem. Students learn to connect subjects and place them in larger contexts. Students also learn to think flexibly and skeptically and to ultimately develop confidence in their own ideas and beliefs.

Location

Colorado College is located in Colorado Springs, a city of about a half million people that is located on the front range of the Rocky Mountains and at the foot of Pikes Peak. The College was founded in 1874, only three years after Colorado Springs itself. Its 90-acre campus is located in what is now downtown Colorado Springs. Because the College is in the downtown area, students are within walking distance of a variety of eclectic cafés, coffee shops, and restaurants; funky clothing stores and mountain outfitters; and theaters and clubs. A museum with a particularly fine collection of Southwestern art is adjacent to the campus. Colorado Springs is also only a 1-hour drive from Denver (metropolitan population of 3 million), the capital of the Rocky Mountain West in many respects. Santa Fe, one of the nation's cultural centers, is just a 5-hour drive to the south.

Students often spend their block breaks—the 4½-day period that separates every block—in the great outdoors. Most excursions are organized informally—groups of friends going camping, hiking, backpacking, climbing, or skiing. Excursions are easy to organize, since the special gear that is often needed is easily obtained from the College. The student-run Outdoor Recreation Committee also organizes First-Year Outdoor Orientation Trips (FOOT) for new students as well as other block break excursions.

Majors and Degrees

Students have more than thirty formal majors from which to choose, twelve of which are interdisciplinary. A student may also choose to double major, take a thematic minor, or even design an independent major. The College also offers a number of special programs for students to complement their liberal arts education. Preprofessional advising programs are available in law, business, medicine, and other health professions. Teacher certification is available through the Education Department, regardless of the student's major. The College also has 3-2 engineering programs with Washington University in St. Louis, the University of Southern California, Rensselaer Polytechnic Institute, and Columbia University.

Academic Program

Students at Colorado College learn under an innovative system called the Block Plan. Under this system, students take eight courses between early September and mid-May, the same number that students take at comparable institutions. Instead of taking four courses at the same time each semester, students study their courses one at a time in eight separate 3½-week periods, called blocks. Most courses last for one block; others may stretch for two or three blocks.

The Block Plan was established thirty years ago to help students devote their full attention to each class. Under the Block Plan, students don't have to juggle classes and assignments and sacrifice their attention to one course to perform well in another. Professors also devote their attention to only one class in any given block. Because of the Block Plan, Colorado College courses have a rhythm different from classes taught under semester systems. Since a class typically meets from 9 a.m. to noon each weekday morning, no bell brings class discussion to a sudden end. Students have the luxury of allowing any topic of discussion to continue without interruption.

Students cover as much material in a class as other students at comparable colleges. While the pace of a class is accelerated, Colorado College students do not have three other classes demanding their time and attention. Under the Block Plan, students learn to focus and work efficiently, organizing their work and time. Field-study opportunities abound. Professors can, and often do, hold classes off campus, sometimes for a day or a week and sometimes for an entire block. Classes go to the mountains for geology study, the Caribbean for research on coral reefs, and Mexico for anthropological work.

Off-Campus Arrangements

About 55 percent of students study abroad for a semester or a year before they graduate. Colorado College offers programs in Costa Rica, the Czech Republic, France, Germany, Great Britain, Hong Kong, India, Italy, Japan, Mexico, the Netherlands, Russia, and Zimbabwe. The majority of these programs cost no more than standard Colorado College tuition. Students who wish to study in a country not available through the College can also attend a nonaffiliated program.

Academic Facilities

Colorado College has some of the most modern equipment and technology available across every discipline. The natural sciences facilities have an electron microscope, a 16-inch reflecting telescope, a computerized microscopic interface, greenhouses with various climates, extensive lab space, and graphics workstations. Facilities for the humanities and social sciences include a language lab with video disk technology, several theaters, and extensive art studios and gallery space. More than 200 computers (PC and Mac) are available for student use. Three fourths of the students living in residence halls have high-speed network access in their rooms. The other fourth have modem access. Tutt Library has nearly 1,300 academic periodicals, more than a quarter of a million government documents, and numerous interlibrary loans. The College maintains two facilities for class retreats. The Gilmore-Stabler Cabin is situated in beautiful, rustic mountain surroundings, just 45 minutes from campus. About 3 hours from campus, the College also maintains the Baca Campus, located near the base of the Sangre de Cristo mountains in the San Luis Valley.

Costs

For the 1999–2000 academic year, tuition was $21,822 and room and board were $5568. Personal expenses and transportation cost $1392, and books and supplies cost $680.

Financial Aid

Colorado College provides need-based financial aid packages to first-year applicants who are U.S. citizens or permanent residents and demonstrate eligibility. Fifty-five percent of Colorado College students receive such aid. To be considered, first-year applicants must mail the FAFSA (code 001347) and PROFILE (code 4072) financial aid applications by February 15. Transfer applicants must mail these forms by April 1. Transfer applicants and international applicants should contact the Admission Office for special financial aid information. A small number of merit-based scholarships are also offered to potential science majors and National Merit Scholars. For more information, students should contact the Financial Aid Office, 14 East Cache La Poudre Street, Colorado Springs, Colorado 80903; telephone: 719-389-6651 or 800-260-6458 (toll-free); fax: 719-389-6173; e-mail: financialaid@coloradocollege.edu; World Wide Web: http//www.ColoradoCollege.edu/Admission.

Faculty

The College strictly limits the size of every class, including introductory-level classes. Almost every class is capped at 25 students, and the average class size is 15. Team-taught classes, classes taught by two professors, are limited to 32 students. With such small class enrollments, almost every class is taught as a seminar. Classes are taught by an accomplished faculty, 97 percent of whom hold the highest degree in their field. Colorado College has no teaching assistants. While professors often lecture, the typical class is primarily a forum for discussion. Students must come to class prepared to ask questions and add insights. Since both students and professors are involved in only one course at any given time, the Block Plan allows for flexibility and innovation. Although most classes meet from 9 a.m. to noon every morning, they are not required to do so. A class might occasionally meet three times in a day or not at all to allow extra time for reading or research. Classes sometimes meet for breakfast in a professor's living room or at midnight in the observatory.

Student Government

The Colorado College Campus Association (CCCA), the College's student government organization, probably has the highest profile among student clubs and organizations. The executive officers and the Student Senate fund student groups and events, discuss campus issues, and represent student opinion to the administration and community.

Admission Requirements

The Colorado College Admission Office enrolls academically accomplished students who have diverse talents, interests, and backgrounds. No one admission factor alone determines whether an applicant is admitted. The Admission Office considers academic record; teacher and counselor recommendations; essays; extracurricular interests, activities, and talents; SAT I or ACT test results; and TOEFL test results (for some international students). Interviews are not part of the admission process, but campus visits are encouraged. Last year, 3,650 students applied and 2,010 were admitted. Of the 550 students enrolled, 30 percent finished in the top 5 percent of their class, 53 percent finished in the top 10 percent, and 85 percent finished in the top 25 percent. The middle 50 percent of ACT scores was 26 to 30; the middle 50 percent of SAT I combined scores was 1200 to 1350.

Application and Information

Regular action first-year applicants have a January 15 postmark deadline and receive a decision by early April. Early action first-year applicants have a November 15 postmark deadline and receive a decision by early January. First-year applicants may use the Common Application. Fall transfer applicants have an April 1 postmark deadline and receive a decision in mid-May. Spring transfer applicants have a November 1 postmark deadline and receive a decision by late December.

For more information, students should contact:

Admission Office
Colorado College
14 East Cache La Poudre Street
Colorado Springs, Colorado 80903
Telephone: 719-389-6344
          800-542-7214 (toll-free)
          800-248-7177 (toll-free in U.S. for video orders)
Fax: 719-389-6816
E-mail: admission@coloradocollege.edu
World Wide Web: http://www.ColoradoCollege.edu/
   Admission

Students on the campus of Colorado College.

COLORADO STATE UNIVERSITY
FORT COLLINS, COLORADO

The University

In 1879, when Colorado State University admitted its first students, it was designated Colorado's land-grant college. The land-grant concept of a balanced program of teaching, research, extension, and public service provides the foundation for the University's teaching and research programs. Today, Colorado State has a commitment to integrating first-rate academic programs with hands-on learning experiences inside and outside the classroom.

Education at Colorado State encompasses the major areas of human knowledge—the sciences, the arts, the humanities, and the professions. The mission of the University is to graduate students who possess the knowledge and skills to compete in a global marketplace and to live full, rewarding lives. The University has historically had a reputation for excellence in its programs, from the baccalaureate to the postgraduate level, and has achieved a worldwide reputation in a number of important fields. Colorado State offers graduate degrees in all eight colleges.

The 22,700 students enrolled at Colorado State represent all fifty states and ninety countries. The variety of students broadens the educational experience for all and enables students to share their backgrounds and heritages and to learn about others in an atmosphere that encourages cultural exchange and an appreciation and respect for diversity. The University provides a wide range of programs to meet the social, recreational, and academic needs of its diverse student population. There are more than 300 clubs and organizations, including student government, honor societies, sororities and fraternities, athletic clubs, cultural and religious organizations, advocacy offices, and major-oriented or professionally oriented clubs. The Lory Student Center, rated one of the ten best student centers in the country, provides a focal point for student life on campus. Many students participate in intramural and club sports. For the more serious-minded athlete, Colorado State offers men's and women's varsity sports in the Mountain West Conference (MWC), Division IA of the National Collegiate Athletic Association (NCAA). All students have access to the sports facilities at the 100,000-square-foot Student Recreation Center, which is open daily for drop-in recreational use. This facility houses a gymnasium with basketball, volleyball, and racquetball courts; an elevated running track; a 10-lane, 25-yard swimming pool and spa pool; and weight, fitness, aerobics, and locker rooms.

Colorado State has ten coed residence halls, each containing dining facilities, recreation and study areas, a laundry room, and vending machines. The halls provide a wide variety of activities, including educational programs, social gatherings, and recreational events. The University's residence hall system received top honors for outstanding programming, leadership development, and dedication shown toward students. Several floors within the residence halls are designated for either specific majors or special interest groups, providing the opportunity to live with people with similar interests. There are fifteen such "Community Living" options, including honors, leadership, engineering, pre-veterinary medicine, performing and fine arts, international awareness, and more. All residence halls are non-smoking.

Location

Fort Collins, a city of more than 108,000 people, provides a unique blend of big-city amenities and small-town friendliness. It is scenically located at the western edge of the plains at the base of the Rocky Mountain foothills and conveniently located 65 miles north of Denver. The wide-open spaces and majestic Rockies make Fort Collins a very attractive place to live and learn. Areas for camping, hiking, skiing, swimming, boating, rafting, climbing, and fishing are within an easy driving distance of campus.

Majors and Degrees

Colorado State University offers bachelor's degrees through eight colleges. Bachelor of Science degrees are granted through the College of Agricultural Sciences in agricultural business, agricultural economics, agricultural education, animal science, bioagricultural sciences, equine science, farm and ranch management, horticulture, landscape architecture, landscape horticulture, and soil and crop sciences; through the College of Applied Human Sciences in apparel and merchandising, construction management, consumer and family studies, exercise and sport science, human development and family studies, industrial technology management, interior design, nutrition and food science, restaurant and resort management, and technology education and training; through the College of Business in business administration, with concentrations in accounting, entrepreneurship, finance–real estate, information systems, management, and marketing; through the College of Engineering in bioresource and agricultural, chemical, civil, electrical, environmental, and mechanical engineering and in engineering science; through the College of Natural Resources in fishery biology, forestry, geology, natural resources management, natural resource recreation and tourism, rangeland ecology, watershed science, and wildlife biology; through the College of Natural Sciences in biochemistry, biological science, botany, chemistry, computer science, mathematics, physical science, physics, psychology, statistics, and zoology; and through the College of Veterinary Medicine and Biomedical Sciences in environmental health and in microbiology.

Bachelor of Arts degrees are offered through the College of Applied Human Sciences in social work and through the College of Liberal Arts in anthropology, art, economics, English, French, German, history, liberal arts, music, performing arts, philosophy, political science, sociology, Spanish, speech communication, and technical journalism. The Bachelor of Fine Arts and Bachelor of Music degrees are offered through the College of Liberal Arts in art and in music.

Teacher licensure at the secondary level is available in biology, biology/natural resources, chemistry, English, French, general science, geology, German, industrial sciences, mathematics, physics, social studies, Spanish, and speech. Teacher licensure in grades K–12 is offered in art, music, and physical education. Vocational secondary education licensure is available in adult technical education, agricultural education, business education, consumer and family studies, marketing education, and trade and industrial education.

Preprofessional programs are offered in dentistry, law, medicine (chiropractic, optometry, osteopathy, physical therapy, physician assistant studies, and podiatry), nursing, occupational therapy, pharmacy, and veterinary medicine.

Academic Program

More than 100 undergraduate programs are offered within the eight colleges and fifty-six departments, allowing students to shape a course of study that best meets their personal and professional goals. Depending on their degree program, students are required to complete a minimum of 128 credit hours for graduation.

Colorado State provides students with a well-rounded education through the All-University Core Curriculum (AUCC), the centerpiece of Colorado State's integrated learning experience. All students are required to complete the AUCC. Students usually meet the AUCC requirements in their freshman and sophomore years and devote their junior and senior years to specialization in their major field. A concentration—a sequence of at least 12 semester credits of selected courses designed to accommodate the specific interests of a student—may be designated within some majors.

1500   www.petersons.com   *Peterson's Guide to Four-Year Colleges 2001*

Students may also choose to pursue a double major, a minor, or an interdisciplinary studies program.

The Colorado State Honors Program provides academically motivated undergraduates in all majors with intellectual stimulation commensurate with their abilities. It fosters a close intellectual association of students and faculty. Independent study is recommended.

Off-Campus Arrangements

The Office of International Programs provides information about and coordinates many study-abroad programs that allow students to study almost anywhere in the world. Study-abroad programs can range from two-week seminars to semester and yearlong periods of study in any major.

Academic Facilities

Colorado State comprises four campuses covering approximately 4,500 acres. The 536-acre main campus, with nearly 100 academic and administrative buildings, is virtually a city within itself. Classrooms and residence halls are in proximity. South of the main campus is the Veterinary Teaching Hospital (107 acres), one of the nation's top facilities for teaching and research in the clinical sciences. A 923-acre agricultural campus supports instruction and research in agronomy and animal science, including the Equine Teaching and Research Center. The Foothills Campus, a 1,730-acre facility located 2 miles west of the main campus, is home to many of the University's renowned research projects. A 1,192-acre mountain campus, Pingree Park, located 55 miles west of the main campus at an elevation of 9,000 feet and bordering Rocky Mountain National Park, is used primarily for summer educational and research programs in forestry and natural resources.

The William E. Morgan Library houses collections totaling more than 3 million items and provides reading areas for more than 1,500 people. The library collections include books, periodicals, newspapers, journals, manuscripts, microfilms, records, and other reference items. The Morgan library has undergone a multimillion-dollar expansion, further enhancing its resources and facilities and enabling it to better serve students.

Costs

All stated costs are per semester. For 1999–2000, tuition and fees for full-time undergraduates were $1527 for Colorado residents and $5370 for nonresidents. The average cost of room and board in on-campus housing was $2451. Books and classroom expenses were estimated at $330. Freshman students, unless they are living at home, married, or over 21 years of age, are required to live on campus and are therefore guaranteed a space in the residence halls. Upperclass students may choose to live in the Colorado State residence halls, in the on-campus apartment housing (for married students, single-parent students, single nontraditional-age students, or single graduate students), or in any of the numerous houses or apartments located nearby.

Financial Aid

Colorado State participates in and administers a wide variety of student financial aid programs, including loans, grants, scholarships, work-study, and student employment. Colorado State's Student Financial Services publishes the *Paying for College* brochure that describes in detail all scholarships and aid offered. In 1998–99, students at Colorado State had more than $131 million in financial resources available; approximately 66 percent of students received some type of financial assistance, and 51 percent of the entering freshman class received some type of scholarship assistance. Student Employment Services assists students with locating part-time positions both on and off campus.

Faculty

The Colorado State faculty teaches both graduate and undergraduate students. There are 1,513 faculty members; 88 percent of the regular faculty hold advanced degrees. The student-faculty ratio is 21:1. Although faculty members are actively engaged in research, the majority of them teach undergraduate classes and serve as advisers.

Student Government

The Associated Students of Colorado State University (ASCSU) comprises all enrolled students. The ASCSU Senate acts as a liaison between the student body and the administration as well as the State Board of Agriculture, the governing body of Colorado State. The ASCSU also offers free legal, consumer, and other services to Colorado State students.

Admission Requirements

Colorado State University selects for admission students who demonstrate the greatest academic potential for successfully attaining a degree and who appear to be the best qualified to benefit from and contribute to the academic and cultural environment of the University. Applications are carefully and individually reviewed. Colorado State is a selective university. In fall 1999, the middle 50 percent of entering freshmen had a GPA range of 3.2 to 3.8, an ACT composite score of 22 to 26, and an SAT I combined score of 1020 to 1200.

Students applying as freshmen must submit a completed application form, a $30 processing fee, official high school transcripts that include high school class rank, college transcripts for any college course work, and scores from either the ACT or SAT I. The personal essay and letters of recommendation from teachers, principals, or counselors are also encouraged. Several factors are considered, including the applicant's grades, class rank, number of completed academic units, scores on either the ACT or SAT I, rigor of high school curriculum, trend in quality of high school performances, leadership qualities, school or community service, and the ability to contribute to an appreciation of diversity on the campus. Minimum freshman admission prerequisites include the completion of 18 units, 15 of which are academic units. Of these 15 academic units, 12 must be composed of 5 units of a social science/natural science combination, with a minimum of 2 units from each area; 4 units of English; and 3 units of mathematics, which includes algebra I, algebra II, and geometry.

Undergraduate students who wish to transfer to Colorado State must submit a completed application form, a $30 application fee, and official transcripts from all colleges and universities attended. The personal essay and letters of recommendation are also encouraged. The admission decision for applicants with 12 or more semester credits is based on college transcripts. Transfer applicants must have a minimum 2.0 GPA (on a 4.0 scale) to be considered for admission; applicants should have at least a 2.5 GPA to be considered strong candidates for admission. Transfer students must have completed a mathematics course at the level of college algebra or above with a grade of C or higher or have completed an intermediate algebra course with a grade of B or higher. Additional factors that are considered include academic rigor; trend in grades; involvement in campus, community, and/or family activities; and an ability to contribute to an appreciation of diversity on the campus.

Students may apply via the World Wide Web at the address listed below. Completed applications with all supporting documents must be received in the Office of Admissions by July 1 for the fall semester and December 1 for the spring semester.

Application and Information

The admissions office is open Monday through Friday, from 7:45 a.m. to 4:45 p.m. during the academic year and from 7:30 a.m. to 4:30 p.m. during the summer. Student-led campus tours are given Monday through Friday at 10 a.m. and 2 p.m. with an admissions/financial aid presentation given half an hour before the tour (9:30 a.m. and 1:30 p.m., respectively). No appointment is necessary.

Additional information and application forms are available by contacting:

Office of Admissions
Colorado State University
Fort Collins, Colorado 80523
Telephone: 970-491-6909
World Wide Web: http://www.colostate.edu

COLUMBIA COLLEGE
COLUMBIA, MISSOURI

The College

Columbia College is a four-year, private, coeducational college offering master's bachelor's, and associate degrees. It was founded in 1851 as Christian College and is affiliated with the Disciples of Christ. The institution is accredited by the North Central Association of Colleges and Schools. Today, students representing twenty-five states and thirty other countries attend the College.

The College's 29-acre campus, located four blocks from the downtown area of Columbia, Missouri, has twenty buildings, ranging from Williams Hall, constructed in 1851, through administration and classroom buildings erected in the early 1900s, to more modern residence halls and classroom facilities completed in the 1960s and 1970s. A gymnasium was erected in 1988, the Stafford Library was erected in 1989, and the Cultural Arts Center was remodeled in 1992. Brown Hall, the arts and humanities building, became operational in 1995. Three spacious residence halls provide housing for students who live on campus. Miller Hall and Banks Hall offer coeducational housing. Banks Hall features a popular Wellness Floor. Every residence hall provides a computer lab and cooking and laundry facilities. Student academic programmers enhance the academic environment within the residence hall system through specialized programming, peer academic counseling, and research and referral information sharing. Any student is entitled to have an automobile, motorcycle, or bicycle on campus. Student service facilities include a Student Center, a central dining facility, a health center, a counseling center, and a career planning and placement center.

Recreational and athletic opportunities are furnished through the College's newly remodeled fitness center, indoor pool, gymnasium, softball field, soccer field, tennis courts, and a large back-campus area for intramural sports programs, which are quite popular. The College is a member of the NAIA Division I and the American Midwest Conference, and its teams compete in men's basketball, volleyball, and soccer and women's softball and volleyball.

Location

Columbia, Missouri (population 75,000 plus 25,000 college students), is situated halfway between St. Louis and Kansas City. The presence of five hospitals, a major mental health center, social service agencies of all kinds, a large network of parks, and a well-educated populace accustomed to a rich cultural life makes Columbia a pleasant place to live, work, and study. *Money* magazine has often ranked it as one of the top twenty cities in the nation.

Majors and Degrees

Columbia College awards the Associate in Arts degree and the Associate in Science degree with majors in business administration, computer information systems, and criminal justice administration. The Bachelor of Arts and Bachelor of Science degrees are awarded with majors in art (history and studio), business administration, computer information systems, computer science, criminal justice administration, education, English, general studies, history, natural science, political science, psychology, and sociology. Preprofessional programs in dentistry, law, medicine, and veterinary science are available. The College also confers the Bachelor of Fine Arts in art and Bachelor of Social Work degrees. Students can choose minors in accounting; biology; chemistry; environmental studies; geology; international business; management; marketing; mathematics; music; philosophy, religious studies, and ethics; physics; and Spanish.

Academic Program

The academic curriculum supports the mission of the College to provide career degree programs based on a solid background in the liberal arts and sciences. Each of the degree programs can include an internship, enabling students to obtain practical experience in addition to the more theoretical classroom instruction.

The College follows a two-semester plan with an eight-week summer session. Each degree program sets its own sequence of requirements. To be eligible for graduation, students pursuing an associate degree must complete 60 semester hours with a cumulative grade point average of 2.0 (C) or better. Each associate degree program has a general education component. To receive a bachelor's degree, students must complete 120 semester hours of credit with a cumulative grade point average of 2.0 (C) or better. Students pursuing a baccalaureate degree must complete a series of general education courses, including 6 semester hours of English composition, and earn at least 39 semester hours of credit in junior- or senior-level courses.

Off-Campus Arrangements

Full-time Columbia College students may enroll, at no extra cost, in courses at two neighboring institutions through a cooperative arrangement. ROTC programs (all branches) are available through this arrangement as well. Study-abroad opportunities are also offered.

Academic Facilities

Stafford Library is fully automated and contains more than 70,000 volumes, 500 periodicals, and 6,000 audiovisual materials. Students also have access to materials through the College's interlibrary loan and exchange program with neighboring institutions.

An art and humanities facility, completed in 1995, provides resources for the art degree programs and a public gallery for promoting cultural growth. The College has a large computer and Internet laboratory; science and psychology lab facilities; an educational curriculum/materials library; the Center for Academic Excellence, which has a variety of individual assistance and tutorial programs; and major classroom buildings for traditional instruction.

Costs

For 1999–2000, student fees included $9808 for tuition and $4904 for room and board. Students should plan to spend about $400 per semester for books, supplies, and incidentals. *The Student Guide to America's Best College Scholarships: 1999–2000* rates Columbia College as one of the top colleges with the lowest costs.

Financial Aid

Most Columbia College students receive some type of financial assistance. The College awards to students more than $4 million annually in federal, state, and institutional funds. Financial aid packages may include need-based and merit-based scholarships, grants, loans, and work-study opportunities in a variety of combinations. The most prestigious awards are the Columbia College Scholarship (full tuition, room, and board) and the Presidential Scholarship (full tuition). Five each are awarded annually. Many other competitive scholarships are available. Some awards and scholarships are automatic if certain criteria are met. Talent awards in athletics, art, and music are also available. Half-tuition scholarships are awarded automatically to upperclassmen who maintain a 3.4 grade point average with 30 hours earned annually.

To be considered for financial assistance, students must complete the Free Application for Federal Student Aid (FAFSA) and submit the Columbia College financial assistance application.

Faculty

Excellence in teaching has been a common goal throughout the history of the College. Teaching is the faculty's primary responsibility. The faculty-student ratio of 1:14 fosters personal attention and animated discussion in the classroom. Faculty members also serve as advisers to students. The relatively small size of the student body promotes excellent communication and rapport among students and faculty members. Nearly eighty percent of the faculty have terminal degrees.

Student Government

All students at Columbia College are members of the Campus Community Government (CCG). The CCG Cabinet, elected from this body, serves as a formal liaison between students and the administration. One branch of CCG, the Student Activities Commission, plans and organizes social activities on campus, from programs of interest to specialized groups to campuswide recreational activities. Each residence hall has representation to CCG through its Hall Council, which is composed of elected students.

Admission Requirements

Columbia College evaluates each applicant individually on the basis of the total application, including academic records, ACT/SAT scores, activities, references, goals, and recommendations of high school counselors. A high school diploma or equivalent certification is required for admission. English and math tests are given on campus to appropriately place students. Admission requirements at Columbia College are moderately selective.

An early-start program is available for students wishing to enter college after their junior year in high school. Transfer students must submit transcripts of all college work attempted in addition to high school academic transcripts. There are no restrictions on the number of transfer students accepted each semester.

Application and Information

Descriptive brochures and application forms are available from the Office of Admissions. A campus visit is highly recommended. The completed application should be returned along with a $25 nonrefundable application fee. There is no fee if the application is submitted before January 1 for the fall semester. Notification of the admission decision is made on a rolling basis following the fulfillment of all admission requirements.

For more information and application materials, students should contact:

Director of Admissions
Columbia College
1001 Rogers Street
Columbia, Missouri 65216
Telephone: 573-875-7352
        800-231-2391 (toll-free in the U.S. and Canada)
E-mail: admissions@email.ccis.edu
World Wide Web: http://www.ccis.edu

Roger Gates at the entrance of the historic Columbia College campus.

COLUMBIA COLLEGE
COLUMBIA, SOUTH CAROLINA

The College

Columbia College, founded in 1854, is a private liberal arts college for women, with a coeducational evening college for working adults and a graduate school attracting professionals from around the world. The College is ranked by *U.S. News & World Report* as one of the top ten regional liberal arts colleges in the South. Among its most notable features are a 14:1 student-faculty ratio, a nationally recognized honors program, an emphasis on leadership development, and unique opportunities for field experience and travel-study in the United States and abroad. Enrollment is 1,373 students from fifteen states and thirteen countries, approximately half of whom live on campus. Forty-five percent of Columbia College alumnae enter graduate, law, or medical school.

The undergraduate curriculum offers thirty-seven majors, twenty-three minors, and five preprofessional programs, including premedicine and prelaw. The graduate school offers master's degree programs in conflict resolution (M.A.) and divergent learning (M.Ed.).

The College's athletics program features National Association of Intercollegiate Athletics competition in cross-country, soccer, tennis, and volleyball. Club-level and intramural opportunities are offered in basketball, camping, canoeing, equestrian, golf, hiking, rowing, scuba diving, skiing, and swimming.

As an institution committed to excellence in teaching—recognized by a 1996 Theodore M. Hesburgh award—the College promotes an environment of participatory learning and openness to ideas. Students are encouraged in every class to discuss, analyze, debate, and consider, with the goal of developing lifelong skills in critical thinking and problem solving. Personal attention from faculty members further enhances students' opportunities for growth, providing custom-designed learning experiences and internship possibilities.

Columbia College advocates a holistic approach to education, emphasizing strong core values, a sense of spirituality, respect for the individual, and service to the campus and the community. Affiliated with the United Methodist Church, the institution seeks students of all religious, geographic, racial, and cultural backgrounds and encourages an understanding of and appreciation for diversity.

The College is accredited by the Southern Association of Colleges and Schools, with additional national accreditation in art, dance, music, education, and social work.

Location

The College is located in Columbia, the capital of South Carolina, with a greater metropolitan population of 583,000. Columbia is the home of nine colleges and universities, including the 27,000-student University of South Carolina; Lake Murray, a 50,000-acre man-made lake accommodating all varieties of water sports; Riverbanks Zoo, one of the top twenty zoos in the country; semi-professional baseball and hockey teams; a thriving cultural arts community; and a wide array of shopping, dining, and entertainment opportunities.

Strategically located midway between New York and Miami at the convergence of Interstate Highways 20, 26, and 77, Columbia is only 2½ hours from both the world-famous South Carolina beaches and the beautiful Blue Ridge Mountains. Mild winters and long summers allow for virtually year-round outdoor activity.

Majors and Degrees

Columbia College awards the Bachelor of Arts degree with majors in accounting, art studio, biology, business administration, chemistry, Christian education, computer information systems, dance, dance education, early childhood education, elementary education, English, English–communication arts emphasis, English–literary studies emphasis, French, French–career development, history, mathematics, music, political science, psychology, public affairs, religion, social work, sociology–deviant behavior emphasis, sociology–family emphasis, sociology–social policy and planning emphasis, Spanish, Spanish–career development, special education, and speech-language pathology. The Bachelor of Science degree is offered in accounting, biology, business administration, chemistry, computer information systems, mathematics, and psychology. The Bachelor of Music degree is offered in music, music education, music performance, and piano pedagogy. The Bachelor of Fine Arts degree is offered in dance performance and choreography. Preprofessional programs are available in dentistry, law, medicine, nursing, and pharmacy.

Certification requirements may be fulfilled for teaching in secondary schools, for teaching the mentally retarded and the emotionally disturbed, and for work in a public school as a speech correctionist. Students interested in teaching in the primary grades, kindergarten, or nursery school are specially trained and certified in these areas.

Academic Program

Candidates for the bachelor's degree must complete 127 semester hours of credit. The student is required to take courses in communications, mathematics, social science, natural science, religion, aesthetics, and physical education. The remaining work is devoted to the selected major and electives. Independent study may be undertaken by qualified students.

The academic year is divided into two semesters. Two summer sessions are also available.

The Center for Contractual Studies offers an individualized curriculum to academically motivated students who are capable of sustained independent inquiry.

Off-Campus Arrangements

With an emphasis on globalization, Columbia College offers semesters at the University of Salamanca (Spain), the University of Angers (France), and Huron University (London), along with travel-study opportunities in Africa, Costa Rica, Greece, and Italy. In addition, scholars and professionals from around the world are invited to campus for interaction with students and faculty.

The College also offers a large number of internships in all areas of study. Internships may be arranged in Columbia; Washington, D.C.; London, England; or other geographic areas, as needed.

Academic Facilities

Columbia College has modern, well-equipped academic facilities. The Barbara Bush Center for Science and Technology, opened in 1997, features state-of-the-art chemistry, physics, biology, geology, and computer laboratories; classrooms; and faculty offices. It is also equipped with 600 data ports throughout the building, whereby students may access the campus computer network and the World Wide Web via laptop computers.

Edens Library houses more than 160,000 bound volumes, along with microfilm, microcard, and microfiche readers and a sophisticated computer catalog and research system. Computer labs, open 24 hours a day for student use, feature both PC-compatible and Macintosh equipment, with a wide variety of general and discipline-based software. The entire campus, including residence hall rooms, is wired for Internet and e-mail use.

Costs

The comprehensive fee for 2000–01, including tuition, room, and board, is $19,750 for a resident student. Tuition for day students is $14,760. The cost of books averages $300 per semester, and the technology fee is $150 per semester. A $20 nonrefundable application fee must be submitted with each application, and a reservation deposit of $200 is required. The deposit is credited toward tuition and fees.

Financial Aid

Financial aid at Columbia College is intended to assist students in meeting normal college expenses. It is the goal of the College to help as many students as possible who wish to attend but cannot do so without financial assistance. Approximately 90 percent of 1999–2000 freshmen received financial aid, with an average one-year award of $14,498. Scholarships, grants, loans, and work opportunities are awarded annually on the basis of financial need and acceptable academic performance. Funds from the Federal Perkins Loan, Federal Work-Study, Federal Pell Grant, Federal Supplemental Educational Opportunity Grant, and Federal Stafford Student Loan Programs are available to qualified financial aid applicants. Students who live in South Carolina and plan to attend Columbia College are eligible to apply for a state-sponsored South Carolina Tuition Grant, based on need and merit. Out-of-state students who plan to live on campus and who meet specified SAT and high school grade criteria may apply for a $3000 Out-of-State Residential Scholarship. Columbia College Presidential, Trustee, and Phyllis O. Bonanno Scholarships, based solely on merit, are available to qualified students on the basis of SAT or ACT scores, high school academic performance, and class rank.

Faculty

Columbia College has a faculty of more than 150 full- and part-time professors, who combine teaching ability and scholarship with a concern for students. Eighty percent of the faculty members hold terminal degrees in their disciplines, and all faculty members are fully engaged in teaching. No classes at Columbia College are taught by graduate assistants.

Student Government

Each student becomes a member of the Student Government Association upon enrollment and participates in the formulation of policies through the association and its committees.

Admission Requirements

The Committee on Admissions seeks to provide Columbia College with a student body that is geographically, socioeconomically, racially, and culturally diverse. A student may be admitted as a member of the freshman class or as a transfer student with advanced standing. Those wishing to transfer must be in good standing at the college last attended. All applications are given individual attention, and special talents are noted.

Columbia College strongly encourages early application and operates on a rolling admissions plan until all available spaces have been filled. Selection to the College is competitive. An applicant should be a graduate of an accredited four-year high school or have equivalent credentials. Admission is based upon the application and personal data sheet filed by the applicant, SAT or ACT scores, the transcript of at least the first three years of high school work, and the recommendations of high school officials. Transfer students must submit transcripts from all colleges previously attended. Columbia College does not discriminate on the basis of race, color, religion, marital status, handicap, or national or ethnic origin.

Application and Information

Application forms and other information about Columbia College may be obtained by contacting:

Office of Admissions
Columbia College
1301 Columbia College Drive
Columbia, South Carolina 29203
Telephone: 803-786-3871
          800-277-1301 (toll-free)
Fax: 803-786-4674
E-mail: admissions@colacoll.edu
World Wide Web: http://www.columbiacollegesc.edu

Barbara Bush Center for Science and Technology.

COLUMBIA COLLEGE CHICAGO
CHICAGO, ILLINOIS

The College

Columbia College Chicago was established during the World Colombian Exposition of 1890. Its original emphasis on communication arts expanded to include media arts, applied and fine arts, theatrical and performing arts, and management and marketing arts. The foundations of a Columbia College education continue to include small class sizes that ensure close interaction with a faculty of working professionals who bring the working world into the classroom, abundant internship opportunities with major employers in the Chicago marketplace, and outstanding professional facilities to foster learning by doing. All students are encouraged to begin course work in their chosen fields immediately, allowing them four full years in which to master their craft and build professional portfolios, audition tapes, resumes, and clip books. The College provides a sound liberal arts background for the developing artist or communicator and supports a student's employment goals through a full range of career services.

Columbia's enrollment of approximately 8,800 students is drawn from the city of Chicago and its suburbs, from across the United States, and from thirty-six other countries. The student body is almost equally divided between men and women. Creative students who enjoy a supportive but challenging environment thrive at Columbia.

At the graduate level, Columbia offers the folowing degrees: Master of Arts in Teaching (M.A.T.), the Master of Arts (M.A.) in arts, entertainment, and media management; teaching of writing; dance/movement therapy; interdiciplinary arts; journalism; multicultural education; and photography. The Master of Fine Arts (M.F.A.) is awarded in creative writing, film and video, and photography.

Outside the classroom, students participate in activities that include the College's student newspaper, radio station, electronic newsletter, two student magazines, cable television soap opera, three theaters, dance center, photography and art museums, and film and video festival. Many of the twenty-eight student clubs on campus are linked to an academic discipline and offer students opportunities to expand their social and professional networking experiences. The Myron Hokin Student Center provides a gallery/café environment in which to relax, study between classes, or meet for lunch. Student artwork is always on display, and daily Hokin Center activities feature live performances of music, comedy, readings, and dance by students and guests.

Just minutes from the main campus, Columbia College's residence hall is an innovation in apartment-style student housing. Groups of 2, 4, or 6 students share fully furnished loft-style apartments. Each apartment contains a spacious living and dining area as well as a full bath and full kitchen. Life in the Columbia College residence hall extends the supportive philosophy of the College, and student residents have access to computer and study rooms, music practice rooms, drawing and painting studio space, and a fitness room as well as recreational and party areas. The Residence Life staff generates a variety of living and learning opportunities to support and enhance student endeavors.

Location

Columbia's campus is set in Chicago's dynamic South Loop neighborhood, near Grant Park and Lake Michigan. Close to the Art Institute, Adler Planetarium, the Field Museum, the Chicago Symphony, and several other colleges and universities, Columbia's faculty members and students effectively utilize the city of Chicago as a social, educational, and professional resource. Convenient public transportation makes all cultural and educational opportunities easily accessible.

Majors and Degrees

At the undergraduate level, Columbia College grants the Bachelor of Arts degree with majors in art and design (concentrations in advertising, art, product design, fashion design, fine art, graphic design, illustration, and interior design), dance (concentrations in choreography, musical theater performance, performance, and teaching), digital media technology (through the Academic Computing Department), early childhood education (Illinois Type IV certification, in conjunction with the Erickson Institute), fiction writing, film/video (concentrations in cinematography, computer animation, directing, documentary, editing, history and aesthetics, producing, screenwriting, sound for film, and traditional animation), interactive multimedia (concentrations in animation, film/video, graphic design, photography, programming for multimedia, project management, and sound), interdiciplinary studies (self-designed major), interpreter training (for the deaf), journalism (concentrations in broadcast journalism, business writing, magazine editing and publishing, news reporting and writing, and reporting in health, science, and environment), management (concentrations in fashion/retail, media, music business, performing arts, small business/entrepreneurship, and visual arts management), marketing communication (concentrations in advertising, marketing, public relations, and sports marketing), music (concentrations in composition, direction, instrumental performance, jazz, musical theater performance, and vocal performance), poetry (through the English Department), photography (concentrations in fine art, photojournalism, and professional), radio/sound (concentrations in acoustics; broadcast journalism; radio management, production, and talent; sound contracting; sound for pictures; and sound recording and reinforcement), television (concentrations in broadcast journalism, interactive TV, postproduction effects, production/directing, and writing/producing), and theatre (concentrations in acting, costume design, directing, general design, lighting design, musical theater performance, playwriting, set design, and technical). Course offerings in the Academic Computing, English, Liberal Education, and the Science and Mathematics Departments support the general studies requirements at Columbia College.

Academic Program

The College supports creative and integrated approaches to education and encourages interdisciplinary study. The Bachelor of Arts degree is awarded to students who successfully complete 124 semester hours of study; 48 of these hours are distributed among courses in the humanities, science, English composition, literature, mathematics, social sciences, and computer applications.

Columbia continues to expand its extensive internship program. Because of the College's location, students can intern with major employers in Chicago's marketplace. From fashion merchandising to film and photography, from computer graphics to illustration, Chicago provides professional settings, classrooms, and employers for Columbia students.

The Career Services office offers a full range of services designed to help students launch their careers. Services include career counseling; seminars on interviewing, resume writing, and job search strategies; internships; placement assistance; job fairs; and alumni activities and assistance.

Off-Campus Arrangements

Cooperative arrangements with other colleges in the Chicago area enable students to take advantage of offerings and facilities at various institutions.

Academic Facilities

Advanced facilities for radio, television, art, computer graphics, photography, fashion design, and film production are available and include professionally equipped color and black-and-white darkrooms, digital imaging computer facilities, photography and film stages, film and video editing suites, and studios for painting, drawing, and 3-D design. The campus also includes the Museum of Contemporary Photography, one of only a few such facilities in the United States to receive accreditation, and the Audio Technology Center, a recording production and research facility. In addition, Columbia has invested in extensive computer facilities that are used by basic computer classes as well as by computer graphics students. The theater/music and dance departments have separate, but conveniently located, centers that have been designed for their specific performance needs. A radio station is managed and operated by Columbia students.

The College's 178,926-volume library and instructional service center provides comprehensive information and study facilities. Reading/study rooms and special audiovisual equipment are available for use in individual projects and research. As a member of a statewide online computer catalog and resource-sharing network, Columbia's library provides students with access to the resources of thirty academic institutions in Illinois, effectively creating an information base of several million volumes. The library also houses several special collections, including the George S. Lurie Memorial collection of books and resource materials on art, photography, and film; the Black Music Resource Center of books and sound recordings; the Screenwriters' Collection of film and television manuscripts; the History of Photography microfilm collection of books and periodicals; and a nonprint collection of 100,000 slides and more than 7,337 videotapes and films. The latest addition to the library is the Albert P. Weisman Center for the Study of Contemporary Issues in Chicago Journalism. The center includes a print and audiovisual collection and a learning center that explores the development of Chicago's political and social history.

Costs

In the 1999–2000 academic year, full tuition (12–16 credit hours) averaged $5345 for each fifteen-week semester, or $10,690 per year. Part-time tuition (up to 9 credit hours) was $365 per credit hour per semester. Summer school tuition was $289 per credit hour.

Some courses require additional service or laboratory fees. There is a nonrefundable registration fee of $50 per semester as well as a $30 library deposit that is refunded when a student leaves the College.

Financial Aid

Columbia College makes every effort to help students seek out and obtain financial assistance, and it also provides information for students seeking part-time employment.

In addition, Columbia offers institution-based scholarships such as Presidential Scholarships for freshmen, scholarships for transfer students, academic excellence awards, leadership awards, housing grants, Fischetti Scholarships for outstanding Columbia journalism students, and Weisman Scholarships for special communications-related projects.

The Financial Aid Office administers federal and state grant and loan programs. Part-time jobs are available in technical, clerical, secretarial, and food service areas. Appropriate application forms for financial aid are provided by the Financial Aid Office and are mailed to students who request them.

Faculty

Many of the 1,167 full- and part-time Columbia faculty members are working professionals (artists, writers, filmmakers, dancers, etc.), and many have national reputations. The College is constantly seeking individuals who are both gifted teachers and talented professionals. Many faculty members work nearby at the disciplines they teach and share practical expertise with students in information workshop settings as well as in the classroom. The interaction with faculty members who are practicing professionals provides students with invaluable access to the latest information in the field. Students also begin developing their own professional network as faculty members share contacts and information on how to break into the business. Columbia keeps class size small to foster these student-teacher relationships.

Student Government

Through the Student Organization Council, students at Columbia are able to sponsor services and activities that address departmental and individual needs. The council works closely with the Office of the Dean of Student Services and serves as a liaison for students in all departments of the College community.

Admission Requirements

At Columbia College, each application is considered individually, and decisions are based on high school records and performance at other colleges. Graduation from high school or evidence of equivalent preparation is required. In some cases, a personal interview may be required. The College has a liberal transfer policy.

Application and Information

Students are encouraged to apply for the fall semester by August 15. Applicants must submit an application for admission, an essay, proof of high school graduation (GED score is accepted), transcripts of previous college work, if any, and a letter of recommendation. Applicants must submit a nonrefundable $25 application fee with the application.

For more information, students should contact:

Undergraduate Admissions
Columbia College Chicago
600 South Michigan Avenue
Chicago, Illinois 60605
Telephone: 312-344-7130
E-mail: admissions@popmail.colum.edu
World Wide Web: http://www/colum.edu

Students at Columbia College Chicago.

COLUMBIA COLLEGE–HOLLYWOOD
TARZANA, CALIFORNIA

The College
Established in 1952, Columbia College–Hollywood (CCH) is a four-year coeducational, professional college offering classes with major course studies in television/video and cinema. Surrounded by such entertainment giants as Disney Studios, Universal City, Warner Studios, and NBC and CBS television studios, the center of the new Tarzana campus is the historic Panavision building. Columbia College–Hollywood is a private, nonprofit institution accredited by the Accrediting Commission of Career Schools and Colleges of Technology.

Since 1952, Columbia College–Hollywood graduates have attained success in their chosen calling all over the world. With the film and television industry poised to enter the twenty-first century in the midst of rapid technical and creative advances, Columbia College–Hollywood is the place for the aspiring film and video student to receive cutting-edge training.

Location
Columbia College–Hollywood makes the most of its location in Los Angeles's San Fernando Valley, the heart of the motion picture and television/video industry. CCH students are frequently invited to work on the many films that are produced daily in the L.A. area. The school's placement director arranges internships for students with production companies and studios, enabling them to gain invaluable experience and make all-important industry contacts. Apart from the excitement that comes from being at the visual media center of the world, there are the well-known physical attractions of Los Angeles itself: its temperate climate, beaches, mountains, and deserts. Los Angeles is a cultural center as well and is home to museums, galleries, concerts (both classical and popular), major-league sports teams, and live theater.

Majors and Degrees
Columbia College–Hollywood offers the Bachelor of Arts (B.A.) degree in cinema and in television/video production. Students who wish may pursue an Associate in Arts (A.A.) degree in television/video production. The A.A. and B.A. degree programs can be attended on a part-time basis.

Academic Program
The Associate in Arts degree requires 96 units of study, of which 48 units are in general education and 48 units are in television production. The Bachelor of Arts degree requires 192 units of study, 48 of which are in general education and 144 of which are in the program major. In the B.A. programs, cinema and television/video students are enrolled in parallel courses of study for the first five quarters. These courses cover both film and video technology, which gives the student a solid foundation. This is beneficial because the two mediums are merging in the professional world. After the fifth quarter, students continue in their major area of study. Most classes are held in the evening.

The program in television/video production is designed to provide students with knowledge and skills in the creative, technical, and operational aspects of the medium. The graduate from this course of study is well-qualified for a variety of entry-level positions in a television broadcast facility, a nonbroadcast video production setting, or an allied industry. Examples of entry-level positions are production assistant, directorial assistant, camera operator, floor director, advertising and sales assistant, copywriter, assistant editor, tape operator, or video engineer.

Through the program in cinema, students learn about the technical and creative aspects of theatrical, documentary, and industrial film production. Graduates from this program are well qualified for entry-level positions such as camera assistant, lighting assistant, grip, dolly grip, budgeting and production assistant, sound recordist, assistant editor, postproduction sound mixer, and assistant director.

Academic Facilities
Columbia College–Hollywood has a nonresidential urban campus with a complete color television studio and control room, videotape and film-editing facilities, and a sound mixing and recording stage. There are also a makeup room, a fifty-seat projection theater, a study area, a scene dock and prop room, well-equipped classrooms, and a 5,500-volume library.

Costs
For the 2000–01 academic year, tuition and fees for full-time attendance are approximately $10,500 per academic year. Laboratory fees vary from quarter to quarter. The estimated living costs for an independent student are approximately $7500 per academic year. Ample housing is available in the vicinity of the College.

Financial Aid
Columbia College participates in the following federal and state financial aid programs: the Federal Pell Grant, Federal Supplemental Educational Opportunity Grant, Federal Work-Study, Federal Family Education Loan (which includes subsidized and unsubsidized Federal Stafford Student Loan), and Cal Grants A, B, and C.

Faculty
The faculty consists of 35 instructors, the majority of whom hold positions in the television, motion picture, or educational fields during the daytime. The majority of classes are held during the evening. The student-faculty ratio is 5:1.

Admission Requirements
Applicants for freshman-level classes must be high school graduates and at least 18 years of age at the time of enrollment. They must have earned a minimum cumulative grade point average of 2.0 or have maintained an overall letter grade of C or better during their high school studies. Transcripts must demonstrate high school graduation. Under special circumstances, a passing score on the General Educational Development test (GED) may be accepted by the College in lieu of high school graduation, provided that the applicant is at least 18 years of age. Applicants for admission to the College on any other level are required to furnish transcripts of previous course work to establish their academic standing. Applicants to the Upper Division programs are required to furnish transcripts verifying completion of an Associate in Arts degree or higher. All transcripts must be sent directly to Columbia College–Hollywood by the educational institutions. Two letters of reference from people, other than relatives, who have been acquainted with the applicant for more than one year and are aware of the applicant's interest in the field of cinema, television, or communications media are required; these letters must be mailed directly to Columbia College–Hollywood by the writers. A 250-word essay concerning why the applicant wishes to study either film or video and describing his or her career goals is required. SAT I scores may be submitted.

Students enrolling in Columbia College–Hollywood for the first time are encouraged to attend an orientation session. Academic objectives and career goals are discussed, school programs and academic requirements are explained, and registration for classes takes place during the course of orientation. To guarantee enrollment, final registration should be completed at least one week prior to the beginning of the quarter.

Advanced standing may be granted to applicants for the programs in television/video production and cinema. Transcripts of the applicants' previous college-level study should be mailed directly to Columbia College by the institution previously attended for evaluation by Columbia College's Admissions Department.

Application and Information

Applications are accepted throughout the year, and applicants may apply to enroll in the fall, winter, spring, or summer quarters. Late registration can occur up to the close of the first week of the quarter; however, acceptance for enrollment in any particular quarter cannot be guaranteed unless the applicant has been fully matriculated at least one week prior to the beginning of that quarter.

A completed application for admission and an application fee of $50 should be mailed to the College or delivered in person by the applicant.

For more information, students should contact:

Admissions Office
Columbia College–Hollywood
18618 Oxnard Street
Tarzana, California 91356
Telephone: 818-345-8414
              800-785-0585 (toll-free)
Fax: 818-345-9053
E-mail: cchadfin@columbiacollege.edu
World Wide Web: http://www.columbiacollege.edu

At Columbia College–Hollywood, students use professional equipment on location for a film production workshop class.

COLUMBIA INTERNATIONAL UNIVERSITY
Columbia Bible College
COLUMBIA, SOUTH CAROLINA

The University

Columbia International University (CIU) has established itself as one of the world's foremost ministry training institutions. The University is a multidenominational, Christian higher education institution that is dedicated to preparing its students to serve God with excellence, whether through full-time ministry or a variety of other vocations. On campus currently, CIU is training students from more than forty-four states and thirty-two other countries. CIU has nearly 15,000 alumni. Alumni serve in various Christian ministry and professional roles in 124 countries.

With an undergraduate student body of 529, CIU's Bible College Division exemplifies a community with diversity in national backgrounds, ages, Christian denominations, and vocational goals. Since its founding in 1923, the institution's objectives for its students remain the same: equipping them for the challenges they will face by offering rigorous academics, practical ministry skills training, and encouragement in spiritual growth.

The Bible College Division offers a one-year Bible certificate, a two-year associate degree in the Bible and thirteen dual-major bachelor's degree programs. Each dual major combines a Bible major with another professional program.

In addition to undergraduate degrees, the University also offers graduate programs through Columbia Biblical Seminary and School of Missions as well as the Graduate School Division. On the same campus as the Bible College Division, students can earn Master of Arts, Master of Divinity, and Doctor of Ministry degrees in areas such as Old Testament, New Testament, Christian education, counseling, missions, intercultural studies, leadership for evangelism and discipleship, and teaching English as a foreign language. The Graduate School Division, also on the campus, offers Master of Arts in Teaching and Master of Education degrees.

The 400-acre, twenty-three-building CIU campus includes residence halls; classroom buildings; Shortess Chapel; Rossi Student Center, which has a dining facility, a post office, and a bookstore; Ridderhof Media and Music Center, including a state-of-the-art computer center; Fleece Library; an alumni center; and a married student housing complex.

Through a wide variety of student activities on the campus, students have the opportunity to develop solid leadership skills. From intramural sports and clubs to small fellowship groups, faculty and student recitals, and on-campus concerts by Christian recording artists, the campus offers something for everyone. Students also have the opportunity to touch lives through actual ministry experience. CIU students learn about their gifts, visions, and values through leading Bible clubs for children, visiting residents of a nursing home, teaching in prisons, and more.

CIU is accredited by the Commission on College of the Southern Association of Colleges and Schools (1866 Southern Lane, Decatur, Georgia 30033-4097; telephone: 404-679-4500) to award degrees at the associate, baccalaureate, master's, first professional, and doctoral levels. The Bible College Division is also accredited by the Accrediting Association of Bible Colleges. The Association of Christian Schools International and the National Association of State Directors of Teacher Education and Certification certify the education programs. The seminary is accredited by the Association of Theological Schools in the United States and Canada.

Location

CIU is located 8 miles from downtown Columbia, South Carolina's 200-year-old capital city. With a growing population of a half million, Columbia offers natural beauty, a moderate climate, entertainment, and cultural activities that one might find in a large city. Community attractions include the Vista, an upscale area of restaurants with a quaint atmosphere and outdoor entertainment; Riverbanks Zoo, one of the South's best; and Lake Murray, an outstanding recreational resource.

The University's campus reflects the charm of the Old South, with towering pines, peaceful lakes, and stately buildings. With the spectacular view overlooking the Broad River, the setting is conducive to life and learning.

An easy day's drive from most of the East Coast and perfectly situated between the mountains and the beaches, Columbia is also less than 100 miles from the beautiful South Carolina beaches, historic Charleston, and the Blue Ridge Parkway.

Majors and Degrees

CIU's majors and degrees provide students with the preparation they require for a large number of careers and callings.

The one-year Bible Certificate Program provides solid Bible training and sharpening of ministry skills for students planning to work in a lay-ministry role.

The two-year Associate of Arts degree provides a biblical foundation for students who are planning to continue their education at a liberal arts institution.

The bachelor's degree ensures that students receive a well-rounded education in the Bible, general education, natural science, social and behavioral science, humanities, and professional instruction. Each student combines a major in the Bible with preparation of a specific field of work through the unique dual-major program. Undergraduate students can choose from a wide variety of majors, including Bible teaching, biblical languages, communication, early childhood or elementary education, family and church education, general studies, humanities, intercultural studies, Middle Eastern studies, music, pastoral studies, psychology, and youth ministry. Teaching English as a Foreign Language (TEFL) is offered as a minor.

In cooperation with Midlands Technical College in Columbia, CIU students can also obtain practical vocational skills, such as nursing, accounting, and more, within the framework of the University's general studies program.

Academic Programs

The goals of CIU's academic programs flow directly from the University's motto, "Preparing World Christians to Know Him and to Make Him Known." Earning a degree at CIU involves more than meeting academic requirements. Personally, students develop a character more like Jesus Christ, know the Bible, and learn to minister to their fellow men and women. Vocationally, each degree program is geared to enable students to fulfill God's purpose for their lives.

CIU's undergraduate curriculum differs from a Christian liberal arts curriculum in the relative amount of study devoted to the Bible versus other disciplines. Each student completes a full major in the Bible in combination with another academic program. The one-year certificate requires 31 hours total, with 14 in the Bible; the associate degree requires 63 hours total and

23 in the Bible; and the bachelor's degree requires 128 hours total, with 32 hours in the Bible and 42 hours in a general education core.

The University provides several flexible-learning formats to accommodate students. Columbia Extension offers several courses by independent learning. The Summer Studies and Winterim programs provide intensive two- to three-week courses between CIU's two academic semesters.

Off-Campus Arrangements

CIU fosters a world vision in many of its students through study-abroad programs at the Jerusalem University College in Israel, EduVenture in Indonesia, a European study tour, cross-cultural internships, and more.

Academic Facilities

CIU provides well-equipped classroom buildings, an outstanding library, and easily accessible computer resources for students. The Fisher Classroom Building was recently renovated and houses the Dean's office, faculty member offices, and classrooms. Another academic building, the Ridderhof Media/Music Center, houses the computing center, the music department (including studios and practice rooms), the field education department, video production and editing studios, radio broadcasting and production studios, a ministry resource center, and a 500-seat concert hall/auditorium.

The G. Allen Fleece Library provides a collection of more than 130,000 book and media items and 10,000 visual aids for student teaching ministries. CIU's unique Ministry Resource Department houses more than 10,000 practical Bible teaching aids for student use. Membership in the Online Computer Library Center (OCLC) network provides interlibrary loan services as well as database access to millions of bibliographic resources through dozens of electronic journal indexes, other area libraries, and nearly 30,000 libraries worldwide. Computer workstations in the library enable students to rapidly search 8 CD-ROM databases that provide more than 2 million bibliographic citations for research purposes.

Costs

Tuition for 2000–01 is $8980. On-campus room and board with a seven-day meal plan average $4520. Additional fees total approximately $150.

Financial Aid

Total financial aid of more than $4 million is distributed to 75 percent of CIU students through scholarships, grants, loans, and work-study programs. Students must complete the Free Application for Federal Student Aid (FAFSA) and a separate CIU scholarship application annually to qualify for financial assistance. In addition, the CIU Financial Aid Office helps students to find other sources of financial aid—including a variety of grants and scholarships. The priority deadline for all financial aid is on or about March 1 annually. The deadline for state aid is June 30.

CIU also offers an interest-free payment plan, which allows students to pay their obligations through monthly installments.

Faculty

Without exception, CIU faculty members choose to teach at CIU because of their desire to be involved in students' lives, both inside and outside of the classroom. Several live on campus with their families, with the goal of being available for students. The Bible College's student-faculty ratio is 19:1, so CIU can offer one-on-one attention for students who desire it. The Bible College Division alone has 17 full-time professors and 27 part-time professors, a full-time equivalency rate of 26.64. Sixty-five percent of the full-time professors have doctorates, and 35 percent have master's degrees only. Fifteen percent of the part-time faculty members have doctorates.

Student Government

Students play an active role in the decisions made on the CIU campus. The Coordinating Council organizes the College Student Association, the Married Student Association, and other organizations that serve as the students' voice to the administration.

Admission Requirements

Columbia International University offers a challenging curriculum that pushes students to be the best they can be. Of those students accepted for the fall 1999 entering class, the average GPA was 3.2 (B/B+), and the average SAT I score was almost 1100. At the same time, CIU recognizes God's power to change lives and help students succeed in an academic environment where perhaps, at an earlier time, they could not or did not. Consequently, the University has chosen to adopt the following criteria to guide the admissions process.

In addition to a solid scholastic background and demonstrated ability to handle college assignments, applicants should demonstrate strong Christian character and commitment. As part of the admissions process, students must submit personal reference forms.

Admission requirements include a transcript from an accredited secondary school, a certificate of high school equivalency or a GED certificate, and SAT I or ACT scores. A minimum high school grade point average of 2.0, a minimum SAT I score of 1000, or a minimum ACT score of 21 is required.

Transfer credits are considered from another accredited college when a student has earned a grade of C or better.

Application and Information

CIU follows a rolling admission policy. Students are highly encouraged to apply early for maximum consideration. Upon receipt of a student's application and all supporting materials, the Admissions Office reviews the application and notifies the prospective student of its decision within a reasonable time frame.

For more information, students should contact:

Bible College Admissions
Columbia International University
P.O. Box 3122
Columbia, South Carolina 29230-3122
Telephone: 800-777-2227 (toll-free)
Fax: 803-786-4209
E-mail: yesciu@ciu.edu
World Wide Web: http://www.ciu.edu

The Ridderhof Memorial Building is a busy center for student activities at Columbia International University. The computer center, music department, and field education offices are housed in this building, along with yearbook offices and a 500-seat auditorium.

COLUMBIA UNION COLLEGE
TAKOMA PARK, MARYLAND

The College

Columbia Union College (CUC) was established in 1904 as the Washington Training Institute. In 1914, the College took the name Washington Missionary College, and in 1942, the College was given accreditation as a four-year, degree-granting institution by the Middle States Association of Colleges and Secondary Schools. In 1961, the College constituency voted to change the name of the school to Columbia Union College.

Columbia Union College is affiliated with the Seventh-day Adventist Church, and, as set forth in the College's Statement of Mission, aims to develop the talent of its students and to instill in them the value of service and the love of truth and learning. The College motto, "Gateway to Service," emphasizes CUC's intent to educate graduates who "bring competence and moral leadership to their communities."

Columbia Union College is a coeducational college that offers degree programs in liberal arts, sciences, and selected professional fields. The College is accredited for granting associate and baccalaureate degrees. CUC offers a combination of spiritual, cultural, academic, athletic, and employment opportunities. CUC is located just outside the nation's capital, which gives students an abundance of hands-on employment, educational, and entertainment opportunities.

Columbia Union College is committed to students. The faculty members of the College are qualified professionals with practical experience. Classes are small (12:1 ratio), and teachers have the time to give students individual attention and training for their futures. CUC takes pride in its graduates and those who instruct them and in its commitment to be more than an institution of higher education. It is a community of spiritual, cultural, athletic, and career opportunities under the spirit of Christianity.

Location

Columbia Union College is located in Takoma Park, Maryland. The College occupies 19 acres in this small community, just minutes from Washington, D.C. A Metrobus stop is located on the campus, and a Metrorail station is just a mile down the road, allowing CUC students access to all parts of the nation's capital, Maryland, and Virginia. Shopping malls, restaurants, recreational resources, and entertainment abound around the campus of CUC. Students frequent the wide variety of interests in the local area and are also employed in prestigious internships and part-time positions in Washington, D.C. The list of employers of CUC students continues to grow and includes the Baltimore National Aquarium, the CIA, Children's Hospital, Seventh-day Adventist World Headquarters, IBM, NASA/Goddard Space Flight Center, National Institutes of Health, Smithsonian Institution, Walt Disney World, the White House, and WTTG–Fox Channel 5. Students and faculty members also take advantage of the educational resources that surround CUC. Visits to an exhibit at a Smithsonian museum or research conducted at the Library of Congress aid in classroom studies.

Majors and Degrees

Columbia Union College grants the Bachelor of Arts degree, with majors in biology, chemistry, communication (emphases in public relations, theory, and journalism–print and broadcast), computer science (emphases in science and information systems), education (emphases in elementary education and early childhood education), English (emphases in English education, prelaw, and writing), foreign language, general studies, history (emphases in American studies, political science, and prelaw), liberal studies, mathematics (emphasis in mathematics education), music, philosophy, prelaw (English or history), psychology, and religion (emphases in religious education, pastoral ministry, and urban ministry). Bachelor of Science degrees are also offered, with majors in accounting, biochemistry, biology, business administration (emphases in finance, human resource management, management, marketing, and prelaw), chemistry, computer science (emphasis in science and information systems), general studies, mathematics (emphasis in mathematics education), nursing, prelaw (business), premedicine, pre–physical therapy, pre–veterinary medicine, and psychology (emphases in counseling and behavioral science). Bachelor of Music degrees are offered in music education and music performance. Associate of Applied Science degrees are offered in accounting, computer science, early childhood education, and respiratory care. An Associate of Science degree is offered in engineering. Columbia Union College also offers Associate of Arts degrees and a Bachelor of Science/Registered Nurse degree. Students may select from several minor concentrations, including accounting, behavioral science, biology, business administration, chemistry, computer science, eclectic communication, English, French, history, marketing, mathematics, music, psychology, religion, and speech communication.

Academic Program

The academic year follows a semester schedule. To graduate, all students must take required core classes. Students must earn 120 to 128 credit hours, including 36 upper-division credit hours, with a minimum GPA of 2.0 and a GPA of 2.5 in the declared major. All traditional students must take general education classes that include 12 hours of religion; 9 of social sciences; 8 of physical sciences, natural sciences, and mathematics; 7 of humanities; 3 of physical education and health; and 6 of practical and applied arts. Courses in English, communication, and computer science are also required. A cooperative education program is required in the business, communication, computer science, English, mathematics, and nursing programs. The cooperative education program aids students in obtaining job placements and internships and also provides career counseling and courses in interviewing, resume writing, and job search strategies. Credit for life experience, nondegree study, and pass/fail options exist at the College. CUC also hosts an Adult Evening Program for degree completion as well as an external (correspondence) degree. Majors in business administration, health-care administration, information systems, and organizational management and a bachelor's degree in nursing program are available through the Adult Evening Program on CUC's main campus and at an off-site location in Gaithersburg, Maryland. Summer courses and special programs are available to give incoming first-year students preparation for college and to aid the progress of students who currently attend.

Off-Campus Arrangements

In conjunction with the University of Maryland, dual majors are available in engineering/chemistry and mathematics. Students may study abroad in Austria, France, and Spain through CUC and Adventist Colleges Abroad.

Academic Facilities

Advanced facilities for radio and television are available. Columbia Union College has its own television studio, online and offline editing suites, and extensive audio technology. The communication department has several high-tech Electronic Field Production (EFP) cameras available for student use. WGTS-FM, a contemporary Christian radio station, is also located on the campus of CUC, and many students work there.

CUC has invested in extensive computer facilities that are used by all students. A large computer laboratory of PCs is available for student use, as are Macintosh computers in other areas of the campus. Each dorm resident has Internet access from his or her room and a personal e-mail account.

Weis Library, on the campus of CUC, has a collection of nearly 130,000 volumes and subscribes to more than 400 periodicals. The library utilizes the services of the Online Computer Library Center (OCLC). OCLC's database contains approximately 38 million bibliographic records from library collections around the world. Interlibrary loan service is expedited through use of this online system. In addition, Weis Library provides Internet and CD-ROM access to many other electronic resources.

Costs

In 2000–01, full tuition (12 to 16 credit hours) averages $12,200 for the academic year, which consists of two semesters. Part-time tuition (up to 9 credit hours) is $510 per credit hour. The general fee is $310 per semester. Summer sessions vary in tuition prices. Some courses require additional service or laboratory fees. There is a nonrefundable application fee of $25.

Financial Aid

Columbia Union College makes every effort to help students seek out and obtain financial assistance, and it also provides information for students seeking part-time employment.

CUC offers institutional scholarships, such as those for musical and athletic groups on campus, as well as scholarships for proven academic excellence. Eighty-five percent of traditional students received some form of financial aid in 1999–2000, and nearly $7 million in financial aid was awarded.

The financial aid office of CUC administers federal and state grant and loan programs. Appropriate application forms for financial aid are provided by the financial aid office and are mailed to students who request them. Students receiving any form of aid, including scholarships, are required to fill out a Free Application for Federal Student Aid.

Faculty

There are 39 full-time and 5 part-time faculty members at Columbia Union College. More than 100 adjunct instructors are employed by CUC. The College prides itself on the integrity of its faculty members and the experience that they bring to the College. The ratio of full-time undergraduate students to full-time undergraduate faculty members is 12:1. Faculty members of CUC are the personal career advisers of students and guide students through their courses of study and preparation for the future. Faculty members share contacts from their professional fields to aid students in obtaining internships and career placement.

Student Government

The Student Association officers are elected yearly. This group leads special activities and plans feature events on and off campus. The Student Government takes interest in general assemblies on informational topics. The editor of the school newspaper, the *Columbia Journal,* and the editor of the College yearbook, *Golden Memories,* also function in the Student Government. Senate meetings are an activity of the Student Government. The Senate includes various representatives of the student body and discusses ideas and concerns of the College, which are then taken to the administration after debate. The Associate Vice President of Student Services directs this special group of leaders as they represent Columbia Union College.

Admission Requirements

A minimum combined score of 800 on the SAT I (or at least 400 in each section) or a minimum composite score of 18 on the ACT is recommended. Applicants must be graduates of an accredited secondary school or have earned a GED certificate. Twenty-one Carnegie units are required, including 4 years of high school English and 2 years each of history, mathematics, and science. An essay is recommended, and an interview, as well as transcripts from previously attended colleges, is required.

Application and Information

Columbia Union College accepts applications on a continuous basis. Applicants must submit an application for admission, two recommendations, transcripts, and proof of high school graduation or successful completion of a GED certificate. Applicants are asked to submit a nonrefundable $25 fee at the time of application.

To receive an application booklet or for additional information, students should contact:

Admissions and Marketing
Columbia Union College
7600 Flower Avenue
Takoma Park, Maryland 20912
Telephone: 800-835-4212 (toll-free)
World Wide Web: http://www.cuc.edu/

Students on the national mall near the Columbia Union College campus.

COLUMBIA UNIVERSITY
NEW YORK, NEW YORK

The University

In 1754 King George II granted a charter to a group of New York citizens to found King's College, dedicated to instruction in "the Learned Languages and the Liberal Arts and Sciences." In its early days, King's College taught such students as Alexander Hamilton, John Jay, Robert Livingston, and Gouverneur Morris. After the Revolution, New York State issued the college a new charter with a more patriotic name—Columbia. In 1897 Columbia moved to a new site on Morningside Heights on the Upper West Side. The architectural firm of McKim, Mead and White, the preeminent architects of their day, designed an open central enclave six blocks long, with a majestic domed and colonnaded library at the center. It remains one of New York's most impressive settings.

Columbia College and the Fu Foundation School of Engineering and Applied Science (SEAS), the two undergraduate schools of Columbia University, today offer their students unique advantages; they are at the same time small (indeed, the Ivy League's smallest), selective colleges and integral components of a major research-oriented university.

The College student body is about 3,900 students; the SEAS student body is about 1,250. Students come from all fifty states and several dozen countries. They represent a dazzling array of ethnic, social, economic, cultural, religious, and geographic backgrounds; year after year, Columbia has the Ivy League's highest percentage of minority students. The diversity of Columbia's student body reflects the diversity of New York City, the world's most international city.

Columbia guarantees four years of on-campus housing to all entering first-year students. More than 90 percent of the undergraduates remain for four years in the residence halls, which are part of the campus' rich and varied extracurricular offerings.

Columbia students take part in extracurricular groups of all kinds: artistic (e.g., many theater groups, musical groups, and dance groups), athletic (twenty-five varsity sports and dozens of club and intramural sports), communications (the *Columbia Daily Spectator* and many other publications, the *Columbian* yearbook, WKCR-FM, a campus television station, and other groups), community service (e.g., Amnesty International, Big Brother/Big Sister programs, tutoring programs, a volunteer ambulance squad, service-to-the-elderly programs, and work in soup kitchens and homeless shelters), and preprofessional (e.g., the Charles Hamilton Houston Pre-Law Association and the National Society of Black Engineers). Other groups represent students' ethnic, religious, political, and sexual identities. There are twelve men's fraternities, five coed fraternities, and seven sororities. A new student center, Lerner Hall, opened in the fall of 1999.

Location

Columbia shares its Morningside Heights neighborhood with a number of other famous institutions: Barnard College, the Cathedral of St. John the Divine, Union Theological Seminary, Jewish Theological Seminary, and the Manhattan School of Music, to name only some of them. Most faculty members from Columbia and other schools make their homes in the neighborhood, and it is an area known for bookstores, wonderfully varied restaurants, and merchants that cater to student tastes, student budgets, and student hours.

Students are encouraged and assisted in making full use of New York's breathtaking variety of cultural, recreational, and professional resources. Columbia students can be found any day of the week exploring the Metropolitan Museum of Art, the Museum of Modern Art, the Guggenheim Museum, the Museum of African Art, the Museo del Barrio, the Asia Society, or another of the city's dozens of museums and galleries. Any evening, they might be discovering the theatrical offerings on, off, or "off-off" Broadway (or on campus); attending the opera, ballet, or symphony at Lincoln Center; taking in a movie on campus or in one of New York's 400-plus cinemas; enjoying jazz in Greenwich Village or blues at the Apollo; sampling *pai gwat* in Chinatown; or biking or boating in Central Park. Columbia's internship programs offer students opportunities to explore in depth a career possibility; nowhere else in the world does the concentration of industries allow such a range of possibilities. New York's public transportation system puts all of the city within easy reach of Columbia students; the campus is served by a subway line and five bus routes.

Majors and Degrees

Columbia College grants the B.A. degree in more than sixty majors in the humanities, social sciences, and pure sciences, including many interdisciplinary majors. SEAS grants the B.S. degree in about twenty engineering fields. A five-year program that begins in either school allows students to receive both degrees.

Joint degree programs offer students the opportunity to combine their undergraduate work with study in Columbia University's schools of law and international affairs and with the Juilliard School in dance and music.

Academic Program

Unlike many other colleges that are attempting to restore structure to their course offerings, Columbia has maintained a coherent and relevant curriculum since the time of the First World War, when it introduced the renowned Core Curriculum, a program of general education that has served as a model for hundreds of colleges around the country. One of the two oldest courses in the core is Contemporary Civilization, a year-long historical survey of western civilization's religious, political, and moral philosophies; the other is Literature Humanities, a year-long introduction to western culture's most seminal and meaningful literary works. A second year of humanities offers a semester each of music and art appreciation, encouraging students to experience the cultural treasures of New York City. The Major Cultures core courses enlarge the scope of inquiry beyond the Western focus in order to promote learning and thought about the variety of cultures and the diversity of traditions that interact in the United States and the world today. The Core Curriculum exposes Columbia's multicultural student body to a variety of disciplines, preparing them for the complex questions and issues of modern society.

One hallmark that distinguishes a SEAS education from that of other prestigious engineering schools is the number of nonengineering courses that every SEAS undergraduate takes; almost a quarter of a student's program is in the humanities and social sciences and includes components of the Core Curriculum. Alumni often cite this feature of their SEAS education as the most important reason for success in their careers.

Off-Campus Arrangements

Columbia maintains at Reid Hall, its Paris campus, several undergraduate programs. Courses at Reid Hall are quite varied, permitting students to work not only in the areas of French language, literature, and culture but also in several other fields throughout the range of the humanities and social sciences. There is additionally a year-long program that includes course work in the French university system.

Columbia was the first U.S. college to offer an integrated year-abroad program with the Universities of Oxford and Cambridge. Students live in a number of residential colleges and study an academic discipline in a tutorial setting. Other programs allow students to work at the University of Kyoto in Japan and at the Free University of Berlin in Germany.

Columbia students may, with the help of a dean, choose from a variety of study-abroad programs around the world in addition to Columbia's own programs.

Academic Facilities

The Columbia University libraries constitute the nation's sixth-largest academic library system, with a collection of more than 6 million volumes and 4 million microunits. There are 26 million manuscript items in 2,500 separate collections. Twenty-six satellite libraries are within the campus. Five of Columbia's libraries are designated Distinctive Collections, so called because their holdings are of unusual depth and nationally significant excellence. All divisions are open to Columbia undergraduates. The Columbia Computer Center has five mainframe computers used for academic research and instruction as well as clusters of microcomputers, terminals, and printers; it has remote units and terminals all over campus, including in residence halls, to guarantee accessibility. The chemistry building, Havemeyer Hall, houses modern laboratory facilities for research and undergraduate instruction. Students may also make use of outstanding facilities throughout the University, including an electronic music lab, a cyclotron, an oral history collection, the facilities and programs of the Lamont-Doherty Earth Observatory, and oceanographic research ships.

Costs

Tuition for the 1999–2000 academic year was $24,150. Room and board for all first-year students were $7700. With typical fees, books, and supplies, the total cost of a year at Columbia was approximately $34,500. This amount does not include travel to and from Columbia.

Financial Aid

All candidates who are U.S. or Canadian citizens or who have U.S. permanent resident status are considered for admission without regard to their financial need, and if admitted they receive financial aid packages to meet their full demonstrated and perceived need for the cost of a Columbia education. Financial aid documents must be filed by January 1 to ensure consideration for financial aid funds. All financial aid packages include a loan and a job (self-help); need not met by the self-help component will be met by grant. All financial aid at Columbia is based on need; no aid is given in the form of academic, athletic, artistic, or other merit awards. More than 50 percent of Columbia students are receiving some form of financial aid. The average financial aid package is more than $21,000. Students who are not U.S. or Canadian citizens and do not have U.S. permanent resident status should be aware that very few such candidates may be admitted to Columbia with financial aid, for which the competition is intense.

Faculty

Because Columbia remains the smallest of the Ivy League schools, class size can be remarkably low, and faculty members are not overwhelmed by the numbers of students they teach. The Columbia faculty is committed to both teaching and research, and students are taught by the most eminent professors as well as young assistant professors. All faculty members maintain office hours, and each student receives a faculty adviser from the department which he or she chooses as a major.

Student Government

Each undergraduate division has its own student council and elects representatives to the Columbia University Senate.

Admission Requirements

The Columbia freshman class of approximately 1,300 students is selected from a much larger pool of applicants by a painstaking process. Candidates for admission are expected to demonstrate the necessary ability and interest to do successful college work in a variety of disciplines as required for the Columbia degree. The following secondary school preparation is recommended: 4 years of English, including meaningful work in literature and writing; 3 (preferably 4) years of mathematics, including precalculus and calculus where offered; 3 (preferably 4) years of history and social studies; 3 or more years of the same foreign language; and 2 or more years of laboratory science (including chemistry and physics where available). The Admissions Committee recognizes that secondary schools vary in offerings and standards; consideration will be given to applicants whose preparations differ from the recommended course of study. Candidates for admission are required to submit test scores from either the SAT I or the ACT as well as from three SAT II Subject Tests, one of which must be Writing. For their other two, SEAS candidates must take any SAT II math test and either physics or chemistry; College candidates may take any two of their choice.

Transfer students may enter the College or SEAS in September only. The College also has a Visiting Students program, which allows students to attend for one or both semesters of their junior year.

Application and Information

The postmark deadline for applications is the first business day after January 1. Candidates are notified of the Admissions Committee's actions on or about April 1. Admitted candidates must respond to Columbia's offer of admission by May 1. Candidates for whom Columbia is their definite first choice may apply under the early decision plan; the deadline is November 1 for all application material, and a decision is rendered by December 15. Candidates admitted to Columbia under early decision are required to withdraw applications at any other colleges. The application fee is $50 for freshman applications postmarked before December 1 and $65 for applications postmarked thereafter and for all transfer applications. The fee may be waived if a school official testifies that the fee would cause the candidate's family financial hardship. For further information or for applications, interested students should contact:

Office of Undergraduate Admissions
Columbia University
1130 Amsterdam Avenue MC2807
New York, New York 10027
Telephone: 212-854-2521
Fax: 212-854-1209
E-mail: ugrad-admiss@columbia.edu

COLUMBIA UNIVERSITY, SCHOOL OF GENERAL STUDIES

NEW YORK, NEW YORK

The University and The School

One of the best kept secrets in American higher education, the School of General Studies at Columbia University is the nation's premier college for returning college students. One of the four undergraduate colleges that grace Columbia, the School of General Studies is the liberal arts division dedicated to those students who have interrupted or postponed their education by at least one academic year.

Unlike the division of the University dedicated to continuing education, the School of General Studies is a degree-granting liberal arts college. Classes are integrated with students from each of the other three undergraduate colleges on campus, allowing students access to world-class professors and an Ivy League education.

General Studies students come from all walks of life and from varied backgrounds, and for that reason may study full- or part-time. Many degree candidates hold jobs as well as study, and many have family responsibilities. Others attend full-time, experiencing Columbia's more traditional college life. It is this diversity in the student body that makes attendance at Columbia so attractive. It is the varied personal experience represented in each classroom that allows for discussion and debate and, in turn, for the academic rigor and intellectual development that characterize a Columbia education. The School has more than 1,100 undergraduate degree candidates and about 250 postbaccalaureate premedical students. The average age of these students is 29. About half are full-time students. Between 80 percent and 85 percent of the School's students go on to graduate and professional schools after graduation. The acceptance rate for General Studies postbaccalaureate students applying to U.S. medical schools and law schools is more than 85 percent.

In addition to its bachelor's degree program, the School of General Studies offers combined undergraduate/graduate degree programs with Columbia's Schools of Social Work, International and Public Affairs, Law, Business, and Dental and Oral Surgery, as well as with Teachers College, the College of Physicians and Surgeons, and the Juilliard School.

Location

Columbia University is located in Morningside Heights, on the Upper West Side of Manhattan. The University's neighbors include the Union Theological Seminary, the Jewish Theological Seminary, the Manhattan School of Music, St. Luke's Hospital, Women's Hospital, Riverside Church, and the Cathedral of St. John the Divine. The diversity of intellectual and social activities these institutions offer in the immediate vicinity is one of Columbia's great assets as a university; another is New York City itself, which offers students at Columbia an almost limitless and astonishingly rich variety of social, cultural, and recreational opportunities that are themselves an education.

Majors and Degrees

The School of General Studies grants the B.A. and B.S. degrees and offers the following majors: African-American studies, ancient studies, anthropology, applied mathematics, archaeology, architecture, art history, astronomy, biology, biology-psychology, chemistry, classics, comparative literature, computer science, dance, earth and environmental studies, East Asian studies, economics, English literature, film studies, French, German, history, Italian, Latino studies, literature-writing, mathematics, Middle East studies, music, philosophy, physics, Polish, political science, psychology, religion, Slavic language, sociology, Spanish, statistics, theater arts, urban studies, visual arts, and women's and gender studies. Individually designed majors are also available. In addition, the School offers two undergraduate dual-degree programs: one in conjunction with Columbia's School of Engineering and Applied Science and the other in conjunction with the Jewish Theological Seminary of America.

Academic Program

The School of General Studies offers a traditional liberal arts education designed to provide students with the broad knowledge and intellectual skills that make possible continued education and growth in the years after college and that constitute the soundest possible foundation on which to build competence for positions of responsibility in the professional world. Requirements for the bachelor's degree comprise three elements: (1) core requirements, intended to develop in students the ability to write and communicate clearly; to understand the modes of thought that characterize the humanities, the social sciences, and the sciences; to gain some familiarity with central cultural ideas through literature, fine arts, and music; and to acquire a working proficiency in a foreign language; (2) major requirements, designed to give students sustained and coherent exposure to a particular discipline in an area of strong intellectual interest; and (3) elective courses, in which students pursue particular interests and skills for their own sake or for their relationship to future professional or personal objectives. Students are required to complete a minimum of 124 points for the bachelor's degree; 60 of these may be in transfer credit, but at least 64 points (including the last 30 points) must be completed at Columbia. In addition to the usual graduation honors (cum laude, magna cum laude, and summa cum laude), honors programs for superior students are available in sixteen of the School's twenty-nine departments.

Off-Campus Arrangements

Columbia offers at Reid Hall in Paris several courses that are open to all undergraduates at the University. Courses at Reid Hall are varied, permitting students to work not only in the areas of French language, literature, and culture but also in several other fields throughout the humanities and social sciences. In addition to the summer program, there is a program during the academic year that includes course work in the French university system. General Studies students also participate in study-abroad programs around the world.

Academic Facilities

The Columbia University libraries constitute the nation's sixth-largest academic library system, with a collection of more than 6 million volumes, more than 4 million microform pieces, and 26 million manuscript items in 850 separate collections. There are twenty-two libraries in the system; five are designated Distinctive Collections because of their unusual depth and nationally significant excellence. All library divisions are open to General Studies students. The University's Computer Center is one of the largest and most powerful university installations in the world and has remote units and terminals in several parts of the campus to enhance its accessibility. The Fairchild Life Science Building houses research facilities, laboratories, electron microscopes, and a vast amount of biochemical equipment used for teaching and research. The University's physics building has been the scene of many important developments in the recent history of physics, including the invention of the laser and the first demonstration in this country of nuclear fission.

Costs

For the 2000–01 academic year, tuition is $808 per point, monthly living expenses are about $1200 for single students and about $1800 for married students, fees are approximately $800, and books cost about $900.

Financial Aid

The School of General Studies awards financial aid based upon need and academic ability. Approximately 70 percent of General Studies degree candidates receive some form of financial aid, including Federal Pell Grants, New York State TAP Grants, Federal Stafford and unsubsidized Stafford Loans, Federal Perkins Loans, General Studies Scholarships, and Federal Work-Study Program awards. Application deadlines are July 1 for the fall 2000 semester and November 15 for the spring 2001 semester.

Faculty

The faculty of the School of General Studies, which is shared with Columbia College, the Graduate School of Arts and Sciences, and the School of International and Public Affairs, includes distinguished scholars in virtually every discipline. Of the School's more than 500 faculty members, more than 95 percent hold a Ph.D. degree. Students, whether full-time or part-time, have many opportunities to work closely with this faculty, both in small classes and in research projects. Faculty members also serve as advisers to students majoring in their area of study and maintain regular office hours to see students.

Student Government

One student of the School represents General Studies students in the University Senate, a decision-making body composed of student, faculty, and administrative staff members from each division of the University. In addition, 2 General Studies students sit as voting members on the Committee on Instruction, which oversees the curriculum of the School. The General Studies Student Council elects officers each year and sponsors activities for students. *The Observer* is published several times each year. The Postbaccalaureate Premedical Program Student Organization sponsors events related to the medical school admissions process.

Admission Requirements

The admission policy of the School is adapted to the maturity and varied backgrounds of its students. Aptitude and motivation are considered together with past academic performance, standardized test scores, and employment history. The School's admission decisions are based on a careful review of each application and reflect the Admissions Committee's considered judgment of the applicant's maturity, academic potential, and present ability to undertake course work at Columbia.

Admission requirements include a completed application form; a 1,000- to 1,500-word autobiographical statement relating the applicant's past educational history and work experience, present situation, and future plans; an official high school transcript; official transcripts from all colleges and universities attended; official SAT I or ACT scores or scores on the General Studies Admissions Examination; and a nonrefundable application fee of $50.

Students from outside the United States may apply to the School of General Studies to start or complete a baccalaureate degree. In addition to the materials described above, international applicants must submit official TOEFL scores.

Application and Information

Application deadlines are July 1 for the fall semester and November 15 for the spring semester. Applicants from countries outside the U.S. are urged to apply by August 15 for the spring semester and April 1 for the fall semester. Applications are reviewed as they are completed, and applicants are notified of decisions shortly thereafter.

For more information, students should contact:

Office of Admissions and Financial Aid
School of General Studies
408 Lewisohn Hall
2970 Broadway
Columbia University, Mail Code 4101
New York, New York 10027

Telephone: 212-854-2772
E-mail: gsdegree@columbia.edu
World Wide Web: http://www.gs.columbia.edu

The Low Memorial Library/Visitors Center and Low Plaza.

COLUMBUS COLLEGE OF ART AND DESIGN
COLUMBUS, OHIO

The College
Founded in 1879, the Columbus College of Art and Design is one of the oldest continuously operating art schools in the country. Located on a three-city-block tract of land adjacent to the Columbus Museum of Art in metropolitan Columbus, the College enrolls 1,220 full-time students. The College is a member of the National Association of Schools of Art and Design.

The Joseph V. Canzani Center, opened in 1993, is the focal point of the seventeen-building campus. The structure houses a large exhibition area, a library and resource center, and an auditorium. A new student recreation center opened in 1996.

A 250-student dorm located next to V-Hall houses all freshmen and first-year transfer students under 21 and offers full cafeteria service. This modern facility has suites that accommodate 4 students with adjoining kitchenettes and bathrooms.

In addition to the regular day-school program, the College conducts an evening program geared primarily to the adult learner, a Saturday program for children 6 to 18 years of age, and summer school classes. The summer school courses are directed toward areas of major concentration. Students generally spend one summer acquiring knowledge in an area of particular interest to them. The College hosts exhibitions throughout the year, sponsors a visiting artist program, and conducts frequent workshops to ensure a rich and exciting environment for the growth of creativity.

Location
Columbus, the capital of Ohio, has a population of more than 1.3 million. Near the College are the Columbus Museum of Art; the Columbus Public Library, housing more than 500,000 volumes; Grant Hospital of Columbus; the Ohio Theatre, a center of cultural activity within the city that showcases the Columbus Symphony Orchestra and Ballet Metropolitan; and the downtown community, rich in social and cultural events.

Majors and Degrees
The Columbus College of Art and Design offers a four-year program leading to the Bachelor of Fine Arts degree. The curriculum features areas of major concentration either in commercial art through the Division of Fashion Design, the Division of Illustration, the Division of Industrial Design, the Division of Interior Design, the Division of Media Studies, and the Division of Visual Communication, or in the fine arts through the Division of Fine Arts, which offers work in ceramics, drawing, glassblowing, painting, printmaking, and sculpture. Integrated within the divisions are specializations in art therapy, computer graphics, fashion illustration, package design, photography, and product design.

Academic Program
The Bachelor of Fine Arts degree requires the completion of 130 semester credit hours (approximately 88 credit hours in art courses and 42 credit hours in general studies courses). During the first year of study, all students are required to take a sequence of core courses in anatomy, color concept, design, drawing, painting, and perspective. In the second year, students choose a major area of concentration and receive instruction in the fundamentals within a specific area. In the third and fourth years, students develop as professionals within their respective fields.

The educational goal of the Columbus College of Art and Design is professionalism. The curriculum is carefully structured so that courses taken at the same time complement each other and courses taken in sequence progress logically from the first year to graduation. Emphasis is placed on skill building, resourcefulness, versatility, and creativity to help students realize their full aesthetic potential. The College stresses the actual work methods used in today's professional art studio, agency, business, or industry, but the curriculum provides a thorough foundation in the methods and concepts of the finer realms of art expression. Students are encouraged to seek the ideal by experiencing the practical.

Qualified students may schedule work in dual divisions. The major divisions are integrated by having similar directions in creative design and related professional courses. The divisions are responsive to contemporary change and continually incorporate new areas of special interest into the curriculum.

Independent study is available in studio courses within the Division of Fine Arts. Specific areas include ceramics, drawing, glassblowing, painting, printmaking, and sculpture.

Academic Facilities
The facilities consist of six large buildings for instruction and six buildings that house the administrative and faculty offices. V-Hall is the largest of the instructional buildings, consisting of space specifically designed for the education of the visual artist. Its features include classroom space; a supply store; glassblowing, ceramics, and printmaking studios; a print shop; a photography lab; exhibition space; and faculty and administrative offices. Battelle Hall, a large two-story building, houses a sculpture studio with an attached foundry and a welding facility on its first floor; on the second floor is a large open space for painting studios. Studio Hall contains two large classrooms for drawing, faculty offices, and the College's in-house print facilities. Beaton Hall is a distinctive building housing classroom space, exhibition areas, and some administrative offices. The Packard Library, located in the Joseph V. Canzani Center, has an open-shelf collection of books and bound periodicals on the arts and subjects offered at the College. The collection is supplemented by slides for classroom use and by circulating files of masterworks on print and picture clippings on all subjects. A copying machine, light tables, and a viewing room with audiovisual equipment are also available for use by students and faculty.

Costs
The tuition for 1999–2000 was $13,400 for the academic year. Room and board for 1999–2000 were $6000 for the academic year. Costs for 2000–2001 are subject to change. Supplies and books are approximately $850 for the first year.

Financial Aid
The College participates in the Federal Perkins Loan Program, the Federal Work-Study Program, the Federal Pell Grant Program, the Federal Supplemental Educational Opportunity Grant Program, the Ohio Instructional Grant Program for Ohio

residents, the Federal Stafford Student Loan Program, and the Federal PLUS loan program. For priority consideration, students should submit applications for these programs before April 15 for the following fall semester and before October 31 for the second semester.

The College also conducts a scholarship competition open to high school seniors entering the freshman class. Art submitted for this competition must be received between February 1 and March 1. After students enter the College, they may also be awarded scholarships through a competition held at the end of each school year. Other scholarship programs include the Scholastic Art Awards, Battelle Scholars Program (for central Ohio students), Art Recognition Talent Search Scholarship, Ohio Governor's Show Scholarship, and industry and foundation scholarships. Applicants should contact the Admissions Office of the College for information about these programs.

Faculty

The College's faculty consists of 130 working professionals (67 full-time and 63 part-time members). The members include a large body of artist-designers who have had extensive professional experience and hold appropriate degrees in the divisions of art offered. Faculty members are professionally oriented, practicing artist-designers with broad teaching experience in diverse areas of the art world. In the General Studies Department, experienced faculty members with graduate degrees teach a wide range of courses in the humanities and sciences. The faculty takes an active interest in the students and is involved in advising them on a one-to-one basis regarding both career decisions and curricular matters. The student-faculty ratio is 9:1.

Student Government

The Student Council is the officially recognized organization that represents the students at the College. Representatives are appointed by the council to sit on most major College committees to ensure that students have a say in the decision-making process. The council also plans social events and organizes art-related activities for the students. Meetings, held each week, are open to all students.

Admission Requirements

Applicants must be high school graduates with a minimum GPA of 2.0 or have received a certificate of equivalence. An official high school transcript must be submitted before acceptance. The submission of ACT or SAT I scores is recommended. Transfer students must also request that an official transcript be sent from each college previously attended. In view of the school's professional goal, it is necessary that examples of artwork be submitted to the Admissions Office for review. A personal interview is also recommended although not required. Application for admission may be made in advance for either the fall semester or the spring semester. Applications should be submitted well before the expected entrance date since the size of all classes is limited.

Application and Information

For information concerning the College and application to its programs, students should contact:

Admissions Office
Columbus College of Art and Design
107 North Ninth Street
Columbus, Ohio 43215
Telephone: 614-224-9101

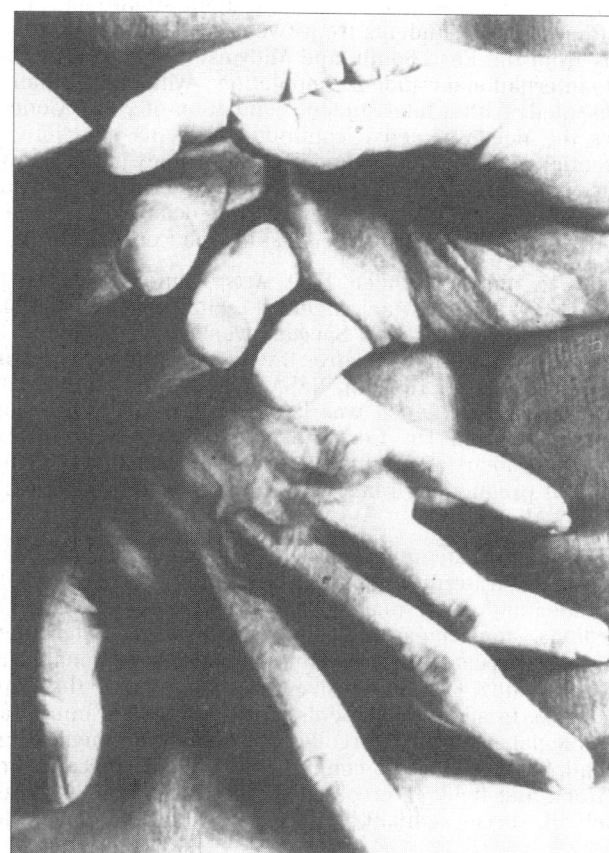

CCAD offers a distinctive education in the visual arts.

CONCORD COLLEGE
ATHENS, WEST VIRGINIA

The College

Concord College, a growing state-supported college committed exclusively to undergraduate instruction, was founded 128 years ago. Concord features accredited career-oriented education with a strong liberal arts base and focuses on the needs of the individual student as its fundamental concern. The beautiful 95-acre campus stands on a ridge of the Appalachian Mountains. Four residence halls and adult studio apartments house up to 1,100 students from twenty-eight states, predominantly from the East, South, and Midwest. Concord also has a large international student population, with thirty nations represented. With a total student population of 2,877, Concord serves the needs of active commuter students who join the residential students in following courses of study in the arts and sciences, business administration, teacher education, and such fields as advertising/graphic design and social work. Preparation for advanced and professional study is a Concord hallmark.

Each year, the Alexander Fine Arts Center presents the Artist-Lecture Series, which includes recitals, plays, art exhibitions, and guest speakers. Special events have included the North Carolina Dance Theatre; the West Virginia Symphony; lecturers Dr. Homer Hickam, NASA scientist and author of the book *Rocket Boys* (which was later made into the hit movie *October Sky*), and Dr. Cornel West, a preeminent African-American scholar from Harvard; and professional art exhibits. Theatrical productions range from Shakespeare and Chekhov to Woody Allen.

Students participate in special interest organizations, honor societies, five fraternities, four sororities, the yearbook, and the newspaper and enjoy many student activities, which include comedians, musicians, magicians, and other entertainers. Concord was recently awarded the Great Lakes Regional Award for Outstanding Comprehensive Programming at the NACA conference. In addition, students participate in intramural and intercollegiate sports. Intercollegiate sports for men include baseball, basketball, cross-country, football, golf, soccer, tennis, and track and field. Intercollegiate sports for women include basketball, soccer, softball, tennis, track and field, and volleyball.

Counseling and tutoring are strongly supported through Student Support Services; faculty-supervised developmental labs in English, reading, and mathematics; and twice-a-year individual counseling with faculty advisers. The Student Needs Assistance Program offers extensive academic support that ranges from time management to reducing stress anxiety to testing at your best.

Location

Athens is a small town in southern West Virginia near the Virginia border. Located near Princeton and Bluefield, West Virginia, Athens is 6 miles from I-77 and not far from I-64 and I-81. Athens has easy access to thriving population centers, such as Roanoke, Virginia; Charleston, West Virginia; and Charlotte, North Carolina. Shopping malls and entertainment are also available nearby, and Pipestem State Park Resort offers many recreational opportunities. WinterPlace ski resort is approximately 20 minutes north of the campus and white-water rafting is also nearby.

Majors and Degrees

Concord offers eighty-four majors, minors, and programs. The degrees offered at Concord are the Bachelor of Science in Computer Information Systems; the Bachelor of Arts in Communication Arts; the Bachelor of Arts/Bachelor of Science in Interdisciplinary Studies; the Bachelor of Social Work; the Bachelor of Science in Education (with a wide selection of teaching fields); the Bachelor of Science in Medical Technology; the Bachelor of Science in Business Administration; the Bachelor of Science, with majors in biology, comprehensive chemistry, GIS and cartography, mathematics, mathematics comprehensive, mathematics/computer science, preprofessional biology, and preprofessional chemistry; and the Bachelor of Arts, with majors in advertising/graphic design, English (with emphases in journalism, literature, and writing), geography, history, history with a concentration in philosophy, political science, preprofessional mentoring program for law, psychology, sociology, and studio art. Concord offers the Regents Bachelor of Arts degree for adults who cannot interrupt their normal activities to attend college but have gained comparable knowledge outside the classroom. Concord also offers a two-year degree, the Associate of Arts in Office Supervision, and five structured interdisciplinary options, including environmental geosciences, health-care management, leadership and entrepreneurial studies, public administration, and sports management.

Academic Program

All students must complete a minimum of 128 semester hours with a grade point average of 2.0 (C) or better to receive a degree. A program of general studies, required of all students, includes courses in communication and literature, fine arts, social sciences, natural sciences, mathematics, foreign languages (optional in most majors), and physical education. Credit is awarded for satisfactory scores on the College-Level Examination Program (CLEP), Advanced Placement (AP), and International Baccalaureate tests. An outstanding honors program is also available to qualifying students. Honors courses and independent study projects are available in most departments. Semesters begin in late August and mid-January; there are summer terms as well.

Off-Campus Arrangements

The Concord College Beckley Center offers a wide range of academic opportunities, from freshman-level courses to the four-year degree in business administration, to students in Raleigh County, West Virginia. Summer internships, which provide valuable professional contacts and experience, are part of the program of study for students majoring in communication arts and advertising/graphic design. Medical technology students must complete a twelve-month internship at an approved hospital. An internship program is available for travel industry management students. Professional fieldwork placements form part of the social work program.

Academic Facilities

An open-stack library and a modern center for academic technologies facilitate research. Students have access to seventeen computer labs, port-per-pillow fiber optics in the residence halls, the observatory, two spacious theaters, and physical education facilities, including gymnasiums, an indoor swimming pool, a dance studio, well-equipped weight rooms, and squash, handball, and racquetball courts. Laboratories are integral components of programs in the natural sciences, psychology, and geography. The Alexander Fine Arts Center houses facilities for art, music, communications, and dramatic arts studies.

Costs

For the 1999–2000 academic year, the tuition and fees for West Virginia residents were $2578, room and board were $4018, books and supplies cost approximately $500, and personal expenses were about $1000. For nonresidents, tuition and fees were $5620 per academic year. All other costs were the same. These figures are subject to change.

Financial Aid

Concord College has the most generous scholarship program in the West Virginia State College System. Merit awards, athletic and talent scholarships, transfer scholarships, and scholarships for nontraditional students are readily available for qualifying students. Federal Pell Grants, Federal Supplemental Educational Opportunity Grants, Federal Perkins Loans, West Virginia Higher Education Grants, Federal PLUS loans, and Federal Stafford Student Loans are available through the College. The State Student Assistance Program and the Federal Work-Study Program offer opportunities for student employment. To receive priority, the Free Application for Federal Student Aid (FAFSA) must be on file by April 15.

Concord offers scholarships to international students. The average scholarship covers about 35 percent of the total institutional cost.

Incoming freshmen who are willing to perform community service may apply for the Bonner Scholars Program, which pays up to $3050 per year for four years as long as its criteria are met. Funded by the Corella and Bertram F. Bonner Foundation of Princeton, New Jersey, the award is primarily based on need and prior service.

Approximately 72 percent of the students receive some form of financial assistance.

Faculty

All members of the faculty teach courses in the program of general studies, and all counsel and advise students. Terminal degrees are held by 61 of the 87 full-time faculty members. In addition, the College employs adjunct instructors who are experts in their fields. The average class size is 17.

Student Government

Concord's Student Government Association (SGA) budgets the student activity fee and plans entertainment. The SGA names students to voting membership on administrative councils and committees. Students also fund the SGA Memorial Scholarship. The College Center Board provides on-campus movies, dances, and special programs. The Concord Office of Student Residential Life offers numerous programs and activities in residence halls.

Admission Requirements

Applicants must have an overall grade point average of at least 2.0 (C) at an approved secondary school or a composite score of at least 17 on the ACT examination or 810 on the SAT I examinations, complete an application form, and send a high school transcript. Applicants may gain admission with advanced standing if they obtain qualifying scores on the College Board's AP tests, CLEP tests, or International Baccalaureate (IB) tests. GED test scores may be considered in lieu of the high school diploma.

Applicants must have completed the following secondary units: 4 in English, 3 in social studies (including U.S. history), 2 in mathematics (algebra I and higher), and 2 in laboratory sciences. Foreign language study is strongly recommended.

Transfer students are encouraged to apply for admission and may be eligible for scholarships. In addition, a limited number of talented high school students can be admitted to the summer school to earn college credit. Talented students who have completed the junior year of high school may be eligible for the College's early admission program.

Application and Information

Applications should be submitted by January 15 for early admission consideration and by August 1 for admission for the fall semester, which begins in late August and ends in December.

For further information, students may contact:
Michael Curry
Vice President for Enrollment Services
Concord College
P.O. Box 1000
Athens, West Virginia 24712
Telephone: 304-384-5248 or 5249
           888-384-5249 (toll-free)
E-mail: admissions@concord.edu
World Wide Web: http://www.concord.edu
               http://www.concord.edu/admissions/
               download.html (to apply on line)

The Administration Building at Concord.

CONCORDIA COLLEGE
BRONXVILLE, NEW YORK

The College

Now in its 120th academic year, Concordia College is a four-year coeducational liberal arts institution in suburban Westchester County, New York. The College is affiliated with the Lutheran Church–Missouri Synod, and while the campus has a gentle, Christian atmosphere, students from all faiths are enrolled and welcomed. As members of a close-knit community, Concordia students are mentored by a dedicated faculty and staff, most of whom live within a 10-minute walk of the campus. Students build relationships that support them as they prepare for fulfilling lives and careers.

Concordia students are active and involved. More than twenty clubs and organizations are supported by the College and the Student Association. Opportunities for participation range from student publications to intramurals, bible study to student government, and drama to social-concern groups. Talented musicians perform both on campus and throughout the United States and Europe with choirs, ensembles, and orchestras. The College's varsity teams compete in the NCAA Division II. Varsity sports include baseball, basketball, soccer, tennis, and volleyball for men and basketball, soccer, softball, tennis, and volleyball for women. Several teams and individual athletes have recently earned national ranking.

College facilities are a pleasant mix of new and newly renovated buildings, primarily in traditional red brick. A standout facility on campus is the Sommer Center for Worship and the Performing Arts, a 650-seat music center that is so acoustically well balanced that artists such as Itzhak Perlman, Yehudi Menuhin, and Harry Connick Jr. have recorded in it. Other special facilities include the newly rebuilt Schoenfeld Campus Center, Scheele Memorial Library, and Meyer Athletic Center, which includes a full-size gymnasium, a weight room, a health club, two squash courts, three indoor tennis courts, and five outdoor tennis courts (three asphalt and two clay). Athletic facilities also include baseball, soccer, and softball fields.

Concordia College is a place where students from many different cultures and geographic locations live, learn, and work together. During their time at Concordia, individuals are encouraged to reach their full academic, spiritual, athletic, and artistic potential.

Location

Concordia's 33-acre campus is set in the small, affluent village of Bronxville. Bronxville is home to 7,000 people, including UN diplomats, investment brokers, and a wide range of other professionals. While entertainment, shopping, and employment opportunities are available within this safe and picturesque village, students also take advantage of the limitless experiences offered in New York City, a 30-minute train ride from Bronxville.

Majors and Degrees

Concordia offers the Bachelor of Arts (B.A.), Bachelor of Science (B.S.), and Bachelor of Music (B.Mus.) degrees. The B.A. program includes majors in behavioral science, biology, education (elementary and secondary, with both state and Lutheran certification), English, history, international studies, mathematics, music (applied, church, and general), and religious studies.

B.S. degrees are offered in arts management, business administration, business education, environmental science, music education, and social work.

The B.Mus. degree is offered in church music.

In addition to majors, the College offers special programs in physical therapy (dual-degree program with New York Medical College), prelaw, premedicine, and nursing (with Dorothea Hopfer School of Nursing).

Academic Program

Concordia College seeks to provide students with an excellent education that strengthens the creative, technical, intellectual, and spiritual aspects of each individual learner. This is accomplished by building each degree program upon a solid foundation of the liberal arts core. To graduate, students must complete requirements in the following three areas: basic skills, knowledge, and values; general studies; and completion of a major and minor. Many of the programs are integrated with field experiences in the Westchester and New York City areas.

Concordia operates on a two-semester calendar with a summer session. A minimum of 122 completed semester hours is required to earn a bachelor's degree.

Guidance through the rigorous academic program includes advising and counseling that are provided for every student by the faculty. Additional assistance is available via peer tutors in most disciplines. The staff members of the Writing Center work with students on various aspects of writing at all levels and offer supplemental instruction to support the Writing Across the Curriculum Program.

The Concordia Honors Program is open (by application) to all students who demonstrate high academic achievement. Honors students are enriched through a variety of special experiences that occur in the classroom and through speakers and trips off campus.

The Concordia Connection is a program for students with diagnosed learning disabilities. Special support services are offered for qualified students who meet regular admission requirements but need specific assistance in order to maximize their academic success.

Concordia offers two other programs. The first is an intensive English as a Second Language (ESL) program. It serves students ranging from beginners to those who simply need some extra support in their study for a degree. The second program is an Accelerated Degree Program (ADP) for adult students over age 25 who have previously earned a minimum of 60 college credits. In the ADP, students who meet the program requirements can complete their degree in one year of intensive study.

The College is accredited by the Middle States Association of Colleges and Schools and by the State of New York.

Off-Campus Arrangements

Concordia is part of the Concordia University System, ten colleges and universities affiliated with the Lutheran Church–Missouri Synod. Students may enroll for up to a year at any of these institutions at no additional charge. Concordia students can also study overseas at Oak Hill College in London.

Academic Facilities

Scheele Memorial Library houses more than 71,500 hardcover volumes, 25,000 pieces of microfiche, and 467 active subscriptions. It is also part of a forty-library online system; this provides students with access to a wide range of academic resources. The library also includes the media center, a long-distance-learning classroom, a curriculum materials center, an art gallery, and individual study rooms.

Newly renovated Brunn-Maier Science Hall contains science laboratories, a computerized writing center, computer laboratories that are equipped with IBM and Macintosh systems, and the Halter Graphics Laboratory, which is equipped for computer graphics, desktop publishing, and music composition.

The Career Development Center provides guidance in career, vocational, and academic choices as well as counseling services, tutorial assistance, and postings for part-time jobs.

The Center for Urban Education provides a forum for research on and exposure to the complexities of teaching within urban settings.

The Sommer Center for Worship and the Performing Arts includes a recital hall and serves as the College Chapel. Private rehearsal rooms for individual and ensemble, vocal, instrumental, and organ practice adjoin the recital hall. Musical and dramatic performances are given in Schoenfeld Campus Center; these performances use the fine acoustics and state-of-the-art lighting and sound systems. Stein Hall houses a number of individual studios, a pipe organ, an electric-piano laboratory, and a language lab for the study of foreign languages and English as a second language.

Costs

Tuition and fees for the 2000–01 academic year are $14,350, and room and board charges are $6200. The cost is the same for in-state, out-of-state, and transfer students.

Financial Aid

Concordia strives to make a college education affordable to students from all backgrounds through an aggressive financial aid program. Both need-based grants and merit-based scholarships are available. Merit awards are available for students with academic, music, and athletic abilities and for students who study in church vocations.

A student's financial aid package may include all or a combination of grants, scholarships, employment, and student loans. Students must file the Federal Application for Federal Student Aid (FAFSA) to be considered for all aid. Concordia's FAFSA code is 002709. Approximately 91 percent of Concordia students receive some assistance.

Faculty

Concordia College's faculty members are committed to student success. The 12:1 student-faculty ratio allows students and faculty members to interact on a personal level. Seventy-nine percent have earned doctoral or terminal degrees. The focus of the faculty is on teaching undergraduate students, and no classes are led by teaching assistants. Professors conduct research with students, some of it at advanced levels.

Student Government

All full-time students are members of the Student Association and elect its representatives each spring. The Student Association organizes and supports campus events and works to provide a voice for all student concerns.

Admission Requirements

Concordia College seeks a student body dedicated to academic excellence and service to one another and society. The applications of students from any race, religion, ethnic background, or creed are welcomed and are given careful consideration. The diverse population comprises students from more than twenty-four states and thirty-five countries.

Each application is considered individually, and all applicants participate in a personal conference (sometimes by telephone) with an admission counselor. The admission decision is based upon the strength of a student's previous curriculum, achievement in that curriculum, personal statement, interview, and SAT I or ACT scores.

Transfer students should have earned a grade point average of at least 2.0.

Application and Information

The application and supporting documents should be received by March 15 for first-year students and July 15 for transfers, although applications are sometimes accepted later. There is a $25 application fee. Early decision applicants should apply by November 15 for the fall semester. All applicants and their families are encouraged to visit the campus. In most cases, students receive an admission decision within three weeks from the date that their file becomes complete.

Requests for information and applications should be addressed to:

Office of Admission
Concordia College
171 White Plains Road
Bronxville, New York 10708
Telephone: 914-337-9300 Ext. 2155
            800-937-2655 (toll-free)
Fax: 914-395-4636
E-mail: admission@concordia-ny.edu
World Wide Web: http://www.concordia-ny.edu

A concert rehearsal in the Sommer Center for Worship and the Performing Arts at Concordia College.

CONCORDIA UNIVERSITY
PORTLAND, OREGON

The University

Concordia University, Portland, is a private, four-year Lutheran university dedicated to the intellectual and professional development of the whole student. Founded in 1905 as an academy, Concordia grew from a junior college to a four-year college in the late 1970s, awarding its first bachelor's degrees in 1980 and graduate degrees in 1996. Concordia attained university status in 1995. The institution's mission statement is, "Concordia University is a Christian University preparing leaders for the transformation of society."

The University is composed of four academic colleges: the College of Education, the School of Management, the College of Arts and Sciences, and the College of Theological Studies. Programmatic development through the 1980s and 1990s increased the University's commitment to local and regional needs through several academic additions. These include a nationally recognized health-care administration program, a concentration in e-business within the bachelor's in business administration, and a progressive program emphasis in environmental management.

Concordia University (CU) further demonstrates its commitment to remain on the cutting edge of program development with its participation in the nationwide Concordia University System. An innovative intercampus partnership of the ten Concordia institutions of The Lutheran Church–Missouri Synod, the system has a combined enrollment of 15,000 students. Opportunities for enrollment in any one of the ten campuses and the benefits of high-tech distance learning and alternative timelines for degree completion are examples of the advantages of a small college within the framework of a nationwide educational system. Through the resource of compressed video, all system campuses are linked to provide academic offerings via a comprehensive telecommunications system. CU's electronic classroom increases educational accessibility and allows students to benefit from the academic expertise at other member institutions.

Concordia graduates meet the professional expectations of the academic, corporate, and church communities by presenting themselves in a focused, experienced, and ethical manner.

Academic focus is provided through the dedication of the University's faculty, whose primary commitment is teaching and instruction. As educators, the faculty members assist students in reaching their full potential; as advisers, they make a conscious attempt to relate to each student's individual needs. Through interaction in and out of the classroom, the student develops personal relationships with instructors who are well versed in their area of expertise. The University's 1:13 teacher-student ratio ensures small classes and intense studies.

Relevant professional experience brings the real world into the classroom. The opportunities to investigate professional applications of a chosen field or career are available to all students. CU sponsors study-abroad opportunities in areas such as Oak Hill College, London; Guangxi Teacher's University in Guilin, China; and Kato School, Japan.

Corporate internships that lead directly to employment consideration and human services practicums that provide a supervised learning experience in a community agency place the student directly in a career path.

Concordia's Lutheran heritage instills within all academic programs an intent to prepare professional leaders with personal attitudes of service and concern. Personal experiences, academic courses, and daily worship opportunities immerse students in a value-centered education grounded in Christian principles.

Concordia offers a full range of resources and activities that help to develop the whole student. Academic and professional needs are met through the Career Resource Center, which provides computerized career search programs, and resume review services. The University's writing center assists students in many academic disciplines. Students who seek a residential experience at college can live in one of five residence halls, each providing a special living situation. Varsity student-athletes compete at the NAIA level in men's baseball, basketball, and soccer and in women's basketball, fast-pitch softball, soccer, and volleyball.

In addition to CU's undergraduate degree programs, the College of Education offers a Master of Arts in Teaching, a Master of Education in curriculum and instruction, and a Master of Education in administration, designed to meet the professional needs of certified teachers.

Location

Concordia University, Portland, is located in the Willamette Valley between the Cascade Mountains and the Coast Range. Situated in the heart of an established residential section of Portland, minutes from downtown and Portland International Airport, Concordia utilizes the exciting resources of the city through internship opportunities, cultural events, and recreational activities. Outdoor recreation opportunities vary from windsurfing in the Columbia Gorge to year-round snow skiing on Mount Hood. The northeast Portland location is also minutes from the Rose Garden, home of the NBA Portland Trail Blazers and venue for major concerts and events. The campus is also well served by public transportation, which connects it to points of interest throughout the city.

Majors and Degrees

Concordia University awards the undergraduate degrees of Associate of Arts, Bachelor of Arts, and Bachelor of Science. The Bachelor of Arts degree is offered in arts and sciences, with emphases in biology, chemistry, English, humanities, interdisciplinary studies, psychology, social science, and theater; business administration, with emphases in accounting–CPA track, e-business, economics, environmental management, international business, marketing, and organizational management; education, with teaching authorization levels 1 (early childhood), 2 (elementary), 3 (middle school), and 4 (high school basic/basic advanced mathematics, biology, chemistry, health, language arts, physical education, and social studies); health and social services, with concentrations in health and fitness management, health-care administration, and social work; and theological studies, with concentrations in the areas of church staff, Christian education, and pastoral studies. Concordia's professional church work programs provide opportunities for Lutheran elementary and secondary school teaching. A degree-completion program for the Bachelor of Science in management, communications, and leadership is available to returning adult students with previous work and college experience.

Academic Program

Concordia operates on a semester calendar with two 15-week semesters. A summer session is offered in selected programs. Academic work is measured in semester hours, and courses are assigned from .5 to 5 semester hours each.

For a baccalaureate degree, 124 semester hours are required; for the associate degree, 63 hours are required. All degree-seeking students, regardless of their major, must complete the general education requirements, which include courses in communications, fine arts, humanities, physical education, religion, science, math, and social science.

In several academic areas, students may earn credit through successful completion of Advanced Placement and College-Level Examination Program (CLEP) tests.

Academic Facilities

Luther Hall contains state-of-the-art physical and life science laboratories, a science library, a greenhouse, an animal room, a long-distance learning classroom, and the University's administrative offices. The primary Luther Hall lecture hall seats 200 students and provides a reverse projection video system that enhances the quality of the learning process.

Hagen Campus Center houses the Sylwester Learning Resource Center, which includes the general library, Educational Media Services, and two student computer labs with Internet and e-mail access.

Costs

Within its commitment to providing a high-quality, affordable education, Concordia's tuition and fees for the 2000–01 academic year total $15,500; annual room and board charges are $3820. The total costs for a student living on campus vary, although average costs, including tuition and fees, room and board, supplies, and personal expenses, are approximately $21,320.

Financial Aid

The Free Application for Federal Student Aid (FAFSA) is used to determine a student's financial need for the awarding of scholarships, grants, work-study programs, and loans. Most awards are made in the spring for the following academic year. Approximately 80 percent of Concordia's students receive some form of financial aid. Merit-based scholarships are awarded based on academic history.

Faculty

Concordia's faculty members are dedicated scholars who are committed to the mission of the institution. Faculty members bring professional and personal experiences to the classroom, which takes learning beyond academic pursuits. Faculty members are also central to the academic advising and mentoring program.

Student Government

Students are elected to serve as hall presidents in the Resident Hall Association. Students also serve as leaders in the areas of intramurals, spiritual life, service and leadership, and student activities.

Admission Requirements

In keeping with its Christian commitment, Concordia University does not discriminate on the basis of sex, race, creed, color, national origin, age, or handicap. All high school graduates or transfer students who have fewer than 12 semester hours of college credit are eligible for admission if they have achieved a cumulative grade point average of at least 2.5 or earned a minimum SAT I verbal score of 480 or a minimum ACT composite score of 18. Transfer students with 12 or more semester hours of college credit should have a cumulative grade point average of at least 2.0. The selection criteria also include references submitted on behalf of a candidate.

Application and Information

Candidates for admission must complete a formal Concordia application for admission, submit test scores and/or high school/college transcripts, and furnish one reference. Applicants are encouraged to apply as early in the academic year as possible. Concordia follows a rolling admission procedure, and candidates are notified of a decision shortly after all the necessary credentials have been received.

For further information and application forms for admission and financial aid, prospective students should contact:

Office of Admissions
Concordia University
2811 Northeast Holman Street
Portland, Oregon 97211
Telephone: 503-288-9371
              800-321-9371 (toll-free)
Fax: 503-280-8531
E-mail: admissions@cu-portland.edu
World Wide Web: http://www.cu-portland.edu

CONCORDIA UNIVERSITY
MONTRÉAL, QUÉBEC, CANADA

The University

Tracing its academic roots over more than 100 years, the University evolved from the 1974 merger of Sir George Williams University and Loyola College. Concordia is a large, urban university, reflecting Montréal's bilingual and multicultural environment. It is set on two campuses: one in the downtown core of Montréal (Sir George Williams) and the other in residential west-end Montréal (Loyola). They are 7 kilometers apart and are connected by a free shuttle-bus service.

The University promotes accessibility, innovation, and an interdisciplinary approach to learning, with a strong tradition of part-time education. Concordia enrolled 25,219 students for the 1999–2000 academic year: 11,432 full-time and 10,314 part-time undergraduates; and 2,812 full-time and 661 part-time graduates. Approximately 90 percent of Concordia's students were Canadians, and 10 percent were international students. Approximately 20 percent listed French as their mother tongue.

Concordia offers more than 150 undergraduate programmes in the Faculties of Arts and Science, Commerce and Administration, Engineering and Computer Science, and Fine Arts.

Through the School of Graduate Studies, the University awards M.A., M.Sc., M.T.M., M.B.A., M.A.Sc., M.Comp.Sc., M.Eng., and M.F.A. degrees in approximately forty subjects. Twenty or more Ph.D. programmes are available, as are twenty Graduate Diplomas.

Concordia Athletics offers extensive opportunities for participation in intramural and intercollegiate sports. Facilities include several full-sized playing fields and a fully equipped physical education centre (Loyola Campus). The centre includes a gymnasium, an ice arena, training and sports medicine areas, an activity room, and a weight-training room.

Location

Concordia counts the city of Montréal as an enhancement to the University experience. Montréal is one of the oldest cities in North America and one of the world's largest French-speaking cities. While French is the predominant language, there is also a large English-speaking population, and the many ethnocultural communities complement the vibrant, cosmopolitan atmosphere. The city is steeped in history and tradition, yet totally "up to the minute." Concerts, films, plays, art shows, and athletic events abound, but if one wishes to get away, there is always the 100-acre Mount-Royal Park set in the heart of metropolitan Montréal. In addition, the nearby Laurentian Mountains and the proximity of New England offer an easy retreat from the urban bustle.

Majors and Degrees

The Bachelor of Administration degree is offered in administration. The Bachelor of Arts degree is offered in anthropology, applied human science, classics, communications studies (including communication/journalism), economics*, education (including child studies and early childhood/elementary education), English (including creative writing, English language, English literature, and English/French), Études françaises (including French/English translation*, French/English literature, French language, and French literature), geography (including human geography, human-environment relationships, and physical geography), history, individual studies, journalism, Judaic studies, leisure science (including therapeutic recreation), linguistics, mathematics* (including actuarial mathematics, pure/applied mathematics, mathematics/statistics, and statistics), modern languages (including German, Italian, and Spanish), philosophy, political science, psychology, religion, science and human relations, sociology (including community/ethnics studies), Southern Asia studies, theological studies, urban studies, Western society and culture, and women's studies. The Bachelor of Commerce is offered in accountancy*, decision sciences (emphasizing operations management), economics, finance*, international business, management (including human resource management*), management information systems*, and marketing*. The Bachelor of Computer Science* degree is offered in the following options: computer applications, computer systems, information systems, and software systems. The Bachelor of Education is offered in the Teaching of English as a Second Language (TESL). The Bachelor of Engineering is offered in building*, civil and environmental*, computer*, electrical*, industrial*, mechanical*, and software engineering*. The Bachelor of Fine Arts degree covers the visual arts and the performing arts. Visual arts offers art education, art history, art history/studio art, cinema (including film animation, film production, and film studies), design art, digital image/sound and the fine arts, interdisciplinary studies, and studio art (including ceramics, fibres, painting and drawing, photography, print media, sculpture, and women in the fine arts). Performing arts offers contemporary dance, music (including electroacoustic studies, integrative music studies, jazz studies, performance studies, selected music studies, and theory/composition), and theatre (including design for theatre, drama for human development, theatre performance, and playwrighting). The Bachelor of Science is offered in biology (including animal biology, botany, cell/molecular biology, and ecology), chemistry* (including biochemistry and biochemistry/molecular biology), exercise science (including adapted physical activity and athletic therapy), geography (including environmental geography and hydrology), individual studies programme, mathematics* (including actuarial mathematics, applied mathematics, and statistics), physics* (including applied physics, physics/marketing, and pure physics), and psychology (including psychobiology). An * denotes work-study programmes.

Academic Programme

The academic year is composed of two terms: a fall term (September to December) and a winter term (January to April), followed by a summer session (early May to mid-August), each fifteen weeks long. Academic activity is measured according to a credit system. Each credit involves a minimum of 45 hours of lectures, tutorials, laboratories, studio or work practicums, examinations, and individual work. Successful completion of a minimum of 90 credits to a maximum of 120 credits (usually 15 credits per term) is required for most undergraduate degrees. In some cases, students must complete additional credits. Undergraduate programmes require a cohesive sequence of courses, and graduation requires completion of one of the following concentrations: honours, specialization, or major (or in fine arts, a double minor).

Off-Campus Arrangements

Concordia recognizes the importance of international academic relations and operates a Centre for International Academic Cooperation to develop and coordinate the University's international orientation. Professors and students travel worldwide, and Concordia continues to play host to visiting students and academics from around the globe. Associations exist with universities in the United States, Central and South America, the Caribbean, Pacific Rim countries, Africa, Great Britain, and most European countries. Research/study programmes have been developed in Costa Rica, England, Greece, and Italy. Concordia was the first Western university to establish a joint doctoral programme with a counterpart in the People's Republic of China, and it maintains exchange programmes with eight PRC academic institutions. The University is a member of the Association of Commonwealth Universities, the Association of Universities and Colleges of Canada, and the American Assembly of Collegiate Schools of Business.

Academic Facilities

The Georges P. Vanier Library and the R. Howard Webster Library house a 2-million-item collection. These include books, monographs, periodicals, government publications, technical reports, microforms, audiovisual material, and special collections. CLUES (the Libraries' catalogue) is accessible by modem and via Gopher and the World Wide Web to assist in identifying and locating materials. Interlibrary Loans Service, giving access to items from virtually any library in the world, is available.

Computing Services provides resources and services to the entire University community. Facilities include a high-speed data communications network linking Concordia to regional, national, and international communities. Concordia offers mainframe-class computers, super-minicomputers, more than 250 public-access personal computers/workstations, timesharing terminals, and vector processing, graphics, and word processing facilities. A comprehensive software library contains numerical analysis routines, statistical processing packages, database products, simulation languages, graphics support, all widely used computer languages, text processing, online news services, and other general-purpose utilities.

The Leonard and Bina Ellen Art Gallery presents a year-round programme. Exhibitions feature material from the University's extensive permanent collection, works produced by the Faculty of Fine Arts professors, or collections from art institutions across Canada and beyond.

The Visual Arts Gallery is devoted to work by Faculty of Fine Arts undergraduates. The Bourget Building Gallery exhibits work by Fine Arts graduate students.

The Faculty of Fine Arts operates several performing arts facilities, including a state-of-the-art concert hall, seating 600, and the Joseph P. Cazalet Studio, a flexible teaching facility serving theatre students. Dramatic productions are staged in the D. B. Clarke Theatre. The Audio Visual Department operates three equipment depots, which are primarily responsible for media services in teaching areas but also provide sales of materials and loan of equipment to the University community.

The Learning Laboratories, media workshops (AVISTAs), television and sound studios, preview and presentation rooms, cinemas, and media library are available to all students, faculty members, and staff for self-instruction, training, and preparation of presentation materials.

The Montréal Conservatory of Cinematographic Art, established in 1968, houses an important collection of films of historic and cultural value. Programmes of public film screenings are offered at nominal prices or free of charge.

Costs

The 2000–01 tuition fees for full-time studies (30 credits) for Canadian citizens and permanent residents are $1668* for Québec residents and $3500* for non-Québec residents. International visa students' tuition fees for full-time studies range from $9100 to $10,500* plus a compulsory $475* for the Canadian Health Insurance. Nonacademic fees may vary depending on the Faculty, but will not exceed $850*. The average total cost for students living on or off campus, including housing and food, was approximately $6600* in 1999. Non-tuition expenses such as transportation, clothing, books, supplies, and miscellaneous items are extra. (*Canadian dollars)

Financial Aid

Students who are Canadian citizens or permanent residents may receive scholarships, fellowships, or loans. Further information is available at the Financial Aid Office. Students from the United States may apply for a Higher Education Loan Plan through their local banking facility and should send their loan forms to Concordia University's Financial Aid Office for processing. Scholarships, bursaries, and loans are generally not available to non-Canadian students. Therefore, visa students should contact their local Department of Education to seek financial assistance, which may be available through the Canadian International Development Agency (CIDA) or other agencies.

Faculty

Concordia employs 751 full-time professors, 1,039 part-time instructors, and 35 professional librarians. Many faculty members are professionals drawn from the artistic or business world who have gained Canadian and international reputations as experts in their fields.

Principal research areas are psychology, electrical engineering, mechanical engineering, computer science, building studies, transportation engineering, cell and molecular biology, behavioural neurobiology, human development, and management studies.

Student Government

Students at Concordia participate in all levels of University government, including departments, Faculty, Senate, and the Board of Governors. Undergraduates belong to the Concordia Student Union (CSU), and each Faculty has one or more associations, as do most academic departments.

Admission Requirements

The University welcomes qualified applicants from all parts of Canada, the United States, and abroad. The basis for admission is completion of the level of secondary education required to apply for university studies in the home province, state, or country. As admission is competitive, students should present strong grades and an appropriate selection of courses relevant to the intended area of study. While letters of recommendation and SAT I/SAT II Subject Test scores are not required, they are recommended to complement the academic transcript. Certain programmes (e.g., visual or performing arts, journalism, creative writing) require auditions, interviews, portfolios, or letters of intent. Students should refer to the Admissions Guide for full details.

Application and Information

September is the normal point of entry for undergraduate studies. Entry in January or the summer session may be possible in certain programmes, where places are available. January entry may require undertaking courses in the subsequent summer session. International students who are not Québec collegial studies graduates are usually not admitted in January.

Application deadline dates for the fall term are March 1 for full-time study and July 15 for part-time study. Applications for the winter term are accepted until October 15 for either full- or part-time study. Late applications will be considered where and when appropriate. The nonrefundable application fee is Can$40 ($25 U.S.). Online application is possible.

Prospective students are encouraged to arrange (one week in advance) a guided tour of the University, including a meeting with an admissions counsellor or an academic adviser. For information concerning admission forms/requirements, or to arrange for tours and appointments, students should contact:

Birks Student Service Centre
1400 de Maisonneuve Blvd West—LB 185
Montréal, Québec H3G 1M8
Canada
Telephone: 514-848-2668
Fax: 514-848-2621
Admissions Information E-mail: admreg@alcor.concordia.ca
Campus Tours E-mail: tours@alcor.concordia.ca
World Wide Web: http://www.concordia.ca

CONCORDIA UNIVERSITY WISCONSIN
MEQUON, WISCONSIN

The University

Concordia University Wisconsin was founded in 1881 as a school of the Lutheran Church–Missouri Synod. Today it is a dynamic, modern university anchored in traditional Lutheran Christian principles. Concordia is part of the Concordia University System, which consists of twelve colleges and seminaries, thus enhancing the resources available for academic and spiritual growth. While Concordia maintains its strong identity as a Lutheran university and embraces its commitment to educating students for service to the church as parochial school teachers and in other ministry-related vocations, Concordia offers a wide variety of exciting and challenging academic fields of study at both the undergraduate and graduate levels.

Students have access to numerous events on campus and in the Milwaukee metropolitan area. While various off-campus activities are organized by the Office of Student Life, on-campus activities are plentiful. There are various athletic fields, drama and music groups, plays, and concerts. The Field House is open to all indoor intercollegiate sports and, with a seating capacity of 2,000, it hosts many activities. The Falcon's Nest offers great fast food in a collegiate atmosphere and serves as a common meeting place for many students.

Since the implementation of various new programs at Concordia and the move to its beautiful 155-acre campus on the shore of Lake Michigan, Concordia University Wisconsin has grown from a total enrollment of 784 students in 1983 to more than 4,500 students today. Concordia is a four-year, NCA-accredited, coeducational liberal arts university that offers more than forty majors to traditional undergraduate, graduate, and adult students.

Various master's degrees are awarded, such as the Master of Business Administration, the Master of Education, and master's degrees in the areas of family nurse practitioner studies, geriatric nurse practitioner studies, nurse educator studies, occupational therapy, physical therapy, and student personnel administration.

Location

Concordia is located just 15 minutes from Milwaukee, a modern commercial center with an old European flavor. This metropolitan area of more than 1.5 million people supports an impressive variety of art and culture. Students may choose to experience the world-renowned Milwaukee Symphony, the Great Circus Parade, ballet, repertory theater, or the Milwaukee Art Museum. In addition to the many cultural experiences available to students, Concordia's spacious, suburban campus on the shore of Lake Michigan provides a quiet, comfortable setting for academic growth and recreational activities.

Majors and Degrees

Concordia University Wisconsin grants traditional baccalaureate degrees, with areas of emphasis in the following major fields: accounting, art, athletic training, biblical languages, biology, business, computer science, early childhood education, economics, elementary education, English, exercise leadership, finance, graphic design, history, humanities, individualized major, interior design, justice and public policy, lay ministry, management, marketing, mass communication, mathematics, missions, music, nursing, occupational therapy, organizational communications, parish music, pastoral ministry, physical education, psychology, radiologic technology, secondary education, social work, Spanish, speech communication, telecasting, theological languages, and theology. Accelerated baccalaureate degrees for adult students are available in health-care administration, liberal arts, management and communications, and management of criminal justice.

Academic Program

As a metropolitan educational institution, Concordia is determined to use all available opportunities and resources provided by the local community to enhance the educational development of its students. Concordia also integrates a global experience into its curriculum so that students can better understand the church and the nation in a truly global environment. Concordia, in turn, within the bounds of its philosophy and resources, is interested in exerting a Christian influence on the community, nation, and world. This is done through traditional and nontraditional University programs, adult and continuing education, graduate programs, and global education.

The requirements for a baccalaureate degree are designed to provide Concordia students with a diverse background in the liberal arts as well as in their chosen fields. At least 126 credit hours must be earned to receive a bachelor's degree. The University operates on a 4-1-4 calendar with a Winterim program. The fall semester is completed before Christmas, and the Winterim takes place in January. The spring semester begins in January and ends in May. The Winterim term provides students with the opportunity to take one concentrated course for three weeks. Opportunities for honors courses and credit by examination are also available.

Academic Facilities

Rincker Memorial Library is available to undergraduates, graduate students, and the faculty as a valuable tool for research and academic growth. Several computer labs, online databases, and state-of-the-art clinical labs are also available for student use.

Costs

Educational fees per semester are $6450, and room and board fees are $2410 for the nineteen-meal plan. Certain programs, such as adult education and various professional programs, have fees that vary from this base fee structure. All students are charged a $30 student activity fee per semester.

Financial Aid

The amount of financial aid awarded is based on the applicant's financial need and scholastic record. As a general rule, the primary financial responsibility lies with the student and his or her parents. Therefore, in order to help determine student need and to make it possible to grant aid fairly, the parents of applicants are asked to file a confidential statement of their income, assets, expenses, and liabilities. On the basis of this financial information, the University is able to determine the difference between University costs and the amount a student and his or her parents can reasonably be expected to provide. The difference is defined as need. There are also various scholarships available, including Presidential, Leadership, Talent, and Church Worker. Five top students receive prestigious Emeritus Scholarships.

Faculty

Concordia University is a teaching university. Of its 123 full-time and 75 part-time faculty members, 67 percent hold a doctorate or terminal degree. Some professors teach at both the undergraduate and graduate levels, and no classes are taught by graduate students. Faculty members also act as academic advisers to students. The student-faculty ratio of 17:1 allows for personalized instruction and small class sizes.

Student Government

The University's Student Government Association (SGA) consists of a president, 3 vice presidents, a secretary, and a treasurer who are elected by the student body to one-year terms. Senators are elected from each residence hall and from commuter seats. Members of the Student Senate may be chosen to serve on committees concerning academic affairs, publications, public relations, the Activities Board, and the Judicial Board. SGA provides a forum for student issues.

Admission Requirements

Students must submit evidence of adequate preparation for college from a regionally accredited high school. A minimum of 16 units of secondary school work is required, of which at least 11 should be in the basic liberal arts areas. SAT or ACT scores are required. Students transferring from other colleges and universities must have official transcripts sent.

Application and Information

Concordia University uses a rolling admission procedure, allowing applicants to receive admission decisions as soon as their files are complete. Files are not considered complete until they contain a completed application form; a $25 nonrefundable application fee; transcripts from all high schools, colleges, and universities previously attended; and standardized test scores. Students are encouraged to apply for admission at any time after completing the junior year of high school. Transfer students should begin the application process at least one semester prior to the anticipated date of entry. Upon acceptance, a $100 tuition deposit is required.

For an application form and further information, students should contact:

Director of Admission
Concordia University Wisconsin
12800 North Lake Shore Drive
Mequon, Wisconsin 53097
Telephone: 262-243-4300
        888-628-9472 Ext. 4300 (toll-free)
Fax: 262-243-4545
E-mail: admission@cuw.edu

Lifelong friendships begin at Concordia University Wisconsin.

CONNECTICUT COLLEGE
NEW LONDON, CONNECTICUT

The College

Long recognized as one of the nation's leading liberal arts colleges, Connecticut College bolsters its tradition of academic excellence with a spirit of cutting-edge innovation. In an effort to ensure that students at the College are prepared to adapt to a rapidly changing world, course offerings at Connecticut College are not constrained by the traditional boundaries created by time, location, or departmental rivalries. Students and faculty members at the College live and learn in a community noted for its commitment to interdisciplinary collaboration, student-faculty cooperation, and academic exploration. Traditional course offerings are supplemented by opportunities for faculty members and students to travel together and conduct research or test findings at the location in the world that best meets their needs. Every student at the College is guaranteed access to funded internships or research opportunities, which can be self-designed in order to help the student prepare for graduate studies or for the career of their choosing when they leave the College.

The learning experience described above and in the paragraphs that follow takes place on a breathtaking campus set on a hill that overlooks the city of New London and the Connecticut shoreline. With nearly all students living on campus, Connecticut College represents the best of a residential liberal arts education. Students and faculty members enjoy close interaction outside of the classroom setting, and the College community gathers throughout the year to support nationally recognized athletic teams and student artists and to welcome distinguished visiting scholars and lecturers.

The 740 acres include a 445-acre arboretum (used extensively by students for research in the biological sciences and environmental studies), an arts center, an auditorium, a large athletic center, an art museum, several computer laboratories, a student center, and a science "triangle" that includes buildings for the biological and physical sciences and an observatory.

Connecticut College is recognized for its scholarship in the arts. The theater department enjoys a partnership with the National Theater Institute of the Eugene O'Neill Theater Center, and modern dance builds on nearly a half century of excellence that dates to the area of Martha Graham and the American Dance Festival. The Lyman Allyn Art Museum, located at the southern edge of campus, offers hands-on instruction in museum studies.

Location

The College is located 2 miles from downtown New London, a city of 35,000 on the southeastern Connecticut seacoast. It is 2 hours by train or car from the urban settings of New York City and Boston. Connecticut College's safe, enclosed campus sits atop a hill that overlooks the city of New London, the Thames River, and Long Island Sound. It is frequently cited as one of the most beautiful college campuses in New England.

Majors and Degrees

Connecticut College awards the Bachelor of Arts degree in more than fifty-eight majors and concentrations, including Africana studies, American studies, anthropology, architectural studies, art, art history, Asian studies, astrophysics, biochemistry, biology, botany, cellular and molecular biology, chemistry, chemistry/biochemistry, Chinese language and literature, Chinese studies, classics, comparative studies in culture (world, image, and text), computer science, creative writing (fiction or poetry), dance, economics, education, English, environmental chemistry, environmental studies, film/media studies, French, gender and women's studies, German studies, government, Hispanic studies, Hispanic studies with concentration in Spanish America, history, human development, international relations, Italian, Italian studies, Japanese language and literature, Japanese studies, mathematical sciences, mathematics, medieval studies, museum studies, music, music with certification in music education, music and technology, neuroscience/psychobiology, philosophy, physics, physics and engineering, physics for education, psychology, psychology-based human relations, religious studies, Russian and East European studies, sociology, sociology-based human relations, theater, theater acting, theater directing, theater dramaturgy, urban studies, and zoology. Students may also minor in the above areas or the following additional areas: astronomy, cognitive science, geophysics, Greek, history of Christian thought, Judaism and culture, Latin, and linguistics.

Academic Program

"The fun within a liberal arts curriculum is at the contact points of the traditional disciplines," says David Lewis, a chemistry professor and the College Provost. His words ring across the curriculum, as students explore majors in emerging fields like neuroscience, architectural studies, dance therapy, or film and media studies. A team of anthropology and physics students, for example, conducts carbon testing on prehistoric New England ceramics from a dig on Cape Cod; advanced courses like Psychohistory and the American Presidency, Environmental Ethics, and The Holocaust push traditional boundaries. In fact, such academic intersections are common at Connecticut College, which is increasingly recognized as one of the most innovative liberal arts colleges in America.

Just as the College has eliminated academic and geographic boundaries, Connecticut has removed the constraints of fixed time frames and fixed credits for courses and takes advantage of all twelve months of the year. This is a logical progression on a campus where every dorm room is wired to the College Ethernet network and the Internet for immediate links to library catalogs, databases, online syllabi, and event listings. The curriculum includes an increasing number of intensive short courses offered at times when many students are studying or working off-campus—in January or June, for instance, or during spring break. An elective Dean's Term each January cuts across traditional curricula, as well, by offering intensive programs in negotiation and conflict resolution, public speaking, and team building.

Off-Campus Arrangements

Connecticut College works diligently to establish relationships with institutions that offer programs of outstanding reputation and quality throughout the world. Students may study at one of these institutions for a semester and receive credit toward their degree. Students may choose from more than 100 institutions for study away from the College.

Every student at Connecticut College is guaranteed a funded work-learning internship experience, either in the U.S. or overseas, between the end of freshman year and graduation. These internships provide crucial opportunities to explore career paths, acquire research skills, interact with a wide range of mentors, and discover new connections between the world of work and the realm of books.

In addition to traditional study-away options, Connecticut College offers an extraordinary range of innovative international experiences. Under the College's new Traveling Research and Immersion Program (TRIP), up to twenty courses per year include an expeditionary component to wherever in the world the subject can be explored and experienced most effectively. Another option is the Study Abroad Teach Abroad (SATA) program, in which small groups of students and professors spend a semester living and working together at a university in a developing country. In addition, each student is offered one funded summer internship, which may take place overseas.

Academic Facilities

The College library houses nearly 500,000 volumes and is part of a consortium with other colleges that makes more than 2 million books available.

Four interdisciplinary centers set Connecticut College apart: the Toor Cummings Center for International Studies and the Liberal Arts (CISLA), the Center for Arts and Technology, the Goodwin-Niering Center for Conservation Biology and Environmental Studies, and the Holleran Center for Community Action and Public Policy. Each pioneers new concepts in interdisciplinary learning and faculty-student collaborative research.

One third of each class majors in science, and the $8-million F. W. Olin Science Center puts freshmen in high-tech research labs and classrooms from the first day of school. The College's unique coastal location and a 435-acre arboretum make marine biology and environmental science natural components of the curriculum; *Newsweek* named the environmental studies major as one of the best in the country.

Costs

The total cost to attend Connecticut College for the 2000–01 academic year is $31,985. This figure includes tuition and room and board.

Financial Aid

All financial aid is based on need, which is determined to be the difference between a family's ability to pay and the cost of education. Connecticut College requires that candidates file the College Scholarship Service (CSS) PROFILE and the Free Application for Federal Student Aid (FAFSA). Copies of parents' and students' most recent income tax returns and W2 forms should be sent directly to Connecticut College. Financial aid deadlines are November 15 for early decision 1 applicants and January 15 for early decision 2 and regular decision applicants. The College offers scholarships, grants, loans, and campus employment, with funds from endowment income, gifts, and budget allocations as well as state and federal programs. For the 1999–2000 academic year, the average grant was $18,056 and the average award was $20,940. More than 50 percent of the College's undergraduates receive some form of financial aid.

Faculty

Professors, 97 percent of whom hold doctoral degrees or the equivalent, are superb teachers as well as renowned scholars and artists. Their dedication to students does not stop at the classroom or laboratory door—it reaches into faculty members' homes, college dining rooms, and residence halls. Undergraduates routinely participate in collaborative research with faculty members, coauthor scholarly papers, and make presentations at academic conferences. A 10:1 student-to-teacher ratio facilitates an interchange in the classroom and a commitment to hands-on learning. The faculty is comprised of 147 full-time and 76 part-time professors.

Student Government

A fundamental distinction of Connecticut College is a nearly 100-year-old Honor Code, one of only twelve entirely student-run honor systems in the country. It underpins all academic and social interactions at the College and creates a palpable spirit of trust and cooperation between students and faculty members. Other benefits of the code include the tradition of shared governance among faculty members and students and self-scheduled, unproctored final exams.

Admission Requirements

Admission to Connecticut College is very competitive and selective. A record pool of more than 4,400 students applied for 475 places in the class of 2004. The acceptance rate for the class of 2004 was 32 percent. Biographical information, extracurricular activities, the high school transcript, standardized test scores, an essay, recommendations, and an optional interview are all components that are taken into consideration when an application is reviewed for admission. Of the admitted students who applied for the class of 2004, 86 percent ranked in the top 10 to 20 percent of their high school class. The medians for the SAT I were 680 verbal and 660 math. The median for the ACT was 28, and the median TOEFL score was 629.

Application and Information

Applicants may choose to apply under one of the two early decision programs or as a regular decision applicant. Early decision is for students who have determined that Connecticut College is their first choice and who will commit to attending if admitted. Regular decision is a nonbinding process. Early decision 1 candidates must submit the Connecticut College Application Part 1 and the Common Application by November 15. Early decision 2 and regular decision candidates must submit the Connecticut College Application Part 1 by December 15 and the Common Application by January 1.

For information about obtaining application materials, students should contact:

Office of Admission and Financial Aid
Horizon Building
Connecticut College
270 Mohegan Avenue
New London, Connecticut 06320
Telephone: 860-439-2200
Fax: 860-439-4301
E-mail: admit@conncoll.edu
World Wide Web: http://www.conncoll.edu

CONVERSE COLLEGE
SPARTANBURG, SOUTH CAROLINA

The College

Converse College is a private, residential liberal arts college for women and the only women's college in the United States with a nationally accredited, comprehensive school of music. From the time a student arrives on campus as a freshman until she completes her requirements for graduation, Converse emphasizes academic quality, personal and social responsibility, experiential learning, leadership development, and career preparation. As a result, Converse has been recognized by *U. S. News & World Report* as one of the top ten colleges and universities in the South. The personal attention resulting from small class sizes, the second-oldest student government association in the Southeast, an 80-year-old honor tradition, and an academic program grounded in the liberal arts all serve to distinguish the Converse experience.

Average enrollment for full-time undergraduates is 750. During the 1999–2000 academic year, Converse enrolled women from twenty-eight states and eight countries. Academic life is enhanced by opportunities to gain valuable leadership experience through participation in student organizations, foreign and domestic study-travel programs, service-learning experiences, and career preparation through an active internship program. All resident students have in-room Internet, cable television, and telephone access. In addition, both resident and commuting students can make use of several state-of-the-art computer labs on campus.

Although academic quality is Converse's first priority, students also benefit from campus life and residential life programs, which are designed to build a sense of community and involvement. The Big Sister/Little Sister student mentoring program, beginning in the freshman year, encourages long-lasting friendships, as do the many student organizations that are an integral part of life at Converse. The College provides numerous opportunities for volunteerism through local civic and church organizations, such as Habitat for Humanity, the Boys and Girls Home, and Mobile Meals. The Office of Career Services offers career counseling, personal interest testing, and current career and graduate school information as well as internship and job placement assistance. The College's NCAA Division II intercollegiate athletics program includes basketball, cross-country, soccer, tennis, and volleyball. A nationally competitive equestrian program is also available. Converse students also have multiple opportunities to participate in social and recreational activities, including intramural sports, whitewater rafting trips, hiking excursions, backpacking tours in the North Carolina Mountains, snow-skiing weekends, and horseback riding trips. Spartanburg's four coeducational colleges provide additional opportunities to develop friendships and participate in social activities. From day one, Converse seeks to produce graduates who are prepared, involved, and accomplished citizens of their communities and the world.

Location

Converse's 70-acre campus is located in Spartanburg, South Carolina, 30 minutes from the Blue Ridge Mountains and the Great Smokies to the northwest and about 4 hours from South Carolina's "Grand Strand" of beaches to the southeast. Atlanta, Charleston, Columbia, Charlotte, and Asheville are all within a few hours' drive. Strategically located along the I-85 business corridor, Spartanburg is also home to approximately ninety international corporations; this makes Spartanburg a true international city and a perfect place for internship and job placement opportunities. Many local and regional companies come to campus each year to recruit Converse graduates. Transportation to and from Spartanburg is easy. Located at the intersection of I-85 and I-26, Spartanburg is only minutes away from the newly expanded Greenville-Spartanburg International Airport, which offers daily service by most major airlines.

Majors and Degrees

Converse students can earn bachelor's degrees in more than thirty areas: accounting; art (art education, art history, art therapy, graphic design, and studio art); biochemistry; biology; business; business administration with concentrations in finance, international business, marketing, and organizational management; chemistry; computer science; economics; education (comprehensive special education, deaf and hard-of-hearing/interpreting, educable mentally handicapped, early childhood, elementary, emotionally handicapped, learning disabilities); English; foreign language (French, German, and Spanish); history, interior design; mathematics; modern languages; music (composition, music education, music history, performance, theory, piano pedagogy); politics; psychology; religion; sociology; and theater.

Preprofessional programs include dentistry, law, medicine, ministry, nursing, pharmacy, and veterinary science. Career programs are offered in arts management, publication and media, and Army ROTC.

Academic Program

The General Education Program, required for each student, introduces Converse women to a variety of subjects, developing an appreciation of Western culture and the liberal arts. Students are then able to choose a major or two in which to specialize. The Converse College Institute for Leadership program is an optional program that emphasizes leadership development, physical fitness, and additional service learning.

An outstanding feature of the Converse curriculum is the double-major program, which allows students to major in two subject areas within the liberal arts or to combine a traditional discipline with a career-related program. Depending on the student's major and course of study, she can earn a Bachelor of Arts, Bachelor of Science, Bachelor of Fine Arts, or a Bachelor of Music. The candidate for the bachelor's degree must complete a minimum of 120 semester hours and have a grade average of no less than C (2.0)

Converse operates on a 4-2-4 academic calendar consisting of two 13-week terms and a 6-week winter term. During the winter term, students can take classes on campus or take advantage of the many opportunities for off-campus study programs, including internships and foreign travel.

Off-Campus Arrangements

Converse offers full-year and semester-long study-abroad programs through which students are able to study in France, Spain, England, Australia, Latin America, and many other countries. One of the highlights of the winter term is the annual study-travel experience in London. Students have also traveled to Budapest, Chile, Germany, Martinique, Morocco, Paris, Peru, Prague, St. Petersburg, Spain, and Switzerland and domestically to New York City, New Mexico's Ghost Ranch, New Orleans, and the American Northwest. A recently established $1-million endowment for the Anne Morrison Chapman Study-Abroad Experience will enable more Converse students to take advantage of international study and travel.

Academic Facilities

Among the twenty-seven buildings on campus are two major classroom buildings with multimedia classrooms and state-of-the-art computer labs as well as facilities for music, the visual and performing arts, physical education, and student activities. The fully automated Mickel Library contains more than 200,000 books, recordings, scores, microfilms, and audiovisual materials and one of the largest music libraries in the Southeast. Converse also maintains five cultural facilities on campus, including Twichell Auditorium, Blackman Music Building, the Milliken Art Building, the Milliken Gallery, and the Hazel B. Abbott Theatre. The College is building a new physical activity complex, which is expected to be ready in the summer of 2001, and is planning to construct a new state-of-the-art teaching and technology building within the next few years.

Costs

For 1999–2000, tuition was $15,230, and room and board costs were $4645 for both in-state and out-of-state residents.

Financial Aid

More than 70 percent of Converse students receive some form of financial assistance through scholarships, federal student assistance programs, loans, and work-study programs. Scholarships and grant awards pay up to the full comprehensive fee. Residents of South Carolina may also qualify for South Carolina Tuition Grants of up to $3360 for freshmen and $3430 for upperclass students. The Free Application for Federal Student Aid (FAFSA) is required of all applicants for financial assistance. Each year, Converse awards $4.8 million in scholarships for academic excellence, musical ability, or leadership. These awards are not based on need, and the FAFSA is not required. The awards are renewable for three additional years. Limited scholarship programs are available to transfer students.

Faculty

Of the College's 81 faculty members, 90 percent hold the Ph.D. or other terminal degree, and full-time faculty members do all student advising. The student-faculty ratio is 9:1 in the undergraduate program and 7:1 in the Petrie School of Music. The College does not employ teaching assistants, and freshman and sophomore classes are taught by senior professors. Faculty members are selected on the basis of teaching proficiency, scholarly competence, character, and ability to impart the excitement and value of learning.

Student Government

The Converse College Student Government Association (SGA) is the second-oldest in the Southeast and has been active for more than ninety years. As an energetic student voice on campus, it serves as an umbrella organization for all campus clubs and organizations. The SGA also maintains important communication links between the College's administration and the students. The Converse Honor Tradition, an integral part of student governance for more than eighty years, ensures that self-discipline, shared confidence, and community integrity are maintained on the campus.

Admission Requirements

Admission to Converse College is an individualized, informative, and interactive process. Students are encouraged to apply as early as possible in their senior year of high school. Early decision admission applications are due by November 15. Sixteen units of high school academic work are recommended. In addition to high school transcripts and SAT I or ACT scores, personal interviews, previous extracurricular activities, demonstrated exceptional talent, and seriousness of purpose may be used as admissions criteria. Converse College participates in the Advanced Placement Program administered by the College Entrance Examination Board. Transfer students are accepted each semester from accredited institutions.

Application and Information

In order to begin the application process, students must send a completed application for admission, a $35 nonrefundable application fee, an official transcript of at least six semesters of secondary school, official SAT I or ACT scores (for freshmen), a graded writing sample, and a teacher recommendation. Applications are accepted on a rolling basis.

All inquiries and requests for application forms should be addressed to:

Office of Admissions
Converse College
580 East Main Street
Spartanburg, South Carolina 29302
Telephone: 864-596-9040
          800-766-1125 (toll-free)
E-mail: info@converse.edu
World Wide Web: http://www.converse.edu

A student relaxes between classes on the 70-acre campus of Converse College.

COOPER UNION FOR THE ADVANCEMENT OF SCIENCE AND ART
NEW YORK, NEW YORK

The College
The Cooper Union for the Advancement of Science and Art occupies a special place in the history of American education. Founded by industrialist and philanthropist Peter Cooper, who believed "education should be as free as water and air," the college opened on a tuition-free, nonsectarian basis in 1859. The Cooper Union continues to fulfill its historic responsibility, offering a full-tuition scholarship education "equal to the best."

Of the 934 students enrolled at Cooper Union, 902 are undergraduates. In the School of Art, there are 148 men and 119 women; in the Irwin S. Chanin School of Architecture, 84 men and 63 women; and in the Albert Nerken School of Engineering, 336 undergraduate men and 120 undergraduate women as well as 23 men and 9 women working toward the Master of Engineering degree. All students take classes in the Faculty of Humanities and Social Sciences.

Most members of the current first-year class are 18 years of age and come from the New York area. About 6 percent of the students are citizens of other countries. There are two fraternities and one sorority on campus in addition to numerous social, special interest, and religious clubs. A strong intramural sports program is available. The college has five buildings, including a full-service cafeteria and student lounges.

Location
Cooper Union is situated on the edge of Manhattan's East Village, within easy walking distance of Washington Square Park and the bookstores, galleries, and film houses of Greenwich Village. Students have the opportunity to take advantage of Cooper Union's location in New York City, an international art center and the information hub of the country. New York offers extraordinary resources and stimuli for learning—great museum collections; performances by orchestras, chamber music groups, jazz musicians, and dance companies; constant exposure to the work of artists from all over the world in the galleries of SoHo, Greenwich Village, and upper Manhattan; the curricula and public programs of nearby colleges and universities; and the ever-changing street life of the city itself.

Majors and Degrees
Degree programs are offered in architecture, fine arts, and engineering. The Bachelor of Architecture is offered in architecture (five-year program); the Bachelor of Fine Arts includes studies in drawing, film/video, graphic design, painting, photography, printmaking, and sculpture; the Bachelor of Engineering in chemical engineering, civil engineering, electrical engineering, and mechanical engineering; and the Bachelor of Science in general engineering. In addition, a certificate program is offered in art.

Academic Program
Cooper Union uses a semester calendar. Each curriculum is designed to meet the professional needs of students entering any of the college's specialized fields. Graduates are well prepared to enter these fields or to continue their education in graduate school. Requirements for the Bachelor of Architecture are 160 credits; for the Bachelor of Fine Arts, 128 credits; for the Bachelor of Engineering, 135 credits; and for the Bachelor of Science, 135 credits. The requirements for the certificate program in art are approximately half the studio course credit requirements of the B.F.A. degree.

In the School of Architecture, an interim year is offered during which students may work in architectural firms or study and travel. In the School of Art, foundation courses in studio art and art history are required, and independent study projects are available. All first-year engineering students in the School of Engineering take core courses in math, chemistry, physics, and computer science. All students also take core courses in the humanities and social sciences. Students have the opportunity for hands-on experience in city agencies, cultural institutions, and the offices and studios of the many professional architects, artists, and engineers who live and work in New York.

Off-Campus Arrangements
A consortium arrangement with nearby Eugene Lang College of the New School for Social Research permits Cooper Union students to take courses for credit not normally offered on their own campus. Limited access to courses at New York University is also available.

The School of Art offers a semester of nonresident study at member schools of the Consortium of East Coast Art Schools and at art schools in Switzerland, England, Italy, France, Germany, and Israel. The School of Engineering offers summer research study at universities in England, Australia, and Hong Kong.

Academic Facilities
The Cooper Union library contains more than 97,000 volumes. The collection also includes 70,000 photographs and 50,000 slides related to fine arts and architecture. There are also studios, a printmaking shop, a full floor devoted to a sculpture and woodworking shop, laboratories, darkroom facilities, an animation room, and lecture halls. The Arthur Houghton Art Gallery, the Center for Design and Typography, the Center for Writing and Speaking, and the historic 900-seat Great Hall auditorium all contribute to the academic and cultural life on campus.

The Computer Center is available to all students and faculty members whenever the Engineering Building is open and provides a centralized resource for technological support of academic computing needs. The center's laboratories contain a variety of minicomputers, including Dell, Pentium II, and Sun SPARC 5, 20, Ultra, and Ultra II workstations; DEC MicroVAX GPX workstations; various Apple Macintosh computers; and Silicon Graphics Indy Octane workstations.

The Computer Center is fully networked and utilizes the UNIX operating system and a high-bandwidth TCP/IP backbone to provide a rich and reliable computing environment. The center is locally accessible through approximately 130 minicomputers, including the Sun SPARC, DEC, and SGI workstations; the Dell PCs, which run the Linux operating system; and the Apple Macintoshes. Data communications with the outside community are maintained via full Internet implementation. E-mail and World Wide Web functions are available at all workstations, PCs, and Macs. Students and faculty members have access to all software packages and programming languages on the local network and can download software from all Internet sites worldwide.

There are currently more than fifty PCs available for student use. Each PC provides DOS, Windows, and Linux environments, which allow students and faculty members to take full advantage of the computer's processing capabilities. A special microcomputer classroom houses thirty Dell PCs. It is designed to be an instructional facility as well as a drop-in facility. Twenty more Pentium-based PCs with higher computational power and CD-ROM capabilities allow a broader range of scientific software applications.

The Mac Room, together with scanners, digital cameras, and CD-ROM burners, provides extra image-processing capabilities to augment the regular academic software. All of the systems are networked together to provide ease of access as well as data and program interoperability.

The new Brooks Design Center includes clusters of seven networked workstations, including SGI Octanes, Sun Ultra SPARCs, IBM RS 6000 workstations, and Intel-based high-end PCs running Windows NT. Advanced design software tools replicate an engineering design office capable of 3-D design and modeling. The center includes project areas (carrels) with videoconferencing equipment and a multimedia presentation room.

Costs

All students admitted to Cooper Union receive a full-tuition scholarship, which is equivalent to approximately $100,000 each in the School of Art or the School of Engineering and $125,000 each in the School of Architecture. Tuition is listed at $8300 per year—a figure that represents the difference between the amount covered by the annual projected endowment income and the actual cost. The annual fee for 2000–01 is $500.

The Cooper Union provides housing for students on a limited basis by lottery at a cost of approximately $6000. The Office of the Dean of Students offers assistance to those who wish to locate other housing accommodations. For students living in New York City and attending the School of Art, $2600 may be required for books, supplies, and personal expenses; approximately $3400 may be required by architecture students, and $1100 may be required by engineering students. Expenses vary greatly depending on the chosen major.

Financial Aid

Aid beyond the full tuition scholarships is available on the basis of need. Students must document need by submitting the Free Application for Federal Student Aid (FAFSA) and the College Scholarship Service's Financial Aid PROFILE. Financial aid is usually offered in the form of packages consisting of grants, loans, and work-study awards. Application for financial aid should be made before April 15.

Faculty

The Cooper Union has a full-time faculty of 55 members and a part-time faculty of 190. Eighty-four percent of the full-time faculty have earned advanced degrees. The faculty-student ratio is 1:7.

The faculty in the School of Engineering is both a teaching and a research faculty, with the former responsibility emphasized. The same faculty teaches undergraduates and graduate students. Graduate students do not serve as instructors. The Cooper Union Research Foundation (CURF), established in 1976 as a not-for-profit corporation, serves as the primary research unit of the School of Engineering. By encouraging and supporting research, the foundation augments the educational opportunities for students, enhances professional development of faculty, and provides services to the community through its research and development efforts. Participation in research activities by faculty and students is essential to the vitality of Cooper Union's educational programs. In attempting to meet this objective, CURF plays an important role for faculty and students having research talent who wish to pursue sponsored research individually or in concert with other faculty members and students. Projects undertaken by CURF are externally funded. Faculty members serve as project directors, assisted by other faculty members, outside consultants, and undergraduate and graduate students of the Cooper Union. Most faculty members in the School of Architecture and School of Art are practicing professionals. The Faculty of Humanities and Social Sciences comprises internationally recognized scholars. All faculty members are expected to counsel students, and many participate as advisers in extracurricular activities.

Student Government

An active student government exists in which representatives are elected by the student body to participate in faculty meetings or to serve on faculty-student committees. Students have full autonomy in the management of student activity funds.

Admission Requirements

The Cooper Union seeks students of exceptional ability and talent. For students in art and architecture, talent is judged in terms of portfolios and home tests; in engineering, ability is judged in academic terms, particularly high school average, SAT I scores, and SAT II Subject Test scores in Mathematics Level I or II and Physics or Chemistry. No special consideration is given to children of alumni or residents of particular areas in the United States. Students who are offered admission may request deferment of enrollment for a period of one year. Specific unit and credit requirements vary in the three schools and are defined in the school catalog.

Application and Information

Architecture freshman applications must be submitted by January 1. Candidates applying to the freshman class as art students must submit their application by January 10. Engineering freshman applications must be submitted by February 1. Transfer applications for art must be submitted by February 10, for architecture by February 15, and for engineering by April 1. Freshman applicants can expect to be notified of the admission decision on or about April 1; art transfer students, on or about April 1; architecture transfer students, about May 15; and engineering transfer students, about May 15.

For further information, students should contact:

Dean of Admissions and Records
Cooper Union for the Advancement of Science and Art
30 Cooper Square
New York, New York 10003
Telephone: 212-353-4120
E-mail: admissions@cooper.edu
World Wide Web: http://www.cooper.edu

CORNELL UNIVERSITY
ITHACA, NEW YORK

The University

Cornell University is unique in American higher education. At once the largest, most comprehensive school in the Ivy League and the public land-grant university for New York State, Cornell is distinct in its combination of privately funded and state-assisted colleges. As a result, Cornell students benefit from outstanding educational programs and are nurtured by the prestigious intellectual tradition of the Ivy League. At the same time, they tap into the democratic spirit and sense of public service that energize the nation's great state universities.

Cornell's thirteen colleges and schools offer instruction in virtually every field, and the University's numerous interdisciplinary programs provide wide-ranging opportunities for study that cuts across traditional department boundaries. Students at Cornell arguably are exposed to the widest arrays of subjects and approaches to learning available anywhere. Moreover, they share the excitement of intellectual discovery with faculty members who are Nobel laureates, Pulitzer Prize winners, and researchers at the forefront of their fields—clear evidence of the University's commitment to undergraduate education. It is not uncommon to find prominent scholars teaching introductory classes and offering courses for general enrollment.

Cornell comprises people of all races, many nationalities, and every social and economic background, and the interplay of differences finds full expression throughout the University and in the surrounding Ithaca community. To put it simply, Cornell offers students the cultural diversity and intellectual vigor often associated with large metropolitan centers as well as the friendly atmosphere and livable pace of a smaller city environment.

Most faculty members live in or near Ithaca and take part in campus activities after classroom hours, and students and faculty members enjoy a sense of community not possible on urban campuses. More than 500 campus clubs and associations allow the development of leadership skills and provide opportunities for students who share interests, concerns, talents, or avocations to find each other.

Cornell's student body numbers about 19,000 students, 13,500 of whom are undergraduates. About 47 percent are women and 53 percent are men. About 37 percent of Cornell's undergraduate students are from New York State, 20 percent are from the Mid-Atlantic and New England states, 36 percent are from elsewhere in the United States, and 7 percent are from outside the country. More than a quarter of students are members of a minority group, and the majority of students attended public high schools.

Students may live on or off campus. In addition to traditional residence halls, Cornell has more than 400 apartments for student families and a variety of small living units and residential program houses that provide an opportunity for cooperative living arrangements. The University has forty-three fraternities and sixteen sororities. About 42 percent of Cornell's students live in University dormitories or apartments, 14 percent live in fraternities or sororities, and 44 percent live off campus.

Cornell maintains one of the most extensive and diversified programs of physical education in the country. The teaching program, which each year offers more than fifty courses ranging from ballroom dancing to rock climbing, emphasizes recreational activities that students can continue to enjoy after they leave the University. The intramural athletics program—the largest in the Ivy League—provides opportunities for members of the University community to compete in more than thirty sports. Cornell also supports eighteen varsity sports for men and eighteen varsity sports for women.

Location

Cornell is on a hillside at the southern tip of Cayuga Lake, the longest of the Finger Lakes of central New York State. Within easy walking distance of the campus is the Cornell Plantations—a living laboratory of natural resources comprising 2,800 acres of woodlands, trails, streams, and gorges. Several ski areas, an extensive system of hiking trails, and three unusually scenic state parks with facilities for hiking, boating, swimming, and camping are a short drive away.

Majors and Degrees

Cornell University offers degrees at the baccalaureate level in seven undergraduate colleges (Agriculture and Life Sciences; Architecture, Art, and Planning; Arts and Sciences; Engineering; Hotel Administration; Human Ecology; and Industrial and Labor Relations). Undergraduates may choose from an impressive range of programs in fields such as agricultural sciences, animal science, architecture, art, behavioral sciences, biological sciences, business management, communications, design and environmental analysis, engineering, environmental studies, food science, government, history, hotel administration, human development, humanities, industrial and labor relations, languages and linguistics, mathematics and computer science, nutritional sciences, physical sciences, plant sciences, policy analysis and management, preprofessional studies, and social sciences.

Academic Program

Although degree requirements vary among the undergraduate units, students are encouraged to take courses in other divisions. This interdisciplinary approach is exemplified by Cornell's nationally recognized ethnic studies programs: Africana studies, Asian studies, Asian-American studies, Latino studies, Latin American studies, and Native American studies. In addition to offering courses, these programs promote multicultural understanding on campus by supporting lectures, conferences, seminars, exhibits, publications, and research projects. Honors programs, independent majors, double majors, and dual-degree programs are available in most areas of study. Entering freshmen may qualify for advanced placement or credit on the recommendation of the appropriate departments of instruction at Cornell.

The academic year is divided into two semesters, which run from late August to mid-December and from January to mid-May. There also are three consecutive summer sessions.

Off-Campus Arrangements

Students in many areas participate in fieldwork programs, internships, engineering cooperative programs, and research projects. They study in Albany; Washington, D.C.; New York City; and other places where they can best learn about the work of government, community organizations, businesses, and industry. Undergraduates participate in Cornell Abroad programs in many countries, including Australia, China, Denmark, Egypt, England, France, Germany, Greece, Indonesia, Israel, Italy, Japan, Kenya, Korea, Mexico, Nepal, Nigeria, Russia, Sweden, and Vietnam.

Academic Facilities

Cornell's library system is one of the ten largest academic research libraries in the United States. Two central libraries and an extensive system of thirteen libraries in the colleges contain more than 6.4 million volumes, subscribe to 63,500 periodicals, and add about 130,000 volumes to their collections each year.

The University's computer resources are important to students in almost every area of study. Cornell Information Technologies operates public terminals and microcomputers, produces documentation, and offers a variety of user education programs. In addition, all of Cornell's undergraduate residence hall rooms have direct Internet connections, enabling residents to log on around the clock.

Costs

Tuition and fees for the 1999–2000 academic year for students enrolled in Cornell's state-assisted units (Agriculture and Life Sciences, Human Ecology, and Industrial and Labor Relations) were $10,418 for New York residents and $19,988 for nonresidents. Tuition and fees for those in the University's privately funded units (Architecture, Art, and Planning; Arts and Sciences; Engineering; and Hotel Administration) were $23,848. Typical room and board costs amounted to $7685 per academic year, and personal expenses, including books, were about $1745.

Financial Aid

Admission decisions are not affected by a prospective student's need for financial assistance, and the University's comprehensive Ways and Means program offers a wide array of financial support options to students and their families. Sixty-two percent of all Cornell undergraduates receive some form of financial aid from University, state, federal, or other sources, and about 50 percent receive Cornell-allocated scholarships, jobs, and/or loans. All financial assistance is awarded on the basis of need, according to the standards of the College Scholarship Service.

Of particular importance to prospective students is Cornell's nationally recognized program of financial assistance known as the Cornell Commitment, which consists of three programs: the Cornell Tradition, which rewards students who demonstrate a commitment to working and funding a portion of their own education; the Meinig Family National Scholars, which rewards outstanding leaders in high school; and the Presidential Research Scholars, which recognizes students who have a strong interest in research.

Faculty

The more than 1,500 members of the Cornell faculty include many men and women who are recognized internationally as leaders in their fields. Among them are Nobel laureates, Pulitzer Prize winners, and scores of individuals who are members of the National Academy of Sciences, the National Academy of Engineering, or the National Academy of Education. Twenty-three members of the faculty have received Guggenheim Fellowships during the past five years, and 3 members of the faculty have received MacArthur Foundation "genius awards."

Nearly all teaching faculty members are involved in research, scholarship, or public service. Maintaining the quality of undergraduate programs is one of Cornell's highest priorities, and there is no distinction between the graduate and undergraduate faculty. Professors act as advisers and keep regular office hours to ensure their availability to students. The University community also enjoys a constant succession of visiting lecturers and professors from other institutions.

Student Government

Cornell students participate in governing the University through the Student Assembly (22 elected students), which has legislative authority over the policies of several campus life departments. Students may also be members of policymaking committees within each undergraduate college, and students sit as voting members on the University's Board of Trustees.

Admission Requirements

Cornell is among the most selective universities in the nation. There were nearly 20,000 applications for the 1999–2000 freshman class. Average combined SAT I scores of entering freshmen are about 350 points above the national average, and more than 80 percent of entering students are in the top 10 percent of their high school classes.

Each undergraduate unit has its own selection committee, and applicants compete only with other students seeking admission to the same division. Intellectual preparedness and evidence of the applicant's abilities in nonacademic areas are important considerations in admission decisions, as are work experience and other activities related to educational or professional objectives. The University seeks individuals with outstanding personal qualities, such as initiative and leadership. Some of Cornell's divisions also require interviews.

All seven undergraduate colleges offer an early decision plan to highly qualified high school seniors whose first preference is Cornell. A few students may be approved for early admission after only three years of secondary school.

Application and Information

Cornell has a two-part application. From freshman applicants, Part 1 is due well before January 1 and Part 2 on January 1. Applicants who wish to be considered under the early decision plan must file Part 1 well before November 10 and Part 2 by November 10; they are notified of decisions in mid-December. From fall transfer students, Part 1 is due well before March 15 and Part 2 on March 15. The spring transfer Part 1 application is due well before November 10 and Part 2 on November 10.

For additional information and application forms, students should contact:

Undergraduate Admissions Office
Cornell University
410 Thurston Avenue
Ithaca, New York 14850-2488

Telephone: 607-255-5241

World Wide Web: http://www.cornell.edu

A student in one of the libraries.

CREIGHTON UNIVERSITY
OMAHA, NEBRASKA

The University

Located in Omaha, Nebraska, Creighton University is a nationally recognized private, Jesuit, Catholic university. Multidimensional programs of study combine challenging academic courses with career development internships, service, and extracurricular opportunities. *U.S. News & World Report* recently ranked Creighton the number one Midwest Regional University for the fourth year in a row. Recognized as a Best Buy by both *Money* and *Kiplinger's Personal Finance* magazines, Creighton was also listed among the nation's top 100 Wired Colleges by *Yahoo! Internet Life* magazine.

The University has a total enrollment of 6,325 students, including 3,875 undergraduates and 2,450 graduate, law, medical, dental, pharmacy, and allied health profession students, who come from nearly every state in the nation and from sixty-eight other countries. Its size allows Creighton to offer ethnic and cultural diversity and a wide variety of course offerings and still provide individual attention with a student-faculty ratio of 14:1.

Creighton strives to educate the "whole student"—academically, spiritually, and physically—in a values-oriented environment. Annually, more than 35 percent of Creighton's graduates enroll in graduate and professional schools. Creighton's highly respected professional schools give Creighton undergraduates preference, annually enrolling about 18 percent of classes from Creighton undergraduate programs.

Creighton University faculty members are internationally recognized for research in such diverse areas as cancer genetics, respiratory diseases, osteoporosis and hard tissue research, laser dentistry and implantology, health policy and ethics, photography, environmental science, international development, Biblical studies, economic forecasting, bankruptcy, and antidiscrimination laws. The University has privately endowed chairs in health sciences, Jewish civilization, communication, theology, accounting, managerial ethics, regional economics, information technology management, legal ethics, medicine, surgery, medical outcomes, humanities, and dentistry and the Clare Boothe Luce Faculty Chair for Women in Science.

The University is committed to and maintains facilities for a fourteen-sport Division I athletic program, including a nationally ranked men's soccer team. Each year, Creighton hosts the men's NCAA College World Series.

Creighton University is accredited by the North Central Association of Colleges and Schools. In addition, all undergraduate and professional programs are individually accredited by the appropriate national and state associations and boards.

Creighton offers doctoral programs in biomedical sciences and medical microbiology. Professional doctoral degrees are also offered in occupational therapy, pharmacology, and physical therapy.

Master of Arts degrees are offered in Christian spirituality, English, international relations, liberal studies, and theology. Master of Science degrees are offered in atmospheric sciences, biomedical sciences, counseling and education, mathematics, medical microbiology and immunology, nursing, pharmacology, and physics. Master's degrees are also offered in business administration, computer science, e-commerce, and information technology management.

Location

Creighton's 92.4-acre campus is intersected by a tree-lined brick mall. It is located within walking distance of downtown Omaha and many recreational, cultural, and entertainment opportunities. Approximately 1,800 students live on campus. Omaha is Nebraska's largest city, with a metropolitan population of 700,000. It offers students outstanding opportunities for internships and employment in city government and leading industries, including telecommunications, insurance, banking, and health care. It has a consistently low unemployment rate and cost of living. The city has its own symphony and opera, numerous theaters and museums, a AAA baseball team, an arena football team, and a minor league hockey team.

Majors and Degrees

The College of Arts and Sciences offers majors leading to the B.A., B.S., and B.F.A. degrees in American studies, applied computer science, art (history and studio), atmospheric sciences, biology, chemistry, classical civilization, computer science, economics, education, English (comparative literature, creative writing, and Irish literature), environmental sciences, exercise sciences, French, German, Greek, history, journalism (news, advertising and public relations, and design production), Latin, mathematics (applied and mathematics/computer science), music, organizational communication, philosophy, physics, political science (legal studies and public policy), psychology, social work, sociology, Spanish, speech communications, statistics, theater, and theology.

A bachelor's degree in emergency medical services is offered through the School of Pharmacy and Allied Health Professions.

Majors in the College of Business Administration lead to a B.S.B.A. degree in accounting, economics, entrepreneurship, finance, international business, management information systems, marketing, and prelaw business. Joint programs between the business college and the School of Law allow students to earn a B.S.B.A. degree and a J.D. in six years or a B.S.B.A., a J.D., and an M.B.A. in seven years. Undergraduate degrees in the College of Arts and Sciences and College of Business Administration are available to nontraditional students through Creighton's University College. Advanced technological training is taught in the Creighton Institute for Information Technology and Management.

A Bachelor of Science in Nursing (B.S.N.) is offered to undergraduates and RN students. The School of Nursing has an accelerated one-year program for students who hold nonnursing degrees and maintains a satellite campus in Hastings, Nebraska. It offers an RN-to-B.S.N. program and a nurse practitioner program.

Academic Program

Undergraduate courses stress a well-rounded liberal arts education, with students fulfilling general education requirements in areas that include theology, ethics and philosophy, cultures and civilizations, natural science, and social and behavioral science and skills. A total of 128 semester hours is required for a bachelor's degree. The University offers unique community living and learning opportunities for upperclass students pursuing special research projects and accepts a select group of students in its honors program.

Academic Facilities

Creighton is committed to providing state-of-the-art facilities, including new and renovated residence halls, the Lied Education Center for the Arts, a modern student center, a 2¼-acre physical fitness center, a Bio-Information Center, and one of the largest artificial turf athletic complexes in the Midwest.

Creighton offers students ample technological support. Campus housing allows for computer hookups as well as cable TV and satellite broadcast reception. Students have access to nearly thirty computer centers, with 24-hour online capability. There are modern desktop design and writing laboratories and broadcast facilities. The University's three libraries include the Reinert Alumni Memorial Library, the Health Sciences Library/Learning Resource Center, and the recently remodeled Klutznick Law Library. Together, they house 746,000 volumes, 7,131 different periodicals, and 1.4 million microforms, including U.S. government documents.

Creighton's health sciences schools are part of the Creighton Medical Center, which includes Saint Joseph Hospital and Creighton Medical Associates. The Ahmanson Law Center houses the School of Law, the local bar association, and the legal clinic.

Costs

Undergraduate tuition for the 2000–01 academic year is $14,312. The average room and board fees for the academic year cost $5720. There is also a University fee of $598.

Financial Aid

In an effort to keep high-quality Jesuit education affordable, Creighton consistently increases the total amount of scholarships and student aid. The student financial aid program totals more than $80 million, including all federal aid. About 81 percent of Creighton undergraduate students receive some type of financial aid.

Scholarships and grants are awarded on the basis of need, academic achievement, and leadership. The University participates in most federally supported financial aid programs. The Free Application for Federal Student Aid (FAFSA) or Renewal Application is to be filed by returning students by April 1 for the next academic year. Renewable, non-need-based scholarships are available to freshmen with outstanding academic and leadership records.

Faculty

Creighton has 695 full-time and 666 part-time faculty members, and several hundred others contribute service. The percentage of those having terminal degrees varies from 85 percent in the College of Arts and Sciences to 100 percent in the School of Law. Senior faculty members conduct most classroom instruction. Forty-three active Jesuit priests live and teach on the Creighton campus, providing spiritual direction as well as guidance in the classroom. Each student has a faculty adviser for individual academic counseling.

Student Government

The Student Board of Governors (SBG) is made up of 32 students elected from the undergraduate and professional schools. As the official student governing body, they serve on University committees, present entertainment events, and provide funding for college government and the more than 130 student clubs and organizations.

Admission Requirements

Creighton University invites men and women of all races, religious faiths, and nationalities to apply for admission. In fall 1998, the mean ACT composite score for incoming freshmen was 25.6. Admission, however, is not based solely on scores but also on the student's personal qualities and leadership potential.

Requirements for freshman admission include high school graduation or equivalent credentials and an indication of college-level ability as reflected in high school grades, ACT or SAT I scores, and recommendations. Freshman applicants should present at least 16 units of high school credit, ideally in English, 4; foreign language, 2; American history, 1; American government, 1; mathematics, 3 (including 1 of algebra); science, 2; and electives, 3.

Students in good standing with a C+ (2.5) average or above at other accredited universities, colleges, or junior colleges may be accepted as transfer students. The College of Arts and Sciences and the College of Business Administration require a minimum of 48 hours to be completed at Creighton. Transfer students are eligible for financial aid.

Application and Information

Completed applications for admission should be submitted to the Director of Admissions. Applications may be submitted any time after completion of the junior year of high school. For priority scholarship consideration, students must apply before February 1. Applicants completing their files after that date are considered for merit scholarships based on availability of funds. The Committee on Applications usually notifies each applicant regarding the decision within three weeks after all credentials have been received by the admissions office.

All requests for information or application forms should be addressed to:

Director of Admissions
Creighton University
2500 California Plaza
Omaha, Nebraska 68178-0055
Telephone: 402-280-2703
         800-282-5835 (toll-free outside Omaha)
Fax: 402-280-2685
E-mail: admissions@creighton.edu
World Wide Web: http://www.creighton.edu

Creighton's tree-lined mall bisects a 92-acre campus that blends new and historic buildings.

CROWN COLLEGE
ST. BONIFACIUS, MINNESOTA

The College

Crown College is a Christian community of higher education dedicated to "Christ-transformation" and the development of servant leaders who will have an impact on their world in a positive and beneficial way. The institution was founded in 1916 in St. Paul, Minnesota, for the purpose of educating men and women for Christian ministry. The mission of Crown College today is to provide a biblically integrated education for Christian leadership in the Christian and Missionary Alliance, the church-at-large, and the world. It is the conviction of the College that the truth of God's Word is an essential ingredient in education. Students not only learn about life, they learn how to live. Crown College is a community of believers desiring to "grow in the grace and knowledge of our Lord and Savior Jesus Christ" (II Peter 3:18).

A recognized leader in biblical higher education, Crown College offers degrees at the associate, bachelor's, and master's levels, preparing students for professions in a variety of fields. A one-year Bible certificate and several teacher education licensures are also offered, the latter through extension courses. The College is accredited by the North Central Association of Colleges and Schools and the Accrediting Association of Bible Colleges. Crown College continues to dedicate itself to the pursuit of educational excellence and to the perpetuation of spiritual fervency.

More than seventeen Christian denominations are represented in the diverse Crown student body that includes more than 1,000 students from approximately thirty states and several countries. Students, faculty members, and staff are vitally involved in a mutual effort to build and maintain a community that reflects and magnifies Jesus Christ.

Most Crown resident students are between 18 and 23 years of age, and 40 percent live off campus (married or single living with family). Residence life at Crown College is intended to provide a meaningful experience in personal growth. By living with others in a residence hall, students can form new friendships, interact with people from different backgrounds, and learn more about themselves. Crown welcomes students with families and provides a fifty-four-unit on-campus housing complex to meet their needs. Crown College is well suited to serve the needs of physically challenged individuals.

Students may participate in a variety of growth opportunities regardless of major. Both men and women are involved in intercollegiate athletics at Crown and participate in baseball, basketball, cross-country, football, golf, soccer, and volleyball. Crown College is part of the National Christian College Athletic Association (NCCAA) and a member of the National Association of Intercollegiate Athletics (NAIA) and the Upper Midwest Athletic Conference. In addition to major music performance groups such as the choir and band, Crown students may audition for several small ensembles that travel and perform throughout the year. Other leadership opportunities include student government, student publications, community service, Students in Free Enterprise (SIFE), and InterCultural Experiences.

In 1995, Crown College began offering Master of Arts degrees in church leadership, ethnomusicology, and missiology. Graduate courses are offered year-round in a modular format. They meet for one week (Monday-Friday) and require preclass and postclass work as described in the course syllabus. Additional information regarding the graduate program is available via e-mail (grad@crown.edu), telephone (612-446-4310), or the World Wide Web (see below).

Location

Situated on a beautiful 193-acre campus west of Minneapolis near the communities of Waconia and St. Bonifacius, Minnesota, Crown College is nestled among the rolling hills of the scenic lake-dotted region west of popular Lake Minnetonka. Just 20 minutes from the bustling Twin Cities of Minneapolis and St. Paul, Crown College offers a place of retreat for learning and growth.

Majors and Degrees

Students may select from more than twenty-five bachelor's degrees, nine two-year associate degrees, and several minors, certificates, and licensures. Majors include biblical and theological studies, business administration, business administration/sports and fitness management, child and family ministries, Christian education, early childhood education, elementary education, English, English education, history, history education, intercultural studies, liberal arts, linguistics, management, music, music education, network administration, New Testament, pastoral ministries, physical education, psychology, social studies education, youth ministry, and youth/social science.

In 1993, Crown began to offer EXCEL, an adult degree completion program for adults ages 25 and older. Four degree completion majors are available for the student who has completed approximately 60 semester credits of college. A major in Christian ministry is designed to equip the students for leadership roles in the church. The management and ethics major is designed to serve adults interested in the integration of the study of the Bible with studies equipping them for effective management and leadership roles in the church, in parachurch ministries, and in the contemporary marketplace. The early childhood and family education major provides course work leading to licensure for prekindergarten, family education/parent educator studies, and family education/early childhood studies. The management and network administration major is designed to serve adults who desire leadership roles in information technology and certification as Microsoft systems engineers. Degree completion classes generally meet one evening per week.

Associate degrees are available for adult students in seven majors: business, Christian studies, early childhood, general studies, liberal arts, network administration, and psychology.

A certificate program is available to nondegree-seeking students in network administration. Crown College is an authorized academic training center for Microsoft Corporation, and as such, the various computer education programs are designed to prepare the learner for Microsoft certification as a user specialist or systems engineer.

Academic Program

Crown College is uncompromising in its commitment to high-quality education with a solid base of studies in the humanities and sciences integrated with enthusiastic biblical studies. Every baccalaureate degree includes a general studies core curriculum and a Christian studies core curriculum in addition to the chosen major.

Practical hands-on experience is built into many of Crown's degrees. For example, the six-month cross-cultural internship for intercultural studies majors is unique at the undergraduate level. Pastoral, youth, and Christian education ministry majors also take a six-month internship during their junior year.

The academic calendar includes two 16-week semesters and two 4-week summer terms. Requirements for graduation are determined by respective departments of the College. The minimum hours required for a baccalaureate degree are 125 semester credits; an associate degree requires a minimum of 66 semester credits; and certificates require 32 semester credits. Students must attain a minimum cumulative grade point average of 2.0 (on a 4.0 scale) in work taken at Crown College.

Matriculated students at Crown College may earn up to 30 semester credits toward degree program requirements with satisfactory results in the following approved testing programs: Advanced Placement examinations of the College Entrance Examination Board (CEEB); College-Level Examination Program (CLEP); or the Crown College Proficiency Exams in math and computers.

Academically exceptional high school students in their junior or senior year may enroll in Crown courses to earn college credit while completing high school graduation requirements. The Learning Assistance Program helps students who need to improve their skills in reading, writing, and math through personal instruction and computer-based tutorials. Career services are available to all students and graduates for counseling concerning career preparation.

Academic Facilities

The Crown College Library contains 105,000 bound volumes, 74,000 titles on microform, 800 periodical subscriptions, and 2,400 records, tapes, CDs, and CD-ROMs. The Academic Computing Center has computers and printers available for student use. Students have access to the Internet, campus e-mail, library card catalog, and other resources through the Academic Computing Center or computers in their residence hall rooms.

Costs

For the 1999–2000 academic year, tuition was $9450 (based on 15 credits per semester), fees were $708, and room and board cost $4316. Students in the Crown Adult Programs (CAP) paid $265 per credit hour.

Financial Aid

In 1999, about 90 percent of Crown students received financial aid. The Financial Aid Office is committed to helping students obtain the maximum amount of financial aid available. The four main categories of aid at Crown College are scholarships, grants, student employment, and low-interest loans. Students needing assistance must submit the Free Application for Federal Student Aid (FAFSA) and request that a copy of the evaluation be sent to Crown College. Through a computer analysis, the FAFSA determines the amount the student and/or family is able to pay for that year's college costs. The Crown College Financial Aid Office subtracts this amount from the student's need and determines the amount of financial aid that the College and government resources attempt to meet. A priority deadline for completion of financial aid is two months before the semester begins.

Faculty

Students find the men and women of Crown's faculty to be mentors, advisers, and friends. Their purpose is not merely to produce well-educated young professionals but to educate Christian leaders who will have an impact for Jesus Christ in the world. Crown's faculty includes 54 full-time and part-time members; more than half have earned doctoral degrees and/or the appropriate terminal degrees in their field. The ratio of faculty to students is 1:14.

Student Government

At Crown College, students have the opportunity to stretch their abilities as leaders by getting involved in any of the cocurricular activities on or off campus. Among the avenues for involvement are Student Services Board, Student Senate, residence hall councils, class offices, resident assistant positions, and Students in Free Enterprise. Students also serve on various academic committees.

Admission Requirements

All applicants must have either graduated from high school or received a certificate of high school equivalency (GED) before registration day of the academic term for which application is made. In addition, all applicants must give satisfactory evidence of Christian conversion by both demonstrating quality Christian character in home and community and by making a positive contribution to the ministry of a local church. Applicants must submit the following: application for admission that includes a spiritual life essay, a Community Covenant response, and a $35 fee; two recommendations, one from a pastor and the other from either a teacher or employer; official transcripts from high school and all previous postsecondary institutions; ACT (preferred) or SAT college entrance exam scores. Standard acceptance requirements include a minimum 2.0 GPA and an ACT composite score of 18. International students, other than Canadians, must also submit a TOEFL score.

Application and Information

Students may submit application for admission any time during the calendar year. Preference for class registration and room assignment is given to those who apply by May 1 for the fall semester. Admissions decisions are made on a rolling basis, and students are informed immediately. For further information on how to apply or to schedule a campus visit, students may contact:

Office of Admissions
Crown College
6425 County Road 30
St. Bonifacius, Minnesota 55375-9002
Telephone: 612-446-4142
            800-68-CROWN (toll-free)
E-mail: info@crown.edu
World Wide Web: http://www.crown.edu

Crown College is situated on a beautiful 193-acre campus near Minneapolis, Minnesota.

THE CULINARY INSTITUTE OF AMERICA
HYDE PARK, NEW YORK

The Institute

The Culinary Institute of America (CIA) is an independent, not-for-profit institution of higher education committed to providing the world's best professional culinary arts and science education. The college's degree and continuing education programs provide students with the opportunity to acquire the general knowledge and practical skills they need to build successful careers in an ever-changing foodservice and hospitality industry.

Originally called the New Haven Restaurant Institute, the college was founded in 1946 to give returning World War II veterans the opportunity to learn a new profession. Founders Frances Roth, an attorney chosen as the first director, and Katherine Angell, first chairman of the board, were instrumental in the college's early growth. A director, a chef, a baker, and a dietitian taught the first class of 50 students in the original sixteen-week program, and the college took off from there. In 1947, the school's name was changed to the Restaurant Institute of Connecticut, and in 1951, as students from all over the country were enrolled, it became The Culinary Institute of America.

In 1972 the college moved to its current home, St. Andrew-on-Hudson, a former Jesuit seminary in Hyde Park, New York. That same year, the Board of Regents of the State of New York granted the CIA the right to confer on graduates the Associate in Occupational Studies degree, and in 1993, the Bachelor of Professional Studies degree. The college currently enrolls more than 2,000 students from around the world.

The CIA offers numerous extracurricular activities, including those sponsored by a variety of student clubs. The college's Student Recreation Center helps students maintain the proper balance between the intensive curriculum and their lives outside of the kitchens, bakeshops, and classrooms. Facilities in the center include a gymnasium, racquetball courts, a natatorium, an aerobics room, an indoor jogging track, a fitness center, a free-weight room, a game room, and a café. The campus also features outdoor tennis courts, a soccer field, a sand volleyball court, and a softball field. A number of fitness and intramural sports programs are offered year round.

Special services include the Marriott Career Planning Center, the Craig Claiborne Bookstore, and the Learning Strategies Center. On-campus residence halls house approximately 1,100 students.

The CIA provides students with two meals per instructional day in specified kitchens and dining rooms, and there is an optional weekend meal plan available.

The Culinary Institute of America is accredited by the Accrediting Commission of Career Schools and Colleges of Technology (ACCSCT). The certificates of accreditation are available for viewing on the wall of the President's Wing on the second floor of Roth Hall. Supporting documentation can be reviewed in the office of the associate vice president of planning, research, and accreditation, also located on the second floor of Roth Hall. Information related to tuition charges, fees, and length of comparable programs at other institutions may be obtained from the Accrediting Commission of Career Schools and Colleges of Technology, 2101 Wilson Boulevard, Suite 302, Arlington, Virginia 22201 (telephone: 703-247-4212).

The Culinary Institute of America is a candidate for accreditation by the Commission on Higher Education of the Middle States Association of Colleges and Schools, 3624 Market Street, Philadelphia, Pennsylvania 19104 (telephone: 215-662-5606). Candidacy was granted in June 1998. Candidacy for accreditation is a status of affiliation with a regional accrediting commission, which indicates that the institution has achieved initial recognition and is progressing toward, but is not assured of, accreditation. It has provided evidence of sound planning and the resources to implement its plans, and it appears to have the potential for attaining its goals within a reasonable time.

Location

The CIA's scenic 150-acre campus is nestled along the east bank of the Hudson River in Hyde Park, New York, conveniently located 1½–2 hours from New York City and Albany.

The Mid-Hudson region's numerous attractions and recreational opportunities offer something for everyone in both rural and urban settings. There are a number of state parks and historic sites throughout the area. Students can taste wines at local vineyards, visit farmer's markets, and pick apples at nearby orchards. Not far to the west lie the Catskill and Shawangunk Mountains, where opportunities for hiking, skiing, rock climbing, mountain biking, and sightseeing abound. Concerts, plays, films, and other cultural and special events are offered regularly at the many colleges, theaters, and community facilities throughout the Hudson Valley and Catskill regions. Students can take advantage of the campus's proximity to New York City and Albany to experience the culture, arts, and nightlife of those exciting cities.

Majors and Degrees

The Culinary Institute of America awards the degree of Bachelor of Professional Studies (B.P.S.) in baking and pastry arts management and in culinary arts management, as well as the degree of Associate in Occupational Studies (A.O.S.) in baking and pastry arts and in culinary arts. A registered certificate program in baking and pastry arts is also offered.

Academic Program

The core of the curriculum at The Culinary Institute of America is the hands-on teaching of cooking and baking as well as the managerial and creative elements that today's culinary professional requires. The unique Progressive Learning Year (PLY) system allows students to build essential culinary skills in a logical sequence during the first five semesters and enables a new class of 72 students to enroll every three weeks. In those five semesters, students take courses that include food safety, product identification, baking, pâtisserie, garde manger, and seafood cookery. They also gain invaluable experience by cooking and serving in the college's bakery café and four fine-dining public restaurants on campus. The upper-level bachelor's courses focus on topics such as marketing, communications, foreign languages, computers in the food business, and history and culture.

The college offers incoming students sixteen entry dates a year for culinary arts and eight entry dates a year for baking and pastry arts. The B.P.S. in culinary arts and baking and pastry arts management programs require four semesters of study on campus and an off-campus externship, followed by four additional on-campus semesters and a wine and food seminar in California. Students must earn 132 total credits in culinary arts management or in baking and pastry arts management to graduate with a bachelor's degree. The A.O.S. programs comprise the first five semesters of the bachelor's degree curricula, including the externship. Students must earn 69 total credits in culinary arts or in baking and pastry arts to graduate with an associate degree.

Off-Campus Arrangements

All students work in externships for a minimum of eighteen weeks (600 hours). These externships provide students with valuable on-the-job experience at CIA-approved foodservice and hospitality establishments—such as hotels, restaurants, and resorts—around the world. B.P.S. students also travel to California's Napa Valley for a four-week wine and food seminar, where they can learn from local purveyors and visit area wineries and vineyards.

Academic Facilities

The CIA campus features thirty-eight professionally equipped production kitchens and bakeshops and five student-staffed public restaurants. The Danny Kaye Theatre regularly hosts culinary events such as the Great Chefs Series, which brings world-renowned chefs to the college for lectures, cooking demonstrations, and discussions. Other valuable resources include the 58,000-volume Conrad N. Hilton Library, containing an outstanding collection of specialized culinary literature; the Learning Resources Center, which provides audiovisual programs to supplement course work; and a host of computer workstations offering Internet access and some of the most advanced technology available today.

Costs

For each semester in academic year 2000–01, tuition is $7700 for the A.O.S. programs and the first half of the B.P.S. programs and $5320 for the second half of the B.P.S. programs. Board is $1050, which includes breakfast and one full-course meal each class day, depending on the session to which the student is assigned. Housing costs range from $1435 to $2170 per semester, depending on the room to which the student is assigned.

Additional required fees for the first five semesters include a confirmation fee of $100, equipment fees of $840 for culinary supplies and $910 for baking and pastry supplies, a second-semester practical exam fee of $135, an externship fee of $350, a fifth-semester practical exam fee of $155, and an A.O.S. graduation fee of $230. Equipment fees for the second half of the B.P.S. programs are about $390 per semester. B.P.S. graduates must also pay a $230 graduation fee. Student activity fees are $75 per semester in both degree programs. The CIA offers students a tuition installment plan. Details are available from the college's Bursar's Office.

Financial Aid

Approximately 89 percent of the CIA's students receive financial aid. Federal programs offered at the college include the Federal Pell Grant, Federal Supplemental Educational Opportunity Grant (FSEOG), Federal Stafford Loan, Unsubsidized Federal Stafford Loan, Federal Perkins Loan, Federal Work-Study Program (which provides a variety of on-campus and community service jobs to eligible students), Federal PLUS Program, and Veterans Administration benefits. Students should also investigate their own state's programs and apply if those grants or scholarships can be used in New York State.

Students who have applied for admission or who are currently enrolled at the CIA may apply for scholarships offered by various organizations in the foodservice industry. A list of these scholarships, which are administered by the college, is available from the Financial Aid Office.

Faculty

The college's faculty is composed of more than 120 chefs and instructors from fifteen countries whose credentials and industry experience are unmatched in culinary education. The faculty also includes the largest concentration of Certified Master Chefs anywhere. The 18:1 student-faculty ratio gives students the opportunity to work in an environment closely representative of the foodservice industry.

Student Government

All students in good standing are members of the Student Council. The council's Executive Board acts as a liaison between students and the administration. The Student Council helps support student activities and funds all student clubs and committees.

Admission Requirements

The Admissions Committee seeks candidates who have demonstrated a commitment to a culinary career and who have the personal initiative, confidence, and motivation to succeed. The basic requirements are successful completion of a secondary school education or its equivalent and some experience in the foodservice and hospitality industry. The applicant's educational record is evaluated on the basis of overall performance and the type of program taken. Academics and leadership ability are key requirements for the B.P.S. programs.

Preference is given to candidates who have worked in foodservice, particularly in a kitchen that offers a varied menu. Before entering the program, students should have had about six months of hands-on food preparation in a non-fast-food environment.

Applicants must submit a formal application for admission, a nonrefundable $30 application fee, a secondary school report, an official secondary school transcript (not a student copy), and an official college transcript, if applicable. The application requirements include an essay of at least 500 words for the B.P.S. or 150 words for the A.O.S. programs. In addition, A.O.S. candidates must provide one recommendation, which may be from an employer in the foodservice industry or a culinary educator, attesting to the applicant's interest in pursuing a culinary career. Two recommendations are required for B.P.S. applicants: one from a guidance counselor or culinary educator describing their academic and leadership potential and the other from an employer describing their foodservice industry experience. Bachelor's degree candidates must also participate in an on-campus or telephone interview.

Application and Information

Because the CIA operates on a continuous admission system, it is recommended that students apply approximately six months prior to the time they wish to enter. Students are notified of an admission decision within a few weeks of the application date. For information or to schedule a tour, students should contact:

Admissions Office
The Culinary Institute of America
433 Albany Post Road
Hyde Park, New York 12538-1499

Telephone: 800-CULINARY (toll-free)
E-mail: admissions@culinary.edu
World Wide Web: http://www.ciachef.edu

Nestled along the banks of the Hudson River, The Culinary Institute of America's campus lies on 150 scenic acres in historic Hyde Park, New York.

CULVER–STOCKTON COLLEGE
CANTON, MISSOURI

The College
Culver-Stockton College was founded in 1853 as the first institution of higher learning west of the Mississippi River chartered expressly for coeducation. Affiliated with the Christian Church (Disciples of Christ), the College is personal (1,000 students) and provides a strong career-oriented education within a liberal arts setting. The College has one of the most attractive campuses in the Midwest, including a Fraternity Park, which was completed in 1997.

Principally residential in character, the College presents a full array of cocurricular activities, including course-related clubs and organizations, an active fraternity and sorority system, a fine intramural program, and a strong intercollegiate athletics program highlighted by baseball, basketball, football, golf, soccer, softball, and volleyball.

Culver-Stockton College has more than 9,000 living alumni, many of whom have achieved distinction in the arts, government, medicine, law, education, and other professional fields. Now in its second century, Culver-Stockton College will move into the twenty-first century as one of the truly distinctive small liberal arts colleges of the Midwest.

Location
Canton, Missouri, a small Mississippi River town of 2,700, is surrounded by the rolling farmland of northeast Missouri. Culver-Stockton is statistically one of the safest college campuses in the United States. The College has close ties with Quincy, Illinois, a progressive, arts-oriented community of approximately 45,000, and is just north of historic Hannibal, home of the famous American author Mark Twain. St. Louis is within a 2½-hour drive, and Chicago and Kansas City are close enough to be significant factors in the cultural life of the College.

Majors and Degrees
Culver-Stockton offers Bachelor of Arts and Bachelor of Science degrees in twenty-four areas, the Bachelor of Fine Art in theater and art, the Bachelor of Music Education, and the Bachelor of Science in Nursing. Study areas include accounting, art, art education, arts management, biology, business administration, chemistry, communication, criminal justice, early childhood development, elementary education, English, history and political science, management, mathematics, medical technology, music, music education, nursing, physical education, psychology, recreation management, religion and philosophy, secondary education, sociology, speech and theater arts education, and theater arts. Preprofessional programs are available in engineering, law, medicine, and the ministry, and the College has cooperative arrangements with Washington University in occupational therapy. The College also has a 2-2 program in engineering with the University of Missouri–Rolla.

Academic Program
The Culver-Stockton emphasis on career preparation is enhanced by the liberal arts. The development of student skills in writing, speaking, critical thinking, and problem solving are critical elements in the liberal arts emphasis. In addition, core courses in composition, speech, and Christian heritage combine with student choices from among five distribution areas to ensure a wide breadth of study. Students must complete 124 credit hours for the bachelor's degree. Major programs require from 26 to 62 credits. Double majors and minors are encouraged, adding further diversity and breadth to graduates' qualifications as they approach the job market.

The College has committed itself to academic distinction. Students are challenged to achieve their maximum potential and to grow in the learned skills, in breadth and depth of knowledge, and in understanding their own values. Each student is assigned an academic adviser prepared to assist the student in achieving his or her educational goals. An individualized plan is developed and then updated each semester until graduation.

For able and highly motivated students, which include freshmen, the College Honors program provides the opportunity to participate in certain specially designated courses and events culminating in an opportunity for independent study or research in an area of the student's special interest. Additional information and research can be secured through the College's connection to the Internet, a computer network of hundreds of thousands of computer systems that allows students, faculty, and staff access to libraries, databases, and fellow researchers throughout the world.

Exploratory and professional internships are available in all majors and are viewed as an important part of the career selection process. Combined with an active career counseling and placement service that includes computerized interest and preference testing, on- and off-campus internships are a key element in the Culver-Stockton approach to addressing the uncertainties of employment after graduation.

Work completed at other colleges and universities is transferable toward Culver-Stockton graduation requirements, and various testing procedures (e.g., CLEP, AP, CPEP) allow credit for equivalent knowledge or experience. Individualized learning options are plentiful; they range from individually negotiated independent study to specially designed degree programs.

The College operates on a two-semester calendar, with the first semester concluding before Christmas and the spring semester ending in early to mid-May. Summer sessions of varying lengths are available to students who wish to overcome deficiencies or accelerate their programs. All programs and classes are characterized by individual attention to the needs and interests of the student.

Off-Campus Arrangements
Culver-Stockton students have continuing opportunities for international experience through an agreement with the Central College at Pella (Iowa) International Program. In addition, off-campus and foreign study experiences, as well as individually designed internship opportunities, are available. Groups of students have traveled with Culver-Stockton faculty members to Eastern Europe, Western Europe, Canada, the Dominican Republic, and Israel. The Concert Choir and the Wind Ensemble tour each year.

Academic Facilities
Culver-Stockton is one of only a handful of colleges its size to put computers at the fingertips of every student. Computer network outlets, which enable students to plug in their personal computers for continuous access to the Internet, World Wide

Web, e-mail, the College network, laser printers, and library holdings, are active in each residence hall room. Culver-Stockton maintains three computer labs with Pentium workstations and Windows 95. Faculty members have integrated computers into the classroom in almost every field, using dedicated computer labs equipped with major-specific software.

The computerized Johann Memorial Library has a collection of 135,924 volumes and also presents comprehensive collections of periodicals, journals, and other materials in both hard copy and microform. Extensive interlibrary loan and electronic bibliographical search capabilities are available to both students and the faculty.

The Robert W. Brown Performing Arts Center and Mabee Art Gallery house professional-quality art and performance studios, computer laboratories, and three performance stages where 200 to nearly 1,000 guests can attend performances.

Costs

The 2000–01 school year costs at Culver-Stockton College are $10,650 for tuition, $4750 for room and board, and approximately $400 for books and supplies. With the exception of students who are married or living with parents, all students receiving college financial aid are required to take room and board contracts.

Financial Aid

Culver-Stockton College has one of the best student financial planning programs available among colleges of comparable size and purpose. The College participates in all federal and state financial aid programs, presenting aid packages that are based on need and merit. The latter include performance—music, art, athletics—awards as well as those based on academic achievement. The College accepts the Free Application for Federal Student Aid (FAFSA). Several Pillars for Excellence full-tuition scholarships are awarded on a competitive basis each year, and the Founders' Scholarship is available to applicants who meet certain GPA and ACT criteria. Other awards are available for students in various other circumstances. All scholarships are renewable. Application procedures are detailed in all admission materials and are subject to certain deadlines.

Faculty

Faculty members with diverse backgrounds, preparation, and interests provide instruction of high quality and individualized attention to students. Faculty members are active in scholarship, professional activity, and service and use College programs to maintain a keen interest and the highest competencies in their fields. Faculty members also take an active role in the advising and sponsorship of student organizations.

Student Government

An active Student Parliament regularly plans campuswide student events and, most important, deals with significant issues of student interest and communicates information about them to the faculty and administration. Students have voting representation on key faculty committees such as the Academic Council, the Student Services Council, the Cultural Events Council, and others that have a direct impact upon the nature and quality of student life.

Admission Requirements

Prospective students are expected to have completed a college-preparatory course of study of 15 units at an accredited secondary school. A proper foundation to facilitate success in college studies includes 4 units of English, 3 units of history, at least 2 units of mathematics (algebra and geometry), and 2 to 4 units of science. Students who intend to major in the science disciplines may wish to select additional high school courses in science and mathematics, and those interested in the humanities and social studies areas typically present additional course work in literature, foreign language, and history. Each applicant for admission is given personal attention and considered on the basis of academic performance, test scores, and personal attributes.

Application and Information

Early application is recommended, as residence halls and classroom space may be limited. For further information, students should contact:

Enrollment Services
One College Hill
Culver-Stockton College
Canton, Missouri 63435

Telephone: 800-537-1883 (toll-free)
E-mail: enrollment@culver.edu
World Wide Web: http://www.culver.edu

Weldon Residence Hall, Culver-Stockton College.

CUMBERLAND COLLEGE
WILLIAMSBURG, KENTUCKY

The College

For more than 100 years, Cumberland College has been committed to providing a superior education in an exceptional Christian atmosphere at an affordable cost. Emphasis is placed on the growth of the individual student. The College strives to instill in students the desire to be agents of change in the world and to use knowledge for the benefit of others as well as themselves.

Cumberland is a four-year, coed liberal arts college offering a broad curriculum with more than forty programs of undergraduate study from which to choose. A graduate program leading to the Master of Arts in Education is also offered.

The student body consists of 1,660 students representing twenty-eight states and twenty-three countries. Most students live on campus in the College's eight residence halls. Each hall is supervised by a director assisted by student staff members.

Extracurricular activities abound, including debate team, theater, musical performance groups, academic societies, Baptist Student Union, Appalachian Ministries, departmental clubs, and intramural sports. Cumberland participates in intercollegiate competition in women's basketball, cross-country, golf, judo, soccer, softball, swimming, tennis, track, volleyball, and wrestling; men's baseball, basketball, cross-country, football, golf, judo, soccer, swimming, tennis, track, and wrestling; and coed cheerleading. The O. Wayne Rollins Convocation/Physical Education Center houses a 2,700-seat athletic arena, a swimming pool, handball courts, an indoor walking/jogging track, and classrooms. The James H. Taylor II Stadium complex includes a football field, an eight-lane all-weather track, and soccer fields.

Students benefit from such special services as the Counseling and Career Development Center, Center for Leadership Studies, Student Health Center, Counseling Office, Academic Resource Center, and free tutorial assistance.

Cumberland College is accredited by the Commission on Colleges of the Southern Association of Colleges and Schools (1866 Southern Lane, Decatur, Georgia 30033-4097; telephone: 404-679-4501) to award Bachelor of Arts, Bachelor of General Studies, Bachelor of Music, Bachelor of Science, and Master of Arts in Education degrees.

Location

Williamsburg is located in southern Kentucky, 185 miles south of Cincinnati, Ohio, and 70 miles north of Knoxville, Tennessee. The campus is easily accessible from Interstate 75, about 1 mile from Exit 11. Williamsburg is one of Kentucky's older towns and is known for its beautiful homes and the hospitality of its people. The College is situated on three hills above the town and has a panoramic view of the surrounding mountains and Cumberland River Valley, an area known throughout the country for its lovely waterfalls, forests, and lakes. The well-kept, historical campus has many trees and lovely lawns. Famed Cumberland Falls State Resort Park is just 20 minutes from campus.

Majors and Degrees

Cumberland College confers the degrees of Bachelor of Arts, Bachelor of Science, Bachelor of General Studies, and Bachelor of Music. Major fields of study are accounting, art, biology, business administration, chemistry, church music, communications and theater arts, computer information systems, education, English, health, history, mathematics, medical technology, movement and leisure studies, music, office administration, philosophy, physics, political science, psychology, religion, social work, and special education.

Minor fields of study can be chosen from major fields or from athletic training (sports medicine), biblical languages, French, geography, philosophy, social work, and Spanish.

Preprofessional and special curricula are offered in medical technology, military science, predentistry, pre-engineering, prelaw, premedicine, prenursing, preoptometry, prepharmacy, pre–physical therapy, pre–veterinary medicine, and religious vocations.

Academic Program

Cumberland seeks to provide academic specialization within the broad framework of a liberal arts education. To supplement the in-depth knowledge acquired within each major, 45 semester hours of general studies from the areas of Christian faith and values, cultural and aesthetic values, the English language, humanities, leadership and community service, natural and mathematical sciences, physical education, and social sciences are required. Students must earn 128 semester hours to graduate with a bachelor's degree.

The academic year begins in late August, with the first semester ending in mid-December. The second semester runs from early January to early May. One 5-week undergraduate summer session and two 4-week graduate summer sessions are also offered. Orientation, preregistration, and academic advising by faculty members begin in the summer preceding entrance.

Students may receive credit for successful scores on the Advanced Placement examinations of the College Board, the College-Level Examination Program (CLEP), and special departmental tests. Through the honors program, highly qualified students have the opportunity to undertake advanced independent study.

Academic Facilities

Cumberland's campus contains twenty-five buildings ranging in architectural style from that of the early 1900s to modern. The science building features well-equipped biology, chemistry, and physics labs providing graduate-level research opportunities. Recent additions to the science facilities include a museum of natural history and a greenhouse.

The McGaw Music Building contains individual rehearsal and studio areas as well as a recital hall. The Norma Perkins Hagan Memorial Library houses more than 150,500 book titles, 1,630 periodical subscriptions, and 715,878 microform titles. Sophisticated computer equipment provides access to an additional 20 million or more items from many of the nation's outstanding libraries. The instructional media center includes a children's library, a computerized language lab, and a listening library.

Other special academic features include a computer center, an art gallery, a word processing center for English composition, a theater, the Counseling and Career Development Center, a 600-seat chapel, two large lecture halls, and the Distance Learning Laboratory.

Costs

For 2000–01, the basic academic-year expenses are $9698 for tuition, $4276 for room and board, $32 for a Student Government fee, and $190 for a technology fee, for a total of $14,196. There are no additional fees for out-of-state students. The average cost for books and supplies is approximately $250 per semester.

Financial Aid

Cumberland sponsors a large financial aid program that coordinates money from federal, state, private, and College sources. Last year, 90 percent of Cumberland students shared more than $15 million in aid.

To apply for financial aid, it is necessary to complete the Free Application for Federal Student Aid (FAFSA). For further information about financial aid opportunities, students should contact the director of financial aid at 800-532-0828. Applications made by March 15 are given priority for the fall semester.

Numerous scholarships and leadership grants are available.

Faculty

There are 95 full-time and 6 part-time faculty members who are respected scholars and whose primary responsibility is to teach. Courses are not taught by graduate assistants. The student-faculty ratio is 15:1, enabling students to receive ample attention and assistance from professors. Faculty members also serve as advisers to help students in planning their academic programs.

Student Government

The Student Government Association acts as a liaison between the students and the College administration. The organization also plans, implements, and governs various activities and special events each year to enhance the quality of campus social life. Members of the executive and legislative branches are elected by the student body.

Admission Requirements

In compliance with federal law, including provisions of Title IX of the Educational Amendments of 1972 and Section 504 of the Rehabilitation Act of 1973, Cumberland College does not illegally discriminate on the basis of race, sex, color, national or ethnic origin, age, disability, or military service in its administration of education policies, programs, or activities; admissions policies; or employment. Under federal law, the College may discriminate on the basis of religion in order to fulfill its purposes. The College reserves the right to discriminate on the basis of sex in its undergraduate admissions programs. Further, the College reserves the right to deny admission to any applicant whose academic preparation, character, or personal conduct is determined to be inconsistent with the purpose and objectives of the College. Where possible, the College will seek to reasonably accommodate a student's disability. However, the College's obligation to reasonably accommodate a student's disability ends where the accommodation would pose an undue hardship on the College or where the accommodation in question would fundamentally alter the academic program. Inquiries or complaints should be directed to the Vice President for Academic Affairs.

The purpose of the admission process is to identify applicants who are likely to succeed academically at Cumberland College and at the same time contribute positively to the campus community. The process considers such factors as high school records (including courses taken, grade trends, and rank in class), college records (if transferring from another institution), scores on the ACT or on the SAT I, application essay, letters of recommendation, extracurricular activities and honors, and personal contact.

Application and Information

Applicants for admission should contact the admissions office for an application form and return the completed form to the College, along with the appropriate application fee. Applicants should also have official transcripts of all high school and college work sent to the College, along with a copy of the ACT or SAT I scores. Each student is notified regarding official admission within ten working days after the application procedure has been completed.

Students accepted for admission must submit the required enrollment deposit.

Additional information may be obtained by contacting:

Office of Admissions
Cumberland College
Williamsburg, Kentucky 40769
Telephone: 606-539-4241
              800-343-1609 (toll-free)
E-mail: admiss@cc.cumber.edu.us
World Wide Web: http://www.cumber.edu

Students on the campus of Cumberland College.

CURRY COLLEGE
MILTON, MASSACHUSETTS

The College

The mission of Curry College, a private institution, is to develop liberally educated persons who are able to gain and to apply knowledge humanely, intelligently, and effectively in a complex, changing world. To achieve its mission, Curry College promotes individual intellectual and social growth by engaging its students in achieving these educational goals: thinking critically, communicating effectively, understanding context, appreciating aesthetic experience, defining a personal identity, examining value systems, and adapting and innovating. The College's curriculum and programs focus on the two hallmarks of the Curry education: a high respect for the individuality of every student and a developmental approach to learning that maximizes opportunities for achievement. One-on-one faculty-student relationships provide ample opportunities for personalized instruction and close interaction. Full student counseling and other support services are provided.

The current undergraduate enrollment is 1,200 men and women (full-time and part-time). Curry students have access to a wide range of cocurricular activities, including the Student Government Association, the student-run newspaper, the yearbook, the Curry *Arts Journal*, several organizations for the performing arts, and the award-winning, student-run radio station. The Office of Student Activities and the Student Program Board provide a variety of special events. A full schedule of men's and women's Division III and intramural sports is also provided. Varsity sports for men are baseball, basketball, football, ice hockey, lacrosse, soccer, and tennis; women's varsity sports are basketball, cross-country, lacrosse, soccer, softball, and tennis.

Now well into its second century of providing distinguished educational service, Curry College was founded in Boston in 1879. It was named in honor of its founders, Samuel Silas Curry and Anna Baright Curry. The College moved to its present site in Milton in 1952. In 1974, it absorbed the Perry Normal School, and, in 1977, it entered into a collaborative relationship with Children's Hospital Medical Center, which resulted in the establishment of Curry's Division of Nursing Studies. Curry College is accredited by the New England Association of Schools and Colleges; the nursing program is accredited by the National League for Nursing Accrediting Commission. Curry offers a Master of Education (M.Ed.) degree and a master's degree in criminal justice.

Location

Curry is ideally situated in Milton, Massachusetts, a largely residential suburb located near the exceptional resources of Boston. The Greater Boston area provides students with a diversity of cultural, educational, recreational, and sports activities. A wide variety of corporations, hospitals, agencies, broadcasting stations, and schools provide excellent opportunities for internships and jobs for Curry students. The College operates a shuttle bus to the MBTA trains, which provide easy access to Boston. Curry students have the benefit of a traditional, wooded New England campus and access to the excitement of a large city.

Majors and Degrees

Curry College awards the Bachelor of Arts (B.A.) and Bachelor of Science (B.S.) in nursing or health education degrees. Majors are biology (with a concentration in biochemistry), business management (with concentrations in accounting, entrepreneurship, finance and economics, human resources, marketing, and sports management), chemistry, communication (with concentrations in film studies, journalism, organizational communication, public communication, public relations, radio broadcasting, television, and theater), criminal justice, education (with concentrations in early childhood education, elementary education, moderate special needs, and preschool education), English (with a concentration in management communication), environmental science, health education, nursing, philosophy, physics, politics and history, psychology (with concentrations in counseling, education, and health), sociology (with concentrations in ethnic and gender studies and service in the community), and visual arts (with concentrations in graphic design and studio arts). Special minors are available in applied computing, dance, music, religion, Spanish, women's studies, and writing. Provision is also made for students to design majors in areas in which they have a special interest.

Academic Program

A central liberal arts curriculum, required for all students, incorporates a variety of academic disciplines into every student's plan of study. Curry's programs also integrate theoretical classroom learning with a wide variety of field internships in the Greater Boston area.

Curry College operates on a two-semester calendar with a summer session. To graduate, students must complete at least 120 credit hours for a B.A. degree or 121 credit hours for the B.S. In both cases, a minimum 2.0 cumulative average must be achieved.

Curry allows students to gain advanced standing in a variety of ways: through successful scores on College-Level Examination Program (CLEP) tests, through credit earned at other accredited colleges and universities, and through end-of-course proficiency examinations. Credit may also be granted for educational experiences that have occurred outside the traditional academic environment.

Many academic programs enrich and facilitate the Curry education. The Freshmen Seminar, the Honors Program, the Women's Studies Program, the Essential Skills Center, and the Field Experience Program are representative of that focus on special interests and diverse learning needs.

The Program for Advancement of Learning (PAL) is a credited program designed to assist intelligent, motivated language-learning-disabled students to achieve at the college level. PAL provides individual or small-group instruction, textbooks on tape, and untimed examinations, as well as other services. Students may take advantage of PAL's services throughout their college careers.

Off-Campus Arrangements

Curry students may earn up to 30 credits for field internships with outside firms, agencies, radio stations, hospitals, schools, or similar organizations. In consultation with faculty members, students develop learning contracts that articulate their educational and personal goals and establish criteria for the evaluation of their field experience. Students may also arrange to study abroad or at another institution within the United States while enrolled at Curry.

Academic Facilities

The Levin Memorial Library houses more than 110,000 volumes, 650 periodicals, and 10,000 microforms. It is a designated depository for U.S. government documents. The library also houses the Essential Skills Center, where students may secure assistance in reading, writing, mathematics, and the development of study skills. Three computer laboratories contain more than 100 Macintosh and IBM computers, laser printers, color printers, and state-of-the-art optical scanning equipment. The entire campus is networked and linked to the Internet.

The Science Building includes five laboratories. Kennedy Academic Center houses a simulated hospital room for use as a nursing laboratory, the Nursing Resource Center equipped with an interactive video lab, and a laboratory for experimental psychology equipped with biofeedback, computer control, and animal and human learning facilities. The Learning Center, with its own computer lab, maintains a complete tape library of all textbooks used at the College. The Hafer Academic Center houses the Experiential Education Office, the Career Planning and Placement Office, the Academic Advising Office, the Educational Technology Center, and the Parents Lounge, which features student art exhibits. In addition, Curry students operate and maintain WMLN-FM, the College's 170-watt Class A FM station.

Costs

Tuition for the 1999–2000 academic year was $16,500. Room was $3490, and board was $2820 (fourteen-meal plan). The cost of the Program for Advancement of Learning was $3575. The cost of books, supplies, and personal expenses was $900 to $1100.

Financial Aid

Curry provides financial assistance for students who need funding in order to attend college. The financial aid program consists of federal, state, and Curry College scholarships, grants, work-study awards, student assistant jobs, and loans. Approximately 60 percent of the student body receive financial aid. All students applying for financial aid must submit the Free Application for Federal Student Aid (FAFSA) and the Curry College financial aid application to the Financial Aid Office by March 1. Students applying for financial aid should contact the director of financial aid.

Faculty

There are 81 full-time faculty members at Curry, many of whom hold earned doctorates. In addition, each year the College hires highly qualified part-time faculty members and visiting lecturers to augment its teaching staff. While Curry's is primarily a teaching faculty, many members are engaged in writing, research, and consulting.

Student Government

The general purpose of the Student Government Association (SGA) is the advancement of the College community and the promotion of the general welfare of the students. The SGA seeks to increase student involvement in the formulation of College policies, to communicate effectively with all constituencies of the College, and to promote student participation within the institution. Members of the SGA serve on the Joint Committee on Communication of the Board of Trustees.

Admission Requirements

Curry College accepts all students who have the necessary preparation and educational background to meet the requirements of the College, regardless of race, religion, national or ethnic origin, age, sex, sexual orientation, or physical handicap. Freshman students are selected on the basis of a combination of the following: secondary school record, scores on the SAT I or ACT, recommendation of the secondary school, and the candidate's readiness for college. To be considered for admission, students must generally present at least 16 units of high school work from an approved secondary school. A recommended program of studies includes 4 years of English, at least 3 years of mathematics, 2 years of a foreign language, 2 years of science (including at least 1 of a laboratory science), and 2 years of social studies. Applicants should contact the Admissions Office to discuss any possible exceptions to these requirements. Nursing applicants are required to have taken high school biology and chemistry. A GED certificate is acceptable in lieu of a high school diploma. Curry College seeks well-rounded students who can contribute to the Curry community in athletic, artistic, and social endeavors as well as in the academic sphere.

Application and Information

Curry's recommended application deadline is April 1. Applicants to the learning disability program (PAL) must apply by March 1. Students are accepted on a rolling basis. Admission options, such as early decision, deferred entrance, and advanced placement, are also available. Students may apply for September or January entrance. Applicants must submit an application and fee, an official high school transcript, scores on the SAT I or ACT, and a counselor's recommendation. In addition, transfer students must submit official college transcripts, and international students must submit results of the Test of English as a Foreign Language (TOEFL). An interview is recommended. The Admissions Committee evaluates each application as soon as all required credentials are received, beginning in January.

Applicants to the Program for Advancement of Learning must submit the application and fee, an official high school transcript, a counselor's recommendation, and the results of a recently administered Wechsler Adult Intelligence Scale (WAIS-R) test. Achievement testing in reading comprehension, written language, and math must also be submitted. Final decisions on admission to the program are made once all credentials are complete.

For more information about Curry College, students should contact:

Michael Poll
Dean of Admission and Financial Aid
Curry College
Milton, Massachusetts 02186
Telephone: 617-333-2210
           800-669-0686 (toll-free)
Fax: 617-333-2114
E-mail: curryadm@curry.edu
World Wide Web: http://www.curry.edu:8080

The suburban campus of Curry College is only minutes from the city of Boston.

DAEMEN COLLEGE
AMHERST, NEW YORK

The College

At Daemen College, degree and student service programs are distinctly designed for the career-minded student. With a student body of 1,800, a low student-faculty ratio (15:1) is maintained in the belief that small classes encourage a better exchange of ideas and knowledge and promote the quality education for which the College is known. Providing more than forty career-oriented majors, this private, four-year, liberal arts college is located on 39 acres in Amherst, New York (a suburb of Buffalo). Daemen's small, friendly campus offers a large selection of cultural, social, fraternal, athletic, and service groups to enrich the college experience, as well as the amenities of a big community nearby. Buffalo offers outstanding cultural and recreational resources plus exciting major-league sports.

On-campus housing is available to all students at any time. A complex of twenty-three modern, two-story apartment-type buildings provides separate housing for men and women; there is also a five-story residence hall for women. The services of the Academic Computing and Resource Center and the Career Development, Health Services, Placement, and Cooperative Education Offices, as well as the Campus Ministry, are always available. Daemen has few architectural barriers; handicapped men and women using wheelchairs find it easy to move throughout the campus.

Along with its bachelor degree programs, the College offers Master of Science degrees in adult nurse practitioner studies, palliative care, physician assistant studies, physical therapy, and special education.

Location

Daemen is located on a 39-acre campus in Amherst, New York, a northern suburb of Buffalo. The campus is easily accessible by the major rail, plane, and motor routes that serve the city of Buffalo. The combination of a beautiful and safe campus and proximity to a bustling city is a definite asset. The area has a rich variety of participatory and spectator sports that range from skiing and swimming to major-league football. The wide range of cultural resources includes the Philharmonic Orchestra, the Albright-Knox Art Gallery, and the Studio Arena Theater. Buffalo, the second-largest city in New York State, is the focal point of the Niagara Frontier, an area that offers many historic and scenic points of interest. The metropolitan facilities offer opportunities in educational, cultural, business, and scientific areas. The many trees and wide open spaces on Daemen's suburban campus are a nice contrast to the nearby cities. Niagara Falls is a short 30-minute drive, and Toronto is only 2 hours away.

Majors and Degrees

Daemen College offers programs that lead to the Bachelor of Arts (B.A.), the Bachelor of Fine Arts (B.F.A.), and the Bachelor of Science (B.S.) degrees. Majors include accounting, art, art education, biology, business administration, business education, business weekend program, chemistry, communications/public relations, drawing/illustration, early childhood, elementary education, English, environmental studies, French, global economics, graphic design, health systems management, history and government, humanities, human resource management, human services, international business, marketing, mathematics, medical technology, natural sciences, nursing, operations management, painting/sculpture, physical therapy, physician assistant studies, predentistry, prelaw, premedicine, pre-veterinary, printmaking, psychology, religious studies, secondary education, social work, Spanish, special education, sport management, travel and tourism, and undeclared/Horizons 2000.

Academic Program

The academic program followed by Daemen College was chosen to provide liberal breadth and great depth simultaneously. This plan is marked by four characteristics: (1) a generous number of courses in the major field; (2) the building of a sequential set of courses in this field so that knowledge is acquired according to a logical progression; (3) a reading list course in the junior year, in which the student reads widely in his or her particular field; and (4) a coordinating seminar in the senior year, which provides an interdisciplinary approach and relates the student's concentration to other components of the curriculum.

A minimum of 122 semester hours is required for a baccalaureate degree. One semester hour represents a lecture period of 50 minutes each week throughout a semester of fifteen weeks or a laboratory or studio period of 100 minutes each week throughout a semester of fifteen weeks.

Off-Campus Arrangements

Internships in various areas, including Washington, D.C., are available for students who major in history and government. Fieldwork at community social service agencies is an option for the psychology or social work major. Internships are available at area hospitals for outstanding applied science students. All students have the opportunity to study in Mexico and Montreal or spend an academic year abroad through the Junior Year Abroad Program. An international studies minor can be combined with most areas of study, and all students can take advantage of travel programs.

Cross-registration arrangements with other colleges and universities enable students to take courses for credit at twenty nearby colleges.

Job search workshops are offered to provide students with the opportunity to write professional resumes and cover letters and to practice effective interviewing and job search techniques.

Through Daemen's Cooperative Education Program, students gain hands-on experience in their chosen field while completing their degree. Academic credit is received for working, many times along with a salary. The program gives students the opportunity to relate classroom theory to actual work experience and, most importantly, enables them to acquire the workplace values that are basic for all career preparations.

Full- or part-time experiences are available in all areas of study, with placements available throughout New York and all over the United States. Co-op assignments include positions in business and industry, banks, hospitals, social service agencies, government agencies, schools and colleges, and cultural organizations. Field placements are incorporated into some of the College's degree programs, including the courses of study in medical technology, physical therapy, and social work.

Academic Facilities

The College's modern library has more than 139,000 volumes, more than 950 periodical subscriptions, a wide selection of musical scores and records, and a complete collection of American Enterprise Institute monographs. A learning resources center augments the library. Art department facilities include ten large studios and one of the largest bronze-casting foundries of any college in the country. Students of French and Spanish find a well-equipped language laboratory in the main classroom building. The beautiful and modern Business Building houses all of the business classrooms, including breakout rooms, which are used for smaller discussion groups. There is also a computer lab, which has fifty Pentium (IBM compatible) computers. All of the business faculty and staff offices are conveniently located on the second floor.

Costs

For 1999–2000, tuition was $11,800, and room and board were $6100. The College fee is $320 per year. It is estimated that an additional $300 per semester for personal expenses enables students to enjoy a typical campus life.

Financial Aid

Daemen believes that students should be able to choose the college that offers the best range of educational opportunities. They should not have to select one simply because its tuition is lower than another. The College, therefore, makes a conscious effort to award financial assistance in three ways: (1) based upon academic achievement, (2) based upon academic achievement and financial need, (3) based upon financial need. Ninety-two percent of all Daemen College students receive financial aid through the New York State Tuition Assistance Program, scholarships and grants, work-study awards, or loans, with the average award totaling about $6200. Daemen College participates in all federal and state financial aid programs and has private sources of scholarship monies to award to eligible students.

Faculty

Class size ranges from about 20 to 30 students, enabling faculty members to get to know the interests and goals of each student. There are 151 full- and part-time faculty members, 81 percent of whom hold terminal degrees.

Student Government

Through the elected Student Governing Board, students are responsible for all nonacademic matters that affect their life at the College. Students serve on advisory committees to the president, the academic dean, and others within the College community.

Admission Requirements

Students applying to Daemen College should have completed four years of college-preparatory studies in secondary school; however, Daemen considers applications from students who have completed only three years and have demonstrated academic strength and social and personal maturity.

Application and Information

For application forms, a catalog, or further information, students should contact:

Maria P. Dillard
Dean of Enrollment Management
Daemen College
4380 Main Street
Amherst, New York 14226
Telephone: 716-839-8225
          800-462-7652 (toll-free in New York, New Jersey, and Pennsylvania)
E-mail: admissions@daemen.edu
World Wide Web: http://www.daemen.edu

While Daemen College is small enough so that all students receive individual attention, it still offers a broad range of programs and facilities.

DALHOUSIE UNIVERSITY
HALIFAX, NOVA SCOTIA, CANADA

The University

Consistently rated as one of the top ten universities in Canada, Dalhousie University offers students quality and tradition in their university education. Founded in 1818, Dalhousie is older than Canada. It is a publicly funded, nondenominational university accredited by the Association of Universities and Colleges of Canada (AUCC) and the Association of Commonwealth Universities (ACU).

Dalhousie is a midsized university with an enrollment of approximately 13,000 students (10,000 undergraduate and 3,000 professional and graduate students). Competitive with much larger universities, Dalhousie offers a wide array of programmes, which means that students benefit from a rich academic environment while enjoying easy access to faculty members and student services. The faculty-student ratio is 1:12.

Dalhousie University is very proud of its long tradition of excellence and leadership. Students go on to assume professional and leadership roles on both the regional and national stage. The range of programmes and (in particular) the obligations assumed for professional and graduate education give Dalhousie a unique role in higher education in Nova Scotia and in the Maritime region. This special niche expanded dramatically in 1997 with the amalgamation of Dalhousie and the Technical University of Nova Scotia (TUNS). This union helps position the province of Nova Scotia as a leader in advanced technical education and research. It opens doors to more students and faculty members, and it establishes the institution as a place where 179 years of history blend with exciting new opportunities for the twenty-first century.

In addition to being a top-ranked Canadian university, particularly for its small class size in students' third and fourth years, Dalhousie offers a variety of student services ranging from career counselling and workshops on exam anxiety to international student advising and support. Students can live in traditional dormitory-style residences, apartment-style houses and buildings, or in the variety of apartments in the residential area surrounding the campus. An off-campus housing office helps students locate apartments nearby.

On the social front, students can participate in varsity and intramural sports, join one of 100 clubs and societies, or get involved in student government. There are many opportunities to meet other Dalhousie students. The International Student Association, with membership from more than eighty countries, provides opportunities to meet new friends and share experiences.

Location

Halifax is the capital city of Nova Scotia and, with a metropolitan-area population of approximately 350,000, can offer students a varied social life. American students like the relaxed East Coast lifestyle, but they still have access to restaurants, movies, pubs, and a variety of cultural activities that provide a range of offerings for all budgets. Halifax is safe and clean, and there are several parks within the city.

Dalhousie's campus is within walking distance of the downtown area. Students enjoy the proximity of services to the campus. There are a metro transit bus system and an out-of-town bus and train service. Getting there is easy: Halifax has an international airport with daily flights to the U.S. and other international destinations. For students in New England, a seasonal ferry service operates daily from Portland and Bar Harbor, Maine. Halifax is an hour and a half by air from Boston and about 2 hours from New York.

Majors and Degrees

Students can complete a variety of degrees in architecture, business, computer science, engineering, law, liberal arts, social sciences, sciences, and health professions.

Within the Faculty of Arts and Social Sciences, students can complete a Bachelor of Arts, Bachelor of Music, or a Diploma/Advanced Diploma in Costume Studies.

Majors available in the Bachelor of Arts include Canadian studies, classics, comparative religion, English, French, German, history, international development studies, linguistics, music, philosophy, political science, Russian studies, sociology and social anthropology, Spanish, theatre, and women's studies. A minor in business administration is also available in any of the above majors.

Within the Faculty of Science, students can complete a Bachelor of Science or Diploma in Meteorology.

Majors available in the Bachelor of Science include biochemistry*, biology, chemistry*, computing science*, earth sciences, economics*, marine biology*, mathematics*, microbiology and immunology, neuroscience, physics*, psychology, and statistics*. A minor in business administration is also available in the above majors.

Within the Faculty of Health Professions, students can complete a Bachelor of Science in recreation or recreation management, Bachelor of Science in health education, Bachelor of Science in kinesiology, Bachelor of Science in nursing, Bachelor of Science in occupational therapy, Bachelor of Science in pharmacy, Bachelor of Science in physiotherapy, Bachelor of Social Work, Diploma in Health Services Administration, and Diploma in Outpost and Community Health Nursing. For the programmes in occupation therapy, pharmacy, and physiotherapy, preference is given to residents of Atlantic Canada.

Within the Faculty of Management, students can complete a Bachelor of Commerce Co-operative (work-study programme), Bachelor of Management, and Diploma in Public Administration.

Within the Faculty of Engineering, students can complete a Bachelor of Engineering. Majors available include biological* (including biosystems and environmental), chemical*, civil*, electrical* (including computer engineering), industrial*, mechanical*, metallurgical*, and mining* engineering.

Within the Faculty of Computer Science, students can complete a Bachelor of Computer Science Co-operative (work-study programme) or a Bachelor of Science with a major in computer science*.

Within the Faculty of Architecture, students can complete a Bachelor of Environmental Design Studies. Within the Faculty of Medicine, students can complete a Bachelor of Science (medicine) or a Doctor of Medicine. Within the Faculty of Law, students can complete a Bachelor of Laws. Within the Faculty of Dentistry, students can complete a Diploma in Dental Hygiene or Doctor of Dental Surgery.

Programmes followed by an * have a cooperative (a combined work-study programme) option available.

Academic Programmes

Students work with their faculty advisers to have their academic programme tailored to their career needs and personal tastes. While each programme has a core of required classes, students are encouraged to choose their electives from liberal arts, social sciences, science, and business.

Cooperative degrees in science generally take five years to complete. Students do not choose their major in the first year. This is done after consultation with an academic adviser upon completion of five credits.

Students applying from other colleges or universities should indicate their intended major on the application form.

Off-Campus Arrangements

Dalhousie participates in a number of exchange programmes with universities in Spain, Mexico, France, Germany, Russia, Sweden, the Commonwealth countries, and the United States.There are fifty exchange/volunteer/work abroad programs available. Advisers in the Registrar's Office help students with this process.

Academic Facilities

Students have access to a range of resources. The Dalhousie University Library consists of the Killam Library, the Sir James Dunn Law Library, the Kellogg Health Sciences Library, and the DalTech Library. The library system is linked with Novanet, a computerized listing of the library holdings of all local universities that gives students access to well over 1.7 million bound volumes.

Computer use is widespread in all academic programmes of study. Undergraduate departments aim to enhance computer fluency regardless of programme choice. There are several computer laboratories (PC and Mac) located throughout the campus, providing students easy access to computers. Dalhousie is linked to the Canadian Universities network, CaNet, and is the hub for Internet service in Nova Scotia.

Students have access to modern laboratories, an aquatron, two electron microscopes, a SLOWPOKE nuclear reactor, the Trace Analysis Research Centre (TARC), and a museum of natural sciences. A language laboratory, a Math Learning Centre, and a variety of other academic workshops (for example, a writing skills workshop) are available to all students.

Costs

In 1999–2000, non-Canadian students paid $7337 for tuition (including a differential fee of $3090; specific cost varies per programme), $5065 for lodging and food, approximately $800 for books, and $416 for health insurance. (All costs are in Canadian dollars.)

Dalhousie's unique Student Employment Assistance programme provides on-campus jobs for students. American students can apply for jobs under this programme, which permits them to work for up to 10 hours per week.

Financial Aid

All applicants from secondary schools are automatically considered for merit-based scholarship awards when they apply. Scholarships range from Can$500 (entrance) to Can$7000 (renewable). The deadline for scholarship consideration is March 15.

Dalhousie University is recognized by both Canadian and American student aid agencies. A bursary or grant programme exists. International students would normally qualify only in emergency situations since, as a requirement for a student visa, students must be able to show evidence of adequate financial support.

Faculty

Dalhousie University has more than 1,000 faculty members, more than 70 percent of whom hold a Ph.D. Professors keep office hours and encourage students to schedule appointments. Professors have an open-door policy for students.

Student Government

The Dalhousie Student Union (DSU) represents students to the University's administration and also organizes social functions, cultural events, and guest speakers for the University community. Elections are held annually for executive positions; many DSU positions carry honorariums. With an operating budget of more than $1 million, the DSU is housed in the Student Union Building (SUB), which offers a number of services to students such as council offices, a radio station, a student newspaper, Lawson Career Centre, restaurants, a game room, and a pub.

Admission Requirements

High school applicants should have a strong academic programme with a minimum B+ average. Applicants must also submit SAT scores. A minimum combined SAT I score of 1100 is required. SAT II requirements are under review.

Students transferring from a college or university must have at least a C+ average. Admission to some majors is particularly competitive. Applicants should provide calendar descriptions for transfer credit assessment.

Since requirements vary among faculties, students are encouraged to contact admissions in the Registrar's Office for information.

Parents, counsellors, students, and student groups are invited to visit the Dalhousie campus. A campus tour may include a visit with an admissions officer, observation of classes in session, and a tour of University facilities and buildings.

Applications and Information

Students are encouraged to apply by March 1 for early admission consideration. The general deadline for applications is July 1, although some programmes have earlier deadlines. International students outside the U.S. or Canada must apply by April 1.

Enrolment limits do not exist for international students.

To contact the Registrar's Office:

Registrar's Office
Dalhousie University
Halifax, Nova Scotia B3H 4H6
Canada
Telephone: 902-494-2450
E-mail: admissions@dal.ca
World Wide Web: http://www.Dal.Ca

Numerous older, attractive buildings are part of the Dalhousie campus.

DALLAS CHRISTIAN COLLEGE
DALLAS, TEXAS

The College
Located in the north Dallas suburb of Farmers Branch, Dallas Christian College (DCC) is one of the fastest-growing colleges in the area. Graduates of the institution can be found in ministries all across the country and around the globe. Dallas Christian College prepares students for Christian leadership in the church, community, and world.

As a Christian college, DCC understands the need for the integration of the Bible into every area of life. All of the courses are taught by professors who have clear biblical principles guiding them both in the classroom and in their personal lives. The College's ultimate goal is to develop Christian leadership in students.

Dallas Christian College is accredited by the Accrediting Association of Bible Colleges (AABC). While the College's primary support base is the Independent Christian Church, DCC is a nondenominational school, with more than a dozen denominations represented in the student body. Dallas Christian College is a small family in a big city. The enrollment is 300 students, triple the enrollment of only four years ago.

There are a variety of social, athletic, and cultural opportunities available. In terms of intercollegiate sports, Dallas Christian College is a member of the NCCAA and NBCAA. The primary sports offerings are men's and women's basketball, men's and women's soccer, and women's volleyball. There are a variety of intramural opportunities as well. The Student Council offers a full selection of service and social projects throughout the year.

Campus housing is provided in dormitories built in a suite format. In addition, there is a full-service cafeteria available to all residential students.

Students may be involved in many ministry opportunities. Among them are some that are officially recognized by the College. Ministry Team is a group of students who travel to church and youth functions with the expressed purpose of teaching the gospel of Jesus Christ. A variety of formats, such as drama, teaching, and music, are used. Urban Team is a select group of students who go into the inner city of Dallas and strive for evangelistic excellence and racial harmony. This group of students was recognized by the North American Christian Convention's Urban Task Force as one of the most productive and evangelistic groups in the country. Worship Team is a music group that travels to church and youth functions in order to lead in worship and bring musical presentations.

Location
Farmers Branch, a quiet suburb of Dallas, is close to anything a student might wish to do in the Dallas–Fort Worth metroplex. The campus is just minutes from the downtown cultural district, which includes the Biblical Arts Center, the Meyerson Symphony Center, and the infamous Dallas Book Depository. There are many concerts at Reunion Arena, the Bronco Bowl, and the Dallas Zoo Amphitheater. Major professional sports teams are nearby, including the NFL Dallas Cowboys, the NHL Dallas Stars, the MLB Texas Rangers, the NBA Dallas Mavericks, the PISL Dallas Sidekicks, and the MLS Dallas Burn.

Majors and Degrees
Dallas Christian College's educational programs seek to produce graduates who take leadership in ministry, management, music, and classroom education.

To fulfill institutional goals, the College offers both Bachelor of Arts (B.A.) and Bachelor of Science (B.S.) degrees with double majors. Degrees are offered in Bible and preaching, business administration, Christian education, cross-cultural missions, general studies, management and ethics (adult and continuing education), ministry and leadership (adult and continuing education), music, psychology, teacher education, and youth and family ministries. All degrees reflect the College's conviction that knowledge of Scripture is basic to education. DCC meets the AABC requirements of a balanced curriculum in Bible, general education, practical ministries, and specialized studies.

Academic Program
Dallas Christian College's academic calendar is based on two semesters, each composed of sixteen weeks of classes, including one week of finals. Courses are offered on a credit-hour basis.

Eighteen credit hours are usually considered the maximum load. To complete a bachelor's degree (130 credit hours) in four years, the student should take 16 to 17 credit hours each semester. A class load of 12 credit hours or more constitutes a full-time load; fewer than 12 credit hours constitute a part-time load, with 7 to 11 credit hours considered a ¾-time load for financial aid purposes. Unless the student's program calls for more than 18 credit hours in a semester, special permission to enroll in additional courses beyond this maximum must be secured through the student's adviser and the Vice President for Academic Affairs. Certain courses in which outside assignments are minimal, such as choir and physical education, require additional class time, labs, or practice time for the credit hours awarded.

Those who must work to help meet college expenses should plan to reduce their credit-hour load. It is recommended that students who work more than 12 hours per week reduce their study load 1 credit hour for each 3 hours of self-support work.

Dallas Christian College welcomes a variety of students of all ages to the campus; many students bring a depth of knowledge to specific subjects. The College recognizes and honors such knowledge by accepting the following examinations through which a student may earn credit: the College-Level Examination Program (CLEP), the Defense Activity for Non-Traditional Education Support (DANTES), and the Advanced Placement (AP) examinations. Assuming that an acceptable grade is attained on an examination, the College grants full degree credit. CLEP, DANTES, and AP credits are accepted for transfer students as well.

Off-Campus Arrangements
In order to graduate with a degree from Dallas Christian College, students must complete an internship in the area of intended service. If a student wants to go into youth ministry, there is a requirement of one summer (or equivalent time) under the tutelage of an experienced professional youth minister.

There are other opportunities off campus, including trips abroad to such places as Israel, Turkey, Mexico, and Europe for class credit.

Academic Facilities

The C. C. Crawford Memorial Library honors the memory of Dr. Cecil Clement Crawford, who, with Mrs. Helen Crawford, came to Dallas Christian College in August 1967. A popular professor during his years at DCC, Dr. Crawford was an honored scholar, educator, preacher, and writer. Before his death in 1976, Dr. Crawford donated his personal library to the College.

The Crawford Memorial Library contains a computer lab with Internet access; electronic databases, which are continually updated on CD-ROM; online database searching; and document delivery. There are also 27,500 volumes, 270 subscribed periodicals, and more than 2,000 audiotapes and videotapes on site.

Costs

The 2000–01 cost for tuition is $190 per credit hour. Room and board charges are $1950 per semester. All freshmen are required to live on campus and participate in the meal plan unless they are living at home with parents or a legal guardian in the Dallas–Fort Worth metroplex.

Financial Aid

Dallas Christian College provides a financial aid program to assist students who need additional resources to meet their educational costs. Students who qualify may be eligible for institutional scholarships and grants based on their talent in the areas of academics and music or on their financial need. Students may also qualify for assistance through federal grant, work, or loan programs. Students applying for financial aid must file the Free Application for Federal Student Aid (FAFSA) and submit an institutional financial aid form to the Financial Aid Offices.

Faculty

Small class sizes (most classes have fewer than 25 students) combined with a teaching rather than research faculty ensure students of personal, high-quality instruction. Eighty percent of full-time faculty members either hold or are completing their doctorates; the student-faculty ratio is 10:1. These elements combined translate into excellent teaching and personal attention. Another advantage of DCC's faculty is that professors are practitioners in their fields—they come with background and experience from the real world, not just from classroom textbooks. This element offers practical, relevant training for students. Faculty members also serve as advisers and mentors to students. They take a sincere and active role in the personal, academic, and spiritual lives of the students.

Student Government

The Student Council (StuCo) of Dallas Christian College represents all registered students. Officers are chosen annually from within the student body and serve through the Student Council. Voicing the concerns and needs of the students to the College administration and providing opportunities for fun and fellowship are at the core of StuCo.

Admission Requirements

Applicants are evaluated on the basis of academic ability, character, and Christian commitment. Those applying are expected to have a high school diploma or the equivalent with a satisfactory grade point average. Students applying as first-time freshmen or those with fewer than 12 transfer credits should submit the Application for Admission, a high school transcript, SAT I or ACT scores, and two letters of recommendation. Students applying for transfer admission should submit the Application for Admission, all college transcripts, and two letters of recommendation.

Home school students are welcome to apply for admission by following the application procedures listed above. A GED diploma may be required of a home school student at the discretion of the Admissions Committee if there is evidence of a discrepancy between the high school transcript and the standardized test scores.

Application and Information

For a viewsheet or catalog, students should contact:

Office of Enrollment Management
Dallas Christian College
2700 Christian Parkway
Dallas, Texas 75234-7299
Telephone: 972-241-3371 Ext. 153
               800-688-1029 (toll-free)
Fax: 972-241-8021
E-mail: dcc@dallas.edu
World Wide Web: http://www.dallas.edu

DANIEL WEBSTER COLLEGE
NASHUA, NEW HAMPSHIRE

The College

Daniel Webster College (DWC) prepares its students for individual excellence through a commitment to individual attention. The College's innovative curriculums in aviation, business/management, computer science, information systems, sport management, and engineering equip students with the knowledge and skills necessary to become tomorrow's industry leaders.

Daniel Webster College is accredited by the New England Association of Schools and Colleges and is a member of the New Hampshire College and University Council. The College holds Federal Aviation Administration Air Agency Certification PSE 15-21 as an approved pilot school. Courses are operated under Part 141 and Part 61 of the FAA regulations.

There is a diverse student population at Daniel Webster College, with twenty-five states and eight countries currently represented. A variety of living options promote comfort and enjoyment. Residential students are housed in four residence halls and in contemporary town house-style apartments on campus. The College Center houses the dining hall, the After Hours Café, the Center for Career Planning and Placement, and the Student Government and Student Life Offices. Movies, dances, and other special events are held at The Common Thread, which contains equipment for pool, darts, and foosball and houses a coffee bar. The Mario J. Vagge Gymnasium has facilities for volleyball and basketball and a weight room. There are plenty of extracurricular activities, including the Student Activities Board, the student newspaper and yearbook, the Jazz Band, the Flight Team, the Professional Pilots Association, a variety of intramural athletics, and other exciting programs. The Leadership Initiative and Student Life Office annually bring nationally renowned speakers and visual performing artists to campus. A rigorous two- and four-year Air Force ROTC program is also available.

Home to the Eagles, Daniel Webster College's men's and women's sports teams compete in the Greater Northeast Athletic Conference at the NCAA Division III level. Men's sports include baseball, basketball, cross-country, golf, lacrosse, and soccer. Women compete in basketball, cross-country, softball, and volleyball. Ice hockey, and skiing are currently available as intercollegiate club sports.

Location

The College is conveniently located in southern New Hampshire in Nashua, the state's second-largest city and twice named "America's Best Place to Live." The city's municipal airport is adjacent to the campus. Nashua is home to a symphony orchestra, theater guild, arts center, and several fine restaurants, shopping areas, and craft centers. Several Fortune 500 companies are nearby, providing employment and internships.

Boston is just 36 miles to the south, and Manchester, New Hampshire, is 20 minutes to the north. Excellent skiing, snowboarding, hiking, and boating and the scenic New Hampshire seacoast are all within an hour's drive.

Majors and Degrees

Daniel Webster College awards Bachelor of Science degrees in aviation/air traffic management, aviation flight operations (professional pilot training), aviation management, computer science, information systems, management and information technology, management and leadership, and sport management.

Associate in Science degrees are awarded in aeronautical engineering, aviation operations, engineering science, general studies, and information systems.

Academic Program

The College operates on a semester system. Courses are designed to provide the highest quality educational opportunities. Independent study, a customized internship program, and advanced-placement programs are available to qualified students. The College is known for its commitment to individual attention.

The College's Aviation Division provides one of the country's most innovative and respected aviation programs and is one of only a few to introduce glider and aerobatic flight into its educational programs. Students can qualify for private single-engine, private glider, instrument, commercial, multiengine, and instructor ratings. A student instructor internship is available to qualified juniors and seniors.

Academic Facilities

Daniel Webster Hall houses several classrooms, laboratories, the College Store, and administrative and faculty offices. The 25,000-square-foot Anne Bridge Baddour Library and Learning Center houses the College's extensive library, the Academic Support Center, and two computer labs. There are also conference and seminar rooms, audiovisual labs, classrooms, and staff offices. The computer facilities include a DUAL PIII 500 PC and RATIONAL APEX and ROSE software, served by a Silicon Graphics Origin 2000 as part of the College's effort and commitment to simulate the professional software engineering environment. The new Eaton-Richmond Building houses offices, multimedia classrooms, and a 350-seat auditorium and features five new state-of-the-art computer labs.

The Tamposi Aviation Center is directly adjacent to Nashua Airport, with its 5,500-foot paved and lighted runway and operating control tower. The College's fleet of aircraft includes Cessna 172 Trainers, Grob G109B motorgliders, Mudry CAP-10 aerobatic trainers, Mooney 201 complex aircraft, and Cessna 303 multiengine Crusaders. The Center is fully equipped with a flight dispatch area, classrooms, offices, and a lab with single- and twin-engine Aviation Simulation Technology flight simulators. It is one of the few aviation schools with its own Air Traffic Control simulators.

Costs

Tuition for 1999–2000 was $15,330. Residence costs, including room and board, were $6001. Books, supplies, and miscellaneous personal expenses were estimated at $2100. There are some fees associated with flight activities. There are no laboratory fees.

Financial Aid

The College is committed to helping students it deems qualified to make a Daniel Webster College education a reality. It offers more than $2 million annually in a variety of financial assistance programs based on analysis of the Free Application for Federal Student Aid (FAFSA), which can be obtained through high school guidance offices. DWC also offers four-year renewable academic performance scholarships to students exhibiting high academic achievement through high school GPA and other test scores. These scholarships range from $500 to $7500. More than 90 percent of the students at Daniel Webster College receive some form of financial assistance.

In addition to providing aid through its own scholarship and work programs, the College administers both federal and local financial assistance programs. For more information, students should call or write the Director of Financial Assistance at the College.

Faculty

The student-faculty ratio at Daniel Webster College is 12:1. This provides the opportunity for individual attention and instruction, tutoring, and advising. While scholarship is encouraged and applauded, the prime focus of the faculty is quality teaching.

Student Government

The Student Activities Board and Office of Student Life coordinate a wide variety of student activities. Student Government represents students' views and facilitates meaningful dialog between the students and the College administration.

Admission Requirements

A student who has graduated from an accredited high school program will be considered for admission. The SAT I or ACT is required for all students interested in earning a Bachelor of Science degree. Consideration is based on high school performance and a letter of recommendation. Transfer students may be admitted to the September and January semesters. Admission decisions are made without regard to race, color, creed, sex, physical handicap, or national origin.

Although not required for acceptance, a personal admission interview is strongly recommended. A campus visit, including an optional tour by air, provides an important opportunity to gain valuable firsthand knowledge of Daniel Webster College.

Application and Information

The application fee is $35. The College operates on a rolling admission basis, and students are notified of a decision within two weeks after their file is complete. Interested students are urged to arrange a campus visit while the College is in session.

For further information, please contact:

Office of Admissions
Daniel Webster College
20 University Drive
Nashua, New Hampshire 03063-1300
Telephone: 603-577-6600
              800-325-6876 (toll-free)
Fax: 603-577-6001
E-mail: admissions@dwc.edu
World Wide Web: http://www.dwc.edu

Daniel Webster College is located in Nashua, New Hampshire—the only city in America twice rated "Number One Place to Live" by *Money* magazine.

DARTMOUTH COLLEGE
HANOVER, NEW HAMPSHIRE

The College

Dartmouth, America's ninth-oldest college, is rich in history and tradition. Founded in 1769 by the Reverend Eleazar Wheelock "for the education . . . of Youth of Indian Tribes, . . . English youth, and others," Dartmouth graduated its first class in 1771. The institution met its greatest challenge in 1819 when Daniel Webster, class of 1801, defended the College against government intervention. This famous dispute, which was finally resolved in the Supreme Court, came to be known as "The Dartmouth College Case." It was Webster's eloquent and convincing oratory that ensured Dartmouth's permanence as a private and independent institution of higher learning. Still appropriately called a college in view of its historic and continuing emphasis on undergraduate education, Dartmouth is actually a small university. Students aspiring to careers in medicine, business, or engineering may find special opportunities at Dartmouth's three professional schools: Dartmouth Medical School, the nation's fourth-oldest school of medicine; the Amos Tuck School of Business Administration, the nation's first graduate school of business administration; and the Thayer School of Engineering, founded more than a century ago.

Undergraduate education provided by an outstanding faculty dedicated to both teaching and research is at the heart of Dartmouth. The College seeks students of outstanding abilities who display curiosity and great intellectual potential and who bring to the community their particular talents and passions. Dartmouth strives for a heterogeneous student body representative of the world's diversity. The College's 4,300 undergraduates represent all fifty states and sixty-two other nations.

All first-year students and a majority of upperclass students live in forty dormitories, all within easy walking distance of other College buildings and facilities. College housing is provided for all registered students, and dormitories contain a mixture of all four classes; no dormitories are reserved for freshmen only. All freshmen and many upperclass students maintain meal contracts through Dartmouth Dining Services.

Dartmouth offers a myriad of extracurricular activities, including more than 250 student organizations. Students participate in theater, music, dance, a daily newspaper, literary publications, student-run AM and FM radio stations, debate, foreign language clubs, service groups, fraternities and sororities, and ethnic, political, and religious organizations. Through the Dartmouth Outing Club, students enjoy bicycling, canoeing, hiking, kayaking, mountaineering, skiing, and other benefits of the North Country. Dartmouth's comprehensive athletics program includes thirty-four men's and women's varsity teams, extensive intramural offerings, and a physical education program.

Location

Set among the rolling hills of Hanover, New Hampshire, the College's beautiful 265-acre campus combines the educational opportunities of one of the nation's most prestigious institutions with an ideal New England setting. While the College itself provides many of the intellectual and cultural advantages usually found only in more urban areas, Dartmouth's proximity to the mountains and rivers of Vermont and New Hampshire allows for a range of outdoor activities. With its 9,000 residents, Hanover provides a comfortable small-town atmosphere for the College community, while the major metropolitan areas of Boston, New York, and Montreal are easily accessible by interstate highways and by regular bus, train, and air service.

Majors and Degrees

Dartmouth College awards a Bachelor of Arts (A.B.) degree in the following areas: African and Afro-American studies; ancient history; anthropology; art history; Asian and Middle Eastern languages and literatures; Asian studies; biochemistry and molecular biology; biology; biophysical chemistry; chemistry; classical archaeology; classical studies; classics; cognitive science; comparative literature; computer science; drama; earth sciences; economics; engineering physics; engineering sciences; English; English—literature and creative writing; environmental and evolutionary biology; environmental studies; film studies; French; genetics, cell, and developmental biology; geography; German; German studies; government; history; Iberian studies; Italian; Latin American and Caribbean Studies; Latino studies; linguistics; mathematics; mathematics and social sciences; music; philosophy; physics and astronomy; psychology; religion; Romance languages; Russian; Russian area studies; sociology; Spanish language, culture, and society; Spanish literatures; studio art; and women's studies. Interdisciplinary programs in education, Jewish studies, Native American studies, and neurosciences may be used to modify or expand on a departmental major.

Academic Program

All Dartmouth students study a broad spectrum of courses fundamental to higher learning and basic to a liberal arts education. Of the thirty-five courses needed for graduation, students must take ten courses distributed across eight intellectual fields: arts; social analysis; literature; quantitative or deductive science; philosophical, religious, or historical analysis; natural science; technology or applied science; and international or comparative study. In addition, students are required to take three courses in world culture, including the culture, ideas, or institutions of the United States, of Europe, and of at least one non-Western society; and a multidisciplinary or interdisciplinary course. All students must become proficient in at least one foreign language and must also complete a major. Majors typically comprise about one third of a student's total course count. Students of exceptional ability may undertake an honors program in the department of major study.

Dartmouth operates on an innovative year-round calendar, which provides unparalleled opportunities for each student to design a formal educational program closely suited to his or her personal goals. Under the Dartmouth Plan, students develop flexible enrollment patterns involving four 10-week terms in each academic year. Dartmouth students take three courses per term, which encourages more intensive study in each subject and allows enough academic variety for challenge and stimulation. Enrollment patterns may include off-campus study and vacation terms in addition to on-campus study.

Off-Campus Arrangements

Off-campus study is available in sixteen countries, and more than half of all Dartmouth students participate in at least one off-campus program. These programs are considered vital extensions of the regular Dartmouth curriculum, offering opportunities both to study other cultures and disciplines in depth and to gain new perspectives on American life. The programs are led by members of the Dartmouth faculty, and students earn full academic credit for their participation. Many of these programs also give students a chance to live with an international family. Foreign language programs are offered in Brazil, France, Germany, Greece, Italy, Japan, Mexico, Morocco, the People's Republic of China, Russia, and Spain. Other off-campus academic programs include the study of religion in Scotland; classics in Greece or Italy; geography in the Czech Republic; government in England or Washington, D.C.; philosophy in Scotland; earth sciences in Mexico; biology in the Caribbean; art history in Florence, Italy; environmental studies in Kenya; and drama, economics, English literature, film studies, history, and music in England.

Academic Facilities

Dartmouth's comprehensive library system includes more than 2.1 million volumes, 170,000 maps, and 2.4 million units of microtext. Collections are housed in Baker Library and in the eight branch libraries on campus. All libraries operate under a policy of open stacks, giving students direct access to their resources.

The faculty members, students, and staff of Dartmouth have a long tradition—spanning nearly fifty years—of envisioning and embracing computing systems and information technologies. Dartmouth's far-reaching computing network touches nearly every activity on campus and allows for wide-ranging access to peers, colleagues, and research associates around the globe. In 1998, Dartmouth was named "the most wired" campus in the nation by *Yahoo! Magazine*. Personal computers, workstations, and central host systems are well integrated at Dartmouth through the computing network. More than 11,000 network ports provide service to more than 120 buildings on campus. All students are required to own personal computers, and Apple Macintosh computers (the recommended system at Dartmouth) number close to 12,000 at the College, professional schools, and the medical center.

Dartmouth's Hopkins Center for the Creative and Performing Arts offers every student participation in and exposure to a broad range of activities, including theater, dance, music, art, exhibits, films, and lectures. The 480-seat Moore Theater is complemented by the flexible, smaller Warner Bentley Theater. Facilities for curricular music and performing organizations include a 1,000-seat concert hall, four recital halls, twelve practice rooms, an extensive music library, and a multistation listening facility. The Student Workshops are fully equipped for woodworking, metalworking, jewelry making, and pottery.

Three facilities have greatly enhanced the College's curricular offerings. Burke Laboratory, the $26-million chemistry facility, houses the most modern equipment and state-of-the-art research technology. The Rockefeller Center for the Social Sciences provides a forum for disciplines concerned with social and political issues. The Hood Museum of Art features additional gallery, classroom, and theater space. Construction of the new $30-million Berry Library began in summer 1998. This undertaking will produce a companion facility to the existing Baker Library and create a new academic hall in the west wing of the Berry Library, which will house the History Department and several high-technology classrooms.

Costs

Expenses for the three-term first year in 2000–01 are as follows: tuition and fees, $25,653; room rent, $4473; board, $3084; and estimated books and personal expenses, $2001. Travel costs vary.

Financial Aid

Dartmouth is committed to providing students with the financial support necessary to enable their attendance. The College wishes to be accessible to the broadest range of students possible such that attendance is based upon an individual's talents and accomplishments, not the ability to pay. For many years, Dartmouth has operated with a need-blind admissions policy, which ensures that admissions decisions are made without regard to the financial circumstances of applicants. Furthermore, the College has guaranteed that 100 percent of a student's demonstrated financial need is met for all four years of enrollment. Currently, 41 percent of the student body receives scholarship assistance, totaling approximately $28 million, with an average scholarship of approximately $16,000 per aid recipient.

Faculty

As an institution devoted to undergraduate education, Dartmouth prides itself on the fact that all senior faculty members teach introductory courses as well as more specialized offerings. For example, all entering first-year students participate in the First Year Seminar Program, which is designed to provide them with experience in independent research and small-group discussion, under the direction of an experienced faculty member.

Student Government

The Student Assembly, Dartmouth's student government, is broadly representative; its membership is drawn from all four classes. Students may also be elected to their respective Class Councils and are eligible for membership on several College-wide committees that have direct bearing upon student concerns, for example, the Trustee Committee on Student Affairs, the Committee on Standing, the Committee on the Freshman Year, and the Council on Budgets and Priorities.

Admission Requirements

Admission to Dartmouth is selective and highly competitive; approximately 10,200 candidates applied for 1,050 places in the entering class last year. Although there are no inflexible subject requirements for admission, candidates are urged to undertake the strongest program of preparation available at their secondary school. Evidence of intellectual capacity, motivation, personal integrity, and involvement in nonacademic areas are all of primary importance. Dartmouth requires all applicants, including all international citizens, to take three SAT II Subject Tests and either the SAT I or the ACT. All tests must be taken no later than January of the senior year in high school. Another important part of the admission process is the interview. All high school seniors are invited to call the Admissions Office to arrange an on-campus interview during their visit to Dartmouth. In addition, most students will have the opportunity to interview with graduates of the College. Group Information Sessions, conducted by admission officers, are offered weekdays January through November on a walk-in basis. Student-guided campus tours are available Monday through Saturday throughout the year.

Application and Information

Under Dartmouth's application procedures, new students are enrolled only at the opening of college in September of each year. Applications may be filed up to January 1 of the calendar year in which the candidate expects to enter college. Admission decisions are announced in mid-April; candidates normally must respond to offers of admission by May 1. Candidates who definitely plan to attend Dartmouth if admitted may request an early decision on their applications, and such requests must be filed by November 1. By mid-December, early decision candidates are notified that they have been accepted, denied, or that a final decision has been deferred until mid-April. Requests for additional information and application forms should be addressed to:

Admissions Office
6016 McNutt Hall
Dartmouth College
Hanover, New Hampshire 03755
Telephone: 603-646-2875
E-mail: undergraduate.admissions.office@dartmouth.edu
WWW: http://www.dartmouth.edu/admin/admissions/

DAVID LIPSCOMB UNIVERSITY
NASHVILLE, TENNESSEE

The University

Lipscomb University is a private, coeducational university of liberal arts and sciences in Nashville, Tennessee, that offers bachelor's and master's degrees. Established in 1891, Lipscomb is a distinctly Christian university with a sterling academic reputation. The University is associated with the Churches of Christ and is committed to providing for its students the finest liberal arts education in a Christian environment. Lipscomb was chosen for inclusion in the 1999–2000 edition of *Peterson's Competitive Colleges*.

Lipscomb University is nestled among towering elm and maple trees in a quiet residential section of Nashville known as Green Hills. Lipscomb's award-winning campus is ideally located within easy driving distance of downtown, new shopping malls, and beautiful state parks and lakes. Lipscomb's 2,500 students represent forty-four states and thirty-nine countries. The majority live on campus in six Georgian-style residence halls. Lipscomb's campus is a beautiful place with a special atmosphere that encourages learning.

Residents and commuters alike enjoy the rich mix of extracurricular activities, from medical missions to "Singarama," a popular musical production involving more than 400 students. Lipscomb has more than fifty academic or service organizations and social clubs. Each year there are activities sponsored by the students and the University, including films, lectures, art exhibits, concerts, theater, recitals, and service projects. There are several campus publications, including a weekly student newspaper, the student yearbook, and a quarterly newspaper for alumni and friends.

Athletics are an integral part of college life at Lipscomb. Lipscomb has a very successful athletics program and an intense intramural athletics program. Lipscomb is moving to NCAA Division I and fields intercollegiate teams in baseball, basketball, cross-country, golf, soccer, softball, tennis, and volleyball. The baseball and men's basketball teams have won national championships, and other sports have produced individual national champions. The men's basketball team has won more games than any other college or university team in the nation since 1986. Lipscomb is also the home of the largest summer basketball camp in the nation.

In addition to the undergraduate degrees described below, the University offers the Master of Arts degree in Bible, the Master of Arts in Religion degree, the Master of Education degree, the Master of Divinity, and the Master of Business Administration.

Location

Lipscomb University is a vital part of Nashville, a city of more than 500,000 residents, the capital of Tennessee, and a regional and national center for education, business, and culture. Recent reports have listed Nashville as one of the top five cities for business opportunity in the country and as one of the most livable cities in the United States. Nashville is centrally located, with half the population of the United States within 600 miles of its borders. Nashville is also easy to reach, with three major interstates leading into the city from six directions. Nashville International Airport is serviced by thirteen airlines. Nashville abounds in history and culture. From such antebellum mansions as the Hermitage, home of President Andrew Jackson, to Cheekwood Botanical Gardens, the Parthenon, and the Tennessee State Museum, Nashville offers abundant resources to strengthen and complement a student's education. The Tennessee Titans NFL franchise and the Nashville Predators NHL franchise provide major-league excitement.

Majors and Degrees

Lipscomb offers the Bachelor of Arts degree in sixty-two fields of emphasis and the Bachelor of Science degree in forty-six fields. These include American studies, art, athletic training, Bible (with concentrations in language, mission, preaching, and youth ministry), biochemistry, biology, business administration (with concentrations in accounting, communication, finance/economics, management, marketing, organizational communication, and professional accountancy), chemistry (applied and professional), communication (with concentrations in mass communication, oral communication, public relations, and theater), computer information systems, computer science, elementary education, engineering science, English, environmental science, exercise science, family and consumer sciences (with concentrations in consumer sciences, dietetics, family relations, fashion merchandising, food systems management, and textiles and apparel), French, general studies, German, government and public administration, history, history–communication, mathematics, music (applied—specializing in brass, percussion, strings, or wind; composition; piano; and voice), philosophy, physics, political science, political science–communication, prearchitecture, pre–dental hygiene, predentistry, pre-engineering, prelaw, pre–medical technology, premedicine, prenursing, pre–occupational therapy, prepharmacy, pre–physical therapy, pre–veterinary medicine, psychology (life-oriented and preprofessional), social work, Spanish, theater, and urban studies. Teaching majors are available in biology, chemistry, English, French, German, health and physical education, history, mathematics, music (instrumental or vocal), physics, Spanish, and theater. A dual-degree program in nursing is offered with Vanderbilt University. Dual-degree programs in engineering are offered with Auburn University, the University of Tennessee at Knoxville, Tennessee Technological University, and Vanderbilt University. Lipscomb's graduates are readily accepted into the nation's finest graduate schools.

Academic Program

Lipscomb requires that students complete general education courses in Bible, communication, humanities, mathematics, natural and social sciences, and physical education. Each student must also satisfy a writing requirement. All degree-seeking candidates must complete a minimum of 132 semester hours of work with a minimum grade point average of 2.0 overall, 2.0 in the major, and 2.0 in the minor. The academic year is on a traditional semester calendar. Lipscomb University is accredited by the Commission on Colleges of the Southern Association of Colleges and Schools (1866 Southern Lane, Decatur, Georgia 30033-4097; telephone 404-679-4500) to award bachelor's and master's degrees. Professional accreditations have been awarded by the National Association of Schools of Music, the Council on Social Work Education, and the Association of Collegiate Business Schools and Programs. The professional chemistry major has been approved by the Committee on Professional Education of the American Chemical Society.

Each student is assigned a faculty academic adviser, who helps the student develop an appropriate academic plan. Advanced placement examinations such as AP and CLEP may be used to establish a maximum credit of 30 semester hours. An Honors Program provides superior students with opportunities for unusual intellectual challenge and growth. Admittance to the Honors Program requires a score of 27 or higher on the ACT or 1210 or higher on the SAT I as well as a high school class ranking in the top 10 percent.

Off-Campus Arrangements

Lipscomb's travel-study programs are highlighted by the semester-long Lipscomb in Vienna program. The University also offers several shorter terms for credit in study abroad. These travel opportunities include such countries as China, England, and Russia and areas such as South America and the Middle East.

Academic Facilities

From the state-of-the-art Axel Swang Center for Business Administration with its interactive classroom to McFarland Hall of Science with its electron microscope to the new Teacher Educational Technology Center in the Burton Bible Building, Lipscomb students enjoy first-class academic facilities. New technology and resources make Lipscomb distinctive. Lipscomb's traditionally strong academic environment includes a campus-wide fiber-optic data network connected to the Internet, microcomputer classrooms, a microcomputer lab in each dormitory, and computer connections in every dormitory room for personal computer use. This system allows Lipscomb University students to access research materials on campus and at other major universities and information systems throughout the world. Lipscomb's online University library contains more than 196,000 bound volumes, periodicals, microform items, records, tapes, and videos. An online electronic catalog allows students to access volumes from a personal computer 24 hours a day or from library computers during operating hours.

Costs

For 2000–01, full-time tuition (based on 15 hours per semester) is $9900; room, a meal plan, and phone are approximately $4570 per year. Part-time tuition for all students is $330 per semester hour.

Financial Aid

The University annually awards approximately $8 million in all types of financial assistance. More than 70 percent of the students receive some form of financial aid. Assistance is based on merit and/or need; awards range from $400 to $13,000 per year. Need is determined by filing a Free Application for Federal Student Aid (FAFSA). Lipscomb provides aid through institutional scholarships and grants; through the Federal Pell Grant, Federal Supplemental Educational Opportunity Grant, and state grants; through the Federal Perkins Loan, Federal Stafford Student Loan, and Federal Parent Loan for Undergraduate Students (PLUS); and through Federal Work-Study and University employment. Information on these and other programs can be obtained through the Office of Student Aid Services.

Faculty

Lipscomb University has a dedicated faculty of 183. Eighty-four percent of the full-time faculty members hold an earned doctorate. Every class is taught by a faculty member, not a teaching assistant. The student-faculty ratio is approximately 17:1.

Student Government

Students participate in the government of campus life through the Student Government Association, the Honor Council, the Inter-Club Council, and various committees. The honor system is a vital part of life at Lipscomb.

Admission Requirements

Lipscomb considers several criteria in the selection of students, including academic achievement, overall creative abilities, and extracurricular activities. Applicants are expected to have followed a college-preparatory course in high school. This track includes at least 4 units of English, 2 units of mathematics (preferably algebra I and II), 2 units of natural sciences, 2 units of history/social sciences, 2 academic electives, and 2 units of the same foreign language. Either the SAT I or the ACT is required.

Application and Information

Tours are given Monday through Friday at 10 a.m. and 2 p.m. and by appointment. Prospective students are encouraged to spend a night in a residence hall, attend classes, and meet with faculty and students. Arrangements must be made in advance through the Office of Admissions.

Priority consideration is given to applicants who submit an application by November 15. Those who apply by November 15 have no application fee and are notified by January 1. Students whose applications are received after the November 15 deadline will be notified by May 1. Accompanying the application must be a $50 fee, an official high school transcript, results from the ACT or the SAT I, and two recommendations. It is highly recommended that application be made by January 1 for priority consideration in admission, financial aid, and awarding of scholarships.

For further information, students may contact:

Scott W. Gilmer
Director of Admissions
Lipscomb University
3901 Granny White Pike
Nashville, Tennessee 37204-3951
Telephone: 615-269-1776
877-LU-BISON (toll-free)
E-mail: admissions@lipscomb.edu

Lipscomb is large enough to provide high-quality resources but small enough that students will not get lost in the crowd.

DAVIDSON COLLEGE
DAVIDSON, NORTH CAROLINA

The College

Founded in 1837, Davidson College consistently ranks as one of the most competitive liberal arts and sciences colleges in the United States. Davidson's student body is made up of 1,600 students from forty-three states and twenty-four other countries, chosen not only for their academic promise but also for their character and leadership.

The liberal arts curriculum at Davidson is designed to give students knowledge and skills that they will put to use throughout their lives. Davidson offers more than 850 courses in twenty major fields and in special interdisciplinary programs. Students benefit from the careful attention of 137 full-time faculty members who are dedicated to teaching and guiding undergraduates. Close relationships between faculty members and students are a hallmark of the Davidson experience.

The Honor System serves as a foundation for life at Davidson. The Honor Code represents a declaration by the entire College community—students, faculty and staff members, and alumni—that an honorable course is the most just and, therefore, the best. The Honor Code promotes trust and respect among all members of the Davidson community.

Student life at Davidson is active and varied. Davidson students participate in a wide range of organizations of special interest and attend cultural and social events offered on campus. From student government to Amnesty International, from the Reach Out service organization to the Black Student Coalition, Davidson's more than fifty campus organizations provide students with opportunities to develop leadership skills, share their talents, and explore new interests. As one of the only colleges of its size in the nation competing in Division I of the NCAA, Davidson supports true scholar-athletes in twenty-one varsity sports. Approximately 25 percent of the student body plays on varsity teams and 80 percent participate in intramural and club sports.

Scheduled to open in 2001, Davidson's new campus center will house, among other facilities, a fitness center, a 25-foot climbing wall, an amphitheater, a bookstore, a café, and offices for student organizations.

Location

Davidson's 450-acre campus is located in Davidson, North Carolina. Davidson students play an integral part in the life of the community. Each day students collect mail from their boxes at the town post office, tutor children at the area elementary school, build houses for Davidson's chapter of Habitat for Humanity, bike and jog throughout the residential neighborhoods, or gather with friends at the local coffee house. Davidson owns 106 acres of waterfront property on Lake Norman, the largest lake in North Carolina, where students participate in a variety of water sports.

Charlotte, North Carolina, one of America's fastest-growing cities, the nation's third-largest banking center, and home to more than 270 multinational corporations, is located 19 miles south of Davidson. From community service projects to internships, from cultural events to professional sports teams, Davidson students draw on Charlotte's advantages for education and entertainment.

Majors and Degrees

Davidson grants the Bachelor of Arts and the Bachelor of Science degrees in twenty major fields: anthropology, art, biology, chemistry, classical studies, economics, English, French, German, history, mathematics, music, philosophy, physics, political science, psychology, religion, sociology, Spanish, and theater. Minors are available in anthropology, chemistry, economics, French, German, music, philosophy, Russian, Spanish, and theater. Students may double major or choose to complement their majors with an interdisciplinary concentration in applied mathematics, Asian studies, computer science, ethnic studies, gender studies, international studies, medical humanities, neuroscience, or Southern studies. Each year a number of students choose to design their own majors through Davidson's Center for Interdisciplinary Studies. Recent self-designed majors have included visual communications, bioethics, comparative literature, and environmental economics.

Academic Program

The liberal arts curriculum at Davidson gives students a broad-based and rich education, exposing them to many different academic areas. Through reading and writing assignments across every discipline, students learn to analyze information, think critically, and communicate effectively.

Davidson requires a total of thirty-two courses to graduate. Through the required core curriculum, every Davidson student takes courses in six areas: the fine arts, natural sciences and mathematics, philosophy and religion, literature, history, and the social sciences. Additional courses are taken in composition, foreign language, cultural diversity, and physical education. In addition to the core curriculum, students choose a major by the end of their sophomore year. A major normally requires up to twelve courses, including at least five upper-level courses. The academic year at Davidson consists of two 15-week semesters. Notably, 92 percent of those who enroll at Davidson graduate within four academic years.

Off-Campus Arrangements

Davidson supports a vigorous program of international education and opportunity for all students. More than half of all Davidson students take part in off-campus study for a summer, a semester, or an academic year. Options include study abroad in England, France, Germany, Ghana, India, Italy, Mexico, Spain, the former Soviet Union, and the Mediterranean region; internship programs in Washington, D.C., and Philadelphia; environmental research with the School for Field Studies in the Virgin Islands, Australia, or Kenya; marine biology off the coast of North Carolina; psychology study at Broughton Hospital in Morganton, North Carolina; exchange programs with Morehouse College and Howard University; and independently arranged programs elsewhere. Davidson's Dean Rusk Program in International Studies provides grants each year to help encourage students to explore their international interests.

In addition to off-campus study programs, the Office of Career Planning and Placement helps students find internships in Charlotte and worldwide. Internships allow students to gain practical, hands-on experience, building on their academic interests. Recent internship sites include the Carolinas Medical Center, the *Charlotte Observer*, NationsBank, the Mint Museum of Art, and the Duke Power Environmental Laboratory.

Academic Facilities

Davidson's campus features seventy-five academic and residential buildings. Chambers Building, with numerous classrooms and administrative and faculty offices, is the central academic building. The E. H. Little Library houses more than 460,000 volumes, 2,100 periodicals, 454,000 microforms, and 100 daily newspapers. The new Baker-Watt Science Complex includes the 32,000-square-foot Watson Life Sciences building (with state-of-the-art biology and psychology laboratories) and the Charles A. Dana Laboratories (housing physics and additional biology laboratories). A 7,000-volume chemistry library, laboratories, and classrooms may be found in the Martin Chemical Laboratories. The Visual Arts Center contains two galleries, a computerized slide library, a lecture hall, and studios for sculpting, painting, and drawing. The Cunningham Fine Arts Building provides space for the performing arts, including theater space for productions, extensive script and music libraries, rehearsal space, and an electronic music studio. The Computer Services Center, with a DEC Alpha 4600, a DEC Alpha 3000-400, network servers, and Internet access from 110 networked personal computers and Macintoshes, provides computer support for the campus.

Costs

Required student charges (tuition, student activity fee, and laundry) for the 2000–01 academic year are $23,094. A room costs $3450, and full board costs $3102.

Financial Aid

Admission decisions are made without regard to a student's financial need. Through a combination of state, federal, and private sources, Davidson grants in excess of $6.5 million to students who qualify. The instructions for applying for need-based aid are included with Davidson's application for admission. Students with financial need are assisted through a combination of Davidson scholarships, federal and state grants, loans, and work-study.

Davidson awards merit scholarships to approximately 15 percent of each entering first-year class. These awards recognize students' academic promise, special talents, and personal qualities. Recipients are selected based on the strength of their admission application. For some scholarships, selection may also be based on the outcome of an audition, interview, portfolio review, or writing sample. Merit scholarships range from $2500 to the comprehensive fee and include the following top awards: the Thomas S. and Sarah B. Baker Scholarship (two awarded, comprehensive fee), the John Montgomery Belk Scholarship (one awarded to a student from the southeastern U.S., comprehensive fee), the William Holt Terry Scholarship (two awarded to students with exceptional leadership qualities, full tuition), the Bryan Scholarship (two awarded to students who contribute in a superlative manner to their sport as well as to the academic and cocurricular life at Davidson), and the Missy and John Kuykendall Scholarship (three awarded to students who provide service leadership).

Faculty

Davidson's 140 full-time faculty members choose to teach at Davidson because they gain their greatest professional satisfaction from working with undergraduates. All classes at Davidson are taught by full professors and 94.3 percent of faculty members have a Ph.D. With a student-faculty ratio of 10.8:1, classes are small (the average class size is 20 students), and individual attention is the norm. Professors' ongoing involvement with students takes many forms: encouraging lively class discussion, including students in their research projects, inviting students to their homes for dinner, and participating in many facets of student life outside of the classroom. Each student is assigned a faculty adviser who provides guidance on academic choices throughout the student's four years.

Student Government

Davidson students have the opportunity to develop valuable interpersonal skills through leadership roles in the Student Government Association, the College Union, the Honor Council, and many special interest organizations. The Honor System governs Davidson's social and academic life, demanding the highest personal and community values and engendering an atmosphere of openness, mutual trust, and integrity among the entire Davidson community.

Admission Requirements

Davidson seeks students of outstanding academic ability and strong character who show promise of leadership. To be considered for admission, a student must have completed at least 16 high school academic units, including 4 units of English, 2 units of intermediate mathematics, 1 unit of plane geometry, 2 units of the same foreign language, and 1 unit of history. Electives should include 3 or 4 years of science and additional courses in mathematics, history, and the same foreign language. In addition to the SAT I or the ACT, the Davidson application requires three essay responses, an official transcript, and recommendations from two teachers, a peer, and a high school counselor. SAT II Subject Tests are recommended but not required. Davidson accepts the Common Application along with required supplemental information.

Admission to Davidson is highly selective. The selection process is composed of three major elements: the evaluation of academic performance and potential, the assessment of individual characteristics, and the recognition of outstanding interests, achievements, and activities. These three elements are used to gain an understanding of each student's academic and personal strengths and give an overall impression of the individual's eligibility for admission. As a college that welcomes students, faculty members, and staff members from a variety of nationalities, ethnic groups, and traditions, Davidson seeks students who will bring diverse and unique talents and strengths to the College community.

Application and Information

Early decision—round one—has an application deadline of November 15 with notification by December 15. Early decision—round two—has an application deadline of January 2 with notification by February 1. Regular decision has an application deadline of January 15 with notification by April 1. To be considered for merit scholarships, students must complete their applications by December 15. Students are encouraged to visit Davidson for a campus tour and an information session with a member of the Admission Office staff. For additional information about Davidson, students should contact:

Nancy J. Cable, Ph.D.
Dean of Admission and Financial Aid
Davidson College
P.O. Box 1737
Davidson, North Carolina 28036
Telephone: 704-892-2230
         800-768-0380 (toll-free)
World Wide Web: http://www.davidson.edu

Chambers Building, Davidson's central academic building, houses classrooms and faculty and administrative offices.

DAVIS & ELKINS COLLEGE
ELKINS, WEST VIRGINIA

The College

A comprehensive liberal arts and sciences education is the hallmark of Davis & Elkins College. Educational programs range from the highly professional, in nursing and teaching, to the innovative, in hospitality management and tourism management, to the traditional, in the liberal arts and sciences.

There are two sororities and two fraternities active on campus and a wide variety of extracurricular organizations, including the Concert Choir, Jazz Choir, radio station, theater, and newspaper.

An extensive schedule of intramural and club athletics is offered for men and women in addition to a sound program of varsity sports. Intercollegiate athletics for women include basketball, cross-country, soccer, softball, tennis, and volleyball. Teams for men include baseball, basketball, cross-country, golf, soccer, and tennis. The College holds membership in the NCAA Division II.

Location

The College is located in Elkins, West Virginia, rated among the top thirty small towns in America. Elkins is situated at the entrance to the Monongahela National Forest and in the center of one of the nation's most prosperous and fastest-growing outdoor recreation areas. Four nearby resorts provide a variety of recreational opportunities, including camping, golfing, hiking, fishing, tennis, and cross-country and downhill skiing.

Majors and Degrees

Davis & Elkins College offers programs of study leading to bachelor's degrees in accounting, art, biology, chemistry, communication, computer science, elementary education, English, environmental science, exercise science, fashion merchandising, health education, history, hospitality management, tourism management, management, marketing, mathematics, music, physical education, political science, psychology and human services, religion and philosophy, religious education, secondary education, sociology, Spanish, sports management, and theater arts.

Preprofessional programs prepare students for admission to schools of medicine, dentistry, forestry, church ministry, occupational therapy, pharmacy, and law. Additional areas of study are available in forestry (3-2 bachelor's-master's programs offered by special arrangement with the State University of New York College of Environmental Science and Forestry at Syracuse), in occupational therapy (3-2 bachelor's-master's program offered by special arrangement with six major universities), and in engineering (3-2 program with West Virginia University).

Associate degrees are available in accounting, computer business systems, marketing, nursing, and psychology and human services.

Academic Program

Davis & Elkins College emphasizes a strong liberal arts and sciences foundation for all students. The Contract Degree Program provides opportunities to design individual programs of study under close faculty supervision. An honors program challenges the more advanced students. The award-winning William James Center provides an academic support program for all students. A Learning Disabilities Program is also available.

Off-Campus Arrangements

Off-campus and independent experiences include cultural studies of the Caribbean, England, Italy, Scotland, and Spain; marine biology courses in Florida; and internships and practicums at several sites throughout Maryland, New Jersey, New York, Pennsylvania, Virginia, West Virginia, and Washington, D.C.

Academic Facilities

An arts center/auditorium complex has a 1,300-seat auditorium for concerts, plays, and other cultural events. The complex also houses the music and theater departments, a swimming pool, and the fitness center. A science center accommodates the business and natural science divisions. The center also contains a planetarium, rooftop greenhouse, promenade room for fashion merchandising majors, computer center, and several microcomputer laboratories. The Booth Library opened in 1992 with a capacity of 300,000 volumes. The library includes a fully equipped media center with computer capabilities and an online computer catalog. One-day calls for materials can be made to three other Mountain State Association of Colleges libraries. Students may also use the resources of the West Virginia University library in Morgantown, West Virginia.

Costs

The comprehensive tuition and fees charge for 2000–01 is $12,724, and room and board costs are $5570. The tuition covers the full cost of student publications, health service, laboratory classes, the Student Union, and athletic contests.

Financial Aid

Scholarships, grants, loans, and campus employment are offered to help students meet financial obligations; a student may be given one award or a combination of several awards. Most financial aid is based on need, but academic, honors, athletic, and performance scholarships are also available; 85 percent of the student body receives some form of financial assistance. Students applying for financial assistance should complete the Free Application for Federal Student Aid by March 1. Forms may be obtained from the Office of Financial Aid.

Faculty

The College has 56 full-time faculty members, of whom 75 percent hold terminal degrees. They include distinguished Fulbright scholars, authors, and lecturers. A student-faculty ratio of 11:1 provides students with ongoing opportunities to interact with instructors on a personal level.

Student Government

Davis & Elkins recognizes through its special governance system the value of student involvement in developing the academic and social policies of the College. Students work alongside members of the faculty and administration in planning and deciding policies in all basic areas of decision making (with the exception of finances) that affect students. Students participating in this process are elected to the Student Assembly by their classmates.

Admission Requirements

Davis & Elkins College seeks to enroll students with academic and personal qualities that indicate potential for intellectual, social, and spiritual growth. A basic premise of the admissions policy is that all applicants are reviewed individually to determine if they are capable of successfully meeting their responsibilities as a Davis & Elkins student and benefiting from the personalized educational experience the College provides. The Enrollment Management Committee establishes guidelines for admission that reflect the College's desire to identify academically capable students who demonstrate potential for further achievement; who are active at school and in the community, with a record of service; and who represent diverse cultures and backgrounds. Freshman applicants are required to submit scores from either the ACT or SAT I and an official high school transcript that demonstrates a solid preparation for college-level work. Transfer applicants are also required to submit official transcripts from all colleges and universities attended.

Davis & Elkins admits students regardless of race, color, sex, handicap, religious affiliation, or national or ethnic origin.

Application and Information

Along with the College application form, prospective students must submit a complete transcript of college-preparatory studies. SAT I or ACT scores are also required. In addition to regular freshman admission, early and deferred admission plans are available. Transfers may be admitted during both the August and January terms. They must have maintained a minimum overall average of C at all colleges attended and must submit satisfactory personal credentials.

Davis & Elkins follows a system of rolling admission. Candidates whose files are completed during the early part of their senior year receive decisions first. Financial aid candidates are requested to complete the application process as early in the calendar year as possible. Admitted students have until May 1, or ten days following notification of a financial award, to present the required advance payment deposit that holds their place in the entering freshman class.

For further information, students should contact:

Office of Admissions
Davis & Elkins College
100 Campus Drive
Elkins, West Virginia 26241-3996
Telephone: 304-637-1230 (call collect)
                800-624-3157 (toll-free)
E-mail: admiss@dne.edu
World Wide Web: http://www.dne.edu

Davis & Elkins College: traditions and values focused on student success.

DEFIANCE COLLEGE
DEFIANCE, OHIO

The College

Defiance College (DC), founded in 1850 and celebrating its sesquicentennial in 2000, is a private liberal arts college related to the United Church of Christ, serving approximately 1,000 students.

Defiance College is one of only 100 colleges and universities nationwide to be named to the Templeton Foundation's Honor Roll for Character-Building Colleges. DC is also currently ranked among *U.S. News & World Report*'s Best Colleges in America. Defiance is accredited by the North Central Association of Colleges and Schools and the Council on Social Work Education.

The College's beautiful campus is located on 150 acres in a residential area of Defiance, Ohio, a short walk from the center of the city. Many of the College's students are from Ohio, with the remaining students representing several states and countries. Fifty-three percent of the College's full-time students live on campus.

Student life is an important part of a Defiance College education. Activities include Greek social organizations; student government; musical and religious groups; theater; the student newspaper, yearbook, multicultural organizations, and service learning activities; honor societies; special interest groups; and intramural athletics. Defiance College is a member of the NCAA at the Division III level. A member of the Heartland Athletic Conference (HCAC), Defiance competes in men's and women's basketball, cross country, golf, indoor and outdoor track and field, soccer, tennis and volleyball, as well as women's softball and men's baseball and football.

In addition to bachelor's and associate degrees, Defiance College awards master's degrees in teacher education and business (organizational leadership).

As a national leader in the field of service learning, DC strives to prepare its graduates not only for the world of work, but also to be active participants in their communities. Students are asked to commit to community service projects throughout the region; many of the students' experiences are tied directly to their major fields of study.

Location

Situated at the historic confluence of the Auglaize and Maumee Rivers, the city of Defiance has a population of about 18,000. Highly diversified industry and some of the richest farmland in the nation contribute to the area's prosperity. Defiance offers excellent shopping and a wholesome living environment. The city is served by daily bus transportation from the Greyhound Bus Lines (Detroit-Toledo-Fort Wayne-Indianapolis). Amtrak service is available into nearby Bryan, Ohio. The metropolitan centers of Toledo and Fort Wayne are approximately 55 miles away. Detroit, Michigan, is 2½ hours away by car, and Chicago is a 4-hour drive from campus. The College is located near the north city limits on Highway 66 just south of U.S. 24.

Majors and Degrees

Defiance College awards bachelor's degrees in forty majors and associate degrees in art, business administration, criminal justice, information technology, and religious education. Areas of study include accounting, art, arts and humanities, athletic training education, biology, business administration, chemistry, Christian education, communication arts, criminal justice, education, environmental science, finance, forensic science, graphic design, history, human resource management, information technology, management, marketing, mathematics, medical technology, natural science, physical education, psychology, restoration ecology, religious studies and design for leadership, social work, sport management, and wellness/corporate fitness. A self-designed major is also an option. Also offered are preprofessional programs in dentistry, law, medicine, veterinary science, and seminary.

Special programs include Freshman Seminar, interdisciplinary studies, cooperative education, internships, field experience, and teaching certification. Recreation and economics are offered as minors only.

Academic Program

Defiance College operates on a semester calendar, consisting of two 16-week semesters. The fall semester runs from late August to mid-December; the spring semester runs from early January to early May. During the fall and spring semesters, students normally take four or five courses, totaling approximately 15 credits. Three 5-week summer sessions are offered. A minimum of 120 semester credits is required for a bachelor's degree; 60 semester credits are required for an associate degree.

Defiance College academic experience includes studies in a major field as well as broad-based studies in the liberal arts. Studies in a major field allow an individual to achieve a level of competence in an area of interest, while studies in the liberal arts broaden the individual's understanding of the world. Core courses are required, and community service is incorporated into the curriculum for all students.

Academic Facilities

Completed in 1993, the College's state-of-the-art Pilgrim Library has shelving for 130,000 volumes and 550 current periodicals, as well as seating for 200 readers. The 30,000-square-foot facility also offers a public access computer lab and an advanced electronic library.

The Carma J. Rowe Science Hall, constructed in 1987, houses laboratories and classrooms. In February 1999, Rowe gained a new science and math computer laboratory. New computer labs have been constructed in Defiance Hall. The McMaster Center, completed in 1988, provides physical education and recreation facilities.

The Justin F. Coressel stadium, dedicated in 1994, features a 5,000-seat football stadium and an eight-lane all-weather track. Training facilities, meeting areas, and locker rooms are available on site.

The Hubbard Hall/McCann Student Activities Center opened in 1996. It features the campus bookstore, a fitness center, a dance room, a snack bar, offices, and meeting rooms.

The new student union, the Serrick Campus Center, was completed in spring 2000 and includes the campus dining complex, admissions and financial aid offices, the registration center, the student health center, and a distance learning classroom as well as banquet and conference spaces.

Costs

Tuition for the 2000–01 academic year is $14,850. Room and board have been set at $4480. There is an additional fee of $100 for student activities and a $75 per-semester technology fee. A student's personal expenses, including books and travel to and from campus, average $1300 per year.

Financial Aid

Defiance College is committed to helping students invest in their future by providing scholarships, grants, loans, and work opportunities. Scholarship eligibility is based upon academic achievements in high school for freshmen and in college for transfer students. The Presidential Service Leadership Award recognizes students with a history of volunteer service. Some financial aid awards are made solely on the basis of merit (academic performance), some are awarded on the basis of financial need, and others are based on both merit and need. Approximately 80 percent of the College's students receive some form of financial assistance, which significantly reduces the cost of tuition and fees. The average financial aid award is $11,000.

Students requesting aid are required to submit the Free Application for Federal Student Aid (FAFSA). Although there is no application deadline, financial aid dollars are awarded on a first-come, first-served basis, so prospective students should file the aid applications as early as possible. DC's Title IV Federal School code is 003041.

Faculty

The 13:1 student-faculty ratio at Defiance College ensures close working relationships between students and faculty members. All of the students at Defiance, from freshmen through seniors, benefit from the faculty's expertise and experience. The College has 40 full-time and 29 part-time faculty members.

Student Government

Student government at Defiance College consists of the Student Senate and the Campus Activities Board. The Student Senate oversees the College's student organizations, while the Campus Activities Board plans and coordinates campuswide events.

Admission Requirements

Defiance College admits students without regard to sex, race, creed, age, national or ethnic origin, color, or disability. Applications are evaluated on an individual basis. Students must be high school graduates or hold an equivalency diploma. Preference will be given to students with a minimum 2.0 GPA and a score of 18 or higher on the ACT or 850 or higher on the SAT I and who rank in the top 60 percent of their class. Other criteria considered are college-preparatory course work, extracurricular activities, the essay, letters of recommendation, and a personal interview. Transfer students will be considered according to their performance at their previous institution. A GPA of 2.0 or higher is necessary to be admitted in good standing.

Application and Information

Applications are reviewed on a rolling basis; therefore, students will be notified of a decision approximately one week after all necessary material is received by the admissions office. Students may apply after completing six semesters of high school. A $25 nonrefundable application fee should accompany the application.

To obtain an application or to receive more information about Defiance College, students should contact:

Admissions Office
Defiance College
701 North Clinton Street
Defiance, Ohio 43512
Telephone: 419-783-2359
               800-520-GODC (toll-free)
Fax: 419-783-2468
E-mail: admissions@defiance.edu
World Wide Web: http://www.defiance.edu

Students enjoy an afternoon with friends near Defiance Hall on the campus of Defiance College.

DELAWARE VALLEY COLLEGE
DOYLESTOWN, PENNSYLVANIA

The College
Founded in 1896, Delaware Valley College is a private, coeducational four-year college enrolling approximately 1,425 full-time students. Over the years, the College has concentrated on producing graduates who can fill employers' needs. Today, DVC's curriculum has expanded to include a broad range of programs in agriculture, business, science, education, and liberal arts.

Students attend Delaware Valley College, first and foremost, to prepare themselves for a professional career. The placement record of Delaware Valley College graduates is outstanding, proving that the time-honored educational philosophy of "scholarship with applied experience" works. An extremely high proportion of graduates find employment in their major field of study or enter graduate school within six months of graduation.

In addition to its academic programs, the College offers a wide range of extracurricular activities and events. A total of thirty-three special interest organizations exist, many of which are linked with a specific major. Student publications include the weekly *RamPages* (newspaper), the *Cornucopia* (yearbook), and the *Gleaner* (literary magazine). The College band and chorale give students the chance to demonstrate their musical talents. There are active minority and international clubs on campus. The DVC Volunteer Corps lines up opportunities for student service to the community in a variety of settings relevant to the student's academic major. A-Day, the student-run campuswide fair, annually attracts 50,000 visitors who enjoy the festival, the entertainment, and the academically oriented projects. Such projects as livestock judging, plant sales, chemistry magic shows, computer-aided design demonstrations, a model rain forest habitat, and equestrian events all demonstrate the expertise of DVC students.

Seventy percent of students live on campus in twelve residence halls. A full range of intercollegiate and intramural athletics programs (NCAA Division III, ECAC, and MAC) for both women and men is offered. All elements of the College's educational and recreational programs are in place to develop students as open-minded professionals who are capable of expanding their horizons in a future of unlimited possibilities.

On the graduate level, Delaware Valley College offers a Master in Business Administration degree program jointly with La Salle University.

Location
The College is located in historic Bucks County, Pennsylvania, approximately 30 miles north of Philadelphia and 70 miles southwest of New York City. Bucks County is one of the fastest-growing areas in the United States, yet it maintains its rich historical and agricultural heritage. The central Bucks County area is also rich in libraries, institutions of higher education, museums, and additional cultural resources, further enhancing the educational opportunities of Delaware Valley College students. The Pennsylvania and New Jersey turnpikes provide quick access to the College. A commuter railway system links the College with Philadelphia, providing daily scheduled arrivals and departures. The College enjoys a mutually beneficial relationship with its surrounding community. Many students find convenient employment opportunities with local businesses, and the community benefits from the many events and activities that are held on campus.

Majors and Degrees
Delaware Valley College awards the Bachelor of Science degree in agribusiness, agronomy and environmental science, animal science, biology, business administration, chemistry and biochemistry, computer information systems management, criminal justice administration, dairy science, food science and management, horticulture, mathematics, ornamental horticulture and environmental design, and secondary education. A Bachelor of Arts degree is awarded in English. The College also offers two-year Associate of Science degree programs in business, equine science, and MIS. Within the degree programs, students are given the opportunity to focus their attention on a number of options, minors, and specializations, such as accounting, business management, computer information systems, ecological landscape design, equine science, floriculture, food service systems management, food technology, landscape contracting and management, livestock management, marketing, microbiology and biotechnology, plant biology, small animal science, sports management, sustainable agriculture, and turfgrass management.

DVC also offers preprofessional preparation in dentistry, law, medicine, optometry, and veterinary medicine.

Academic Program
All courses are taught from a liberal arts perspective, which broadens the students' appreciation of their cultural heritage. The College is committed to producing graduates who are not only technically competent but also skilled in the use of language, mathematics, and computers. The entire academic program is designed to contribute to the total educational growth of the student and provides him or her with the opportunity to participate in special methods and techniques courses that coordinate theory with practice. The College stresses a practical, hands-on approach to learning. The curriculum includes a required 24-week Employment Program through which students gain practical work experience in their field while still in college. The Employment Program provides valuable entries on student resumes as it builds meaningful skills.

The academic calendar consists of two 15-week semesters, a January term, and two 6-week summer sessions.

Academic Facilities
Many of the courses taught at Delaware Valley College are laboratory or field oriented. Facilities include many lecture rooms, laboratories containing the most up-to-date equipment, and approximately 550 acres of cultivated and forested lands, which offer a variety of field laboratory situations. In addition, the recently acquired 174-acre Roth Farm is being developed and maintained with the help of students and various DVC departments as a "working history farm" to demonstrate agricultural and food production practices from the 1890–1910 era.

Delaware Valley College students benefit from the low student-laboratory ratio. This enables ready access to equipment, which is imperative to learning. Specifically, the College utilizes biology, chemistry, physics, plant science, and animal science laboratories. Facilities include a tissue culture laboratory, a food processing plant, a greenhouse-laboratory complex, a dairy, a small-animal science center, equine breeding barns, and an indoor equestrian center. The campus is itself a recognized arboretum managed by students and faculty members. These facilities are all supported by the Krauskopf Memorial Library, which houses some 80,000 publications.

Costs

For 2000–01, tuition and fees are $17,050, room is $2790, and board is $3550 for a twenty-one-meal plan.

Financial Aid

The College is committed to providing financial assistance so that every student is able to meet the costs of obtaining a college education. DVC offers to students of academic promise faculty scholarships and faculty grants. It participates with the federal government in the Federal Pell Grant Program, the Federal Supplemental Educational Opportunity Grant Program, the Federal Perkins Loan Program, and the Federal Work-Study Program. More than 80 percent of the College's total student body receives some type of financial aid; the average award package totaled $11,400 for 1998–99.

Faculty

All courses at Delaware Valley College are taught by faculty members who combine professional expertise with deep theoretical knowledge and are devoted to the teaching profession. Courses are never taught by graduate students. The faculty numbers approximately 80 instructors, who are friendly and accessible and always ready to help individual students make the most of the educational opportunities offered by the College. The teacher-student ratio is 1:16.

Student Government

Students are encouraged to make the most of extracurricular activities to ensure that their education includes as many different experiences as possible. The student government acts to coordinate the activities of all organizations on campus and sponsors a variety of mixers, movies, concerts, and speakers.

Admission Requirements

In reviewing applications for admission, the College takes into consideration the quality of a student's high school work, scores on the SAT I or ACT, class rank, the guidance counselor's recommendation, and the level of a student's motivation, as determined by extracurricular activities. A personal interview is recommended.

Application and Information

For more information about Delaware Valley College and its academic, athletic, and financial aid programs, the student should contact:

Office of Admissions
Delaware Valley College
700 East Butler Avenue
Doylestown, Pennsylvania 18901-2697
Telephone: 215-345-1500 Ext. 2211
              800-2DELVAL (toll-free)
Fax: 215-230-2968
E-mail: zenkos@devalcol.edu
World Wide Web: http://www.devalcol.edu

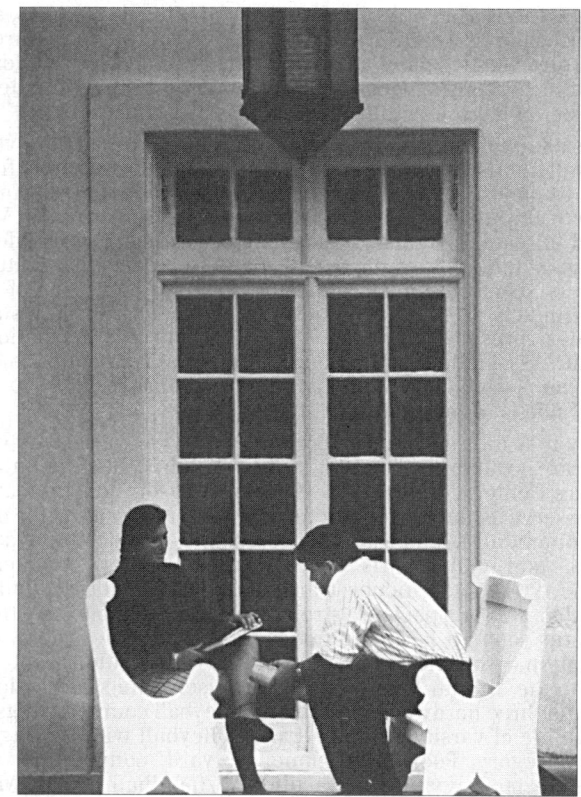

Students relaxing in front of Lasker Hall.

DENISON UNIVERSITY
GRANVILLE, OHIO

The University

Denison is a private four-year liberal arts university that provides a rigorous and challenging education while preparing students for lives of leadership and service. The University dates back to 1831, when the Ohio Baptist Education Society established the Granville Literary and Theological Institution. The University was given its present name and moved to its current location in the 1850s. Denison has nearly 26,000 alumni, an endowment of $441 million as of December 30, 1999, and total assets of $493 million as of June 30, 1999. It has achieved a national reputation based upon its lengthy cultural heritage, the vitality of its intellectual and ethical concerns, and the performance of its graduates. Extensive personal, career, and professional school counseling is available to students. Fifty-nine percent of Denison's graduates earn a graduate or professional degree within fifteen years of graduation.

As a residential college, Denison requires its students to live in University housing and offers a variety of housing options from which to choose. Within residential units, students have input and/or vote on policy questions and internal governance. Very limited off-campus housing is available for upperclass students through a lottery system. A full slate of social and cultural events is scheduled each semester. Forty-two percent of the approximately 2,100 students join the different fraternities and sororities present on campus. The Denison International Student Association, the Black Student Union, the Asian American Association, and La Fuerza Latina respond to the special needs of multicultural students.

Twenty-two intercollegiate sports and a wide variety of club sports are available. The $7.2-million Mitchell Recreation and Athletics Center, completed in 1994, and the Physical Education Center serve as the focal point for intercollegiate sports for men and women, all student athletic recreation, physical education classes, and club sports. The Mitchell Center includes a six-lane, 200-meter indoor track, four state-of-the-art indoor tennis courts, a spacious strength room, a modern fitness apparatus room, a large multipurpose and aerobics room, and international squash courts. The Physical Education Center is home to the Alumni Memorial Field House with its recreational track and three hardwood basketball/volleyball courts; Livingston Gym, home of varsity basketball and volleyball with seating for 3,000; Gregory Pool, a six-lane, 25-yard competition and recreation facility; and five racquetball/handball courts. More than 75 percent of Denison students participate in athletics or recreational activities and DU's varsity teams have collected back-to-back conference All-Sports titles, setting new point records each year.

Location

The 1,200-acre Denison campus is located on a hill overlooking the village of Granville, in central Ohio. Founded in 1805 by settlers from Massachusetts, Granville bears a marked resemblance to a New England village. Columbus, the state capital, 27 miles to the west, is the nearest large city and is served by numerous national airlines. Newark, 7 miles to the east, is an industrial city of 50,000 people. Granville has several fine restaurants and adequate shopping facilities, but those seeking the larger department stores go to Newark or Columbus. The University is a cultural and recreational center for the local community, and the Denison Community Association encourages student participation in community service activities, providing nearly 10,000 hours of volunteer fieldwork each year. State parks, lakes, bike trails, and ski areas are nearby.

Majors and Degrees

Denison offers the degrees of Bachelor of Arts, Bachelor of Science, and Bachelor of Fine Arts. Departmental, interdepartmental, and individually designed majors, as well as concentrations within departments, are available within the degree programs. The B.A. can be earned through departmental programs in art (history or studio), biology, chemistry, communication, computer science, dance, economics, education, English, environmental studies, geology, history, international studies, mathematical sciences, modern languages (French, German, and Spanish), music, philosophy, physical education, physics, political science, psychology, religion, sociology/anthropology, and theater and cinema and through interdepartmental programs in black studies, classical studies, East Asian studies, educational studies, and women's studies. Interdisciplinary programs leading to a B.A. in philosophy, political science, and economics (PPE) and media, technology, and arts (MTA) have recently been added. The B.S. is offered in biochemistry, biology, chemistry, computer science, geology, mathematical sciences, physics, and psychology. The B.F.A. majors are art (studio) and theater. Concentrations can be arranged in astronomy, geophysics, Latin American and Caribbean studies, and neuroscience. Certification is available in secondary education and organizational studies.

Preprofessional preparation is available in business, dentistry, engineering, forestry, law, medicine, nursing, occupational therapy, and veterinary medicine. Denison offers 3-2 programs in engineering with Rensselaer Polytechnic Institute, Washington University, Case Western Reserve University, and Columbia University; in forestry and environmental studies with Duke University; in natural resources management with the University of Michigan; and in medical technology with Rochester General Hospital.

Academic Program

Denison expects its students to profit from exposure to a broad liberal arts education and to achieve proficiency in a major field. Degree requirements include successful completion of approximately thirty-five courses (127 semester hours) with a 2.0 or better average, both overall and in the major and minor fields; fulfillment of all general education requirements; passing comprehensive examinations if required in the major; and fulfillment of minimum residence requirements. About one third of a student's course work (thirteen courses) must be chosen from core course offerings in the humanities, sciences, social sciences, and fine arts. Another third is in the major field of study, and the remainder is in electives. There are opportunities for directed and independent study. Students may receive advanced placement or credit through College Board Advanced Placement (AP) tests or proficiency examinations. Credit is automatically given for an AP score of 4 or 5. Denison's academic calendar consists of two semesters and an optional May Term, which includes internships and travel seminars. The academic year begins in late August and ends in mid-May.

Off-Campus Arrangements

Denison cooperates in off-campus study programs sponsored and supervised by recognized American colleges and universities and by the Great Lakes Colleges Association. Qualified students may participate for a semester or a year of international study in Europe, Latin America, Asia, Africa, or the Middle East. Domestic programs, offered on a one- or two-semester basis, include the Washington Semester, the Urban Semester in Philadelphia, the Fine Arts Program in New York City, the Oak Ridge Science Semester, the Newberry

Library Program in Chicago, the Border Studies Program, and linkages with historically black universities.

Academic Facilities

Prominent among the nine academic and administrative buildings on the academic quadrangle are the Denison University libraries. As a member of the Five Colleges of Ohio consortium and OhioLink, the library offers access through a combined state-of-the-art online catalog to collections of more than 1.25 million and 18 million volumes, respectively. In addition, the Denison library offers reference assistance, library instruction, interlibrary loan service, government documents, archives, and a comprehensive Learning Resources Center. On-campus collections include more than 340,000 volumes, 315,000 government documents, 1,200 periodical subscriptions, 18,000 sound recordings, and 4,000 videocassettes. The fully automated library can be reached from computers anywhere on campus via the campus network. Denison students have access to more than 175 microcomputers in eight public clusters, 225 computers in departments labs, and network outlets in every residence hall, all of which provide 24-hour access to the network. In addition to the libraries, network services include central servers where students can keep files and programs, e-mail and access to the Internet and the World Wide Web. Purchase of a computer is not required, but about two thirds of Denison's students opt to own a computer, almost all of which are connected to the campus network. More detail is available on the Denison website under /computing/. The Chemistry Center contains well-equipped laboratories and a 292-seat circular auditorium. Features of the two-year-old $7.2-million F. W. Olin Science Hall include a 42-seat planetarium with a Zeiss Skymaster projector, a laser spectrometer, and computer-based learning centers for physics and astronomy, geology and geography, and mathematics and computer science. The Fine Arts Center is made up of six buildings containing classrooms and performance facilities for art, music, theater and cinema, and dance. Burke Hall contains a recital hall, the theater workshop, and an art gallery. Other buildings are the Theatre Arts Building; the Doane Dance Building; Burton Hall, that houses the Department of Music; Cleveland Hall, for studio art courses; the Art Annex; and the Film Annex, the center of Denison's nationally recognized cinematography program.

Costs

Annual charges for the 2000–2001 academic year are as follows: tuition, $20,680; room and board, $5760; and student fees, $1010. An estimated $1800 for books, travel, and personal expenses brings the total annual cost to $29,250.

Financial Aid

Denison's financial assistance program awards more than $33 million annually to 96 percent of the undergraduates. Financial aid packages based on need are composed of grants, loans, and employment on campus. Applicants for both federal and Denison grant aid must complete a Free Application for Federal Student Aid (FAFSA) as early as possible after January 1 and request that the information be sent to Denison. In addition to the institutional need-based grants, Denison offers more than 1,000 merit-based scholarships ranging from full- to half-tuition. Alumni awards in the amounts of one-fifth to one-third tuition, recognizing academic achievement, leadership, and talent, are also offered. The average need-based aid award (including loans and work) received by 1999 entering freshmen was $21,325. The financial aid decision is entirely separate from the admission decision. For more information, students should write to Denison's Office of Financial Aid and ask for the financial aid brochure.

Faculty

Denison's 167 full-time and seven part-time faculty members are deeply committed to teaching and to students. Many have national reputations in their fields; each year faculty members win national awards for teaching excellence. Ninety-eight percent of faculty members have an earned doctorate or terminal degree in their field. The faculty-student ratio is 1:12. Small classes (average class size is 20) and unique opportunities for one-on-one research with a faculty member encourage active learning. All incoming first-year students are assigned a faculty adviser to assist with course selection and to ease the transition to college life.

Student Government

Through the Denison Campus Government Association, students budget and direct such campus organizations as the Student Senate, FM radio station, Denison Film Society, and campus newspaper. Students are strongly represented on the governance councils of the University.

Admission Requirements

Entering first-year students should have earned at least 16 academic credits in secondary school, including 4 years of college-preparatory English. Strongly recommended are 3 years each of mathematics, science, foreign language, and social studies. A candidate for admission must file a formal application and submit scores on either the SAT I or ACT. The Admissions Committee is particularly interested in the quality of the academic program, the grade point average, and test results from the SAT I or ACT. Other selection criteria are written references from a college adviser and an academic teacher, extracurricular and personal accomplishments, and the student's essay on the application. An interview is recommended. It is Denison's goal to enroll a broad cross section of students. Denison University admits students of any race, color, religion, age, personal handicap, sex, sexual orientation, veteran status, and national or ethnic origin.

Application and Information

First-Choice Early Decision candidates should apply by January 1. The merit-based scholarship deadline is also January 1. Early Decision applicants will be notified within two weeks of completing their applications of admission or of deferment of a decision until April. All admitted Early Decision candidates must send an enrollment deposit within two weeks. Candidates for regular admission should apply by February 1. Those deferred under Early Decision and all regular applicants are given a final decision by April 1. Candidates admitted in April must respond to the admission offer by May 1.

Director of Admissions
Denison University
Box H
Granville, Ohio 43023
Telephone: 740-587-6276
          800-336-4766 (toll-free)
E-mail: admissions@denison.edu
World Wide Web: http://www.denison.edu

Denison...preparing you for a lifetime of leadership and learning.

DEPAUL UNIVERSITY
CHICAGO, ILLINOIS

The University

Founded by the Vincentian Order of Priests in 1898, DePaul is the second-largest Catholic university in the country and has a diverse student body enrolled on six campuses. DePaul's location in Chicago—a world-class center for business, finance, government, law, and culture—and its partnership with the city provide students with exceptional career-related job experiences, internships, mentorships, services, and cultural opportunities.

The Loop campus, including the DePaul Center, Computer Science and Telecommunications Center, O'Malley Place, the Merle Reskin Theatre, and the Frank J. Lewis Center, is home to the Colleges of Law and Commerce, the School for New Learning, and the School of Computer Science, Telecommunications, and Information Systems and is located in the heart of downtown Chicago. The College of Liberal Arts and Sciences, the School of Music, the School of Education, and The Theatre School are located on the 36-acre campus in the historic Lincoln Park neighborhood. About 11,775 of DePaul's 19,549 students are undergraduates. In a typical year, 1,500 first-year students, about 40 percent of whom are from outside the Greater Chicago area, come from approximately 200 high schools. Though exhibiting a wide variety of backgrounds, DePaul students share a willingness to work hard in order to achieve their educational and career goals. Few undergraduate classes are scheduled in the afternoon, allowing time for study, extracurricular involvements, and part-time employment.

More than 120 student organizations provide opportunities for participation in personal, community, and University activities. There are music performance groups, student publications, and honor and service societies. Women's NCAA Division I sports include basketball, cross-country, riflery, soccer, softball, tennis, track, and volleyball. Men's NCAA Division I sports include basketball, cross-country, golf, riflery, soccer, tennis, and track. Intramural sports programs are available throughout the year. Facilities include two gymnasiums, a swimming pool, handball and tennis courts, basketball and volleyball courts, weight rooms, and a soccer/softball field. In fall 1999, the Ray Meyer Athletic and Recreation Center, a 120,000-square-foot facility, was opened. In fall 2000, the University will open a new state-of-the-art varsity athletic center and a conference center.

Thirteen residence halls and off-campus housing are available at Lincoln Park. Two new semi-suite residence halls will open in fall 2000. Both campuses have student centers and career counseling and placement offices.

The following graduate degrees are offered: master's degrees in liberal arts and sciences, accountancy, business, computer science, education, and music; the M.F.A. in theater; the J.D. in law; the Master of Law in taxation; and the Ph.D. in computer science, philosophy, and psychology.

Location

DePaul is located in a culturally and academically rich urban environment. The University has six campuses: the Loop campus in downtown Chicago, the Lincoln Park campus, and four suburban campuses. The downtown campus is just blocks from the Art Institute, Orchestra Hall, Grant Park and Lake Michigan, and the LaSalle Street business district. Since 70 percent of DePaul's students work to help finance their education, they find that the downtown location provides many professional employment opportunities. At the Lincoln Park campus, the potpourri of stores, theaters, restaurants, and music clubs reflect the broad spectrum of interests of the people who live and work in the area. A short walk or local bus ride enables students to browse through neighborhoods of unique shops and fine old Victorian homes or visit the area's conservatory, zoo, two museums, and professional sports arenas.

The University serves the needs of the Chicago community in many ways, such as providing the public with theater, music, and the resources of the Mental Health Center and its Learning Disabilities Center, the Legal Clinic, and the Monsignor John Egan Urban Center. There are also courses in several adult and graduate programs that are offered at all of the University's campuses.

Majors and Degrees

Bachelor of Arts and Bachelor of Science degrees are offered through six undergraduate colleges. The College of Liberal Arts and Sciences provides programs of study in the following fields: American studies, art, biological sciences, chemistry, clinical laboratory science, communication, comparative literature, economics, English, environmental science, French, geography, German, history, international studies, Italian, Jewish studies, Latin American studies, mathematical sciences, nursing (R.N. completion only), philosophy, physics, political science, psychology, religious studies, sociology and anthropology, Spanish, urban studies, and women's studies. The School of Computer Science, Telecommunications and Information Systems provides programs of study in computer science, data analysis and database information systems, and human-computer interaction. The College of Commerce offers programs of study in accountancy, business administration, economics, finance, management, and marketing leading to a bachelor's degree, as well as a five-year program leading to both a bachelor's and a master's degree in accountancy. The School of Education offers programs of study in early childhood education, elementary education, physical education, and secondary education. The School of Music provides programs of study in applied music (performance), composition, jazz studies, music/business, music education, and sound recording technology. The Theatre School (founded in 1925 as the Goodman School of Drama) offers programs of study in acting, costume design, costume technology, dramaturgy/criticism, general theater studies, lighting design, playwriting, production management, scene design, theater management, and theater technology. Certificate programs are offered in acting and costume construction.

Double majors and minors may be taken in many areas of study. Preprofessional programs include dentistry, engineering, law, medicine, optometry, osteopathy, pharmacology, and veterinary medicine.

A 3-2 option and a 2-3 option in pre-engineering, which result in a B.E. from Illinois at Urbana-Champaign, Illinois at Chicago, Detroit, Southern California, Northwestern, Iowa State, Ohio State, or the University of Notre Dame, are available.

Academic Program

To be eligible for a degree, a student must complete at least 188 quarter hours of college academic work with a grade point average of at least 2.0. Each college has its own liberal studies program, consisting of courses taken in five divisions: English and history, philosophy-religion, fine arts and literature, behavioral-social sciences, and natural sciences–mathematics. Typically, thirteen courses are required for a major. The academic year is composed of three quarters.

Outstanding students may enter with credit earned through selected Advanced Placement (AP) Program tests. Up to 50 percent of the total credits necessary for graduation can be earned through CLEP, Advanced Placement, and University tests. In some cases, degree requirements can be completed in three years. Advanced undergraduates may take graduate courses. Honors programs are also offered in accountancy and in liberal arts; an honors degree is awarded.

The School for New Learning is DePaul's nontraditional college for adults 24 years of age or older. The school offers a competency-based program featuring contract learning and individualized curricula. Students are responsible for designing their own programs and may receive credit for life experience.

Off-Campus Arrangements

The University has study-abroad programs that are available in Argentina, China, England, France, Germany, Greece, Hungary, Ireland, Israel, Italy, Japan, Malta, Mexico, Poland, Russia, South Africa, Spain, Thailand, Vietnam, and Zimbabwe.

Academic Facilities

The DePaul Center, a $70-million teaching, learning, research, and student services complex, is the cornerstone of the Loop campus. The DePaul Center Library at the Loop campus and the Lincoln Park Library contain 738,072 volumes, 15,890 periodical subscriptions, and extensive microcard and microfilm collections. The Law Library has 183,187 volumes and 10,356 periodical subscriptions. Among the outstanding holdings are the Dickens, Napoleonic, Horace, and Irish collections; the Farthing Collection of Illinois Sessions and Statutes; the antiquarian treasury of St. Thomas More's works; and the Verrona Williams Derr–African/American Collections. The libraries have reciprocal borrowing agreements with six other universities and are members of major cooperative lending groups.

The facilities and equipment of the Academic Computing Services include two VAX-11/780 central processors (the nation's largest DEC system), two 9-track magnetic tape drives, and three additional disk drives. These systems, along with an AT&T system 3B2/300, a Harris system HCX-9, and an IBM 4381 system, provide a total of 609 ports for student input through 800 campus terminals. Also available are 144 dial-in telephone lines for students with home computers who prefer to complete course work on the University computer from their homes. Student computer facilities, including more than 850 microcomputers, are located on all six DePaul campuses.

Among the other academic facilities are a 140-seat lecture/recital hall, the Concert Hall with a seating capacity of 500, and the 1,400-seat Reskin Theatre for stage productions. In 1999, the McGowan Center for Biological and Environmental Sciences, a three-story state-of-the-art facility, was opened at the Lincoln Park campus.

Costs

For the 2000–01 academic year, tuition is $15,390 for the Schools of Education, New Learning, and Computer Science and the Colleges of Liberal Arts and Sciences and Commerce; $18,700 for the School of Music; and $19,600 for The Theatre School. The tuition amounts for The Theatre School and the School of Music are guaranteed for four years. The registration fee (included in the tuition amount) is $30; books are estimated at $600. Average housing costs in 2000–01 are $4450 for room (double occupancy) and $1800 for board. A required resident health-care fee is $126 per year; waiver of this cost is possible if the resident is covered by private insurance.

Financial Aid

DePaul has planned its financial aid program to assist as many students as possible. Scholarships, grants, loans, and work-study opportunities are awarded singly or, more commonly, are combined in a financial aid package to meet the demonstrated financial need of the student. About 70 percent of full-time DePaul students receive some form of financial aid; 68 percent of the recipients receive gift assistance.

Merit scholarships for freshmen and transfer students, with values ranging from $6000 to full tuition for four years (approximately $56,000), are based on academic and extracurricular accomplishments. Institutional competitive scholarships are based on equal consideration of class rank, grade point average, and SAT I or ACT scores, without regard to need. Out-of-state and Illinois applicants are treated equally. All other financial aid programs, except athletic, music, and theater talent awards, are based primarily on need.

Students who wish to apply for aid must complete the Free Application for Federal Student Aid (FAFSA) and the DePaul application for admission. Applications and information can be obtained by contacting the Office of Student Aid. Application and notification of decisions are on a rolling basis. Financial aid programs are available to transfer students on the same basis as they are for regular upperclass students. Students are encouraged to apply before April 1 to receive maximum consideration.

Faculty

Approximately 88 percent of the full-time faculty members hold the Ph.D. or the terminal degree in their field. Faculty members are selected for their teaching ability and conduct all University classes. In addition to teaching, DePaul's faculty members are also engaged in research, publishing in their fields of expertise, and service. Graduate assistants do not teach classes at DePaul.

Student Government

The Student Government Association offers students the opportunity to become involved in representative government. The student-operated Activities Board also provides services and programs.

Admission Requirements

A candidate for freshman admission to DePaul University should be a graduate of an approved secondary school and should have taken a minimum of 16 academic units. It is recommended that the academic work emphasize English, mathematics, laboratory science, social studies, and college-preparatory electives. Applicants should rank in the upper half of their class and present strong SAT I or ACT scores. Recommendations are required, and interviews are recommended. The School of Music and The Theatre School require auditions and interviews for admission. Early action, advanced placement, a cooperative high school–college program, and deferred entrance are available.

Transfer students are welcome. To be considered, transfers must be in good academic standing at the last college attended and must have earned a minimum cumulative GPA of 2.0 (C) in transferable courses at all colleges attended. Commerce applicants must have a cumulative GPA of 2.5 or better; registered nurses interested in the B.S.N. completion program must have at least a 2.5 cumulative GPA. At least 30 semester (44 quarter) hours of transferable credit must have been completed; those who have completed fewer than 30 semester hours must also meet the requirements of freshman applicants.

Rolling admission is on a space-available basis. The early action deadline is December 1. It is strongly recommended that freshman applicants apply by February 1.

Application and Information

Applicants are notified of the disposition of their applications soon after their application files are completed.

Campus visits and overnight stays are regularly scheduled for prospective students. Interested students and their families are encouraged to call the admission office to arrange for an individual tour.

For further information, prospective students should contact:

Office of Admission
DePaul University
1 East Jackson Boulevard
Chicago, Illinois 60604-2287

Telephone: 312-362-8300
        800-433-7285 (toll-free outside Illinois)
E-mail: admitdpu@wppost.depaul.edu

DEPAUW UNIVERSITY
GREENCASTLE, INDIANA

The University

"DePauw is not a spectator sport" is the way one graduate described the DePauw experience. Indeed, DePauw students expect and seek a challenge. In small classes, students are challenged by professors who are leading scholars with a passion for teaching. There are countless opportunities to excel in more than fifty programs of study, four honors programs, numerous leadership positions with student organizations and living units, athletic programs, and more. DePauw students have a tradition of volunteerism, as demonstrated by the fact that three fourths of the student body of 2,200 participate in community service each year. In the first annual *Guide to Campuses Where You Can Make a Difference*, DePauw ranked among the top fifteen colleges where students are truly making a difference in terms of service, both on campus and in the community. In brief, DePauw provides a broad, liberal arts education that is intended to serve as a foundation for the student's lifetime of learning and growth.

At DePauw, the traditional liberal arts curriculum is complemented by perhaps the largest per capita student internship program in the country. Sixty-nine percent of DePauw students complete at least one internship during a semester, Winter Term, or summer, and 27 percent of students complete at least two internships. As a result, DePauw offers a unique opportunity for students to explore various interests and career possibilities, and that has a significant impact for students following graduation. More than 96 percent of DePauw graduates are employed or in graduate/professional school within nine months of graduation. The figure increases to more than 99 percent after one year. Of those students obtaining employment after graduation, approximately 1 out of 4 students accept jobs at companies and organizations where they served a student internship.

Much of DePauw's reputation for excellence can be attributed to the uncommon success of its alumni. DePauw ranked eleventh in the nation in terms of the likelihood that its graduates will become chief executive officers of major American companies, according to *Fortune* magazine in 1990. DePauw ranked eighth in the nation and first in the Midwest as the undergraduate origin of the nation's top executives, according to a 1994 study by Standard & Poor's Corp. DePauw also ranked sixteenth as a baccalaureate source for Ph.D. degree recipients in all fields, according to a 1998 survey by Franklin and Marshall College.

DePauw guarantees graduation in four years for students in forty standard programs, or the University waives tuition and fees for any subsequent course work necessary for graduation.

Location

DePauw is located in a town of 10,000 people set amid the gently rolling hills of west-central Indiana. The campus is exceptionally well maintained, blending new, state-of-the-art facilities with buildings, such as the historic East College, that exemplify the University's heritage. DePauw students are very active in the community, as indicated by the fact that about three fourths of the student body volunteers each year for public service in twenty-five community organizations. Greencastle is 45 miles west of Indianapolis and within a 4-hour drive of Chicago, St. Louis, Louisville, Cincinnati, and Columbus.

Majors and Degrees

DePauw offers the Bachelor of Arts (B.A.), Bachelor of Music (B.Mus.), Bachelor of Musical Arts (B.M.A.), and Bachelor of Music Education (B.M.E.). DePauw offers majors in more than fifty areas, including anthropology, art (history), art (studio), biological sciences, chemistry, classical civilization, classical languages, communication, computer science, conflict studies, earth sciences, East Asian studies, economics, elementary education, English (literature), English (writing), French, geography, geology, German, Greek, health and physical performance (sports medicine and sports science), history, interdisciplinary, Latin, mathematics, modern Romance languages, music and a second major, music-business, music composition or performance, music education, philosophy, physics, political science, psychology, religious studies, Russian studies, sociology, sociology and anthropology, Spanish, and women's studies. Preprofessional programs are available in dentistry, law, medicine, and secondary education. In addition, DePauw offers 3-2 programs in medical technology, pre-engineering, and prenursing.

Academic Program

DePauw is committed to providing its students with a traditional, liberal arts education complemented by internship opportunities, and degree requirements reflect this approach. The University follows a 4-1-4 calendar, with four-month fall and spring semesters and a January Winter Term. The normal course load in a semester is four courses, but course load may vary from three to 4½ courses. During the January Winter Term, first-year students study on campus, and upperclass students participate in research, internships, and travel abroad. DePauw's distinctive honors programs include Honor Scholars, Management Fellows, Media Fellows, and Science Research Fellows.

During the 1999–2000 academic year, DePauw began a new first-year experience program, called depauw.year1, that is designed to build a sense of community among first-year students. The program includes special seminars, speakers, programs, and other activities.

Thirty-one courses are required for students earning a Bachelor of Arts, Bachelor of Music, or Bachelor of Musical Arts degree. The Bachelor of Music Education degree requires thirty-two courses. Each student must complete a major, achieve at least a 2.0 GPA (on a 4.0 scale) in that major, and satisfy the senior major requirement. Students must attain a minimum cumulative GPA of 2.0, while students in the B.M.A. and B.M.E. programs need a minimum 2.5 GPA. Fifteen courses leading to a bachelor's degree, including six of the last eight courses, must be completed in residence at DePauw or in a University-approved program. Students in the College of Liberal Arts must achieve certification in writing (W), quantitative reasoning (Q), and oral communication skills (S). Students must complete three Winter Term projects with satisfactory grades, including an on-campus Winter Term for first-year students. A maximum of 3 internship course credits and five internship experiences (including Winter Terms) may be applied toward the bachelor's degree.

Off-Campus Arrangements

DePauw offers extensive off-campus study programs. Domestic programs include the Washington Semester, United Nations Semester, Sea Semester, New York Arts Program, Newberry Library Program, Oak Ridge Science Semester, and Philadelphia Urban Semester. Study abroad is available in Africa, Australia, Austria, Belgium, the Caribbean, China, Denmark, England, France, Germany, Greece, India, Indonesia, Ireland, Italy, Japan, Latin America, Mexico, the Middle East, the Netherlands, Scotland, Singapore, the former Soviet Republics, Spain, Switzerland, Vietnam, and the former Yugoslav Republics. Many students also participate in off-campus Winter Term projects.

More than 40 percent of students study off-campus as part of their DePauw experience. In order to receive course credit, a student must have approval from the International Center; other restrictions may apply.

Academic Facilities

The new blends with the old on DePauw's 175-acre campus, which features sixty-two buildings and a nearby 40-acre nature preserve. DePauw's facilities provide an excellent environment for teaching and learning. The physical plant is equal to or superior to that of other liberal arts universities.

The centerpiece of the campus is historic East College, built in 1877 and listed on the Register of Historic Landmarks. Newer buildings on campus include the F. W. Olin Biological Sciences Building, which features state-of-the-art facilities for science research, teaching, and study. The Center for Contemporary Media has superb facilities and equipment for *The DePauw*, the oldest student newspaper in the state; student-operated WGRE-FM radio; and a television unit in which students produce programs for broadcast statewide and nationwide. The Grover L. Hartman Center for Civic Education and Leadership serves as a coordinating center for student volunteer programs. The Performing Arts Center is home to the School of Music and features outstanding performance halls.

Costs

Expenses for the 2000–01 academic year include $20,200 for tuition, $6324 for room and board, and $310 in fees for health services and activities. Books and supplies are approximately $550 per year, and personal expenses are approximately $700 per year.

Financial Aid

Admission to DePauw is need-blind. Ninety-six percent of all DePauw students receive scholarships, grants, loans, or work-study assistance. The average financial aid package covers slightly more than half of total costs. DePauw's financial aid program is designed to recognize achievement and potential and to assist students who otherwise would be unable to attend the University due to financial constraints. DePauw maintains its own scholarship, work, and loan programs and participates in all traditional forms of state and federal financial aid.

February 1 is the priority filing date for applications for fall financial aid. FAFSA and institutional financial aid applications are required. Scholarships/grants available include federal and state scholarships/grants, University scholarships/grants, private scholarships/grants, ROTC scholarships, academic merit scholarships, and activity scholarships. Approximately 32 percent of students work on campus during the academic year. DePauw participates in the Federal Work-Study Program, and 51 percent of students who receive financial aid participate in work-study.

Faculty

DePauw professors are devoted to teaching students. The University has 191 full-time equivalent faculty members, and 93 percent have the terminal degree in their field. The student-faculty ratio is 11:1. All classes at DePauw are taught by professors and not by graduate assistants. Ninety-seven percent of full-time faculty members serve as academic advisers to students.

Student Government

Leadership opportunities in a wide variety of organizations are an integral part of the DePauw experience. Students have numerous opportunities to be involved in student government as well as committees and councils representing student concerns. The president of the student body presides over the many committees of the Student Congress; each committee has several student representatives as members. Sororities, fraternities, and residence halls all have annual elections of officers and representatives to various campus organizations.

Admission Requirements

DePauw does not conduct admission by the numbers. Along with grades and SAT I or ACT scores, the University looks at the required student essays, record of other achievements, and examples of any special talent a student may have. Also considered are the high school attended, the quality of courses selected in high school, and the recommendations of high school counselors, teachers, coaches, and employers. DePauw examines each individual's application carefully.

To be admitted to the first-year class at DePauw, students must have graduated from an accredited secondary school or offer evidence of equivalent education. Students should have completed the following work in a college-preparatory program: 4 units of English, 4 units of mathematics, 3 units of a foreign language, 4 units of social science, and 3 units of science (2 or more laboratory sciences). In addition, School of Music candidates must audition.

Application and Information

Prospective students can obtain an application for admission by calling or writing the Office of Admission. DePauw also is a member of the Common Application Group and gives the common application the same consideration as the University's application.

Students interested in early decision must submit applications by November 1, and students interested in early notification must submit applications by December 1. Admission decisions are mailed in mid-December for early decision applicants and in mid-February for early notification applicants. Early decision applicants who are admitted must respond by February 15; other admitted applicants who decide to enroll must submit an enrollment deposit by May 1. Students should contact:

Madeleine R. Eagon
Vice President for Admission and Financial Aid
DePauw University
P.O. Box 37
Greencastle, Indiana 46135-0037
Telephone: 765-658-4006
          800-447-2495 (toll-free)
Fax: 765-658-4007
E-mail: admissions@depauw.edu
World Wide Web: http://www.depauw.edu

Historic East College is the centerpiece of DePauw University's campus. The East College bell summons students to class and also signals victories in football.

DESIGN INSTITUTE OF SAN DIEGO
SAN DIEGO, CALIFORNIA

The Institute

Design Institute of San Diego is a private, independent college founded in 1977 and devoted exclusively to professional education in interior design. Enrollment is approximately 290 students.

The Bachelor of Fine Arts degree program at Design Institute is nationally accredited by the Foundation for Interior Design Education Research (FIDER). FIDER accreditation is important because it is recognized by the profession's principal design organizations, such as the American Society of Interior Designers (ASID), the International Interior Design Association (IIDA), the Interior Design Educators Council (IDEC), and the National Council of Interior Design Qualification (NCIDQ).

Design Institute is approved to operate under the Education Code of the State of California as a degree-granting educational institution. The Institute is accredited as a Senior College by the Accrediting Council for Independent Colleges and Schools.

Students are encouraged to join such organizations as ASID and participate as student chapter members. Student contact with working professional interior designers provides insight and understanding of professional standards and practices and serves as an important reinforcement of classroom learning.

Design Institute students have won numerous national and regional portfolio and design competitions, including the ASID Yale R. Burge portfolio competition, the ASID/Villeroy and Boch "Designing with Tile" competition, the Halo/Metalux Annual Lighting competition, the ASID Interior Design Excellence Award, and IIDA CALIBRE awards.

Location

Design Institute of San Diego is located within a few miles of the Pacific beaches of La Jolla. Southern California has always been a mecca for artists and designers who find the ocean, the desert, and the California sunlight conducive to the creative life.

San Diego has become one of America's largest cities, but it has retained the character of a small, seaside community. Its lifestyle is casual while offering a wealth of cultural and intellectual resources, including major museums, galleries, opera, dance, and theater.

Recreational opportunities abound. The city has long been the home and training ground for many of the world's finest athletes. Biking, surfing, jogging, boating, and hiking are a part of San Diego life.

The city is alive with visual interest, from its gracious old missions to the stark beauty of the Salk Institute designed by Louis Kahn. All of this, combined with an almost perfect climate, makes San Diego an ideal city in which to learn and work.

Major and Degree

Design Institute of San Diego offers a single program of study leading to a Bachelor of Fine Arts degree in interior design.

Academic Program

The Bachelor of Fine Arts degree program prepares students for careers in interior design. It balances the two most important aspects of the profession: interior design as creative and technical ability and interior design as professional business practice.

The creative aspects of interior design are part of an ongoing dialogue with culture. Through formal education, students gain insight into the historical development of furniture, decorative objects, and the interior architectural features of the built environment.

The social sciences have a profound influence on design. Design Institute students study the needs, values, behavior patterns, perceptions, and responses of people as the basis on which to create environments for living and working.

The design process requires more than aesthetic and social decisions. Specialized knowledge of structural principles, details and drawing, programming, building codes, energy conservation, safety regulations, lighting, and methods of construction are all part of the vocabulary of today's interior designer.

The curriculum at Design Institute is carefully organized to introduce these concepts in logical sequence, continually layering and overlapping basic design principles as their levels of complexity increase, providing the student with a firm framework on which to build a professional practice.

The Bachelor of Fine Arts degree is awarded upon completion of three years of study in interior design (90 credit units) and one year of study in general education (36 credit units).

Design Institute operates on a semester basis, fall and spring. The program is offered both day and evening.

Academic Facilities

Academic facilities are of a high-tech contemporary style and include spacious classrooms, drafting studios, exhibition space, a computer lab, a student lounge, and administrative offices. A library containing books, periodicals, samples, catalogs, and slides is available for student use. All facilities offer convenient parking.

Costs

Tuition for 2000–01 is $10,200 for the academic year. Books and supplies are estimated at $400 per semester. Beginning students should budget an additional $400 for the purchase of equipment.

Financial Aid

Approximately 60 percent of students attending Design Institute in 1999–2000 received some type of financial assistance. Types of aid included Federal Pell Grants, Federal Supplemental Educational Opportunity Grants (FSEOG), Federal Stafford Student Loans, California Workstudy, and Cal Grants A and B. All awards are made on the basis of eligibility.

Faculty

The faculty at Design Institute includes 40 practicing interior designers, architects, artists, historians, environmental psychologists, lighting engineers, computer technologists, and business consultants—all working professionals who bring to the classroom practical instruction based on current professional knowledge.

Student Government

The college does not have a student government. All matters of interest to students are welcomed by the administration and faculty at any time.

Admission Requirements

All candidates for admission must possess a high school diploma or its equivalent. Previous training in art or design is not essential as this training is provided within the program. The school welcomes applications from those whose personal goals are consistent with the educational objectives of the school and whose previous background indicates a reasonable opportunity to benefit from the curriculum offered. A personal interview is advised but not required.

Transfer students may receive credit for courses, completed at an accredited institution, that are similar to courses at Design Institute. In some cases the transferring student may need to submit actual work for evaluation. A grade of C is required to transfer credit, and official transcripts must be presented.

Design Institute welcomes applications from international students. Those from non-English-speaking countries must present evidence of English language proficiency at a level that will allow them to proceed without difficulty. Certified translations of official transcripts are also required. A Certificate of Eligibility Form (I-20) will be issued after the applicant has submitted all admissions material and has been accepted by the school.

Application and Information

Admission decisions are made on a rolling basis for both the fall and spring semesters. Applications are evaluated upon the receipt of the completed application for admission, the application fee of $25, and official transcripts. Applicants will be notified of the school's decision in writing within thirty days of the completion of the admission procedures.

For a catalog and application, students should contact:

Paula Parrish
Director of Admissions
Design Institute of San Diego
8555 Commerce Avenue
San Diego, California 92121
Telephone: 858-566-1200
              800-619-4337 (toll-free)
Fax: 858-566-2711
E-mail: disdadm@msn.com
World Wide Web: http://www.disd.edu

Design Institute's faculty of active professionals provides a wealth of exposure to diverse design philosophies and experiences.

DICKINSON STATE UNIVERSITY
DICKINSON, NORTH DAKOTA

The University

Student success, both inside and outside the classroom, has been the focus of Dickinson State University since 1918 when the University was established as Dickinson Normal School and Model High. The tradition continues today, allowing easy access and meaningful relationships with qualified professors, supportive and comfortable living arrangements on campus, and with student activities, providing something for everyone.

Dickinson State, with an enrollment of approximately 1,800 students, is the only comprehensive, four-year public university in West River North Dakota. The University is proud of its safe campus. Its location offers students a secure environment in which to pursue their educational and social interests.

The University's mission, as dictated by the North Dakota University System, is to provide high-quality, accessible programs; to promote excellence in teaching and learning; to support scholarly and creative activities; and to provide service relevant to the economy, health, and quality of life of the citizens of North Dakota.

Dickinson State University is accredited by the North Central Association of Colleges of Schools (NCA), the North Central Association for Teacher Education (NCATE), and the National League for Nursing Accrediting Commission (NLNAC).

At Dickinson State, there are approximately forty-five different organizations to help every student find a niche. Students choose from intramural sports, band, chorus, drama, art, forensics, student government, honorary societies, academic clubs, and cheerleading, to name just a few.

Living in a residence hall at Dickinson State offers many conveniences and countless opportunities to build friendships in an exciting environment close to classes and University activities. Meal plans are available on campus for five or seven days per week. For added ease, students can also opt to purchase meals at the snack bar. Rooms have free access to the campus computer network and cable television. Features in each hall include game room, exercise equipment, computer stations, laundry facility, and kitchenette. Students can select to live in women's, men's, or coed halls. Three family student housing complexes provide 66 apartments at reasonable housing rates to nontraditional students.

Location

Dickinson State is located in Dickinson, North Dakota, near the rugged and beautiful Badlands. With a population of more than 18,000, Dickinson is the hub of West River North Dakota. The community lies only 30 miles from Theodore Roosevelt National Park, and it is just one hour's drive south of Lake Sakakawea. Dickinson is served by both commercial air and bus transportation.

Dickinson's location provides abundant opportunities for people to enjoy outdoor recreational activities year-round. The area's picturesque rivers, lakes, and Badlands are ideal for hiking, fishing, boating, hunting, cross-country skiing, and much more.

As the state's fifth-largest community, Dickinson offers a wide array of restaurants, shopping malls, specialty stores, historic landmarks, museums, movie theaters, and other entertainment outlets. The region offers abundant dinosaur fossils and geological phenomena for explorers of all ages. Many of these treasures are displayed in Dickinson's impressive Dakota Dinosaur Museum.

Health-care services are provided by a 109-bed acute-care hospital, two major clinics, and numerous specialty clinics. The University's Student Health Service provides prompt care on campus for routine health concerns.

Majors and Degrees

Programs offered at Dickinson State University include liberal arts along with specialized programs in education, business, health services, agriculture, and computer science. There are opportunities for preprofessional study and vocational training in selected areas as well.

Dickinson State offers Bachelor of Arts and Bachelor of Science degrees in 10 departments, including majors and/or minors (indicated with a *) in accounting, agriculture, art, biology, business administration (with concentrations in accounting, agribusiness, banking and finance, business management, computer science, management information systems, manufacturing technology, marketing, and office administration), business education, chemistry, coaching*, computer science, earth science*, elementary education, English, geography*, German*, graphic design, history, journalism*, mathematics, music, music education, nursing, physical education, political science, psychology*, science composite, secondary education, social science composite, social science (elementary education)*, sociology*, social work (linked with University of North Dakota), Spanish, speech and theater, university studies, and writing.

Associate degree programs include agriculture with specialty areas in agriculture sales and service or farm and ranch management, nursing, office administration (with concentrations in accounting, agribusiness, computer, legal, management, and medical studies), and university studies.

Preprofessional programs include chiropractic, dentistry, engineering, forestry, home economics, law, medicine, medical/lab technology, mortuary science, optometry, physics, social work, veterinary, and wildlife management.

Academic Program

While many of the majors that Dickinson State University offers have unique academic requirements, the basic baccalaureate degree academic curriculum consists of approximately 39 semester hours of general education courses from the areas of communications, scientific inquiry, expression of human civilization, understanding human civilization, multicultural studies, and physical education; a specific major core curriculum of 32 to 60 or more semester hours; approximately 24 semester hours of credit in a minor field of study (when a minor is required); and professional education course work for those students entering the teaching profession. Students seeking a Bachelor of Arts degree must also complete a minimum of 16 semester hours of a foreign language. A minimum of 128 semester hours is required for graduation in a baccalaureate degree program. Associate degree programs require 64 credit hours for graduation.

Academic Facilities

The commitment to technology at Dickinson State is evident in the number of cutting-edge computers provided for student use.

There is an outstanding student-to-personal computer ratio, resulting in easy access to the type of technology students need to excel. Computer labs are located in academic areas, the library, and all residence halls. Students also have free access to e-mail and the Internet, including the World Wide Web.

Stoxen Library is proud of its highly sophisticated automated library. The On-line Dakota Information Network allows students to access resources from across the United States.

Costs

For North Dakota residents, tuition and fees are $1189 per semester; for Minnesota residents, they are $1258 per semester; for residents of Montana, South Dakota, Manitoba (Canada), and Saskatchewan (Canada), they are $1437 per semester; for residents of Alaska, Arizona, California, Colorado, Hawaii, Idaho, Nevada, New Mexico, Oregon, Utah, Washington, and Wyoming, they are $1685 per semester; and for residents of other states, tuition and fees are $2844 per semester. Room and board costs range from $1358 to $1650 per semester. Books are approximately $300 per semester. These figures reflect current costs, which are subject to change.

Financial Aid

College is a valuable investment in the future, and Dickinson State realizes financing it can be challenging. One of the best college buys in the region, Dickinson State's tuition and housing rates are among the lowest in the upper Midwest. In addition, attractive tuition rates are offered for students living in states and provinces bordering on North Dakota. Special rates also exist for students who live in those states participating in the Western Undergraduate Exchange (WUE). These include Alaska, Arizona, California, Colorado, Hawaii, Idaho, Nevada, New Mexico, Oregon, Utah, Washington, and Wyoming.

The Office of Financial Aid is ready to help ease the cost of a college education through a number of financial aid programs, including scholarships, grants, loans, student employment opportunities, cultural diversity awards, and international awards. More than 85 percent of Dickinson State's students received financial assistance last year.

Faculty

Dickinson State University has 75 full-time and 30 part-time faculty members. Students develop close relationships with their teachers since three fourths of classes have fewer than 30 students.

Student Government

The Student Senate is the governing body and official voice of Dickinson State University students. The Senate is composed of a cross-section of students elected by the campus community. The Campus Activity Board (CAB) offers a broad range of social and recreational activities, including dances, films, comedians, and other special events. The Campus Programming Committee (CPC) provides a variety of educational, instructional, and cultural programs. Residence Hall Councils are made up of elected student residents and deal with matters relating to campus housing. The Student Policies Council is composed of students, faculty, and staff members. The Council recommends policies and programs related to student affairs.

Admission Requirements

Dickinson State's admission policy allows students to enroll if they are high school graduates or have successfully completed the GED examination along with completion of the ACT. The completion of a high school college-preparatory course core curriculum is also required for admission into a baccalaureate program.

The nursing program has special enrollment and admissions requirements. Students should apply early for this program.

All students under the age of 21 who have not completed 60 credit hours are required to live on campus. Exceptions to this policy include married students; students living locally with parents, grandparents, or a legal guardian; students who live with a brother or sister who is a head of a household; and single parents with one or more dependents.

Application and Information

The admissions staff is anxious to discuss the variety of programs the University has to offer and give a tour of the beautiful campus, its classrooms, facilities, and residence halls. When students are on campus, they should meet with the financial aid staff to discuss concerns about financing an education. Admissions representatives are available Monday through Friday, 8 a.m. to 4 p.m., Mountain Time. Students should contact:

Office of Admissions
Dickinson State University
Dickinson, North Dakota 58601-4896
Telephone: 800-279-HAWK (toll-free)
E-mail: dsuhawks@eagle.dsu.nodak.edu
World Wide Web: http://www.dickinsonstate.com

Dickinson State University students have the opportunity to participate in a myriad of activities.

DOMINICAN COLLEGE OF BLAUVELT
ORANGEBURG, NEW YORK

The College

Dominican College, an accredited four-year institution for men and women, reflects the traditions of its founding Dominican order in its emphasis on a value-centered, liberal arts–based education. The College offers thirty undergraduate programs and four master's degree programs in special education, occupational therapy, physical therapy, and nursing. Its 1,800 students represent a diverse ethnic population and include both campus residents and commuters.

Dominican's campus is growing. The Hennessy Student Center, completed in 1995, contains a 1,000-seat gymnasium, a physical fitness room, a suspended running track, athletic training facilities, athletic offices, and all-purpose meeting rooms. Hertel Hall, a residence center completed in 1996, contains social areas, computer-equipped study lounges, a kitchenette, student meeting rooms, and computer- and cable-equipped double and suite-type dorm rooms. Resident students eat in the Granito Center, which was also built in 1996. Seven other buildings comprise the campus. Cooke Hall houses administration offices; the admissions office is in De Porres Hall. Doyle Hall is the teacher education facility, and the library is located in Pius X Hall. Casey, Rosary, and Forkel Halls contain classrooms. Casey Hall also houses the dean's office and the offices of the arts and sciences, business administration, and social sciences faculties.

There are a number of social, athletic, and academic activities on campus through which students can satisfy personal interests. Student organizations include the yearbook, the College newspaper, the drama club, Alpha Chi honor society, the Council on Student Activities (COSA), and academic clubs. To help students take advantage of the region, the College organizes outings, including ski trips to the Berkshires and theater evenings in Manhattan. Varsity sports include men's baseball, basketball, cross-country, golf, and soccer and women's basketball, cross-country, soccer, softball, and volleyball. Dominican College is a member of the National Collegiate Athletic Association (NCAA), the National Association of Intercollegiate Athletics (NAIA), and the Central Atlantic Collegiate Conference (CACC). In addition, many community service–oriented activities are available through academic departments of the College and through the campus ministry program.

In order to serve the adult and nontraditional student, the College offers an Accelerated Evening Program, a Weekend College, and an Evening Program. Students enrolled in these programs may pursue full-time study while maintaining full-time employment. Academic support services, career counseling, co-op education, internships, and placement opportunities are provided for all students. Continuing education programs for professional development and cultural enrichment are also offered.

In addition to its undergraduate degrees, Dominican offers a five-year Bachelor of Science/Master of Science degree in occupational therapy; a Family Nurse Practitioner Program leading to a Master of Science (M.S.) in Nursing degree; a Master of Science in Education (M.S.Ed.) degree leading to certification in special education, with an emphasis on teaching students with multiple needs; and a Master of Science (M.S.) in physical therapy.

Location

Dominican College is located in Rockland County, New York, 17 miles north of New York City and approximately 3 miles north of Bergen County, New Jersey. This convenient suburban location offers easy access to the outstanding cultural and educational resources of New York City.

Majors and Degrees

Dominican College awards B.A., B.S., B.S.Ed., B.S./M.S., and B.S.N., degrees. The areas of concentration in the liberal arts are American studies (with programs in education only), biology (which includes a premedicine track and pre–physical therapy studies), English, history, humanities, mathematics, natural sciences, psychology, and social sciences. In business administration, areas of concentration include accounting, computer information systems, economics, health service administration, and management, and there are specializations in financial management, human resource management, information systems management, international management, and marketing management. Business course clusters are also available in personal computers and supervisory management.

Other areas of concentration are elementary education, secondary education, special education/elementary education, special education for teachers of the visually impaired/elementary education, and special education/secondary education.

Also offered are programs in athletic training and generic and upper-division nursing and an Accelerated Bachelor of Science in Nursing program (accredited by the National League for Nursing Accrediting Commission) as well as programs in occupational therapy (accredited by the Accreditation Council for Occupational Therapy Education) and social work (accredited by the Council on Social Work Education). A five-year integrated program in engineering offers a Bachelor of Arts degree in mathematics from Dominican and a Bachelor of Engineering degree from Manhattan College.

Academic Program

The degree programs at Dominican College have been designed to give students the benefit of a continuum of study in the liberal arts disciplines and in professional preparation. A purposely flexible approach to the requirements for the baccalaureate degree accommodates varied learning styles, previous academic backgrounds, divergent learning and career goals, and prior experience.

To receive a degree, students must complete a minimum of 120 semester hours, 30 of which must be earned at Dominican College. The College will grant up to 60 credits for achievement on proficiency examinations administered by American College Testing, Inc.; the New York State Regents' External Degree Program; and the College-Level Examination Program. Learning acquired through experience may also be validated by the submission of a portfolio demonstrating that the student has acquired knowledge that corresponds to courses required at Dominican College.

Placement testing and a coordinated advisement process provide students with information and guidance for the effective use of the resources of the College. Support for the ongoing development of academic skills is provided through the Learning Resources and Writing Center, which offers tutoring in basic mathematics, writing, and other subjects. Opportunities for elective internships and independent study enable students to pursue a wide range of career and academic interests. An Honors Program provides innovative learning opportunities for qualified students.

Academic Facilities

The College library, located in Pius X Hall, provides more than 103,000 volumes and approximately 640 periodical titles, with more than 14,300 volumes of additional back files on microfilm. The collection includes reference sources, basic indexes, and other bibliographic aids, including computerized search programs with remote access.

Forkel Hall contains science laboratories and a nursing practicum lab. Casey Hall houses the Learning Resources and Writing Center. Students may use computer labs in Casey and Rosary Halls; the residence center is also equipped with computers.

Costs

Dominican College offers a fixed tuition rate under which new full-time students registered in the fall or spring semester are guaranteed tuition protected from increases for the entire period of continuous enrollment. The tuition for 2000–01 is $12,660 per academic year. Room and board are $7000 per academic year. For part-time and weekend students, the undergraduate tuition is $422 per semester hour.

Financial Aid

Dominican College administers four types of aid: scholarships, grants, loans, and work-study programs. Scholarships are awarded on the basis of a student's academic record and financial need. Athletic grants are awarded to men and women on the basis of athletic ability, financial need, and academic record. Leadership Incentive Grants are awarded to students who demonstrate leadership skills and potential. Students applying for aid should file the Free Application for Federal Student Aid (FAFSA) by February 15. Transfer students are required to submit a transcript of all financial assistance received at institutions previously attended.

Supplementary aid opportunities are available through the New York State Tuition Assistance Program (TAP), the Federal Pell Grant Program, the Federal Family Education Loan Program, the Federal Supplemental Educational Opportunity Grant Program, Nursing Student Loans, Nursing Scholarships, the Federal Perkins Loan Program, the Federal Work-Study Program, and veterans' benefits.

Faculty

The Dominican faculty has 160 members, and the present student-faculty ratio is about 12:1. Faculty members hold degrees from thirty different universities and colleges located in fourteen states and three other countries. Many have had varied experiences prior to teaching at the college level. Faculty members work with students as academic advisers and as advisers for nonacademic activities.

Student Government

The Dominican College Student Government Association is the official representative of the students. It approves charters for clubs and organizations, helps to plan the cultural and social calendar, aids in directing and coordinating social activities, and manages the student activity budget.

Admission Requirements

Entering freshmen are expected to have completed a secondary school program or its equivalent. The recommended preparation includes 16 academic units distributed among English, mathematics, natural sciences, social sciences, and foreign languages. All applicants for admission as freshmen are required to take the SAT I or the ACT. TOEFL scores are required for international applicants. Test results submitted from comparable national testing programs will also be accepted. Admission to the Honors Program is available to students who rank in the upper levels of their high school graduating class and who achieve acceptable scores on entrance examinations. A minimum cumulative index of 2.0 is required for transfer students, with a maximum of 70 credits accepted from accredited two-year colleges and 90 credits from four-year colleges.

A personal interview is recommended in order to allow the applicant to become better acquainted with the College and to exchange information with a member of the admission staff. Dominican College does not discriminate on the basis of sex, race, color, age, national origin, religious affiliation, or physical limitation and is an Equal Opportunity/Affirmative Action employer.

Application and Information

An applicant should submit the completed Dominican College application form to the Office of Admissions.

Application forms and additional information may be obtained by contacting:

Director of Admissions
Dominican College
470 Western Highway
Orangeburg, New York 10962
Telephone: 914-359-7800
           201-476-0600
E-mail: admissions@dc.edu
World Wide Web: http://www.dc.edu

Dominican College fosters relationships between students and faculty members through small, personal classes. Students also benefit from an array of academic programs and Dominican College's Fixed Tuition Plan. The College's Fixed Tuition Plan means no increase in tuition dollars over four continuous years of full-time enrollment.

DOMINICAN UNIVERSITY
RIVER FOREST, ILLINOIS

The University

Dominican University is a Catholic university with a total enrollment of 2,300 men and women. Rosary College of Arts and Sciences, the undergraduate college of the University, offers a liberal arts curriculum with a career orientation in a personalized, value-centered environment. Exciting and diverse course work—from international business to communication arts and sciences, from chemistry to fashion design and merchandising—encourages individuality and independence. Special programs, such as study abroad and honors seminars, challenge students to reach their highest potential as scholars, as professionals, and, most important, as individuals.

The emphasis on a strong liberal arts curriculum began in Wisconsin in 1848 when Fr. Samuel Mazzuchelli, O.P., founded St. Clara Academy, a frontier school for young women. Father Mazzuchelli offered instruction in astronomy, logic, history, and natural philosophy—courses considered revolutionary for women at the time. Administered by the Dominican Sisters of Sinsinawa, St. Clara College was established in 1901. In 1918, on the invitation of Archbishop Mundelein of Chicago, the school was incorporated in River Forest as Rosary College. The institution has been coeducational since 1970. In 1996, the Board of Trustees formally approved changing the name of the institution to Dominican University.

The atmosphere on the 30-acre wooded campus is close-knit. The ivy-covered Gothic buildings are impressive; they include a 287,000-volume library, a Fine Arts Building with a recital hall and auditorium, two fully-networked residence halls, and the Student Center, home to the men's and women's basketball and volleyball teams. Alive with activity, the center has an elevated running track, an indoor swimming pool, and a student grill that overlooks the glass-enclosed racquetball courts. Other varsity sports include men's baseball, soccer, and tennis and women's soccer, softball, and tennis.

Rosary College of Arts and Sciences offers more than forty major fields of study. The University also has three graduate schools: Business, Education, and Library and Information Science. Approximately 50 percent of the corporate librarians or information specialists in the Chicago area are graduates of Dominican University.

In addition to a solid academic program and respected, dedicated instructors, the University offers innovative learning opportunities. For example, Dominican University was one of the first colleges in the United States to offer study-abroad programs. Just 4 students participated in that first Fribourg semester; today, University undergraduates earn college credits through programs based in London, Strasbourg, Florence, Milan, and Salamanca.

Spring Fling, Founder's Day Celebration, and the inspiring Candle and Rose ceremony—Dominican University's traditions make a student's college life rewarding and memorable. A variety of clubs and honor societies also offer the opportunity for students to get involved. Students often travel off campus, perhaps to a Cubs baseball game at Wrigley Field or perhaps to a Chicago soup kitchen as a Campus Ministry volunteer. The University also sponsors a wide range of cultural programs on campus, ranging from lectures, plays, and concert performances by the Vienna Boys Choir and the Chicago Sinfonietta, the orchestra-in-residence, to an appearance by Danny Glover. Recent theater productions include *Godspell*, *The Crucible*, and *A Chorus Line*.

At Dominican, opportunities to grow are limited only by the student's imagination.

Location

Dominican University is located in River Forest, a residential suburb just 10 miles west of Chicago's Loop. Students can take advantage of city offerings by using nearby public transportation, or they can enjoy the surrounding Oak Park–River Forest residential community, which, among other attractions, is home to the largest number of Frank Lloyd Wright houses in the country. These include Wright's first home and studio.

Majors and Degrees

Dominican University awards both the Bachelor of Arts and the Bachelor of Science degrees. Programs include accounting, American studies, art, arts and media management, biology, biology-chemistry, business administration, business writing, chemistry, communication arts and sciences, computer graphics, computer information systems, computer science, corporate communication, criminology, economics, education, engineering, English, environmental management, environmental science, fashion design, fashion merchandising, fine arts, food science and nutrition, food service management, French, gerontology, graphic design, history, international business, international relations and diplomacy, Italian, mathematics, mathematics and computer science, nursing, nutrition and dietetics, pastoral ministry, philosophy, photography, political science, psychology, social science, sociology, Spanish, theater arts, and theology.

The Bachelor of Arts Honors Degree is awarded to students who complete the interdisciplinary Honors Program. Preprofessional programs are available in dentistry, law, library and information science, and medicine. In cooperation with Rush University, Dominican University offers the first two years of study in nursing and medical technology. Engineering students complete a five-year degree program, earning a Bachelor of Arts degree from Dominican University and a Bachelor of Science degree from Illinois Institute of Technology.

Academic Program

The curriculum of Rosary College of Arts and Sciences is built around a core of interdisciplinary seminars and liberal arts requirements. One interdisciplinary seminar is taken at each academic level. The liberal arts core requirements include history, philosophy, social sciences, natural sciences, literature and fine arts, and religious studies. In addition, students must demonstrate proficiency in writing, mathematics, computer applications, research, and a foreign language. The language requirement can be met in a variety of ways, including study abroad. Service learning and experiential learning opportunities are available to all students. Students must complete 124 credit hours to graduate.

The Honors Program is designed to adapt the strengths of a small institution to the special needs of superior students. Students invited to participate in the program take four honors seminars during their years at Dominican University. In their senior year, honors students complete special projects in their major fields.

Off-Campus Arrangements

Students have a variety of opportunities to study off campus, ranging from the study-abroad programs described below to the Washington Semester, a semester of study at the Washington (D.C.) Center for Learning Alternatives. Students in the sciences and mathematics have the opportunity to do research at Argonne National Laboratory, one of the outstanding research centers in the country. Juniors and seniors who have fulfilled any prerequisites set up by their major department may earn credit through internships. The internships provide on-the-job experience that gives students a realistic view of their field.

Students are encouraged to deepen their understanding of other peoples and cultures through study-abroad programs. The semester in London includes 6 to 8 semester hours of British life and culture and 6 to 8 semester hours of independent study. The Strasbourg experience is a two-semester program. During the first semester, students continue their language and civilization studies while participating in internships in business, political, or other organizations. Other study-abroad programs are available in Florence, Milan, and Salamanca. In addition, Dominican University faculty members assist students who wish to study in other countries.

Academic Facilities

At the heart of academic life is the Rebecca Crown Library, with more than 287,000 volumes, 1,200 periodicals, and 70,000 federal government documents. The library's membership in LCS (an online network of more than thirty academic libraries in Illinois) and ILLINET-ON-LINE (a network of 600 public and academic libraries) provides access to more than 10 million volumes and 10,000 current periodicals. The University also provides computer laboratories and classrooms where students may do classwork or personal projects. In the Fine Arts Building, students may attend lectures, plays, and musical performances in the auditorium and recital halls or view exhibitions in the art gallery. The Science Building is also home to the Junior Citizens' Child Development Center, a licensed day-care facility for children of faculty, staff, students, and community residents.

Costs

Tuition and fees for 2000–01 are $14,820 for full-time students. Room and board charges are estimated at $5030 (costs vary depending on type of room and meal plan selected). Part-time students are charged $490 per credit hour. The cost of books averages $700 per academic year.

Financial Aid

Dominican University supports both merit-based and need-based financial aid programs. Academic scholarships are offered to qualified full-time incoming freshmen based on grades and ACT/SAT I scores and to full-time transfer students who have a minimum cumulative 3.5 grade point average at previous institutions. Parish Leadership Awards are available to full-time incoming students.

Need-based financial aid programs include grants, loans, and campus employment. Students apply for financial aid by submitting the Free Application for Federal Student Aid (FAFSA). Aid awards are made on a rolling basis, but early application is encouraged. Institutional grants, as well as Federal Supplemental Educational Opportunity Grant (FSEOG) and Federal Pell Grant funds, are available to students. State grants are available to Illinois residents through the Illinois Student Assistance Commission. Federal Perkins Loans and Federal Stafford Loans are offered to eligible students. The University also offers monthly payment plans.

Approximately 70 percent of undergraduate students receive some form of financial assistance.

Faculty

Excellent teachers ensure the excellence of education. At Dominican University, more than 70 percent of the faculty hold doctoral degrees. With a student-faculty ratio of 12:1, individualized attention is the norm.

All classes at Rosary College of Arts and Sciences are taught by faculty members of the University; there are no teaching assistants. The highest priority of the University is teaching. In addition, faculty members do research and publish works in their academic disciplines.

All advising is done by members of the faculty, who guide students in choosing their courses, selecting majors, and developing career interests. Close interaction between faculty members and students is the hallmark of the undergraduate program.

Student Government

Members of the Student Government Association (SGA) represent students on various official committees such as the board of trustees, educational policies committee, and judicial review board. In addition, SGA sponsors educational and social events for students and distributes student activities fees to the clubs and organizations.

Admission Requirements

Graduation from an accredited secondary school is required for admission. In addition, the academic record in high school, class rank, and test scores on the ACT or SAT I are considered. Generally, students who rank in the upper half of their high school class, have a composite score of 20 or above on the ACT or a combined score of 950 or above on the SAT I, and have a minimum 2.5 GPA are eligible for admission. Currently, more than 50 percent of entering freshmen rank in the upper 25 percent of their class. Sixteen units of college-preparatory work are required; 14 of the units must be in the areas of English, mathematics, social studies, laboratory science, and foreign language.

Generally, applicants wishing to transfer from another college or university must have a cumulative grade point average above 2.3 in order to qualify for admission.

Application and Information

Rosary College of Arts and Sciences operates on a rolling admissions program. However, early application is recommended to ensure that financial aid and housing are available. A $20 application fee is charged, and a $100 tuition deposit is required after acceptance. The tuition deposit also serves as a housing deposit for students who plan to live on campus.

Office of Undergraduate Admissions
Dominican University
7900 West Division
River Forest, Illinois 60305
Telephone: 708-524-6800
                800-828-8475 (toll-free)
Fax: 708-366-5360
E-mail: domadmis@email.dom.edu
World Wide Web: http://www.dom.edu

Dominican University's Lewis Hall.

DOMINICAN UNIVERSITY OF CALIFORNIA
SAN RAFAEL, CALIFORNIA

The University
Dominican University of California (formerly Dominican College of San Rafael) is an independent, Catholic, learning-centered university. It offers a beautiful setting, a close-knit community of approximately 1,400 students, and an intimate social environment that is an important context for academic goals and personal development.

The Office of Student Development coordinates many services that support the University's educational programs. It provides life-planning, career, and personal counseling without charge to Dominican students; offers housing, health, and job placement services; and helps students make the most of their college experience by its readiness to assist them in resolving problems.

The University and the Associated Students of Dominican University sponsor a number of campus activities each year for both resident and nonresident students. Dominican supports eight intercollegiate teams that compete in the NAIA Far West Region, California Conference: men's and women's basketball, soccer, and tennis and women's softball and volleyball. Students can participate in the chorus, drama group, literary magazine, newspaper, campus ministry activities, special interest clubs, dances, and other social events.

Campus Ministry responds to the spiritual needs of Catholic and non-Catholic members of the University community. Catholic liturgies, ecumenical activities for students of all faiths, and community service projects are scheduled throughout the year.

Graduate degrees (M.A., M.S., and M.B.A.) and credentials are granted in counseling psychology, education, humanities, international business with a Pacific Basin focus, nursing, strategic leadership.

Three residence halls of varied architecture accommodate 250 students; there is a dining hall for resident students and others who wish to purchase meals on campus. Forest Meadows, which comprises approximately 25 acres, is the site of the new Conlan Recreation Center, a soccer field, and an outdoor amphitheater where commencement exercises are held. The Recreation Center features regulation basketball and volleyball courts, two cross-courts for volleyball and basketball, and 1,285 spectator seats. It also features a weight-training and fitness room, a multipurpose room, lockers, athletic department offices, and conference rooms. Outside is a six-lane recreational swimming pool and grassy patio area.

Location
The University is located on 80 wooded acres in scenic Marin County, 17 miles north of San Francisco and less than an hour's drive from Pacific Ocean beaches.

Majors and Degrees
A broad range of degrees and certificate and credential programs are offered in letters, the arts and sciences, and professional and preprofessional disciplines.

Undergraduate degrees (B.A., B.S., B.S.N., and B.F.A.) are awarded in the academic areas of art, art history, biology, business (accounting and finance, information business systems, international business, management, and marketing), communications (journalism and marketing), e-studies (e-art and e-commerce), English, English with a writing emphasis, environmental science, history, humanities, interdisciplinary studies, international studies, liberal studies, music, music with a performance concentration, nursing, occupational therapy, politics, prelaw, premedicine, psychology, and religion.

Academic Program
The General Education Program offers more than a brief exposure to the major areas of knowledge in the humanities, arts, and natural and social sciences. It is designed to provide a sequence of courses with a thematic focus that integrates the wisdom and perspectives of several disciplines. The focus assists students in discovering relationships between areas of knowledge, beliefs, cultures, and peoples that differ globally and historically, as well as in acquiring an awareness of tradition, a love of discovery, a respect for the diversity of the human condition, and a realization of human interdependence. Courses within the General Education Program also expose students to a variety of learning experiences that includes discussion, lectures, seminars, simulations, practicums, and quiet reflection.

A strong internship program offers students job experience in areas of their choice.

An evening degree-completion program (Pathways) for adult learners is also available.

The ELS Language Centers program provides intensive, high-quality English instruction to prepare international students to enter American colleges and universities. Completion of the ELS Language Centers' program Level 201 satisfies Dominican's English requirement for admission.

Off-Campus Arrangements
Dominican offers exchange programs with Aquinas College, Grand Rapids, Michigan; Barry University, Miami, Florida; and St. Thomas Aquinas College, Sparkill, New York. These programs enable students matriculated at any one of the four colleges to spend a semester on a campus in a different part of the country, taking advantage of its location and programs. Students pay tuition on their home campus and room and board on the host campus. Further information about the program, recommended for students in the sophomore or junior year, is available from the Office of the Vice President for Academic Affairs.

Individualized programs for study in other countries may be planned in consultation with Dominican's Center for International Programs, the adviser, and the transcript evaluator. Dominican grants credit for international study only after a student who obtained prior approval of the program of study has returned to the campus and enrolled for the following year.

Arrangements are available whereby Dominican students can participate in Army ROTC at the University of San Francisco, Air Force ROTC at San Francisco State University, or Naval ROTC at the University of California at Berkeley. Students interested in the ROTC programs should request further information from the appropriate ROTC recruiting officer.

Academic Facilities
Archbishop Alemany Library houses approximately 100,000 volumes in open stacks, almost 3,000 reels of microfilm,

subscriptions to nearly 500 periodicals in print, and another 1,200 in full-text online. The library also houses the Fletcher Jones Computer Laboratory, an art gallery, a listening room, and a fireplace corner.

Guzman Hall, Albertus Magnus Hall, Bertrand Hall, and the San Marco Art Gallery together house faculty offices, science laboratories, lecture halls, a computer center, art galleries and studios, and classrooms. Angelico Hall houses an 850-seat concert auditorium and theater, music studios and practice rooms, and faculty offices.

Costs

Undergraduate full-time tuition (12–17 units per semester) is $17,256 per year for 2000–01; part-time tuition is $719 per unit. Fees are $350; room and board (a nineteen-meal-per-week plan) are $8440 annually.

Financial Aid

Financial aid is awarded on the basis of need and merit. Dominican University participates in various federal and state need-based financial aid programs and also has its own financial aid funds, donated by generous alumni and friends, available to help meet University costs.

Need-based financial aid comes in the form of scholarships, grants, part-time employment, and loans. The federal and state financial aid programs are the Federal Supplemental Educational Opportunity Grant, Federal Pell Grant, Federal Work-Study, Federal Stafford Student Loan, CLAS/PLUS loan, and Cal Grants A and B. Eligibility for need-based aid is determined after the student, who must be a citizen or permanent resident of the United States, files the Free Application for Federal Student Aid (FAFSA). The need-based financial aid deadline for first priority consideration is February 1, although late applications are accepted. Student assistantship positions are also available for graduate students.

Faculty

Students find themselves intellectually challenged by the faculty members, who hold degrees from colleges and universities throughout the world and who are committed to individualized teaching and careful supervision of students' development. The majority of the faculty hold Ph.D.'s. The student-faculty ratio is 13:1.

Student Government

The primary vehicle through which students plan and provide activities, distribute activity funds, and represent themselves to the University's administration and broader community is ASDU—the Associated Students of Dominican University. ASDU is the student association and the student government body. Through elected and appointed representatives to various Dominican committees and governing groups, students may voice their opinions on institutional matters.

Admission Requirements

Dominican University welcomes applications from prospective students of all ages, religions, races, and national origins. Although the University prefers that candidates have a grade point average of at least 2.5 (a minimum of 2.0 for non-nursing/occupational therapy transfer students), the University believes that academic potential is measured by more than grades alone. Each candidate for admission is given individual consideration and is evaluated by the Admissions Office on the basis of his or her past scholastic record, present motivation, and potential intellectual development as indicated by all of the admission materials submitted.

Recommended for undergraduate admission are graduation from an accredited high school with a total of at least 15 units in college-preparatory subjects, to include the following: 4 years of English, 2 years of one foreign language, 2 years of college-preparatory mathematics (algebra, geometry, trigonometry), 1 year of laboratory sciences to be taken in grades 10–12, and 1 year of U.S. history (1 year of world history or Western civilization is an acceptable alternative for international students). The University encourages students to choose additional courses in at least two of the following areas: English, history, foreign language, fine arts, social science, advanced mathematics, laboratory science, introductory music, art, computer science, and typing.

Dominican University admits highly qualified students after the completion of their junior year in high school if they have fulfilled all admission requirements for freshman standing or passed an equivalency exam and arranged a conference with a member of the admission staff prior to acceptance.

High school seniors wishing to take up to two Dominican University courses per semester to meet high school graduation requirements may do so with the written permission of their high school principal or counselor. Arrangements must be made through the Office of Admissions.

Application and Information

The Admissions Office makes its decision on each freshman candidate after receiving his or her completed application form with a $40 nonrefundable fee; an official high school transcript to date; one recommendation from a teacher, administrator, or counselor; scores from either the Scholastic Assessment Test (SAT I) or the American College Testing (ACT) exam; and a personal essay as described in the application. (For information about the SAT I, students should write to Educational Testing Service, 1947 Center Street, Berkeley, California 94704 or P.O. Box 592, Princeton, New Jersey 08541. For information about the ACT, students should write to American College Testing Program, Operations Division, P.O. Box 168, Iowa City, Iowa 52243.)

Transfer students must also submit the application form, a $40 fee, and their high school transcript (if they have fewer than 24 transfer units). In addition, they must send official college transcripts to date and one academic letter of recommendation or one professional letter of reference.

International students should fulfill the admission requirements for native students; however, an SAT I or ACT score is not required. A score of at least 550 on the Test of English as a Foreign Language (TOEFL), administered by the Educational Testing Service, or official certification of achieving Level 201 in the ELS program may be submitted in lieu of SAT I or ACT scores.

An interview with a member of the admission staff is strongly recommended to enable the candidate and the University to become acquainted with one another.

Students may obtain application forms and information by contacting:

Office of Admissions
Dominican University of California
50 Acacia Avenue
San Rafael, California 94901-2298
Telephone: 415-485-3204
        888-323-6763E (toll-free)
Fax: 415-485-3214
E-mail: enroll@dominican.edu
World Wide Web: http://www.dominican.edu

DORDT COLLEGE
SIOUX CENTER, IOWA

The College

Dordt College is a Christian liberal arts college with an enrollment of more than 1,400 students from more than thirty states, seven Canadian provinces, and a dozen other countries.

Dordt College seeks to provide a complete Christian context for learning and equips its students to enter careers and face the challenging issues of the world with a deeper understanding of God's will.

Dordt is accredited by the North Central Association of Colleges and Secondary Schools. Dordt's social work program is accredited by the Council on Social Work Education, and the engineering program is accredited by the Engineering Accreditation Commission of the Accreditation Board for Engineering and Technology, Inc.

Dordt's students are mostly of traditional college age, and about 85 percent live in campus residence halls and apartments. Since a majority come to Dordt from a distance, the campus is a busy place, both during the school week and on weekends.

Dordt seeks to provide a wealth of opportunities for spiritual growth. Each school year begins with an all-College retreat, and throughout the year, students can take advantage of Bible study groups, twice-weekly chapel services, lecture and film series, residence hall devotions, and other opportunities for spiritual refreshment and sharing. Excellent opportunities for Christian growth and service are available through student-run volunteer organizations, which annually involve 15–20 percent of the student body in outreach projects.

Dordt College is a member of the National Association of Intercollegiate Athletics (NAIA). Intercollegiate competition for men is scheduled in baseball, basketball, cross-country, golf, hockey (club status), soccer, tennis, and track. Women compete in basketball, cross-country, soccer, softball, tennis, track, and volleyball. Club teams and a program of intramural sports offer competitive recreational activities for all students.

Dordt College has an active theater program that involves students of many majors. A campus newspaper, a yearbook, and a literary magazine are published by students. Students interested in music may audition for a place in one of two choral groups, the college band, or the orchestra.

Location

Sioux Center is an attractive, growing community of 6,000 about 45 minutes northeast of Sioux City, Iowa, and 60 minutes southeast of Sioux Falls, South Dakota. Both Sioux City and Sioux Falls offer major airline connections as well as entertainment options that are near enough to be convenient but distant enough to provide a getaway from campus life.

Sioux Center has a vigorous, diversified economy that provides students with numerous opportunities for part-time employment. Public parks, an indoor swimming pool, a golf course, and a full-service shopping district are a few of the attractive features of the city. Most important is the attitude of the people of Sioux Center, who warmly welcome the participation of students in the life of the community.

Majors and Degrees

Dordt offers a Bachelor of Arts degree, a Bachelor of Science in Engineering degree, and a Bachelor of Social Work degree, along with a two-year Associate of Arts degree.

Majors in the bachelor's degree program are accounting, agribusiness, agriculture, animal science, art education, art history, biology, business administration, chemistry, communication, computer science, Dutch, education, engineering, engineering science, English, environmental studies, exercise science, fine arts studio, general science, German, graphic arts, history, individual studies, management information systems, mathematics, medical technology, music, philosophy, physical education, physics, plant science, political science, psychology, public relations, radio/television communication, recreation, social studies, social work, Spanish, special education, theater arts, theology, and youth ministry.

Preprofessional programs are offered in dentistry, law, medicine, nursing, occupational therapy, optometry, pharmacy, physical therapy, seminary, and veterinary medicine.

Associate of Arts degree areas of concentration are agriculture, general studies, secretarial science, special education aide studies, and teacher aide studies.

Academic Program

Dordt College offers a dynamic liberal arts education that is permeated by a Christian world view. That distinctive educational approach places a particular major or academic discipline within a larger context, helping students see how different areas of life work together to reflect the wholeness of God's creation. Along with this broad perspective, Dordt College students develop the tools they need to function effectively in today's complicated world—the ability to distinguish sharply, to think critically, and to judge wisely.

In the eight semesters it typically takes to earn a bachelor's degree at Dordt, students take at least forty courses. Fourteen of those are general education requirements, such as communication, literature, natural science, history, and philosophy. General education also includes a cross-cultural component, which most students complete by participating in a study-abroad program or by taking one of a variety of courses with a strong cross-cultural component. Students who are earning a bachelor's degree must take ten or more courses in a major area. Programs such as secondary and elementary education require ten to fifteen professional courses in addition to the major. Other students may choose to take additional courses in their major, declare a minor or a second major, or take electives in areas that interest them.

In the two-year A.A. program, students take fewer general education courses plus twelve courses in an area of concentration that prepares them to enter a career field. Because students in the A.A. program take many of the same courses that are required for the B.A. degree, they are more broadly prepared than graduates of many two-year technical school programs. If they choose, students can go on and earn their bachelor's degrees with an additional two years of study.

Some majors require qualified students to complete an internship or practicum. In other majors, internships are available but optional. Some majors require senior research or design projects; other majors offer the option of pursuing a personal interest through an individual studies project.

Off-Campus Arrangements

Credit is offered for study off campus in the following programs: The American Studies Program, Washington, D.C.; the AuSable Institute of Environmental Studies; the Chicago Metropolitan Center Program; the China Studies Program; the German Overseas Program; the Latin American Studies Program, Costa Rica; the Los Angeles Film Studies Program; the Middle East Studies Program; the Netherlandic Studies Program in Contemporary Europe; the Oxford Honors Program and Summer School; the Russian Studies Program; the Semester in Spain; the Summer Institute of Journalism; and the Summer Study Program in Mexico.

Academic Facilities

Twenty-three well-equipped buildings occupy Dordt's 50-acre campus. Some of the College's specialized facilities include the Science and Technology Center, which houses a large greenhouse and accommodates the engineering, agriculture, chemistry, biology, and physics departments. Science students have the advantages of various modern laboratory facilities, including an electron microscope lab and a nuclear magnetic resonance lab. The library has study space for more than 350 students and houses more than 130,000 holdings. The library features a variety of computer applications, including an online catalog, online periodical indices, CD-ROM reference sources, and Internet access. The B. J. Haan Auditorium, with seating for 1,500, is home to the thirty-seven-stop, fifty-seven-rank Dordt College Casavant Organ, one of the finest organs in the Midwest. The auditorium adjoins the music building, which provides generous facilities for large group rehearsal, individual practice, classes, and labs.

Dordt's recreation complex is a full-featured fitness and physical education facility that includes a 2,500-seat gymnasium, a 200-meter indoor track, indoor tennis courts, racquetball courts, a weight room, three basketball/volleyball practice courts, and other facilities.

The Agriculture Stewardship Center, located two miles north of the campus, includes a dairy and 160 acres of farmland used for production, crop testing, and research for the College's agriculture program.

Costs

For the 2000–01 academic year, tuition is $13,200 per year. Room and board total $3800 per year, which included $1980 for a residence hall room and $1820 for a full meal plan. Other costs include a mandatory student activity fee of $150 and estimated annual student expenses of $600 for books, supplies, and personal items.

Financial Aid

About 95 percent of Dordt College students receive some form of financial aid, which may include scholarships, grants, loans, or a work-study position. In addition to participating in the full range of available federal and state programs for students with financial need, Dordt provides its own need-based aid as well as an extensive scholarship program, which is based on superior academic potential and performance.

Students applying for financial aid must complete the Free Application for Federal Student Aid (FAFSA) and the Dordt College Supplemental Data Form. These forms should be filed as soon as possible after January 1 and not later than April 1.

Faculty

Dordt College has 75 full-time faculty members. About 70 percent hold the highest degree in their teaching areas. Teaching is the primary task of the faculty, and the 15:1 student-faculty ratio means that personal attention to the needs of the student is a hallmark of education at Dordt College. Dordt also has the excellent services of a number of adjunct professors; however, since an exceptionally high percentage of faculty members are full-time, professors are readily available outside of class hours to answer questions and give advice.

Student Government

The student government organization at Dordt College, Student Forum, is an elected body that represents the opinions of the student community to the College administration through its own deliberations and through the placement of its members on various decision-making bodies on campus. In addition to student input via Student Forum, virtually every College committee has student representation. Elected residence hall councils are also part of the student government picture at Dordt College.

Admission Requirements

Dordt College seeks as students men and women who are committed to the biblical, Christian principles that undergird the College's academic program and campus life. Applicants for admission agree to live within the expectations and policies of the College.

For regular admission status, Dordt requires a cumulative GPA of at least 2.25 on a 4.0 scale and an ACT composite score of 19 or above or an SAT score of 910 or above. Required high school transcripts should show the following minimum course work: 3 years of English, 2 years of mathematics (algebra and/or geometry), and a half year of word processing/keyboarding. Recommended preparation includes an additional year of English and math, plus 2 years of science, social science, and foreign language.

Students whose records indicate that they may have difficulty with college-level work may be admitted with special provisions.

College credits presented by transfer students are evaluated on the basis of the quality of the student's work and the relationship of the subject matter to the Dordt curriculum. A maximum of 61 semester hours of credit is granted to graduates of junior colleges.

Application and Information

Application for admission should be made well in advance of the semester that a student wishes to enter Dordt College. Students are considered for admission after they have submitted the application for admission, a transcript of their high school record (and a college transcript in the case of transfer students), and results of the ACT. A $100 tuition deposit, refundable until May 1, is due within 21 days of acceptance.

For more information, students should contact:

Quentin Van Essen
Admissions Office
Dordt College
498 4th Avenue, NE
Sioux Center, Iowa 51250
Telephone: 712-722-6080
        800-34-DORDT (36738) (toll-free)
Fax: 712-722-1967
E-mail: admissions@dordt.edu
World Wide Web: http://admissions.dordt.edu

Dordt College graduates consistently rank faculty availability among the College's greatest strengths.

DRAKE UNIVERSITY
DES MOINES, IOWA

The University

A Drake University education offers a unique mix of advantages for future success. More than seventy major programs of study—including top-notch professional and preprofessional programs and options for undecided students—create lively and diverse learning opportunities. Drake's outstanding faculty members are renowned scholars and experts whose top priority is teaching. The student-faculty ratio is 14:1, and no graduate assistants teach classes. Drake's 4,900 students, including 3,100 full-time undergraduates and 400 full-time graduate and law school students, represent forty-six states and more than fifty countries. Approximately 1,700 students live on campus. Drake provides full high-speed connections to the University's telecommunications and fiber-optic systems and the Internet and World Wide Web in every residence hall room, with an Ethernet port for every resident. More than 95 percent of Drake graduates find career employment or enter graduate school within six months of earning their degrees.

In addition to its undergraduate degrees, Drake offers master's degrees in accounting, biology, business administration, education, mass communication, nursing, and public administration, as well as Doctor of Pharmacy, Doctor of Jurisprudence, and Doctor of Education degrees. The following joint degrees also are offered: M.B.A./J.D., M.B.A./Pharm.D., M.P.A./J.D., and M.A. in mass communication/J.D.

Location

Drake University's 120-acre campus is located in Des Moines, Iowa's capital and largest city. Des Moines offers numerous internship and employment opportunities in all fields, including government, banking, insurance, publishing, nonprofit organizations, and health care. More than 70 percent of Drake students graduate having had one or more internships. With a metropolitan population of approximately 400,000, Des Moines also offers diverse cultural and entertainment options, a convention center, a nationally known art center, a civic center, professional athletics, parks and bike trails, and a downtown skywalk system.

Majors and Degrees

The College of Arts and Sciences offers degree programs and liberal arts education experiences that equip students to apply knowledge and skills to the scientific, mathematical, literary, and artistic tasks that will confront them in all careers. The college awards Bachelor of Arts and Bachelor of Science degrees with majors in anthropology and sociology; astronomy; biochemistry, cell and molecular biology; biology; chemistry; computer science; economics; economics with business emphasis; English; environmental science; French; German; history; international relations; law, politics, and society; mathematics; mathematics education (secondary); military science; philosophy; physics; politics; psychology; religion; rhetoric and communication studies; sociology; and Spanish. The college offers individualized majors and an open enrolled (undeclared) option. Preprofessional study and combined-degree programs are available in church vocations, dentistry, law, marine science, medicine and allied fields, physics/engineering, and social work. Concentrations are available in aging studies, cultural studies, Latin American studies, multicultural studies, neuroscience, and women's studies. Through the School of Fine Arts, the College of Arts and Sciences awards Bachelor of Arts, Bachelor of Fine Arts, Bachelor of Music, and Bachelor of Music Education degrees, offering programs in art, music, and theater arts with a dual focus on teaching excellence and artistic creativity. The Department of Art and Design, which is accredited by the National Association of Schools of Art and Design, provides degree programs in art history, drawing, graphic design, interior architecture, painting, printmaking, and sculpture. The Department of Music provides degree programs in church music, music education, music performance, and piano pedagogy. Students may earn a Bachelor of Arts degree with a music major and a Bachelor of Music degree with elective studies in business. The Department of Theatre Arts offers majors in musical theater, theater arts, and theater education. The undeclared option is available in art, music, and theater arts.

Drake University's College of Business and Public Administration provides a four-year undergraduate program leading to the Bachelor of Science in Business Administration, with majors in accounting, accounting/other business major, actuarial science, actuarial science/finance, finance, general business, information systems, insurance, international business, management, and marketing. Interdisciplinary majors, combinations of majors, and open business (undeclared) enrollment are also available. The college is one of only 315 colleges in the nation that are accredited by the AACSB–The International Association for Management Education. Drake's College of Pharmacy and Health Sciences offers a two-year prepharmacy program as part of the six-year Pharm.D. program. The college is accredited by the American Council on Pharmaceutical Education and is a member of the American Association of Colleges of Pharmacy. The School of Journalism and Mass Communication offers a Bachelor of Arts in Journalism and Mass Communication with majors in advertising (management and creative tracks), electronic media (broadcast news and radio/television), magazines, news/Internet, and public relations. An open enrolled (undeclared) option is also available. The school is accredited by the Accrediting Council on Education in Journalism and Mass Communications. Drake's School of Education offers professional programs in elementary education, secondary education, and rehabilitation services. The University awards the Bachelor of Science in Education for teaching at the elementary level and the Bachelor of Arts or Bachelor of Science for teaching at the secondary level. Drake University has been a member of the American Association of Colleges for Teacher Education since the association's inception.

Undergraduate programs are offered through evening and/or weekend courses in accounting, finance, general business, information systems, insurance, international business, management, marketing, psychology, and sociology.

Academic Program

What makes the Drake experience so exceptional is the wide variety of accessible, hands-on learning opportunities students have both in class and out of class, beginning in their first year. Drake students conduct real research with top-notch faculty members and many students present and publish their work. They student-teach in local schools; participate in and lead more than 160 campus organizations; perform in campus and community theater productions and music ensembles; and work on the campus newspaper and radio/TV station and award-winning magazines. Students also gain invaluable experience in career-related internships in all fields and they network with Drake's 45,000 alumni worldwide, many of whom are business and civic leaders in central Iowa and beyond.

A Drake education combines a foundation in the liberal arts and sciences with professional programs. The Drake curriculum offers extraordinary preparation for the varied challenges of career and life, with discussion-based first-year seminars, individualized plans for achieving educational goals, and a Senior Capstone—a research project, thesis, or other major work that demonstrates a student's ideas and abilities. Candidates for an undergraduate degree are required to successfully complete a minimum of 124 semester hours. Exceptional students may participate in Drake's Honors Program, a challenging interdisciplinary program of study. Students also have many opportunities for internships, undergraduate research, independent study, and combined bachelor's and master's degree programs.

Qualified Drake students may earn credit through the College Board's Advanced Placement Program, the International Baccalaureate, College-Level Examination Program, and the Modern Language Association's Cooperative Foreign Language Tests.

The academic year is divided into two semesters; summer terms are also offered.

Off-Campus Arrangements

Through the Center for International Programs and Services, which maintains affiliations with several institutions and consortia, students can arrange to study overseas for a semester or a year. Programs are available in Argentina, Australia, Austria, Belgium, Belize, Bolivia, Botswana, Brazil, Cameroon, Canada, Central America, Chile, China, Costa Rica, Cuba, Czech Republic, Dominican Republic, Ecuador, England, France, Germany, Ghana, Greece, Hong Kong, Hungary, India, Indonesia, Ireland, Israel, Italy, Jamaica, Japan, Kenya, Latin America, Madagascar, Mali, Malta, Mexico, Morocco, Namibia, Nepal, the Netherlands, New Zealand, Nicaragua, Northern Ireland, Poland, Russia, Scotland, South Africa, Spain, Switzerland, Taiwan, Tanzania, Thailand, Tibet, Tunisia, Turkey, Uganda, Venezuela, Vietnam, Wales, Western Samoa, and Zimbabwe and on a cruise around the world.

Academic Facilities

Cowles Library contains more than 553,000 books and journals and more than 94,000 government documents. Specialized collections are also maintained by Drake's colleges and schools, including the Law School, the College of Pharmacy and Health Sciences, the Center for Teacher Education, and the School of Fine Arts. The multimillion-dollar Harmon Fine Arts Center includes the Studio Theatre, the Monroe Recital Hall, and the 600-seat Hall of the Performing Arts. The 775-seat Sheslow Auditorium in Old Main also provides a beautiful performance hall. The Dwight D. Opperman Hall and Law Library contains a computer resource facility, study rooms, and more than 250,000 volumes.

Costs

For the 2000–01 school year, tuition and fees are $16,980; room and board are $4870. Full-time students also pay a $110 technology fee annually.

Financial Aid

Drake University's financial aid program is designed to offer, within the University's resources, all capable and deserving students the opportunity for higher education. The average financial aid package awarded to Drake students in 1999–2000 was $14,290. Approximately 95 percent of full-time Drake students receive some form of financial aid; Drake provides more than 5,000 grants and scholarships on a merit and need basis and $40 million in financial assistance annually. Students interested in applying for financial aid should contact Drake's Office of Student Financial Planning and should file the Free Application for Federal Student Aid (FAFSA) by March 1. Students may apply for all federal, state, and institutional awards on this form.

Faculty

Drake's 267 full-time faculty members are accomplished in their fields and dedicated to their professions, yet they are primarily teachers. Full professors, including department chairs, regularly teach introductory-level courses. Each student works with a faculty adviser. The student-faculty ratio is 14:1.

Student Government

Drake offers students a wide variety of opportunities for campus involvement. Students play an active role in academic planning and campus governance through the Student Senate and its committees as well as through representation on some committees of the Faculty Senate. Students are elected to the senate by the student body. Students are also elected to the Student Activities Board, which plans cultural, social, educational, and special events. The Residence Hall Association is a network of student representatives who plan activities, address concerns, and provide information about residential life.

Admission Requirements

Admission to Drake University is competitive. Because the University prefers students with varied talents and interests, there is no single, inflexible set of admission standards; however, the essential criterion is a high school scholastic record that gives evidence of the student's capacity to do satisfactory college work. The Admission Committee grants or denies admission by reviewing each candidate's total record. Drake University admits students without regard to age, sex, sexual orientation, race, religion, color, national or ethnic origin, or disability.

To be considered for admission, first-year applicants must submit a completed application form, the $25 nonrefundable application fee, the High School Report and Counselor Recommendation Form, an official high school transcript, and ACT or SAT I scores. Applicants are also encouraged to submit a sample of their written work. An interview with a member of the admission staff is recommended but not required. Transfer applicants are considered for admission on the basis of all college work attempted. Transfer students must provide official transcripts from all colleges and universities attended previously; high school transcripts may also be requested.

Application and Information

Application for admission to undergraduate degree programs may be made for any fall, spring, or summer term. Beginning November 1, students are notified of the admission decision within three weeks of the date that all credentials are received. March 1 is the priority deadline for consideration for admission and merit- and need-based aid. Candidates should contact:

Thomas F. Willoughby
Dean of Admission
Drake University
Des Moines, Iowa 50311
Telephone: 515-271-3181
        800-44-DRAKE (toll-free)
Fax: 515-271-2831
World Wide Web: http://www.drake.edu

DREW UNIVERSITY
MADISON, NEW JERSEY

The University

Drew prepares students for personal and professional growth in a rapidly changing world. It provides a rigorous liberal arts education characterized by inspiring teaching, close student-faculty relationships, the integration of modern technology into the study of the traditional arts and sciences, widespread opportunities for experiential learning, and the cultivation of interdisciplinary and global perspectives. Students become fluent in the use of electronic information systems, explore the ideas and methodologies of diverse fields of study, sharpen the critical thinking and communications skills essential to success in all professions, and learn to place subjects of inquiry into larger intellectual and cultural contexts.

The use of the computer, as well as specialized equipment in the Academic Computer Center and the multimedia Language Resource Center, is integrated into the curriculum. All students, faculty members, and staff have access, from their rooms and offices, to a campuswide information system that includes the Internet, electronic mail, campus information, and the library catalog. Students also have access from their rooms to voice mail and broadband cable television with college, local, national, and international channels. In 1996, the University began operating a network in its academic and administrative buildings, allowing for high bandwidth communication and shared access to software and video, audio, graphic, and textual data, stored locally or on the Internet.

Drew is committed to providing students with a global perspective through special off-campus programs, a variety of area studies programs, and curricular opportunities to investigate the history, economics, politics, literature, religions, and cultures of other nations and heritages. In addition, student-organized clubs and activities promote and celebrate the multicultural and international diversity of the campus community. Along with the faculty and staff, Drew students (coming from thirty-nine states and ten countries) help create a stimulating and supportive campus community. Drew's enrollment totals more than 2,300 students, of whom close to 1,500 are undergraduates.

Ninety percent of Drew students live on campus in traditional residence halls or in special theme/language houses (ASIA Tree House, Umoja House, Environmental Concerns House, Spanish House, Spirituality House, and Women's Concerns House). Fifteen percent of Drew students are members of American ethnic minority groups. Drew students exert extraordinary influence on student affairs and provide leadership in seventy clubs and organizations, including a highly-rated newspaper, a radio station, a television station, a literary magazine, a prelaw society and law journal, cultural clubs, a social committee, service organizations, an environmental action group, political clubs, fine and performing arts groups, and intramural sports programs. In addition, students may attend more than 300 free lectures, concerts, exhibits, conferences, films, dances, parties, and performances each year. Speakers appearing in Drew's Forum have included Shimon Peres, Colin Powell, Barbara Bush, Gerald Ford, Mario Cuomo, George Bush, Mike Wallace, and Elizabeth Dole. First Lady Hillary Rodham Clinton spoke at Drew's 1996 commencement. The University also sponsors varsity sports (NCAA Division III), which include men's and women's basketball, cross-country, lacrosse, soccer, swimming, and tennis; women's field hockey and softball; men's baseball; and coed equestrian riding (IHSA) and fencing.

Drew has maintained a historical affiliation with the United Methodist Church since the school's founding in 1867 and provides a chaplain who, along with Roman Catholic and Jewish clergy, conducts worship services and oversees various student religious groups, including Catholic Campus Ministry, Hillel, Hindu Gathering, Methodist Ministry, and others.

Drew also has a graduate school, which offers eleven master's and eight doctoral programs in the humanities, as well as a theological school, which offers four professional degrees.

Location

Drew's undergraduates enjoy a location that affords a wide variety of academic, cultural, and recreational opportunities. Just 30 miles west of New York City, the quaint, small town of Madison, New Jersey, provides a safe home to Drew's beautiful, heavily wooded, 186-acre campus. The immediate area has the highest concentration of headquarters for international corporations and research companies in the nation. Proximity to these resources, and to those provided by New York City, makes special semesters, academic internships, research assistantships, field trips, and guest speakers important parts of all department curricula. In addition, numerous parks and recreational areas, including the Jersey Shore, several ski resorts, Giants Stadium, and the Meadowlands, are all within a 1-hour ride by car, commuter train, or bus.

Majors and Degrees

The College of Liberal Arts awards the Bachelor of Arts degree in anthropology, art, behavioral science, biochemistry, biology, chemistry, classics, computer science, economics, English, French, German, history, mathematics, mathematics and computer science, music, neurosciences, philosophy, physics, political science, psychology, religious studies, Russian, Russian area studies, sociology, Spanish, theater arts, and women's studies. Interdisciplinary and other special majors may be arranged. Minors are available in major subject areas (except behavioral science and neurosciences) as well as in African-American/African studies, American studies, archaeology, arts administration and museology, Asian studies, business management, comparative literature, environmental studies, European studies, humanities, Jewish studies, Latin American studies, linguistic studies, Middle East studies, Russian studies, Western heritage, and writing. Nonmajor offerings include international relations, marine biology, and foreign languages, including Arabic, Chinese, Hebrew, and Italian.

A seven-year, dual-degree program (including three years of study at Drew) leads to a B.A. from Drew and a medical degree (M.D.) from the University of Medicine and Dentistry of New Jersey–New Jersey Medical School (UMDNJ–NJMS) in Newark. An articulation agreement with the Graduate School of Management of Rutgers University offers qualified Drew graduates guaranteed admission to the M.B.A. program in professional accounting. Five-year cooperative programs lead to a B.A. from Drew and a master's degree in forestry from Duke University, a B.S. in engineering from Washington University in St. Louis or Columbia University in New York, or a B.S. in chemical engineering from Stevens Institute of Technology. Through a cross-registration agreement with the College of St. Elizabeth, students may earn teacher certification in several areas.

Academic Program

Drew operates on a two-semester calendar. To graduate with the bachelor's degree, students must complete 128 credit hours, including a major, the First-Year Seminar, and, as part of the general education program, a minor. The major is chosen by the end of the sophomore year. Independent study, a regular offering in some departments, is an option in all departments. Up to 8 semester hours may be earned in off-campus internships for academic credit. General and specialized honors are awarded in the major field. Drew has one of New Jersey's three Phi Beta Kappa chapters as well as chapters of twelve other national honor societies: Alpha Kappa Delta (sociology), Beta Beta Beta (biology), Omicron Delta Epsilon (economics), Delta Phi Alpha (German), Phi Alpha Theta (history), Pi Delta Phi (French), Pi Mu Epsilon (mathematics), Pi Sigma Alpha (political science), Sigma Pi Sigma (physics), Psi Chi (psychology), Sigma Delta Pi (Spanish), and Dobro Slovo (Russian). There is also Epsilon Omega Psi, Drew's Educational Opportunity Scholars honors program, and Pinnacle, for nontraditional continuing education students.

Off-Campus Arrangements

The Drew International Seminars Program was established to allow as many students as possible to study, on location, a culture other than their own. In small groups, students and faculty members engage in course work on campus combined with three to four weeks of on-site, interdisciplinary study during January or May. Subjects and locations vary each year, depending on interest. In 1999–2000, programs were held in Egypt, the Galapagos Islands, Greece, Ireland, Paris, Spain, and Ghana. In 2000–01, programs will be held in Egypt, Chile, Ireland, Cuba and Puerto Rico, Eritrea, Russia, and Tunisia. Students receive 8 credits for the entire program. The University subsidizes all travel, room, and board costs for the seminar; students are only charged tuition. Drew sponsors a summer program on the arts and culture of Western Africa in Côte d'Ivoire and semester-long programs that offer on-site study of British politics, history, literature, and theater in London; the new Europe in Brussels; American politics and public policy in Washington, D.C.; and theater, contemporary art, the United Nations, or Wall Street in New York City. Several of these programs include internship opportunities. A full-year exchange program is available with Marburg University in Germany. Students may also participate in off-campus programs sponsored and supervised by other recognized American colleges and universities. University-approved marine biology programs are available at such institutions as the University of Miami, University of Hawaii, Duke University, and the Marine Biological Laboratory at Woods Hole. Closer to campus, credit-bearing internship opportunities in business, communication, industry, government, social service, and the arts and entertainment provide students with professional experiences that allow them to apply theories and skills learned in the classroom.

Academic Facilities

The University library complex, which houses more than 470,000 volumes, 2,600 periodicals, and 358,583 microforms, is a federal, state, and United Nations depository. Drew's library is automated. Students and faculty have 24-hour direct access from personal computers to the Drew library card catalog and selected journal indexes as well as to other bibliographic databases across the nation. Drew maintains open computer labs for multimedia, foreign languages, computer graphics, and general use. The University's DEC VAX and DEC Server systems provide mainframe computing power for instruction and research. The Hall of Sciences contains impressive research-grade equipment, including a scanning electron microscope; an observatory with solar radio and optical telescopes; a greenhouse; a laser holography laboratory; nuclear magnetic resonance, infrared, ultraviolet-visible, and mass spectrometers; and a chemistry and physics library. The William E. and Carol G. Simon Forum and Athletic Center is open to the entire University community. There is seating capacity for 4,000 people in its indoor forum, featuring a Cybex fitness room; an eight-lane, 25-yard pool; a six-lane, 200-meter indoor track; and an indoor area with four multipurpose courts for basketball, tennis, or volleyball. Other major facilities include the Lena C. Coburn Media Resource Center, the Elizabeth Korn Art Gallery, the Commons Theater, and the recently expanded and renovated Kirby Shakespeare Theatre.

Costs

Tuition for the 2000–01 academic year is $23,472, fees are $546, and room and board are $6782.

Financial Aid

Drew offers a comprehensive program of need-based and merit-based financial assistance. Last year, 80 percent of the first-year class received some form of assistance. Need-based aid is available in the form of University grants, campus employment, loans, or a combination of these. The Federal Pell Grant, Federal Supplemental Educational Opportunity Grant, Federal Work-Study, state grant, and federal and state loan programs are also sources of aid. A completed Free Application for Federal Student Aid (FAFSA) and a completed PROFILE form of the College Scholarship Service are required of all applicants for need-based aid. The on-time filing deadline is February 15; aid applicants are notified in early April. No special application is necessary for Drew's various academic merit awards, including academic scholarships of between $6000 and full tuition and Thomas H. Kean Minority Scholarships of between $1000 and $15,000. Students must submit a portfolio for the $10,000 awards for artistic talent.

Faculty

Of the University's 117 full-time faculty members, 93 percent hold the Ph.D. or highest degree in their fields. All college faculty members teach undergraduates, including the dean and the president, Thomas H. Kean, the former Governor of New Jersey, who teaches a course on state politics and government. In addition, the Charles A. Dana Research Institute for Scientists Emeriti (RISE) has brought 10 select and prominent scientists, recently retired from the area's corporate community, to campus to continue their work. With hundreds of patents and publications to their credit, RISE scientists serve as mentors and provide research assistantships for undergraduates.

Student Government

The student government is active in shaping institutional policy, academic and nonacademic. Students sit as voting members on the University Senate and on many college faculty committees, administer their own social program, manage the extracurricular budget, and participate in the judicial process.

Admission Requirements

Applicants for admission are strongly encouraged to complete a minimum of 16 academic units, including 4 in English, 3 in mathematics, 2 in foreign language, 2 in laboratory sciences, 2 in social studies, and 3 in other academic areas. SAT I or ACT scores are required. Admission is based principally on academic performance in high school. Typically, nearly 50 percent of Drew's first-year students graduated in the top 10 percent of their high school class; nearly 75 percent graduated in the top 25 percent. Personal qualities and special talents are also considered. About 10 percent of each freshman class enter under Drew's Early Decision Plan, and early admission is also available. Applications from transfer and international students are encouraged. A campus interview is required for transfer students and strongly recommended for first-year candidates. Interviews are offered between May and January. Overnight accommodations are available on campus for visiting candidates. Tours are offered throughout the year.

Application and Information

The application deadline for first-year admission is February 15. Candidates are notified after mid-March. Accepted students are expected to respond to an offer of admission by May 1. The early decision application deadlines are December 1 and January 15. Transfer applications are reviewed on a rolling basis beginning April 1. The final deadline for transfer students for the fall semester is August 1. For information and application forms, prospective students should contact:

Dean of College Admissions
Drew University
Madison, New Jersey 07940
Telephone: 973-408-DREW
Fax: 973-408-3068
World Wide Web: http://www.drew.edu

DREXEL UNIVERSITY
PHILADELPHIA, PENNSYLVANIA

The University

Drexel is a private, nonsectarian, coeducational university that has maintained a reputation for academic excellence since its founding in 1891. Its academic programs offer students practical preparation for graduate school and a variety of careers. Full-time, paid professional experience through Drexel's cooperative education program is a vital part of a Drexel education. Students gain professional experience in jobs related to their career interests by alternating classroom study with periods of employment in business, industry, and government. More than 2,300 employers from twenty-eight states and ten other countries participate in this program. Another distinctive element is the University's microcomputer requirement, through which all undergraduates participate in a computer-enhanced education.

Drexel University grants bachelor's, master's, and doctoral degrees. The undergraduate enrollment is 6,800 full-time students, who represent all fifty states and numerous other countries. Seven modern coed residential halls house more than 2,200 students on campus. In addition to the challenging academic atmosphere, Drexel offers its students social, cultural, athletic, and community service opportunities. In conjunction with Drexel's fourteen fraternities and four sororities, the Campus Activities Board sponsors a host of events, including dances, lectures, excursions, and films. Students can also take part in a variety of extracurricular activities, including musical groups, a dance ensemble, theatrical productions, a computer users' group, and a student-run newspaper, radio station, and cable TV station. Drexel offers nine intercollegiate sports for men and nine for women and is a Division I member of the NCAA, competing in the regional conference, AMERICA EAST. Drexel also sponsors a variety of intramural and club sports.

Location

Drexel is located in the University City area of Philadelphia, a growing educational and residential community. The museums, theaters, restaurants, historic attractions, and recreational facilities of one of the nation's top cities can be reached easily from Drexel's campus. Year-round recreational opportunities can also be found in the Pocono Mountains and at the New Jersey shore, both within 2 hours of the campus.

Majors and Degrees

The College of Arts and Sciences awards Bachelor of Arts and Bachelor of Science degrees with majors in applied sociology and participatory research, biological sciences, chemistry, communication, computer science, history-politics, international area studies, literature, mathematics, nutrition and food science, physics, psychology, and unified science.

Due to Drexel's recent alliance with MCP Hahnemann University, students in the College of Arts and Sciences may study art or family therapy, medicine, mental health technology, nursing, psychology, physical therapy, and public health or in the physician assistant studies program. These programs allow students to begin their studies at Drexel University before continuing at MCP Hahnemann University.

The College of Business and Administration awards the Bachelor of Science in Commerce and Engineering and the Bachelor of Science in Business Administration degrees. Both degrees are offered with concentrations in accounting, economics, finance, general business, human resource management, international business, management information systems, marketing, and operations management.

The College of Engineering awards the Bachelor of Science in appropriate technology, architectural engineering, chemical engineering, civil engineering, computer engineering, electrical engineering, environmental engineering, materials engineering, and mechanical engineering.

The College of Information Science and Technology awards a Bachelor of Science in Information Systems with concentrations available in areas such as analysis and design, distributed systems, information resource management, and knowledge-based systems.

Nesbitt College of Design Arts offers a Bachelor of Architecture program and Bachelor of Science degree programs in culinary arts, design and merchandising, digital media, dramatic writing, fashion design, film and video production, graphic design, hotel and restaurant management, interior design, music, and photography.

The School of Environmental Science, Engineering and Policy offers a Bachelor of Science in environmental science and environmental engineering. The School of Biomedical Engineering and Science, in conjunction with the College of Engineering, offers a Bachelor of Science in biomedical engineering. The School of Education offers preparation in teacher education.

Academic Program

Drexel's distinguishing feature is Drexel Co-op: "The Ultimate Internship"™. Combined with rigorous academic programs, this feature provides an education that enables students to bridge the gap between academic studies and the working world. The co-op/internship program generates a two-way educational force: academic knowledge finds concrete form in the workplace, while personal growth and experiential learning on the job enrich the academic experience.

All undergraduates are prepared for full-time professional internships through Drexel's cooperative education program. With the new flexible degree programs, studies in engineering, information systems, and commerce and engineering, as well as science programs in the College of Arts and Sciences, are designed to be completed in four or five years, including eighteen months of co-op experience. Design arts programs require four years to complete and include six months of co-op. Business, humanities, and social science programs offer both four-year and five-year co-op/internship options.

Each college has its own sequence of graduation requirements, including a common core of subjects and the opportunity for specialization after the core is complete. All engineering and science students share a common program for the first year and part of the second. Specialization begins in the fourth term through elective course work and also allows students to acquire background in related fields. In the College of Business and Administration, 40 percent of the graduation requirements are in business subjects and 40 percent in liberal studies. Nesbitt College of Design Arts has a common program with course work in the humanities, the arts, and the physical and social sciences through the first two years. Students then choose an area of professional specialization.

The College of Arts and Sciences provides students with a broad and useful preparation for a variety of careers, as well as preparation for graduate and professional schools. The College of Information Studies provides a foundation program in the liberal arts, sciences, and computers. This foundation prepares students for a choice of specializations within the information systems major, which can lead to careers in such fields as computer education, database administration and design, or information management consulting in business and industry, health and medicine, government, libraries, or education.

The University offers an honors program, open to students in every major. Qualified students take part in special sections of general and required courses as well as in honors colloquia and seminars. They are also encouraged to undertake ambitious independent projects under the supervision of a faculty adviser. Beginning in the third year, qualified students in most of Drexel's engineering and science specialties may take graduate courses along with their undergraduate curricula and graduate with B.S. and M.S. degrees. The University also offers a B.S./M.B.A. program.

Academic Facilities

Drexel has twenty buildings that are used for teaching; these contain dozens of state-of-the-art laboratories for classes and research. The W. W. Hagerty Library (1983) houses 493,537 volumes and maintains subscriptions to 3,435 periodicals. The LeBow Engineering Center (1989) forms a state-of-the-art engineering education complex with the Center for Automation Technology. The Design and Imaging Studio supports programs in the design arts. Instructional Media Services, Drexel's media production center, offers a variety of audiovisual and graphic design services. An electronic-music laboratory provides facilities for creating, modifying, and recording sound and music.

In 1983, Drexel became the nation's first university to require all entering students to have personal access to a microcomputer. As a result, there are more than 13,000 personal computers on campus. Drexel's mainframe system is an IBM 9121-320. Minicomputers include a Prime 6450 and an AT&T 3B15. The IBM and Prime systems have access to the Internet and the World Wide Web.

Costs

In 2000–01, the tuition for full-time freshmen enrolled at Drexel ranges from $15,744 for a student in the five-year program to $21,506 for a student in the four-year program. Fees are $1169 per year. The cost of on-campus housing ranges from $5025 to $5715. Board costs are $3295 per year. Books and supplies are approximately $500 annually and miscellaneous expenses are about $1600 for commuting students and $1100 for resident students.

Financial Aid

Approximately 87 percent of all freshmen receive financial aid. The aid package may contain academic, athletic, or performing arts scholarships; grants; or loans; or part-time employment. Federal programs are also included. All students applying for aid must submit the Free Application for Federal Student Aid by May 1. Notification of incoming freshmen and transfer students begins about March 1.

Drexel offers a unique achievement-based award, the A. J. Drexel Scholarship, to all qualified incoming freshmen and transfer students. With an annual award value of up to $8000, the A. J. Drexel Scholarship is renewable on a yearly basis, provided the student maintains a 3.0 grade point average and full-time status. Criteria include a strong academic record and involvement in extracurricular and community service activities.

Faculty

Approximately 97 percent of Drexel's more than 400 full-time faculty members hold the Ph.D. or the highest degree in their field. Many of the engineering faculty members are registered professional engineers. As a matter of policy, faculty members engaged in research and graduate teaching are required to teach at the undergraduate level as well. Thus, the undergraduate student benefits from the research activities of the faculty. Specially selected faculty members serve as advisers for freshmen.

Student Government

Drexel's student congress is composed of representatives from each of the colleges, student organizations, and special interest groups. The congress is structured so that all key administrators and deans in the University have student counterparts. Students take part in the governance and other decision-making processes of the University through joint committees and advisory boards.

Admission Requirements

All colleges within the University require completion of a college-preparatory program in high school that includes at least 3 years of mathematics and 1 year of laboratory science. Students applying to major in engineering, the sciences, and commerce and engineering are required to take 4 years of mathematics through trigonometry and 2 years of laboratory science; more advanced math, chemistry, and physics are strongly recommended. The quality of academic performance is more important than merely meeting minimum requirements. The strength of preparation is judged primarily by rank in class or relative grade point average, by the degree of improvement in the quality of the academic record, and by the comments and recommendations of the principal, guidance counselor, or teacher. Freshman applicants are required to take the SAT I or the ACT. Freshman applicants in engineering are required to take the SAT II Math II C test.

Transfer applicants must have a 2.5 cumulative average or better for consideration and generally are expected to complete at least 15 credits at a four-year college or community or junior college in a program of study comparable to the one being sought at Drexel.

Application and Information

Application forms with complete instructions for admission and financial aid and the appropriate college prospectus may be obtained by writing to the address given below. Each application must be accompanied by a nonrefundable application fee of $35; however, the fee may be waived in cases of extreme hardship if requested by the secondary school or if the student visits the campus. Students may access Drexel's online application at the Web site listed below.

Applications for regular full-time undergraduate status are accepted throughout the senior year. Drexel subscribes to the College Board's Candidates Reply Date of May 1. Transfer students should apply at least three months before the beginning of the term in which they wish to enroll.

Office of Undergraduate Admissions
Drexel University
3141 Chestnut Streets
Philadelphia, Pennsylvania 19104
Telephone: 800-2-DREXEL (toll-free)
World Wide Web: http://www.drexel.edu

In Drexel Co-op: "The Ultimate Internship,"™ Drexel students practice what they learn in the classroom in a professional setting while earning a salary and building a resume.

DUKE UNIVERSITY
DURHAM, NORTH CAROLINA

The University

Duke University is an independent, comprehensive, coeducational research university. It was founded in Randolph County, North Carolina, in 1838 as Union Academy. It became Trinity College in 1859 and moved to Durham in 1892. In 1924, in recognition of the Duke family, Trinity College became Duke University.

Duke offers undergraduate programs in two schools—Trinity College of Arts and Sciences and the Pratt School of Engineering. The University's professional schools in business administration, divinity, the environment, law, medicine, and nursing and the graduate schools of Arts and Sciences and Engineering rank at or near the top of their fields.

Duke's limited enrollment of 11,170 full-time students (6,367 undergraduates: 6,316 full-time and 51 part-time) places it among the smallest of the nation's major universities, and students enjoy an academic community that maintains a commitment to individual education and an appreciation of academic and individual diversity. Because approximately 87 percent of the undergraduates come from states other than North Carolina, the University population bears no special regional mark, although it derives direct benefit from the climate and culture of one of the most rapidly developing areas in the country.

Predominantly residential, the University provides housing and classrooms for undergraduate men and women on both the East and West campuses and some housing on the North Campus and in the Central Campus Apartments. First-year students are housed together on East Campus. Living units provide the focus for much of the social activity on campus, and residence halls differ in nature, providing a variety of residence styles for all students. Fraternities have traditionally been housed in sections of residence halls, while sororities observe no special housing arrangements. Approximately 36 percent of the undergraduate men and women belong to fraternities or sororities. Students are guaranteed four years of on-campus housing and must sign a three-year housing agreement. First-year students participate in a modified board plan. The University Union, the University-sponsored Artists Series, the Broadway at Duke Series, a variety of independent organizations, and varsity, club, and intramural sports provide a rich calendar of activities.

Location

Durham, a city of nearly 200,000, is about 250 miles south of Washington, D.C. Durham and nearby Raleigh and Chapel Hill constitute the three points of the Research Triangle, one of the nation's foremost centers for research-oriented industries and government, research, and regulatory agencies. Two interstates and the Raleigh-Durham International Airport (20 minutes from the campus) make Durham easily accessible.

Majors and Degrees

Trinity College of Arts and Sciences offers programs leading to the A.B. degree or the B.S. degree in African and Afro-American studies, art history, Asian and African languages and literature, biological anthropology and anatomy, biology, Canadian studies, chemistry, classical languages and classical studies, comparative area studies, computer science, cultural anthropology, drama, economics, English, environmental sciences, environmental sciences and policy, French studies, geology, Germanic languages and literature, history, Italian and European studies, linguistics, literature, mathematics, medieval and Renaissance studies, music, philosophy, physics, political science, psychology, public policy studies, religion, Russian, sociology, Spanish, visual arts, and women's studies. Minors are also available in a number of these fields.

Special nonmajor interdisciplinary programs are available in the applied sciences; arts; education; film and video; genetics; health policy; human development; Judaic studies; Latin American studies; markets and management studies; neurosciences; perspectives on Marxism and society; primatology; science, technology, and human values; and study of sexualities.

First-year students are encouraged to participate in the FOCUS program, which features seminar courses clustered around such topics as Evolution and Humankind, The Arts in Contemporary Society, Twentieth-Century America, Exploring the Mind, Twentieth-Century Europe, Changing Faces of Russia: Redefining Boundaries, Diversity and Identity: Unstable Labels, Computers and Society, and Visions of Freedom.

The Pratt School of Engineering offers accredited four-year programs leading to the B.S.E. in biomedical, civil, electrical, and mechanical engineering.

Academic Program

The University observes a two-semester calendar; first-semester exams fall before the winter break. Students in the liberal arts plan their own courses of study, with the counsel and approval of an adviser, according to guidelines rather than specific course requirements. The University Writing Course, a one-semester class in expository writing, is the only course required of all undergraduates. The general studies requirement for students in Trinity College consists of courses in four areas of knowledge: arts and literatures, civilizations, social sciences, and natural sciences and mathematics. In addition, through general studies courses and courses in the major, students meet requirements in modes in inquiry (quantitative, inductive, and deductive reasoning; interpretive and aesthetic approaches), focused inquiries (cross-cultural inquiry; science, technology, and society; ethical inquiry), and three areas of competency (foreign language, writing, research). Students with interests that cannot be met within an established major may apply to enter Program II, a specialized curriculum adapted to their particular interests. Thirty-four courses are required for graduation.

Seminars, tutorials, preceptorials, and discussion sections, ranging from 1 to 15 students, supplement the classes of the first two years and lead to advanced seminar and independent study courses in the junior and senior years. When students declare a major—no later than the end of the sophomore year—a faculty member from the major department becomes their permanent adviser. Superior work in the major field qualifies students to be invited to participate in special departmental programs leading to graduation with distinction.

Those who plan to continue their study in a professional school need not follow a prescribed curriculum at Duke. Instead, faculty advisers assist them in planning a program of study that provides an appropriate foundation for advanced work and that also takes into account their own special interests.

Off-Campus Arrangements

Duke offers an unusually comprehensive study-abroad program. Students may take advantage of opportunities organized by the University or those that are sponsored by other American schools. Students may also receive credit through arrangements made directly with foreign universities. In certain cases, scholarship aid may be applied to study abroad. Approximately 40 percent of all undergraduates take advantage of study-abroad opportunities.

Students take part in local internships and in other internship programs sponsored by the Career Development Center. Internships sponsored by the Institute of Policy Sciences and Public Affairs provide field training in such areas as the administration of justice, communication policy, environmental policy, and health policy.

Academic Facilities

With more than 4.8 million volumes, more than 16 million manuscripts, 1.3 million public documents, 22,588 audio and 18,701 film and video recordings, 3.9 million microforms, and 40,000 current serials, Duke University's library holdings are among the most extensive in the nation. Although the University's most sophisticated research facilities (a phytotron, a hyperbaric unit, and a free-electron laser facility) are used primarily for graduate and postgraduate research, they are also available to the undergraduate student who has reached a level of study requiring their use. Undergraduates may choose to spend a semester at the Duke University Marine Laboratory, which is located on a small island off the coast of North Carolina and includes laboratories, a natural history center, and two seagoing research vessels. Reciprocal arrangements with the Consolidated University of North Carolina permit the sharing of both library and classroom facilities of the various schools.

All students have access to extensive computing facilities and services supported by Duke's Office of Information Technology (OIT). Services include free accounts on Duke's main computer system, which provides access to the Internet for activities such as e-mail and browsing the World Wide Web. OIT maintains a number of campus computer clusters for use by the Duke community. Students find IBM personal computer clusters in ten campus locations and Macintosh clusters in seven. A number of applications, including word processors and spreadsheets, are installed on these computers. More than 100 Sun workstations occupy seven clusters; students may access UNIX software applications from these computers. All campus clusters are equipped with laser printers and provide Internet access. DukeNet is a campuswide fiber-optic network designed to provide high-speed data communications among computers on campus and to serve as Duke's connection to the Internet. All undergraduate residence hall rooms are wired for DukeNet access.

Costs

For 1999–2000, the cost of a year in Trinity College was $33,830, with $24,740 allotted for tuition and fees and an average of $7088 for room and board (although costs vary with accommodations). Tuition and fees for the School of Engineering were $24,840, for a total cost of $33,930. These total yearly estimates include miscellaneous expenses. All fees are subject to change; the Office of Undergraduate Financial Aid can provide up-to-date information.

Financial Aid

Duke University is committed to meeting 100 percent of the demonstrated need of all admitted students. Applying for financial aid has no bearing on the admissions decision. The comprehensive aid program includes honorary and need-based scholarships, both federal and institutional college work-study program awards, Federal Perkins Loans, Federal Stafford Student Loans, and University-sponsored internships. Students applying for financial aid should submit the Profile Application provided by the College Scholarship Service and the Free Application for Federal Student Aid (FAFSA). For further information, students should contact the Office of Undergraduate Financial Aid. Duke offers a limited number of merit and athletic scholarships. All students are automatically considered for all appropriate scholarships.

Faculty

Duke has a faculty of 2,168 full-time and part-time members. The student-faculty ratio is 11:1. More important than the favorable student-faculty ratios is the nature of the faculty: every department or division can claim individuals of national or international prominence; among the faculty members are current or past presidents of nearly all of the major academic societies; many professors have received presidential appointments to federal advisory positions; and more than 130 hold faculty chairs that have been named or endowed to attract or retain professors of extraordinary ability. In the arts and sciences, nearly every faculty member teaches undergraduates, and a great many make time available for service as first-year student and departmental advisers.

Student Government

Students at Duke are regarded as mature individuals capable of governing their own actions and at the same time furthering the best interests of the broader University community. The Duke Student Government and various student-faculty-administration committees provide a number of avenues for student involvement and interaction with the faculty and administration. Since 1972, Duke undergraduates have served as voting members of the Board of Trustees.

Admission Requirements

The Committee on Admissions selects students on the basis of their academic record, standardized test scores, and nonacademic accomplishments. Duke University does not discriminate on the basis of race, color, national or ethnic origin, gender, handicap, sexual orientation or preference, age, or financial need in the administration of its admission policies. No geographic quotas are imposed. Candidates for admission should present a minimum of 4 years of English and at least 3 of mathematics, natural science, a foreign language, and social studies. Students are encouraged to enroll in advanced level work in as many of these areas as possible since this provides the best preparation for the Duke curriculum. Most engineering applicants present 4 units in mathematics and at least 1 unit in physics and/or chemistry. Students should submit either ACT scores or SAT I and SAT II Subject Test scores, including the Writing Test. Applicants for the Pratt School of Engineering who choose to take the SAT I and II must take the SAT II: Subject Test in Mathematics. Personal interviews are recommended but not required. Most applicants are interviewed in their home regions by members of the Alumni Admissions Advisory Committee since the availability of on-campus interviews is limited. On-campus interviews may be scheduled from June 1 to November 30.

Application and Information

The application deadlines for first-year students are November 1 for early decision and January 2 for regular decision. Students who want to arrange an alumni interview should file Part I of their application by October 1 for early decision or by December 1 for regular decision. For transfer students the deadline is March 15 for fall admission. Students must choose to apply to either Trinity College of Arts and Sciences or the Pratt School of Engineering at the time of application. Required tests should be taken no later than January of the senior year (October of the senior year for early decision applicants). Duke accepts the Common Application.

For additional information, students should contact:

Office of Undergraduate Admissions
Duke University
2138 Campus Drive, Box 90586
Durham, North Carolina 27708-0586

Telephone: 919-684-3214
Fax: 919-681-8941
E-mail: undergrad-admissions@duke.edu

D'YOUVILLE COLLEGE
BUFFALO, NEW YORK

The College
D'Youville College is a private, coeducational, liberal arts and professional college that has offered students an education of high quality since 1908. The College was the first in western New York to offer baccalaureate degrees to women. Its current enrollment is 1,900 men and women. Students may choose from thirty undergraduate and graduate degree programs that are enhanced by a 14:1 student-faculty ratio. The College is committed to helping its students to grow not only in academics but in the social and personal areas of their college experience as well.

The multiple-option Nursing Degree Program is one of the largest four-year private-college nursing programs in the country. Available nursing programs include B.S.N., B.S.N./M.S. (five years), and RN to B.S.N. D'Youville also offers five-year combined bachelor's/master's (B.S./M.S.) degree programs in physical therapy, occupational therapy, international business, and dietetics. Master's degree programs are offered in special education, community health nursing, and health services administration. Ninety-four percent of D'Youville's 1998 graduates are employed in their field or are in graduate school.

Students residing in Marguerite Hall have a scenic view of the Niagara River and Lake Erie, which separate the U.S. and Canadian shorelines. The Koessler Administration Building contains the Offices of Admissions, Financial Aid, the President, Student Accounts, and the Registrar; the Learning Center; and the Kavinoky Theatre. The Student Center, the focal point of leisure and extracurricular activities, has a gymnasium, a swimming pool, a weight-training room, a dance studio, a general recreation center, a pub, and dining facilities. Student organizations and regularly scheduled activities, including intramural sports, NCAA Division III intercollegiate sports (baseball, basketball, volleyball, golf, cross-country, soccer, and softball), a ski club, the College newspaper, the yearbook, and social organizations, as well as academic programs, all help to make up an active campus life.

Location
D'Youville is situated on Buffalo's residential west side. The College is within minutes of many local attractions, including the downtown shopping center, the Kleinhans Music Hall, the Albright-Knox Art Gallery, two museums, and several theaters that offer stage productions. Seasonal changes in the area offer a variety of recreational opportunities. Buffalo is only 90 miles from Toronto and 25 minutes from Niagara Falls, making it a gateway to recreation areas in western New York and Ontario. Holiday Valley, a skier's paradise, is an hour's drive away. The city is served by the New York State Thruway, Amtrak, Greyhound and Trailways bus lines, and most major airlines.

D'Youville enjoys a diversified interchange with the community due to its affiliations with schools, hospitals, and social agencies in the area. College students in the Buffalo area number more than 60,000.

Majors and Degrees
D'Youville offers the degrees of Bachelor of Arts (B.A.), Bachelor of Science (B.S.), and Bachelor of Science in Nursing (B.S.N.). Majors include accounting, biology, business education, dietetics, education (elementary, secondary, and special), English, history, management, nursing, occupational therapy, philosophy, physical therapy, physician assistant studies, preprofessional studies (dental, law, medicine, and veterinary studies), and sociology. Five-year combined B.S./M.S. programs are offered in dietetics, international business, nursing, occupational therapy, and physical therapy.

Academic Program
The area of concentration recognizes individual differences and varying interests but still provides sufficient specialization in one discipline to form a foundation for graduate studies and professional careers. Students attending D'Youville are expected to complete the requirements of their chosen concentration while earning a minimum of 120 credit hours. Core requirements include humanities, 24 hours; social science, 12 hours; science, 7 hours; mathematics/computer science, 6 hours; and electives, 9 hours. A cumulative average of at least 2.0 must be maintained to meet graduation requirements. Sixteen credit hours, or five or six courses per semester, are considered a normal work load. Internships to meet specific career goals may be arranged in any major.

The College offers a Career Discovery Program that was purposely designed for the undecided student. This program, which can last for two years, offers credit courses and internships.

The academic year is composed of two semesters, each lasting approximately fifteen weeks. The first semester, including final examinations, ends before the Christmas holidays. During the eight-week summer sessions, programs of selected courses are given at all levels on a daily basis.

Off-Campus Arrangements
The baccalaureate program in nursing is affiliated with thirteen area hospitals and public health agencies. The education program is affiliated with local elementary, junior high, and secondary schools and with special education centers in the area for purposes of student teaching. The social work program cooperates with fifteen social welfare agencies for student case-study work. The occupational therapy, physical therapy, and physician assistant programs are affiliated with appropriate clinical settings throughout the United States.

Academic Facilities
D'Youville's new, modern Library Resources Center, which was completed in fall 1999, contains 154,000 volumes, including microtext and software, and subscriptions to 870 periodicals and newspapers. The multimillion-dollar Health Science Building houses laboratories, including those for anatomy, organic chemistry, and gross anatomy; activity and daily living labs for the health professions; and additional laboratories for physics, chemistry, quantitative analysis, and computer science. It also houses classrooms, faculty member offices, and development centers, including one for career development.

Costs
For 1999–2000, tuition was $5450 per semester, and room and board cost $2690 per semester. A general College fee is required and is based on credit hours taken; a Student Association fee of $40 per semester is applied toward concerts, yearbooks, activities, and guest lectures. A $100 deposit ($150 for dietetics,

physician assistant studies, occupational therapy, and physical therapy programs), credited toward tuition, must be submitted by all candidates who accept an offer of admission.

Financial Aid

D'Youville attempts to provide financial aid for students who would not otherwise be able to attend. Determination of aid is based on the Free Application for Federal Student Aid. Aid is available in the form of grants, loans, and employment on campus. In addition, D'Youville offers scholarships for academic achievement to incoming students. High school students with a minimum B+ average and an SAT I combined score of at least 1000 or an ACT composite score of at least 22 are automatically considered for D'Youville scholarships.

The six academic divisions of the College also award scholarships that range from $1000 to $6000 per year, which are renewable for three to four years. Outstanding students who wish to live on campus may be eligible for a D'Youville Resident Scholarship, which provides students with a one-half total room and board waiver ($1345 per semester) for up to four semesters.

Faculty

The ratio of faculty members to students is 1:14. All members of the full-time instructional staff hold a doctorate or another advanced degree. Faculty members act as advisers and are available for consultation with students.

Student Government

The Student Association (SA), a representative form of student self-government, seeks to inspire in its members dedication to the intellectual, social, and moral ideals of the College and works closely with the administration and faculty. All students of D'Youville are considered members of the SA and may be elected to the executive council and the student senate. There are seventeen academic and social clubs affiliated with the SA.

Admission Requirements

An applicant must be a high school graduate or have a high school equivalency diploma before matriculating. The applicant should have a college-preparatory background, including required English and history courses and a sequence in either mathematics or science. Scores on the SAT I or the ACT are also required for admission. High school advanced placement credit is acceptable and transferable. The admission decision is based on high school grade point average, rank in class, and scores on the SAT I or ACT. Students who have difficulty meeting normal admission standards may be admitted with a reduced academic load.

The College Learning Center offers academic assistance to students whose education has been interrupted or has not prepared them adequately for college courses. The Tutor Bank, a system of peer tutoring, offers the assistance of qualified students to those who need help in specific academic disciplines.

Superior high school students should investigate D'Youville's Honors Program. The program guarantees all participating students a scholarship valued at more than $18,000. Students with at least a 90 percent high school average and an SAT I combined score of at least 1100 or an ACT composite score of at least 25 are automatically evaluated for this scholarship.

Application and Information

D'Youville admits students on a rolling admission basis; therefore, applications are reviewed as they are received by the admissions office. Transfer students who have a quality point average of at least 2.0 are encouraged to apply by December 1 for the spring semester and by July 1 for the fall semester. A brochure listing course offerings and giving details about costs and room and board is available upon request.

R. H. Dannecker
Director of Admissions and Financial Aid
D'Youville College
One D'Youville Square
320 Porter Avenue
Buffalo, New York 14201-1084
Telephone: 716-881-7600
 800-777-3921 (toll-free)
E-mail: admiss@dyc.edu

EARLHAM COLLEGE
RICHMOND, INDIANA

The College

Earlham College, founded in 1847 by the Society of Friends, is an independent, liberal arts college. Earlham enrolls approximately 1,123 students—590 women and 533 men—representing forty-eight states and twenty-two countries. Seventy-five percent of Earlham's students are from outside Indiana, and 50 percent come from at least 500 miles away. Students are of many races, religious backgrounds, economic levels, and ethnic traditions. Earlham believes that a strong liberal arts education is the best intellectual preparation for a satisfying and successful life. Graduates have distinguished themselves in careers in science, medicine, law, business, higher education, and social and humanitarian service.

Student activities and groups are as varied as the students themselves. There are numerous extracurricular programs in music, theater, dance, social and political action, ethnic and international awareness, and intramural and varsity athletics. Students manage an FM public radio station, food co-op, equestrian program, newspaper, and literary magazine. Activities are coordinated by the Student Activities Board, the Earlham Events Committee, and various special interest groups, such as the Black Leadership Action Coalition, Women's Program Committee, International Club, and Earlham Service Learning Center. Students are very active in community service and donated more than 20,000 hours worth of time to the Richmond community during the 1998–99 school year.

Earlham is a member of Division III of the NCAA and the North Coast Athletic Conference. The College offers seven intercollegiate sports for men (baseball, basketball, cross-country, football, soccer, tennis, and track) and eight intercollegiate sports for women (basketball, cross-country, field hockey, lacrosse, soccer, tennis, track, and volleyball). Club sports available are swimming, ultimate frisbee, and men's lacrosse and volleyball. Twenty percent of the students participate in intercollegiate athletics, and many more participate in an extensive intramural program. Earlham's athletic facilities include indoor and outdoor tennis courts; football, baseball, soccer, and hockey fields; an all-weather track; and a $13-million athletic and wellness center.

Earlham is a residential college. Students live in the seven residence halls and in twenty-three College-owned houses near the campus. Five smoke-free residence halls are available.

Location

Earlham's tree-shaded campus lies at the southwestern edge of Richmond, Indiana, a city of 40,000 people. Richmond is 70 miles from Cincinnati, Ohio, and Indianapolis, Indiana, and 40 miles from Dayton, Ohio. Many students find opportunities to join in local activities. Auctions, the city's arboretum, the symphony orchestra, theater and opera companies, and the art association all offer extra dimensions to student life.

Majors and Degrees

Earlham College awards the B.A. degree in twenty-nine majors: African/African-American studies, art, biology, chemistry, computer science, economics, education, English, French, geology, German, history, human development and social relations, international studies, Japanese studies, Latin American studies, management, mathematics, music, peace and global studies, philosophy, physics/astronomy, politics, psychology, religion, sociology/anthropology, Spanish, theater arts, and women's studies. There are also special academic programs in athletics, physical education, and wellness; environmental sciences; humanities; languages and literatures; museum studies; studio art; and wilderness. Many students also create their own majors, and it is possible to complete a degree in three years. Minors are available in most major areas of study, plus Jewish studies, legal studies, and teaching English to speakers of other languages (TESOL).

Cooperative programs are offered in architecture, engineering, forestry, management, and teacher education. Excellent preprofessional programs are available in law, medicine, and the ministry.

Academic Program

Earlham introduces students to concepts and methods of inquiry in the humanities, social sciences, natural sciences, fine arts, and foreign languages through a program of subject area requirements, stressing both broad exposure and personal flexibility in course scheduling. An interdisciplinary humanities program provides a common intellectual experience for all students in their first year.

Students gain an in-depth understanding of one or more disciplines in their major area of academic concentration. An academic major usually consists of eight to ten courses in one department, a senior research project or seminar, and a departmental comprehensive examination.

Earlham grants credit for Advanced Placement examinations and higher-level International Baccalaureate subjects. Students may also receive credit for independent studies and academic internships.

The academic year consists of two semesters plus an optional May term. There is no on-campus summer session.

Off-Campus Arrangements

More than 65 percent of Earlham's students participate in at least one off-campus study program. Academic credit is earned, and, except for transportation costs, no extra charge is incurred for off-campus study. Earlham College students can study abroad in Austria, China, Colombia, the Czech Republic, England, France, Germany, Greece, Hong Kong, India, Israel/Palestine, Japan, Kenya, Martinique, Mexico, Northern Ireland, Russia, Scotland, Senegal, and Spain. Earlhamites also participate in American programs in the southwestern United States, Philadelphia, New York, Chicago, and Oak Ridge, Tennessee. The academic focus of programs vary, and students in all majors are encouraged to participate in at least one off-campus program. Earlham offers a one-month wilderness experience backpacking in the Uinta Mountains in Utah or canoeing in the boundary waters of Canada.

Academic Facilities

The Earlham College library is composed of two nationally renowned teaching libraries—Lilly Library and Wildman Science Library. The combined collections contain more than 350,000 volumes and 1,300 current periodicals, as well as maps, music, and works of art. Special collections include the Herbert

Hoover Peace Studies Collection, the Quaker Collection, and the Government Documents Collection.

Modern, well-equipped science laboratories for biology, chemistry, geology, and physics are found in Stanley and Dennis halls. Dennis Hall is also the location of the Joseph Moore Natural History Museum and the Ralph Teetor Planetarium. Earlham's observatory has a 14-inch Schmidt-Cassegrain telescope. Extensive computing facilities include a VAX cluster providing e-mail, Net News, and Internet access via LYNX; five microcomputer labs with 100 workstations (Macintosh, PC-DOS and Windows, UNIX, and NexTs) for word processing, programming, and Internet access. One mixed-platform lab is available 24 hours a day.

Music and art studios are found in the Runyan Student Center, which also houses a modern theater, the campus radio station, and the College bookstore. Other studios and Goddard Auditorium are located in Carpenter Hall.

Earlham owns and operates a living-history museum—the Conner Prairie Pioneer Settlement—near Indianapolis. Museum staff members teach academic courses, and students can work at the museum or do historical research there.

Costs

Tuition, fees, and room and board charges for 2000–01 total $26,006. Students have free admission to the Earlham Artist Series, athletic events, speaker series, and numerous lectures, concerts, and dances.

Financial Aid

Most financial aid is awarded on the basis of demonstrated need; more than 70 percent of Earlham's students receive financial assistance. Earlham usually meets the full need of all accepted students with a combination of Earlham Grants, endowed scholarships, loans, federal and state grants, and campus work. Students must file both the Free Application for Federal Student Aid (FAFSA) and a special Earlham form.

Scholarships are awarded without regard to financial need and recognize achievement in all areas of the liberal arts. The Carleton B. Edwards scholarship is available for students planning to major in chemistry. Earlham also offers scholarships through the National Merit Scholarship Corporation. Special scholarships are available to members of the Society of Friends and students who will enhance the diversity of the student body. There are scholarships and limited financial aid for international students (non-U.S. citizens).

Faculty

The faculty is composed of 108 women and men; 98 percent of the full-time faculty members hold the doctoral degree. Current faculty members have been recognized for teaching and scholarly excellence by receiving awards or fellowships from the Ford Foundation, Danforth Foundation, IBM, Woodrow Wilson Foundation, Fulbright-Hays Program, Kellogg Foundation, Japan Foundation, Lilly Endowment, National Endowment for the Humanities, National Science Foundation, and Carnegie-Mellon Foundation. The student-faculty ratio is 11:1.

Student Government

Students are encouraged to share in and contribute to the Earlham community as a whole, while also respecting individual differences. All academic and social life is governed by the Community Code, which is based on the principles of respect for persons, building community, academic integrity, peace and justice, and simplicity. Campus organizations reach decisions by consensus, and conflicts between members of the community are resolved through direct discussion, sometimes including mediated meetings. A judicial board of students and faculty members hears cases of serious Community Code violations.

Admission Requirements

Admission decisions are based on more than SAT I scores or high school grades, as important as these criteria are. Earlham pays close attention to teacher and counselor recommendations, application essays, and personal interviews. Applicants should have had an academic or college-preparatory high school program, with a minimum of 15 academic units from the ninth through twelfth grades. The SAT I is the preferred required test, although the ACT may be substituted. Campus visits are strongly recommended, although not required.

Application and Information

Earlham offers several admission options: the early decision deadline is December 1 (notification by December 15); the early action deadline is January 1 (notification on February 1); the regular decision deadline is February 15 (notification by March 15); and the transfer deadline is April 1. International students (non-U.S. citizens) should apply by March 1. Applications are accepted after these deadline dates as long as places remain in the entering class. Students who submit applications after April 1 are notified of the admission decision approximately two weeks after their application is complete.

Students wishing additional information or materials on Earlham College should contact:

Office of Admissions
Earlham College
Richmond, Indiana 47374
Telephone: 765-983-1600
         800-EARLHAM (toll-free)
Fax: 765-983-1560
E-mail: admission@earlham.edu
World Wide Web: http://www.earlham.edu

Earlham has a long, rich history of joint student-faculty collaborative research, mostly sponsored by the Ford and Knight Foundations. Here, Nelson Bingham, professor of multidisciplinary studies and psychology, meets with students after class.

EASTERN COLLEGE
ST. DAVIDS, PENNSYLVANIA

The College
Eastern College brings a special purpose to its mission as a Christian institution of higher education. The College wants to produce world Christians, capable of confronting injustice and indifference with the character, competence, and commitment Eastern has helped them develop. First and foremost, Eastern remains true to its biblical heritage. The power of the prophetic Word and the Lordship of Jesus Christ provide the context for the College's theological position. The College is sure of its Christian stand, and this encourages it to strengthen its faith by confronting serious contemporary issues. Neither narrow-minded nor staid, the College affirms and embraces Christians whose doctrinal positions may be broader or more restrictive. As a result, those at the College can actively pursue the full dynamic of an abundant Christian life and take an obedient walk with Him. In addition, the academic process revolves around a curriculum that emphasizes foundational skills as well as the understanding and application of knowledge in an increasingly complex society. Classroom experience is intellectually rigorous. A creative core curriculum builds on basic truths and continually challenges the potential of an expanding mind. Practical experience is generated through an extensive internship program as well as through relationships with established ministries such as World Vision, Young Life, Youth for Christ, foreign missions, and Christian outreach programs. The academic climate is enhanced through the presence of graduate programs. Knowledge, ultimately, is written as indelibly on the heart as it is on the mind. Justice and a will obedient to the Lord result from such an academic experience.

More than 1,200 full-time undergraduates and 700 graduate students are enrolled at Eastern. The graduate program includes an M.B.A./M.S. in the economic development of Third World nations and an additional emphasis in urban America and a traditional M.B.A. with concentrations in finance, marketing, human resource management, and health administration. An M.B.A. in nonprofit management and an M.S. in health services management are also offered. In addition, M.Ed. degrees in multicultural education and school health services, M.A. degrees in educational counseling and counseling, and an M.S. in school psychology are offered. Students from more than thirty other countries are represented in these programs.

On-campus housing accommodates 1,000 students. Students may select from seven residence halls. Air-conditioned suites and apartments are available as well as single rooms and the traditional double arrangement. For students who wish to connect a personal computer, each residence hall room is connected to the campus computer network. Intercollegiate teams for men are fielded in baseball, basketball, cross-country, lacrosse, soccer, tennis, and volleyball (club). The intercollegiate program for women offers basketball, cross-country, field hockey, lacrosse, soccer, softball, tennis, and volleyball. An intramural program offers opportunities for participation in basketball, soccer, softball, touch football, and volleyball.

The goal of the Student Ministry Program is to provide a varied and comprehensive structure of organizations and activities that will help students become effective disciples of Jesus Christ. Student ministries include residential ministries such as weekly chapel, a Sunday-night worship led by students, grow groups, and student chaplains. Strong outreach ministries provide students with opportunities to minister to a needy world. Among the opportunities available are Evangelicals for Social Action, Fellowship of Christian Athletes, and a chapter of Habitat for Humanity. Although it is an independent missions organization, the Evangelical Association for the Promotion of Education (EAPE) works closely with the Student Ministry Program. EAPE uses student volunteers to staff its programs in inner-city Philadelphia and Camden.

Location
Eastern College is located near Philadelphia, one of America's educational centers, and is only 2 hours from Washington, D.C., and New York City. Eastern's immediate community is Philadelphia's Main Line. This residential area is ½ mile north of Lancaster Pike (U.S. Route 30) at the eastern edge of the town of Wayne. Eastern's convenient suburban setting provides easy access to Philadelphia. SEPTA trains run every half hour from the St. Davids station to downtown Philadelphia. The traveling time is under 30 minutes.

Eastern has one of the most picturesque campuses in America. At the same time, it is within minutes of a variety of intellectual and cultural resources, including Philadelphia, historic Valley Forge, and the Amish country of rural Pennsylvania. The seashore and the Pocono Mountains can be reached in an hour or two. Nearby Philadelphia is an incomparable educational and cultural center. Rare collections of historical and anthropological interest are displayed in the University of Pennsylvania Museum. Facilities at the Franklin Institute and Fels Planetarium promote the physical sciences, those at the Academy of Natural Sciences and Wistar Institute, the biological sciences. The exhibits of the Museum of Art of the Parkway and of the Pennsylvania Academy of Fine Arts are open to the public. The Philadelphia Orchestra is world renowned. Tickets to its concerts are available to students at special rates.

Majors and Degrees
Undergraduate degrees include the Associate of Science, Bachelor of Arts, Bachelor of Science, Bachelor of Science in Nursing, and Bachelor of Social Work degrees. Majors are offered in accounting, art history, astronomy, biblical studies (biblical languages, without biblical languages), biology, biochemistry, chemistry, communication arts (film, intercultural, journalism, public relations/advertising, speech, theater), economics and finance, elementary education (early childhood, special education), English (English–communications for secondary education, English for secondary education, literature, writing), environmental studies, French, health administration, health and exercise science (exercise science, sport and fitness, sports medicine/pre–occupational therapy/pre–physical therapy), history, management (five-year M.B.A. option), marketing, mathematics, missions, music (church music, composition/electronic music, cross-cultural music, performance, teaching), philosophy, political science, psychology, secondary education, social work, sociology, Spanish, studio art, theological studies (theology, theology and Bible, theology and philosophy), urban economic development, and youth ministry. Minors are offered in accounting, American history, anthropology, astronomy, biblical studies, biology, chemistry, communication arts, dance, English as a second language, English literature, English writing, environmental studies, European history, fine arts, French, French civilization, gender studies, language, Latin American studies, leadership, mathematics, missions, music, philosophy, political science, psychology, social welfare, sociology, Spanish, sport and coaching, and theological studies.

Academic Program
In the core curriculum, students take courses designed to fulfill the basic mission of Eastern: to provide biblical foundations to which all learning and action can be related, to ensure acquisition of certain basic skills, and to broaden the student's view of the world. Courses in the breadth area of the core are planned and taught in such a way that central themes of the

Christian faith are integrated into the course content. The Fixed Core includes courses such as justice and diversity in a pluralistic society and science, technology, and values.

Eastern enrolled its first class into the Templeton Honors College in fall 1999. This college within a college offers a rigorous, classically oriented curriculum designed to challenge the most academically gifted students and prepare them for leadership and service at the very top of culture and society and in the professions linked to their academic majors. The honors college includes a required study-abroad, study-away semester. Enrollment in the honors college is highly competitive and limited to 24 new students each academic year. Students qualify to apply to the honors college by achieving a combined score of 1300 or higher on the SAT I or 30 or higher on the ACT or by ranking in the top 9 percent of their high school class.

Off-Campus Arrangements

Eastern students are encouraged to study abroad or in culturally different settings or to participate in one of several special programs recognized by the College. Academic Study Abroad is required of language majors. They are advised by the chairperson of the language department on various study options in France, Spain, and Mexico. Non–language majors may select from many options, including (but not limited to) Canada, England, Israel, Kenya, Peru, South Africa, and Uganda. AuSable Institute, located in Mancelona, Michigan, serves evangelical Christian colleges by offering courses that provide academic content, field experience, and practical tools for the stewardship of natural resources. Programs are offered in January, May, and during summer sessions. Students may apply for certificate programs leading to the designation of naturalist, land resources analyst, water resources analyst, or environmental analyst. The American Studies Program, sponsored by the Christian College Coalition, provides an opportunity for students to spend time in Washington, D.C., exploring national and international issues at public policy seminars led by leading Washington professionals. Students also serve as interns in various positions. This program, open to juniors and seniors, is of special interest to political science majors. The Latin American Studies Program, also sponsored by the Christian College Coalition, is based in Costa Rica. Students live with native families; study Spanish and the local culture, history, politics, economics, and religious life; participate in service projects; and travel in Central America. In addition, the Coalition operates a films study center in California and offers Russian studies and Middle East studies programs.

The Oregon Extension offers a semester of community living and liberal arts studies. Thirty-two students from across the nation earn college credit in eight disciplines while living in wood-heated cabins in the Cascade mountains of southern Oregon. Open to juniors and seniors with a GPA of 3.0 or better, the program relates Christian truth to academic study. The Honors Research Program at the Argonne National Laboratory in Chicago provides junior and senior biology, chemistry, and math majors an opportunity for advanced research at a nationally recognized laboratory. Argonne work is taken for a sixteen-week term during the academic year or an eleven-week term between the junior and senior years. The Goshen Study Service Trimester is a ten-week program open to students and faculty through Goshen College in Indiana. Participants study the history and culture of Caribbean nations and engage in a service project. Exchange programs with selected American Baptist colleges allow upperclass students to spend a semester or a year at another college. May Term opportunities include special courses, seminars, and study tours. Eastern Baptist Theological Seminary offers students the chance to take selected course work along with their college work.

Academic Facilities

Of Eastern's twenty-six buildings, the primary academic facility is the McInnis Learning Center. In addition to classrooms and offices for faculty and administrators, the main floor includes a 300-seat auditorium and several music practice rooms. Other features are the biology science center, a highly regarded curriculum laboratory for those preparing to be teachers, a technology classroom for distance learning, a planetarium, the media services center, a computer-assisted language laboratory, and a student computer center. Eastern recently added a state-of-the-art observatory on the roof of the McInnis Learning Center. In any liberal arts setting, the library and its resources are a critical component in the learning process. The Warner Library is a comfortable facility housing more than 130,000 volumes, 725 periodicals, and hundreds of microforms and audio recordings. In addition to on-campus resources for most research needs, Eastern students have access to libraries throughout the region both directly and via computer. Facilities for chemistry, physics, and computer science are located in Andrews Hall. In addition to offices and classroom space, Andrews houses six teaching laboratories, a computer center, and scientific equipment generally found only at larger colleges and universities.

Costs

For the academic year 1999–2000, tuition was $13,728, room and board were $5878. Total costs for the year were $19,606.

Financial Aid

Eastern is committed to providing education to qualified students regardless of their means. The financial aid program offers scholarships, grants, loans, and employment. The College utilizes the Pennsylvania Higher Education Assistance Agency (PHEAA) for needs analysis forms processing. The student is required to complete the Free Application for Federal Student Aid (FAFSA) to determine financial aid eligibility. Overall, the College views financial assistance to students as a cooperative investment. If parents contribute to the maximum of their ability and if the student contributes his or her fair share through earnings and personal savings, the College attempts to complete the partnership. In addition, estimates of financial aid eligibility may be obtained from the Financial Aid Office whether or not the student is an applicant. Non-need academic scholarships ranging from $500 to $6000 are available. These scholarships are awarded on the basis of SAT I or ACT scores and high school class rank information. Music, leadership, honors college, and church-matching grants are other college-based grant programs that are available.

Faculty

Eastern employs more than 75 full- and part-time faculty members. More than 80 percent have doctorates. Some faculty members teach both graduate and undergraduate courses. They are primarily a teaching faculty. Almost all serve as academic advisers. The student-faculty ratio is 14:1.

Student Government

As a Christian college and community, Eastern is concerned with establishing standards of conduct that are consistent with a Christian lifestyle and in the best interests of each student and the community. These standards flow from biblical values and form the community's commitment to be witnesses to each other.

Admission Requirements

The College seeks applicants who present acceptable academic records: most applicants rank in the top half of their class and have combined SAT I scores of at least 1080 or comparable ACT scores. A campus visit and interview are recommended. One reference is required. Transfer applicants are welcome.

Application and Information

Applications are generally accepted until the beginning of each term. Admission decisions are made within 48 hours of receipt of all materials. Students should see Eastern's Web site for more information.

Mark Seymour
Executive Director of Enrollment Management
Eastern College
1300 Eagle Road
St. Davids, Pennsylvania 19087-3696

Telephone: 800-452-0996 (toll-free)
E-mail: ugadm@eastern.edu
World Wide Web: http://www.eastern.edu

EASTERN CONNECTICUT STATE UNIVERSITY
WILLIMANTIC, CONNECTICUT

The University

Eastern Connecticut State University, Connecticut's public liberal arts university, offers twenty-nine undergraduate majors as well as graduate degrees in accounting, education, and organizational management. Eastern has all the advantages of a small school combined with "large-university resources." The University's concern for the individual student, along with its small classes, personalized counseling, and independent study opportunities, encourages intellectual and personal growth and development. The student body (3,428 full-time undergraduates) is heterogeneous, a mixture of various ethnic and socioeconomic groups. Students attending Eastern hail from 158 Connecticut towns, twenty states, and thirty-seven countries. There are six residence halls and three apartment complexes on campus. Housing is available to students who have been admitted to the University and have paid the tuition and housing-binder fees. Sixty percent of undergraduate students live in on-campus residence halls. The main cafeteria serves meals seven days per week. Cars are permitted for all students except for freshmen living on campus. There are more than forty special interest clubs and organizations on campus, as well as a student newspaper, a yearbook, and a literary and arts magazine. Extracurricular events include concerts, dances, films, intramural sports, lectures, musical and dramatic productions, and bus trips to Boston and New York City. Varsity sports for men include baseball, basketball, cross-country, lacrosse, soccer, and track. Women participate in intercollegiate basketball, cross-country, field hockey, lacrosse, soccer, softball, swimming, track, and volleyball. Sports facilities include an athletic center with a 2,800-seat gymnasium for badminton, basketball, tennis, and volleyball; a six-lane swimming pool; handball and squash courts; saunas; a fitness center and rooms for physical conditioning, modern dance, and gymnastics; and a new athletic complex that includes a state-of-the-art baseball field with a 1,500-seat grandstand as well as field hockey and multipurpose fields.

Location

Willimantic, Connecticut, a small city of diversified interests and many styles of living, has a population of 22,000. It has convenient shopping centers and a growing community of ambitious and ecology-minded individuals who are concerned with the city's future. The eastern Connecticut region is famous for its rolling hills, forests, state recreational areas, nature trails, clear lakes and streams, and beaches. Skiing areas are nearby. Hartford is 40 minutes away, and New Haven and Boston are both less than an hour and a half from Willimantic by car. The University of Connecticut, only 8 miles away, also presents noteworthy cultural events.

Majors and Degrees

Eastern offers four undergraduate degrees: the Bachelor of Arts, the Bachelor of General Studies, the Bachelor of Science, and the Associate in Science. The Bachelor of Arts degree is awarded with majors in computer science, economics, English, environmental earth science, fine arts (academic tracks in art history and criticism, dance, fine arts history, individualized major, interior design, music history and literature, music performance, music theory, theater, and theory and criticism), history, history and social sciences, mathematics, predentistry, prelaw, premedicine, psychology, public policy and government, social work, sociology and applied social relations, studio art, and Spanish. The Bachelor of Science degree programs include accounting, biology, business administration (concentrations in the areas of finance, management, and marketing), communication, early childhood education, elementary education, middle school/junior high school education, physical education, secondary education, and sports and leisure management. Certification in secondary education is available in biology, English, environmental earth science, history, and mathematics. Special four-year degree programs are also available for the following health professionals: dental hygienists, licensed practical nurses, medical laboratory technicians, radiological technologists, registered nurses, and respiratory therapists. The associate degree program is available in the arts and sciences. The Bachelor of General Studies is a flexible degree program for adults who are 25 or older. Such students may design a program integrating life experience into major or minor concentrations through a learning contract developed with their departmental adviser.

Academic Program

The basic graduation requirements for a bachelor's degree are a minimum of 120 hours of credit and completion of a major program (30–48 hours of credit in one specific field). In addition, all degree candidates must take a freshman English composition course and three physical education courses and fulfill specified credit hours in the humanities, natural sciences, social sciences, interdisciplinary courses, and computer competence (usually during the first two years). To earn an associate degree, students must complete 60 credit hours, which include credit hours in general education requirements, 15 credit hours in a concentration, and 5–9 credit hours in electives. The University operates on a two-semester system. The fall semester usually starts the first week in September and ends in mid-December; the spring semester, which includes a one-week vacation, runs from the third week of January to the middle of May. One 6-week and two 3-week sessions are offered during the summer. An Intersession program is offered in January of each year.

Eastern offers an Honors Program for academically talented students; this program emphasizes independent study. The Contract Admissions Program (CAP) is an educational support service that offers counseling, tutoring, developmental courses, and financial assistance to highly motivated students who might otherwise have been denied admission on the basis of traditional criteria. Cooperative Education (Co-op) is an optional work-study program; students may choose to participate in the program for one or more periods.

The University grants credit for Advanced Placement Program examination in all the subject areas tested and accepts up to 60 credit hours earned through the College-Level Examination Program (CLEP). Persons with a minimum of five years of successful work experience in areas of specialization taught by the University may qualify for advanced placement through credit for life experience and learning.

U.S. Army and Air Force ROTC programs, offered by the University of Connecticut at Storrs, are available to qualified Eastern students.

Off-Campus Arrangements

All formal opportunities for off-campus study available through the University carry credit. These include off-campus internships, study abroad, and consortium arrangements with the University of Connecticut and other institutions in the Connecticut State University System. Internships are available in the academic areas of applied social relations, biology, business administration, communication, computer science, economics, education, environmental earth science, psychology, public policy and government, and Spanish. Biology majors may study in Belize or in Bermuda through the tropical biology program, which involves a ten-day trip. There are also opportunities to join international study groups for one semester, one academic year, or a summer session. Eastern also participates in the National Student Exchange program (NSE), which allows students to attend other public colleges and universities across the United States while still paying tuition and fees to Eastern.

Academic Facilities

The J. Eugene Smith Library contains more than 500,000 volumes and 127,000 square feet of educational learning space. The Media Building contains a color television studio, a recording studio, an FM radio station, an electronic auditorium, a computer center, darkrooms, and graphic arts areas and serves as the hub of the audiovisual distribution system. The planetarium contains two electron microscopes and a geology laboratory. The Science Building provides modern, well-equipped laboratories for biology, chemistry, and physics. There is a fully equipped early childhood center. A four-story, 72,000-square-foot classroom building and the library and clock tower serve as the academic hubs of the campus.

Costs

For 1999–2000, tuition and fees for a Connecticut resident were $3634, and nonresident tuition and fees were $9174 on an annual basis. The fees included an admission binder fee of $90, which is required to secure a place in the University, and a $100 housing binder fee. Room was estimated at $3075 and board at $2390 for two semesters. Payments should be made as soon as possible after receipt of the bill for these charges. Books and supplies average $600 a year. The schedule of tuition and fees is subject to change as warranted.

Financial Aid

Financial aid includes grants and scholarships, low-interest loans, student employment opportunities, and special programs for veterans and their families. The University participates in the Federal Perkins Loan, Federal Pell Grant, Federal Supplemental Educational Opportunity Grant, and Federal Work-Study programs. In addition, it provides aid through alumni funds and other resources of its own. Approximately two thirds of all Eastern students receive financial aid. Awards are based primarily on demonstrated financial need. All students who wish to apply for financial assistance are required to complete the Free Application for Federal Student Aid (FAFSA) and send it to the processing agency by March 15 for the fall semester or by November 15 for the spring semester.

Faculty

The friendliness and approachability of the University's professors are usually noted by the students enrolled at Eastern. Faculty members are concerned primarily with teaching, although many write and carry on significant research. Faculty members hold advanced degrees from leading American and foreign colleges and universities; 81 percent hold terminal degrees. All of them serve as academic counselors. Full-time advisers and counseling services are available to assist students in matters of personal and academic concern.

Student Government

An organized plan of student government and student representation on University committees permits students to solve campus problems and develop basic policies for student life. The Student Senate is the governing body; it supervises and coordinates all student activities and serves as a liaison with the faculty, administration, and Board of Trustees.

Admission Requirements

Eastern maintains a selective admission policy, and applicants are considered on an individual basis. The criteria used are an applicant's personal accomplishments and motivation, the secondary school record, satisfactory SAT I scores, rank in class (preferably in the upper half of the high school graduating class), and a teacher's or guidance counselor's recommendation. Applicants must be secondary school graduates or have received a high school equivalency diploma. Their secondary school program should include 16 academic units of college-preparatory work, with the following divisions: English, four years; mathematics, three years; science, two years (including one year of laboratory science); social sciences, two years (including U.S. history); and foreign language, two years. Students who are admitted without having fulfilled the language requirement must complete one year of a foreign language (6 credits) at Eastern. Early acceptance is offered to outstanding high school students. Deferred entrance is also available. A campus interview is suggested, although not required.

Highly motivated students who do not qualify for admission if traditional criteria are used may be admitted through the Contract Admissions Program described above.

Application and Information

Application should be made after the first quarter of the senior year of high school. Applicants must submit previous academic records, an admission application, a $40 nonrefundable application fee, a complete transcript of high school grades and rank in class, a recommendation from a guidance counselor or teacher, and an official copy of the SAT I or ACT college report. The University adheres to a rolling admission policy. Applicants are usually notified of the admission decision within one month after their application folder is complete. Application forms and information may be requested from:

Kimberly Crone
Director of Admissions and Enrollment Management
Eastern Connecticut State University
Willimantic, Connecticut 06226

Telephone: 860-465-5286
Fax: 860-465-5544
World Wide Web: http://www.ecsu.ctstateu.edu

Eastern's J. Eugene Smith Library, with more than 500,000 volumes and 127,000 square feet of educational space, serves as the academic hub of the campus.

Peterson's Guide to Four-Year Colleges 2001   www.petersons.com

EASTERN MENNONITE UNIVERSITY
HARRISONBURG, VIRGINIA

The University

Eastern Mennonite, a private Christian university founded in 1917, provides a high-quality liberal arts education that emphasizes spiritual growth and cross-cultural awareness. The nurturing environment of EMU's student-oriented campus not only prepares students for a wide variety of careers but also challenges students to answer Christ's call to a life of nonviolence, witness, service, and peacebuilding. The undergraduate experience is enriched by the recent addition of graduate programs in business administration, conflict transformation, counseling, and education. The University also has a seminary. EMU is accredited by the Southern Association of Colleges and Schools. In addition, the nursing, teacher education, and social work programs are accredited by their specialty organizations at the national level.

Undergraduate students make up about 1,000 of the 1,400 students. Of the undergraduates, 60 percent are women and 7 percent are American multiethnic students. Nine percent come from international settings. Students represent thirty-seven states and twenty-two other countries. Most students are traditional college age. Religious backgrounds vary widely, with 60 percent representing Mennonites.

EMU is a residential community in which students live on campus until age 21 (unless they are married or live at home). Housing options include traditional residence halls, coed buildings, suite arrangements, apartments for upperclass students, and group houses. An energetic residence staff provides a dynamic residential life program focused on education and support. After the freshman year, a housing lottery is used to determine certain housing options.

The cocurriculum at Eastern Mennonite affords numerous opportunities to develop skills, express creativity, or just have fun. Students are active in intramurals, music ensembles, theater, and the more than twenty-five campus organizations that vary from Peace Fellowship to the Judo Club. Some students help operate the school radio station or edit the student newspaper or yearbook. Most students stay on campus on the weekend to enjoy movies, concerts, celebrative worship, and many other activities. Both men and women compete as members of the NCAA Division III and the Old Dominion Athletic Conference. EMU fields varsity teams for men and women in basketball, cross-country, soccer, tennis, track and field, and volleyball. Additional teams include baseball for men and field hockey and softball for women.

The dining hall offers many food choices and two meal plans (twenty-one or fourteen meals). Open hours are 7 a.m. to 7 p.m. The snack shop is the other eating facility on campus where students may use a Lion's Share account. Fast food restaurants and grocery stores are nearby. Other services offered by the University include career services, health and counseling services, a Learning Center, and a multicultural program. The Director of Career Services helps students to explore ways to use their education in the workplace.

Location

Eastern Mennonite's 92-acre campus on the edge of the growing town of Harrisonburg is located in the scenic Shenandoah Valley, with a view of the famous Blue Ridge Mountains. With only a 2-hour drive to the nation's capital or the state capital of Richmond, students have access to both urban and rural America. Skiing, hiking, the beach, and major cultural opportunities are all within easy reach. Three other institutions of higher learning are located nearby. With its growing ethnic diversity, Harrisonburg's many restaurants provide a variety of cuisines. Local businesses are the sites for EMU business student internships. Students also carry out numerous volunteer activities with local charities.

Majors and Degrees

The University offers Bachelor of Arts, Bachelor of Science, and associate degrees, as well as a one-year certificate. The Bachelor of Arts degree requires intermediate-level competency in a foreign language. Majors are offered in accounting; art; art education; biblical studies; biochemistry; biology; business administration; camping, recreation, and outdoor ministries; chemistry; communication; computer information systems; computer science; congregational and youth ministries; culture, religion, and mission; economic development; economics; English; environmental science; French; German; health and physical education; history; history and social science; international agriculture; international business; justice, peace, and conflict studies; liberal arts; mathematics; medical technology; music; nursing; philosophy and theology; psychology; recreation and sports leadership; social work; sociology; Spanish; and theater. Professional certification programs are available in early, elementary, secondary, and special education. Preprofessional programs are offered in engineering, law, and health sciences. Transfer agreements facilitate articulation with engineering schools. A liberal arts major allows students to design their own programs. Minors include many of the above areas plus church music, coaching, exercise science, family studies, finance, journalism, marketing, missions, physics, political science, socioeconomic development, and teaching English as a second language. Associate in Arts degrees are offered in Bible studies and general studies. An Associate in Applied Science degree focuses on paraprofessional education. One-year certificates may be earned in Bible or general studies.

Academic Program

The academic calendar consists of two 15-week semesters from late August to late April. The baccalaureate degree requires 128 semester hours. All students complete a major, the Global Village general education curriculum, and electives. The Global Village curriculum is a sequence of courses consisting of 49 semester hours distributed as follows: faith (11), humanities (9), cross-cultural studies (9), math/natural science (9), social science (3), writing (3), speech (2), physical education (2), and the first-year experience (1).

Associate degrees require 64 semester hours of general education requirements, a concentration in a major, and electives. Thirty semester hours are needed to complete a certificate.

Cross-cultural studies take students to another culture for a semester or a three- to nine-week summer session. An honors program provides academic challenges and leadership opportunities for a select group of students through faculty mentoring, seminars, research opportunities, and special projects. Twelve honors students are selected from each first-year class. Two of the 20 receive full-tuition scholarships, and 10 are awarded half-tuition scholarships. Other special academic opportunities include credit by examination and extension credit for special programs with outside organizations.

Off-Campus Arrangements

Eastern Mennonite is one of the few universities to include a cross-cultural study requirement of 9 semester hours as part of the general education curriculum. The program takes students and teaching faculty members to settings that include Central America, the Middle East, Africa, Europe, Russia, China, Japan, Native American reservations, and Washington, D.C. The program, which is community-based, usually includes living with local families. Students also study the historical, geographical, social, economic, religious, and artistic forces that shape the culture. Students may also spend nine months in the Washington study service year program. A dozen students live in a community and put knowledge into practice through internships, group living, and a student-centered seminar. Students also take courses at a local university. Other students spend a semester or year in the Brethren Colleges Abroad Program. Foreign language majors spend a full year in a country where the target language is spoken.

Academic Facilities

Academic facilities include a modern science building equipped with laboratories for study and research. The building also houses a planetarium and a museum with impressive collections of mounted animals and insects, minerals, fossils, and artifacts from distant locations. The modern library is fully automated with a state-of-the-art computer system. In addition to the usual resources, the library houses a large historical collection pertaining to Mennonite faith and life. Several campus buildings have laboratories equipped with computers for student use. Residence halls are connected to the campus network, providing students who purchase computers with access to the library and the Internet. The network accommodates both PCs and Macintosh computers.

Other special facilities and programs include a campus radio station, an arboretum, an observatory, Park Woods, a music program for young children, a kindergarten for student practicums, an intensive English program, and the Orie Miller Global Village Center, which provides resources for mission, service, and peacebuilding endeavors.

Costs

Tuition and fees for 2000–01 are $14,150. Room and board are estimated at $5170. Additional expenses for books, transportation, and incidental costs are estimated at $1250. Special fees are charged for applied music instruction and certain physical education courses.

Financial Aid

More than 90 percent of EMU students receive financial aid. Scholarships include those given for academic achievement and an award of $1000 given to new first-year students who are children of alumni. Other grant aid, given to meet financial need, includes federal aid, endowed scholarships, foundation grants, and aid from the operating budget. Admission is need-blind. In addition, students with financial need may obtain federal loans or participate in the work-study program. Virginia residents receive the Virginia Tuition Assistance Grant, regardless of need, which amounts to $2700 or more annually. If students receive grants from their churches, EMU matches up to $500 per year. No application is needed for academic scholarships except for honors awards. Students applying for need-based aid must complete the Free Application for Federal Student Aid (FAFSA). Applications should be completed by February 15.

Faculty

Faculty members at Eastern Mennonite are devoted first to teaching. Sixty percent hold doctorates or terminal degrees in their fields. Most faculty members are full-time. A faculty-student ratio of 1:13 provides for small classes and out-of-class relationships. All classes are taught by faculty members rather than graduate assistants, and 75 percent of classes have 25 or fewer students. In some disciplines, students participate in faculty research and publication. All faculty members serve as academic advisers to students.

Student Government

All students are members of the Student Government Association (SGA), which is led by the Senate and its Executive Committee. The Senate is composed of students elected from the residence halls. SGA coordinates student involvement in the campus community, communicates concerns to and from the administration, and aids in decision making. Students also hold representation on some faculty and administrative committees.

Admission Requirements

Admission to EMU is moderately competitive. Factors considered include high school or previous college GPA, high school rank, SAT I or ACT scores, support from a reference, and commitment to uphold the lifestyle expectations of EMU. Applicants should rank in the upper half of their high school class. Some majors have specific GPA requirements to enter the upper-level courses. Recommended high school units include English (4), math (3), science (2), foreign language (2), social studies (2), and electives (6). Transfer students are welcome. The University seeks to be an inclusive community that welcomes students from diverse backgrounds and various religious and ethnic groups. Campus visits are encouraged. Students should apply by May 1.

Application and Information

The freshman application priority filing date is March 1. The final filing date is August 1. The application deadline for transfer applicants is thirty days prior to the start of the term for both fall and spring. Notification of admission is sent on a rolling basis. Inquiries and application materials should be sent to:

Ellen B. Miller
Director of Admissions
Eastern Mennonite University
Harrisonburg, Virginia 22802

Telephone: 800-368-2665 (toll-free)
Fax: 540-432-4444
E-mail: admiss@emu.edu
World Wide Web: http://www.emu.edu

Each fall, Student Orientation Staff (SOS) members help first-year students move into residence halls and get accustomed to campus life.

EASTERN NAZARENE COLLEGE
QUINCY, MASSACHUSETTS

The College

Eastern Nazarene College (ENC) is a coeducational liberal arts school, founded in 1900, that has been located in Quincy, Massachusetts, since 1919. It pursues a mission of educational excellence in an atmosphere of a Christian worldview and life view. It is one of nine liberal arts colleges supported by the International Church of the Nazarene in the U.S. and one of a network of institutions supported by the church around the world. The campus, three blocks from Quincy Bay, is located in a suburb of Boston, just a 10-minute walk from the Boston subway system and literally on the doorstep of the city.

Eastern Nazarene College offers resources and opportunities to students of all races, creeds, and colors. Approximately one half of ENC students come from Nazarene Church backgrounds; the remainder is comprised of students from more than thirty denominations and some from other faiths. A school ENC's size, with a 15:1 student-faculty ratio, allows students to get to know their professors personally and fosters contact between student and teacher both academically and in matters of life and faith. An NCAA Division III athletic program and numerous other campus organizations, including service opportunities with ministry, are available to ENC students. The undergraduate student body of more than 1,300 is made up of an equal number of traditional students and nontraditional adult learners.

Location

Quincy, a city of 85,000, is a southern suburb of Boston within easy reach of the city by all modes of transportation, both public and private. As a result, many opportunities are available in this historic region, from cultural events and major league sporting attractions to internships and joint ventures with major universities.

Majors and Degrees

The College offers Bachelor of Arts or Bachelor of Science degrees to students completing a prescribed four- to five-year course of study and Associate of Arts degree to those completing a two-year program. Major fields of concentration are accounting, advertising and public relations, athletic training, biology, business administration, business management, chemistry, child and adolescent development, church music, clinical and research psychology, communication arts, computer engineering, computer science, early childhood education, electrical engineering, elementary education, engineering, English, English as a second language, environmental science, French, general science, general studies, health sciences, history, journalism, lay ministries, liberal arts, literature, marine biology, marketing, mathematics, middle-school education, movement arts, music, music business, music education, music performance, pharmacy, physical education, physics, prelaw, premedical studies, premedical technology, pre–physical therapy, psychology, radio and television broadcasting, recording arts, religion, secondary education, social relations, social work, sociology, Spanish, special education, speech communication, sports therapy, theater arts, urban ministry, writing, youth and Christian education, and youth ministry.

The Division of Social Sciences offers the Bachelor of Arts with concentrations in accounting, business administration, child and adolescent development, clinical and research psychology, history, movement arts, prelaw, psychology, social relations, social work, sociology, and urban ministry in conjunction with the Division of Religion. The Associate of Arts is also available with a concentration in business administration.

The Division of Arts and Letters offers the Bachelor of Arts with concentrations in advertising and public relations, church music, communication arts, English, French, journalism, literature, music, music business, music performance, radio and television broadcasting, recording arts, Spanish, speech communication, theater arts, and writing. The Bachelor of Science with a concentration in church music is also available.

The Division of Natural Sciences offers the Bachelor of Science with concentrations in athletic training (in conjunction with Social Sciences), biology, chemistry, computer engineering, computer science, electrical engineering, engineering (in a cooperative program with Boston University), engineering physics, environmental science, general science, marine biology, mathematics, physics, premedical studies, premedical technology, pre–physical therapy, psychology, and sports therapy (in conjunction with Social Sciences). The Bachelor of Arts is also available, with concentrations in biology, chemistry, computer science, general science, marine biology, mathematics, physics, and psychology.

The Division of Religion and Philosophy offers the Bachelor of Arts with concentrations in religion and youth ministry and the Associate of Arts with concentrations in lay ministries and youth and Christian education.

The Division of Teacher Education offers teacher certification in conjunction with a liberal arts major in one of the following fields: elementary education, English as a second language, middle school education, music education, physical education, secondary education, and special education. An Associate of Arts is also offered in early childhood education.

Academic Program

Each student seeking a bachelor's degree completes a general liberal arts core curriculum combining academics with a Christian education as part of a 130-semester-hour program. A grade of C or better must be obtained for all courses in the selected major, in which the student must complete at least 32 hours. Electives completing the total number of semester hours needed must also be fulfilled. The senior year's work and that of the chief concentration of the major subject must be completed in residence at ENC. A comprehensive examination in the major field must be completed to the satisfaction of the major department, and a cumulative grade point average of 2.0 or better must be maintained. Dual-degree programs leading to both a B.A. and B.S. in a concentration require 162 semester hours. Most ENC students are able to complete bachelor's studies in four or five years.

The Associate of Arts requires the completion of a minimum of 65 total credits, of which 21 are a liberal core curriculum, and a minimum of 24 in the major area of study. A cumulative grade point average of 1.8 or better is required.

Academic counseling is available through the Center for Academic Services to provide services to students who may need additional guidance to maintain satisfactory progress in their course work. Students interested in these services make an appointment with the Director of Academic Services.

Off-Campus Arrangements

ENC has a diverse off-campus study program, the centerpiece of which is ENC Romania. The program is located in the city of Sighișoara, in the heart of Transylvania. The focus of the semester in Romania is 8 credits of cross-cultural service learning, involving reading and reflection on the dynamics of cross-cultural ministry and extensive volunteer work in such facilities as orphanages and geriatric centers. The service-learning aspect of the program taps the expertise of Romanian professionals.

Through the Coalition of Christian Colleges and Universities, ENC is able to offer an American studies program in Washington, D.C.; a Latin American studies program in Costa Rica; a program at the Los Angeles Film Studies Center; an environmental studies program; and a summer semester at Great Britain's University of Oxford.

Academic Facilities

A center for on-campus study is the state-of-the-art Nease Library, which houses 115,000 volumes and more than 600 periodicals. Reference service is available for all materials, and a full-service Resource Center, featuring MacIntosh and DOS computers, is available for student use.

Costs

Tuition for the 2000–01 academic year is $13,236; room and board are $4550. Other student fees total $826. Various payment plans are offered. For information, students can contact the Office of Student Accounts at 800-510-3495 (toll-free).

Financial Aid

Eastern Nazarene College encourages any prospective student to consider its sources of aid. Both the Free Application for Federal Student Aid (FAFSA), which can be obtained from the ENC Financial Aid Office, and the ENC Application for Financial Aid must be submitted by February 28 for priority consideration.

About 400 institutional scholarships and grants dealing with academics, activities, and need are available, as are several open to members of the Nazarene Church. A family grant program also operates. These can be mixed with Pell Grants; the FSEOG program; state grants; Federal Stafford, Perkins, and PLUS loans; and work-study programs.

For further details, students can write (Financial Aid Office, Eastern Nazarene College, 23 East Elm Avenue, Quincy, Massachusetts 02170) or call (800-883-6288; toll-free).

Faculty

At ENC, the faculty is committed to fostering excellence in students. The professors value their work with academics in a Christian environment. More than 70 percent hold doctoral degrees in their field of concentration. Many have authored or contributed to numerous books and articles in addition to having presented at regional and national conferences. Two faculty members currently hold or have held joint teaching appointments at Harvard University and Massachusetts General Hospital.

Student Government

Student life and activities at ENC are entrusted to a large degree to the students themselves. The Executive Council of the student organization, a representative group of students and one faculty adviser, discusses campus problems and ideas suggested by the student body. The council works with the administration for the solutions to these problems and assists in coordinating and implementing the intramurals of the College.

Admission Requirements

All applicants are encouraged to have completed a high school curriculum that prepares students for college in English, history, foreign language, mathematics, social sciences, and sciences and must submit a high school transcript, SAT I or ACT scores, two letters of recommendation, and an essay before an application for admission is reviewed by the admission committee. Admission is normally granted on a rolling basis to students who rank in the upper half of their high school class and score 480 or above on both the math and verbal sections of the SAT or 18 or above on the English section and 20 on the math section of the ACT.

Applicants who do not meet the above standards can be considered for admission through the College Achievement Program (CAP). The Committee of Admissions, before considering an application for the CAP, might require additional grade reports, placement testing, a campus visit, and an interview and references attesting that the student is ready for college. The number of applicants accepted through CAP is limited, and some may be denied admission or placed on wait-list status for the fall semester.

International applicants should consult the special admissions instructions for international students.

Application and Information

Applications are available from the Office of Admissions upon request. Applications mailed early in the senior year of high school help ensure priority consideration for fall registration, residence hall preference, and financial aid. An acceptance tuition deposit of $250 and a room deposit fee of $250 must be submitted by May 1 by all students accepted for, and planning to attend, the fall semester.

Office of Admissions
Eastern Nazarene College
Quincy, Massachusetts 02170
Telephone: 617-745-3000
800-88-ENC-88 (toll-free)
E-mail: admissions@enc.edu
World Wide Web: http://www.enc.edu

"We seek that wisdom which goes beyond knowledge, that meaning which goes beyond facts, that purpose which comes only from a relationship with Jesus Christ as Lord."—Dr. Kent R. Hill, President

EASTERN NEW MEXICO UNIVERSITY
PORTALES, NEW MEXICO

The University

Eastern New Mexico University (ENMU), a regional state institution, combines a traditional learning environment with twenty-first century technology to provide a rich educational experience. Eastern emphasizes liberal learning, freedom of inquiry, cultural diversity, and whole student life. Excellent teaching and active learning define campus relationships. Student learning is at the center of Eastern's decision-making process. Scholarship (both primary and applied), cultural enrichment, and professional service are also important contributions of the University community. Educational programs are offered at the Portales campus and also by interactive distance education; public broadcast television; a branch/community college in Roswell, New Mexico; and a University center in Ruidoso, New Mexico. Eastern's focus is to prepare students for careers and advanced study, impart citizenship and leadership skills and values, support and expand the role of education and excellent teaching at all levels, and enable citizens to respond to a rapidly changing world.

In 1997, Eastern was granted unconditional, ten-year reaccreditation by the North Central Association. It is also accredited by the National Association of Schools of Music, the Association of Collegiate Business Schools and Programs, the American Speech-Language-Hearing Association, and the National League for Nursing Accrediting Commission. Geology and chemistry programs are approved by the American Institute of Professional Geologists and the American Chemical Society, respectively.

Eastern's diverse student population of approximately 3,600 includes students from across the nation and around the world. Forty percent are nontraditional students, and 24 percent are Hispanic. About one fourth of the student population lives on campus in the four residence halls and the apartments, which provide a variety of living arrangements for single students, families, and commuters. All freshmen not living with their parents live on campus. Eating facilities include the Dining Room, the Zia Room, and the Cafe Down Under (CDU), which features fast-food choices. Students can select specific meal plans, Flex dollars (an account with a decreasing balance), or a combination of the two.

Eastern is the home of the New Mexico Center for Teaching Excellence (CTE), a state-funded program designed to promote practices of fine teaching across the state, from kindergarten through higher education. Eastern's graduate programs in education, with emphases in bilingual education, education administration, elementary education, reading, counseling and guidance, and special education, complement the CTE's program to give students a wide range of learning experiences. Because of Blackwater Draw, the world-famous archaeological site near Portales where evidence of some of the earliest Americans has been found, ENMU's graduate and undergraduate programs in anthropology draw students interested in the Clovis man and his culture from around the world. Eastern's Speech, Language and Hearing Clinic provides support for the graduate program in communicative disorders required for speech pathology licensure in the state of New Mexico.

More than 80 social, service, professional, religious, political, arts, athletic, and special interest student organizations provide students with numerous opportunities for leadership and development. As a member of the NCAA Division II and the Lone Star Conference, Eastern participates in baseball, basketball, cross-country, and football for men and in basketball, cross-country, softball, tennis, and volleyball for women. In addition, Eastern's rodeo teams (men's and women's) participate in the Southwest Region of the National Intercollegiate Rodeo Association. Eastern also has an extensive intramural athletics program. Student services provide a nationally certified tutoring program free of charge as well as counseling, health, career, testing, advising, and orientation services.

Location

Bright blue skies, clean air, sunshine, moderate temperatures, and spectacular sunsets characterize the high plains (elevation 4,200 feet) of eastern New Mexico, where Portales is located. Just 20 miles from Clovis, New Mexico, Eastern is accessible by air from Amarillo and Lubbock, Texas (2 hours' driving time northeast and southeast, respectively), and from Albuquerque, New Mexico, a 4-hour drive to the northwest. Portales is a farming and ranching community where Valencia peanuts (the small red-skinned ones), cattle, and milk (dairies) are the major products. Roosevelt County, where Portales is located, is considered a very safe place to live.

Majors and Degrees

Undergraduate degrees granted at Eastern are the Bachelor of Arts, the Bachelor of Applied Science, the Bachelor of Business Administration, the Bachelor of Arts in Education, the Bachelor of Fine Arts, the Bachelor of Music, the Bachelor of Music Education, the Bachelor of Science, the Bachelor of Science in Education, the Bachelor of Science in Nursing, and the Bachelor of University Studies. Majors in the College of Business include accounting, agricultural business, applied economics and finance, business administration, business education, computer information systems, human resource management, marketing, and marketing education. In the College of Education and Technology, the majors include agriculture education, early childhood education, elementary education, family and consumer sciences, physical education, and special education. The College of Fine Arts majors are art, music, music education, and theater. The College of Liberal Arts and Sciences offers majors in allied health services, anthropology, biology, chemistry, communication, communicative disorders, computer science, criminal justice, English, geology, history, mathematics, nursing, physics, political science, psychology, religion, social studies, sociology, Spanish, technology, university studies, and wildlife and fishery sciences. Eastern also offers a student-designed degree option.

Academic Program

The purpose of the undergraduate programs at Eastern is to prepare students for careers, advanced study, and an environment where change makes lifelong learning imperative. Degrees require a minimum of 128 hours, which includes 53–56 hours of general education courses, 36 hours in a major, 15–24 hours in a minor, and elective credit. Eastern does offer credit by examination (CLEP, AP, ACT) and honors courses for students whose ACT scores exceed 25. Eastern is on a semester calendar, with the fall semester finishing before end-of-the-year holidays and the summer session being eight weeks in length.

Off-Campus Arrangements

Eastern participates in the International Educational Exchange (IEE), National Student Exchange (NSE), and the Western Interstate Commission of Higher Education (WICHE) and is New Mexico's pilot institution for the Western Governors' Virtual University. Students participating in the exchange programs attend institutions abroad (IEE) or in the U.S. (NSE) but are only required to pay Eastern tuition and fees. WICHE allows New Mexico resident students to study at out-of-state institutions that offer programs unavailable in New Mexico and to pay New Mexico in-state tuition rates at the out-of-state institution. Eastern also offers cooperative education and internship opportunities. Stipends and/or credit hours are available in many of those placements.

Academic Facilities

Eastern's instructional buildings boast some of the finest resources available at any university. Scientific research activities are located in the newly renovated Roosevelt Hall, where transmission and scanning electron microscopes are used by students and faculty members. The Broadcast Center houses two 100,000-watt stations (KENW-TV, the Public Broadcasting Station, and KENW-FM, the National Public Radio affiliate), where students gain hands-on experience in television and radio operation. Golden Library has more than 900,000 volumes, including books, films, and thousands of U.S. and New Mexico government documents for which Golden serves as a selective depository. The library can be accessed from off-campus sites, residence halls, and the University Computer Center, which houses three student computer labs with more than thirty stations each that are open 21 hours a day. Other resources include the University Bookstore, the Health Service Center, an indoor swimming pool, four museums, and the University Theatre Center, which houses a 420-seat proscenium theater and a 125-seat experimental theater.

Costs

In-state tuition for 1999–2000 was $636 per semester for 12–18 credit hours (a full-time student course load). Fees for 1999–2000 were $279 per semester for full-time students. Housing costs for double occupancy rooms were $770 per semester, and a fourteen-meal food plan was $885 per semester. Books and supplies are estimated at $374 per semester. Out-of-state tuition for 1999–2000 was $3078 per semester, and fees were $279. The 1999–2000 annual total for an in-state student was $6080; for an out-of-state student, the annual total was $10,964.

Financial Aid

More than 85 percent of the students at Eastern derive financial assistance from four basic types of aid—scholarships, grants, employment, and loans. Scholarships are awarded for academic achievement and/or special talent—artistic or athletic, for example. The Office of Admissions and individual academic departments award scholarships. Application deadlines are March 1. Students are encouraged to seek scholarship opportunities from hometown and professional organizations as well. Federal or state grants, work-study, and many loans are accessible through the Free Application for Federal Student Aid (FAFSA), which determines eligibility for those funds. The priority packaging deadline for the FAFSA is also March 1. Some non–work-study employment is available on campus as well as off campus.

Faculty

Eastern employs about 180 faculty members, 86 percent of whom are full-time with doctoral or terminal degrees and all of whom are active instructional staff. Although Eastern faculty members are active researchers, Eastern is a teaching institution where the focus is on student learning. Faculty members serve as academic advisers and organization sponsors. They also often invite students to work with them in their laboratories and on their research projects. Graduate teaching assistants teach some labs and freshmen-level classes; however, most are taught by faculty members. The average class size is 22.

Student Government

Associated Students of Eastern New Mexico University (ASENMU), patterned on the federal government, has executive, legislative, and judicial branches. The student senate has representatives, who are elected at the beginning of each academic year. ASENMU appoints student representatives to twenty-three University committees, appoints a lobbying group that prepares a platform of requests and lobbies the New Mexico Legislature on behalf of the students, and also determines, through a proposal and review board of students, how the student fees will be spent. Student government representatives also take part in the discussions regarding tuition and fee changes each year. Finally, one of the five Board of Regent members at Eastern is a student. Students apply for the position through a rigorous selection process, which culminates in gubernatorial appointment.

Admission Requirements

Eastern requires high school graduation or the completion of a GED diploma. Admission begins with the submission of a completed application for admission, all high school and/or college transcripts, and ACT/SAT I scores. Students are admissible based on the following criteria: 1) a score of 21 or higher on the ACT or a score of 990 or higher on the SAT I, 2) a 2.0 high school GPA and either a minimum score of 15 on the ACT or a minimum score of 720 on the SAT I, or 3) a 2.0 college GPA. Students are strongly encouraged to visit Eastern so that they can tour the campus, stay in a residence hall, eat in the dining hall, and meet with a faculty adviser, a financial aid officer, and an admissions representative. Following acceptance, students attend a one- or two-day orientation prior to the semester in which they begin.

Application and Information

Admission application materials should be submitted as early as possible to facilitate the awarding of scholarships and financial aid. Course work of students transferring to Eastern is evaluated by the Office of Admissions to determine what classes will be accepted by the University. The individual college also evaluates transferrable credits to determine how those classes will fit into the student's desired degree plan. Transfer students should submit transcripts of all completed courses during the semester prior to desired attendance. Transcripts of courses completed during the semester in which the student applied to ENMU should be forwarded as soon as possible thereafter.

Inquiries and applications should be sent to:

Douglas Dobbins, Director of Admissions
Office of Admissions, #7
Eastern New Mexico University
Portales, New Mexico 88130
Telephone: 800-FOR-ENMU or 800-367-3668 (toll-free)
Fax: 505-562-2118
Email: johnlowry-king@enmu.edu
World Wide Web: http://www.enmu.edu

Students learn technical skills in the state-of-the-art Broadcast Center as they produce *Scene 3 News*, a comprehensive 30-minute news program each evening on KENW-TV, Eastern's Public Broadcasting Station.

EASTERN WASHINGTON UNIVERSITY
CHENEY, WASHINGTON

The University

Established in 1882 as the Benjamin P. Cheney Academy, Eastern Washington University has grown from a premier teachers' college into a comprehensive state university focused on small classes, active learning, and a commitment to teaching. The University retains the charm and personality of its founding on the parklike campus in Cheney. It also exhibits the distinctive marks of the modern comprehensive university in its newer facilities and the expansion of higher educational opportunities into downtown Spokane and other sites through eastern Washington. Eastern is fully accredited by the Northwest Association of Schools and Colleges and by numerous professional accreditation agencies in specific disciplines.

In addition to the undergraduate degrees listed below, Eastern offers master's degrees in the arts and sciences, business, education, nursing, physical therapy, public administration, social work, and urban and regional planning.

Eastern's 8,200 students come from more than thirty-five states and twenty-four countries. Students of color make up about 12 percent of the student body and international students about 3.5 percent. About 58 percent of Eastern's students are women. Educational and support services are available through the American Indian Studies, Chicano Education, and African American Education Programs and the English Language Institute. The University's proximity to Spokane allows it to serve a diverse population that includes residential students on campus, students who commute to Cheney from Spokane, and students who complete their studies at the University's Spokane facilities. Six residence halls can accommodate 1,900 students on campus. Additional housing is available for married students and students with children. Fraternity and sorority housing, as well as off-campus housing within walking distance in Cheney, affords a variety of housing options. All residence halls are smoke-free.

Students and the University community enjoy unparalleled facilities for fitness and recreation. The PHASE complex includes a 5,500-seat pavilion, an indoor aquatics center, a field house with indoor track and tennis, and the main PHASE building, which houses indoor courts for basketball, volleyball, and racquetball; dance studios; a fitness center; and a large, multisurfaced rock for climbing practice. These facilities and Woodward Field are the venues for the NCAA Division I Eagles who compete in the Big Sky Conference.

Location

The University's campus is in Cheney, a comfortable and compact city of 8,500, where students may find a variety of services, facilities, and shopping while enjoying the pleasant, secure feel of a small town. Spokane, the state's second-largest city and a regional hub for manufacturing, business, transportation, and health services for more than 400,000 residents, is just 17 miles away and offers a full range of social, cultural, recreational, and consumer opportunities. The Inland Northwest Region offers virtually unlimited scenic and recreational attractions in a four-season climate. There are more than seventy-six lakes within 50 miles of the campus, easy access to the mountains, and many rivers. Other outdoor activities include world-class skiing within a short drive in nearly every direction. The University sits amid fascinating geological and geographic diversity, with the arid high country to the west, the rich Palouse farming area to the south, and the fir-covered mountains climbing from Spokane into Idaho and Montana. The region is served by the Spokane International Airport, rail and bus service, and interstate access.

Majors and Degrees

The University comprises four colleges: Business and Public Administration; Education and Human Services; Letters, Arts, and Social Sciences; and Science, Mathematics, and Technology. These colleges award the Bachelor of Arts, Bachelor of Science, Bachelor of Dental Hygiene, Bachelor of Business Administration, Bachelor of Arts in Education, Bachelor of Fine Arts, Bachelor of Nursing, and Bachelor of Music in more than sixty-five degree programs; many specialized options are offered. The following majors are available: anthropology; applied psychology; art; biology (including medical technology); business administration (including accounting, business economics, finance, human resource management, management information systems, marketing, and operations management); chemistry/biochemistry; communication disorders; communication studies; computer information systems; computer science; criminal justice; dental hygiene; earth science; economics; education (including early childhood education, gifted/talented education, library science education, and reading); English; geography; geology; government; health services administration; history; international affairs; journalism; liberal studies; mathematics; military science; modern languages and literatures; music; natural science; nursing; occupational therapy; philosophy; physical education, health, and recreation (including community health education, exercise science, health education, physical education, recreation and leisure services, and sports medicine/athletic training); physics; psychology; radio-television; social science education; social work; sociology; technology (including computer engineering technology, construction, design, electronics, graphic communications, manufacturing, mechanical engineering technology, and organizational and mass communication); theater; and urban and regional planning.

Academic Program

Eastern's graduates must have well-developed skills in critical thinking and the ability to express themselves in oral, written, and quantitative forms of communication. The liberal arts core curriculum extends throughout the student's four-year program and includes both breadth and depth requirements as well as writing instruction and assessment in all areas of the curriculum. Small classes, a low student-faculty ratio, and facilities like the Writing Center, a drop-in help center for students, offer the student the resources to meet high expectations. Eastern's core curriculum and liberal arts goals are unique in that their design was a direct response to input from Eastern alumni, employers, and students. Students who select a major early may take advantage of Eastern's "Finish in Four" program that guarantees graduation in four years in more than fifty majors. Minors are available in many areas of study, and teacher certification requirements and specific endorsements are available in conjunction with academic disciplines. The University Honors Program offers motivated students the opportunity to challenge their limits through special honors courses that are part of the core curriculum. University and departmental honor societies continue to provide these opportunities in the major fields. Career preparation is a focus during each student's entire program. Internships and career exploration opportunities for freshmen and sophomores assist in early career and major selection, enhanced employment skills, and locating professional internships as upper-division students.

Off-Campus Arrangements

Study-abroad opportunities are available for Eastern students as well as for students from other campuses. A variety of programs are available in more than twenty-five countries. The University maintains official agreements with institutions in Ghana, Canada, Thailand, and elsewhere. In addition, internships are available in all of the University's colleges both in the Inland Northwest and beyond.

Academic Facilities

Eastern's campus includes more than 300 acres in Cheney. The University also maintains classroom, office, and laboratory/clinic facilities in downtown Spokane and shares facilities at the new Riverpoint Higher Education Center, also in downtown Spokane. The University libraries include the Kennedy Library on the Cheney campus, with more than 800,000 items, online catalogs, and computer search capabilities covering Eastern as well as other Washington State libraries. A downtown library facility is jointly supported by Eastern and Washington State University. The student computing laboratories are located throughout the academic departments. The residence halls are wired for both voice and data communications. The Pence Union Building houses the main computer lab center, with Macintosh and IBM-compatible systems, on-site assistance, DEC mainframe access with faculty sponsorship, and Internet access. Additional facilities for learning and teaching include the planetarium, a speech and hearing clinic, and the Turnbull Laboratory for Ecological Studies.

Costs

Undergraduate tuition and fees for 1999–2000 were $2700 for Washington State residents and $9594 for nonresidents. Typical on-campus room and board cost about $4498.

Financial Aid

The Financial Aid and Scholarship Office assists students in identifying the most appropriate sources of funding for their college education. Students who are admitted to the University may apply for federal, state, and University funds by using the Free Application for Federal Student Aid and by applying before the priority deadline of February 15. Although most financial aid is based entirely on need, a number of scholarships are available for students who meet competitive academic criteria. Academic scholarships also reward outstanding performance by continuing students at Eastern. Awards, which provide a reduction of the nonresident tuition, are available to qualified students from Alaska, Arizona, California, Colorado, Hawaii, Idaho, Montana, Nevada, New Mexico, North Dakota, Oregon, South Dakota, Utah, and Wyoming through the Western Undergraduate Exchange Program. Applicants interested in need-based financial aid and academic scholarships should contact the Financial Aid and Scholarship Office, Sutton Hall, M.S. 142, Eastern Washington University, 526 5th Street, Cheney, Washington 99004.

Faculty

More than 600 faculty members provide highly personalized instruction to undergraduates at Eastern. Faculty members are committed to keeping class sizes small and to helping students graduate in a timely manner, as stated in the "Finish in Four" guarantee available in many majors. Eastern's faculty members are teachers and take pride in innovative curricula, in maintaining close relationships with the community and with professionals outside of the University for the benefit of their students, and in their research, which brings new information and methods into the classroom.

Student Government

All students are members of the Associated Students of Eastern Washington University. A president, executive officers, and a 12-member council are elected annually. The 12 council members represent the students' interests in every facet of student life at Eastern. The student government is responsible for budgeting and managing student fees collected from all students. These funds are used for the operation of the student union, the Pence Union Building, athletic and intramural programs, and the more than seventy-five clubs and organizations that provide opportunities for involvement of students both on campus and in the community.

Admission Requirements

Freshman applicants are admitted on the basis of their high school GPA and test scores on the SAT I or ACT. Applicants also must meet the following core requirements in high school: English, 4; math, 3 (algebra I and II and geometry); social science, 3; science, 2 (including 1 lab science); foreign language, 2 (same language); and fine arts (or elective from above subject areas), 1. Students who do not meet the academic criteria for admission may be considered on the basis of additional evidence of potential presented to the Office of Admissions.

Transfer students must meet a minimum grade point average of 2.0 for consideration. Many majors require considerably higher grade point averages for entry into the major field. Transfer students should consult the University Catalog or contact the Office of Admissions for specific program requirements.

Application and Information

All freshman applicants should submit an application, complete high school (and any college) transcripts, and SAT I or ACT scores to the Office of Admissions. Decisions for fall freshmen are made on December 1 and on a rolling basis thereafter. Transfer students should submit an application, an official high school transcript, and official transcripts from all colleges and universities attended. A nonrefundable application fee of $35 is required of all applicants. A campus visit or participation in an overnight on-campus program is the best way to learn more about Eastern. Students should contact the Office of Admissions to find out more about these and other programs designed to provide an opportunity to explore Eastern Washington University. Additional information and application materials may be obtained from:

Office of Admissions
Sutton Hall
M.S. 148
Eastern Washington University
526 5th Street
Cheney, Washington 99004

Telephone: 888-740-1914 (toll-free)
Fax: 509-359-6692
E-mail: admissions@mail.ewu.edu
World Wide Web: http://www.ewu.edu

The size of the newly expanded and renovated John F. Kennedy Library has been doubled, making it a state-of-the-art facility with fifty different databases available, 500 study carrels, and more.

ECKERD COLLEGE
ST. PETERSBURG, FLORIDA

The College
Eckerd College, a liberal arts institution of distinctive quality, was founded in 1958 as Florida Presbyterian College. Its first freshman class entered in 1960. Eckerd College is related by covenant to the Presbyterian Church (U.S.A.), and it is governed by a self-perpetuating Board of Trustees. Dedicated to excellence, Eckerd College has in its short history established a national reputation as a leading innovative liberal arts college. Its student body, faculty, and program attest to the high expectations of its founders and to a remarkable degree of fulfillment in the years that have followed. Eckerd College currently enrolls 1,560 students (685 men and 875 women) from forty-nine states and fifty-seven countries. Seventy percent of the student body comes from out of state.

Campus life includes a multitude of activities that assist students with their intellectual, social, physical, and spiritual growth. Dormitory life is one hub of the College social environment. More than 80 percent of students live in dorms, and the majority live on campus all four years. The dorms are small and informal; friendships are easily developed in this setting. Upperclassmen may choose to live in the apartment-style town houses located right on campus. Through the Eckerd College student government, social and cultural programs are planned for the College community. Four buildings in the center of campus have been recently transformed into the Hough Campus Center, with snack bars, lounges, student offices and meeting rooms, and a fitness center. The Campus Center is designed to accommodate meaningful interactions between all members of the College community. Many special interest clubs are available, as is a range of intramural sports programs. NCAA Division II intercollegiate athletics for men are baseball, basketball, board sailing, golf, sailing, soccer, tennis, and waterskiing and for women, basketball, board sailing, cross-country, sailing, soccer, softball, tennis, volleyball, and waterskiing. Club volleyball is available for men, and club swimming and rugby are available for men and women. In addition, students have the opportunity to get involved with the campus television and radio stations, the yearbook, and the weekly newspaper.

Location
The 281-acre campus, bordered in part by a 1¼-mile waterfront, is located in a suburban setting on the southern tip of the peninsula that makes up Pinellas County. This peninsula is bounded on the west by the Gulf of Mexico and on the east by Tampa Bay. St. Petersburg is a city of approximately 425,000 people and is a major part of the rapidly growing Tampa Bay metropolitan area. The area has become the national and regional headquarters for many major corporations. Cultural and recreational opportunities abound, including art museums, symphony orchestras, professional theater and road-show engagements of Broadway plays, concerts, and year-round professional sports attractions.

Majors and Degrees
The Bachelor of Science is offered in biology, chemistry, computer science, environmental studies, marine sciences, mathematics, physics, and psychology. The Bachelor of Arts is offered in American studies, anthropology, biology, business administration, comparative literature, creative writing, economics, French, German, history, human development, humanities, international business, international relations and global affairs, international studies, literature, management, modern languages, music, philosophy, political science, psychology, religious studies, Russian studies, sociology, Spanish, theater, visual arts, and women's and gender studies.

In addition to the list of approved majors given above, Eckerd offers flexible concentrations of study so that the student may design his or her own program, either in a traditional field or in an interdisciplinary field. Some typical concentrations include biological illustration, human services management, Latin American development studies, management information systems, organizational dynamics, and personnel and global human resources management. Preprofessional programs include dentistry, engineering and applied science (a 3-2 program), law, M.B.A. studies, medicine, theology, and veterinary medicine.

Academic Program
The student pursues the study of a major field by joining a Collegium, a group of like-minded scholars who view their subjects, however diverse, in the same way. Each Collegium has its own decision-making group composed of professors and students.

Eckerd operates on the 4-1-4 calendar system. Among the many programs that illustrate the innovative nature of Eckerd are the mentorship program, a special training program for faculty members to enable them to help students in their academic progress, career planning, and personal growth; Autumn Term, a three-week orientation program for freshmen, designed to provide an intensive foretaste of college living and college academic work; Winter Term, a one-month midyear program especially adaptable to independent study and off-campus projects, first designed and implemented by Eckerd; a series of interdisciplinary seminars to explore issues related to aesthetics, cross-cultural interaction, environmental concerns, and social relations; and a senior capstone experience involving a choice of thesis, creative project, or comprehensive examination.

Eckerd College has pioneered a residential Academy of Senior Professionals on campus, which prominent retired men and women from around the world are invited to join. These distinguished persons come from professions to which Eckerd students aspire and are available for lectures, advising, career counseling, and mentoring. The academy now comprises more than 300 distinguished professionals.

Off-Campus Arrangements
Various kinds of off-campus opportunities are available. Among the many options for international education are the Eckerd College Study Centre in London, yearlong exchange programs in Japan and Korea, and semester-long exchange programs on every continent through Eckerd's affiliation with the International Student Exchange Program. The Sea Semester Program is available for marine science students, and an exchange program with students on other campuses across the country can be arranged for January or for a semester. As part of a Career Service program, many internship and field experience placements are available. These can be taken for credit upon satisfactory completion of an Independent-Study Contract.

Academic Facilities

The library at Eckerd has more than 140,000 volumes, 1,000 periodicals, and 13,000 items on microfilm. Its reading room is a favorite place for study and research. Complete laboratory facilities are available for language, marine science, chemistry, physics, biology, and experimental psychology. Two state-of-the-art science buildings opened in 1993: a $2.5-million waterfront marine science laboratory and a marine mammal pathobiology laboratory. The 375-seat Bininger Theatre provides professional facilities for theatrical productions. The Roberts Music Center houses classrooms, practice studios, and acoustically insulated listening rooms. The Griffin Chapel has one of the finest Flentrop organs in the country, and a smaller Flentrop is located in the Music Building. Both instruments are used by students studying the organ. Facilities for physical education include a modern gymnasium and basketball court; a swimming pool; a renovated weight room; tennis and volleyball courts; a new complex for soccer, softball, and baseball fields; and a fleet of canoes, kayaks, sailboats and power vessels equipped for waterskiing that are used in an extensive waterfront program. The waterfront program also includes the newly constructed Wallace Boat House and a fully equipped and nationally acclaimed Water Search and Rescue Team. The Ransom Center for Visual Arts provides studios for painting, sculpting, silkscreening, weaving, pottery, photography, video graphics, and other media. The Elliot Gallery is a part of the largest building in the art complex and features continuous showings of visiting exhibits as well as exhibits of work by students and faculty members. The Science Auditorium is equipped for films and demonstrations, and films are shown at Dendy McNair auditorium both for entertainment and for academic courses. The Computer Center houses a Sun SPARCserver 10 and twenty computers that are linked to more than 500 terminals around the College. Students have access to more than 200 personal computers, both Macintosh and IBM compatible, in several laboratories and in all the dormitory lounges throughout the campus. Each dormitory room is wired for access to the Internet and the campus intranet, which includes the library. There is also a Writing Center available to all students, which features desktop publishing capabilities.

Costs

For 2000–01, tuition is $18,565. Room and board total $5110. Books are about $900 per year.

Financial Aid

Twenty-five scholarships of $8000 to $10,000 per year are available to entering freshmen regardless of financial need. These Presidential Scholarships are awarded to outstanding freshmen with strong scholastic records and leadership potential, as demonstrated in a special competition. Other scholarship programs for outstanding students include Church and Campus Scholarships for Presbyterian students recommended by their pastor, Byars Scholarships for Florida residents, Honors and Special Talent Scholarships for outstanding applicants for admission, and full tuition Special Honors Scholarships for National Merit, National Achievement, and National Hispanic Scholars and Semifinalists. Additional details on these and other programs are available from the College's admissions office.

More than 88 percent of all students at Eckerd receive scholarships and/or financial aid. Academic performance, personal development, and potential contribution to the College communiity are important considerations. Financial need is determined by an evaluation of the Free Application for Federal Student Aid (FAFSA). A student's total financial aid package ordinarily consists of a scholarship or grant, work aid, and a loan. As a rule, the mix of grant and loan funding contains a more favorable grant component when the student's academic performance is strong.

Faculty

The faculty has 130 professors (100 full-time and 30 part-time). Ninety-five percent have earned a Ph.D. or a terminal professional degree; their average age is 45. The faculty-student ratio is 1:14. No graduate assistants teach courses.

Student Government

Student activities at Eckerd College are administered by the Eckerd College Organization of Students (ECOS). ECOS conducts campus social programs, including dances, concerts, and films; works to create special events and bring speakers to campus to address issues important to students; and represents student interests in academic policy decisions. Students have voting membership on all major faculty committees.

Admission Requirements

Scores on either the SAT I or ACT are required for admission. No specified high school subjects are required, but the following are recommended as minimal: 4 units in English, 3 in mathematics, 2 in a foreign language, 3 in science, and 3 in social studies. Although no minimum high school average or rank is required, students with less than a 2.5 average are seldom admitted. In last year's freshman class, 60 percent of the members ranked in the top fifth of their high school graduating class. An interview is recommended but not required. Geographical location and religious preference are not admission factors. Early admission is available to promising high school juniors. In addition, credit and advanced standing are offered through the Advanced Placement Program of the College Board or the International Baccalaureate Program.

Application and Information

Application may be made at any time and should include a $25 application fee. A rolling admission policy is practiced. For more complete information and to make arrangements to visit the campus, students should contact:

Dean of Admissions
Eckerd College
4200 54th Avenue South
St. Petersburg, Florida 33711
Telephone: 727-864-8331
              800-456-9009 (toll-free)
Fax: 727-866-2304
E-mail: admissions@eckerd.edu
World Wide Web: http://www.eckerd.edu

Eckerd's waterfront campus on Boca Ciega Bay.

EDGEWOOD COLLEGE
MADISON, WISCONSIN

The College

With a progressive and challenging curriculum, Edgewood offers the advantages of a small private college in a university-oriented city. The result is a stimulating learning environment rich in academic and recreational resources.

Edgewood's 55-acre wooded campus is situated on the shore of Lake Wingra in a residential neighborhood of Madison near parks and an arboretum. The College has three residence halls and one apartment building for students, a new student center/union, the new Sonderegger Science Center, a new library, classrooms, athletic facilities, a chapel, and a theater. Campus organizations include the student newspaper, student government, professional groups, and a variety of clubs to meet personal interests. There are intramural athletics and intercollegiate teams in men's baseball, basketball, cross-country, golf, soccer, and tennis and women's basketball, cross-country, golf, soccer, softball, tennis, and volleyball.

Edgewood is near the end of a major building program that has added several campus improvements, including the new Sonderegger Science Center and the Henry J. Pradolin Humanities Center. The Sonderegger Science Center has been designed to be a national model for science education and collaboration. The Henry J. Pradolin Humanities Center, which will be completed on August 1, 2000, consists of state-of-the-art classrooms, offices, and, most importantly, a student center/union.

Edgewood collaborates with the University of Wisconsin–Madison, located only a few blocks away, in a program of shared resources that gives students opportunities that are not usually available at a college of Edgewood's size. Edgewood students may enroll in one university class per semester and have access to the university's library system and art museum. Guest lecturers, concerts, athletic events, and special programs are all readily available on a regular basis.

The current undergraduate population is 1,200. The student body includes both residents and commuters. Although the majority of students come from the Midwest, about 15 percent are from states other than Wisconsin or from countries outside the United States.

The College is accredited by the North Central Association of Colleges and Schools, and its programs in education are accredited by the National Council for Accreditation of Teacher Education. The nursing program is approved by the Wisconsin State Board of Nursing and the National League for Nursing Accrediting Commission.

Location

Madison is a growing and exciting community, with a colorful assortment of art fairs, outdoor markets, festivals, sporting events, and concerts taking place throughout the year. As Wisconsin's state capital, Madison is home to a vigorous state legislature and a politically active community at all levels. The city has a stable economy driven by a broad base of educational, medical, and financial institutions as well as light industry. While Madison is renowned for its scenic beauty, it is also the gateway to hundreds of vacation, park, and lake areas in northern and central Wisconsin.

Majors and Degrees

Edgewood College offers baccalaureate degrees with majors in accounting, art, art therapy, biology, broad-field social studies (concentration in economics, history, political science, or sociology/anthropology), business (concentration in financem management, or marketing), chemistry, child life, computer information systems, criminal justice, cytotechnology, early childhood–exceptional needs, economics, elementary education, English (writing or literature), French, graphic design, history, international relations, mathematics, medical technology, music, natural science and mathematics, nursing, performing arts, psychology, public policy and administration, religious studies, sociology, and Spanish. Preprofessional programs are available in dentistry, engineering, law, medicine, pharmacy, and social work. Individualized majors and minors may also be arranged. Minors include many traditional areas, plus computer science, environmental science, philosophy, secondary education, and women's studies.

Class scheduling alternatives provide nontraditional students with an opportunity to obtain B.A. or B.S. degrees in accounting, business, computer information systems, criminal justice, industrial/organizational psychology, nursing, or religious studies, with courses taken in the evenings or on two weekends per month on a semester basis. Many people also attend classes for personal enrichment or professional development or participate in a separate continuing education program of noncredit short courses.

The Associate of Arts degree in liberal studies is offered, with credits applicable to the College's four-year programs if students decide to continue their studies after earning the two-year degree.

Academic Program

The curriculum includes a foundation for all students in composition, logic, mathematics, speech, foreign language, arts, sciences, and perspectives, with an advanced sequence designed for honors students. Departmental course requirements for majors and minors are added to the above. The human issues project, a multidisciplinary study or activity, requires every student to apply knowledge and experience to the examination of a selected aspect of the human condition and the values involved.

Students are encouraged to participate in field experiences, internships, and independent studies, regardless of major. Education students begin classroom observation and practice as early as the freshman year. Nursing, medical technology, and cytotechnology students engage in clinicals in hospitals and laboratories as juniors and seniors.

The College is on a 4-1-4 calendar that consists of four months of classwork each semester and the Winterim, an optional educational and cultural program held each January between semesters, during which credit may be earned or independent pursuits followed. An eight-week summer session and special summer or spring break workshops are also available.

Edgewood offers alternative routes to credit for its degrees through the College-Level Examination Program (CLEP), the College Board's Advanced Placement (AP), the ACT Program's Proficiency Examination Program (PEP), locally administered programs of retroactive credit for foreign language proficiency, and credit for work experience that closely matches the content of a course.

Off-Campus Arrangements

Collaboration with the University of Wisconsin–Madison enables Edgewood students to take one course per semester at the university under Edgewood's tuition. This relationship greatly broadens the scope of courses, libraries, museums, and faculty members available to students of the College.

Edgewood encourages students to take advantage of community resources. Arrangements with a children's hospital, a local nursing home, a school for exceptional children, and a school for juvenile offenders provide education, psychology, and sociology majors with opportunities for off-campus experiences. Volunteerism at community meal programs, local prisons, shelters, centers for at-risk children, and public health agencies is also encouraged.

Qualified students may plan for special one- or two-week courses abroad or for a semester or year at an international institution of higher learning.

Academic Facilities

The College library is a comfortable facility with a reading atrium and group study rooms. Its collection includes books, periodicals, videotapes, audio recordings, and CD-ROM databases in several fields, including business. In addition, microcomputers, CD players, tape recorders, photocopiers, video equipment, and microform readers are available for student and faculty use. The library offers direct computerized access to the catalog of the University of Wisconsin libraries and to other library catalogs through the Internet. An interlibrary loan delivery service connects hundreds of libraries in the state.

Computer labs on campus have both Apple and PC equipment that connects to a local access network. Student rooms in the residence halls are also joined to the network. The foreign language lab has audio and videotape equipment and receives international programs via satellite.

Costs

Edgewood's tuition and fees were $11,600 per year for 1999–2000. The complete cost of room and board in a campus residence hall averaged $4250 per year. Other expenses, including books, travel, and supplies, averaged $1500.

Financial Aid

Edgewood's financial aid program combines innovative merit-based assistance with traditional need-based assistance to make the Edgewood experience affordable. Institutional merit awards are available based on academic, leadership, science, and fine arts skills. More than 90 percent of freshman aid applicants receive some form of grant or scholarship. The College administers traditional federal and state programs, including the Federal Pell Grant and the Wisconsin Tuition Grant. Campus employment is available along with Federal Stafford Student Loans, Federal Perkins Loans, and supplemental loans. To apply for assistance, students must complete the Free Application for Federal Student Aid (FAFSA). Students may arrange with the College to pay tuition in monthly installments.

Faculty

The College currently has a full-time teaching faculty of 76, of whom 80 percent have doctoral or terminal degrees in their fields. While some Sinsinawa Dominicans continue to teach at the College, most of the faculty are lay members. All classes and labs are taught by the primary professor and not by graduate students. The favorable student-faculty ratio allows good rapport between professors and students. Faculty members take a keen interest in their students, serving as academic advisers and becoming involved in student activities. The full-time faculty is supported by a cadre of part-time instructors who bring added expertise to the classroom.

Student Government

Through their participation in various committees and organizations and through the Student Senate, students have the opportunity to take part in determining scholastic, intellectual, recreational, social, and cultural activities both on and off campus. Students have a voice and vote on the commencement, curriculum and education policy, library policies, student affairs, and teacher education programs.

Admission Requirements

Edgewood accepts applicants on the basis of the amount and kind of ability a student possesses, as reflected in scholastic standards that have been met, high school and community activities, and employment. Candidates for admission to Edgewood must submit 16 units of high school study, including 12 units in English, speech, mathematics, history, natural science, social science, and foreign language. High school grade point average, rank in class, ACT or SAT I scores, and recommendations are considered in determining the applicant's potential to do college work. Applicants from nontraditional high schools are welcome to apply.

Transfer students are evaluated on the college-level work they have done as well as on the standard criteria for admission. Each department determines transferability of credits, but a minimum of 52 hours must be completed in residence, including the major requirements.

Application and Information

Dean of Admissions
Edgewood College
855 Woodrow Street
Madison, Wisconsin 53713
Telephone: 608-663-4861
800-444-4861 (toll-free)
World Wide Web: http://www.edgewood.edu

Students in front of the Sonderegger Science Center, a state-of-the-art facility that has already become a national model for science and education collaboration.

EDINBORO UNIVERSITY OF PENNSYLVANIA
EDINBORO, PENNSYLVANIA

The University

Edinboro University, a part of the Pennsylvania State System of Higher Education, is located in the borough of Edinboro, Erie County, Pennsylvania. It is the oldest teacher-training institution in Pennsylvania west of the Allegheny Mountains and the second oldest in the state. Edinboro Academy was chartered in 1856. After the passage of the State Normal Act in 1857, the school opened as Edinboro Normal School for the preparation of teachers. Under its original charter, the school was privately administered until 1861, when the commonwealth chartered it as a state normal school. The school was purchased by the commonwealth of Pennsylvania in 1914. The state recognized Edinboro State Teachers College as a four-year college in 1926 and granted it the right to offer a Bachelor of Science in Education degree in the areas of elementary, secondary, and art education. The name of the institution was changed to Edinboro State College in 1960. In 1983, university status was given to each of the state colleges, and a comprehensive commonwealth university system was established.

Edinboro's graduate school offers the graduate degrees and certifications of postbaccalaureate certification, Edinboro University graduate certificate, Master of Arts, Master of Fine Arts, Master of Education, Master of Science, Master of Science in Nursing, and postmaster's certification.

The University is accredited by the Commission on Higher Education of the Middle States Association of Colleges and Schools (3624 Market Street, Philadelphia, Pennsylvania 19104; telephone: 215-662-5606). The commission is an institutional accrediting agency that is recognized by the U.S. Secretary of Education and the Commission on Recognition of Postsecondary Accreditation. Other University accreditations and program approvals include the National League for Nursing Accrediting Commission, the American Dietetic Association, the Council on Rehabilitation Education, the Council for Accreditation of Counseling and Related Educational Programs, the American Speech-Language-Hearing Association, the Council on Social Work Education, the National Association of Schools of Music, the Pennsylvania State Board of Nursing, and the Pennsylvania Department of Education.

Of the 7,079 students at Edinboro, 6,400 are undergraduates. The University maintains eight on-campus residence halls for approximately 2,500 students. There are more than forty buildings situated on the spacious 585-acre campus, which includes open fields, a lake, and many acres of woods.

Edinboro University in Erie–The Porreco Center serves as the site of day and evening classes, conferences, and informal gatherings. Donated to the University as part of its first-ever capital campaign and valued at $1.1 million, the 27-acre estate has eleven buildings.

Location

Located adjacent to the business district of Edinboro, Pennsylvania, the University is accessible by automobile from all sections of the state and is near the intersection of Interstates 90 and 79. Passenger service of all kinds operates on frequent schedules, connecting Edinboro with nearby cities and towns, including Erie, Pennsylvania's third-largest city. The Erie Airport is just 30 minutes away by automobile or bus. Within walking distance of the campus, the community of Edinboro has eight churches of various denominations.

Majors and Degrees

The University awards the Associate of Arts, Associate of Engineering Technology, Associate of Science, Bachelor of Arts, Bachelor of Fine Arts, Bachelor of Science, Bachelor of Science in Nursing, and Bachelor of Science in Education. These permit majoring in the following areas: anthropology, applied media arts (with concentrations in animation, cinema, graphic arts, and photography), fine arts/crafts (with concentrations in ceramics, drawing, jewelry/metalry, painting, printmaking, sculpture, textile design, weaving/fibers, and wood/furniture design), art education, art history, biology, biology/premedical LECOM, biomedical equipment technology, business administration/accounting, business administration/administration, business administration/financial services, business administration/marketing, chemistry, chemistry/forensic sciences, chemistry/industrial biochemistry, communication studies (with concentrations in broadcasting, organizational communication, and public relations/advertising), communication speech and hearing disorders, computer science, computer science/application, computer science/theoretical, criminal justice (A.A. and B.A.), drama, earth sciences, economics, elementary education, elementary/early childhood education, elementary/special education, 3/2 engineering/natural science and math, English/literature, English/writing/journalism, environmental science/biology, environmental science/geology, environmental studies/geography, foreign language, general business administration, general studies, geography, geology, German, health and physical education, history, humanities, human services/social services, human services/developmental disabilities, industrial trades leadership, innovative nursing, liberal studies, manufacturing engineering technology, mathematics, medical technology, music, music education, natural science and math, natural science and math/wildlife, nuclear medicine technology, nursing, nursing/RN, nutrition, philosophy, physics, political science, preschool education, psychology, secondary education (biology, chemistry, earth and space science, English, general science, German, mathematics, physics, social studies and Spanish), social science, social work, sociology, Spanish, special education, special education/elementary education, and specialized studies. Preprofessional programs are offered in dentistry, law, medicine, pharmacy, and veterinary science. Minors also exist in fifty-three specializations.

Academic Program

Associate degrees require a minimum of 60 semester hours of credit, including a general education component.

Baccalaureate degrees require a minimum of 128 semester hours of credit. A general education requirement of 60 semester hours is distributed among the arts, humanities, and science and technology to ensure a basic liberal arts foundation. The remaining 68 semester hours are devoted to specialization and may include major and professional courses, a minor, and other concomitant courses.

Advanced placement credit and honors courses are available.

The Office of Continuing Education offers a variety of workshops and special interest courses. The Office of Adult Student Information Services enables nontraditional students to enroll for academic programs at convenient times and locations on a full- or part-time basis.

An Army Reserve Officers' Training Corps (ROTC) program is available.

The Office for Students with Disabilities provides services essential for physically disabled, hearing-impaired, visually impaired, and learning-disabled individuals.

Academic Facilities

The seven-story Baron-Forness Library is the focal point of the University campus. The library houses more than 440,000 bound volumes and more than 1.3 million microform units. The University has one of the largest and most powerful educational computer systems in northwestern Pennsylvania. State-of-the-art computers provide support for the instructional and administrative needs of the University.

Costs

For 1999–2000, the tuition fee for a resident of Pennsylvania was $1809 per semester; for nonresident students, the cost per semester was $2714. For a semester, room rent was $1054, and meals were $840. Additional fees included a student activity fee of $75, a University Center fee of $64, a health fee of $50, and an instructional service fee of $180. The cost of books and supplies varies with the academic major. (Costs are subject to change for 2000–01.)

Financial Aid

The types of financial aid offered by Edinboro include student employment, loans, grants, and scholarships. In most cases, Pennsylvania State Grant and Free Application for Federal Student Aid forms are used to determine eligibility for these programs. Federal aid administered by the University is available for both the regular academic year and the summer sessions. The application deadline for upperclass students for these programs is normally May 1 for the following academic year. Freshmen may apply for aid upon acceptance by the University. Financial aid is also available through the University's ROTC program. For additional information, students should contact the Director of Financial Aid (814-732-5555 Ext. 266).

Faculty

Edinboro's student-faculty ratio of 18:1 makes it possible to maintain close interaction between students and the highly qualified faculty members. A large percentage of the faculty have completed terminal degrees in their area of specialization.

Student Government

The Student Government Association is a vital and active organization on the campus and serves as the official student voice in all University matters. Student Government Association representatives serve on nearly all University committees and participate in the University governance system. This organization sponsors special events, activities, and student clubs to satisfy a variety of student interests. The Student Government Association participates in the annual budget recommendations regarding the budgeting of the Student Activity Fund.

Admission Requirements

To satisfy the requirements for admission to Edinboro University, candidates must be graduates of an approved high school or an institution of equivalent status or have equivalent preparation (GED) as determined by the Credentials Division of the Department of Education. Applicants must file a high school transcript, and they must give evidence of scholastic aptitude, as measured by satisfactory scores on the SAT I or ACT. An audition is required of students applying for admission to the music curriculum. Transfer students from other postsecondary institutions must file grade transcripts from each institution attended. Applicants may have the SAT I or ACT requirement waived on the basis of maturity, life experiences, or other factors through a personal interview with the Admissions Office.

Application and Information

Students may make application for admission as early as July 1, after finishing the junior year of high school, and may request this application form in writing from the Admissions Office.

Requests for application papers, viewbooks, financial aid forms, and further information should be addressed to:

Admissions Office
Biggers House
Edinboro University of Pennsylvania
Edinboro, Pennsylvania 16444

Telephone: 814-732-2761 (TTY/voice)
           800-626-2203 (toll-free)
Fax: 814-732-2420

An aerial view of Edinboro University of Pennsylvania.

ELIZABETH CITY STATE UNIVERSITY
ELIZABETH CITY, NORTH CAROLINA

The University

Elizabeth City State University (ECSU) was founded on March 3, 1891, as a two-year normal school to train teachers of African-American heritage. In 1937, the institution became a four-year teacher's college and two years later was renamed Elizabeth City State Teacher's College. In 1969, the institution was dedicated as a regional university. In 1971, ECSU became a constituent institution of the sixteen-campus University of North Carolina system.

ECSU is a public university offering baccalaureate programs in the basic arts and sciences and in selected professional and preprofessional areas and the master's degree in elementary education. Credit hours required to earn a master's degree are 36 semester hours.

Elizabeth City State University is accredited by the Commission on Colleges of the Southern Association of Colleges and Schools to award baccalaureate degrees and is a candidate for accreditation to award the master's degree. The University currently offers twenty-six academic majors and many associated minors and concentrations in two divisions and twelve departments.

ECSU enrolls nearly 2,000 students: 75 percent of students are African American, 24 percent are Caucasian, and 1 percent are students from other cultural and ethnic backgrounds. The student body is almost equally divided between residential and commuting students. Ninety percent of students are pursuing their education full-time. Students come from seventy-one of North Carolina's 100 counties, twenty-two states, the District of Columbia, and four other countries.

At ECSU, nearly half of the students choose to live on campus. These students live in a number of residence halls and one apartment complex. Each facility is staffed by administrators and student assistants who help provide and maintain a high-quality experience for students. Students who live on campus are automatically enrolled in a campus meal plan that provides all meals. The campus dining hall features an array of freshly prepared entrees, salads, sandwiches, and snack items. Snack bars are also located around campus. ECSU strives to consistently provide a safe environment. Campus police officers and security guards patrol the campus at all hours. The Vikings Patrol, an auxiliary unit of students trained in police communications, helps the campus police staff the 24-hour security phone system. In addition, the residence halls are monitored 24 hours a day by student service professionals. The Commuter Center gives students a place to relax or study between classes.

Participation in extracurricular activities brings students' leadership skills to the surface. There are more than sixty officially recognized social, service, and interest-related organizations on campus. They range from professional and academic clubs to religious groups and service organizations, including fraternities and sororities. Activities like these bring students with similar interests together and add an extra measure of fun and camaraderie to the college years. Some of the organizations available include Greek fraternities and sororities, the Art Guild, Cheering Squad, Commuter Student Club, Criminal Justice Club, Dance Group, Residence Hall Council, Industrial Arts Club, NAACP, NABA, Panhellenic Council, Majorettes, University Band, University Choir, University Players, Gospel Choir, Viking Yearbook, Social Sciences Club, Spanish Club, Students in Free Enterprise, Student Government, and Usher's Guild.

ECSU is a Division II university and is affiliated with both the CIAA Conference and the NCAA. ECSU has one of the highest graduation rates of athletes attending NCAA Division II colleges. Men's varsity teams include baseball, basketball, cross-country, football, tennis, and track and field. Women's teams include basketball, cross-country, softball, track and field, and volleyball.

For students who want to play sports for fun, the campus offers numerous intramural sports activities and recreational and leisure activities. The campus also has an Olympic-size indoor swimming pool and a six-lane bowling alley.

Location

Elizabeth City State University is nestled in the historic Albemarle area near the mouth of the Pasquotank River in northeast North Carolina. This location is only minutes from Virginia Beach, Norfolk, and the Tidewater region. To the south lies the beautiful Outer Banks, a spot for vacationers from all over the country.

Majors and Degrees

ECSU offers the following degrees and their prospective majors: the Bachelor of Science degree in accounting, applied mathematics, biology, business administration, chemistry, computer information sciences, criminal justice, geology, industrial technology, mathematics, music industry studies, physics, and psychology; and the Bachelor of Arts degree in art, English, history, music, political science, sociology, and sociology/social work curriculum.

ECSU also offers the Bachelor of Science degree in elementary education (K–6) and special education (K–12) and the Bachelor of Science degree with teacher licensure in basic business education/comprehensive business education, biology, chemistry, mathematics, physical education and health, and technology education. The Bachelor of Arts degree with teacher licensure is offered in art (minor in education K–12), English, history, music (minor in education K–12), political science, and sociology. ECSU also offers a host of concentration alternatives for students, designed to provide preparation in a specialty within the major discipline. Some examples include airway science, athletic coaching, black studies, environmental science, prelaw, and speech/drama.

Academic Program

Elizabeth City State University awards twenty-six bachelor's degrees to students who have successfully completed all courses and other requirements prescribed by the major department and all of the general education courses prescribed by the University for all students. Credit hours required to earn an undergraduate degree vary from 124 to 130 semester hours. The University Honors Program is designed to challenge students with high academic potential at an accelerated rate and to provide them with exposure to a wide variety of in-depth academic experiences. The ROTC program is also available and is based on a four-year curriculum integrated with the normal baccalaureate degree program.

Academic Facilities

ECSU is an ever-growing campus, with more than fifty buildings spread over 114 acres in historic Elizabeth City, North Carolina. The beautiful and modern campus has many unique facilities, including the state-of-the-art G. R. Little Library, which utilizes a computerized catalog system and contains close to 1 million items, including books, microfilms, audiotapes, videotapes, films, and periodicals. Online services are also available to provide connection to the limitless resources of the Internet, scholarly research, and computer software. The Jimmy R. Jenkins Science Center houses the University's state-of-the-art planetarium, the first in the surrounding North Carolina area. Some of the building's most significant features include seminar and lecture rooms, instrumentation laboratories, an aquarium, and an appended greenhouse. For students in the music industry studies program, facilities include a comprehensive twenty-four-track recording studio. More facilities are on their way toward completion. The current Academic Computing Center was expanded in 1998, and the new music and art complex opened in 1999.

Costs

Tuition and fees per semester in 1999–2000 for North Carolina residents were $925.70 for commuters and $2874.70 with room and board. Out-of-state tuition and fees per semester were $4205.50 for commuters and $6154.50 with room and board. Approximately $250 can be estimated per semester for books and other supplies.

Financial Aid

Of all ECSU students, 86 to 90 percent receive some form of financial aid. Assistance available to eligible students consists of grants, loans, scholarships, and part-time employment. Students applying for financial aid must complete the Free Application for Federal Student Aid (FAFSA). Deadline dates for priority consideration are March 1 (fall semester), November 1 (spring semester), and April 1 (summer semester).

Faculty

Elizabeth City State University employs 120 full-time faculty members; 72 percent hold doctoral degrees, while the remainder hold master's degrees. Many professors are nationally respected scholars who conduct in-depth research and have published numerous works. The faculty-student ratio is 1:15.

Student Government

The Student Government Association (SGA) of Elizabeth City State University is composed of students who are elected by the student body. The SGA's primary goal is to attend to the students' needs and development. It is the duty of the SGA to maintain a certain level of communication with students, faculty members, and the administration.

Admission Requirements

To be considered for admission to ECSU, applicants must have graduated from an approved or accredited high school and have achieved at least a 2.0 grade point average. Applicants should have a minimum SAT I score of 700 or minimum ACT score of 16 for in-state residents and a minimum SAT I score of 800 or minimum ACT score of 18 for out-of-state residents. Students who graduated from high school after June 1990 must meet the following requirements: 4 units of English, emphasizing literature, composition, and grammar; 3 units of mathematics (including algebra I and II and geometry); 3 units of science (including at least 1 unit of a life or biological science, at least 1 unit of a physical science, and at least one laboratory course); and 2 units of social studies, including U.S. history. Two units of the same foreign language are not required but are highly recommended.

Transfer students must satisfy all entrance requirements; their transcripts are evaluated in relation to the requirements of the specific program for which they are applying.

Application and Information

High school students should apply in the fall of their senior year. All students are encouraged to apply before May 1 for the fall semester and before December 1 for the spring semester. Summer session students may register up to the first day of classes.

Official notification of admission eligibility is sent to each applicant immediately after all credentials have been thoroughly evaluated.

The Office of Admissions is open Monday through Friday between 8 a.m. and 5 p.m. For further information about Elizabeth City State University, students should contact:

Office of Admissions
Elizabeth City State University
Campus Box 901
1704 Weeksville Road
Elizabeth City, North Carolina 27909
Telephone: 252-335-3305
         800-347-3278 (toll-free)
World Wide Web: http://www.ecsu.edu

The Jimmy R. Jenkins Science Complex houses a state-of-the-art planetarium, the first of its kind in northeastern North Carolina.

ELIZABETHTOWN COLLEGE
ELIZABETHTOWN, PENNSYLVANIA

The College
Founded in 1899 to provide a high-quality higher education to men and women, Elizabethtown College maintains its commitment to an academic program that combines a traditionally strong liberal arts core curriculum with a career and professional orientation. The students at Elizabethtown come from twenty-nine states and twenty-five countries, providing a diversity of backgrounds that enhances the College as a whole.

A residential college, 87 percent of E-town students live on the 185-acre campus in six dormitories and senior townhouses. Student-run residence hall councils plan programs and provide leadership opportunities. A wide variety of campus cultural events and other activities draw 80 percent student participation every weekend. The College maintains an active intramural sports program and fields nine NCAA Division III teams for men (baseball, basketball, cross-country, golf, soccer, swimming, tennis, track and field, and wrestling) and nine for women (basketball, cross-country, field hockey, soccer, softball, swimming, tennis, track and field, and volleyball), several of which contend for national titles each year.

The College offers an effective personal and career counseling service, which encourages students to make use of its office as early as their freshman year. The employment and graduate school placement rate for students within eight months after graduation has averaged 90 percent for the past several years.

Location
Elizabethtown is a community of 20,000 people, located in south-central Pennsylvania, within 20 minutes of Hershey, Lancaster, and Harrisburg, the state capital. Philadelphia and Baltimore are within 2 hours of Elizabethtown; New York and Washington are within 4 hours. Elizabethtown is served by Amtrak train service from Philadelphia and Pittsburgh, and the Harrisburg International Airport is 15 minutes away.

Majors and Degrees
Bachelor of Arts degrees are awarded in art, communications, economics, English, history, modern languages, music, philosophy, political philosophy, political science, psychology, religious studies, social work, and sociology-anthropology. Bachelor of Science degrees are offered in accounting, biochemistry, biology, biotechnology, business administration, chemical physics, chemistry, chemistry management, computer engineering, computer science, early childhood education, elementary education, engineering physics, environmental science, industrial engineering, international business, mathematics, medical technology, music education, music therapy, occupational therapy, and physics. Fifty-two minors/concentrations as well as eight certification programs in secondary education are available.

The College offers joint institutional (3-2) programs with Duke University, leading to a master's degree in forestry or environmental management; 3-2 programs in engineering with Pennsylvania State University are offered, leading to a Bachelor of Arts in physics and a Bachelor of Science in engineering. Cooperative (2-2) programs with Thomas Jefferson University in diagnostic imaging, laboratory sciences, and nursing lead to a Bachelor of Science, and 2-3 or 3-3 programs in physical therapy lead to a Master of Science. A joint program with Widener University also leads to a physical therapy degree.

Preprofessional majors are offered in dentistry, law, medicine and osteopathy, the ministry, and veterinary medicine.

The Pre-Medical Primary Care Program through the Pennsylvania State University College of Medicine at the Milton S. Hershey Medical Center provides options for Elizabethtown students pursuing careers in internal medicine, family practice, and pediatrics.

Academic Program
Elizabethtown's core program of traditional and innovative liberal arts areas complements both the intensive studies in the academic major/minor and the wide selection of elective courses. Students develop skills for critical analysis, effective communication, and habits of mind that ensure adaptability in the ever changing global job market.

Independent and directed studies and extensive internship and externship possibilities are available.

The College operates on a semester calendar. Freshmen arrive in the last week of August, and examinations are given prior to the winter break. The spring semester begins in the middle of January and runs through early May. Intensive summer-session courses are available for students who wish to accelerate their academic program. Students may earn credit toward graduation through Advanced Placement examinations, College-Level Examination Program tests, or tests administered by the individual departments.

Off-Campus Arrangements
Through the Brethren College Abroad (BCA) Program, students may spend all or part of a year studying in China, Ecuador, England, France, Germany, Greece, India, Japan, Mexico, or Spain. Study and internships in major U.S. cities and abroad are also available through cooperative programs with Boston, American, and Fordham Universities. Social work majors are required to complete 600 hours of field instruction in off-campus agency settings. Medical technology students spend their senior year studying at AMA-approved cooperative hospital programs. Both occupational therapy and music therapy students must complete six months of fieldwork in an approved health-care setting.

Academic Facilities
The nine academic buildings on campus include the Leffler Chapel/Performance Center, seating 900 for arts, religious, and cultural events; the High Library, with 161,989 bound volumes; two science halls, Esbenshade (biology, engineering, math, occupational therapy, and physics) and Musser (chemistry); a music building; and three other classroom buildings, one of which houses the College's VAX 3100 computer, which is connected to the $3.25-million campuswide network. Steinman Center houses the offices, classrooms, and facilities of the Department of Communications.

Costs
Tuition, room, board, and fees for 1999–2000 were $23,600; $18,220 of this was tuition. Students should also plan on an

additional cost of about $1500 for books, transportation, and personal expenses, for a total cost of about $25,100. Financial aid is based on this figure.

Financial Aid

Financial aid packages are typically a combination of scholarships, grants, loans, and student employment; 92 percent of the students receive some form of aid. To apply for financial aid, students must file the Free Application for Federal Student Aid (FAFSA) and the Elizabethtown College Verification Form. Estimated data should not be filed. Signed copies of the parent's (and student's, if applicable) most recent federal income tax form, including all schedules, must also be submitted to the financial aid office.

About 160 freshmen with the strongest academic credentials receive academic scholarships, awarded on a competitive basis and without regard to need. The deadline for all financial aid is April 1.

Faculty

Elizabethtown has a teaching faculty of 179 full- and part-time professors. The student-faculty ratio is 12:1. Eighty-five percent of the faculty hold a Ph.D. or the highest earned degree in their field. After the freshman year, students who have declared a major are assigned a faculty adviser within the department.

Student Government

Students play an active role in campus governance through the Student Senate, the Residence Hall Association, and other organizations. Members of the Student Senate are elected from each class to voice student concerns, coordinate special events, and allocate funds for student activities and more than sixty student-run clubs and organizations. The Activities Planning Board, also a student group, provides weekend programs, campus social activities, and entertainment for the College community.

Admission Requirements

Decisions about admission to Elizabethtown are made without regard to sex, race, religion, physical handicap, or place of residence. Approximately 74 percent of all applicants are accepted. Students should have followed an academic curriculum, with the completion of at least 18 college-preparatory units recommended. Fifty-eight percent of the students admitted are in the top 20 percent of their high school class, and 37 percent are in the top tenth. Transfer students are encouraged to apply.

The College seeks diversity, and students who display leadership abilities or special talents are considered highly desirable. Campus interviews are recommended but not required for most students, although the College reserves the right to require interviews in special cases. Music students are required to have auditions, and occupational therapy students must have an interview at the invitation of the department.

Early acceptance is available for highly qualified high school juniors.

Application and Information

The College operates on a rolling admission basis and does not specify a deadline for application, except in the case of occupational therapy students, who must submit a completed application by December 15. Students can apply using the common application or on line at the Web site listed below. Applicants must submit a high school transcript, SAT I or ACT scores, two letters of recommendation, and a personal statement, essay, or graded paper. Early application is strongly recommended. Accepted students should notify the College of their decision to attend by May 1; matriculation after that date is on a space-available basis. Students interested in the Hershey Foods Honors Program must submit a completed application by January 15.

For more information, students should contact:

Office of Admissions
Elizabethtown College
One Alpha Drive
Elizabethtown, Pennsylvania 17022-2298
Telephone: 717-361-1400
Fax: 717-361-1365
E-mail: admissions@etown.edu
World Wide Web: http://www.etown.edu

The Elizabethtown men's soccer team, with forty-five winning seasons, won the NCAA Division III championship in 1989 and captured its record seventeenth Middle Atlantic Conference championship in 1996.

ELMHURST COLLEGE
ELMHURST, ILLINOIS

The College

Elmhurst College is a private, comprehensive liberal arts college that is located near the geographic center of metropolitan Chicago. Founded in 1871, the College advances the practical and professional relevance of the liberal arts tradition. The faculty and staff members assume that one's work is a central concern of an educated person. The academic programs are characterized by their connections with the professional world and their responsiveness to the intellectual needs to today's diverse student population. In forty-nine undergraduate majors and five graduate programs, Elmhurst students strengthen their skills of critical and creative inquiry and develop their capacity for lives of learning, service, and meaningful work.

The College enrolls 2,800 undergraduate and graduate students. Sixty-five percent are full-time undergraduates; 31 percent are over age 25. Twenty-two states and seventeen countries are represented in the student body. More than one third of Elmhurst's undergraduates live on campus in one of five residence halls.

The Center for Professional Excellence (CPE) is a distinctive component of an Elmhurst education. Established in 1997, the CPE offers internships, mentorships, international study programs, service-learning opportunities, guidance through career launches and transitions, and other student-centered programs. The goal of this innovative center is to enhance the traditional college experience with additional, purposeful challenges, both intellectual and professional, on campus and beyond.

While Elmhurst is small enough to offer students opportunities to make real contributions to campus life, it also is large enough to offer an extensive range of choices among cocurricular and extracurricular activities. Eighty-seven registered clubs, organizations, and athletic teams are active on campus. The jazz band, radio station, and student newspaper, *The Leader*, have a professional edge. The Mill Theatre, in its seventieth year, presents dramas, musicals, and student-directed productions of original scripts. The Elmhurst College Jazz Festival is an annual, nationally recognized celebration of the supremely American artform. Eminent artists and business, political, and religious leaders regularly speak to campus audiences. Examples include Lech Walesa and Elie Wiesel, winners of the Nobel Prize for Peace; the acclaimed poets Maya Angelou and Gwendolyn Brooks; and the explorer Robert Ballard, who discovered the wreckage of the *R.M.S. Titanic*.

The College fields sixteen teams in NCAA Division III and is a charter member of the highly competitive College Conference of Illinois and Wisconsin (CCIW). During the 1990s, the Bluejays won CCIW championships in baseball, softball, and volleyball and qualified for postseason play in men's basketball and women's volleyball.

Elmhurst is affiliated with the United Church of Christ. Like the church, the College is open, welcoming, and ecumenical. Nearly half of the students are Roman Catholic. Jews, Muslims, Orthodox, and many Protestant denominations are represented on the faculty and in the student body. In short, people of all creeds (and of none) come to the campus to learn and thrive.

Master's degrees are offered in five disciplines: computer network systems, early childhood special education, industrial/organizational psychology, professional accountancy, and professional writing.

Location

Elmhurst's handsome suburban campus, located 16 miles west of Chicago's Loop, is a registered arboretum, with twenty-three red-brick buildings and more than 600 varieties of trees and other plants. The students benefit enormously from the College's location near the heart of one of the world's most important and appealing urban regions. The Chicago area offers world-class opportunities for internships and other professional opportunities and for cultural, social, and sporting events. A commuter railroad stops two blocks from campus, and city and suburban attractions also are accessible via several interstate highways. The city of Elmhurst, a charming suburb with 42,000 residents, is located on the eastern edge of DuPage County, which is 6 miles southwest of O'Hare International Airport.

Majors and Degrees

Undergraduates at Elmhurst can choose from among forty-nine majors. Through the interdepartmental major, students can develop individualized programs of study, with the guidance of a faculty adviser. The College awards the Bachelor of Arts, Bachelor of Liberal Studies, Bachelor of Music, and Bachelor of Science degrees.

Elmhurst offers undergraduate degree programs in accounting; American studies; art; athletic training; biology; business administration; chemistry; communication studies; computer science; early childhood education; economics; elementary education; English; environmental management; exercise science; finance; fitness management; French; geography and environmental planning; German; history; information systems; interdepartmental, interdisciplinary communication studies; international business; logistics and transportation management; management; marketing; mathematics; music; music business; music education; musical theater; nursing; philosophy; physical education; physics; political science; professional communication; psychology; secondary education; sociology; Spanish; special education; speech-language pathology; speech–theater education; theater; theology; and urban studies.

The College offers preprofessional programs in actuarial science, allied health services, dentistry, engineering, law, library science, medicine, seminary, and veterinary medicine.

Academic Program

Undergraduates must complete a minimum of thirty-two courses for graduation; the last eight courses must be completed at Elmhurst College. Up to six courses may be taken on a pass–no pass basis.

About one third of Elmhurst students are transfers from other four-year institutions or community colleges. The Office of Admission addresses specific policies regarding transfer credit with students on an individual basis. Elmhurst provides alternatives by which students may obtain credit for areas of study in which they demonstrate prior competence. Such programs include advanced placement, departmental examinations, the College-Level Examination Program (CLEP), credit for experiential learning, and credit for noncollegiate instruction.

Academic Facilities

The A. C. Buehler Library, the academic heart of the College, contains more than 225,000 books and subscribes to more than 1,000 periodicals. Through computer-supported consortia, students have access to 20 million books and other resources. The campus has state-of-the-art academic technology. It includes PC and Macintosh laboratories; mainframe, graphics, robotics, and cartography laboratories; an instructional media center; a weather station; a 24-track digital music recording studio; and a 750,000-volt proton accelerator. All students have Internet access. The Deicke Center for Nursing Education occupies its own well-equipped building, Memorial Hall, and uses healthcare facilities throughout metropolitan Chicago. One of the nine academic buildings, Old Main, is listed on the National Register of Historic Places.

Costs

Tuition and fees for full-time students totaled $13,900 for 1999–2000. Room and board were $5266; books and other expenses averaged $1500. Part-time tuition was $405 per semester hour. Tuition at Elmhurst is low for private colleges in Illinois.

Financial Aid

In 1999, Elmhurst awarded about $10.5 million in grants and scholarships. About 75 percent of full-time students received some type of aid. The typical package offered to eligible full-time students was about $13,800. Approximately 65 percent of all aid is in the form of grants and scholarships. Roughly 30 percent of all freshmen who received aid were awarded additional grant assistance based on prior academic accomplishments. All awards are renewable. To apply for financial aid, students should complete the Elmhurst Application for Financial Aid and the Free Application for Federal Student Aid (FAFSA). New students must be admitted before an aid offer is made.

Faculty

Elmhurst College has 107 full-time faculty members. More than 90 percent hold the highest academic degree in their field. The College has 226 adjunct faculty members. The academic atmosphere attracts scholars who love to teach, on a campus where they can work with students as individuals. The average class has 19 students; the largest class has about 35 students. The student-faculty ratio is 14:1. A faculty member, not a teaching assistant, teaches every class.

Student Government

Elmhurst College believes in shared governance. Students are voting members of such important groups as the College Council. The Student Government Association (SGA) is the primary avenue through which students make recommendations to faculty members and administrators. The SGA consists of an elected student chairperson, 14 student members, 3 faculty members, 4 administrators, and the Dean of Student Affairs.

Admission Requirements

Elmhurst seeks students whose academic profile provides a sound basis for success in the classroom and the larger College community. Typically, successful applicants for freshmen admission rank in the top half of their high school class; present a college-preparatory curriculum, including at least 3 units in English and 2 or more in laboratory science, in math, and in social studies (foreign language is recommended but not required); and score at or above the national average on the ACT or SAT I. The most important single element in admission review is the quality of a student's classroom performance. A faculty committee reviews applicants who fall short of the stated criteria. This committee may issue a positive decision with certain conditions, such as requiring the student to take a lighter full-time course load.

Transfer applicants should present an overall college grade point average of 2.7 or higher on a 4.0 scale and be in good standing at the college they most recently attended. High school records are required. As part of the admission process, the College provides an evaluation of previous credits, in relation to both graduation requirements at Elmhurst and major department regulations. Thus, official transcripts from each college attended are required with the application.

Elmhurst College does not discriminate on the basis of race, color, creed, age, gender, disability, marital status, sexual orientation, national origin, or ethnic origin.

Application and Information

Elmhurst College admits freshman and transfer students to both the fall and spring terms. Most new students enroll in the fall. Admission decisions are made on a rolling basis. For fall term, the preferred application deadline is April 15 for freshman admission and July 1 for transfer admission. For the spring term, the preferred application deadline is January 15 for all applicants.

For additional information and admission materials, students are encouraged to contact:

Office of Admission
Elmhurst College
190 Prospect Avenue
Elmhurst, Illinois 60126-3296
Telephone: 630-617-3400
          800-697-1871 (toll-free)
E-mail: admit@elmhurst.edu

A picturesque, traditional college setting.

ELMIRA COLLEGE
ELMIRA, NEW YORK

The College
Elmira College is a small, independent college that is recognized for its emphasis on education of high quality in the liberal arts and preprofessional preparation. One of the oldest colleges in the United States, Elmira was founded in 1855. The College has always produced graduates interested in both community service and successful careers. Friendliness, personal attention, strong college spirit, and support for learning beyond the classroom help to make Elmira a special place. Elmira College is one of only 255 colleges in the nation to be granted a chapter of the prestigious Phi Beta Kappa honor society.

The full-time undergraduate enrollment is about 1,150 men and women. The students at Elmira represent more than twenty-seven states, primarily those in the Northeast, with the highest representation coming from New York, New Jersey, Massachusetts, Connecticut, Maine, and Pennsylvania. International students from twenty-three countries were enrolled in September 1999. Ninety-five percent of the full-time undergraduates live in College residence halls.

The intercollegiate sports program includes men's and women's basketball, soccer, and tennis; men's golf, ice hockey, and lacrosse; and women's field hockey, lacrosse, softball, and volleyball. An intramural program is also available. Emerson Hall houses the student fitness center, a pool, and a gym capable of seating 1000, as well as the Gibson Theatre, which has a state-of-the-art sound and lighting system. Professional societies; clubs; music, dance, and drama groups; a student-operated FM radio station; and the student newspaper, yearbook, and literary magazine also provide numerous opportunities for extracurricular activity.

Location
Elmira College is located in the city of Elmira, which has a population of 35,000, in the Finger Lakes region of New York. The campus is a 10-minute walk from downtown Elmira. The relationship between the College and the local community is excellent, and numerous community activities and facilities are open to students, including the Elmira Symphony and Choral Society, the Elmira Little Theatre, clubs and civic groups, museums, movies, and a performing arts center. Excellent recreational areas are available in upstate New York and nearby Pennsylvania.

Majors and Degrees
Elmira College offers programs leading to the bachelor's degree in more than thirty-five majors, including accounting, American studies, art/art education, biochemistry, biology, business administration, chemistry, classical studies, computer information systems, criminal justice, economics, elementary education, English literature, environmental studies, fine arts, French, history, human services, individualized studies, international business, international studies, mathematics, medical technology, music, nursing, philosophy/religion, political science, psychology, public affairs, social studies, sociology/anthropology, Spanish, speech and hearing, and theater. The Critical Language Program is available for the study of Chinese, modern Greek, modern Hebrew, Japanese, and Russian on an independent study/tutorial basis. Secondary teaching certification is offered in several areas. A 3-2 program in chemical engineering with Clarkson University is available.

Preprofessional preparation is offered in education, medical technology, nursing, and speech pathology and audiology. Faculty advisers assist those who seek preparation for graduate study in dentistry, law, or medicine in choosing appropriate course work. More than 50 percent of Elmira graduates pursue graduate study.

Academic Program
The College's calendar is composed of two 12-week terms followed by a 6-week spring term. Students enroll for four subjects during the 12-week terms, completing the first term by mid-December and the second during the first week of April. The 6-week term, from mid-April through May, may be devoted to a particular project involving travel, internship, research, or independent study. Students are required to participate in internships in order to gain practical and meaningful experience related to their program of study. Credit is awarded for these projects.

Special opportunities for outstanding students include participation in ten national honorary societies on campus and a chance to assist faculty members in teaching and research. The College also offers an accelerated three-year graduation option for outstanding students.

Army and Air Force ROTC are available.

Off-Campus Arrangements
Through the Junior Year Abroad programs, students may study in the United Kingdom, France, Spain, and Japan, as well as in other countries throughout Europe and Asia. Elmira students may participate in American University's Washington Semester or Drew University's United Nations Semester, or they may study at the Washington Center for Learning Alternatives. Students from Elmira may spend the third term studying marine biology or doing sociological research on the island of San Salvador in the Bahamas. Education majors may work as student teachers in the Bahamas and in England.

Academic Facilities
The Elmira campus offers exceptional academic facilities in a beautiful setting. The modern Gannett-Tripp Library houses more than 389,000 volumes, receives 852 periodicals, and includes a special Mark Twain collection room and photography and audiovisual facilities.

The College Computer Center features a Digital VAX 4000-600 minicomputer. The Computer Center also offers IBM PC and Apple Macintosh microcomputers for student use. Dormitory rooms are equipped to provide access to the Internet.

A Center for Mark Twain Studies has been established at Quarry Farm, the author's summer home, which is located a few miles from campus. The College also operates a Speech and Hearing Clinic on campus, which serves the public and provides valuable internship experience for students. Excellent facilities for drama and music are available.

Costs
Tuition for 2000–01 is $21,960, room is $4450, board is $2830, and fees are $580.

Financial Aid

Financial aid is available for both freshmen and transfer students. Awards are based upon the Free Application for Federal Student Aid (FAFSA) and Financial Aid PROFILE as well as the student's academic potential. Types of aid include grants, scholarships, federal loans, Elmira College loans, and work opportunities. In addition, superior students may qualify for no-need Elmira College Honors Scholarships. For 1999–2000, the average freshman aid package (including all types of aid) amounted to more than $19,000. Transfer students applying for financial aid must submit a financial aid transcript from all colleges previously attended, whether or not they received financial aid. About 80 percent of the full-time undergraduates receive financial aid.

Faculty

Members of the faculty are chosen for their ability in and dedication to teaching. All full-time faculty members serve as advisers, and the faculty approves all academic programs. Currently, the full-time faculty consists of 11 full professors, 25 associate professors, 32 assistant professors, and 10 instructors. Ninety-eight percent of the faculty hold the Ph.D. or highest degree in their field.

Student Government

Student government, an important part of the educational system at Elmira College, prepares students for active and responsible citizenship in society. Student government organizations include the Student Senate, the Judicial Board, and the Student Activities Board.

Admission Requirements

The Office of Admissions at Elmira College uses a rolling admission system. Each applicant is evaluated individually on the basis of his or her total application, including academic record, rank in class, SAT I or ACT scores, essay, activities, references, and goals. The College strongly advises a personal interview. The recommendations of teachers and guidance counselors are also important. Special consideration is given to applicants from distant states and other countries, applicants with special skills, and applicants who are prepared to become actively involved in designing their own programs.

Elmira has early decision, early admission, and advanced placement programs.

Application and Information

For further information, applicants should contact:

Dean of Admissions
Elmira College
Elmira, New York 14901
Telephone: 800-935-6472 (toll-free)
World Wide Web: http://www.elmira.edu

The Mark Twain Study is one of the most famous literary landmarks in America.

ELON COLLEGE
ELON COLLEGE, NORTH CAROLINA

The College

Elon was founded in 1889 by the United Church of Christ and remains a church-related rather than a church-controlled institution. The beautiful 500-acre campus is graced by ancient oak trees, well-kept lawns, brick sidewalks, a fountain, and two lakes. Visitors to Elon's campus often remark on the friendliness of the people and the strong sense of community. Elon is accredited by the Southern Association of Colleges and Schools. At the graduate level, it offers master's degrees in business administration, education, and physical therapy.

With a student body of 3,900, Elon offers the varied opportunities of a university as well as small classes and individual attention. The members of the diverse student body come to Elon from forty-two states and thirty-five countries. Seventy percent of Elon's students come from out of state, primarily the Eastern Seaboard. Student satisfaction is consistently high: 91 percent of students eligible to return to Elon do so. Students are housed in one of the twenty-two residence halls on campus. In addition, there are thirteen fraternity and sorority houses. Freshmen and sophomores are required to live on campus. Students with at least junior standing may choose to live in nearby apartments. All students may have cars on campus.

In addition to a challenging academic curriculum, Elon encourages students to participate in five programs known as the Elon Experiences: student undergraduate research, study abroad, internships, volunteer service, and leadership. Elon is ranked number one nationally among comprehensive colleges for the percentage of students who participate in study-abroad programs. Sixty-seven percent of Elon students complete internships, compared to approximately 33 percent nationally, and approximately two-thirds of Elon students volunteer in the community. Students can record their participation on an Elon Experiences transcript, which is issued as a companion to the traditional academic transcript.

Elon's exceptional sports facilities include three gymnasiums, a baseball stadium, a field house, six athletic fields, and an Athletic Center. A new on-campus stadium will be constructed in 2001. The Athletic Center features the 2,400-seat Alumni Gym, an aerobic fitness center with a weight room, racquetball courts, and an indoor pool. The Jimmy Powell Tennis Center is a twelve-court state-of-the-art complex. A member of the Big South Conference, Elon competes in NCAA Division I (I-AA in football). Before becoming a member of the NCAA, Elon won two NAIA national football titles as well as national championships in golf and tennis. In NCAA Division II, Elon teams won eight straight conference excellence awards, emblematic of the league's top athletic program. Intercollegiate sports are baseball, basketball, cross-country, football, golf, soccer, and tennis for men and basketball, cross-country, golf, soccer, softball, tennis, and volleyball for women. Campus Recreation administers an extensive intramural program with seven multipurpose recreational fields. Other components include aquatics, fitness, open recreation, outdoor programs, special events, wellness, and sports clubs such as field hockey, lacrosse, rugby, and swimming.

The College has 100 organizations, which include seven national fraternities, ten national sororities, the weekly student newspaper, the yearbook, an FM radio station, a student-run cable channel, a dance organization, the Black Cultural Society, the Student Union Board, the Catholic Campus Ministry, Intervarsity Christian Fellowship, Elon Hillel, Model UN, Habitat for Humanity, and Elon Volunteers. Ninety-seven percent of seniors report having been involved in at least one organization, and 70 percent were involved in more than one.

Through the Elon Career Center, students can enroll in 1-credit-hour courses such as Choosing a Major and Securing a Job. The center also sponsors a Transition Tactics mentoring program, job fairs, and on-campus interviews with employers and helps students arrange internships and cooperative education experiences. More than 92 percent of the students who work with the Career Center have jobs within six to nine months of their graduation.

The beautiful 75,000-square-foot Moseley Campus Center includes a concert/banquet hall, campus shop, food court, radio station, space for all campus organizations, post office, TV and game room, and lounge areas.

Location

The campus is located in the town of Elon College, adjacent to Burlington, in the Piedmont region of North Carolina. The College is surrounded by a quiet, residential neighborhood yet is accessible to the major universities and private colleges of Greensboro, Durham, Chapel Hill, and Raleigh. Beaches and mountains are only 3½ hours away by car. Major bus, train, and airline transportation is nearby. Interstate 85/40 is within 2½ miles of the campus.

Majors and Degrees

Elon confers the Bachelor of Arts (B.A.) degree in art, biology, chemistry, communications (broadcast, corporate, and film), computer science, economics, education (elementary, middle, secondary, and special education/learning disabled), English, French, history, human services, international studies, journalism, mathematics, music, music performance, philosophy, physics, political science, psychology, public administration, religious studies, science education, social sciences education, sociology, Spanish, and theater arts. An independent major is also available. A Bachelor of Fine Arts (B.F.A.) is offered in music theater. The Bachelor of Science (B.S.) degree is offered in accounting, biology, business administration (finance, information systems, international business, management, and marketing), chemistry, computer science/engineering, engineering mathematics, engineering physics, environmental studies, health education, leisure/sport management, mathematics, medical technology, music education, physical education, physics, and sports medicine.

Elon offers preprofessional advising programs in dentistry, engineering, law, medicine, optometry, physical therapy, theology, and veterinary science.

Minor fields of concentration are offered in all major areas and also in African/African–American studies, anthropology, Asain/Pacific studies, computer information systems, criminal justice, dance, geography, non-violent studies, and women's/gender studies.

Academic Program

Elon's academic program is distinguished by a philosophy of learning that integrates academic and experiential activities. The recently revised curriculum features a general studies core and experiential learning in a 4-hour course design. Innovative teaching methods encourage independent thinking and active learning, especially through the Elon Experiences, a program that promotes the values of independent learning, intercultural understanding, work experience, volunteer service, and leadership. Students complete 132 hours of credit for the bachelor's degree.

Academic scholarship programs, known as the Elon Fellows programs, feature study/travel grants, mentor relationships, and some paid internships and research assistantships, as well as additional scholarships for selected participants. Programs include Science Fellows, Honors Fellows, Journalism/Communications Fellows, North Carolina Teaching Fellows, Jefferson-Pilot Business Fellows, and the Isabella Cannon Leadership Fellows.

The College operates on a 4-1-4 academic calendar consisting of 2 four-month semesters of classwork divided by a one-month winter term during January. The winter term allows students to gain added experience through additional course work, internships, study abroad, special research, or cooperative education programs in industry.

Off-Campus Arrangements

Elon offers numerous opportunities for international study/travel: a year in Japan; a semester in Australia, Ecuador, England, France, Japan, Spain, or Sweden for the same tuition, room, and board cost as at Elon; winter term study/tours to Australia and Europe and countries such as Belize, Costa Rica, England, Ghana, Italy, and Mexico; summer programs in Israel, India, and China; and exchange programs with universities in Japan and Sweden. In addition, the Office of International Programs assists students in joining study-abroad programs offered by other universities. Each year, approximately 46 percent of the graduates have participated in a study-abroad experience, which ranks Elon number one for study abroad among comprehensive colleges.

Academic Facilities

Known for its beautiful campus, Elon has some of the finest academic facilities in the region. The most recent additions include the new 74,000-square-foot McMichael Science Building, the new 75,000-square-foot Belk Library, and more than 150,000 square feet of activity space in the Koury Athletics Center and Moseley Campus Center. Classroom facilities offer interactive multimedia and teleconferencing capabilities with computer and satellite links, Internet access, laser disc technology, and cable television. A new communications facility that will open in 2001 will include two television studios, nonlinear digital audio/video editing equipment, and cameras to support a student-run cable channel that features programs of news, music videos, sports broadcasting, and social issues.

The Belk Library contains 214,727 volumes and 8,248 serial subscriptions and has an online catalog. It has 400 CD-ROM products and subscribes to twelve online commercial services. Facilities include spaces for private or group study, 150 PCs, exhibit areas, and microfilm and microfiche readers. The LaRose Resources Center in Belk Library provides free tutorial assistance in most academic areas, computer-assisted instruction, videotaping, satellite and cable television facilities, and an extensive variety of audiovisual equipment and materials. Computer resources on campus include IBM labs, Macintosh labs, and an Apple lab. There are more than 600 microcomputers linked to a Novell network and to a Hewlett-Packard (HP) system. The majority of residence halls are wired to the campus and Internet networks.

The Faith Rockefeller Model Center for the Arts features many outstanding theatrical and musical presentations. Classrooms for art, music, drama, communications, and dance programs are located here, as well as a 600-seat theater, a 125-seat recital hall, and a black box theater.

Costs

Elon College is one of the most reasonably priced private colleges in North Carolina. The 2000–01 tuition is $13,556, room is $2120, board is $2540, and fees are $225, for a total cost of $18,441, including the winter term. Additional estimated average costs for books, transportation, and personal expenses are $2748.

Financial Aid

Approximately 60 percent of Elon students receive some form of financial assistance. The College Scholarship Service's Financial Aid PROFILE is used to determine eligibility for institutional need-based aid. The Free Application for Federal Student Aid is used to determine eligibility for federal aid programs. The College participates in all federal and state grant and loan programs, including the Federal Pell Grant, Federal Supplemental Educational Opportunity Grant, Federal Perkins Loan, Federal Stafford Student Loan, Federal Work-Study, North Carolina Legislative Tuition Grant, and several outside loan and payment programs. Scholarships are available for athletic and fine arts achievement and through Army ROTC. Free room and board are provided for recipients of a four-year ROTC scholarship. Presidential Scholarships of $2000 to $3000 are awarded to approximately the top one quarter of each freshman class. Selected candidates are nominated by the Admissions Office. Such scholarships are renewable for up to four years. For further information regarding any aid programs, students should contact the Office of Financial Planning.

Faculty

Elon has 272 full-time and part-time faculty members. Eighty-four percent have earned the highest degree in their field. The primary emphasis is on teaching, although many faculty members participate in research. Faculty members enjoy a close rapport with the students. A 16:1 student-faculty ratio promotes a high level of faculty participation in student programs.

Student Government

All Elon students are members of the Student Government Association (SGA) and have a vote through their elected executive officers, class officers, and student senate members. The SGA has the full support and cooperation of the faculty and administration. Students are encouraged to participate in the governance of the College and have an active role on all faculty administrative committees.

Admission Requirements

Every student who applies to Elon College is evaluated individually. Campus interviews are not required. Secondary school courses recommended for admission include 4 units of English, 2 or more units of one foreign language, 3 or more units of math (algebra I and II and geometry are required), 2 or more units of science (including at least one laboratory science), and 2 or more units of social studies, including U.S. history.

Application and Information

An application should be accompanied by a nonrefundable $25 fee, SAT I or ACT scores, an official secondary school transcript, and a completed counselor evaluation form. Transfer students should, in addition, submit a transcript from every college previously attended and a dean's evaluation form. The minimum GPA for transfer students is 2.0. Elon has a rolling admission policy with a February 1 priority deadline. Students are notified of a decision four to eight weeks after receipt of all application materials. The early decision application deadline is November 15 of the year prior to enrollment. Notification of the decision is made within three weeks of receipt of the completed application.

Nan P. Perkins
Dean of Admissions and Financial Planning
2700 Campus Box
Elon College, North Carolina 27244
Telephone: 800-334-8448 (toll-free)
E-mail: admissions@elon.edu
World Wide Web: http://www.elon.edu

The Alamance Building with Fonville Fountain at Elon College.

EMBRY-RIDDLE AERONAUTICAL UNIVERSITY
PRESCOTT, ARIZONA

The University

Students at Embry-Riddle Aeronautical University–Arizona (Embry-Riddle/AZ) receive a comprehensive, technical, and applied education geared toward designing the next generation of aviation and aerospace vehicles and the systems that support them. Embry-Riddle's reputation is based upon its leadership role in aviation education as well as its commitment to a strong academic preparation and learning environment. Embry-Riddle is a private, independent four-year university and is accredited by the Commission on Colleges of the Southern Association of Colleges and Schools.

The campus team takes pride in providing Embry-Riddle/AZ students with a unique combination of features not readily found on other campuses. A sense of belonging exists, with the total focus on undergraduate education. Students share a love of aviation and a special motivation to succeed and become experts in their field. There is a close-knit residential atmosphere; nearly 800 students live in ten on-campus residence halls, which offer both suites and apartments. Housing priority is given to freshmen and sophomores. Most students take advantage of on-campus dining facilities and a variety of meal-plan options. The coed (17 percent female) student population of 1,600 undergraduates comes from fifty states and territories and twenty-three other countries. Four percent of the students are international.

Students' pride in their campus experience is reflected in the enthusiasm and diversity of activities available. There are more than fifty student clubs and organizations, five professional associations, three fraternities and two sororities, three sports clubs, and thirty-five intramural sports. The NAIA men's wrestling team, the NAIA women's volleyball team, and the intercollegiate flight team compete with other regional and national universities. The student precision flight team has consistently ranked among the top in the country in the SAFECON competitions, sponsored by the National Intercollegiate Flying Association (NIFA).

The extended Embry-Riddle family consists of more than 20,000 students and 38,000 alumni. The Embry-Riddle Daytona Beach, Florida, campus, with 4,500 undergraduate and 250 graduate students, offers additional resources. At Extended Campus Centers around the U.S. and the world, 9,000 undergraduate and 5,000 graduate students find Embry-Riddle's programs geared toward the needs of adult and part-time learners. Guided by its worldwide network of alumni, Embry-Riddle's reputation has grown steadily throughout the aviation, aerospace, and business communities. Embry-Riddle's placement rate for residential campus students one year after graduation is 91 percent. Since its inception in 1926, the flight-related school has added engineering and related majors, as well as six master's degree programs, to become the world-renowned university it is today.

Location

Just like the people, the University's location is warm and friendly. Prescott is a mile-high city on the Colorado Plateau, a beautiful geologic region that is home to the largest stand of ponderosa pine trees in the world. The campus is about 100 miles northwest of Phoenix, 260 miles southeast of Las Vegas, and 375 miles east of Los Angeles. Prescott's climate reflects seasonable weather, with daytime averages of 80 degrees in the summer and 45 degrees in the winter. The local mountains exhibit the spirit of the rugged West, and students enjoy taking off for snow skiing, hiking, and tours of the Grand Canyon.

Known as a vacation getaway, Prescott offers shopping, entertainment, health, and recreational options and a friendly small-town atmosphere. For a flavor of city lights, Phoenix is a 2-hour drive away. The campus is situated on 510 acres, but campus life is centered within a 1-mile walking radius. Most of the eighty-four individual buildings are interconnected by walkways and indoor and outdoor lounging areas, making it easy to bump into friends and faculty members. The campus Flight Training Center is located nearby at the Prescott Municipal Airport.

Majors and Degrees

The B.S. in aeronautical science (professional pilot program) emphasizes multiengine training and prepares students for a career as an airline, military, or corporate pilot. The first two years include courses leading to FAA certification as an instrument-rated commercial pilot, with the last two years stressing professional-level courses in aircraft systems and flight methodology. Training in the late-model fleet is combined with the use of simulators, including two Level A Boeing 727 motion simulators.

Both the B.S. in aerospace engineering and in electrical engineering are approved by the Accreditation Board for Engineering and Technology (ABET). Aerospace engineering centers on the design of aircraft and spacecraft; electrical engineering focuses on circuits, communication and control systems, and electronic/avionics materials and devices. Embry-Riddle is consistently rated as one of the country's best engineering schools by *U.S. News & World Report*'s "America's Best Colleges."

In the B.S. in computer science program, studies consist of graphics, simulation, computer architecture, database management, operating systems, software engineering, artificial intelligence, and applications to the aviation industry.

The B.S. in computer engineering program prepares students for life and work in the twenty-first century by emphasizing the use of information technologies in the curriculum. The faculty and staff members and students in this program are located at any of Embry-Riddle's campuses across the U.S. and around the world; Embry-Riddle's computer engineering program is believed to be the first truly multilocation program. Program participants teach, learn, and interact via personal telecommunications and electronic teleconferencing systems. This feature prepares students to fulfill industry's need for engineers who can work successfully in international design teams. The program provides a broad background in computer design, software engineering, electronic circuit theory, network theory, and programming languages. An avionics focus is added to courses, which places the Embry-Riddle computer engineering graduate in a unique position to increase career opportunities in the aerospace industry. The computer engineering major was designed in consultation with major computer and engineering companies, including IBM, with whom Embry-Riddle has a partnership program.

The B.S. in science, technology, and globalization (STG) is an interdisciplinary program for the global work environment. The program is based primarily on humanities and social sciences in conjunction with the hard sciences and technology. STG students specialize in one of three significant areas for the aviation and aerospace industries: security, environment, and technology policy and management.

The B.S. in aerospace studies is an interdisciplinary program that draws upon a strong core of general education and advanced-level courses in a variety of areas to enhance communication, critical thinking, and technical skills; students also choose three minor areas of study.

Academic Program

The undergraduate academic preparation provides a strong foundation for all students, whether or not they choose a career in aviation. Each major is a combination of general education, specialized aviation focus, and applied technology. The general education component consists of courses in communication skills, social sciences/humanities, mathematics, computer science, and physical science.

Along with the major, students may opt to select a minor from the following fields: aviation safety, aviation weather, computer applications, computer science, environmental studies, humanities, mathematics, psychology, security studies, and technology, policy, and management. Army and Air Force Reserve Officer Training Corps (ROTC) courses are also available to all Embry-Riddle students and may lead to a position as a commissioned officer. Entering high school students with selected ROTC scholarships receive full room and board subsidies from Embry-Riddle.

Through additional participation in internships and cooperative education (co-op) arrangements, Embry-Riddle/AZ students gain valuable work experience. These opportunities are open to students in all fields of study, and many companies have co-op agreements to provide these opportunities: Allied Signal, Continental Airlines, Delta AirLines, Federal Aviation Administration (FAA), Honeywell, Gulfstream Aerospace Corporation, Lockheed Martin, NASA, Northwest Airlines, the Naval Air Systems Command, and Raytheon.

The academic year is divided into two semesters of fifteen weeks each. The average course load is 12–18 semester hours of credit. Two summer terms of approximately seven weeks each allow for additional enrollment.

Many support programs exist to encourage students' development. The Student Success Center offers the college success course, orientation programs, academic advisement and counseling, and tutoring and supplemental instruction. In the Career Placement and Co-Op Services Office, students find assistance through job fairs, resume preparation and referral, the job bank and interviews, and the careers library.

Academic Facilities

Tucked into the rolling hillsides, the campus blends nature with the layout of the eighty-four buildings. Landmarks include the King Science and Technology Center; Davis Learning Center, with its auditorium and classrooms; the Bookstore; and the Visitor Center. Students and faculty members stroll down the many pathways and past outdoor lounging areas. The center of campus focuses on student life and services such as the library, cafeteria, the radio station and student government offices, student activities and financial aid offices, and the post office. The recreational facilities—a pool, tennis and basketball courts, a gym, and hiking trails—are located at the edges of the campus.

Most of the classrooms, laboratories, and faculty offices are situated between the middle of campus and the hillside residence halls. These buildings house specialized labs, including the Airway Science Lab, Robertson Aviation Safety Center, Physics Lab, Engineering Graphics Lab, Aerospace Engineering Wind Tunnel, Aerospace Engineering Structures, and Aerospace Engineering Materials Lab.

Halfway up the sloping hillside stands the 22,000-square-foot King Engineering and Technology Center, which opened in 1995. The center's computer science classroom, the Computer-Aided Engineering Lab, and the UNIX Lab provide students with the latest in computer technologies. This center also houses the Linear Lab, Senior Design Lab, Electronics Power Lab, Honeywell Control and System Integration Lab, and Communications Lab. Here, too, the distance learning classroom connects Embry-Riddle/AZ students to faculty members and students at other Embry-Riddle sites as well as to worldwide teleconferencing facilities.

The campus computer network links all student rooms, an e-mail system, library resources, engineering research labs, and distance learning facilities. The Embry-Riddle libraries are known for their outstanding aviation collections, which can be utilized by either visiting the facility or accessing the World Wide Web.

Three miles from campus, the Embry-Riddle Flight Training Center occupies several buildings at the Prescott Municipal Airport. Embry-Riddle owns and maintains about fifty aircraft at Prescott. Currently, the Prescott fleet includes Cessna 150, Cessna 172, Cessna 182, Cessna 340, and twin-engine Beechcraft BE76 Duchess aircraft.

Costs

The 2000–01 academic-year tuition for all programs is $7250 per semester. Flight fees are charged in addition to tuition. On-campus housing accommodations range from $1350 to $1500 per semester, depending upon the accommodations; meal-plan options are an approximate $1200 per semester addition to these charges. Students also need to include costs for books, transportation, and personal expenses. Since the tuition is similar for all students, in many instances these costs are lower than out-of-state tuition for state universities and are in the lower tier of costs for all national private universities.

Financial Aid

Students and their families find many sources of aid available to assist with paying the costs of a private university; more than 81 percent of students receive financial assistance. Embry-Riddle participates in all national and state assistance programs. The completion of the Department of Education's Free Application for Federal Student Aid (FAFSA) forms assures students consideration for these funds. In addition, Embry-Riddle/AZ provides assistance in the form of on-campus jobs, academic scholarships, veterans' educational benefits, and ROTC room and board stipends.

Faculty

Easy access to faculty members is another strength of Embry-Riddle/AZ. Faculty members, not graduate students, teach classes. The average class size is 25, with an overall student-faculty ratio of 17:1. Faculty members keep regular office hours and consider it their most important role to enhance the individual learning of each student. As academic advisers, faculty members help in course selection and career guidance.

Faculty members bring both teaching and industry backgrounds to the classroom; most have extensive practical experience in their field along with outstanding academic credentials. The faculty participates with members of Advisory Boards, consisting of experts from their field, to continually update the curriculum and technology.

Student Government

The Student Government Association (SGA) has an extremely important role. It provides many student activities, including service and community organizations, Activities Planning Board, *Horizons* newspaper, and representation and funding for clubs and committees. Also, the SGA is the key communication link to the University administration, and the council president serves as a member of the University Board of Trustees.

Admission Requirements

Each student receives individual consideration for admission based upon a variety of factors and circumstances. Completion of the Embry-Riddle/AZ Application for Admission begins this process; official transcripts and score reports for either the SAT I or ACT should also be submitted. Notification takes place throughout the year.

Application and Information

A virtual tour of Embry-Riddle/AZ is available on the World Wide Web (see address below). For additional information, including information on campus visits, and application forms, students may contact:

Embry-Riddle Admissions
3200 Willow Creek Road
Prescott, Arizona 86301
Telephone: 520-708-6600
        800-888-ERAU (toll-free)
E-mail: admit@pr.erau.edu
World Wide Web: http://www.pr.erau.edu

EMBRY–RIDDLE AERONAUTICAL UNIVERSITY
DAYTONA BEACH, FLORIDA

The University

The purpose of Embry-Riddle Aeronautical University is to provide a comprehensive education of such excellence that graduates are responsible citizens and well prepared for productive careers in aviation and aerospace.

In addition to its traditional residential campuses in Daytona Beach, Florida, and Prescott, Arizona, Embry-Riddle serves the continuing education needs of the aviation industry through an extensive network of off-campus centers in the United States and Europe and through its division of continuing education's training seminars and management development programs. The total University enrollment (full-time and part-time) is more than 12,000. Approximately 4,500 undergraduate students are currently enrolled at the Daytona Beach residential campus, and more than 6,000 students are enrolled in graduate programs University-wide. Students come from all fifty states and more than 100 countries, which makes Embry-Riddle truly an international university.

Graduate programs leading to the degrees of Master of Science in Aerospace Engineering, Master of Business Administration in Aviation, Master of Aeronautical Science, Master of Science in Technical Management, Master of Human Factors and Systems, Master of Industrial Relations, and Master of Software Engineering are available at the Daytona Beach campus as well as at many college of continuing education locations.

Embry-Riddle provides cocurricular activities that appeal to almost every taste. Students take advantage of the many opportunities for personal growth and development through social and preprofessional fraternities and sororities and cultural and recreational activities. Embry-Riddle's award-winning Precision Flight Demonstration teams offer students the opportunity to compete nationally in air and ground events. Embry-Riddle also has the largest all-volunteer Air Force ROTC detachment in the country and the fastest-growing Army ROTC detachment. Embry-Riddle athletes participate in intercollegiate and intramural competitions in many sports, including baseball, basketball, cross-country, golf, lacrosse, rugby, soccer, tennis, volleyball, and wrestling.

Location

The year-round clear flying weather and the resort communities surrounding Embry-Riddle's residential campus in Daytona Beach, Florida, offer students an excellent environment in which to study, fly, and enjoy recreational activities. The campus, located adjacent to the Daytona Beach International Airport, contains more than twenty main buildings set on 211 acres and is only 3 miles from what is called the world's most famous beach. The high-technology industries located in Daytona Beach and in nearby Orlando provide the University with an outstanding support base. In addition, the Kennedy Space Center is less than two hours' drive away.

Majors and Degrees

Embry-Riddle awards undergraduate degrees at the associate and baccalaureate levels. Degree programs are grouped into six areas. The business administration degree program options are the B.S. in business administration, the B.S. in management of technical operations, and the B.S. in aviation management. The engineering degree program options are the B.S. in aerospace engineering, civil engineering, and engineering physics. The computer science degree program offers the B.S. in computer science and computer engineering. The aerospace studies degree program offers a B.S. in aerospace studies. The flight degree program offers the A.S. and B.S. in aeronautical science. The aviation maintenance, avionics, and technology degree programs offer the A.S. in aircraft maintenance, the Associate in aviation maintenance technology, the B.S. in aviation maintenance management, the B.S. in aviation technology, the A.S. in avionics technology, the B.S. in avionics engineering technology, and the B.S. in aircraft engineering technology. The human factors degree program offers the B.S. in applied experimental psychology. The University also offers a B.S. in air traffic management, a B.S. in applied meteorology, a B.S. in communications, and a B.S. in safety science.

The college of continuing education is specifically attuned to the educational needs and challenges of the adult, part-time student. Embry-Riddle's degree programs can be pursued at more than 100 locations throughout the continental United States, Alaska, Hawaii, and Europe. The department of independent studies offers Embry-Riddle undergraduate degree courses especially designed to serve the needs of the student who cannot attend regularly scheduled classes. These courses are used to fulfill the requirements of the A.S. and B.S. degrees in professional aeronautics and the Bachelor of Science in business administration. Embry-Riddle's center for professional programs offers a series of seminars, conferences, and hands-on training for the aviation professional.

Academic Program

Even a field as specialized as aviation requires a broad background. General education courses required of all students who are pursuing a baccalaureate program include communication skills, such as English composition, literature, and technical report writing; humanities; social sciences; mathematics; physical science; economics; and computer science. To ensure academic success, Embry-Riddle provides free tutorial services.

The calendar year is divided into two semesters of fifteen weeks each, with the summer session divided into two terms. The average course load for each fall or spring semester is 15 credit hours.

Academic Facilities

Embry-Riddle's multimillion-dollar Airway Science Simulation Laboratory (ASSL) provides an unsurpassed environment for aviation education and research. The ASSL duplicates the components and functions within the national airspace system. Included in the simulation laboratory are various functions that demonstrate the weather reporting, airports, airways, air traffic control, flow control, and pilot and aircraft performance found in the actual nationwide system.

The Jack R. Hunt Memorial Library is a 48,000-square-foot facility with a seating capacity of 800. The library houses more than 50,800 books and more than 83,000 items of microfiche, periodicals, documents, newspapers, and media programs. Among the library's resources is a historical aviation collection that includes materials dating from 1909 to the present. A computer link is maintained with the Southeastern Library Network, connecting 6,000 libraries nationwide for shared cataloging and rapid interlibrary loans. The library also utilizes Dialog Information Retrieval Service, a service that provides access to more than 200 databases that list documents, reports, doctoral dissertations, and many other kinds of information.

The Gill Robb Wilson Aviation Technology Center houses classrooms, single-engine and multiengine simulators, a weather room, and dispatch headquarters. Flight instruction is given in the Embry-Riddle fleet of eighty-nine aircraft. The Advanced Flight Simulation Center gives Embry-Riddle students the opportunity to train in world-class simulators not available at any other private university in the United States. The center, with more than 20,000 square feet of space and four high bays, currently houses two FAA Level "D" simulators, the Boeing 737-300 and Beech 1900D airliners. These simulators offer full-motion training and exact duplicates of actual cockpits. They can duplicate adverse weather conditions, a full range of emergency situations, and virtually any flight pattern. In addition to the four high bays, the center offers briefing rooms, a conference room, classrooms, a self-learning laboratory, offices, an instructor bay, a reception area, a lounge, maintenance facilities, and space for computers and hydraulic systems for the simulators.

The Samuel Goldman Aviation Maintenance Technology Center houses facilities to support instruction in maintenance and repair of fixed-wing and helicopter airframes and power plants (reciprocating and turbine). Avionics maintains an FAA-certified repair station, which affords avionics students the opportunity to learn the theory and practice of the trouble analysis and repair of airworthy aircraft and equipment. The advanced reciprocating engine lab (FAA Certified Repair Station 708-55) overhauls engines for the Embry-Riddle fleet. Engine test cells allow students to check the effectiveness of their repairs.

The Lehman Engineering and Technology Center houses subsonic and supersonic wind tunnels and a smoke tunnel; structures, materials, and aircraft design and composite materials laboratories; and a computer-aided design/computer-aided manufacturing system. Embry-Riddle is also the country's first university to use its own rapid prototyping stereolithography for design instruction. Additional facilities to support instruction include the Lindbergh Center, which provides modern classroom facilities and chemistry and physics laboratories; the academic computing center, which provides hands-on experience with both mainframe and personal computers; and the Center for Aerospace Research, which supports both undergraduate and graduate research and other creative activities.

The 5,300-square-foot interfaith chapel accommodates the variety of faiths represented by the student body of Embry-Riddle. It consists of a 140-seat nondenominational worship area, four prayer rooms (Catholic, Jewish, Muslim, and Protestant), and administrative spaces for Campus Ministry's 2 chaplains and student assistants.

The 18,500-square-foot lecture auditorium and classroom complex provides space for large audience events, including presentations by distinguished lecturers and speakers. A discussion/demonstration room is also equipped to facilitate distance teaching/learning and to enhance hands-on demonstrations.

The 50,000-square-foot field house contains two full-size NCAA basketball courts, a fitness center, and a weight room. The field house allows the University to consolidate its recreation/intramural activities and provide a place to host events and assemblies.

Costs

The 2000–01 tuition is $7250 per semester. Flight fees are charged in addition to tuition. On-campus room and board costs are approximately $3035 per semester. Personal expenses are in addition to the above. (Costs are subject to change.)

Financial Aid

Applicants for financial aid are required to complete the Department of Education's Free Application for Federal Student Aid (FAFSA) and any other documents requested by the University. Students are encouraged to apply early if they wish to be considered for all types of programs. Florida residents may also apply for several additional programs available through the state.

Faculty

The faculty members provide an excellent balance of professional experience and academic achievement. There is also a healthy balance between maturity and youth among the faculty. Faculty members who teach in the specialized and major programs have had professional experience in their areas of instruction. The student-faculty ratio is 18:1, and the primary concern of each faculty member is personalized teaching in classrooms and laboratories, on the flight line, and in student advising.

Student Government

The University places great emphasis upon student self-government. The Student Government Association has 2 voting members on the Board of Trustees and also supports publication of the weekly newspaper and the *University Annual*.

Admission Requirements

Admission is open to any qualified applicant, regardless of creed, sex, race, national origin, handicap, or geographical location. Admission decisions are based on high school work, college courses attempted, and SAT I or ACT scores. Embry-Riddle encourages every student to visit the campus and have a personal interview prior to making the decision to attend the University.

A student who is transferring from a community college or from a four-year institution and who has completed at least 12 semester hours immediately prior to applying at Embry-Riddle is considered a transfer applicant.

Application and Information

Embry-Riddle requires each applicant to submit an application form and fee, SAT I or ACT scores, and an official high school/college transcript. Flight students must provide an FAA Class I or Class II medical certificate. When a student is accepted for admission, tuition and housing deposits are required by May 1. For further information, interested students should contact:

Director of Admissions
Embry-Riddle Aeronautical University
P.O. Box 11767
Daytona Beach, Florida 32120-1767
Telephone: 904-226-6100
        800-862-2416 (toll-free nationwide)
E-mail: admit@db.erau.edu
World Wide Web: http://www.embryriddle.edu

Embry-Riddle Aeronautical University's Daytona Beach, Florida, campus.

EMERSON COLLEGE
BOSTON, MASSACHUSETTS

The College

Emerson College is the nation's only four-year college devoted exclusively to the study of communication and performing arts. As an independent, privately supported coeducational college, Emerson engages students as active participants in learning by providing unique opportunities to explore their fields of interest. On a daily basis, theory and experience are linked in the classroom and in applied learning settings such as television and radio studios, stages and performance spaces, digital production labs, editing booths, writing workshops, and observation areas in the Robbins Speech, Learning and Hearing Center—just some of the options on campus. Strong student-faculty interpersonal communication also creates avenues for students to explore career interests. An internship program, with 1,500 positions in Boston, Los Angeles, and other locations across the country and in Europe, is integrated with the academic course work, which enables students to gain professional experience and develop skills in a hands-on environment.

Emerson's graduate programs enrich the academic climate and heighten the level of inquiry and creativity for the College community. Graduate programs include communication disorders, communication industries management, creative writing, global marketing communication and advertising, health communication, integrated marketing communication, journalism, management communication, media arts, political communication, speech communication studies, theater education, and writing and publishing.

Founded in Boston in 1880, Emerson College has been a pioneer in the fields of communication and performing arts. Notable moments in the College's history include the establishment of the first children's theater (1919), the first professional training program in speech pathology (1935), the first undergraduate programs in broadcasting and broadcast journalism (1937), the first educational FM radio station at a New England college (1949), and the first speech and hearing clinic in a Boston college (1953).

An active and diverse student body represents every region of the U.S. and more than seventy-five countries. There are more than fifty student organizations on campus, including AHANA (African, Hispanic, Asian and Native American), EBONI (Emerson's Black Organization with Natural Interests), Amigos, Emerson Independent Video, *The Berkeley Beacon* (student newspaper), the Emerson Film Society, the Musical Theatre Society, the Society for the Advancement of Management, and the Forensics Society. The athletic program fields six men's and seven women's teams participating in Division III athletics.

The Learning Assistance Center provides academic support services to all students and gives them the opportunity to develop skills and abilities necessary for academic success at the college level. Individual and group tutorials are available as well as peer tutoring.

First-year students are expected to live in student residence halls unless they commute from home.

Career planning is an integral part of an Emerson education. From self-assessment through consideration of job offers, the Career Services Office assists students and alumni in career planning and job search strategies, beginning in the first year and continuing throughout the Emerson experience.

The College is accredited by the New England Association of Schools and College.

Location

Emerson College's walking campus is located in the heart of Boston near Beacon Hill and the Boston Common. The greater Boston area's thriving business district includes radio, television, and publishing markets; outstanding speech and hearing clinics; and world-renowned hospitals that make this city an ideal setting for the College. A lively and thriving theater district and a vast array of other cultural as well as professional opportunities provide an extended campus.

Majors and Degrees

Within the School of the Arts, the following majors are available: acting, audio/radio, dance, film, musical theater, new media, television/video, theater design/technology, theater education, theater production/management, theater studies, and writing, literature, and publishing.

Within the School of Communication, Management and Public Policy, majors include broadcast journalism; communication, management, and public policy studies; communication, politics, and law; management communication and public relations; marketing communication and advertising; and print journalism.

The School of Communication Sciences and Disorders offers the major of communication disorders.

Interdisciplinary and self-designed majors, as well as the honors program, are available through the Institute for Liberal Arts and Interdisciplinary Studies.

Academic Program

Emerson College operates on a calendar of two 15-week semesters, plus two 6-week summer sessions. The requirements for graduation combine a liberal arts curriculum with various communications core curricula specific to individual departments. Within the Institute for Liberal Arts and Interdisciplinary Studies, freshman seminars and innovative courses supplement communication specializations. A four-year honors program challenges students through interdisciplinary seminars and independent study. Students are also given the flexibility to design a program of study according to their individual interests.

Off-Campus Arrangements

Study abroad in Europe is offered during both the academic year and the summer at Emerson's Castle in Well, the Netherlands. An L.A. Semester Program is available for students who seek an intensive internship-based experience. Programs are also offered in affiliation with Suffolk University, Wheelock College, Berklee College of Music, School of the Museum of Fine Arts in Boston, Massachusetts College of Art, Boston Architectural Center, and Boston Conservatory. Internships, practica, directed study, and independent study are available to second-, third-, and fourth-year students.

Academic Facilities

Among the outstanding multimedia facilities available to the Emerson community are two radio stations (WECB-FM and the award-winning WERS-FM, 88.9); television studios; Emerson Independent Video, a student-run production company; the Emerson Majestic Theatre, a 975-seat proscenium house; the Robbins Speech, Language and Hearing Center; and the Thayer Lindsley Parent-Centered Preschool Nursery for the Hearing Impaired. All radio and television facilities are operated by students.

The Academic Computing Centers have more than 120 workstations, including high-end Macs, PCs, and compatibles; twenty-eight Media 100 digital video editing stations; one Avid Media Composer workstation for nonlinear digital editing; and peripherals, including color printers, CD burners, and digital video I/O devices. Additional labs include an Advanced Projects Lab, a Hypermedia Lab, and a Digital Production Lab. All College buildings, including residence halls, are wired with T1 high-speed access to the Internet.

The Emerson College Library, which houses more than 160,000 volumes, has its own media center and computer facility. The Student Union offers a variety of student services. The athletic facilities include a 10,000-square-foot fitness center that features top-notch fitness equipment and a variety of aerobics and group exercise classes as well as one-on-one assistance with training and conditioning.

Costs

Tuition for the 1999–2000 academic year was $18,816. Room and board were $8734. The activities fee, the cost of health insurance, and the orientation fee totaled approximately $900. Expenses for books, lunches, transportation, and personal fees were estimated at $1800.

Financial Aid

All financial aid applicants are required to apply for the Federal Pell Grant, local state scholarships, and various other sources of funding. Students applying for September admission who wish to apply for financial aid should submit all appropriate forms to the College Scholarship Service six weeks prior to the Emerson College financial aid deadline of March 1. Students who seek January admission should submit these forms to the College Scholarship Service six weeks prior to the Emerson College deadline of December 1. All accepted first-year applicants are considered for merit-based aid in recognition of their academic and personal achievements. Students who plan to apply for financial aid should contact the Financial Assistance Office at Emerson College (telephone: 617-824-8655) for complete information.

Faculty

There are 101 full-time faculty members, of whom more than 79 percent have a doctorate or terminal degree in their field. In addition, each year part-time faculty members and visiting lecturers augment the teaching staff. Many of these professional men and women are nationally recognized and award-winning authors, producers, directors, consultants, and researchers. The faculty-student ratio is 1:17.

Student Government

Students are encouraged to participate in the Student Government Association (SGA). Students serve on various committees of the College and vote on issues that affect the College community. All students who have paid their activities fees are members of SGA.

Admission Requirements

Admission is competitive and is determined on the basis of both academic and personal qualifications. Emerson seeks the student who is able to accept the responsibility and challenge of active participation in the learning experience. In general, an applicant should have had 4 years of college-preparatory English and 3 years each of mathematics, science, social science, and foreign language. Each applicant works with an admission counselor who functions as the student's personal contact with the College throughout the admission process. Although personal interviews are not required, a tour of the College is strongly recommended. Admission to the College is need-blind.

Emerson College admits qualified students regardless of race, color, religion, national and ethnic origin, sex, sexual orientation, age, or disability to all the rights, privileges, programs, and activities generally accorded or made available to students at the College. It does not discriminate on the basis of race, color, religious beliefs, national and ethnic origin, sex, sexual orientation, age, or disability in the administration of its educational policies, admissions policies, scholarship and loan programs, and athletic and other College-administered programs.

Application and Information

To apply, an applicant must submit an application and fee, an official high school transcript, results of the SAT I or ACT, two letters of recommendation, and an essay. Emerson also welcomes transfer students, who must submit official college transcripts in addition to the above materials, and international students, who must submit results of the Test of English as a Foreign Language (TOEFL). Acting, musical theater, and dance applicants are required to audition/interview.

For the fall semester, Emerson offers first-year applicants both an Early Action Plan (application deadline November 15) and Regular Admission (priority deadline February 1). The priority deadline for international applicants is February 1 and March 1 for transfer students. For the spring semester, the priority deadline is November 1 for first-year, transfer, and international applicants.

For application information, prospective students should contact:

Director of Admission
Emerson College
100 Beacon Street
Boston, Massachusetts 02116-1596

Telephone: 617-824-8600
Fax: 617-824-8609
E-mail: admission@emerson.edu
　　　　international@emerson.edu (international students)
　　　　transfer@emerson.edu (transfer students)
World Wide Web: http://www.emerson.edu/admiss/

The all-College television studio in the Media Services Center.

EMMANUEL COLLEGE
BOSTON, MASSACHUSETTS

The College
Founded in 1919 by the Sisters of Notre Dame de Namur, Emmanuel College is known for the quality of its academic programs, its focus on developing the talent and abilities of its students, and its Catholic heritage, which fosters the development of intellectual integrity and a strong social conscience.

Emmanuel's traditional undergraduate college for women offers a four-year liberal arts program in the arts and sciences. Essential to the College's mission is its commitment to provide an excellent liberal arts education with a solid career orientation. The College offers these academic opportunities to qualified students of all economic, religious, racial, and ethnic backgrounds.

Enrollment in 1999–2000 was more than 1,600 students, of whom 753 were undergraduates studying on the Boston campus. Emmanuel's diverse student population includes students from all over the United States and more than thirty-six other countries. Approximately 64 percent of the College's traditional undergraduate students reside in Emmanuel's residence halls on campus, while the rest commute from the local area.

The Internship and Career Development Office offers a four-year career development program for all Emmanuel students. Starting in their first year and continuing until graduation, students are exposed to career planning, assessment, and goal setting. Workshops on resume writing, job/internship search skills, the Internet job search, and interviewing skills are some of the services that are offered to students. The Internship and Career Development Office also maintains a Career Advisory Network of more than 300 committed alumnae who are available to students for networking, career advice, and mentorship. Other services include job and internship postings, individual career counseling, and career planning programs and events.

Emmanuel College offers state-of-the-art computer classrooms and computer labs in a powerful campuswide communications network that provides students access to the Internet, voice mail, e-mail, and cable television. The computer classrooms, both IBM and Macintosh, are used to teach basic computer skills such as word processing and creating spreadsheets as well as a wide variety of academic subjects, such as mathematics, sociology, and art. In the computer labs, students have access to powerful IBM and Macintosh computers and peripherals for their studies and outside interests.

A wide variety of academic clubs, honor societies, and social and special interest organizations is available for student participation. Intercollegiate athletics include Division III varsity basketball, soccer, softball, tennis, and volleyball. Sports facilities on campus include a gym, tennis courts, and exercise room. Swimming, softball, and golf are nearby.

A leader in adult education for more than twenty years, Emmanuel College also offers women and men excellent undergraduate, graduate, and professional degree programs through the Center for Adult Studies. The College offers these academic programs in flexible formats on the Boston campus; some are also available at satellite campuses in several convenient locations across Massachusetts. Graduate degree programs include the M.A. in Human Resource Management, M.S. in Management, Master of Education, and the Urban Clinical Pastoral Education Program.

Emmanuel College is fully accredited by the New England Association of Schools and Colleges.

Location
Located on The Fenway in the heart of Boston's cultural, medical, and educational communities, Emmanuel's secure 16-acre campus is the only self-contained college campus in Boston. The College is within walking distance of the Museum of Fine Arts, the Gardner Museum, Fenway Park (home of the Boston Red Sox), Symphony Hall, and a variety of the world's most renowned medical institutions. Proximity to numerous colleges and universities as well as public transportation offers Emmanuel students additional academic, social, and cultural opportunities.

Majors and Degrees
Emmanuel College confers bachelor's degrees in the following areas: art, biology, chemistry, economics and management, educational studies, English, history, mathematics, physics (interinstitutional), political science, psychology, sociology, and Spanish. Students may also design individualized majors, which reflect particular academic and career interests. The College confers a Bachelor of Fine Arts in painting/printmaking and in visual communication/graphic design. Tracks within majors allow students with specialized interests to pursue concentrations in accounting, art therapy, biochemistry, communication arts, counseling and health psychology, developmental psychology, information technology, and medical technology. The education program provides provisional certification for elementary and secondary teachers.

Academic Program
The bachelor's degree requires completion of thirty-two courses, divided among general requirements, major requirements, and electives. Students may choose a minor within any department that offers a major and in the following areas: music, philosophy, religious studies, speech, theater arts, and women's studies. Internships are an integral part of most majors and provide students with opportunities for career exploration and the acquisition of professional skills. The honors program provides highly qualified and motivated students with opportunities for additional intellectual exploration and challenge. Students with Advanced Placement scores of 3, 4, or 5 may receive credit and advanced placement.

Off-Campus Arrangements
Emmanuel College is a member of the Colleges of the Fenway collaboration, which allows Emmanuel students to take courses at five institutions within close walking distance: Simmons College, Wheelock College, Massachusetts College of Pharmacy and Allied Health Sciences, Wentworth Institute of Technology, and Massachusetts College of Art. Students are encouraged to spend a semester or year abroad in any approved program. In addition, the College participates in an exchange program with sister colleges in California and Japan and provides opportunities for internship and study semesters in Washington, D.C.

Academic Facilities
In addition to administrative and faculty offices, the administration building houses a chapel, auditorium, exercise room, lecture and conference rooms, bookstore, art and music studios, and state-of-the-art computer classrooms (IBM and Macintosh platforms).

The Cardinal Cushing Library, which holds 93,000 volumes, includes listening, viewing, and editing rooms; an art gallery; a language laboratory; a computer laboratory (IBM and Macintosh platforms); and a lecture hall. The library also has four indexes on CD-ROM, EPIC, and FirstSearch database online searching and a connection with OCLC. Through the College's membership in the Fenway Library Consortium, all students have use of fourteen area libraries that collaborate to exchange information and optimize resources. The library's online catalog is provided through Fenway Libraries Online, which contains the holdings of eight academic libraries in addition to Emmanuel's. The Emmanuel College Academic Resource Center (ARC) offers a wide variety of programs and resources that help students reach for excellence in achieving their academic goals. The writing center, peer tutor program, and specially designed workshops are a few of the varied programs available. The Academic Resource Center includes classroom space; tutorial areas for all subjects, study skills, and reading and writing; and the computer-aided instruction laboratory. Practice software and exam manuals for graduate school exams also are available, as is graduate school information. All ARC programs focus on providing the individual attention that is the hallmark of Emmanuel College.

Marian Hall contains the physics, biology, and chemistry departments and the psychology laboratories. This state-of-the-art science center is well-equipped for both laboratories and lectures. In addition to science facilities, Marian Hall also houses a renovated dining hall and a gymnasium.

Costs

Tuition for the 2000–01 academic year is $16,112. Room and board costs in the College residence halls are $7390 per year. There are additional fees of approximately $300 per year.

Financial Aid

Emmanuel College is committed to meeting the financial need of its students, insofar as funds permit, based on a careful analysis of the information that is provided by students and their families, regardless of race, color, religion, sex, age, national or ethnic origin, or the presence of any handicap. Eighty percent of current traditional Emmanuel students receive financial aid through a combination of scholarships, grants, loans, and Federal Work-Study Program awards.

The amount of financial aid that is granted to students is based on individual need, as determined by the College. Entering students who seek financial assistance should file the Free Application for Federal Student Aid (FAFSA). The FAFSA may be obtained from a secondary school or from the College. Also, a completed copy of the parents' and student's federal income tax forms must be forwarded to the financial aid office.

Students who complete the requirements for admission to Emmanuel College are considered for special scholarships, which are awarded on the basis of academic achievement and specific eligibility requirements. These include the Presidential, Dean's, Women in Arts and Sciences, Transfer, and Cardinal Medeiros Scholarships. Of note is the Sisters of Notre Dame Scholarship program, in which a $2500 scholarship is awarded to any student recommended by a Sister of Notre Dame at the time of application. Additional scholarships, grants, or loans may be awarded by the director of financial aid upon receipt of the FAFSA.

Faculty

The College has 45 full-time faculty members, 76 percent of whom have a doctorate or other terminal degree. Faculty members, who have degrees from diverse national and international universities, share in a free exchange of ideas and ideals with students. The student-faculty ratio is 13:1. All classes are taught by faculty members, not teaching assistants.

Student Government

Emmanuel students have the opportunity to participate in decision-making processes that affect the College. The student governing body is the Student Government Association (SGA), which is composed of student representatives from each class. The SGA provides a channel of communication for expressing the needs and opinions of the students to the College community.

Admission Requirements

An applicant's academic achievements, creativity, initiative, and involvement in her community are considered. No single standard measure for determining ability is used in accepting applicants to the College. The admissions committee reviews each applicant's high school curriculum and record, recommendations, and test results. It is recommended that applicants submit a strong academic program.

Candidates for admission as first-year students are required to take either the SAT I or ACT. A personal interview with a representative of the admissions office is suggested. Applicants are encouraged to visit the campus during their junior and senior years of high school so that they may visit classes and talk with students and faculty members.

Application and Information

To apply, a student must submit an application with a $40 nonrefundable fee, SAT I or ACT scores, an official copy of her high school transcript, and two letters of recommendation. International students must submit the TOEFL score and Certification of Finances. The College operates on a rolling admissions policy; the applicant is notified of the admission decision as soon as her file is complete, after December 1. Emmanuel observes the College Board's Candidates Reply Date of May 1. The College also subscribes to the early decision plan. All admissions requirements should be completed before November 1 of the applicant's senior year to be considered for early decision.

Students who apply for transfer admissions must submit an application; a nonrefundable fee of $40; official secondary school and postsecondary school transcripts, including scores on the SAT I or ACT; and two letters of recommendation, at least one from a recent college professor. Transfer students must have a minimum grade point average of 2.0. An interview with a transfer counselor is recommended.

For further information or an application, students should contact:

Meg Miller
Director of Admissions
Emmanuel College
400 The Fenway
Boston, Massachusetts 02115

Telephone: 617-735-9715
Fax: 617-735-9801
E-mail: enroll@emmanuel.edu
World Wide Web: http://www.emmanuel.edu

Emmanuel students enjoy the campus setting of 16 secure acres in the heart of Boston's academic, medical, and cultural communities.

EMORY & HENRY COLLEGE
EMORY, VIRGINIA

The College
Since its founding in 1836, Emory & Henry College has instilled a strong sense of values in students and has prepared them for lifelong learning and success. Among the College's alumni have been congressmen, businesspeople, scientists, teachers, artists, ministers, authors, and many public servants. The College's 900 students (almost equally divided between men and women) constitute a diverse group, coming from rural areas of southwestern Virginia as well as from urban centers nationwide. They represent more than twenty states and several countries. The campus stretches over 150 acres of rolling hills and has many trees and broad open spaces. The buildings are a mixture of historic structures renovated for contemporary use and modern facilities designed to blend with the environment. The College was named in honor of Bishop John Emory, an outstanding United Methodist churchman, and Patrick Henry, a Revolutionary War patriot from Virginia.

The King Health and Physical Education Center enhances the College athletics program. Varsity sports for men are baseball, basketball, cross-country, football, golf, soccer, and tennis; women compete in basketball, cross-country, tennis, and volleyball. Several sports are played on a club basis. In addition, a wide-ranging intramural program enrolls nearly 70 percent of all boarding students. Students have opportunities for involvement in a variety of campus activities: Christian fellowship, fraternities, sororities, sports clubs, honor groups, multicultural groups, and service clubs. Student staffs produce a yearbook, a newspaper, and a literary magazine; others operate an educational FM radio station. Musically talented students have opportunities to participate in a choral program and a pep band. The prestigious Concert Choir has toured throughout the United States and in parts of Europe. The Barter Theatre Conservatory at Emory & Henry College, officially established in spring 2000, provides a theater education program that integrates college-level drama study with the benefits of experience on a professional stage. A chapter of Alpha Phi Omega and the Appalachian Center for Community Service are available for students committed to community service.

Location
Emory & Henry is located in Emory, Virginia, which is approximately 25 miles north of Bristol, a city that offers large shopping areas, movies, and restaurants. The area surrounding Emory is known for its scenic beauty, recreational opportunities, and talented craftsmen. Within an hour's drive are slopes for snow skiing, lakes for waterskiing, the Appalachian Trail for hiking, and locations for horseback riding, canoeing, and many other sports. The historic town of Abingdon, Virginia, which lies just 7 miles south of Emory, is the home of the renowned Barter Theatre, the oldest professional theater in the United States. Abingdon's downtown district includes shopping areas, movie theaters, restaurants, and museums. The city also hosts the annual Virginia Highlands Festival, bringing together musicians, artists, and craftsmen for exhibitions and competition.

Majors and Degrees
Emory & Henry College offers programs of study in Appalachian studies, art, biology, chemistry, classical studies, computer science, economics and business, elementary and secondary education, English, environmental studies, French, geography, history, international studies, land-use analysis and planning, mass communications, mathematics, medical technology, music, philosophy, physical education, physics, political science, psychology, public policy and community service, religion, sociology, Spanish, sports medicine, and theater. In addition, the College offers a cooperative program in engineering in conjunction with Tulane and North Carolina State. A cooperative program in forestry is available through an agreement with Duke University.

The Bachelor of Arts degree is awarded in all programs of study and the Bachelor of Science degree in selected areas. Individualized programs of study may be developed in consultation with a faculty adviser. Preprofessional preparation in dentistry, law, medicine, ministerial studies, and veterinary medicine may be completed within several of the programs.

Academic Program
Emory & Henry offers a liberal arts program with emphasis on writing, reasoning, value inquiry, and knowledge of global concerns, as well as a broad introduction to liberal arts subjects. All students complete a core curriculum, which includes a yearlong, interdisciplinary Western Tradition course and a writing course for all first-year students. Sophomores complete an ambitious Great Books program, and upperclass students take courses related to value inquiry and global studies. Along with the core curriculum, each student completes a major and a minor or a combined program referred to as an area of concentration. Students also have the opportunity to choose elective courses and to participate in international exchange programs.

Emory & Henry operates on a semester calendar from late August to mid-December and from mid-January to mid-May. A summer session runs from late May to early July. Freshmen typically carry a four-course load of 13–14 credit hours per semester, including the yearlong course on Western tradition. Upperclass students carrying a full load will complete five courses (15–17 credit hours) each semester. Thirty-eight courses are required for graduation. Classes meet on Monday-Wednesday-Friday or Tuesday-Thursday schedules.

One important feature of the Emory & Henry curriculum is its orientation toward helping students make a smooth transition from high school to college. A Center for Academic Support and Career Services aids students in developing strong study skills. The Writing Center helps students in every department to use writing for effective communication. Introductory courses in the modern foreign languages are taught by the Dartmouth Intensive Model, emphasizing concentrated study and drills that develop conversational skills in two semesters of work.

Off-Campus Arrangements
Many faculty members encourage students to get involved in community projects or research that will benefit the region. Internship opportunities are available for students in most of the College's programs, providing academic credit for off-campus work in community agencies and businesses. Many students have completed internships in the surrounding communities, while others have opted for internships outside the region, including several in Washington, D.C., in positions related to Congress or the federal government.

The College offers certain travel/study options regularly and can arrange other opportunities for interested students. Each year, a faculty member leads a monthlong study program in Rome, Italy, that provides 2 course credits in Roman art and archaeology. The College has exchange agreements with colleges and universities in Africa, Asia, Europe, the Middle

East, and South America. In addition, the Department of Modern Languages cooperates with the Vanderbilt-in-France program, which gives students the opportunity to live and study in France for varying periods of time. Students who desire other types of travel/study are assisted by faculty and staff members in locating suitable programs.

Academic Facilities

McGlothlin-Street Hall is a 70,000-square-foot academic center currently under construction that will house the Departments of Biology, Business, Chemistry, Education, Environmental Studies, Geography, International Studies, and Psychology and a 104-seat auditorium and a tiered 60-seat auditorium. Classrooms and laboratories in McGlothlin-Street Hall will be equipped with the most current technological equipment, including Internet access and interactive TV. Kelly Library currently holds more than 250,000 volumes and maintains subscriptions to 1,063 periodicals; the library features a computer center with PCs and terminals available for student use. Residence halls are wired for Internet access. Miller-Fulton Hall contains computerized classrooms used for instruction in such fields as accounting and computer science. Another computerized classroom in Byars Hall is used for instruction in writing, desktop publishing, and related fields. Science departments located in Miller-Fulton Hall and Gibson Hall feature a variety of equipment, such as a microcomputer-based laboratory for physics students, computerized chromatography for chemistry students, a DNA sequencer in the Biology Department, and biofeedback equipment. Art students have access to studios, an exhibition area, and printing equipment, and music students make use of practice rooms and a recital hall.

Costs

For 2000–01, the comprehensive fee for a resident student is $18,472 (includes tuition, room, and board). For a commuter student, the charge for tuition and fees is $12,950. There is a technology fee of $200 for resident students and $100 for commuter students.

Financial Aid

Forms of aid include need-based and non-need-based scholarships, loans, and part-time jobs. A Bonner Scholars program provides substantial scholarships for selected students who do volunteer work in the surrounding region. Virginia residents are eligible for a special grant based on residence. Merit scholarships are awarded based on academic performance, and many can be renewed based on continued academic success. Ninety-six percent of fall 1999 undergraduates received financial aid. The average aided first-year student received an aid package worth $12,696, meeting 91 percent of need. The priority application deadline for financial aid is April 1 and the deadline is August 1.

Faculty

Emory & Henry has 68 full-time faculty members, and the current faculty-student ratio is 1:14. More than 80 percent of the faculty members hold terminal degrees. Every student is provided with a faculty adviser who assists in the selection of courses. While the faculty members are encouraged to continue study and research, their primary function is teaching. Many professors live near the campus, and they make their homes open to students for special events, informal class meetings, or other activities.

Student Government

Students at Emory & Henry are encouraged to take part in campus decision making. They have voting representatives on nearly every faculty committee and on the Board of Trustees. The central body in campus government is the Council on Student Affairs, which brings together representatives of the student body, faculty, and administration.

Admission Requirements

Admission to Emory & Henry is determined on the basis of both academic achievement and personal qualifications. An applicant's secondary school preparation must include the following: 4 years of English, 3 years of mathematics (at least through algebra II), 2 years of laboratory sciences, 2 years of a single foreign language, and 2 years of history and social studies. It is strongly recommended that 1 year of study in the fine arts be included.

Application and Information

To apply for admission, students should submit the basic application form, an essay, a copy of the high school transcript, scores from either the SAT I or the ACT, and a nonrefundable $25 fee. Transfer applicants must submit a transcript from any college previously attended and a statement of good standing. A rolling admission policy allows notification of the admission decision within two weeks after a file has been completed.

Students who have thoroughly researched their college options and have determined that Emory & Henry College is their first choice are encouraged to consider applying under the Early Decision Plan. Although these students may file regular applications with other colleges, it is understood that they are applying for Early Decision only at Emory & Henry College and intend to enroll if admitted.

To be considered for Early Decision, a student should submit the completed Application for Admission, including the Early Decision Agreement; the secondary school transcript; and a report of either SAT I or ACT test scores by December 1. The College agrees to notify candidates of their admission by December 20. The $200 enrollment deposit deadline for Early Decision is January 20. Under Early Decision, students will either be admitted or deferred to regular admission, for which they will receive full and unbiased consideration.

Application forms and other information may be obtained by contacting:

Office of Admissions and Financial Aid
Emory & Henry College
P.O. Box 947
Emory, Virginia 24327-0947
Telephone: 540-944-6133
     800-848-5493 (toll-free)
Fax: 540-944-6935
E-mail: ehadmiss@ehc.edu
World Wide Web: http://www.ehc.edu

Kelly Library.

EMORY UNIVERSITY
Emory College
ATLANTA, GEORGIA

The University

Founded by the Methodist Church in 1836 as a college at Oxford, Georgia, Emory University received its university charter in 1915 and in the same year moved to the present campus in northeast Atlanta. The original campus is now Oxford College of Emory University, a two-year liberal arts division. The main campus occupies 631 acres. The original structures are of Italian Renaissance design and have red-tiled roofs and marble facades. In recent years, Emory has engaged in an extensive building and renovation campaign. The University is currently building nine new facilities ($250 million), including a performing arts center, chemistry and physics facilities, and a nursing school.

Emory offers a stimulating intellectual environment in one of America's most exciting cities. The undergraduate college provides the advantages of a small college and the resources of a major university. Selective and innovative, with an emphasis on excellent teaching, Emory offers a rewarding environment for the student with serious intellectual and professional interests. Of the more than 10,000 men and women enrolled at Emory University, more than 4,500 are undergraduates in the College. Geographic distribution of students is diverse; approximately 55 percent are residents of states outside the South. Seventy percent of the students go on to graduate or professional school, and academic competition is keen. At the same time, the campus is a friendly one where students and faculty members may interact in a casual atmosphere. A majority of the students live on campus in residence halls, fraternity houses, or sorority lodges. Extracurricular activities are plentiful and include lectures, concerts, movies, musical groups, theater, journalism, debate, volunteer groups, intramural sports, such as lacrosse and rugby, and intercollegiate sports. There are more than 200 student organizations that encourage widespread involvement.

Emory athletes compete in ten varsity sports for men and women in the Division III University Athletic Association. Varsity sports include baseball (men's), basketball (men's and women's), cross-country (men's and women's), golf (men's), soccer (men's and women's), softball (women's), swimming and diving (men's and women's), tennis (men's and women's), track and field (men's and women's), and volleyball (women's). Seventy percent of the students participate in intramural, club, and recreational sports.

Emory ResNet provides Ethernet connections in each residence hall room, giving students access to the Internet via the campus computer network. Cable television is also available in each room. First-year students are required to live on campus. Housing is guaranteed for four years. Approximately 65 percent of undergraduates live on campus.

Other than Emory and Oxford colleges, major University divisions include the Graduate School of Arts and Sciences; the Schools of Business, Law, Medicine, Nursing, Public Health, and Theology; and the Division of Allied Health Professions.

Location

Emory University's wooded campus is in the rolling hills of Atlanta in an attractive residential section called Druid Hills. Adjacent to the campus is Emory Village, a small, neighborhood complex of shops and restaurants. Downtown Atlanta, easily accessible by rapid transit from Emory, provides an exciting, progressive atmosphere in which students can enjoy many recreational and cultural activities, often at reduced rates. In addition, Atlanta is just a few hours from the mountains of north Georgia and the Carolinas and from the Georgia and Florida beaches.

Majors and Degrees

Emory College, the undergraduate arts and sciences school of Emory University, offers the B.A. degree in forty-two areas of study and the B.S. degree in seven areas. B.A. programs are offered in African/Afro-American studies, anthropology, art history, Asian studies, biology, chemistry, classical civilizations, classical studies, classics, computer science, creative writing, dance, economics, educational studies, English, film studies, French, French cultural studies, German studies, Greek, Hispanic/Latin American studies, history, interdisciplinary studies in culture and society, international studies, Italian studies, Judaic language and literature, Judaic studies, Latin, literature, mathematics, medieval and Renaissance studies, Middle Eastern studies, music, neural biology and behavior, philosophy, physics, political science, psychology, religion, Russian, sociology, Spanish, theater, and women's studies. Joint concentrations are available in art history and history, classics and English, classics and history, classics and philosophy, economics and history, English and history, mathematics and computer science, mathematics and economics, philosophy and religion, and religion and classical civilizations. The B.S. degree is offered in anthropology and human biology, applied physics, biology, chemistry, computer science, mathematics, neural biology and behavior, and physics. Four-year combined bachelor's-master's degree programs are offered in biology, chemistry, English, history, mathematics, philosophy, physics, political science, and sociology. Students may apply for admission to the School of Business or the School of Nursing upon completion of two years of undergraduate work. Emory offers minors in Japanese studies, journalism, linguistics, and studio art.

A 3-2 program in engineering is offered in cooperation with the Georgia Institute of Technology.

Academic Program

The Bachelor of Arts and Bachelor of Science degree programs combine general education in six broadly defined areas with advanced study in a subject of special interest to the individual student. The six areas of general education are (1) seminars and writing, including instruction in English composition and seminars representing a wide range of fields and topics designed to engage students in various aspects of inquiry and research; (2) natural and mathematical science (three courses); (3) social sciences (two courses); (4) humanities (two courses); (5) historical, cultural, and international perspectives, including courses covering western and nonwestern cultures, history, and a year of foreign language study; and (6) health and physical education (4 semester hours). To fulfill these area requirements, a student may choose from a wide variety of courses. In addition to the area requirements, a student must complete a concentration in at least one major field. To graduate, a student must complete satisfactorily a total of 132 semester hours.

The academic calendar is divided into two semesters from September to May, and there is a limited third semester during the summer months. Several special programs are available, including honors programs, independent study, internships, combined-degree programs, and the opportunity to take courses in the graduate divisions of the University. Five courses may be taken on a satisfactory-unsatisfactory grading basis.

Off-Campus Arrangements

Emory participates in cross-registration through the University Center in Georgia, an eighteen-member consortium of colleges and universities in the Atlanta area. A semester in Washington, D.C., is available for economics and political science students, and Georgia government internship programs are available for political science majors. Study abroad is encouraged and can be taken in a wide variety of programs for a semester or a year.

Academic Facilities

Emory's five libraries hold 2.4 million volumes plus access to thousands of electronic information resources. Woodruff Library, the central library, which supports the social sciences and humanities, provides an integrated service environment, joining technology and media specialists with librarians. The facility includes an information commons, electronic classrooms, group study rooms, and data-wired seating and is open 24 hours a day Sunday through Friday. The $40-million O. Wayne Rollins Research Center houses biology, physiology, physics, and biomedical research facilities. Biology laboratories are equipped for teaching all aspects of biology, from molecules to populations. Students learn independent research techniques in neurobiology, cell physiology, ecology, genetics, and developmental biology. The chemistry building houses modern laboratories, including undergraduate teaching laboratories and research facilities in many specialized areas of analytical, inorganic, organic, and physical chemistry. Undergraduates are encouraged to participate in research projects. Wired with state-of-the-art technology, the $25-million Goizueta Business School building is considered one of the most technologically advanced business schools in the U.S. Scattered throughout this facility are more than 1,000 data ports. For teleconferencing, distance learning, or satellite feeds, the auditorium is equipped with ISDN lines that feed video transmission to any room in the building.

Costs

For the 2000–01 academic year, tuition is estimated at $24,240, and room and board are estimated at $7870.

Financial Aid

Emory makes every effort to help students who need financial aid. Grants, loans, employment, and deferred payment plans are available. The amount of each grant is determined by financial need, and financial aid decisions are made independently of admission decisions. Merit scholarships (not based on need) are also available. In addition, Emory offers non-need institutional loans. The state of Georgia provides Tuition Equalization Grants to legal residents of Georgia who enroll at Emory; approximately 60 percent of the students in the College receive aid. More than 2,000 students have part-time employment at the University, including federally funded work-study. Applications from high school seniors for financial assistance and copies of the Financial Aid PROFILE and the Free Application for Federal Student Aid (FAFSA) are accepted between January 1 and April 1. Priority attention is given to applications filed before February 15.

Faculty

Emory College has approximately 700 faculty members and a student-faculty ratio of 10:1. Senior faculty members teach courses at all levels, including first-year courses. Every student is assigned a faculty adviser for assistance in course selection and academic counseling. Faculty members are encouraged to work closely with students, as well as conduct research.

Student Government

Emory has always assumed that its students are responsible individuals. Students are involved at various levels of government in the University. Governing organizations with student representation include the Student Government Association (for the entire University), the College Council (primarily undergraduate), and the University Senate (predominantly faculty). Students also serve on all standing committees of the Emory College faculty. Students have a strong voice in residence life governments, social activities, and publications.

Admission Requirements

Admission to Emory is very selective. The Admission Committee evaluates applicants on the basis of secondary school records, SAT I or ACT scores, and recommendations from teachers and counselors. The College requires 4 years of high school English, 2 years of algebra and 1 of geometry, and at least 2 years of a foreign language. It strongly recommends that the remaining units include 2 or more years of history or social science, 3 years of laboratory science, and an additional year of mathematics. Students who wish to enter college before high school graduation are considered as early admission candidates. The middle 50 percent of freshmen entering in 1999 scored in the 630–700 range on the verbal portion of the SAT I and in the 650–710 range in the math section and completed high school programs with at least a B+ average. Average ACT scores ranged from 27 to 30. Emory seeks students who have not only academic ability but also talent and diversity. Students are encouraged to provide an overall view of themselves in their application, including extracurricular activities and interests and academic goals. The Admission Office encourages visits to the campus and arranges tours and focus sessions with staff members. Representatives from the Admission Office visit many high schools during the year to increase contact with students.

Application and Information

Applicants may apply as either early decision or regular decision candidates. Emory offers two rounds of early decision, both of which are binding. Early decision I postmarked deadline is November 1, and decisions are mailed by December 15. Early decision II postmarked deadline is January 1, and decisions are mailed by February 1. Regular decision applicants are encouraged to apply in the fall of the senior year of secondary school, but no later than the postmarked deadline of January 15. Applicants for regular decision are notified by April 1. Materials required for application include the completed application form, $40 application fee, an official secondary school transcript, a letter of recommendation, and standardized test scores (SAT I or ACT). SAT II subject tests are recommended but not required. Test scores should be sent by the applicant's school or the testing center. Emory videos are available on a complimentary loan. Students may call 800-255-0384 (toll-free) or go to the Web site (http://www.videc.com) to order the video.

Daniel C. Walls
Dean of Admission
Boisfeuillet Jones Center
Emory University
Atlanta, Georgia 30322

Telephone: 800-727-6036 (toll-free)
E-mail: admiss@learnlink.emory.edu
World Wide Web: http://www.emory.edu

Emory's Italian Renaissance campus is just 5 minutes north of downtown Atlanta.

ENDICOTT COLLEGE
BEVERLY, MASSACHUSETTS

The College

Founded in 1939 and named for John Endicott, the first colonial Governor of Massachusetts Bay Colony, Endicott is an independent, coeducational institution. The College is approved to offer the Bachelor of Science, the Bachelor of Arts, the Bachelor of Fine Arts, and the Master of Education degree. Accredited by the New England Association of Schools and Colleges, the College holds the following accreditations in individual academic programs of study: the Commission on Accreditation of Allied Health Education Programs (athletic training), Commission on Accreditation in Physical Therapy Education, Foundation for Interior Design Education and Research (FIDER), National Association of Sport and Physical Education and North American Society for Sport Management (NAPSE-NASSM), and the Sport Management Review Council (SMPRC).

More than 1,200 students from twenty states and thirty countries are currently enrolled at the College. More than 80 percent of Endicott's students reside on campus. On the campus are fifteen residence halls with architectural styles ranging from Colonial to Gothic to modern townhouses, several newly renovated residence halls, and an apartment-style residence hall accommodating 125 students. A new apartment residence hall accommodating first-year and upperclass students opened in fall 1999.

Participation in campus clubs and organizations allows students to develop new interests and skills. Among some of the many clubs and student organizations are the Endicott Players (drama club), the Endicott Review (literary magazine), Student Government Association, chorus, Sports Management Club, Sailing Club, Ski Club, the Outdoor Adventure Interest Group, Intercultural Club, the Endicott Community Television, Athletic Training Club, Health Science Club, the Peer Learning Program, and Phi Theta Kappa and Alpha Chi (national honor societies).

NCAA Division III intercollegiate teams and intramural sports for men and women include baseball, basketball, cross-country, equestrian, field hockey, golf, lacrosse, soccer, softball, tennis, and volleyball. Endicott is a member of the Commonwealth Coast Conference. Approximately 18 percent of Endicott students participate in competitive athletics and/or intramural and club sports.

Endicott was the first college in the country to require internships in which students gain professional, hands-on experience in their chosen fields while pursuing their degrees.

A popular area within the Academic Center is the Courtyard Café, a convenient gathering place for students to meet socially or talk with their professors. The café offers soups, salads, sandwiches, and snacks throughout the day.

Location

Located 20 miles north of Boston, Massachusetts, the "college capital" of the world, Endicott's beautiful oceanfront campus is recognized as one of the most scenic campuses in the country. The campus is surrounded by 200 parklike acres of woods, trails, lawns, lakes, and islands, and the peninsula of Marblehead shelters the College's three private beaches, bordering on historic Massachusetts Bay. This expanse of water is ideal for pleasure boating and is the scene of frequent yacht races.

The campus offers easy access to beaches, historic towns and sites, and Boston. As a cultural and educational center, Boston provides diverse entertainment and leisure-time resources, including fine museums, theater, excellent shopping, concerts, sporting events, and a wide variety of restaurants.

Majors and Degrees

The College offers baccalaureate programs of study, which include advertising, athletic training, business administration, communications, creative arts therapy, criminal justice, elementary and early childhood education, English/creative writing, entrepreneurial studies, fine arts, graphic design/visual communications, hotel-restaurant-travel administration, human services, interior design, international business, international hospitality program (includes culinary arts), law and government, liberal studies, management, marketing, nursing, photography, psychology, and sports management. The College offers associate degrees in business administration, liberal arts, and physical therapist assistant studies.

Academic Program

Endicott offers a wide range of professional and liberal arts majors designed to meet the needs of today's students. Bachelor's degree candidates are required to complete two 140-hour internships for 2 credits each and one full-semester, 12-credit internship. The semester-long internship within the student's major highlights the final year for most Endicott students. This fourteen-week, full-time, field-based professional experience is individually planned and supervised by faculty members through regular on-site visits. Students participate in biweekly on-campus seminars designed to support experience in the field. Nursing, physical therapist assistant, and athletic training internship credits are earned in clinical education experiences over the course of the length of the program. Education students devote their internship hours to student teaching in their final year at Endicott.

The College Honors Program is designed to afford qualified students the opportunity to undertake independent study and research above and beyond normal requirements of the major and the College. First-year students with distinguished high school records are admitted into the honors program. To remain in the program, students are evaluated by the Honors Council each year, based on academic record, leadership, community service and character.

Off-Campus Arrangements

International study-abroad programs can be applied for through the International Office of Studies and Programs. Dozens of international study, internship, and community service options may include the College's annual monthlong London Internship program; the annual community service internship project in Mexico City and Puebla, Mexico; and semester-long educational experiences in Florence, Italy, and Perth, Australia. Through the College's affiliation with Les Roches School of Hotel Management and the Hotel Institute Montreux, both in Switzerland, students in the hospitality major may choose to study for a semester abroad. Endicott has a collaborative relationship with the College for International Studies (CIS) in Madrid, Spain, where students have the opportunity to study language, culture, humanities, economics, and political science while living with families in Madrid. Additional study-abroad programs can be individually arranged according to the student's interests.

Endicott is a member of the Northeast Consortium of Colleges and Universities in Massachusetts (NECCUM). Under the cross-registration program, students may take a course not offered at Endicott at a member college. The member colleges include Salem State, Merrimack College, Gordon College, North Shore Community College, Marion Court College, University of Massachusetts Lowell, Northern Essex Community College, Montserrat School of Art, and Middlesex Community College. This option is on a space-available basis for full-time students.

Academic Facilities

The Fitz Memorial Library accommodates Endicott students in its reading rooms and computer labs. The Academic Computing Center is composed of four state-of-the-art labs and equipped with

IBM-compatible and Apple Power Mac computers as well as laser printers and scanning equipment. All the labs provide access to the World Wide Web. Similarly, all classrooms and residence halls are connected to the network with fiber-optic cable. On the building's terrace level, the Little Theatre provides space for campus events, lectures, and drama productions. On the same level is the Academic Support Center, which provides a wide range of services to all students seeking a successful academic experience.

The Art Center houses a gallery, an auditorium, and studios for graphic and interior design, ceramics, sculpture, and painting. Art exhibits from both students and local artists are regularly on display for the College community and local city residents.

The Samuel A. Wax Academic Center has classrooms, labs, and offices for the Arts and Sciences, Business, Nursing, Communications and Education Divisions. A large auditorium is located on the first floor and is equipped for musical and dramatic performances as well as the College's lecture series. The Scangas Center for Media and Learning, located on the ground level, is equipped with interactive technology, which provides creative new ways to link programs both on and off campus. The technology classroom makes possible the delivery of course content off the Internet through CDs and videotapes and through audio conferencing and videoconferencing using phone lines. Video technology enables students to develop video editing and composition skills for application to distance learning and video production. The television and radio studios are also located within this media center and the photography studio is situated on this same ground level.

The Callahan Center, situated across Endicott Pond from the Academic Center, houses the Student Development and Student Activities Departments, Dining Hall Services (which include an extensive food court), the Career Counseling Center, and a solarium-style recreation center where light meals and refreshments are served.

The $10 million Post Sports Science and Fitness Center, which opened in fall 1999, includes a competition gym with a seating capacity of 1,200; a separate field house; an elevated running track; weight, fitness, and aerobics studios; two racquetball courts; trainers' rooms; laboratories for the physical therapist assistant studies and athletic training programs; and academic classrooms.

The Hospitality School, located on the South Campus at Tupper Hall, is the site of the gourmet-style international restaurant, La Chanterelle, run by an international professional staff and the hospitality students.

Costs

For the 1999–2000 academic year, tuition was $14,000, room and board rates were $7410, and general fees were approximately $600. Fees vary by major.

Financial Aid

Seventy-seven percent of the College's students receive aid through scholarships, grants, loans, or work-study programs. More than $4 million of Endicott scholarship funds are offered on the basis of need and/or merit. To qualify for financial aid, a student must be a U.S. citizen and be enrolled in an approved program. Most of the aid programs require that a student demonstrate financial need, which is defined as the deficit between the cost of the education and the amount that the student's family can be expected to contribute. A copy of the Free Application for Federal Student Aid (FAFSA) and an institutional financial aid questionnaire are required to be submitted to the financial aid office. Every applicant's financial aid situation is evaluated individually so that a financial aid award accommodates the student's particular needs. The financial aid office has set a priority deadline of March 15 for financial aid applications; however, applications arriving after that date are processed throughout the remainder of the year prior to enrollment. All forms of Endicott's financial assistance are renewable each year upon application.

Faculty

Endicott has a faculty of 144 members, 62 of whom are full-time and involved in research and publishing. Forty percent have doctorates or terminal degrees in their appropriate field. In addition to fulfilling their teaching responsibilities, faculty members serve as academic advisers to the students enrolled in their departments. Part-time faculty members total 82.

Student Government

The Student Government Association is the controlling body for student governance at Endicott. The association is chaired by student officers who are selected through campuswide elections. It brings together representatives from all areas of student interest and responsibility. Programs are carried out by many groups, including campus organizations, clubs, College committees, and residence halls. The group most concerned with the College's entire yearly program is a student-run Activities Committee, which plans cultural, educational, social, and other special events. Each subcommittee has a chairperson and elected representatives from each residence hall. Meetings are open to all students, and students are encouraged to become involved in planning and implementing programs of interest to them.

Admission Requirements

Applicants are evaluated according to their past academic performance and their potential for achievement. Requirements for admission include an official secondary school transcript, a letter of recommendation from a high school or college guidance/academic counselor and/or a teacher, and two essays. SAT I or ACT scores are required and evaluated on an individual basis. The admission committee reviews each applicant's file and bases its admission decision on the applicant as a total individual. Factors such as motivation, academic progress, extracurricular activities, community service, and employment history are considered. Students are encouraged to visit for an information session with a member of the admissions staff and to have a student-guided campus tour.

Application and Information

The application form should be submitted with a $25 application fee, and the applicant should ensure that all required documents be forwarded to the College. Endicott has a policy of rolling admissions, and most applicants are notified of the admission decision within three to four weeks of the time their application is complete.

Interested students are encouraged to contact:

Admissions Office
Endicott College
376 Hale Street
Beverly, Massachusetts 01915
Telephone: 978-921-1000
              800-325-1114
Fax: 978-232-2520
E-mail: admissio@endicott.edu
World Wide Web: http://www.endicott.edu

The Endicott College oceanfront campus has been noted as one of the most scenic in the United States.

ERSKINE COLLEGE
DUE WEST, SOUTH CAROLINA

The College

At Erskine, students can become a part of a 160-year-old legacy of academic strength and traditions. As an institution devoted to Christian commitment and excellence in learning, Erskine prepares students for responsible living, service, and community in both church and society. Erskine was founded in 1839 by the Associate Reformed Presbyterian (ARP) Church, a denomination begun by Scottish immigrants in the eighteenth century. In 1927, the Due West Women's College, which was founded before the Civil War, merged with Erskine. Erskine College is nonsectarian. A number of faiths are represented in the College's student body. Most students belong to the following denominations (ranked in order from most to least number of students): Baptist, Presbyterian, Associate Reformed Presbyterian, United Methodist, Catholic, Episcopalian, and Lutheran. The current enrollment is approximately 500 men and women. About 90 percent of the College's students live in the residence halls; the other 10 percent commute from home and nearby communities or are married students who rent local homes or apartments. Students come from numerous other states and several other countries.

The Carnegie Foundation for the Advancement of Teaching lists Erskine as a "BA-1" institution, the highest classification for liberal arts institutions offering primarily undergraduate degrees.

Erskine is a member of the NCAA Division II and is a charter member of the Carolinas-Virginia Athletic Conference. Women's teams at Erskine compete in basketball, cross-country, soccer, softball, and tennis. Men compete in baseball, basketball, cross-country, soccer, and tennis. The Robert Stone Galloway Physical Activities Center contains two gymnasiums, a dance studio, a weight room, handball/racquetball courts, and other facilities. The M. Stanyarne Bell Sports Center includes excellent facilities for outdoor sports. The comprehensive intramural schedule at Erskine enables every interested student to participate in the excitement of competition.

Other extracurricular activities are numerous, and students must be careful to budget their time so that studies will not be neglected. As many as 15 percent of the student body have been involved in student dramatic presentations. The fine arts are an important part of the academic and extracurricular life at Erskine. Private applied instruction in all musical instruments is accessible to the entire student body. Participation in a variety of choral and instrumental ensembles is available to all students through audition, and at least one instrumental and one choral ensemble are open to participants without a required audition. Ensembles tour domestically and internationally and perform at state and regional conventions of musicians. Programs in visual art are open to all students. Students may participate in and view musicals, operas, an extensive concert series, and exhibits of visual art in the Bowie Art Center. The equestrian club competes with other colleges throughout the South. Literary societies provide student activities comparable to those provided by fraternities and sororities at other colleges. Movies, dances, and other activities take place in Watkins Student Center, in the dining facility, and in the student canteen/campus shop. Three student publications have won numerous state and regional awards. The *Arrow* is the student yearbook, the *Tower Times* is the biweekly newspaper, and the *Review* is the student literary magazine, published yearly.

The ARP Church's seminary, founded in 1837, is governed by the same board as the College and has an enrollment of nearly 400 men and women. The seminary is located in Due West and shares the McCain Library and dining facilities with Erskine.

Location

The academic village of Due West, South Carolina, is more than a small college town with a distinctive name. When driving into Due West, people can get out of their cars and walk anywhere, or jog and bike through the fresh air of the rural countryside. Due West is 15 minutes from a great waterskiing lake, and seven 18-hole golf courses are within 30 miles of the College. Due West and Erskine include the best of both worlds: a small-town atmosphere for daily living with urban and recreational opportunities just a short drive away. Professional sports, opera, and other major recreational and cultural events and facilities are a 2-hour drive away in Atlanta, Georgia, or Charlotte, North Carolina. By car, Due West is an hour from Greenville, 2 hours from Columbia, and 20 minutes from Anderson and Greenwood.

Majors and Degrees

The Bachelor of Science (B.S.) degree is awarded with majors in athletic training, biology, business administration (concentrations in accounting, economics, and management), chemistry, early childhood education, elementary education, music education, music management, physical education, special education, sports management, and sports medicine. The Bachelor of Arts (A.B.) degree is awarded with majors in American studies, behavioral science, Bible and religion, biology, chemistry, Christian education, English, French, history, mathematics (including an emphasis in computer science), medical technology, music, natural science, physics, psychology, social studies, and Spanish. Preprofessional programs are available in dentistry, law, medicine, pharmacy, and veterinary medicine.

A 3-2 engineering program is offered in cooperation with Clemson University. A program in health-related fields is offered in cooperation with the Medical University of South Carolina.

Erskine offers a program leading to certification in athletic training.

Students may choose among the following minors: Bible, business administration, Christian education, computer science, economics, elementary education, English, family studies, French, history, mathematics, music, non-Western studies, philosophy, physical education, physics, psychology, secondary education, sociology, Spanish, special education, and theater.

Academic Program

Erskine's course of study includes a traditional basic curriculum of courses in the natural sciences, modern languages, English, Bible, history, mathematics, social studies, fine arts, and physical education. This general education curriculum requires about two years of study. Students usually select a major during or before their sophomore year. During the last two years, the curriculum consists of major and minor fields of study. To graduate, students must achieve competency in word processing, complete the basic education requirements, satisfy an academic department's requirements for a major, satisfy requirements for a minor field of study or 12 semester hours of electives, and complete 124 semester hours of work. The major and minor fields of study and all 124 semester hours must be completed with at least a C average (2.0 GPA).

Placement in a course beyond the freshman level may be approved on the basis of qualifying scores (generally 3 or higher) on the Advanced Placement tests of the College Board. Credit may also be granted for such scores at the discretion of the appropriate department head and the dean of the College.

Erskine has a 4-1-4 academic calendar. The four-month fall term begins in early September and ends in December; the spring term begins in February and ends in May. Students normally take four or five courses each during the fall and spring terms. January is set aside as a one-month winter term, during which students enroll in one nontraditional or specialized course not available in the fall and spring terms. This period also provides a time when students in preprofessional programs can work off campus with physicians, attorneys, teachers, veterinarians, or other professionals in order to gain insight into the practical work encountered in a specific profession.

Off-Campus Arrangements

Travel courses are offered each winter term. These may include a fine arts tour of New York; tours of Russia or China or countries in the Near East, Europe, or Africa; or a study tour to an area within the Western Hemisphere (such as Mexico, the Caribbean, or the western United States). Tours are offered for credit in art and music appreciation, biology, education, foreign language, and history. Winter term courses may also be taken at other 4-1-4 colleges. Erskine offers a junior year abroad with cooperative programs at the University of St. Andrews in Scotland; the Institute for American Universities at Aix-en-Provence, France; and Tandem Escuela Internacional in Madrid, Spain. One Erskine student per year qualifies for study in each of the three programs.

Academic Facilities

Belk Hall houses administrative offices, faculty offices, and classrooms. Memorial Hall houses the music department and an auditorium with seating for 175. The Erskine Building contains the education department, the psychology department, and an auditorium with seating for 800. The Robert Stone Galloway Physical Activities Center houses the physical education department. The new Daniel-Moultrie Science Center provides state-of-the-art facilities for instruction in biology, chemistry, and physics, as well as in psychology and sociology.

Defining marks of the McCain Library include a user-friendly environment, an excellent collection of more than 200,000 bound volumes, subscriptions to more than 800 journals, many CD-ROM and online resources, Internet access, a popular fiction and nonfiction collection, one-on-one and group library instruction, an online catalog (SCOTTY) and cost-free searches of the sixty OCLC FirstSearch databases and 450 databases available on Dialog. The library is a select depository for U.S. government documents and has an extensive religion collection. The multimedia room is heavily used by McCain Library patrons.

Erskine helps see to it that students are ready for life in the information age. Fifty-two miles of fiber-optic cable connect a student's dorm room to every room and office on campus and to the rest of the world. Full Internet access is available for every student in the residence halls, and numerous computers are available throughout campus for student use. Most academic departments utilize computers in laboratories to give students experience in interfacing computers and scientific equipment, beginning in freshmen courses. Erskine's Mentoring Networked Classrooms enhance the learning process for students at the College. The classrooms have computers that are networked with the instructor's computer in order to maximize the mentoring process. There are also computer laboratories for word processing and business-related or science-related applications located in Belk Hall and the Daniel-Moultrie Science Center.

Costs

The cost of tuition ($14,697), fees ($1015), and room and board ($5094) at Erskine for the 2000–01 academic year total $20,806. Indirect expenses for books and supplies, personal expenses, and transportation are approximately $1825.

Financial Aid

Erskine attempts to meet every applicant's financial need, as determined by the Free Application for Federal Student Aid. Approximately 90 percent of the students enrolled in 1999–2000 received financial aid, including academic and special ability scholarships; state, federal, and private grants; government and private loans; and work-study awards. The College gives money for academic and athletic scholarships. Those who are interested in the academic advantages of a small private college should contact the Director of Financial Aid at Erskine for further information.

Faculty

Faculty members at Erskine hold doctoral degrees from major public and private universities throughout the United States. In disciplines where the Ph.D. is generally considered to be needed, nearly 90 percent of the faculty have earned that degree. The most important characteristics of the members of the faculty are competence in their discipline, teaching effectiveness, and concern for students as individuals. The student-faculty ratio is about 12:1.

Students are assigned a freshman adviser who is a faculty member interested in helping freshmen adjust to the demands of the College curriculum. Once the student selects a major course of study, a faculty adviser in the major area is assigned to the student.

Student Government

Erskine's Student Government Association is virtually autonomous, and student representatives sit on the Board of Trustees, in faculty meetings, and on all College committees. The Student Senate consists of elected representatives from each class and from every dormitory. The student-elected Entertainment Board manages a large budget and provides various forms of entertainment throughout the year. One adult resident director lives in each of the six single-sex dormitories. Behavior in the dormitories is regulated by Student Life Assistants, who may take cases involving unsatisfactory behavior to the Judicial Council or to the deans of students.

Admission Requirements

Erskine admits all qualified persons regardless of race, creed, or national origin. Applicants should have 14 units of college-preparatory courses, including 4 units in English, 2 in math, and at least 5 other units (required) from the following areas: history, science, Latin, modern foreign languages, advanced math, and English. In judging candidates for admission, the Admissions Committee emphasizes the high school academic record. Scores on the SAT I or ACT are required of students whose first language is English. Students whose first language is not English may submit scores on the Test of English as a Foreign Language (TOEFL) in lieu of SAT I or ACT scores. A recommendation from the high school guidance counselor is required and is an important part of the candidate's file. Applicants' interests and extracurricular activities are also considered in making the admission decisions. Students applying for regular admission are not required to have an interview, but a campus visit and interview are strongly recommended. Transfer applicants must submit a transcript from every college previously attended, as well as a completed recommendation from the last college attended.

Application and Information

The Admissions Committee has a rolling admission policy. After all of a candidate's application materials have been received, a decision is made and the candidate is notified promptly. Upon acceptance, a student is expected to pay a $150 deposit, refundable until May 1, to be applied to his or her account. There is no application deadline, but early applicants are eligible for scholarships and other benefits not available to late applicants. A nonrefundable application fee of $15 is required. The application for admission to Erskine is now available on line at the Web site listed below.

For additional information, prospective students should contact:

Admissions Office
Belk Hall
Erskine College
Due West, South Carolina 29639

Telephone: 800-241-8721 (toll-free)
E-mail: admissions@erskine.edu
World Wide Web: http://www.erskine.edu

EUGENE LANG COLLEGE, NEW SCHOOL UNIVERSITY
NEW YORK, NEW YORK

The College

Eugene Lang College is the distinctive liberal arts division of New School University, formerly known as the New School for Social Research. It is a major urban university with a tradition of innovative learning. The College offers all the benefits of a small and supportive college as well as the full range of opportunities found in a university setting.

Lang students are encouraged to participate in the creation and direction of their education. The desire to explore and the freedom to imagine shared by students and faculty members contribute to a distinctive academic community.

Eugene Lang College students currently come from thirty-one states and twelve countries. The ratio of men to women is approximately 1:3. About 45 percent of the College's 500 students come from outside the New York metropolitan area; 4 percent hold foreign citizenship, and 23 percent are members of minority groups. The student body is composed of both residential and day students. The university operates residence halls within walking distance of classes; incoming freshmen and transfer students are given housing priority within these facilities. Great diversity in interests and aspirations is found among the students. Through the Office of Student Services, students produce a student newspaper and an award-winning literary magazine. They organize and participate in dramatic, musical, and artistic events through the "Lang in the City Program," as well as numerous political, social, and cultural organizations at the university and throughout New York City.

The New School for Social Research was founded in 1919 by such notable scholars and intellectuals as John Dewey, Alvin Johnson, and Thorstein Veblen. It has long been a home for leading artists, educators, and public figures. For example, the university was the first institution of higher learning to offer college-level courses in such "new" fields as black culture and race, taught by W. E. B. DuBois, and psychoanalysis, taught by Freud's disciple Sandor Ferenczi. Among the world-famous artists and performers who have taught at the New School are Martha Graham, Aaron Copland, and Thomas Hart Benton. Today, such noted scholars as Robert Heilbroner, Eric Hobsbawm, Jerome Bruner, and Rayna Rapp are among the hundreds of university faculty members accessible to Lang College students.

The other divisions of the university include the Adult Division, which offers more than 2,000 credit and noncredit courses to students each semester; the Graduate Faculty of Political and Social Science (founded in 1933 as the University in Exile), which grants M.A. and Ph.D. degrees; the Robert J. Milano Graduate School of Management and Urban Policy, which awards the M.A. and M.P.S. degrees; Parsons School of Design, one of the oldest and most influential art schools in the country; and Mannes College of Music, a renowned classical conservatory. The total university enrollment in 1999–2000 was approximately 6,000 degree-seeking students.

Location

The university is located in New York City's Greenwich Village, which historically has been a center for intellectual and artistic life. This slower-paced, more personal New York City neighborhood of town houses and tree-lined streets offers students a friendly and stimulating environment. Over and above the resources of Greenwich Village, New York City offers virtually unlimited cultural, artistic, recreational, and intellectual resources that make it one of the world's great cities.

Majors and Degrees

Eugene Lang College awards the Bachelor of Arts degree. Students are encouraged to design their own program of study, which includes an area of concentration, in consultation with their faculty adviser. Lang offers five broad areas of concentration within which a student maps out an individual path: cultural studies; mind, nature, and values; social and historical inquiry; urban studies; and writing, literature, and the arts. A student's concentration consists of eight to ten courses (32–40 credits) leading to relatively advanced and specialized knowledge of an area of study. In addition, students are encouraged to pursue an internship, where appropriate.

Students may also apply to a five-year B.A./B.F.A. program in conjunction with Parsons School of Design or in jazz studies at New School University, and advanced students may apply to the five-year B.A./M.A. and B.A./M.S.T. programs offered in conjunction with the university's graduate divisions. The College also offers a joint B.A./J.D. program with Benjamin Cardozo School of Law.

Academic Program

When planning a program of study, Eugene Lang College students are encouraged to reflect on what their education means to them. Their program should parallel their own academic and personal development. By actively participating in the process of their education, students gain the knowledge to make informed choices about the direction of their studies with the help of their advisers and peers.

Small seminar classes serve as the focus of the academic program at the College. The maximum class size is 15 students. Classes are in-depth, interdisciplinary inquiries into topics or issues selected each semester by the College's outstanding faculty. Most importantly, the classes engage participants in the study of primary texts, rather than textbooks, and emphasize dialogue between teacher and student as a mode of learning. Here, not only is intellectual curiosity fostered by the small classes, but a genuine sense of community develops as well.

Although the College does not emphasize course requirements outside the area of concentration, freshmen are required to take one writing course and three other seminars of their choice in each of their first two semesters at the College. Upper-level students create their programs by selecting seminars from the College's curriculum, or they may combine offerings of the College with courses and workshops given by the New School's Adult Division, Graduate Faculty of Political and Social Science, Robert J. Milano Graduate School of Management and Urban Policy, and Parsons School of Design.

The College operates on a semester calendar; the first semester runs from September through mid-December and the second, from late January through mid-May. Students generally earn 16 credits per semester; a minimum of 120 credits is required for graduation.

Off-Campus Arrangements

Eugene Lang College recognizes the immense value of work undertaken beyond the classroom. The College arranges appropriate projects—internships with private and nonprofit organizations—which serve to strengthen the connection between theoretical work in the classroom and practical work on the job. Sophomores and juniors have the option of spending a year on a sponsored exchange with Sarah Lawrence College and the University of Amsterdam. Other exchanges, both American and abroad, are available.

Academic Facilities

Eugene Lang College is located on 11th Street between Fifth and Sixth Avenues in Greenwich Village. The university includes twelve academic buildings, including a student center, a Computer Instruction Center with more than seventy-five IBM personal computers and Macintosh systems, a 500-seat auditorium, art galleries, studios for the fine arts, classrooms, a writing center, and faculty offices. Lang College students have full and easy access to the Raymond Fogelman Library and the Adam and Sophie Gimbel Design Library. In addition, the university participates in the South Manhattan Library Consortium. Together, the libraries in the consortium house approximately 3 million volumes covering all the traditional liberal arts disciplines and the fine arts.

Costs

Tuition and fees for the 2000–01 academic year are $20,910. Room and board cost approximately $9005, depending upon the specific meal plan and dormitory accommodations chosen. University fees are $115 per year.

Financial Aid

Students are encouraged to apply for aid by filing the Free Application for Federal Student Aid (FAFSA) and requesting that a copy of the need analysis report be sent to the New School (FAFSA code number 002780). Qualified College students are eligible for all federal and state financial aid programs in addition to university gift aid. University aid is awarded on the basis of need and merit and is part of a package consisting of both gift aid (grants and/or scholarships) and a self-help component (loans and Federal Work-Study awards). Aid is renewable each year as long as need continues and students maintain satisfactory academic standing at the College. Special attention is given to continuing students who have done exceptionally well.

Faculty

At Eugene Lang College, the faculty-student ratio is 1:9. Class size ranges from 8 to 15 students. Faculty members are graduates of outstanding colleges and universities and represent a wide variety of academic disciplines; 95 percent hold Ph.D.'s. College faculty members also serve as academic advisers, who are selected carefully in order to ensure the thoughtful supervision of students' programs and academic progress.

Well-known faculty members from other divisions of the university teach at the College on a regular basis. In addition, every semester, the College hosts distinguished scholars and writers as visiting faculty and guest lecturers who further enrich the academic program of the College and the university.

Student Government

There is a student union at the College, which is an organized vehicle for student expression and action as well as a means of funding student projects and events. Students are encouraged to express their views and concerns about academic policies and community life through regular student-faculty member meetings.

Admission Requirements

Eugene Lang College welcomes admission applications from students of diverse racial, ethnic, religious, and political backgrounds whose past performance and academic and personal promise make them likely to gain from and give much to the College community. The College seeks students who combine inquisitiveness and seriousness of purpose with the ability to engage in a distinctive, rigorous liberal arts program. Each applicant to the College is judged individually; the Admissions Committee, which renders all admission decisions, considers both academic qualifications and the personal, creative, and intellectual qualities of each applicant. A strong academic background, including a college-preparatory program, is recommended. An applicant's transcript; teacher and counselor recommendations; SAT I, ACT, or SAT II Subject Test scores; and personal essays are all taken into consideration. In addition, an interview is required. A tour of university facilities and a visit to Lang College seminars are recommended. High school students for whom the College is their first choice are strongly encouraged to apply as early decision candidates and will be notified early of an admission decision. Early entrance is an option for qualified high school juniors who wish to enter college prior to high school graduation. Candidates for early entrance must submit two teacher recommendations. Students who have successfully completed one full year or more at another accredited institution may apply as transfer candidates. If accepted, transfer students may enter upper-level seminars and pursue advanced work. International students may apply for admission as freshmen or transfers by submitting a regular application to the College. If English is spoken as a second language, TOEFL scores are required. The "New York Connection" program invites students from other colleges to Eugene Lang for a semester and incorporates an internship into their studies.

Students interested in applying for the combined B.A./B.F.A. degree program in fine arts or jazz studies are encouraged to apply for admission as freshmen to these special five-year programs. In addition to the admission requirements outlined above, a home exam and a portfolio are required for fine arts, and an audition is required for jazz studies.

Application and Information

Freshmen, transfers, and visiting students may apply for either the September (fall) or January (spring) semester. To apply for admission to the College, students must request an application packet and submit the required credentials and a $30 application fee by the appropriate deadline. (The application fee may be waived in accordance with the College Board's Fee Waiver Service.) For the semester beginning in January, the required credentials must be submitted by November 15, with notification by December 15. For the September semester, early decision candidates must submit the required credentials by November 15, with notification by December 15; for freshman candidates applying for general admission, the deadline is February 1, with notification by April 1; for freshman early entrants, transfers, and visiting students, the deadline is rolling to May 15, with notification rolling until July 1.

For further information, students should contact:

Jennifer Gill Fondiller
Director of Admissions
Eugene Lang College, New School University
65 West 11th Street, Third Floor
New York, New York 10011
Telephone: 212-229-5665
Fax: 212-229-5355
E-mail: lang@newschool.edu
World Wide Web: http://www.lang.edu

THE EVERGREEN STATE COLLEGE
OLYMPIA, WASHINGTON

The College

"Unique," "innovative," and "challenging" are all words that have been used to describe the curriculum offered by the Evergreen State College, a public liberal arts and sciences college offering undergraduate and graduate studies. Established in 1971 to provide innovation in higher education, Evergreen is the smallest and newest four-year public institution in the state of Washington. Since its beginning, Evergreen has designed and refined a format for higher education that has been recognized nationally and internationally as remarkable and exciting. Evergreen seeks qualified students who demonstrate a spirit of inquiry and a willingness to participate in their educational process within a collaborative framework. The College desires students who also express an interest in campus or community involvement, a respect and tolerance for individual differences, and a willingness to experiment with innovative modes of teaching and learning.

An education at Evergreen emphasizes interdisciplinary studies and collaborative learning. Instruction relies heavily on seminars—small discussion groups that involve students and faculty members in active participation. A state-supported college that offers the advantages of a small private liberal arts college, Evergreen is fully accredited by the Northwest Association of Schools and Colleges.

Graduate programs in public administration, environmental studies, and teaching are available.

Nearly 3,900 undergraduates from almost every state in the Union are enrolled at Evergreen; 43 percent are men, 57 percent are women, and 16 percent are students of color. The average age of the student body is 22. About 1,000 students live on campus in apartment-style units. Accommodations include single and double studios as well as one- to six-bedroom apartments. Housing is within walking distance of classrooms and other campus facilities. Campus life is centered in academic programs, the residence halls, student clubs, and special-interest groups. On-campus activities include dances, plays, films, distinguished visiting speakers, concerts, and a variety of recreational activities. Notable among campus activities and services are those sponsored by the First Peoples Community, a network of minority student groups that offers peer support, guest speakers, and campus ethnic festivals.

Evergreen's women's and men's intercollegiate teams compete in swimming, soccer, tennis, and basketball and have recently joined the NCAA Division III athletic conference. Numerous intramural sports are also available. The Campus Recreation Center is equipped with an eleven-lane swimming pool, a separate diving well, a sun deck, five racquetball/handball courts, a gymnasium, a wellness center, a challenge course, a rock-climbing practice wall, two multipurpose rooms for dance and the martial arts, and exercise/weight-training rooms/classes with the latest in weight training equipment.

Location

The College is just outside Washington's capital city of Olympia in the midst of 1,000 acres of woods, with a 3,300-foot waterfront on Puget Sound. The campus is heavily forested with alder, maple, cedar and Douglas firs and has trails for walking, jogging, and bicycling. The beachfront provides a delightful place for strolling, sunbathing, or marine research.

Olympia is a seaport community of about 70,000, located at the southernmost tip of Puget Sound. The Pacific Ocean is about an hour's drive to the west. The rain forests and mountains of the Olympic Peninsula lie to the north, and the Cascade mountain range is 2 hours east. Seattle, 60 miles north of the campus by freeway, offers all the cultural and recreational activities typically found in a large city, while Portland, Oregon, is less than a 2-hour drive south.

Majors and Degrees

Evergreen awards the Bachelor of Arts and Bachelor of Science degrees. Students are able to design undergraduate academic concentrations in American studies, anthropology, art, biology, business management, chemistry, communications, community service, comparative literature, computer science, creative writing, cultural studies, ecology, economics, energy studies, English, environmental studies, ethnic studies, European studies, film and television, French, general science, history, human development, humanities, Japanese, literature, marine biology, marine sciences, mathematics, music, Native American studies, natural sciences, performing arts, philosophy, photography, physical sciences, physics, political science, prelaw, premedicine, psychology, public administration, Russian, small-scale agriculture, social sciences, sociology, Spanish, urban studies, and visual arts.

Academic Program

Evergreen provides innovative academic programs that enable students to enroll each quarter in a single comprehensive program rather than in several separate courses. These coordinated programs bring a group of students and faculty members into extended contact, allowing them to work intensively in ways that encourage intellectual growth and friendship. The study of one topic at a time from a variety of perspectives provides students an excellent opportunity to combine the elements of an undergraduate education into a meaningful, cohesive whole.

The curriculum is founded on (1) collaborative, interdisciplinary teaching and learning; (2) small classes and close personal interaction of students and faculty members; (3) studies and group projects that encourage the understanding of theory as well as the development of practical applications; (4) narrative evaluations of the student's academic achievement; and (5) areas of concentration designed jointly by students and faculty members.

Studies at Evergreen are interdisciplinary. Students master one or more major fields of study by drawing knowledge from several different academic disciplines to develop an understanding of the relationships between the arts, the humanities, and the natural and social sciences. The academic program is based on the conviction that coordinated interdisciplinary study produces better conceptualizers, analysts, and problem-solvers and ultimately better citizens. A student's academic progress is assessed through narrative evaluations written by faculty members that describe in detail each student's academic activities, objectives, area of concentration, and degree of success in the attempted program. Narrative evaluations provide a comprehensive and insightful analysis of every student's work.

Each bachelor's degree requires the completion of 180 quarter credit hours. The academic calendar consists of three 10-week quarters and a summer session.

Off-Campus Arrangements

Evergreen offers an extensive internship program for advanced students. Placements are sponsored by faculty members and may be located anywhere in the world, although most are located in the Pacific Northwest. An international student exchange program exists with Miyazaki and Kobe Universities in Japan. Each year, Evergreen offers coordinated programs that enable students to spend a portion of the year overseas. Other study-abroad arrangements can also be made.

Academic Facilities

As the state's newest four-year college, Evergreen offers undergraduates some of the most modern academic facilities in the Pacific Northwest. The regional accreditation team that reviewed Evergreen described its scientific and artistic plant as "superior to that which can be found in any institution of which we have knowledge." Some of the resources available include a library containing 250,000 books, 30,000 reference volumes, 2,000 periodical subscriptions, and 4,000 items of media loan equipment. The science laboratory buildings house a lab supply store, a number of teaching and research laboratories, an advanced microscopy laboratory, and several instrument laboratories that feature spectrophotometers, chromatographs, ultracentrifuges, scintillation counters, and other equipment necessary for advanced work in the sciences. The computer applications lab is a facility designed to provide students in the laboratory science curriculum with language instruction, experiment and instrument interfacing, high-resolution color graphics, simulations, complex calculations, scientific software development, local networking, linear and digital electronics, and microprocessor applications.

The art facility includes ceramics, painting, and drawing studios; areas for weaving, batik, jewelry, drawing, and design; and a large high-ceilinged area for sculpture, casting, welding, glassblowing, lapidary work, spray painting, shop, and sheet-metal work. The communications laboratory building is a comprehensive instructional, performance, and production facility for audio and video communications, including dance, film, music, speech, theater, and two-dimensional design. This state-of-the-art facility also includes equipment for the performance of electronic music and for conventional filmmaking and previewing.

All Evergreen students have free access to computer facilities. The computer center's resources include microcomputer laboratories, clusters of microcomputers, 150 computer workstations, and minicomputers. Other on-campus computer facilities include NOVA minicomputers, micro-Plato workstations, plotters and graphic terminals, a hybrid analog/digital system, and additional scientific data acquisition devices. An extensive computer science teaching lab provides microcomputing resources and overhead display projection systems. The graphics imaging lab provides facilities for graphics and imaging projects.

Costs

Annual undergraduate tuition for 1999–2000 was $2757 for Washington State residents and $9759 for nonresidents. The estimated cost of books and supplies was $780. The cost of room and board was $5136, and personal living expenses were estimated at $1971.

Financial Aid

Evergreen's goal is to provide sufficient financial aid to make it possible for all qualified students to attend. Awards from Evergreen's aid programs, which are based on financial need, are designed to supplement the contribution of the student and his or her family. Once a student's level of financial need has been determined, his or her application is reviewed to evaluate eligibility for all programs. A financial aid package, which may combine a grant, scholarship, loan, and work opportunity, is then offered to meet the student's needs as closely as possible. Financial aid applications received by the processor by February 15 will have priority.

A variety of scholarships funded by the College's Foundation and private donors are available. Most of these scholarships are awarded on the basis of merit, high academic achievement, community service, and artistic or musical talent. For more information about these scholarships, students should write to the Office of the Dean of Enrollment Services or call 360-866-6000, Ext. 6310.

Faculty

Evergreen has a dedicated faculty committed to teaching. Eighty-six percent of faculty members hold the Ph.D. or other terminal degree; 45 percent are women, and 26 percent are people of color. The favorable faculty-student ratio of 1:22 ensures close interaction between students and faculty members. Faculty members teach in one full-time program at a time, enabling them to have direct contact with a small group of students. Students work in small seminar groups from their freshman through their senior year and engage with academic content in unique ways. Faculty members strive to foster the environment of a learning community where common goals can include working across cultural and personal differences, engaging with difficult intellectual ideas through discussion, and making the abstract real and applicable to true-life situations. At Evergreen, students spend an average of 12–16 hours a week in direct contact with faculty members.

Student Government

Students at Evergreen have chosen to actively serve on a variety of campuswide committees and task forces rather than participate in a more traditional student government. With direct access to governance policies and resolutions, all Evergreen students are encouraged to become involved with campus issues. Students also directly administer the funds collected from the student services and activities fees, which are used to support a wide variety of student organizations.

Admission Requirements

First-year students are admitted on the basis of their high school GPA and test scores (SAT I or ACT). Essays and letters of recommendation are not required. First-year students are required to have completed the following college-preparatory program in high school: 4 years of English courses designed to develop college-level reading and writing proficiencies (composition, creative writing, and literature); 3 years of mathematics selected from algebra, geometry, trigonometry, advanced algebra, and higher-level courses; 3 years of social studies; 2 years of science, including 1 year of laboratory science (biology, chemistry, or physics); 2 years of the same foreign language; and 1 year in the visual/performing arts or in any of the aforementioned areas.

Students with at least 40 transferable credits are considered under transfer admission criteria. Transfer students are admitted on the basis of their cumulative college GPA, good standing at the last institution attended, and satisfactory completion of a variety of courses in the liberal arts and sciences.

Because Evergreen seeks to achieve a diverse student body, special consideration is given to applicants who are Vietnam-era veterans, adults 25 years of age and older, and students whose parents do not have a baccalaureate degree. In addition, special recognition is given to applicants who have 90 quarter credits of transferable work, an Associate in Arts degree from a Washington community college, or an Associate in Technical Arts degree from a Washington community college with which Evergreen has negotiated an "Upside Down" degree program.

Application and Information

Applications for fall entrance are accepted from September 1 to March 1; applicants are notified by April 1. Applications for winter entrance are accepted from April 1 to October 1; applicants are notified by November 1. Applications for spring entrance are accepted from June 1 to December 1; applicants are notified by January 1. Applications received after the deadline are considered on a space-available basis.

For more information about Evergreen, students should contact:

Office of Admissions
The Evergreen State College
Olympia, Washington 98505

Telephone: 360-866-6000 Ext. 6170
E-mail: admissions@evergreen.edu
World Wide Web: http://www.evergreen.edu

FAIRLEIGH DICKINSON UNIVERSITY
FLORHAM–MADISON AND TEANECK–HACKENSACK, NEW JERSEY, AND OXFORDSHIRE, ENGLAND

The University

Founded in 1942, Fairleigh Dickinson University (FDU) is one of New Jersey's leading private universities. It is comprised of two strategically located and uniquely different campuses in northern New Jersey—Teaneck–Hackensack and Florham–Madison—offering both undergraduate and graduate programs. Building on its long history of international outreach and its proximity to New York City, FDU is dedicated to preparing students with a highly focused, career-oriented education that will enable them to fully participate as world citizens in the global marketplace of ideas, commerce, and culture.

Both its Teaneck–Hackensack and Florham–Madison campuses offer students a distinctive living and learning environment and a wide range of academic choices within an intimate university setting. Residence halls and off-campus housing are available on both campuses. FDU has nearly 100 active academic, social, political, and professional student organizations; sororities and fraternities; and sports at the varsity, intramural, club, and intercampus levels. Lectures, seminars, concerts, performances, and special events are also an intrinsic part of University life.

Location

Less than ten miles from New York City, Teaneck–Hackensack is FDU's larger and more comprehensive campus, attracting a diverse and international student population to its open, cosmopolitan campus. Its programs are designed to encourage students to take advantage of the many career and cultural opportunities of New York. The Florham–Madison Campus is located near historic Morristown in New Jersey's "Silicon Valley," 35 miles from Manhattan. The campus is situated on a former estate of 200 private, wooded acres, yet its students find countless internship and learning opportunities at the many major national and international corporations that surround it.

FDU also owns and operates an overseas campus—Wroxton College—in Oxfordshire, England, and has a location in Israel on the campus of the Bio Technical Institute in Tel-Aviv.

Majors and Degrees

Bachelor of Arts degrees are offered in art, communication, communication arts, criminal justice, economics, electronic filmmaking and digital video design, English language and literature, fine arts, French language and literature, general studies, history, humanities, international studies, mathematics, philosophy, political science, psychology, sociology, Spanish language and literature, and theater.

Bachelor of Science degrees are offered in accounting; biochemistry; biology; business management; chemistry; civil engineering technology; clinical laboratory science; computer science; construction engineering technology; economics and finance; electrical engineering; electrical engineering technology; entrepreneurial studies; environmental science; hotel, restaurant, and tourism management; marine biology; marketing; mathematics; mechanical engineering technology; medical technology; nursing (including a one-year accelerated program); radiologic technology; and science.

QUEST, FDU's five-year teacher certification program, allows students to earn a bachelor's degree in a field of their choosing in the liberal arts or sciences as well as dual teacher certification in one or two high-demand specifications and a Master of Arts (M.A.T.) degree. Preprofessional studies are offered in chiropractic, law, medicine, optometry, and veterinary.

Accelerated degree programs include a five-year bachelor's/Master of Business Administration degree (B.A./M.B.A. or B.S./M.B.A.); a five-year bachelor's/master's degree in psychology (B.A./M.A.); a seven-year bachelor's/Doctor of Dental Surgery with New York University (B.S./D.D.S.); a five-year bachelor/Master of Arts in Teaching (B.A./M.A.T. or B.S./M.A.T.); a 150-credit-hour bachelor's/master's degree in accounting (B.S./M.S.); a five-year bachelor's/Master of Arts in Public Administration (B.A./M.P.A.); a six and one-half-year bachelor's/Doctor of Chiropractic (B.S./D.C.); a seven-year bachelor's/Doctor of Medicine (B.S./M.D.), offered in cooperation with the Karol Marcinkowski University of Medical Studies in Poland; and a five-year bachelor's civil engineering technology or construction engineering technology/master's in systems science with a concentration in pollution studies (B.S.Civ.E.T./M.S. or B.S.Con.E.T./M.S.)

Associate in Science degrees are offered in physical therapy assistant studies and radiography. In addition, the Edward Williams program offers an Associate in Arts degree in liberal arts.

Academic Program

Candidates for the degree of Bachelor of Arts or Bachelor of Science must complete a minimum of 128 credit-hours of course work, maintain a minimum 2.0 CGPR (individual colleges have minimum CGPRs for course work within their majors), and complete the University Core Curriculum—a sequence of four courses designed to provide all FDU undergraduates with a solid foundation in the liberal arts, sciences, and humanities. The Core provides students with a common base of knowledge; improves skills in communications and analysis; promotes understanding of individual, societal, and international perspectives; and inculcates an appreciation for the interrelationship among bodies of knowledge. Candidates for the B.A. must take 30 to 44 credits in the major, 40 to 63 credits in distribution requirements (19 to 23 credits in foundation courses; 15 to 30 credits in humanities and social and behavioral sciences; and 6 to 10 credits in laboratory science), and the University Core; the remainder of credits may be taken as free electives. Candidates for the B.S. degree must complete 54 to 60 credits in the major and the University Core; the remaining credits are taken in foundation and free elective courses. The undergraduate program includes all courses needed to meet graduate and professional school requirements.

FDU offers a University Honors Program and a Cooperative Education program, and many departments have internships and work-experience programs. More than forty undergraduate concentrations have been developed to enhance a student's major—including American minority studies, biotechnology, criminal justice, entrepreneurial studies, electronic filmmaking and digital video design, environmental science, international business, and public relations. Mature adult students may participate in the SUCCESS program of personalized learning that leads to the B.A. in humanities.

Through FDU's Regional Center for College Students with Learning Disabilities, students can receive academic support within the regular college curriculum (enrollment is selective and limited). The Freshmen Intensive Studies program is designed to assist a limited number of promising students who require focused support as they begin their college careers. FDU also offers English Language Centers (a division of Berlitz, Inc.) on both campuses as a service to international students.

Off-Campus Arrangements

FDU strongly encourages all students to incorporate an international learning experience as part of their education. For example, students can spend a semester or year at Wroxton College, the historic British campus located 70 miles from London that FDU has owned and operated since 1965. A variety of other international experiences are also available based on student interests and career goals.

Domestic learning experiences available to students include the well-known Semester in Washington; in addition, the marine biology curriculum includes laboratory field experiences that are available at the University of Hawaii at Hilo, Shoals Laboratory of Cornell University, and Duke University's Marine Laboratory in Beaufront, North Carolina.

Academic Facilities

The University maintains comprehensive libraries on each campus and a business reference library on the Teaneck Campus. The libraries have combined holdings of 445,718 volumes and subscriptions to 2,235 periodicals. Each library provides computer search services and access to subject CD-ROMs to augment in-house print resources. FDU is a participating member of the Online Computer Library Center and maintains a University-wide online catalog to facilitate intracampus library loans. Each FDU library has a number of distinguished special collections on subjects such as the Columbia film archives, the Kahn Memorial Collection on the History of Photography, and the Harry Chesler Collection of comic art, graphic satire, and illustration.

Students have access to more than 200 minicomputers and microcomputers on campus as well as to programming languages and software. In addition, there are state-of-the-art computer graphics laboratories for the production of professional quality, computer-generated art. Computer, software, and Internet training is offered through the campus Computer Center. Resident students with their own computers can link to the campus computer network from their rooms. Student e-mail and Internet access accounts are also offered to all students.

Costs

Based on a flat-fee structure, tuition in 1999–2000 was $14,732; campus and academic fees were $987; room and board were $6536; and the estimated cost of books and supplies was $623.

Financial Aid

FDU awards more than $23 million in financial aid annually, including a generous scholarship program for academically outstanding students. To be considered for financial aid, students should file the Free Application for Federal Student Aid (FAFSA) and FDU's University Financial Aid Application. Applications for aid should be filed by March 15 for priority consideration. Applications filed after this date are processed subject to availability of funds. The average financial aid award in 1997–98 to first-year students was $15,750. Under Fairleigh Dickinson's Family Plan—one of the first of its kind—families with two or more children attending the University at the same time qualify to receive additional financial incentives of $2500 or more.

Faculty

There are 262 full-time and 574 part-time faculty members at Fairleigh Dickinson University. Of the full-time faculty members, 85 percent hold a doctoral or the highest terminal degree in their field. The student-faculty ratio is approximately 14:1 on the Madison Campus and 15:1 on the Teaneck–Hackensack Campus. All courses are taught by faculty members. Members of the faculty and administration participate in advising students as well as in planned activities that concern the student body as a whole. All first-year students are assigned faculty mentors to help develop class schedules and assess students' academic progress.

Student Government

Each FDU campus has a student council that acts as the governing body to enforce student regulations and to plan social club activities. The student council serves as a liaison with the faculty and administration of both the campus and the University. It offers students' opinions as an aid in developing University curricular and extracurricular policies. The University Senate, which formulates University policies, includes voting representatives from the student body.

Admission Requirements

The University recommends at least 16 units of full-credit work from an accredited secondary school, including 4 years of English, 2 years of history, 1 year of a laboratory science, 2 years of college-preparatory mathematics, 5 to 7 elective units (4 should be academic), and 2 or 3 years of a foreign language. Additional science and mathematics units are required for some majors. The criteria that are used for University-wide admission are the high school record, SAT I or ACT scores, and counselor recommendations. SAT II Subject Test scores are used for placement only. Freshmen may submit scores on the SAT II: Writing Test. Foreign Language Subject Test scores may be submitted by those applicants who intend to continue study of the language they took in high school. The Mathematics Level I or II Subject Test may be taken by prospective chemistry, physics, mathematics, and engineering majors. The SAT I may be taken as early as July preceding the senior year and as late as March of the senior year, but the November or December test dates are preferred. Campus visits are strongly recommended. Interviews may be required in select cases and are available to all students.

Application and Information

Students must submit a completed and signed application form, a secondary school record form listing all courses and grades, SAT I or ACT scores, and a nonrefundable $40 application fee (which can be waived in cases of hardship). Freshmen and transfer students are admitted in September, January, and during summer sessions. Applicants for regular admission are reviewed on a rolling basis and are notified after receipt of all credentials. Information on filing an online application can be found by visiting the University's Web site at http://www.fdu.edu.

For application forms, financial aid information, and other materials, students should contact:

Office of University Admissions
Fairleigh Dickinson University
1000 River Road—H335C
Teaneck, New Jersey 07666
Telephone: 800-FDU-8803 (toll-free)
World Wide Web: http://www.fdu.edu

FAIRMONT STATE COLLEGE
FAIRMONT, WEST VIRGINIA

The College
Fairmont State College (FSC) is the largest state-supported four-year college in West Virginia, with an enrollment of 6,627 students. Founded in 1867, the College is located in the north-central portion of the state in the city of Fairmont, West Virginia. In addition to the main campus, which includes thirteen major buildings, classes are also offered at the FSC Robert C. Byrd National Aerospace Education Center in Bridgeport as well as at the FSC Gaston Caperton Center, a new 36,000-square-foot state-of-the-art facility in Clarksburg. The College also has satellite facilities reaching across the north-central region of West Virginia and at the Center for Workforce Education at the I-79 Technology Park.

Fairmont State College has a rich and proud athletic tradition. The College is a member of NCAA Division II and offers men's teams in baseball, basketball, cross-country, football, golf, tennis, and swimming. The College sponsors women's teams in basketball, cross-country, golf, softball, swimming, tennis, and volleyball. Fairmont State's cheerleaders are consistently among the top teams in the state and the nation. FSC also has an extensive and well-organized intramural program and provides other recreational facilities across campus.

Students who live on campus are housed in one of three residence halls and take their meals at a centrally located dining hall or at the food court in the student center. For those students who prefer to live off campus, private accommodations close to the College are available. Parents who are taking classes at the College may find it convenient to enroll their young children in the day-care center located on the main campus.

The Newman Center and the Wesley Foundation are available to minister to the spiritual needs of students; both organizations are adjacent to the FSC campus. There are also various student organizations, honor societies, and social fraternities and sororities to enhance extracurricular life at the College.

Location
Fairmont is the county seat of Marion County and has a population of approximately 20,000. Located along Interstate 79 approximately 90 miles south of Pittsburgh, the city and College are easily accessible to all travelers.

Fairmont State College and the city of Fairmont share a long history of mutual cooperation and respect. Shopping malls, restaurants, cultural entertainment, and nightlife are easily found throughout the city, while countless outdoor recreational pleasures are offered by such places as Pricketts Fort State Park, Valley Falls State Park, and a variety of city and county parks nearby.

Majors and Degrees
Fairmont State College offers one-year certificates, two-year associate degrees, and four-year baccalaureate degrees, as well as a wide range of continuing education classes. FSC offers courses of study leading to baccalaureate degrees in the humanities, social and natural sciences, teacher education, business, industrial technology, and the fine arts.

Academic Program
Fairmont State College offers 127 program areas in the Schools of Business and Economics, Education, Fine Arts, Health Careers, Language and Literature, Science and Mathematics, Social Science, and Technology.

Special degrees such as the Regents Bachelor of Arts degree offer nontraditional approaches for individual career or personal requirements. Certificate programs are designed to provide basic skills or increased proficiency in specific occupational areas. Preprofessional studies are designed to prepare students for a wide variety of professional programs beyond a four-year degree.

Academic Facilities
The Ruth Ann Musick Library has a collection of more than 200,000 books and more than 15,000 bound periodicals, microfilms, and other materials. The Learning Resource Center, located on the first floor of the library building, offers a large collection of audiotapes and videotapes to supplement and enhance learning. The Computer Center allows students to use the latest in technology, including free access to the Internet. Music, theater, and other fine arts are showcased in Wallman Hall Theatre and the Gallery.

Costs
Fairmont State College remains a very financially affordable institution. Tuition and fees for the 1999–2000 academic year were $2244 for West Virginia residents and $5228 for out-of-state residents. Average room and board costs were $3882 per year. Textbooks cost approximately $500 per year.

Financial Aid
About 53 percent of Fairmont State College students receive some form of financial aid. Guidelines and forms for West Virginia and out-of-state residents are available from high school guidance counselors or FSC's Financial Aid Office.

Faculty
Fairmont State College employs 204 full-time faculty members, ensuring a student-teacher ratio of 20:1. Each student is assigned a faculty adviser who helps schedule courses, oversees classroom performance, and offers academic counseling.

Student Government
Student Government at Fairmont State College actively seeks to supplement the academic atmosphere with intellectual, cultural, and social activities. Student Government members are involved in all aspects of life on campus and work cooperatively with the College administration.

Every segment of the student body is represented in the Government. Members are elected each spring by the student body and receive special training for these positions. Members include a president, vice president, secretary, treasurer, parliamentarian, and representatives of the four classes and other groups. An adviser is assigned by the Vice President for Student Affairs.

Admission Requirements
Students must indicate on the admission application their degree or program objective—a four-year baccalaureate degree, two-year associate degree, or one-year certificate program. Admission is granted to Fairmont State College for

baccalaureate degree programs and to the Fairmont State Community and Technical College component for associate degree and certificate programs.

Admission to Fairmont State College does not guarantee admission to specific programs, which may be restricted based on qualifications and available space.

Application and Information

Campus tours are available Monday through Friday by appointment. Fairmont State College also sponsors a Saturday Campus Visitation Day once each fall and spring semester. For more information or to schedule a tour, students should contact:

Office of Student Affairs
Fairmont State College
1201 Locust Avenue
Fairmont, West Virginia 26554
Telephone: 304-367-4892
         800-641-5678 (toll-free)
         304-367-4141 (admissions and records)
         304-367-4213 (financial aid)
         304-367-4216 (housing)
         304-367-4000 (campus operator)
         304-623-5721 (Caperton Center)
         304-842-8300 (Aerospace Education Center)

Fairmont State College students have an opportunity to relax and socialize in the inviting plaza in front of the newest building on campus.

FASHION INSTITUTE OF TECHNOLOGY
NEW YORK, NEW YORK

The Institute

Today, to know the Fashion Institute of Technology (FIT) only by name is not to know it very well at all. The name reflects back fifty years to the college's origins when it was devoted exclusively to educating students for careers in the apparel industry. But the name no longer tells the whole story.

A "fashion college" that offers programs in interior design, jewelry design, advertising and communications, and even toy design; a community college that offers bachelor's and master's degree programs in addition to the traditional two-year associate degree, FIT is an educational institution like no other.

FIT is rooted in industry and the world of work. Industry visits by students and lectures by many different leaders in the field provide a cooperative and creative bridge between the classroom and the actual world of work. Although the college is now associated with many industries and professions, FIT's commitment to career education is still its hallmark and a source of pride to an institution whose industry connection is an integral part of its history. FIT counts among its alumni such luminaries as Calvin Klein and Norma Kamali, as well as successful and talented professionals in advertising, packaging, television, the design fields, merchandising, manufacturing, public relations, and retailing.

Founded in 1944, FIT today is a college of art and design and business and technology of the State University of New York. More than fifteen majors offered through the School of Art and Design and ten through the School of Business and Technology lead to the A.A.S., B.F.A., or B.S. degrees. (The School of Graduate Studies offers programs leading to the Master of Arts or Master of Professional Studies degree.) FIT is an accredited institutional member of the Middle States Association of Colleges and Schools, the National Association of Schools of Art and Design, and the Foundation for Interior Design Education Research. The eight-building campus includes classrooms, studios, and labs that reflect the most advanced education and industrial practices. FIT serves more than 5,700 full-time and 5,400 part-time students, who come not only from within commuting distances, but from all fifty states and sixty-five other countries. Three dormitories serve approximately 1,250 students and offer various accommodations. Student participation is encouraged through more than sixty campus clubs, organizations, and athletic teams.

With a consistent job placement rate of 88 percent, FIT graduates are well prepared to meet employers' needs. Working with both undergraduates and graduates, placement counselors develop job opportunities for full-time, part-time, freelance, and summer employment.

Location

The campus leaves behind the rolling green lawns of the more traditional college campus in favor of the challenges and excitement of "unique New York." FIT's location in the heart of Manhattan on Seventh Avenue at 27th Street—where the worlds of fashion, art, design, communications, and manufacturing converge—permits an exceptional two-way flow between the college and industries and professions it serves. Students are encouraged to participate in the cultural activities of New York, where opera, dance, theater, and the art world are readily accessible. Education, career direction, technical skills, and the liberal arts combine to take full advantage of New York's special offerings.

Majors and Degrees

The college offers both a two-year program leading to the Associate in Applied Science (A.A.S.) degree and an upper-division program leading to the Bachelor of Fine Arts (B.F.A.) or Bachelor of Science (B.S.) degree. Associate-level art and design majors are offered in accessories design, advertising design, display and exhibit design, fashion design, fine arts (with a career-exploration component), illustration, interior design, jewelry design, menswear, photography, and textile/surface design. In the business area, majors are offered in advertising and marketing communications, fashion merchandising management, manufacturing management, patternmaking technology, and textile development and marketing. Bachelor of Fine Arts degrees are awarded in advertising design, computer animation and interactive media, fabric styling, fashion design, illustration, interior design, packaging design, restoration, textile/surface design, and toy design. (Transfer students wishing to enter B.F.A. programs may have to complete the one-year A.A.S. program described below prior to entry into the upper division.) The Bachelor of Science degree is offered in advertising and marketing communications; cosmetics and fragrance marketing; direct marketing; fashion merchandising management; home products development and marketing; international trade and marketing for the fashion industries; product management: textiles; production management: apparel; and textile development and marketing. The B.S. program is open to students who hold an associate degree from the college or an equivalent degree from another accredited institution. Graduates of other accredited institutions of higher learning or transfer students who have a minimum of 30 transferable credits and can satisfy the liberal arts requirements may enter one-year A.A.S. programs in accessories design, advertising and marketing communications, advertising design, fashion merchandising management, fashion design, jewelry design, manufacturing management, textile development and marketing, and textile/surface design.

Academic Program

Programs are designed to prepare students for creative and/or executive careers in the fashion and related professions and industries. To qualify for the A.A.S., a student must satisfactorily complete the credit hours prescribed for a given major with approximately one third of all required credits in the liberal arts, achieve a minimum GPA of 2.0, and receive the recommendation of the faculty. To qualify for the B.S. or B.F.A., a student must satisfactorily complete the credit and course requirements prescribed by the major, achieve a minimum GPA of 2.0 on all work completed, and receive the recommendation of the faculty. A minimum of 60 approved credits is required; at least half of the credits required in the major area must be earned in residence at the upper-division level. If the student has an appropriate Fashion Institute of Technology associate degree, a minimum of 30 approved credits must be earned in residence at the upper-division level. Most majors offer internship programs in their courses of study.

Saturday Live programs are available during the fall, spring, and summer. These twenty-five programs offer high school students the chance to learn in a studio environment, to explore the business and technology sides of the fashion industry, and to discover natural talents and creative abilities. Classes are taught by a faculty of artists, designers, and other professionals. High school credit may be earned at the discretion of each student's high school.

Off-Campus Arrangements

The "FIT International Program in Fashion Design/Florence and New York" provides an international experience for students interested in careers in the global fashion industry. Offered to full-time, matriculated FIT students as two distinct programs leading to the A.A.S. and B.F.A. degrees, the curricula are taught in both New York City and Florence, Italy, with students completing a year of study in one city and then the other.

Textile/surface design majors may apply for a semester abroad at Winchester School of Art or Chelsea School of Art near London or at the Nova Scotia College of Art and Design in Halifax. Fashion merchandising management majors may apply for semester-abroad study in merchandising at RMIT in Australia, Manchester Metropolitan University in England, or Scuola Lorenzo de' Medici in Italy; seventh-semester advertising design students may study at the London College of Printing's School of Graphic Design or Nottingham Trent University in England; and seventh-semester students may study international marketing at the American University in Rome or business at Middlesex Polytechnic in London. A semester at the Institut Commercial de Nancy in Nancy, France, or at CELSA, Université de Paris IV, Sorbonne, is available for a limited number of advertising and marketing communications students with a working knowledge of French. Selected upper-division students majoring in fashion design may study for one semester at Nottingham Trent University, at Esmod, a college of fashion in Paris, or at the Polimoda in Florence, Italy. Brief off-campus courses are offered for credit during summer and Winterim semesters and include the fashion industry in Asia; French costumes and interiors in Paris; fashion and fabric in France and Italy; public relations in Britain; French in Paris; and art and design in Italy.

Academic Facilities

The campus, a modern plant with outstanding facilities for studying all aspects of a dynamic industry, covers almost two square blocks. The Fred P. Pomerantz Art and Design Center offers up-to-date facilities for design studies: photography studios with color and black-and-white darkrooms, painting rooms, a sculpture studio, a printmaking room, a graphics laboratory, display and exhibit design rooms, life-sketching rooms, and a model-making workshop. The Shirley Goodman Resource Center houses the Museum at FIT and the Library/Media Services, with references for history, sociology, technology, art, and literature; international journals and periodicals; sketchbooks and records donated by designers, manufacturers, and merchants; slides, tapes, and periodicals; and a voluminous clipping file. The Instructional Media Services Department provides audiovisual and TV services and has modern facilities and equipment, including 16-mm films, filmstrips, slides, audiotapes and videotapes, and a complete in-house TV studio. The Museum at FIT is the repository for the world's largest collection of costumes, textiles, and accessories of dress (with an emphasis on twentieth-century apparel), and is used by students, designers, and historians for research and inspiration. The museum's galleries provide a showcase for a wide spectrum of exhibitions relevant to fashion and its satellite industries. The annual student art and design exhibition is shown here, as are other student projects. Student work is also displayed throughout the campus. Fashion shows of menswear, womenswear, and accessories occur each academic year.

The Design/Research Lighting Laboratory features more than 400 commercially available lighting fixtures controlled by a computer. The Peter G. Scotese Computer-Aided Design and Communications Facility provides art and design students with the opportunity to explore technology and its integration in the design of textiles, toys, interiors, fashion, and advertising as well as photography and computer graphics. Also located on campus is the design/research lighting laboratory, an educational and professional development facility for interior design and other academic disciplines. The Gladys Marcus Library houses more than 110,000 titles, including books, periodicals, and nonprint materials.

Costs

An unusual program of sponsorship, shared by the city and State of New York, makes a comparatively low tuition rate possible. The 1999–2000 tuition per semester for New York State residents was $1250 for associate-level programs and $1492.50 for baccalaureate programs; for out-of-state residents, it was $2925 for associate-level programs and $3400 for baccalaureate programs. Dormitory fees ranged from $1976.50 to $2346 per semester, and meal plan fees were $1202 per semester. The Student Association fee was $105, books and supplies were $400–$800, and personal expenses were about $500. Costs are subject to change.

Financial Aid

The Fashion Institute of Technology attempts to remove financial barriers to college entrance by providing scholarships, grants, loans, and part-time employment for students in financial need. Approximately 64 percent of the 5,700 full-time students receive some type of financial aid. The college directly administers its own institutional grants and scholarships, which are provided by the Educational Foundation for the Fashion Industries. College-administered federal funding includes Federal Pell Grants, Federal Supplemental Educational Opportunity Grants, Federal Perkins Loans, and Federal Work-Study Program awards. New York State residents who meet state guidelines for eligibility may also receive TAP and/or Educational Opportunity Program grants. The college will try to meet students' needs by forming a financial aid package from institutional scholarships and federal grants, loans, and Federal Work-Study Program awards. Financial aid applicants must also apply to all available outside sources of aid and must file the Free Application for Federal Student Aid (FAFSA), on which they apply for the Federal Pell Grant. Other material must be requested from the Financial Aid Office.

Applications for financial aid should be completed prior to March 1 for fall admission or prior to November 15 for spring admission.

Faculty

Those who do, teach at FIT. Members of the FIT community have considerable experience and are on the cutting edge of their various fields and industries.

Student Government

The Student Council, the governing body of the Student Association, gives all students the privileges and responsibilities of citizens in a self-governing college community. Many faculty committees include student representatives.

Admission Requirements

Because the college prepares students for creative and executive positions in the fashion industries, it selects candidates with aptitude in these areas. For the Art and Design Division, demonstrated artistic talent and achievements that predict success on the college level are valued. Candidates for admission to the A.A.S. two-year degree programs must possess a high school diploma or its equivalent or be a candidate for a diploma, and they must submit a high school transcript showing class average or rank in class. A portfolio evaluation is required of all students who apply for an art or design program. Recommendations of teachers, guidance counselors, and principals are considered. The bachelor's degree programs have been structured as an additional two years of study in the upper division for specific majors in the associate-level programs. External applicants will be considered for the upper division if they have completed an associate degree or at least 60 credits in an equivalent program. A departmental recommendation is required of all B.S. candidates; B.F.A. candidates must submit a portfolio for review by a departmental committee. Academic standing and personal interviews are considered in evaluating applications for admission to either program.

Application and Information

Candidates who have graduated from a New York State high school should obtain applications from the high school guidance office. Candidates from out-of-state high schools should request applications by writing the Office of Admissions.

Director of Admissions
Fashion Institute of Technology
Seventh Avenue at 27 Street
New York, New York 10001-5992
Telephone: 212-217-7999
        800-GO-TO-FIT (toll-free)
E-mail: fitinfo@fitsuny.edu
World Wide Web: http://www.fitnyc.suny.edu

FELICIAN COLLEGE
LODI, NEW JERSEY

The College
Felician College is a Catholic/Franciscan college serving more than 1,400 men and women. Its mission is to provide a values-oriented education based in the liberal arts while it prepares students for meaningful lives and careers in contemporary society. To meet the needs of students and to provide personal enrichment courses to matriculated and nonmatriculated students, Felician College offers day, evening, and weekend programs. The College is accredited by the Middle States Association of Colleges and Schools, and carries program accreditation from the National League for Nursing Accrediting Commission and the National Accrediting Agency for Clinical Laboratory Sciences.

In addition to its undergraduate degree programs, Felician College offers a Master of Science in Nursing (M.S.N.), a Master of Arts degree in catechism, and a Master of Teacher Education.

Felician College competes in Division II of the National Collegiate Athletic Association (NCAA). The Felician teams, called the Golden Falcons, compete in men's baseball, men's and women's basketball, men's and women's soccer, and women's softball. The Athletic Department also sponsors numerous intramural sports activities, such as indoor soccer, faculty-student softball and volleyball games on the quad.

Students may elect to reside in one of the spacious suites in Elliott Hall or Milton Court Residence, both located on the new Rutherford Campus, a 10-minute shuttle bus ride from the main campus in Lodi. The campuses offer comfortable student lounge areas, student meeting rooms, dining halls, a gymnasium, a fitness center, and grassy areas for outdoor recreation.

Location
Felician College is located on two beautifully landscaped campuses in Lodi and Rutherford, in Bergen County, in northern New Jersey. Both campuses, nestled in suburban towns, are a 30-minute bus or train ride from New York City and a few miles from the New Jersey Meadowlands sports complex.

Majors and Degrees
Felician College offers programs of study in the arts and sciences, health sciences, and teacher education.

A liberal arts program leading to the Bachelor of Arts, Bachelor of Science, Bachelor of Science in Nursing, or Associate in Arts degree is designed to provide students with a broad general education and concentrated preparation in a major area. For the B.A. degree, a student may choose a departmental major in art, biology, business administration, computing science, English, history, management and marketing, mathematics, philosophy, psychology, or religious studies. A student may choose an interdisciplinary major in one of three liberal arts areas: humanities, natural sciences and mathematics, or social and behavioral sciences. Concentrations are available in accounting, biochemistry, communications, environmental science, fine arts, general science, gerontology, graphic design, international education and foreign languages, mathematical sciences, political science, and sociology. Bachelor of Arts degree programs in elementary education and special education enable students to seek New Jersey certification in elementary education (K–8) and teaching of the handicapped.

The Bachelor of Science degree is offered in nursing and in business administration. A program leading to the Bachelor of Science degree in clinical laboratory science and eligibility for national certification is offered in collaboration with the University of Medicine and Dentistry of New Jersey's School of Health-Related Professions. For this degree, a student may concentrate in cytotechnology, medical technology, or toxicology.

Two-year programs are offered leading to the Associate in Arts degree in liberal arts, the Associate in Applied Science degree in nursing, the Associate in Applied Science degree in medical laboratory technology, and the Associate in Science degree in psychosocial rehabilitation. A student who completes the two-year nursing program is eligible to take the examination for licensure as a registered nurse given by the New Jersey Board of Nursing; a student who completes the medical laboratory technology program is eligible to take the nationally administered examination for certification by the Board of Registry of the American Society of Clinical Pathologists.

Academic Program
A candidate for the B.A. in liberal arts is required to complete an organized program of study comprising 120 semester hours distributed among prescribed and elective courses. Eleven interdisciplinary courses in the College's Core Curriculum focusing on the theme "The Good Life" are included in the prescribed courses. Each baccalaureate degree student in arts and sciences is required to prepare a written and oral senior research project. A minimum of 45 credit hours must be earned at the College. A student who pursues an A.A. degree is required to complete 64 to 66 credits in an approved program of studies.

A candidate for the B.A. in elementary or special education is required to complete a program of 126 to 130 semester hours, including credits in general education, professional education, and a major in the arts and sciences. Field experience begins in the freshman year, students participate in a practicum in the junior year, and there is supervised teaching during the senior year in a public elementary school. The education programs are approved by the National Association of State Directors of Teacher Education and Certification (NASDTEC).

Students working toward an Associate in Applied Science degree in nursing start clinical experience in the freshman year. Clinical experiences in medical laboratory techniques begin during the first semester, continue throughout each semester, and include a summer internship. The Associate in Applied Science programs require 70–71 credit hours.

Field experiences, career seminars, and internships are integral parts of the career focus in the liberal arts curriculum.

An evening and weekend college program provides adults with the opportunity to earn associate and baccalaureate degrees offered at Felician College. Students may take courses through the traditional semester format and through an accelerated trimester format. Distance learning courses are also offered.

The Honors Program for students with strong academic records provides an opportunity to conduct scholarly research and develop leadership skills through service learning. Upon successful completion of the program students graduate as Honors Scholars.

The Service Learning Program allows students to be of service to others while learning the value of citizenship and responsibility through action and reflection.

Academic Facilities

Seminar rooms, multimedia and learning resource centers, and laboratories in accounting, computers, psychology, science, and writing are updated annually the latest instructional technology. Through the Internet Laboratories, all students have access to e-mail and the World Wide Web. The College auditorium comfortably seats 1,500 people; its large stage with modern theatrical features hosts performing groups from all parts of the country. The College library has a selective collection of more than 110,000 volumes, as well as periodicals, cassettes, records, microfilms, and ultrafiche. A curriculum library serves as a resource center for the teacher education programs. The Child Care Center, the Felician School for Exceptional Children, the Lourdes Health Care Center, and the Nursing Skills Laboratory, all located on the Lodi campus, furnish convenient facilities for observation, application of learning, and field experiences.

Costs

Undergraduate tuition in 1999–2000 was $10,560 per year for full-time students. The annual cost of room and board was $5600.

Financial Aid

Felician College participates in federal, state, and institutional programs of financial assistance. To determine the amount and type of aid needed, applicants must file a Free Application for Federal Student Aid (FAFSA) with the Department of Education. The College participates in the Federal Work-Study, Federal Pell Grant, and Federal Supplemental Educational Opportunity Grant programs. Students who do not receive state scholarships may be considered for New Jersey tuition aid grants. Through a state-guaranteed loan program, students may also take out low-interest bank loans. A number of institutional scholarships are available for qualified students in need of financial assistance. To take advantage of federal financial aid programs exclusively for veterans, a certificate of eligibility should be submitted to the director of financial aid at Felician College. Outstanding high school students who have completed their junior year may inquire about the Summer Scholars Program grants awarded to students interested in taking a course for college credit during the summer session. More than half of the students attending Felician receive financial aid.

Faculty

All courses are taught by fully qualified faculty members with advanced degrees, who are dedicated primarily to teaching, advising, and continued involvement in their disciplines. The student-faculty ratio of 15:1 facilitates a close working relationship, as well as individualized programs of instruction. The faculty is composed of lay and religious men and women.

Student Government

All students participate in the Student Government Organization (SGO). The governing body of the SGO, composed of elected representatives from various student groups, coordinates activities on and off campus, including community service, campus ministry, and social, cultural, civic, and athletic events. Student representatives also serve on College committees with faculty members and administrators.

Admission Requirements

Applicants must be graduates of an accredited high school and must present 16 academic units or the high school equivalency certificate, character references, satisfactory SAT I or ACT scores, and a physician's certificate of health. A personal interview with the College's director of admissions or division director is considered an important factor in the admission procedure.

Students graduating with an associate degree from a recognized junior college are eligible for admission into the upper division of Felician College. Applications for transfer are considered for both fall and spring semesters. Admission requirements may be adjusted for adults on the basis of maturity and experience.

Felician College offers credit and advanced placement for acceptable scores on the College Board Advanced Placement tests and the College-Level Examination Program tests. Superior high school students who have completed their junior year may be granted part- or full-time admission to Felician College upon recommendation by their high school principal and guidance counselor.

Application and Information

Applications, accompanied by a $25 fee, should be made during early fall of the senior year. The Admissions Office evaluates applicants' credentials on a rolling basis. However, applicants for the fall semester are strongly encouraged to apply as early as possible.

Director of Admission
Felician College
262 South Main Street
Lodi, New Jersey 07644
Telephone: 201-559-6131
Fax: 973-778-4111
World Wide Web: http://www.felician.edu

At Student Orientation. It's easy to make friends at a small college.

FERRIS STATE UNIVERSITY
BIG RAPIDS, MICHIGAN

The University

Ferris State University is Michigan's foremost professional and technical university, providing career-oriented education to nearly 10,000 students. Accredited by the North Central Association of Colleges and Schools, the University offers more than 120 programs through the Colleges of Allied Health Sciences, Arts and Sciences, Business, Education, Pharmacy, Technology, University College, and the Michigan College of Optometry. These offerings lead to bachelor's and associate degrees and certificates, master's degrees in accountancy, criminal justice administration, information systems management, and career and technical education, and doctorates in optometry and pharmacy.

One of Michigan's fifteen public universities, Ferris State University is recognized for its career-oriented educational programs that are designed to meet the technology and workforce demands of business and industry, the health-care professions, and society in general through applied research and practical education. Ferris was founded in 1884 by Woodbridge N. Ferris (1853–1928), a distinguished Michigan educator and politician who served two terms as the state's governor and was elected to the United States Senate. Ferris was a private institution until 1950 when it joined the state higher education system. The college obtained university status in 1987.

The student body consists primarily of Michigan residents (about 91 percent), with about 6 percent from out of state and 3 percent from other countries. Students who are members of minority groups represent about 21 percent of the enrollment. Nearly 36 percent of Ferris students live on campus. The University's eighteen residence halls can accommodate 4,346 students, and married students or students with dependents may apply for one of the nearly 400 one-, two-, and three-bedroom apartments located on campus. The University also maintains dining service facilities for students.

Services available to Ferris students include academic and personal counseling, tutoring, the collegiate skills program, aptitude and CLEP testing, career study classes, career planning and placement, and a variety of programs and seminars on crime prevention, safety, and substance abuse prevention and education.

In addition to an extensive academic support system characterized by close student-faculty interaction, Ferris also offers positive experiences to help students grow socially and culturally as well as academically. Students may choose to participate in any of more than 210 student organizations, including an extensive intramural program, fifteen varsity sports, and theater and musical activities, as well as many social and academic fraternities and sororities that are open to students majoring in any field. Ferris is a member of the NCAA and competes in Division I hockey and in Division II basketball, cross-country, football, golf, tennis, and track for men and basketball, cross-country, golf, soccer, softball, tennis, track, and volleyball for women.

Ferris graduates consistently have experienced high job placement rates because Ferris programs are tailored to the needs of employers. The most recent annual survey of graduates showed that 98 percent of Ferris's 1997–98 graduates were employed or continued as full-time students. Of those in the job market, 88 percent found employment in a position related to their major field of study.

Location

FSU's 600-acre campus is located in Big Rapids, a city of about 12,600 on the banks of the Muskegon River in Mecosta County, midway between Grand Rapids and Cadillac in west-central Michigan. Big Rapids' major economic base is the University, which employs 1,283 faculty and staff members. Known as the "tubing capital of Michigan," the Big Rapids area provides a wide array of recreational activities and community events with more than 100 lakes, thousands of acres of rolling terrain and woodlands, and creeks and rivers throughout the county.

Majors and Degrees

The College of Allied Health Sciences awards Bachelor of Science degrees in health care systems administration, industrial and environmental health management, medical records technology, medical technology, nuclear medicine technology, and professional nursing. Associate degrees are offered in dental hygiene, medical laboratory technology, nuclear medicine technology, opticianry, radiography (X-ray), respiratory care, and technical nursing.

The College of Arts and Sciences offers Bachelor of Science degrees in applied biology, applied mathematics, applied speech communication, biotechnology, new media printing and publishing, public administration, and technical and professional communication, as well as a Bachelor of Social Work degree. Associate degrees are offered in applied speech communication, industrial chemistry technology, and ornamental horticulture technology. Preprofessional programs include liberal arts, engineering, law, mortuary science, optometry, and pharmacy.

The College of Business awards Bachelor of Science degrees in accountancy, advertising, a dual accountancy-computer information systems degree, a dual accountancy-finance degree, business administration, computer information systems (CIS), dual degrees in CIS-management and CIS-marketing, finance, hotel management, human resource management, insurance, insurance–real estate, international business, management, marketing, marketing-sales, music industry management, operations management, professional golf management, professional tennis management, public relations, resort management, small-business management, and visual communication. Associate degrees are offered in general business, restaurant and food industry management, legal assistant studies, real estate, and visual communication.

The College of Education awards Bachelor of Science degrees in allied health education, biology education, business education, chemistry education, criminal justice, English education, mathematics education, recreation leadership and management, technical education, television production, training in business and industry, and wage-earning home economics. Associate degrees are offered in child development, pre–criminal justice, and preteaching in elementary education and secondary education.

The Michigan College of Optometry offers the Doctor of Optometry degree.

The College of Pharmacy offers the Doctor of Pharmacy degree.

The College of Technology awards Bachelor of Science degrees in automotive and heavy equipment management; computer networks and systems; construction management; electrical/electronics engineering technology; facilities management; heating, ventilation, air-conditioning, and refrigeration engineering technology; heavy equipment service engineering technology; manufacturing engineering technology; plastics engineering technology; printing management; product design engineering technology; quality engineering technology; rubber engineering technology; surveying engineering; and welding engineering technology. Associate degrees are awarded in architectural technology; automotive body; automotive service technology; building construction technology; civil engineering technology; heating, ventilation, air-conditioning, and refrigeration technology; heavy equipment technology; industrial electronics technology; manufacturing tooling technology; mechanical engineering technology; plastics technology; printing and digital graphic imaging technology; printing technology; rubber technology; surveying technology; technical drafting and tool design; and welding technology.

University College is the newest college on the Ferris State campus, starting its inaugural year fall 1996. University College provides a variety of academic and career selection services and opportunities to students enrolled in the other seven colleges. Among those housed under the University College umbrella are the Honors Program, Career Exploration program, educational and career counseling, the Collegiate Skills and Directed Studies Programs, the Academic Support Center, the Special Needs Counselor, the Structured Learning Assistance Workshops, and freshmen seminars.

Ferris State University has announced that it will merge with Kendall College of Art and Design of Grand Rapids. This merger, which will be final by the year 2000, will bring together the most prestigious art school in Michigan and Ferris State's world-class technology programs to expand academic options for students interested in a wide variety of careers.

Academic Program

Ferris is dedicated to the ideal of blending career-oriented professional training with a solid base of general education. While major programs of study provide graduates with the skills and knowledge required to enter a chosen career, general education provides graduates with the academic skills, analytic flexibility, and broad base of knowledge required for continued learning, performance, and advancement in their personal and professional lives. Ferris currently is on the semester system, and the minimum requirement for a baccalaureate degree is 120 semester hours. The average program requires between 120 and 130 semester hours. The minimum number of hours required for an associate degree is 60. The University's academic year begins in August and ends in early May.

Off-Campus Arrangements

Off-campus sites include Ferris State University–Grand Rapids; the University Center for Extended Learning, with classes in Big Rapids and Alma; the Northern Michigan Regional Center, with classes in Traverse City and Ludington; the Southeast Michigan Regional Center, with classes in Flint, Dearborn, Monroe, Clinton Township, and Lansing; and the Southwest Michigan Regional Center, with classes in Dowagiac, Niles, Jackson, and Muskegon. Selected classes are also offered over the Internet.

Academic Facilities

Ferris State's strikingly modern physical plant of 114 buildings contains numerous special-purpose classroom buildings to support its distinctive course offerings and includes only one structure predating a 1950 fire that destroyed the former buildings. The Abigail S. Timme Library is the University's information resource center, serving as the gateway to sources available through the Internet/World Wide Web. On-site, the Automated Reference Center features more than 20 CD-ROMs in a networked environment. Collections include more than 750,000 books, periodicals, documents, and other materials. The library is also designated as a patent and materials trademark depository.

Costs

For 1999–2000, tuition and fees for undergraduate Michigan residents were $2059 per semester or $4118 per year and $8726 per year for out-of-state residents. The 1999–2000 yearly room and board rate for the seven-day meal plan was $5110. Books and supplies are estimated at $800 per year. Ferris State honors the Midwest Student Exchange Program (MSEP), which allows nonresident students from Illinois, Kansas, Minnesota, Missouri, Nebraska, Indiana, Ohio, and Wisconsin to pay tuition in an amount equal to 150 percent of the resident tuition rate. Under MSEP, nonresident students from participating states pay tuition and fees of $6177 per year and $5110 for yearly room and board.

Financial Aid

Approximately 70 percent of Ferris students receive some type of financial aid through federal, state, and University programs. In 1999–2000, student financial aid included more than $43 million in scholarships, grants, loans, work-study, or a combination of these. The Free Application for Federal Student Aid (FAFSA) must be submitted by April 1 to receive priority consideration for need-based financial aid. The University also provides merit-based scholarships in recognition of superior academic performance and residence-based scholarships for students living on campus who maintain high academic grades. The Woodbridge N. Ferris Scholarship Program offers competitive awards ranging from $500 to $6000 per year to those who qualify. The Residential Life Scholarship offers $2000 per year for entering students who live in a residence hall on campus, have a 3.0 or better high school GPA, and have a minimum score of 20 on the ACT. Information and counseling are available from the Office of Scholarships and Financial Aid (telephone: 231-591-2110 or 800-940-4-AID, toll-free).

Faculty

There are 476 full-time faculty members teaching at Ferris State University. Many have earned doctorates and have come to Ferris from positions with other colleges and universities, government, and business. Most of the faculty members in technical programs offer their students practical expertise derived from working in the fields they teach.

Student Government

The Associated Student Government is the elected student governing body that represents student concerns to the University administration and Board of Trustees and works toward improvement of student life.

Admission Requirements

The Admissions Office receives and reviews all applications and credentials for admission. The University has a rolling admission policy in which applications are reviewed and decisions made on a continual basis. Diverse academic offerings and a flexible admission policy allow for the admission of most serious-minded applicants to FSU. Some programs are selective in nature and require the completion of specific courses and a minimum grade point average in high school or previous college work. High school applicants are encouraged to apply any time after the end of their junior year and are strongly advised to submit the application and all credentials during the first semester of their senior year. Applications should be completed carefully, with the $20 application fee (check or money order) attached, and returned to the high school guidance officer for processing. The high school will complete the second page and attach an official academic transcript before sending the application to Ferris. Freshmen are also required to submit their ACT test results (Ferris ACT code #1994) prior to enrollment. The ACT results are used for advising, course placement, and scholarship consideration. The application for admission should not be delayed if ACT scores are not available prior to application time.

Transfer students should apply by the beginning of the last semester or quarter at their transferring institution. Completed applications for admission, the $20 application fee, and one official academic transcript from each college or postsecondary institution previously attended must be submitted. Transfer students are required to submit ACT test results for advising and course placement, except if the student (1) has had both a college English and algebra or higher math class, (2) has completed at least 60 semester hours or 90 quarter hours of college work, or (3) has an associate degree or higher from a regionally accredited college.

Application and Information

Admission applications may be obtained from high school or college counselors or by contacting:

Admissions Office
Ferris State University
420 Oak Street, PRK 101
Big Rapids, Michigan 49307-2020
Telephone: 231-591-2100
        800-4FERRIS (toll-free)
E-mail: admissions@ferris.edu

FERRUM COLLEGE
FERRUM, VIRGINIA

The College

Ferrum College is a four-year, independent, coeducational college situated on a 700-acre wooded campus in the foothills of southcentral Virginia's Blue Ridge Mountains. Ferrum is a self-contained community; 81 percent of the student body lives on campus, and many faculty members live on or near campus and are closely involved in campus life. Ferrum also provides in-room Dell computers at no extra charge.

Founded in 1913 by the United Methodist Church, Ferrum is a comprehensive liberal arts college accredited by the Southern Association of Colleges and Schools. Ferrum's student body of about 950 (56 percent men, 44 percent women) is a diverse group; while the largest contingent comes from Virginia, twenty-five other states and more than a dozen other countries are also represented.

Ferrum's curriculum provides solid career preparation that includes rigorous academics, a strong experiential learning component, and a practical, broad-based, "real-life" emphasis. Ferrum students take what they learn in the classroom and apply it in the community through internships, volunteer opportunities, and fieldwork.

The result: a successful start to a meaningful career. Ferrum recently surveyed the graduating class of 1997 and 96 percent of the respondents reported being either employed, attending graduate school, or both.

In addition to academic facilities—including Stanley Library and the Academic Resources Center, which offers tutoring services free of charge to all students—there are three freshman and two upperclass residence halls; a popular, busy student center and dining hall; a student fitness center with basketball and racquetball courts and a Nautilus weight and fitness room; a high and low ropes leadership training course; an on-campus co-ed riding center; fine arts facilities; three student computer labs; and a comprehensive intercollegiate and intramural athletic complex.

Ferrum College students take advantage of a variety of extracurricular activities offered throughout the year. There are more than sixty student clubs and organizations, and many Ferrum students take part in the wide-ranging intramural sports program. Ferrum also has one the region's top NCAA Division III athletic programs, offering baseball, basketball, cross-country, football, golf, soccer, and tennis for men; basketball, cross-country, field hockey, lacrosse, soccer, softball, tennis, and volleyball for women; and co-ed equitation and cheerleading opportunities.

The Dell OptiPlex computers feature an Intel Pentium Processor and Windows 98. Ferrum students now have free hardware and access to the best research libraries in the world, the most up-to-date databases, and computer word processing capabilities.

Location

Ferrum's residential campus, while just a 15-minute drive from the town of Rocky Mount and only 35 miles from the city of Roanoke, provides a measure of peace that is ideal for thoughtful study and quiet introspection. Opportunities for hiking, swimming, rock climbing, mountain biking, and camping are available minutes from campus; those seeking the amenities of urban life will find an array of shops, restaurants, and cultural offerings in Roanoke. Interstate 81 and the Roanoke Regional Airport are 45 minutes to the north, while Interstates 85 and 40 and the Piedmont Triad International Airport lie 90 minutes to the south.

Majors and Degrees

Ferrum College awards the Bachelor of Arts, Bachelor of Science, and Bachelor of Social Work degrees. Students may choose from the following majors: accounting, agriculture, art, biology, business administration (emphasis areas: decision support systems, financial management, management, or marketing), chemistry, computer science, criminal justice, dramatic and theater arts, English, environmental science, fine arts, foreign languages (French, Russian, Spanish), history, information systems, international business, international studies, liberal arts (teacher education), liberal studies, mathematical science, medical technology, outdoor recreation, philosophy, physical education (emphasis areas in sports medicine and teaching/coaching), political science, preprofessional science, psychology, recreation and leisure, religion/philosophy, religious studies (Christian ministries), social studies, and social work.

Minors include agriculture, art, biology, business, chemistry, computer science, criminal justice, drama, economics, educational theater, English, environmental science, fine arts, folk studies, foreign languages (French and Spanish), history, horse science, international studies, journalism, mathematical science, music, outdoor recreation, philosophy, political science, psychology, recreation and leisure, religion, and sociology.

Students may also pursue a program in teacher education.

Academic Program

Ferrum College's comprehensive approach to higher education provides the benefits of liberal arts education with solid, practical career preparation. To graduate, students must complete 127 semester hours of academic work, meet the appropriate distribution and major/minor requirements, and achieve a cumulative grade point average of at least 2.0.

Faculty members encourage students to take advantage of the wide variety of experiential learning opportunities available. Internships are required for programs such as environmental science, agriculture, teacher education, social work, recreation and leisure, and sports medicine and strongly recommended for all others, reflecting the College's belief in the value of hands-on learning. Ferrum students can also do volunteer work, join student government and/or the residence life staff, or work on campus in jobs ranging from student trainers to ropes course facilitators to public relations interns.

The College's innovative teacher education program is a single multisemester course designed to encourage participants to develop a personal philosophy of education. Students receive more than 500 hours of teacher training over the course of the program and can become certified at the elementary, middle school, and/or secondary levels.

Ferrum operates on a two-semester academic calendar.

Off-Campus Arrangements

Through a number of cooperative programs, Ferrum students can study abroad in a range of countries, including England, France, and Russia.

Academic Facilities

Ferrum's Stanley Library, which was renovated and expanded in 1995, contains approximately 109,000 volumes and maintains subscriptions to 581 periodicals as well as more than 7,500 online journals, all of which are easily accessible through a computerized card catalog system. The library offers direct Internet access. Other campus facilities include Garber Hall, which has a science annex (housing a greenhouse, classroom, and laboratory space); a performing arts center; a chapel; and the Grousbeck Music Center. Direct access to the Internet and e-mail is available to all students, and a multiyear plan to network campus buildings and residence halls is complete.

Costs

The 1999–2000 comprehensive annual fee for resident students was $15,990, which included tuition, room, board, student activities fees, laboratory fees, and medical fees. The comprehensive annual fee for commuting students was $10,990 and included tuition, student activities fees, laboratory fees, and medical fees. There is no added cost to out-of-state students.

Financial Aid

In 1999–2000, 95 percent of Ferrum students were offered some form of financial assistance. For the 81 percent of students receiving need-based aid, the average financial aid package totaled $10,975, or 69 percent of total costs for the year. Ferrum makes every effort to provide financial assistance consistent with the ability of students and their families to meet college expenses. A comprehensive assistance program includes campus jobs, scholarships, grants, and loans. A typical package consists of 60 percent scholarships and grants, 34 percent low-interest loans, and 6 percent campus-based jobs.

Ferrum College is one of a small group of colleges nationwide that offers a unique financial aid opportunity known as the Bonner Scholars Program, which gives qualified students a chance to receive scholarship funds and to become involved in various service projects.

The Free Application for Federal Student Aid (FAFSA) and forms concerning grants and scholarships are sent to all applicants and should be completed and submitted no later than April 1 for priority consideration. Virginia residents are eligible for grants under the Tuition Assistance Grant (TAG) Program, and out-of-state students receive a comparable TAG offered by the College.

Faculty

There are 67 full-time teaching faculty members, most of whom hold doctorates or terminal degrees in their fields. Faculty members are dedicated to providing students with in-depth, one-on-one assistance, and frequently involve students in their own research projects. Ferrum's "total community" concept makes close relationships between students and teachers possible. The student-faculty ratio is 13:1.

Student Government

The Student Government Association (SGA) enables students to assume a measure of responsibility in the organization of campus life. Through the SGA, students implement their own activity programs, enforce regulations governing student life, and assist in the development of College policy. Students are actively involved in the workings of the Honor Board, which deals with academic violations, and the Campus Judicial System, which has jurisdiction over nonacademic violations on campus.

Admission Requirements

Students who wish to apply for admission are encouraged to call, write, e-mail, or visit Ferrum College. The staff of the Admissions Office, which is open Monday through Friday, 8 a.m. to 5 p.m., and on Saturday from 9 a.m. to noon, welcomes the opportunity to talk and/or meet with applicants. Personal interviews are recommended and may be required for some students. Appointments for conferences and tours of the campus may be arranged by contacting the Admissions Office. The applicant's complete high school record is the most important factor considered by the Admissions Committee, and class rank, grades, courses completed, and test scores are evaluated. The College requires that each applicant for admission as a full-time student take either the SAT I or the ACT. The test should be taken either late in the junior year or early in the senior year, and the student should request that the results be sent to Ferrum College.

Application and Information

Applicants should submit a completed application (available on request from the Admissions Office), a high school transcript (and a college transcript, if applicable), and scores from the SAT I or ACT.

Further information may be obtained by contacting:

Director of Admissions
Spilman House
Ferrum College
Ferrum, Virginia 24088-9000
Telephone: 800-868-9797 (toll-free)
 540-365-4614 (TDD)
E-mail: admissions@ferrum.edu
World Wide Web: http://www.ferrum.edu

Schoolfield Hall, Ferrum College's performing arts center, is reflected in the water of Adams Lake in the center of Ferrum's campus.

FINLANDIA UNIVERSITY
HANCOCK, MICHIGAN

The University

Founded in 1896, Finlandia University brought hope of a new future to many of the Finnish immigrant mine workers in the Upper Peninsula. These immigrants brought with them a heritage of learning with good character, a tradition of literacy, and a love for freedom and faith. Finlandia University still thrives on these principles.

Finlandia, formerly Suomi College, has been a college of the Lutheran church since its inception. In 1988, the College became affiliated with the Evangelical Lutheran Church in America. The curriculum, campus events, and the community explore the value of faith, vocation, and service. The North Central Association of Colleges and Schools, the Michigan Commission on College Accreditation, and the Michigan Department of Public Instruction accredit the University.

Serving more than 390 students from eight states and four countries, Finlandia University celebrates the diversity of its student body through education and experience with others. Twelve percent of Finlandia University students are members of minority students and 6 percent are international. Approximately one-third of all students live in the coed residence hall.

Students also enjoy the benefits of the Paavo Nurmi Athletic Center, including the fitness center, swimming pool, full-size gymnasium, and bowling alley. Many students participate in intramural sports, campus clubs, and student senate activities. The campus chaplain holds chapel services twice a week, while artists, scholars, and performers present topics of interest during the Campus Enrichment Hour twice each month. Special academic programs include learning disabilities and the English Language Institute (ELI).

In addition, Finlandia's new chapel will provide an enhanced spiritual atmosphere. The new intercollegiate athletic program consists of men's and women's basketball, men's and women's cross-country running, men's ice hockey, and women's volleyball.

Location

Finlandia University's campus is located in Hancock, Michigan. The University is 2 hours west of Marquette, Michigan; 4 hours north of Green Bay, Wisconsin; 6 hours northeast of Minneapolis, Minnesota; and 8 hours north of Chicago, Illinois. The Houghton County Memorial Airport is 5 miles north of the campus, and Mont Ripley, the area ski hill, is about a mile from the campus. Nestled on a hill across the Portage Lake from Houghton, Michigan, the campus offers an incredible view. Fall colors, winter snowfalls, and spring flowers guarantee a dynamic panorama year-round. Hancock and Houghton also offer students social opportunities for shopping, theater, and dining, all in the natural setting of the Copper Country.

At the turn of the century, the Keweenaw Peninsula was the single greatest supplier of copper in the world. Old mine shafts act as a living history of the industry and civilization of the area. The area id rich in Finnish culture; one can still order Pannakuken (Finnish pancakes) for breakfast at the Kaleva Café or listen to a Kantele concert (Finnish string instrument) performed in the Finnish American Heritage Center Theater.

The rugged terrain of the Keweenaw Peninsula extends into Lake Superior, making it great for outdoor activities such as hiking, swimming, canoeing, and camping. From the top of Brockway Mountain to the shores of Lake Superior–on both sides of the peninsula–waterfalls, streams, and wildlife make viewing the area a spectacle. The winter season is also very active, as students enjoy ice-skating, snowmobiling, hockey, and both downhill and cross-country skiing.

Majors and Degrees

Finlandia University offers the Bachelor of Arts degree in elementary education (seeking accreditation for fall 2001); liberal studies and general studies with concentrations in environmental science, Finnish studies, history, international studies, literature, music, philosophy, psychology, religion, and sociology; and rural human services; the Bachelor of Business Administration degree in accounting, criminal justice, entrepreneurial studies, international business and small-business management; and the Bachelor of Fine Arts degree in ceramic design, fiber design, product design, studio arts, and visual communication design.

Finlandia University also awards the Associate in Applied Science degree in criminal justice, nursing, and physical therapist assistant studies; the Associate in Arts in pre-education; and the Associate in General Studies degree.

Academic Program

Graduates of Finlandia University are prepared for professional careers requiring academic competence, responsible citizenship, and service to others. The entire campus participates in the learning process in a community dedicated to excellence in teaching and service. The University offers two academic semesters per year, with two shorter sessions in the summer. All programs at Finlandia University require completion of a liberal arts core curriculum, including courses in English, humanities, mathematics, natural sciences, physical education, and social sciences.

All baccalaureate degrees require completion of at least 120 credits (at least 60 credit hours must be earned at the University) with a cumulative grade point average of at least 2.0 and completion of a program approved by the University. All associate degrees require completion of at least 60 credits (at least 30 credit hours must be earned at the University) with a cumulative grade point average of 2.0, and completion of a program approved by the college. Students may earn college credit through Advanced Placement, College-Level Examination Program, the Institutional Challenge Examination, or experiential learning.

Off-Campus Arrangements

All students enrolled in a baccalaureate degree program are required to complete practicum or internship experiences as part of their educational experience. Students in the art and design and business administration programs are encouraged to consider completing this requirement at a location overseas, such as Suomi's sister college, the Kuopio Academy of Craft and Design in Finland. Students in the rural human services, nursing, and physical therapist assistant studies programs typically find clinical placements in community or regional health-care agencies.

Academic Facilities

The newly renovated Sulo Aileen Maki Library houses more than 30,000 books, 350 journal titles, and 15,000 audiovisual materials and provides Internet access to several educational research Web servers. The Art Design Center is home to a ceramics lab, a woodworking shop, and studio arts, fiber, and graphic design areas, as well as studios for individual student work. Nursing and physical therapist assistant studies clinical labs are located on campus, along with biology and chemistry lab facilities. The nursing labs are also conducted in area hospitals. Two computer labs are available for student use. The Finnish American Heritage Center hosts visual and performing arts exhibitions as well as theater and music productions.

Costs

Full-time tuition and general fee charges for the 2000–01 academic year are $5850 per semester; part-time tuition and general fee charges are $390 per credit hour. Room and board charges are $2170 per semester. Approximately $1000 should be allowed for other costs, such as books, supplies, the application fee, and personal expenses. Additional fees include $250 for art and design students and $100 for nursing and physical therapist assistant studies students per semester.

Financial Aid

Finlandia University offers competitive merit-based scholarships as well as substantive need-based grants for new and transfer students. Qualified international students are eligible for a limited number of scholarships. More than 97 percent of students who attend Finlandia University receive some form of financial aid. Entrance Scholarships ($2000 to $5000) are renewable each year, while Campus Housing Scholarships ($1000 to $2000) and Endowed Scholarships ($300 to $5000) are awarded for one year only. Institutional grants are also renewable pending financial need.

Finlandia University students are eligible for the Federal Pell Grant, the Federal Supplemental Educational Opportunity Grant, and the Federal Work-Study Program as well as the Stafford, PLUS, and Perkins loan programs. State residents are also eligible for the Michigan Tuition Grant, the Michigan Competitive Scholarship, the Michigan Merit Award and State Work-Study Programs. The priority date for full financial aid consideration is May 1; however, Michigan residents have a priority date of February 21 for full Michigan Tuition Grant consideration.

Faculty

The 31 full-time and 9 part-time faculty members at Finlandia University hold degrees from more than twenty-five different universities; 79 percent hold earned advanced degrees. Faculty members typically also have extensive practical experience in their field, making them knowledgeable about theory and application in the workplace. The faculty focuses more on teaching and service than on research and publication. The faculty at Finlandia University believes that active participation is an essential component in the learning process. Small class sizes (most between 8 and 12 students) enhance the meaningful exchange of ideas and stimulate thought-provoking discussions.

There are no graduate assistants at Finlandia University, and, with a 11:1 student-faculty ratio, professors are available to work individually with each student. Every student is assigned a faculty adviser to assist in course selection, academic progress, and career placement. Whether during an experiment in the biology lab or over lunch in the cafeteria, faculty members express their commitment to helping students on a daily basis.

Student Government

The student senate of Finlandia University plays a vital role in the development of the campus community. The elected members of the student senate respond to requests and concerns submitted by the student body and promote academic, spiritual, social, cultural, and recreational activities.

Admission Requirements

Finlandia University seeks applications from students who have strong academic credentials and a variety of extracurricular experiences and abilities. The University's desire is to see students excel in their program of study as they contribute to the diversity and personal growth of the student body. Although regular admission decisions are based mostly on the cumulative high school grade point average and the ACT or SAT I scores, all information provided on the application for admission is considered. Students applying to Finlandia University should submit an application for admission, the $20 application fee, and official transcripts from all high schools and colleges attended.

Students applying to the nursing program are required to have completed high school courses in algebra and chemistry with a grade of at least a B. In addition, students must present a cumulative high school GPA of at least 3.0. Students applying to the physical therapist assistant studies program are required to have completed one year of high school algebra and biology with a grade of at least a B as well as one course that incorporates the use of computers. Students must also present a cumulative high school GPA of at least 3.0.

Application and Information

Admission decisions are made on a rolling basis; however, the priority date for full financial aid consideration is May 1. The application deadline for the nursing and physical therapist assistant studies programs is March 1. Once all required materials are received, admission decisions are made within five working days.

All inquiries should be made to:

Office of Admissions
Finlandia University
601 Quincy Street
Hancock, Michigan 49930-1882
Telephone: 906-487-7274
          877-202-5491 (toll-free)
Fax: 906-487-7383
E-mail: admissions@finlandia.edu
World Wide Web: http://www.finlandia.edu

FISHER COLLEGE
BOSTON, MASSACHUSETTS

The College

Fisher College, a private college for men and women, was founded in 1903 and has been a leader in preparing students for challenging careers. Currently, 600 students come from all parts of the United States and twelve different countries. The student body is composed of 210 men and 390 women. Five percent are part-time, 95 percent are full-time, 60 percent are state residents, and 60 percent live on campus. Nine percent of the students are international, 4 percent are 25 or older, 11 percent are Hispanic, 18 percent are black, and 5 percent are Asian or Pacific Islander. Ninety percent of all students enter Fisher immediately after high school. Ninety-eight percent of all students find jobs upon graduation.

The Student Activities Office is the focal point of campus life and offers a full range of extracurricular activities, including the yearbook, the Volunteer Community Service Club, a fashion show, the Performing Arts Club, Phi Theta Kappa, the Women's Issue Support Group, and the Multi Cultural Club.

Fisher College offers intercollegiate men and women's basketball, golf, and cross-country. Men's soccer and baseball and women's softball and volleyball are also available.

Fisher College is accredited by the New England Association of Schools and Colleges.

Location

Fisher is a small college in a world-class city. Boston is the student capital of the Northeast—there are countless schools and colleges in Boston, drawing sustenance from one another. Boston is a place where numerous educational, cultural, and social opportunities can be found. A particular attraction for Fisher students is the College's proximity to the many points of interest for which Boston is famous. Some of the country's finest facilities for drama, art, and music are within walking distance of the College. The College's classroom buildings and dormitories overlook the Charles River and its beautiful esplanade. Students can explore "Beantown" itself. They can hike the Freedom Trail to Old North Church and wander through the Boston Museum of Fine Arts. They can browse the designer shops along Newbury Street, enjoy a bowl of chowder at Quincy Market, experience the thrill of Harvard Square, or get acquainted with Boston by attending a Red Sox game with their roommates or a mixer with other students from colleges all over the city. Fisher College is located on Beacon Street in the Back Bay, one of the most exclusive and historic parts of the city. Beacon Street is bustling, and Fisher College occupies one of its elegant brownstones.

Excellent transportation facilities link the College to the center of Boston and the surrounding communities. Interstate bus terminals are within walking distance, and Boston's Logan International Airport is only 15 minutes away by taxi. Fisher's accessibility is a great convenience for students living outside New England.

Majors and Degrees

Fisher College awards a Bachelor of Science degree in management. Fisher also offers associate degree programs in administrative assistant studies, with executive, international, legal, mass communication, and medical concentrations; business administration, with an accounting concentration; computer technology; early childhood education; fashion merchandising, with a fashion design concentration; liberal arts, with humanities, social science with a justice studies option, and women's studies concentrations; medical assistant studies; paralegal studies; physical therapist assistant studies; and travel hospitality management. Certificate programs are also available.

Academic Program

Fisher College offers a core interdisciplinary program. In 1999–2000, 310 courses were offered. To earn a bachelor's degree, students must complete 121 credits. A faculty adviser is assigned to each student with the selection of courses.

Fisher College offers an Academic Support Center that is staffed by a learning skills specialist and Fisher faculty members. It provides a supportive environment where students may receive assistance in reading, writing, and test-taking skills and strategies as well as content tutoring in specific areas. Fisher also offers an English as a second language program during the academic year and summer.

Fisher College is the first in the country to include an international trip as part of its educational process. Euroweek takes second-year students to a new destination each year for one week of international adventure. Students traveled to Rome, Italy, in 1999 and will travel to Athens, Greece, in 2000.

Fisher College's location offers students a wide range of internship choices. Some internship locations include Walt Disney World, Boston Children's Hospital, the Park Plaza Hotel, and Saks Fifth Avenue.

Fisher College's Placement Office offers students a full range of professional services designed to help guide students along the path to a successful career. With a 98 percent effective placement rate and lifetime assistance, the Placement Office is an invaluable resource.

Academic Facilities

The Fisher College Library contains more than 30,000 volumes and 450 periodicals as well as a comprehensive supply of audiovisual materials. The library also provides students with Internet access. Students also use the Boston Public Library, located only a few blocks from the College.

Costs

In 1999–2000, tuition for full-time students was $12,800. The annual room and board charge was $7000. There was a comprehensive fee of $1100. The total annual expense for resident students, including fees, was $20,900. The total annual expense for resident students, including fees, was $20,900. The total annual expense for commuting students, including fees, was $13,900.

Financial Aid

A high percentage of students at Fisher receive some forms of financial aid. These include the Fisher Trustee Scholarship, Fisher Honor Scholarship, Federal Pell Grants, Federal Perkins Loans, Federal Stafford Student Loans, the Federal Work-Study Program, Fisher Dean Scholarship, and Fisher Urban Scholarship. All students who wish to apply for aid must submit the Free Application for Federal Student Aid (FAFSA).

Faculty

The faculty at Fisher is aware of and sensitive to students' needs and aspirations. Faculty members are chosen for their academic qualifications and experience. Students find that the faculty is involved in promoting the progress and success of each student. The student-faculty ratio is approximately 20:1, and faculty members and course advisers counsel students both during posted office hours and informally throughout the day. There are 60 faculty members (25 full-time, 30 percent with terminal degrees).

Admission Requirements

The admissions process at Fisher may be best described as individualized. The College advocates an admission policy that accentuates positive attributes in a student's record. Applicants are evaluated objectively on the basis of their performance in secondary school and their supporting credentials. They are evaluated subjectively on the basis of their character and motivation to attend college. Applicants who have successfully completed the General Educational Development test (GED) are also considered for admission if they present evidence of the potential to perform successfully in college-level courses. Scores on the SAT I are not formally required. TOEFL scores are required for international students. An interview, SAT I or ACT scores, and placement exams are required for some applicants. Recommendations and interviews are strongly recommended.

Application and Information

Fisher College operates under a rolling admission program that enables the College to take action on an application as soon as a student's credentials have been received and reviewed. To obtain an admission application form and a College catalog, prospective students should contact:

Director of Enrollment Management
Fisher College
118 Beacon Street
Boston, Massachusetts 02116
Telephone: 617-236-8818
         800-821-3050 (toll-free in-state)
         800-446-1226 (toll-free out-of-state)
Fax: 617-236-5473
E-mail: admissions@fisher.edu
World Wide Web: http://www.fisher.edu

FISK UNIVERSITY
NASHVILLE, TENNESSEE

The University
Money magazine recently listed Fisk University as the nineteenth-best bargain for the dollar among 1,011 public and private colleges and universities in America. Founded in 1866, the University is coeducational, private, and one of America's older historically black universities. It serves a national student body, with an enrollment of 820 students for academic year 1998–99. There are two residence halls for men and three for women. The focal point of the 40-acre campus and architectural symbol of the University is Jubilee Hall, the first permanent building for education of blacks in the South. The Victorian-Gothic structure is named for the internationally renowned Fisk Jubilee Singers, who continue their tradition of singing the Negro spiritual. The original Jubilee Singers toured this country and abroad in 1871. Their selflessness is the saga of Fisk.

From its earliest days, Fisk has played a leadership role in the education of African Americans. Faculty and alumni have been among America's intellectual, artistic, and civic leaders. Among them are W. E. B. DuBois, the great social critic and cofounder of the NAACP, and the distinguished artist of the Harlem Renaissance, Aaron Douglas, who taught at Fisk. In proportion to its size, Fisk continues to contribute more alumni to the ranks of scholars pursuing doctoral degrees than any other institution in the United States.

In addition to the undergraduate degrees listed below, Fisk offers the Master of Arts in biology, chemistry, physics, psychology (general or clinical), social gerontology, and sociology. Fisk also offers a master's degree in business administration in cooperation with Owen School of Management at Vanderbilt University, as well as an early admission program with Meharry Medical College.

The mission of the University is to prepare students to be skilled, resourceful, and imaginative leaders who will address effectively the challenges of life in a technological society, a pluralistic nation, and a multicultural world.

Location
The campus is located 1.9 miles north of downtown Nashville, the capital of Tennessee. Known as the Athens of the South for its academic and artistic attributes and Music City for its music and recording industry, the city has become a mecca for students and tourists. The twenty-third-largest metropolitan area in the United States, Nashville is an easy drive from several major cities.

Majors and Degrees
At the undergraduate level, the Bachelor of Arts, Bachelor of Science, and Bachelor of Music are offered. Academic majors for the B.A. degree include biology, chemistry, dramatics and speech, English, French, history, mathematics, music, physics, political science, psychology, religious and philosophical studies, sociology, and Spanish. B.S. degrees are offered in accounting, art, chemistry, computer science, economics, elementary education, finance, international business relations, management, and music education. The B.Mus. degree in performance is for the student who plans to pursue graduate or additional studies leading to a career in performance as a teacher or as a professional singer or instrumentalist.

Academic Program
The academic year comprises two semesters. All undergraduates are required to complete the core curriculum, which provides a common intellectual background for all students. Its purposes include developing a level of skill in written and oral communication and in quantitative thinking that is appropriate to support a lifelong program of study in the liberal arts. Requirements for graduation vary by program but are approximately 120 credit hours.

Fisk is accredited by the Southern Association of Colleges and Schools.

Off-Campus Arrangements
The following programs are offered with neighboring institutions: Fisk—Meharry Medical College Joint Program in Biomedical Sciences; Nursing and Medical Technology—Rush Medical Center in Chicago; Engineering—Vanderbilt, University of Alabama in Huntsville, and Florida Agricultural and Mechanical University; and Pharmacy—Howard University in Washington, D.C.

Academic Facilities
The University campus is designated as a historic district, and eight buildings are on the National Register of Historic Places. One of the more modern and functional facilities in the area, the University Library houses almost 200,000 volumes and includes the Aaron Douglas Gallery of African American Art, one of the foremost collections in America. The Carnegie Building houses faculty offices, computer laboratory facilities, and various administrative offices. The campus radio station, WFSK-FM, is housed in DuBois Hall. Talley-Brady Hall houses the chemistry and physics departments. It includes seven student laboratories and nine smaller research laboratories, as well as classrooms, a lecture hall, and faculty offices. The Carl Van Vechten Gallery houses the nationally famous Stieglitz Collection, one of the more important collections of modern art in this country, which includes original works by Cézanne, Picasso, Renoir, and others. Among other campus buildings are the Little Theatre, Fisk Memorial Chapel, and Park-Johnson, an academic building. In sum, the Fisk campus is a fine mixture of historic and modern facilities.

Costs
Tuition for 2000–01 is $8740; room is $2920, and board is $2110. Fees are $300, and new students are assessed a matriculation and room reservation fee of $125. Costs are subject to change. The cost of books is estimated at $400 per semester.

Financial Aid
Student financial aid is based on the principle that all qualified and motivated students who earnestly seek an education should be able to attend college, regardless of the economic status of the student's family. Aid is awarded on an individual basis, and the amount to be offered is determined by an examination of the family's financial position. Assistance is offered to the student from grants, loans, or work, or from a combination of funds. Eligibility requirements vary depending on the financial aid source. Applicants are urged to complete financial aid forms by April 20 to receive consideration while funds are available.

Faculty

A student-faculty ratio of 14:1 allows for individualized instruction and small classes. More than 60 percent of the faculty hold the doctorate or an equivalent degree.

Student Government

The University is proud of its democratic traditions and communications, even to the extent of having a student representative on the Board of Trustees.

Admission Requirements

Admission to Fisk is, and traditionally has been, selective. Today's entering students are typically ranked in the top fifth of their high school class; almost all rank in the top half. Some students, however, may be admitted to Fisk despite gaps in their previous educational background or record if the University judges them to show strong promise in other ways. Fisk's enrollment has been growing in recent years, though the University remains deliberately small and cultivates a family feeling on its campus.

The University seeks students who will benefit from and contribute to a University community that offers a liberal arts program and seeks to equip students for intellectual and social leadership in the modern world. Admission is granted to those applicants who show evidence of adequate preparation and ability to pursue college studies successfully at Fisk. The admission staff, in recommending candidates to the director of admissions, considers rank in class, high school grades, the quality of the high school, type of high school program, personal record, assessment and subject test scores, the student's written personal statement, and any demonstrated talent or achievement showing leadership ability and the probability of success in college. Also considered, when available, is information on the applicant's personality, character, and (where relevant to the student's prospects for successful performance) health. Fisk actively discourages applications from students who do not meet the basic qualifications for admission.

To qualify for admission to the freshman class, candidates should present the following credentials: graduation, by date of matriculation at Fisk, from an accredited secondary school with a scholastic record sufficient to predict success at Fisk; strong endorsements from the high school principal, headmaster, counselor, or teacher, with regard to the applicant's academic ability, motivation, character, citizenship, and leadership qualities; and a minimum of 15 acceptable units of high school credit properly distributed in the curriculum. Although applicants with a variety of patterns of study in high school are considered for admission, the following high school preparation is generally recommended: 4 years of English, including ninth grade; 1 year each of algebra and geometry; 1 year of foreign language; 1 year of history; 1 year of laboratory science; and at least 6 units (6 full-year courses or the equivalent) of elective studies. High school electives should be in fields related to college work, such as English, dramatics, mathematics, the natural sciences, history, the social sciences, and foreign language.

In addition, the following are special recommendations for high school preparation appropriate to applicants expecting to major in selected disciplines at Fisk: mathematics and natural science majors should have chemistry and biology, and if possible also physics, while in high school; music majors should have several years of previous study in musical performance, preferably piano, and should have participated in a variety of musical activities. A statement of musical experience, lists of musical compositions recently studied and of those performed publicly, and the names of recent teachers should accompany the application for admission. During freshman orientation week, tests of musical aptitude, ability, and general musicianship are administered.

Prior to full admission to the freshman class, the University also requires candidates to present results of a recent health examination.

Application and Information

Applications are processed on a rolling basis; that is, the application is acted upon when the file is complete.

For an early decision, applications should be filed prior to November 15; students are notified by January 17. Early decision applicants must then notify the University of their decision by January 30.

For further information, students should contact:

Director of Admissions
Fisk University
Nashville, Tennessee 37208-3051
Telephone: 615-329-8665
        800-443-5475 (toll-free)

FITCHBURG STATE COLLEGE
FITCHBURG, MASSACHUSETTS

The College

Fitchburg State College, the Leadership College, is a liberal arts institution where career-oriented and professional education programs thrive. Under the leadership of its president, Dr. Michael Riccards, Fitchburg State has undertaken a number of major initiatives. The College now offers a three-year baccalaureate program, more internship opportunities, a substantially increased Merit Scholarship program, and a guarantee that its graduates will be qualified for jobs in their fields. The College is investing in new technologies in every curriculum to assure that Fitchburg State continues to place more than 85 percent of its graduates in their chosen professions.

Fitchburg State's excellent academic reputation and graduate placement can be attributed to a nationally recognized faculty and a commitment to teaching that is unparalleled in Massachusetts. The College serves 3,000 students in its day division and another 4,000 students in its evening and graduate programs. The average class size is 25, and the overall student-teacher ratio remains low at 15:1. Each student is assigned to an academic adviser to assist with the planning of a program of study. In addition, each department has access to state-of-the-art equipment and an internship network that spreads throughout New England.

Student life at Fitchburg State is friendly and informal. There are numerous and varied opportunities for student leadership through the Student Government Association, the Athletic Council, the All-College Committee, the Campus Center Advisory Committee, the Residence Hall Councils, publications, and student-faculty-administration committees. Three student publications offer creative opportunities—the *Point*, a weekly newspaper; the *Scrimshaw*, a literary magazine; and the *Saxifrage*, the College yearbook. A number of special interest clubs are open to all students. Several sororities and fraternities contribute to the social and recreational life of the campus. Hundreds of popular and well-attended activities take place during the year, including films, lectures, concerts, seminars, coffeehouses, pub entertainment, recreational tournaments, performing arts series, and visual arts exhibits.

In addition to the bachelor's degrees listed below, Fitchburg State confers the Master of Arts in Teaching (M.A.T.), the Master in Business Administration (M.B.A.), the Master of Education (M.Ed.) in several disciplines, and the Master of Science (M.S.) in communications media, computer science, counseling, and management. Several Certificate of Advanced Graduate Studies (C.A.G.S.) programs are available as well.

Location

The College is located in a residential area near the center of Fitchburg, a city with a population of 43,000, which serves as the hub of the commercial and industrial life of north-central Massachusetts. The Wallace Civic Center and Planetarium, located within walking distance of the College, provides a variety of activities, such as exhibits, fairs, performances, ice-skating, hockey, light shows, astronomy demonstrations, and lectures. Fitchburg offers many opportunities for study and practical experience in the areas of sociology, psychology, health, computer technology, business, industry, political organization, and community service. Outdoor activities, including skiing, camping, hiking, canoeing, and fishing, are just minutes away from campus.

The historic and literary centers of Lexington and Concord and the widely varied cultural advantages of Boston are approximately an hour's travel from the College. Worcester is a half hour to the south. Both train service and bus service are available.

Majors and Degrees

Fitchburg State College confers the Bachelor of Arts and the Bachelor of Science degrees. Undergraduate majors are offered in biology, business administration, communications/media, computer information systems, computer science, criminal justice, early childhood education, economics, elementary education, English, geography, history, human services, industrial technology, mathematics, medical technology, middle school education, nursing, political science, psychology, sociology, special education, and technology education/industrial arts.

Academic Program

The College operates on a two-semester basis. The first semester begins in early September and ends in mid-December, and the second semester begins in mid-January and ends in mid-May.

The curriculum has a strong liberal arts and sciences requirement, providing a strong foundation for either further academic study or a career. Students may obtain practical experience through volunteer placement in social agencies, government offices, and businesses related to their interests. Some major programs require an extensive supervised practicum to complete degree requirements. For education majors, a broad spectrum of student-teaching experiences is available. The four-year honors program, for students with excellent high school records, culminates in a senior thesis or project.

Off-Campus Arrangements

Fitchburg State is one of nine state colleges under the jurisdiction of the Massachusetts Board of Higher Education. Through this affiliation, students may participate in the College Academic Program Sharing program, which allows study for a semester or a year at another college. The College also participates in a regional compact under the auspices of the New England Board of Higher Education, which enables Fitchburg students to attend certain programs in other states at in-state tuition rates.

A junior-year-abroad program is available in conjunction with universities in France, Poland, Russia, Scotland, and Spain.

Academic Facilities

The College has a number of special facilities. An unusually well-equipped Academic Skills Center is part of the College library in the Hammond Building. The McKay Campus School Teacher Education Center is specifically designed for observing pupil development and instructional techniques. An Instructional Media Center is located in the Conlon Building. Modern, well-equipped shops support the industrial education and industrial technology programs. Two lecture halls, one in each of the College's newest academic buildings, are equipped for multimedia presentations.

Costs

Tuition for residents of Massachusetts was $1090 per year in 1999–2000; nonresidents paid $7050. Residence hall and meal plan fees have not been set. Required fees, including the student activity fee, Campus Center fee, and athletic fee, totaled $1976. Books and supplies were estimated at $750, depending on the student's major. Fees are subject to change.

Financial Aid

Many sources of financial aid are available to Fitchburg State students. The College participates in federal and state programs, including the Federal Direct Student Loan Program. Packages consisting of grants, loans, work-study awards, and scholarships are given to students demonstrating financial need. Financial aid applications for the fall semester must be completed by the preceding March 15 to be given priority consideration.

Faculty

The full-time Fitchburg State faculty numbers 240 men and women, more than 65 percent of whom hold earned doctoral degrees. Full professors teach freshman sections as well as advanced courses.

Student Government

All full-time undergraduate students are members of the Student Government Association (SGA). The purposes of the SGA are to encourage responsibility and cooperation in democratic self-government; to form an official body for expressing the judgments of students and fostering activities and matters of general student interest; and to promote full understanding and cooperation among the students, the faculty members, and the administration in order to further the welfare of the College.

The governing body of the SGA consists of 6 SGA officers and a General Council, which includes these officers and 28 elected representatives of classes and residence halls, as well as the commuter student body. The SGA operates through a number of standing and ad hoc committees, membership on which is open to all students.

An 11-member All-College Committee, representing students, the faculty, and the administration, makes recommendations to the president of the College concerning matters of campuswide policy.

Admission Requirements

The College seeks to admit, without regard to race, religion, or ethnic background, students who are capable of success. To this end, significant attention is given to the student's high school record and SAT I scores. The record of achievement in high school is the single most important item in the applicant's academic credentials. Freshman applicants should have completed a college-preparatory program that includes 4 units in English, 2 units in a foreign language, 2 units in social studies, 3 units in mathematics, and 3 units in the natural sciences.

An essay is required. Interviews are not required but are recommended. Applicants who have questions about the programs and procedures at the College or about matters of housing and financial aid are encouraged to request an interview through the Admissions Office.

Transfer students are welcome to apply to Fitchburg. A transcript from each college previously attended must be submitted.

International students are encouraged to apply; applications should be completed at least nine months before the desired date of enrollment. Scores on the Test of English as a Foreign Language (TOEFL) must be submitted.

Application and Information

Acceptance of qualified applicants begins in January and proceeds on a rolling basis until all available spaces are taken. Students should apply by April 1 for the fall semester and by December 1 for the spring semester.

For further information, students should contact:

Director of Admissions
Fitchburg State College
Fitchburg, Massachusetts 01420
Telephone: 978-665-3144
Fax: 978-665-4540
E-mail: admissions@fsc.edu
World Wide Web: http://www.fsc.edu

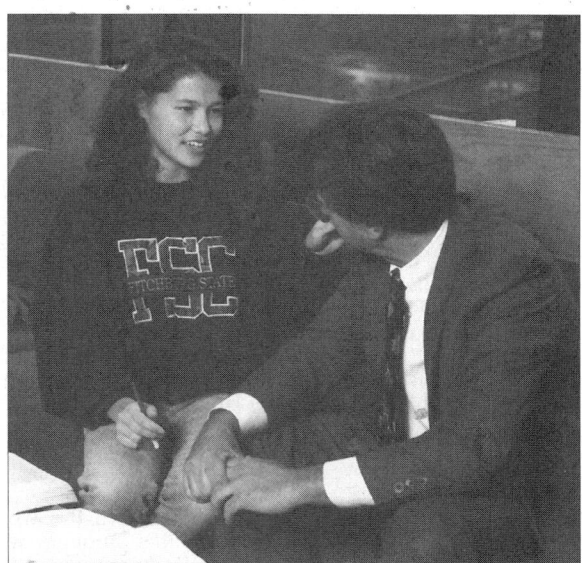

One of the hallmarks of education at Fitchburg State College is close student-faculty member interaction.

FIVE TOWNS COLLEGE
DIX HILLS, NEW YORK

The College

Nestled in the rolling hills of Long Island's North Shore, Five Towns College offers students the opportunity to study in a suburban environment that is close to New York City. Founded in 1972 by a group of educators and community leaders, Five Towns College is an independent, nonsectarian, coeducational institution that places its emphasis on the student as an individual. Many students are drawn to the College because of its strong reputation in music, media, and the performing arts. The College offers associate, bachelor's, and master's degrees. The College also offers programs leading to the Master of Music (M.M.) degree in jazz/commercial music and in music education.

From as far away as England and Japan and from as close as Long Island and New York City, the 750 full-time students reflect a rich cultural diversity. The College's enrollment is 64 percent men and 36 percent women, with a minority population of approximately 27 percent. The College's music programs are contemporary in nature, although classical musicians are also part of this creative community. The most popular programs are audio recording technology, music performance, music business, teacher education, theater, and film/video production.

Coeducational living accommodations are available just a short distance from the Five Towns College campus at the State University of New York at Farmingdale. Students reside in a modern dormitory, with SUNY student privileges. A regularly scheduled shuttle bus connects both campuses. Five Towns College has announced plans to construct residential facilities on campus. A construction time schedule will be posted on the College's Web site once it becomes available.

The College's Athletic Center is home to the Five Towns College "Sound." The Soundmen and Soundwomen play intercollegiate sports as members of the National Association of Intercollegiate Athletics (NAIA). The Athletic Center includes facilities for basketball and volleyball, a dance studio, and locker and equipment rooms. The College offers the following intercollegiate sports: men's basketball, cross-country, and soccer and women's basketball, cross-country, and volleyball. The following intramural sports are also offered: basketball, flag football, soccer, and volleyball. A growing number of students are interested in lacrosse.

Location

The College's serene 40-acre campus, located in the wooded countryside of Dix Hills, New York, provides students with a parklike refuge where they can pursue their studies. Just off campus is Long Island's bustling Route 110 corridor, the home of numerous national and multinational corporations. New York City, with everything from Lincoln Center to Broadway, is just a train ride away and provides students with some of the best cultural advantages in the world.

Closer to campus, the many communities of Long Island abound with cultural and recreational opportunities. The College is located within the historic town of Huntington, which is home to the Cinema Arts Center, InterMedia Arts Center, Hecksher Museum, Vanderbilt Museum, numerous restaurants, coffeehouses, and quaint shops. The nearby shores of Jones Beach State Park and the Fire Island National Seashore are world renowned for their white, sandy beaches.

Majors and Degrees

The College offers the Associate in Arts (A.A.) degree in liberal arts, with concentrations in communications arts, literature, and theater arts; the Associate in Science (A.S.) degree in business administration, with a concentration in telecommunications; the Associate in Applied Science (A.A.S.) degree in business management and in jazz commercial music, with concentrations in accounting, audio recording technology, broadcasting, computer business applications, marketing/retailing, and video arts; the Bachelor of Music (Mus.B.) degree in music education and in jazz/commercial music, with concentrations in audio recording technology, composition/songwriting, music business, musical theater, performance, and video music; the Bachelor of Fine Arts (B.F.A.) degree in theater, with concentrations in acting, film/video, and theater technology; and the Bachelor of Professional Studies (B.P.S.) degree in business management, with concentrations in audio recording technology, music business, and video arts.

Academic Program

The following describes some of the more popular programs at Five Towns College. For a complete description of the College's academic program, students should visit the Five Towns College Web site at the address listed below.

The music education program is designed for students interested in a career as a teacher of music in a public or private school. The undergraduate program leads to New York State provisional certification, while the graduate program leads to permanent certification. The course work provides professional training and includes a student-teaching experience. Music students are required to complete at least 40 credits, achieve a GPA of at least 3.0, and pass a piano qualifying examination before being admitted to this program. The audio recording technology concentration is designed to provide students with the tools needed to succeed as professional studio engineers and producers in the music industry. The music business concentration is designed for students interested in a career in entertainment-related business fields. The course work includes the technical, legal, production, management, and merchandising aspects of the music business. The composition/songwriting concentration provides intensive instruction in a core of technical studies in harmony, orchestration, counterpoint, MIDI, songwriting, form and analysis, arranging, and composition for those who intend to pursue careers as composers, arrangers, and songwriters. The performance concentration includes a common core of technical studies and a foundation of specialized courses, such as music history, harmony, counterpoint, improvisation, ensemble performance, and private instruction. The video music concentration includes professional training in music scoring and compositional techniques and in the artistic and technical skills required for the creation of synchronized music. The theater arts program is designed for students interested in careers as actors, entertainers, scenic designers, directors, stage managers, lighting or sound directors, filmmakers, and videographers. The film/video concentration includes extensive technical preparation in videography, filmmaking, linear and nonlinear editing, storyboarding, scriptwriting, producing, and directing.

To earn a bachelor's degree, students must accumulate between 120 and 128 credits, depending upon the program of study, with a proper distribution of courses and a GPA of at least 2.0. To earn an associate degree, students must accumulate between 60 and 64 credits.

Off-Campus Arrangements

Off-campus internship opportunities are available to Five Towns College students who have fulfilled the necessary prerequisites, including a cumulative grade point average of at least 2.5., with a 3.0 in their major. In recent semesters, students have interned for major corporations such as MTV,

Atlantic Records, Polygram Records, CBS, ABC, EMI Records, MCA Records, SONY Records, The Power Station, Pyramid Recording Studios, Channel 12 News, and many others.

Academic Facilities

Five Towns College occupies a multiwinged facility that comprises approximately 120,000 square feet and includes a 500-seat auditorium, production studios, athletic and dining facilities, classrooms, computer labs, and a student center. Four T-1 lines connect the College's completely fiber-optic computer network to the Internet. All students have access to this network and are provided with an e-mail account.

The Five Towns College Library has more than 35,000 print and nonprint materials. These include nearly 30,000 books and print items, 464 periodical subscriptions, and approximately 5,000 audiovisual materials. Through its membership in the Long Island Library Resource Council (LILRC), students have access to other libraries around the country.

The Technical Wing at Five Towns College consists of eleven studio/control rooms. These facilities house the College's state-of-the-art 48-track SSL and 24-track digital recording studios and the Electronic Music-MIDI Studio. The Film/Video Studio utilizes Beta Sp, SVHS video formats, and the 16mm film format. Nonlinear edit suites utilize the Media 100 XS and XR operating systems on Macintosh G3 and G4 platforms. Students utilize these facilities to develop their skills while creating professional quality productions, both in the studio and on location, under the supervision of industry professionals. Student productions include CDs, music videos, documentaries, sitcoms, public service announcements, commercials, and talk shows, among many others.

The Dix Hills Center for Performing Arts at Five Towns College is an acoustically "perfect" venue, with digital lighting systems, digital sound reinforcement for concert production, and a Barco 6300 digital projection system for multimedia productions. The professional stage is 60 feet wide, with a proscenium opening of 16 feet and 32 feet of fly space. Students utilize this facility to produce live concerts, plays, musicals, and other performances and special presentations.

Costs

The tuition for 2000–01 is $9900 per year. Miscellaneous fees are approximately $400, and books are about $700. Private instruction fees for performing music students are $525 per semester.

Financial Aid

The annual tuition at Five Towns College is among the lowest of all the private colleges in the region. Nevertheless, approximately 68 percent of all students receive some form of financial assistance. Need-based and/or merit-based grants, scholarships, loans, and work-study programs are available to qualified recipients, including transfer students. Prospective students are urged to contact the Financial Aid Office as early as possible.

Faculty

The College's growing faculty consists of 68 full- and part-time members. The student-faculty ratio is 14:1. While the faculty is more strongly committed to teaching than to research, many members continue to be active in their respective areas of expertise.

Student Government

The Student Council (SC) serves as the representative governance body for all students. The SC consists of an elected president and vice president and 9 elected at-large representatives who select from among themselves a secretary and a treasurer. The Student Council charters clubs and organizations, allocates student activity fees, and recommends policies that affect student life.

Admission Requirements

The College encourages applications from students who will engage themselves in its creative community and who will contribute to the academic debate with honor and integrity. Students seeking a seat in the entering class of students should have attained a minimum high school grade point average of 78 percent or a GED score of not less than 280. The SAT I or ACT exam is required for all freshmen entering the College after the spring 2001 semester. Transfer students must also submit official transcripts of all college-level work attempted. International students from non-English-speaking countries must submit a TOEFL score of at least 500 or its equivalent. Students may be admitted for deferred entrance or with advanced standing. The College does not accept students on an early admissions basis, although early decision is available. Candidates for admission must submit a completed Application for Undergraduate Admission, official high school transcripts, at least one letter of recommendation, and a personal statement. International students must submit additional information and should contact the Foreign Student Advisor.

Application and Information

Admission into any music program is contingent upon passing an audition demonstrating skill in performance on a major instrument or vocally. Music students must also take written and aural examinations in harmony, sight singing, and ear training in order to demonstrate talent, well-developed musicianship, and artistic sensibilities. Admission into any theater program is also contingent upon passing an audition. In some cases, the Admissions Committee may request an on-campus interview with an applicant. Music, theater, video arts, and film/video students are encouraged to submit a portfolio tape or reel, if available.

Except for applicants applying on an early decision basis, new students are accepting on a rolling basis, with decisions for the fall and spring semesters mailed starting January 15 and September 15, respectively. There is an application fee of $25.

For further information, students should contact:

> Director of Admissions
> Five Towns College
> 305 North Service Road
> Dix Hills, New York 11746-5871
> Telephone: 631-424-7000 Ext. 110
> Fax: 631-424-7008
> E-mail: admissions@ftc.edu
> World Wide Web: http://www.ftc.edu

The Dix Hills Center for the Performing Arts.

FLAGLER COLLEGE
ST. AUGUSTINE, FLORIDA

The College

Founded in 1968, Flagler College is an independent nonsectarian college that offers a four-year program leading to the baccalaureate degree in selected preprofessional and liberal studies. The College is coeducational, predominantly residential, and small by intent—enrollment is limited to 1,650 students. Flagler is governed by a Board of Trustees of 15 members and is accredited by the Commission on Colleges of the Southern Association of Colleges and Schools (1866 Southern Lane, Decatur, GA 30033-4097; telephone 404-679-4501), one of the six nationally recognized regional accrediting associations.

The campus is situated in the heart of historic St. Augustine, 4 miles from the Atlantic beaches. The focal point of the campus is Ponce de Leon Hall, formerly a famous resort hotel. Described as a masterpiece of American architecture, the Ponce de Leon is listed on the National Register of Historic Places. Ponce de Leon Hall contains a residence hall for 500 students, the dining hall, the student center, the infirmary, and some administrative offices. The 19-acre campus includes a men's residence hall, a technologically advanced library, and ten other buildings that are used for classrooms, faculty and administrative offices, and recreational and athletic facilities.

The College strives to develop the qualities that smallness fosters. These qualities include, but are not limited to, civility, integrity, loyalty, dependability, and affection. An atmosphere of friendliness and respect prevails throughout the College. Students come from forty-three states and twenty-two countries or territories; 62 percent of the students are from Florida. The student body is composed of traditional college-age students; most are between the ages of 18 and 22. Approximately 60 percent of the students live on campus. Students indicate that its size, location, cost, and programs of study are the major reasons for their choosing Flagler.

The College offers a wide range of extracurricular activities that are designed to enrich the student socially, culturally, and physically. Activities include working on the College newspaper or the yearbook, performing in a theatrical production, or attending College-sponsored movies, lectures, dances, or concerts throughout the year. In addition, some of the favorite pastimes of Flagler students are biking around town, walking through the restoration area, surfing at the beach, competing in a sports event or being a spectator, or just sunning by the pool. Athletics play an important role in campus life. Intercollegiate sports for men are baseball, basketball, cross-country, golf, soccer, and tennis. Intercollegiate sports for women are basketball, cross-country, golf, soccer, tennis, and volleyball. A lively intramural sports program is available for both men and women. Athletic and recreational facilities include a gymnasium, eight tennis courts, and a swimming pool. A 19-acre athletic field for baseball, soccer, softball, and intramurals is located 2 miles from the campus.

Location

St. Augustine is located on the northeast coast of Florida, about midway between Jacksonville and Daytona Beach. Famous as a tourist center, rich in history, and beautifully maintained in all its storied charm, St. Augustine provides an attractive environment for a liberal arts college. Community resources complement the programs offered by the College. Flagler is an important part of the St. Augustine community and seeks to use the educational, cultural, and recreational resources of the community to supplement and enhance the quality of life and the quality of education at the College.

Majors and Degrees

Flagler College awards the Bachelor of Arts degree in the following areas: accounting, art education, business administration, communication, deaf education, elementary education, English, fine art, graphic design, history, Latin American studies–Spanish, philosophy-religion, political science, psychology, secondary education, social sciences, Spanish, sport management, and theater arts. In addition, the College offers preprofessional programs in fashion, human services, law, and youth ministries.

Academic Program

The principal focus of the College's academic program is undergraduate education in selected liberal and preprofessional studies. The purposes of the academic program are to provide opportunities for general and specialized learning, to assist students in preparing for careers, and to aid qualified students in pursuing graduate and professional studies.

Flagler operates on a semester calendar with two 14-week semesters. The fall term is completed prior to Christmas, and the spring term ends in late April. All students must complete 36 semester hours in general education requirements, including 6 hours in English composition, 6 hours in mathematics, 3 hours in computer science, 3 hours in speech, and 18 hours in three broad areas: humanities, social sciences, and natural sciences/mathematics. The normal academic load is 15 semester hours, which generally represents five courses per term. The number of credits required for a major varies by department. Education majors are required to complete a highly prescribed course of study leading to certification in two or more areas (e.g., elementary education and specific learning disabilities). A student must complete a minimum of 120 semester hours to satisfy graduation requirements. Business administration and education are the two most popular majors at Flagler.

Advanced placement may be awarded to entering freshmen on the basis of scores earned on the tests of the College-Level Examination Program (CLEP) and/or the Advanced Placement Program (AP Program) of the College Board.

Off-Campus Arrangements

Students majoring in deaf education have the benefit of working with faculty members and students at the Florida School for the Deaf and the Blind (FSDB), the largest school of its type in the nation. The FSDB is located in St. Augustine, approximately 2 miles from the College campus. Flagler is certified by the Council on the Education of the Deaf and holds membership in the Northeast Florida Consortium for the Hearing Impaired. In addition, Flagler serves as the Southeast Regional Extension Center for Gallaudet University.

Students may study abroad for a semester, a year, or a summer in one of the established international study groups. Students majoring in Latin American studies–Spanish usually participate in a study-abroad program in Guanajuato, Mexico. Students enrolled in this program audit courses offered by the University of Guanajuato. Each student lives with a Mexican family and is counseled and assisted by a local adviser.

A joint program with the Fashion Institute of Technology in New York City is available to business administration majors. Students who participate in this program spend their junior year at the Institute and upon graduation from Flagler receive both a bachelor's degree from the College and an associate degree from the Institute. At the Institute, students may major in fashion buying and merchandising, advertising, or communications. Arrangements may be made to major in fashion design in the year at the Institute by also engaging in appropriate work in the art department at the College.

Academic Facilities

The William L. Proctor Library building has three floors. The first two floors are devoted to the library with a capacity for 125,000 volumes. At present the library houses 71,413 volumes, 62,616 microform items, 1,451 audiovisual materials, and subscriptions to 425 periodicals. Interlibrary loan service is available for items that the library does not own. Also included on these two floors are study carrels, computer catalog stations, database stations, and an Internet lab. The third floor of the Proctor Library building is devoted to computer laboratories for computer science and graphic arts courses. There is also a computer lab for students' word processing needs.

Costs

For 2000–01, costs are $6320 for tuition and fees and $3910 for room and board. While other costs may vary according to the student's lifestyle, the estimate for books, supplies, and miscellaneous expenses is about $1000 per year.

Financial Aid

Financial aid is awarded primarily on the basis of proven need, as demonstrated by the information given by the applicant on the College application for financial aid and on the Free Application for Federal Student Aid (FAFSA). Awards may consist of grants, loans, campus employment, or some combination of the three. In addition to providing institutional grants, the College participates in all federal programs. Some aid may be awarded solely on the basis of academic achievement, talent, athletic ability, leadership, or character. Approximately three fourths of the student body receives some form of aid from the College. Only those students who have applied for admission and have been accepted are considered for aid. It is recommended that all the necessary forms be submitted by March 15.

Students who have resided in Florida for at least one year are eligible to receive a tuition offset grant of approximately $2700 per year to attend a private college or university in Florida. Funds for the Florida Resident Access Grant are appropriated by the state legislature, and awards are not based on academic merit or financial need.

Faculty

Teaching is central to Flagler's mission. The College seeks to attract and retain a professionally competent faculty dedicated to the art of teaching and advising. Faculty members at Flagler are committed to high standards of performance and are concerned for the welfare of the College and its students. Faculty members are readily available and meet regularly with students outside the classroom. Many faculty members advise student clubs and organizations and take an active role in student life.

The teaching staff is composed of 59 full-time and 52 part-time faculty members. Half of the full-time faculty members hold earned doctorates. A favorable 20:1 student-faculty ratio ensures small classes, individual attention, and interaction between the faculty and students. The average class size is approximately 22 students; 93 percent of classes have 35 or fewer students.

Student Government

The Student Government Association (SGA) plays an important role in planning and implementing a varied program of campus activities at Flagler. Elected student representatives are responsible for voicing student ideas and opinions in matters of general student concern. The SGA also serves as the coordinating unit for many social, academic, and recreational activities. Members of the SGA serve on several committees of the College and participate in many community services and projects.

Admission Requirements

Flagler seeks students from diverse geographical backgrounds who can benefit from the educational experience offered by the College. Flagler welcomes applications from all qualified men and women without regard to age, sex, race, color, marital status, handicap, religion, or national or ethnic origin. Each applicant is evaluated individually, and admission is determined on the basis of the student's academic preparation, scholastic aptitude, and personal qualities. Other factors taken into consideration are the student's motivation, initiative, maturity, seriousness of purpose, and leadership potential. All admission decisions are made on a "need-blind" basis. The College offers an early decision plan.

For freshman applicants, the high school record remains the most important factor in determining admission to the College. The admission staff takes into consideration the quality of courses selected, grade point average, class rank, test scores, a recommendation from a secondary school counselor, a narrative, and participation in extracurricular activities. All freshman applicants are required to submit scores from either the SAT I or the ACT. A minimum of 16 high school units is required; at least 13 must be academic units. The College does not prescribe a particular course of study, but prospective applicants are advised to take 4 units of English, 4 units of social studies, 3 units of mathematics, 2 units of science, and 3 units of academic electives.

Transfer students who have completed at least 24 semester hours of transferable college credit are required to submit an official transcript from each institution attended. In addition, all transfer applicants are required to submit scores from either the SAT I or the ACT. Transfer students are expected to have a minimum 2.5 grade point average and may transfer up to 64 semester hours of credit from a community college. Those who have earned fewer than 24 semester hours of credit must satisfy requirements for freshman admission. In addition to fulfilling the above requirements, international students must submit scores from the TOEFL or demonstrate proficiency in the English language.

An interview is not required as part of the admission process, but many students regard on-campus interviews as valuable experiences because of the exchange of information. Arrangements for a campus visit should be made with the Admissions Office at least one week in advance.

Application and Information

Applications for admission should be submitted in the fall or the winter of the year prior to the desired term of enrollment. Applicants must arrange for transcripts and recommendations to be sent directly to the Admissions Office. The deadline for submitting an application is January 15 for early decision candidates and March 1 for all others.

Application forms and related materials should be sent to:

Director of Admissions
Flagler College
King Street
St. Augustine, Florida 32084

Telephone: 800-304-4208 Ext. 220 (toll-free)
E-mail: admiss@flagler.edu
World Wide Web: http://www.flagler.edu

Flagler students in front of Ponce de Leon Hall.

FLORIDA AGRICULTURAL AND MECHANICAL UNIVERSITY
TALLAHASSEE, FLORIDA

The University

For more than a century, the primary goals of the Florida Agricultural and Mechanical University (FAMU) have been to promote academic excellence and to improve the quality of life for those it serves. Founded in 1887 as the State Normal School for Colored Students, FAMU opened its doors with 2 instructors and 15 students. It was designated a land-grant institution in 1890 and became a university in 1953. It is a full and equal partner in the ten-member State University System. The FAMU campus, covered by lush shrubbery, flowering plants, and massive oaks, covers 419 acres. Valued at $119 million, the University campus has 111 buildings. Although historically black, the University seeks qualified students from all racial, ethnic, religious, and national backgrounds without regard to age, sex, or physical handicap. The current enrollment is 12,000 (84 percent black, 56 percent women). Graduate degrees in twenty disciplines are coordinated through the School of Graduate Studies, Research and Continuing Education.

The School of Journalism, Media and Graphic Arts publishes a weekly student newspaper and operates an FM radio station. There are more than 100 student organizations on campus, including nationally affiliated fraternities and sororities, honor societies, religious groups, fashion/modeling clubs, the Literary Guild, Orchesis Contemporary Dance Theatre, the Playmakers Guild, and the FAMU Gospel Choir, which released its first album in 1985. The Marching 100, FAMU's 300-member marching band, has received national television and magazine coverage and, in 1985, became the first band outside the Big 10 Conference to earn the Sousa Foundation's prestigious Sudler Trophy. The University, a member of the Mid-Eastern Athletic Conference (MEAC), sponsors seventeen NCAA Division I teams for men and women and operates a I-AA football program within that division. Athletic facilities include Bragg Stadium (25,600), with a field house, locker rooms, weight room, and training facility; a track and field complex with an eight-lane, all-weather, 400-meter track; competition-grade tennis courts; two outdoor pools; baseball and softball fields; and a complex that serves as headquarters for the largest women's athletic program at any historically black institution in the country. The intramural sports program is divided into informal free play, competitive sports, and sports clubs.

Location

The University is located on the highest of seven hills in Tallahassee (population 200,000) among the heavily wooded, rolling hills of northwest Florida and only 22 miles from the Gulf of Mexico. There are more than 1,000 acres of public parks and land and numerous lakes nearby. Programs at FAMU, Florida State University, and Tallahassee Community College provide top-name entertainment, much of which is offered free, or at reduced prices, to students. Students in various disciplines intern or are employed in community businesses and agencies of all three levels of government. The University is located eight blocks from the Capitol Complex, and bus service is available from campus to shopping malls; state, county, and city offices; and recreational areas. An intercampus shuttle (between FAMU and FSU) and an on-campus shuttle run during class hours daily.

Majors and Degrees

The College of Arts and Sciences offers baccalaureate majors and degrees in Afro-American studies, chemistry, computer information systems, criminal justice, economics, English, fine arts, foreign languages, general biology, history, mathematics, music, philosophy and religion, political science and public management (prelaw and urban studies), physics, predentistry, premedicine, psychology, social work, sociology, and theater. The College of Education offers baccalaureate degrees in business teacher education; elementary education; health, physical education, and recreation; industrial arts education; office administration; secondary education; and vocational-industrial education. The FAMU/FSU College of Engineering offers baccalaureate degrees in chemical, civil, electrical, industrial, and mechanical engineering. The College of Engineering Sciences, Technology and Agriculture offers baccalaureate degrees in agribusiness, agricultural science, agricultural engineering, animal science (pre–veterinary medicine), architectural and construction technology, civil engineering technology, electronic engineering technology, entomology and structural pest control, landscape design, and ornamental horticulture. The College of Pharmacy and Pharmaceutical Sciences offers three professional degrees. The School of Allied Health Sciences offers baccalaureate degrees in health-care management, health information management, occupational therapy, physical therapy, and respiratory therapy. The School of Architecture offers a four-year, preprofessional baccalaureate degree in architectural studies and a five-year, professional baccalaureate degree in architecture. The School of Business and Industry offers baccalaureate and five-year M.B.A. degrees in accounting and business administration. The School of Journalism, Media and Graphic Arts offers baccalaureate degrees in broadcast journalism, photography, graphic design, magazine journalism, newspaper journalism, printing management, printing production, and public relations. The School of Nursing offers a baccalaureate degree program in nursing.

Academic Program

The School of General Studies facilitates and monitors the general education of all matriculating undecided students. All students take core courses in English, mathematics, humanities, health, American history, natural sciences, and social and behavioral sciences. After completing these core requirements, students select an area of specialization in a major offered in one of the other colleges and schools. A minimum of 120 semester hours is required for the baccalaureate degree. Students who meet test and grade point average requirements and write an acceptable honors thesis are selected for the Honors Program, which enables them to accelerate completion of the basic requirements, enroll in classes of reduced size, develop leadership skills, have honor courses identified as such on their transcript, and be recognized at the annual All-University Convocation. FAMU offers Army and Naval ROTC.

Off-Campus Arrangements

The School of Architecture has a center in Washington, D.C., where students may study for one or two semesters. Architecture students have also worked on special projects in Florida and other parts of the continental United States. The College of Pharmacy and Pharmaceutical Sciences has a component in Miami, Florida, through which students receive clinical training in the hospitals of the Miami Medical Center. The College of Pharmacy also operates the Clinical Pharmacology Research Unit in Jackson Towers, Miami, Florida, for human drug studies and other research and research training. Through the University's Cooperative Education Program, students receive internships and other short-term work-study opportunities in business and industry, education, and government. The Cooperative Education Program has placed students in most of the fifty states. Individual schools and colleges provide undergraduate internships, usually for upper-division students. Students have interned in such places as London, England; San Juan, Puerto Rico; Sydney, Australia; and Geneva, Switzerland. FAMU has three cooperative programs with Florida State University, which is also located in Tallahassee. The general program enables students to take a limited academic load at the other institution. The Program in Medical Science (PIMS) provides a special route to medical school for students by allowing them to complete the first year of medical study in Tallahassee before transferring to a medical school. The joint FAMU/FSU College of Engineering program enables students to earn an engineering degree at FAMU while giving them access to course offerings at FSU.

Academic Facilities

The Coleman Memorial Library encompasses Library Service and Instructional Media Services. The library has 400,000 bound volumes, 3,640 periodicals, and 84,500 microfilms; a complete line of audiovisual equipment; a fully equipped television studio; and a photography laboratory. The Florida Black Archives, Research Center and Museum, located on campus, complements academic studies in history and has become a popular tourist attraction. Students have access to the R. A. Gray State Archives, the Leon County Public Library, the Robert Strozier Library at FSU, and the FSU Law Library.

Costs

In 1999–2000, basic registration fees for Florida-resident undergraduates were approximately $74 per semester hour and for nonresidents, $307. The basic cost of University housing is approximately $1169 per semester. Other estimated expenses are board (University Commons), $799 per semester for nineteen meals; books, $250; orientation, $15; and health fee, $52. For the most current information, students should contact the admission office.

Financial Aid

Financial aid is awarded according to each student's need in relation to college costs. Awards are available as need-based and non-need-based grants, loans, part-time employment (work-study), and scholarships. These awards may be offered singly or in various combinations. High-achieving high school and transfer students may be eligible for awards under special programs such as Presidential Scholars, Distinguished Scholars Award, and Life Gets Better scholarships. The priority deadline for financial aid application completion is March 1.

Faculty

Approximately 60 percent of the University's 463 faculty members hold doctoral degrees. Faculty members are expected to teach, conduct research, and provide public service. They are heavily involved with student affairs and serve as sponsors and advisers to clubs, student organizations, and professional societies. The overall student-faculty ratio is approximately 29:1; it varies by discipline and course level.

Student Government

Student Government Association officers are elected late in the spring semester and serve for the ensuing academic year. Representatives serve on University committees and advisory groups; each class has elected officers.

Admission Requirements

Florida A&M University encourages applications from qualified students of all national, racial, religious, and ethnic groups. Admission is selective; subject to limitations of curricula, space, and fiscal resources; and based on such factors as grades, test scores, educational objectives, pattern of courses completed, past conduct, recommendations, and personal records. Although requirements are subject to change without notice, current policy allows students to be considered for admission if they have graduated from an accredited high school or approved GED program and earned at least 19 units of academic credit, of which 4 must be in English (3 with substantial writing requirements), 3 in mathematics (algebra I and higher levels), 3 in natural sciences (2 with substantial lab requirements), 3 in social sciences, and 2 in foreign language. The remaining 4 elective units must come from these subject areas or other courses approved by the State Department of Education and the Florida Board of Regents. Students must submit ACT or SAT I scores. Applicants with at least a B average (3.0 on a 4.0 scale) in the required high school academic units who submit other evidence of successful academic progress are academically eligible for admission regardless of standardized test scores. Academic eligibility for students with less than a B average is determined on a sliding scale, published in the University catalog, that relates GPA to SAT I or ACT scores. Students who do not meet these requirements but who bring to the University other important attributes or special talents may be admitted by the University Admissions Committee. Outstanding students may submit an application for early admission during their junior year in high school (without having completed all credit requirements), along with a high school transcript (a B average or better), SAT I (at least 1010 combined) or ACT (at least 21 composite) scores, and a recommendation from the principal or designated representative.

Applicants who have attended any accredited institution of higher education and earned 12 or more semester hours are considered transfer students. Undergraduate transfers who enter FAMU with junior-class standing must have passed the College Level Academic Skills Test (CLAST) to be admitted to upper-level courses and degree programs. Transfer applicants with fewer than 60 semester hours of credit must meet first-time-in-college admission requirements. Undergraduate transfer applicants who have not earned the A.A. degree from a Florida community/junior college or from a state university must be in good standing and eligible to return to the last institution attended, must have earned a minimum of 60 semester hours and maintained at least a C (2.0) average, and must present passing scores on the Florida CLAST before admission to FAMU's upper division. Students who have earned an A.A. degree from an accredited state institution are automatically eligible for admission to nonlimited-access programs, under the Florida Community College–State University System Articulation Agreement. International transfer applicants who are not native English speakers must present a minimum score of 500 on the Test of English as a Foreign Language (TOEFL).

Admission to certain programs is highly selective. These limited-access programs tend to reach enrollment capacity before the cutoff dates for general admission, so interested students should apply early. Admission to the University does not ensure access to on-campus housing.

Application and Information

Office of Admissions
Florida Agricultural and Mechanical University
Tallahassee, Florida 32307
Telephone: 850-599-3796
E-mail: admissions@famu.edu
World Wide Web: http://www.famu.edu

FLORIDA ATLANTIC UNIVERSITY
BOCA RATON, FLORIDA

The University

Florida Atlantic University (FAU) ranks among the top universities in the nation in *U.S. News & World Report* and is one of the top 100 college buys in the country, according to *America's 100 Best College Buys® 2000*.

Florida Atlantic University was established in 1961, making it the fifth-oldest university in the state system. As an upper-division and graduate state university, FAU admitted its first students in September 1964. In 1984, FAU accepted its first freshman class, instituting a comprehensive four-year undergraduate program. Enrollment has increased from 867 in the first year to 20,313 in 1999.

FAU is a midsize comprehensive university located in the heart of a rapidly expanding metropolitan area, encompassing cities and towns from Fort Lauderdale to Port St. Lucie. The original campus is located in Boca Raton, and the University expanded to six other campuses in south Florida: Dania Beach (SeaTech), Davie, Fort Lauderdale (two locations: Reubin O'D. Askew Tower and Commercial Boulevard), Jupiter (John D. MacArthur Campus/Honors College), and Port St. Lucie (Treasure Coast).

The residential campus in Boca Raton accommodates more than 1,500 students in seven residence halls and a student apartment complex. The Student Services Building and a completely renovated cafeteria are adjacent to the residence halls. On the east side of the campus is the athletic complex, with its 5,000-seat gymnasium, field house, state-of-the-art weight room, swimming and diving complex, and athletic fields and courts (baseball, soccer, and softball). The main academic areas of the campus are grouped around the centrally located library and learning resources buildings. A 24-hour study area is connected to the library. The south campus of Palm Beach Community College is also located on the University's grounds.

FAU campuses can be found throughout the southeast Florida region. One of FAU's newest campuses is located in Dania Beach. Known as SeaTech, the campus is a marine and ocean engineering facility. The University's 110,000-square-foot facility in Davie, adjacent to the central campus of Broward Community College, houses the Liberal Arts College. In addition, an Education and Science Building on the Davie campus is home to programs in education and science as well as state-of-the-art laboratories. A University Tower campus joins the Fort Lauderdale skyline, offering primarily graduate programs in the busy city center. A third campus in Broward County is located on Commercial Boulevard. The Honors College of Florida Atlantic University opened in fall 1999 in Jupiter; this is the first public honors institution in the United States to be built from the ground up. To the north, the University provides classes and services at its Port St. Lucie campus, with extension classes in Belle Glade and Okeechobee.

At the graduate level, FAU offers Master of Arts and Master of Science degrees in most academic areas. The Education Specialist degree is offered in curriculum and instruction, educational leadership, and guidance and counseling. The Doctor of Education degree is awarded in administration and supervision, elementary education, and exceptional student education. The University also offers the Ph.D. in business administration; complex systems and brain sciences; computer, electrical, mechanical, and ocean engineering; mathematics; physics; psychology; and public administration.

Florida Atlantic University is accredited by the Commission on Colleges of the Southern Association of Colleges and Schools to award associate, bachelor's, master's, and doctoral degrees. In addition, it is accredited by twelve professional agencies. FAU is also a member of the National Association of State Universities and Land-Grant Colleges and the Council of Graduate Schools in the United States. The University offers fifty-six bachelor's, forty-nine master's, three specialist's, and fifteen doctoral degrees.

Location

The 850-acre Boca Raton campus, located on a former U.S. Army airfield, is inhabited by a variety of wildlife, including burrowing owls. The University's athletic teams have taken the feisty bird as their mascot. The campus was designated as a burrowing owl sanctuary by the Audubon Society in 1971. The FAU–Boca Raton campus is 3 miles west of the Atlantic Ocean and midway between Palm Beach and Fort Lauderdale. The University is easily accessible from major north-south highways. By car, the University is off Exit 39 of I-95 on Glades Road; by air, the University is 25 miles from both the West Palm Beach and Fort Lauderdale airports.

South Florida's climate is subtropical, with an average year-round temperature of 75 degrees. FAU's campuses are within easy driving distance from some of the most beautiful beaches and recreational facilities to be found anywhere.

Majors and Degrees

Florida Atlantic University offers programs leading to the Bachelor of Arts and Bachelor of Science degrees, as well as twelve specialized bachelor's degrees. A minimum of 120 credit hours is required for a bachelor's degree.

The College of Architecture, Urban and Public Affairs, offers majors in architecture (upper division only), criminal justice, public management, social work, and urban and regional planning. The Dorothy F. Schmidt College of Arts and Letters offers a general college major and majors in anthropology, art, communication, English, history, languages and linguistics (French, German, Italian, Japanese, and Spanish), music, philosophy, political science, sociology, and theater. The College of Business offers majors in accounting, computer information systems, economics, finance, health administration, international business, management, marketing, and real estate. The Honors College in Jupiter offers a liberal arts education for first-time freshmen. The College of Education offers majors in elementary education, exceptional student education, exercise science and wellness education, medical technology, and physical therapy. Secondary education majors enroll in the college of their main subject. The College of Engineering offers majors in computer science and computer, electrical, and ocean engineering. The College of Liberal Arts in Davie (upper division only) offers majors in biological sciences (biotechnology, ecology and organismic biology, marine biology, microbiology, and molecular biology), communication, English, geography, graphic design, history, interdisciplinary studies, music (chamber music/accompanying emphasis or piano performance emphasis), political science, psychobiology, psychology, social psychology, and sociology. The College of Nursing offers the Bachelor of Science in Nursing degree. The College of Science has majors in biological science (biotechnology, ecology and organismic biology, marine biology, microbiology, and molecular biology), chemistry, geography, geology, mathematical sciences, physics, psychology, and social psychology. Preprofessional programs are available in medicine, veterinary medicine, dentistry, optometry, and pharmacy. Certificate programs are available in classical studies, environmental studies, ethnic studies, film and video, gerontology, Judaic studies, Latin American studies, statistics, and women's studies.

Academic Program

The University offers a baccalaureate program designed for highly motivated and well-qualified applicants. The rigorous core of courses prepares all students for the challenges of today's rapidly changing society.

Off-Campus Arrangements

Florida Atlantic University has established a work-study program between its nine colleges and cooperating businesses, industries, and government laboratories. This permits a student to divide his or her program into six-month periods of study at the University and on-the-job experience in participating organizations for the duration of the course. Cooperative work-study classes normally start in the fall and spring semesters each academic year. FAU has exchange agreements with international schools ranging from China to Germany. Students spend one or two semesters abroad, or they enroll in study tours or six-week summer programs. Arrangements must be made through the Office of International Programs.

The University Center at FAU provides the Off-Campus Housing Guide for upper-division transfer students seeking housing.

Academic Facilities

The Boca Raton campus resources feature the five-story S. E. Wimberly Library with more than 1 million holdings. The Dorothy F. Schmidt College of Arts and Letters features a 75,000-square-foot three-building complex encompassing a performing arts center, art gallery, experimental theater, visual arts center, lecture halls, classrooms, and offices. The College of Business occupies a four-story classroom/office building. The College of Education's four-story, 90,000-square-foot facility houses its five academic apartments and offers a teaching gymnasium, an early childhood center, and the A. D. Henderson University School, a public elementary school located on the campus and operated by the College of Education. There are five buildings dedicated entirely to engineering and science disciplines. The Science and Engineering and Social Science Buildings were recently joined by a Physical Science Building. There is also a marine sciences center located between the Intracoastal Waterway and the Atlantic Ocean. The Gumbo Limbo Nature Center provides teaching and research facilities.

Costs

For the 1999–2000 academic year, in-state tuition for full-time students was $2253; out-of-state tuition was $9241. (A full-time course load is 24 to 30 semester hours per academic year.) Average room and board costs totaled $4993. Additional expenses were approximately $610 for books, $1230 for personal items, and $1338 for transportation. Fees are subject to change at any time by action of the Florida legislature. FAU offers one of the lowest tuition rates and expense costs available today.

Financial Aid

Approximately $50 million in financial aid is awarded each year. A comprehensive program of student financial aid includes scholarships, grants, loans, and employment that may provide assistance from initial enrollment through graduate study. Assistance is tailored to fit each student's requirements and may vary during his or her enrollment. As a member of the College Scholarship Service of the College Board, the University is guided by the principles and policies of that organization.

Students who are interested in applying for need-based aid must complete the Free Application for Federal Student Aid (FAFSA), which is available in all U.S. high schools, colleges, and universities. Students are strongly encouraged to complete the FAFSA in January for fall admission. The process of applying for aid normally takes six to eight weeks. The priority deadline is March 1. Students must be notified of their acceptance to the University before award allocations can be made.

FAU recognizes and rewards high achievement. There is a wide variety of scholarships available for academic, athletic, or artistic talent (refer to the FAU catalog under Financial Assistance).

Faculty

Recognizing that the excellence of its faculty is the true measure of the worth of a university, FAU has brought together a distinguished group of scholars who hold a balanced dedication to both teaching and research. The members of the faculty come from more than thirty states and several countries. The majority hold the doctorate or a professional degree. They all represent a high level of professional experience and academic attainment and are committed to the development of a vigorous educational program of high caliber.

The University community has benefited from the presence of 12 Eminent Scholars, distributed over seven colleges. In addition, two Endowed Chairs have been fully funded and five others partially funded. The presence of these distinguished scholars and researchers has greatly enhanced the academic climate of the University and has provided focal points for the development of new programs, particularly at the graduate level.

Student Government

Florida Atlantic University's student government has been recognized by *Florida Leader—Best of Florida Schools 1999 Magazine* as the "Best Student Government" in Florida public universities. FAU gives students an active role on virtually all University and faculty committees, including the Curriculum Committee. They serve on college advisory councils and operate the Student Government Association and Residence Hall Councils, as well as the interclub, interfraternity, and Panhellenic groups. Students also serve on the University Senate along with members of the faculty and staff.

Admission Requirements

Florida Atlantic University welcomes applications from talented students. Applications are reviewed on a rolling basis beginning in October and extending until the admission deadlines. Freshmen may apply for fall or spring semester admission, transfer students for fall, spring, and summer admission. Preferred application filing dates are June 1 for the fall term and October 15 for the spring term; international students must file by April 1 for the fall term and October 1 for the spring term.

Freshman admission is competitive. Admission decisions are based primarily on a combination of the high school average and the SAT I or ACT. Students must have completed a minimum of 19 academic units in high school to be eligible for consideration. These units should include English (4 units), math (3 units, Algebra I and above), social science (3 units), science (3 units, 2 with a lab), foreign language (2 units, 1 language sequence), and academic electives (4 units). Electives are chosen from the above areas, computer science, fine arts, and humanities. Students who have completed more demanding courses receive added consideration. Students may also be considered on the basis of outstanding abilities or extraordinary circumstances that indicate the potential to benefit from a competitive university curriculum and environment. The University is firmly committed to affirmative action policies and equal access.

Students who have completed fewer than 60 semester hours (fewer than 90 quarter hours) prior to entry into FAU must meet the freshman admission requirements and have maintained a GPA of 2.0 (on a 4.0 scale) in the college or university previously attended. Students who have completed 60 or more semester hours (90 or more quarter hours) are eligible for admissions as upper-division students (junior level or higher) if they have maintained a minimum GPA of 2.0 in their college-level work and are in good academic standing at each institution they have attended. Students with an A.A. degree from a Florida community college are guaranteed admission with upper-division status, with the exception of limited-access programs. Limited-access programs at FAU are architecture, education, nursing, and physical therapy. These programs have a higher standard for admission.

Students can take the FAU online campus tour by going to http://www.fau.edu/alumni/camptour.htm.

Application and Information

Director of Admissions
Florida Atlantic University
777 Glades Road
P.O. Box 3091
Boca Raton, Florida 33431-0991
Telephone: 800-299-4FAU (toll-free)
World Wide Web: http://www.fau.edu

FLORIDA INSTITUTE OF TECHNOLOGY
MELBOURNE, FLORIDA

The Institute
Florida Institute of Technology was founded in 1958 for the purpose of offering science and engineering courses to specialists working on the space program at Cape Canaveral. The primary aim of the university has been to keep abreast of current and anticipated needs in the developing fields of high technology. This philosophy is reflected in Florida Tech's response to the nation's growing need for qualified specialists trained in the fields of science and engineering. Other degree programs offered at Florida Tech (aviation, business administration, psychology, and business and technical communication) give the university a well-rounded approach to higher education.

There are more than 4,000 graduate and undergraduate students currently enrolled at Florida Tech. On-campus housing is provided for all freshmen. Limited space is available for upperclass and graduate students. On- and off-campus fraternity housing is also available. Motor vehicles are allowed on campus. Men's intercollegiate sports are baseball, basketball, crew, cross-country, and soccer. Women's sports are basketball, crew, cross-country, softball, and volleyball. Intramural basketball, football, racquetball, softball, and volleyball are played throughout the year. There are seven national fraternities, two national sororities, and one local sorority. Student chapters of professional and social organizations include the American Institute of Aeronautics and Astronautics, Society of Physics Students, and Blue Key National Honor Fraternity. Student services include the Campus Ministry, Counseling Center, Veterans Administration Office, Placement and Cooperative Education Office, Health Service, Individual Learning Center, and Freshman Counseling. The Division of Language and Linguistics provides the university's international students with intensive instruction in English.

Approximately 2,000 students at Florida Institute of Technology are pursuing undergraduate studies. Sixty-nine percent are men. The average class size is 30, and the average laboratory size is 15. Although Florida residents comprise a large portion of the population, there are students from every state, many from the Eastern Seaboard of the United States, and international students from more than ninety countries.

Location
The Florida Tech campus is located in Melbourne, Florida, a safe, residential community on the Space Coast of Florida. Melbourne is the high-technology center of Florida, with many companies that serve, support, and complement the efforts of the space program. Melbourne is home to approximately 65,000 residents, representing many U.S. states and other countries. The city is in east-central Florida, approximately 1 hour southeast of Orlando and 3 hours north of Miami. The beaches are 4 miles from the campus and provide opportunities for all water sports. Central Florida attractions such as Walt Disney World, Sea World, and the Kennedy Space Center are nearby.

Majors and Degrees
The College of Engineering, the College of Science and Liberal Arts, the School of Aeronautics, the School of Psychology, and the School of Business award the Bachelor of Science degree in aerospace engineering, biological sciences, business administration, business communication, chemical engineering, chemistry, civil engineering, computer engineering, computer information systems, computer science, computer software development, electrical engineering, environmental sciences, humanities, mathematics, mechanical engineering, meteorology, ocean engineering, oceanography, physics, psychology, science education, space sciences, and technical communication. Students may tailor their curricula for specific majors in aquaculture; astronomy; astrophysics; environmental engineering; general biology; marine biology; molecular biology; preprofessional biology, chemistry, and physics; or oceanography. The School of Aeronautics grants the Bachelor of Science degree in aeronautical science (with an option in flight), aviation computer science, aviation management (with an option in flight), and aviation meteorology.

Academic Program
The university operates on a calendar of two semesters and three summer sessions. Programs in the pure sciences prepare the student for graduate or professional work. Practical aspects of computer science and engineering can be combined with management science for the business minded, and a wide variety of programs are available for the environmentalist. Baccalaureate programs are completely outlined for each discipline; opportunity for diversification is provided by the technical and humanities electives offered during the junior and senior years. Substitutions or specialized programs require the approval of the student's faculty adviser and the appropriate department heads. All majors participate in research, internships, or senior projects.

In the School of Aeronautics, the bachelor's programs provide a strong business or science background in the first two years and concentrate on specialized knowledge in the aviation industry during the final two years. Students can select from seven accredited aviation bachelor's degrees, including aeronautical science, aviation computer science, aviation management, and aviation meteorology. Flight training is an integral part of the aviation management and aeronautical science programs, but both can be completed without flight. Flight students earn their FAA commercial, instrument, and multiengine flight certificates and can earn their instructor, air taxi, and airline transport pilot ratings and the flight dispatcher certificate.

Students at Florida Tech may qualify for advanced placement through English and mathematics examinations administered by the university. Advanced credit is awarded for Advanced Placement (AP) exams and higher-level International Baccalaureate subjects.

The university offers a four-year Army ROTC program, and it rewards ROTC scholarship winners with a generous supplemental scholarship package. Prospective students should contact an ROTC representative at the university.

Academic Facilities
The university is home to the Claude Pepper Institute for Aging and Therapeutic Research and a Genetic Engineering Research Center. Computer facilities include the Harris Lab, with SunSPARC and GSI workstations; the Quad Lab, with Internet

access terminals; and the MicroCenter, which offers PCs and Macintosh computers for student use. A variety of word processing, spreadsheet, database management, and graphics software is also available. The F. W. Olin Engineering Complex and the F. W. Olin Life Sciences Building incorporate the latest in multimedia and information technology, including advanced computer teaching and research classrooms, laboratories, and conference centers. The Applied Research Laboratory for Research in Space Science and Electrical and Computer Engineering is located 1 mile from campus. Extensive laboratory facilities are located throughout campus for chemistry and biological sciences. The physics department operates a 14-inch Schmidt telescope. A 15-acre botanical garden is maintained in support of biological studies. A fleet of more than forty-five aircraft is available at Melbourne International Airport, 3 miles from the campus. The School of Aeronautics uses 20,000 square feet of administrative and instructional facilities on airport property. This site serves as headquarters for flight and simulator training and ground-school instruction.

Costs

Tuition for the 2000–01 academic year is $18,000 for science and engineering majors and $16,500 for all other majors. Students pursuing aviation majors with flight training can expect an additional cost of $7000 per year in flight fees. Room and board costs for the year are approximately $5000.

Financial Aid

Awards are based on academic promise, need, college costs, and the availability of funds. Approximately 80 percent of the university's students receive grants, scholarships, loans, and employment, either in a single award or in various combinations. Several kinds of monthly installment plans are available for tuition and other expenses. The priority deadline for financial aid is March 15. Students eligible for Veterans Administration benefits may contact the VA representative on the Melbourne campus.

Faculty

The student-faculty ratio is 11:1. Eighty-nine percent of the full-time faculty members hold doctoral degrees and are closely involved with student life, serving as counselors and advisers. In general, freshman- and sophomore-level instructors carry full-time teaching loads. Upper-level and graduate instructors are involved with both teaching and research responsibilities. Some undergraduate labs are taught by graduate students. Adjunct faculty members, who bring skills and expertise from area businesses and industries, are also utilized.

Student Government

The Student Government functions as the vital link between the administration and the student body, as the liaison between the university and the community, and as the catalyst for social change. The organization promotes new ideas and encourages student participation at all levels of university involvement.

Admission Requirements

Applicants should have a strong background in science and mathematics. The ACT or SAT I is required of all incoming freshmen (the ACT code ensuring the receipt of test results is 0716; the SAT I code is 5080). Personal recommendations by counselors or faculty members are not required but are taken into consideration in certain circumstances. Early admission is possible, provided that formal application procedures are followed, and is contingent upon approval by the Admission Committee. Transfer students are considered individually on the basis of transcripts and overall performance. Prospective applicants who do not meet the standardized admission requirements but are interested in attending Florida Tech are urged to arrange a personal interview with the admissions counselor to receive individual attention.

Application and Information

The university encourages applicants from every social, ethnic, racial, and religious background. Florida Tech practices a rolling admission policy. The application fee is $35. Completed applications, high school and college transcripts, and standardized test results should be sent to the office below.

For further information, students may contact:

Office of Admissions
Florida Institute of Technology
150 West University Boulevard
Melbourne, Florida 32901-6988
Telephone: 321-674-8030
        800-888-4348 (toll-free)
E-mail: admissions@fit.edu

Florida's subtropical weather allows year-round fun on and off campus.

FLORIDA INTERNATIONAL UNIVERSITY
MIAMI, FLORIDA

The University

Florida International University (FIU), established by the Florida state legislature in 1965, is a member of the State University System of Florida. The University offers a variety of academic programs and courses that lead to bachelor's, master's, and doctoral degrees. Major University divisions are the Colleges of Arts and Sciences, Business Administration, Education, Engineering, Health Sciences, and Urban and Public Affairs, as well as the Schools of Accounting, Architecture, Computer Science, Hospitality Management, Journalism and Mass Communication, Music, Nursing, Policy and Management, and Social Work. The Southern Association of Colleges and Schools accredits all academic programs. The professional programs of the respective colleges and schools are accredited or approved by the appropriate professional associations or are pursuing full professional accreditation or approval. The University has three major goals: to provide students with a university education, to serve the broad community, and to become a major international education center by helping to create greater understanding among the people of the Americas and the world.

The University has two campuses and two academic centers. The University Park campus in southwest Miami-Dade County is about 10 miles west of downtown Miami. The North Campus is located on Biscayne Bay in North Miami. Both campuses operate under a central administration. Two centers are located in Broward County—one on the central campus of Broward Community College in Davie, the second at University Tower in downtown Fort Lauderdale.

The University has a diverse population of students. There are more than 31,000 men and women enrolled. Eight percent of the enrollment consists of international students who represent 110 countries. The University currently has more than 200 registered student organizations, which enrich campus life and contribute to the social, cultural, and academic growth of students. Nationally recognized lecturers appear regularly, and concerts and movies are offered, usually at no cost.

Athletic opportunities are numerous. Students can participate in intercollegiate, intramural, and recreational sports. NCAA Division I intercollegiate athletics are available for men in baseball, basketball, cross-country, soccer, and indoor and outdoor track and field. Women can participate in NCAA Division I intercollegiate athletics in basketball, cross-country, golf, soccer, softball, tennis, indoor and outdoor track and field, and volleyball. A Nautilus Fitness Center is available on both campuses.

The University offers apartment-style housing for students at both the University Park and North Campuses. The facilities provide students with the opportunity to live with others in a convenient and supportive residential setting. A special program exists for interested first-year students. The newest residence hall, University Park Towers, opens in fall 2000. Most of the residence halls offer a full range of amenities to students, including cable television, computer connectivity, study rooms, computer labs, and various recreational areas, including a swimming pool.

Location

Both campuses are close to concert halls, theaters, libraries, and museums as well as recreational and ecological facilities. Award-winning performances can be seen regularly at Gusman Cultural Center, the Dade County Auditorium, Jackie Gleason Theatre of the Performing Arts, and the Coconut Grove Playhouse. Well-known personalities appear throughout the year at area concert halls and hotels.

Disney World, the Everglades, marine and state parks, Seaquarium, Metro Zoo, Fairchild Tropical Gardens, and the Parrot Jungle are popular student attractions. Other favorite year-round activities include swimming, waterskiing, scuba diving, sailing, tennis, golf, and horseback riding. Occasionally, students head south for a weekend in the Florida Keys or the Bahamas.

Majors and Degrees

The School of Architecture offers a Bachelor of Science in architectural studies and a Bachelor of Science in interior design.

The College of Arts and Sciences offers programs of study that lead to the Bachelor of Arts in art history, chemistry, dance, economics, English, environmental studies, French, geology, history, humanities, international relations, liberal studies, philosophy, political science, Portuguese, psychology, religious studies, sociology/anthropology, Spanish, theater, and women's studies. The Bachelor of Science is offered in biology, chemistry, environmental studies, geology, mathematical sciences, mathematics, physics, and statistics. A Bachelor of Fine Arts is offered in theater and visual arts. The School of Music offers a Bachelor of Music and a Bachelor of Science in music education. The School of Computer Science offers a Bachelor of Science in computer science.

The College of Business Administration offers a Bachelor of Business Administration with majors in finance, international business, logistics, management, management information systems, marketing, personnel management, and real estate. The School of Accounting offers a Bachelor of Accounting.

The College of Education offers the Bachelor of Science in art education (1–12), biology education, chemistry education, elementary education, emotional disturbance education, English education, French education, health education, health occupations education, history education, mathematics education, mental retardation education, parks and recreation management, physical education (K–8 or 6–12), physics education, social studies education, specific learning disabilities education, technical education, vocational home economics education, and vocational industrial education.

The College of Engineering offers programs of study that lead to the Bachelor of Science in chemical engineering, civil engineering, computer engineering, construction management, electrical engineering, environmental and urban systems, industrial and systems engineering, and mechanical engineering.

The College of Health Sciences offers programs of study that lead to the Bachelor of Science in dietetics and nutrition, health information management, occupational therapy, and physical therapy. The School of Nursing offers a Bachelor of Science in nursing. The school is accredited by the National League for Nursing Accrediting Commission and is open to generic and RN students.

The School of Hospitality Management offers an academic program of study that leads to the Bachelor of Science with a major in hospitality management. With the cooperation of industry executives, the school has an internship program that utilizes hotels, motels, restaurants, clubs, airlines, travel agencies, and cruise lines as practice labs for students.

The School of Journalism and Mass Communication offers a Bachelor of Science in communication.

The College of Urban and Public Affairs offers programs of study that lead to a Bachelor of Science in criminal justice, a Bachelor of Health Services Administration, and a Bachelor of Public Administration. The School of Social Work offers the Bachelor of Science in Social Work.

Preprofessional programs are offered in dentistry, law, medicine, and veterinary medicine.

Academic Program

At the undergraduate level, all students complete 36 semester hours of general education requirements before graduation. These consist of 6 semester hours each in the areas of humanities, mathematics, natural science, social science, and English composition and 6 semester hours in courses that require 6,000 words of writing. The academic programs are planned in such a manner that students may tailor academic programs to fit their personal goals.

There are three terms in the academic calendar year: fall, spring, and summer. Two terms (or semesters) of full-time attendance constitute an academic year; a normal course load is defined as at least 12 semester hours per term. Miniterms are also available within each semester.

Academic Facilities

The buildings at University Park house classrooms, lecture halls, offices, laboratories, computer facilities, student recreational facilities, an international conference theater, an auditorium, music and art studios, an experimental theater, and the Media Center. A three-story library opened in 1975, and a five-story addition was completed in 1997. On the North Campus, an administrative building houses offices, a library, media services, and a computer center. In 1986, the University dedicated the teaching gym and the Golden Panther Arena at University Park. Buildings currently under construction or recently completed are transforming the campus into a major collegiate center, as envisioned in the University's Master Plan. Newer structures include the College of Education, which contains two case study rooms and nineteen laboratories; the North Campus Kovens Conference Center, a state-of-the-art facility that accommodates up to 1,100 people; the Wertheim Performing Arts Center; expansion of the University Park Green Library; the National Hurricane Center; the Graham Center Student Union (expansion) and Multi-Purpose Complex; and a baseball stadium.

Costs

Tuition for undergraduate courses during academic year 1999–2000 was $72.14 per credit hour for Florida residents and $305.09 for non-Florida residents. A health fee of $36 and an athletic fee of $10 per term were also assessed. (These costs are subject to change.)

Financial Aid

The University adheres to the philosophy that a student is entitled to a university education regardless of his or her financial status. The financial aid program at the University includes scholarships, grants, loans, and employment. Awards are based on need, and individual attention is given to each applicant. To apply for aid, students should submit the Free Application for Federal Student Aid (FAFSA) and a University institutional financial aid application. Students are advised to apply before March 1.

Faculty

The University has more than 1,800 full-time and adjunct faculty members; more than 80 percent hold terminal degrees in their fields. The faculty works across disciplinary boundaries in dealing with issues that are central to the environmental, urban, and international missions of the University. The University gives primary consideration to selecting faculty members who have a strong sense of commitment to teaching, research, and counseling students.

Student Government

FIU's Student Government Association (SGA) seeks to include all interested students on University-wide committees and task forces to ensure student representation. In developing the governing policies, the SGA strives to set up programs that entertain, educate, and challenge FIU's community.

Admission Requirements

Applicants are encouraged to apply as soon as possible prior to their intended term of enrollment. All applications are carefully reviewed. Applicants are notified of their admission status once a completed application, nonrefundable $20 application fee, and all supporting documents have been received. It is the applicant's responsibility to request transcripts and test scores, when applicable, from all previously attended schools. All applicants are considered for admission without regard to race, creed, age, disability, gender, marital status, or national origin.

The University seeks highly motivated students with strong academic backgrounds and exceptional test scores for its freshman class. Competition for a place in the freshman class is created by the quality and number of applicants. Freshman admission requires graduation from an accredited secondary school, at least 19 academic units in college-preparatory courses, and official SAT I or ACT scores. Decisions are based on the student's academic preparation.

Transfer applicants from accredited Florida public community colleges should have an Associate of Arts (A.A.) degree. Applicants who do not hold an A.A. degree must complete at least 60 semester hours of transferable credit, with a minimum grade point average of 2.0, based upon a 4.0 scale. Applicants transferring from a Florida community college or university are required to take the College Level Academic Skills Test (CLAST) prior to entering. For students transferring from out-of-state or private colleges, the test can be taken during the first semester of enrollment. All applicants must meet the criteria published for limited-access programs and should consult the specific college and major for requirements.

International students must submit a Declaration of Finance that shows financial resources sufficient for attending the University and for all living expenses. Students from non-English-speaking countries must also submit a score of 500 or higher on the TOEFL.

Application and Information

Additional information may be obtained from the Office of Admissions.

If an alternative format of materials is necessary or sign language interpreter services are needed, students should notify the Office of Admissions five days in advance so that appropriate arrangements can be made with the Office of Disabled Student Services.

Office of Admissions
University Park, PC 140
Florida International University
Miami, Florida 33199
Telephone: 305-348-2363
Fax: 305-348-3648
E-mail: admiss@fiu.edu
World Wide Web: http://www.fiu.edu

FLORIDA SOUTHERN COLLEGE
LAKELAND, FLORIDA

The College

Florida Southern College was founded in 1885 by the Methodist Church and has remained an affiliate throughout its 113-year history. The original campus was in Leesburg, but the College moved to Palm Harbor in 1902 and finally settled in Lakeland in 1922. Florida Southern is an intentionally interactive, residential, coeducational college of liberal arts and sciences. Although 60 percent of the 1,700 students come from Florida, the remaining 40 percent represent forty-six states and thirty-five other countries. All ages and economic strata are represented. Students come to Florida Southern because they want a liberal arts education and believe a smaller campus is the best place to find it. The atmosphere is relaxed and personal, fostering a very close-knit student body and faculty.

All members of the academic community take pride in the campus, a historic landmark and site of the largest collection of buildings designed by renowned architect Frank Lloyd Wright. Annie Pfeiffer Chapel, the first of the Wright buildings to be completed, hosts regular worship services at which students of all denominations are welcome. Specific residence halls are reserved for freshmen. Upperclass students, whether members of fraternities and sororities or independent students, are housed in a variety of on-campus accommodations, including the newly constructed Publix Commons. There is limited visitation in the residence halls. The George Jenkins Field House, which seats 3,000 people, includes a three-court gymnasium, a weight room, and a sports equipment room. Facilities for tennis, racquetball, dance, swimming, and waterskiing are also available. Opened in 1997, the Nina B. Hollis Wellness Center features a fully equipped fitness center, an aerobics/dance studio, an intramural gymnasium, and a wide-screen TV/lounge area. There are branches of six national Greek fraternities and six national Greek sororities on campus. Each of these organizations defers rush to the second semester. Student activities include intercollegiate and intramural sports, drama and music groups, publications, and various clubs and organizations related to academic, political, religious, and social interests. In addition, many students are involved in volunteer programs and internships in the surrounding community.

Location

Florida Southern's campus consists of approximately 100 acres on the shore of Lake Hollingsworth in Lakeland, Florida, a pleasant community of about 90,000 residents in the heart of Florida's citrus belt. Lakeland is 45 minutes from Tampa and an hour from Orlando. Within an hour's drive of the state's major recreational attractions, including Disney World and major beaches, the College is ideally situated for internships and job opportunities with leading corporations that tap into one of the largest markets in the U.S. Members of the community come to the College campus to attend Fine Arts Series performances in music, dance, and drama; to hear distinguished speakers; and to participate in College and business symposiums. The Lakeland Center also offers many cultural and entertainment opportunities.

Majors and Degrees

Florida Southern College offers a Bachelor of Arts, Bachelor of Music, Bachelor of Music Education, Bachelor of Sacred Music, or Bachelor of Science degree in the following majors: accounting, art (art education, graphic design, and studio art), athletic training, biology, business administration (concentrations in computer information systems, finance, hotel/resort management, human resource management, international business, marketing, and paralegal law office studies), chemistry, citrus and environmental horticulture, communication (advertising business, advertising design, broadcasting, communication art, journalism, and public relations), criminology, economics, elementary education (including specific learning disabilities), English (dramatic arts, literature, and writing), history, mathematics, music (music education, music management, performance, and sacred music), physical education (sports management), physics, political science, prekindergarten/primary education, psychology, religion (Christian education and philosophy), sacred music, secondary teacher certification (biology, English, history, mathematics, political science, social science, and Spanish), sociology, Spanish, and theater arts (performance and technical). Divisional majors are available in humanities, science, and social science.

Preprofessional programs are offered in dentistry, engineering, law, medicine, physical therapy, theology, and veterinary medicine. The professional programs include accounting, business administration, citrus marketing, journalism, music management, and teacher education (elementary, health and physical, prekindergarten/primary, and secondary education as well as specific learning disabilities). Students who wish to teach at the secondary level choose a major in a subject area and complete the requirements for certification by the state of Florida.

An honors program provides special opportunities for a select group of entering freshmen to explore topics of common interest in an integrated and interdisciplinary fashion. Selection to the honors program is highly competitive; the program is limited to approximately 10 percent of the entering class.

Academic Program

All degree programs require the satisfactory completion of a minimum of 124 semester hours with a minimum grade point average of 2.0. (The Bachelor of Music Education degree requires a minimum of 140 semester hours.) Grading is traditional, with a pass/fail option available. The College operates on the semester system with two 15-week semesters, one 4-week May Option Term, and two 4-week summer sessions. The average course load is 15 hours per semester. Students are required to complete a core curriculum of liberal arts and science courses in addition to their major course work. Credit by examination is awarded on the basis of successful scores on Advanced Placement tests, the International Baccalaureate (I.B.), and College-Level Examination Program (CLEP) tests. Scores on both the general and subject examinations of CLEP are acceptable.

Florida Southern has a Career Center that assists students in clarifying their career and life goals and that provides opportunities for them to explore these goals. Approximately 20 percent of Florida Southern graduates go immediately on to graduate work. Internship experiences help to place the vast majority of other graduates in field-related jobs within a few months of graduation.

Off-Campus Arrangements

The Year Abroad Program allows students to spend their junior year studying in one of several countries in Western Europe.

Florida Southern participates in the Washington Semester of American University in Washington, D.C., through which selected students spend a semester in Washington studying government and international relations. Selected students may also spend one semester at Drew University in Madison, New Jersey, studying various aspects of the United Nations through Drew University's United Nations Semester.

The May Option Program is a short term designed to enable students to enrich their educational experiences by combining study and travel. Courses may be offered abroad at sites such as Harlaxton, England, or at off-campus sites in the United States.

Academic Facilities

Florida Southern's Roux Library houses a collection of 136,629 volumes, nearly 400,000 microform pieces, more than 7,000 video and audio titles, and 715 periodical subscriptions. The Branscomb Memorial Auditorium seats 1,800 and is nationally known for its nearly perfect acoustical properties. The Ludd M. Spivey Humanities and Fine Arts Center includes the Marjorie M. McKinley Music Building, the Melvin Art Gallery, and the Loca Lee Buckner Theater. The theater seats 350 and is equipped with a hydraulic thrust stage, a computer-controlled lighting system, and laboratories for costume, makeup, and set design. The Polk Science Building houses the College's newly renovated, state-of-the-art science laboratories and one of the few planetariums in central Florida. The Pre-School Laboratory provides an opportunity for students majoring in prekindergarten/primary education to observe and teach preschoolers.

Costs

The comprehensive cost for 2000–01 is $18,540 ($12,950 for tuition and standard fees and $5550 for room and board). There are additional fees for individual music instruction and the use of practice rooms. Florida Southern estimates that another $500 is adequate for books and supplies, and $500 should cover personal expenses, exclusive of travel to and from home. Members of fraternities and sororities have additional expenses related to membership in these organizations.

Financial Aid

The Student Financial Aid Office offers students its counsel and assistance in meeting their educational expenses. Aid is awarded on the basis of an applicant's need, academic performance, and promise. Ninety-three percent of the students at Florida Southern receive financial assistance. To demonstrate need, an applicant is required to file the Free Application for Federal Student Aid (FAFSA). Various forms of aid, such as scholarships, grants, loans, and campus employment, are used to help meet students' needs. Merit scholarships are available, and awards are based on academic promise; performance ability in music, theater, or art; or athletic ability in baseball, basketball, cross-country, golf, soccer, softball, tennis, or volleyball. Applicants for aid must reapply each year. Florida Southern participates in the Federal Perkins Loan, Federal Supplemental Educational Opportunity Grant, and Federal Work-Study college-based programs. All applicants are expected to apply for any entitlement grant for which they are eligible, such as a Federal Pell Grant and, for Florida residents, a Florida Student Assistance Grant and the Florida Tuition Voucher. The Federal Stafford Loan Program is also available. There are extensive on-campus employment opportunities. The completed FAFSA and the College's financial aid application must be filed with the Student Financial Aid Office by April 1. Early application is encouraged for students seeking academic scholarships.

Faculty

Eighty percent of Florida Southern's faculty members have doctoral or other terminal degrees in their respective fields. The faculty is primarily a teaching faculty; all faculty members have posted office hours and are available for consultation and advising. Faculty members are selected not only for their teaching ability but also for their ability to relate to the needs and concerns of college students. The student-faculty ratio is 16:1.

Student Government

The Student Government Association represents the student body in matters involving the College administration, faculty, and student body and is responsible for coordinating student government. Each full-time student is a member of the association and has a vote in its affairs. The subsidiaries of the association are the Association of Campus Entertainment (ACE), the House of Representatives, the Student Senate, and the four classes: freshman, sophomore, junior, and senior. Students hold membership on all major College committees as well as on the Board of Trustees.

Admission Requirements

Florida Southern looks for two things in applicants: performance and promise. The majority of applicants who have been admitted as freshmen have had a grade of B or better in college-preparatory courses (including four courses in English, three in mathematics, and the balance divided among science, foreign language, and social science), have ranked in the upper half of their graduating class, and have earned scores of at least 500 on each of the verbal and math portions of the SAT I or a composite score of at least 23 on the ACT. Nevertheless, the Admissions Office is committed to reviewing individual applicants on their own merits, based on the level of challenge attempted, patterns of grades over time, recommendations from appropriate references, and an applicant's own assessment of the learning environment ideally suited to his or her needs. Applicants must graduate from an accredited high school with a minimum of 19 credits, 16 of which must be academic. Qualified high school juniors may apply for early admission if they have the recommendation of their secondary school and have had a personal interview with the Director of Admissions. Applications from transfers are welcome, as are those from students resuming their education and from older students who have delayed their entrance into college. Transfer applicants should have a minimum 2.5 grade point average and be graduates of or eligible to return to their former institutions. Transfer students with fewer than 25 semester hours must submit high school transcripts and standardized test scores. Applicants who hold Associate of Arts degrees from regionally accredited two-year institutions are typically granted junior standing. Three references (2 academic and 1 personal) are required. All applicants are encouraged to interview; an interview may be required for some candidates.

Application and Information

An application is ready for consideration by the Admissions Committee when it has been received with the $30 application fee, required test scores and references, and transcripts from each school attended. Since all students are required to live on campus unless they are seniors, married, or living with their parents, early application is desirable to ensure that housing will be available. The freshman application deadline is April 1. The deadline for applications for athletic training and pre–physical therapy is February 1.

For more information about Florida Southern College, prospective students should contact:

Director of Admissions
Florida Southern College
111 Lake Hollingsworth Drive
Lakeland, Florida 33801-5698

Telephone: 800-274-4131 (toll-free)
E-mail: fscadm@flsouthern.edu
World Wide Web: http://www.flsouthern.edu

Joseph Reynolds residence hall.

FLORIDA STATE UNIVERSITY
TALLAHASSEE, FLORIDA

The University

Florida State University (FSU) is one of the nation's most popular universities, enrolling students from all fifty states and more than 100 countries. Its goals are to give students the best possible education while continuing a program of service to the people of Florida and to the nation. The University strives to maintain an intellectual climate of learning in which students develop respect for and become excited about the discovery of truth. Florida State's diverse student population participates in a Liberal Studies Program that has been nationally recognized for its effectiveness in fostering a spirit of free inquiry into humane values and for developing strong written analytical skills. The aim of the University is excellence and distinction in all pursuits. Home of the National High Magnetic Field Laboratory, the Supercomputer Computations Institute, and other internationally acclaimed research centers, Florida State is one of only eighty-eight institutions in the Research I category as classified by the Carnegie Foundation for the Advancement of Teaching. Florida State University's academic programs are fully accredited by the Southern Association of Colleges and Schools.

Established as the Seminary West of the Suwannee by act of the Florida legislature in 1851, the institution has undergone various changes in name and mission. It was designated the Florida State College for Women from 1909 until 1947, when it became coeducational and was given its present name. Today, Florida State University is a nationally recognized comprehensive, public, coeducational research institution with a strong liberal arts base. Current enrollment is 32,878, which includes 25,965 undergraduates. The average freshman is 19 years old; the average undergraduate is 22. Minority students comprise 22 percent of the total undergraduate student population.

The main campus of FSU is composed of 456 intensely utilized acres, making it convenient for students to get to and from classes. About 63 percent of the freshman class lives on campus in one of fourteen residence halls. Housing is available for upperclass and transfer students as well. Students may also live in nearby fraternity and sorority houses or in one of the many scholarship houses surrounding the campus.

Florida State University offers a wide variety of extracurricular activities. Student clubs and organizations range from academic and professional to cultural and special interest, honorary and religious to recreational and athletic, political and theatrical to social and service. Facilities supporting student activities and recreation are extensive, including a completely equipped University Union, a Student Recreation Center, and the Seminole Reservation (a lakefront recreation area). Florida State's men's and women's athletic teams compete at the NCAA Division I level and are part of the Atlantic Coast Conference.

Location

Florida State University is located in historic Tallahassee, the capital of Florida, a city of approximately 242,000 residents. A classic college town, Tallahassee is part of the "other" Florida, with its rolling hills, canopy roads, mild climate, and Southern hospitality.

Majors and Degrees

The College of Arts and Sciences offers baccalaureate programs with majors in actuarial science, American and Florida studies (American studies), anthropology, biochemistry, biological sciences (cell biology, ecology and evolution, environmental science, genetics and molecular biology, marine biology, physiology, plant sciences, preprofessional health sciences, and zoology), chemical science, chemistry (analytical chemistry, biochemistry, chemistry, environmental chemistry, inorganic chemistry, nuclear chemistry, organic chemistry, and physical chemistry), classics (classical archaeology, classical civilizations, classics, classics and religion, and Greek and Latin), computer and information science (computer science), English (creative writing, English, English/business, linguistics, and literature), French (French, French/business, French and German, French and Italian, French and Russian, and French and Spanish), geology, German (German, German/business, German and Italian, German and Russian, and German and Spanish), Greek, history, humanities (humanities and women's studies), Italian (Italian, Italian/business, Italian and Russian, and Italian and Spanish), Latin, Latin American and Caribbean studies (Latin American and Caribbean studies and Latin American and Caribbean studies/business), mathematics (applied mathematics and mathematics), meteorology, philosophy, physics, physics-interdisciplinary (physics/biology, physics/biology–premed, physics/biophysics, physics/computer science, physics/education, physics/environmental science, physics/geology, physics/government, physics/health physics, physics/management, physics/music technology, physics/oceanography, and physics/philosophy), psychology (clinical psychology, general experimental psychology, and psychology), religion (religion and religion and classics), Russian (Russian, Russian/business, and Russian and Spanish), secondary science and/or mathematics teaching, Spanish (Spanish and Spanish/business), and statistics.

The College of Business offers programs in accounting, business administration (business administration and entrepreneurship and small-business management), finance, hospitality administration, management (human resource management, management, and operations management), management information systems, marketing, multinational business (multinational business operations), real estate, and risk management–insurance.

The College of Communication offers programs in audiology and speech pathology and in communication (advertising, communication for business, communication studies, communication theory and research, communications/art, communications/science, general communication, interpersonal communication, mass communication, media communication, media performance, media production, public relations, and speech communication).

The School of Criminology and Criminal Justice offers a program in criminology.

The College of Education offers programs in early childhood education, elementary education, emotional disturbances/learning disabilities, English education, health education (community health education and health education), mathematics education, mental retardation, multilingual/multicultural education, physical education (physical education and sports management), recreation and leisure services administration, rehabilitation services, science education, social sciences education, and visual disabilities.

The College of Engineering offers programs in chemical engineering (bioengineering, chemical engineering, environmental engineering, and materials engineering), civil engineering (civil engineering, environmental engineering), electrical engineering (electrical engineering, computer engineering), industrial engineering, and mechanical engineering.

The College of Human Sciences offers programs in clothing, textiles, and merchandising (apparel design and technology, clothing and textiles, merchandising, and textiles); family and consumer sciences education; family, child, and consumer sciences (child development; family, child, and consumer sciences; and housing); food and nutrition (dietetics, food and nutrition, food and nutrition science, and nutrition and fitness); and human sciences (exercise science, human science).

The School of Information Studies offers a program in information studies.

The School of Motion Picture, Television, and Recording Arts offers a program in motion picture, television, and recording arts.

The School of Music offers programs in music composition, music education (music education, choral music education, instrumental music education), music history and literature (music history), music–liberal arts (music–liberal arts, jazz and contemporary media), music performance (brass, guitar, harp, harpsichord, music performance, music theater–music, organ, percussion, piano, piano pedagogy, strings, voice, and woodwinds), music theory, and music therapy.

The School of Nursing offers a program in nursing.

The College of Social Sciences offers programs in Asian studies (Asian studies and Asian studies/business), economics (applied economics and economics), geography (environmental studies and geography), international affairs, political science, Russian and East European studies (Slavic and East European studies), social science, and sociology.

The School of Social Work offers a program in social work.

The School Theatre offers a program in theater (acting, design/technology, musical theater–theater, and theater).

The School of Visual Arts and Dance offers programs in art education, dance, history and criticism of art (art history), interior design, and studio art.

Preprofessional programs are offered in dentistry, law, medicine, the ministry, optometry, pharmacy, physical therapy, and veterinary medicine.

Academic Program

The liberal studies program for undergraduates provides for the study of the natural environment; the social sciences; the historical background of present-day civilization; and cultures, past and present, as expressed through language, literature, art, music, and philosophy. Undergraduate students may earn by examination a maximum of 60 of the minimum total 120 semester hours of credit required for graduation. Examinations may include departmental examinations administered by the academic departments in lieu of course work and examinations administered by national testing agencies. To encourage liberal education and to emphasize learning, the University permits limited enrollment in elective courses outside the major and minor fields on a satisfactory/unsatisfactory grading basis.

FSU recognizes scholastic excellence in a number of ways, including the announcement of deans' lists for undergraduates who achieve the required average for their school or college and honors programs for qualified upper-division students and qualified freshmen entering the Division of Undergraduate Studies.

The University seeks to facilitate the transfer of community college students at the upper-division level from public schools in Florida. Students who earn an Associate in Arts degree from a Florida public institution in a university-parallel program and who are applying for a non-limited access program are eligible to be admitted to the upper division of Florida State University. In general, transfer credit is allowed for courses completed at all other regionally accredited institutions of higher learning.

Off-Campus Arrangements

The University maintains cooperative programs with Florida Agricultural and Mechanical University and Tallahassee Community College, both located in Tallahassee. These programs permit students to take courses that are not readily available at the home institution. Students may study internationally with FSU in Italy, England, Spain, Costa Rica, France, Russia, or Vietnam. Participants can choose from a wide variety of liberal arts classes to satisfy graduation requirements while experiencing the rich cultures that these countries have to offer. The Office of Cooperative Education arranges for students to find employment in education, industry, business, government, or social-action work situations to enrich their on-campus learning experiences.

Academic Facilities

The University libraries are completely air conditioned and have more than 2.3 million book titles, 5.7 million microforms, 9,800 current serials, and 43,000 sound recordings. The Super FN accelerator plays an important role in the University's long-standing leadership in nuclear research. The Edward Ball Marine Laboratory on the Gulf Coast provides extensive facilities for teaching and research in the marine sciences. The FSU College of Computation Science and Information Technology serves research and training needs of the faculty and students in Florida and offers services to researchers throughout the country. In addition, the National High Magnetic Field Laboratory (the only national laboratory in Florida), plays a major role in the advancement of fields as diverse as biology, medicine, physics, chemistry, engineering, superconductivity, and materials science.

Costs

The typical basic expenses for one semester in 1999–2000 for an undergraduate student living in a University residence and participating in a campus food plan were a registration fee for Florida residents of $73.19 per credit hour ($306.14 per credit hour for non-Florida residents); books and supplies (estimated), $350; housing in residence halls, $1347–$1630; housing for married students, $290–$470 a month; and food (estimated), $1129–$1369.

Financial Aid

Florida State University believes that the primary purpose of financial assistance is to provide aid to students who, without assistance, would be unable to attend. Thus, financial aid is awarded based on an individual's need and the costs incident to attending the University. The Office of Financial Aid administers money from federal, state, and University sources in the form of loans, grants, scholarships, and part-time employment. Some merit scholarships are available for academically outstanding students.

Faculty

FSU employs 1,679 traditional faculty members, whose academic backgrounds reflect both diversity and quality. Approximately 90 percent of the teaching faculty members hold doctorates or other terminal degrees. Faculty members are expected to demonstrate an effective balance between classroom instruction and research.

Student Government

The student government plays an active and significant role in the development of policy. Elected and appointed officials are involved in all aspects of University life and have budget authority over activity and service fees, which total about $5.4 million.

Admission Requirements

Most Florida residents accepted to the University have at least a B+ average in their academic subjects and a combined score of at least 1100 on the SAT I or a composite score of 25 on the ACT. Out-of-state students must meet somewhat higher standards. Freshmen must have earned at least 4 units of English, 3 units of mathematics (algebra I and above), 3 units of natural science (at least 2 units with laboratory), 3 units of social science, 2 units of the same foreign language, and 4 units of academic electives. Transfer applicants with fewer than 60 transferable semester hours must meet freshman admission criteria and have a cumulative college grade point average of at least 2.5 (on a 4.0 scale). Transfer applicants with 60 or more transferable semester hours must have a 2.5 minimum cumulative college grade point average unless they will receive an Associate in Arts degree from a Florida public institution immediately prior to transferring. All transfer applicants must submit official transcripts from each institution previously attended. Access to a number of degree programs is limited at the junior year to those students meeting additional criteria. They are programs in the College of Business; College of Communication; College of Education; School of Motion Picture, Television, and Recording Arts; and School of Nursing and the majors in computer science and psychology. Auditions are required for programs in dance, music, and B.F.A. theater.

Application and Information

Office of Admissions
Florida State University
Tallahassee, Florida 32306-2400
Telephone: 850-644-6200
Fax: 850-644-0197
E-mail: admissions@admin.fsu.edu
World Wide Web: http://admissions.fsu.edu

FORDHAM UNIVERSITY
NEW YORK, NEW YORK

The University

Fordham, New York City's Jesuit University, offers a distinctive educational experience that is rooted in the 450-year-old Jesuit tradition of intellectual rigor and personal respect for the individual. The University enrolls 13,551 students, of whom 6,578 are undergraduates.

Fordham has four undergraduate colleges and six graduate schools. In addition to its full-time undergraduate programs, the University offers part-time undergraduate study at Fordham College of Liberal Studies and during two summer sessions.

Fordham College at Rose Hill and the College of Business Administration, located on the Rose Hill campus, are adjacent to the New York Botanical Garden and the Bronx Zoo. The Rose Hill campus is a self-contained 85-acre campus with residential facilities for 2,520 students and ample parking for commuters. It is easily accessible by public and private transportation. Fordham also provides an intercampus van service to transport students to and from Manhattan. Fordham College at Lincoln Center is located in Manhattan, overlooking the famous Lincoln Center for the Performing Arts complex. The Lincoln Center campus houses McMahon Hall, a new 850-bed apartment-style residence, and is accessible via the West Side Highway and major subway lines.

The University has an extensive athletics program that consists of twenty-two varsity sports, ten club sports, and numerous intramural sports. The newly renovated Murphy Field is the heart of intramural and recreational sports at Fordham, hosting softball, soccer, and flag football games. The Vincent T. Lombardi Memorial Center provides sports facilities to the campus for basketball, squash, swimming and diving, tennis, track, and water polo.

Location

With one campus in Manhattan and another only 30 minutes away, Fordham offers its students the unparalleled cultural, recreational, and academic advantages of one of the world's great cities. The University provides unusual opportunities for participating in activities of direct service to the city, ranging from small-group community projects in the Bronx to large government-sponsored projects in Manhattan. The internship program makes ample use of the advantages of Fordham's New York City location.

Majors and Degrees

Fordham University offers undergraduates more than sixty-five majors. Fordham College at Rose Hill offers programs of study leading to the B.A. or B.S. in African and African American studies, American studies, anthropology, art history, biological sciences, chemistry, classical civilization, classical languages (Latin and Greek), communication and media studies, comparative literature, computer and information sciences, economics, English, fine arts, French language and literature, French studies, general science, German, German studies, history, information systems, international political economy, Italian, Italian studies, Latin American and Latino studies, mathematics, mathematics/economics, medieval studies, Middle East studies, music, philosophy, physics, political science, psychology, religious studies, sociology, Spanish language and literature, Spanish studies, theology, urban studies, and women's studies.

Also at the Rose Hill campus, the College of Business Administration offers programs leading to the B.S. in accounting (public or management) and business administration, with areas of concentration in business economics, finance, human resource management, information and communications systems, management systems, and marketing. The G.L.O.B.E. Program provides business students with an international study option that incorporates course offerings from both Fordham College at Rose Hill and the College of Business Administration.

Special programs at Rose Hill include a cooperative engineering program, double major or individualized majors, interdisciplinary studies, the B.S./M.B.A. program, and honors programs. Preprofessional programs are offered in architecture, dentistry, law, medicine, and veterinary medicine, and a program for teacher certification is offered in elementary and secondary education.

Fordham College at Lincoln Center offers the B.A. in African and African American studies, anthropology, art history, classical civilization, classical languages (Latin and Greek), communication and media studies, comparative literature, computer and information sciences, economics, English, French language and literature, French studies, history, information systems, international/intercultural studies, Italian, Italian studies, Latin American and Latino studies, mathematics, mathematics/economics, Middle East studies, philosophy, political science, psychology, religious studies, social science, social work, sociology, Spanish language and literature, Spanish studies, studio art, theater, theology, urban studies, visual arts, and women's studies. Special programs at Fordham College at Lincoln Center include extensive offerings in the performing arts (including a new B.F.A. in dance with the Alvin Ailey Dance Company), a cooperative engineering program, creative writing, double major or individualized majors, independent study, and interdisciplinary studies. Preprofessional studies are offered in business, dentistry, health, and law. A teacher certification program is offered in elementary and secondary education.

Academic Program

Students in all the undergraduate colleges pursue a common core curriculum designed to provide them with the breadth of knowledge necessary for life in twenty-first century. Drawn from nine disciplines, the common core curriculum includes the study of philosophy, English composition and literature, history, theology, mathematical reasoning, natural science, social sciences, the fine arts, and foreign language. Business students benefit from the common core as well as additional business core courses.

Off-Campus Arrangements

Fordham participates in an exchange program with major U.S. universities and in special programs that provide opportunities to study abroad at universities in England, Ireland, Italy, Korea, Mexico, and Spain.

Academic Facilities

The outstanding libraries on the two campuses have combined holdings of more than 1.7 million volumes and 13,000 periodicals. On the Rose Hill campus, the $54-million William D. Walsh Family Library, which serves the entire Fordham community, has seating for 1,500 and a state-of-the-art Electronic Information Center, as well as media production laboratories, studios, and auditoriums. Students also have access to the vast library facilities of New York City, neighboring universities, and the various specialized collections maintained by numerous local museums and other institutions. Among laboratory facilities utilized by undergraduates are Mulcahy Hall (chemistry), Larkin Hall (biology), and Freeman Hall (physics and biology). The University has more than forty buildings that provide ample space for classrooms, science laboratories, theaters, and athletics facilities.

Costs

At the Rose Hill and Lincoln Center campuses, undergraduate costs for the 1999–2000 academic year were $19,200 for tuition and fees and between $6485 and $9580 for room and board. Residence halls are available at both campuses. Chemistry, physics, and biology fees were approximately $50 per laboratory course. Nominally priced meals are available in cafeterias on both campuses. Such incidentals as transportation and laundry vary in cost. There is no difference in fees for out-of-state students.

Financial Aid

More than 80 percent of the entering students enroll with aid from Fordham and from outside sources. Among the major aid programs are the Federal Pell Grants, Federal Supplemental Educational Opportunity Grants, Federal Perkins Loans, work grants sponsored by both the government and the University, and University grants-in-aid. Outside sources of aid include state scholarships (more than 20,000 are awarded to students entering colleges in New York State each year), the New York State Tuition Assistance Program (TAP), privately sponsored scholarships, state government loan programs, and deferred-payment programs. The University also offers academic scholarships ranging from $7500 to the full cost of tuition and room.

Applicants for aid must submit the Free Application for Federal Student Aid (FAFSA) and the College Scholarship Service PROFILE. Inquiries should be directed to the Fordham Office of Undergraduate Admission.

Faculty

The University has a full-time faculty of 594 and a student-faculty ratio of 10:1. Most members of the undergraduate faculty also teach at the graduate level, and 96 percent of the full-time faculty members hold doctoral or other terminal degrees.

Student Government

The traditional student governing body at Fordham is the United Student Government, composed of undergraduates attending the University.

Admission Requirements

Admission is based on academic performance, class rank, secondary school recommendation, and SAT I or ACT scores. Religious preference, physical handicap, race, or ethnic origin are not considered; out-of-state students are encouraged to apply. More than 57 percent of the students accepted for the freshman class ranked in the top fifth of their secondary school class, and the average combined SAT I score was 1170. Normally required are 22 high school units, including 4 in English, 3 in mathematics, 3 in science, 2 in social studies, 2 in foreign language, 2 in history, and 6 electives. For regular admission, the SAT I or the ACT should be taken no later than the January preceding entrance. Candidates for early decision should complete the examinations by October of their senior year. The University participates in the College Board's Advanced Placement Program. Personal interviews are not required but may be arranged by contacting the Office of Undergraduate Admission.

Application and Information

Application may be made for either September or January enrollment. The application deadline is February 1 for fall admission. The completed application, the secondary school report, the results of the SAT I or ACT, all financial aid forms, and an application fee of $50 (check or money order made payable to Fordham University) should be submitted by this date. Students are notified by April 1. Candidates for early decision should apply by November 1 and receive notification by December 15. Transfer students must apply by December 1 for spring admission or by July 1 for fall admission.

For additional details and application forms, students should contact:

Office of Undergraduate Admission
Thebaud Hall
Fordham University
441 East Fordham Road
New York, New York 10458-9993

Telephone: 800-FORDHAM (367-3426) (toll-free)
E-mail: enroll@fordham.edu

The William D. Walsh Family Library at Fordham University.

FORT VALLEY STATE UNIVERSITY
FORT VALLEY, GEORGIA

The University
Fort Valley State University, founded in 1895, is a unit of the University System of Georgia. Located in central Georgia, it is one of two land-grant universities in the state. Since its founding, the University has developed a comprehensive and stimulating curriculum that offers educational experiences in the liberal arts, education, and sciences as well as in selected vocational and technical fields. The student body (1,682 women and 1,141 men) represents more than fifteen states and five countries; the majority of the students come from Georgia. The University's physical facilities range from older buildings constructed by students in the early 1900s to the modern buildings constructed in the 1990s.

There are seventy-three approved organizations on campus through which students are able to make practical application of knowledge gained in the classroom or pursue a personal interest. Opportunities for travel, interaction with students from other colleges and universities, and participation in community affairs provide valuable experiences. Departmental organizations, service organizations, hometown organizations, scholastic honoraries, social fraternities and sororities, special interest organizations, religious organizations, and varsity athletics are among the areas of involvement provided for students.

Graduate degrees are conferred in counseling and guidance, early childhood education, mental health counseling, middle grades education, and vocational rehabilitation. A collaborative Ed.D. program with the University of Georgia is also available.

Location
Fort Valley, Georgia, is located 12 miles west of I-75 between Macon and Perry. The area is known throughout the world for its camellias and peaches and pecan industry.

Majors and Degrees
Fort Valley State University awards the undergraduate degrees of Associate of Science, Bachelor of Arts, Bachelor of Science, Bachelor of Business Administration, and Bachelor of Social Work. Majors are offered in accounting, agricultural economics, agricultural education, agricultural engineering technology, animal science, chemistry, commercial design, computer information systems, computer science, criminal justice, early childhood education, economics, electronic engineering technology, elementary education, English, food and nutrition, French, general business, home economics education, infant and child development, management, marketing, mass communication, mathematics, middle grades education, office administration, ornamental horticulture, physical education, physics, plant science, political science, psychology, social welfare, sociology, veterinary technology, and zoology.

Academic Program
The academic year consists of two 16-week semesters. There are also three- and six-week summer sessions. A full academic load is 12–18 hours. Most courses are offered on a 2- or 3-semester-hour basis.

The foundation upon which all degree programs are built is the core curriculum of the University System of Georgia. Baccalaureate degree candidates must complete 60 hours in this general education program during the freshman and sophomore years in humanities, mathematics and sciences, social sciences, and other major-specific courses. The total number of hours required for graduation varies according to the program; however, most require 120 hours.

Credit may also be obtained through the College-Level Examination Program (CLEP) or through a proficiency examination administered by the department in charge of the discipline involved. A maximum of 30 semester hours of credit by examination may be applied toward graduation requirements.

Off-Campus Arrangements
Students at Fort Valley State may participate in cooperative training programs with local agencies and industries and receive up to 3 credit hours per semester for co-op experience or a maximum of 12 hours for the total program.

In addition, students may enroll in courses at Macon, Dublin, and Robins Residence Center, which operates as an educational consortium and offers courses to academically qualified military and civilian employees of Robins Air Force Base. As a part of this center, Fort Valley State University offers academic programs leading to the Associate of Science and Bachelor of Science degrees in electronic engineering technology and computer science.

Academic Facilities
The Henry Alexander Hunt Library/Learning Resources Center is the chief information/support services facility on campus. Located centrally to all dormitories and classrooms, it has a seating capacity of 625, open stacks, computers for word processing, and a 24-hour study room. The center, which includes the Curriculum Materials Center and Media Services, has 190,062 volumes, 1,213 current periodical subscriptions, 50 newspaper subscriptions, CD-ROM computer workstations to access bibliographic information, a black heritage archival collection, and a growing video collection. The staff offers students point-of-use reference experiences, bibliographic instruction, and online capabilities for accessing databases for interlibrary loan.

Costs
In 1999–2000, matriculation and other fees were $1147 per semester, a room was $850 per semester, and board was $866 per semester. Costs per semester for 2000–01 are not available.

Financial Aid
Almost 95 percent of all Fort Valley State University students receive financial aid through federal and state grants. Aid includes Federal Pell Grants, Hope Grants, Federal Supplemental Educational Opportunity Grants, Federal Perkins Loans, Federal Stafford Student Loans, Federal Work-Study awards, Georgia Incentive Grants, Georgia Higher Education Assistance Corporation awards, and work opportunities provided by the University. Presidential Scholarships are available to Georgia residents who demonstrate outstanding scholarship. CDEP scholarships are available to students in engineering, math, and geophysics. Students requesting financial aid are required to file the appropriate forms by April 1. Further information may be obtained from the Financial Aid Office.

Faculty
Fort Valley State University has a full-time faculty of 152 members and 22 part-time members, 63 percent of whom hold an earned doctorate.

Student Government

The Student Government Association (SGA) of Fort Valley State University is the official body through which students participate in the creation and administration of the policies and regulations by which they are governed. The SGA is the organization through which students make known their needs and wishes on all matters of concern to them. The SGA recommends students to serve on all student-faculty committees, the channels through which policy is formally initiated.

Admission Requirements

All applicants are required to present acceptable scores on the SAT I or ACT. A transcript of high school credits from an accredited secondary school or a high school equivalency certificate is required. In addition to meeting regular admission requirements, transfer students must submit transcripts of all college-level work.

Students may apply for temporary enrollment as transient students at Fort Valley State University. A statement of permission to enroll as a transient student must be obtained from the Registrar or dean of a student's home institution and submitted to the registrar at least ten work days prior to the beginning of the semester in which the student wishes to enroll.

Application and Information

All applications for admission should be received at least ten work days prior to the beginning of the semester in which the applicant wishes to enroll. A $20 application fee is required.

Office of Admissions and Enrollment Management
Fort Valley State University
Fort Valley, Georgia 31030
Telephone: 912-825-6307
          800-248-7343 (toll-free in Georgia)
E-mail: admissap@mail.fvsu.edu
World Wide Web: http://www.FVSU.edu

The C. W. Pettigrew Farm and Community Life Center.

FRAMINGHAM STATE COLLEGE
FRAMINGHAM, MASSACHUSETTS

The College

Founded in 1839 as the first public college in the United States for the education of teachers, Framingham State College has a well-established tradition of academic excellence. Students discover a challenging curriculum firmly based in the liberal arts tradition, combined with many exceptional social and cocurricular activities designed to enhance their educational experience. Today, Framingham State College is known for its emphasis on undergraduate education and its commitment to "university learning in a college environment." It has become a comprehensive arts and science college with several career-related majors that serve an enrollment of 5,315 full- and part-time students. Forty percent of day-division students live on campus. Students of color represent 9 percent of the student body, while students over the age of 25 represent 20 percent of the undergraduates.

Framingham State College offers residential housing to 1,400 students in seven residence halls: four coed and three all-female. On-campus housing is guaranteed for four years. Resident students are required to purchase either a ten-, fourteen-, or nineteen-meal-per-week plan. Both the resident and commuter cafeterias are located in the D. Justin McCarthy College Center, the hub of all student activities. The College Center is the home for the campus art gallery, game room, meeting rooms, pub, radio station, college newspaper, club and organization offices, and offices for student services and student activities.

The Student Union Activities Board (SUAB) is one of the largest and most active clubs on campus. It plans the majority of campus events. There are several different committees, each with its own programming purpose, including concerts, films, special social programs, and travel and recreation. They have sponsored major concerts, dances, lectures, films, spring break events, cultural activities, and much more. SUAB also sponsors the Fall Street Fair and Spring Sandbox Weekend.

The College competes on the NCAA Division III level in a number of intercollegiate sports for men and women, including baseball, basketball, cross-country, field hockey, football, ice hockey, soccer, softball, and volleyball. A number of intramural sports are also offered. Several club sports are offered, including cheerleading, equestrian, and rugby.

Location

Located in Framingham, the largest town in Massachusetts with a population of 68,000, Framingham State College is situated 20 miles west of Boston and is accessible from all major highways (Exit 12 on I-90, the Massachusetts Turnpike). Public transportation on both train and bus lines is readily available. The 73-acre campus is in a prime residential location, offering students a small to medium-sized suburban campus with access to the cultural, social, and educational opportunities of Boston and the New England region.

Majors and Degrees

Framingham State College confers the Bachelor of Arts and Bachelor of Science degrees. Undergraduate majors are offered in art history, biology, business administration, chemistry, clothing and textiles, communication arts, computer science, consumer and family studies, early childhood education, economics, elementary education, English, food and nutrition, food science, French, geography, history, mathematics, nursing (post-RN program), politics, pre-engineering, psychology, sociology, Spanish, and studio art. Within the twenty-five major programs are a variety of concentrations and minors. The following preprofessional programs are also offered: dental, law, medical, and veterinary.

Academic Program

The mission of Framingham State College is to offer a dynamic and affordable program of educational excellence to its students. The College emphasizes a broadly based curriculum that blends the liberal arts and sciences with several professional fields.

Each student must satisfy a thirty-two-course requirement for completion of any degree program. Up to twenty courses form the basis of a student's major area of study. The other twelve courses are used to fulfill the general education requirement, which encompasses the humanities, social sciences, natural and physical sciences, mathematics, and computer science. The general education requirement ensures that students will experience the benefits of a liberal arts education through familiarity with a variety of curricula. Each student is assigned a faculty member in his or her major as an academic adviser. Undeclared students are assigned advisers through the Center for Academic Support and Advising (CASA). Selected students may participate in departmental and College-wide honors programs.

The College operates on the traditional two-semester calendar, with two optional summer sessions as well as a winter intersession.

Off-Campus Arrangements

Framingham State College students may choose to participate in one or several College-affiliated programs, allowing them to take credit-bearing courses outside of the College. Among the most popular are internships, the CAPS (College Academic Program Sharing) program, the Massachusetts Bay Marine Studies Consortium, the Washington (D.C.) Internship, and study abroad.

Internships are available in most majors at the College. Annually, hundreds of FSC students serve as interns in the State House, town and city governments, museums, and a variety of businesses and high-technology firms in the greater Boston area. Internships allow students the opportunity to gain direct, practical experience, while applying the knowledge and skills they have acquired in the classroom.

Through the CAPS program, Framingham State College students may take up to 30 semester hours of college credit at one of the other eight Massachusetts state colleges. Students who participate in the Massachusetts Bay Marine Studies Consortium may also attend a variety of credit-bearing classes and symposia at other schools.

For those students who seek an international dimension to enhance their undergraduate program, study abroad for a summer, semester, or academic year is an option. In the past, students have studied in Canada, England, France, Ireland, Italy, Mexico, New Zealand, and Spain.

Academic Facilities

The Henry Whittemore Library houses 200,000 bound volumes, 60,000 volume equivalents in microforms, and 1,600 current periodicals in subscriptions. Four online computer systems supplement the present publications, giving students access to materials from other libraries, such as the Minuteman Library Network. The College provides extensive computing capabilities for its students. The primary delivery vehicle is a LAN of nearly 100 486DX personal computers running under Novell NetWare version 3.12. The file server for the LAN is capable of storing two gigabytes of data. To ensure high availability, the server's disk drives are mirrored and the disk controllers duplexed. All workstations contain eight megabytes of RAM and are Windows capable. Academic departments have computer systems and software available to their students.

A child-care center, planetarium, and greenhouse, housed in Hemenway Hall, provide students with the opportunity to gain practical experience in related studies. Likewise, the radio station and television studios serve as forums to apply textbook knowledge.

The Challenger Learning Center, established in memory of Christa Corrigan McAuliffe, the nation's first teacher astronaut and a 1970 graduate of the College, is located on campus. The Center provides a unique hands-on learning experience designed to foster interest in mathematics, science, and technology.

Costs

Tuition and fees for the 1999–2000 academic year were $2976 for in-state students and $8936 for out-of-state students. Yearly residence hall charges were $2399, and the yearly meal plan was $1660. Students should anticipate additional expenses for books, supplies, transportation, and personal items. All costs are subject to change.

Financial Aid

Sources of financial aid available to Framingham State College students include federal, state, and institutional programs. Framingham State College students were the recipients of more than $10.5 million last year in loans, scholarships, grants, and work-study.

Federal programs incorporate the Federal Work-Study program, the Federal Pell Grant, Federal Supplemental Educational Opportunity Grant, the Federal Perkins Loan, and both subsidized and unsubsidized Federal Stafford Student Loans. State-funded aid includes state scholarship grants and a No-Interest Loan Program. Institutional funds mainly provide scholarships.

All students applying for financial aid must file the Free Application for Federal Student Aid (FAFSA), designating Framingham State College as the recipient. Transfer students must submit financial aid transcripts documenting all previous aid received. The priority filing deadline for fall entrance is March 1.

Faculty

There are more than 165 full-time faculty members, all of whom are dedicated to upholding the undergraduate mission of the College. More than 70 percent of them hold the doctoral degree in their field. The active involvement of many professors in research and writing complements their primary commitment and dedication to teaching excellence at the undergraduate level. With an impressive student-faculty ratio of 15:1, Framingham is able to offer a variety of programs in a challenging academic atmosphere.

Student Government

The Student Government Association (SGA) is the center of all political and social activity of the students of Framingham State College. The primary duties of SGA are to provide funding for more than thirty organizations through the student activity fee, to ensure representation of the Framingham State College students in the state student organization, and to act on all other matters that concern the students of the College. SGA also plays a major role in the formulation of College policies, which are of mutual concern to the students, the faculty, and the administration, through the All College Governance system. All students who pay activity fees are eligible to seek one of the many positions within SGA and are encouraged to do so.

Admission Requirements

Framingham State College seeks to enroll students with a strong academic background who possess the necessary skills to succeed in college. Admission decisions are based primarily on the strength of the high school record and test scores. Secondary school students are required to pass 16 college-preparatory units: 4 years of English; 3 years of math, including algebra I and II and geometry; 3 years of science, including 2 years of laboratory science; 2 years of history/social science, including 1 year of U.S. history; 2 years of the same foreign language; and two college-preparatory-level electives. High school students are encouraged to elect additional courses in music, art, and computer science.

Students in the upper 50 percent of their class with a B average or higher are encouraged to apply. Recommendations, essays, and personal statements are not required but may be submitted as part of the applicant's materials. International and transfer students, as well as adults returning to college (ARC), are also encouraged to apply.

To be considered for admission to a degree program at the College, all applicants must submit a completed application along with the application fee ($10 for in-state and $25 for out-of-state student), an official high school transcript, and official SAT I scores. Transfer students must submit official transcripts from all colleges previously attended.

Application and Information

It is recommended that students apply by the priority filing date of March 15 for fall admission (December 1 for spring admission). Interviews are not required, but students are encouraged to attend an admissions information session and tour. The information sessions are presented by a member of the admissions staff and are followed by a tour of the campus conducted by a student admissions representative. Students should call the Office of Admissions to arrange an appointment.

For further information, application materials, or to schedule a campus visit, students should contact:

Office of Admissions
Framingham State College
100 State Street
P.O. Box 9101
Framingham, Massachusetts 01701-9101
Telephone: 508-626-4500
E-mail: admiss@frc.mass.edu
World Wide Web: http://www.framingham.edu

FRANCISCAN UNIVERSITY OF STEUBENVILLE
STEUBENVILLE, OHIO

The University

The College of Steubenville was founded in 1946 by the Franciscan Friars, T.O.R., to fulfill the need for an institution of higher learning in the Steubenville area. What began as a hometown storefront college is today a 114-acre hilltop campus drawing 1,691 undergraduate students from fifty states and thirty-five countries. In 1980, the Ohio Board of Regents granted university status to the College of Steubenville. In becoming a university, the institution has diversified and broadened the educational opportunities available to students while continuing to offer all the advantages of a small private college. The University is fully accredited by the North Central Association of Colleges and Schools and approved by the Department of Education of the state of Ohio. Its nursing program is approved by the National League for Nursing Accrediting Commission.

Franciscan University of Steubenville is nationally and internationally known as a center of Christian renewal. It is committed to providing high-quality academics in a Catholic environment.

A "household" system within the residence halls brings students together to form close personal relationships. Sharing a section of a hall, they also share their ideas, questions, and problems in a supportive manner that benefits every member of the group.

In addition to bachelor's and associate degrees, the University also offers a Master of Arts in Counseling, Master of Arts in Philosophy, Master of Arts in Theology and Christian Ministry, Master of Business Administration, Master of Science in Education, Master of Science in Educational Administration, and Master of Science in Nursing.

Franciscan University also offers an external Master of Arts in Theology and Christian Ministry through its Distance Learning Program. Students may complete 30 of the 36 graduate credits through audiotaped courses; 6 credits must be earned on campus during summer sessions.

Location

The University is located an hour's drive west of Pittsburgh, 2½ hours south of Cleveland, and 2½ hours east of Columbus and is easily accessible from major highways, turnpikes, and the Pittsburgh International Airport. Steubenville is a small urban community with a population of 22,000. Because of the town's proximity to metropolitan areas, students at the University can have the advantages of a large city as well as the atmosphere of a small community.

Majors and Degrees

Franciscan University of Steubenville grants the Bachelor of Arts degree in biology, chemistry, classics, communication arts (journalism and TV/radio), economics, English (drama, literature, Western and world literature, and writing), French, history, humanities and Catholic culture, philosophy, political science, psychology, sociology, Spanish, and theology. The Bachelor of Science degree is granted in accounting, anthropology, business administration (economics, finance, management, and marketing), computer information science, computer science, education (with twenty different licensure programs), engineering science, mathematical sciences, mental health and human services, nursing, and social work. Associate degrees are awarded in accounting, business administration, child development, general studies, and theology. Minors are offered in Franciscan studies, human life studies, and music. The special honors program in the Great Books of Western Civilization is offered to highly qualified candidates and is limited to 40 students. A pre-theology program and an M.B.A. 4+1 program are also offered.

The University also offers the following preprofessional programs: dentistry, law, medicine, occupational therapy, optometry, pharmacy, physical therapy, and veterinary medicine.

Academic Program

Whatever the major, a student's education is made richer, broader, and more valuable through the study of a variety of academic disciplines. Students take classes that help develop their communication skills while expanding their knowledge of the humanities, the natural sciences, the social sciences, and theology. These requirements, plus the electives chosen, allow students to explore new areas and to deepen their knowledge and understanding of the fields outside their major that interest them most.

The academic curriculum is divided into three main categories. The first category, courses in the major program, consists of introductory courses and a minimum of 24 credit hours in upper-level courses, in which the student must maintain at least a C average.

Courses in the Core Program, the second main category, broaden students' interests; expose them to different points of view; challenge them to rethink their positions on questions of values, religion, society, nature, and self; and enable them to communicate their thoughts, beliefs, questions, and opinions effectively.

Elective courses, the third main category of the curriculum, permit students to sample courses that seem interesting, that may complement their major, or that may prepare them for alternative careers in the future. Students take sufficient elective courses to complete the 124 credits needed for graduation. The actual number of electives varies with each major program.

Through consultation with a faculty adviser, a student may select courses that fulfill requirements in a second field (for a minor or a double major).

Franciscan University of Steubenville actively participates in the Advanced Placement and College-Level Examination programs and gives credit by examination in a number of subjects.

Academic Facilities

Through the John Paul II Library's OPAL Catalog and OhioLINK Network, students have access to more than 6.4 million books and journals in addition to the University's own collection of 200,000 books, 30,000 bound periodicals, and subscriptions to more than 900 current periodicals. Online databases include the OhioLINK catalog for online searching and borrowing from more than seventy Ohio libraries; access to more than eighty specialized databases in social sciences, the sciences, and humanities; nearly 2,000 full-text journals on line; and ATLA Religion Indexes, Catholic Periodical and Literature Index, Philosopher's Index, and other CD-ROM databases.

Egan Hall houses classrooms, a theater, and special laboratories for the education, computer science, and psychology departments. Franciscan University opened an $11-million state-of-the-art science building in fall 2000. This 43,000-square-foot, four-story campus addition furnishes extensive classroom, laboratory, and storage space for the departments of biology; chemistry, physics, and engineering science; and computer science and mathematical science. It will enormously enhance the University's ability to give its growing number of students in sciences the first-class education they need to thrive in the highly sophisticated and increasingly complex scientific fields.

A simulated nursing clinic, equipped with examining room, tables, beds, and lab equipment, gives nursing students the opportunity to practice their skills. Nursing students gain clinical experience in hospitals and health-care facilities in the tri-state area of Ohio, West Virginia, and Pennsylvania.

Costs

For the 2000–01 academic year, tuition for full-time students is $12,690, room and board costs are $5070, and the activity fee is $280.

Financial Aid

The University participates in all available federal, state, and local financial aid programs. More than 80 percent of the students receive assistance through grant, scholarship, loan, and work programs. Application for assistance is made by means of the Free Application for Federal Student Aid (FAFSA). Academic scholarships are awarded on the basis of merit, without consideration of financial need.

The University has several special programs that increase the amount of institutional aid available to qualified students. The Student Work Opportunity Program puts students to work helping with important operations of the University while they earn money to be applied toward their tuition and fees. An institutional loan program makes additional self-help funds available at a reasonable rate of interest.

Faculty

Both lay and religious faculty members willingly invest their talents and energies in a people-building process that takes place in and out of the classroom. There are 149 full-time and part-time faculty members who make personal attention the rule rather than the exception. The student-faculty ratio is 16:1.

Student Government

The heart of student participation in the decision-making process of the University is in the Franciscan University Student Association. Other organizations and committees address the needs of specific constituencies of the student body. The Student Activities Board, along with its specific committees, provides for social and cultural activities. Chapel Ministry addresses pastoral concerns involved in meeting students' spiritual needs.

Admission Requirements

The University has a rolling admission policy. The application deadline for fall resident student enrollment is June 1. No single factor determines admission. The decision is based on a satisfactory high school record and recommendation, and satisfactory entrance examination scores (SAT I or ACT), all in relation to the student's proposed major.

A student must present a minimum of 15 high school units with at least 10 units in four of the following fields: English, foreign language, social science, mathematics, and natural sciences. The remaining 5 units may be in other subjects counted toward graduation. Students applying for admission with a major in chemistry, engineering science, or mathematical sciences should have 2 units in algebra and 2 units in geometry and trigonometry combined.

Transfer students must also submit a transcript from every college previously attended; once accepted, they may request preliminary evaluations of these transcripts. Full credit is given for courses transferred from an approved institution, provided the grade for each course is a C or better. No correspondence courses are accepted, but a maximum of 30 credits is allowed for extension work from an approved institution.

Application and Information

Prospective students are encouraged to apply as early as possible. Applicants must submit a completed application with the $20 application fee, official high school (and previous college) transcripts, and scores on the SAT I or ACT (which may be included on the high school transcript).

More information about Franciscan University of Steubenville is available by contacting:

Director of Admissions
Franciscan University of Steubenville
1235 University Boulevard
Steubenville, Ohio 43952
Telephone: 740-283-6226
           800-783-6220 (toll-free)
E-mail: admissions@franuniv.edu
World Wide Web: http://www.franuniv.edu

Saints Cosmas and Damian Science Hall, scheduled for completion by fall 2000.

FRANCIS MARION UNIVERSITY
FLORENCE, SOUTH CAROLINA

The University

Francis Marion University (FMU), established by the South Carolina legislature in 1970, is a four-year coeducational comprehensive institution with a growing number of graduate programs. Named for one of South Carolina's greatest heroes, General Francis Marion of Revolutionary War fame, the University has shown the same qualities of strength attributed to the patriot general.

The institution believes that all qualified South Carolina students and a number of out-of-state and international students should have the privilege of formal academic university training at Francis Marion University at a level consistent with their talents. This belief is the basis of the University's intention to attract students with a wide range of abilities and preparation and to provide them with academic experience that will permit them to contribute to the well-being of their community, state, and nation. To achieve these ends, Francis Marion offers numerous programs of study in the liberal arts and professional programs in education, business, the sciences, and technology. Although the teaching mission of Francis Marion University is paramount, research programs are also supported in order to sustain faculty vigor and to enhance the quality of teaching. Much of the University's research is related to faculty development.

Francis Marion is accredited by the Commission on Colleges of the Southern Association of Colleges and Schools (SACS) to award bachelor's- and master's-level degrees. The business programs are accredited by AACSB–The International Association for Management Education. The teacher education programs of the University are approved by the National Council for Accreditation of Teacher Education (NCATE). The chemistry program is approved by the Committee on Professional Training of the American Chemical Society, and the psychology program meets the standards of training approved by the Council of Applied Master's Programs in Psychology (CAMPP). The Master of Science in Applied Psychology Program is accredited by the Interorganizational Board for Accreditation of Master's in Psychology Programs (IBAMPP). The theater arts program is accredited by the National Association of Schools of Theatre (NAST), and the visual arts and art education programs are accredited by the National Association of Schools of Art and Design (NASAD). The University is approved by the South Carolina State Board of Education and is a member of the American Council on Education and the American Association of State Colleges and Universities.

The Francis Marion athletic program is a member of the NCAA Division II Peach Belt Athletic Conference, which consists of twelve members in Florida, Georgia, North Carolina, and South Carolina. The school sponsors seven intercollegiate men's sports (baseball, basketball, cross-country, golf, soccer, tennis, and track and field) and seven women's sports (basketball, cross-country, soccer, softball, tennis, track and field, and volleyball). In addition to a 3,027-seat gymnasium, the Smith University Center houses an eight-lane pool, racquetball and handball courts, a fitness room, lockers and showers, a sauna, the University Center Cafe, a television lounge, and the Patriot Bookstore.

Students are informed through the campus newspaper, *The Patriot;* animated electronic signboards; a cable education access channel; and a travelers' information radio station operated by the institution. The institution also provides artistic, scientific, and literary programs for the public, both on campus and in the various communities the University serves.

In addition to the undergraduate majors and degrees listed below, graduate degrees are offered in business administration, education, and applied psychology.

Location

Located on a 300-acre tract of land originally included in a grant by the King of England and later made a cotton plantation, Francis Marion University is situated 7 miles east of Florence in the beautiful northeastern section of South Carolina. The University is located on U.S. Highways 76 and 301 and is just more than an hour's drive from Myrtle Beach and the Grand Strand and 4 hours from the Blue Ridge Mountains. With a metropolitan-area population of 125,000, the city of Florence is nestled alongside Interstate Highway 95, the main north-south corridor from the New England area to Miami, and at the eastern end of Interstate Highway 20. The city is served by Amtrak, bus service, and a regional airport.

Majors and Degrees

Francis Marion University offers four undergraduate degrees: Bachelor of Arts, Bachelor of Business Administration, Bachelor of General Studies, and Bachelor of Science. Twenty-eight majors (accounting, art education, biology, business economics, chemistry, computer information systems management, computer science, early childhood education, economics, elementary education, English, finance, French, general business administration, history, international studies, management, marketing, mass communication, mathematics, physics, political science, psychology, secondary education certification, sociology, Spanish, theater arts, and visual arts) are available in addition to cooperative programs with other institutions and several preprofessional programs. The health physics program prepares students for careers in nuclear physics and is one of only three such programs in the Southeast.

Academic Program

The usual course load for Francis Marion University students is 15 to 17 hours per semester. The University offers four undergraduate degrees, each of which requires a minimum of 120 semester hours of approved credit. This includes those hours required for completion of the General Education Program (48 to 60 hours) and those required for majoring in a particular area or areas of concentration. To meet the special needs of students with superior academic ability, the University has an honors program, which is implemented through honors sections of regular courses, an interdisciplinary honors colloquium, and an honors independent study.

The fall academic semester begins in late August and continues through early December. The spring semester begins in early January and runs through the end of April. A three-week late spring term is available for students, in which they are allowed to take one course. The University also offers two 5-week summer terms: early June through early July and mid-July through mid-August.

The University gives credit for courses in which College Entrance Examination Board Advanced Placement Examinations have been given and in which appropriate levels of competence have been demonstrated. The score necessary for credit for a particular course is determined cooperatively by the Advanced Placement Committee of the University and the appropriate department or school.

Academic Facilities

The University's physical plant includes nine major buildings: J. Howard Stokes Administration Building; James A. Rogers

Library, which houses more than 355,000 volumes; Robert E. McNair Science Building; Hugh K. Leatherman, Sr. Science Facility; Walter Douglas Smith University Center; Founders Hall; John K. Cauthen Educational Media Center; Peter D. Hyman Fine Arts Center; and the Thomas C. Stanton Academic Computer Center. Francis Marion is also home to a two-story observatory, equipped with a 14-inch reflecting telescope, and a planetarium, which offers public shows twice monthly.

Costs

University fees for the 1999–2000 academic year were $3260 for in-state undergraduate students and $6520 for out-of-state undergraduate students. Housing fees per year were $1650 for a 4-person, four-bedroom apartment; $1750 for a 2-person, one-bedroom apartment; and $3550 for a 2-person dormitory room (which includes a meal plan). For interested students, the University offers a Living Learning Residence Hall. These figures do not include the cost of books and miscellaneous expenses and are subject to change.

Financial Aid

The University administers a variety of scholarship, grant, loan, and work programs. Presidential Scholarships, Francis Marion Scholarships, and Francis Marion Academic Excellence Scholarships in varying amounts are made possible by numerous organizations and individuals. Federal Pell Grants, Federal Supplemental Educational Opportunity Grants, Federal Perkins Loans, Federal Stafford Student Loans, Federal Work-Study Program, South Carolina Need-Based Grants, South Carolina Teacher Loans, and institutional work-study programs are also available.

Students must complete and file the Free Application for Federal Student Aid (FAFSA) as soon as possible after January 1 of the year in which the students want to receive fall semester financial assistance. The FAFSA is required for most types of financial assistance and is available from high school counselors and the University Office of Business Affairs–Financial Assistance after January 1. Priority processing is given to students who file prior to March 1. To be considered for an institutional scholarship, the FMU Application for Institutional Scholarship Application must be submitted to the Office of Financial Assistance by March 1, and students are encouraged to file a FAFSA.

Faculty

Francis Marion University employs 159 full-time faculty members, about 85 percent of whom hold doctoral degrees, and 42 part-time faculty members. The average class size is 21 students. All students are assigned a faculty adviser (in their curriculum) to assist them with class scheduling and academic planning. Incoming freshmen are required to take the Freshman Seminar course, an introduction to the opportunities available at the University.

Student Government

Upon enrollment, all full-time students automatically become members of the Student Government Association, the organization that represents all students in planning, organizing, and directing the student organizations and programs on campus. The Student Government Association consists of an executive council, a legislative assembly, and a judicial council and provides an early experience in self-government, which, in turn, serves as a useful background for later public service. The Student Government Association jointly participates with the faculty and administration in certain designated areas of governance of the University.

Admission Requirements

Francis Marion University encourages all qualified students to apply. Equal educational opportunities are offered to students regardless of race, sex, religion, color, or national origin. Incoming freshmen are required to have a high school diploma or its equivalent and a satisfactory high school record, including completion of the following college-preparatory courses: English (4 courses), mathematics (3), laboratory science (2), foreign language (2), U.S. history (1), physical education or ROTC (1), social studies (2), and mathematics, computer science, or social sciences (1). Applicants must also have satisfactory scores on the SAT I or ACT in addition to the proper completion of all application material and a recommendation from their high school. Transfer students with at least 24 transferable hours must present proof of eligibility to return to the last school attended and satisfactory grades on all academic work attempted at previous institutions. All international student applicants must meet regular admission requirements and must submit satisfactory scores on the Test of English as a Foreign Language (TOEFL) and verification that adequate financial resources are available for expenses while attending the institution. Admission of adult students is by special action of the Admissions Committee. Francis Marion also offers admission, for one or more courses, to high school seniors of exceptional ability.

Although interviews are not required for admission, prospective students may arrange a visit and tour of the campus by contacting the Office of Admissions. The University holds three open house programs for high school juniors and seniors during the academic year, one in the fall and two in the spring.

Application and Information

Prospective students are encouraged to take the SAT I or ACT (and request that the score be sent to Francis Marion University) and to complete and return to the Office of Admissions an application form with the $25 nonrefundable application fee. Students may also apply on line. They should request that their high school principal or guidance counselor send a transcript of their high school record through their junior year, their class rank, courses enrolled in as a senior, and an evaluation and recommendation.

Application forms and other information about Francis Marion University may be obtained by contacting:

Office of Admissions
Francis Marion University
P.O. Box 100547
Florence, South Carolina 29501-0547

Telephone: 800-368-7551 (toll-free)
Fax: 843-661-4635
E-mail: admission@fmarion.edu
World Wide Web: http://www.fmarion.edu

The Leatherman Science Facility.

FRANKLIN COLLEGE OF INDIANA
FRANKLIN, INDIANA

The College
Founded in 1834 as one of Indiana's first and finest coeducational liberal arts institutions, Franklin College has a long tradition of excellence in education, leadership, and professional preparation. A Franklin education revolves around the broad goal of achieving wealth of mind, health of body, and strength of character while developing sensitivity to others through close personal relationships with classmates and faculty members. Franklin's commitment together with the faculty's support for this focus on leadership and professional development, curriculum, and internship programs support this goal. While the majority of the 900 students come from Indiana, many other states and countries are represented. Seven residence halls (including the newly renovated Freshman Residence Center) provide a variety of living arrangements on the Franklin College campus.

The 74-acre campus currently includes seventeen buildings and the houses of five national fraternities. The Student Entertainment Board (SEB) is responsible for scheduling campuswide social events. The Eli Lilly Campus Center, with its student lounge, recreation room, snack shop, bookstore, and campus dining facility, serves as a center for numerous student activities. Franklin College sponsors more than seventy academic, social, and religious extracurricular groups. Additional campus involvement includes intercollegiate athletic competition at the NCAA Division III level for both men and women. Involvement in many activities enhances a student's personal growth and fulfills the "Franklin College Experience."

Location
An excellent relationship exists between the city of Franklin (population 15,000) and the College. The campus is a 20-minute drive south from downtown Indianapolis. The Indianapolis International Airport is a 25-minute drive from campus.

Majors and Degrees
Franklin College confers the Bachelor of Arts degree in the following areas: accounting, American studies, biology, business (finance, general, international business, management/industrial relations, and marketing), Canadian studies, chemistry, computing/computer information systems, economics, education (elementary, middle school, and secondary), English, French, history, journalism (advertising/public relations, broadcasting, and news-editorial), mathematics, philosophy, physical education, physics, political science, psychology, religious studies, sociology (criminal justice and social work), Spanish, and theater. Minors are also offered in many of these areas and in fine arts.

Students considering a career in dentistry, forestry, medical technology, medicine, nursing, optometry, or veterinary medicine arrange their program with the advice of the Pre-Professional Advisor of the science division. Students seeking a career in law plan their program in consultation with Pre-Law Advisors. Students planning a career in secondary education may elect an academic area of concentration that will satisfy the state requirements for a teaching major. The education department is endorsed and approved by the Indiana Professional Standards Board and the National Council for Accreditation of Teacher Education (NCATE).

Franklin College offers cooperative programming in various areas of study. A combined-degree program in medical technology is offered in cooperation with two nearby hospitals. A cooperative B.S. degree program in engineering is available through Washington University; a combined B.S. degree in nursing is available through a cooperative arrangement with Rush University; a combined B.S. and graduate degree program in public health is available through the University of South Florida.

Academic Program
The current academic program is the result of the faculty's plan to meet the express needs of students; the primary emphasis is on the unity of knowledge. Franklin believes in the importance of providing students with a liberal arts background while they develop talents for a particular professional career. Approximately one third of each student's total course work is composed of the prescribed and exploratory courses that make up the general education core curriculum.

All of Franklin's academic departments offer individualized study, allowing a student to pursue his or her field of interest in depth.

As part of the 4-1-4 calendar, students complete up to 8 hours of credit in a special four-week winter-term program in January. The winter term is designed to allow students to study in areas of particular interest to them, either within or outside their major field of study. A large number of internships are available during the winter term and the summer, offering practical experience under the supervision of a professional. The fall semester ends before Christmas; the spring semester begins in February and ends in May. An eight-week summer session beginning in mid-June allows students to take up to 9 additional credit hours.

Franklin gives credit in seventeen academic areas for successful scores on CLEP subject examinations; credit is also granted for successful scores on the Advanced Placement tests of the College Board. The Running Start Program enables talented high school students to get an early start on their college education.

Off-Campus Arrangements
Franklin College students participate in a variety of off-campus study experiences, including a year or a semester of study through Acadia University of Nova Scotia, Telemark University of Norway, and Hong Kong Baptist University. Other off-campus study programs include the American University Washington Semester; a junior year abroad; programs at Harlaxton College in England, Franklin College of Switzerland, and Brethren Colleges Abroad; and specific exchange programs in Japan and Taiwan.

Academic Facilities
Franklin College has two campus buildings listed on the National Historic Register. Old Main, the original home of the College, and Shirk Hall, home of the Pulliam School of Journalism, are footholds of the rich past and recent renovation of the Franklin College campus. Classrooms and administrative, business, and professorial offices, along with computer laboratories, occupy Old Main; Shirk Hall also houses classrooms and the radio and television stations.

A. A. Barnes Science Building, also recently renovated, houses all science, biology, and chemistry department classrooms and laboratories. The newly renovated Spurlock Center gymnasium and fitness center provides increased classroom and office space and an improved weight room.

The newest addition to the academic facilities on campus is the Dietz Center for Professional Development, home of the Professional Development Program and the program's epicenter. State-of-the-art conference rooms and computer facilities enhance Franklin's career programming commitment to its students.

The B. F. Hamilton Library, containing more than 117,000 volumes and collections of microfilm, slides, art reproductions, recordings, and periodicals, is a member of P.A.L.N.I. (Private Academic Library Network of Indiana) and continues to grow and house additional classrooms and computer facilities. The 2001 completion of the Center for Learning and Fine Arts will provide new classrooms and practice and performance accommodations, and it will house the facilities and meeting rooms for the Leadership and Professional Development program.

Costs

The total cost of the 2000–01 academic year is $19,100. This amount is derived from tuition ($14,100), room and board ($4800), an orientation fee ($50), and the student activity fee ($150), which entitles a student to admittance to all athletic contests and winter events.

Financial Aid

The Franklin College financial aid program assists students who might not otherwise be able to attend college and also rewards applicants for excellent academic achievement in high school. Awards are based on scholarship, curricular and extracurricular activities, and financial need. Aid involving financial need includes Franklin College grants, loans, and employment. Franklin participates in the Federal Stafford Student Loan, Federal Perkins Loan, and Federal Work-Study programs. Ben Franklin Distinguished Scholarships, President's Scholarships, Academic Excellence Scholarships, and Dean's Scholarships are awarded on the basis of academic performance, activities, and standardized test scores. The Ben Franklin Scholarship covers the full cost of tuition, room, and board; the President's Scholarship is a full-tuition award; and Academic Excellence and Dean's Scholarships are awarded automatically on the basis of specified criteria. Scholarships are renewable for each of the recipient's four academic years at Franklin, provided students maintain a minimum GPA of 3.0 and advance in class status each year. The Free Application for Federal Student Aid (FAFSA) is required.

Faculty

The 13:1 student-faculty ratio allows Franklin faculty members to provide excellent instruction in small classes that promote participatory learning. Eighty percent of current faculty members have obtained the highest degree in their field. Faculty members serve as advisers, and the majority reside in the city of Franklin, which enables them to provide supplemental attention outside the classroom. While many faculty members carry on research and publish their work, their main emphasis is teaching. No classes are taught by graduate students or teaching assistants.

Student Government

The Student Congress is composed of representatives elected by the student body. The congress provides a forum for student concerns and is the most important governmental communication link among students, faculty, and administration. Student government also includes the Judicial Board and the Residence Hall Council. These groups have jurisdiction over certain questions concerning the social standards and regulations of the College.

Admission Requirements

Applications for admission to Franklin College are evaluated on an individual basis. A student's potential academic and personal contributions to the College, recommendations, school and community activities, academic record, and standardized test scores are taken into consideration by the Admissions Committee. A student should complete a strong college-preparatory program. Candidates for admission are urged to visit the campus in order to experience the College community.

Application and Information

To be considered for admission, an applicant must submit a completed application, a transcript of all secondary school and college work attempted, and either SAT I or ACT scores. A decision regarding acceptance is made after the College receives all necessary credentials. Notification is sent immediately after the Admissions Committee has acted.

For further information, students should contact:

Admissions Office
Franklin College
501 East Monroe Street
Franklin, Indiana 46131
Telephone: 317-738-8062
　　　　　　800-852-0232 (toll-free)
Fax: 317-738-8274
E-mail: admissions@franklincollege.edu
World Wide Web: http://www.franklincollege.edu

The bell tower on top of "Old Main" on the Franklin College campus.

FRANKLIN COLLEGE SWITZERLAND
LUGANO, SWITZERLAND

The College

Franklin College has a single specific mission: to provide students with an educational experience that is in every significant respect international. Students live in a vigorous Swiss city and mix freely with its population, as well as with their fellow students and faculty members who come from more than fifty different countries. Most of Franklin's courses are cross-cultural in content or perspective or both.

Named for the United States' first and most illustrious ambassador to Europe, Franklin College was founded in 1969 as a non-profit and independent postsecondary institution that takes as its cornerstone Benjamin Franklin's vigorous support of intellectual interchange between nations. Franklin students want their college education to be international, partly because the need for people with an international competence is great. Many have a cross-cultural background from parents or relatives born or raised in another country; all share the desire to let their college studies take them beyond national boundaries. Franklin College is the "international alternative" in education.

One third of the students come from the United States and two thirds from Europe, Asia, Africa, South America, and the Middle East. Bringing a variety of experiences and perspectives to college life, they live in College apartment residences on and near the campus. The apartments all have kitchenettes, though the campus cafeteria also provides regular meal service, and there is a residence supervisor for each of the five buildings.

Campus activities are varied. The College Student Union promotes a student newspaper, a literary magazine, a theater group, language and sports clubs, and a variety of social events that take advantage of southern Switzerland's extensive recreational resources. For sports, the Dean of Students enrolls interested students in the considerable number of local Swiss clubs and teams that welcome newcomers—especially basketball, football, ice hockey, soccer, and volleyball teams, but also clubs for crew, fencing, flying, golf, hang gliding, ice-skating, judo, parachuting, riding, rock-climbing, sailing, swimming, tennis, track, and windsurfing. By joining the local groups, Franklin students become part of the region's life; they are themselves essential to the cross-cultural learning the College promotes.

Location

The Franklin College campus is in the Sorengo section of the city of Lugano, southern Switzerland's principal business, banking, medical, and cultural center. Accessible from campus either by public transportation or on foot, downtown Lugano and its surrounding lakeside villages are renowned for their scenic beauty and Mediterranean climate. Palm trees line lakefront piazzas, and an outdoor life-style is typical of Ticino, the Italian-speaking canton of Switzerland that best exemplifies Swiss versatility in all three of the national languages—Italian, German, and French.

Throughout the year, Lugano features outstanding cultural activities at the world-famous Thyssen art collection, the Swiss-Italian radio station with its own permanent symphony orchestra, and the International Convention Center, which attracts guest performers from around the world. Three public museums, many art galleries, several movie houses, and a multitude of restaurants and discotheques make for a range of recreational choices normally found only in a large city. A covered ice rink, swimming pools, and a wide range of other sports facilities are maintained by local sports clubs; Lugano and the southern part of Switzerland offer access to an extraordinary variety of sports activities. In the spring and fall, Ticino's most popular recreation is hiking. In winter, skiing is available on Mount Tamaro, 20 minutes' drive from campus, or in the fabled St. Moritz, Davos, Klosters, and Zermatt.

Majors and Degrees

The Bachelor of Arts program offers majors in history and literature, international banking and finance, international communications, international economics, international management, international relations, literature, modern languages, and visual and communication arts, with combined and double majors in two of nine subject areas. The Associate in Arts degree program provides a strong liberal arts foundation for students who usually continue their education in a baccalaureate degree program. The Institute for Modern European Studies, the Institute for International Management, and the Institute for Political Science and Economics offer specialized, one-year diploma programs for students coming to Franklin from colleges and universities in the United States.

Academic Program

Franklin's curricula promote international awareness and integrative thinking by being interdisciplinary in the highest tradition of liberal education. The courses of study explore the diverse disciplines that inform an educated human being. Students must complete at least 126 credit hours to be eligible for the B.A. degree (64 for the A.A. degree) and must maintain a minimum cumulative grade point average of 2.0 on a 4.0 scale.

As an integral credit-bearing part of the academic program, students participate twice a year (in mid-October and mid-March) in faculty-led academic travel-study programs to various destinations in Eastern and Western Europe, Africa, Asia, and the United States.

All degree candidates must demonstrate a foreign language proficiency equivalent to three years of university-level instruction in a language taught at Franklin. They meet this requirement, in a language other than their mother tongue, by successfully completing appropriate courses at Franklin or by passing an equivalency test administered by the language department.

In addition to their major field of study, students may add courses within another discipline to form a minor. The number of credit hours (12 to 15) and the program of courses are subject to departmental approval.

Students enrolled in one of the institutes must complete 30 semester hours in two consecutive semesters at the College with a minimum grade point average of 2.0. For students enrolling at Franklin for only one semester, completion of a specified distribution of courses with a grade point average of 2.0 or better leads to a Certificate of Studies.

The College operates on a two-semester calendar, with classes starting in late August and mid-January; two summer sessions are also available. A weeklong required orientation program for all new students is held in August and mid-January.

A cooperative agreement exists between Franklin College and the C. W. Post School of Business of Long Island University for a one-year (36-credit) graduate M.B.A. program. Students majoring in international management are treated on equal terms with C. W. Post students with regard to entry. Courses in this special M.B.A. program are taught on the Franklin College campus in Lugano and on the C. W. Post campus in New York.

Off-Campus Arrangements

The Academic Travel Program is a fully integrated part of the regular curriculum. Each semester, students participate in two weeks of faculty-led academic travel. More than any other program of study, it gives students an opportunity to learn the "other way"—by experience. Travel destinations for 1999–2000 included Rome and southern Italy, Sicily, England, Germany, Paris, Greece, Madrid, Prague, Budapest, southern France, Namibia, South Africa, and the United States.

Internships are also available. Students with academic interest in any area may apply for an internship after two semesters of residence at Franklin, either by asking to be considered for one of the internships provided by the College or by arranging for an appointment themselves. The internship program is coordinated by a member of the Franklin faculty; a student may earn a maximum of 3 credit hours in an assignment.

Students in good standing who major in modern languages are eligible for study in a country where the target language is spoken; such study is limited to one semester at an approved institution.

Academic Facilities

The Franklin College Library contains 28,600 volumes and offers numerous English and foreign-language periodicals. The library also participates in the Swiss interlibrary loan system linking major Swiss university libraries. Microcomputers are available for student use; students also have access to the Internet.

Costs

The comprehensive fee for the 2000–01 academic year is $28,010. This figure includes the cost of tuition, the room and board charge, and student fees. The estimated cost of incidentals is $4000 per year. The estimated cost to fly round-trip from the United States is $1100.

Financial Aid

Franklin College offers need- and merit-based financial aid to qualified students. Applicants for financial aid must submit the FAFSA to the College Scholarship Service for evaluation. Veterans' and Social Security benefits are available to eligible students. Federal Stafford Student Loans may be obtained through local lenders. On-campus employment is available to students who demonstrate need. Students interested in applying for on-campus employment should notify the campus Financial Aid Office at the beginning of each semester.

Faculty

The Franklin College faculty numbers 34 full-time and part-time teachers, approximately half of whom are American or British; the other half are of various European nationalities. The majority have advanced degrees from American universities, the others from English and Continental universities, and most have lived, studied, and taught in a variety of countries. The teaching staff represents the cross-cultural aims of the College. Faculty members are committed to the European arena of study, are familiar enough with particular countries to organize and lead academic travel, are competent in more than one language, and are dedicated to the personal, discursive style of teaching demanded by a small liberal arts college with small classes. These teachers also advise the various student activities, lead local excursions, and regularly contribute to the College's cocurricular program of lectures. In addition, each faculty member acts as academic counselor to a number of students. The faculty-conducted Academic Travel Program promotes the intellectual friendship between teacher and student essential to a liberal arts education. The student-faculty ratio is approximately 10:1.

Student Government

The student body elects the members of the Student Union. In addition to sponsoring interest groups and arranging social events, the Student Union appoints members to attend meetings of the College faculty and the Appeals Board.

Admission Requirements

Franklin College seeks students who are eager to meet the challenge of studying and living in Europe, serious about undertaking college-level learning, and prepared to contribute positively to the intellectual life of the College. To identify such students, and also to ensure a diverse student population, the College Admissions Committee considers both academic and personal facts, including the student's academic record, evaluations by teachers and counselors, test scores, extracurricular interests and talents, and academic distinctions. Admission to the College is limited and therefore competitive. To achieve the best match between the student and Franklin, a personal interview is strongly recommended; one can be arranged by contacting the Admission Office in Lugano or New York. Applicants to the freshman class must submit a completed application form and a nonrefundable fee of $40; an official transcript of their secondary school record; SAT I or ACT scores, either included on transcripts or forwarded by the testing service to Franklin College (code number 0922); and three letters of academic evaluation. Applicants are advised to take the College Board SAT II: Writing Test given in December. Applicants whose first language is not English must submit their score on the Test of English as a Foreign Language (TOEFL); a score of at least 550 is required. Transfer applicants and institute applicants are required to submit a completed application and a nonrefundable application fee of $40, an official transcript of their college record, and one letter of academic recommendation.

Application and Information

The priority application deadline is March 15 for applicants to the freshman class and June 15 for transfer and institute applicants. Admission decisions are made on a rolling basis. Applicants can usually expect a decision within three weeks from the time their application is completed. All inquiries and applications should be directed to the nearest Admission Office.

U.S. Admissions Office
Franklin College
135 East 65th Street
New York, New York 10021
Telephone: 212-772-2090
Fax: 212-772-2718
E-mail: info@fc.edu

Karen Ballard
Director of Admissions
Franklin College
via Ponte Tresa, 29
6924 Sorengo/Lugano
Switzerland
Telephone: 41-91-985-2260
Fax: 41-91-994-4117
E-mail: info@fc.edu
World Wide Web: http://www.fc.edu

FRESNO PACIFIC UNIVERSITY
FRESNO, CALIFORNIA

The University

Fresno Pacific University, founded in 1944, is a Christian university of the arts and sciences. Fresno Pacific University (FPU) provides a complete education for students through excellence in Christian higher education. The academic program at FPU features a unique sequence of courses that challenge the student to develop academically, emotionally, and spiritually. Fresno Pacific University emphasizes faculty-student interaction, practical service, professional internships, and building a strong educational community in a Christian context.

Sponsored by the Mennonite Brethren Church, the University offers a distinctively Christ-centered vision of community and society. Through the pursuit of the knowledge of God and God's creation and using the tools of theology, science, and the arts, the University provides a stimulating center where students will be challenged to shape their thought, character, and lifestyle in a way that will prepare them for meaningful vocations and service in the world.

The 2,000 students at FPU (half undergraduates) form a rich community of different cultures, ethnicities, and religious denominations that bring the wider world to the student. Minority enrollment is 27 percent; international students make up 6 percent of the student body. On-campus living arrangements include apartments and residence halls as well as University-sponsored houses. Apartment living is available near the University. Host family arrangements can be made for international students. Students are involved in many clubs, organizations, and activities. Christian growth opportunities include various settings for worship, prayer, Bible study, and discipleship training. University Hour, a twice-a-week gathering of the campus community, offers students and faculty members a look at a variety of issues from a Christian perspective, as well as the sights and sounds of cultural and artistic presentations.

The Sunbird athletic teams of Fresno Pacific University are members of the National Association of Intercollegiate Athletics (NAIA) and compete at the intercollegiate level in men's basketball, cross-country, soccer, and track and women's basketball, cross-country, track, and volleyball. Intramural sports programs for both men and women are active throughout the school year. The theater department produces a variety of dramatic productions: full-length stage productions, readers theater, and one-act plays and hosts a traveling drama group. The music program offers a variety of musical opportunities: the Concert Choir, which takes a major tour each year, and many smaller vocal and instrumental ensembles.

The parklike 42-acre FPU campus has fourteen major buildings that include a unique outdoor amphitheater, Special Events Center/Gymnasium, a well-supplied bookshop, and a swimming pool. The campus provides convenient access for handicapped people.

The Student Life office provides personal, job, and career counseling and information on work and service opportunities as well as other support to students.

The graduate school offers five master's degrees, twelve credentials in education, and six graduate certificates.

Location

Fresno Pacific University is the only accredited, private, residential four-year Christian university of the liberal arts and sciences in central California. FPU is located in the heart of California, in the Great Central Valley. The Fresno metropolitan area has an ethnically and culturally diverse population of 500,000. Yosemite, Kings Canyon, and Sequoia National Parks; ski areas; beaches; and cultural and entertainment attractions of San Francisco and Los Angeles are all accessible from Fresno.

Majors and Degrees

Fresno Pacific University offers the Bachelor of Arts (B.A.) degree in applied mathematics, biblical and religious studies, biology, business accounting, business finance, business information systems, business marketing management, business nonprofit administration, chemistry, child development, church music, contemporary Christian ministries, English communication, English drama, English education, English literature, English writing, environmental science, environmental studies, history, intercultural studies, international business, mathematics education, music education, music performance/composition, philosophy, physical education exercise science, physical education health fitness, psychology, social science education, social work, Spanish language and culture, and teaching/liberal studies. Preprofessional programs are available in law and medicine.

Academic Program

An FPU education begins with a broad foundation exposing the student to many areas of study. From this foundation, students learn the intellectual skills necessary to begin study in a major and a minor. Fresno Pacific University operates on a two-semester plus summer academic calendar. The academic year consists of an early fall semester, which ends before the Christmas holiday, and a spring semester, which concludes in May. The minimum number of units for a Bachelor of Arts degree is 124 units. The General Education Program includes four courses in biblical studies and religion. FPU grants credit for certain scores on Advanced Placement tests and College-Level Examination Program (CLEP) tests.

Off-Campus Arrangements

FPU offers special experiences in off-campus education. The University is part of several consortia that offer international and U.S. settings for education. Study-abroad programs are available in many countries of the world, including China, Ecuador, England, France, Germany, Greece, India, Japan, Mexico, Russia, and Spain, to name a few. An American studies program is available in Washington, D.C., as is a film study program in Los Angeles, California. Short-term study-abroad programs that are led by FPU faculty members are also available to various countries in May of each year.

Academic Facilities

Hiebert Library is owned and operated jointly with the Mennonite Brethren Biblical Seminary. There are currently 140,000 volumes, 1,100 journal subscriptions, 200,000 microforms, and an audiovisual collection of 4,000 items. Three computer laboratories are available to all students, where they can access word processing, e-mail, Internet, spreadsheet, database, and other software for their use in class work, research, and writing, using either MS-DOS or Macintosh equipment, including Power Macs.

Costs

The tuition and fees for 2000–01 are $14,248, and room and board for the academic year are $4290.

Financial Aid

Fresno Pacific University offers a variety of federal, state, and private financial aid programs to assist students who would benefit from an education but need financial aid. Such students are encouraged to apply for assistance. More than 95 percent of FPU students receive financial assistance in the form of loans, grants, scholarships, and many on-campus employment opportunities. Merit scholarships are awarded to students based on academic achievement. Other scholarships include service/leadership, music, drama, and athletics awards. Students wishing to apply for financial aid must be accepted for admission and complete the Free Application for Federal Student Aid (FAFSA) and the FPU Financial Aid Application. California students should complete the FAFSA before the March 2 California Grant deadline and submit the Cal Grant GPA Verification Form in order to be considered for the Cal Grant program. Financial aid for international students is also available on a limited basis. International students should complete the FPU Financial Aid Application only.

Faculty

The FPU mentor-collegium program for incoming freshman students assigns a faculty mentor to each incoming student. This faculty member becomes an adviser/counselor, and the small group of students guided by the mentor forms a collegium. The collegium meets periodically for academic, social, and other activities. A special collegium—or core—course helps freshmen adjust to university life.

As a further expression of the conviction that interpersonal relationships are essential to the total educational process, the University encourages "Noon Hour Encounters," in which faculty members invite students to lunch for conversation in a local restaurant. Relationships that are developed in this informal setting are valuable to both faculty members and students.

More than 60 percent of the faculty members have earned doctorates. The student-faculty ratio is 15:1, with the average class size being 16 students. FPU's small class sizes promote discussion. Students know their professors up close and on a first-name basis.

Student Government

Fresno Pacific University is committed to helping students develop character and competence in order to become effective leaders who inspire, empower, and serve others. The Associated Students of Fresno Pacific University offers a variety of services, provides student representation to the University, and gives many opportunities for personal, social, spiritual, and political growth for students. Members of the Student Executive Council also serve as members of standing staff and faculty committees within the University governance structure. The Student Executive Council is composed of the following positions: president, vice president, business manager, student ministries, social affairs, commuter representative, secretary, and class senators. Appointment to these leadership roles is conducted through student body elections and personal interviews.

Admission Requirements

Fresno Pacific University welcomes students who qualify academically, who demonstrate the physical and emotional capacity for university work, who accept the purposes and standards of the University, and who would benefit from a Christian liberal arts education.

Acceptance for admission as a freshman student is based on an eligibility index score determined by a formula using the high school grade point average (excluding physical education, military science, and applied courses) and the total score from either the SAT I or the ACT.

Transfer students may bring in a maximum of 70 units of credit from an accredited postsecondary institution. To be granted admission solely on college-level academic work, a minimum of 24 transferable units must have been completed with at least a 2.4 academic GPA.

International students are valuable to the richness of the University's community. For those seeking improvement in their English language skills, the Intensive English Language Program (IELP) offers various levels of English language instruction. Students may receive university credits for language courses or may enroll in the Language and Culture Studies Program (LCS) to receive only a certificate. International students need good English skills in order to succeed in undergraduate studies. To study in regular undergraduate courses, students must reach a score of at least 500 (with 50 or higher on each section) on the TOEFL. SAT I or ACT scores are useful in considering students for scholarships. An application file can be complete without TOEFL and SAT I or ACT scores, although the University strongly recommends that they be submitted.

Application and Information

U.S. students entering directly from high school must submit an application for admission, a $30 nonrefundable application fee, official high school transcripts, SAT I or ACT scores, and at least one letter of recommendation.

U.S. transfer students need to submit an application for admission, a $30 nonrefundable application fee, official transcripts from high school verifying graduation, official transcripts from each college attended, and at least one letter of recommendation. Test scores are not required, but they are recommended.

Requirements for international students include the international application form, a $30 nonrefundable application fee, certified and translated transcripts from all secondary schools and postsecondary institutions certifying academically acceptable marks/grades, a completed financial certification form, two letters of recommendation, and a TOEFL score.

For more information, students should contact:
Jon Endicott, Director of College Admission
Fresno Pacific University
1717 South Chestnut Avenue
Fresno, California 93702
Telephone: 559-453-2039
          800-660-6089 (toll-free)
E-mail: ugadmis@fresno.edu
World Wide Web: http://www.fresno.edu/undergrad/

For international student information, students should contact:
International Programs and Service Office
Fresno Pacific University
1717 South Chestnut Avenue
Fresno, California 93702
Telephone: 559-453-2069
Fax: 559-453-5501
E-mail: ipso@fresno.edu
World Wide Web: http://www.fresno.edu/undergrad/

Fresno Pacific University provides a complete education for students through excellence in Christian higher education.

FROSTBURG STATE UNIVERSITY
FROSTBURG, MARYLAND

The University

A state-supported liberal arts institution, Frostburg State University has gone through a series of transitions since its founding in 1898. Established originally as a normal school, the University has expanded to a campus of more than 200 acres and a student body of more than 5,400. During the past decade, the most significant one in the University's history, the academic offerings have been expanded and enrollment has increased. Eleven residence halls provide sufficient on-campus housing to meet the needs of entering students.

The University offers extensive extracurricular activities. There are about 100 student organizations on campus, including sororities and fraternities, honor societies, professional organizations, communications and media-related groups, athletic clubs, Little Sister programs, and special-interest groups. The University offers twenty intramural sports. Intercollegiate sports for men are baseball, basketball, cross-country, football, soccer, swimming, tennis, and track and field; 10 percent of the men participate in these. Intercollegiate sports for women are basketball, cross-country, field hockey, lacrosse, soccer, softball, swimming, tennis, track and field, and volleyball; 5 percent of the women participate.

Location

Located in the mountains of western Maryland, the University campus is bordered on one side by the city of Frostburg (population 7,500), an attractive community that offers a range of activities, from dining at a gourmet restaurant to a community club social. Neighboring scenic and recreational areas are enjoyed throughout all four seasons of the year. Skiing is a popular winter activity, along with other traditional outdoor sports. The surrounding area has numerous historic sites, such as the C & O Canal and Fort Necessity. The history of the growth of Allegany County can be seen in the Allegany Museum, which is located in Cumberland, Maryland (population 25,000), just a short distance from the campus. Baltimore, Maryland, and Washington, D.C., are 150 miles east of the campus. Pittsburgh, Pennsylvania, is 100 miles to the northeast.

Majors and Degrees

Students completing an undergraduate program of study at the University may earn the Bachelor of Arts (B.A.), the Bachelor of Science (B.S.), or the Bachelor of Fine Arts (B.F.A.) degree. The diversity of the University's academic program is reflected in the majors that are available: accounting, actuarial science, biology, business administration, business education, chemistry, computer science, early childhood education, economics, elementary education, English, environmental analysis and planning, fine arts, foreign languages and literature, general science (earth science concentration), geography (cartography and urban geography concentrations), health and physical education, history, international studies, justice studies, liberal studies, mass communications, mathematics, music, philosophy, physics, political science, psychology, recreation, social science, social work, speech communication, speech communication and theater, theater, and wildlife-fisheries management.

Frostburg offers preprofessional programs in dentistry, law, medicine, and diverse other areas. Frostburg also participates in cooperative preprofessional programs with the University of Maryland. These include several allied health programs (nursing, pharmacy, and physical therapy). These programs involve preprofessional study at Frostburg and professional training at the University of Maryland. Through a collaborative program with the University of Maryland, mechanical and electrical engineering majors are offered at Frostburg. This program offers the opportunity to attend a small university and receive a degree from the University of Maryland, College Park's established and nationally accredited engineering program.

Academic Program

A student's program of study begins with the General Education Program (GEP), which is designed to provide the foundation for educational development. Through three components, a unified concept of general education is developed to meet the special needs of each student. The first of these components provides a common core of essential tools for further learning; primary among these tools are skills of verbal and symbolic communication. Another component of the GEP offers exposure to broad fields of knowledge through study of the humanities, social sciences, and natural sciences. The third component helps the student gain an understanding of the interrelationship of various disciplines. Each student selects specific courses and develops a common theme to aid in his or her understanding.

The significant distinction of the B.A. degree program is that it requires a student to become competent in a foreign language at the intermediate level. Students who are contemplating additional study beyond an undergraduate degree are strongly encouraged to obtain the B.A. degree, since it is of particular value in a graduate program. Many students are able to combine specific graduate school goals with their major by tailoring their program to meet specific needs. Serious students, with the assistance of their adviser, are able to arrange a program that will help them achieve a high degree of success in acceptance to a variety of professional and graduate schools.

The offerings of an honors program provide the challenge that will make the serious student aware of his or her potential as an individual. Superior performance in a secondary school program will encourage the student to participate in this demanding curriculum.

Off-Campus Arrangements

Frostburg State University offers students a variety of opportunities for off-campus learning. The largest of these is the internship program. Internships are a required part of several major programs (i.e., education, accounting, and political science) but are also available to students in most other majors. An internship allows students to gain practical experience and earn credit in their chosen field. Off-campus centers have been opened in Hagerstown and Frederick. For students who wish to study abroad, Frostburg participates in the International Student Exchange Program, which allows students to select the country in which they wish to study abroad and, if qualified, to be assigned to an institution in that country. Students majoring in education or physical education have the opportunity to study in England through special exchange programs in those majors.

Academic Facilities

As a residential campus, the University has grown physically in order to maintain pace with an expanding academic program.

Academic facilities include eleven classroom buildings. Compton Hall was recently renovated to accommodate three computer laboratories. The campus radio station, WFWM, was also renovated and electronically updated recently. An addition to the campus is the Nelson P. Guild Human Resources Center. This building houses the psychology, economics, political science, sociology, social work, and computer science departments. A beautiful performing arts building provides an exciting cultural center for the campus.

Costs
In 2000–01, the annual cost of tuition and fees is $4132 for Maryland residents and $9282 for nonresidents. The cost of room and board is $5229 per year. Semester charges for room, board, tuition, and fees are payable at or prior to registration in the fall and in the spring.

Financial Aid
Financial aid available for eligible students includes need-based grants, merit-based academic scholarships, Federal Stafford Student Loans, and Federal Work-Study Program awards. Approximately 65 percent of the University's students receive financial aid.

Faculty
Frostburg's faculty consists of 233 full-time and 70 part-time members. Seventy percent of the faculty members hold a Ph.D. degree. The student-faculty ratio is 17:1. All professors have weekly office hours during which they are available to students.

Student Government
A tripartite student government system allows students and members of the faculty and administration to become involved together in deciding the direction the University should take.

Admission Requirements
Applicants are considered for admission on the basis of their high school record and SAT I scores. A strong emphasis is placed on the high school transcript. High school equivalency certificates are accepted. An interview is not required, but the Admissions Office encourages students to visit the campus and talk with a member of the admission staff.

Application and Information
Students may apply to Frostburg State University by submitting an application along with official copies of their SAT I scores and high school transcript. Frostburg is on a rolling admissions program. The University must close admission when no further space is available. Students are strongly advised to make a college choice early in their high school career. Notification of admission decisions begins in mid-November for the fall semester.

For further information, prospective students should contact:

Admissions Office
Frostburg State University
101 Braddock Road
Frostburg, Maryland 21532

Telephone: 301-687-4201
Fax: 301-687-7074
E-mail: wblair@frostburg.edu
World Wide Web: http://www.frostburg.edu

A view of the campus.

GANNON UNIVERSITY
ERIE, PENNSYLVANIA

The University

Gannon University is dedicated to excellence in holistic education. The oldest part of the University is Villa Maria College, founded in 1925 by the Sisters of St. Joseph. In 1933, Archbishop John Mark Gannon established Cathedral College, a two-year institution, which by 1941 had evolved into a four-year college, the Gannon School of Arts and Sciences. The name Gannon College was adopted in 1944, and Gannon achieved university status in 1979. Villa Maria College subsequently joined Gannon as one of the colleges of the University in 1989.

Gannon's campus is located in the heart of downtown Erie, giving students the benefit of being within walking distance of stores, shops, restaurants, and theaters. The campus consists of thirty-four buildings located within six city blocks. Among these buildings is the Student Recreation Center, which has a pool; three gyms; a running track; a weight room; courts for racquetball, handball, volleyball, and basketball; and other facilities. Also on campus are an additional gymnasium, which is open to students during posted hours; two residence halls; six apartment buildings; classroom and faculty-office buildings; an administration building; and a multipurpose chapel building. The new Student Campus Center is a place that gives students the opportunity to meet and socialize between classes with faculty members and other students. Each residence hall also has a game room.

Gannon offers students a broad intramural sports program that runs throughout the entire year. In intercollegiate athletics, Gannon offers men's baseball, basketball, cross-country, football, golf, soccer, water polo, and wrestling, along with women's basketball, cross-country, golf, lacrosse, soccer, softball, volleyball, and water polo. There is also an intercollegiate coed swimming team.

There are approximately 3,300 students at Gannon, more than 2,600 of whom are undergraduates. The ratio of commuting to resident students is approximately 1:4. The University has a placement office to aid students in finding part-time work during school and full-time work after graduation.

Location

Erie is Pennsylvania's third-largest city and is located in the northwestern corner of the state on the shore of Lake Erie. Erie is approximately 120 miles north of Pittsburgh, Pennsylvania; 90 miles east of Cleveland, Ohio; and 90 miles west of Buffalo, New York. The campus is within 5 miles of Interstates 79 and 90 and 5 miles from Erie International Airport. Erie is also serviced by rail and bus transportation.

Majors and Degrees

The College of Humanities, Business and Education awards the Bachelor of Arts and Bachelor of Science degrees.

In the School of Humanities the areas of study from which students may select a major are communication arts, criminal justice, English (with concentrations in applied communications, literature, and writing), foreign language business option, foreign language and international studies, foreign language and literature, foreign language teaching, history, liberal arts, mortuary science, paralegal studies, political science, prelaw, prelaw 3/3 early admissions, psychology, social science, social work, theater and communications arts, and theater.

In the School of Business the areas of study from which students may select a major are accounting, advertising communications, business administration, finance, international business, management, management information systems, marketing, and risk management.

In the School of Education the areas of study from which students may select a major are early childhood education, elementary education, secondary education (in biology, chemistry, communications, English, foreign language, mathematics, science, and social studies), and special education.

The College of Sciences, Engineering and Health Sciences awards the Bachelor of Science degree.

In the School of Sciences and Engineering the areas of study from which students may select a major are biology, chemistry, chemical engineering, computer science, earth science, electrical engineering, electrical engineering five-year co-op, environmental science, mathematics, mechanical engineering, mechanical engineering five-year co-op, and science. A minor is offered in environmental and occupational science and health. Preprofessional and accelerated programs of study are offered in prechiropractic, predentistry, premedicine, preoptometry, preosteopathy, prepharmacy, pre–physical therapy, prepodiatry, pre–veterinary medicine, seven-year optometry, and seven-year podiatry.

In the School of Health Sciences the areas of study from which students may select a major are dietetics, medical technology, nursing, occupational therapy, physician assistant studies, radiologic sciences, respiratory care, and sport and exercise science.

The associate degree program offers Associate of Science and Associate of Arts degrees. Areas of study in which students may major are accounting, business administration, early childhood education, paralegal studies, radiological sciences, and respiratory care.

Academic Program

Each undergraduate program has its own sequence of requirements. Students in all programs must complete credits in liberal studies. A faculty adviser is assigned to each student to assist in academic planning. A department chairperson and faculty adviser also assist each student in selecting courses that fulfill requirements and best meet the student's desired career objectives. The basic graduation requirements for bachelor's degree candidates are 128 credit hours, including completion of requirements for their major and the liberal studies program. Students must also have quality point averages of at least 2.0 in their senior year and 2.0 in their field of concentration. To earn an associate degree, students must usually complete 60–68 credit hours, depending on the program. Students may receive credit through the Advanced Placement Program or the College-Level Examination Program.

Gannon offers a program for students with learning disabilities.

Gannon University has an Army ROTC program that is open to any interested students.

Gannon's academic calendar consists of two full semesters, running from August to December and from January to May. There are also optional summer sessions.

Academic Facilities

The Nash Library currently has more than 250,000 bound volumes. The library subscribes to more than 1,000 periodicals and has book and periodical materials on various forms of microfilms and microcards. The library contains a personal computer lab, a lecture room, a curriculum library, the Founder's Room for fine and rare books, lounges, study rooms, typing rooms, an information-retrieval system, a TV studio, the latest audiovisual and tape equipment, and a multimedia studio classroom. In addition, students may use the facilities and resources of the Erie County Law Library and the Erie County Library. For specialized research projects, an efficient interlibrary loan service is available.

The A. J. Palumbo Academic Center houses the Schools of Health Sciences, Education, and Humanities, and offers the finest laboratories, technology, and classrooms available today. From education to nursing to foreign language programs, the faculty and facilities in Palumbo provide the highest quality education. Other notable programs of interest are the University's Honors Program, Program for Students with Learning Disabilities, and the Teaching and Learning Enhancement Center and Freshmen Focus Program. The Offices of Admissions and Financial Aid are also housed in this multilevel building.

The Zurn Science Center has laboratories for research in biology, anatomy, physics, chemistry, and engineering. The building also houses three computer laboratories, including the Computer Integrated Enterprise Center and an IBM PC lab. There are numerous classrooms and two auditoriums in the building. Among other University facilities are additional classroom buildings, a TV and radio station, a theater, and the Career and Counseling Center.

Costs

For 2000–01, full-time tuition is $6705 per semester ($7115 for engineering and health sciences) or $13,410 per academic year ($14,230 for engineering and health sciences). Tuition for part-time students is $365–$385 per credit hour. Room and board are approximately $2600 per semester. The total cost for the academic year at Gannon, including books and supplies, is between $13,800 and $15,200 for commuting students and $18,883 and $20,323 for resident students, depending on the program of study.

Financial Aid

In order to bring a Gannon education to qualified students who could not otherwise afford it, the University offers an integrated financial aid program of scholarships, grants, loans, and employment. An application for financial aid must be filed with the application for admission. The filing has no effect on the decision of the Committee on Admissions. Gannon's financial aid program is open to all full-time students attending classes during the nine-month period from September to May. All students seeking financial aid should file the admission and financial aid applications no later than March 1.

Faculty

Gannon's faculty consists of 325 lay and religious men and women. Fifty-three percent of the full-time faculty members have doctoral degrees. The student-faculty ratio is about 13:1, and there are approximately 25 students in each class. Most faculty members assist in the faculty-adviser program, giving each student individual attention and counseling on academic and personal matters.

Student Government

The Student Government Association (SGA) is composed of students elected by members of their class. Through SGA, students can play a responsible role in the planning and working of the University. SGA has voting representatives on all the standing committees of the University. Members of SGA not only research existing policies and problems but they also look for new ways to improve the academic life of students. The SGA also plans social events for the student body.

Admission Requirements

Gannon University actively recruits students of all races, creeds, and ages from all geographic regions. Transfer and international students are encouraged to seek admission. Applicants are required to submit scores (including senior-year scores) on either the SAT I or ACT, an up-to-date transcript of the high school record showing rank in class (plus a college transcript for transfer applicants), a completed application form, and a nonrefundable $25 fee. Admission decisions are based upon numerous factors, central of which is the strength of the high school record, as demonstrated through grades and relative class standing. Less critical, although significant, are the SAT I or ACT scores and other test scores that may be available. Recommendations and personal statements also affect admission decisions. Transfer and international students should check with the admissions office for special application procedures.

Application and Information

Students applying for admission in the fall semester should start the application process at the beginning of their senior year in high school. Gannon operates on a rolling admission basis, which means that there is no deadline for filing applications (for most programs). However, early applications are recommended, as are enrollment deposits. Several health science programs have application deadlines; students should contact the admissions office for additional information.

For further information, students should contact:

Director of Admissions
Gannon University
109 University Square
Erie, Pennsylvania 16541
Telephone: 814-871-7240
          800-GANNON-U (toll-free)
Fax: 814-871-5803
E-mail: admissions@gannon.edu
World Wide Web: http://www.gannon.edu

Gannon University's faculty advisers are always available to help students chart their personal, educational, and professional accomplishments and potential.

GARDNER–WEBB UNIVERSITY
BOILING SPRINGS, NORTH CAROLINA

The University

Gardner-Webb University was founded in 1905 as a private high school by a group of Baptist associations. It became a junior college in 1928, was renamed Gardner-Webb College in 1942 in honor of former governor O. Max Gardner, and became a fully accredited senior college in 1971. Gardner-Webb moved to University status in 1993. The most outstanding characteristics of the University are its Christian environment, sense of community, and proven record of academic distinction. Its origins are obviously deep in Christian tradition, which is exemplified in the lives of staff and faculty members. Because the University is small, students can be well known by a large percentage of the faculty and administration. The cosmopolitan student body (more than 3,040 men and women, of whom nearly 2,600 are undergraduates) represents twenty-eight states and twenty-one other countries and gives an added, valuable dimension to a student's educational experience. Cars are permitted for all.

The heritage of the University is reflected in its beautiful landscape and stately brick buildings. However, the University is constantly forging ahead with advanced technology and state-of-the-art facilities. There are several social and service clubs on campus, including the Drama Club, Fellowship of Christian Athletes (FCA), Campus Ministries United, student government, and various University and student committees. There are many extracurricular activities for those who are interested. The Student Entertainment Association offers a full program of social events and entertainment. The Gardner-Webb Theatre offers a full season of plays. There are a student newspaper, a literary magazine, and a yearbook. Students may also participate in community projects or in various kinds of off-campus ministries, including those to the deaf and to prison inmates.

The Master of Arts degree is awarded in counseling (school counseling and agency counseling), elementary education, English, middle school education, physical education, and school administration.

Gardner-Webb also offers an M.B.A. degree and a Master of Divinity degree.

Intramural sports, in which all students are urged to participate, include basketball, racquetball, softball, tennis, touch football, and volleyball. Intercollegiate sports include baseball, basketball, cross-country running, football, golf, soccer, softball, swimming, tennis, track, volleyball, and wrestling. A modern physical education building, an indoor heated pool, and an athletic field amply accommodate these programs. A new wellness center and an Alpine Tower are being added as well.

The Program for the Blind at Gardner-Webb University has been developed to allow students with visual handicaps to receive a liberal arts education. Special support services and job opportunities are provided for every entering student who is visually impaired.

The Degree Program for the Deaf provides interpreters, note takers, and tutors skilled in sign language so that hearing-impaired students have full access to all University programs.

Location

The University is located at the foot of the beautiful Blue Ridge Mountains in Boiling Springs, North Carolina, a university town of about 3,000 people. The campus comprises 200 acres of land in an area of gently rolling, wooded hills. Nine miles away is Shelby, a town of about 20,000 people. There are a Greater Shelby Community Theatre and a Community Concert Series, and restaurants abound in the area. Charlotte, an area of about 400,000 people only 50 miles away, offers many other opportunities for cultural, social, and recreational activities. Several nearby lakes and Asheville and Beech Mountain, an hour and a half away in the heart of the mountains, provide facilities for summer and winter sports. Greenville, South Carolina, is 55 miles away and Spartanburg, 36 miles. Shelby is served by Greyhound-Trailways bus lines, and the Charlotte airport is served by major airlines. Interstate 85 is only 15 miles away, and Highway 74 runs through Shelby.

Majors and Degrees

The degrees of Bachelor of Arts, Bachelor of Science, and Associate in Arts are offered. Fields of concentration are available in the following subjects: accounting, American sign language, athletic training, biology, business administration, chemistry, communications, computer science, early childhood education, English, French, health education, history, intermediate education, international business, interpreter training, management information systems, mathematics, medical technology, music, nursing, physical education, physician assistant studies, political science, psychology, religion, sacred music, social sciences, sociology, Spanish, and sports management.

A dual-degree program is available in engineering with the University of North Carolina at Charlotte and Auburn University.

Preprofessional programs are available in dentistry, law, medicine, ministry, pharmacy, and veterinary medicine.

Academic Program

The total program is marked by flexibility for the student but encourages, through active faculty advisement, choosing a substantial course of study. Elements of the humanities, the social and physical sciences, and mathematics or related disciplines must be taken. A typical bachelor's degree program requires 128 semester hours for graduation: 59 to 63 in the core (humanities and social and physical sciences), 30 in the major, and 39 to 42 in supporting subjects and free electives. Requirements for science curricula vary somewhat. The associate degree requires the completion of 64 semester hours. A cumulative average of C (2.0 on a 4.0 scale) or better is required for graduation.

Gardner-Webb grants advanced placement and credit on the basis of the College-Level Examination Program (CLEP), the Advanced Placement (AP) tests of the College Board, and the International Baccalaureate Program.

Off-Campus Arrangements

Students in the Departments of Business, Fine Arts, Foreign Languages and Literature, and Religious Studies and Philosophy are given the opportunity to enrich their educational experiences through travel and study in Europe, Latin America, and the Holy Land.

Academic Facilities

The University's library currently holds 200,000 volumes. There are fully equipped biology, chemistry, and physics laboratories as well as computer and learning-assistance laboratories. A special-events/convocation center houses a theater and an athletics arena. The University also has a 50,000-watt FM stereo radio station.

Costs

Costs for the 1999–2000 academic year were $10,780 for tuition and $4630 for room and board. Part-time tuition was $230 per semester hour for 1 to 9 hours. Books and supplies averaged $500.

Financial Aid

Gardner-Webb University makes available to its students a variety of scholarships, loans, grants-in-aid, and work-study awards. Prospective applicants with financial need should contact the financial aid director early in their senior year of high school for a financial need estimate. Applications received after April 1 can be considered only in terms of available funds. An applicant must be accepted for admission before being awarded aid. Students must file the Free Application for Federal Student Aid (FAFSA). Scholarships and other types of aid include academic awards, Christian service awards, endowed scholarships, and annual scholarships. There are several Gardner-Webb loan funds. The University also administers aid from the full range of federal programs: Federal Pell Grants, Federal Work-Study Program awards, Federal Perkins Loans, and federally guaranteed Federal Stafford Student and Federal PLUS loans. North Carolina students have access to state grant funds administered by the University. Scholarships based on academic promise are also granted each year. Of all students, 90 percent receive aid in some form. The two criteria for receiving financial aid are financial need and academic promise.

Faculty

The faculty-student ratio is 1:15. Faculty members engage both formally and informally in student advising and counseling. A staff of professional counselors is also available. Faculty members teach at all class levels without regard to academic rank or length of service. Graduate assistants are not used to teach classes.

Student Government

The University has a student government whose members are elected by the student body. This organization, set up with executive, legislative, and judicial branches, is very influential in campus affairs. In addition, students have voting positions on all standing committees of the University.

Admission Requirements

Although a fixed pattern of high school credits is not prescribed, the following minimum course distribution is recommended: 4 units in English, 2 in a foreign language, 2 in social science, 2 in algebra, 1 in geometry, and 2 in natural science, plus electives. The University requires each applicant to submit an application form, a high school transcript, and SAT I scores. ACT scores are also acceptable. Acceptance to Gardner-Webb is based on the applicant's high school record, rank in class, SAT I or ACT composite scores, and extracurricular activities. Transfer students' course credits are evaluated on courses as credit only, not on grade point average. An interview is recommended but not mandatory.

Gardner-Webb admits students of any race, color, and national or ethnic origin to all the rights, privileges, programs, and activities generally accorded or made available to students at the University.

Application and Information

Applications, together with a nonrefundable $25 application fee, may be submitted for either semester. Early application is advised. Notification of the admission decision is given on a rolling basis upon receipt of all application data. A $150 room deposit for boarding students is due thirty days after acceptance and is refundable until May 1. A $50 deposit is required of commuting students.

For further information, students should contact:

Director of Admissions
Gardner-Webb University
Boiling Springs, North Carolina 28017
Telephone: 704-434-4GWU
        800-253-6472 (toll-free)
World Wide Web: http://www.gardner-webb.edu

Gardner-Webb University students enjoy a safe, real-world Christian environment where people really care.

GENEVA COLLEGE
BEAVER FALLS, PENNSYLVANIA

The College

Founded in 1848, Geneva is a Christian, coeducational college whose purpose is to develop servant-leaders who will transform society for the kingdom of Christ. The College's mission is to educate and minister to a diverse community of students through biblically based programs and services that are marked by excellence and anchored by the historic evangelical and reformed Christian faith. The curriculum is rooted in the liberal arts and sciences, vocationally focused, and delivered through traditional and innovative programs.

Geneva College has been accredited by the Middle States Association of Colleges and Schools since 1923.

The current enrollment is 1,799 men and women, including 224 part-time students. In addition to the undergraduate degrees listed below, Geneva offers Master of Arts degrees in professional counseling and higher education, a Master of Science in organizational leadership, and a Master in Business Administration. The Student Center, which is the hub of campus life, provides a common meeting place for the College's students, 20 percent of whom are commuters. The remainder of the students come from thirty-five states and thirty-two countries. Student organizations include the Student Senate, an FM radio station, a cable-TV station, the campus newspaper (the *Cabinet*), the yearbook, the concert band, the marching band, the a cappella choir, a literary magazine, and more than fifty interest groups. Geneva has an active intercollegiate and intramural athletics program and holds membership in the National Association of Intercollegiate Athletics and the National Christian College Athletic Association. Varsity sports are baseball, basketball, cross-country, football, soccer, tennis, and track for men and basketball, cross-country, soccer, softball, tennis, track, and volleyball for women.

Location

Geneva College has been an important part of the Beaver Falls community since 1880. The campus covers more than 55 acres overlooking the Beaver River. It is 3 miles south of the Beaver Valley Interchange of the Pennsylvania Turnpike, near I-79 and I-80, and 20 miles from the Greater Pittsburgh Airport. Beaver Falls is a quiet, friendly community of 10,000, and about the same number of people live in residential areas surrounding the city. Pittsburgh is 40 miles to the southeast, and there are numerous resort areas within 50 miles that offer a wide range of year-round activities.

Majors and Degrees

The College offers the degrees of Bachelor of Arts, Bachelor of Science, Bachelor of Science in Education, Bachelor of Science in Business Administration, Bachelor of Science in Engineering, Associate in Business Administration, Associate in Engineering, Associate in Biblical Studies, and Associate of Arts. Majors are offered in accounting, applied mathematics, applied music, biblical studies, biology, business (with concentrations in accounting, aviation, finance/economics, human resource management, management, management information systems, and marketing), chemical engineering, chemistry, Christian ministries (with concentrations in missions, pastoral studies, and preseminary studies), communications, computer science, elementary education, engineering (with concentrations in civil, electrical, and mechanical engineering), English, history, human services, math education, music, music business, music education, philosophy, physics, political science, psychology, sociology, Spanish, special education, speech communication, speech pathology, writing, and youth ministry. Minors are available in many of the above areas, as well as in Christian school teaching, oral communication in business and industry, public administration, public relations, theater, visual communication, writing for business, writing for publication, and youth ministries. There are preprofessional programs in law, medicine, and affiliate programs in cardiovascular technology, criminal justice, and medical technology. Special programs are also offered in art and in business aviation (with concentrations in aerospace management, air traffic control, and professional piloting).

Geneva College offers a 1-2-1 dual-degree program in aviation/business administration in cooperation with the Community College of Beaver County (CCBC) through which students earn the Associate in Applied Sciences in Aviation degree in aerospace management, air-traffic control, or professional piloting from CCBC plus the B.S.B.A. degree from Geneva. The B.S.B.A. program includes study in Geneva's liberal arts core curriculum. Students receive the appropriate Federal Aviation Administration (FAA) licenses and certification, and the combination of the two degrees enhances students' career potential for administration and management positions. Students in the program are part of the Geneva College community all four years and may participate in cocurricular activities. Other cooperative programs with CCBC are in business administration/business management, business education, criminal justice, or data processing.

In 1983, Geneva College and the FAA signed an agreement that provides a cooperative work-study program. Recommended electrical engineering majors can train with the FAA in the computerized control of air traffic. In cooperation with the Inova Fairfax Hospital of Falls Church, Virginia, Geneva offers a Bachelor of Science degree with a major in biology that is geared toward cardiovascular technology. This program involves three years of study at Geneva and one calendar year at Fairfax. Geneva has formal affiliations for medical technology with the University Hospitals of Cleveland (Case Western Reserve University), St. Joseph's Hospital (Lancaster), and St. Vincent Health Center (Erie). For juniors and seniors interested in an art concentration, Geneva offers opportunities through the Art Institute of Pittsburgh.

Academic Program

Candidates for baccalaureate degrees complete 126–39 hours of course work. Study in the major area may begin immediately. Thus, students are able to relate their primary field of study to the core curriculum. The core requirements include one semester each of English and speech, four semesters of humanities, three semesters of biblical studies, three semesters of social science, two lab sciences or one lab and two non-lab sciences, and two semesters of physical education.

Geneva College also has an honors program that is designed to meet the needs of the ablest and most highly motivated students at Geneva.

The first semester runs from late August to the week before Christmas, the second semester from early January to early

May. During May, the academic calendar features an optional Experimester, in which students and faculty members test innovative approaches to learning. One 3-week and two 5-week summer sessions, from May and early June to early August, offer up to 12 semester hours of credit.

Academic Facilities

McCartney Library is the major information resource center, with a 160,891-volume collection of books and bound periodicals, 168,665 microbooks, 855 periodicals, thirty-five computer information workstations, 23,403 media units, and various other microfilm and media materials. Total library holdings are 353,412. The Science and Engineering Building has well-equipped laboratories for biology, chemistry, engineering, and physics; two public networked computer labs containing PCs and several discipline-specific PC labs; and a library of science and technology resources. The Brooks Curriculum Center provides resource materials for education majors. Northwood Hall, home to business and psychology, features smart classrooms, seminar rooms, 100 computers for student use, and a conference center.

Costs

For the academic year 2000–01, tuition and fees are $13,350. Housing (including board) costs range from $5390 to 5690. The estimated cost of books and supplies is $600. For Evening and Summer School, tuition and fees are $433 per semester hour.

Financial Aid

The rising cost of education is of major concern to everyone. Through careful expense control and an adequate financial aid program, Geneva College seeks to provide an opportunity for higher education for every qualified student. More than 90 percent of the College's students receive financial aid. Geneva offers financial assistance through scholarships, grants-in-aid, student loans, and employment. Students who are in an academic program and have a minimum combined SAT I score of 1150 and a minimum 3.0 GPA receive an honor scholarship to be applied toward their tuition each semester, regardless of need. Other awards are determined on the basis of financial need. Several local, regional, industrial, and foundation scholarships are available and are assigned on the basis of each scholarship's specific requirements. Geneva participates in the Federal Perkins Loan, Federal Pell Grant, Federal Supplemental Educational Opportunity Grant, and Federal Work-Study programs. Students may also receive help through part-time employment. The College urges students to file the Free Application for Federal Student Aid (FAFSA). For further information, students should write to the director of financial aid at Geneva College.

Faculty

The Geneva College faculty is composed of evangelical Christians who believe that liberal arts and professional studies must be integrated with the values and morality of historical Christianity. The faculty consists of 75 full-time professors (71 percent of whom have earned doctorates), 5 professional librarians, and 76 ancillary personnel who come to the College from their regular pursuits in education and industry to offer their special skills to the academic program. At Geneva, professors also serve as academic advisers to students in their respective major areas. Interpersonal relationships are easily formed between students, faculty members, staff members, and the administration. Faculty members place high priority on being available to students for counseling and academic assistance.

Student Government

The chief agency of student government is the Student Senate. Its membership consists of 4 officers elected by the day-school student body, 3 elected representatives from each of the four classes, 2 elected commuter representatives, and 1 nontraditional student representative. Two elected faculty members are advisory members of the senate. The senate deals with matters of interest to the student body and assists in matters of student discipline. In addition, most regular committees of the College have student representatives who are recommended by the Student Senate president as regular participants with equal voting privileges.

Admission Requirements

Geneva seeks students who are qualified for rigorous study in a Christian, liberal arts atmosphere. Approximately 60 percent of the freshmen admitted are in the upper two fifths of their class. Admission requirements include SAT I or ACT scores (the middle 50 percent of SAT I scores range from 960 to 1170, and the median SAT I verbal score is 530, the mathematics score, 520), a counselor/teacher recommendation, high school transcripts, and college transcripts (for all transfer prospects). The usual high school preparation includes the following units: English, 4; social studies, 3; foreign language, 2; mathematics, 2; science, 1; and electives, 4. Early admission is possible after the junior year of high school.

Credits and grades earned elsewhere by transfer students are, when necessary, converted to semester hours and Geneva's 4.0 grading system but remain otherwise unchanged. Credit for college-level work may be obtained through the College Board's Advanced Placement Program, the College-Level Examination Program, or departmental examinations.

Application and Information

Geneva College admits students of any race, color, sex, religion, handicap, or national or ethnic origin. All applicants are encouraged to visit the campus. Transfers and high school seniors are urged to submit their applications (students may apply on-line) with the $25 application fee as early as possible; admission decisions are made on a rolling basis. After a student is accepted, a $25 tuition deposit and a $75 room reservation deposit (for residential students) confirm intention to enroll.

Counselors are available weekdays from 8 a.m. to 4:30 p.m. for phone inquiries at the toll-free numbers given below. Written requests for information and application forms should be sent to:

David Layton
Director of Admissions
Geneva College
3200 College Avenue
Beaver Falls, Pennsylvania 15010-3599
Telephone: 800-847-8255 (toll-free)
E-mail: admissions@geneva.edu
World Wide Web: http://www.geneva.edu

GEORGE FOX UNIVERSITY
NEWBERG, OREGON

The University

George Fox University was founded 109 years ago by the Society of Friends (Quakers) with the purpose of providing students a challenging academic atmosphere and a commitment to Christian faith. From a modest beginning of 15 students in 1891, George Fox has grown to an enrollment of 2,300 students from thirteen countries.

Students find George Fox to be a place where the integration of spiritual and intellectual challenge takes place in a friendly, caring environment. This tradition of integration has been recognized by the Templeton Foundation by naming George Fox University to the honor roll of character-building colleges. National recognition for academic reputation has also been given by *U.S. News & World Report*.

Seventy-five percent of George Fox students live in campus residence halls, suites, and apartments. Opportunities for extracurricular involvement are available in music, drama, journalism, student government, radio, clubs, and athletics. George Fox is a member of the NCAA Division III and competes in six men's sports (baseball, basketball, cross-country, soccer, tennis, and track) and seven women's sports (basketball, cross-country, soccer, softball, tennis, track, and volleyball). A number of intramural sports are also available.

Regular chapel services bring the campus community together in worship. Students have the opportunity to put their faith into action on volunteer mission trips and during community outreach activities.

In addition to its undergraduate degrees, George Fox confers the Master of Business Administration, Master of Education, Master of Arts in Teaching, and Doctor of Psychology degrees, and seven master's degrees through Western Evangelical Seminary, a graduate school of George Fox University.

Location

George Fox University is located in Newberg, a residential community of 16,500 people. The 75-acre tree-shaded campus is a 30-minute drive from the major metropolitan environment of Portland. The University is situated in the beautiful Pacific Northwest, with scenic Mt. Hood and the rugged Pacific coastline within short driving distances.

Tilikum Retreat Center, set on a 90-acre lake and just 10 minutes away, provides students a change of pace from the classroom. Students enjoy hiking, canoeing, and fishing at the camp. Tilikum has an extensive summer day camp program that employs many University students.

Majors and Degrees

George Fox confers the Bachelor of Arts and Bachelor of Science degrees. The following undergraduate majors are available: art, biblical studies, biology, business and economics, chemistry, Christian educational ministries, cognitive science, communication arts, communication/video production, computer and information science, electrical engineering, elementary education, family and consumer science, fashion merchandising, foods and nutrition in business, history, interdisciplinary studies, interior design, international studies, mathematics, mechanical engineering, music, philosophy, physical education, religion, secondary education, social work, sociology, and writing/literature.

Academic Program

The academic year at George Fox University is divided into two semesters of fifteen weeks. In addition to the two semesters, the University sponsors a three-week May Term. For graduation, students are required to earn 126 credit hours, including 54 general education and 42 upper-division credits.

Students may reduce the number of required courses and add flexibility to their undergraduate years with credit earned through Advanced Placement, the College-Level Examination Program, and credit by examination.

An innovative program called "Computers Across the Curriculum" expands the computer literacy of students. The University issues every incoming freshman a computer for school and personal use. The computer becomes the property of the student upon graduation. To meet the needs of this program, the University has a full-service computer store, a campus network, and a CD-ROM computer center on campus.

George Fox demonstrates its commitment to freshmen by providing a Freshman Seminar Program to assist students as they integrate themselves into the academic and social life of the University community.

Off-Campus Arrangements

The importance of international study is shown through a variety of programs. Each year during May Term, George Fox sponsors a number of three-week study tours led by University faculty. These international learning experiences are designed for students completing their junior year. Through the Coalition for Christian Colleges and Universities, students are also given the opportunity to study for a semester in China, Costa Rica, England, Kenya, Russia, and countries in the Middle East, as well as Washington, D.C.

Membership in the Christian College Consortium enables George Fox University students to attend for a semester one of twelve colleges located throughout the United States.

Academic Facilities

The three-story, $2.25-million Murdock Learning Resource Center houses more than 175,000 books and periodicals. Its features include rare book collections, study carrels, computer and audiovisual laboratories, a recording studio, and a darkroom.

The $5.3-million Edwards/Holman Science Center brings a new dimension to the University's science programs. The 36,000-square-foot building provides classrooms, offices, and laboratories for biology, chemistry, premedicine, mathematics, computer science, and engineering programs.

The William and Mary Bauman Auditorium seats 1,150 people in a facility that is among the finest in the Northwest. Rotating art exhibits appear in the large corridor-gallery along the east side of the building.

Costs

Tuition for the 2000–01 year is $17,300. Room and board are $5550. Fees are $310. Books are estimated to cost $600 per year.

Financial Aid

George Fox maintains that every qualified student should be able to attend the university of his or her choice without letting limited finances stand in the way. To this end, federal, state, and institutional need-based funds are available, as are merit awards in academics, music, and drama. About 87 percent of all students receive financial aid.

Faculty

The faculty at George Fox University fosters an atmosphere of discussion and independent thinking in the classroom. Faculty members have found a healthy balance between teaching and research by devoting a majority of their time to educating students. For students, the result is a passport to a career as well as an enriched life.

The University employs 117 full-time and 53 part-time faculty members. Seventy-five percent of the full-time faculty hold earned doctoral degrees. Faculty members are personally committed Christians who are involved in the lives of their students. The student-faculty ratio is 16:1.

Student Government

The Associated Student Community of George Fox University serves as a unifying force and voice for the campus student community and plays a significant role in organizing cultural, social, and recreational activities.

Admission Requirements

Students admitted to George Fox University must show academic ability, high moral character, and social concern. These qualities are evaluated by consideration of each applicant's academic record, test scores, recommendations, interview reports, and participation in extracurricular activities. The priority application deadline is February 15.

In order to provide a solid foundation for college-level work, it is recommended that the applicant present the equivalent of 16 academic units from an approved high school. The following units are suggested: English, 4; social studies, 2; science, 2; mathematics, 2; foreign language, 2; and health and physical education, 1.

Application and Information

For additional information, students should contact:

Office of Undergraduate Admissions
George Fox University
Newberg, Oregon 97132-2697

Telephone: 800-765-4369 Ext. 2240 (toll-free)
E-mail: admissions@georgefox.edu
World Wide Web: http://www.georgefox.edu

GEORGE MASON UNIVERSITY
FAIRFAX, VIRGINIA

The University

Originally a college of the University of Virginia, George Mason University was established as an independent, coeducational institution in 1972. The University offers a full schedule of daytime, evening, and off-campus courses as well as a wide variety of workshops and institutes, thus providing a broad range of educational opportunities for its students and the surrounding community. Its academic programs are offered through seven divisions: the College of Arts and Sciences, the School of Management, the Graduate School of Education, the School of Information Technology and Engineering, the School of Law, the College of Nursing and Health Science, and University Institutes and Centers. In the development of George Mason University's 661-acre campus, care has been taken to preserve the natural beauty of the Virginia countryside. The University's buildings are surrounded by groves of trees and parklike recreational sites, and parking areas are located on the perimeter of the campus.

The George W. Johnson Center provides students with a total learning experience through interaction with books, technology, peers, and faculty and staff members. The $50-million building with 8 acres of interior space is the first of its kind on a college campus to combine a 100,000-square-foot state-of-the-art open-space library facility with the meeting, activity, and food service space normally associated with a student union. The Student Housing Office handles arrangements for on-campus housing and also assists students who prefer to live off campus in finding suitable accommodations in the local area.

Student activities at Mason focus on the Student Unions, which include comfortable lounges, video games, rooms for billiards and TV, and quiet study areas. The Student Union also houses the student newspaper, *Broadside*, and the Student Government offices. Clubs, fraternities, and sororities are also based in the Student Union. The clubs range from those for special interest groups, such as international students, to honor, athletics, and political clubs. The Union has a more serious side, too. Students needing assistance in a variety of areas can find it at such Student Affairs Offices as Counseling, Career Services, and Cooperative Education. A second Student Union building provides many similar facilities and features two large dining areas with adjacent outdoor patios. The University's athletic and recreational facilities include a gymnasium, a field house with an indoor track, a 10,000-seat arena, and a new aquatic center. The Aquatic and Fitness Center is designed to provide aquatic opportunities for the broadest spectrum of campus life. The center hosts world-class swimming events and offers state-of-the-art recreational facilities. Two pools are contained within the center—a 50-meter Olympic pool and a 25-yard recreation pool. The Fitness Gallery contains treadmills, rowing ergometers, stair-climbing equipment, exercise bikes, and strength-conditioning equipment.

Location

Located just outside the city of Fairfax and with campuses in Arlington and Prince William Counties, George Mason University benefits by its proximity to both urban and rural areas. To the west are the forested Blue Ridge Mountains, perfect for hiking, camping, and fishing, with skiing an added attraction in winter. Just 16 miles to the east is downtown Washington, D.C., offering a wealth of theaters, shops, museums, art galleries, and historic sites. Fairfax County and its surrounding areas are also rich in history. Manassas Battlefield Park, in nearby Prince William County, marks the site of Thomas J. "Stonewall" Jackson's heroic stand. Historic houses are located throughout the region. One of these is Gunston Hall, once the home of the University's namesake, George Mason.

Majors and Degrees

George Mason University awards B.A., B.F.A., B.M., B.S., B.S.Ed., and B.S.N. degrees in the areas of accounting; administration of justice; anthropology; art history; art studio; biology; business administration; chemistry; classical studies; communications; computer engineering; computer science; dance; decision sciences; earth systems sciences; economics; electrical engineering; English; finance; French; geography; German; government and international politics; health, fitness, and recreation resources; history; interdisciplinary studies; management; marketing; mathematics; medical technology; modern and classical languages; music; nursing; philosophy; physics; psychology; public administration; Russian studies; social work; sociology; Spanish; systems engineering; teacher certification; theater; and urban systems engineering.

As an alternative to traditional degree programs, the University also offers the Bachelor of Individualized Study degree. Designed especially for the needs of the mature student, the program gives credit for nontraditional instruction and life experience as well as for actual courses taken.

Academic Program

New Century College is a new undergraduate B.A. or B.S. degree program based on the belief that education is most effective when small groups of faculty members and students concentrate together on genuine intellectual problems. The curriculum stresses an integrative learning experience that is more active, collaborative, interdisciplinary, and self-reflexive than traditional degree programs. Students develop learning strategies appropriate to their individual learning styles and to the particular problem or issue they are studying.

Classes are in session the year round. The fall semester runs from late August to mid-December, the spring semester runs from late January to early May, and the summer sessions begin in late May. Programs are flexible, allowing students to take courses as electives in most of the University disciplines while majoring in another particular area.

Off-Campus Arrangements

Through the University's membership in the Consortium for Continuing Higher Education in Northern Virginia, a broad base of learning opportunities is available for upper-level undergraduates on a space-available basis through the participating members. To broaden and enrich their undergraduate education, Mason students may undertake programs of study abroad through George Mason University's Center for Global Education. The University also offers an Extended Studies Program, which is administered through the Office of Admissions.

Academic Facilities

Fenwick Library, Johnson Center Library, Arlington Campus Library, and Prince William Library comprise the George Mason University Libraries. Together, the libraries hold 500,000 volumes of books and periodicals as well as extensive collections of microforms, maps, videocassettes, sound recordings, and videodiscs. The libraries are also depositories for U.S., Virginia, and European union materials. Special Collections and Archives holds manuscripts and papers from prominent Virginians as well as more than fifty collections, including the Ollie Atkins Photographic Collection, the Robert Breen Theatre Collection, and the Planned Community Archives. The Law School, located in Arlington, has its own library, which houses an additional 195,000 volumes. The campus libraries—Fenwick, Johnson Center, Prince William, and Arlington—share a common library information system, Polaris, which provides access to the collections of the libraries. Available via the World Wide Web, the Polaris system is also enhanced by access to more than 300 databases worldwide. More than 150 workstations are available in the campus libraries, and all provide access to Polaris as well as to the Internet. More information about computing and libraries at George Mason can be found at the University's Web site (http://www.gmu.edu/).

Clarence Robinson Hall houses a fully equipped theater, additional classrooms, laboratories, and departmental offices. Another modern building, David King Hall, houses research centers and laboratories for the Departments of Physics, Geology, and Biology. An important University facility is the Child/Youth Study Center, where the learning disabilities of handicapped children are studied and diagnosed. The Center for the Arts, noticeable at the entrance of the campus, includes classrooms, offices, rehearsal rooms, and a 2,000-seat theater. The Science and Technology II Building gives more classroom and research space for high-tech studies.

George Mason has more than 500 computer workstations (PCs, Macs, SGIs, and X-terminals) available for student use in the public computer labs. PC, Mac, and UNIX applications are available in the computer labs. Access to the central computer systems (MASON, a system cluster consisting of multiple DEC Alpha machines, a DEC 3000/300, and HP K420, and an IBM ES9000) is available to all workstations on campus through MASONet, the campuswide data network. All residence hall rooms have access to MASONet. Through MASONet, all campus computers can access Network Virginia, the state ATM network, as well as the Internet. In addition to the above, specialized UNIX-based workstations (Sun, DEC, HP, and SGI) are installed in various computer labs throughout the University.

Costs

The basic expenses for the 2000–01 academic year (August to May) for in-state undergraduate students are $4468 for tuition, room, and board per semester ($8848 for out-of-state students), plus approximately $610 for books and supplies. Students who reside in residence halls must purchase one of three meal plans. Student health insurance is available if desired.

Financial Aid

George Mason University students receive financial aid from grants, loans, scholarships, and part-time employment sources. Students who require financial aid must complete the Free Application for Federal Student Aid (FAFSA). The FAFSA should be mailed as soon as possible after January 1 to receive priority consideration. George Mason University, Fairfax, Virginia (school code 003749), must be clearly indicated on the college release. Further information may be obtained by contacting the Office of Student Financial Aid, telephone: 703-993-4350.

Faculty

Of the 1,920 faculty members at George Mason University, approximately 85 percent hold doctoral degrees. The student-faculty ratio is 17:1, allowing faculty members to develop personal involvement with and concern for each student. All classes are taught by qualified faculty members.

Student Government

George Mason University's Student Government provides students with an opportunity to participate actively in the administration of their affairs through its three branches—executive, legislative, and judicial—and through student membership on many University committees. It also acts as a link in fostering student-faculty relationships and in providing effective representation on the students' behalf.

Admission Requirements

Admission to George Mason University is selective. The number of new students admitted each year is limited by the availability of instructional space. All applications for admission are reviewed individually.

Applicants for admission to the freshman class are considered in accordance with the following criteria: (1) a complete record of academic achievement from an accredited secondary or preparatory school, where graduation is based on no fewer than 15 units, distributed as follows: 4 units of English, 3 units of mathematics—algebra I, algebra II, and geometry (plus an additional unit of advanced mathematics for business, computer science, engineering, and mathematics majors), 2 units of the same foreign language (not required of business, computer science, engineering, or mathematics majors), 1 unit of social science, 1 unit of laboratory science (2 units for computer science, engineering, and mathematics majors—chemistry and physics are recommended), and 4 to 5½ units in academic electives and (2) satisfactory scores on the SAT I or the ACT examination. Interviews are available for freshman applicants. Transfer applicants must have a minimum cumulative GPA of 2.0 (C) for consideration; however, transfer admission is competitive. Guided tours are available Monday through Friday at 10:30 a.m. and 2:15 p.m. and on Saturdays at 10 and 11:30 a.m. from the admissions office, Finley Building, and Room 119.

Application and Information

A nonrefundable fee of $30 is required with each application. The deadlines for filing a freshman application are February 1 for the fall semester and November 1 for the spring semester. Transfer applicants should apply by March 15 for the fall and by November 1 for spring. An official transcript is required from each collegiate institution attended. Applications may be accepted after the fall deadline on a space-available basis. Applications and information may be obtained via e-mail or the World Wide Web (addresses below).

A written request for material may be made to:

Office of Admissions MSN 3A4
Finley Building
George Mason University
Fairfax, Virginia 22030-4444

Telephone: 703-993-2400
E-mail: admissions@gmu.edu
World Wide Web: http://www.admissions.gmu.edu

The Center for the Arts at George Mason University.

Peterson's Guide to Four-Year Colleges 2001 www.petersons.com

GEORGETOWN COLLEGE
GEORGETOWN, KENTUCKY

The College

Chartered in 1829, but with origins dating to 1787, Georgetown College is one of the oldest Baptist-affiliated colleges in America. The coeducational undergraduate student body of about 1,350 comes primarily from Kentucky, Ohio, and Indiana, but twenty-seven other states and ten other countries are also represented. The standard of excellence maintained since the College began has helped to channel more than 10,000 alumni into medicine, law, diplomacy, teaching, business, the ministry, social work, and countless other occupations all over the world. In addition to its undergraduate programs, the College offers a graduate program leading to the Master of Arts in Education.

The academic reputation of the College is the primary reason given by freshmen for selecting Georgetown. The College's Christian commitment is another strong influence among a majority of students. By combining strong academics, a Christian emphasis, and a comprehensive extracurricular program that provides many opportunities for student involvement and leadership, Georgetown is able to offer a distinctive living and learning community. This program has brought Georgetown national recognition in publications such as *U.S. News & World Report, Peterson's Competitive Colleges, Barron's 300 Best Buys,* and *Templeton Foundations' Top Character Building Colleges.* The Carnegie Foundation has also recognized Georgetown as a Baccalaureate I institution.

Membership in local chapters of national honoraries is available in most academic disciplines. Georgetown's chapter of Phi Beta Lambda (the honorary business fraternity) has achieved distinction on the state and national levels. The Association of Georgetown Students sponsors concerts, films, dances, and special events, and the Office of Campus Ministries organizes religious activities.

Kentucky's oldest drama group still resides on campus along with a nationally recognized forensics team. One of Georgetown's choral groups performs on tour in Europe every third summer. A 50,000-watt stereo FM radio station, concert and pep bands, a weekly student newspaper, a yearbook, fraternities and sororities, and many other extracurricular activities provide opportunities for all students, regardless of major. The Academic Team has won the Kentucky state championship three out of the past five years.

More than 90 percent of Georgetown's students live on campus in the College's fourteen dormitories or four modern apartment-style townhouses. Most of these residence halls house fewer than 80 students each. This housing arrangement promotes a friendly, family atmosphere and demonstrates the College's personal approach to education.

The College fields athletic teams in seven NAIA intercollegiate sports for men (baseball, basketball, cross-country, football, golf, soccer, and tennis) and in seven NAIA sports for women (basketball, cross-country, golf, soccer, softball, tennis, and volleyball) and offers cheerleading and dance teams. Georgetown's teams regularly participate on the national tournament level, and in the 1990s, the Tigers captured two national championships. Team members regularly receive national recognition. The athletic facilities are among the best of comparable institutions. Rawlings Stadium and nearby apartments host the summer camp of the NFL's Cincinnati Bengals.

Location

Recognized as one of the safest cities in Kentucky, historic Georgetown is in the Lexington metropolitan area. Some of the world's most famous horse farms are very close to the campus, and the Kentucky State Horse Park (open the year round and offering 100 riding horses) is only 5 miles south of the College. Major industrial facilities are also located nearby. The Toyota Motor Manufacturing Company plant is 4 miles north of the campus, and LexMark's facility is about 11 miles to the south. The community is served by all major airlines at the Lexington Bluegrass and Greater Cincinnati airports and is readily accessible by the interstate highway system (I-75 and I-64).

Majors and Degrees

Georgetown College confers the degrees of Bachelor of Arts, Bachelor of Science, Bachelor of Music, and Bachelor of Music Education. Major programs are available in accounting; American studies; art; biological sciences; business administration and communication arts; business administration and ethics; chemistry; church music; communication arts; computer science; elementary education; English; environmental science; European studies; finance; French; German; history; international business management; kinesiology; management; management information systems; marketing; marketing/finance; mathematics; medical technology; music; music education; philosophy; physics; political science; psychology; religion; sociology; and Spanish. Preprofessional preparation is offered in dentistry, engineering, kindergarten education, law, medicine, the ministry, nursing, pharmacy, physical therapy, teacher education, and veterinary science.

Georgetown offers dual-degree programs in nursing (with the University of Kentucky), engineering arts (with Washington University and the University of Kentucky), and ministerial education (with Regent's Park College of Oxford University).

Academic Program

The College operates on a semester-hour system of two 15-week semesters, a summer session of two 5-week terms, and three miniterms. Students may study abroad in College-sponsored programs in England, France, Mexico, Chile, or Hong Kong. Arrangements through the Kentucky Institute for International Studies and the Consortium for Global Education provide additional study opportunities throughout Central and South America, Europe, Africa, and Asia.

To qualify for graduation, students must complete a minimum of 128 semester hours, including major and minor field requirements and up to 56 semester hours of general education. The general education requirements are distributed as follows: Christian faith and values, 6 hours; effective communication, 8 hours; natural sciences, 9 hours; social sciences, 6 hours in two fields; cultural and aesthetic values, 16 hours; foreign language and culture, 9 hours; and physical education, 2 hours. Any of these general education requirements may be satisfied by examination.

Students may be granted college credit for satisfactory performance on the Advanced Placement tests given by the College Board. They may also earn credit in twenty subjects and a waiver of certain requirements by taking the College-Level Examination Program (CLEP) subject examinations. The College also recognizes credit earned through the International Baccalaureate program.

Both Air Force and Army ROTC programs are available for Georgetown College students through an agreement with the University of Kentucky. Cadets are full-time students at Georgetown and take one course session weekly at UK. Applicants are considered on the basis of their ACT or SAT I scores, high school academic record, extracurricular and athletic activities, personal references, and a medical examination.

Academic Facilities

Georgetown's academic commons includes ten classroom buildings. From historic Pawling Hall, built in 1844 and completely renovated in 1991, to the modern Wilson Fine Arts Building, each facility has special features that enhance the learning process.

The George Matt Asher Science Center is the largest classroom building on campus. In addition to the eleven science laboratories located in the center, students also have access to a foreign language lab, a botanical greenhouse, a 24-foot-screen planetarium, and one of five computer science labs.

The Ensor Learning Resource Center (library), completed in 1998, encompasses more than 55,000 square feet, including space for 220,500 books and 1,050 periodicals, and features state-of-the-art electronic research technology. Other features include study tables with computer hookups and a replica of the Yale Law Library study room, complete with a 14-foot-high fireplace.

The Nunnelley Music Building, Wilson Fine Arts Building, and Wilson Theatre, all located on the campus's west side, provide a focal point for the arts. The Nunnelley Music Building's features include private-lesson studios, ensemble rehearsal rooms, and computer facilities for music students. The theater seats up to 150 and offers a fully equipped workshop for set construction. The Anne Wright Wilson Fine Arts Building, featuring lecture and gallery space, a sculpture yard, a modern computer graphics lab, and photography, printing, painting, and design labs, opened in 1996.

Costs

The 2000–01 academic-year expenses are $12,140 for tuition, $4610 for room and board, and $240 for additional fees, for a total of $16,990.

Financial Aid

Approximately 94 percent of the College's students receive some form of financial assistance. Academic or need-based scholarships, departmental grants, Federal Perkins Loans, Federal Stafford Student Loans, Federal Pell Grants, Federal Work-Study Program awards, athletic scholarships, and Christian Service Grants are available. To be considered for assistance, students should file the Free Application for Federal Student Aid (FAFSA). Priority consideration is given to those who file before February 15. A number of awards, some paying up to the full cost of tuition, fees, and room and board, are made on the basis of academic ability alone; the application deadline for these is February 1.

Faculty

Georgetown has an outstanding faculty; 91 percent of its members hold the terminal degree in their area of expertise. The student-faculty ratio is 13:1, and the average class size is 15. No academic classes are taught by graduate students, and full professors teach freshman-level courses. Faculty members are readily accessible to any student both in and out of the classroom, and they interact freely with one another across disciplinary lines.

Student Government

The Association of Georgetown Students (AGS) actively represents the voice of the students in nearly all campus matters. It has a major responsibility in coordinating campus life and activities and regularly encourages interaction between students, the faculty, and the administration to enhance student development.

Admission Requirements

Applicants for admission to Georgetown are considered individually on the basis of a combination of academic records. All applicants must submit high school transcripts, official score reports of the ACT examination or the SAT I, and a brief written essay. International students must also present scores on the Test of English as a Foreign Language.

Other materials the student feels would be helpful in evaluating his or her potential for success, such as recommendations, tapes, and the like, are welcome. Evidence of creativity and leadership is also considered. Applicants should generally be in the upper half of their graduating class and have taken a strong college-preparatory program.

Admission and financial assistance are awarded by Georgetown College without regard to race, sex, national origin, or handicap.

Application and Information

Application should be made in the senior year, and students are notified of the admissions decision on a rolling basis. Georgetown endorses the NACAC common Candidates Reply Date of May 1.

Further information may be obtained from:

Director of Admissions
Georgetown College
400 East College Street
Georgetown, Kentucky 40324-1696
Telephone: 502-863-8009
          800-788-9985 (toll-free)
E-mail: admissions@georgetowncollege.edu
World Wide Web: http://www.georgetowncollege.edu

The Ensor Learning Resource Center contains more than 290,000 book volumes and microfilm and audiovisual titles as well as more than 170 computers and 185 data drops throughout the 55,000-square-foot building.

GEORGETOWN UNIVERSITY
School of Nursing
WASHINGTON, D.C.

The University and The School

Georgetown is an international university located in Washington, D.C. As the nation's capital, Washington attracts people from all over the country and from all parts of the world. The University has played a key part in the city's life since 1789, the year in which George Washington was inaugurated President. The School of Nursing, founded in 1903, has achieved the goal of excellence enunciated by its founders. Today, it ranks among the country's most respected university programs.

The diversity of the student population at Georgetown provides a stimulating environment for student life and study. All fifty states and more than 100 countries are represented by the 6,000 men and women currently enrolled at the undergraduate level. Outside opportunities and extracurricular activities offer students a chance to broaden their horizons in many directions. Popular entertainers and renowned speakers provide students with a diverse selection of both social and intellectual pursuits. Campus life includes such activities as dramatics, several journalistic publications, choral and instrumental groups, intramural and varsity sports, and student government. Campus ministries reflect the religious pluralism of the University, as clergy from the major faiths work together with students in organizing a vibrant religious and socially active life on campus.

Location

The University is located in historic Georgetown. Students come to the University recognizing the special opportunities, the wealth of experience, and the insights and exposure that life in Washington will provide. Located less than 2 miles from the White House and 3 miles from the Capitol, the University is set high on a bluff overlooking picturesque Georgetown and the Potomac River. The Lauinger Library provides a panoramic view of Washington's skyline, including the Washington Monument, the Lincoln and Jefferson memorials, and the John F. Kennedy Center for the Performing Arts. More than 240 other libraries, museums, and research facilities in the city are open to Georgetown students, including the world-famous Library of Congress, National Archives, Smithsonian Institution, Folger Shakespeare Library, and National Gallery of Art. Most foreign embassies and federal government agencies have library facilities with staff members who are willing to help students.

Majors and Degrees

Georgetown University School of Nursing offers two majors for students interested in health-care–related fields. The Bachelor of Science in Nursing (B.S.N.) degree prepares students as generalists who are able to practice nursing in any health-care setting. The RN-B.S.N. and RN-M.S. tracks enable registered nurses to complete their bachelor's degree or master's degree programs in advanced practice nursing graduate courses. There is also an accelerated second-degree program for college graduates who wish to pursue a bachelor's degree in nursing upon completion of the prerequisite courses. The Bachelor of Science degree in health studies is the second major offered and is designed for students who aspire to careers in health policy, public health, law, medicine, health education, health administration, international health, and many other related fields. This innovative curriculum includes three tracks of concentration from which to choose (health systems, international health, and science). Premedical or other preprofessional courses may be taken in addition to the curriculum of either nursing or health studies upon admission. Preprofessional advising is available. Transfer students are welcome to apply for admission in either major. Prerequisite courses are not required. Graduate programs for advanced practice in nursing are available to college graduates in acute-care nurse practitioner studies, family nurse practitioner studies, management of integrated health systems/clinical care coordination, nurse anesthesia, and nurse midwifery. For more information regarding the courses of study, students should go to the School of Nursing Web site (listed below).

Academic Program

The School of Nursing is one of four undergraduate schools at Georgetown University, which is internationally recognized for its excellence in the fields of government, science, and the humanities. Graduates of the School of Nursing at Georgetown receive an education that prepares them to begin professional practice and provides the basis for ongoing professional development. The curriculum is four academic years in length and is based upon a core of courses in three broad areas of knowledge: the humanities, the behavioral sciences, and the physical sciences. The study of nursing and health studies is initiated in the freshman year, continued throughout the sophomore year, and concentrated in the junior and senior years. A variety of minor concentrations are available in such fields as English, fine arts, philosophy, psychology, and sociology through courses taken in other undergraduate schools of Georgetown University.

Students study the curative and restorative aspects of health care, as well as health maintenance and health education. Freshman- and sophomore-year courses provide the foundation common to all health-care professionals. Junior- and senior-year courses provide the student with the knowledge and skills necessary to become a competent practitioner and health-care provider. Practical clinical exposure, which begins in the first year and increases in the sophomore and junior years, culminates in the senior practicum. This practicum is designed to ease the transition of the individual from the role of student to that of a professional health-care provider. Students are permitted to choose an area of concentration for the senior practicum based upon the clinical settings available to the School of Nursing. In keeping with the University's commitment to international work and study, students have opportunities for intercultural clinical experiences; to date, these have included work in Appalachia, England, Guatemala, and Ireland.

A significant topic included in the curriculum is bioethics, within the field of philosophy. Opportunities are available for students to participate in interdisciplinary courses offered at the Kennedy Institute of Bioethics. Other relevant areas of study are computer technology, management, research, and community-based care.

Qualified applicants may be admitted to the Army Reserve Officers' Training Corps, which supports a unit (the Hoya Battalion) on the Georgetown campus. Tuition assistance and subsistence allowances are available. Graduates serve as commissioned officers in the U.S. Army Nurse Corps for their obligation period and receive consideration in choice of location and clinical assignment.

Academic Facilities

The School of Nursing is an integral part of the University as well as of the Medical Center, which is adjacent to the main campus. The School's classrooms, faculty, and administration are located in St. Mary's Hall. Students also have classes and laboratories on the main campus and in the medical school. In addition to using the Lauinger Library, students in the School of Nursing use the rich resources of Dahlgren Library in the University Medical Center.

The Georgetown University Hospital is located on the main campus adjacent to the School of Nursing. The hospital's exciting research, innovative techniques, and sophisticated instrumentation provide an exemplary background for student clinical practice. Opportunities for professional practice are also available at other excellent health-care facilities in the Washington area.

Costs

Tuition for the 1999–2000 academic year was $21,466; room and board costs were $8670. Other expenses, which included lab fees, books, personal expenses, and travel, were approximately $2800. There are three board plans available: nineteen meals per week, fourteen meals per week, or any of seven meals. Other plans enable students who do not wish these options to choose lunch only or plan their board charges on a pay-as-you-go basis. University housing includes apartments, dormitories, town houses, and college houses. The University guarantees housing for three out of four years. Accommodations are also available in apartments and houses in the Georgetown area of Washington, within blocks of the University. Both the University and the public transportation system provide excellent facilities to meet students' needs.

Financial Aid

In cases of economic need, the University makes every effort to provide financial aid in the form of scholarships, grants, loans, and jobs to enable students to come to Georgetown. The amount of financial assistance given varies with the demonstrated financial need of the applicants. Students must submit the Free Application for Federal Student Aid (FAFSA) of the College Scholarship Service as soon after January 1 as possible. All forms must be completed and received at Georgetown from the College Scholarship Service by March 1 to ensure full consideration for financial aid. Awards based on need are generally presented in packages of grants, loans, and/or work-study jobs. It is vital for students who wish to be considered for financial aid to mark the appropriate box on the admission application.

Faculty

Faculty members are renowned for their academic specialty and profession. Certified nurse practitioners, including nurse-midwives and specialists at the Georgetown University Hospital, are among the members of the clinical faculty. At Georgetown, meaningful contact between professor and student is encouraged and emphasized. Senior members of the faculty teach introductory courses as well as advanced seminars. The student-faculty ratio in the clinical setting is 8:1, and the average class size is 20.

Student Government

In order to maintain communication on academic affairs among the students, faculty, and administration, the student body in each school at Georgetown elects a Student Academic Council annually. This provides a mechanism for student representation in matters concerning the students in the School. The council is composed of elected representatives from each class. These representatives and council members also hold positions on the Executive Council and on the Committees on Curriculum and Students. Each representative has voting privileges as set out by each group's constitution.

Students have opportunities to join the Georgetown chapter of the National Student Nurses Association, where students are actively involved in current issues and concerns of the profession and in community issues, both on campus and in surrounding areas. Sigma Theta Tau, a professional honor society, recognizes practitioners and students of nursing who exemplify outstanding qualities of leadership, scholarship, and service to the profession of nursing. The Health Studies Society offers camaraderie for students interested in all aspects of health care. A seminar series brings experts in the field of health for lecture and discussion. The Yes! to Success Program is designed to enrich the four-year curriculum by providing students with advanced skills for learning and professional practice. A series of seminars focuses on learning strategies, preparation for national certification exams, and readiness to enter health-care professions or graduate studies.

Admission Requirements

The University and the School of Nursing welcome applications from men and women of character, motivation, and intelligence, without distinction on the basis of race, sex, or religious belief. Transfer students and candidates with degrees in fields other than nursing are encouraged to apply.

All candidates are required to take the SAT I offered by the College Board or the ACT Assessment offered by American College Testing. Candidates are requested to submit results of at least three SAT II Subject Tests, including the Writing Test and two others appropriate to their area of interest. A student's test results, academic record, teacher and counselor recommendations, alumni interview, essays, and extracurricular activities (i.e. medical explorers, hospital volunteer, community service) provide the basis for the admissions committee review. All applicants to the School of Nursing are encouraged to take 3 years of mathematics and are required to complete 1 year of biology and 1 year of chemistry.

Students interested in Georgetown are strongly encouraged to visit the campus. Personal interviews are not required but may be scheduled at the School of Nursing. Tours of the campus and information sessions are available Monday through Friday and on Saturday mornings through the Office of Undergraduate Admissions.

Application and Information

For general information and application materials, students should contact:

Office of Undergraduate Admissions
Georgetown University
P.O. Box 37455
Washington, D.C. 20013
Telephone: 202-687-3600
World Wide Web: http://www.georgetown.edu (to download applications)

For specific information regarding nursing or health studies, students should contact:

Michelle Harvin
Coordinator of Admissions and Recruitment
Georgetown University School of Nursing
3700 Reservoir Road, NW
Washington, D.C. 20007
Telephone: 202-687-2781
        800-89NURSE (toll-free)
E-mail: harvinm@gunet.georgetown.edu
World Wide Web: http://www.georgetown.edu/schnurs/

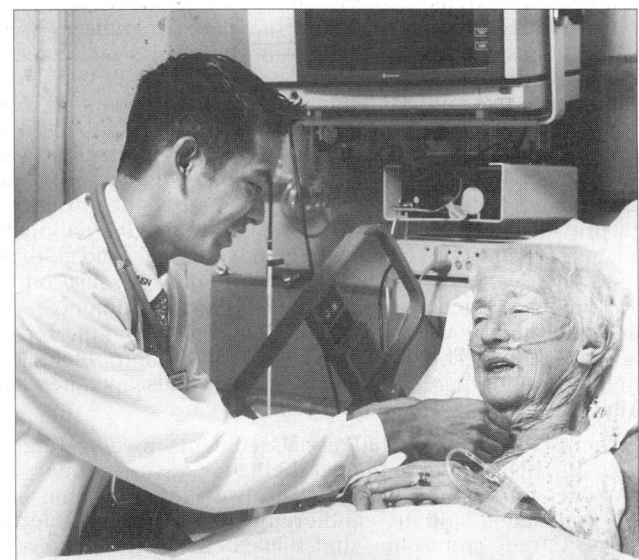

Clinical experiences for students take place in various health-care facilities, particularly at the Georgetown University Medical Center, conveniently located on the Georgetown campus.

GEORGIAN COURT COLLEGE
LAKEWOOD, NEW JERSEY

The College

Georgian Court College (GCC), founded by the Sisters of Mercy of New Jersey, began in 1908 as a liberal arts college for young women. The current undergraduate enrollment in the women's college is 1,070. In 1976, the College expanded to include a Graduate School of Education. In 1979, the coeducational Undergraduate Evening Division was established to provide both men and women the means to pursue a baccalaureate degree while being involved in full- or part-time employment; it now enrolls 512 students. The College's strong academic program aims not merely to educate competent professionals but, more importantly, to develop students' potential and to deepen their understanding of society and commitment to its future. Georgian Court students follow a curriculum broad enough to be truly liberal, yet specialized enough to provide preparation in depth for further study and future careers. The mission of Georgian Court is the education of creative and responsible leaders who have a firm sense of moral, spiritual, and intellectual values.

The College's beautifully landscaped 150-acre campus on the former George Gould estate provides an impressive setting for college life. The campus has seventeen buildings. The majority of the College's students come from New Jersey. A small percentage come from surrounding states and other countries. Twenty-two percent of the students enrolled in the women's college are resident students. St. Joseph Hall and Maria Hall provide private or semiprivate dormitory rooms situated around comfortable lounges. Kitchenettes are located on each floor.

Both resident and commuting students participate in a wide variety of activities, including numerous cultural and social functions. There are a number of College-sponsored trips to New York and Philadelphia to visit museums, attend the theater, and shop. In addition, social activities are planned on campus, with invitations extended to area colleges. The Patrick and Julia Gavan Student Lounge is the gathering place for students in all divisions. Seasonal parties, live entertainment, and special events make the student lounge a popular place to be. There are also thirty-five cultural, educational, honorary, and service-oriented clubs and organizations. Two student publications provide opportunities for students who enjoy photography or writing. For students who are musically inclined, the Court Singers, Court Notes, and the Georgian Court College Concert Band provide opportunities. Women's intercollegiate competition is offered in basketball, cross-country, soccer, and softball. The varsity teams compete in the National Association of Intercollegiate Athletics, the National Collegiate Athletic Association, the Central Atlantic College Conference, and the Jersey Nine Association. The facilities at Georgian Court include a heated swimming pool, tennis courts, and landscaped acreage ideally suited for jogging and bicycling.

The Counseling Center staff assists students in adjusting to college life, helps them to budget their time, gives seminars on leadership and personal growth, and provides individual and group counseling and psychotherapy in addition to referral services. Career counseling and placement services are also offered to all students and alumni. Students needing extra assistance with course work may take advantage of the tutorial aides available through Student Support Services. The Health Center, staffed by registered nurses throughout the day and evening, provides general health care and arranges for medical treatment as needed. Campus ministers are available to provide spiritual counseling. The Eucharistic Liturgy is offered on campus. In addition, the Lakewood area has a wide variety of churches and synagogues to serve non-Catholic students. The Learning Center (TLC) is an assistance program designed to provide an environment for students with mild to moderate learning disabilities. Emphasis is placed on developing self-help strategies and study techniques.

Location

Bordering the north shore of Lake Carasaljo, the campus is situated in a quiet, residential neighborhood of Lakewood, New Jersey. Centrally located in the state, Georgian Court is convenient to the Route 9 corridor, the Garden State Parkway, and Interstate 195. New York City, Philadelphia, and Atlantic City are each less than 1½ hours by car from the campus. The distance to the seashore is approximately 10 miles.

Majors and Degrees

The Bachelor of Arts degree is awarded in art, art history, biology, chemistry, English, French, history, humanities, mathematics, music, physics, psychology, religious studies, sociology, Spanish, and special education. The Bachelor of Fine Arts is awarded in general fine arts and graphic design/illustration. The Bachelor of Science degree is awarded in accounting, biochemistry, biology, business administration, chemistry, and physics. Students planning a career in social work can obtain the Bachelor of Social Work degree.

Teacher certification programs in elementary education, subject areas (N–12), and special education are available at Georgian Court.

A dual-degree program in engineering is offered with George Washington University. Students in this program take specified courses during three years at Georgian Court and then transfer to George Washington University for two years of engineering study. At the completion of the program, students obtain a B.A. in mathematics from Georgian Court and a B.S. in engineering from George Washington University.

Academic Program

Successful completion of 132 credit hours is required for a B.A., B.F.A., B.S., or B.S.W. degree. With departmental approval, students may elect a second major. All students must complete general education requirements, which are designed to provide the breadth essential for complete development of the truly liberally educated person. These consist of nine approved semester courses in the humanities, five in the social sciences, and three in the natural sciences/mathematics.

Many departments offer minor field sequences, certification programs, or concentrations. These include anthropology, bilingual/bicultural studies, commercial art, computer science, economics, English as a second language, gerontology, holistic health, marketing, medical technology, nuclear medicine technology, philosophy, and political science. Preprofessional programs include chiropractic, dentistry, law, medicine, and veterinary. In addition, interdisciplinary minors are available in American studies, international area studies, Latin American studies, and women's studies. Internships, externships, and practicums are offered in most majors, and independent studies are available in many.

Off-Campus Arrangements

Students are permitted to enroll in an accredited college or university offering a study-abroad program. Georgian Court

College credits are offered for Autumn Semester in Quebec and study abroad in a Spanish-speaking country.

Academic Facilities

The Arts and Science Center contains classrooms, seminar rooms, offices, studios for the fine arts, the Little Theatre, a radioisotope laboratory, a computer laboratory, an anthropology laboratory, and modern laboratories and equipment for instruction and research in the biological, chemical, and physical sciences. The library houses a collection of more than 200,000 items in print and nonprint format, including 1,070 periodical titles. An online library system, CD-ROM network, and Internet capability provide students with access to a wide variety of information resources both local and worldwide. A multimedia classroom enhances instruction in the use of electronic resources, and a computer lab permits students to use these resources as well as e-mail, course-related software, and general software such as word processing and spreadsheets. The library catalog and many CD-ROM databases can be utilized from any networked computer on campus. The library is open 80 hours weekly, with reference assistance available at all times. Hamilton Hall houses the Learning Center and the program in special education. Residence halls are wired for room telephones, and data lines are connected by fiber-optic cable.

Costs

Tuition for the 2000–01 academic year is $12,742. Residence and board are $4700 (seven-day meal plan) or $4550 (five-day meal plan). General fees are $200.

Financial Aid

Georgian Court College has endeavored to keep the cost of attending an independent college affordable. A large percentage of its students receive financial assistance. Financial aid consists of all scholarships, grants, loans, or campus jobs offered to the applicant to help meet education-related expenses. Eligible students may be aided through a combination of these items, called a financial aid package. Georgian Court offers both need-based and no-need financial aid. For example, some scholarships are granted on the basis of a superior academic record, SAT I or ACT scores, and financial need; other scholarships are based on academic excellence only. Athletics grants of variable amounts are available to students who qualify for admission and demonstrate the ability to participate in the sports program while advancing their college career. Georgian Court financial aid is available to U.S. citizens and eligible noncitizens. The College also participates in the New Jersey Educational Opportunity Fund program. In order to be considered for any financial aid, all students must submit a Georgian Court financial aid form to the Financial Aid Office. All applicants must also submit the Free Application for Federal Student Aid (FAFSA). This analysis indicates the student's degree of financial need. The data are evaluated by the Financial Aid Committee, beginning February 15. An award letter and acceptance statement are then sent to students who qualify for aid, indicating the assistance provided to meet the student's financial need. Acceptance statements must be returned to the Financial Aid Office to finalize the awards. Financial aid information is included in the viewbook and on the GCC Web site (under Admissions).

Faculty

Seventy-one percent of the full-time teaching faculty members hold doctoral degrees. From the freshman year on, students have the opportunity to take courses with department chairpersons and other faculty members in the upper professional ranks. The student-faculty ratio is 12:1. The average class size is approximately 15. Individual counseling by the faculty adviser is an integral part of the educational process at Georgian Court.

Student Government

The Student Government Association, composed of elected students, organizes extracurricular activities for students. Through the student government structure, students take leadership roles in shaping student life and participate in all major College committees in conjunction with the faculty and administration.

Admission Requirements

Georgian Court College welcomes applications from students who desire a liberal arts education and have the necessary qualifications to benefit from the College's program. Entrance is based on individual merit. The high school record of achievement is of primary importance and must reflect solid performance in a college-preparatory program. Candidates for admission must have completed 16 academic (Carnegie) units. The majority of students attending Georgian Court ranked in the upper half of their senior class in high school. All candidates are required to take the SAT I or ACT, preferably by December of the senior year. Further consideration is given to the applicant's extracurricular activities and letters of recommendation submitted by teachers, counselors, employers, or similarly qualified people. A campus interview is highly recommended. The interview focuses primarily on a discussion of the student's experiences and interests and allows the interviewer to explain the College's current offerings. A guided tour of the campus is also offered.

Well-qualified applicants whose first choice is Georgian Court College and who apply no later than November 15 may be considered for early decision. A mature, well-qualified student who wishes to enter college after three years of high school may apply for early entrance. Transfer students are accepted into the freshman, sophomore, and junior classes for the fall and spring semesters. All students must be in good standing at their former college. Applicants with fewer than 24 credits must fulfill all requirements for admission to the freshman class. International students in need of an I-20 student visa must present official documents at least six months prior to the semester's start and must have a minimum TOEFL score of 550. International students must complete a GCC financial support form and should be prepared to assume full financial responsibility for educational and personal expenses in the United States.

Application and Information

To apply for admission, regular freshman applicants should send an application, high school transcript, and nonrefundable $30 application fee. Transfer students should submit an application, the fee, and transcripts from high school and all colleges attended. Freshman applicants are urged to file an application as early as possible in their senior year of high school. Freshman and transfer applications must be received by August 1 for the fall semester and by January 1 for the spring semester. The College has a rolling admissions policy; however, transfer and freshman applications should be received by August 1 for the fall semester and December 15 for the spring semester for the best course selection.

Marjorie J. Cooke
Director of Admissions
Georgian Court College
900 Lakewood Avenue
Lakewood, New Jersey 08701
Telephone: 732-364-2200 Ext. 760
          800-458-8422 (toll-free)
Fax: 732-364-4442
E-mail: admissions-ugrad@georgian.edu
World Wide Web: http://www.georgian.edu

GEORGIA SOUTHWESTERN STATE UNIVERSITY
AMERICUS, GEORGIA

The University

Georgia Southwestern State University is a four-year liberal arts and professional university of the University System of Georgia. Through the School of Arts and Sciences, the School of Business, the School of Computer Sciences, the School of Education, and the School of Nursing, the University prepares students for selected career fields while providing them with the knowledge to adapt to the ever-changing work force. Southwestern offers more than thirty academic programs. These programs are enhanced by the state-of-the-art Research and Technology Center that is bringing Georgia Southwestern into the twenty-first century with the latest in fiber optics and computer technology.

The personalized atmosphere of Southwestern gives students a chance to interact with their professors, thus creating a dynamic learning environment.

All degree programs at Georgia Southwestern State University are accredited by the Southwestern Association of Colleges and Schools. The programs in education and nursing are accredited by the National Council for Accreditation of Teacher Education and the National League for Nursing, respectively.

Most of the 2,600 students enrolled at Georgia Southwestern State University are Georgia residents, although twenty-two states and thirty-one other countries are represented. In a campus atmosphere that is both relaxed and friendly, students can enjoy the variety of choosing from more than sixty social and academic organizations that are available at Georgia Southwestern, making campus life at Southwestern an ever-changing mix of activities and events. Intramural and intercollegiate sports are very popular. Student athletes compete on the varsity level in baseball, basketball, softball, tennis, and volleyball. As a member of NAIA Division I and a candidate for NCAA Division II, Georgia Southwestern offers athletic scholarships.

In addition to the undergraduate degrees offered through the five schools, Southwestern also offers graduate programs at the master's and specialist levels in education, business, computers, and social administration. Plans are in place for a master's program in nursing.

Location

Georgia Southwestern in nestled on 225 wooded acres in the beautiful south Georgia community of Americus. With a county population of 30,000 that is continually growing, Americus exemplifies true "down home" southern hospitality.

Founded in 1832, Americus has a rich history and is an eclectic example of the fanciful Victorian architecture of the 1800s. Americus and Sumter County boast two national historic sites, Andersonville Civil War Village and the Jimmy Carter National Historic and Preservation District. The county also houses Souther Field Airport, home of Lindbergh's first flight; the 1892 vintage Windsor Hotel; the International Headquarters for the highly respected Habitat for Humanity volunteer organization; and high-tech industrial firms such as Martin Marietta, Cooper Lighting, TEXTRON automotive exteriors, and Mulcoa.

Long, warm summers and short, mild winters are characteristics of the area's climate, making for pleasant living conditions and year-round recreation. Sumter County has three golf courses, a recreation facility, and a lake. As the roots for Georgia Southwestern State University, Americus provides an atmosphere of tranquility that is conducive to learning. Americus is proud of its true southern hospitality and community pride.

Majors and Degrees

Georgia Southwestern State University's five schools provide a highly respected faculty and a variety of academic choices. The School of Arts and Sciences offers programs that lead either to a Bachelor of Arts, Bachelor of Fine Arts, or Bachelor of Science degree in art, biology, chemical technology, chemistry, earth sciences, English, French, geology, history, mathematics, music, political science, psychology, social science, sociology, or Spanish. Preprofessional programs are offered in dentistry, law, medicine, pharmacy, and veterinary medicine.

The School of Business offers programs that lead to a Bachelor of Business Administration degree in accounting, business education, general business, human resource management, or marketing. The School also offers the Associate of Science degree in accounting.

The School of Computer and Applied Sciences offers programs that lead to a Bachelor of Science degree in computer science, computer information systems, computer science technology, or comprehensive business education. A special dual-degree program in cooperation with the Georgia Institute of Technology Engineering School is available.

The School of Education offers programs that lead to Bachelor of Science degree with eligibility for teacher certification in art, business, early childhood, English, French, health and physical education, history, mathematics, middle school, music, science, Spanish, special education, secondary education, and social science.

The School of Nursing offers a program leading to the Bachelor of Science in Nursing.

Academic Program

The core curriculum of the University System of Georgia was established for the general purpose of aiding and facilitating the educational progress of students as they pursue baccalaureate degrees within and among the units of the University System. All candidates for a baccalaureate degree must earn a minimum of 120 semester hours of academic credit and complete five specified courses in physical education. A quality point average of 2.0 (C) or higher and completion of the minimum requirement of the core curriculum and of the specific degree programs are required for graduation. Candidates for the associate degree programs must earn a minimum of 60 semester hours and fulfill the above requirements. Candidates for the B.S. in education degree must successfully complete the Georgia Teacher Certification Test (TCT) in their specific area of certification.

The University operates on the semester system with each semester being fifteen weeks, except for the summer semester, which is eight weeks long. Normally, the baccalaureate degree is earned in eight semesters, and the associate degree is earned in four semesters. The normal course load for students is 15 semester hours in academic subjects. A student is considered to be carrying a full load if he or she is enrolled for 12 semester hours of academic credit, with the maximum load being 18 semester hours.

Southwestern may grant credit for satisfactory scores on selected tests of the College-Level Examination Program

(CLEP) and Advanced Placement (AP) tests and for work completed at military service schools or military experience as recommended by the Commission on Accreditation of Services Experiences of the American Council on Education.

Academic Facilities

The James Earl Carter Library (named in honor of President Carter's father) is an attractive two-story rectangular structure completed in 1971. The library is fully climate controlled and is acoustically treated and carpeted throughout. It houses more than 190,000 volumes, 140,575 government document items, and 618,842 units of microtext and can seat more than 650 persons. Library holdings are supplemented by GALILEO (Georgia Library Learning Online), which provides access to computer data and to the Internet.

The Rosalynn Carter Institute for Human Development was established on campus in 1987. The Institute was formed in honor of former First Lady Rosalynn Carter, an alumni of Georgia Southwestern, to enhance development and mental health. The Rosalynn Carter Institute provides research, public administration, and clinical training opportunities for students. Conferences and workshops offer students an opportunity to encounter nationally recognized figures in the human development and mental health fields.

Georgia Southwestern State University was designated by the Board of Regents of the University System of Georgia as the Asian Language and Culture Center in 1988. The Center for Asian Studies sponsors the Japanese Language Teacher Training Program in cooperation with a Japanese intercultural exchange organization. The Center also sponsors a Summer Study Program in Japan.

Costs

In 1999–2000, tuition and fees for Georgia residents were $1156 per semester or $2312 for the academic year. Room and board were $3540 for the academic year. For non-Georgia residents room and board were the same, but tuition and fees were $3876 per semester or $7752 for the academic year. Books and supplies cost approximately $200 per semester.

Financial Aid

For the 1999–2000 academic year, 78 percent of all undergraduate students received some form of financial aid. Georgia Southwestern participates in both the federal and state loan and grant programs, as well as college work-study, work-aid, academic scholarships, talent scholarships, and athletic scholarships. Students requesting financial aid are required to submit the Free Application for Federal Student Aid (FAFSA) and the University's institutional aid form.

Faculty

Georgia Southwestern State University has a full-time faculty of 122 members, 81 percent of whom hold an earned doctorate. The full-time student-faculty ratio is 15:1.

Student Government

The Student Government (TSG) consists of 4 elected officers (President, Vice President of Academic Affairs, Vice President for Student Life, and Secretary Treasurer), 11 elected senators, and 1 appointed senator. This organization is influential in campus affairs and is the chief student organization on campus. The Student Government is responsible for meeting the activity needs of the student body.

Admission Requirements

In assessing a student's readiness for admission to Georgia Southwestern, the Admission Office reviews his or her high school grades and curriculum, test scores, previous college work (if applicable), and other qualifications. For admission consideration to the freshman class the SAT I or ACT is required. Completion of the College Preparatory Curriculum (CPC) is required for regular admission. Transfer students must have been in good standing at their last college attended and have a minimum GPA of 2.0.

Joint enrollment and early admission are available for high school students who have completed their sophomore year. There is a special application process for this option. Minimum standards include a cumulative high school grade point average of at least 3.0 (B) in academic subjects and either a minimum combined SAT I score of 1050 or an ACT composite score of 23 or better.

Application and Information

Application can be made anytime following completion of the junior year. Students are notified on a rolling admission basis throughout the year. Upon receipt of the completed application and supporting documents, an admission decision will be made and communicated to the student.

Further in-depth information about Georgia Southwestern can be obtained by contacting:

Admissions Office
Georgia Southwestern State University
800 Wheatley Street
Americus, Georgia 31709
Telephone: 912-928-1273
              800-338-0082 (toll-free)
Fax: 912-931-2059
E-mail: gswapp@canes.gsw.peachnet.edu
World Wide Web: http://www.gsw.edu

Students relaxing on the campus of Georgia Southwestern State University.

GEORGIA STATE UNIVERSITY
ATLANTA, GEORGIA

The University

Established in 1913, Georgia State University is an urban institution where more than 23,000 students are provided unique academic experiences and diverse cultural and social events, as well as numerous business and professional offerings. At Georgia State University, classroom walls blend into the city, fusing educational and career opportunities. Located in the heart of downtown Atlanta, the University's campus offers a vibrant learning atmosphere where traditional education is enhanced through hands-on learning internships, guest lectures, and employment in the region's thriving financial, legal, communications, entertainment, hospitality, and business centers. All the cultural advantages and conveniences of big city living are only a short walk or shuttle ride away. The transformation of the historic Rialto Theater in the Fairlie-Poplar District into a first-class performance venue for music, dance, and drama; the expansion of the College of Business Administration; and the relocation of the School of Music comprise a major contribution by the University to the revitalization of Atlanta's city center.

This close-knit relationship between the University and the city of Atlanta was on full display as the Georgia State University Sports Arena served as the site of the 1996 Olympic badminton competition. Athletes from many of the 195 participating countries lived in the Georgia State University Village, which now provides housing for 2,000 students. This state-of-the-art apartment-style residence hall is among the nation's most unique college housing, offering students a safe community atmosphere for living, learning, and making lasting friendships in the world's newest international city.

While the University is widely recognized for its statewide, regional, and national contributions, students worldwide are drawn by the school's international focus. Students from 127 countries and all fifty states come each year to take part in the multicultural experience of living and learning at Georgia State. Minorities make up more than 30 percent of the student body and are well represented in student organizations and leadership roles. With more than 200 majors in fifty-two degree programs and an abundance of extracurricular activities, ranging from social and service clubs to athletic teams to political and professional groups, opportunities abound for both educational and personal enrichment.

Georgia State continues to build on its tradition of solid teaching and real-world education. The University is comprised of five colleges, including arts and sciences, business administration, education, health sciences, law, and a school of policy studies. Students are assured a comprehensive and well-rounded education in choosing from fifty-two nationally recognized and accredited degree programs encompassing 217 fields of study leading to bachelor's, master's, specialist's, and doctoral degrees. With a strong commitment to research that makes a difference, as well as accessible, high-quality academic programs, the University is taking a leading role in the progression toward the twenty-first century. These commitments are evident in the fact that the Biomechanics and Ergonomics Laboratory served as an official research facility for the Summer Olympic Games. In addition, the Computer Science Program consistently ranks among the finest in the country, while the Master of Business Administration program was recently ranked by *U.S. News & World Report* as one of the nation's top ten part-time M.B.A. programs. The College of Education confers more education degrees than most colleges in the Southeast and claims a 100 percent pass rate in several majors among students taking the Georgia Teacher Certification Test. With more than 4,500 alumni, the College of Health and Human Sciences is the major provider of allied health and nursing professionals for the state of Georgia.

The College of Law offers the Juris Doctor degree, as well as a joint Juris Doctor/Master of Business Administration degree, with a pass rate among the highest of all law schools in Georgia on the Bar examination in recent years.

Location

The city of Atlanta is the capital of Georgia as well as the cultural and economic center of the nation's fastest-growing region. With its diverse population, thriving business and industry, and exceptional educational and research universities, Atlanta is quickly establishing itself as the newest international city. Located just a short drive from mountain ranges and beaches and coastal regions, Atlanta offers a myriad of experiences. The Georgia State University campus is alive with the energy and excitement that characterizes the city that hosted the 1996 Summer Olympic Games.

Majors and Degrees

The broad range of disciplines includes accounting, actuarial science, African-American studies, anthropology, art, art (studio), art education, biology, chemistry, computer information systems, computer science, criminal justice, decision sciences, early childhood education, economics, English, exercise science, film and video, finance, French, geography, geology, German, health and physical education, history, hospitality administration, interdisciplinary studies, journalism, management, marketing, mathematics, middle childhood education, music, nursing, nutrition and dietetics, philosophy, physics, political science, psychology, real estate, recreation, religious studies, respiratory care, risk management and insurance, social work, sociology, Spanish, speech, theater, and urban policy studies.

Academic Program

Georgia State University offers a highly accessible academic program operating on the semester system with a year-round schedule that includes both day and evening courses. The academic programs emphasize real-world preparation to enhance the educational experience.

Georgia State University presents the student with a comprehensive curriculum focusing on developing the requisites for competence, personal fulfillment, and responsible leadership in business and the professions, in the sciences, in the creative and performing arts, in government, and in public service. The University requires each student seeking the baccalaureate degree to satisfactorily complete a basic core of general education subjects. This core serves as the learning foundation that prepares students to excel in their chosen field of study. In addition to the core, undergraduates at Georgia State must take and pass the Regent's Test, which evaluates a student's competency level in reading and writing. Graduation requirements include a minimum 2.0 cumulative grade point average for an undergraduate degree. In addition, the University requires each candidate for a baccalaureate degree who has transfer credit from another institution to have completed a minimum of 39 semester hours in residence (enrolled in one or more courses at Georgia State University).

The University recognizes that learning can take place in various modes and places other than the traditional classroom. Knowledge gained through experiential learning and other means is evaluated for possible credit through examination. The Cooperative Education Program is another example of Georgia State's devotion to providing students with a real-world education by administering periods of paid work experience related to the student's academic studies.

Off-Campus Arrangements

Georgia State University's expanding Distance Learning Program provides interactive classes and allows participants to register for challenging courses that are conveniently offered near their home or work. Courses are taught from the downtown campus and reach other sites throughout the state. Additionally, Georgia State offers a limited number of courses at two satellite locations.

Georgia State University is also a participant in the Georgia Statewide Academic Medical System, the world's largest and most comprehensive distance learning and health-care network. From on-site locations, the University delivers classes, training, conferences, and meetings locally and internationally.

Academic Facilities

With thirty buildings, Georgia State University is a prominent fixture in the downtown community. Georgia State's more than 255 acres (24 acres located downtown and more than 200 acres elsewhere in the metropolitan area) include centers for recreation, research, and academic instruction.

The Language Research Center at Georgia State University is an interdisciplinary biobehavioral laboratory known for basic and applied research in language and cognition. Its projects focus on language and cognitive development of the rare Bonobo, the common chimpanzee, and human children. Researchers in this program developed the first computer-based communication system for language research with apes.

Georgia State is also the only university in the U.S. to house a biosafety level 4 laboratory. This state-of-the-art facility enables Georgia State scientists to work on vaccine development for viruses, including the herpes B virus. The lab also tests thousands of samples from people all over the world who may have contracted herpes B.

The combined holdings of Georgia State's Pullen and Law Libraries total more than 1.3 million volumes, as well as more than 2 million microtext units. Government documents number approximately 800,000, and an additional 64,000 audio unit titles are available. The carefully selected collections are designed to serve not only the varied needs of undergraduate students but also the special needs of professional and graduate students engaged in research.

Costs

The cost of attending Georgia State University for the 1999–2000 academic year (two semesters) for students classified as Georgia residents was $2886 for tuition and fees. For students classified as nonresidents of the state of Georgia, these basic costs were $10,128 for two semesters of attendance. Supplemental costs (transportation, room and board, etc.) averaged $3890 for students living at home and $13,400 for students living away from home. The fee for residing in the University Village averaged $2095 (billed per semester), a price that included all utilities, cable television hookup, computer ports, local phone service, and transportation to and from campus.

Financial Aid

There are several sources of financial aid available, ranging from federal and state grants or loans to institutional scholarships (including seventy-five non-need-based). In 1999, more than $93.7 million in aid was awarded to Georgia State students. The HOPE Scholarship rewards graduates of Georgia high schools who have at least a 3.0 grade point average and enabled 4,898 students to attend Georgia State tuition free in 1999. In addition to the scholarships, loans, and grants, additional aid is available via part-time Federal Work-Study and on- and off-campus employment. GSU 62 is an institutional program allowing senior citizens full or partial tuition waivers. To apply for financial aid, students must complete a FAFSA. The priority application deadline for financial aid is April 1, and notification is continuous.

Faculty

Of the 982 full-time faculty members at Georgia State University, 85 percent hold terminal degrees in their fields. In addition, there are 483 part-time faculty members who help keep the average class size at Georgia State at approximately 25 students. Though teaching is the top priority for the faculty, many instructors are involved in scholarly and professional pursuits such as authoring textbooks and trade publications, administering multimillion-dollar research projects, and acting as consultants to professional organizations.

Student Government

The Student Government at Georgia State University actively represents the students' interests in all areas of college life. Elected student leaders enjoy a close working relationship with the administration and play an important role in structuring University policy.

Admission Requirements

The current minimum requirements for freshman admission to Georgia State University include successful completion of a college-preparatory curriculum (4 units in English, 3 units in mathematics, 3 units in lab science, 3 units in social science, and 2 units in the same foreign language). Beginning summer semester 2001, 4 mathematics units will be required, plus 4 additional academic units, for a total of 20 academic units in a college-preparatory curriculum. Freshman admission is also determined by the applicant's high school grade point average and scores on the SAT I or ACT and TOEFL. Typically, a high school grade point average of 3.0 in the college-preparatory curriculum combined with SAT I scores of 500 verbal and 500 math meet the minimum freshman requirements.

Transfer admission requirements include successful completion of 30 semester hours (45 quarter hours) of college-level, core curriculum course work at an accredited college or university. The cumulative grade point average from all transferable course work must be at least 2.2, and good academic standing at the last accredited institution attended is required.

Application and Information

More information is available by contacting:
Undergraduate Admissions
Georgia State University
P.O. Box 4009
Atlanta, Georgia 30302-4009
Telephone: 404-651-2365

The Georgia State University Village, which houses 2,000 students.

GODDARD COLLEGE
PLAINFIELD, VERMONT

The College
Goddard College was chartered in 1938, the seventy-fifth anniversary of its parent institution, Goddard Seminary. The new Goddard was to be coeducational, experimental, and progressive. For its first twenty-one years, Goddard College was unaccredited and laid the groundwork for an educational experience unique to higher education. As a result, it became known as one of the most interesting colleges in the country. In 1959, the New England Association of Schools and Colleges accepted Goddard's application for accreditation. Goddard has since continued to experiment with various styles of learning. Educators at Goddard are known as leaders in such areas of progressive education as discussion-based learning, self-designed majors, and narrative evaluation.

Goddard has an undergraduate residential program serving approximately 200 students; six off-campus, low-residency programs at the undergraduate and graduate levels serve an enrollment of approximately 325 adults. In addition to the individually designed B.A. and M.A. programs, Goddard offers M.A. degrees in education, health arts and sciences, psychology and counseling, and social ecology and M.F.A. degrees in interdisciplinary arts and writing.

Location
The Goddard campus is 250 acres of rolling Vermont forest and pasture land, with three clusters of buildings. One cluster was once the headquarters of Greatwoods Farms, an early-twentieth-century showplace built on the site of an eighteenth-century farmhouse, one of the first in Plainfield. Another nearby cluster includes a dozen small student houses known as The Village for Learning, a student-built, multiuse design center from the 1960s, and the student-built solar greenhouse for biological experiments. The third cluster, built in the late sixties and early seventies, is a 5-minute walk along a forest path. It includes two student-built visual arts buildings and the Eliot Pratt Center.

Plainfield is 8 miles from Montpelier, the state capital, and about 50 miles from Burlington, the largest city in Vermont. The campus is approximately 2½ hours from Montreal, 3 hours from Boston, and 6 hours from New York City. The closest major airport is in Burlington, and an Amtrak station is located in Montpelier.

Majors and Degrees
Goddard College offers a Bachelor of Arts degree that is designed by the individual student. This liberal arts degree is usually composed of group studies selected by students. The studies are categorized under the following areas: writing and literature, performing arts, and visual arts; cultural anthropology and multicultural studies, feminist studies, and history and social inquiry; education and teaching, psychology and counseling, and media studies and communication; leadership, community organization, and business; health arts; social ecology; and the natural, physical, and ecological sciences. Goddard is approved by the Vermont State Department of Education to recommend initial Vermont teacher licensure in early childhood, elementary, and middle grades education; in art education at all school levels; and in secondary English and social studies.

Goddard also offers, through its off-campus, low-residency model, an individually designed Bachelor of Arts degree program for adult learners.

Academic Program
The ideals and instruments of progressive education create the atmosphere for learning at Goddard. Students find a process that is designed to allow them to explore what is important to them as individuals. Students are empowered to create their own Bachelor of Arts degree program and, as a result, there are no required courses. Students work with faculty advisers in creating a broad, liberal arts education. Group studies replace traditional classes, and discussion replaces lecture as the primary teaching method. This, coupled with a narrative evaluation process instead of a grading system, creates a serious learning environment. As a result, Goddard attracts mature, independent thinkers who are very serious and creative about learning.

The work program, part of the holistic curriculum at Goddard, requires students to work 8 hours per week for the benefit of the whole. This community emphasis is designed to encourage a greater sense of responsibility for one's own well-being and allows students to work and learn in a variety of settings. Consistent with the Goddard mission, the work program lays the foundation for students to graduate and continue to work and provide leadership for the benefit of other communities and the earth as a whole.

Off-Campus Arrangements
Students are encouraged to explore and utilize resources outside of Goddard by participating in internships, study leaves, and field semesters. The study leave mode allows students to transfer to other colleges for one semester and apply those credits toward their Goddard education. A field semester involves committing an entire semester to a pre-arranged study plan in conjunction with immersion in another country, culture, or resource area.

Academic Facilities
The Eliot Pratt Center houses the William Shipman Library, the photography and holography labs, a computer center, video and recording facilities, and the radio station, WGDR. The library contains approximately 75,000 volumes and nearly 300 active periodical subscriptions and subscribes to an online database vendor for access to more than 400 online databases. Many areas on campus have Internet access.

The Sculpture Building has many open areas for large work, and the Painting Building contains a weaving studio, ceramics studio, and printing equipment among the three floors of open space. Musicians have access to a piano practice room and a gamelan (an Indonesian percussion instrument) in the music building.

Flanders Day Care Center provides a learning laboratory for students interested in child psychology and early childhood education.

Costs
The comprehensive fee of $20,592 for the 1998–99 campus program included tuition, room, and board. Books, travel, and personal expenses were not included and varied by individual.

Financial Aid

Goddard participates in a variety of financial aid programs, including Federal Pell Grants and Federal Supplemental Educational Opportunity Grants, student and parental loan programs, college work-study, institutional aid, and various state, private, and College scholarships. Seventy-two percent of all students receive some form of financial aid. Applicants are encouraged to file early using the Free Application for Federal Student Aid.

Faculty

The faculty consists of 18 core and 6 associate faculty members. The Goddard faculty practices progressive education by experimenting and creating new methods of teaching that encourage experiential learning. Seventy-two percent of the faculty members hold terminal degrees, and the faculty-student ratio is 1:7.

Student Government

Students are encouraged to participate in all aspects of the governance at Goddard. Students have representatives on most committees at the College, including the Board of Trustees, the executive committee, and all hiring committees. The College's governance structure emphasizes collaboration and consensus building among all constituencies. Monthly community meetings provide additional opportunities for input, ideas, and constructive criticism.

Admission Requirements

Goddard welcomes applications from individuals of all ages and encourages diversity. Goddard does not discriminate on the basis of race, sex, age, sexual orientation, or handicap. The campus environment is very liberal, and Goddard seeks candidates with open, inquisitive minds. All applicants must write a personal statement and interview on campus or over the phone. Goddard seeks creative students with strong writing skills, maturity, and self-motivation.

Application and Information

Admission is rolling, and applications will be accepted up to thirty days prior to the beginning of the semester. This is due in large part to the high number of transfer students applying to Goddard in the spring.

Application forms and information may be obtained by contacting:

Office of Admissions
Goddard College
Plainfield, Vermont 05667
Telephone: 802-454-8311
           800-468-4888 (toll-free)
E-mail: admissions@earth.goddard.edu
World Wide Web: http://www.goddard.edu

Goddard student John McKenna and faculty member Diane Felicio practice Indonesian music on a Javanese gamelan.

GONZAGA UNIVERSITY
SPOKANE, WASHINGTON

The University
Gonzaga, founded in 1887, is an independent, comprehensive university with a distinguished background in the Catholic, Jesuit, and humanistic tradition. Gonzaga emphasizes the moral and ethical implications of learning, living, and working in today's global society. Through the University Core Curriculum, each student develops a strong liberal arts foundation, which many alumni cite as a most valuable asset. In addition, students specialize in any of more than seventy-five academic majors.

Gonzaga's 108-acre campus is characterized by sprawling green lawns and majestic evergreen trees. Towering above the campus are the stately spires of St. Aloysius Church, the well-recognized landmark featured in the University logo.

Because personal growth is as important as intellectual development, Gonzaga places great emphasis on student life outside of class. Ten of the fourteen residence halls house only 25 to 35 students each, providing an intimate atmosphere. Each hall has a chaplain or a resident Jesuit. Since 98 percent of the freshmen and 43 percent of the total undergraduate student body live on campus, campus-based activities ranging from current affairs symposiums to intramural sports keep students informed and entertained. Students in all academic majors integrate with the Spokane community through a variety of activities, such as volunteer opportunities and internships at numerous businesses and agencies. Gonzaga provides both career and counseling centers.

Gonzaga enrolls approximately 5,000 students, of whom about 3,000 are undergraduates. About 50 percent of the students come from Washington State, with forty-six other states and forty-six other countries also represented. In addition to its undergraduate colleges and schools, Gonzaga University has a Graduate School that includes more than twenty master's programs and a doctoral program in Educational Leadership, and a School of Law.

Location
Located along the banks of the Spokane River in a quiet, turn-of-the-century neighborhood, Gonzaga University is just a 15-minute walk from downtown Spokane, a city with a metropolitan area population of 392,000. Spokane's beautiful 100-acre Riverfront Park, in the heart of downtown, is close to the Spokane Arena, Opera House, and Convention Center. Fine restaurants and an assortment of shops and department stores, many of which can be reached through a convenient, weatherproof skywalk system, are also in the city's core. For mall shoppers, the Northtown Mall is a 15-minute drive from campus.

Majors and Degrees
Gonzaga's undergraduate school awards the B.A., B.B.A., B.E., B.Ed., B.G.S., B.S., and B.S.N. degrees. Majors offered in the College of Arts and Sciences are advertising, art, Asian studies, biochemistry, biology, broadcast studies, chemistry, classical civilization, classics (Latin and Greek), computer science, criminal justice, economics, English, exercise science, French, German, German studies, history, integrated studies, international studies, Italian studies, journalism, Latin, literary studies, mathematics, mathematics/computer science, music (performance), music education, music theory and literature, philosophy, physics, political science, psychology, public relations, religious studies, sociology, Spanish, speech communications, and theater arts. The School of Business Administration, accredited by the American Assembly of Collegiate Schools of Business, offers a Bachelor of Business Administration degree with a major in accounting or a major in business administration with concentrations in economics, entrepreneurship, finance, human resource management, individualized program, international business, law and public policy, management information systems, marketing, operations management, and real estate. As well as granting teacher certification on both the elementary and secondary levels, the School of Education offers degrees in physical education and special education. The School of Engineering has degree programs in civil, electrical, general, and mechanical engineering as well as concentrations in environmental and computer engineering. The general engineering degree allows attainment of the M.B.A. in five years of study. All engineering programs are professionally accredited by the Accreditation Board for Engineering and Technology, Inc. (ABET). The School of Professional Studies offers degrees in general studies and nursing.

Academic Program
Gonzaga University believes that it is necessary for all students, regardless of their chosen major or profession, to attain an education that goes beyond specialization. Therefore, all students attending Gonzaga receive a strong liberal arts background as well as depth in their major. The Core Curriculum is a very important component of the 128 semester units a student must earn for graduation.

The Honors Program challenges special achievers with an integrated curriculum compatible with any major and most double majors. The program requires a separate application. Gonzaga also offers a Dual Enrollment Program that gives qualified Spokane-area high school seniors an opportunity to enroll in classes at the University. Credits earned through the Washington State Running Start Program or International Baccalaureate (IB) program are accepted on a class-by-class basis. College credit is given for certain test scores in most Advanced Placement (AP) subjects.

The academic year follows a two-semester system beginning in early September. Two summer sessions also are available.

Off-Campus Arrangements
Gonzaga University offers qualified students the opportunity to study abroad through programs in Africa, Australia, British West Indies, China, Costa Rica, England, France, Germany, Ireland, Italy, Japan, Mexico, and Spain.

Academic Facilities
Gonzaga's "library of the future," the Ralph E. and Helen Higgins Foley Center, is a $20-million window to worldwide information resources. The library features more than 300 specialized databases, satellite capabilities, an advanced computer-controlled video editing system, a rare book room, computerized retrieval services, and beautiful views.

Foley Center holdings include 782,000 volumes and microform titles, with two special collections of materials especially rich in the areas of philosophy and classical civilization, as well as the nation's most extensive collection of works by the famous Jesuit poet Gerard Manley Hopkins. The School of Law maintains its own library of 130,000 volumes. The historic Administration Building houses the student-operated FM radio station, KAGU; a television broadcasting studio; the offices of the *Bulletin,* a weekly, student-published newspaper; the Russell Theatre; the Computer Center; a 24-hour computer lab; the University Chapel; and the main administrative offices and classrooms.

Campus computing services include more than 250 PC and Macintosh computers and Sun Workstations dispersed throughout a dozen computer labs across campus. An HP9000/K100 minicomputer provides central academic services and student electronic mail. Students have access to the Internet, library, and central academic services from their dorm rooms or from off campus. The Herak Center, the engineering building, houses a state-of-the-art CAD/CAM center, an electronics/circuit lab, a digital electronics lab, a microwave/communications lab, an electrical power lab, a microprocessor lab, an electronics repair shop and controlled-environment calibration lab, and the Materials Science and Materials Testing Center. Hughes Hall for biology and chemistry contains the Chemistry Library, Hughes Auditorium, the Live Sciences Museum, and the laboratories for chemistry, anatomy and physiology, comparative anatomy, spectrographics, aquatic ecology, embryology, genetics, microbiology, organic chemistry, and zoology.

Costs

Tuition and fees for the 2000–01 academic year are $17,460. Room and board costs are $5730 for the year.

Financial Aid

Gonzaga University offers many different types of financial aid to qualified students, including scholarships, Federal Pell Grants, Federal Supplemental Educational Opportunity Grants, work-study jobs, Federal Perkins Loans, Federal Stafford Student Loans, and on- and off-campus employment. In order to apply for financial aid awards, a student must first be accepted by the University and must see that the Free Application for Federal Student Aid (FAFSA) is submitted by February 1. After this date, awards are made on a funds-available basis. Approximately 90 percent of the students at Gonzaga receive some sort of financial assistance.

Faculty

The student-faculty ratio is 16:1, and the average class size is 22, allowing close, mentoring relationships to develop. Faculty members serve as academic advisers, an integral part of the relationship with students. All classes at Gonzaga are taught by faculty members. Eight percent of the faculty members are Jesuits, and 88 percent of the 273 full-time faculty members hold the highest degree in their fields.

Student Government

The Gonzaga Student Body Association provides the means for students to participate in making decisions about student life at Gonzaga. The 5-member Executive Council, an elected board of students that administers and initiates programs, also serves as a liaison between the administration and the students. The Student Senate, a legislative body consisting of 24 senators, is responsible for sounding out the needs of the student body and directing this information to the Executive Council. Students also serve on the Board of Regents, search committees, budget committee, and many other University committees.

Admission Requirements

Gonzaga requires freshman applicants to have at least 17 academic units of completed high school work and strong test scores on the ACT or SAT I. Transfer students who have earned 30 semester credits or 45 quarter credits do not need to submit a high school transcript or test scores. The admission process is selective, and applicants are considered individually. The Admissions Committee seeks motivated, well-rounded students and considers the rigor of academic study in high school, in addition to grades and test scores, as well as personal characteristics, awards and activities, and an essay.

Application and Information

Gonzaga University's priority deadline for admissions applications is March 1. The final deadline is April 1 for freshmen and July 1 for transfer students. The nonbinding early action application deadline is November 15. Students may also apply by using the Common Application, APPLY!, CollegeLink, and the Catholic College Common Application. It is recommended that all students applying for financial aid for the fall semester submit their application materials by March 1.

All requests for further information or materials should be addressed to:

Dean of Admission
Gonzaga University
Spokane, Washington 99258-0102

Telephone: 800-322-2584 (toll-free)
E-mail: ballinger@gu.gonzaga.edu
World Wide Web: http://www.gonzaga.edu

Gonzaga University: Education for the mind and spirit.

GORDON COLLEGE
WENHAM, MASSACHUSETTS

The College

Gordon College is a traditional New England liberal arts college with a difference. Founded in Boston in 1889 as a missionary training institute, the College today offers the solid liberal arts foundation that distinguishes the best of New England's small colleges. Decidedly residential, Gordon College fosters the development of an inclusive Christian community. Nearly 84 percent of the College's 1,500 students live on campus in residence facilities ranging from small houses to a new residence hall that houses 150 students.

What sets Gordon apart from other New England colleges is that the liberal arts and sciences are taught from a Christian perspective. Gordon attempts to expand, not hinder or ignore, students' understanding of God and his purpose for their lives. Because of the integral relationship between faith and learning on this campus, Gordon has been described as a "major intellectual bastion of Protestant evangelicalism" where "religious commitment is seen as an enhancement rather than a threat to free and rigorous academic inquiry." There is also a commitment to a multicultural approach to learning that reflects the diversity of the world.

In addition to the undergraduate degree programs described below, Gordon offers a Master of Education program in curriculum and instruction.

The practice of the Christian faith and the pursuit of academic excellence go hand in hand at Gordon. The College has won widespread recognition for the quality of its programs. The John Templeton Foundation has selected Gordon as one of the 100 best colleges and universities in North America for character building. College president R. Judson Carlberg was recognized by Templeton for his character-based approach to leadership and education. Several programs have also been nationally honored for their spiritual and character-building focus. Gordon is also regularly listed among Barron's "best buys" for colleges and is one of Edward Fiske's choices for his *Selective Guide to Colleges*. *U.S. News & World Report* also ranks Gordon among the top national liberal arts colleges in the nation.

For many students, Gordon's residential life is as important as the College's academic reputation. Within this Christian community there is considerable diversity: more than sixty denominations, as well as forty states and eighteen other countries, are represented. Regular chapel and convocation services bring the campus community together in worship, and a wide range of student ministries provides ample opportunities for putting faith into practice. Hundreds of Gordon students are involved in off-campus volunteer ministries such as hunger action, prison outreach, nursing home visitation, and working with the hearing impaired.

Gordon also offers a variety of recreational and social opportunities, including sixteen varsity sports, a strong intramural athletics program, ten music ensembles, and four theater troupes. Concerts, movies, coffeehouses, and occasional day trips are scheduled on weekends. In addition, a lake for swimming and miles of hiking and cross-country ski trails are available on the College's expansive, wooded campus on Boston's North Shore. During the 1999–2000 school year, a new music building and a new center for the fine arts were opened. These buildings make Gordon one of the premier venues for the fine and performing arts in the greater Boston area. The College has also opened a new residence hall (1998) and an athletic and recreation center (1996). In recent years the College has renovated the student center and modernized several of its residence halls.

Location

Less than 3 miles from the Atlantic Ocean, Gordon is situated in a suburban community near beautiful coastal towns like the artist colony of Rockport and picturesque Manchester, a favorite location for Hollywood film crews. Boston, which is just 25 miles south and less than an hour away by train, offers numerous cultural and recreational opportunities as well as many historic attractions: the Boston Symphony, the Museum of Fine Arts, the Freedom Trail, the Isabella Stewart Gardner Museum, Copley Square, and colorful Faneuil Hall Market. Gordon's proximity to Boston and its high-technology metropolitan area provides many employment and internship possibilities.

Majors and Degrees

The Bachelor of Arts degree is awarded to students who graduate with the following majors: accounting, biblical and theological studies, business administration, communication arts, economics, English, foreign languages (combined), French, German, history, international affairs, international business, Jewish studies, leisure studies and recreation, music, philosophy, political studies, psychology, social work, sociology, Spanish, special education, visual arts, and youth ministries. The Bachelor of Science degree is awarded to students who graduate with the following majors: biology, chemistry, computer science, early childhood education, elementary education, mathematics, middle school education, movement science, and physics. The Bachelor of Music degree is awarded to students who concentrate in music performance. In addition, the following programs are offered in conjunction with Thomas Jefferson University's College of Allied Health: cytotechnology, dental hygiene, medical technology, nursing, occupational therapy, physical therapy, and radiological technology. There is also a five-year program that allows students to earn a liberal arts degree at Gordon (A.B. or B.S.) and an engineering degree in selected fields from the University of Massachusetts at Lowell. A broad-range Cooperative Education program is available to give students salaried on-the-job training related to their studies.

Academic Program

The four-year baccalaureate degree program is conducted within the context of a semester academic calendar, and the academic year is divided into two 15-week semesters. Sixteen semester hours per term constitute a normal registration, and courses normally carry 4 semester hours of credit.

Graduation requirements include a minimum of 124 semester hours of credit, 32 of which must be taken at Gordon, the last 16 in residence; a grade point average of 2.0 or above; fulfillment of the liberal arts core curriculum; and fulfillment of the course requirements specified for the major, with no fewer than 18 semester hours in the major earned at Gordon.

The Kenneth L. Pike Honors Program provides exceptional students with an opportunity to design a flexible, individualized academic program. To enter the Pike program, a student must have completed at least one term at Gordon and have a cumulative grade point average of at least 3.5. Gordon accepts a limited amount of credit validated by the College-Level Examination Program (CLEP). Students may also take placement tests in writing and/or foreign languages to determine whether they may waive, respectively, the basic writing requirement and/or one or more of the foreign language courses.

Off-Campus Arrangements

One of Gordon's strengths is the number and quality of its off-campus programs, which include Latin American studies in Costa Rica and the International Seminar, a four-week summer course abroad. Students can also study in England, at Oxford University, through Gordon's program there. Several marine biology field courses are also offered for credit, including a January tropical coastal waters course off the coasts of Kenya or Venezuela. In addition, Gordon participates in the Christian College Consortium, the Coalition for Christian Colleges and Universities, and the Northeast Consortium of Colleges and Universities in Massachusetts. As a result, the following opportunities are available to students: American Studies Program, featuring political and governmental affairs internships in Washington, D.C.; study at Jerusalem University College in Israel; a Middle East Studies Program, based in Cairo; semesters at Daystar University College in Nairobi, Kenya; Au Sable Trails Institute, a cooperative environmental studies program; and Urban Studies, a cooperative residential study program in San Francisco.

Academic Facilities

The Phillips Music Center is the newest academic building on campus. Opened in 2000, it contains an intimate recital hall, an instrument repair shop, electronic studios, and ample classroom, office, and practice space for the College's many music majors. In late 1999, Gordon opened the Barrington Center for the Arts. This building, home to the communications, theater, and visual arts departments, contains two art galleries, a studio theater, set construction space, a video screening room, and many other artistic touches that make this building one of the best of its kind north of Boston. The next new academic building will be a science center, tentatively planned for 2002. The campus is fully wired for individual student access to e-mail, the Internet, and the intranet.

Costs

The following rates are for the 2000–01 academic year, which is divided into two 15-week semesters. Annual tuition (16 hours per semester) is $16,550, board is $1700, room (double occupancy) is $3550, and the comprehensive fee is $720. The total for two semesters is $22,520.

Financial Aid

Students who demonstrate financial need normally receive a combination of grants, loans, and student employment opportunities. Nearly 80 percent of Gordon students receive financial aid, which includes federal, state, private, and institutional awards.

The A. J. Gordon Scholarship Program awards approximately twenty-five $8000 scholarships per year to incoming freshmen who show promise of leadership and academic achievement. There is a separate application that requires a prearranged visit to campus on one of the special A. J. Gordon Scholarship days. Gordon has also begun a Choral Scholars Program, which provides a number of $6000 renewable scholarships to students who are focusing on choral studies and who have solid academic records. A competitive audition and an interview are required.

Faculty

Nearly 97 percent of the full-time faculty of 84 have earned doctorates. Faculty members are professing Christians who seek to integrate their faith with their discipline. Although the first priority of the faculty members is teaching, many distinguish themselves in research and publications. A faculty-student ratio of 1:18 contributes to considerable interaction, both formal and informal, outside of class.

Student Government

The Student Government Association, whose primary officers receive stipends, plays a significant role in campus events, programs, and student publications. The student government president, a voting member of the Campus Advisory Council, represents student concerns directly to the president and administrative officers of the College.

As a Christian community, Gordon attempts to achieve a balance between individual freedom and the need for clear standards that are in harmony with the Christian character of the College. Practices clearly prohibited in Scripture are not condoned, and smoking and alcohol consumption are not permitted on campus.

Admission Requirements

A successful applicant must give evidence of both strong academic promise and a decision to follow Christ. Other factors that contribute to an applicant's chances of acceptance include musical, dramatic, or athletic experience; cross-cultural perspective; and proven leadership ability in service to church, community, or school. Applicants are expected to have successfully completed courses in the following areas at the college-preparatory level: English (4 years), mathematics (2 years), science (2 years, including at least 1 year of a laboratory science), social studies (2 years), and 5 units of acceptable electives. It is recommended that 2 or more years of foreign language be among these electives.

Credentials required for freshman applicants include an application, a $40 nonrefundable application fee, a high school transcript, SAT I or ACT scores, a personal reference, and an admission interview. Applications from transfer and international students are welcome. Interviews are required of transfer applicants, who must also submit an application, a $40 nonrefundable application fee, a college transcript, a college catalog for transfer credit evaluation, SAT I or ACT scores, a personal reference, and a high school transcript if less than one collegiate academic year has been completed. International applicants must submit TOEFL or SAT I scores, the Foreign Students' Financial Aid Form of the College Scholarship Service, a second personal reference from a school official in lieu of an admission interview, and all other regular admission credentials. Canadian students may apply upon completion of grade 12 or 13. For music applicants, an audition is required in addition to the regular admission requirements.

Application and Information

Regular admission is on a rolling basis; the application deadline for early decision is December 1.

For further information, students may contact:

Silvio Vazquez
Dean of Admissions
Gordon College
Wenham, Massachusetts 01984-9988

Telephone: 800-343-1379 (toll-free)
E-mail: admissions@hope.gordon.edu
World Wide Web: http://www.gordon.edu

In addition to obtaining a top-notch education, Gordon students also have the opportunity to live in one of the most beautiful parts of the United States.

GOSHEN COLLEGE
GOSHEN, INDIANA

The College
Goshen College (GC) is a fully accredited national liberal arts college that is known for leadership in international education, service-learning, and peace and justice issues in the Anabaptist-Mennonite tradition. Founded in 1894 by the Mennonite Church, one of the historic peace churches, GC serves more than 1,000 students in both traditional and nontraditional programs. While students from Mennonite backgrounds represent more than half of the student body, about twenty-five denominations are represented. Students come from more than thirty states, every Canadian province, and more than thirty countries. Goshen College was one of five liberal arts colleges recognized in 1999 by the Knight Foundation's Presidential Leadership Award Program for liberal arts excellence. Goshen's track record of sustained excellence has attracted national attention. Goshen is one of 300 schools included in *Barron's Best Buys in College Education* for offering a high-quality education at below-average prices. *Money* magazine listed GC fourteenth in the nation for educational value when financial aid is taken into account. For 2000, a study by *U.S. News & World Report* includes GC among the top 140 national liberal arts colleges. Ernest L. Boyer, in *Smart Parents' Guide to College*, praises GC's Study-Service Term (SST) program. GC was named one of *The 100 Best Colleges for African-American Students* in a book by Erlene B. Wilson. A study by Franklin and Marshall ranked GC in the top sixth of liberal arts colleges in the number of its graduates who go on to complete doctoral degrees. Among the top 100 schools in its category, GC has the lowest cost among national colleges in the Great Lakes region. Peterson's lists GC among its 190 *Top Colleges for Science*.

In a highly energetic environment, students have plenty of opportunities to cultivate leadership skills and assume responsibility. Students edit a weekly newspaper and a yearbook, operate a radio station, produce a campus television program, serve on campus publishing editorial boards, and work and perform in theater and musical groups. Representatives of the student body are elected to serve on the Student Senate, Campus Ministries team, and Campus Activities Council. Campus groups also include the Student Women's Association, Black Student Union, PAX, Latino Student Union, Nursing Students Association, Fellowship of Christian Athletes, Social Work Action Association, International Students Club, Business Club, and Pre-Med Club. GC belongs to the National Association of Intercollegiate Athletics and the Mid-Central College Conference and competes intercollegiately in men's and women's basketball, cross-country, soccer, tennis, and track and field; men's baseball and golf; and women's softball and volleyball. More than 60 percent of GC students participate in intramural athletics. All students have free access to the Gingerich Recreation-Fitness Center.

Most Goshen students live in one of the College's five residence halls, which were made accessible, one port per pillow, to the campus computer network in 1997. Small-group housing is available to upper-level students. College-owned houses are available for married students and families.

With a long history of emphasis on experiential learning, Goshen College's Applied Learning programs encourage partnerships between the College and the community by placing students in practicum, internship, and service experiences. In addition, the College inaugurated its first Service-Learning Day in 1999; classes were suspended so that students and faculty and staff members could participate in community service projects. Students also benefit from Multicultural Education Office programs that emphasize meaningful ways to address issues of diversity in order to prepare students for life in an increasingly interconnected, multicultural world.

Location
The campus is on the south side of Goshen, a city of 25,000 in north-central Indiana, 2 hours east of Chicago and 45 minutes east of South Bend. Known as the Maple City for its many maple trees, Goshen is part of Elkhart County, one of the fastest-growing counties in the nation during the 1980s and 1990s. The county enjoys its rich Mennonite and Amish heritage while serving as home to major corporations in the recreational vehicle, medical diagnostics, and automotive component industries.

Majors and Degrees
The Bachelor of Arts is awarded in accounting; art; Bible and religion; biology; business; business information systems; chemistry; communication; computer science; computer science and applied mathematics; early childhood education; economics; environmental studies; elementary education; English; environmental science; family life; French; German; Hispanic ministries; history; history and investigative skills; management information systems; mathematics; molecular biology; music; natural science; peace, justice, and conflict studies; physical education; physics; psychology; social work; sociology/anthropology; Spanish; and theater. A Bachelor of Science in Nursing or a Bachelor of Science in organizational management is also awarded. Interdisciplinary majors usually combine work in three different departments and allow students to tailor their studies to individual interests. Preprofessional programs in engineering, law, medicine, occupational therapy, physical therapy, seminary, and veterinary medicine are available as well. The College also offers minors in more than thirty areas. With concentrations in several areas, the College offers more than seventy programs of study, leading to thirty majors and thirty minors.

Academic Program
The College calendar consists of two 15-week semesters and a 3½-week May term. A total of 120 semester hours (124 for nursing majors) is required for graduation. One third are usually in general studies courses, including art, Bible and religion, history, literature, philosophy, physical education, science, and social science; another third are courses in the student's major. Most majors require a practicum for graduation. All students must complete a course of international study. Most students choose to participate in the Study-Service Term (SST) program abroad, a thirteen-week term, including course work and field experience in a service assignment, in a significantly different country. Students also can fulfill the requirement by taking courses on campus or by participating in other study-abroad programs.

Off-Campus Arrangements
Goshen is one of the very few U.S. colleges that requires international education. Most students complete this requirement by going on SST, while others choose to take classes with an international emphasis on campus. Since the SST program began in 1968, more than 6,000 GC students have benefited from it tremendously, both academically and personally. The program has served as the model for international education programs across the country. In the SST program, students spend six weeks together focusing on the study of one country while immersed in its language and culture. The six-week SST field experience gives students a chance to develop interpersonal skills and to serve others. The field experience often relates to the students' major areas of study. During both parts of the program, students live with host families. Most SST units cost the same as a semester on campus. GC students earn 13–14 hours of credit for SST; however, the benefits continue for a lifetime. SST gives students a broader context for living their lives while helping them set an appropriate

individual direction. The growing internationalization of U.S. business and culture amplifies SST's benefits; now, more than ever, foreign language skills and knowledge of other cultures are advantages in the job market.

Other off-campus programs include spring term courses in marine biology at the College's center in the Florida Keys and courses in Europe in theater history, art history, and literature. Students in the environmental studies minor are able to take courses at the Au Sable Institute, an environmental studies institute in Mancelona, Michigan.

Academic Facilities

On its 135-acre campus, Goshen College has eighteen major buildings and laboratories. The newest building on campus, opened in 1994, is the Gingerich Recreation-Fitness Center. The center features a swimming pool, running track, and gymnasium. The building houses the physical education department, student health center, and intramural and intercollegiate athletics. Plans for a $22-million music facility are in progress, with completion set for 2001. Another recent addition to the campus is an annex to the Science Building, which contains modern science classrooms, laboratories, and equipment. It also contains the Turner Precision X-Ray Measurements Laboratory and the Biological Research Laboratory. The Turner Laboratory gives physics majors a rare opportunity to assist in basic research on crystals. The Biological Research Laboratory, equipped with an electron microscope, Geiger system, climate chambers, incubators, and microtechnique systems, is also open to qualified students. The College regularly does research for larger universities and major industries.

The Harold and Wilma Good Library houses a collection of 120,000 volumes and 800 periodicals, the Mennonite Historical Library, and the Art Gallery.

At the Goshen College Laboratory Kindergarten, psychology and education majors can observe and participate in activities. The Merry Lea Environmental Learning Center, an 1,150-acre nature preserve, offers internships in environmental and elementary education and is a key site for the College's environmental studies major and minor. Goshen College has a progressive attitude concerning technology in an effort to encourage students to learn how to use technology intelligently and effectively. Ranked by *Yahoo!* as one of the country's Most Wired Campuses, computer facilities include three modern student labs, one of which is located in a residence hall, with one computer for every 7.6 students as well as printers, scanners, digital cameras, and other equipment. Computers in student labs are upgraded annually. Multimedia classrooms feature integrated technology as well as media production facilities. All residence hall rooms are connected to the campus network and the Internet; account and course information is available on the College intranet. The John S. Umble Center for the Performing Arts includes an auditorium for drama and music performances, classroom space, a scene shop, and a costume-property shop. Umble Center has been recognized internationally for its exceptional acoustics.

Costs

Costs for 1999–2000 included tuition, $12,320; room, $2150; board, $2190; and tech fee, $260. The total for a residential student was $16,920. Costs included two 15-week semesters and one 3½-week May term.

Financial Aid

Almost 90 percent of the College's students receive some type of financial assistance through federal, state, and Goshen College programs. The average award is more than $12,900. GC offers more than 130 different scholarships. College aid includes ten half-tuition scholarships, an unlimited number of four-year Merit Scholarships of up to $2000 for National Merit Finalists, four-year Menno Simons Scholarships of up to $3500 per year, four-year Honors Scholarships of up to $3000 per year, a Service/Involvement Recognition Award of up to $2500 per year, and numerous one-year endowed scholarships. About 60 percent of incoming students receive renewable academic scholarships. Work-study jobs and other on-campus jobs are available.

Faculty

The faculty includes about 80 full-time and 30 part-time members. Most have lived or worked abroad. The student-faculty ratio is 13:1.

Student Government

The Student Senate acts as an advocate of student concerns and corresponding policy changes and works with the administration. The Campus Activity Council plans student activities. Most College committees include 1 or 2 voting student members.

Admission Requirements

Applicants should rank in the upper half of their high school graduating class and may apply for admission at any time after the junior year and up to one month before they wish to begin college. ACT or SAT I scores are required. Recommended high school work includes 4 years of English, 2 years of science, 2 years of social science, 2 years of mathematics, and 2 to 4 years of a foreign language. Prospective students are encouraged to visit the campus and meet with faculty, students, and administrators. Special campus open houses scheduled throughout the year provide excellent opportunities for visits.

Application and Information

Students who would like more information may contact:
Office of Admissions
Goshen College
Goshen, Indiana 46526
Telephone: 219-535-7535
          800-348-7422 (toll-free)
Fax: 219-535-7609
E-mail: admissions@goshen.edu
World Wide Web: http://www.goshen.edu

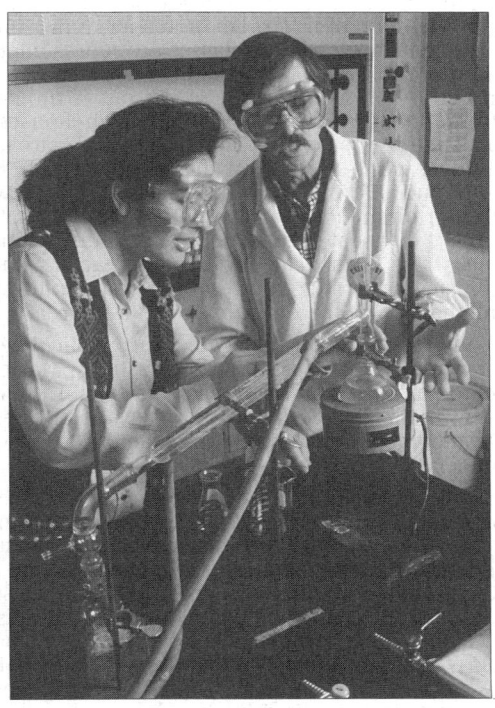

Research and hands-on learning serve students well, especially those who go on to graduate school.

GOUCHER COLLEGE
BALTIMORE, MARYLAND

The College

Since its inception in 1885, Goucher College has maintained a reputation for academic excellence and a tradition of high quality combined with flexibility. The past few decades have seen many changes in academic programs and the student population, during which time Goucher has held fast to its commitment to a superior liberal arts education designed to help students achieve their fullest potential. The 1,100 men and women enrolled as undergraduates come from all parts of the United States and many other countries; they represent diverse backgrounds, interests, and points of view.

Goucher's strength in the liberal arts comes from its attention to learning both inside and outside the classroom. Academic departments are organized into five divisions: arts, humanities, interdisciplinary studies, natural sciences and mathematics, and social sciences. The Goucher College curriculum encompasses courses from all five divisions; a freshman colloquium; an off-campus learning experience that is satisfied through an internship, study abroad, or an independent research project; and demonstrated proficiency in writing, computers, and a foreign language.

Goucher's fieldstone buildings on a 287-acre wooded, residential campus provide an ideal setting for learning. The residence halls are an important part of the students' educational and social experience. Residence on campus is generally required of all students who do not live at home. The four halls are divided into fifteen residential houses of about 50 students each; housing space is guaranteed for all four years. There are areas for socializing, meeting rooms, and kitchenettes in each hall, and there is one main dining room. A kosher dining hall is also available. Students from all four classes are represented in each house, and there is a staff of 15 resident assistants to serve as peer counselors. The social center of campus is the Pearlstone Student Center (refurbished in 1997), which houses a cafe, lounge, bookstore, post office, commuter study area, student activities office, game room, and the popular Gopher Hole, a nonalcoholic pub offering space for casual conversations and featuring entertainment several nights a week. The cultural center is the 1,000-seat Kraushaar Auditorium. Lectures and performances at Kraushaar by leading actors, actresses, dancers, musicians, writers, and political and cultural figures attract audiences from the entire metropolitan area.

Goucher confers a postbaccalaureate, a premedical certificate, and postbaccalaureate teaching certification. Master's programs include a Master of Teaching, a Master of Education in collaboration with the Sheppard Pratt National Center for Human Development, and a limited-residency Master of Arts in historic preservation.

Athletic facilities include a 50,000-square-foot Sports and Recreation Center, the Welsh gymnasium, and the von Borries swimming pool. The sports center features a field house, sauna, wellness laboratory, weight-training room, squash and racquetball courts, lockers, and offices. There are two dance studios, 4 miles of wooded riding and jogging trails, six tennis courts, riding rings, and stables. Goucher belongs to NCAA Division III. Varsity sports for men are basketball, cross-country, lacrosse, soccer, swimming, and tennis. Women's varsity sports are basketball, cross-country, field hockey, lacrosse, soccer, swimming, tennis, and volleyball. The College competes on a coeducational basis in equestrian sports.

Location

In the 1950s, the College moved from its original site in downtown Baltimore to a 287-acre campus 8 miles north in suburban Towson. Since Goucher is near Baltimore and Washington, D.C., students enjoy cultural offerings and the social advantages provided by both cities as well as nearby colleges and universities. An hour's drive west of Baltimore are the resort areas of the Catoctin Mountains, near Camp David, while to the east the shores of the Chesapeake Bay and Atlantic Ocean make Maryland one of the world's greatest fishing, swimming, and sailing centers.

Majors and Degrees

Goucher awards the Bachelor of Arts degree. Areas of study and concentration include American studies, art, arts administration, biological sciences, chemistry, cognitive studies, communication, computer science, dance, economics, education, English, historic preservation, history, international relations, international and intercultural studies (British, European, Latin American, and Russian), management, mathematics, modern languages (French, German, Russian, and Spanish), music, peace studies, philosophy, politics and public policy, prelaw studies, premedical studies, psychology, religion, sociology-anthropology, special education, theater, and women's studies. Goucher students are free to tailor their studies to their own goals and interests through traditional, double, or individualized majors or by taking a major and a minor. There is also a dual-degree program in science and engineering with Johns Hopkins University. Entrance to the Johns Hopkins Whiting School of Engineering is guaranteed for students with a minimum 3.2 GPA in Goucher science classes.

Academic Program

The core curriculum is the foundation for a Goucher education. Recently revised, the core retains Goucher's tradition of academic rigor while becoming more relevant to a changing world. There is a strong emphasis on both interdisciplinary study and the development of a global perspective. Requirements include a demonstrated proficiency in a foreign language, English composition, and computer technology, along with courses in the arts, natural sciences, humanities, social sciences, and mathematics as well as a 3-credit off-campus requirement that reflects the College's belief in balancing classroom theory with real-world experience and that may take the form of an internship, a period of study abroad, or an independent project. All freshmen take the semester-long Freshman Colloquium. Taught in small sections, the course integrates humanities and social sciences perspectives. There is an interdisciplinary honors program in addition to honors courses in each department. The Goucher degree requires 120 semester hours of credit. The departmental major consists of at least 30 credits (about ten courses); the double major requires 60 credits. Goucher's calendar is based on the semester system.

Off-Campus Arrangements

For a number of years, Goucher College and Johns Hopkins University have had a reciprocal agreement by which qualified students at either institution may elect courses at the other without payment of additional fees. The College has similar agreements with Loyola College; Maryland Institute, College of Art; Towson University; Morgan State University; the College of Notre Dame of Maryland; Baltimore Hebrew College; and Essex Community College.

Study-abroad programs are available at the University of Exeter, Great Britain; University of Salamanca, Spain; Eberhard-Karls Universität, Germany; the Sorbonne, France; Hebrew University, Israel; and National Autonomous University of Mexico. International summer programs are available in Greece and Great Britain. An exchange program exists with the

Roehampton Institute in London. January programs include trips to Honduras, England, and within the European community.

Academic Facilities

Julia Rogers Library, whose services include literature search by computer, contains more than 282,000 volumes and has seating for 540 students. Students work in excellent dance studios, language and drama laboratories, and acoustically engineered music practice rooms. The Jane and Robert Meyerhoff Arts Center offers space for both studio art and theater teaching. Computer literacy is required of all Goucher graduates, and the College has committed itself to combining computer technology with liberal arts education. Computer and technological resources are concentrated in the Thormann International Technology and Media Center and the Advanced Technology Laboratory and enable students to move beyond basic familiarity with computers to explore areas ranging from artificial intelligence to computer music. The Thormann Center uses satellites, international networking, and other technologies to bring students into immediate contact with other nations and cultures. The Hughes Field Politics Center offers internships in a variety of government and private settings. The science facilities include modern teaching laboratories, extensive faculty and student research space, computer centers, an observatory, specimen preparation rooms, a plant laboratory, an NMR spectrometer, and an electron microscope, plus a psychology area with numerous experiment rooms. The communication program stresses the use of audiovisual technology, equipment, and software. There is a campus television studio, and students also take applied courses at a local professional studio. Computers are used extensively by students in all areas. There are terminals in every student-centered building on campus, including the residence halls (the student-computer ratio is 9:1). Goucher also has time-sharing arrangements with other area colleges and universities and belongs to a national computer network.

Costs

Tuition for 2000–01 is $21,000 for two semesters. The cost per credit hour is $735. For two semesters, the cost for room is $5090, and the cost for board (nineteen-meals-per-week plan) is $2560. Students residing on campus pay a health fee of $135. A student activities fee of $150 is required of all students.

Financial Aid

In an average year, more than half of Goucher's students receive some form of aid; 45 percent are awarded grants, ranging from $400 to the total cost of the education. The average financial aid award is more than $15,000. Goucher participates in the Federal Work-Study Program and helps students benefit from Federal Supplemental Educational Opportunity Grants, Federal Pell Grants, Federal Perkins Loans, Federal Stafford Student Loans, and College loans. Goucher also offers a competitive merit award program.

Faculty

There are approximately 150 full- and part-time members of the faculty; most have doctorates or the highest attainable degree in their field. While Goucher professors are encouraged in their research work, their primary efforts are directed toward teaching. It is not unusual for full professors to teach freshmen. The student-faculty ratio of 11:1 and the size of the student body combine to make for an excellent and easy rapport between students and faculty members. Goucher faculty members are known not only for their dedication to teaching but also for their willingness to spend many out-of-class hours counseling or just talking with students.

Student Government

The Student Government Association, to which all students belong, coordinates social activities, dispenses student activity funds, and formulates and enforces social regulations and the academic honor code. Students are represented on faculty and administrative committees. Students have begun departmental clubs in such fields as chemistry, computer science, French, history, math, political science, and Russian. Special interest groups include UMOJA–The African Alliance, Community Auxiliary for Service (CAUSE), International Students' Club, Environmental Concerns Organization (ECO), and Commuting Students' Organization. Student publications include a yearbook, literary magazine, and newspaper.

Admission Requirements

The Goucher Admissions Committee seeks to enroll students with strong academic ability who represent a variety of talents, ambitions, backgrounds, and experiences. Each candidate is considered individually. An application complete for review consists of the following: application form (Goucher or Common Application); one essay; a nonrefundable $40 application fee (or fee waiver form); recommendations from 1 teacher who has taught the applicant in an academic subject; a recommendation from a counselor or school principal; the official school transcript, including senior courses and first-term grades; and SAT I or ACT scores (TOEFL for international students), sent directly from the testing agency to Goucher. The SAT II: Writing Test is required for home-schooled students. Goucher accepts for admission to the freshman class a number of carefully selected students who have completed the eleventh grade and are ready to begin college a year early. Admission criteria are reviewed and weighed in the following order of importance: (1) the quality and level of secondary courses selected (AP or honors-level classes carry more weight than regular level); a sound preparation includes at least 15 units of college-preparatory subjects; (2) grades received in grades 9–12; (3) essay; (4) SAT I or ACT scores; the average score for entering freshmen is 605 verbal (recentered), 571 math (recentered); (5) letters of recommendation; and (6) activities, special interests, and awards. Applicants are encouraged to apply as early in the fall as possible. The application closing deadline is February 1. Applications are reviewed by the Admissions Committee, and the candidate is notified on or about April 1. Candidate reply date is May 1. Applications from transfer students filed by April 1 are given priority. Those filed after that date are considered on a rolling admissions basis.

Application and Information

Director of Admissions
Goucher College
1021 Dulaney Valley Road
Baltimore, Maryland 21204-2794
Telephone: 410-337-6100
          800-GOUCHER (toll-free)
E-mail: admissions@goucher.edu
World Wide Web: http://www.goucher.edu

On the campus of Goucher College.

GRACE COLLEGE
WINONA LAKE, INDIANA

The College

Grace College is a Christian undergraduate college of arts and sciences founded in 1948 and affiliated with the Fellowship of Grace Brethren Churches, a conservative evangelical denomination. Grace College attracts students from a variety of conservative evangelical backgrounds and from around the United States and several other countries. The College offers an environment and academic program that are conservative in theology and progressive in spirit and that emphasize three qualities for students as they reach adulthood—mature Christian character, academic and career competence, and a heart for service to mankind. Enrollment at Grace College is 953, providing an ideal atmosphere in which students can learn, grow, and develop lasting friendships.

Grace College has a campus of 160 acres. Approximately 69 percent of the College's students live on campus. The majority of students range in age from 18 to 23 years. More than 50 percent of the students come from Indiana; students also come from thirty-three other states and ten countries. Approximately one third of the students are affiliated with the Fellowship of Grace Brethren Churches; the other two thirds are from other conservative Christian denominations, particularly Baptist and independent church backgrounds.

Grace College's intercollegiate sports are men's baseball, basketball, golf, soccer, and tennis and women's basketball, soccer, softball, tennis, and volleyball as well as cross-country and track and field for both men and women. The men's basketball team won the NAIA Division II national championship in 1992.

All major campus buildings at Grace College are centrally located, and most were constructed within the past thirty years. One exception is Westminster Hall, which was built in 1905 and is listed on the National Register of Historic Places and on the Indiana State Historical Register.

In addition to bachelor's and associate degrees, Grace College offers a Master of Arts degree in counseling.

Location

Grace College is located in the heart of historic Winona Lake. The town is in the midst of a major restoration that includes a boat-in restaurant, a hotel, and artisan shops as well as parks and museums. The lake itself offers a variety of activities, including waterskiing, swimming, and boating, and the region surrounding Winona Lake provides a number of recreational and cultural opportunities for students. The beaches of Lake Michigan and cities such as Chicago and Indianapolis are within 2 or 3 hours of the campus and make a great day trip.

The town of Winona Lake is approximately 40 miles west of Fort Wayne and 50 miles southeast of South Bend. Travel to the College is facilitated by the proximity of major highways and regional airports. The region has experienced unprecedented economic growth in recent years and offers a host of career opportunities, as well as excellent positions for part- and full-time student employment.

Majors and Degrees

Grace College offers the following majors leading to the Bachelor of Arts degree: biblical studies, Christian ministries, English, English education, French, French education, German, German education, international languages, music, Spanish, and Spanish education. In addition, all majors leading to the Bachelor of Science degree may also lead to the Bachelor of Arts degree, provided that the student fulfills the second-year proficiency in a foreign language requirement.

Grace College offers the following majors leading to the Bachelor of Science degree: accounting, art, art education, biology, business administration, business education, communications, counseling, criminal justice, general science, graphic design, international business, management information systems, mathematics, mathematics education, music education, music performance, physical education, psychology, science education, social work, sociology, and youth ministries.

Preparation for graduate study in professional programs is available in dentistry, medicine, pharmacy, and veterinary medicine through the Department of Biological Science. Preparation for law school is available through the Division of Social Sciences.

Grace College offers the Associate of Science degree in biblical studies and information processing.

Academic Program

The Christian liberal arts philosophy of Grace College pervades each program of study and reflects the College's recognition that a broad common core of course work is central to each student's education. When combined with detailed study in a major field, this core establishes the foundation for successful graduate study and for a career.

The requirements for the bachelor's degree include the successful completion of one major (36–56 semester hours) and one minor (20–28 semester hours) area of concentration in addition to the specified program of general education courses. Students are required to complete a total of 124 semester hours of course work.

Through the January session (Winterim) offered each year, students have an opportunity to take courses off campus as well as on the campus.

Grace College operates on a two-semester calendar and offers a summer session in addition to Winterim. Advanced Placement (AP) and College-Level Examination Program (CLEP) test scores are considered for college credit and advanced placement.

One outstanding strength of Grace College is the Student Academic Counseling Center. The center offers academic advising and tutorial services.

Off-Campus Arrangements

Students majoring in a foreign language spend their junior year or its equivalent studying at a university located in a country where that language is spoken.

Academic Facilities

The Morgan Library contains classrooms, faculty offices, the Archives and Special Collections area, and the Computer Center, as well as the libraries of Grace College and Grace Theological Seminary. The combined collections total approximately 155,000 volumes. Students receive assistance through interlibrary lending and computer-based research services available in the library.

The Cooley Science Center serves the needs of the departments in the natural sciences, as well as those of the business and mathematics departments. The center houses faculty offices, classrooms, and laboratories.

The Education, Behavioral Science, and Art Departments are located in Mount Memorial Hall. The building also houses classrooms, offices, and a graphic design computer laboratory. The graphic design computer lab is among the most up-to-date computer graphics labs on any college or university campus in the United States and utilizes hardware and software based on the PowerMac computer system.

Rodeheaver Auditorium seats 1,400 and is used for special activities, including concerts, chapel services, and special conferences.

Costs

For full-time students, tuition for the 2000–01 academic year is $10,700. Room and board charges in Grace College residence halls total $4983 for the two-semester academic year, which brings the total charges for tuition, room, and board to $15,683 for the academic year.

Financial Aid

The College offers extensive financial assistance to qualified students. Most students receive some sort of financial assistance—in the form of a scholarship, grant, loan, or campus employment—to help pay college costs. The average amount of financial aid awarded to a Grace College student totals $6500 per year.

To be considered for financial assistance at Grace College, students must submit the Free Application for Federal Student Aid (FAFSA). Students may receive Federal Pell Grants, Federal Perkins Loans, and Federal Supplemental Educational Opportunity Grants. In addition, students may be eligible for Federal Work-Study Program awards.

The FAFSA should be on file by March 1 for priority consideration. To renew financial aid, students must refile the FAFSA each year.

Faculty

Forty full-time and 33 part-time faculty members teach at Grace College; 27 full-time faculty members hold earned doctorates. Several Grace College faculty members are involved in various forms of research and writing, but their primary function is teaching. Every student has a faculty adviser in the academic major. Grace's student-faculty ratio is 17:1.

Student Government

Each of the four classes elects officers and plans activities. The College administration appoints one faculty adviser for each class and one for the student governing body. The Student Senate, consisting of student officers and representatives from each class, guides the student body by encouraging actions and activities beneficial to the College and students. Other student organizations are the Social Activities Board and Grace Ministries in Action, a group that coordinates student involvement in Christian service work.

Admission Requirements

Any individual who is in harmony with the evangelical Christian viewpoint of Grace College and possesses high academic and social standards is invited to apply. Graduation from an accredited high school or its equivalent is required. Each candidate completes an application that provides the Admissions Committee with pertinent information. The prospective student must secure recommendations from a guidance counselor and his or her pastor. All freshman applicants are required to take either the ACT or the SAT I. Students transferring from other colleges should request a transcript of their academic record from each college attended since high school.

Application and Information

Students may apply for admission to any semester. Applications are accepted on a rolling basis until January 1 for the spring term and August 1 for the fall term. There is a $20 nonrefundable application fee.

Interested students and their parents are encouraged to visit the campus and to arrange for an interview at that time in order to get a clear picture of Grace College. Arrangements can be made for housing and meals for applicants by contacting the Grace College Visitor's Center.

Catalogs, application forms, and additional information may be obtained from the address below.

Grace College
200 Seminary Drive
Winona Lake, Indiana 46590
Telephone: 800-54-GRACE (toll-free)
World Wide Web: http://www.grace.edu

The Center for Intercultural Studies is a new facility that houses the Department of Foreign Languages and Cultures at Grace.

GRACELAND UNIVERSITY
LAMONI, IOWA

The University

Graceland University offers students a strong academic program firmly rooted in the liberal arts tradition with an emphasis on career preparation. Since its founding in 1895 as a private, coeducational University, Graceland has maintained a tradition of academic excellence based on a commitment to the Christian view of the wholeness, worth, and dignity of every person. The University, sponsored by the Reorganized Church of Jesus Christ of Latter Day Saints, is nonsectarian and offers a varied religious life program for those who wish to participate. Thirty-one percent of Graceland students come from Iowa, and the remaining 69 percent represent forty states and thirty nations.

Graceland believes that an important part of a student's learning experience is achieved through association with other students in residence hall living. This belief is supported by an on-campus housing system that provides students with the camaraderie of a fraternity or sorority without the competition. Within the residence halls, there are men's and women's houses. Members of each house elect a House Council to plan social, intramural athletic, religious, and academic support activities. Residence halls are equipped with voice mail, e-mail, Internet connections, and cable TV.

The North Central Association of Universities and Schools accredits Graceland as a bachelor's and master's degree–granting institution. Graceland's teacher-education program has been approved by the Iowa Department of Education and is accredited by the National Council for Accreditation of Teacher Education (NCATE). The nursing program is accredited by the National League for Nursing Accrediting Commission and the Missouri Board of Nursing and is approved by the Iowa Board of Nursing.

In addition to its undergraduate programs, Graceland offers a Master of Science in Nursing and an RN to M.S.N. course of study through the Outreach Program. Graceland also offers a Master of Education degree program.

Location

Lamoni, in south-central Iowa, is on Interstate 35 three miles north of the Missouri border. It is located in the heart of the Golden Triangle, 1 hour from Des Moines, 2 hours from Kansas City, and 3 hours from Omaha. Lamoni is the home of Liberty Hall Historic Center, antique shops, and, within 10 miles, a county lake, Slip Bluff County Park, and Nine Eagles State Park.

Majors and Degrees

Graceland awards the degrees of Bachelor of Arts, Bachelor of Science, and Bachelor of Science in Nursing. These degrees represent study in liberal arts with a concentration of courses in a major. The majors and concentrations offered in the Bachelor of Arts programs are accounting, art, athletic training, business administration, chemistry, commercial design, communications, criminal justice, economics, elementary education, English–literature, English–writing, entrepreneurship and free enterprise, finance, German, health, history, human services, information technology, international business, international studies, management, management of information systems, marketing, mathematics, modern foreign language, music, music education, peace studies, philosophy and religion, physical education and health, political science, psychology, publications design, recreation, religion, secondary education, social science, sociology, Spanish, speech communication, theater, and wellness program management. Bachelor of Science programs and majors are addiction studies, basic science, biology, chemistry, clinical laboratory science/medical technology, computer science, nursing, pre-engineering, premedicine/predentistry, and pre–veterinary medicine. In addition, a special liberal studies program is offered at Graceland allowing individualized program design by students. Nursing majors complete their last two years at the Graceland Independence Campus in Independence, Missouri.

Graceland offers five undergraduate Outreach Programs: a Bachelor of Science in Nursing (B.S.N.), a Bachelor of Science in addiction studies, a Bachelor of Arts in liberal studies (with emphases in health-care administration and health-care psychology), and an RN to B.S.N. program. (Applicants for the B.S.N. must be registered nurses.) These programs allow individuals to complete their degrees through a combination of directed independent study, preceptor-guided practicums, and short residences. For more information, students interested in the addiction studies major should call 800-585-6310 (toll-free); those interested in the nursing and health-care programs should call 800-537-6276 (toll-free).

Academic Program

Graceland is committed to helping develop the lives of its students—intellectually, socially, physically, and ethically. Its curriculum is strongly rooted in the liberal arts. The general education requirements include course selections ranging from writing, speech, history, and humanities to mathematics, science, biology, and economics. Graceland offers majors that foster conceptual thinking, emphasize general principles, develop communication skills, and accommodate growth and enrichment.

Two programs at Graceland give attention to the special needs of students. The honors program is designed for highly motivated students who want to expand their learning beyond the regular academic curriculum. Honors students are required to develop and complete an honors thesis or project. Chance is a program for bright students who have the aptitude for University education but have experienced learning difficulties. The Lindamood-Bell clinical model is used for remediation in reading, spelling, and language comprehension.

The University operates on a 4-1-4 academic calendar. The regular semesters are separated by a one-month Winter Term in January. Full tuition for either the fall or the spring semester includes Winter Term. This program is geared toward innovative and exceptional approaches and action-oriented learning experiences. On-campus programs vary from dance basics to science fiction to philosophy. Off-campus Winter Term experiences range from scuba diving in Grand Cayman to touring Italy. Winter Term is also the ideal time to explore career interests through an internship.

Off-Campus Arrangements

Many students see the world during Winter Term by visiting such places as Australia, China, England, France, Grand Cayman Island in the British West Indies, Hungary, Italy, India, Israel, Japan, and Mexico. Students who major in a foreign language may study abroad during their junior or senior year under the auspices of a recognized study program.

Academic Facilities

The Shaw Center for the Performing Arts includes an 800-seat auditorium, a 150-seat studio theater, a 40-foot proscenium stage with orchestra pit, a Casavant pipe organ, a full fly gallery, a spacious scene shop, an art gallery, classrooms, rehearsal rooms, and faculty offices.

Computer facilities include three primary microcomputer laboratories with Macintosh and IBM-compatible computers. Students have access to equipment of commercial quality for desktop publishing and graphics design, and to a music laboratory that provides computer-assisted tutoring, synthesis, and composition as well as professional-quality manuscript printing. The centerpiece of this laboratory is the Kurzweil synthesizer. Graceland's Enter.Net.C@fe provides 24-hour Internet access for student research and recreation.

The Frederick Madison Smith Library uses the latest technologies to provide the information services that students need. Ten fully networked computer workstations offer access to the Internet and many research databases, including 2 databases that provide full-text newspaper articles and periodicals for online reading. Access to LIBBIE, the computerized library catalog, is available from residence hall rooms. Articles and books may be ordered from a worldwide network of research libraries. Students log on to the library's home page to ask reference questions. Holdings include approximately 116,840 books and bound journals, 2,845 audiovisual materials, 76,350 government documents, 582 magazine and newspaper subscriptions, and 5,194 items in the Teacher Curriculum Lab. Three microcomputer labs and the Iowa Communications Network (ICN) classroom are located in the library. Students throughout the state take classes from Graceland via the ICN.

Students have the opportunity to use the ABT 32 scanning electron microscope, nuclear magnetic resonance spectroscope, Fourier transform infrared spectroscope, and a computer lab with state-of-the-art PCs that provide access to a multiple-operating system environment.

Eugene E. Closson Physical Education Center includes an indoor junior Olympic-size pool; an indoor track; a weight room; basketball, tennis, and volleyball courts; and a racquetball court. The Bruce Jenner Sports Complex contains the outdoor track, the football stadium, the soccer field, intramural fields, eight tennis courts, and two sand-volleyball courts. The campus borders on a nine-hole golf course and two small ponds for fishing and canoeing.

Costs

Full-time tuition for 2000–01 is $12,230. Tuition per credit hour is $380. All freshmen and sophomores are required to live on campus. The room fee is $1530, and board is $2570. The social activities fee is $120.

Financial Aid

Graceland's financial aid program is designed to assist qualified students in attending University. Ninety-four percent of Graceland's students receive financial aid such as academic scholarships, performance grants, work/study, federal and state grants, and government loans. Academic scholarships are based on high school GPA and composite ACT or combined SAT I scores for entering freshmen and on cumulative GPA for transfer and continuing students. Grants are available for achievement in athletics and performing arts and for international students. The University matches a grant up to $1000 annually for a contribution made by a church and designated for a student attending Graceland.

Faculty

Eighty percent of faculty members on the Lamoni campus have earned a doctorate or the highest degree in their field. Faculty members are active in their professional fields, but consider teaching their primary responsibility. The student-faculty ratio is 16:1.

Student Government

Students are actively involved in the decision-making process of the University. Executive members of the Graceland Student Government attend faculty meetings and participate with voice and vote. Each academic department has student representatives who participate in business sessions and serve on faculty search committees. Students provide leadership for the housing system and for the campus social program. There are many avenues through which students can gain practical leadership experience.

Admission Requirements

Admission to Graceland is competitive. To be considered, high school graduates must qualify in two of the following three areas: (1) rank in the upper 50 percent of their class; (2) have a minimum 2.0 GPA, based on a 4.0 system; and (3) have either a minimum composite ACT Assessment score of 21 or a minimum combined SAT I score of 960. No one is denied admission to the University on the basis of race, color, religion, age, sex, national origin, disability, or sexual orientation. Prospective students and their families are encouraged to visit the campus.

Application and Information

Students are encouraged to apply as early as possible. For more information and application materials, students should contact:

Bonita Booth
Vice President for Enrollment Management and
 Dean of Admissions
Graceland University
700 University Avenue
Lamoni, Iowa 50140
Telephone: 515-784-5196 (local)
  800-346-9208 (toll-free in the United States)
  800-638-0053 (toll-free in Canada)
Fax: 515-784-5480
E-mail: admissions@graceland.edu
World Wide Web: http://www.graceland.edu

From computer labs with Internet access to thousands of books, journals, and periodicals, the Frederick Madison Smith Library provides students with free access to a world of information.

GRAND CANYON UNIVERSITY
PHOENIX, ARIZONA

The University

Grand Canyon University is Arizona's only private, Christian, liberal arts university. The purposeful integration of faith and learning has made Grand Canyon the distinguished university it is today. Since the University's founding by the Arizona Southern Baptist Convention in 1949, professors at Grand Canyon have believed in a rare holistic approach to education wherein the mind, the body, and the spirit are seen as essential partners in the learning experience. With more than 2,000 students, Grand Canyon University is committed to providing students with individual attention from faculty members and administrators. Grand Canyon offers more than sixty programs of study that all have their foundation in a core of liberal arts courses.

As a member of the Council of Christian Colleges and Universities, Grand Canyon University belongs to an elite group. Less than 3 percent of all colleges and universities in the United States are Christ-centered, providing a value-added educational environment that synthesizes faith, learning, and life. At Grand Canyon, students seeking to learn and grow within a Christian value system find a sense of community, a demanding academic curriculum, and countless opportunities for community leadership and service both on and off campus. Grand Canyon University is open to students from all faith perspectives.

In an era of the ever-escalating costs of higher education, Grand Canyon University offers an excellent education with outstanding value. Grand Canyon is among a select group included in the *Student Guide to America's 100 Best College Buys*. *U.S. News & World Report* ranks Grand Canyon in the top five Western liberal arts colleges for "Getting Your Money's Worth." *U.S. News & World Report* also continues to rank Grand Canyon University in the top Western liberal arts colleges for quality—regardless of cost. Grand Canyon University is the only Arizona school to be recognized in the John Templeton Foundation's guidebook, *Honor Roll for Character-Building Colleges*.

A degree from Grand Canyon University represents a well-rounded education. The Grand Canyon curriculum is challenging and radiates from a strong core of liberal arts and sciences. The University provides both traditional and innovative programs that enable students to think critically and creatively, solve problems through open-minded analysis, and communicate effectively. Academic habits acquired at Grand Canyon University stay with Grand Canyon graduates, enabling them to live flexible lives, to be open to new career opportunities, and to develop confidence in their ability to learn and adapt.

Grand Canyon University offers graduate degrees that include the Master of Arts in Education, Master of Arts in Teaching, Master of Education, and Master of Business Administration.

Location

Grand Canyon University is located just minutes from central Phoenix, Arizona's state capital and sixth-largest city in the United States. Phoenix is the nerve center of the Southwest, one of the fastest-growing regions in the nation. The greater Phoenix metropolitan area, known as the Valley of the Sun for its more than 300 days of sunshine each year, offers numerous educational, social, cultural, and recreational activities that enhance university life. Phoenix is a major-league city in many ways. The city is one of only eleven in the nation to be home to four major-league sports teams—the Phoenix Suns, Arizona Cardinals, Phoenix Coyotes, and Arizona Diamondbacks. The valley also provides opportunities for hiking, camping, cycling, golf, water sports, and virtually any other activity all year long. Also within a 2-hour drive of the Grand Canyon campus is some of the best snow skiing in the Western United States. Grand Canyon University students flourish in the school's southwestern environment. Surrounded by rugged mountains, lush valleys, and the arid beauty of the Sonoran Desert, Grand Canyon students feel a part of the larger human experience. Grand Canyon University and the Grand Canyon State are wonderful places in which to learn.

Majors and Degrees

Grand Canyon University awards bachelor's degrees in more than sixty areas of study. Specific degrees awarded are the Bachelor of Arts, Bachelor of Business Administration, Bachelor of Liberal Studies, Bachelor of Music, Bachelor of Science, and Bachelor of Science in Nursing.

Specific study areas include accounting, allied health, applied management, applied music, art education, athletic training, biblical/theological studies, biochemistry, biology (environmental/general/human/secondary teaching), chemistry (general/secondary teaching), Christian education, church music, communications (with emphasis in broadcasting/journalism/photojournalism/public relations), computer information systems, corporate fitness and wellness, creative arts in worship, elementary education, English literature, English teaching, finance, fine arts management, graphic design, history, international business, international studies, justice studies, management (with emphasis in human resource development/information systems), marketing, martial arts, mathematics (engineering/general/secondary teaching), music education, physical education (teaching), physical science, physics (secondary teaching), piano performance, political science, predentistry, premedical technology, premedicine, pre-occupational therapy, pre-optometry, pre–osteopathic medicine, prepharmacy, pre–physical therapy, pre–physician assistant studies, prepodiatry, pre–sports health care, pre–veterinary medicine, psychology, reading education, recreation, science for elementary teachers, secondary education, social sciences, sociology, special education (emotional handicapped and learning disabilities), speech teaching, speech/theater, studio art, teaching English as a second language, theater/drama, and vocal performance.

Academic Program

Grand Canyon University is accredited by the Commission on Institutions of Higher Education of the North Central Association of Colleges and Schools (30 North LaSalle Street, Suite 2400, Chicago, Illinois 60602-2504; telephone: 800-621-7440, toll-free). Grand Canyon Bachelor of Business Administration and Master of Business Administration degree programs are additionally accredited by the Association of Collegiate Business Schools and Programs. The work of Grand Canyon students seeking certification as elementary, secondary, and special education teachers, or for the renewal of teaching certificates, is approved by the Arizona State Department of Education. Over the past fifteen years, 92 percent of Grand Canyon University College of Education graduates have been placed in teaching positions. Grand Canyon University Samaritan College of Nursing is accredited by both the National League for Nursing and the Arizona State Board of Nursing for the Bachelor of Science in Nursing degree. Over the past five years, 94 percent of nursing program graduates have passed the state board exams on their first attempt.

Graduates of Grand Canyon University's College of Science and Allied Health benefit from Grand Canyon's relationship with the Kirksville College of Osteopathic Medicine. Kirksville's southwest center, Arizona School of Health Sciences, located on Grand Canyon's campus, reserves a large number of admission slots in each of its programs exclusively for qualified Grand Canyon students. These programs include physical therapy, occupational therapy, and physician assistant studies. Grand Canyon graduates are also in demand at a national level, with approximately 150 reserved admission slots in health-care programs across the country. The California College of Podiatric Medicine and Butler University

College of Pharmacy and Health Sciences both have offices on campus, with other professional schools seeking the opportunity to have firsthand access to Grand Canyon students.

Off-campus internships are an important educational experience available to Grand Canyon students. Classroom sessions are more relevant when subject matter is seen in the light of the work environment. Students from all disciplines hone their skills through off-campus clinical and intern programs. Some internships result in permanent positions after graduation, an invaluable benefit.

Grand Canyon University is also a member of the Coalition of Christian Colleges and Universities and the Association of Southern Baptist Schools and Colleges. While exploring a major field of study in-depth at Grand Canyon, students are exposed to a wide range of experiences both on and off campus. This diversity is a key element of Grand Canyon's vision of educating students for successful careers and lives. Students benefit from Grand Canyon's blend of characteristics for a high-quality Christian education—small classes, accessible faculty members, a challenging curriculum, and hands-on learning experiences.

Academic Facilities

Grand Canyon University consists of thirty-three buildings on a 90-acre campus. The campus features the Fleming Library, which houses a collection of more than 166,000 volumes, 700 periodicals, newspapers, microfilm, and audiovisual materials. Fleming Library is a member of the CCLC network and as a designated depository receives a variety of government documents. Library holdings are expanded by CD-ROM databases, computerized database searches, and interlibrary loans. Computers housed in the library have Internet access to assist students.

The majority of classes are held in the Fleming Classroom Building, with additional classes held in the Weidenaar Classroom Building, Wallace Building, and College of Business. Ethington Memorial Theatre sets the perfect stage for drama and other productions, with more than 300 seats. The C. J. and Thema Smith Arts Complex houses the A. P. Tell Gallery and other tailored creative spaces. The Tell Science Building and Samaritan College of Nursing are both equipped with state-of-the-art laboratory, computer, multimedia, and clinical learning spaces.

Grand Canyon University features two microcomputer laboratories utilizing IBM-compatible personal computers and a separate Macintosh computer laboratory.

Costs

An estimated budget for a full-time resident student (15 hours) for the 2000–01 academic year is $15,157 per year (two semesters). This includes tuition and fees ($10,911) and room and board ($4246).

Financial Aid

Grand Canyon University has made a commitment to its students by keeping costs down year after year and focusing its dollars on what will benefit students directly. The result of this effort yields an educational experience that offers high value and quality for the investment students make. The Office of Financial Aid and the Business Office at Grand Canyon University are committed to working with students and their families. They can help explain various options and ensure that every available resource is utilized to meet individual financial needs. More than 85 percent of Grand Canyon students receive some form of financial assistance to help meet the cost of their education. In addition to federal and state financial aid, Grand Canyon University has academic and other specific-criteria scholarships and aid available. Students wishing to apply for financial aid must be accepted for admission and complete the Free Application for Federal Student Aid (FAFSA) and have it on file in the Office of Financial Aid.

Faculty

Faculty members are drawn to Grand Canyon University due to a love of teaching. Rather than concentrating mainly on research and publication, Grand Canyon faculty members focus on assisting students to acquire knowledge and attain higher standards that help them reach their potential as people and as scholars. More than three quarters of Grand Canyon faculty members have earned doctoral or terminal degrees from some of the nation's most prestigious universities, and many are considered experts in their field. Beyond their academic qualifications, Grand Canyon faculty members are good friends. They help students become involved in the community and guide them through further explorations of their faith.

Student Government

Grand Canyon University understands that student involvement is essential in the university experience. Grand Canyon's Campus Leadership Council (CLC) is student led and staff supported. CLC is responsible for developing student leaders and programs that provide opportunities for contribution to the Grand Canyon campus and surrounding community. Interviews for CLC are held in the spring semester of each year for the following student positions: Chief Executive Officer, Chief Financial Officer, Director of Marketing, Director of Clubs and Organizations, Director of Intermurals, Director of Traditional Events, Director of Student Activities, and Director of Ministries.

Admission Requirements

For admission to Grand Canyon University, students should submit an application for admission with a $25 nonrefundable application fee to the Grand Canyon University Office of Admission. Freshmen must submit their official high school transcript and/or GED scores plus have their ACT or SAT I scores submitted to Grand Canyon University. Transfer students must have their transcripts forwarded to Grand Canyon University. Both freshman and transfer students must bring a health history, with proof of immunization for mumps, measles, and rubella, to put on file.

Application and Information

Grand Canyon operates on a rolling admission system. Applicants generally receive an admission decision within two weeks after all required documents are on file in the Office of Admission. It is to the student's advantage to apply as early as possible. Applications for financial aid and housing cannot be completely processed and transcripts are not evaluated until the admission application is complete.

For further information and application materials, students should contact:

Office of Admission
Grand Canyon University
3300 West Camelback Road
P.O. Box 11097
Phoenix, Arizona 85061-1097
Telephone: 602-249-3300
    800-800-9776 (toll-free)
E-mail: prvogel@grand-canyon.edu
World Wide Web: http://www.grand-canyon.edu

Students in front of Fleming Library at Grand Canyon University in Phoenix, Arizona, experience the integration of faith in their learning process while surrounded by the beauty of the Southwest.

GRAND VIEW COLLEGE
DES MOINES, IOWA

The College

Grand View is a four-year liberal arts college affiliated with the Evangelical Lutheran Church in America. Founded 100 years ago, Grand View offered a high-quality education to all students who sought the opportunity. Today, Grand View continues the tradition, educating a diverse student body in a career-oriented, liberal arts–grounded curriculum at three campus locations in greater Des Moines. Grand View welcomes traditional students and adult learners representing a wide range of religious and cultural backgrounds.

At Grand View College, students find a winning combination of high-quality programs, experienced professors, and caring individuals. With 1,400 students and a 15:1 student-faculty ratio, students get to know their professors and other students well. They learn independence and seek responsibility in Grand View's educational environment. Learning is an interactive process at Grand View—students engage in lively discussions, work on real-world projects, and participate in career-related work experiences.

Grand View College stands out from other colleges because of its partnerships with leading businesses and organizations in Des Moines, which has led to 95 percent of students finding jobs right after graduation. Grand View is known for its ability to connect students with exciting and challenging career opportunities.

Students are encouraged to develop leadership and team skills through involvement in campus organizations, which include intercollegiate and intramural athletics, speech and theater groups, major department clubs, student government, and the Grand View College Choir. Active honorary societies include Alpha Chi, Alpha Mu Gamma, Alpha Psi Omega, Alpha Sigma Lambda, Beta Beta Beta, Phi Eta Sigma, Sigma Theta Tau, and Theta Alpha Kappa. Grand View's student leadership program provides opportunities for students without leadership experience to seek and develop critical thinking, interpersonal, and networking skills.

Student athletes compete in men's baseball, basketball, and soccer and women's basketball, soccer, softball, and volleyball. Grand View participates in the Midwest Classic Conference of the National Intercollegiate Athletic Association.

Three locations offer Grand View students convenient scheduling options for their program of study. Weekend and evening classes are offered at the main campus in Des Moines and also at Grand View West in West Des Moines. For motivated students seeking to complete their degree quickly, an accelerated program leading to a business administration degree and an individualized degree in organizational and technical studies are offered at Grand View's Camp Dodge Campus in Johnston, Iowa.

Location

Grand View is located in Des Moines, a metropolitan area of nearly 495,000 people in central Iowa. Des Moines is the state capital and serves as the communications hub for Iowa. Nationally recognized organizations that have their corporate offices in Des Moines include Pioneer Hi-Bred International, Inc.; The Principal Financial Group; Meredith Corporation; and The Des Moines Register and Tribune Company.

Grand View College's campus is Des Moines—and as part of the Grand View community, students are not limited by the confines of a small college or small town. In a given day, students can catch an Iowa Cubs professional baseball doubleheader, head down to the Court Avenue district for great food and nightlife, or take in a concert at the Civic Center.

A thriving arts program in Des Moines features the Des Moines Metro Opera, Ballet Iowa, The Des Moines Symphony, the Des Moines Art Center, and the Des Moines Playhouse.

Des Moines features four distinct and beautiful seasons. Except for a month or so of bundle-up, see-your-breath weather, the climate is ideal for outdoor activities. Grand View students can take advantage of terrific recreational opportunities, including several golf courses, Saylorville Lake, and many city parks and state forests.

Easily accessible from Interstates 35 and 80, Grand View is 4 hours from Minneapolis, 6 hours from Chicago, and 4 hours from Kansas City.

Majors and Degrees

Grand View College grants the Bachelor of Arts degree and offers majors in accounting, applied math, biology, business administration, computer science, creative and performing arts, criminal justice, elementary education, English, graphic design, graphic journalism, human services, individualized major, journalism, liberal arts, mass communication, organizational and technical studies, physical science, political studies, psychology, radio-TV, religion, secondary education, and visual arts. Grand View also offers a Bachelor of Science degree in nursing. In addition, the College offers certificate programs in art therapy, business information systems, corporate communication, international business, and sport management and postbaccalaureate certificates in accounting and management in accounting.

Academic Program

Grand View operates on a 4-4-1 academic calendar. The first semester runs from September to December. The second semester begins in early January and ends in late April. Three 1-month summer sessions are offered in May, June, and July, as is a summer trimester evening program.

Grand View College has adopted a competency-based General Education Core. Requirements for the core are defined in student learning goals. Completion of the educational core enables students to achieve a measurable level of competency in key skill and knowledge areas, such as writing, critical analysis, oral communication, and computer proficiency.

The Logos Honors Program provides an alternative to the General Education Core. By invitation, freshman and sophomore students enrolled in this program complete a series of courses designed to challenge exceptional students.

The Grand View academic mission is to serve a diverse student body by providing a variety of learning environments and teaching techniques. In order to meet this commitment, Grand View provides academic support programs and services designed to enable students to master skills essential for success in college-level courses. Special programs and services include a mathematics lab for drop-in tutoring, a writing lab to assist students in honing their skills, reading and study skills assessment and planning, and individual tutorial programs.

Costs
For 2000–01, the comprehensive cost for freshmen on campus is $16,776, which includes tuition, the activity fee, and room and board. Health services and computer access are also included in the comprehensive fee.

Financial Aid
More than 90 percent of all full-time Grand View students received financial assistance in 1999–2000. The average freshman full-time award package for 1999–2000 was $13,080, which included grants, scholarships, work-study, and student loans. The amount of aid is determined through a combination of merit and analysis of need as determined through the Free Application for Federal Student Aid. The priority deadline for financial aid is March 1. Students receive notification of financial aid packages following acceptance of admission to the College and receipt of their financial aid analysis of need.

Faculty
There are 67 full-time faculty members and 65 part-time faculty members. Fifty-five percent hold terminal degrees. All classes are taught by professors; no graduate or teaching assistants instruct Grand View classes.

Student Government
Students participate in College governance. The Student Activities Council and Viking Council plan student activities that promote educational, social, cultural, and recreational aspects of student life. Students serve as representatives on faculty and staff search committees, programming committees, and student life committees.

Admission Requirements
In keeping with its tradition, Grand View provides an opportunity to enroll for all graduates of accredited high schools. Applicants' files are reviewed to determine their preparedness for a Grand View education. Official copies of high school transcripts and submission of ACT or SAT I scores are required for first-time freshman applicants. Applicants transferring from another college are required to submit official transcripts from all colleges previously attended.

Application and Information
For more information about Grand View, students should contact:

Admissions Office
Grand View College
1200 Grandview Avenue
Des Moines, Iowa 50316

Telephone: 515-263-2810
              800-444-6083 (toll-free)
Fax: 515-263-2974
E-mail: admiss@gvc.edu
World Wide Web: http://www.gvc.edu

Grand View College's Humphrey Center, formerly Old Main, is listed on the National Register of Historic Places.

GREENSBORO COLLEGE
GREENSBORO, NORTH CAROLINA

The College

Established in 1838, Greensboro College is a four-year coeducational liberal arts college that is affiliated with the United Methodist Church. It is located in the College Hill Historic District of Greensboro, North Carolina. With an enrollment of approximately 1,000 men and women, the College stresses a small community atmosphere and maintains a student-faculty ratio of 13:1.

The College has completed an exciting $10-million building and renovation program that provides new classrooms and laboratories and transforms the gardens and grounds in a way that preserves and enhances the special character of the campus setting. The 40-acre campus serves both the academic and the recreational needs of the students. Its architecture is in the traditional Georgian style. The buildings include a student center, three residential halls, classroom buildings, a chapel, an auditorium, a library, a student services center, and a main administrative building.

The James G. Hanes gymnasium houses an indoor pool, weight-training room, dance gymnasium, athletic training room, and basketball court. Through a cooperative agreement with a nearby YMCA, full-time students have free access to racquetball and additional basketball courts, four additional weight rooms, another indoor pool, aerobics classes, Jacuzzi, and sauna. Intercollegiate sports include baseball, basketball, cross-country, football, golf, lacrosse, soccer, and tennis for men and basketball, cross-country, lacrosse, soccer, softball, swimming, tennis, and volleyball for women. Greensboro College is a member of the NCAA Division III and competes in the Dixie Intercollegiate Athletic Conference. An extensive intramural program is also offered for students.

There is great religious and ethnic diversity at Greensboro College, where students come from more than thirty states and twenty-four other countries. Many graduates have brought distinction to the College and themselves by furthering their studies in graduate and professional schools in all parts of the United States and abroad. Recent Greensboro College graduates have been accepted into the graduate schools of the College of William and Mary; the Universities of Chicago, Hawaii, North Carolina at Chapel Hill, and Virginia; and Duke, Eastman School of Music, Emory, Georgetown, Johns Hopkins, North Carolina State, Princeton, St. Andrews University in Scotland, Temple, Vanderbilt, and Wake Forest Universities. Most graduates pursue careers in business, education, health care, and the arts.

Extracurricular activities are designed to supplement and reinforce academic study at the College. More than 100 student leadership positions are available in more than forty-five different student organizations, enabling most students to be as active in campus life as they wish. An innovative Cocurricular Portfolio Program, which is part of the Greensboro College leadership development program, is available to all students.

Location

The city of Greensboro, located near the center of North Carolina, has a rich variety of resources. There are major industries, including insurance companies and textile manufacturers, and many cultural, social, and athletic opportunities. With a population of more than 1 million people in the Triad region, the city is a major business center. More than 20,000 college students study at the six colleges and universities within the city. Greensboro College is at the heart of this community.

Majors and Degrees

Greensboro College awards the Bachelor of Arts and Bachelor of Science degrees. Students can major in the following areas: accounting, art, biology, birth-through-kindergarten teacher education, business administration and economics, chemistry, education or special education, English, French, history, history and political science, mathematics, middle school education, music, physical education, political science, psychology, religion and philosophy, secondary education, sociology, Spanish, sports and exercise studies, and theater. Minors are available in child and family studies, computer science, ethics, interdisciplinary studies, legal administration, and other areas in which majors are offered. Combined-degree programs are offered in medical technology, physician's assistant studies, and radiological technology.

Academic Program

All students are required to take courses in the humanities, the natural sciences, the social sciences, and the arts. The general education requirements for both the B.A. and B.S. degrees total 52 semester hours. Graduation requires the completion of 124 semester hours.

Greensboro College offers an honors program for superior students who qualify on the basis of SAT I or ACT scores, high school grade point averages, or AP examination results. Students enrolled in the program must complete requirements in addition to those expected of students in the regular B.A. and B.S. degree programs.

First-year students at Greensboro College may elect to participate in a multifaceted freshman-year experience program, which includes the Precis, a three-day excursion designed to help new students begin building friendships, as well as specialized opportunities to join many campus clubs and organizations.

Because Greensboro College recognizes that people must learn not only how to live but also how to make a living, the liberal arts curriculum and setting provide the context for a variety of professional programs, including accounting, business, and legal administration, as well as preprofessional programs in law, medicine, and theology. Besides providing career and academic counseling, the College seeks to ensure that its graduates acquire the basic intellectual and communications capabilities to enable them to cope with the changing demands of a specific career or the unpredictability of employment opportunities. The College also seeks to develop in its graduates a philosophy of life and an appreciation of Judeo-Christian values that transcend particular vocational skills.

Greensboro College believes that all students have potential for leadership. The central component of the Leadership Program is the Cocurricular Portfolio. This program is a way for students to assess skills, set goals, and deliberately design and record activities in a professionally printed portfolio that is used upon graduation. An internship program during the junior and senior years places students in business and agency settings that are related to the major and to career aspirations.

Off-Campus Arrangements

Greensboro College is a member of the Greater Greensboro Consortium and the Piedmont Independent Colleges Association, which provide for arrangements with Bennett College, Elon College, Guilford College, Guilford Technical Community College, High Point College, North Carolina Agricultural and Technical State University, Salem College, and the University of North Carolina at Greensboro. With permission from the academic dean, students at Greensboro College may take courses offered at any of the other campuses. Library resources are shared.

Academic Facilities

The James Addison Jones Library has approximately 102,000 volumes, periodicals, CD-ROMs, and microfilm reels. The computerized card catalog system allows students to access the holdings of other area colleges. Interlibrary loan among the colleges is permitted. Four levels of open stacks include extensive resources in juvenile literature and in religion. There are also reading rooms, periodical and browsing rooms, and the Sternberger Cultural Center, a multipurpose meeting room for College and community events.

One of the College's goals is to be sure that every student develops a broad range of technical skills in order to flourish in the twenty-first century. State-of-the-art computer labs are available for all students, and students can access the Internet and World Wide Web from most points on campus. All dorm rooms provide access to e-mail and the Internet. Other facilities include a modern computer laboratory, a computerized writing laboratory, natural science laboratories, the Parlor Theater, and the Gail Brower Huggins Performance Center, one of the most elegant and state-of-the-art performance facilities in the Triad area. Music facilities include a computerized music laboratory, practice rooms, two recital areas, thirty-nine pianos (including a 9-foot concert grand), and a concert stage. In addition, Greensboro College is one of only three colleges in the state to have a Fisk organ. There are two large art studios, one for the teaching of two-dimensional media and one for the teaching of three-dimensional media. Students in the education department are served by the Curriculum Materials Center, which contains audiovisual equipment, books, teaching kits, and a variety of other special supplies.

Costs

For 1999–2000, the total cost of tuition, fees, room, and board was estimated at $16,600. A private room was estimated to cost an additional $1250. Greensboro College estimates that an additional $800 to $1500 is adequate for books, clothing, entertainment, and other incidental expenses.

Financial Aid

Greensboro College participates in many federal programs of student aid, including the Federal Pell Grant, Federal Work-Study, Federal Perkins Loan, Federal Supplemental Educational Opportunity Grant, Federal Parent Loan for Undergraduate Students, and Federal Stafford Student Loan programs. Authorized state programs include North Carolina Legislative Tuition Grants, the State Contractual Scholarship Fund, North Carolina Prospective Teacher's Scholarships/Loans, and North Carolina Student Incentive Grants. Institutional programs funded by Greensboro College include the College work-study program, grants, scholarships, and loans. Full- and partial-tuition scholarships are awarded to students based on merit. United Methodist Church scholarships and grants, based on both financial need and merit, are available. Full merit-based Presidential Scholarships, valued at more than $66,000 each, are available. Approximately 85 percent of the students at Greensboro College receive some form of financial assistance. All students are encouraged to apply for financial aid, and the College accepts the Free Application for Federal Student Aid (FAFSA). Applications for United Methodist Church scholarships and grants are available from the financial planning office. A career development office on campus is available to aid all students seeking a part-time job, regardless of their financial need.

Faculty

Greensboro College has 105 full- and part-time faculty members. Almost 90 percent of the full-time faculty members hold the highest degree in their areas of study. Although some faculty members have distinguished themselves by their research, scholarship, and creativity, all are deeply committed to undergraduate teaching and the personal welfare of the students. Every student has a faculty adviser, and there is a favorable student-faculty ratio of 13:1.

Student Government

The College Council of Greensboro College, acting within the policies and regulations of the College, is the main representative voice of the students. The College Council serves the student body by addressing various policy decisions that affect the students and by acting as a sounding board for student opinions. The College Council is the communication link between student organizations, the student body, the administration, the staff, and the faculty. The College Activities Board (CAB) plans and executes student events on campus.

Admission Requirements

Admission decisions are based on all available information. Although applicants are asked to submit scores from the SAT I and ACT, the high school record is actually the most important single factor. There is no exact formula that can be applied to all applications, but acceptable scores on the SAT I or ACT, rank in class, grade point average, and high school program form the basis for evaluation. Candidates for admission should demonstrate academic achievement in a select academic program in high school, although completion of a given program of study is not as important as evidence of intellectual curiosity and emotional and social maturity. A curriculum that provides good preparation for Greensboro College might include 4 units of English, 3 units of college-preparatory math (algebra I, II, and geometry), 2 units of science (including one laboratory science), 2 units of history, 2 units of the same foreign language, and electives chosen from art, music, physical education, and social science. An interview on campus is very helpful to the student and to the College. Arrangements may be made for the interview at the student's convenience.

Greensboro College accepts transfer credits on a case-by-case basis. Credit will be given for courses successfully completed at accredited universities, senior colleges, junior colleges, community colleges, and technical colleges.

Application and Information

Students should submit an application for admission and immediately ask high schools and any colleges they have attended to forward official transcripts to Greensboro. SAT I or ACT scores should be forwarded to Greensboro College by the testing agency or the student's high school. Reference letters may be requested by the Admissions Committee, which reviews all applications on a rolling basis. As soon as a decision is reached, the student is notified. Greensboro College has no closing date for applications, but those received before March 31 are given priority.

Inquiries and application materials should be sent to:
Director of Admissions
Greensboro College
815 West Market Street
Greensboro, North Carolina 27401-1875
Telephone: 800-346-8226 (toll-free nationwide)
Fax: 336-378-0154
E-mail: admissions@gborocollege.edu

Greensboro College students frequently gather in front of historic Main Building.

GREENVILLE COLLEGE
GREENVILLE, ILLINOIS

The College

Since 1892, Greenville College has provided high-quality Christian higher education. Accredited by the North Central Association since 1948, the College is affiliated with the Free Methodist Church but welcomes students of any denomination. Its mission is to equip students for lives of effective leadership and redemptive servanthood. Students help with homeless projects in St. Louis and flood relief, forego vacations to minister in the inner city, raise funds for missions, work in big brother/sister programs, donate blood, sponsor needy children, tutor area youth, and lead discipleship groups.

Greenville's 850 students come from thirty-six states and nine countries. Numbers of men and women are about equal, and most students are 18–22 years old. Nearly half of them graduated in the top quarter of their high school classes. Ten percent of the student body are members of ethnic minority groups.

Greenville College's familylike atmosphere communicates a clear message that faculty, administration, and students care for each other. New students participate in a freshmen-year experience led by professors and designed to help them get acquainted, learn time management, establish priorities, and set goals. Career services personnel help seniors with resume writing and job placement. Faculty and students are always ready to help a fellow student with small and large concerns. Late in the evening, professors often stop by the library to help students preparing for their exams the next day. Because of the large number of musically talented students, everyone grows accustomed to hearing good music in many styles.

Unmarried students live in non-coed residence halls (freshman roommates are usually assigned by the College). Students attend chapel—a time of community and worship—three times a week. Students agree to a Christian code of conduct. Covenant groups and opportunities for personal growth abound.

A large dining commons provides full food service, while the Student Union offers a variety of fast foods. The bookstore offers Christian books, magazines, and CDs as well as many varieties of "GC wear," gifts, and vital college gear. The school sponsors movies, concerts, and many other activities, and residence halls often plan activities with the brother or sister floors. Dinners, parties, and ball games appeal to many.

The first weekend in May each year is AGAPÉ weekend at the local county fairgrounds. Billed as the Midwest's largest Christian music festival, AGAPÉ provides two days of the biggest names in Christian music. Students organize all details and coordinate the event.

Through regular and postseason competition with both NCAA Division III and the National Christian College Athletic Association (NCCAA). Greenville offers fifteen intercollegiate sports. Men have baseball, basketball, cross-country, football, golf, soccer, tennis, and track; women have basketball, cross-country, soccer, softball, tennis, track, and volleyball. Intramural tournaments between dorm floors are common; Scott Field, located in the center of the campus quad, is often the site of ultimate Frisbee or touch-football games. Two large gymnasiums allow for athletic activities year-round. A fully equipped health club offers exercise, swimming, and weight training; all students have complimentary memberships.

Location

Greenville is located on I-70, 45 miles east of St. Louis. The historic southern Illinois town (population 6,400) provides a picturesque public square just two blocks from Greenville College's campus. In addition to visiting or working in the numerous shops and restaurants downtown, students can drive 20 minutes south to the Carlyle Lake water recreation area or 45 minutes west to major shopping malls in St. Louis.

Majors and Degrees

The College grants Bachelor of Arts and Bachelor of Science degrees. Students major in accounting, adult fitness/recreation, art, biology, business management, chemistry, communication, computer science, contemporary Christian music, early childhood education, education, elementary education, engineering (3-2), English, environmental biology, French, history and political science, leadership/recreation, management information systems, marketing, mass communication, mathematics, modern languages, music, pastoral ministries, philosophy, physical education, physics, predentistry, predietician, prelaw, premedicine, pre–medical technology, pre-nursing, pre-occupational therapy, preoptometry, prepharmacy, pre–physical therapy, pre–veterinary medicine, psychology, psychology-religion, public relations, recreation, religion, religion-philosophy, secondary education, social work, sociology, Spanish, special education, speech communication, sports management/recreation, theater, urban ministries, or youth ministries.

Greenville offers fully certified teacher training in early childhood through high school as well as in all levels of special education. It also has a 3-2 engineering co-op with the University of Illinois and Washington University in St. Louis and a 2-2 program with Mennonite College of Nursing.

Students with varied interests occasionally pursue multiple majors and/or participate in honors programs. In addition, the school offers an individually tailored education plan (ITEP), which allows qualified students to design their own majors.

Academic Program

The liberal arts core includes courses in fine arts, humanities, religion, science and mathematics, and social sciences. Each year, at least 500 courses are offered; the minimum required for graduation is at least thirty-three courses.

Classes meet during two semesters, three summer sessions, and a January Interterm. Interterm allows students to take nontraditional courses or travel to England, Ireland, Australia, Russia, and other countries. Classes in English as a second language are available, as is free tutoring for many classes. The College allows advanced accelerated degree and multiple degree programs. Most departments encourage or require an internship, co-op experience, or senior project or recital.

Greenville graduates do well. Teacher-education graduates are placed at more than twice the national average. The strong premedical program places more than 90 percent of its graduates into medical school, again twice the national average. Business students often find that summer-long internships lead to jobs after graduation.

An honors program is available for students who wish to enhance their academic program.

Off-Campus Arrangements

Through associations with other Christian colleges and organizations, students may spend a semester, at little or no additional charge, at international locations, including Costa Rica, Egypt, England, Israel, Kenya, Russia, and Ukraine. In the United States, students may study government in Washington, D.C., social programs in Chicago, film at the Los Angeles Film Center, ecology at the Au Sable Institute in Michigan, or psychology at the Focus on the Family Center in Colorado. Students may also spend a January Interterm at any of several sister schools.

Academic Facilities

Greenville's recently completed library addition houses 120,000 bound volumes, plus more than 4,000 microforms. Students have access to all library facilities, including online computer catalog searches. The educational media center contains thousands of current textbooks for teacher training.

The College provides computers with Internet access for student use; computer labs are staffed with tutors, and one is open 24 hours a day. Freshmen composition classes are taught in a fully equipped computer classroom.

The Business Department has completed a model office, which includes the latest electronic equipment used in the commercial world. Science classes have well-equipped laboratories for physics, chemistry, biology, and the physical sciences. Their equipment includes ion accelerators, scanning tunneling microscopes, and several large telescopes. Music practice rooms have pianos (both acoustic and electronic) or organs. The College has a digital recording studio, a full 24-track recording studio for advanced students, and a smaller 8-track facility for beginners.

Costs

Greenville's comprehensive fee for 1999–2000 was $17,446. This included $12,586 for full-time tuition (12–17 credit hours) and $4850 for room and board. Books, supplies, and laboratory fees are extra, averaging $500.

Financial Aid

Students receive financial aid based on merit, need, or a combination of both. Each year, 100 highly qualified high school seniors come to campus to compete for honor scholarships of $14,000 to $24,000. Other aid is available for leadership and service in high school.

Many students receive need-based scholarships as well. Students complete the Free Application for Federal Student Aid (FAFSA) by June 1 to determine their eligibility for college, state, and federal assistance during the academic year. The Student Financial Services Office assists students in getting loans from the College and external sources and in obtaining campus employment. Early estimator forms allow students to know their approximate financial aid award early in their application process.

Faculty

Greenville's teaching faculty consists of 53 full-time members and 15 adjuncts; the student-faculty ratio is 14:1. All professors teach and advise students and, although their primary function is teaching, faculty members regularly publish articles in scholarly journals and author textbooks. Professors spend summers and sabbatical leaves working in major industries, theaters, and laboratories to keep fully aware of changes in their fields. Sixty percent have doctoral or terminal degrees in their specialties. Faculty members always have time to talk with a student who needs help or advice.

The Council of Independent Colleges identified Greenville as one of the top ten liberal arts colleges in the nation for excellence in the academic workplace and for an extraordinarily high level of faculty involvement. Recently, the Coalition for Christian Colleges and Universities recognized Greenville College for meeting students' expectations for a caring faculty. Faculty members coach sports, advise clubs, and help in all areas of campus life. Most live less than 1 mile from campus, so it is common for them to have student groups in their homes. Students and faculty form friendships that often last far beyond college years.

Student Government

The Senate is the student governing body. Its elected president is an ex-officio member of Faculty Council, the faculty governing body. Most faculty committees have at least one student member. Students manage the College newspaper and yearbook, radio station, AGAPÉ music festival, homecoming, concerts, social activities, and all clubs and student organizations.

Admission Requirements

In addition to an application, prospective students submit ACT or SAT I scores, high school transcripts, and two references. The College encourages all prospects to visit the campus prior to making a final enrollment decision. It may require a personal interview and/or testing for some.

Students are recommended to follow a college-preparatory program in high school that includes four years of English and three years each of science, math, and foreign language. The College accepts satisfactory Advanced Placement examinations. For a nonprobationary acceptance, students generally need a minimum ACT score of 18 or SAT I composite of 860 and a 2.0 GPA (on a 4.0 scale). Transfer students need similar requirements plus a transcript of college courses. International students receive individual evaluation and may need to take the TOEFL test.

Application and Information

Students may call or write the College for application materials. Greenville encourages students to apply as early as possible during their senior year, although there is no official application cutoff. Applicants generally hear from the admissions committee within two weeks of the school's receiving all necessary materials. For further information, applicants should call or write:

Mr. Randall C. Comfort
Dean of Admissions
Greenville College
P.O. Box 159
Greenville, Illinois 62246
Telephone: 618-664-2800 Ext. 4401
              800-345-4440 (toll-free)
E-mail: admissions@greenville.edu
World Wide Web: http://www.greenville.edu

GRINNELL COLLEGE
GRINNELL, IOWA

The College

Grinnell College has been named one of the fifteen best liberal arts colleges in the country for the past fifteen years by *U.S. News & World Report*. The 95-acre campus is located in the heart of the Midwest, and its student body comes from forty-eight states and forty-six countries. Founded in 1846—the first four-year liberal arts college west of the Mississippi to grant a B.A. degree—Grinnell is described today in the Yale publication, *The Insider's Guide to the Colleges*, as "one of the most enlightened, progressive colleges in the Midwest—or the entire country, for that matter." Innovative from the beginning, Grinnell was the first college to establish an undergraduate department of political science (in 1883), and the school's travel-service program preceded the establishment of the Peace Corps by many years. The first-year tutorials, cooperative preprofessional programs, and a comprehensive program in quantitative studies and the impact of technology on society are examples of current innovations.

The College is a cultural and recreational resource for the local community as well as for its 1,345 students, the faculty, and the staff. More than 500 events during the academic year include plays, concerts, art exhibitions, dance recitals, lectures, discussions, and intramural and intercollegiate sports, all of which are free to the College community and general public. The Rosenfield Program in Public Affairs, International Relations, and Human Rights brings many outside lecturers to campus to enhance current-events programming. Facilities for sports and recreational activities are provided by the Physical Education Complex. The new Bucksbaum Center for the Arts, which opened in 1999 with a $22-million addition, more than doubles existing arts space on campus, offering a new recital hall, art gallery, theater, scene shop, studio theater, and classroom and studio space.

Location

Named one of the twenty-five best small towns in America, Grinnell is located in central Iowa, 55 minutes east of downtown Des Moines, off Interstate 80, in a prosperous and picturesque agricultural area. Stores, personal and professional services, a modern hospital, churches, restaurants, and other community features are available in addition to opportunities for community involvement. A landscape of rolling hills is a ten-minute bike ride from campus, and nearby Rock Creek State Park offers hiking, swimming, and sailing. In town, Grinnell students can enjoy the classic soda fountain and a five-cent cup of coffee at Cunningham Drug or the local bakery's freshly made sweets at 2 a.m.

Majors and Degrees

Grinnell offers an integrated and highly disciplinary four-year undergraduate liberal arts program leading to the Bachelor of Arts degree. Majors available in the humanities are art, Chinese, classics (Greek and Latin), English, French, German, music, philosophy, religious studies, Russian, Spanish, and theater. In science, the majors are biology, chemistry, computer science, general science, mathematics, physics, and psychology. Majors in social studies are American studies, anthropology, economics, history, political science, and sociology. Interdepartmental majors and independent majors may be arranged.

Nonmajor programs and concentrations are offered in alternative language studies, education (elementary and secondary certification), general literary studies, humanities/social studies, and physical education. Interdisciplinary concentrations include Africana studies, Chinese studies, environmental studies, gender and women's studies, global development studies, Latin American studies, linguistics, Russian and Eastern European studies, technology studies, and Western European studies.

In cooperation with other institutions, the College offers preprofessional programs in architecture, engineering, and law.

Academic Program

A Grinnell education is anchored in intense, active learning that occurs in one-on-one interactions between faculty members and students. The school is known for its rigorous academic and diverse extracurricular program. Its open curriculum enables students to learn initiative and leadership by assuming responsibility for their individual courses of study, which are developed under the guidance of a faculty adviser to reflect each student's goals for the future, including graduate school. This process challenges students to define their academic goals.

Outside of the First-Year Tutorial (a one-semester special topics seminar that stresses methods of inquiry, critical analysis, and writing skills), there are no core requirements. To graduate, students are expected to complete at least 32 credits in a major field and a total of 124 credits of academic work, with no more than 48 credits in one department and no more than 92 credits in one division. In the humanities, arts, and social and natural sciences at Grinnell, students have opportunities to conduct original research and undertake advanced study through independent and interdisciplinary projects that foster intellectual discovery. Course exemptions and advanced placement are also available. Students usually take 16 credits of course work during each of the two semesters in the academic year, which begins in late August and ends in mid-May.

Off-Campus Arrangements

Grinnell's commitment to the importance of off-campus study reflects the school's emphasis on social and political awareness and the international nature of its campus. More than 100 off-campus study opportunities are available to Grinnell students, including the Grinnell-in-London program and study tours of China, France, Greece, and Russia. These study programs in Europe (including Russia), Africa, the Near East, and Asia, as well as nine programs in Central and South America, provide the opportunity for research and enrichment in many disciplines, from archaeology to education. In addition to off-campus programs, Grinnell offers an extensive internship program in such areas as urban studies, art, and marine biology for students interested in field-based learning and experience in professional settings. Second- and third-year students may apply for summer internship grants and receive credit for the experience. Semester programs in the United States include those at the Oak Ridge National Laboratory, Newberry Library, and National Theatre Institute.

Academic Facilities

The eleven academic buildings on campus include the Grinnell College libraries—consisting of Burling Library, the Windsor Science Library, and the Music Library—which hold 423,068 volumes, 24,313 sound recordings, 12,185 microforms, 485,285 state and federal documents, and 2,700 serials, with an online catalog system and CD-ROM databases. The Black Library offers a special collection of works related to Africana studies. A recent $15.3-million renovation and addition to the College's science facilities in the Robert N. Noyce '49 Science Center has equipped lab facilities and classrooms with research tools that encourage hands-on experience and collaborative work. These include sophisticated laboratories, aquaria, a herbarium, scanning and transmission electron microscope facilities, a nuclear magnetic resonance spectrometer, a physics historical museum, and other specialized resources. An observatory houses a computerized, research-quality, 24-inch reflecting telescope with sophisticated auxiliary devices and a lab, classroom, and darkroom. More than 1,000 PCs, Macintoshes, and workstations, linked to a variety of servers over a campus network, are used for teaching, research, and administrative computing. Near Grinnell, the biology department maintains the widely recognized 365-acre Conard Environmental Research Area, which has a fully equipped field-research laboratory for studies in ecology. Programs in art, music, and theater are housed in the new Bucksbaum Center for the Arts. The center includes the Roberts Theatre, the Flanagan Arena Theatre, the Scheaffer Gallery for art exhibitions, a studio for modern dance, music rooms, a scene shop, and art studios. The College Forum (student union) and the Harris Center, both centers for cultural activity and social and recreational events, serve all members of the College community.

Costs

The comprehensive fee of $26,320 for 2000–01 includes $19,982 for tuition, $3110 for board, $2710 for a room, and $518 for activities, health, and other fees. Students should allow for the additional costs of books, supplies, travel, laundry, and personal expenses.

Financial Aid

Grinnell has a long-standing commitment to both a need-blind admission policy and to providing 100 percent of institutionally calculated need to each qualifying student. To that end, more than $13 million is budgeted annually for grants and scholarships. Grinnell also offers further assistance through campus employment opportunities, loans, and numerous payment options. Students wishing to be considered for financial aid should, along with their parents, file the Free Application for Federal Student Aid (FAFSA) by February 1.

Faculty

The Grinnell faculty consists of 134 men and women. Ninety-three percent hold Ph.D. degrees, and among the members are scholars, writers, and artists of established reputation who are active in producing original, significant work. All classes are taught by professors, not teaching assistants, and the student-faculty ratio of 10:1 means that Grinnell students can work closely with their instructors, who view classroom teaching as their top priority.

Student Government

Self-governance is a guiding principle at Grinnell College. Students serve on departmental educational policy committees and the Faculty Curriculum Committee. Students regulate the residence halls in consultation with residence life coordinates and serve on committees that determine social policy and regulations. The organizational structure of the Student Government Association covers almost all aspects of student activity and campus life. There are no sororities or fraternities.

Admission Requirements

Academic promise and intellectual self-reliance are qualities sought in students applying to Grinnell. Requirements are a scholastic record and class standing that show ability to do college work; graduation from an accredited secondary school with 4 units of English, 3 units of mathematics, and 9 other units of electives; satisfactory results on the SAT I or the American College Testing (ACT) examination; recommendation of the secondary school counselor; and recommendation of a secondary school teacher and an English instructor. Interviews on campus or with alumni are strongly recommended.

Application and Information

Students may apply for early decision if Grinnell is their school of first choice. Students applying for early decision–first choice should submit their applications by November 20; they will be notified by December 20 regarding both admission to the College and financial aid. Early decision is a commitment to enroll, and those accepted must withdraw all other applications.

Students may file applications for regular admission by January 20. Those filing by this date will be notified of the decision on admission and financial aid by April 1. Applications received after the January 20 deadline will be considered only if all spaces in the entering class have not been filled.

Grinnell College offers early admission to superior college-bound students who have completed the junior year of secondary school but who will neither complete their senior year nor receive a secondary school diploma.

For an application form and more information about Grinnell, students should contact:

Office of Admission
Grinnell College
P.O. Box 805
Grinnell, Iowa 50112-0807
Telephone: 641-269-3600
          800-247-0113 (toll-free)
E-mail: askgrin@grinnell.edu
World Wide Web: http://www.grinnell.edu

The Grinnell campus is considered to be one of the most attractive of American collegiate landscapes, as depicted in this photograph of North Campus near Gates-Rawson Tower.

GROVE CITY COLLEGE
GROVE CITY, PENNSYLVANIA

The College

The beautifully landscaped campus of Grove City College stretches more than 150 acres and includes twenty-seven neo-Gothic buildings valued at more than $100 million. The campus is considered one of the loveliest in the nation. While the College has changed to meet the needs of the society it serves, its basic philosophy has remained unchanged since its founding in 1876. It is a Christian liberal arts and sciences institution of ideal size and dedicated to the principle of providing the highest-quality education at the lowest possible cost. Wishing to remain truly independent and to retain its distinctive qualities as a private school governed by private citizens (trustees), it is one of the very few colleges in the country that does not accept any state or federal monies. Affiliated with the Presbyterian Church (U.S.A.) but not narrowly denominational, the College believes that to be well educated a student should be exposed to the central ideas of the Judeo-Christian tradition. A 20-minute chapel program offered Tuesday and Thursday mornings, along with a Sunday evening worship service, challenge students in their faith. Sixteen chapel services per semester are required out of forty opportunities. Religious organizations and activities exist to provide fellowship and spiritual growth.

Ninety-one percent of the 2,300 students live in separate men's and women's residence halls. All others are regular commuters or married students. A full program of cultural, professional, athletic, and social activities is offered. An arena, Crawford Auditorium, and the J. Howard Pew Fine Arts Center are used for athletics, concerts, movies, plays, and lectures. The Physical Learning Center is one of the finest among the nation's small colleges. A student union, bowling alleys, handball/racquetball courts, playing surfaces, a bookstore, and Ketler Recreation Lounge are also available. There are more than 100 organizations and special interest groups, including local fraternities and sororities. No alcohol or drugs are permitted on campus. The athletics activities include an extensive intramural and recreational program and twenty intercollegiate varsity teams for men and women.

The College's well-established placement services are used constantly by students interested in business and industrial employment and by those seeking educational positions in the teaching field. A complete file of personal data, scholastic records, and recommendations is prepared for each registrant. These files are available to the scores of prospective employers who visit the campus annually to interview the graduating seniors. One of Grove City's strengths is placing students in business, industrial, and teaching positions, as well as in professional institutions such as medical schools.

Location

Grove City, a town of 8,000 people, is 60 miles north of Pittsburgh. Convenient to I-79 and I-80, Grove City is only a day's drive from Chicago, New York City, Toronto, and Washington, D.C. The municipal airport has a 3,500-foot runway, and there is bus service to Pittsburgh.

Majors and Degrees

Grove City College offers undergraduate degrees in liberal arts, sciences, engineering, and music. The Bachelor of Arts is offered with majors in Christian thought, communication, economics, English, English/communications, history, modern language (French, Spanish, and international studies), philosophy, political science, psychology, secondary education, and sociology. Preprofessional students in Christian education, law, or theology usually earn the B.A. degree. Interdisciplinary major programs are also available for qualified students.

The Bachelor of Science is granted with majors in accounting, applied physics, applied physics/computer, biochemistry, biology, business, business/computer, business management, chemistry, early childhood education, elementary education, financial management, industrial management, international business, marketing management, mathematics, mathematics/computer, and molecular biology. Preprofessional students often select one of these majors for dentistry, medicine, or other health fields.

The Bachelor of Science in Electrical Engineering degree is also offered. The electrical engineering major has concentrations in computer engineering and electrical engineering. The Bachelor of Science in Mechanical Engineering major provides for mechanical systems design and/or thermal systems design. The electrical and mechanical engineering programs are accredited by the Accreditation Board for Engineering and Technology, Inc. (ABET).

The Bachelor of Music degree is awarded to those who major in music. Programs may also include concentrations in business, education, performing arts, or religion.

Academic Program

Grove City College's goal is to assist young men and women in developing as complete individuals—academically, spiritually, and physically. The general education requirements provide all students with a high level of cultural literacy and communication skills. They include 38–50 semester hours of courses with emphases in the humanities, social sciences, and natural sciences and in quantitative and logical reasoning, as well as a language requirement for nonengineering and science majors. Degree candidates must also complete the requirements in their field of concentration, physical education, electives, and convocation. To graduate, a student must have completed 128 semester hours (136 in engineering) plus 4 convocation credits. About 80 percent of those entering as freshmen stay and receive a diploma.

A distinctive liberal arts–engineering program includes engineering courses plus courses in the humanities to provide students with a well-grounded preparation for entering the engineering field, as well as the civic and cultural life of society. The economics program exposes students to all economic philosophies, yet strongly advocates economic freedoms and free markets.

Grove City follows the early semester calendar plan. Academic credit may be granted to incoming freshmen on the basis of scores on appropriate Advanced Placement tests, International Baccalaureate tests, or on the College-Level Examination Program tests. Honors courses, independent study, seminars, and the opportunity for juniors to study abroad for credit are also offered.

Academic Facilities

The College library houses 158,000 books and 270,000 microfilm/microfiche units. Modern, well-equipped laboratories for biology, chemistry, engineering, and physics are available, as are facilities for language and piano studies. The Technological Learning Center, which consists of 40 microcomputers and three big-screen projection systems, has received national recognition. The mainframe is a VAX 6250. All freshmen receive their own color notebook-sized computer and printer.

The J. Howard Pew Fine Arts Center has art, photography, and music studios; a rehearsal hall; a little theater; a museum; an art gallery; music practice rooms; and an auditorium and stage large enough to accommodate the most elaborate drama productions and concerts.

Costs

As a relatively small, financially sound college, Grove City is able to charge an unusually low tuition in comparison to other independent institutions of similar quality. The 1999–2000 annual tuition charge was $6976 for B.A. degree students, $7506 for B.S. and B.M. degree students, and $7864 for B.S.E.E. and B.S.M.E. degree students. The cost of a color notebook computer and printer for all freshmen is included in the tuition fees. There is no comprehensive fee. Room and board were $4048. Expenses for books, laundry, transportation, and personal needs vary considerably with the lifestyle of the individual.

Financial Aid

Because the College's tuition charges are low, every student, in effect, receives significant financial assistance. Fifty-seven percent of the freshmen receive additional aid from GCC. Students applying for financial assistance must complete Grove City College's financial aid form. Job opportunities are available both on and off campus.

Faculty

The focus of the Grove City faculty members is on teaching students, although many members are involved with research and writing. Seventy-four percent of the faculty members hold doctorates. Most of the administrative staff also teach part-time in various departments. The student-faculty ratio is approximately 20:1. Faculty members emphasize teaching and attention to the students' individual needs; they also participate extensively in the College's extracurricular programs.

Student Government

The Student Government Association provides an opportunity for direct student interaction with the faculty members and administration in matters relating to campus activities. Students serve on regular College committees (library, publications, religious activities, and student activities) and also on the Men's and Women's Governing Board and the Discipline Committee.

Admission Requirements

An applicant for admission should be a high school graduate with the following recommended units: English, 4; foreign language, 3; mathematics, 3; history, 2; and science, 2. Engineering, science, and mathematics majors should have 4 units each in both mathematics and science. Auditions are required for music majors. An interview is highly recommended, especially for those who live within a day's drive.

The College seeks academically qualified students without regard to race, color, sex, religion, or national or ethnic origin. Grove City students generally come from middle-income families. The greatest number come from Pennsylvania, Ohio, New Jersey, and New York, although forty-six states and eleven countries were represented in 1999–2000. Ninety-six percent of the women and 68 percent of the men in the most recent freshman class ranked in the top fifth of their high school class. Their average SAT I combined score was 1258; the average ACT composite score was 27.

Transfer students may receive advanced standing if they have been in good standing at their previous institutions and have maintained a minimum grade point average of 2.0 (on a 4.0 scale).

Application and Information

A regular admission applicant should take the SAT I or ACT by October or November of the senior year in high school. The application should include scores on the SAT I (preferred) or the ACT, a high school transcript, references, a recommendation from the student's principal or counselor, and a nonrefundable application fee of $30. An application may be submitted after the eleventh grade. An early decision applicant should take the entrance test in the eleventh grade, visit the College for an interview, and submit the application by November 15; notification of the admission decision is mailed on December 15. Approved early decision applicants must accept by January 15 and submit a nonrefundable deposit of $200.

Applicants seeking regular decision must submit the completed application and supporting documents by February 15 of their senior year. Notification of the admission decision is mailed on March 15. Students who are offered admission should reply as soon as possible, but no later than May 1, and include a nonrefundable deposit of $150. Applications received after February 15 will be considered as space permits. The College receives five applications for every freshman vacancy.

Additional information may be obtained from:

Jeffrey C. Mincey
Director of Admissions
Grove City College
100 Campus Drive
Grove City, Pennsylvania 16127-2104
Telephone: 724-458-2100
Fax: 724-458-3395
E-mail: admissions@gcc.edu
World Wide Web: http://www.gcc.edu

Crawford Hall.

GUILFORD COLLEGE
GREENSBORO, NORTH CAROLINA

The College

Founded on its present site in 1837 as the Quaker New Garden Boarding School, Guilford College, with its Georgian buildings set on 340 wooded acres on the western edge of Greensboro, North Carolina, retains a sense of tranquility and tradition. Guilford is the third-oldest coeducational college in the nation and has a long-standing history of commitment to the individual student.

Guilford's 1,250 students come from more than forty states and thirty other countries. In addition, there are approximately 150 adult students enrolled in day and evening classes. The College's size ensures the academic community's commitment to personalized education without giving up academic diversity. Students are encouraged to take an active part in extracurricular activities on campus, including seminars and lecture series, interest and service clubs, wide-ranging cultural opportunities, and an extensive program of intramural and intercollegiate athletics for both men and women. The Student Union, a student organization, sponsors many of the social, recreational, and cultural programs offered at the College. Many students participate in a variety of community service projects and volunteer programs.

There are frequent exhibitions featuring distinguished artists as well as College faculty members and students. Dramatic presentations range from *Romeo and Juliet* to *Waiting for Godot*. A touring choir and opportunities for individual lessons complement the music program. Each summer, Guilford is the home of the Eastern Music Festival. Orchestral, dramatic, operatic, and balletic opportunities are also available in the city of Greensboro.

Guilford has twelve intercollegiate athletic teams that compete at the NCAA Division III level and in the Old Dominion Athletic Conference (ODAC). The sports include women's basketball, lacrosse, soccer, tennis, and volleyball and men's baseball, basketball, football, golf, lacrosse, soccer, and tennis. More than 70 percent of Guilford students take part in a diverse intramural program and in club sports such as rugby, swimming, and cross-country. Sports programs are coupled with special academic opportunities in sports medicine, sport management, and physical education.

Primarily residential in nature, Guilford provides dormitory accommodations for 960 students. About 150 nontraditional (adult) students are enrolled through the College's Center for Continuing Education.

Location

Greensboro, North Carolina, is a city of 200,000 people, located midway between Washington, D.C., and Atlanta, Georgia. The greater metropolitan area has a population of more than 1 million. The city is served by two interstate highways, and the Piedmont Triad International Airport is less than 5 miles from campus. Numerous historic sites and recreational parks—local, state, and national—are within day-trip distance of the College. Greensboro's central location in the state allows easy access both to the coast and to several major ski areas in the mountains. The amenities of life in the Southeast—climate, pace, and friendliness—coupled with rich cultural opportunities and sound economic growth make the Sun Belt an attractive area in which to study and to live.

Majors and Degrees

Guilford College offers B.A. or B.S. degrees in accounting, African-American studies, art, biology, chemistry, criminal justice, economics, education studies, English, environmental studies, exercise and sports studies, French, geology and earth sciences, German, history, integrative studies, international studies, justice and policy studies, management, mathematics, music, peace and conflict studies, philosophy, physics, political science, psychology, religious studies, sociology/anthropology, Spanish, sport management, theater studies, and women's studies. The B.F.A. is offered in art.

Additional concentrations are available in applied ethics, communications, computing and information technology, creative writing, forensic science, intercultural studies, Japanese, medieval studies, money and finance, and sport administration.

Dual-degree programs are available in forestry and/or environmental science with Duke University and in physician's assistant studies with Bowman Gray School of Medicine of Wake Forest University.

Preprofessional programs are offered in dentistry, law, medicine, ministry, and veterinary science.

Academic Program

Each student works closely with a faculty adviser to select courses that meet his or her individual educational and career goals. Thirty-two semester courses are required for graduation, eight of which are generally in the major field of study. Required courses are few but represent a distribution over the principal fields of the arts and sciences. Flexible requirements allow for interdisciplinary and double majors.

Incoming first-year students and transfer students have an opportunity to participate in Avanti, a summer preorientation program that includes computer training, learning skills, academic advising, self-awareness workshops, and Outward Bound–style outdoor experiences.

Independent study, off-campus internships, and off-campus seminars are open to all students. An expanded honors program includes a variety of honors courses for students with exceptional academic credentials and motivation. One pass/fail elective course may be taken each semester.

Entering students may waive courses through advanced-placement examinations in English, history, laboratory science, mathematics, and foreign languages. Advanced placement requires an AP score of 3 or better or a general CLEP score of 500 or better; credit requires an AP score of 4 or better or a general CLEP score of 550 or better. Subject CLEP scores must be at least 50 for advanced placement and at least 55 for credit.

Guilford College has a two-semester calendar. The first semester ends before winter break, and the second semester ends in early May.

Off-Campus Arrangements

Semester abroad programs enable students to study in Africa, China, England, France, Germany, Italy, Japan, and Mexico. Students may also participate in programs sponsored by other American colleges and universities. A full year of academic credit for study in Japan is available through a cooperative program with International Christian University in Tokyo.

Guilford participates in two consortia that allow open registration in seven area colleges and universities without additional fees. Other member schools are Bennett College, Elon College, Greensboro College, Guilford Technical Community College, High Point University, North Carolina A&T State University, and the University of North Carolina at Greensboro.

An on-campus programs director assists students who wish to study abroad. An internship director helps to place students who wish to study elsewhere in the United States. Course credit is given for all approved off-campus study. One-week off-campus seminars are sponsored by the College throughout the regular academic year in such locations as New York City, Washington, the Outer Banks, and Florida. These seminars focus on urban problems, education, government, the arts, religion, geology, ecology, and marine life. The Washington Semester in Washington, D.C., supplements the academic program and helps students develop professional skills and career potential through internships with the federal government, lobbying organizations, or public agencies.

Internships may be done in any discipline. Locally, students may pursue internships as part of their academic and career development in business, education, government, health services, law, medicine, scientific research, and social services. In addition, the Internship and Service Learning Office sponsors a variety of community service activities, such as the Student Literacy Corps and Project Community.

Academic Facilities

Stately Georgian-style buildings in excellent condition house classrooms, a spacious auditorium, the library, a well-appointed student center, administrative offices, and residence halls. The 65,000-square-foot Frank Family Science Center opened in March 2000 and features fourteen laboratories (with twenty-four workstations each), 1,600 computer connections, a rooftop observatory with a computer-driven telescope, and a 150-seat multipurpose auditorium/planetarium. Multiple studio space is available to students in the fine arts. Guilford's Hege Library is one of the three largest private libraries in North Carolina. The library contains 250,000 volumes and includes an art gallery, a media center, and the only Friends Historical Collection in the Southeast. Hege Library is fully automated and is linked to buildings across the entire campus. Students also have library privileges at six colleges within 20 miles that have an additional 1.3 million volumes. In the near future, Guilford will complete construction of a new 38,000-square-foot fitness and recreation facility. It will complement the renovations made to the existing athletic facilities, which contain a swimming pool, racquetball courts, and additional multipurpose courts.

The state-of-the-art Bauman Telecommunications Center houses two computer-equipped classrooms, faculty offices, and three computer labs that contain ninety-one personal computers; these labs are open 24 hours a day. In addition, there are 200 public terminals in the Center and other terminals in academic buildings around the campus. Fiber-optic hookups link Bauman Telecommunications Center to most academic buildings on campus, and all students living on campus can access the facility from their residence hall rooms. In addition, satellite connections make it possible to bring in foreign language programming from around the world. In 1995, Guilford acquired twenty state-of-the-art computers from AT&T to establish a multimedia learning center for cultures and languages. Approximately 450 students have PCs in their residence hall rooms, and the College has full Internet access. All students have e-mail accounts, and, through an interdisciplinary course, students are playing an active role in developing the College's World Wide Web home page.

Costs

Basic expenses for the 1999–2000 academic year were $16,400 for tuition, $5610 for room and board, $270 for the student activity fee, and $300 for the technology fee. Personal expenses, book costs, and transportation expenses vary according to individual need.

Financial Aid

Guilford College tries to meet the demonstrated financial need of all students, as determined by the Free Application for Federal Student Aid (FAFSA). More than $13 million in scholarships, loans, grants, and work-study opportunities was awarded to students last year. Academic scholarships are awarded on a competitive basis. Guilford offers six merit-based and special interest scholarship programs, including the Guilford College Scholarships, which provide full tuition, room and board, books, and two trips home annually to up to 5 students. About 82 percent of last year's student body received some form of merit- or need-based assistance. The average need-based award was $14,300 a year per recipient.

Faculty

The faculty has superior credentials; 89 percent have a Ph.D. or the terminal degree in their field. The College seeks faculty members who value the sense of community and concern for individuals that are part of Guilford's heritage. Currently, 89 full-time and 34 part-time teachers provide a student-faculty ratio of 13:1.

Student Government

Guilford entrusts its students with responsibility for governing their own actions and furthering the best interests of the entire College community. The student Community Senate is composed of representatives from residence halls and the day-student organization, a member of the administration, and 2 faculty members. Students serve on all faculty and administrative committees and on the College's Board of Trustees and Alumni Board. Since 1982, the student government has sponsored fund-raising activities to set up and maintain the first student-initiated loan fund in the country.

Admission Requirements

Each applicant is considered on an individual basis. The Admission Committee examines each applicant's academic potential as predicted by performance on the SAT I or ACT and by his or her high school record. The committee selects from among academically qualified students those whose particular backgrounds and talents might enrich the College's educational community. The committee looks for students whose energies and concerns promise constructive leadership and useful service in their own lives and in society. Interviews, although not required, are strongly recommended so that the applicant can become better acquainted with Guilford and so that the admission staff can better evaluate the candidate. Guilford is competitive with respect to admissions.

Application and Information

Admission plans include early decision, early action, and regular decision. Early decision applicants must apply by November 15 and are notified by December 15. Early action and merit scholarship applicants must apply by January 15 and are notified by February 15. The regular decision priority deadline is February 15, and applicants are notified by April 1. After February 15, applications are considered on a space-available basis. Candidates admitted for regular decision must reply to their offers of admission by May 1.

Early entrance applicants are considered after their junior year of high school. They must have an outstanding academic record and must be sufficiently mature socially to adjust to college life.

Transfer candidates should apply for admission by December 1 for the spring semester and by April 1 for the fall semester.

The priority deadline for applying for financial aid is March 1.

For further information and application forms for admission and financial aid, students should contact:

Admission Office
Guilford College
5800 West Friendly Avenue
Greensboro, North Carolina 27410
Telephone: 336-316-2100
         800-992-7759 (toll-free)
E-mail: admission@guilford.edu
World Wide Web: http://www.guilford.edu

GUSTAVUS ADOLPHUS COLLEGE
SAINT PETER, MINNESOTA

The College

Gustavus Adolphus College was founded in 1862 by Swedish Lutheran settlers for the education of teachers and pastors. Gustavus has since become a nationally ranked undergraduate college of the liberal arts and sciences. Affiliated with the Lutheran Church (ELCA), Gustavus is dedicated to helping students attain their full potential as persons, developing in them a capacity and passion for lifelong learning and preparing them for fulfilling lives of leadership and service to society. Although the student body is primarily midwestern, Gustavus draws its 2,492 students from forty-two states and seventeen other countries; 6 percent are persons of color. A Phi Beta Kappa institution, Gustavus typically sends 35 percent of each graduating class directly to graduate school. Gustavus students have won Fulbright, Goldwater, Marshall, Rhodes, Truman, Watson, and Younger Scholarships and National Science Foundation Pre-doctoral Fellowships. Students also benefit from the annual Nobel Conference on science and values, which brings world-renowned scholars to the campus for a two-day symposium. Nobel Conference XXXVI, "Globalization 2000: Economic Prospects and Challenges," will be held October 3–4, 2000.

Campus life is central to the Gustavus experience. More than 90 percent of the students live on campus in eleven residence halls and share their meals at the Market Place. "Gusties" are typically active in campus student groups, choosing from thirty music organizations (including concert bands, choirs, a symphony orchestra, and jazz bands); ten religious groups; local fraternities and sororities (25 percent of students are members); nine service organizations; student media, including a weekly newspaper, radio station, literary magazine, and yearbook; and more than sixty other special interest clubs. The student-run Campus Activities Board brings speakers, bands, and other entertainment to campus throughout the year. Gustavus competes at the NCAA Division III level and is a member of the Minnesota Intercollegiate Athletic Conference. Twenty-five varsity sports are offered for men and women, along with ten club sports and thirty-one intramural sports. All students may use the multimillion-dollar Lund Center, which contains an indoor track and forum, 50-meter by 50-yard pool, weight room, racquetball courts, gymnastics facilities, and an indoor ice rink. The nearby Swanson Tennis Center houses six indoor courts for year-round use. Additions to the campus include an international center and residence hall, a nine-lane outdoor track, an international soccer field, and the Campus Center, which houses the Market Place and Courtyard Café, the diversity center, the student activities and ticket center, the book store, the health center, and student organization offices.

Location

The 340-acre Gustavus campus overlooks the town of Saint Peter (population 9,000) and the scenic Minnesota River Valley, 65 miles southwest of the Twin Cities of Minneapolis and St. Paul. Saint Peter is a historic residential community set among river bluffs and rolling farmland, where the College serves as a cultural and recreational resource. Outdoor activities such as biking, running, hiking, skiing, camping, and canoeing are popular in the area. Ten miles south of Saint Peter lies Mankato (population 40,000), a regional business center providing nearby internship sites as well as a variety of shopping and dining choices. The campus "Gus Bus" offers transportation to the Twin Cities and Mankato on different weekends each month, although students may have cars on campus after their first year. Students arriving at the Minneapolis/St. Paul International Airport can reach Saint Peter by taking Land to Air bus transportation.

Majors and Degrees

Gustavus awards the Bachelor of Arts degree in accounting, art, art history, athletic training, biochemistry, biology, chemistry, classics, communication studies, computer science, criminal justice, economics, education (elementary and secondary; coaching certification also offered), English, environmental studies, financial economics, French, general science, geography, geology, German, health fitness, history, international management, Japanese studies, management, mathematics, music, nursing, peace studies, philosophy, physical education and health, physical science, physics, political science, psychology, religion, Russian studies, Scandinavian studies, sociology/anthropology, Spanish, speech, and theater.

Preprofessional programs are available in actuarial science, architecture, arts administration, church vocations, dentistry, engineering, law, medicine, ministry, occupational therapy, optometry, peace studies, pharmacy, physical therapy, veterinary medicine, and women's studies. Special degree opportunities include 3-2 engineering degree programs with Washington University in St. Louis, the University of Minnesota, and Mankato State University; a 3-2 occupational therapy program with Washington University in St. Louis; and a 3-2 environmental management program with Duke University.

Academic Program

Gustavus operates on a 4-1-4 academic calendar. The first semester runs from September through December, followed by a monthlong January Term and a second semester extending from February through May. Students typically enroll in four courses each semester and one in January Term. To graduate, students must complete 35 credits (1 credit per full course) with a cumulative grade point average of at least 2.0, including three January Term courses, an approved major, and general education requirements. A major takes roughly one third of a student's courses, with another third required for distribution among the general education areas of the arts, religion, humanities, math and science, social science, foreign cultures, and personal fitness. Students may choose from two different tracks to fulfill general education course work. Curriculum I includes a First-Term Seminar and requires that students complete at least three writing-intensive courses; Curriculum II explores the interrelatedness of the disciplines and incorporates writing in every class. (Gustavus has gained national recognition for its Writing Across the Curriculum program.) Remaining classes are taken as electives. There are opportunities for independent study and individualized majors. Gustavus credit is granted to students who earn a 4 or 5 on the College Board Advanced Placement exams or to students scoring 4 or above on the International Baccalaureate higher-level exams. Gustavus offers Army ROTC through Minnesota State University, Mankato.

Off-Campus Arrangements

About one third of Gustavus students have studied abroad before graduating. Students may study abroad for credit for a full year, a semester, or a January Term. International study programs are offered in forty different countries through Gustavus-sponsored programs, through the Institute for European Studies, or through approved programs sponsored by other colleges and universities.

Students may apply for a number of seminar/internship programs, including the American University Washington Semester Program; Metro-Urban Studies Term or City Arts Term in Minneapolis/St. Paul through the Higher Education Consortium on Urban Affairs; the Research Volunteer Program at the National Institutes of Health in Bethesda, Maryland; and European work experiences through Boston University International Programs. Internships may be conducted for credit during a semester, over the summer, or during January Term; they occur in the Twin Cities metropolitan area, the Saint Peter/Mankato area, and at other sites nationwide and worldwide. Gustavus has a comprehensive Career Center with three full-time professional staff members to assist students in securing internships and employment.

Academic Facilities

The Folke Bernadotte Memorial Library houses 260,758 volumes, 1,445 current periodical subscriptions, 31,381 microform items, 278,178 government documents, and 13,389 recordings and videotapes. Gustavus also subscribes to the PALS online catalog and LEXIS-NEXIS, giving students access to additional millions of volumes and periodical holdings.

The Gustavus computing network is comprised of 1,000 computers using TCP/IP protocols running over a fiber-optic backbone. Students have direct network access from any of 424 public access computers, the majority of them Macintoshes or IBM/PCs, but also including SGI, NeXT, and Linux machines. Computer labs or clusters are located in the library and in eight academic buildings (open 100 hours/week), and in all residence halls (open 24 hours/day); all residence halls are hardwired for direct network access from individual student rooms and provide full Ethernet connectivity from every student room on campus. The campus network gives students full access to library holdings, the Internet, and printing from laser printers in the computer labs.

Gustavus is recognized for having science facilities that are "the envy of other small schools in its class" (*National Review College Guide*). Facilities include two electron microscopes, a 300-MHz NMR spectrometer, molecular biology and materials research laboratories, a five-section greenhouse, an herbarium, and the 55-acre Linnaeus Arboretum. The 15,000-square-foot F. W. Olin Hall for physics, math, and computer science also provides student research offices, along with a 16-inch computer-guided Meade LX-200 telescope, artificial intelligence laboratory, and laboratories in electronics and instrumentation, optics, solid state, and nuclear physics that have recently been enhanced by equipment grants.

Other facilities of note include the award-winning Christ Chapel, which seats 1,500 and is the site of voluntary daily chapel and the annual Christmas in Christ Chapel services, as well as concerts and lectures; the two-building Schaefer Fine Arts Complex, which features an art gallery, art and music studios, a MIDI computer lab, Björling Concert Hall, Anderson Theatre, Kresge Dance Studio, and an outdoor amphitheater; and the Culpepper Language Laboratory, which provides multimedia language study capability and SCOLA television programming in Confer Hall.

Costs

Tuition, room, and dining service fees for 2000–01 are $22,575. This amount also includes campus health service and laboratory costs. Additional fees are charged to incoming students to cover technology, student government, and orientation. Private music lessons are $200 per semester; music majors receive instruction free of charge. Students should allow an estimated $1630 for expenses.

Financial Aid

More than 70 percent of Gustavus students receive financial assistance based on the College's analysis of the Free Application for Federal Student Aid (FAFSA) and Gustavus Supplement. Need-based packages in most cases contain a combination of federal (such as Pell) and/or state (for in-state residents) grants; scholarships and/or grants from Gustavus; subsidized federal loans; and student employment. The priority deadline for submission of the FAFSA is April 15.

Gustavus awards the following scholarships purely on the basis of merit, although they might be part of an overall need-based package: Partners in Scholarship Awards, which offer faculty mentorships for research and graduate school preparation ($10,000/year); Presidential Scholarships, awarded to students who, as National Merit Finalists, select Gustavus as their first-choice college ($7500/year); and Trustee Scholarships, which recognize academic achievement in high school ($1000 to $5000/year). Other merit-based scholarships are given for music, service, and theater/dance.

Faculty

Gustavus has 170 full-time and 66 part-time faculty members; 88 percent have earned the Ph.D. or a terminal degree. Teaching is the first priority of the faculty. All classes are taught by professors, with a student-faculty ratio of 13:1 and an average class size of 17. Professors serve as academic advisers to first-year students as well as to majors.

Student Government

All Gustavus students are represented by the Student Senate, whose members are elected by class and by residence hall. The Senate serves as a student voice in campus policy by fielding student representatives for campus committees such as strategic planning, personnel, and academic policy. Members of the Senate also meet regularly with the Board of Trustees. The Senate annually administers a budget of more than $250,000, which is disbursed to petitioning student organizations.

Admission Requirements

Gustavus seeks academically well prepared students from a broad range of backgrounds. Successful applicants will have completed a college-preparatory sequence of courses, including 4 years of English and social studies, 3 to 4 years of math and science, and preferably 2 or more years of a foreign language. While the difficulty of and achievement in high school classes is the most important consideration in admission, scores on either the ACT or SAT I, letters of recommendation, the essay, and out-of-class activities are also carefully considered.

Application and Information

The early decision deadline is November 15, with notification December 1 and a reply expected by January 1. Thereafter, applications are reviewed on a rolling basis, with early action between January 1 and February 15 and regular decision between February 15 and April 15, both with a reply expected by May 1. Transfer students and international students complete separate application forms and may enroll in either semester. Interviews on campus are recommended but not required. For more information about Gustavus, students should contact:

Mark H. Anderson
Dean of Admission
Gustavus Adolphus College
800 West College Avenue
Saint Peter, Minnesota 56082
Telephone: 507-933-7676
        800-GUSTAVUS (toll-free)
Fax: 507-933-7474
E-mail: admission@gustavus.edu
World Wide Web: http://www.gustavus.edu

GWYNEDD-MERCY COLLEGE
GWYNEDD VALLEY, PENNSYLVANIA

The College

The dedication of the Sisters of Mercy to higher education led to the founding of Gwynedd-Mercy College in suburban Philadelphia in 1948. Gwynedd-Mercy is a four-year coeducational college with majors in both the liberal arts and professional fields of study.

Although it is intended that Gwynedd-Mercy remain a college of approximately 1,800 students, its size does not inhibit its ability to innovate. Gwynedd-Mercy was the first Catholic college in the United States to establish a sequential associate degree to bachelor's degree program in nursing, and it has recently established the first such progressive program in health information technology.

U.S. News & World Report's Best Colleges 2000 recently named the College number one in the state of Pennsylvania for freshmen retention (93 percent) and a Best Value College. Students at Gwynedd-Mercy establish strong cooperative relationships, encouraging and tutoring one another at all levels. A high degree of interaction and cooperation is also evident between faculty members and students. This may help to explain the high retention rate.

Gwynedd-Mercy offers participation in eighteen NCAA Division III athletic teams—ten for women, eight for men. Two sports boast conference Coaches of the Year. Men's basketball garnered its first-ever PAC Championship in 1999, while the women's basketball team won its first-ever NCAA bid. Gwynedd-Mercy's recognized excellence in the health fields provides a basis for its commitment to physical as well as spiritual wellness.

A special effort is made to encourage the participation of all students in activities and student government. Opportunities are available through drama club, campus ministry, a nationally renowned choir, yearbook staff, and social committees. The first Catholic college chapter of Habitat for Humanity, endorsed by former President Jimmy Carter, gives students the chance to help in the actual construction of homes for the less fortunate. Students can write for the college newspaper, the *Gwynmercian*, which has received a first-place rating with special merit from the American Scholastic Press Association. Through the on-campus chapter of Mercy Corps, students can help the poor with fund-raising efforts and adopt-a-family programs at Thanksgiving and Christmas holidays. Some students decide to give a year of service, after graduation, to Mercy Corps' nationwide outreach program.

A student lounge dedicated as an International Center for Understanding and Culture (ICUC) was opened in 1986. It gives American students the opportunity to meet, socialize with, and get to know young people from other countries. This diversified international student group includes 63 international students representing thirty countries. The ICUC quickly became a popular campus meeting place for students to confide their hopes and dreams.

On the graduate level, Gwynedd-Mercy offers a master's degree program in education (educational administration, mental health, reading, school and community counseling, school counseling, and a Master Teacher program) nursing (geriatrics, oncology, and pediatrics), and an M.B.A. (in cooperation with Allentown College).

Location

Gwynedd-Mercy's idyllic 160-acre campus is located in Gwynedd Valley, Pennsylvania, a suburb 20 miles from Center City Philadelphia. Old City, South Street, and sports arenas are a 25–30 minute car ride from campus. The College is situated just minutes from several major highways, including the Pennsylvania Turnpike. The immediate area is rich in the history of Colonial America, and two of the oldest homes in Pennsylvania are located on the Gwynedd campus.

Majors and Degrees

Gwynedd-Mercy offers baccalaureate degrees in accounting, behavioral/social gerontology, biology, business administration, business education, computer information sciences, elementary education, English, history, mathematics, nursing, psychology, sociology, and special education. Seven certification options are available through the School of Education.

Associate in Science degrees are awarded in the allied health fields of cardiovascular technology, health information technology, and respiratory care. Associate degrees are also granted in accounting, business administration, computer programming, liberal studies, natural science, and nursing.

Academic Program

The school year is divided into two semesters, and most baccalaureate degree programs require the completion of a minimum of 125 credit hours. Gwynedd-Mercy maintains a strong liberal arts component in all its degree programs. Whether the student chooses to major in one of the liberal arts or to pursue a professionally oriented degree, courses are required in language, literature and the fine arts, humanities, and behavioral, social, and natural sciences.

Individualized internships and work-experience programs are available and recommended in all majors to give students first-hand experience in their chosen major. Nearby Fortune 500 companies offer a wide variety of experience to students in business and accounting. TAP, the Teacher Assistant Program, places every education major in the classroom one day a week beginning in the freshman year. All allied health and nursing programs require clinical experience. The 2+2 programs—those with an associate degree to bachelor's degree progression—offer allied health and nursing students the opportunity to gain employment in their field while continuing toward the baccalaureate degree. The School of Business and Computer and Information Sciences maintains a successful work-experience semester. Through this paid internship, students earn credit while gaining valuable experience in challenging positions.

The tutoring program begun for science and health majors has expanded so that free tutoring is now available in other academic areas for students who need it. This complements the close student-faculty relationship that is part of the Gwynedd-Mercy milieu.

Off-Campus Arrangements

The excellent on-campus laboratory facilities are extended by affiliations with more than 200 hospitals and health-care agencies in Pennsylvania, New Jersey, and Delaware, where students may complete their clinical experience. Merck provides a one-semester industrial laboratory experience for qualified biology majors. Gwynedd maintains a close relationship with nearby companies, such as Unisys, McNeil, and Sun Company, for work-experience programs.

Academic Facilities

Gwynedd-Mercy has expanded its physical facilities as its student enrollment has increased. The Sister Isabelle Keiss Center for Health and Science opened in fall 1999 and houses the Schools of Nursing and Allied Health and the Division of Natural Sciences. The 50,000-square-foot state-of-the-art facility offers laboratories for areas such as nursing skills, respiratory care, cardiovascular technology, radiation therapy, health information technology, organic chemistry, and microbiology. The College's Griffin Complex houses the College's Student Union—equipped with a game room, a full gymnasium and track, racquetball court, and weight room. Also open for 2000 is a new residence hall, Loyola Hall Suites. Lourdes Library houses the Lincoln Library, which is a large adjunct collection of books on Lincoln and the Civil War, is housed in Assumption Hall. Theaters include the Julia Ball Auditorium, a small in-the-round theater, and a TV production studio. One computer laboratory is reserved for computer majors. A separate facility is maintained for use by the general student body. Both are staffed and open at hours convenient to student use. Hobbit House, a private school for preschoolers, is situated on campus, where students in the School of Education are trained.

Costs

The estimated 1999–2000 academic-year tuition (two semesters) for full-time students (12 to 18 credits per semester) was $13,500. Allied health and nursing students paid $14,500. Room and board were, on average, $6300. Professional liability fees for students enrolled in clinical components and lab fees are extra. There is no parking or student activities fee.

Financial Aid

Gwynedd-Mercy's financial aid program is designed to provide financial assistance to academically qualified students whose resources are inadequate to meet the costs of attending the College. The student financial aid committee endeavors to assist as many students as possible, using Gwynedd-Mercy funds as well as federal, state, and other available funds. Aid is awarded on the basis of demonstrated financial need, academic proficiency, and responsible campus citizenship.

A financial aid packet is sent, with instructions, to those who request it on their application form. High school students should request the Free Application for Federal Student Aid (FAFSA) from their guidance office. In 1999–2000, 91 percent of Gwynedd-Mercy full-time students received some form of financial aid. March 15 is the deadline for freshmen entering in the fall semester. The deadline for Academic Scholarships is February 15.

Faculty

The student-faculty ratio is 15:1, allowing for personal contact, advising, and after-class instruction. This is a widely acknowledged strength of the Gwynedd-Mercy experience. For nursing students in the clinical setting, there are never more than 8 students to 1 clinical adviser; in the allied health programs, there often is one-to-one instruction. The quality of teaching is enhanced by the diversified interests of the faculty. The 181 faculty members (90 part-time) teach both day and evening classes, allowing students the greatest flexibility in scheduling. Free tutoring is available in many disciplines.

Student Government

All students are encouraged to take part in the responsibilities of student government. This student participation and shared responsibility for the welfare of the College are promoted through a framework of committees. The student government president and 3 other students are members of the College Council, which is responsible for the continuing self-evaluation of the College and for policy formation. In addition, students share membership in the Educational Planning Committee, Faculty/Student Committee, Financial Aid Committee, and Library Committee.

Admission Requirements

Admission to Gwynedd-Mercy is based on a student's high school record, rank in class, SAT I or ACT scores, counselor's recommendation, and choice of major. Entrance requirements vary with the program. The rolling admission policy allows the student to be informed of the admission decision within two to three weeks after the file is complete.

Gwynedd-Mercy awards College credit for satisfactory completion of Advanced Placement courses. The exam score must be 3 or above.

A minimum 2.0 grade point average (on a 4.0 scale) is generally required to transfer from another college. Gwynedd-Mercy does, however, retain the right to require a higher GPA for admission to some programs.

Gwynedd-Mercy selects all students on the basis of academic achievement and does not discriminate on the basis of race, religion, gender, handicap, or sexual orientation.

Application and Information

All prospective applicants are urged to visit the campus to meet and talk with an admission counselor, a dean, or a program director. To apply for admission, applicants should complete the application form and submit it to the admissions office along with the required nonrefundable $25 application fee. First-time freshmen must also submit an official high school transcript or equivalency certificate; a written recommendation from a principal, teacher, guidance counselor, or employer; and results of the SAT I or ACT (for recent high school graduates). All applicants should verify that they meet the specific requirements and have the necessary high school prerequisites for admission.

Students wishing to transfer to Gwynedd should complete the application form and submit it to the admissions office along with the required nonrefundable $25 application fee, high school and college transcripts, and a letter of recommendation.

For additional information or to schedule campus tours and visits, students are encouraged to contact:

Office of Admissions
Gwynedd-Mercy College
1325 Sumney Town Park
P.O. Box 901
Gwynedd Valley, Pennsylvania 19437

Telephone: 800-DIAL-GMC (toll-free)
E-mail: admissions@gmc.edu
World Wide Web: http://www.gmc.edu

Students at Gwynedd-Mercy College.

HAMILTON COLLEGE
CLINTON, NEW YORK

The College
Chartered in 1812, Hamilton College is the third-oldest college in New York State. Originally a frontier school for the native Oneida Indians and children of early settlers, and later an all-male college, today Hamilton is a private, nonsectarian liberal arts institution enrolling 1,740 men and women from around the country and the world. As a small residential college, Hamilton is dedicated to offering its students the opportunities and facilities necessary to achieve a well-rounded education both inside and outside the classroom. Because of its comfortable size, students come to know their professors as colleagues and often as friends.

A weekly newspaper, several literary and humor publications, a campus radio station, a student-produced television program, musical and drama groups, academic clubs, active religious and volunteer service organizations, and other special interest groups provide opportunities for student leadership. The College has a large student-run public affairs council, a program board, and two active film societies; lectures, films, and other cultural activities are an integral feature of the weekly schedule.

A high percentage of students at the College enjoy intercollegiate, intramural, and recreational athletics. Fourteen men's and fourteen women's varsity teams participate in NCAA Division III competition, and the College is a charter member of the New England Small College Athletic Conference. Hamilton's facilities include the oldest indoor collegiate hockey arena, a multipurpose field house, a gymnasium, weight rooms, a fitness center with state-of-the-art exercise equipment, 20 acres of playing fields, an all-weather track, an artificial-surface field, a high ropes course, a nine-hole golf course, and the William M. Bristol Jr. Swimming Pool.

Residential life at Hamilton provides opportunities for students to learn from classmates in a positive environment of community living conducive to academic achievement, personal growth, and a respect for the rights of all residents. Traditional residence halls, suites, campus apartments, and substance-free, smoke-free, and quiet housing are among the available living arrangements.

Hamilton sponsors a complete range of student services, including opportunities to meet with professionals trained to provide extensive career planning, personal counseling, and general and women's health-care services.

Location
Hamilton is situated on a 1,250-acre hilltop campus overlooking the Mohawk and Oriskany Valleys of scenic central New York. Hamilton's two campuses, consisting of the original college campus and the former Kirkland College campus (which merged with Hamilton in 1978) reflect a blend of the traditional and the contemporary. The village of Clinton still retains much of the New England flavor brought to it by eighteenth-century settlers. While the city of Utica is within a 15-minute drive and Syracuse is situated less than an hour to the west, many rural areas also surround Hamilton. The Adirondack Mountains, ideal for hiking and skiing, are within an hour's drive.

Majors and Degrees
Hamilton offers the Bachelor of Arts degree with concentrations in Africana studies, American studies, anthropology (archaeology or cultural anthropology), art, art history, Asian studies, biochemistry/molecular biology, biology, chemistry, classical languages, classical studies, communication studies, comparative literature, computer science, creative writing, dance, East Asian studies, economics, English, foreign languages, French, geoarchaeology, geology, German, government, history, mathematics, music, neuroscience, philosophy, physics, psychology, public policy, religious studies, Russian studies, sociology, Spanish, theater, women's studies, and world politics. In consultation with the faculty, students may design their own concentrations.

Academic Program
Hamilton strives to provide its students with a broad liberal arts education. In addition to course work in an academic concentration, the academic program includes general education courses, electives, and distribution requirements of two courses in each of four academic divisions: science and mathematics, historical studies and social sciences, the humanities, and the arts. Some students choose to meet the requirements of two separate concentrations or choose a concentration and a minor.

The general education program reflects an appropriate respect for breadth and depth in the study of the liberal arts. The essential goals of this education include achieving proficiency in the fundamental skills of written, oral, and quantitative work; a variety of course work among the four academic divisions; a knowledge of others and an awareness of the diversity of the human condition; and a familiarity with ethical issues and how such issues may be evaluated.

In addition, Hamilton offers an increasing number of interdisciplinary concentrations, including American studies, East Asian studies, public policy, and women's studies, as well as minors in Africana studies, astronomy, environmental studies, and Latin American studies.

Three times during the past ten years, a Hamilton student has been a finalist for the Apkar Award, signifying the best undergraduate research paper in physics completed during the previous year. A Hamilton student won the award in 1994. Funding for students to conduct collaborative summer research with the faculty has expanded greatly in recent years.

Off-Campus Arrangements
Each academic year, Hamilton offers many educational opportunities at international and domestic sites away from campus. The Junior Year in France, pioneered by Hamilton more than thirty years ago, is today one of the most widely respected programs of its kind and enrolls students from many colleges. A parallel program allows students conversant in Spanish to spend a year or semester in Madrid, Spain. Hamilton's newest program, the Associated Colleges in China program (with Williams and Oberlin Colleges), offers intensive summer and/or semester-long study of Chinese in Beijing. Students also participate in programs sponsored by other colleges and universities, providing study-abroad opportunities in more than 100 countries.

Within the United States, the Term in Washington allows qualified students to spend a semester of their junior or senior year in the nation's capital, serving internships in the executive and legislative branches of the federal government. Hamilton is also a member of the American Maritime Studies Program, in conjunction with Williams College and Mystic Seaport. Approximately 40 percent of all Hamilton students study off campus at some point during their academic career.

Academic Facilities

Library facilities include the main Daniel Burke Library, the Dana Science Library, a music library, and the Audiovisual Services Division in the Christian A. Johnson Building. Circulation, reference, and interlibrary loan services are available to all in the community. Access to 546,816 volumes can be obtained through an online computer catalog. The Hans H. Schambach Center for the Performing Arts is home for much of the music program, containing ample classroom and rehearsal space, as well as the 700-seat Carol Woodhouse Wellin Hall. The adjacent List Studio provides rehearsal areas for dance and space for studio art. The Minor Theater offers a more intimate setting for rehearsal and the study of drama.

The campus computer network provides faculty and staff members and students with high-speed access to e-mail, College information, library databases, software, and information resources on the Internet. More than 950 institutionally owned computers and 1,200 student computers are connected to the network through 3,000 "information outlets" located in all College buildings, including one outlet per student in residence halls. More than 550 computers are available to students in public and departmental computing facilities.

The Saunders Hall of Chemistry contains laboratories that are well adapted to student experimentation and research. Geology, biology, psychology, and physics, housed in the Science Building, utilize such sophisticated equipment as two electron microscopes, robotics and laser laboratories, experimental rooms for psychology, and additional facilities for specific research.

Costs

Tuition and fees for 2000–01 are $26,100; room and board in College facilities are $3320 and $3120, respectively.

Financial Aid

Hamilton awards financial assistance on the basis of need to more than half of its 1,740 students. In addition, eight to ten awards of between $7500 and $10,000 are given to the most outstanding members of the first-year class, without consideration of need. Through a comprehensive program of scholarships, loans, and jobs, Hamilton attempts to meet the full financial need of all students admitted to the College. In addition to the PROFILE form of the College Scholarship Service, candidates for assistance must file the FAFSA and a Hamilton financial aid form by February 1. All admission decisions are determined without reference to a student's financial need.

Faculty

The 187 full-time members of Hamilton's faculty are committed to excellence in teaching, learning, and creativity. They are not only teachers and mentors, but are also friends and academic colleagues who are admired and respected by their students. Often their scholarly achievements outside the classroom contribute to their disciplines. Professors frequently share research with students and encourage them to participate as well. For example, students have recently accompanied faculty members on scientific expeditions to the Antarctic and to present papers at professional meetings throughout the United States. Because the student-faculty ratio is 10:1 and because all courses are taught by faculty members, both students and professors do their best to meet each other's expectations. Faculty members are easily accessible to students needing help, for academic advising, or to those simply wishing to discuss their work or whatever else may be on their minds. Most students leave the campus having made at least one lasting friend among the faculty.

Student Government

The Student Assembly, which administers a $275,000 budget for students programs, represents the functions of student government at Hamilton, and students often join with faculty members, administrators, and trustees on other College-wide committees to set policy.

Admission Requirements

Hamilton seeks to enroll intelligent, well-prepared, and strongly motivated students from as great a variety of backgrounds as possible. The admission staff and the College are dedicated to finding candidates who will contribute a wide diversity of talents, interests, and experiences to campus life. Applicants are expected to have taken advantage of the strongest academic curriculum available at their high schools. A strong record of personal accomplishment—taking into consideration the opportunities available—is also an important gauge of the candidate's ability to contribute to the life of Hamilton. Although a strong academic preparation is the most important consideration for admission, other special talents and interests may be considered. Outstanding achievement or potential demonstrated in the arts, music, and athletics may be influential in the admission process. Scores on the SAT I or ACT are required for admission. Candidates should keep in mind that while test scores are a part of Hamilton's evaluation, a student's overall academic record in high school is far more important.

Application and Information

Application materials may be requested directly from the College, or students may apply using the Common Application Form. The deadline for regular admission is January 15, and decisions are mailed by early April. There is a $50 application fee. Candidates who have chosen Hamilton as their first-choice college may apply for early decision by one of two possible deadlines, November 15 and January 10. Decisions are mailed by December 15 and February 15, respectively. Early decision acceptance is binding. A $200 deposit is required to ensure the accepted student's place in the class.

Dean of Admission
Hamilton College
198 College Hill Road
Clinton, New York 13323
Telephone: 315-859-4421
          800-843-2655 (toll-free)
Fax: 315-859-4457
World Wide Web: http://www.hamilton.edu

The Bienecke Student Village provides a variety of opportunities for student interaction.

HAMPDEN-SYDNEY COLLEGE
HAMPDEN-SYDNEY, VIRGINIA

The College

Hampden-Sydney, a four-year liberal arts college for men, has been in continuous operation since January 1776, six months before Jefferson wrote the Declaration of Independence. The tenth-oldest college in the country, Hampden-Sydney was formed with the guidance of such men as James Madison and Patrick Henry, who were members of the first Board of Trustees. The College was modeled after the Presbyterian College of New Jersey (now Princeton), and the same curriculum was chosen, except that at Hampden-Sydney there was to be a "greater emphasis upon the cultivation of the English language." Throughout its history, Hampden-Sydney College's mission has been "to form good men and good citizens."

Today, the College has a total enrollment of 996 students, representing thirty-four states and several other countries. Students enjoy a complete and diverse campus life, with an active student government and honor court. Interest clubs, literary organizations, and performing societies, as well as intellectual and social gatherings, enhance the extracurricular offerings. Hampden-Sydney's Union Philanthropic Society is the oldest active debate club in the country. Approximately 30 percent of the students belong to the twelve social fraternities. Eight varsity teams enjoy spirited NCAA Division III competition as members of the Old Dominion Athletic Conference, while club and intramural teams draw strong participation.

As a wholly undergraduate institution, Hampden-Sydney is committed to the belief that liberal education provides the best foundation not only for a professional career but also for the challenges of life. Nearly half of the graduating seniors enter graduate or professional school within five years. Basic to the College's program and success are the faculty members, 87 percent of whom hold earned doctorates in their fields. The student-faculty ratio is 12:1, and the average class size is 15 to 20. It is in this setting that the true value of the Hampden-Sydney education shines through. Students work closely with professors, learning to think critically and analytically, to assimilate and interpret information, and to express themselves cogently and coherently. Beyond the classroom, faculty-student relationships flourish as well. Faculty members and students jointly contribute to the community in a wide variety of service activities and share social and enrichment opportunities.

Hampden-Sydney faculty members are nationally recognized as inspired teachers and productive scholars in such diverse fields as NASA-sponsored gamma ray research, environmental economics, and cetacean (whale and dolphin) evolution.

Hampden-Sydney is fully accredited by the Southern Association of Colleges and Schools and is a member of the Association of Virginia Colleges, the Association of American Colleges, the Southern University Conference, the College Entrance Examination Board, the American Chemical Society, and the College Scholarship Service.

Location

Hampden-Sydney is an hour from Richmond, Charlottesville, and Lynchburg. Its stately Federal-style buildings have earned designation as a National Historic Preservation Zone. Southern Virginia's rolling countryside and temperate climate are delightful year-round and especially in the spring and fall. The College's rural setting and tree-studded campus provide miles of jogging and bicycling trails and excellent fishing. Hampden-Sydney has a picture-perfect 660-acre campus, with a wonderful feel of community.

Majors and Degrees

Students may choose one of twenty-six established majors, plus custom programs, which lead to the degree of Bachelor of Arts or Bachelor of Science: applied mathematics, biology, chemistry, classical studies, economics, economics and mathematics, English, fine arts, French, German, Greek, Greek and Latin, history, humanities, Latin, management economics, mathematics, mathematics and computer science, philosophy, physics, political science, psychology, religion, religion and philosophy, and Spanish.

Academic Program

The curriculum is divided into three principal areas of study: humanities, social sciences, and natural sciences (including mathematics). The study of the humanities allows students to gain an understanding of the intellectual and literary influences that have shaped culture. Exposure to the humanities also increases students' appreciation of the importance of ideas and expands their ability to communicate. Studying the social sciences gives insight into human behavior and institutions and is central to the liberal arts education. The world's increasing reliance on scientific and technological advances—and the practical and ethical problems that accompany them—makes a general understanding of natural science indispensable.

To ensure that individual programs are broadly based, students are required to study in each division. Students take at least two semesters of English composition and rhetoric and study a foreign language through the second-year level. The College requires that students complete 120 semester hours for graduation.

In addition to the curriculum offerings, students may profit from one of Hampden-Sydney's special academic options, such as the Honors Program, study-abroad program, or business internship programs. Students may take courses at six other private colleges in Virginia, pursue a public service concentration, study foreign policy in Washington, or engage in international studies at Oxford University. Faculty advisers help develop programs suited to individual interests.

Academic Facilities

Hampden-Sydney is committed to providing state-of-the-art facilities. The J. B. Fuqua Computing Center contains a variety of computer systems for student use. Students can access the campus network and the Internet with their own computers from their dormitory rooms or by using one of the computing laboratories located in Bagby Hall, Eggleston Library, Gilmer Hall, Morton Hall, and the Computing Center.

Eggleston Library is one of the College's most valuable academic resources; its collection was specifically selected to support Hampden-Sydney's liberal arts curriculum. Eggleston Library contains 220,172 volumes, 58,000 periodical titles, microform, and government documents arranged in open stacks or computerized for ease of use. Also located in Eggleston, the Fuqua International Communications Center houses the newest electronic equipment to support learning. It maintains a collection of more than 10,640 videodiscs, videotapes, compact discs, sound recordings, and computer software programs. Study carrels and viewing-listening rooms hold a variety of hardware for individual and group use. Two antennae for reception of satellite television broadcasts from around the Western Hemisphere add an international dimension to the center.

Costs

Tuition for the 1999–2000 academic year was $16,048. Room and board for the academic year averaged $5898. Other College fees (telecommunications, parking, and student activities) ranged between $600 and $1000. Books and miscellaneous expenses were estimated at $1500.

Financial Aid

Hampden-Sydney College offers financial aid to students who can make the most of the education that the College offers. Both academic achievement and promise, as well as financial need, are considered in the initial award of College funds. Similarly, financial aid for returning students is based upon both academic performance and demonstrated need. Approximately 87 percent of students receive financial aid based upon academic scholarship and need. The average need-based award of $12,600 consists of approximately 72 percent grant/scholarship funds. Financial aid in 1999–2000 totaled nearly $11.8 million, including all federal aid awarded.

Entering students who wish to be considered for financial aid must complete two forms—the Free Application for Federal Student Aid (FAFSA), which determines eligibility for federal programs, and the CSS PROFILE, which is used for consideration for College funds. These forms may be obtained from high school guidance offices or Hampden-Sydney and must be submitted between November 1 (for early decision) and March 1 of the senior year.

Faculty

Hampden-Sydney has 100 faculty members (62 full-time and 38 part-time). While the College places primary emphasis on teaching skills, faculty research is encouraged as an aid to improving the quality of teaching. Eighty-seven percent of faculty members have terminal degrees, and 90 percent are involved in academic advising. With more than 40 percent maintaining campus housing, faculty members are involved with students in a full range of academic, social, and recreational activities.

Student Government

Hampden-Sydney has a long tradition of student involvement in College affairs. Students serve as members of the faculty's Academic Affairs, Student Affairs, Lectures and Programs, and Athletic Committees. In addition, students are often named to various task forces, ad hoc committees, and search committees seeking key College officials. The Student Court, elected by classes, is the judicial arm of Student Government. The court tries cases arising from breaches of the Code of Student Conduct and Honor Code, assisted by a corps of student investigators and advisers. The College Activities Committee keeps an active calendar of events, planning dances, concerts, movies, and other activities for students.

Admission Requirements

Prospective students are expected to have mastered a solid, demanding college-preparatory program, including at least 4 units of English, 2 units of one foreign language, 3 units of mathematics, 2 units of natural science (one of which must be a laboratory course), and 1 unit of social science. In addition, a third unit of foreign language and a fourth unit of mathematics are recommended. Hampden-Sydney also considers SAT I or ACT scores and looks closely at recommendations from guidance counselors, teachers, and other people who know the applicant well. The records of successful applicants often include examples of impressive school and community extracurricular contributions in addition to their academic preparation.

There are two admission plans. If Hampden-Sydney is the student's first-choice college, he should apply under the early decision plan by November 15. The deadline for the regular decision program is March 1. Application forms are available on request from the Admissions Office. Hampden-Sydney also accepts the Common Application in lieu of its own form and gives equal consideration to both.

Students may apply electronically at the Hampden-Sydney World Wide Web site or on the CollegeLink and Apply! computerized application forms. Though not a requirement, the College encourages campus visits as the one true way to witness the spirit and community of Hampden-Sydney.

The College also welcomes armed service veterans and students who wish to transfer from another college or university. Students must be in good standing, with a C average or above.

Hampden-Sydney College, while exempted from Subpart C of the Title IX regulation with respect to its admissions and recruitment activities, does not discriminate on the basis of race, color, sex, religion, age, national origin, handicap, or veteran status in its educational programs and with respect to employment.

Application and Information

Completed applications for admission should be submitted to the Dean of Admissions before the noted deadlines for each admission plan. Notification for early decision candidates is mailed on December 15. Regular decision notification begins on March 1 and continues through April 15. The candidate's reply date is May 1.

All requests for information or application forms are welcomed and should be addressed to:

Dean of Admissions
Hampden-Sydney College
Hampden-Sydney, Virginia 23943
Telephone: 800-755-0733 (toll-free)
Fax: 804-223-6346
World Wide Web: http://www.hsc.edu

Hampden-Sydney's campus has 660 wooded acres. Near several big cities, the campus is quiet, safe, and busy, with lots of room in which to work and play.

HAMPSHIRE COLLEGE
AMHERST, MASSACHUSETTS

The College

Hampshire College was founded in 1965 through the cooperative efforts of educators at Amherst, Mount Holyoke, and Smith colleges and the University of Massachusetts. (These colleges comprise Five Colleges, Inc., one of the nation's oldest and most successful educational consortia.) The mandate of Hampshire College was to provide a model of innovative liberal arts education. Individualized programs of study, close collaboration between faculty members and students, multidisciplinary learning, and an emphasis on independent research and creative work have been the foundation of Hampshire's program since its opening in 1970. Today, more than 7,000 Hampshire alumni provide convincing evidence of the soundness of the founders' vision. Nearly a fifth of Hampshire's graduates have started their own businesses, while others are pursuing successful careers in medicine, law, education, publishing, finance, public service, and the arts.

Hampshire's 1,100 men and women students come from across the United States and from Europe, Africa, Asia, and Latin America. Despite their varied backgrounds and career aspirations, they share a spirit of open-mindedness and intellectual curiosity and a strong desire to take part in Hampshire's distinctive approach to education.

Hampshire's campus consists of 800 acres of orchards, forest, and open land. Five residential areas provide both dormitory and apartment-style accommodations, most with single rooms. The Robert Crown Center, Hampshire's main athletic facility, houses a swimming pool, a playing floor, a bouldering cave, a rock-climbing wall, and weight-training equipment. The Multisports Center includes four indoor tennis courts, a jogging track, a weight-training room, and a playing area for soccer, volleyball, and aerobics classes. The Outdoors/Recreational Athletics Program offers courses in a variety of athletic activities, provides support to students who wish to play informal team sports such as soccer, basketball, and softball, and sponsors frequent backpacking, rock-climbing, bicycle, and canoe trips. Students also organize and participate in about eighty-five varied social and cultural organizations on campus.

Location

Hampshire College is located in the Pioneer Valley of western Massachusetts, an area known for its pastoral beauty and its extraordinary educational and cultural offerings. The nearby towns of Amherst and Northampton offer shops, restaurants, and entertainment, and the Five Colleges sponsor concerts, film series, lectures, theater and dance performances, and gallery exhibitions throughout the year. The surrounding New England countryside provides year-round opportunities for outdoor recreation. Hampshire is located 2 hours from Boston and 3 hours from New York City by car or public transportation.

Majors and Degrees

Hampshire College confers the Bachelor of Arts degree on students who successfully complete an individualized program of study that is designed and carried out in close collaboration with faculty members. Areas of study are organized within three multidisciplinary schools: Humanities, Arts, and Cultural Studies (architecture and environmental design, art history, classics, comparative religion, critical theory, dance, digital imagery, film, history, journalism, literature, media and cultural studies, music, painting, philosophy, photography, and video), Natural Science (agriculture, alternative technology, biomedical science, botany, chemistry, environmental science, geology, human and molecular biology, mathematics, physical anthropology, physics, physiology, science education, science and public policy, and women's health); and Social Science (African-American studies, anthropology, Asian-American studies, economics, history, Latino studies, legal studies, political science, psychology, sociology, and urban geography). Two experimenting schools reflect the faculty's desire to collaborate in new ways. The School of Cognitive Science includes aspects of biology (animal behavior and cognition, animal communication, evolution of behavior and cognition, and functional neuroscience and neural network theory); communications (sociology of information technology and new media study and practice); computer science; philosophy of mind, language, and science; linguistics; and several areas of psychology (cognitive psychology, cognitive development, cognitive neuroscience, experimental psychology, physiological psychology, and psychology of language). The Interdisciplinary Arts School encourages students and faculty members to work within and across the boundaries of such art forms as sculpture, painting, theater, and writing and to explore the relationship between artistic production and social action.

Academic Program

Hampshire's distinctive academic structure offers every student the benefits of small classes, close contact with faculty members, individualized programs of study, and multidisciplinary learning. Students complete three divisions of study, rather than the traditional freshman–senior sequence. In Division I, Basic Studies, students explore their interests by taking courses and pursuing research or creative projects across Hampshire's schools. In Division II, the Concentration, they gain mastery of their chosen field through continued course work and independent study, internships, or study in other countries. Students are also expected to study some aspect of the Third World as part of their Division II work and to perform community service. In Division III, Advanced Studies, students complete a major academic or creative project—a written thesis, artistic exhibition or performance, or scientific experiment. Division III students are also required to participate in an interdisciplinary seminar with other advanced students or assist a faculty member in teaching a course.

Students at Hampshire receive extensive written evaluation of their work instead of traditional letter or number grades. Passage from one division to the next is marked by a final meeting in which a faculty committee reviews the student's activities and accomplishments. A transcript portfolio consisting of evaluations of course work and independent projects, as well as grades for Five College courses, provides a detailed record of the student's Hampshire education. The portfolio may also include letters of recommendation from faculty members and samples of the student's written work.

Off-Campus Arrangements

Hampshire students take courses and use the academic facilities at the other four schools of Five Colleges, Inc., at no extra cost; they regularly participate in theater and dance productions at the other colleges as well. A free bus system provides easy transportation among the five campuses.

The Five Colleges offer cooperative programs in African studies, astronomy, black studies, coastal and marine sciences, dance, East Asian languages, international relations, Latin American studies, Middle Eastern studies, Native American

Indian studies, peace and world security studies, and women's studies. Students have access to more than 8 million volumes in Five College libraries, and each year more than 6,000 courses are offered on the five campuses.

Academic Facilities

Hampshire's modern academic buildings provide superior facilities and equipment for a full range of intellectual and artistic activity. The Harold F. Johnson Library Center houses book and media collections, a computer laboratory, a fully equipped television production studio, and an art gallery. The Cole Science Center includes two floors of open laboratories with the most advanced chemistry instrumentation currently available in any undergraduate liberal arts college in the U.S. An attached 1,800-square-foot greenhouse supports research in aquaculture and energy use. The Longsworth Arts Village houses sophisticated film and photography facilities, art studios, and music and dance studios. In Emily Dickinson Hall, the Performing Arts Center includes two theaters. Franklin Patterson Hall contains classrooms, lecture halls, and faculty offices. Adele Simmons Hall houses a psychology research laboratory, a state-of-the-art video and film screening auditorium, computing facilities, and a digital design center. The Lemelson Fabrication Shop supports projects in innovation and applied problem solving. The Hampshire College Farm Center, a nationally recognized agricultural research and teaching facility, is located on 220 acres adjacent to the main campus.

Costs

In 2000–01, tuition is $25,709, room is $4331, board is $2483, the activities fee is $316, and the health service fee is $100.

Financial Aid

Hampshire has developed a generous financial aid program, which awards more than $9 million in grant aid annually. To be considered for an award, applicants must demonstrate financial need and submit all required materials by the stated deadline. Financial aid for international students is competitive, with maximum awards covering only up to tuition.

Approximately half of Hampshire's students receive financial aid with award packages that average about two thirds of Hampshire's total cost. Financial aid packages consist of income from on-campus employment (work-study), student loans, and grant assistance. In recent years, grant assistance has accounted for two thirds of the average aid package, and self-help funds (loans and employment) have made up the remaining third.

Hampshire also offers a merit scholarship program, consisting of several named scholarships designed to honor academic achievement, leadership, and a commitment to social concerns and the arts among students from all ethnic and socioeconomic backgrounds. Scholarships range from $2500 to $7500 per year over a four-year period.

Hampshire was the first college in the country to offer matching grants to students who have earned National Service Education Awards. Hampshire matches National Service Awards, spread over a four-year period. Students can receive up to $2365 per year from Hampshire.

Students wishing to apply for financial aid at Hampshire College must do so at the same time they apply for admission. Any student applying for financial aid must complete the Hampshire financial aid application, a PROFILE application, a Non-custodial Parent Statement (if applicable), and the Free Application for Federal Student Aid (FAFSA). Applicants register to receive a customized PROFILE application from the College Scholarship Service (CSS) and return the completed PROFILE application to them. The FAFSA and PROFILE registration forms are available from high school guidance offices. All financial aid information is considered strictly confidential by the College.

Faculty

Hampshire's faculty has 92 full-time members, 81 percent of whom hold Ph.D. or other terminal degrees, and 8 part-time members. They are accomplished scholars and artists whose primary commitment is to teaching and academic advising. The student-faculty ratio at Hampshire is 12:1.

Student Government

Students at Hampshire serve with faculty, administrators, and staff on all of the College's governing bodies. Seven students serve on the College Senate, which approves the curriculum, academic calendar, degree requirements, and academic standards. Seventeen students are elected to Community Council, which oversees the quality of student life and manages a large student activities budget. The Judicial Council, which interprets the Hampshire Constitution and considers cases involving infractions of College regulations, includes 3 student members. Hampshire is one of the few colleges where students play a central role in the promotion and reappointment of faculty members. As members of Hampshire's schools, they also help determine curricular development and academic policy. One student is elected every two years to serve on the Board of Trustees, and students sit on seven committees of the board.

Admission Requirements

Hampshire College seeks students who are willing to assume substantial responsibility for shaping their own education. Applicants are asked to submit a personal statement, a critical essay or an academic paper, and a detailed description of their interests and activities, in addition to academic transcripts and recommendations. Transfer students must also provide a general outline of the program of study they intend to pursue at Hampshire. Interviews are strongly recommended; students who live far from Massachusetts may arrange an interview with a local Hampshire representative by calling the admissions office. Hampshire does not require SAT I or other standardized test scores for admission. Applicants are expected to demonstrate strong academic achievement and the potential to undertake Hampshire's individualized educational program.

Application and Information

Applications for September admission are due February 1 for first-year students and March 1 for transfer students. Notification is mailed on April 1; accepted students must respond to Hampshire's offer of admission by May 1. International students, whether first-year or transfer, must apply by February 1.

Hampshire offers Early Decision and Early Action plans for first-year students only. The Early Decision application deadline is November 15, with notification on December 15. Early Action applications are due by January 1, with notification after January 21. While Early Decision candidates promise to attend Hampshire if admitted, Early Action candidates have until May 1 to notify Hampshire of their intention to enroll.

Spring term admission is available to first-year and transfer students. Students should apply by November 15, with notification to follow on December 15.

Under its Early Entrance plan, Hampshire admits a limited number of high school juniors who show exceptional academic and personal maturity. An interview is required.

For complete information and application materials, students should contact:

Director of Admissions
Hampshire College
Amherst, Massachusetts 01002-5001
Telephone: 413-559-5471
E-mail: admissions@hamp.hampshire.edu
World Wide Web: http://www.hampshire.edu

HAMPTON UNIVERSITY
HAMPTON, VIRGINIA

The University

Hampton University is a privately endowed, nonsectarian coeducational institution. Its population of almost 6,000 students comes from nearly every state and thirty-nine other countries and territories. The campus is one of the most picturesque in the South. Its 204 acres of waterfront property accommodate 155 buildings that include academic buildings, staff residences, and other structures. Founded in 1868, the University looks back on more than a century of outstanding contributions in higher education; it now has the buildings, the equipment, the faculty, and the administrative leadership to meet the challenges of its second century.

Challenge as a form of motivation is always present in a student's life at Hampton. Students' minds are stimulated and seasoned by contact with scholars, and their skills are sharpened by learning to use the most modern tools available anywhere.

The College of Continuing Education is a major academic unit of Hampton University. Its purpose is to provide instruction of high quality to the nontraditional student at the undergraduate and graduate levels, locally and at distant learning centers.

The programs of the Graduate College are designed to prepare students for professional competence in a specific field and for prospective graduate study. Graduate programs leading to the Master of Art (M.A.) degree are offered in biology, communicative sciences and disorders, counseling, elementary education, museum studies, and special education. The Graduate College also offers the Master of Science (M.S.) degree in applied mathematics, biology, chemistry, computer science, nursing, and physics; the Master of Business Administration (M.B.A.) degree; the Ph.D. degree in physics; and the Doctor of Physical Therapy (D.P.T.) degree.

Location

Hampton University is located in the Hampton Roads area of southern Virginia. The area's rich social heritage includes places and reminders of events that contributed to making our nation great. There are numerous opportunities for community involvement, and students are able to work on a voluntary or assigned credit basis on many of the problems in the surrounding community. Both faculty members and students participate in community planning and in ongoing community programs. The well-known annual Hampton Jazz Festival, which originated at and through the efforts of Hampton University, is now a community-wide event sponsored jointly by the city and the University. This marvelous musical experience, attended by thousands of patrons from around the world, annually revives and renews the best in the African-American cultural heritage.

Majors and Degrees

Bachelor of Arts (B.A.) and/or Bachelor of Science (B.S.) degrees are offered in the following majors: accounting, art, aviation (air traffic control, aviation computer science, electronic systems, flight education, and management), banking and finance, biology, business management, chemistry, communicative sciences and disorders, computer science, early childhood education, elementary education, engineering, engineering electronics/chemical engineering, English, entrepreneurial studies, finance, fine and performing arts, history, marketing, marine and environmental science, mass media arts, mathematics, middle school education, music engineering, nursing, physics, political science, professional tennis management, psychology, recreation, secondary education, sociology, and special education.

A Bachelor of Architecture degree is granted to those completing the five-year program in architecture.

The School of Pharmacy offers an innovative entry-level professional program leading to the Doctor of Pharmacy (Pharm.D.). The program requires six years for completion. The first two years consist of preprofessional pharmacy education followed by four years of professional pharmacy education. For additional information, students should contact the Office of the Associate Dean for Student and Academic Affairs, School of Pharmacy (757-727-5071).

The School of Science offers an entry-level Doctorate of Physical Therapy (D.P.T.) program to be completed in three years. The University has updated its plans for the D.P.T. program to meet the changes mandated by the American Physical Therapy Association requiring that the physical therapy degree be offered at the postbaccalaureate level by the year 2002. Therefore, all freshmen who are interested in pursuing a graduate degree in physical therapy must obtain a baccalaureate degree in another major while completing prerequisites for application to the doctorate program. Students who obtain undergraduate degrees at Hampton University will be given preference for admission to the Physical Therapy program. For more detailed information on the D.P.T. program, students should call 757-727-5260.

Academic Program

Requirements for receiving an undergraduate degree from Hampton University include completion of the following: a minimum of 120 semester hours with a cumulative grade point average of 2.0 or higher and a grade of no less than C in all courses in the major; courses in the general education sequence totaling 46–48 semester hours; and courses in the major field, related subjects, and free electives totaling at least 74 semester hours. The total number of semester hours required for the various majors differs from department to department. In each major program, students have a number of free electives. Students must be in residence the final 30 semester hours prior to the completion of degree requirements. English 101–102 and Speech 103 must be passed with a grade of at least C. Remedial or developmental work does not count toward graduation.

The University operates under a 4-4 academic calendar.

Off-Campus Arrangements

A cooperative work-study program is designed to tie together a student's education and his or her future employment.

Academic Facilities

Special research laboratories are available for faculty members and for advanced students in the natural sciences. The Peabody Collection in the main library is one of America's outstanding sources of information on African-American culture and history. The Hampton University computer center is available for research purposes to faculty members and advanced students.

In projecting Hampton into the twenty-first century, the Academic Technology Mall (ATM) has been established. The ATM is located on the fifth floor of the Harvey Library, housing sixty-one computers for use by students, the public, faculty members, and staff members. Funded by a grant from the Kellogg Foundation, the ATM is designed to acquire and integrate a wide variety of technology resources. The five components of the ATM are the resource management system, telecommunications, multimedia productions lab, foreign language laboratory, and electronic classroom.

Costs

The annual costs in the 1999–2000 academic year were $15,334 for on-campus students and $10,580 for off-campus students. Upon notification of acceptance, students must pay a $600 advance deposit fee.

Financial Aid

Students who are unable to meet the total cost of their college education may receive aid in the form of scholarships, grants-in-aid, loans, or part-time employment. Seventy-three percent of all Hampton students receive financial aid in amounts ranging from $500 to $14,518 per academic year.

Faculty

The members of the distinguished Hampton faculty come from the United States and from a number of countries around the world. The favorable faculty-student ratio permits a great deal of individualized instruction. The designers of Hampton's curriculums believe that living is learning and learning is living and that the learning process, as the Hampton faculty views it, must happen in the lives of the students.

Student Government

The Student Government, which is self-perpetuated by democratic student elections, is the recognized governing agency for the student body. The Student Government cooperates with the administration and faculty in the formulation of policies affecting the general welfare of the college, shares in the implementation of these policies, and works with all student organizations in stimulating student initiative and responsibility in campus affairs. Each year a student is democratically elected to serve as a representative to the Hampton University Board of Trustees.

Admission Requirements

A total of 17 Carnegie units of secondary school work are required for consideration as an applicant for admission (a unit represents a year's work in a subject-matter area). While the Committee on Admissions is more interested in the quality of the applicant's academic preparation and in his or her general promise as a college student than in the total number of such units offered, the core units must include 4 in English, 3 in mathematics (algebra 1, algebra 2, and geometry), 2 in science (biology and chemistry), 2 in social science, and 6 academic electives.

Hampton University requires that the student must have a cumulative grade point average of at least 2.0 in the core requirements. A combined SAT I score of 920 is required. Those students taking the ACT must have minimum scores of 20 on the English section and 20 on the math.

Transfer applicants must submit official transcripts of all previous college work and their secondary school report along with SAT I or ACT scores. In addition, transfer students must have a minimum of 15 hours of college credit along with a 2.3 cumulative grade point average. All credits earned must satisfy Hampton University's entrance requirements and must be equivalent to the general average at the institutions previously attended.

Application and Information

Applications, furnished by the director of admissions upon request, should be filled in completely and returned with the required nonrefundable application fee of $25 (money order made payable to Hampton University).

Applications for the fall term must be submitted by March 15; notification of the admission decision is made on a rolling basis. Applications for admission to the second semester should be completed by December 1. The applicant is expected to reply within thirty-five days after receiving a statement of acceptance. Students who have satisfactorily completed courses at an accredited institution may be admitted with such advanced standing as their previous records warrant.

An application form, additional information, and literature may be obtained by contacting:

Leonard M. Jones Jr.
Director of Admissions
Hampton University
Hampton, Virginia 23668
Telephone: 757-727-5328
    800-624-3328 (toll-free)
E-mail: admit@hamptonu.edu
World Wide Web: http://www.hamptonu.edu

The University chapel.

HANOVER COLLEGE
HANOVER, INDIANA

The College

Hanover College is a private, independent, undergraduate liberal arts college related to the Presbyterian Church (U.S.A.). A Hanover education offers more than academic knowledge. It encourages students to explore ideas and make their own decisions. A Hanover education is preparation for the future. It stimulates the development of personal responsibility and sound judgment.

Hanover succeeds by emphasizing timeless standards: a strong, traditional liberal arts education; a rigorous curriculum within the academic community; and an open forum for spirited, independent discussion of ideas. For more than 170 years, Hanover College has remained an institution with a firm sense of its identity, its purpose, and its mission.

Those looking for a close, friendly relationship between faculty members and students will find just that at Hanover. The campus is truly an academic community, with 95 percent of the students and 50 percent of the faculty members and their families residing on the College grounds. In this setting of open dialogue and respect, students find many informal opportunities to discuss class work, career goals, and subjects of mutual interest. Interaction is not restricted to the hours spent in classes. The average size of classes is less than 16. Students find plenty of opportunities at Hanover for open group discussion and the informal sharing of ideas.

Hanover is committed to the liberal arts in the finest sense and for good reason. The College understands that there is more to higher education than facts, tests, and grades. Today's careers demand that students not only possess a broad range of human knowledge but that they also know how to apply that knowledge logically and independently.

Hanover provides an educational kaleidoscope for creating future opportunities. Students learn highly sought, adaptable skills required in the field of their choosing. A liberal arts education prepares them to think critically and communicate effectively.

Location

Hanover College is located on 650 acres overlooking the Ohio River. The campus consists of beautifully landscaped grounds, with thirty-five major buildings designed in Georgian architecture. The town of Hanover is located in southeastern Indiana, a scenic area of natural beauty. Neighboring, historic Madison is minutes away; Louisville, 45 miles; Cincinnati, 70 miles; and Indianapolis, 95 miles from campus. Chicago, St. Louis, and Nashville are an easy day's drive from campus.

Majors and Degrees

The Bachelor of Arts degree is awarded in the following major fields of study: art, biology, business administration, chemistry, classical studies, communication, computer science, economics, elementary education, English, French, geology, German, history, international studies, Latin American studies, mathematics, Medieval-Renaissance studies, music, philosophy, physical education, physics, political science, psychology, sociology-anthropology, Spanish, theater, and theological studies. Teacher certification is available in both elementary and secondary education.

Academic Program

Hanover's academic program includes a 4-4-1 yearly calendar of four courses during each of the fall and winter terms (fourteen weeks each). One course on or off campus during the spring term (four weeks) gives students the opportunity for intensive study of a subject.

Hanover students earn the Bachelor of Arts degree. The Hanover faculty placed the College in the forefront of national curricular reform by adopting a new system of general degree requirements for students in 1992. The professors have ensured that the liberal arts core of an education at Hanover is both substantial and flexible, strong in fundamentals and full of opportunity for experimentation and innovation.

The faculty has also created a structure for multidisciplinary courses that allows students to complete two requirements with a single course. For example, a course in architecture jointly taught by an artist and a physicist might count toward the completion of the fine arts and natural science requirements. A course in Latin American social movements and literature jointly taught by faculty members in political science and Spanish might fulfill requirements both in literature and in cultures other than the West.

Major and minor programs provide students both breadth and depth of understanding within a given field. Majors culminate in either an internship, an independent study, or other form of directed or specialized study. All major programs prepare students for graduate studies. Preprofessional advising is available in dentistry, education, law, medicine, and other fields.

Off-Campus Arrangements

One aspect of Hanover's personal approach to education is the many specialized study opportunities that exist for students. Students are encouraged to apply to the College for funds granted from the Richter Trusts. These funds support study projects students have designed and planned. Projects are often undertaken during semester breaks or over the summer. These funds have allowed students to pursue specialized educational interests such as making stained-glass windows, building robots, studying koalas in Australia, and examining education in Soviet schools.

During the four-week spring term, many departments offer distinctive study programs. Students have studied Spanish in Spain and Latin America; Asian cultures in India and China; Dante in Florence, Italy; art, economics, and business in New York City; politics in Washington, D.C.; sociology at the East-West Center in Hawaii; theater in Canada and England; and international economics in Canada.

Exciting off-campus offerings include the junior-year-abroad program, the government-oriented Washington Semester Plan in cooperation with American University, and the Philadelphia Center Internship Program relating city and human interaction.

Hanover participates in a spring term consortium with seven other colleges and universities. Approved courses are taught on college campuses throughout the Midwest and East, as well as in Belgium, England, France, Italy, Greece, Germany, Spain, Mexico, and Canada.

Academic Facilities

The Multicultural Center, located in the heart of campus, serves the entire community as a support facility for students from other countries and for members of American minority groups. With its fully equipped kitchen, spacious lounge, and meeting and dining areas, the Center is ideal for dinners, lectures, studying, or getting together with friends. The student-operated center is open evenings and weekends.

The Writing Center and the Mathematics Center are housed adjacent to the DOS Laboratory in the Center for Fine Arts. These centers offer students tutorial assistance in writing and mathematics at every stage of their undergraduate careers.

Hanover has three Academic Computing Centers in addition to various departmental facilities. The PC lab is located in the Center for Fine Arts; the Mac lab can be found in the Computing Center. There are twenty-one pieces of equipment in each lab that are kept fully operational by the academic computing staff. Electronic mail accounts, in addition to modems, are available for dial-in access to the on-campus network and the Internet. Both labs are open evenings and weekends and are staffed by student lab assistants. The Academic Computing Centers offer training and support services for both students and faculty members.

Costs

Hanover's costs reflect its commitment to providing a high-quality education at a reasonable cost. Direct student expenses for a year at Hanover, including tuition, general fees, room, and board, are $16,700 for 2000–01. The most current cost information is always available from the Office of Admission.

Financial Aid

More than 70 percent of Hanover students receive some form of direct financial assistance. College aid is available in the form of scholarships, grants, loans, and campus employment. Every effort is made to meet all demonstrated need of every student. The College offers three types of competitive scholarships based on merit, regardless of financial need. All Hanover scholarships are awarded on the basis of financial need and/or academic merit.

Faculty

Hanover professors are accessible, dedicated, and knowledgeable. Nearly 90 percent hold a doctorate or other terminal degree. A third of the faculty members have been at the College for more than fourteen years.

The faculty members at Hanover want to teach. Though substantial scholars by any standards, they are not subjected to the "publish or perish" existence found on many campuses. To the contrary, Hanover's small-college experience offers one-on-one academic advising as an integral part of the student-faculty member relationship.

Student Government

Student Senate is the campuswide organization of student government. Through representative and advisory means, it provides input into the decision-making processes of the College. Student Senate promotes mutual cooperation among various campus constituencies in pursuit of its goals.

The Interfraternity Council and the Panhellenic Council are the governing bodies of the Greek social organizations at Hanover College. Composed of representatives of each fraternity and sorority, the councils promote a cooperative spirit and encourage mutual support among the organizations. They collectively serve the campus and wider community through activities and philanthropic projects.

Admission Requirements

To be considered for admission at Hanover, a prospective student must have the appropriate academic preparation and complete the required credentials by the dates listed below. The Admission Committee of Hanover College reserves the right to waive and/or alter requirements.

Students must graduate from an accredited secondary school and successfully complete a college-preparatory curriculum. The committee will consider applications from home-schooled students or others who have completed virtually all graduation requirements; an on-campus interview is always a requirement in such cases. The recommended curriculum for high school includes the following: English—4 units, with an emphasis on college-level writing; math—a minimum of algebra I and II and geometry (a fourth year of math is strongly recommended); science—2 units of laboratory science (a third unit is strongly recommended); foreign language—2 units of the same foreign language in consecutive years (a third unit is strongly recommended); social studies—2 units (3 units are recommended); and electives—a well-rounded selection, ideally including some units in the fine arts, religion, and philosophy.

Hanover accepts the SAT I or the ACT for admission purposes. Hanover will take the highest set of test scores; therefore, it may be advantageous to students to sit for these exams more than once. Standardized test scores are accepted directly from the test corporations or as a part of official transcripts mailed directly from the high school. SAT II: Subject Tests are not required but are considered if submitted.

Hanover offers two admission options, each with specific deadlines by which all required materials must be postmarked.

Early Action (nonbinding) admission candidates who have submitted completed application materials postmarked by December 1 are notified of their admission status by December 20, although some candidates may be deferred for later consideration. Students who are admitted through Early Action admission and who enroll by the May 1 National Reply Date receive priority consideration for housing assignments and class preregistration. The application for admission serves as the application for merit-based scholarships, including the prestigious Scholarships for Merit Competition. Those who qualify to apply for the merit competition must submit all admission materials postmarked by January 15.

Regular admission candidates who submit completed application materials after December 1 are notified of their admission status on a rolling basis, beginning January 20 and ending when the freshman class is full. Applications received after the March 1 application deadline are considered on a space-available basis only.

Application and Information

For more information, students should contact:

Office of Admission
Hanover College
P.O. Box 108
Hanover, Indiana 47243-0108

Telephone: 800-213-2178 (toll-free)
Fax: 812-866-2164
TDD: 812-866-7047
E-mail: admissions@hanover.edu
World Wide Web: http://www.hanover.edu

Brown Memorial Chapel is a landmark on the Hanover campus and is one of thirty-five buildings designed in classic Georgian-style architecture that contribute to Hanover's reputation as one of the most beautiful campuses in the country.

HARDING UNIVERSITY
SEARCY, ARKANSAS

The University

Harding University is known for its outstanding liberal arts program and for its training of leaders. Students attend from nearly every state in the Union and about forty countries. Affiliated with the Church of Christ, Harding is a selective-admission university with a total enrollment of 4,415.

Harding University was established as a senior college in 1924 when two junior colleges, Arkansas Christian College and Harper College, merged to form Harding College. Originally founded in Morrilton, Arkansas, the school moved to its present Searcy campus in 1934. Harding officially became Harding University in 1979 in order to better serve its constituency.

Harding has six divisions: the College of Arts and Humanities, the College of Bible and Religion, the College of Sciences, the School of Business, the School of Education, and the School of Nursing. Students can select from more than seventy undergraduate majors. The Master of Business Administration, Master of Education, Master of Science in Education, and Master of Science in Nursing are awarded. In addition, there are a number of graduate degree programs offered at Harding Graduate School of Religion located in Memphis, Tennessee. Many of the more than 30,000 alumni have pursued careers throughout the world.

Harding University is a member of the NCAA Division II. Men compete in baseball, basketball, cross-country, football, golf, soccer, tennis, and track. Women's teams compete in basketball, cross-country, soccer, track, and volleyball. The University also has an excellent intramural program that involves a large number of students.

Most students live in campus housing. The University has thirteen residence halls and several apartment complexes for student use. An application for housing should be filed when the student applies for admission.

Location

Harding is located in Searcy, Arkansas, a town of nearly 20,000. The small-town setting allows students to enjoy the beauty of the Ozark Mountains while being only 50 miles northeast of Metropolitan Little Rock, the state capital, and within 100 miles of Memphis. Camping, canoeing, backpacking, cycling, and a host of outdoor activities are available to Harding students. The Buffalo River, Greer's Ferry Lake, and Blanchard Springs Caverns are all located within a short driving distance of the campus. Proximity to Little Rock and Memphis allows students to enjoy the cultural and social activities associated with these cities.

Majors and Degrees

Harding University awards the Bachelor of Arts, Bachelor of Business Administration, Bachelor of Fine Arts, Bachelor of Music Education, Bachelor of Science, Bachelor of Science in Medical Technology, Bachelor of Science in Nursing, and Bachelor of Social Work. Majors are offered in the following fields: accounting, advertising, advertising art, American studies, art, athletic training, Bible and religion, biblical languages, biochemistry, biology, business education, ceramics, chemistry, child development, communication, communication disorders, communications management, computer science, computer information systems, criminal justice, dietetics, economics, education (elementary, kindergarten, secondary, and special), English, family and consumer science, fashion merchandising, food merchandising, French, general science, health-care management, history, home economics, human resources, interior design, international business, international studies, journalism, management, marketing, mass communication, mathematics, mathematics education, missions, music (voice and string instrument), music education (instrumental and voice/choral), nursing, office systems, oral communication, painting, physical education, physics, political science, professional sales, psychology, public administration, public relations, radio and television, religious education, social science, social work, sociology, Spanish, sports management, theater, and theater management.

Academic Program

Harding's academic year is composed of two semesters, an optional thirteen-day intersession following the spring semester, and two optional five-week summer sessions. The University grants college credit for Advanced Placement courses successfully completed with an examination score of 3 or higher. A maximum of 32 semester hours can be earned on the basis of the scores reported in the College-Level Examination Program. An honors program admits students by invitation. Harding has an Early Entrance Program for students who have not finished high school and who meet stated criteria.

Each student is assigned an academic adviser to help plan an individualized program of study. In order to graduate, 128 credit hours are required, including a core of general education courses.

Off-Campus Arrangements

Harding offers four outstanding study-abroad programs. Harding University–Florence gives students a chance to spend a semester in Europe. The University owns a sixteenth-century villa near Florence, Italy, that serves as the students' headquarters. Harding University–Greece is located in the seaside resort town of Glyfada just 45 minutes from Athens. This program focuses on the culture of Greece, Turkey, and Israel. Harding University–England is located in the Hyde Park area of London. Harding University–Australia is the most recent addition to the study-abroad program. It is located in Brisbane. All four programs set aside ample time for travel, which allows students the opportunity to acquire a world vision in the course of their academic studies.

Academic Facilities

Brackett Library is at the center of the academic training available to Harding students. With more than 487,000 volumes and 1,330 periodicals, the recently renovated library gives students immediate access to vast research sources. The campus has forty-seven buildings strategically placed on a beautiful 200-acre campus. These include the J. E. and L. E. Mabee Business Center, which houses the School of Business faculty and provides classrooms equipped with color video monitors; the John Mabee American Heritage Center, designed as a continuing education complex with an auditorium, a hotel that can accommodate 150 visitors, and facilities for seminars, workshops, and conventions; and the George S. Benson Auditorium, which seats 3,539 and provides additional classroom space. There are three computer laboratories with extensive equipment available for student use.

Costs

Tuition and fees for the 2000–01 school year are $8425 per year, based on a course load of 30 semester hours. Room and board cost $4438 per academic year. The total for the school year is $12,863.

Financial Aid

Approximately 80 percent of the students at Harding University receive some form of financial aid. Harding tries to meet all its students' demonstrated need. The College accepts the Free Application for Federal Student Aid (FAFSA).

Academic scholarships are given to students who show outstanding promise. Various departments award departmental scholarships to students who show a particular aptitude for a given subject.

Students may qualify for loans, grants, and work-study programs by submitting the FAFSA to the Harding University Financial Services Office. Upon filing this form, a student is considered for all the federal financial aid programs. It is recommended that a student apply for financial aid as soon as possible after January 1 and before May 1.

Faculty

The student-faculty ratio is 18:1. No graduate students teach any undergraduate courses. On staff there are more than 200 full-time faculty members, with approximately 75 percent holding earned doctorates or terminal degrees.

Student Government

The student government at Harding University is called the Student Association. Officers are elected each year to represent the student body. Class representatives are also selected to serve the interests of their respective classes. Various committees help to involve students in all aspects of student life and community service.

Admission Requirements

The Office of Admissions Services reviews several criteria in the selection of applicants. All students must submit the application with a fee of $25, a housing form with a housing confirmation fee of $125, official transcripts, official ACT or SAT I scores, and an educational reference and a character reference. All academic and personal qualifications are considered in granting admission.

Application and Information

Students should apply soon after the completion of the junior year of high school. Although the deadline for applications is May 1, all admission materials should be submitted early because of the limited number of places in the freshman class. To arrange a campus tour or to receive additional information, students should contact:

Office of Admissions Services
Harding University
Station A, Box 12255
Searcy, Arkansas 72149
Telephone: 501-279-4407
              800-477-4407 (toll-free)
Fax: 501-279-4865
E-mail: admissions@harding.edu

The administration building on the campus of Harding University.

HARRINGTON INSTITUTE OF INTERIOR DESIGN
CHICAGO, ILLINOIS

The Institute

Harrington Institute is dedicated exclusively to professional education in interior design. It is a private, coeducational, urban college that enrolls 525 students. Since its founding in 1931, the Institute has consistently advanced its position to become internationally recognized for the quality of the education it offers and the success of its graduates.

The Institute is recognized by the Illinois Board of Higher Education as a private college authorized to award the Bachelor of Fine Arts in interior design and Associate of Technology in interior design degrees. The Institute is accredited by the National Association of Schools of Art and Design (NASAD). The Day Division bachelor's degree program is accredited by the Foundation for Interior Design Education Research (FIDER), the nationally recognized accrediting agency for interior design. The Institute is also authorized under federal law to enroll international (alien nonimmigrant) students.

The Institute attracts and maintains a diversified student body, which consists of high school graduates and transfer students who are preparing to begin a career, working adults who want to move ahead in the field or make a career change, and returning adults whose education was interrupted or postponed earlier in life. The student body reflects a rich variety of backgrounds and generates a spirit that is lively, collaborative, and informal. Although competition to excel is keen, individual talents, unique strengths, and creativity are respected. Opportunities for personal and professional growth, development, and advancement are plentiful. Students need bring only the initiative and determination to succeed.

The American Society of Interior Designers (ASID) sponsors a student chapter at the Institute, which offers students opportunities to meet practicing professionals and gain a firsthand understanding of professional standards and practices. Harrington Institute students are frequent award winners in national competitions sponsored by ASID, the Institute of Store Planners, and the Institute of Business Designers.

The Institute maintains a placement service that has an outstanding record in assisting graduating students and alumni to find rewarding positions in the profession.

Location

Harrington Institute's location in the heart of Chicago, a world center of design, is of inestimable value. Students have access to important designers' resources at the Chicago Merchandise Mart to supplement their studies. Its showroom galleries, exhibiting the best of contemporary furnishings, textiles, and accessories of every description, are a magnet for designers from around the world. The Chicago School of Architecture is internationally famous, and students have daily contact with its finest examples, from landmark architecture to the most dynamic of twentieth-century design. The downtown Loop is a living museum of public art. Works of art by Picasso, Calder, Matisse, Bertioia, Chagall, and Miró further enrich the student's design experience. Libraries, galleries, museums, theaters, the Chicago Symphony Orchestra, and the Lyric Opera are within easy walking distance, and the proximity of the campus to Grant Park, Buckingham Fountain, and Lake Michigan enhances its atmosphere of beauty and tradition.

Majors and Degrees

Harrington Institute of Interior Design offers a full-time program leading to either the Bachelor of Fine Arts in Interior Design or the Associate of Technology in Interior Design degree. The Institute also offers an Associate of Applied Science in Interior Design and a Professional Diploma of Interior Design through a part-time evening program.

Academic Program

The exclusive mission of Harrington Institute is professional education in interior design, serving students who seek career preparation. The goal of the Institute's curriculum is to produce practicing interior designers who are proficient in residential, commercial, and institutional design. Because successful practice is grounded in sound theory, instruction at Harrington Institute strives for balance between content and method, knowledge and skills, creativity and discipline, problem solving and decision making. Each course in the curriculum articulates with other courses in an intensive, structured, comprehensive, and integrated program of studies.

Classwork combines conventional methods of presentation, such as lecture, discussion, and audiovisuals, with studio courses in which a critic-instructor guides students through a problem-solving process of experimentation and exploration of alternative solutions to a wide variety of design problems. Field trips and guest lecturers augment classwork to take maximum advantage of Chicago's renowned architecture and interior design resources. Computer-aided drafting (CAD) courses prepare students to generate graphic displays of design projects through hands-on computer training.

As the profession of interior design evolves, so does the Harrington Institute curriculum. It continues to undergo regular reevaluation to ensure the continuation of its reputation for high quality education.

The bachelor's degree is awarded upon completion of 123 semester hours of credit, 30 of which are earned in liberal arts and general education courses. The Associate of Technology degree program requires six semesters of full-time study and 93 semester hours of credit. The Associate of Applied Science degree is awarded upon completion of 64 credit hours, including 21 in liberal arts and general education courses. The Professional Diploma of Interior Design requires 43 semester hours of credit earned over six semesters of part-time study.

Off-Campus Arrangements

Harrington Institute's full-time upperclassmen students may apply to participate in an annual spring term student exchange program conducted for credit with the Department of Interior Architecture of the Rotterdam College of Design in the Netherlands. The program has stimulated the exchange of ideas and interest in different approaches to interior design for students of both countries and has proved to be of great benefit to participating students.

Academic Facilities

The Institute's specially designed facilities, spreading over five floors of the historic Fine Arts Building, add a special flavor to the student's experience. An architectural landmark and center of artistic tradition in Chicago, the building offers well-lighted, spacious studio classrooms overlooking Grant Park, Buckingham Fountain, and Lake Michigan. Facilities also include the Design Library, computer lab, photography lab/darkroom, design workshop, and auditorium as well as staff and faculty offices, a student lounge, a school store, and display areas for student work.

The Design Library's continually expanding collections consist of more than 22,000 volumes and 23,000 slides, which support every aspect of the curriculum. The library subscribes to ninety international and domestic professional journals, magazines, and indexes in interior design, architecture, and art. Four full-time professional librarians and staff members serve students, faculty, and alumni on an extended schedule. The library also houses the Products Library of current catalogs, product information, color and fabric samples, and tile and laminate samples from more than 3,000 manufacturers. Use of this collection of resources is integral to interior design studio course projects. The library holds memberships in ILLINET/OCLC and the Chicago Library System, which enable staff to search and borrow nationwide, via computer, from the holdings of almost 5,000 libraries containing 14 million volumes.

Costs

Tuition and fees per semester for the 1999–2000 academic year were $5738 in the full-time Day Division and $2689 in the part-time Evening Division. Students should budget an estimated $350 for textbooks and materials per academic year and an estimated $550 for the initial purchase of equipment and textbooks. A monthly tuition payment plan is available.

Financial Aid

In 1999–2000, more than 60 percent of the full-time student body received loans and grants to help them meet the costs of education. Harrington Institute administers these funds through the Federal Pell Grant, Federal Stafford Student Loan, and Federal PLUS loan programs as well as the privately funded Excel Student Loan program. International students are not eligible for financial aid or for part-time employment. Students should contact the director of financial aid for application materials.

Faculty

The Harrington Institute faculty is composed of more than 50 experienced educators, each of whom is also a professional interior designer, architect, space planner, artist, or technician. Because of the Institute's Chicago location, prominent practitioners who might otherwise be unavailable are able to serve on the faculty while continuing professional practice. The resulting mix of professional and academic involvement is one of Harrington's most valuable assets. Each faculty member is knowledgeable about his or her own specialization as well as its relationship to the total profession. Together, the faculty demonstrates an exceptional ability to motivate students to acquire and refine the knowledge and skills they will need to function as competent professionals.

Student Government

The Harrington Institute Student Council consists of elected representatives who serve to facilitate communication with the administration and to sponsor professional and social events.

Admission Requirements

The Institute maintains a selective admission policy and encourages students with creative aptitude to apply. No previous training in art or design is required because the program assumes progression from beginner to advanced and professional proficiency. A high school diploma or its equivalent is a prerequisite for admission. As part of the admission procedure, each applicant participates in a personal interview. Early application is advised.

Credits of transfer students are accepted as the courses apply to the Harrington Institute curricula. A grade of C or better is required for consideration as transfer credit. A portfolio must be presented prior to the beginning of the semester for each studio course for which transfer credit is requested.

International students are advised to complete admission procedures far enough in advance of the expected date of enrollment to fulfill all requirements. They must demonstrate proficiency in English by presenting an acceptable score on the Test of English as a Foreign Language (TOEFL). They must also provide certified English translations of official transcripts of credit.

Application and Information

To apply, each prospective student must submit a completed application for admission, official transcripts of high school or college credits, and a $50 application fee.

To receive a college catalog and an application for admission, students should contact:

Director of Admissions
Fine Arts Building
Harrington Institute of Interior Design
410 South Michigan Avenue
Chicago, Illinois 60605-1496
Telephone: 877-939-4975 (toll-free)
Fax: 312-939-8005
E-mail: hiid@interiordesign.edu

Small classes provide students with individual faculty attention.

HARTFORD COLLEGE FOR WOMEN
of the University of Hartford
HARTFORD, CONNECTICUT

The College

Hartford College for Women (HCW) is at the forefront of women's education as it prepares the leaders of tomorrow.

Since its founding in 1933, Hartford College for Women has been dedicated to raising the aspirations of women and equipping those women with the skills and the confidence they need to turn their aspirations into achievements. It is no accident, then, that Hartford College for Women was established during the Great Depression, when more than 1,500 schools and colleges across the United States had closed their doors.

At a time when many young women found they couldn't afford to go to college, two progressive leaders of the YWCA, Blanche Babcock and Bess Graham, set out to make a college education available to young women in the Hartford area. With the help of Mary Wooley, president of Mount Holyoke College, they opened what was originally called "Mount Holyoke in Hartford."

Six years later, the school received its own charter, and Hartford College for Women was born. Dedicated to meeting the ever-changing educational needs of women of all ages and backgrounds, HCW has a sixty-year reputation for exceptional faculty members, small classes, individualized attention, and commitment to the success of every student.

Today, Hartford College for Women offers its students more opportunities for growth than ever before. In 1991, Hartford College for Women became part of the University of Hartford, one of the finest comprehensive universities in the eastern United States. HCW offers its students the unique combination of classes on a small, intimate campus with the comprehensive academic, social, and recreational resources of a large coeducational university. HCW students are eligible to take courses on the main University campus, participate in all academic support resources and extracurricular social and cultural activities, and have access to a fully equipped sports center. The 320-acre main University campus is located just 1½ miles from the HCW campus, and frequent shuttle service is available.

The students who are enrolled at HCW come from many diverse backgrounds and cultures.

Single-sex housing for University of Hartford female students is available on the HCW campus, with two choices for living arrangements. The town-house residences provide housing for the students in adjoining apartment-style units. Each house has four or five private bedrooms, two bathrooms, a living room, and a furnished kitchen/dining area. The town houses are built around a common courtyard and are connected to the central campus by a wooden footbridge. Johnson House serves as a residence for 18 students. The house includes kitchen and laundry facilities, a student TV room, the Office of the Resident Director, and students' mailboxes.

HCW is accredited by the State of Connecticut to award the two-year associate degree and the four-year bachelor's degree.

Location

The campus is located at the intersection of Asylum Avenue and Elizabeth Street in Hartford's historic West End. The triangular 13-acre campus, which is listed on the National Register of Historic Places and has been described as one of the most beautiful in New England, combines the gracious architecture of the early 1900s with contemporary classrooms, a science center, a library, computer facilities, and dining services. Just minutes away are all the social and cultural activities of Hartford: the professional Hartford Stage Company, the Bushnell Memorial Hall (which hosts traveling Broadway shows as well as performances by the Hartford Symphony and Connecticut Opera), the Wadsworth Atheneum, and many other entertainment options. The campus is just hours away from popular East Coast destinations, such as New York City, Boston, New England's ski resorts, and the Atlantic seaboard. The University of Hartford is only 1½ miles away, and HCW is linked to the main campus by shuttle-bus service. Hartford College for Women shares fully in the academic resources, sports facilities, cultural events, and social activities of the University of Hartford, while maintaining its own activities and programs that support women.

Majors and Degrees

Academic Express is an innovative redesign of the HCW curriculum from a conventional 14-week semester system into 7-week term courses offered in the evenings and on weekends year-round. It is an accelerated program for both full- and part-time students pursuing liberal arts, women's studies, and legal studies. Advising, registration, counseling, financial aid, library, and student life services are available to students during the evenings and on weekends. It is the only evening/weekend program of its kind in the area for women who want single-gender education and offers the same excellent teaching and personal attention that HCW is known for in a format and schedule geared to the motivated, mature student of both traditional and nontraditional age. By attending classes only two nights per week, or one night and one Saturday morning, a student can obtain an A.A. or A.S. degree in two years or a B.A. or B.S. degree in four years.

At the core of the College is its dedication to a quality liberal arts Associate in Arts degree program. In this program, women can begin a major in many different areas, including business, literature, mathematics, the natural and social sciences, and philosophy. Qualified students who receive an associate's degree from HCW are eligible to transfer to a four-year program at one of the University of Hartford's eight other nationally recognized schools and colleges.

The legal studies program offers bachelor's and associate degrees and a certificate for students interested in a career as a paralegal. All three courses of study are accredited by the American Bar Association.

Women's studies is an interdisciplinary major offered jointly by HCW and the College of Arts and Sciences of the University of Hartford. The Bachelor of Arts degree is embedded in a rich array of courses that focus on women's contributions to culture and society as well as the historical and social impact of gender, race, and class.

Academic Program

HCW students develop the skills that are valued in today's workplace and that are necessary to live and work in the twenty-first century, including critical thinking, problem solving, oral and written communication, leadership, and team building.

To qualify for the Associate in Arts degree, a student must attain a minimum grade point average of 2.0 with at least 60 credits in academic courses, in order to provide a wide distribution of academic experience. For the bachelor's degree, a student must attain a minimum grade point average of 2.0 with at least 120 credits.

The college education necessary to prepare students for today's rapidly changing world demands more than "book learning." Students need real connections to career and business opportunities. A wide range of internships that are designed to complement course work provide work-based learning opportunities to acquire career advancement skills in the public, private, and nonprofit sectors.

Academic Facilities

The College offers ongoing academic counseling through the faculty advisers.

Student Support Services is composed of multifaceted educational support programming designed to assist students in completing their academic course work. This full range of alternative educational delivery systems emphasizes the development of independent and lifelong learning skills. Emphasis is placed on providing support at the individual level.

Academic Assessment and Placement Services provide initial academic placement testing and advising for all new HCW students and assure that students are placed appropriately in academic courses.

HCW students are encouraged to use the Academic Support Services on the main campus of the University of Hartford. These services include the Center for Reading and Writing; Peer Tutoring through the Student Government Association; the Math, Physics, and Computer Science Tutoring Laboratory; and the Chemistry Tutoring Laboratory. Information concerning Academic Support Services is posted in the Bess Graham Library on the HCW campus and on student bulletin boards. Students who seek additional help in arranging tutoring can contact the librarian.

Personal computers in the Resource Center of the library link the campus to the electronic library system at Mortensen Library on the main campus of the University of Hartford. This system provides HCW students with up-to-date research tools, including the online catalog for both libraries, a variety of citation and full-text databases, and Internet access. These computers are also available for word processing.

Costs

The Academic Express program costs $345 per credit hour; most courses are 3 credits.

Financial Aid

HCW is very sensitive to the financial commitment families make in providing for the expenses associated with undergraduate education and welcomes the opportunity to counsel students and their families about financial assistance policies and procedures.

Cooperative efforts between the University and a student's family may resolve what may appear to be financial obstacles. Students applying for financial assistance must complete the appropriate information on the application for admission.

The Free Application for Federal Student Aid (FAFSA) must be filed in order for a student to be considered for all need-based aid. In addition to the above procedures, transfer students must submit copies of financial aid transcripts from each institution previously attended, whether or not the student has received financial aid.

Faculty

To facilitate close interaction between the faculty members and students, HCW keeps its student-faculty ratio to a low 8:1. Class sizes are small, with an average of 11 students and a range of 6–25 students per class. There are 7 full-time and 47 part-time faculty members. In recent years, 5 of the instructors named Connecticut Professor of the Year have been members of the University of Hartford teaching faculty, including a professor at HCW. This statewide recognition is only one indication of the extraordinary academic credentials, coupled with personal dedication, found among the HCW and University faculties in all disciplines. HCW students are never a number or a face in a crowded classroom. The HCW faculty is committed to providing the education and guidance students need to achieve their goals, no matter what their age, background, or aspirations.

Student Government

Students are actively involved in and concerned with the affairs of the College. They are regularly invited to informal discussions on academic and extracurricular matters. The student body is also represented on various College committees, and students are involved in making important decisions that affect the entire student body and College community. All students have the opportunity to participate in the governance of the student body.

Admission Requirements

As classes begin every seven weeks, HCW operates on a rolling admission basis. Applications for admission are considered on a weekly basis. Applicants should arrange to have official high school or college transcripts sent to HCW. School profiles, including an explanation of grading, ranking, and course levels, are also helpful. Students are encouraged to supplement application credentials by submitting a personal statement, a resume, and recommendations and by scheduling an interview. A $35 nonrefundable fee must accompany the application for admission.

Transfer students who have completed 24 semester hours of transferable college work are not required to submit admission test scores or a high school transcript. It is the responsibility of the student to ensure that transcripts from all postsecondary institutions of higher education are forwarded directly from the institution to the Admissions Office, whether or not transfer credit is desired.

Application and Information

To find out more about Hartford College for Women, or to apply, students should contact:

Annette Rogers, Director of Admissions
Hartford College for Women
1265 Asylum Avenue
Hartford, Connecticut 06105-2299
Telephone: 860-768-5600
           800-582-6118 (toll-free)
E-mail: hcwinfo@mail.hartford.edu

HARTWICK COLLEGE
ONEONTA, NEW YORK

The College

Hartwick College, a private college located in the northern foothills of the Catskill Mountain region of New York State, was founded in 1797 as the first Lutheran seminary in America. Hartwick became a four-year coeducational liberal arts and sciences college under its present charter in 1928. The current enrollment is 1,444 students (685 men and 759 women).

Approximately 62 percent of Hartwick's students come from New York State, and about 38 percent come from elsewhere in the Northeast or from outside the Northeast. The student body represents thirty-four states and twenty-five countries. The majority of students live on campus and eat together in the College Commons. Residence halls are coeducational by floor or wing. Adjoining the campus are four special interest houses. As an alternative to downtown living, the College has twenty self-contained town houses on campus that house 80 students. Each two-story unit has one double and two single bedrooms, two baths, a living room, a study area, and a kitchen. About 75 students live in the five fraternity and four sorority houses. Other off-campus housing includes facilities at the Pine Lake environmental campus.

There are more than sixty student clubs and organizations on campus. A variety of social and cultural events, including special weekends, are offered throughout the academic year.

More than three quarters of the students participate in recreational, intramural, or intercollegiate sports. Hartwick is well known for its NCAA Division I soccer program, and the College has exciting prospects for its new NCAA Division I women's water polo team. Women's soccer and field hockey and men's and women's basketball, lacrosse, and swimming are also successful programs.

The Trustee Center for Professional Development begins working with first-year students in developing career goals. One innovative program offered by the center is the Guaranteed Placement Program. If, after completing a checklist of activities and cocurricular experiences while maintaining a 3.0 grade point average, a student does not have a job within six months of graduation from Hartwick, the College's Board of Trustees guarantees the student a paid internship in his or her chosen field. The center also coordinates Metrolink, an award-winning program that connects students with Hartwick alumni and parents for shadow experiences and career advice. Metrolink is conducted in New York City, Boston, and Washington, D.C.

Location

The city of Oneonta, with a population of 14,000, is a college town. Hartwick College and the State University of New York College at Oneonta are located in the city. Students have access to the libraries on both campuses, and cross-registration for courses is also possible. Hartwick College is an integral part of the Oneonta community, and many area residents share in campus activities. Oneonta has a variety of shops, restaurants, and theaters. Many cultural and recreational resources exist in the city and throughout the area, including the Catskill Symphony Orchestra, the Catskill Choral Society, the Orpheus Theatre, several ski centers, city and state parks, golf courses, tennis courts, and lakes. Oneonta is also home to the National Soccer Hall of Fame and is near Cooperstown, the site of the Baseball Hall of Fame.

Majors and Degrees

Hartwick students may select courses from thirty areas offered by nineteen departments, they may pursue independent study or create an individual student program, or they may take advantage of numerous special study options on and off campus available through Hartwick and cooperating educational institutions. Hartwick awards the B.S. degree in accounting, biochemistry, chemistry, computer science, information science, medical technology, music education, and nursing. It awards the B.A. degree in anthropology, art, art history, biology, chemistry, economics, English, French, geology, German, history, management, mathematics, music, philosophy, philosophy/religious studies, physics, political science, psychology, religious studies, sociology, Spanish, and theater arts. An accelerated B.A./B.S. option is available.

Preprofessional programs in engineering are offered in cooperation with Clarkson University and with Columbia University School of Engineering and Applied Science. In these programs, a student spends three years at Hartwick and two at the other institution, earning a B.A. from Hartwick and a B.S. from the cooperating university. Hartwick also participates in a cooperative 4+1 M.B.A./M.S. program with Clarkson University and a 3-3 cooperative law program with Albany Law School. Nursing students, upon graduation, are qualified to take the New York State Board Examination for licensure as registered professional nurses. Students graduating with a medical technology major are qualified to take the National Registry Examination for the professional certification MT (ASCP).

Academic Program

Several years ago, Hartwick College launched an academic program called Curriculum XXI. The result of careful study and planning by the faculty, this program redefines the basic elements of a college education. Its starting point is the simple fact that those who are entering college now will spend much of their lives and nearly all of their productive careers in the twenty-first century. Its requirements include courses in history, literature, social and behavioral analysis, non-Western culture, science, and mathematics—courses that provide a variety of ways of learning about humanity and nature, a grounding in our cultural heritage, and a knowledge of other cultures. A second element of Curriculum XXI involves in-depth study in a major program and a baccalaureate thesis in the major field. Seminars that emphasize student involvement are a third element of the curriculum. A first-year seminar introduces the tradition of liberal education through the critical examination and analysis of a fundamental dilemma or problem. A contemporary issues seminar, taken in the junior or senior year, offers an interdisciplinary exploration of a contemporary issue and demonstrates how liberally educated people can responsibly address complex problems. The faculty and staff at Hartwick assist students in identifying and achieving their goals through instruction, advice, guidance, and example. Independent study, directed study, internships, and off-campus programs are integral parts of the curriculum for many students. Writing competence is required for graduation.

Hartwick offers both advanced placement and credit for scores of 3 or better on the Advanced Placement tests (4 or 5 in the Departments of French and Music). Advanced placement for credit is also offered through the College-Level Examination Program (CLEP) to students who have acquired mastery of a subject in ways other than the traditional classroom experience.

The College has a 4-1-4 calendar, consisting of two 15-week terms and one 4-week term in January.

Off-Campus Arrangements

Hartwick offers numerous opportunities for off-campus study. In 1999–2000, students participated in semester-long programs in Hawaii, New York, Massachusetts, Colorado; Argentina and Colombia; Ireland, Italy, England, Austria, Spain, and the Netherlands; India; Kenya; Queensland, Australia; and Chiapas, Mexico. January Term programs were scheduled for South Africa; Banaras; Thailand; Austria, England, France, Greece, Ireland, and Spain; the Bahamas, Costa Rica, Cuba, and Guatemala; and New York City, Hawaii, the Grand Canyon, and the Florida Keys. Independent study and year-abroad programs are also available. By participating in the College's Early Experience Program, Hartwick first-year students have opportunities to study abroad during the January term.

Academic Facilities

The Anderson Center for the Arts is an attractive and highly functional building that houses facilities for the fine arts. The complex includes studios and classrooms, soundproof practice rooms, a theater, and the Foreman Gallery. Yager Hall houses the College's 284,000-volume library, the Yager Museum, the College archives, classrooms, a computing lab, and laboratory and office space. The Yager Collection contains more than 6,000 American Indian artifacts covering a period of 10,000 years. It has been described as one of the largest and most important collections of its kind in New York State. Arnold and Bresee Halls contain several classrooms, faculty and administrative offices, and a small theater. Recently constructed Clark Hall is home to computer and information sciences, English, the writing center, math, foreign languages, psychology, and the College's Media Center. The Binder Physical Education Center provides facilities for recreation, physical education classes, intramurals, and club and intercollegiate sports, in addition to a fitness center. The Miller Hall of Science provides offices, classrooms, and laboratory facilities for the study of the physical and life sciences. Special features include a tissue-culture laboratory, electron microscopes, a greenhouse, a herbarium, and an extensive shell collection. The building is undergoing a $12-million addition and renovation that will provide shared spaces for cross-disciplinary teaching and research. The Ernest B. Wright 16-inch Telescope and Observatory is located on the western edge of the campus. In addition, the Pine Lake environmental campus, a 918-acre site 8 miles from the main campus, serves as an important resource for environmental study as well as for recreation.

Costs

Tuition for 1999–2000 was $23,745, room was $3175, board was $3165, and student fees were $325. The estimated cost of books, personal expenses, and transportation was $1200.

Financial Aid

Hartwick College grants financial aid on the basis of both academic merit and financial need. Scholarships based on merit are awarded to prospective students, including transfers, and are based upon outstanding academic achievement and leadership in high school and/or college. The average amount of a financial aid award to first-year students is nearly $17,000. Approximately 75 percent of Hartwick students receive some form of aid.

Aid based on financial need is offered in the form of grants, scholarships, student loans, and part-time employment. Aid offered through grants that do not have to be repaid includes Hartwick College grants-in-aid, College-sponsored scholarships, Federal Pell Grants, and Federal Supplemental Educational Opportunity Grants. Loan programs include the Federal Nursing Student Loan, Federal Perkins Loan, and Federal Stafford Student Loan programs. Other sources of financial aid include state grants and scholarships, Vocational Rehabilitation Grants, and New York State Tuition Assistance Program awards.

A Hartwick College Conversion Loan is available to the families of first-year students. The interest rate is variable, to be paid while in college, with repayment of the loan commencing three months after graduation. If a student finishes the first year with a minimum 2.5 cumulative grade point average, one half of the loan will be converted to a grant for the second year.

Students requesting financial aid must file a Hartwick College financial aid application with the College, accompanied by a copy of their parents' federal income tax return and W-2 statement. They must also submit the Free Application for Federal Student Aid (FAFSA). The deadline is February 15. All forms should be mailed by mid-January. Approximately 75 percent of Hartwick's new students receive financial aid. Some work opportunities are also available for students not receiving financial aid.

Faculty

The Hartwick faculty is a teaching faculty, with principal responsibilities and commitments to students in the classroom. Faculty members serve as student advisers, share committee assignments with students and staff members, and act as advisers to various student organizations. The student-faculty ratio is 12:1. Ninety-four percent of the faculty members hold the Ph.D. or other terminal degrees.

Student Government

The Student Senate serves as the central voice of the student body and carries out executive and legislative functions of the Hartwick College student government. Students share responsibilities with faculty, administrators, and trustees on a number of committees established by the faculty and Board of Trustees, as well as on the Judicial Board and the College Traffic Court.

Admission Requirements

Hartwick College seeks secondary school graduates who demonstrate academic competence and show evidence of being able to benefit from, and take full advantage of, the living and learning experience at Hartwick. Applicants are evaluated not only on class rank and test scores but also on personal qualities, activities, special talents, and recommendations. Applicants are required to submit a secondary school transcript, an essay, and two recommendations. Transfer students must submit official transcripts of work at other institutions, a secondary school transcript, and a letter of recommendation from an official of the college previously attended. On-campus interviews and scores on the SAT I or ACT are strongly recommended for all applicants but are not required.

Application and Information

Applications for regular admission must be filed by February 15 in the year of expected college entrance in the fall. Requests for early decision may be made up to January 15 of the year of entrance. Admission decisions for early decision are made within two weeks after the complete application is on file. Other candidates for fall admission are notified on or about March 15. A nonrefundable fee of $35 must accompany the application. The College accepts the Common Application and online applications (on the College's Web page).

Prospective students may obtain application forms and additional information by contacting:

Susan Dileno
Dean of Admissions
Hartwick College
Oneonta, New York 13820
Telephone: 607-431-4150
      888-HARTWICK (toll-free)
E-mail: admissions@hartwick.edu
World Wide Web: http://www.hartwick.edu

HARVARD UNIVERSITY
Harvard College
CAMBRIDGE, MASSACHUSETTS

The University

Harvard University includes Harvard College and the following graduate and professional schools: the Graduate School of Arts and Sciences, the Business School, the Design School, the Divinity School, the School of Education, the John F. Kennedy School of Government, the Law School, and the Schools of Dental Medicine, Medicine, and Public Health.

The residential plan for undergraduate students is an essential part of the Harvard experience. Every student is assured a place in College housing for four years. Freshmen live in one of the several dormitories in Harvard Yard, the oldest and most central part of the campus. At the end of the freshman year, students move into residential Houses in which they will live for the remainder of their undergraduate careers. The House system provides a smaller community for students within the larger University environment. Each House has a resident senior faculty member who is called the master, a senior tutor or dean, a tutorial staff, a library, and dining facilities. All Houses are coeducational, and much of the social, athletic, extracurricular, and academic life centers on the House.

Harvard offers more than 250 student organizations. Some groups are long-established, such as the Hasty Pudding Club and Phillips Brooks House; others reflect the changing interests, attitudes, and politics of the times. Students find organized activities in dance, drama, government, journalism, music, religion, social service, visual arts, and a variety of other special interest areas.

The Department of Athletics offers forty-one intercollegiate sports programs for men and women—more than any other college in the country. In addition, there is a comprehensive system of intramural and recreational sports. The extensive athletic facilities include six basketball courts, forty squash courts, two swimming pools, and forty-eight tennis courts. Also available are facilities for aerobics, baseball, fencing, football, hockey, lacrosse, martial arts, racquetball, rowing, soccer, track, water polo, weight lifting, and wrestling. Houses have their own intramural teams, and there are sports clubs run by students.

Location

Harvard College is located in Cambridge, a city on the banks of the Charles River, across from Boston. Metropolitan Boston is a pleasant mixture of New England culture and urban vitality. Both Boston and Cambridge enjoy a history of tradition and innovation, as illustrated by their concert halls, libraries and bookstores, museums, theaters, coffeehouses, shops, and sports arenas. The cultural and recreational opportunities are countless and easily accessible. Beaches and mountains are both conveniently near.

Majors and Degrees

Harvard offers more than forty areas in which an undergraduate may specialize. Some of these fields of concentration are Afro–American studies, anthropology, applied mathematics, astronomy, biochemical sciences, biology, chemistry, classics, computer science, East Asian studies, economics, engineering and applied sciences, English, environmental science and public policy, fine arts, folklore and mythology, geological sciences, Germanic languages and literatures, government, history, history and literature, history and science, linguistics, literature, mathematics, music, Near Eastern languages and literatures, philosophy, physics, psychology, religion, Romance languages and literatures, Sanskrit and Indian studies, Slavic languages and literatures, social studies, sociology, statistics, visual and environmental studies, and women's studies. Within fields, there are various options for specialization, and it is possible to combine major fields or to devise special concentrations. Almost all undergraduates pursue an A.B. degree (only the engineering and applied sciences concentration offers an S.B. degree program).

Academic Program

Harvard's goal is to provide students with the freedom to design individual academic programs within the structure of a broadly based liberal arts curriculum. Students must complete at least thirty-two 1-semester courses during their four years, chosen from the 3,000 courses available in the humanities, social sciences, and natural sciences. A one-semester course in expository writing is required of all freshmen.

At the end of the freshman year, students choose a field of concentration. During the next three years, they take a minimum of twelve 1-semester courses chosen from that field and related fields. Except in a few fields, sophomores are assigned a tutor within their chosen field of concentration. The tutorial group meets weekly to investigate assigned topics or areas of special interest. Juniors and seniors may elect to pursue tutorials on an individual basis, thus enabling them to study an issue in depth. The culmination of the tutorial program is the senior thesis. Cross-registration in other faculties of Harvard University and with the Massachusetts Institute of Technology is also available.

The Core Curriculum courses are specially designed to fulfill students' requirements outside of their fields of concentration. Eight 1-semester courses are required, chosen from seven areas of intellectual inquiry: literature and arts, historical study, social analysis, moral reasoning, science, foreign cultures, and quantitative reasoning. This core program gives students an appreciation of disciplines other than their chosen concentration. Before graduation, students are also required to demonstrate proficiency in a foreign language and competence in certain areas of data analysis.

Freshmen who have earned a score of 4 or 5 on each of four or more College Board Advanced Placement examinations may be eligible for sophomore standing. Students who accept sophomore standing may complete requirements and receive an A.B. degree in three years or remain a fourth year to pursue further academic interests.

Each year, about one quarter of the freshmen elect to participate in the Freshman Seminar Program. The seminar format is designed for those freshmen who are eager to work independently or within small groups on special topics, under the guidance of a professor well known in his or her field.

Off-Campus Arrangements

A large number of students receive credit each year for work done away from the Harvard campus under the auspices of a variety of programs that are sponsored by foreign and American universities. Undergraduates interested in study-abroad programs are counseled on an individual basis about program applications, academic credit, and financial assistance.

Courses (including ROTC programs) are also available through the Massachusetts Institute of Technology.

Academic Facilities

The University library system consists of the Harvard College Library and the libraries of the graduate and professional schools. Together these libraries house more than 13 million volumes, constituting the largest university library collection in the world.

The University Museum includes the Peabody Museum of Archaeology and Ethnology, the Botanical Museum, the Museum of Comparative Zoology, and the Mineralogical Museum. The Fogg and Sackler museums house a collection of paintings, drawings, and sculpture. Contemporary exhibits are featured regularly at the Carpenter Center for Visual Arts. The Loeb Drama Center seats 500 in the auditorium and houses a small experimental theater.

More than a dozen buildings are used exclusively for the classrooms, laboratories, and museums of the natural sciences. There are microcomputers available for use in the science center and all residence halls. All student rooms have Internet network access.

Costs

Costs for 2000–01 are tuition and fees, $25,128, and room and board, $7982. Estimated personal expenses, books, supplies, and similar costs are $2290; travel expenses vary.

Financial Aid

All financial aid awards at Harvard College are based on need. Approximately two thirds of the undergraduates receive some form of financial assistance. Financial aid is provided in the form of scholarships, loans, and term-time employment. Family income and a number of other factors are considered in determining need. Admissions decisions are need blind. Any students who feel they may need financial assistance are encouraged to apply. Financial aid applicants are required to submit the CSS PROFILE, the FAFSA, and copies of their family's tax returns by February 1. Applicants are usually notified of their aid awards at the same time they are notified of the admission decision.

Faculty

Harvard's faculty is an outstanding group of scholars, teachers, and researchers. The Faculty of Arts and Sciences consists of about 700 full-time members, all of whom hold the highest degree in their fields; they may be assisted by teaching fellows who are doctoral candidates. In a typical course, a faculty member teaches a group of about 25 students. Course enrollments may range from 50 to 500 or more students, but many of the courses with the largest enrollments are taught entirely in small sections of about 20. In contrast, the great majority of classes are taught with very small enrollments, and the tutorial system provides individual instruction. Because teaching and scholarship are both highly valued at Harvard, a freshman may well be taught by a Nobel Prize winner or a distinguished scholar.

Student Government

A freshman may participate in the Freshman Council. Representatives are elected from each dormitory in Harvard Yard. A freshman may also participate in the Undergraduate Council, the main student government organization. Upperclass men and women who reside in the Houses elect members for their respective House committees as well as for the Undergraduate Council, the Committee on Housing and Undergraduate Life, and the Committee on Undergraduate Education.

Admission Requirements

Undergraduates come from every state and nearly 100 countries. Over 18,000 applicants from both public and private schools compete for 1,650 places in the freshman class. The Admissions Committee seeks a diverse group of students who are intellectually capable, socially aware, and mature. The committee considers not only academic achievement but also students' extracurricular talents and potential for contributing to the Harvard community.

Applicants should present a high school transcript, two letters of recommendation, scores on the SAT I (or the ACT) and any three SAT II: Subject Tests, and scores on the TOEFL if English is not their first language. They must also submit a series of personal essays and, if at all possible, meet with an alumnus or alumna for an interview in their local area. The credentials of all applicants are considered in depth, and full attention is given to each candidate's particular strengths and abilities as well as personal qualities.

Application and Information

Students may apply to Harvard College under the early or regular action programs. Final application deadlines are November 1 and January 1, respectively; however, the preferred deadline for early action is October 15 and for regular action is December 15. Early action decision letters are mailed in early December. Applicants who are deferred in the early action process are automatically considered in the regular action process. Regular action decision letters are mailed in early April. Students who apply to transfer into the sophomore or junior year should submit their applications by the preferred deadline of February 1, if at all possible. They may express a preference to enter in the fall or the spring. The College also accepts a few visiting students each fall and spring from well-qualified candidates who are currently matriculated at another college and wish to spend a term studying at Harvard. Requests for application forms should be directed to:

Harvard College Office of Admissions
Byerly Hall
8 Garden Street
Cambridge, Massachusetts 02138
Telephone: 617-495-1551 (for freshman admissions)
617-495-9707 (for transfer and visiting student admissions)
E-mail: college@fas.harvard.edu
World Wide Web: http://www.college.harvard.edu

HARVEY MUDD COLLEGE
CLAREMONT, CALIFORNIA

The College

Harvey Mudd College was founded in 1955. Its mission is to educate undergraduate men and women in a rigorous academic environment, focusing on mathematics, science, and engineering, and also to provide a rich background in the humanities and social sciences. The faculty members are eminent, experienced professionals—humanists who are aware of technological needs and engineers and scientists who have an abiding faith in liberal learning. Small classes, the excellent faculty, and exceptional students create a setting that is conducive to both teaching and learning. An attitude of mutual trust prevails in all aspects of campus life and is amplified by a spirit of cooperation among students and faculty members and encouraged by the student-directed honor code. Harvey Mudd students deal daily with high standards, demanding course loads, and intense pressure, but in an atmosphere void of intimidation and unreasonable competition. The current undergraduate enrollment is 184 women and 511 men. In addition to the advantages that all small colleges share, Harvey Mudd has the advantage of being a part of the Claremont Colleges system, which has a total enrollment of approximately 5,000. Students in the Claremont Colleges share many opportunities in course offerings, facilities, and extracurricular activities. The cluster of adjacent colleges also offers a well-integrated social life and a rich intellectual atmosphere, supported by lectures, concerts, dramatic productions, seminars, colloquia, and festivals. Harvey Mudd has a joint program of intercollegiate and intramural athletics, physical education, and recreation with Claremont McKenna and Scripps colleges. The varsity athletic teams compete in the Southern California Intercollegiate Athletic Conference. Varsity teams compete in basketball, cross-country, soccer, swimming, tennis, track, and water polo, plus men's baseball, football, and golf and women's volleyball. Intramural teams are fielded in basketball, flag football, floor hockey, inner-tube water polo, soccer, softball, and volleyball. The culmination of the intramural season is a weekend playoff tournament, known as the Mudd Bowl. There are also club sports and recreational activities indigenous to the terrain and climate of the region. There is an active sailing club with a 30-foot racing sloop, located at Newport Harbor, and two other sailboats. Campus activities include the student newspaper, the *Compass;* the Claremont College Players, a dramatics group; the Forensic Society; the Symphony Orchestra; departmental organizations; religious activities; a stage band; a jazz band; a brass ensemble; the yearbook; two radio stations; and political clubs. The seven residence halls tend to be the center of social life on campus. All halls are coed and house students of all class levels. Freshmen are required to live on campus, and 97 percent of all students typically reside on campus.

Upon graduation, about 50 percent of Harvey Mudd's students enter graduate school at some of the nation's most prestigious universities. Virtually all of these students receive fellowships and assistantships. In a typical year, twice as many corporate recruiters visit the campus as there are seniors seeking employment, and it is not uncommon for seniors to have between ten and fifteen job interviews. More than 40 percent of Harvey Mudd alumni hold Ph.D.'s, the highest percentage in the country.

The Master of Engineering degree and the Master of Arts degree in mathematics are awarded jointly by Harvey Mudd and the Claremont Graduate University to Harvey Mudd alumni who complete a fifth-year program of study.

Location

The town of Claremont is located at the base of Mount Baldy. It takes 30 minutes to get to the ski slopes and 45 minutes to an hour to get to the Pacific Coast beaches, the desert, and the center of Los Angeles, where unlimited social, sports, and cultural activities are available. The town is served by the Ontario International Airport, a 15-minute drive away. With a population of 37,000, Claremont is known throughout southern California for its active support of educational and cultural programs. Adjacent to the Claremont Colleges is Claremont Village, a friendly community featuring sidewalk cafés, specialty shops, tree-lined streets, and Victorian homes. The weather in Claremont is warm and dry, with mild winters.

Majors and Degrees

The Bachelor of Science degree is awarded in biology, chemistry, computer science, engineering (nonspecialized), mathematics, physics, a joint major in computer science and mathematics, an off-campus major (at another one of the Claremont Colleges), and IPS (individual program of study). An IPS degree may be built around the College's programs and other interdisciplinary fields.

Academic Program

The College is an autonomous member of a much larger center of learning, the Claremont Colleges. Cross-registration at the other six Claremont Colleges (Claremont Graduate University, Claremont McKenna, Keck Graduate Institute, Pitzer, Pomona, and Scripps) is encouraged. Thus, students may experience the best that each Claremont College has to offer.

Harvey Mudd students devote one third of their study to a common technical core curriculum in mathematics, physics, chemistry, biology, computing, and engineering design. Another third of the course work is devoted to the humanities and the social sciences, an emphasis that is unsurpassed by any accredited engineering college in the nation. The final third of the work is taken in the student's major, which is not declared until the middle of the sophomore year. The College uses a High Pass/Pass/No Credit grading system in the first semester of the freshman year.

Unique in higher education, Harvey Mudd's Clinic Programs expose advanced students to real, unsolved problems that require them to investigate alternatives, exercise judgment, and put into practice what they have learned. Clinic teams usually consist of 4 juniors and seniors. They work under the direction of a student leader, a faculty member, and a liaison from a sponsoring company and are responsible for conducting the work, monitoring the project's progress, managing a budget, and following it through to satisfactory completion. This hands-on experience has created numerous summer and full-time employment opportunities for students. More than thirty-five corporations participate in the Clinics annually.

A broad range of undergraduate research opportunities is available in theoretical and experimental sciences and mathematics, and all students must carry out research or clinic projects for at least one year. It is not uncommon for undergraduate students at Harvey Mudd to author or coauthor scientific papers that are published in national journals.

Academic Facilities

Classroom and laboratory facilities are modern and extensive and are available 24 hours a day. The academic buildings are within a 5-minute walk of all other facilities on campus. Central in both function and location is the Sprague Library, which houses more than 60,000 bound reference works and 6,800 periodicals in engineering, mathematics, and science. A computerized catalog system gives Harvey Mudd students immediate online access to all the holdings of both the Harvey

Mudd library and the Seeley Mudd Science Library at Pomona College. Altogether, Harvey Mudd students have open-stack access to more than 1.9 million volumes in the library system of the seven Claremont Colleges.

The College has a distributed model of computing, with some resources located centrally, but with specialized resources distributed to the various academic departments. The central facilities include SPARC and UltraSPARC systems manufactured by Sun Microsystems running UNIX; VAX and Alpha systems manufactured by Digital Equipment Corporation running VMS; and file servers running Novell NetWare. Also available centrally are three public access laboratories housing more than fifty Apple PowerMacintoshes and DELL Pentium personal computers. In addition, each of the academic departments has computing facilities, the three largest belonging to the computer science, engineering, and mathematics departments. Computer science's resources include a multiprocessor Sun SPARC 1000 and Sun UltraSPARC 3000 servers, two ATM switches, and clusters of SGI Indigo 2 and Sun SPARC workstations of various vintages. All are accessible from a local cluster of color X terminals as well as the campus network. The Engineering Computing Facility, which is part of the Engineering Design Center, includes a cluster of Hewlett-Packard workstations and Hewlett-Packard Pentium personal computers. The mathematics department also has an HP workstation-based facility and a lab of DEC VMS workstations. There are numerous other personal computers and workstations in the labs around the College. All resources are attached directly to the campus network. Although this is done mostly via Ethernet or fast Ethernet, some of the major resources are attached directly to the combination ATM and FDDI backbone. Running through a fiber cable plant, the network includes all the student residence halls and all academic and administrative buildings. It is also connected to the central library, the other Claremont campuses, and the national and international Internet. From their rooms, through a direct twisted-pair Ethernet connection, students can access any of these resources in addition to databases in the library, software on servers, compute cycles on supercomputers, and archives of public domain software, and they can send electronic mail and surf the Web. They can even create their own resources, such as a Web server, and attach it to the Net for others to access.

Physics laboratory facilities support student instruction and experimental research in astronomy, electronics, optics, condensed matter, low-temperature physics, atomic physics, nuclear physics, geophysics, and biophysics. Nearby Table Mountain Observatory is available for astronomy observation. Chemistry research in the areas of synthetic and physical chemistry, organic and inorganic chemistry, biochemistry, crystallography, and liquid crystals is supported by extensive research instrumentation. Biology facilities include apparatus for molecular biology, neurobiology, artificial intelligence, and robotics.

Costs

The total expenses for the 1999–2000 academic year were tuition, $21,584; fees, $499; room, $4077; and board, $3940 (nineteen-meal plan). The total cost was $30,100. Travel costs are additional, and an estimated $1700 should be allowed for personal expenses and books.

Financial Aid

About 80 percent of the students at Harvey Mudd receive some type of financial aid. Scholarships and loans are awarded on the basis of financial need. All students are expected to contribute a portion of their summer earnings toward the cost of attending HMC. On-campus jobs are available; however, freshmen are discouraged from working during their first semester. Harvey Mudd sponsors National Merit Scholarships, and one third of the current freshman class are Merit Scholars. All aid applicants must file the Free Application for Federal Student Aid (FAFSA) and the College Scholarship Service (CSS) Financial Aid PROFILE. California residents applying for aid must also apply for the Cal Grant.

Faculty

Harvey Mudd's student-faculty ratio is 9:1. All courses, laboratories, and recitation sessions are taught by full-time faculty members with a Ph.D. Excellence in teaching is the primary criterion for the reappointment and promotion of faculty members, but most members are also actively involved with students in research. Professors are accessible, and close relationships are formed between students and faculty mentors.

Student Government

Elected officers participate in the Associated Students of Harvey Mudd College Council. The Student Affairs Committee coordinates most extracurricular and social activities in conjunction with the Dorm Affairs Committee. The student Judicial Board interprets the College's constitution and enforces the honor code. More than 10 percent of the student body is involved in some form of student government.

Admission Requirements

Admission is highly competitive. For fall 1999, 1,642 applicants applied for admission to a freshman class limited to approximately 175 students. The most important aspects of a candidate's application are the courses that were taken and the grades that were earned in secondary school. To be competitive for admission, candidates must excel in a rigorous college-preparatory program, with a heavy emphasis on mathematics and science. Students interested in attending Harvey Mudd must take at least 1 year each of chemistry and physics. A year of high school calculus or its college equivalent is required. Even though the major thrust of Harvey Mudd's program is in mathematics and science, particular attention is focused on a student's proven talents in English and communication skills. Typical candidates have taken several Advanced Placement (AP) or even college-level courses; however, candidates who have not had the opportunity to take honors, accelerated, or AP courses are given every consideration and should not hesitate to apply. Scores on the SAT I and three SAT II: Subject Tests are required for admission. Two of these SAT II tests must be Writing and Mathematics Level IIC. Because Harvey Mudd desires a multidimensional student body, serious consideration is given to an applicant's extracurricular and leadership activities. Interviews are not required, but a personal interview is strongly recommended and can influence a final decision. Teacher and counselor recommendations are essential to the admission decision.

Of the entering freshmen in 1999–2000, 41 percent were from California. Twenty-nine percent were National Merit Scholars and 24 percent ranked first in his or her high school class. Students who scored in the middle 50 percent (from the 25th percentile to the 75th percentile) on the SAT I achieved verbal scores from 660 to 770 and math scores from 730 to 800; Subject Test scores in the middle 50 percent ranged from 650 to 760 in Writing and from 730 to 800 in Mathematics Level IIC.

Application and Information

Early decision candidates must complete their application by November 15; notification is mailed by December 15. The deadline for receipt of regular applications is January 15. Applicants for regular decision are notified April 1.

Deren Finks
Dean of Admission and Financial Aid
Harvey Mudd College
Claremont, California 91711

Telephone: 909-621-8011
E-mail: admission@hmc.edu

HAVERFORD COLLEGE
HAVERFORD, PENNSYLVANIA

The College
Haverford is the first college established by members of the Society of Friends (Quakers). Founded in 1833, Haverford has chosen to remain small, undergraduate, and residential to carry out its educational philosophy and to maintain a strong sense of community. An Honor Code is created and directed by students and is an important element of the Haverford community. The Honor Code allows students to directly confront academic and social issues in a spirit of cooperation and mutual respect.

Haverford's 1,100 students represent forty-five states, Puerto Rico, the District of Columbia, and twenty countries. Nineteen percent of the students are students of color, while an additional 4 percent are international students.

Haverford is a residential campus with 98 percent of the students and 70 percent of the faculty living on campus. Students may also choose to live at nearby Bryn Mawr College. Housing on Haverford's campus is single-sex or coed, and residence halls vary in accommodations from 4-person apartments to suites and singles. Other choices of residence facilities include the Ira De A. Reid House (Black Cultural Center), La Casa Hispanica, and an environmental house.

Haverford's athletic teams participate in Division III of the NCAA. Intercollegiate sports include baseball, basketball, cricket, cross-country, fencing, field hockey, lacrosse, soccer, softball, squash, tennis, track and field, volleyball, and wrestling. Haverford also sponsors several junior varsity, club, and intramural sports teams. Athletic facilities include the Alumni Field House and Ryan Gymnasium.

Location
The College is located 10 miles (16 kilometers) west of Center City Philadelphia on a wooded campus of 204 acres. Haverford's proximity to the fifth-largest city in the United States allows its students to take advantage of the many social, cultural, and educational resources that this historic area offers. Extensive public transportation allows students easy access to the city and environs.

Majors and Degrees
Majors leading to a B.A. or B.S. degree are offered in twenty-nine departments: anthropology, archaeology, astronomy, biology, chemistry, classics, comparative literature, East Asian studies, economics, English, fine arts, French, geology, German, growth and structure of cities, history, history of art, Italian, mathematics, music, philosophy, physics, political science, psychology, religion, Romance languages, Russian, sociology, and Spanish. Students may minor, arrange an interdepartmental or double major, or design an individual major. Twenty-five to 30 percent of the students major in the sciences or mathematics, 30–35 percent in the social sciences, and 35–40 percent in the humanities. Approximately 15 percent have double, interdepartmental, or special majors. A 3-2 engineering program is offered with the University of Pennsylvania.

Further areas of study, called concentrations, include Africana studies, biochemistry and biophysics, computer science, East Asian studies, educational studies, feminist and gender studies, Latin American and Iberian studies, mathematical economics, neural and behavioral science, and peace studies. Secondary school teacher certification can be arranged in conjunction with several major subjects; additional course work and practice teaching are required.

Academic Program
Students plan their programs using established guidelines and with the help of faculty advisers. They must have at least three courses in each of the divisions of the College: humanities, social science, and natural science. In addition, they must fulfill requirements in foreign language, social justice, writing, and quantitative course work. Flexibility in the curriculum allows opportunities for independent study, foreign study, and noncollegiate academic study. Majors are selected at the end of the sophomore year. Normally, students take four courses per semester and thirty-two courses over four years. Scheduling is flexible, however, and students may arrange programs to meet individual needs, including six-semester, seven-semester, and five-year programs. Credit is given on the basis of Advanced Placement (AP) examinations, A-Level examinations, and International Baccalaureate Higher Level examinations.

One of Haverford's distinctive features is its extensive academic and social cooperation with Bryn Mawr College. Students may take courses or major at either school, live on either campus, and eat on either campus. There are more than 3,500 cross-registrations annually. Extracurricular activities, such as a weekly newspaper, a drama club, a radio station, an orchestra, social action groups, and intramural sports, operate jointly. A free bus service between the two campuses, which are a mile apart, facilitates cooperative arrangements. Haverford and Bryn Mawr also share library resources with nearby Swarthmore College. All three college libraries are linked electronically, and students have instant access to library resources through the campus computer network. Combined holdings are in excess of 1.5 million volumes.

Off-Campus Arrangements
Haverford students may take advantage of the course offerings at Swarthmore College and the University of Pennsylvania in addition to courses at Bryn Mawr. Students may also enhance their college experiences by arranging study abroad in forty-five programs overseas or study away at Claremont McKenna, Fisk, Spelman, or Pitzer colleges.

Academic Facilities
Major facilities include the James P. Magill Library (445,000 volumes), computer centers, Stokes Hall for the physical sciences, Sharpless Hall for biology and psychology, the Strawbridge Observatory for astronomy, the Music Center, Gest Center for Cross-Cultural Study of Religion, the Fine Arts Center, Marshall Auditorium, and the Language Learning Center. Academic buildings and dormitories are linked by a campuswide computer network.

Costs
The total approximate costs for 2000–01 are $33,000 for new students and $32,850 for returning students. This consists of $24,706 for tuition, $7910 for room and board, and a student association fee of $234. New students have a one-time orientation fee of $150.

Financial Aid

The College has an extensive financial aid program. Approximately 38 percent of Haverford's students receive College grant aid. Candidates for Haverford College funded aid must file the Financial Aid PROFILE with the College Scholarship Service, along with the FAFSA. Applicants may register for the PROFILE by completing a short form, available from their local high school guidance office, and sending it to the College Scholarship Service. Regular decision students should complete the PROFILE registration process by January 2, so the College Scholarship Service can send the form and have students complete it by the January 31 deadline. The FAFSA is also available from high school guidance offices and must also be filed by January 31. Early decision candidates should complete the PROFILE registration process by October 15 and file the PROFILE form with the College Scholarship Service by November 15.

Further details are given in the leaflet "Financial Aid at Haverford," which is included in the admission application booklet. Haverford's College Scholarship Service PROFILE code number is 2289, and the FAFSA code number is 003274.

Faculty

The student-faculty ratio is 10:1. The faculty devotes its full teaching time to undergraduates. There are no graduate assistants. The regular faculty is supplemented by 90 to 100 scholars, artists, and public figures who visit the College annually under the auspices of seven specially endowed funds.

Student Government

The Students' Association has responsibility for nearly all aspects of student life. The Haverford Honor Code, established and administered by students, has been in existence since 1897. The Honor Code makes possible a climate of trust, concern, and respect, which produces a campus atmosphere conducive to learning and personal growth. The code provides for students' academic and social freedom within the confines of agreed-upon community standards. Exams are not proctored, and the students schedule their own final exams. The code is administered by an elected Honor Council of 16 students—4 from each class at the College. Each year, the students meet to discuss resolutions and changes in the Honor Code and to approve its adoption. The students also elect several members of the student body to serve on faculty committees and as nonvoting representatives to the Board of Managers (trustees).

Admission Requirements

Admission to Haverford is highly competitive. Admitted students have strong academic records and represent a diversity of backgrounds and interests. The primary criteria for admission are academic and personal qualities as shown by the school record, College Board test scores, extracurricular achievement, and personal recommendations. A combination of qualities that indicates academic and personal promise and potential for growth at Haverford is more significant than any single factor. Of the most recent first-year class, 97 percent rank in the top fifth of their high school class; their SAT I scores range from 400 to 800; the recentered mean SAT I ranges are 640–720 (verbal) and 630–730 (math). All candidates are required to take the SAT I and three SAT II Subject Tests, including the Writing Test. The ACT may be substituted for the SAT I. A visit to campus to meet students, observe classes, and have an interview is strongly recommended, and students who live within 150 miles of the campus are required to arrange an on-campus interview. A first-choice early decision plan and a deferred matriculation plan are offered.

Admission of transfer students to Haverford is also highly competitive. A limited number of transfer students are accepted each year. Candidates must have completed one full year of college, with a minimum grade point average of 3.0 (B). Campus visits are strongly recommended for those wishing to transfer. A transfer student must spend a minimum of two years at Haverford in order to receive a degree.

Application and Information

The application deadlines for admission are November 15 for early decision candidates, January 15 for regular decision candidates, and March 31 for transfer candidates. Haverford also accepts the Common Application, which is available in school guidance offices. The admission office is open from 9 a.m. to 5 p.m. on weekdays (8:30 a.m. to 4:30 p.m. from June to August) and, during the fall, from 9 a.m. to noon on Saturday. For more information or to arrange an interview or tour appointment, students should contact:

Office of Admission
Haverford College
370 Lancaster Avenue
Haverford, Pennsylvania 19041-1392
Telephone: 610-896-1350
           610-896-1436 (TTY/TDD)
Fax: 610-896-1338
E-mail: admitme@haverford.edu
World Wide Web: http://www.haverford.edu

HAWAII PACIFIC UNIVERSITY
HONOLULU, HAWAII

The University
Hawaii Pacific University (HPU) is an independent, coeducational, career-oriented comprehensive university with a foundation in the liberal arts. Undergraduate and graduate degrees are offered in close to fifty different areas. Hawaii Pacific prides itself on maintaining small class size (averaging 25 students) and individual attention to students.

Students at HPU come from every state in the union and more than ninety countries around the world. The diversity of the student body stimulates learning about other cultures firsthand, both in and out of the classroom. There is no majority population at HPU. Students are encouraged to examine the values, customs, traditions, and principles of others to gain a clearer understanding of their own perspectives. HPU students develop friendships with students from throughout the United States and the world, important connections for success in the global economy of the twenty-first century.

In addition to the undergraduate programs described below, HPU offers several graduate programs: the M.B.A. (with twelve concentrations), the M.S. in Information Systems (M.S.I.S.), and the M.A. in human resource management, management, and organizational change.

HPU has a dual affiliation with both NCAA and NAIA intercollegiate sports. Men's athletic programs include baseball, basketball, cheerleading, cross-country, soccer, and tennis. Women's athletics include cheerleading, cross-country, soccer, softball, tennis, and volleyball.

The Housing Office at HPU offers many services and options for students. Residence halls with cafeteria service are available on the Windward campus, while University-sponsored apartments are available in the Waikiki area for those seeking more independent living arrangements.

Location
With two campuses linked by shuttle, Hawaii Pacific combines the excitement of an urban, downtown campus with the serenity of the Windward residential campus, which is set in the lush foothills of the Koolau mountains. The main campus is located in downtown Honolulu, the business and financial center of the Pacific. Eight miles away, situated on 135 acres in Kaneohe, the Windward campus is the site of the School of Nursing, the marine science program, and a variety of other course offerings. Students may take classes on whichever campus is most convenient. The beautiful weather, for which Hawaii is famous, allows for unlimited recreation opportunities year-round. The emphasis on a career-related curriculum keeps students focused on their academic goals. The economy in Hawaii makes cooperative education and internship opportunities hard to beat. Students desiring to expand their horizons in preparation for the changing global economy find Hawaii a working laboratory. The many opportunities available at HPU provide for a healthy combination of school, work, and fun.

Majors and Degrees
Hawaii Pacific University offers programs that lead to the degrees of Bachelor of Arts (B.A.), Bachelor of Science in Business Administration (B.S.B.A.), Bachelor of Science in Computer Science (B.S.C.S.), Bachelor of Science in environmental science, Bachelor of Science in marine science, Bachelor of Science in Nursing (B.S.N.), Bachelor of Science in premedical studies, and Bachelor of Social Work (B.S.W.).

Undergraduate majors include the B.A. in anthropology, communication (concentrations in journalism, public relations, speech/theater, and visual communication), economics, engineering (a 3-2 program), environmental studies, history, humanities, human resource development, human services, international relations, international studies (concentrations in American, Asian, comparative, European, and Pacific studies), justice administration, literature, military studies, political science, psychology, social sciences, sociology/anthropology, and teaching English as a second language. The School of Business programs include the B.S. in accounting, business economics, computer information systems, corporate communication, entrepreneurial studies, finance, human resource management, international business, management, marketing, public administration, and travel industry management. The B.S. is also available in computer science, environmental science, marine biology, military studies, nursing, oceanography, and premedical studies. The Bachelor of Social Work is also available. Dual degrees, double majors, and minors are also offered.

Academic Program
The baccalaureate student must complete at least 124 semester hours of credit. Forty-five of these credits provide the student with a strong foundation in the liberal arts, with the remaining credits composed of appropriate upper-division classes in the student's major and related areas. The academic year operates on a modified 4-1-4 semester system, featuring a five-week winter intersession. The University also offers extensive summer sessions. A student can earn up to 15 semester hours of credit during the summer. By attending these supplemental sessions, a student may complete the baccalaureate degree program in three years. A five-year B.S.B.A./M.B.A. program is also available.

Off-Campus Arrangements
Hawaii Pacific's academic and cocurricular programs are intertwined with the world of work. The University offers a comprehensive cooperative education/internship program in which a student may enroll throughout his or her course of study. This program enables students to gain significant experience in a career-related position as well as earn academic credit and a salary. At the upper-division level, the position is generally an internship with a leading Honolulu firm. Recent internship employers have included Aloha Airlines; the Bank of Hawaii; the city and county of Honolulu; the state of Hawaii; Hilton Hawaiian Village Hotel; IBM; KGMB-TV and Radio; Merrill Lynch; New York Life; Ogilvy & Mather; Price Waterhouse; Sears, Roebuck and Company; Sheraton; Starr, Siegle, McComb; and U.S. agencies and departments.

Academic Facilities
The downtown campus comprises six buildings in the center of Honolulu's business district. HPU's newest facility is the Multi-Media and Technology Center, which houses state-of-the-art classrooms, a communication lab, a robotics lab, and a graduate M.S.I.S. high-tech classroom. Hawaii Pacific's Meader Library provides a large collection of circulating books, special reference resources, newspapers from around the world, and periodicals. A number of special collections are housed with extensive business collections and a separate career development section. Meader Library has a tutoring center that

provides free tutoring in all core subjects, a graduate reading room, and ample study space. A computerized search system allows students access to information from libraries throughout the nation. The Learning Assistance Center is the home of language labs and an audiotape and audiovisual library as well as the multimedia lab with the latest in interactive computer and CD-ROM technology. The recently expanded computer lab has more than 125 IBM-compatible PCs.

On the suburban and residential Windward campus, academic life revolves around the Amos N. Starr and Juliette Montague Cooke Academic Center (AC). The AC houses faculty and staff member offices, classrooms, an art gallery, and the Atherton Learning Resources Center, which includes a library with extensive collections in the areas of Asian studies, marine science, and nursing. The Boyd MacNaughton Pacific Resource Room houses the Hawaiiana and Pacific special collections. The Academic Computer Center provides access to IBM computers.

Costs

For the 2000–01 academic year, tuition is $8920 (for most majors), and books and supplies cost approximately $1400. For students who live in residence halls, room and board are $8520. University-leased apartments rent for $3035 per semester. (There is an additional $400 refundable security deposit required for residence halls and University-leased apartments.) Tuition for marine science majors is $10,920, and tuition for nursing majors who are in their junior or senior year is $13,100.

Financial Aid

The University provides financial aid for qualified students through institutional, state, and federal aid programs. Approximately 50 percent of the University's students receive financial aid. Among the forms of aid available are Federal Perkins Loans, Federal Stafford Student Loans, Guaranteed Parental Loans, Federal Pell Grants, and Federal Supplemental Educational Opportunity Grants. To apply for aid, students must submit the Free Application for Federal Student Aid (FAFSA). The FAFSA may be submitted at any time, but the priority deadline is March 1.

Faculty

Hawaii Pacific's dedicated professors put a priority on teaching. At HPU, teaching assistants are not found in the classroom, only qualified professors. The student-faculty ratio is 18:1, and class size averages 25 students. Students get to know their professors as colleagues and mentors. HPU faculty members are actively involved in their academic fields and bring this experience to the classroom. Many of them are renowned leaders in their particular disciplines. The University has 145 full-time and 281 part-time faculty members. Seventy-seven percent have earned Ph.D.'s or terminal degrees in their fields. Hawaii Pacific has a staff of professional academic advisers whose primary responsibility is to assist students with academic programs and guide students toward their individual goals. Students meet with an adviser prior to every semester's registration.

Student Government

All registered students are members of the Associated Students of Hawaii Pacific University (ASHPU), which is headed by elected officers and class representatives. ASHPU supervises many clubs, organizations, and activities, including a literary magazine; a student newspaper; a pep band; preprofessional, cultural, and social organizations; service societies; dances; luaus; and cheerleading.

Admission Requirements

Hawaii Pacific seeks students who are motivated and show academic promise. The admissions office requires that applicants complete and forward the admission application and high school transcripts. Transfer students should also submit college transcripts. While ACT and SAT I scores are not required, the University recommends that test results be submitted for placement purposes.

First-time freshmen are expected to have a minimum GPA of 2.5 (on a 4.0 scale) in college-preparatory courses. Students with less than a 2.5 may be considered for admission but should also submit three letters of recommendation and a short essay on educational and personal objectives. HPU recommends that students complete 4 years of English, 2 years of math and social studies, and at least 1 year of history and science.

Transfer students with 24 or more postsecondary credits are required to have a 2.0 or above. For students with less than 24 credits, a combination of college and high school GPA is used.

The Marine Science and Environmental Science Programs require a high school GPA of 3.0 or above and 3 years of science, including biology, chemistry, and physics, as well as mathematics through precalculus (trigonometry). Transfer students must demonstrate ability in science and math at the college level. Students not meeting the above criteria are encouraged to enroll at HPU without declaring a major to demonstrate the ability to do college-level work in science and math.

Application and Information

Candidates are notified of admission decisions on a rolling basis, usually within two weeks of receipt of application materials. Early entrance and deferred entrance are available. HPU accepts the Common Application form.

For further information and for application materials, students should contact:

Office of Admissions
Hawaii Pacific University
1164 Bishop Street, Suite 200
Honolulu, Hawaii 96813
Telephone: 808-544-0238
           800-669-4724 (toll-free)
Fax: 808-544-1136
E-mail: admissions@hpu.edu
World Wide Web: http://www.hpu.edu/

Students on the HPU downtown campus.

HEIDELBERG COLLEGE
TIFFIN, OHIO

The College

Heidelberg College, founded in 1850, is a selective, private coeducational liberal arts college that is affiliated with the United Church of Christ. Believing that a liberal education is the best career preparation a person can have to confront the challenges of the future creatively, Heidelberg College offers students a solid base on which to grow in their professional and personal lives. Heidelberg's dynamic community maintains a touch of its Old World heritage yet continually brings innovative ideas into the classroom.

The current undergraduate enrollment is about 1,200 men and women. Students come to Heidelberg from twenty-two states and nine other countries. This cross-cultural mix helps to keep the campus diverse and to broaden students' knowledge and understanding of ethnic and cultural differences.

Heidelberg has more than sixty campus organizations that offer opportunities for leadership, service, and fellowship. Included in these organizations are thirteen departmental clubs and fifteen departmental honorary societies that sponsor discussions, lectures, and field trips. Other cocurricular activities include a student-edited and student-managed newspaper, a television station that broadcasts daily news, forensic programs, choral and instrumental groups, and intramural sports. The Communication and Theatre Arts Department presents four or more dramatic productions each year.

A member of the Ohio Athletic Conference, NCAA Division III, Heidelberg offers nine varsity men's sports: baseball, basketball, cross-country, football, golf, soccer, tennis, track, and wrestling. The women's varsity sports program, among the first in Ohio to be affiliated with the NCAA Division III, fields eight intercollegiate teams: basketball, cross-country, golf, soccer, softball, tennis, track, and volleyball. Athletic facilities include a weight room, handball/racquetball courts, locker rooms, and an eight-lane, all-weather track, which is considered one of the finest in Ohio.

Heidelberg College also offers Master of Arts degree programs in counseling and education as well as a Master of Business Administration (M.B.A.) degree program.

Location

Heidelberg's 110-acre campus is located in Tiffin, Ohio, a town of 20,000. It is the center of a prosperous agricultural and business area. Downtown Tiffin, within half a mile of campus, is traditional in appearance; its charming brickwork stores and large lampposts trimmed in wrought iron resemble an old German town. Four metropolitan areas are within easy driving distance: Toledo, 50 miles; Columbus, 86 miles; Cleveland, 92 miles; and Detroit, 103 miles.

Majors and Degrees

Heidelberg offers a wide variety of undergraduate majors and several preprofessional programs within nineteen academic departments. It awards the Bachelor of Arts, Bachelor of Science, and Bachelor of Music degrees. Majors are available in accounting, anthropology, athletic training, biology, business administration, chemistry, communication and theater arts (communication/media, theater), comprehensive science, comprehensive social studies, computer information systems, computer science, economics, education (early childhood, middle childhood, adolescence to young adult, intervention specialist studies, multiage German, multiage Spanish, multiage health and physical education, multiage music education), English (literature, writing), environmental biology, German, health–physical education and recreation, health services administration, history, international studies (international relations, cross-cultural studies), management science, mathematics, music, music industry, music performance, music performance pedagogy, music theory/composition, philosophy, physics, political science, psychology (child and adolescent, mental health, biopsychology, general), public administration, public relations, religion, Spanish, and water resources (biology, chemistry, geology). Preprofessional and cooperative degree programs include dentistry, engineering, environmental management, law, medical technology, medicine, nursing, occupational therapy, optometry, osteopathy, physical therapy, physician assistant studies, podiatry, and veterinary science.

Academic Program

To graduate, a student must complete 120 academic semester hours, comprising 36–45 semester hours of general education, 40 semester hours in a selected major, and 35–44 hours of electives. Four activity credits in health and physical education and 1 credit for Total Student Development (TSD) are also required.

Off-Campus Arrangements

To supplement their course work, students may choose from a variety of off-campus study programs that provide practical, career-related experience. For example, students interested in studying habitats not found in northwestern Ohio may do on-site field research in Caribbean biogeography in Belize and on-site field research in the Appalachian mountains of West Virginia. Students may also participate in the excavation of an archaeological site.

Opportunities for practical experience in research are also available through Heidelberg's nationally recognized Water Quality Laboratory, which has ongoing research in water-quality studies involving both northern Ohio streams and Lake Erie. Heidelberg's internship program also enables students to participate in on-the-job internships in several area businesses and industries.

Students interested in studying in Washington, D.C., may take part in the Washington Semester at American University; those interested in studying abroad may participate in Heidelberg's own programs in Germany (at Heidelberg University) and Spain or may participate in programs arranged cooperatively with other colleges and universities in such locations as England, Latin America, Africa, and the Far East.

Heidelberg also has cooperative degree programs in engineering with Case Western Reserve University and in forestry with Duke University.

Academic Facilities

Beeghly Library, containing 154,000 volumes, is the intellectual heart of Heidelberg College. The three-story circular library holds a seventy-seat audiovisual room, a seminar and computer room, the Rickard-Mayer Rare Books Room, and the Besse Collection of Letters. Bareis Hall of Science has excellent laboratories and facilities where students may observe demonstrations and experiments. Also located in Bareis Hall are the computer center and the Heidelberg Water Quality Laboratory. The computer center provides access to Macintosh and PC-compatible computers. All of these systems are connected to a campuswide network providing e-mail, file transfer, World Wide Web, and full access to the Internet. The high number of computers and terminals available for student use in addition to the convenience of the computer center hours are outstanding strengths of the College. Additional computer facilities are located in Brenneman Music Hall, the Pfleiderer Center for Religion and the Humanities, and the Aigler Alumni Building. Founders Hall houses a 250-seat performance theater and a rehearsal theater; an FM radio station, WHEI; television studio WHEI-TV; video taping rooms; costume rooms; a dance studio; and offices and classrooms for the Departments of Communication and Theatre Arts and the Languages.

Costs

For the academic year 2000–01, tuition and fees are $16,998; room and board cost $5474.

Financial Aid

More than 95 percent of the undergraduate student body at Heidelberg receive financial aid. College and government programs—including scholarships, grants, loans, and jobs—total about $11.3 million annually. Government assistance includes the Federal Pell Grant, direct loan programs, the Federal Supplemental Educational Opportunity Grant, and the Federal Work-Study Program. Heidelberg offers students who meet various academic requirements a number of grants and scholarships that are renewable if eligibility is maintained.

Faculty

Close personal interaction between students and professors is one of Heidelberg's primary strengths. With a faculty-student ratio of 1:12, 62 full-time professors serve the student body. More than 80 percent of the faculty members hold doctoral degrees in their disciplines. Heidelberg's faculty members are readily available to answer questions and meet with students outside of the classroom.

Student Government

Because students are voting members of 90 percent of the faculty committees, their concerns are heard and have an impact on academic standards, athletics, educational policies, and religious life. Heidelberg's Student Senate is made up of 25 students and a Student Affairs adviser.

Admission Requirements

Heidelberg's selective admission policy seeks to admit those students who will benefit from the educational offerings of the College and who will contribute to the shared life of the campus community. The Admission Committee considers each applicant individually to determine if the student will be able to successfully fulfill the academic responsibilities of a Heidelberg student. The applicant's high school achievement record is the single most important factor considered. Other factors considered are ACT or SAT I scores, cocurricular involvement, character, talent, and teacher recommendations.

Application and Information

Although Heidelberg follows a rolling admission policy, applicants are strongly encouraged to complete this process before January 1. Once all admission credentials are received, applicants are notified of the College's admission decision within two weeks.

For additional information, students should contact:

Office of Admission
Heidelberg College
310 East Market Street
Tiffin, Ohio 44883
Telephone: 419-448-2330
800-HEIDELBERG (toll-free)
Fax: 419-448-2334
E-mail: adminfo@heidelberg.edu

Founders Hall (1851), the oldest building on the Heidelberg campus, is one of ten listed on the National Register of Historic Places.

HENDRIX COLLEGE
CONWAY, ARKANSAS

The College

Hendrix is an undergraduate, residential, coeducational liberal arts college that is affiliated with the United Methodist Church. Hendrix is a vibrant community of learners that includes outstanding students and a distinguished faculty that is dedicated to teaching. Hendrix is located on a campus setting that engenders an inclusive and value-laden community. Students who enroll at Hendrix discover one of the nation's finest liberal arts colleges.

Enrollment at Hendrix is 1,150. Eighty-five percent of Hendrix students live on campus, and all freshmen live on campus. Approximately 35 percent of the students come from states other than Arkansas. Students who choose to attend Hendrix are highly motivated to excel. Hendrix students share an earnest enthusiasm for ideas and a respect for individual differences. The faculty, staff, and the campus itself work to foster a closely knit community. At Hendrix, one can immediately observe the shared sense that what is going on is an important enterprise without undue formality. It is readily apparent that all members of the community enjoy what they are doing.

Life at Hendrix is characterized by informality, a sense of belonging, and a high level of participation. The social life is coordinated by the Social Committee. There are no fraternities or sororities on campus, so each event is open to all members of the Hendrix community. Most students are involved in intramural sports, volunteer service, clubs and organizations, music, theater, and a variety of other activities. The Outdoor Activities and Recreation (OAR) program provides hiking, canoeing, camping, and many other outdoor opportunities.

Location

Conway is located 30 miles northwest of Little Rock, the capital city of Arkansas, and at the foothills of the Ozark Mountains. The cultural amenities of a dynamic metropolitan area are easily accessible (restaurants, concerts, clubs, and much more), yet within 45 minutes students can canoe the Buffalo River or enter the trailhead at Petit Jean Mountain. Conway, a pleasant community of 40,000 people, is home to three colleges.

Majors and Degrees

Hendrix awards the Bachelor of Arts (B.A.) degree. Under the umbrella of the B.A., Hendrix offers twenty-three different majors. Programs of study include anthropology, art, biology, chemistry, computer science, economics and business, English, French, German, history, interdisciplinary (self-designed) studies, international relations, mathematics, music, philosophy, philosophy and religion, physical education, physics, politics, psychology, religion, sociology, Spanish, and theater arts. Minors are offered in these areas as well as in gender studies. Hendrix offers exceptional preprofessional programs in dentistry, engineering, law, medicine, ministry, pharmacy, social work, and veterinary medicine.

Academic Program

Hendrix offers a distinguished liberal arts curriculum. While pursuing a major field of study in any one of two dozen disciplines in the humanities, the natural sciences, or the social sciences, Hendrix students also study broadly in the tradition of the West, non-Western cultures or foreign languages, and a variety of disciplines essential to the perspectives of educated persons in the contemporary world. All students are encouraged to design independent studies and tutorials in conjunction with faculty mentors.

In order to offer new students a common beginning, the College requires all first-year students to take a two-term sequence that is intended to introduce the major issues, problems, and achievements in the development of Western culture. Western Intellectual Traditions (WIT) concentrates on classical Greece, the High Middle Ages, the seventeenth century, and the late nineteenth century. Students read and discuss key works of philosophy, political theory, drama, and literature in small sections of 25 students. Beginning with readings from Plato, Locke, or Aristophanes, lively discussions often ensue and may lead to a greater insight into contemporary issues. Through a series of lectures, developments in music, art, science, and history are also presented.

The College utilizes a 3-3 calendar, also called the term system. Students take three classes per term, and classes meet four or five days per week. Each term is approximately eleven weeks long. In 2002, the College will move to a traditional semester calendar, with students completing four courses each term.

Hendrix offers several special learning opportunities in which a great many students participate. The Steel Center sponsors conferences on issues on the cutting edge of religion and philosophy. The Murphy Program for the Study of Language and Literature brings novelists, poets, and playwrights to campus, sponsors the language house and study-abroad programs, and funds a writing center on campus. Research and independent study opportunities are an integral part of the learning experience at Hendrix. Students have taken part in projects at colleges and universities around the nation. Many of these projects have culminated in presentations at the annual meetings of such organizations as the National Conference on Undergraduate Research, the American Chemical Society, and the Arkansas Academy of Science. Through the interdisciplinary studies program and with the assistance of faculty advisers, students are encouraged to design their own programs of study leading to interdisciplinary majors by combining courses from a variety of departments.

Off-Campus Arrangements

Hendrix encourages students to take advantage of the many opportunities for off-campus study. The Hendrix-in-London program is an annual term of study in British literature and history, including excursions throughout the British Isles. The Hendrix-in-Oxford program allows students to spend their junior year taking part in an individual program of study under the direction of Dr. Francis Warner, British playwright and Oxford University don. The College also participates in the International Student Exchange Program, through which students may study all over the world.

Students may also take part in the Washington Semester and the Gulf Coast Research Laboratory program. Students may choose to spend a semester at the American University in Washington, D.C., observing governmental operations and pursuing internships. The Gulf Coast Research Laboratory in Ocean Springs, Mississippi, provides an opportunity for students who are interested in marine biology to study in a field laboratory. Each summer Hendrix students take part in internships at a variety of businesses, organizations, and government agencies. In the past, students have been placed at Arkansas Educational Television Network, the U.S. Senate office, the University of

Arkansas for Medical Sciences Biomedicine Research facility, the National Center for Toxicological Research, the Savannah River Atomic Energy Laboratories, and the School for Field Studies in the Central American Republic of Belize. Students have also participated in summer research projects on the Hendrix campus and at Harvard, Brown, Vanderbilt, University of Tulsa, and Washington University.

Academic Facilities

The 58-acre main campus is the location of twenty-one of the twenty-three College buildings, three of which are on the National Register of Historic Places. The College is currently engaged in a $30-million construction program. Six new residence houses, configured in suites with space for approximately 20 students in each house, opened in fall 1999. A 30,000-square-foot addition to the Physical Sciences Center also opened in fall 1999, and the existing facility will be thoroughly renovated in 1999–2000. A $10.6-million grant from the Donald Reynolds Foundation will fund a new 60,000-square-foot life sciences center, which will open in 2001. The Bailey Library and Academic Resource Center, a 60,000-square-foot facility with a shelf capacity of 300,000 bound volumes, opened in 1994. Bailey houses the computer lab, with more than fifty Macs and personal computers available to students 24 hours a day.

The Cabe Theatre Arts Center is an outstanding teaching theater. Cabe is equipped with a thrust stage with a pneumatic turntable center, a computer-driven lighting system, and makeup and set construction areas.

The Language House provides a total immersion opportunity for 10 students interested in a particular foreign language. The language of focus rotates each year among French, Spanish, and German. An educator who is a native speaker of the chosen language lives in the house with the students. The residents concentrate on the culture of the language by eating indigenous meals, celebrating national holidays, and sharing in other activities designed to deepen each student's insight into the way of life of the people who speak the studied language.

The College is fortunate to have high-quality science equipment to support the outstanding scholarship in these areas. The chemistry department has recently implemented a gas chromatograph–mass spectrometer that was obtained through a grant from the Hewlett-Packard Foundation. Hendrix is one of only twenty colleges to have received such a grant. Chemistry students are using a new laser in the physical chemistry lab and a new high-field nuclear magnetic resonance spectrometer. The chemistry and physics departments continue to solicit and receive grants so that Hendrix students can work on the most modern equipment. The biology department has state-of-the-art laboratories with research equipment that includes growth chambers and tissue culture and animal facilities. The math department utilizes the newest in computer programs, such as Mathematica, to enhance the students' learning experience.

Costs

Hendrix tuition for the 1999–2000 academic year was $11,440. Room and board were $4415. There is a one-time $250 orientation fee for new students. The fees for an auto decal, post office box, and student activities totaled $133. The cost of books averages $600 a year.

Financial Aid

Through a combination of merit-based and need-based assistance, Hendrix has a firm commitment to help those students who desire a Hendrix education. By interviewing scholarship candidates, the scholarship committee is able to gain insight into what makes each student unique. Scholarship awards are made on the basis of a student's academic record, extracurricular activities, leadership qualities, and an on-campus interview. Each year the College hosts a Scholar Recognition Day on campus. Awards range from $1500 to full tuition, room, board, and fees.

Approximately 90 percent of the student body receives financial assistance. To apply for financial assistance, students must complete the Free Application for Federal Student Aid (FAFSA). Financial aid may come in the form of grants, student loans, or work-study (approximately 450 students work on campus). To receive priority consideration for financial aid, students must submit the FAFSA by February 15. Awards are made in late March.

Faculty

The College has a teaching faculty of 80 professors, 100 percent of whom have Ph.D.'s or the appropriate terminal degrees in their fields. Hendrix has no graduate students teaching on campus. There is a 12:1 student-faculty ratio. Therefore, students receive personal attention from faculty members with degrees from such American schools as Yale, Duke, Chicago, Tulane, Emory, and Claremont and European universities such as Oxford and London.

Teaching is the faculty's top priority. Small interactive classes (the average size is 15) encourage discussion and challenge students to think clearly. The mutual respect born in the classroom and the accessibility of the faculty often lead to lasting friendships.

Student Government

The Student Senate, through a number of committees, has the opportunity to help determine the academic and social climate of the campus. The Senate is responsible for distribution of proceeds from the student activities fee. The activities fee funds the campus radio station, newspaper, yearbook, literary magazine, and social events. The Social Committee sponsors such events as comedy nights, dances, parties, concerts, and many other social functions. The Senate recommends the appointments for student representation on faculty committees. Hendrix students are represented on most faculty committees.

Admission Requirements

Hendrix considers applicants on the strength of their academic records. Students should submit a high school transcript, ACT or SAT I test scores, an essay, and a record of extracurricular activities. It is recommended that applicants complete 4 units of English, 3 units of social studies, 3 units of mathematics, 2 units of natural sciences, and at least 2 units of foreign language. Special consideration is given to students taking Advanced Placement, International Baccalaureate, and honors courses. The recommended deadline is February 15 for regular admission and January 15 for merit scholarship consideration. Applications are reviewed on a rolling basis, and students are notified within four weeks of application completion.

Application and Information

For more information and application materials, students should contact:

Mr. Rock Jones
Vice President for Enrollment
Office of Admission
Hendrix College
1600 Washington Avenue
Conway, Arkansas 72032

Telephone: 800-277-9017 (toll-free)
Fax: 501-450-3843
E-mail: adm@hendrix.edu
World Wide Web: http://www.hendrix.edu

HESSER COLLEGE
MANCHESTER, NEW HAMPSHIRE

The College

The primary purpose of Hesser College is to provide a high-quality education that is highly personalized, cost-effective, and employment oriented. Hesser's innovative approach to higher education provides students with increased flexibility over traditional colleges. After two years of college, students earn an associate degree and are prepared to enter the workplace, or they can continue their studies in one of Hesser's bachelor's degree programs.

Hesser College was established in 1900 as Hesser Business College, a private, nonsectarian college. Since 1972, Hesser has expanded and enriched its curriculum in keeping with its tradition of providing an affordable career education of high quality. The physical building encompasses more than fifteen different businesses, all of which create the Hesser Center of Commerce and Education. This is an unusual and beneficial partnership of business and education.

Nearly 85 percent of the students work in the afternoons, evenings, or weekends while attending Hesser College. The 890 men and women currently enrolled represent several states and more than fifteen countries. A large part of the student population comes from the New England and mid-Atlantic states.

Hesser offers intercollegiate sports in men's and women's basketball and volleyball, men's soccer, and women's softball. The basketball team has consistently been a major power in the Northern New England Small College Conference. Students also participate in a number of intramural sports programs. Extracurricular activities are varied and include social activities, clubs, trips, and educational programs in the residence halls. A freshman orientation program is conducted each fall before classes begin.

The College has developed a number of learning assistance programs to help students succeed in their studies. Tutoring and special classes are provided by the faculty throughout each semester. In addition, several departments offer honors programs and special opportunities for independent study. The College also sponsors an active chapter of the national honor society, Phi Theta Kappa, which promotes scholarship and service to the College and the community. The Bachelor Degree Programs Coordinator assists students who wish to continue their education beyond the associate degree level.

Hesser College is fully accredited by the New England Association of Schools and Colleges. The association is the official accrediting agency for schools and colleges in the six New England states and is widely considered to hold the strictest academic standards. Students who choose Hesser are assured of a high-quality education.

Location

Hesser College is located in Manchester, New Hampshire. With a population of more than 100,000, Manchester is a medium-sized city that offers many cultural, historical, and social events. Hesser's central location provides easy access to entertainment, shopping, and a variety of part-time jobs and academic work experiences. Manchester is within 1 hour of Boston, and the mountains and major ski resorts are within 1 to 2 hours of Hesser's campus. Manchester has been called the "Gateway to Northern New England," and several major carriers serve the Manchester Airport.

Manchester was recently named by *Money* magazine as the number one small city in the Northeastern United States. In addition, Manchester was recently named one of the best cities in the United States for business. According to *U.S. News & World Report*, it is "at the hub of things" in the fast-growing high-technology and financial industries of southern New Hampshire.

Majors and Degrees

Hesser College offers the Bachelor of Science degree in business administration, with specializations in accounting, management, and marketing, and in criminal justice. Based on the innovative 2+2 academic model, Hesser's programs offer students great flexibility in their academic pursuits.

In addition, Hesser offers a wide range of associate degree programs that are intended to prepare students for high-demand careers. They include accounting; business administration; business computer applications; business science/individualized studies; child-care studies; communications and public relations; corrections, probation, and parole; early childhood education; graphic design; hotel/restaurant management; human services; interior design; international business; law enforcement; liberal studies; marketing; medical assistant studies; medical office management; microcomputer support specialist studies; network engineer; occupational therapy assistant studies; paralegal studies; pharmacy technician studies; physical therapist assistant studies; psychology; radio/video production and broadcasting; small-business management/entrepreneurship; solutions developer studies; sports management; and travel and tourism.

Academic Program

The primary goal of the curriculum is to prepare students for success in specific career areas. The general education requirements are designed to provide the skills necessary for career growth and lifelong learning. Internships, practicums, and opportunities for part-time work experience are available in all majors. An education from Hesser College provides a solid career foundation. The College's goal is quite simple: to prepare people for careers and career advancement.

Many of the Hesser College programs are for the career-minded student who wants to concentrate on the skills required to be successful in the workplace. Seventy-five percent of the courses that students take are directly related to their career choices.

Hesser College follows a traditional semester calendar.

Off-Campus Arrangements

The College offers opportunities for cooperative education and internships in most of its academic programs. The early childhood education program includes practicums and supervised fieldwork in the freshman and senior years, utilizing a variety of child-care facilities. In addition, several programs' curricula incorporate short-term study tours: the business and hotel restaurant management program studies on a trip to Walt Disney World, the travel and tourism program studies on a cruise to the Bahamas, and the criminal justice program studies on a trip to Washington, D.C. The occupational therapy assistant studies and physical therapist assistant studies programs require students to participate in at least 265 hours of clinical experience in a health-care setting under the direct supervision of a certified instructor or therapist.

Hesser College has relationships with many businesses, and internship sites have been located in the Hesser Center of Commerce and Education, in nearby downtown Manchester, and throughout the region.

Academic Facilities

The academic facilities located within the Hesser Commerce and Education Center include several networked computer labs, an automated office simulation lab, the online American Airlines reservation system (SABRE) computer lab, the court reporting computer-assisted transcription lab (X-Scribe), a medical assistant lab, an occupational therapy assistant lab, and a physical therapist assistant lab. The College library contains more than 40,000 titles. The Academic Support Center provides special tutoring and programs in study skills, reading, writing, math, and computer skills.

The College includes dormitories for approximately 70 percent of the 890 students. A wide range of resources are located on campus. Academic advising is coordinated through department chairpersons and the Academic Support Center, and the size of the College allows for individual attention to the financial and career counseling needs of each student.

Costs

Part-time students are billed at the rate of $320 per credit for all majors. Full-time expenses per semester in 1999–2000 were $4320 for tuition (12–16 credits), $1550 for room, and $950 for the optional meal plan.

Financial Aid

Hesser College offers financial assistance to students based on demonstrated financial need. Seventy percent of the students receive some form of aid. More than fifty scholarships are awarded each year to freshman and senior students. The College offers low-interest loans from both internal and external sources. Federal Supplemental Educational Opportunity Grants, Federal Work-Study, Federal Perkins Loans, Federal Direct Student Loans, and state scholarship programs are available to those who qualify. Awards are made on a rolling basis and are subject to availability. In order to apply for financial aid and scholarships at Hesser, students must complete the FAFSA form and a Hesser College Institutional Financial Aid Application.

Faculty

The faculty members of Hesser College consistently receive high student evaluations for their interests in each student's success and for the high quality of their teaching. The majority of the faculty members have completed programs of advanced study, and all have practical experience in business or other career fields. Faculty members participate in national and regional conferences and associations and are continually involved with program review and curriculum development. The student-faculty ratio is 18:1.

Student Government

Hesser College students are invited to participate in the President's Advisory Board meetings, which convene several times throughout the year to facilitate communication between College students and the administration.

Admission Requirements

Admission to Hesser College is made by a committee of administrators and admission personnel. A high school transcript must be submitted, and international students must also submit TOEFL scores. SAT I scores are not required but may be considered in the admission decision if submitted. Transfer students are required to submit high school and college transcripts, with a minimum 2.0 grade point average for all previous college work.

It is recommended, but not required, that applicants come to Hesser for an interview and that they submit recommendations from counselors, teachers, and employers. The College operates on a rolling admissions basis, and notification is continuous.

Application and Information

Applicants must submit an application form with a $10 nonrefundable fee. Applications are reviewed on a first-come, first-served basis and normally take seven to fourteen days to be fully reviewed upon receipt of all required information.

Requests for additional information and application forms should be addressed to:

Director of Admissions
Hesser College
3 Sundial Avenue
Manchester, New Hampshire 03103
Telephone: 603-668-6660
        800-526-9231 (toll-free)
Fax: 603-666-4722
E-mail: admissions@hesser.edu
World Wide Web: http://www.hesser.edu

Students at Hesser College.

HIGH POINT UNIVERSITY
HIGH POINT, NORTH CAROLINA

The University

High Point University is a private university related to the United Methodist Church. With more than 3,000 students, the University is large enough to guarantee quality and diversity in programs and services, yet small enough to enable community among students, faculty members, and staff members. Approximately 2,500 students are enrolled at the High Point campus, and about 500 students are enrolled at the Madison Park campus in Winston-Salem, North Carolina. In a typical year, students come from forty-one states and thirty-four countries, making the campus a microcosm of the nation and the world, thereby creating an ideal learning environment.

The University fully recognizes its responsibility to provide the best liberal arts education possible, but faculty and staff members also recognize that education, as often defined, is not sufficient. Therefore, the University intentionally seeks to develop character by encouraging personal responsibility and by inculcating values through curricular and cocurricular programs and services, including the University chapel where services are offered each week.

In addition to the bachelor's degrees described below, the University offers the Master of Science in management and international management and the Master of Business Administration.

Location

Together, High Point, Greensboro, and Winston-Salem form the Golden Triad of North Carolina, a metropolitan area of approximately 1.4 million people, 73,000 of whom live within the city of High Point. Both Winston-Salem and Greensboro are 20 minutes from campus, as is the Piedmont Triad (Greensboro-High Point) International Airport. Both Raleigh and Charlotte are 1½ hours away, the Appalachian Mountains are 2 hours away, and the Atlantic Ocean is 4 hours away.

The region is known, nationally and internationally, for the quality of its institutions of higher education. Within a 60-mile radius are Duke University, UNC-Chapel Hill, and Wake Forest University, along with sixteen other colleges and universities. Obviously, such an area is replete with athletic, cultural, recreational, and social activities for young adults.

Majors and Degrees

High Point University awards the Bachelor of Arts degree in art, art education, computer technology, criminal justice, elementary education, English: literature, English: media, English: writing, French, history, human relations, international studies, middle grades education, North American studies, philosophy, political science, religion, sociology: cultural studies, sociology: general studies, sociology: social work, Spanish, special education, and theater arts. The University awards the Bachelor of Science degree in accounting, biology, business administration (accounting, economics, finance, international management, management, and marketing), chemistry, chemistry: business, computer information systems, computer science, exercise science, forestry, home furnishings management, home furnishings marketing, interior design, international business, mathematics, medical science, medical technology, physical education, psychology: general studies, psychology: industrial/organizational, psychology: mental health, recreation, sports management, and sports medicine. Within the liberal arts major, students can complete the requirements for admission to professional schools, including dentistry, law, medicine, pharmacy, theology, and veterinary medicine.

Academic Program

The academic program is administered through fourteen academic departments that offer forty-five majors, primarily in the liberal arts. In addition, the University allows students with well-defined objectives that cannot be satisfied within the regular curriculum to design their own individualized majors. An honors program recognizes and encourages creativity and academic achievement.

The curriculum emphasizes the study of the liberal arts in the belief that there is no better way to encourage communication skills, critical thinking, and personal integrity and in the belief that in the process of acquiring these skills students become self-learners who are equipped to succeed in life and work. Within the liberal arts framework, the University provides several professional programs, including business administration, computer information systems, computer science, computer technology, exercise science, home furnishings marketing and management, human relations (a program affiliated with American Humanics, Inc.), international business, sports management, and sports medicine. Cooperative baccalaureate programs are offered in forestry, medical science, and medical technology.

The curriculum prepares students to pursue graduate programs consistent with the majors enumerated above and professional programs beyond the baccalaureate degree in areas that include, but are not limited to, dentistry, law, medicine, ministry, physical therapy, and sports medicine.

Through the Student Career Intern Program, juniors and seniors at High Point University are able to explore career opportunities outside the classroom. The program enables a student to assume the responsibilities of a regular employee in a local business or agency before graduating from High Point, thereby enabling the student to evaluate his or her career choice prior to graduation.

Students who have completed Advanced Placement courses in high school and who have achieved a score of 3, 4, or 5 on the Advanced Placement tests administered by the College Board may receive credit at High Point University. Applicants may also receive credit for university-parallel courses successfully completed prior to enrollment at High Point, including courses completed while in high school.

Off-Campus Arrangements

Students may choose to study abroad for a year, a semester, or a summer through the High Point University in England program offered in cooperation with the University of Leeds or through the University's program at Westminster College, Oxford. The University's affiliation with international study programs administered by other institutions also makes it possible for students to study in Canada, France, Germany, Spain, and Mexico, and, subject to prior approval, transfer credit may be awarded for university-parallel work offered by institutions other than those with which the University has formal affiliation.

Students enrolled at High Point University may cross-register on the campus of any other member institution in the Greater Greensboro Consortium, including two state institutions and a women's college.

Academic Facilities

The Herman and Louise Smith Library has 48,000 square feet of floor space and storage capacity for more than 250,000 volumes. Services include a computerized integrated library system that enables patrons to access both the University's holdings and the holdings of other libraries through local, regional, and national networks. Access to information is facilitated by a number of bibliographic databases on a CD-ROM local network as well as by online services that offer more than 200 databases. The learning assistance center, located in the library, provides tutoring and other programs designed to facilitate learning. The academic computing center provides a microcomputer laboratory and access to a mainframe system and supports the major in computer information systems, the minor in computer science, and the programs of the learning assistance center. The Horace S. Haworth Hall of Science provides science laboratories and modern equipment. The James H. and Jesse E. Millis Athletic and Convocation Center houses a state-of-the-art sports medicine center, along with facilities for physical education that include, but are not limited to, the aerobic center, an Olympic-size pool, racquetball courts, and tennis courts.

Costs

For 2000–01, tuition, room, board, and general fees for full-time boarding students are $18,210.

Financial Aid

Students who require financial assistance should complete the Free Application for Federal Student Aid (FAFSA). The FAFSA indicates how much the student and the parents/guardians of dependent students can contribute toward the cost of attending High Point University. The University subtracts that amount from the cost of attending and attempts to underwrite the difference through a financial aid package that consists of one or more of the following: scholarships, grants that do not have to be repaid, loans, and/or college work-study.

Presidential Scholarships, ranging from $5500 to full tuition ($12,440), are awarded on a competitive basis to entering freshmen. Phi Theta Kappa National Scholarships ranging from $2500 (GPA: 3.0–3.49) to $5000 (GPA: 3.5–4.0) are awarded automatically to Phi Theta Kappa alumni who have earned the associate degree in a university-parallel program, and full-tuition scholarships ($11,760) are awarded to Phi Theta Kappa alumni on a competitive basis.

Faculty

High Point University has a student-faculty ratio of 15:1 and an average class size of 22 students. More than 75 percent of faculty members have earned either the Ph.D. or another terminal degree. All members of the faculty teach classes and advise students, and faculty members routinely interact with students on a regular basis.

Student Government

High Point University intentionally seeks to involve students in campus life through Student Government, service on University-wide committees, and student activities, including fourteen NCAA Division I athletic teams, eight Greek organizations, and more than fifty other campus organizations. In addition, in a typical year, High Point University students provide more than 25,000 hours of voluntary service to the community of High Point.

Admission Requirements

Freshman applicants must be graduates of an accredited secondary school and must exhibit satisfactory performance in a college-preparatory curriculum of 16 units distributed as follows: English, 4; foreign language, 2; mathematics, 2; history, 1; laboratory science, 1; and electives, 6. Every freshman applicant must submit scores on the SAT I or the ACT. International applicants may submit TOEFL scores as an alternative to the SAT I or ACT; however, students who wish to play on an athletic team must take the SAT I. Campus visits and personal interviews are strongly recommended.

Application and Information

Application forms must be completed by the student and sent to the Office of Admissions, along with a nonrefundable $25 processing fee. Official transcripts (high school and college, where applicable) must be sent directly to the University by the appropriate school official. Students should request that a copy of their SAT I, ACT, or TOEFL scores be sent to the Office of Admissions at High Point University by the testing agency. High Point University operates under a rolling admission plan and accepts applications at any time. However, because enrollment is limited by available residential spaces, early application is encouraged. All requests for application materials and information should be directed to:

Office of Undergraduate Admissions
High Point University
University Station, Montlieu Avenue
High Point, North Carolina 27262-3598
Telephone: 336-841-9216
           800-345-6993 (toll-free)
E-mail: admiss@highpoint.edu
World Wide Web: http://www.highpoint.edu

High Point University, located on a 77-acre campus, enrolls 3,000 students from forty-one states and thirty-four countries.

HILBERT COLLEGE
HAMBURG, NEW YORK

The College
Since its founding in 1957, Hilbert College has provided challenging academic programs and close personal attention to its students. The College is a coeducational, independent, four-year institution that grants degrees on both the baccalaureate and associate levels. There is a strong commitment to the philosophy that the liberal arts are the cornerstone of a Hilbert College education. In harmony with its Franciscan Spirit, the College provides individual counseling and support services for students whose diversified needs are best met in this small-college setting. Hilbert College's campus consists of seven buildings: Bogel Hall, which is the academic building; the Francis J. and Marie McGrath Library; the Campus Center; the residence hall; the grounds and maintenance building; the Hafner Recreation Center; and Franciscan Hall, which is the student services and administration building.

Hilbert College has a student body of approximately 900 students. There is an on-campus residential population of 100 students. All students are offered a myriad of social activities that range from academic and student clubs to NCAA Division III athletics. Student government takes an active role in the planning and operation of most campus events. The College's Division III athletics program offers intercollegiate competition in men's baseball, basketball, golf, and soccer. Women's sports include basketball, soccer, softball, and volleyball. Programs in men's volleyball, women's cross-country, and women's lacrosse are to be added for the 2001 season.

Location
Hilbert College's 40-acre campus is located in the town of Hamburg in western New York State on the shore of Lake Erie. The campus is approximately 15 miles south of Buffalo, a city of 350,000 people.

Hilbert College's proximity to Buffalo makes many cultural and recreational resources easily accessible to its students. Downtown attractions include Kleinhans Music Hall, Studio Arena Theatre, the Albright-Knox Art Gallery, the Museum of Science, and the Buffalo Zoo. The historic Shea's Theatre is also located downtown and is Buffalo's home to many concerts, operas, and Broadway shows. Niagara Falls, one of the nation's greatest natural attractions, is just a 35-minute drive from the campus. Buffalo also provides professional sports in football, hockey, lacrosse, and triple-A baseball. Hamburg also is located a short distance from several cross-country and downhill ski resorts.

Majors and Degrees
Hilbert College offers programs of study leading to the Bachelor of Arts (B.A.) degree in English, liberal studies (city planning, government, and law), and psychology. The Bachelor of Science (B.S.) degree is offered in accounting, business administration, criminal justice, economic crimes investigation, human services, and paralegal studies. The College also offers the Associate degree programs (A.A. and A.A.S.) in accounting, banking, business administration, criminal justice, human services, liberal arts, management information systems, and paralegal studies.

Academic Program
The Bachelor of Arts and Bachelor of Science degrees are granted upon completion of 120 credit hours.

The Associate in Arts, the Associate in Applied Science, and the Associate in Science degrees are granted upon completion of 60 credit hours.

Common to all academic programs is the completion of the Liberal Arts Core Curriculum. All students must fulfill the following graduation requirements: basic skills courses, liberal arts requirements (vary according to program), and an interdisciplinary core course. The purpose of the Liberal Arts Core Curriculum is to develop the habits of thought, methods of critical investigation, and ethical perspectives that enable students to make reasoned judgments and increase their capacity for leading fuller lives. By studying the various liberal arts disciplines, students should achieve a greater awareness of their cultural and social identity while cultivating the intellectual skills and competence that allow them to perform successfully in their chosen careers.

Hilbert has developed a serious of transfer agreements with most two-year colleges in New York State. These agreements allow two-year college graduates to move directly into a four-year program at Hilbert College as full juniors and with no course duplication. In addition, since Hilbert is accredited by the Commission on Higher Education of the Middle States Association of Colleges and Schools; therefore, its credits are readily transferable nationwide to other four-year colleges and universities.

Academic Facilities
Bogel Hall, the academic building, contains the Palisano Lecture Hall, faculty offices, two computer labs, the Academic Services Center, the chapel, and most classroom space.

McGrath Library, an expansive building consisting of a two-level core housing the library collection, a seminar wing, and a conference wing, maintains a collection approaching 34,000 volumes, more than 340 periodicals, and a large selection of microforms and audio/video materials. The first floor houses the reference, index, and periodical collections. Computer workstations with the library catalog and numerous full-text databases, which enormously supplement the periodical collection, are also available on this floor. The circulating book collection begins on this level and continues in the stacks located on the second floor. The second level primarily houses the McGrath Library Law Collection in support of the paralegal studies and liberal studies programs on the campus. This collection ranks as one of the largest academic law collections open to the public in western New York State. The library's seminar wing houses video-equipped classrooms and the Legal Research Lab. Ample study space is available throughout the library with both private carrels and group-study tables available for student use.

Costs
For 2000–01, tuition and fees are $11,300, and room and board are $4670. The approximate cost for books and supplies is $700 and for travel and miscellaneous expenses, $1000.

Financial Aid
Eighty percent of the members of the current freshman class receive financial aid. Financial aid packages consist of loans, scholarships, grants, and jobs. Awards are provided on the basis of need, as established by the Free Application for Federal

Student Aid (FAFSA), and as funds are available. There are several merit-based scholarships for academic and leadership talents as well as transfer articulation and minority scholarships.

Faculty

Hilbert has a faculty of 78 men and women. Fifty-five percent of the full-time faculty members hold doctoral or terminal degrees; 45 percent hold master's degrees. The student-faculty ratio is 19:1, with an average class size of 25.

Student Government

The largest student organization on campus is the Student Government Association (SGA). Headed by student-elected officers, this representative organization acts on the behalf of the entire student body. The SGA administers student funds to sponsor on-campus activities and events that range from intimate concerts to larger campuswide festivities. The SGA is comprised of two bodies, the association and the student senate. The association contains elected students who represent the needs of different classes, residents, and commuters. The Student Senate is a smaller group that is comprised of the student government elected officers and individual class representatives. The Senate is responsible for the disbursement of funds to student-run clubs and organizations.

Admission Requirements

Hilbert College is open to men and women regardless of faith, race, age, physical handicap, or national origin. All students have an equal opportunity to pursue their educational goals through programs available at the College.

The College considers for admission to regular degree study those applicants who have been awarded a high school diploma or a New York State High School Equivalency Diploma.

Application and Information

The closing date for the receipt of applications is August 20. Admission decisions are made on a rolling basis.

For a catalog or an application, students should contact:

Office of Admissions
Hilbert College
5200 South Park Avenue
Hamburg, New York 14075
Telephone: 716-649-7900
          800-649-8003 (toll-free)
World Wide Web: http://www.hilbert.edu

Franciscan Hall, the Student Services Center.

HILLSDALE COLLEGE
HILLSDALE, MICHIGAN

The College

Hillsdale College is a private, independent, nonsectarian institution of higher learning founded in 1844 by men and women who described themselves as "grateful to God for the inestimable blessings" resulting from civil and religious liberty and as "believing that the diffusion of learning is essential to the perpetuity of those blessings." The College has maintained institutional independence since its founding by refusing to accept aid from or control by federal authorities. Far-reaching private support from a national constituency has enabled Hillsdale to continue its trusteeship of the intellectual and spiritual inheritance derived from the Judeo-Christian faith and Greco-Roman culture.

The current undergraduate enrollment is 543 men and 566 women. The College draws students from forty-eight states and eleven countries. About half come from Michigan. The entering freshman class in 1999 had an average high school grade point average of 3.55 and mean ACT and SAT I scores well above the national averages. Hillsdale students are housed in dormitories, fraternity and sorority houses, and various off-campus dwellings. Single and double rooms are available on campus; there are no coed dormitories. Each College-owned residence hall is supervised by a resident director and student staff members. All freshmen (except commuters) are required to live on campus; upperclass students seeking to live off campus must apply to the dean of men or dean of women for this privilege.

Hillsdale's athletes participate in eighteen intercollegiate varsity sports (the College belongs to the NCAA Division II and the Great Lakes Intercollegiate Athletic Conference), and a vigorous intramural program is also available. The College emphasizes the concept of the student-athlete and is proud of the national recognition won by a number of its athletes for academic achievements. Four national fraternities, four national sororities, and about forty other social, honorary, and service organizations provide Hillsdale students with an array of cocurricular opportunities. A resident drama troupe, a bagpipe and drum corps, a wind ensemble, a concert choir, a chorale, and a College-community orchestra constitute the College's performing arts organizations.

Special student services provided by the College include career planning and placement counseling, academic advising and tutoring, and a health service staffed by a physician and a resident nurse.

Location

Hillsdale College is located amidst the hills and lakes of south-central Michigan. The Indiana and Ohio turnpikes are each 30 minutes away, and the College is easily reached from such metropolitan areas as Detroit, Chicago, Cleveland, Toledo, and Indianapolis. The town of Hillsdale is a county seat with a population of 9,000. Stores, churches, restaurants, and a movie theater are all within walking distance of the campus.

Majors and Degrees

Hillsdale awards the Bachelor of Arts or Bachelor of Science degree in accounting, art, biology, chemistry, computational mathematics, economics, education, English, financial management, French, German, history, marketing management, mathematics, music, philosophy, physical education, physics, political science, psychology, religion, sociology, Spanish, speech, and theater. Interdisciplinary majors in American studies, Christian studies, classical studies, comparative literature, European studies, international studies, and political economy are also available. Preprofessional programs are offered in dentistry, engineering, forestry, law, medicine, optometry, osteopathy, pharmacy, theology, and veterinary medicine.

Hillsdale offers a 3-2 (B.A./B.S.) or 4-2 (B.A./M.S.) cooperative program in engineering science with Northwestern University and Tri-State University.

Academic Program

Hillsdale operates on a two-semester schedule, with the fall term beginning in late August and ending in mid-December and the spring term beginning in mid-January and ending in mid-May. Two 3-week summer sessions are also offered.

The College believes that a sound liberal arts education includes study in the humanities, natural sciences, and social sciences, and each student is required to complete core courses in these areas. Students are also required to declare a major by the end of their sophomore year. To graduate, they must complete at least 124 hours of course work and fulfill the requirements of at least one major field. It is not unusual for a student to complete two majors or a major and a minor. Each baccalaureate program is based on the completion of four years of study in the liberal arts. The B.A. program stresses language (and includes a foreign language requirement), literature, and the arts. The B.S. program stresses mathematics and the natural sciences. Both programs equally emphasize the social sciences.

The honors program enables exceptionally talented students to develop their intellectual potential through special honors classes, available all four years, and to participate in yearlong colloquia in the junior and senior years.

The Center for Constructive Alternatives conducts four weeklong symposia during the academic year. These programs, dealing with themes that have contemporary significance and application, are of major importance in the intellectual life of the College. Each brings to the campus distinguished scholars and public figures chosen for their ability to contribute to the theme.

Off-Campus Arrangements

Two internship programs in Washington, D.C., place students at the ERI National Journalism Center or in congressional and government offices for a summer of work and study. Additional internships may be established in the fields of business and communication arts in consultation with the academic department concerned.

Hillsdale College is one of five American colleges affiliated with Keble College of Oxford University. This affiliation enables Hillsdale students to study abroad for a summer or a year at Oxford. Hillsdale offers a summer business program in cooperation with Regents College in London, England. The College also offers qualified students the opportunity to study in Seville, Spain, and France and Germany. Qualified individual students who wish to study in another country for a semester or a year are assisted by their faculty adviser and the registrar in planning a program that enables them to gain full credit as well as a rewarding experience. Students majoring in international studies are encouraged to participate in internships abroad.

Academic Facilities

Kresge Center for Traditional Studies contains classrooms, research facilities, language laboratories, faculty offices, and special laboratory facilities for experimental psychology. Mossey Learning Resources Center, a library and learning center, houses more than 150,000 books and about 14,000 periodicals (both bound and microfilmed volumes), along with the Richardson Heritage Room, a special collections library for first editions. Hillsdale also participates in the general interlibrary loan program, which offers computerized access to 13 million bibliographical records (books, periodicals, and microfilm). Computer terminals for word processing and other functions, videocassette and videodisc players, record and tape players, and a large collection of recordings, audiotapes, and videotapes are available in the Mossey Center.

Strosacker Science Center has well-equipped facilities for biology, chemistry, mathematics, and physics. Special research areas and departmental libraries are also available. The recently completed, 32,000-square-foot Herbert Henry Dow Science Building provides additional classrooms, research laboratories, animal rooms, and a computer lab. Perhaps the most widely known of Hillsdale's academic facilities is the Mary Randall Preschool, a circular laboratory school in which nursery school children are taught by students specializing in early childhood education and psychology. Experts in the field have called this building "a model for the nation." The Hillsdale Academy, a K–12 private model school, provides additional opportunities for classroom observation. The indoor facilities of the Athletic Complex include a field house with a swimming pool, a six-lane indoor track, basketball courts, volleyball courts, tennis courts, and handball and racquetball courts. A prescription turf football field, ringed by an all-weather, Pro-turf, eight-lane running track, is in a lighted stadium that seats 7,000 people. Baseball and softball diamonds and ten lighted tennis courts complete the outdoor facilities of the College's Athletic Complex.

The Sage Center for the Arts, which houses the departments of art, music, and theater, opened in 1992. The 47,000-square-foot facility features eight practice rooms, a 350-seat auditorium with a complete scene shop, makeup room, costume shop, and hydraulic orchestra pit that can be raised to provide additional seating for nonmusical events.

Costs

Tuition for 1999–2000 was $13,220, room was $2630, board was $3000, and mandatory fees were $240. Books, supplies, and personal expenses (including travel, recreation, and clothing) are estimated at $1200 per year.

Financial Aid

Financial aid at Hillsdale is available in many forms. Academic scholarships are awarded on a competitive basis, regardless of financial need, to students who rank in the top 10 percent of their high school class and have standardized test scores in the top 10 percent according to national test norms. The priority deadline for academic scholarship consideration is January 1. Athletic scholarships are also available on a competitive basis in men's baseball, football, and soccer; men's and women's basketball and track and cross-country; and women's swimming, tennis, and volleyball. To apply for aid on the basis of financial need, students are required to file Hillsdale's Confidential Family Financial Statement (CFFS) and (for Michigan residents) the Free Application for Federal Student Aid (FAFSA) in January or February of the year of prospective enrollment at Hillsdale. Grants and loans are available from the College and from state sources. Students may also earn up to $1000 per year in various campus jobs.

Faculty

The faculty consists of 89 full-time members (75 of whom have doctorates) and 38 part-time members. No classes are taught by graduate students. The size and closeness of the College community enable faculty members and students to get to know each other well in and out of the classroom. Each student has a faculty adviser who directs the program of study and provides academic and career counseling. Hillsdale's faculty is dedicated primarily to teaching and to students' personal development. Many faculty members also engage in research and scholarly writing, supported by summer and sabbatical leaves funded by the College.

Student Government

Hillsdale's student government and campus organizations offer students special opportunities to develop leadership skills that enrich their collegiate experience and their lives after graduation. The governing organization of the student body is the Student Federation, which is composed of 16 elected representatives. This group funds student organizations, sponsors all-College entertainment, and acts upon matters of concern to the student community. The Men's Council and Women's Council serve as legislative and judicial bodies within their respective domains in cooperation with members of the administration. The Leadership Workshop, which works closely with the administration, faculty, and community organizations, provides an additional forum for students to cultivate and perfect their leadership skills.

Admission Requirements

Admission is a privilege extended to students who are able to benefit by, and contribute to, the academic and social environment of the College. Important determinants for admission are intellectual curiosity, motivation, and social concern. Accordingly, grade average, test scores, class rank, strength of curriculum, extracurricular activities, interviews, self-evaluations, and recommendations from high school counselors or teachers are all reviewed carefully and are important in the evaluation process. Although some factors are necessarily more important than others, seldom is any single criterion, however important, decisive.

Transfer students must submit the standard application, including the high school record, SAT I or ACT scores, and transcripts from all colleges previously attended. Applications by transfers are evaluated similarly to nontransfers. A transfer form is also required from the dean of students of the most recent college attended.

Candidates for admission from other countries follow the customary entrance procedures. Students who come from a non-English-speaking culture must demonstrate proficiency in English by satisfactory performance on the Test of English as a Foreign Language (TOEFL) or the Michigan Test of English Proficiency or at an ESL Center.

Application and Information

Students may apply to Hillsdale College any time after the completion of the junior year of high school. A formal application includes a completed application form accompanied by a nonrefundable fee of $15 and all required credentials. Applications are accepted on a rolling basis, and applicants are usually notified of the decision of the Admissions Committee within six weeks after all necessary information has been received. Hillsdale College has been distinguished since its founding by voluntarily adhering to a nondiscriminatory policy regarding race, religion, sex, or national or ethnic origin—long before government began regulating such matters.

All records and forms should be mailed to:

Admissions Office
Hillsdale College
Hillsdale, Michigan 49242-1298
Telephone: 517-437-7341
E-mail: admissions@ac.hillsdale.edu
World Wide Web: http://www.hillsdale.edu

HIRAM COLLEGE
HIRAM, OHIO

The College
Founded by the Christian Church (Disciples of Christ) in 1850, Hiram College cherishes its heritage, while remaining free from sectarian doctrine or denominational control. Hiram's 900 students come from twenty-five states and several countries and represent more than twenty-five different religions. SAT I and ACT scores of Hiram's entering freshmen exceed national norms: in 1999, SAT I medians were 580 (verbal) and 560 (math); the ACT composite median was 24. Between 50 and 60 percent of the College's graduates go on to graduate school or professional school within five years. The College was awarded a Phi Beta Kappa chapter in 1971.

Ninety-three percent of Hiram's students live in the eleven residence halls and eat their meals on campus. Newer College buildings are designed to complement Hiram's old, distinguished Western Reserve architecture. Student services include a health center, a fitness center, a sports medicine clinic, a career placement office, professional counseling on a wide range of personal and academic concerns, optional religious services and activities, and sports for everyone. There are honorary societies, social clubs, music and drama groups, student publications, religious groups, and student government and political and social-action groups. The campus radio station and student publications are directed by the students themselves.

Location
Hiram's campus is in the scenic, rural Western Reserve area of northeastern Ohio. Located in Portage County, the campus is about 35 miles southeast of Cleveland. The area is served by excellent state and federal highway systems, which make the College easily accessible. Cleveland Hopkins Airport is an hour's drive from Hiram, and campus cars can be commissioned on advance request, providing transportation to and from the airport. The campus is a day's drive or less from New England and northern East Coast cities and about a 6-hour drive from Baltimore, Chicago, and Washington, D.C. By air, it is an hour from the East Coast and less than an hour from Chicago and the Middle Atlantic coast.

Majors and Degrees
Hiram College awards the Bachelor of Arts (B.A.). Areas of major concentration are art; art history, biology, biomedical humanities, chemistry, classical studies, communication, computer science, economics, elementary and secondary education, English, environmental studies, French, German, history, integrated language arts, integrated social studies, international economics and management, management, mathematics, music, philosophy, physics, political science, psychobiology, psychology, religious studies, social science, sociology, Spanish, and theater arts. Minors are available in most areas of study as well as in exercise and sport science, health care humanities, international studies, photography, and writing.

Preprofessional programs offer preparation for study in a wide variety of fields, including dentistry, engineering, law, medicine, physical therapy, and veterinary medicine.

Hiram also offers a cooperative, dual-degree program in engineering with Case Western Reserve University and Washington University, leading to a Bachelor of Arts degree from Hiram in a field of science or mathematics and a Bachelor of Science in engineering from the cooperating engineering school.

Academic Program
Hiram's academic calendar, the Hiram Plan, is unique among colleges and universities. Each fifteen-week semester is divided into a twelve-week and a three-week session. During the three-week session, students take only one intensive course. The plan provides two formats for learning, which increases opportunity for small group study with faculty, study in special topics, hands-on learning through field trips and internships, and study abroad.

Hiram College's commitment to the liberal arts is manifested in a core curriculum required of all students. Required courses include the Freshman Colloquium, a small, seminar course on a special topic taught by a student's adviser; First Year Seminar, providing an introduction to Western thought and emphasizing critical thinking, effective writing, and speaking; and a sequence of interdisciplinary courses.

The course of study in most areas of major concentration is specified by the departments and divisions. Students generally take ten courses from within a department, as well as two or three courses from related or supporting departments. Alternatively, a student, with the assistance of the adviser, may develop an area of concentration that consists of related courses from different academic areas, crossing departmental lines to focus on particular needs or interests. A student may also submit a proposal for an individually designed program to the Area of Concentration Board.

Off-Campus Arrangements
A number of domestic and international off-campus programs and study opportunities are available. Programs in Australia, England, France, Germany, Italy, Mexico, Turkey, and other locations are conducted by the College's own teaching staff. Study-abroad programs are available to students regardless of their major discipline, and more than 50 percent of the College's graduates have participated. Hiram students may also spend a semester at the School of Social Sciences and Public Affairs of the American University in Washington, D.C. Another facet of Hiram's off-campus opportunities is study at John Cabot University, a Hiram affiliate, which is the major American university in Rome. Students may also take advantage of exchange programs with Mithibai College of the University of Bombay, India, and Kansai University of Foreign Studies in Osaka, Japan. Other opportunities are offered through the College's affiliation with the Institute for European Studies and the Institute for Asian Studies.

Internships with corporations and agencies are also available in all academic departments, and arrangements are made for students on an individual basis.

Other opportunities for off-campus study in marine science are described in the section below.

Academic Facilities
A new science building, the Esther and Carl Gerstacker Science Hall, opened in January 2000. This $6.2-million state-of-the-art facility includes modern chemical laboratories specially designed for undergraduate instruction and research, plus a substantial amount of new chemical instrumentation. Hiram also opened a $7.2-million library in 1995. This five-level facility contains nearly 180,000 volumes in open stacks and features a reference area that includes recent government documents (the library is one of only 1,400 federal depositories in the U.S.); a media center featuring a listening library, videotape collection, and video production room; a computer area equipped with CD-ROM and printers, with access to the Internet and other resources on the information superhighway; and an archival pavilion that houses a number of special collections relating to the history of the Western Reserve, including the papers of notable Hiram alumni James A. Garfield, twentieth president of the United States, and poet Vachel Lindsay.

Other resources include the Stephens Memorial Observatory; Center for International Studies; Center for Literature, Medicine, and the Health Care Professions; Writing Center; InterVIEW™, a PC-based video conferencing and interview system; and SIGI Career Guidance System. The computer facilities include a fiber-optic network, Ethernet, two microcomputer laboratories, three student terminal rooms with laser printers, and a microcomputer center. Students have 24-hour access from their dormitories to Hiram's DEC VAXcluster as well as other computer systems on the network. Hiram is one of only a few undergraduate colleges in Ohio directly connected to the Cray Supercomputer at the Ohio Supercomputer Center in Columbus.

The 260-acre James H. Barrow Field Station encompasses a diversity of habitats that allow for the investigation of both aquatic and terrestrial ecosystems. These include permanent and temporary ponds, a natural and a simulated stream, old fields, and early- and late-successional forests, including a unique beech-maple climax forest. Facilities at the station include the Frohring Laboratory Building, which houses laboratories as well as natural history display areas open to the public; an observation building; a solar-heated, earth-bermed Aquatics Building that houses an experimental stream; and the Ruth E. Kennedy Memorial Nature Trail. The station buildings and the nature trail were built and are maintained by faculty members and students. Recent independent and/or team research projects involving students and faculty members from a variety of disciplines include examinations of the effects of fertilizer enrichment on an old-field ecosystem, the distribution of blood parasites in natural populations of small mammals, and the nesting success of bluebirds.

Northwoods Field Station in upper Michigan, a day's drive from Hiram, offers an additional facility for field trips, summer course work, and research activities.

Students interested in marine science have opportunities for advanced work at Shoals Marine Laboratory off the coast of New Hampshire and at the Gulf Coast Research Laboratory in Mississippi. The College's affiliations with these facilities provide students with field experience in Hiram courses and the opportunity to enroll in any of more than twenty specialized summer courses.

Costs

Costs for 1999–2000 were $17,230 for tuition and $5954 for room and board. Fees were $705, including a one-time fee of $225 that was charged to freshmen for the orientation program.

Financial Aid

More than 75 percent of Hiram's students receive financial aid based on need. All financial aid awards are made on a one-year basis, and each year a new Free Application for Federal Student Aid (FAFSA) must be submitted to determine eligibility. Most financial aid at Hiram is a combination of a loan, a job, and a scholarship or grant-in-aid. Scholarships awarded on the basis of merit are also available and range from $3000 to $12,000 per year. Aid includes Federal Pell Grants, Federal Supplemental Educational Opportunity Grants, Federal Perkins Loans, Federal Stafford Student Loans, state grants, Federal Work-Study awards, and veterans' benefits. Campus employment is available regardless of aid eligibility.

Faculty

Hiram has a teaching faculty of 68 full-time members, 95 percent of whom hold earned doctorates or the appropriate terminal degree. The student-faculty ratio is 12:1. The ideal of a "community of scholars" thrives at Hiram, where students engage in research side by side with their professors, enjoy extracurricular activities with their teachers, and reach out with the faculty to serve the community. Faculty concern and guidance begin even before the formal opening of the academic year. One week prior to opening, faculty members work with their advisees, groups of about 15 freshmen, as part of the first-year orientation program. This one-week program, the New Student Institute, is followed by a semester-long seminar in which the freshmen continue to meet as a group. Seminar topics introduce students to scholarship in the liberal arts tradition. Approximately twenty seminars are offered each year.

Student Government

The student governing body, or Student Senate, composed in part of members elected from the academic departments and residence halls, is very active at Hiram. The Senate administers a $150,000 student activities budget and is involved in almost all aspects of college policymaking and governance. It holds seats with faculty, staff, and administrators on most College committees, the College Executive Committee, and the Student Life Subcommittee of Hiram's Board of Trustees. The Kennedy Center Programming Board, an arm of the student government, plans recreational and cultural activities for the campus community.

Admission Requirements

Admission to Hiram College is competitive. The admission process attempts to bring to Hiram students who have the ability and desire to benefit from the College's educational programs. Candidates should have pursued a strong secondary school program of college preparation in the humanities, sciences, and social sciences. All applicants are required to submit SAT I or ACT scores.

Application and Information

Application materials include the completed application form and a nonrefundable $25 application fee; a secondary school report, which must be completed and returned to Hiram directly by the high school guidance counselor; the results of the SAT I or ACT; and an essay. Teacher recommendations are also required. The application deadline is March 15. Applicants are encouraged to visit the campus. The Office of Admission, located in Teachout-Price Hall, is open year-round for interviews from 9 a.m. to 4 p.m. on weekdays and from 9 a.m. to noon on Saturday (except during the summer months). Prospective students should address questions to:

Dean of Admission
Hiram College
Hiram, Ohio 44234
Telephone: 330-569-5169
          800-362-5280 (toll-free)
E-mail: admission@hiram.edu
World Wide Web: http://www.hiram.edu

Esther and Carl Gerstacker Science Hall.

HOBART AND WILLIAM SMITH COLLEGES
GENEVA, NEW YORK

The Colleges
Hobart and William Smith are independent, coordinate liberal arts colleges in Geneva, New York. Hobart College for men was founded in 1822; William Smith College for women, in 1908. The two Colleges have the same faculty; men and women attend all classes together and share one campus. Each College, however, awards its own degrees, has its own dean's office, and maintains its own student government and athletic programs. Residential options include both coeducational and single-sex housing, small houses, cooperatives, and theme houses. A number of residence halls, academic buildings, two gymnasiums, and numerous athletic fields are part of the Colleges' facilities. The Colleges' newest buildings include Rosenberg Hall (biology and chemistry) and the Melly Academic Center.

Location
Geneva, New York, a city of 15,000 people, is located on the northern shore of Seneca Lake, the largest of the scenic Finger Lakes. Rochester, Syracuse, and Ithaca are all within an hour's drive. Twenty-seven other colleges and universities are located in the Finger Lakes area.

Majors and Degrees
Hobart and William Smith Colleges offer Bachelor of Arts and Bachelor of Science degrees. Programs leading to provisional certification in elementary, secondary, and special education are offered. Departmental majors include anthropology, art (history and studio), biochemistry, biology, chemistry, classics, comparative literature, computer science, dance, economics, English, French, geoscience, history, mathematics, modern languages, music, philosophy, physics, political science, religious studies, sociology, and Spanish. Interdisciplinary and individualized majors have been developed in Africana studies; American studies; architectural studies; arts and education; Asian studies; critical social studies dialogues; environmental studies; European studies; Latin American studies; lesbian, gay, and bisexual studies; media and society; public policy studies; Russian area studies; urban studies; and women's studies.

The Colleges offer dual-degree programs in engineering in cooperation with Columbia University, Dartmouth College, Rensselaer Polytechnic Institute, and the University of Rochester. A 4-1 M.B.A. program is offered in conjunction with Clarkson University and the Rochester Institute of Technology. In addition, the Colleges offer a 3-4 degree in architecture with Washington University in Saint Louis. A five-year M.A.T. program is offered.

Academic Program
At the heart of a Hobart and William Smith education is the requirement that each student complete a major and a minor or two majors, one of which must be disciplinary and the other interdisciplinary. The first option gives a student depth of knowledge; the latter gives breadth by reaching across traditional disciplines. Each student must also address the Colleges' educational goals and objectives, which represent an understanding of the skills, areas of knowledge, and qualities of mind and character that identify a liberally educated man or woman. Students must demonstrate the following abilities: critical reading and listening; effective speaking and writing; skills for critical thinking and argumentation; experience with scientific inquiry; quantitative reasoning; an appreciation of artistic expression based in experience; an intellectually grounded understanding of race, gender, and class; critical knowledge of the multiplicity of world cultures; and an intellectually grounded foundation for ethical judgment and action.

The academic year is divided into two 14-week semesters. Students normally take four courses each semester.

Off-Campus Arrangements
There are a number of opportunities for off-campus study. Hobart and William Smith offer terms abroad on six continents, with programs in Australia, China, Denmark, the Dominican Republic, Ecuador, England, France, Germany, Iceland, India, Ireland, Israel, Italy, Japan, Korea, Mexico, Russia, Scotland, Senegal, Spain, Switzerland, and Vietnam. Domestic programs are also offered in Los Angeles, New York, and Washington, D.C. Many off-campus programs include internships. Hobart and William Smith participate in cooperative programs in architecture and engineering and in a 4-1 M.B.A. program.

Academic Facilities
Among the major academic and administrative buildings on the campus is the Warren Hunting Smith Library. The library contains more than 345,661 volumes, 2,056 periodicals, and 76,243 microform titles as well as classrooms, study areas, and audiovisual facilities. As a member of the Rochester Regional Resources Library Council, the library provides students with access to holdings in excess of 5 million volumes in other library collections through the interlibrary loan system. The Colleges' science facilities include modern laboratories, a 110-acre research preserve, a science library, and a 65-foot research and laboratory vessel that is used for studies on Seneca Lake. Science students regularly participate in research projects at Geneva's New York State Agricultural Experiment Station, a world-class facility. A computer center and the Houghton House arts center are also part of the Colleges' facilities.

Costs
The total annual cost of $31,224 for the 1999–2000 academic year included tuition of $23,865, room and board of $6882, and fees of $477. Personal expenses were about $800 per year, and books and supplies were approximately $750.

Financial Aid
More than 65 percent of Hobart and William Smith students receive financial aid. Hobart and William Smith Colleges' Scholarships, Federal Pell Grants, Federal Supplemental Educational Opportunity Grants, Federal Perkins Loans, Federal Work-Study Program awards, loans through the Federal Family Education Loan programs, and part-time employment are the most frequent sources of financial aid. New York State residents may be eligible for the New York State Tuition Assistance Program.

To determine financial need, the Colleges rely on an evaluation of the Free Application for Federal Student Aid (FAFSA) and the College Scholarship Service's Financial Aid PROFILE. Both forms should be filed before February 15. Financial aid awards are adjusted annually to meet changing needs.

Faculty

The full-time teaching faculty numbers 134 members, of whom more than 98 percent hold Ph.D. degrees. The student-faculty ratio is 13:1.

Student Government

There are two student governments at Hobart and William Smith. All Hobart students are members of the Hobart Student Association. All William Smith students are members of the William Smith Congress. These student governments each maintain legislative, judicial, and committee functions that provide for student self-determination at the Colleges. The student governments are also responsible for appropriating student financial resources to support the numerous cultural and social activities on campus.

Admission Requirements

Admission to the Colleges is based on demonstrated potential to undertake college-level work and to contribute to life on campus. The Committee on Admission is most interested in students with comprehensive high school programs. Applicants are expected to have had a minimum of 4 years of English, 2 years of algebra, 1 year of plane geometry, two laboratory sciences, and 2 years of a modern or classical language. Other units could come from social studies and from additional work in mathematics, science, literature, and languages. Two personal recommendations and scores on either the SAT I or the ACT examination are required. Candidates submitting scores on the SAT I are encouraged to submit the results of any SAT II Subject Tests. Campus tours and personal interviews are available throughout the year and may be arranged by contacting the appropriate admissions office.

Application and Information

Application should be made early in the senior year of high school and not later than February 1. A nonrefundable $45 fee must accompany each application. A campus visit, which may include an interview, is strongly recommended. First-year candidates are notified of their application results in late March and must respond by the Candidates Reply Date of May 1. Two early decision plans are offered to students who name Hobart or William Smith as their first-choice college. Under these plans, students must apply before November 15 of their senior year in high school and are notified of the admission decision by December 15; students applying before January 1 are notified by February 1. The Colleges also offer an early admission plan to selected high school juniors as well as a deferred entrance plan, under which students may delay the start of their college education for up to two years.

For more information, students should contact:

Mara O'Laughlin
Director of Admissions
Hobart and William Smith Colleges
629 South Main Street
Geneva, New York 14456
Telephone: 800-852-2256 (toll-free) (Hobart)
               800-245-0100 (toll-free) (William Smith)
E-mail: hoadm@hws.edu (Hobart)
        wsadm@hws.edu (William Smith)

Coxe Hall, on the campus of Hobart and William Smith Colleges.

HOFSTRA UNIVERSITY
HEMPSTEAD, NEW YORK

The University

Hofstra University is traditional, contemporary, and innovative. As universities go, Hofstra is young, but the extraordinary vigor and growth shown in the brief span of its life have marked it as an educational phenomenon. The University offers the student with ability a good education and unusual opportunities for choice. In many fields, special facilities—clinics, Hofstra's Television Institute, the radio station, a reading center, and a playhouse—enrich the curriculum. Hofstra's philosophy is to provide a strong foundation in the liberal arts and sciences. The University's ultimate goal for its students is "the pursuit of knowledge, understanding, and wisdom upon which a good life can be built." The extracurricular program is full and varied. As a result of the Program for the Higher Education of the Disabled, Hofstra is 100 percent accessible to persons with disabilities. Necessary services are provided for wheelchair-bound and other disabled students who meet all academic requirements for admission.

Students attending Hofstra come from forty-four states and sixty-four countries. The freshman class numbers more than 1,500. The total enrollment at Hofstra is approximately 13,000; there are 9,316 full-time undergraduates and 3,824 part-time undergraduates. Major University divisions are the College of Liberal Arts and Sciences, the School of Communication, the School of Business, the School of Education and Allied Human Services, New College, the School of Law, University Without Walls, and the Division of Continuing Education. Residential facilities accommodate 4,100 students in modern on-campus residence halls.

Location

Hofstra's campus, covering 240 acres, is situated 25 miles east of New York City. The surrounding Long Island area offers recreation of all kinds and includes boating facilities, beaches, golf courses, and theaters. Cultural and educational facilities in New York City are readily accessible by car or railroad.

Majors and Degrees

The Bachelor of Arts (B.A.) is awarded in Africana studies, American studies, anthropology, art history, Asian studies, biology, chemistry, classics, communication, computer science, dance, drama, economics, education (dual enrollment required), engineering science, English, fine arts, French, geography, geology, German, Hebrew, history, Italian, Judaica, Latin, liberal arts, mathematics, music, philosophy, physics, political science, psychology, Russian, social science, sociology, Spanish, speech arts, and speech therapy. The Bachelor of Business Administration (B.B.A.) is awarded in accounting and business law, finance, business computer information systems, international business, management, and marketing. The Bachelor of Science (B.S.) is offered in applied economics, applied physics, applied social science, biochemistry, biology, chemistry, communication arts, computer science, computer science/mathematics, economics/business, electrical engineering, environmental resources, exercise specialist studies, fine arts, geology, industrial engineering, mathematics, mechanical engineering, and music. The Bachelor of Science in Education (B.S.Ed.) is offered with specializations in fine arts, music, physical education, and secretarial and office studies. The Bachelor of Engineering (B.E.) is offered in engineering science with specializations in bioengineering, civil engineering, electrical engineering, environmental engineering, and mechanical engineering. The Bachelor of Fine Arts (B.F.A.) is awarded in theater arts.

The School of Education and Allied Human Services also offers a program leading to the degree of Associate in Applied Science (A.A.S.) with a specialization in elementary education. The objective of this curriculum is to encourage the acquisition of skills and to broaden the backgrounds of personnel engaged in auxiliary roles in the elementary school. The courses are given during evening and summer sessions and may be taken on a part-time basis.

The Hofstra-Columbia Cooperative Program in Engineering is a 5-year program leading to a B.A. degree from Hofstra and a B.S. from Columbia University or to a B.E. from Hofstra and an M.S. from Columbia University.

Academic Program

The requirement for the B.A. degree is 124 semester hours, of which 94 must be in liberal arts and 30 in free electives. Successful completion of at least 124 semester hours with a quality point average of 2.0 or better is required for graduation. For the major, each academic department defines the special pattern of required and suggested study that suits its discipline. Beyond this major requirement, five general requirements in humanities, natural sciences, social sciences, English, and foreign languages must be fulfilled. A candidate for graduation with the degree of B.B.A. must successfully complete at least 125 semester hours with a quality point average of 2.0 or better, completing at least 62 hours in liberal arts subjects (humanities, mathematics, natural sciences, and social sciences), 30 hours in general business courses (accounting, business law, quantitative methods, business writing, finance, and general business), and all major and additional requirements as listed under the department of specialization. Each of the scientific-technical programs leading to the B.S. degree requires a total of 124 to 134 semester hours, of which approximately half must be in liberal arts courses exclusive of those offered by the academic department of major specialization.

The School of Education and Allied Human Services is a professional school to which undergraduate students are admitted only after they have established a broad liberal arts foundation. All undergraduate candidates for enrollment in the elementary education program must have an overall quality point average of at least 2.5 at the time of enrollment in the School of Education and must complete a dual-degree B.A. program with majors in elementary education and a liberal arts area. Candidates for the secondary education program must have an overall average of 2.5 or better. Frequently, students must take more than the minimum 124 semester hours for graduation in order to meet the subject requirements of their academic departments.

New College is one of the two Bachelor of Arts degree–granting colleges for full-time day students at Hofstra. Founded in 1959, New College aims to provide contemporary programs to fulfill the academic needs and interests of students within the traditions of the liberal arts. Emphasizing small, faculty-offered classes and, as adjuncts, independent study and off-campus education, New College has elective programs in the humanities, social sciences, natural sciences, and interdisciplinary studies. Within this context of "area studies," students may also participate in programs for preprofessional study, the study of the creative arts, and, through a coordination of resources from all "area studies," programs emphasizing human services. To graduate from New College, a student must successfully complete 120 credits in a manner consistent with general graduation requirements and those contained within an area of study.

Candidates for the A.A.S. degree must complete at least 60 semester hours with a grade point average of at least 2.0. The student must complete 40 credits in liberal arts plus all the departmental major requirements and additional requirements for the major in elementary education.

College credit may be granted to qualified students passing such external examinations as the College Board Advanced Placement tests, the CLEP tests, and the New York State College Proficiency Examination. A maximum of 30 credits may be granted for external credit by examination.

A preprofessional adviser provides a direct link between students and medical, dental, and law schools.

Off-Campus Arrangements

Hofstra sponsors summer study-abroad programs in such places as China, England, France, Germany, Italy, Korea, the Netherlands, and Spain. Students wishing to pursue such study may consult with the Advisement Office. Other overseas courses are organized by faculty members as part of credit-bearing courses. Recent courses have been held in Mexico and Egypt; similar courses are being planned for India and China.

Academic Facilities

Hofstra's fully computerized library has seating for 1,200 students and contains more than 1.4 million volumes (including law), as well as special units for periodicals, reserve books, documents, curriculum materials, special collections, and microfilm. The University's computer facility is designed to provide the latest in time-sharing capability in a multiprogramming environment for both academic and administrative purposes. The Language Laboratory has modern tape-recording and playback facilities for perfecting foreign language skills. Other facilities include the Television Institute, Hofstra Museum, Career Center, Career Development Center, Psychology Evaluation and Research Center, radio station, Reading Center and Clinic, Speech and Hearing Center, Physical Fitness Center, Hofstra Stadium, and Olympic-size indoor swimming pool.

Costs

Tuition per semester (12–17 credits) was $6875 in 1999–2000. A University fee of $275 per semester covered certain University services, such as campus activities, admission to theatrical productions, and publication subscriptions. Tuition and fees totaled about $14,400 per college year; room and board averaged $7350. A tuition deposit of $250 and a room reservation fee of $100 are required; these fees are applied to tuition and room and board, respectively. Off-campus housing is also available. New College tuition was approximately $340 more per semester for 12–20 credits. (These costs are subject to change for 2000–01.)

Financial Aid

Financial aid options range from scholarships through assistance grants to loans and part-time jobs. About 84 percent of all students receive financial help, and almost 65 percent work to earn part of their expenses. Scholarships average $3825 per year; loans average $2625 per year. Hofstra subscribes to the principles of the College Scholarship Service in determining the amount of awards. Federal funds include Federal Perkins Loans, Federal Pell and Federal Supplemental Educational Opportunity grants, and Federal Work-Study Program awards. To be considered for financial aid, completed financial aid applications and credentials (including the Free Application for Federal Student Aid) should be received on or before March 1.

Faculty

Hofstra's faculty numbers 1,176 members, including 489 full-time members; 90 percent of the full-time faculty members hold the highest degree in their field. All faculty members are expected to serve the undergraduate and graduate schools as both teachers and academic counselors. Their primary function is to teach. Nevertheless, individual members find the time to write and carry on significant research. Hofstra has some distinguished teachers, and nationally known scholars fill special chairs in economics and literature. The student-faculty ratio is 13:1. The average class size is 24.

Student Government

The chief instrument of government is the Student Government Association, which supervises and coordinates all student activities and serves as a liaison with the faculty and administration. The Student Government Association sends representatives to the committees of the University Senate—Executive, Curriculum, Standards, Faculty, University Planning, and Scholarship and Student Aid. It supervises student activities through nine standing committees. The Judiciary Board has responsibility for promoting justice in the conduct of student affairs.

Admission Requirements

Admission to Hofstra is very competitive. Hofstra employs joint criteria for the admission of freshman candidates. The high school rank in class is considered of primary importance, and SAT I and/or ACT scores are given secondary consideration. The mean combined SAT I score (verbal and math) for the class entering in the fall of 1999 was 1092. Of these freshmen, 50 percent scored in the top fifth. To be considered, an applicant should rank in the top third of his or her graduating class and present a minimum of 16 academic units: 4 of English, 3 of history and social studies, 2 of foreign language, 2 of mathematics, 1 of science, and 4 of electives in other academic subjects. Prospective engineering majors need at least 3 years of mathematics and considerably more science, including physics. SAT I or ACT scores must be submitted, preferably in December of the senior year. Interviews are recommended for freshman applicants. Hofstra accepts applications from freshman, transfer, international, and disabled students, regardless of their place of residence.

The University has an early decision plan for students whose first choice is Hofstra. The completed application must be submitted before December 1. Early admission may be granted, on completion of three years of secondary school, to students with extraordinary maturity and promise. A personal interview is required for early admission. Transfer students with a cumulative grade point average of 2.5 or better (on a 4.0 scale) from a fully accredited institution are considered for admission. Transfer credit is granted for all appropriate courses completed with a grade of C or better (D or better if 30 credits have been completed with a grade point average of 3.0 or better).

Application and Information

Freshman applicants must submit the application, a $40 application fee, the high school transcript, test scores, and a guidance counselor's recommendation. Transfer students must submit an application, the application fee, high school and college transcripts, and test scores (if fewer than 24 semester hours were attempted at the previous college). For additional information, students should contact:

Dean of Admissions
Hofstra University
Hempstead, New York 11549
Telephone: 516-463-6700
       800-HOFSTRA (toll-free)
Fax: 516-463-5100
E-mail: hofstra@hofstra.edu
World Wide Web: http://www.hofstra.edu

HOLLINS UNIVERSITY
ROANOKE, VIRGINIA

The University

Hollins University was founded in 1842 as Virginia's first chartered women's college. Today, Hollins is an independent arts and sciences university that enrolls approximately 1,100 students in its undergraduate programs for women and its coed graduate programs. Hollins is proud of its creative writing program, career internships, average class size of 14, and study-abroad opportunities. Hollins prepares its students for career excellence in the sciences, humanities, and business. In addition to the Bachelor of Arts degree in thirty major fields, Hollins awards a Master of Arts degree in children's literature, creative writing, liberal studies, screenwriting and film studies, and teaching. With a coeducational, graduate creative writing program long acknowledged to be one of the best of its size in the country, Hollins students are exposed to the creative genius of Pulitzer- and Nobel-prize-winning writers. A 10:1 student-faculty ratio enables students to work closely with their professors both inside and outside the classroom.

Situated on a 475-acre campus in the Shenandoah Valley of the Blue Ridge Mountains, Hollins is a quiet campus for the serious student looking to broaden her mind through a rigorous academic program. Students come to Hollins from forty-two states and nine countries and bring with them cultural and ethnic diversity. Nontraditional-age women can earn their bachelor's degrees in the Horizon Program.

Because approximately 95 percent of Hollins women live on campus in dormitories, language houses, or University apartments, a large family of friends develops in the first year and replaces the need for sororities. However, for those interested in group activities, there are nearly fifty clubs and organizations, including a multicultural club, Black Student Alliance, a literary society, and political, environmental, women's, and volunteer organizations. Each year, 40 percent of the student body volunteers in social service agencies locally and internationally, including a Jamaica service project. The $14-million Wyndham Robertson Library features state-of-the-art technology and is a National Literary Landmark. An $8-million athletic complex enables Hollins to compete and train its athletes more effectively for NCAA Division III competition in basketball, fencing, field hockey, golf, lacrosse, riding, soccer, swimming, tennis, and volleyball. Hollins's strong riding program offers top facilities, including stables where collegiate riders may board their horses. The academic program is enriched by guest lectures, dance and theater productions, and the annual Literary Festival.

Location

Hollins is located on the outskirts of Roanoke, a cosmopolitan center with a population of approximately 225,000. Roanoke has its own opera, ballet, and orchestra. Mill Mountain Theatre, the Science Museum, and the Center in the Square cultural center provide entertainment for the area. The historic downtown market, with fresh flower and fruit stands and specialty shops, is a favorite spot on the weekends. Hollins is a 3½-hour drive from both Washington, D.C., and Richmond, 5 hours from Virginia Beach, and within easy driving distance of more than a dozen other colleges. The Roanoke Regional Airport is a 10-minute drive from campus. The campus has been described as "achingly picturesque." The Front Quadrangle is listed on the National Register of Historic Places. The Blue Ridge Mountains are minutes from campus and ideal for hiking the Appalachian Trail, camping, caving, and skiing.

Majors and Degrees

Hollins grants the Bachelor of Arts degree in art history, biology, business, chemistry, classical studies, communications studies, computational sciences, computer science, creative writing, dance, economics, English, film and photography, French, German, history, interdisciplinary studies, international studies, mathematics, music, philosophy, physics, political science, psychology, religious studies, sociology, Spanish, studio art, theater, and women's studies. Minors are offered in most major areas, and preprofessional programs are offered in education, law, medicine, and veterinary science. The Rubin Writing Semester offers women from other colleges and universities who want intensive study in creative writing and contemporary literature with Hollins's lively community of writers an opportunity to become visiting student writers.

Hollins has a 3-2 engineering program with Washington University and Virginia Tech and a six-year dual-degree architectural program with Virginia Tech.

Academic Program

Candidates for the Bachelor of Arts degree normally follow a four-year program. They are required to complete 128 credits of academic work and 16 Short Term credits. The Short Term begins in January and lasts four weeks. First-year students are required to take a seminar on campus. Students may spend subsequent Short Terms pursuing career internships, independent study, outward bound experiences, or service projects. Every student is required to take 8 credits in each of the four divisions: humanities, social sciences, natural sciences and mathematics, and fine arts, and must demonstrate competency in oral communication, quantitative reasoning, and information technology. In addition to divisional requirements, two regular terms of physical education or varsity sport participation are required. Students must choose a major by the end of their sophomore year and complete a minimum of 32 credits in the major field prior to graduation. Each first-year student must meet a writing requirement. Hollins grants 4 academic credits for Advanced Placement examination scores of 4 or 5 and in some cases for a score of 3. Hollins grants 8 academic credits for International Baccalaureate scores between 5 and 7 and up to 32 credits for an I.B. diploma.

Off-Campus Arrangements

In 1955, Hollins was one of the nation's first colleges to establish a program that enabled students to study overseas. For semester or full-year study, Hollins has its own programs in England and France and consortium programs in Germany, Ireland, Japan, Mexico, and Spain. Hollins's link with Christie's Education in London provides art history students with an extensive year of study abroad and hands-on experience in museums and auction houses. Hollins's program is Christie's first educational connection with an American college or university. Forty-four percent of Hollins students study abroad before graduation. Domestic exchange programs are possible with members of the six-college exchange: Hampden-Sydney College, Mary Baldwin College, Randolph-Macon College, Randolph-Macon Woman's College, Sweet Briar College, and Washington and Lee University. The Washington Semester at American University and the United Nations Semester provide juniors with an opportunity to study the political process in more detail.

Academic Facilities

The library collection is one of the largest private undergraduate collections in Virginia. The entire collection—books, documents, audiovisual materials, and periodicals—contains more than 372,000 items, including 256,000 books, 3,000 audiovisual titles, and 7,000 current journal titles, many with electronic full-text access. The microforms area holds more than 100 million microform pieces. The library has been a selective depository for U.S. government documents since 1968. The Dana Science Building houses modern laboratories and research facilities for computerized online recording and analysis of physiological and behavioral data, plant and animal tissue culture, photomicroscopy and electron microscopy, biochemistry and molecular biology, chromatography, spectrophotometry, electrochemistry, gas kinetics, and centrifugation. A tower with 20-cm reflecting telescopes enables students to make astronomical observations, and up-to-date minicomputer and microcomputer hardware gives every student easy access to a broad range of software. A state-of-the-art computer network has been developed to link individual student rooms to the library, to laboratories, and to college and universities nationwide. Computer Services operates a VMS and UNIX cluster, a fiber-optic-based data communications network, six computer labs that are open seven days a week, and sophisticated software, including word processing, multimedia, and graphics. The campus also has a state-of-the-art library, an art gallery, a writing center, a preschool, a women's center, and a career development center. Every dormitory room has cable and Internet access.

Costs

The 2000–01 costs are $16,960 for tuition and $6415 for room and board, which includes telephone, cable television, and computer network connections for each student's room. The Student Government Association fee is $250. The University estimates a budget of $600 for books and $800 for personal expenses, excluding travel costs.

Financial Aid

All students are admitted without regard to financial need. Financial aid is awarded on the basis of both academic merit and need. Sixty percent receive need-based aid in the form of grants, merit scholarships, low-interest loans, and campus jobs. The average award in 1999–2000 was $14,846, which included allowances for books, transportation, and personal expenses. The types of scholarships and grants available to undergraduates are Federal Pell Grants, Federal Supplemental Educational Opportunity Grants (FSEOG), state grants, University scholarships and grants, private scholarships and grants, academic merit scholarships, and aid for undergraduate students who are members of a minority group. Federal Perkins Loans, Federal PLUS, and Federal Stafford Student Loans are also available. Tuition Plan Inc., Knight Tuition Plans, deferred payment plans, and guaranteed tuition help ease tuition payments. A financial aid form should be filed with the financial aid office by March 1. Notification of awards is on a rolling basis.

Faculty

Faculty members are committed to teaching and are dedicated to their students. Although scholarly research and writing is emphasized, primary attention is placed on education. Currently, there are 82 full-time and 13 part-time faculty members, of whom 56 percent are women; 94 percent of the full-time faculty members hold the doctoral or corresponding terminal degree in their fields. With a student-faculty ratio of 10:1 and an average class size of 14, students have considerable opportunity for personal attention. No courses are taught by graduate assistants, and 51 percent of freshman classes are taught by tenured faculty members.

Student Government

Each year, students sign the honor code, pledging not to lie, cheat, or steal. Hollins is thereby able to conduct daily operations with a great deal of trust. Final exams are freely scheduled and administered by students under the Independent Exam System. The campus judicial system is run by the students. Students who are elected to the Student Government Association have the authority to administer all student-related activities. Weekly Senate meetings are open to the entire campus. Students are represented on policymaking faculty committees and the Board of Trustees. Most students participate in some form of student government committee work.

Admission Requirements

To be considered for admission, a student must have completed a minimum of 16 secondary school units in English, mathematics, science, social studies, and foreign language. All students must take the SAT I or the ACT; three SAT II Subject Tests, including the Writing Test with essay, are recommended. In addition to standardized test scores, the Admissions Committee takes into account an applicant's secondary school record, class rank, essay, recommendation, and personal interview. Transfer students are accepted in both semesters. International applicants can submit TOEFL scores in place of the SAT I or ACT.

At Hollins, the application process is very personal. The admissions officers go to great lengths to ensure that Hollins and the applicant are a good match.

Application and Information

Hollins has a formal early decision plan. The early decision application deadline is December 1; the deadline is February 15 for regular admission. Notification of admission is on a rolling basis beginning December 15 for early decision candidates and January 15 for regular admission candidates. The application fee is $25. A $400 tuition deposit must be made by May 1. For more information, students should contact:

Office of Admissions
Hollins University
P.O. Box 9707
Roanoke, Virginia 24020
Telephone: 540-362-6401
           800-456-9595 (toll-free)
E-mail: huadm@hollins.edu
World Wide Web: http://www.hollins.edu

A view of part of Hollins's historic Front Quadrangle.

HOOD COLLEGE
FREDERICK, MARYLAND

The College

Hood College, founded in 1893 as a private residential college for women, offers majors in twenty-six fields of study. Hood prepares talented students to excel in their areas of academic interest and to achieve their personal and educational goals. The College's teaching, curriculum, and on-campus facilities, together with the resources available in the Washington, D.C., and Baltimore areas, enable Hood students to apply their strengths most effectively and to set a clear direction for their futures.

Hood graduates, with their strong backgrounds in the liberal arts, have proven exceptionally successful in their career fields and in graduate or professional study. At Hood, students develop every facet of themselves—the ethical, the intellectual, the physical, and the emotional. Hood students, as the College motto suggests, are educated in "heart, mind, and hand."

In Hood's classrooms, laboratories, library, and discussion groups, students acquire a depth of knowledge and a repertoire of skills that serve them well throughout their lives. Opportunities to link classroom learning with practical experience are ample. Internships, research projects, travel grants, and international experiences enable Hood students to study and work independently or as team members to address the complex issues of the twenty-first century. Frederick, the second-largest city in Maryland; the Washington, D.C., and Baltimore areas; and locations abroad provide a rich mix of settings in which Hood students may explore, learn, and shape lifelong values, as well as acquire hands-on career experience.

The heart of Hood College is its faculty—women and men chosen both for their command of their disciplines and for their love of teaching. Hood's classes are small and the atmosphere is one of respect for the viewpoints of others. Students often work with a faculty member to explore areas of specific academic interest or to collaborate on a plan, a project, or an analysis. At Hood, the faculty members serve as undergraduate advisers, guiding students in course selection, in planning a four-year program of study, and in reaching long-term academic and career goals.

The College offers graduate degrees in eight programs of study: biomedical science, business administration (M.B.A.), computer science, curriculum and instruction, education, environmental biology, management of information technology, and psychology. Undergraduates may take graduate-level courses in their senior year; students may earn a combined bachelor's/master's degree in one of several fields in five years.

Hood College is accredited by the Commission on Higher Education of the Middle States Association of Colleges and Schools and is approved by the Maryland Higher Education Commission. Graduates of the teacher education program receive certification to teach in Maryland as well as reciprocity to teach in thirty-five other states. The social work program is accredited by the National Council on Social Work Education.

Location

Hood occupies a beautiful, tree-shaded 50-acre campus in the northeast section of Frederick, just a few minutes' walk from the historic district. Less than an hour's drive from the Hood campus is Washington, D.C., which offers a remarkable range of cultural, educational, and recreational opportunities as well as many internship sites. Hood provides easy access to Washington through its shuttle bus to the metrorail system, which services the metropolitan area. The international port of Baltimore, the historic cities of Gettysburg and Annapolis, and more than thirty colleges and universities are all within an hour's drive of the campus. College-sponsored excursions include outdoor recreation such as skiing and white-water rafting.

Majors and Degrees

The Bachelor of Arts degree is offered in the following majors: art history, biochemistry, biology, chemistry, communication arts, early childhood education, economics, English, environmental science and policy, French, French-German, history, information and computer science, Latin American studies, law and society, management, mathematics, philosophy, political science, psychology, religion, social work, sociology, Spanish, and special education. The Bachelor of Science degree is offered in computer science. Hood students often undertake two majors or a major and one or two minors. Secondary education certificate programs are available in biology, chemistry, English, French, history, mathematics, and Spanish.

Preprofessional preparation and advisement is available to students who wish to pursue advanced degrees in dentistry, law, medicine, or veterinary medicine. Hood offers an active Pre-Law Society for students interested in careers in the legal profession, as well as an undergraduate chapter of the American Medical Student Association for those who are pursuing the premedicine program.

Hood College and George Washington University in Washington, D.C., offer a dual-degree program that includes civil, electrical, and mechanical engineering and operations research and computational science. A student who completes this jointly sponsored 3-2 engineering program receives a B.A. degree in mathematics from Hood College and a B.S. degree in engineering from George Washington University.

Academic Program

Hood provides a wide range of programs supported by a fully networked campus with Internet access, sophisticated science laboratories, a fully computerized library, and advanced computer equipment. Hood's core curriculum exposes students to a range of academic disciplines and helps them to understand the connections and tensions among those disciplines. Reading, writing, analytical, and computing skills are refined and strengthened as students complete the carefully conceived core requirements. Each year a limited number of highly talented new students are invited to participate in Hood's Honors Program. The College provides special grants for creative writing studies, research and travel, and summer projects, to name a few.

Off-Campus Arrangements

Students in every major may earn academic credit by completing an internship. Students also use internships to explore career options and gain practical experience in their chosen fields. Hood's internship locations have included embassies, congressional offices, nationally recognized cancer research laboratories, major corporations, museums and art galleries, financial institutions, government agencies and nonprofit organizations, hospitals, radio and television stations, newspapers, and magazines.

Hood offers study-abroad opportunities through its own program at the Université de Strasbourg in France and the Hood/CIEE Program in Seville, as well as exchange programs with Seoul Women's University and the Universidad de Chile. Students may also arrange for study in other countries. In addition, Hood is affiliated with the Public Leadership Educational Network (PLEN), which offers seminars and internships in Washington, D.C., and several international locations. Through the Duke University Marine Sciences Education Consortium, Hood students may use marine laboratory facilities for independent study projects or course work in Beaufort, North Carolina.

Academic Facilities

The traditional redbrick, white-columned buildings on the Hood campus house excellent classroom and laboratory facilities. A library/information technology center contains more than 165,000 volumes as well as 220,000 microform items and 950 periodicals. Students have access to national and international library databases from various locations on campus through the College's electronic network.

Facilities include an academic computing center that houses a VAX-6210 computer, a 24-hour computing lab, terminal access in academic departments and laboratories, a Netscape lab, an observatory, an audiovisual-tutorial biology laboratory, individual psychology laboratories, a child development laboratory and nursery school, simultaneous-translation and language laboratories, a visual-communications studio, art and photographic studios, an art gallery, music practice rooms and three organs, the Huntsinger Aquatic Center, an Academic Services Center, and a Career Planning and Placement Center, which houses a state-of-the-art videoteleconferencing computer that allows students to interview face-to-face with potential employers. Hood's new Hodson Science and Technology Center, scheduled for completion for the fall 2001 semester, will complement Hood students' traditional grounding in the liberal arts with strong preparation for success in many science-related fields.

Costs

In 2000–01, the comprehensive cost for resident students, which includes tuition, room, and board, is $25,520. Tuition for commuting students is $18,620.

Financial Aid

More than half of Hood's students receive institutionally funded financial aid. Grants; low-cost, long-term loans; and on-campus work opportunities are available for eligible students. Hood offers a comprehensive program of merit-based scholarships. Selection for these scholarships is generally based upon academic accomplishment, contribution to school and community, leadership ability, or unique talents and special achievements. Merit Scholarships are renewable during the undergraduate program. A brochure entitled *Financing Your Education* is available from the College.

Faculty

Hood's student-faculty ratio is 10:1, and there are 73 full-time professors, 96 percent of whom hold the terminal degree in their fields. In addition, professionals and specialists with particular areas of expertise are brought to campus to teach individual courses. Hood has one of the highest percentages of women faculty members of any independent college in the United States.

Student Government

Through Hood's Student Government Association, students are involved in every aspect of community life, from academic affairs to residential life. Hood students enjoy an unusual degree of responsibility for their own governance. Hood's Honor Code embodies principles to which its students subscribe and promotes mature consideration of and respect for the needs and rights of all members of the College community.

Admission Requirements

Hood College seeks a talented and diverse student body whose members demonstrate academic achievement and potential, leadership ability, contributions to their communities, concern for the rights of others, and respect for their viewpoints. Admission to the College is selective and is based upon the quality of the secondary school record, standardized test scores, recommendations from counselors and classroom teachers, and special talents. Candidates for freshman admission should submit the Hood Application for Admission, Hood's electronic application, or the Common Application; SAT I scores; appropriate recommendations; an official high school transcript; and any other supporting material that demonstrates the quality of the candidate's preparation to undertake a challenging curriculum at Hood College. ACT and TOEFL scores are accepted. Interviews are highly recommended and campus visits are strongly recommended.

Application and Information

Applications and the $35 application fee should be filed no later than February 15 for fall entrance. Students are encouraged to apply as early reply candidates. The deadline for early reply admission is November 1. Notification for early reply admission is December 15. The deadline for regular decision admission is February 15. Notification for regular decision admission is March 15.

A student viewbook, financial aid information, an application form, and other materials may be obtained by contacting:

Director of Admissions
Hood College
401 Rosemont Avenue
Frederick, Maryland 21701-8575
Telephone: 301-696-3400
           800-922-1599 (toll-free)
Fax: 301-696-3819
E-mail: admissions@hood.edu
World Wide Web: http://www.hood.edu

Hood College's 50-acre campus features broad lawns, flowering trees, and stately redbrick buildings.

HOPE COLLEGE
HOLLAND, MICHIGAN

The College

Founded in 1862, Hope College has always promoted, in a liberal arts setting, the dual concept of preparation for life and vocation. The demanding academic program is supported by an accepting Christian campus community. Students from all walks of life are welcomed, respected, and given freedom to grow in this vibrant environment. Preparation for a career and for life in general involves both classroom and extracurricular activities. Hope sponsors seven local fraternities and six local sororities. Other activities include student publications, musical groups, and political organizations. Students manage an FM radio station, and their cable TV shows are broadcast weekly to the Holland community. There are four major theater productions each year as well as a film series, a Great Performance Series, and lectures by outstanding speakers. Many Christian activities broaden the range of student involvement, including Chaplain's Office Ministries, Fellowship of Christian Athletes, Intervarsity Christian Fellowship, and similar organizations. Voluntary chapel is offered three weekdays and Sunday, and is well attended. Intercollegiate sports include baseball, basketball, cross-country, football, golf, soccer, swimming, tennis, and track for men and basketball, cross-country, golf, soccer, softball, swimming, tennis, track, and volleyball for women. Club sports include lacrosse, ice hockey, sailing, men's volleyball, and Ultimate Frisbee. An extensive program of intramural sports is also maintained. An excellent health and recreation facility is available for student use. As Hope is a residential college, 78 percent of the students reside on campus. The College has eleven residence halls, with capacity ranging from 40 to 300 students. Styles include corridor, cluster suite, coed, and single-sex residence halls. In addition, upperclass students have the option of living in seven apartment buildings or fifty-five cottages, which are houses on or near campus that have been refurbished to accommodate students. The services of a well-developed Career Services Center are available to students and alumni for help with everything from assessing interests to arranging job interviews. The current enrollment is 2,943; 6 percent are part-time students. The student body represents thirty-eight states and thirty countries. Approximately 55 percent of the College's graduates become candidates for higher degrees within five years.

Location

Hope College's 45-acre wooded campus is in a residential area two blocks from the central business district of Holland, Michigan, a community that was founded by Dutch settlers and now has a population of 35,000 within city limits and a total area population of 100,000. The town is only a 30-minute drive from Grand Rapids and a 3-hour drive from Chicago and Detroit. An 85-acre biological field station is located on the shores of Lake Michigan, 5 miles from campus. Holland has long been known as a summer resort area, but it is also a fine spot for winter sports. Excellent relations exist between town and College. They have cooperated on the building of a municipal stadium for football and a Civic Center for Hope's intercollegiate basketball program.

Majors and Degrees

Hope College awards the Bachelor of Arts, Bachelor of Science, Bachelor of Music, Bachelor of Science in Engineering, and Bachelor of Science in Nursing degrees. Major programs include accounting, art, biology, business administration, chemistry, classical languages, communication, computer science, economics, engineering, engineering physics, English, environmental studies, French, geochemistry, geology, geophysics, German, history, kinesiology (physical education, exercise science, and athletic training), Latin, mathematics, music (church music education, instrumental education, literature and history, performance, theory, and vocal education), nursing, philosophy, physics, political science, psychology, religion, social work, sociology, Spanish, special education, and theater. Hope is fully accredited for certification in elementary, secondary, and special (emotionally impaired and learning disabilities) education. Preprofessional programs are offered in dentistry, law, medical technology, medicine, the ministry, and physical therapy. Alternatives to departmental majors include the composite major and contract curriculum major. The composite major is concentrated study in any approved combination of majors related to a particular academic or vocational objective of the student that meets Hope's educational objectives. The contract curriculum major allows a student to develop his or her own plan of study within the educational objectives of the College.

Academic Program

To graduate, students must pass all College-required courses, earn at least 126 credit hours, and meet minimum GPA requirements. A Phi Beta Kappa institution, Hope is widely respected as a liberal arts college that balances academic excellence with a deep concern for the quality of life of its students and alumni. Hope's commitment to the Christian faith provides an incentive for academic excellence and rigorous inquiry and a perspective on the wholeness and value of life. A core curriculum brings teachers and students together for the purpose of facilitating student growth in seven areas: communication skills, social adaptation, an understanding of our heritage and society, a respect for science and discovery, an awareness of other cultures, an understanding and appreciation of the arts, and an understanding of religion and its impact on society. To accomplish this, students select course work in the following disciplines: English, fine arts, foreign language, kinesiology, mathematics, natural science, philosophy, religion, and social science.

Off-Campus Arrangements

Hope College participates in off-campus programs sponsored and supervised by the Associated Colleges of the Midwest (ACM), the Institute for Asian Studies (IAS), the Institute for European Studies (IES), and the Great Lakes Colleges Association (GLCA). Students may study for a semester or a year in fifty-two countries; some continents and countries included are Africa, Austria, China, France, Germany, Great Britain, India, Japan, Latin America, Russia, Spain, the Middle East, and the Netherlands. Hope also runs a summer school in Vienna, Austria. The College's director of international education assists students in arranging programs in other countries. Domestic programs of one or two semesters' duration include the Washington Semester, Urban Semester in Philadelphia, Semester at the Chicago Metropolitan Center, Arts Program in New York City, Oak Ridge Science Semester, and Newberry Library Program in the Humanities.

Academic Facilities

The campus library contains more than 320,000 volumes, 1,550 periodical subscriptions, approximately 290,000 microforms, 11,800 video and audio recordings, and a 19,000-volume set in ultrafiche from the Library of American Civilization. The Peale

Science Center, containing the most modern laboratory equipment available, facilitates close working relationships between faculty and students. The physics laboratories include a 2.7-MeV Van de Graaff accelerator. Students from many academic disciplines take advantage of state-of-the-art computer facilities. Access to computing facilities is excellent across the campus. Theater, music, dance, and art departments have excellent facilities. The DePree Art Center is a $1.3-million facility that contains a major art gallery, classrooms, and studios.

Costs

Annual charges for the 2000–01 academic year are tuition, $16,554; room, $2382; board, $2842; and activity fee, $90, for a total fixed cost of $21,868.

Financial Aid

Types of aid include academic scholarships, grants, loans, and campus employment. Approximately 55 percent of Hope's students receive need-based aid. All accepted students may be considered for federal and Hope-funded assistance. Michigan residents may apply for state-funded programs. Applicants for aid should be accepted for admission and should submit the Free Application for Federal Student Aid (FAFSA) and the CSS PROFILE by February 15 to receive priority consideration for need-based aid. Hope sponsors National Merit Scholars with a $14,000-per-year tuition scholarship. Other academic awards range from $3000 to $14,000. Talent awards of $2500 are also available in the fine arts and creative writing. Seventy-three percent of 1999 freshmen received a merit award. Consideration for merit awards requires submission of all completed application for admission documents by February 15.

Faculty

Hope's 204 full-time faculty members hold degrees from more than 115 different universities; 80 percent hold a Ph.D. or terminal degree in their field. In addition, there are 84 part-time faculty members who teach in a broad range of disciplines, many of whom also teach, perform, and work outside the campus community. The student-faculty ratio is 14:1. Members of the faculty are dedicated to maintaining excellence in both teaching and scholarship and to taking a personal interest in students. Many conduct research programs in which students actively participate, sometimes as early as their freshman year. Faculty members also serve as academic advisers and frequently host student groups in their homes.

Student Government

Hope has an established community governance system. Decisions that concern the College community are made primarily by boards and committees composed of students, faculty, and administrators. The Academic Affairs, Administrative Affairs, and Campus Life boards bear the major responsibility for policy decisions, while subcommittees of each deal with more specific areas. Residence hall units elect representatives to Student Congress; these representatives are then appointed to the major boards. A Judicial Board of 7 students, 2 faculty members, and 1 staff person is charged with maintaining high standards of student life.

Admission Requirements

Hope is interested in students who seek the rigors of a proven, demanding academic program and feel comfortable in an open, supportive, Christian campus community. A complete admission file includes the completed application form, the application fee, high school/college transcripts, and either ACT or SAT I scores. Primary factors considered are the applicant's high school course selection, grades, rank, test scores, counselor's recommendation, essay, and involvement in extracurricular/ leadership activities. The College prefers that its students enroll having completed at least four college-preparatory classes per semester in the ninth through twelfth grades, including a variety of subject areas. The minimum background includes 4 years of English, 2 years of mathematics, 2 years of foreign language, 2 years of history or social studies, and at least 1 year of laboratory science. For fall 1999, freshmen had a mean GPA of 3.6 (on a 4.0 scale), and their average rank was in the 80th percentile. Campus visits are not required but are strongly recommended for interested students and their parents.

Application and Information

Most students apply for the fall semester, but applications are accepted for the spring semester or other sessions. Admission decisions are made on a rolling basis as applicants' files become complete. Students must submit the application form, official high school transcript, results of the SAT I or ACT, and $25 application fee. Prospective freshmen are encouraged to submit applications during the first semester of their senior year in high school. Completed applications for admission must be on file by February 15 to ensure consideration for merit scholarships. A $300 deposit is requested by May 1.

Hope College Admissions
69 East 10th Street
P.O. Box 9000
Holland, Michigan 49422-9000
Telephone: 616-395-7850
　　　　　　800-968-7850 (toll-free)
E-mail: admissions@hope.edu
World Wide Web: http://www.hope.edu

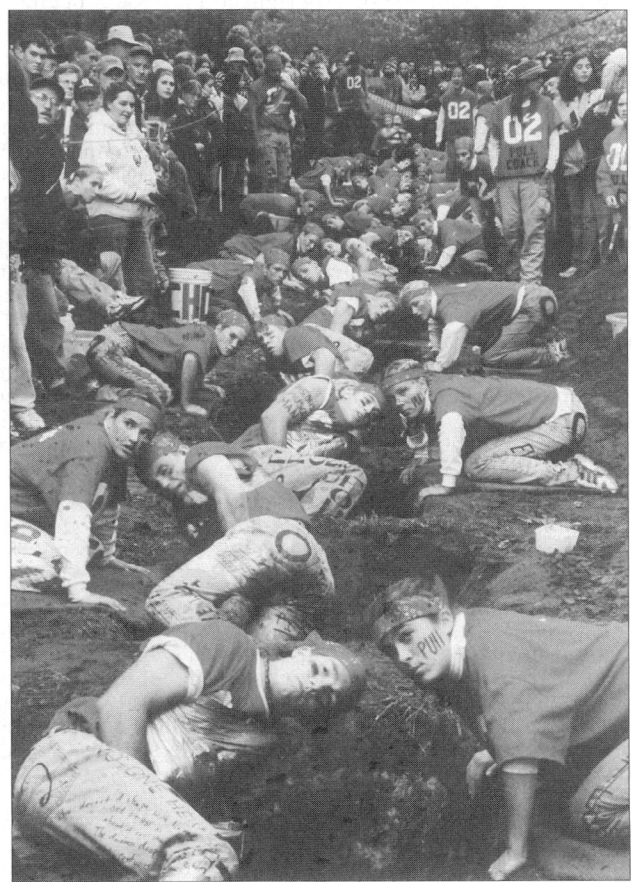

The Pull, an annual tug-of-war between freshmen and sophomores, has been called "the most unique sporting event in the nation" by *Sports Illustrated*.

HOUGHTON COLLEGE
HOUGHTON, NEW YORK

The College

Founded in 1883, Houghton College is one of America's most highly regarded Christian liberal arts colleges. Sponsored by the Wesleyan Church, Houghton attracts students from more than forty evangelical denominations. Houghton has an enrollment of 1,230 full-time undergraduate students who represent forty states and twenty-five countries. Most students live in College housing within the distinctly residential environment, while many faculty members live within walking distance of the campus. Houghton's 1,300 acres in the scenic Genesee Valley of western New York offer students various recreational opportunities. The College operates a 386-acre equestrian center and both downhill and cross-country ski facilities.

Accredited by the Middle States Association of Colleges and Schools and the National Association of Schools of Music, Houghton's selective admission ensures an academically able student body. Most students represent the top 20 percent of their high school's graduating class, possess SAT I or ACT scores commensurate with a competitive college, and are active in their churches and communities. Houghton offers more than forty majors and programs in an undergraduate-only atmosphere, a commitment that allows students to benefit from the instruction and guidance of experienced professors beginning with their first year of study.

Extensive cocurricular opportunities at Houghton include a competitive NAIA intercollegiate athletic program that fields ten teams for men and women, a wide array of intramural leagues, numerous Christian service organizations, student publications, music groups, and student government, to name a few. Houghton's Artist Series brings well-known classical performers to campus several times a year. The student-guided Campus Activities Board sponsors regular Christian contemporary concerts and other student-oriented activities. Student chapel services meet three times per week. *The Star*, the College's weekly student newspaper, offers practical journalism experience. The student radio station is popular with those students who are interested in broadcasting.

The residential experience is at the heart of a Houghton education. Freshmen and sophomores are required to live in a College residential hall. Juniors and seniors may also choose from several recently constructed town houses and approved community houses for off-campus living.

All resident students are required to participate in the College's board plan. Most students enjoy Houghton's twenty-one-meal-per-week plan, while those living in a town house may opt for a reduced meal plan.

Widespread national recognition has characterized Houghton for many years. *The National Review*, for example, has included Houghton in its recent listing of "America's Top Liberal Arts Colleges," recognizing the College as one of the country's leading fifty-eight liberal arts institutions. Several other publications have noted Houghton's outstanding faculty, placement of students in the nation's premier graduate schools, and the College's relative value.

Location

Houghton students benefit from the College's location in the rolling hills of western New York. The College's vast property—among the nation's leaders in campus acreage—offers numerous recreational opportunities, while nearby Letchworth State Park is one of the state's natural treasures. The metropolitan cities of Rochester and Buffalo, within an hour and a half drive of Houghton, offer cultural, entertainment, and shopping venues.

The West Seneca Campus of Houghton College is located in a suburb of Buffalo, New York. This campus is used primarily as a residential and instructional location for academic internships and student teaching as well as for the College's adult degree completion program. The College's two campuses are connected via an interactive TV link.

Majors and Degrees

Houghton grants Bachelor of Arts, Bachelor of Science, and Bachelor of Music degrees. Majors and programs are available in accounting, art, Bible, biology, business administration, chemistry, communication, computer science, educational ministries, elementary education, English, French, general science, history, humanities, international studies, mathematics, medical technology, ministerial studies, music education, music performance, music theory, philosophy, physical education, physics, political science, predentistry, pre–engineering, prelaw, premedicine, prenursing, preoptometry, pre–physical therapy, preseminary, pre–veterinary science, psychology, recreation, religion, secondary education, social science, sociology, Spanish, and writing.

An adult degree completion program (B.S. in organizational management), designed for those with 62-plus credit hours and suitable work experience and who are at least 25 years old, is offered at the College's campus in West Seneca, New York, and at extension sites in Olean and Arcade, New York.

A 3-2 engineering program is available through cooperation with Clarkson University in Potsdam, New York, and Washington University in St. Louis, Missouri.

Academic Program

Most bachelor's degrees at Houghton consist of 125 credit hours. As a traditional liberal arts institution, Houghton requires all students to complete an extensive general education curriculum in addition to courses in their major and minor fields of study. Included in the 55-credit-hour general education requirements are courses in composition, communication, foreign language, social science, history, mathematics, natural science, biblical literature, religion/philosophy, music, and art. Lecture and seminar courses with classes averaging 21 students create a positive learning environment with daily interaction between professors and students.

Houghton offers the First-Year Honors Program for approximately 30 students. Students spend the second semester of their first year studying in London, England, with Houghton faculty members. Independent study and honors projects are also available.

The College follows a 4-4-1 calendar. In addition to the fall and spring semesters, the College offers May Term, a two- to four-week term where students may enroll in one concentrated course. Both on- and off-campus courses are available during May Term.

Houghton accepts credit from the Advanced Placement Program of the College Board. Students must achieve a final exam score of 4 or higher to receive credit from Houghton. CLEP credit may also be accepted for subject exams only. Students wishing to challenge the College's foreign language requirement may take a College-administered placement test. A portion or all of the foreign language requirement may be waived, although no credit hours are granted.

Army ROTC is offered through cooperation with nearby St. Bonaventure University.

Off-Campus Arrangements

As a member of the Coalition for Christian Colleges and Universities, Houghton is able to offer many off-campus opportunities, including the American Studies Program in Washington, D.C.; the Latin American Studies Program in Costa Rica; the Film Institute in Los Angeles, California; the Russian Studies Program in Moscow; and the Middle Eastern Studies Program in Cairo, Egypt. Houghton also operates the Oregon Extension Program in Lincoln, Oregon, as well as programs in London and Tanzania. Education majors may also complete their student teaching requirement in an overseas school.

Academic Facilities

The Willard J. Houghton Library contains more than 220,000 volumes, 26,000 microfilm titles, and 3,036 periodical subscriptions. The College's online catalog, which uses the Virginia Tech Library Systems software, offers easy access to the College's holdings. Membership in a regional library consortium helps ensure optimum interlibrary loan service.

The Stephen Paine Science Building offers 65,000 square feet of animal, instructional, and research laboratories; a greenhouse; computer facilities; and lecture classrooms.

A comprehensive academic building completed in 1989 offers 49,000 square feet of classrooms, learning resource facilities, laboratories, faculty offices, media services, and an interactive TV link with the College's Buffalo Suburban Campus. Other major facilities at Houghton include a modern Physical Education Center, four major residence halls and eighteen town houses accommodating more than 900 students, the 1,300-seat Wesley Chapel, the Reinhold Campus Center, the Stevens Arts Studios, a 386-acre equestrian center, and several outdoor athletic and recreational areas. Houghton's new Center for the Arts features an acoustically designed recital hall, a music library, numerous practice rooms, spacious teaching studios, an instrumental rehearsal hall, and a professional digital recording studio.

The Educational Technology Initiative is a campuswide commitment that provides the latest technology within the context of a traditional liberal arts institution. Each first-year student obtains a laptop computer and printer, with on-campus technical support provided. Students connect to the College network from their residence hall rooms and many other locations for such purposes as communication with professors and fellow students and high-speed access to the Internet.

Costs

Houghton's tuition and fees are $15,140 for the 2000–01 academic year; this includes a laptop computer. Room and board (twenty-one meals per week) total $5400. Other indirect expenses, including books, supplies, and travel, average $1500.

Financial Aid

Houghton administers more than $15 million in aid annually, benefiting nearly 90 percent of the student body. Traditional federal and New York State aid, including Federal Pell Grants, TAP, FSEOG, work-study, and Federal Perkins Loans, is available for students demonstrating need through the Free Application for Federal Student Aid (FAFSA) and the Houghton College Financial Aid Application. The priority application deadline for financial aid is March 1. Houghton also offers merit-based scholarships for excellence in academics, athletics, music, and art. Students should contact the Financial Aid Office for specific information regarding merit-based scholarships.

Faculty

The College's faculty currently totals approximately 100 members, nearly 80 of whom are full-time. More than 80 percent hold the terminal degree in their discipline. Since Houghton is an undergraduate institution, all courses are taught by qualified professors, not teaching assistants or graduate students. All full-time students work directly with a faculty adviser in their area of study. The College maintains a student-faculty ratio of 14:1, with classes averaging approximately 21 students.

Student Government

The Houghton Student Government Association (SGA) consists of elected student representatives. This College-sponsored organization allows students to have a direct impact on their college experience in areas ranging from academics to residence life to cocurricular activities. Most College committees include student representatives.

Admission Requirements

Houghton's competitive admission process seeks to select applicants who clearly possess the academic and spiritual qualities necessary for a successful experience at Houghton. Candidates for admission should submit a high school transcript indicating at least 16 units of college-preparatory course work. The academic evaluation of each applicant includes a review of the quality of the high school curriculum, grade point average, rank in class, and scores from the SAT I or ACT. Other important application materials include the applicant's pastor's recommendation and an essay regarding the student's desire to attend an evangelical Christian institution. Transfer students are evaluated on the basis of the above information in addition to the college-level course work completed to date.

The Admission Office responds to applications for admission on or about January 1 (for files completed by November 15) and on a rolling basis beginning February 1 for all other applications. The College subscribes to and supports the national Candidates Reply Date of May 1.

Application and Information

For application materials, students should contact:

Admission Office
Houghton College
1 Willard Avenue
Houghton, New York 14744
Telephone: 716-567-9353
                800-777-2556 (toll-free)
E-mail: admissions@houghton.edu
World Wide Web: http://www.houghton.edu

The Quad at Houghton College.

HOWARD UNIVERSITY
WASHINGTON, D.C.

The University

Howard University, founded in 1867, is a coeducational private institution of higher learning located in the northwestern section of Washington, D.C. Since its founding, Howard University has grown from a single-frame building to a campus of 241 acres with buildings and equipment valued at more than $820 million. The University has been expanded to include a 22-acre West Campus on which the School of Law is located, a 22-acre School of Divinity campus and support service facility in northeast Washington, and a 108-acre tract of land in Beltsville, Maryland. Howard University consists of twelve schools and colleges: the Graduate School of Arts and Sciences; the Schools of Business, Communications, Divinity, Education, Law, and Social Work; and the Colleges of Arts and Sciences; Dentistry; Engineering, Architecture and Computer Science; Medicine; and Pharmacy, Nursing and Allied Health Sciences. The University offers baccalaureate, master's, Doctor of Dental Surgery, Doctor of Education, Doctor of Medicine, Doctor of Ministry, Doctor of Pharmacy, Doctor of Philosophy, Doctor of Social Work, and Juris Doctor degrees. The total fall 1999 enrollment at Howard was 10,248. Approximately 13 percent of the students are from Washington, D.C.; 74 percent are from other states; 7 percent are international students representing 104 countries and U.S. possessions; and 5 percent are international students who are permanent U.S. residents.

The University's physical plant consists of more than ninety buildings, including the Howard Plaza Towers and the Bethune Hall Annex, a theater, two dormitories for women, two dormitories for men, and five coed dormitories. Student organizations include religious groups, special interest clubs, honor societies, sororities, fraternities, the band, the chorus, a string ensemble, student weekly publications, a debating group, and service clubs. Varsity athletics include men's baseball, basketball, cross-country, football, indoor and outdoor track, soccer, and wrestling; women's basketball, bowling, cross-country, indoor and outdoor track, and volleyball; and coed swimming and tennis. The intramural program includes all of these sports.

There are a variety of styles and locations of University housing, ranging from standard double rooms to shared apartments with full kitchens. Early housing applicants, once admitted to the University, are given priority for spaces most favored by new students. Freshman students admitted by May 1 are guaranteed housing, and all entering freshman students are required, as long as space is available, to reside in University housing for their first two years. The residential life experience contributes to the educational and personal development of students. Students living in the local area and certain other categories of students may request an exception to the residential requirement. Certain residence halls (dormitories) are part of the combined room and board plan; residents of other halls may opt to purchase a meal plan. There are lively and diverse activities sponsored in the residence halls, and students in the residence halls are also encouraged to involve themselves in community service as part of their college experience. Each undergraduate residence hall has well-trained live-in staff members as well as front-desk monitors 24 hours a day. Residence counselors are aided by graduate assistants and resident assistants.

Location

The Howard University campus is situated on one of the highest elevations in the District of Columbia, overlooking downtown Washington. The White House, the Capitol, and all the cultural and historic institutions of the city are within minutes of the campus. Many of the University's academic programs are designed to make use of these institutions and to serve the needs of the immediate community as well as the entire Washington metropolitan area.

Majors and Degrees

The University offers the following undergraduate degrees: Bachelor of Architecture, Bachelor of Arts, Bachelor of Business Administration (nine options available), Bachelor of Fine Arts, Bachelor of Music, Bachelor of Music Education, Bachelor of Science, Bachelor of Science in Chemical Engineering, Bachelor of Science in Civil Engineering, Bachelor of Science in Nutritional Sciences, Bachelor of Science in Systems and Computer Sciences, Bachelor of Science in Electrical Engineering, Bachelor of Science in Mechanical Engineering, Bachelor of Science in Clinical Laboratory Science, Bachelor of Science in Nursing, Bachelor of Science in Occupational Therapy, Bachelor of Science in Radiation Therapy, and Bachelor of Science in Physician Assistant. The major areas of undergraduate study are accounting, administration of justice, African studies, Afro-American studies, anthropology, architecture, art, biology, chemical engineering, chemistry, civil engineering, clinical laboratory science, communication studies, computer-based information systems, consumer affairs management, dental hygiene, design, drama, economics, education, electrical engineering, English, fashion merchandising, finance, fine arts, French, German, Greek, history, hospitality management, human development, insurance, interior design, international business, journalism, management, marketing, mathematics, mechanical engineering, music, nursing, nutritional science, occupational therapy, pharmacy, philosophy, physical education, physical therapy, physician assistant studies, physics, political science, psychology, radio/television/film, recreation, Russian, sociology, Spanish, systems and computer science, theater arts, and visual arts. The University offers degrees in ninety-three undergraduate areas and certificates in dental hygiene, music therapy, and radiation therapy.

Academic Programs

The requirements for a bachelor's degree vary among the University's schools and colleges. A core of courses is required for each major.

The University awards credit for successful scores on Advanced Placement tests as well as credit for the International Baccalaureate program.

The University offers cooperative education programs in the College of Arts and Sciences; the College of Engineering, Architecture and Computer Sciences; the School of Business; and the School of Communications. Departmental honors programs are also offered for students with exceptional ability. Special remedial services are provided through the Center for Academic Reinforcement. Domestic and international exchange programs are also available for sophomores, juniors, and first-semester seniors.

Howard University is accredited by the Commission on Higher Education of the Middle States Association of Colleges and

Schools, and its programs in specialized fields are accredited by numerous professional agencies.

Academic Facilities

There are separate classroom and laboratory facilities for each major discipline. The University library houses more than 2 million bound volumes, 26,000 current serial subscriptions, 3.5 million microforms, a media center, a microfilm preparation center, and the Moorland-Spingarn Research Center, which has the largest collection of black literature in the United States. The University also operates a radio station (WHUR-FM) on a 24-hour basis. The radio station and a TV station (WHUT-TV) serve as laboratories for the School of Communications.

Costs

Tuition is $8750 and fees are $487 for the 2000–01 academic year. Room and board costs vary, depending upon the assigned accommodations and selected meal plan. The average annual cost of room and board is $5000. The approximate annual cost of books and supplies is $800.

Financial Aid

The University's financial aid program is designed to aid the maximum number of students. Every effort is made to assist needy and qualified students through scholarships, loans, grants, and part-time employment. The amount of aid granted is determined by the availability of funds, the extent of the student's need, and his or her academic performance. Most financial aid awards are given for the academic year and are divided equally between the two semesters. All undergraduate students seeking financial aid must file the Free Application for Federal Student Aid (FAFSA), which can be obtained from the University's Office of Financial Aid and Student Employment. Applications must be filed by February 15.

Faculty

The University's faculty consists of 451 full professors, 551 associate professors, 597 assistant professors, 174 instructors, 190 lecturers, 50 adjunct professors, and 114 teaching assistants, making a total of 2,127. The normal teaching load is 12 credit hours, but professors also spend time advising, doing research and committee work, and undertaking administrative duties.

Student Government

Student government has many levels and branches and is concerned with all aspects of student life. Students hold voting memberships on the Board of Trustees.

Admission Requirements

All applicants must be graduates of accredited high schools and must present acceptable high school records, SAT I or ACT scores, and SAT II: Writing Test scores. Students who have studied a foreign language for 2 years and intend to continue study of that language should also take the SAT II Subject Test in that language. Applicants seeking admission to the Department of Music must audition in person or send a tape, those seeking admission to the Department of Art must submit a portfolio, and drama applicants must submit two letters of reference and a resume. Enrollment Management/Admission will notify applicants of any additional requirements upon receipt of an application.

Application and Information

Guided tours of the campus are conducted, by appointment, Monday through Friday, beginning at 10 a.m. The last tour begins at 3 p.m. Students who wish to schedule a tour should contact the Office of Admission and Recruitment at the numbers below. All students seeking admission for the fall semester should apply by April 1. Those seeking admission for the spring semester should apply by November 1. A nonrefundable application fee of $45 is required of all applicants.

For further information, students should contact:

Enrollment Management/Recruitment
Howard University
2400 Sixth Street, NW
Washington, DC 20059
Telephone: 202-806-2900
World Wide Web: http://www.howard.edu

HUNTER COLLEGE
OF THE CITY UNIVERSITY OF NEW YORK
NEW YORK, NEW YORK

The College

Hunter College is committed to the achievement of a pluralistic community; it offers a curriculum designed to meet the highest academic standards while fostering understanding among individuals from different racial, cultural, and ethnic backgrounds. The goal of a Hunter College education is to encourage the fullest possible intellectual and personal growth in each student. Originally called Normal College, the school was founded in 1870 by Thomas Hunter to educate young women who wished to be teachers. Today Hunter is a coeducational, fully accredited college with a large, distinguished faculty in the liberal arts and sciences and several professional schools. Hunter offers both undergraduate and graduate degrees and enrolls more than 19,000 students.

Location

Hunter students study at the center of one of the most magnificent cities in the world. Within easy walking distance are many of the world's finest museums, libraries, concert halls, cultural centers, and theaters.

Majors and Degrees

Hunter College offers several types of degrees, including the Bachelor of Arts (B.A.), Bachelor of Science (B.S.), Bachelor of Fine Arts (B.F.A.), Bachelor of Music (B.Mus.), the combined Bachelor of Arts/Master of Arts (B.A./M.A.), and the combined Bachelor of Arts/Master of Science (B.A./M.S.). The following programs of study are available: accounting, anthropology, archaeology, art history, art (studio), biological sciences, black and Puerto Rican studies, chemistry, Chinese language and literature, classical studies, community health education, comparative literature, computer science, dance, economics, elementary education, energy and environmental studies, English language arts, English literature, film, French, geography, German, Greek, Hebrew, history, honors curriculum, Italian, Jewish social studies, Latin, Latin and Greek, Latin American and Caribbean Studies, mathematics, media studies, medical laboratory sciences, music, nursing, nutrition and food science, philosophy, physical education, physics, political science, psychology, religion, Romance languages, Russian, secondary education, sociology, Spanish, statistics, theater, urban studies, and women's studies. Secondary education programs are for grades 7–12 unless otherwise noted; programs are offered in biology, chemistry, Chinese, dance (K–12), English, French, German, Greek, health education (K–12), Hebrew, Italian, Latin, mathematics, music (K–12, accelerated B.A./M.A. program only), physical education (K–12), physics, Russian, social studies, and Spanish.

Special programs in anthropology, biology/biopharmacology, biology/environmental and occupational health sciences, economics, English, history, mathematics, music, physics, and sociology/social research lead to the combined bachelor's/master's degree, enabling highly qualified students to earn both degrees in a shorter period of time than is required for taking the degrees separately.

Hunter College also provides preprofessional advisement and preparation for advanced study in chiropractic, dentistry, law, medicine, osteopathy, pharmacy, podiatry, and veterinary medicine.

Academic Program

A liberal education should help men and women to bring a rich and informed sense of the possibilities of humanity to their careers, their public responsibilities, and their personal lives. This goal is basic to Hunter's educational philosophy. The College offers training in both the sciences and the humanities and schooling in a number of professional fields. As they work toward their career goals, students are expected to reach a broader understanding of the place of their chosen fields of study and work in the wider realms of knowledge and of society.

The program of study for an undergraduate degree at Hunter consists of four parts totaling 120 credits: a distribution requirement, a pluralism and diversity requirement, a concentration of in-depth study, and elective courses.

Sophomores whose performance indicates intellectual curiosity and exceptional ability may apply to the Thomas Hunter Honors Program. This interdisciplinary program provides exceptional undergraduate students in B.A.-granting disciplines with an individualized course of study suited to their needs and interests.

Subject to departmental approval, students may be awarded sophomore standing (up to 30 credits) for successful scores on examinations, including the College Level Examination Program (CLEP) subject tests, the Advanced Placement examinations of The College Board, and the Regents College Examination (RCE) Program of New York State.

Off-Campus Arrangements

Hunter College's location in the heart of Manhattan allows innumerable possibilities for internships. Hosts have included Atlantic Records, CNN, Council on Foreign Relations, DreamWorks SKG, Madison Square Garden, Metropolitan Museum of Art, New York City Council, Simon & Schuster, and many more. Interns have performed curatorial and administrative work in museums; research and production work on TV news shows and newspapers; design work in commercial graphics; booking, managing, and technical work in theaters; and many other jobs.

Academic Facilities

The College comprises five sites in Manhattan. The largest, at 68th Street and Lexington Avenue, is a modern complex of buildings interconnected by skywalks. Especially convenient for students from all five boroughs is a direct entrance to Hunter College from the New York City Subway System. Programs in the arts and sciences and in teacher education are conducted at this campus.

The Division of the Schools of the Health Professions, which includes the Hunter-Bellevue School of Nursing, one of the nation's largest nursing programs, and the School of Health Sciences, noted for its outstanding programs, is located at the Brookdale Campus on East 25th Street. The Hunter College School of Social Work, recently listed among the top ten schools of its kind in the nation by *U.S. News & World Report,* is uptown at East 79th Street. On Manhattan's West Side, Hunter's Studio Art Building houses an 8,000-square-foot gallery and provides M.F.A. students with individual studios that are among the best in the city. The Campus Schools at Park Avenue and East 94th Street—an elementary school and a high school for the intellectually gifted—are renowned, as is the College itself, for a long tradition of academic excellence. All locations are minutes from Grand Central Terminal, Penn Station, and the New York/New Jersey Port Authority Bus Terminal, making Hunter easily accessible from Connecticut, Westchester, New Jersey, and Long Island.

The collections of the Hunter College libraries are housed in the Jacqueline Grennan Wexler Library and the Art Slide Library (located at the main campus), as well as at the branch libraries at the Brookdale Campus and the School of Social Work. The libraries hold 735,000 volumes, 2,300 periodicals, a nonprint collection of more than 1 million microforms, and 130,000 art slides in addition to records, tapes, scores, music CDs, and videos. Recently, new computer, multimedia, and Internet labs were installed, and the first CD-ROM network was created. The CD-ROM network provides access to indexes, abstracts, and complete texts and multimedia resources. Access to the information superhighway is available through Internet labs.

Costs

The reasonable tuition and fees at Hunter College make a quality undergraduate education affordable. In 1999–2000, New York State residents who enrolled as full-time, matriculated students paid $1600 per semester ($135 per credit part-time). Nonresidents who enrolled as full-time, matriculated students paid $3400 per semester ($285 per credit part-time). All students paid a Student Activity Fee ($61.60 per semester for full-time students and $46.30 per semester for part-time students) and a $5 per-semester Consolidated Fee.

Financial Aid

Hunter College participates in all state and federal financial aid programs. Financial aid is available to matriculated students in the form of grants, loans, and work-study. Grants provide funds that do not have to be repaid. Loans must be repaid in regular installments over a prescribed period of time. Work-study consists of part-time employment, either on campus or in an outside agency. More information is available from the Office of Financial Aid at 212-772-4820.

Entering freshmen whose high school records indicate a high level of academic achievement may apply to the Hunter College Scholarship Program. The scholarships awarded through this program are independent of any financial assistance a student may receive from other sources and are made possible through alumni donations to the Hunter College Scholarship and Welfare Fund and anonymous donations to the Hunter College Foundation. The Scholars Award pays $3200 per year for a maximum of four years. A limited number of Scholars Award recipients may also be eligible for a Dormitory Award, which provides a free room at the Hunter College Residence Hall for a maximum of four years. The Athena Award is a $10,000-a-year scholarship granted for a maximum of four years. More information on the Scholarship Program is available from the Office of Admissions.

Faculty

Thanks in great part to its cosmopolitan and central location, Hunter College attracts a special kind of faculty member. Some are well-known scholars and researchers in their fields—for example, biologists involved in advanced research on genetic structure. Others are professionals with active careers in the city: well-known painters and sculptors; architects and urban design experts; environmental health scientists engaged in ensuring occupational health and safety; theater critics, film directors, and musicians; or nursing administrators in some of the country's leading hospitals. The nationally renowned members of the faculty maintain Hunter's reputation for academic excellence through accomplishments in teaching, publications, and research made possible by millions of dollars in grants awarded annually.

Student Government

Hunter College has several governing assemblies, most of which provide for student participation. The College Senate serves as the legislative body of the College and is composed of faculty members, students, and administrators. Hunter also has two Student Governments (undergraduate and graduate) that play essential roles in the life of the College. Students also sit, with voting power, on faculty and administrative committees.

Admission Requirements

Candidates for freshman admission are considered based on the overall strength of their academic preparation, grades in individual subjects, cumulative high school averages, and SAT or ACT scores. The College recommends completion of 4 years of English, 4 years of social studies, 3 years of mathematics, 2 years of a foreign language, 2 years of laboratory sciences, and 1 year of performing or visual arts as the minimum academic preparation for success in college. Transfer applicants with fewer than 24 credits must have a cumulative grade point average (GPA) of at least 2.0 and must meet the freshman criteria previously outlined. Those with 14–23.9 credits and a GPA of 2.5 as well as those with 24 or more credits and a GPA of 2.0 are eligible, regardless of high school average. The School of Health Sciences and the School of Nursing offer several upper-division programs that have special admission criteria. For more information, applicants should contact the Office of Admissions.

Application and Information

Requests for further information and for application materials should be sent to:

Office of Admissions
Hunter College of the City University of New York
695 Park Avenue
New York, New York 10021-5085
Telephone: 212-772-4490
              212-650-3188 (TTY)
Fax: 212-650-3336
E-mail: admissions@tzayid.hunter.cuny.edu
World Wide Web: http://www.hunter.cuny.edu

Students at Hunter College enjoy the convenience of skywalks, which connect all four buildings at the 68th Street campus. Hunter's Upper East Side location provides easy access to some of New York's finest offerings: Central Park and the Metropolitan Museum of Art are just blocks away.

HUNTINGDON COLLEGE
MONTGOMERY, ALABAMA

The College

To be successful in the twenty-first century, college graduates must be prepared to assume the role of world citizen, must be adept at using information and communication technology, and must have real-world experience in addition to a broad undergraduate education. Huntingdon College's outstanding liberal arts program provides travel/study, internships and hands-on learning opportunities, a computer for each entering freshman, and direct connections to the Internet and Campus Intranet in a port-per-pillow arrangement as part of its innovative Huntingdon Plan.

Founded in 1854, Huntingdon is a private liberal arts college related to the United Methodist Church. More than 700 students represent twenty-four states and twelve countries. Huntingdon has been recognized as a "Best Buy" by *Money* magazine, an "up and coming" college by *U.S. News & World Report*, and as a "hidden gem" by Kaplan/*Newsweek* and has been included in *Templeton's Honor Roll of Character-Building Colleges*. In recent years, 96 percent of Huntingdon students applying to law school have been admitted; and 89 percent of those applying to medical school have been admitted (the national averages are 56 percent and 41 percent respectively). The mean grade point average among the 1998 freshman class was 3.42, the mean ACT score was 25, and the mean combined SAT I score was 1123; 75 percent of applicants were admitted.

Huntingdon provides a wide range of clubs, organizations, and activities, including national fraternities and sororities, special interest groups, performing groups, the Campus Ministry Association, service clubs, publications, and intramural sports. NCAA Division III intercollegiate athletics include men's varsity baseball, basketball, cross-country, golf, soccer, and tennis and women's varsity basketball, cross-country, soccer, softball, tennis, and volleyball. Huntingdon is a residential campus. About 69 percent of full-time students live in campus residence halls.

The College's Academic Services Center provides academic counseling, career planning, job placement, and internships. The center conducts workshops in personal growth and careers, maintains a library of graduate and professional school information, and offers computer-assisted career planning. Placement services range from summer jobs to permanent employment after graduation. Staff members provide resume assistance, career contacts, and background on employers. Representatives from government, business, and nonprofit organizations are invited to campus to recruit. More than 90 percent of all Huntingdon graduates are either employed in their chosen fields or enrolled in graduate or professional schools within 6 months of graduation.

Location

Huntingdon's 58-acre campus is a naturally picturesque park. Centrally located on the edge of one of Montgomery's most beautiful neighborhoods, Old Cloverdale, campus buildings of primarily Gothic design extend along a semicircular ridge, overlooking a lush wooded area and natural amphitheater. Montgomery enjoys a pleasant climate with warm summers and mild winters and is not far from Gulf beaches, mountains, rivers, and parks.

A variety of cultural and educational activities take place in Alabama's capital city, just minutes from the campus, including the Alabama Shakespeare Festival, concerts, and performances of the civic ballet. State archives, state government offices and laboratories, the capitol building, the fine arts museum, and countless historic landmarks are also nearby. Montgomery is within easy driving distance of Birmingham (90 miles), Atlanta (170 miles), the Gulf of Mexico (160 miles), and New Orleans (300 miles).

Majors and Degrees

Huntingdon College offers the Bachelor of Arts degree with majors in art, art education, biology, business administration, chemistry, communication studies, computer science, dance, dance education, dance management, digital art, early childhood education, elementary education, English, environmental chemistry, European studies, history, human performance and kinesiology, international studies, mathematics, music, music education, musical theater, physical education, political science, psychology, public administration, public affairs, public policy, religion and philosophy, Spanish, and theater. Huntingdon is the only college that offers tri-subject majors combining the study of political science with two of the following: economics, history, philosophy, psychology, and public communication.

Preprofessional programs in dentistry, law, medicine, optometry, pharmacy, physical therapy, theology, and veterinary medicine have excellent placement rates.

Teacher education programs are offered in early childhood education and elementary education. Secondary education programs are offered in biology, chemistry, English language arts, history, mathematics, psychology, and social sciences. Preschool through grade 12 programs in art, dance, physical education, and vocal/choral music are also offered.

A dual-degree program in engineering is offered in cooperation with Auburn University.

Academic Program

Huntingdon's core curriculum includes unique interdisciplinary liberal arts courses, a senior capstone course, and freedom of choice in the selection of distribution courses within topic areas such as aesthetic expression, science and technology, and social and self-awareness. Credit is available for Advanced Placement and International Baccalaureate students.

Superb lecture and cultural programs bring current issues, topics of interest, and the arts to life for Huntingdon students. A long list of notable Huntingdon lecturers includes Elizabeth Dole, Bob Hope, Beverly Sills, animal behaviorist Dr. Jane Goodall, Susan Rook, dinosaur expert Dr. Jack Horner, paleoanthropologist Dr. Donald Johanson, and Dr. Henry Kissinger. The College's Performing Arts Series offers dance, music, and theatrical performances throughout the year.

The College operates on a 4-1-4 system, with a two-week January Term and two 6-week summer sessions. Classes begin at the end of August. Freshman registration is held in June, July, and August. The College also offers a Summer Scholars Program, a six-week summer session for high school juniors who have a 3.0 academic grade point average or higher.

Off-Campus Arrangements

Huntingdon students may participate in the Marine Environmental Sciences Consortium on Dauphin Island in Alabama. Participation in Air Force ROTC at Alabama State University or in Army ROTC at Auburn University at Montgomery is also available to students enrolled at Huntingdon. Through a consortial agreement with local colleges, Huntingdon students may take courses at Auburn University at Montgomery and at Faulkner University.

The College offers a travel/study opportunity as part of the Huntingdon Plan. Students who enter as freshmen may choose from a menu of travel/study programs during the January term of the junior or senior year. Many opportunities are offered within regular tuition and fees, while others require marginal additional costs. Past study opportunities have included the Caribbean; Mexico; New York; Washington, D.C.; the Bahamas; Los Angeles; England; Ireland; Italy; Spain; Belize; Peru; the Galapagos Islands; and the Holy Land. The College is also a member of the Center for Cooperative Study Abroad (CCSA), which offers study programs in English-speaking countries and a four-college archaeological consortium in Sepphorus. All study experiences sponsored through the Huntingdon Plan or through CCSA are faculty-directed and are offered for academic credit.

Academic Facilities

The Houghton Memorial Library holds nearly 150,000 volumes, periodicals, audiovisual materials, and microforms. The Wilson Center accommodates studies in business, mathematics, and computer science and houses state-of-the-art computing equipment, including a network of more than fifty PCs and Macintoshes available 24 hours a day. Since each student is also provided with a computer, the student-computer ratio is 1:more than 1. No extra charges are made for the use of these facilities. The Smith music building has a 120-seat recital hall, music studios, a library, rehearsal and practice rooms, four pipe organs, and twelve grand pianos. Huntingdon's chemistry instrumentation is outstanding.

Costs

Tuition for the 2000–01 school year (two semesters) is $11,000; room and board are approximately $5500. Books, supplies, and fees, including a $910 student fee, average about $1700 per school year.

Financial Aid

At Huntingdon, financing an education is a cooperative effort. Through a variety of resources, Huntingdon College administers more than $6 million in aid to more than 90 percent of its students. These resources include institutional scholarships, gifts, and endowments as well as federal grants, loans, and work-study assignments. In addition, the school benefits from the Alabama Student Assistance and the Alabama Student Grant programs. To apply for financial aid, students must apply for admission, complete a Huntingdon College Financial Aid Application, and complete the Free Application for Federal Student Aid (FAFSA). Although the majority of financial aid is based upon demonstrated financial need, Huntingdon awards scholarships for academic merit, leadership, or performance skills in art, dance, drama, and music. The priority deadline for the completion of the financial aid process is April 15. The scholarship application deadline is January 31.

Faculty

The faculty is composed of 45 full-time and 32 part-time teaching members; approximately 85 percent hold Ph.D. degrees or the highest degrees in their fields. In addition to teaching, the faculty's major responsibility is advising students. Faculty members work closely with students to plan and develop individual programs to fulfill the student's career interests. The student-faculty ratio is 12:1, and the average class size is 15 students.

Student Government

The Student Government Association, authorized by the College administration, embraces the entire student body. Based upon the honor system, it places responsibilities for the enforcement of regulations and the safeguarding of standards upon the individual. The association encourages student leadership and good citizenship through communication, cooperation, and endeavors among students, faculty, administrators, and other officials. The legislative powers of the association are vested in the Senate, which is composed of representatives from other leading organizations on campus. The Executive Cabinet members are elected by the student body each spring. The Student Government Association and the College Programming Council, funded by the activity fee, present a variety of activities throughout the year. These include dances, festivals, parties, movies, special programs, and many other social events as well as such special events as the Presidential Banquet, Homecoming, pageants, and Parents Weekend.

Admission Requirements

Huntingdon College is an equal opportunity educational institution and, as such, does not discriminate in its admission policy on the basis of race, color, sex, creed, national origin, or handicap. The Faculty Committee on Admissions places primary emphasis on the strength of the student's secondary school record. Required test scores (ACT or SAT), school recommendations, and other personal qualifications as demonstrated by extracurricular activities are also carefully evaluated by the Faculty Committee on Admissions. Secondary school graduation or an equivalency diploma is required.

Prospective students and their parents are encouraged to call the Admission Office to plan a visit to the campus, observe a class, and meet with an admission counselor.

Transfer applicants must meet freshman admission standards and have at least a C average (2.25 on a 4.0 scale) with a minimum of 15 hours of academic work. Applicants must be in good standing from the last college attended. If the applicant has attended more than one college, the overall grade point average obtained at these schools must meet the minimum academic average required at Huntingdon. Transfer students may enroll at the beginning of any semester.

Application and Information

Applications are processed and notification is given on a rolling basis. Early admission is available after the junior year of high school for students of exceptional ability. Materials to be sent include the completed Application for Admission, a $25 application fee, an official high school transcript, and scores on either the ACT or SAT I.

For more information, students should contact:
Suellen Ofe
Vice President for Enrollment Management
Huntingdon College
1500 East Fairview Avenue
Montgomery, Alabama 36106-2148
Telephone: 334-833-4497
        800-763-0313 (toll-free)
Fax: 334-833-4347
E-mail: admiss@huntingdon.edu
World Wide Web: http://www.huntingdon.edu

Social and academic activity flourish in the parklike setting affectionately known as Huntingdon's Green.

HURON UNIVERSITY
HURON, SOUTH DAKOTA

The University
Huron University was founded in 1883 and for 117 years has continued to be a viable and relevant educational resource in the Upper Midwest. The mission of Huron University, an institution of higher education, is to provide career-oriented education by teaching applied, real-world, state-of-the-practice programs in selected technical, business, teacher education, and health science fields. The University serves the needs of the students for employment and career advancement and the needs of industry for qualified professionals prepared at the associate, bachelor's, and master's levels. In the world of business, companies retain their leading edge through continuous commitment to improvement in technology and updates of equipment, hardware, and software. Huron University stays in touch with these changing needs to ensure that the students' education is based on current industry standards. State-of-the-practice equipment and learning tools support the educational experience. This commitment is the students' assurance that their degree from Huron University is a symbol of industry relevance and technological achievement.

Recently a $1.5-million renovation to both the Kerr and Churchill residence halls was completed. Included in the list of updated items are the carpeting, furnishings, fire alarms, and security lights in both of the dorms.

The Commission on Institutions of Higher Education of the North Central Association of Colleges and Schools (NCA) accredits Huron University and its degree programs. Inquiries can be directed to NCA at 30 North LaSalle Street, Suite 2400, Chicago, Illinois 60602; telephone: 312-263-0456.

Location
Huron University is in Huron, South Dakota, which is a community of 13,000 located in the east-central part of the state. The campus is centered nicely in the middle of town. Huron is known for being a safe and friendly community whose residents have held a long and intense interest in the University and its students.

Majors and Degrees
Huron University offers many different Bachelor of Science degree programs, including athletic training, computer science, criminal justice, financial management, general education, management (concentrations in business, human resources, marketing, and sports), management information systems, managerial accounting, nursing, and teacher education (with majors in elementary education, physical education with a minor in coaching, history education, and science/biology education). The Associate of Science degrees are designed to provide initial skill-building preparation for a career. The associate degrees and the bachelor's degrees include foundational courses as well as job-specific knowledge courses designed to prepare students to enter a career field. A student may earn an Associate of Science degree in the following areas: accounting, business management, criminal justice, management information systems, and nursing.

Academic Program
At Huron University, students find a dynamic roster of rigorous degree programs designed to introduce them to some of the most exciting and fastest-growing career fields. Huron's curricula, faculty members, and facilities are pathways to career worlds in the high-tech universe designed to meet the standards of excellence in the technological marketplace. The University offers a learning environment that revolves around the students. The students learn firsthand the importance of keeping technical skills sharp and industry knowledge current. They understand the challenge of staying on the leading edge of their careers. Huron offers degree programs that meet those needs and presents them in a supportive, adult-oriented atmosphere geared to academic and career success. From business and computer science to nursing and education, Huron offers the educational programs students need to discover their potential and meet their destiny. Regardless of the degree program chosen, the student benefits from the University's century-long foundation of educational excellence and its revitalized environment. Innovative approaches to learning, an outstanding faculty, and a student-centered philosophy of personalized service are offered. The faculty plays a crucial role. Students continually give professors high ratings in areas such as clarity, ability to use examples and stimulate thinking, and communication skills.

Academic Facilities
The focal point of academic life is the Ralph Voorhees Hall, which was constructed in 1909. Located at the center of campus, this hall contains many of the administration offices essential to campus life, including Academic Services. The majority of the new high-tech classrooms are also located in Voorhees Hall. These classrooms are small to encourage interaction between students and professors. Some of the classrooms are equipped for high-tech presentations and demonstrations, featuring document cameras, overhead projectors, and video and computer equipment. Found on the lower level of the Ella McIntire Resource Center is the largest computer lab on campus. The entire resource center is continually enhanced to provide ready access to a wealth of resource materials and information. From extensive volume collections to CD-ROM databases and online search services, the resource center has become a virtual library with a supportive environment geared toward career-oriented education. Among the resource center's capabilities and features are reference collections, major CD-ROM databases, online services, and ProQuest Direct. ProQuest has 3,607 journals electronically delivered over the Internet and includes such topics as business, research, education, computer science, and legal issues. A recent completion of rewiring of the entire campus with both category 5 and fiber-optic cabling is the latest of the technological advancements on the campus. This addition provides high-speed Internet and network access to every classroom, office, and dorm room. Eventually, this will allow the students' use of laptop computers in the classroom, linked to both the professor's laptop and the Internet.

Costs
To assist students in planning for their educational expenses, Huron University offers a guaranteed tuition plan for up to four years of undergraduate study, providing the student remains a full-time student in good standing at the University. Each undergraduate credit hour costs $200. The 2000–01 cost for a

full-time student averages $11,050. This amount includes $7200 for tuition, $2850 for room and board, and approximately $1000 for books and fees.

Financial Aid

Huron University is committed to assisting students in developing financial plans for their educational goals. The University participates in many federal and state financial aid programs as well as providing some institutional aid. Additional and specific information on financial aid programs can be obtained through the financial aid department. Institutional scholarships are available for academics, cheerleading/flag, athletics, and band. The University also provides commitment and special situation scholarships on a case-by-case basis.

Faculty

Huron University employs 18 full-time professors; among these are 2 Professors Emeriti. Along with these, there are 4 dean/chairs, 8 part-time professors, and, at minimum, 35 adjunct professors. On an average, the student-faculty ratio is 12:1. The courses are taught by professors only; no teaching assistants are employed.

Huron University professors consider themselves mentors as well as educators. Professors view students as customers, and they are eager to share their experiences.

Student Government

Just as the real world changes quickly, campus life evolves and changes, too. A small community means that students get heard, and their concerns can be addressed immediately. Students and their organizations are the driving force behind nearly every student activity on the campus. At the top of the list is Student Senate, an organization that represents every student on campus. In addition, there are many clubs specifically designed to meet every student's needs.

Admission Requirements

Admission to the University is based, in part, on documented ability to perform college-level work. A high school diploma or GED is required, as are a completed application and fee. ACT or SAT I scores are accepted. Interviews with admission advisers may be in person or via telephone. Campus tours and personal interviews are available at any time and can be arranged by contacting the admissions office.

Application and Information

Each year, Huron University accepts a limited number of new students. To be considered for one of the available openings, it is strongly recommended that application be made in the fall of the student's senior year of high school. Applications and additional information about the University can be obtained by contacting:

Admissions Department
Huron University
333 9th Street SW
Huron, South Dakota 57350
Telephone: 800-710-7159 (toll-free)
E-mail: admissions@huron.edu
World Wide Web: http://www.huron.edu

Ralph Voorhees Hall.

HUSSON COLLEGE
BANGOR, MAINE

The College
Husson College was founded in 1898 as a commercial college committed to the development of business skills of a practical nature. The decades following the College's establishment were characterized by continuing growth and expansion. In 1968, the College moved to its present location, a beautiful 200-acre campus on the edge of the city of Bangor, approximately 1 mile from downtown. Modern residence halls provide comfortable living quarters for students. The total enrollment of 2,005 includes 952 undergraduate students.

Campus life accommodates a wide range of interests. Women's intercollegiate sports are basketball, field hockey, soccer, softball, and volleyball. Men compete in baseball, basketball, lacrosse, and soccer, and golf is a coed intercollegiate sport. The athletic teams have competed in national tournaments and have had an outstanding record of success over the years. There are honor societies, an a cappells choir, prayer groups, sororities, fraternities, professional business societies, a student government, a student newspaper and yearbook, Campus Crusade for Christ, and WHSN, the student radio station. Events at the College include concerts, movies, lectures, and similar activities. Residential life also plays an important role in the education of the students. On-campus housing is guaranteed for four years. Student residence halls are coeducational by floor, and there are no triples. Each residence hall room is equipped with a telephone jack, cable TV outlet, and two data ports. The College has a nearly barrier-free campus.

Husson is accredited by the New England Association of Schools and Colleges, the American Association of Medical Assistants, and the National League for Nursing Accrediting Commission. After filing a Declaration of Intent for Accreditation, the Husson College physical therapy program has received approval to proceed with the accreditation process. This approval was granted by the Commission on Accreditation in Physical Therapy Education (CAPTE). The occupational therapy program has applied for developing program status with the Accreditation Council for Occupational Therapy Education.

The Husson College Dining Service, located in the Dickerman Dining Commons, has been recognized as one of the best in the business by the National Association of College and University Food Services for its efforts to meet the needs of a diverse student population.

Husson places a great deal of emphasis on equipping the student with marketable job skills. The professionally staffed Office of Career Counseling assists students in making career choices and in finding jobs. Husson College has an excellent placement record because employers appreciate the Husson educational program and the sound professional training of the College's graduates.

Master's degrees are offered in business (M.S.B.), nursing (M.S.N.), physical therapy (M.S.P.T.), and occupational therapy (M.S.O.T.). The M.S.B. program is designed for individuals in supervisory or administrative positions in business and education who have not had previous business or managerial training, as well as for business college graduates who desire more advanced education in their areas of expertise. The M.S.N. program (family and community nurse practitioner studies and advanced practice psychiatric nursing) reflects Husson's ongoing commitment to educate nurses for the challenges of the twenty-first century. Graduates are eligible to sit for the American Nurses Credentialing Center Family Nurse Practitioner certification exam. Husson also offers a B.S./M.S.B. degree in accounting. The M.S.P.T. and M.S.O.T. programs are five-year entry-level master's programs.

Location
Bangor is a city of 33,000 people on the Penobscot River, about 40 miles from the Atlantic Ocean and famed Bar Harbor and Acadia National Park to the south and equidistant from the Canadian border on the east and New Hampshire on the west. Mount Katahdin, Baxter State Park, Moosehead Lake, and several well-known ski areas are within a 1- to 3-hour drive of the campus. The region abounds in recreation opportunities.

Majors and Degrees
Husson College offers programs of study leading to the Bachelor of Science (B.S.) and Associate of Science (A.S.) degrees. B.S. degrees are offered in accounting, biology, biology teacher education, business administration (family business, finance, general, international, management, or sports management), business technology education, computer information systems, criminal justice, elementary education, executive administration, hospitality management, nursing, occupational therapy, paralegal studies, physical education, psychology, and science and humanities.

In addition, Husson offers A.S. degree programs in accounting, business administration, computer information systems, executive administration, medical assisting, and paralegal studies. A one-year undeclared major is offered.

Academic Program
A cooperative education option, allowing students to combine job experience with the opportunity to earn up to 12 academic credits, is available in most four-year programs.

Academic Facilities
Peabody Hall contains classrooms, computer labs, a library, administrative offices, a campus center, an art gallery, and a chapel. Bell Hall houses the Physical Therapy, Occupational Therapy, and Nurse Practitioner Labs. The Newman Athletic Center has a double gymnasium, an Olympic-size swimming pool, tennis courts, a weight room, an exercise room, and other facilities.

The computer labs are open 24 hours a day and are equipped with Pentium computers; students work in a Windows NT environment. All students have e-mail addresses and access to the Internet. Computer kiosks are located in the administration building for easy access.

Costs
The basic academic-year expenses in 2000–01 for undergraduate students are $9480 for tuition, $5150 for room and seven-day board, and $100 for the comprehensive fee. Even though the cost of living in the area is somewhat lower than that in other parts of the country, students should plan to have sufficient funds available for books and personal expenses.

Financial Aid

The majority of Husson students receive some form of financial aid. The dollar amount of financial aid to be offered to the student is determined by the Free Application for Federal Student Aid (FAFSA). On the basis of this review, financial aid is authorized in the form of Federal Pell Grants, Federal Supplemental Educational Opportunity Grants, Federal Perkins Loans, and Federal Work-Study awards. There are several academic scholarships awarded annually on a competitive basis. The College strives to help each student find whatever financial aid is available and appropriate to help reduce the cost of education. Part-time jobs off campus are also available.

Faculty

The Husson faculty is oriented toward teaching rather than research. There are 49 full-time and 29 part-time professors. The small size of classes enables students to develop academic relationships with their professors. Husson's small-college environment attracts and holds highly dedicated faculty members who share a commitment to the students' whole development.

Student Government

There is an elected Student Senate, and students serve on many committees across the College. The President of the Student Senate is a voting member of the College Board of Trustees.

Admission Requirements

Husson College believes that all individuals who have the desire to further their education should have the opportunity to develop college-level competence. Admission is refused to applicants who do not demonstrate the potential to succeed in a college program. All applicants are considered on an individual basis.

Applicants to the freshman class are admitted on the strength of their secondary school curriculum, grade point average, class rank, counselor recommendations, and SAT I or ACT scores in relation to their intended major. Students whose high school transcripts show limited academic performance may be accepted on a conditional basis if they have a favorable recommendation from a high school guidance counselor or principal and show evidence of potential for success.

Transfer students are welcome and must present transcripts of their high school and college records. Transfer applicants should be in good academic standing and generally need a grade point average of at least 2.0 to be eligible for admission.

Application and Information

Husson College's rolling admission program allows applications to be reviewed as soon as they are complete. Application may be made for either the September or January term; there is no January entry for physical or occupational therapy majors. Applications for physical therapy should be received by January 15. There is a $25 application fee. All applicants should have copies of their transcripts sent to the Admissions Office as soon as possible after applying for admission.

Applicants are encouraged to get to know Husson College. Campus tours and open house programs, including the Fall Open House on November 18, 2000, and the Spring Open House on March 24, 2001, provide candidates with an opportunity to visit the College and experience campus life. Prospective students may also visit at other times, and personal interviews are recommended.

Additional information and application materials are available by contacting:

Director of Admissions
Husson College
One College Circle
Bangor, Maine 04401
Telephone: 207-941-7100
           800-448-7766 (toll-free)
Fax: 207-941-7935
E-mail: admit@husson.edu
World Wide Web: http://www.husson.edu

An aerial view of the Husson College campus.

IDAHO STATE UNIVERSITY
POCATELLO, IDAHO

The University

Idaho State University (ISU) has existed as an institution since 1901, when it was first established as the Academy of Idaho. It gained university status in 1963. Offering instruction in nearly every area of the arts and sciences, the University also conducts well-rounded programs of training in vocational and technical fields. Bachelor's and master's degrees in a variety of areas are awarded by the College of Arts and Sciences, the College of Business, the College of Education, the College of Engineering, the College of Health Professions, the College of Pharmacy, and the Graduate School. Doctoral degrees offered at ISU include the Doctor of Philosophy, Doctor of Arts, and Doctor of Education. Certificate programs of varying lengths, an Associate of Technology degree, an Associate of Applied Science degree, and a Bachelor of Applied Technology degree are included in the curricula of the School of Applied Technology.

Because of its location and character, ISU serves a diverse population that includes traditional-age students, nontraditional students, working professionals, and senior citizens. ISU has a total enrollment of 12,739 (10,144 undergraduate); they represent nearly every state in the Union and forty-seven countries. U.S. and international students attend the University because of its reputation as an academic and vocational institution of high quality; its relaxed, safe, and rural atmosphere; and its location at the foot of the Rocky Mountains.

Through its programs in pharmacy and other health-related professions, ISU is a center for education in the health field. Its programs in education, business, and engineering respond to a variety of current and emerging demands. It serves as a national center for Doctor of Arts degree programs. ISU also has responsibility for Idaho's dental education program. Several of the programs in the School of Applied Technology, the largest such school in the state, are nationally recognized.

ISU is accredited by the Northwest Association of Schools and Colleges. In addition, the University is accredited or approved for specific programs by the following organizations: AACSB-The International Association for Management Education; the Accreditation Board for Engineering and Technology, Inc.; the Accreditation Council for Graduate Medical Education; the American Association for Accreditation of Laboratory Animal Care; the American Association of Colleges of Nursing; the American Association for Health Education; the American Association of Medical Assistants; the American Association of Museums; the American Chemical Society; the American Council on Pharmaceutical Education; the American Dental Association Commission on Dental Accreditation; the American Dietetic Association; the American Health Information Management Association; the American Speech-Language-Hearing Association; the Association of University Programs in Health Administration; the Automotive Standard Excellence; the Commission on Accreditation in Physical Therapy Education; the Commission for the Accreditation of Allied Health Education Programs; the Council for the Accreditation of Counseling and Related Educational Programs; the Council on Education of the Deaf; the Council for Education in Public Health; the Council on Social Work Education; the Federal Aviation Administration; the Idaho Board of Nursing; the Idaho Board of Pharmacy; the Idaho Bureau of Occupational Licenses; the National Accrediting Agency for Clinical Laboratory Sciences; the National Association of Radio Telecommunication Engineers; the National Association of School Psychologists; the National Association of Schools of Music; the National Association of State Directors of Teacher Education and Certification; and the National Council for Accreditation of Teacher Education.

Location

Idaho State University is located in a residential section of Pocatello, the state's second-largest community. With an area population of 60,000 people, Pocatello provides all the amenities of a good-sized town without the usual urban difficulties. ISU is near the Utah and Wyoming borders and in the middle of some of the most beautiful country in the United States. Within driving distance are Yellowstone National Park, Sun Valley, Salt Lake City, and Jackson Hole. Pocatello and the surrounding area offer year-round recreational, cultural, and social opportunities. ISU also has two outreach campuses in Idaho Falls, Boise, and Twin Falls and offers a variety of distance learning options.

Majors and Degrees

Bachelor of Science and Bachelor of Arts degrees are offered in American studies, anthropology, art, biochemistry, biology, botany, chemistry, computer science, corporate training, dental hygiene, dietetics, early childhood education, ecology, economics, educational interpreting, elementary education, engineering (with options in civil, electrical, and mechanical engineering), engineering management, English, family and consumer sciences, French, general studies, geology, German, health-care administration, health education, history, human exceptionality, international studies, junior high/middle school education, mass communication, mathematics, medical technology, microbiology, music, nursing, philosophy, physical education, physician assistant studies, physics, political science, psychology, radiography, secondary education, social work, sociology, Spanish, speech communication, speech pathology and audiology, theater, vocational teacher education, and zoology. Bachelor of Fine Arts degrees are offered in art and theater. Bachelor of Music Education and Bachelor of Music in performance degrees are offered. Bachelor of Business Administration degrees are offered in accounting, computer information systems, finance, management, and marketing. ISU also offers a Bachelor of University Studies. The Bachelor of Applied Technology is offered for all State Board of Education–approved A.A.S. programs. A six-year Doctor of Pharmacy program is also available to undergraduates. Academic associate degrees are available in art, biology, business administration, chemistry, criminal justice, English, foreign languages, general studies, geology, history, math, physics, political science, radiographic science, sign language studies, and speech communication. Applied technology associate degrees are available in aircraft maintenance, automotive collision repair and refinishing, building construction technology, child development, civil engineering technology, computer software engineering technology, culinary arts technology, dental laboratory technology, design drafting technology, diesel electric technology, electrical apprenticeship, electromechanical technologies, electronic radio frequency/telecommunications technology, electronics technologies, fire service technology, graphic arts/printing technology, health information technology, hospitality management technology, instrumentation technology, laser/electrooptics technology, machining technology, marketing technology, management technology, medical assistant studies, occupational therapy assistant studies, office technology, physical therapist assistant studies, and welding.

Academic Program

Idaho State University requires a broad liberal arts education of all candidates for the bachelor's degree. Students are required to complete credits in math, English, speech, the physical and natural sciences, the humanities, and the social sciences before concentrating on their major field. All bachelor's degree candidates must complete a minimum of 128 credit hours. ISU operates on the semester system; opportunities are available for receiving credit by examination or tailoring a degree through the Bachelor of

University Studies program. Internships are also arranged for students through the Career Development Center and individual departments.

Off-Campus Arrangements

For premedical students, Idaho State University is a participant in the Washington-Alaska-Montana-Idaho (WAMI) medical education program at the University of Washington School of Medicine; ISU also has a contractual agreement with the University of Utah School of Medicine, reserving a specified number of seats in these respective medical school classes. Students in the University's Idaho Dental Education Program (IDEP) may complete their first year of professional training in Pocatello and finish their studies at Creighton University in Omaha, Nebraska. ISU participates in the Western Interstate Commission for Higher Education's (WICHE's) Western Undergraduate Exchange (WUE), Professional Student Exchange Program (PSEP), Western Regional Graduate Program (WRGP), and Doctoral Scholars Program under the Compact for Faculty Diversity. ISU is also a member of the National Student Exchange Program.

Academic Facilities

Facilities at Idaho State University combine a mixture of modern and traditional architecture, from the Eli M. Oboler Library, one of the largest education buildings in the state of Idaho, to the Holt Arena, the first covered athletics stadium on a U.S. college campus. The library houses more than a million volumes, bound periodicals, microtexts, and government documents and has the finest medical collection in the state. It is also home to a comprehensive media center and a satellite classroom facility. Since 1908, the library has been a depository for U.S. government publications, and in 1966 it became a depository for all nonsecret publications of the Atomic Energy Commission. Modern classroom and laboratory facilities in the University's more than twenty other buildings provide an excellent learning environment for the academic student, while up-to-date vocational classrooms effectively replicate the work environment for career-oriented students. A Physical Science Building with nine classrooms, fourteen labs, and state-of-the-art technical facilities is now operational.

Costs

Resident fees were $2398 and nonresident tuition was $6240, for a total out-of-state cost of $8638 per year for 1999–2000. Room and board costs were approximately $3580 per year, depending upon the meal plan chosen. A 5 percent increase is anticipated in fees and tuition and room and board costs for the 2000–01 academic year. Miscellaneous costs average $600 for books and supplies, $1890 for personal expenses, and $810 for transportation.

Financial Aid

The goal of Idaho State University's financial assistance program is twofold: to reward those students who demonstrate outstanding academic, leadership, or other talents and to aid those students unable to bear the costs of attending the University. In keeping with these goals, ISU provides financial assistance for some 80 percent of its students through grant, loan, work, and scholarship programs. ISU accepts the Free Application for Federal Student Aid (FAFSA). The priority deadline for mailing the FAFSA is March 1. The scholarship application deadline for new and transfer students is February 20. A number of competitive out-of-state-student tuition and reduced fee waivers are also available to domestic and international students, as are campus and off-campus job placement programs.

Faculty

Idaho State University has a 17:1 student-faculty ratio across its 225 disciplines. Because ISU's faculty members emphasize teaching, classes are generally taught by professors, not graduate students. More than 64 percent of ISU's 536 full-time and 60 part-time faculty members hold the doctoral degree, first professional degree, or terminal degree in their field. Teaching, advising, research, and service are faculty priorities at ISU. Many of the University's faculty members are nationally recognized for their expertise in accounting, biology, electronics, geology, mathematics, and pharmacy.

Student Government

There are more than 120 student organizations at ISU. The Associated Students of Idaho State University (ASISU) is the official governing body for students. A president, a vice president, and a 20-member senate are elected by the students each February. ASISU is an effective and vocal organization that sets policy in many aspects of life at ISU. It administers a budget of more than $1 million and has recently funded completion of a Child Care/Student Activities Center. ASISU is currently engaged in funding a new student union to be built on the Idaho Falls campus. Student leaders also work on a statewide level with the State Board of Education and the Idaho Legislature.

Admission Requirements

To be admitted, prospective freshmen must demonstrate a minimum earned 2.0 GPA in the following core curriculum high school courses: 8 credits in English; 6 credits in math (algebra I and higher); 6 credits in natural sciences; 5 credits in social sciences; 2 credits in humanities/foreign language; and 3 credits in other college-preparatory courses. Those not meeting these requirements may be accepted provisionally; they should write to the Director of Admissions, Campus Box 8270, Idaho State University. An application, a final high school transcript or GED certificate, an ACT or SAT I score, and a $30 application fee are required. Transfer students to ISU must have a minimum 2.0 cumulative GPA and should provide transcripts of their previous college courses as well as a high school transcript if they have fewer than 25 earned college credits. An ACT or SAT I score is also required of transfer students under 21 years of age who have fewer than 14 earned college credits. International students must demonstrate satisfactory to above-average performance in their previous secondary or postsecondary educational experiences. A minimum TOEFL score of 500 is required, along with proof of financial support.

Application and Information

Deadlines for submission of all application materials are August 1 for the fall semester and December 1 for the spring semester. Notification is made within two weeks of application. For additional information and application materials, students should contact:

Office of Enrollment Planning and Academic Services
Campus Box 8054
Idaho State University
Pocatello, Idaho 83209-0009

Telephone: 208-236-3277
Fax: 208-236-4314
E-mail: isuinfo@isu.edu
World Wide Web: http://www.isu.edu

Natural beauty can be experienced on the campus of Idaho State University, located in a mountain valley.

ILLINOIS INSTITUTE OF TECHNOLOGY
CHICAGO, ILLINOIS

The Institute

Illinois Institute of Technology (IIT) is a private, Ph.D.-granting research university with programs in architecture, business, design, engineering, law, psychology, and science. One of the sixteen institutions in the Association of Independent Technological Universities (AITU), IIT offers exceptional preparation for professions that require technological sophistication. Through a committed faculty and close personal attention, IIT provides a challenging academic program focused on the rigor of the real world. The internationally famous main campus is based on a master plan developed by the late Ludwig Mies van der Rohe, one of the most influential architects of the century, who served for twenty years as director of IIT's College of Architecture. An independent university, the Institute includes the College of Architecture, the Armour College of Engineering, the Institute of Psychology, the Stuart School of Business, the Institute of Design, and the Chicago-Kent College of Law.

The more than 6,000 students at IIT (more than 1,700 of whom are undergraduates) are encouraged to participate in the many social, cultural, and athletic opportunities available. Student activities include the campus newspaper, the radio station, special interest clubs, theater and music groups, intramural and varsity athletics, fraternities and sororities, honor societies, professional societies, student government, residence hall organizations, and the student-run Union Board. Campus facilities include the union building, which has its own bowling alley and recreation area; a convenience store and campus book store; a gymnasium; and seven residence halls and eight resident fraternity houses. Counseling, job placement, and student health services are included in the various campus services.

Location

IIT stands in the midst of a developing urban area. It is 1 mile west of Lake Michigan and 1 block from the White Sox ballpark. The campus is located approximately 3 miles south of the Chicago Loop, offering students unlimited opportunities to enjoy art, music, drama, films, museums, and other entertainment. Also convenient to the campus are a number of recreational areas, including McCormick Place exhibition hall, Soldier Field, Grant Park, Lincoln Park Zoo, various bicycle paths, and lakefront beaches. IIT is easily accessible to the rest of Chicago via two major expressways. Bus and elevated railroad lines have stops on campus, and the IIT bus provides free transportation between the campus and the university's Downtown Center in Chicago's West Loop area.

Majors and Degrees

The Armour College of Engineering offers the Bachelor of Science in Engineering with specializations in aerospace, architectural, chemical, civil, computer, electrical, environmental, mechanical, and metallurgical and materials engineering, as well as a B.S. in computer science. IIT also offers the Bachelor of Science degree in biology, chemistry, computer information systems, Internet communications, mathematics, molecular biochemistry and biophysics, physics, political science, professional and technical communication, and psychology.

The College of Architecture awards the Bachelor of Architecture degree through its five-year professional degree program. A fifth-year option in city and regional planning is also available for students pursuing a degree in architecture.

There are various options and minors available within each curriculum, such as bioengineering, business, computer-aided drafting, ethics and morality, law, management, manufacturing technology, military science, psychology, public policy, and technical communications. Other individualized specializations may be arranged with approval of the dean. Combined undergraduate/graduate degrees include those offered in conjunction with business administration (B.S. and M.B.A.), law (B.S. and J.D.), and public administration (B.S. and M.P.A.).

Along with its traditional premed program, IIT has also established an honors combined program in engineering and medicine (B.S. and M.D.) with the Finch University of Health Sciences/Chicago Medical School and Rush Medical College. IIT also offers an honors combined program in law (B.S. and J.D.) with the Chicago-Kent College of Law. Students interested in an honors program must submit an undergraduate application and a supplemental application for the graduate portion of the program. All application materials are available on line.

Academic Program

While requirements vary according to the major, all IIT students complete a general education core, which includes a minimum of 7 semester hours in mathematics and computer science, 11 semester hours in natural science or engineering, 12 semester hours in the humanities, and 12 semester hours in the social sciences. Students pursuing a Bachelor of Science in Engineering or in the physical sciences take, in addition, a program that includes further study in mathematics and computer science, chemistry, and physics.

IIT's mission is to educate students for complex professional roles in a changing world and to advance knowledge through research and scholarship. The Institute is committed to the educational ideal of small undergraduate classes and individual mentoring. IIT's unique Introduction to the Professions program brings students and senior faculty members together each week in small groups, where students interact with their advisers as both teachers and mentors. Throughout the curricula, the IIT interprofessional projects provide a learning environment in which interdisciplinary teams of students apply theoretical knowledge gained in the classroom and laboratory to real-world projects sponsored by industry and government. Many IIT students further enhance their education through a wide variety of research and entrepreneurial projects.

Cooperative education is encouraged. This career development program begins with a freshman year of full-time study and then alternates semesters of study and employment in industry for approximately four additional years. Placement services are provided by the university. Ninety-two percent of recent graduates were placed in jobs in the fields of their majors or went on to graduate or professional schools.

Study abroad is available in several academic disciplines.

Academic Facilities

As the central library, the Paul V. Galvin Library provides a broad range of services, including information on engineering, business, science, mathematics, the humanities, architecture, and design via the Internet; numerous electronic and paper-based databases; a document delivery service; interlibrary loan; and special collections. The main campus operates DEC minicomputers, a Silicon Graphics "Challenge" UNIX multiprocessor, and local UNIX servers. Terminals and microcomputers are located in most academic buildings across the campus, in residence halls, and in Galvin Library. Seminars, tutorials, and computer lab work are conducted in microcomputer classrooms. Among IIT's thirty-two research centers are the Center for Synchrotron Radiation Research, the Fluid Dynamics Research Center, and the Research Laboratory in Human Biomechanics. Most research centers offer undergraduates opportunities to participate on their projects.

Costs

Annual tuition for 2000–01 is $18,000. Other expenses are $5428 for room and board and approximately $1000 for books, $1200 for transportation costs, and $2100 for personal expenses. Additional fees are $100. The estimated annual total for freshmen is $27,828. Annual tuition covers the fall and spring semesters.

Financial Aid

Most full-time undergraduates at IIT receive financial aid from a variety of sources. IIT participates in the Federal Perkins Loan, Federal Work-Study, Federal Pell Grant, Federal Supplemental Educational Opportunity Grant, federally insured student loan, Illinois State Scholarship Commission Monetary Award, Illinois Guaranteed Loan, and Federal PLUS loan programs and similar programs. In addition, IIT provides generous merit-based and need-based scholarships and loans from its own funds and from those supported by a number of companies and other organizations. The NEXT Initiative offers five-year scholarships ranging from $64,000 to $110,000 for the study of engineering. All admitted students are automatically reviewed for tuition scholarships. More than 500 are awarded each year. Athletic scholarships are also available for qualified students. Two other programs may be utilized by students working to supplement their financial aid: on-campus employment and the cooperative education program. IIT requires the Free Application for Federal Student Aid (FAFSA). No additional applications or forms are required.

Army, Naval, and Air Force ROTC programs are offered. ROTC scholarship winners receive supplemental scholarships from IIT.

Faculty

There are about 334 full-time faculty members; the student-faculty ratio is approximately 11:1. All members of the senior teaching faculty instruct in both upper- and lower-division courses. Ninety-nine percent hold doctoral degrees or the highest professional degree in their area.

Student Government

The Student Leadership Committee (SLC) is a vital force in the IIT community. It acts as the students' official voice in communications with faculty and administration, and it plans, develops, and supervises most of the activities pertaining to campus life. In addition to having its own standing committees, SLC is represented on seven of the ten institutional committees pertaining to undergraduates.

Admission Requirements

Admission evaluation is a thorough, personal process. Of paramount consideration is the student's academic performance in high school, specifically in areas that are vital to the student's major at IIT. Minimum high school preparation includes 16 units of credit, including at least 4 units in English, 4 units in mathematics, and 2 units in laboratory sciences (including physics). High school preparation in mathematics through the precalculus level is required. Calculus is encouraged but not required. Chemistry is strongly recommended.

A completed application, recommendations, test scores—either SAT I or ACT—and an official high school transcript are required for admission. Interviews are not required. Supplemental applications and materials are required for the Honors Program in Engineering and Medicine, the Honors Law Program, and for the NEXT Initiative Scholarship Program. Special deadlines apply to these programs. All materials are available on line.

Application and Information

Applications are reviewed on a rolling basis. Students are encouraged to apply as early as possible; an online application is available on IIT's Web site. In general, applicants can expect notification within two weeks after their completed applications are received.

For further information, students should contact:

Office of Admission
Illinois Institute of Technology
10 West 33rd Street
Chicago, Illinois 60616-3793
Telephone: 312-567-3025 (from Chicago)
              800-448-2329 (toll-free outside Chicago)
Fax: 312-567-6939
E-mail: admission@iit.edu
World Wide Web: http://www.iit.edu

IMMACULATA COLLEGE
IMMACULATA, PENNSYLVANIA

The College
Immaculata, a comprehensive Catholic liberal arts college for women of all faiths, offers a high-quality education firmly grounded in values and tradition. Immaculata graduates are known for their skills and knowledge but also for their desire to serve. The College was founded in 1920 and has since grown to enroll 3,200 students in bachelor's, master's, doctoral degree programs, and accelerated degree completion programs. The College has the programs and resources of a university in the intimate atmosphere of a small women's college; in fact, Immaculata College is known as The University Within A College™.

Approximately 400 traditional-age women attend the day division, with 85 percent of them living in campus housing. The evening division includes both graduate and undergraduate programs that are open to both men and women, most of whom commute. Traditional-age students represent eighteen states and fifteen countries, giving the campus both ethnic and geographic diversity. Eight percent of the traditional-age students are members of minority groups. Resident students live in four dormitory buildings containing both double and single rooms. Both resident and nonresident students participate in more than thirty student clubs and organizations that represent interests in athletics, student government, academic disciplines, community action, music, dance, theater, and student publications.

Intercollegiate sports include basketball, cross-country, field hockey, lacrosse, soccer, softball, tennis, and volleyball. Athletic fields, gymnasiums, a weight room, and an Olympic-size swimming pool are available for student use and provide numerous opportunities for physical activities and wellness programs. The Student Association of Immaculata College provides the unity, enthusiasm, and leadership that are representative of the students who choose the College.

Immaculata College offers unique traditions as a part of the overall collegiate experience. The College celebrates Freshman Investiture, the academic capping of the newest members of the College community; the Sophomore Pinning Ceremony; the Junior Ring Ceremony; and the Senior Hooding Ceremony. Carol Night, one of Immaculata's best-loved traditions, involves students, faculty members, and alumnae singing around the Christmas tree in the Rotunda of Villa Maria Hall.

The main building, Villa Maria Hall, is of neo-Renaissance architecture in gray stone with a red tile roof. The other thirteen major campus buildings are likewise of gray stone with red tile roofs, unifying the aesthetic appearance of the campus. Renovations of the three main buildings, Villa Maria, Lourdes, and Nazareth halls, are scheduled for completion in December 2000.

Graduate degrees offered include the Master of Arts in cultural and linguistic diversity, counseling psychology, educational leadership and administration, music therapy, nutrition education, and organization leadership. Doctoral degrees are offered in clinical psychology, school psychology, and educational administration. ACCEL® degree completion programs are offered in nursing, organization dynamics, and human performance management; this program also offers an Associate of Science degree in business administration.

Location
Immaculata's 400-acre campus is located in historic Chester County, 20 miles west of Philadelphia and 10 miles south of Valley Forge. The area is primarily suburban, with numerous colleges and universities offering a wide range of cultural and social activities. The many places of interest in Philadelphia and Lancaster are easily reached by car or train. Southern New Jersey shore resorts and New York City are within 2 hours by car, with Pocono Mountain ski resorts and Washington, D.C., only 2½ hours away by car or train. The College provides numerous opportunities for internships in the business, educational, and scientific communities throughout the area.

Majors and Degrees
Immaculata offers the Bachelor of Arts, Bachelor of Music, Bachelor of Science, Associate of Arts, and Associate of Science degrees as well as certification in education for nursery school through grade 12. Undergraduate major fields of study include accounting, biology, biology/chemistry, biology/psychology, business administration, chemistry, dietetics, economics, education certification, English, environmental science, exercise science, family consumer sciences/home economics education, fashion marketing, foods in business, French, German, history, history–international studies, history–politics, information technology, international business/foreign language, international studies, mathematics, mathematics/computer science, mathematics/physics, music, music therapy, politics, prelaw, premedicine, psychology, sociology, sociology/social work, Spanish, Spanish/psychology, and Spanish/social work. Most of the majors at Immaculata can be combined with certification in early childhood, elementary, secondary, or special education.

Academic Program
Two factors are emphasized in the educational program at Immaculata: a comprehensive liberal arts background and a major field of concentration that prepares students to begin a career or to attend graduate school. Degrees in all majors require 126 credits. This number includes 54 credits in a liberal arts core, which is required of all students. The honors program, an option for gifted students, offers an array of courses designed to give those who participate a special involvement in the learning process.

The Mary Bruder Center houses the offices for personal, career, and graduate study counseling and for educational and career testing. Workshops and seminars in resume writing, interviewing, career options, internship opportunities, and graduate fellowships are offered at regular intervals.

The College operates on a four-day week class schedule, with Wednesday as an open day, allowing opportunities for educational observations and junior-senior internships. The academic schedule is traditional—spring and fall semesters with two summer sessions.

Off-Campus Arrangements
Both summer-abroad and junior-year-abroad programs combine travel with academic study to broaden the experience of students who seek these opportunities. Immaculata, as one of the sponsoring institutions for the International Studies Association, offers four-week, credit-bearing summer programs in France, Germany, Italy, Mexico, and Spain.

Every undergraduate major department offers internship opportunities for students in agencies, businesses, institutions, or corporations related to their study. Some majors—dietetics, nutrition, fashion marketing, and music therapy—require a multiweek internship for the degree.

Academic Facilities

The Gabriele Library, dedicated in 1993, houses 130,000 volumes and offers 714 periodical subscriptions and 3,609 units of microfiche. In addition to the computer center, students have access to networked computers in the library, an interactive language lab with a video screen, and a multifacet science lab with computer-simulated experiments; they also have Internet/Intranet access from their dorm rooms. Well-equipped laboratories, art studios, media centers, and an 1,150-seat theater give students more than adequate facilities with which to pursue their interests.

Four state-of-the-art computer labs were recently added: the Campus Learning and Language Laboratory, the Sister Maria Socorro Studio Laboratory for Mathematics and Science, a new Biology Laboratory, and the Loyola Executive Technology Center. The fiber-optic backbone of the campus was also completed, connecting all administrative, academic, and residential buildings.

Costs

For 2000–01, tuition and fees are $13,950, and room and board are $6800. An additional $1000 is estimated to cover books and personal spending.

Financial Aid

Financial aid is available in the form of scholarships, grants, loans, and part-time campus employment through the resources of Immaculata, federal and state governments, and private endowments. Presidential and Immaculata scholarships are awarded for academic excellence. Approximately 90 percent of the students receive some form of aid, and all students who demonstrate need are offered financial aid packages. Beginning March 1, the College sends financial aid packages to accepted students as their files are completed. The Free Application for Federal Student Aid (FAFSA) reporting code is 003276.

Faculty

The faculty has 70 full-time and 120 part-time members, more than half of whom hold doctorates. All others have at least one master's degree. Although several members of the Immaculata faculty have conducted research and presented papers in various disciplines, both nationally and internationally, high-quality teaching is of the greatest importance to Immaculata's academic program. Full-time faculty members serve as academic counselors and activity moderators. The student-faculty ratio is 11:1.

Student Government

The Student Association of Immaculata College (SAIC) governs most aspects of student life for both resident and commuter students. The resident-assistant program moderates dorm life by holding open meetings to discuss safety issues and to set dorm regulations. Students serve on the various College policymaking committees and handle all student activity funds. The College aims to develop leadership in women by providing as many leadership opportunities as possible.

Admission Requirements

In order to be considered for admission to the Women's College at Immaculata, students must submit an official secondary school transcript indicating course selection for the senior year. They also must include their class standing, submit SAT I or ACT scores, and send at least one letter of recommendation. The reporting code for the SAT I is 2320, and the reporting code for the ACT is 3596. Writing samples and an admission interview, while not required, can enhance a candidate's application. The Admission Committee requires a minimum secondary school GPA of 2.5 in 16 or more course units as follows: 4 units of English, 2 units of social science, 2 units of mathematics, 2 units of science (1 lab), and 2 consecutive years of the same foreign language. Most candidates exceed this curriculum. The application fee can be waived for students with high financial need.

Application and Information

Applications are accepted from prospective freshmen and transfer students until May 1 for the fall semester and until December 1 for the spring semester. Decisions are made on a rolling basis three to four weeks after an applicant's file is complete. All admission credentials should be sent to the address below. For further information, students should contact:

Office of Undergraduate Admission
Immaculata College
P.O. Box 642
Immaculata, Pennsylvania 19345-0642
Telephone: 610-647-4400 Ext. 3015
        877-IC TODAY (toll-free)
Fax: 610-640-0836
E-mail: admissions@immaculata.edu
World Wide Web: http://www.immaculata.edu

Students at Immaculata College.

INDIANA STATE UNIVERSITY
TERRE HAUTE, INDIANA

The University

Indiana State University (ISU) is a publicly assisted, comprehensive, residential institution offering instruction at the associate, bachelor's, master's, and doctoral levels. It was founded in 1865 as the Indiana State Normal School. Through the years, it evolved through successive stages as the Indiana State Teachers College and Indiana State College. It attained university status in 1965. University enrollment stands at 10,985. In fall 1999, undergraduate enrollment was 9,334 students, of whom 4,573 were men. Graduate enrollment was 1,651. The ISU educational experience is enriched by the presence of a diverse student body drawn from throughout Indiana and the rest of the country and more than seventy other countries.

Indiana State's identity and its vision for the future are based on a historic embrace of the values of opportunity and success for all of its students. In seeking to extend this vision into the twenty-first century, the University, through its Strategic Plan, is promoting excellence in areas such as technology; the student experience, particularly in the first year; teaching and learning; outreach; scholarships; and partnerships with educational institutions, government agencies, business and industry, and individuals.

ISU is committed to providing a high-quality educational experience in a student-centered learning environment. The student-faculty ratio is 16:1, and approximately 75 percent of classes at ISU have 25 or fewer students. Seventy-eight percent of classes are taught by full-time faculty members; 67 percent are taught by tenure-track faculty members with terminal degrees in their respective fields. Students can choose from more than 115 majors, ranging from criminology to packaging technology, athletic training to geography, teacher education to insurance, and safety management to nursing. The Graduate School offers master's and doctoral programs in a number of the areas listed in the Majors and Degrees section.

Many of ISU's academic programs are nationally known, and some are the only ones of their kind in the state. The insurance and risk management program is listed as one of the top four programs in the nation by the *Journal of Risk and Insurance* in terms of the breadth of courses offered. It also is listed as one of the top eight programs in the country by *Independent Agent* magazine. The safety management program is one of twelve in the nation accredited by the American Society of Safety Engineers. The campus's undergraduate and graduate programs in athletic training were the first in the nation to be accredited. ISU also is one of only four institutions in the country that has accredited graduate and undergraduate programs in this field. The Doctor of Psychology in clinical psychology program is the only program of its kind in the state accredited by the American Psychological Association. The criminology program has the largest graduate program in the state and is the only four-year program in the state with a criminalistics lab. The principal intern program has been recognized as the outstanding school administrator preparation program in America by the American Association of School Administrators. The Department of Geography, Geology, and Anthropology ranks third in the nation among Ph.D.-granting departments in student enrollment, and its program in the application of remote sensing and geographic information systems is internationally recognized. The School of Technology has several programs—biomedical electronics technology, computer hardware technology, and instrumentation and control technology—that are the only accredited programs of their kind in the nation. ISU's programs in industrial automotive technology and packaging technology are the only ones of their kind in the state.

The Hulman Memorial Student Union Board provides cultural, social, educational, and recreational programming for the Student Union and for the entire campus. As the primary all-campus programming board, the Union Board produces events that involve the whole student body, such as Homecoming and Tandemonia, a weeklong spring festival featuring a tandem bike race. Students at ISU can choose from among nearly 200 organizations and clubs. Students can compete in intramural sports. ISU's athletic teams compete in the NCAA Division I.

Location

Indiana State University's scenic campus is adjacent to the downtown area of Terre Haute, which comprises a metropolitan area of 100,000 people in west-central Indiana. The University's proximity to downtown Terre Haute helps to foster a number of partnerships between the campus and local businesses, government agencies, and civic organizations. Terre Haute serves as the fine arts, cultural, and athletic center of west-central Indiana and east-central Illinois. Terre Haute has the Sheldon Swope Art Museum, the Eugene V. Debs Museum, the Terre Haute Symphony Orchestra, Community Theatre, and the historic Indiana Theater. The city also has an extensive and excellent parks system. It is convenient to four major metropolitan areas: Indianapolis is within 75 miles, and St. Louis, Chicago, and Cincinnati are each only 180 miles away.

Majors and Degrees

Indiana State's undergraduate academic programs are offered through its College of Arts and Sciences and its professional Schools of Education, Business, Nursing, Technology, and Health and Human Performance.

College of Arts and Sciences programs include African and African-American studies; anthropology; art; art history; chemistry; child development and family life; clinical laboratory science; communication studies; computer science; criminology (two- and four-year programs); dietetics; economics; English; English teaching; family and consumer science education; fine art; food and nutrition; food service management; foreign language concentration (international studies); French; French teaching; general family and consumer science; general studies (two-year program); geography; geology; German; German teaching; history; interdisciplinary studies (humanities); interior design; journalism; Latin; life sciences; mathematics; mathematics education; music; music business administration; music education; music history; music merchandising; music performance; music theory; philosophy; physics; political science; pre-dental hygiene; predentistry; pre-engineering; prelaw; premedicine; preoptometry; prepharmacy; pretheology; pre-veterinary medicine; psychology; public relations; radio/television/film; Russian; science education; social studies education; social work; sociology; sociology long-term health care; Spanish; Spanish teaching; speech communication and theater teaching; study of religion; textiles, apparel, and merchandising; theater; visual arts education; and women's studies.

The School of Business offers programs in accounting, administrative office systems, business administration, business education, finance, insurance, management, management information systems, marketing, office support and technology (two-year program), and quality and decision systems.

The School of Education has programs in child development and early childhood education (two-year program); communication disorders; counseling; curriculum, instruction, and media technology; early childhood education; educational and school psychology; elementary education; kindergarten–primary education; special education; and speech-language pathology.

The School of Health and Human Performance has programs in athletic training, community health, environmental health, health-safety education, physical education, pre–occupational therapy, recreation and sport management, safety management, and sports studies–fitness and exercise science.

The School of Nursing has two- and four-year nursing programs.

The School of Technology offers programs in aerospace administration, architectural technology (two-year program), biomedical electronics technology, computer hardware technology, computer-integrated manufacturing technology, construction technology, electronics and computer technology, electronics technology, general aviation–flight (two-year program), general industrial technology, human resource development, industrial automotive technology, industrial supervision, industrial technology (two-year program), instrumentation and control technology, manufacturing technology, mechanical technology, packaging technology, printing management, professional aviation flight technology, technology education, trade and industrial education (two-year program), vocational trade-industrial teaching, and vocational trade-industrial-technical laboratory.

Academic Program

ISU's academic strength lies in its liberal arts and professional programs of study, its interdependent undergraduate and graduate programs, and its extensive student development programs. Undergraduate programs combine general education with majors and minors. All students working toward a bachelor's degree at Indiana State must take a minimum of 42 semester hours of general education course work, including 11 to 26 hours of basic studies and 31 hours of liberal studies. Most degree programs require 124 semester hours and a minimum 2.0 grade point average for graduation. Baccalaureate degree candidates must have earned at least 50 semester hours of residence credit at Indiana State. The academic calendar includes fall and spring semesters and summer sessions of varying lengths.

The University Honors Program, which offers special courses, colloquia, seminars, and independent study, is designed to challenge the talented student and help him or her broaden and enhance their education. DegreeLink, a partnership with other public colleges and universities, makes an ISU degree available statewide by means of satellite technology. The transformation of student life through the development of learning communities is the result of the First-Year Experience Program, which was funded by a $2-million grant from the Lilly Endowment. The Student Academic Services Center offers a number of programs for students with special needs. Indiana State's Career Center helps students formulate career goals, gain career-related work experience while in school, and find employment. An Air Force ROTC program is available.

Academic Facilities

Indiana State is committed to providing students with facilities that match the excellence of its academic programs. Over the past several years, the University, through its Campus Master Plan, has completed a number of building projects, including the Center for Fine and Performing Arts, which combines state-of-the-art performance facilities and an art gallery; the John T. Myers Technology Center, which features specially designed laboratories and classrooms in a high-technology setting; and Root Hall, a classroom building for the humanities. The Student Computing Complex offers students access to computers 24 hours a day. Computer clusters are also located in residence halls and other buildings throughout campus. All residence hall rooms are wired for Internet access.

With more than 1 million books and more than 5,000 subscriptions to periodicals and journals, the Cunningham Memorial Library ranks as one of the finest collegiate libraries in the Midwest. The library was one of the first in the state to computerize its card catalog and continues to be a leader in making information available in various electronic formats, including CD-ROM and the Internet.

The University also has laboratories and other learning resources such as computer-integrated manufacturing, a remote sensing and geographic information systems laboratory, the Writing Center, specially designed rehearsal rooms, fully equipped science laboratories, an observatory, and a human performance laboratory.

Costs

Fees for full-time undergraduate students who are Indiana residents are $3564 per year and $8898 per year for out-of-state residents. Housing costs are $4604 per year. ISU charges no additional fees for computer use, activities, admission to athletic events, or health services.

Financial Aid

ISU awards financial aid to about 76 percent of freshman students. Indiana State University offers financial assistance to students in a number of forms, including loans, grants, scholarships, and work-study. Payment plans are also available. ISU awards more than $1 million in scholarships each year. Prestigious scholarship programs such as the President's Scholars and the Alumni Scholars are available to outstanding high school students. Those students who meet the minimum academic requirements for a scholarship are mailed a scholarship application after they have been admitted. Students also may be considered for financial assistance such as loans and grants after gaining admission to the University. Those who apply for assistance before March 1 are given priority. Students should file the Free Application for Federal Student Aid and an Indiana State Financial Aid Application.

Faculty

Indiana State's instructional programs are carried out by its 650 faculty members. As a teaching university, ISU expects its faculty members to give highest priority to instruction and the intellectual and personal development of students. Faculty members, however, also are expected to be engaged in meaningful and productive scholarship and professional service and to integrate what is learned from these activities into their teaching. Faculty members also serve as student advisers and assist students in the planning of their academic programs.

Student Government

The Student Government Association (SGA), of which every student is a member, is the governing body for all ISU students. SGA operates under its own constitution and consists of three branches: legislative, executive, and judicial.

Admission Requirements

Admission applications are reviewed as they are received. Students are considered for admission after receipt of complete credentials—an application, a nonrefundable $20 processing fee, and official transcripts from all schools and colleges previously attended. Freshman and transfer students who have completed fewer than 24 transferable semester credit hours must submit scores from either the SAT I or ACT. In general, freshman applicants are expected to rank in the upper half of their high school graduating class and have completed Indiana Core 40 for regular admission. Additional information is available from high school counselors or the ISU Office of Admissions. It is suggested that prospective students visit the campus and talk with a member of the admissions staff.

Application and Information

High school students should complete an application in the fall of their senior year. To ensure full consideration, applications and official transcripts must be received in the Office of Admissions by August 1 for the fall semester, December 1 for the spring semester, May 1 for the first summer session, and July 1 for the second summer session. Indiana State encourages all prospective students to visit campus. Requests for appointments and information should be addressed to:

Director of Admissions
Tirey Hall
Indiana State University
Terre Haute, Indiana 47809
Telephone: 812-237-2121
        800-742-0891 (toll-free)
E-mail: admisu@amber.indstate.edu
World Wide Web: http://www.indstate.edu

INDIANA UNIVERSITY OF PENNSYLVANIA
INDIANA, PENNSYLVANIA

The University

Founded in 1875, Indiana University of Pennsylvania (IUP) draws its 14,000-plus enrollment from nearly every state and from scores of other countries. With three campuses located in the foothills of the Allegheny Mountains, IUP is the largest of the fourteen universities in the State System of Higher Education and the only one that grants doctoral degrees.

Recognized as a "public Ivy," the University sustains a tradition of high academic quality at an affordable cost. In forty-five academic departments located within six colleges and two schools, IUP offers more than 100 major fields of study. Graduate programs in many professional and applied areas are available, as are seven doctoral programs. IUP has one of the largest internship programs in Pennsylvania, providing students with professional experience to supplement their classroom learning.

The following publications have recognized IUP for its high academic standards and competitive costs: *Arco's Dollarwise Guide to American Colleges*; *Barron's 300 Best Buys in College Education*; *The Best Buys in College Education* by Edward Fiske, education editor of the *New York Times*; *Changing Times: How to Get an Ivy League Education at a State University* by Martin Nemko; *Money* magazine's Money Guide; *Two Hundred Most Selective Colleges: The Definitive Guide to America's First-Choice Schools*; and *U.S. News & World Report*.

In addition to accolades for its academic programs, IUP has been recognized as the safest campus location in the entire Northeast and as the fifth safest in the nation by *Crime at College: A Student Guide to Personal Safety* (1994).

Location

Located 50 miles northeast of Pittsburgh in the borough of Indiana, the seat of Indiana County, IUP is just three blocks from the town's business district. The University is easily accessible by automobile from all sections of the state. Passenger services of various kinds operate on frequent schedules, connecting Indiana with all nearby cities and towns, including Pittsburgh, Altoona, and Johnstown. Bus service connects Indiana with the main line of the Pennsylvania Railroad at Johnstown and Pittsburgh. The community of Indiana has more than thirty churches that represent all major faiths. All churches are within walking distance of the campus.

Majors and Degrees

IUP awards B.A., B.S., B.F.A., B.S.Ed., and B.S.N. degrees in approximately 100 majors in the areas of the arts and sciences, business, consumer services, elementary and secondary education, fine arts, food and nutrition, health and physical education, home economics, medical technology, nursing, respiratory therapy, and safety sciences. IUP also offers the Associate of Arts degree in business. Dual majors are available to students who wish to augment their academic background.

Academic Program

IUP provides for the nourishment of the whole person through its Liberal Studies Program. In addition to fulfilling the 53-semester-hour Liberal Studies requirement, each student must complete the necessary major and minor requirements to reach the minimum total of 124 credits necessary for graduation.

Courses taken by students under the Advanced Placement Program of the College Board prior to admission may be recognized by the awarding of college credit or by the exemption of required subjects from the students' curriculum. For students who have acquired learning in nontraditional or other ways or who have advanced in a given field, an opportunity to gain exemption from a course is offered through examinations given at the discretion of each department.

The University offers an Army Reserve Officers' Training Corps (ROTC) program.

IUP operates on two 14-week semesters—September through December and January through May—plus two 5-week summer sessions.

Off-Campus Arrangements

The University participates in joint programs with other colleges and universities. Included in these cooperative programs are one in family medicine with Jefferson Medical College of Thomas Jefferson University, one in forestry with Duke University, two in engineering with Drexel University and the University of Pittsburgh, one in graphic arts with the Art Institute of Pittsburgh, one in jewelry with the Bowman Technical School, one in optometry with Pennsylvania College of Optometry, and one in podiatry with Philadelphia School of Podiatry.

The Office of International Affairs has arrangements for students to study in numerous countries. Each year, approximately 200 students study abroad. Other opportunities for off-campus study include the marine science consortium, graphic arts exchange program, internships, and studies in the health services, which are offered through the University's affiliations with hospitals and other universities.

Academic Facilities

The Information Systems and Communications Center, established in 1963 on the ground floor of Stright Hall, provides computational support for undergraduate and graduate courses, faculty and student research, and the administrative requirements of the University. Terminals are located in the center and in various other locations on campus.

The University's campuswide cable system and fiber-optic backbone are fully connected to all academic buildings and each residence hall room, allowing immediate connection to the University's mainframe computer and access to the University's television station and educational programming.

The library complex, completed in 1981, provides study room for about 1,200 students. The total library holdings of 835,378 volumes are housed in the main library building. The well-organized general holdings are enhanced by the reference collection, 3,854 current magazines, extensive files of bound magazines, 1.7 million units of microforms, and varied media holdings exceeding 30,000. The IUP libraries are fully automated.

Costs

The basic costs that a student who is a resident of Pennsylvania could expect to incur per semester while enrolled at IUP in 1999–2000 included $1809 for tuition, $1877 for room and board, $400 for fees, and approximately $500 for books and supplies. Additional costs include $500 to $1000 for personal expenses. Tuition for out-of-state students was $4523 per semester. All costs are subject to change.

Financial Aid

The types of financial aid offered by IUP include student employment, loans, grants, and scholarships. In most cases, the PHEAA and Federal Pell Grant application forms are used to determine eligibility for these programs. Federal aid administered by the University is available for both the regular academic year and the summer sessions. The application deadline for upperclass students for these federal aid programs is normally May 1 (preferred deadline is March 15) for the following academic year. Freshmen may apply for aid upon acceptance by the University. For the summer sessions, the application deadline is May 1. Financial assistance is also available through IUP's ROTC program.

Faculty

There are 768 full-time and 87 part-time teaching faculty members. In addition, there are 218 people serving in the administration. The student-faculty ratio is 19:1. While primarily serving as instructors, faculty members also aid students in course selections and career planning and advise student organizations and clubs.

Student Government

IUP students actively participate in the governance of the University through the Student Congress and through elected representatives to the University Senate.

Admission Requirements

Any graduate of an accredited four-year high school or holder of a high school equivalency diploma is qualified to apply for admission to IUP. Applicants are reviewed by the Admissions Committee on the basis of high school records, recommendations, and scores earned on the SAT I or the ACT. Applicants are expected to name their major field upon application, but a change in major can be made prior to or during the freshman year.

Application and Information

Applications are accepted for consideration for the fall and spring semesters after July 1 of the preceding year. Applications are reviewed on a rolling basis, beginning in September, until vacancies are filled.

To request an application, catalog, or further information, students should contact:

Office of Admissions
Pratt Hall, Suite 216
Indiana University of Pennsylvania
201 Pratt Drive
Indiana, Pennsylvania 15705
Telephone: 724-357-2230
               800-442-6830 (toll-free)
Fax: 724-357-6281
E-mail: admissions_inquiry@grove.iup.edu
World Wide Web: http://www.iup.edu/admiss

INDIANA WESLEYAN UNIVERSITY
MARION, INDIANA

The University

Indiana Wesleyan University (IWU), founded in 1920, has maintained its affiliation with the Wesleyan Church and strives to meet the needs of the total person by providing challenging opportunities for students spiritually, intellectually, and socially. Uniqueness, a distinctly Christian approach, and dynamic growth characterize Indiana Wesleyan University. Integration of biblical principles and faith in Christ occurs in classrooms, athletics, and extracurricular activities. Bible classes and chapel, along with accountability, discipleship, and Bible study groups, also enhance spiritual growth.

There are more than fifty majors offered to a student body of more than 2,000. In addition to associate and bachelor degrees, Indiana Wesleyan offers the Master of Science (M.S.) degree and the Master of Arts (M.A.) degree. Approximately 1,500 students live on campus in University housing; there are residence halls, small unit apartments, duplex apartments, and town houses available.

Numerous activities are sponsored by the University, such as drama-theater, choral and ministry groups, a student-run newspaper, a radio and television station, and student government opportunities.

The campus is approximately 150 acres in size, including a 65-acre outdoor athletic complex that features a Mondo track, one of the best running surfaces in the world. A wellness/recreation center includes Luckey Gymnasium, three auxiliary gyms, a 25-yard swimming pool, a fitness center, a climbing wall, four racquetball courts, an elevated track, and eight lighted tennis courts.

Indiana Wesleyan University is dedicated to "helping you discover God's direction for your future."

Location

Located in east-central Indiana, Marion is approximately 1 hour north of Indianapolis and 1 hour south of Fort Wayne, just off of Interstate 69. Marion is a community of approximately 32,000.

Majors and Degrees

Indiana Wesleyan confers the following degrees: Associate of Arts (A.A.), Associate of Science (A.S.), Bachelor of Arts (B.A.), and Bachelor of Science (B.S.). Majors are offered in accounting, addictions counseling, art*, art studio, athletic training, biblical literature, biology*, business administration, ceramics, chemistry*, Christian education, Christian ministries, church music, communication arts, computer graphics, computer information systems, computer science, criminal justice, economics, elementary education, English*, finance, general studies, health promotion and wellness, history, illustration, intercultural studies, management, marketing, mathematics*, medical technology, music*, music theory/composition, nursing, painting, photography, physical education*, political science, pre–art therapy, prelaw, printmaking, psychology, recreation management, religion and philosophy, social studies*, social work, sociology, Spanish, special education, sports management, writing, and youth ministries.

Those areas of study marked with an * indicate that teaching certificates are also available.

IWU offers premedical programs in dentistry, medicine, optometry, pharmacy, physical therapy, physician assistant studies, and veterinary medicine. A 3-2 program for Salvationists allows three years of study at Indiana Wesleyan followed by two years of study at the College for Officer Training.

Academic Program

The academic year at Indiana Wesleyan is composed of two semesters. Credit is computed in semester hours—the equivalent of one 55-minute class per week for approximately fourteen weeks. A student successfully completing work in a course that meets 165 minutes per week will receive 3 semester hours of credit at the end of the semester. Classification is based on progress toward meeting degree requirements in semester hours earned (freshman, 0–28; sophomore, 29–59; junior, 60–89; senior, 90 or more). A total of 124 semester hours of credit is needed for graduation.

Institutional general education requirements include humanities (12 hours), Bible (6 hours), physical education (3 hours), English composition (3 hours), communication (3 hours), literature (3 hours), lab science (4 hours), science/math (6 hours), social science (9 hours), and intercultural experience (3 hours).

Indiana Wesleyan University launched the Wesley Honors College in fall 1998. This program offers a select group of talented students a challenging academic environment in which they can stretch their minds and prepare for leadership roles in the Christian community and in society at large. Honors College students complete a rigorous program of honors courses in addition to meeting the requirements of an academic major. Students take at least 16 hours of Honors College courses during their four-year college career. Students admitted to the Honors College are selected from students who have been admitted to the University as freshmen and who have achieved a combined score of at least 1250 on the SAT I or 28 on the ACT. Honors College students receive an annual merit scholarship of $1000 in addition to any other academic scholarships they might receive.

An Honor Society is also active on campus. All students who are admitted with an honor status are eligible to participate. This organization sponsors events outside the classroom that appeal to students with intellectual interests. Most Honors Seminars are open to all students who participate in the Honor Society.

A Summer Honors Program was designed for students preparing to enter their senior year of high school. Students receive 6 credit hours toward graduation at IWU; this credit can be transferred to other institutions.

Off-Campus Arrangements

As a member of the Council of Christian Colleges and Universities, Indiana Wesleyan University participates in the following programs: the American Studies Program, for students to expand their world by studying in Washington, D.C.; the Los Angeles Film Studies Center, for study in the center of the film industry; the Middle East Studies Program, for students to explore the Middle East; the Russian Studies Program, which combines academics and adventure; the Latin American Studies Program, in which students live and learn in Latin America; the China Studies Program, in which students experience China; and the Oxford Honors Program, in which students study at Oxford University. Summer opportunities include the Oxford Summer School Program and the Summer Institute of Journalism.

Academic Facilities

Library and media services include the interlibrary loan services, an online catalog, access to other library catalogs around the state and nationwide, periodical indexes, Internet access, and reference assistance by professional librarians. The expanded Burns Hall of Science (adding approximately 42,000 square feet to the facility) opens in fall 2000. The Beard Arts Center includes art studios, two art galleries, radio broadcast studios, and the LPTV station, WIWU. The Phillippe Performing Arts Center, completed in 1996, includes an auditorium, recital hall, theater, and classrooms. This 65,000-square-foot building houses the music and theater departments and serves as the spiritual and cultural hub of the campus and community. The Noggle Christian Ministries Center offers classrooms, a large lecture hall, and conference areas. The existing 72,000-square-foot Student Center, which houses offices for student services (Records, Financial Aid, Business Office, Student Development, and Student Support Services), the Baldwin Dining Room, student lounges, and student government offices, will be expanded to include a theater, a coffee shop, and an enlarged game room and University bookstore. This state-of-the-art facility meets students' needs and provides a central meeting location on campus.

Costs

Tuition for the 2000–01 school year is $12,250, room cost is $2070, and board is $2670. The total cost of tuition, room, and board is $16,990.

Financial Aid

The Financial Aid Office at Indiana Wesleyan University works diligently to make financial awards available to students to help them meet the cost of a high-quality Christian education. More than $39 million per year in financial aid from state, federal, and institutional sources is awarded to students. Eighty-five percent of all students receive an average financial aid package of $11,000.

Among the wide range of financial awards for which a student may qualify are scholarships recognizing academic, musical, art, or athletic achievement; need-based awards, such as grants, education loans, or work-study employment; and special church matching scholarships and family tuition discounts that are not offered at many other schools. National Merit finalists/semifinalists receive the equivalent of 100 percent of tuition.

To apply for financial assistance, students must submit the Free Application for Federal Student Aid (FAFSA) to the federal processor after January 1. The FAFSA must be postmarked by March 1 to receive priority consideration. Students must be accepted for admission by March 1 prior to fall enrollment to receive maximum financial assistance. Each student receiving aid is required to reapply yearly and meet the criteria to continue eligibility.

Faculty

Indiana Wesleyan University's faculty is dedicated to the integration of faith and learning. Classes are taught from a biblical Christian perspective, and professors are actively involved in the lives of their students. The student-faculty ratio is 17:1. There are 105 full-time and 54 part-time faculty members. The faculty members at Indiana Wesleyan are committed to teaching and also have the responsibility of advising incoming freshman students and students in their major. Although teaching is their primary scholarly activity, many are also engaged in writing books and articles that are published in leading journals and periodicals and traveling around the world for speaking engagements.

Student Government

The Indiana Wesleyan University Student Government Organization (SGO) plays a major role in matters of self-government and areas of mutual interest to the student body and the University. Student government is made up of an executive board and a senate. The senate gives immediate direction to student committees that assist in problems of social and religious activities, student organizations, and community service. The SGO represents the concerns of the students to the University administration and elects students to sit as members on University faculty committees.

Admission Requirements

It is strongly recommended that applicants have taken at least 10 units in university-preparatory courses in high school. These should include English, science, social science, mathematics, and foreign language. No specific distribution of these courses is required. Applicants must submit an official transcript of all high school course work along with scores on the SAT I or ACT.

Students must achieve at least a 2.8 GPA (on a 4.0 scale) and 960 on the SAT I or 21 on the ACT to be considered for regular admission. Students who have not achieved these levels may be accepted on a conditional status. This conditional status restricts the credit hours for which students may register in their first semester. Other conditions may also apply, depending on the evaluation of the students' academic achievements.

Any student considering transferring from an accredited institution will be considered for admission, provided he or she has at least a 2.0 GPA (C average) and is in good academic and social standing. An official transcript from each institution attended is required.

Application and Information

Applicants are encouraged to submit an application as early as possible following completion of their junior year. A student must submit a completed application; a high school transcript, which must include at least six semesters; scores from the SAT I or ACT; a recommendation; a community values expectations form; and a nonrefundable $25 application fee. In addition, a transfer student must submit official transcripts from all colleges or universities previously attended and a transfer information form. A tuition deposit of $100 is required and is refundable until May 1.

For additional information, students should contact:
Office of Admissions
Indiana Wesleyan University
4201 South Washington Street
Marion, Indiana 46953-4974
Telephone: 765-677-2138
   800-332-6901 Ext. 2138 (toll-free)
E-mail: admissions@indwes.edu
World Wide Web: http://www.indwes.edu

The Phillippe Performing Arts Center on the campus of Indiana Wesleyan University.

Peterson's Guide to Four-Year Colleges 2001 www.petersons.com

INTERNATIONAL COLLEGE OF THE CAYMAN ISLANDS
NEWLANDS, GRAND CAYMAN, CAYMAN ISLANDS

The College
International College of the Cayman Islands (ICCI), situated in one of the world's premiere banking and financial business centers, is ideally located to prepare students for business careers. The school was founded in 1970 and operates as a nonprofit, privately controlled, American-style senior college at Newlands, Grand Cayman.

The international student body is made up of about 200 men and women each quarter and usually includes representatives from other Caribbean islands and from every continent in the world. This cultural diversity enhances class discussions and is an integral part of the educational goals of ICCI. ICCI offers the flexibility of allowing students to enroll at any of four times during the year.

The College is accredited as a senior college to award associate's, bachelor's, and master's degrees by the Accrediting Council for Independent Colleges and Schools (ACICS), Washington, D.C. In addition to its undergraduate programs, the College offers a Master of Business Administration degree program and a Master of Science degree program in management.

Location
The Cayman Islands, located in the Caribbean Sea between Cuba and Jamaica, are internationally famous for exceptional water sports. The 80-plus degree clarity of the ocean waters makes underwater photography and fishing major attractions for the more than 1 million visitors to the Cayman Islands each year. The islands are an English-speaking British Overseas Territory, known for the friendliness of their approximately 30,000 citizens. The temperature averages 85 degrees year-round with sunshine and gentle tradewinds.

The College is about 15 minutes from the capital of George Town, located in the quiet rural village of Newlands. Caribbean flavor permeates the College campus, with its tropical bungalow-style buildings and colorful flowers and palm trees. The rich cultural heritage of the Cayman Islands, available to students through the Queen Elizabeth Botanic Park, environmental tours on land and sea, and local art and craft production of all kinds, enhances the educational experience at ICCI.

Majors and Degrees
The Associate of Science degree is offered in business, with concentrations in accounting, banking, broadcasting, finance, hotel and tourism management, and information systems. General studies and office administration are also offered at the associate degree level.

Bachelor's degrees are offered in business administration, community service, liberal studies, and office administration. Several concentrations are available within these major areas, including elementary and secondary business teacher education.

For those employed in the banking industry, the Bachelor of Science degree in business administration with a concentration in international finance meets the requirements for direct entry into the associateship program of the British Chartered Institute of Bankers (ACIB). The business administration program also has an accounting concentration.

Academic Program
The academic year consists of four quarters—fall, winter, spring, and summer. A full academic load is 10–15 credits each quarter. A typical course is 5 credits.

A minimum of 180 credit hours is required for the Bachelor of Science degree with no fewer than 60 credits earned in upper-division (300- and 400-level) courses and at least 55 credits in general education courses outside the major field. The specific requirements for each major vary. Credit by examination is available.

A minimum of 90 credit hours is required for the Associate of Science degree. No fewer than 25 credits must be earned in general education courses.

A cumulative grade point average of 2.0 or higher is required of all students in undergraduate programs at the College. To fulfill degree residence requirements, the equivalent of three quarters of full-time study must be taken at International College of the Cayman Islands.

The College also offers developmental studies in English, reading, math, and English as a second language courses.

Off-Campus Arrangements
Students who have earned at least 45 credits may participate with permission in internship programs with businesses and agencies and receive up to 5 credits for participation in a program. Each quarter, one or more seminars are offered over a long weekend in Miami. Two Miami seminars are required for graduation.

Academic Facilities
A computer laboratory, equipped with Pentium 133 personal computers, is provided by the College. The library houses a constantly updated collection of books, 140 periodicals, CD-ROM subscriptions to ProQuest and SIRS, an Internet subscription to LIRN, and a multimedia center, which includes computers with CD-ROM and Internet access. The Cayman Islands' first radio station, ICCI-FM, 101.1 MHz, is owned and operated by the College and is staffed by students and community volunteers as a workshop for the school's Broadcasting Department. This department is one of the very few in the Caribbean that trains radio students for careers in this field and offers the Associate of Science degree in business with a concentration in broadcasting management.

Costs
In 1998–99, tuition per course was $375. Total tuition cost for three quarters was $3375. A registration fee of $62.50 and other fees of about $21.25 were charged each quarter. A dorm room for the school year cost between $2157 and $2438, with a $250 deposit. Kitchen and dining facilities are provided. Books cost approximately $750 for the school year. (All costs are in U.S. dollars.)

Financial Aid

Three kinds of financial assistance are available for students who qualify when funding permits: grants, grants-in-aid, and loans. (Grants-in-aid include campus work assignments.) Approximately 15 percent of the students at International College of the Cayman Islands receive financial assistance.

Faculty

International College of the Cayman Islands has a full-time and adjunct faculty of 40. Adjunct faculty members are generally working full-time in the area in which they teach, giving students the benefit of current, hands-on business experience tested in the marketplace. About 40 percent of the full-time faculty members hold earned doctorates. Guest lecturers, drawn to the Cayman Islands from around the world, share their expertise with students. Classes are small, enabling the students to receive individual attention and to participate extensively. All full-time faculty members act as academic advisers, and most instructors know their students by name. The student-faculty ratio is 11:1.

Student Government

The Academic Council includes student representation. Student committees plan boat cruises, beach picnics, banquets, and dances for the enjoyment of students and faculty members. The island is full of recreational and cultural events and activities such as volleyball, softball, netball, basketball, cricket, rugby, soccer, SCUBA diving, golfing, bike races, miniature golf, drama, musicals, concerts, and art shows. The school is less than 4 miles from Spotts Public Beach and Pedro St. James Castle, the site of the "birthplace of democracy in the Cayman Islands." Annual festivities, such as International Happening, Agricultural Fair, Batabano Festival, and Pirates Week, are part of the island and campus life.

Admission Requirements

Requirements for regular admission to a degree program include completion of an application form and payment of the application fee, submission of an official high school transcript that evidences graduation or its equivalent, a minimum SAT I recentered score of 1010 or ACT composite score of at least 21, and two letters of reference. Mature students, A-level students, or students transferring with credits from accredited or internationally recognized colleges or universities are exempt from submitting SAT I scores. A TOEFL score of at least 550 is required for students whose native language is not English. Continuing education or transient students are only required to provide a completed, paid application form. Overseas students should request a Student Visa Application Packet and return all completed application materials at least four months before the beginning of the quarter in which they wish to enroll.

Application and Information

Applications for any quarter are considered at any time up to the opening of the quarter; however, overseas students must submit an application at least four months before the quarter in which they wish to enroll. Overseas applications must be sent via international airmail and include a nonrefundable application fee of $37.50 (U.S. dollars).

For application forms and additional information, students should contact:
Director of Admissions
International College of the Cayman Islands
P.O. Box 136 Savannah
Grand Cayman, Cayman Islands
Telephone: 345-947-1100
Fax: 345-947-1210
E-mail: icci@candw.ky
World Wide Web: http://cayman.com.ky/pub/icci

ICCI's Caribbean-style campus.

IONA COLLEGE
NEW ROCHELLE, NEW YORK

The College

Iona College takes its name from the island of Iona in the Inner Hebrides, just off the west coast of Scotland. It was to this tiny island that the Irish monk Columba came in A.D. 563 to establish an abbey from which missionaries went forth to teach and evangelize. The island of Iona became a center of faith and culture that contributed significantly to the civilization of Western Europe. In 1940, the Congregation of Christian Brothers founded Iona College in New Rochelle, New York.

Iona College has as its mission the education of its students through classroom instruction and actual experience to develop ethical and skilled decision makers enriched by the liberal arts. Iona has emerged as a prominent member of the academic community in the New York metropolitan area. The College is accredited by the Middle States Association of Colleges and Schools. Master of Arts degrees are offered in English, history, and Spanish, and Master of Science degrees are offered in communication arts, computer science, criminal justice, educational computing, health services administration, journalism, pastoral and family counseling, school administration and supervision, secondary education, telecommunications, and multicultural education. A Master of Science in Teaching degree is offered for those who wish to prepare for careers in kindergarten through twelfth grade education but who did not study education at the undergraduate level. Post-master's diplomas and certificates are also available in some areas of study. A Master of Business Administration degree is available through Iona's well-known John G. Hagan School of Business Administration, which also offers programs in advanced business studies beyond the M.B.A. level.

Outstanding physical facilities complement Iona College's beautiful 35-acre suburban campus in Westchester County. Forty-seven buildings provide modern equipment and a fine learning environment for a diverse student population of approximately 4,900, of whom 2,500 are undergraduate day students. Georgian architecture dominates the Iona campus, which has undergone extensive expansion and revitalization over the past decade. Some of the major academic buildings, including the John G. Hagan Hall, Myles B. Amend Hall, and Doorley Hall, have been completely renovated. The John A. Mulcahy Campus Center includes a multipurpose arena, an Olympic-size swimming pool, a Nautilus center, conference areas, and administrative offices. An 800-car parking garage accommodates the commuting students and the large crowds that come to the Mulcahy Campus Center for basketball games, concerts, and academic award assemblies. Mazzella Field is centrally located on Iona's campus and has artificial turf for football, soccer, and other intercollegiate and intramural sports. The Murphy Science and Technology Center includes the adjoining 349-seat Joyce Auditorium and is a state-of-the-art facility complete with science, communications, and computer labs; classrooms; a technological library; a student lounge; and administrative offices. The Arrigoni Center is a multipurpose space for exhibits, conferences, liturgies, student events, and other activities. The Brother Arthur A. Loftus Residence Hall houses 320 students. Each floor in Loftus has a lounge and kitchenette. Also available in this residence are a study lounge, a game room, a snack/TV room, a computer lab, an exercise room, a meditation lounge, a mailroom, and a laundry room. Rice Hall, which accommodates 100 students, has an exercise room, a TV/game room, a study room with computer facilities, and a laundry room for residents.

Location

Iona's New Rochelle campus is not far from Long Island Sound. The area offers the sophistication of an established suburb as well as easy access to New York City by automobile or public transportation. Iona also has campuses in Manhattan and Rockland County.

Majors and Degrees

Iona College offers the Bachelor of Arts, Bachelor of Science, and Bachelor of Business Administration degrees in more than forty majors, including accounting, behavioral sciences, biochemistry, biology, business administration, chemistry, computer and information sciences, computer applications and information systems, computer science, criminal justice, ecology, economics, elementary education, English, finance, French, health care, history, humanities, information and decision technology, interdisciplinary science, international business, international studies, Italian, management, marketing, mass communication (advertising, broadcasting, journalism, and public relations), mathematics, medical technology, philosophy, physics, political science, psychology, religious studies, social science, social work, sociology, Spanish, speech and dramatic arts (speech arts and humanistic communication, speech/language pathology and audiology, and theater arts), and teacher certification (elementary and secondary subjects). Five-year combined bachelor's and master's degree programs are available in accounting, computer science, education/reading, history, and psychology. There are also minors available in business, classical humanities, fine arts, German, gerontology, peace and justice studies, and women's studies. Students may concentrate in health profession preparation (chiropractic, dental, medical, physical therapy, and veterinary) or prelaw.

Academic Program

For completion, a minimum of 120 credits is required for the majority of B.A. and B.S. degrees, and a minimum of 126 credits is required for all B.B.A. degrees. All students must complete the core curriculum and their school requirements, achieve a scholastic index of at least 2.0, satisfy course requirements in the major field, and secure a satisfactory score on a comprehensive examination or such substitutes as may be specified in the major field of study. The normal course load is five courses per semester. Juniors and seniors usually carry 15–18 credits per semester. A credit corresponds to 1 hour of class work or 2 hours of laboratory work plus 2 hours of supplementary assignments per week for fifteen weeks. Students are considered to be in good academic standing if, in the judgment of the Committee on Academic Standing, they are able to complete their programs of study within four years with a cumulative scholastic index of at least 2.0.

An honors program is available for students who want a stimulating learning experience that will permit them to pursue some of their own interests.

Off-Campus Arrangements

Iona College encourages students to broaden their educational experience and to gain cultural enrichment through study and travel abroad. Iona sponsors summer, semester, and intersession programs in Ireland, Belgium, Spain, Italy, Mexico, Morocco, and France. Medical technology students spend their fourth year in residence at a hospital approved by the American Society of Clinical Pathologists.

Academic Facilities

Iona's main library is the Ryan Library on the New Rochelle campus. The library system houses approximately 221,000 volumes, 984 periodical titles, and a resource center for audiovisual materials. In addition, Iona students have access to the library at the College of New Rochelle and to the New Rochelle Public Library, as well as to the fine public library system in Westchester County. Access to the College library holdings is available through a campuswide computer network. Online reference and information retrieval service to major databases is available. Opened in 1995, the Helen Arrigoni Library/Technology Center links Iona to the world through the Internet and has CD-ROM and multimedia capabilities. A film/video theater and a radio laboratory, as well as classrooms utilized for instruction in the arts and sciences, are available in various buildings on the Iona College campus. Students have access to an IBM mainframe located in the Computer Center, and a network of more than 500 microcomputers covers the New Rochelle campus. In addition to the computer facilities for administrative, academic, and research purposes, public computing laboratories are available throughout the day and evening.

Costs

For 1999–2000, the tuition charge was $14,700 per year for full-time students enrolled for 15 credits. Students carrying fewer than 12 credits per semester paid tuition at the rate of $490 per credit plus the appropriate fees.

Financial Aid

The financial aid program at Iona exists to assist students who would be unable to pursue an education without some form of economic assistance. Scholarships are available for students who have demonstrated strong academic ability throughout high school. Scholarship amounts range from $4000 to full tuition. Students who have been accepted for admission or are in attendance and who demonstrate financial need and academic potential are eligible to be considered for financial aid. Financial need is the difference between the total cost of attendance (which includes tuition, fees, books and supplies, room and board, transportation, and a minimum amount for personal expenses) and the resources that the family can be expected to provide. Iona attempts to assist the largest possible number of qualified students with its limited resources. Nearly 90 percent of Iona students receive some form of financial aid. The average financial aid package is $9500 per year. Financial aid includes Iona scholarships and grants-in-aid, Federal Pell Grants, Federal Supplemental Educational Opportunity Grants, Federal Stafford Student Loans, Federal Perkins Loans, New York State Tuition Assistance Program awards, and on- and off-campus employment through the Federal Work-Study Program. Deferred tuition payment plans are also available. Applicants for financial aid should file the Free Application for Federal Student Aid (FAFSA) as soon after January 1 as possible for the following fall semester.

Faculty

Iona College has approximately 170 full-time and 200 part-time faculty members. Undergraduate classes are not taught by graduate students. The College encourages a close relationship between faculty members and students, and full-time faculty members are available for student conferences. First- and second-year students are assigned to faculty advisers, and upperclass students to advisers in their major fields. Counselors and advisers assist the students in the preparation of their programs. The student-faculty ratio is 16:1.

Student Government

The Student Government Association (SGA) is a service organization that coordinates, supervises, and promotes student activities. The SGA also provides a necessary degree of leadership and coordination for the more than seventy student clubs and societies that are part of the student life at Iona College. Such student groups further the ideals and spirit of the College, attend to particular student interests, and present a definite opportunity for individual growth and development.

Admission Requirements

Iona College seeks individuals who are challenged to be ethical and skilled decision makers motivated to leadership and service. Freshmen are selected based on competitive high school grades, SAT I/ACT scores, academic program, class rank, extracurricular experiences, and letters of recommendation. Personal character and potential to succeed are highly valued.

Applicants to the baccalaureate program must be graduates of a secondary school or must demonstrate equivalent preparation. The College prefers applicants who are in the upper 50 percent of their high school class and have 16 acceptable units of credit, including English, 4; mathematics, 3; foreign language, 2; American history, 1; natural science, 1; and social studies, 1. Results of either the SAT I or ACT are required; the test should be taken in the spring of the junior year or the fall of the senior year.

Admission to Iona College for transfer students is based on the number of credits completed and the student's cumulative grade point average. For students who have completed fewer than 24 college credits, the high school academic record is also evaluated.

Application and Information

Iona's rolling admissions policy enables year-round applications. In addition, Iona has an Early Action Plan. Students who apply under this plan must have completed their application by December 1. Decisions will be mailed by December 20. To ensure acceptance into certain academic programs, however, applications should be filed no later than March 15. Completed applications are reviewed immediately upon receipt, and acceptances are mailed in the spring.

The Committee on Admissions requires applicants to submit a completed College application form along with an application fee of $25. A student fills in part of the application and gives the form to his or her high school counselor to be completed. The applicant must also request the secondary school to forward to the College a transcript of grades and a recommendation from a high school official. Veterans are required to supply a copy of their Separation Qualification Record, showing service training and schools completed. Transfer students must supply an official transcript of grades from high school and each college attended.

Office of Undergraduate Admissions
Iona College
New Rochelle, New York 10801
Telephone: 914-633-2502
          800-231-IONA (toll-free)
World Wide Web: http://www.iona.edu

IOWA STATE UNIVERSITY OF SCIENCE AND TECHNOLOGY
AMES, IOWA

IOWA STATE UNIVERSITY

The University

Iowa State University of Science and Technology (ISU), a public, broad-based international university of 25,000 students, was established in 1858 as one of the first U.S. land-grant colleges. It is a member of the prestigious Association of American Universities and is accredited by the North Central Association of Colleges and Schools. All fifty states and more than 100 other countries are represented in the student body, exposing students to ideas from other cultures both in and out of the classroom.

Iowa State has grown in size and reputation to become one of the nation's leading educational institutions and has made significant contributions to the development of the United States and the world. Revolutionary innovations include the world's first electronic digital computer, the digital encoding process that led to the development of facsimile machines, and LoSatSoy, a new cooking oil low in saturated fat. Iowa State's graduates include George Washington Carver, one of the nation's most distinguished educators and plant scientists; Carrie Chapman Catt, a leader in the women's suffrage movement; and John Vincent Atanasoff who, as a faculty member at Iowa State, invented the electronic digital computer.

Nearly 8,000 students live on campus in nineteen residence halls, each divided into houses, which are small-group living arrangements of about 60 residents. Wellness houses, learning communities, honors houses, and alcohol- and smoke-free houses are a few of the options available. The Department of Residence is in the midst of a $105-million renovation and improvement project. In addition, thirty-four fraternities and twenty sororities provide an attractive option for 3,000 undergraduates and an immediate network of 30 to 100 peers per house.

More than 500 clubs and organizations provide unlimited leadership, social, and cultural opportunities. Annually, 3,000 teams participate in fifty intramural sports, 2,500 people participate in forty sports clubs, and 20,000 students, staff members, and faculty members participate in outdoor recreation activities. Facilities include the Lied Recreation/Athletic Center, which houses twenty courts for basketball and volleyball, a 300-meter track, artificial turf area, and a weightlifting and fitness center; Beyer Hall; the Physical Education Building; the State Gym; and many outdoor facilities. The Cyclones have twenty Division I intercollegiate men's and women's sports and belong to the Big 12, one of the premier sports conferences in the country.

Outstanding facilities for the cultural and performing arts include the 2,700-seat Stephens Auditorium, the 452-seat Fisher Theater, and the 15,000-seat Hilton Coliseum. Iowa State attracts the top entertainment acts. Recent performers include Shermie Alexie, Bill Cosby, Simon Estes, Billy Joel, Mae Jemmison, George Strait, Jars of Clay, Prince, Wynton Marsalis, Nikki Giovanni, The Washington Week in Review, Michael W. Smith, Yanni, Sarah McLachlan, Aerosmith, and Harry Connick Jr.

Personal support services, available to help students become their best, include the following: assertiveness training; career counseling; communication skills workshops; medical, physical, and learning disabled services; and stress management, study skills, and test-taking workshops.

Location

Iowa State is located in Ames, just 30 minutes north of Iowa's capital, Des Moines. Minneapolis, Chicago, Kansas City, St. Louis, Omaha, and other metropolitan areas are a short drive from Ames or easily accessible by plane and train.

The campus environment rates high with students and faculty and staff members. The book *The Campus as a Work of Art* rated Iowa State among the twenty-five most beautiful campuses in the nation. The American Society of Landscape Architects recently chose Iowa State as a "medallion site," one of only three central campuses in the nation. Students spend most of their time on the 24-acre central campus.

Ames was recently ranked the second-best "micropolitan" area (population 50,000 or fewer) in the nation. Students take advantage of arts groups, recreational facilities, biking and hiking trails, more than eighty restaurants, a great downtown, many shopping areas, and twenty-five movie theaters.

Majors and Degrees

Iowa State University offers more than 110 undergraduate and more than 100 graduate degree programs in eight colleges.

The College of Agriculture includes programs in agricultural biochemistry, agricultural business, agricultural education, agricultural extension education, agricultural studies, agricultural systems technology, agronomy, animal ecology, animal science, dairy science, dietetics, entomology, environmental science, food science, forestry, genetics, horticulture, international agriculture, microbiology, nutritional science, pest management, plant health and protection, professional agriculture, public service and administration in agriculture, seed science, and zoology.

The College of Business offers programs in accounting, finance, management, management information systems, marketing, and transportation and logistics.

The College of Design offers programs in architecture, art and design, community and regional planning, graphic design, interior design, and landscape architecture.

The College of Education offers programs in community health education, early childhood education, elementary education, environmental studies, exercise and sports science, industrial technology, and secondary education.

The College of Engineering offers programs in aerospace engineering, agricultural engineering, ceramic engineering, chemical engineering, civil engineering, computer engineering, construction engineering, electrical engineering, engineering operations, engineering science, industrial engineering, mechanical engineering, and metallurgical engineering.

The College of Family and Consumer Sciences offers programs in apparel merchandising, design, and production; child and family services; dietetics; early childhood education; family and consumer sciences education; family resource management and consumer sciences; food science; hotel, restaurant, and institution management; housing and the near environment; nutritional science; and studies in family and consumer sciences.

The College of Liberal Arts and Sciences is the largest college and offers programs in advertising, African-American studies, American Indian studies, anthropology, astronomy, biochemistry, biology, biology/premedical illustration, biophysics, botany, chemistry, classical studies, computer science, earth science, economics, English, environmental science, environmental studies, French, genetics, geology, German, gerontology, history, interdisciplinary studies, international studies, journalism and mass communication, Latin, liberal studies, linguistics, mathematics, meteorology, music, naval science, performing arts, philosophy, physics, political science, Portuguese, psychology, religious studies, Russian, secondary education, sociology, Spanish, speech communication, statistics, technology and social change, women's studies, and zoology.

Academic Program

Each college provides academic support through advising offices. Additional academic services include academic learning labs, learning communities, learning teams, peer education, supplemental instruction, and tutoring services. The University Honors Program provides academically talented students an opportunity to stretch their minds through individualized programs, special courses and seminars, unique off-campus opportunities, and 24-hour access to Osborn Cottage, home of the honors program.

The academic year is divided into two semesters of sixteen weeks each, beginning in late August and ending in early May.

Soar in Four guarantees graduation in four years in all majors except architecture and landscape architecture.

Off-Campus Arrangements

Students take advantage of internships, cooperative education programs, and research programs, which provide the opportunity for professional work with national and international companies. International exchange programs are available at more than 100 colleges and universities in forty countries. The National Student Exchange program provides students an opportunity to study at one of 148 reciprocating universities around the country.

Academic Facilities

Iowa State facilities include 173 campus buildings, including several recent state-of-the-art additions. Among the newest are the Durham Center for Computation and Communication, the Molecular Biology Building, the Center for Designing Foods, and Howe Hall, the $61-million engineering facility that is the home of the Engineering Teaching and Research Center (ETRC). Construction will soon begin on new buildings for the College of Business and the University Honors Program.

Technology is utilized to provide students the resources to succeed in a competitive global market. Iowa State is home to C2, one of the world's most advanced virtual reality rooms, and is soon to be home to C6, a fully immersed virtual reality environment. Students are provided free e-mail and Internet access and space to create their own Web page. Students use AccessPlus via the Web or at kiosks for instant access to jobs, grades, schedules, and more. Computing resources include thousands of workstations, 24-hour availability, and mainframe/Internet access from residence hall rooms.

Costs

For the 2000–01 academic year, in-state tuition and fees are approximately $3132 and out-of-state tuition and fees are approximately $9748 (based upon full-time undergraduate status for two semesters). Room and board are approximately $4360 for two semesters. Books and supplies are estimated at $704 per year.

Financial Aid

Need- and merit-based financial assistance is available to qualified applicants. Approximately 66 percent of students receive some type of financial aid (grants, scholarships, loans, jobs). Students should apply for admission early to receive maximum consideration for merit scholarships. All applicants are encouraged to file the FAFSA by February 14 (for fall semester enrollment). ISU's Web site (http://www.public.iastate.edu/~fin_aid_info/) provides links to scholarships and financial aid resources.

Faculty

Iowa State has 1,797 faculty members, 85 percent of whom hold doctorates. The student-faculty ratio is 15:1.

Student Government

The Government of the Student Body (GSB) legislates and administers student policy and provides services to meet the needs of students. The functions of GSB are carried out by executives and senators elected by ISU students. GSB's primary function is the allocation of student activity fees, through which a number of diverse services and student organizations are funded.

Admission Requirements

Students seeking admission directly from high school (or transferring from another college or university with fewer than 24 semester hours of transferable college credit) must have a minimum of 4 years of English, 3 years of math (including 1 year each of algebra, geometry, and advanced algebra), 3 years of science (including 1 year each of courses from two of the following fields: biology, chemistry, and physics), and 2 years of social studies. In addition, students applying to the College of Liberal Arts and Sciences must have completed an additional year of social studies, for a total of 3 years, plus 2 years of a single foreign language. Grades, class rank, and quality of course work are the most important criteria in the admissions decision.

Transfer applicants are admitted if they have a minimum of 24 semester hours of graded transferable credit from regionally accredited colleges or universities and have achieved for all college work previously attempted the GPA required by ISU for specific programs. A 2.0 GPA (on a 4.0 grading scale) is the minimum transfer grade point average requirement. Some programs may require a transfer grade point average higher than this minimum. Applicants with fewer than 24 semester hours of graded transferable college credit prior to their enrollment at Iowa State must also meet the admission requirements for students entering directly from high school.

Application and Information

Students interested in applying for the fall semester should apply during the fall of the year preceding their entry to Iowa State. Students should submit applications for other terms six to nine months in advance. Applicants must submit an application along with a $20 application fee ($50 for international students) and have their secondary school provide an official transcript of their academic record, including credits and grades, rank in class, and certification of graduation.

Applicants must also arrange to have their ACT or SAT I scores reported to Iowa State directly from the testing agency. The Test of English as a Foreign Language (TOEFL) is required of international students whose first language is not English. Applicants may be required to submit additional information or data to support their applications.

To visit the campus and experience firsthand the benefits of an Iowa State education, students should call 800-262-3810 (toll-free) to receive an application and additional enrollment information and to arrange a customized visit. Students can also visit the University's Web site listed below and use the online application or download the application to their personal computer.

Office of Admissions
Alumni Hall
Iowa State University of Science and Technology
Ames, Iowa 50011-2010
Telephone: 800-262-3810 (toll-free)
           515-294-3094 (TTY/TDD)
Fax: 515-294-2592
E-mail: admissions@iastate.edu
World Wide Web: http://www.iastate.edu/~admis_info/

ITHACA COLLEGE
ITHACA, NEW YORK

The College

Coeducational and nonsectarian since its founding in 1892, Ithaca College enrolls approximately 5,900 students—about 2,600 men and 3,300 women. The College community is a diverse one; virtually every state is represented in the student population, as are more than seventy-five other countries. Students come to Ithaca College to get active, hands-on learning that brings together the best of liberal arts and professional studies. The program is offered in five schools: the School of Humanities and Sciences (2,100 students), School of Business (500 students), Roy H. Park School of Communications (1,200 students), School of Health Sciences and Human Performance (1,300 students), and School of Music (500 students). There are approximately 300 graduate students.

Freshmen and most upperclass students (with some exceptions) must live on campus, and all students are guaranteed continuous campus housing. There are thirty-one residence halls, which range from garden apartments to fourteen-story towers. Extracurricular life is largely self-contained. There are more than 140 student organizations, a strong Division III intercollegiate athletic program (twenty-five teams) as well as extensive intramural and club sports programs, and daily dramatic and music performances. A wide range of services is available, beginning with summer orientation for new students and including career planning and placement assistance, a counseling center, and a health center that is staffed by 4 physicians.

According to College surveys completed in the past three years, 98 percent of first-year graduates are employed or are full-time graduate students.

The School of Business offers a one-year M.B.A. program.

Location

Ithaca College is in Ithaca, New York. Approximately 90,000 people live in the surrounding county, about a quarter of whom are Ithaca College or Cornell University students. The city combines the cultural and commercial features of a diverse, multicultural, mostly youthful population with the spectacular scenery of central New York's Finger Lakes.

Majors and Degrees

Ithaca awards the Bachelor of Arts, Bachelor of Science, Bachelor of Fine Arts, and Bachelor of Music degrees in the more than 100 degree programs offered through its five schools.

The School of Business offers a B.S. in business administration, with concentrations in accounting, finance, human resource management, international business, legal studies, management, and marketing, as well as a B.S. degree in accounting for those pursuing CPA licensure.

The Roy H. Park School of Communications offers the B.A. in journalism and media studies. Also offered are the B.S. in cinema and photography; organizational communication, learning, and design; telecommunications management; and television-radio and the B.F.A. in film, photography, and visual arts.

Through the School of Health Sciences and Human Performance, students can earn the B.S. in athletic training/exercise science, community health education, exercise science, fitness and cardiac rehabilitation/exercise science, health and physical education, health services administration, health teacher K–12 studies, leisure services, physical education teacher K–12 studies, speech-language pathology and audiology, sport management, sport studies, sports information and communication, teachers of speech and hearing handicapped studies, and therapeutic recreation, or they can enroll in the five-year B.S./M.S. clinical science/physical therapy or occupational science/occupational therapy programs.

The School of Humanities and Sciences offers the B.A. in anthropology, art, art history, biochemistry*, biology*, chemistry*, computer science, drama, economics, English*, environmental studies, French*, German*, history, mathematics*, mathematics-economics*, mathematics-physics*, philosophy, philosophy–religion, physics*, planned studies, politics, psychology, social studies*, sociology, Spanish*, and speech communication; the B.S. is offered in applied economics, applied psychology, chemistry*, computer information systems, computer science, mathematics–computer science*, planned studies, speech communication*, and theater arts management; the B.F.A. is offered in acting, art, musical theater, and theatrical production arts. The * indicates areas that have a teacher certification option or teaching degree available.

Students in the School of Music can earn the B.A. in music and the Mus.B. in composition, jazz studies, music education, music in combination with an outside field, performance, performance/music education, recording, and theory.

Special programs offered by Ithaca include the Exploratory Program for undecided majors; a 3-1 program in optometry offered in conjunction with the Pennsylvania College of Optometry and the State University of New York College of Optometry; 3-2 programs in chemistry-engineering and in physics-engineering, offered in cooperation with Cornell University, Rensselaer Polytechnic Institute, and other schools; and M.B.A. 4+1 programs offered with Clarkson University, the Rochester Institute of Technology, and the American Graduate School of International Management (Thunderbird).

Academic Program

Undergraduate programs of study address two primary issues: the need for rigorous academic preparation in highly specialized professional fields and the need for students to prepare for the complex demands of society by acquiring an intellectual breadth that extends beyond their chosen profession. Each degree offered requires a minimum of 120 credit hours and a specified number of liberal arts credits. Minors, academic concentrations, and numerous teacher certification programs are available. Exceptionally qualified applicants to the School of Humanities and Sciences will be invited to apply to the honors program, an intensive four-year program of interdisciplinary seminars. The writing center offers assistance to students at any stage of the writing process, and Academic Computing and Client Services aids students in the use of personal and College computers. The Gerontology Institute provides opportunities for students to work with the elderly in a variety of community settings. The Center for Teacher Education serves to coordinate the fifteen courses of study leading to a teaching certificate.

The academic year comprises two 15-week semesters, from late August to mid-December and from mid-January to mid-May.

ROTC programs are offered in conjunction with Cornell University.

Off-Campus Arrangements

The College maintains a center in London, England, and offers courses in the liberal arts, business, communications, music, and theater arts. Study-abroad programs are also available in Australia, the Czech Republic, Scotland, and Spain or in more than forty-five countries through affiliate arrangements with the Institute for European and Asian Studies, the Institute for American Universities, and the School for International Training. Communications students may choose to spend a semester in Singapore at the Nanyang Technological University, and selected juniors and seniors in communications may study at the Ithaca College Communications Program in Los Angeles, which offers outstanding internship opportunities.

Academic Facilities

All academic facilities have been constructed since 1960, and three new major buildings have opened this year: a health sciences facility, a 69,000-square-foot addition to the music building, and a fitness center. The Roy H. Park School of Communications contains television and radio studios, a film and photography complex, and a variety of digital laboratories. The College's two science buildings house state-of-the-art physics, biology, chemistry, mathematics, computer, and psychology laboratories. Additional campus facilities include theaters, auditoriums, concert halls, and research laboratories. Computing facilities include mainframes, several computer networks, and hundreds of computers in satellite stations, laboratories, and classrooms, allowing easy access to e-mail and the Internet. The library contains approximately 500,000 materials in various formats.

Costs

For 1999–2000, tuition was $18,410, room was $3980, board was $3976, and the health and accident insurance fee was $255.

Financial Aid

Financial aid, which totals more than $75 million from all sources, is extended to approximately 75 percent of Ithaca students. To apply for financial aid, students should check the proper space on the College's admission application, and if seeking federal aid, submit the Free Application for Federal Student Aid (FAFSA) by February 1 with the U.S. Department of Education at the address indicated on the form. Early decision and physical therapy candidates should follow the time line outlined under the Application and Information section below. All accepted applicants are considered for merit aid in recognition of their academic and personal achievement. Programs providing grants and loans include the Federal Work-Study, Federal Pell Grant, Federal Perkins Loan, Federal Stafford Student Loan, and Federal Supplemental Educational Opportunity Grant.

Faculty

There are 447 full-time and 122 part-time faculty members; the overall student-faculty ratio is 12:1. Ninety percent of the full-time faculty members have a Ph.D. or a terminal degree in their field. While the faculty is principally devoted to teaching at all levels, there is also significant publishing and research in various disciplines. Faculty members serve as academic advisers to students and are active in the community.

Student Government

The student government is composed of the student congress, all-College committee representatives, executive officers and assistants, and the student government executive board. Students administer a budget of approximately $400,000. The student congress includes representatives from each residence hall and school as well as students who live off campus. There is a student member of the Ithaca College Board of Trustees, and the student government appoints representatives to several standing all-College committees, including the Academic Policies Committee. The College encourages and expects student participation in governance.

Admission Requirements

Admission is based on the high school record, personal recommendations, SAT I or ACT scores, and, for some programs, auditions or portfolios. Campus visits are recommended but not required. Admission is selective and competitive; individual talents and circumstances are always given serious consideration. Transfer students must also submit official transcripts from each college or university they have attended. Applicants whose native language is not English must take the Test of English as a Foreign Language. Typically, there are about 8,500 applicants for 1,400 places in the freshman class.

Application and Information

For freshman regular decision, prospective students should apply by March 1; applicants are notified of a decision on a rolling basis no later than April 15 and must confirm their enrollment by May 1. Freshman applicants seeking institutional and federal aid should file the FAFSA by February 1 with the federal processor.

For freshman early decision, which is binding, students should apply by November 1; applicants are notified by December 15 and must confirm their enrollment by February 1. Early decision applicants seeking institutional and federal financial aid should submit the Financial Aid PROFILE, available from the College Scholarship Service, by November 1 and the FAFSA by February 1.

For physical therapy (both freshman and transfer), students should apply by January 15; applicants are notified by March 10 and must confirm their enrollment by May 1. Applicants seeking institutional and federal financial aid should submit the CSS PROFILE and the FAFSA by January 15.

Students who want to transfer into Ithaca College should apply by July 15 for fall admission and by December 1 for spring admission. Applicants seeking institutional and federal financial aid should file the FAFSA by February 1.

All applicants must submit a $45 application fee. Ithaca's application for admission is available on line (http://www.ithaca.edu/admission).

For additional information and application forms, students should contact:

Paula J. Mitchell
Director of Admission
Office of Admission
Ithaca College
100 Job Hall
Ithaca, New York 14850-7020
Telephone: 800-429-4274 (toll-free)
          607-274-3124
Fax: 607-274-1900
E-mail: admission@ithaca.edu
World Wide Web: http://www.ithaca.edu

The Ithaca College campus.

JACKSONVILLE UNIVERSITY
JACKSONVILLE, FLORIDA

The University

Jacksonville University (JU) is a private, independent, coeducational institution. Originally founded in 1934 as a junior college, the institution served local commuter students for the first twenty-eight years of its existence. In the 1950s, the institution moved to its current location and expanded its courses and degree offerings. With this change, the institution became Jacksonville University. The University's current enrollment is approximately 2,100 undergraduate and graduate students. Students come from forty-seven states and forty-four countries. JU accommodates more than 1,000 students in its residence facilities, which include apartments with kitchenettes, and guarantees housing for all four years. Fifty-two percent of the students are women. The average class size is 15 students, and most classes are limited to 40 students.

Campus facilities include a gymnasium, a nine-hole golf course, tennis courts, a baseball stadium, intramural fields, a football/soccer/track complex, and handball/racquetball courts, all useable throughout most of the year. Ocean beaches are only minutes away by car. Students pursue their creative talents and special interests by participating in cocurricular activities, such as student publications, chorus, orchestra, band, dance, and theatrical productions. Six sororities and seven fraternities, as well as numerous academic, service, and social organizations, are active on campus. NCAA Division I sports include men's baseball and basketball; women's basketball and volleyball; men's and women's crew, cross-country, golf, indoor and outdoor track and field, soccer, and tennis; and coed sailing. Intercollegiate athletics also include men's nonscholarship football, competing at the NCAA Division I-AA level. Active intramural sports competition is available to interested students.

Jacksonville University is accredited by the Commission on Colleges of the Southern Association of Colleges and Schools. Programs in music and dance are accredited by the National Association of Schools of Music and the National Association of Schools of Dance, respectively. The nursing program is accredited by the Commission on Collegiate Nursing Education and the National League for Nursing Accrediting Commission. Teacher education programs are approved by the Florida Department of Education for the purposes of teacher certification.

Graduate programs are available leading to the Master of Business Administration degree in five concentrations and the Master of Arts in Teaching degree in eleven areas.

Location

The University occupies a 260-acre suburban riverfront campus across the St. Johns River from downtown Jacksonville and 12 miles from the Atlantic Ocean beaches. Jacksonville is the home of a professional symphony orchestra, a performing arts center, theaters, art museums and galleries, the NFL Jacksonville Jaguars, and minor-league baseball and ice hockey teams. Major airlines serve the Jacksonville International Airport. The region's year-round climate is mild and pleasant, permitting outdoor activity throughout the year.

Majors and Degrees

Jacksonville University offers the following degrees through the Colleges of Arts and Sciences, Business, and Fine Arts: B.A., B.F.A., B.M., B.M.E., B.S., and B.S.N.

Undergraduate academic programs of study include accounting, art, art history, aviation management, aviation management and flight operations, biology, business administration, chemistry, communication, computer art and design, computer information systems, dance, economics, engineering (various disciplines through dual-degree programs), elementary education, English, environmental studies, finance, French, geography, history, international business, management, marine science, marketing, mathematics, music, music education, music performance, nursing, philosophy, physical education, physics, political science, psychology, secondary education, sociology, Spanish, studio art, and theater arts. Students may also pursue preprofessional programs in dentistry, law, medicine, pharmacy, and veterinary medicine.

Academic Program

Students enrolled in baccalaureate programs enjoy broad exposure to the liberal arts through a core curriculum. The core provides a foundation for study in the various major fields and is usually completed during the freshman and sophomore years. The core includes courses in English composition and literature, mathematics and computer science, the social sciences, the humanities, history, fine arts, philosophy or religion, the natural sciences, foreign language, and physical education. The core also requires community service for graduation.

Baccalaureate majors require a minimum of 128 semester credits. Generally, students acquire these credits in four years, although year-round enrollment makes it possible to earn a bachelor's degree in three years. All programs require a minimum 2.0 (C) grade point average for graduation. A pass-fail option is also available.

Undergraduate research, internships, study abroad, and an active honors program enhance the educational experience of JU students. Independent study programs enable promising students to pursue individual work in areas of special interest within and outside their major fields of study. In the departmental honors program, advanced study may be concentrated in the major.

JU also awards undergraduate credit through advanced placement and credit by examination. Such credit requires the achievement of satisfactory scores on the College Board's Advanced Placement tests or CLEP examinations.

Jacksonville University has a Naval ROTC unit. Successful completion of the program leads to an officer's commission in either the U.S. Naval Reserve or U.S. Marine Corps Reserve.

Off-Campus Arrangements

Approved study abroad may be integrated as a part of the baccalaureate program. The University is affiliated with the American Institute for Foreign Study (AIFS), which offers study-abroad experiences in nine countries on all continents. Summer language programs are popular with many students. JU faculty members also lead travel-study courses to many countries and regions of the world. With the help of advisers, JU students may also plan individual programs of study abroad.

Academic Facilities

The Carl S. Swisher Library houses a collection numbering more than 500,000 bibliographic items and a PC lab with forty-two computers. The Swisher/Merritt-Penticoff/Nelms science complex, along with the Millar Wilson Laboratory, Reid Medical Science Building, and Charter Marine Science Center, house modern laboratories and facilities for biological, chemical, and physics study and research. Marine science facilities include an operational wet lab. The Phillips Fine Arts Building houses the Alexander Brest Museum, two large rehearsal halls, music studios, and practice rooms. Swisher Auditorium is used for operas, musicals, and plays, while the Terry Concert Hall is an acoustically balanced facility for orchestra, choral, and band concerts. Studios house painting, ceramics, glassblowing, photography, sculpture, jewelry making, and other art activities. The Alexander Brest Dance Pavilion includes two large dance studios, offices, and dressing rooms. The J. Arthur Howard Administration Building centrally locates most administration and student service offices. The J. Henry Gooding Social Science Building contains classrooms, offices, and the Urban Studies Center. Wilma's Little People's School, a child development facility, supports teacher education programs. The Davis Building houses the College of Business.

Costs

For 1999–2000, full-time (12–16 credit hours) tuition per year was $14,390. For students taking more than 16 credit hours, there was an additional fee of $240 per credit hour. Mandatory fees for full-time students totaled $560 per year. Residence hall room rental was $2430 per year, and a seven-day meal plan was available at $2780 per year.

Financial Aid

The University has a strong financial assistance program based upon both merit and need. Merit scholarships range in amounts from $500 to full tuition, room, and board. Fine arts scholarships are offered on a competitive basis to students excelling in art, theater, dance, and music. Athletic awards are offered based on talent and skill in NCAA Division I sports (except for men's football and sailing). JU also participates in a broad range of federal and state programs that include loans, grants, and work-study opportunities. The University requires financial aid applicants to complete the Free Application for Federal Student Aid (FAFSA). The deadline for submission of all forms to ensure the availability of aid for the fall term is March 15.

Faculty

Jacksonville University employs more than 100 full-time faculty members. Faculty members are readily accessible to students and take an active role in the lives of students as teachers, mentors, and friends.

Student Government

Student participation in University governance is a function of the Student Government Association (SGA), a constitutional legislative body composed of representatives elected at large by the student body. The SGA places student members on important University committees and boards. Dolphin Productions, operating under SGA auspices, schedules concerts, lectures, films, and other cultural and entertainment activities.

Admission Requirements

Jacksonville University seeks qualified students from diverse social, geographic, cultural, religious, and socioeconomic backgrounds. The Admissions Committee evaluates each applicant on an individual basis. Students applying as freshmen should have satisfactorily completed, or be in the process of completing, a standard college-preparatory curriculum. The University requires that applicants complete a minimum of 4 years of English, 3 years of mathematics, 3 years of science, 3 years of social science, and 2 years of foreign language. Freshman applicants also must submit scores from either the SAT I or ACT, the application form with essays, and at least one letter of recommendation. Admission interviews and campus visits are recommended but not required.

The University welcomes applications from transfer and international students; transfers comprise approximately one third of the entering class each year. To be considered for transfer admission, applicants must submit the application form with essays, one letter of recommendation, and official copies of transcripts from all colleges attended. Transfers must have a minimum 2.0 college GPA and be in good standing at their previous institution. International applicants should contact the Office of Admissions for further information.

Students interested in dance, music, or theater arts may be required to audition separately for admission to those programs. Students who plan to major in visual arts may be required to submit a portfolio of their work. Admission to nursing, teacher education, and fine arts programs occurs after the student is admitted to the University.

New students may enroll for the fall, spring, or summer terms. Students are notified of acceptance beginning on November 1 for the fall term, and on a rolling basis thereafter.

Individuals, families, and groups may visit the campus throughout the year, both during the week and on scheduled Saturdays. Campus visits include a meeting with an admissions counselor and a campus tour. Invitations to a series of open houses are extended to prospective students and parents. On-campus overnight visits are arranged for interested students. Students or parents should call the Admissions Office to make visit arrangements.

Application and Information

Application for freshman admission should be filed as soon as possible after the completion of the junior year in high school. Forms are available from the JU Internet Web site and the admissions office by calling or writing:

Office of Admissions
Jacksonville University
2800 University Boulevard North
Jacksonville, Florida 32211-3396
Telephone: 904-745-7000
           800-225-2027 (toll-free)
E-mail: admissions@ju.edu
World Wide Web: http://www.ju.edu

JAMES MADISON COLLEGE
Michigan State University
EAST LANSING, MICHIGAN

The College and The University

James Madison College (JMC) is a small, student-centered, undergraduate college in a large, land-grant research university that offers a rigorous, residential, liberal education in public affairs. It has an enrollment of approximately 1,000 students. Faculty members are dedicated to the highest standards of excellence, and their primary activity is undergraduate teaching. The curriculum and individual courses are multidisciplinary and are intended to cultivate the skills of rigorous thought, lucid prose writing, and articulate speech. Since it was established in 1967, the College has graduated 5 Rhodes scholars, 6 Truman scholars, 4 Marshall scholars, 6 Fulbright scholars, and 4 National Science Foundation fellows. Madison students and faculty members learn and teach in a residential setting that nurtures a collegium of scholars among students, the faculty, and the staff. The College draws on the resources of the wider University to enrich the programs.

Michigan State University (MSU), founded in 1855 as the Agricultural College of the State of Michigan, was the prototype for sixty-nine land-grant institutions that were established under the Morrill Act of 1862. Today, instruction is offered in more than 200 programs of undergraduate and graduate study, all of which are taught by nearly 4,000 academic staff members in fourteen degree-granting colleges.

MSU operates the largest on-campus residence hall system in the United States, with a capacity of more than 16,000 students. James Madison students live and take most classes in Case Hall, where the College's faculty and staff offices are housed.

Students participate in the Big Ten tradition as competing members or as cheering fans of Michigan State University's twenty-four intercollegiate athletic teams. The campus affords numerous recreational opportunities, including golf courses, indoor and outdoor tennis courts, hiking trails, bike paths, the Kresge Art Museum, the MSU Museum, and the Wharton Center for Performing Arts.

Location

MSU is essentially an arboretum-park that has long been recognized as being among the most beautiful campuses in the United States. Complementing campus life is the adjacent city of East Lansing, which is noted for its vibrant atmosphere, shops, restaurants, malls, houses of worship, and convenient mass transit. Lansing, the state capital, is only 10 minutes away.

Majors and Degrees

James Madison offers a unique Bachelor of Arts degree in public affairs that especially appeals to students who hope to be leaders in the public or the private sector. Its curriculum also serves as an excellent prelaw program. Drawing on fields such as economics, sociology, history, and political science, students learn how public policy is made and how solutions are found to contemporary social problems. There are four areas of concentration: international relations, political economy, political theory and constitutional democracy, and social relations.

Academic Programs

Madison's program in international relations trains students to think imaginatively and in depth about the problems of world society and the opportunities for solving them. It is a sophisticated program whose graduates have gone on to careers in the foreign service, politics, international organizations, national security, the news media, and international business. It also provides excellent preparation for law school and graduate study in international affairs or international business. It is organized around four themes: the making of foreign policy, both in the United States and elsewhere; the causes of war and the means for resolving conflicts; the economic, political, and social problems of developing countries and proposed strategies for overcoming them; and the politics and organization of international economic relations.

The political economy program offers a broad course of study in economic theory and applied economics. The aim of the program is to foster a critical understanding of economic forces and their relationship to issues of social justice and prosperity. In the tradition of classical political economy, the curriculum examines the interconnectedness between economic organizations, social forces, political institutions, and government policy. The field embraces the mathematical, statistical, and modeling techniques of contemporary economic analysis while emphasizing the rediscovery of the roots and traditions of economic thought. The curriculum is designed to provide students with a systematic grounding in the major paradigms of economic analysis. The curriculum is also dedicated to empowering students with the capacity to analyze real-world developments in business, society, and government policy. Communication and computer skills are stressed, and students receive extensive experience in writing and speaking. It is this combination of technical expertise with the humanistic tradition of the liberal arts that makes political economy an excellent preparation for careers in business, law, and government. It also provides the foundation in economic and quantitative analysis now expected of entering students in many graduate programs in business, public administration, urban planning, and labor and industrial relations.

Madison's program in political theory and constitutional democracy (PTCD) is concerned with the major competing principles that have animated political communities and the attempts made to translate these principles into practice. Complex, fundamental questions are raised in the search for the values and principles that have been most important in the formation of governments. The College does not teach that there are right or wrong answers to these questions but rather that there are ways to approach them in a productive and intellectually exciting manner. The PTCD curriculum emphasizes both philosophy and history. Course readings range from Plato and the classical poets to contemporary political theory, literature, and U.S. Supreme Court decisions. The introductory course sequence is a consideration of the ways that politics and morality have been thought about at different times and places. These case histories are then used in a comparative analysis of the American experience. In other required core courses, students are confronted with philosophical systems that champion various and diverse concepts of justice. In senior seminars, students explore a focused topic in ways that shed new light on many of the themes and questions that have been raised by the curriculum.

The social relations program focuses on enduring issues in public affairs as they are shaped by the relations among individuals and groups of people in their social and historical settings. Topics of inquiry include the influences on intergroup relations of such factors as class, race, ethnicity, sex/gender, age, political and religious belief, and national identity. The program is also explicitly comparative, looking at social relations within the United States and abroad. The goals of the program are to provide a liberal education that is focused on the study of the relations among groups of people; to cultivate the research, reasoning, methodological, and analytical skills needed to interpret these relations; and to nurture capacities for normative judgment, informed decision making, and sophisticated problem solving. Classical and contemporary social theory as well as social history provide foundations for study of such issues as individual and social identity, social structure and labor market experiences, inequality and social mobility, poverty and wealth, assimilation and pluralism, prejudice, discrimination and civil rights, intergroup conflict and conflict resolution, social movements, and contemporary politics.

Quantitative and qualitative methods are used to provide experience in original research and social analysis in such policy areas as immigration, civil rights, family and children, education, residential segregation and exclusion, urban policy, social security, and social welfare.

One special feature of the first year at Madison is the writing program. MC 111–112 (Identity and Community: An Approach to Writing) is a yearlong course whose goal is to improve students' skills in reading, thinking, speaking, and writing and to increase students' understanding of themselves, of American culture, and of their place in American society.

The course is two semesters long and earns students 6 credits in writing. During the first semester (MC 111), students examine the themes of individuality, identity, and community in American life. Readings in MC 111 come largely from the American humanities, including autobiographies, biographies, history, fiction, and essays. Written assignments may include personal essays, narratives, summaries, analytic and interpretive essays, and critical reviews. Instruction in writing stresses the process of writing from invention to revision—including conferences, peer critiques, and collaborative learning—and the principles of writing, such as telling facts, thesis, clarity, unity, and vitality.

During the second semester (MC 112), students focus on specific themes or periods in American history. Students examine the impact of change, how individuals and groups of people react, and how American society is reconstructed during periods marked by social change. Cross-cultural comparisons may also be in order. Assignments include using the library, doing research in primary documents, and presenting the results to an audience of one's peers. Oral tasks may include public speeches, creative oral presentations, interviews, and simulated presentations at conferences. In MC 112, students learn to do research, document material effectively, and speak in different contexts—skills that are necessary in more advanced courses at Madison and in their careers after they graduate.

The academic year consists of two semesters of approximately fifteen weeks each. Two sessions are scheduled during the summer. To qualify for graduation, students must complete approximately 120 credits, a minimum of 51 of which must be in Madison courses (41 if transferring from another MSU major or from another college or university).

Academic Facilities

James Madison students live and take most classes in Case Hall, where the College's faculty and staff offices and a College library are housed. A collection of more than 4 million volumes is located in MSU's main library and in fourteen branch libraries. Electronic databases provide access to abstracts in agriculture, education, law, and medicine; citation indexes; and full-text articles in selected periodicals.

The first and only unit-level satellite writing center on campus, the Madison Writing Consultancy weaves the philosophy of the MSU Writing Center into the specific needs of JMC to provide writing support to all students free of charge.

Costs

Michigan State University is consistently listed in national publications as one of the best values in American higher education. For the 1999–2000 academic year, in-state tuition per credit hour for freshmen and sophomores was $147.25 and for nonresidents was $394 per credit hour. Juniors and seniors paid $164 for in-state tuition and $408.25 for out-of-state tuition. Matriculation fees, which included the student information technology fee and the infrastructure/technology fee, were assessed at $288 for students enrolling in more than 4 credits and at $238 for students enrolling in 4 credits or fewer per semester.

Financial Aid

MSU offers one of the most extensive merit scholarship programs in the nation. Need-based grants, loans, and part-time jobs can be combined in financial aid packages to help all qualified students afford MSU.

Faculty

James Madison College has an outstanding teaching faculty. Each faculty member serves as an academic adviser to students. In first-year courses, the average section size is about 20. Sophomore and junior courses enroll approximately 35 students each. Senior seminars are confined to 20 students.

Student Government

The James Madison College Student Senate advises the Dean and faculty on College issues, provides leadership opportunities to students, and sponsors extracurricular and cocurricular activities.

Admission Requirements

Admission to Michigan State University is based on academic preparation and ability and, in the case of transfer students, availability of space in the desired academic program. Admission decisions are made without regard to race, color, gender, religion, creed, national origin, political persuasion, sexual preference, marital status, handicap, age, or (in the case of U.S. citizens and permanent residents) financial need. In keeping with its land-grant tradition, MSU is committed to providing opportunities to students from a full range of socioeconomic backgrounds.

Application and Information

Students who are interested in admission to James Madison College must apply to Michigan State University and indicate on the application that they wish to be admitted to James Madison College. In recent years, the number of qualified freshman applicants has exceeded available spaces. The freshman class is filled initially by those persons who qualify for admission after having completed grade 11. For fullest consideration, students should apply by October 1. The application and nonrefundable $30 application processing fee must be received before the established deadline. The admissions committee reviews applications once all required materials are received and usually notifies prospective students of their decision within four to six weeks, although notification may take up to eight weeks.

For more information about James Madison College, students should contact:

Admissions
James Madison College
Michigan State University
356 South Case Hall
East Lansing, Michigan 48825-1205
Telephone: 517-353-5260
Fax: 517-432-1804
E-mail: jmcadmissions@www.jmc.msu.edu
World Wide Web: http://www.jmc.msu.edu

or

Office of Admissions and Scholarships
Michigan State University
250 Administration Building
East Lansing, Michigan 48824-0590
Telephone: 517-355-6470

Beaumont Tower.

JEWISH THEOLOGICAL SEMINARY OF AMERICA
Albert A. List College of Jewish Studies
NEW YORK, NEW YORK

The College and The Seminary

The Albert A. List College of Jewish Studies of the Jewish Theological Seminary is a four-year, private, coeducational liberal arts college. List College offers qualified men and women a full spectrum of courses in Jewish studies and grants the Bachelor of Arts degree. Students can earn two undergraduate degrees—one in Jewish studies from List College and one in the liberal arts major of their choice from Columbia University's School of General Studies or Barnard College.

Since the College has a current enrollment of 190, students can benefit from the small classes and intimate atmosphere, which offer them an opportunity to interact with faculty members beyond the classroom.

To complement the strong academic program at List, there is an array of extracurricular activities, including sports, performing musical groups, dancing, student government, theater, and community service projects. Shabbat and holidays are celebrated by the community, and religious observance is voluntary. Students also enrolled at Columbia or Barnard participate in many of the additional activities on those campuses, such as intercollegiate athletics, campus newspapers, musical and drama groups, and Greek life.

After earning two undergraduate degrees, more than 80 percent of List students continue their education at the most competitive graduate and professional schools. Many have achieved prominence in the fields of business, law, medicine, education, the rabbinate, and community service.

Founded in 1886, the Jewish Theological Seminary is the academic and spiritual center of Conservative Judaism worldwide. The Seminary's New York campus includes five separate yet integrated schools: the Albert A. List College of Jewish Studies, the Graduate School, the Davidson School of Education, the Rabbinical School, and the Cantorial School. The full range of programs the Seminary offers has established its reputation as a leading academic institution for Jewish studies on the undergraduate and graduate levels.

Location

List College is located on the vibrant Upper West Side of New York City. Its affiliation with Columbia and Barnard and its proximity to Teachers College, Union Theological Seminary, and the Manhattan School of Music puts List in the heart of a close-knit and dynamic academic community. Students are encouraged to explore the wealth of cultural activities New York offers—from music and dance at Lincoln Center to theater on and off Broadway; from art at the Metropolitan or Whitney Museum to the galleries in SoHo and Greenwich Village.

Majors and Degrees

Students may major in Bible, Jewish history, Jewish literature, Jewish music, Jewish philosophy, Midrash, or Talmud and Rabbinics. An interdisciplinary major, consisting of courses from more than one department, may be proposed by the student for the dean's approval. Approved interdisciplinary majors have included ancient Jewish studies and liturgy and American Jewish studies. All majors at List College consist of seven courses or 21 credits taken in a chosen department. Each department determines the specific distribution of courses and requirements for majors. During the sophomore year, students may choose a major field. With approval, an initial declaration of major may be modified at any time up to registration for the fall semester of the senior year. A Bachelor of Arts degree is offered for all of the majors listed above.

A unique feature of the Joint and Double-Degree programs with Barnard College and Columbia University's School of General Studies is that students have the opportunity to study two major subjects in great depth. Thus, these students choose a second major enabling them to receive a second bachelor's degree. These majors include architecture, biology, computer science, economics, English, history, political science, premedicine, psychology, and many others. Two majors provide both an enriched education and an opportunity for a wider range of career options.

Academic Program

The course of study leading to the degree of Bachelor of Arts is usually completed in four years. Students must take a minimum of 96 credits in Judaica at List College and a minimum of 60 credits in liberal arts at another accredited college or university to qualify for the degree. Of the 96 List College credits, 51 are required of all students, 21 comprise the major, and 24 are taken as electives. The required credits are distributed among the following subjects: Bible, Hebrew language, Jewish history, Jewish literature, Jewish philosophy, and Talmud and Rabbinics.

Of the 60 required liberal arts credits, 18 must be distributed as follows: 6 in English; 6 in history, philosophy, or the social sciences; and 6 in mathematics or laboratory sciences. The remaining 42 credits may be taken in electives. The Joint Program, a cooperative arrangement with Columbia University, and the Double-Degree Program, a cooperative arrangement with Barnard College, are two ways of fulfilling this requirement. Students at Columbia or Barnard may apply up to 18 credits toward the electives required by List College.

Applicants who, through their academic achievement in high school, have demonstrated exceptional promise and a commitment to serious study may be invited to join the Honors Program. These students participate in a series of stimulating interdisciplinary seminars during their first and second years. Senior honors students are guided through their theses in a small seminar. These students graduate with honors, appropriately concluding this challenging experience. In recognition of their outstanding achievements, honors students, regardless of financial need, are awarded a significant annual stipend.

The Day School Teacher Training Program offers qualified students an opportunity to prepare for careers as members of Jewish-studies faculties in the growing North American network of Jewish day schools, especially the Solomon Schechter Day Schools. This List College program consists of a specially designed curriculum with a minor in Jewish education. Students are encouraged to spend a year of study in Israel. Undergraduates who are selected must spend a year as full-time interns after the completion of the B.A. program. This experience culminates with the awarding of certification. Students who are selected for the Day School Teacher Training Program receive substantial fellowships.

Off-Campus Arrangements

Students may vary their studies and enrich their educational experience by spending a semester or a year at a university abroad. Many students choose to study at the Hebrew University in Jerusalem. Other accredited Israeli universities provide additional opportunities. Students may also take advantage of the *ulpan* (Hebrew language study groups) offered. Faculty advisers help students plan their programs so that they receive full credit for their study abroad.

Through Columbia University, students in the Joint or Double-Degree Program may elect to participate in additional international study programs such as the Reid Hall Program in Paris or the Study in Great Britain Program.

Academic Facilities

Students have access to the library of the Jewish Theological Seminary, which houses the largest collection of Judaica in the Western Hemisphere and a state-of-the-art Jewish music center, as well as to Columbia University's extensive library system and computer facilities.

Costs

For 1999–2000, full-time tuition and fees were $8320. Tuition fees for part-time students (taking fewer than 9 credits) were $445 per credit. Tuition costs for students attending the combined programs with Columbia University or Barnard College were an additional $12,276. Housing fees were $4700, although students are not required to live in College housing. Annual miscellaneous costs were estimated to be $2500. This figure includes food, personal expenses, and supplies.

Financial Aid

The Seminary is committed to meeting 100 percent of each student's demonstrated financial need. Approximately two thirds of all List College students receive financial aid. Applications for financial aid have no bearing on admission. In order to determine what their need is, applicants for financial assistance are required to complete the Free Application for Federal Student Aid (FAFSA) as well as the PROFILE of the College Scholarship Service and indicate on the form that the information should be forwarded to the Jewish Theological Seminary (code number 2339); Columbia University, School of General Studies (code number 2095); and/or Barnard College (code number 2038). Students must also submit a Jewish Theological Seminary Financial Aid Application and a copy of their parents' and/or their own income tax return to the Seminary Financial Aid Office. In addition to scholarships available from JTS, Columbia, and Barnard, students may be eligible for low-interest loans. Students who receive financial aid are required to secure a Federal Stafford Student Loan from their local bank as part of the financial aid package.

March 1 is the financial aid application deadline for the fall semester; November 1 is the deadline for the spring semester.

Faculty

The Seminary has the largest faculty in North America devoted solely to Jewish studies. Ninety percent of the full-time faculty members have doctoral degrees from renowned universities. In addition to teaching, all faculty members are available for advising and counseling.

Student Government

An active student government is responsible for coordinating social, cultural, educational, and community service programs. It also serves as a vehicle for List College students to express their ideas and concerns to the administration. Each class elects representatives to the Student Council and to the Student-Faculty Committee, which brings professors and students together to discuss matters of mutual concern.

Admission Requirements

High school graduates, regardless of race, color, religion, gender, or national origin, who have demonstrated academic promise, intellectual curiosity, and personal motivation are invited to submit an application for admission to List College. Applicants should submit a completed application form, the fee, and an essay. An official high school transcript, official SAT I scores, scores from the SAT II: Writing Test, and two letters of recommendation should be provided by the appropriate sources. A Hebrew high school transcript, where available, should also be provided. Admission to List College is on a need-blind basis. For students applying for the fall semester, all materials are due by February 15; for the spring semester, by November 1.

Well-qualified high school seniors who have selected List College as their first choice may apply under one of two early decision plans. To be considered under the fall early decision plan, candidates should submit required materials by November 15; they are notified no later than December 15. For the winter early decision plan, materials are due by January 15 for notification no later than February 15. Both Columbia University's School of General Studies and Barnard College will consider applicants for the Joint and Double-Degree programs under these early decision programs.

Applicants are strongly encouraged to arrange for a personal interview at List, Columbia, and/or Barnard. These interviews should be scheduled during the fall semester but no later than March 1. The College visit can include interviews and a tour of JTS and the surrounding area, as well as an overnight stay in a residence hall.

For application to the Joint Program with Columbia University, students must submit a Joint Program application according to the instructions above and may arrange for an interview. For application to the Double-Degree Program with Barnard College, students must submit applications to both List College and Barnard College and arrange for an interview at each college.

Application and Information

For additional information, students should contact:

Reena Gold
Director of Admissions
Albert A. List College of Jewish Studies
Jewish Theological Seminary of America
3080 Broadway, Box 32
New York, New York 10027-4649
Telephone: 212-678-8832
Fax: 212-678-8947
E-mail: lcadmissions@jtsa.edu
World Wide Web: http://www.jtsa.edu

Students at the Albert A. List College of Jewish Studies.

JOHN BROWN UNIVERSITY
SILOAM SPRINGS, ARKANSAS

The University

John Brown University (JBU) was founded in 1919 by evangelist and lecturer Dr. John E. Brown Sr. JBU is a private, interdenominational Christian university that provides top-quality higher education. The University's mission is to provide a Christ-centered higher education that contributes dynamically to the intellectual, spiritual, and occupational effectiveness of men and women in God-honoring service. This commitment is clearly articulated in the University's educational philosophy and adopted motto of "Head, Heart, and Hand." "Head" refers to the mind and academic excellence, "Heart" refers to spiritual growth, and "Hand" refers to a readiness to enter the workplace in professions, careers, and service activities, leading and serving in useful and responsible ways. Taken as a whole, "Head, Heart, and Hand" represents a commitment to educate the whole person for effective living and leadership, honoring God, and serving and leading others.

JBU's student body represents more than 1,500 students from forty-seven states and thirty-three countries. The average 1999–2000 freshman scored 25 or higher on the ACT, had a score of 1180 on the SAT I, had a GPA of 3.51, and came from the top third of his or her class. The average age of full-time students is 25, with 73 percent of the student body composed of traditional students 18 to 24 years old. Sixty-eight percent of the student body lives on campus, and international and U.S. students from minority groups make up 15 percent of the student body.

The University's Advance Degree Completion Program offers working adults with prior college experience the opportunity to earn a bachelor's degree in organizational management by attending classes one night per week for eighteen months. The University also offers three Master of Science degrees in counseling education, licensed professional counseling, and pastoral counseling.

Students are required to attend chapel services twice weekly. Student groups include the Student Government Association, sixteen CAUSE Ministry groups that minister to hundreds of people in the surrounding area, clubs in eleven different academic departments, the African Heritage International Fellowship, the Council for International Friendship, the Married Students Fellowship, Mu Kappa (for missionary kids), the honors program, the student newspaper and yearbook, and three different choirs.

JBU offers men's and women's varsity basketball, swimming, and tennis, as well as men's varsity soccer and women's varsity volleyball. Most students participate in the intramural sports program or in the sports clubs for men's baseball, rugby, and volleyball and women's soccer and softball. Students reside in either the men's J. Alvin Residence Hall, the women's Mayfield Residence Hall, or the California Residence Hall, which houses men on one side and women on the other. There are six town houses for upperclass students and twenty duplexes for married students and their families.

The University is accredited by the North Central Association of Colleges and Schools; the National Council for the Accreditation of Teacher Education; the Accreditation Board for Engineering and Technology, Inc.; the American Council for Construction Management; and the International Assembly for Collegiate Business Administration.

Location

John Brown University is located in the historic community of Siloam Springs, Arkansas. The first resident in 1837 was a German immigrant named Simon Sager. His homestead, Simon Sager Cabin, is located on the campus of JBU and is on the National Register of Historic Places. The main street of Siloam Springs is on the National Register of Historic Districts and consists of sixty-five original buildings, with seven of those buildings on the National Register of Historic Places. Siloam Springs is near the natural beauty of the Ozarks, with Fayetteville, Arkansas, 30 minutes to the east and Tulsa, Oklahoma, 1 hour to the west.

Each fall, freshman orientation groups spend a "Day of Caring" all over Siloam Springs, washing windows for the elderly, painting city park benches, and helping United Way agencies.

Majors and Degrees

The University awards B.S., B.A., B.S.E, B.Mus.Ed, A.S., and A.A. degrees in more than fifty major fields, including accounting, art/fine arts, athletic training, biblical studies, biochemistry, biology/biological sciences, broadcasting, business administration (with concentrations in economics, information systems, management, and marketing), business education, chemistry, commercial art, communication, construction management, digital media, early childhood education, education, elementary education, engineering (with concentrations in electronic and mechanical engineering), English, graphic arts, health education, health services administration, history, interdisciplinary studies, international business, international studies, journalism, liberal arts/general studies, mathematics, medical technology, middle school education, ministries, music, music education, organizational management, pastoral studies, physical education, physical fitness/exercise science, piano/organ, premedicine sequence, psychology, public relations, radio and television studies, recreational facilities management, religious education, religious studies, secondary education, social sciences, special education, sports medicine, theology, and voice. Students may double major in any two fields.

Academic Program

Each undergraduate student of the University must complete a minimum of 124 semester hours of academic credit, including 54 semester hours of general (core) curriculum course work that covers the areas of mathematics, natural and social sciences, human wellness, humanities, and biblical studies. Each bachelor's degree program requires a minimum of 24 or more semester hours in the major field of study, and most curricula require a minor field of study consisting of 18 to 27 semester hours. Students earning two bachelor's degrees must complete 154 semester hours, incorporating all requirements for both degrees. The University offers a nationally recognized honors program, consisting of a variety of enriched courses in the general education curriculum that have been developed especially for gifted and motivated students. Students accepted into the honors program must substitute these courses for at least 18 semester hours of the regular general education curriculum in order to receive a University Honors Degree. JBU offers Army and Air Force ROTC programs.

Off-Campus Arrangements

The University offers several opportunities for students to earn credit hours and study off campus and abroad. These include the American Studies Program in Washington, D.C., sponsored by the Council for Christian Colleges and Universities (CCCU); the Institute of Holy Land Studies in Jerusalem; the Latin American Studies Program in San Jose, Costa Rica, sponsored by the CCCU; the National Collegiate Honors Council Semesters Program, which offers off-campus semesters in locations such as the Czech Republic, Maine, Texas, Mexico, Washington, and Appalachia; the Russian Studies Program; the Oxford Honours Programme at the Centre for Medieval and Renaissance Studies, Keble College, Oxford University; the Los Angeles Film Studies Center; the Au Sable Institute of Environmental Studies in Michigan; JBU's Irish Study Abroad Program in Belfast, Ireland; and JBU's Mexican Study Program in Pueblo, Mexico.

Academic Facilities

The Walton Lifetime Health Complex, completed in 1989, is outfitted with three basketball/volleyball courts, four racquetball courts, an aerobics room, a large Nautilus weight room, a $\frac{1}{10}$-mile jogging track, Murray Sells Gymnasium, a snack bar, Bynum Theatre and Lecture Hall, and the health promotion/human performance classrooms and labs. The Cathedral of the Ozarks houses the Bible, English, psychology, history, art, and music departments, as well as the 100-seat Jones Recital Hall, twelve soundproof music practice rooms, and the 1,100-seat main auditorium, which is used for chapel services and concerts. The Mabee Center houses the teacher education, business, and communications departments, as well as several lecture rooms, three state-of-the-art IBM computer labs with fifty-five computers, and one Macintosh computer lab with twenty computers. The Arutunoff Learning Resource Center holds more than 100,000 books, microfilms, sound recordings, music scores, videotapes, curriculum media, and archival materials, as well as an extensive CD-ROM database capable of accessing more than 32 million items held in thousands of libraries across the nation and abroad.

Costs

The cost to attend JBU in 2000–01 is $15,970 for the year. Full-time tuition and fees are $11,492, and room and board are $4478. The cost of books is estimated at $300 per semester, and certain classes and labs charge an extra fee. The typical annual cost per student for books, supplies, personal expenses, and travel is about $3000.

Financial Aid

In 1999–2000, JBU awarded institutional need-based scholarships to more than 600 students (averaging $3620) and institutional non-need-based scholarships to 270 students (averaging $1510). Loans from external sources averaged $4762, and more than 475 students took advantage of the Work-Study Program. The average total aid for freshmen was $10,060, meeting 80 percent of need; aid was provided to all those who qualified. Students applying for financial aid must submit the Free Application for Federal Student Aid (FAFSA). The priority deadline is March 1. Tuition repayment and installment payment plans are available. There are full and partial waivers for employees, children of employees, and senior citizens.

Faculty

There are 114 faculty members (90 full-time, 24 part-time). Sixty-five percent of the faculty members have doctoral or terminal degrees, and 100 percent of the faculty members advise undergraduate students in their respective departments. While many faculty members perform research in their field of expertise, all full-time faculty members teach undergraduate courses throughout the year. The undergraduate student-faculty ratio is 16:1. A faculty association meeting is held monthly.

Student Government

The Student Government Association (SGA) is the student voice to the faculty and administration and is the organization responsible for all-campus activities. Officers and senators are elected each spring by the entire student body. Senators represent each academic area and each of the four classes. SGA officers meet regularly with the president and cabinet members to discuss campus topics. JBU's administration views the SGA as a representative voice for the student body and listens to concerns and suggestions.

The University has written policies against drugs, narcotics, tobacco, alcoholic beverages, social dancing, profane languages, pornography, and harassment of any kind.

Admission Requirements

JBU recruits students from all over the United States and abroad. To be admitted as a first-time freshman, applicants must present a transcript showing graduation from high school or GED scores, class rank, and the score and percentile achieved on the ACT or SAT I. To be admitted as a regular freshman, an applicant must have scored at or above the 40th percentile on the ACT or SAT I, have a high school cumulative GPA at or above 2.5 (excluding remedial course work), and have a high school class ranking at or above the 50th percentile. Applicants must also submit two references: one from a high school counselor or teacher and the other from a church leader. Academic, social, and spiritual factors are also considered by the admissions staff to help determine an overall "fit" between the student and the University. Transfer students must present a transcript showing 12 or more units of previously completed college work with an overall GPA of at least 2.0. At least 9 units must be transferable, and a high school transcript and standardized test scores may also be required. Transfer students with more than 12 semester hours of transfer credit receive scholarship consideration on the basis of college credit.

Application and Information

There is a limited number of residence hall spaces available for new students, so early application to JBU is advised. JBU admits the number of qualified candidates from the applicant pool for whom available spaces exist. Remaining applicants are placed on an active waiting list. Students receive notice of official acceptance as soon as space is available. As long as housing space is available, students receive acceptance notification by May 1. For information about enrolling at John Brown University, students should contact:

Don Crandall
Vice President for Enrollment Management
John Brown University
Siloam Springs, Arkansas 72761-2121
Telephone: 877-JBU-INFO (toll-free)
Fax: 501-524-4196
E-mail: jbuinfo@acc.jbu.edu
World Wide Web: http://www.jbu.edu

John Brown University, founded in 1919.

JOHN CARROLL UNIVERSITY
UNIVERSITY HEIGHTS, OHIO

The University

In the Jesuit tradition of leadership, faith, and service, John Carroll University provides its students with a rigorous education, rooted in the liberal arts and focused on questions of moral and ethical value. The University wants its graduates to make a difference in their chosen careers and in bettering their communities. One of twenty-eight Jesuit colleges and universities in the United States, John Carroll offers degree programs at the undergraduate and graduate levels in fifty-four arts and sciences, business, and preprofessional fields.

John Carroll was founded in 1886 as St. Ignatius College. In 1923, its name was briefly changed to Cleveland College. Later it became John Carroll University, named after the first Catholic bishop of the United States. In 1934, the University moved from its original location on Cleveland's near west side to its current location in University Heights. Originally a men's college, the University and all its programs officially became coeducational in 1968.

In 1999–2000, the enrollment was 4,389, with 3,295 students enrolled in full-time undergraduate programs and 862 in graduate programs. Students come from thirty-two states, the Virgin Islands, Puerto Rico, and seven other countries. The student body is 48 percent men, 52 percent women, and 9.7 percent minority group members. The University's eight residence halls house 1,850 students.

A well-rounded education includes learning and leadership activities outside the classroom. The University owns Thorn Acres, a 30-acre recreational facility used for fishing, canoeing, retreats, and student-group meetings. John Carroll offers more than eighty student organizations and clubs, as well as community volunteer-service opportunities, men's and women's varsity and intramural sports, and academic honor societies. A natatorium, racquetball and tennis courts, two gymnasiums, and weight-training and fitness facilities are located in the Student Center. Office space is set aside for a host of student activities, including the newspaper, radio station, yearbook, Student Union, fraternities and sororities, and various student organizations. University Counseling Services provides free personal and psychological counseling, therapy, in-depth analysis of academic and vocational concerns, and testing.

Students at John Carroll, in the Jesuit spirit of "making a difference," volunteer to help improve the local community. Each year, students paint the homes of the elderly or underprivileged, feed the homeless, and aid the dying. Student-organized Project Gold, a community service program, has supplemented University-run community service projects such as Christmas in April and Meals on Wheels.

The Graduate School at John Carroll offers Master of Science degree programs in biology, chemistry, mathematics, and physics; Master of Arts degree programs in communications management, counseling and human services, English, history, humanities, and religious studies; Master of Education; and Master of Business Administration degree programs. In addition, Economics America (the Cleveland Center for Economic Education), a nonprofit educational organization located on John Carroll's campus, provides advanced course work in economics for educators.

Location

Just 30 minutes from downtown Cleveland, John Carroll is located in the quiet, residential Heights neighborhood; it is surrounded by Shaker Heights, University Heights, and Cleveland Heights. The graceful walkways, rich landscape, and Gothic and contemporary architecture of the campus complement the surrounding community beautifully. The campus is easily accessible by bus, rapid transit, and car. Two shopping centers are within walking distance, so restaurants, theaters, banks, department stores, grocery stores, and specialty shops are all nearby. University Circle, 10 minutes from campus, is the home of the Cleveland Symphony Orchestra; Cleveland Museums of Art, Natural History, and Health Education; and Garden Center of Greater Cleveland. Downtown Cleveland offers comedy clubs; world-class shopping; theater; the Flats, an extensive entertainment district located on the Cuyahoga River; the Rock and Roll Hall of Fame; the Great Lakes Science Center; Jacobs Field, home to the Cleveland Indians; Gund Arena, home to the Cleveland Cavaliers, Rockers, and Lumberjacks; and the new Cleveland Stadium, home to the Cleveland Browns.

Majors and Degrees

The Bachelor of Arts degree is awarded in art history, classical languages (Greek and Latin), communications, economics, education and allied studies (prekindergarten, elementary education, secondary education, and certain disabilities), English, French, German, Greek, history, humanities, mathematics teaching, modern languages (French, German, and Spanish), philosophy, physical education, political science (with an optional concentration in public administration and policy studies), religious studies (with an optional concentration in religious education), sociology, and world literature. The Bachelor of Science degree is awarded in biology, chemistry, computer science, engineering physics, mathematics, physics (with optional concentrations in computer engineering, electrical engineering, and engineering physics), and psychology. The Bachelor of Science in Business Administration degree is granted from John Carroll's Boler School of Business in accounting, business logistics, economics, finance, management, and marketing. Optional minors are offered in the American political system, art history, business, chemistry, communications, computer science, economics, engineering physics, English, foreign affairs, French, German, Greek, history, humanities, Latin, mathematics, philosophy, physical education, physics, probability and statistics, psychology, public administration and public policy, religious education, religious studies, sociology, and Spanish.

The University is well known for its preprofessional programs, including dentistry, engineering, law, and medicine. Interdisciplinary concentrations for students interested in exploring selected topics in several academic disciplines are available. These include East Asian studies, economics and mathematics, environmental studies, gerontology, humanities, international economics and modern language, international studies, neuroscience, perspectives on sex and gender, and public administration and policy studies.

Academic Program

In keeping with the Jesuit tradition of liberal arts education, every undergraduate takes a core curriculum that includes a single-theme first-year seminar course, four courses in humanities, four in science and mathematics, three in philosophy, three in social sciences, two in religious studies, one in English composition and rhetoric, and one in speech communication. Therefore all students enroll in the College of Arts and Sciences for their first two years. After the first two years, students select a major and are admitted to their respective degree programs.

To earn a degree, a student must complete a minimum of 128 credit hours with a grade point average of at least 2.0 (C) for all course work. The last 30 hours of instruction must be completed at John Carroll. Candidates for graduation must complete all the courses and proficiency requirements for the degree, and they must complete all the major requirements with an average of at least 2.0. All course work required for a declared minor or concentration must be completed with at least a 2.0.

A number of special programs are available, including ROTC and student exchange. The University operates on a semester calendar, with three 5-week summer sessions offered between academic years.

Off-Campus Arrangements

John Carroll offers many special educational opportunities. Exchange programs are available with two universities in Japan, and students annually participate in archaeological explorations in Tel el-Hesi and Ashkelon in Israel. There are other approved programs as well.

John Carroll University is a member of the Northeast Ohio Commission on Higher Education and offers students the opportunity to take one course per semester at one of the other sixteen area universities while enrolled full-time at John Carroll. There is no additional charge for tuition; the only stipulation is that the course may not be offered at the home institution. Students often take courses in the performance-based arts or in specific engineering fields through this cross-registration program.

Academic Facilities

The recently completed $6.8-million expansion of Grasselli Library has doubled the capacity of the building and has enhanced accessibility of electronic databases. The library currently has more than 616,000 cataloged holdings. Students interested in computers have more than 100 microcomputers in four computer labs available for their use. The O'Malley Center for Communications and Language Arts features a television studio and newsroom, computer-assisted and audio language laboratories, and a center for writing instruction. Those who are studying radio broadcasting may work in the radio station, and dramatic presentations are given in both Kulas Auditorium and the Marinello Little Theatre. The Boler School of Business's Bruening Hall houses high-tech presentation classrooms featuring computerized audiovisual technology. The University earned a Kresge Challenge Grant and purchased science instrumentation and has endowed future laboratory upgrades.

Costs

Tuition is $16,334 for the 2000–01 academic year. Room and board are $6128. The average cost for books and supplies is $800 per year.

Financial Aid

In 1999–2000, 70 percent of the student body received some type of need-based financial assistance. Qualified students may be awarded scholarships, honor awards, grants, work-study employment, and loans or a combination of these to help offset the cost of their education. Merit-based scholarships, such as the President's Honor Award, National Merit Scholarship, and the Mastin Scholarship are given to a number of outstanding high school students based solely upon their academic achievement. Most students, however, apply for need-based aid by completing the Free Application for Federal Student Aid (FAFSA). The financial aid application deadline is March 1.

Faculty

The majority of John Carroll's 410 faculty members teach undergraduate classes, although some teach graduate programs as well. Of the full-time faculty, 90 percent hold doctorates or the appropriate terminal degree in their field, and 65 percent are tenured. The faculty's primary focus is teaching and scholarship. Counseling of students, research and publication, and community service are also important pursuits. John Carroll's faculty includes 15 resident Jesuit priests. The student-faculty ratio is 15:1.

Student Government

The John Carroll student body is self-governed, with the elected Student Union officers actively representing all students—undergraduate, graduate, full- and part-time, and day and evening—in all academic, social, religious, and disciplinary matters. Fifty-six men and women are elected to Student Union service for one-year terms.

Admission Requirements

Applications for admission from all serious candidates are welcome. John Carroll attracts students of diverse geographic, economic, racial, and religious backgrounds. Admission criteria in descending order of importance are the quality of the high school curriculum, grade point average, test scores on either the SAT I or ACT, extracurricular activities, and the recommendation of a high school counselor or teacher. Personal interviews are recommended, though optional, and are taken into consideration when admission decisions are made.

The deadline for applications to John Carroll is February 1. Candidates are informed of decisions on a rolling basis and should be notified within four weeks of applying.

Application and Information

John Carroll subscribes to the Candidates Reply Date of May 1. Accepted students who wish to reserve their place in the freshman class must submit their tuition deposit (and room deposit, if they wish to reserve on-campus housing) by May 1 to ensure their place in the class. All deposits are refundable by written request up to the May 1 deadline.

To request a viewbook and a current application, students are encouraged to contact:

Thomas P. Fanning
Director of Admission
John Carroll University
University Heights, Ohio 44118-4581
Telephone: 216-397-4294

Grasselli Tower stands behind the bust of Archbishop John Carroll, the University's namesake, along the main quadrangle.

JOHN JAY COLLEGE OF CRIMINAL JUSTICE OF THE CITY UNIVERSITY OF NEW YORK
NEW YORK, NEW YORK

The College

Founded in 1964, John Jay College of Criminal Justice is the unit of the City University of New York that emphasizes as its special mission criminal justice, fire science, and other related public service fields. The institution developed out of a recognition of the increasing complexity of law enforcement and the need for professionalization at all levels of the criminal justice system. Intended at its founding, as the College of Police Science, for members of the New York City Police Department, the College nevertheless has always welcomed civilian students with an interest in criminal justice. At present, approximately 20 percent of the College's 10,000 students are members of uniformed criminal justice and fire service agencies; the majority of the students are civilian preprofessionals, many of whom plan careers in these areas.

Most of the College's students are residents of New York City and of surrounding communities in New York, New Jersey, and Connecticut. All students commute to the College directly from their homes or from their places of employment. To accommodate students, such as police officers, who work rotating tours of duty, both day and evening courses are offered. A student may attend a class in the daytime or, with the same professor covering the identical material, in the evening, depending on his or her work assignment.

The College also offers master's degrees in criminal justice, forensic psychology, forensic science, protection management, and public administration. The Ph.D. in criminal justice is awarded through the Graduate School and University Center of the City University of New York and John Jay College of Criminal Justice.

Location

John Jay College occupies two buildings on the West Side of Manhattan at 59th Street and 10th Avenue—John Jay Square. One of the buildings was recently renovated and houses new classrooms, a theater, the world's largest criminal justice library, administrative offices, and an extensive athletic facility. Within a radius of a mile are Lincoln Center for the Performing Arts, the New York theater district, Carnegie Hall, and numerous other cultural facilities. The College's location not only makes access to major criminal justice agencies convenient but also offers all the aspects and resources of one of the most fascinating cities in the world as the background for its programs.

Majors and Degrees

The Bachelor of Arts degree is granted in criminal justice, criminology, deviant behavior and social control, fire service administration, forensic psychology, government, judicial studies, justice studies, and public administration. The Bachelor of Science degree is offered in computer information systems, correctional studies, criminal justice, criminal justice administration and planning, fire science, forensic science, legal studies, police studies, and security management.

A B.A./M.A. program, which enables particularly well-qualified students to earn both degrees in a shorter time than would be required to earn them individually, is offered in criminal justice and forensic psychology. A similar B.A./M.P.A. program in public administration is available.

The A.S. degree is granted in correction administration, police science, and security management.

Academic Program

As a specialized college, John Jay emphasizes the particular areas of its mission—all aspects of the broad fields of criminal justice and fire science—against a background of the liberal arts. Thus, the humanities, physical sciences, and social sciences contrast and integrate with the practical and theoretical components of the study of these public service fields. Since most students at John Jay College are planning to enter or already are employed in public service fields, the interdisciplinary approach to education that is the basis of the College's philosophy aims at a broadening and a further professionalization of their careers.

Candidates for the baccalaureate degree at John Jay College must fulfill certain broad educational requirements during the first half of their degree program (40–60 credits). In addition, all candidates must complete a major field of study of at least 36 credits. A minimum of 32 of the candidate's total credits and at least 50 percent of the selected major must be completed in residence. The associate degree at John Jay requires completion of basic distribution requirements and a specialization program (64–67 credits).

The Thematic Studies Program offers an alternative way of meeting basic course requirements and of completing the liberal arts portion of the baccalaureate and associate degree programs. Students who enroll in Thematic Studies take a package of classes related to a specific theme, combining literature, sociology, psychology, ethnic studies, history, writing, philosophy, government, and criminal justice. Each course centers on a broad topic or theme, to which all classwork and projects are related. These interdisciplinary courses are taught by teams of 6 to 8 professors. Students undertake individual or group projects, supplementary lectures, readings, discussions, and papers.

With departmental approval, students may be awarded credit for successful scores on the College-Level Examination Program (CLEP) subject tests, the College Proficiency Examinations (CPE), the Regents External Degree Examinations (REDE), and College Board Advanced Placement (AP) tests. Students may apply for and may be granted up to 32 credits for external and/or equivalent learning experiences.

The John Jay Curriculum in Alcohol Studies and Research is designed to help present and prospective alcoholism counselors, personnel directors, program administrators, and healthcare professionals in the public and private sector complete the educational component required to obtain the New York State credential in alcoholism counseling.

The Certificate Program in Dispute Resolution is also available. This 30-credit, multidisciplinary program responds to the needs of personnel working in the criminal justice system as well as of those in other public and private sectors for training in the techniques of dispute resolution.

Programs are also offered in African-American studies and in Puerto Rican studies.

Off-Campus Arrangements

The College's location in midtown Manhattan and its special focus on criminal justice and related fields offer unparalleled opportunities for students to earn academic credits while gaining experience. Internship courses, which provide 3 credits each, combine classes and supervision with practical experience in criminal justice and government agencies, cultural organizations, private businesses, and health, research, and nonprofit institutions. Internships are available in such places as legislators' offices, hospitals, courts, New York City agencies, district attorneys' offices, juvenile-diversion programs, museums, legal societies, fire and police departments, social service agencies, and federal agencies.

The cooperative education program provides alternating periods of paid employment and college work. Juniors and seniors with satisfactory college records may enter into this program with such employers as IBM, the U.S. Customs Service, the U.S. Marshalls Service of the Department of Justice, and the Inspector General's Office of the Department of Health and Human Services. No college credit is offered for this off-campus employment.

Academic Facilities

The library collection consists of more than 250,000 books, periodicals, microforms, and cassette tapes and supports the full range of the College's curriculum and educational mission. The main strength of the collection is the holdings in the social sciences and criminal justice, public administration, and related fields and the growing bodies of material dealing with forensic science, fire science, and forensic psychology. Holdings in these areas are extensive and support the research needs of students and faculty members and of criminal justice agency personnel who are engaged in planning and development.

Five specially equipped laboratories are used to educate students in the professionally oriented forensic science program. In addition, research rooms are available for use by forensic science majors and faculty.

The Security Management Lab provides hands-on training in computer security and other modern security systems and techniques applicable in the field.

The Microcomputer Laboratory consists of four separate labs for classroom instruction and individual assignments. The labs are staffed with supervisors and consultants who assist students in their individual projects.

Costs

For New York State residents, tuition costs for 1999–2000 were $135 per credit hour or a maximum of $1600 per term. Tuition costs for out-of-state residents were $285 per credit hour or a maximum of $3400 per term. (Tuition may be increased at any time by action of the Board of Trustees.)

Financial Aid

Financial aid programs are available to assist students who would not otherwise be able to obtain a college education. John Jay College makes every effort to help as many students as possible with a combination of financial aid awards, such as Federal Pell Grants, Federal Work-Study program employment, Tuition Assistance Program (TAP) awards, Federal Stafford Student Loans, Federal Perkins Loans, Federal Supplemental Educational Opportunity Grants (FSEOG), veterans' benefits, and scholarships through the Mayor's Scholarship Program.

Faculty

The faculty consists of 260 full-time and 300 part-time members. All faculty members teach undergraduate courses, and teachers of graduate courses are drawn from the same group. Of the full-time faculty members, approximately 80 percent hold doctoral degrees.

While the John Jay College faculty has a representative background in the humanities, social sciences, and natural sciences, the special emphasis of the College has established as members of the faculty experienced practitioners in the fields of criminal justice and fire science, a large number of whom hold earned doctorates as well. Faculty members are encouraged to function as academic counselors to their students.

Student Government

The student government consists of an executive board of elected representatives from each class, including graduate students. Among the chief functions of the student government are the allocation of student fees, the chartering of campus clubs and monitoring of their activities and expenditures, and the selection of students to serve on College Council committees. Members also serve as student advocates before faculty and administrators.

The College Council is composed of faculty members, students, and administrators. Students are also voting members of College committees on personnel and budget, curriculum, retention, and other areas of College governance.

Admission Requirements

An applicant for freshman admission must present evidence of having received a high school diploma from an accredited high school or a New York State Equivalency Diploma or have passed a General Educational Development (GED) examination during or after June 1970. Students from non-English-speaking countries must submit TOEFL scores.

Effective as of September 2000, admission to the baccalaureate program for recent graduates of domestic high schools will be determined using an index that weights specific performance indicators. The indicators weighted include college admission average, number of academic courses completed in high school, and SAT I or ACT scores. SAT I or ACT scores are required for admission to the baccalaureate program.

Applicants to the baccalaureate program who are not recent graduates of domestic high schools must have a high school academic average of at least 80 and a minimum of 16 academic units with a combined total of 4 units of English and math, with at least 1 unit in each discipline, or an SAT I score of at least 1020.

Applicants who do not meet the baccalaureate criteria may be admitted to the associate degree program provided that they have an SAT I score of at least 900 or a minimum high school academic average of 72 or a GED score of at least 300. Associate degree applicants with lower academic averages may be considered provided that they have higher numbers of academic units, including English and math units. Course work in the associate degree program is applicable toward bachelor's degree requirements.

Students who have attended a college or postsecondary institution must have a minimum cumulative GPA of 2.0 based on the total number of credits attempted and completed. Prospective transfer students with fewer than 12 credits must have a minimum GPA of 2.0 and the prerequisite high school average and academic units for admission to the baccalaureate program.

Application and Information

Applicants who have attended college since graduation from high school may apply for admission with advanced standing.

For application materials and additional information, requests should be made to:

Office of Undergraduate Admissions
John Jay College of Criminal Justice
445 West 59th Street, Room 4205
New York, New York 10019
Telephone: 212-JOHNJAY
World Wide Web: http://www.jjay.cuny.edu

JOHNS HOPKINS UNIVERSITY
School of Nursing
BALTIMORE, MARYLAND

The University and The School

Since its founding in 1876, Johns Hopkins University has been in the forefront of higher education. Originally established as an institution oriented toward graduate study and research, it is often called America's first true university. Today, Johns Hopkins' commitment to academic excellence continues in its eight academic divisions: Nursing, Medicine, Public Health, Arts and Sciences, Engineering, Continuing Studies, Advanced International Studies, and the Peabody Conservatory of Music. With a full-time enrollment of approximately 6,570 students, it is the smallest of the top-ranked universities in the United States and, by its own choice, remains small. The School of Nursing attracts a national and international student body of about 500 students.

The School of Nursing was established in 1983 by Johns Hopkins University, in affiliation with three Baltimore hospitals: Church, Johns Hopkins, and Sinai. Together, these institutions formed the Consortium for Nursing Education, Inc., united for innovation and excellence in teaching, research, and patient care.

By choosing to attend Johns Hopkins University School of Nursing, students will become leaders in the nursing profession. A Hopkins education will provide a solid foundation on which to base a lifelong career in the ever-growing field of nursing. Hopkins students enjoy the advantages of an education at an institution with a worldwide reputation and an outstanding network of alumni who are willing to serve as guides and mentors. Students at the School of Nursing are given the opportunity to participate in designing an educational program tailored to their individual needs. A rigorous academic curriculum, which includes a strong scientific orientation, gives students the background to understand the health-care decisions they will make as professionals. Students learn in an atmosphere where excellence is expected, valued, and reinforced.

The School of Nursing is one of only a few in the country that emphasizes undergraduate research. Its graduates are prepared for professional practice through an educational process that emphasizes clinical excellence, critical thinking, and intellectual curiosity. In addition to the undergraduate program, a graduate program is offered that offers a number of majors, including nurse practitioner studies.

Guest speaker programs, concerts, lacrosse, and other sports are just a few of the activities that enrich life at Hopkins. There are more than seventy student organizations on campus, including fraternities and sororities and social, religious, and cultural groups.

Location

The School of Nursing is located on the campus of Johns Hopkins Medical Institutions, including the School of Medicine, the School of Hygiene and Public Health, and Johns Hopkins Hospital. Located 10 minutes away is the Homewood Campus of Johns Hopkins University, which is accessible to students via a free shuttle service.

Often referred to as "the biggest small town in America," Baltimore has undergone one of the most successful transformations of any city in the nation. Baltimore's famous Inner Harbor and the National Aquarium are focal points of this revitalization. Washington, D.C., is less than an hour away by car or train.

Major and Degree

The School of Nursing offers an NLNAC-accredited upper-division program that leads to a Bachelor of Science degree with a major in nursing. An accelerated program of study makes it possible for students who hold a bachelor's degree in another discipline to receive a nursing degree within thirteen months. Students who hold a bachelor's degree in another discipline are also eligible to apply to the Direct Entry Combined B.S./M.S.N. program. The Bachelor of Science degree is also available for registered nurses.

Academic Program

Johns Hopkins University School of Nursing prepares students for professional nursing practice through an educational process that combines a strong academic curriculum with intensive clinical experience. The program is built on the University's commitment to research, teaching, patient service, and educational innovation and the consortium hospitals' commitment to excellence in clinical practice. The School's mission is to prepare its students academically and technologically for challenges of the future and to graduate professional nurses who can participate in all aspects of modern health care.

The upper-division courses in the baccalaureate nursing program are planned to meet the nursing needs of people in a complex and rapidly changing health-care system. The program is built on the liberal and general education prerequisites. The curriculum is planned to provide a balance among technologies, the theories of nursing, and the caring functions of the nurse. A high priority is placed on educating the nurse to practice in a variety of health-care settings as they exist today and in the future.

Students who are already registered nurses may enter with 33 credits of the ACT challenge examinations. A minimum of 30 of the 63 credits in the upper division must actually be taken at Johns Hopkins University.

Johns Hopkins University School of Nursing has a collaborative program of study that integrates academic study at Johns Hopkins University and volunteer service in the Peace Corps. The Peace Corps Preparatory Program combines four semesters of academic course work followed by Peace Corps training and two years of volunteer service. Registered nurses who are interested in obtaining a B.S. degree may challenge approximately 35 of the upper-division credits upon acceptance to the Peace Corps program. Students who already possess a Bachelor of Science degree in a major other than nursing are eligible for the thirteen-month accelerated program at the School of Nursing prior to Peace Corps service. A Peace Corps Fellows Program is offered to returned Peace Corps volunteers.

The Army Reserve Officers' Training Corps (ROTC) is the principal source of commissioned officers for the Active Army, Army Reserve, and Army National Guard. All Army nurses are officers. Johns Hopkins University offers two- and three-year scholarships to students enrolled in Army ROTC, which is located on the Homewood Campus of Johns Hopkins University.

Academic Facilities

The William H. Welch Medical Library is the central resource library serving Johns Hopkins Medical Institutions. Students have free 24-hour-per-day access to the Welch Library Gateway, which leads users to local and remote bibliographic databases, full-text journals, and other resources available locally and on the Internet. The Nursing Information Resource Center (NIRC), located in the School of Nursing, is managed by the Welch Library. The NIRC maintains a core collection of books to support student course work, a reprint file of material used in the students' courses, a pamphlet file of material from the National League for Nursing, and clinical skills videocassettes. In addition, the facilities and 2 million volumes of the University's Milton S. Eisenhower Library, on the Homewood Campus, are available to School of Nursing students.

Three microcomputer, computer/interactive video laboratories are equipped with a computer network that contains seventy IBM-compatible microcomputers and laser printers. Several classrooms and the auditorium have PC hookup and distance learning capabilities. Additional computer resources are available throughout the campus.

Three nursing practice labs are available to provide the student with an opportunity to gain experience and confidence in performing a wide variety of nursing technologies. Students practice basic nursing technologies at numerous patient care stations designed to closely approximate hospital inpatient areas. Practice using actual medical equipment is an integral part of the laboratory experience, and patient simulators are provided to facilitate clinical skill mastery.

The clinical facilities of the three consortium hospitals, as well as a variety of other acute, long-term community and specialty health-care institutions, are available for student clinical education.

Costs

For the 1999–2000 academic year, undergraduate tuition was $17,250.

Financial Aid

Johns Hopkins University School of Nursing attempts to provide financial assistance to all eligible accepted students. The School of Nursing will assist those students who qualify for need-based aid. Such assistance is usually in the form of loans, grants, scholarships, and work-study programs. While most of the financial aid received by students is based on financial need, many students also benefit from awards based on academic merit and achievement.

Faculty

The faculty members view professional nursing as a unique health service offering effective, humane, and competent care to individuals, families, groups, and communities. Nurses function in independent, interdependent, and dependent roles to promote and improve delivery of health care. The faculty members view education as a process and as an enriching interaction in which both the teacher and learner must actively participate in an atmosphere of mutual trust. They believe that it is the responsibility of the teacher to guide the teaching-learning process and to develop the potential of each individual student to the highest level possible. The student-faculty ratio is 8:1.

Student Government

Each class within the School of Nursing has a government board and a president. There is also the Student Government Association (SGA), which includes all divisions of the entire University. Each class has 2 representatives to the SGA, and anyone may attend the meetings.

Admission Requirements

The School seeks individuals who will bring to the student body the qualities of scholarship, motivation, and commitment. The Committee on Admissions is interested in each applicant as an individual and will consider both academic potential and personal qualities. Therefore, school records, test scores, recommendations, a personal statement about goals and interests, and an interview are all important.

A complete application consists of an application form and nonrefundable $50 application fee; recommendations from 3 persons, 2 of whom must be instructors in current or recent courses; official college transcripts; an official high school transcript (unless the applicant has already completed a college degree); and SAT or ACT scores, if they are not more than five years old and the student does not already hold a bachelor's degree. A grade point average of at least 3.0 (on a 4.0 scale) is recommended.

In addition to the above requirements, registered nurses must send a copy of their Maryland nursing license. Applications are accepted for both the spring and fall semesters.

Students are required to spend two years in a liberal arts setting either at Johns Hopkins University or another accredited university or college offering the prerequisite courses essential for entry into an upper-division nursing curriculum. This includes course work in anatomy and physiology, microbiology, the humanities, social sciences, chemistry, and nutrition. In addition, the School of Nursing has articulation agreements for direct transfer with the College of Notre Dame of Maryland; Gettysburg College, Pennsylvania; Juniata College, Pennsylvania; Mount Holyoke College, Massachusetts; Mount Saint Mary's College, Maryland; Pennsylvania State University; Randolph-Macon Woman's College, Virginia; State University of New York College at Oneonta; Virginia Polytechnic Institute and State University, Virginia; Washington College, Maryland; and Wittenberg University, Ohio.

International students must submit official test score reports of the Test of English as a Foreign Language (TOEFL). In order to be considered for admission, non-permanent residents must establish their ability to finance their education in the United States. International students must submit official records of all university-level course work. To be considered for transfer toward a degree, any courses listed on an international transcript must be submitted by the student to the World Evaluation Service (WES). WES must then send the official results to Johns Hopkins University School of Nursing.

Johns Hopkins University is an affirmative action/equal opportunity institution.

Application and Information

All inquiries concerning the School of Nursing should be directed to:

Office of Admissions and Student Services
Suite 113
School of Nursing
Johns Hopkins University
525 North Wolfe Street
Baltimore, Maryland 21205-2110
E-mail: jhuson@son.jhmi.edu
World Wide Web: http://www.son.jhmi.edu

JOHNS HOPKINS UNIVERSITY
School of Arts and Sciences and
G. W. C. Whiting School of Engineering
BALTIMORE, MARYLAND

The University

Privately endowed, the Johns Hopkins University was founded in 1876 as the first American institution committed to the idea that knowledge should be discovered, rather than merely transmitted, in a university setting. Daniel Coit Gilman, the first president of Johns Hopkins, stated that the object of the University was "not so much to impart knowledge as to whet the appetite, exhibit methods, develop powers, strengthen judgment, and invigorate the intellectual and moral forces." Today, Johns Hopkins continues to stress "creative scholarship" by providing graduate-style education for undergraduates.

Johns Hopkins seeks diversity in its student body, which comes from all over the United States and from many other countries. Of the total undergraduate enrollment of approximately 3,800, about 41 percent are women and 59 percent are men. All out-of-town freshmen and sophomores must live in campus dormitories. In addition, University residences, located directly across from the library on Charles Street, are available for upperclass students. Students may also live in private housing or in fraternity housing. Hopkins has twelve fraternities and four sororities.

Films, concerts, seminars, and athletic events are offered on campus. The Student Union provides places for students to meet, such as the Glass Pavilion, where larger group activities are held, and the Arellano Theater, which is used for theater and films and contains lounges and music rooms. The Student Council runs a number of activities, including an annual spring fair featuring outdoor concerts and exhibits. Men's varsity teams compete in fourteen sports. In the fall, there are crew, cross-country, football, soccer, and water polo. In the winter, there are basketball, fencing, swimming and diving, and wrestling. The big sports season at Hopkins is spring, with baseball, crew, indoor track, tennis, and track, as well as lacrosse. The men's and women's lacrosse teams compete at the Division I level, and the men have won the NCAA lacrosse championships thirty-seven times. Women's varsity sports include basketball, crew, cross-country, fencing, field hockey, indoor track, soccer, squash, swimming, tennis, track and field, and volleyball. An extensive intramural program is also available.

Location

Johns Hopkins's Homewood campus is 140 acres of lush, peaceful greenery, bounded on all sides by residential areas. Hopkins offers the best of both worlds—the tranquil seclusion of the campus plus the adjacent urban environment. Restaurants, grocery stores, and other shops are nearby. The Baltimore Museum of Art, which is on the southwest corner of the campus, is well known for its collection of primitive and modern art. The Walters Art Gallery, a 10-minute drive away, has a collection that spans civilization from Egypt to the nineteenth century, and many smaller museums, galleries, and outdoor showings feature local artists. The University is located just 4 miles from the heart of downtown Baltimore; the theater, symphony, and opera are 10 minutes away, as are Oriole Park at Camden Yards and Baltimore's PSINet Stadium at Camden Yards, home of the Baltimore Ravens. Weekend activities include shopping at Harborplace, visiting the National Aquarium, enjoying an ethnic festival by the water, sailing on the Chesapeake Bay, and hiking around the Maryland countryside. Washington, D.C., with such resources as the Smithsonian Institution, the National Gallery of Art, and the Kennedy Center, is a 40-mile drive by car or a 50-minute train ride. Baltimore is readily accessible by train, plane, bus, and boat.

Majors and Degrees

Bachelor of Arts degrees are awarded in anthropology; astronomy and physics; biology; biophysics; chemistry; classics; computer science; earth and planetary sciences; economics; English; environmental science; film and media studies; French; geography; German; Hispanic and Italian studies; history; history of art; history of science, medicine, and technology; humanities; Iberian and Latin American studies; international studies; mathematics; Near Eastern studies; philosophy; political science; psychology; sociology; and writing. A Bachelor of Arts degree in engineering is also available for students who seek preparation for professional careers (such as law or business) with technological orientation. Bachelor of Science degrees are awarded in biomedical engineering, chemical engineering, civil engineering, computer engineering, computer science, electrical engineering, geography and environmental engineering, materials science and engineering, mathematical sciences, and mechanical engineering. Area majors are available in humanistic studies, natural sciences, and social and behavioral sciences. Accelerated B.A./M.A. programs are offered in chemistry, earth and planetary sciences, economics, French, German, Hispanic and Italian studies, history, humanistic studies, international studies, mathematics, and psychology. Accelerated B.S./M.S. programs are offered in all engineering departments. A dual-degree program leading to a Bachelor of Arts or Bachelor of Science degree and a Bachelor of Music degree is available in cooperation with the University's Peabody Conservatory of Music.

Academic Program

The departments in the School of Arts and Sciences and G. W. C. Whiting School of Engineering comprise four general areas for undergraduate programs: engineering, humanistic studies, natural sciences, and social and behavioral sciences. If a student has special interests that fall outside the bounds of the departmental and area majors, an individual program can be devised, or a student may study independently with the guidance of a faculty member. Qualified students may complete their degree requirements in fewer than four years. In a number of departments, undergraduates of exceptional ability and motivation may in some cases engage in graduate work with the object of qualifying for the simultaneous award of the bachelor's and master's degrees at the end of four years.

Students may select either a departmental major or an area major. The departmental majors attract those who wish to specialize in a particular discipline. The area majors are interdepartmental in nature and are broader and more flexible than most departmental majors. The area majors are also adaptable for students who plan to enter business, law, medicine, or theology. Johns Hopkins has an extremely flexible program. There are no required freshman courses. All students must fulfill distribution requirements as well as the requirements for their major; the distribution requirements include a writing course. In most majors, 120 credits are required for graduation. Johns Hopkins has a 4-1-4 calendar.

The University offers the Army ROTC program on campus and the Air Force ROTC program in cooperation with the University of Maryland College Park.

Off-Campus Arrangements

If qualified, a student may undertake a program for study abroad, normally during the junior year. The School of Arts and Sciences also offers a one-year program of study for selected upper-level undergraduates at the Bologna Center of the Johns Hopkins University in Bologna, Italy. The University participates in a cooperative program with the following colleges in the

Baltimore area: Goucher College, Loyola College, Morgan State University, College of Notre Dame of Maryland, Towson State University, Baltimore Hebrew University, and Maryland Institute, College of Art. Undergraduates may also take courses at the other divisions of the Johns Hopkins University, including the Peabody Conservatory, the School of Nursing, the School of Public Health, the School of Advanced International Studies, the School of Continuing Studies, and the School of Medicine.

Academic Facilities

The University's major library collection is housed in the Milton S. Eisenhower Library on the Homewood campus. Not only is this the University's major research, teaching, and cultural resource, but the quality and quantity of its collections (2.3 million volumes) and services rank it as one of the country's major research libraries as well. The University's other libraries are the Welch Medical Library and the Library of the School of Advanced International Studies in Washington, D.C. Evergreen House contains the majority of the University's rare books, including incunabula, editions with fine bindings, products of famous printers, and several special subject collections. Host systems and microcomputer terminal access and user support are provided by Homewood Academic Computing. Host systems, including an IBM 3081 running VM/CMS, a VAX 6000/420 running VMS, and a Silicon Graphics server running UNIX, provide users with extensive software offerings and the computation cycles necessary for both instruction and research. Networked to these systems are three terminal rooms that provide a full array of laser and line printers, graphics devices, microcomputers, and terminals. Off-campus access is provided through a 1200-, 2400-, 9600-, and 14,400-baud modem pool.

The Association of Universities for Research in Astronomy (AURA) designated the Homewood campus as the site of the Space Telescope Science Institute. The Institute serves as the ground base for NASA's Space Telescope Project.

Costs

Estimated costs for 2000–01 are $24,930 for tuition, $8185 for room and board, and an estimated $1600 for books and personal expenses. Travel expenses vary.

Financial Aid

Financial aid is based on demonstrated eligibility, as determined by the Free Application for Federal Student Aid (FAFSA) and the Hopkins Financial Aid Form. Financial aid programs include Hopkins scholarships, Federal Pell Grants, Federal Supplemental Educational Opportunity Grants, Federal Perkins Loans, Federal Stafford Student Loans, and Federal Work-Study Program awards. The application deadline for freshman applicants is February 1. Students are notified of their financial aid award at the time of their acceptance. Approximately 60 percent of the students receive financial assistance. Students must reapply for financial aid each year with the FAFSA and the Johns Hopkins Supplemental Application.

Johns Hopkins also awards scholarships through Merit Program Scholarships and the National Achievement Scholarship Program for Outstanding Negro Students, as well as through ROTC. To be considered for the approximately seventeen Hodson Trust Scholarships, which are based on merit and provide $17,000 toward tuition per year, students must be nominated by their high school counselor.

Faculty

The University's intellectual reputation is based on the strength of its faculty, of whom 99 percent hold a doctorate. The student-faculty ratio is 8:1 in the G. W. C. Whiting School of Engineering and 10:1 in the School of Arts and Sciences. The well-known professors at Johns Hopkins teach both undergraduate and graduate students, which means that students receive a great deal of personal attention, both in and out of the classroom. Hopkins has a large number of notable professors, including Alice McDermott (professor of writing seminars), winner of the 1998 National Book Award for Fiction; Saul Roseman (professor of biology), a molecular biologist, who is a principal authority on the biochemistry of complex carbohydrates and on cell membrane functioning and serves as a consultant to the American Cancer Society and the National Academy of Science; and Charles O'Melia (professor of geography and environmental engineering), who specializes in aquatic chemistry, water and wastewater treatment, and modeling of natural surfaces and subsurface waters and is a member of the National Academy of Engineers. Faculty members are always accessible to advise and assist students and to work with them on independent research projects.

Student Government

Johns Hopkins students enjoy the benefits of a well-organized and far-reaching student government, which is led by a powerful Student Council. The council is composed of elected class representatives and officers, but it relies on the active participation of many students in its numerous committees, boards, and commissions. Through the Student Activities Commission, the University encourages initiative and independence by giving students full responsibility and control of funds for various clubs and organizations.

Admission Requirements

In choosing from a large number of applicants, the University selects those men and women who will benefit from a Johns Hopkins education. A student's intellectual interests and accomplishments are of primary importance, and the Admissions Committee carefully examines each applicant's scholastic record, standardized test results, and recommendations from secondary school officials and other sources about the student's character, intellectual curiosity, seriousness of purpose, and range of extracurricular involvement. Scores on the SAT I and three SAT II: Subject Tests, one of which must be the Writing Test, are required; however, ACT scores are acceptable in lieu of these. The secondary school report and an essay must also be submitted. Every year, the University enrolls a first-year class of approximately 980 men and women from all parts of the United States and a number of other countries. In addition, transfer students from other colleges and universities are admitted to the sophomore and junior classes.

Advanced-standing credit is granted for college-level work completed at an accredited college or through the Advanced Placement Program.

Application and Information

The application deadline is January 1. Notification is given by April 15. Johns Hopkins has an early admission policy under which students who have accelerated their high school preparation and are ready to undertake full-time university studies before completing high school may apply. Also, if applicants consider Hopkins their first choice, they may apply under the early decision plan. This requires that the application be filed by November 15. Students are notified of the decision of the Admissions Office by December 15. Accepted students who wish to postpone their college studies for one year after graduation from high school may do so provided that they notify the director of admissions and submit the nonrefundable $600 deposit by May 1.

Director of Admissions
140 Garland Hall
Johns Hopkins University
3400 North Charles Street
Baltimore, Maryland 21218
Telephone: 410-516-8171
E-mail: gotojhu@jhu.edu
World Wide Web: http://apply.jhu.edu

JOHNSON & WALES UNIVERSITY
PROVIDENCE, RHODE ISLAND

The University

Founded in Providence in 1914, Johnson & Wales University (J&W) is a private, career-oriented institution offering programs that are geared to the success of a range of students. The University's 12,338 students attend classes at campuses in Providence, Rhode Island; Charleston, South Carolina; Norfolk, Virginia; North Miami, Florida; Denver, Colorado; and Worcester, Massachusetts. Most are recent graduates of high school business, college-preparatory, and vocational/technical programs, representing fifty states and eighty-one countries. The academic focus of the University is on two- and four-year degree programs in business, food service, hospitality, and technology. Graduate programs in accounting, educational leadership, hospitality administration, international business, organization and management, teaching, and teacher certification are also offered.

Students are involved in a variety of extracurricular activities. The Student Activities Office and fraternities and sororities are among the many groups that schedule social functions throughout the academic year. Sports and fitness programs include aerobics, baseball, basketball, soccer, tennis, and volleyball.

The University maintains eleven residence halls. Student services include academic counseling and testing, a tutorial center, and health services. The University's Career Development Office provides extensive career planning and placement services, including a telephone hireline. Since 1979, 98 percent of J&W's graduates from the fifty states seeking employment within 60 days of graduation have been employed within that time.

Johnson & Wales is accredited by the New England Association of Schools and Colleges and is accredited by the Accrediting Council for Independent Colleges and Schools. The court reporting program is approved by the National Court Reporters Association. The hospitality programs in Providence are accredited by the Accreditation Commission for Programs in Hospitality Administration.

Location

The urban location of the University's Providence, Rhode Island, campus enables students to take advantage of internship and part-time work activities offered by the city's many nearby business and community groups and government agencies. The Charleston, South Carolina campus is located in the Port City Center of that historic city, which is home to numerous special events each year. The Norfolk, Virginia campus is in the heart of the Hampton Roads area. Norfolk is one of Virginia's most accessible cities, near to the many yearly festivals and activities of the region. In North Miami, Florida, the J&W campus is a short trip from the sun and fun of Fort Lauderdale and the culture and diversity of Miami. All of Johnson & Wales' city campuses retain a small-town feel and easy accessibility to students.

Majors and Degrees

Johnson & Wales University's Providence campus offers Bachelor of Science degree programs in accounting; baking and pastry arts; court reporting; criminal justice; culinary arts; culinary nutrition; direct response retailing; electronics engineering; entrepreneurship; equine business management; equine business management/riding; financial services management; food marketing; food service entrepreneurship; food service management; hospitality management; hotel management; information science; international business; international hotel and tourism management; management; marketing; marketing communication; paralegal studies; retail marketing and management; sports/entertainment/event management; travel-tourism management; Web management and Internet commerce; and Web site development.

The Associate in Science degree is awarded in accounting, advertising/communications, applied computer science, business administration, communications, computer drafting, computer/business applications, court reporting (legal assistant studies), criminal justice, electronics engineering, electronics technology, entrepreneurship, equine business management, equine studies, fashion merchandising, financial services management, food and beverage management, hotel management, management, marketing, paralegal studies, recreation/leisure management, restaurant management, retailing, sales management, and travel-tourism management.

The Associate in Applied Science degree is awarded in culinary arts and in baking and pastry arts. In its Continuing Education division, Johnson & Wales' Providence campus also offers certificate programs in computer-aided drafting and paralegal studies (a bachelor's degree is required for acceptance into the paralegal studies program), diploma programs in baking and pastry arts and culinary arts, and associate and bachelor's degrees in electrical engineering technology and mechanical engineering technology.

The University's campus in Charleston, South Carolina, offers Bachelor of Science degree programs in food service management, hospitality management, hospitality sales and meeting management, and hotel-restaurant/institutional management. It also offers the Associate in Applied Science degree in baking and pastry arts, culinary arts, food and beverage management, hotel-restaurant management, restaurant/institutional management, and travel-tourism management. The campus at Norfolk, Virginia, offers associate degrees in culinary arts and food and beverage management (first year only) and a one-year certificate program in culinary arts. The North Miami, Florida, campus offers associate degrees in accounting, baking and pastry arts, business administration, criminal justice, culinary arts, fashion merchandising, food and beverage management, hotel-restaurant management, management, marketing, restaurant/institutional management, and travel-tourism management and bachelor's degrees in accounting, culinary arts, food service management, hospitality management, hotel-restaurant institutional management, management, and marketing. The Denver campus offers associate's degrees in business administration, culinary arts, and marketing. Bachelor's degrees are offered in culinary nutrition, food service management, international business, management, and marketing.

Academic Program

Johnson & Wales University offers programs in business, food service, hospitality, and technology within an academic structure of three 11-week terms. Classes generally meet four days a week, Monday through Thursday. The "upside-down" curriculum of the University provides immediate concentration in the student's chosen major. The associate degree is awarded after two years of successful study, at which time the student may continue studies toward the baccalaureate degree or seek immediate employment. Two degrees, the associate and the bachelor's, can result from a complete four-year course of study.

Learning by doing is an important part of career training at J&W, and many programs include laboratory studies as well as formal internship requirements. Special advanced placement programs are featured for high school seniors with exceptional skills in culinary arts or baking and pastry arts. In addition, the University grants credit and/or a waiver of certain courses on the basis of CLEP and challenge examinations. All degree candidates must successfully complete the required number of courses and/or quarter credit hours, as prescribed in the various curricula, with a minimum average of 2.0.

Off-Campus Arrangements

Learning at Johnson & Wales University is not limited to the classroom. Culinary arts majors enjoy selective career co-ops with prestigious food service establishments that include, among others, Legal Sea Foods, Boston Harbor Hotel in Massachusetts; Keystone Resorts in Colorado; Walt Disney World in Florida; the Ritz-Carlton in Washington, D.C.; and Trump Hotels & Casino in New Jersey. The hotel-restaurant management program features an internship at the Johnson & Wales Inn and the Radisson Airport Hotel, which are full-service hotel complexes owned and operated by the University (the Radisson is a corporate franchise). Fashion merchandising and retailing majors spend their eleven-week internships at Gladding's, a women's specialty store also owned by the University. Students majoring in travel-tourism management participate in an internship at American Express Travel Service, the University's travel agency, while optional selective career co-ops are available with cooperating businesses for students in other programs. Most internships and co-ops are one term in duration and carry 13.5 quarter hours of credit. A student foreign exchange program is available to culinary arts majors and a term-abroad program to senior hospitality majors.

Academic Facilities

The facilities of the Providence campus are located throughout the intimate state of Rhode Island and in nearby Massachusetts. The downtown Providence campus is home to the University's College of Business, Hospitality College, and School of Technology. A number of academic and residential facilities are located at this campus, as well as several training facilities. The Harborside Campus, located a short distance away and also in Providence, houses the University's College of Culinary Arts. This campus has four student residence halls as well as specialized classrooms and laboratories, production kitchens, bakeshops, dining rooms, a storeroom, and meat-cutting facilities. This campus is also home to the new University Recreation and Athletic Center, a student activities office, a bookstore, a gymnasium, a dining center, a snack bar, and an arcade.

The academic facilities of the Charleston, South Carolina campus are housed in a five-story brick building constructed in 1881 as part of the Reconstruction. Facilities include academic classrooms, demonstration/production kitchens, bakeshops, dining rooms, a storeroom, a mixology laboratory, a resource center, computer laboratories, and a public training food service facility.

The Norfolk, Virginia campus is located in the Westgate Center in the Norfolk Commerce Park and includes several classrooms, production/demonstration kitchens, a bakeshop, and a resource center. The University provides transportation to and from student residence facilities.

In North Miami, Florida, the campus is located at a former hospital and office complex. There are academic, administrative, and residential facilities and the building has been converted to include a number of classrooms, production/demonstration kitchens, a bakeshop, and a specially designed conference center.

The Denver, Colorado, campus, located in the Park Hill neighborhood, combines old-world charm with the latest technological resources, including stately turn-of-the-century buildings and newer student centers, in a quiet park landscape. The traditional residential campus is fully wired with computers in every classroom and laboratory.

Costs

Tuition at the Providence campus for 2000–01 is $13,275–$16,320. The basic four-day room-and-board plan is $5970–$7290. An optional weekend meal plan is available for $735. Each student is also charged a general fee of $525, and there is an orientation fee of $140 for new students. Books and supplies are estimated at $600 to $800 per year, depending upon the program. The Guaranteed Tuition Plan guarantees students no tuition increases while they are continuously enrolled at the University.

Tuition and fees vary at other campuses. Students should consult the respective campus catalogs for further details.

Financial Aid

Johnson & Wales students are eligible to apply for a variety of financial aid programs, including the Federal Pell Grant, Federal Supplemental Educational Opportunity Grant, Federal Work-Study, and Federal Perkins Loan programs. They are also eligible for University-based student scholarship and loan programs and state-supported grants and scholarships. In the past, approximately 80 percent of the University's entering students have received some sort of financial assistance. Students must submit the Free Application for Federal Student Aid (FAFSA) to the Federal Student Aid Processor to be considered for financial aid. Although there is no deadline, early application is strongly suggested for full consideration.

Faculty

The University's 325 full-time and 149 part-time undergraduate faculty members (all campuses) are oriented toward instruction rather than research. Many are chosen for their professional experience in business, culinary arts, and hospitality services. The student-faculty ratio is 30:1.

Student Government

Student Government Association (SGA) representatives serve as the link among students, faculty, and administration to bring student body concerns to the awareness of the University community.

Admission Requirements

Johnson & Wales University seeks students who have a true desire to succeed. Academic qualifications are important, but an applicant's motivation and interest in doing well are given special consideration. Graduation from high school or equivalent credentials are required for admission. It is recommended that students applying for admission into the culinary arts and baking and pastry arts programs have some prior education or experience in food service. Although no tests are required, all applicants are encouraged to submit scores from the SAT I or ACT. High school juniors may apply for early admission under the ACCESS Program. Transfer students are required to submit official high school and college transcripts and to have a minimum GPA of 2.0. Credits to be transferred from other institutions are evaluated on the basis of their equivalent at Johnson & Wales.

Application and Information

Johnson & Wales does not require an application fee. After submitting the application, the student is responsible for requesting that appropriate transcripts be forwarded to the Admissions Office of the University. While there is no deadline, students are advised to apply as early as possible before the intended date of enrollment to ensure full consideration of their application. Applications are accepted for terms beginning in September, December, and March and for the summer sessions.

Inquiries and applications should be addressed to:

Kenneth DiSaia
Dean of Admissions
Johnson & Wales University
8 Abbott Park Place
Providence, Rhode Island 02903-3703

Telephone: 401-598-1000
800-DIAL-JWU (toll-free)
Fax: 401-598-2948
E-mail: admissions@jwu.edu
World Wide Web: http://www.jwu.edu

JOHNSON C. SMITH UNIVERSITY
CHARLOTTE, NORTH CAROLINA

The University

Johnson C. Smith University (JCSU), established in 1867 as a college for African Americans, is a small coeducational university under private control and formerly affiliated with the Presbyterian Church (U.S.A.). The general purpose of the University is to provide an environment in which men and women may realize as fully as possible their individual potential for intellectual, social, spiritual, emotional, and physical growth and well-being. The University is a fully accredited member of the Southern Association of Colleges and Schools, and its Department of Education is nationally accredited by the National Council for Accreditation of Teacher Education (NCATE). The campus buildings and grounds occupy 100 acres in the city of Charlotte. There are forty-six buildings, including the University chapel, administration and classroom buildings, modern residence halls, faculty houses, and the Honors College Center.

The University provides an environment in which students can fulfill their physical, social, cultural, spiritual, and other personal needs and in which they can develop a compelling sense of social and civic responsibility for leadership and service in a dynamic, multicultural society. Currently, there are 621 men and 925 women enrolled at the University. Students hail from the majority of the fifty states and several other countries. At the end of the freshman year, about 75 percent of the freshmen register for further study at the University. Fifteen percent of the University's graduates go on to graduate or professional school. More than 90 percent of the students reside on campus.

In addition to ten honor societies that are open to qualified students, there are numerous opportunities for social, religious, and cultural activities. Ten percent of the women and 11 percent of the men belong to the four sororities and four fraternities on campus. Students may participate in varsity basketball, football, golf, tennis, track, and volleyball. Intramurals are offered in basketball, flag football, recreational games, tennis, volleyball, and water sports. The modern gymnasium contains an Olympic-size pool. In 1995, Mecklenburg County voters approved a bond referendum for construction of a $2.3-million Olympic-size track, which, through a public-private partnership, has been built with county money on University-owned land and will be operated for the school and the community with JCSU funds.

Johnson C. Smith University is an Equal Opportunity/Affirmative Action institution.

Location

Charlotte, the largest city in the Carolinas, with a population of more than 500,000, is a commercial, banking, and cultural center of the South. The city has an impressive skyline, a revitalized uptown, numerous industries and factories, and a diverse residential community. The area is rich in historic landmarks. Charlotte offers all the cultural and recreational facilities of any large city, including professional and other sports events; excellent shopping and dining facilities; rock, popular, jazz, and classical music concerts; theater; art; and exceptional gardens. The area is served by an international airport and Amtrak railway service. Major highways provide easy access to beach and mountain areas.

Majors and Degrees

Johnson C. Smith University offers the Bachelor of Arts, Bachelor of Science, and Bachelor of Social Work degrees. Majors are offered in applied mathematics, biology, business administration, chemistry, communication arts, computer engineering, computer science/engineering, computer science/information systems, criminal justice, economics, elementary education, English, English education, general science, health education, history, liberal arts, mathematics, mathematics education, physical education, political science, psychology, social science, social studies education, social work, and sociology. Preprofessional programs are offered in dentistry and medicine. In addition, a student may minor in most areas where majors are offered, as well as in African-American and African studies, French, prelaw, and Spanish. Students may also complete courses in military science as part of either the Army ROTC program or the Air Force ROTC program.

Johnson C. Smith University, through a collaborative relationship with several other institutions, offers programs leading to degrees in civil, electrical, and mechanical engineering.

Academic Program

To be eligible for a bachelor's degree, students must complete a minimum of 122 hours with a minimum grade point average of 2.0 overall and in the major area and must satisfy all requirements of the curriculum of the Liberal Studies Program. Those Liberal Studies requirements include successful completion of a Competency Testing Program, the Learning Across the Curriculum Program, and a senior investigative paper. A minimum of the last 32 of the required graduation hours must be earned at the University.

The University offers the following special programs designed to assist students to both build upon their current understandings and expand into new areas of inquiry: the Teaching and Learning Center provides various academic support programs to aid students in their interactions with the academic demands of the college curriculum; the Honors College provides specially designed curricular and extracurricular experiences for students who are highly motivated, superbly prepared, and sufficiently dedicated to the highest levels of scholarship and academic achievement; the Division of Lifelong Learning provides college credit and personal enrichment courses to meet the needs of adult students through evening courses and/or workshops; and the program in international affairs provides both a formal program of study in various approaches to the analysis of international relations and opportunities for international educational experiences.

Academic Facilities

Construction on a new track and field academic sports complex is expected to be completed in fall 2000. The James B. Duke Memorial Library, a fully automated facility with more than 115,000 volumes and subscriptions to 252 periodicals, has been completely renovated and was dedicated in March 2000. The $7.7-million project was completed in summer 1999.

Library resource materials include materials directly related to classroom work as well as general and recreational reading materials. The collection includes valuable reference books, periodicals, pamphlets, and audiovisual materials. Books and periodicals that are not available in the James B. Duke Memorial Library may be obtained through interlibrary loans.

The Rufus Patterson Perry Science Building and the George E. Davis Science Hall contain twelve institutional laboratories, five research laboratories, five lecture rooms, an auditorium, and a computer center. The science complex was designed to provide facilities for high-quality training in the traditional subjects as well as opportunities for research on subjects of current interest. The equipment available for instruction and research includes a superconducting 300-MHz Fourier Transform (FT)-Nuclear Magnetic Resonance spectrometer with multinuclear detection and variable temperature capabilities, computer-controlled UV-visible-near-IR spectrometers, FT-infrared spectrometers, gas-liquid and high-pressure liquid chromatographs, various incubators and biological hoods for providing up-to-date instruction and state-of-the-art research in biology and chemistry and related fields.

The University completed construction in 1997 on a state-of-the-art technology center. The $2.6-million facility has educational, research, and community outreach components. A facility with nine laboratories (analog electronics, digital electronics and microprocessors, telecommunications and computer networks, digital signal processing, automatic control and robotics, computer graphics, numerical analysis and high-level programming languages, commercial data processing, and general computing), the Technology Center provides technical support and expertise to faculty members and students in all disciplines as new technologies are infused into the University curriculum. Special emphasis on research in the areas of applied mathematics, computer science, and computer and electrical engineering characterize the recently completed facility.

Computer science classrooms, located in the Rufus Patterson Perry Science Building, were designed to provide hands-on experience for students training for various computer fields; to aid in the instruction of chemistry, physics, biology, economics, psychology, business administration, and mathematics; and to provide assistance in research activities. Many biology and chemistry majors benefit from courses in computer science and programming. The University Computer Center, also housed in the Rufus Patterson Perry Science Building, contains an IBM System/AS400, which is used for administrative computing. A state-of-the-art computer room, housing eighteen computers for student use, operates in Biddle Memorial Hall. Computers are also available for student use in the Honors College Center, residence halls, the University Library, and all classroom buildings. Additionally, all departments have one or more microcomputer systems to support the instructional and research activities of the unit.

Costs

For 1999–2000, tuition, fees, room, and board totaled $13,849 per year for all students. Residents of the Honors College Center and the two newest residence facilities pay additional housing fees.

Financial Aid

Loans, grants, and scholarships are available and are awarded on the basis of need or special achievement. In recent years, the average amount of aid awarded to members of the freshman class has been $3500 per student. Forms of aid include Federal Pell Grants, Federal Supplemental Educational Opportunity Grants, Federal Perkins Loans, Federal Stafford Student Loans, Federal Work-Study awards, North Carolina state grants (for North Carolina residents only) and institutional awards. There are also a variety of scholarships and other aid programs. In order to be considered for financial aid, students must file the Free Application for Federal Student Aid (FAFSA). Applications are available at high school guidance offices or through the University's Student Financial Aid Office. All students are urged to file applications as early in the year as the forms are made available. Applications for financial aid should be filed by May 1; the school code (002936) should be included on application. The University does not use an institutional financial aid application.

A limited number of academic scholarships (Duke Scholars) are offered in the freshman year, primarily to participants in the Honors Program. Recipients are selected from high school seniors who earned high scores on the SAT I and who have a minimum grade point average of 3.0.

For outstanding students in the sciences, the Minority Biomedical Research Support Program and other programs provide a variety of services and salaried positions during the academic year and summer. These students participate in research projects and seminars and attend meetings of national scientific importance.

Faculty

The University has 89 faculty members, approximately 75 percent of whom hold doctorates. The student-faculty ratio is 17:1.

Student Government

Opportunities for student participation in policymaking are provided through membership in the Student Government Association, the Student Christian Association, the Residence Halls Council, the Pan Hellenic Council, and the Board of Trustees.

Admission Requirements

Candidates for admission should be graduates of accredited high schools and should rank in the upper 50 percent of their class and have a minimum average of C. They should have completed 16 academic units, consisting of at least 4 in English, 2 in mathematics, 2 in social science, 2 in science (at least 1 in a laboratory science), and 6 in electives. The recommendations and reputation of the high school; the student's record in extracurricular activities, athletics, and achievement in advanced placement or honors courses; evidence of leadership potential; and impressions made during an optional interview are all factors that affect the admission decision. Students are required to have the official report of their SAT I or ACT scores forwarded directly to the University. The University accepts approximately 40 percent of the students who apply for admission.

Application and Information

Applications for admission should be submitted by June 15 for full consideration. Each student who is accepted must pay a $100 nonrefundable matriculation fee and a nonrefundable $100 room reservation fee to reserve his or her place in the class.

Application and financial aid forms may be obtained by contacting:

Director of Admissions
Johnson C. Smith University
100 Beatties Ford Road
Charlotte, North Carolina 28216-5398
Telephone: 704-378-1010
           800-782-7303 (toll-free)
E-mail: webmaster@jcsu.edu
World Wide Web: http://www.jcsu.edu

JOHNSON STATE COLLEGE
JOHNSON, VERMONT

The College

Founded in 1828, Johnson State College served as a school for the training of teachers until the 1960s, when it expanded into the liberal arts and the sciences. The current enrollment is more than 1,500 men and women. Sixty-five percent of the College's students are Vermonters, with the balance coming from twenty-three states and ten other countries. The campus has modern facilities, including a new state-of-the-art Library and Learning Center, Dewey Campus Center, the beautiful Dibden Center for the Fine and Performing Arts, a visual arts building, an excellent science facility, a health/athletics complex, and well-equipped residence halls and College apartments. The College is surrounded by 350 acres of meadowland and forest, and there are two ponds. Located on a hill overlooking the village of Johnson, the campus commands a breathtaking view of the Green Mountains. The College is accredited by the New England Association of Schools and Colleges and is approved by the Vermont State Board of Higher Education.

At the graduate level, the College offers the Master of Arts in Education degree in administration and supervision, early childhood education, elementary curricula, reading and language arts, special education of the gifted and talented, and special education of the handicapped; the Master of Arts in counseling; and the Master of Fine Arts in studio arts.

More than thirty clubs and organizations provide a variety of student activities. These include *Basement Medicine* (the student newspaper), *Stoneboat* (the literary magazine), the Dance Ensemble, the Theater Club, the radio station (WJSC-FM), the College Concert Band, and the Outing, Earth Awareness, Snowboarding, and International Clubs. Varsity athletic competition is available for women in basketball, cross-country running, soccer, softball, and tennis and for men in basketball, cross-country running, lacrosse, soccer, and tennis. Many intramural and club sports, including indoor soccer, baseball, golf, hockey, lacrosse, rugby, swimming, and volleyball, are also available. Johnson State College's health education/sports complex includes two weightlifting areas, a basketball court, a gymnasium, racquetball courts, a swimming pool, a training room, and a human performance lab. Also on campus are outdoor tennis courts, cross-country running and ski trails, a snowboard park, and large playing fields. The gymnasium and outdoor athletic facilities also provide recreational outlets for many individuals in the campus community. The Stearns Center houses the Base Lodge Snackbar, a post office, the Summit Book Store, and a spacious dining room. The College also has a Counseling Center, an Advising Center, and a Career Resource Center.

Location

The College is just 20 minutes from Stowe, the ski capital of the East; 45 minutes from Burlington, Vermont's largest city; and 90 minutes from Montreal, Canada. Other attractions near the College are Smugglers' Notch ski area, Jay Peak ski area, Ben and Jerry's ice cream factory, and Lake Champlain. The College can be reached by rail (Amtrak) or air (Burlington International Airport).

Majors and Degrees

Johnson State College offers major academic programs leading to the Bachelor of Arts or Bachelor of Science degree in anthropology/sociology, art, athletic training, biology, business management, drama and theater, English, environmental sciences, health sciences, history, hospitality and tourism management, journalism, mathematics, music, outdoor education, performing arts, performing arts management, physical education, political science, and psychology. The Bachelor of Fine Arts degree is offered in studio arts and writing.

The Bachelor of Arts or Bachelor of Science degree leading to state teacher certification is offered in art education (K–12), dance secondary education, elementary education, health and physical education (K–12), life sciences (biology) secondary education, mathematics secondary education, middle school education, music education (K–12), physical sciences (chemistry) secondary education, and social studies.

Associate of Arts or Associate of Science degrees are offered in accounting information systems, business information systems (computers), business management, and general studies.

Certificate programs, leading to business certification, are offered in accounting, French for business majors, and small-business management.

Minors are available in anthropology/sociology, arts management, biology, business, chemistry, dance, environmental education, French, gender studies, history, literature, mathematics, music, natural resources, political science, prelaw, psychology, Spanish, studio art, and theater.

Academic Program

The Johnson State curriculum provides students with a general liberal arts background and the opportunity for career preparation in a specific area. All students in four-year programs are required to complete at least 120 credit hours in the selected program of study. Those studying for the associate degree must complete at least 60 semester hours of credit in the selected program of study. Students may transfer internally from two-year to four-year programs.

Transfer credit is awarded for college courses in which a grade of C– or above was earned. Accepted transfer students receive a credit evaluation.

The academic year consists of fall and spring semesters of fifteen weeks each and a six-week summer session. The College offers courses in the evening and on weekends through the External Degree Program.

Off-Campus Arrangements

Johnson State College provides internship opportunities in all degree programs, including student teaching for education majors.

The College offers study abroad opportunities through the National Student Exchange, New England–Quebec Student Exchange, and Semester in London programs.

Academic Facilities

The 350-acre, hilltop campus houses modern, well-equipped buildings. College facilities include an art gallery, a greenhouse, art studios, dance studios, the Visual Arts Center, three computer centers, a library, a student center, the Child Development Center, and the Dibden Center for the Fine and Performing Arts, which contains a theater. The new Library and

Learning Center contains more than 96,000 volumes, an audiovisual department, microfilm and microfiche units, government documents, periodicals, journals, records, the Vermont Room, the Art Room, the Ellsworth International Room, and the Children's Library. The Babcock Nature Preserve, a 1,000-acre tract of forests and ponds, serves as an outdoor laboratory for scientific and educational research.

Costs

Tuition and fees for the academic year 1999–2000 for Vermont residents were $5009 and for nonresidents, $10,505. Room and board expenses were $5298. Costs are subject to change for 2000–01.

Financial Aid

Sixty-seven percent of Johnson's students receive financial assistance from federal, state, College, or other sources. Grants, loans, and work-study jobs are available for qualified students. Applicants for financial aid should file the Free Application for Federal Student Aid (FAFSA) by March 1 of the year preceding anticipated enrollment. All financial aid awards are based on need. The College offers renewable academic scholarships for both freshmen and transfers. Special scholarships are also available.

Faculty

The full-time faculty at Johnson consists of 65 men and women, 91 percent of whom hold a Ph.D. or equivalent degree. Adjunct faculty members, many of whom are local professionals, complement the full-time faculty. The student-faculty ratio is 17:1. Each student has a faculty member serving as an academic adviser.

Student Government

The Johnson State College Student Association is a vital and active organization that has a strong voice in College affairs. Student representatives are elected to the Student Assembly, which helps plan curriculum and program developments. The association coordinates student social and cultural activities, including dances and numerous clubs.

Admission Requirements

Admission to Johnson State College is granted to applicants who have demonstrated the potential to succeed at the college level. They are evaluated on the basis of their high school transcripts, letters of recommendation, standardized test scores (SAT I or ACT), and class rank. The College emphasizes course selection, grades, and participation in extracurricular activities in reviewing applications.

All candidates should successfully complete a college-preparatory program that includes 4 years of high school English, 3 years of mathematics, 3 years of social science, and 2 years of science (one course with a laboratory).

Applicants who do not qualify for regular admission may receive a conditional acceptance to the College.

A campus visit and an interview are strongly recommended.

Application and Information

The College has a rolling admission policy and processes applications throughout the year. However, high school students seeking fall enrollment are encouraged to apply early in their senior year. The College admits first-year and transfer students regardless of their state of residence. Notification dates are also rolling. Students may enter at the beginning of the fall or spring semester.

The student's application file is complete when the following items have been received: a completed application form, a $30 nonrefundable application fee, a transcript from the high school and any colleges previously attended, a writing sample, standardized test scores, and a reference from a teacher, a college adviser, or an employer. An enrollment deposit of $200 is required by May 1 or within two weeks of notification of acceptance if the applicant applies after May 1.

For application forms and further information, students should contact:

Penny P. Howrigan
Associate Dean of Enrollment Services
Johnson State College
337 College Hill
Johnson, Vermont 05656
Telephone: 802-635-1219
              800-635-2356 (toll-free)
Fax: 802-635-1230
E-mail: jscapply@badger.jsc.vsc.edu
World Wide Web: http://www.jsc.vsc.edu

A view from campus overlooking the town of Johnson.

JUDSON COLLEGE
ELGIN, ILLINOIS

The College

Judson College is an evangelical Christian college of the liberal arts, sciences, and professions. Founded in 1963, Judson College was named for the first missionary from North America, Adoniram Judson, and the spirit of Christian service that he embodied is very evident on Judson's campus. The College offers residential living in an environment that encourages and supports Christian growth. At Judson, it is believed that all truth is God's truth, and that the honest search for truth in any subject area will lead a student to God the Creator.

Judson's students have chosen the College for a number of reasons, but two are consistently mentioned: the vibrant Christian community and a liberal arts curriculum that is practical. They expect to be encouraged to grow in their faith, while being prepared to succeed in a career. The College expects students to be actively involved in their education both inside and outside of the classroom.

Student activities are coordinated by the Student Senate and involve many on- and off-campus opportunities. Concerts, films, dramatic productions, athletic contests, banquets, and outings to Chicago all make for a complete social calendar. Students also may choose to be involved in choir, chamber singers, the newspaper (*Eagle Outlook*), the yearbook (*Lantern*), intramurals, Christian ministry groups, academic clubs, service clubs, and the international club (United Cultures of Judson).

Judson is a member of the NAIA, NCCAA, and the Chicagoland Collegiate Athletic Conference (CCAC). Intercollegiate sports include baseball, basketball, cross-country, soccer, softball, tennis, and volleyball. The intramural program includes basketball, flag football, softball, volleyball, and other sports. The Lindner Fitness Center offers three basketball courts, two racquetball courts, an elevated running track, a Nautilus room, and a free-weight room.

The present College enrollment is approximately 1,300 students. Sixty-five percent of the more than 810 traditional students live in residence halls; married student housing is also available. The remaining 500 students are enrolled in the Division of Continuing Education. Forty-one states are represented on campus, as are twenty countries.

Location

Judson College is located in Elgin, Illinois, a northwest suburb only 40 minutes from Chicago. The scenic campus covers 84 acres of rolling hills nestled alongside the Fox River. This location provides the maximum opportunity for internships and employment. With all of Greater Chicagoland at the College's doorstep, the social opportunities are innumerable. Similarly, the service and ministry options are boundless.

Majors and Degrees

The College grants the Bachelor of Arts degree in the following majors: architecture (five-year program leading to a master's in architecture in addition to baccalaureate degree), art (pre-master's), biblical studies, biology, business (accounting), business management, chemistry, early childhood education (prekindergarten–grade 3), elementary education (kindergarten–grade 9), English (language and literature), English education (grades 6–12), general art, history, human services, international business, management information systems, marketing, mathematics, mathematics education (grades 6–12), media studies, music, music education (grades 6–12), music ministry, music performance, physical education (grades 6–12), psychology, speech communications, sports management, visual communications (graphic design), worship arts, and youth ministry. International studies, missionary/intercultural studies, and philosophy are available as minors.

Students also may design their own major, with the assistance of an adviser, should they wish to do so.

Preprofessional programs are available in dentistry, law, medicine, nursing, occupational therapy, physical therapy, physician's assistant studies, and seminary studies.

Academic Program

The goal of the College's academic program is to integrate faith and learning. Judson College has instituted a unique program for freshmen that combines small-group mentoring by faculty and staff members and upperclassmen with their college success course. The Bachelor of Arts degree requires completion of 126 semester credit hours. The College operates on a 4:4:1:1 calendar. May post-terms, lasting approximately three weeks, each feature conventional and travel courses. In addition, students may choose to take additional course work offered on an open-entry, open-exit basis through the Customized Learning Center or through Judson online.

Off-Campus Arrangements

Through its affiliation with the Council for Christian Colleges and Universities, Judson provides an opportunity for students to study from two to four months in a variety of settings. Students may earn credit in the American Studies Program in Washington, D.C., by serving as interns and participating in an issue-oriented seminar program. The Latin American Studies Program is located in San Jose, Costa Rica; students live with a Costa Rican family while studying in a wide variety of subject areas. Seminar courses and internships in the film industry are available through the Los Angeles Film Studies Center. For the student who wishes to relate to the Muslim world, study the Arabic language, and serve as an intern, there is the Middle East Studies Program. The Russian Studies Program provides the opportunity to study the Russian language and culture while spending a portion of the time living with a Russian family. In addition to the established summer studies program at Oxford, there are now traditional semester programs available. There is also the Council's new China Studies Program in addition to a separate exchange program, cosponsored by Judson, at Hong Kong Baptist University.

Academic Facilities

The centerpiece of any academic institution is its library. Judson's library contains 118,000 volumes, 8,000 musical scores, 10,000 recordings, and current subscriptions to 520 journals, periodicals, and newspapers. The college is a member of ILCSO, a computer catalog of the holdings of all state universities and many private colleges in Illinois. This network, when combined with OCLC, can provide an additional 39 million titles on a free interlibrary loan basis. Online computer searching is available using Dialog, First Search, and the following CD-ROM products: Compact Disclosure (company reports), Academic Abstracts (index to periodical articles), ERIC (education database), CD-Word (Bible text and concordance), Oxford English Dictionary, Religious and Theological Abstracts, and three online newspapers.

Four computer labs are available for students, which also provide data and Internet access to each residence hall room. The chapel and performance hall are available for services, concerts, and drama productions.

Costs

Tuition and fees for the 2000–01 academic year are $13,990. Room and board are $5360. The cost for books varies dramatically, but students spend an average of $600 per year.

Financial Aid

Scholarships, grants, loans, and church matching grants are available for students who need assistance in meeting college expenses. Academic scholarships are available to incoming freshmen and transfer students who meet the necessary standards. Talent scholarships are also available in athletics, art, communications (newspaper, yearbook, video), drama, and music. In addition, on-campus jobs are available and the local community has a high number of well-paying options available to college students. More than 90 percent of Judson's students receive some form of financial aid.

Faculty

Judson has an outstanding, creative, and dedicated faculty. Faculty members exemplify high standards of academic excellence in the context of the Christian faith. They place a high priority on teaching and relating personally with students, and the favorable student-faculty ratio of 16:1 facilitates such mentoring relationships.

Student Government

A wide range of opportunities to develop leadership ability are available to students through involvement in the following student government committees: Academic Life, Communications, Community Outreach, Concert, Elections, Homecoming, Missions, Social Activities, and Spiritual Life.

Admission Requirements

Judson seeks students with academic ability, personal promise, strong motivation, and high moral character. The following are the minimum standards for regular admission as a freshman: class rank above the 50th percentile, composite ACT of 18 or composite SAT of 840, and GPA of 2.0 (on a 4.0 scale). Transfer students must have a 2.0 (on a 4.0 scale) for regular admission. Applicants who do not meet these standards may be admitted on probation after being evaluated by the Admissions Review Committee.

Application and Information

An application packet or information on visiting the College can be obtained from the Admissions Office. Judson uses a rolling admission procedure, which means that decisions are mailed to applicants within a short period of time after all application materials have been received.

For further information, students should telephone, write, or e-mail:

Director of Admissions
Judson College
1151 North State Street
Elgin, Illinois 60123
Telephone: 847-695-2500 Ext. 2310
              800-879-5376 (toll-free)
E-mail: admissions@judson-il.edu

Judson College's Lindner Fitness Center.

JUNIATA COLLEGE
HUNTINGDON, PENNSYLVANIA

The College

Juniata College is an independent, coeducational college of liberal arts and sciences, founded in 1876 by members of the Church of the Brethren to prepare individuals "for the useful occupations of life." Juniata College holds a place of national prominence in higher education. Recent studies rank the College highly in the percentage of graduates that eventually earn doctoral degrees; one, in fact, ranked Juniata in the top 10 percent in the nation among all four-year private undergraduate institutions. Juniata's national reputation is strongest in several fields, including chemistry, environmental science and education, health sciences, peace and conflict studies, and prelaw. The College is known for the personal attention it gives students. Each student is assigned 2 faculty advisers, and the average faculty-student ratio is 1:14.

As a community that focuses on the whole person, Juniata recognizes the importance of both curricular and cocurricular aspects of student development. Juniata has bridged the traditional higher education dichotomy between academic affairs and student affairs by merging these two branches of the College, a structural move that integrates the student's total college experience. A Student Development Council composed of both academic affairs and student services staff members meets regularly to coordinate efforts, as staff members cross conventional boundaries to meet student needs.

Location

Juniata is located in Huntingdon, which lies in the scenic Allegheny Mountains of central Pennsylvania. The 110 acres on College Hill have allowed for careful expansion, and the thirty-one buildings blend well with each other and the spaciousness of the campus. Juniata's campus also consists of a 665-acre field station and a 315-acre nature preserve. The surrounding area is suited for many outdoor activities such as swimming, boating, fishing, hunting, skiing, and hiking. Raystown Lake, the largest recreational lake wholly in Pennsylvania, is only 15 minutes from Juniata. Several major cities lie within a short drive of the campus—3 hours to Pittsburgh, Baltimore, and Washington; 4 hours to Philadelphia; and 5 hours to New York City. The nearest commercial airport is in State College, the location of Penn State University. In addition, Huntingdon is on the main U.S. east-west railway line, with travel by train to East and West Coast cities available.

Majors and Degrees

Juniata awards B.A. and B.S. degrees in the arts, humanities, natural sciences, and social sciences. Rather than complete a traditional major, each Juniata student designs a Program of Emphasis (POE) that is tailored to the student's own goals and often crosses departmental lines. Working closely with 2 academic advisers, students select courses for either a designated or an individualized POE. Current areas of study include accounting, anthropology, art (art history; museum studies, with an art history focus; and studio fine arts), biological sciences (biochemistry, biology, botany, ecology, microbiology, molecular and cell physiology, and zoology), business management (international business, management, and marketing), chemistry, communication, computer science, criminal justice, early childhood education, early childhood and special education, economics, elementary education, elementary and special education, English, environmental science, environmental studies, exploratory studies, geology, health communication, history, interdisciplinary studies (humanities, liberal arts, natural sciences, and social sciences) international politics, international studies, languages (French, German, Russian, and Spanish), marine science, mathematics, peace and conflict studies, physics, politics, pre–allied health (biotechnology, cardiovascular technology, cytogenetics, diagnostic imaging/radiography, medical technology, nursing, occupational therapy, and physical therapy), pre-engineering, pre–health professions (dentistry, medicine, optometry, pharmacy, podiatry, and veterinary science), prelaw, preministry, psychology, public administration, secondary education (biology, chemistry, communication, earth and space science, English, French, German, general science, mathematics, physics, social studies, and Spanish), social work, and sociology. The pre–allied health and pre-engineering programs are cooperative programs. A new program in information technology beings in fall 2000. Information technology incorporates business, communication, and computer science to help students meet the technology needs of tomorrow.

Academic Program

Designed to foster individual responsibility, Juniata's flexible and academically rigorous program allows both acquisition of a broad range of knowledge and in-depth examination of a particular field. Almost 60 percent of the students attending Juniata develop their own program through a flexible program of emphasis (POE). The POE allows Juniata students to develop programs in environmental politics/peace studies, premed/theater, and many more.

Students must satisfactorily complete 120 semester credit hours. Writing, computer and bibliographic skills, and college transition issues are addressed in the freshman year. Graduation requirements also include a two-course cultural analysis sequence, advanced communication/writing skills, quantitative studies, social sciences, humanities, international, fine arts, and natural sciences and an optional service learning component. In addition, all students complete a 45–60 credit POE, and many choose to complete an integrative senior project to graduate with distinction.

Many students include independent study and independent research in their POEs. Participation in internships is also encouraged. In fact, 63 percent of the class of 1999 participated in at least one internship throughout their four-year experience; many participated in more than one.

Juniata accepts AP credit for a score of 4 or better on the AP exam. In addition, students with an International Baccalaureate Diploma receive sophomore standing.

Academic Facilities

Juniata's academic programs are facilitated by up-to-date technology, labs, and bibliographic resources. In addition to the College's Academic Computer Center, the campus has high-tech classroom/laboratory and computer labs devoted specifically to business and psychology, education and foreign languages, and writing. A human interaction lab offers students the opportunity to study communication and group interaction. In addition, the College has a distance learning and teleconferencing facility, multimedia classrooms, and a teaching and learning technology center (TLT Center) for both student and faculty member use. The TLT Center was designed to give faculty members and students the resources for utilizing advanced technology in their course work and presentations. In summer 2000, the College breaks ground for the von Liebig Center for Natural Sciences. The $20-million facility will be complete in fall 2002. The original Brumbaugh Ellis Science Center will continue to house the environmental sciences, physical sciences, information technology, mathematics, computer science, and information technology departments.

For research projects, students in the natural sciences use laboratories equipped with sophisticated instrumentation typically reserved for graduate students. The Raystown Field Station, 665 acres that include a complete watershed, serves as an ecology and environmental science laboratory site. Upcoming renovation of

Brumbaugh Science Center ensures that this facility will meet the learning needs of students into the twenty-first century.

Juniata's Beeghly Library provides the College with an online public access catalog that is accessible campuswide and an extensive CD-ROM network.

Costs

For 2000–01, the general fee is $24,650, consisting of tuition of $18,940 and room, board, and fee costs of $5710. There are several special and occasional fees (e.g., for laboratory or studio use, $30–$100).

Financial Aid

The Juniata College Office of Student Financial Planning is committed to building relationships with families striving to meet the long-term investment needs associated with quality education. Juniata succeeds by maximizing available assistance opportunities from Juniata programs as well as state and federal government programs in the form of grants, loans, and work-study initiatives. The College's commitment extends to academic scholarship assistance as well. Juniata offers aggressive scholarship programs designed to recognize and reward academic achievement. Students who exhibit promise of future success may be eligible for academic awards ranging from $5000 to full tuition. Students who wish to be considered for Nomination Scholarships should have their admission applications postmarked no later than January 15 of the senior year.

Juniata representatives work with each family, matching their individual circumstances to all applicable aid programs. For need-based aid, individual plans are developed using the Free Application for Federal Student Aid (FAFSA) as the basis for determining need. The results of the FAFSA needs analysis should reach Juniata by March 1.

Juniata College offers all students who submit an application the opportunity to gain an early understanding of their eligibility for assistance through its Early Financial Aid Assessment (EFAA) Program. The EFAA is available in September; those submitting a completed form receive a response within two to three weeks. The financial assistance programs are designed to reassure students that a four-year commitment to Juniata College will be reciprocated through the College's commitment to meeting the needs of its students.

Faculty

Juniata has 77 full-time and 17 part-time faculty members, of whom 81 percent (63 of 77 full-time faculty members) hold a doctoral or terminal degree in their field. The student-faculty ratio is 14:1. Although faculty members engage in numerous scholarly pursuits and maintain professional ties to their academic fields, they consider teaching and advising their primary functions.

Student Government

Juniata seeks to provide an environment within which students can mature intellectually, socially, and personally in a manner consistent with academic programs. In campus life as well as in the classroom, many opportunities for growth and self-exploration exist. Students have a voice—and in most cases a vote—in all essential areas of campus governance.

Admission Requirements

Juniata seeks students who show strong academic promise, motivation, and maturity. The College seeks a wide geographic representation and a variety of cultural, social, and economic backgrounds. Selection is made without regard to race, sex, religion, creed, color, handicap, or the ability to afford a private college education. Careful consideration is given to the academic record, test results, and personal qualities of applicants. Applicants should have completed a minimum of sixteen college-preparatory courses in mathematics, social studies, foreign language, and laboratory science. SAT I or ACT scores are required. International student candidates may be required to submit a TOEFL score. Interviews and campus visits are strongly recommended.

Transfer students who have completed A.A. or A.S. requirements in an approved collegiate transfer program at an accredited community or junior college may enter Juniata with junior-class standing and receive transfer credit for two years of course work. Students who transfer without a degree receive credit on a course-by-course basis. Students whose college has a formal transfer agreement with Juniata College should consult with their transfer coordinator to review requirements for that agreement. It is strongly recommended that transfer students have an interview.

Application and Information

Students may apply to Juniata after completion of their junior year in secondary school. A nonrefundable $30 fee must accompany the application. A complete secondary school transcript that indicates courses and grades (with a list of senior courses, if known) must be sent from the applicant's guidance office along with SAT I or ACT scores, an essay, and a letter of recommendation. An on-campus interview is highly recommended but not required. Transfer students must complete the normal application requirements and submit an official transcript from each college previously attended.

Candidates for freshman admission can choose from two application deadlines. Early decision is designed for students who believe that Juniata College is their first choice. The early action application deadline is November 15 of the student's senior year in secondary school, with notification no later than December 31. Early decision admission gives a student his or her admission decision, financial aid award, and priority housing early in the senior year. The student is asked to complete Juniata's institutional aid form in order to receive an early financial aid award. Students are strongly encouraged to submit a nonrefundable $200 matriculation deposit as soon as they have had the opportunity to inspect program and financial aid information.

Students who wish to be considered for all merit awards offered by Juniata need to have their application postmarked by January 15 of the senior year.

The rolling admission deadline is March 15 of a student's senior year. Students can expect an admission decision within three to four weeks of receipt of all necessary information and completion of the application file. Financial award packages are determined after the FAFSA has been completed. In addition, students may choose to complete the College Scholarship Service PROFILE form; however, it is not required.

Juniata accepts applications for transfer admission for either the spring or fall semesters. The application due date for fall applicants is June 1; the due date for spring applicants is December 1. It is to the student's benefit to submit all application materials before the due date. Juniata's transfer admission policy is rolling. In most cases, transfer students receive an admission decision within one month of receipt of all credentials. Necessary credentials include an essay, a statement of interest, a secondary school transcript, SAT I or ACT scores, and college transcripts.

Application forms and additional information may be obtained from:

Enrollment Center
Juniata College
1700 Moore Street
Huntingdon, Pennsylvania 16652
Telephone: 814-641-3420
        877-JUNIATA (877-586-4282, toll-free)
Fax: 814-641-3100
World Wide Web: http://www.juniata.edu/

On the campus of Juniata College.

KANSAS STATE UNIVERSITY
MANHATTAN, KANSAS

The University

Founded in 1863, Kansas State University (K-State) is a nationally recognized comprehensive university with more than 200 undergraduate programs and options, sixty-two master's degree programs, and forty doctoral programs.

K-State ranks first nationally among state universities in its total of Rhodes, Marshall, Truman, and Goldwater Scholars since 1986. K-State scholars have been awarded six Rhodes, nine Marshall, sixteen Truman, twenty-four Fulbright, thirty-six Goldwater, and thirteen Phi Kappa Phi scholarships.

Approximately 3,500 students live in the nine residence halls, and more than 2,700 students are members of eleven national sororities and twenty-three national fraternities. Six national African-American and two Latino fraternities and sororities have K-State chapters. The University maintains 552 apartments for students. More than 325 student organizations are available, and 88 percent of K-State students participate in recreational activities. K-State is a member of the NCAA (Division I) and the Big Twelve Conference.

The College of Arts and Sciences offers strong programs in the natural sciences, communications, humanities, fine arts, social sciences, and the health professions. College of Engineering student teams regularly compete and win national competitions and have a high pass rate on the fundamentals of the engineering licensing exam. The College of Business Administration is one of 326 American colleges and universities to hold accreditation from AACSB–The International Association for Management Education at both the undergraduate and graduate levels; the accounting department is also separately accredited by AACSB–The International Association for Management Education. The College of Agriculture offers fifteen majors and the only programs worldwide in bakery, feed, and milling science and management, and the College of Education offers the most comprehensive teacher education program in the state. The College of Human Ecology is one of the oldest and largest such colleges in the nation. The College of Architecture, Planning, and Design, where every program is professionally accredited, is one of a small number of public, comprehensive design schools in the nation. The College of Veterinary Medicine is internationally recognized as a center for the study of livestock diseases. The College of Technology and Aviation has the only FAA-approved bachelor's degree in aviation in the state and more than forty aircraft for training.

Location

The 668-acre campus is located in Manhattan, Kansas, a city with a population of approximately 45,000. A satellite campus, Kansas State University at Salina, is located 60 miles west in Salina and is the home of the College of Technology and Aviation. Nicknamed "The Little Apple," Manhattan is 125 miles from Kansas City. Local attractions include Aggieville, one of the oldest campus shopping areas in the nation, and the Sunset Zoo. Tuttle Creek Reservoir offers opportunities for waterskiing, fishing, boating, swimming, and camping. An active community arts program features outstanding performances in McCain Auditorium and Nichols Theatre. The Beach Museum of Art features traveling exhibits and houses the University's collection of Regionalist art and Gordon Parks photographs.

Majors and Degrees

The College of Arts and Sciences offers majors in anthropology, art, biochemistry, biology, chemical science, chemistry, criminology, dance, economics, English, fisheries and wildlife biology, geography, geology, history, kinesiology, mass communications, mathematics, microbiology, modern languages, music, philosophy, physics, political science, psychology, social work, sociology, speech, statistics, and theater. Interdisciplinary majors are humanities, life sciences, physical sciences, and social sciences. Secondary majors, which can be taken only in addition to a primary major, are American ethnic studies, gerontology, industrial and labor relations, Latin American studies, natural resources and environmental sciences, and women's studies. Preprofessional programs are law and options in the health professions that include dentistry, health information management, medical technology, medicine, nursing, occupational therapy, optometry, pharmacy, physical therapy, respiratory therapy, and veterinary medicine.

The College of Business Administration confers a B.S. with majors in accounting, finance, management, management information systems, and marketing. Management options available are general management, human resource management, and operations management. Marketing offers an agribusiness option. Finance options include financial services, financial management, and controllership.

The College of Engineering offers degree programs in architectural engineering, biological and agricultural engineering, chemical engineering, civil engineering, computer engineering, computer science, construction science and management, electrical engineering, industrial engineering, information systems, manufacturing systems engineering, mechanical engineering, and nuclear reactor technology. Options and concentrations are available in aerospace engineering, bioengineering, construction engineering, engineering materials, environmental engineering, food engineering, nuclear engineering, and power systems.

The College of Agriculture offers degree programs in agribusiness, agricultural economics, agricultural education, agricultural communications and journalism, agricultural technology management, agronomy, animal sciences and industry, bakery science and management, feed science and management, food science and industry, horticultural therapy, horticulture, milling science and management, park management and conservation, and recreation and park administration. The College also has a preprofessional program in veterinary medicine and a secondary major in natural resources and environmental sciences.

The College of Education administers programs in elementary, secondary, and special education. Secondary education programs are agriculture, art, biological science, business, chemistry, earth/space science, English, family and consumer economics, geography, history, journalism, mathematics, modern languages, music, physical science, physics, political science, sociology, and speech. Additional endorsements in computer studies, English as a second language, health education, and psychology are also available. Areas for K–12 certification are art, foreign language (French, German, or Spanish), and music.

The College of Human Ecology offers majors in apparel marketing and design, communication sciences and disorders, dietetics, early childhood education, family and consumer economics (financial planning), family life and community services, general human ecology, hotel and restaurant management, human ecology and mass communications, interior design, life span human development, nutritional sciences (premedical, pre-dental, medically related fields), public health nutrition, and textiles. Dual degrees are offered in family studies and human services and social work and in nutrition and exercise sciences. Family and consumer sciences education and early childhood education certification programs are offered.

The College of Architecture, Planning, and Design offers nationally accredited professional five-year degree programs in architecture, interior architecture, and landscape architecture. Before entering one of the three professional programs, the student completes a one-year common environmental design studies program.

The College of Technology and Aviation offers the bachelor's degree in aeronautical technology, electronics engineering technology, land information technology, mechanical engineering technology, and technology management and associate degrees in aviation maintenance, avionics, civil engineering technology, computer engineering technology, computer information systems, computer science technology, electronic engineering technology, environmental engineering technology, geographic information systems, industrial engineering technology, mechanical engineering technology, professional pilot, and surveying technology. The College also offers a certificate in aviation maintenance.

Academic Program

The common requirements for all curricula leading to an undergraduate degree are English composition and public speaking. To graduate, a student must complete a prescribed curriculum and 18 hours of approved general education courses. The total credit requirement for a bachelor's degree ranges from 120 to 167 hours, according to the curriculum taken.

Academic Facilities

The University's library system contains more than 1.4 million volumes, 13,063 journals and serials, more than 4.4 million government publications, and computerized information retrieval for all academic curricula. There are branch libraries for architecture and design, chemistry, math/physics, veterinary medicine, and technology (at Salina). Computing and Network Services provides an IBM S/390 Enterprise server, and computer laboratories all across the campus are available to students. The J. R. Macdonald Laboratory is one of the nation's leading laboratories in research in heavy-ion and atomic physics. Among K-State's research and laboratory facilities are the 8,616-acre Konza Prairie Research area, the Center for Basic Cancer Research, a NASA Center for Gravitational Studies in Cellular and Developmental Biology, the Center for Science Education, an Environmental Protection Agency center for hazardous substance research, a laser center, a population and demographics lab, a heliodon and wind tunnel, the Sensory Analysis Center, the Institute for Environmental Research, and the Institute for Social and Behavioral Research.

Costs

Projected tuition for 2000–01 is approximately $2620 for Kansas residents and $8935 for nonresidents. Books and supplies average $685, room and board average $4610, and personal expenses and transportation average $2855. Total costs for state residents are approximately $10,440, and for nonresidents they are $17,085. All figures are subject to change.

Financial Aid

Approximately 70 percent of the University's students receive some form of financial assistance. During 1999–2000, K-State students received more than $85 million through federal, state, and institutional student aid programs, including scholarships and veterans' benefits. About 80 percent of all scholarships are awarded on the basis of merit; in 1999–2000, K-State awarded approximately $6 million in scholarships. K-State recognizes the importance of high-quality leadership by awarding a Leadership Scholarship for students with an ACT composite score of 26 or higher. National Merit Semifinalists and Finalists are considered for Presidential Scholarships, and other top scholars may receive the Putnam, Foundation, Honors, or Medallion scholarships. All federal need-based programs are available at K-State, and application for them should be made by filing the Free Application for Federal Student Aid prior to March 1 preceding fall enrollment. The freshman priority deadline for scholarship applications is November 1.

Faculty

K-State has 1,214 full-time instructional, research, and extension faculty members, of whom 84 percent have doctorates or comparable advanced degrees. A K-State professor was named the 1996 national Professor of the Year for research/doctoral universities by the Carnegie Foundation for the Advancement of Teaching. Faculty members have received recognition in such diverse areas as atomic physics, aviation, biotechnology, cancer research, career education, creative writing, environmental research, grain science, military history, robotics, science education, space technology, and veterinary medicine.

Student Government

In 1995, 1997, and 1998, the National Association for Campus Activities honored K-State for having the nation's best large-school student government.

Admission Requirements

In-state students may be eligible for admission if they meet one of three academic criteria. A high school graduate with an ACT composite score of 21 or higher or an SAT I score of 990 or higher or a student who is ranked in the upper third of the high school class is considered admissible. In addition, Kansas residents who are high school graduates may be admitted if they are unable to meet the above requirements but have a 2.0 or higher GPA in a set of core courses. Out-of-state students need a minimum GPA of 2.5 if they attempt to qualify on the basis of core curriculum completion. All students are required to take either the ACT or SAT I regardless of the criteria used for admission, since the test results are also used for academic advising purposes.

Transfer students with 24 or more credit hours must have a 2.0 or higher GPA on their transfer work. Students with less than 24 credit hours are required to have a minimum GPA of 2.0 on their transfer work plus meet one of the three requirements for high school graduates.

International students must submit a $45 application fee and all required credentials before their records are assessed. Students applying directly from their home country are evaluated based on K-State's interpretation of academic credentials and comparison of education systems. International students applying after attending other U.S. institutions must demonstrate comparable academic potential.

Application and Information

Entering freshmen are encouraged to apply early in their senior year of high school. High school graduates must complete the application form and submit official ACT results. Transfer students should begin the application process at least one semester prior to their anticipated date of entry; they must submit a completed application form and official transcript from each institution previously attended. Only transcripts received directly from credit-granting institutions are considered official and acceptable for admission purposes. There is a $20 application fee for freshman and transfer students. All credentials are evaluated as they are received on a rolling basis. Students are notified in writing of their admission status within five working days of the receipt of required documents.

For application forms and information, students should contact:

Director of Admissions
Kansas State University
119 Anderson Hall
Manhattan, Kansas 66506-0102
Telephone: 785-532-6250
          800-432-8270 (toll-free in Kansas only)
E-mail: kstate@ksu.edu
World Wide Web: http://www.ksu.edu/Consider

KEAN UNIVERSITY
UNION, NEW JERSEY

The University
Established in 1855, Kean University has undergone continuous growth. In 1958 it moved to its present campus, where modern facilities and spacious grounds help it to fulfill its many educational goals. A delightful contrast to the surrounding urban area, the campus consists of 120 acres of rolling lawns and wooded areas, bisected by a gracefully flowing stream. An additional 28 acres on the East Campus are used both for intercollegiate and intramural recreation and for other student activities.

The University's approximately 12,000 full- and part-time graduate and undergraduate students form a heterogeneous student body representing diverse cultural backgrounds. About 90 percent of the full-time undergraduates commute to school.

Kean University offers students a broad extracurricular program of cultural, social, and athletic activities. Among the offerings on last year's schedule were several guest-lecturer series; a program of classical and contemporary music, dance, and drama; jazz concerts with regional jazz artists; and monthly art exhibitions in the Gallery. Varsity, intramural, and lifelong sports activities also enjoy wide popularity.

Location
Kean University is located in Union, New Jersey, which has been named an All-America City by the National Municipal League. New York City is approximately 10 miles away. Facilities for all forms of surface and air transportation, including an international airport, are within minutes of the campus.

Majors and Degrees
Kean University awards baccalaureate degrees in forty-six majors and more than seventy options and collateral programs.

Bachelor of Arts degrees are offered in accounting, art history, biology, chemistry, communications, criminal justice administration, early childhood education, earth science, economics, education of the hearing impaired, elementary education, English, fine arts, foreign languages (Spanish), history, industrial education, industrial technology, interior design, mathematics, music, music education, philosophy and religion, physical education, political science, psychology, public administration, recreation administration, sociology, special education, speech and hearing, studio art, theater, and visual communication.

Bachelor of Science degrees are offered in accounting, chemistry, computer science, finance, graphic communication, health information management, industrial technology, management science, marketing, medical technology, occupational therapy, and psychology/psychiatric rehabilitation. Bachelor of Fine Arts, Bachelor of Social Work, and Bachelor of Science in Nursing (for RNs only) degree programs are also offered.

Physical therapy is a dual M.S. program that is available to Kean University undergraduates; it is offered in cooperation with the University of Medicine and Dentistry of New Jersey (UMDNJ).

Academic Program
All degree programs include a 52-semester-hour general education requirement, including 18 credits in a humanities-based core curriculum and 34 credits distributed among courses that clearly meet the University's goals of a general education. These goals are designed to foster a broad liberal arts education as the foundation for specialized studies. Each degree program includes individual major requirements and free electives. A minimum of 30 semester hours is required for each major.

Internships are available to juniors and seniors in many degree programs.

The University calendar is based on a two-semester system with two summer sessions.

Off-Campus Arrangements
Kean University offers a variety of travel/study programs in which students may participate for a semester or for shorter periods of time. Programs include travel to all areas of the world. Travel/study programs may be taken for credit or for personal enrichment. Selected courses are also offered in nontraditional formats, such as distance education and service learning.

Academic Facilities
The Nancy Thompson Library is a comprehensive learning center with 270,000 volumes, 14,200 microfilms, and 1,350 subscription journals. Included are rare books and printed materials. The library has an online catalog, Voyager, and some CD-ROM databases. Kean University participates in an interlibrary loan system through which books and other materials not available in the University library may be borrowed. The library has a journal document delivery service available for a fee. The Instructional Resource Center (IRC) provides a variety of nonprint materials, electronic and conventional audiovisual equipment, and comprehensive media services, all of which support the academic programs at the University.

Laboratory facilities include the Reading Institute, the Institute of Child Study, and the Clinic in Learning Disabilities. The University has an electron microscope and operates a meteorological station. Students have access to a statewide computer network whose facilities exceed demands in virtually all cases.

Costs
Full-time undergraduate tuition and fees in 1999–2000 for New Jersey residents were $4383.50 and for out-of-state students were $6080.50. (Tuition is subject to change for 2000–01.) Housing costs for full-time students were $4322 per academic year. Apartment-style housing is available on the campus for 1,000 full-time students. Three traditional dormitories house 260 students, who pay an additional food plan cost of $600 per semester. Other students may participate in a variable-cost food plan. Commuting students pay a $15 annual parking registration fee.

Financial Aid
Approximately 59 percent of all full-time undergraduate students receive some form of financial aid. Federal aid is available in the form of Federal Perkins Loans, Federal Pell Grants, Federal Supplemental Educational Opportunity Grants, Federal Work-Study Program awards, and Federal Direct Loans. State aid includes Garden State Scholarships, Educational Opportunity Fund awards, and Tuition Aid Grants.

Students should complete and mail the Free Application for Federal Student Aid (FAFSA) to the processing center by March 15.

Faculty

Kean has 353 full-time faculty members, 13 part-time faculty members, and 454 adjunct faculty members. The faculty's regularly scheduled office hours and participation in virtually all areas of campus governance and operations ensure that they have continual interaction with students. Part-time and adjunct faculty members, including elected officials, business leaders, and industry representatives, provide valuable links with the community at large. Graduate assistants are not given primary instructional responsibility for any undergraduate course.

Student Government

The Student Organization, a truly autonomous body, is incorporated and is composed entirely of students chosen through campuswide elections. The student officers administer an annual budget that is derived from student activity fees and receipts. The Student Organization's responsibilities include providing cultural programming, cocurricular activities, entertainment, and athletics.

The University wholly supports the concept of students' rights of self-determination, and student participation in all areas of campus governance is traditional.

Admission Requirements

Admission to Kean University is based on a student's projected ability to complete a degree program, without regard to age, sex, race, color, creed, or national origin. Freshman applicants are expected to have a cumulative grade point average of at least 2.5. SAT I scores are required; the suggested combined score is 1020. The student is also expected to have completed 16 high school units. Exceptions to standards may be made in some individual cases. Highly qualified high school juniors may apply for early admission if they have a recommendation from their high school guidance counselor. Advanced standing based on CLEP scores and/or an evaluation of life experience is available for entering freshmen.

Transfer applicants are required to have a minimum grade point average (GPA) of 2.0, but some academic programs require a higher GPA; occupational therapy, for example, requires a GPA of at least 2.8.

Application and Information

The application deadline for freshman applicants is May 31 for fall admission and November 1 for admission in the spring. Students are accepted on a rolling basis. Application deadlines for all international (F-1 visa) students are March 1 for fall admission and November 1 for spring admission. The Kean University application, a $35 application fee, high school and college transcripts, and SAT I results (freshman candidates only) should be forwarded to the admission office. Campus visits are recommended. Tours are given on Friday at 10 a.m. from October to April.

For additional information and application forms, students should contact:

Director of Admissions
Kean University
Union, New Jersey 07083

Telephone: 908-527-2195
Fax: 908-351-5187
E-mail: admitme@turbo.kean.edu
World Wide Web: http://www.kean.edu

Students on the Kean University campus.

KEENE STATE COLLEGE
KEENE, NEW HAMPSHIRE

The College

Keene State College is a coeducational residential college with an enrollment of approximately 3,700 full-time undergraduate students and 1,000 part-time and graduate students. Founded in 1909, the College enrolled 27 students its first year. From its original 20 acres, the campus has expanded to 160 acres and more than seventy-six buildings that feature an attractive blend of traditional and contemporary architecture.

The superb physical facilities on campus include living accommodations ranging from traditional older residence halls to apartments and suites. The College has three buildings registered as National Historic Landmarks and numerous recently completed facilities, including Rhodes Hall academic building, the Thorne-Sagendorph Art Gallery, and the Lloyd P. Young Student Center. The College also owns the College Camp on Wilson Pond, a short drive from the campus, and the 400-acre Louis Cabot Preserve on Lake Nubanusit in Nelson and Hancock, New Hampshire.

Today, Keene State College is a vibrant educational community that provides the people of New Hampshire with an extensive range of educational opportunities, awarding associate, bachelor's, and master's degrees. Students come to Keene State College for its small size and friendly atmosphere, the choice of thirty-five major programs, a location in the heart of New England, and a private feeling at a public price.

Keene State is part of the University System of New Hampshire. It is also affiliated with CoPLAC (the Council for Public Liberal Arts Colleges) and Campus Compact: the Project for Public and Community Service. Valuing service to the community, the College strives to prepare the next generation of leaders for the state, the region, and the nation.

Location

Keene, New Hampshire, at the geographic center of New England—only 84 miles from Boston and 200 miles from New York City—is a thriving, prosperous city of 22,000. The Keene State campus is bordered by Main Street on one side and the Ashuelot River on another. It is only four blocks from the town's Central Square, which offers a variety of shops, restaurants, and theaters. The surrounding New England landscape includes the foothills of Mount Monadnock (the second-most-climbed mountain in the world) only 18 miles to the southeast of Keene. Opportunities for skiing, mountain climbing, camping, swimming, and hiking are all within a short drive of the campus.

Majors and Degrees

Bachelor of Arts and Bachelor of Science degrees are granted in American studies; applied computer science; art; biology; chemistry; chemistry-physics; communication; computer mathematics; economics; education; English; environmental studies; French; geography; geology; graphic design; health science; history; journalism; management; mathematics; mathematics-physics; music; physical education; psychology; safety studies; social science; sociology; Spanish; technology studies; theater, dance, and film; and vocational teacher education. An individualized B.A. or B.S. major is available for students who wish to design their own interdisciplinary program. Music education and music performance students are awarded the Bachelor of Music degree. Minors in thirty-five areas make it possible for students to supplement and strengthen their program. A strong cooperative education program provides work/credit opportunities in many majors.

Two-year degree programs offered are the Associate in Arts in general studies and Associate in Science in applied computer science, chemical dependency, general studies, and technology studies.

Academic Program

Education in the liberal arts and sciences and in several professional fields is provided through associate and baccalaureate degree programs. These programs include three basic components: breadth and balance achieved through general education requirements, depth of scholarship developed through specialization in a major field, and an opportunity to elect a minor or courses in other areas of interest. The College's areas of emphasis include teacher education, science and technology, and the fine and performing arts.

All baccalaureate programs have the same general education requirements, which are intended to broaden, deepen, and integrate the student's understanding of the most significant aspects of humanity's heritage. These studies also enhance the capacity for aesthetic enjoyment, critical thinking, creativity, abstract and logical reasoning, and oral and written communication.

A total of at least 120 credit hours is required to graduate, including 3 in English composition, 15 in arts and humanities, 12 in social sciences, and 12 in science/mathematics.

The academic year at Keene State consists of fall and spring semesters, plus two optional summer sessions.

Off-Campus Arrangements

Students are encouraged to study for a semester or a year at national and international exchange programs. The National Student Exchange is a domestic alternative to study abroad, with programs at 149 colleges and universities in the U.S., Guam, the Virgin Islands, and Puerto Rico. Keene State has ten Direct Exchange Programs with institutions in Canada, Ecuador, England, France, Ireland, and Russia and more than sixty consortium programs in such popular destinations as Austria, Costa Rica, Israel, Italy, and Spain.

Academic Facilities

The Wallace E. Mason Library houses approximately 210,000 paper volumes and has active subscriptions to more than 1,200 periodicals, newspapers, and annual publications. The microform collection of more than 550,000 items includes the Library of American Civilization, the Library of English Literature, ERIC, Envirofiche, various newspapers, and a collection of college catalogs. Students also have access to the 100,000 volumes available at Keene Public Library. Mason Library has direct online access to more than 4,000 libraries through OCLC, an international library network, and also subscribes to EPIC, which provides subject access to the OCLC database. The fully automated library supplies several CD-ROM indexes and provides online access to more than 400 databases. Mason Library houses the Holocaust Resource Center, with materials for those who wish to study, teach, or commemorate the Holocaust; it also houses the Curriculum Materials Library, which provides elementary and secondary education teaching materials for student teachers and classroom teachers across the state.

Other academic resources include the Arboretum and Gardens, the BodyWorks Fitness Center, the Film Studies Center, the Language Learning Center, and the Writing and Math Centers.

The Redfern Arts Center on Brickyard Pond houses classrooms and performance spaces for the art, music, and theater programs. Thorne-Sagendorph Art Gallery hosts exhibits by KSC students and faculty members, as well as regional, national, and international artists.

Keene State operates Wheelock Elementary School, which serves as a laboratory for students studying education, psychology, or recreation, and the Child Development Center, which offers direct experience for majors in early childhood education.

Computer equipment is available in all academic areas. A network connects student rooms and the offices of full-time faculty members and administrative personnel to the online library catalog, e-mail, and the World Wide Web.

Costs

Tuition for the 1999–2000 academic year was $3830 for New Hampshire residents and $9140 for out-of-state students. Room and board cost $4938, and mandatory fees totaled $1216. Books and supplies cost about $500 per year.

Financial Aid

Financial assistance is available in three basic forms: grants and scholarships, loans, and part-time employment. Grants and scholarships do not have to be repaid. Educational loans must be repaid, but such loans are made on a long-term, low-interest basis. Additional aid consists of part-time, on-campus employment. At Keene State, aid can be based on merit or need or a combination of both. Matriculated students are eligible to apply for assistance if they are enrolled for at least 6 credits per semester. Currently, approximately 70 percent of Keene State students receive some sort of financial aid. Interested students should write to the Office of Student Financial Management for more information.

Faculty

The resident faculty numbers more than 180 individuals who value personal attention to students and a commitment to academic advising. They are also active in their academic fields—writing books and articles, serving as consultants, presenting papers and seminars, participating in exhibits, and performing in concerts.

Student Government

The 27-member Student Assembly is the official student government organization of Keene State College. Its members are elected by the student body, with representatives for each academic class, off-campus students, and adult learners. A student body president and vice president are elected by the entire student body, while the chair of the Student Assembly, the secretary, and the treasurer are elected by Student Assembly members. Members of the Student Assembly serve on student committees and College Senate committees. The Student Assembly allocates student activity fee money and recognizes and sets policies for official student organizations.

Admission Requirements

The following requirements apply to all undergraduate programs except the Associate in Science in technology programs. Applicants should provide (1) an application accompanied by the application fee; (2) an official high school transcript and evidence of high school graduation or a satisfactory high school equivalency certificate; (3) scores on the SAT I (applicants are responsible for making arrangements to take the test and for having the results forwarded to Keene State College); and (4) a satisfactory evaluation from the high school guidance counselor or principal (applicants who have been out of high school for several years do not need to submit this evaluation; questions regarding this requirement should be addressed to the director of admissions).

Applicants should have completed college-preparatory course work, ensuring competence in English grammar and composition, college-level reading speed and comprehension, and a distribution of courses in the humanities (English literature, a foreign language, history, and philosophy), the social sciences (political science, sociology, anthropology, psychology, economics, and geography), the sciences (2 years required, 1 of which must be a lab), and mathematics (algebra I, algebra II, and geometry).

A personal interview is not required, although all applicants are encouraged to visit the campus. Visits are arranged through the Admissions Office.

Application and Information

To receive an application form and additional information, students should contact:

Kathryn G. Dodge
Director of Admissions
Elliot Hall
Keene State College
Keene, New Hampshire 03435-2604
Telephone: 603-358-2276
    800-KSC-1909 (toll-free)
Fax: 603-358-2767
E-mail: admissions@keene.edu
World Wide Web: http://www.keene.edu

Appian Gateway serves as a gathering place for students and welcomes visitors to Keene State College's traditional New England campus.

KENDALL COLLEGE
EVANSTON, ILLINOIS

The College
For more than sixty-five years, Kendall College has provided its students with a small, personal, and supportive academic environment. Kendall's reputation for distinctiveness and relevance is based on the College's understanding of career opportunities. Kendall requires actual work experience as part of each degree and certificate program. As a result, Kendall's students graduate with a solid liberal college education and hands-on internship experience in their chosen field. The College uses the rich resources of its metropolitan environment to relate academic theory to experience.

As a private, four-year, coeducational institution, Kendall College offers associate and bachelor's degrees in business, business information technology, culinary arts, early childhood education (state certification), hotel and restaurant management, human services, and several liberal arts majors. The faculty advisers encourage and offer assistance to students in planning and preparing for their careers while attending the College.

In 1997–98, Kendall College introduced varsity sports; men's and women's teams are fielded in basketball, cross-country, soccer, track and field, and volleyball. Kendall is committed to building better citizens through a healthy combination of academics and athletics.

Kendall College is accredited by the Commission on Institutions of Higher Education of the North Central Association of Colleges and Schools to offer programs leading to certificates, associate degrees (arts and sciences), and bachelor's degrees (arts and sciences). The College is also accredited by the University Senate of the United Methodist Church. The Culinary School is accredited by the American Culinary Federation Accrediting Commission.

Location
Kendall College is situated in the beautiful city of Evanston, Illinois, the first city north of Chicago. The College, just two blocks from the shores of Lake Michigan, provides a natural setting near sandy beaches, historic homes, tree-lined bicycle paths, and a variety of parks for recreational activities. A train station two blocks from the campus and a network of expressways link Kendall with the Chicago metropolitan area. Kendall's proximity to Chicago offers numerous opportunities for internships and job placement after graduation.

Evanston is a cosmopolitan city with a myriad of entertainment. From Big Ten athletics at Northwestern University (one block east of Kendall's campus) to dozens of art galleries, museums, and theaters, Kendall students have a variety of activities available to them.

Majors and Degrees
Kendall's Bachelor of Arts degree programs include American studies, business, early childhood education (with state certification), e-commerce/Web development, hotel/restaurant management, human services (with elective concentrations in gerontology and substance abuse), liberal arts, social sciences, and system administration. Kendall also offers a Bachelor of Science program in culinary management.

The Associate in Applied Science (A.A.S.) degree program includes the culinary arts degree. Culinary certificates are available in baking and pastry and professional cookery. Students can also pursue certificates in addiction counseling, e-commerce/Web development, and system administration.

Academic Program
Kendall College operates on a quarters program. The first quarter term extends from September to early December, the second extends from January to March, and the third extends from April to June. Summer sessions are offered from July to September. A student must fulfill a minimum of 92 quarter hours for an associate degree and a minimum of 184 quarter hours for a bachelor's degree and maintain a 2.0 GPA.

Academic Facilities
Kendall's library has a comfortable atmosphere, conducive to work and study. It contains a conference room, worktables, and individual study carrels. Copy machines are available, as is a video player. The library currently has more than 37,000 books, 250 periodicals, and a growing video collection. It also houses special collections of culinary, business, early childhood, human services, hospitality, and Native American materials. The library offers other excellent resources through local consortia and electronic connections.

The campus also houses a Montessori demonstration school and seven laboratory kitchens, including a fine dining restaurant for the training of culinary and hotel/restaurant management students; it is also located near a wide range of athletic facilities. The Kendall College Mitchell Indian Museum is located near the campus for the education of students and the community at large.

Costs
In 1999–2000, full-time tuition for the Liberal and Professional Studies Program was $10,746 for three quarters, and College room and board were $5008.50 for three quarters. Part-time tuition was $325 per credit hour. Full-time tuition for the culinary arts program was $19,764 for four quarters and included culinary facilities usage and equipment and two meals per day, five days per week. Room and board for the culinary arts program were $4190 for four quarters. Part-time culinary arts tuition was $354 per credit hour.

Financial Aid
The College offers institutional awards. A needs analysis and the determination of eligibility culminate in the financial aid package, which comprises different types of financial aid combined to meet the student's demonstrated need. The financial aid packaging process ensures effective use of available funds and provides fair and equitable treatment of all applicants. It is the goal of Kendall College to seek funding and to package aid to fully meet the needs of all applicants. Awards are made giving priority to applicants who meet the March 15 preferential filing date. The Kendall College Financial Aid Office believes that self-help (loan and work) should be a part of the Kendall aid package. Students are encouraged to make a commitment of current and future earnings to their education. The College administers aid for undergraduates, including need-based scholarships, non-need scholarships, state and federal awards, Federal Supplemental Educational Opportunity Grants, Federal Work-Study, and campus employment.

Faculty

The undergraduate academic faculty has 27 full-time and 40 part-time members; 55 percent of the full-time faculty members have doctoral and/or professional degrees. The student-faculty ratio is 17:1. The faculty members at Kendall College believe that students work best when they are actively involved in making choices about their own learning. As Kendall students develop clear ideas of what they wish to study, they are provided with the opportunities to use tutorials to continue their education.

Student Government

Kendall College's Student Government Committee was designed to give students a leadership role and voice in building and improving their campus community. The Kendall College Student Government Committee is appointed by the Dean of Students on a yearly basis based upon the recommendations of faculty and staff members in the Kendall community. This group serves as an advisory group to the Dean of Students Office regarding student activities and services and participates in various campus decision making.

Admission Requirements

Kendall assesses its entrance difficulty level as moderate. Admission to Kendall College is open to men and women of all races and religious affiliations. Each applicant is considered on the basis of probable success at Kendall, as indicated primarily by high school grades, class rank, and ACT or SAT I test scores. A minimum GPA of 2.0 and an 18 on the ACT or an equivalent SAT I score are required for acceptance. Qualities of character are also important at Kendall. Therefore, personal interviews and campus visits are encouraged, though not required, to help determine admission.

Application and Information

High school seniors may obtain applications from the Office of Admissions and may submit the admission application at any time. The Office of Admissions must be sent an official transcript of high school records.

Students in good standing at a previous college at the time of application to Kendall are admitted through normal admission procedures. Some students may be admitted on probation after consultation with the Admissions Committee.

For further information, students should contact:

Amy G. Bhote
Dean of Admissions
Kendall College
Evanston, Illinois 60201-2899
Telephone: 847-866-1304
              847-866-1300
Fax: 847-733-7450
E-mail: admissions@kendall.edu
World Wide Web: http://www.kendall.edu

Kendall College, located just north of Chicago, has been educating students for more than sixty-five years.

KENT STATE UNIVERSITY
KENT, OHIO

The University
Situated on a 1,200-acre campus, Kent State University is a medium-sized state university that offers educational opportunity, intellectual adventure, and academic stimulation to its more than 20,700 students. Chartered in 1910, the University provides more than 170 fields of study in a wide range of undergraduate programs as well as numerous graduate and noncredit programs. Two-year associate degree programs are offered through seven regional campuses in Ashtabula, Geauga, Stark, Trumbull, and Tuscarawas counties and in the cities of Salem and East Liverpool.

As a residential campus, Kent requires students to reside in one of twenty-eight residence halls until junior academic standing is achieved. Exceptions include commuting and nontraditional students. Students can easily walk to any of the more than 100 academic, residential, administrative, and recreational buildings. The University has an eighteen-hole golf course, a 291-acre airport, a two-rink indoor ice arena, and three on-campus theaters. There are 230 student organizations, nineteen fraternities, nine sororities, and eighteen varsity sports. The Career Service Center provides career counseling and job placement assistance for students and alumni.

Location
Kent, Ohio, a city with a population of 30,000, is within easy traveling distance of the major metropolitan areas of northeastern Ohio. Within a 20-mile radius are concerts, cultural events, numerous amusement parks, museums, nature preserves, recreational areas, and year-round sports.

Majors and Degrees
The College of Arts and Sciences awards Bachelor of Arts, Bachelor of Science, and Bachelor of General Studies degrees. Major fields of concentration are American studies, anthropology, applied conflict management, applied mathematics, biology, botany, chemistry, classics, computer science, conservation, criminal justice studies, earth science, economics, English, ethnic heritage studies, French, French translation, geography, geology, German, German translation, history, international relations, Latin, Latin American studies, management and industrial studies, mathematics, Pan-African studies, philosophy, physics, political science, psychology, Russian, Russian translation, sociology, Soviet and East European studies, Spanish, Spanish translation, and zoology. Numerous interdisciplinary and preprofessional programs are available, including general studies, integrated life sciences, predentistry, pre-engineering, prelaw, premedicine, preosteopathy, prepharmacy, and pre–veterinary medicine. Students may also design their own individualized major.

The College of Business Administration awards the Bachelor of Business Administration degree. Major fields of concentration are accounting, business management, computer information systems, economics, finance, marketing, and operations management.

The College of Education offers the Bachelor of Science in Education and Bachelor of Science degrees, with licensure programs available in adolescence/young adult education, early childhood education, intervention specialist studies (majors include deaf education, gifted, mild/moderate needs, and moderate/intensive needs), middle childhood education, multi-age education, and vocational education.

The College of Fine and Professional Arts offers the degrees of Bachelor of Architecture, Bachelor of Arts, Bachelor of Fine Arts, Bachelor of Music, and Bachelor of Science. The college also offers multiple-degree programs. The academic divisions are the Schools of Architecture and Environmental Design; Art; Communication Studies; Exercise, Leisure, and Sport; Family and Consumer Studies; Fashion Design and Merchandising; Journalism and Mass Communication; Music; Speech Pathology and Audiology; and Theatre and Dance.

The College of Nursing awards the Bachelor of Science in Nursing degree. The four-year program includes clinical practicums in the Cleveland-Akron-Warren area.

The School of Technology offers associate, bachelor's, and master's degree programs throughout Kent's eight-campus system. Students can select from a number of specialized academic programs in aeronautics, industrial, electrical, manufacturing, or educational technologies.

Academic Program
Kent State University's colleges and schools all maintain separate academic programs; completion of 36 credits of liberal education course work is a University requirement for all students. The number of credit hours required for graduation varies but is generally 121 semester hours. Credits can be transferred from previous college work satisfactorily completed or earned through courses taken at one of Kent State University's regional campuses. Credit by examination is available. Generally, to earn a degree, students must earn at least 30 semester hours in residence.

The Honors College provides opportunities for students and faculty members to develop and implement special learning experiences. It offers four-year programs of undergraduate study with concurrent enrollment in one of the University's degree-granting programs. In addition, the Honors College awards advanced-placement credit, early admission to high school students, and specialized academic advising. Its Experimental and Integrative Studies Division offers nontraditional learning experiences for students and faculty members of the entire University community.

Support services are available for students needing assistance to ensure a successful college experience. The Academic Success Center Program offers tutoring, and Student Disability Services provides assistance to students with various physical disabilities and specific learning disabilities.

Army and Air Force ROTC programs are offered on campus.

Off-Campus Arrangements
Through the Center for International and Comparative Programs, Kent State University offers students a variety of overseas academic programs that provide a balance of academic, linguistic, and cross-cultural experiences and learning opportunities. Credit is granted toward degrees.

Academic Facilities
The collections of the University libraries total more than 2.4 million bound volumes, 12,600 periodicals, and 1.2 million microform pieces. Computer Services makes available an instructional laboratory that accepts FORTRAN, Pascal, BASIC, LISP, C, Ada, and assembly languages. An IBM 2003 mainframe computer is available for advanced work and research. The Department of Mathematics and Computer Science operates computer laboratories with Sun-4/670 and HP/Apollo 700 workstations as well as a Wavetracer DTC SIMD machine.

These are connected to the campus network, which includes macrocomputer and microcomputer facilities. The Honors Center is a living-learning residential complex that houses undergraduate students as well as staff offices, a library-seminar room, a student computer facility, and an audiovisual center. The Center for Applied Conflict Management is an academic unit offering programs of study, research, and service activities that focus on the dynamics of change in human systems. The Instructional Television Service operates a closed-circuit, campuswide network and a production center for NETO, Inc., Channels 45 and 49, northeastern Ohio's public television stations. Audiovisual services support regularly scheduled classes with films and other educational materials. The Instructional Resources Center assists students in the production of educational media materials. The Language Laboratory provides tapes and other tools to assist students in foreign language studies. The Academic Testing Services Office offers test administration, test scoring, and research activities. The School of Fashion Design and Merchandising sponsors a working museum of fashion for students and the general public. This school houses classrooms, labs, a library, and a collection of costumes donated from the Silverman-Rogers estate for hands-on study.

As a recognized leader in liquid crystal technology, Kent's Glenn H. Brown Liquid Crystal Institute is the nation's only center devoted solely to liquid crystal research. With a recent grant from the National Science Foundation, Kent became the home of Ohio's first Science and Technology Research Center for the Study of Advanced Liquid Crystalline Optical Materials.

Costs

Instructional and other fees for Ohio residents for 1999–2000 were $5014 per year. For students residing outside Ohio, instructional and other fees were $9918 per year. Although room rates vary, costs for board and a double room average $4530 per year. The average student spends $710 per year for books and supplies and should budget extra money for personal needs and expenses. All fees and charges are subject to change.

Financial Aid

The University's financial aid program assists promising students who lack the funds necessary to finance a college education. This program, which serves nearly two-thirds of Kent's student body, consists of four basic sources of financial aid: scholarships, loans, grants-in-aid, and part-time employment. To be considered for financial aid awards, students must be admitted to the University and must submit the Free Application for Federal Student Aid (FAFSA). Ohio students should also check the Ohio Instructional Grant (OIG) box on the FAFSA if they are interested in being considered. Students planning to attend the fall semester as freshmen should apply for financial aid after January 1 and before March 1 of the same year. In order to meet the March 1 priority deadline, it is recommended that all financial aid forms be completed and mailed no later than February 1. Applications received after March 1 are considered, but sufficient funds to assist all late applicants may be lacking. Additional information and forms are available from the Office of Student Financial Aid, P.O. Box 5190.

Kent State University's Honors College awards merit scholarships to selected individuals who have the potential for superior scholarly and creative work at the University as determined by academic performance and creative artist competitions. For additional information, students should write to the Dean, Honors College, P.O. Box 5190. The Office of Student Financial Aid also administers numerous private scholarships, including the President's Scholarship for out-of-state students, the President's Grant for out-of-state students who are children of alumni, and various departmental scholarships. Kent also administers the Oscar Ritchie Memorial Scholarship competition for qualified high school juniors who are members of underrepresented minority groups, including African Americans, Latinos, and Native Americans. Kent offers the Founders Scholarship Program for academically talented freshmen entering the University in the fall. Qualified students are invited to campus to participate in an examination and meetings with faculty members. Scholarships range from full tuition, fees, room, and board to partial scholarships of varying amounts. Students should contact the Office of Admissions for a comprehensive scholarship application at the address or phone numbers listed below.

Faculty

The University's commitment to scholarship and teaching excellence is enhanced by a full-time faculty of approximately 976 members, of whom 87 percent hold a Ph.D. or the highest degree in their field. Some of the faculty members are research oriented, and others publish widely.

Student Government

Students have leadership opportunities through residence hall and Greek organizations and the undergraduate Student Senate. The senate is responsible for allocating student activity fees to registered undergraduate organizations, appointing undergraduates to all University committees and to other positions, conducting elections, and polling student opinion. Two students serve on Kent's Board of Trustees.

Admission Requirements

Kent State University's freshman admission policy differs for students with varying degrees of preparation for college studies. The students most likely to be admitted and to succeed at the Kent campus are those who have graduated with at least 16 units of the recommended college-preparatory curriculum in high school, achieved a high school grade point average of 2.5 or higher, and acquired an ACT score of 21 or better (or a combined SAT score of 980).

Students who do not meet the above criteria but who have graduated with a cumulative grade point average of at least 2.2 (on a 4.0 scale) at a chartered or accredited high school or who have passed the GED may be admitted. High school course selection, class rank, recommendations, and ACT or SAT I scores are closely examined when making admission decisions for such students. Transfer students are required to have a cumulative 2.0 GPA for admission to the University.

Because special facilities and available faculties are limited, admission to certain academic programs requires special procedures and superior credentials. For freshmen, selective admission requirements apply to aeronautics flight technology, architecture, dance, education, fashion design and merchandising, interior design, journalism and mass communication, music, nursing, theater, and the six-year medical program with the Northeastern Ohio Universities College of Medicine. For transfer students, selective requirements apply to all of the preceding and to art and business. Students should contact the Office of Admissions for information.

Application and Information

Application forms are available from the Office of Admissions upon request. A $30 nonrefundable application fee is required. Application early in the senior year helps ensure priority consideration for fall registration, residence hall preference, and financial aid. Students may also access Kent's online application at http://www.kent.edu/admissions. Applications are processed on a rolling basis.

Office of Admissions
Kent State University
P.O. Box 5190
Kent, Ohio 44242-0001
Telephone: 330-672-2444
        800-988-KENT (toll-free)
E-mail: kentadm@kent.edu
World Wide Web: www.kent.edu

KENTUCKY STATE UNIVERSITY
FRANKFORT, KENTUCKY

The University

Kentucky State University (KSU) is a liberal studies public institution that offers a friendly, individualized education with excellence as its ultimate goal. Founded in 1886, the University is located in the historic capital city of Frankfort. While the University has changed to meet the needs of the society it serves, its basic goal has remained unchanged since its founding. It is a liberal studies institution of ideal size that is dedicated to the principle of providing the highest-quality education at the lowest possible cost.

Kentucky State University's enrollment for fall 1999 was 2,194 students. The primary source of students is the state of Kentucky, but more than thirty states and territories are represented on the campus; students also come from twenty-seven other countries and bring to the campus a regional, national, and global cultural and ethnic diversity. Nontraditional students may earn a degree at Kentucky State University through several programs.

The University believes that the on-campus residential experience is an essential part of student life. Freshman and sophomore students are required to live on campus. Residential living space is reserved for freshmen and other upperclass students who wish to live on campus.

KSU has about sixty student organizations—ranging from social fraternities and sororities to departmental clubs, literary groups, and political organizations. Students enjoy intramural sports as well as intercollegiate men's baseball, football, and golf; women's softball and volleyball; and men's and women's basketball, cross-country, tennis, and track. KSU offers convocations, special lectures, art exhibits, fine arts performances, and many other activities designed to complement classroom learning. It also offers personal and career counseling, helps students prepare resumes, arranges job interviews, and provides testing to help students assess their interests and abilities. Placement activities include an annual career fair. Health care is available on campus. KSU offers a Master of Public Administration degree program, and, through KSU's Interinstitutional Graduate Center, three other state institutions offer graduate classes and programs.

KSU offers a Master of Science in Agriculture.

Location

KSU is located at the western edge of the Bluegrass region in Kentucky's capital city (population 27,500). The Frankfort area offers historic, scenic, and recreational attractions. Activities in the area include boating, camping, fishing, golfing, horseback riding, and water and snow skiing. Frankfort is between Kentucky's two largest cities, 25 miles west of Lexington and 50 miles east of Louisville. It is on Interstate 64, less than an hour's drive from Interstates 71, 65, and 75, the Bluegrass Parkway, and the Mountain Parkway. Bluegrass Airport, near Lexington, is 20 miles from Frankfort; Standiford Field in Louisville is approximately 55 miles away. Bus transportation to and from both cities is available.

Majors and Degrees

Kentucky State University awards the degrees of Bachelor of Arts, Bachelor of Science, Bachelor of Music Education, and Bachelor of Music in Performance. Majors offered are applied mathematics (3-2 engineering); art (studio); art education; biology (options in general biology or health sciences); business administration (specialization in accounting, business administration, economics, management, or marketing); chemistry; child development and family relations; computer science; criminal justice; early elementary education (grades K-4); English; history; liberal studies (including a student-designed liberal studies major); mathematics; medical technology; microcomputers; music education; music performance (options in vocal or instrumental music); physical education (nonteaching or teaching); political science; psychology; public administration; social studies education; social work; sociology; and textiles, clothing, and merchandising (options in art or business). Secondary teacher certification is offered in biology, English, history, and mathematics. The Associate in Applied Science degree is offered in administrative support services, computer science, drafting and design technology, electronics technology, and nursing. An Associate of Arts degree is offered in liberal studies. In cooperation with various professional schools in Kentucky and other states, KSU offers preprofessional study in community health, cytotechnology, dentistry, engineering (3-2 program), law, medical technology, medicine, nuclear medicine technology, optometry, physical therapy, and veterinary medicine.

Academic Program

KSU provides a full liberal studies experience. Central to KSU's academic program are courses called the Liberal Studies Requirements. These 53 credit hours, required of all baccalaureate students, provide the broad, basic knowledge necessary in a rapidly changing world. The Liberal Studies Requirements include courses in English, speech, mathematics, and foreign language; in the behavioral, social, and natural sciences; and in health and safety education and physical activity. At least 128 hours are required for a bachelor's degree; at least 64 hours are required for an associate degree. KSU awards up to 64 credit hours based on examinations and certifications. The academic year is divided into two semesters—fall and spring—and a six-week summer session. KSU's Whitney M. Young, Jr., College of Leadership Studies is believed to be unique in U.S. public higher education. The college is a division in which students study the Great Books—enduring works of literature, including those on history, philosophy, mathematics, and sciences. Intensive work in writing is required. After two years, students may continue the study of the Great Books, which constitutes a liberal studies major, and minor in another area; they may major in an area in one of the University's other colleges and schools and minor in the Great Books study; or they may select both a major and minor in other areas after completing the equivalent of their Liberal Studies Requirements in Whitney Young College. Students may cross-enroll in Air Force ROTC classes at the University of Kentucky in nearby Lexington. Completion of the ROTC program leads to a commission as a second lieutenant in the appropriate branch of service.

Off-Campus Arrangements

Some students may qualify for internships in which they can test vocational preferences and develop job skills in work situations and may earn credit toward graduation. KSU also offers cooperative education opportunities that enable students to work off campus as a required part of an academic program. Students receive credit each semester for the paid work assignments. Through the Cooperative Center for Study in England, KSU students can study abroad between semesters, in the summer, or during their junior year.

Academic Facilities

The University has thirty-three buildings on its 485-acre campus. Blazer Library houses nearly 300,000 volumes and subscribes to hundreds of periodicals and journals. Students have access to the nearby Kentucky Historical Society Library, which has 50,000 volumes, and State Library of the Kentucky Department of Libraries and Archives, which has more than 125,000 volumes, 87,000 U.S. government documents, and hundreds of periodicals and journals. KSU also has four auditoriums, used for concerts, plays, lectures, films, and other cultural activities; biology, chemistry, physics, computer, music, and language laboratories; art studios; darkrooms; an art gallery; and a research farm and a fish hatchery.

Costs

In 2000–01, for full-time undergraduate residents of Kentucky, tuition, room (double occupancy), board, and fees total $5746 per year. For full-time undergraduate out-of-state students, the total is $9786. Books, supplies, and personal expenses cost an estimated $600–$900 a year. KSU offers one meal plan, required of students in residence halls. Certain laboratory courses require small additional fees.

Financial Aid

Eligibility for financial assistance is based on demonstrated financial need, scholastic ability, useful talent, training, and experience. Students can apply for State Student Incentive Grants, Federal Pell Grants, Federal Supplemental Educational Opportunity Grants, Federal Perkins Loans, Kentucky Stafford Student Loans, Federal PLUS loans, part-time employment awards, and Federal Work-Study Program awards. Approximately 90 percent of KSU's students receive some form of financial assistance. To be considered for need-based financial assistance, prospective students must submit a KSU financial aid application and a Free Application for Federal Student Aid (FAFSA) and signed copies of their and their parents' federal income tax return from the previous year. The FAFSA, which can be obtained from high school guidance counselors or the KSU Office of Admission, should be mailed directly to the College Scholarship Service in Cahokia, Illinois. Students who complete the application process by the priority date of February 15 receive consideration for both the fall and spring semesters. For students who do not qualify for need-based aid but who have demonstrated specific academic, artistic, musical, or athletic skills or talent, scholarships and grants-in-aid are available. Students may qualify for Full Presidential Scholarships (tuition, room, and board), Partial Presidential Scholarships (tuition, plus one half the cost of room and board), or Presidential Tuition Scholarships (tuition only). Residents of the Kentucky counties of Anderson, Franklin, Scott, Shelby, Owen, and Henry may qualify for Service Area Scholarships. Other scholarships are available as well. Prospective students must submit an Application for Scholarship and a FAFSA by March 15 of the year they plan to enter KSU. Application forms can be obtained from the Office of Admissions.

Faculty

In 2000–01, KSU has 123 full-time and 7 part-time faculty members; 99 percent hold advanced degrees. Faculty members who teach graduate classes also teach undergraduate classes. Qualified professors, not graduate students, teach all classes. While faculty members represent a broad range at KSU, they share a commitment to close student-teacher relationships and to the value of a liberal education as preparation for graduate and professional school and career employment.

Student Government

The Student Government Association gives students a voice in campus affairs, plays a part in scheduling and sponsoring campus activities, and enacts legislation in matters of student concern, subject to ratification by the President's Cabinet and Board of Regents. SGA and the Cabinet have joint jurisdiction in regulating and promoting student activities and organizations. An SGA member serves as a voting member of the Board of Regents.

Admission Requirements

KSU seeks serious students who are committed to excelling in college studies. The University requires that all prospective students complete a precollege curriculum of 21 high school units, with at least 4 units in English; 3 in mathematics; 2 in sciences, including at least one laboratory course; and 2 in social sciences. Additional units in foreign languages, mathematics, sciences, arts, and computer literacy are highly desirable. New freshmen from Kentucky must have graduated from an accredited high school and taken the ACT. (Under recently enacted legislation, Kentucky State University may accept up to 10 percent of first-time freshmen, enrolled in baccalaureate programs, based on SAT I, rather than ACT, scores.) Any graduate of an accredited high school will be unconditionally admitted if they meet the precollege curriculum requirements established by the Kentucky Council on Higher Education and have an admission index of 430. The admission index is a numerical score determined by multiplying the cumulative grade point average (on a 4.0 scale) by 100 and the ACT Composite (or converted SAT I) by 10, and adding the two numbers. Nontraditional applicants (25 years of age or older) may substitute results of the Career Planning and Placement Test (CPP-II) for ACT or SAT I results if pursuing an associate degree. Students applying for admission to the Whitney M. Young, Jr., College of Leadership Studies should have taken sound academic courses in high school and have a strong interest in learning (transfer students will be considered, but they must start at the beginning of the Whitney Young program).

Application and Information

High school students should complete and submit an admission application early in their senior year. An official high school transcript and ACT or SAT I scores should be sent to KSU during the senior year. A final high school transcript, including class size and rank, grade point average, and date of graduation, should be sent to KSU after graduation and by July 1. Transfer students must submit official transcripts and statements of good standing from each college attended. Students dismissed less than honorably from other institutions may not enroll at KSU until they qualify for readmission to the college or university from which they were dismissed. Applicants are encouraged to visit the campus. Requests for a student prospectus, application forms, and further information should be directed to:

Office of Admission
Kentucky State University
400 East Main Street
Frankfort, Kentucky 40601-9957
Telephone: 502-227-6349
        800-633-9415 (toll-free in Kentucky)
        800-325-1716 (toll-free outside Kentucky)
Fax: 502-227-6239
World Wide Web: http://www.kysu.edu

KENTUCKY WESLEYAN COLLEGE
OWENSBORO, KENTUCKY

The College
The tradition of high-quality teaching and a talent for translating a liberal arts education into usable and useful service have long been hallmarks of Kentucky Wesleyan College (KWC). Founded by the United Methodist Church in 1858, the College's mission is to prepare leaders for the twenty-first century through a coordinated and integrated liberal arts education.

To fulfill its mission, Kentucky Wesleyan offers Leadership KWC, a nationally recognized leadership program established with an $800,000 grant from the W.K. Kellogg Foundation. Liberal arts course work forms the basis of Leadership KWC and represents the College's belief that a solid liberal arts education provides the communication, problem-solving, and creative-thinking skills necessary for tomorrow's leaders. To specifically explore leadership, students may enroll in special courses with a leadership emphasis, such as Profiles in Leadership, Women in Leadership, or the Psychology of Leadership. Students put leadership theory into practice through internships, community service, and workshops such as the College's summer sailing experience. Students may choose to participate in Leadership XXI, a more extensive cocurricular leadership program that involves leadership courses, community service, leadership workshops, campus activity participation, and a senior thesis or project. Students who successfully complete Leadership XXI receive a leadership citation at graduation.

There are more than forty campus organizations, including two national sororities, three national fraternities, several campus ministries, the *Panogram* (newspaper), the *Porphrian* (yearbook), 90.3 FM (WKWC), and the Kentucky Wesleyan Singers. The College also supports an extensive intramural athletics program.

Kentucky Wesleyan participates in the NCAA Division II and the Great Lakes Valley Conference. The men's basketball program is one of the top programs in the nation. With national championships in 1966, 1968, 1969, 1973, 1987, 1990, and 1999, Kentucky Wesleyan is the only school in NCAA Division II to win national championships in each of the past four decades. The College leads the nation with seventy-eight NCAA wins and seventeen NCAA regional championships.

Kentucky Wesleyan is home to more than 700 students from twenty-three states and several other countries. There are one women's, one men's, and two coed residence halls. Each residence hall room is air conditioned and has a cable television hookup and access to the campus computer network.

Location
Kentucky Wesleyan College is located on 70 beautiful acres in Owensboro, Kentucky's third largest city. Owensboro is located on the southern bank of the Ohio River, and the College is in a safe, residential neighborhood. The College is 45 minutes east of Evansville, Indiana; 2 hours north of Nashville, Tennessee; 2 hours west of Louisville; 4 hours east of Cincinnati; and 4 hours west of St. Louis.

A growing community of more than 60,000 people, Owensboro is the cultural and industrial centerpiece of western Kentucky. Owensboro provides students with many opportunities for part-time employment and internships as well as easy access to museums, parks, shopping malls, theaters, and an excellent symphony orchestra. There are opportunities for outdoor activities such as fishing, hiking, cycling, and water skiing.

The College and the Owensboro community share a warm relationship. Many students are employed by local businesses and some remain in Owensboro after graduation. In addition, many local businesses and shops offer discounts on goods and services to students.

Majors and Degrees
Kentucky Wesleyan College offers the Bachelor of Arts and/or Bachelor of Science degrees with majors in accounting, art, art education, biology, business administration and economics, chemistry, communication arts, computer science, criminal justice, education (elementary, middle grades, and secondary), English, fitness and sports management, history, human services administration, mathematics, medical technology, physical education, physics, political science, psychology, religion and philosophy, sociology, and Spanish. In addition, the College offers the Bachelor of Music, Bachelor of Music Education, Bachelor of Nursing, and a 3-2 combined engineering degree program in cooperation with the University of Kentucky and Auburn University.

Preprofessional programs are offered in Christian ministries, dentistry, environmental science, law, medical technology, medicine, optometry, pharmacy, physical therapy, physicians assistant studies, and veterinary medicine.

Academic Program
There are three academic divisions in the Kentucky Wesleyan College curriculum: the Natural Sciences, the Humanities and Fine Arts, and the Social Sciences. The requirements for the degrees of Bachelor of Science and Bachelor of Arts are based on the principle of a broad distribution of studies among the representative fields of human culture and a concentration of studies in a specific field. In most cases, 128 semester hours are required to obtain a bachelor's degree.

Students have the opportunity to develop and carry out individual programs of studies related to their particular vocational or professional goals through the Interdisciplinary Studies (IDS) Program. By combining courses from two or more departments, the IDS student works toward a specially tailored area of concentration.

Kentucky Wesleyan operates on a semester calendar with classes from late August to mid-December and from mid-January to mid-May. A limited summer term is offered from late May to late June. Credit and/or advanced placement is offered through CLEP, Advanced Placement courses, and the International Baccalaureate.

Off-Campus Arrangements
Students learn outside of the traditional classroom through a variety of off-campus study opportunities. Students may arrange to study overseas on an individual basis for a summer, a semester, or a year. During spring break, students may choose to study business institutions, take urban studies, or observe plays and playwrights in New York City for credit. Marine biology in Belize is also offered each year during spring break. Other coordinated trips have included travel to Estonia, Israel, London, and Mexico.

Academic Facilities

Kentucky Wesleyan's academic facilities include the Library Learning Center, the PLUS Center, the Criminal Justice Research Center, a 5,000-watt student-programmed FM radio station (WKWC), the KWC Playhouse (theater), extensive natural science laboratories, a greenhouse, and an animal colony.

The library houses more than 100,000 bound volumes, 10,938 government titles, and 61,945 microform items and subscribes to more than 450 periodicals. Also located in the library is the campus computer laboratory. The campus computer network links all academic buildings and residence halls and features a variety of popular software programs, a campuswide electronic mail system, and access to the Internet and World Wide Web. Each residence hall room is equipped with a network hookup; this allows students access to the computer network 24 hours a day.

The Criminal Justice Research Center allows students to conduct criminal justice research, including pilot studies, survey research, program evaluations, and theoretical studies. Students and faculty members work together in designing, presenting, and publishing research data.

Natural science laboratory equipment includes a purge and trap gas chromatography system, a Fourier transform infrared spectrometer, an atomic absorption spectrometer, a high-performance liquid chromatography system, and an ultraviolet visible spectra photometer.

Costs

The total cost for attending Kentucky Wesleyan College is well below the national average for private colleges. Tuition for the 2000–01 academic year is $10,070. Annual room and board charges are $2250 and $2580, respectively. The student activity fee is $150 and the technology fee is $100. Students and parents should also consider expenses for books, transportation, and personal and miscellaneous items.

Financial Aid

Kentucky Wesleyan participates in all federal student aid programs and is committed to helping each student meet his or her demonstrated financial need. No student should hesitate to apply for admission due to financial reasons. Kentucky Wesleyan awards more than $6.2 million each year in financial aid to eligible students. Kentucky residents may qualify for Kentucky Higher Education Assistance Authority Grants.

In addition to federal and state financial aid programs, Kentucky Wesleyan invests more than $2.6 million annually in scholarships and grants for its students. Academic scholarships are awarded to students who attend one of several on-campus scholarship days. These scholarships range from $2000 to full tuition and are renewable annually. Students who demonstrate a strong record of leadership in their school, church, place of employment, or community are encouraged to apply for Stanley Reed Leadership Awards. These awards range from $2000 to $4000 and are renewable annually (applications are available from the Office of Admission).

For maximum financial aid consideration, students are requested to submit the Free Application for Federal Student Aid (FAFSA) and the Kentucky Wesleyan College Financial Aid Application by March 1. Kentucky Wesleyan is need-blind in its admission process.

Faculty

Kentucky Wesleyan's 71 faculty members (44 full-time, 27 part-time) combine scholarship and teaching ability with a genuine concern for students. Seventy percent of faculty members have the doctorate or a terminal degree in their fields. A student-faculty ratio of 15:1 and small class size (15–25 students) ensure that students and faculty members develop the rapport crucial to an effective learning environment. All faculty members teach and advise students; there are no graduate teaching assistants.

Student Government

Students elect at-large members and officers on an annual basis to represent the student body in all areas of College life. The vice president of the Student Government Association also serves as an ex-officio member of the College's Board of Trustees. All policy and disciplinary issues are reviewed by the Dean of Student Life and by elected members of the Student Judiciary Board. The student handbook contains established guidelines for student life on campus.

Admission Requirement

Each applicant is considered individually on the basis of his or her academic record, ACT and/or SAT I scores, extracurricular involvement, essay, and recommendations. Freshman applicants should generally be in the top half of their class and have taken a strong college-preparatory curriculum. Applicants are considered for admission upon receipt of their completed application, a $20 application fee, official high school transcripts, and ACT or SAT I scores.

Kentucky Wesleyan also seeks to enroll transfer, international, and adult students who have demonstrated the ability to succeed in a competitive academic environment. Transfer applicants should submit a completed application, a $20 application fee, official high school transcripts, and official transcripts from all colleges attended. International applicants must submit a $50 application fee, TOEFL scores (500 or better required) and/or SAT I or ACT test scores, and an English translation of their high school transcript.

Application and Information

The Office of Admission is open from 8 a.m. to 5 p.m., Monday through Friday, and on Saturday by appointment. Interested students are encouraged to visit the campus during one of the College's weekend open houses in the fall and winter or by individual appointment during the week. Students who wish to stay on campus overnight are welcome to do so at no charge.

Students may apply for admission after completing their junior year. Applications are evaluated on a rolling basis, and students can expect to be notified of a decision within two weeks of completing their application for admission.

To arrange a campus visit or request application materials, students should contact:

Office of Admission
Kentucky Wesleyan College
3000 Frederica Street
Box 1039
Owensboro, Kentucky 42302-1039
Telephone: 270-926-3111
          800-999-0592 (toll free)
E-mail: admitme@kwc.edu
World Wide Web: http://www.kwc.edu

KETTERING UNIVERSITY
FLINT, MICHIGAN

The University

Kettering University (formerly GMI Engineering & Management Institute) offers education for the real world. Nearly 100 percent of Kettering's students receive a job offer or are accepted by graduate schools before receiving their diplomas. Kettering University has a unique partnership that offers students, business, and industry an opportunity found at no other undergraduate college in America. Kettering, a five-year cooperative engineering, management, science, and math university, is the only institution that assists incoming freshmen to be selected by companies for cooperative employment, a process initiated for all accepted students. Kettering University successfully integrates the practical aspects of the workplace into the world of higher education through its more than 750 corporate partners, corporations, and agencies located throughout the United States, Canada, and selected countries. Kettering's corporate partners represent most major industrial groups; many are recognized as worldwide leaders in business innovation and manufacturing technology. These corporations share a commitment to "grow their own" engineers and managers by employing exceptionally talented young men and women in one of the ten baccalaureate degree programs. Kettering's corporate partners invest in students' futures by providing a five-year program of progressive work experience that exposes them to processes, products, corporate culture, and the technology necessary to compete in tomorrow's business environment.

Founded in 1919, Kettering University is private and enrolls about 2,400 undergraduate students. The University is accredited by the North Central Association of Colleges and Schools. Its engineering curricula are accredited by the Accreditation Board for Engineering and Technology, Inc. (ABET). The management program is accredited by the Association of Collegiate Business Schools and Programs (ACBSP).

The combination of academics and professional, paid work experience offered through Kettering University is not only highly effective, it is without equal, even among other cooperative education programs. The advantages of a Kettering education have enabled thousands of graduates to rise to key executive leadership positions in the world's finest corporations.

A varied program of sports, fitness, and recreational activities is offered. A 445-student residence hall and a 120-student apartment complex are located on campus. Campus facilities include athletic fields, tennis courts, and a recreation center with an Olympic-size, six-lane swimming pool, aerobic fitness rooms, a full line of Nautilus equipment, and basketball, tennis, and racquetball courts. A public golf course is adjacent to the campus.

Professional counseling, support services, and health care are available.

Location

Located in east-central Michigan, 60 miles west of Lake Huron and Canada and 60 miles north of Detroit, Flint is a city of 135,000 residents with a metropolitan area population of 450,000. Flint is particularly proud of its distinctive College and Cultural Center Complex, which is about 1½ miles from campus. Built and endowed entirely by the gifts of private citizens, the center includes the Alfred P. Sloan Museum; the Whiting Auditorium, home of the Flint Symphony and host to leading stage shows and entertainers; the Robert T. Longway Planetarium, Michigan's largest and best-equipped sky show facility; the Flint Institute of Arts; the F. A. Bower Theatre; the Dort Institute of Music; the University of Michigan–Flint Campus; the C. S. Mott Community College; and the Flint Public Library. The IMA Sports Arena is home to the Flint Generals professional hockey team, as well as the University hockey club, and is the site of many special events.

Outdoor and indoor recreational opportunities are abundant. Within a few minutes' drive are downhill and cross-country skiing facilities, several fine lakes for the entire range of water sports, a wide selection of good golf courses open to the public, and excellent indoor and outdoor skating rinks.

Majors and Degrees

Kettering University offers a five-year, professional cooperative program with curricula leading to designated Bachelor of Science degrees in Computer Engineering, Electrical Engineering, Industrial Engineering, Manufacturing Systems Engineering, and Mechanical Engineering degrees; a designated Bachelor of Science in Business and Industrial Management degree with concentrations in accounting/finance, information systems, manufacturing management, marketing, and materials management; and designated Bachelor of Science degrees in applied mathematics, applied physics, computer science, and environmental chemistry. Minors are available in applied chemistry, applied mathematics, applied optics, computer science, liberal arts, and management.

Academic Program

Although each program at Kettering University has its own sequence requirements, 180 credit hours are generally required, including thesis credit hours. The program involves nine academic terms and up to eleven co-op terms, two of which are focused on the capstone fifth-year thesis project, which is done on behalf of the student's co-op employer. Students alternate between twelve-week periods of academic study on the campus in Flint and twelve-week periods of related work experience with their corporate employer. The academic year consists of two 12-week academic terms on campus and two 12-week terms of paid work experience. A typical Kettering University cooperative student may earn up to $65,000 in co-op wages through the complete program.

Academic Facilities

Classrooms, laboratories, and offices of the academic departments are located in the Academic Building, with more than 95,000 square feet devoted to laboratories. In addition to the traditional laboratory facilities expected of any top engineering school, Kettering University has labs to demonstrate and experiment with a wide range of technologies found in industry—from basic machining to emerging technologies. The instrumentation in some labs is generally found only in graduate school facilities at other colleges. There are manufacturing, laser, radioisotope, heat transfer, electricity and solid-state electronics, metallurgy, computer-aided design (CAD), computer-integrated manufacturing (CIM), acoustics, mechatronics, human factors, digital and analog computer, robotics, holography, and electron microscopy laboratories and the Polymer Optimization Center. The campus is fully networked and allows access to computer resources from dormitory rooms, dedicated labs, and other locations. Sun servers, networked SPARC stations for high-end CAD/CAE applications, and more than 300 microprocessors of various types allow students to use all major operating systems and applications. Each student has unlimited 24-hour access to computer resources and the World Wide Web. The library contains more than 94,000 cataloged volumes and currently subscribes to more than 540 periodicals and various online services. Special facilities include a microfilm area, database search services, record and tape listening and videocassette viewing facilities, and a special collection of SAE, SME, and ASME technical papers.

Costs

Tuition in 2000–01 is $15,965 per year plus a $65 student activity fee per term. The orientation fee is $75 (first term only). Books and supplies are approximately $750. Room and board are $4120 per year (fifteen meals per week).

Financial Aid

In addition to all traditional sources of aid, all Kettering students benefit from a special resource that is significant and not need based. One of the many advantages of attending Kettering University is the opportunity for students to earn a salary during their co-op work terms. Co-op income is substantial and can help cover part of the cost of a Kettering education by supplementing the family contribution, and the standard forms of need-based and merit-based financial aid. Students who live at home during work experience periods are able to contribute a greater proportion of earnings directly to educational expenses. About 70 percent of students are able to live at home during work terms. The typical range of co-op earnings over the five-year program is $40,000 to $65,000.

Kettering University offers all the traditional forms of financial aid, both need- and merit-based. The new Kettering Scholarship program, with awards up to $60,000, is available to qualified applicants. Because of their talents, many students win scholarships from agencies and organizations from their local communities. Michigan residents are often recipients of the Michigan Competitive Scholarship/Tuition Grant. More than 92 percent of the 1999 entering class received some form of financial aid, making a private education at Kettering very affordable.

The primary purpose of financial aid at Kettering University is to supplement a student's unmet financial need after cooperative earnings and parents' contributions. Students who wish to apply for financial aid should complete the Free Application for Federal Student Aid (FAFSA) and request that a copy of the analysis be sent to Kettering University. Aid is given as grants, scholarships, loans, and work-study awards.

Faculty

Kettering University's full-time faculty of 144 have teaching as their prime responsibility. Most professors in degree disciplines have industrial experience in addition to academic credentials and maintain contact with industry through consulting, sponsored research, and advising on fifth-year student thesis projects. More than 80 percent hold the doctorate. Because only half of the students are on campus at any one time, class sizes are small and opportunities for enrichment and extra help are readily available. Kettering faculty members find the challenge of teaching talented students who share their experiences from co-op especially refreshing and rewarding.

Student Government

Kettering University students enjoy an active college life with a wide range of clubs and organizations and an exciting intramural athletic program. Eleven professional societies are active on campus, and there are fourteen national fraternities and six sororities. More than half of all students are active in fraternities and sororities. Kettering students tend to enjoy competition, whether it be in service activities or on the athletic field. The student government represents the interests and needs of the students and contributes to their educational development in the areas of leadership skills, self-confidence, interpersonal relations, and organizational operations.

Admission Requirements

Admission to Kettering University is competitive and based on scholastic achievement and nonscholastic interests, activities, and achievements. Applicants are required to have earned the following credits (a credit represents two semesters or one year of study): algebra, 2 credits; geometry, 1 credit; trigonometry, ½ credit; laboratory science, 2 credits (physics and chemistry are strongly recommended for all students; at least 1 credit of chemistry or physics is required); and English, 3 credits. A minimum of 16 credits is required; however, the University encourages students to complete at least 20 credits. Applicants must submit results of the SAT I or ACT. (Kettering's ACT code number is 1998; the SAT I code number is 1246.) The staff of the Corporate Relations Office initiates the process and assists all enrolled students with the process of securing cooperative employment. The process begins upon confirmation of enrollment and continues until each student is employed. Many students are able to secure co-op employment before classes begin.

Most Kettering University students achieve at or near the top 10 percent of their graduating class on traditional criteria such as grades, rank, and test scores. Corporate employers are also very interested in activities, career goals, experiences, leadership, and other personal qualities. Kettering University also welcomes students wishing to transfer from other colleges and universities. The transfer alternative is an excellent way to gain admission for students who do not enroll as freshmen.

Application and Information

Prospective freshmen are encouraged to file their application early in their senior year. Admission decisions for transfer applicants are based on college record for those who have completed at least 30 credits. Applications are accepted all year long; however, early application greatly increases visibility for early employment possibilities in the co-op search process. The application fee is $25.

Admissions Office
Kettering University
1700 West Third Avenue
Flint, Michigan 48504-4898
Telephone: 810-762-7865
          800-955-4464 (toll-free in the United States and Canada)
E-mail: admissions@kettering.edu
World Wide Web: http://www.kettering.edu

Kettering University graduates expect a good job or entrance into a top graduate school.

KING'S COLLEGE
WILKES-BARRE, PENNSYLVANIA

The College

King's College is an independent four-year Catholic college with more than 2,200 men and women students. Founded by the Holy Cross Fathers of the University of Notre Dame in 1946, King's prepares students for a purposeful life with an education that integrates the human values inherent in a broadly based curriculum with programs in humanities, sciences, and social sciences and specialized programs in business, health care, and other professions. In an open Catholic tradition, the College encourages the religious, moral, personal, and social development of its students.

In addition to the undergraduate degrees listed below, King's College also offers Master of Science degrees in finance (with tracks in accounting and taxation) and health-care administration, a Master of Education (M.Ed.) degree (with a concentration in reading), and a five-year physician assistant studies program.

Academic advising begins before students enroll and continues throughout their four years of study. King's Academic Skills Center includes a nationally certified tutoring program and a faculty-staffed writing center. More than 80 percent of King's first-year students return for their sophomore year, a percentage well above the national average. In comparison to the national average of 54 percent, 63 percent of King's students who enter as first-year students graduate within four years, and 99 percent are employed within the first six months of graduation.

Campus features include the Charles E. and Mary Parente Life Sciences Center, the Mulligan Physical Sciences Center, the William G. McGowan School of Business, and a 33.5-acre athletic complex, which includes a field house and fields for baseball, softball, men's and women's soccer, football, and field hockey. The 15-acre campus also includes five residence halls; two dining halls; the Sheehy Student Center, which houses the College's FM radio station; the J. Carroll McCormick Campus Ministry Center; and the William S. Scandlon Physical Education Center, which includes a 3,200-seat basketball arena, wrestling facilities, racquetball and handball courts, an Olympic-size swimming pool, a rifle range, and a strength and fitness center as well as a state-of-the-art sports medicine facility. The College also has a 5,000-square-foot weight room with more than 13,000 pounds of free weights that is approved by the American Weightlifting Federation. The student health center is located in Hafey-Marian Hall, a modern six-story building for classrooms and faculty offices, and a consulting physician is on call at all times. The six-story administration and science buildings form a unit that houses the College's theater, a cafeteria, administrative offices, science laboratories, and classrooms.

More than fifty student organizations provide King's students with the opportunity to explore interests outside the classroom. Student athletics include intercollegiate competition in men's baseball, basketball, football, golf, lacrosse, soccer, swimming, tennis, and wrestling; women's basketball, field hockey, lacrosse, soccer, softball, swimming, tennis, and volleyball; and coed cross-country, riflery, and cheerleading. Intramural and club sports include basketball, bowling, field hockey, flag football, racquetball, riflery, softball, street hockey, and volleyball. Other cocurricular activities include academic clubs in almost every department, the King's Players (theater), the nationally ranked debate team, Christian Voices, Campus Ministry, the Experiencing the Arts Series, the *Crown* (student newspaper), the *Regis* (yearbook), and *SCOP* (literary magazine).

Location

The King's campus is located in a residential area near downtown Wilkes-Barre, a city of approximately 50,000 on the banks of the Susquehanna River in the Pocono Mountains. Once noted for its anthracite coal industry, Wilkes-Barre has developed both economically and culturally, yet it has avoided many typical urban problems. The crime rate in the city is one of the lowest in the nation. Local events include the Cherry Blossom Festival, a national ice carving competition, and the Fine Arts Fiesta. Shopping malls, movie theaters, parks, art galleries, and restaurants are nearby. Two blocks from King's is the F. M. Kirby Center, which has hosted such performers as Bill Cosby, the Spin Doctors, and Howie Mandel. National recording acts regularly perform in the area.

King's is a short drive from several well-known ski resorts, state parks, and major lakes, as well as the stadium of the Phillies' AAA baseball team, the Pocono International Raceway, and an arena/convention center that is home to the Pittsburgh Penguins' minor-league ice hockey team. New York City and Philadelphia are within a 2½-hour drive; Harrisburg, Pennsylvania, and Morristown, New Jersey, are within 2 hours; and New England and Washington, D.C., are within 4 hours.

Majors and Degrees

King's awards Bachelor of Arts, Bachelor of Science, Associate in Arts, and Associate in Science degrees. The College's thirty-seven major programs are offered by the College of Arts and Sciences and the William G. McGowan School of Business, which is a candidate for AACSB–The International Association for Management Education accreditation. The College of Arts and Sciences includes the humanities and social sciences division (corporate communications, criminal justice, English, French, gerontology, history, human resources, mass communication/media technologies, philosophy, political science, psychology, sociology, Spanish, theater, and theology), the education division (early childhood, elementary, secondary certification and special education), the science division (biology, chemistry, computer science, environmental studies, general science, mathematics, and neuroscience), and the allied health division (clinical lab science, physician assistant studies, and sports medicine). Available majors in the William G. McGowan School of Business are accounting, business administration, computers and information systems, economics, finance, health-care administration, international business, and marketing. King's offers preprofessional programs in dentistry, law, medicine, pharmacy, and veterinary science.

Academic Program

The general education program at King's was recognized with the presentation of the Hesburgh Award Certificate of Excellence at the annual meeting of the American Council on Education. King's was among the top institutions in the nation to be included in the last six editions of *Barron's Best Buys in College Education* and six consecutive issues of *U.S. News & World Report's Best Colleges Guide*. The College was also featured for its efforts in the assessment of student learning in the *Chronicle of Higher Education*, *Change: The Magazine of Higher Learning* and three times by inclusion in the John Templeton Foundation Honor Roll for Character-Building Colleges. The core curriculum is recognized as a model curriculum. It incorporates traditional and new concepts in liberal arts education, develops competence in such areas as communications and problem solving, and measures students' progress throughout the program.

The honors program offers highly motivated students the challenge of learning in discussion-centered courses that explore distinctive subject matter with exciting and innovative approaches. Sixteen honor societies encourage students to excel in their chosen fields and recognize students for their academic distinction; members are honored each year at the All-College Honors Convocation. Science students receive hands-on lab training much earlier than students at other institutions and work together with faculty members on real-world research projects.

Off-Campus Arrangements

Experiential learning (via internships) is available in conjunction with almost every major. Placement possibilities include CNN, Coopers & Lybrand, the New York Stock Exchange, the Pennsylvania Department of Education, the Pennsylvania State House of Representatives, the U.S. House of Representatives, U.S. Senators' offices, U.S. Department of Energy, Walt Disney World, and Xerox Corporation. Every year students are placed with local, regional, and national companies around the globe.

The International Internship Program and Study-Abroad Program are also options for King's students. Participants spend fourteen weeks in cities working at a variety of professions. An agreement with Webster University provides study opportunities on campuses throughout Europe.

Academic Facilities

King's facilities include the 51,000-square-foot, three-story D. Leonard Corgan Library, which contains several study rooms, a 100-seat auditorium, and a 160,000-volume collection accessed by a computerized catalog. The library uses its affiliation with the Online Computer Library Center to provide students and faculty members with access to college and research libraries throughout the United States. The library provides full-text databases from every computer on campus. Students and faculty members have direct access to more than 1 million volumes through the local library cooperative (NEPBC). Residence halls have cable television and individual phone service in rooms. King's features ten IBM computer labs with more than 200 PCs; 24-hour labs in three residence halls; a networked campus with full access to the Internet and the World Wide Web; networked residence hall rooms; e-mail accounts for all students; computerized library databases; multimedia classrooms with a variety of instructional aids; course discussions on course listservs outside of the traditional classroom; a technology component of the core curriculum that requires all students to learn to access, process, and develop their own computer and information presentation skills; distance learning facilities for teleconferencing; satellite downlink capabilities in the 220-seat Burke Auditorium of the William G. McGowan School of Business; and cross-registration with area colleges that enables students to take courses complimentary to their majors. The $6.4-million Charles E. and Mary Parente Life Sciences Center, which contains a molecular biology laboratory, includes computer facilities, instrumentation rooms, a rooftop greenhouse, and environmental chambers. The $6-million Physical Sciences Center includes modern research laboratories, computer facilities, and state-of-the-art instrumentation used for molecular identification. Over the past five years, King's has spent more than $400,000 on new equipment for the sciences.

Costs

For the 2000–01 academic year, tuition for full-time students is $16,000. Room and board totals $3260. There is a comprehensive College fee of $700.

Financial Aid

King's attempts to financially assist all qualified students; more than 85 percent of King's students currently receive financial aid. Aid is awarded on the basis of documented need, the difference between the expected cost of the college education and the expected family contribution toward this education. According to a recent study, grants and scholarships funded by King's comprise 40 percent of all financial aid sources available to its students; this figure exceeds the national average of 18.5 percent.

Four types of financial aid are available at King's: grants, loans, work-study programs, and scholarships ranging from $5000 to full tuition. Usually a combination of the sources is used in a financial aid package. A deferred-payment program, through which students and/or their families make scheduled payments to the College, is also offered. Students who desire financial aid must fill out the Free Application for Federal Student Aid (FAFSA), as well as the College's application. Forms are mailed to students accepted for admission.

Faculty

King's College has 106 full-time and 77 part-time faculty members. Eighty-five percent of the full-time faculty have a Ph.D. or an equivalent terminal degree. Graduate assistants do not teach courses. The student-faculty ratio is 15:1.

Student Government

The student government coordinates and participates in numerous activities for both the student body and the surrounding community. It regularly holds open forums for students and senior administrators at the College, coordinates informal socials for the students with the College president, and makes presentations at each meeting of the Board of Directors. In addition, the student government sponsors such events as AIDS Awareness Week, Hunger Week, Earth Day, and a celebration of cultural diversity. Community projects include Make a Difference Day, the Great American Smokeout, National Collegiate Alcohol Awareness Week, and fund-raisers for the United Way. The Association for Campus Events, a student-operated organization, also sponsors comedians, movies, and performers throughout the year.

Admission Requirements

King's encourages applications from qualified individuals who are seniors in high school and those who wish to transfer from another institution. To be considered for admission, students must be prepared to pursue successfully a program of study at the College, as evidenced by the quality of previous academic and extracurricular performance, the recommendation of school officials and character references, and the student's display of personal promise, maturity, and motivation. King's admits students of any race, sex, color, creed, or national or ethnic origin. Admission decisions are made for both high school students and transfer students with the understanding that all current courses and examinations will be completed satisfactorily. Candidates should complete 4 years of mathematics (through trigonometry or precalculus); a year of high school chemistry and physics is also strongly recommended. High school students must take either the SAT I or the ACT. Test scores are used primarily for advisement and placement.

Application and Information

Applicants should forward a completed application and the $30 fee to the Admissions Office. Secondary and postsecondary (if applicable) transcripts must be sent. High school students must also submit SAT I or ACT scores. Admission decisions are not made until these credentials are received. King's subscribes to a rolling admission policy with priority acceptance in March; decisions are announced within two to four weeks from the date of application. Upon notification of acceptance, a $100 nonrefundable deposit is requested to reserve a place in the class. The deposit deadline is May 1 but may be extended upon request. The acceptance deposit for the professional phase of the physician assistant program is $300. To schedule an interview or to obtain an application form or more information, students should contact:

Admission Office
King's College
133 North River Street
Wilkes-Barre, Pennsylvania 18711
Telephone: 570-208-5858
          800-955-5777 (toll-free)
          888-KINGS-PA (toll-free)
E-mail: admssns@kings.edu
World Wide Web: http://www.kings.edu

KNOX COLLEGE
GALESBURG, ILLINOIS

The College

Knox College is a vital community of teachers and students that provides a challenging liberal arts curriculum, a faculty of national distinction, and a campus atmosphere noted for its informality. Knox invites students who seek a strong education and who relish the chance to explore their own ideas within a community of friends and mentors. Founded in 1837, Knox is one of the Midwest's great liberal arts colleges and among the nation's best. Site of the fifth Lincoln-Douglas debate, Knox has enrolled women and African-American students since the 1850s and international students since the 1860s. Knox has been known for its high academic quality since the nineteenth century and has many distinguished alumni in the professions, business, journalism, the natural sciences, and higher education.

Knox is an independent, coeducational four-year college. The student body of 1,220 comes from forty-seven states and forty-one countries. There are roughly equal numbers of men and women; 12 percent of students are members of American minority groups (5 percent Asian, 3 percent Hispanic, 3 percent African-American, and 1 percent Native American), and 11 percent are international students. Knox is very much a residential college, with more than 90 percent of students living on its spacious 82-acre campus. Most student residences are organized in 8- to 15-person suites with double and single rooms; options include coeducational residence halls, former private homes, and apartment-style units. Campus life is characterized by wide participation in more than seventy-five student organizations and extracurricular activities. The student-run Union Board provides a full entertainment calendar throughout the year. Musical groups run the gamut from rock, folk, and jazz combos to the Chamber Singers and the Knox-Galesburg Symphony. There are frequent theater productions and a modern dance ensemble. Knox has a 1,000-watt FM station, a biweekly student newspaper, and a student literary magazine twice named the nation's best. Student groups provide activities ranging from political activism to community service to religious meditation. There are five fraternities and two sororities. Knox competes at the NCAA Division III level in eleven men's and ten women's sports. Varsity sports are baseball, basketball, cross-country, football, golf, indoor and outdoor track, soccer, swimming, tennis, and wrestling for men and basketball, cross-country, golf, indoor and outdoor track, soccer, softball, swimming, tennis, and volleyball for women.

Location

Galesburg is an historic city of 33,000 located about 180 miles west of Chicago, 200 miles north of St. Louis, and about an hour away from the Mississippi River. It is accessible by transcontinental Amtrak trains, commercial airlines, bus lines, and interstate highways. Community service and internship and employment opportunities are available in local social service agencies, hospitals, financial institutions, and a variety of manufacturing firms. The campus is located three blocks from downtown shops, movie theaters, and restaurants. Notable features are the Orpheum Theater (a restored 1,000-seat concert hall), specialty shops on historic Seminary Street, and Lake Storey on the city's north side.

Majors and Degrees

Knox awards the Bachelor of Arts degree in the following major fields: American studies, art (history and studio), biochemistry, biology, Black studies, chemistry, classics, computer science, economics, education (elementary and secondary), English (literature and creative writing), environmental studies, French, German, German area studies, history, integrated international studies, international relations, mathematics, modern languages, music, philosophy, physics, political science, psychology, Russian, Russian area studies, sociology-anthropology, Spanish, theater, and women's studies. Students may also design their own interdisciplinary major. Nonmajor concentrations are offered in Black studies, environmental studies, Latin American studies, religious studies, and women's studies and preprofessional course sequences are identified for dentistry, engineering, law, medicine, and veterinary medicine. In addition, Knox offers teacher certification in art and in elementary and secondary education.

Knox offers special programs in cooperation with several other institutions, including dual-degree programs in the following fields, all of which include the Knox B.A. degree: architecture (M.A.), engineering (B.S.E.), environmental management (M.E.M.), forestry (M.F.), law (J.D.), and nursing/medical technology (B.S.).

The Knox-Rush Early Identification Program identifies selected Knox first-year students for admission to Rush Medical College upon completion of their Knox degree.

Academic Program

The goal of Knox College is to provide students with a strong education in the liberal arts and to prepare them for rewarding professional and personal lives. The curriculum is designed to integrate the skills of critical inquiry and communication with study in breadth and depth. The required First-Year Preceptorial encourages students to engage the fundamental questions and concerns of a liberal education and fosters thoughtful debate, careful reasoning, and clear writing. Other requirements include the achievement of competence in mathematics and in one foreign language (these may be fulfilled by examination), the selection of two courses from each academic division to satisfy distribution requirements, and the completion of a major field. A new requirement is the completion of an Advanced Preceptorial course, selected from a designated group of interdisciplinary courses, where students bring the perspective of their major to a cross-disciplinary topic in order to integrate their specialized study with the larger concerns of a liberal education. The academic calendar is three 10-week terms, with a normal load of three 1-credit courses per term. Thirty-six credits are required for graduation. There is an optional three-week Mini-Term offered during the month of December.

The close relationship of faculty and students is key to Knox's program. Students work with faculty advisers to develop their programs of study; the ratio of first-year students to faculty advisers is held to no more than 8:1, while the overall student-faculty ratio is 12:1. Students with declared majors work with an adviser in their major field. Small classes (averaging 18 students) are the rule, and independent study is common in every department. Student research is a distinctive feature at Knox, which regularly sends one of the largest contingents to national conferences on undergraduate research. Promising students are encouraged to apply for one of the several available research opportunities, including the Ford Research Fellows, Richter Fellows, and ACM Minority/McNair Fellows Programs, to pursue an independent project under the supervision of a faculty mentor. Similarly, seniors are encouraged to pursue College Honors. Other special features worthy of note are the nationally recognized Writing Program, the theater department's Repertory Term, and the art department's Open Studio experience.

Off-Campus Arrangements

Knox maintains its own programs abroad in Buenos Aires, Argentina; Besançon, France; and Barcelona, Spain, in cooperation with the universities of those cities. In addition, Knox recognizes and gives credit for thirty-one programs in twenty countries, as well as eight programs in the United States. Students normally participate in these programs during the junior year.

Academic Facilities

The Knox campus has forty-two academic and residential buildings. Old Main, built in 1857, is the sole intact site of the 1858 Lincoln-Douglas debates and is on the National Register of Historic Buildings. Library holdings include more than 285,000 volumes and 685 periodicals in addition to OCLC interlibrary loan, online databases, and an automated catalog accessible from remote workstations around campus. Seymour Library's Special Collections Center houses manuscripts and rare book collections of national importance, such as the Finley Collection on the Old Northwest and the Hughes Collection on Hemingway and the "Lost Generation." Umbeck Science-Mathematics Center contains spacious teaching and research labs, extensive research equipment including electron microscopes and NMR, and a science library. Computer technology features a campuswide fiber-optic network, Internet access, five student computer labs (including 24-hour access), several specialized departmental labs, and more than 200 Macintosh and IBM-compatible PCs for student use. Davis Hall, housing the social sciences and modern languages, includes a data analysis microcomputer lab and a language center equipped with audio, video, and computer equipment. The Fine Arts Center contains two theaters, a recital hall, music rehearsal studios, and art studios for painting, drawing, sculpture, printmaking, and ceramics. In addition, there is a Student Union, an outstanding gymnasium, and a recreational field house.

Costs

The comprehensive fee for 2000–01 is $26,610. This includes $20,940 for tuition, $5436 for room and board, and a $234 student activities fee. Extra expenses for books, travel, supplies, laundry, and incidentals are estimated at $1200.

Financial Aid

Knox is committed to being accessible to all qualified students. Admission decisions are made without regard for ability to pay, and Knox awards need-based financial aid according to each student's eligibility. Financial aid awards may include federal and state grants, student loans, and campus employment. New students must file an official financial aid application by March 1 for priority consideration. Knox offers a number of supplemental loan options as well as a variety of payment plans.

Knox also awards merit-based scholarships that are not based on financial need to recognize outstanding academic achievement as well as special abilities in art, chemistry, mathematics, music, theater, and writing.

Faculty

Knox has 99 full-time and 13 part-time faculty members, of whom 92 percent hold the Ph.D. or equivalent. Faculty members teach all courses. More than two thirds have published or presented scholarly or creative work in the past five years. National recognition includes major research awards from the National Science Foundation, the National Institutes of Health, and the National Endowment for the Humanities; a 1997 ASCAP Award–winning composer; and a 1994 NSF Shannon Award–winning geneticist.

Student Government

At Knox, students are treated as full members of the community. Students administer the campuswide honor and judicial systems, regulating academic and social behavior. They are appointed to all faculty committees (except two personnel committees), have formal observer status to the Board of Trustees, and are a majority of the members on the committee regulating student affairs. In addition, there is an elected Student Senate.

Admission Requirements

Applicants to Knox must demonstrate the ability to do successful college-level work and to make a positive contribution to the campus community. The fundamental requirement is successful completion of a challenging college-preparatory program. Of the 1999 first-year students, 46 percent were in the top tenth of their high school class and roughly 75 percent were in the top quarter. The middle 50 percent of students scored between 550 and 650 on the mathematics portion of the SAT I and between 550 and 680 on the verbal; on the ACT composite, the mid-50 percent range was 24 to 29. Applicants must complete the application form, file a nonrefundable $35 fee, and provide Knox with their SAT I or ACT scores, their academic transcripts, and recommendations from a teacher and counselor. Interviews are strongly recommended. Applications from transfer and international students are strongly encouraged.

Application and Information

For more information, students should contact:
Paul Steenis
Director of Admission
Knox College
Galesburg, Illinois 61401
Telephone: 309-341-7100
              800-678-KNOX (toll-free)
Fax: 309-341-7070
E-mail: admission@knox.edu
World Wide Web: http://www.knox.edu

Knox College's Old Main, the last remaining site of the Lincoln-Douglas debates of 1858.

KUTZTOWN UNIVERSITY OF PENNSYLVANIA
KUTZTOWN, PENNSYLVANIA

The University

In a recent independent survey, 93 percent of students and recent alumni rated their education at Kutztown University (KU) as excellent or good in regard to their overall college experience, the quality of instruction they received, and the quality of the faculty. Kutztown offers excellent academic programs through its undergraduate Colleges of Liberal Arts and Sciences, Visual and Performing Arts, Business, and Education and through its graduate studies program. A wide range of student support services complements the high-quality classroom instruction.

In addition, Kutztown students have the advantage of a well-rounded program of athletic, cultural, and social events. At Kutztown, there are clubs, organizations, and activities to satisfy nearly every taste. Currently, some 7,900 full-time and part-time students are enrolled at the University. About half of the full-time undergraduates live in residence halls; the rest live at home or in apartments in nearby communities.

Kutztown University's attractive 325-acre campus includes a mix of old and new buildings, including stately Old Main, the historic building known to generations of Kutztown's students; University Place, a modern residence hall in a courtyard setting; and the Student Union Building.

Location

The University is located in a beautiful rural Pennsylvania Dutch community midway between the cities of Allentown and Reading. Both cities are a short drive from campus and have major shopping and recreational facilities. Kutztown borough, an easy walk from campus, has ample stores and shops to meet the needs of students. Philadelphia is about 1½ hours away, and New York City, about 2½.

Majors and Degrees

The Bachelor of Arts is awarded in American studies, anthropology, economics, English, French, general studies, geography, German, history, mathematics, music, philosophy, political science, psychology, Russian, Russian and Slavic studies, social welfare, sociology, Spanish, speech communication, and theater. The Bachelor of Fine Arts is available with majors in communication design, crafts, related arts, and studio art. The Bachelor of Science is offered in biology, chemistry, computer and information science, criminal justice, environmental science (concentrations in biology, chemistry, and geology), general studies, geology, marine science, mathematics, medical technology, nursing (at the upper-division level—for RNs), physics, psychology, public administration, and telecommunications. The Bachelor of Science in Business Administration is offered with majors in accounting, economics, finance, general business, international business, management, and marketing. The Bachelor of Science in Education is awarded with concentrations in art education, early childhood education, elementary education, and library science and, on the secondary level, in biology, chemistry, communication, earth-space science, English, French, general science, German, mathematics, physics, Russian, social studies (anthropology, economics, geography, history, political science, psychology, and sociology), Spanish, and special education (concentrations in mentally/physically handicapped/elementary education, speech-language pathology, and visually impaired/elementary education).

Academic Program

The University observes a two-semester calendar, and first-semester examinations are completed by late December. A minimum of 128 semester hours and a cumulative quality point average (QPA) of at least 2.0 are required for graduation. In the College of Liberal Arts and Sciences and College of Business, a quality point average of at least 2.0 in the major is also required. Core curricula vary for specific majors.

Students seeking admission to teacher education must complete a three-stage process. (1) Applicants must have a projected grade point average (PGPA) of at least 2.0. Students with less than a 2.0 PGPA may be granted admission on a conditional basis and are required to schedule and pass appropriate developmental education courses. (2) During the fourth semester (or after completing 64 credits), applicants must present evidence of 30 hours of classroom observation, achieve at least a 2.5 overall average, pass a speech screening test, and complete basic speech, mathematics, English composition, EDU 100, student teaching, and professional education courses as determined by each major with a minimum grade of C. (3) Prior to student teaching, applicants must complete a professional semester or early field experience, have achieved at least a 2.5 QPA as well as a 2.5 QPA in all courses in the major required for student teaching, and be recommended by the department screening committee. Students are required to pass the National Teachers Examination (NTE) (three core batteries and a specialty area) at the end of their academic program before the Pennsylvania Department of Education will issue an Instructional I (Probationary) Certificate.

The distinctive University Honors Program is available to qualified students in all areas of study. Freshmen who have been identified as potential honors students based on their high school records and SAT scores, transfer students from other honors programs, and incumbent students who have at least a 3.25 GPA are invited to enroll in the program. The 21 credits in honors work, which include a senior thesis project, count toward the 128 credits required for graduation. Honors students select specially designed courses, independent study, and internships. The Honors Program awards several merit-based scholarships, and students who complete the program receive an honors diploma upon graduation.

Kutztown University and the Colleges of Engineering and Earth and Mineral Studies of Pennsylvania State University cooperate in a 3-2 program in liberal arts and engineering. Three years or the equivalent are spent at Kutztown University, where the student takes liberal arts courses along with pre-engineering courses. Upon satisfactory completion of this program and recommendation by the faculty, the student enters Pennsylvania State University and fulfills the specified course requirements. Successful completion of these programs leads to appropriate baccalaureate degrees from both institutions.

Kutztown University provides an opportunity for higher education for students who, because of economic need, cultural disadvantage, or inadequate preparation, have previously been unable to attend college. Students admitted to Kutztown University under the Developmental Summer Program attend a preparatory program designed to introduce them to university study and to provide supportive services in counseling and tutoring as well as special instruction in study skills, reading, and writing.

Off-Campus Arrangements

Students majoring in education spend one semester of their senior year student teaching in area schools under the guidance of an experienced teacher. Additional teaching field experiences are available in the junior year during the "professional semester." Internships in other programs provide students with one semester of practical experience in their specialty. For example, political science students may work in local, state, or federal government agencies; psychology students in area psychiatric hospitals, clinics, and rehabilitation centers; social welfare and criminal justice students in various social agencies; telecommunications students in commercial or public broadcasting, cable television, and industrial, medical, or institutional television; and medical technology students in area hospitals.

Kutztown University has exchange and study-abroad programs with colleges and universities in fourteen countries. In addition, through the International Student Exchange Program, KU students may study for a year in any of sixty institutions in twenty-seven countries. Kutztown is now in its sixth year of a cooperative program with the Diplomatic Academy of the Russian Foreign Ministry, Moscow, in which prominent Russian scholars and foreign affairs experts visit KU to meet with classes and give public lectures.

Through consortium arrangements with colleges and universities in three states, Kutztown participates in the operation of a marine science research center at Wallops Island, Virginia, which has laboratories, research equipment, and coastal research ships. Through this facility, students in marine science classes are able to gain firsthand knowledge of the ocean environment. The University's participation in the Pennsylvania Consortium for International Education provides opportunities for study abroad during the summer.

Academic Facilities

In 1998, Rohrbach Library doubled in size with the completion of a new addition and the modernization of nearly the entire library complex. Now, Rohrbach Library provides many attractive and functional areas that greatly enhance the learning environment for all students. More than 500 computer connection points have been installed with full access to the Internet. The library has more than 400,000 books and bound periodicals, subscriptions to 2,000 current periodicals and newspapers, and more than 1 million microform units. The map collection is one of the finest in Pennsylvania, with more than 20,000 sheets, and includes Braille maps, city plans, and topographic and raised-relief maps. The library also houses the Audiovisual Center, which is administered by the Audiovisual Communications Department. The AV Center maintains a comprehensive collection of more than 15,000 media items that includes microcomputer software, films, filmstrips, videocassettes, records, and audiocassettes. A well-equipped microcomputer laboratory is located in the center. The Curriculum Materials Center provides preservice and in-service teachers with current teaching and learning resources. More than 11,000 carefully chosen volumes on Russian culture symbolize Kutztown's support of the State System of Higher Education's World Culture Program. Kutztown's resources are supplemented by interlibrary loans through a nationwide computerized network of libraries. Electronic access to library materials is provided through Quincy (the online catalog), Infotrac, which provides full-text journal articles, and many other online resources. Computerized database search enables students and faculty members to obtain customized bibliographies on complex subjects. Other resources include a modern science complex, an astronomical observatory and planetarium, a seismic observatory, the Sharadin Art Gallery, a television studio, a modern language laboratory, and a speech clinic. All residence hall rooms are wired for Internet usage, and new multistation computer labs are available in buildings across the campus.

Costs

In 1999–2000, tuition was $3618 for Pennsylvania residents and $9046 for out-of-state residents. Room and board were $4352. Other fees were $782.80. Books and supplies average $500. Clothes and travel expenses are additional.

Financial Aid

Kutztown University believes that no student who is eligible to enroll at the University should be denied the opportunity for an education solely because of lack of funds. Financial assistance is available through grants, private and institutional scholarships, military officer training programs, on-campus part-time employment, and loans. A booklet describing financial aid opportunities may be obtained by writing to the director of financial aid. Any student wishing to investigate financial aid opportunities should do so when applying for admission, as most programs have application deadlines.

Faculty

Although many professors at Kutztown University are involved in important research and are leaders in their fields, their primary interest is in the classroom. The University has more than 330 full-time instructors and a favorable student-faculty ratio. Upon enrollment in the University, each student is assigned a faculty adviser to help plan his or her academic career. Many faculty members are active in campus groups as members or advisers, creating a close and friendly working relationship with students.

Student Government

All students are members of the Student Government Association and elect representatives who form the Student Government Board (SGB). Students at Kutztown are regarded as mature individuals who can be, in great measure, responsible for the control of their own environment. For that reason, the SGB exercises considerable discretion in coordinating and funding student organizations. Most University committees, including the Council of Trustees, have student members with full voting rights.

Admission Requirements

The main criteria for admission are achievement as indicated on scholastic records, standardized and aptitude tests, and recommendations. Candidates must have graduated from an approved secondary school or demonstrate equivalent preparation. Scores on either the SAT or the ACT are required and are regarded as evidence of ability to do university-level work. It is the responsibility of the applicant to request that his or her scores be forwarded to the admissions office. Either test should be taken no later than the fall of the senior year, and sitting for these exams during the junior year is encouraged. For admission to a special curriculum, the candidate may be required to take an appropriate aptitude test or to supply additional evidence of ability to succeed in the given field. Specific requirements and instructions are included in the admission application materials.

Application and Information

The completed application and all other required materials must be mailed to the director of admission. No action will be taken by the admission committee until all necessary steps have been completed. For additional information and application forms, students should write to:

Dr. Robert McGowan
Director of Admissions
Kutztown University of Pennsylvania
Kutztown, Pennsylvania 19530
E-mail: admission@kutztown.edu

LABORATORY INSTITUTE OF MERCHANDISING
NEW YORK, NEW YORK

The College

Situated in a lovely town house in the center of the fashion capital of the world, the Laboratory Institute of Merchandising (LIM) has been a major force in fashion and business education for six decades. Its graduates can be found throughout the reaches of the industry, and its high standards of education have earned LIM accreditation from the Middle States Association of Colleges and Schools.

LIM is a highly personal college where students learn about the business of fashion with an emphasis on academic and professional study. Lifelong friends are made at LIM as well as lifelong careers. While most students come to the college directly from high school or transfer from other colleges, there are also those of nontraditional college age who enter LIM. Students come to LIM from many parts of the country and the world. The current enrollment at LIM is 267.

LIM prides itself on its placement record. Prior to graduation, the Placement Office undertakes the important task of counseling each student with regard to her or his career. The Office has had outstanding success in helping both four- and two-year graduates obtain positions relevant to their studies. More than 90 percent of the graduates available for placement have been placed in positions related to their studies within ninety days of graduation.

The unique nature of LIM's curriculum provides students with a foundation of core courses in liberal arts and business while offering diverse and intensive hands-on preparation in the fashion industry. This affords graduates the opportunity to accept executive training, merchandising, management, marketing, and communications positions in a wide variety of areas within the fashion and business worlds.

Support services are important at LIM. In addition to academic and career advising, personal counseling is provided through the Dean of Student Services' office. Because of the college's small size and the close relationships between students and staff, any faculty member or administrator, including the president, is readily accessible to help and advise all students. LIM's advisory board members, all successful fashion industry executives, serve as mentors to junior and senior students, offering additional guidance and advice.

Aside from the Student Government and the Fashion Club, other clubs are formed in accordance with student interest. Students have responsibility for *LIMLIGHT*, the college yearbook, and for fashion shows and other social and cultural events.

While most students commute, many live in apartments and student residences near the campus. LIM recommends the Educational Housing Service, as well as several other private dormitory residences in New York City, for off-campus housing. These facilities, which broaden the social experiences and friendships for LIM students, are safe, convenient, and located just minutes from the college.

LIM's unique open-house program, called Student-For-a-Day, offers students and their families the opportunity to tour the college and learn not only of LIM's unique academic programs, but also of the vast array of careers found in the fashion industry. The day also includes a special presentation on visual merchandising and financial aid information on a group or individual level. Current LIM students assist in hosting the event and are available to answer questions. Lunch is provided, and, immediately following, students are invited to stay for a personal interview, which is a requirement for admissions, and sit for the LIM Competitive Scholarship exam.

Location

LIM is fortunate to be able to call New York City its campus. A whole world of fashion is at the college's doorstep and includes such famous stores as Saks Fifth Avenue, Bloomingdale's, Henri Bendel, Armani, and Ralph Lauren. Some of the most exciting buildings in the world are within walking distance—Trump Tower, Rockefeller Center, St. Patrick's Cathedral, and the Metropolitan Museum of Art, with Broadway just a few blocks away. New York City is the headquarters for the garment, cosmetics, advertising, publishing, and textile industries, all of which are essential to the fashion industry and are visited regularly by LIM students. The college incorporates all of these resources into the curriculum. For example, the course The Performing Arts involves going to the theater, the ballet, concerts, and the opera. Another course, Fashion Magazines, includes trips to photography studios and modeling agencies, as well as tours of magazine and advertising firms. New York City offers LIM students an unparalleled learning experience.

Majors and Degrees

LIM offers four-year programs in fashion merchandising and marketing leading to a Bachelor of Business Administration (B.B.A.) or a Bachelor of Professional Studies (B.P.S.) degree and a two-year program leading to the Associate in Applied Sciences (A.A.S.) degree. Qualified transfer students may also apply to a one-year program (ACCESS) leading to the associate degree. Students have the option to study either fashion merchandising or visual merchandising.

Academic Program

LIM offers a combination of classroom education and supervised practical fieldwork that has been designed to prepare students for executive training programs and other entry-level executive positions in various areas of the fashion industry.

The curriculum has three divisions: fashion/visual, business, and arts and communications. Classroom study is supplemented by weekly field trips into the heart of the fashion industry and guest lectures by luminaries from the fashion world.

Work-study is an integral part of an LIM student's education. During the four-year bachelor's degree program, a student will enter the fashion industry three times. Each of the first two years of study contains a five-week, 3-credit work project. During Work Project I, freshmen are placed in paid, full-time selling positions in order to learn the basics of retailing. Work Project II, sophomore year, continues the retailing experience. Qualified sophomores may choose an internship in more glamorous areas such as cosmetics, magazines, designer showrooms, and fashion forecasting companies.

The third and most significant work experience is the senior co-op. Students spend one semester working full-time in the fashion industry in an area relevant to their career goals and ambitions. This program earns 13 credits and is required for graduation from the bachelor's degree program. The responsibility, challenge, and fun of this semester prepare students for their next step—the business world.

Students who are applying to the associate degree program follow the first two years of the bachelor's degree program, including the required Work Projects.

To graduate, students must complete 126 credits for the bachelor's degree or 66–67 credits for the associate degree (33 for one-year ACCESS students), achieve a grade point average of at least 2.0, and satisfactorily complete the cooperative work assignments.

LIM accepts qualified students as transfers throughout the four years. Those with an associate degree in fashion merchandising or related field or with 60 acceptable college credits from a regionally accredited college are usually eligible for junior-year status. Transfer students must complete a minimum of 33 semester hours in addition to the co-op semester at LIM.

LIM's calendar runs on a traditional semester format, offering both fall and spring start dates. Also offered is a summer program in July for both high school and college students. The specially selected courses, such as Display Workshop, Cosmetics Marketing, and Fashion Magazines, blend academics with hands-on experience. Three college credits can be earned for any of these courses.

Off-Campus Arrangements

Study-abroad options are available, including study in London and Paris.

Academic Facilities

LIM's specialized resource center contains 11,000 volumes pertaining to the liberal arts, fashion merchandising, and related fields, as well as 110 professional and academic journals. The library connects to the Internet and accesses worldwide information sources. Students also have Internet access via AOL (America Online). Videocassettes and other multimedia items useful for fashion-related studies are also at students' disposal. A distinctive feature of the video collection is a major group of tapes of the Institute's guest-lecture series, an important reference source for use by students and faculty alike. Personal computers are available for use in the library and classrooms. The student-to-computer ratio is 7:1. The Tutoring Center offers peer-tutoring and special computer programs to supplement and reinforce other learning.

Costs

In 2000–01, tuition is $12,800. Books, supplies, and fees are about $750. Other expenses vary, depending on residence. Students who commute spend from $550 to $1500 for transportation. In 1999–2000, off-campus room and board were about $6000. Personal expenditures are about $1000 a year.

Financial Aid

LIM believes that lack of funds should not keep students from attending college. Thus, admissions decisions and financial aid are totally separate, and a request for aid has no effect on admissions. About 85 percent of LIM's students receive some form of financial aid. Institutional scholarships, Federal Pell Grants, Federal Perkins Loans, Federal Supplemental Educational Opportunity Grants, and New York State TAP grants are all available for eligible students. In addition, LIM is qualified to certify Federal Stafford Student Loans. The Free Application for Federal Student Aid (FAFSA) should be filed by all applicants by April 1. Aid is granted on the basis of need and scholarships on the basis of need and ability. Details of the financial aid program are available on request from the Financial Aid Office.

LIM features a Merit Scholarship Program for incoming freshmen and transfer students. These scholarship monies are awarded for academic achievement in high school or college. Students can remain eligible for their scholarship throughout their stay at LIM by maintaining a GPA of 3.0 or above. The Merit Program also includes a one-time award exclusively for incoming freshmen who attain a combined SAT I score of 1000 or higher.

The catalog discusses other available scholarship opportunities, including the Minority Scholarship and the LIM Competitive Scholarship exam. LIM's Fashion Education Foundation also administers a limited number of grants other than direct institutional awards.

Faculty

LIM prides itself on its faculty members. More than a third of the teaching staff, including all members of the liberal arts faculty, have advanced degrees; all professional subject faculty members have wide business and professional experience. Many, through their business contacts, bring guests to class to share in the lectures and discussions. The student-faculty ratio is 8:1.

Each student is assigned an adviser from the faculty or administrative staff. Work-study and career guidance is given to students by the Placement Office, with conferences held before, during, and after the cooperative work assignments and prior to permanent placement interviews. Students are always welcome to discuss career options at any other time as well.

Student Government

The Student Services Office is the center of all student activities at LIM. This facility supports student government and approves other student organizations and establishes their operating budgets.

Admission Requirements

Applicants must hold a high school or equivalency (GED) diploma and submit SAT I or ACT scores. International students must achieve a TOEFL score of at least 550. Great emphasis is placed on the required personal interview, which the college prefers to conduct on campus. Transfer students' records will be evaluated individually with liberal interpretation placed on course equivalencies. Transfer students may enter LIM in either semester and with any amount of credits accumulated. Students applying for junior year status must hold either an associate degree or have at least 60 acceptable semester hours of credit. Transfer students with more than 30 acceptable semester hours of credit are eligible for the one-year ACCESS program. LIM's admissions committee recognizes that many intangibles go into the making of a successful fashion merchandising student, and it evaluates each application individually.

Application and Information

The application should be accompanied by the $35 fee, an official high school transcript, an official college transcript (if applicable), SAT I or ACT scores, and TOEFL scores (if applicable). Letters of recommendation are recommended. Applicants must also make an appointment for a personal interview. The college uses a rolling admission policy. Applicants are informed of the admission decision within approximately two weeks after all admission requirements have been fulfilled. Application materials may be obtained from the address below:

Andrew Ippolito
Director of Admissions
Laboratory Institute of Merchandising
12 East 53rd Street
New York, New York 10022-5268
Telephone: 212-752-1530
        800-677-1323 (toll-free outside New York City)
Fax: 212-421-4341
E-mail: admissions@limcollege.edu
World Wide Web: http://www.limcollege.edu

LAFAYETTE COLLEGE
EASTON, PENNSYLVANIA

The College
Founded in 1826, historically affiliated with the Presbyterian Church (U.S.A.), and named after the Revolutionary War hero, the Marquis de Lafayette, Lafayette College is committed to providing the best possible undergraduate education in the liberal arts, sciences, and engineering for men and women who can benefit most from the Lafayette experience. The current undergraduate enrollment is 2,244 men and women. Students from thirty-nine states and forty-one other countries currently attend Lafayette. They represent a wide range of interests, special talents, and aspirations. The College draws strength from the diversity of its students.

Primarily residential in nature, Lafayette guarantees on-campus housing to all students who choose to take advantage of the varied living options available to them. More than 96 percent of the students live on the 110-acre main campus in single-sex or coeducational residence halls, social residence halls, fraternities, or sororities, and another 2 percent live close to campus. An array of student organizations, cultural events, social opportunities, and varsity and intramural sports programs are available to all students.

Recent trends indicate that approximately two thirds of Lafayette graduates go on to obtain a graduate or professional degree. About 20 percent pursue full-time graduate or professional study immediately. A large and growing number obtain practical experience through employment and then undertake full-time study for an advanced degree, often with an employer's financial support. Others continue academic pursuits on a part-time basis.

Location
Lafayette College is located in a picturesque setting atop a hill overlooking the Delaware and Lehigh Rivers and Easton, a progressive city of 30,000 people. Allentown and Bethlehem are located near Easton, and, together with the city and adjacent areas, they make up the Lehigh Valley, the third-largest metropolitan area in Pennsylvania. Various business establishments that serve the needs of students are available near the campus and in downtown Easton. Beyond Easton to the west and north are rolling farmland, beautiful countryside, and the Pocono Mountains. New York City is 70 miles east of the campus, and Philadelphia is 60 miles south.

Majors and Degrees
Lafayette awards the Bachelor of Science (B.S.) degree in the following fields: behavioral neuroscience, biochemistry, biology, chemical engineering, chemistry, civil engineering, computer science, electrical and computer engineering, geology, mathematics, mechanical engineering, physics, and psychology. The Bachelor of Arts (A.B.) degree is awarded in the following majors: American studies, anthropology and sociology, art, biochemistry, biology, chemistry, computer science, economics and business, engineering, English, French, geology, German, government and law, history, international affairs, mathematics, mathematics/economics, music, philosophy, physics, psychology, religion, Russian and East European studies, and Spanish.

In addition, Lafayette students may enroll in a five-year program leading to either a B.S. and an A.B. or two B.S. degrees.

Academic Program
Students work together one-on-one with faculty advisers to ensure the planning of a program that is both educationally sound and responsive to the student's individual interests and needs. Each academic department specifies core curriculum requirements for its majors. All A.B. candidates must satisfy a course-distribution requirement, which can be met through advanced placement, transfer credit, or a broad selection of college course work.

In combining arts, sciences, and engineering in one undergraduate institution and in having one faculty with a unified educational approach, Lafayette has a distinctive capability to exercise a broadening influence on all students. Approximately one half of Lafayette's students major in the humanities and social sciences, while the other half specialize in the natural sciences and engineering. Flexible curricular arrangements enable students to defer their final decision on a major until the end of the sophomore year.

In addition to the formal majors offered at the College, interdisciplinary minor programs are offered in ten areas: Black studies, classical civilization, East Asian studies, environmental science, ethical studies, health care and society, Jewish studies, Latin American and Caribbean studies, technology studies, and women's studies. A number of internships can also be arranged through the various academic departments.

Students planning to continue their study in a professional school are assisted by faculty preprofessional advisers in designing a program of study that provides an appropriate foundation for advanced work.

Army ROTC programs are offered for both men and women.

The College observes a two-semester academic calendar. An optional January interim session is offered. Classes are available on campus as well as off campus, including study overseas.

Off-Campus Arrangements
Students are encouraged to spend a semester or a year in a study-abroad program sponsored by the College or another institution. The College has recently established affiliations with four universities overseas. Groups of students led by Lafayette professors attend Vesalius College at the University of Brussels, l'Université de Bourgogne in Dijon, Middlesex University in London, the University College in London, and the Sweet Briar junior-year-abroad program in Paris.

Students also travel widely during the Lafayette interim session. Two faculty members have accompanied each group of students in their pursuit of knowledge in China, England, Germany, France, Israel, and Russia as well as in Eastern Europe and sub-Saharan Africa.

Lafayette is a member of the American Collegiate Consortium, an association of some sixty American colleges and universities that operates a prestigious study-abroad program at the Universities of Voronezh and Yaroslavl in Russia. Students may take a full semester of courses in the fields of their choice alongside Russian students.

Academic Facilities
Skillman Library, a building that has won awards for its architectural design and functional effectiveness, contains more than 482,000 hardbound volumes, as well as numerous pamphlets, periodicals, electronic databases, CD-ROMs, electronic journals, microfilms, audiovisual materials, and special collections. The library operates on an open-stack policy. Cooperative arrangements with other Lehigh Valley colleges make more than 1 million books available to Lafayette students.

Ten additional classroom, laboratory, and departmental buildings house specialized libraries, modern scientific and engineering equipment, studio rooms, galleries, classrooms, seminar rooms, and faculty offices.

The College's rapidly growing Academic Computing Services facilities include a campuswide network with connections in every residence hall, office, and classroom; a VAX 6310, an ARIX, and an IBM 9375 minicomputer; and more than 150 public IBM-compatible microcomputers available for student use, many of them 24 hours a day. At no charge, students can have access to electronic mail and the Internet and to general and course software from the computing sites or from their rooms.

Costs

The comprehensive fee for 2000–01 is $23,758. Additional costs include a room fee of $4095, a board fee of $3318, and an estimated $1625 for books, travel, and miscellaneous expenses.

Financial Aid

Substantial amounts of financial aid are available for students with demonstrated need. Approximately 60 percent of the student body receives financial aid: more than 40 percent of Lafayette's students receive financial aid directly from the College in the form of grants, loans, and work opportunities, and almost 20 percent are assisted by government grants or other awards not funded by the College. Detailed information regarding financial assistance is available from the Office of Student Financial Aid, Lafayette College, Easton, Pennsylvania 18042-1777 (telephone: 610-330-5055). Each year, through the Marquis Scholars Program, Lafayette offers merit scholarships to 60 entering first-year students who have demonstrated academic excellence. Each recipient is awarded a minimum of $12,500 each year with a scholarship to full need each year if need exceeds $12,500. In addition, 32 entering freshmen receive $7500 Trustee Scholarships.

Faculty

One hundred percent of the College's 183 faculty members hold the doctoral degree or the terminal degree in their field. Many have earned wide recognition for their research and scholarship or have won awards for superior teaching. Some hold faculty chairs endowed to attract or retain professors of exceptional ability. Students benefit from a student-faculty ratio of about 11:1 and from the fact that all faculty members—full professors and heads of departments, as well as junior faculty members—teach classes and advise students on an individual basis.

Student Government

Traditionally, students have contributed to major policy decisions at Lafayette. Student Government is responsible for formulating student activity policy, distributing funds to student organizations, and maintaining liaison with the Board of Trustees, the faculty, and the administration. Voting student members sit on four trustee committees and on almost all faculty committees, and student representatives participate in faculty meetings.

Admission Requirements

Lafayette admits students without regard to sex, race, religion, or physical handicap. All Lafayette students pursued a strong college-preparatory program of studies, and approximately one half graduated in the top tenth of their secondary school class. Many held leadership positions in school or community organizations or on sports teams. They are encouraged—and expected—to assume major responsibility for all aspects of their lives at the College and to continue to develop those attributes and talents on which their admission was based.

Lafayette requires submission of SAT I or ACT scores. Three SAT II Subject Tests, one of them Writing, are recommended. It is also recommended that B.S. degree candidates take Subject Tests in Mathematics and Physics or Chemistry in addition to the Writing Subject Test. Students are strongly encouraged to visit the Lafayette campus for an admission interview and a student-guided tour.

Application and Information

Applications for admission should be filed by January 1. Candidates are notified of the admission decision around April 1. If a student requests consideration of their application under the Early Decision Plan, a decision is normally made within thirty days of receipt of completed application forms. February 15 is the deadline to request early decision. Applicants accepted under early decision are obligated to enroll at Lafayette unless their financial needs are not met.

Office of Admissions
Lafayette College
Easton, Pennsylvania 18042-1770

Telephone: 610-330-5100
World Wide Web: http://www.lafayette.edu

A class on the quad of Lafayette College.

LAGRANGE COLLEGE
LAGRANGE, GEORGIA

The College

Founded in 1831, LaGrange College is the oldest private college in Georgia. Affiliated with the United Methodist Church, LaGrange College seeks to admit any qualified student. With an enrollment of approximately 1,000 men and women and only 17 students in the average classroom, LaGrange College provides a challenging and supportive academic environment. Students live in college residence halls that provide 24-hour access to the College's fiber-optic computer network. This network provides continuous access to the Internet and the World Wide Web, e-mail, computer games, and the online files of the College library. In addition to computer network access, each room is also outfitted with central air-conditioning, cable television, and local telephone service. The College is fully accredited by the Commission on Colleges of the Southern Association of Colleges and Schools as well as the University Senate of the United Methodist Church.

Students come from nineteen states and twenty-five other countries. The Master of Education (M.Ed.) degree, the Master of Arts in Teaching (M.A.T.) degree, and the Master of Business Administration (M.B.A.) degree are offered in addition to the Bachelor of Arts (B.A.), Bachelor of Science (B.S.), Bachelor of Science in Nursing (B.S.N.), and Associate of Arts (A.A.) degrees. The College is located in a residential section of LaGrange, Georgia, which has a population of 28,000. Nearby are the world-famous Callaway Gardens, the Warm Springs Foundation, and Franklin D. Roosevelt's Little White House. The West Point Dam on the Chattahoochee River provides one of the largest lakes in the region; waterfronts and a marina are within the city limits of LaGrange. The city of LaGrange is 65 miles southwest of Atlanta and 55 miles southwest of Hartsfield Atlanta International Airport.

Intercollegiate athletic teams for men include baseball, basketball, cross-country, golf, soccer, swimming, and tennis. Women's teams include basketball, cross-country, fast-pitch softball, soccer, swimming, tennis, and volleyball. The College's athletic facilities include an indoor competitive swimming pool, an outdoor recreational swimming pool, a fully equipped fitness center, two lighted softball fields, a lighted soccer field, a lighted baseball park, three gymnasiums, and a training facility.

One of the most original activities LaGrange students enjoy is "Dive-in movies," in which second-run movies are beamed onto a 35-foot screen in the College's indoor pool, and students watch the movie while drifting about in floats, inner tubes, and rafts supplied by the College. Other on-campus activities include intramural sports tournaments, theater performances, karaoke and "Open Mic" competitions, "Fall Festival," art exhibitions, "Vegas on the Hill," and Greek Week. The College regularly hosts guest lecturers. Recent lecturers include Truett Cathy, founder and chairman of Chick-Fil-A, Inc.; Edwin Newman, retired NBC News anchor; Scott Carpenter, former Mercury astronaut; and Larry Mize, PGA golfer. The College hosts one semiformal dance each quarter—homecoming in the fall, the quadrangle dance during the winter, and May Day festivities in the spring. Many off-campus excursions are planned each quarter, such as snow-skiing trips to North Carolina, trips to Atlanta to visit "Planet Hollywood" or a Braves game, and overnight camping trips.

Majors and Degrees

LaGrange offers the Bachelor of Arts (B.A.) degree in accounting, art and design, art education, biochemistry, biology, business administration, chemistry, Christian education, computer science, early childhood education, English, history, mathematics, middle grades education, music, political science, psychology, religion, secondary education, social work, social work/criminal justice, and theater arts. The Bachelor of Science (B.S.) degree is available in chemistry, computer science, and mathematics. The Bachelor of Business Administration (B.B.A.) degree is available with concentrations in accounting, economics, international business, and management. The Bachelor of Science in Nursing (B.S.N.) degree is also offered. The Associate of Arts (A.A.) degree is offered in business administration, criminal justice, and liberal studies. Preprofessional programs of study, as preparation for graduate and professional study, are available in dentistry, journalism, law, medicine, optometry, pharmacy, physical therapy, and theology/seminary. Dual-degree (3-2) programs in engineering have been established with Georgia Institute of Technology and Auburn University.

Academic Program

Each program of study contains a substantial interdisciplinary liberal studies component and extensive specified course work in the discipline in which the student has selected a major. A minimum of 108 semester hours are required to earn a bachelor's degree; 48 semester hours of liberal studies courses are required for all bachelor's degrees. Most majors require an additional 36 to 56 semester hours of credit beyond the liberal studies curriculum. Students may be eligible for credit and/or exemption in certain areas through the Advanced Placement (AP) tests or the College-Level Examination Program (CLEP).

Academic Facilities

The William and Evelyn Banks Library is a modern academic learning center that provides more than 125,000 volumes of books, periodicals, and multimedia. The College participates in Galileo, an online collaborative offering approximately 1,800 full-text journals as well as extensive abstracts. The periodical collection is activated through the Academic Abstracts CD System. The circulation system is fully automated, and the library recently installed a local area CD-ROM network.

The campuswide fiber-optic computer network provides network and PC access in every dorm room and in all eleven computer labs on campus. Students are able to access the College library files, the Internet, the World Wide Web, e-mail, and other resources from any of the computer labs. The Price Theater is a state-of-the-art proscenium theater with seating for 280, thirty-six fly lines, electronic sound and lighting systems, computer design capabilities, a full costume and scenery shop, and an actors' lounge. The Lamar Dodd Art Center is a $2.5-million facility for the study of art and design and includes a gallery for the College's outstanding art collection.

Students who are majoring in biochemistry conduct research in the College's DNA fingerprinting lab, which was established with a National Science Foundation grant. The College's music facilities, which are home to the creative music technologies program, include a fully equipped MIDI recording studio, MIDI workstations, isolation rooms, and an electroacoustic multimedia recital hall, while the entertainment/music library is home to many original Hollywood music scores.

Costs

Tuition and fees for 1999–2000 were $11,001 and room and board were $4656 for the year, bringing the total costs for 1999–2000 to $15,657. Book costs ranged from $600 to $800 per year.

Financial Aid

As a private college, LaGrange is committed to helping meet the difference between the funds any student has available and the cost of attending LaGrange College. More than 80 percent of LaGrange students receive some combination of financial awards. These awards may include grants, loans, scholarships, and employment opportunities. Federal financial aid and institutional funds are available to all students who qualify. The state of Georgia provides additional funding for Georgia residents. All Georgia residents who enroll as full-time students receive the Georgia Tuition Equalization Grant in the amount of $1000 per year. The HOPE Scholarship, which totals $3000 per year, is awarded to all Georgia residents who have graduated from high school since 1996 with a B average and who enter as freshmen. Georgia residents who do not qualify for the HOPE Scholarship as freshmen may be able to obtain the HOPE Scholarship by maintaining a 3.0 grade point average through the freshman and sophomore years. Academic scholarships that range from $1000 to full scholarships are also awarded. All accepted students are considered for scholarships; a separate application is not required. In 1999–2000, all financial aid applicants were awarded financial aid.

Faculty

All courses at LaGrange College are taught by professors, 88 percent of whom hold terminal degrees. Faculty members are rewarded for teaching and are not required to conduct research, although many do conduct research. All faculty members teach undergraduates and serve as academic advisers. Full-time faculty members number 60; 22 are part-time. The student-faculty ratio is 12:1, and the average class contains 17 students.

Student Government

The LaGrange College Student Government Association (SGA) exists to serve as a medium for student expression, to coordinate campus activities, and to govern within the parameters granted by the President. Student publications are supported by the SGA; these include the newspaper, yearbook, and magazine. The SGA oversees more than forty clubs and organizations in all, including three national fraternities and three national sororities, as well as service clubs, religious organizations, honorary organizations, and departmental/special interest groups.

Admission Requirements

LaGrange College seeks to admit any qualified student who desires to study on the LaGrange campus. Preference is given to applicants who have had strong preparation in high school. A typical matriculant should have completed a total of 16 units of college-preparatory courses at an approved high school, including 4 units of English, 4 units of college-preparatory mathematics, 3 units of social science, 3 units of laboratory science, and 2 units of a foreign language.

Freshman applicants should submit a completed application for admission, a $20 nonrefundable application fee, official high school transcripts, and official SAT I or ACT scores. Transfer students should submit an application, the application fee, and official transcripts of all college work attempted. Transfer students who have earned fewer than 30 semester hours of credit must also submit official high school transcripts.

Application and Information

Applications for admission are evaluated on a rolling basis and should be submitted at least one month prior to the beginning of the quarter in which entrance is desired. Applicants can expect to receive notification within two to three weeks of the date that all documents are submitted. Weekday campus visits are encouraged, and appointments can be arranged by contacting the Admission Office. For additional information, students should contact:

Office of Admission
LaGrange College
601 Broad Street
LaGrange, Georgia 30240
Telephone: 706-812-7260
 800-593-2885 (toll-free)
Fax: 706-812-7348
E-mail: lgcadmis@lgc.edu
World Wide Web: http://www.lgc.edu

The William and Evelyn Banks Library overlooks the College's main entrance.

LAKE ERIE COLLEGE
PAINESVILLE, OHIO

The College

Lake Erie College, founded in 1856, is an independent, coeducational institution located in the city of Painesville in northeastern Ohio. Instruction is provided at the baccalaureate and master's degree levels to academically qualified individuals. Programs of study, founded in the liberal arts, are offered in the arts and sciences, humanities, equestrian studies, teacher education, and business administration. Lake Erie College accommodates both residential and commuting students of various ages on a full-time and part-time basis. Local, national, and international students benefit from the College's traditional emphasis on intercultural programs.

Intercollegiate sports play an important role in student life. Lake Erie College athletics are exciting for competitors and spectators alike. The College is a member of the Allegheny Mountain Collegiate Conference and competes at the NCAA Division III level. Men compete in basketball, cross-country, golf, soccer, and tennis. Women compete in basketball, golf, soccer, softball, tennis, and volleyball. The College also sponsors an intercollegiate equestrian team.

Location

Lake Erie College is located on 48 acres of naturally wooded land in Painesville, Ohio. Painesville is an attractive community in northeast Ohio 28 miles east of Cleveland and 3 miles south of Lake Erie. The Cleveland Museum of Art, Playhouse Square, Lake Metro Parks, Holden Arboretum, professional baseball and basketball teams, theaters, comedy clubs, and other recreational attractions are located nearby.

The area is served by two national highways, U.S. 90 and U.S. 20, and state routes 2 and 44.

Majors and Degrees

At the undergraduate level, Lake Erie College offers the Bachelor of Arts, Bachelor of Science, and Bachelor of Fine Arts degrees. Majors are available in accounting, biology (predentistry, premedicine, and pre–veterinary science), business administration, chemistry, communications, criminal justice, dance, elementary education, English, environmental science, equestrian facilities management, equestrian teacher/trainer, equine stud farm management, fine arts (multidisciplinary), fine arts (with concentration), international business, legal studies, mathematics, modern foreign language, music, psychology, and social sciences (history, prelaw, sociology). Students may also pursue an individualized academic major.

Academic Program

The philosophy of Lake Erie College is that the well-being and enrichment of society are dependent upon the abilities of individuals to think both creatively and critically, to make reasoned and informed decisions, and to assume responsibility for their personal actions and continuing education.

Education at Lake Erie College promotes the knowledge and understanding of various cultures and the growth of personal and social responsibilities associated with the acquisition of knowledge and the mastery of skills. The liberal arts and career-oriented disciplines the College offers are not mutually exclusive bodies of knowledge, and the best education is one that promotes the integration of both types of disciplines. The process of education is as vital as the subject matter communicated. It is through intercultural awareness, directed practice in discerning relationships among disciplines, and making informed judgments that a person becomes educated and acquires the flexibility necessary to meet the rapidly changing demands of the marketplace and the world.

One hundred twenty-eight semester hours are required to earn a bachelor's degree.

Off-Campus Arrangements

Through the College's Academic Program Abroad, students live and study with a native family in the Netherlands, France, England, Austria, Italy, or Spain while earning Lake Erie College credits. This affords students the opportunity to study within the special educational experience that is part of living in another country, speaking another language, and learning another culture. Academic experiences abroad range in duration from two weeks to an entire semester, depending upon individual schedules. Following the fourth semester of full-time study, students are offered a free study trip abroad.

Academic Facilities

The scenic and peaceful Lake Erie College campus provides the ideal setting to pursue an academic career; it reflects the College's commitment to provide a high-quality education in a personalized environment. The focus of the campus is College Hall, completed in 1859. College Hall is a center for classroom and office activities.

Four residence halls are located on campus. Each contains a computer facility, kitchen, TV lounge, exercise room, and a laundry room. The Arthur S. Holden Center, dedicated in 1997, houses a telecommunications center, a computer center, computerized classrooms, conference rooms, faculty offices, student life offices, a dining center, student government offices, a bookstore, and study areas.

The Fine Arts Building houses the 200-seat C. K. Rickel Theatre, the B. K. Smith Gallery, art studios, the dance studio, photography laboratories, faculty offices, and classrooms. The Austin Hall of Science includes laboratories, classrooms, and offices. The Jane White Lincoln Center for Physical Education and Recreation includes a gymnasium with pro-turf flooring, a conditioning center with a Universal weight room, a free weight room, first aid training rooms, classrooms, and offices. Adjacent to the center is Hitchcock Field, with a field for soccer and softball. Kilcawley Hall houses the President's Office and the Institutional Advancement offices.

The Lincoln Library/Learning Resource Center maintains a collection of more than 90,000 books and subscribes to more than 750 periodicals. Audiovisual services, educational media and media production centers, two computerized indexes, and three computer laboratories are also located in the library.

The 150-acre George M. Humphrey Equestrian Center is located just 5 miles from the campus. Served daily by the College van, the equestrian center includes an indoor arena of 100 feet by 225 feet, with seating for 1,000 spectators, and an indoor warm-up area of 75 feet by 130 feet. The Clarence T. Reinberger Equestrian Work Center has an additional indoor ring of 80 feet by 96 feet. Other facilities include the Equine

Stud Farm Laboratory and breeding facilities as well as stabling for 100 horses. The equestrian center also features outdoor riding rings and a hunt field.

Costs

Tuition per semester for 2000–01 is $7570 for full-time students and $415 per credit hour for part-time students. The room charge is $1450 for a double room and $2000 for a single per semester. The cost for board is $1160 for ten meals per week and $1260 for fourteen meals per week per semester. Fees total $460 for full-time students and $30 per credit hour for part-time students per semester. Academic Program Abroad costs at the established sites are comparable to a semester's costs on the Lake Erie campus.

Financial Aid

Lake Erie College offers a number of competitive scholarship programs that are not based on need. Other forms of financial aid, all based on need, include scholarships, grants (federal, state, local, and College), loans (federal and state), and work-study programs; the application deadline for need-based aid is March 1. Approximately 85 percent of full-time students receive financial aid. Estimates of the expected family contribution are available from the Office of Financial Aid. To apply for aid, students must submit a Free Application for Federal Student Aid (FAFSA), Form 1040, and other documents required by Lake Erie. The deadline for priority consideration is March 1.

Faculty

The Lake Erie College faculty is well qualified, capable, and eager to teach. Eighty-five percent of the faculty members hold doctoral or terminal degrees in their field. Many bring firsthand experiences in their disciplines to the classroom. They remain active in their respective academic disciplines and are able to provide students with information on current research, new trends, and career opportunities. Class size ranges from 4 to 30, and the student-faculty ratio is 15:1.

Student Government

Students at Lake Erie College play an important role in decision making in many aspects of campus life. Students retain membership on most faculty and administrative committees. The Student Government Association provides a means for students to govern their nonacademic lives and to maintain channels of communication with the faculty and administration.

Admission Requirements

A composite evaluation is made of each applicant, with special attention given to high school credentials. A college-preparatory background is necessary and should include 4 units of English, 3 units of mathematics, 3 units of science, 3 units of social studies, and 6 additional units from other academic areas; 2 units of foreign language are advised. Scores on the ACT or SAT I are recommended; students may submit a portfolio of representative work or come to campus for a formal interview in lieu of test results. Lake Erie College welcomes students of all races and backgrounds.

Application and Information

Lake Erie College operates with a rolling admission policy; however, application by March 1 is necessary for scholarship and/or financial aid candidates. Applicants are notified of the admission decision within three weeks of receipt of all materials.

All correspondence should be directed to:

Office of Admissions
Lake Erie College
391 West Washington Street
Painesville, Ohio 44077
Telephone: 440-639-7879
              800-533-4996 (toll-free)
E-mail: lecadmit@lakeerie.edu

The Arthur S. Holden Center, dedicated in 1997, houses a telecommunications center, a computer center, computerized classrooms, conference rooms, faculty offices, student life offices, a dining center, student government offices, a bookstore, and study areas.

LAKE FOREST COLLEGE
LAKE FOREST, ILLINOIS

The College
Lake Forest College is a coeducational undergraduate community of 1,200 students that celebrates the personal growth accompanying the quest for excellence. Founded in 1857, Lake Forest provides a secure residential campus of great beauty and enriches its curriculum with the vibrant resources of Chicago.

A national liberal arts college, Lake Forest prides itself on diversity, with students representing forty-four states and forty-five other countries. Members of minority groups make up more than 28 percent of the Lake Forest student body. With 82 percent of its students living in residence halls, Lake Forest fosters interaction and shared experiences among its diverse population. Lake Forest offers each student the opportunity to develop a variety of life skills.

More than eighty student organizations, groups, and clubs provide the campus with a wide range of extracurricular opportunities. These enriching experiences work in unison with Lake Forest's commitment to high standards of academic excellence and integrity. Ultimately, Lake Forest endeavors to help individuals develop lives of leadership, service, and personal fulfillment.

Location
Thirty miles north of Chicago on Lake Michigan's famed North Shore, Lake Forest College is situated on 107 scenic wooded acres in a residential community. The town of Lake Forest is 25 miles from O'Hare International Airport. Students are within an easy commute to Chicago, a world-class city of nearly 3 million people and a treasure of cultural locations. Chicago has become an extension of the campus. Internships, independent study, research projects, and field trips are readily available through Chicago's vast resources.

Majors and Degrees
Lake Forest College awards the Bachelor of Arts (B.A.) degree in eighteen departments and six interdisciplinary majors spanning more than 500 courses. Departmental majors are art, biology, business, chemistry, communications, computer science, economics, education (in conjunction with another major), English, French, German, history, mathematics, music, philosophy, physics, politics, psychology, sociology and anthropology, and Spanish. The interdisciplinary majors are American studies, area studies, Asian studies (including Japanese language), comparative literature, environmental studies, and international relations. Course work is also available in religion and theater.

Students may create their own majors through the independent scholar program, which enables qualified and motivated students to design and pursue individual degree programs that focus on particular topics or themes rather than on single academic disciplines.

In addition, the College also offers minors. Students can declare a minor in those departmental and nondepartmental programs that have a major, as well as in religion, theater, African-American studies, French civilization, metropolitan studies, and women's studies. A minor requires at least six and no more than eight courses.

Lake Forest offers cooperative degree (3-2) programs with the School of Engineering of Washington University (St. Louis) and the University of Illinois at Urbana–Champaign. Cooperative programs allow students specializing in narrow fields to broaden their studies. Students may receive a Bachelor of Arts degree from Lake Forest after earning a Bachelor of Science degree from Washington University or the University of Illinois at Urbana–Champaign.

Academic Program
Lake Forest College bases its academic calendar on two 15-week semesters, from late August through mid-December and from mid-January through early May. The curriculum establishes an integrated framework for the general education of undergraduate students across four years of study. The curriculum includes general education requirements, which ensure that students receive educational breadth as well as depth while allowing considerable latitude in designing individual programs of study. Also included are requirements for writing and cultural diversity. Students are expected to pass thirty-two courses, fulfill the general education requirements, and complete the requirements of a major.

Off-Campus Arrangements
In addition to the Chicago Internship Program, Lake Forest College provides students with a wide variety of opportunities for off-campus study. Semester-long options also include the Washington Semester Program, the Chicago Semester in the Arts, the Oak Ridge Science Semester, the Wilderness Field Station, the Urban Studies Program, and the Newberry Library Program in the Humanities.

There are many options for international study, such as Lake Forest's own international internship programs in Paris and in Santiago (Chile), as well as the Ancient Mediterranean Civilizations Program in Greece and Turkey and the Marine Biology Program in the Bahamas. As a member of the Associated Colleges of the Midwest, Lake Forest also offers programs in such countries as China, Costa Rica, the Czech Republic, England, India, Italy, Japan, Russia, Tasmania, and Zimbabwe.

Academic Facilities
Donnelley Library contains almost 400,000 books and documents and 1,300 current periodicals. It is one of the few college libraries nationally where students and faculty members can borrow books on line from other libraries—now forty-six statewide. The library provides access to CD-ROM and electronic databases and the Internet. The Special Collections Unit includes the College Archives and houses rare books and manuscripts.

Information Services and Technology provides services and support for all technology on campus, including more than 140 public-access computers located in two residence hall computer labs and a main computer teaching lab. All residence hall rooms, as well as faculty offices, laboratories, and classrooms, have direct access to the College's fiber-optic network. Students also have direct access to the Internet, including World Wide Web, Gopher, FTP, and Usenet news groups, through their residence hall rooms and the public-access computer labs.

Among the fifty-five buildings on campus is the Dixon Science Research Center, designed for student-faculty research. The modern three-story, 7,500-square-foot facility contains thirteen laboratories and two animal holding facilities. State-of-the-art equipment includes a nuclear magnetic resonance spectrometer with a 400-megahertz superconductivity magnet and an electron microscope.

Costs

Comprehensive fees for 2000–01 are $27,300, including $21,190 for tuition and fees, $5000 for room and board, $550 for books, and $560 for miscellaneous costs.

Financial Aid

Lake Forest College's comprehensive financial aid is offered to students who are financially unable to pay the full cost of a college education. Approximately 75 percent of students receive financial aid, with the average aid package totaling $18,500.

More than $7 million is awarded annually in the form of Lake Forest College grant and scholarship assistance. Lake Forest College honors students distinguish themselves through academic achievement and leadership activities with the Deerpath Merit Scholarship Program and the Presidential Scholarship Competition. The Deerpath Scholarship, renewed annually, recognizes applicants who have excelled in the areas of visual or performing arts, music, leadership, science, or academics. The Presidential Scholarship offers full- and half-tuition awards, renewed annually, to a distinctive group of students. The average total in grants and scholarships is $13,375.

Faculty

At the center of Lake Forest College stands its distinguished faculty members. They are first and foremost teachers. The College seeks and retains faculty members principally because they enjoy and excel at teaching undergraduates. Faculty members, not graduate assistants, teach the College's courses and provide academic advising. A student-faculty ratio of 12.5:1 gives students easy access to their teachers, while providing opportunities for informed counsel about individual programs of study.

The faculty's tradition of teaching excellence is matched and supported by its achievement in scholarly research. More than 96 percent of Lake Forest College's faculty members hold a Ph.D. or its equivalent. Faculty members are active as lecturers, consultants, critics, artists, editors of journals, and authors of books, scholarly articles, and newspaper opinion pieces. Among the faculty's many published books in recent years, five titles have appeared on the Outstanding Books List of *Choice* magazine. Many faculty members are recognized authorities in their fields and are sought by the news media to provide expert commentary on current events. Lake Forest faculty members consistently receive a vast array of fellowships and grants.

Student Government

The first Lake Forest College student body self-governing organization was the Student Council, established in 1917. Today, Student Government is composed of the General Assembly and its subcommittees, the Executive Committee and the four Student Government officers: the president, vice-president, treasurer, and secretary. Student members of other College governing committees also play an active and important role in the Student Government.

Ultimate responsibility for guiding Lake Forest College rests with the Board of Trustees. The Student Government president and vice-president serve as voting members on the full board.

Students at Lake Forest College advise the administration through representation on a variety of committees that deal with the hiring of faculty members, allocation of the budget, department course offerings, and administering a judicial system while also taking a prominent role in enhancing the educational growth and social life of the campus community.

Admission Requirements

Admission to Lake Forest College is competitive and based on a record of achievement in academic studies and extracurricular activities. Selection includes assessment of a student's program of study, academic achievement, aptitude, intellectual curiosity, qualities of character and personality, and activities both within and outside the school setting. Lake Forest College unequivocally selects its students without regard to social background, religious affiliation, race, national origin, gender, handicap, or financial position. This admission policy is manifest in the diverse nature of the student community.

Students are urged to begin the application procedure early in their final year of secondary school. There is no formal closing deadline for receipt of the application. The early notification deadline is December 1. This option is nonbinding but allows the student to receive an admission decision as early as December 20. The early decision (binding) deadline is January 1. Admission decisions are announced no later than the third week of March for all freshman candidates whose applications are complete as of March 1.

Lake Forest recommends a precollege program that includes a minimum of 4 years of English; 3 or more years of mathematics, including trigonometry; in-depth study in one or more foreign languages; and 2 to 4 years of work in both the social and natural sciences. All candidates are required to present the results of either the SAT I or the ACT. The tests may be completed in the candidate's junior or senior year of secondary school. Although an interview is not required, the admission staff welcomes and encourages visits to the campus by prospective students and their families.

Candidates for undergraduate admission may obtain the required application forms by contacting the Admission Office. Lake Forest College also accepts the Common Application in lieu of its own form and gives equal consideration to both. Students may obtain copies of the Common Application from their high schools.

Students who wish to defer enrollment should complete the application procedure during the final year of secondary school.

Transfer students are admitted at the beginning of each semester. Transfer applicants should have achieved an overall college average of at least a C or its equivalent and be eligible to return to their previous institutions. When a transfer student is admitted to the College, the maximum credit accepted in transfer is 60 semester hours. All transfer students are required to submit the following credentials: an application for admission, a secondary school transcript, transcripts of all college work completed through the most recent term, and a letter of recommendation from the academic dean or a professor at the current college.

Application and Information

The Admission Office is open from 8:30 a.m. to 5 p.m. on weekdays and 9 a.m. to 1 p.m. on Saturdays throughout the year. For further information, including a campus tour, interview, or an application form, prospective students should contact:

Admission Office
Lake Forest College
555 N. Sheridan Road
Lake Forest, Illinois 60045
Telephone: 847-735-5000
          800-828-4751 (toll-free)
Fax: 847-735-6271
E-mail: admissions@lfc.edu

LAKEHEAD UNIVERSITY
THUNDER BAY, ONTARIO, CANADA

The University

Lakehead University was established in 1946 as the Lakehead Technical Institute and became the Lakehead College of Arts, Science and Technology in 1956. The Lakehead University Act was given Royal Assent by the Lieutenant Governor of Ontario in 1965, and the first degrees in arts and science were granted in May 1965.

Lakehead University is committed to excellence and innovation in undergraduate and graduate teaching, service, research, and scholarly activity. Dedicated to a student-centred learning environment, Lakehead celebrates its people and their diversity. Recognizing its place in northwestern Ontario, the University partners with others to reach out to the region, the province, and beyond as a global participant. Lakehead is especially committed to working with aboriginal people in furthering their aspirations. Accountable in their actions to the highest standards of quality, Lakehead's graduates demonstrate leadership, independent critical thinking, and social and environmental responsibility.

Lakehead is situated on approximately 150 hectares of wooded land that overlooks the city of Thunder Bay. Most of the University's administrative and instructional buildings are grouped around Lake Tamblyn; the residence buildings are located along the McIntyre River. The Student Centre is a focal point of campus life and provides an assortment of student facilities, which include banking services, restaurants, and campus stores. Many of the campus's building are connected by underground tunnels that allow for comfortable walking between classes during cold winter days. In addition to its academic facilities, Lakehead has provided a number of scenic paved trails on and around the campus for walking, jogging, biking, and cross-country skiing. The campus is within walking distance of the edge of the city and is serviced regularly by public transit service.

Lakehead offers excellent recreational and sporting facilities to all of its students. Students have access to the University pool, saunas, the fitness centre, courts, the gymnasium, and the track. Lakehead's varsity teams are members of the CIAU Interuniversity League and compete in basketball, cross-country, track and field, and wrestling.

There are approximately thirty active academic, social, recreational, and international clubs on campus.

Lakehead offers a wide variety of programs and courses that are designed to meet the needs of almost any student and has developed an extensive range of educational options that extend from two-year diploma courses to graduate programs. Graduate programs include master's degrees in applied sport science and coaching, biology, chemistry, economics (co-op option available), education, engineering, English, forestry, geology, history, mathematical sciences (co-op option available), philosophy, physics (co-op option and honours degree available), psychology, social work, and sociology and the Doctor of Philosophy in clinical psychology.

Location

Thunder Bay, with a population of about 125,000 people, is located on the northern shore of Lake Superior, the world's largest lake, making Thunder Bay Canada's largest inland port. Thunder Bay is the commercial, educational, and recreational centre of northwestern Ontario and offers historic Old Fort William and the Thunder Bay Symphony Orchestra. Thunder Bay and its surrounding areas provide an array of outdoor recreational opportunities. Although self-contained, Thunder Bay is within a day's driving distance of Winnipeg, the capital of Manitoba.

Majors and Degrees

The University currently offers the following undergraduate majors: anthropology, biology, business (co-op option available in commerce), chemistry, computer science (co-op option available), economics, economics and geography, economics and mathematics, education, engineering, English, environmental studies and biology, environmental studies and geography, environmental studies and earth science, environmental studies and physics, environmental studies (forest conservation), forestry (co-op option available), French, general arts, general science, geography, geography with an honours Bachelor of Outdoor Recreation, geology, history, history with an Honours Bachelor of Outdoor Recreation, indigenous learning, kinesiology, mathematical sciences, medical laboratory sciences, music, natural science, nursing, outdoor recreation, philosophy, philosophy and religious studies, physics (co-op option available), political science, political science and history, psychology, psychology and philosophy, social work, sociology, and visual arts.

Cooperative programs are available that lead to the Honours Bachelor of Commerce (with majors in human resources management/industrial relations, management systems, and marketing), the Bachelor of Science in computer science, the Honours Bachelor of Science in computer science, the Honours Bachelor of Science in forestry, and the Bachelor of Science in physics.

Minor programs are offered in art history, classics, computer science, drawing, economics, Finnish, French, German, gerontology, indigenous learning, international politics, law and politics, native language, Northern studies, occupational ethics, Ojibwe, philosophy, religious studies, Spanish, statistics, and women's studies. Undergraduate diplomas are available in engineering technology, integrated forest resources management, native language instructor studies, and library and information studies. Certificate programs are offered in aboriginal languages, environmental assessment (distance education only), French proficiency, indigenous learning, Northern clinical practice, primary health-care nurse practitioner studies, and tourism and recreation resources management.

Academic Programs

The academic year consists of the fall term (September to December), winter term (January to April), and spring/summer term (May to August).

Off-Campus Arrangements

Through its extensive exchange programs, Lakehead's students have the opportunity to travel and study abroad. Students are prepared for increasing globalization and the various challenges of the next millennium.

Lakehead University offers an extensive range of programs and courses (undergraduate, graduate, diploma, and certificate) through distance education. Courses are delivered using various distance education formats, such as print packages, audio/videocassettes, audioconferencing, videoconferencing, computer conferencing, the World Wide Web, and other Internet services. Courses commence in January, February, May, and September, providing an opportunity for year-around study.

Academic Facilities

The University Library consists of the Chancellor Norman M. Paterson Library and the Education Library. Together, these serve the needs of students and faculty members on campus as well as those students taking courses at off-campus locations and through distance education. The University library collection contains 696,499 books, journals, and other documents as well as more than 354,500 microform volumes. Access to the collection is provided through the multiLIS automated library management system. The library has an ERL server that provides University access to some of its CD-ROM databases. A number of academic resources, including electronic journals, are available through the library's Web page. Services provided by the library include computerized literature searching as well as interlibrary loan service.

The Counselling and Career Centre is home to the University chaplain, two student counsellors, and a career information library. Students receive personal and career counselling at the centre throughout the year. The centre organizes a series of seminars on a variety of topics.

The Learning Assistance Centre is available to help students who are experiencing academic difficulties. Tutoring is available in a variety of subjects, and students with special needs can arrange for additional support services.

Lakehead has become a centre of research in the northwestern Ontario region, and the facilities available to students and research industries reflect this. Facilities relevant to environmental and scientific research and study have benefited not only the programs in forestry and environmental studies but also the inhabitants of Thunder Bay and the area in general.

Costs

For the 2000–01 academic year, full-time undergraduate tuition and fees range from Can$2510 to Can$3950 for residents of Ontario and Can$5475 to Can$7900 for international students. There are other costs for books, course materials, and lab instruments as well as compulsory health insurance for international students. On-campus and off-campus accommodations and the residence meal plan are additional costs. Other personal expenses, such as clothing, travel, and recreation, are extra.

Financial Aid

Students who are Canadian citizens or permanent residents of Canada and who are also considered residents of Ontario may qualify for financial assistance through the Ontario Student Assistance Program (OSAP). These students should refer to the OSAP Web site at http://osap.gov.on.ca for more details on eligibility. International students are not eligible for entrance scholarships, bursaries, and awards, but they are eligible to apply for these forms of assistance once they are registered as full-time students. Scholarships are based on academic merit while bursaries, although they may have an academic component, are mainly based on financial need. Students are encouraged to contact the Financial Aid Office at 807-343-8206 for further information.

Faculty

Relatively small class sizes at Lakehead encourage communication between students and faculty members. One-on-one interaction is available, providing students with opportunities for hands-on experiences in labs and with easier accessibility to a wide range of facilities.

Student Government

The Lakehead University Student Union (LUSU) provides students with a variety of activities with clubs, programming, and special events and with support in many academic areas of the University. LUSU has representation on the University's Board of Governors and Senate.

Admissions Requirements

As admission requirements vary by department and program, applicants are encouraged to contact Lakehead regarding specific program requirements. In general, applicants are expected to have completed an Ontario Secondary School Diploma (OSSD) with an overall average of 60 percent or its equivalent. Certain degree and diploma programs require specific course prerequisites for admission.

Admissions to the cooperative education programs are more selective due to the limited number of positions available. Admissions decisions for co-op programs are based on academic standing and background information that points to a competency level and background experience appropriate to the co-op position.

International students seeking admission to regular study are normally required to have a TOEFL score of at least 550. International inquiries should be addressed to the Department of International Activities.

Application and Information

Students apply to Lakehead using the General Application form for Ontario universities, which is available from the Ontario Universities Application Centre, the Office of the Registrar at Lakehead, or from high schools around Ontario. Applicants must specify the program and major to which they wish to be admitted and whether they plan to study on a full- or part-time basis.

The application deadline for Canadian and international students is July 1 for the fall term. This may vary by program.

For information about scheduling a visit or applying to Lakehead, please contact:

For Canadian residents:
Office of the Registrar
Lakehead University
955 Oliver Road
Thunder Bay, Ontario P7B 5E1
Canada
Telephone: 807-343-8500
            800-465-3959 (toll-free in Ontario, Manitoba, and Saskatchewan)
Fax: 807-343-8023
E-mail: liaison@lakeheadu.ca
World Wide Web: http://www.lakeheadu.ca

For international inquiries:
Department of International Activities
Lakehead University
955 Oliver Road
Thunder Bay, Ontario P7B 5E1
Canada
Telephone: 807-343-8133
Fax: 807-346-7829
E-mail: international.activities@lakeheadu.ca
World Wide Web: http://www.lakeheadu.ca

LAKE SUPERIOR STATE UNIVERSITY
SAULT SAINTE MARIE, MICHIGAN

The University

Lake Superior State University is surrounded by the scenic beauty of Michigan's eastern Upper Peninsula and northern Ontario. There are many opportunities for outdoor sports that offer students personal challenges. The University encourages students to find a balance between personal growth and academic achievement. Many graduates have commented that not only do they feel exceptionally qualified for either careers or graduate school after their educational experience at Lake Superior State University, but they also leave with a greater awareness of their abilities.

The University's enrollment of 3,200 is for many the ideal size, large enough to offer more than sixty excellent bachelor's and associate degree programs and two certificate programs, yet small enough for students to receive personal attention from faculty and staff. Counseling, financial aid, and placement services provide students with the support they need to succeed at Lake Superior State University.

The James Norris Physical Education Center offers recreation for all students, whether they enjoy the excitement of watching nationally ranked ice hockey teams compete, the challenge of participating in varsity sports, playing or watching some of the twenty-five intramural sports with friends, or just having fun while keeping fit. The center's facilities include an ice arena; swimming and diving pools; tennis, racquetball, and basketball courts; a dance studio; and weight rooms. In addition, a new 66,000-square-foot intramural building opened in February 1999.

The University offers a wide range of extracurricular activities, including student branches of professional societies, clubs, a literary society, sororities, fraternities, musical groups, and a student newspaper. Because the University is located on the Canadian border, there is an international atmosphere on campus. In addition to the advantage of personal contact, which is permitted by its relatively small size, the University offers students opportunities to assume leadership positions, to make lasting friendships, and to succeed in their academic and career pursuits.

Location

The attractive campus overlooks both Sault Sainte Marie, Michigan, population 16,000, and Sault Sainte Marie, Ontario, population 83,000. Also within view are the famous "Soo Locks," which make it possible for freighters to pass between Lake Huron and Lake Superior.

The immediate area offers active students many outdoor opportunities, including cross-country and downhill skiing, backpacking, canoeing, and hunting and fishing along miles of lakeshore beaches and forest trails. The Sault Sainte Marie sister cities provide a variety of cultural and recreational activities such as concerts, plays, cinemas, shopping malls, and restaurants.

All students, including freshmen, may have cars on campus. Cars are convenient for exploring the surrounding area, but they are far from necessary. Downtown is only a 10-minute walk, and an international bus offers service from campus to Sault Sainte Marie, Ontario. A ride board is available for students to find rides home for weekends and holidays.

Majors and Degrees

Lake Superior State University offers Bachelor of Arts and Bachelor of Science degrees with majors in accounting, biology, business administration, clinical laboratory sciences, computer and mathematical sciences, criminal justice (corrections, criminalistics, generalist, law enforcement, loss control, and public safety), early childhood education, electrical engineering (digital systems, robotics, electrical-mechanical), elementary and secondary teacher education for selected curricula, engineering management, English language and literature, environmental chemistry, environmental engineering technology, environmental geology, environmental science, exercise science (athletic training), finance and economics, fine arts, fire science (engineering technology, generalist, and hazardous materials), fisheries and wildlife management, geology, history, human services, legal assistant studies, manufacturing engineering technology, mathematics, mechanical engineering, nursing (B.S.N., B.S.N. completion), parks and recreation management, political science (general, prelaw, and public administration), psychology, recreation management, social science, sociology, and therapeutic recreation. Preprofessional programs (in dentistry, medicine, optometry, pharmacy, and veterinary science) and transfer programs are also available. Selected degrees are offered through extension centers in Alpena, Escanaba, Petoskey, and Traverse City.

Two-year associate degree programs are offered in business, chemistry, corrections, early childhood education, exercise science and health fitness, fire science, law enforcement, legal assistant studies, liberal arts, manufacturing engineering technology, natural resources technology, office administration, personal computer specialist studies, substance abuse prevention and treatment, technical accounting, and telecommunications engineering technology. One-year certificate programs are available in information processing and personal computer specialist studies. Associate of Applied Science degrees in machine tool technology and construction are available through a joint program with a local area career center.

Academic Program

A minimum of 124 semester hours is required for a baccalaureate degree, and a minimum of 62 semester hours is required for an associate degree. The Bachelor of Arts and Bachelor of Science degrees require 33 semester hours of general education courses and a minimum of 50 hours in departmental courses. As many as 30 semester hours may be earned by credit by examination through the College-Level Examination Program (CLEP), the College Board's Advanced Placement tests, or departmental examinations. The University begins instruction in early September and ends its regular academic year during the first week in May. Four-, eight-, and twelve-week academic sessions are offered during the summer months. The baccalaureate degree program in nursing is accredited by the National League for Nursing. The National Accrediting Agency for Clinical Laboratory Sciences has accredited the clinical laboratory sciences program. All engineering technology programs are accredited by TAC/ABET (Technology Accreditation Commission of the Accreditation Board for Engineering Technology, Inc.). The University is fully accredited by the North Central Association of Colleges and Schools.

To prepare students for successful careers and/or graduate studies, Lake Superior State University encourages students to gain practical experience in their fields of study. Many academic majors feature independent research courses and internships at the junior and senior levels. In addition, cooperative education programs are available to students majoring in engineering and engineering technology programs.

Academic Facilities

The many state-of-the-art learning facilities on campus contribute to the academic excellence of Lake Superior State University. Students are encouraged to learn through hands-on experience with the resources available to them. The Kenneth J. Shouldice Library houses more than 135,000 volumes, an audiovisual center, classrooms, and an auditorium. An interlibrary loan service is also available. A major addition, nearly doubling the size of the library, was completed in 1997.

Two academic computer centers provide all students with access to IBM and IBM-compatible microcomputers. In addition, students majoring in psychology, mathematics, or a discipline from the department of biology/chemistry, business/economics, criminal justice/fire science, engineering technology, nursing, or recreation studies have their own computer labs. These labs have special software related to specific fields of study, and some of the labs are also available for general student use.

The Crawford Hall of Science, with a recently completed $23-million renovation, contains fifteen fully equipped biology, chemistry, geology, and physics labs; the Ben Long Planetarium; an auditorium; and a natural history museum. The Center for Applied Science and Engineering Technology is equipped with computer-aided-design (CAD) and computer-aided-manufacturing (CAM) facilities, digital electronics facilities, Fanuc Staubli Adept industrial robots, metal-machining tools, materials testing, and other labs. The James Norris Physical Education Center houses, in addition to its sports facilities, a firing range, classrooms, and a criminalistics laboratory.

Lake Superior State University is able to provide many opportunities for study of the natural environment. The Aquatic Research Laboratory, just minutes from campus on the St. Mary's River, is the only fully operating fish hatchery in all of Michigan's colleges and universities. State and federal grants make it possible for students to participate in research while also learning about the daily operations of a hatchery. Students also participate in water quality research at the lab.

Costs

The basic costs for 1999–2000 were as follows: Michigan resident tuition, $4030 per year; nonresident tuition, $7735 per year; room and board, $4931 per year; books, $500 per year; and parking fee, $50 per year. (Tuition and room and board rates are subject to change through action by the Board of Trustees.)

Financial Aid

The University is committed to rewarding academic achievement as well as to meeting the needs of the many students who apply for financial assistance. Through University, state, and federal programs, about three quarters of full-time U.S. students in 1999–2000 received a financial aid package, which may have included a scholarship, a grant, work/study employment, a loan, or a combination of these. Students must consider carefully the full cost of college and the support available from parents, savings, and summer employment in determining their need for financial aid. In order for their need to be assessed, applicants must submit the Free Application for Federal Student Aid (FAFSA) to the appropriate processing center and have it be received by March 21. However, FAFSAs for Michigan Competitive Scholarship semifinalists must be received by February 21. Application forms for all financial aid programs are available from the Financial Aid Office, and the office's staff can give counsel and information. Students with superior high school or community college academic records are encouraged to apply for scholarships regardless of need. Financial assistance is limited to citizens and permanent residents of the United States. Wishing to recognize high achievers and the University's out-of-state connections, LSSU provides resident tuition for dependents of LSSU alumni, Ontario residents, and U.S. high school students who rank in the top 20 percent of their graduating class or those who have a 3.0 overall grade point average and an ACT or SAT I composite in the 75th percentile. Nonresident transfer students may qualify for resident tuition if they have been granted the in-state tuition rate while attending a Michigan community college.

Faculty

Lake Superior State University emphasizes teaching and personal contact between faculty and students. The student-faculty ratio is 19:1. All instruction is done by faculty members, who also serve as advisers to students. Additional assistance is available from the counseling center and the learning center. Computer aide instruction modules and tutors are available.

Student Government

Student Government is the chief student governing body on campus. Its president is a member of the Administrative Council, which advises the president of the University. Students also act as voting members of all councils and committees on campus. Student appointments to University committees are made by Student Government, which also oversees all clubs, organizations, and social events on campus.

Admission Requirements

High school students who apply during the senior year may be granted tentative acceptance based on work completed in grades 9 through 11 and their ACT or SAT scores. For final acceptance as freshmen, applicants must be graduates of accredited secondary schools with an acceptable overall grade point average and ACT or SAT scores. Secondary school preparation should consist of a full four-year curriculum of at least 15 acceptable entrance credits, which should include 4 years of English, 3 years of math to algebra II, 3 years of social science, 2 years of science, and 3 years of electives.

Students out of high school for at least twenty-four months need not take the SAT or ACT.

Transfer students are those who are attending or who have attended another college or university. Acceptance of transfers to LSSU is based on a 2.0 or higher cumulative GPA. Transfers who have fewer than 19 semester hours (29 quarter hours) of transferable credit must also submit official high school transcripts. Transfer students who graduated less than twenty-four months prior to enrollment at the University must also submit ACT or SAT scores.

Application and Information

High school seniors are encouraged to apply for admission early in the senior year. Both financial aid and scholarship applicants should have their completed applications in the admissions office by April 1. The application for freshman admission should include an official transcript of grades and a $20 (U.S. currency) nonrefundable application fee. Transfer applications should include an official transcript from every college or university attended, a high school transcript, if applicable, plus the $20 nonrefundable application fee. Notification of the admission decision is normally sent within three weeks.

Admissions Office
Lake Superior State University
Sault Sainte Marie, Michigan 49783
Telephone: 906-635-2231
        888-800-LSSU Ext. 2231 (toll-free)
World Wide Web: http://www.lssu.edu

LAMBUTH UNIVERSITY
JACKSON, TENNESSEE

The University

Lambuth University is an independent, undergraduate, church-related liberal arts institution supported by the Memphis Annual Conference of the United Methodist Church. Lambuth has a limited enrollment with small classes and much responsibility for students in the areas of academic and social life. One of the hallmarks of a Lambuth education is the way students are encouraged to think for themselves. Lambuth is committed to academic excellence, and the curriculum expands rather than limits students' choices. Liberal arts core courses, which are taken by students in all majors, enable students to become proficient in areas beyond their majors—from reading and writing to science and math to religion and philosophy. Through these core courses, students receive a well-rounded education that serves them throughout college and into the future. In providing an academic atmosphere for students, any institution must have faculty members who support the purpose of the university and who respond to students. Lambuth University knows that the faculty and students are the most important part of the University's existence. Even though faculty members participate in research and scholarship, their primary responsibilities are teaching and advising.

Lambuth's 1,000 students come from across the nation and the world, representing twenty-six states and nineteen countries. Most students live on campus in modern, well-equipped residence halls. An infirmary is also located on campus.

The Lambuth experience is not all study. The more than twenty-six clubs and organizations available on campus meet almost every interest. National fraternities and sororities, a wide variety of musical and dramatic activities, and special interest groups (including the Black Student Union) give students plenty of opportunities to participate, acquire leadership skills, and expand their horizons. Intercollegiate sports include basketball, cheerleading, cross-country, golf, soccer, softball, tennis, and volleyball for women and baseball, basketball, cross-country, football, golf, soccer, and tennis for men.

On-campus facilities include an athletic center with an Olympic-size indoor swimming pool, two gymnasiums, a weight room, a handball/racquetball court, and outdoor lighted tennis courts. The Wilder Student Union houses a cafeteria, bookstore, media center, career center, and cardiovascular wellness center. The 50-acre campus provides a naturally beautiful setting, with broad expanses of green lawns shared by tall trees. The R. E. Womack Chapel sits in the heart of a parklike quadrangle that is bordered by buildings of Georgian Colonial design.

Location

Jackson, Tennessee, is a lively town of about 80,000 people, with five colleges and universities located in and around this growing community. Jackson's vitality can be seen in its symphony orchestra, bookstores, and civic center and coliseum. The West Tenn Diamond Jaxx, the AA minor-league baseball team for the Chicago Cubs, provides local sports entertainment. Jackson has been the home of such legendary figures as Davy Crockett, Casey Jones, Thomas Edison, and Carl Perkins. Nearby lakes, rivers, and state parks offer waterskiing, canoeing, hiking, and camping. Memphis and Nashville, both easily accessible by interstate highways, provide two different views of an exciting and revitalized mid-South.

Majors and Degrees

Lambuth University offers the degrees of Bachelor of Arts, Bachelor of Science, Bachelor of Business Administration, and Bachelor of Music. Majors and concentrations are available in accounting, art, biology, chemistry, church music, communication, computer information systems, criminal justice, elementary education, English, fashion merchandising, foreign languages, general business, general music, health and physical education, human ecology, interior design, international relations, management, marketing, mathematics, music (performance), music education, philosophy, piano pedagogy, political science/history, psychology, religion, sociology, special education, special major (self-designed), speech and hearing therapy, and theater. Preprofessional programs are offered in dentistry, engineering, health information management, law, medical technology, medicine, ministry, nursing, optometry, pharmacy, physical therapy, and veterinary science.

Academic Program

To earn a bachelor's degree, students must complete 128 semester hours. All students must also complete core requirements in the liberal arts, consisting of three courses in English, one course in speech, two courses in religion, two courses in physical education, two courses in natural science, two writing courses, one math course, one course in computer science, and two interdisciplinary courses. A minor course of study is also required. Lambuth offers students with special career goals the opportunity to design their own interdisciplinary major by combining areas of specialization. Lambuth does accept credit through CLEP and Advanced Placement.

Honors study is available in most departments for students who have a cumulative GPA of 3.25 or higher at the end of the first semester of the junior year. The honors program consists of an 8-semester-hour sequence of research or the equivalent carried out over the last three semesters of study in a particular discipline. Each year, each division of the University also selects two Lambuth Scholars, who receive credit for course work while freed of the usual requirements of test taking and class attendance to pursue more independent study.

Lambuth follows a 4-4-1 academic calendar, with a one-month optional May term. The University also offers three sessions of summer school.

Off-Campus Arrangements

Through a cross-enrollment arrangement that greatly expands course offerings, students may take courses at two other four-year colleges in the city of Jackson. Speech and hearing therapy majors enroll in a clinical practicum, which includes 150 hours of work in speech and hearing testing and therapy under the direct supervision of a speech pathologist. Students majoring in interior design participate in the Interior Design Show House and also work for one semester as apprentices with professional interior designers. Under the Tennessee Legislative Intern Program, political science and prelaw students have the opportunity to work in the Tennessee legislature. Students in all disciplines are encouraged to engage in internships both in the Jackson area and further afield. Lambuth students also participate in study-abroad programs in various countries, including England and France.

Academic Facilities

The Luther L. Gobbel Library houses more than 237,000 items and is a depository for U.S. government documents. The M. D. Anderson Planetarium, adjacent to Hyde Science Hall, houses a Spitz Space System A3P projector, which can project more than 2,000 stars on a 10-meter dome. Other facilities and equipment in Hyde Science Hall include a gas chromatograph and ultraviolet and infrared spectrophotometers. The University offers multiple computer labs that contain various personal computers for student access. A fine arts wing, located in the chapel building, contains music studios, practice rooms, and rehearsal rooms. The Hamilton Theatre for the Performing Arts is home to musical and theatrical events throughout the year. Other campus facilities include the Learning Enrichment Center, Interior Design House, and Dunlap-Williams Log House Museum. The Oxley Biological Field Station, a facility located on Kentucky Lake and open year-round, is used by faculty members and students to study freshwater and terrestrial ecology in a natural habitat. Students also have access to the Gulf Coast Research Lab at Ocean Springs, Mississippi, which specializes in marine and estuarine biology.

Costs

For the 2000–01 academic year, tuition is $8498 and room and board are $4432, for a total cost of $12,930. (Out-of-state students are not charged additional fees in any category.)

Financial Aid

Lambuth University offers a comprehensive program of financial assistance to students who otherwise would be unable to continue their education beyond the secondary level. An essential part of the financial aid program at Lambuth is the individual attention given to students in their financial planning. Academic scholarships are awarded based upon ACT or SAT I scores and academic performance in high school. Performance awards in athletics, music, and drama are available on a limited basis. United Methodist scholarships are also available, as are preministerial grants. State and federal financial aid resources include Federal Supplemental Educational Opportunity Grants, Tennessee Student Assistance Awards, Federal Pell Grants, and loans (Federal Perkins, Federal Stafford Student, and Federal PLUS). The University also offers a variety of on-campus jobs. To enable the University to determine the level of need, financial aid applicants must submit the Free Application for Federal Student Aid (FAFSA) and request that a copy of the needs analysis report be sent to Lambuth. Financial need is not a factor in determining admission. The priority deadline for all types of aid is February 15.

Faculty

The student-faculty ratio is 15:1. No graduate teaching assistants conduct classes at Lambuth. The University has 70 full- and part-time faculty members, with the majority of the full-time faculty possessing terminal degrees. Faculty members have earned distinction by publishing, consulting, and lecturing on a national scale, yet they remain deeply committed to teaching. They have studied and earned degrees at more than eighty of the most prestigious institutions of higher learning. Many write textbooks and professional articles, and many share their time and knowledge by serving in professional and community organizations. Students have direct access to their instructors for advice and help in their studies.

Student Government

Lambuth has an active Student Government Association (SGA), which is divided into three branches: executive, legislative, and judicial. The SGA represents students on University committees and presents their interests and concerns to the Board of Trustees. The Student Activities Committee coordinates numerous activities of social and educational value each year.

Admission Requirements

In keeping with Lambuth's personalized approach to education, the University's Admissions Committee carefully evaluates each applicant's file for strengths, weaknesses, and exceptional circumstances. Items required for the file include an application for admission, an official high school transcript, ACT or SAT I scores, and at least one recommendation for admission (emphasis is placed on grades in college-preparatory courses). Transfer students must submit an application for admission, an official college transcript from each college attended, and a letter of good standing from the most recent college attended. On-campus interviews are strongly recommended.

Application and Information

Lambuth has a rolling admission policy. Beginning October 1, students are notified of the admission decision as soon as all application materials have been received. A $25 application fee should be submitted with the application. Interviews and campus tours are available through the Office of Admissions.

For further information, students should contact:

Office of Admissions
Lambuth University
705 Lambuth Boulevard
Jackson, Tennessee 38301
Telephone: 901-425-3223
      800-LAMBUTH (toll-free)
E-mail: admit@lambuth.edu
World Wide Web: http://www.lambuth.edu

Founded by the Methodist Church in 1843, Lambuth is one of the most time-honored universities in the South.

LA ROCHE COLLEGE
PITTSBURGH, PENNSYLVANIA

The College
Founded in 1963 by the Sisters of Divine Providence, La Roche College has distinguished itself as a growing institution that offers students academic challenge in an atmosphere of support and encouragement. The College was recently named for having the thirteenth-safest college campus in the United States by the APBnews.com/CAP Index study. Students at the College number more than 1,800, including over 300 graduate students.

La Roche is a Catholic, coeducational, international four-year institution and is fully accredited by the Middle States Association of Colleges and Schools. It is chartered by the Commonwealth of Pennsylvania, and its programs have been approved by the Pennsylvania Department of Education. The College holds memberships in the Council for Independent Colleges, the National Association for Independent Colleges and Universities, the American Council on Education, the Pittsburgh Council on Higher Education, and the National Collegiate Athletic Association (NCAA). La Roche's nursing program is accredited by the National League for Nursing Accrediting Commission (NLNAC). Its interior design and graphic design majors are accredited by the National Association of Schools of Art and Design (NASAD), and its interior design major is also accredited by the Foundation for Interior Design Education Research (FIDER). The Center for Teacher Education is fully accredited by the Pennsylvania Department of Education in elementary education, early childhood education, nursing education, secondary mathematics, secondary science, secondary English, Spanish (K–12), and special education.

Campus clubs and organizations give students an opportunity to participate in a variety of activities, including athletic associations, social clubs, academic societies, and student chapters of professional associations. In addition to intramural sports, La Roche participates in eleven NCAA intercollegiate sports, including men's varsity baseball and golf; women's softball, tennis, and volleyball; and men's and women's basketball, cross-country, and soccer.

The 38,000-square-foot College Center is the focal point of the La Roche campus. The building houses a dining room, an art gallery, a bookstore, admissions offices, student activity offices, and other student service offices. The Kerr Fitness and Sports Center, with facilities for basketball, volleyball, racquetball, dance, karate, and weight training, opened in June 1993.

Students are encouraged to live on campus in one of four residence halls, where apartment-style suites promote group interaction and a sense of community. With the guidance of a residence life director, students plan a variety of programs, including guest speakers, recreational events, and social activities. The College recently opened a new state-of-the-art residence hall. The 154-bed structure contains furnished 2-person suites with private baths, wall-to-wall carpeting, and microwave and refrigerator units and provides free laundry services.

Location
La Roche College's attractive 80-acre wooded campus is located in the North Hills of Pittsburgh, just 10 minutes from the center of the city. Pittsburgh is the second-largest city in Pennsylvania and the headquarters for several of the largest corporations in the United States, including USX and US Airways. A lively, dynamic city, Pittsburgh has outstanding facilities and attractions, including the Pittsburgh Symphony, the Civic Light Opera, Carnegie Music Hall and Museum, Three Rivers Stadium, Mellon Arena, Heinz Hall for the Performing Arts, and professional sports teams: the Steelers, the Penguins, and the Pirates.

Majors and Degrees
La Roche awards the Bachelor of Arts, Bachelor of Science, and Bachelor of Science in Nursing degrees in five academic divisions with thirty-nine majors: administration and management, with majors in accounting, administration and management, computer information systems, finance, and international management; graphics, design, and communications, offering majors in communication design, graphic design, and interior design; humanities, with options in education (early childhood, elementary, and English), English studies—language and literature, English studies—professional writing, liberal studies, performing arts/dance, history, human services, political science, psychology, science, sociology, religious education/catechetics, and religious studies and a certificate program in modern language; sciences, with majors in applied mathematics, biology, chemistry, education (biology, chemistry, general science, and mathematics) environmental studies, medical technology, natural sciences, psychobiology, radiography (for registered radiographers), and respiratory therapy (for certified respiratory therapists); and social sciences. A baccalaureate completion program for RNs is offered through the Division of Nursing. A Bachelor of Arts in international studies is offered as a cross-divisional major.

Academic Program
La Roche offers students a rare blend of liberal arts studies and professional preparation. This combination permits students to develop broad perspectives and understanding while acquiring particular professional skills. Opportunities for research and in-depth study are available through independent study, directed research, and an honors program. In each of these activities students work closely with faculty members who guide and direct their research. Students can gain practical field experience through an internship in one of Pittsburgh's many businesses or corporations. Students pursuing internships work closely with experienced professionals in the field. In addition, a faculty adviser monitors the student's progress and may require a paper, journal, and/or practicum work samples. Study-abroad programs are also available.

In La Roche's highly individualized program, students work with faculty mentors who help identify and foster each student's talents and assist students in applying knowledge acquired at La Roche to the world of work. New students meet with an adviser/mentor during orientation to select courses for their first term. The mentor works with students in selecting a major and appropriate courses and advises students on their graduation requirements.

Degree requirements in most majors include a minimum of 120 credits. Students must demonstrate competence in English, mathematics, and practical computer application and must complete a core curriculum.

Academic Facilities
The John J. Wright Library and Learning Center is fully equipped to support every academic major. The library is an official repository for government documents and participates in an interlibrary loan system that circulates materials through the ten higher education institutions in Pittsburgh.

La Roche has four computer labs that house IBM and IBM-compatible personal computers for student use. Students can sharpen their computer skills with a variety of software, including WordPerfect, Lotus, D-base, MS-DOS, and Norton Utilities. For graphic design students, the design complex includes studios for sculpture, figure drawing, and painting. Darkroom and lighting studios are also available for photography students. Two computer labs provide students access to Macintosh systems that use QuarkXpress, Illustrator, and Photoshop, among others. Each student also has access to the Internet at any of La Roche's state-of-the-art computer labs and in their residence halls.

Costs

Full-time tuition for the 1999–2000 academic year was estimated at $11,025. Room and board costs were approximately $5910.

Financial Aid

At La Roche, every student who qualifies and meets the appropriate deadlines is offered a financial aid package. The College strives to meet each student's demonstrated financial need. Ninety-five percent of La Roche's full-time students receive some form of financial assistance. Aid is available through various scholarships, grants, loans, work-study awards, and special benefits made available by the federal and state governments, La Roche College, and private organizations. In addition, the College awards full and partial tuition scholarships to students who qualify on the basis of academic achievements. Financial aid counselors are available to answer questions and assist students. The College provides a free financial aid estimating service to all students who apply to La Roche. La Roche also offers several payment plans. Information on these options can be obtained from the College's admissions office.

All students who intend to apply for financial aid must submit the Free Application for Federal Student Aid (FAFSA). Students who live outside of Pennsylvania should also submit their own state grant form, if applicable. All students are encouraged to submit the proper forms as soon after January 1 as possible so that they are processed prior to La Roche College's May 1 deadline.

The Pacem In Terris (Peace on Earth) Institute at La Roche College provides scholarship assistance and collegiate opportunities to young women and men from war-ravaged regions of the world with the provision that they return to their homelands upon graduation to put their skills to work. The institute was established in 1993 by Monsignor William A. Kerr, President of La Roche College, and the name is derived from the last encyclical of Pope John XXIII. He expressed his vision in a letter entitled "Pacem In Terris" during Easter week in 1963, less than two months before his death. He asked all men and women of goodwill, from all parts of the globe, to work together for a world community with an enhanced appreciation of human rights.

Faculty

At La Roche, faculty members are an acclaimed international group. They work closely with students to provide both challenge and encouragement. In addition, they are experts in their fields. Many have earned distinguished honors, including a history professor who won a Christopher Award, an artist/teacher who was recognized for her achievements in computer graphics, and a sociology professor who completed a fellowship with the prestigious Heritage Foundation.

Student Government

The Student Government Association (SGA) is a central and vital organization at the College. It is a legislative body responsible for all areas of student life. All enrolled students are represented by the SGA, and all full-time students are eligible for election. Students are also represented on various administrative committees within the College, including the Academic Senate, Administrative Council, and Planning Commission.

Admission Requirements

La Roche is selective in its admission process. The College seeks students who demonstrate a strong desire to fulfill their academic potential and have a clear commitment to personal growth and achievement. Because the College values a commitment to community and lifelong learning, the admission staff also considers a student's extracurricular and volunteer activities in such areas as school, church, and community.

The admission committee reviews each applicant individually, assessing personal and academic strengths in light of a student's background and opportunities. Committee members carefully examine high school records (course work, grade point average, and class rank), letters of recommendation, and SAT I or ACT scores. La Roche's code numbers are 2379 for the SAT I and 3607 for the ACT.

Application and Information

Candidates for admission should submit a completed application, a copy of their high school transcript, a school report completed by a guidance counselor, and a $25 nonrefundable application fee. SAT I and ACT scores should be sent directly to the College. La Roche adheres to a rolling admission system by which students receive decisions once their application credentials are complete. To ensure appropriate financial aid and housing opportunities, students are encouraged to apply no later than March 31 for fall and December 31 for spring semester.

For additional information regarding La Roche admission, prospective students should contact:

Office of Admissions
La Roche College
9000 Babcock Boulevard
Pittsburgh, Pennsylvania 15237
Telephone: 412-536-1270
          800-838-4LRC (toll-free)
Fax: 412-536-1048
E-mail: admsns@laroche.edu
World Wide Web: http://www.laroche.edu

President Msgr. William A. Kerr and students on the campus of La Roche College, where students experience personalized attention and quality education.

LASELL COLLEGE
NEWTON, MASSACHUSETTS

The College

Founded in 1851, Lasell College is a coeducational, independent, nonsectarian institution of higher education and offers career-oriented bachelor's and associate degree programs. Predominantly a residential college, Lasell seeks to provide its students with the experience of living and learning in a community organized around a central educational purpose that Lasell calls "connected learning." Central to the Lasell plan of education is the belief that students acquire and retain knowledge most effectively when classroom theory is reinforced by regular application under direct faculty supervision. Students are supervised at any number of Lasell's on- and off-campus laboratories and internship and externship sites.

Lasell's students are encouraged to participate in a wide variety of campus organizations and to take an active role in developing new interests. Among Lasell's organizations are the Business Club, the Fashion Forum, the Drama Club, and the Lasell Center for Public Service. All clubs organize and sponsor their own activities, including health fairs, fashion shows, trips, and various lectures and presentations. Lasell publications, run by the students themselves, include a newspaper and a yearbook. Each year the students and staff of the College plan a series of programs and events designed to inform and involve members of the Lasell community. These include lectures, Diversity Week, International Week, and highlighting the roles of men and women in society and the world at large. Other annual events include the Commencement Ball, the Torchlight Parade, and River Day. Athletic teams compete in a number of NCAA Division III sports, including men's basketball, cross-country, lacrosse, soccer, and volleyball and women's basketball, cross-country, field hockey, lacrosse, soccer, softball, and volleyball.

Resident students may choose to live in Victorian houses or modern residence halls. More than 85 percent of residence rooms are double occupancy, and all rooms are cable- and Internet-ready. Each residence hall plans its own activities and participates in all College programs. Resident staff members are on hand to provide support when necessary. Special emphasis is placed on the advantages of the College as a close-knit community in proximity to Boston.

Location

Lasell's campus is 15 minutes from downtown Boston in the suburb of Newton, Massachusetts. The "T", or Mass Transit, is conveniently located within walking distance of the campus. The College has 50 acres of land, with forty-three residential and academic facilities. Students experience the advantages of a suburban setting with all of the social and cultural attractions offered in the city of Boston.

Majors and Degrees

Lasell offers Bachelor of Science and Bachelor of Arts degree programs in accounting, athletic training (pending accreditation), business administration, business management, criminal justice, day-care program administration, early childhood education (N–3), elementary education, exercise physiology, fashion design and production, fashion/retail merchandising, finance, general studies, health-care administration, hotel and travel/tourism administration, human services, legal studies (prelaw), liberal arts, management information systems (MIS), marketing, paralegal studies, psychology, sociology, special education, and sports management.

Associate in Science degree programs are offered in health science, nursing, occupational therapy assistant studies, and physical therapist assistant studies.

Academic Program

Candidates for a bachelor's degree complete between 123 and 128 semester hours of course work. Candidates from associate degree programs at other colleges may transfer up to 45 semester hours toward a Lasell bachelor's degree. Lasell College recognizes that students must be exposed to a wide breadth of liberal arts courses to have a well-rounded education and function in the twenty-first century. Lasell's core curriculum integrates writing across the curriculum, oral communication skills, critical and quantitative reasoning, computer literacy, and ethical development.

Academic Facilities

Lasell College's buildings feature the Heath Management Center, Wass Science Building, the Brennan Library, the Yamawaki Art and Cultural Center, the Learning Center, an Academic Computer Center, various laboratory facilities, and an athletic center.

The Heath Management Center, Wolfe Hall, is highlighted by a mock boardroom, modern seminar room, travel classrooms, and a fashion design lab. Wolfe also has a Business Computer Lab, which houses state-of-the-art computers that run business software. The Wass Science Building has laboratories for anatomy, biology, chemistry, and physical science. The Brennan Library, a modern multimedia center, contains 51,000 volumes, 400 periodical subscriptions, and a large record and videocassette collection.

The Yamawaki Art and Cultural Center, a three-story building with Victorian flair, provides students with labs, studios, classrooms, exhibit areas, and a theater. The Learning Center assists all students with any academic need. The center provides students with tutorial services in several areas, including reading, writing, study skills, and mathematics.

The Academic Computer Center is a College-wide facility that provides direct instruction and support. More than 100 computers are available for student use, and the staff of the center offers courses and workshops to enhance computer literacy.

On-site laboratory facilities provide realistic settings where students practice theories from the classroom. Those available for students include a retail management center, two child-study centers, a travel agency, PC labs, a computer-aided design system, a bed-and-breakfast, and an advertising agency.

Lasell's athletic center, which opened in May 1997, features a suspended indoor track, competition-size basketball court, cardiovascular exercise room, and dance studio.

Costs

For the 2000–01 academic year, tuition for full-time students is $14,700. Room and board charges are $7700.

Financial Aid

More than 85 percent of the students at Lasell receive some form of financial aid. Programs include Lasell grants, Federal Pell Grants, Federal Supplemental Educational Opportunity

Grants, Federal Perkins Loans, Federal Stafford Student Loans, Federal Work-Study, awards, state scholarships, and Lasell alumnae scholarships.

Lasell uses the Free Application for Federal Student Aid (FAFSA) to determine eligibility for federal programs and the CSS Profile to determine a student's eligibility for its financial aid programs. Applicants for aid who wish to enroll in September should mail the FAFSA to the appropriate processing centers as soon as possible after January 1. In 1998–99, the average financial aid package, including loans, grants, and work-study totaled $11,000. Lasell guarantees all financial aid packages for four years if a family's financial situation and a student's academic record remain the same.

Faculty

Lasell has a total of 155 faculty members (48 full-time, 107 part-time), many of whom are practicing professionals in their respective fields and bring their experience to the classroom. The student-faculty ratio is 10:1. The student-faculty bond, strengthened by faculty members acting as academic advisers, is considered a vital element in the social, academic, and cultural growth and development of students. Faculty members serve as role models for success, and particular emphasis is placed on their availability for individual and group conferences.

Student Government

Students are elected in the fall and spring of each year to the association's Executive Council and Executive Board. The elected officials represent the student body and govern and coordinate College activities. All students are encouraged to participate in the association and to use it as an effective agency for communicating their concerns and interests.

Admission Requirements

Applicants are evaluated on the basis of their academic achievement, overall initiative, and SAT I or ACT scores. Prospective students are urged to visit the Lasell campus for a tour and interview. Appointments may be scheduled Monday through Saturday by calling the Admissions Office. Several open house programs are scheduled throughout the academic year so that prospective students may have an in-depth visit at Lasell.

Application and Information

Candidates for admission should submit an application and $25 fee, a high school transcript, SAT I or ACT scores, and a letter of recommendation. Lasell has a rolling admission policy, and an applicant will receive a decision shortly after their application has been completed. Transfer applicants must submit high school and college transcripts and a letter of recommendation.

For further information, students should contact:

David Eddy
Director of Admission
Lasell College
1844 Commonwealth Avenue
Newton, Massachusetts 02166

Telephone: 617-243-2225
Fax: 617-796-4343
E-mail: info@lasell.edu
World Wide Web: http://www.lasell.edu

Lasell's theory of connected learning gives students the opportunity to immediately apply what they have learned in the classroom.

LAWRENCE TECHNOLOGICAL UNIVERSITY
SOUTHFIELD, MICHIGAN

The University

Founded in 1932 as Lawrence Institute of Technology by brothers Russell and E. George Lawrence, Lawrence Technological University has more than 22,000 alumni worldwide. The curriculum at Lawrence Tech is diverse, but the University has traditionally given students a high-quality, affordable education with an emphasis on theory and practice. The University, including the graduate programs in business, architecture, and engineering, is accredited by the North Central Association of Colleges and Schools. Appropriate national professional agencies provide additional accreditation to various degree programs in architecture, interior architecture/design, illustration, administration and management, chemistry, and engineering. The University offers graduate degree programs in architecture, automotive engineering, business administration, civil engineering, computer science, industrial operations, information systems, manufacturing systems, and science education.

An independent university, Lawrence Tech offers a highly competitive tuition rate, modern facilities, and real-world application of textbook knowledge. The 115-acre campus is situated at a hub of American business and industry and near sites of some of the world's most significant manufacturing and engineering accomplishments.

There are approximately 5,000 students at Lawrence Tech; more than 500 live in on-campus housing; 23 percent are women.

Numerous fraternities, sororities, and social and professional organizations sponsor a variety of activities during the year. Intramural sports teams involve nearly 25 percent of the student body, and recreational facilities include the 38,000-square-foot Don Ridler Field House, which features a running track, a gymnasium, racquetball courts, saunas, and a weight and conditioning room. Lawrence Tech's campus includes eight major buildings, all built since 1955. The campus has more than doubled in size since 1981.

Location

Southfield is a suburb of 76,000 people, a center of corporate and industrial activity, and a city offering a pleasant balance between big-city entertainment opportunities and a quiet residential atmosphere. Southfield's daytime population of commuting workers swells to 275,000. Oakland County has the third-highest per capita income in the country. The Lawrence Tech campus is conveniently adjacent to major freeways and about a 30-minute drive north of downtown Detroit. Southeastern Michigan offers a rich variety of recreational and cultural activities, with public transportation making most areas accessible to students. Within a few miles of the campus, students can find many restaurants, parks, shopping areas, and recreational facilities. Research, manufacturing, scientific, and business enterprises are also located nearby, aiding co-op students as well as those who work full- or part-time while attending classes. More than 200 Fortune 500 companies have headquarters or business operations here.

Majors and Degrees

Lawrence Tech offers more than forty majors or course concentrations. Most programs are available day or evening. Dual-degree programs combining the associate and baccalaureate programs are also available. Postgraduate preparation includes premedicine, predentistry, prelaw, and pre-biomedical engineering programs.

The College of Architecture and Design offers Bachelor of Science degrees in architecture and interior architecture/design. A Bachelor of Fine Arts degree is also offered in architectural illustration.

The College of Arts and Sciences awards the Bachelor of Science in administration, chemistry, computer science, environmental chemistry, humanities, mathematics, mathematics and computer science, physics, physics and computer science, and technical communication; and an associate degree in chemical technology.

The College of Engineering confers Bachelor of Science degrees in civil engineering, computer engineering, electrical engineering, engineering technology, industrial management, information technology (new program), mechanical engineering, and technology management. The college also offers evening associate programs in construction, electrical, manufacturing, and mechanical engineering technology.

The College of Management awards graduate degrees.

Academic Program

Graduation from Lawrence Technological University requires completion of a degree program with an overall GPA of at least 2.0. Most disciplines combine a strong concentration in the major with basic science, humanities, and mathematics requirements. Engineering students share a core program the first two years, as do administration, industrial management, architecture, and interior architecture majors. The University operates on a semester calendar.

Off-Campus Arrangements

Lawrence Tech engineering and technology students may participate in a co-op program, alternating semesters of classes and work.

Academic Facilities

Lawrence Tech has an extensive network of computers based on the University's VAXcluster, PCs, workstations, and hundreds of terminals and microcomputers in various labs on campus. Each student has his or her own account and is encouraged to make use of it. The library houses a broad selection of books, periodicals, CD-ROM databases, and microforms and is part of a nationwide network of more than 6,000 libraries that share resources via computer terminals and phone lines. Lawrence Tech is also surrounded by many outstanding municipal and research libraries. The campus houses many research labs, including an 18,000-square-foot manufacturing engineering lab. Lawrence Tech also owns a nearby Frank Lloyd Wright-designed home that is used as a study center. Beginning with the fall 2000 semester, incoming freshmen are required to use laptop computers in the classroom.

Costs

The 1999–2000 tuition for freshmen and sophomores majoring in arts and sciences and engineering technology areas was $330 per credit hour. For juniors and seniors, tuition was $346 per credit hour. In architecture and engineering, tuition for freshmen and sophomores was $346 per credit hour; for juniors and seniors, it was $362 per credit hour. A normal course load was 12–17 credit hours per semester. The undergraduate registration fee was $100 each semester. International students on temporary visas must deposit the first semester's tuition and fees at the time of first registration.

Financial Aid

Approximately two thirds of the student body receive financial assistance at Lawrence Tech. Through various University, state, and federal programs, the Student Financial Aid Office administers more than $12 million annually. Federal and state grants are available based upon need. Many privately funded scholarships are awarded to qualified students, based on need and/or scholastic performance. Part-time employment is available at the University on a first-come, first-served basis for full-time students. Student loans are also available from a variety of sources—state, federal, and private. Prospective students are urged to contact the Student Financial Aid Office for information on deadlines and requirements for eligibility.

Faculty

Approximately 350 full-time and part-time faculty members teach at Lawrence Tech. Many part-time faculty members hold full-time jobs in industry and bring their real-world perspective to the classroom. About 60 percent of the full-time faculty members hold a doctoral degree or the terminal degree in their field. Faculty involvement is extensive in student chapters of professional associations, which meet on campus. Many faculty members are professional engineers or registered architects in Michigan and elsewhere. To promote a low student-faculty ratio, approximately 70 percent of the undergraduate classes at Lawrence Tech have 19 or fewer students; 2 percent of the classes have more than 50.

Student Government

The Student Government sponsors and supports a variety of campus activities. It oversees expenditures, meets regularly to plan events, and is authorized to levy fines for minor, on-campus infractions. More than forty student clubs and organizations, including fraternities, sororities, honor societies, and student chapters of professional groups, are active on campus.

Admission Requirements

A high school diploma or the equivalent is required of all students applying to baccalaureate or associate degree programs. Most baccalaureate applicants must have a minimum 2.5 overall GPA in academic subjects and a minimum 2.0 average in subject areas pertaining to the desired program of study. Applicants to associate degree programs are required to have a minimum 2.0 average in the three academic areas (humanities, mathematics, and science) combined. ACT results are required of all entering freshmen. Required high school courses vary with the curriculum, and Lawrence Tech offers a number of basic studies courses designed to augment incoming students' backgrounds if deficiencies exist.

Application and Information

Programs start in August and January. An optional summer semester begins in May or July. Entry in the fall semester is advised but not required. Students must submit transcripts from all schools attended, along with a nonrefundable $30 admission fee. To obtain a University catalog and an application form, students should contact:

Admissions Office
Lawrence Technological University
21000 West Ten Mile Road
Southfield, Michigan 48075-1058

Telephone: 800-CALL-LTU (toll-free)
E-mail: admissions@ltu.edu
World Wide Web: http://www.ltu.edu

The Wayne H. Buell Management Building, housing the library, dining, and bookstore facilities, as well as the College of Management.

LAWRENCE UNIVERSITY
APPLETON, WISCONSIN

The University

Lawrence University offers a distinguished education in the liberal arts and sciences that blends study in the traditional disciplines with programs that address contemporary issues. Its 1,200 undergraduate men and women, from fifty states and forty countries, participate in a curriculum that not only promotes in-depth study within a single area but also invites exploration of the connections among different academic fields. Bright, motivated students are attracted to Lawrence by the exceptional level of student-faculty interaction both inside and outside the classroom.

Lawrence offers a number of meaningful differences that set it apart from other colleges. Among the most important are Freshman Studies, a two-term seminar-style course that, through major works of literature, art, and music, develops the ability to think critically, write cogently, and argue persuasively; Individualized Study, which encourages and requires intellectual maturity and self-direction and emphasizes the application of knowledge over the simple rote learning of facts; Bjorklunden, Lawrence's 400-acre estate on the shore of Lake Michigan, where students and faculty members gather every weekend of the academic year for relaxed yet focused discussions on issues and ideas covering a wide range of topics; the Conservatory of Music, which not only provides intensive training in performance, theory-composition, and music education, but also provides musical opportunities to all Lawrence students and supports performances of a quality and frequency not found in other colleges of similar size; and the Honor Code, which ensures academic integrity, promotes mutual trust and respect, and values cooperation and collaboration over competition in all aspects of campus life.

Lawrence offers an active social life and a full range of recreational and athletic opportunities. Six residence halls on campus offer living arrangements from single and double rooms to 4-person suites. A women's residence, theme houses, and a co-op house provide alternative living arrangements. Thirty percent of Lawrence's students belong to five national fraternities and three national sororities. More than 100 student clubs and organizations provide a wide variety of activities ranging from performances by major music ensembles, an international film series, and Celebrate! (a spring festival attended by more than 50,000) to the annual Trivia Weekend (the longest-running and most notorious trivia contest in the country), crew on the Fox River, and winter camping along Lake Michigan. The Buchanan Kiewit Recreation Center offers an indoor track; swimming pool; weight/exercise room; dance room; racquetball, handball, and walleyball courts; gymnasium; and saunas. Alexander Gymnasium, Whiting Field, and the Banta Bowl (a 5,300-seat football stadium) house twenty-three varsity and four club sports teams (NCAA Division III). The spirit of volunteerism flourishes at Lawrence, with more than ten campus organizations devoted to tutoring local school-age children, committing to Habitat for Humanity, serving as Big Brothers/Sisters, and other volunteer activities. A staffed volunteer bureau assists students in finding volunteer opportunities.

Location

Lawrence is in Appleton, a city of 70,000 people, located on the banks of the historic Fox River in northeast Wisconsin. The Fox Cities area (population 200,000), of which Appleton is the center, has been considered one of the three best medium-sized metropolitan areas in the United States, based on "quality of life" indicators and has been cited as among the safest for cities its size. The 84-acre Lawrence campus overlooks the river and is situated adjacent to the city's downtown area. Appleton is accessible by car, bus, and plane and offers the commercial/retail advantages of a larger urban area and the recreational opportunities and safety of a Midwestern town.

Majors and Degrees

Lawrence awards the Bachelor of Arts (B.A.), the Bachelor of Music (B.Mus.), and the five-year B.A./B.Mus. The more than thirty areas of study include anthropology, art history, biology, biomedical ethics, chemistry, Chinese, classics, cognitive science, computer science, East Asian languages and cultures, economics, English, environmental studies, French, gender studies, geology, German, government, history, international studies, linguistics, mathematics, mathematics-economics, music, music education, music performance, music theory-composition, natural sciences, neuroscience, philosophy, physics, psychology, religious studies, Russian, studio art, and theater and drama. Preprofessional education is available in business, law, and medicine. Cooperative degree programs are available in engineering, environmental management, forestry, medical technology, nursing, and occupational therapy.

Academic Program

The academic program not only emphasizes in-depth work within a single discipline but also encourages breadth by exposure to many fields of inquiry. Distribution requirements for both B.A. and B.Mus. candidates promote exposure to all areas of the arts and sciences. Working with their faculty advisers, students are encouraged to take initiative and responsibility for selecting a course of study best suited to them. More than 90 percent of Lawrence's students take advantage of tutorials and independent study, working one-on-one with faculty members. The Honors in Independent Study Program culminates in a written thesis or piece of work in the creative or performing arts and an oral examination.

Lawrence operates on a three-term calendar, with students taking three courses in each ten-week term. The academic year begins in late September and ends in mid-June.

Off-Campus Arrangements

More than half of all Lawrence students take advantage of a wide variety of both domestic and international off-campus study opportunities. The value of participating in off-campus opportunities is supported by the faculty through a resolution encouraging all students to do so. Many choose to attend Lawrence's program with its own campus in London, which operates all three terms of each academic year. Others choose from programs in cities such as Beijing, Florence, Munich, Rome, and Tokyo; countries such as the Cayman Islands, Costa Rica, the Czech Republic, France, India, Peru, Russia, Senegal, Spain, Tanzania, and Zimbabwe; and domestic programs in Chicago; Washington, D.C.; Woods Hole, Massachusetts; and the Boundary Waters in northern Minnesota. Need-based financial aid is available to assist students with the additional costs of attending an off-campus program sponsored by or endorsed by Lawrence.

Academic Facilities

Seeley G. Mudd Library has 370,000 volumes, 300,000 government documents, 1,400 current periodical subscriptions, 16,000 recordings and videotapes, and more than 102,000 microform items. In addition to the online catalog, the library can access national computerized bibliographic databases. The library houses the Media Center, with its listening facilities, audiovisual equipment, and video studio, and the Career Center. There are more than 250 terminals and PC and Macintosh computers located across the campus, providing round-the-clock access to the campuswide computing system. Fiber-optic cabling interconnects all principal stations and residence halls by room and all halls have central computer lounges available around the clock. Science facilities include twenty-three general laboratories for student use; twenty-five special laboratories for research, including a laser physics lab; a graphics and computational physics lab; four environmentally controlled rooms; animal rooms for psychology and biology; a greenhouse; two electron microscopes; a nuclear magnetic resonator; and a variety of spectrometers. Briggs Hall, the new facility for the social sciences and math, opened in 1997. Main Hall houses humanities classrooms, seminar rooms, a computer text laboratory, a language acquisition center, and the Hiram A. Jones Latin Library. The Music-Drama Center and the Shattuck Hall of Music house private practice studios, classrooms, a recital hall, large and small ensemble rehearsal halls, a digital recording studio, performance facilities for the theater department, and WLFM, Lawrence's FM radio station affiliated with Wisconsin Public Radio. Lawrence has two theaters: the first, with a proscenium stage, seats 500 people; the second is an experimental theater, adaptable to arena- or thrust-stage productions. The Memorial Chapel seats 1,250 people and is the primary venue for convocations, performances by Lawrence's large ensembles, and other public events and concerts. The Wriston Art Center offers a first-rate facility for the studio art and art history programs. It includes an outdoor amphitheater, three galleries, and two- and three-dimensional art studios and houses the University's outstanding permanent collection.

Costs

For 2000–01, annual tuition is $21,717, room and board average $4791, and the activity fee is $138. Books, travel, and living expenses are estimated at $1800 per year.

Financial Aid

Lawrence adheres to a need-blind admission policy. For U.S. citizens and permanent residents, the Financial Aid Office makes awards on the basis of the candidate's need, as determined from the Free Application for Federal Student Aid (FAFSA) and the Lawrence University Application for Financial Aid. Lawrence is committed to meeting the full demonstrated financial need of every admitted student. Nearly two thirds of Lawrence's students receive grants, long-term loans, and work-study packages, totaling more than $12 million. In 1999, the average aid package exceeded $18,000. To apply for financial aid, students must submit the FAFSA, the Lawrence Application for Financial Aid, a photocopy of their parents' IRS 1040 forms and schedules, and a photocopy of their own IRS 1040 form. Non-need-based scholarships and conservatory performance awards ranging from $1000 to $10,000 per year are awarded primarily to strongly recommended applicants ranking in the top 5 percent of their class and to exceptional musicians by audition.

Faculty

Lawrence has 140 full-time faculty members; 93 percent hold a Ph.D. or the highest degree in their field; 30 percent are women. The student-faculty ratio is 11:1, and the median class size is 15. The faculty plays a central role in guiding students' experiences. Active scholars and artists, the faculty members encourage students to join with them in academic pursuits, many of which have led to collaborative faculty-student published works. Lawrence was recently ranked fifth nationally among 205 small, private undergraduate institutions in the total amount of awards received from the Research Corporation's Cottrell College Science Program for faculty and student participatory research. Members of the Lawrence faculty have received seven National Endowment for the Humanities fellowships in the last six years.

Student Government

The Lawrence University Community Council governs most nonacademic matters. It has a student president, vice president, and treasurer; 12 student representatives; and 4 faculty representatives.

Admission Requirements

The admission staff considers the strength of an applicant's course of study (16 units of English, math, history, social studies, physical sciences, and foreign languages are recommended), grades, standardized test scores (ACT or SAT I), recommendations, and extracurricular activities. Candidates for the B.Mus. degree are judged additionally on musicianship, performance potential, recommendations of teachers, and general academic ability. All music applicants must audition. More than half of Lawrence's students graduated in the top 10 percent of their high school class. A personal interview is not required, but a campus visit is strongly recommended and is required for merit award consideration.

Application and Information

Two binding early decision plans, as well as the regular application procedure (deadline January 15, notification by April 1), are available for high school seniors. (International students should not apply under the early decision plans.) A $200 nonrefundable enrollment deposit is due two weeks after notification of admission under either of the early decision options or on or before the Candidates Reply Date of May 1 under the regular application procedure. A completed application consists of the personal application form with essay, the secondary school report form and official transcript, the teacher's report form, official ACT or SAT I scores, and the application fee of $30. In addition, Conservatory of Music applicants must complete a supplementary music form, submit a music teacher's recommendation, and audition on campus or at a regional site. Transfer applicants are considered and notified on a rolling admission basis and should submit high school and college transcripts and ACT or SAT I scores. Lawrence accepts the Common Application form for high school seniors.

Office of Admissions
Lawrence University
P.O. Box 599
Appleton, Wisconsin 54912-0599
Telephone: 920-832-6500
        800-227-0982 (toll-free)
E-mail: excel@lawrence.edu
World Wide Web: http://www.lawrence.edu

LEBANON VALLEY COLLEGE
ANNVILLE, PENNSYLVANIA

The College

More than 130 years of tradition, an outstanding student body and faculty, and exceptional facilities make this private liberal arts college stand out among other schools. Founded in 1866, Lebanon Valley is steeped in a tradition of providing students with an educational foundation that transcends time and embraces new technology. The College has instilled in its graduates the desire and ability to think, ask questions, solve problems, and communicate effectively. These qualities, combined with a love for education and learning, prepare students to be competitive in a world that is constantly changing. A supportive community provides the final ingredient students need to achieve success in the job market and professional or graduate school.

The Lebanon Valley College family of 1,340 students is growing. The new freshmen and transfer students have become part of a student body that represents eighteen states and twelve countries. Technology wires them to the world and prepares them for the future. Beautiful spaces foster quiet reflection, where students work and play together, building friendships that last a lifetime.

Students' efforts and accomplishments are being recognized. Few other small colleges have received more Fulbright awards than Lebanon Valley College—ten awards in the past nineteen years—with mathematics majors receiving five during that period. *U.S. News & World Report* ranks Lebanon Valley College as one of the top ten regional liberal arts colleges in the North. It is also featured annually in *101 of the Best Values in America's Colleges and Universities*.

Lebanon Valley's tree-lined campus feels like a college of yesteryear—with twenty-first-century accoutrements. Students enjoy state-of-the-art facilities whether they are studying in the atrium of the Bishop Library or using a workstation in the molecular modeling lab. The College's forty-one buildings provide for every facet of college life with nineteen residence halls, including two condominium-style halls; classroom buildings; a student center; a recreational sports center; a varsity gymnasium; a library; a music center; an art gallery and recital hall; an art studio; and a chapel. One of the keys to providing students with a rich, well-rounded experience is to offer a wealth of opportunities for learning and growth beyond the classroom. There are new athletic fields, gardens and plazas, baseball and softball parks, and a physical therapy facility.

The staff of the Career Services Office helps students to research careers and establish contacts with potential employers. Seminars are offered on resume writing and interviewing skills. An alumni database provides students access to individuals who are working in their prospective field.

The College's mission is to continue to carry out the art of teaching and learning with the same dedication and love that has come to be identified with the educators of the Valley.

Master's programs are offered in business administration, physical therapy, and science education.

Location

Annville, founded in 1799, is a small town of approximately 5,000 people. Located in the heart of Pennsylvania Dutch country, the town is just 10 minutes east of Hershey and within a 2- to 3-hour drive of Philadelphia, Baltimore, New York, and Washington, D.C. Nestled in a valley, the College sits on 235 beautiful acres. A wide variety of cultural events and activities are offered on campus and within the community.

Majors and Degrees

The College confers five baccalaureate degrees. The Bachelor of Arts is available in the following major programs: American studies, economics, English, French, German, historical communications, history, music, philosophy, political science, psychology, religion, sociology, Spanish, and certain individualized majors. The Bachelor of Science is available in the following major programs: accounting, actuarial science, biochemistry, biology, business administration, chemistry, computer science, cooperative engineering, cooperative forestry, elementary education, health-care management, hotel management, international business, mathematics, music education, physics, psychobiology, and certain individualized majors. The Bachelor of Science in chemistry, the Bachelor of Science in medical technology, and the Bachelor of Music (with an emphasis in music recording technology) are also available. In addition to its thirty-three majors, Lebanon Valley offers preprofessional programs in dentistry, law, medicine, ministry, pharmacy, and veterinary science.

Academic Program

Lebanon Valley has long been known for the strength of its academic programs and the achievement of its faculty members and alumni. The science program is particularly strong, with exceptionally well equipped laboratories. The U.S. Office of Technology Assessment chose Lebanon Valley for its select list of the 100 most productive colleges and universities nationally in science, and Peterson's identifies Lebanon Valley as one of 200 colleges and universities in America offering outstanding programs in the sciences and mathematics. Lebanon Valley's mission arises directly from its historical traditions and a relationship with the United Methodist Church. The College's aim is to enable its students to become people of broad vision capable of making informed decisions and prepared for a life of service to others. To that end, the College provides an education that helps students to acquire the knowledge, skills, attitudes, and values necessary to live and work in a changing, diverse, and fragile world. The general education core provides students with the breadth of knowledge and experience across the curriculum, in addition to their major course work. Each student's academic program is fully complemented by a wide range of extracurricular activities, including guest lectures; concerts; Division III athletics; trips to New York and Washington, D.C.; and a variety of cultural activities.

Off-Campus Arrangements

Domestic students are encouraged to take advantage of the numerous study-abroad opportunities to England, France, Germany, the Netherlands, New Zealand, and Spain. Scholarship money and financial aid can be transferred to the programs, making the cost of studying abroad the same as the cost of attendance at Lebanon Valley. Students can focus on becoming fluent in a language or join their classmates and a faculty adviser in a classroom experience. Internships both abroad and in the U.S. are a very popular method for students to research possible professions, establish early contacts, and gain valuable experience within their professional field.

Academic Facilities

Lebanon Valley has beautiful facilities and provides a safe environment in which students can live and learn. The Bishop

Library, built in 1995, houses 183,500 cataloged items, including books, journals, microfilm, and media collections. Most importantly, the library, residence halls, classrooms, and administrative offices are linked to the campus network, providing state-of-the-art technology and Internet access. A videoconferencing center not only brings guest lecturers "virtually" to campus but also allows students to interview with a company overseas or in another city. Well-equipped laboratories provide students with hands-on experience and numerous opportunities for research.

Costs

Annual tuition and fees for the 2000–01 school year are $17,925. Room and board charges are set at $5680.

Financial Aid

Lebanon Valley is committed to helping families finance a college education and has received national recognition for being one of the first colleges to offer merit-based scholarships. High school achievement is rewarded at Lebanon Valley. Students who graduate in the top 30 percent of their high school class automatically receive one of the College's academic scholarships for up to half of the cost of tuition. Additional need-based financial aid is available, and 90 percent of students receive some form of financial aid. The College has committed more than $9 million to institutional aid. The Free Application for Federal Student Aid (FAFSA) and the Undergraduate Financial Aid Application must be completed to determine eligibility. The priority deadline for filing for financial aid is March 1 of the senior year of high school.

Faculty

Lebanon Valley College's faculty members are dedicated to teaching. The close-knit community and an opportunity to be actively involved in the students' educational growth have drawn talented, multifaceted faculty members from all over the country. Many professors choose to live in the area and take an active role in supporting students' growth and development both in and out of the classroom. Faculty members are very involved in professional organizations and play an active role in helping students find internships and get started with research. Of the 81 professors at Lebanon Valley, 82 percent have earned a Ph.D. or equivalent terminal degree. The College is committed to maintaining a low student-teacher ratio of 16:1. The average class size is 16.

Student Government

Lebanon Valley students participate in the College's governing system through the Student Government Association. This group includes 25 students who are elected from the student body each year for a one-year term beginning in September. Among the government's major responsibilities is fostering understanding, communication, and cooperation among the students, faculty members, and administration. It serves as the channel for all students' recommendations for establishing or changing policy and routes these recommendations to the appropriate administrative offices or faculty committees. The Student Government Association is a highly visible group on campus.

Admission Requirements

The admission process is selective, and the student's academic record is the most important factor. Lebanon Valley seeks students from diverse backgrounds and those who display leadership abilities, a commitment to community service, and special talents. All applicants should have completed 16 credit units and graduated from an accredited secondary school or present an equivalency certificate (GED). Of the 16 units, 4 should be in English, 2 in foreign language, 2 in mathematics, 1 in science, and 1 in social studies. Additional course work in math and science is strongly recommended. More than 75 percent of the freshman class rank in the top 30 percent of their high school class. Advanced standing is offered through CLEP and AP examinations.

Application and Information

To apply, students should submit a completed application, a $25 application fee, and official copies of their high school transcript and SAT I or ACT scores. Lebanon Valley has a rolling admission process. However, students are encouraged to apply early during the fall of their senior year. The Admission Advisory Group gives careful consideration to scholastic credentials such as grades and test scores as well as to the nonacademic qualities of each applicant. Personal visits to the campus may also be arranged.

For more information, applicants should contact:

William J. Brown Jr.
Dean of Admission and Financial Aid
Lebanon Valley College
101 North College Avenue
Annville, Pennsylvania 17003-0501
Telephone: 800-445-6181 (toll-free)
Fax: 717-867-6026
E-mail: admiss@lvc.edu
World Wide Web: http://www.lvc.edu

"Hot Dog" Frank Aftosmes, who opened his hot dog shop a block from Lebanon Valley's campus in 1928, still keeps watch in the Peace Garden. Funded by hundreds of graduates, the life-size bronze statue commemorates his lifelong friendship with the Lebanon Valley community.

LEHIGH UNIVERSITY
BETHLEHEM, PENNSYLVANIA

The University

Lehigh was founded in 1865 by industrialist and philanthropist Asa Packer, whose vision for the University, to provide a "classical education for a useful life," is still adhered to today. Lehigh's four colleges offer students an integrated education that is both liberal and technical. An intellectually stimulating combination of disciplines is a trademark of a Lehigh education. This is evident both in academic programs and in the flexibility students have to take courses among the different colleges.

More than 100 buildings dot the wooded hillside of the Asa Packer Campus, Lehigh's original location, now one of three contiguous campuses encompassing more than 1,600 acres. The Asa Packer Campus is a mixture of stunning old and new structures, from fraternity and sorority houses and residence halls to athletic and academic buildings. The Mountaintop Campus provides additional teaching and research space. The Murray H. Goodman Campus features the 16,000-seat Goodman Stadium for football; the 5,600-seat Stabler Arena for athletic contests, concerts, and special events; the Rauch Field House; and outdoor athletic fields for intercollegiate and intramural sports. Lehigh enrolls about 4,500 undergraduate students, 40 percent of whom are women. Lehigh's growing minority population currently stands at 12 percent. Roughly 68 percent of the students come from Pennsylvania, New Jersey, and New York, with the rest hailing from nearly every state and more than forty countries. Fifty-six percent of freshmen ranked in the top tenth of their high school class. Approximately 70 percent of all undergraduates live on campus in residence halls, fraternity or sorority houses, apartments, and specialty housing, such as the Umoja House, the Creative Arts House, ROTC, and the Impact House. There are twenty-eight fraternities and eight sororities on campus. Twenty-three varsity athletic teams compete in the Patriot League, which emphasizes the scholar-athlete. An intramural program of thirty sports and other activities is also offered; 80 percent of the students participate. There are about twenty-five club sports and 130 other student clubs, honor societies, and religious organizations.

Students must work hard to meet stringent academic demands, but the University provides support services to ensure each student ample opportunity to succeed. Lehigh's Student Life Office directs students toward help with academic or personal problems, legal issues, or general concerns. Lehigh offers a health center, fitness center, counseling service, drug and alcohol counseling service, testing service, and learning center. The University provides career planning and placement throughout students' undergraduate years and offers comprehensive support services for minority students.

Location

Bethlehem, the "Christmas City," is an ethnically diverse community of 78,000. Founded in 1741 by Moravian missionaries seeking religious freedom, the original settlement had a simple beauty that has been preserved in the city's historic section. Bethlehem is part of the picturesque Lehigh Valley and is ideally located 60 miles from Philadelphia and 90 miles from New York City. About 775,000 people live in the Lehigh Valley, and students have many cultural events, ethnic restaurants, and sources of entertainment from which to choose.

Majors and Degrees

In the College of Arts and Sciences, the Bachelor of Arts degree is offered in the following major fields: Africana studies; American studies; anthropology; architecture; art; Asian studies; behavioral neuroscience; biology; chemistry; classical civilization; classics (Latin, Greek, or both); cognitive science; computer science; earth and environmental science; economics; English; French; German; history; international careers; international relations; journalism; journalism/science writing; mathematics; molecular biology; music; natural science; philosophy; political science; physics; pre–dental science; premedical science; preoptometry; psychology; religion studies; Russian studies; science, technology, and society; social psychology; social relations; sociology; Spanish; theater; and urban studies. In addition, the Bachelor of Science degree is offered in behavioral neuroscience, biochemistry, biology, chemistry, computer science, earth and environmental science, mathematics, molecular biology, physics, and statistics. The college offers minors in most major fields and in special areas such as actuarial science, astronomy, education, Jewish studies, Latin American studies, public administration, and women's studies.

In the College of Business and Economics, the Bachelor of Science degree is offered with majors in accounting, business information systems, finance, management, and marketing.

The College of Education offers an undergraduate minor in education and a five-year program leading to a combined B.S. or B.A./M.Ed. with teaching certification in elementary or secondary education.

In the P. C. Rossin College of Engineering and Applied Science, the Bachelor of Science degree is offered in biochemistry, chemical engineering, chemistry, civil engineering, computer engineering, computer science, electrical engineering, engineering mechanics, engineering physics, fundamental sciences, industrial engineering, materials science and engineering, and mechanical engineering. Students pursuing a B.S. degree in the college can organize a special studies program in the humanities and social sciences. Environmental engineering is offered through civil engineering or a special studies program.

A popular five-year curriculum in arts and engineering leads to a B.A. or B.S. degree from the College of Arts and Sciences and a B.S. degree from the P. C. Rossin College of Engineering and Applied Science.

Academic Program

Lehigh's academic programs encourage development of oral and written communication skills, analytical and problem-solving abilities, and interpersonal skills. Frequent well-known guest speakers, seminars, plays, concerts, and art exhibits complement in-class learning. There are various opportunities for advanced international and experiential study. Lehigh also encourages students in all disciplines to integrate humanistic, social, and cultural values with technological utility. In the College of Arts and Sciences, students must complete a minimum of 121 credit hours to earn either a B.A. or B.S. degree. The College Scholar Program offers exceptional breadth and rigor to invited top students, and the Freshman Seminar Program exposes all first-year students to small seminars with senior faculty members. In the College of Business and Economics, students must complete a minimum of 124 credit hours to earn the B.S. degree. The curriculum proceeds from a strong liberal arts base, blending theoretical foundations with practical business applications. The program has been accredited since 1938 by AACSB–The International Association for Management Education. Lehigh is one of about 100 colleges to have both its business and accounting programs accredited. Several interdisciplinary academic centers enrich programs for students through conferences, visiting experts, courses, and faculty and student research in the areas of business communications, economic education, entrepreneurship, innovation management, private enterprise, and real estate. In addition, the Iacocca Institute is now an integral part of the College of Business and Economics. In the P. C. Rossin College of Engineering and Applied Science, students must complete a minimum of 133 credit hours to earn a B.S. The college's thirteen programs combine sciences and mathematics with general studies in the humanities and social sciences. In addition to interdisciplinary research projects with faculty members, the college offers a co-op program for select engineering students. Students still graduate in four years while working in industry the fall of their junior year and the summer before their senior year.

Off-Campus Arrangements

Semester and yearlong study-abroad programs are available in Australia, Austria, Belgium, China, Costa Rica, the Czech Republic, Denmark, Egypt, England, France, Germany, Ghana, Greece, Ireland, Israel, Italy, Japan, Kenya, Korea, Mexico, Russia, Scotland, Senegal, Spain, Sweden, and Taiwan. Lehigh's own summer-study programs are available in London and Paris and at various other locations in Europe and China. All programs are approved for credit. Some internships in other countries are also available. Each of the three colleges offers hands-on learning experiences, including internships, co-ops, and externships. Credit for off-campus study may be earned through Urban Semesters in Philadelphia and Washington, D.C., and by cross-registration through cooperative arrangements with a consortium that includes five other Lehigh Valley colleges.

Academic Facilities

Students can draw upon well-equipped laboratories and faculty experts who welcome undergraduate involvement in research and scholarship. Lehigh was one of the first U.S. institutions to install a campuswide telecommunications network with telephone and computing network capabilities in every student residence and faculty and staff office. The system provides access to the Internet and the World Wide Web, as well as e-mail and campus computing services. The network allows library users access to the University's online catalog and to several hundred national and international electronic databases. From their rooms, students can use this system to submit reference inquiries, place orders, and request media services and delivery of documents electronically. The University is connected through the network to the Library of Congress. The University library system provides users access to 1,238,837 books and journals, electronic databases, microfilm, computer software, and media collections. A 25,000-volume Special Collections Division includes a rare book collection featuring three copies of the first edition of Charles Darwin's *On the Origin of Species* and an original edition of John James Audubon's *Birds of America*. The Zoellner Arts Center opened in January 1997 and showcases dynamic arts programs in music and theater.

Costs

Tuition in 1999–2000 was $23,150. The average room and board cost was $6630.

Financial Aid

Lehigh offers almost 100 merit scholarships each year based on academics, leadership, or talent in music or theater. Top Lehigh students who graduate with a 3.5 GPA can take a fifth year of courses tuition free. Many students use this program to earn a master's degree or a second bachelor's degree. Lehigh is committed to providing need-based financial aid, and more than half of the undergraduate students receive some financial assistance. Lehigh awards more than $33 million annually in University grants and scholarships.

The Office of Financial Aid coordinates aid sources to assist students, including University, state, and federal grants and loans and campus employment. The applications required include the CSS Financial Aid PROFILE, which must be filed with the College Scholarship Service by February 1, and the Free Application for Federal Student Aid (FAFSA), which is accepted between January 1 and April 15 (must be filed by March 1). The FAFSA is used to qualify for federal and state student aid. When filing the PROFILE registration form, determination will be made if it is also necessary to submit (directly to Lehigh) either the Business/Farm Supplement—for the self-employed—or the Noncustodial Parent Statement—to be filed by the noncustodial parent when the applicant's parents no longer live together. Notification of aid is sent in late March or early April. Acceptances must be received postmarked by May 1.

Faculty

Of Lehigh's 391 full-time faculty members, 99 percent hold the terminal professional degree in their field. Many are leaders in research and scholarship and hold national, international, and honorary positions with professional societies; however, they are committed first and foremost to undergraduate teaching and advising. It is common for a senior faculty member to teach a freshman course, and close student-faculty advising is the norm. Faculty members often meet with individual students and small groups outside of class, accompany students abroad, and participate in student governance and other activities. The undergraduate student-faculty ratio is 11:1. There are 77 part-time faculty members, and some graduate students are involved in undergraduate laboratory assistance and review session teaching.

Student Government

Students participate in the Student Senate, an elected deliberative body that addresses student life and campus issues. Students are ensured access to the highest levels of decision making through 2 nonvoting representatives to the Board of Trustees.

Admission Requirements

Lehigh encourages men and women of all backgrounds to consider study at the University. All applicants should have completed 4 years of English, 3 or 4 years of mathematics, 2–4 years of history and social studies, 2–4 years of laboratory science, and 2 years of foreign language. Because an individual's potential for success cannot be fully reflected in the mere accumulation of units in a four-year college-preparatory program, the Office of Admissions takes into account a number of criteria in evaluating applicants, first and foremost of which is the strength of the high school record. The University requires either the SAT I or ACT, and they must be taken by December of the senior year. Lehigh encourages candidates to arrange an interview and a campus visit and to talk with faculty members and students. The Office of Admissions is pleased to assist in making arrangements. A visit to the campus for an interview or an information session is highly recommended.

Application and Information

Early decision applications are due by November 15, with notification sent by December 25. All applications must be in by January 1. Notification is given by April 1, and accepted applicants must reply by May 1. Transfer students who have attended other colleges and universities are admitted with advanced standing each January and August. The deadline for transfer applications is April 1 for fall enrollment and November 1 for January admission. Financial aid and guaranteed housing are available for transfer students.

Lorna J. Hunter, Dean of Admissions and Financial Aid
Office of Admissions
Lehigh University
27 Memorial Drive West
Bethlehem, Pennsylvania 18015
Telephone: 610-758-3100
Fax: 610-758-4361
E-mail: admissions@lehigh.edu
World Wide Web: http://www.lehigh.edu

LEHMAN COLLEGE OF THE CITY UNIVERSITY OF NEW YORK
BRONX, NEW YORK

The College

Established in 1968 as a senior college of the City University of New York (CUNY), Lehman offers nearly 90 undergraduate and graduate degree programs and specializations in business, liberal arts, natural and social sciences, education, nursing and health professions, and the fine and performing arts. Many programs provide training for particular careers and lead to professional degrees, preparing students for positions in private, nonprofit, and government organizations, as well as for graduate study.

Lehman offers an active, diversified, and supportive campus life. Organized around various cultural, religious, political, academic, and personal interests, more than sixty clubs are housed in a Student Life Building that also features computer, conference, kitchen, and recreation areas. Many of these activities give students valuable experiences both for careers and for life. Through counseling and additional support services, students find the answers to academic and career questions, while a Child Care Center, Student Health Center, and Office of Disabled Student Services help meet a variety of other needs.

Lehman serves as a regional center for the arts and recreation. The campus has a 2,300-seat Concert Hall, a 500-seat theater, a 150-seat recital hall, and an art gallery. In addition, the campus publishes several newspapers and hosts a radio station and a cable television station. The APEX, a sports and recreation facility, includes a fully equipped fitness center; a free-weight room; two full-size gymnasiums; four racquetball courts; a two-lane, 1¼-mile indoor track; an aerobics/dance studio; a ballet studio; an Olympic-size indoor swimming pool; and five outdoor tennis courts.

Location

Lehman College is located in a quiet residential neighborhood in the northwest Bronx. Convenient to major highways and multiple bus and subway lines, this location offers students easy access to the cultural, social, and academic resources of a city that is world renowned for its opportunities in almost every field of endeavor.

Majors and Degrees

Majors at Lehman College include accounting (specialties in industrial and government accounting and accounting and business practice); American studies; anthropology; anthropology (physical), biology, and chemistry; art (specialties in art history and studio art in ceramics, computer imaging, painting, photography, printmaking, and sculpture); biology; black studies; business education; chemistry (specialty in biochemistry); comparative literature; computer science; computing and management; dance; dance-theater; dietetics, foods, and nutrition; economics (specialty in business management); English (specialties in creative writing, literature, and professional writing); French; geography; geology; German; Greek; Greek and Latin (specialty in classical culture); health education and promotion (options in community health and community health and nutrition); health N-12 teacher studies; health services administration; Hebraic and Judaic studies (specialties in Hebraic and Judaic studies); Hebrew; history; Italian; Italian-American studies; Latin; Latin American and Caribbean studies; linguistics; mathematics; multilingual journalism; music; nursing; philosophy (specialties in ethics and public policy); physics; political science; psychology; Puerto Rican studies; recreation education; Russian; social work; sociology; Spanish; speech; speech and theater (specialties in communication arts—mass communications and public and group communications); speech pathology and audiology; and theater.

Academic Program

Lehman College offers 120-credit Bachelor of Arts, Bachelor of Science, and Bachelor of Fine Arts degree programs in the liberal arts and sciences as well as a dual Bachelor of Arts/Master of Arts in mathematics. Many of these programs include course work and fieldwork that lead to professional certification. These programs include the B.S. in accounting–certified public accountant; dietetics, foods, and nutrition–dietitian; education (elementary)–elementary school teacher (N–6); education (secondary)–secondary school teacher in academic subjects; health education and promotion–health education specialist and health N–12 teacher; health services administration–nursing home administrator; professional nursing–registered nurse; recreation education–therapeutic recreation specialist and certified leisure professional; and speech education–teacher of the speech and hearing handicapped. Lehman also offers courses that lead to graduate programs for professional certification, including predentistry, prelaw, premedicine, prepharmacy, pre–veterinary science, and social work; these Lehman programs include a professional option that allows students to complete the undergraduate degree at an accredited professional school in their senior year. In addition, a pre-engineering transfer program is offered in cooperation with the School of Engineering at City College.

Lehman also offers an array of programs designed for specific needs and interests. These include the Freshman Year Initiative, which helps students make the transition from high school to college; the Individualized Baccalaureate Program for students who wish to design their own majors; the Lehman Scholars Program for honors students; the Adult Degree Program for returning students; ESL and Language Transition Programs; and study-abroad programs. Students can earn transferable credits through high school Advanced Placement examinations, the College Level Examination Program, internships, and fieldwork and through an evaluation of their life experience and achievement.

The 120-credit baccalaureate program includes core curriculum courses in the humanities, social sciences, the modern age, natural sciences, and problem solving through quantitative reasoning. Students must also complete distribution courses in seven major areas of study as well as courses in English composition, oral English, and foreign language. They also must fulfill major requirements, and minor fields of study are required of most students, although students in certain majors are exempt from the minor requirement. In addition, all students are required to pass Skills Assessment Tests before registering for their sixty-first credit.

The academic calendar is divided into fall and spring semesters, with two summer sessions. Classes are offered days, nights, and weekends to accommodate students with work and family responsibilities.

Off-Campus Arrangements

Through a cooperative arrangement, students may take courses at other colleges within the City University of New York, one of the nation's most distinguished and extensive university systems. Off-campus internships are available through the academic departments and the Career Services Office. Opportunities for overseas study are available for an intersession, a semester, or an academic year through sponsored trips and the study-abroad and Paris/CUNY Exchange Programs.

Academic Facilities

Lehman's 37-acre campus is dominated by Gothic towers and tree-lined walks, where a blend of traditional and modern design helps reinforce the College's sense of community. This sense of community is further enhanced by the computers (including personal and multiuser systems) available for student use in the new Information Technology Center, the library, and departmental facilities. They provide access to general-purpose and specialized-application software, local and regional networks, and the Internet. Audio/video reception/distribution capability via satellite and other means is available in many classrooms, as are specialized facilities to support multimedia, distance learning, and high-end graphics capabilities. The library offers 546,000 books, 574,000 microforms, and 1,300 periodicals in open stacks and a fully automated CUNY-wide book catalog with a remote-access circulation system, periodical indexes, electronic full-text databases, a CD-ROM LAN, and large video and audio collections.

Costs

Eligible New York State residents who are matriculated students pay $1600 per semester for full-time study (at least 12 credits or credit equivalents), $135 per credit for matriculated part-time study, or $160 per credit for nonmatriculated study. Nonresidents and international students pay $3400 per semester for full-time study, $285 per credit for part-time matriculated study, and $325 per credit for nonmatriculated study. Each semester, all students must pay a student activity fee ($55 for full-time students and $35 for part-time students during the fall and spring semesters and $29 during the summer sessions) and a $5 Consolidated Service Fee.

Financial Aid

Lehman College participates in federal and New York State financial aid programs. Students may request aid by filing a Free Application for Federal Student Aid (FAFSA), which may make them eligible for Federal Pell Grants, FSEOG, SEEK, the Federal Work-Study Program, and student loans. New York State residents may also file a Financial Aid Supplemental Information Request (FASIR), which may enable them to participate in New York State's Tuition Assistance Program (TAP). The College also offers various scholarships, including a renewable Academic Achievement Award Scholarship for entering students. Other scholarships and awards are tied to specific areas of study; students in eligible fields of study are given assistance in pursuing federal scholarship programs.

Faculty

The College has more than 300 full-time faculty members, of whom 85 percent hold doctoral degrees or their equivalent. Many have been recognized nationally and internationally for their scholarship and research through grants and awards; a significant number serve as faculty members at CUNY's graduate center. Most important, faculty members work closely with students outside the classroom in individual and group settings to support their academic, professional, and personal growth. The faculty-student ratio is 1:15.

Student Government

Lehman's student government is divided into the Campus Association for Student Activities (CASA), the programming arm of the student government, and the Student Conference, the legislative arm of the student government. CASA officers are responsible for the appropriation and management of student funds for clubs, cultural programs, entertainment, and other activities. The Student Conference makes up approximately one third of the Lehman College Senate, the decision-making body on matters of academic policy.

Admission Requirements

Due to a recent change in the city of New York's admissions policies, all freshman applicants who graduate from high school on or after June 2000 must submit an SAT or ACT score as part of their application package. This score, along with three other components, determine a student's admission eligibility. The first of these is submission of the total number of College Preparatory Initiative (CPI) units. In evaluating high school transcripts, CUNY assigns CPI units to Regents-level courses indicated on the student's high school transcript. Second, CUNY evaluates the College Academic Average (the high school academic average earned only in CPI English, a foreign language, social studies, mathematics, science, and fine arts courses). Third, CUNY evaluates a student's earned average in English CPI courses. Students who do not meet these freshman admission requirements but who satisfy particular academic and economic criteria may be eligible for admission through the SEEK Program, the City University's opportunity program for its senior colleges.

Transfer students who have earned at least 13 credits must have an overall cumulative index of at least 2.0 in all previous college work. Students transferring with fewer than 13 credits must have an overall cumulative index of at least 2.5 or meet the requirements for freshman admission. Students transferring from CUNY community or comprehensive colleges must also pass the Skills Assessment Tests prior to their admission to the College.

Applicants with student or other nonimmigrant visas who were not educated in an English system are required to score at least 500 on the TOEFL.

Application and Information

Applicants are encouraged to submit their completed applications with all official documentation and fees by March 15 for fall admission or by November 1 for spring admission.

The staffs of the Recruitment and Admissions Offices are available to answer questions and provide assistance with the admissions process. Students may request application materials, speak with an Admissions Counselor, or schedule a campus tour by contacting:

Office of Recruitment
Shuster Hall, Room 158
Lehman College
250 Bedford Park Boulevard, West
Bronx, New York 10468-1589
Telephone: 877-LEHMAN-1 (toll-free)
E-mail: enroll@lehman.cuny.edu
World Wide Web: http://www.lehman.cuny.edu

LE MOYNE COLLEGE
SYRACUSE, NEW YORK

The College

Le Moyne College is a four-year Jesuit college of approximately 2,000 undergraduate students that uniquely balances a comprehensive liberal arts education with preparation for specific career paths or graduate study. Founded by the Society of Jesus in 1946, Le Moyne is the second-youngest of the twenty-eight Jesuit colleges and universities in the United States.

The campus environment is one of a closely knit community. Le Moyne's personal approach to education is reflected in the quality of contact between students and faculty members. A wide range of student-directed activities, athletics, clubs, and service organizations complement the academic experience. Intramural sports are very popular with Le Moyne students, and approximately 75 percent of the students participate in athletics. Le Moyne also has sixteen NCAA intercollegiate teams (eight for men and eight for women). Athletic facilities include lacrosse, soccer, and baseball fields; tennis, basketball, and racquetball courts; a weight training and fitness center; and two gymnasiums. A recreation center houses an Olympic-size indoor swimming pool, a jogging track, indoor tennis and volleyball courts, and additional basketball, racquetball, and fitness areas. More than 80 percent of students live in residence halls and town houses on campus. The Residence Hall Councils and the Le Moyne Student Programming Board organize many campus activities, including concerts, dances, a weekly film series, student talent programs, and special lectures as well as off-campus trips and skiing excursions.

Location

Le Moyne's 150-acre tree-lined campus is located in a residential setting 10 minutes from Syracuse, the heart of New York State, whose metropolitan population is about 240,000. Syracuse is convenient to most major cities throughout the Northeast, New England, and Canada, and has a wide array of shopping centers and restaurants, many near Le Moyne. Syracuse offers year-round entertainment in the form of rock concerts at the Carrier Dome and Landmark Theatre; professional baseball, hockey, and lacrosse; Bristol Omnitheatre, one of only nineteen omnitheaters in the country; the Syracuse Symphony; Syracuse Stage; Everson Museum of Art; and the completely transformed Armory Square area downtown, offering one-of-a-kind eateries, pubs, and coffee houses in addition to a wide variety of social and cultural events. All are easily accessible via the excellent public transportation service, which schedules regular stops on Le Moyne's campus.

Just a few miles outside the city are the rolling hills, picturesque lakes, and miles of open country for which central New York is renowned. State parks, recreational areas, and other facilities for swimming, boating, hiking, downhill and cross-country skiing, snowboarding, and golf are nearby.

Majors and Degrees

Le Moyne College awards the Bachelor of Arts degree in biology, economics, English, English/communications, English/creative writing, English/drama, English/literature, French, history, international studies, international studies/global studies, mathematics, mathematics/actuarial science, mathematics/statistics, philosophy, political science, psychology, religious studies, sociology, sociology/anthropology, sociology/criminology and criminal justice, sociology/human services, sociology/research and theory, and Spanish. The Bachelor of Science degree is awarded in accounting, biology, business administration, business/finance, business/management information systems, business/marketing, business/operations management, business/organization and management, chemistry, industrial relations and human resources management, multiple science, physics, and psychology.

Students may minor in communications, drama, fine arts, management information systems, urban studies, or women's studies as well as in any of the major fields of study offered. Preprofessional programs are offered in dentistry, law, medicine, optometry, pharmacy, and veterinary medicine. Students may prepare for teaching careers through certification programs in elementary education, secondary education, special education, and TESOL.

Formal accelerated 3-4 programs are offered in dentistry, optometry, and podiatry in cooperation with SUNY at Buffalo School of Dental Medicine, Pennsylvania College of Optometry, and the New York College of Podiatric Medicine. Predental students may also participate in an early assurance program with SUNY at Buffalo School of Dental Medicine. Cooperative 3-2 dual-degree programs in engineering are available with both Clarkson University and Manhattan College. A 3-2 program in engineering with the University of Detroit Mercy is also offered to Le Moyne students. A 2-2 program in environmental science and forestry is available in cooperation with SUNY College of Environmental Science and Forestry in Syracuse.

SUNY Health Science Center at Syracuse offers students pursuing careers in the health-related professions 2-2 programs in physical therapy, medical technology, respiratory care, and cytotechnology and also offers premedical students at Le Moyne the opportunity to participate in a medical school early assurance program. An early assurance program for premedical students is also available through SUNY at Buffalo School of Medicine.

Academic Program

While each major department has its own sequence requirements for the minimum 120 credit hours needed for the Le Moyne degree, the College is convinced that there is a fundamental intellectual discipline that should characterize the graduate of a superior liberal arts college. Le Moyne's core curriculum provides this foundation by including studies of English language and literature, philosophy, history, religious studies, science, mathematics, and social sciences.

For exceptional students, Le Moyne offers an integral honors program that includes an interdisciplinary humanities sequence as well as departmental honors courses. Le Moyne also offers a part-time course of study during evening hours through its Center for Continuous Learning.

Le Moyne students may enroll in Army and Air Force ROTC programs at Syracuse University.

Off-Campus Arrangements

The study-abroad program allows students to spend semesters in Australia, Japan, and exciting European locations such as England, France, Ireland, Italy, and Spain. Le Moyne is a participant in the sixty-member New York State Visiting Student Program.

For career preparation, Le Moyne's strong emphasis on internships has been a continuing and expanding source of resume-building and real-world experiences for students from several different majors, all of whom have gained invaluable credentials to take to their first interviews. In addition, science interns have been given extraordinary access to research opportunities with some of the leading labs and companies.

Externships let a student observe alumni who work in the student's area of interest. This program has taken students to places such as the White House and Capitol Building in Washington, D.C.; New York State's seat of government in Albany; and hospitals, Fortune 500 companies, and a wide array of small businesses.

Many student-teaching opportunities also exist. In every education class, from freshman year through senior year, students are required to spend time in a classroom.

Academic Facilities

Le Moyne students benefit from an ongoing commitment to technological excellence. The College's thirty buildings are equipped with accounting, biology, chemistry, computer science, physics, psychology, and statistics laboratories. There is a newly created Academic Support Center. A new performing arts center houses generous production, performance, and classroom space; the latest light and sound technology; scene and costume shops; an aerobics and dance studio; and rehearsal rooms for instrumental and choral music. There are also an extensively renovated color television studio; a radio/recording studio; a receiver-antenna satellite dish; an electronic ultramicrotome; a nuclear magnetic resonance spectrometer; a Carl Zeiss electron microscope; an AMRAY 1000B scanning electron microscope; a 231,283-volume, open-stack library; and extensive on-site computer facilities. In addition, with a newly installed fiber-optic network, students can access the Library's system, the campus network, and the Internet from several computer labs around campus or from their rooms if they have computers of their own. All classrooms are being converted to "smart" classrooms, with multimedia capabilities that are transforming the learning process. Le Moyne students have access to the libraries of many other institutions through the Central New York Library Resources Council.

Costs

For 1999–2000, Le Moyne's tuition was $14,580. Room and board charges were $6320. Additional fees amounted to approximately $360, and books and supplies cost approximately $500.

Financial Aid

Financial aid is offered to 95 percent of Le Moyne's students through scholarships, grants, loans, and work-study assignments. Le Moyne offers a generous program of merit-based academic and athletic scholarships as well as financial aid based on a student's need and academic promise. Federal funds are available through the Federal Pell Grant, Federal Work-Study, Federal Supplemental Educational Opportunity Grant, and Federal Perkins Loan programs. A student's eligibility for need-based financial aid is determined from both the Free Application for Federal Student Aid (FAFSA) and the Le Moyne Financial Aid Application Form. It is recommended that these forms be mailed by February 1.

Faculty

The Le Moyne full-time faculty numbers 126 men and women; 92 percent have earned the highest degree in their field. With an average class size of 21 students, a student-faculty ratio of 14:1, and private offices for all full-time faculty members, the College promotes a personal as well as an academic relationship between students and faculty. Le Moyne has no graduate students or teaching assistants instructing students in any department. Faculty members are happy to assist and encourage students who wish to do undergraduate research through tutorials or senior research projects. These projects are carried out in an atmosphere free of competition from graduate students for books, laboratories, or professors' time. Le Moyne emphasizes advising and academic counseling for students throughout their four years.

Student Government

The College encourages student leadership in all activities. Positions of leadership are open to students in all class years. Students are represented by a Student Senate and have formal representation through the senate on most College-wide committees involved in decision making and policy formation.

Admission Requirements

Le Moyne seeks qualified students who are well-prepared for serious academic study. Secondary school preparation must have included at least 17 college-preparatory high school units, 4 of which must be in English, 3–4 in social studies, 3–4 in mathematics, 3 in foreign language, and 3–4 in science. It is also recommended that prospective science and mathematics majors complete 4 units of mathematics and science. The SAT I or ACT is required and should be taken by December or January of the senior year in high school. Campus visits are strongly recommended, as the admission process is a personal one. As bases for selection, academic achievement and secondary school recommendations are of primary importance; SAT I or ACT scores are important as they relate to the record of achievement and to recommendations. Out-of-state students are encouraged to apply.

Application and Information

The Admission Committee reviews applications and mails decisions on a rolling admission cycle beginning January 1. The priority deadline for applications is March 1; all students who wish to be considered for academic non-need scholarships should have a completed application on file in the Office of Admission before this date. Students who wish to be considered under the early decision program must have a completed application submitted by December 1. Early decision applicants will by notified by December 15. Transfer students are encouraged to apply before May 1 for the fall semester and December 1 for the spring semester. A fun-filled two-day orientation program takes place in mid-summer.

Dennis J. Nicholson
Director of Admission
Le Moyne College
Syracuse, New York 13214-1399
Telephone: 315-445-4300
         800-333-4733 Ext. 4300 (toll-free)
E-mail: admsoffc@maple.lemoyne.edu
World Wide Web: http://www.lemoyne.edu

Grewen Hall, the oldest building on campus, has opened its doors to students for more than fifty years.

LENOIR–RHYNE COLLEGE
HICKORY, NORTH CAROLINA

The College

Lenoir-Rhyne College, founded by 4 Lutheran ministers in 1891, is accredited by the Commission on Colleges of the Southern Association of Colleges and Schools. The College's facilities have grown from one building on a small tract of land to more than twenty major structures on a 100-acre campus. The College seeks to liberate mind and spirit, clarify personal faith, foster physical wholeness, build a sense of community, and promote responsible leadership for service in the world. The campus population of 1,481 (64 percent women, 36 percent men) includes a wide range of ethnic, cultural, and religious backgrounds. An outstanding faculty, student selectivity, reputation for academic excellence, financial resources, and ability to retain and graduate students make Lenoir-Rhyne one of North Carolina's premier small liberal arts colleges.

More than forty campus organizations, including academic honoraries, religious organizations, special interest clubs, four fraternities, and four sororities, invite students to participate and develop their leadership potential. There are intercollegiate teams for men in baseball, basketball, cross-country, football, golf, and soccer and for women in basketball, cross-country, golf, soccer, softball, and volleyball.

Lenoir-Rhyne offers master's degree programs in four areas: education (birth–kindergarten), master teacher (elementary, middle school, reading, gifted), counselor education (school counseling, community/agency counseling), and Master in Business Administration.

Location

Lenoir-Rhyne College is located in the western Piedmont of North Carolina and is readily accessible by car, airline, and bus. Hickory, an All-America City, provides many cultural events as well as winter and water sports.

Majors and Degrees

The College grants the undergraduate degrees of Bachelor of Arts, Bachelor of Science, and Bachelor of Music. Majors are offered under the Divisions of Humanities, Natural Sciences and Mathematics, Social and Behavioral Sciences, and Professional Programs.

A student in the Division of Humanities may major in art education, classics, communication, English, English–theater arts, French, German, music (applied music, music education, and sacred music), philosophy, religious studies (parish education and pretheology), Spanish, or theater arts. The Division of Natural Sciences and Mathematics offers programs of study in biology, chemistry, computer science, environmental studies, mathematics, physics, preforestry, prepharmacy, prephysician's assistant studies, and science (for medical technologists, for teachers, and premedical). A student in the Division of Social and Behavioral Sciences may major in economics, environmental studies, history, human and community services, political science, psychology, or sociology. The Division of Professional Programs offers majors in accounting, business administration, education (business, elementary, birth–kindergarten, intermediate, secondary, and special education for the hearing impaired), health and exercise science, health and physical education (pre–physical therapy, sports management, sports medicine, and teaching), international business, nursing, and occupational therapy.

Under the general studies program, a qualified student may formulate his or her own area of concentration. Concentrations already planned include American studies, chemical technology, comparative literature, international relations, and preprofessional programs in engineering, environmental management, forestry, and law.

Programs in medical technology, pharmacy, and physician's assistant studies are offered in cooperation with a number of outstanding hospitals and medical schools. In addition, Lenoir-Rhyne offers 3-2 programs in computer technology and engineering in cooperation with North Carolina State, Clemson University, UNC–Charlotte, and North Carolina A&T that allow a student to combine three years of liberal arts study with two years of specialized work. A similar program, offered in cooperation with Duke University, results in both a bachelor's and a master's degree in environmental management or forestry.

Academic Program

The College operates on a semester calendar. A two-term summer session is also offered.

Regardless of their major, Lenoir-Rhyne students complete specified courses designed to provide a foundation upon which to build their liberal arts education. The core curriculum includes courses in English, science and mathematics, social and behavioral sciences, humanities, computer science, religion, and physical education. A student may choose a variety of courses within these disciplines to fulfill core requirements. There is a formal final examination period at the end of each term.

An honors program is offered in many disciplines at Lenoir-Rhyne. Courses in the honors programs are designed to provide students of exceptional ability with an intellectual challenge and to encourage academic excellence and creativity. Honors work is also available in special sections of the core curriculum. Lenoir-Rhyne subscribes to the College Board's Advanced Placement Program and provides the opportunity for students to earn credit for many courses through the College-Level Examination Program and through a College credit-by-examination program.

In cooperation with the North Carolina School for the Deaf in nearby Morganton, Lenoir-Rhyne offers a program in which a student may gain certification to teach students in schools for the deaf throughout the United States or to teach hearing-impaired students in public schools. The College accepts a number of hearing-impaired students in its regular undergraduate program.

Lenoir-Rhyne is one of only a few colleges in the nation that has implemented the innovative Dartmouth Model in its program of foreign language instruction.

A business internship program offers students hands-on experience while they earn credit toward their degree. The international business major is comparable to many graduate programs in the field.

Students have opportunities to attend various programs and

seminars sponsored by Lenoir-Rhyne's Lineberger Center for Cultural and Educational Renewal and its Broyhill Institute for Business Leadership.

Off-Campus Arrangements

Through an arrangement with American University, a student may spend a semester in Washington, D.C., to study and observe the federal government in operation and to earn credit toward a Lenoir-Rhyne degree. A study-abroad program at Harlaxton College in Grantham, England, is available during the fall semester. Students may also engage in overseas study through the foreign language and business departments, as well as choose from more than twenty-five sponsoring universities in eighteen countries through the College Consortium of International Study programs.

Academic Facilities

The Carl Augustus Rudisill Library houses 141,781 accessioned volumes, 37,613 audiovisuals, and 436,307 microform titles; it subscribes to 5,059 periodicals, including 17 daily newspapers. A learning resource center in the library includes an audiovisual distribution center, darkrooms, curriculum and computer laboratories, a television studio, and other instructional resources. The Minges Science Building contains modern facilities for the study of the natural sciences, including an environmental chamber, cell and molecular biology equipment, instruments for measuring radioactivity, an atomic absorption spectrophotometer, and an observatory with a photometrically equipped 12.5-inch Cassegrainian telescope. The campus also includes an instructional building and the Belk Centrum. Another classroom facility has been completely renovated. The physical education center includes classrooms, racquetball courts, a gymnasium, and a swimming pool.

Costs

Tuition and fees are $13,356 for the 2000–01 academic year. Residence costs, including room and board, are $4920. Personal expenses, including books and supplies, are estimated at $1500.

Financial Aid

Lenoir-Rhyne College makes every effort to assist students through a program of scholarships, loans, and work-study awards. Last year, more than 90 percent of the student body received financial aid through an aid program totaling approximately $13.9 million. The amount of aid awarded to a student is determined by need, as indicated on the Free Application for Federal Student Aid (FAFSA). The priority filing date for the FAFSA and the Lenoir-Rhyne Scholarship Application is March 1. In addition to need-based aid, Lenoir-Rhyne College also offers academic, athletic, honors, and music scholarships.

Faculty

With a full-time faculty of 107 members, Lenoir-Rhyne College has a full-time student-faculty ratio of about 12:1. Approximately 73 percent of the faculty members hold earned doctorates. No graduate students serve as instructors at Lenoir-Rhyne. Lenoir-Rhyne was recently named one of ten independent colleges and universities in the nation that are exemplary academic workplaces. The Council of Independent Colleges bases these awards on faculty morale and sense of job satisfaction.

Student Government

Every Lenoir-Rhyne College student is a member of the Student Government Association (SGA). A student who maintains at least a 2.0 grade point average is eligible for elective and appointive offices. A student may also serve on faculty committees and participate in meetings of the faculty assembly as a representative of the SGA. All students adhere to an honor code.

Admission Requirements

Lenoir-Rhyne accepts students to all programs without regard to sex, race, handicap, or religion. To qualify for admission, an applicant should have graduated from high school with at least 4 units in English, 3 in mathematics (2 in algebra and 1 in geometry), 1 in a laboratory science, 1 in American history, and, preferably (although they are not required), at least 2 years of a foreign language. Nursing majors must have completed a chemistry course. Applicants must also submit SAT I or ACT scores.

The Admissions Committee gives each application individual attention; primary emphasis is placed on the student's record of achievement in high school. Interviews are recommended but not required. Arrangements for an interview at the College and a campus tour may be made through the Admissions Office. Admission representatives also visit high schools all along the Eastern Seaboard.

Lenoir-Rhyne accepts transfer students from accredited community, junior, and senior colleges and universities throughout the nation. Transfer students should have transcripts from all colleges previously attended forwarded to the Admissions Office.

Application and Information

Application for admission may be made by submitting a high school transcript showing rank in class, the completed application and $25 fee, and SAT I or ACT scores. Candidates are encouraged to apply early in their senior year of high school. The College accepts students on early acceptance or a rolling basis. Deferred enrollment is available.

For additional information, students should contact:

Rachel Nichols
Director of Admissions and Financial Aid
Lenoir-Rhyne College
Hickory, North Carolina 28603
Telephone: 828-328-7300
          800-277-5721 (toll-free)
E-mail: admission@lrc.edu

Students gathering on the Lenoir-Rhyne College campus.

LESLEY COLLEGE
CAMBRIDGE, MASSACHUSETTS

The College

Lesley College offers academic programs in art therapy, counseling, education, human services, liberal arts, and management. Central to the mission at Lesley is a commitment to excellent and creative instruction offered in an intimate college environment in which each student is a valued, significant, and contributing member. Education at Lesley combines theoretical and practical approaches to learning, blending a strong liberal arts foundation with substantial professional preparation. Beginning with their freshman year, Lesley students have direct field exposure in their chosen fields. The result is a balanced integration of theory and practice.

Lesley is a small, independent women's college, where students enjoy the warmth and informality of a close-knit community. The 600 full-time undergraduate students enrolled live on the 5-acre campus, an urban academic village, set in the heart of the Cambridge intellectual community and minutes from downtown Boston. Students benefit from a cosmopolitan environment that encourages creativity and provides easy access to a wide range of opportunities for fieldwork and practical experience. Lesley College as a whole is a large, comprehensive institution of more than 7,000 students, the majority of whom are studying in one of Lesley's many graduate or adult baccalaureate programs. Undergraduate women's college students benefit tremendously from the resources and the breadth of opportunities that come from being part of a much larger institution.

The College is accredited by the New England Association of Schools and Colleges. The teacher certification programs have been approved by the Interstate Certification Compact (ICC). The ICC is a reciprocity agreement in which more than thirty states have established standards for granting certification.

In addition to the degrees offered through the Women's College, Lesley also offers Bachelor of Fine Arts degree programs at the Art Institute of Boston, as well as adult baccalaureate and graduate programs for both men and women.

Location

Cambridge and Metropolitan Boston are famous for their educational, cultural, and business resources. Historically a center of finance and business, Boston has one of the most concentrated enclaves of high-tech industry in the nation, supported by a sophisticated, university-based research and development community. Cultural life in the Boston area is rich and varied. More than 100 museums, dedicated to virtually every artistic, cultural, and scientific discipline, provide ample opportunities for student involvement on many levels. There are shops and restaurants of every ethnic variety, first-run films, theater, and famed professional sports teams. In addition, the Boston area has an efficient public transportation system for travel within the metropolitan area and easy, direct transportation to and from all regions of the United States.

Majors and Degrees

The Women's College offers Bachelor of Science degrees in the following areas: art therapy, counseling, education, human services, management, and several interdisciplinary liberal arts majors.

Students in the education program may choose to concentrate in one of the following areas: day-care leadership, early childhood education, elementary education, middle school education, and special education. Students may also choose to specialize in early care and education, early intervention, integrating media into the curriculum, mathematics education, science education, multicultural education, and teaching reading. Students are required to elect an interdisciplinary liberal arts major in one of three broad fields: humanities, natural sciences, or social sciences. Completion of the education program qualifies the student to be recommended for certification in Massachusetts and the other states in the Interstate Certification Compact.

Students pursuing a bachelor's degree in art therapy, counseling, or human services have a liberal arts minor. Options include art, computer technology, drama, environmental studies, health, history, literature and writing, mathematics, music, psychology, sociology, and women's studies. Human services majors may also choose specializations in health-care administration, management, and social work.

Students in the management program may choose to combine a management major with a liberal arts minor or a management minor with an interdisciplinary liberal arts major. Within the management major, students may also elect a healthcare administration, human resource management, or marketing focus. Management programs at Lesley emphasize general management preparation, with a focus on preparing women for leadership positions in a wide variety of management settings.

Students can also choose a major in the following liberal arts areas: Humanities: The Arts, Literature and History; Natural Science: Mathematics, Science and Computer Technology; Social and Cultural Studies; or Human Development and Family Studies. Like all Lesley students, those selecting a liberal arts major also integrate internship experiences through an individualized professional minor in order to prepare for professional careers after graduation.

In addition, the following accelerated bachelor's/master's degree programs are offered in conjunction with Lesley's graduate programs: a B.S./M.A. in counseling psychology or clinical mental health counseling; a B.S./M.Ed. in early childhood education, elementary education, middle school education, or special education; and a B.S./M.S. in management.

Academic Program

Practical field exposure begins in the freshman year and complements classroom instruction throughout the undergraduate program. Students also take required liberal arts courses in the humanities, sciences, and social sciences as well as electives, which they may choose to suit their own interests. The four-year sequence of professional studies offers field experiences in the student's area of special interest, related seminars, and general theoretical courses.

Off-Campus Arrangements

Lesley College participates in student exchange programs with Bradford Ilkley Community College in England and Örebro University in Sweden. Students enrolled in the human services and management degree programs may also participate in an exchange with the American University in Washington, D.C.

Academic Facilities

The Eleanor DeWolfe Ludcke Library is a state-of-the-art multimedia resource center supporting the academic programs of the College through a collection of electronic, journal, and monographic resources. Located at the center of campus, the

Ludcke Library also houses the Kresge Center for Teaching Resources and the Microcomputer Center, as well as a computer lab and three computer classrooms. A fully automated online catalog also gives students access to holdings at fifteen other academic and special libraries through the Fenway Library Consortium. The main library collections contain materials basic to a general liberal arts education, as well as specialized materials relevant to education, human services, and management.

The Kresge Center for Teaching Resources, on the second floor of the Ludcke Library, offers one of the finest collections in the Northeast of juvenile literature, as well as teaching aids; video, audio, and film collections; and media services. Students may produce teaching materials, using the center's equipment, and professional staff offer support in children's literature, media materials, and production of teaching materials.

The Microcomputer Center is on the top floor of the Ludke Library. It contains three classrooms and more than seventy Apple II, Macintosh, and IBM-compatible computers, as well as software, CD-ROM's, videodiscs, and productivity tools.

The Wordprocessing Center is on the third floor of Doble Hall, adjacent to the Ludcke Library. Facilities include Macintosh and IBM-compatible computers and printers. The center is open 24 hours a day.

Costs

Fees in 2000–01 for enrollment in Lesley College include tuition, $16,300; room and board, $7520; a health services fee, $750; and a student activity fee, $165. Costs are subject to change without prior notice. (Students should call the College to confirm current expense figures.)

Financial Aid

No student should fail to consider Lesley College because of financial considerations. More than 75 percent of the undergraduates receive financial aid from one or more sources. The average amount received by newly enrolled students was $16,000 in a combination of scholarships/grants, loans, and work-study jobs. The College participates in all federal aid programs, including the Federal Pell Grant, Federal Supplemental Educational Opportunity Grant, Federal Perkins Loan, and Federal Work-Study programs. The College also offers its own grants and need-based scholarships as well as a number of merit scholarships.

Students applying for financial aid must submit the Free Application for Federal Student Aid (FAFSA) and request that copies of the analyses be sent to Lesley College. In addition, students must complete the Lesley College financial aid application and submit it to the College's Financial Aid Office. Students must send a signed photocopy of their own and their parents' federal 1040 income tax forms to the Financial Aid Office. Students are advised to file all financial aid forms and documents as early as possible. The FAFSA should be filed by February 1 and the Lesley form by February 15.

Faculty

Faculty members appointed to the professional programs are skilled practitioners whose academic training enables them to help students make the necessary connections between theory and practice. The members of the liberal arts faculty are scholars in their specialized disciplines, yet they are also generalists who can teach introductory and interdisciplinary courses. More than two thirds of the faculty members hold Ph.D.'s.

Student Government

The Student Senate is the representative governing body of the College's undergraduate student population. Through the sponsorship of the senate, numerous organizations, activities, seminars, and conferences are brought to the Lesley campus.

Admission Requirements

Lesley's Women's College admits qualified women regardless of race, religion, color, national origin, sexual orientation, age, or handicap. Students may be admitted to the Women's College on either a full-time or a part-time basis. All freshman candidates for admission must submit scores on the SAT I or the ACT. Graduates of accredited secondary schools who present a total of 15 units earned in a college-preparatory program of study are qualified to apply for admission. Candidates must present 15 units, including English, 4 units; mathematics, at least 2 (but preferably 3) units; American history, 1 unit; and science, at least 2 (but preferably 3) units, with at least 1 being a laboratory science. Scholarship, character, personality, and relevant experience are basic considerations. The College recommends a personal interview. A tour of the College campus is normally a part of the interview procedure. Family and friends are welcome to accompany the applicant.

Students who have successfully completed 12 or more hours of college work may apply for admission as transfers. The maximum number of hours that may be transferred is 65. Transfer applicants must present a minimum cumulative grade point average of 2.5. Advanced standing is determined by the nature and quality of the work offered for credit.

Application and Information

Applications are reviewed on a rolling basis beginning January 15 with a preferred freshman deadline of March 15 and a transfer application deadline of June 1 for the fall semester. All applications for the spring semester are due by December 15. An early decision plan is available for qualified students. The deadline for early decision applications is December 1. A $35 application fee must accompany all freshman and transfer applications.

For further information about Lesley College, students should contact:

Director of Undergraduate Admissions
Lesley College
29 Everett Street
Cambridge, Massachusetts 02138-2790
Telephone: 617-349-8800
        800-999-1959 Ext. 8800 (toll-free)
E-mail: ugadm@mail.lesley.edu

LEWIS & CLARK COLLEGE
PORTLAND, OREGON

The College
Founded in 1867 in a small town south of Portland, Lewis & Clark College moved to its present location in Portland's southwest hills in 1942. The 115-acre campus is situated in a wooded residential area 6 miles from the center of the city and overlooks the lush Willamette Valley and Mount Hood in the distance. The student body is known for its geographic diversity. Of the nearly 1,800 undergraduates, 27 percent are from Oregon and 73 percent come from forty-eight other states and thirty-four countries. Approximately 55 percent live in housing on campus, most of which is coed (92 percent). Residence halls allow for interaction among students, and the units are governed through student representation and hall councils. There are no fraternities or sororities. The College offers numerous cocurricular activities, including athletics and cultural events such as lectures, symposia, art exhibits, theater productions, concerts, recitals, and dance performances. Currently, there are eighteen NCAA Division III teams, thirteen club teams, and eight intramural sports. Athletic facilities include three basketball courts, a competition-size swimming pool, a weight-training room, a stadium, a baseball/softball complex, and six tennis courts, three of which are covered by an airdome. The renowned College Outdoors Program offers backpacking, rafting, skiing, and sea kayaking in Oregon's nearby wilderness areas.

Location
Portland has long been known for its livability and its excellent transportation service. Public buses and a College shuttle run from the Lewis & Clark campus to the center of Portland. The metropolitan area (population 1.8 million) is bisected by the Willamette River. Mount Hood, offering year-round skiing, is 50 miles away, and Oregon's rugged coastline lies 90 miles to the west. The city has 1,200 acres of parks, 33 music associations, 35 theater and dance companies, more than 50 galleries and museums, and more than 1,000 restaurants. Professional sports teams compete in arena football, baseball, hockey, indoor soccer, and NBA and WNBA basketball.

Majors and Degrees
Lewis & Clark offers programs leading to the Bachelor of Arts degree. Academic majors include art, biochemistry, biology, business/economics, chemistry, communications, computer science and mathematics, East Asian studies, economics, English, environmental studies, foreign languages, French, German, Hispanic studies, history, international affairs, mathematics, music performance (composition, education, and general music theory), philosophy, physics, political science, psychology, religious studies, sociology/anthropology, and theater. Students may also design a major or pursue a double major and numerous minors. Preprofessional programs are available in dentistry, education, law, and medicine.

Dual-degree (3-2 and 4-2) programs in engineering are offered in cooperation with Columbia University, Washington University (St. Louis), the University of Southern California, and the Oregon Graduate Institute.

Academic Program
The liberal arts curriculum offers sufficient structure to ensure depth and breadth of study, but it also incorporates a high degree of freedom in order to promote creative and critical thinking. The required General Education Curriculum emphasizes critical and analytical thinking in a first-year common syllabus course, "Inventing America," and a formalized international studies requirement, satisfied either by participating in an approved overseas program or by taking two courses on campus. In the four-year plan of study, approximately one third of a student's time is devoted to general education, one third to a major program, and one third to elective courses. Students are also encouraged to participate in departmental honors programs, undergraduate research, independent study, and internships.

The academic calendar consists of two 15-week semesters. A normal load is four 4-semester-hour academic courses, plus one or more activity courses. By graduation a student is expected to have earned at least 128 semester hours—equivalent, roughly, to eight different classes a year. The fall semester begins early in September and ends before Christmas, and the spring semester begins in mid-January and ends in early May. There are also a limited number of courses offered during two summer sessions.

The community of scholars at Lewis & Clark College is dedicated to personal and academic excellence. Joining the Lewis & Clark community obligates each member to observe the principles of mutual respect, academic integrity, civil discourse, and responsible decision making.

Off-Campus Arrangements
Lewis & Clark offers nationally recognized international and off-campus study opportunities that have been in existence for thirty-eight years. Fifteen to eighteen different overseas study programs and two domestic programs are available annually. Usually, 20 to 24 students, plus a faculty leader, participate in each program. More than 50 percent of the College's graduates have taken advantage of these outstanding programs, often satisfying General Education or major requirements at the same time.

Overseas study may have either a general-culture focus or a specialized academic focus. On general-culture programs, students become immersed in the everyday life of the host country by living with local families, traveling, studying in classes and seminars, and working on independent projects. Programs with a more specific academic focus may include studying German language and literature in Munich; perfecting language skills in France, Ecuador, Russia, Japan, or China; or studying literature in England. Sites for overseas study programs in 2000–01 are Australia, Chile, China, Colombia, Dominican Republic, Ecuador, England, France, Germany, India, Ireland, Italy, Japan, Kenya/Tanzania, Poland, Romania, Russia, Scotland, Senegal, Spain, Vietnam, and Zimbabwe. Domestic programs are available in New York or Washington, D.C., for those interested in economics, political science, theater, or art. All programs, both overseas and domestic, are for credit and are similar in cost to full-time, on-campus study for the same period. Students with financial aid or scholarships can apply their assistance to the expenses of these programs.

Academic Facilities
The Aubrey R. Watzek Library (open 24 hours per day during the week when school is in session) houses approximately 251,542 volumes, 1,820 periodical subscriptions, 398,855 microforms, and 9,000 units of audiovisual materials. Its mission is to provide a solid core of materials designed to support the curriculum and the research needs of the Lewis & Clark community. The library offers individualized reference assistance in the use of both print and electronic resources. The library's Web site provides access to its catalog as well as to a full range of electronic databases and links to useful Internet resources. The library is a member of Orbis, a consortium of fourteen academic libraries that have a unified catalog that enables students to request and receive materials from member libraries within two days.

Music department facilities include Evans Auditorium, a 400-seat recital hall equipped with an orchestra pit and stage elevator; an extensive record, CD, and tape collection; twenty-two practice rooms; forty-three pianos, including several 6-foot and 7-foot concert grands; two harpsichords; two organs; an electronic music studio with CD production capability; and an Indonesian gamelan orchestra. The 600-seat chapel houses an 85-rank Casavant organ. A $20-million construction project resulted in a new art building that is equipped with expanded studios for ceramics, sculpture, painting and drawing, calligraphy, design, and printmaking. The department also has a library of 50,000 art history slides. The arts center contains two gallery spaces as well. A three-story humanities center also opened its doors in 1996.

The biology/psychology complex is equipped with newly renovated research laboratories, a newly constructed greenhouse, teaching laboratories, a human-computer interaction laboratory, a psychophysiology research laboratory, a controlled-environment chamber, a scanning electron microscope equipped with an EDX analyzer, extensive field sampling equipment, and facilities for tissue culture, computer-based data acquisition and analysis, and molecular biology recombinant DNA experiments. The Olin Physics-Chemistry Laboratory Building has more than 40,000 square feet of classroom, laboratory, and study space, with special facilities and equipment for such areas as inorganic chemistry, biochemistry, organic chemistry, physical chemistry, spectroscopy, X-ray analysis, and nuclear physics. Scientific research equipment includes diode array UV/visible spectrometers, a gas chromatography–mass spectrometer, HPLC, two FT-IRs, a 300-MHz FT-NMR, an X-ray fluorescence spectrometer, and an atomic absorption spectrometer. The electronics laboratory workstations are equipped for training in analog and digital circuitry as well as computerized data acquisition via A/D converters and IEEE-488 bus devices and analysis using LabView software. The Molecular Modeling Laboratory has ten SGI O2 computer workstations, and the computer science classroom/lab is equipped with ten UNIX/Windows computers. The electronics and machine shops are professionally staffed. The Karle Observatory houses a number of telescopes: a 10-inch Newtonian, 8- and 11-inch Cassegrains, and a solar coelstat with a spectrograph. In addition, there are student-faculty research laboratories designed for independent undergraduate research, a three-dimensional seismograph, a holography laboratory, an imaging laboratory with a high-resolution optical microscope, a biophysics laboratory equipped to study collective phenomena in proteins and macromolecules, a solid-state laboratory equipped with recycling liquid helium refrigeration and superconducting magnet (9T), and an advanced physics laboratory for ongoing student projects.

Computer facilities include several computer laboratories in academic buildings and residence halls that are for student use. More than 150 Macintosh, IBM, and compatible computers are available for student use. These machines are an integral part of the first-year General Education requirement, "Inventing America." The College operates two Digital Equipment Corporation servers alongside a pair of Sun SPARCstations.

Costs

Tuition and fees for 2000–01 are $21,520. The room and board charge is $6100 for fourteen meals per week; other meal plans are also available. The estimate for books and personal expenses is $1500.

Financial Aid

In 1999–2000, 69 percent of the College's students received some form of financial assistance. Institutional, state, and federal resources, including Federal Pell Grants, Federal Supplemental Educational Opportunity Grants, Federal Perkins Loans, and Federal Work-Study awards, may be part of an aid award. Other options include low-interest Federal Stafford Student Loans and opportunities to work on and off campus. To receive priority consideration for financial aid, students must meet appropriate deadlines for admission and should submit the Free Application for Federal Student Aid (FAFSA) by early February. Merit-based awards are offered to exceptional students who are selected as Neely Scholars (ten full-tuition scholarships), Trustee Scholars (fifteen half-tuition scholarships per year), and more than a hundred Dean's Scholars ($3000–$7000 scholarships per year). Students designated as National Merit Finalists with Lewis & Clark officially named as their first choice receive up to $2000.

Faculty

The 168-member faculty, which is committed to undergraduate teaching and advising, is also active in research, writing, and publishing. Involving students in the research process is of high priority. Ninety-two percent of the faculty members hold a Ph.D. or the highest advanced degree in their discipline. The student-faculty ratio is approximately 13:1. The average class size is 17, with an average size of 25 for first-year-level courses and of 15 for upper-division courses.

Student Government

The Associated Students of Lewis & Clark (ASLC) has a decentralized structure that encourages cocurricular participation by students and places a high priority on participation with faculty and staff in the process of enriching the academic environment. ASLC consists of an Executive Council, governing boards, and appointed students who serve on faculty constitutional, standing, and special committees. The 24 members of the Student Academic Affairs Board (SAAB) are appointed on a departmental basis to solicit, evaluate, and support undergraduate and faculty research, instruction, curriculum, and program enhancement. One quarter of the total ASLC budget of nearly $330,000 is used by SAAB in support of undergraduate research grants and speakers.

Admission Requirements

Lewis & Clark College seeks first-year and transfer applicants who are committed to academic excellence and personal growth. Admission is competitive. Applications are carefully reviewed and examined for degree of academic preparation, ability to express ideas in essay form, participation in activities, citizenship and community service, and support given by the school through recommendations. Interviews and campus visits are encouraged but are not required. Recommended high school preparation includes 4 years of English, 4 years of history or social science, 3 to 4 years of mathematics, 3 years of laboratory science, 2 to 3 years of foreign language, and 1 year of fine arts. The SAT I or ACT is required, unless the student is applying via the Portfolio Path.

Application and Information

First-year applicants should submit the Lewis & Clark or Common Application; a personal essay; an official academic transcript, including senior grades from the first marking period; one recommendation from a counselor; and at least one reference from an academic teacher. Lewis & Clark's application form can be found on line at the College's Web site (address below). Application deadlines are December 1 for early action (notification by January 15) and February 1 for regular admission (notification by April 1). The optional Portfolio Path Admissions Program provides an opportunity for applicants who have shown exceptional academic initiative to demonstrate the full extent of their pursuits by presenting a portfolio of their academic work. Under this plan, SAT I or ACT scores are optional. For more information about Lewis & Clark College or to arrange a visit, students should contact:

Office of Admissions
Lewis & Clark College
0615 Southwest Palatine Hill Road
Portland, Oregon 97219-7899
Telephone: 503-768-7040
          800-444-4111 (toll-free)
Fax: 503-768-7055
E-mail: admissions@lclark.edu
World Wide Web: http://www.lclark.edu

LEWIS UNIVERSITY
ROMEOVILLE, ILLINOIS

The University

A Christian Brothers university, Lewis University is the twelfth-largest private college or university in Illinois. More than 4,100 students are enrolled, with 1,000 residing on campus. A comprehensive, Catholic university, Lewis is large enough to offer the resources of a dynamic university yet small enough to give each student personal attention. The student-faculty ratio of 15:1 ensures that each student experiences interaction with teachers and mentoring in the classroom. The success of the University is based on its heritage and the strength of its sponsors, the Christian Brothers and their founder, St. John Baptist de la Salle. The Christian Brothers have a long history of providing excellence in education and being responsive to individual and social needs. Teaching all over the world, they operate sixty high schools and seven colleges and universities in the United States.

Lewis offers small classes, relevant programs in more than sixty majors, an active campus life, service learning opportunities, dedicated faculty members, a sense of community, an ideal location, exciting athletic competition, and a beautiful campus. These elements are combined to provide high-quality, values-based educational experiences that focus on academic choices, career preparation, service to the community, and lifelong learning.

While the majority of the student body are Illinois residents, the Lewis enrollment includes men and women from more than twenty-five states and twenty-nine countries. Eight residence halls offer various styles of living, including suite arrangements and quiet areas, among others. Campus residents report that the close-knit resident population helps to create a friendly and supportive atmosphere. More than fifty student clubs and organizations provide each student with the opportunity to pursue a variety of academic, career- or hobby-related, social, and athletic interests. Sororities and fraternities offer social and volunteer opportunities. The University has a strong intramural program in which 80 percent of resident students participate. There are eighteen intercollegiate sports, including men's and women's basketball, cross-country, golf, soccer, swimming, tennis, track, and volleyball plus men's baseball and women's softball. All teams compete in NCAA Division II. Lewis teams have captured the Great Lakes Valley Conference All Sports Trophy twelve times in the past sixteen years. At the same time, 95 percent of student athletes at Lewis earn the bachelor's degree, and a high percentage make the Deans' List.

On the graduate level, the University offers degree programs leading to the Master of Business Administration (M.B.A.); the Master of Arts (M.A.) in education, leadership studies, counseling psychology, and school counseling and guidance; the Master of Science in Nursing (M.S.N.); the Master of Education; and the Master of Science (M.S.) in criminal/social justice.

Location

Located in Romeoville, Illinois, Lewis is only 35 minutes southwest of Chicago. This allows students to take advantage of the resources of one of the world's largest cities while enjoying the beautiful suburban campus. Shopping and recreational facilities are located nearby.

Majors and Degrees

Lewis University offers programs leading to the Bachelor of Arts (B.A.) degree in accountancy, American studies, art studio, athletic training, biochemistry, biology, broadcast journalism, business administration, business studies, chemistry, communications technologies, computer graphic design, computer science, criminal/social justice, drawing, economics, education, English, environmental science, finance, history, human communication, human resources management, illustration, liberal arts, management information systems, marketing, mathematics, multimedia production, music, music merchandising, painting, philosophy, physics, political science, print journalism, private security/loss prevention management, psychology, public relations, radio/television broadcasting, religious studies, social work and human services, sociology, special education, speech education, sport management, and theater. Programs leading to a Bachelor of Science (B.S.) degree include biochemistry, biology, chemistry, computer science, mathematics, physics, political science, and public administration. Preprofessional programs are offered in dentistry, engineering, law, medical dietetics, medicine, meteorology, optometry, pharmacy, physical therapy, physician's assistant studies, and veterinary science. In addition to its more than sixty majors, Lewis offers interdisciplinary courses in women's studies and ethnic studies. Accelerated programs for working adults are available in business, computer network administration, social and community studies, and aviation maintenance management. The Bachelor of Science in Nursing (B.S.N.) degree is offered in the College of Nursing.

The Scholars Academy allows eligible students in every major to enhance their educational opportunities through intensive projects arranged by contract with faculty members, conferences, immersion seminars, and travel. To prepare students for careers in aviation, the University offers Bachelor of Science degree programs in aviation administration, aviation flight management, and aviation maintenance management as well as Associate of Science degree programs in aviation flight and aviation maintenance. Certificate programs are offered in aviation flight dispatch and aviation maintenance technology.

The Bachelor of Elected Studies (B.E.S.) degree and a liberal arts degree may be pursued by students whose educational and career goals lead them to combine course work from several areas. The B.E.S. degree allows students to develop their own major by choosing a concentration from any area of the University. The liberal arts degree permits them to combine two minors into a major.

Academic Program

The Lewis curriculum has three components: general education requirements, requirements in a major, and elective courses. The general education requirements include specific courses in the humanities and the social or natural sciences designed to introduce the student to liberal culture. Requirements for the student's chosen major provide the opportunity for a greater depth of study in one academic field. Electives allow the student to select additional courses suited to his or her educational needs. The emphasis on humanities and communication arts in the undergraduate curriculum provides students with the knowledge of history and of the human experience necessary to develop an awareness of and responsiveness to contemporary social issues. Qualified students may receive academic credit through Advanced Placement, through CLEP testing, or for prior learning.

Students selecting majors in the College of Arts and Sciences discover that course work has been developed to foster critical thinking, open inquiry, precision in thought and expression, and familiarity with a broad range of knowledge. The College of

Business seeks to educate individuals who are competent in the functional areas of business and who can recognize the responsibilities of business to the political, social, and economic segments of society. Many of the courses taken by business students are selected from the liberal arts area. Similarly, the College of Nursing builds on a foundation of liberal education. During the first two years, nursing students concentrate in the natural and behavioral sciences and the humanities. In the third and fourth years, advanced nursing science courses are taken, while clinical experience is acquired in hospitals and other health-care facilities. The nursing program prepares professional nursing practitioners who are competent to deliver health-care services in many situations.

The University operates on a semester system. The fall semester begins the Monday before Labor Day, and the spring semester starts in mid-January. Summer school sessions are six, eight, or ten weeks in length, depending on the program.

Academic Facilities

The academic facilities of the campus include a library, classrooms, labs, an aviation complex, a modern computer laboratory, and various studios (music, art, theater, radio, and television). Computer equipment consists of IBM, Macintosh, and Apple stand-alone computers as well as an IBM Risc System/6000 Powerserver 550 running AIX (UNIX) operating system, teletypes, CRTs, high-speed printers, and calculators. A microcomputer lab is available to all students, and additional computer facilities are open in the Art, Education, and Aviation departments and the Colleges of Business and Nursing.

The University library houses more than 186,000 volumes and an extensive microfiche and microfilm collection and is a depository for U.S. government documents. Besides housing a specialized music collection and an art-print collection, the library is home for the Archives of the Illinois & Michigan Canal Heritage Corridor.

The Aviation Department is housed in the $2.5-million Harold E. White Aviation Center next to the Lewis University Airport. The airport, which houses more than 300 aircraft, is the site of flight-training and management programs.

Costs

Tuition for 1999–2000 for full-time students (32 credits) was $13,664 ($427 per credit), while yearly room and board costs averaged $5730, depending on room size and the meal plan chosen. General service fees and student activity fees are included in the tuition.

Financial Aid

Lewis University is committed to helping all students who need financial assistance. Besides assisting students in obtaining federal and state grants, Federal Work-Study jobs, or loans (repayable after graduation), the University offers academic and athletic scholarships as well as additional Lewis grants to students with demonstrated financial needs. To be considered for any aid, a student must apply for federal, state, and Lewis aid, using the appropriate forms. Additional information is available from the Office of Admissions.

Faculty

The Lewis University faculty places a strong emphasis on scholarship and personal contact. Approximately 60 percent of the members of the general faculty hold doctoral degrees, and 100 percent of the members of the aviation faculty hold FAA-approved licenses. In addition, because the student-faculty ratio is 15:1, classes tend to be close-knit, enhancing the opportunities for extensive interaction between faculty members and students, both in class and through office hours.

Student Government

The Student Governing Board (SGB) consists of presidents of each of seven councils: the commuter, cultural awareness, honorary organization, interfratority, interorganizational, Pan Hellenic, and residence hall councils. Four at-large members are appointed by the Office of Student Affairs. The SGB works in the development of an effective activity program, reviews the quality of student life, oversees the effective functioning and financing of student organizations, represents student needs and concerns to the administration of the University, and serves as the judicial body in overseeing organizational conduct.

Admission Requirements

Lewis University welcomes candidates for admission who present a strong record of academic success and/or high motivation. Freshman candidates are required to present ACT or SAT I results, as well as a record of high school work. Students whose main language is not English must also present a score of at least 500 on the Test of English as a Foreign Language (TOEFL). In addition to the above requirements, applicants for the nursing program must have taken 1 year of chemistry, 1 year of biology, and at least 1 year of algebra.

Transfer students with fewer than 12 credits should apply in the same manner as freshman applicants. Transfer students who have completed 12 or more college credits may be admitted to the College of Arts and Sciences if they have maintained an overall GPA of 2.0 or higher. (The Colleges of Nursing and Business have additional transfer requirements. For further information, students should contact the transfer coordinator in the Office of Admissions.) Most transfer students have all their college credits accepted. However, for the Lewis degree, a maximum of 72 credit hours may be transferred from community colleges.

Application and Information

Application forms for admission and financial aid may be obtained from the Office of Admissions. Freshman applicants should submit the application for admission, ACT or SAT I scores, and high school transcripts. Transfer applicants who have earned 12 or more credit hours should submit transcripts from each college or university attended and the completed admission application.

Director of Admissions
Lewis University
Route 53
Romeoville, Illinois 60446-2298
Telephone: 800-897-9000 (toll-free)
E-mail: admissions@lewisu.edu
World Wide Web: http://www.lewisu.edu

Lewis University students enter data in the modern computer laboratory.

LIBERTY UNIVERSITY
LYNCHBURG, VIRGINIA

The University

Founded in 1971 by Dr. Jerry Falwell, Liberty University (LU) provides a Christian, comprehensive, coeducational environment committed to serious scholarship at the undergraduate and graduate levels. The University is situated on a 160-acre campus with complete classroom, dormitory, study, leisure, and recreational facilities. Liberty University is approved by the State Council of Higher Education for Virginia and is accredited by the Commission on Colleges of the Southern Association of Colleges and Schools to award associate, bachelor's, master's and doctoral degrees. There are more than 5,100 undergraduate and graduate students in the traditional resident program. The student body represents all fifty states and more than seventy-four countries.

In addition to the 4,000-seat Earl H. Schilling Center, Liberty's facilities include the 12,000-seat football stadium and the 9,000-seat Vines Convocation Center. Also in use is Matthes-Hopkins Field, a superb outdoor track facility. Intercollegiate athletic competition is in NCAA Division I. Men compete in baseball, basketball, cross-country, football, golf, indoor track, soccer, tennis, and track and field. Women compete in basketball, cross-country, soccer, softball, track and field, and volleyball. Other sports programs include ice hockey, lacrosse, and volleyball for men at the club level, as well as intramural competition in several sports for both men and women.

Location

The University is located in the heart of Virginia in Lynchburg (population 68,000), with the scenic Blue Ridge Mountains as a backdrop. The city is more than 200 years old and is noted for its culture, beauty, and educational advantages. Nearby are such sites as Appomattox Court House; Natural Bridge; Thomas Jefferson's Monticello; historic Lexington; Washington, D.C.; and other places of interest.

The city of Lynchburg offers a wide variety of activities for recreation and entertainment. Excellent sports facilities and programs, cultural events at the Lynchburg Fine Arts Center, beautiful lakes and streams, and many other local attractions enhance the lives of Lynchburg residents. Lynchburg also has more than 2,000 hotel rooms, numerous outlets and malls, and a number of restaurants that serve a wide variety of cuisines. Lynchburg is accessible by air, train, and bus.

Majors and Degrees

The Bachelor of Science degree is offered in accounting, athletic training, biology, business (economics, finance, management, management information systems, and marketing), communication studies (advertising/public relations/media management, media graphic production, print and electronic journalism, and speech communication), computer science, elementary education, English, exercise science and fitness programming, family and consumer sciences, general studies, government (administration of justice, general, and prelaw), health promotion, history, interdisciplinary studies, mathematics, multidisciplinary studies, nursing, physical education, psychology (human services/counseling, child/adolescent development, and clinical/experimental), religion (biblical studies, missions, pastoral ministries, and youth ministries), social sciences, special education, and sport management.

The Bachelor of Arts degree is offered in English, general studies, history, interdisciplinary studies, philosophy, and religion (biblical studies).

The Bachelor of Music degree is offered in choral and instrumental music.

Minors are available in accounting, athletic training, aviation, biblical Greek, biblical studies, biology, business, chemistry, coaching, communication studies (journalism and speech), English, exercise science, family and consumer sciences, French, government, health promotion, history, mathematics, missions, music, philosophy, physical education, psychology, Spanish, sport management, theology, and youth ministries.

The Teacher Licensure Option is available at the elementary level in general studies; at the secondary level in biology, computer science, English, history/social sciences, mathematics, and work and family studies; and at both levels in music (choral or instrumental), health/physical education, special education, and teaching English as a second language.

Academic Program

A minimum of 120 semester hours is required for the B.S., while a minimum of 123 semester hours is necessary for the B.A. In addition to the major, the student must complete general education courses in humanities, natural sciences and mathematics, social sciences, physical education, and religion. The A.A. requires a minimum of 64 semester hours.

Liberty is on the early semester calendar. During the summer, there are several one- and two-week modular classes offered. Winter modulars are also offered between semesters.

The University also offers higher education degrees for the adult learner through home study. Liberty's External Degree Program (EDP) is a distance learning program that is accredited by the Commission on Colleges of the Southern Association of Colleges and Schools to award associate, bachelor's, master's, and doctoral degrees. For more information on the External Degree Program, students should call 800-424-9595 (toll-free).

Academic Facilities

Currently, 283,000 bound or microfilmed volumes are contained in the library. The LU library participates in an area library cooperative program. Students may find employment or volunteer their services in the University's 50,000-watt FM radio station or student-run radio and TV stations. The Fine Arts Hall houses the Lloyd Auditorium, which has a seating capacity of 315, as well as a recital hall and several practice rooms. The Arthur S. DeMoss Learning Center houses several large lecture halls, modern classrooms, and labs. The Science Hall houses biology, chemistry, and computer labs. Liberty's student center, David's Place, provides a place for students to relax and offers such amenities as TV lounges; a game room; a multipurpose room for films, aerobics, and banquets; and a snack shop.

Liberty is in the process of revamping the entire computer structure of the campus and overhauling all systems. Upon completion, each student will be able to reach their professors, various campus offices, and the Internet from individual dorm rooms.

Costs

Tuition for 1999–2000 was $285 per credit hour; the room and board cost was $2400 per semester and included twenty-one meals per week. A technology fee of $100 per semester provided each student with an e-mail address and access to the Internet.

The estimated cost for books per semester is $350. Additional fees (such as lab fees) are required for specific classes and are listed in the class registration book. Automobiles are permitted if they are registered and a fee of $30 per semester has been paid.

Financial Aid

A variety of grants, scholarships, and on-campus jobs are available at Liberty. All federally funded student financial aid programs, except the Federal Perkins Loan Program, are available. Athletic, academic, merit, talent, Association of Christian Schools International (ACSI), National Merit, and other Liberty University assistance grants are also available for qualified candidates. Students are required to provide the University with a copy of the Free Application for Federal Student Aid (FAFSA). Approximately 90 percent of the student body received some type of aid last year. An annual review of each student's financial aid award is made upon request.

Faculty

About 300 different colleges and universities worldwide are represented in the education of the Liberty faculty. The average Liberty faculty member has more than thirteen years of teaching experience. Courses are taught by faculty members, not graduate assistants. All members of the faculty serve as advisers to the students in their discipline, and many also serve as dorm parents.

Student Government

Students elect representatives to serve on the Student Senate. This group provides recommendations and suggestions to the student development staff. Student Senate members also organize and direct activities and civic programs.

Admission Requirements

All applicants should be familiar with Liberty's philosophy and expectations before applying. Applicants to the A.A., B.A., and B.S. programs must be high school graduates and must submit two official copies of the high school transcript, indicating graduation date (or GED test scores, if applicable). Applicants must also submit either ACT or SAT scores, which are used for academic counseling and placement. The applicant must demonstrate the ability to do college work. Three personal references may be requested if needed. Although interviews are not required, prospective students are encouraged to visit the campus. Four College-for-a-Weekend programs are available each year, giving prospective students an opportunity to participate in classes, attend social and athletics events, experience dorm life, and converse with students and faculty members.

Application and Information

All admission materials should reach the Office of Admissions by June 15 for fall enrollment; however, applicants are encouraged to complete the application process by January 1 to be considered for maximum scholarship opportunities. Applicants for the spring term should complete the process by December 1, although early October is preferred.

To learn more about Liberty University, students should contact:

Office of Admissions
Liberty University
1971 University Boulevard
Lynchburg, Virginia 24502

Telephone: 800-543-5317 (toll-free)
Fax: 800-628-7977
E-mail: admissions@liberty.edu
World Wide Web: http://www.liberty.edu

The Court of Flags on the lower campus of Liberty University.

LIMESTONE COLLEGE
GAFFNEY, SOUTH CAROLINA

The College
Founded in 1845, Limestone is a fully accredited, private, coeducational liberal arts college. The College maintains a small student body and a well-qualified faculty in order to create an atmosphere in which each student will develop intellectually, physically, and socially. The College endeavors to help students prepare for a satisfying, useful life through the development of meaningful leisure-time activities, effective communication skills, responsible decision-making abilities, and lifelong aspirations. In addition to its programs on campus, Limestone offers several of its academic majors in an accelerated evening and Saturday format (Block Program) at several locations throughout South Carolina. These programs are intended primarily for working adults.

Extracurricular activities play a vital part in the development of all students at Limestone College. Among these activities are intercollegiate athletics in men's baseball, basketball, golf, lacrosse, soccer, and tennis and in women's basketball, lacrosse, soccer, softball, swimming, tennis, and volleyball. Students who are interested in music have the opportunity to participate in several instrumental and choral ensembles. A theater program is also available.

The 115-acre Limestone campus is well laid out for pleasant college living. The classrooms, library, laboratories, auditorium, bookstore, post office, and administrative offices are housed in buildings that border the central and circular drives, making each easily accessible to the others. The back campus has a plaza of four dormitories, and a cafeteria is located nearby. The Timken LYFE Center is a physical education complex that houses the gymnasium, an AAU-size swimming pool, and athletic training facilities. The College also has eight lighted tennis courts, a baseball field, a softball field, and a soccer/lacrosse field.

Location
Gaffney, a small city with a population of 25,000, provides an ideal setting for a college campus. Whereas the distractions associated with a large city are absent from daily life, the cultural programs and services offered in such places are within a 50-mile radius of the cities of Charlotte, Spartanburg, and Greenville. All are connected to Gaffney by Interstate 85.

The climate is free from extremes of heat or cold. The well-known resort areas of the Blue Ridge Mountains, the Great Smoky Mountains, and the beaches of the Atlantic Coast are accessible for weekend visits. In the immediate area, facilities are available for all water sports, horseback riding, golf, tennis, and skiing.

Majors and Degrees
Limestone College offers the Bachelor of Arts, Bachelor of Science, and Associate of Arts degrees with majors in art education, biology, business administration (concentrations in accounting, biology, computer science, economics, general business, management, management information systems, and marketing), chemistry, computer science, counseling and human services, elementary education, English, history, liberal arts, mathematics, music, music education, physical education (concentrations in athletic training and general physical education), prelaw, psychology, secondary education, social work, and studio art. Majors approved for South Carolina teacher certification are art education, biology, elementary education, English, mathematics, music education, physical education, secondary education, and social studies.

Academic Program
The course of study leading to the B.A., B.S., or A.A. degree consists of four elements: requirements in communication and quantitative skills; a general liberal arts program, involving five different subject groups; courses in the major; and appropriate electives. The baccalaureate degree programs require the completion of a minimum of 120 semester hours.

Advanced placement and credit are given for scores of 3 or higher on the Advanced Placement examinations of the College Board.

An honors program involving special courses, seminars, and lectures is available for exceptional students. Admission to this program is contingent upon outstanding high school grades and scores on the SAT I of the College Board, the completion of a special application, and an interview. Almost 10 percent of all Limestone students are enrolled in this rigorous academic program.

A Program for Alternative Learning Styles (PALS) is available for qualified students with certified learning disabilities who might not otherwise succeed at the college level.

Academic Facilities
Limestone has outstanding computer facilities, including a DEC Alpha 2000 and a Novell network with more than 100 nodes. The A. J. Eastwood Library, a modern, air-conditioned structure, houses approximately 60,000 volumes and is fully computerized. Fullerton Auditorium, with a seating capacity of 975, serves for drama and musical productions and is one of the finest such facilities in the state of South Carolina. There are also well-equipped science and computer laboratories.

Costs
The direct costs for a student at Limestone College for the 2000–01 school year are $14,900. The cost of tuition is $10,100, and room and board are $4800. In addition, the cost of books, supplies, laundry, travel, and personal expenses is estimated at $1500 per year.

Financial Aid
Limestone College endeavors to meet the financial need of any qualified student through scholarships, grants, loans, work-study opportunities, or a combination of these. Limestone offers merit scholarships to students with outstanding academic, leadership, or athletic abilities as well as to those who have exceptional talents in such areas as art and music.

More than 90 percent of Limestone College students receive some type of financial aid. Because institutional financial aid is limited, students are urged to submit their applications for admission and financial aid as early as possible.

Faculty
Personal attention to students and instruction of high quality characterize the faculty at Limestone College. Two thirds of the faculty members hold Ph.D.'s or other terminal degrees in their fields. The student-faculty ratio is 11:1. Students and instructors work closely together in both learning and counseling situations. Each student has an assigned faculty adviser for assistance in course selection and for personal counseling.

Student Government
The Student Government Association exemplifies the College's democratic tradition and the principles of honor and individual responsibility. It is every student's privilege and responsibility to

participate in the government of the learning community of which he or she is a member. The more highly organized activities, including student organizations and social events, are coordinated through the association. The College also has a literary magazine and a yearbook.

Admission Requirements

Limestone College does not discriminate on the basis of race, color, creed, national origin, financial need, or physical handicap. Each candidate for admission is evaluated as an individual. The College recommends that applicants have the following high school preparation: English, 4 units; mathematics, 3 units; foreign language, 2–4 units; laboratory science, 2 or more units; and social sciences, 2 units.

Applicants must submit an official transcript of the secondary school record, scores on the SAT I, and a nonrefundable $25 application fee. Transfer applications are encouraged.

Application and Information

Completed application forms for admission and for financial aid should be sent to the director of admissions at Limestone College. It is recommended that applications be submitted by May 1. Any admission applications received after that date are considered on a space-available basis. The College practices a rolling admissions policy. As soon as the application, high school transcript, and test scores have been received, the applicant is notified of his or her status. Upon acceptance, a student is required to submit a $100 deposit.

Director of Admissions
Limestone College
1115 College Drive
Gaffney, South Carolina 29340
Telephone: 864-488-4554
           800-795-7151 (toll-free)
Fax: 864-487-8706

The Winnie Davis Hall of History, named in honor of the daughter of Jefferson Davis, was completed about 1904 and is listed on the National Register of Historic Places.

LINCOLN UNIVERSITY
LINCOLN UNIVERSITY, PENNSYLVANIA

The University

Lincoln University is a nonsectarian, coeducational, state-related, four-year liberal arts institution. Founded in 1854, it is the oldest college in the United States to have as its original purpose the higher education of youth of African descent. Today, it provides a superior education to people of all races.

On Lincoln's well-maintained campus, modern architectural styles blend with designs from an older era. There are eighteen residence halls (eleven for women, seven for men); a student union building with a bookstore, a snack bar, and activity rooms; many modern facilities such as Manuel Rivero Hall, which houses an Olympic-size swimming pool, a 2,400-seat gymnasium, a bowling alley, a dance studio, and a large game room; and John Miller Dickey Hall, a $5.4-million computer center, a humanities complex, and the $17-million state-of-the-art Thurgood Marshall Living and Learning Center. A $13-million International Cultural Center with a 2,000-seat auditorium will open in the near future. Students may also use one of the twelve well-equipped computer labs, which have a 6:1 student-computer ratio. The current enrollment is approximately 2,000.

Lincoln's Division III intercollegiate varsity sports program consists of baseball, basketball, cross-country, soccer, tennis, and track. In addition, the University sponsors a drama group, a dance troupe, a student radio station, a student newspaper, and an active music program, which includes several choral groups and a jazz band. The campus is the scene of frequent concerts, lectures, and a variety of cultural and recreational programs.

At the graduate level, the University offers five master's degree programs in administration, education, human services, mathematics, and reading, with concentrations in educational administration, human resource management, and budget and financial management. Certification programs are available in reading and teacher certification.

Location

The campus is surrounded by the rolling farmlands and hills of southern Chester County in Pennsylvania. It is located on Old U.S. Route 1, approximately 45 miles south of Philadelphia; 25 miles west of Wilmington, Delaware; and 55 miles north of Baltimore, Maryland. These three major cities provide excellent cultural and recreational resources. Oxford, Pennsylvania, the town nearest to Lincoln University, is located 4 miles south of the campus. There are shopping areas, banks, churches, and restaurants. Lincoln opened an Urban Center campus in Philadelphia for its master's degree programs.

Majors and Degrees

Lincoln University offers four-year programs leading to the undergraduate degrees of Bachelor of Arts and Bachelor of Science. Majors available to students are as follows: accounting, biology, business administration and economics, chemistry, computer science, criminal justice, education, English, finance, history, human services, international relations, journalism and communications (in cooperation with Temple University), mathematics, modern languages, music, philosophy, physical education, physics, political science, psychology, public affairs, recreational leadership, religion, sociology/anthropology, and therapeutic recreation. Preprofessional programs in dentistry, engineering, law, medicine, nursing, and veterinary science are also offered.

Lincoln offers a 3-3 program in engineering in cooperation with Drexel University and 3-2 programs in engineering in cooperation with Pennsylvania State University, Lafayette College, New Jersey Institute of Technology, the University of Delaware, Howard University, and Rensselaer Polytechnic Institute. These programs lead to a B.A. from Lincoln University and a B.S. degree from one of the engineering schools.

Academic Program

The University operates on a semester calendar system. It is accredited by the College and University Council of the State of Pennsylvania and by the Middle States Association of Colleges and Schools, and its health-related programs are accredited by the American Medical Association.

Lincoln requires the study in depth of a single field of concentration. New students are assigned faculty advisers by the registrar when they enroll, based upon their career intent as expressed in their application for admission. The normal load for a full-time student each semester is 15 credit hours plus physical education. The minimum load necessary to be registered as a full-time student is 12 credit hours. Students are not permitted to carry more than 5½ courses or 18 credit hours without the consent of their adviser and the approval of the registrar. Upon satisfactory completion of 120 to 128 credit hours, the student is recommended by the faculty to the Board of Trustees for the degree of Bachelor of Arts or Bachelor of Science.

The Lincoln Advanced Science and Engineering Reinforcement program (LASER) is one of the most successful engineering and science training programs in the nation.

The T.I.M.E. (Talent Improvement and Motivational Experience) Program, funded by the Commonwealth of Pennsylvania Legislative Act 101, is one of Lincoln University's supportive services programs providing counseling and tutorial support in mathematics, reading, writing, and content courses.

Off-Campus Arrangements

Through a study-abroad program, students are offered the opportunity to visit a number of other countries, including the People's Republic of China, the Commonwealth of Independent States, Taiwan, and several African and European countries.

Academic Facilities

The 422-acre campus contains a library with 178,750 volumes, 580 current periodicals, and 45,104 microforms. Lincoln's up-to-date facilities also include Harold Grim Hall, a life science building; Ware Center, dedicated to the fine arts; Wright Hall; a learning resource center; and John Miller Dickey Hall.

Costs

Tuition and fees for 1999–2000 were $5404 for Pennsylvania residents and $8296 for out-of-state students. Total costs, including room and board, were $10,638 for Pennsylvania residents and $13,530 for out-of-state students. Tuition and fees are subject to change without notice.

Financial Aid

Financial aid awards are based on need. An applicant for aid is required to file the Free Application for Federal Student Aid (FAFSA) and mail the application to the Central Processor. Lincoln University's federal code is 003290. The financial aid application deadline is March 15.

More than 90 percent of the students at Lincoln receive some type of financial assistance. Aid is awarded in the form of packages, which may include scholarships, federal grants, state grants, Federal Perkins Loans, Federal Stafford Student Loans, Federal Work-Study Program awards, and institutional aid.

Scholarships are offered to prospective students with outstanding academic potential. The minimum requirements are a combined SAT score of 900 or above, at least a 3.0 or B average, and significant school and community involvement. Students should write to the Director of Admissions for further information.

Faculty

The student-faculty ratio is 16:1. There are 97 full-time and 34 part-time faculty members. Seventy-four (77.9 percent) of the full-time faculty members have doctorates.

Student Government

The members of the Student Government Association are elected by the student body as representatives of and for all the students. It is the responsibility of the Student Government Association to make use of all channels of communication between the student body and its elected officials and between the Student Government Association, the administration, and the faculty for the purpose of alleviating campus problems and for the implementation of programs, regulations, and long- and short-range planning.

Admission Requirements

It is desirable that students be graduates of accredited high schools. The University admits candidates who rank in the upper 50 percent of their graduating class, have a 2.7 average or higher, show evidence of leadership qualities, and have completed 21 Carnegie units, including 4 of English, 3 of mathematics, 3 of social science, and 3 of science. Applicants generally submit a combined SAT score of 850 or higher and two letters of recommendation. Lincoln reviews each application to find acceptable students.

Application and Information

Lincoln University has a rolling admissions policy. For application forms and further information, students should contact:

Office of Admissions
MSC 147
Lincoln University
P.O. Box 179
Lincoln University, Pennsylvania 19352-0999
Telephone: 610-932-8300 Ext. 3994
        800-790-0191 (toll-free)
E-mail: admiss@lu.lincoln.edu
World Wide Web: http://www.lincoln.edu

Thurgood Marshall Living and Learning Center on the campus of Lincoln University.

LINDENWOOD UNIVERSITY
ST. CHARLES, MISSOURI

The University

An independent liberal arts university founded in 1827, Lindenwood University is the second-oldest university west of the Mississippi River. It originally opened as a college for women and became coeducational in 1969. Lindenwood remains committed to the overall development of young people. Combining traditional liberal arts studies with internships and work experience, Lindenwood students are able to take an active place in the work force upon graduation.

Lindenwood's student development programs enhance the academic experience. Students may participate in the "Talent Accomplishment Program," an innovative academic- and career-advising program.

Lindenwood offers a strong residential life program to foster the academic and personal development of all of its students. The University encourages the work-service experience as part of the learning process and as a valuable dimension of the liberal arts education.

Lindenwood is accredited by the Commission on Institutions of Higher Education of the North Central Association of Colleges and Schools and is a member of the Teacher Education Accreditation Council. The University has a historical relationship with the Presbyterian Church and is committed to the values inherent in the Judeo-Christian tradition. Welcoming students from all religious denominations, Lindenwood offers a value-oriented educational experience.

The University's athletic teams compete in the National Association of Intercollegiate Athletics (NAIA) Division II. Lindenwood's men and women athletes participate in baseball, basketball, cross-country, field hockey, football, golf, soccer, softball, tennis, track, volleyball, and wrestling. University sports facilities include the Harlen C. Hunter Stadium with an artificial turf field, an outdoor all-weather track, baseball and softball fields, and the University's newest building, the 3,000-seat Robert F. Hyland Performance Arena. It is home to the Lions and Lady Lions basketball, volleyball, and wrestling teams. Students may also participate in an assortment of intramural sports at the fitness center.

Student organizations and clubs provide avenues for extended personal growth, leadership, and community service. The University radio station, 35,000-watt KCLC-FM, is staffed by students.

Residential students may live in dormitories, houses, and apartment-style accommodations. All residential buildings are located on Lindenwood's wooded campus and are easily accessible from University facilities. Two new residence halls will open in fall 2000.

Lindenwood University offers graduate and undergraduate degrees in more than fifty majors, including twenty-three master's programs. Accelerated programs are available in both areas.

Location

The 368-acre campus is located in St. Charles, Missouri, a city of about 40,000 people situated 20 miles from downtown St. Louis. Resting on the banks of the Missouri River just south of the Mississippi, St. Charles is the site of Missouri's first state capital. The area offers a wide range of opportunities for all types of interests and is particularly rich in state heritage and attractions associated with the history of America's westward expansion. Lindenwood's proximity to a major city allows students to enjoy theme parks, a world-class zoo, professional sports events, Broadway plays and theater, performances of a world-renowned symphony orchestra, state parks, and lakes. St. Louis–Lambert International Airport is located just 5 miles from Lindenwood University on Interstate 70.

Majors and Degrees

With a foundation as solid as the campus' century-old linden trees, the academic programs of Lindenwood University have a tradition of excellence and innovation. Lindenwood awards Bachelor of Arts, Bachelor of Fine Arts, and Bachelor of Science degrees with majors in accounting, art (studio), art history, biology, business administration, chemistry, computer science, corporate communications, criminal justice, early childhood education, elementary education, English, finance, French, general studies, history, human resource management, human service agency management, management, marketing, mass communications, mathematics, medical technology, music, performing arts, physical education, political science, pre-engineering, psychology, public administration, religion, retail marketing, secondary education, social work, sociology, Spanish, special education, theater, and writing. Preprofessional courses are offered in dentistry, engineering, law, medicine, and veterinary medicine. Also, programs in engineering are available in conjunction with Washington University in St. Louis and the University of Missouri–Columbia.

Academic Program

The emphasis at Lindenwood University is on an individualized liberal arts education with career-oriented preparation. Students fulfill general education requirements, participate in the Work and Learn program when qualified, and acquire an in-depth knowledge of at least one area of study as a major. Lindenwood requires the completion of 128 credit hours to earn a bachelor's degree.

Academic Facilities

The Margaret Leggat Butler Library contains bound volumes, microfilm items, periodicals, and computers. Young Science Hall houses an auditorium, laboratories, and classrooms for natural sciences, mathematics, and computer science. A Macintosh and personal computer lab is located in the Lillie P. Roemer Memorial Arts Building, also home to KCLC-FM, an independent radio station owned and operated by Lindenwood University. Harmon Hall provides students with art, photography, dance, music, and performing arts studios; classrooms, practice rooms, a recital and lecture hall, and the Downstage Theatre; and the Harry D. Hendren Gallery, which attracts local and national art exhibits. In addition, Lindenwood Studio East offers expanded space for art studios. The 450-seat Jelkyl Theatre is located in Roemer Hall, home to administration and faculty offices, as well as classrooms. The Lindenwood Cultural Center provides a forum for the University's music and adult education programs. An auditorium seats 750 people. Sibley Hall, named for founders Mary Easton Sibley and George C. Sibley, was built in 1860 to replace the original log cabin that served as the first University building. Sibley Hall is listed on the National Register of Historic Places.

Costs

For the academic year 2000–01, tuition is $10,800. Students who choose to live on campus pay $5600 for room and board, including all local telephone service. There is a nonrefundable $150 room deposit. Books cost about $750 per academic year.

Financial Aid

Financial aid is available to all qualified students. A student must submit the Free Application for Federal Student Aid (FAFSA). As determined by the evaluation, a student's financial need may be met with a combination of federal, state, and institutional sources of aid. In addition, institutional awards are available in the areas of academics, leadership, athletics, drama, yearbook/newspaper, and music. Resident students may earn $1800 toward their expenses by working on campus.

Faculty

Lindenwood has 130 full-time faculty members, who advise students regarding majors and other matters to help them succeed academically.

Student Government

The Lindenwood Student Government Association (LSGA) is made up of representatives elected by the student body. LSGA has the responsibility of providing a balanced program of cultural, social, and recreational events and activities throughout the year.

Admission Requirements

Applicants are evaluated on an individual basis, and admission is based on an analysis of the student's grade point average, ACT or SAT I scores, extracurricular activities, recommendations, and personal qualifications. Students are admitted without regard to race, sex, or national origin.

Application and Information

Although admission to Lindenwood is on a rolling basis, students are encouraged to apply by April 15 for the fall semester and by December 1 for the spring semester. To qualify for the full amount of financial aid, students must submit their federal financial aid forms before April 15.

To apply for admission, a student should submit a completed application form with a nonrefundable $25 application fee, a transcript of high school and/or college work, and ACT or SAT I scores. Notification of the admission decision is mailed soon after all required materials are received and evaluated by the Director of Undergraduate Admissions.

An application for admission, financial aid, and scholarships and other information about Lindenwood University can be obtained by contacting:

Director of Undergraduate Admissions
Lindenwood University
209 South Kingshighway
St. Charles, Missouri 63301

Telephone: 636-949-4949
Fax: 636-949-4924
World Wide Web: http://www.lindenwood.edu

Students look over class notes in the shade of the linden trees at Lindenwood University.

LINFIELD COLLEGE
MCMINNVILLE, OREGON

The College
Linfield College (1849) is an independent, coeducational, residential, comprehensive liberal arts college dedicated to providing an educational environment conducive to learning and participation. There are 1,518 full-time students on the McMinnville campus. These students come primarily from the thirteen Western states (thirty states overall) but also from twenty-three countries. Members of minority groups make up 11 percent of the student body, and 4 percent of students are international. Most students are between 18 and 22. Linfield is primarily residential, with one residence hall for men, six for women, and nine that are coeducational, each accommodating between 10 and 100 residents. There are also four fraternity houses. Each hall establishes its own calendar of social, educational, and recreational events throughout the year. Students who reside on campus eat their meals in the College dining hall. Houses and apartments are available for upper-division students. Social clubs, professional organizations, sororities (one local and three national: Alpha Phi, Phi Sigma Sigma, and Zeta Tau Alpha) and fraternities (one local and three national: Kappa Sigma, Pi Kappa Alpha, and Theta Chi), service clubs, and almost forty other organizations play an important role in the daily life of a Linfield student. Linfield's winning athletics tradition fosters participation at all levels of competition. Women compete in intercollegiate basketball, cross-country, golf, lacrosse, soccer, softball, swimming, tennis, track and field, and volleyball. Men compete in intercollegiate baseball, basketball, cross-country, football, golf, soccer, swimming, tennis, and track and field. Water polo, Ultimate Frisbee, and men's lacrosse are club sports. Linfield also has an extensive and active year-round intramural program.

Linfield hosts the Oregon Nobel Laureate Symposium. (There are only five such symposiums worldwide.) At each symposium, several Nobel laureates come to share their backgrounds and expertise within the context of a basic theme.

The Linfield–Good Samaritan School of Nursing, an academic unit of the College at its Portland campus, prepares students for the B.S.N. This campus, at the Good Samaritan Hospital and Medical Center, has residence facilities, food service options, and a residence life program. The Portland campus median age is 24.

Location
Located in McMinnville, 36 miles southwest of Portland, Linfield College is a leader in the cultural, educational, and recreational events of the fast-growing community of 24,000. The seat of county government, McMinnville provides Linfield faculty and students with many opportunities to participate in community service activities. Four cinemas, a community playhouse, bowling alleys, coffeehouses, and a wide variety of restaurants welcome Linfield students. Shopping is within walking distance. The central Oregon coast is an hour to the west, and the outdoor activity areas of the Oregon Cascade mountains, including year-round skiing at Mt. Hood, are 2 hours to the east. Salem, the state capital of Oregon, is 23 miles to the southeast, and Eugene is 80 miles south. Rainfall in western Oregon averages 42 inches annually, and the winter temperature averages 41°F.

Majors and Degrees
The Bachelor of Arts degree is awarded in art, communication, creative writing, elementary education, English, French, German, history, mathematics, music, philosophy, political science, psychology, religious studies, sociology, Spanish, and theater arts. The Bachelor of Arts or Bachelor of Science degree is offered in accounting, anthropology, applied physics, athletic training, biology, business, chemistry, computing science, economics, elementary education, exercise science, finance, general science, health education, international business, mathematics, medical technology, physical education, and physics. The College has programs to prepare students for advanced study in dentistry, law, and medicine. The education department offers a strong program of teacher certification at the secondary and elementary levels. A 3-2 engineering program is available with Oregon State University, Washington State University, and the University of Southern California. A 3-2 forestry program is also available with Oregon State University.

Academic Program
The academic year is divided into two 15-week semesters (fall and spring) and an optional four-week winter term in January. (Tuition for January term is included in the fall and spring costs.) The January term offers regular departmental courses and cultural-epochs study. Academic courses are assigned 1–5 semester credit hours each; 125 credits are required for a B.A. or a B.S. degree. Students divide their time equally among required general education courses, a major area of study, and elective subjects. The Linfield Curriculum courses, selected to provide a solid foundation in the liberal arts, require students to take 6 semester hours in at least two courses in each of the five areas of inquiry. These areas of inquiry are as follows: the Vital Past; Ultimate Questions; Individual, Systems, and Societies; the Natural World; and Images and Arts. In addition, students are required to take a writing-intensive course, a course addressing global diversity, and a course dealing with American pluralism. Major requirements differ from department to department. Individually designed majors are available with faculty approval. Students majoring in a foreign language spend an academic year in a country in which the language being studied is the native tongue. Language majors have recently studied in such cities as Avignon, Guadalajara, Nantes, Munich, Quebec, and Valencia. The Advanced Placement (AP) Program of the College Board is recognized, and 5 semester hours of credit are granted for a score of 4 or 5 on an AP test. AP examinations do not satisfy general education requirements. The College recognizes the International Baccalaureate Diploma and awards up to 30 semester hours of credit for higher-level courses on a course-by-course basis. Total credit awarded by AP or I.B. may not exceed 30 semester hours.

The College offers an intensive course in English as a second language. It is designed to help international students whose native language is other than English to achieve competence in academic and social English skills, so that they can work effectively in their undergraduate classes at Linfield.

Off-Campus Arrangements
Off-campus educational experiences include the Semester Abroad Program, involving four months of study in San José, Costa Rica; Paris, France; Vienna, Austria; Yokohama, Japan; Hong Kong, China; Seoul, South Korea; Beijing, China; Galway, Ireland; or Nottingham, England. Sophomores, juniors, and seniors are encouraged to participate, and approximately 20 students are selected for each country each year. The program is designed to serve students who have successfully completed one year of study at Linfield in the appropriate language and who will return to the campus to share their international experiences with the College community. Transportation is included in the cost of tuition, and most of these study programs cost the same as a semester on campus. January term study-abroad programs for four weeks are also offered. Recent offerings included Jane Austen (England); Mainland Southeast

Asia History (Cambodia, Vietnam, China, and Hong Kong); European Community: Structure and Economic Perspectives (Belgium, France, and Luxembourg); Medieval Philosophy (Spain, France, Belgium, and England); and History of World War II (Hawaii, Japan, and the Philippines).

Academic Facilities

Murdock Hall houses the biology and chemistry departments and up-to-date laboratories and equipment. Laboratory and research space is provided for general and advanced chemistry and biology, organic chemistry, biochemistry, microbiology, bacteriology, immunology, ecology, botany, physiology, embryology, and gross and microscopic anatomy. Taylor Hall houses the economics and business departments, a computer center, a resource library, a seminar room, and classrooms. The physics and mathematics departments are housed in Graf Hall. There are 144 IBM and Macintosh computers on campus readily available for access by students. Services on the network that students can use include the two UNIX hosts (available for programming, e-mail, and other communication services), a connection to the Internet, file servers, and both laser and dot-matrix printers. Linfield students benefit from a communications and technology network, including phone service, voice mail, e-mail, and Internet connections in each residence hall room.

The Health and Physical Education/Recreation Complex houses three gymnasiums; weight rooms; fitness laboratories with a hydrostatic weighing tank, a metabolic and pulmonary measuring system, and an electrocardiovascular exercise ECG system; an eight-lane, 25-yard-long indoor pool; handball and racquetball courts; classrooms; offices; and a 28,000-square-foot field house.

The Linfield College Library has more than 145,000 volumes in open stacks. It has 116,420 units of microforms and subscribes to 1,173 periodicals. Students may request materials not available at Linfield from libraries throughout the world through an interlibrary loan system. The library provides an online catalog with Internet connections. Other facilities include art galleries and studios, a 250-watt FM radio station, an experimental psychology laboratory, dance and music studios, a theater, a preschool, and a 425-seat auditorium that houses a three-manual, 48-rank Casavant pipe organ.

Costs

For 1999–2000, tuition and fees were $17,720 per two-semester year; board was $2740, and a double room was $2560.

Financial Aid

Eligibility for most of Linfield's assistance programs is based on need as determined by a federally approved needs analysis processor. The only form required for need-based programs is the Free Application for Federal Student Aid (FAFSA). Linfield participates in the Federal Perkins and Federal Stafford Student Loan programs, Federal Supplemental Educational Opportunity Grants, Federal Work-Study, and other forms of financial assistance on the basis of demonstrated need.

The College awards a number of scholarships to full-time students based on scholastic achievement, independent of financial need. These academic scholarships vary from 20 percent to full tuition. To be considered, students must have a minimum GPA of 3.4. A number of other criteria are used when determining scholarships. Linfield sponsors National Merit Scholarships. The minimum award is 50 percent of tuition. Awards can range to full tuition, depending on financial need, provided the student has indicated that Linfield is his or her first-choice college. The College also sponsors the annual Academic Competitive Scholarship Program in early March of each year. Participation is limited to high school seniors who meet particular academic requirements. Each academic department offers prizes ranging from $10,000 to $16,000, divided over the student's four years at Linfield, provided the student maintains a grade point average of at least 3.0. Scholarships of varying amounts are awarded to entering students who are particularly talented in music performance. Amounts range from $1500 to $2500 annually. Interested students are required to audition either in person or by cassette tape by February 15. Financial assistance for non–U.S. citizens is limited to partial tuition scholarships and the opportunity to work part-time on campus. Other scholarships are available for students who demonstrate outstanding leadership and community service and who show an interest in study abroad.

Faculty

There are 132 full-time faculty members, who are committed to undergraduate teaching and scholarship. Ninety-five percent have doctoral or other terminal degrees within their field. The faculty-student ratio is 1:13. Faculty members serve as academic advisers. There are no teaching assistants.

Student Government

Students have a significant voice in establishing and changing College policies and regulations. The Student Senate, chosen through campus elections, is the focus of student opinion and debate. Students are represented on most College governing councils and committees, with faculty members and trustees, and are encouraged to express and implement their ideas on academic or extracurricular matters.

Admission Requirements

Admission to Linfield College is selective. Admission is granted to students who are likely to grow and succeed in a personal and challenging liberal arts environment. Each applicant is judged on individual merit. A faculty admissions committee evaluates candidates in a number of areas that commonly indicate academic potential. These include high school performance, a writing sample, recommendations from teachers and counselors, and precollege standardized test results (ACT or SAT I). The committee also considers the depth and quality of an applicant's involvement in community and school activities. It reviews all applications as a group, selecting those students who show the greatest likelihood of benefitting from and contributing to the Linfield community. Linfield is a member of the Common Application Association.

International students whose education has been in a language other than English must submit certified English translations of their academic work. Proficiency in English is required, as demonstrated by an official TOEFL score report, including a Test of Written English (TWE) score. Admitted international students must show evidence of financial responsibility and submit a $2000 deposit before a Certificate of Eligibility I-20 is issued.

Early action applicants must apply by November 15, and notification is made by January 1. The preferred application deadline for regular admission is February 1, with notification made on or before April 1.

Application and Information

Interviews are not required, but students are encouraged to visit. Appointments should be made in advance. The Office of Admissions is open Monday through Friday, 8 a.m. to 5 p.m. The Linfield Web site provides students with information on student life, academic programs, and athletics. Students may also complete their application for admission on line or ask for additional information. Interested students are encouraged to contact:

Director of Admissions
Linfield College
McMinnville, Oregon 97128
Telephone: 503-434-2213
         800-640-2287 (toll-free)
Fax: 503-434-2472
E-mail: admissions@linfield.edu
World Wide Web: http://www.linfield.edu

LOCK HAVEN UNIVERSITY OF PENNSYLVANIA
LOCK HAVEN, PENNSYLVANIA

The University

Founded as the Central State Normal School in 1870, Lock Haven University (LHU) is part of Pennsylvania's State System of Higher Education. The enrollment is 3,700—an ideal size for a high-quality, personalized education. Students represent twenty-six states across the nation, and the International Education program, one of the finest in the state, attracts students from twenty-nine countries around the world. The University has seven residence halls, which house approximately 1,600 students. Six of the residence halls are coeducational; one is all-female. All residence halls are equipped with kitchens, storage and vending areas, and both recreational and study lounges; individual rooms receive basic telephone and cable TV service at no charge. There are also hundreds of rental units—apartments and houses—within easy walking distance of the campus. In addition to the full meal plan for resident students, the University dining hall offers flex accounts and several partial meal plans for off-campus and commuting students. Social and extracurricular offerings at Lock Haven University are exhaustive and exciting. Lock Haven's nationally recognized athletic teams include NCAA Division I men's wrestling; Division II men's and women's basketball, track and field, and cross-country; men's soccer (former national champions), football, and baseball; women's soccer, softball (former national runners-up), lacrosse (former national champions), volleyball, swimming, and field hockey (six-time national champions between 1981 and 1995). Other extracurricular offerings include an active student government and a residence hall council that both governs and promotes on-campus life, Greek life (seven national fraternities, four national sororities, and a variety of honorary and professional Greek-letter societies), and more than sixty recognized clubs and organizations.

More than seventy-five academic programs are offered through the College of Arts and Sciences and the College of Education and Human Services. Widely respected programs in international education, health sciences/athletic training, and computer science attract acclaim from across the state and the country. Master's programs are offered in education (curriculum and instruction), health science (physician assistance in rural primary care), and liberal arts. Lock Haven University is accredited by the Middle States Association of Colleges and Schools, the National Council for Accreditation of Teacher Education, the National Athletic Training Association, and the Council on Social Work Education.

Lock Haven's branch campus in Clearfield, Pennsylvania, has grown steadily since opening in 1989. Construction is underway on a new facility that will allow the Clearfield Campus to accommodate many more students and programs. Currently, more than 200 students attend the Clearfield Campus. The Associate of Science in nursing, the Associate of Applied Science in management, and many general education programs are offered there.

Location

The University is located on 165 acres in Lock Haven, Pennsylvania, a pleasant town of about 10,000 full-time residents. The town is resplendent with meticulously restored Victorian homes and turn-of-the-century architecture. Located on a hill overlooking the Susquehanna River, the campus is adjacent to all the outdoor wonders the area has to offer. During late spring and summer, the river is dotted with boats, rafts, and inner tubes. There are opportunities for swimming, fishing, hiking, hunting, skiing, camping, and hang gliding. The Millbrook Playhouse provides professional summer-stock theater, and the Ross Library is noted for its collection of artwork by John Sloan, a Lock Haven native for whom the University's fine arts and performing center is named. Lock Haven is within easy reach of Pittsburgh (3½ hours), Philadelphia and New York City (under 4 hours), and Washington, D.C. (about 4 hours). Lock Haven is accessible via Interstate Route 80 and U.S. Routes 15 and 220 and is served by the State College and Williamsport airports and by a Trailways bus station.

Majors and Degrees

The Bachelor of Arts degree is offered in economics, engineering (a cooperative five-year dual-degree program with Pennsylvania State University), English, environmental geology, French, general studies, German, history, humanities (English, philosophy, and speech/theater), international studies, journalism/mass communication, Latin American studies, mathematics, natural sciences (biology, chemistry, and physics), philosophy, political science, psychology, social sciences (economics, history, political science, and sociology/anthropology), sociology (with optional concentration in the administration of criminal justice), Spanish, speech communications, and theater. The Bachelor of Fine Arts is offered in music. The Bachelor of Science degree is offered in accounting, applied geology, biology, biology/chemistry, biology/chemistry with a medical technology emphasis, chemistry, computer information science, computer science, general studies, geography, management science, physics, preprofessional preparation (dentistry, medicine, pharmacy, and veterinary medicine), and social work. The Bachelor of Science degree in recreation is offered with concentrations in fitness management, leisure and commercial management, outdoor management, and therapeutic recreation. The Bachelor of Science degree is offered in early childhood education, early childhood/special education, elementary education, health and physical education (with optional concentrations in aquatics, coaching, sports and physical education in a correctional institution, and sports administration), and secondary education (with concentrations in biology, chemistry, earth and space science, English, French, general science, geography/social science, German, mathematics, physics, social sciences, and Spanish), and there is a dual-degree program in elementary and special education. The Bachelor of Science degree in health science is offered with concentrations in community health, general (preprofessional), pre–physical therapy, and sports medicine/athletic training. The sports medicine/athletic training program at LHU is one of only seventy programs nationwide accredited by the National Athletic Training Association.

Academic Program

Candidates for graduation from Lock Haven University must have completed at least 128 credits, including a minimum of 60 credits of general education course work. The two-semester academic year is supplemented by optional summer sessions. Internships and independent study are frequently part of a well-balanced degree program. Credits from many accredited institutions are accepted, contingent upon a minimum grade point average of 2.0. Educational experiences gained while in the armed services will be evaluated for credit. Lock Haven University maintains a Veterans' Affairs Office to provide counseling and assistance in financial aid and other matters. The Army Reserve Officers' Training Corps offers a full program in military science to supplement the educational experience.

Off-Campus Arrangements

The Bachelor of Science in Education degree program includes one semester of student teaching, which can be done in the Lock Haven area, elsewhere in Pennsylvania, or—through the Office of International Education—in Australia, Austria, Belgium,

Ecuador, England, Germany, or Scotland. Any student may study abroad for a semester or more and have those credits accepted toward graduation. Exchange programs exist with universities in Australia, Canada, Costa Rica, England, Finland, France, Germany, Italy, Japan, Mexico, Morocco, the People's Republic of China, Poland, Russia, Scotland, Spain, Taiwan, Tunisia, and Ukraine. Students may apply for a semester overseas during any year at Lock Haven.

Academic Facilities

The Robinson Hall Learning Center is a multimillion-dollar research learning facility that houses five academic departments, as well as a full-production radio station, a full-production color-TV studio, the academic computing center, a multipurpose Model United Nations auditorium, and a psychological behavior laboratory outfitted for primate study. The Stevenson Library has more than 360,000 volumes and an extensive collection of periodicals, microfilm, and microfiche. The University belongs to the state's Inter-Library Loan system, the Ohio College Library Center, and the Susquehanna Library Cooperative. Two large auditoriums are used for plays, concerts, and other performances. The John Sloan Fine Arts Center includes a theater, an art gallery, classrooms, art and pottery studios, and music practice rooms. Akeley Hall houses a complete student computing center. Sixty-four PCs attached to the University network are available for use by all students. Raub Hall houses another computer lab with thirty PCs for general student use. Each residence hall also houses computers for student use. Raub Hall houses a smaller computer center with thirty IBM PCs for general student use. The Sieg Conference Center, several miles from the main campus, is used as a retreat by classes, clubs, and other campus organizations.

Costs

For the 1999–2000 academic year, tuition was $3618 for in-state students and $7046 for out-of-state students. Room and board added up to $4136 for the year. In addition, students paid $642 in fees, which included a student activity fee, a student center fee, and an educational services fee. Thus, in-state on-campus students paid a total of $8396, and out-of-state on-campus students paid $11,824.

Financial Aid

Approximately 80 percent of the students at Lock Haven University receive financial aid. Aid is divided into grants, loans, and work programs. Available grants include the Federal Pell Grant, a federally funded program awarding students from $400 to $2340 per academic year; the Pennsylvania Higher Education Assistance Agency (PHEAA) grant, through a state program that awards students (in-state only) up to $2600 per academic year; the University-administered Federal Supplemental Educational Opportunity Grant (FSEOG), which provides up to $600 per academic year in addition to other financial aid when a need still exists; and other state grant programs. Loans available through the Office of Financial Aid include Federal Perkins Loans, federally insured Federal Stafford Student Loans, and parents' loans, which vary according to the lending institution. Work programs are divided into the Federal Work-Study Program, which requires demonstration of financial need, and campus employment, which is open to most students to help defray college expenses. Most of the above aid may be applied for by filling out the Free Application for Federal Student Aid (FAFSA), which may be found in most high school guidance offices. The deadline is April 15, but it is recommended that applications be filed sooner. A University financial aid form is sent to all newly admitted students and should also be filled out by April 15 for full consideration. Most award programs are operated on a first-come, first-served basis from a limited amount of available funds. Questions should be directed to Dr. William Irwin, Director of Financial Aid, 877-405-3057. The Lock Haven University Foundation offers an extensive scholarship program, including the Presidential Scholars Program for incoming freshmen who have exhibited exemplary academic and leadership performance in high school. Application forms for this scholarship program may be requested in advance, along with information about other LHU Foundation scholarships, by writing to Mrs. Lynn Lytle, Director of Foundation Development, Akeley Building.

Faculty

The student-faculty ratio at Lock Haven University is a comfortable and personal 18:1. The faculty of 211 full- and part-time professors includes both career-long educators and professionals who bring experience and practical know-how to the classroom. Most faculty members have an advanced degree in their field, and 55 percent of the tenure-track faculty have earned a Ph.D. The diversity and competence of the faculty round out the education students receive at Lock Haven University.

Student Government

Upon payment of the semestral activity fee, each student enrolled at Lock Haven University automatically becomes a member of the Student Cooperative Council, Inc. (SCC), the governing student body. The SCC owns and manages the Parsons Union Building, the student bookstore, and the campus snack bar. The SCC also controls the budgeting of athletics and of the on-campus clubs and organizations. Students are elected by popular vote to represent each of the residence halls and the commuting population. A high percentage of the campus cultural and entertainment events, as well as campus improvements that affect the day-to-day function of the University, are funded exclusively through the SCC.

Admission Requirements

As part of the State System of Higher Education, Lock Haven University has established four general requirements for admission: (1) scholarship, as evidenced by graduation from an approved four-year high school or institution of equivalent grade or equivalent preparation as determined by the Credentials Division of the Pennsylvania Department of Education; (2) integrity and appropriate personality, as shown in estimates by secondary school officials of the applicant's trustworthiness, initiative, industry, and social adaptability; (3) satisfactory command of English, as evidenced by the secondary school record and verbal ratings in standardized tests; and (4) satisfactory performance on either the SAT I or the ACT. Preference is given to students who have a combined SAT I score of 1000 or better and rank in the top 40 percent of their class. Transfer students with 24 or more transferable credits and a cumulative grade point average of 2.0 or better may be considered for admission.

Application and Information

Applicants should send their secondary school transcript, a completed application form, and a $25 processing fee to the address below. In addition to the application form, transcripts, and fee, transfer students must submit transcripts of all previous college and college-level work and—if fewer than 24 credits are being transferred—a copy of their SAT I or ACT results. Students seeking admission from other countries should send their request for application materials six to twelve months prior to their intended matriculation date. All international students whose primary language is not English are required to take the Test of English as a Foreign Language (TOEFL) and achieve a score of 550 or better before being admitted for study. TOEFL information may be obtained by writing to TOEFL, Box 899, Princeton, New Jersey 08541, USA. High school seniors should submit formal application materials in early fall for the fall semester and by December 1 for the spring semester. Transfer students must submit materials by June 1 for the fall semester and by December 1 for the spring semester. Once a student has been admitted to the University, he or she must submit a deposit ($100 for on-campus students and $50 for off-campus students) and a physical examination report. For more information, students should contact:

James C. Reeser
Dean of Admissions and Financial Aid
Lock Haven University of Pennsylvania
Lock Haven, Pennsylvania 17745
Telephone: 570-893-2027
           800-332-8900 (toll-free in Pennsylvania)
           800-233-8978 (toll-free outside Pennsylvania)
E-mail: admissions@lhup.edu
World Wide Web: http://www.lhup.edu

LONG ISLAND UNIVERSITY, BROOKLYN CAMPUS

BROOKLYN, NEW YORK

The Campus

Students who wish to be in a metropolitan setting during their years of higher education make up the student body of Long Island University's Brooklyn Campus. The proximity of many cultural, commercial, educational, and governmental institutions is reflected in the University's curricula and activities. The 11,230 students represent every region of the United States and many other countries. Even though most students commute, many live and work on or near campus.

An integrative approach to undergraduate education known as The Long Island University Plan (LIUPlan) includes the Freshman Experience Program, comprehensive academic advisement, cooperative education and career development, and an innovative, integrative curriculum in the University Honors Program. Through workplace experiences, workshops, development of technological skills, consultation services, integrative seminars, and tools for self-assessment and exploration, the LIUPlan enables students to develop skills and talents that can lead to coherent, well-informed, and successful lives. Cornerstones of the LIUPlan are: (1) expanded academic and personal counseling from application to graduation; (2) enhanced academic and career opportunities—to give students decisive advantages in career fields of their choice by providing an option for well-paid, professional-level work or other types of special semesters that build professional connections, credentials, and experience; and (3) essential literacies—to hone students' analytic and writing skills and to familiarize them with the fundamental languages of culture and science. For further information about the LIUPlan, students should contact the Brooklyn Campus Office of Admissions at 718-488-1011.

In addition to its undergraduate degree programs, the Brooklyn Campus also offers forty-five master's-level programs leading to the M.A., M.S., M.S.Ed., M.B.A., and M.P.A. degrees as well as Ph.D. programs in clinical psychology and pharmaceutics.

Location

The 11-acre campus is located in downtown Brooklyn, 20 minutes from midtown Manhattan and convenient to public transportation that serves all parts of the metropolitan area. Within walking distance are excellent shopping areas, restaurants, and entertainment.

Majors and Degrees

The Bachelor of Arts degree is granted in the following areas: economics, English, English teacher studies (7–12), history, jazz studies, journalism, media arts, modern languages (French, German, Spanish), music (applied), music theory, philosophy, political science, psychology, social studies teacher studies (7–12), sociology-anthropology, social work, speech, and visual arts. The Bachelor of Science degree is granted in the following areas: accounting, bilingual teacher of special education studies, bilingual teacher of speech and hearing handicapped studies, biology, biology teacher studies (7–12), business finance, business management, chemistry, chemistry teacher studies (7–12), cytotechnology, elementary education, health science, humanities, integrated information systems, marketing, mathematics, mathematics teacher studies (7–12), medical technology, nuclear medicine technology, nursing, physical education teacher studies (K–12), physician's assistant studies, physics, respiratory care, social science, sports science, and teacher of speech and hearing handicapped studies. The Bachelor of Fine Arts degree is granted in the following areas: dance, music (jazz studies), and studio art. The Associate of Applied Science degree is offered in business administration; the Associate of Arts degree is offered in social science, science, and humanities. Five-year dual B.S./M.S. degree programs are offered in accounting, nursing (executive program for nursing and health-care management), adult nurse practitioner studies, occupational therapy, and physical therapy. The Arnold & Marie Schwartz College of Pharmacy offers a six-year Pharm.D. program.

Academic Program

All undergraduate students are required to complete a core curriculum in the liberal arts and sciences in order to acquire the general background of ideas and knowledge that an educated person must have. The core curriculum consists of courses in the humanities, the natural sciences, mathematics, and the social sciences. Specific requirements may vary depending on the major. Of the 128 credits required for graduation, a student must take 24 or more credits of advanced work in the major and have at least 48 credits in upper-division work. The minimum number of credits required in the liberal arts and sciences varies from 64 to 96, depending on the degree awarded. Qualified students in any major may arrange for independent studies and honors work.

The University Honors Program, open to all majors, offers academically qualified students core courses, designed for cross-disciplinary inquiry, and advanced seminars, which are theme oriented and field based. The program also allows for creative, as well as research, projects for independent study. Members of the program are eligible for Distinction in Honors when they write a thesis. All members may extend independent study beyond the stated limits through the Honors Program.

All students may enroll in the Cooperative Education Program, gaining valuable field experience and pay for employment related to their major field of study.

In the Arnold & Marie Schwartz College of Pharmacy and Health Sciences, degree requirements vary according to the individual program.

The commitment of the University to the support of each student's individual learning needs is reflected in the number of counseling and academic support services it offers. Instructional resources include the Academic Advisement Center, Achievement Studies, and Freshman Guidance, all of which are for students who require close program supervision and counseling, and the Academic Reinforcement Center, which provides free tutoring for nearly all undergraduate disciplines. Other academic support services include the Writing Center, the Mathematics Center, the Academic Computing Center, and the Apple Macintosh Computer Skills Lab. Special programs include the Higher Education Opportunity Program (HEOP) and the Special Educational Services Program for Disabled and Academically High Risk Students. For specific academic majors, faculty advisers and/or professional academic counselors are provided. A 1-credit course, Freshman Orientation Seminar, familiarizes incoming students with the academic and cultural resources of the University and the community.

Academic Facilities

The Salena Library Learning Center combines the traditional materials of a library with modern educational technology. Computer-assisted instruction and audiovisual materials are available to each student to facilitate individual research and self-paced instruction. Database searching is available to faculty and students. Cooperative agreements make the resources of the Academic Libraries of Brooklyn (ALB) available to LIU students. The Brooklyn Campus of Long Island University is part of a University-wide electronically linked library/resource network of 2.6 million volumes. Special library collections are in law, transportation, pharmacy, and the Weinberg Archives of Architecture and City Planning.

The Academic Computing Center supports teaching, research, and student computer needs. Staff members are available to support the microcomputing environment and to help with connections to the wide-area network LIUNET, the CLSI library system, and Internet. LIUNET consists of DEC VAX computer systems, IBM RS 6000 UNIX systems, and hundreds of PCs (IBM and Apple). On campus, there are eighteen computer labs, including special labs for writing, science, and other disciplines, as well as general access labs utilizing the latest in Macintosh and IBM technology.

The state-of-the-art Health Sciences Center housing programs in pharmacy, physical therapy, respiratory therapy, and nursing was recently constructed on campus.

Costs

Tuition for 1999–2000 was $478 per credit hour plus University and Student Activity fees, which vary with the number of courses for which the student is enrolled each semester. The 1999–2000 cost for a residence hall room ranged from $1285 to $2825 per semester, apartments ranged from $2395 to $2925 per semester, suites ranged from $1895 to $2095 per semester, and board costs ranged from $600 to $1250 per semester. Apartments, suites, and standard rooms are available on a first-come, first-served basis. The Residence Hall has a 24-hour study lounge, an IBM computer lab, and an on-site dining hall.

Financial Aid

Long Island University has a no-need-test scholarship program, which awards scholarships on the basis of academic qualifications or talent and skills. Financial aid is awarded on the basis of need and includes combinations of grants, loans, and work-study programs. Cooperative education placements are available to all students and serve as a valuable resource in meeting the cost of tuition. The entitlement programs of the Tuition Assistance Program and Federal Pell Grant Program form the foundation of a student's financial aid package. Applicants must file a Free Application for Federal Student Aid (FAFSA), a New York State TAP Application, and a Long Island University Application for Financial Aid, all obtainable from either the Admissions Office or Financial Aid Office. Students are assisted in securing part-time employment by the Office of Cooperative Education and Career Development.

Faculty

Most faculty members teach both graduate and undergraduate courses. Students have the opportunity to work with senior faculty members early in their college career. Although engaged in research projects of varying types, the faculty's primary focus is the students' academic development.

Student Government

The Student Government Association, the Campus's governing body of student life and its functions, consists of all registered students. The executive council includes president, vice president, treasurer, secretary, and 4 representatives from each academic class. Graduate, evening, and part-time students are represented on the council. The council's prime responsibility is to allocate funds to the various student organizations, thus assuring a full range of student activities.

Admission Requirements

Admission requirements are a high school average of 80 or above and/or an SAT I combined score of at least 850. A limited number of students who present credentials below these minimums may be accepted in programs designed to assist them to reach their full potential. Students should present 16 units of high school work, including 4 years of English, 3 of social studies, and 2 of mathematics (including geometry). GED (high school equivalency) scores can be accepted in lieu of a high school diploma for older students or service veterans. Credit for life experience may be awarded to qualified applicants.

Long Island University does not discriminate on the basis of sex, handicap, race, national origin, religion, political belief, or sexual preference in any of its educational programs and activities, including employment practices and policies relating to recruitment and admission of students.

Application and Information

Admission applications should be completed by August 15. Late applications are considered.

Forms may be requested from:

Undergraduate Admissions Office
Long Island University, Brooklyn Campus
1 University Plaza
Brooklyn, New York 11201
Telephone: 718-488-1011
World Wide Web: http://www.liu.edu

The state-of-the-art William Zeckendorf Health Sciences Center.

LONG ISLAND UNIVERSITY, C.W. POST CAMPUS
BROOKVILLE, NEW YORK

The Campus

C.W. Post Campus is one of the six campuses of Long Island University (LIU), the eighth-largest independent university in the U.S. It is situated on the North Shore of Long Island, approximately 25 miles from mid-Manhattan, on the former estate of cereal heiress Marjorie Merriweather Post. At the graduate level, the Campus offers numerous master's degree programs as well as doctorates in clinical psychology and information studies.

Ninety-one percent of the 4,628 undergraduates are from New York; the remainder come from all parts of the United States and thirty-four other countries. More than 1,400 students live in residence halls. On-campus organizations are numerous and include the traditional interest-oriented activities. Students also frequently take an active part in local or national public affairs. Ten percent of the students join fraternities and sororities. Intercollegiate and intramural sports for men and women include basketball, football, horseback riding, and others. Many cultural and entertainment activities are offered on campus throughout the year, and most are open to the general public. The Hillwood Commons campus center has an outstanding art museum and film theater. Musical and dramatic presentations are offered in the Little Theater, Great Hall, and Tilles Center.

Since 1959, Long Island University has also been offering upper-division and graduate programs at its Brentwood Campus. Undergraduate programs at Brentwood combine liberal arts and sciences with professional education in fields such as business administration and education. Master's degree programs include business administration (fast-track M.B.A.), health administration (M.P.A.), public administration (M.P.A.), special education and reading, school administration and supervision, school counseling, elementary education, and classes in TESOL and bilingual and middle school education.

C.W. Post also offers a Psy.D. in clinical psychology, a Ph.D. in information studies, a J.D./M.P.A. in public administration, and a J.D./M.B.A. in business administration in association with the Touro's law school.

Location

C.W. Post's spacious 307.9-acre campus is nestled in the quiet, safe suburban community of Brookville. Bus transportation is available to the Long Island Rail Road's stations in Greenvale and Hicksville and to nearby communities. Two major shopping centers in the immediate area include good restaurants, movie theaters, and department stores. The cultural opportunities in New York City are also easily accessible to students.

Majors and Degrees

The major areas of study are accounting, acting, anthropology, applied art, applied mathematics, art, art education, art history and theory, arts management, art studio, art therapy, biology, biology education, broadcasting, business administration, cardiovascular perfusion, ceramics, chemistry, chemistry education, clinical laboratory sciences (medical technology), communication arts, comparative languages, computer art, computer science, criminal justice, dance studies, earth science education, economics, educator in non-school settings, elementary education, English, English education, environmental science, film, finance, fine arts, French, geography, geology, German, graphic design, health-care administration, health education, health and physical education, health information management (medical records), history, history education, information systems, information transfer, interdisciplinary studies, international studies, Italian, Italian education, journalism, management, marketing, mathematics, mathematics education, medical biology, molecular biology, music, music education, nursing (for RNs only), nutrition, painting, philosophy, photography, physical education, physical education in a non-school setting, physics, political science, pre-engineering math, pre-engineering physics, prelaw, premedicine, prepharmacy, pre-respiratory therapy, psychology, public administration, public relations, radiologic technology, sculpture, social studies education, social work, sociology, Spanish, Spanish education, special education, speech-language pathology and audiology, theater, and theater arts.

There are also the following accelerated five-year dual-degree programs: B.S./M.S. in biology, B.A./M.S. in criminal justice, B.A./M.B.A. in international studies/business administration, B.A./M.A. in political science, B.S./M.S. in accounting, B.S./M.S. in accounting/taxation, B.S./M.P.A. in health-care administration, B.S./M.P.A. in public administration, and B.S./M.P.A. in political science/health-care administration.

Academic Program

To be eligible for a bachelor's degree, a student must complete at least 129 credits, 44 of which must be taken in general core courses. The B.F.A. degree programs require between 134 and 136 credits. All students in good academic standing, including freshmen, may take two elective courses per academic year (including summer school sessions) on a pass/fail basis for regular credit. A total of 24 credits may be taken on this basis.

The Long Island University Plan offers C.W. Post students a complete counseling network that ties together all academic, career, and financial counseling for students, beginning before enrollment and extending throughout the undergraduate years. Freshmen meet with faculty mentors and peer counselors twice a week for seven weeks in a 1-credit freshman seminar, College 101. The plan also emphasizes essential literacies and provides opportunities to earn income while gaining career-related experience. In addition, this is the first four-year institution in the New York area to offer the option of a fully integrated program of alternating full-time work and study, known as experience-enriched or cooperative (co-op) education. Through co-op, students build a resume, explore potential careers, establish contacts through networking, and earn money to defray the cost of a college education. C.W. Post places more than 250 students in paid cooperative education positions each year.

An outstanding honors and merit scholarship program provides talented students with an academic environment designed to help them achieve their greatest potential. Approximately 8 percent of undergraduates who have demonstrated outstanding intellectual potential and academic achievement are selected to participate in this nationally respected program. The objective of the program is enrichment, not acceleration. In the first two years, honors students take some basic courses in special limited-enrollment honors sections, where the approach to the material is more sophisticated than in regular classes. During the junior and senior years, honors students, as part of their program, participate in an interdepartmental lecture and in tutorial courses in their major and write a thesis or engage in the production of an equivalent project in their major. As the honors students progress through their college career, the program of study becomes increasingly independent and more related to personal needs.

Off-Campus Arrangements

C.W. Post has affiliations with such institutions as Regents College in London, Franklin College in Switzerland, and Meiji Gakuin University in Japan. Post students can also participate in Long Island University's Friends World Program. This program operates throughout the world in places such as Costa Rica, India, and China and allows students to study in as many as four different countries throughout their college careers. This respected program attracts individuals from every corner of the globe and brings them together for an academically and culturally rewarding experience.

Academic Facilities

The B. Davis Schwartz Memorial Library, one of the finest library facilities on Long Island and part of the Long Island University System, houses 2.6 million volumes as well as a fully equipped Instructional Media Center and Tax Library. The Center for Business Research, formerly the Nassau County Research Library, was established in 1978 and is a specialized business reference library offering a wide variety of research services for the business, financial, and professional communities in the New York metropolitan area. It has an extensive research collection, including books, microfilm, and microfiche. All students have free access to the Internet and the World Wide Web. More than 400 Macintosh and IBM computers are available in several buildings. Science and professional education laboratories are fully equipped. Other facilities include an interfaith center, a modern student center, an interactive technologies center, and a modern concert theater.

Costs

For 1999–2000, tuition was $15,340, room and board averaged $3270 per semester, and student activity/University fees were $720.

Financial Aid

C.W. Post participates in all major federal and New York State financial aid programs. Aid includes Federal Pell Grants, Federal Supplemental Educational Opportunity Grants, Federal Perkins Loans, Federal Direct Loans, Federal Work-Study Program awards, and institutional grants and scholarships. Students should consult the admissions office for specific criteria and deadlines for a wide range of academic scholarships.

The LIU Plan combines scholarships and cooperative education to provide a high-quality education at an affordable cost. All C.W. Post students are strongly encouraged to participate in paid professional internships (also known as cooperative education). Students gain work experience related to their major, begin to build a resume, and help reduce their costs by supplementing financial aid with co-op earnings.

The C.W. Post Campus requires all applicants for financial aid to submit the Free Application for Federal Student Aid (FAFSA), Financial Aid PROFILE, and New York State TAP Application (New York State applicants only), in addition to the application for admission. In addition, transfer students may need to obtain financial aid transcripts from all previously attended colleges and universities before new federal assistance may be disbursed at C.W. Post. All applicants seeking financial assistance are strongly urged to apply early in order to be assured of full exposure to the funding possibilities. The recommended submission date for application is March 1 in order to meet the University's deadline of May 15 each year. Financial aid is granted only after a student has been offered admission. All aid is granted for one year but is renewable, based on published criteria and federal and state eligibility guidelines.

Faculty

C.W. Post has 311 full-time faculty members. The undergraduate and graduate faculty are essentially the same group. Eighty-two percent of the full-time faculty members have the highest degree in their fields.

Student Government

The Student Government Association is the representative body of all students and is composed of three branches: the executive, the legislative, and the judicial. The Student Government Association works closely with the administration on many student-life issues such as recognition and funding of student clubs and organizations, special events, faculty evaluations, and campus issues that affect the academic life of the C.W. Post student.

Admission Requirements

A minimum of 16 units, accumulated in the four years prior to graduation from an accredited secondary school or the equivalent, is required. These units should consist of English, 4; social studies, 3; a foreign language, 2; mathematics through plane geometry or intermediate algebra, 2; a laboratory science, 1; and 4 units in electives distributed among social studies, language, mathematics, science, and other preparatory subjects acceptable for graduation from a secondary school. The high school average, rank in class, and SAT I or ACT scores are all evaluated for an admission decision.

Application and Information

Applicants must take either the SAT I or the ACT and have the scores forwarded directly to the C.W. Post Campus. On-campus interviews are strongly recommended. Admission decisions are made on a rolling basis, but those wishing to be considered for scholarships should consult with the admissions office for application deadlines. Transfer students are encouraged to apply and constitute a large percentage of the undergraduate population at the C.W. Post Campus. Classes are offered year-round. Students may begin studies in the fall, winter, spring, or summer semesters. Campus tours are available daily. The Office of Admissions, located in College Hall, is open Monday through Thursday, 9 a.m. to 8 p.m. and Friday and Saturday, 9 a.m. to 5 p.m. For additional information and to schedule interviews and campus visits, students are encouraged to contact:

Office of Admissions
Long Island University, C.W. Post Campus
720 Northern Boulevard
Brookville, New York 11548-1300

Telephone: 516-299-2900
           800-LIU-PLAN (toll-free)
Fax: 516-299-2137
E-mail: enroll@cwpost.liu.edu
World Wide Web: http://www.liu.edu

A view of the C.W. Post Campus.

LONG ISLAND UNIVERSITY, FRIENDS WORLD PROGRAM

SOUTHAMPTON, NEW YORK

The Program

With eight program centers and campuses around the world and a student body and faculty drawn from twenty-two countries, Friends World Program is uniquely international. There are 243 students currently enrolled. The Program is designed for students who are capable of assuming greater responsibility for their own lives and learning. The Program's worldwide facilities offer students the opportunity to live, study, and work in two or more other cultures while earning an accredited B.A. degree; to design individual programs of study based on their personal interests and goals; and to combine academic study with field experience and internships. While acquiring a balanced liberal arts education, including the development of practical fluency in one or more foreign languages and an appreciation of the culture and values of several world regions, students have the opportunity to carry out in-depth study and gain practical experience in their chosen field. In addition, they develop a deeper understanding of and a broader perspective on current world issues.

The Program began as Friends World College, founded on Long Island, New York, in 1965, under the sponsorship of the New York Yearly Meeting of Friends, and became part of Long Island University in 1991. While its beginnings were Quaker and North American, the Program is nonsectarian and has a student body and faculty drawn from many parts of the world. The purpose of the Program is to encourage men and women from every nation to treat the entire world as a university, to take the most urgent human problems as one basis of their curriculum, to seek designs together for a more humane future, and to consider all humanity the focus of their ultimate loyalty.

Location

Since 1965, Friends World students have carried out studies in more than seventy-five countries, making a reality of the phrase "The World Is Your Campus." Friends World maintains faculty and program centers in eight world regions. In 1991, the Program affiliated with Long Island University and relocated to the Southampton College campus in Southampton, Long Island, 90 miles from New York City. This campus serves as the joint home of the North American center and the world headquarters. An urban center in London, England, is home base for students working on projects throughout the British Isles and on the European Continent. The Latin American center in San José, Costa Rica, serves Central America, South America, and the Caribbean. The ancient city of Kyoto, considered the "heart of Japan," is the location of the East Asian center. Jerusalem, crossroads of the Middle East, is the site of the program in that region. The center in Bangalore, India, helps students carry out programs in South Asia. Zhejiang University in Hangzhou is the center for studies in the People's Republic of China. In addition, students have the opportunity to study in three distinct areas in one year by opting for the year-long program in Comparative Religion and Culture. Selected students focus on beliefs and religious practices in Taiwan, India, and Israel. Thus, while the headquarters of the Program is in the United States, students carry out their learning all over the world. In the truest sense, the Program's "community" is the entire globe.

Majors and Degrees

The Bachelor of Arts (B.A.) degree is awarded by Long Island University. Students have designed individual programs of study in most of the liberal arts fields, including African-American studies, animal behavior/wildlife studies, anthropology, archaeology, area studies (African, Asian, European, Latin American, and Middle Eastern), communications (film, journalism, photography, and video), community health, community organization and development, criminal justice and comparative legal systems, economics, education, environmental studies/ecology, fine arts and crafts, gender studies, holistic and natural healing, human services, languages, music, Native American studies, nutrition, peace studies and conflict resolution, philosophy, psychology/counseling, religion, sociology, sustainable development, theater/mime, and United Nations studies.

Academic Program

The learning process is a carefully planned combination of academic study and field experience. The Program involves classroom study, immersion language training (often including homestays), and independent fieldwork in at least two other countries. Under the guidance of an international faculty, students develop skills and competence in a major academic field by combining reading and library research, hands-on experience, and analytical writing. Friends World students typically spend at least two years abroad working with center faculty members to design and carry out field studies (such as internships, apprenticeships, and investigative research) in several cultural settings. For example, they have studied Gandhian nonviolence in India, desert agriculture in Israel, animal behavior in Kenya, and holistic healing and acupuncture in Japan and China. Students have worked with a feminist publishing cooperative in Paris, interned with a U.S. Congressman in Washington, researched agrarian economic development in Costa Rica, apprenticed with a modern dance company in Munich, worked with the United Nations in New York, and interned with a legal center in London. Many other projects range from anthropology to zoology.

Freshmen from North America spend the first year in the United States. The fall semester is spent in residence on the campus in Southampton, New York. While participating in a core program of seminars and studies in the liberal arts, students work closely with a faculty adviser to define their educational interests and goals and to design an individual learning plan for the second semester of independent field studies in the United States, which takes place January through April. Students then return to campus in mid-April for a monthlong residential program to reflect on their experiences, complete their portfolios, have their year's work evaluated, and prepare for study at the overseas center of their choice the following year.

As a record of their learning and growth, students maintain journals or portfolios of their work. The portfolio replaces the usual assignments and examinations of traditional colleges. The B.A. degree is conferred by Long Island University after successful completion of 120 credits, the preparation of a senior thesis or senior project report, and an external evaluation. Long Island University is accredited by the Middle States Association of Colleges and Schools.

Up to 60 semester hours of credit are accepted toward the B.A. degree from the following sources: transfer credits from other accredited institutions of higher education, College-Level Examination Program (CLEP) tests, military service, and College Board Advanced Placement examinations. Credit may also be awarded for learning acquired through life experience. Such learning must be documented and evaluated by the Friends World faculty.

Academic Facilities

Each of the regional centers maintains a small library of books and materials relating to the regional culture, as well as a resource file of individual and institutional contacts and advisers that students use in developing and carrying out their field studies. In addition, the centers often make cooperative arrangements with local facilities in the region, such as libraries, language institutes, research laboratories, and other colleges and universities.

Costs

For 1999–2000, tuition was $15,340 per year. Tuition usually increases about 5 percent each year. Room and board costs vary from center to center. Books, supplies, and personal expenses (exclusive of international travel) average $1625 per semester.

Financial Aid

Aid is awarded on the basis of need, as determined by the College Scholarship Service, using the Free Application for Federal Student Aid (FAFSA). Long Island University participates in most of the federal and state programs of aid for U.S. students, including the Federal Pell Grant, Work-Study, Direct Student Loan, and Perkins Loan programs. Students who are not U.S. citizens are ineligible for the aid programs listed above. They may be given partial tuition grants but will need to cover the balance of tuition and all living and travel costs from their own resources.

Merit scholarships are awarded to entering first-year students with a cumulative high school average of 90 percent or above and a demonstrated commitment to community service work. The merit grant is also offered to students transferring into Friends World who have completed at least 24 credit hours in the past academic year and who have at least a 3.0 cumulative academic average. Nontraditional credit is also accepted.

Faculty

Friends World Program has a 35-member faculty (supported by a Southampton College faculty of 72) drawn from ten countries and commanding twenty-five languages. A worldwide 7:1 (15:1 in the U.S.) student-faculty ratio emphasizes Friends World's commitment to personalized learning. Each of the Program centers is staffed by a core group of faculty advisers and draws adjunct faculty members from other institutions and professional groups in the region. In addition, scores of field advisers provide supervision and support for individual students during field studies.

Student Government

Students and faculty members participate together in the governance of each regional learning community. The "World Conference" of the Program includes faculty and student representatives from each regional center. This weeklong gathering produces a series of recommendations on educational and governance matters.

Admission Requirements

The Program seeks self-reliant, mature, intelligent, and world-minded men and women of all nationalities, races, and socioeconomic groups. Completion of a college-preparatory high school program is generally required, although applicants presenting a passing score on the GED test or life experience credit are also considered. Early admission is offered to qualified high school juniors. Programs are also available for transfer students and for visiting students from other colleges and universities who desire a semester or year of study abroad.

Application and Information

Friends World Program operates on a rolling admission basis with no application deadline. Information can be obtained by writing or calling the admissions office.

Admissions
Friends World Program
Long Island University-Southampton College
239 Montauk Highway
Southampton, New York 11968

Telephone: 631-287-8474
Fax: 631-287-8463
E-mail: fw@southampton.liunet.edu
World Wide Web: http://www.liu.edu

A Friends World student makes his way up the Ganges River in India.

LONG ISLAND UNIVERSITY, SOUTHAMPTON COLLEGE

SOUTHAMPTON, NEW YORK

The College

Southampton College, with a current undergraduate enrollment of 1,476, is one of three residential campuses of Long Island University, the eighth-largest independent university in the country. Its blend of strong academic programs, personal attention, and spectacular location has attracted students from the Northeast, across the United States, and around the globe. Southampton's 110-acre campus is nestled in the Shinnecock Hills of beautiful eastern Long Island and is surrounded by pristine bays and the Atlantic Ocean. The campus's forty-three modern buildings house spacious classrooms, state-of-the-art laboratories, comfortable dormitories, and social and administrative facilities. Dormitories consist of suites with four (in most cases double) bedrooms, a living area, and a bath. Students have the option of choosing co-ed or single-sex dorms. Smoke-free and honors dorms are also available.

The College's gymnasium, with a capacity of 1,400, is the site of many concerts and athletic events.

A wide range of intercollegiate NCAA Division II sports are available, including basketball, lacrosse, soccer, tennis, and volleyball for men and basketball, soccer, softball, tennis, and volleyball for women. Intramural and club sports are also available.

Students may have cars and motorcycles on campus. Student resident assistants are available at all times for assistance. Medical, counseling, and placement services are also available. In addition, Southampton's Student Activities Office provides students with the opportunity to organize on-campus events, ranging from informal poetry readings to large concerts.

A variety of noncredit continuing education courses and lectures are offered. At the graduate level, Southampton offers Master of Science degrees in accounting and in education (elementary and reading), a Master of Professional Studies in gerontology, a Master of Fine Arts in English and writing, and a five-year B.S./M.S. dual degree in accounting.

Location

Southampton's location offers the best of both worlds, the spectacular beaches, fine dining, and shopping of a world-renowned summer resort combined with the excitement, culture, and employment opportunities of New York City only 90 miles away (1¾ hours by car, 2 hours by Long Island Railroad). The surrounding Hamptons are a haven for famous artists and writers, many of whom teach at the College. During the fall, winter, and spring, Southampton's shops, restaurants, museums, and art galleries remain open, providing a sophisticated and stimulating yet peaceful environment for living and learning. As the oldest English settlement in New York State (1640), the town of Southampton also offers a rich historical setting to enjoy and explore.

Majors and Degrees

Southampton offers the Bachelor of Arts degree in fine arts, elementary education (N–6), English and writing, environmental studies, history/political science, liberal studies, psychology, secondary education (biology, 7–12; English, 7–12; social studies, 7–12), and sociology. The Bachelor of Science degree is offered in accounting and chemistry, art teaching (K–12), environmental science and marine science (each with concentrations in biology and chemistry), interdisciplinary psychology/biology, and psychology/biology. Both the Bachelor of Arts and the Bachelor of Science degrees are offered in biology and business. The Bachelor of Fine Arts degree is offered in art and communication arts.

Students may minor in all major areas as well as in languages, music, and theater. Those who major or minor in secondary education are eligible to apply for certification from New York State upon graduation.

Academic Program

Southampton's academic year is based on a two-term fall/spring calendar, with a winter intersession and two summer sessions offered from May through August.

Basic curriculum requirements include two courses in fine arts, three courses in English, and two courses each in humanities, natural science, and social science. Requirements for graduation include 128 semester hour credits with a grade point average of at least 2.0 (on a 4.0 scale).

The Long Island University Plan offers Southampton students a program of classroom study combined with professional work experience to help them gain the hands-on experience that is so critical to prospective employers while defraying the cost of their college education. Academic, career, and personal counseling, as well as development of essential literacies in writing, technology, science, and culture, are also stressed. Cooperative education, a combination of classroom learning and major-related employment experience, is also available for all areas of study. Co-op students may choose from more than 3,000 paid professional positions.

Students who perform at a superior level are invited to be part of Southampton's Honors Program. The College's Freshman Program, designed to ease the transition from high school to the college environment and to enhance a student's opportunities for success, includes an extended 1-credit orientation course, intense advising, upperclass peer counseling, and freshman dormitory clusters.

Off-Campus Arrangements

Southampton offers a wide range of off-campus learning experiences, including the Friends World Program, which provides opportunities to study in China, Costa Rica, England, India, Israel, Japan, and across the United States; SEAmester, a nine-week sailing adventure aboard a schooner with ports of call from Maine to the Bahamas; Tropical Marine Biology, an exploration of Australia's Great Barrier Reef and other exotic South Sea environments through snorkeling, SCUBA diving, and lectures; Spring in Australia, the study of Australia's environment through field trips, site visits, research, and extended travel; Australearn, the study of the ecosystems of the tropical coastal regions of Australia; and exchange programs with Southampton University and Winchester College in England as well as Queensland University in Australia.

Internships that are specifically tailored for marine and environmental science students include work at Brookhaven National Laboratory, Skiowa Institute for Oceanography, Osborne Laboratories, National Oceanic and Atmospheric Administration, and Woods Hole Laboratories. Internships are also available for business, education, social science, English and writing and science majors.

Academic Facilities

Southampton's library houses more than 145,000 volumes, 10,000 pamphlets, 140,400 microforms, and nearly 900 recordings and subscribes to 660 periodicals. Long Island University's 2.6-million volume collection is also available to Southampton students through an automated information retrieval system.

The College offers state-of-the-art computer facilities, including the Academic Center Computer Lab, a twenty-five-station Pentium II lab; the Queen Anne Computer Center, with twenty-two Pentium PCs, four Macintosh Computers, and a Macintosh color scanner in addition to twenty Pentium 200MMX multimedia computers, a color flatbed scanner, and a PostScript Laser Jet printer; the Ada Lovelace Computer Off-center with a twenty-station Pentium, 200MMX multimedia classroom, LaserJet PostScript printer, a 37" screen faculty presentation system, and a flatbed color scanner; the Business Center Computer Lab, which features ten Pentium multimedia computers; the Fine Arts Computer Lab, including fourteen Power Macintoshes, five Pentium PCs, a networked Epson Stylus Color 3000 printer, two flatbed scanners, and a slide scanner; the H.E.O.P. Computer Lab with eight Pentium PCs and a networked LaserJet printer; the Library Computer Lab, which contains four multimedia 586 class computers, four Pentium-class PCs, and a networked laser printer; and the Technology Center's Island Room, which has twenty Silicon Graphics workstations, a dedicated Silicon Graphics Origin200 server, and a large assortment of scanners, VCRs, and printers.

Southampton students can connect from their dorm rooms to the College's campuswide computer network, which offers Internet access at more than twenty times the speed of a modem connection. Students provide their own computers, and a one-time fee is charged for network card and installation. No additional fees are charged for online time or usage.

Teaching facilities include Chancellors Hall, the academic center; an on-campus Marine Station; a fleet of twelve marine research vessels, including the 44-foot RV Paumanouk; psychology/biology laboratories; photography, sculpture, welding, painting, and ceramics studios; a metal-casting facility; music practice studios; computer laboratories; chemistry, biology, geology, and statistical laboratories; a learning laboratory; and WPBX, a 25,000-watt National Public Radio affiliate. The 440-seat Avram Theatre and the Avram Art Gallery are the sites of lectures, dramatic productions, concerts, and art exhibits.

Costs

The tuition for 1999–2000 was $15,340. The standard room and board fee, based on a double-occupancy room and nineteen meals per week, was $7500 per year; other options are available. Tuition usually increases by approximately 5 percent each year. Room and board charges usually increase by approximately 5 percent each year. To estimate charges for 2000–01, add to the charges above by using these estimated percentage increases. The cost of books is about $500 per year. Laboratory fees, travel expenses, and incidental costs vary.

Financial Aid

Scholarships based on academic merit range from $1000 to full tuition, renewable annually. Talent scholarships of $1000 to $6000 are offered in art and writing. Athletic scholarships are also available and are based on talent, determined by Southampton coaches.

Other financial aid awards administered by the College are based on financial need and academic promise. These include special scholarships and state and federal assistance, including Federal Supplemental Educational Opportunity Grants, Federal Work-Study awards, and Federal Perkins Loans.

Candidates for admission requesting financial aid should submit their application, along with the College's aid form, well in advance of the March 1 deadline. All students applying for financial aid must also submit the Free Application for Federal Student Aid (FAFSA), which can be obtained from any high school guidance office or college financial aid office. Southampton's FAFSA code is 002755.

Faculty

Southampton has an accomplished teaching faculty with a strong sense of obligation to and interest in their students. Eighty-eight percent of the faculty members hold appropriate terminal degrees. Faculty members also serve as advisers to students. Most classes are small. Individualized attention from the faculty helps students realize their maximum academic potential. The student-faculty ratio of 11:1 allows for student-oriented courses and policies.

Student Government

Southampton has a representative student government that deals with all aspects of student life. Student committees meet with faculty committees to help formulate academic and fiscal policies. Students are also represented in a University-wide student government organization.

Admission Requirements

Admission to Southampton is based upon the College's evaluation of the applicant's potential for a profitable experience. The Admissions Office feels it is essential not only that the applicant meet the College's standards but also that the College meet the applicant's expectations. Therefore, an interview is recommended. The applicant's performance in secondary school (and college, if applicable) and a counselor's remarks are perhaps the most important considerations for admission. SAT I or ACT scores are required for all students, and TOEFL scores are required for students whose native language is not English.

Southampton offers early admission to qualified high school juniors. Through prior arrangement with his or her high school, a student can receive a secondary school diploma upon completion of the freshman year of College.

New undergraduate applicants must have graduated from high school or have qualified for an equivalency diploma. Transfer students with an A.A. or A.A.S. degree receive credit for all courses (including grades of D) taken as part of the associate degree program. Transfer students without an associate degree receive transfer credit for all liberal arts courses completed with a grade of C (2.0) or higher. Up to 68 credit hours may be transferred from any accredited two-year institution. Up to 98 credit hours may be transferred from an accredited four-year institution. Transfer students must submit a transcript from every college attended as well as proof of high school graduation.

A total of 64 hours of credit by examination can be accepted under the following programs: CLEP (administered by the College Board) with a grade of C or above; CPEP (administered by the New York State Department of Education) with a grade of C or above; and the GED college-level examination (administered by DANTES, formerly the United States Armed Forces Institute) with a score in the 50th percentile or above. Credits earned by examination may lead to a waiver of course requirements or be accepted as elective credits. It is also possible to receive credit for life experience.

Application and Information

Applications for fall entry should be completed prior to August 15; for spring entry, by January 15. Completed applications for admission and financial aid, transcripts, SAT I or ACT scores, TOEFL scores for students whose native language is not English, school recommendations, and all inquiries should be sent to:

Admissions
Long Island University
Southampton College
239 Montauk Highway
Southampton, New York 11968
Telephone: 631-283-4000
Fax: 631-287-8125
E-mail: info@southampton.liu.edu

LORAS COLLEGE
DUBUQUE, IOWA

The College

Loras College, Iowa's oldest college, was founded in 1839. Loras' liberal arts curriculum promotes learning of the broadest kind. The Catholic-Christian tradition of Loras nourishes heart and soul, while its small, comfortable size gives students room to discover themselves. The College's 1,800 men and women students come from thirty-two states and sixteen countries. Included in *Barron's Best Buys in College Education* and *Ruggs Recommendations*, Loras ranks thirty-seventh among the nation's 232 Catholic colleges in the total number of students later earning a doctorate. Of those students who received B.A. degrees from Loras over the last three years, 94 percent were employed full-time or attending graduate school within one year of graduation.

In addition to its academic strength, Loras offers a variety of activities for students to engage in outside of the classroom. Sixty organizations, including social and service sororities and fraternities, encourage involvement and provide a sense of belonging to college life. Student services include the international and multicultural affairs office, personal and psychological counseling offices, a career services center, and campus ministry, all housed in a $7-million campus center. Also in the center are recreational facilities that host weekly activities such as dances, contests, game shows, concerts, and guest speakers. One of the nation's leading intramural sports programs is organized from the beautiful Graber Sports Center, a $4-million complex. Loras athletes compete in twenty-one intercollegiate sports affiliated with the NCAA Division III. Each year, Loras hosts the National Catholic Basketball Tournament. This tournament attracts teams from across the nation to compete for the championship title.

A variety of residence hall living options are available for Loras students, including three coeducational residence halls, an all-women's residence hall, and an all-men's residence hall. An apartment-style complex, new residence hall and arts complex, and fifteen houses are also available to juniors and seniors.

Location

Loras College's 60-acre campus stands atop one of the Mississippi River's highest bluffs in historic Dubuque, at the junction of Iowa, Illinois, and Wisconsin. The campus is situated in a residential area, 10 blocks from the center of town, and is a relatively short drive from Chicago, the Twin Cities, Madison, and Des Moines. The picturesque city of Dubuque, Iowa's oldest city, has been nurtured through the years by men and women who have left a rich legacy in Victorian mansions, Tiffany-windowed churches, and grand public buildings. Today, many historic structures are restored as museums, art galleries, hotels, restaurants, and antique and specialty shops. With the Five Flags Civic Center, the Grand Opera House, greyhound racing, cable cars, trolleys, riverboats, 26 miles of biking and hiking trails, and downhill skiing, Dubuque offers natural beauty, historical significance, and year-round fun and excitement.

Majors and Degrees

Loras College offers four-year undergraduate programs based in a liberal arts tradition and leading to the Bachelor of Arts, Bachelor of Science, and Bachelor of Music degrees. Majors offered include accounting, art (education and studio), biochemistry, biological research, biology, business (finance, human resource management, management, management information systems, and marketing), chemistry, classical studies, computer science, criminal justice, electromechanical engineering, economics, education (early childhood, elementary, secondary, and special), engineering physics, English (literature and writing), general science, history, international business, international studies, mathematics, medical technology, modern foreign languages (French, German, and Spanish), music (applied and education), parish ministry, philosophy, physical education, physics, political science, psychology, psychology/gerontology, religious studies, social work, sociology, speech communication (journalism, media—radio and TV, public address, and public relations), sports management, and sports science. In addition, individualized majors may be arranged.

Loras offers the following preprofessional programs in cooperation with other institutions: architecture, dentistry, ecclesiastics, engineering, law, medicine, nursing, optometry, osteopathy, physical therapy, and veterinary medicine.

Academic Program

Requirements for the Bachelor of Arts or Bachelor of Science degree include completion of core courses that demonstrate effective communication in critical thinking, oral expression, and written expression. Students must also complete an additional distribution of credits in their area of concentration; 12 credits each in the social and behavioral studies, natural science, and philosophy and religious studies divisions; and 15 credits in the humanities division. A minimum of 120 credits is required for a bachelor's degree. Successful completion of a thesis and/or a comprehensive examination is required, according to the department or division in which a student takes an area of concentration.

Advanced standing, accelerated degree programs, honors programs, and graduate courses that are open to undergraduates for credit are all available. Most students take 15 credits of course work during each of the two semesters in the academic year, which usually begins in late August and ends in May.

Off-Campus Arrangements

In addition to opportunities for internships in 80 percent of all academic majors, Loras provides a wide range of opportunities through its Center for Experiential Learning. The center sponsors programs for credit that combine classroom work, internships, and service learning on five continents. Nationally, Loras students may study and intern with peers in Dubuque and Chicago. Internationally, they study and learn through service in Dublin, Ireland; Santiago, Spain; Lviv, Ukraine; and Pretoria, South Africa. They may also intern and serve at sites in Bangladesh, Colombia, England, and Japan.

Academic Facilities

The Wahlert Memorial Library, which opened in 1960, is currently one of the three largest private collections in Iowa, with holdings of 431,445 items, subscriptions to more than 1,100 periodicals, a depository for state and federal documents, and a collection of maps numbering about 5,000. The library houses an outstanding rare book collection that includes, among other items, a manuscript collection dating back to the twelfth century and sixty-one incunables printed through the year 1500, giving Loras College the largest such collection in the state. In 1995, the Horizon Automated Library Software System was installed.

There are approximately 120 microcomputers located in various labs around campus available for student use. These include approximately ninety Compaq DeskPro 2000s and thirty Power Macintosh computers connected to scanners and laser and dot-matrix printers. Dial-up access as well as Internet access are available.

Loras College is connected to the Internet, allowing students to communicate with friends and relatives at other institutions also connected to the Internet through e-mail. There are also a number of bulletin board systems and libraries available via the connection. There are no time limits or charges for this service.

The computer center staff is available to help students select, purchase, and use microcomputer hardware and software to meet their personal computing needs. Students and faculty and staff members are eligible for discounts on purchases.

Costs
Estimated costs for 2000–01 are $15,100 for tuition and $5600 for room and board.

Financial Aid
Loras is committed to helping its students. Eighty percent of Loras students receive more than $17 million in scholarships, grants, loans, and employment. Both need-based and merit-based programs are available. Students seeking assistance should apply as soon after January 1 as possible and no later than April 15. Most types of financial assistance require completion of a need analysis form—the Free Application for Federal Student Aid (FAFSA). Loras College grants provide qualified students with as much as $8000 per year, for which students may reapply each year. Academic scholarships based on class rank, test scores, and competition can supply from $2500 to full tuition, room, and board per year. State of Iowa Scholarships, Federal Stafford Student Loans, Federal Perkins Loans, Iowa PLUS loans, Federal Pell Grants, Federal Supplemental Educational Opportunity Grants, Iowa Tuition Grants, and Iowa Supplemental Grants may also help make up a student's financial assistance package. Campus employment is available to those demonstrating financial need.

Faculty
The outstanding Loras teaching faculty of 120 full-time and 25 part-time members is composed of laymen, laywomen, priests, and sisters. More than 80 percent of the full-time faculty members hold the highest degree in their field. The student-faculty ratio of 13:1 ensures students individual attention from instructors in an open, friendly, and responsive atmosphere. All students are taught by Loras teaching faculty.

Student Government
Students may serve on College-wide committees with faculty members and administrators. Leadership of the student body is vested in the Student Senate and various class officers. The College Activities Board (CAB) offers additional opportunities for student involvement.

Admission Requirements
Each year, more than 1,200 applicants seek admission to Loras College. The approximately 450 first-year students selected each year have an average composite ACT score of 23. It is preferable that the high school program include 4 units of English and 3 units each in mathematics and natural science.

Early entrance and deferred entrance may be arranged.

Application and Information
Applications are processed on a rolling basis, and prospective students may apply to Loras anytime after their junior year of high school. Loras makes every effort to process applications within three weeks. Transfer students' credits are evaluated on an individual basis.

The College's innovative registration program allows first-year and transfer students to register on a one-to-one basis with their faculty adviser.

For more information about Loras College, students should contact:

Tim Hauber
Director of Admissions
Loras College
1450 Alta Vista
Dubuque, Iowa 52004-0178
Telephone: 319-588-7236
          800-245-6727 (toll-free nationwide)
World Wide Web: http://www.loras.edu

The benefits of being in a smaller college community include accessible classes, approachable professors, and the opportunity to make friends easily and get involved in a variety of activities.

LOUISIANA SCHOLARS' COLLEGE AT NORTHWESTERN STATE UNIVERSITY OF LOUISIANA

NATCHITOCHES, LOUISIANA

The College

Established in 1987 by the Louisiana Board of Regents for Higher Education, the Louisiana Scholars' College at Northwestern State University serves as the state's designated honors college. For the modest cost of tuition at a public institution, the College offers highly motivated students a unique educational opportunity designed specifically to meet their needs. An important part of the four-year Common Curriculum is the opportunity to work with faculty mentors and bright undergraduate colleagues as they explore the best that has been thought, written, and created. In seminars, directed study, and laboratory sessions, students are intellectually challenged by faculty members whose primary responsibility is honors education. The Common Curriculum is built around the liberal arts tradition and is completed by all students. Each student designs an individual plan of study with his or her faculty adviser, focusing on a traditional major or one of the three areas of concentration: humanities and social thought, scientific inquiry, or the fine and performing arts.

Living together in an honors residence hall and attending most of their classes in Morrison Hall, students with diverse interests but similar abilities make up a distinctive community of some 250 within the larger University community of more than 8,500. The residence hall has suites with two bedrooms and a bath. One floor houses men, and two floors are reserved for women. Its lounges are frequently the setting for functions, from seminars to informal chats with professors. A computer lab was installed in the dormitory in fall 1999.

Students in the College actively participate in the full range of University activities, including student government, athletics, media, and social organizations. From football games to soccer matches to rowing races on the Cane River, students have a variety of sporting events to choose from, all of which they are admitted to free of charge. Students who wish to participate rather than watch can take advantage of bicycles, canoes, paddle boats, and other equipment available for their use, or they may join one of the many intercollegiate and intramural teams. Golfers, swimmers, tennis players, and others enjoy the athletic facilities available on campus.

More than 130 clubs and organizations offer a range of other activities as well. Students in the Scholars' College participate in theater, play in the state's largest marching band, join fraternities and sororities, become disc jockeys for KNWD (the campus radio station), or write for the campus paper, just to name a few.

Location

Scholars' College borders the historic district of Natchitoches, the oldest permanent European settlement in the Louisiana Purchase, today a pleasant town of 20,000 and the parish seat. Nearby are the plantations of the Cane River and the Kisatchie National Forest. Interstate 49 connects Natchitoches with Alexandria, 50 miles to the south, and with Shreveport, Louisiana's third-largest city, 60 miles to the north. New Orleans, Dallas, and Houston are approximately 4 hours away.

Majors and Degrees

Students complete a four-year undergraduate program designed in a liberal arts tradition, which leads to a Bachelor of Arts or Bachelor of Science degree. Students choose between an individually designed plan of study and a more traditional major. The majors include accounting, anthropology, art, biology, business administration, chemistry, computer information systems, English, history, journalism, mathematics, music, physics, political science, psychology, social sciences, sociology, and theater. An important part of an academic plan is the senior thesis or project that is required of all students.

The individualized plan of study includes one of three concentration areas: Humanities and Social Thought, Scientific Inquiry, and Fine and Performing Arts. Each concentration emphasizes the flexibility of mind, breadth of experience, and solid grounding in the liberal arts and sciences increasingly demanded by professions such as medicine, law, business, and scientific research. Students, under the guidance of one or more faculty advisers, define a principle of coherence in their studies and seek to gain a wide experience of the disciplines in one of the concentrations.

Each concentration demands that students complete at least 45 credits in the appropriate disciplines. Students in Humanities and Social Thought choose from courses in such fields as history, literature, economics, philosophy, classics, sociology, and modern languages. Those in Scientific Inquiry select from offerings in biology, chemistry, mathematics, physics, and related fields. Students in the Fine and Performing Arts focus on the history and performance of music, art, dance, and theater.

Academic Program

While students deepen their understanding of a specific area of inquiry, they take part in an extensive four-year Common Curriculum. Central to this curriculum is a series of seminars devoted to great works and significant ideas that have shaped the world. In the first two years, students in Texts and Traditions: The Shaping of Western Culture move chronologically from antiquity through the twentieth century, reading works by such major figures as Homer, Plato, Dante, Galileo, Shakespeare, Jefferson, Mozart, Darwin, Dostoyevsky, and Woolf. Subject to periodic revision, the reading list, like the title of the course, emphasizes that our cultural inheritance consists of conflicting ideas and sharply antagonistic perspectives.

With an increased awareness of the importance of independent analysis and lively debate, juniors continue their study of central texts in a one-semester seminar, Democratic Vistas: The Idea of America. Seniors participate in a two-semester colloquium in which they examine from their many disciplinary perspectives an issue of contemporary concern. Topics such as "Liberty and the First Amendment" and "Crime and Punishment" are chosen and developed each year by the faculty and the senior class.

To ensure a comparable understanding of the methods and accomplishments of the sciences, students also enroll in majors'-level courses in the physical and life sciences. While developing skill in quantitative reasoning and experimental procedure, together with an understanding of the main theoretical postulates of modern science, students explore important areas of knowledge in biology, chemistry, physics, and mathematics. Their study emphasizes the complex relationships between and among these disciplines as well as those techniques of inquiry common to all scientific learning.

Other requirements of the Common Curriculum include the study of a modern or classical language and writing-intensive seminars on a variety of topics. A special orientation seminar and a computer applications course prepare entering students for the demands of the curriculum.

Off-Campus Arrangements

Through the International Student Exchange Program, students are eligible to study for a semester or year at any of more than 100 institutions abroad. Students choose to go for any of the three semesters, fall, spring, or summer, or combine the semesters for up to a year abroad at the same cost as residential study on the NSU campus. Also available in the summer are courses taught abroad by the University's faculty members for credit. A trip to Italy to study the classics in depth or a trip to northern Europe's leading businesses are examples of what these courses have to offer.

Academic Facilities

Centrally located between the honors dorm, Watson Library, and laboratory facilities, Scholars' College is housed in its own academic building on a tree-shaded quadrangle. Serving as the center of the College, it contains classrooms, faculty members' offices, administrative support, a networked PC lab with Internet connections, and a language room equipped with an international satellite downlink. The University is the home of the Williamson Museum, which specializes in the anthropology of the region. The Louisiana Folklife Center, also on campus, documents and preserves Louisiana's traditional arts. In addition, the campus houses the National Center for Preservation Training and Technology, administered by the National Park Service.

Costs

For the 1999–2000 academic year (fall and spring semesters), in-state tuition and student fees were $2287 plus a student-assessed technology fee of $5 per credit hour. Room and board, based on double occupancy, were $2756. Out-of-state tuition was $6577 plus the technology fee. A student can expect to pay $400 each semester for books.

Financial Aid

Students admitted to the Louisiana Scholars' College are candidates for the University's most prestigious academic scholarships, including the Academic Excellence Award and the Board of Trustees scholarships. Work-assistantships are also available; students who qualify receive campus jobs, for example, as computer-room tutors, laboratory aides, and research assistants. Non-Louisiana residents may also qualify for out-of-state fee waivers.

Faculty

Fourteen full-time faculty members, all of whom hold doctorates, represent the traditional disciplines of the liberal arts and sciences. They were selected, in national searches, for their scholarly achievements and their dedication to teaching and learning with undergraduates in a liberal arts setting. Courses are typically taught as seminars and have limited enrollment, usually no more than 20, so that each student can participate actively and receive individual attention. Faculty members are readily available for consultation.

Student Government

Students in the College regularly serve as leaders in the University's Student Government Association and Student Activities Board. In the College itself, students take primary responsibility for fostering a community of scholars. College Forum meetings are held regularly for all students and faculty members to discuss matters of mutual concern, including course offerings, reading lists, and faculty appointments.

Admission Requirements

The Selection Committee seeks highly motivated students who wish to pursue a multidisciplinary liberal arts education. Applicants first submit an application, which includes an essay, and are then interviewed by a member of the faculty. The committee examines high school transcripts, academic honors, extracurricular achievements, standardized test scores (SAT I or ACT), and letters of recommendation. Campus tours and class visits are strongly recommended.

Application and Information

More information concerning the College curriculum is available. Admission decisions are made on a rolling basis as applicants' files are completed. Students are encouraged to complete their admission and scholarship applications by December 1 in order to make the first scholarship priority deadline, but applications are considered until the freshman class is filled. Inquiries from transfer students are welcome.

Inquiries and application requests should be directed to:

Admissions Coordinator
Louisiana Scholars' College
Northwestern State University of Louisiana
Natchitoches, Louisiana 71497
Telephone: 318-357-4578
                800-838-2208 (toll-free)
Fax: 318-357-5908
E-mail: lscrecruits@nsula.edu
WWW: http://vic.nsula.edu/scholars_college/

One of the advantages of the Scholars' College is the opportunity for hands-on experience in a number of disciplines.

LOUISIANA STATE UNIVERSITY AND AGRICULTURAL AND MECHANICAL COLLEGE

BATON ROUGE, LOUISIANA

The University

Louisiana State University (LSU), the state's oldest and largest institution of higher learning, was founded in 1860 and moved to Baton Rouge in 1869. The campus occupies 2,000 acres on the southern edge of the city, just east of the Mississippi River. More than 250 buildings make up the central part of the campus.

From its initial emphasis on agriculture and engineering, the University has evolved into a major research institution, the state's only Carnegie Research I University. LSU's Center for Advanced Microstructures and Devices, an Aquaculture Research Facility, a Students Recreational Sports Complex, and a Computer Center are just a few examples of the rapid expansion the University is experiencing. LSU also holds the distinction of being one of a select number of universities in the country with both land-grant and sea-grant status and is actively pursuing space-grant status.

The campus community offers a wide variety of social, cultural, and recreational opportunities and is enriched by the presence of a number of nationally recognized writers, musicians, and artists who serve on the humanities faculty. The University has a predominantly Louisianan student community, but many of LSU's nearly 30,000 students come from all fifty states and 120 other countries. There are numerous extracurricular activities that range from sailing to billiards. LSU fields NCAA Division I men's and women's teams in basketball, golf, swimming, tennis, and track and field; women's teams in gymnastics, soccer, softball, and volleyball; and men's teams in baseball and football. Club sports include karate, rugby, soccer, tae kwon do, volleyball, and waterskiing. LSU supports one of the largest coeducational intramural sports programs in the country. The LSU Union's facilities provide areas for eating and studying, meeting rooms, two theaters, an art gallery, a bookstore, and a U.S. post office. More than 250 student organizations serve as focal points for specific interests and social activities. There are social fraternities and sororities on campus as well as churches, religious centers, and nondenominational units. LSU residence halls offer a variety of accommodations.

At the graduate level, Louisiana State University offers programs that lead to the degrees of Doctor of Philosophy, Doctor of Musical Arts, Master of Arts, Master of Arts in Liberal Arts, Master of Fine Arts, Master of Landscape Architecture, Master of Science, Master of Science in Biological and Agricultural Engineering, Master of Science in Chemical Engineering, Master of Science in Civil Engineering, Master of Science in Electrical Engineering, Master of Science in Industrial Engineering, Master of Science in Mechanical Engineering, Master of Science in Petroleum Engineering, Master of Science in Engineering Science, Master of Education, Master of Library and Information Science, Master of Natural Sciences, Master of Mass Communication, Master of Music, Master of Business Administration, Master of Public Administration, and Master of Social Work. In addition, the degrees of Juris Doctor, Master of Public Administration/Juris Doctor, Master of Laws, and Master of Civil Law are offered through the Paul M. Hebert Law Center, and the degree of Doctor of Veterinary Medicine is offered through the School of Veterinary Medicine; both schools are located on the campus. The University also awards the Certificate of Advanced Study in Library and Information Science and the Certificate of Education Specialist.

Location

Louisiana State University is located in Baton Rouge, Louisiana, the state's capital and second-largest city. Baton Rouge has a rapidly growing metropolitan area population of 500,000. The mild Baton Rouge climate makes it possible for students to enjoy outdoor sports and activities all year long. The city of New Orleans is within an hour's drive.

Majors and Degrees

Bachelor's degrees are awarded for the following general curricula (students should consult the LSU *General Catalog* for a complete list of curricula concentrations): accounting; agricultural business; animal, dairy, and poultry sciences; anthropology; architecture; biochemistry; biological engineering; chemical engineering; chemistry; civil engineering; communication disorders; computer engineering; computer science; construction management; dietetics; economics; electrical engineering; elementary grades education; English; environmental engineering; environmental management systems; family, child, and consumer sciences; finance; forestry (forest management); French; general business administration; general studies; geography; geology; German; history; industrial engineering; information systems and decision sciences–management information systems; information systems and decision sciences–operations management; interior design; international studies; international trade and finance; kinesiology; landscape architecture; Latin; liberal arts; management; marketing; mass communication; mathematics; mechanical engineering; microbiology; music; music education; nutrition, food, and culinary sciences; petroleum engineering; philosophy; physics; plant and soil systems; plant biology; political science; psychology; Russian area studies; secondary education; sociology; Spanish; speech communication; studio art; textiles, apparel, and merchandising; theater; vocational education; wildlife and fisheries; and zoology.

Preprofessional programs that do not culminate in a degree from LSU but that enable students to be placed in professional programs are dental hygiene, medical records administration, occupational therapy, ophthalmic medical technology, physician's assistant studies, premedical technology, prenursing, radiological technician studies, rehabilitation counseling, and respiratory therapy.

Academic Program

LSU operates on a traditional two-semester plan with a multiple-session summer term. All students complete a 39-hour general education curriculum in English composition, analytical reasoning, arts, humanities, natural sciences, and social sciences. Freshmen are admitted to the University College Center for the Freshman Year, which is an academic division similar to a medium-sized college in a large university setting. The Center provides individual, academic, and career counseling as well as developmental education courses. Students remain in the Center until they have earned at least 24 semester hours of college-level credit and have met requirements for admission to a senior college. Credit-hour requirements for graduation vary between 128 and 170 semester hours, depending upon the curriculum chosen. Students with strong high school preparation can obtain University credit for Advanced Placement courses. An honors curriculum is available for superior students. A noncredit fourteen-week intensive English and orientation program is offered for international students that begins in January, April, and September.

Off-Campus Arrangements

LSU participates in a cross-registration program with Southern University in Baton Rouge and Baton Rouge Community College. Several cooperative programs either exist or are currently under development. The University also participates in the Academic Common Market, an interstate agreement among thirteen Southern states for sharing special programs. Up to one fourth of the number of hours required for the bachelor's degree may be taken through the Division of Continuing Education by correspondence study, extension courses, or both. The Evening School program provides educational opportunities for students not in residence, and the Office of Academic Programs Abroad administers a number of summer and exchange programs for undergraduate students in various fields and countries.

Academic Facilities

The University libraries offer students and faculty members strong academic support through collections that contain more than 3 million bound volumes, more than 5 million microform holdings, and a manuscript collection of more than 12 million items. The library catalog is computerized and accessible from terminals around campus. Supercomputer facilities are available on campus through the System Network Computer Center (SNCC), which provides computer resources for instruction, research, and administrative data processing. The staff conducts seminars, maintains a broad selection of software, consults with the center's clients, assists with and promotes the use of microcomputers and data communications, and manages distributed computer centers.

Computing supported by SNCC includes microcomputers, superminicomputers, supercomputers, terminals, two major I/O rooms, and data communications. An IBM 3090-600J mainframe computer supported by the MVS/TSO operating system is used for research, administrative data processing, and instruction. An IBM 3084 QX6 processor supported by the VM/CMS operating system and a Data General ECLIPSE MV/10000 are used predominantly for interactive student support. A VAX 8800 processor is available to support interactive graphics.

The LSU museum complex includes the LSU Museum of Art, the Museum of Geoscience, and the Museum of Natural Science. In the Nuclear Science Center, specialized radiation detection and measuring equipment and labs accommodate educational and research activities using nuclear energy technology. The University has extensive studios and practice rooms for the art and performance disciplines and two theaters for performances.

Costs

University fees for 1999–2000 were $1442 per semester for Louisiana residents and $3542 for out-of-state students. There are special fees for graduation, registration of motor vehicles, and advanced standing examinations. Louisiana resident expenses are estimated at $9250 per academic year for fees, room and board, books, and personal expenses. Nonresident expenses are estimated at $14,000 per academic year.

Financial Aid

More than 55 percent of LSU's students receive financial assistance in the form of scholarships, federal and state grants, loans, and student employment. Students should submit the LSU Application for Admission and Scholarship as soon as possible after their junior year of high school. Those students who wish to apply for all of the federally funded financial aid programs (grants, loans, and Federal Work-Study) should complete the Free Application for Federal Student Aid (FAFSA) as soon as possible after January 1 of their senior year. Once enrolled, students are eligible to apply for a number of scholarships that are awarded by specific academic departments. Details are available from LSU's Office of Student Aid and Scholarships, which is located at 202 Himes Hall.

Faculty

LSU's faculty totals 1,345 members. The student-faculty ratio is 18:1. More than 80 percent of the full-time faculty members hold terminal degrees; many have earned national and international distinction. Members of the graduate faculty also teach undergraduate courses. Some undergraduate courses are taught by advanced graduate students who hold teaching assistantships.

Student Government

The Student Government Association is a policymaking body that is composed of students who represent most campus organizations and groups. The Board of Supervisors of the LSU System includes an elected student member. Students serve on a number of faculty senate committees.

Admission Requirements

Starting in fall 2000, students will be automatically admitted to LSU if they meet one of the following three requirements: 1) if they have a high school GPA/ACT score combination of at least 3.5/28 or a GPA/SAT score combination of at least 3.5/1260 and if they have undertaken a rigorous college-preparatory curriculum at an accredited state-approved high school; 2) if they have completed 17.5 specified high school units and have a high school GPA/ACT score combination of at least 2.5/20 (LSU has determined that the following combinations of GPA/ACT scores will be accepted as equivalent: 2.3/23, 2.4/21, and 2.6/19) or a GPA/SAT score combination of at least 2.5/950; or 3) if they have completed 16 of 17.5 specified high school units and have a GPA/ACT score combination of 2.5/22, 2.7/21, or 3.0/20 or a GPA/SAT score combination of at least 2.5/1030, 2.7/990, or 3.0/950. All other students will be considered for admission based on an evaluation of their likelihood of success at LSU.

The specified high school units that are required for automatic admission to LSU are 4 years of English composition and literature, 3 years of college-preparatory mathematics (algebra I and II and geometry, trigonometry, calculus, or another advanced mathematics course), 3 years of natural sciences (biology, chemistry, and physics), 3 years of social studies (1 unit in American history; 1 unit in world history, world geography, or history of western civilization; and 1 unit consisting of courses such as civics, free enterprise, economics, sociology, psychology, and American government), 2 years of the same foreign language, 2 years of approved academic electives, and one semester of computer science. More detailed information is available upon request.

LSU offers early and concurrent admission programs for exceptional students who choose to enroll on a full-time basis or who want to take University courses while still in high school.

Students with previous college or university work from regionally accredited institutions are considered for admission if they have an overall GPA of at least 2.0 on all college work attempted. Transfer students who have earned fewer than 24 semester hours of college-level work (excluding remedial) must also meet the requirements for freshman admissions.

Application and Information

A nonrefundable application fee of $25 must accompany the application for admission. Application deadlines are May 1 for the fall semester and summer term and December 1 for the spring semester. The application deadline for international students is November 1 for the fall semester. Students are encouraged to apply well in advance of the deadlines. Prospective freshmen are advised to apply upon completion of their junior year in high school.

For application forms and additional information, students should contact:

Office of Undergraduate Admissions
110 Thomas Boyd Hall
Louisiana State University
  and Agricultural and Mechanical College
Baton Rouge, Louisiana 70803

Telephone: 225-388-1175
E-mail: lsuadmissions@lsu.edu
World Wide Web: http://www.lsu.edu

LOUISIANA TECH UNIVERSITY
RUSTON, LOUISIANA

The University
Louisiana Tech University, founded in 1894, is a state-supported coeducational university that is accredited by the Commission on Colleges of the Southern Association of Colleges and Schools to award associate, baccalaureate, master's, and doctoral degrees. Enrollment is approximately 10,000 students, and the physical plant has grown to more than 130 buildings. There are approximately 255 acres on the main campus.

Louisiana Tech University competes in Division I athletics, including baseball, basketball, cross-country, football, golf, indoor and outdoor track, softball, tennis, and volleyball. The 84,000-square-foot Lambright Sports Center offers students an opportunity to participate in intramural and fitness programs. The center consists of six basketball courts, twelve racquetball courts, two saunas, two weight rooms, and an indoor jogging track. The natatorium offers year-round swimming in the Olympic-size T-shaped pool. Students have the opportunity to play golf on the University course. They are admitted free of charge to intramural and varsity sports events. More than 180 student organizations (Greek, honors, academic, performing arts, sports, residence hall, and other special interests) are active on campus and in the Ruston community. Popular entertainment and concerts are brought to the campus by the Union Board and Louisiana Tech Concert Association. Approximately 3,000 students reside in University housing. The health center, counseling center, and career planning and placement center are available for use by all students.

In addition to its undergraduate programs, Louisiana Tech University offers numerous master's and doctoral degree programs. Doctoral degrees are awarded in applied computational analysis and modeling, business, counseling psychology, education, and engineering. A specialist's degree is awarded in counseling.

Location
Ruston is located in north-central Louisiana between the cities of Shreveport and Monroe. These nearby cities offer a wide selection of stores, theaters, and fine restaurants and pubs. The Louisiana Downs (horse racing), Red River Revel (festival), Louisiana State Fair, and Independence Bowl are a few of the annual attractions. Because of the mild climate, outdoor recreational opportunities—including hunting, fishing, boating, skiing, tennis, and golf—can be enjoyed throughout most of the year.

Majors and Degrees
Louisiana Tech University awards the Bachelor of Arts, Bachelor of Science, Bachelor of Fine Arts, and Bachelor of General Studies degrees. Majors are offered in accounting, agricultural business, animal science (dairy production, equine studies, livestock production, and pre–veterinary medicine), architecture, art education, aviation, biology (animal biology and molecular biology), biomedical engineering, business administration (business analysis, computer information systems, and general business administration), business economics, chemical engineering, chemistry, civil engineering, computer science, construction engineering technology, elementary education, English (technical writing), environmental science (biological sciences, earth and agricultural sciences, and environmental and occupational health sciences), family infancy and early childhood education (child life, consumer affairs merchandising, early childhood education, family and consumer sciences education, and family studies), finance, fitness/wellness (clinical health fitness), forestry (business management and natural resources management), French, French education, general studies, geography, geology, graphic design, health and physical education, health information administration, history, industrial engineering, interior design, journalism, management (business management and entrepreneurship, human resource management, and production/operation management), marketing, mathematics, mechanical engineering, merchandising and consumer affairs, music, music education (instrument and vocal), nutrition and dietetics, photography, physics, plant sciences (agronomy and horticulture), political science (prelaw), preprofessional speech-language pathology, psychology, secondary education (business, English, mathematics, social studies, and vocational agriculture), Spanish, special education (mild moderate elementary, mild moderate secondary, preschool handicapped, and severe-profound), speech (speech communication and theater), studio, and wildlife conservation (aquatic ecosystems, pre–graduate school, and terrestrial ecosystems). An associate degree is awarded in business technology, general studies, health information technology, and nursing (two-year RN program).

Academic Program
All baccalaureate degree programs include a minimum of 126 semester hours. Minimum graduation requirements include a grade point average of 2.0 (C) on all earned curricular course work. Additional GPA performance may be required in certain colleges. All curricula contain a general education core of 45 semester hours, distributed as follows: 12 of humanities, 9 of natural sciences, 9 of social sciences, 6 of English, 6 of mathematics and computer literacy, and 3 of art. Credit for selected courses may be earned through credit examinations administered by the academic departments, through the Advanced Placement Program of the College Board, and through subject examinations of the College-Level Examination Program.

In its fifty years at Louisiana Tech, the Air Force ROTC has commissioned more than 1,000 graduates into the Air Force. The honors program offers small classes, intellectually challenging professors, and greater interaction with faculty members, while also sponsoring special social, academic, and cultural events.

Louisiana Tech University operates on a quarter calendar with four terms (fall, winter, spring, and summer), and students earn semester-hour credit.

Off-Campus Arrangements
The University has offered an on-base degree program at Barksdale Air Force Base in Bossier City, Louisiana, since 1965. Louisiana Tech University participates in a cross-registration program with Grambling State University and Northeast Louisiana University that makes it possible for students to enroll at any of the universities. The University also participates in the Academic Common Market, an interstate agreement among thirteen Southern states for the sharing of special programs. International study opportunities are available through enrollment in the Tech Rome Program and the London Seminar in International Finance.

Academic Facilities
Prescott Memorial Library offers a full array of informational resources and services. TECHNET is the automated library system that provides access to the Tech Library online catalog and to additional electronic research resources. Located in the library are more than 1.5 million volumes and 2,500 current periodical subscriptions. Tech's library is one of only fifty-three U.S. government regional document depositories, and it is a depository for Louisiana state documents, USGS maps, and Department of Energy contractor reports. Other facilities include the Student Technology Laboratory, with fifty computer workstations providing Internet access and productivity soft-

ware; the Electronic Reference Center, with twenty computer workstations providing electronic catalogs, indexes, and full-text databases; and the Media Center, which includes audio and video services as well as satellite teleconferencing. The library's home page is found at http://www.latech.edu/tech/library.

The Louisiana Tech Computing Center provides centralized computing and consulting support for University activities in areas of instruction, research, and administration. Approximately 1,500 computer nodes are located in college buildings, dormitories, and microcomputer labs. In addition, ninety-six dial-in phone lines (33.6 kbs) are available.

The Center for Rehabilitation Science and Biomedical Engineering (housed in a 63,000-square-foot complex including dormitory space) is recognized at the state, national, and international levels for its work, ranging from the study of disabilities to the application of technology to assist disabled people.

Costs

University tuition for the 2000–01 academic year is $2379 for Louisiana residents, $5799 for nonresidents, and $5919 for international students. These figures are based on 8 semester hours, which is the course load for a full-time student. The cost of room and board is approximately $3030. Special fees are assessed for particular colleges, vehicle registration, and certain academic curricula and courses. All fees are subject to change.

Financial Aid

In 1999–2000, approximately 80 percent of Louisiana Tech students received more than $40 million in student aid funds. Financial assistance includes scholarships, grants, student loans, and student jobs. Students should apply by April 1.

Faculty

The instructional faculty consists of 386 full-time members, 78 percent of whom possess terminal degrees in their respective fields. Most faculty members are actively involved in instruction, research, University service, and student-related activities. The student-faculty ratio is 26:1.

Student Government

Every student enrolled at Louisiana Tech University is a member of the Student Association (SA). The Student Government Association (SGA) is an organization of the SA whose purposes are to serve as a channel of communication to the faculty and administration and to all levels of state government regarding the opinions, wishes, and needs of the SA; to establish, in cooperation with the administration, faculty, and the state of Louisiana, policies affecting the University community; to establish and execute such programs and other projects beneficial to the students; and to promote and improve relations between the Ruston area and the students of Louisiana Tech University. Elections to choose SGA officers are held each spring.

Admission Requirements

Applicants for freshman admission must graduate from an accredited high school and possess an overall 2.0 grade point average (on a 4.0 scale) on the following courses: English, 4 units in courses emphasizing grammar, composition, and literature (English I, II, III, and IV); mathematics, 3 units (2 units of algebra and 1 unit of geometry or a higher level of mathematics for which algebra is a prerequisite); social studies, 3 units (1 unit must be American history); science, 3 units (chemistry, physics, and biology are preferred); and electives, 4½ (foreign languages, social studies, science, mathematics, speech, advanced fine arts, and computer literacy are recommended; no more than 3 elective units may be taken in vocational subjects). Otherwise, students must either rank in the upper 50 percent of their graduating class or have a composite ACT score of at least 22 or a combined SAT I score of at least 1010. All students are encouraged to apply for admission. Louisiana Tech University may admit students not meeting all stated requirements. In such cases, the admission decision is affected by the student's potential for degree completion and the need to enhance the University's demographically diverse student population. Some factors to be considered may include age, experience, ethnic background, and creative talent. Applicants are encouraged to take the ACT or SAT I in their junior year of high school and send scores to the University as soon as possible. An application form and admission information will be sent to the student when scores are received.

Students desiring to transfer to Louisiana Tech University with fewer than 24 semester hours of course work must meet the same requirements as an entering freshman and be eligible to reenter the institution from which he/she is transferring. Students with 24 hours or more must have a 2.0 grade point average (on a 4.0 scale) on all transfer work. Students transferring should submit an application and a complete, official transcript from each college attended, whether or not credit was earned or is transferable.

High school students may be considered for early admission to the University if they meet the following requirements: achieve an overall academic average of 3.0 (B) or better on all work pursued during three years (six semesters) of high school, earn a minimum ACT composite score of 24 or a minimum SAT I combined score of 1090 to be submitted prior to June 1, and receive a recommendation from their high school principal. The student may be enrolled full-time or part-time. Upon completing a minimum of 24 semester hours at the University, the student will be issued a diploma by the high school last attended.

Summer Enrichment at Louisiana Tech is designed to enable students to pursue college credit between their junior and senior years. Students have the option of validating grades and credits received during the summer. The Summer Scholars Program for exceptional students awards scholarships to entering freshmen who want to get an early start by enrolling in the summer quarter.

International applicants must have a minimum 2.5 GPA on all work pursued and an official TOEFL score report of 500 or better. International students must also submit a financial statement. Detailed information regarding international admission may be obtained by contacting the Office of Admissions.

Application and Information

The application and nonrefundable $20 application fee should be submitted to the Office of Admissions by August 1 for admission in the fall quarter, November 1 for the winter, February 1 for the spring, and May 1 for the summer. Deadlines for international students are June 1 for the fall quarter, September 1 for the winter, December 1 for the spring, and March 1 for the summer.

Students with inquiries and requests for application materials should contact:

Office of Admissions
Louisiana Tech University
P.O. Box 3178, Tech Station
Ruston, Louisiana 71272-0001
Telephone: 318-257-3036
        800-LATECH-1 (toll-free)
World Wide Web: http://www.latech.edu

On the campus of Louisiana Tech University.

LOYOLA COLLEGE IN MARYLAND
BALTIMORE, MARYLAND

The College
Loyola College is a private, liberal arts college with the Catholic traditions of the Jesuits and the Sisters of Mercy. It is an educational community of students and faculty cooperating for the intellectual, spiritual, and professional enrichment of all its members and for the improvement of the local community and society in general. The intellectual enterprise is a joint creation of the faculty members and the students. Loyola's current full-time undergraduate enrollment is 3,200 men and women; more than 75 percent of the student body live on campus.

Loyola encourages cocurricular activities that contribute to the academic, social, and spiritual growth of the student. These include social and cultural organizations, Student Government activities, military science activities, national honor societies, and Division I athletic programs such as basketball, crew, cross-country, golf, lacrosse, soccer, swimming and diving, tennis, and volleyball. The majority of the student body participates in the wide variety of intramural sports offered.

In recent years, the College's campus has undergone significant expansion. Completed in 1998, Charleston Lower Courtyard, a town-house complex, is the most recent housing addition. Six apartment complexes and three freshman dormitories also provide Loyola students with on-campus housing. Completed in fall 1999, the Andrew White Student Center provides more dining choices and expanded meeting and recreational space, making it a popular hub of the remodeled campus. The Student Center also provides facilities for athletics and the fine arts, including the McManus Theatre, the 4,000-seat Reitz Arena, and an Olympic-size pool. The center also has an art gallery, classrooms, and music, photography, and studio art labs. Adding to Loyola's sports facilities will be the new Recreation and Sports Complex, scheduled for completion in December 2000. This 110-square-foot athletic facility will provide another Olympic-size pool, squash courts, a climbing wall, running tracks, and outdoor playing fields.

Location
The Loyola College campus is located in a lovely residential area of north Baltimore, 5 miles from the Inner Harbor area. This location offers the student the advantages of quiet residential living with the attractions of city life. The metropolitan area has a wide variety of theaters, museums, professional and intercollegiate sports events, and historical points of interest. Other colleges and universities in the vicinity help to expand the social calendar.

Majors and Degrees
Loyola College offers programs in thirty-three majors. The Bachelor of Arts degree is awarded in classics, communications, economics, education, English, fine arts, French, German, history, Latin, philosophy, political science, psychology, sociology, Spanish, speech pathology/audiology, theology, and writing. The Bachelor of Business Administration degree is awarded in accounting, business economics, finance, general business, international business, management, management information systems, and marketing. The Bachelor of Science degree is awarded in biology, chemistry, computer science, electrical engineering, engineering science, mathematical science, and physics.

Academic Program
The curriculum at Loyola College is divided into three parts: the core, the major, and electives. The core contains those courses that Loyola College considers essential to the liberal arts curriculum. These courses, which are required of all students regardless of major, are completed during the freshman and sophomore years. The core consists of a classical or modern language, English literature, poetry and drama, writing, mathematics and natural science, social science, fine arts, history, philosophy, ethics, and theology. The major enables students to pursue in depth their specialized area of study. Electives give students the opportunity to broaden their intellectual and cultural background in areas of special interest. To prepare for graduate study, students may enroll in one of the four preprofessional programs: dental, law, medical, or veterinary.

An honors program and honors housing are available to outstanding students. The honors program stresses independent work by specially grouped students in many of the core courses. Honors housing provides an environment conducive to study and close social interaction.

Off-Campus Arrangements
Loyola College participates in a cooperative program with the College of Notre Dame of Maryland, Johns Hopkins University, Goucher College, Morgan State University, Towson University, the Peabody Conservatory of Music, and the Maryland Institute of Art. Loyola students may cross-register at any of these area colleges and universities.

Students in good academic standing may pursue studies abroad through Loyola's programs in Leuven, Belgium; Bangkok, Thailand; Alcalá, Spain; Melbourne, Australia; and Newcastle, England. Loyola has programs available in twenty-eight other countries in conjunction with other schools.

Academic Facilities
The Donnelly Science Center has recently been expanded, making it the largest academic building on the Evergreen campus. It features state-of-the-art laboratories for tomorrow's scientists and health-care professionals and new classrooms and offices that give faculty members even more space for instruction and research.

With the opening of the spring 2000 semester, Loyola welcomes the new Sellinger School of Business. For the first time since its formation in 1980, the School of Business and Management is headquartered in one central location on the Evergreen campus. Highlights of this newest academic addition include eleven classrooms, five seminar rooms, fifty-two faculty and departmental offices, and an information center. Also, 90 percent of Sellinger classes are taught in Internet-linked, multimedia classrooms.

A modern library shared by Loyola College and the College of Notre Dame of Maryland has a capacity of 349,000 volumes, making it one of the largest college libraries in the country.

Costs
For 2000–01, tuition for all undergraduate students is $21,230 per year. Room is $5040, optional board is estimated at $2400, and student fees are $570. The approximate cost of books and supplies is $400.

Financial Aid

It is the intent of Loyola College to assist qualified students who might not otherwise be able to provide for themselves an opportunity for higher education. Financial aid is awarded on the basis of academic ability and financial need. Two thirds of the student body receive financial assistance in the forms of Loyola College scholarships, state scholarships, Federal Pell Grants, Federal Supplemental Educational Opportunity Grants, Federal Perkins Loans, and Federal Work-Study Program opportunities. To apply for financial assistance, students must submit the Free Application for Federal Student Aid and the Financial Aid PROFILE through the College Scholarship Service in Princeton, New Jersey. The financial aid application deadline is February 1.

Faculty

Loyola College intends to remain a relatively small college and continue to have a faculty-student ratio similar to the current one of 1:14 in order to ensure interest in the individual student. The members of the administration and the full-time faculty of 230 hold degrees from seventy-three different colleges and universities. All of the full-time faculty members serve as student advisers. More than 90 percent of the course work in the Day Division of Loyola College is taught by full-time faculty members. No classes are taught by graduate students.

Student Government

The Student Government serves three chief functions, which make its existence not only valuable but necessary. These functions are to represent the student body outside the College, to provide leadership within the student body, and to perform services, both social and academic, for the students. Responsibility for budgeting activities also rests with the Student Government. The president of the Student Government is a member of the College Academic Council.

Admission Requirements

Applicants for admission to Loyola College are evaluated according to their academic qualifications. The most important academic criteria include the secondary school record, performance on the College Board's Scholastic Assessment Test (which is the College's required entrance examination), and the recommendations of the principal or guidance counselor. The College welcomes applications from men and women of character, intelligence, and motivation, without discrimination on the grounds of race or religious belief.

Application and Information

Interested students seeking to enroll at Loyola College may obtain the application form by writing to the address listed below. Each applicant must instruct the College Board to send his or her Scholastic Assessment Test scores to the Admissions Office. Applicants for all forms of financial aid must submit the Financial Aid PROFILE of the College Scholarship Service and the Free Application for Federal Student Aid. A $30 application fee must accompany the application for admission.

For additional information, students are encouraged to contact:

Admissions Office
Loyola College in Maryland
4501 North Charles Street
Baltimore, Maryland 21210-2699
Telephone: 410-617-5012
 800-221-9107 Ext. 5012 (toll-free)
World Wide Web: http://www.Loyola.edu

Loyola's campus offers the freedom of a residential setting, yet it is only minutes away from the resources of a major metropolitan area.

LOYOLA MARYMOUNT UNIVERSITY
LOS ANGELES, CALIFORNIA

The University
Loyola Marymount University, situated on a picturesque campus, offers competitive students an education of high quality in a friendly and relaxed atmosphere. As successor of the oldest institution of learning in southern California, St. Vincent's College, the University is steeped in a tradition and history of dedication to academic excellence and the total development of its students. Although the emphasis is within the undergraduate school (enrollment 4,567), 1,234 students attend the Graduate Division, primarily in the evening hours, working toward master's degrees in the fields of arts, arts in teaching, business administration, education, and science (including engineering). The School of Law, situated at a separate campus, has both day and evening divisions and offers the Juris Doctor degree. Law school enrollment is 1,345.

Almost 60 percent of the undergraduate students live on campus and are able to choose accommodations in one of ten residential halls or five apartment complexes. Students have access to a sports pavilion, two swimming pools, baseball and soccer fields, tennis and volleyball courts, and four indoor racquetball courts. A new recreation center (due to open in fall 2000) will include additional courts and a fitness center. LMU fields teams in eleven intercollegiate sports (baseball, basketball, crew, cross-country, golf, soccer, softball, swimming, tennis, volleyball, and water polo) and has club teams in lacrosse and rugby. More than 2,000 undergraduate students participate in the active intramural program, which includes coed sports. Student organizations include the AM/FM radio station (KXLU), Biology Society, Black Students Freedom Alliance, Chinese Club, MEChA, Pre-Legal Society, Student Activities Board, University Choruses, fraternities and sororities, and various honor and service groups. The Debate Squad and LMU's Air Force ROTC detachment have received national recognition in their respective areas.

Location
LMU is ideally located on a 152-acre mesa that overlooks the southwest section of Los Angeles and the Pacific Ocean from Malibu to Santa Monica. The campus is close to the beach, and the University community enjoys a cool, clean, coastal climate. LMU is near the metropolitan complex, but it has the benefits of the slower pace of its residential community, Westchester. Los Angeles International Airport is 10 minutes away, and nearby freeways provide easy access to the city and its cultural and recreational activities.

Majors and Degrees
Loyola Marymount University offers the B.A. in the fields of Afro-American studies, animation studies, art history, Asian Pacific studies, biology, Chicano studies, classics, communication studies, dance, economics, English, European studies, film studies, French, history, humanities, Latin, liberal studies, music, philosophy, political science, psychology, recording arts, screenwriting, sociology, Spanish, studio arts, television production, theater arts, theology, and urban studies. The College of Business Administration offers the Bachelor of Science degree in accounting and the Bachelor of Business Administration degree with emphases in business law, computer information systems and operations management, finance, international business, management, marketing, and travel and tourism. The College of Science and Engineering offers bachelor's degrees in biochemistry, biology, chemistry, computer science, engineering (civil, electrical, and mechanical), engineering physics, mathematics, natural science, and physics. Areas of emphasis can include such fields as computer engineering, environmental science, and marine biology.

Academic Program
While premajor and major requirements differ with each area of study, a core curriculum is maintained as a degree requirement in the fields of American cultures, communication skills, fine arts, history, literature/psychology, mathematics/science, philosophy, social science, and theology, thus ensuring each student a balanced education. The maximum requirement in each of the core fields is 6 units of academic work. The interdepartmental honors program provides challenges for the exceptional student.

The academic calendar consists of two semesters and a six-week optional summer session. The fall semester begins in late August and ends before Christmas. The spring semester begins in mid-January and ends in mid-May. Students may earn credit through Advanced Placement examinations. In addition, it is possible for students to earn credit by examination for any course offered by LMU.

Off-Campus Arrangements
Students interested in studying abroad have a choice of several University-sponsored programs. LMU offers programs in Africa, China, England, France, Germany, Ireland, Italy, Japan, Korea, Mexico, the Philippines, and Spain; the University also has numerous affiliated programs, including the Rome Center of Loyola University of Chicago and the American Institute for Foreign Study. Choice of programs is made on the basis of the student's interest and ability or skill. Courses may be conducted in English, the language of the country in which the student elects to study, or both. In addition, LMU offers internship programs through which students can earn course credit for independent study that has been approved by the dean of the college in which the student is enrolled. The programs range from student involvement in political campaigns to the counseling of underrepresented youths to professional work at TV studios.

Academic Facilities
The completely automated Charles Von der Ahe Library contains the undergraduate library collections, which total approximately 350,000 books and bound periodicals, 135,000 microforms, 3,100 subscriptions, and 13,000 recordings. Among the special collections are materials on St. Thomas More, Oliver Goldsmith, Spanish culture and civilization, and German and American philosophy. The library is also a federal depository for government documents. The undergraduate library includes a Learning Resource Center, a multimedia area for audiovisual materials and equipment. Study carrels are equipped for using a variety of formats, such as videocassettes, 8-mm and Super-8 film, audiotapes, turntables, filmstrips, and slides—both with and without cassettes. Instructional media related to classwork and individualized study are available. The Law School Library, located within the School of Law in downtown Los Angeles, contains more than 500,000 volumes and microforms and is a

depository for government documents of the state of California and the United States. It also has complete holdings of all publications relating to California law. All students have at their disposal an IBM 360/30 computer that is equipped to program five languages. The communication arts complex houses the Louis B. Mayer Motion Picture Theatre, a full-size color-television studio, a motion-picture soundstage, an HS-200 (instant-replay) machine, and other modern equipment. Strub Theatre offers excellent theatrical facilities for the performing arts of drama and dance.

Costs

Tuition for the 2000–01 academic year is $19,100. The cost of room and board varies with options that students select—for example, a full or partial meal plan, an apartment on campus, or a dormitory. However, the average yearly cost is approximately $7000. Students should expect to spend about $680 for books and supplies and $1360 for additional miscellaneous expenses.

Financial Aid

Approximately 77 percent of the University's undergraduate students receive some type of financial assistance. The total amount of financial aid awarded to students is approximately $60 million. Students applying for aid must file the Free Application for Student Aid (FAFSA) and the CSS PROFILE. All students are expected to apply for the Federal Pell Grant, and California residents must apply for the California grants. Most aid is awarded on the basis of need, but the University does offer merit scholarships (including full-tuition scholarships). The priority date for financial aid is February 15. Aid is awarded after that date on a funds-available basis.

Faculty

LMU's faculty is dedicated to undergraduate teaching and is easily accessible to students. Eighty-five percent of the faculty members hold a Ph.D. in their area of instruction.

Student Government

The University believes that active student input is an essential part of the undergraduate years. Students sit on every University committee, including the Board of Trustees, with full voting rights. Students operate the campus recreation centers, manage the dormitories as resident advisers, operate a used-book store, and serve as advisers to their academic departments. Student actions have resulted in the development of such things as a campus recreation center, the water polo team, and the complete semester calendar.

Admission Requirements

Admission to LMU is selective, and a candidate is expected to present a better-than-average record in college-preparatory courses. Minimal achievement and limited preparation narrow the candidate's chances for acceptance into the University and into specific programs. In determining an applicant's eligibility, the University gives careful consideration to the student's academic preparation, national test scores, letters of recommendation, extracurricular activities, and family relationships to the University. A personal interview is not required but is recommended if it is convenient. Prospective candidates are always welcome to visit the campus, and personal tours or overnight stays can be arranged upon written request. Students who, for academic reasons, were not acceptable for admission as freshmen may be admitted to advanced standing if they have completed at least the equivalent of 30 semester hours of transferable college work with better than a B– average. Business and communications majors need at least a B average in transferable courses.

Application and Information

Applicants must submit official transcripts from the last high school attended and from each college attended, arrange for SAT I or ACT scores to be sent to the Office of Admissions, submit a recommendation form from an official of the last school attended, and file an application with the $40 nonrefundable fee. Applications are considered when all necessary documents have been received prior to the deadline of the semester for which application is made. The deadlines are February 1 for the fall semester and December 1 for the spring semester.

International students who are not legal residents of the United States must follow the same admission procedure but are required to submit all completed data before the following deadlines: fall semester, July 1; spring semester, December 1. International students must also submit scores on the Test of English as a Foreign Language (TOEFL), submit a statement of financial responsibility for all obligations covering the full period of time for which the student is making application, be certain all records of previous academic training are original or authentic copies with notarization, and have notarized English translations of all the required records.

For more information about Loyola Marymount University, prospective students should contact:

Matthew X. Fissinger
Director of Admissions
Loyola Marymount University
7900 Loyola Boulevard
Los Angeles, California 90045
Telephone: 310-338-2750
              800-LMU-INFO (toll-free)
Fax: 310-338-2797

Between classes at Loyola Marymount University.

LOYOLA UNIVERSITY CHICAGO
CHICAGO, ILLINOIS

The University

Loyola University Chicago is the most comprehensive Jesuit university in the United States. Founded in 1870 by priests of the Society of Jesus, Loyola continues the Jesuit commitment to education, which is well-grounded in the liberal arts and based on excellence in teaching and research.

Loyola attracts students from all fifty states and seventy-four countries to its nine schools and colleges: the Stritch School of Medicine, the School of Law, the College of Arts and Sciences, the School of Business Administration, the Niehoff School of Nursing, the School of Education, the School of Social Work, the Graduate School, and Mundelein College (for adult and lifelong learning).

Each year, Loyola enrolls 1,100 freshmen and 450 transfer students. These students choose Loyola because of its personal attention, its environment of academic excellence, and its reputation for career preparation. Loyola students take advantage of Chicago as an educational resource, often combining their studies with internships and part-time work experience.

The University seeks to provide an environment that will enhance the academic, social, and spiritual growth of students. More than 100 student organizations, including fifteen national fraternities and sororities, and extensive recreational sports programs and facilities are provided. NCAA Division I teams include basketball, cross-country, golf, soccer, track, and volleyball for men and basketball, cross-country, golf, soccer, softball, track, and volleyball for women.

The University provides twelve undergraduate residence halls on the Lake Shore Campus. There are both coed and single-sex halls. Freshmen and sophomores are expected to live on campus. There is also convenient and affordable off-campus housing in the immediate vicinity of campus for upperclass students.

Location

The Lake Shore Campus is located 8 miles north of the city's center and sits on the shore of Lake Michigan in the Rogers Park/Edgewater area, a desirable residential neighborhood where many Loyola faculty and staff members reside. Students at the Lake Shore Campus take advantage of the tranquil lakeside setting but can enjoy the bustle of downtown within minutes by riding either the University-run shuttle bus or convenient public transportation.

Loyola's Water Tower Campus is located on Chicago's "Magnificent Mile," a fashionable area on the near north side. Close to theaters, museums, major corporate and financial institutions, and some of Chicago's most elegant shops and boutiques, the Water Tower Campus is a vibrant educational center.

Majors and Degrees

Loyola's four undergraduate colleges offer the Bachelor of Arts (B.A.), Bachelor of Science (B.S.), Bachelor of Business Administration (B.B.A.), Bachelor of Science in Education (B.S.Ed.), and the Bachelor of Science in Nursing (B.S.N.) degrees. The College of Arts and Sciences offers majors in anthropology, biology (neuroscience), chemistry (biochemistry), classical civilization, communication (communication and social justice), computer science, criminal justice, economics, English (creative writing), environmental sciences/studies, fine arts (art history, studio art, and visual communication), French, German, Greek (ancient), history, international studies, Italian, Latin, mathematics, mathematics and computer science, music, philosophy, physics, political science, psychology, social work, sociology, Spanish, statistical science, theater, theology, theoretical physics and applied mathematics, and women's studies. The School of Business Administration offers majors in accounting (public), economics, finance, human resource management, information systems management, international business, managerial accounting, marketing, and production management. The School of Education offers a major in elementary education as well as secondary school certification in fourteen majors. The Niehoff School of Nursing offers the Bachelor of Science in Nursing and a baccalaureate completion program for registered nurses as well as a major in food and nutrition/dietetics. Five-year dual-degree (bachelor's/master's) programs are available in accounting, applied social psychology, computer science, criminal justice, environmental studies/management, information systems management, mathematics, political science, and sociology.

Minors are available in most of the fields listed above as well as in Asian and Asian-American studies, black world studies, international studies, Latin American studies, medieval studies, neuroscience, peace studies, psychology of crime and justice, Rome studies, and women's studies.

Preprofessional programs offered at Loyola include dentistry, law, medicine, optometry, osteopathic medicine, pharmacy, podiatry, and veterinary medicine. A 3+3 Law Program, in conjunction with the Loyola University School of Law, allows talented undergraduates to enter law school at the conclusion of their junior year of college. Loyola also offers a 3+2 Engineering Program with Washington University in St. Louis, the University of Illinois at Urbana-Champaign, and other universities.

Academic Program

Jesuit educators believe that a solid foundation in the liberal arts and sciences is essential for students entering all professions. Loyola's Core Curriculum is designed to give students this foundation. The core requirements vary by college but usually include courses in literature, expressive arts, history, social sciences, mathematical and natural sciences, philosophy, and theology. The core allows students who are undecided about their majors to explore all possibilities before deciding upon a field of study.

Most majors require 128 semester hours for graduation. Exceptionally well qualified students may apply to the Honors Program. Students may receive credit through the Advanced Placement Program (AP Program) tests, the International Baccalaureate (I.B.), and certain College-Level Examination Program (CLEP) tests are accepted. Loyola students may participate in the Air Force, Army, and Naval ROTC programs through neighboring universities.

Off-Campus Arrangements

Students can choose to attend Loyola's Rome Center of Liberal Arts in Rome, Italy, for a semester or year, or they can choose to enroll in Loyola's study-abroad programs in Belgium, Great Britain, Israel, Korea, Mexico, and Spain.

Academic Facilities

The University's library system, including the Cudahy Library at the Lake Shore Campus and the 25 E. Pearson Building Library at the Water Tower Campus, contains more than 1.3 million books and 12,000 periodical subscriptions. Other academic facilities include extensive laboratories for the biology, chemistry, and physics departments; a nursing resource center; and computing facilities on all campuses, including IBM and VAX mainframe computers and hundreds of microcomputers. These and other computing facilities were part of a $19-million plan for resources that has been installed over the past few years.

The School of Business is located in a $38-million building on the Water Tower Campus.

The Martin D'Arcy Gallery of Medieval and Renaissance Art is located on the Lake Shore Campus along with the Fine Art Department's gallery and studios. The theater department's facilities include the Mullady Theatre, where the most sophisticated computerized lighting system in Chicago was recently installed, and the Studio Theatre, an experimental black-box facility. Loyola's FM radio station and TV production studios provide communication majors with extensive on-campus experience.

The Medical Center Campus in Maywood, a suburb of Chicago, consists of the Foster G. McGaw Hospital and the Stritch School of Medicine. Recently added to this campus were the Mulcahy Outpatient Center, the Russo Surgical Pavilion, and the Cardinal Bernardin Cancer Center.

The Mallinckrodt Campus in suburban Wilmette, Illinois, is home to the School of Education.

Costs

For the 2000–01 academic year, tuition for full-time undergraduates is $18,270. Based on double occupancy, room and board costs average $7400. Books and fees total about $1580 per year.

Financial Aid

Loyola attempts to meet the financial need of as many students as possible. Seventy-five percent of Loyola students receive some form of aid, including University-funded scholarships and grants, federal and state grants, work-study, and loans. Students are encouraged to file the Free Application for Federal Student Aid (FAFSA) by mid-February in order to receive consideration for all types of aid.

Merit scholarships are awarded to entering freshmen who have outstanding academic records. Presidential, Damen, and Loyola scholarships are awarded to students who rank at the top of their high school graduating class and score well on the ACT or SAT I. Scholarship amounts for these programs are $5000–$10,000 per year. These awards are renewable for up to three years.

Other scholarships available include competitive awards for students admitted to the Honors Program and students from Jesuit/BVM/Sisters of Christian Charity high schools, National Merit/National Achievement finalists, theater scholarships (awarded by audition), and debate, leadership, nursing, and public accounting awards.

Transfer students who have completed 30 hours of college credit with an outstanding record of academic achievement may receive a Transfer Academic Scholarship. These awards are renewable for up to three years.

Faculty

More than 95 percent of the University's full-time faculty members hold the Ph.D. or the terminal degree in their field. Faculty members generally teach both graduate and undergraduate students, and senior faculty members often teach Core Curriculum courses. The student-faculty ratio is far below the national average, giving undergraduates ready access to faculty members both as teachers and as advisers.

Student Government

Student government at Loyola provides a liaison between students and administration, emphasizes concerns for student rights, and provides a forum for debate, recommendation, and action on issues that pertain to students. Students also take an active role on University policy and advisory committees and as elected representatives in the residence halls.

Admission Requirements

Students seeking admission to Loyola University Chicago are evaluated on the basis of the overall academic record, including ACT or SAT I scores. Most Loyola students rank in the upper quarter of their graduating class, but consideration is given to students in the upper half. Candidates should be graduating from an accredited secondary school with a minimum of 15 units, including courses in English, math, social studies, and science. Study of a foreign language is strongly recommended. Students must submit the application for admission along with high school transcripts, test scores, and a secondary school counselor recommendation. Admission counselors are available to meet and talk with students individually either before or after the application is submitted.

Transfer students with 20 semester hours or more of acceptable credit are evaluated on the basis of their college work only. Minimum acceptable grade point averages are 2.0 (C) for the College of Arts and Sciences and the School of Education and 2.5 (C+) for the Schools of Business Administration and Nursing. Candidates must also have been in good standing at the last college attended.

Application and Information

Applicants are notified of the admission decision three to four weeks after the application, supporting credentials, secondary school counselor recommendation, and $25 application fee are received.

Prospective students are encouraged to visit the campus. The Undergraduate Admission Office encourages students to schedule individual appointments and campus tours or to participate in one of the many campus programs offered throughout the year.

To obtain an application and further information and to arrange a visit, students should contact:

Undergraduate Admission Office
Loyola University Chicago
820 North Michigan Avenue
Chicago, Illinois 60611
Telephone: 312-915-6500
         800-262-2373 (toll-free)
E-mail: admission@luc.edu
World Wide Web: http://www.luc.edu/

LOYOLA UNIVERSITY NEW ORLEANS
NEW ORLEANS, LOUISIANA

The University

Founded by the Jesuits in 1912, Loyola University's more than 35,000 graduates have excelled in innumerable professional fields for more than eighty years. Approximately 3,500 undergraduate students enjoy the individual attention of a caring faculty in a university dedicated to creating community and fostering individualism while educating the whole person, not only intellectually, but spiritually, socially, and athletically. Loyola students represent forty-nine states and forty-eight countries. This diversity is found in a setting where the average class size is 22 students. More than 53 percent of the students permanently reside outside Louisiana, and 30 percent belong to minority groups.

Loyola's 20-acre main campus and 4-acre Broadway campus are located in the historic uptown area of New Orleans and are hubs of student activity. The University's residence halls, equipped with computer labs, kitchen, laundry, and study facilities, are home to almost 1,000 students. The Joseph A. Danna Center, the student center, houses four food venues, including the remodeled Orleans Room, Pizza Hut, N'Awlins Poboys, and a gourmet coffee shop. Also found in the Danna Center are an art gallery, travel agency, microcomputer center, hair salon, concierge desk, post office, and game room. Nationally affiliated fraternities and sororities are among Loyola's more than 120 student organizations. During the fall's Organizational Fair, students can join the award-winning newspaper, the Loyola University Community Action Program (a volunteer community service organization, the largest such club on campus), or one of the many special interest groups. Students can also take this opportunity to sign up for one of Loyola's club sports. Every year students participate in club cheerleading, crew, cycling, golf, men's and women's rugby, and soccer (men's). For the more serious-minded, Loyola participates in the National Association of Intercollegiate Athletics (NAIA) men's baseball, basketball, and cross-country and women's basketball, cross-country, soccer, and volleyball. The Recreational Sports Complex offers six multipurpose courts, an elevated running track, an Olympic-size swimming pool, weight rooms, and aerobics and combat-sports facilities.

The University Counseling and Career Services Center provides personal, educational, and vocational counseling and testing services for all students. The center coordinates an active employer-recruitment program that helps students find internships, summer jobs, and career employment after graduation. The center brings more than 200 businesses and graduate/professional schools to campus to interview Loyola students. The office also maintains close contact with the New Orleans Chamber of Commerce, which includes more than 500 businesses.

The Joseph A. Butt, S.J., College of Business Administration is fully accredited at both the undergraduate and graduate levels by the AACSB–The International Association for Management Education and houses the Mildred Soule and Clarence A. Lengendre Chair in Business Ethics.

Location

Loyola's main campus fronts oak-lined St. Charles Avenue in uptown New Orleans. Its red-brick, Tudor-Gothic buildings overlook Audubon Park, home of the famous Audubon Zoo. The downtown area is a 20-minute streetcar ride away, allowing students to take advantage of the city's broad cultural and artistic environment. Considering that New Orleans enjoys an average temperature of 70 degrees, students can enjoy year-round outdoor activities in a city famous for its food, music, and cultural festivals. Lake Pontchartrain is within the city limits and provides facilities for water sports.

Majors and Degrees

Loyola University grants degrees in four-year undergraduate programs. The College of Arts and Sciences grants the B.A. degree in classical studies, communications (advertising, broadcast journalism, broadcast production, communications studies, film studies, photojournalism, print journalism, and public relations), criminal justice, drama, drama communications, economics, English, French, German, graphic arts, history, philosophy, political science, psychology (also premedicine), religious studies, Russian, sociology, Spanish, theater arts, and visual arts and grants the B.S. in biology (predentistry, premedicine, prepharmacy, and pre–veterinary studies), chemistry (premedicine), computer information systems, computer science, elementary education, mathematics, and physics. The College of Business Administration awards the B.B.A. degree in accounting, economics, finance, international business, management, and marketing, as well as the Bachelor of Accountancy. The College of Music grants the B.M. in jazz studies, music education, music history, music therapy, piano pedagogy, theory and composition, and vocal and instrumental performance; the B.S. in music business; and the B.M.E. in instrumental and vocal performance. City College, which offers the evening program, confers bachelor's degrees in communications science, computer information systems applications, criminal justice, humanities/art, organizational science, religious education/ministry, and social/behavioral sciences, as well as the B.S.N. (a degree-completion program for RNs) and a degree-completion program in radiologic technology.

Academic Program

Once enrolled at Loyola, students are introduced to the common curriculum, designed to give them a well-rounded preparation in their major field of concentration, as well as the ability to understand and reflect on disciplines allied to or outside their major. The curriculum is divided into four categories: major, minor, common curriculum, and elective courses. Students must meet the requirements of their degree program as specified by their particular college; the minimum four-year program requires 128 hours. Common curriculum courses include seven introductory courses in English composition, math, science, philosophy, religion, literature, and history and nine upper-division courses in humanities, social science, and natural science. Through the Early Scholars/Early Artists Program, academically gifted and artistically talented local high school sophomores, juniors, and seniors may participate in challenging college courses and earn academic credit. (Interested students should contact the Office of Admissions for more information.) The College of Arts and Sciences also requires a minimum of one year of study in a modern foreign language. The honors program and independent studies provide special opportunities for qualified students.

Off-Campus Arrangements

Through the international studies program, students may spend their junior year in Rome. Summer programs in Mexico, Ireland, Greece, and London are also available, as well as opportunities to study in Belgium and Japan. Through consortium arrangements, students may cross-register for courses for credit at Xavier University, Tulane University, and Notre Dame Seminary and participate with these institutions in joint social-cultural events. In addition, the University offers a rigorous internship program in New Orleans at businesses, institutions, and schools to give students practical experience in their fields, including business administration, communications, education, modern foreign languages, music, and writing. Loyola offers a 3-3 program with the Loyola School of Law for students interested in pursuing a prelaw tract, as well as a 3-2 program in engineering with Tulane University and an early acceptance program with Tulane University Medical School.

Academic Facilities

A $13-million Communications/Music Complex includes classrooms, offices, specialized instructional facilities for the College of Music and the Department of Communications, and a 600-seat performing arts facility for the College of Music. It also houses fully equipped TV and radio studios. The communications department, which has one of the most comprehensive programs in broadcasting and print journalism in the United States, operates its own closed-circuit broadcasting studio in TV and radio and publishes its own newspaper.

Computing is an integral part of campus life at Loyola. In addition to the campus academic minicomputer network that supports an IBM SP2 system, ten microcomputer labs—located throughout the campus—provide students with access to Intel- and Macintosh-based computers and MS-DOS technology. A noteworthy characteristic of Loyola's computing resources is its student-centered emphasis. For example, specialized computer labs exist in the Writing Across the Curriculum Center, English and Math Basic Skills Labs, Poverty Law Clinic, and Business Solutions Center.

The Broadway campus, approximately two blocks down St. Charles Avenue, houses the Loyola School of Law, the visual arts department, the Institute of Human Relations, the Institutional Advancement Office, and a residence hall.

Other facilities on campus include the University libraries, which contain more than 559,000 volumes and hold subscriptions to more than 6,500 periodicals and journals. The main library also offers more than 250,000 microform units and 2,200 media titles. There are specialized libraries for music, law, media, and government documents. Music-listening carrels are available in the Music Library. The 150,000-square-foot J. Edgar and Louise S. Monroe library contains 630 simultaneous computer links, a media center, a visual arts center, and the Lindy Boggs National Center for Community Literacy.

Costs

For the full-time undergraduate student attending during 1999–2000, tuition was $14,140 for the year, plus a $592 student activity fee. Day-division part-time students were charged $500 per credit hour, while evening-division part-time students were charged $207 to $500 per credit hour. The cost of residence halls (double occupancy) and a complete meal plan was $6245 for the year.

Financial Aid

Loyola University's endowment provides money for financial aid in addition to that provided by federal funding. Assistance in the forms of merit- and talent-based scholarships, loans, work-study program awards, and grants is awarded on the basis of academic achievement and need. More than 450 scholarships are awarded annually to students with competitive grades and test scores. To apply for one of the scholarships, students must have a GPA of at least 3.2 and competitive standardized test scores. Offers of financial aid are not made until after admission. Notifications of awards are sent within four weeks of the receipt of completed financial aid applications. Awards of need-based financial aid packages are made on a first-come, first-served basis.

Faculty

Behind every program at Loyola is a faculty of Jesuit and lay professors who are especially well qualified in their particular fields. The Jesuit Order, recognized throughout the world for its educational contributions over the centuries, administers the University's faculty of 246 full-time professors, of whom 89 percent hold the terminal degree in their field. Loyola also employs 138 part-time instructors. No graduate assistants teach classes. The student-faculty ratio of 12:1 emphasizes the University's special quality of personal involvement and concern for each student and his or her particular needs.

Student Government

Loyola's Student Government Association consists of representatives elected by the student body from each of the four colleges and the law school. The association conducts general meetings, elections, and student activities. Student representatives sit on nearly all University committees.

Admission Requirements

Prospective students must submit an application, resume, and essay; have a high school transcript or GED test results sent; submit ACT or SAT I scores; and have their counselor or teacher send a recommendation. Individual attention is given to each application form. Final selection is based on high school grades, test scores, and counselor or teacher recommendations. Significant community involvement and demonstrated leadership abilities are recommended. Auditions are required for final acceptance to the College of Music. Portfolios are required for final acceptance to the Department of Visual Arts.

Transfer students are required to submit an application and an official transcript from each institution previously attended. To be selected, students must have a minimum cumulative GPA of 2.25 when transferring from an accredited institution.

Decisions are made on applications on a rolling basis during the students' senior year in high school. December 1 is the priority deadline for merit-based scholarships.

Application and Information

Interested students are encouraged to contact:
Office of Admissions
Loyola University
6363 St. Charles Avenue, Box 18
New Orleans, Louisiana 70118
Telephone: 504-865-3240
          800-4-LOYOLA (toll-free)
Fax: 504-865-3383
E-mail: admit@loyno.edu
World Wide Web: http://www.loyno.edu

The Communications/Music Complex overlooks Audubon Park and affords a view of Most Holy Name of Jesus Catholic Church, located on Loyola's campus.

LUTHER COLLEGE
DECORAH, IOWA

The College

As an academic community, the students and faculty of Luther College are committed to liberal learning in the arts and sciences. Founded in 1861 by Norwegian immigrants, Luther is a college of the Evangelical Lutheran Church in America. Most students live on campus in the seven residence halls. Eighty-eight percent of the 2,550 students come from Iowa, Minnesota, Wisconsin, and Illinois. All together, thirty-eight states and forty-five other nations are represented in the student body.

Throughout the year, the College provides a stimulating cultural and educational atmosphere by bringing distinguished public figures, theater groups, musicians, and educators to the campus. Luther has an active Phi Beta Kappa chapter and several departmental honor societies as well. There are seven local social organizations for both men and women, in addition to one national service fraternity. Extracurricular activities are an important part of campus life. A full theater and dance program and thirteen performing music ensembles, including two bands, seven choirs, two orchestras, the Opera Workshop, the Jazz Band, and the Collegium Musicum, are major cocurricular interests.

Men may participate in ten intercollegiate sports: baseball, basketball, cross-country, football, golf, soccer, swimming, tennis, track and field, and wrestling. Women compete in nine intercollegiate sports: basketball, cross-country, golf, soccer, softball, swimming, tennis, track and field, and volleyball. Club sports include fencing, rugby, and volleyball, and 64 percent of the student body are involved in an extensive intramural and recreational sports program. Available for recreational use and for the physical education program are twelve outdoor tennis courts, an eight-lane polyurethane 400-meter track, a downhill ski area, numerous cross-country ski trails, canoes, and 15 acres of intramural fields. The extensive field house contains a 25-yard indoor pool, four racquetball courts, four hardwood basketball courts, a wrestling room, a weight-training room, a dance studio, and a 3,000-seat gymnasium. A sports forum houses a six-lane 200-meter indoor track, six indoor tennis courts, locker rooms, and athletic training facilities.

Location

The College is located in Decorah, a city of 8,000 people in the scenic bluff country of northeast Iowa. The Upper Iowa River, which runs through the campus, is one of twenty-seven rivers throughout the country designated as a National Scenic and Recreational River. Rich in Scandinavian heritage, Decorah is a popular recreation area, providing opportunities for spelunking, fishing, hunting, cross-country and Alpine skiing, camping, hiking, cycling, and canoeing. Three airports are located within a 75-mile radius of Decorah: in Rochester, Minnesota; Waterloo, Iowa; and La Crosse, Wisconsin.

Majors and Degrees

Luther College grants the Bachelor of Arts (B.A.) degree and offers majors in accounting, Africana studies, anthropology, art, Biblical languages, biology, business, chemistry, classical languages (Greek and Latin), classical studies, communication, computer science, economics, elementary education, English, health, history, management, management information systems, mathematics, mathematics/statistics, modern languages (French, German, Norwegian, and Spanish), music, nursing, philosophy, physical education, physics, political science, psychobiology, psychology, recreation, religion, Scandinavian studies, social work, sociology, sociology/political science, speech and theater, and theater/dance. Interdisciplinary majors are arts management, international management, museum studies, Russian studies, Scandinavian studies, and sports management.

Preprofessional preparation is offered in cytotechnology, dentistry, engineering, environmental management, forestry, law, medical technology, medicine, music therapy, optometry, physical therapy, theology, and veterinary medicine.

Academic Program

Luther operates on a 4-1-4 academic calendar. The first semester runs from September to December, followed by a 3-week January Term and the second semester, which runs from February to May. Two 4-week summer sessions are offered, one in June and the other in July. Each candidate is required to complete satisfactorily a total of 128 semester hours of credit with a C average or better. At least 76 of the required 128 semester hours must be earned outside the major discipline. Each senior writes a research paper in his or her major. Students are required to complete the following number of semester hours of credit in designated areas: 12 of Paideia, an interdisciplinary course; 9 of religion/philosophy; 8 of natural science (4 of which may be in mathematics); 8 of social science; 3–9 of foreign language or culture (proficiency based); 3 of fine arts; and 2 of physical education. Demonstration of competency in mathematics is required. Advanced placement and credit by examination are available. A qualified student may develop an interdisciplinary major in consultation with a faculty adviser.

Off-Campus Arrangements

Students may participate in off-campus programs during the fall and spring semesters, the January Term, and summer sessions. All of the programs carry academic credit. Luther participates in the Iowa General Assembly Legislative Intern Program during the spring semester of each year. Urban studies semesters may be arranged in conjunction with other colleges. The Washington Semester gives qualified juniors the opportunity to study at American University and work within one department of the federal government. Luther College also co-sponsors a semester program in Washington, D.C., through the Lutheran College Washington Consortium. Students may elect to be exchange students at other colleges for one semester or a January Term.

Luther is an affiliate of the Institute of European Studies, which has centers in over twenty European and Asian countries; students studying at one of these centers receive credit in accordance with the provisions for transfer credit for study abroad under the Junior Year Abroad programs. A community studies program in Nottingham, England, is staffed by a Luther professor each year. In alternate years, a Luther professor directs on-site programs in Münster, Germany, and in Malta. In addition, opportunities for study are available in a variety of settings such as the Bahamas, China, Russia, Tanzania, and Norway.

Academic Facilities

The 800-acre campus includes the Preus Library, housing 340,000 volumes, 1,058 periodicals, and the College art collection. The library offers five on-line indexes and ten commercial on-line services and provides access to more than 480 other libraries. Modern, well-equipped laboratories in the Valders Hall of Science are supplemented by several other science-teaching facilities on campus: a planetarium, a greenhouse, a herbarium, a live-animal center, a human anatomy laboratory, a natural history museum, and a psychology sleep laboratory. The science facilities also include an extensive field study area and two electron microscopes. Within easy walking distance of the campus, the field study area offers an ideal setting for studies in aquatic biology, ecology, and field biology. Five ponds, two reestablished prairies, marshes, woodlots, and agricultural lands are available for classwork and independent study. The College has a fiber-based campus network connecting a variety of PC and Macintosh computers (in several environments) to shared computing resources and to the Internet. An HP 3000/957 and an HP 9000 as well as two terminal servers that provide dial-up access are included on the network. More than 400 microcomputers and terminals are available for student use throughout the campus.

Luther College maintains radio station KWLC-AM, and the College's affiliate station, KLSE-FM, is part of the Minnesota Public Radio network. Luther also maintains the largest archaeological research center in Iowa. The Norwegian American Museum in Decorah, one of the finest ethnic museums in the country, provides an invaluable resource for museum and Scandinavian studies. The foreign language departments maintain a twenty-five-station electronic classroom, and the psychology department houses a twenty-station IBM interactive computer network.

The impressive F. W. Olin Hall houses the economics and business, mathematics, and computer science departments. Among its technological wonders is the Luther Round Table Room, where students experience simultaneous decision making via a computer network.

The award-winning Jenson Hall of Music contains state-of-the-art computer facilities, a recording studio, and four pipe organs: 23-stop/34-rank and 42-stop/61-rank tracker organs for practice and performing and two Schlicker practice organs of 8 and 5 ranks, respectively. Jenson Hall of Music also contains 32,000 square feet of classrooms, studios, practice rooms, and rehearsal rooms for keyboard, vocal, and instrumental music. The Center for Faith and Life (CFL) houses a 42-stop/62-rank organ in the 1,600-seat auditorium for the performing arts. The CFL also houses the offices of the campus ministry, a 24-hour meditation chapel, a 200-seat recital hall, and one of four campus art galleries.

Costs

For 2000–01, the comprehensive fee is $21,950, which includes tuition, general fees, facilities fees, room, board, subscription to student publications, and admission to College-supported concerts, lectures, and other events. A room telephone and a health-service program are also included. Private music lessons are $175 per semester. Luther estimates that an additional $2000 is adequate for books, clothing, entertainment, and other personal expenses.

Financial Aid

More than 90 percent of all Luther students receive some financial aid in the form of grants, such as the Federal Pell Grant; scholarships from Luther and other sources; loans; and jobs on campus. Luther awards Regents and Presidential scholarships to applicants demonstrating superior academic achievement. The amount of aid given is determined by the College's analysis of the Free Application for Federal Student Aid. The priority deadline for a financial aid application is March 1 each year. Students receive notification of financial aid awards after their acceptance for admission.

Faculty

There are 185 full-time and 60 part-time faculty members; 76 percent hold a Ph.D., and an additional 13 percent hold other terminal degrees. The ratio of students to faculty is 12:1.

Student Government

Students share in the governance of the College. They participate in social and cultural programming and all kinds of College activities; they have full membership on most College committees, majority representation in the Community Assembly, and nonvoting representation on the Board of Regents.

Admission Requirements

Admission is selective. An applicant must be a graduate of an accredited high school and have completed at least 4 units of English, 3 units of mathematics, 3 units of social science, and 2 units of natural science. It is strongly recommended that the applicant have at least two years of a foreign language. Seventy percent of entering students rank in the top quarter of their high school class. Transfer students may enroll either semester. Early admission and admission with honors are available. The priority deadline to apply for admission is March 1 each year.

Application and Information

An application, SAT I or ACT scores, an educator's reference, a transcript of previous academic work, and a $20 application fee are required for admission. On-campus interviews are recommended but not required. For more information about Luther, students should contact:

Admissions Office
Luther College
Decorah, Iowa 52101-1042
Telephone: 319-387-1287
          800-458-8437 (toll-free)
Fax: 319-387-2159
     319-387-1060 (international)
E-mail: admissions@luther.edu (admissions)
        lutherfa@luther.edu (financial planning)
        lundsony@luther.edu (international)
World Wide Web: http://www.luther.edu

Luther College's spacious 800-acre campus in the scenic bluff country of northeast Iowa.

LYNCHBURG COLLEGE
LYNCHBURG, VIRGINIA

The College

Lynchburg College is a fully accredited, coeducational, nonsectarian liberal arts college related to the Christian Church (Disciples of Christ). It offers undergraduate programs in the liberal arts, sciences, and professional disciplines (including business, communications, education, and nursing) and graduate programs in business and education. The College is committed to the principle that every individual is of infinite worth, and it endeavors to provide a program of liberal education consistent with the needs of contemporary society. It draws its undergraduate student body of 2,025 men and women from thirty-one states and nineteen countries. The College community is largely residential, with approximately 64 percent of the full-time undergraduate student body living on campus. Approximately 50 percent of the undergraduates are from out of state.

The 214-acre campus has long been considered one of the most beautiful in the South. Thirty-two buildings of mostly Georgian Colonial design have the majestic Blue Ridge Mountains as a backdrop. The Claytor Nature Student Center, a 470-acre farm in nearby Bedford County, is utilized for environmental and educational purposes as a learning laboratory to promote the property as a model of environmental management in cooperation with various organizations locally and nationally.

A wide variety of activities are available in the Lynchburg College community: service and honor organizations, more than 50 clubs, four fraternities, and four sororities, as well as opportunities to participate in dramatic productions, student publications, religious activities, and musical performances. New Horizons provides adventure-based leadership and team-building opportunities for individuals and groups.

Community service is a distinguishing feature of the Lynchburg College students, who annually contribute more than 15,000 volunteer hours to the community through such projects as Habitat for Humanity, Camp Jaycees, Special Olympics, and other programs.

The varsity athletics program is diverse and includes baseball, basketball, cross-country, equestrian sports, golf, indoor and outdoor track and field, lacrosse, soccer, and tennis for men and basketball, cross-country, equestrian sports, field hockey, lacrosse, soccer, softball, tennis, track, and volleyball for women. In addition, an intramural program exists for interested men and women along with various club sports. Lynchburg College possesses some of the finest athletics facilities of any private college in Virginia. The College participates in NCAA Division III and is a charter member of the Old Dominion Athletic Conference (which includes Bridgewater, Eastern Mennonite, Emory & Henry, Guilford, Hampden-Sydney, Hollins, Lynchburg, Mary Baldwin, Randolph-Macon, Randolph-Macon Woman's, Roanoke, Sweet Briar, Virginia Wesleyan, and Washington and Lee).

Location

Lynchburg College is located in central Virginia, 100 miles from Richmond, 180 miles southwest of Washington, D.C., and 50 miles east of Roanoke. Greater Lynchburg is a growing business and industrial center with a population of more than 220,000. The city is noted for its climate, culture, and historic landmarks. It is within an easy drive of the Blue Ridge Mountains, where many popular lakes and resorts are located. Air, bus, and railroad transportation place Lynchburg within easy reach of any urban center.

Majors and Degrees

Lynchburg College offers the degree of Bachelor of Arts in the following fields: accounting, art (applied or education), business administration, chemistry, child development (elementary, middle, secondary, or special education), communication, economics (liberal arts or business), English, European literature, French, health and movement science, health promotion, history, international relations, management, marketing, mathematics, music, philosophy, physics, political science, psychology, psychology–special education, religious studies, social studies, sociology, Spanish, sports management, sports medicine, and theater. The degree of Bachelor of Science is offered in the following fields: accounting, biology, chemistry, child development (elementary, middle, secondary, or special education), computer science, economics (liberal arts or business), engineering (dual-degree program), English, environmental science, health and movement science, health promotion, history, international relations, management, marketing, mathematics, nursing, physics, psychology, psychology–special education, religious studies, sociology, sports management, and sports medicine.

A candidate for a B.A. degree may elect to take a joint major in foreign language–business management, philosophy–political science, psychology–special education, religious studies and another field, or sociology/religious studies. B.S. degree joint majors are available in foreign language–management, and psychology–special education. Double majors and minors may also be taken in many areas of study. Advanced undergraduates may also take some graduate courses.

Preprofessional and professional courses are available for students who want preparation for careers in dentistry, forestry and wildlife management, law, library science, medicine, the ministry and ministry-related occupations, optometry, pharmacy, physical therapy, social work, teaching, and veterinary medicine.

Academic Program

To be eligible for a degree, a student must complete at least 124 semester hours of college-level academic work. In addition, a degree candidate must have a grade point average of at least 2.0 on all work undertaken, plus an average of at least 2.0 on all work undertaken in the major field.

The curriculum at Lynchburg College is divided into two general areas; some additional hours are available for students to explore course work in free elective areas of their choice. The first of the two areas of study consists of General Education Requirements (GERs) selected from the broad disciplines of world literature, fine arts, philosophy, religious studies, mathematics, history, social science, laboratory science, foreign languages, and health and movement science. All students are exposed to each of these academic areas. The second of the two general areas is the major. The College offers thirty-nine majors, ranging from education and business to the sciences and the humanities, as well as twelve preprofessional programs. This curriculum offers students breadth (GERs) as well as depth (the major). Students may devote their free elective hours to one of thirty-nine minor programs to further enhance their education.

Outstanding students may be selected to participate in the College's Westover Honors Program, the purpose of which is to attract, stimulate, challenge, and fulfill academically gifted students. The program offers a challenging curriculum that promotes intellectual curiosity and independent thinking and places strong emphasis on creative problem solving.

The College operates on an early semester calendar. The first semester begins in late August and ends before Christmas, and the second semester runs from mid-January to early May. An optional three-week winter term is also offered. An Advanced Placement Scholars Program permits some students to enter with advanced standing, credit, or both. Credit is also awarded on the basis of satisfactory scores on the CLEP subject exams. Early admission is available for the talented student. Eligible students who want to accelerate their program may meet degree requirements in three years.

Lynchburg offers entry-level computer courses to all students, and students are strongly encouraged to become computer literate. New students may bring a computer of their own or utilize one of the many available on campus. All students are assigned an e-mail account and have access to the Internet. In addition, all students are allowed to develop their own home pages on the World Wide Web, which they have access to through the computer resources provided by the College. All residence hall rooms are wired for network access.

Off-Campus Arrangements

Various agency and intercollege exchange programs are available for interested students. Language students may engage in foreign-study programs and are encouraged to do so. In addition, any student who wishes to study abroad may do so as part of the College's study-abroad program.

Internships, organized through the Career Development Center, are available locally, nationally, and internationally. More than 800 internships are already established, and new sites are developed each year. Cooperative programs exist for some departments, such as political science, where full credit is granted for study at another college or university. Specific guidelines for these programs are set forth by each department. In addition, Lynchburg College, Randolph-Macon Woman's College, and Sweet Briar College, as members of the Tri-College Consortium of Virginia, maintain cooperative relationships for the sharing of facilities and offerings. Students at each of the colleges are granted access to the libraries of the other two, and a student may enroll in a course on either of the other campuses without payment of additional tuition.

Academic Facilities

As a result of a $6.1-million renovation and expansion, the Hobbs Science Center is the nucleus for technology-assisted learning. In addition to excellent resources (including a scanning electron microscope) for biology, chemistry, physics, mathematics, and computer science, Hobbs Science Center provides integrated technology support and facilities for all students at Lynchburg College. There are fifteen computer laboratories on campus (including designated laboratories in the education and nursing buildings and a desktop publishing center in the communication department), three networked classrooms, and more than 200 computers available for student use. The Wilmer Writing Center is part of the Learning Center, a focal point for tutoring, study areas, language learning, and academic support in Hopwood Hall, the main classroom building on campus.

The Knight-Capron Library is the center for undergraduate research, providing reference and study areas, rare books and documents, and other resources. By being linked electronically to other libraries in the community and beyond, the Knight-Capron Library's considerable holdings (206,537 volumes, 414,581 microfilm items, and more than 600 periodicals subscriptions) are greatly enhanced.

The Daura Art Gallery has been expanded and is now the major repository of more than 1,000 works of the Catalan-American artist, Pierre Daura. The expansion of this facility makes the Daura Gallery the largest visual art exhibit center in the city of Lynchburg. Each year, it is the site for the Senior Art Show in which chosen student works are exhibited.

Costs

For resident students entering in the 2000–01 session, total charges are $22,380; this includes $17,980 for tuition, $2600 for room, $1800 for board, and $125 for a student activity fee.

Financial Aid

Lynchburg College administers a financial aid program of more than $20 million. These resources are awarded to students as a result of meritorious achievement and/or demonstrated need. Lynchburg College offers academic and achievement scholarships that range from $3000 to $10,000 and are based on performance and accomplishments at the high school or community college level. These awards are renewable each year until the student graduates, as long as the recipient maintains a qualifying minimum academic average each year. Students are identified to receive these scholarships through the admission application; no separate application is necessary. Free early aid estimates are available for students.

To determine eligibility for need-based financial aid, the student should complete the Free Application for Federal Student Aid (FAFSA), which may be obtained at most high schools and at Lynchburg College. The FAFSA results determine the student's eligibility for federally funded grants and loans and other support such as work-study opportunities. In addition, students from Virginia are eligible to apply for the Virginia Tuition Assistance grant.

Faculty

The Lynchburg College faculty has 108 full-time members, 81 percent of whom hold the doctorate or terminal degree in their field, and 82 part-time members. The student-faculty ratio is 15:1. While many faculty members are involved in research projects, it is a College policy that the faculty's top priorities must be in the classroom.

Student Government

The student government of Lynchburg College is regulated by agreements determined by the students, faculty, and administration. It is felt that the College should not be run by the faculty alone, nor by students alone, but through the cooperative interest of all. Campus government is vested in the Student Government Association, the Judicial Boards, the Campus Life Policies Committee, and the Office of the Dean of Student Development. The Student Government Association is also responsible for the Academic Honor Code, a prominent part of campus life.

Admission Requirements

A candidate for admission to Lynchburg College should be a graduate of an approved secondary school with a minimum of 16 academic units or the equivalent, as shown by examination. It is strongly recommended that the academic work include major emphases in the areas of English, foreign language, social science, natural sciences, and mathematics. An applicant must demonstrate above-average academic ability in all areas of study, as admission is competitive. In support of the record, a student must present satisfactory scores on the SAT I or ACT. It is strongly recommended that all students have a personal interview and visit the campus before their first semester at Lynchburg College. Enrollment Office hours during the academic year are 9 a.m. to 5 p.m., Monday through Friday, and 9 a.m. to noon on Saturday.

Application and Information

Early decision admission applications must be received by November 15; notification of acceptance will be made by December 15. All other applications are processed on a rolling admissions basis. Applicants will be notified of the status of their application usually within two weeks of the date their application file is completed.

For information, students should contact:

Sharon Walters-Bower, Director of Recruitment
Lynchburg College
1501 Lakeside Drive
Lynchburg, Virginia 24501
Telephone: 804-544-8300
          800-426-8101 (toll-free)
Fax: 804-544-8653
E-mail: admissions@lynchburg.edu
World Wide Web: http://www.lynchburg.edu

LYNDON STATE COLLEGE
LYNDONVILLE, VERMONT

The College

Situated on picturesque Vail Hill in Lyndonville, Vermont—the heart of the Northeast Kingdom—few campuses in the country can match the sheer beauty of Lyndon State College's location. Established in 1911 as a one-room teacher-training college, Lyndon has grown to a fully accredited, comprehensive, four-year college serving more than 1,200 students in liberal arts and preprofessional programs. Lyndon provides two- and four-year degree programs that prepare students for a wide choice of careers and graduate study. LSC's program includes traditionally structured lecture/discussion courses as well as self-directed, highly individualized learning experiences.

Lyndon State College is accredited by the New England Association of Schools and Colleges, which accredits schools and colleges in the six New England states. Membership in the association indicates that the institution has been carefully evaluated and found to meet standards agreed upon by qualified educators. Lyndon's three degree programs in recreation resource and ski resort management are accredited by the National Recreation and Park Association.

Lyndon's Academic Support Center, Career Planning and Placement Office, Project EXCEL, Health Services, Cooperative Education Office, and Student Activities Program serve the needs and promote the well-being of the students. Student publications include a biweekly newspaper and an annual literary magazine.

Location

Lyndon State College is situated high on a hillside overlooking magnificent Burke Mountain and the picturesque Passumpsic Valley in the heart of Vermont's scenic Northeast Kingdom. It is located 1 mile west of Lyndonville and 9 miles north of St. Johnsbury and is easily accessible from all points by Interstate 91. The College is a 3-hour drive from Boston and Springfield, Massachusetts, and 2 hours from Montreal.

Facilities for such recreational sports as Alpine and cross-country skiing, hiking, fishing, and swimming are available within minutes of the College.

Majors and Degrees

Lyndon State College offers the Bachelor of Arts or Bachelor of Science degree in interdisciplinary studies (an individually designed program). The Bachelor of Arts degree is offered in design and graphic communications, English (literature and journalism and writing), interactive digital media, liberal studies, mathematics, psychology, and social sciences, including history (interdisciplinary). The Bachelor of Science degree is offered in allied health sciences (athletic training, health sciences, and preprofessional study in health sciences), business administration (accounting, business administration, and small-business management and entrepreneurship), education (early childhood, elementary education, middle grades, and reading teacher studies), English (secondary education 7–12), human services, meteorology, natural science (environmental science, natural science, and secondary education 7–12), physical education (activities programming, sports management, and teacher education K–12), recreation resource and ski resort management (adventure-based program management, recreation resource management, and ski resort management), social science (secondary education 7–12), special education/teacher of the handicapped, and television studies (broadcast news and broadcast design and production). The Associate of Science degree is offered in business administration (business administration and small-business management and entrepreneurship), computing, design and graphic communications, interactive digital media, television news, and television production. The Associate of Arts degree is available in general studies.

Academic Program

Lyndon operates on a two-semester calendar and a six-week summer-session schedule. To graduate with a bachelor's degree, a student must complete 122 semester hours of credit and meet College and program requirements. Sixty-two semester hours are required for an associate degree. Each student is tested for competence in writing and mathematics at entry to the College; any deficiencies noted must be made up in noncredit classes during the first two semesters. The College has a general education (distribution) requirement of 37 semester hours.

For two-year programs, students are accepted into a concentration upon admission; for four-year programs, in the fourth semester. Academic departments are responsible for advising and for planning the student's core courses within the concentration. In bachelor's degree programs, most concentrations require at least 42 credits of junior- and senior-level course work. The College requires that 30 of the last 39 hours toward any degree be spent in residence. Leaves of absence are granted to students in good academic standing.

Lyndon recognizes learning acquired from previous experience through an assessment course that documents nontraditional learning. The College offers fieldwork and practicums in most academic programs through the Cooperative Education Office.

Off-Campus Arrangements

Lyndon offers a variety of opportunities for off-campus study for credit, on either a full-time or part-time basis. Students can apply professional theories and principles through full-time cooperative education internships in behavioral science, business, education, meteorology, physical education, recreation, social science, and television production or technical support programs. Students in elementary education participate in a sophomore-year exploratory field experience (a full semester of work blending on-campus study and off-campus experience), a junior-year field experience (two half-days a week), and a full semester of student teaching. Students majoring in psychology complete required fieldwork related to their particular studies at least twice during their upperclass years.

Lyndon grants credit for study in other countries through an approved program such as the Experiment in International Living or the American Institute for Foreign Study.

Academic Facilities

Lyndon State College's exciting Academic Center—located atop the Samuel Read Hall Library—features state-of-the-art academic and computer classrooms and laboratories, including a fully equipped computer laboratory that is linked to the College's expanding computer information network.

The library maintains a collection of more than 90,000 circulating volumes, as well as periodicals, audio and video materials, and microfiche collections. The library also participates in the Inter-Library Loan System, which allows students more extensive access to reference materials. The library's electronic catalog allows access to the collections of many other Vermont colleges, the Vermont Department of Libraries, and the University of Vermont. The language and science laboratories, the computer center and laboratories, and the music rooms are available to students for study, experimentation, and practice.

The meteorology laboratory, staffed by a technician, prepares weather information and forecast information that is broadcast over Vermont radio and television stations. Meteorology students also operate a 24-hour weather-reporting telephone line.

Operated daily by students, LSCTV/NewsCenter 2 is a noncommercial, public-service television facility that provides local news and educational, cultural, and public-service programs. Radio station WWLR-FM is staffed by student volunteers who provide local communities with programs of news, music, and interviews.

Costs

The 1999–2000 tuition for Vermont residents was $4092 per year; for nonresidents, $9588. Room and board (twenty-one-meal plan) for one academic year were $5298. Required College fees, including health and accident insurance, totaled $1125. Total expenses for a Vermont resident living on campus were $10,515; for a nonresident, $16,011. Miscellaneous expenses were estimated at $1000. The estimate for these expenses is included in the financial aid budget.

Financial Aid

Financial aid is available in the form of loans, grants, and campus employment under the Federal Work-Study Program. Approximately 80 percent of the student population receives some type of financial aid from institutional and outside sources. Approximately 35 percent of the students are employed by either the Federal Work-Study Program or the College dining hall.

Applicants for aid are required to complete the Free Application for Federal Student Aid (FAFSA). In addition to filing the FAFSA, transfer students are required to have a financial aid transcript completed by the financial aid officer of each college they attended. For a student to be considered an on-time applicant, the FAFSA should be filed in early February in order to reach the College's Financial Aid Office by the March 15 deadline.

Faculty

Lyndon's excellent faculty consists of 63 full-time members and 53 part-time members. The student-faculty ratio is 17:1. The faculty is dedicated fully to undergraduate teaching. Full-time faculty members serve as academic advisers to students and as advisers to student organizations. Student evaluation of teaching is a formal process and is used in personnel decisions. Faculty members participate in dramatic, musical, and intramural athletic activities on campus and in many civic and community organizations.

Student Government

Students play an important role in Lyndon's internal organization. Students actively represent Lyndon on the Vermont State Colleges' Board of Trustees, in the Vermont State Colleges' Student Association, and on many campus committees.

The Student Senate heads the student organizations. It has jurisdiction over all student affairs and is responsible for addressing student issues and concerns, evaluating all campus clubs and organizations, and allocating Student Activities moneys.

Admission Requirements

Each application for admission is evaluated on its individual merits. Applicants for admission are expected to successfully complete a college-preparatory program and rank in at least the upper 60 percent of their graduating class. Recommended secondary school preparation includes 4 years of English and 2 years each of mathematics, science, and history. Admission decisions for first-year students are determined on the basis of the student's application, a copy of the secondary school transcript, the recommendation of the secondary school principal or guidance counselor, performance on the ACT or the SAT I, and, if possible, a personal interview. Although applicants' scores on the ACT or the SAT I are reviewed, more emphasis is placed on transcripts, class rank, and recommendations than on test scores.

Applicants who have completed examinations taken through the College Board's Advanced Placement Program with a grade of 3 or higher are granted both advanced placement and course credit after evaluation by the academic dean and appropriate department chairpersons. Advanced standing is awarded for successful performance on the tests of the College-Level Examination Program. Lyndon will grant up to 60 college credits for scores above the 40th percentile on the five general examinations in English composition, humanities, mathematics, natural science, and social science/history and for scores at or above the minimum score established by the College Board for a wide variety of subject examinations.

Transfer students are encouraged to apply. A minimum 2.5 cumulative grade point average is recommended for consideration. Admission requirements for transfer students are the same as those for freshman applicants, but an official transcript must also be obtained from each college-level institution that the applicant has attended. Transcripts are required even if no credit is being transferred from a particular institution. Transfer credit may be given at Lyndon for courses completed with the equivalent of a grade of C or better at accredited or officially approved institutions.

The College may permit candidates to defer their enrollment for a period of two semesters.

Application and Information

A nonrefundable $30 fee must accompany each application. Lyndon uses a rolling admission system, and applicants may apply and be accepted throughout the year. All applications are given prompt attention, and applicants (except those applying under the NEBHE Regional Student Program) may expect a decision within two weeks of the date the application process has been completed.

For further information, students should contact:

Director of Admissions
P.O. Box 919
Lyndon State College
Lyndonville, Vermont 05851
Telephone: 802-626-6413
        800-225-1998 (toll-free in New England)
Fax: 802-626-6335
E-mail: admissions@mail.lsc.vsc.edu
World Wide Web: http://www.lsc.vsc.edu

LYNN UNIVERSITY
BOCA RATON, FLORIDA

The University

Founded in 1962, Lynn University is a private, coeducational institution located in Boca Raton, Florida. The University, small by design, provides an environment within and outside the classroom in which a community of learners can pursue academic excellence. Faculty, staff, and students contribute to an atmosphere that nurtures creativity, fosters achievement, and values diversity.

Accredited in 1967 by the Southern Association of Colleges and Schools, Lynn University has steadily grown to become a comprehensive university offering undergraduate and graduate programs in more than thirty disciplines. Lynn leads the country in offering majors in many of the world's fastest-growing professions, thus preparing its students to meet the career demands of the twenty-first century. The 2,000 students who are currently enrolled come from all parts of the United States and nearly seventy nations.

Lynn is a residential institution with four air-conditioned residence halls that house 65 percent of the undergraduates. The residence halls include study lounges, computers, and recreation areas as well as health and fitness facilities that offer free weights, exercise machines, and cardiovascular equipment. The Lynn Student Center, the "living room" of the University, houses the dining room and the auditorium. Students study or relax outside on the patio or on comfortable sofas in the lounge. Also in the student center are the University Grill, a popular "snacking spot" for students, faculty members, and staff, and WLYN!, the campus radio station. Laundry facilities, mailboxes, the University bookstore, and a variety of athletic facilities are all located on campus.

University life is designed to provide a learning situation through which students are guided toward responsible decision-making and leadership. An extensive program of activities complements the academic program at Lynn, ensuring the development of the whole person. Students may choose from a variety of campus organizations and activities, including student government, the newspaper or yearbook, cocurricular clubs, leadership groups such as the Knights of the Roundtable, and fraternities or sororities.

Lynn University holds membership in the National Collegiate Athletic Association (NCAA) Division II and the Sunshine State Conference. Lynn has won 15 national championship titles in many sports. The intercollegiate athletic program includes men's and women's basketball, crew, golf, soccer, and tennis; men's baseball; and women's softball and volleyball. An even wider range of athletic opportunities are available for students through the intramural athletic program.

Location

The University is located in Boca Raton, one of the most vibrant communities in the state of Florida. Its location provides a wide variety of cultural and recreational opportunities to students. Boca Raton is a progressive community with tremendous economic potential and is quickly becoming one of the nation's leading centers of commerce. Facilities of IBM, Siemens, MBNA Marketing Systems, Sony, Pratt and Whitney, Motorola, Sensormatic, and other similar companies are located just a few miles from the University, providing excellent opportunities for internships and employment after graduation. The picturesque 123-acre campus is positioned 3 miles from the Atlantic Ocean and 2 miles from the heart of Boca Raton. The campus is set among freshwater lakes, palms, and lush tropical foliage, providing the peace and quiet that is necessary to concentrate on academics.

Majors and Degrees

Bachelor of Science, Bachelor of Arts, and Bachelor of Music degrees are available in accounting; aviation management; business management and entrepreneurship; communications; culinary arts management; elementary education; English; fashion design; fashion marketing; funeral service/business management; graphic design; history; hotel, resort, and food service management; human services; international business; international communications; international golf management; international hotel and tourism management; international relations/political science; Irish studies; liberal arts; marketing; natural sciences (environmental/premedicine); pre–primary/primary education; psychology; secondary education; sports and recreation management; tourism management; and visual design. Associate degree programs offered include fashion merchandising, funeral service, liberal arts, and pre–primary education.

Academic Program

The University is committed to student-centered learning, where faculty and staff members provide personalized attention to students who have varying levels of academic proficiency with a motivation to excel. A full range of academic and support programs is coordinated to serve the increasingly diverse needs of all students. These are enhanced by the favorable 19:1 student-faculty ratio.

The Freshman Seminar is the cornerstone to freshman advising at Lynn and provides an introduction to college life for all new students. The course includes academic success strategies, time management, communication skills, study and test-taking techniques, academic advisement, and career development. The course is taught by select members of the faculty and staff who serve as mentors to new students throughout their freshman year.

The Honors Program strives to create a dynamic academic environment that will serve to heighten intellectual curiosity, promote free and active inquiry, and stimulate creative discovery among students with particularly strong academic promise. The innovative curriculum, team-taught by faculty members, encompasses the full breadth of the liberal arts and sciences while promoting both an in-depth exploration and a broad intellectual synthesis of the ideas and concepts that have shaped the dilemmas and choices of the past, present, and future.

The Freshmen Frontiers Program provides a smooth transition to college life for incoming students. Specialized assistance and support enable a student to be successful in the first and most critical semester of their college careers. Students become involved in tutorials that provide the academic foundation of good study habits and meet weekly mentors who deal with any problems that arise. The Dean of Freshmen reviews the academic background and preparation of all incoming students in order to individualize learning by selecting a blend of university-level courses to address identified needs.

The Advancement Program is designed for students with specific learning differences who have the motivation and intellectual capacity for college-level work—students whose skill and performance levels indicate that without support, their chances of success at the college level would be at risk. Various accommodations are available, including content area tutorials given in specific subjects by tutors with advanced degrees. Untimed and verbal examinations, taped lectures, and textbooks on tape are also available. All students admitted to the Advancement Program are required to take a 3-credit course titled Language and Learning.

Lynn University's approach to the development of academic programs has been one that focuses on the balance of a carefully selected core of liberal arts subjects within the framework of a curriculum that is career-oriented and provides both theoretical and practical preparation. Upon this solid liberal arts foundation, students build special competence in their chosen fields of concentration. The practical application of knowledge is a vital component of Lynn's academic program; therefore, residencies, student teaching, community service projects, and internships are required for many degrees.

The University follows a semester calendar and offers a summer session. Most graduate programs are scheduled on ten-week term cycles.

Off-Campus Arrangements

At Lynn University, great importance has been placed on bringing together students of various nationalities and cultures in an effort to foster greater understanding of diversity. Through a commitment to international education, students are empowered with the knowledge and understanding to effectively and peacefully deal with the challenges that face them in today's world. Recently, the University broadened its global perspective through the development of a number of study-abroad programs and the School of International Studies.

Study abroad is an integral part of a Lynn University education. The American College-Dublin in Ireland, an affiliate of Lynne University, welcome students for a semester of study abroad. Both campuses provide quality international education to Lynn University students interested in expanding their horizons. These are two examples of Lynn's commitment to expanding educational opportunities for students in the global market. Through an exchange agreement with the Trident School of Languages in Nagoya, Japan, the Lynn student can experience the customs, cultures, and languages of Asia.

The College of International Communications, established in 1996, has as its dean Mr. Irving R. Levine, the renowned NBC News Chief Economics Correspondent. Under the school's umbrella, the three undergraduate departments share a common core curriculum and the development of internationalized field experiences. Community service educational experiences, symposia, workshops, lectures by visiting scholars, and international internship opportunities are also offered within this degrees.

Academic Facilities

Recently, the University has seen the completion of four multimillion-dollar projects, made possible through the support of local community leaders. These include the Lynn Residence Hall, a dormitory for upperclassmen; the de Hoernle Sports and Cultural Center; and the Sensormatic Wing of the Assaf Academic Center. The Lynn Library, completed in early 1996, is a state-of-the-art facility providing reference materials in print and visual media, learning resources, computer facilities, and connection to online services. The de Hoernle International Center, a $3-million multipurpose academic center, was completed in fall 1997.

The Ritter Academic Center is home to the School of Business and houses classrooms, computer labs, and faculty offices. Art and photography studios and science laboratories can be found in the Assaf Academic Center, where most of the classes for the College of Arts and Sciences are taught.

Costs

Tuition for the 2000–01 academic year is $18,500. Yearly room and board fees total $6800. The service and technology fee is $750. Books are purchased separately.

Financial Aid

A student's education is not only a commitment of intellect and time, but a substantial financial investment as well. The University has a broad program of student financial aid, including scholarships, grants, work-study, and loans. Academic, athletic, and need-based scholarships are awarded. Inquiries may be made to the Office of Financial Aid.

Faculty

Faculty members are thoroughly committed to teaching and are readily accessible to students. The University has a very favorable student-faculty ratio of 19:1. Seventy percent of full-time faculty members hold doctoral degrees. Individualized attention is emphasized, and students are challenged as well as nurtured. A freshman mentoring program ensures a solid transition to University life.

Student Government

Officers of the student body, elected annually by the students, are involved in a wide variety of activities and interests.

Admission Requirements

All candidates for admission must be graduates of an accredited high school or must present formal evidence of having completed high school graduation requirements. Applicants are required to take the SAT I or ACT. Greater emphasis is placed on the recommendation of the applicant's guidance counselor than on standardized test scores. An early admission program is available for exceptionally strong students.

The University participates in the Advanced Placement Program. High school students who have taken an advanced placement test and scored 3 or higher may earn both credit and placement in a higher level course. University credit may also be earned by taking the College-Level Examination Program (CLEP) tests. International Baccalaureate credit is also granted.

All international applicants are expected to complete an undergraduate application for international admission. Applicants for whom English is not a first language must submit results from the TOEFL. All transcripts of previous academic work must be accompanied by certified English translations.

Transfer students who have completed a minimum of 15 academic college credits are expected to submit an official transcript from each college attended, along with a recommendation from the dean of students at the institution most recently attended. Those who have accumulated fewer than 15 credits are asked to also submit high school transcripts. Every effort is made to facilitate the transfer of credit from other institutions, and a special transfer adviser is available to ensure proper placement.

Application and Information

There is no formal deadline for admission, and applicants are notified on a rolling basis upon receipt of all credentials. The application fee is $25. For additional information about admission, to obtain an application packet, or to arrange for an interview and tour of the campus, prospective students should contact:

Office of Admission
Lynn University
3601 North Military Trail
Boca Raton, Florida 33431-5598
Telephone: 561-237-7900
              800-544-8035 (toll-free)
Fax: 561-237-7100
E-mail: admission@lynn.edu
World Wide Web: http://www.lynn.edu

A part of the campus of Lynn University, in Boca Raton, Florida.

MAHARISHI UNIVERSITY OF MANAGEMENT
FAIRFIELD, IOWA

The University

Since its founding in 1971 by Maharishi Mahesh Yogi, the goal of Maharishi University of Management (Maharishi International University, 1971–95) has been to make education complete so that every student may enjoy academic excellence, consciousness, and creativity and a high quality of life in accord with Natural Law. The University achieves its goal by offering new disciplines along with traditional studies and by incorporating the daily practice of the Transcendental Meditation® and TM-Sidhi® programs into its rigorous yet achievable academic schedule. This Consciousness-Based^{SM} (enlightenment-based) approach is unique, as it adds to traditional education scientifically validated programs for students to develop their full potential for inner and outer success. Scientific research demonstrates that students make rapid progress in academic achievement and in developing their creativity, intelligence, and good health.

The University is an accredited, private college offering bachelor's, master's, and doctoral programs in a broad range of disciplines. It developed its reputation for academic excellence through outstanding faculty members who are committed to the University's unique and innovative education. Faculty members include internationally recognized scholars and researchers who teach both undergraduate and graduate programs and conduct groundbreaking research in affiliated institutes. For example, the National Institutes of Health (NIH) allocated substantial funds for the creation of the University's Center for Natural Medicine and Prevention (CNMP). The CNMP is one of eight NIH-funded centers focusing on research in natural medicine and prevention and the only one specializing in minorities. Its research collaborators include the University of Iowa College of Medicine, Morehouse School of Medicine, Charles R. Drew University of Medicine and Science, and Cedars-Sinai Medical Center. The CNMP and the University attract significant, prestigious grants and peer recognition for continuing the extensive scientific research on the benefits of practice of the Transcendental Meditation program and Maharishi Vedic Medicine^{SM}.

Students find study here more effective and enjoyable because systematic programs for complete personal development enhance learning. Both students and alumni find the structured daily routine of all programs, which includes a professional dress code and punctual, full attendance at classes, helps prepare the ground for personal and career success. Graduates are accepted at leading professional schools and universities and are successful in careers in business, government, natural health care, the arts, and other fields. Students gain a head start in their careers through internship opportunities in challenging roles in business or in research projects, for example, studying the ecology of areas such as Arizona, Costa Rica, or Ecuador.

Students come to Maharishi University of Management from every state and more than ninety countries. The student body is a world family, excited about knowledge, open-hearted and friendly, and dedicated to world peace and making the world a better place. Most of the University's undergraduate students live on campus in single rooms. There are 200 units of housing available in the adjoining Utopia Park for students with families. Students enjoy a positive and nourishing atmosphere that is virtually crime free and drug free and without other problems that plague many university campuses. Alumni surveys conducted through ACT, Inc., indicate a remarkably high level of satisfaction with the education received at the University, in contrast to the national reference group.

There are numerous student clubs representing the variety of student backgrounds, including international student groups, an active student environmental organization, sports clubs, cultural clubs, a chess club, and many others, such as the unique Yogic Flying Club, whose members demonstrate the TM-Sidhi program, including Yogic Flying (an advanced technology of consciousness), in many locations around the U.S. Activities also include a wide variety of sports, public interest, and recreational events, including movies, dances, visiting speakers, and Student Government–sponsored conferences. Sports include aerobics and fitness training, basketball, golf, gymnastics, soccer, skiing, swimming, tennis, volleyball, and adventure sports, such as kayaking, mountain biking, rock climbing, and white-water rafting.

Location

Set in a rural Iowa community, Fairfield is within a 1-hour drive of Iowa City, home of the University of Iowa, and is approximately a 4-hour drive from Chicago, Kansas City, or St. Louis. Students enjoy a wide variety of shops and restaurants, including a dozen serving international cuisine, and take advantage of diverse cultural and recreational activities and a community that is a lively center for the arts. Students benefit from the dynamic local business and entrepreneurial community, which offers opportunities for field trips, projects, internships, consulting, and careers for graduates. Because of the local, national, and international success of Fairfield businesses, the former governor of Iowa called Fairfield the "entrepreneurial capital of Iowa."

Majors and Degrees

The University offers a comprehensive range of bachelor's degree programs, including the B.A. in fine arts or the B.F.A. with emphases, majors, or minors available in visual arts, theater arts, film video arts, 3-D animation, Web design, digital media, intermedia, and music; the B.A. or B.S. in chemistry, computer science, and psychology; the B.S. in biology, which qualifies as premedicine and includes emphases in environmental studies and sustainable agriculture (organic farming); the B.S. in mathematics and physics; and the B.A. in education, electronics, literature (emphasis available in writing), Maharishi Vedic Medicine^{SM}, management, and the Science of Creative Intelligence®. Undergraduate minors include creative writing, exercise and sport sciences, and most bachelor's degree areas. Associate of Arts degree programs are also available in most areas.

Nondegree programs offered at the University include certificate programs in Maharishi Vedic Science^{SM}, Sanskrit and Reading the Vedic Literature, English as a Second Language, and Maharishi Gandharva Veda^{SM} music, as well as technical training certificates in the Maharishi Rejuvenation^{SM} program and in Fine Furniture and Woodworking.

Academic Program

Students study one subject at a time through a four-week block system in a forty-four-week academic year. This allows in-depth focus on each subject and greater retention of knowledge without the conflicting demands of other classes. Students enjoy a learning experience giving the wholeness of knowledge in every class—faculty members relate every part of each discipline students study to the whole of the discipline, and the whole to the deepest level of the student's own intelligence. This approach makes learning personally relevant—students feel at home with all knowledge. First-year undergraduate students explore up to twenty disciplines in light of the interdisciplinary principles of the Science of Creative Intelligence, a new discipline connecting each branch of knowledge to the whole tree of knowledge. Through these first-year Natural Law Seminars, students thoroughly prepare to choose their major fields of study.

Off-Campus Arrangements

With the University's unique block system, study-abroad programs can be easily arranged. The Rotating University program offers courses in some of the world's most beautiful settings, such as the Swiss Alps, India, and Italy.

Academic Facilities

The University's 262-acre campus includes 1.2 million square feet of academic, research, residential, administrative, and recreational facilities. The campus provides accommodation in "no-alcohol" dormitories and features dining halls that serve natural foods and a rich and wholesome vegetarian and dairy menu, research and teaching laboratories, a library offering the latest computer technology, a radio station, a student union building, movie and drama theaters, recreational and sports facilities, a nondenominational chapel, and an outstanding elementary and secondary school. All buildings on campus are smoke free. The redevelopment of the campus began in 1998 with the construction of the first building designed according to the principles of Natural Law (Maharishi Sthapatya Veda^{SM} design), so that the architecture of the campus will be more than environmentally friendly and will actually promote clearer thinking, better health, and good fortune.

The library provides excellent resources for study and research, including access to extensive databases, the Internet, and CD-ROM reference sources, and houses tape, record, and CD collections. The library oversees a campuswide, closed-circuit television network offering videotaped and audiotaped courses, conferences, and presentations, along with live satellite broadcast receiving and Internet videoconferencing capabilities. The library's catalog and serials list is accessible on line, as are many items in its expanding electronic library.

The University is equipped with a campus computing network using fiber-optic cable to connect academic buildings and providing access to the Internet. Current development of a campus intranet will allow online access by students to Registrar's Office information. All student dorms have Ethernet connections. Tuition and fees allow free e-mail and voice mail accounts and free access to the World Wide Web. There are five computer laboratories available to students, as well as a bank of library computers and an array of modems enabling remote access to the network, also at no additional charge. The University has more than one computer in departmental and public access labs for every 4 on-campus students. (This compares to an approximate ratio of 1:16 at other universities.) Students also have access to specialized laboratories within their major departments, such as a state-of-the-art digital media laboratory.

Costs

Undergraduate tuition and fees for 2000–01 (for a forty-four-week academic year) total $15,630. A single room is $2720, and board is $2480. The total cost, including tuition, fees, room and board, books and supplies, and travel and personal expenses, is estimated at $23,730.

Financial Aid

The financial aid priority filing date is April 15, and the deadline for fall admission is July 15. Notification of awards is given on a rolling basis. Filing a Free Application for Federal Student Aid (FAFSA) is required. Federal Work-Study, Federal Pell Grant, FSEOG, Federal Stafford Student Loan, and Federal Perkins Loan programs are available, as are state grants, loans, and/or work-study. The University also provides institutional funds for grants and loans and both merit- and need-based scholarships. The average full-time undergraduate financial aid package for U.S. students is approximately $18,500.

Faculty

Maharishi University of Management has 87 full-time teaching and research faculty members and more than 23 adjunct and visiting faculty members. Almost 70 percent of the full-time faculty members have a Ph.D. or the highest degree in their field. The faculty members include internationally recognized scholars and researchers. With the University's 8:1 student-faculty ratio, students are assured maximum access to faculty members. Eighty-five percent of undergraduate courses and all of the first-year Natural Law Seminars are taught by senior faculty members, including the most distinguished professors in every academic department. The University has been awarded grants and contracts in excess of $32 million since 1977 from federal, state, and private sources, including prestigious research grants for which the University has competed successfully with large state universities and major research institutions.

Student Government

The Student Government Executive Committee, together with its sister organizations, World Congress and Student Senate, represents the official voice of the University's students. It provides communication channels between students, the faculty, the administration, and the staff; includes various committees to enhance the quality of student life; and sponsors and funds student clubs, movies, concerts, dances, speakers, and many other activities. Its 9-member executive committee is elected every spring by the student body.

Admission Requirements

Applicants are considered for admission after a comprehensive evaluation of their completed application. While an applicant's previous academic performance is a primary consideration, commitment to gaining maximum benefit from the educational opportunities offered at the University is also an important consideration in the admission decision.

For bachelor's programs, a high school diploma, SAT I or ACT test scores (SAT I required for engineering majors), and essays are required. Three high school units each of English, mathematics, science, and social studies are recommended. For admission requirements for nondegree programs, students should contact the Office of Admissions.

Application by April 15 for fall admission and October 15 for spring admission ensures maximum financial assistance and space availability. Applications are accepted after those dates but are then considered on a space-available basis. Acceptance is on a rolling basis.

Application and Information

Applicants may download, print, and mail application forms from the University's Web site or may submit their application on line. For more information, students should contact:

Brad Mylett, Director of Admissions
Maharishi University of Management
Fairfield, Iowa 52557

Telephone: 515-472-1110
Fax: 515-472-1179
E-mail: admissions@mum.edu
World Wide Web: http://www.mum.edu

Students gain the practical knowledge they need to succeed in their personal and professional lives.

MAINE COLLEGE OF ART
PORTLAND, MAINE

The College
Maine College of Art (MECA) is northern New England's only professionally accredited four-year college of art and design offering the Bachelor of Fine Arts degree in eight studio majors and the Master of Fine Arts degree in studio arts. Founded in 1882, the College is a nationally accredited, independent college with an enrollment of approximately 400 students who come from New England and throughout the United States as well as other countries.

The College has earned a reputation for an intimate learning atmosphere with a low student-faculty ratio of 10:1. Its urban location on the coast of Maine combines many cultural activities with a superb natural environment, and its accomplished faculty members, who are often found working alongside their students, are uniquely dedicated to the students' goals.

Extracurricular activities at Maine College of Art are largely informal. They revolve around departmental events, which include field trips and work with visiting artists, as well as larger all-College occasions, such as exhibition openings and visiting artist lectures. The College calendar is full from Orientation Week in September to the Senior Thesis Exhibition and commencement in May. First-year students begin their MECA education with a workshop at Haystack Mountain School of Crafts in Deer Isle.

Location
Located only a 2-hour drive from Boston and accessible by six major airlines, Portland is a small, cosmopolitan city on a peninsula in Casco Bay. While Portland has remained a working port, it has undergone a vast rebirth during the last fifteen years. Its waterfront, the Old Port, has been restored and is a thriving area of shops, bookstores, restaurants, and galleries a short walk from Maine College of Art. The College's buildings are all located in the downtown Arts District along with museums, theaters, concert halls, artists' studios, and cafés.

There is a high quality of life in Portland. A short distance inland are lakes and mountains that invite camping, hiking, and downhill and cross-country skiing. The coast offers pine forests, sandy beaches, rocky outcroppings, and breathtaking ocean vistas.

In the immediate vicinity of the College, the Portland Museum of Art offers free admission to MECA students, and the YWCA offers swimming privileges. Within walking distance, students can find a number of swimming pools, gyms, tennis courts, and health clubs.

Students become involved in the community through Art in Service internships that follow service learning techniques in placing students with local schools and health agencies. Students may also participate in credit-earning internships with area businesses and service agencies ranging from film studios to museums.

Majors and Degrees
Maine College of Art offers the Bachelor of Fine Arts degree in ceramics, graphic design and media arts, metalsmithing and jewelry, painting, photography, printmaking, sculpture, and self-designed studies. Students may also minor in art history.

Academic Program
The structured four-year B.F.A. degree curriculum develops students' abilities in perception, organization, and expression and increases their self-understanding, oral and written skills, and sense of personal place in human thought and cultural accomplishment. The academic year consists of two 15-week semesters. A comprehensive Thesis Exhibition of work accomplished during the fourth year in the student's major area is shown at the end of the school year.

Maine College of Art is noted for its strong foundation program in drawing and two- and three-dimensional design, which precedes study in the major. The mastery of these fundamentals permits students to devote the greater part of their time in the second two years to the major. Throughout the four years, art history and liberal arts studies are critical elements of the educational program. Such knowledge fosters and enriches ideas for the artist's work. The program is designed to equip students with the skills, visual insights, self-confidence, and self-discipline traditionally associated with the professional artist or designer.

An exchange program with Bowdoin College, located 20 miles north of Portland, allows full-time students at Maine College of Art to take academic courses at Bowdoin College at no additional tuition charge. The College belongs to the Greater Portland Alliance of Colleges and Universities, which allows exchanges for credit at four different area institutions. Prior to taking such courses, interested students must fulfill their English composition and art history survey requirements at Maine College of Art and must have the approval of the appropriate department head. Advanced MECA students are also eligible for the exchange program with the Hanoi Fine Arts College in Vietnam.

The College offers a summer Early College Program for high school students, which bears college credit. For the month of July, high school students participate in an intensive foundation program in a professional art college environment while earning 3 college credits. This structured experience is taught by Maine College of Art faculty members and distinguished visiting artists. Planned activities such as field trips and visits to museums add to the enjoyment of the summer program. Students from outside Portland may live in the College's supervised dormitory residences; a full meal plan is provided. Scholarships for the high school Early College Program are available.

Maine College of Art's year-round Continuing Studies Program offers credit courses in a variety of disciplines for adults. All classes are taught by practicing artists, including members of the faculty in the B.F.A. program. Noncredit workshops are also offered in the evenings and on weekends for adults seeking enrichment programs. Classes for students in grades 4–12 are offered on Saturdays during the academic year as well as on weekdays in the summer. Emerging and professional graphic designers expand their design vocabulary with workshops at the Maine Summer Institute in Graphic Design, three 5-day workshops led by internationally acclaimed designers during July and August. The 2000 faculty included Bruno Monguzzi, Melle Hammer, Nancy Skolos, and Thomas Wedell. MECA also sponsors a week-long summer fellowship for high school art teachers.

Academic Facilities
The College's physical plan currently includes five buildings; of these, two house the instructional and studio activities, two serve as residence halls, and one is an administration building. In 1993, MECA acquired the landmark Porteous department store, a 148,000-square-foot building in the heart of the city's Downtown Arts District. Open 24 hours a day, the Porteous Building includes individual studio spaces for majors. Three of the five stories of this elegant building have been renovated to house five of the seven studio departments as well as foundation classrooms. The ground floor includes the ICA@MECA (the College's professional gallery

of contemporary art), the Student Gallery, ArtWorks (a student sales gallery), and an independent art supply store.

Renovations to the second floor of the Porteous Building are now under way to house the new Joanne Waxman Memorial Library, one of the largest art libraries in New England and currently the beta testing site for an innovative software that links art text with images.

The Porteous Building has a state-of-the-art ventilation system for a safe and healthy environment for studio arts. Its tall windows, high ceilings, and commanding views of the city and coast make it an exceptional location for the College.

Costs

The cost of tuition for 1999–2000 was $16,530. Other costs, such as housing and art supplies, varied greatly from student to student. The cost of books and art supplies ranged from $800 to $1650 and room and board, from $3000 to $7042. Fees and insurance were $70. The total expenses were estimated to range from $20,397 to $24,300.

Financial Aid

Maine College of Art offers a wide range of financial aid programs and services to assist students and families with paying for college. The College participates in all federal and state financial aid programs and also offers a significant amount of institutional grant and scholarship funding. The Free Application for Federal Student Aid (FAFSA) is the only application required for both federal and institutional aid. Alternative loan programs based on student and/or family credit are available to supplement traditional forms of financial aid. The deadline for preferential consideration of financial aid requests is March 1.

Faculty

There are 20 full-time and 34 part-time faculty members teaching in the B.F.A. program. Faculty members are professional artists, designers, and scholars who are also devoted to teaching, to which they bring experience, vision, and inspiration. Faculty members also serve as advisers to students, which adds to the personal atmosphere of the College.

Student Government

Student representatives are elected annually by each class. They plan and organize traditional events, help with the art auction and student art show, and are responsible for allocating the student activities fee. This fee funds projects and activities that range from subsidizing the College newspaper to sponsoring visiting lecturers. Student representatives serve on many of the committees involved in the College's decision-making process.

Admission Requirements

The portfolio is considered central to application for admission. A written statement of purpose, high school records, SAT I scores, and the recommendations of teachers, guidance counselors, or employers are also required. An on-campus interview is strongly encouraged. Admission is competitive and on a rolling basis, with priority given to applications completed before March 1. Students may enter the B.F.A. program in September or January.

Application and Information

A complete packet of materials may be obtained by contacting:

Admissions Office
Maine College of Art
97 Spring Street
Portland, Maine 04101
Telephone: 207-775-3052
           800-639-4808 (toll-free)
E-mail: admissions@meca.edu
World Wide Web: http://www.meca.edu

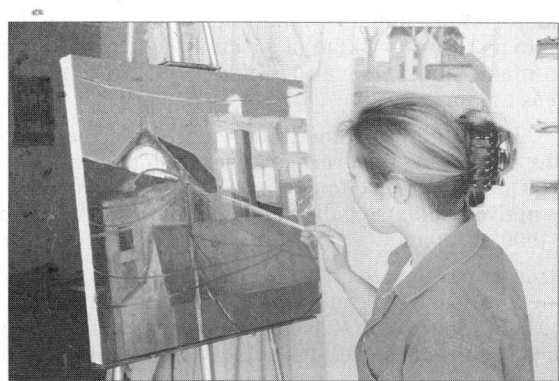

The low student-faculty ratio (10:1) encourages individual attention and a dynamic relationship between students and faculty members.

MALONE COLLEGE
CANTON, OHIO

The College

Malone College is a Christian college for the arts, sciences, and professions. The College was founded and established in 1892 by Walter and Emma Malone as the Cleveland Bible College. In 1957, the College moved to Canton, Ohio, and assumed the name Malone College. Today, Malone is one of four Christian colleges in Ohio that is a member of the Council for Christian Colleges and Universities. Malone also belongs to the thirteen-member Christian College Consortium.

At Malone College, students are challenged to grow in three vital aspects of life. Spiritually, students are placed in an environment that lends itself to cultivating a deeper relationship with God. Academically, students encounter rigorous challenges offered by a strong faculty, of whom 58 percent hold doctoral, first professional, or terminal degrees. Socially, Malone offers students a chance to experience the real world through on-campus and off-campus activities in which they are exposed to almost every kind of social influence. This requires them to make vital personal decisions and to formulate their own ideas and moral values.

Malone's 2,200 students come from twenty states and six other countries. At Malone, the average undergraduate class size is 21 students. Of the total enrollment, more than 850 students live on campus in five residence halls, the newest of which just opened for fall 1999 occupancy.

Students can participate in a variety of clubs and activities, including Christian organizations and thirteen intramural sports. Malone also offers strong varsity programs, including nine men's sports (baseball, basketball, cross-country, football, golf, indoor track, outdoor track, soccer, and tennis) and nine women's teams (basketball, cross-country, golf, indoor track, outdoor track, soccer, softball, tennis, and volleyball). Students may also participate in the campus radio station, newspaper, yearbook, student government, and marching band.

Malone also offers the opportunity for students to earn a master's degree in business, Christian ministries, and education.

Location

Malone College sits on a 78-acre campus in a quiet, residential area of Canton, Ohio. This setting lends itself to a variety of cultural experiences, including the Professional Football Hall of Fame; the ballet, symphony, and theater; museums; and professional sports teams. There is also easy interstate access to the metropolitan areas of Cleveland, Akron, and Youngstown.

Majors and Degrees

The Bachelor of Arts is offered in accounting, art, Bible/theology, biology, biology–clinical laboratory science, business administration, chemistry, church music, commercial music technology, communication arts, computer science, educational ministries, English, health education, history, integrated language arts, integrated science, integrated social studies, interdisciplinary social science, international affairs, law and society, liberal arts, life science/chemistry education, mathematics, music, physical education, physical science, psychology, social work, Spanish, sports ministry, sports science, urban studies, and youth ministry.

Many of these majors and several other fields are available as secondary education fields.

The Bachelor of Science is offered in early childhood education, health education, middle childhood education, music education, nursing, physical education, Spanish education, special education, and visual arts education.

Malone also offers degree-completion programs in nursing and management.

Academic Program

Since Malone is a college for the arts, sciences, and professions, there is a comprehensive general education requirement regardless of the chosen course of study. Students must meet requirements in each of Malone's academic areas, including communications, science, English, Bible/theology, and social science.

Malone students must meet a total of 60 semester credit hours in the aforementioned areas. A minimum of 124 credit hours is required to graduate. This is an accumulation of the major requirements, general education curriculum, and, in most cases, a series of electives. Malone offers forty-four undergraduate degree opportunities, the most popular of which are education, nursing, and business administration.

Malone's academic calendar is based on two semesters, with a summer school that includes three sessions.

Off-Campus Arrangements

Malone students are given the opportunity to spend a semester on another Christian college campus through the Christian College Consortium Visitor Program. Other off-campus opportunities include programs sponsored by or affiliated with the Council for Christian Colleges and Universities: American Studies (Washington, D.C.), China Studies (Shanghai), Latin American Studies (San Jose, Costa Rica), Middle East Studies (Cairo, Egypt), Russian Studies (Moscow, Nizhni Novgorod, and St. Petersburg), Los Angeles Film Studies (Los Angeles, California), Global Stewardship Studies (Belize, Central America), and Oxford Summer School Program (Oxford, England). Malone also provides international study opportunities in Costa Rica (for tropical ecology), Guatemala (for teacher education), and Kenya (at Daystar University).

Academic Facilities

The Cattell Library contains 110,546 books, 569,182 microfilm units, 1,524 periodicals, 105 CD-ROMs, and 9,653 records, tapes, and CDs. Communication majors also have a television studio on campus. There are 140 computers available for general student use in the library, residence halls, and the three computer labs.

Costs

The cost for one year at Malone is $17,810, which includes $12,150 for tuition and $5480 in room, board, and fees.

Financial Aid

Affordability is one of the strengths of Malone College. The College holds the belief that a college education is a family investment that requires realistic support. Nearly 95 percent of traditional Malone students receive some form of financial aid.

This is offered through federal grants and loans, state grants, work opportunities both on and off campus, or Malone College scholarships. These scholarships are awarded on the basis of one or more of the following: need; academic, musical, or athletic talent; or Christian perspective and leadership ability. Malone requires the completion of the FAFSA (Free Application for Federal Student Aid). The average financial aid package amounts to approximately $10,785 per year.

Faculty

Fifty-eight percent of Malone College faculty members hold doctoral, first professional, or terminal degrees. The undergraduate student-faculty ratio is 15:1. This allows students to learn and achieve in a comfortable setting and gives them easy access to assistance from professors.

Student Government

Malone's student organizations are directed by the Student Senate, which in turn is guided by a president and a vice president. The Senate is represented at nearly all of the institution's committee meetings, including the Board of Trustees' meetings. Working through committees, the Senate plays a significant role in shaping the total academic, spiritual, and social life of the Malone community. In addition, positions on the Senate are paid positions.

Admission Requirements

Malone welcomes applications for admission from bright, qualified high school graduates who want to attend college in an atmosphere of high academic standards and evangelical Christianity. Admission is based on objective evaluation of an applicant's motivation, maturity, and other personal qualifications and the applicant's academic credentials, with an emphasis on high school grade point average (2.5 or higher), ACT composite results equal to or above the national mean, class rank, standardized test scores, and depth of high school courses. Other applicants may be accepted by committee approval. A personal interview and campus visit are required in such instances. Malone admits students of any race, color, religion, sex, and national or ethnic origin who meet the academic requirements.

Application and Information

Applications for admission to Malone College are accepted until July 1, and there is a $20 fee required with the application. The Malone Admissions Office is open for campus visitation Monday through Friday from 8:30 a.m. to 5 p.m. The visitation includes a one-on-one interview with an admissions counselor and an individual tour of Malone's campus.

For more information about Malone College, students should contact:

John A. Chopka
Dean of Admissions
Admissions Office
Malone College
515 25th Street, NW
Canton, Ohio 44709
Telephone: 330-471-8145
           800-521-1146 (toll-free)
E-mail: admissions@malone.edu
World Wide Web: http://www.malone.edu

The Brehme Centennial Center is home to Malone's cafeteria, bookstore, and instrumental music department.

MANCHESTER COLLEGE
NORTH MANCHESTER, INDIANA

The College
Manchester College, founded in 1889, is an independent, coeducational, liberal arts college of the Church of the Brethren. Throughout its history, the College has held that values are central in the study of all majors and that the liberal arts provide a foundation of critical skills and sound scholarship.

An emphasis on service produces exceptional graduates who possess both professional ability and personal convictions, prepared for responsible lives that make a difference in the world.

Located at the edge of North Manchester, Indiana, Manchester College is primarily a residential school; 75 percent of the students live on the beautiful 124-acre campus. The academic buildings are constructed around a tree-lined central mall, and manicured flower gardens dot the campus. In addition, the resource-rich 100-acre Koinonia Environmental Retreat Center is located 12 miles from the academic campus.

The undergraduate enrollment is 1,100. Most students are between the ages of 18 and 22. Approximately 85 percent of the full-time students are from Indiana. Students from twenty-three states and twenty-three countries were also enrolled during 1999–2000. Sixteen percent of the students are members of the Church of the Brethren, but many different religious backgrounds are represented, and all are welcomed.

At Manchester, students get to know the members of the College's well-trained, concerned faculty on both a personal and an academic level. Faculty members take the time to assist students in a caring way, both in the classroom and as advisers.

There are five residence halls on campus, two of which are less than five years old, which provide a variety of living experiences for students to choose from.

Manchester is a member of the National Collegiate Athletic Association Division III and offers nine men's and eight women's sports. The Physical Education and Recreation Center houses physical education classes, a fitness center, intercollegiate and intramural sports, and recreational activities. The College has a very strong intramural program that involves about 80 percent of its students.

In addition to its undergraduate program, Manchester College offers the Master of Accountancy degree.

Location
Located in the heart of Indiana's beautiful lake country, North Manchester is a thriving community of 6,000 people. It is within a half hour's drive of the Fort Wayne metropolitan area and is only 3½ hours from Chicago. Wide streets with large shade trees, graceful homes, and a beautiful park combine to provide a setting for classic college living.

Majors and Degrees
Manchester College grants Bachelor of Arts and Bachelor of Science degrees. Areas of study include accounting, adapted physical education, art, athletic training, biology, business administration, chemistry, coaching, communication studies, computer science, corporate finance, criminal justice, early childhood education, economics, elementary education, engineering science, English, environmental studies, exercise science, French, gender studies, German, gerontology, health and fitness instruction, history, journalism, mathematics, media studies, medical technology, music, nonprofit management, peace studies, philosophy, physical education, physics, political science, prelaw, premedicine, prenursing, pre–occupational therapy, pre–physical therapy, psychology, religion, secondary education, small-business administration, social work, sociology, Spanish, and theater arts. Individualized interdisciplinary majors can also be arranged to meet a student's particular goals.

Academic Program
The curriculum reflects a commitment to sound training in a specific area of study, the major, and broad development of skills and understanding through the liberal arts. In addition, students may explore interests different from specific career or professional areas through elective courses. This combination prepares students for careers or graduate school immediately after graduation and equips them for the challenges and changes of the coming century.

Manchester College operates on a 4-1-4 calendar and offers three summer sessions. Qualifying scores on the Advanced Placement Program and College-Level Examination Program tests of the College Board are recognized for college credit or advanced placement.

Off-Campus Arrangements
Manchester College students may study abroad for a semester or year in thirteen countries: at Philipps-Universität Marburg in Marburg/Lahn (Germany), the Institut International d'Études Françaises of the University of Strasbourg (France), the University of Nancy (France), the University of Barcelona (Spain), St. Mary's College in Cheltenham (England), Hokkai Gakuen University in Sapporo (Japan), the Dalian Institute of Foreign Languages in Dalian (People's Republic of China), the University of La Verne Athens Center (Greece), the Catholic University of Ecuador, the Federal University of Ouro Preto (Brazil), Satya Wacana University (Indonesia), Marmara University (Turkey), Cochin (India), and Universidad Veracruzana (Mexico).

During the January term, numerous classes are held off campus. In the past several years, professors have taken classes to India, Africa, England, Mexico, Russia, France, Ghana, Vietnam, Nicaragua, Haiti, Germany, Costa Rica, Cuba, and Hawaii as well as to destinations in the continental United States.

Field experiences and internships are offered for credit in accounting, broadcasting, business, criminal justice, early childhood education, elementary education, forensic chemistry, gerontology, health sciences practicum, journalism, peace studies, physical education, political science, psychology, secondary education, and social work.

Academic Facilities
Manchester College has a local area network of 165 IBM-compatible workstations, one for every 6 students. In addition, the Clark Computer Center houses file servers, three computer labs, and an AS400 for student use. PC labs tied to the network are located in each residence hall and the library.

Cordier Auditorium, dedicated in 1978, seats 1,300 people and has modern facilities for staging, lighting, and sound.

The Holl-Kintner Hall of Science has extensive laboratory facilities for biology, botany, physics, and geology as well as four separate chemistry laboratories and a number of research laboratories. Students in astronomy use the 10-inch Newtonian reflector telescope in the Charles S. Morris Observatory.

The Funderburg Library is a newly renovated, three-story building that houses more than 170,000 books, 800 periodicals, and 4,500 audio recordings available for student use. Computer connections allow access to major libraries across the country.

Costs

Tuition for 2000–01 is $14,610 for full-time students. Room and board costs for the residence halls (double occupancy) are $5360. The total charges are $19,970 for the academic year.

Financial Aid

Manchester offers extensive scholarship and grant assistance through institutional resources. Academic awards include Presidential, Honors, and Dean's Scholarships. Special scholarships based on academic merit and interest are awarded in art, broadcasting, journalism, music, theater, and the video arts. Service scholarships, modern language scholarships, and honors stipends are also awarded. Scholarships based on merit and need are available to international students. Manchester also gives need-based grants. More than $6 million in institutional funds and more than $9 million in total aid were awarded in 1999–2000.

Approximately 97 percent of Manchester's students have some type of financial assistance, whether it is a scholarship, a grant, a loan, or campus employment. Questions about financial aid should be referred to the Office of Admissions.

Faculty

Manchester's faculty consists of 72 full-time and 18 part-time members. Eighty-eight percent hold earned doctorates or terminal degrees in their field. The main mission of the faculty members is to teach, although they do participate in research projects. All classes are taught by these members of the faculty. They also advise students in academic matters. There is a 14:1 student-faculty ratio.

Student Government

Students at Manchester assume responsibility for the governmental and judicial activities of the College. The Community Council provides a forum for discussion and investigation of community concerns and a channel for evaluating and solving community problems.

Each of the residence halls elects a governing body, which is responsible for providing leadership.

The judicial system of the College includes three courts: the Judicial Board, the Community Court, and an administrative hearing panel. The Student Budget Board is charged with responsibility for receiving requests for funds to support the activity program of the College and for making the necessary appropriations.

The Manchester Activities Council organizes programming of student events. Students are offered a wide variety of leadership and participation opportunities as part of the College's student development program.

Admission Requirements

Manchester College seeks to enroll students whose scholastic record, test scores, and personality give promise of success in college. Graduation from an accredited high school or its equivalent is required.

The College recommends that students take 4 years of English, 3 years of laboratory science, 3 years of mathematics, 2 years of foreign language, and 2 years of social studies in high school. Students may take either the ACT or the SAT I, and personal recommendations from a high school principal or guidance counselor are required.

For transfer students, transcripts of all previous college work are required.

Application and Information

Students may apply for admission prior to each term. Applications are accepted on a rolling basis until thirty days before the term begins. There is a nonrefundable $20 application fee.

Interested students and their parents are encouraged to visit Manchester College and meet faculty members, coaches, and current students; sit in on classes; and take a campus tour. Arrangements can be made by writing or calling the Office of Admissions.

Application forms and further information may be obtained from:

> Office of Admissions
> Manchester College
> North Manchester, Indiana 46962-0365
> Telephone: 800-852-3648 (toll-free)
> E-mail: admitinfo@manchester.edu
> World Wide Web: http://www.manchester.edu

Students from the First Year Colloquium course Bodies in Motion lead residents of Peabody Retirement Community in Tai Chi.

MANHATTAN COLLEGE
RIVERDALE, NEW YORK

The College

Manhattan College was founded by the Brothers of the Christian Schools in 1853 and chartered by the state of New York in 1863. Traditionally a private men's college, in 1964 it began a student-faculty exchange program with the College of Mount Saint Vincent. Manhattan became fully coeducational in 1973. The College has an enrollment of more than 3,200, of whom 2,400 are undergraduates. Approximately 82 percent of Manhattan's students come from New York State; 17.3 percent represent thirty-nine other states and the remainder represent fifty other countries. Approximately 1,500 housing units are available, consisting of on-campus residence halls and off-campus apartments. Sixty percent of the students reside on campus. Manhattan offers seventy extracurricular organizations and five student publications and fields twenty varsity and club sports teams.

Of Manhattan's 40,000 living alumni, more than 18,000 work in the New York City area. Manhattan graduates are prominent leaders in business, government, education, the arts, the sciences, and engineering.

Location

The main campus of the College is located 12 miles north of midtown Manhattan in the suburban Riverdale section of the Bronx, about a mile from Westchester County. Riverdale is an upper-middle-class community, the home of many New York business, political, and education leaders. The area offers the calm and quiet of a residential, suburban setting as well as easy access to the many advantages of New York City. The College is easily accessible by subway, bus, or highway.

Majors and Degrees

The liberal arts curriculum of the School of Arts provides programs that lead to a Bachelor of Arts or Bachelor of Science with majors in the humanities and the social sciences, including communications, economics, English, fine arts, government, history, modern foreign languages, philosophy, psychology, religious studies, and sociology. Interdisciplinary majors include international studies, peace studies, and urban affairs. In the School of Science, programs lead to a Bachelor of Science or Bachelor of Arts with majors in biochemistry, biology, chemistry, computer science, mathematics, and physics.

The School of Engineering has a day session with programs leading to a Bachelor of Science in chemical, civil, computer, electrical, environmental, and mechanical engineering.

The School of Business has programs leading to a Bachelor of Science in Business Administration with majors in accounting, computer information systems, economics, finance, global business, managerial sciences, and marketing.

The School of Education offers a curriculum leading to a Bachelor of Arts for teachers of English, foreign languages, and social studies and to a Bachelor of Science for teachers of biology, chemistry, computer science, general science, mathematics, physics, and special education. The physical education curriculum leads to a Bachelor of Science in physical education in one of three concentrations: teaching, pre–physical therapy, or sports medicine. The health education curriculum leads to a Bachelor of Science in health education or community health. Curricula in radiological and health sciences lead to a Bachelor of Science in radiation therapy or nuclear medicine technology.

Academic Program

The core curriculum shared by the School of Arts and the School of Science studies some of the vital works of humankind, explores new ideas, examines the meaning of scientific experimentation, and encourages a student to develop his or her thinking and leadership abilities. The major programs offer advanced work in specific humanistic and scientific disciplines and opportunities to work on research projects in collaboration with faculty scholars.

In the School of Engineering, all engineering students follow a common core curriculum during the first two years and choose a major at the beginning of the junior year. Each curriculum includes a generous selection of courses in basic sciences, the engineering sciences, humanistic studies, and mathematics.

The School of Business prepares students for positions of executive responsibility in business, government, and nonprofit organizations. The business curriculum is based on a strong commitment to liberal education and is well balanced between professional business courses, humanities, sciences, and social sciences. This is a reflection of the School's belief that executives should be broadly educated and should involve themselves, as well as their organizations, in efforts to solve social problems.

The School of Education prepares students for teaching, counseling, and health professions. Students complete the College's core curriculum in liberal arts and sciences and then complete a major in various programs in the School's three departments: Education, Physical Education & Human Performance, and Radiological & Health Professions. All programs include internships/practicums in schools, hospitals, or other institutions. Graduates of the school's teacher-preparation programs receive New York State provisional teaching certification. The school also offers a five-year B.A./M.S. program in elementary or secondary education and special education.

Off-Campus Arrangements

Students in the liberal arts curricula who have demonstrated superior achievement in their first two years are encouraged to spend their junior year studying abroad. Manhattan College offers study-abroad programs; arrangements can be made to a country of choice. Students in the School of Business may participate in the International Field Studies Seminar. As participants in the seminar, students spend time in another country studying the effect of that environment on international firms.

Career services and co-op education integrate classroom theory with the practical experience of a job in industry, business, the social services, the arts, or government. Portions of the education courses are conducted in New York City schools, in order that student teachers may gain experience in urban education at an early stage.

Manhattan College and the neighboring College of Mount Saint Vincent collaborate in an exchange of students and facilities to provide more extensive opportunities for academic development.

Academic Facilities

There are more than forty scientific and engineering laboratories at Manhattan, including the Research and Learning Center, as well as a modern language laboratory and a computer information systems laboratory. A psychology laboratory is located on the campus of the College of Mount Saint Vincent. Manhattan College's libraries house 200,000 volumes and 1,590 periodical titles.

Costs

For 1999–2000, the tuition for all curricula was $7950 per semester. A fee that varied among programs was added. The rate per credit was $440. Room and board came to $3725 per semester for a seven-day meal plan.

Financial Aid

Manhattan grants or administers financial assistance in the form of tuition awards to students on the basis of need and/or ability. Need is evaluated through the FAFSA. In addition to a general scholarship fund, Manhattan offers endowed scholarships, special-category scholarships and grants, student athletic grants, Federal Pell Grants, Federal Supplemental Educational Opportunity Grants, student loans, Federal Work-Study Program awards, and New York State financial assistance. A total of 1,650 students receive financial aid from Manhattan College, and approximately 87 percent receive financial aid from government or private agencies.

Faculty

Manhattan's faculty has 190 full-time and 82 part-time teachers. The faculty-student ratio is approximately 1:15. Almost 95 percent of the faculty members hold doctorates. The maximum teaching load on the undergraduate level is 12 credit hours per semester. Faculty members serve on the College Senate, the Council for Faculty Affairs, and numerous faculty and campus committees. In addition, they are available to students for informal guidance and counseling and also serve as official moderators of many campus organizations.

Student Government

The Manhattan Student Government is composed of students elected annually by their peers to fill posts outlined in the Student Government Constitution. The Student Government allocates funds to all student organizations. Members of the Student Government are also full voting members of the College Senate.

Admission Requirements

Manhattan has a long-standing policy of nondiscrimination. No applicant is refused admission because of race, color, religion, age, national origin, sex, or handicap. All applicants must present an academic diploma from an accredited high school and must offer a minimum of 16 credits in academic subjects. Liberal arts candidates must be proficient in at least one foreign language. At the discretion of the Committee on Admissions, quantitative requirements may be modified for applicants with especially strong records who show promise of doing well in college. In the selection process, attention is given to scholastic ability as indicated by grades and rank in class, as well as to standardized test scores and recommendations from principals and counselors. All candidates must submit either SAT I or ACT results. An interview with a member of the admission staff is recommended. Applicants may submit scores on the General Educational Development test in lieu of a formal high school diploma. However, all such applicants must submit the results of the appropriate College Board tests. Manhattan College offers early acceptance for high school seniors, admission to advanced standing, advanced placement, and credit by examination. Junior college or other transfer students are welcome. There are also three special-status categories for students: nonmatriculated, nondegree, and noncredit. Manhattan College requires applicants whose native language is not English to take the Test of English as a Foreign Language as well as the SAT I. The average SAT I scores of entering freshmen in 1999 were 550 in mathematics and 550 in the verbal portion; 50 percent of the incoming class ranked in the upper quarter of their high school class.

Application and Information

Application forms are furnished by the Admission Office on request. The Common Application Form, which is available in many high school guidance offices, may also be used. After supplying the information required, students must send the application for admission to the Admission Office at Manhattan College. The high school report and the student evaluation and transcript must be submitted by the high school guidance counselor. This should be done after six terms of high school or right after the seventh term. There is a rolling admissions policy and a March 1 deadline for financial aid applications. A nonrefundable application fee of $35 is required.

William J. Bisset
Dean of Admissions and Financial Aid
Manhattan College
Riverdale, New York 10471
Telephone: 718-862-7200
        800-MC2-XCEL (toll-free)
E-mail: admit@manhattan.edu

Students entering the quadrangle of the Manhattan College campus.

MANHATTAN SCHOOL OF MUSIC
NEW YORK, NEW YORK

The School
Since 1917, Manhattan School of Music has been preparing gifted young musicians to assume places on the great stages of the world. When they select Manhattan School of Music, students choose to work with faculty members who are themselves performers with international reputations. In addition, they choose to be with exceptional students from around the world who come together to create an environment remarkable not only for its intensity, but also for its genuine friendliness and sincere cooperation. When students choose Manhattan School of Music, they also choose New York itself, the very heart of music and art in America.

While all music conservatories of the first rank are acknowledged for their ability to develop talents and refine skills, Manhattan School of Music has a particular combination of strengths that makes it something more—an unrivaled place from which to launch a career.

Performance is the vital expression of a musician's life. At Manhattan School of Music, performance is not simply the goal for students, it is at the center of their lives. With extensive performance opportunities on campus and the chance to freelance and begin to develop a network of professional contacts, students undergo remarkable changes; they start to think and function as professional musicians while they are still in school. It is this powerful convergence of unmatched opportunity and rigorous training that gives these students the best chance to go as far as their talent, their intelligence, and their courage can take them.

Manhattan School of Music enrolls 800 students, approximately 50 percent of whom are undergraduates. They come from more than forty states and more than forty countries. Twenty percent of the students are people of color and nearly 40 percent are international students.

Student groups include Student Council, Composers Now, Pan-African Student Union, Korean Students Association, Chinese Student Association, and Lesbian and Gay Student Association.

Students must live in residence housing for the first and second years of their study and may apply to stay longer. The School will open a new residence facility during the 2001–2002 academic year.

Location
For musicians and other artists of great ability and ambition, New York is universally acknowledged as the best place to be. Around the corner and down every street there are opportunities to see and hear the best music in the world every night of the year. With Broadway and off-Broadway theaters, world-famous jazz clubs, and countless museums, New York remains what it has always been—the most extraordinary city on earth. The names of the legendary places and performers that make New York what it is are the very definition of excellence. Carnegie Hall, Lincoln Center, the Blue Note, the Metropolitan Opera, the New York Philharmonic, the American Ballet Theater, the New York City Ballet, the New York City Opera, the Alvin Ailey American Dance Theater, and the Metropolitan Museum of Art are all accessible from campus.

As part of New York's "Academic Acropolis," Manhattan School of Music shares its student-oriented, Upper West Side location with Columbia University, Barnard College, Union Theological Seminary, Jewish Theological Seminary, Bank Street College, the Cathedral of St. John the Divine, and Riverside Church.

Majors and Degrees
Manhattan School of Music offers Bachelor of Music degrees in classical composition, classical performance (guitar, orchestral instruments, piano, and voice), jazz composition, and jazz performance.

Academic Program
The degree requires completion of a four-year program of study, with a required humanities core sequence, a music history and music theory core sequence, required courses relevant to each instrument/major, and large and small performance ensembles. Faculty members provide weekly, private, one-on-one instruction in each major. The number of credits required to graduate depends on the instrument/major but is no fewer than 120.

Because the School is dedicated to training outstanding performing artists, performance is at the core of most courses. Appropriate assignments to symphony orchestras, opera studios and workshops, jazz ensembles, and chamber music ensembles evolve into more than 400 public performances per academic year by students. Performance opportunities include Symphony Orchestra, Philharmonia Orchestra, Chamber Sinfonia, Opera Theater, American Musical Theater Ensemble, Percussion Ensemble, Guitar Ensemble, Baroque Aria Ensemble, Jazz Orchestra, Concert Jazz Band, Afro-Cuban Ensemble, and more than seventy-five jazz combos and chamber music groups.

A cross-registration program between Manhattan School of Music and Barnard College of Columbia University enables qualified undergraduates to have access to a wide variety of academic courses. Musically qualified Barnard students may enroll in lessons with Manhattan School of Music faculty members.

Academic Facilities
Facilities at Manhattan School of Music include a 1,000-seat auditorium for symphony, opera, and jazz performances; a 250-seat recital hall; a 75-seat recital hall; a 35-seat recital hall/recording studio; three electronic music studios; and an 82,000-volume library, which includes more than 20,000 recordings.

Costs
Tuition for the 2000–01 academic year (12–18 credits per semester) is $20,100. Annual fees required of all students are $530, including a health insurance fee. Housing costs are $5900 to $7200 per year, and food costs are approximately $4000 per year.

Financial Aid
Manhattan School of Music offers federal and state financial assistance as well as its own institutional resources in the form of scholarships and grants. Federal and state aid is administered in accordance with federal and state laws and regulations. The majority of institutional scholarships are awarded on the

basis of audition results, financial need, previous academic work, and the School's need for particular instruments/majors. Each year the School also awards approximately 5 percent of its resources on the basis of merit alone. Forty percent of the School's students receive scholarships. The financial aid deadline is March 15 for both government and institutional aid.

Faculty

The faculty forms the essential core of any school, but at a conservatory, faculty members take on an additional importance, for it is not simply what they know but what they do that helps to transform their students.

Manhattan School of Music's 250 faculty members are soloists and chamber and jazz artists as well as members of the New York Philharmonic, the Metropolitan Opera Company, the Chamber Music Society of Lincoln Center, New York City Opera, and the Orpheus Chamber Orchestra. Artists-in-residence include American String Quartet and Windscape.

Regular faculty members teach 98 percent of all courses and 100 percent of private lesson instruction.

Each year Manhattan School of Music brings more than 50 internationally renowned conductors and performing artists to the School. Selected conductors during 1998–2000 have been Kurt Masur, George Manahan, Zdenek Macal, James Paul, Jerzy Semkow, Graziella Contratto, Lawrence Leighton Smith, Elizabeth Schulze, Jorge Mester, Stanislaw Skrowaczewski, Samuel Cristler, James Judd, Sergiu Commissiona, Steven Crawford, and Yuri Temirkanov. Selected master classes during 1998–2000 have been conducted by Elly Ameling, voice; Robert Mann, violin; Elvin Jones, jazz drum set; Midori, violin; Costas Cotsiolis, guitar; David Wonsey, percussion; Byron Janis, piano; Steve Wilson, jazz saxophone; Charles Reicker, voice and auditioning; David Friesen, jazz double bass; Eduardo Isaac, guitar; Alicia de Larrocha, piano; David Russell, guitar; Amy Putnam, percussion; Martin Katz, voice and accompanying; Eugene Istomin, piano; Justin DiCioccio, The Complete Jazz Artist of the Twenty-first Century; Sherrill Milnes, voice; William Westney, an "un-masterclass"; Zoran Dukic, guitar; Dimitry Markevitch, cello; Peter Norton, trombone; Glen Velez, percussion; Billy Watrous, jazz trombone; Susan Cheng, Music from China; Vladimir Feltsman, piano; Lynn Harrell, cello; Marzio Conti, flute; Dr. Don Greene, performance enhancement; Dusan Bogdanovic, guitar; David Amram/Ludmila Ulehla/Susan Botti, composers forum; members of the St. Petersburg Philharmonic, sectionals; Ruth Laredo/Frank Morelli, Programming and Audience Development; David Russell, guitar; Kadar Khan, Music from India; Ellen Shade, voice; Andy Narell, percussion; Warren Vache, jazz trumpet; John Duarte, guitar; John O'Conor, piano; Pulse Percussion Ensemble, percussion; David Epstein, Career Advice for Musicians in the Twenty-first Century; Kakraba Lobi, percussion; Tilman Hoppstock, guitar; Miriam Fried, violin; Joseph Seiger, Art of the Sonata; Robert Levin, African Drumming; Glenn Dicterow, violin; Goran Sollscher, guitar; Lorin Hollendar, The Healing Power of Music; members of the Berlin Philharmonic, sectionals; Marni Nixon, voice; Rolando Morales, percussion; and Leo Brouwer, guitar.

Student Government

The Manhattan School of Music Student Council serves as the voice of the student body. Made up of both undergraduate and graduate students, the council voluntarily serves a one-year, renewable term and serves as an advisory body to the administration. The council also sponsors various social activities at the School.

Admission Requirements

Manhattan School of Music requires an in-person audition in New York City during one of the two audition periods (March and May). Cellists, bassists, and tubists may submit a videotape in lieu of a live audition. A high school transcript or an official high school equivalency diploma is required of all applicants. Additional requirements can be found on the application.

Manhattan School of Music is a highly selective college and admitted only 40 percent of the freshman applicants for admission for the 1999–2000 academic year. Manhattan School of Music seeks a geographically and ethnically diverse student body.

International applicants residing outside of North America may submit a videotape (U.S. format only) in lieu of a live audition. In addition, applicants whose first language is not English must take the TOEFL or the IELTS and submit their scores before consideration for admission.

Recognition of transfer credits from other institutions of higher education in theory, sight singing, dictation, keyboard harmony, required piano, and music history is determined by placement tests given during new student orientation before the first semester. Credit for other courses completed with a minimum grade of C or its equivalent depends upon the extent to which these subjects satisfy the curricular requirements of the School.

Application and Information

Applications for both freshmen and transfer students must be received by December 15 for the March audition period and by April 1 for the May audition period. Notification of admission status is sent by mail two to four weeks after each audition period.

For more information, please contact:

Lee Cioppa
Director of Admission
Manhattan School of Music
120 Claremont Avenue
New York, New York 10027
Telephone: 212-749-2802 Ext. 2
Fax: 212-749-5471
E-mail: admission@msmnyc.edu
World Wide Web: http://www.msmnyc.edu

The Manhattan School of Music building as viewed from across Broadway.

MANHATTANVILLE COLLEGE
PURCHASE, NEW YORK

The College
Manhattanville, a coeducational, independent liberal arts college, attracts bright students who seek the challenge of a demanding curriculum at a small college that stresses individual attention and humanistic values. Founded in New York City in 1841, the College moved to its present location in 1952. The 1,070 undergraduate students come from across the United States and from twenty-five countries.

Most students live on campus in one of four residence halls. Clubs and organizations center on particular interests but open their programs to all students. These groups include the College Orchestra and Chorus; Student Government; *Touchstone*, the student newspaper; and the Player's Guild (dramatics). Students may also participate in eighteen NCAA Division III varsity athletic teams and intramural sports or may become involved in the yearbook, literary magazine, and radio station. There are a health service, dining service, post office, college store, fully equipped fitness center and pool, and campus café. A career planning and fieldwork office assists students in the search for future job opportunities and helps students secure more than 250 internships and off-campus jobs that relate to their academic pursuits.

Location
Manhattanville's campus—100 acres of suburban countryside—is located in New York's Westchester County, just minutes from White Plains to the west and Greenwich, Connecticut to the east. It is 25 miles from the heart of Manhattan, the home of some of the world's foremost museums and theaters, Lincoln Center, the New York Public Library, and Madison Square Garden. Nearby shopping, dining, and entertainment facilities are excellent. Students who wish to become involved in local community programs can find opportunities to volunteer their services. The campus van transports students directly to New York City on weekends and to Manhattan-bound commuter trains on other days. Public transportation stops within the campus and transports students to White Plains, the Westchester (mall), the Galleria (mall), and the train station.

Majors and Degrees
Manhattanville College offers the undergraduate degrees of Bachelor of Arts, Bachelor of Fine Arts, and Bachelor of Music.

For the Bachelor of Arts degree, students may choose from the following major fields of study: anthropology, art, art history, biochemistry, biology, chemistry, computer science, dance and theater, economics, English, French, history, management, mathematics, music, music management, neuroscience, philosophy, physics, political science, psychology, religion, sociology, and Spanish.

For the degree of Bachelor of Music, the major areas are instrumental music or voice, music education, music history, music management, music theory, and sacred music.

For the Bachelor of Fine Arts degree, students may specialize in design, drawing, painting, photography, printmaking, and sculpture.

Interdisciplinary programs are offered in American studies, Asian studies, biochemistry, environmental studies, German studies, international studies, preprofessional studies, Romance languages, and women's studies. A self-designed program is also available.

Other undergraduate programs include prelaw and premedicine, teacher education (leading to New York State provisional certification), two five-year combined-degree programs (B.A./M.A.T. and B.A./M.P.S.) in teaching offered with Manhattanville's Graduate School of Education, a five-year combined-degree program (B.A./M.B.A.) in business administration offered with New York University, a five-year program in prenursing with New York University, and courses in English language training, Italian, and Japanese.

Academic Program
Manhattanville operates under a traditional liberal arts program. At the core of Manhattanville's undergraduate curriculum is the portfolio. Working closely and meeting regularly with an adviser, the student discusses and plans his or her program to fulfill graduation requirements. Students establish a major and a minor from the different branches of the liberal arts, and they submit academic evidence of proficiency in written critical analysis and qualitative research. Study plans, annual evaluations, transcripts, and examples of the students' best work are part of the portfolio and are evaluated by a College-wide review board.

A special option open to B.A. candidates is the self-designed major. If students' interests direct them outside or beyond existing departmental majors, they may propose a program of study to the Board of Academic Standards, delineating their goals and the means by which they will be achieved. A double major is also possible.

Off-Campus Arrangements
Students interested in literature, history, and philosophy may take part in Manhattanville's exchange program with St. Clare's College in Oxford, England. In addition, students may spend their junior year abroad in Bath, Florence, Madrid, Paris, St. Petersburg, or Vienna under programs conducted by other American colleges and universities, and they may participate in a program at the Université de l'Ouest at Angers, France.

Manhattanville conducts an exchange program with Sacred Heart University (Tokyo, Japan) and the Catholic University of Korea/Songsim (Seoul, South Korea). In addition, Manhattanville is affiliated with the New York State Visiting Students Program, through which students enrolled at a New York State college or university may spend a semester or a year at another participating institution. Manhattanville and the State University of New York College at Purchase also cooperate to enable students to enroll in courses on each other's campus that are not given at the home campus.

Academic Facilities
The Manhattanville library is considered one of the foremost undergraduate teaching libraries in the country. It has a general collection of more than 275,000 volumes and bound periodicals and an evolving array of electronic databases, journals, and full-text research tools. The library subscribes to many publications, including those of distinguished learned societies,

and has a substantial and growing collection of books and newspapers on microtext. Its excellent reference facilities and extensive bibliographical holdings include the printed catalogs of such major libraries as the Bibliothèque Nationale, the British Museum, and the Library of Congress. The Menendez Language Laboratory includes tapes and record libraries that provide materials for class instruction and individual practice in French, Spanish, Russian, Italian, German, Chinese, Japanese, Hindi, Marathi, modern Hebrew, and English as a second language. In addition, the College provides a writing clinic, audiovisual facilities, a reading clinic, a bibliographic instruction program, and approximately fifty microcomputers available for student use.

Costs

For the 1999–2000 academic year, tuition was $18,860. Average room and board costs were $8000.

Financial Aid

Manhattanville offers both merit scholarships and need-based financial aid. More than 65 percent of Manhattanville students receive financial awards. The institutional form and the Free Application for Federal Student Aid (FAFSA) are required. The types of awards available are honors, merit, and leadership scholarships, Manhattanville grants and scholarships, Federal Perkins Loans, Federal Stafford Student Loans, Federal Pell Grants, Federal Supplemental Educational Opportunity Grants, and Federal Work-Study Program awards as well as Tuition Assistance Program awards and Higher Education Opportunity Program awards for eligible New York State residents.

Faculty

As a result of the advising system under which faculty members serve as advisers who guide and counsel students throughout their undergraduate careers, student-faculty relationships are very strong. Seventy-five percent of the faculty members hold doctorates, and 50 percent serve full-time. The faculty-student ratio is 1:10. There are three faculty members in residence, and many more live on campus in faculty housing.

Student Government

Students, in large measure, shape the quality of life on the Manhattanville campus. Elected representatives of the student body run the Student Government, which serves as a principal means of communication among the administration, faculty, and students. Its Board of Directors is responsible for formulating policy on student life and for implementing this policy through various committees. Student Government members also serve on the College's policymaking and ad hoc committees.

Admission Requirements

Manhattanville College admits men and women as candidates for undergraduate degrees if their academic records indicate the competence to engage in a challenging liberal arts curriculum. Admission to the College is selective, and the most important consideration is the student's secondary school performance. When weighing this, the Admissions Committee evaluates the quality of the school, the strength of the student's program, and his or her success in those studies. Next, the committee considers the various recommendations that are submitted on behalf of the student along with scores on required standardized tests. The SAT I and/or the ACT are required. A campus interview is strongly recommended. Students who plan to specialize in music should come to Manhattanville for an audition or should secure permission to submit a tape. Students who plan to apply for the B.F.A. degree program should present portfolios to the art department for evaluation. The portfolios are not required for admission to the College.

Manhattanville offers both early decision admission and rolling admission. In both cases, advanced standing is given to accepted applicants who obtain scores of 4 or 5 on Advanced Placement examinations or whose secondary school records warrant it.

Application and Information

The deadline for early decision applications is December 15, and the deadline for regular admission is March 1. The College subscribes to the Candidates Reply Date. Applications should be submitted as early in the senior year as possible. The application fee is $40. All application decisions are made without regard to race, religion, sex, national or ethnic origin, or handicap.

For further information, students should contact:

Office of Undergraduate Admissions
Manhattanville College
2900 Purchase Street
Purchase, New York 10577
Telephone: 914-323-5464
800-32-VILLE (toll-free)

Reid Hall ("The Castle") at Manhattanville College.

MANNES COLLEGE OF MUSIC, NEW SCHOOL UNIVERSITY
NEW YORK, NEW YORK

The College

Founded in 1916 by David and Clara Damrosch Mannes, who were then world renowned as a violin-piano duo, the Mannes College of Music is recognized—nationally and internationally—as being among the finest professional music conservatories.

As such, its primary focus is on the training of outstanding young musicians who are preparing for professional careers in performance. This contrasts with college and university music departments, which more often prepare students for careers in fields such as music education, scholarly disciplines such as music history and research, and music-related fields such as music therapy or music journalism. Mannes is also distinguished by a relatively small enrollment that permits the close and supportive environment of a craft shop.

Mannes is a member of the Association of Professional Schools of Music (APM), is accredited by the Middle States Association of Colleges and Schools, and is chartered by New York State to award the degrees of Bachelor of Music, Bachelor of Science, and Master of Music, as well as undergraduate and graduate diplomas.

Mannes has about 300 students enrolled in its degree-granting College Division. They are from twenty-five states and twenty-four countries in Europe, the Orient, and South America. The vast majority are of traditional college age, although a small number who have significant professional career experience and wish additional certification or training enroll in the Master of Music degree program.

In order of percentage of the student body, students major in stringed instruments, voice, piano, winds, brass, percussion, choral and orchestral conducting, composition, guitar, historical performance, and music theory.

The number of internationally prominent artists who are Mannes graduates contrasts dramatically with the school's relatively small size. Graduates include Frederica von Stade, Julius Rudel, Murray Perahia, Richard Goode, Eugene Istomin, Anthony Newman, Eve Queler, the winners of both the 1985 and the 1986 Stokowski Conducting Competition, and Semyon Bychkov, who was appointed successor to Daniel Barenboim as music director of L'Orchestre de Paris. Others who trained at Mannes include Burt Bacharach, June LeBell, Ruggiero Ricci, Gerard Schwarz, Mimi Benzell, and Mitch Miller.

Location

Mannes's location is particularly well suited for both students and musicians. Manhattan's West Side is one of the most vibrant areas of New York and is the site of most of the city's major musical and other cultural activities. Within blocks of the College are Lincoln Center, Merkin Hall, Symphony Space, the Museum of Natural History, and the New York Historical Society, as well as recreational centers such as Central Park and Riverside Park. Easily accessible by public transportation of every kind, the College is also near restaurants of every cuisine and price range.

Majors and Degrees

Undergraduate degrees offered by Mannes College of Music are the *Bachelor of Music* and the *Bachelor of Science*.

Students may major in composition, conducting, guitar, historical performance, piano, theory, voice and opera, and all orchestral instruments.

Academic Program

Mannes is one of seven academic divisions of the New School for Social Research. Its musical strengths are therefore linked to a university known for its progressive outlook and deep commitment to the arts. Mannes students may take advantage of the complete range of course offerings at the New School, and Mannes's position within the university provides academic and cultural resources that are unobtainable at most independent colleges of music.

Within the music profession, Mannes is especially noted for its intensive training. All students take rigorous and extensive courses in theory, ear training, harmony, analysis, and counterpoint. Mannes's pioneering curriculum in these areas is heavily influenced by Schenker's analytic approach and is now being emulated by many music schools throughout the world.

In order to graduate with an undergraduate degree, students must complete a minimum of 131 hours of study. Mannes College of Music operates on the semester system.

Academic Facilities

In 1984, Mannes College moved to new quarters on Manhattan's West Side. The Federal-style building, erected in 1928, was completely rebuilt to serve the needs of a modern conservatory population, but it still retains the informal ambience that characterizes life at Mannes. In addition to classrooms, practice rooms, and offices, the building houses two student lounges and a spacious library, which provides study carrels and a listening room. Two concert halls are available; the larger seats 300, the smaller, suitable for student recitals, seats 50. Dormitory accommodations for approximately 30 students are available.

Costs

In 1999–2000, full-time tuition was $18,000; part-time tuition was $500 per credit. Application and College fees totaled $390. A registration deposit of $500 is required of new, full-time students; returning students pay $150. Annual dormitory fees are approximately $6800.

Financial Aid

In any given year, more than 80 percent of the students qualify for tuition assistance on the basis of financial need, level of achievement, and talent. U.S. citizens draw from federal financial aid programs: the Federal Supplemental Educational Opportunity Grant, Federal Pell Grant, Federal Work-Study Program, and Federal Perkins Loan. The College itself allocates generous scholarship support.

Faculty

Throughout its history, Mannes has attracted the world's foremost teaching artists to its faculty. Musicians such as Alfred Cortot, George Szell, Vladimir Horowitz, Sylvia Marlowe, and Judith Raskin are among those who have been affiliated with Mannes; Rise Stevens was president of Mannes College from 1975 through 1978.

Faculty members today include Peter Serkin, Felix Galimir, Richard Goode, Ruth Falcon, Vladimir Feltsman, Walter Trampler, Grant Johannesen, Theodor Uppman, Timothy Eddy, and principal players from the New York Philharmonic, Metropolitan Opera Orchestra, and New York City Opera and Ballet orchestras. Among the guest artists who frequently teach master classes are Elisabeth Schwarzkopf, Joseph Gingold, Yo

Yo Ma, James Galway, Gaby Casadesus, Hakan Hagegard, Andras Schiff, Arleen Auger, Regine Crespin, and Judith Blegen.

Student Government

Students at Mannes College of Music are at liberty to organize a student government association that meets their needs.

Admission Requirements

The most important element of training prior to entry into Mannes is previous study in the student's field of concentration. All entering students must be high school graduates and are required to pass entrance examinations in their major fields of study. (Accompanists are provided for students auditioning in voice and orchestral instruments.) Placement tests in theory, ear training, dictation, and piano are also required.

Mannes does not accept students at a "beginner's" level. A significant number of undergraduate students transfer to Mannes after they determine, based upon education elsewhere, that they should be in a specialized and intensive institution such as a conservatory.

Application and Information

Upon receipt of the completed application, prospective students are notified of the examination times. A prospective student may audition only once for admission in a given academic year. Midyear applicants may be permitted to reaudition for the following academic year.

Prospective students are asked to file completed application forms by the prescribed deadlines. The nonrefundable $100 application fee must be accompanied by a letter of recommendation from a recent music teacher or an evaluation by a professional musician and all high school and college transcripts.

Applications and further information may be obtained by contacting:

Admissions Office
Mannes College of Music, New School University
150 West 85th Street
New York, New York 10024
Telephone: 212-580-0210
          800-292-3040 (toll-free)
Fax: 212-580-1738

Mannes College of Music, New School University, located on Manhattan's Upper West Side.

MANSFIELD UNIVERSITY OF PENNSYLVANIA
MANSFIELD, PENNSYLVANIA

The University

Mansfield University traces its heritage back to 1857, when Mansfield Classical Seminary opened. In 1862, Mansfield became a state normal school. In 1927, it became Mansfield State Teachers College, and in 1960, it broadened its degree offerings and became Mansfield State College. In 1983, it became Mansfield University. A four-year, coeducational, fully accredited institution, Mansfield offers more than eighty undergraduate degree programs. Through its Office of Graduate Studies, the University also offers master's degree programs in art education, education, elementary education, library science and information technologies, music education, and special education. The University offers the advantages of a private-college environment at a public-school cost.

Three quarters of the students enrolled at Mansfield are Pennsylvanians, many from the Williamsport-Scranton-Harrisburg triangle, but Mansfield is represented nationally by nineteen states and internationally by thirteen countries. Most students live in residence halls that are centrally located on campus. Single or double rooms are available in coed or single-sex residence halls.

Mansfield students are physically active; more than half participate in organized athletics, and one in five participates in intercollegiate sports. There are more than seventy clubs and organizations for interests such as mathematics, dramatics, politics, and music. The forensic team has traditionally ranked among the top fifteen such teams from colleges and universities throughout the country. There are five national men's fraternities and four national women's sororities. The University also provides counseling, career development, and placement services. On-campus interviews are scheduled and are conducted by representatives of business, industry, public schools, and civil service agencies.

Location

The borough of Mansfield is situated in the Endless Mountains of Pennsylvania, 22 miles from the New York State border. The University's campus is at the northern edge of town, near community stores and restaurants. The natural environment of the area provides numerous opportunities for outdoor recreation. The Pennsylvania State Grand Canyon, approximately 15 miles from campus, offers opportunities for rafting, canoeing, boating, hiking, and picnicking. The Tioga-Hammond Dam offers miles of hiking shores, a marina, and unlimited camping facilities. Transportation by bus is available to downtown Mansfield. Nearby airports include both the Elmira–Corning Regional Airport, between Elmira and Corning, New York, and the Lycoming County Airport, located in Montoursville, Pennsylvania.

Majors and Degrees

Mansfield University offers the following degrees for undergraduates: the Bachelor of Arts, the Bachelor of Science, the Bachelor of Science in Education, the Bachelor of Music, the Bachelor of Science in Nursing, the Bachelor of Science in Social Work, the Associate of Applied Science, the Associate of Arts, and the Associate of Science. Programs of study leading to a baccalaureate degree include accounting, art (studio), art education, art history, biochemistry, biology, broadcasting, business administration, cell and molecular biology, chemistry, communications, computer science, criminal justice administration, dietetics, earth and space science, economics, elementary education, engineering (in conjunction with Pennsylvania State University, George Washington University, the University of Rochester, and the University of Pittsburgh), English, environmental science, fisheries biology, French, geography, German, history, human resource management, information systems, international business, international studies, journalism, liberal studies, marketing, mathematics, medical technology, music, music business electives, music education, music performance, music therapy, nursing, philosophy, physics, political science, prelaw, premed, psychology, public relations, regional planning, secondary education, social studies, social work, sociology/anthropology, Spanish, special education, speech, sports nutrition, theater, and travel and tourism. Preprofessional programs are also available.

Two-year Associate of Applied Science degree programs in respiratory therapy and radiology technology are offered in conjunction with the Robert Packer Hospital in Sayre, Pennsylvania. Students in these programs attend classes and are housed at the Robert Packer facility after one semester at the Mansfield University campus. Additional two-year programs are offered in accounting, art, business administration, criminal justice, geography/mapping technology, information systems, liberal studies, and travel and tourism.

Academic Program

The general education program offers alternative course selections in order to provide students with courses of study to meet individual needs, career goals, and the basic requirements for the major. Faculty advisers are available to assist students in their course selection. To graduate with a baccalaureate degree, a student must pass at least 120 semester hours, earn at least a 2.0 quality point average in all work attempted and in the major, and complete the requirements for general education and for the major. To graduate with an associate degree, a student must successfully complete at least 64 semester hours. For the baccalaureate degree, a minimum of 32 semester hours of work earned on campus will meet the requirement for one year of residence. For the associate degree, at least 15 semester hours must be taken through Mansfield University.

Independent study is available in each curricular field and allows qualified students to increase their knowledge in a particular academic discipline by examining it in an intensive manner with guidance from a faculty member who has special expertise in that subject. Students in good academic standing may request permission to take a comprehensive examination in a particular course offered by the University. Students may also take tests of the College-Level Examination Program by contacting the counseling center. Opportunities to study abroad also exist.

The honors program offers a special academic opportunity for superior students; it is an enhancing, intellectually challenging college experience. Students enrolled in the honors program supplement their regular studies with honors courses in the humanities, the physical sciences, and the social sciences. The program's interdisciplinary emphasis is perhaps its most distinctive feature. All honors work is identified as such in each student's academic record.

The two-semester academic year runs from early September to mid May, with Thanksgiving, Christmas, and spring breaks.

Academic Facilities

Buildings on campus, a mixture of traditional and modern architecture, are set among open lawns and tree-shaded walks. The campus covers approximately 175 acres. Allen Hall houses the University's high-tech lecture room and TV studio. The Grant Science Center has a planetarium, solar collector, science museum, and animal collection. Decker Gymnasium, the athletic center, has an Olympic-size swimming pool. There are three auditoriums on campus as well as an art gallery, located in North Hall. The University's student-operated radio station broadcasts from South Hall.

The University library contains more than 225,000 volumes, 707,763 volume equivalents in microfilm, and 2,200 serial subscriptions. Approximately 19,645 audiovisual materials are held. More than 13,000 records and cassettes are available for student use. A significant collection of material is also available on CD-ROM.

Costs

In 1999–2000, tuition for Pennsylvania state residents was $3618 a year. Tuition for out-of-state students was $9046 a year. The cost of room and board was $3852 per year. Students also paid an additional $942 per year in fees. Books and supplies were estimated at $750 per year. (Costs are subject to change.)

Financial Aid

The Office of Financial Planning exists to provide information and financial assistance to students. It attempts to inform the student population of application procedures and deadlines, the types of aid available, the eligibility requirements, and other pertinent data. Students should file for financial aid immediately upon receiving confirmed admission to Mansfield University. To apply for aid, all students, regardless of the state in which they live, must file the Free Application for Federal Student Aid (FAFSA) and the institutional application. The filing of these two documents constitutes a completed application for all available types of aid except Guaranteed Student Loans; applications for these loans may be obtained from a student's hometown bank.

Part-time employment is available at the University through state and federal work-study programs for students who have shown evidence of financial need. Details can be obtained by contacting the Office of Financial Planning (570-662-4878). Approximately 80 percent of Mansfield's students receive some form of aid.

Faculty

Mansfield's faculty is composed of approximately 200 members. The student-faculty ratio is about 16:1, allowing for extensive classroom interaction. All faculty members maintain office hours during which they are available to students. Faculty members also serve as academic advisers in the Counseling Center. Graduate students are not used in a teaching capacity. Although Mansfield's faculty is primarily concerned with teaching excellence, many members publish extensively and are actively involved in their fields.

Student Government

The Student Government Association (SGA), of which every student is a member, has an Executive Council and a Senate. The Executive Council consists of a president, a vice president of academic affairs, a vice president of administrative affairs, and a vice president of social affairs. The Senate is composed of one senator for every 100 students. The Senate chooses its own officers, and the chairperson may vote only when the Senate is equally divided. SGA's Committee of Finance, whose members are appointed by the president of SGA, is responsible for appropriating the Student Activity Fee, with final approval from the Senate. Various other committees of SGA are responsible for initiating change on Mansfield's campus. Any student may find out about the various faculty, administrative, or student committees by expressing interest at the SGA office. Appointments to each committee are made by the president of SGA with the confirmation of the Senate.

Admission Requirements

Applicants for admission must have graduated from an approved secondary school or have equivalent preparation, as determined by the Credentials Evaluation Division of the Pennsylvania Department of Education, and should have earned a combined score of 920 or better on the SAT I or a composite score of 19 or better on the ACT. Applicants should have been enrolled in a college-preparatory curriculum and ranked in the top three fifths of their class. Letters of recommendation are preferred, as are any personal attributes that may contribute to the University community.

Mansfield offers an Equal Education Opportunity Program for students who do not qualify under regular admissions. The program is designed to meet the needs of students who have college potential but who are financially or academically deprived. Students are sometimes required to have a personal interview to be considered for this program.

Mansfield University is committed to ensuring equal opportunity for all persons regardless of race, sex, handicap, or other legally protected classifications.

Application and Information

Students interested in applying to Mansfield University should return a completed application form with a $25 nonrefundable application fee. Applicants will be accepted, beginning July 1, following the junior year of high school. Applicants must submit an official high school transcript and the results of the SAT I or ACT to the Admissions Office.

Admissions Office
Mansfield University of Pennsylvania
Mansfield, Pennsylvania 16933
Telephone: 570-662-4243
          800-577-6826 (toll-free)
Fax: 570-662-4121
E-mail: admissions@mnsfld.edu
World Wide Web: http://www.mnsfld.edu

MARIAN COLLEGE
INDIANAPOLIS, INDIANA

The College

Marian College, founded in 1851 by the Sisters of St. Francis, is a Catholic, ecumenical, coeducational, comprehensive liberal arts college. Located in the northwest suburbs of Indianapolis, the scenic 114-acre campus is composed of three turn-of-the-century estates, a lake, and a waterfall. The campus is heavily wooded and has twenty-four buildings, including a Physical Education Center. Swimming pools, tennis courts, gymnasiums, and student lounges are part of the campus setting.

The close contact between students and faculty at Marian College provides an exceptionally enriching experience for the 1,339 students. Building on a strong tradition of invaluable personal attention, the College has developed a distinctive mentor's program. Classes are small enough to permit seminars, group discussions, laboratories, and individual conferences. The goal is a true liberal arts education—broad acquaintance with varied disciplines, expertise in a chosen specialty, and an insatiable appetite for more knowledge. Marian's small population creates a friendly campus where personal attention abounds. The students bring with them the ideas and cultures of eighteen states and several other countries, representing many religious and ethnic traditions. This cosmopolitan atmosphere is enhanced by such world-view courses as Eastern literature and history, comparative religions, and Jewish studies.

Extracurricular and social activities are an important part of life at Marian, giving students the opportunity to develop leadership abilities in a variety of ways. Theater students present at least four departmental productions annually. The madrigal singers, chorus, wind ensemble, and band may interest musically inclined students. Noteworthy films sponsored by student groups, as well as dances, mixers, field days, Homecoming, and sports, provide other social opportunities. Departmental clubs support classroom instruction. Three student publications provide vital campus communication channels.

Marian College is a member of the National Association of Intercollegiate Athletics. The College provides opportunities for men to compete in intercollegiate baseball, basketball, cross-country, cycling, golf, soccer, tennis, and track. Women may compete in intercollegiate basketball, cheerleading, cross-country, softball, tennis, and volleyball. In addition to the intercollegiate sports program, the College provides numerous sports for both men and women through the intramural sports program. About 90 percent of the students on campus participate in this College-organized program and have the use of all facilities.

Located near the campus is the Major Taylor Velodrome, built for the 1982 Summer Sports Festival. Students train at the velodrome. Marian has won four national track championships.

Location

Some of the necessities for a complete education can be found only in metropolitan areas. Despite its small-town atmosphere, the campus is a 10-minute drive from Indianapolis and such places as Clowes Hall, where Broadway plays and musicals, top entertainers, ballet, Shakespearean drama, and lecturers are scheduled regularly. Further exposure to the fine arts is provided by the Indianapolis Museum of Art, within view of the campus, and by the Indianapolis Symphony Orchestra, one of the best in the nation. Because Indianapolis is the state capital and also the largest city in the state, students interested in government and politics have superb opportunities to observe and participate. Professional basketball, baseball, football, and hockey are all 10 minutes away, and each May the city is the site of the Indianapolis 500. The NASCAR Brickyard 400 takes place at the Indianapolis Motor Speedway in August. Large shopping centers are also within minutes of the campus.

Majors and Degrees

The College offers programs leading to the Bachelor of Arts or the Bachelor of Science degree. Programs are offered in accounting, art, art history, biology, business administration, chemistry, communications, early childhood education, elementary education, English, environmental studies, finance, food and nutrition sciences, French, German, history, mathematics, medical technology, music, musical theater, nursing, philosophy, physical education, psychology, religious education, secondary education, sociology, Spanish, sports management, theater, and theology. Minors are available in most of these areas, as well as in athletic training, computer studies, economics, physics, and political science. Courses are also offered in humanities, journalism, and non-Western studies.

The Associate of Arts degree is offered in accounting, art, business administration, early childhood education, history, liberal arts, music, pastoral leadership, psychology, religious studies, and theater. Licensed practical nurses (LPNs) with one year of experience may earn an associate degree in nursing.

Teacher education programs in early childhood, elementary, secondary, and special education lead to certification. Combined programs in engineering are available with cooperating institutions. Preprofessional programs are available in dentistry, law, and medicine. Registered nurses (RNs) with one year of experience may earn a bachelor's degree in nursing.

Academic Program

Marian students build their major and minor areas of study on a foundation of courses in the humanities and the social and natural sciences. Students design their academic program with the help of their academic adviser. While general education requirements, as well as those for major and minor fields of study, are outlined by the faculty, students do arrange their schedules from a group of courses in fulfillment of the requirements. Because students enter college at differing levels of academic achievement, advanced placement or preparatory course work is available to freshmen and upperclass students. The Honors Program with its enriched curriculum also provides special opportunities for academically promising students.

Juniors and seniors may elect four courses (no more than two per semester) on a pass/fail basis. Seminars or comprehensives are required of seniors for academic assessment in their major field. Juniors and seniors in the Division of Business may participate in a cooperative education program, which is designed to integrate classroom learning with practical work experience.

Freshmen who do well on the general examinations portion of the College-Level Examination Program test may receive up to 30 hours of credit toward their degree requirements. Other credit and Advanced Placement examinations are available.

Off-Campus Arrangements

Students interested in international study may spend a semester or two and/or a summer abroad. Marian College will assist these students in finding programs compatible with their degree requirements. Some courses not offered at Marian may be taken at any of the cooperating institutions in the Indianapolis area. Practical experience in special education programs prepares students to teach the educable and trainable mentally handicapped.

Academic Facilities

A 35-acre wetland ecological laboratory containing a small lake, a stream, a mature and second growth of hardwood forests, marshland, and a diverse assortment of wildlife is utilized by students. The area also serves as a resource for Marian's Environmental Studies Program. Laboratories in psychology, music, science, special education, and computer science are open to students for work in these fields. The ultramodern library, containing more than 125,000 volumes and serving the Marian College community, could easily serve the needs of an institution many times the size of Marian. The Learning and Counseling Center offers such services as personal counseling, skill development, tutoring, and reentry support for nontraditional students.

Costs

For 2000–01, tuition is $14,432 per year, services and fees are $404, books and supplies are approximately $700, and room and board (twenty meals per week) are $5046 per year. (A fifteen-meal-per-week plan is available.) Average personal expenses are $1260.

Financial Aid

The College awards yearly scholarships to outstanding students based on their academic records without regard to financial need. Athletic grants are awarded in all varsity sports for men and women. Indiana residents may qualify for state scholarships and grants. Marian College offers a full range of comprehensive academic scholarships. The College also participates in the Federal Pell Grant, Federal Perkins Loan, Federal Stafford Student Loan, Federal Work-Study, and Federal Supplemental Educational Opportunity Grant programs. Applicants for aid must file the Free Application for Federal Student Aid (FAFSA) to establish eligibility for these programs. The FAFSA may be obtained from a high school counselor or the Financial Aid Office of the College. The average 1999–2000 financial aid package from all sources for enrolled freshmen was $13,118.

Faculty

Diversity in faculty members' educational and personal backgrounds contributes to the learning experience at Marian. Each faculty member, whether instructor or professor, teaches general education courses as well as specialized subjects; thus, that crucial initial contact of students and scholars begins in the freshman year. The faculty numbers 124, and the student-faculty ratio is 12:1. The close personal relationship among students, faculty members, and administrators is a particular strength of the education offered at Marian. The inclusion of part-time members—professional educators and businesspersons—in the faculty provides opportunities for students to become personally acquainted with leaders in the Indianapolis community.

Student Government

All students at Marian are members of the Student Association. The legislative arm of the association is the Executive Board, an elective body that chooses students to serve on various College committees, initiates activities of interest to students, and works for changes in College policies concerning students. The College believes that students should be involved in the affairs and decisions of the College community and encourages such involvement by inviting students to serve on its legislative body and on the majority of the College committees.

Admission Requirements

Marian College believes the goals and purposes of a liberal arts education are best attained within a heterogeneous community and encourages applications from members of all cultural, racial, religious, and ethnic groups. Each year the Admissions Committee selects for admission men and women representing a wide variety of interests and backgrounds, from all parts of the United States and from several other countries.

Every applicant is expected to present 16 acceptable units of secondary school work, 3 of which should be in English, 2 or more in mathematics (algebra and geometry are recommended), 1 or more in a laboratory science, and 1 or more in social studies. Two years of a foreign language are strongly recommended. Important factors in considering the applicant for admission are the quality of academic achievement, including rank in the secondary school class; academic potential, as reflected by the results of the SAT I and/or the ACT; and evidence of leadership and service, as indicated by curricular and extracurricular contributions in the secondary school and community. Marian College also gives consideration to any student who has completed high school by passing the GED examination.

Transfer students are considered if they meet all the requirements stated above and are in good standing.

Application and Information

Applications for admission and other materials may be secured by contacting:

Office of Admissions
Marian College
3200 Cold Spring Road
Indianapolis, Indiana 46222
Telephone: 317-955-6300 (call collect from out-of-state)
　　　　　　800-772-7264 (toll-free in Indiana)
E-mail: admit@marian.edu
World Wide Web: http://www.marian.edu

Students enjoy Marian College's park-like campus.

MARIAN COLLEGE OF FOND DU LAC
FOND DU LAC, WISCONSIN

The College

Marian College is a welcoming community of students and faculty and staff members working together to make a difference. Founded in 1936 by the Sisters of the Congregation of Saint Agnes as a school for teacher education, Marian now offers more than forty majors and minors in professional and preprofessional programs. A strong liberal arts curriculum, combined with experiential education, gives students the thinking, speaking, and writing skills essential for any career choice.

Whether students are in the Cardinal Meyer Library, looking at plans for the new Technology and Executive Learning Center, relaxing in campus housing, using one of the campus's many computer labs, or enjoying coffee in the Common Grounds Coffeehouse, they can be assured that they are continuing in their quest for wider knowledge.

The Marian campus is comprised of 1,000 traditional undergraduate students, 600 adult completion students, and an additional 700 students who are pursuing master's degrees. Students at Marian welcome an active campus life with involvement opportunities in many social organizations and clubs as well as one of twelve NCAA Division III athletic programs. Men's intercollegiate sports include baseball, basketball, golf, ice hockey, soccer, and tennis. Women's intercollegiate sports include basketball, golf, soccer, tennis, and volleyball.

Students enjoy a variety of modern housing options. Two traditional residence halls, as well as town house and courtyard complexes with spacious living rooms, kitchens, bedrooms, and private bathrooms, are where Marian students make their home away from home. The Todd Wehr Alumni Center and coffee house, where students and faculty and staff members can relax and socialize, further enhance the beautiful 97-acre campus.

There are six instructional divisions at Marian: the Division of Arts and Humanities, the Division of Business, the Division of Educational Studies, the Division of Mathematics and Natural Science, the Division of Nursing, and the Division of Social and Behavioral Science. In addition to the undergraduate degrees listed below, Marian offers degree completion programs for adults and master's degrees in education and organizational leadership and quality.

Location

Marian College is located on the edge of Fond du Lac (French for "bottom of the lake"), a small city of 40,000 in a wide Wisconsin valley that stretches from the southern end of Lake Winnebago, the largest lake in the state, to rolling hills farther south. Students at Marian College have the privilege of living in a year-round recreational area where many people choose to vacation. The College is located only one hour from both Milwaukee and Madison, and 2½ hours from Chicago. Marian College has a long history of attachment to its local community, which in turn takes great pride in the College and supports it strongly.

Majors and Degrees

Marian College of Fond du Lac awards bachelor's degrees with majors in accounting, administration of justice, applied information technology, art, art therapy, biology, business management, chemistry, communication, cytotechnology, education (art, early childhood, elementary, music, and secondary), English, history, human relations, marketing, mathematics, medical technology, modern languages, music, music industry, nursing, political science, psychology, radiological technology, social work, Spanish, and sport and recreation management. Preprofessional majors are available in dentistry, law, medicine, pharmacy, and veterinary medicine. Students may also design a major to fit their own needs and interests.

Academic Program

All programs are based upon common general requirements. All students, regardless of their specific degree program, must successfully complete 48 credits in liberal arts, complete at least one major program, and have taken at least 128 hours of credit with a minimum average of 2 grade points for each credit hour. The senior year, or at least the last 32 credit hours, must have been completed at Marian College. Credit is awarded for CLEP subject and general examinations according to the current criteria and policies of Marian College. Details may be obtained from the assistant dean of academic affairs.

The College conducts traditional academic programs in two semesters, the first from late August to mid-December and the second from mid-January to mid-May. There is also a two-week Maymester in mid-May and a two-week winterim in December. Students may also take advantage of extensive summer school sessions.

Off-Campus Arrangements

Marian offers a cooperative education program that allows students to integrate classroom theory with practical work experience. Students have extraordinary opportunities to test the appropriateness of their career choices to their interests, their abilities, and their temperaments while developing new knowledge, understanding, and skills. Cooperative education is open to all junior and senior students in good academic standing. Students must meet the specific requirements established by their major academic department. A student can earn a maximum of 12 credits for professional or paraprofessional work related to his or her academic and career interests. Students work under the close supervision of an employer, with coordination provided by a faculty member. In the professional programs of education, nursing, and social work, students complete extensive clinical experiences that prepare them to be skilled professionals upon graduation. There are also a number of immersion experiences available and a study-abroad program at Harlaxton College in England.

Academic Facilities

The Cardinal Meyer Library is the physical and intellectual center of campus. The library contains more than 95,000 volumes and microforms and subscribes to more than 650 periodicals. The library is fully automated, with CD-ROM and Internet access capabilities. In addition, the library belongs to netLibrary, an Internet-based collection of e-Books. NetLibrary allows students access to the full text of scholarly, reference, and professional e-Books online. Respected presses, including many notable university presses, publish in the netLibrary collection. Learning resource centers, located throughout the campus, supplement the library's collection in academic areas such as art, education, music, nursing, science, and social work.

As of fall 2000, a campus-wide fiber-optics network will be in place, thus providing access to the Internet, e-mail, and a multitude of other information resources from every office, classroom, and residence hall room on the campus. Personal computers may be configured for direct access to the system, or students may utilize fully equipped computer labs around campus. Slated to open in spring 2001 is a new Technology and Executive Learning Center. The first floor of the building will house computer labs and classrooms for the Applied Information Technology courses as well as a 250-seat auditorium. Conference and executive training rooms will be located on the second floor, while the third level will provide additional classrooms.

The Todd Wehr Alumni Center houses the Common Grounds Coffeehouse and the Marian College History Room. The new coffee house lends itself to the course work that students practice daily in the classroom. Students serve in roles such as accounting manager, staff manager, and public relations and marketing specialist. An additional 20 student baristas (servers) are gaining experience in this unique learning laboratory.

Costs

Annual full-time undergraduate tuition for 2000–01 is $12,624. Housing costs range from $2100 to $4700, depending on the student's choice of accommodations. Students may select from a variety of meal plans ranging from $1975 to $2400 per year. The cost of books is not included in the tuition figure.

Financial Aid

The Marian College Financial Aid Office coordinates an active program of financial assistance for students. Aid is based on need and/or academic merit. The principle sources of aid include the Federal Pell Grant Program, the Federal Work-Study Program, and Marian Assistance. Academic scholarships, including the Academic Achievement Award ($7500), the Presidential Scholarship ($5000), the Naber Leadership Award ($3000), as well as the Sister Shelia Burns Award and Regional Awards, are available to entering students and are renewable.

Faculty

A hallmark of Marian College is its faculty's mission to teach. With a student-faculty ratio of 14:1, professors regard their students' success as a measure of their own and provide individualized attention to help students attain their academic, personal, and career goals. All classes are taught by faculty members with no use of graduate assistants.

Student Government

The Student Senate is the largest and most influential student organization on campus. It is the governing body of the students and their representative body in College governance. All registered students are members of the Student Senate. This body is responsible for initiating activities that are beneficial to the spiritual, intellectual, personal, and social development of every Marian student. Every registered student helps elect officers of the Student Senate to represent all other student groups, living units, clubs, and organizations. There are more than thirty student clubs and organizations represented in the Student Senate. A hallmark of the College is service to the community. Students are encouraged to participate and earn a service transcript indicating the hours provided.

Admission Requirements

Marian College encourages students who show evidence of academic motivation and ability to undertake baccalaureate-level studies to apply. In judging an applicant's eligibility, the College gives consideration to the entire secondary school record, ACT or SAT I test scores, and any academic credit earned after high school graduation. The ACT test is preferred. Admission decisions are made on a rolling basis, and applicants usually receive a response to their application within two or three weeks after all credentials have been received. When the application materials are reviewed by an admissions committee, the committee may direct the Admissions Office to accept the student, accept with provisions, or deny acceptance until evidence of academic potential is provided. Each applicant is considered on an individual basis, and an interview may be required.

Admission to freshman standing at Marian presupposes at least 16 units of high school credit, including at least 3 units of English, 2 of mathematics, 1 of laboratory science, and 1 of history. Biology and chemistry are prerequisites for the nursing program. Physics and a foreign language are recommended.

Students who have acquired academic credits at another accredited college may be admitted to Marian with advanced standing. Only college credits with a grade of C or better are accepted in transfer. The grade point average at Marian is based solely on courses taken at Marian College.

Marian College admits qualified students regardless of race, sex, creed, color, ethnic origin, or disability to all rights, privileges, and activities generally made available to students at the College.

Application and Information

For additional information regarding the application process or for other information, students may contact:

Stacey Akey
Dean of Enrollment Management
Marian College of Fond du Lac
45 South National Avenue
Fond du Lac, Wisconsin 54935
Telephone: 920-923-7650
        800-2-MARIAN (toll-free)
E-mail: admissions@mariancollege.edu
World Wide Web: http://www.mariancollege.edu

Marian College of Fond du Lac—a stimulating place to learn and grow.

MARIST COLLEGE
POUGHKEEPSIE, NEW YORK

The College

Marist College is located on the Hudson River, just north of the city of Poughkeepsie, midway between New York City and Albany. The 150-acre riverside campus comfortably accommodates 3,500 full-time undergraduates. The campus has twenty-eight buildings, including nine residence halls, three major classroom buildings, library facilities, and a student center, which includes a bookstore, music rooms, a theater, and a cafeteria. Town house residences and garden apartments are also available for upperclass students. There are three major athletic fields and a boathouse and waterfront facilities for sailing and crew. The James J. McCann Recreation Center, one of the largest collegiate sports complexes in the Mid-Hudson Valley, houses a 4,000-seat field house and a natatorium with a diving well and spectator space for 700, as well as an indoor track, a crew tank, handball and racquetball courts, a weight room, a dance studio, and other facilities for recreation and competition.

Campus life accommodates a wide range of interests and talents. The student-administered College Union Board annually presents a full schedule of films, concerts, and social activities. More than sixty clubs and organizations are available in many areas, including theater, drama, music, debate, publications, and volunteer programs. Varsity sports for men are sponsored in baseball, basketball, crew, cross-country, diving, football, lacrosse, soccer, swimming, tennis, and track. Varsity sports for women are offered in basketball, crew, cross-country, diving, lacrosse, soccer, softball, swimming, tennis, track, and volleyball. Ice hockey, skiing, an equestrian team, rugby, and soccer are available as club sports. The Marist Red Foxes compete in NCAA Division I in the Metro-Atlantic Athletic Conference (MAAC). An extensive intramural program encourages all students to participate in athletic recreation, and more than 80 percent of Marist students take part in club or team activities.

Special student services are offered in the areas of academic advising, counseling, career development, campus ministry, veterans' affairs, financial aid, health, residence living, and support of disabled students.

Graduate degrees are available in business, computer science, educational psychology, management information systems, psychology, public administration, and school psychology.

Location

Marist's location in the historic and scenic Hudson Valley provides access to many cultural and recreational opportunities. The Franklin D. Roosevelt Home and Presidential Library and the original plant of the IBM Corporation attest to the national and international significance of the region and its people and organizations. The river also serves as a focus for the College's Environmental Studies program, while the nearby Catskill Mountains provide areas for such outdoor activities as hiking, skiing, and rock-climbing. A short distance from the campus, the city of Poughkeepsie offers a major civic center that consolidates many of the area's cultural programs and expands leisure-time choices. With Amtrak and Metro North railroad stations only minutes from campus, students also have convenient access to New York City, Albany, Boston, and other major metropolitan areas.

Majors and Degrees

The College is organized into six academic areas: the School of Computer Science and Math; the School of Science and Environmental Studies; the School of Management and Management Studies; the School of Social and Behavioral Sciences; the School of Communication and the Arts; and the Division of Humanities. The Bachelor of Arts is awarded in American studies, communication arts, computer mathematics, economics, English, fine arts, French, history, mathematics, political science, psychology, psychology/special elementary education, Russian, and Spanish. The Bachelor of Science is offered in accounting, biology, business administration, chemistry, computer science, criminal justice, environmental science, information systems, information technology, medical technology, and sociology/social work. The Bachelor of Professional Studies is offered in fashion design/fashion merchandising. Concentrations are offered in Jewish studies, Latin American studies, paralegal studies, and public administration. In order to provide greater academic opportunities for students, the College offers two combined B.A./M.A. programs (one in psychology and one in teacher education) and two combined B.S./M.S. programs (one in information systems and one in computer science). These accelerated programs allow students to graduate with both degrees in five years.

Preprofessional programs in law, medicine, dentistry, and pre–veterinary medicine and other allied health professions are available. Marist's teacher education program qualifies students for secondary education teacher certification in biology, chemistry, English, French, history, mathematics, social studies, and Spanish and for teacher certification in special/elementary education.

Academic Program

Central to academic planning at Marist is the core curriculum, a program that provides all students with a solid educational foundation in the liberal arts. Students can take advantage of the double-major option that allows equal study in two subject areas. They can also choose a major in one subject and a minor in another area of interest. The Honors Program, the Marist Abroad Program, the Center for Estuarine Studies, and special academic advising are available for students wishing to enhance the academic experience. Faculty members help all students identify areas of academic interest and then continue to support students as that interest is developed and explored.

Off-Campus Arrangements

Through the international study options offered, students can spend their junior or senior year abroad. Marist students, representing a cross section of majors, have studied in many countries in Europe, as well as in Africa, Australia, and Latin America. Through the College's membership in the Associated Colleges of the Mid-Hudson Area, Marist students may cross-register at any one of four other institutions: Culinary Institute of America, Dutchess Community College, State University of New York College at New Paltz, and Ulster Community College.

A comprehensive program of off-campus internships is offered in all majors, and Marist has one of the largest communication arts internship programs in the Northeast. Cooperative education opportunities (paid work experiences) are currently available in a number of majors.

Academic Facilities

The James A. Cannavino Library opened its doors in January 2000. This 83,000-square-foot, three-story facility integrates traditional books and periodicals with IBM digital technology. A robust network (three LAN rooms) capable of transmitting large video files to 24 simultaneous users supports an array of servers, collaborative digital workrooms (ten), five classrooms fully computerized for teaching and learning, and about 400 network jacks for student laptops, available for rental at the main desk. The third floor of the library houses the Collaborative Learning Center, which offers academic support functions ranging from a writing center to multimedia classrooms and language labs. The two-story atrium entrance and lobby have a coffee bar to provide students a place to relax and meet with faculty members and friends. By combining areas for academic research with classrooms and an array of student support services, the Cannavino Library offers new opportunities for collaborative learning and educational innovation.

The Computer Center, which may be used by all students for course work, provides up-to-date technology as well as the use of an IBM 9672-S390 mainframe system. Through a joint study with the IBM Corporation, Marist offers more than $15 million in state-of-the-art computer technology. Facilities include 200 terminals and 250 online personal computers in PC labs located across campus. A campuswide telecommunications network allows students to access the mainframe, conduct library research, and communicate with faculty members, all from their residences. Students have access to the ROLM PhoneMail System and the IBM Token-Ring local area network (LAN), as well as the Internet, World Wide Web, Prodigy, and other electronic information exchange systems. Cabling extends to every faculty and administrative office, every classroom building, the library, and every residence hall; all student rooms are equipped with data jacks to connect personal computers to the system. A mid-rise residence hall overlooking the Hudson River, town houses, expansion of the student center and bookstore, a 4-acre campus green, and an outdoor performing arts area are among recent additions to campus.

The Lowell Thomas Communications Center links the study of communications with computer technology. It features two sets of television and radio broadcast studios, computer-equipped classrooms, and print journalism areas, as well as a public gallery displaying memorabilia of the late Lowell Thomas, the legendary broadcaster and explorer.

The Instructional Media Center's functions include consultation on media methods; production of films, slides, and videotapes; dispensing of audiovisual hardware; and distribution of video programming to classrooms. Group work and individual study in German, Italian, French, Russian, and Spanish, as well as in English for non-English-speaking students, are available.

The Charles H. Dyson Center incorporates some of the most advanced technologies in education and houses the College's undergraduate and graduate programs in business, social and behavioral sciences, public administration, and public policy. The center is also used for innovative computer simulations and computer-assisted group learning and problem solving. In addition, it houses the School of Adult Education and the Office of Graduate Admissions.

Costs

Tuition and fees for 1999–2000 were $14,490 for a full year. Room and board for a full year were $7714. The additional costs of transportation, clothes, and spending money usually amount to several hundred dollars. Students should plan on books and supplies costing an estimated $500 per year.

Financial Aid

Approximately 70 percent of the College's full-time students receive aid from Marist and outside sources, including New York State Tuition Assistance Program (TAP) grants, Federal Pell Grants, Federal Supplemental Educational Opportunity Grants, Federal Perkins Loans, Federal Stafford Student Loans (Subsidized and Unsubsidized), and Federal Work-Study Program awards. Marist also has Merit Awards for outstanding students, which are not based on financial need. Overall, Marist annually awards more than $10 million in grants and scholarships from its own funds. For a student to be considered for assistance, the Free Application for Federal Student Aid (FAFSA) should be filed as soon as possible after January 1. The financial aid staff is available to discuss financial aid possibilities with all prospective students.

Faculty

The College has 159 full-time faculty members, approximately 90 percent of whom either hold doctorates or are doctoral candidates. A strong working relationship between students and faculty is an important aspect of the learning process at Marist. The student-faculty ratio is currently 15:1.

Student Government

Student representation in decisions affecting the College is a tradition at Marist. Through Student Government committees, the student body is given a role in both administrative and academic policymaking.

Admission Requirements

Applicants must have graduated from an accredited high school. Rigor of high school curriculum and rank in class are primary considerations; admission is based on a review of the high school transcript, scores on the SAT I or ACT, and the recommendation of the guidance counselor or college adviser. Marist has an early decision policy, as well as a flexible transfer policy. Details about either of these procedures may be obtained from the Admissions Office.

Application and Information

Application may be made for either September or January enrollment, depending on the choice of the applicant. Students can apply on line through Marist's Web pages at the address listed below. The College notifies regular candidates of the admission decision in early March. The completed application form, the secondary school transcript, results of the SAT I or ACT, the recommendation of the guidance counselor or college adviser, and an application fee of $35 must be submitted before a decision on admission can be made. Candidates for early decision should apply by December 1.

Additional details and application forms are available by contacting:

Admissions Office
Marist College
290 North Road
Poughkeepsie, New York 12601
Telephone: 914-575-3226
           800-436-5483 (toll-free)
E-mail: admissions@marist.edu
World Wide Web: http://www.marist.edu

MARLBORO COLLEGE
MARLBORO, VERMONT

The College

Marlboro College, tucked away in the foothills of the Vermont Green Mountains, is unlike any other college in the country. Liberal by nature, Marlboro's rigorous, self-designed liberal arts curriculum is taught in small classes and advanced one-on-one instruction, called tutorials, that emphasize creative and independent thinking by mature, self-motivated students. Marlboro's goal is to teach students to think clearly and learn independently, develop a command of concise and correct writing, and aspire to academic excellence, all while participating responsibly in a self-governing community. The College's 7:1 student-faculty ratio sparks dynamic exchanges between students and faculty members both in and out of the classroom and fosters a close-knit community in which academic work is respected and ideas are appreciated. About 60 percent of all Marlboro students go on to graduate study. The Marlboro Graduate Center in nearby Brattleboro, Vermont, offers the Master of Arts in Teaching with Internet Technologies and the Master of Science in Internet Strategy Management.

Marlboro opened in fall 1947. The campus was originally a cluster of barns and other farm buildings that the first students converted into classrooms and dormitories. The fields and woodlands that make up its rural 350-acre campus are perfect for cross-country skiing and other outdoor activities. Equipment for and instruction in rock climbing, backpacking, canoeing, kayaking, and cross-country skiing are available through the College's Outdoor Program. The soccer team competes with other colleges, and more impromptu volleyball, basketball, softball, and hackey-sack teams compete intramurally. In addition, Marlboro's broomball (a game akin to hockey) tournament takes place each winter, with prizes not only for the team that wins the most games but also for the team with the best costumes. The Student Activities Office organizes many events both on and off campus, including concerts, lectures, poetry and fiction readings, art shows, and trips to Boston, Montreal, and New York for museum visits, shopping, and baseball games. Other activities that enrich campus life include parties, dances, plays, and film screenings.

Marlboro is—and intends to remain—one of the nation's smallest liberal arts colleges, with fewer than 300 students at any given time. Students come from about forty states and approximately five other countries. Transfer students are a vital group on campus; roughly one third of Marlboro's students are transfers from other colleges. Seventy percent of all students live in campus housing, which consists of small dormitories (both single-sex and coed), several four-bedroom cottages, and a renovated country inn.

Location

The village of Marlboro, whose center lies 2 miles from the College, consists of a post office, a town clerk's office, and an inn. About 600 full-time residents live within the 36-square-mile township. During the summer, the village swells to accommodate the famous Marlboro Music Festival. The town of Brattleboro, 12 miles away, is a lively cultural and commercial center located on the first Vermont exit off Interstate 91. The College is 2 hours by car from Boston, 3½ from New York City.

Majors and Degrees

Marlboro confers the Bachelor of Arts degree in American studies, anthropology, art history, ceramics, classics, creative writing, cultural history, dance, drawing, economics, film/video studies, history, languages, literature, music, painting, philosophy, photography, political science, psychology, religion, sculpture, sociology, and theater. The Bachelor of Science is offered in astronomy, biochemistry, biology, chemistry, computer science, environmental sciences, mathematics, and physics. Marlboro students frequently combine areas of study and work toward interdisciplinary degrees. Students in the College's World Studies Program may earn the Bachelor of Arts in International Studies.

Academic Program

Marlboro's Plan of Concentration, more than any other academic component, sets the College apart from other liberal arts institutions. Undertaken by all Marlboro students in their junior and senior years, the plan is a two-year pursuit, focused, often cross-disciplinary, culminating in a project that is designed by the student and carried out with close guidance from one or more faculty sponsors. Final evaluation of the student's plan is conducted by a faculty committee and an outside examiner, usually a recognized expert in the student's field.

Marlboro's intimate advising system takes the place of formal distribution requirements. Freshmen and sophomores are advised to take a wide range of liberal arts courses. Increasingly, as students progress within fields of particular interest, they take individual tutorials that make it possible to work one-to-one with faculty members of their choice.

Operating under the assumption that clear writing and clear thinking are inseparable, Marlboro requires each student to pass a Clear Writing Requirement, usually by the end of the freshman year. Expository writing assignments, tutorials, and a variety of designated writing courses distributed throughout the curriculum help students meet the requirement.

Off-Campus Arrangements

Students working on the Plan of Concentration often travel abroad or attend other institutions for a period of time to augment their academic work. Marlboro faculty members may help plan these pursuits and frequently aid students in securing internships in academic fields. The College also sponsors several field trips each year, such as scientific expeditions to tropical, desert, or mountain environments and outdoor adventures in mountain climbing or white-water rafting.

The World Studies Program (WSP) is a four-year program leading to a Bachelor of Arts in International Studies. The program involves intensive study on campus, as well as a six- to eight-month internship abroad. In addition, WSP sponsors regular International Nights, which generally include a themed dinner, music from other countries, and lectures or films.

In March 1998, Marlboro, with approval from the New England Association of Schools and Colleges, extended its accreditation to Huron University in London, effectively forming an academic partnership. Huron, with 260 students who represent 60 other countries, offers an American-style liberal arts education and is especially strong in undergraduate and graduate business education and undergraduate international area studies. The two institutions have created a series of programs and exchanges for students and faculty members in all curricular areas.

Academic Facilities

In keeping with a spirit of community trust and academic inquiry, Marlboro's computer labs, updated with T-1 lines that equip the campus with the World Wide Web, and the 52,000-volume Howard and Amy Rice Library are open to students around the clock. In addition to classroom buildings, the College has a 270-seat theater; the Brown Science Building, with its recently completed Integrated Science Lab; art and pottery studios; music practice rooms; remodeled photographic darkrooms; a dance studio; and a small astronomical observatory that was designed and built by a student. The Campus Center houses a coffee shop, a recreation room, and the small, but well-stocked, college bookstore. Most public buildings are open 24 hours a day.

Costs

Tuition at Marlboro was $18,800 for the 1999–2000 academic year. Room and board cost $6750, and required fees were $860. Fees include a first-time orientation fee of $100 and an annual health fee of $430.

Financial Aid

No one should refrain from applying to Marlboro because of perceived inability to meet costs. More than 80 percent of all Marlboro students receive financial help. The College is committed to helping any student who qualifies for admission assemble the financial resources necessary to attend, and need is not a factor in the admission decision. Non-need scholarships are available.

Faculty

Marlboro's 41 full-time faculty members are committed first and foremost to teaching, rather than to publishing or research. The lively exchange of ideas between teachers and students is the cornerstone of the Marlboro curriculum.

Student Government

All students and faculty and staff members are equal members of the College Town Meeting. Since the opening of the College in 1947, the community has come together every few weeks to debate budget initiatives, College policies, and other issues. A board of Selectpersons elected by the College community serve the College's interests and are responsible for drafting Town Meeting rules and regulations. Students serve on more than thirty College committees, including those that review admissions and make faculty-hiring decisions. Other important committees include the social committee and the Community Court, which is responsible for enforcing the bylaws of the Town Meeting.

Admission Requirements

The admission committee seeks students with intellectual promise; a high degree of self-motivation, self-discipline, personal stability, and social concern; and the ability and desire to contribute to the College community. All applicants are considered without regard to race, creed, sex, sexual orientation, national or ethnic origin, age, or disability. Transfers and older or returning students are encouraged to apply.

Like most colleges, Marlboro requires students to submit a variety of documentation, from high school transcripts to teacher recommendations. Unlike most colleges, however, Marlboro's review process is conducted by an Admissions Committee composed of students, faculty members, and staff. This committee evaluates each applicant as a unique individual who possesses qualities that are not necessarily quantifiable.

An interview is required of all applicants. When a visit to the campus is not possible, alternative arrangements can be made. Most campus interviews are conducted by faculty members in the applicant's area of interest. Marlboro does not use a formulaic approach in making admission decisions. Applicants are encouraged to demonstrate their particular strengths; the goal is a successful match between the student and the College.

Application and Information

New students and transfers are admitted for either the spring or fall semester. Applicants for the fall semester have a choice of three admission plans. Early decision is for those students who have thoroughly researched Marlboro and for whom Marlboro is the first choice. Applicants should be aware that early decision is binding. The deadline for submitting application materials is November 15, and applicants are notified by December 15. Early action, a nonbinding plan, has a deadline of January 15. These applicants are notified of a decision on February 1. The recommended regular admission deadline is March 1.

An application for admission must include a completed application form with a $30 fee, complete transcripts from all secondary schools and colleges, SAT I or ACT scores, an analytical writing sample, an autobiographical statement, an interview, and one recommendation. Interviews and campus visits can be scheduled at any time during the application process. The Admissions Committee welcomes applications from home-schooled students. In lieu of a high school transcript, home-schooled students must submit a detailed description of their curriculum.

A 15-minute Marlboro College videotape is available on loan by calling or writing to Marlboro College.

Office of Admissions
Marlboro College
Marlboro, Vermont 05344
Telephone: 802-257-4333
          800-343-0049 (toll-free)
Fax: 802-257-4154
E-mail: admissions@marlboro.edu
World Wide Web: http://www.marlboro.edu

On the campus of Marlboro College.

MARSHALL UNIVERSITY
HUNTINGTON, WEST VIRGINIA

The University

Marshall University is a public institution, established as Marshall Academy in 1837 and granted university status in 1961. Assigned a major role as an urban-oriented university by the West Virginia Board of Trustees, it is devoted to offering both undergraduate and graduate courses of study to accommodate both full-time students and employed persons who wish to pursue studies on a part-time basis. The Community and Technical College of the University provides two-year associate degree programs and prebaccalaureate courses. The health-care expertise of the medical staff and faculty has given rise to a concentration of undergraduate programs in allied health technologies and sciences. The school has been recognized as a "best value" based on academic quality and moderate cost.

The Graduate School offers various master's degree programs and a Ph.D. in biomedical sciences; the M.D. is available at the Marshall University School of Medicine. Marshall offers a master's degree in adult and technical education; art; biological sciences; biomedical sciences; business administration; business foundations programs; chemistry; communication disorders; communication studies; counseling; criminal justice; early childhood, elementary, or secondary education; educational specialist studies; engineering; English; environmental science; exercise science; family and consumer science; family nurse practitioner studies; forensic science; geography; health and physical education; health-care administration; history; humanities; industrial and employee relations; information systems; journalism; leadership studies; mathematics; music; nursing; physical science; political science; psychology; reading education; safety; school psychology; sociology; special education; teaching; and technology management.

The Ed.D. degree is offered in educational administration in cooperation with West Virginia University. A master's degree in forestry and in environmental management is offered in cooperation with Duke University.

All of the University's academic programs are highly regarded by professional schools and educators and business, industry, and government. The University is fully accredited by the North Central Association of Colleges and Schools. AACSB–The International Association for Management Education accredits the Lewis College of Business.

Eighty percent of Marshall's students are residents of West Virginia. Approximately 2,000 live in campus housing. The informal and relaxed atmosphere of the six residence halls, single sex and coed, contributes an important focus to life at Marshall. The University offers more than 100 student organizations that provide excellent opportunities for extracurricular involvement. Twelve national fraternities and seven national sororities represent social organizations, with the majority having houses. Clubs, organizations, intramural athletics, theater, musical ensembles, student government, religious groups, and Black United Students provide many cultural and social activities. Marshall is a member of the NCAA-1A Mid-American Conference. Intercollegiate sports include men's baseball, basketball, cheerleading, cross-country, football, golf, soccer, and track and field and women's basketball, cheerleading, cross-country, soccer, softball, tennis, track and field, and volleyball.

Location

Huntington, with a population of 55,000, is the second-largest urban center in West Virginia. It is located on the banks of the Ohio River in the Tri-State region, bordering eastern Kentucky and southern Ohio. The area has many good shopping centers, theaters, parks, swimming pools, golf courses, churches, and art galleries. Huntington's Civic Arena is host to some of the top names in entertainment. Many of these activities are within walking distance of the Marshall University campus. The city and the University work effectively together to provide the best educational and cultural opportunities possible. A regional airport, Amtrak, and Greyhound Bus Line provide transportation to and from the city.

Majors and Degrees

The Bachelor of Arts (B.A.) degree is offered in basic humanities, classical or modern languages (French, German, Latin, and Spanish), communication disorders, communication studies, counseling, criminal justice, economics, education (elementary and secondary), English, family and consumer science, geography, geology, history, international affairs, journalism and mass communications, multidisciplinary studies, physical education, political science, psychology, and sociology. The B.A. degree is also available through the Board of Regents External Degree Program. The Bachelor of Science (B.S.) degree is offered in biological science, botany, chemistry, computer science, cytotechnology, dietetics, environmental biology, geography, geology, integrated science and technology, mathematics, microbiology, park resources and leisure services, physics, physiology/molecular biology, safety technology, and zoology. The Bachelor of Business Administration (B.B.A.) degree is awarded in accounting, economics, finance, management, management information systems, and marketing. The Bachelor of Fine Arts (B.F.A.) is offered in music, theater, and visual arts. The Bachelor of Science in Medical Technology (B.S.M.T.), the Bachelor of Science in Nursing (B.S.N.), and the Bachelor of Social Work (B.S.W.) degrees are also offered.

The Associate of Applied Science degree is offered in automotive technology, banking and finance, computer technology, electronics technology, engineering technology, general studies, health information technology, hospitality management, interior design, legal assistant studies, management technology, medical assistant studies, medical lab studies, occupational development technology, office technology, physical therapist assistant studies, police science, radiologic technology, respiratory therapy assistant studies, and technical studies. The Certificate of Proficiency is offered in emergency medical technology.

Academic Program

Each undergraduate division specifies its own sequence requirements, but all baccalaureate degree students must complete a minimum of 128 credit hours with an overall GPA of at least 2.0. All students must complete general requirements in humanities, social sciences, science, and mathematics. To qualify as full-time, the undergraduate student must carry at least 12 credit hours per semester. Permission from the academic dean is required for students who wish to enroll for 19 hours or more in one semester.

Students may receive credit through Advanced Placement or College-Level Examination Program tests. Marshall University offers the following special programs: Public Service Internship, Honors Program, Semester Abroad Program, National Student Exchange, Academic Common Market, Cooperative Work-Study Program, U.S. Army Reserve Officers' Training Corps (ROTC), remediation services, academic assistance, counseling, and job placement.

The Marshall Plan for Quality Undergraduate Education went into effect in 1995. Designed to provide Marshall graduates with a competitive advantage, it includes science/computer literacy, global studies, intensified writing courses, and a capstone experience for all baccalaureate students entering at that time and later.

Academic Facilities

Facilities on the Marshall University campus include the Center for Academic Excellence; Center for the Fine and Performing Arts;

Birke Art Gallery; H.E.L.P. Center for those with learning disabilities; Center for International Programs; Psychology Clinic; Fitness and Wellness Center; Speech and Hearing Clinic; Writing Center; Learning Resource Center; language, mathematics, chemistry, and physics laboratories; WPBY-TV and WMUL-FM studios; and the Center for Academic Support. The John Deaver Drinko Library, an ultramodern library and information center that opened in 1998, provides 390 computer stations, group study rooms, a reading lab, a 24-hour computer lab, and a café among its many features.

Costs

Tuition and fees for the 1999–2000 academic year were $2440 for West Virginia residents, $4456 for Metro students (residents of the counties adjacent to Huntington, West Virginia), and $6512 for out-of-state students. Room and board were $4620, and books averaged $600.

Financial Aid

Approximately 50 percent of the student body receives some type of financial assistance. Students who are admitted by February 1 and submit the application for financial aid by March 1 will be considered for some type of financial aid. Marshall University participates in the following programs: Federal Pell Grant, Federal Supplemental Educational Opportunity Grant, West Virginia Higher Education Grant, Federal Work-Study, Federal Stafford Student Loans, Federal Perkins Loans, and Federal PLUS. Scholarships of $500 are guaranteed to students with a minimum ACT composite score of 19 (or an SAT I composite score of 910) and a 3.0 GPA. Scholarships of $1250 are guaranteed to students with a minimum ACT composite score of 25 (or an SAT I composite score of 1140) and a 3.5 GPA; a tuition waiver and $1250 are guaranteed to students with a minimum ACT composite score of 30 (or an SAT I composite score of 1340) and a 3.5 GPA. There is no separate application for scholarships at the University; however, students should apply for admission to Marshall prior to February 1 of their senior year.

Faculty

Marshall University has 699 full-time faculty members. Eighty-three percent hold a doctorate or terminal degree in their field. The student-faculty ratio is approximately 23:1.

Student Government

Marshall University sponsors the Student Government Association (SGA), a student-oriented organization that ensures practical and creative interaction among those students interested in administration and campus politics. The SGA consists of four executive members (president, vice president, treasurer, and secretary) and an equal number of representatives from among residence hall students, off-campus students, and transient students. All officers and representatives serve from the spring of their election year until the following spring. The executive members receive a small monthly salary. Only full-time students with an overall GPA of 2.25 or higher are eligible for office. The goal of the SGA is to provide students with a number of important services, including off-campus housing assistance, a student consumer liaison, health insurance, legal aid, and various entertainment opportunities. The SGA sponsors the Muscular Dystrophy Dance and appoints students in the University community to various planning and organizational positions and committees on campus. The SGA also accepts requests for special project funding from recognized groups or clubs throughout the year. The SGA is active and viable at Marshall University, helping students and the University to grow together.

Admission Requirements

The average ACT and SAT I scores of entering freshmen at Marshall University are 21.2 and 990, respectively, and the average high school GPA is 3.24. Students seeking a baccalaureate degree must have the following high school preparation: 4 units of English, 3 units of social studies, 2 units of laboratory science, and 2 units of mathematics (algebra I or higher). In addition, they must graduate from an approved high school with either a minimum GPA of 2.0 and a minimum composite score on the ACT of 19 (a minimum composite score of 910 on the SAT I). The Marshall University Community and Technical College has an open admissions policy for students desiring a two-year associate degree and/or career training. Applications from transfer students and nontraditional or returning students are welcome. Transfer applicants are required to have earned a cumulative GPA of at least 2.0 (C) on all previous college work. Academically superior high school students may be admitted to Marshall University on a part-time basis, provided they have a GPA of at least 3.0 (B) and the recommendation of a high school counselor or principal. Campus visits for prospective students are conducted daily, Mondays through Fridays at 10 a.m. and 1 p.m. and on some Saturdays through the Welcome Center. Students may call the Welcome Center at 304-696-6833, or the toll-free number listed below, to make arrangements.

Admission to the University is not necessarily admission to a particular college or curriculum within the University. Applicants for the nursing program should apply a year in advance and show satisfactory scores on the ACT; an interview is required. Entry into the music program requires an audition.

Application and Information

Applicants to the freshman class should submit the Undergraduate Application for Admission and have their high school counselor or principal forward a transcript of grades to the Office of Admissions. Scores on the ACT should be forwarded to Marshall (code number 4526 on the ACT form). High school students who have not been admitted to Marshall and who have their ACT scores forwarded to the Office of Admissions will receive a preprinted application form approximately six weeks after the test scores are received. This form takes the place of the regular application for admission. The student should complete the designated sections of the form and take it to the high school counselor, who should then certify the student's GPA and return the form to Marshall. Transfer applicants should submit an application and request that official transcripts from each college previously attended be forwarded to the Office of Admissions. Prospective students are notified as soon as action is taken on their application. For more information, students should contact:

Director of Admissions
Marshall University
Huntington, West Virginia 25755-2026
Telephone: 304-696-3160
        800-642-3499 (toll-free)
Fax: 304-696-3135
E-mail: admissions@marshall.edu
World Wide Web: http://www.marshall.edu

Drinko Library.

MARS HILL COLLEGE
MARS HILL, NORTH CAROLINA

The College

Mars Hill College (MHC), an academic community rooted in the Christian faith, challenges and equips students to pursue intellectual, spiritual, and personal growth. This growth is grounded in a rigorous study of the liberal arts, connected with the world of work, and committed to character development, service, and responsible citizenship in the community, the region, and the world. Mars Hill College is the oldest educational institution in western North Carolina. It was founded by a small group of pioneer citizens who were descendents of the original settlers of the area. The school opened in 1856 as the French Broad Baptist Academy. On February 16, 1859, the school was chartered by the North Carolina General Assembly as Mars Hill College, a name suggested from the verse in the Bible at Acts 17:22, "Then Paul stood in the midst of Mars Hill. . . ."

Students are at the center of the educational program at Mars Hill College. The College is committed to their academic, social, spiritual, and personal growth and development. The educational program is student oriented and tailored to meet the individual needs of each person as well as possible. Mars Hill College offers students a well-rounded education. Through the general education program, the College helps students acquire the abilities and knowledge needed to be responsible and successful and provides a sound foundation for a major. Through a carefully chosen major, students gain the knowledge and skills needed to be successful in a vocation or graduate study related to the major they choose. Some students choose to major in more than one area or to minor or concentrate in additional areas in order to be more versatile.

Cocurricular activities support, and in some cases are responsible for, the goals of general and specialized education. Many such activities complement and enrich classroom studies. They also lead to individual growth and development in being responsible and accountable, setting priorities, developing leadership, and expressing creativity. The College's LifeWorks Learning Partnership involves students and faculty members in creating connections between faith and learning, between service and learning, and between learning in and out of the classroom. Through LifeWorks, students explore their roles in the community through tutoring and mentoring children, building a Habitat for Humanity house, participating in a community-based research project, or doing an internship at one of more than seventy-five sites, or through many other opportunities. Making these connections helps students develop the knowledge, skills, and values that will enable them to make a life as well as to make a living.

Mars Hill currently has 1,256 students enrolled. As part of its strategic plan, the College plans to increase the enrollment to 1,500 students by 2006.

Athletics are a major aspect of campus life at Mars Hill College. Intercollegiate competition, including men's baseball, basketball, cross-country, football, golf, lacrosse, soccer, and tennis and women's basketball, cross-country, soccer, softball, tennis, and volleyball, is offered through College teams that are affiliated with the NCAA Division II and the South Atlantic Conference. Hiking, snow skiing, white-water rafting, and golf are popular off-campus activities.

Social activities and entertainment are important to a student's life at Mars Hill. There is a great diversity of student organizations at Mars Hill College, through which a student can find personal, social, professional, and educational fulfillment. These include honor organizations such as Alpha Chi National Honor Scholarship Society, Beta Beta Beta, and the Business Honor Club. Professional organizations include Music Educators' National Conference, Music Teachers' National Association, American Guild of Organists, Alpha Psi Omega Theatre Fraternity, Delta Omicron Music Fraternity, and Phi Mu Alpha Sinfonia. Interest groups include Bailey Mountain Cloggers, Fellowship of Christian Athletes, Young Democrats, College Republicans, and Christian Student Movement. Greek organizations that are active in campus life include two national and four local fraternities and sororities.

Location

Mars Hill College is located in the mountains of western North Carolina, one of the most beautiful regions of the United States. The town of Mars Hill has a population of approximately 3,000. It is 18 miles north of Asheville via highway 19-23. The closest interstates are I-40, I-26, and I-240. Atlanta, Georgia, is 227 miles away; Roanoke, Virginia, is 264 miles away; and Charlotte, North Carolina, is 162 miles away. Asheville was recently named an All-American City and one of the top twenty-five cultural cities in America. Asheville has the sophisticated attractions of a major metropolis, including theater and a symphony, and is known for its high-quality arts, crafts, and musical offerings. Scenic attractions such as Mount Mitchell, Great Smoky Mountains National Park, Craggy Gardens, Linville Falls and Caverns, Biltmore House and Gardens, and the Blue Ridge Parkway are within easy driving distance.

Majors and Degrees

The College awards the Bachelor of Arts degree in art, communication, education/elementary (K–6), education/middle grades (6–9), English, history, international studies, music, political science, psychology, religion and philosophy, sociology, Spanish, and theater arts; the Bachelor of Science in accounting, athletic training, biology, botany, business administration, chemistry, computer science, fashion and interior merchandising, mathematics, medical technology, physician assistant studies, physical education/sports management, physical education/sports science, physical education/teacher education, recreation, and zoology; the Bachelor of Science–Allied Programs in allied business and computer technology, allied health, allied management and community science, allied natural science, allied public services, allied social science, and allied technology and modern life; the Bachelor of Music in music education and performance; the Bachelor of Social Work; and the Bachelor of Fine Arts in musical theater. Preparatory programs for postgraduate study are available in dentistry, law, medicine, and veterinary medicine.

Academic Program

The academic program, which leads to a degree, is composed of four related parts: general education, community life, the major, and electives. Courses taken as electives may be in the student's major, in related disciplines, or in other areas of special interest. A maximum of 9 semester hours of credit for developmental courses may be applied toward graduation as electives. To receive a degree from Mars Hill College, a student must complete the general education and major requirements specified in the student's catalog of entry and earn a minimum of 128 semester hours of credit. Sixty semester hours, including 12 semester hours in the major, must be earned at a senior-level institution. The last 32 semester hours must be earned at Mars Hill. The student must earn a cumulative grade point average of 2.0 for all courses attempted at Mars Hill.

There are opportunities in most academic departments for students to engage in independent study, research, seminars, and directed readings. Such opportunities are open to all students in accordance with policies established by the Curriculum Committee. Independent study is defined as a program of study designed by a student and faculty member to achieve mutually agreed-upon objectives. Independent study and directed reading projects are designed to allow students to engage in research or study not available in regularly scheduled courses or to pursue in greater depth a subject or interest to which the student was introduced during a regular course.

Off-Campus Arrangements

The College recognizes the importance of global awareness and supports academic programs that emphasize international/intercultural education. Study-abroad opportunities are an essential feature of an international education, and students and faculty members are encouraged to participate in them. Students are eligible to study at more than 100 international universities through the International Student Exchange Program (ISEP). The College strongly encourages all foreign language majors to spend at least one semester of their training abroad.

Academic Facilities

Renfro Library supports the Mars Hill College curriculum by serving the research and information needs of the students, faculty members, and staff members of the College. The MHC computer network provides access to the Renfro Library catalog and direct access to encyclopedias, atlases, literary and biographical indexes, and other online information sources. The network is also used to search for indexes, abstracts, and full-text journals. The library contains more than 90,000 books and periodical volumes and provides in-house access to more than 700 journals. Interlibrary loan services are available through network agreements with regional and national consortia.

The Harris Media Center is designed to serve the audiovisual needs of students and faculty members. The passive solar facility includes teaching darkrooms for photography classes and a projection room for viewing films, videotapes, multi-image programs, and computer presentations. Two viewing classrooms, an area for individual listening and viewing, a video studio with taping and editing facilities, and storage and maintenance facilities for audiovisual materials are also located in the Media Center. The College ranks high among North Carolina campuses with its computer-student ratio of 1:6. More than 180 computers are available for student use on the campus. Students with computers can access the network by modem from both on and off campus 24 hours a day.

Costs

For the 2000–01 academic year, tuition is $12,000, and room and board are $4500. Fees are $800, and books are estimated at $600.

Financial Aid

Mars Hill College offers students a variety of grants, scholarships, loans, and employment opportunities to assist with the cost of college. Prospective students may contact the school beginning in the fall to inquire about the merit scholarship and award program. Students must file the Free Application for Federal Student Aid (FAFSA) in order to be considered for financial aid. The school code for Mars Hill College is 002944. Federal aid is administered through the following programs: Federal Pell Grants, Federal Supplemental Education Opportunity Grants (FSEOG), the Federal Work-Study Program, Federal Perkins Loans, Federal Stafford Student Loans, and Federal PLUS Loans. North Carolina residents qualify for the North Carolina Legislative Tuition Grant (NCLTG) and/or the need-based Contractual Grant (NCCG). Eighty percent of students receive some form of aid.

Faculty

The members of the faculty at Mars Hill College are very accomplished in their respective fields and skilled in the art of teaching. There are 81 full-time and 69 part-time faculty members. Of the full-time faculty members, 68 percent hold a doctorate or terminal degree in their discipline or specialty. The student-faculty ratio is 13:1.

Student Government

The students of Mars Hill College voted for a self-governing unit to be known as the Student Government Association (SGA). SGA is the students' voice to the faculty members, the administration, and those outside the academic community. The students are encouraged to support the organization and to communicate their needs to the elected leaders of the SGA. The Student Government Association is organized into three branches: the Executive, the Judicial, and the Legislative. The SGA constitution provides for 4 student body officers—president, vice president, secretary, and treasurer—and for other legislative, judicial, and programming units.

Admission Requirements

Candidates submit an application, a $25 application fee, an official high school transcript, and official SAT or ACT scores. A minimum of 18 units is required. These units should include 4 in English, 2 in history, 2 in natural science, and 3 in mathematics. It is recommended that the balance include 2 foreign language units and/or 1 computer science unit. Acceptance is based on the applicant's high school grade point average, rank in class, SAT or ACT scores, and extracurricular activities. Transfer candidates submit an application, a $25 application fee, and official college transcripts from all institutions previously attended. A General Educational Development (GED) certificate is accepted. All rights accorded to students are made without regard to race, color, national or ethnic origin, gender, or impairment of the student.

Application and Information

Applications may be submitted to Mars Hill College for either semester. Notification of the admission decision is given on a rolling basis upon receipt of all application data. A $250 deposit is required for boarding students, and a $150 deposit is required for commuting students. The deposit is due three weeks after acceptance and is fully refundable until May 1 for fall applicants and December 1 for spring applicants.

For further information, students should contact:
Admissions Office
Mars Hill College
Mars Hill, North Carolina 28754
Telephone: 828-689-1201
          800-543-1514 (toll-free)
Fax: 828-689-1473
E-mail: admissions@mhc.edu
World Wide Web: http://www.mhc.edu

On the campus of Mars Hill College.

MARYCREST INTERNATIONAL UNIVERSITY
DAVENPORT, IOWA

The University
Marycrest International University (MIU) is an independent, co-educational university that prepares students of all faiths in liberal and professional studies. MIU provides programs, facilities, and resources that foster the development of knowledge, abilities, and values appropriate to world citizens. Extracurricular activities include the Student Government Association for developing leadership skills; *The Crest*, the University's national-award–winning student magazine, and its online version; and numerous academic clubs and service organizations. Marycrest is a member of the NAIA and sponsors intercollegiate sports, including men's basketball, soccer, and volleyball and women's basketball, soccer, softball, and volleyball. In addition, MIU offers a wide range of recreational and intramural activities and access to a first-class fitness center on campus.

Location
Marycrest International University is a 22-acre campus nestled among trees on the bluffs overlooking the Mississippi River in Davenport, Iowa, one of the four clustered cities known as the Quad Cities. With a population of more than 350,000, the Quad Cities area is one of the safest and most affordable and dynamic metropolitan areas in the Midwest. The Quad Cities provide many cultural events, including one of the oldest symphony orchestras in the U.S., and professional baseball, hockey, and basketball. The Davenport riverside is home to the Bix 7, an internationally known 7-kilometer race, and the Bix Beiderbecke Jazz Festival. The Quad Cities are easily reached by eight major highways and rail, bus, and air. The Quad City International Airport, a 20-minute drive from MIU, is served by major and commuter airlines.

Majors and Degrees
MIU offers sixteen undergraduate academic majors. Undergraduate majors include accounting, American language and culture, biology, business, computer graphics/multimedia, computer science, education, English, environmental science, history, mathematics, nursing, psychology, social and behavioral sciences, social work, and special studies.

MIU was the first private institution in the United States to offer computer graphics as a major. This program has been awarded recognition by the National Graphics Association for its creative approaches. The University's computer graphics/multimedia major features a project-based arena involving computer graphics, broadcast, print, and art media, within which students, faculty members, and staff members work as a team on interactive multimedia projects. The business major at MIU provides the knowledge and practical skills necessary to develop business contacts, conduct practical business research, utilize information to identify business opportunities, and help solve real operational business problems. The computer science major has a computer systems/systems management focus and a software development cluster of courses that allow a student to emphasize certain aspects of programming. The teacher education program is approved by the Iowa Department of Education and includes elementary education and endorsements in secondary education. MIU also is the first private university in Iowa to have professional development schools, an innovative approach to teacher education at the elementary school level. Many of the education courses are taught at Truman Elementary School and Blue Grass Elementary School with the collaboration of MIU education faculty members and Truman School faculty members.

Other majors at MIU include communication and preprofessional tracks.

Academic Program
Academic programs at MIU feature a curriculum that integrates liberal arts, professional studies, and experiential education. Innovative learning methods are tailored to individual students' needs. The University's international focus offers the opportunity for global experience and learning through travel and interpersonal relationships. The academic calendar consists of two semesters, as well as summer sessions.

Candidates for the Bachelor of Arts, Bachelor of Science, Bachelor of Science in Nursing, and Bachelor of Social Work degrees must successfully complete at least 124 semester hours. This includes the University's general education requirements, at least one major and any required supporting courses, the Capstone Seminar, and other graduation requirements. Some majors require more than 124 hours.

MIU is notable in that more than 95 percent of its alumni survey respondents are employed in the fields for which they studied.

Off-Campus Arrangements
As leaders in the implementation of technological innovation and distance education, Marycrest International University encourages students to expand their concept of education and to avail themselves of the various networks with which Marycrest is linked, both within and outside the United States.

MIU students learn about other cultures in many of their day-to-day experiences and interactions on campus. They also have the opportunity to link technologically with other sites and cultures through the MIU Videoconferencing Center. In addition, students may choose to study for a semester at affiliated institutions in the Netherlands, Germany, and Japan or at other U.S. and international sites with which MIU is networked. Students receive academic credit from Marycrest International University for these off-site experiences.

Academic Facilities
Marycrest's wooded hilltop campus includes historic and contemporary academic buildings, comfortable residence halls, and a spacious Activities Center. The Cone Library contains 150,000 books. It is possible to withdraw information from other local, state, and national libraries through affiliation with the River Bend Library System as well as from other information centers by computer. The Nursing Building has an academic auditorium, a television and multimedia production studio, nursing laboratories, and the Rita Koenigsaecker Language Institute. Walsh Hall has a journalism and photography studio laboratory; a computer graphics laboratory; a computerized collaborative classroom; biology, physics, and chemistry laboratories; the campus bookstores; and a post office. The campus maintains the Babcock acres as an environmental laboratory for research and study.

Costs
The 1999–2000 band tuition (12–17 semester hours) was $12,400. Double-occupancy room and board were $4840 per year. Books, fees, and supplies vary according to major and average $1000.

Financial Aid
Marycrest International University participates in all federal and state financial aid programs and offers a variety of institutional grants and scholarships based upon merit, talent, and need. To receive financial assistance, students must complete and submit the Free Application for Federal Student Aid (FAFSA). Once the University determines a student's need, an award letter will be mailed listing all financial aid resources for which the student is

eligible. Only students who have been accepted into the University may receive a financial aid award.

Faculty

Marycrest International University maintains a professionally distinguished faculty dedicated to the art of teaching. More than 60 percent of the full-time faculty members hold terminal degrees. A 14:1 student-faculty ratio ensures close interaction between students and faculty members. MIU's graduates and students have historically expressed great satisfaction with their instruction and with the high quality of the faculty at MIU.

Student Government

The MIU Student Government Association (SGA) enables every student to be actively involved in the determination of activities that are sponsored by the University and in the overall governance of the University. The SGA has been instrumental in providing leadership in all areas of the institution. Representatives have seats on all campus committees.

Admission Requirements

Freshman applicants coming directly from high school, along with submitting an application for admission and a nonrefundable $25 application fee, must provide a copy of their high school transcript, official documentation of ACT or SAT I scores (except if applying for admission more than a year after leaving high school), and official transcripts for any college course work completed during high school. Transfer applicants also need to submit an application for admission and pay a nonrefundable $25 application fee, provide official transcripts from each college or university attended, and submit evidence of high school or equivalency test completion. International applicants must submit a completed application for international student admission (which includes the Educational Background form), a nonrefundable $50 application fee, a completed Declaration of Finances form with a certified bank statement from each sponsor, an official transcript of all high school records, an official transcript of each college attended, and an official score of at least 500 on the Test of English as a Foreign Language (TOEFL). Any documents not in English must be accompanied by English-language translations.

Application and Information

Marycrest International University accepts applications for consideration throughout the calendar year. Early admission secures benefits for students, such as priority in registration and earlier consideration for financial aid. Prospective students are encouraged to visit the campus. Admission representatives schedule an interesting and informative day for students and families, during which they may meet faculty members, current students, and a financial aid officer. Meals on campus and an overnight residence hall stay may also be arranged. For an application and information about the University or to make an appointment for a campus visit, students should contact:

Office of Admission
Marycrest International University
1607 West 12th Street
Davenport, Iowa 52804-4096

Telephone: 319-326-9225
              800-728-9705 (toll-free)
Fax: 319-327-9620
E-mail: admission@mcrest.edu
World Wide Web: http://www.mcrest.edu

Marycrest International University students enjoy the scenic beauty of the campus as they take a stroll past Petersen Hall.

MARYGROVE COLLEGE
DETROIT, MICHIGAN

The College

Marygrove College is a professionally oriented, Catholic, coeducational, liberal arts college located in northwest Detroit. The Sisters, Servants of the Immaculate Heart of Mary (IHM), founded Marygrove College in 1905 in Monroe, Michigan, as St. Mary College. When the College needed more room to grow, the new College opened in Detroit in September 1927 with 287 female students.

Marygrove proudly affirms its rich heritage of Roman Catholicism. The Catholic intellectual tradition informs its general education curriculum and shapes the organizational culture of its community by educating the students toward the mission of the College. The College is proud, however, to practice its "catholicity" in the spirit of the Vatican Council II by welcoming and embracing persons from diverse ethnic and religious backgrounds, by supporting ecumenical and interfaith services and activities, and by striving to be as inclusive as possible in service to metropolitan Detroit.

The fundamental purpose of Marygrove College is to educate each student toward intellectual and professional competence, toward career flexibility through grounding in the liberal arts, and toward active compassion and commitment.

Marygrove has approximately 400 full-time and 600 part-time undergraduate students. The College received national recognition for the diversity of its student body. The 1999 edition of America's Best Colleges by *U.S. News & World Report* lists Marygrove as the ninth most diverse institution in the Midwest. While many undergraduates arrive directly from high school and live on campus, many come with years of professional experience. Many students have jobs, families, and very full lives outside of class and enjoy the interaction with traditional-age students. Marygrove recruits purposeful, career-minded, highly motivated people who take their responsibilities and aspirations seriously.

Students have access to a coeducational residence facility, Florent Gillet Hall, which opened in 1958. The spacious suites are composed of two bedrooms, a bathroom, and a study area. Depending on availability of space, a student may arrange for private accommodations. Florent Gillet Hall also contains a large lounge area for student events.

The College offers a variety of academic services, including advising, career counseling and placement, a cooperative education program, student support services, computer labs, a writing assistance program, and campus ministry. Campus housing, study abroad, service learning, team sports, and honors programs are currently under expansion at Marygrove.

Marygrove College is accredited by the Commission on Institutions of Higher Education of the North Central Association of Colleges and Schools (NCA), 30 North LaSalle Street, Suite 2400, Chicago, Illinois 60602-2504; telephone: 312-263-0456. The education unit at Marygrove College is accredited by the National Council for Accreditation of Teacher Education (NCATE).

Location

The only small, private, liberal arts college in Detroit, Marygrove sits on 50 beautiful, wooded acres. Two classic Tudor Gothic buildings—the Liberal Arts Building and Madame Cadillac Hall—are set amid groves of towering trees and expansive lawns. This idyllic setting creates a perfect atmosphere for learning.

Located in the northwest corner of Detroit, Marygrove is within easy reach of cultural, entertainment, and sporting events. Students may visit the world-renowned Detroit Institute of Arts, famed Greenfield Village, or African American Museum or shop at local malls within easy access. They may also listen to cool jazz at one of the nearby jazz clubs or drive 10 minutes to the downtown area and observe a play at the State or Fox Theatre or watch the Tigers in the beautiful new stadium.

Majors and Degrees

Marygrove College offers Bachelor of Arts (B.A.), Bachelor of Science (B.S.), Bachelor of Applied Science (B.A.S.), Bachelor of Business Administration (B.B.A.), Bachelor of Fine Arts (B.F.A.), Bachelor of Music (B.Mus.), and Bachelor of Social Work (B.S.W.) degrees.

The majors offered in the Bachelor of Arts program include accounting, art, art therapy, business, business administration, chemistry, child development, dance, early childhood education, English, family and consumer sciences, financial planning, foods and nutrition, food service management, history, language and international business, language arts, marketing, mathematics, music, political science, psychology, religious studies, social science, social studies, and special education. The Bachelor of Science program includes majors in biology, computer information systems, environmental science, foods and nutrition, general science, and mathematics. Bachelor of Applied Science majors include allied health, computer information systems, and radiology imaging. The education department certifies majors for elementary and secondary education in more than sixteen major and minor areas of study. Preprofessional programs offered at Marygrove include law, medicine, and dentistry.

The Associate of Arts degree (A.A.) in liberal studies is also offered, as is the Associate of Science (A.S.) in general science and specialized programs.

Academic Program

At Marygrove, the courses offered assist in the development of skills used in the personal and professional lives of students. They are designed to establish standards for the ethical decisions students will be called on to make, foster appreciation for the dignity of the individual, expand the essential skills needed for continued self-development and independent learning, and increase cognitive, communicative, judgmental, and interpersonal powers.

As part of the general education plan, the whole College curriculum includes the following emphases: writing, information literacy, oral/visual presentation, cultural diversity, critical thinking, social justice, and learning to learn.

Because Marygrove expects that each graduate should be able to effectively interpret and express ideas in writing, the College emphasizes writing across the curriculum.

Most majors require 128 semester hours for graduation. Exceptional students may qualify for the Honor's Program. Students may receive credit through the Advanced Placement

(AP) Program, credit by examination and portfolio (CLEP), and the Proficiency Examination Program (PEP).

Off-Campus Arrangements

Study-abroad opportunities are offered each year. Numerous internships are available for students in selected programs. Students may also choose to attend classes through one of the College's satellite programs.

Academic Facilities

The Michigan Library Association honored the Marygrove Library program with two awards. In 1995, it received Outstanding Program Recognition for its excellent bibliographic instruction program, and in 1998, it was awarded the association's Information Literacy Award.

The library is a complete student resource center occupying a wing of the Liberal Arts Building. It is replete with a beautiful oak-paneled reading and group study room, a spacious reference/reading room, four floors of stacks, individual study carrels, a library instruction classroom, meeting rooms, and media facilities. Students have online access from the library or home to the library's catalog and electronic databases and its extensive print, electronic, microform, and audiovisual learning resources, which are carefully selected to support course-related endeavors.

Costs

For the 2000–01 academic year, tuition for full-time undergraduates is $10,140. Based on double occupancy, room and board costs average $6000. Books and fees total about $900 per year.

Financial Aid

The Marygrove community believes that talent, not money, should open the doors of the College. By offering scholarships, work-study opportunities, grants, loans, and flexible payment plans, the College does all it can to make a Marygrove education financially available to all qualified students.

About 95 percent of Marygrove students (enrolled at least half-time) receive some form of financial assistance. Many students with limited personal resources receive enough financial help to cover their basic college costs, including tuition and fees.

Each fall semester, Marygrove awards scholarships to recent high school graduates and transfer students who demonstrate excellence in academics and the visual and performing arts. These awards range from $3000 to full tuition and are renewable each year, provided the student maintains his or her grade point average.

Faculty

The undergraduate division has 55 full-time and 13 part-time faculty members. The student-teacher ratio is 17:1. The average class size is 15 students. Faculty members, not teaching assistants, teach all courses.

With about 1,000 undergraduates, Marygrove is an intimate learning environment—a place where every student counts.

Faculty members and students often collaborate on college projects and committees. All students have facutly advisers to help them and challenge them to succeed. Faculty members are available to consult with students after class, during office hours, and by appointment.

Student Government

The Marygrove Student Government is the official representative of the College student body. The goal of the Student Government is to enhance the quality of student life at Marygrove. Student Government plans, supports, and promotes student activities; surveys students and works to resolve student concerns; and represents the student body on college-wide committees.

Admission Requirements

Students seeking admission to Marygrove College are evaluated on their overall academic record, including ACT and SAT I scores. Applicants should submit a completed application, a letter of reference from a secondary school counselor, and school transcripts. An interview is recommended.

Admissions advisers are available to meet students and give them tours of the campus on a walk-in basis or from scheduled appointments.

Transfer students with 24 semester hours or more of acceptable credits are evaluated based on their previous academic record. The minimum acceptable grade point average for admission to the College is 2.0 (C). However, students must adhere to each department's standards for specific majors. The Education and Social Work Departments accept a minimum grade point average of 2.7 and 2.5, respectively.

Application and Information

Applicants are notified of the admission decision one week following receipt of the completed application, supporting credentials, and secondary counselor recommendation and payment of the $25 application fee.

The Office of Admissions encourages prospective students to visit the campus. Students may participate in the Touring Tuesday's Program, schedule individual appointments at other times, or tour the facilities during campus event programs scheduled throughout the year.

To obtain an application or arrange a campus visit, students should contact:

Office of Admissions
Marygrove College
8425 West McNichols Road
Detroit, Michigan 48221-2599
Telephone: 313-927-1240
Fax: 313-927-1345
E-mail: info@marygrove.edu
    sfrank@marygrove.edu
World Wide Web: http://www.marygrove.edu

MARYLAND INSTITUTE, COLLEGE OF ART
BALTIMORE, MARYLAND

The College

Established in 1826, the Maryland Institute, College of Art, is the oldest independent, fully accredited art college in the nation. Because of its belief in the vital role of art in society, the Institute is dedicated to the education of professional artists and to the development of an environment conducive to the creation of art. The College has a well-equipped network of studio facilities, an exceptional faculty, extensive exhibition space, and an impressive art college library. A unique on-campus residential environment is provided, designed with the artist in mind. The College offers many options not fully available at a liberal arts college, including a visiting artists program that welcomes more than 100 artists a year to the campus; 24-hour-a-day access to well-designed and fully equipped studios; the opportunity to exhibit work in numerous galleries, starting in the freshman year; the opportunity to study, through College-sponsored programs, at art colleges throughout the United States and abroad; a challenging liberal arts program that is integrated into and expands upon the studio program; and the opportunity to study with other students who are serious about their art.

In addition to the undergraduate degrees described below, the Institute offers the Master of Fine Arts in painting, sculpture, and photography; the Master of Arts in Teaching; and the Master of Arts in Digital Arts.

The faculty comprises 180 professional artists, designers, art historians, writers, and scholars—an assemblage of dedicated, working professionals who share the insights and experiences they have gained as practicing artists and scholars.

The College's 1,254 students represent forty-five states and fifty-seven countries. They are marked by their intellectual curiosity, creativity, motivation, and self-discipline. Students develop a body of work that prepares them for a variety of career paths. The Maryland Institute experience, which includes internship programs and other reality-based opportunities, develops a firm base upon which students can launch and build their careers.

The Office of Multicultural Affairs coordinates programs, services, and activities for international students. The College provides specific services to international students such as orientation, immigration advisement, personal counseling, and host families.

The Maryland Institute is a residential campus providing apartment-style housing that includes laundry facilities and is wired for Internet access. Additional benefits of 24-hour-a-day project rooms and studio facilities are incorporated into the residence. The Commons offers independence, privacy, and a lively sense of activity generated by a community focused on art. Student life is also focused at the College Center, which houses the Center Café, Java Corner, and meeting rooms for student organizations. The campus also includes a health center, and students have access to an athletic facility.

The College is accredited by the Middle States Association of Colleges and Schools and the National Association of Schools of Art and Design.

Location

The Maryland Institute is an urban campus that is located in a historic and beautiful neighborhood, surrounded by many cultural and educational institutions. These include the Meyerhoff Symphony Hall, the Lyric Opera House, and the Theatre Project. Baltimore has been cited as a city especially attractive to artists because of its vibrant and supportive atmosphere and its low cost of living. In addition to four world-class museums—the Contemporary Museum, the Walters Art Gallery, the Baltimore Museum of Art, and the American Visionary Art Museum—Baltimore features a wide range of alternative art spaces and galleries that present classical and nontraditional works by acclaimed and emerging artists. It is also ideally situated for an artist because it is at the center of the Washington–New York art corridor. By train, Washington, D.C., is 40 minutes to the south; New York City, less than 3 hours to the north. The Institute offers frequent inexpensive bus trips to New York studios, galleries, and museums.

Majors and Degrees

The Maryland Institute offers the Bachelor of Fine Arts degree in the following studio majors: ceramics, drawing, fibers, general fine arts, illustration, interior architecture and design, painting, photography/video, printmaking, sculpture, sculptural studies, and visual communications graphic design. Electronic media concentrations are offered in animation, digital multimedia, and video. The College offers an art history minor, a language and literature minor, and a cross-disciplinary minor. Students may also pursue double majors. Five-year combined Bachelor of Fine Arts/Master of Arts degrees are offered in teaching and in digital arts.

Academic Program

To receive the Bachelor of Fine Arts degree, students must complete a minimum of 126 credits, including 42 liberal arts credits. Students participate in a foundation program during their freshman year and then select a studio major. During the first year, the curriculum is well structured to provide the vocabulary and technical skills necessary for further specialized study. By the end of four years, students are expected to be able to work independently in their chosen medium. The program integrates writing and academic inquiry with studio practice. This combination reflects the need for artists to pursue intellectual concepts as well as aesthetic principles.

Off-Campus Arrangements

The Maryland Institute participates in a cooperative exchange program with Goucher College, the Johns Hopkins University, Loyola College, the Peabody Conservatory, Notre Dame College, and the University of Baltimore. This program makes it possible for full-time students at the Institute to enroll in one course per semester at one of the cooperating institutions without incurring an additional tuition charge. This option has proved to be exceptionally useful in offering studies not available at MICA, such as languages, the sciences, and business.

The Maryland Institute is a member of the Alliance of Independent Colleges of Art and Design (AICAD), which has cooperatively developed a program of study in New York City for eligible second-semester juniors and first-semester seniors. The Maryland Institute New York Studio Program's center, a loft facility in the Tribeca area of lower Manhattan, is home base for the semester-long program. Students may pursue either an independent study or, as apprenticeship students, they may work with a professional artist, museum, gallery, or an art-related business.

The Institute encourages young artists to work and live in other cultural settings so that they will better understand the universality of the language of art. Junior-year-abroad opportunities in England, France, Israel, Italy, Japan, the Netherlands, and Scotland allow third-year students to study for one semester at colleges and universities noted for their strength in the visual arts. Summer study in specialized subjects has been designed to provide students an opportunity to work closely with senior faculty members in locations that offer diverse cultural, environmental, and philosophical experiences. Greece, Italy, Canada, and Mexico are the current sites for two- and four-week programs. Exchange programs in China and Germany are also options for students.

The director of career development arranges job internships for juniors and seniors. These internships provide educational experiences that bridge the worlds of academics and work. There are more than 800 local and national listings.

Academic Facilities

The urban campus includes sixteen buildings with 235,000 square feet of studio and classroom space. The studios are fully furnished with state-of-the-art equipment for each area of concentration. The Decker Library includes more than 50,000 volumes, 300 current periodical subscriptions, and 120,000 slides of artwork. It is one of the largest art college libraries in the country.

The Maryland Institute has taken a leadership role in integrating new technologies into its programs of study. Within a very short time, the oldest degree-granting college of art in the United States has developed its facilities to provide more than one computer and/or video workstation for approximately every 4 students. The College's faculty has introduced computer-based courses in all of the professional studio majors, and the computer is also an important resource in the liberal arts area, whether as a tool for word processing or as a research medium for accessing images and information in a variety of forms. In some departments, such as interior architecture and design, graphic design, or photography, competency in the creative use of digital technologies is considered fundamental to the curriculum.

In addition to using the computer as a powerful imaging tool, the Maryland Institute is using the virtual space of the Internet as a site for new educational experiences. Using its own site on the World Wide Web as a model, the Institute is training many of its students to design web pages for themselves or clients. The College's students are also using the Internet to engage in interactive studio projects with other student groups in both the United States and Europe. From employment searches to virtual exhibitions, students are using cyberspace for extended communication and creative opportunities.

Exhibitions play a major role in the artistic and intellectual life at the Institute. Each year, more than ninety public exhibitions are featured in the Institute galleries, which are unrivaled by any art college. They bring the work of regional, national, and international artists, as well as faculty members and students, to the public year-round.

Costs

For the 2000–01 academic year, tuition is $19,800. Room is $4500 and board is $2040. There is an activities fee of $120 and a health center fee of $170.

Financial Aid

Each year approximately 65 percent of the full-time students receive $4 million in financial assistance. The College administers a variety of programs, including need-based grants and scholarships, government-related loans, and college work-study programs. The College also awards more than $300,000 through competitive, merit-based scholarship programs. Students who are not U.S. citizens or permanent residents are not eligible for financial aid.

Faculty

The faculty consists of 91 full-time and 89 part-time professional artists, designers, art historians, writers, and poets. Their work is represented in more than 250 public and private collections from the Museum of Modern Art to the Stedelijk Museum in Amsterdam and the Victoria and Albert Museum in London. They have won individual honors and awards from notable foundations, such as the National Endowment for the Arts and the Guggenheim Foundation. They are Fulbright Scholars and recipients of the Prix de Rome, the Louis Comfort Tiffany Award, and the MacArthur Fellowships. The faculty-student ratio is 1:10.

Student Government

The Student Voice Association represents the interests and viewpoints of students to the faculty, administration, and board of trustees. The student activities staff works closely with the Programming Arts Committee to plan interesting activities, entertainment programs, and trips for the Institute community. The Student Exhibition Committee organizes exhibitions in student-space galleries throughout the campus.

Admission Requirements

Students applying to the Maryland Institute must have made a serious commitment to art; therefore, a portfolio of artwork that demonstrates talent, ability, and experience is required for admission to the College. The portfolio is very important; however, evidence of academic ability as determined by level of course work, grades, test scores, and class rank are also weighted heavily in the admission decision. Individual interests and accomplishments, revealed in the personal statement, letters of recommendation, and lists of extracurricular and volunteer activities beyond classroom instruction, strengthen the application. The required personal essay is seriously considered. A TOEFL score of 550 or above is required of students whose native language is not English.

Application and Information

Students interested in early decision must complete all requirements for admission by November 15. Freshmen applicants for the fall term should complete the application process by March 1 for priority admission and financial aid consideration. Those who wish to be considered for Merit Scholarships must complete the application procedures by January 15; transfer students have a March 15 deadline. Applicants for admission in January are asked to complete the application process prior to December 1. For an application, catalog, and further information, students should contact:

Office of Undergraduate Admission
Maryland Institute, College of Art
1300 Mount Royal Avenue
Baltimore, Maryland 21217
Telephone: 410-225-2222
Fax: 410-225-2337
E-mail: admissions@mica.edu
World Wide Web: http://www.mica.edu

MARYLHURST UNIVERSITY
MARYLHURST, OREGON

The University

The oldest private Catholic liberal arts university in Oregon, Marylhurst University was established in 1893 by the Sisters of the Holy Names of Jesus and Mary. Marylhurst's founders believed in offering educational choices to people who had few—and that belief forms the cornerstone of its mission today.

Students come to Marylhurst for its student-centered philosophy—the small class sizes, the emphasis on classroom interaction and participation, and the practicing professionals who make up the majority of its faculty. Marylhurst attracts students who want to grow from their experiences and be challenged by what they are learning—who expect the best from themselves and their education. In return, Marylhurst expects their active participation in the learning process and a high level of commitment to their own intellectual goals.

Marylhurst's graduate programs include Master of Business Administration, Master of Arts in art therapy, Master of Arts in interdisciplinary studies, Master of Arts in applied theology, and Doctor of Ministry (through a cooperative program with the San Francisco Theological Seminary).

Marylhurst University is accredited at the baccalaureate and master's level by the Northwest Association of Schools and Colleges (NASC) and at the baccalaureate level by the National Association of Schools of Music.

Approximately 1,500 students of all ages and backgrounds attend Marylhurst. About 16 percent of Marylhurst's freshman class comes from out-of-state. Seventy-eight percent of undergraduate students are over the age of 25; approximately 8 percent are members of minority groups. The University has a growing population of international students, representing over thirty countries from around the world, such as Thailand, Japan, France, Taiwan, and Turkey.

Student organizations include OASIS (Organization Against Social Injustice and Suffering), Student Ambassadors, Association of Women in Communication, Student Association of Marylhurst Musicians, Toastmasters, and the Marylhurst University student chapter of the Gerontological Society of America.

Marylhurst's popular art gallery, the Art Gym, is known for displaying the work of some of the Pacific Northwest's finest contemporary artists. Portland's city life is just 20 minutes away by car and offers an endless variety of cultural and social activities.

On-campus housing is available in Villa Maria and Thompson Residence Halls for fall, winter, and spring terms. Both residence halls are substance-free. All rooms are single occupancy and open to full-time undergraduate and graduate students. The residence hall contract includes a meal plan in Clark Commons. Payments for the residence halls must be made in full prior to occupancy.

Marylhurst offers dining services for students in Clark Commons, which is open from 7:30 a.m. to 6:30 p.m. Monday through Friday; 8 a.m. to 6:30 p.m. on Saturday; and 12:30 to 6:30 p.m. on Sunday. Hot lunches are available Monday through Saturday, 11:30 a.m. to 1 p.m., and Sunday from 12:30 to 1:30 p.m. Dinner is available daily from 5 to 6:15 p.m. A salad bar and deli bar are available from 11:15 a.m. to 6:30 p.m.

A weekly mass is offered on campus at 4 p.m. on Wednesday in St. Anne's Chapel. An ecumenical meditation service is offered at varying times throughout each term. Counseling and spiritual direction are available by appointment.

Location

Marylhurst University is just 20 minutes from downtown Portland, Oregon. Portland, known as the City of Roses, is a friendly, attractive river city of about 550,000, with many parks and a casual, cosmopolitan air. Situated in the northwestern corner of the United States, the region receives a lot of rainfall but offers generally mild temperatures year-round. The Cascade mountain range runs through the center of Oregon; to the east, the climate is high desert; to the west, the Oregon coastline is known for its rugged and dramatic beauty. The area is very favorable for outdoor activities and Portland offers many cultural and social opportunities as well. For those who wish to explore the region more extensively, a number of national parks, and several larger cities such as Seattle and San Francisco, are within easy traveling distance.

Majors and Degrees

Marylhurst University is organized into three undergraduate colleges. The Division of Applied Sciences and Natural and Social Sciences offers a Bachelor of Science degree in management and Bachelor of Arts degrees in communication, organizational communication, science, psychology and social sciences. The Division of Fine Arts offers a Bachelor of Fine Arts degree in art, a Bachelor of Arts in art and art and music therapy, a Bachelor of Music in music, and a Bachelor of Arts in music. The Division of Liberal Studies offers Bachelor of Arts degrees in English, global studies, liberal studies, and religious studies and philosophy.

Academic Program

In addition to general education and major requirements, all degree-seeking students are required to complete the following requirements: math and writing assessment tests in the first or second quarter at Marylhurst; Integrated Learning I: Entering Student Seminar (1 credit) within the first two quarters; Information Studies (3 credits) during the first year (most beneficial if taken with a class that requires a research paper); and Integrated Learning III: Senior Seminar (4 credits) as a senior.

International students may receive assistance with their English skills through the Pacific International Academy, which also offers a detailed orientation to Marylhurst University and the United States for international students.

Marylhurst also offers, both on site and on line, a writing center for students, which provides guidance at all stages of the writing process and helps develop prewriting, revising, and editing skills.

Academic Facilities

Shoen Library has an on-site collection of approximately 100,000 books, 475 print journal subscriptions, and 3,000 online full-text journal subscriptions, as well as CDs, videos, and access to electronic and Internet databases. In addition, the library has just joined the Orbis Consortium—a library consortium consisting of, in addition to the University of

Chicago, fifteen colleges and universities in the Pacific Northwest. Schoen Library also provides computer clusters throughout the facility. Its teaching lab features seventeen PC workstations and digital projection capabilities; a drop-in lab equipped with PCs; a reference area equipped with PCs; a fine arts area (Whipple Room) with PC and Mac G4 capabilities; and selective semiprivate "nooks" for PC users who want to get away from it all. All PCs have full Internet access and laser printing options. The library provides some media equipment and also collaborates with the Instructional Technology and Information Systems Departments to provide media services and resources.

Costs

Undergraduate tuition for the 2000–01 academic year is $249 per credit hour. The student services fee is $17 per quarter and the technology fee is $4 per credit hour (maximum $48 per quarter). A late registration fee of $25 is charged for those who register more than one week after the beginning of the term. Tuition and fees are subject to change.

Financial Aid

Students are eligible for the standard range of federal aid programs, including the Pell Grant program and the Work-Study program. Additional opportunities for aid are available through state-sponsored programs and University and private scholarships. In 1998–99, approximately $6.3 million was awarded to Marylhurst students from these combined sources. Sixty-five percent of Marylhurst students receive financial aid of some kind.

Faculty

The majority of Marylhurst faculty members are successful professionals with advanced degrees in their fields of study. Eighty-five percent of undergraduate faculty members and 95 percent of graduate faculty members hold doctoral degrees. Marylhurst's student-faculty ratio is 8:1.

Admission Requirements

Marylhurst University has an open admissions policy for most undergraduate programs. Prospective students must complete and return an application form and a $20 nonrefundable processing fee, submit their high school diploma or equivalent, and have official transcripts sent directly to the Office of Admissions from all colleges attended. Incomplete files are closed after six months and individuals are required to reapply.

Marylhurst University's Early Scholars Program (an undergraduate honors program), and the undergraduate online degree-completion program (a Bachelor of Arts in Organizational Communication or a Bachelor of Science in Management, which is offered to students who have already completed two years of college work) are selective.

Applicants to the Early Scholars program must complete the application process by April 15; preferred selection goes to those who complete the process by February 15. The University reviews all Early Scholar applicants and selects those who demonstrate the likelihood of benefiting from and contributing to the academic opportunities of the program. Applicants are encouraged to visit the campus and meet the director of the program, faculty members, and students. For more information, students should call 503-636-6319.

International applicants are considered for enrollment or admission as degree students if they meet the following requirements: appropriate academic background, demonstrated proficiency in speaking and writing English as evidenced by the results from a number of standardized tests, documentation of adequate funding to complete a full course of study at Marylhurst, submission of official copies of previous college and/or high school documents as well as official translations of the original document, completed admission form(s) and fee, proof of health and accident insurance, and proof of measles immunization. Transfer students must provide a formal release from the college previously attended. Within the first quarter of arrival at Marylhurst, an evaluation of language proficiencies is required, which may result in required remedial work and additional English or math assessments as necessary.

Application and Information

With the exceptions of the Early Scholars program and the undergraduate online degree-completion program, applications for undergraduate studies are accepted continuously throughout the year; students may enroll in courses or begin a degree program at any time during the year.

Upon acceptance, students receive a letter from the Office of Admissions. They will then be admitted to a regular degree program and assigned an academic adviser.

For more information or to request materials, please contact:
Office of Admissions
17600 Pacific Highway (Highway 33)
Marylhurst, Oregon 97036-0261
Telephone: 800-634-9982 Ext. 3317
Fax: 503-635-6585
E-mail: admissions@marylhurst.edu
World Wide Web: http://www.marylhurst.edu

Marylhurst University students enjoy a quiet moment between classes.

MARYMOUNT COLLEGE
TARRYTOWN, NEW YORK

The College

Founded in 1907, Marymount is an independent, four-year liberal arts college whose mission is to prepare women for leadership in the twenty-first century. A pioneer in women's education for more than ninety years, the College encourages women to explore their goals and ideas. Marymount also offers a special weekend session to serve the needs of working women and men wishing to pursue a bachelor's degree. The College enrolls 700 students in the Women's College and 300 in the Weekend College. Marymount accommodates both commuting and residential students.

The College's physical facilities consist of twelve buildings, seven of which have been constructed since 1950. The facilities include new computer labs, a newly renovated athletic center with an Olympic-size pool, and a science building with state-of-the-art laboratory equipment. The four dormitories accommodate approximately 650 students.

Students come from many parts of the country to take advantage of the academic facilities of the College and the cultural offerings of New York City. Student organizations include numerous special interest clubs, community service programs, and honor societies. The College provides frequent social and cultural activities in which students may participate, as well as dramatic performances, art exhibits, film festival series, and dance concerts. Café Eclipse is a popular meeting spot. Marymount has intercollegiate teams and an extensive intramural program.

Location

The campus is located along the Hudson River in suburban Westchester County, just 25 miles north of New York City. Students enjoy the scenic countryside and residential village life as well as the convenience of being close to a major metropolitan center.

Majors and Degrees

Women's College students can receive the degrees of Bachelor of Arts or Bachelor of Science. Major fields of concentration include American studies, art (art education, art history, interior design, studio art), biology, business (accounting, economics/finance, management, marketing), chemistry, education (corporate training and development, dual certification in elementary/special education, home economics education, secondary education), English (creative writing, English literature, journalism), fashion design, fashion merchandising, foods and nutrition, French, history, information systems, interior design, international studies (business, economics, history, politics, sociology), mathematics, politics (public policy), psychology (art therapy), social work (B.S.W. equivalent), sociology, Spanish, and speech and drama (acting/directing, communication, history/criticism, theater management). Minors are available in anthropology; cognitive neuroscience; computer science; diversity and globalism; ethics, religion, and spiritual values; music; philosophy; race and ethnic studies; religious studies; and women's studies.

Students in the Weekend College can receive the degrees of Bachelor of Arts or Bachelor of Science. The major programs offered are business, corporate training and development, economics, education, English, foods and nutrition, history, information systems, legal and policy studies, liberal studies, and psychology.

Academic Program

Marymount students have great flexibility in their course selection, although there is a general education requirement. In consultation with their academic adviser, they may choose from the wide variety of courses offered in some thirty majors. From this broad background, they are guided in their choice of a major field, which comprises ten to twenty-one of their courses. Candidates for a bachelor's degree must complete 120 semester credits and fulfill the requirements of their major program. Students are also encouraged to participate in our internship program for college credit.

The College awards credit for successful scores on the College-Level Examination Program (CLEP) general and subject examinations. Students may also earn credit through Advanced Placement (AP) examinations. Credit for life/work experience is also available to adult students on presentation of a portfolio.

Off-Campus Arrangements

The flexibility that is built into the curriculum allows students to take advantage of less traditional learning experiences. Marymount has study-abroad programs in the United Kingdom and Australia, which are open to both Marymount students and students from other colleges. In addition, Marymount students may study in Austria, France, Italy, and Spain with affiliated programs. The opportunity to gain on-the-job experience for credit is available through an extensive internship program, which places students both locally and internationally.

Academic Facilities

The Marymount library has a collection of more than 117,100 volumes and lists 750 periodical titles and 7,529 microfilms. A fully equipped, multimedia, interactive language laboratory includes tapes and records for the study of French, Italian, Spanish, and English as a second language. The College has a science building, a state-of-the-art CAD computer lab, audiovisual facilities, a writing center, mathematics laboratories, computer centers, a teacher education center, art studios that include a darkroom for photography, and foods and clothing laboratories.

Costs

For the 2000–01 academic year, the total cost is $22,930. Tuition is $14,700, fees are $430, and room and board are $7800. Additional costs are estimated to be $1625.

Financial Aid

In 1999–2000, Marymount students received more than $8.8 million in student financial aid. Of this, $5.1 million came from federal programs, $810,000 from state programs, and more than $2.8 million from Marymount. Trustee grants and scholarships are also available. Financial aid applicants are required to file the FAFSA. It is recommended that the form be submitted by February 1. Early applicants can expect to receive their award notifications beginning April 15.

Faculty

The faculty has 59 full-time and 70 part-time members; 98 percent of the faculty members hold terminal degrees in their discipline. The student-faculty ratio is 12:1.

Student Government

An active Student Government Association (SGA) is composed of elected student representatives from each of the four classes. SGA members serve on policymaking committees with faculty and administrators and represent the student body in planning for all aspects of student life at Marymount.

Admission Requirements

Candidates for admission are required to be graduates of an accredited high school and must submit a completed application for admission, present a letter of recommendation from a guidance counselor, have a B or better average, rank in the top two fifths of their graduating class, and complete 16 academic high school units. The College requires that the SAT I or ACT be taken in the junior year of high school or in the fall semester of the senior year. Other factors important to admission officers are the reputation of the applicant's school, advanced placement or honors courses that have been taken, and the student's involvement in school and community activities.

Admission to the Weekend College may be in the fall, spring, or summer term. Procedures and criteria vary from those of the Women's College, and applicants are encouraged to write or call for an academic counseling session.

Application and Information

The application, a $30 fee, official high school records and recommendation, and test scores should be submitted by May 1 for admission to the fall term or by December 1 for the spring term. Notification of the admission decision, which is given on a rolling basis, begins in the late fall. Deferred admission and early admission are available.

For further information, prospective students should contact:

Daniela Esposito, Director of Admissions
Dean of Admissions
Marymount College
100 Marymount Avenue
Tarrytown, New York 10591-3796
Telephone: 914-332-8295
　　　　　　800-724-4312 (toll-free)
Fax: 914-332-7442
E-mail: admiss@mmc.marymt.edu
World Wide Web: http://www.marymt.edu

Butler Hall was named for the founder of the College, Mother Marie Joseph Butler, R.S.H.M.

MARYMOUNT MANHATTAN COLLEGE
NEW YORK, NEW YORK

The College

Marymount Manhattan College (MMC) is an urban, independent undergraduate liberal arts college. The mission of the College is to educate a socially and economically diverse population by fostering intellectual achievement and personal growth and by providing opportunities for career development. Inherent in this mission is the intent to develop an awareness of social, political, cultural, and ethical issues in the belief that this awareness will lead to concern for, participation in, and the improvement of society. To accomplish this mission, the College offers a strong program in the arts and sciences to students of all ages as well as substantial preprofessional preparation. Central to these efforts is the particular attention given to the individual student. Marymount Manhattan College also seeks to be a resource and learning center for the metropolitan community.

The social and extracurricular life of the student body of approximately 2,300 students centers on a number of clubs and organizations sponsored through the Student Affairs Office, including the International Students Club, Amnesty International, the French Club, the television station WMMC-TV, the Nature/Science Club, the student newspaper and magazine, Student Government, the student volunteer organization, and the Student Development Committee. MMC has an indoor swimming pool for student use. Students attend musical events, and MMC's own off-Broadway theater, the only one on the Upper East Side of Manhattan, offers students an opportunity to participate in student productions.

The Residence Life Office at Marymount Manhattan College is committed to providing residents with numerous opportunities and experiences that foster intellectual achievement and social and personal growth. Students are encouraged to become involved in the many activities that are sponsored by Residence Life and are assisted with assuming responsibility for their own lives and living environment. In the summer of 2000, the College will open a new dormitory. It will house 500 students on thirty-three floors in apartment-style living. Located in a luxury midtown building, amenities at this location include a concierge, lecture rooms, and a health club.

The Office of Academic and Career Advisement serves the entire College community by providing an integrated program of academic and career counseling. The office helps students by offering internship opportunities and workshops in job placement, resume writing, and graduate school preparation. For the past five years, 90 percent of biology majors who apply are accepted to advanced professional schools, including Mt. Sinai School of Medicine and Cornell Medical College. Other College services include personal and financial aid counseling, health services, and campus ministry.

Location

Marymount Manhattan College is centrally located on Manhattan's Upper East Side at 221 East 71st Street between Second and Third avenues. Within walking distance of the campus are the Frick, Metropolitan, Whitney, and Guggenheim museums; the French Institute and National Audubon Society; Central Park; New York Hospital and Sloan-Kettering Research Center; the United Nations; and public libraries. All forms of public transportation are easily accessible. Within minutes of the College are shops, restaurants, and movie theaters. This location gives students the opportunity to take advantage of New York City's rich culture and to explore a variety of neighborhoods.

Majors and Degrees

Marymount Manhattan College offers programs leading to the Bachelor of Arts, Bachelor of Science, and Bachelor of Fine Arts degrees. Majors are offered in accounting, acting, art, biology, business management, communication arts, dance (B.A. and B.F.A.), English, history, international business communications, international studies, liberal arts, political science, psychology, sociology, speech-language pathology and audiology, and theater arts (B.A. and B.F.A.). Some of the minors offered are business, business communications, creative writing, education, French, mathematics, media studies, religious studies, Spanish, and writing. Certificate programs are offered in alcoholism counseling, business management, computer information management, gerontology, industrial organizational psychology, and teacher certification.

Academic Program

Marymount Manhattan College has designed its programs to enable students to meet the challenges of contemporary society. MMC is committed to the belief that a liberal arts education provides students with the ability and the flexibility to manage change and with broad understanding and the communication and problem-solving skills that are essential for success in any career and in life. To accomplish its goals, the College offers a liberal arts education, integrated with preprofessional training opportunities and individualized attention. The curricula are organized into six divisions: humanities; fine arts, performing arts, and communication arts; natural sciences and mathematics; social sciences; business management; and psychology and education. Also offered are special-interest sequences that complement the student's major and minor with added concentration in such areas as prelaw, premedicine, social work, marketing, international business, finance and investments, and creative writing. Cooperative programs with the American Institute of Banking, China Institute, Deutsches Haus Goethe Institute at New York University, Iona at Marymount Manhattan College, Jewish Chautauqua Society, Laboratory Institute of Merchandising, Mannes College of Music, Martha Graham School of Dance, New York Institute of Finance, and St. John's University (B.S./M.B.A. program) are also options for MMC students. The College's small size provides students with an individually planned academic career, reflects students' academic needs and interests, and supports their career goals.

Candidates for the Bachelor of Arts, Bachelor of Science, and Bachelor of Fine Arts degrees must complete 120 credits. To qualify for a degree, a student must maintain an overall scholastic average of at least 2.0. Requirements for certificate programs vary.

The College recognizes various types of nontraditional credit, including credit for acceptable scores on the Advanced Placement (AP), College-Level Examination Program (CLEP), and New York State College Proficiency Examination (CPE) tests and credit for life experience.

MMC encourages its students to participate in internship programs in New York City that range from work at hospitals, financial institutions, magazines, and publishing houses to HBO and CBS.

Off-Campus Arrangements

The College's Academic Year Abroad offers an opportunity for students to broaden their educational experience and to gain cultural perspectives through study at other colleges in the Americas and overseas. Students may spend one or both semesters of their junior year in this program. MMC summer sessions and January intersessions also offer students opportunities in travel/study-abroad courses in Egypt, France, Great Britain, Eastern Europe, Ireland, Russia, and Spain.

Academic Facilities

The Thomas J. Shanahan Library at MMC is a library/learning center. It contains more than 100,000 volumes in open stacks and maintains an extensive periodical collection. The media center, on the main library floor, houses nonprint materials, microfiche, microfilm, filmstrips, slides, tapes, videotapes, and records. Through the library's affiliation with the New York Metropolitan Reference and Research Library Agency, MMC faculty members and students have access to the materials of the member libraries. The library also participates in the Online Computer Library Center (OCLC), a computerized database of the holdings of some 4,000 libraries that is currently being used for cataloging and reference purposes.

The modern 250-seat Marymount Manhattan Theatre is equipped with an orchestra pit capable of accommodating 40 musicians. The theater has a special acoustical design, a sprung dance floor, a full technical balcony with equipment for lighting and sound, thirty-five counterweighted-line sets in the fly system, dressing rooms with showers, and a scene shop. Students benefit from exposure to the numerous professional dance, opera, and theatrical groups that perform at the College.

Recently, two completely remodeled laboratory facilities were opened to strengthen education in two areas in which MMC has always excelled—science and communication arts.

MMC's science facilities in biology, chemistry, and physics underwent a total reconstruction valued at close to $1 million, thanks to the generosity of the Samuel Freeman Charitable Trust and the Ira De Camp Foundation. The new Samuel Freeman Science Center opens many new doors of opportunity to students who are biology/premedicine majors or who are interested in pursuing careers in other science or health-related fields.

The College's new Multimedia Suite, featuring the latest in digital computer technology, is one of the most advanced facilities of its kind in New York City. With digital multimedia capability, a decor inspired by top television postproduction houses, and access to the public library's new B. Altman Advanced Learning Superblock, the Multimedia Suite will further enhance students' skills in traditional video and television production and allow them to develop, design, and evaluate cutting-edge multimedia projects. In conjunction with the Communication Arts Department, the College offers students the Media Library, where many videos and screening computers are available to students.

The Writing Center at MMC provides a range of services and activities, including career-based courses, personal critiques and one-on-one assistance, lectures, workshops, and special events such as the Best-Selling Author Series and Annual Writers' Conference, as well as a minor in creative writing. This enables students to be a part of the highly respected New York City writing community.

Costs

For the 1999–2000 academic year, full-time tuition was $13,550. The fee for a space in a residence provided by the College was approximately $7000 per year. For part-time students, tuition was $365 per credit. Additional fees are applicable for various laboratory and studio classes.

Financial Aid

The College administers a variety of financial aid programs, including scholarships sponsored by the College. Some of the awards are based on academic achievement; others are based on financial need. Students are also eligible for aid through a wide variety of state and federal programs. In addition, a number of jobs are available for students on campus, and the Offices of Financial Aid and Academic and Career Advisement can help students locate part-time off-campus jobs to help finance their education. More than 90 percent of MMC students receive some form of financial assistance. Therefore, limited finances alone need not prevent any student from attending the College. The suggested deadlines for applying for financial aid are April 15 for the fall semester and before November 15 for the spring semester.

Faculty

Marymount Manhattan College's student-faculty ratio is 18:1. In addition to the staff of the advisement office, faculty members act as advisers to students. Full-time faculty members teach in all sessions and divisions (days, evenings, and weekends). Part-time instructors, who are drawn from the wealth of experienced teaching professionals in New York City, supplement the full-time faculty.

Student Government

The Student Government Association responds to three areas of concern at MMC. The association primarily serves the needs of its constituents by managing the student government budget, planning and publicizing events, and establishing organizations that reflect the interests of the students. In addition, the association assists faculty and administrative groups and committees in their policy and procedural tasks and communicates the results of committee work to the student body. Finally, the Student Government Association provides special representatives for students' rights and freedoms through established and clearly defined channels of authority.

Admission Requirements

Marymount Manhattan College seeks candidates with qualities that indicate potential for success in higher education and the ability to contribute to the College community. Admission is based on a combination of factors: the student's academic program, including scholastic average and rank in class; two recommendations from teachers, counselors, or employers; and activities. SAT I scores are required for general admission.

Each year the College enrolls an increasing number of transfer students. Transfer students may receive up to 90 credits for course work completed in an accredited postsecondary institution with a grade of C- or better. Transcripts are evaluated on a course-by-course basis. In addition, the College has articulation agreements with several accredited business colleges and grants full or partial credit for many business and liberal arts courses taken at those schools.

Prior to registering, all new students are required to take placement examinations in the basic subject areas of English composition, reading, and mathematics.

Application and Information

The admissions application must be received by February 1 for MMC scholarship consideration. For application forms and for more information about Marymount Manhattan College, students should contact:

Office of Admissions
Marymount Manhattan College
221 East 71st Street
New York, New York 10021
Telephone: 212-517-0555
              800-MARYMOUNT (toll-free)
E-mail: admissions@mmm.edu
World Wide Web: http://marymount.mmm.edu

Marymount Manhattan College, in the heart of Manhattan.

MARYMOUNT UNIVERSITY
ARLINGTON, VIRGINIA

The University

Marymount University is a comprehensive, coeducational Catholic institution, founded in 1950. Marymount emphasizes excellence in teaching, attention to the individual, and values and ethics across the curriculum. The University enrolls approximately 2,100 undergraduate and 1,600 graduate students. Marymount offers thirty-eight undergraduate majors and twenty-five graduate degree programs through the Schools of Arts and Sciences, Business Administration, Education and Human Services, and Health Professions. The University is located in a residential neighborhood of Arlington, Virginia, adjacent to Washington D.C.

The University's focus on ethics and values has received national recognition. The John Templeton Foundation lists Marymount in its *Guide to Colleges That Encourage Character Development*. The University's Center for Ethical Concerns provides a forum for the exchange of ideas about ethical issues and problems; faculty members incorporate the teaching of ethics across the curriculum.

Through Spirit of Service (SOS), the community outreach center of the University's Campus Ministry Association, students have the opportunity to serve the community in diverse ways. They work with children, at-risk youths, and homeless people; they participate in food drives and neighborhood beautification projects; and they help build homes. Service components are also part of the curriculum in a number of Marymount courses, from paralegal studies to fashion design. At Marymount, both faculty members and students seek ways to reach out to the community.

Marymount considers living on campus to be an important aspect of campus life. The University operates four residence halls, which house approximately 600 students. Two halls house women students exclusively; two house men and women on separate floors. Most rooms are double occupancy.

The Rose Benté Lee University Center opened in fall 1999. The Lee Center is a multipurpose facility where faculty members, students, and all members of the Marymount community come together to hold meetings, study, get a bite to eat, purchase books, exercise, play sports, and share thoughts and ideas. The center includes a spacious café, the campus bookstore and marketplace, the 1,000-seat Bell Atlantic Sports Arena, a swimming pool, recreational gym, fitness center, and meeting rooms and lounges. Special events, such as an Honors Convocation and academic conferences, also take place in the Lee Center.

Marymount is an NCAA Division III institution and a member of the Capital Athletic Conference. The women's basketball team has been invited to the NCAA national championships for the past eight years. Intercollegiate sports for men and women include basketball, lacrosse, soccer, swimming, and tennis. Men also have golf; women have volleyball.

Location

With Marymount's proximity to the nation's capital, students enjoy the cultural and educational advantages of Washington, D.C. Museums, galleries, theaters, the Capitol, the Library of Congress, and the National Archives are all easily accessible, and Marymount shuttle buses provide service to the public Metro system. Union Station and Reagan National Airport are also within easy reach. The resources of Washington, whether for research, recreation, or internships, are right next door, while students enjoy the benefits of a peaceful, residential campus.

Majors and Degrees

The University awards the undergraduate degrees of Bachelor of Arts, Bachelor of Science, Bachelor of Science in Nursing (B.S.N.), and Bachelor of Business Administration (B.B.A.). Thirty-eight majors are available. Programs include art, biology, communications, computer information systems, computer science, criminal justice, economics, economics and public policy, English, environmental science, fashion design, fashion merchandising, graphic design, health and fitness management, history, interior design, liberal studies, mathematics, paralegal studies, philosophy, political science, psychology, secondary education, sociology, and theology and religious studies. Bachelor of Business Administration programs include accounting, business administration, business law, finance, health-care administration, human resource management, international business, management, management science, marketing, and retail management. Bachelor of Science and Associate in Applied Science programs are offered in nursing. Education licensure programs are available for undergraduates in art education, early childhood education, and secondary education. The course work for these programs is in addition to the courses required for a student's major discipline.

Academic Program

Marymount University's goal is to help each student achieve his or her full potential. While students study a liberal arts core curriculum plus the required elements of their discipline, they are able to work with their faculty adviser to tailor an academic program that fits their personal and career objectives. Small classes and personal attention help ensure student success and a strong sense of community. An honor system guides academic and social conduct. Cultural and educational resources of the nation's capital add to the curriculum through off-campus activities.

The balancing of academics and hands-on, practical experience is a cornerstone of Marymount's commitment to providing students with a well-rounded education. All students complete an internship as part of their program of study. High-quality academics, ethics across the curriculum, and a focus on service complete the solid foundation Marymount provides students.

Off-Campus Arrangements

Undergraduate degrees require completion of an internship in the chosen field in addition to all necessary course work in the major and a required core of liberal arts courses. Marymount students intern regularly in Senate and Congressional offices on Capitol Hill, in the State Department, in the Smithsonian Institution museums, and with corporate and association offices and major public relations and media organizations in and around Washington, D.C. Internships can lead to permanent employment after graduation. Through Marymount's London program, students have the option of doing their internship abroad in the London offices of international business firms, the British Court system, and Parliament, to name just a few of the opportunities available.

Academic Facilities

The main campus includes classrooms, computer labs, science labs, seminar rooms, language labs, nursing autotutorials, and studios for fine and graphic arts, fashion design, and interior design. The Ballston Campus, an eight-story building just minutes from the main campus by free shuttle bus, also houses classrooms, seminar rooms, and computer labs, in addition to physical therapy labs and the Truland Auditorium.

Emerson G. Reinsch Library is home to 176,986 volumes and is connected via computerized resources to the Washington Research Library Consortium, which includes thirteen area universities. The Instructional Media Center, also housed in the Reinsch complex, provides audiovisual support for instruction; the Learning Resource Center offers both group and individualized tutorials and functions as a test center. Events, from academic conferences to concerts, are held in the 190-seat Reinsch Auditorium, described by the *Washington Post* as "visually and acoustically elegant."

Costs

Tuition for 2000–01 is $14,300 for the academic year (September to May). Room and board for the academic year are $6350 for a double room; single rooms cost $600 extra per semester.

Financial Aid

Marymount provides an extensive scholarship and grant program and participates in all federal and state aid programs. To be considered for aid, students must file the Free Application for Federal Student Aid (FAFSA) with the College Scholarship Service and Marymount's financial aid application with the University's Financial Aid Office. Approximately 80 percent of full-time undergraduate students receive aid in the form of scholarships, grants, loans, work-study awards, or on-campus employment. Academic scholarships are available for freshmen and are renewable each year.

Faculty

There are 146 full-time faculty members. In addition, visiting lecturers, representing the business and professional world of the nation's capital, complement the full-time staff. The undergraduate student-faculty ratio is 14:1. Classes and seminars are small, and professors are available for counseling and advice.

Student Government

The student government acts as the official liaison between students, faculty, and the administration. It may make policy recommendations related to student issues. The Activities Programming Board plans and implements a variety of events, including comedy nights, movies, theme parties, dances, concerts, and trips.

Admission Requirements

To be eligible for admission, a candidate must be a graduate of an accredited high school and have a minimum of 15 credits. The quality of the student's preparation is more important than the precise distribution, but the following credits are recommended: English, 4; foreign language, 3; mathematics, 3; social sciences, 3; and science, 2. It is strongly recommended that applicants for the nursing program have credits in high school biology and chemistry. Other secondary-level science backgrounds are considered in special cases. The Admissions Committee bases its evaluation of the high school record on both the student's educational objectives and specific needs. The candidate must also present a letter of recommendation from a high school counselor (or another appropriate school official) and scores on the SAT I or on the ACT, taken in the senior year. A campus interview is not required but is strongly recommended as it is beneficial to the applicant and helpful in the admission process. The University holds campus visit days in the fall and spring for prospective students and their families. Visitors to the campus are welcome at any time. Appointments with admissions personnel may be made by calling in advance.

Application and Information

High school students seeking admission are advised to apply early during their senior year. They should submit an application, a nonrefundable fee of $35, a high school transcript, SAT I or ACT scores, evidence of expected graduation from an accredited high school, and a recommendation from a high school counselor or an appropriate school official. Those who have attended another college or university must submit the application, $35 fee, test scores, evidence of high school graduation, transcripts of college-level study, and a recommendation from the Dean of Students at the previous institution. The University has a rolling admission policy and notifies applicants soon after the application process is completed and the Admissions Committee has acted on the application.

An application form, a catalog, curriculum brochures, and other information may be obtained by contacting:

Chris Domes, Dean of Enrollment Management
Marymount University
2807 North Glebe Road
Arlington, Virginia 22207-4299
Telephone: 703-284-1500
              800-548-7638 (toll-free)
E-mail: admissions@marymount.edu
World Wide Web: http://www.marymount.edu

Marymount University's historic 21-acre campus is only 10 minutes away from Washington, D.C.

MARYVILLE COLLEGE
MARYVILLE, TENNESSEE

The College

Founded in 1819, Maryville College is among the fifty oldest institutions of higher education in the United States and one of the fifteen oldest in the South. Related to the Presbyterian Church (U.S.A.), the College welcomes students of all faiths. The current enrollment is about 1,000 men and women; students come from twenty-seven states and twenty countries. There is a strong community feeling on campus, and social activities include all students.

Facilities include twenty-four structures, of which nine are residence halls. Centrally located on the 300-acre campus is the Cooper Athletic Center, which contains three full-size gymnasiums, an indoor pool, racquetball courts, and a weight room. The College is a member of NCAA Division III. It fields men's varsity teams in baseball, basketball, football, soccer, and tennis. Women's varsity sports are basketball, soccer, softball, tennis, and volleyball. A wide range of team and individual intramural sports are also offered. The College provides numerous social and special interest organizations.

Maryville College's Mountain Challenge Program is among the finest outdoor programs in the nation. On-campus facilities include a low-ropes course, an indoor climbing wall, and a climbing tower that is accessible to persons with disabilities. Equipment is available to students for rock climbing, hiking, camping, canoeing, biking, and white-water rafting in the nearby Great Smoky Mountains National Park.

Location

The city of Maryville is part of the metropolitan Knoxville area in eastern Tennessee. Maryville and Alcoa are side-by-side communities with a combined population of 30,000. The campus is 15 minutes south of Knoxville, a city of 500,000 people and the home of the University of Tennessee. Twenty minutes east of the campus are the Great Smoky Mountains, which provide ample opportunities for hiking, camping, snow skiing, and sightseeing. Maryville offers the best of both worlds—access to the city and to the mountains.

Majors and Degrees

Maryville College awards the Bachelor of Arts and Bachelor of Music degrees. Areas of study are American Sign Language, art, biochemistry, biology, business and organization management, chemical physics, chemistry, child development, computer science/business, computer science/mathematics, economics, education, English, environmental studies, history, human services, international studies, literature, mathematics, music, outdoor recreation, physical education, political science, psychology, religion, sign-language interpreting, sociology, Spanish, theater, and writing/communication. Students may also design individualized programs that combine two or more disciplines. Certification is available in both elementary and secondary education.

Maryville College is one of very few colleges in the United States to offer four-year majors in American Sign Language and sign-language interpreting.

Minors are offered in most major areas as well as areas in which majors are not available. They include accounting, American studies, German, medieval studies, philosophy, and physics.

Preprofessional study is offered in dentistry, law, medicine, pharmacy, and physical therapy. The College offers dual-degree programs in engineering in association with several regional universities. A dual-degree program is offered in nursing with Vanderbilt University (B.S. in Health Care and M.S. in Nursing). The Graduate School of Business at the University of Tennessee, Knoxville, has entered into an agreement with the College that will allow top students in business to complete the Master of Business Administration degree program in five years.

Academic Program

Course requirements for the baccalaureate degrees may usually be completed in four years. Maryville operates on a semester-hour system with a minimum of 128 hours required for graduation. Students must satisfy general education requirements, which account for about half the total number of courses. Each major has specific course requirements, which vary according to the program. Faculty academic advisers are assigned to all incoming students.

A senior thesis is required of every student. Internships and practicums are available in conjunction with all majors. All students must pass an English proficiency test in their sophomore year and a comprehensive examination in their major in the senior year.

Credit by examination is available through CLEP tests, AP tests, I.B. courses, and institutional examinations.

The College calendar includes two traditional semesters with a three-week January term.

Off-Campus Arrangements

Affordable study abroad is available through sister school tuition arrangements in France, Japan, Korea, Puerto Rico, and Wales and through cooperative arrangements in Europe and Africa. The College is a member of the Oak Ridge Associated Universities, which affords multiple opportunities for research and study. Students participate in field study in biology and natural history in the Great Smoky Mountains and the lakes of east Tennessee. Internships and summer programs are available at such sites as the Woods Hole Oceanographic Institution in Massachusetts, the Savannah River Ecological Station in South Carolina, and several national laboratories, such as Argonne, Lawrence Livermore, and Los Alamos. Student interns also study in Washington, D.C., at the Washington Center for Learning Alternatives, in Nashville in the Tennessee State Legislative Intern Program, and with several international corporations in the United States and abroad. The International Programming Committee and the student's major department assist in arranging study abroad, internships, and other off-campus experiences.

Academic Facilities

The Sutton Science Center is a modern, well-designed, and well-equipped facility for the sciences, computer science, mathematics, and psychology. Private study carrels are available to many students in the sciences. The Fine Arts Center provides a 250-seat recital hall, an art gallery, classrooms, and private studios for both art and music students. Other classroom facilities are located in a mixture of older and newer buildings. The Lamar Memorial Library is fully automated with an online catalog and access to libraries throughout the world.

Costs

For 2000–01, tuition is $16,224; room and board costs are $2550 and $2760, respectively; and the student activity and technology fees total $425, for a total of $21,959. The College estimates a cost of $2125 annually for books, supplies, transportation, and personal expenses.

Financial Aid

Approximately 85 percent of Maryville's students receive financial assistance through scholarships, grants, loans, or employment. The Presidential Scholarships are the College's most prestigious merit awards; these renewable awards are $15,000 annually. The MC Scholar award of $4000 to $8000 is available to students with outstanding academic and personal achievement. Maryville participates in the Bonner Scholars program, which provides scholarship assistance in exchange for community service. Transfer students who have an associate degree and are members of Phi Theta Kappa may compete for scholarships. The College also offers scholarships in art, music, and theater. Federal aid programs include the Federal Pell Grant, Federal Supplemental Educational Opportunity Grant, Federal Perkins Loan, and Federal Work-Study programs. Tennessee residents may qualify for the Tennessee State Grant. To apply for financial aid, students should complete the College's scholarship application and the Free Application for Federal Student Aid (FAFSA) before February 1.

Faculty

The student-faculty ratio is 14:1; average class size is 20. Nearly 90 percent of the 60 full-time faculty members hold doctoral or terminal degrees in their fields. Faculty members are committed to teaching in the undergraduate setting but are also involved in research and the publication of books and articles.

Student Government

The Student Government represents the entire student community and is involved in college-wide policy making, judicial issues, and student programming.

Admission Requirements

Admission to Maryville is selective. Students applying from high school are expected to have successfully completed a strong college-preparatory program. Factors evaluated in the admission decision include courses taken, grade point average, test scores (either SAT I or ACT), and teachers' recommendations. An admissions essay or a graded writing sample is also encouraged. The majority of entering students rank within the top 25 percent of their high school graduating class. An on-campus interview is strongly recommended but is not a requirement for admission.

Application and Information

To apply to Maryville College, a student should submit the application for admission, an official high school transcript, and scores on either the ACT or SAT I. The application fee is $25. Transfer students must submit a high school transcript plus official transcripts from each college previously attended. The application deadline for early action is September 15. The application deadline for early decision is November 15. The deadline for regular admission is March 1.

Maryville College does not discriminate on the basis of race, color, gender, ethnic or national origin, religion, sexual orientation, age, disability, or political beliefs in its admission procedures and educational programs.

For further information regarding admissions, financial assistance, academic programs, and campus visits, students should contact:

Office of Admissions
Maryville College
502 East Lamar Alexander Parkway
Maryville, Tennessee 37804
Telephone: 423-981-8092
           800-59-SCOTS (toll-free)
Fax: 423-981-8005
E-mail: admissions@maryvillecollege.edu
World Wide Web: http://www.maryvillecollege.edu

Maryville students work together to reach the peak on the climbing tower.

MARYVILLE UNIVERSITY OF SAINT LOUIS
ST. LOUIS, MISSOURI

The University

Maryville University of Saint Louis is an independent coeducational university with an enrollment of more than 3,000 undergraduate and graduate students. The quality and variety of its curriculum—solid liberal arts studies and professional programs covering more than fifty fields (undergraduate and graduate)—have attracted an increasing number of students in recent years. A special feature is the large measure of personal concern for each student demonstrated by everyone on campus, from the faculty members through the administrative staff to the president.

The University was founded in 1872 by the Religious of the Sacred Heart, moved to its present site in suburban St. Louis in 1961, became an independent college in 1972, and became a university in 1991. The two residence halls house 350 students.

Maryville University is committed to the education of the whole person through programs designed to meet the needs of traditional and nontraditional students offered in day, evening, and weekend formats. Primarily an undergraduate teaching university, Maryville offers select, high-quality graduate programs in professional fields where there is evidence both of need and of corresponding institutional strength. The liberal arts and sciences are recognized as the foundation of all academic programs, including those leading to professional degrees. True to its heritage, Maryville is resolutely committed to being a university where excellence is preeminent in all endeavors, and where the Judeo-Christian tradition of the University is honored in symbol and in substance.

At the graduate level, Maryville offers a Master of Business Administration degree, with concentrations in accountancy, information systems, international business, management, and marketing; a Master of Arts in Education degree, with areas of concentration in art, early childhood (with certificate), educational leadership (with principal certification), elementary or secondary generalist studies, environmental, gifted (with certificate), the middle-level teacher (with certificate), secondary teaching and inquiry (with certificate), teaching diverse populations, and the renewing teacher; a Master of Physical Therapy; a Master of Science in Nursing; and a Master of Science in Rehabilitation Counseling.

Consistent with its mission, Maryville University is committed to achieving the following goals: to serve as a model for the integration of liberal and professional learning; to provide a people-oriented campus environment that encourages responsible interaction, personal growth, and development of character; to become a more heterogeneous academic community where people of diverse cultures, ethnicity, and ages are understood and valued; to internationalize the campus, including providing opportunities for travel and study abroad; to make leadership development a prominent aspect of the undergraduate experience; to increase the residential population and expand the geographic base of the student body; to be a highly focused, student-centered, value-oriented university dedicated to empowering its members, eliminating bureaucracy, and being incomparably responsive; to aid students in fashioning a personal philosophy of life that is reasoned, decent, and civilized; to maintain a collegial environment embracing the values of academic freedom and participatory university governance; and to be an active participant in the life of the metropolitan St. Louis community, particularly the Maryville Centre, by offering varied and enriching educational, cultural, and recreational services.

Athletic facilities include three outdoor tennis courts, intercollegiate soccer and softball fields, a lighted baseball complex, and a handsome multipurpose gymnasium that includes a fully equipped fitness center. Maryville is a member of NCAA Division III and the Saint Louis Intercollegiate Athletic Conference. The University fields women's teams in basketball, cross-country, golf, soccer, softball, tennis, and volleyball and men's teams in baseball, basketball, cross-country, golf, soccer, and tennis.

Location

Maryville's suburban campus is located at Highway 40/I-64 and Woods Mill Road, 2 miles west of I-270 in West St. Louis County. The campus is nestled on 130 acres of rolling hills, with wooded areas, creeks, and two lakes. It is within 30 minutes of downtown St. Louis and its international airport. The University maintains a close association with its neighbors at the Maryville Centre, a unique educational, corporate, cultural, and residential complex, and St. Luke's Hospital. Within easy driving distance of the campus are many of the social, cultural, athletic, and entertainment facilities of the metropolitan area, including the St. Louis Art Museum; St. Louis Symphony Orchestra; Missouri Botanical Garden; Municipal Opera; ballet, opera, and rock performances; world-renowned zoo; touring, repertory, and dinner theaters; professional baseball, hockey, and football; large park systems; many movie theaters; St. Louis Science Center; and Museum of Science and Natural History.

Majors and Degrees

The University offers undergraduate programs leading to the Bachelor of Arts, Bachelor of Science, Bachelor of Science in Clinical Laboratory Science, Bachelor of Science in Nursing, Bachelor of Science in Occupational Therapy, and Bachelor of Fine Arts degrees. Courses of study include accountancy, accounting information systems, actuarial science, art education, art-studio, biology, business administration, chemistry, clinical laboratory science, communications, education (early childhood, elementary, middle-level, and secondary), English, English as a second language, environmental sciences, environmental studies, graphic design, health-care management, health science, history, humanities, information systems, interior design, liberal studies, management, marketing, marketing information systems, mathematics, music, music therapy, nursing, occupational therapy, organizational leadership, paralegal studies, philosophy, political science, preprofessional studies (dentistry, engineering, law, and medicine), psychology, psychology/sociology, religious studies, science, and sociology. Physical therapy is now a five-year master's degree program.

Academic Program

The academic curriculum and programs are based on a semester calendar with a summer session. Professional programs combine education toward a career with a strong liberal arts base to ensure that students in all fields develop a high degree of competence in professional areas closely related to their academic interests. A cooperative education program combines supervised, paid work experience with classroom studies. An intensive English program is offered for international students.

Weekend College enables students to attend classes on alternate weekends to earn a bachelor's degree in accountancy, accounting information systems, business administration, communications, health-care management, information systems, liberal studies, management, marketing, nursing (one of the nation's few weekend programs in nursing; it includes a B.S.N. degree-completion program for RNs), organizational leadership, psychology, psychology/sociology, and sociology.

Corporate and Continuing Education offers a variety of classes on personal and professional development and computing. Regularly scheduled classes are available on topics such as management, supervision, leadership, communication, sales and marketing, career adaptations in the workplace, and many other areas. Customized classes, seminars, and workshops can be arranged on all business topics as well as most computer software programs. Fees are determined by course length, required materials, and instructional expenses.

Off-Campus Arrangements

Maryville encourages students in good academic standing to expand their perspectives of themselves and of the world by studying abroad for a summer, a semester, or a year. With adequate planning, the experience can be integrated with the academic program in such a way that the student can progress toward graduation. Most financial aid (excluding work-study) is usually applicable to study abroad. Maryville participates in a consortium with other area colleges and universities that enables each school to supplement its own offerings in various fields while avoiding duplications. Maryville students may take courses at the other campuses at no additional cost.

Academic Facilities

The University Library's collection includes access to more than 75 databases. Most of the databases and the library catalog are accessible through remote sites. The collection includes 207,000 volumes, 1,500 current serials, 1,500 videos, and 775 annual reports and 10Ks from major corporations. Other facilities include laboratories for the natural sciences, occupational therapy, physical therapy, nursing, teacher education, and computers; an art gallery; art and design studios and laboratories; multimedia-ready classrooms; an observatory; and outdoor trails for ecological studies.

Costs

For 1999–2000, tuition and fees were $12,280 per year, and room and board were $5400. The cost of books and supplies varies with the program of study. There are extra fees for private music lessons and laboratory courses.

Financial Aid

Financial aid is available in the form of employment, loans, and grants; awards are based on need as determined by the FAFSA and University-administered forms. Scholarships, which are awarded on merit rather than on a need basis, are also available. Students are free to accept employment or a grant without being obligated to accept a loan, which may be offered as part of a financial aid package. Last year, more than 80 percent of the University's full-time students received financial aid; the average award was $9654. Deferred payment plans are available through arrangements with the University for those who wish to pay their educational expenses in installments.

Faculty

A faculty of more than 280 includes 96 full-time professors and instructors, most of whom hold a Ph.D. or the appropriate terminal degree. Practicing professionals supplement the full-time staff. Faculty members serve as academic advisers, counselors, and members of University committees. No classes are taught by graduate students.

Student Government

Maryville University is committed to providing leadership opportunities for its students. There are more than thirty clubs and an active student government association, through which students participate in sponsoring a wide range of social, cultural, ethnic, religious, community service, and intellectual events.

Admission Requirements

The University seeks to admit students who give evidence of their ability to achieve academic success at Maryville. Students are selected without regard to race, age, religion, sex, national origin, disability, or Vietnam-era veteran status. Admission decisions are made by means of a review of each applicant's school record, ACT or SAT I scores, recommendations, and other information provided. A personal interview is recommended. For new freshmen, the record of achievement in high school is the single most important item in an applicant's academic credentials.

Graduates of accredited associate degree transfer programs are accepted with advanced standing and are granted full credit for academic courses taken in a transfer program. Transfer students from four-year colleges and universities are welcome; credits from other institutions are evaluated individually because of the integrated nature of Maryville's program. Transfer students must take at least 30 credit hours at Maryville in order to receive a bachelor's degree.

Application and Information

Freshman applicants must submit an application for admission with a $20 application fee, an official high school transcript, and ACT or SAT I scores. Under Maryville's rolling admission policy, applications are reviewed immediately upon receipt of all necessary material.

Transfer students must submit an application for admission with a $20 application fee and high school and college transcripts.

Certain programs require additional credentials. The physical therapy and occupational therapy programs require submission of a letter of recommendation; physical therapy also requires a personal interview. Admission of students to the B.F.A. or B.A. in art program requires a portfolio evaluation by the art and design faculty. Acceptance into the nursing program requires a personal interview. Applications may be submitted by mail or electronically. All admission applications are available on the Maryville Web site listed below.

For further information, students should contact:

Dr. Martha Wade
Vice President for Admissions and Enrollment Management
Maryville University of Saint Louis
13550 Conway Road
St. Louis, Missouri 63141-7299
Telephone: 314-529-9350
        800-627-9855 (toll-free)
Fax: 314-529-9927
E-mail: admissions@maryville.edu
World Wide Web: http://www.maryville.edu

Students enjoy comfortable accommodations for small group or individual study in the University Library.

MARY WASHINGTON COLLEGE
FREDERICKSBURG, VIRGINIA

The College

Mary Washington College (MWC) is one of the nation's top undergraduate colleges. It has distinctive academic programs, a beautiful campus, a sharp and diverse student body that knows how to study and have fun, and a unique sense of friendship and camaraderie that makes MWC very special. The College is entirely coeducational and enrolls 4,000 full-time students. It is accredited by the Southern Association of Colleges and Schools. A number of honorary groups, including Phi Beta Kappa, have chapters on campus.

Numerous leadership opportunities are available within the student government and the College's Honor System. There are more than ninety-five clubs and organizations on campus, representing ethnic, religious, political, social, and academic interests. Performance opportunities include three major singing groups, an eighty-piece College/Community Orchestra, and a jazz ensemble. Other popular activities include a nationally prominent debate team, a literary magazine, an award-winning newspaper, and a student-run radio station. In addition, fine arts and cultural events are brought to campus from nearby Washington, D.C., and Richmond and include theater productions, concerts, dance groups, art exhibits, and lectures.

Many social activities take place each week. An active schedule of events, including concerts, dances, movies, comedians, and other talent, provides social opportunities throughout the week and during the weekends.

Approximately 70 percent of the full-time students live on campus. With nearly twenty different residence halls, a variety of living arrangements are available. There are special housing areas for students who are studying a foreign language, desire a quiet environment, or distinguish themselves through leadership, service, or academic honors.

Mary Washington College is a member of NCAA Division III. The College offers intercollegiate athletic teams for men in baseball, basketball, crew, cross-country, horseback riding, lacrosse, soccer, swimming, tennis, and track and field and for women in basketball, cross-country, field hockey, horseback riding, lacrosse, soccer, softball, swimming, tennis, track and field, and volleyball. Intramural athletic opportunities include badminton, basketball, field hockey, flag football, inner tube water polo, racquetball, soccer, softball, Ultimate Frisbee, and volleyball. Club sports include rugby and volleyball for men and crew, rugby, and synchronized swimming for women. Indoor facilities include a 64,000-square-foot physical education building with courts for basketball, volleyball, racquetball, and badminton; two dance studios; a six-lane, 25-yard swimming pool; and a fully equipped weight room. The College has a lighted tennis complex; fields for field hockey, lacrosse, rugby, soccer, and softball; and an eight-lane, 400-meter synthetic-surface track. The baseball stadium provides one of the nation's finest collegiate facilities for players and fans.

Location

Fredericksburg, Virginia, is a city of 25,000, with a metropolitan-area population of more than 100,000. It is located along Interstate 95 and is only 50 miles south of Washington, D.C., and 50 miles north of Richmond, Virginia. Public transportation to and from Fredericksburg is available by bus and Amtrak. Fredericksburg is conveniently reached from Washington's Ronald Reagan National Airport or Richmond International Airport and is served by a regularly scheduled commuter rail to Washington. The historic Old Town district of Fredericksburg and modern shopping centers are within easy walking distance of the campus.

Majors and Degrees

Mary Washington College offers programs of study leading to the Bachelor of Arts and Bachelor of Science degrees with majors in American studies, art history, art (studio), biology, business administration, chemistry, classical civilization, classics (Latin), computer science, economics, English, environmental sciences, French, geography, geology, German, historic preservation, history, international affairs, Latin, mathematics, music, philosophy, physics, political science, psychology, religion, sociology, Spanish, and theater and dance, with additional program options in predental, prelaw, and premedical preparation. There are additional course offerings in anthropology and Italian.

The course work for teacher licensure, including student teaching, leads to the award of an elementary or secondary school teaching license in Virginia. The program in education has been approved by the National Association of State Directors of Teacher Education and Certification.

In addition to the B.A. and B.S. degrees, the College offers a Bachelor of Liberal Studies, which is directed toward the educational needs of students who are 24 years of age and older.

Academic Program

The curriculum is made up of three parts. To fulfill general education requirements, the student must complete courses in the areas of natural and social sciences, the arts, literature, humanities, and mathematics. These courses make up about one third of the 122 semester hours needed for the degree. A second third of the degree must follow one of the thirty-two major programs available, which students officially select upon completion of 28 semester hours. For the remaining third, the student chooses electives that allow the pursuit of the major in greater depth, the study of other areas of interest, or the development of career skills. Each student also must demonstrate competence in a foreign language and in English composition. Competence in the foreign language may be demonstrated by earning a score of 4 or better on the AP exam, earning a score of 620 or better on the SAT II: Subject Test, or completing the intermediate level of a language in college. Students must also take five designated Writing Intensive courses. Across-the-curriculum courses are required in four areas: oral communication, race and gender, global awareness, and the environment.

The College operates on a semester plan. First-semester classes begin in late August and end in early December. The second semester begins in mid-January and ends with graduation in early May.

Off-Campus Arrangements

Mary Washington College sponsors study-abroad programs in Europe, the West Indies, Mexico, and southern Africa. Students may also participate in various study-abroad programs sponsored by other institutions and receive credit toward a degree at Mary Washington, provided that this work is approved in advance. The College provides advising for study abroad through the Office of International Programs. Through the Academic Internship Program, students may supplement classroom learning by participating in interesting off-campus work experiences for which they earn college credit. The internship is chosen during the junior or senior year and relates to the student's major or career path.

Academic Facilities

The Simpson Library, a modern facility that opened in 1989, houses a collection of more than 335,000 volumes, 520,000 microforms, and 1,700 periodical subscriptions, which may be accessed through an online computer catalog. The College has more than 2,000 CD-ROMs, and commercial online services are also available. In addition, the College is within an hour's travel time of the Library of Congress in Washington, D.C. The science department is located in the Jepson Science Center, where modern laboratories and facilities are available for student instruction and research. Students have full access to computer facilities in the Jepson Science Center, Trinkle Hall, and other campus locations. Facilities for the performing arts, art galleries, and language laboratories are located in DuPont and Goolrick halls and in the Phyllis Ridderhof Martin Art Gallery.

Costs

The charges for the 1999–2000 nine-month term for a resident of Virginia were $1550 for tuition, $1398 for fees, and $5158 for room and board. For a residence hall student who is not a legal resident of Virginia, the tuition charges were an additional $6430. Books cost about $720 per year, and personal expenses for a residence hall student are approximately $1400.

Financial Aid

Scholarships, loan funds, and part-time student employment opportunities are available and, in most cases, are awarded on the basis of financial need. The Free Application for Federal Student Aid (FAFSA) is required to determine eligibility for funds and should be filed prior to March 1. General scholarships are available to all students who can demonstrate financial need. Federal financial aid funds are also available. Grants to students average $2000 per nine-month session, loans range from $500 to $5500 per session, and part-time employment pays from $675 to $2250 for the session. In addition to these forms of aid, the College has established the merit-based Alumni Scholarship Program, with awards ranging from $500 to more than $3500. Inquiries about aid should be sent to the associate dean for financial aid.

Faculty

The faculty is a teaching faculty. About 90 percent hold a Ph.D. or terminal degree, and the faculty-student ratio is 1:18. No classes are taught by graduate students or teaching assistants. A faculty mentor assists each student in selecting appropriate subjects during his or her first two years; a faculty adviser chosen in the major department assists the student during the last two years.

Student Government

The Student Government Association is divided into three branches: executive, legislative, and judicial. The executive cabinet is the major link with the administration; the legislative branch is composed of the student senate and its committees; and the judicial branch includes three levels of student courts. In addition, the Honor System, which is administered by students through an elected Honor Council, provides a code of personal integrity at the College.

Admission Requirements

The minimum academic requirements for admission are graduation from an accredited secondary school (or equivalent credentials) and credit for at least 16 academic units, with an emphasis on college-preparatory work. Applicants should complete, as a minimum, 4 years of English, 3 years of mathematics (including algebra II), and 3 or more years of laboratory science, social studies, and a foreign language in order to be competitive for admission. The results of a recent SAT I or ACT are also required. All testing should be completed by the January test date of the applicant's senior year in high school. Applicants are strongly encouraged to submit SAT II: Subject Test scores in their areas of special interest and ability.

Mary Washington College seeks to attract a diverse student body whose members have demonstrated academic achievement and leadership. The College is strongly committed to providing a campus atmosphere in which ethnic and cultural diversity is appreciated and valued. Transfer students and international students are encouraged to apply. The Committee on Admissions considers the quality of an applicant's college-preparatory work, test information, recommendations, and personal qualifications. Admission is very competitive; almost all freshmen in a recent entering class were in the upper one third of their high school graduating class.

Application and Information

Interested students should request application materials early in their senior year. The high school transcript form should be given to the appropriate person in the secondary school, who should complete it and return it directly to the College. Students are urged to submit their applications as early as possible. The suggested filing date for August admission is February 1 for freshmen and March 1 for transfer students. Applications received after the filing dates are considered if space permits. Students are notified of August admission by April 1.

Honors Admission is offered to high school students with exceptionally strong academic records who apply by January 15. These students are chosen on the basis of their high school program of studies, grades, class rank, and test scores.

Students selecting Mary Washington as their first choice may wish to apply under the early decision program, in which case the application must be filed by November 1. Notification is made by December 15.

Students admitted under the early decision and Honors Admission plans are automatically considered for the Alumni Scholarship Program, Mary Washington's most prestigious academic scholarship award.

Requests for admissions catalogs, application forms, and additional information should be directed to:

Dr. Martin A. Wilder Jr.
Vice President for Admissions and Financial Aid
Mary Washington College
1301 College Avenue
Fredericksburg, Virginia 22401-5358
Telephone: 540-654-2000
          800-468-5614 (toll-free)
          540-654-1105 (TTY)
E-mail: admit@mwc.edu
World Wide Web: http://www.mwc.edu

Mary Washington College's Monroe Hall houses Departments of Business Administration, Political Science and International Affairs, History, Economics, Geography, and Sociology and Anthropology.

MARYWOOD UNIVERSITY
SCRANTON, PENNSYLVANIA

The University

Marywood University is coeducational, comprehensive, residential, and Catholic. Founded in 1915 by the Sisters, Servants of the Immaculate Heart of Mary, the University serves men and women from a variety of backgrounds and religions. The University enrolls nearly 3,000 students in an array of undergraduate and graduate programs. Committed to enriching human lives through ethical and religious values and a tradition of service and motivated by a pioneering, progressive spirit, Marywood provides a framework for educational excellence that enables students to develop fully as persons and to master professional and leadership skills necessary for meeting human needs.

The central focus of the undergraduate curriculum is expressed in the phrase "living responsibly in an interdependent world." Students are encouraged to incorporate a concern for the responsible use of resources into their personal and professional lives. Marywood's historic concern for the enrichment of human life through honoring religious values and a tradition of service also extends to programs at the graduate level. Programs leading to master's and doctoral degrees are offered in the Graduate School of Arts and Sciences and the School of Social Work.

The athletic program for women and men at Marywood provides students with opportunities to play on competitive intercollegiate, club, and intramural teams. Students compete on an intercollegiate basis in baseball, basketball, cross-country, field hockey, soccer, softball, tennis, and volleyball. Marywood is a member of the NCAA Division III and the Pennsylvania Athletic Conference (PAC). Marywood's teams have been successful, winning titles in basketball, field hockey, softball, tennis, and volleyball. In addition, Marywood teams and individuals have participated in tournaments at the national level.

Marywood is fully accredited by the Middle States Association of Colleges and Schools, and its programs are accredited by the Pennsylvania Department of Education, the National Association of Schools of Music, the National Council for Accreditation of Teacher Education, the American Dietetic Association, the Council on Social Work Education, the National Association of Schools of Art and Design, the National League for Nursing Accrediting Commission, and the American Bar Association.

Location

Situated on a hilltop, Marywood's scenic 115-acre campus is part of an attractive residential area of the city of Scranton in northeastern Pennsylvania. With a population of 70,000, Scranton is the fifth-largest city in Pennsylvania and is the county seat of Lackawanna County (the county population is approximately 212,000). Marywood is relatively close to many major cities of the Northeast; traveling by car, it is 1 hour to Binghamton, 2½ hours to New York and Philadelphia, 4 hours to Washington, D.C., and 5½ hours to Boston. Several airlines serve the Wilkes-Barre/Scranton International Airport, which is 20 minutes from campus. The Pocono Mountains, offering spectacular scenery and an abundance of outdoor recreational opportunities including downhill skiing, are only a few minutes from campus.

Majors and Degrees

Marywood University offers a variety of majors and minors at the undergraduate level. Individually designed majors, developed with faculty guidance, and double and interdisciplinary majors are also available. A five-year bachelor's/master's degree program is offered in special education.

At the undergraduate level, Marywood University awards the Bachelor of Arts (B.A.), Bachelor of Business Administration (B.B.A.), Bachelor of Fine Arts (B.F.A.), Bachelor of Music (B.M.), Bachelor of Science (B.S.), Bachelor of Science in Nursing (B.S.N.), Bachelor of Social Work (B.S.W.), and the Associate of Arts (A.A.).

Marywood offers majors and minors in the following areas of study: accounting, advertising and public relations, art (studio: ceramics, painting, sculpture; design: graphic design, illustration, interior design, photography), art education, art therapy, arts administration (art, music, theater), aviation management, biology, chemistry (minor), church music, communication sciences and disorders (audiology, deaf studies, speech/language pathology), computer information and telecommunications systems, computer science (minor), criminal justice, education (elementary, secondary), English, environmental science, family and consumer sciences education, finance, French, general science education, gerontology, health and physical education (athletic training, education, physical activity), health services administration, history/political science, hotel and restaurant management, industrial/organizational psychology, international business, journalism (minor), legal assistant studies (associate and baccalaureate programs), legal studies, management, marketing, mathematics, medical technology/clinical laboratory science, multimedia (minor), music, music education, music therapy, nursing, nutrition and dietetics, performance, performing arts, philosophy (minor), physician assistant studies, psychology, psychology/clinical practice, public administration, radio/television, religious studies, retail business management, science, social sciences, social work, sociology, Spanish, special education, telecommunications: broadcast and corporate communications, theater, and women's studies (minor).

Preprofessional programs are offered in chiropractic, communication sciences and disorders, dentistry, medicine, physician assistant studies, and veterinary medicine. A joint seven-year bachelor's/doctoral program in chiropractic involves three years of study on the Marywood campus and additional work at New York Chiropractic College, located in Seneca Falls, New York.

Academic Program

Marywood's programs are administered through four degree-granting schools. The Undergraduate School offers degrees in nearly sixty academic disciplines including the arts, sciences, music, fine arts, social work, and nursing. All students are required to complete a core curriculum in the liberal arts in addition to the courses in their major. Opportunities for undergraduates abound through double majors, honors and independent study programs, practicums, internships, and study abroad. Army and Air Force ROTC programs are available.

Off-Campus Arrangements

Study-abroad opportunities are available in such countries as Australia, Canada, England, France, Mexico, and Spain. A visiting student program allows Marywood retail business management students to study at the Fashion Institute of Technology in New York City. Students can also earn a degree through Marywood's distance learning program.

Academic Facilities

A multimillion-dollar Center for Natural and Health Sciences houses state-of-the-art science laboratories, a multimedia computer lab, a lecture hall, and three computer labs connected to the campus fiber-optic network. More than 300 microcomputers, located in nine instructional labs and eleven clusters, are found in the Center for Graduate and Professional Studies, Performing Arts Center, Visual Arts Center, and Liberal Arts Center, giving students access to the library's online catalog, CD-ROM databases, and Internet resources.

Marywood's Learning Resources Center (LRC) houses library services, media services, and academic computing services. The library collection includes more than 212,000 volumes, 1,008 current journal subscriptions, and more than 43,000 audiovisual items. The LRC provides CD-ROM databases and a full text database. It also participates in the interlibrary loan network with 8,650 libraries. The research collection includes many index and abstract services.

Costs

Tuition for full-time students (32 credit hours at $495 per credit hour) for the 2000–01 academic year is $15,840. There is also a general fee of $558 for full-time students. Costs for room and board for a full academic year are approximately $6900, depending on which meal plan is selected and desired room occupancy. Costs of books and supplies are estimated at $700.

Financial Aid

Marywood offers a comprehensive program of financial aid to assist students in meeting educational costs. Eligibility for federal and state-funded programs is based on demonstrated financial need. In determining financial need, a federal eligibility formula is used to analyze family income and assets. In addition, the University awards hundreds of scholarships and grants from institutional funds on the basis of academic merit. Applicants to Marywood are considered for all financial assistance programs for which they qualify. Candidates are required to submit the Free Application for Federal Student Aid (FAFSA) and the Marywood application form, preferably by February 15.

Faculty

Of the 247 faculty members at Marywood, 125 are full-time and 90 percent of these hold the Ph.D. or the highest degree in their field. Sixty-one percent of the faculty members advise freshmen, and 83 percent advise undergraduates. The student-faculty ratio is 12:1. Faculty members are evaluated on both their teaching and their scholarly and artistic activities.

Student Government

All matriculated students in the Undergraduate School are members of the Student Government Association. The SGA operates with a number of committees including the Student Council, the Resident Committee, and the Commuter Committee. The association plays a key role in establishing a positive campus environment.

Admission Requirements

Candidates for admission should demonstrate reasonable progress toward graduation in an accredited secondary school, have graduated from a secondary school, or offer evidence of an equivalent secondary education. Each candidate should show satisfactory academic preparation in 16 units of subject matter, including 4 units of English, 3 units of social studies, 2 units of mathematics, 1 unit of science with laboratory, and 6 additional units. Either SAT I or ACT scores are required for those who wish to enter as freshmen.

In addition to fulfilling general admission requirements, candidates for admission to a degree program in art, education, music, nursing, and pre-physician assistant studies must meet special standards established by the department. Prior to enrollment, art and music candidates are required to audition on a major instrument or to present an art portfolio. Candidates for pre-physician assistant studies are required to have an interview.

For certain programs, candidates without the recommended distribution of units may be eligible for admission if their course work as a whole and the results of their tests offer evidence of a strong foundation for college work. Candidates who are deficient in required course work may complete the appropriate work during the summer or the first year in college.

A student who demonstrates satisfactory academic performance at another college may apply for admission as a transfer student. Academic courses presented for transfer should be equivalents of courses required by the programs of study at Marywood. Students should have earned a grade of C or higher in their course work; C– will not transfer. A student should expect to earn a minimum of 60 credits at Marywood University; ordinarily at least one half of the credits required for a major must also be earned at Marywood.

International candidates are required to meet the academic standards for admission, demonstrate proficiency in the use of the English language, and submit documentation of having sufficient funds to cover educational and living expenses for the duration of study. To certify proficiency in the use of English, international applicants whose native language is not English must submit scores from the Test of English as a Foreign Language (TOEFL).

Application and Information

Applications for admission are considered on a rolling basis; however, candidates are encouraged to submit applications by March 1. Applications received after March 1 are considered on the basis of available space in particular programs. To be considered for admission, applicants must submit to the Office of Admissions a completed application, a nonrefundable $25 application fee, an official high school transcript with an indication of class rank, an official report of scores from the SAT I or ACT, and at least one letter of recommendation.

Transfer students must submit a completed application, a nonrefundable $25 application fee, an official high school transcript, official academic transcript(s) reflecting all college course work for which the candidate has enrolled, and at least one letter of recommendation.

All submitted credentials become the property of Marywood and are not returnable to the applicant. Admission standards and policies are free of discrimination on grounds of race, color, national origin, sex, age, or disability.

For further information, interested students should contact:

Mary Anne Fedrick, Director
Office of Undergraduate Admissions
Marywood University
2300 Adams Avenue
Scranton, Pennsylvania 18509
Telephone: 570-348-6234
              800-346-5014 (toll-free)
Fax: 570-961-4763
E-mail: ugadm@ac.marywood.edu
World Wide Web: http://www.marywood.edu

Students at Marywood enjoy a break between classes.

MASSACHUSETTS COLLEGE OF LIBERAL ARTS
NORTH ADAMS, MASSACHUSETTS

The College

Massachusetts College of Liberal Arts (formerly North Adams State College) was founded in 1894 as North Adams Normal School. There are approximately 1,500 undergraduate students enrolled and an additional 200 part-time students who are graduate students, evening students, and special program students.

Massachusetts College of Liberal Arts (MCLA), a four-year, residential, coeducational liberal arts college, offers numerous baccalaureate degrees and a Master of Education degree with concentrations in three areas.

The College is located on 80 acres and includes an athletic complex with softball, baseball, and soccer fields; tennis courts; and a cross-country course. There are three residence facilities that hold more than 1,000 students. Nine intercollegiate athletic programs including baseball (men), basketball (men/women), cross-country (men/women), hockey (men), soccer (men/women), softball (women), and tennis (women) are available. In addition, there are forty-five clubs, organizations, and intramural activities.

The Amsler Campus Center, a four-story complex, houses one of the three residence gymnasiums, a state-of-the-art fitness center, a swimming pool, a dance complex, racquetball and handball courts, two cafeterias, and a counseling center, as well as the bookstore and an athletic training center.

Additional services offered through the College include health services, academic support services, tutorial centers, and the First Year Seminar, an academic and social support service for incoming freshmen.

Location

MCLA is located in North Adams, Massachusetts, 1 mile from the downtown area of 15,000, in the northwestern corner of the state, bordering both Vermont and New York. Centered in the heart of the Berkshires, North Adams offers numerous cultural, historical, and recreational opportunities. Cultural attractions in the Berkshires include Tanglewood Theater, Jacob's Pillow, the Sterling and Francine Clark Art Institute, and the Williamstown Theater Festival. Approximate travel time from Boston is 2½ hours; from New York City, 3 hours; from Albany, New York, 1 hour; from Burlington, Vermont, 3 hours; and from Hartford, Connecticut, 2 hours.

Majors and Degrees

MCLA confers the Bachelor of Arts and Bachelor of Science degrees. Undergraduate programs are offered in biology, business administration, computer science, education, English/communications, fine and performing arts, history, interdisciplinary studies, mathematics, philosophy, physics, psychology, and sociology. Teacher certification is offered in the areas of early childhood education (grades N–3), elementary education (grades 1–6), middle school education (grades 5–9), and secondary education (grades 9–12).

Concentrations include accounting, anthropology, art, arts management, broadcast media, computer science, crime and delinquency, finance/economics, journalism, literature, medical technology, music, political science, prelaw, public relations, social work, sociology, sports medicine, theater studies, and writing. There are twenty-six minors offered through the College.

Academic Program

MCLA operates on a two-semester basis with the first semester running September through December and the second running January through May. Classes are available to all students through both day and evening offerings.

A minimum of 120 semester hours of credit, including major requirements and achievement of a quality point average of at least 2.0, is necessary for completion of a bachelor's degree. At least 39 of the 120 credits must be in upper-division work. MCLA offers a course of study divided into three segments: a general education program, major and minor fields of study, and elective areas in which students have the opportunity to pursue additional academic interests. This program reflects the College's intention that its graduates acquire a sound general education foundation, master in considerable depth one or more integrated areas of human knowledge, and enjoy the freedom to explore fields of personal interest.

College credit is awarded to students with successful scores on the Advanced Placement examinations of the College Board and the College-Level Examination Program (CLEP) tests.

Off-Campus Arrangements

The College participates in the College Academic Program Sharing (CAPS), enabling a student to study at another state college and to earn up to 30 credits while maintaining degree status at MCLA. Students are also offered the opportunity to cross-enroll at Williams College and Berkshire Community College. Travel courses are offered during school breaks, and students are encouraged to explore other cultures while earning course credits. Internships are also offered to students in any major program, both on campus and off campus. Local businesses, such as General Electric, Community Development Corporation, Channel 7 in Boston (a CBS-affiliated station), the Museum of Contemporary Art, and the Berkshire Mall, routinely offer one-semester internships to qualified students.

As a member of the College Consortium for International Studies (CCIS), MCLA offers its students the opportunity to study abroad in sixteen countries throughout the world for a semester or for an entire year.

Academic Facilities

The holdings of the Eugene Lawrence Freel Library include 192,000 book volumes, 544 current journals and newspaper subscriptions, more than 300,000 microform units, and approximately 6,500 nonbook items. College facilities also include television and radio production facilities; biology, chemistry, and physics labs; three computer labs; two amphitheaters; a performance theater; the Career Services Center; and the Center for Academic Advancement.

Costs

In 1999–2000, annual tuition was $1090 for in-state students and $7050 for out-of-state students. Room and board per year were approximately $4800, fluctuating with the choice of housing and meal plans. Additional academic and miscellaneous expenses, including books and travel, averaged $2500 for the year.

Financial Aid

The Office of Financial Aid helps students remove financial obstacles that stand between them and their educational goals. The College's financial aid philosophy is that it should make every effort to enable attendance for students who have financial need remaining after their families have met as much of the cost as is reasonably possible. Need is calculated by subtracting the family's contribution from the total cost of attendance. Those students whose need is greatest may expect to receive priority in the awarding procedure if they meet published deadlines. Although the financial aid programs operate under specific federal and state constraints, every effort is made to consider each student's family financial situation individually. Typically, the student's financial aid award consists of a package composed of a combination of grant, loan, and part-time employment. The deadline for applying for financial aid is April 1 for priority review; however, applications will be accepted on a rolling basis until funds are exhausted.

Faculty

The College currently employs 84 full-time and 50 part-time faculty members; of these, 73 percent hold a doctoral degree. The student-faculty ratio is 13:1, and all classes are taught by faculty members. Working with a diverse student body, the faculty and staff aim to develop liberally educated individuals who have the knowledge, perspectives, critical thinking abilities, and ethical values necessary to become active citizens and leaders within their chosen field.

Student Government

The Student Government Association (SGA) has been in existence at MCLA since 1909. It was formed in order to coordinate and unify matters of student governance on campus, allowing students to have input in all College policies. The SGA administers the Student Activities Trust Fund to all recognized clubs and organizations and sponsors additional Massachusetts College events.

Admission Requirements

All freshman applicants must submit an official copy of their high school record, including at least the first-quarter senior grades. The primary emphasis in evaluating a candidate is on the total high school profile, consisting of overall grade point average, the applicant's curriculum, SAT I/ACT scores, and the level of competition in the individual high school. The unit requirements for freshman admission are English, 4; mathematics, 3; science, 3; history/social science, 2; foreign language, 2; and electives, 2.

Transfer students are strongly encouraged to apply for admission. To be eligible for admission, a student must have a cumulative grade point average of at least 2.0 on a 4.0 scale and submit an official transcript from each college attended. Transfer students are notified at the time of acceptance of the number of credits accepted and how they transfer into their program of study. MCLA has developed transfer articulation agreements with many community and junior colleges to ensure admission and maximum transferability of credit. MCLA offers joint admission to transfer students from Massachusetts community colleges.

International students must submit a record of secondary work along with scores on the Test of English as a Foreign Language (TOEFL).

Consideration is given to applicants regardless of their race, religion, national origin, sex, age, color, ethnic origin, or handicap. Admission interviews are recommended for all applicants.

Application and Information

The application for admission to Massachusetts College of Liberal Arts requests information regarding a student's academic background, extracurricular activities, and personal data.

Applications are reviewed on a rolling admission schedule, and students are accepted by the College until all spaces are filled. Tours of the campus are provided daily and on specific weekends.

Application materials and additional information, including tour dates and times, may be obtained by contacting:

Denise Richardello
Dean of Enrollment Management
Massachusetts College of Liberal Arts
375 Church Street
North Adams, Massachusetts 01247-4100
Telephone: 413-662-5410
           800-292-6632 Ext. 5410 (toll-free)
E-mail: admissions@mcla.mass.edu
World Wide Web: http://www.mcla.mass.edu

Historic Murdock Hall on the Massachusetts College of Liberal Arts campus.

MASSACHUSETTS COLLEGE OF PHARMACY AND HEALTH SCIENCES
BOSTON, MASSACHUSETTS

The College

Founded in 1823, the Massachusetts College of Pharmacy and Health Sciences (MCPHS) is well into its second century as one of the nation's oldest schools of pharmacy. One of only a few that remain private and independent, the College has the distinct advantage of quickly responding to change. That flexibility has allowed the College to expand its mission and programs over time to include nursing and the allied health sciences.

With its distinguished history and an international reputation, the Massachusetts College of Pharmacy and Health Sciences is helping to redefine the roles of pharmacists, nurses, and allied health professionals in health-care delivery. The College's unique programs integrate theoretical and applied knowledge in the health professions with general education in the arts and sciences, so that graduates may become enlightened citizens as well as competent practitioners.

The curriculum at MCPHS is designed to develop active thinkers and learners who are prepared for changing professions and a complex world. A core of liberal arts and sciences courses, or "science building blocks," are built into all bachelor's degree programs. Developed by scholars and working professionals, these courses are often custom-tailored to give students practical information and valuable insights into today's health-care concerns.

The College has a growing athletic program with affiliations in the NCAA Division III, the Southern New England Athletic Conference, and the Massachusetts Association of Intercollegiate Athletics for Women. MCPHS intercollegiate athletics include men's and women's basketball, cross-country, and soccer; men's baseball, and women's softball. In addition, cheering is offered as a club activity and students may participate in a variety of intramural sports. Other student activities include the Academy of Students of Pharmacy, Black Student Union, the Indian Student Organization, the International Student Association, the Republic of China Student Association, the Vietnamese Student Association, the College yearbook, and the *Dispenser* (student newspaper). There are also five professional fraternities—two for men, two for women, and one coed.

The College also offers the Master of Science and Doctor of Philosophy degrees in chemistry (analytical or organic/medicinal), pharmaceutics/industrial pharmacy, and pharmacology.

Location

Dedicated solely to health education, the College is a highly respected institution in Boston's world-renowned Longwood Medical and Academic Area (LMA). Its location alone gives MCPHS students resources unmatched by any other program. The LMA is home to the nation's premier medical centers and educational and research institutions—a highly stimulating and inspiring environment in which to learn.

Boston is a college town in the best sense of the word—cultural, accessible, and pulsing with activity. Students can experience Boston's history along the Freedom Trail, enjoy its seafood on the waterfront, or explore its ethnic neighborhoods such as the Italian North End. Favorite spots include Faneuil Hall Marketplace; the Esplanade along the Charles River for outdoor concerts and movies, biking, jogging, and in-line skating; and the Public Gardens and Boston Common for walks, picnics, and just relaxing. The city's elaborate public transportation network (the "T") connects students to all these places and many more, such as Cambridge and Harvard Square, where students might browse in bookstores and enjoy a sidewalk performance; Newbury Street for shopping and distinctive galleries; the Fleet Center where the Celtics and Bruins play; and Symphony Hall, home of the Boston Pops and the Boston Symphony Orchestra.

In fall 2000, the College will open a campus in Worcester, Massachusetts, the second-largest city in New England. The new campus is located adjacent to the Worcester Medical Center and is close to the Fallon Clinic, St. Vincent's Hospital, and the medical school at the University of Massachusetts.

Majors and Degrees

The Massachusetts College of Pharmacy and Health Sciences offers the following undergraduate degrees and programs: Bachelor of Science degrees in allied health sciences, chemistry, health communications, health psychology, nursing (for RNs only), pharmaceutical sciences, pharmacy, physician assistant studies (six-year master's program), and radiologic sciences (concentrations in nuclear medicine technology, radiation therapy, and radiography). All pharmacy students admitted to the College are directly enrolled in the Doctor of Pharmacy (Pharm.D.) program. Premedicine concentrations are also offered.

MCPHS Worcester offers an accelerated pharmacy program for students who have already completed two years of preprofessional requirements at MCPHS-Boston or at another undergraduate institution.

Academic Program

Students in each of the undergraduate programs begin their studies in the basic sciences, humanities, and social sciences. First-year classes include two semesters of English, math, biology, and chemistry. After completing basic science courses, Bachelor of Science degree candidates progress to advanced courses in chemistry, psychology, pharmaceutics, and pharmacology. Students are also required to complete professional development courses such as interpersonal communications, ethics, and law courses. In addition, students must complete 12 semester hours of elective courses in the humanities, social sciences, and behavioral sciences, as well as 12 semester hours of general elective course work.

A significant aspect of every student's education at MCPHS is the application of theoretical knowledge in a clinical setting. For example, the sixth year of the Pharm.D. program is devoted to clinical clerkships comprised of required rotations in general medicine and ambulatory care and several elective rotations.

Off-Campus Arrangements

The externship/clinical experience is a very important part of an MCPHS education and is built into most programs. The programs place students in professional settings for firsthand learning and guidance as they work with a mentor from the sponsoring institution's staff. Students may choose from among more than 55 hospitals and 100 community practice sites in and around Boston. The College's affiliations with Boston's high-caliber medical centers, top teaching hospitals, and pharmacies ensure students the highest quality experience.

As part of its pharmacy curriculum, the College offers an optional radiopharmacy externship program in conjunction with the Massachusetts General Hospital. The program consists of an academic phase based at the College and an experiential component performed at the hospital.

In 1996, the College officially entered into a consortium called the Colleges of the Fenway. In addition to MCPHS, the Colleges of the Fenway include Emmanuel, Simmons, and Wheelock Colleges; the Wentworth Institute of Technology; and Massachusetts College of Art. Students of each of the participating institutions may take courses at any of the others, as well as use the facilities of each. In effect, the collaboration has created a "mega-campus" for MCPHS students.

Academic Facilities

In 1996, the College completed construction of an eight-story, 230,000-square-foot mixed-use facility. Connected to the existing George Robert White Building by a sky-lighted atrium, the new building includes sophisticated research facilities, modern laboratories, faculty offices, classrooms, a 166-student residence hall, and dining commons. A portion of the facility's research space has been leased to the Brigham and Women's Hospital, solidifying the College's nearly half-century-old education union with that distinguished institution.

The MCPHS Sheppard Library is a pharmaceutical and medical information center that maintains a working collection of more than 70,000 catalogued print and nonprint materials, and an archives collection that documents the history of the College. The library receives approximately 800 serial subscriptions annually.

Costs

Tuition for the preprofessional curriculum is $16,900 per academic year. Tuition for the professional curriculum is $19,000. Room and board costs are $8000. Additional fees and the cost of books are estimated at $800.

Financial Aid

Financial aid is both merit- and need-based. A combination of various forms of aid is usually offered to meet the established needs of each qualified student. The College administers Federal Work-Study Program awards, Health Professions Student Loans, Federal Pell Grants, Federal Supplemental Educational Opportunity Grants, and Federal Perkins Loans as well as in-house scholarships. The priority deadline for application is March 1, and notification is made on a rolling basis. Approximately 83 percent of the students at the College receive financial aid.

Faculty

There are 64 full- and part-time faculty members; 61 percent of the full-time and 44 percent of the part-time faculty members have an earned doctorate or other terminal professional degree.

Student Government

The Student Government is an elective body charged with appropriating funds for and monitoring student activities, overseeing class elections, and functioning as the voice of the students and their interests. Its membership includes the dean of students, 18 student representatives, and 2 faculty representatives.

Admission Requirements

No single standard is used in the admission decision-making process. All applicants are considered without regard to race, sex, color, or creed. Each applicant's high school record, curriculum, and class standing are evaluated along with official test scores. The required secondary school background is 4 years of English, 3 years of college-preparatory math, 2 years of a laboratory science (biology and chemistry), and 1 year of history. Applicants must also submit scores on the SAT I or the ACT. The TOEFL is required if English is not the applicant's first language. An interview is highly recommended.

Advanced standing of up to one year may be given on the basis of results on the College Board's Advanced Placement examinations. The College subscribes to the early decision plan.

Transfer students are accepted into all of the undergraduate majors, provided they have completed high school biology, chemistry, and algebra II (or its equivalent at the college level). Students must submit official transcripts from all colleges attended. Recommendations and personal statements are required. A student with less than 30 semester hours of college course work must submit a high school transcript. Application deadline is March 1.

Application and Information

For application forms or information, students should contact:
Office of Admission
Massachusetts College of Pharmacy
  and Health Sciences
179 Longwood Avenue
Boston, Massachusetts 02115

Telephone: 617-732-2850
 800-225-5506 (toll-free outside Massachusetts)
Fax: 617-732-2801
World Wide Web: http://www.mcp.edu

The George Robert White Building on the campus of the Massachusetts College of Pharmacy and Health Sciences.

MASSACHUSETTS INSTITUTE OF TECHNOLOGY
CAMBRIDGE, MASSACHUSETTS

The Institute

Massachusetts Institute of Technology was chartered in 1861 to create a new kind of university at which students could be educated in the application as well as the acquisition of knowledge. Education and related research continue to be MIT's central purpose, with relevance to the practical world as a guiding principle. The campus is located on 142 acres in Cambridge, Massachusetts, bordering the Charles River for a mile and overlooking downtown Boston.

The total Institute enrollment is 9,885; 1,776 women and 2,596 men are enrolled as undergraduates. Ninety-five percent of all undergraduates live in a mixture of coed and single-sex housing that consists of ten dormitories and thirty-five independent living groups. The independent living groups include twenty-seven nationally affiliated fraternities, five coed fraternity-like groups, five sororities, and the Women's Independent Living Group (WILG). All freshmen are guaranteed a room on campus for four years.

Location

Located in the city of Cambridge, directly across the Charles River from Boston, MIT is one of fifty colleges and universities within a 20-mile radius. As a result, in the area there is an extraordinary variety of young people from all over the world as well as an impressive range of facilities and activities available to all students. Within 2 miles of the Institute are the Museums of Science and Fine Arts, the Gardner Museum, the New England Conservatory of Music, the New England Aquarium, and the Boston Public Library. Students can easily travel by bus or subway to the theater district for pre-Broadway and local productions, the Boston Symphony Orchestra, the Boston Pops, the Boston Ballet Company, and the Opera Company of Boston. An hour or two from MIT by car are the mountains of Vermont and New Hampshire, the ocean beaches of Cape Cod, and the lakes and rivers of Maine. The Boston area is where the American Revolution began, and historic sites are numerous.

Majors and Degrees

Some of the more common disciplines for which a B.S. is offered are American studies, anthropology/archaeology, architecture, astronomy, biology, chemistry, cognitive science, earth and planetary sciences, economics, engineering (aeronautics and astronautics, chemical, civil, electrical and computer science, environmental engineering science, materials science, mechanical, nuclear, and ocean), foreign literatures, history, humanities, interdisciplinary science, life sciences, linguistics, literatures, management, mathematics, music, philosophy, physics, political science, Russian studies, urban studies and planning, visual design, and writing. Many students earn a B.S. in either a preexisting interdisciplinary program or one of their own design; biomedical engineering is one of the most frequently chosen. Large numbers of MIT graduates go on to medical, law, and business schools; although there are no programs in premedicine or prelaw, there is a Preprofessional Advising Office.

Academic Program

The undergraduate programs at MIT are designed to help students develop the understanding, maturity, and capabilities to meet the challenges of modern society. Students base their studies on a core of subjects in science, mathematics, and the humanities (General Institute Requirements), usually begun the first year, and then slowly go on to concentrate in their departmental or interdepartmental programs. There is considerable time to take elective subjects each year. For most students, the program for the B.S. requires four years of full-time study. The freshman year at MIT is on a pass/no-credit basis.

One of the most exciting features of undergraduate education is the opportunity for students to join with faculty members in ongoing research projects (Undergraduate Research Opportunities Program, or UROP). Eighty percent of all undergraduates are involved in active research in the MIT tradition of learning by doing.

Advanced placement may be granted to entering freshmen through College Board Advanced Placement tests, college transcripts, and advanced-standing examinations at MIT.

Air Force, Army, and Naval ROTC subjects are available without academic credit.

There is a cross-registration program with Wellesley College and Harvard University.

Academic Facilities

The Institute has an extensive library system that includes 2.4 million volumes, more than 20,000 current journals and serials, and numerous back files. The Institute has well-equipped facilities to support all its programs.

At least sixty interdisciplinary and interdepartmental facilities provide opportunities for faculty, students, and staff to join together on projects that cross traditional disciplinary lines. Some of these are the Artificial Intelligence Laboratory, Bates Linear Accelerator, Center for Advanced Visual Studies, Center for Cancer Research, Center for International Studies, and Whitehead Institute.

Costs

The tuition for 2000-01 is $26,050. The standard cost for room and board is $7175, and $2850 can be estimated for books, materials, clothing, entertainment, and personal expenses. A range of options is available in housing and dining arrangements; most students pay a total of about $36,075 per year, excluding travel expenses.

Financial Aid

Financial aid is awarded on the basis of need and is dependent on an objective analysis of family finances. Financial aid packages take into account the family contribution (including the parents' contribution, student's summer earnings, and student's assets), the student's self-help (loan and/or part-time job), and MIT grant money, if necessary, to meet the established costs. The CSS Financial Aid PROFILE and the Free Application for Federal Student Aid (FAFSA) are required to apply for financial aid.

More than 59 percent of the undergraduates received financial aid last year.

Faculty

A single faculty of approximately 1,000 members teaches undergraduate and graduate students and engages in research.

Seven hundred graduate students and teaching assistants are on the staff, bringing the total of the Institute's teaching staff to 1,700. The Institute is characterized by one-on-one interaction between students and professors, and most of the faculty members participate in UROP. All students are assigned to faculty members who serve as their advisers throughout their undergraduate years.

Student Government

The Undergraduate Association is the major undergraduate governmental body. Its functions are divided among committees that allocate funds to student organizations, manage social and musical events, operate certain facilities on campus, improve classroom and living conditions in the dormitories, propose educational reforms, sponsor feedback programs, operate free computer services, and recommend student representatives for more than fifty faculty and administrative committees.

Admission Requirements

Ideal preparation for study at MIT would include English (4 years), history/social studies (2 or more years), mathematics through calculus (4 years), laboratory sciences (biology, chemistry, and physics), and a foreign language. Applicants are required to take the SAT I or the ACT, as well as three SAT II Subject Tests–Writing or History, Science, and Mathematics Level I, Ic, or IIc. The December testing date is the last one for which SAT I, SAT II, and ACT scores are considered. Interviews are also required but are conducted in the applicant's home area by a member of the MIT Educational Council. All interviews must be completed between May 1 of the junior year and December 15 of the senior year in high school. The deadline for submission of regular admission applications is January 1.

Application and Information

Candidates who wish to apply for early action must submit an application and all materials by November 1 as well as have tests completed on or by the November testing date. They can expect to hear from the admission committee by mid-December.

Freshmen are admitted for September only. Transfer students are accepted for September and February.

Requests for additional information and application forms should be addressed to:

Admissions Office
Room 3-108
Massachusetts Institute of Technology
Cambridge, Massachusetts 02139-4307
Telephone: 617-253-4791
E-mail: mitfrosh@mit.edu
World Wide Web: http://web.mit.edu/admissions/www/

Spring in the Great Court, Massachusetts Institute of Technology.

MASSACHUSETTS MARITIME ACADEMY
CAPE COD, MASSACHUSETTS

The Academy

As the oldest continuously operating maritime academy in the United States, Massachusetts Maritime Academy is a coeducational state college with both maritime and nonmaritime curricula. Graduates of Massachusetts Maritime Academy have traditionally been recognized for their excellence. Naval admirals and government and business leaders are prominent among the Academy's alumni.

In addition to a Bachelor of Science degree and a professional license, students achieve a sense of self-confidence and competence—qualities important to success in any career.

A clear statement of approval regarding the Academy is made by employers within both maritime and shoreside industries. Nearly 100 percent of the senior class find high-paying employment within a few months of graduation.

The approximately 800 men and women have in common an interest in hands-on activities, an aptitude for mathematics and science, leadership potential, and an interest in, or experience on, the ocean. They recognize the value of a regimented campus life-style for developing decision-making skills, discipline, and the ability to assume responsibility. The Academy attracts most of its students from the Northeastern states, with Massachusetts residents making up two thirds of the total. However, students from across the nation as well as seven other countries are in attendance. The great majority of students live in traditional college dormitories as a part of the requirements to obtain a professional maritime license. Some students commute to the campus as participants in the Facilities and Environmental Engineering Program.

The Regiment of Cadets is divided into companies and is administered by student leaders as well as by full-time staff members. All students wear uniforms daily and participate in various activities, such as flag formation (morning colors) and inspection of quarters.

MMA has a fine athletics complex and a highly competitive athletics program; the Academy fields varsity teams in baseball, crew, cross-country, football, lacrosse, rifle marksmanship, sailing, soccer, softball, and volleyball. Academy teams have won All–New England titles in baseball and football. A vigorous intramural athletics program spans the academic year. The Academy also has active programs through the aviation, boxing, Catholic Newman, floor hockey, Knights of Columbus, minority awareness, photography, pistol and rifle, propeller, rugby, scuba, swimming, wrestling, and yachting clubs.

Massachusetts Maritime Academy is for the well-directed, environmentally conscientious, motivated young man or woman who loves the ocean and travel and who desires a thorough education to prepare for engineering, business, and maritime-related professions or for the armed forces. For students who are talented in mathematics and science, mature, and self-disciplined and who enjoy travel, the Academy can provide tradition, a fine education, and optimum hands-on training.

Location

The Academy is located on Taylor's Point, a peninsula at the western mouth of the scenic Cape Cod Canal where it joins Buttermilk Bay. Cape Cod is one of the most beautiful resort areas of the United States. Massachusetts Maritime Academy is located at the gateway to the cape, and it is less than an hour from the cities of Boston and Providence, Rhode Island, and from the Cape Cod National Seashore.

Majors and Degrees

Massachusetts Maritime Academy provides graduates with twofold credentials: a fully accredited Bachelor of Science degree and a professional license, which enables graduates to seek employment within the various maritime industries and within the stationary power plant industry. To achieve this end, students can major in facilities and environmental engineering, international maritime business, marine engineering, marine safety and environmental protection, or marine transportation. A five-year dual major program allows students to obtain both marine transportation and engineering licenses. The marine safety and environmental protection major, conducted with Woods Hole Oceanographic Institution, is designed to present the opportunity for preparation in the scientific, management, and legal foundations of environmental protection. A variety of minor concentrations in such areas as business management, commercial fisheries, mechanical engineering, and environmental/facilities engineering also broaden employment options for graduates.

Academic Program

Two academic terms on campus separated by a winter Sea Term make up the ten-month academic year. Approximately six months of sea time aboard the Academy's training ship are required. This time is divided into four cruises of approximately seven weeks each. Countries visited during Sea Term have included Barbados, Mexico, Portugal, England, Ireland, Italy, Germany, and Greece; cadets cruise to twelve to fifteen countries before graduating. During Sea Term, cadets apply classroom lessons to the operation of a large oceangoing vessel. The cadets have the opportunity to ship commercially with a variety of shipping companies or participate in paid co-op programs and internships throughout the world. Cadets have the summer off.

The academic program involves extensive study and emphasizes a blend of mathematics and sciences with technical and professional studies. Each career program provides a solid foundation in mathematics, physical science, humanities, and social studies in addition to a core of required professional subjects. Maritime majors are eligible to sit for U.S. Coast Guard license examinations as a Third Mate (Deck Officer) or Third Assistant Engineer of steam and motor vessels of unlimited tonnage. Facilities and environmental engineering majors are eligible for state licensure. Although there is no military obligation, some students select service in the U.S. Navy, U.S. Army, Coast Guard, or Marine Corps or in other military branches. Courses offered through the Department of Naval Science qualify cadets to apply for an officer's commission in the U.S. Naval or Coast Guard Reserve upon graduation. Graduates hold positions throughout the maritime industry as well as in government administration and land-based industries, and they have had great success in many fields unrelated to the maritime profession, such as power-plant operations and industrial and mechanical engineering.

Academic Facilities

Massachusetts Maritime Academy has facilities representing state-of-the-art technology in order to provide cadets with the finest training available. An All Weather Navigation and Radar Training Simulator coupled with a prototype of a "Schoolship"

Full-Function Video Shiphandling Simulator is the most modern instruction device for commercial marine navigation available in the world today. The system features not only video but also realistic radar, loran C, and depth-finding and radio-direction-finding capabilities. The Center for Marine Environmental Protection and Safety provides state-of-the-art oil spill response management and tanker liquid cargo simulators for student and industry training. The library computer lab makes personal-application equipment, along with modems, databases, and a wide variety of popular software applications, available to faculty, staff, and cadets.

Costs

In 2000–01, tuition, fees, room, board, and Sea Term are $9248 for residents of Massachusetts, Connecticut, Delaware, Florida, Maryland, New Jersey, Pennsylvania, Rhode Island, Virginia, and Washington, D.C.; $9818 for certain New England residents; and $16,108 for out-of-state residents. These figures do not include uniforms, books, or incidental personal expenses.

Financial Aid

Massachusetts Maritime Academy offers its 800 students more than $350,000 per year in merit awards based on academic achievement, leadership, and community activities. Most of these awards are renewable for four years.

In addition, the Academy assists families with federal and state need-based programs, which include grants, scholarships, work opportunities, and student loan programs. Students apply for the need-based programs by completing the Free Application for Federal Student Aid (FAFSA). The Academy's priority deadline for submission of the FAFSA and other application materials is March 15.

Faculty

The faculty is known for its high academic standards. Seventy-five percent of the academic faculty have doctoral degrees or top professional licenses. In the marine transportation department, there are 8 Ship Masters; in the marine engineering department, there are 8 Chief Engineers and 3 Ph.D.'s. These figures compare favorably with those at any similar academy in the country. The student-faculty ratio is a low 13:1 to ensure that all students receive personal attention commensurate with their academic and professional needs. The Academy also provides a strong support and tutorial program to ensure that every student may have an optimum opportunity for success.

Student Government

A student government is elected to help meet the extracurricular needs of the student body, and its members participate with faculty members and administrators on various all-Academy committees. Students are also represented on the Massachusetts Maritime Academy Board of Trustees.

Admission Requirements

Massachusetts Maritime Academy seeks applicants who have demonstrated an aptitude for mathematics and science. SAT or ACT scores are required of all applicants. In making admission decisions, the admission committee considers important criteria to be the applicant's class standing, SAT or ACT scores, and high school average, stressing college-preparatory mathematics and laboratory sciences (such as chemistry and physics). The rest of the evaluation considers the student's leadership potential, athletics or extracurricular participation, church and community involvement, employment, maritime experience, and letters of recommendation. At least two letters of recommendation are required. A personal interview is strongly recommended.

Application and Information

The application should be submitted as soon as possible but no later than June 1 for the class entering in September. Early decision deadline is November 1. Throughout the year, applicants and their families are invited to visit the Academy. Successful applicants receive a timely decision as well as follow-up communication throughout the year.

Application forms may be obtained by contacting:

Office of Admissions
Massachusetts Maritime Academy
101 Academy Drive
Buzzards Bay, Cape Cod, Massachusetts 02532
Telephone: 508-830-5000
          800-544-3411 (toll-free)
Fax: 508-830-5077
E-mail: admissions@mma.mass.edu
World Wide Web: http://www.mma.edu

Located at the gateway to Cape Cod, Massachusetts Maritime Academy is the oldest continuously operating maritime academy in the United States.

McGILL UNIVERSITY
MONTRÉAL, QUÉBEC, CANADA

The University

Founded more than 175 years ago, McGill University is named for the Honourable James McGill, a Scottish fur trader who became a leading Montréal merchant and philanthropist. McGill College received its royal charter from George IV in 1821.

Classes began in 1829 when the teaching wing of the Montréal General Hospital was incorporated into the College. The Faculty of Arts opened its doors in 1843. During the next ten years, the University added modern languages, commercial studies, and the sciences. In 1884, the first female students were admitted, and classes for men and women gradually merged.

In 1906, Sir William Macdonald endowed a college at Ste. Anne de Bellevue, a village about 25 miles west of downtown Montréal. The Macdonald campus buildings are now the site of the Faculty of Agricultural and Environmental Sciences, which includes the School of Dietetics and Human Nutrition. The Macdonald farm, the Morgan arboretum, the St. Lawrence Valley Ecomuseum, and the Avian Science and Conservation Centre provide the livestock and field facilities used in teaching and applied research and offer students the opportunity to gain hands-on knowledge in an agricultural milieu.

McGill is a comprehensive, publicly funded private university with a diverse student population. The full-time student body is 20,959 registrants: 58.1 percent from Québec, 26 percent from other provinces in Canada, and 15.9 percent from the United States and some 120 other countries. One in every 5 students lists French as his or her mother tongue. The language of instruction at McGill is English; however, students may write term papers and examinations in French.

McGill is composed of twelve faculties, ten schools, and four institutes: the Faculties of Agricultural and Environmental Sciences, Arts, Dentistry, Education, Engineering, Graduate Studies and Research, Law, Management, Medicine, Music, Religious Studies, and Science; the Schools of Architecture, Communication Sciences and Disorders (graduate programs only), Computer Science, Dietetics and Human Nutrition, Nursing, Physical and Occupational Therapy, Social Work, and Urban Planning; the Graduate School of Library and Information Studies; McGill School of Environment; and the Institutes of Air and Space Law, Comparative Law, Islamic Studies, and Parasitology. The University offers degrees at the bachelor's and master's levels and offers doctorates in all major areas. Professional degrees in dentistry and medicine are also offered.

Residence accommodation downtown is available for 1,400 students in six buildings; all but one are coed. The Macdonald campus has a coed residence for 240 students. Most first-year students stay in residence for one year and then move to an apartment.

Extracurricular activities are an important part of University life—they provide recreation and instruction, enhance a sense of independence, and offer experience in leadership. More than 100 student-run clubs support specialized interests, the largest being the McGill Outing Club, where members arrange skiing, canoeing, climbing, and hiking excursions.

Indoor and outdoor men's and women's intercollegiate teams challenge the teams of other universities. Intramural athletics provide competition with fellow students, and instructional programs offer opportunities to improve standards and abilities in a wide choice of activities.

Location

Montréal is distinctly North American, yet it also has a very European atmosphere. The University gates open onto one of the main downtown avenues with restaurants and outdoor cafés, high-rise office buildings, boutiques, and underground shopping malls. On the north side, beyond the residences and sports facilities, a mountain park offers immediate access to the outdoors. Each of Montréal's four distinct seasons brings its own special pleasures of indoor and outdoor activities.

Majors and Degrees

The Bachelor of Arts degree is offered in African studies; anthropology; art history; Canadian studies; classics; computing (foundations of); East Asian studies; economics; English (literature, drama, and theatre, and cultural studies); environment (faculty program); French language and literature (literature, literature and translation); geography (geography/urban systems); German (language and literature, literature and culture); Hispanic literature and culture/languages; history; humanistic studies; industrial relations (faculty program); international development studies; Italian studies (Italian studies/Medieval and Renaissance periods); Jewish studies; Latin American studies; linguistics; mathematics; Middle East studies; music; North American studies; philosophy; political science; psychology; Québec studies; religious studies; Russian; sociology; and women's studies.

The Bachelor of Science degree is offered in anatomy and cell biology; atmospheric science; atmospheric science and physics; biochemistry; biology; biology and mathematics; chemistry (bioorganic, environmental, and materials options); chemistry and biological sciences; chemistry and mathematics; computer science; earth and planetary sciences; environment; geography; mathematics; mathematics and computer science; mathematics, statistics, and computer science; mathematics, chemistry, and physics; microbiology and immunology; physics; physics and geophysics; physiology; physiology and mathematics; physiology and physics; psychology; and science for teachers. The Bachelor of Science (agriculture) degree is offered in agricultural economics (agribusiness, agricultural systems, and natural resource economics options), animal biology, animal science, applied zoology, botanical sciences, environmental biology, general agricultural sciences, microbiology, plant science, resource conservation, soil science, and wildlife biology. Bachelor of Science degrees are offered in agricultural engineering, architecture, food science, nursing, nutritional science, occupational therapy, and physical therapy.

The Bachelor of Commerce degree is offered in accounting, economics, entrepreneurship, finance, information systems, international business, international management, labour-management relations, management science, marketing, mathematics, operations management, organizational behaviour and human resource management, psychology, and strategic management.

The Bachelor of Education degree is offered in kindergarten and elementary education (also Jewish studies option), general secondary two-subject option, vocational secondary education (one subject), physical education, physical activity and health sciences, and teaching of English as a second language (ESL) or French as a second language. Also offered are the B.Ed. for certified teachers, a concurrent B.Ed./B.Mus., and a B.Ed./B.Sc.

The Bachelor of Engineering is offered, with specializations in chemical engineering, civil engineering, computer engineering, electrical engineering, mechanical engineering, metallurgical engineering, and mining engineering (co-op).

Bachelor of Law degrees are offered in civil and common law.

The Bachelor of Music is offered in composition, music education, music history, music technology, performance, performance (church music, early music, or jazz), and theory.

The Bachelor of Social Work (B.S.W.) degree is offered; a special one-year B.S.W. degree program (application deadline is December 1, entrance is in May) is offered for applicants who already hold a degree in another area.

The Bachelor of Theology degree is offered in religious studies.

The professional degrees of Doctor of Dental Surgery and Doctor of Medicine, Master of Surgery are also offered. The Bachelor of Architecture is offered.

Academic Program

The academic year has two regular semesters: fall term (September to December) and winter term (January to May). There are four months of summer sessions (May, June, July, and August). Applicants who have completed an appropriate level of education outside Québec may be considered for entrance to a University program that usually requires a minimum of eight semesters (four years), or 120 credits, of study. A few programs require longer periods of study.

Applicants who have completed a Québec Diploma of Collegial Studies, Advanced Level Examinations, or the French or International Baccalaureate normally are admitted to a three-year, 90-credit program.

Off-Campus Arrangements

McGill students may participate in a variety of official exchange programs with more than 280 universities worldwide or make independent arrangements to spend a year elsewhere.

Academic Facilities

With holdings of more than 5.7 million items, the McGill network of sixteen libraries is the largest in Montréal and the fourth largest in Canada. The six major areas encompass the humanities and social sciences, law, life sciences, medicine, music, and physical sciences and engineering. The network features easy physical access to all of the resources; automated computer entry into the catalogue from library, office, or home; quiet study areas; and workshops for new students. There are extensive computing facilities to meet undergraduate, graduate, faculty, and research needs. The campuswide mainframe service provides interactive and batch services and e-mail. A number of departments operate their own local systems to provide specialized services to their researchers, staff members, and students. Microcomputer laboratories and terminals connected to both the central mainframe and the departmental systems are located throughout the campus. The McGill high-speed fibre optics–based backbone network interconnects all these facilities and is available to all staff members and students. University archives, two major museums, and many unique and rare collections and exhibitions offer valuable resources for research. Most areas are open to the public.

Costs

For 1999–2000, tuition fees for a normal full-time course load of 30 credits were $1668 for Québec residents, $3168 for other Canadian citizens and permanent residents, and $8268 to $13,500, depending on the program, for visa students. There are other miscellaneous University charges for course materials, books, and instruments, and there is a compulsory health insurance for visa students. Room and board plus additional meals or off-campus housing and food amounted to approximately $7512 in 1999–2000. Personal expenses, such as transportation, clothing, and amusements, are extra. (All figures are in Canadian dollars.) Tuition fees may increase in 2000–01.

Financial Aid

Scholarship awards range in value from $2000 (renewable) to $10,000 (renewable) and are based on outstanding academic achievement or a combination of outstanding academic achievement and leadership qualities. Further information is available in the application for admission package.

Faculty

Research has always supported and enhanced teaching at McGill. Knowledge gained in the laboratory and in the library enlightens the practices of lectures and theoretical discussions. The great majority of McGill's full-time professors hold a Ph.D. degree, and almost all classes are taught by full-time, regular staff members.

Student Government

Students participate in the governance and administration of the University, with representation on both the Senate and the Board of Governors. The Undergraduate Students' Society manages its own building and all the various facilities it contains, including food services. Different academic areas also have their own undergraduate societies.

Admission Requirements

Admission is based on a review of the whole academic dossier, including academic performance over the past three years, strength of programs, rank in graduating class, and scores on standardized tests (if applicable). Students are expected to have a minimum B+ average or the equivalent, depending on where they have completed their studies. Admission is competitive. Transfer applicants are evaluated on the basis of their university/college record and the criteria listed above.

Application and Information

Applications for first-year admission in September should be completed and forwarded to McGill by January 15 for international and U.S. applicants, by February 1 for applicants from Canadian provinces other than Québec, by March 1 for applicants from Québec, by May 1 for exchange students, and by July 1 for special and visiting students.

While the majority of students enter in September, it is possible to be considered for admission to some undergraduate programs in January. For January admission, applications must reach McGill by September 1 for international, U.S., and Canadian (from provinces other than Québec) applicants and by November 1 for applicants from Québec and for special and visiting students. For further information about January admission and the programs to which it applies, students should contact the Admissions Office.

McGill welcomes applications from all interested students regardless of race, religion, age, handicap, nationality, or sex.

Admissions information and University calendars are available on the admissions Web site. An online application can be accessed, completed, and submitted via the World Wide Web (http://www.aro.mcgill.ca/admissions).

Prospective applicants are encouraged to visit the McGill campus. One-hour walking tours, which are conducted in the morning or afternoon, are led by McGill students. Applicants are also invited to attend selected classes in most faculties during the months of October, November, February, and March.

For more information about visits and tours, students should contact:

The Welcome Centre
Burnside Hall, Room 115
805 Sherbrooke Street, West
Montréal, Québec H3A 2K6
Canada
Telephone: 514-398-6555
Fax: 514-398-2072
E-mail: welcome@aro.lan.mcgill.ca
World Wide Web: http://www.mcgill.ca

To receive a regular application form or for additional information, students should contact:

Admissions, Recruitment, and Registrar's Office
McGill University
845 Sherbrooke Street, West
Montréal, Québec H3A 2T5
Canada
Telephone: 514-398-3910
Fax: 514-398-4193
E-mail: admissions@aro.lan.mcgill.ca
World Wide Web: http://www.aro.mcgill.ca

McKENDREE COLLEGE
LEBANON, ILLINOIS

The College

McKendree College has evolved from the Lebanon Seminary, founded by Methodist circuit riders in 1828. Later the institution's name was changed to McKendree in honor of Bishop William McKendree, America's first native-born Methodist bishop, who fought with Washington in the Revolutionary War. McKendree also has campuses in Louisville and Radcliff, Kentucky.

McKendree's liberal arts core fosters qualities that employers and graduate school programs are seeking, such as critical thinking, problem solving, and verbal and written communication. Built on this classic foundation, a McKendree College education stands the test of time. Because the College's general education curriculum encompasses several key disciplines, students can more easily understand the relationships among literature, art, history, economics, and the natural and social sciences. A student's ability to recognize these decisions, and to make decisions based upon them, makes him or her a better employee.

Students' voices are heard at McKendree, and their viewpoints are important. Much time is spent outside the classroom. One way for students to enhance their lives is by helping others improve their lives. Community service is a key part of the College's institutional mission and a commitment shared by its students. Students build houses in the U.S. and abroad, work on Indian reservations in the Southwest, tutor children, assist the elderly, and visit homeless shelters.

Because many McKendree activities are run by students, leadership opportunities are available. Students can organize the Model United Nations program, a semiannual campus program for high school students; direct a community service program; serve on student government; be a resident assistant; manage the orientation program for new students; or find their own niches. Opportunities for activities are further enriched by the 1,200 campus-based students.

A variety of student services are available, including a career, personal counseling, and placement center. This center offers many psychological and career-oriented tests that assist students in making career choices and successfully finding employment.

Many students choose to live on campus to more fully experience the benefits of a traditional campus environment. Residence halls are equipped with private phone lines, cable television access, microfridges (combination microwave/refrigerator units), and computer terminals networked to the College mainframe and the Internet. On-campus apartments feature a clubhouse and a swimming pool. Dining options are available in Ames Dining Hall and the Lair snack bar.

Classic facilities at McKendree include Old Main and Bothwell Chapel, which were completed in 1851 and 1858, respectively. Other traditional facilities include the Lair (student union); Holman Library; a fitness center, track, and field; and the College's convocation center, which features a 1,600-seat gym. Presently under construction, the new Marion K. Piper Academic Center will house state-of-the-art classrooms and a computer center, faculty and admission offices, and a large student lounge.

Participation in athletics is a tradition at McKendree. The College fields intercollegiate teams in baseball, basketball, bowling, cross-country, football, golf, soccer, swimming, tennis, and track and field for men and in basketball, bowling, cross-country, golf, soccer, softball, swimming, tennis, track and field, and volleyball for women. It also offers intramural activities. The playing fields, Melvin Price Convocation Center, and the fitness center are usually available for student recreation from 9 a.m. to 11 p.m. daily. In addition, there are five fraternities, three sororities, and many other social, specialized, and honors organizations that provide a rich social and academic atmosphere.

Location

Combining a rural setting with proximity to Fairview Heights and St. Louis, McKendree provides an ideal balance. The College is in the heart of a quiet community where safety and serenity are easy to find. Lebanon offers shops and entertainment establishments, including the Looking Glass Playhouse community theater. The exciting cultural, recreational, and professional opportunities of St. Louis are less than 25 minutes from campus. St. Louis also features Fortune 500 companies, professional sports teams, shopping, and entertainment. The nearby city of Fairview Heights offers many facilities for shopping, entertainment, and part-time employment. St. Clair Square, a shopping mall with more than ninety stores, is only 15 minutes from Lebanon. Major rail, bus, and air transportation serve St. Louis. Lebanon is within 20 miles of Interstate Highways 70, 64, and 55.

Majors and Degrees

McKendree College awards the Bachelor of Arts degree with majors in biology, English, history, international relations, mathematics, music, organizational communication, philosophy, political science, psychology, psychology with an emphasis in social work, religious studies, religious studies with an emphasis in Christian studies, social science, sociology, sociology with an emphasis in criminal justice, sociology with an emphasis in social work, speech communication, and speech with an emphasis in public relations; the Bachelor of Business Administration with majors in accounting, business administration, economics/finance, management, and marketing; the Bachelor of Fine Arts with majors in art and art education; the Bachelor of Science with majors in athletic training, biology, chemistry, computing and information science, mathematics, medical technology, and physical education; and the Bachelor of Science in Education with a major in business education and elementary education. An upper-division Bachelor of Science in Nursing program is open to currently licensed RNs. McKendree offers preprofessional programs in dentistry, law, medicine, optometry, theology, and veterinary medicine. A 3-2 program with Washington University offers occupational therapy as an option. In addition to these academic areas, minors are offered in coaching, French, gender studies, German, journalism, Spanish, and theater.

Academic Program

McKendree College endorses the philosophy of a career-oriented liberal arts education. A broad-based core program promotes skills in oral and written communication and in analytical and comprehensive thought. Course work in the majors covers theory and current practice relevant to each area. Emphasis is placed on special projects, as well as on individually designed majors and individualized instruction. The spring and fall semesters are supplemented by a summer session. The College also provides courses on a one-month, six-week, and eight-week format.

All candidates for a Bachelor of Arts or a Bachelor of Science degree must complete a minimum of 128 semester credits and maintain a minimum grade point average of 2.0. A general education core curriculum of 40 credit hours is also required.

Credit can be applied toward a degree through the College-Level Examination Program (CLEP). Credit earned through the

United States Armed Forces Institute or through DANTES can also be applied toward a degree provided that the credits are not duplicated and are normally acceptable for a liberal arts degree.

McKendree cooperates with Parks College of Saint Louis University and Southern Illinois University at Edwardsville in offering Air Force and Army Reserve Officer Training Corps (ROTC) programs.

Academic Facilities

Voigt Science Hall, the first building to be completed in McKendree's expansion during the mid-sixties, houses laboratories and lecture rooms for biology, chemistry, and mathematics as well as classrooms for other liberal arts programs. Clark Hall provides general classroom space, offices, and computer laboratories. Benson Wood Art Building offers studio space for painting, sculpture, and ceramics. The new Piper Center will enhance present facilities, with state-of-the-art classrooms and computer facilities.

Holman Library, one of the most beautiful of the modern buildings on campus, holds more than 74,000 microfilm titles, periodicals, volumes, and audiovisual aids and is linked to ILLINET (an automated library system that enables students to borrow books from most Illinois colleges). Individual study carrels, special facilities for a videotape laboratory, and several seminar rooms in which small classes or study groups meet make Holman adaptable and one of the more frequented buildings on campus.

Costs

Tuition is $410 per hour or $13,120 for 32 semester hours, the regular full load, in 2000–01. Room and board costs are $4570 for a double room and fifteen meals a week. Private rooms are available at a higher cost. The average cost for books is $876 per year.

Financial Aid

More than 85 percent of McKendree's students receive financial aid. Students may receive Federal Pell Grants, Illinois Student Assistance Commission MAP Grants, Federal Perkins Loans, Federal Stafford Student Loans, and Federal Work-Study Program awards. McKendree students are eligible for need-based grants and for academic, community service, and athletic scholarships. All students applying for scholarships, need-based grants, or student loans are required to complete the Free Application for Federal Student Aid (FAFSA). Financial aid application forms are available at McKendree's Financial Aid Office. Students are advised to complete all forms as soon as possible before enrolling in classes. The announcement of financial aid packages is usually made within two weeks after all material has been received by the College. All financial aid packages are computed on an individual basis.

Faculty

The majority of McKendree's full-time faculty members hold terminal degrees. Some specialized courses are taught by part-time faculty members, who lend their expertise in various one-month and one-semester programs. The student-teacher ratio is 15:1; the average class size is 20. All full-time faculty members are trained in academic counseling and advising. Faculty members also sponsor and participate in various student organizations and activities. McKendree students do not receive instruction from graduate assistants.

Student Government

McKendree offers an ideal atmosphere for student involvement. Members of the College's student body participate actively in all facets of academic and social life. Students are represented on committees ranging from entertainment and the Model United Nations to instructor-evaluation groups and the Board of Trustees.

Admission Requirements

The primary criterion for admission as a freshman is the student's cumulative high school record, as evidenced by his or her transcript. Applicants must satisfy two of the following: a minimum of 2.5 on a 4.0 scale, a minimum score of 20 on the ACT, or ranking in the top 50 percent of their class. In special circumstances, students without these qualifications may be considered for admission if, by test or other evidence, they show promise of being able to do college work successfully. The College may require an interview as part of the admission process.

McKendree welcomes transfer students. They must submit records of all postsecondary work, plus high school transcripts, and must have a cumulative college GPA of 2.0 or better. No course completed with a grade below C will be accepted for transfer.

All applicants are encouraged to visit the campus to speak with counselors, faculty members, and students and should notify the Office of Admissions in advance of their visit. Questions concerning admissions or campus visits should be directed to the Office of Admissions.

Application and Information

Students are encouraged to apply early in their senior year of high school. Transfer students may apply at any time before the start of the fall or spring semester. Inquiries, application materials, transcripts, and test scores should be addressed to:

Office of Admissions
McKendree College
701 College Road
Lebanon, Illinois 62254
Telephone: 618-537-6831
         800-BEARCAT (toll-free)
E-mail: scordon@atlas.mckendree.edu
World Wide Web: http://www.mckendree.edu

McKendree's new pep band performs at a football game.

McMURRY UNIVERSITY
ABILENE, TEXAS

The University

Founded in 1923 and affiliated with the United Methodist Church, McMurry University is a four-year, coeducational, liberal arts college that strives to maintain the highest academic standards possible while building its liberal and professional programs. Although most of the 1,400 students come from Texas and New Mexico, a total of twenty-three states and seven countries are represented in the student body. The students at McMurry also represent a wide range of religious affiliations: United Methodist, 31 percent; Baptist, 26 percent; Catholic, 11 percent; others and no preference, 32 percent.

Fifty-four percent of the full-time students live on campus in the residence halls. Approximately 39 percent of the eligible full-time students are members of local fraternities or sororities. All students are allowed to have cars.

McMurry University is active in the American Southwest Conference, a pioneering conference that has successfully implemented the student-athlete concept. The University is also a member of NCAA Division III. Baseball, basketball, cross-country, football, golf, swimming, tennis, and track are offered for men; basketball, cross-country, golf, swimming, tennis, track, and volleyball are offered for women. An active intramural sports program in both team and individual competition is available for students year-round.

All students are encouraged to try out for one of the choirs, the band, or theatrical productions. Each program offers a limited number of scholarships based on talent. Art exhibits of work by students and faculty members, as well as various invitational and traveling shows, are shown regularly in the art gallery of the Ryan Fine Arts Center and the Gypsy Ted Gallery.

Location

McMurry University is an important part of Abilene, Texas, a 114-year-old community of about 110,000 people. Abilene is centrally located in west-central Texas, 151 miles west of Fort Worth, 250 miles northwest of San Antonio, and 165 miles southeast of Lubbock.

Concerts; the Civic Ballet; the Philharmonic Orchestra; the Abilene Zoo; the Abilene Community Theatre; the Intercollegiate Orchestra and Opera; a children's, historical, and art museum; and the Abilene Repertory Theatre are some of the cultural and recreational resources to which McMurry students have access and in which many participate. Three local television stations and a morning newspaper provide excellent coverage of McMurry events. Abilene also has a shopping mall, movie theaters, and fine restaurants. Lakes in the area offer many opportunities for outdoor activities.

Majors and Degrees

Seven undergraduate baccalaureate degrees are offered: the Bachelor of Arts, Bachelor of Business Administration, Bachelor of Fine Arts, Bachelor of Music, Bachelor of Music Education, Bachelor of Science, and Bachelor of Science in Nursing.

The B.A. is offered in art, chemistry, communication, English, French (intercollege program), German (intercollege program), history, mathematics, music (church, instrumental, organ, piano, and vocal), philosophy, political science, psychology, religion, sociology, Spanish, and theater. The B.F.A. is offered in painting, ceramics, and theater. The B.S. is offered in biochemistry, biology, chemistry, computer science, education, environmental science, exercise and sports studies, mathematics, mathematics-computer science, natural science, and physics. The B.B.A. offers areas of concentration in accounting, computer information systems, economics, finance, general business, health-care administration, management, marketing, and multimedia studies. The B.M. is offered in music with an emphasis in church music. The B.M.E. is offered with concentrations in instrumental music (secondary level) and vocal music (all levels).

Preprofessional programs are offered in dentistry, engineering, law, medicine, the ministry, pharmacy, physical therapy, and veterinary medicine.

Academic Program

All degree programs at McMurry University are built upon a liberal arts core curriculum of three interdisciplinary courses as well as general education requirements in six areas: written and oral communication, health fitness, fine arts, humanities, science and mathematics, and social sciences.

Because the core curriculum was designed to expand students' choices in meeting basic degree requirements, students are strongly urged to consult with their faculty advisers regarding course selections. Core curriculum requirements in specific areas may be met by earning acceptable scores on the College Board's Advanced Placement (AP) examinations or College-Level Examination Program (CLEP) subject examinations.

Although requirements vary within departments, a candidate for the baccalaureate must complete satisfactorily not fewer than 126 semester hours of work, including the core curriculum requirements.

Opportunities for innovative and concentrated study are available to students in the May Term, a three-week miniterm following the spring semester. Courses are designed to explore, in experimental and innovative ways, academic areas not normally treated in the regular semesters. The May Term is followed by two 5-week summer terms.

The Servant Leadership Program promotes the idea that Servant Leaders will lead others by being servants first, seeking the best for those they lead. It is a unified curricular and cocurricular program, combining ethics, leadership, and service to the community.

Off-Campus Arrangements

Through a consortium agreement with Abilene Christian University and Hardin-Simmons University (both in Abilene), McMurry students may take course work for credit at any of the three institutions. In addition, library holdings at McMurry and the two other universities are available to students from any of the three institutions through a shared online computerized system.

Academic Facilities

The University provides excellent opportunities for academic growth, including a fully equipped science center containing laboratory facilities for biology, chemistry, geology, and physics; fine arts facilities; two theaters, a recital hall, rehearsal rooms, and a band hall; and physical education facilities, including the physical education center, auxiliary gymnasium, football field, field house, track, tennis courts, a baseball field, and an indoor swimming pool.

McMurry's computer center has a DEC computer system and microcomputer labs with Macintosh and PC-compatible microcomputers. There are student computer facilities in the Jay-Rollins Library; the Education Building; the Academic Enrichment Center; biology, chemistry, foreign languages, computer science, and psychology labs; and the writing and math classrooms. Numerous software packages are available for student use at these locations. The computer-to-student ratio on campus is 1:6. All students have access to the Internet through University labs and from their residence hall rooms.

The Jay-Rollins Library at McMurry University has more than 143,000 volumes and offers access to more than 900,000 additional volumes in Abilene through the Abilene Library Consortium. The library is also a member of the Online Computer Library Center and the AMIGOS Bibliographic Council. An interactive distance learning classroom, an observation classroom, and a faculty lab for interactive research were added in fall 1999.

The McMurry student affairs division provides most student services under the direction of the Dean of Student Affairs. Among the offices and services provided are residential life, new student orientation, judicial affairs, the United Methodist Campus Center, the Office of Student Activities, campus recreation, career services, counseling, and handicapped student services. The health service, security office, international student affairs, and a wellness center also fall within student affairs. The University also provides an Academic Enrichment Center that provides both tutoring and access to state-of-the-art computing equipment.

Costs

The average yearly costs for a student entering in the 1999–2000 academic year, including tuition, fees, books, supplies, room, and board, were $14,519. Personal expenses and transportation costs obviously vary a great deal but can be estimated at $2349 a year.

Financial Aid

Financial aid is awarded by the Office of Financial Aid and includes Federal Pell Grants, Federal Supplemental Educational Opportunity Grants (FSEOG), Texas Tuition Equalization Grants (TEG), TEXAS Grants, State Student Incentive Grants (SSIG), College Access Loans (CAL), academic scholarships, transfer scholarships, honors scholarships, ministerial scholarships, Federal Perkins Loans, Federal Work-Study awards, Texas Work-Study, Institutional Work Program, Federal Stafford Student Loans (subsidized and unsubsidized), PLUS Loans, and endowed scholarships. In addition, activity scholarships are available in art, music (instrumental and vocal), speech, and theater. An international scholarship is also awarded annually. Students applying for financial aid should submit the Free Application for Federal Student Aid (FAFSA) and a McMurry Financial Aid Request Form and be approved for admission.

Faculty

Classes and laboratories at McMurry University are taught by regular faculty members, and those holding earned doctorates teach at all levels. Approximately 83 percent of the faculty has earned a doctorate or an equivalent terminal degree. The student-faculty ratio is 17:1. Each student is assigned a faculty member who serves as an academic adviser for individual counseling on degree planning, and members of the faculty are involved in many other phases of student life.

Student Government

The most inclusive of the McMurry University student organizations is the Student Association. Composed of all students at the University, this organization exists primarily to promote democratic expression and exercise of student opinion and to represent, serve, and assist students in matters relating to student social life, activities, and elections. The leadership of the Student Association is vested in the McMurry Student Government, which is divided into executive, judicial, and legislative branches. Student Government provides student representation on the University's Board of Trustees as well as on many faculty committees. All officers of the Student Association are elected by the student body or appointed by the Executive Council with Senate confirmation.

Admission Requirements

Candidates for admission should be graduates or prospective graduates of an accredited secondary school. Students are eligible to apply at any time after completion of the junior year in high school. The high school transcript and scores from the ACT or SAT I are required for consideration. High school grades and class rank, quality of high school program, test scores, extracurricular activities, and leadership potential are all considered in the admission decision. Although not required, an on-campus interview is strongly recommended. Sixty-seven percent of the entering students in 1999 graduated in the top third of their high school class, and 53 percent were in the top quarter. The College-Level Examination Program (CLEP) subject exams may be taken to earn course credit and advanced placement. McMurry University welcomes applications for admission from all qualified students regardless of sex, age, race, color, national origin, religion, or handicap.

Application and Information

A completed admission application form, a $20 nonrefundable application fee, scores on the ACT or SAT I, and a high school transcript or a transcript from each college attended must be submitted to McMurry University. Each application is considered as it is completed, with earlier applications receiving preference. Housing and financial aid cannot be guaranteed until the student has been approved for admission.

Director of Admissions
Box 278
McMurry University
Abilene, Texas 79697
Telephone: 915-793-4700
           800-460-2392 (toll-free)
Fax: 915-793-4718
E-mail: admissions.mcm.edu
World Wide Web: http://www.mcm.edu/

MCP HAHNEMANN UNIVERSITY
College of Nursing and Health Professions

PHILADELPHIA, PENNSYLVANIA

The University and The School

MCP Hahnemann University (MCPHU) is an academic health center that includes more than 2,700 students in its School of Medicine, College of Nursing and Health Professions, and School of Public Health. The University grants degrees from the associate through the doctorate in more than forty programs. It has a rich heritage spanning two centuries of health-care education. Hahnemann University was founded in 1848, while Medical College of Pennsylvania was founded in 1850. In 1993 the two schools consolidated into one institution.

The student population is not only culturally diverse but also age-diverse, ranging from high school graduates to older adults. The University is also sensitive to the many time constraints placed on today's students, so many programs offer flexible scheduling.

MCPHU has adapted to changing health-care and health-system trends via continually updated curricula, leading-edge technology and equipment, and continuing education and development for its faculty members. The University is accredited by the Middle States Association of Colleges and Schools.

The University offers undergraduate and graduate programs in the College of Nursing and Health Professions as well as graduate programs in the School of Public Health. Biomedical graduate programs are offered through the University's School of Medicine.

The College of Nursing and Health Professions offers students an opportunity to develop an understanding of the roles, responsibilities, and interrelationships of all members of the health-care team. Students interact with other University members through classroom and clinical experiences and through student activities such as lectures and films, social events, intramural sports, publications, and student government and organizations. Assistance is provided through the Student Counseling Center, the Office of International Programs and Services, Student Health Services, Multicultural Programs and Services, and the Office of University Student Life. A one-year nondegree program, HEART (Health Education And Related Training), is available to strengthen academic skills. Tutorial and counseling support are offered by Academic Enrichment Services/Act 101 for state residents and through the Student Resource Center for other students.

Stiles Alumni Hall, a sixteen-story building, is the University's housing facility, located one block north of the Center City campus. It contains 195 carpeted apartments, furnished and unfurnished, with various floor plans to accommodate single or shared occupancy. Information about off-campus housing may be obtained from the Office of Residential Life.

Location

All undergraduate programs are offered in Philadelphia on the University's Center City campus, while the Emergency Medical Services' baccalaureate, bachelor's degree completion programs, and the Master of Science program are also offered at Allegheny on the University's Pittsburgh campus. On the Center City campus, students have easy access to all the attractions of central Philadelphia and can partake of the many historic, cultural, scientific, sports, entertainment, and dining advantages of the city—many within walking distance. MCPHU is convenient to and accessible by bus, rail, and subway lines. New York City, Atlantic City and other New Jersey shore points, the Pocono Mountains, and Washington, D.C., are but a few of the recreational areas within a 1- to 3-hour commute of the University.

Majors and Degrees

The Associate of Arts degree is available in humanities and sciences. The Associate of Science degree is offered in emergency medical services, humanities and sciences, and radiologic technology.

The Bachelor of Arts degree is available in humanities and sciences. The Bachelor of Science degree is offered in addictions counseling sciences, biomedical sciences preprofessional studies, cardiovascular perfusion technology, emergency medical services, humanities and sciences, mental health technology, physician assistant studies. Nursing B.S.N. and RN-B.S.N. programs are also available.

A certificate is available in radiologic technology. A postbaccalaureate certificate of completion option is offered in physician assistant studies.

Academic Program

Candidates for graduation must have fulfilled all course requirements in the major curriculum prescribed by the program director. Associate degree candidates must have completed course work equivalent to a minimum of 60 semester hours with a minimum cumulative grade point average of 2.0 on a 4.0 scale. In addition, the following distributional requirements must be met: 3 semester hours each of social sciences, humanities, and natural sciences and 6 semester hours of English (6 semester hours in college-level composition, 6 semester hours in combined college-level composition and literature, or 3 semester hours in college-level composition and 3 semester hours in literature).

Bachelor's degree candidates must have completed course work equivalent to a minimum of 120 semester hours with a minimum cumulative grade point average of 2.0. In addition, the following distributional requirements must be met: 3 semester hours each of mathematics/statistics and computer science; 6 semester hours each of humanities and natural sciences; 6 semester hours of English (see above); and 12 semester hours of social sciences (3 semester hours of health administration and management may be selected in lieu of 3 semester hours of a social science at the program director's discretion).

Academic Facilities

For clinical experience and research, students have ready access to the University's comprehensive system of health care, including tertiary-care adult hospitals, a specialty children's hospital, community hospitals, and a large number of practice sites. The libraries and supporting services provide specialized facilities for a variety of research projects, and microcomputer facilities, including word processing, graphics and computer-assisted instruction, and online search capabilities, are available to all students. Photocopiers, group study rooms, individual study carrels, and a 24-hour study lounge are available. The University's location in Philadelphia provides access to other excellent science and medical libraries.

Costs

The cost of tuition for 1999–2000 ranged from $4880 to $5735 per semester for full-time students and from $390 to $480 per credit for part-time students. The certificate program in radiologic technology was $1000 per semester for full-time students. There was a $40 laboratory fee for certain lab courses. Room and board costs ranged from $7200 for off-campus commuters to $8550 for University housing. Books and supplies were estimated at $650 per year.

Financial Aid

MCPHU awards funds to students from loan programs and numerous scholarship and grant programs. Awards are based on financial need, with the neediest students funded first. Some scholarship funds are awarded to students based on both financial need and academic merit. Students must complete the Free Application for Federal Student Aid (FAFSA) form to be considered for any aid from the University.

Faculty

The College of Nursing and Health Professions graduate and undergraduate faculty members are the same group in many cases, but generally are program-specific at the graduate or undergraduate level. It is primarily a teaching faculty, although the University does have a mandate to increase its research base; several departments are already well funded and others are making strides in that direction.

The faculty members are not resident. Many are involved in research or scholarship that may enable them to hold such voluntary positions as board members and editors of journals. Generally, the faculty members are involved with and participate in student activities and events. Sixty percent of the full-time faculty members hold advanced degrees. The student-faculty ratio varies according to teaching modality. In the didactic setting the ratio can be as high as 20:1, but in the clinical setting it ranges between 8:1 and 1:1, according to specific program accreditation standards and requirements. The counseling duties of the faculty members primarily involve course and thesis/dissertation advisement, but often include career advisement. This varies according to departmental needs.

Student Government

Students are encouraged to express their views. The student-run Student Senate is the governing body of the school and is composed of 5 officers and a representative from each class of each program. It represents student views and speaks to the faculty members and administration regularly. Students must maintain at least a 3.0 grade point average to hold committee positions.

In addition to appointing student representatives to University committees, the Senate also participates in the Student Council, which involves student leaders from each of the three student governments at MCPHU. Active membership on faculty, University, and School administrative committees provides students with a forum in which to express their views and vote on matters of student interest, including institutional and academic policies.

Admission Requirements

In general, applicants must submit a completed application form along with official high school transcript(s) or a GED certificate, official transcript(s) from each college and/or university attended, and scores from the SAT I or ACT. Students should check the application for more specific information on which applicants are required to submit SAT I and/or TOEFL scores.

Each request to apply transfer credits is considered individually. Only credits in which the applicant has earned a grade of 2.0 (C) or higher on a 4.0 scale will be considered. A passing grade is acceptable for courses taken on a pass/fail basis.

Applicants who are not United States citizens must submit all necessary documentation to satisfy U.S. Immigration and Naturalization Service requirements before admission is offered. All international applicants must provide proof of their ability to cover tuition and all living expenses while in student status.

Application and Information

For specific application deadlines for the various programs, interested students should contact the Office of Enrollment at the address below.

Admission information and material can be requested from:

Office of Enrollment
MCP Hahnemann University
245 North 15th Street
Mail Stop 472
Philadelphia, Pennsylvania 19102-1192
Telephone: 215-762-8288
E-mail: enroll@mcphu.edu
World Wide Web: http://www.mcphu.edu

MEMORIAL UNIVERSITY OF NEWFOUNDLAND
ST. JOHN'S AND CORNER BROOK, NEWFOUNDLAND, CANADA

The University

Memorial University is the only university in the Canadian province of Newfoundland and Labrador. Established as a college in 1925, the institution became a full-fledged university in 1949. Today Memorial is the largest Canadian center of research east of Montreal. Much of that research focuses on the North Atlantic Ocean, which has dictated the province's history and evolution. Publicly funded, Memorial University recognizes in its mission statement a special obligation to serve its home province. In meeting that obligation, Memorial has fostered groundbreaking research in areas ranging from marine biology to maritime history, folklore to aquaculture, and naval architecture to linguistics.

There are approximately 16,000 students at Memorial University. About 90 percent come from Newfoundland and Labrador; the remaining 10 percent includes students from every province in Canada, the United States, and about 100 other countries.

Most of the programs are based at the largest campus, in the center of St. John's, close to recreation, sports facilities, cultural outlets, and the city's historic downtown. Almost all the buildings are linked by a system of skywalks and underground tunnels, allowing resident students to wear shorts to class even in the middle of winter.

Also located in St. John's is the Marine Institute, a center for training in ocean-related careers, from navigation to aquaculture. Officially merged with Memorial University in 1992, the Marine Institute has won international acclaim for its innovation and research.

Sir Wilfred Grenfell College, in Corner Brook, is a small liberal arts college with about 1,200 students. Memorial's fine arts degree programs are offered here, as are interdisciplinary degrees in arts and sciences. The college is known for its intimate atmosphere and the personal attention and assistance given to each student.

Location

Newfoundland is Canada's easternmost province. Physically separated from the rest of the country, it has a distinct cultural identity. The music, art, and theater reflect a culture tied to the land and, especially, the ocean. St. John's, the capital at the extreme eastern edge of the country, has a population of about 175,000. Corner Brook, on the west coast of the island portion of the province, has about 25,000 people. Both cities are home to professional theater companies. The spectacular and unspoiled terrain draws tourists from all over the world for activities such as whale watching, hiking, skiing, canoeing, and photography. Newfoundlanders are famous for their friendliness, and the cultural and social opportunities are well known.

The province has a very low crime rate and numerous parks, and even from the densest urban centers, open country is never more than a few minutes' drive.

Majors and Degrees

The general Bachelor of Arts and the Bachelor of Arts (Honors) degrees at the St. John's campus are offered with majors in anthropology (archaeology/physical or social/cultural), Canadian studies (general only), classics (classical studies, Greek, or Latin), computer science, drama and music (general only), economics, English language and literature (language and theater/drama specializations), folklore, French, geography, German, history, linguistics, mathematics, medieval studies (general only), philosophy, political science, psychology, religious studies, Russian, sociology, sociology/anthropology, and Spanish. Degrees can be completed with joint majors or with a major and minor. Minors can be taken in most of the areas above or in aboriginal studies, business administration, law and society, medieval studies, music, Newfoundland studies, Russian studies, women's studies, or any of Memorial's science departments.

The interdisciplinary Bachelor of Arts degree at Sir Wilfred Grenfell College is offered in English (Canadian literature, dramatic literature, or modern literature), environmental studies (environmental perspectives or environmental pursuits), historical studies, humanities, psychology, and social/cultural studies. The Bachelor of Fine Arts degree is offered in theater (acting or stagecraft) and visual arts. A Bachelor of Science degree in environmental science is also offered. In addition, students may complete the first two years of the University of New Brunswick's Bachelor of Science program in forestry. The four-year Bachelor of Nursing Collaborative Program is available at the Western Regional School of Nursing in Corner Brook.

Memorial's Faculty of Business Administration offers the Bachelor of Business Administration as well as the Bachelor of Commerce, a cooperative degree, with concentrations available in accounting, finance, human resources and labor relations, information systems, management science, marketing, and small business/entrepreneurship. In addition, a Bachelor of Arts/Bachelor of Commerce co-operative program is now offered.

The Bachelor of Education is offered with degree options in primary education, elementary education, intermediate/secondary education, music education, Native and northern education, postsecondary education, and special education.

The Bachelor of Engineering, a co-op degree, is offered in the disciplines of civil engineering (construction and structural or environmental and municipal options), electrical engineering (computer and communication or electrical options), mechanical engineering (design or manufacturing options), and ocean and naval architectural engineering.

The Bachelor of Music degree is offered with majors in music history and literature, performance, theory and composition, and general music studies. The conjoint B.Mus./B.Mus.Ed degree is available as a five-year program in cooperation with the Faculty of Education.

The Bachelor of Science and Bachelor of Science (Honors) degrees are offered in biochemistry, biology, chemistry, computer science, computer science and geography, computer science and physics, earth sciences, earth sciences/physics, environmental sciences (Grenfell College only), geography, mathematics and statistics, physics and physical oceanography, psychology, pure mathematics/computer science, and statistics/computer science. Bachelor of Science (Joint Honors) degrees are offered in applied mathematics/chemistry, applied mathematics/physics, behavioral neuroscience, biology and earth sciences, biology/psychology, cell biology/microbiology and biochemistry, chemistry/biochemistry, computer science and geography, computer science and physics, dietetics, earth sciences/chemistry, earth sciences/physics, geography/earth sciences, nutrition, physics/biochemistry, physics/chemistry, pure mathematics/computer science, pure mathematics/statistics, statistics/biology, and statistics/computer science.

The University also offers the degrees of Bachelor of Kinesiology, Bachelor of Maritime Studies, Bachelor of Nursing, Bachelor of Physical Education/Bachelor of Physical Education (Honors) (general or teaching options), Bachelor of Recreation, Bachelor of Science (Pharmacy), and Bachelor of Social Work.

Academic Program

The academic year has three semesters: fall (September to December); winter (January to April); and spring (May to August). Some programs admit students in September only, while others can be started in any semester. Two 6-week sessions in the spring semester offer concentrated study opportunities; however, course offerings in the spring semester are limited in number. Most programs take four years (eight semesters) to complete. Exceptions include the B.Eng., which takes six years, including six co-op work terms; the B.Comm., which takes five years, including three work terms; and the B.S.W., which takes a total of five years to complete.

Off-Campus Arrangements

In addition to its three campuses in Newfoundland, Memorial University has a campus in Harlow, England. The Harlow campus is used by various faculties to give students the opportunity of a semester's study abroad. Memorial also operates Institute Frecker on the French island of St-Pierre, just 14 miles off the coast of Newfoundland. A semester of French cultural immersion is available to students of French. The University is a member of CUSEC, an agreement under which students can spend a semester at another Canadian university. Memorial also has about a dozen formal exchange agreements with universities in other countries. Some programs, largely in arts and science, offer "field schools" for credit; students spend several weeks getting credit in other countries for program-related fieldwork. Past field schools have been held in Malta, Greece, Russia, Germany, and Barbados, among other areas.

Academic Facilities

The University has six libraries. The largest, on the St. John's campus, has 1.2 million bound volumes and 17,000 periodical subscriptions. Other Memorial libraries include those at Grenfell College and the Marine Institute, plus specialized libraries for education, medicine, and music. The University is home to several archives and collections. The on-campus computer network is among the most advanced of any educational institution in the world, with more than 100 courses that include some Internet component, and several offered entirely on line. Laboratory and research facilities include the Ocean Sciences Center, a wave tank, and a marine simulator. Theaters, used for student productions, are located in both Corner Brook and St. John's.

Costs

Tuition costs for Canadian students for the 1999–2000 academic year were Can$1650 per semester for a normal five-course program; tuition for international students was Can$3300 per semester. Student organization fees, which include a health and dental plan, were Can$177 per semester for Canadian students; international students must purchase additional health insurance, which costs approximately Can$500 per year. The cost of books and supplies varies by program. The cost of room and board in the St. John's campus residences was about Can$2000 per semester, depending on the meal plan selected.

Financial Aid

Canadian students are eligible for government loans and grants. Memorial University offers scholarships in many areas; a complete listing is found in the University *Calendar*. Renewable scholarships valued up to Can$5000 per academic year are available and are generally awarded on the basis of academic merit. Memorial's award-winning on-campus work experience program provides students with jobs related to their areas of study. In extreme cases, emergency short-term loans are available through the Council of the Students' Union.

Faculty

Memorial University has 1,188 full-time and 143 part-time faculty members, many of whom are world-renowned researchers; all teach at both the graduate and undergraduate levels. The faculty-undergraduate student ratio is about 1:14.

Student Government

There are several student unions at Memorial University. The largest is the Memorial University of Newfoundland Students Union (MUNSU) on the larger St. John's Campus. MUNSU has voting representation on the University's senate and board of regents. It also owns and operates a food court, bar, games room, student-run newspaper, radio station, and child care center. MUNSU funds approximately seventy student organizations, with focuses from the academic to the political and including special interest groups such as student parents and international students.

Admission Requirements

A minimum 70 percent, computed from the grades received on selected final year high school courses (or their equivalents in other provinces and countries), is required for admission to the University. Complete information for specific provinces and countries is available in the University *Calendar* (available on the Web site). Applicants with a first language other than English must have a TOEFL score of 550 or above. Auditions, portfolios, or personal interviews are required for fine arts and music programs. Some programs require a separate application form in addition to the University General Application form. While most qualified applicants are accepted to the Faculties of Arts and Sciences, some departments may limit enrollment. Entry is competitive in other faculties and schools. In the Schools of Social Work, Nursing, Pharmacy, and Medicine, preference is given to applicants from within Newfoundland. Enrollment is also limited in the Faculties of Business Administration, Education, and Engineering, so minimally qualified candidates will not always be accepted.

Application and Information

The general deadline for application for September admission is March 1; applications received after this time are processed as time permits. Deadlines are earlier for some disciplines (e.g., medicine and social work) and later for others (e.g., B.Rec.). Students are advised to contact the University as early as possible to allow sufficient time for applications to be sent, completed, and evaluated and for supporting documentation, where necessary, to be gathered and evaluated.

To inquire or to request application materials, students should contact:

Office of Student Recruitment and Promotion
Memorial University of Newfoundland
St. John's, Newfoundland A1C 5S7
Canada
Telephone: 709-737-8896
Fax: 709-737-8611
E-mail: new.students@mun.ca
World Wide Web: http://www.mun.ca

MENLO COLLEGE
ATHERTON, CALIFORNIA

The College

Menlo College, an independent, coeducational, nonsectarian institution, stands out among institutions of higher education in four exciting ways. First, rather than offer a traditional set of majors as many institutions do, Menlo concentrates on providing excellent programs in liberal arts, management, and mass communications. Menlo's location in the heart of the Silicon Valley allows the College to train tomorrow's leaders in an intimate, student-centered, academically challenging environment. The College is small enough to be a real community but large enough to support a wide array of intercollegiate sports, student organizations, and internship opportunities, giving students the confidence and breadth of experience to flourish after graduation. The College's distinguished alumni provide a strong base of support for graduates, which helps students make the transition from college to career with great success.

A Menlo education is a process of training and cultivating leaders. This process begins with a broad-based liberal arts foundation in the humanities, mathematics, sciences, and social sciences. At the same time, students are challenged to enrich and develop their writing, critical-thinking, and decision-making skills. The result is rich programs staffed with seasoned practitioners who are experts in their respective fields. The advantage is a cutting-edge curriculum that equips students to succeed. In recognition of Menlo's superior business program, the College has earned its place in the *U.S. News & World Report*'s America's Best Colleges edition for four consecutive years. Other programs have been singled out by business executives, entrepreneurs, and industry leaders as illustrations of the type of preparation needed to succeed in the twenty-first century.

The learning process does not end in the classroom. Students are encouraged to participate in internships and study programs that bridge the gap between theory and practice. These opportunities range from Fortune 500 companies to innovative start-up enterprises, from San Francisco to South America, Asia, and Europe. Not only do participants gain hands-on experience, but they also grow personally as they encounter diverse peoples, cultures, and values, whether at home or 10,000 miles away.

As a whole, College-sponsored activities promote self-exploration and often lead to the discovery of hidden talents. Students can participate in a variety of clubs or organizations, ranging from the Alpha Chi National Honor Society and the Poetry, Art, and Music Society to the Menlo Oak Newspaper and the Outdoor Club. Leadership skills are cultivated through an activist student government and student life positions and special workshops that tackle pressing contemporary issues.

This commitment to personal and intellectual growth, coupled with Menlo's ideal location in a major metropolitan area, draws students from all over the United States and all around the world. The global village is a reality at Menlo, given the broad social, religious, cultural, and national makeup of the student body. The appreciation of different cultures that results becomes a tremendous advantages in the marketplace.

Menlo's warm, friendly atmosphere is enhanced by its residential status. Nearly two thirds of all students live in one of five residence halls. Off-campus apartments (for students who are older than 21 or married) are also an option.

For those who enjoy the exhilaration of intercollegiate competition, Menlo offers men's baseball, basketball, cross-country, football, golf, soccer, tennis, and track and field, and women's sports include basketball, cross-country, softball, tennis, track and field, and volleyball. The College competes in the NAIA Pacific Conference and the NCAA Division III. Intramural sports are also available. Almost 30 percent of all students participate in sports.

To meet students' health needs, the College provides care via the Menlo Medical Clinic. Counseling services are offered by faculty and resident life staff members and the Counseling Services Office.

Whether in the classroom, in the laboratory, or on the playing field, Menlo College nurtures students by creating programs, activities, and services that foster individual success.

Location

Menlo College is located on the San Francisco peninsula in the town of Atherton, a residential community near the cities of Menlo Park and Palo Alto. Major freeways do not pass near the campus, nor is heavy industry nearby. The area ranks among the most attractive and exciting in the world, with numerous cultural resources and a temperate climate. San Francisco lies 30 miles to the north. Many other important educational centers are within an hour's drive of Menlo, making the area an exciting place in which to study and live. To the south is Silicon Valley, where high-tech companies in the electronics, computer, aerospace, biotechnology, and pharmaceutical industries are literally transforming the world in which we live and work. Surrounding the San Francisco Bay Area is the great natural beauty of northern California, extending from the spectacular California coast to the majestic Sierra Nevada. Favorite spots such as Big Sur, Monterey Bay, Lake Tahoe, Napa Valley, and Yosemite National Park can be reached in a half-day's drive from Menlo.

Majors and Degrees

Menlo College offers a Bachelor of Science in Management degree program with concentrations in environmental resource management, general management, international management, management information systems, and sports management. The Bachelor of Arts degree is offered in the fields of mass communications, with emphases in electronic communication arts, media management, and media studies, and in the field of liberal arts, with specializations in environmental policy and planning, humanities, international policy studies, and psychology.

Academic Program

Menlo College operates on a semester calendar. To earn a bachelor's degree, students must complete 124 units of credit and maintain good academic standing.

The Management Program provides a comprehensive management education based on a rigorous core modeled after the M.B.A. program.

The Mass Communications Program gives students a broad understanding of communication processes through a carefully selected core curriculum. Students are encouraged to pursue their studies with managerial and leadership goals in mind.

The Liberal Arts Program affords an interdisciplinary foundation and the intellectual essence of the management curriculum while integrating the humanities and social sciences.

The Academic Success Program and Learning Resource Center provide dynamic resources for increasing students' academic ability and morale. Included are innovative approaches to tutoring and developmental courses. The goal is to assist faculty members in meeting the needs of a varied student population using an assortment of individualized, small-group, and computer-based instruction. This method facilitates study and discussion of course material, tutoring, and test preparation.

Off-Campus Arrangements

The difference between obtaining an exciting professional position with opportunity for advancement and growth and settling for second best often comes down to experience. Internships enable students to apply theory to practice—to take classroom knowledge and test its relevancy. Through the Career Services Office and each academic department, qualified students are urged to participate in local, national, or international internships. As juniors or seniors, students spend one or more semesters working off campus in their fields of study obtaining academic credit and/or financial compensation and valuable insight.

Academic Facilities

Bowman Library maintains a superb collection of books and periodicals, supplemented by holdings in microform, computer software programs, and videocassettes. Networked CD-ROM workstations provide access to general and specialized periodicals and reference resources as well as the Internet and World Wide Web. Other workstations provide access to electronic databases offering abstracts and images of selected journal articles. Students can tap into the resources of academic, technical, and public libraries in the surrounding area and nationwide through Menlo's membership in a number of library cooperative networks. The library contains rooms for group study, viewing videocassettes and microforms, and photocopying.

Menlo College's four computer labs provide students with access to state-of-the-art PC and Macintosh hardware, software, and networking capabilities. All computer-lab equipment is connected to the campus network as well as the Internet and World Wide Web. Classroom labs include both individual workstations and presentation facilities. The Open Access lab is available more than 95 hours per week and is staffed by experienced monitors who are familiar with all lab equipment and applications and are able to provide students with the best possible technical and instructional services. With a 5:1 student-computer ratio, Menlo College offers students ample access to a wide range of computing resources for both classroom assignments and personal use.

Costs

Tuition for 1999–2000 was $16,800. Residence costs, including room and board, were $6800. Student body fees were $200.

Financial Aid

Menlo is noted for a strong program of merit and need-based aid. Approximately 70 percent of Menlo's students enroll with financial assistance, including Menlo scholarships, achievement awards, and on-campus employment as well as Federal Pell Grants, Federal Stafford Student Loans, State of California Grants, Federal PLUS loans, and others. Students transferring to Menlo are fully eligible to be considered for financial aid. Merit scholarships of up to $10,000 per year are available for both domestic and international students.

Faculty

Menlo's faculty members devote their full attention to teaching. The College faculty is composed of approximately 60 educators, both full- and part-time. Guest lecturers from business, industry, and other professions add to the breadth of instruction. Faculty members are readily available to give students personal help and counseling. A student-teacher ratio of 10:1 allows for small classes and individual attention to students' progress.

Student Government

Students elect their own representatives to student government, which is responsible for legislative and executive decisions affecting student activities and the coordination of student affairs. At Menlo, students take the lead in shaping their education and the future of their college.

Admission Requirements

The Admission Committee considers each candidate individually, through the assessment of academic achievement and personal qualities, talents, and interests. There is an early decision plan for entering freshmen, and transfer students are welcome. Applicants are evaluated on the basis of their academic record (minimum 2.5 GPA), course of study, personal recommendations, school activities, essay, and scores on either the SAT I or ACT. A personal visit is strongly recommended but not required. The College looks for freshmen with both breadth and depth of academic background in college preparatory subjects. Transfer students are evaluated on the strength of their college programs. Applicants are considered without regard to age, race, color, creed, gender, sexual orientation, national origin, marital status, disability, or any other characteristic protected by law.

Application and Information

Students may enter Menlo College at the opening of the fall or spring semester. For further information concerning admission, students should contact:

Office of Admission
Menlo College
1000 El Camino Real
Atherton, California 94027-4301
Telephone: 650-688-3753
               800-55-MENLO (toll-free)
Fax: 650-617-2395
E-mail: admissions@menlo.edu
World Wide Web: http://www.menlo.edu

MERCER UNIVERSITY
MACON, GEORGIA

The University

Mercer University, a church-related institution founded by Georgia Baptists in 1833, serves a function performed neither by secular institutions nor by churches. It is composed of the College of Liberal Arts, the Stetson School of Business and Economics, the School of Engineering, the Walter F. George School of Law, the School of Medicine, the School of Education, the Southern School of Pharmacy, and the McAfee School of Theology. The College of Liberal Arts, founded more than 160 years ago, is the oldest of the University's schools and remains the center of the educational programs. The Stetson School of Business and Economics was established in 1984 and offers the B.B.A. and M.B.A. degrees in both Macon and Atlanta. The School of Medicine was established in 1982 to provide primary-care physicians for rural, medically underserved areas. The School of Education, established in 1995, is the training school for future educators and teachers. It also works to improve the quality of adult education and to enhance the University's ability to serve the adult student. The School of Engineering opened in 1985 and offers both bachelor's and master's degrees. The School of Law was established in 1873 and was named the Walter F. George School of Law in 1947 in honor of one of its most distinguished alumni. The Southern School of Pharmacy, which is located in Atlanta, was founded in 1903 and became a part of Mercer University in 1959. The McAfee School of Theology (Atlanta) began in 1996 by offering the Master of Divinity degree.

Two residence halls for men, two for women, four coed halls, and on-campus apartments house approximately 1,400 students. Other facilities on campus include living accommodations for married students and faculty members, the library, science building, infirmary, fraternity and sorority lodges, college bookstore, cafeteria, and recreation areas.

Mercer's undergraduate daytime enrollment is approximately 2,400; 80 percent of the students come from Georgia, and thirty-seven other states and thirty other countries are also represented in the student body. The total undergraduate and graduate enrollment is approximately 7,000. Students are kept informed about special events and programs by the University calendar. The Lamar Lectures and the Insight Lecture Series, for example, bring well-known lecturers and public figures to the campus throughout the year.

In addition to the undergraduate programs listed below, Mercer's School of Education awards Master of Education and Specialist in Education degrees. The Eugene W. Stetson School of Business and Economics awards Master of Business Administration, Master of Science in Health Care Policy and Administration, and Master of Science in Technology Management degrees. The School of Engineering awards the Master of Science in Software Systems, Master of Science in Engineering, and Master of Science in Engineering/Technical Management degrees. The Walter F. George School of Law awards the Juris Doctor (J.D.) and combined J.D./M.B.A. degrees. The School of Medicine awards the Doctor of Medicine (M.D.), Master in Family Therapy (M.F.T.), Master in Family Services (M.F.S.), and Master of Public Health (M.P.H.) degrees. The Southern School of Pharmacy awards the Doctor of Pharmacy (Pharm.D.), Doctor of Philosophy (in pharmaceutical science), Master of Pharmacy Administration, and combined Pharm.D./M.B.A. degrees. The McAfee School of Theology awards the Master of Divinity (M.Div.) degree.

Location

Macon is everything a college town should be; its central location allows easy access to the Georgia coast, the Florida beaches, and the north Georgia mountains. Macon is 75 miles south of Atlanta and is served by two interstate highways, I-75 and I-16. The Macon airport is served by two commuter airlines. Macon is a blend of the old (many historic mansions and sites) and the new. The metropolitan area population is approximately 350,000.

Majors and Degrees

Mercer offers programs of study leading to the Bachelor of Arts, Bachelor of Music Education, Bachelor of Music in Performance, Bachelor of Music in Sacred Music, Bachelor of Science, Bachelor of Business Administration, and Bachelor of Science in Engineering degrees. Majors offered in the College of Liberal Arts include African-American studies, art, biology, chemistry, Christianity, classical studies, communication and theater arts, computer science, earth science, economics, English, environmental science, history, individualized, leadership and community service, mathematics, modern foreign languages (French, German, and Spanish), music (education, performance–vocal and instrumental, and sacred music), natural science, philosophy, physics, political science, psychology, social science, and sociology. Students may elect to minor in anthropology, criminal justice, health physics, photography, women's and gender studies, and most of the major study areas. Within the Stetson School of Business and Economics, students can earn a B.B.A. in accounting, business administration, computer information systems, economics, finance, individualized, international business, management, or marketing.

The School of Engineering offers specializations in nine different areas: biomedical engineering, computer engineering, electrical engineering, environmental engineering, environmental systems technology, industrial engineering, industrial management, mechanical engineering, and technical communication. Minors are available in aerospace engineering and manufacturing.

The School of Education awards degrees in early childhood, middle grades, secondary, and specific learning disabilities.

Students who have successfully completed all appropriate academic requirements at Mercer in a two-year program are automatically eligible for admission to the Southern School of Pharmacy. Preprofessional work is offered in the University for students expecting to enter any of the following professions: dentistry, law, medicine, medical technology, pharmacy, physical therapy, or theology.

Academic Program

The University's curriculum comprises two options in the general education program. In the distributional track, the student takes courses that provide an introduction to some of the major areas of human knowledge and endeavor. Most of this work, which lays the foundation for continued study and for the student's own contribution to society, is carried out during the freshman and sophomore years. During the junior and senior years, the student takes specialized courses in major fields in the upper-division curriculum.

The second option, the Great Books Program, consists of eight courses to be taken in sequence, each course carrying 3 hours of credit. Great Books offers the student a traditional approach to learning. Students read works of such classic thinkers as Plato, Socrates, Milton, and Freud—the works about which textbooks are written. The sequence can begin in the first semester of the freshman year and continues through the first semester of the senior year.

While students at Mercer University are required to complete a major, they are encouraged to explore the many fields of knowledge open to the inquiring mind. A number of special studies courses—often topical and interdisciplinary—are offered each semester. All students have the option of taking two courses each year on a satisfactory/unsatisfactory basis. Many departments offer courses in special topics, independent research, and independent reading. In addition, a student who has a special interest not filled by the traditional majors may apply for permission to complete an independent major, subject to the approval of the dean of the college and a faculty committee.

The usual load is 15 semester hours (five courses) for students in the College of Liberal Arts, the Stetson School of Business and Economics, and the School of Education and 15–18 semester hours (five to six courses) for students in the School of Engineering. A student who maintains a B average may, with the adviser's permission, take an additional course. A student may receive up to 30 hours of credit through the College-Level Examination Program (CLEP). Credit is usually awarded to those who score a 3, 4, or 5 on the Advanced Placement tests of the College Board.

Academic Facilities

Mercer is located on a 130-acre campus. The University's administration building, which overlooks the campus, is listed on the National Register of Historic Places. The University library provides 95,000 square feet of space, has the capacity to house 500,000 books, and contains 24-hour study rooms. Of great importance in the field of English literature are the Shelley and Burns collections. Both are considered the most extensive in the South and are probably among the largest in the United States. The microfilm collection includes a file of the *New York Times* dating from 1951 to the present. The Hugh M. Willet Science Center is equipped with superior scientific equipment and houses the Departments of Biology, Earth Sciences, Chemistry, and Physics. New additions to Mercer's campus include the engineering and classroom building and Stetson Hall, which houses the schools of business and education.

Costs

For 1999–2000, the total cost for a year at Mercer University was $21,617, exclusive of clothes and major travel expenses; $16,290 of this was for tuition and health fees and $5327 was for room and board. The cost of books and academic supplies is estimated at $600 a year.

Financial Aid

Mercer University endeavors to meet the financial aid needs of every qualified student through scholarships, grants, loans, work-study opportunities, or a combination of these. Approximately 65 percent of the student body receives some need-based financial assistance each year. All applicants for financial aid are asked to submit the Free Application for Federal Student Aid (FAFSA) and the Mercer University financial aid form. Mercer also offers non-need-based academic scholarships up to full tuition. Those students who are eligible for scholarships will be notified by letter after acceptance to the University. Georgia residents may be eligible for the Georgia Tuition Equalization Grant and the HOPE Scholarship, which are set by the state each year.

Faculty

There are more than 500 full-time faculty members at Mercer. Faculty members teach at all levels, so that an entering freshman takes courses from professors who also teach graduating seniors. The majority of the faculty members serve as student advisers. The advisory system and the relatively small classes mean that students and faculty members come to know each other well, with the resulting benefits of a cooperative educational endeavor. The faculty-student ratio is 1:18.

Student Government

Recognized student activities at Mercer are directed and sponsored by the Student Government Association. Elected representatives include the president, vice president, secretary-treasurer, and freshman adviser; representatives from each of the four classes and from the University at large; the editors of the three student publications; and the Student Union Activities Board. All of these officers are chosen in a campuswide election each spring. Liberal arts, business, engineering, and education students are equally represented on most major school committees.

Admission Requirements

Mercer is interested in academically well-rounded students. Therefore, no rigid formula for admission is used, and there is flexibility in the admission requirements. The University recommends that a student complete an academic program of 4 years of English, 3 years of math (including Algebra II), 3 years of science, 3 years of social science, and 2 years of foreign language. A student must submit an application and a $25 application fee, a complete high school record showing rank in class, scores on the SAT I of the College Board or the ACT examination, a guidance counselor evaluation, and a list of all extracurricular activities. In 1998–99, approximately 80 percent of all freshman applicants were accepted.

Application and Information

Inquiries regarding admission should be addressed to the director of undergraduate admission. The formal application must be accompanied by a nonrefundable fee of $25; there is no provision for waiver of this fee. The applicant should request that a full record be sent to the director of undergraduate admission by the appropriate officials in his or her high school. Because enrollment at Mercer is limited, students should submit an application as early as possible during the senior year of high school.

For more information, students should contact:

Donna Haley, Associate Director of Undergraduate Admission
Mercer University
1400 Coleman Avenue
Macon, Georgia 31207
Telephone: 912-301-2650
        800-342-0841 (toll-free in Georgia)
        800-637-2378 (toll-free outside Georgia)
E-mail: admissions@mercer.edu
World Wide Web: http://www.mercer.edu

The administration building at Mercer University is on the National Register of Historic Places.

MERCY COLLEGE
DOBBS FERRY, NEW YORK

The College

The history of Mercy College is built upon traditional educational foundations and is rich in progressive achievements and community service. The College is characterized by its innovative approach to education, which is reflected in its responsive and dynamic curriculum that allows the College to provide relevant educational service in rapidly changing times. The student body of 8,359 men and women is a microcosm of the communities the College serves, being diverse in ethnic origin, social background, age, and goals.

The many intellectual interests and social concerns of the student body are fostered by the wide range of extracurricular organizations and activities. Student publications that address these interests and concerns are *Reporter's Impact*, the College newspaper; *The Blue Max*, the College yearbook; and *The Spoken Wheel*, the literary magazine. The Concert and Lecture Bureau, the Women's Forum, and individual departments and programs frequently sponsor outstanding speakers, performances, films, and colloquia. The Mercy College Players and Mercy College Community Chorus provide showcases for students' talents. In addition to having athletic facilities available for recreational purposes, the College sponsors NCAA Division II teams in baseball, basketball, golf, soccer, softball, tennis, and volleyball. In recent years, Mercy teams have won conference and regional championships in soccer, golf, and women's softball.

To meet the multifaceted needs of students, the College provides academic, career, and personal counseling and health services. The flexible scheduling options, weekend classes, distance learning by modem, accelerated B.S. program, home-study programs, writing center, and tutoring services are available to all students. The main campus has a student activities center, a dining hall, a residence hall, a television studio, and a graduate center.

The College offers M.S. degrees in acupuncture and Oriental medicine; human resource management; nursing, with a specialization in family health nursing; organizational leadership; and physical and occupational therapies. Mercy also offers master's degree programs in banking, education–learning technology, education-tricertificate, and organizational leadership.

Location

The College's main campus in Dobbs Ferry is situated on 60 acres of beautifully landscaped grounds overlooking the Hudson River. A sanctuary in the region made famous by Washington Irving, the College enjoys all of the benefits of close community ties in Westchester County and of proximity to New York City. The College is just a 40-minute train ride from Grand Central Station and is easily accessible by car from New York City; Westchester, Rockland, Putnam, and Orange counties; northern New Jersey; and southern Connecticut.

Majors and Degrees

Mercy College offers programs leading to the Master of Arts, Bachelor of Arts, Bachelor of Science, Associate in Arts, and Associate in Science degrees and certificate programs. The major degree program offerings include accounting, behavioral science (specializations in community health, gerontology, and health services management), biology, business administration (specializations in banking, direct marketing, finance, general business administration, industrial and labor relations, international business, management, marketing, office information, and systems and technology), communications studies/television and media, communication disorders, computer information systems, computer science, criminal justice, English literature, film studies, history, interdisciplinary studies, journalism, mathematics (specializations in actuarial science, computer science, and operations research), medical technology, music, nursing (post-RN), occupational therapy, paralegal studies, physical therapy, psychology (specialization in computer research applications), public accounting, public safety (specializations in occupational safety and health administration, and safety administration), social work, sociology (specialization in computer applications), therapeutic recreation, and veterinary technology. Interdisciplinary programs are available in American studies, business leadership, Third World studies, and women's studies. Preprofessional programs are offered in chiropractic, dentistry, law, medical technology, medicine, optometry, nursing, and pharmacy.

Teacher certification is offered in early secondary education, elementary education, music education, secondary education, special education (specializations in teaching of the mentally retarded, the emotionally handicapped, and the learning disabled), teaching English as a second language, and teaching of the speech and hearing handicapped. Tricertification is available in elementary and special education and bilingual education.

Career-oriented certificate programs include accounting, business management, child care, computer science, criminal justice, direct marketing, fire science, general business administration, gerontology, human behavior, journalism and media, liberal studies, management, marketing, occupational safety and health administration, personnel management, pet-assisted therapy facilitation, private security, public safety, Spanish language and culture, and substance abuse counseling. Mercy's innovative majors with unique scheduling also include five-year B.S./M.S. programs in acupuncture and Oriental medicine, occupational therapy, and physical therapy and a B.S./M.D. program.

Academic Program

Mercy College offers a full range of undergraduate programs within fifteen academic departments. To be eligible for graduation with a bachelor's degree, a student must accumulate 120 academic credits and must fulfill one of the major curricular distributions. A dual major or a minor concentration is possible. To earn an associate degree, a student must complete 60 academic credits and must satisfy the appropriate curricular distribution.

The College offers a program for students with learning disabilities. A program in English as a second language offers instruction for those students whose native language is not English, and many courses are taught in Spanish and Korean through the Bilingual Education Program.

Students receiving satisfactory scores on College-Level Examination Program (CLEP) tests, the New York State Regents College Examinations, or College Board Advanced Placement

(AP) examinations are eligible for advanced placement. Up to 30 credits for life achievement may also be awarded to qualified students. Entering students selected on the basis of past achievement and motivation may be invited to participate in the Mercy College honors program.

Off-Campus Arrangements

Through its membership in several interinstitutional cooperative programs, Mercy College is able to offer students a variety of off-campus learning opportunities. The Westchester Consortium of Colleges, the Westchester Conservatory of Music, and Long Island University's Arnold & Marie Schwartz College of Pharmacy and Health Sciences allow for the sharing of faculty and resources in many programs. In addition, degree programs at Mercy College are enriched through joint ventures with private businesses, industries, and research facilities such as the Institute of Continuing Biomedical Education, the New York Medical College Graduate School, and the Karol Marcinkowski University of Medical Sciences in Poznan, Poland. Juniors and seniors are eligible to participate in the College's cooperative education program, through which they gain paid, professional work experience in conjunction with classroom work in their major fields of study.

Academic Facilities

The main campus occupies six modern, fully equipped, air-conditioned buildings housing classrooms and administrative offices, science laboratories, psychology laboratories, the library, an audiological laboratory and clinic for speech pathology, a center for journalism studies, TV studio, acupuncture clinic, veterinary clinic, recording studio, computer facilities, a theater and auditorium, a gymnasium, a residence hall, and a graduate center. The College also houses the Lower Hudson Valley Environmental Center. The Yorktown Heights campus and branch campuses in Westchester County and the Bronx offer a range of facilities and services to meet the needs of each student population.

The Dobbs Ferry campus library serves as the nucleus for the Mercy College library system, which houses a collection of more than 315,000 volumes. The system also includes extensive audiovisual materials, a federal depository for government publications, and interlibrary loan capabilities. Library materials are cataloged by means of a national online computerized system (OCLC), using the modern COM (computer output microfilm) catalog.

Costs

Tuition in 1999–2000 for a full-time student was $7800 per year (based on 12 to 18 credits per semester) or $310 per credit.

Financial Aid

Financial assistance is available in the form of scholarships, grants, loans, and employment for all eligible matriculated students. All students requesting financial assistance are requested to file the Free Application for Federal Student Aid (FAFSA) by July 1 for the fall semester and by November 1 for the spring semester. Mercy College provides $310,000 in scholarships and $1.5 million in grants to students per year.

Faculty

Of the 670 faculty members, 157 are full-time and more than 60 percent hold doctorates. Faculty members are actively involved in academic advisement and are dedicated to providing all students with teaching of the highest quality and preparation for life. The student-teacher ratio of 17:1 ensures a personalized atmosphere and individualized attention.

Student Government

It is the responsibility of the Student Association (SA) to represent the voice of the student body. Besides providing liaison between students and the faculty, the SA, in conjunction with the College Council for Student Affairs, determines policy with regard to student behavior. In addition, it administers the activities funds and approves budgets for student organizations and clubs whose existence it has authorized.

Admission Requirements

Qualified high school students may apply for early admission or advanced study before completion of their high school education. Once admitted, all applicants must score satisfactorily on the College's placement examination.

Application and Information

To be considered for admission, freshman candidates must submit an application for admission, an application fee of $35, and an official high school transcript. Transfer students should submit the application with a fee of $35 and an official transcript from each college or university previously attended. There is a graduate application fee of $60. Transfer students who have completed fewer than 15 college credits must submit a copy of their high school record in addition to their college transcripts. All applicants are encouraged to visit the campus to discuss their college plans with an admission counselor or to have an interview by phone with an admission counselor.

An application form and additional information may be obtained by contacting:

Joy Colelli
Dean for Admissions
Mercy College
555 Broadway
Dobbs Ferry, New York 10522
Telephone: 914-674-7600
          800-MERCY-NY (toll-free)
E-mail: admission@merlin.mercynet.edu
World Wide Web: http://www.mercynet.edu

The College's main campus in Dobbs Ferry overlooks the Hudson River.

MERCYHURST COLLEGE
ERIE, PENNSYLVANIA

The College

Mercyhurst College is a distinctive Catholic liberal arts college with excellent programs in the arts and sciences, professional preparation, and technology. As a college that believes in an academically challenging environment, it has worked hard to create strong academic programs, satisfying student-life activities, and career-preparation options. Founded in 1926 by the Sisters of Mercy, Mercyhurst College is a fully accredited, primarily undergraduate, four-year institution for men and women. Located on an 84-acre campus in Glenwood Hills, in Erie, Pennsylvania, Mercyhurst currently enrolls more than 3,000 students in liberal arts and career programs. Entering its seventy-fourth academic year in 2000, Mercyhurst College continues to offer distinctive programs that reflect a rich liberal arts tradition while responding to the career needs of a changing society.

At Mercyhurst College, small classes enable the faculty to give maximum attention to each student. At the same time, students are challenged to develop and grow through active participation in the classroom. The belief at Mercyhurst is that given various academic programs of high quality and a personal atmosphere in which to pursue them, students will receive meaningful preparation, whether it be for further studies, a career, or living a wholesome life. Mercyhurst students develop socially by meeting new people and participating in exciting activities. Interacting daily with other students, the faculty, and administrators, Mercyhurst students gain valuable interpersonal and organizational skills that they can carry into their professional and personal lives.

Mercyhurst has intercollegiate sports programs in baseball, basketball, crew, cross-country running, football, golf, hockey, lacrosse, soccer, softball, tennis, volleyball, and women's field hockey. Students can participate in more than twenty clubs, intramural sports, the student government, publications, theater, and the campus ministry. At the heart of student life are the residence halls, the bookstore, and the student union.

Mercyhurst offers three graduate degrees in administration of justice, special education, and organizational leadership.

Location

Erie, the third-largest city in Pennsylvania, has been well described as "a city of all seasons." Located on the shore of Lake Erie, the city has many recreational, social, and cultural activities in an environment rich with heritage. Erie combines the positive elements of a big city with the good points of a small town to create an attractive life-style for its residents and visitors.

Presque Isle, located 20 minutes west of the College, attracts millions of people yearly to its sandy beaches and beautiful bay waters, while the winter snows draw downhill and cross-country skiers to nearby slopes. The Erie area has a great variety of activities in the arts, sports, and entertainment fields during all seasons.

Majors and Degrees

Mercyhurst College awards primarily the Bachelor of Arts degree. The Bachelor of Arts majors are accounting; archaeology/anthropology; art (art education, art therapy, graphic design, and studio); biochemistry; biology (biology education, environmental science, medical technology, neuroscience, predental, premedical, prenursing, prepharmacy, and preveterinary); business (advertising, business/chemistry, business education, business–sports marketing, finance, management, and marketing); business/chemistry; chemistry (business/chemistry, chemistry education, computational chemistry, and environmental); communications (electronic media and print media); computer systems; criminal justice (corrections, juvenile justice, and law enforcement); dance; early childhood education (elementary education and special education); earth/space science education; elementary education (special education); elementary education/special education dual certification; English (creative writing, English prelaw, and English writing); English education; facilities and property management; foreign languages and cultures; foreign language education; forensic science; general science education; geology (environmental geology/hydrogeology); history (Research/Intelligence Analyst Program and social science education); hotel, restaurant, and institutional management (professional clubhouse and golf management and professional convention management); mathematics (actuarial science and mathematics education); music (applied music); philosophy; political science (environmental studies and politics and prelaw); psychology (neuroscience); religious education/lay ministry; religious studies; Russian studies; social work (gerontology); sociology; and special education (elementary education). The Bachelor of Science degree is awarded in earth–space science education, general science education, human ecology (dietetics, family and consumer science education, family ecology, fashion merchandising, and interior design), and sports medicine (athletic training, premedical, pre–physical therapy, and wellness/health promotion). Mercyhurst College also offers a Bachelor of Music degree program in applied music and music education.

Academic Program

In keeping with a renewed emphasis on the liberal arts, in 1997–98, Mercyhurst adopted new core requirements, which include a select, limited number of courses, primarily from the liberal arts disciplines, that are designed to furnish students with a broad base of skills and liberalizing knowledge. In addition to completing the core program, students must complete a major. Graduation requirements for the Bachelor of Arts degree are 120 credits; for the Bachelor of Music degree, 128 credits; and for the Bachelor of Science degree, 120 credits. The Associate of Science degree requires that a minimum of 60 credits be successfully completed.

Mercyhurst College offers an honors program, cooperative education, contract majors, independent/tutorial study, and off-campus study. Students may earn credit or advanced placement through challenge examinations, life experience, Advanced Placement tests, and CLEP tests.

The College operates on a three-term calendar.

Off-Campus Arrangements

The Mercyhurst College Term Abroad program allows students to develop an awareness of other cultures and life styles.

Academic Facilities

Academic facilities at Mercyhurst College include the Hammermill Library, which contains more than 170,000 volumes and 850 periodical subscriptions. In addition, the library maintains an archive of northwestern Pennsylvania history and the Tullio Room for Urban Politics. WMCE-FM radio and HURST-TV, the College's radio and cable television stations, are located in Baldwin Hall. Zurn Hall is home to four floors of art studios and science laboratories, including the world-class Mercyhurst Archeological Institute paraformalien facilities, a state-of-the-art computer laboratory featuring Gateway Pentium computers, an astronomical observatory, and a greenhouse. The D'Angelo School of Music provides modern facilities, including a three-level music building with twenty-five practice rooms, a class piano lab with MIDI capabilities, instrument lockers, classrooms, offices, rehearsal spaces, and a music library. The 850-seat Mary D'Angelo Performing Arts Center, completed in 1996, has hosted some of the world's finest artists. There are numerous computer centers spread across campus for student use. A $2.8-million addition to the library was completed in November 1997.

Costs

Tuition for 2000–01 is $13,290. Room and board charges are $5364. Student fees are estimated at $900. Students should budget about $1500 for books, supplies, and personal expenses.

Financial Aid

Eighty-five percent of Mercyhurst's students receive financial aid. Academic scholarships include valedictorian/salutatorian scholarships and Egan Honor Scholarships. Special institutional grants include Presidential Service Grants, athletic grants, D'Angelo Music Scholarships, and institutional employment grants. Programs of special interest include the Mercyhurst Family Plan and Mercyhurst three-year degree program. Government aid programs include Federal Pell Grants, state grants and loans, Federal Supplemental Educational Opportunity Grants, Federal Stafford Student Loans, Federal Perkins Loans, Federal PLUS loans, and Federal Work-Study employment. The Mercyhurst College financial aid application must be filed by every student seeking any type of financial assistance through the College, whether merit- or need-based. The preferential filing deadline is March 15 of each academic year.

Faculty

There are 119 full-time and 75 part-time faculty members who staff undergraduate programs at Mercyhurst. Fifty percent of the faculty hold a Ph.D. or the terminal degree in their field of study. The primary faculty function is teaching, but faculty members are also active in research, publishing, and service to their community. The faculty-student ratio is 1:17.

Student Government

A student government organization is designed to help meet the academic, cultural, and social needs of the student body and is financed by an activity fee. Student government comprises an Executive Committee, a Student Activities Committee, representatives from each major and club on campus, and 7 College senators.

Admission Requirements

Individual initiative and academic capability are the bases of the Mercyhurst admission policy. Emphasis is placed on the strength of the secondary school preparation and on the personal qualities of applicants. Grades, rank in class, recommendations, standardized test scores, interviews, and the demonstration of specific talents and abilities are used as measures of achievement and potential. Typically, one half of Mercyhurst students are A to B+ students, one quarter are B students, and one quarter are C students.

Application and Information

Mercyhurst College follows a rolling admission policy. Students must file a completed application form, along with a $30 nonrefundable application fee, and arrange with the high school and/or other appropriate educational institutions to have a complete transcript and SAT I or ACT scores mailed to the Admissions Office.

For additional information about Mercyhurst College, students should contact:

James Breckenridge, Director of Admissions
Mercyhurst College
501 East 38th Street
Erie, Pennsylvania 16546
Telephone: 814-824-2202
          800-825-1926 (toll-free)
E-mail: admug@mercyhurst.edu
World Wide Web: http://www.mercyhurst.edu

The tower of Mercyhurst College, added to Old Main in 1932.

MEREDITH COLLEGE
RALEIGH, NORTH CAROLINA

The College

Meredith College, chartered in 1891 by North Carolina Baptists to provide excellence in education for women, is today the largest private women's college in the Southeast. Even as the College has grown to 2,166 undergraduate degree candidates, the faculty-student ratio of 1:14 offers individual attention and advising, with an emphasis on the liberal arts, career preparation, and personal development. The College retains an appreciation of its Baptist heritage and is now independently governed. Degree candidates choose from more than thirty major fields.

The faculty is dedicated to teaching and advising and to challenging the students to meet their academic and personal goals. Undergraduate students pursue programs leading to Bachelor of Arts, Science, and Music degrees; the College also offers Master of Business Administration, Master of Education, Master of Health Administration, and Master of Music degrees. College programs are accredited by the Southern Association of Colleges and Schools, the National Council for the Accreditation of Teacher Education, the Council on Social Work Education, the Foundation for Interior Design Education and Research (FIDER), and the National Association of Schools of Music. The College also has an approved American Dietetic Association Plan V Program. It is also the home of the Fletcher School of Performing Arts, which brings renowned performers and master classes to the campus.

The College focuses heavily on leadership development for women. Students participate in a wide variety of campus activities, including performing groups, sports, publications, academic and personal interest clubs, and student government. More than 500 leadership positions are available for women to fill. A member of NCAA Division III, Meredith fields five intercollegiate sports teams in basketball, fast-pitch softball, soccer, tennis, and volleyball.

Location

Meredith's beautiful 225-acre campus is on the western edge of Raleigh, North Carolina's capital city, and is adjacent to the booming Research Triangle area of Raleigh, Durham, and Chapel Hill. A total of eleven colleges and universities that serve approximately 90,000 students can be found here. Raleigh, a city of 266,000 people, is centrally located between the North Carolina coast and the mountain ranges of the western part of the state. Two interstates and the Raleigh-Durham International Airport (15 minutes from the campus) make Raleigh easily accessible.

Majors and Degrees

Meredith confers three baccalaureate degrees. A candidate for the Bachelor of Arts degree can select her major from American civilization, art, biology, chemistry, dance, economics, English, French, history, international studies, mathematics, music, musical theater, political studies, psychology, public history, religion, social work, sociology, Spanish, speech communication, and theater. The Bachelor of Science degree is available in accounting, biology, business administration, chemistry, child development, clothing and fashion merchandising, computer information systems, computer science, exercise and sports science, family and consumer science, foods and nutrition, health science, interior design, international business, and mathematics. The Bachelor of Music degree candidate can major in performance or music education. A student may also work with the faculty to create a self-designed major.

Licensure programs taken in addition to a major are offered in school social work and teacher education. Teacher education licensure is offered in birth to kindergarten (B–K), elementary (K–6), middle grades (6–9), secondary (9–12), art (K–12), business (9–12), dance (K–12), French/Spanish (K–12), home economics (7–12), music (K–12), and theater arts (K–12).

Preprofessional preparation is available in medicine, dentistry, law, and veterinary medicine. Minors are offered in most major fields and in some other areas such as professional communications, criminal justice, cross-cultural skills, physical education, philosophy, and women's studies. Concentrations are also available within most departments. A five-year B.S. and Master of Business Administration program is an option for outstanding accounting majors.

Academic Program

Meredith's academic program blends a strong liberal arts foundation with opportunities for career and preprofessional preparation. To achieve breadth in her education, each student must fulfill general education requirements in humanities and arts, social and behavioral sciences, mathematics and natural sciences, and health and physical education. By the end of her sophomore year, she declares a major and begins to study her chosen field in depth. She may round out her program by completing options such as a second major, a minor or a concentration, a teacher education program, an experiential learning component (an internship, co-op, or field work), or a study-abroad program.

There are opportunities for advanced placement with credit for those who show by examination (AP, I.B., CLEP, and/or departmental examinations) that they have mastered the material for any college-level course. Each year approximately 25 entering students are invited to participate in the Honors Program. About 30 entering students participate in the Teaching Fellows Program, which provides special seminars, mentors, honors classes, and cultural opportunities for the winners of the prestigious North Carolina Teaching Fellows Scholarship/Loan.

Off-Campus Arrangements

Through the Cooperating Raleigh Colleges consortium, students may take courses at no extra cost at North Carolina State and Shaw Universities and at Peace and St. Augustine's Colleges.

Women who are interested in expanding their international horizons can participate in either summer or academic-year inter-cultural programs in almost any country. Every summer, students and faculty members travel to England, Italy, and Switzerland for five or ten weeks of study. It is possible to earn an entire semester of credit through this summer study at approximately the same price as a regular semester on campus in Raleigh. Art students above the freshman level may study in Florence, Italy. Students of French may study at the Université Catholique de l'Ouest in Angers, France, and students of Spanish may study at Universitas Nebrissensis in Madrid, Spain. Students of almost any major can study in the United Kingdom and Australia. Those seeking a less traditional venue can study at Meredith affiliates in the People's Republic of China or can work with the Office of Study Abroad to find a program appropriate to their academic or travel interests.

Students may take advantage of opportunities within the United States by completing a United Nations Semester at Drew University, a federal government semester through the Washington Semester program at American University, and a capital city semester in state government through Meredith's own program in Raleigh.

Academic Facilities

The Carlyle Campbell Library contains 134,414 volumes, 1,943 periodicals, 43,200 titles on microform, and 11,751 records, tapes,

CDs, and videos. As part of its academic department facilities, the campus also houses a music library, art galleries, a research greenhouse, music practice rooms, a state-of-the-art language lab, an autism lab, computer labs, a child-care lab, an indoor swimming pool, lighted outdoor tennis courts, a putting green, and a soccer field. The campus is also cabled to provide network and e-mail access in classrooms, computer labs, and residence halls.

Costs

For 2000–01, the cost of a year at Meredith is $14,100, including $9840 for tuition and $4260 for room and board. The comprehensive cost ($14,100 for on-campus and $9840 for commuting students) covers most course, laboratory, library, and student activity fees. The cost does not include personal expenses, transportation, or books. For part-time students, costs are $295 per credit hour.

Financial Aid

Meredith's financial aid program is designed to meet a high percentage of the analyzed need of the student. Approximately 55 percent of undergraduate students receive need-based assistance; when competitive scholarships and state entitlement grants are added, approximately 74 percent of Meredith students receive some form of financial assistance. The Free Application for Federal Student Aid (FAFSA) and a Meredith financial aid application are used to determine eligibility for need-based federal, state, and institutional funds that include grants and scholarships, loans, and work-study. A freshman candidate may also file special application forms for the competitive scholarships that recognize students for superior academic ability and talent in art, music, or interior design. A North Carolina Teaching Fellow who is selected for Meredith's program may use her scholarship at the College and will have other gift assistance coordinated to match the stipend provided by the state.

Faculty

The College has 268 full-time and part-time faculty members. Seventy-nine percent of the full-time faculty members have earned doctoral degrees. The student-faculty ratio is 14:1, and the average class size is 19. Sixty-nine percent of the full-time faculty members are women.

Student Government

Meredith has one of the oldest student government associations in the South and has an honor code that is a key ingredient of the Meredith community. Through the Student Government Association, students assume primary responsibility for making and enforcing regulations. Every student is a member of SGA.

Admission Requirements

Along with academic achievement, Meredith values individuality, integrity, and diversity. Each application is evaluated to determine how the student's academic preparation and ability match Meredith's requirements and challenges and to assess motivation, special talents, and commitment to learning. A freshman candidate is expected to have at least 16 units of credit earned in grades 9–12, with at least 14 in the academic subjects. Her program should include English (4 units), history/social studies (3), mathematics (3 in algebra I, algebra II, and geometry or a higher level course), science (3), foreign language (1, with 2 recommended), and electives (2, preferably from the academic subjects). Careful attention is given to an unweighted grade average on the academic subjects and to class rank; test scores (SAT I preferred, or ACT) are reviewed in relation to the high school record; recommendations from a school official and a teacher are also required. An interview may be requested in some instances, and students are encouraged to visit for an admissions conference and campus tour.

For transfer admission from an accredited college or university, the student needs at least an overall C average in transferable courses, must be eligible to return to the college attended, and must be recommended by college officials. If the student has fewer than 30 semester hours of transferable work, she must also meet Meredith's freshman admission requirements. Nontraditional students and international students should contact the Office of Admissions.

Application and Information

An application for admission should be sent to the Office of Admissions along with a nonrefundable $35 processing fee (or acceptable fee-waiver request). Electronic filing is available. The student is responsible for requesting that her official high school transcript, SAT I or ACT scores, and recommendations be sent to the admissions office. A transfer student must file an official transcript from each postsecondary institution attended.

Meredith has two freshman admission plans: early decision and rolling admissions. An early decision candidate must apply by October 15; this "first choice" plan means that if accepted under early decision, the student fully expects to enroll and will withdraw any other pending applications. The student is notified by November 1. A candidate under the rolling plan is encouraged to file early in the senior year, with February 15 as the recommended deadline. Notifications under this plan begin in early November. The candidates' reply dates are December 1 for early decision and May 1 for rolling admission candidates.

Transfer applicants are encouraged to apply by February 15. Notifications begin in late January, and May 1 is the candidates' reply date. For admission to the spring semester, a freshman or transfer student should apply by December 1.

For additional information and for planning a campus visit, students should contact:

Office of Admissions
Meredith College
3800 Hillsborough Street
Raleigh, North Carolina 27607-5298
Telephone: 919-760-8581
          800-MEREDITH (toll-free)
Fax: 919-760-2348
E-mail: admissions@meredith.edu
World Wide Web: http://www.meredith.edu

Meredith College's beautiful 225-acre campus is located on the edge of North Carolina's capital city near urban activity and eleven other colleges and universities.

MERRIMACK COLLEGE
NORTH ANDOVER, MASSACHUSETTS

The College

Founded in 1947 by the Augustinian Order, Merrimack College is now recognized as a superior Catholic coeducational institution of higher learning. The 2,000 undergraduates come from more than twenty-three states and more than twenty countries. The College is located in the suburban towns of Andover and North Andover, Massachusetts, 25 miles north of Boston. Merrimack is a small college of liberal arts and professions; however, it is its size, personalized academic and social environment, and campus location that attract many students. Seventy-five percent of the students reside on campus in the College's residence facilities, town houses, or apartment-style housing. The College strives to provide continued growth in its academic, professional, and support services. These services include a director of academic support services; the Faculty Advisement Program; a Cooperative Education Office; the Student Services Office; the Placement Services Office, which is concerned with career development and job placement; the Counseling and Health Offices, which are concerned with personal counseling and health services; the Campus Ministry Office, which is involved with social-action projects through its Merrimaction Corps; and the Student Activities Office. A writing center, a math resource center, and a science help center offer students additional assistance in academic areas.

The College offers a full calendar of cultural, governmental, athletic, and social activities. The Student Government Association sponsors a film series and hosts leading musical artists and prominent lecturers on campus. Students also may participate in the On-Stagers, one of the College's seventeen cocurricular activities; join a sorority or fraternity; or become involved in the many class-sponsored events. The College also has a student newspaper and a choir. Athletic programs are offered at both the intercollegiate and intramural levels. As a member of the Hockey East Conference, NCAA, ECAC, and Northeast Ten Conference, Merrimack has varsity teams in eight sports for men and eight sports for women. The S. Peter Volpe Physical Education Center has exercise rooms, squash and racquetball courts, a 3,600-seat hockey rink, and a 1,700-seat gymnasium for basketball. Outdoor facilities include athletic fields and eight tennis courts.

Location

Merrimack College is located in northeastern Massachusetts, an area that is close to cultural opportunities and filled with historic sites. The campus is a half-hour's drive from Boston and within easy driving distance to the lake, shore, and mountain region of New Hampshire, Vermont, and Cape Cod.

Majors and Degrees

Merrimack College awards the B.A. and B.S. degrees through both day and evening programs, as well as the A.A. and A.S. degrees within the Division of Continuing Education. Bachelor of Arts degree programs in the liberal arts include communication, digital media/graphic design, economics, English, fine arts, French, history, modern languages, philosophy, political science, psychology, religious studies, self-designed major, sociology, and Spanish. Teacher certification is available for elementary, middle, and secondary education.

Students in the sciences or engineering may attain the Bachelor of Arts degree in biology and mathematics and the Bachelor of Science degree in biochemistry, chemistry, civil engineering, computer science, electrical engineering, environmental science, health science, physics, and sports medicine.

Bachelor of Science degrees are offered in business administration with academic concentrations in accounting, business economics, finance, international business, management, and marketing.

Cooperative (work-study) degree programs may be elected by students majoring in biology, all business programs, chemistry, civil or electrical engineering, computer science, health science, math, physics, and select liberal arts.

The Division of Continuing Education offers programs leading to either the associate or the bachelor's degree in accounting, computer and information sciences, human services administration, liberal arts, and management. The associate degree only may be earned in engineering science and the ministry. The bachelor's degree only may be earned in electrical engineering.

Academic Program

The Merrimack College academic calendar consists of two 15-week semesters, beginning in early September and mid-January. Summer sessions are also available.

To receive a bachelor's degree, all students must complete forty semester courses with a final quality point average of 2.0 or better. Students usually take five academic courses each semester. All bachelor's degree programs revolve around a fifteen-course liberal arts core curriculum. The remaining semester courses in a student's program, following completion of core, major, and cognate requirements, are open electives. The liberal arts core curriculum consists of courses in religious studies and philosophy, humanities, the social sciences, and mathematics and science.

Merrimack College also offers interdisciplinary courses, Junior Year Abroad programs, and internships through the departments of English, history, political science, psychology, and sociology. Special academic programs include a double major in the Division of Arts and Sciences; a contract Bachelor of Arts or Bachelor of Science degree, consisting of a special interdepartmental program in two or more fields; and a double-degree program, usually involving five years, through which the student earns two bachelor's degrees (B.A. and B.S.).

Academic Facilities

The McQuade Library's book collection now stands at more than 130,000 volumes, and more than 1,000 journals are received, with access to the Noble Database, a source of more than seventy Boston libraries. The library offers a computerized catalog, circulation, and acquisition system. It provides 450 private study carrels, seminar rooms for small classes and group study, and a collection of tapes and records in audio rooms for either private or group listening. The library also houses Alumni Hall, a 200-seat auditorium that is used for film shows and lectures, and an art gallery, in which artwork by faculty, students, and local artists is displayed. The Information Technology Center, which features a Digital Equipment Corporation VAXcluster, is now located in McQuade Library. It accommodates multiple languages, including BASIC-Plus, FORTRAN, COBOL, APL, Pascal, C, Ada, MODULA-2, and LISP. The center is also equipped with microcomputers, Digital Equipment Corporation Gigi graphics terminals, and CRTs. The microcomputers can be used as stand-alone systems or as devices to access the VAX system. A group of twenty-five Macintosh personal computers are available to students for word processing. The Gregor Johann Mendel, O.S.A., Center for Science, Engineering and Technology provides students with state-of-the-art laboratory equipment and facilities. Extensive renovations have been completed in two additional academic buildings and are planned for 2000 for the Campus Center. The Deegan Residence Hall, accommodating 300 freshmen, was completed in fall of 1998. The Rogers Center for the Arts was completed in 1999. The College is also a host site for the American Language Academy, one of the largest national companies specializing in English language instruction for international students.

Costs

Tuition for the 2000–01 academic year is $16,200; room and board costs are $7700. These costs are exclusive of books, supplies, travel, and personal expenses.

Financial Aid

Merrimack College sponsors financial aid through federally and state funded grants, loans, and work-study awards. Merrimack also provides scholarships and campus employment from College operating funds. To be eligible for any scholarship or financial aid program, an applicant must file the Free Application for Federal Student Aid (FAFSA) and PROFILE by February 15. Students who receive scholarships or other financial aid through Merrimack College are notified between March 15 and April 30. Currently, 80 percent of all Merrimack students receive scholarships and financial assistance through federal, state, and College funds.

Faculty

The Merrimack faculty is committed to the academic and personal growth of undergraduate students. The 118 full-time faculty members, of whom more than 75 percent hold a Ph.D. degree, are supplemented by 100 lecturers. The faculty-student ratio is 1:14. Faculty interaction with students, through small classes and the availability of teachers, is a hallmark of the College. Faculty members also participate in a Student-Faculty Advisement Program to provide for students' individual academic guidance; they also serve on many College-wide academic and student affairs committees.

Student Government

The Student Government Association has a twofold purpose. This democratic body represents all students' rights by concerning itself with all policy matters that affect the student body and by serving as a primary liaison between students and the administration. The association also conducts and coordinates a varied program of social and cultural events for the College community.

Admission Requirements

Merrimack College seeks academically prepared students who are eager to improve themselves intellectually and socially within the College community. The Admission Committee considers each applicant on an individual basis and evaluates a candidate's strengths in light of personal accomplishments, motivation, and the academic major selected. The Admission Committee places primary emphasis on the secondary school record (courses selected and rank in class), SAT I or ACT scores, and a teacher's or a guidance counselor's recommendation. Applicants are encouraged, but not required, to visit the campus for an interview. The Admission Committee does not discriminate against applicants on the basis of race, sex, religion, or national origin; in fact, the College welcomes diversity among students. Applicants must have earned the following high school units: 4 years of college-preparatory English, 2 years of social studies, 3 years of mathematics (including algebra II), 2 years of science, and 5 electives. Applicants for the sciences or engineering programs, however, are expected to have at least 4 years of mathematics and 3 years of science (including physics for engineering) but need have only 3 electives.

Merrimack offers early decision and deferred admission to properly qualified applicants. Merrimack also gives credit and advanced placement for scores of 3 or better on the Advanced Placement examinations sponsored by the College Board.

Transfer applicants for the fall or spring semester should be in good academic standing at the institution last attended, not be on academic or disciplinary probation at that institution, and have a quality point average of at least 2.5 on the Merrimack College scale.

International applicants must also submit the results of the Test of English as a Foreign Language (TOEFL) with a minimum score of 550.

Application and Information

Application for entrance for the fall term should be made by February 15. Once all proper materials are received, the Admission Office informs the applicant of the College's decision, beginning January 30. All applications for the spring term should be made by December 1. Merrimack College adheres to the NACAC deposit deadline of May 1.

For more information, students should contact:

Office of Admission
Merrimack College
North Andover, Massachusetts 01845
Telephone: 978-837-5100
Fax: 978-837-5133
E-mail: Admissions@Merrimack.edu

MESSIAH COLLEGE
GRANTHAM, PENNSYLVANIA

The College

Messiah College is a coeducational Christian college of the liberal and applied arts and sciences. Founded in 1909 by the Brethren in Christ Church, Messiah offers a high-quality academic program among the rolling hills of south-central Pennsylvania.

More than 2,700 students come to Messiah from thirty-eight states and twenty-two other countries. They represent more than sixty different denominations, and approximately 6 percent are ethnic minorities. Messiah is a residential college; more than 90 percent of students live on campus, creating a real sense of community.

The College has a vibrant campus life. Most students supplement their classroom experience by participating in one or more of the fifty extracurricular activities on campus. Organizations range from national honor societies to special interest clubs to service/outreach teams. Student government, the yearbook, a student-run weekly newspaper, and a College radio station offer additional opportunities for involvement.

Messiah fields twenty intercollegiate sports teams—ten for men and ten for women. Several of these NCAA Division III teams enjoy national rankings each year. Athletic facilities include a competition-size indoor pool, a diving pool, two gymnasiums, an artificial turf field hockey field, a weight room, exercise machines, competition tennis courts, a demonstration tennis court, and an indoor track as well as an expansive soccer stadium, manicured baseball and softball diamonds, and outdoor track and field areas.

Location

Messiah's beautiful 400-acre campus is located in suburban south-central Pennsylvania. The campus is only 10 miles from the cultural resources of Harrisburg, the state capital, and 2 hours from Philadelphia, Baltimore, and Washington, D.C. The Yellow Breeches Creek running through campus and the nearby Susquehanna River provide many recreational opportunities, while Harrisburg and its environs offer internship and service possibilities.

Majors and Degrees

Messiah awards both Bachelor of Arts and Bachelor of Science degrees. The College offers more than fifty majors, including accounting; art; art history; Bible; biochemistry; biology; broadcasting, telecommunications, and mass media; business administration; business information systems; chemistry; Christian ministries; civil, electrical, and mechanical engineering; communication; computer science; economics; education; English; environmental science; family studies; French; German; history; humanities; human resource management; international business; journalism; marketing; mathematics; music; nursing; nutrition and dietetics; philosophy; physical education; physics; political science; psychology; religion; social work; sociology; Spanish; sport and exercise science; sports medicine; theater; and therapeutic recreation.

In addition, Messiah offers several preprofessional programs, including dental, law, medical technology, medicine, ministerial, pharmacy, physical therapy, and veterinary science.

Messiah also has a satellite campus in Philadelphia. Additional majors are offered at the Philadelphia campus in cooperation with Temple University, including art education; art history; broadcasting, telecommunications, and mass media; civil engineering; journalism; physics; social work; and therapeutic recreation.

Among the fifty different minors offered at Messiah are coaching, criminal justice, horticulture, peacemaking, and urban studies.

Academic Program

Messiah's curriculum consists of general required courses in writing, the sciences, the arts, language and culture, Christian faith, and physical education; courses required in the major field of study; and elective courses to fill the 126 credit hours necessary for graduation.

The College's academic year consists of two semesters, fall and spring, with a January Term between the two; students concentrate on one course during the monthlong term.

Specialized programs of study include the College Honors Program, individualized majors, independent study, service-learning, and internships.

Off-Campus Arrangements

In addition to the Philadelphia campus, Messiah offers many opportunities for students to receive credit for study at other locations. As a member of the Coalition for Christian Colleges and Universities, the College participates in the following semester-long programs: American Studies Program (Washington, D.C.), AuSable Institute of Environmental Studies (Michigan), Central American Study and Service, Global Stewardship Study Program, Jerusalem University College, Latin American Studies Program (Costa Rica), Los Angeles Film Studies Center, Oxford Semester (England), Russian Studies Program, Middle East Studies Program, Oregon Extension, and International Business Institute (Europe and Russia).

Messiah also participates in the Brethren Colleges Abroad program. Study-abroad locations include China, Ecuador, England, France, Germany, Japan, and Spain. The College also participates in a student-faculty exchange each year with Daystar University College in Kenya.

The College sponsors several cross-cultural study tours every January Term and Summer Term to various locations, including Greece, Guatemala, Israel, and the Bahamas.

Academic Facilities

In addition to a 250,000-volume library, academic facilities include a science center; a renovated and expanded nursing hall; a hall of engineering, mathematics, and business; a fine arts center; and a sports center. All of these were constructed within the last twenty-five years. Computer facilities include twelve labs with 400 computers, all of which are connected to the campus network. Some labs are located in residence halls. Each room has a connection to the campus network and to the Internet.

Costs

Tuition and fees in 1999–2000 totaled $15,096, and room and board averaged $5500. The estimated cost of books is $500, travel costs about $550, and personal expenses cost roughly $1100.

Financial Aid

The College tries to make a Messiah education affordable for all who want it. First, tuition, room, and board are consistently priced at or below the average cost of attending a four-year private college.

Second, in addition to federal and state grants, loans, and on-campus employment programs, Messiah students benefit from about $12 million in institutional merit scholarships and need-based aid. Approximately 90 percent of students receive financial aid, with the average annual award per recipient being $11,900. The deadline for application for institutional aid is March 1 for the following fall semester.

Messiah also offers both a semester and a monthly payment plan. The latter option allows students to divide payments into ten smaller portions over the course of the year instead of paying in a lump sum at the beginning of each semester.

Faculty

Messiah College is a teaching (as opposed to research) institution. Its mission is to educate undergraduate students. Faculty members are chosen for their scholarship, Christian commitment, and teaching ability. All classes are taught by professors, 73 percent of whom have received the terminal degree in their field. All 141 full-time professors (and some of the 104 part-time faculty members as well) serve as advisers to students. The student-faculty ratio is 15:1.

Student Government

The Messiah College Student Association (MCSA) is self-governing and controls its own budget of more than one quarter of a million dollars. It promotes social events on campus and provides a number of services to students, including outreach opportunities, social events, and book sales. MCSA's judicial branch, J-Council, is responsible for hearing cases of rule violations so that students are tried by their peers, not the College administration. The College values student input—student representatives are found on almost every standing and ad hoc committee on campus.

Admission Requirements

Students who are serious about learning and agree with the College's aim to make Christ preeminent are invited to apply for admission. Transfer, international, and ethnic minority students are welcome and encouraged to apply.

Messiah College is selective in its admissions policy. More than half of last year's freshman class ranked in the top 20 percent of their high school class; one fifth ranked in the top 5 percent. Sixty-nine were valedictorians or salutatorians, 13 were National Merit Scholars, and 75 had SAT I scores of more than 1300 or ACT scores of more than 28.

The College expects that applicants will have taken at least 4 years of English, 2 of mathematics, 2 of science, 2 of social studies, and six electives, preferably two in foreign language. The large majority of accepted students exceed these minimum requirements. The SAT I or ACT should be taken by January of the senior year. On-campus information sessions and tours are recommended but not essential. Two recommendations are required.

Application and Information

Messiah has a rolling admissions policy; applications are reviewed and acted on as they are received. The Admissions Office is open from 8 a.m. to 5 p.m. on weekdays. For more information, to arrange a campus tour and an interview, or to request a catalog and application, students should contact:

Admissions Office
Messiah College
Grantham, Pennsylvania 17027
Telephone: 717-691-6000
           800-233-4220 (toll-free)
Fax: 717-796-5574
E-mail: admiss@messiah.edu
World Wide Web: http://www.messiah.edu
America Online keyword: Messiah

Built in 1991, Frey Hall houses computer labs, sculpture and ceramic studios, and state-of-the-art engineering facilities comparable to those found at large universities.

MIDDLEBURY COLLEGE
MIDDLEBURY, VERMONT

The College
Middlebury's current high rank among national liberal arts colleges rests on achieved excellence and leadership, especially in the areas of literary study, language study and pedagogy, global understanding, and environmental awareness and study. The goal of a Middlebury education is to prepare students to respond throughout their lifetimes as responsible citizens of a changing world.

Those admitted to Middlebury have in common a high degree of intelligence and the commitment to fulfilling its potential. Beyond that, the coeducational student body of 2,265 pursues a wide range of interests and comes from fifty states and more than seventy countries.

With 94 percent of the students living on campus—in houses and dorms holding from 3 to 240 students—the interaction outside of the classroom forms a vital part of the learning experience. Faculty members participate with students in the Commons System, each group with its own events and system of self-governance. Activities are campus-centered, and more than 1,500 cultural, social, and club events take place each year. Many students also participate in athletics, with the seasons organized to allow two- and three-sport athletes to compete throughout the academic year without jeopardizing their academic standing.

Founded in 1800 and coed since 1883, Middlebury awarded the first bachelor's degree by an American college to an African American in 1823. Summer programs, including eight Language Schools, the Bread Loaf School of English, and the Bread Loaf Writers' Conference, complement the undergraduate program during the academic year.

Location
Middlebury's handsome campus sits in central Vermont at the edge of a classic New England small town between the Green Mountains and Lake Champlain. Burlington International Airport is less than an hour away; students can drive to Montreal in 2½ hours, Boston in 3½ hours, and New York City in 5 hours.

Majors and Degrees
Undergraduate students earn a bachelor's degree based on concentration in a single field, an interdisciplinary program, or an individually created major as an independent scholar. Joint and double majors are common. Majors include American civilization; American literature; art (history, studio); biology; chemistry and biochemistry; Chinese; classical studies; classics; computer science; economics; English; environmental studies; French; geography; geology; German; history; international studies (East Asian studies, European studies, international politics and economics, Latin American studies, Russian and East European studies); Italian; Japanese; literary studies; mathematics; molecular biology and biochemistry; music; philosophy; physics; political science; psychology; religion; Russian; sociology-anthropology; Spanish; theater, dance, and film/video; and women's studies. Students may earn teacher certification, and special advising is available to prepare for professional programs in architecture, business management, dentistry, engineering, law, medicine, nursing, and veterinary science.

Academic Program
Middlebury's mission, "to educate students in the tradition of the liberal arts," receives its practical expression through the curriculum, which helps students develop a pool of specific knowledge while learning to think critically and articulate thoughts clearly. Middlebury emphasizes the connections across disciplines that characterize a liberal arts education.

Students typically take four courses in the thirteen-week fall semester, one course in the month-long winter term in January, and four courses in the thirteen-week spring semester. Among their thirty-six courses required for graduation, they take at least one course in seven of eight academic categories: literature, the arts, philosophical and religious studies, historical studies, physical and life sciences, deductive reasoning and analytical processes, social analysis, and foreign language. Students take at least one course introducing them to each of three cultural themes: one course focusing on the United States, one on Europe, and one on another part of the world. Their course work also includes at least two writing program courses and a major. Many students also participate in career internships and summer science research programs.

Off-Campus Arrangements
Before graduation, nearly two thirds of each class spends at least one term studying off campus. Approximately half of those going abroad study at one of the Middlebury Schools Abroad, in Florence, Italy; Getafe, Logroño, Madrid, and Segovia, Spain; Mainz, Germany; Paris, France; or Irkutsk, Moscow, Voronezh, or Yaroslavl, Russia. The remaining students going abroad study at approved programs all over the world, with the largest numbers in Australia, China/Taiwan, the former Soviet Union, Japan, Latin America, and the United Kingdom.

In the United States, Middlebury also offers participation in off-campus study programs, including the Washington Semester Program, the SEA Education Association's Seminar Program, the Williams College–Mystic Seaport Program in American Maritime Studies, and the Semester at Woods Hole Biological Laboratory, as well as exchange programs with Berea College, St. Mary's College, and Swarthmore College.

Academic Facilities
The libraries house more than 1.2 million holdings and provide online access to resources worldwide. Similarly, advanced computer technology connects the students and faculty members with information and colleagues globally. Special scientific equipment includes the Geographic Information Systems laboratory, a rooftop observatory with a computer-controlled 16-inch telescope, and a 32-foot research vessel on Lake Champlain. The arts take advantage of an interactive, contemporary center with conventional and experimental venues. Language studies are enhanced by multimedia workstations and satellite reception of live international broadcasts. A spacious new science facility opened in 1999. Overlooking the Champlain Valley and the Adirondack Mountains, Bicentennial Hall is be one of the best technologically equipped academic buildings in New England.

Costs
In 2000–01 the comprehensive fee, including tuition, room, board, and other fees, is $32,765. Another $1700, plus travel costs, should be budgeted for additional expenses.

Financial Aid
Middlebury admits students without consideration of their financial aid requirements. Approximately 40 percent of the student body receives financial aid, which through grants, loans, and work-study programs meets their assessed need to the full extent that resources permit. The average aid package (grant, loan, and/or job) equals about 75 percent of the comprehensive fee. The College is committed to keeping at a

minimum the amount students are expected to borrow, and nearly two thirds of all students have campus jobs. Students must apply for financial aid by November 15, December 15, or December 31—depending on whether they seek early or regular decision—and submit the College Scholarship Service PROFILE, Free Application for Federal Student Aid, federal income tax returns, and other documents as appropriate.

Faculty

Of the College's 283 faculty members (204 full-time equivalents) who are joined by others in visiting residencies, more than 95 percent have terminal degrees in their fields, and all serve as student advisers. Whereas they are teachers first, their research, creative, and publishing activities often involve students directly, who thus graduate with professional listings on their resumes. The student/faculty ratio is 10:1.

Student Government

Through the Student Government Association students participate in forming College policy affecting academic and student affairs, as well as expressing their views collectively on matters of general interest. The Student Judicial Council has jurisdiction for cases involving violations of College rules or regulations or the undergraduate honor system (except plagiarism); the Community Council handles nonacademic issues; and the Student Finance Committee allocates activity fees to student organizations. The dean of students and faculty representatives meet with the councils as appropriate.

Admission Requirements

Admission is competitive at Middlebury, with almost three fourths (73 percent) of those admitted ranking in the top tenth of their high school classes and 26 percent of those applying receiving offers of admission.

Middlebury recommends students present high school backgrounds with 4 years each of English, one foreign language, and mathematics or computer science; 3 years each of laboratory sciences and history; and some study of music, art, or drama.

Students submit the following application materials: Middlebury's preapplication supplement (available in the College's prospectus or on its Web site) and fee, the Common Application, high school transcript, and a guidance counselor recommendation and two teacher recommendations. Standardized test scores must be submitted using one of the following two options: the ACT or three exams that must include a writing test, a quantitative test, and a test of the student's choice. Tests may be selected from the SAT II, Advanced Placement (AP), or International Baccalaureate (IB) exams. Students may submit exams that are all of one type (e.g., three SAT IIs, three APs, or three IBs) or combine tests of different types (e.g., two SAT IIs and one AP). The following tests satisfy the writing and quantitative requirements: writing—SAT II Writing, AP English Language and Composition, and IB Language (A1, A2, or B English); quantitative—SAT II Chemistry, Math, or Physics; AP Computer Science, Chemistry, Economics, Math, or Physics; or IB Chemistry, Computing Studies, Economics, Math, Physics, or Physical and Chemical Systems. (Students should note that the SAT I math exam does not satisfy the quantitative testing requirement, and the SAT I verbal exam does not satisfy the writing requirement.) Students for whom English is not their first language are required to demonstrate English proficiency. Middlebury considers either the TOEFL or the results from a number of other standardized assessments, including SAT I, SAT II: Writing Test, IELTS, CPE, MELAB, APIEL, and ELPT. Predicted grades in I.B. A1 or A2 English or in A-level English are also considered. Campus visits are not required, but they are recommended as the best way to learn about the College. Group information sessions and tours are available. Interviews are offered but are not required. Students should call the Admissions Office for further information on scheduling a visit.

Application and Information

Those applying for Early Decision I must submit materials postmarked by November 15 and are notified by late December; for Early Decision II and regular decision, the preapplication supplement must be postmarked by December 15 and all other materials by December 31. Candidates for Early Decision II are notified of the decision in early February, and regular candidates by early April.

Students can visit Middlebury's home page on the World Wide Web at the address listed below and write, phone, or fax the Admissions Office for further information:

Admissions Office
The Emma Willard House
Middlebury College
Middlebury, Vermont 05753

Telephone: 802-443-3000
Fax: 802-443-2056
World Wide Web: http://www.middlebury.edu/

The centerpiece and symbol of Middlebury College.

MIDLAND LUTHERAN COLLEGE
FREMONT, NEBRASKA

The College

Midland Lutheran College is committed to providing a value-based education that prepares students for success in a variety of careers. While the College is related to the Evangelical Lutheran Church in America, it actively seeks and celebrates religious diversity. Students represent the full range of the Judeo-Christian tradition.

Midland's 1,036 men and women come from twenty-three states and four countries. With a 15:1 student-faculty ratio, the College emphasizes close relationships between teachers and students. Faculty members at Midland make teaching and advising a priority, keeping generous office hours and making themselves available at home during evenings and weekends. Students at Midland receive the close attention that makes for a satisfying college career.

Midland balances a fine liberal arts tradition with a forward-looking commitment to achievement in vocation. The College's Career Planning and Resource Center assists students from their first days on campus. The full-time center aids freshmen and sophomores with major and course selection as well as career choice; juniors and seniors receive help in resume writing, interview skills, and job placement. Workshops and seminars are held throughout the year to provide specialized help in planning a career. Recruiters from major corporations regularly visit the campus to seek Midland graduates for employment.

The College provides a strong cocurricular program that complements its academic offerings. More than 90 percent of the College's students are involved in cocurricular activities, including athletics, drama, music, speech, student government, religious organizations, academic societies, and fraternity/sorority life.

Students may choose to live in one of five dormitories on campus. Upperclass students have the option of living off campus in homes or apartments in the community. Either way, students are integrated into the academic and cocurricular life of the campus.

Location

Located in Fremont, a town of 25,000 in eastern Nebraska, Midland is only 35 miles from Omaha and 50 miles from Lincoln. Fremont is a quiet, residential, tree-filled town offering a variety of restaurants, movie theaters, and shops. Omaha and Lincoln provide the cultural advantages of major metropolitan areas, including museums, symphonies, theater, the opera, fine dining, and major shopping facilities. Students regularly take advantage of what Omaha and Lincoln have to offer.

Majors and Degrees

Midland offers four baccalaureate degrees: Bachelor of Arts, Bachelor of Science, Bachelor of Science in Business Administration, and Bachelor of Science in Nursing. In addition, the College offers a two-year Associate of Arts degree.

The Bachelor of Arts degree is available in art, behavioral science, communication arts, education, English, history, language arts, music, performing arts, philosophy/religion, physical education, and social science. The Bachelor of Science degree is available in biology, chemistry, math/computer science, natural science, and physical science.

Academic Program

Midland seeks to provide every student with the breadth of study important to a liberal arts education. All students are required to take the yearlong interdisciplinary humanities course, Odyssey in the Human Spirit. The award-winning Odyssey is taught by a team of humanities professors who present major themes in Western cultural heritage through the study of individual personalities. Students in the course also learn basic research and writing skills. Odyssey was honored in 1986 by the National Endowment for the Humanities as an outstanding course in the liberal arts.

Students meet general education requirements in seven general education areas. By taking courses in each of these areas, students are exposed to a variety of disciplines and ways of thinking. These courses become the foundation for more specialized learning in the student's academic career.

Midland operates under the 4-1-4 academic calendar. The fall and spring semesters are separated by the one-month Interterm in January. Interterm provides unusual on-campus and off-campus study opportunities for the faculty and students. Faculty members often teach courses in special areas of interest; students take courses on the Midland campus or elsewhere. Recent Interterm courses have included Theatre in New York City, touring children's theater productions, Halley's Comet and Other Space Debris, and Literature of World War II.

Off-Campus Arrangements

During the January Interterm, students may arrange to take classes for credit at any of a number of colleges using the 4-1-4 calendar or undertake independent study throughout the United States and abroad in Europe, South America, and other parts of the world. In cooperation with Central College, Midland offers additional study-abroad programs in Austria, England, France, Germany, Mexico, Spain, and Wales. The College participates in the Evangelical Lutheran Church in America/African Study program, providing opportunity for study in Liberia.

Academic Facilities

The Anderson Complex houses faculty and administrative offices, conference areas, and departmental space for the business, journalism, nursing, humanities, and education departments. The building's contemporary design blends with existing campus architecture, creating a mall effect. The complex also contains up-to-date computer facilities for general use, as well as fine journalism and darkroom facilities. The journalism lab has been called the envy of many a professional newsroom.

Luther Library contains more than 100,000 volumes and subscribes to hundreds of foreign and domestic periodicals. The library features an audiovisual center with computers, video equipment, and tape machinery to complement student work.

Swanson Hall of Science houses the campus computer center, laboratories for student use, and the Behlen Observatory and Lueninghoener Planetarium. The observatory and planetarium receive full use by campus and community. Credit and noncredit courses are regularly offered to permit students to use these outstanding astronomy facilities.

Costs

For 2000–01, tuition and all fees total $13,940. Room and full board are $3760. Private music lessons are an additional cost. Books and supplies are estimated to cost $500 per year.

Financial Aid

More than 90 percent of Midland's students receive financial assistance. The deadline for application is May 1, but awards are made on a rolling basis. Applications received prior to the May 1 deadline receive priority examination. Midland requires that students complete the College's own financial aid application along with the Free Application for Federal Student Aid (FAFSA). Students must be accepted for admission before financial aid can be awarded.

Scholarships are awarded on the basis of academic achievement and special abilities in athletics, music, art, and drama. Scholarship assistance may range from $500 to $6400 per year. Lutheran students are automatically eligible for a $500 Lutheran Student Award. In addition, funded scholarships ranging from $100 to $1000 provide assistance for students in a variety of areas.

Federally funded programs provide assistance to students in the form of Federal Pell Grants, Federal Supplemental Educational Opportunity Grants, Federal Stafford Student Loans, Federal Perkins Loans, and a variety of other kinds of aid.

Students may be eligible to receive work-study assignments that provide on-campus employment opportunities often related to their major.

Midland is committed to providing adequate sources of financial aid for deserving students. Contributions to the College's endowment have provided ever-increasing sources of revenue to students requiring aid to receive a Midland education. Midland aims to increase its endowment in the coming years to ensure that financial aid will be available for those students who need it.

Faculty

Midland's faculty members are committed to teaching and advising. With a student-faculty ratio of 15:1, students are assured of close contact with full-time faculty members. Class sizes are deliberately kept small, especially at the upperclass level. Almost 50 percent of the faculty have earned the Ph.D. or another terminal degree, many from the leading colleges and universities in the nation. All faculty members are responsible for advising a small group of students, guiding them in course selection, and helping them to plan majors and careers. In addition, faculty members serve on various campus committees responsible for promoting aspects of campus life. Faculty members also serve as advisers to student organizations.

Student Government

Midland's Student Senate is made up of elected representatives from the student body. The senate provides input on matters of concern to students and is committed to enhancing the social, cultural, intellectual, and spiritual life on campus. The senate sponsors a full calendar of social and entertainment activities for students, and representatives from the senate serve on various College committees.

Admission Requirements

Midland Lutheran College admits students without regard to race, color, sex, religion, handicap, or national origin. While many students are from Nebraska, the College encourages diversity in its student population. Applicants are evaluated on the basis of personal and academic ability and on their potential to succeed at Midland.

Most applicants rank in the top half of their high school graduating class, but others will be considered on the basis of their personal educational objectives and their ACT scores. A personal interview for all prospective students is recommended but not required.

Application and Information

Students are encouraged to apply as early as possible to Midland. Applications are reviewed on a rolling basis, and students are notified of acceptance as soon as possible after all of their application materials are received. Along with a completed Midland application form and a $30 application fee, students should submit ACT scores and a copy of their high school transcript. Transfer students should also submit copies of transcripts from all colleges or universities attended.

For more information, students should contact:
Roland R. Kahnk
Vice President for Enrollment Services
Midland Lutheran College
900 North Clarkson
Fremont, Nebraska 68025
Telephone: 402-721-5480 (call collect)
           800-642-8382 (toll-free in Nebraska)

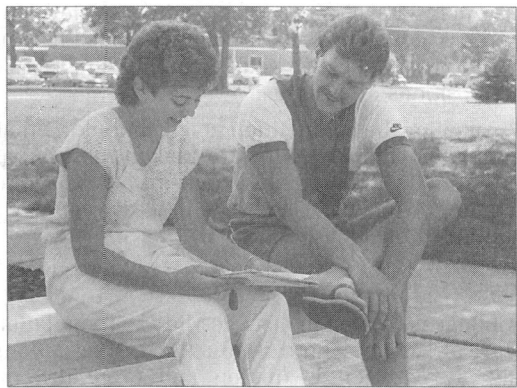

Midland Lutheran College is small enough for students to form close relationships with classmates and faculty members.

MIDWAY COLLEGE
MIDWAY, KENTUCKY

The College

Midway College, Kentucky's only women's college, was established in 1847 as the Kentucky Female Orphan School to prepare financially disadvantaged women for teaching careers. Since 1988, Midway has served as an independent, residential four-year college that emphasizes career preparation based on a liberal arts background and is fully accredited by the Southern Association of Colleges and Schools.

An education at Midway is designed specifically to educate and empower women for achievement and leadership. The women's college offers nine baccalaureate degree programs and eight associate degree programs. Midway College is dedicated to providing a living and learning environment that enables students to assume roles of responsibility as contemporary women.

Learning at Midway is hands-on. Many of the College's programs require internships, which give students the opportunity to apply knowledge gained in the classroom in a professional setting. Experience gained at Midway is valuable when students begin their job searches after graduation.

Students continuously cite small, interactive classes and individualized faculty attention as their primary reasons for selecting Midway. Enrollment at Midway is approximately 1,000 traditional residential, commuter, and nontraditional students. Approximately thirty states and seven other countries are represented in the College's student population.

Opportunity for involvement is one of the factors that makes an education at Midway such a rewarding experience. With various athletic teams, activities, clubs, and organizations at Midway, students have many opportunities to develop talents and leadership skills. The small college atmosphere makes it easy for students to get involved in campus life or to assume leadership positions on campus.

Students can enjoy the competition and camaraderie that comes with participation in intercollegiate and intramural sports. A variety of athletic scholarships and grants are offered to talented young women in basketball, cross-country, riding, soccer, softball, tennis, and volleyball.

Location

Midway College is located in historic Midway (population 1,400) in the heart of scenic central Kentucky. Nestled among horse farms halfway between Lexington and Frankfort, the state capital, Midway is a picturesque, friendly community full of stately homes, restaurants, and antique and gift shops. Downtown Lexington is 15 minutes away and offers students many cultural and social opportunities, such as shopping, dining, movies, and theater. Louisville and Cincinnati are less than 80 miles away by interstate, and Lexington is served by major airlines through Bluegrass Field.

Majors and Degrees

Bachelor's degrees are available in biology, business administration, English, environmental science, equine studies, liberal studies, nursing, paralegal studies, psychology, and teacher education. Areas of concentration include a liberal studies degree with concentrations in art studio, communication, English, music, natural sciences, philosophy and religious studies, or social and psychological sciences; an equine studies degree with concentrations in equine management, equitation instruction, or equine therapy; and a business administration degree with concentrations in accounting and equine business.

The College offers associate degrees in business administration, computer information systems, early childhood education, equine management, general studies (science), in-home child care, nursing, and paralegal studies.

Academic Program

The College calendar includes a fall and spring semester and a summer program. Midway College offers discussion and study groups, an Arts and Lecture Series, seminars, films, and chapel services to enrich the academic program of any student who wishes to participate. Students must complete requirements designed for a liberal knowledge of the major areas of learning in the humanities and arts, social and behavioral sciences, natural sciences, and mathematics. All incoming first-year students must enroll in a seminar entitled "College and Life Success Strategies for Women." Students may receive college credit or advanced course placement from the College-Level Examination Program (CLEP). Any student who wishes to receive credit from a CLEP or Advanced Placement (AP) examination should contact the Office of Student Development.

Off-Campus Arrangements

Qualified equine students at Midway may vary their studies and enrich their educational experience by studying abroad at prestigious Bishop Burton College in England during their junior year. Bishop Burton specializes in show jumping, dressage, and combined training. Midway College is a member of the Kentucky Institute for International Studies, a consortium of colleges and universities, that organizes and coordinates a group of summer and semester study-abroad programs for college students throughout the world.

Academic Facilities

Midway's 105-acre campus includes eight administrative, classroom, and residential buildings; an amphitheater; tennis courts; soccer and softball fields; and the Keeneland Equine Education Center, a 35,000-square-foot equine education complex with indoor and outdoor riding facilities and 50 acres for cross-country riding. Several of the College's Georgian-style buildings have been renovated in recent years.

The Little Memorial Library was completed in summer 1997. The state-of-the-art facility houses 70,000 volumes, 400 current periodicals, and 150 study stations and is home to the college computer center.

In spring 2000, ground was broken for the $6–million Anne Hart Raymond Center for Mathematics, Science and Technology. Completion of the project is scheduled for 2001.

The College's bookstore and café, Eagle Trading Company, is located among quaint shops and restaurants just off campus in downtown Midway. The Trading Company is a social hub where students can relax, socialize, or grab a sandwich. A wide variety of cards, souvenir gifts, books, magazines, and Midway College clothing is available. Students can also participate in a creative writing workshop and attend literary readings or musical performances at the bookstore.

Costs

Tuition for the 1999–2000 academic year was $9062. Room charges totaled $2275. Students have two board options; a nineteen-meal plan costs $2575, and a fifteen-meal plan costs $2325. Costs of books, travel, and personal expenses may vary with each student.

Financial Aid

Families representing many income levels qualify for financial assistance at Midway. More than 90 percent of Midway students traditionally receive financial aid. In an effort to assist all families in budgeting their educational expenses, Midway offers a variety of payment plans, including a no-interest monthly payment plan.

Financial aid is available through scholarships, grants, loans, and campus work-study. Awards are based on scholarship potential, merit, and individual need. The size of each award may vary with need. Further information on special scholarships may be obtained from Midway's Office of Financial Aid.

Students seeking financial assistance at Midway College must complete the Free Application for Federal Student Aid (FAFSA). This form may be obtained from any high school guidance office or from the Office of Financial Aid at Midway College. The FAFSA should be filled out as soon as possible after filing taxes from the previous year. Forms completed by April 1 are given higher priority.

Faculty

Small classes guarantee personal attention from professors and create a comfortable environment for discussion and debate. Midway professors make every effort to help students succeed and graduate. Faculty members know their students well and work with them to ensure that their program of study meets their individual interests and career objectives.

Midway College faculty members come from a variety of graduate and professional schools, creating a well-rounded intellectual base for students. Approximately 70 percent of the baccalaureate and general education faculty members have a doctorate or terminal degree.

Student Government

Midway's Student Government Association (SGA) serves as an intermediary for the consideration of college issues that are of vital interest to students, faculty members, and staff while developing principles of democratic self-government and encouraging and promoting cooperation between faculty, staff, administration, and students. All students enrolled at Midway College are members of the SGA. Elections are held throughout the year for representative positions. SGA meetings are held weekly, and student attendance is encouraged and welcomed.

Admission Requirements

Midway College considers the sum of a student's total experiences and achievements when considering admission. The College seeks students who have a strong academic background and varied talents, interests, and backgrounds. Every applicant is considered individually based on academic record, college entrance test scores, recommendations, interviews, and extracurricular background.

To apply, students should send a completed application, an official transcript and/or GED scores, and the results of her ACT or SAT I to the admissions office. Minimum admission requirements include graduation from an accredited high school with a minimum 2.2 grade point average (on a scale of 4.0) or satisfactory completion of the GED and an ACT composite score of 18 or its equivalent. Specific programs may have additional requirements. Applications are accepted on a rolling basis until the beginning of the fall and spring semesters.

Application and Information

Candidates for admission are encouraged to apply for admission at the end of their junior year or in the early part of their senior year. Students are encouraged to visit the College for a personal interview, a tour of the campus, and discussions with admissions staff members, faculty members, and students. The Office of Admissions is open Monday through Friday from 8 a.m. to 5 p.m. and by appointment on weekends and evenings. For more information or application materials or to arrange a campus visit, interested students should contact:

Director of Admissions
Midway College
512 East Stephens Street
Midway, Kentucky 40347-1120
Telephone: 800-755-0031 (toll-free)
Fax: 606-846-5823
E-mail: admissions@midway.edu
World Wide Web: http://www.midway.edu

Internationally known for equine studies, students at Midway College can concentrate on equine management, equitation instruction, equine therapy, or equine science (pre-veterinary).

MILLERSVILLE UNIVERSITY OF PENNSYLVANIA
MILLERSVILLE, PENNSYLVANIA

The University

Millersville University is a multifaceted public institution with a wide range of programs and a primary commitment to high-quality undergraduate instruction. Millersville's student body of approximately 7,400 is large enough for the University to offer a wide variety of programs. The University is small enough, however, to provide friendly service and individual attention. Students report that the relaxed, friendly campus atmosphere is one of the things they like best. The Millersville campus features a beautiful green and flowered landscape, a lake with two resident swans, and clean, well-maintained facilities.

Millersville University was established in 1855 as a normal school, the first one in Pennsylvania. It remained a teachers' college until 1962, when it was authorized to offer liberal arts degrees. It has been Millersville University of Pennsylvania since 1983.

The two reasons students most frequently cite for choosing Millersville are its excellent academic reputation and low tuition. The most popular majors are elementary education, business administration, biology, and psychology. Millersville's undergraduates are diverse; 1 in 5 students attends part-time, 1 in 10 is a member of a racial/ethnic minority, and 15 percent are more than 25 years old. Thirty-five percent of Millersville undergraduates are from Lancaster County, 60 percent from elsewhere in Pennsylvania, 4 percent from out of state, and 1 percent from other countries.

The University offers a wide range of intercollegiate varsity, intramural, and club sports; special interest clubs; and fraternities and sororities, to which 10 percent of undergraduates belong. A broad program of cultural events is offered, with alcohol-free nightclubs particularly popular.

Thirty-six percent of undergraduates live in campus residence halls, with the rest commuting from home or living nearby. Men's, women's, and coed dormitories are provided and special interest housing is available. University-affiliated apartments are adjacent to campus. Noncommuting freshmen and sophomores are required to live on campus.

Special services provided for students include tutoring, academic advisement, career planning and placement, personal counseling, health services, wellness activities, child care, and special facilities for commuters.

Location

Millersville, in the heart of Pennsylvania Dutch country, is 3 miles from Lancaster, a growing metropolitan area. Lancaster County is an exceptionally friendly and beautiful area with a large number of stores, restaurants, theaters, parks, and tourist attractions. The campus is served by the area bus system, and Lancaster has train and air service.

Lancaster County is one of the fastest-growing counties in Pennsylvania and has one of the lowest unemployment rates in the state. The local economy is unusually sound and diverse. Sixty percent of Millersville graduates settle within the county.

Majors and Degrees

Millersville offers the Bachelor of Arts degree in anthropology, art, biology, chemistry, earth sciences, economics, English, French, geography, German, history, international studies, mathematics, music, philosophy, physics, political science, psychology, social work, sociology, and Spanish.

The Bachelor of Science degree is offered in biology, business administration, chemistry, computer science, geology, industrial technology, mathematics, meteorology, occupational safety and hygiene management, oceanography, physics, and speech communications.

The Bachelor of Science in Education degree with teaching certification is offered in art education, biology, chemistry, earth sciences, elementary education, English, French, German, mathematics, music education, physics, social studies, Spanish, special education, and technology education.

The University also offers the Bachelor of Fine Arts degree in art, the Bachelor of Science in Nursing degree, the Associate of Arts degree in applied American history, and the Associate of Science degree in chemistry, computer science, and gerontology.

Most majors offer several options that permit specialization. More than thirty minors are offered along with 3-2 engineering programs for chemistry and physics majors. Special advisement is available for students interested in premedicine and prelaw.

Academic Program

Millersville University places a strong emphasis on the liberal arts. Half the courses required for all its undergraduate degrees, including those with technical or professional majors, are in the liberal arts. This prepares students for a lifetime of learning and gives them a background in writing, speaking, analysis, and critical thinking across a broad range of subjects.

Millersville's baccalaureate degree programs have four common curricular elements: proficiency requirements in English composition and speech; the general education program, which constitutes about half the curriculum; the major field of study; and elective courses if needed to meet the minimum of 120 credits required for graduation. Within this framework, students have many choices in developing programs of study.

The general education program has requirements in writing, speaking, humanities, natural sciences and mathematics, social sciences, and interdisciplinary and/or multicultural study. There is also a health and physical education requirement.

Millersville offers a University honors program, departmental honors programs, independent study, a pass/fail option, remedial courses, and special advisement to students undecided about a major.

The University operates on a 4-1-4 academic calendar with summer sessions.

Off-Campus Arrangements

An exchange agreement with Franklin and Marshall College allows Millersville students to take Franklin and Marshall courses not offered at Millersville. Cooperative education internships are available to students in most majors, and some majors offer or require specialized internships. Millersville has study-abroad programs in England, Germany, Japan, Peru, and Scotland. Qualified students who wish to study abroad elsewhere may do so through cooperative arrangements with other colleges and universities.

Academic Facilities

Ganser Library houses more than 490,000 books and more than 558,000 other items and subscribes to more than 2,400 periodicals. Materials from other libraries are available through interlibrary loan. The library also houses computerized database-searching facilities, a curriculum center, a listening room, and archives.

Millersville's computing facilities include IBM and VAX mainframes and SUN Workstations. There are 450 terminals and microcomputers available, including IBM and Macintosh models. Users with their own microcomputers can access University mainframes through telephone lines. Access to the Internet is available for all faculty members and students.

Other University facilities include an extensive scientific instrumentation inventory, industry and technology laboratories, a variety of art studios, a large auditorium and a small theater, two gymnasiums and swimming pools, radio and television production facilities, and a language laboratory. The University's day-care center and prekindergarten provide field experiences in early childhood education.

Costs

Annual tuition and fees in 1999–2000 were $4595 for Pennsylvania residents and $10,023 for out-of-state students. Annual room and board charges for 1999–2000 were set at $4730. All students were expected to pay approximately $600 for books and incidentals.

Financial Aid

About 70 percent of Millersville undergraduates receive financial aid through grants, scholarships, employment, and loans. Scholarships are available on the basis of academic performance. Federal Pell and Federal Supplemental Educational Opportunity grants and Pennsylvania Higher Education Assistance Agency (PHEAA) grants are awarded on the basis of need. Students may also qualify for Federal Perkins Loans and Federal Stafford Student Loans. On-campus and off-campus job opportunities are plentiful.

Students applying for a federal or state grant, Federal Work-Study, or a Federal Perkins Loan must complete the Free Application for Federal Student Aid, which is available from high school guidance offices or the Financial Aid Office. Deadlines are given in the forms' instructions.

Faculty

Millersville University faculty members are dedicated to teaching and to offering individual attention. They take a personal interest in their students' lives and careers and are solely responsible for providing academic advisement. The University keeps a relatively low student-faculty ratio of 17:1 and an average class size of 25. No classes are taught by graduate assistants. Eighty-five percent of the 324 full-time faculty members hold a doctorate or the terminal degree in their field.

Student Government

Millersville University students participate in University governance through the Student Senate, faculty-student committees, and representation on the Faculty Senate and the Council of Trustees. The Student Senate works with faculty members and the administration on major University policies.

The possession, use, or sale of alcoholic beverages and illegal drugs is prohibited on the University campus. Smoking is prohibited in all academic buildings on campus except for specifically designated areas. Freshmen and sophomores living on campus are not permitted to have motor vehicles.

Admission Requirements

Millersville University admits approximately half its applicants. More than 80 percent of its full-time freshmen rank in the top 40 percent of their high school class. Academic records are the most important factor in admission decisions. Applicants must have successfully completed at least 4 years of high school English, 3 years of social studies, 3 years of mathematics, 2 years of history, and 2 years of science. In addition, 2 years of foreign language and 1 additional year each of math and science are strongly recommended.

Because an important part of the college experience is meeting people with backgrounds and interests different from one's own, Millersville University is committed to recruiting a diversified student body. SAT I or ACT scores are required. Interviews, recommendations, and essays are not required. Out-of-state, international, and transfer applicants are welcome. Exceptional high school students may apply for early admission at the end of their junior year. Admitted applicants may defer their admission. Advanced standing is offered through CLEP and AP examinations.

Application and Information

To apply, students should submit a completed application form along with a $30 fee and official copies of the high school record and SAT I or ACT scores. The University has a rolling admission policy, and students are encouraged to apply early in their senior year for fall admission. Applicants are usually notified of a decision within a month after a completed application is received.

Requests for application forms and additional information should be directed to:

Darrell C. Davis
Director of Admissions
Millersville University of Pennsylvania
P.O. Box 1002
Millersville, Pennsylvania 17551-0302
Telephone: 717-872-3371
        800-MU-ADMIT (toll-free)
E-mail: muadmit@marauder.millersv.edu
World Wide Web: http://www.millersville.edu

Millersville University's campus includes shaded lawns that invite students to study or relax with friends.

MILLIGAN COLLEGE
MILLIGAN COLLEGE, TENNESSEE

The College
From its beginning in 1866, Milligan College has offered students an education that integrates academic excellence with Christian values. A four-year liberal arts college, Milligan provides a broad education while also offering twenty-eight majors of specialization and two master's degree programs. Christian perspectives are integrated into everything, from classes to student activities, as students find the academic and spiritual foundation necessary to build a successful and sound future.

A student body of more than 900 students represents thirty-six states and eleven countries. Sixty percent of the students come from outside Tennessee. Eighty percent of traditional students live on campus in one of six residence halls, creating a true collegiate environment. Milligan offers a richly diverse college atmosphere with a true family feeling. With more than twenty-five clubs and organizations on campus, there are many opportunities to develop leadership skills and to make a difference through ministry and service to the community and the world. A wide variety of activities and campus events encourage social, cultural, and spiritual growth. Milligan College is affiliated with the Christian Churches/Churches of Christ, but the interdenominational student body is diverse.

Students enjoy a number of athletic and recreational opportunities, including intercollegiate and intramural sports. A member of the NAIA and the Tennessee-Virginia Athletic Conference, Milligan maintains a very competitive, successful, and nationally recognized athletic program. Since 1995, Milligan teams have won ten NAIA National Championship berths. Men's varsity teams include baseball, basketball, cross-country, golf, soccer, and tennis. Women's varsity teams include basketball, cross-country, soccer, softball, tennis, and volleyball.

Milligan is accredited by the Commission on Colleges of the Southern Association of Colleges and Schools and the National Council for Accreditation of Teacher Education. Milligan College is listed in *U.S. News & World Report* as one of the best regional liberal arts colleges in the South and in *The Student Guide to America's 100 Best College Buys*.

In addition to undergraduate majors, Milligan offers Master of Education and Master of Science in Occupational Therapy degrees.

Location
Milligan's 145-acre campus is located in the foothills of the beautiful Appalachian Mountains in northeastern Tennessee. Outdoor activities, such as hiking, camping, white-water rafting, snow skiing, and mountain biking, are just minutes away from the campus. The Tri-Cities area offers all the benefits of a growing region, including historical locations, theaters, parks, restaurants, shopping malls, golf courses, and other urban attractions. Students are active in local civic clubs, churches, and service projects, and many are employed in internships or part-time work in area businesses. Business and civic leaders serve on the Milligan College President's Executive Council as community liaisons.

Majors and Degrees
Bachelor of Science, Bachelor of Arts, Bachelor of Science in Nursing, and Associate of Science degrees are offered. Undergraduate majors include accounting, Bible/ministry, biology, business administration (seven emphases), chemistry, Christian education, communications (five emphases), computer information systems, computer science, early childhood education, English, fine arts (three emphases), history, humanities, humanities: French, humanities: Spanish, human performance and exercise science (four emphases), human relations (two emphases), mathematics, middle grades education, missions, music, music ministry, nursing, psychology, sociology, and youth ministry. Teacher licensure is available in early childhood, middle grades, secondary, and special education. Cooperative programs in engineering, mortuary science, ROTC, and medical technology and preprofessional programs in medicine and law are also available. A special Business Administration Major for Adults program allows adults who have completed sixty or more semester hours of college credit to complete a 48-semester-hour major in about eighteen months.

Academic Program
Milligan College offers students a liberal arts education in a community of inquiry, responsibility, and caring. Learning occurs in an atmosphere of Christian commitment that integrates the Scriptures with humanities, sciences, social studies, professional studies, and fine arts. The candidate for the bachelor's degree must have completed a major, a minor, and electives to total 128 semester hours of credit, with at least a 2.0 GPA. Core curriculum requirements include courses in humanities, the Bible, the social sciences, ethnic studies, laboratory science, speech communication, mathematics, and health/fitness.

Realizing that not all college-level learning occurs in a college classroom, Prior Learning Assessment programs provide a method by which other modes of learning can be evaluated for college credit. The Advanced Placement Program (AP), the College-Level Examination Program (CLEP), and DANTES are available to all students interested in receiving college credit for studies or work experience already completed.

Milligan College is on a semester system. Semesters begin in August and January, and there are also two 4½-week summer sessions that last from early June until early August. New student orientation is held in August and January.

Rising juniors are required to take the Academic Profile, a test covering general knowledge, and graduating seniors are required to take a test to demonstrate knowledge in their major field of study.

Off-Campus Arrangements
Students can go beyond geographical and cultural boundaries and earn up to 16 hours of credit with Milligan's Study Abroad Program or with the many off-campus learning opportunities sponsored by the Coalition for Christian Colleges and Universities. These include an American Studies Program in Washington, D.C.; a Latin American Studies Program in Costa Rica; the Los Angeles Film Studies Center; and an increasing number of overseas travel programs, which include studies in China, the Middle East, and Russia and at Oxford University or Springdale College in England. Through an affiliation with the International Business Institute, Milligan business majors can earn college credit through a ten-week summer program of intensive study and travel throughout Russia and Europe. Milligan also offers a four-week summer Humanities Tour in Europe, during which students explore the origins of Western civilization. In addition, internship opportunities offer students college credit and work experience in their field of interest prior to graduation.

Academic Facilities
MCNet, a campuswide computer network system that consists of unlimited Internet availability through fiber-optic cabling, is accessible from each residence hall and three on-campus, fully

equipped, student computer labs. In addition to the more than 140,000 materials (books, periodicals, microform documents, and computer information databases) in Milligan's P. H. Welshimer Library, students and faculty members have unlimited access to the holdings of four other local colleges through the Holston Associated Libraries (HAL), an interlibrary network on the Internet. Special collections within the library contain materials on the history of the College, the Restoration Movement, and the local area. The library also participates in resource-sharing agreements with the libraries of Emmanuel School of Religion and East Tennessee State University. A Writing and Study Skills Center offers access to resources, instruction, and tutoring for academic success. Television and radio production studios and an FM radio station provide on-site training for communication students. A darkroom, a theater, and an art gallery feature works by fine arts students. Standardized laboratory facilities are available for general and advanced work in various science departments, including a gross anatomy lab.

Costs

Tuition for 2000–01 is $11,900. Room and board are $4200. Additional fees are approximately $400. Typical annual miscellaneous costs (books, supplies, etc.) are approximately $1000 per year. As a private institution, Milligan supplements student fees with income from endowments and gifts from alumni, friends, and churches in order to keep tuition below the national average of similar private institutions.

Financial Aid

Approximately 90 percent of all students at Milligan College receive federal, state, and/or institutional aid in the form of need- and merit-based grants and scholarships, work-study programs, and low-interest educational loans. Financial assistance is allocated on the basis of need demonstrated by information supplied on the Free Application for Federal Student Aid (FAFSA), which should be completed by February 1 for priority consideration, and the Milligan College Financial Aid Application, which is due by March 1. The Milligan College Office of Financial Aid begins mailing award letters on or before March 15. The average aid package ranges from $7500 to $8500.

Faculty

In addition to their career-based experience, nearly 70 percent of Milligan's quality faculty members (64 full-time; 40 part-time), hold a Ph.D. or the equivalent. As active Christians, professors integrate Biblical truths into their classes and are active leaders both on and off campus. The 12:1 student-faculty ratio and small classes put the student at the center of attention and allow faculty members to cultivate special mentoring relationships with students. Faculty members serve as advisers to students, from registration to graduation, and are often instrumental in helping students find employment or gain admission to graduate school following graduation. Faculty members lead study groups in their homes, support students in extracurricular activities, provide friendship and moral support, and challenge students to stretch their minds in all areas of academic, spiritual, and professional growth.

Student Government

The Student Government Association (SGA) serves as the official representative voice of Milligan students and promotes academic, social, and spiritual activities for the campus community. SGA operates under a constitution approved and supported by the administration of the College and cooperates with the administration in promoting well-ordered conduct among students and in enforcing the regulations of the College. SGA leadership is provided by an executive council and representatives from each class, each dorm, and the non-traditional student body (commuters and married students). As a Christian college, Milligan adopts basic moral and social principles and expects students to serve Christ in an atmosphere of trust, encouragement, and respect for one another.

Admission Requirements

Character, ability, preparation, and seriousness of purpose are the qualities emphasized in considering applicants for acceptance to Milligan College. Overall excellence of performance in high school subjects as well as evidence of Christian commitment and academic potential provide the basis for admission to Milligan College. These qualities are evaluated by consideration of each applicant's academic record (based on transcripts), two personal references, essays, test results, and participation in extracurricular activities. Some majors, such as music, require auditions and interviews. All applicants should have a high school diploma or equivalent and have completed a college-preparatory curriculum with course work in English, math, science, and history as well as in social sciences, foreign language, and some work in speech, music, or art in preparation for study in a liberal arts curriculum. Satisfactory scores on the ACT or SAT I are required of all applicants to the freshman class. The average ACT score for those enrolled is 23. Transfer students must have a grade point average of 2.0 or above and must follow the same application procedures as first-time students; however, ACT or SAT I scores are not required for transfer students.

Application and Information

Applications are processed on a rolling basis, and early application is encouraged. Notification is also given on a rolling basis. An application packet, complete with detailed instructions and requirements, can be obtained from the Admissions Office.

For further information, students should contact:

Admissions Office
Milligan College
P.O. Box 210
Milligan College, Tennessee 37682
Telephone: 423-461-8730
         800-262-8337 (toll-free)
Fax: 423-461-8982
E-mail: admissions@milligan.edu
World Wide Web: http://www.milligan.edu

Milligan College is a Christian liberal arts college that unites humanities, sciences, and fine arts with a Christian worldview. It believes in encouraging the academic, spiritual, and personal growth of students so they can shape their futures successfully.

MILLS COLLEGE
OAKLAND, CALIFORNIA

The College

Mills is the only women's college among the many fine educational institutions in the San Francisco Bay Area. Founded in 1852 as the first women's college west of the Rockies, it is committed to remaining a women's college because it believes that such an environment offers women special advantages in preparing for new roles and responsibilities.

A small, liberal arts college, Mills enrolls more than 700 undergraduate women and 300 graduate women and men. The faculty is equally divided between women and men, and the ratio of students to faculty is approximately 11:1. The College has remained small because ideas and enthusiasm are more readily transmitted in a community of this size. Classes are normally small; 84 percent have 20 or fewer students. Faculty members observe each person's work closely, encouraging high performance and offering individual instruction when appropriate.

Although the College is a diverse community that serves many interests, it is built to a human scale. The 135-acre campus includes rolling meadows, peaceful woods, and a meandering creek. Mills is essentially a residential campus; 53 percent of its undergraduates live in four attractive residence halls, two small apartment buildings, and a co-op house. Undergraduate housing is guaranteed. Residence halls and classrooms are all within easy walking distance. The opportunities for discussion and discovery continue naturally outside the classroom: learning is at the center of everyday life. Conversations over dinner, in the residence halls, or during evening study in the library can sharpen and refine ideas that spring to life in a morning class. The Persis Coleman Organization and the Mary Atkins Organization provide a similar focus for commuting, older, and married students.

The student population offers many avenues for challenge and discovery. There is a variety of ethnic, national, economic, religious, and cultural backgrounds, which gives vitality and texture to campus life. Students come from forty states and twelve countries; 32 percent are women of color, 2 percent are international students, and about 23 percent are women over 23 who are returning to college.

Academic, creative, and athletic abilities are cultivated and prized at Mills. Students participate in extensive intramural programs and seven intercollegiate sports (basketball, crew, cross-country, soccer, swimming, tennis, and volleyball). Mills is a member of NCAA Division III. Athletic facilities include a well-equipped gymnasium, a sauna and weight room, outdoor tennis courts, a cross-country running trail, a soccer field, and the Trefethen Aquatic Center, which includes a state-of-the-art competition swimming pool. Other facilities include the Art Museum, a student center, restaurant, bookstore, and post office.

Location

The San Francisco Bay Area offers an exciting, cosmopolitan context for classroom work. Students may explore this larger "classroom" by taking internships with corporations and other organizations in San Francisco, Oakland, and elsewhere. They may also hike through the wild and beautiful East Bay parklands; enjoy symphonies, operas, theaters, and museums; or ski in the Sierras.

Majors and Degrees

The Mills curriculum includes thirty-four majors in the social sciences, English literature and creative writing, modern languages and cultures, the natural sciences, mathematics, and the fine arts. This breadth gives students chances to pursue interests outside their chosen academic fields as well as to test the waters of completely unfamiliar subjects.

Mills offers the Bachelor of Arts degree in American studies; anthropology and sociology; art (history and studio); biochemistry and molecular biology; biology; business economics; chemistry; child development (2); communication; comparative literature; computer science; dance; dramatic arts; economics; English (2); environmental studies; ethnic studies; French studies; German studies; government; Hispanic studies; history; international relations; liberal studies; mathematics; music; philosophy; political, legal, and economic analysis; psychology; sociology; and women's studies.

Students who choose to create their own major work with 2 faculty advisers to plan an individual program that draws courses from across the curriculum and knits them into a coherent whole.

Preparation for teaching and for California state teaching credentials is available at all levels, from nursery school to junior college. Special prelaw and premedicine advising is available.

Academic Program

To earn a Mills B.A., students must take thirty-four semester courses (usually four courses each semester). Grading is traditional, and a pass-fail option is available outside the major. First-year students take interdisciplinary seminars on such topics as Science and Pseudoscience, Tribal Cultures in Fact and Fiction, and Music and the Written Word. Students are also expected to choose two courses from each of four areas (natural sciences and mathematics, social sciences, humanities, and fine arts), a one-semester multicultural or cross-cultural course, and one course that heavily stresses writing skills. They also must choose at least half their courses from outside their major field. Students complete their chosen major with a senior project or thesis. A comprehensive program in mathematics and computer science offers basic grounding in mathematics for women who have had insufficient high school preparation but need math skills for their prospective careers.

The Career Center offers a four-year counseling program to assist students in clarifying their career and life goals. Workshops, individual counseling sessions, an extensive internship program, a strong "old girl" alumnae network, and special opportunities to meet Bay Area business leaders and top professional women in every field all help students to focus their interests and plan career goals.

Off-Campus Arrangements

Mills has exchange or visiting programs with fifteen American colleges and universities: Agnes Scott, Barnard, Manhattanville, Mount Holyoke, Simmons, Spelman, Swarthmore, Wellesley, and Wheaton Colleges and Howard University. American University's Washington Semester program is available for qualified students. Students with a spirit of adventure and a 3.0 GPA may participate in eleven study-abroad programs in Austria, England, France, Germany, Ireland, Israel, Italy, Japan, Scotland, Spain, and Wales.

Sophomores, juniors, and first-semester seniors may cross-register for one course per semester at the University of California at Berkeley, California College of Arts and Crafts, the Graduate Theological Union, Holy Names College, and St. Mary's College of California, or they can pursue a subject as an independent study project under the supervision of a Mills professor, who will guide their work.

Academic Facilities

The beautiful, open-stack, computerized F. W. Olin Library attracts students to study as well as research among its 248,238 volumes, 22,000 rare books and manuscripts, and 816 periodicals. Students may also use most of the library resources on site at the University of California at Berkeley to supplement the Mills collections. The academic computer center (Mills was a women's college pioneer in computer study), electronic music studio, and excellent laboratory facilities in the physical and life sciences are widely used by students in all majors. The highly regarded Children's School provides a daily laboratory for students interested in early childhood education. Lisser Hall contains a flexible proscenium stage as well as a small experimental theater; graduates in theater design as well as in performance have made names for themselves in professional theater and films.

Costs

For 2000–01, tuition is $18,000, and room and board are $7588. Medical care, insurance, and Associated Student fees total $1056 for resident and commuting students. Students should calculate the costs of travel, books, and personal expenses on an individual basis.

Financial Aid

More than 80 percent of Mills students are awarded a financial aid package that includes a loan, campus work-study, and a scholarship grant from Mills, outside sources, or both. Awards are based on both need and academic merit. Scholarship grants range from $200 to full tuition per year. Mills makes a special effort to provide financial aid to members of minority groups who demonstrate need.

Almost 90 percent of Mills undergraduates who apply for financial aid are offered assistance. Financial aid applicants are expected to apply for assistance from appropriate outside sources, such as the National Merit Scholarship, Federal Pell Grant, and California State Grant programs. More than 40 percent of Mills students have some of their determined need offset by such outside awards. Loans may be obtained by most students, and 45 percent of undergraduates are offered campus work opportunities; some students take off-campus jobs.

All freshman and transfer candidates who are California residents must file the Free Application for Federal Student Aid (FAFSA) to be considered for all types of government aid and must also file the Cal Grant GPA Verification Form. Students who seek Mills scholarship funds must also file the Mills Financial Aid Form. Priority is given to applicants who meet the published deadlines.

Faculty

The Mills faculty is evenly divided between women and men and offers students the chance to work with professional women mentors in every academic area. Faculty members are selected for teaching ability and scholarly achievement; 95 percent of full-time faculty members hold the top degree in their field.

Student Government

Student government plays a strong and active role in Mills life. Mills students establish the form of their own government and regulate all nonacademic aspects of their lives. The Honor System places the responsibility for upholding the social and academic standards of the College on the individual. Students serve as members of most faculty committees and also participate in curriculum planning.

Admission Requirements

Most freshmen admitted to Mills have a strong B average and have followed a full college-preparatory course in their secondary school, including English, 4 years; mathematics, 3 to 4 years; foreign languages, 2 to 4 years; social sciences, 2 to 4 years; and laboratory science, 2 to 4 years. Many have special talents or have taken course work in the fine arts. Mills is interested in individuals, not statistical averages, so each application is carefully reviewed. Credit for precollege courses is granted under certain conditions, and students are encouraged to take the College Board Advanced Placement tests. Applications from transfers are welcome, as are those from students resuming their education or older women who have delayed their entrance to college or who wish to continue work on the B.A. The SAT I or ACT is required of all applicants. For women resuming their studies with at least 12 units of college credit, the SAT I/ACT requirement may be waived. For international applications, both the SAT I/ACT and the TOEFL are necessary. Applications should be accompanied by transcripts and three letters of recommendation. An interview, either on campus or with an alumna representative, is strongly recommended for all applicants.

Application and Information

The priority deadline for admission applications is February 1. Applicants are notified by the Admission Committee in late March. All students are encouraged to meet this deadline; however, international students, merit scholarship applicants, and all other financial aid applicants must apply by February 1. Financial aid is awarded on a first-come, first-served basis, starting with those who meet the deadline. Financial aid awards are made after admission decisions.

For admission to the spring term, the deadline is November 1, and admission decisions are mailed in late December. Students who want to be considered for a California State Grant for the spring semester must apply by the previous March 2 deadline.

For more information, students should contact:

Avis E. Hinkson
Dean of Admission
Mills College
5000 MacArthur Boulevard
Oakland, California 94613
Telephone: 510-430-2135
              800-87-MILLS (toll-free)
Fax: 510-430-3314
E-mail: admission@mills.edu
World Wide Web: http://www.mills.edu

Mills students in front of Concert Hall.

MILWAUKEE SCHOOL OF ENGINEERING
MILWAUKEE, WISCONSIN

The School

Milwaukee School of Engineering (MSOE) is a member of, and accredited by, the North Central Association of Colleges and Schools. Discipline-specific accrediting agencies are identified in the MSOE academic catalogs. Advancing beyond acquisition to the highly sophisticated application of knowledge has been the foundation of MSOE's educational philosophy for more than ninety-five years. This approach, the university's educational niche, produces graduates who are fully prepared to begin their first jobs and pursue challenging careers. MSOE graduates start their careers as work-ready problem solvers and develop into leaders: creating new products, starting or heading companies, and working to better their communities. MSOE is governed by a more than 50-member Board of Regents elected from leaders in business and industry nationwide who are members of the more than 200-member MSOE Corporation.

The student body of more than 2,700 men and women comes from throughout the United States and numerous countries. Since its founding, the university has encouraged the enrollment of students of any race, color, creed, or gender. Approximately half of the full-time students live in three modern high-rise residence halls.

Representatives of firms from throughout the country, including representatives from Fortune 500 companies, visit MSOE during the academic year to interview graduating students for employment and to discuss career opportunities. The University has a 98 percent placement rate. MSOE's Counseling Services Office provides individual assistance for students with educational, personal, or vocational concerns. Free, on-campus tutoring is provided by the Learning Resource Center and Tau Omega Mu, an honorary fraternity founded in 1953 for the purpose of aiding students who need extra help with their studies.

The Student Life and Campus Center provides on-campus recreational activities. This facility houses student activity rooms, student organization offices, a TV viewing area, a cafeteria, and a game room. Additional recreation areas can be found in the residence halls and the MSOE Sports Center.

There are more than fifty professional societies, fraternities, and other special interest groups on campus. Many students participate in intramural sports programs. MSOE is a member of the National Collegiate Athletic Association (NCAA) Division III Lake Michigan Conference. The Athletic Department sponsors NCAA student teams in men's baseball, basketball, cross-country, golf, ice hockey, soccer, tennis, track and field, volleyball, and wrestling and women's basketball, cross-country, soccer, softball, tennis, track and field, and volleyball that compete with teams from other private colleges and universities in the Midwest.

In addition to the undergraduate degree programs listed below, MSOE offers six Master of Science degree programs: architectural engineering, engineering, engineering management, environmental engineering, medical informatics (jointly offered with the Medical College of Wisconsin), and perfusion.

Location

The MSOE campus is located in the East Town section of downtown Milwaukee. Nearby are the Bradley Center, the Midwest Express Center, the Marcus Center for the Performing Arts, the theater district, churches of most denominations, major hotels and office buildings, restaurants, and department stores. Famous for its friendly atmosphere, Milwaukee offers students many opportunities for educational, cultural, and professional growth. The metropolitan area has more than 13,000 acres of parks and river parkways. A few blocks east of the MSOE campus is Lake Michigan, a place of year-round natural beauty. MSOE also offers classes in Appleton, Wisconsin, for students who wish to pursue select graduate degrees in the evening on a part-time basis.

Majors and Degrees

Four-year programs are offered that lead to Bachelor of Science degrees in business and computer systems, construction management, engineering (architectural, biomedical, computer, electrical, industrial, mechanical, and software), engineering technology (electrical and mechanical), management systems, and nursing. A Bachelor of Science or Bachelor of Arts degree is offered in technical communication. A two-degree, five-year option is available in a combination of engineering, business, and technical communication programs. An engineering/environmental engineering degree (B.S./M.S. combination) is also available.

Academic Program

MSOE guarantees graduation in four years for full-time undergraduate students who start on track as freshmen, follow the prescribed curriculum, and meet graduation requirements.

The degree programs at MSOE combine study in degree specialty courses with basic study in sciences, communication, mathematics, and humanities in a high-technology, applications-oriented atmosphere. Students who are admitted with advanced credit to a program leading to a bachelor's degree must complete at least 50 percent of the curriculum in residence at MSOE. MSOE operates on a quarter system. Students average between 16 and 19 credits per quarter, which represent a combination of lecture and laboratory courses.

MSOE offers students the opportunity to participate in the Air Force Reserve Officer Training Corps (AFROTC) program or the Army ROTC program, which are offered in conjunction with Marquette University.

Academic Facilities

The Fred Loock Engineering Center adjoins the Allen-Bradley Hall of Science, forming a prime technical education and applied research complex. The Walter Schroeder Library houses more than 60,000 volumes, with collections that represent the specialized curricula of the university. Electronic technology enables the library to connect with libraries, government agencies, and other sources of information throughout the world. Academic computing facilities, which are available to all MSOE students and faculty on an unlimited basis, are administered by the Computer and Communication Services Department (CCSD). Full-time freshmen are required to participate in a Technology Package program that includes a notebook computer and affiliated services. A full range of software is available on these systems and via the local area network linked by a fiber-optic ring around the campus. State-of-the-art electrical, mechanical, industrial, and nursing laboratories complement the respective areas of study. The Applied Technology Center (ATC) utilizes faculty and student expertise to solve technological problems confronting business and industry. The ATC is heavily involved in the transferring of new technologies into real business practice through the Rapid Prototyping Center (MSOE is the only university in the world to possess the four leading rapid prototyping technologies), Fluid Power Institute, Photonics and Applied Optics Center, High Impact Materials and Structures Center, Construction Science and Testing Center, and the Center for Biomolecular Modeling.

There are more than sixty laboratories at MSOE, many with industrial sponsorship from such companies as Johnson Controls, Aeroquip-Vickers, Harley-Davidson, Wisconsin Bell, Rockwell Automation/Allen-Bradley, Master Lock, Snap-On Tools, General Electric, and Outboard Marine Corporation. The key to the Rapid Prototyping Center's success is a high level of industrial parts design and fabrication activity using stereolithography, laminated object manufacturing, and fused deposition modeling systems.

Costs

For 2000–01, tuition is $19,845 per year, plus $1140 for the Technology Package (notebook computer, software, insurance, maintenance, Internet access, and user services). The cost of room and board in the residence halls is approximately $4530 per year. Books and supplies average $370 per quarter but may be somewhat higher the first quarter.

Financial Aid

Qualified students are assisted by a comprehensive financial aid program, including MSOE and industry-supported scholarships, student loans, and part-time employment; Federal Perkins Loan, Federal Stafford Student Loan, Federal Work-Study, Federal Pell Grant, and Federal Supplemental Educational Opportunity Grant programs; and state-supported grant programs.

Faculty

There are 244 men and women on the MSOE faculty (full-time and part-time). Many are registered professional engineers, architects, and nurses in Wisconsin and other states. They and their colleagues in nontechnical academic areas are active in related professional societies. The student-faculty ratio is 12:1; MSOE does not utilize teaching assistants.

Student Government

The MSOE Student Government Association (SGA) represents clubs and fraternities as well as residence halls and commuting students. SGA appoints representatives to the Campus Security and Disciplinary Hearing committees and the Alumni Association's Board of Directors.

Admission Requirements

Each applicant to Milwaukee School of Engineering is reviewed individually on the basis of his or her potential for success as determined by academic preparation. Admission may be gained by submitting an application for admission and the appropriate transcripts. Transcripts indicating graduation from an approved high school or high school equivalency are required of all applicants. In addition, transfer students are required to submit transcripts from all prior institutions attended. An applicant's prior course work is reviewed to determine eligibility for admission. Required course work varies depending on the desired course of study. Students are encouraged to complete math through precalculus (including algebra and geometry), chemistry, biology (nursing), physics, and 4 years of English. All entering freshmen are also required to provide results from the ACT or the SAT I unless they have completed 15 or more college credits or have been out of high school for two or more years. Entering freshmen are given placement tests to determine their exact standing in mathematics and science.

Transfer opportunities exist into the junior year of the Bachelor of Science in management systems and the Bachelor of Science/Bachelor of Arts in technical communication programs with the appropriate associate degree or equivalent credits.

Application and Information

Classes start in September, November, March, and June. Freshmen and transfer students may enter at the beginning of any quarter; however, entry in the fall quarter is recommended. An application for admission may be obtained by contacting the address below or by visiting MSOE's Web site listed below. Applicants are encouraged to visit the MSOE Admission Office to obtain the form and have a preadmission counseling interview. Procedures for admission are included with the application.

Admission Office
Milwaukee School of Engineering
1025 North Broadway Street
Milwaukee, Wisconsin 53202-3109
Telephone: 414-277-6763
               800-332-6763 (toll-free)
E-mail: explore@msoe.edu
World Wide Web: http://www.msoe.edu

Students and their families, faculty, and staff get together to begin the new school year during orientation festivities in "The Mall" at MSOE.

MINNEAPOLIS COLLEGE OF ART AND DESIGN
MINNEAPOLIS, MINNESOTA

The College

The 113-year-old Minneapolis College of Art and Design, along with The Minneapolis Institute of Arts and the Children's Theatre Company, occupies three square blocks in a residential neighborhood just south of the downtown district. The three institutions constitute one of the largest art centers in the nation.

There are currently 324 men and 213 women enrolled in the B.F.A. program. The College maintains furnished apartments in modern residences, which can accommodate approximately 185 students (35 percent of the entire student population).

In addition to its regular academic program, the College offers evening, Saturday, and summer school classes and art-related films, lectures, performances, and conferences through the Continuing Studies Office. The MCAD Gallery hosts exhibitions during the academic year, providing students with an excellent opportunity to view the work of important contemporary artists and designers. As part of a visiting artists program, nationally prominent artists, designers, and critics visit the campus for varying periods of time to teach, lecture, and work with students and faculty.

Although there are a variety of campus social events each year, students who apply to the College should be aware that its standards of professionalism and performance demand a significant commitment.

In addition to its undergraduate programs, the Minneapolis College of Art and Design offers the Master of Fine Arts degree in visual studies.

Location

Minneapolis and St. Paul have a combined population of 2 million. The Twin Cities are rich in cultural resources, which include the Guthrie Theatre, the Walker Art Center, the Minnesota Orchestra, the Hennepin Center for the Arts, and the University of Minnesota. The area has major-league sports teams in baseball, basketball, and football. There are beautiful city lakes, bike paths, ski slopes, and city and state parks.

Majors and Degrees

The Minneapolis College of Art and Design offers the Bachelor of Science degree in visualization and the Bachelor of Fine Arts degree with majors in advertising design, animation, cartooning/comic illustration, drawing, film/video, fine arts studio, furniture design, graphic design, illustration, interactive multimedia, painting, photography, printmaking, and sculpture.

Academic Program

In order to be awarded the B.S. degree, students are required to complete 120 semester credits, 36 of which concentrate in courses relating to visualization (e.g., communication theory and marketing: history, strategies, forms and perceptions, media analysis, hypermedia), and 18 credits, which are taken within MCAD's studio offerings. Students are also required to participate in team-based projects, an externship or study abroad program, and a senior project/exhibit. This degree program offers course work in visual persuasion and information techniques applicable to the fields of advertising/marketing, science/technology, entertainment, education, and corporate communications.

The B.F.A. program requires students to complete 120 semester credits. Eighteen of these are in the first-year Foundation Studies program, 39 are in the liberal arts area, and 63 are in the studio. To facilitate the growth of the perception and judgment necessary for meaningful creative endeavor, the College has developed a curriculum that stresses critical thinking, artistic inquiry, professional responsibility, and interdisciplinary dialogue. The goals of the first-year Foundation Studies Program are to develop a student's ability to integrate verbal and visual communication skills and enhance personal expression while preparing for the major areas of study. Course work within the various majors provides students with a solid foundation in craftsmanship and offers both technical and conceptual information. All students are encouraged to expand their interests and technical abilities in other disciplines through elective courses. Complementing work in the studio courses, the Liberal Arts Division offers study in history, criticism, literature, philosophy, religion, and the social and behavioral sciences.

Off-Campus Arrangements

Internships and independent study are available. Mobility programs with other colleges in the Association of Independent Colleges of Art and Design, the four art colleges in Canada, Osaka University of Arts, and Macalester College allow students to take advantage of academic offerings at other institutions while pursuing a degree at the College. The College offers study abroad opportunities in Denmark, England, France, Germany, Ireland, Italy, Japan, and Mexico, and a New York studio semester. In addition, a Student-at-Large Program permits students who are not pursuing a degree to enroll in day classes on a space-available basis.

Academic Facilities

The College's glass-walled main building features a remarkable flexible architectural plan that integrates studios, lecture-critique rooms, auditoriums, offices, the Media Center, and exhibition spaces. Personal, individual student workspaces are available to all students upon completing their foundation requirements. The College's seven computer labs, with more than 110 stations, offer a variety of software and hardware that support all academic areas. The Computer Center is connected to the global network Internet, which provides public information and e-mail access. The College library contains 50,000 volumes with emphasis on the visual arts; an extensive picture file; a collection of more than 130,000 slides; an audiocassette, videocassette, and CD-ROM collection; and periodical files. The Minneapolis Institute of Arts, a major American museum, and the Children's Theatre, an internationally acclaimed professional theater, are located adjacent to the College campus.

Costs

Tuition for 2000–01 is $19,060. Art supplies and books average $1500, and housing is approximately $3650. Students should allow about $500 for personal expenses and about $300 for transportation locally.

Financial Aid

More than 72 percent of the College student body receive financial aid to meet education costs. Financial aid administered by the College comes from federal, state, and private sources and includes Federal Pell Grants, Federal Stafford Student Loans, Federal Supplemental Educational Opportunity Grants, Federal Perkins Loans, and Minnesota State Scholarships and Grants-in-Aid. College-controlled aid includes a variety of College grants, scholarships, and work-study contracts. Aid from private sources is also available. To qualify, applicants must submit the Free Application for Federal Student Aid (FAFSA).

Faculty

The College has a faculty of 92 working professional artists and designers (38 full-time, 54 part-time). Sixty-six percent of full-time faculty members have earned terminal degrees. Members of the fine arts and media arts faculty generally have their own studios and exhibit works locally, nationally, and internationally. Members of the design faculty have professional responsibilities apart from their teaching, as many of them are employed by corporations, agencies, and design firms. The faculty-student ratio of 1:12 and the small size of the student body support excellent communication and rapport among students and faculty members.

Student Government

MCAD's student government includes a chairperson, a secretary, a treasurer, and the elected student representatives to the regular College standing committees. The government meets officially each week in open forum and sponsors a variety of activities and organizations, including membership passes to the Walker Art Center and the Minneapolis YMCA, a student gallery in the Calhoun Square Mall, film series, and social activities.

Admission Requirements

Admission to the College is based on a student's previous academic performance, creative abilities, and degree of personal motivation. All applicants must have graduated from an accredited public or private secondary school, in the upper half of their class, or have received a certificate of equivalence. To apply for admission, every candidate must submit a completed application form, an application fee, letters of recommendation, and a portfolio of creative work. SAT I, PSAT, or ACT scores are also required. A B.F.A. applicant who has had art-related courses should submit one letter from an art instructor. An applicant who has had no art-related courses should submit a letter from an instructor in an academic area other than art or from a counselor. All freshman applicants who are applying for the first time must submit a high school transcript. Transfer applicants must submit high school and college transcripts. High school transcripts are not required for applicants who have received a four-year undergraduate degree. Portfolios are required of all B.F.A. transfer applicants desiring studio credit transferral.

Recognizing the value of a truly pluralistic academic community, the College strives to attract qualified men and women from all cultural, racial, religious, and economic backgrounds, from this country and abroad.

Application and Information

For a College catalog and an application form, students should write to the following address:

Admissions Office
Minneapolis College of Art and Design
2501 Stevens Avenue South
Minneapolis, Minnesota 55404

Telephone: 612-874-3760
                800-874-6223 (toll-free)
Fax: 612-874-3701
E-mail: admissions@mcad.edu
World Wide Web: http://www.mcad.edu/

The North Studio, one of the painting and drawing classrooms where students take advantage of the large spaces and natural lighting.

MISSOURI SOUTHERN STATE COLLEGE
JOPLIN, MISSOURI

The College

Missouri Southern State College is a four-year institution that specializes in undergraduate university education with an international perspective. The College focuses on classroom teaching, resulting in a tradition of small classes and close, personal interaction between faculty members and approximately 5,600 students. This approach is maintained through an 18:1 student-teacher ratio. Southern's faculty members come from all over the world, with degrees from prestigious universities and professional experience in the disciplines they teach.

Southern stresses the development of independent learners and their ability to conceptualize, solve problems, manipulate thoughts and patterns, and work cooperatively. Those elements, coupled with an international emphasis, enable Southern's graduates to compete successfully in the rapidly changing world. This international emphasis, a distinctive theme of the College's mission, is the focus of the Institute of International Studies, which coordinates all international programs and activities, including a pervasive global dimension in all curricula, study-abroad opportunities for faculty members and students, internships abroad for students, and expanded foreign language offerings.

A wide range of extracurricular activities, designed to support the academic experience and develop leadership abilities, is available for both resident and commuting students. More than eighty-five organizations, including departmental groups, Greek fraternities and sororities, religious and professional organizations, and honor societies invite involvement and camaraderie. Also available are music and theater performance activities and many other opportunities. Varsity athletes in fourteen men's and women's sports compete in NCAA Division II. Athletic facilities include a new multipurpose 80,000-square-foot athletic center, with comfortable chair-back seating for approximately 3,500. The facility features a six-lane, 200-meter indoor track and will be home to the Missouri Southern men's and women's basketball teams, who will play on the arena's parquet floor. Other facilities include an artificial turf stadium with an all-weather running track, a swimming pool, racquetball courts, and lighted tennis courts and softball and soccer fields.

The 600 students who live on campus enjoy air-conditioned residence halls. The Student Life Center offers a cafeteria, an aerobics room, a weight/exercise room, laundry facilities, a computer lab, a video game room, and a lounge with a big-screen television and surround sound.

Location

Missouri Southern's 341-acre campus is located in what has been known as the "Crossroads of America." Two major cross-country highways intersect in Joplin—U.S. 71 north to south and I-44 east to west. This location allows easy access to major metropolitan cities around the Midwest. However, the College is also in ideal surroundings on the edge of the Ozarks, where recreational opportunities abound. The beautifully landscaped and extremely safe suburban campus rests on the edge of town within walking distance of the region's largest mall. Many movie theaters, restaurants, and athletic and cultural activities provide entertainment throughout the year. Students find employment in businesses throughout Joplin, which is Missouri's fourth-largest metropolitan region, and the surrounding communities. Area businesses also provide internships for students in a variety of disciplines and recruit graduates for permanent positions.

Majors and Degrees

Missouri Southern offers more than 100 degree options for the Bachelor of Science, Bachelor of Arts, Bachelor of Science in Business Administration, Bachelor of Science in Education, and Bachelor of General Studies. Also offered are Associate of Arts and Associate of Science degrees. Bachelor's degrees are awarded in accounting, art, athletic training, biology, chemistry, communications, computer-assisted manufacturing technology, computer information science, criminal justice administration, data processing, economics and finance, elementary education, English, environmental health technology, French, general business, German, health promotion and wellness, history, international business, international studies, management, management technology, marketing, mathematics, medical technology, music, nursing, paralegal studies, physical education, physics, political science, psychology, secondary education, social studies, sociology, Spanish, and theater. Associate degrees are awarded in accounting, computer-aided drafting and design, computer analysis, computer-assisted manufacturing technology, computer programming, dental hygiene, environmental health technology, law enforcement, pre-engineering, radiologic technology, and respiratory therapy. Certificate programs include basic police recruit studies, computer science and information systems, emergency medical technician studies, and EMT-paramedic studies. Preprofessional programs are offered in agriculture, dentistry, engineering, medicine, optometry, pharmacy, and veterinary medicine.

Academic Program

Because graduates may change occupations and careers several times during their working lives, all students pursuing a degree complete the core curriculum, a series of courses carefully designed to instill certain lifelong thinking and learning skills. Core courses emphasize critical thinking, problem-solving, and communications skills; a general understanding of scientific and artistic aspects of this culture; and the ability to function in a global society through knowledge and understanding of other cultures. In both the core and major studies, writing skills and computer literacy are developed, and an international perspective is stressed in every possible course. The baccalaureate degree requires 51 credit hours of the core with a total of 124 hours; the Associate of Arts degree requires 64 hours, with 42 hours from the core; and the Associate of Science degree requires 64 hours, with 26 hours from the core curriculum.

Several degree programs are designed to provide a seamless path for students wishing to transfer from a two-year institution to Missouri Southern, to transfer from Missouri Southern to another institution to continue undergraduate studies in areas such as engineering or medicine, or to proceed to graduate school in an area such as environmental health.

Many broad-based majors offer emphases that allow students a more specialized direction of study. A prestigious Honors Program provides special challenges and opportunities for qualified students who may receive full scholarships for their academic studies.

Off-Campus Arrangements

Study abroad is an integral part of the College's international approach to education. A summer-study program at Oxford and Cambridge Universities in England is available to qualified students for three-week sessions on various subjects. Many other travel/study opportunities developed by departments last a week to a semester and include language studies, business practices, art, law enforcement, teacher education, and many other disciplines. A significant number of students receive financial assistance for these programs. In addition, students can pay Missouri Southern fees and study abroad for a semester or year in more than 100 colleges and universities throughout the world as part of the International Student Exchange Program (ISEP).

Using telecommunications technology, students in several area towns can take classes via interactive television and the Internet. Courses for dual credit are available in selected high schools in the area.

Academic Facilities

More than $35 million in construction will be completed or underway by 2001, including a current major expansion of Spiva Library that will double its size. Also scheduled for construction is a $12 million health sciences building that will be home to the nursing, kinesiology, and health and wellness programs, among others. Other recent construction includes a new 80,000-square-foot athletic center that features a 200-meter indoor track and a parquet basketball floor, a 250-seat black box theater (opened in fall 1999), a new cafeteria, a major expansion of the Mills Anderson Justice Center, and extensive remodeling of the Ummel Technology Building.

Southern has a safe, modern, and beautifully landscaped campus. The George A. Spiva Library houses more than 238,000 books and 1,200 periodicals. A state and federal government documents collection, a law library, and a 584,000-item microform collection provide additional reference materials for student research. A world of materials and services are available through the library's link with a nationwide computer network of libraries. All functions of the library are automated so students or professors can access library functions via modem. A vast array of resources is also available on CD-ROM format. State-of-the-art computer labs are located in the library and throughout the campus for student use.

Taylor Auditorium is a 2,000-seat facility equipped with state-of-the-art computerized sound and lighting systems. Theater students train and perform there, as do the College's music groups. Both Matthews Hall Auditorium and Mills Anderson Justice Center Auditorium have 300 seats and are equipped for multimedia presentations, films, and other events. Webster Hall Auditorium, seating 400, provides performance space for small musical presentations, lectures, and satellite conferences. Webster Hall also has a variety of facilities that give students extraordinarily valuable experience. Communications students have hands-on opportunities in the production studios of Missouri Southern Television, which broadcasts over the air and on cable. KXMS-FM broadcasts classical music to the region—and around the world on the Internet—24 hours a day.

Costs

Tuition for 2000–01 is $79 per credit hour for Missouri residents and $158 per credit hour for out-of-state students, the lowest in the state of Missouri. Residence halls cost $1805 per semester (including twenty meals per week). An added cost-saving feature is the rental of textbooks for $5 per credit hour per semester.

Financial Aid

A wide variety of financial aid options assist students with college costs. Approximately $14 million is distributed each year to 70 percent of the students, with an average award of approximately $3500. Federal programs include the Federal Pell Grant, Federal Supplemental Educational Opportunity Grant, Federal Work-Study Program, Federal Perkins Loan, and Federal Stafford Loan, among others. Several state programs aid prospective teachers and students with high academic standing. In addition, the College provides a wide range of academic scholarships, performing awards, and student employment. Special scholarships are available for qualified junior college transfer students, and out-of-state tuition waivers are offered to students in a designated surrounding area.

Faculty

The whole focus of Missouri Southern's faculty is teaching and advising undergraduate students. With an 18:1 faculty-student ratio, close personal attention to the individual student's success is integral to the teaching process. Faculty members serve as personal advisers and mentors. Of the 204 full-time faculty members, 62 percent have doctoral or terminal degrees. Faculty members are actively involved in other campus activities as well as many community endeavors and encourage their students to participate in their communities.

Student Government

The Student Senate is the student governing body of the College. Senate members serve on various Faculty Senate committees as voting members, serve as liaisons with the College administration, and initiate new programs for the academic and cultural benefit of all students. The Campus Activities Board organizes social and cultural activities for the students.

Admission Requirements

Students are admitted to Missouri Southern if they are in the top half of their high school graduating class or have a minimum composite score of 18 on the ACT test or 850 on the SAT. Students are strongly encouraged to complete a 16-unit high school core curriculum consisting of 4 units of English, 3 units each of math and social science, 2 units of science, 1 unit of visual/performing arts, and 3 units of additional core electives (2 years of foreign language is highly recommended). Students whose ACT scores and class rank are below those stated may request a review by the admission selection committee.

Application and Information

The College has a priority deadline of August 1. Students may apply any time during their senior year of high school. There is a $15 nonrefundable application fee. Information on specific academic areas and other College programs is readily available from the Admission Office and online by contacting:

Admission Office
Missouri Southern State College
3950 East Newman Road
Joplin, Missouri 64801-1595

Telephone: 417-625-9378
           800-606-MSSC (6772) (toll-free)
Fax: 417-659-4429
E-mail: admissions@mail.mssc.edu
World Wide Web: http://www.mssc.edu

MISSOURI VALLEY COLLEGE
MARSHALL, MISSOURI

The College

Missouri Valley College is a private, coeducational, liberal arts college related to the Presbyterian Church (U.S.A.). It is committed to preparing young people to take their place as active and contributing members of their community. The College was founded in 1889 by a group of Presbyterian and civic leaders in Marshall, Missouri. It has been fully accredited by the North Central Association of Colleges and Schools since 1916. Missouri Valley College is approved by the Missouri State Department of Education and the Board of Christian Education of the Presbyterian Church (U.S.A.). The College is governed by a Board of Trustees consisting of successful individuals from the fields of business, law, medicine, the ministry, education, and the arts and sciences. The premedical courses meet the requirements of the Council on Medical Education of the American Medical Association.

The 1,300 students come from some thirty-five states and several countries, although the majority are from Missouri. Most students live in the ten residence halls located on the College's attractive 150-acre campus.

Membership in the nine social or service fraternities and sororities is open to any student. There are also several service organizations, departmental clubs, honor societies, and recreational groups.

Students may participate in a variety of social, cultural, and recreational programs provided by the College. Intramural and intercollegiate athletics are enjoyed by both men and women. Intramural sports are baseball, basketball, football, softball, and volleyball. Intercollegiate sports are baseball (men), basketball (men and women), football (men), golf (men and women), rodeo (men and women), soccer (men and women), softball (women), track and cross-country (men and women), volleyball (women), and wrestling (men). Students also staff the College newspaper, yearbook, radio station, and television studio.

Missouri Valley is home to the region's newest state-of-the-art multipurpose athletic complex. The Georgia Robertson Burns Complex hosts basketball, indoor track competition, volleyball, and wrestling, as well as indoor physical education and intramural activities. Other features include an extensive weight room, a wooded cross-country course, practice fields, and locker facilities.

Other athletic facilities on campus include Gregg-Mitchell Field, the College's home football and outdoor track field; two soccer fields; three outdoor tennis courts; an intramural field; a weight room housed within the largest women's residence hall; and a forty-stall stable with riding arena to accommodate the rodeo team.

The Ferguson Center houses the central dining room, bookstore, snack bar, lounges, recreation room, radio station, television studio, business and campus life offices, and offices for student organizations.

Location

The College is located in Marshall, Missouri, a city of about 15,000 people, approximately 80 miles east of Kansas City and 180 miles from St. Louis. The Missouri River valley provides a setting rich in the history of the Western Movement and the Civil War. Nearby are the restored historic town of Arrow Rock, an archaeological site, and a Civil War battleground. The Marshall Habilitation Center and several agriculture-related industries provide additional opportunities for education outside the classroom. Indian Foothills Park has softball and baseball fields, a swimming pool, tennis courts, a golf course, and a picnic and recreation area. The Missouri River valley and nearby state parks provide opportunities for camping, hiking, canoeing, and fishing. Students may also participate in the programs of the Marshall Symphony Orchestra and are welcome to join the local YMCA.

Majors and Degrees

Missouri Valley College awards Bachelor of Arts and Bachelor of Science degrees with majors in accounting, actuarial science, alcohol and drug studies, art, biology, business administration (agribusiness, finance, management, and marketing), computer science, criminal justice, economics, elementary education, English, exercise science, general studies, history, human services agency management, mass communications (journalism, radio, and TV), mathematics, philosophy/religion, physical education, political science, psychology, recreation administration, sociology, and speech communications and theater. In addition, the College offers Bachelor of Science degree programs leading to teacher certification in early childhood education, secondary education (English, math, social studies, and speech/theater), and special education.

The Associate of Arts degree is offered in liberal arts and small-business administration.

Preprofessional courses are available in dentistry, engineering, law, medicine, pharmacy, theology, and veterinary medicine.

Academic Program

The emphasis at Missouri Valley College is on a personalized liberal arts education with a focus on career preparation. Students are expected to meet general education requirements in basic skills, gain a wide perspective on the breadth of human knowledge, and acquire an in-depth knowledge of at least one area of study as a major.

Basic requirements for graduation include 128 semester hours of credit. The College has a strong Student Outreach Services Program for those students needing help to achieve success in college academics.

Academic Facilities

The Murrell Memorial Library houses more than 70,200 volumes, 500 periodicals, online data search facilities, and a computer lab. The Collins Science Center contains modern laboratories for biology, chemistry, and physics and houses a computer center. The Mabee Memorial Auditorium provides facilities for the speech communications and theater department. The College operates a television studio and maintains a darkroom, a ceramics workshop with a kiln, and a greenhouse.

Costs

Tuition and fees for the academic year 2000–01 are $11,500. Room and board are $5000 per academic year. Books and supplies cost about $500 per semester, and there is an activity/computer fee of $400 per year. Miscellaneous personal expenses, such as transportation, are not included and vary according to the individual student.

Financial Aid

Financial aid is available to all qualified students, and financial need may be met through a combination of federal, state, and institutional sources of aid. Federal grants and loans help a large number of Missouri Valley College students. Institutional awards and grants are made in the areas of academics, leadership, athletics, drama, and music. To be eligible for financial assistance, a student must be admitted to the College and must submit the Free Application for Federal Student Aid (FAFSA).

Faculty

Faculty members serve as advisers to students in their major fields and work closely with students to help them achieve success in their academic programs. Approximately 60 percent of the faculty members have earned a doctorate or the highest academic degree offered in their field.

Student Government

The Student Senate is made up of representatives elected by the student body and has responsibility for providing a balanced program of cultural, social, and recreational events and activities throughout the school year.

Admission Requirements

Applications for admission to Missouri Valley College are reviewed individually. The College desires to select freshmen and transfer students who will benefit from Valley's full-service program and who demonstrate the potential for academic and personal success.

It is suggested that prospective students make an appointment to visit the campus. Students will have the opportunity for a personal interview with a member of the admission staff and the occasion to tour the College's facilities. Appointments may be arranged by contacting the Admissions Office at the address below.

Students are admitted without regard to race, sex, color, or national origin. Admission status is based upon an analysis of the student's adjusted GPA, ACT or SAT I scores, and personal characteristics.

Application and Information

Students seeking freshman admission should make known their intentions as early as possible in the school year prior to the academic year for which admission is sought. While there is no stated deadline for application, students are encouraged to apply by August 15 for the fall semester or by December 15 for the January term or spring semester. The priority date for submitting the application for admission and the financial aid application is April 1 for fall enrollment.

Students need to take the following steps to satisfy admission procedures: (1) An application form should be completed and submitted in person or by mail to the Admissions Office. (2) The high school principal or counselor should forward an official transcript to the Admissions Office. Applicants may provide a copy of a General Educational Development (GED) certificate in lieu of transcripts. (3) A copy of the results of either the ACT or SAT I test should be provided. A student's high school counselor can assist in arranging for the test and obtaining the results. (4) There is a nonrefundable $10 application fee. (5) Students should submit any other material documenting successful experiences that demonstrate their ability to make satisfactory progress in Missouri Valley College's academic programs. This documentation might include but is not limited to letters of recommendation from teachers, counselors, or principals.

An application form, financial aid information, and other information about Missouri Valley College may be obtained by contacting:

Admissions Office
Missouri Valley College
Marshall, Missouri 65340
Telephone: 660-831-4114

MVC's recently completed Burns Athletic Complex, home of the Vikings.

MITCHELL COLLEGE
NEW LONDON, CONNECTICUT

The College

Mitchell is a private, coeducational four- and two-year residential college. With 500 full-time students and a 14:1 student-faculty ratio, the College provides a supportive student-centered learning environment that addresses the educational needs of all students, including those with learning disabilities. Mitchell is especially proud of its success in working with students who have yet to reach their full academic potential. To that end, the College maintains access for students with varied academic abilities who are highly motivated to succeed.

A student's potential is developed through the College's unwavering commitment to individual asset development. This philosophy comes to life through the College community: a faculty that embraces the task of developing students' intellectual capabilities, a staff specifically trained for programs and services that encourage academic and personal growth, and fellow students who are also exploring their own potential.

Mitchell's nationally recognized student support program, C.A.R.E.S. (Career Preparation, Academic Advisement, Retention, Education, and Support), includes extensive hands-on internship experiences; a Freshman Seminar helps students successfully make the transition to college; and career and transfer assistance helps students plan the next step in their learning adventure.

More than 90 percent of the full-time students live in three traditional residence halls, each housing 100 students. Each building has three floors with double rooms and common baths. The College also offers four historic Victorian and Colonial waterfront residence halls, accommodating between 20 and 30 students each. Other facilities include a fully-equipped gymnasium, a fitness center, athletic fields, a sailing dock, and indoor recreation areas.

Nearly all full-time students are of traditional college age, 18 to 22, and come from throughout the country and around the globe. Most students come from New England states, with about 60 percent from Connecticut, 30 percent from other New England states, and the remaining 10 percent from other states. International students and representatives of multicultural groups comprise approximately 25 percent of the student population. About 150 part-time students, many of whom are adults commuters, enhance the classroom experience.

Clubs for students interested in biking, business, community service, choir, Hillel, music, the newspaper, the yearbook, skiing, multicultural affairs, psychology, and history bring together students with similar interests. Weekends are filled with guest comedians, bands, formal and casual dances, lectures, and organized trips to Boston and New York City.

Rolling lawns, the 26-acre Mitchell Woods, and the waterfront beaches offer plenty of opportunities to outdoor enthusiasts.

Mitchell College is a member of the National Junior College Athletic Association and fields thirteen intercollegiate teams. Men play baseball, basketball, cross-country, lacrosse, and soccer; women play basketball, cross-country, soccer, softball, and volleyball; men and women compete together in cheerleading, golf, sailing, and tennis. The College has a history of athletic excellence, winning many national and New England championships. A full schedule of intramural sports is organized for students of all athletic experience and ability.

Location

New London, Connecticut, where Mitchell College makes its home, is a major center of activity in southeastern Connecticut, a region rich in historic significance. This small but sophisticated city, also home to Connecticut College and the U.S. Coast Guard Academy, is a maritime and resort center located midway between Boston and New York City on the main rail line.

The campus is situated in the city's most scenic residential section. Bordered by a long stretch of sandy beach, the campus consists of 65 acres of gently sloping hillside and forest.

Places for shopping, banking, dining, and fun are within easy walking distance or can be accessed by buses that pass the College entrance. A major shopping mall, factory outlets, and fine and casual dining are minutes from the campus. The region is also home to major tourist attractions, such as the U.S.S. Nautilus and Submarine Museum, Mystic Marinelife Aquarium, Mystic Seaport, Olde Mystic Village, Ocean Beach Park, Stonington Vineyards, Foxwoods Resort and Casino, the Mohegan Sun Casino, and the Essex Steam Train.

Majors and Degrees

Baccalaureate degrees are offered in human development and liberal studies (concentrations are in behavioral science, history, and management). Early childhood education and criminal justice are expected to be added as degree programs during the 2000–01 academic year. Associate degrees are offered in athletic training, business administration–accounting, business administration–management (also available with a computer and information systems concentration), criminal justice, early childhood education, general engineering (a 2-3 program with the University of New Haven), graphic design, human development, human services, liberal arts, marine science, physical education, sports management, and therapeutic recreation.

Students undecided about their academic majors are enrolled in the Discovery Program, which is specially designed to provide special courses, additional advising and services to explore their full potential, and assistance in choosing a major.

Academic Program

The academic calendar consists of two full semesters that run from September to December and from January to May. A mini January term and two summer sessions are also offered.

All students must complete the core curriculum, which consists of expository writing, composition and literature, effective speaking, introduction to computer and information systems, an introductory psychology or sociology course, a mathematics course, a lab science, and either U.S. history I and II or Western civilization I and II.

If a student is having difficulty, it is recognized early. Mitchell grades at five-week intervals rather than just at midterms and finals. If a student is experiencing a problem, faculty members and the student's academic adviser work with the student to get back on course.

Mitchell's Tutoring Center provides free, unlimited individualized tutoring by trained professionals (not peer tutors) in every academic discipline. It also offers assistance in improving writing, research, and computer skills, as well as test and exam preparation and study skills development. Some of Mitchell's most successful students are regular users of the Tutoring Center, and they attribute much of their success to its programs.

Students with diagnosed learning disabilities may enroll in the College's nationally recognized Learning Resource Center, which provides supplemental instruction and support along with a student's regular academic program. Each student is assigned two learning specialists to work one-on-one with the student and in small-group settings. The program is designed to teach the learning strategies a student needs to gain independence.

Following completion of their associate degree, students continue in one of Mitchell's baccalaureate programs or successfully transfer to the four-year college or university of their choice.

Off-Campus Arrangements

When not in class, Mitchell students gain the skills and experience they need to succeed in their careers and to make a difference in their communities. These learning experiences are an increasingly important element of a Mitchell education. Nearly all academic programs require or encourage students to participate in volunteer opportunities, internships, or practical experiences as part of their curriculum.

Some of the opportunities include exploring the seacoast with a nationally recognized scientist, teaching at a local elementary school, partnering with a local police officer, helping to negotiate a bill through the state legislature, assisting with advertising campaigns, coaching developmentally challenged athletes or practicing the skills of injury prevention, and sparking the imagination of local school children through storytelling sessions.

Academic Facilities

Mitchell's unique 65-acre waterfront campus includes a 45,000-volume library and two primary classroom buildings.

Students have full use of Mitchell's state-of-the-art computing facilities, with high-speed, full T-1 Internet access. Staffed and open seven days a week with fully trained help-desk consultants, students may use the computer labs to e-mail, scan images, print documents, and complete academic assignments. This same high-speed network and Internet access is also available in each student's residence hall room. For those who do not own a computer, Mitchell offers a computer purchasing plan and service agreement for students.

Costs

Tuition, room, board, and fees for the 2000–01 year are $22,700. Additional annual miscellaneous expenses, including books, are estimated at $1500 per year. Students enrolled in the Learning Resource Center pay an additional $2600 per semester.

Financial Aid

Mitchell annually awards more than $3 million in financial aid, both in need-based and merit-based scholarships and in grant programs designed to recognize academic, athletic, and leadership abilities. Accepted students may qualify for grants and scholarships that do not need to be repaid. They include the Connecticut Independent College Student Grant Program, Federal Pell Grants, Federal Supplemental Educational Opportunity Grants, and Mitchell Scholarships. Self-help aid in the form of loans is also available. They include Federal Stafford Student Loans (subsidized and unsubsidized), Federal PLUS Loans, and Federal Perkins Loan programs. On-campus job opportunities are plentiful for students regardless of their financial aid status.

Mitchell Valued Potential (MVP) scholarships are awarded based on an individual student's ability to contribute to the College. They may be given to students who demonstrate potential in leadership, volunteerism, and involvement in school activities. Athletic scholarships are available to students who participate in men's and women's baseball, basketball, soccer, and softball; women's volleyball; and men's lacrosse. Various payment plans are available.

Faculty

Twenty-two full-time and 30 part-time faculty members teach in Mitchell's classrooms. The student-faculty ratio is 14:1.

Student Government

The Student Government Association (SGA) is comprised of officers and senators who represent the residents and commuters. It addresses issues with campus administration, organizes community projects, serves as the active voice for the student body, and sponsors at least one campuswide program each semester. The SGA also works in tandem with the Student Activities Office concerning club funding and overall programming.

Student involvement is not only encouraged but also expected of all Mitchell students. The College considers participation in campus life the significant edge up for all Mitchell graduates as they enter the workforce in comparison to their peers at other colleges. An active student leads to a well-rounded person. Students enhance their life with self-discipline skills, demonstrate selfless service, and become happier members of the College family through involvement in student activities, athletics, campus employment, and community service opportunities.

Admission Requirements

Each student is evaluated individually as soon as the completed application, along with the official transcript, is received. Admission is based on academic preparation, scholastic aptitude, personal character, and potential to be academically successful. Other important factors taken into consideration include the student's motivation, initiative, maturity, seriousness of purpose, and leadership potential. SAT I or ACT test scores are required. A campus visit and admissions interview are strongly encouraged. Open houses are held in October, January, and April.

Application and Information

Mitchell uses a rolling admission policy. Students can expect to be notified of decisions within weeks of the College's receipt of completed applications and official transcripts sent directly from the students' high schools.

For more information, students should contact:

Kevin Mayne
Vice President for Enrollment Management and Marketing
Mitchell College
437 Pequot Avenue
New London, Connecticut 06320-4498
Telephone: 800-443-2814 (toll-free)
Fax: 860-444-1209
E-mail: admissions@mitchell.edu
World Wide Web: http://www.mitchell.edu

MOLLOY COLLEGE
ROCKVILLE CENTRE, NEW YORK

The College
In 1955, 44 students became part of an exciting new tradition in higher education on Long Island. As the first freshman class of Molloy College, these young students made a commitment to academic excellence. So did the College, which had a distinguished faculty of 15 and a library containing 5,000 books.

Today, Molloy College has become one of the most respected four-year private coeducational institutions of higher learning in the area. It provides academic programs in both day and evening divisions. The Molloy population consists of recent high school graduates, transfer students, and graduate students whose average age is 24. Molloy College is accredited by the Board of Regents of the University of the State of New York and the Middle States Association of Colleges and Schools, and its programs in nursing and social work are accredited by the National League for Nursing Accrediting Commission and the Council on Social Work Education.

Despite its growth over the years, Molloy College retains an intimate and personal atmosphere. It encourages the 2,500 students to develop close working relationships with the faculty. The student body represents many ethnic and socioeconomic groups; to meet their varied needs, the College offers thirty-three undergraduate majors and programs.

The key word at the College is involvement. Student-run clubs and organizations offer a variety of planned activities. Student publications, which include the yearbook, a literary magazine, a newspaper, and a weekly newsletter, provide an outlet for students who want to share their literary and journalistic talents.

Molloy College offers opportunities for students to exercise their leadership abilities, contribute their special talents, utilize their initiative, and expand their social horizons through the variety of activities made conveniently available to them. Athletics, an integral part of student life, are represented at Molloy College on the varsity level by women's basketball, cross-country, soccer, softball, tennis, and volleyball. These teams compete in the NCAA, the ECAC, and the NYCAC. The women's equestrian team holds membership in the Intercollegiate Horse Show Association. Men's baseball, basketball, cross-country, lacrosse, and soccer are played at Division II level.

Student services include the Counseling and Career Services, the Campus Ministry, the Siena Women's Center, health services, and referrals for off-campus housing.

On the graduate level, Molloy College offers a Master of Science degree in nursing and education and post-master's certification in nursing.

Location
Located on a 25-acre campus in Rockville Centre, Long Island, Molloy College is close to metropolitan New York and all its diverse and rich resources. The College is easily accessible from all parts of Nassau, Suffolk, and Queens counties.

Majors and Degrees
Molloy College offers the A.A. degree in liberal arts; the A.A.S. degree in cardiovascular technology, health information technology, nuclear medicine technology, and respiratory care; and B.A. or B.S. degrees in accounting, art, biology, business management, communications, computer information systems, computer science, criminal justice, English, environmental studies, French, history, interdisciplinary studies, international peace and justice studies, mathematics, music, music therapy, nursing, philosophy, political science, psychology, social work, sociology, Spanish, and theology. Teacher certification programs are available in elementary (pre-K–6), secondary (7–12), and special education dual certification.

Special advisement is offered for students interested in predental, prelaw, premedical, or preveterinary programs.

The internship program at the College offers students the opportunity for on-the-job experience along with the classroom exposure so essential to the completely educated person. Internships are available in accounting, art, business management, communications, computer science, criminal justice, English, history, IPJ studies, mathematics, music therapy, political science, psychology, social work, and sociology.

Academic Program
Molloy College, dedicated to the total development of the student, offers a strong liberal arts core curriculum as an integral part of all major fields of study. A minimum of 128 credits is required for a baccalaureate degree. Double majors can be chosen, and numerous minors are available.

Advanced placement credit is granted for a score of 3 or better on the AP exam. CLEP and CPE credit is also given. Qualified full-time students may participate in the Army ROTC program at Hofstra University or St. John's University on a cross-enrolled basis. Molloy students may also elect Air Force ROTC on a cross-enrolled basis with New York Institute of Technology.

Molloy has a 4-1-4 academic calendar.

Academic Facilities
Molloy's James Edward Tobin Library has 133,500 books, 650 periodical subscriptions, 13,500 bound periodicals, 2,950 microfilms, 1,200 microfiches, and four OCLC computer terminals. The Media Center houses 500 pieces of hardware and 9,700 pieces of software.

The College computer labs house 260 microcomputers. In addition, many academic departments have their own computer labs. For example, the International Business Center has sixteen state-of-the-art microcomputers with Internet and e-mail accessibility for students to communicate internationally.

The Wilbur Arts Center features numerous art studios, music studios, a cable television studio, and the Lucille B. Hays Theatre.

Kellenberg Hall houses six science labs, a language lab, and the education resource center. Casey Hall houses two nursing labs and the behavioral sciences research facility.

Costs
For 1999–2000, tuition and fees were $12,470. The cost per credit for part-time students was $395.

Financial Aid
More than 85 percent of the student body of Molloy College is awarded financial aid in the form of scholarships, grants, loans,

and Federal Work-Study Program employment. Financial aid awards are based on academic achievement and financial need. Completion of the Molloy College Application for Financial Aid/Scholarship and the Free Application for Federal Student Aid (FAFSA) is required. No-need scholarships and grants are also available. Students who have attained a 95 percent or better high school average and a minimum combined score of 1250 on the SAT I are considered for the Molloy Scholars' Program, which awards full tuition scholarships. Partial scholarships are available under the Board of Trustees Scholarships, Dominican Scholarships, and the Fine and Performing Arts Scholarships. The Transfer Scholarship Program grants partial tuition scholarships to students transferring into Molloy College with at least a 3.0 cumulative average. Athletic grants (Division II only) are awarded to full-time students based on athletic ability in baseball, basketball, cross-country, equestrian, lacrosse, soccer, softball, tennis, and volleyball.

Faculty

The 290 full-time and part-time faculty members at Molloy are dedicated as much to the students as to their respective fields. The 9:1 student-faculty ratio allows for small classes where students can receive the individual attention they deserve.

In addition to their teaching responsibilities, faculty members advise students in their fields to help them select courses that both satisfy major course requirements and lead to the attainment of career goals.

Student Government

Every member of the Molloy College student body belongs to the Molloy Student Association, whose elected leaders form the Molloy Student Government. This group of students provides the leadership necessary to keep extracurricular life at Molloy College alive, productive, and practical.

Admission Requirements

Recommended admission qualifications include graduation from a four-year public or private high school or equivalent (GED test) with a minimum of 16 units, including 4 in English, 3 in social studies, 2 in a foreign language, 2 in mathematics, and 2 in science. Nursing applicants must have taken courses in biology and chemistry. Mathematics applicants must have taken 4 units of math and 2 of science (including chemistry or physics). Biology applicants must have credits in biology, chemistry, and physics and 4 units of math. A portfolio is required of art applicants, and music students must audition. Social work applicants must file a special application with the director of the social work program.

The admissions committee bases its selection of candidates on the secondary school record, SAT I or ACT scores, class rank, and the school's recommendation. A particular talent or ability can be important. Character and personality, extracurricular participation, and alumni relationships are all considered. On-campus interviews are recommended but not required.

The St. Thomas Aquinas Program, which houses both HEOP and the Albertus Magnus Program, may be options for students not normally eligible for admission.

An early admission plan is available.

Application and Information

To apply to Molloy College, students should submit the following credentials to the Admissions Office: a completed application for admission, a nonrefundable $25 application fee, an official high school transcript or GED score report, official results of the SAT I or ACT, and official college transcripts (transfer students only).

The College uses a rolling admission system. Students are advised of an admission decision within a few weeks after the application filing process is complete.

For further information, prospective students should contact:

Director of Admissions
Molloy College
1000 Hempstead Avenue
Rockville Centre, New York 11570
Telephone: 888-4-Molloy (toll-free)
World Wide Web: http://www.molloy.edu

An aerial view of Molloy College.

MONMOUTH UNIVERSITY
WEST LONG BRANCH, NEW JERSEY

The University

Monmouth University is a private, moderate-sized coeducational institution committed to providing a learning environment that enables men and women to pursue their educational goals and realize their full potential for making significant contributions to their community and society. Small classes, which allow for individual attention and student-faculty dialogue, together with careful academic advising and career counseling, are hallmarks of a Monmouth education.

The student body is diverse, with a population of 4,004 undergraduates and 1,421 graduate students. Although most are from the Northeast, nineteen states and thirty-five nations are represented, and there is a rich ethnic mix. Of the 3,400 full-time students enrolled, more than 1,600 live on campus in traditional residence halls and garden apartment complexes. Both resident and commuting students have a wide variety of extracurricular activities to choose from: an active Student Government Association; the campus newspaper and FM radio station; the yearbook and the literary magazine; the African-American Student Union; Hillel and Christian Ambassadors organizations; almost twenty-five special interest groups; theater; intramurals; and sororities and fraternities that engage in service work on behalf of the University and of the community.

The University's NCAA Division I intercollegiate athletics program includes nine men's teams—baseball, basketball, cross-country, football, golf, indoor track, outdoor track and field, soccer, and tennis—and nine women's teams—basketball, cross-country, field hockey, indoor track, outdoor track and field, soccer, softball, lacrosse, and tennis. The gymnasium has an Olympic-size indoor pool, three regulation-size basketball courts, and a recently expanded training room and fitness center. Outdoor facilities include six tennis courts, an eight-lane all-weather track, baseball, football, soccer, and softball fields, and in-line skating courts.

Many special events are planned each year, including art exhibits, concerts, films, lectures, public-issues forums, entertainment programs, and sightseeing excursions and shopping and museum-hopping trips to cities in the metropolitan area.

Monmouth students are accorded many special services, including the full resources of the Learning and Career Advising Center, which is staffed by academic and other professional personnel who offer academic advising in addition to individual personal and career counseling. Academic skills services, including the Math Center, the Reading Center, the Writing Center, and the Peer Tutoring Office, provide personalized academic assistance. There are offices to serve students with disabilities and international students. Employment counseling is available through the Placement Office. The Health Center makes available basic medical care.

In addition to its undergraduate degree programs, Monmouth also offers eighteen graduate degree programs in business administration, computer science, corporate and public communication, criminal justice, education, electrical engineering, health-care management, history, liberal studies, nursing, psychological counseling, social work, and software engineering.

Location

The location of the University—in a quiet residential area of an attractive community near the Atlantic Ocean, yet little more than an hour's drive from the metropolitan attractions of New York and Philadelphia—is an appealing feature. The University's safe and secure 147-acre campus, considered one of the most beautiful in New Jersey, includes among its forty-five buildings a harmonious blending of traditional and contemporary architectural styles. The centerpiece building is Woodrow Wilson Hall, a National Historic Landmark that houses administrative offices and humanities classrooms. Monmouth's $6.5-million business administration building, Bey Hall; a $4-million renovation of the technology building, Howard Hall; and a $4.7 million renovation of the Edison Science Hall provide students with a first-class learning environment. Restaurants, shops, and theaters are within easy reach, and several large shopping malls and the PNC Bank Arts Center, an entertainment hub, are only a few miles away. Another advantage the University has is proximity to many high-technology firms, financial institutions, and a thriving business-industrial sector. These provide not only employment possibilities for Monmouth University graduates but also the opportunity for undergraduates to gain practical experience through various internships and the cooperative education program conducted by the University.

Majors and Degrees

Monmouth University offers twenty-six baccalaureate degree programs within five schools. The School of Business Administration awards bachelor's degrees in business administration with concentrations in accounting, economics, finance, management, and marketing. The School of Education awards bachelor's degrees that allow students to earn certification as a nursery and elementary teacher (N–8), as a subject teacher (K–12), or as a special education teacher. The School of Humanities and Social Sciences awards bachelor's degrees in the areas of anthropology, art, communication, criminal justice, English, foreign language (Spanish concentration), history, history–political science, music/theater arts, political science, psychology, and social work. The School of Humanities and Social Sciences includes the Department of Interdisciplinary Studies. The School of Science, Technology and Engineering awards bachelor's degrees in biology, chemistry, clinical lab sciences, computer science, mathematics, medical technology, and software engineering. This school houses the Center for Technology Development and Transfer. The School of Nursing and Health Studies awards the Bachelor of Science in Nursing to upper-division transfer students. A preprofessional advising program is available for students who intend to pursue careers in medicine, dentistry, or other health-care fields. Monmouth also offers an accelerated degree program, the Graduate Scholars Program, to enable students to achieve both a bachelor's and master's degree in just five years.

Academic Program

The curriculum is attuned throughout to today's globally oriented technological society while retaining a strong grounding in the liberal arts. Under the General Education Curriculum, students in all degree programs acquire a breadth of knowledge beyond their major fields of study, including an appreciation of world culture. Monmouth University also emphasizes writing, speaking, and other interpersonal skills that are critical to personal and professional success. Monmouth requires all students to fulfill computer literacy and experiential education requirements. Experiential education is a real-world experience related to the academic major.

Monmouth University believes that, while providing sound preparation for successful careers, a major goal of higher education is to help students develop important values. These include a keen sense of citizenship, social responsibility, and the leadership qualities that will equip graduates to contribute actively to the democratic society in which they live. Academic programs at Monmouth stress the importance of thinking in a global context, preparing students for life in an increasingly complex, multicultural world.

An honors program is available for all students who meet the academic requirements.

Genuine concern for the individual student characterizes the Monmouth University educational program. Professors—not teaching assistants—conduct all courses and supervise all laboratories. Students benefit from direct interaction with professors, who are recognized for their scholarly expertise.

Cooperative education is available to students, enabling them to gain practical experience in jobs related to their majors while completing their studies. Internships are available in criminal justice, medical technology, and social work; special off-campus programs are offered for biology and political science majors; and all education majors are required to complete a semester of student teaching. All of these programs carry college credit. The University also participates in the Washington Center, which offers programs in which students may earn credit from their own institution for experiential learning gained through internships and symposia in the nation's capital.

Monmouth University offers a program for students who have not met regular admission requirements but who appear to have the potential for success in college. The Edward G. Schlaefer School is designed to give special attention to incoming students who need extra support and a more structured learning environment in the freshman year.

Academic Facilities

The Guggenheim Library holds 248,000 volumes and 1,300 periodicals. There are excellent computer facilities. Academic programs are supported by state-of-the-art computer hardware and software and classroom/laboratory facilities. The major components supporting Monmouth's academic programs include UNIX, Windows NT, and Novell server systems connected by a sophisticated campus Ethernet network spanning twenty-three buildings and encompassing more than 1,000 workstations campuswide. Workstations that are specifically dedicated to student use are distributed among thirty instructional and open-use laboratories and include DEC-Alpha servers, Silicon Graphics servers and workstations, SUN servers and workstations, Pentium servers and workstations, and Macintosh workstations. Laptop plug-in ports are available in convenient locations across campus. A campus communications network (HawkNet) connects all Monmouth University computing resources to the Internet. All students receive a computer account that provides them with e-mail, World Wide Web browsing and authoring tools, and electronic access to the Guggenheim Library catalog. The Lauren K. Woods Theatre offers students an opportunity to experience all phases of the theater arts, from acting to lighting. The multifunction stage is adaptable to any type of performance, from conventional to theater-in-the-round. All control of the various aspects of a theatrical performance is maintained by students. There are communications facilities for both radio and television, and the University supports a student-run FM radio station. There are also a student-run greenhouse and studios for art and music majors.

Costs

For 2000–01, tuition is $15,758 per year. Room and board are $6690 per year, depending on the type of room and meal plan selected. Costs are subject to change for 2001–02.

Financial Aid

Monmouth University believes that qualified students should not be denied an educational opportunity due to lack of financial resources. The financial aid staff counsels students and their families and assists them in obtaining the maximum financial aid to which they are entitled. In a cooperative effort, the University utilizes institutional, federal, and state resources and expects a reasonable family contribution toward the student's cost of attendance. In developing each student's award package, all resources available are utilized to address individual circumstances and to provide equitable treatment for all applicants.

A wide range of institutional scholarships and grants is offered to the incoming class each year. Award amounts vary according to the quality of the student's previous academic record and housing status. They range up to a maximum of tuition and fees. The scholarship and grant program is available to all prospective full-time freshman and transfer students. Award amounts are renewed at the same level each year for the student's four-year undergraduate career. Scholarship recipients are required to maintain a minimum 3.0 cumulative GPA; merit grant recipients must maintain a minimum 2.5 cumulative GPA; incentive grant recipients must maintain a minimum 2.0 cumulative GPA. Grants and scholarships for this program are offered without regard to financial need. Since resources are not unlimited, priority is given to students who are in full-time attendance and have filed in a timely fashion. All awards are subject to the availability of funds. Students and their families are strongly encouraged to call or visit the Financial Aid Office for assistance.

Faculty

The University's professors are leaders in their fields and contribute through research, publishing, and consulting to their respective academic areas. There are 196 full-time and 262 part-time faculty members. Approximately 85 percent of the full-time instructional faculty have doctorates. The average class size is 22, and the student-faculty ratio is 19:1. The largest class section at Monmouth is 35. Professors are able to know each student by name, and faculty members are available to students for office consultation and extra help.

Student Government

Monmouth's Student Government Association is an important and necessary voice in the University community. Seven senators from each class, along with certain elected officials, express clear and definite opinions and cast votes on University policy. Student representatives are present at all faculty meetings and other resolution-adopting events to present the opinions of the student body. All students are strongly encouraged to participate in these activities.

Admission Requirements

A number of factors are taken into consideration by the Admission Committee when it evaluates candidates for admission. When considering freshman applicants, the committee evaluates grades and test scores. High school transcripts and SAT I or ACT scores must be sent with the application. Counselor recommendations and other information supporting the application are welcome.

Transfer students must submit official transcripts from all colleges attended. If they have earned fewer than 24 transferable credits, they must fulfill freshman admission requirements as well.

An interview is highly recommended. Campus tours are conveniently arranged to meet various schedules.

Application and Information

The deadline for freshman applicants who want to enroll in the fall semester is April 1. For spring semester, the deadline for applications is January 1. Applications received after due dates will be considered on a space-available basis. As housing is somewhat limited, the ideal application time is prior to March 1. When all necessary materials have been submitted, a decision and notification are made as quickly as possible. For further information, students should contact:

Office of Undergraduate Admission
Monmouth University
400 Cedar Avenue
West Long Branch, New Jersey 07764-1898
Telephone: 732-571-3456
           800-543-9671 (toll-free)
Fax: 732-263-5166
E-mail: admission@monmouth.edu
World Wide Web: http://www.monmouth.edu

MONROE COLLEGE
BRONX, NEW YORK

The College

Founded in 1933, Monroe College is a private, coeducational, nonsectarian institution that offers associate and bachelor's degree programs in a unique 2+2 format in accounting, business, computer science, health information management, hotel and hospitality management, information systems, and office technologies. Monroe College is committed to providing a high-quality education, coupled with individualized attention and preparation for today's business world, to serious-minded students who understand the true value of such an education. The Monroe College student is given the opportunity to gain academic and professional competency through comprehensive curricula and is also offered a support system that provides those services essential for academic and professional success. Monroe College, which has campuses in both the Bronx and New Rochelle, is accredited by the Commission on Institutions of Higher Education of the Middle States Association of Colleges and Schools.

Monroe enrolls approximately 4,000 students on its two campuses and at the distance learning sites in Brooklyn and Manhattan. The diverse student population includes recent high school graduates as well as more mature students who are returning to the educational forum. International students, who have access to an International Students' Center and counselors at the New Rochelle campus, make up 5 percent of the total student body. Members of minority groups are well represented on both campuses, as well. The students are primarily commuters, but housing facilities are available at the New Rochelle campus.

Social activities are centered around the Student Activities Committee (SAC) and the athletic program. They seek to provide an opportunity for the future development of the whole student. The student-run newspaper and drama, cheerleading, and dance groups, as well as SAC, are open to all students. Monroe participates in intercollegiate basketball, soccer, and volleyball. Intramural sports include fencing, basketball, volleyball, track, and bowling. Cultural activities include Latino Month and Black History Month, among many others. Professional clubs are available for students in each major. The rich cultural treasures and tourist attractions found in New York City are easily accessible by public transportation.

Location

Monroe is part of the metropolis of New York City, with an urban campus in the Fordham district of the Bronx. The campus is easily accessible by car or public transportation. Its locale is near the Yankees, the Bronx Zoo, and the New York Botanical Gardens. A short train ride away is Manhattan, which is known for Central Park, Broadway, Wall Street and the Financial District, many museums, the Statue of Liberty, the Empire State Building, the World Trade Center, the Staten Island Ferry, and the South Street Seaport.

Monroe's suburban New Rochelle campus is located in the heart of the Sound Shore Corridor in bustling Westchester County. The campus offers convenient and spacious housing that is directly adjacent to the site of New Roc City, a multimillion-dollar development that includes recreational facilities, shops, and restaurants. Within a short distance is the Long Island Sound, with abundant opportunities for recreation and leisure-time activities. Students can make use of a multitude of cultural facilities in New Rochelle and the surrounding communities. Students can also easily travel into New York City by inexpensive public transportation.

Majors and Degrees

Monroe College confers the Bachelor of Business Administration degree in accounting, business management, and information systems and associate degrees in accounting, business administration, computer science, health information management, hospitality management, and office technologies.

Academic Program

Monroe College's bachelor's and associate degree programs emphasize study in the liberal arts as well as in-depth immersion in each academic major. Applicants may be admitted to either the associate or bachelor's degree program upon acceptance. Upon the completion of 60 credits, all Monroe students receive an associate degree. Bachelor's programs, leading to the Bachelor of Business Administration (B.B.A.), require completion of 60 credits beyond the associate degree. Those interested in continuing for a bachelor's degree must apply for admission to the upper division. Monroe operates on a three-semester calendar. The fifteen-week semesters begin in early September, early January, and late April.

There are also distance learning opportunities through Internet courses. Video teleconferencing opportunities are currently offered to all public-sector workers and their families at sites in Brooklyn and Manhattan. Three centers are provided by the Department of Citywide Administrative Services. Classes are offered in the evening during the week and carry college credit. The department plans to expand this program to include sites in all five of the New York City boroughs within the next year.

Advanced placement is available for CLEP, transfer credit, prior learning experience (life experience evaluation), and proficiency examinations. Students can receive advanced-standing placement for up to 50 percent of the required credits for their chosen degree program.

Off-Campus Arrangements

Internship and co-op programs are conducted by the College in cooperation with businesses, industries, government agencies, and nonprofit organizations. They integrate on-campus study with off-campus work-study experience. The programs complement and reinforce the professional curriculum studied in the class, providing a broader comprehension of the context in which the student will be employed.

Academic Facilities

Both campuses have complete libraries with Online Computer Library Center (OCLC) access to other metropolitan New York and Westchester college libraries. The Learning Resource Centers, which are available to all students from early in the morning to late at night, are equipped with state-of-the-art computers and academic enrichment computer programs and videos. Staff tutors are available on a daily basis to reinforce classroom lectures in all subjects. In addition, Monroe has more computers per student than any other college of its size in the area. Student Services provides close educational advisement as well as health clinics and primary-level psychological counseling. Students are also urged to take advantage of the Lifetime Career Placement Service. This program evaluates the academic performance and personal attributes of the student in order to identify skills and career goals so they may obtain a position in their field of study upon graduation. Career services also assists students in obtaining part-time employment during their college careers. Workshops are provided on self-assessment, resume preparation, interview skills, and job search strategies. Currently the College has a 95 percent placement rate.

Costs

Tuition for the 2000–01 academic year is $6920, and individual courses cost $865, plus a College fee of $65 for up to 6 credits and $130 for more than 6 credits. Boarding students pay an additional residence fee of $1600 per semester (double room) with a nonrefundable $100 application fee. Books cost approximately $275 per semester.

Financial Aid

Financial assistance is determined by the need of the student along with the availability of funds from federal, state, and institutional sources. More than 90 percent of the students receive some type of financial aid. The College takes into account the objective facts and the financial circumstances of the student and family, recognizing the differences of each family situation. Available assistance includes Federal Pell Grants, Federal Supplemental Educational Opportunity Grants, Federal Stafford Student Loans (subsidized and unsubsidized), Federal PLUS Loans, Federal Perkins Loans, and the Federal Work-Study Program. For those students who have been New York State residents for one year or more, TAP may also be available. In addition, the College offers institutional aid (grant-in-aid), scholarships, loans, and employment to students, as well as funding for the purchase of some special equipment and services for the disabled.

Faculty

Monroe has more than 200 full-time faculty members and adjunct faculty members who are experts in their fields, as well as an excellent tutorial staff. They work closely with their students, both inside and outside the classroom, to help them make the most of their talents, interests, and dreams. The student-faculty ratio is 15:1.

Admission Requirements

Monroe College seeks serious individuals who demonstrate that they have the interest, ability, and potential to successfully complete appropriate requirements for the course of study selected. Graduation from an accredited high school, two-year college, or the equivalent; a personal interview; and SAT I scores and/or an entrance exam are the basic requirements for admission to Monroe College.

Application and Information

Submission of the following credentials is required: a completed application, a transcript of all prior formal education, SAT I or ACT scores if available, two letters of recommendation, and an essay on a topic provided to all applicants. The College actively seeks applications from international students.

Applications are accepted on a rolling basis. Students are informed of the decision by the Admission Committee within two weeks of submission of all required documentation.

Students interested in applying to the Bronx campus should contact:

Peter Vida
Director of Admissions
Monroe College–Bronx Campus
Monroe College Way
Bronx, New York 10468
Telephone: 718-933-6700
            800-55-MONROE (toll-free)
Fax: 718-364-3552
E-mail: admissions@www.monroecoll.edu
World Wide Web: http://www.monroecoll.edu

Students interested in applying to the New Rochelle campus should contact:

Rhoda Kaufman
Director of Admissions
Monroe College–New Rochelle Campus
434 Main Street
New Rochelle, New York 10801
Telephone: 914-632-5400
            800-55-MONROE (toll-free)
Fax: 914-632-5462
E-mail: admissions@www.monroecoll.edu

International students should contact:

Gersom Lopez
Director of International Student Admissions
Monroe College–New Rochelle Campus
434 Main Street
New Rochelle, New York 10801
Telephone: 914-632-5400
            800-55-MONROE (toll-free)
Fax: 914-632-5462
E-mail: glopez@www.monroecoll.edu
World Wide Web: http://www.monroecoll.edu (select International Admissions)

MONTANA STATE UNIVERSITY–BILLINGS
BILLINGS, MONTANA

The University

Montana State University–Billings (MSU–Billings) is set under the Rimrocks, sandstone cliffs that shadow the Yellowstone River. The University draws its inspiration and strength from the city of Billings and the mountains and prairies of the Yellowstone region.

The environment, adventure, practicality, hard work, community, and diversity are the values of the Yellowstone region and are the values of the University. Committed to a curriculum anchored in the liberal arts, the University offers students the specific knowledge and skills conducive to success in a career, be it in business, education, technology, or some other field. With an enrollment of 4,200, the University offers degrees in five colleges: Arts and Sciences, Business, Education and Human Services, Professional Studies and Lifelong Learning, and Technology.

The College of Arts and Sciences provides quality programs in the arts, humanities, and sciences that meet the needs of the state and region, including the number one–ranked communication arts department in the nation. This College also offers a rich menu of general education courses for the University's baccalaureate students.

As Billings has evolved into the major business center in the region, the business programs at Montana State University–Billings have grown and prospered. The College of Business is now second to the College of Education and Human Services in the number of degrees it awards. The College's graduates enjoy a high placement rate and outstanding success on the CPA exam.

The College of Education and Human Services has earned a reputation as regional leader. Faculty members and student teachers remain current in their fields through site work in area professional development schools that cover elementary, middle, and high school education. It has exclusive responsibility in the state of Montana for the undergraduate and graduate degree programs in special education, special education supervision, and rehabilitation counseling. The undergraduate degree in human services is also unique within the state system.

The College of Professional Studies and Lifelong Learning, the newest college at MSU–Billings, represents the institution's commitment to respond to the needs of changing academic expectations in higher education. The College extends the boundaries of MSU–Billings by delivering classes in the community via traditional classes, interactive television, and the Internet.

The College of Technology offers certificate and associate degree programs. Its primary mission is to equip or retrain its students with the applied academic and technical skills to enter the job market successfully. These career opportunities emphasize technical components and immediate hands-on applications.

MSU–Billings students enjoy modern and spacious living quarters in Rimrock and Petro residence halls, which feature all the comforts of home, including free cable TV hookups, kitchen facilities, comfortable lounges, and free access to laundry machines. The residence hall complex also includes The Rimrock Cafe and Stingers Espresso Bar, the student union offices, the Book Depot, and meeting rooms.

Location

The largest city in Montana, Billings (population 100,000) is the primary medical center for a multistate area and serves as a regional center for business, transportation, education, and agriculture. The Yellowstone area offers students an array of cultural and recreational opportunities. Hiking, biking, camping, canoeing, fishing, rock climbing, white-water rafting, skiing, snowmobiling, and many more activities are available to students. Within 45 minutes of the campus, the 12,000-foot Beartooth Mountains rise from the Yellowstone Valley and feature breathtaking views and incredible ski slopes.

Majors and Degrees

Bachelor's degrees are offered in accounting, applied science, art, art teaching (K–12), biology, biology teaching, business economics, chemistry, chemistry teaching, communication and theater, elementary education, English, English teaching, environmental studies, finance, general business administration, health administration, health and physical education (K–12), health promotion, history, history teaching, human services, information systems, liberal studies, management, marketing, mathematics, mathematics teaching, music, music performance, music teaching (K–12), psychology, public relations, rehabilitation and related services, social science teaching, sociology, Spanish, Spanish teaching (K–12), and special education (elementary or secondary).

Preprofessional programs are available in art therapy, engineering, family and consumer science, law, medicine, nursing, pharmacy, and physical therapy.

A two-year associate degree is also available with a variety of thematic concentrations.

Two-year Associate of Applied Science degrees include options in accounting technology, administrative assistant studies, drafting technology, heating/ventilation and air-conditioning technology, medical secretary studies, microcomputer operations, paramedics, and process plant technology.

Certificates are available in accounting assistant studies, assistant drafter studies, automobile collision repair, automobile collision repair and refinishing, automobile refinishing, automotive technology, computer assistant studies, computer-assisted drafting (CAD), diesel technology, major appliance repair, office assistant studies, paramedics, practical nurse studies, and welding/metal fabrication technology.

Academic Program

Access and excellence are fostered through quality instruction at Montana State University–Billings.

Because the University is concerned that its graduates experience practical aspects of the subject matter in which they specialize, the University offers internships, research opportunities, teaching experiences, clinics, hands-on work assignments, and other practical activities. A Cooperative Education Program further increases students' opportunities to apply classroom learning to the demands of specific work assignments.

The University is also strongly committed to providing developmental and other academic support programs necessary to assist promising students.

Academic Facilities

The senior campus, which houses the Colleges of Arts and Sciences, Business, Education and Human Services, and Professional Studies and Lifelong Learning, is located on the northern edge of Billings. The MSU–Billings library features a computerized card catalog, interlibrary loans, and CD-ROM and laser-disc systems. Utilizing computer connections, students can access Internet subscribers worldwide, including other state university sources. The Computer Annex maintains a full complement of computer hardware and software for student use. Open weekdays, evenings, and weekends, the Annex features a programming classroom, an open-access lab, a software library, and personal computer classrooms. Career Services, the Advising Center, Financial Aid, Admissions, and Records are all conveniently located on the first floor of McMullen Hall. Cisel Recital Hall has soundproof practice rooms, an acoustic recital hall, and exceptional facilities for students. Alterowitz Gymnasium houses a 4,000-seat arena, a practice gym, a collegiate-size swimming pool, an enclosed running track, and racquetball courts. All twenty-two buildings are within a short walking distance across the senior campus.

The College of Technology is located on the west side of Billings, 7 miles from the senior campus. This 18-acre site contains a 100,000-square-foot classroom, lab, and shop area.

Costs

The estimated 2000–01 tuition for Montana residents is $2908; for nonresident students, it is $7871. Other fees include an optional health insurance fee ($440), books and supplies ($800), room ($2060 for double occupancy), and meals ($1200).

Financial Aid

Approximately 60 percent of Montana State University–Billings students receive some form of financial aid, including loans, grants, and work-study jobs. The scholarship deadline is March 1. Financial aid has a March 1 priority date for filing. Students applying for scholarships and financial aid need to complete the admissions process in advance of those dates. The University also has a job locator program to assist students in finding employment off campus.

Faculty

At Montana State University–Billings, students are taught and mentored by talented professors (not graduate assistants). The faculty members, 90 percent of whom have earned the highest degrees in their fields, are at the forefront of their academic disciplines. Each year, they receive Fulbright fellowships and other prestigious grants to further their professional development. They explore innovative teaching approaches and include students in their research, presentations, and published works.

Student Government

The Associate Students of Montana State University–Billings (ASMSU–Billings) represent student interests, needs, and welfare within the University system and provide for the expression of student opinion and interests to the community at large on issues affecting student life. ASMSU–Billings also serves to protect the privileges and rights of students.

Admission Requirements

For admission to the College of Arts and Sciences, the College of Business, the College of Education and Human Services, and the College of Professional Studies and Lifelong Learning, applicants must submit an application for admission with a nonrefundable fee of $30.

Freshmen must submit their high school transcript (indicating class rank, graduation date, and cumulative grade point average) and scores from either the ACT or the SAT I. A graduate of any accredited high school is eligible for admission provided he or she has obtained a minimum score of 22 on the ACT or 1030 on the SAT I, has at least a 2.5 high school grade point average, or ranks in the upper half of the graduating class and has completed the prescribed college-preparatory curriculum (4 years of English; 3 years of math, including algebra I, algebra II, and geometry; 3 years of social studies; 2 years of laboratory science; and 2 years of electives chosen from foreign languages, computer science, visual or performing arts, or vocational education).

Transfer students must submit their college transcript and have at least a 2.0 cumulative grade point average based on transferable credits from all colleges or universities previously attended.

For the College of Technology, applicants must submit an application for admission with a nonrefundable fee of $30. To be eligible for admission, applicants must have earned a high school diploma from an accredited institution or a GED certificate.

Application and Information

For further information and application materials, students should contact:

Office of Admissions and Records
Montana State University–Billings
1500 North 30th Street
Billings, Montana 59101-0298

Telephone: 406-657-2158
                800-565-MSUB (toll-free)
Fax: 406-657-2302
E-mail: admissions@msubillings.edu
World Wide Web: http://www.msubillings.edu

Montana State University–Billings, "the University of the Yellowstone," provides students with serene surroundings and academic excellence.

MONTANA STATE UNIVERSITY–BOZEMAN
BOZEMAN, MONTANA

The University

Montana State University in Bozeman is the largest, most comprehensive Land Grant university in the state, with undergraduate and graduate programs offered in the Colleges of Agriculture; Arts and Architecture; Business; Education, Health, and Human Development; Engineering; Letters and Science; and Nursing. Undecided students can explore all of their academic interests through the General Studies program prior to selecting a major.

"Mountains and minds" is a slogan especially appropriate to Montana State University. Nestled in the beautiful ranges and wilderness areas of the Rocky Mountains, the campus environment of clean air, uncrowded classes, and wide open spaces creates a collegiate atmosphere unrivaled in most of the United States.

MSU is unique in that it is not an overgrown and impersonal institution. The enrollment of 11,753 students (10,542 undergraduates) allows for much closer student-faculty interaction than is possible at many schools, ensuring each student the individual attention and academic counseling that are so important in achieving a meaningful college education. Its 1,170-acre campus and the surrounding area offer unlimited opportunities for combining academic and recreational experiences.

Location

Few geographical locations offer the broad range of recreational opportunities found in Bozeman. A community of about 50,000 people in a broad valley surrounded by the magnificence of the northern Rockies, Bozeman is a university town, the social and economic center for a large agricultural area, and a major tourist destination. Outstanding outdoor recreation is at the town's doorstep. Two challenging ski areas (Big Sky and Bridger Bowl), world-class fly-fishing streams, and a multitude of hunting, hiking, camping, mountain climbing, ice-skating, snowmobiling, boating, swimming, and waterskiing opportunities are within minutes of Bozeman. In addition, the gateway to the phenomenally breathtaking Yellowstone National Park is less than an hour away. The community, in cooperation with the University, offers a variety of cultural activities throughout the year, including opera, symphony, ballet, and various festivals. The Museum of the Rockies, which houses nationally known dinosaur exhibits, is also located on the campus.

Majors and Degrees

The College of Agriculture offers degrees in agricultural business (options in agribusiness management and farm and ranch management), agricultural education (options in agricultural education teaching, agricultural education broadfield teaching, and extension), agricultural operations technology, animal science (options in livestock management and industry and science), biotechnology (options in animal systems, plant systems, and microbial systems), environmental science (options in environmental biology and soil and water science), horticulture (options in horticulture, landscape design, and turfgrass science), land rehabilitation, land resource sciences (options in agroecology and land resources analysis and management), plant science (options in crop science, plant biology, and plant protection), and range science.

The College of Arts and Architecture offers degrees in architecture (five-year master's), arts (options in art education K–12 broadfield and art history), environmental design, fine arts, media and theater arts (options in motion picture/video/theater and photography), and music education (options in music K–12 broadfield and studio teaching).

The College of Business offers degrees in business with options in accounting, finance, management, and marketing.

The College of Education, Health and Human Development offers degrees in elementary education (options in early childhood education, K–8 education, instructional media K–12, mathematics, music, reading K–12, science education, and special education), health administration, health and human development (options in biomechanics, community health, exercise and wellness, exercise physiology, family and consumer sciences, food and nutrition, health enhancement K–12, and pre–physical therapy studies), health promotion, secondary education (options in general science broadfield, physical science broadfield, social studies broadfield, and departmental teaching options), and technology education (options in industrial technology, technology education teaching, and technology education broadfield teaching).

The College of Engineering offers degrees in chemical engineering, civil engineering (options in bioresources and civil engineering), computer engineering, computer science, construction engineering technology, electrical engineering, industrial and management engineering, mechanical engineering, and mechanical engineering technology.

The College of Letters and Science offers degrees in biological sciences (options in biology, biology teaching, biomedical science, and fish and wildlife management), chemistry (options in biochemistry, chemistry laboratory, chemistry professional, and chemistry teaching), earth sciences (options in geography, geohydrology, and geology), economics (options in economic science and general economics), English (options in literature and English teaching), history (options in history and history teaching), mathematics (options in applied mathematics, mathematics, mathematics teaching, and statistics), microbiology (options in environmental health, medical laboratory science, and microbiology), modern languages and literatures (options in commerce, French, French teaching, German, German teaching, Spanish, and Spanish teaching), philosophy (options in philosophy and philosophy and religion), physics (options in interdisciplinary physics, physics teaching, and professional physics), political science, psychology (options in applied psychology and psychological science), and sociology (options in anthropology, justice studies, and sociology).

The College of Nursing offers degrees in nursing. Bachelor of Arts and Bachelor of Science degrees are also offered in directed interdisciplinary studies. Nondegree programs are offered in military aerospace studies (Air Force) and military science (Army). A general studies program is available for students who are undecided about a major.

Montana State University offers direction in several preprofessional disciplines, including dentistry, medicine, occupational therapy, optometry, physical therapy, and veterinary science.

An intensive English language program is also available to students.

The three smaller units of the Montana State University system: MSU–Billings, MSU–Northern, and the Great Falls College of Technology offer a wide variety of additional academic programs.

Academic Program

Although there is no rigid four-year sequence, all freshmen and sophomores in bachelor's degree programs must fulfill the prescribed University-wide core curriculum. The amount and type of other requirements vary among the departments.

An interdisciplinary University honors program is a significant addition to the curricular and community life of Montana State. Students from various academic fields take part in innovative seminars and research projects. Teaching is primarily Socratic in method.

MSU is ranked among the top in the nation for the number of Goldwater Fellowships in the sciences.

Included among the special programs at MSU are various internships and cooperative education opportunities.

The University operates on a semester system, and a summer session is available.

Off-Campus Arrangements

MSU offers opportunities for off-campus study, including the National Student Exchange Program, which allows students to attend one of more than 140 other colleges and universities for up to one year, and an international study program, which offers opportunities for study in 220 locations in fifty countries.

Academic Facilities

The University has many special facilities that are used for undergraduate education and research. The foremost of these is a 1.4-million-volume library that receives more than 3,500 periodicals on a regular basis and also serves as a depository for U.S. government documents. The newest addition to the facilities on campus is the Ag BioScience building, which opened in 1999. This building houses one of the two largest biocontainment facilities in the nation. It is a research unit for plants and the diseases that affect them. The Engineering and Physical Sciences building houses state-of-the-art laboratories, classrooms, lecture halls, and a National Engineering Research Center. Since its completion in 1997, this building has been recognized and utilized by various national entities, including NASA. The area surrounding the University is utilized as a natural laboratory by students in such academic areas as agriculture, botany, fish and wildlife management, geology, and geophysics.

Costs

University tuition and fees for the 1999–2000 academic year for out-of-state students were $8714; board and a double room, $4650; and books and supplies, about $750. Personal expenses and transportation costs were estimated at $2250. The estimated total for an out-of-state student was $16,364 per year. Residents of Montana paid one third the cost in tuition and fees, with all other expenses remaining constant.

Financial Aid

Montana State University maintains a comprehensive program of financial assistance for both freshmen and upperclass students, including scholarships, loans, grants, and work-study opportunities. Such aid is intended to recognize and assist students who otherwise would not be able to begin or continue their education. Approximately 75 percent of the students attending Montana State University receive some form of financial aid. Approximately 25 percent earn part of their expenses through part-time employment.

Faculty

There are 685 resident faculty members at Montana State who are teachers and hold their scholarly relationship with their students as a priority above all else. For example, 5.1 percent of lectures/seminars are taught by graduate teaching assistants (GTAs) and 36.1 percent of labs are taught by GTAs. Members of the faculty serve as advisers to undergraduate and graduate students, and many also serve as faculty advisers for student clubs, organizations, and committees.

Student Government

Student government at MSU has a long history of responsible leadership and service to the campus. As a result, students actively participate in the administration of the University as well as of student organizations.

Admission Requirements

All applicants must file an application for admission with a nonrefundable $30 fee. Freshmen must submit their high school record (posting date of graduation and rank in class) and scores from either the SAT I or ACT. Transfer applicants must submit official transcripts from each college or university attended. Transfer applicants who have earned fewer than 12 postsecondary quarter or semester credits must also submit an official high school transcript and test scores.

A graduate of any high school that is accredited by the Board of Public Education is eligible for admission as a first-time full-time undergraduate student provided he or she has obtained a minimum score of 22 on the ACT or 1030 on the SAT I or at least a 2.5 high school grade point average or ranks in the upper half of the school's graduating class and has completed the prescribed college-preparatory curriculum. Entering students are required to have completed the following courses in high school in order to be eligible for admission: 4 years of English, 3 years of mathematics (algebra I and II and geometry), 3 years of social studies, 2 years of laboratory science, and 2 years of electives chosen from foreign languages, computer science, visual or performing arts, or vocational education.

Transfer students must present at least a 2.0 (C) cumulative GPA based on transferable credits from all colleges or universities previously attended.

Application and Information

For answers to admission questions and to request an application form, a University *Bulletin*, or information about financial aid, housing, or specific programs, students should contact:

Office of New Student Services
Montana State University
P.O. Box 172190
Bozeman, Montana 59717-2190
Telephone: 406-994-2452
          888-MSU-CATS (toll-free)
E-mail: admissions@montana.edu
World Wide Web: http://www.montana.edu

Montana State University in Bozeman.

MONTANA TECH OF THE UNIVERSITY OF MONTANA
BUTTE, MONTANA

The College

Surrounded by the ore-rich mountains that give Butte, Montana, the name "the richest hill on earth," Montana Tech opened its doors in 1900 as the Montana School of Mines. Nearly 100 years later, the school remains one of the most respected mining and engineering schools in the country. Montana Tech's original minerals curriculum has evolved to include programs on the technological edge of resource recovery, environmental protection, business management, communication, and computer science. These programs attract hard-working, practical students from all over the country and many parts of the world. Curriculums designed for hands-on learning support the overall job placement rate of 98 percent in 1999. Montana Tech has long been recognized as one of the premier small colleges in the United States, with national recognition from *U.S. News & World Report*, *Barron's Best Buys*, and *The Princeton Review*, among others. Montana Tech offers a proven curriculum along with the outdoor adventure of the rugged Rocky Mountains.

The undergraduate student body is composed of 739 women and 1,121 men. There are 105 graduate students.

M.S. degrees are offered in all engineering programs as well as in industrial hygiene and technical communications.

The Montana Tech faculty members, aware of their school's reputation for academic excellence, endeavor to ensure that students receive a strong educational background and good career preparation. As a result, Tech graduates are sought by recruiters from industry and government. The 1999 Graduate Survey shows a 98 percent placement rate for members of the class of 1998. The average starting salary for engineering graduates was $41,458.

The Student Union Building, the property of the Associated Students of Montana Tech (ASMT), houses the dining area, a game room, a bookstore, offices and conference rooms, and the students' own FM radio station, KMSM. A variety of athletic and recreational activities are offered, such as varsity and intramural team sports, hiking and backpacking, and downhill and cross-country skiing. ASMT provides rental equipment for some of these activities.

Location

Built upon rich deposits of gold, silver, copper, molybdenum, and manganese, the city of Butte has earned and maintained worldwide fame for mining and is now in the process of diversifying. Not only is the city becoming a research and silicone processing center as well as a transportation hub, but it is also attracting world-class athletes who train at the United States High Altitude Speed Skating Center. Butte's historical heritage and traditional charm have also encouraged a new industry—tourism. Butte's population of 35,000 is its richest resource. Visitors always receive a warm welcome from friendly people who take a great deal of pride in Butte, which was named an All-America City in 1988. In addition to Butte's theaters, restaurants, and symphony orchestra, there is a community concert organization that brings visiting performers to the city during the academic year.

Majors and Degrees

Bachelor of Science (B.S.) degrees are offered in biology, business and information technology, chemistry, computer science (options in math, business, and engineering), environmental engineering, general engineering (emphases in civil engineering, mechanical engineering, systems/control, and welding engineering), general science, geological engineering, geophysical engineering, liberal studies, mathematics (emphases in applied mathematics and pure mathematics), metallurgical engineering, mining engineering, occupational safety and health (emphases in applied health science and science and engineering), petroleum engineering, professional and technical communications, and software engineering. A program of course work is available in pre–health sciences/biology and a nursing program is offered in cooperation with Montana State University.

Associate of Science/Engineering, Associate of Science, or Associate of Arts degrees are also offered upon completion of two years of prescribed college work.

Students may obtain the equivalent of the first two years of course work required for most degrees not offered at Montana Tech.

Academic Program

B.S. degrees in engineering require the completion of a minimum of 120 to 140 semester credit hours, the number depending upon the specific discipline. All other degrees require a minimum of 120 semester credit hours, with the exception of occupational safety and health, which requires 135 semester credit hours.

Montana Tech offers both parallel and alternating cooperative education in all degree programs. Co-op education students gain valuable professional experience in their chosen field, make contacts for future employment, and may earn money to help finance their education.

Students are strongly advised to seek summer employment in their chosen career field as a matter of orientation and practical experience. Individual departments offer assistance in securing such experience to augment the course of study.

Students may receive credit through successful performance on Advanced Placement (AP) or College-Level Examination Program (CLEP) tests. In addition, comprehensive challenge examinations may be taken by students who have mastered the content of a college course of instruction on their own time, provided that the student's adviser agrees and approval is given by the course instructor and department head.

Montana Tech is accredited by the Commission on Colleges of the Northwest Association of Schools and Colleges. All engineering curricula are accredited by the Accreditation Board for Engineering and Technology, Inc. (ABET), and the chemistry program is accredited by the American Chemical Society.

Academic Facilities

Montana Tech's campus reflects a blend of the traditional and the modern, ranging from the first campus structure, Main Hall (1900), to a modern health, physical education, and recreation complex. The modern library has an attached 260-seat auditorium that is used for both instruction and theatrical performances. The library participates in the Washington Library Network, which allows access to a large number of volumes in other libraries throughout the Pacific Northwest. Montana Tech recently finished $20 million in construction and remodeling.

A fully integrated computer system connects the College's mainframe computers with more than 500 on-campus workstations accessible to students. In the Microcomputer Laboratories, students may use a variety of machines for word processing, business applications, and engineering data acquisition and analysis. Tech's computer labs feature IBM-compatible 586, Pentium, and Sun computers; these labs are open 24 hours a day. In addition to the on-campus network, Tech's computer system is linked to the larger Montana University System network and several national networks. The Montana Tech Learning Center provides students with college survival programs through study skills development, tutorial assistance, computer software, videotapes, and faculty and staff support for students wishing to develop skills for academic success.

The Museum Building houses one of America's outstanding mineral collections as well as the Earthquake Studies Office, which records tremors telemetrically from seismic monitors throughout southwestern Montana. The Montana Bureau of Mines and Geology, a research department of the College, is a source of geological and mineralogical maps and publications. The bureau also provides educational employment for a number of students interested in its various research fields.

Costs

The 1999–2000 tuition and fees for Montana residents were $2862. Tuition and fees for nonresidents were $8162. Room and board cost $3940. Residents of states participating in the WICHE/WUE program (Alaska, Arizona, Colorado, Hawaii, Idaho, Nevada, New Mexico, North Dakota, Oregon, South Dakota, Utah, Washington, and Wyoming) pay approximately 150 percent of Montana resident tuition and fees. The number of students applying for WICHE/WUE status will be limited.

Financial Aid

More than 65 percent of Montana Tech's students receive some form of financial assistance while working toward a degree. In 1999, $500,000 in scholarships to new students was awarded, with an average award of $1800. Other federal student aid is available at Tech through the Federal Pell Grant, Federal Supplemental Educational Opportunity Grant, Federal Perkins Loan, and Federal Work-Study programs. There are also opportunities for part-time employment on campus and in Butte enterprises.

Faculty

Although Montana Tech's faculty members engage in research and consulting activities, they are all teaching faculty. Approximately 85 percent hold a doctoral degree in the discipline they teach. Faculty members serve as advisers to students enrolled in degree programs in their field. Undergraduate faculty members also teach graduate courses. Most faculty members in science and engineering have had industrial experience in addition to their years of teaching service. The 16:1 student-faculty ratio at Montana Tech provides ample opportunity for students to receive individual attention from faculty members.

Student Government

All Montana Tech students are members of the Associated Students of Montana Tech. This student governing body elects its own officers in an annual spring election. The president of ASMT is a voting member of the Montana Tech Administrative Board. Committees are appointed by ASMT to provide leadership and coordination in various student functions.

Admission Requirements

Both Montana residents and nonresidents applying for full-time freshman status must satisfy one of the following three requirements: an ACT Assessment minimum composite score of 22 or an SAT I minimum combined score of 1030; a high school grade point average of 2.5 (on a 4.0 scale) or better; or a ranking in the upper half of their high school graduating class.

Freshman applicants' college-preparatory program must include 4 years of English; 3 years of mathematics (2 years of algebra and 1 of geometry); 3 years of social studies, including a year of U.S. history and a year of world history; 2 years of laboratory science, 1 of which must be in earth science, biology, chemistry, or physics; and 2 years chosen from foreign language, computer science, visual and performing arts, or vocational education units. Transfer students normally are required to have a minimum cumulative grade point average of 2.0, based on a 4.0 system, for all college work attempted.

Montana Tech does not discriminate on the basis of race, color, age, religion, sex, or national or ethnic origin in administration of its educational and admission policies, scholarship and loan programs, athletic programs, or other school-administered programs. The College is also committed to providing equal opportunities for the physically or mentally handicapped, in compliance with federal regulations.

Application and Information

A $30 application fee must be sent with the application for admission. For further information, interested students should contact:

Office of Admissions
Montana Tech of the University of Montana
1300 West Park Street
Butte, Montana 59701-8997
Telephone: 406-496-4178
           800-445-TECH (toll-free)
World Wide Web: http://www.mtech.edu

The Main Hall, which was built in 1895 as the "School of Mines."

MONTCLAIR STATE UNIVERSITY
UPPER MONTCLAIR, NEW JERSEY

The University

Founded in 1908 as a normal school for the education of future teachers, Montclair State has evolved into a four-year comprehensive public university that offers a broad range of educational and cultural opportunities. Montclair State is composed of the School of Business, the School of the Arts, the College of Humanities and Social Sciences, the College of Science and Mathematics, the College of Education and Human Services, and the Graduate School and confers degrees in forty-three undergraduate majors and thirty-four graduate majors. Through its diverse programs and services, Montclair State seeks to develop educated men and women who are inquiring, creative, and responsible contributors to society.

Montclair State has been designated a Center of Excellence in the fine and performing arts in northern New Jersey. It is accredited by the Middle States Association of Colleges and Schools, and its teacher education, administrative, and school service personnel programs are approved by the National Council for Accreditation of Teacher Education.

The total enrollment was 13,285 in fall 1999; 6,234 women and 3,925 men were enrolled as undergraduates. The majority of students are from New Jersey, and approximately 80 percent commute. The remainder live in campus residence halls or apartments or in University-approved off-campus housing. Approximately 70 percent belong to student organizations. Some of the organizations that are involved in student life are the College Life Union Board, which is responsible for coordinating all social, cultural, educational, and recreational student programs; the Intercollegiate Athletic Council, which provides men and women of all the schools with the opportunity to participate in many varsity sports; and the Student Intramural and Leisure Council, which runs one of the country's few student-controlled intramural programs.

Location

Montclair State has the advantage of being situated on a 200-acre suburban campus, only 14 miles west of New York City. This proximity to the city gives students the opportunity to take advantage of the unusually rich cultural, social, and educational environment of the metropolitan area, while Montclair's suburban setting offers a nice contrast to city life. Mountain resorts and ocean beaches are also nearby.

Majors and Degrees

Montclair State offers programs of study leading to the Bachelor of Arts degree in anthropology, broadcasting, classics, economics, English, fine arts, French, general humanities, geography, history, human ecology, Italian, justice studies, linguistics, music, music therapy, philosophy, political science, psychology, religious studies, sociology, Spanish, speech communication, and theater studies. The Bachelor of Science degree is offered in allied health services, biochemistry, biology, business administration, business education, chemistry, computer science, geoscience, health education, human ecology, mathematics, molecular biology, physical education, physics, recreation professions, and technology education. The Bachelor of Fine Arts degree is awarded in dance, fine arts, and theater. The Bachelor of Music is awarded in music, and there is a five-year combined B.Mus./B.A. program. There is a special 4½-year degree program in music therapy. Combined Bachelor of Science/Doctor of Dental Medicine and Bachelor of Science/Doctor of Medicine degrees are also offered with the University of Medicine and Dentistry of New Jersey–New Jersey Dental School and University of Medicine and Dentistry of New Jersey–New Jersey Medical School, respectively.

A teacher certification program is offered in many of the subject areas mentioned above, generally for grades K through 12.

Minors are available in many of the majors listed. There are also several interdisciplinary academic programs, such as African–American studies, archaeology, criminal justice, film, Hispanic community affairs, international studies, paralegal studies, prelaw studies, public administration, Russian, Russian area studies, and women's studies. Part-time bachelor's degree programs are available.

Academic Program

Successful completion of a minimum of 128 semester hours is necessary for graduation. Course requirements include general education (34–58 semester hours), comprising communication, humanities and the arts, pure and applied sciences, social and behavioral sciences, a physical education requirement, and a multicultural awareness requirement; courses in the major field of study in arts and sciences programs (a minimum of 33–82 semester hours); and electives (12–37 semester hours).

The academic calendar is organized into two semesters (fall and spring) and summer sessions.

Montclair State also offers undergraduate degrees through the Second Careers Program (for students over 25 years of age) and the Weekend College.

Off-Campus Arrangements

Through the Cooperative Education Program, a student may receive academic credit for a full-time job and earn a full-time salary. This program gives a student the opportunity to receive on-the-job training in his or her prospective career area. Internships—work for credit, not pay—are available through many major departments.

Through programs offered by the New Jersey State College Council for International Education, the International Student Exchange Program, and the College Consortium for International Studies, students have the opportunity to study abroad in the continent of Australia and such countries as Argentina, Austria, Belize, China, Colombia, Denmark, Ecuador, France, Germany, Great Britain, Greece, Hungary, Ireland, Israel, Italy, Jamaica, Korea, Mexico, the Netherlands, Portugal, Spain, and Uruguay. In addition, foreign language majors may spend a year, a semester, or a summer in French-, German-, Italian-, or Spanish-speaking countries.

The University is a charter member of the New Jersey Marine Sciences Consortium, through which students may take field-oriented courses in the marine sciences. The New Jersey School of Conservation, located in Stokes State Forest, is the largest university-operated environmental education center in the world. Through this facility, students may take courses relating to the environment in the humanities, social sciences, and natural and physical sciences and in outdoor pursuits.

Academic Facilities

The holdings of the Harry A. Sprague Library include 352,998 books, 2,778 periodical subscriptions, 23,000 government publications, and more than 1.5 million nonprint items. The Nonprint Department has equipment for viewing and listening to videocassettes, records, audiocassettes, compact discs, soundslide sets, and a variety of microforms. As a designated government publications depository, the library receives and makes available for use its collections of federal and New Jersey publications.

Sprague Library provides computerized access to its holdings, interlibrary services, and information retrieval. Online database searching and compact disc database searching are available for most subjects and disciplines.

Students are also encouraged to use the resources of the Media Center, which provides audiovisual materials, equipment, and services. The center contains a film library, videotaping equipment, and a wide range of other audiovisual equipment and provides custom graphic and photographic services. The Computer Center offers computer services to students and incorporates the latest advances in technology in its facilities. Also included among the University's facilities are two modern theaters, a recital hall, a theater-arts workshop, and science, language, and computer laboratories.

Costs

In 1999–2000, undergraduate tuition was $105.16 per semester hour for New Jersey residents and $165 per semester hour for out-of-state students. Room rent for dormitory students was $2080 per semester; meal plans cost $1026 per semester. An additional estimated $1500 per year was needed for fees and textbooks. (Costs are subject to change.)

Financial Aid

Four major types of financial aid programs are available at Montclair State: loans, grants, scholarships, and employment. Within each of these categories, funding may be available through federal, state, and/or institutional sources. State aid programs include Tuition Aid Grants, Educational Opportunity Fund Grants, Bloustein Distinguished Scholars awards, Public Tuition Benefits awards, and N.J. CLASS loans. Federal sources of aid include Federal Pell Grants, Federal Supplemental Educational Opportunity Grants, Federal Perkins Loans, Federal Work-Study, Federal Stafford Student Loans, Federal PLUS loans, and programs for veterans. Approximately 75 percent of undergraduates receive financial aid. Students should contact the Financial Aid Office regarding application materials and deadline dates.

Faculty

Faculty members teach both graduate and undergraduate courses, with few departments employing graduate assistants. More than 90 percent of the faculty members hold doctorates or the appropriate terminal degree in their disciplines. A faculty-student ratio of 1:15 permits considerable interaction between students and professors. All faculty members have posted office hours in order to provide students with assistance in course material and in planning a program of study. In addition, faculty members participate actively in student-oriented activities, serve as advisers to student clubs, and conduct extracurricular workshops and field trips.

Student Government

The Student Government Association (SGA), a parent corporation that includes within its structure various class organizations and services for the student body, is composed of all undergraduates. The substantial budget of the SGA allows for the development and financing of student activities and services, such as concerts, film series, intramural sports, a drop-in center, legal aid services, a student-run radio station, and a student newspaper. The Student Government Association Legislature acts as the final representative for the entire undergraduate student body and is composed of elected representatives from each class and major curriculum.

Admission Requirements

Montclair State is an Equal Opportunity/Affirmative Action institution and does not discriminate on the basis of sex, race, color, national origin, age, or physical handicap in providing access to its benefits and services, in compliance with relevant federal and state legislation.

Applicants must present a certificate of graduation from an approved secondary school (or a high school equivalency certificate), showing the following minimum college-preparatory units: English, 4; history, 2; mathematics, 3; laboratory science, 2; foreign language, 2; and electives in English, social studies, science, mathematics, or foreign languages, 3. Full-time freshman applicants must take the SAT I or ACT; Subject Tests are not required. Admission to the programs in dance, fine arts, music, and speech/theater depends upon successful completion of departmental tests, auditions, or interviews.

Application and Information

Applicants must submit a completed application form, a nonrefundable application fee of $40, a copy of their official high school transcript, and copies of their SAT I or ACT scores. Admission decisions are announced on a rolling basis until all spaces are filled.

For application forms and additional admission information, students should contact:

Office of Admissions
Montclair State University
Upper Montclair, New Jersey 07043-1624
Telephone: 800-331-9205 (toll-free)
World Wide Web: http://www.montclair.edu

MONTREAT COLLEGE
MONTREAT, NORTH CAROLINA

The College

Montreat is a four-year Christian liberal arts college affiliated with the Presbyterian Church (USA). At Montreat College, a student's experience is enhanced by an education of value, grounded in a strong liberal arts core, taught by an outstanding Christian faculty, and prized by today's employers and graduate schools. Students benefit from Montreat's small classes where their opinions matter, and they grow through one-on-one interaction with professors and classmates. Studies challenge them to integrate faith and learning while considering subjects in ways never thought possible. Hands-on experiences in the majors (internships, field studies, mission programs, community service, and independent research) enable students to gain practical career and life preparation.

Montreat College enrollment is rapidly growing. Enrollment is more than 1,000 in the traditional Montreat campus program and in the off-campus School of Professional and Adult Studies. The student body typically represents approximately thirty states and ten other countries.

The natural beauty of the Montreat campus both calms the spirit and awakens the senses. In a diverse and multicultural environment, students learn how to investigate the unfamiliar, think critically, and communicate and clarify their ideas. In the process, they develop the skills, personal values, and faith to take their places in the world with confidence.

Montreat College welcomes students of many denominations and cultural backgrounds, including students from all corners of the world. In the dorm or over dinner at a professor's house, students find themselves sharing perspectives and exchanging ideas. The distinct spirit of community goes beyond the faculty, staff, and students and extends to visiting Christian conference members and residents of the neighboring towns of Montreat and Black Mountain, as well as to the "cottagers" who vacation there throughout the seasons.

Students enjoy living in the beautiful stone residence halls that provide views of the mountains surrounding the campus. The air-conditioned residence halls provide cable TV, computer networking, phone installation, laundry facilities, and kitchen areas.

Montreat College is also a place where students can set themselves apart through an extraordinary range of leadership opportunities. At Montreat College, a special emphasis is placed on the concept of servant leadership. Students participate in Servanthood and Leadership Training (SALT) Week each January. A nationally recognized Discovery/Wilderness Program takes advantage of the mountain location and offers a unique twenty-one day adventure for academic credit. Outdoor recreation opportunities ranging from hiking to white-water adventures to snow skiing are available to students. The students also choose from a variety of off-campus volunteer service opportunities such as area nursing homes, churches, children's homes, and shelters.

Montreat College is a member of the National Association of Intercollegiate Athletics (NAIA). Men compete in baseball, basketball, cross-country, golf, soccer, and tennis. Women compete in basketball, cross-country, soccer, softball, tennis, and volleyball. Students enjoy an active intramural program where exciting competition takes place throughout the year.

Location

Montreat College is located in the beautiful Blue Ridge Mountains of western North Carolina. The scenic main campus is nestled into sloping woods just 15 miles east of Asheville, North Carolina, and 2 miles from I-40. Students enjoy the proximity of Asheville, one of North Carolina's most architecturally and culturally diverse cities. Adjacent to Montreat is the historic town of Black Mountain, with picturesque avenues, stores, and restaurants.

Montreat College's off-campus School of Professional and Adult Studies has permanent campus facilities in Charlotte and Asheville and holds classes in a number of additional North Carolina locations.

Majors and Degrees

Montreat College is accredited by the Commission on Colleges of the Southern Association of Colleges and Schools to award the Master of Business Administration degree, bachelor's degrees, and associate degrees. Students can choose to pursue a Bachelor of Arts, Bachelor of Science, or Bachelor of Music degree with a wide variety of majors, minors, and concentrations. Teacher certification is available in elementary education, English education, and history–social studies education.

Students pursuing a Bachelor of Arts degree may choose to major in American studies, Bible and religion (liberal arts), English (communications, literature, or secondary education), history (historical studies or social studies education), human services, and mathematics.

Majors available in the Bachelor of Science degree program are American studies, Bible and religion (Christian education or Christian ministries), business administration (accounting, information systems, international business, management, marketing, quality management, or sports management), environmental studies, history (historical studies or social studies education), human services, mathematics, and outdoor education.

A Bachelor of Music degree is offered with concentrations in music business, organ performance, piano performance, and voice performance.

Montreat College's School of Professional and Adult Studies is designed especially for the adult learner who has completed some college work and desires to finish a degree in an accelerated program. This off-campus program offers the Master of Business Administration, Bachelor of Business Administration, and Associate of Science degrees.

Academic Program

Upon enrollment, students are assigned a faculty adviser to assist them in clarifying their educational objectives and meeting the requirements for graduation. Students and faculty advisers work together in arranging a program of study leading to graduation. Graduation requirements are a minimum of 126 semester hours, cumulative quality point average of at least 2.0, completion of the general education core requirements, 33 semester hours in 300-level or above courses, completion of all major requirements, a grade of C or better in courses needed for the major or minor, and completion of at least 31 semester hours at Montreat College.

Students interested in careers in medicine, law, criminology, and other professional areas are reminded that the best preparation, according to graduate school advisers in these areas, is a solid liberal arts degree program such as that found at Montreat College.

Off-Campus Arrangements

Off-campus academic experiences are utilized by Montreat students through programs in Chicago, Illinois; Colorado Springs,

Colorado; Washington, D.C.; Los Angeles, California; AuSable, Michigan; Oxford, England; Jerusalem, Israel; Cairo, Egypt; Moscow, Russia; and Costa Rica. Local and international service and internship opportunities are also available to students.

Academic Facilities

Classrooms are conveniently located close to dormitories. Morgan Hall provides modern classroom space for the environmental studies, science, and math departments. The natural environment of Montreat, North Carolina, offers a broad, living laboratory close at hand for highly specialized majors in environmental studies and outdoor education. The library belongs to a coalition of college libraries, which greatly enhances study and research by making even more resources available from colleges throughout western North Carolina. The College has installed a campuswide fiber-optic computer network linking the campus and providing access to the Internet. The centrally located L. Nelson Bell Library houses one of the College's computer labs and the spacious Hamilton Gallery. The Belk Campus Center contains a computer lab, classrooms, campus store, lounges, and mailboxes. Gaither Hall houses the administration offices, the Chaplain's office, and state-of-the-art music laboratories and rehearsal rooms. The Christian Studies Center features the beautiful Chapel of the Prodigal, with an original fresco by internationally known artist Ben Long, and the McGowan Center for Christian Studies, which houses the Christian Ministries division.

Costs

Tuition, room, and board for the 2000–01 school year are $16,344. This cost includes all fees except for a few selective courses requiring a registration fee. There is no out-of-state tuition fee. Basic fees for each semester are due at registration. Tuition payment plans are available through Academic Management Services (AMS).

Financial Aid

Through generous financial aid and scholarship packages, deserving students receive the quality academics of a private college at a modest cost. Each year, more than 90 percent of Montreat students receive some form of financial aid. Working individually with each student, the College awards financial aid packages that include scholarships, grants, loans, and work-study jobs. Scholarships are also made available to transfer students. All students must submit the Free Application for Federal Student Aid (FAFSA) and the Montreat College Application for Scholarship and Financial Assistance. To drastically reduce processing time, the FAFSA can be electronically submitted by the College to the federal government for students who have applied, been accepted, and submitted a $100 deposit. For more information, students should call the Financial Aid Office at 800-545-4656 (toll-free).

Faculty

Montreat College seeks to provide an education that is constantly informed by Christian insights. All faculty members are professing Christians committed to teaching, learning, and investing themselves in the lives and futures of their students. More than half of the full-time faculty members hold a doctorate or the highest degree in their field. Students benefit from small classes and a very favorable student-faculty ratio of 12:1.

Student Government

An active Student Government Association (SGA) is composed of all the full-time students at Montreat College. It carries out its responsibilities through its executive, legislative, and judicial branches, which operate at all levels of campus living. It plays a primary role in interpreting the needs of students and in determining the quality of student life. The SGA works closely with the Director of Student Services and holds the authority to implement and make effective its responsibility to the College community. Officers are elected by the students.

Admission Requirements

To be accepted, a student must have a minimum score of 860 on the SAT I and a minimum cumulative 2.25 GPA (on a 4.0 scale). An ACT composite score of at least 18 is acceptable in lieu of the SAT I score. Montreat welcomes transfer students. Home-schooled students are also welcomed and encouraged to apply. International students from countries where English is not the primary language must score a minimum of 500 on the Test of English as a Foreign Language (TOEFL).

Application and Information

Students are required to submit a formal application accompanied by a $15 application fee. The common application is accepted. An official transcript of high school credits must be submitted directly from the high school to the College Office of Admissions. SAT I/ACT verification is also required. Montreat College's school code is 005423.

For more information, students should write or call:
Office of Admissions
Montreat College
P.O. Box 1267
Montreat, North Carolina 28757
Telephone: 828-669-8012 Ext. 3781
              800-622-6968 (toll-free)
Fax: 828-669-0120
E-mail: admissions@montreat.edu
World Wide Web: http://www.montreat.edu

Students on the campus of Montreat College.

MONTSERRAT COLLEGE OF ART
BEVERLY, MASSACHUSETTS

The College
Students come to Montserrat College of Art for many reasons—to gain professional competence, to develop special talents, and to engage in new areas of experience. Whatever the personal goal, students find an environment in which their visions, aspirations, and commitments are nurtured and refined.

Founded in 1970 by a group of artists seeking new solutions, Montserrat possesses a variety of advantages that distinguish it from the nation's other schools of art and design. With an enrollment of 385 students of diverse cultural and artistic backgrounds, the College is large enough to offer the wide array of courses and concentrations that comprise a strong visual arts curriculum, yet small enough to provide the personal attention that is often difficult to find in larger educational environments. Montserrat is a residential college that encourages a student's sense of belonging to the college community and a greater involvement in its cultural life. The College is accredited by the New England Association of Schools and Colleges (NEASC) and the National Association of Schools of Art and Design (NASAD).

Location
Many Montserrat students reside on campus in the historic city of Beverly, located 30 minutes north of Boston along the coast of the Alantic Ocean. Beverly was founded in 1626 and was home to George Washington's naval base. Student housing is nestled among the homes of downtown Beverly and is within walking distance of all College facilities. The main academic building faces the newly landscaped public common and the Beverly Public Library. The Cabot Street Cinema screens popular, foreign, and art films and is the home of the Le Grand David Spectacular Magic Company. Shops, cafes, and restaurants line nearby Cabot Street where Montserrat's two other studio buildings are located. The public beach at Dane Street and tranquil Lynch Park, site of President Taft's summer White House, are just steps away. The renowned Peabody Essex Museum, the House of the Seven Gables, and other sites related to the infamous Witch Hysteria of 1692 are located in the neighboring city of Salem.

Boston and Cambridge are easily accessible by car or commuter train. More than 100 colleges and universities are located in the Boston metropolitan area. World-class museums, such as Boston's Museum of Fine Arts, galleries, libraries, shopping, sports, and a variety of entertainment options provide a stimulating intellectual, cultural, and social environment in which to live and learn.

Majors and Degrees
There are two 4-year options for study at Montserrat. Students may apply as a candidate for either the Bachelor of Fine Arts (B.F.A.) degree or the Diploma of the College. Both options offer the same challenging studio program but a different curriculum of liberal arts study.

Following the first year of art foundation studies, a student may choose to concentrate in fine arts, graphic design, illustration, painting and drawing, photography, printmaking, or sculpture and can also prepare for a career in art education. To earn the B.F.A. degree, a student must earn 120 credits—78 credits of studio course work and 42 credits in liberal arts, including a minimum of 12 credits in art history and 6 credits in English. A student is awarded the Diploma of the College upon completion of 108 credits—a minimum of 78 credits of studio course work and a minimum of 6 credits in both art history and English. The balance of credits required for the Diploma of the College may be earned in either studio or liberal art courses. The art education program complements a studio concentration and prepares students to qualify for provisional certification with advanced standing in Massachusetts public schools and other states with reciprocity agreements.

Academic Program
Art is born of a rich variety of human experience and inquiry. Montserrat's unique curriculum engages both faculty and students in discovering new ways for the liberal and visual arts to work together to educate the total artist. During the first year of foundation studies, students are introduced to the various studio concentrations at Montserrat. The foundation curriculum is a carefully crafted sequence of varied but complementary courses that emphasize the visual, technical, written, and verbal skills essential to a successful art college experience.

Once a student has earned 90 credits, completed required course work, and demonstrated sufficient media skills in the chosen studio concentration, entry into the Senior Seminar is determined by a faculty panel. Students in Senior Seminar have the opportunity to delve independently into a significant, coherent body of work. Aided by a faculty mentor, students work intensely to articulate their unique voice and visual language. Seniors exhibit seminar work throughout the spring in the Montserrat Gallery at 301 Cabot Street. This revelatory experience helps students mature as artists and designers and, ultimately, make the transition into professional life.

Off-Campus Arrangements
Montserrat offers students a variety of opportunities to broaden their horizons and earn credits towards the B.F.A. degree or Diploma through, local, national, and international study.

The College is a member of the Northeast Consortium of Colleges and Universities in Massachusetts. Students may take classes and use the library facilities of member colleges.

Through Montserrat's affiliation with the Association of Independent Colleges of Art and Design (AICAD), students may spend a semester or a year in comparable studies at a member institution. Students remain registered at Montserrat, retaining residency and student aid eligibility. The AICAD New York Studio Program offers third-year students the opportunity to spend a summer in New York City either as a professional intern or attending weekly seminars while working independently in a semiprivate studio. Students may choose to spend a month in the walled, papal city of Viterbo in Italy while attending Montserrat's summer residential program. Intensive courses in painting, drawing, photography, art history, and writing are offered.

Academic Facilities
Montserrat's main building, the historic Hardie Building, houses four floors of newly renovated studios, classrooms, exhibition spaces, the Paul Scott Library, and offices. Specially equipped studios for printmaking, photography, painting, and

illustration, as well as video and computer labs, are located here. Graphic design students work in an environment similar to a professional design studio, with computers, access to the Internet, and a meeting area. The Paul Scott Library contains a collection of more than 12,000 books, numerous art and related periodicals, videos, CDs, and other resources. The library also offers Internet access and houses a slide collection of more than 37,000 slide images. The library is a member of the North of Boston Library Exchange consortium of academic and public libraries, including the Beverly Public Library located across the street from Montserrat's Hardie Building.

The Montserrat campus offers four galleries that feature an exciting array of exhibitions by artists within the Montserrat community of students, alumni, faculty, and staff and also professional artists of regional and national note.

Montserrat's Cabot Studio Building offers spacious facilities for sculpture students and semiprivate studios for seniors concentrating in painting, photography, printmaking, sculpture, and mixed media.

Across Cabot Street are the newly renovated studios for illustration students, including semiprivate studio spaces for seniors in the department. Adjacent to the studios are reproduction equipment and an extensive collection of research materials.

All students are entitled to free admission to the Boston Museum of Fine Arts, one of the finest collections of art in the world. The museum houses permanent exhibits of art and artifacts representing virtually all periods and civilizations, as well as changing exhibitions of art.

Costs

Tuition and general fees for the 2000–01 academic year are $13,830. Other annual direct costs of attendance, including supplies, health insurance, and on-campus housing in a shared room, are estimated at $5000. Indirect costs of attendance, such as food, transportation, and other personal expenses, are estimated at $3500.

Financial Aid

Nearly 80 percent of Montserrat students receive financial assistance (grants, loans, and employment). Sources include the federal government, state government, the College, and corporate and civic sponsors. Most financial aid is awarded on the basis of demonstrated need. To apply for financial aid, students must complete the Free Application for Federal Student Aid (FAFSA). Applications filed by March 1 receive priority consideration. Each year a select number of exceptional applicants for fall admission are nominated to compete for renewable merit scholarships. Candidates in the competition must complete all requirements for admission and be accepted at the College by March 1.

Faculty

The faculty of Montserrat comprises professional artists and designers and accomplished scholars. There are 19 full-time faculty members and 45 part-time instructors. Fifty-nine percent of faculty members have earned a master's degree and 29 percent hold doctorates. The student-teacher ratio is 14:1.

Student Government

Students have a voice in College policies, events, and activities through the Student Council, which maintains close communication with College administrators and faculty. Each year, a student elected by the Student Council serves as a representative at all faculty meetings. Student Council members are active in the programming and planning of social activities and College events designed to enhance student life.

Admission Requirements

The Admissions Committee is interested in the unique interests, experiences, and abilities of each applicant. The portfolio of artwork is the most significant part of a prospective student's application, and it is highly recommended that it be presented in person during an on-campus interview. Applicants who reside more than 150 miles from the campus may present the portfolio during an off-campus meeting or may mail the portfolio in slide form. Academic transcripts, standardized test scores, letters of recommendation, and an artist's statement help the Admissions Committee to assess an applicant's potential for success at the College.

Application and Information

Admissions decisions are made on a rolling basis, and applicants are notified of a decision within two to three weeks of completing all application requirements. For complete information on admission, financial aid, studio and academic programs, student and residential life, and campus visits, prospective students may contact:

Admissions Office
Montserrat College of Art
23 Essex Street
Beverly, Massachusetts 01915
Telephone: 978-921-4242 Ext. 1153
          800-836-0487 (toll-free)
Fax: 978-921-4241
E-mail: admiss@montserrat.edu
World Wide Web: http://www.montserrat.edu

MOORE COLLEGE OF ART AND DESIGN
PHILADELPHIA, PENNSYLVANIA

The College
America's only college of art and design for women, Moore College of Art and Design originated in 1848 as a school to educate women for practical careers in art. Moore has a long-standing commitment to both fine and professional arts. The College moved to its present location on the Benjamin Franklin Parkway in 1959.

College-managed residence halls, located conveniently at or near the main campus, house most of the students. Student services include the Health Office and Infirmary and an active career center that brings together qualified seniors and prospective employers during the students' final year of study. Faculty advising and psychological counseling services are also available.

The College is accredited by the Middle States Association of Colleges and Schools, the National Association of Schools of Art and Design, and by FIDER.

Location
Moore is located in the cultural heart of Philadelphia, on Logan Circle, within sight of the Academy of Natural Sciences, the Franklin Institute, and the Philadelphia Free Library. Within short walking distance are the Philadelphia Museum of Art and the Rodin Museum. Surrounded by this artistic and cultural vitality, Moore's students have ready access to fine artistic offerings in a stimulating urban setting. More than forty nearby colleges and universities, including the University of Pennsylvania, Temple University, and Drexel University, form the largest higher-education community in the nation.

Philadelphia is only 90 minutes from New York City. Public transportation makes the journey practical for organized or informal trips, and classes frequently convene in New York for professional critiques of student artwork.

Majors and Degrees
Moore College of Art and Design offers a four-year program leading to the Bachelor of Fine Arts degree in the professional and fine arts, with concentrations in the following areas: communication arts (emphasis in graphic design or illustration), fashion design, general fine arts (with art teacher certification), interior design, textile design, three-dimensional fine arts, and two-dimensional fine arts. Moore also offers the Bachelor of Fine Arts degree in studio art with an emphasis in art history. The College also offers certificates in art teacher certification and desktop publishing/computer graphics.

Academic Program
The College operates on a two-semester academic year. Of the total number of hours required for completion of the B.F.A. degree program, approximately two thirds are in a studio area and one third in academic courses.

A student's first year includes a broadly based core of studies in art history, basic design, color, drawing, and the humanities. Introductory courses to the fine and professional arts are also offered. Tutorial support is available for all students. At the end of her first year, the student chooses a professional or fine arts concentration in which she can pursue her personal art objectives.

While instruction in the core studies is highly directive, advanced studio courses require more initiative and self-discipline as the College provides each student with an increasingly personal program of study and assistance. Seniors in both the fine arts and professional arts acquire practical experience in their fields through internships, apprenticeships, and the College's cooperative education program.

The College participates in the Association of Independent Colleges of Art and Design (AICAD) Student Mobility Exchange Program. A student who meets eligibility requirements may apply for one semester's study at an AICAD member school's program.

In addition to the Bachelor of Fine Arts degree, Moore offers a wide variety of programs for adults and young people, grades K–12. The Division of Continuing Studies provides courses in the fine arts, professional arts, and electronic arts, given primarily at night and on weekends. The Young Artists' Workshop is held on Saturdays during the fall and spring and weekdays during the summer. The summer program has a residency component for 11th and 12th grade young women, which incorporates a full day of studio classes and evening activities. For more information on these programs, students should call the Division of Continuing Studies at 215-568-4515, Ext. 1122.

Academic Facilities
The Moore College of Art and Design complex is a quadrangle of academic buildings and student housing surrounding an interior courtyard. Three art galleries, an auditorium, a library, and classrooms are housed in this complex. Most studio classrooms offer extensive natural lighting. Library holdings include more than 33,000 volumes, 73,000 slides, 1,500 recordings, 340 periodical subscriptions, picture files, and exhibition catalogs. Students in all disciplines have access to an extensive computer graphics lab.

The College Gallery program presents a wide range of exhibitions in the three College galleries and other display areas. The work of outstanding artists, often including works by Moore faculty members, alumnae, and students, is exhibited.

Costs
Estimated tuition and fees for 1999–2000 were $15,975; room and board fees for students living in College residence halls were approximately $6100. Books, supplies, and personal expenses (excluding transportation) are estimated to be between $1600 and $1800 per year for most students.

Financial Aid
The College offers financial aid based on financial need as established by information provided on the Free Application for Federal Student Aid (FAFSA).

The principal forms of financial aid are Federal Pell Grants, Federal Supplemental Educational Opportunity Grants, Federal Perkins Loans, and Moore College of Art and Design scholarships and grants. Assistance is also available through the Federal Work-Study program. For full consideration, students are encouraged to apply for financial aid by April 1.

Moore College annually grants $1 million in scholarship aid to incoming and continuing students who demonstrate excellence in art. Awards are granted on the basis of the portfolio review and academic merit.

Faculty

Moore College of Art and Design has 70 faculty members, 10 in academic and 60 in studio areas. All studio classes are taught by practicing professionals. The student-faculty ratio is approximately 13:1.

Student Government

Moore's student government includes the following student organizations: the Black Student Union, Moore Environmental Action Now, the Asian Student Union, the Hispanic/Latina Student Group, the Re-Entry Women's Group, and the Social Committee.

Admission Requirements

The admission decision is based on an evaluation of the following required materials: transcripts from high schools and any colleges attended, SAT I or ACT examination scores, and a portfolio of eight to twelve original pieces of art. International students should submit scores on the Test of English as a Foreign Language (TOEFL) instead of SAT I or ACT scores.

Freshmen may enter in the fall and spring semesters.

Transfer students are encouraged to apply for advanced class standing at Moore. Class standing is determined on the basis of acceptable transfer credits and an evaluation of the applicant's portfolio. Upper-level transfers may enter in the fall or spring semester.

Application and Information

Although Moore has no application deadline, students seeking admission in the fall semester are encouraged to submit applications to the Admissions Office by April 1.

For application forms, catalogs, and additional information, students should contact:

Director of Admissions
Moore College of Art and Design
20th and the Parkway
Philadelphia, Pennsylvania 19103-1179
Telephone: 215-568-4515 Ext. 4015
          800-523-2025 (toll-free)
Fax: 215-568-8017
E-mail: admiss@moore.edu

Moore College of Art and Design has the unique distinction of being the only art college for women in the United States.

MORAVIAN COLLEGE
BETHLEHEM, PENNSYLVANIA

The College

Moravian College is the nation's sixth-oldest college, tracing its origins to a women's program begun in 1742. Settlers from Eastern Europe, known as Moravians, founded both the College and the community of Bethlehem and brought to America a rich cultural heritage of architecture, music, scholarship, and craftsmanship. The strength of Moravian's music program and the community's famed Bach Choir are aspects of the continuing influence of this heritage. Moravian College is a selective, coeducational institution offering more than forty programs with foundations in the liberal arts and sciences. Among its strengths and distinctions are an outstanding faculty with a personal and professional commitment to teaching, a demanding academic program recognized for its excellence and high standards, and close working relationships among students, faculty members, and staff. Moravian has won national recognition for the depth and effectiveness of its career-counseling and placement programs. Opportunities for field studies and internships enhance career preparation in much the same way that independent study and honors programs enhance all aspects of the academic program.

The majority of the 1,280 students enrolled come from Pennsylvania and New Jersey, but approximately twenty-five states and twelve countries are represented in the student body. Moravian's students are involved in a wide range of activities and athletics. Men compete in intercollegiate baseball, basketball, cross-country, golf, soccer, tennis, and track and field; women compete in basketball, cross-country, field hockey, soccer, softball, tennis, track and field, and volleyball. Intramural sports include basketball, indoor soccer, softball, and touch football. Club sports include equitation, ice hockey, lacrosse, and skiing. Activities range from participation in an outing club to modern dancing. There are departmental clubs, honor societies, fraternities, sororities, and service organizations. Communications opportunities include a student newspaper, a yearbook, WRMC (radio station), a literary magazine, and work in the Media Center. Performance groups include the Moravian College Theatre Company, a wind ensemble, an orchestra, and the Moravian College Choir, which in recent years has toured Europe, Israel, the Caribbean, Scandinavia, and England and performed at the Kennedy Center in Washington, D.C. Nationally known lecturers, scholars, authors, and artists are brought to campus, and, through the College-Community Concert series, many major European and American touring orchestras have appeared on campus. Many students participate in volunteer activities related to political, social welfare, health, and teaching fields. Approximately 85 percent of Moravian's students reside on campus in housing that ranges from traditional dormitory to apartment and town-house accommodations.

An M.B.A. degree is offered by the Department of Economics and Business through the Division of Continuing Studies. Moravian College as a corporate institution also includes a theological seminary offering programs leading to the Master of Divinity, M.A. in Theological Studies, and M.A. in Pastoral Counseling degrees; a cooperative program leading to the M.A. in Christian Education is also offered. While campus facilities are shared with the undergraduate program, the faculty, the administration, and fee schedules are separate.

Location

Moravian College is located in Bethlehem, Pennsylvania, a city of 75,000 people. Bethlehem's location in the Lehigh Valley area (Allentown-Bethlehem-Easton) and its proximity to New York and Philadelphia allow it to combine the advantages of these cities with the accessibility and friendliness of a smaller community. Moravian shares its Lehigh Valley location with the world headquarters of Bethlehem Steel Corporation, Air Products, Mack Truck, Rodale Press, Union Pacific, and other businesses and industries, as well as with five other private colleges: Lafayette, Muhlenberg, Cedar Crest, and Allentown colleges and Lehigh University. Bethlehem, with its distinctive history, is carefully preserving its past while engaging in twentieth-century expansion.

Majors and Degrees

Moravian College offers the Bachelor of Arts, Bachelor of Science, and Bachelor of Music with programs of study in forty areas. The following programs of study are offered: accounting, art, art history and criticism, biology, chemistry, classics, computer science, criminal justice, drama and theater, economics, engineering, English, French, geology, German, graphic and advertising design, history, information systems, international management, journalism, management, mathematics, medical technology, music, natural resource management, nursing, philosophy, physics, political science, psychology, religion, social science, sociology, and Spanish. (Engineering, geology, medical technology, natural resource management, occupational therapy, and physical therapy are offered in cooperation with other institutions.) The College offers preprofessional programs in law, medicine, teacher education (elementary, secondary, and music), and theology. Students can also structure interdepartmental majors, individually designed majors, double majors, and minors in all areas.

Academic Program

The academic year consists of fall and spring terms of fifteen weeks each. The typical course load per term is 4 course units equivalent to 4 semester-credit hours per unit.

To earn a baccalaureate degree, students are required to complete 32 course units (128 semester-credit hours). By following Moravian's new general education curriculum, Learning in Common, students are given a coherent introduction to the liberal arts and sciences. Special programs available include independent study, field study, and a special honors program in the senior year. Through its Division of Continuing Studies, Moravian offers both degree and nondegree programs. Day students may elect courses in the evening or summer session to accommodate their schedules or to have the opportunity to share classes with adults who bring a wide range of experiences and perspectives to classroom discussions.

Off-Campus Arrangements

Moravian students may participate in the Washington Semester, study at Oxford University, and experience a variety of other study-abroad opportunities for a summer, a term, or a full academic year. In addition, through the Lehigh Valley Association of Independent Colleges, students may cross-register for courses offered by Lehigh University and Lafayette, Muhlenberg, Cedar Crest, and Allentown colleges. Two- and four-year U.S. Army ROTC programs are available through cross-registration with Lehigh University. All programs carry academic credit. Students may also participate in courses and programs offered through the Lehigh Valley Center for Jewish Studies.

Academic Facilities

Reeves Library houses 245,332 volumes and operates on an open-stack policy, with reading areas throughout the building. Cooperation with other Lehigh Valley colleges makes more than 2 million volumes readily accessible to Moravian College students. An automated online catalog with remote access is available, as are other online reference services. The library is open until midnight.

Collier Hall of Science, which has been recognized for its architectural design and function, provides lecture halls, teaching laboratories, specialized collections and reading rooms, a greenhouse, and individual research laboratories for faculty members and advanced students in physics, earth science, chemistry, biology, and computer science. All members of the Moravian College community have access (except for scheduled laboratory class times) to networked DOS/Windows and Apple Macintosh microcomputers in the academic computing laboratory in Hamilton Hall from 8 a.m. to 12 midnight. The lab provides laser printing capabilities for Macintosh and Windows computers. Students with their own computers who purchase a network kit from the Center for Information Technology may connect to the campus network directly from their dormitory rooms. This connection provides 24-hour access to network services, including printing, file servers, e-mail, and the Internet. The network provides storage for personal files and access to campus software such as Microsoft Word, Excel, and PowerPoint; Minitab; SPSS; WordPerfect; and various other programs needed for academic pursuits. The Center for Music and Art is located on the College's historic Church Street campus, in an area that reflects the grace of Colonial and Victorian architecture. The center has been extensively renovated for practice and performance needs and includes a changing-exhibition art gallery.

Costs

The comprehensive fee for 2000–01, which includes a student activity fee, is $19,400. Additional costs include a room fee of $3330 and a board fee of $2790. Books, travel, and miscellaneous expenses are estimated at $2130 for resident students, $3650 for students commuting from home, and $4770 for off-campus residents. International students' expenses are the same as those for resident students with additional expenses for airfare. A one-time freshman orientation fee of $30 is also charged.

Financial Aid

Moravian College, together with state and federal programs, offers financial aid to qualified students through scholarships, loans, grants, and employment. The purpose of these programs is to provide financial assistance to supplement that given by the student's family. Applications for financial aid, filed with the College and with state and federal agencies, allow students to be considered for each program for which they are eligible. The Comenius Scholar program awards grants that range from one quarter to one half of the tuition to a limited number of high-achieving students. All financial aid awards generally involve both grants and student self-help in the form of loans and student employment. Endowed scholarships are also available in several areas of study. Academic achievement, future promise, and contributions to the College play a role in the type of award made. The College also awards up to two full tuition scholarships to qualified international students each year.

The College awards approximately $15 million annually in financial aid (grants, campus jobs, and loans from public and private sources) to an average of 80 percent of the student body. Incoming freshmen and upperclassmen are required to file the College Scholarship Service Financial Aid PROFILE with signed copies of federal income taxes for both parents and student, and the Free Application for Federal Student Aid (FAFSA).

Faculty

Ninety-two percent of Moravian's 105 full-time faculty members hold earned doctoral or other terminal degrees. The student-faculty ratio is 14:1. Many Moravian faculty members have distinguished themselves in research, publication, and public service, but the primary focus of their endeavors is on effective teaching and advising of students.

Student Government

The United Student Government represents students' interests, allocates activity funds to student organizations, and appoints students to student-faculty committees. Self-governance is developed through the appointment of an undergraduate resident staff and a student-dominated College Discipline Committee. Two students are elected annually as voting members of the Board of Trustees. The Haupert Union Program Board, composed entirely of students, provides a major part of the College's social program and, through its various committees, is a vehicle for the development of leadership.

Admission Requirements

Moravian welcomes students from diverse backgrounds and geographic locations. The Admissions Committee carefully evaluates the preparation and potential of each applicant, placing emphasis on academic achievement in secondary school. Other factors considered include a student's test scores, recommendations, extracurricular activities, major interests, and demonstrated interest in the College. Graduation from an accredited secondary school or a high school equivalency certificate is required. Eighty percent of the students entering Moravian in 1999 graduated in the top two fifths of their secondary school class, 50 percent in the top fifth. Of the 1,356 applicants, 995 were accepted. Of those that were accepted, 318 enrolled. Applications for early admission and early decision are recommended, and deferred admission can be arranged. Transfer and international students are welcome and are encouraged to apply. International applicants must demonstrate English proficiency and the ability to assume expenses and must provide transcripts (originals and certified translations) documenting secondary and postsecondary school study. Each transfer student's credentials are considered individually to determine the number of credits to be accepted. Transfer applicants must present a minimum 2.5 grade point average (4.0 scale). Students are strongly encouraged to visit the Moravian campus. Interviews, tours of the College, and visits with faculty members may be arranged by contacting the Admission Office prior to the visit.

Application and Information

Each prospective student should submit a completed application and a nonrefundable $30 application fee as early as possible in the senior year, preferably by January 1. The deadline is March 1. An official high school transcript, an essay, letters of recommendation, and reports from either the SAT I or ACT are required. The TOEFL is required of all applicants for whom English is not the native language. Applicants are notified of the Admissions Committee decision beginning March 15. Early decision applicants must apply by January 15. The committee notifies these applicants of its decision between December 15 and February 1.

For an application form or additional information, students should contact:

James P. Mackin
Director of Admission
Moravian College
Bethlehem, Pennsylvania 18018

Telephone: 610-861-1320
Email: admissions@moravian.edu
World Wide Web: www.moravian.edu

MOREHEAD STATE UNIVERSITY
MOREHEAD, KENTUCKY

The University

Historically, Morehead State University (MSU) traces its lineage to the Morehead Normal School, which opened its doors in 1887. The private school closed in spring 1922 when the Kentucky General Assembly established Morehead State Normal School. Since then, the University has grown from a teachers' college to a regional university that serves Kentucky and Appalachia. Until university status was granted in 1966, the institution's primary mission was the training of teachers. However, the curriculum now embraces nearly 120 academic programs on the associate, baccalaureate, and graduate levels. Physically, the University consists of more than fifty major structures valued at more than $144 million. There are more than 42,000 MSU alumni. Administratively, the University operates under an 11-member Board of Regents that consists of 8 citizens appointed by the governor of Kentucky, with three other seats held by elected faculty, staff, and student representatives. The administrative structure covers primarily four areas: academic affairs, administration and fiscal services, student life, and university advancement. Each of these units is headed by a vice president.

MSU has twenty-four master's degree programs, plus two graduate-level nondegree programs designed especially for professional educators. A post-master's–level degree in education specialist studies, along with a joint doctoral degree with the University of Kentucky, are offered on the campus.

There are approximately 8,200 men and women enrolled at Morehead State University, of whom about 6,800 are undergraduates. The University recognizes more than 100 student organizations, including twenty-one nationally chartered fraternities and sororities, and sponsors a full program of intercollegiate and intramural athletics for men and women. MSU is basically a residential campus and has fourteen residence halls. About 90 percent of its students are Kentuckians. Graced by a large lake, the campus sits in the foothills of the Daniel Boone National Forest. Among the University's facilities are an experimental farm and a nine-hole golf course.

Location

The University is located near the main shopping area of Morehead, a city of about 12,000 people that lies midway between Ashland, Kentucky, and Lexington, Kentucky, on Interstate 64. Commercial airline service is available in Lexington and in Huntington, West Virginia, which is also on the I-64 corridor. Nearby recreational areas are Cave Run Lake and Rodburn Park, which are owned by the U.S. Forest Service. Three Kentucky state parks—Natural Bridge, Carter Caves, and Greenbo—are within an hour's drive. The city of Morehead is served by a 150-bed hospital and functions as the medical, educational, cultural, and commercial center of northeastern Kentucky.

Majors and Degrees

Morehead State University awards the following undergraduate degrees: A.A., A.B., A.A.B., A.D.N., A.A.S., B.B.A., B.M., B.M.E., B.S., B.S.N., B.U.S., and B.S.W.

The College of Science and Technology offers the Bachelor of Science (B.S.) degree in agricultural education, agricultural science (with options in agribusiness, agricultural economics, agronomy, animal science, general agriculture, golf-course management, and horticulture), biology, chemistry, environmental science, geology, human sciences (with options in dietetics, hotel/restaurant and institutional management, child development, and vocational family and consumer sciences) industrial technology (with options in construction/mining technology, electricity/electronics technology, graphic communication technology, and manufacturing/robotics technology), industrial education (with options in industrial education/orientation exploration and industrial education preparation), mathematics, mathematics and computer programming, mathematics/physical science teaching (with options in chemistry, mathematics, and noncalculus- or calculus-based physics), medical technology, physics, and secondary science teaching (with options in biology, chemistry, earth science, and physics). The college also offers a Bachelor of Science in Nursing (B.S.N.), a Bachelor of Radiological Sciences, and a Bachelor of Arts (A.B.) degree in geology.

Two-year programs include the Associate of Applied Science (A.A.S.) degree in agricultural technology (with options in agribusiness, agricultural production, equine technology, and ornamental horticultural), human sciences (with options in food service management and child development), industrial technology (with options in construction/mining technology, electricity/electronics technology, graphic communication technology, and manufacturing/robotics technology), and veterinary technology. An associate degree in nursing (A.D.N.) is also available. Preprofessional programs are available to prepare students for careers in chiropractic medicine, dentistry, engineering, forestry, law, medicine, optometry, pharmacy, physical therapy, and veterinary medicine.

The College of Business offers the Bachelor of Business Administration (B.B.A.) degree with options in accounting, business and marketing education, business information systems, computer information systems, economics, finance, management, marketing, and real estate. The Associate of Applied Business (A.A.B.) degree includes options in business information systems, computer information systems, and real estate, with specialty areas in administrative legal support, administrative medical support, and administrative support management.

The College of Education and Behavioral Sciences offers the Bachelor of Arts (A.B.) degree in elementary education (P–5 and 5–9), health and physical education (P–12), psychology, recreation, sociology (with an emphasis on criminology), and special education (options in learning and behavior disorders (P–5 or 5–8) and moderate and severe disabilities (P–5 or 5–8)). The Bachelor of Science (B.S.) degree in exercise science and the Bachelor of Social Work (B.S.W.) degree are also available. Secondary teacher certification can be obtained through programs in many subject matter disciplines.

The Caudill College of Humanities offers the Bachelor of Arts (A.B.) degree in art, communications (emphases in advertising–public relations, electronic media news, electronic media production and management, and journalism), English, French, geography, government, history, paralegal studies, philosophy, social science teaching, Spanish, speech, speech/theater, and theater. Three degrees are available in music: the Bachelor of Music (B.M.) in music performance, the Bachelor of Music Education (B.M.E.) in teaching, and the Bachelor of Arts (A.B.) for the study of music within the liberal arts curriculum.

Academic Program

Morehead State University requires the successful completion of a minimum of 64 semester hours for an associate degree and a minimum of 128 semester hours for a bachelor's degree. The bachelor's degree programs include 42 semester hours of general education requirements, and at least 43 of the 128 semester hours must be in junior- and senior-level courses. A minimum of one year in residence at MSU is required. Bachelor's degree programs also require the completion of an area of concentration of not fewer than 48 semester hours or a major of not fewer than 30 semester hours and a minor of not fewer than 21 semester hours. For associate degrees, at least 16 semester hours must be earned in residence. Students must have a minimum average standing of 2.0 (on a 4.0 scale) to earn any undergraduate degree at Morehead State University.

MSU awards credit by examination through CLEP and other programs and credit for certain life experiences, such as military service. The University has an academic honors program for top students. Honors students may exceed the maximum course load with permission.

MSU operates under a calendar with two 17-week semesters—from mid-August to mid-December for the fall semester and from early January to mid-May for the spring semester. The summer session is divided into two 4-week sessions that begin in early June and end in late July.

In addition to the main campus, classes are taught in Ashland, Jackson, Maysville, Pikeville, Prestonburg, West Liberty, Whitesburg, and other locations. Also, the University offers a number of distance learning classes throughout the region via the Internet and interactive compressed video.

Morehead State University sponsors study tours in the United States and abroad.

Academic Facilities

Morehead State University's academic facilities include Camden-Carroll Library, which has 291,000 volumes; 2,600 serial subscriptions; 7,300 microform titles; 7,700 recordings; 10,200 audiovisual items, including CD-ROMs and other computer software; and nearly 10,000 government documents. With forty-five terminals to access the online catalog, the library also has a variety of other computers, including multimedia workstations and Internet workstations.

The Lappin, Cassity, Reed, Ginger, Baird, Claypool-Young, and Combs buildings provide modern classroom and laboratory facilities. In addition, the University has extensive agricultural facilities at the Derrickson Agricultural Complex north of Morehead. Theaters include Kibbey (100 seats) and Button Auditorium (1,300 seats). Media facilities include two television production studios, a 50,000-watt public radio station, and complete darkroom and composition laboratories for the student newspaper and yearbook. Computer facilities are available to students. Other specialized laboratories are used by students in food service, music, art, recreation, energy studies, Appalachian studies, graphic arts, health sciences, teacher education, and water testing. MSU has a 10:1 student-computer ratio.

Costs

For residents of Kentucky, the average cost of the 1999–2000 academic year for undergraduate study was approximately $7300. Out-of-state students paid approximately $11,000. These costs include tuition, books, activity fees, supplies, room, meals, transportation, and personal expenses. Certain laboratory courses require additional fees.

Financial Aid

Morehead State University offers qualified applicants a wide variety of financial assistance, including loans, grants, scholarships, and work opportunities. In addition, students are encouraged to investigate the possibility of getting aid through veterans' benefits, rehabilitation grants, and other private and public sources. Seventy percent of the students at MSU receive financial assistance. Aid renewal is generally based on various eligibility factors, including grades and financial need. April 1 is the priority filing deadline for the financial aid application.

Faculty

The University has 328 full-time faculty members and about 100 part-time (lecturers) faculty members. Faculty members are encouraged to concentrate on teaching duties while still devoting appropriate energies to research and public service. Graduate students are rarely used as instructors. Academic advisement is provided by full-time faculty members. About 62 percent of the faculty members hold earned doctoral degrees, and the student-faculty ratio is about 17:1.

Student Government

The Student Government Association, of which all full-time students become members, elects its executive branch and the Student Congress, and the judicial branch is appointed by elected student leaders. The Student Government Association has complete control of the entertainment series and has representatives on all standing committees of the University. A student serves as a voting member of the MSU Board of Regents.

Admission Requirements

All applicants must score above a minimum admissions index. Their score is calculated by multiplying the high school grade point average (on a 4.0 scale) by 100 and adding the result to the ACT composite score multiplied by 10. For example, a student has a high school GPA of 3.0 and an ACT composite score of 20; his or her admissions index would be 500 (300 + 200). The minimum admissions index is 400 for unconditional admission or 350 with at least an ACT composite score of 14 for provisional admission.

Students must also have completed the "Pre-College Curriculum" as defined by the Kentucky Council on Higher Education. Students failing to meet the admissions index and/or the precollege curriculum may be admitted to Morehead State University on a conditional basis.

Transfer applicants must have a minimum grade point average of 2.0 (on a 4.0 scale) and be in good standing with all previous institutions for unconditional acceptance.

Selected high school students within the service region of MSU are given an opportunity to enroll in college-level courses while still in high school.

Application and Information

MSU does not assess an application fee or an admission fee. Students applying for the fall semester are requested to submit all materials by June 1. Response from the Office of Admissions generally occurs within ten days. Students may be admitted temporarily during processing of the complete application. New students admitted for the fall are invited to participate in a summer orientation and registration program (SOAR).

Director of Admissions
Howell McDowell 301
Morehead State University
Morehead, Kentucky 40351
Telephone: 606-783-2000
        800-585-6781 (toll-free)
World Wide Web: http://www.moreheadstate.edu

MORGAN STATE UNIVERSITY
BALTIMORE, MARYLAND

The University

Morgan State University, a coeducational institution, is located in a residential section of Baltimore, Maryland. The compact campus of twenty-nine academic buildings, service facilities, and residence halls covers an area of more than 143 acres. The University offers both graduate and undergraduate programs of study. Recently, emphasis has been placed on the urban orientation of the University. This emphasis has been incorporated in the graduate programs in particular. At the graduate level, the University offers the Master of Arts degree in African-American studies, economics, English, history, international studies, mathematics, music, sociology, and teaching. The Master of Business Administration is offered in accounting, finance, international management, management, and marketing. The Master of Science degree is offered in educational administration and supervision, elementary and middle school education, engineering, science, and transportation. Professional degrees are offered in architecture, city and regional planning, and landscape architecture. The Doctor of Education degree is offered in mathematics education, science education, and urban educational leadership. In addition, the Doctor of Philosophy degree is offered in history and the Doctor of Engineering degree is offered in civil, electrical, and industrial engineering. The Doctor of Public Health is now being offered in the School of Education and Urban Studies.

Morgan State University does not discriminate against applicants because of race, sex, religion, or nationality. The institution was chartered in 1867 and was built on its present site in 1890. From 1867 to 1890, it was known as the Centenary Biblical Institute; from 1890 to 1938 as Morgan College; and from 1938 to 1975 as Morgan State College. In 1975, the college became Morgan State University.

The McKeldin Center, often called the "living room of the campus," is the focal point of cultural and social activity for the University community. Its purpose is to provide all members of the University community with programs and facilities to satisfy a variety of out-of-classroom tastes and needs. The McKeldin Center is utilized according to individual interests for meetings, lectures, music, movies, reading, and other forms of indoor recreation or simply for relaxing over a cup of coffee or casual conversation with friends.

The University is a member institution of several consortia, including the National Student Exchange, a consortium of twenty-two state colleges and universities across the country.

Location

The University has the advantages of both suburban life and proximity to an urban center. Built on two slopes, the campus is strategically located in the picturesque northeastern section of Baltimore, a city with a population of more than 657,000, and is surrounded by rapidly growing residential communities. The center of the city is easily accessible from the University campus.

Majors and Degrees

The Bachelor of Arts degree is offered in economics, English, fine art, history, international studies, music, philosophy, political science, sociology, speech communication, telecommunications, and theater arts. The Bachelor of Science degree is offered in the fields of accounting, biology, business administration, chemistry, computer science, economics, elementary education, engineering (civil, electrical, and industrial), engineering physics, finance, health education, home economics, hospitality management, information science and systems, management, marketing, mathematics, medical technology, mental health, physical education, physics, psychology, social work, and telecommunications.

Academic Program

Students admitted to Morgan to study for a Bachelor of Arts or Bachelor of Science degree are generally expected to adhere to the accepted standards of higher education. Honors programs, independent study, and cooperative education programs are available in most areas. For those students requiring special placement and/or special assistance, support services and programs are provided.

To earn a bachelor's degree, students must generally complete a minimum of 120 semester hours, depending on the program. Engineering students should expect to earn 135 semester hours to qualify for the degree.

Through the Continuing Studies Program, students can pursue an education outside traditional daytime classwork. Students in the program include part-time students, as well as many full-time students who have been away from a formal educational experience for two or more years and want to pursue courses for personal fulfillment or career advancement. The Continuing Studies Program includes Summer School, Weekend University, noncredit courses, extension programs, conferences, and workshops.

Morgan State's Weekend University is designed for working adults and others who are unable to attend weekday classes. Classes are scheduled on Friday evenings and Saturdays, providing students the opportunity to earn a bachelor's degree in accounting, business administration, social work, or telecommunications in approximately five to six years.

Off-Campus Arrangements

The Cooperative Education Program is a special program that permits students to extend their chosen major program by working in business, industry, or government agencies, alternating a semester of study with a semester of work while studying for undergraduate and graduate degrees. This program enables students to gain experience in an area close to their chosen field and to understand the requirements of that chosen field. A Cooperative Work-Study Program allows students who qualify to gain financial support while learning.

Through cooperative education projects, students may participate in specific seminars cooperatively planned and implemented by the Maryland state colleges or may take courses on other state college campuses. In addition, a cooperative project with Goucher College, Towson State University, Loyola College, and Johns Hopkins University provides an opportunity for students to enroll in courses not offered on the home campus.

Academic Facilities

The Departments of Biology, Chemistry, Physics, and Mathematics and the School of Engineering have specialized research facilities. Modern science and engineering facilities have been completed recently. In addition, two supercomputers were acquired by the University to support instruction and research.

The modern Soper Library's holdings constitute more than 660,000 volumes, including works in special collections. One such collection includes books on Africa, with an emphasis on sub-Saharan Africa. The African-American collection is a body of historically significant and current books by and about African Americans and includes papers and memorabilia of such persons as the late Emmett P. Scott, secretary to Booker T. Washington, and Arthur J. Smith, who was associated with the Far East Consular Division of the State Department. The Forbush Collection, named for Dr. Bliss Forbush, is composed of materials associated with the Quakers and slavery. The Martin D. Jenkins Collection was acquired in 1980. Together, these collections provide both a contemporary and historical view of African Americans in education, military service, politics, and religion.

Costs

In 2000–2001, tuition and fees are $4388 for residents of Maryland and $10,358 for nonresidents. Room and board, with a nineteen-meal plan, ranges from $5730 to $5940, depending upon the dormitory. Thus, tuition, fees, board, and room for a student who is a Maryland resident range from $10,118 to $10,328; for a nonresident student, they range from $16,088 to $16,298. Costs are subject to change without prior notice.

Financial Aid

Scholarships, loans, and campus employment are available, and awards are made on the basis of student merit and financial need. Information on these as well as on Federal Pell Grants, other federal grants, and Federal Work-Study awards may be obtained by writing to the Financial Aid Office.

Faculty

A majority of the University's 276 faculty members hold doctoral degrees. Many faculty members have attained national and international distinction for their research and creative work, and a number are officers of state, regional, national, and international professional organizations.

Student Government

Student government at Morgan State University is part of the student activities program, which is considered a vital element of the total educational program.

Admission Requirements

Applicants whose academic and personal qualifications show promise of success in college are considered on the basis of their high school grades, rank in class, personal recommendation, and scores on the SAT I or ACT.

Application and Information

Applications for August entrance should be submitted no later than April 15; those for January entrance should be submitted no later than December 1. Applications to Morgan State University are accepted as far as the facilities will permit. Transfer students must submit a transcript from every college previously attended. A limited number of out-of-state and international students may be accepted. All application forms must be accompanied by a $25 application fee and should be forwarded to:

The Office of Admissions
Morgan State University
Cold Spring Lane and Hillen Road
Baltimore, Maryland 21251
Telephone: 443-885-3000

MORNINGSIDE COLLEGE
SIOUX CITY, IOWA

The College

For more than 100 years, the goal of Morningside College has been to provide students with an education of the highest quality. Morningside is rooted in a strong church-related, liberal arts tradition, and its challenge is to prepare students to be flexible in thought, open in attitude, and confident in themselves.

Founded in 1894, Morningside College is a private, four-year, coeducational, liberal arts institution affiliated with the United Methodist Church. The College seeks both students and faculty representing diverse social, cultural, ethnic, racial, and national backgrounds.

At the graduate level, Morningside confers a Master of Arts in Teaching, with specialization in elementary education, special education in learning disabilities, and computer-based learning.

Morningside College's approximately 1,200 students are encouraged to participate in a wide variety of activities, including departmental, professional, and religious organizations; honor societies; and sororities and fraternities. A newspaper, literary magazine, yearbook, and campus radio station are all under student direction. These activities provide students with many opportunities to develop leadership, interpersonal, and social skills. Since nearly all activities on campus are student initiated and student directed, ample opportunities for leadership development exist. Music recitals and concerts, theater productions, and lecture and convocation series are held each semester. Intercollegiate athletics are available in NCAA Division II for men in baseball, basketball, cross-country, football, and track and field and for women in basketball, cross-country, golf, soccer, softball, track, and volleyball. Intramural sports include baseball/softball, basketball, football, swimming and diving, and volleyball.

The Hindman-Hobbs Recreation Center includes an Olympic-size pool, saunas, racquetball courts, a weight room, three basketball courts, and a jogging track.

Location

Morningside College is located on a 41-acre campus in Sioux City, the fourth-largest city in Iowa. The campus is based in a residential section of the community, adjacent to a city park, swimming pool, and tennis courts and within 5 minutes of a major regional shopping mall. The Sioux City metropolitan area offers a blend of urban shopping, commerce, and recreation in a scenic, rural setting. Students find Morningside's Sioux City location to be advantageous in seeking internship opportunities and full- or part-time employment.

Majors and Degrees

The five undergraduate degrees conferred by Morningside College are the Bachelor of Arts, Bachelor of Science, Bachelor of Science in Nursing, Bachelor of Music, and Bachelor of Music Education. Career programs consist of accounting, art, biology, biopsychology, business administration, chemistry, computer science, corporate communications, criminal justice, drama, early childhood education, economics, elementary education, English, French, graphic arts, history, Indian studies, industrial psychology, interdisciplinary studies, mass communications, mathematics, music, nursing, philosophy, photography, physical education, physics, political science, psychology, recreation management, religious studies, sociology, Spanish, special education, and speech-drama. Students choosing to teach in secondary school may be certified in all academic majors.

In cooperation with other institutions, Morningside offers preprofessional programs in dentistry, engineering, environmental science, law, medical technology, medicine, the ministry, physical therapy, and veterinary medicine.

Academic Program

Morningside operates on a two-semester system; sessions are held from late August to December and from January to early May. Evening school is offered each semester. A 3-week May interim and two 5-week summer sessions are also available.

Morningside College is committed to the liberal arts as a foundation for every field of concentration at the undergraduate level. Requirements in general education consist of a distribution of studies in the humanities, natural sciences, social sciences, and physical education. Some interdisciplinary courses are also required.

Special opportunities include a voluntary Honors Program, in which students meet weekly to discuss such focus topics as Ancient Rome and the Eighteenth Century. Friday is Writing Day, a weekly discussion format that allows students and faculty to read aloud and react to one another's writing.

The College's commitment to technology cuts across the academic divisions. In the music and art departments, for example, students produce movies and multimedia productions, arrange music, and create CD-ROMs. Mass communication majors work in state-of-the-art radio and television studio environments. Engineering, physics, and chemistry students learn through computerized labs beginning their first year, and behavioral and health studies majors gain clinical experience in the computerized animal laboratory.

Virtually all Morningside students use computers to complete papers and projects. The College also provides student computer facilities on campus (including in the residence hall rooms) that link students to the world via free e-mail and Internet use.

Off-Campus Arrangements

Morningside students who qualify have the opportunity to take advantage of special programs for off-campus study. Programs are available for a summer session, a semester, or the entire school year. The College has agreements with schools in Spain, England, France, Austria, Germany, Mexico, Israel, Japan, and Taiwan.

Students participate in exchange programs with Edgehill College in Oxford, England; University of Caen in France; and Kansai Gadai University in Japan.

In addition, Morningside has opportunities for students to enroll for a semester at American University to study the U.S. government in action. Students can also enroll for a semester at Drew University to study the United Nations. Students who participate in these programs maintain their enrollment at Morningside College.

Academic Facilities

Each resident Morningside student is provided with a personal computer for his or her use. After eight consecutive semesters of residence-hall living, students own their computers and software and take them along after graduation. The College's microcomputer support staff maintains and services student computers as long as students are living in the residence halls. All Morningside students and faculty members have full Internet access through which they have e-mail, library access, the World Wide Web, and ISCA.

The Hickman-Johnson-Furrow Library has over 117,000 volumes, more than 5,000 audio recordings and video materials, and over 600 current print periodical subscriptions. The library also subscribes to a database indexing 1,700 journals, of which 700 are full-text and available online to students in the library and in their residence hall rooms. In addition, the library houses a closed-circuit television system, a television studio, a microcomputer lab, and classrooms.

The Eugene C. Eppley Fine Arts Building is one of the finest music and art facilities in the Midwest. The auditorium seats 1,500 people and is noted for its acoustical qualities and the majestic Sanford Memorial Organ. The MacCollin Classroom Building, adjoining the auditorium, houses offices, art studios, practice rooms, and classrooms for music and art students.

The Robert M. Lincoln Center houses the College's division of economics and business and contains a library, auditorium, microcomputer lab, conference room, and several classrooms.

Costs

Tuition and fees for 1999–2000 were $13,146, and room and board were $4636. These figures do not include books and personal expenses.

Financial Aid

In 1998–99, more than $13 million was awarded in financial aid to Morningside students, with an average financial aid package of $13,400. The financial aid resources of federal, state, and College programs are available to Morningside students through a combination of scholarships, grants, loans, and work-study employment. Morningside values students who achieve both in and out of the classroom—people who are thinkers and doers. Morningside Celebration of Excellence Scholarships recognize academic excellence and outstanding service, and awards of up to $6000 per year are renewable for four years. Morningside also values its ties with alumni, the region, and the United Methodist Church, and those awards (up to $3000 per year) are also renewable for four years. Students are encouraged to submit the Free Application for Federal Student Aid (FAFSA) as early as possible. The College's code number is 001879. The annual priority deadline for need-based financial aid is March 1.

Faculty

Seventy-nine percent of Morningside College's 72 full-time faculty members have earned the terminal degree in their chosen field. The College also employs 58 part-time instructors and has a 12:1 student-faculty ratio.

Student Government

Student government is directly responsible for regulation, supervision, and coordination of student campus activities. The president of the student body is a voting member of the Board of Directors, allowing for student input in decisions facing the Board.

Admission Requirements

Morningside College selects students for admission whose scholastic achievement and personal abilities provide a foundation for success at the college level. While the College seeks students who rank in the upper half of their graduating class, each application is considered on an individual basis. The student's academic record, class rank, and test scores are considered. Transfer students must have a minimum 2.0 GPA on previous college work to qualify for automatic admission. It is the policy and practice of Morningside College to not discriminate against persons on the basis of age, sex, religion, creed, race, color, national or ethnic origin, sexual orientation, or physical or mental disability.

Application and Information

Rolling admission allows for flexibility; however, prospective students are encouraged to apply as early as possible before the semester in which they wish to enroll. Transfer and international students are welcome. Catalogs, application forms, and financial aid forms are available from the Office of Admissions.

For further information, students should contact:

Office of Admissions
Morningside College
1501 Morningside Avenue
Sioux City, Iowa 51106
Telephone: 712-274-5111
           800-831-0806 (toll-free)
E-mail: mscadm@morningside.edu
World Wide Web: http://www.morningside.edu

Students and professor at work in chemistry lab.

MOUNT ALOYSIUS COLLEGE
CRESSON, PENNSYLVANIA

The College

Founded in 1853 as Mount Aloysius Academy by the Sisters of Mercy, Mount Aloysius was established as a junior college in 1939. Since then, 10,019 students have graduated with associate degrees. In 1992, Mount Aloysius began a new chapter in its history, offering upper-division courses to students interested in pursuing a Bachelor of Arts or a Bachelor of Science degree. Since 1997, many students have received their baccalaureate degree. Most Mount Aloysius students come from Pennsylvania, but more students are coming from other states. Seventy-three percent of the Mount's day students are women, 49 percent are 25 years of age or older, 10.6 percent live on campus, and 3.4 percent are from out of state. In addition, there are approximately 400 students enrolled through the Center for Life Long Learning.

Mount Aloysius believes that students must be able to evaluate ethical issues and form a sound moral character consistent with traditional Judeo-Christian values. Social growth is also seen as a vital element of a complete education, encompassing the important ability to relate closely with people.

The College recognizes that student activities play a distinctive role in the total educational program. There are approximately twenty organized groups on campus, including a newspaper, a resident hall association, and a student activities planning board. Student activities include social events, intramural sports, intercollegiate sports, cultural events, functions of campus organizations, and forums and lectures by guest speakers.

Mount Aloysius College is adjacent to U.S. Route 22 between Altoona and Johnstown. Twelve buildings comprise the administration, academic, and residence areas of the Mount's 90-acre campus. The Main Building, a picturesque structure dating to 1897, houses the administrative and academic offices, classrooms, laboratories, art studio, Health Services Department, and Career Services Department. Cosgrave Center, a modern fieldstone building, is the Student Union and contains the dining hall, bookstore, commuter lounge, snack bar, day-care center, student mailboxes, and several administrative offices. The College's Health and Physical Fitness Center is adjacent to Cosgrave Center. The center has a seating capacity of 1,800 and serves as the home of intercollegiate basketball and volleyball as well as most intramural programs and fitness activities. The facility provides space for three basketball courts, three volleyball courts, a tennis court, a weight and exercise room equipped with a sauna, two locker rooms, an office area, two changing rooms for sports officials, storage rooms, public rest rooms, a lobby, and a vestibule. Ihmsen Hall is the housing facility for resident students. Alumni Hall is a multipurpose room that is used for performing arts series. The Mount's facilities are open twelve months per year and are made available to outside groups as scheduling permits.

Mount Aloysius is fully accredited by the Middle States Association of Colleges and Schools and approved by the Pennsylvania Department of Education. Its programs in medical assistant studies, occupational therapy assistant studies, nursing, and surgical technology are accredited by the American Association of Medical Assistants, the American Occupational Therapy Association, the National League for Nursing Accrediting Commission, and the Committee on Allied Health Education and Accreditation, respectively.

Location

Mount Aloysius is located in Cresson, Pennsylvania, in the southern Allegheny Mountains of central Pennsylvania. The College's setting is rural, although two middle-sized cities, Altoona and Johnstown, are within a short distance. The area has warm summers, brisk autumns, and snowy winters. Facilities for such outdoor activities as boating, hiking, horseback riding, swimming, skiing, fishing, and golf abound in central Pennsylvania.

Majors and Degrees

Mount Aloysius College awards bachelor's degrees, associate degrees, and diplomas of performance in the arts and sciences in both career-oriented and traditional programs of study. Baccalaureate degrees are available in accounting, business administration, criminology, early childhood education, medical imaging, nursing, occupational therapy, and professional studies. The Mount's associate degree programs are offered in accounting, applied technology, business administration, criminology, early childhood education, general studies, human services, interpreter training for the deaf, legal assistant studies, liberal arts, medical assistant studies, microcomputer applications, nursing, occupational therapy assistant studies, pharmacy technician studies, physical therapist assistant studies, radiography, and surgical technology. The College's two diploma programs are offered in psychiatric technician studies and surgical technology.

Academic Program

Whether preparing students for careers upon graduation or for its baccalaureate-level programs, Mount Aloysius recognizes the importance of a broad education. Thus, in addition to receiving solid preparation for a chosen career, every student at the College receives a foundation in the arts, the sciences, and the humanities through a core curriculum.

Credits and degree requirements at Mount Aloysius vary from program to program. Students must complete between 60 and 71 credits to earn an associate degree and a minimum of 120 credits to earn a bachelor's degree. Strong emphasis is placed on the specialized courses within each program of study, and many academic programs combine classroom experience with related training at area clinical sites, agencies, and institutions.

In addition to its regular academic programs, Mount Aloysius offers independent and directed study and an educational enrichment service.

The academic calendar includes two semesters and two optional summer sessions.

Off-Campus Arrangements

An important feature of many academic programs at Mount Aloysius is off-campus training. Many of the College's programs of study require credit-yielding practicums, through which students work and receive training at local hospitals, schools, or agencies. Students in the medical assistant studies, nursing, occupational therapy assistant studies, occupational therapy studies, pharmacy technician studies, physical therapist assistant studies, radiography, and surgical technology programs participate in required on-the-job training during their time at the Mount.

Academic Facilities

In 1995, Mount Aloysius College opened both a new library and a new era signifying greater access to information for the Mount community. The library's growing collection of approximately 70,000 print and nonprint titles is now housed in a state-of-the-art, 31,000-square-foot facility with ample seating space, four group study rooms, a reading lounge, a Law Library and classroom, and additional room for future expansion. This facility is also completely automated, with an online catalog and access to remote libraries and the World Wide Web at more than thirty public workstations. Also located in the library is the Information Technology Center, home to fifteen multimedia computer workstations and some of the latest offerings in educational software.

Academic Hall is an instructional facility housing classrooms, labs, seminar rooms, and faculty offices. Pierce Health and Science Hall is a 31,000-square-foot facility that houses all laboratory science courses and certain allied health programs. The facility has state-of-the-art instructional resources and allows the Mount to continue educating health and science professionals well into the twenty-first century.

Costs

Annual tuition and fees in 2000–01 for full-time students at Mount Aloysius are $10,780, and room and board are $4830. Annual tuition for the nursing, occupational therapy, occupational therapy assistant studies, pharmacy technician studies, physical therapist assistant studies, and radiography programs is slightly higher.

Financial Aid

Mount Aloysius recognizes the expense involved in acquiring a college education and encourages students to apply for all available financial aid. Through its financial aid office, the Mount assists students in applying for state and federal grants, loans, work-study awards, and MAC Merit Scholarships. MAC Merit Scholarships are awarded based on GPA and SAT scores. They are renewable on a yearly basis. Scholarships range from $1000 to $5000 per year. Mount Aloysius participates in all federal and state student grant programs, including the Federal Pell Grant, Federal Supplemental Educational Opportunity Grant, and Pennsylvania Higher Education Assistance Agency Grant programs. In 1999–2000, the Mount awarded an estimated $9.2 million in student financial aid. Eighty percent of the College's students received some form of financial aid.

Faculty

The Mount Aloysius faculty consists of 58 full-time and part-time members, whose primary responsibility is teaching. Most MAC faculty members hold advanced degrees at the master's or doctoral level, and all faculty members are expected to maintain close instructional ties with students. Many members hold national professional certificates in such disciplines as nursing, medical assistant studies, and occupational therapy. The Mount Aloysius student-faculty ratio of 12:1 allows close contact between students and faculty and is an important element of the College's overall academic philosophy.

Student Government

The Student Representative Council represents students on all issues that concern them at the College. The association appoints student representatives to all student-oriented College committees. The College encourages active student participation in the general governance structure and in other matters concerning the development and implementation of policies on resident student life.

Admission Requirements

The College admits a freshman class of about 500 students. Admission is selective and is based primarily on academic promise, as indicated by a student's secondary school performance and activities, standardized test scores, and special experience and talents. Applicants are required to have, or expect to earn, a diploma from an approved secondary school or a GED diploma and must submit a transcript of grades from the secondary school and SAT I or ACT scores. Prospective students are invited to visit the College to speak with students, faculty, and staff. Visits can be arranged for a day or a weekend by contacting the admissions office.

In addition to the general College entrance requirements, specific admission requirements exist for applicants to some of the Mount's health-related programs. Prospective applicants should contact the Office of Admissions for detailed information.

Application and Information

To apply for admission to Mount Aloysius, candidates are encouraged to submit their application and $25 application fee to the Office of Admissions during the fall semester of their senior year in high school. They must also arrange to have their secondary school send their transcript and to have either the school or the testing agency send their SAT I or ACT scores to the Office of Admissions.

For further information, students should contact:

Office of Admissions
Mount Aloysius College
7373 Admiral Peary Highway
Cresson, Pennsylvania 16630
Telephone: 814-886-6383
          814-88MOUNT
          888-823-2220 (toll-free)
E-mail: admissions@mtaloy.edu
World Wide Web: http://www.mtaloy.edu

The historic Main Building, located on the scenic campus of Mount Aloysius College.

MOUNT HOLYOKE COLLEGE
SOUTH HADLEY, MASSACHUSETTS

The College

Long distinguished for the quality of its curricular and cocurricular life, as well as for the diversity of its student body and the success of its alumnae, Mount Holyoke is an independent college of liberal arts and sciences for women. The student body, numbering 2,000, comes from forty-nine states and seventy-one countries. One out of every 4 students is an international student or an African-American, Latina, Asian, or Native American woman from the United States. Between 25 and 30 percent of each graduating class enter graduate or professional school immediately after graduation; 70 percent do so within ten years. Law and medical programs attract approximately 40 percent of those who enroll in professional school directly from college. More than half of those who go directly to work upon graduation join corporate training programs or take entry-level management positions in banking, insurance, retailing, and the nonprofit sector.

Mount Holyoke is committed to maintaining small classes and individualized academic advising. The College's faculty-student ratio is 1:10. More than half of Mount Holyoke's classes enroll fewer than 15 students, and one third enroll fewer than 10. All students are advised by members of the faculty. Non-Western cultures are a focus of the College's curricular life. Most students pursue interdisciplinary courses, some taught by teams of faculty members from different fields. Use of computers, proficiency in foreign languages, and development of writing skills are stressed throughout the curriculum.

Mount Holyoke participates in the Five College Consortium, which also includes Amherst, Hampshire, and Smith colleges and the University of Massachusetts at Amherst. Students enrolled at any one of the five colleges can take the courses as well as participate in the cultural and social offerings of the other four. In addition, the five institutions' faculty and classes are coordinated in areas of common interest such as African studies, coastal and marine biology, design, environmental studies, film studies, Judaic and Near Eastern studies, legal studies, neuroscience, and Slavic studies.

Forming a vital part of Mount Holyoke's offerings are diverse cocurricular opportunities—concerts, conferences, exhibitions, films, and social events. Noted actors, dancers, and musicians perform at Mount Holyoke and within the Five College area. In addition, there are performance opportunities through chamber ensembles, dance groups, theater productions, and an active choral program. These opportunities are supplemented by groups such as the Five College Dance Department, the Five College Orchestra, and the New World Theatre. More than 100 clubs and organizations at Mount Holyoke provide creative outlets, leadership experiences, and service opportunities.

The residence halls complement the liberal arts experience, co-ordinating cultural and social events and providing a home away from home for all students. Almost all students live on campus in the residence halls, each of which accommodates between 65 and 130 students. All four classes are mixed in each hall, and housing is guaranteed for all four years.

A comprehensive sports complex has indoor and outdoor facilities. The field house includes tennis, volleyball, squash, and racquetball courts; a 200-meter track; and an eight-lane swimming pool with a separate diving tank. The field house adjoins the newly renovated gymnasium and dance studios. There are also sixteen tennis courts, an eighteen-hole golf course, lakes for canoeing, a 400-meter track, and four varsity fields. A 20-acre equestrian center provides a fifty-seven-stall barn and large indoor and outdoor riding arenas. This center is one of the finest available to students anywhere. Mount Holyoke is an NCAA Division III school and offers fifteen intercollegiate teams as well as intramural and club sports.

Location

South Hadley, Massachusetts, is about 20 minutes from Springfield, 1½ hours from Boston, and 3 hours from New York City by car. Convenient bus, plane, and train service to the College is available. Bradley International Airport, 40 minutes away by car, serves Hartford and Springfield; Amtrak train stations are located in Amherst and Springfield. Restaurants, shops, and theaters are within walking distance of campus, and Northampton and Amherst are minutes away via the Five College bus.

Majors and Degrees

Mount Holyoke offers the Bachelor of Arts degree. Majors include African studies, African-American studies, American studies, anthropology, art (history and studio), Asian studies, astronomy, biochemistry, biological sciences, chemistry, computer science, critical social thought, dance, economics, English, environmental studies, European studies, French, geography, geology, German, Greek, history, international relations, Italian, Latin, Latin American studies, mathematics, medieval studies, music, neuroscience and behavior, philosophy, physics, politics, psychology, psychology and education, religion, Romance languages and literatures, Russian, Russian and European studies, sociology, Spanish, statistics, theater arts, and women's studies. Students whose interests uniquely cross departmental lines may design their own majors.

Academic Program

Within the framework of the liberal arts and sciences, Mount Holyoke offers students considerable freedom of choice in the academic program. The basic plan of study includes a distribution of courses among at least seven disciplines, courses in language, courses in a major and minor field, and at least one course dealing with an aspect of Africa, Asia, Latin America, the Middle East, or the nonwhite peoples of North America. Ordinarily, distribution and language course requirements are completed within the first two years. A normal schedule is four 4-credit courses per semester, each meeting one to four times per week. By graduation, a student has completed 128 credits of academic work in courses that provide exposure to a variety of disciplines, as well as specialization in a major and a minor field. Independent study, honors work, and self-scheduled examinations are among the options available. The Frances Perkins Program is designed for women beyond the traditional undergraduate age who wish to initiate, continue, or enrich their undergraduate education.

The academic calendar consists of two semesters separated by an active January Term program. During January Term, students may take a single intensive course, pursue an independent project, or conduct a Career Exploration Project in a professional setting with alumnae or friends of the College.

Off-Campus Arrangements

The Mount Holyoke student lives and studies in an area where four independent colleges and a large university enroll a total of nearly 30,000 students. Amherst College, Hampshire College, Mount Holyoke College, Smith College, and the University of Massachusetts at Amherst participate in an extensive Five College cooperative exchange program. Free buses run among the institutions (all within a 10-mile radius) every 20 minutes from morning to late evening, seven days a week, during the school year. Mount Holyoke is a member of the Twelve College

Exchange Program, and students can spend a year or semester at any of the other participating institutions (Amherst, Bowdoin, Connecticut, Dartmouth, Smith, Trinity, Vassar, Wellesley, Wesleyan, Wheaton, and Williams). The Twelve College Exchange includes the Williams/Mystic Seaport Program in American Maritime Studies and the National Theatre Institute Program. Mount Holyoke also has its own exchange programs with Mills College in Oakland, California; Spelman College in Atlanta, Georgia; the Universities of Kent and Essex in England; and the University of Bonn in Germany.

Large numbers of students study abroad in such countries as Brazil, France, Greece, India, Israel, Italy, Japan, Kenya, Mexico, Nepal, Senegal, the former Soviet Union, Spain, Sri Lanka, and the United Kingdom.

Internships involve full-time work for eight to twelve weeks over the summer. The College has five major internship programs: the Washington Internship Program, the International Internship Program, the Complex Organizations Program, the Science Internship Program, and the Special Internship Program.

Academic Facilities

The Williston Memorial Library houses 649,000 volumes, 1,636 periodicals, extensive archives, and an audiovisual center, which includes a recording studio, film information, and rental services. The new Science Library houses all holdings in the sciences and in psychology. Three buildings house science classrooms and laboratories and an extensive array of sophisticated equipment. There are also a Laboratory Theatre with a 200-seat auditorium and complete production facilities; a music building with its own auditorium; an observatory with numerous telescopes, including a 24-inch reflecting telescope and an 8-inch Alvan Clark refracting telescope; and an art building with studios, a bronze-casting foundry, a library, an auditorium, and a museum. In addition, the College has a psychology building with a vivarium, the Gorse Child Study Center, Talcott Arboretum, a Japanese meditation garden and teahouse, and the Skinner Museum complex, which contains a remarkable collection of nineteenth-century Americana and a kosher/hallal kitchen.

The Joan E. Ciruti Center for Foreign Languages is a state-of-the-art language learning center. Its three levels of classrooms and laboratory space enable language instructors to integrate traditional methods of teaching with the latest in audio and video equipment plus computers. The College's computing facilities include a variety of PCs for word processing, programming, statistics, and computer-aided instruction; a network of DEC and Sun computers for programming, statistics, electronic mail, and other standard time-sharing functions; access to the powerful University of Massachusetts CYBER systems and to national networks; stand-alone systems, computers for instrumental control and data analysis, and PC labs to support research and curricular work in departments; and dormitory word processing sites. Students use the College's computers free of charge. Seminars on computer services and facilities are available.

Costs

For 2000–01, tuition is $25,220 and room and board are $7410, for a total of $32,630. Health insurance and an activity fee total $785, books and supplies are $750, and personal expenses are $750.

Financial Aid

Financial need should not discourage any student from applying to Mount Holyoke. The College administers a program of need-based aid. Students are funded to the extent of demonstrated need, and 65 percent receive some form of assistance, such as loans, employment, and grants.

Faculty

Mount Holyoke's faculty of more than 200 members has national and international distinction. Approximately 98 percent hold the highest degree in their field. All courses are taught by faculty members; professors are also active in advising students about classes, cocurricular opportunities, and careers. While teaching and advising undergraduates are their primary functions, faculty members are active in research, writing, and publishing. Two have won Pulitzer Prizes, and numerous others have received grants from major corporations and foundations.

Student Government

Mount Holyoke students, together with the faculty and administrators, have a strong hand in shaping campus life. Students sit on several committees, including the Academic Policy Committee, the Committee on Academic Responsibility, and the Board of Admissions. The Student Government Association allows students to govern their cocurricular lives and to maintain communication with the faculty and administration. Students have an effective honor code of long standing.

Admission Requirements

Mount Holyoke seeks young women of outstanding intellectual ability and personal qualities, varied in their interests and talents, desirous of a liberal education, and representative of many public and independent schools. Mount Holyoke welcomes students of all economic, ethnic, geographic, religious, and social backgrounds. To make the College a truly multiracial community, students from minority groups have been actively sought for many years. A high school program providing a good preparation for Mount Holyoke includes 4 years of English, either 4 years of one foreign language or a combination of 3 years of one language and 2 years of another, and 3 years each of mathematics, history, and laboratory sciences. SAT I or ACT scores are required for freshman and transfer applicants. The Test of English as a Foreign Language (TOEFL) is recommended for students for whom English is not a primary language. Personal interviews are highly recommended for all candidates either on campus or with an Alumna Admissions Representative.

Application and Information

Two rounds of early decision are available: the deadline for Round I is December 1, with notification by January 1; the deadline for Round II is January 1, with notification by February 1. The deadline for regular admission is January 15, with notification by April 1. Other admission options, such as early entrance, deferred entrance, and advanced standing, are available.

The admission office is open all year, Monday through Friday, from 9 a.m. until 5 p.m., and Saturday mornings from 9 a.m. until noon. Visitors are welcome to come to the admission office to take a campus tour, obtain admission materials, or meet with a staff member if available. For more information about Mount Holyoke, students should contact:

Board of Admission
Mount Holyoke College
South Hadley, Massachusetts 01075-1496

Telephone: 413-538-2023
Fax: 413-538-2409
E-mail: admissions@mtholyoke.edu

MOUNT IDA COLLEGE
NEWTON CENTRE, MASSACHUSETTS

The College

Mount Ida College has just finished celebrating its centennial. Founded in 1899, Mount Ida has been one of the Northeast's most innovative postsecondary institutions, evolving from a junior college to a four-year institution offering applied arts, sciences, and technology with a liberal arts core.

Approximately 1,400 full-time students are enrolled at Mount Ida. About 75 percent of these students represent New England, New York, New Jersey, and Pennsylvania. The international population represents approximately 15 percent of the full-time population. Approximately 800 men and women reside in five College dormitories, four of which are coed and one of which is all women.

Mount Ida's beautiful 85-acre campus was once an elegant country estate. Academic, administrative, and residential buildings are surrounded by playing fields, a pond, and wooded areas in a comfortable, self-contained environment. Over the last ten years, more than $16 million in new construction has been expended, providing dormitories, classrooms, and other buildings and an expansion of the Learning Resource Center. In 1994, construction was completed on a $2.5-million student center. A new academic technology building and a new Gymnasium were completed in spring 1999.

At Mount Ida College, where each student is known by name and recognized as an individual, students find it easy to become involved. Students are encouraged to start new positive groups on campus that will enrich the College community. Campus organizations and clubs reflect the diversity of the student body and afford wonderful opportunities for creative expression and leadership development. Some of these are the Student Government, the Residence Hall Council, the Judicial Board, Phi Theta Kappa, Alpha Chi, and Phi Theta Delta Honor Societies, the International Student Club, the Drama Club, the student newspaper, the yearbook, the literary magazine, the Veterinary Technology Club, A.S.I.D., the Fashion and Design Club, and the Communications Club. A variety of social, cultural, and recreational activities are also an important part of student life. These include intercollegiate mixers, Parents Weekend, international dinners, a faculty lecture series, Winter Carnival, a Spring Semi-Formal, the Spring Fling Weekend, the Annual Fashion Show, and Senior Week.

Various intercollegiate sports are offered during the school year, including basketball, football, lacrosse, and soccer for men and basketball, cross-country, soccer, softball, and volleyball for women. There is also a coed equestrian team. Mount Ida College is currently a provisional member of the NCAA Division III. Many of Mount Ida's teams have enjoyed national rank and tournament action.

Location

Newton, a city of 90,000, is located only 8 miles (13 kilometers) from the center of Boston. College shuttle buses connect students with the Newton Centre business district, where there is MBTA subway service to Boston. The Boston metropolitan area is home to more than sixty other institutions of higher learning, numerous historic sites, a wide variety of shops, and diverse cultural and social opportunities. Local industrial parks, business districts, and shopping malls provide a wide variety of easily accessible employment opportunities.

Majors and Degrees

Mount Ida grants B.S., B.L.S., A.A., and A.S. degrees. Majors and areas of study include accounting, advertising and sales, bereavement studies, business administration, child study, communications, computer systems management, criminal justice, dental hygiene, early childhood teacher (N–3) certification, equine studies, exercise science, fashion design, fashion merchandising, funeral service, graphic design, health/fitness, hotel/restaurant management, human services, individualized studies, interior design, legal studies, liberal arts, management, marketing, psychology, science, sports management, travel/tourism, and veterinary technology.

Academic Program

Mount Ida's academic and social support systems help students navigate the college world and maximize potential. Prime examples are the Learning Opportunities Program (professional and comprehensive support for learning disabled students) and the Academic Success Center (tutoring and skills development). Each student has both an academic adviser and a personal adviser.

Off-Campus Arrangements

An option available to qualified students is a semester of study abroad at Regent's College in London, England. Students take a broad range of courses in art, literature, the social sciences, and business. Students may also participate in Regent's Internship Program, obtaining field experience in areas such as business and retailing, medicine and social work, advertising and public relations, law and politics, the performing arts, journalism, education, and environmental service. Placement in museums and living history projects is also possible.

Many programs include either a required or option internship that provides the opportunity to gain valuable practical experience. For example, the Veterinary Technology program includes several rotations at a variety of facilities, including the Tufts University School of Veterinary Medicine Teaching Hospital, Massachusetts Institute of Technology, Harvard Primate Center, New England Aquarium, and approximately seventy other sites.

Academic Facilities

The Learning Resource Center and the NCDE Library house more than 66,000 volumes, 560 periodicals, and a variety of media, including video disks and educational software programs. The Learning Resource Center is a member of the Minuteman Library Network, which also includes thirty-four public libraries, in a collaborative effort to provide excellence in information resources and services. Other on-campus facilities include a nursery school, a dental laboratory and clinic, computer laboratories, art studios, a communications laboratory, and facilities for the programs in veterinary technician studies and veterinary technology, including animal kennels, laboratories, and a surgical operating theater.

In 1995, the College purchased a farm in Dover, Massachusetts, only 4 miles from campus. The Mount Ida College Equestrian Center is a 4-acre facility that backs up to miles of trails abutting conservation land. The Equestrian Center consists of several barns, outdoor arenas, and turnout areas, as well as stalls for thirty-two horses and a 120-foot by 60-foot indoor arena with an observation area. The instructional activities at the facility include community riding lessons, children's equestrian summer camp, and the Collegiate Equestrian Team. Teaching emphasis is on hunters, jumpers, dressage, and combined training, and a number of horses at the facility compete effectively on various regional circuits. Transportation is provided for students traveling to the facility.

Costs

Tuition for the 2000–01 academic year is $13,300. Room and board charges are $8950, and books and supplies range between $500 and $750, depending on the program of study.

Financial Aid

Mount Ida supplements federal, state, and private funding with a substantial commitment of College funds. As a result, about 70 percent of Mount Ida's students received financial assistance during the academic year 1999–2000. Grants, scholarships, campus employment, and loans are utilized to enable students to afford the College's opportunities. Mount Ida does not have a financial aid application deadline.

Faculty

Mount Ida's faculty consists of approximately 200 members, 75 percent of whom hold a master's or higher degree in their field of concentration. Each student is assigned a faculty adviser in the major field of study. Freshmen and transfer students are also assigned Personal Advisors for Leadership (PAL) who meet with them throughout the year to discuss issues ranging from student life to career goals. There are full-time career services counselors, a health center counseling staff, and a residence counseling staff. Most classes at Mount Ida have fewer than 25 students; such small classes are conducive to the individual attention to students for which Mount Ida is renowned. The student-faculty ratio is 9:1.

Student Government

Through the Student Government Association, the student body is able to share with the administration and faculty the establishing and administering of rules essential for successful group living. The system of student government is based on the assumption that each student will take responsibility for group behavior on the College campus and in the community. The College supports a Student Leadership Program, which includes both an academic and cocurricular component.

Admission Requirements

A composite evaluation is made of each applicant. Official college and high school transcripts are required, as are recommendations, a personal statement, and SAT I or ACT scores. Transfer students must submit official transcripts of all completed college course-work. Transfer credit for fashion design, graphic design, and interior design studio courses may depend on a portfolio review.

Application and Information

Mount Ida has a rolling admissions policy. Although there is no deadline for the submission of applications, applicants are encouraged to apply as early as possible. Applications are considered as long as there is space in the desired program of study. Applicants are notified within three to four weeks after all credentials have been received.

All correspondence should be directed to:

Judith A. Kaufman, Dean of Admissions or
Nancy Lemelman, Director of Admissions
Mount Ida College
777 Dedham Street
Newton Centre, Massachusetts 02459
Telephone: 617-928-4553
Fax: 617-928-4507
E-mail: admissions@mountida.edu
World Wide Web: http://www.mountida.edu

Carlson Student Center.

MOUNT MARTY COLLEGE
YANKTON, WATERTOWN, AND SIOUX FALLS, SOUTH DAKOTA

The College

Named one of America's Best Christian Colleges by Institutional Research & Evaluation, Inc., of Gainesville, Georgia, Mount Marty College was founded in 1936 as a Benedictine, Catholic liberal arts college by the Sisters of Saint Benedict of Yankton, South Dakota. The College is named in memory of Martin Marty, a Benedictine missionary to the Indians who came to Dakota Territory in 1876 and became the territory's first Catholic bishop.

The College began as a junior college for women. After fifteen years, it offered its first Bachelor of Arts and Bachelor of Science degrees in 1951. In 1969, Mount Marty College became coeducational. Associate of Arts degrees were added in 1975, and the first Master of Science degree was awarded in 1985.

By 1998, Mount Marty College had grown to include campuses in Watertown and Sioux Falls, South Dakota. The Watertown campus offers a variety of degree programs that are in high demand in the area. The Sioux Falls campus is home to two graduate programs, nurse anesthesia and pastoral ministries. The total student population of the three campuses in fall 1999 was 1,015 students, with more than 600 at the Yankton campus.

The primary emphasis at Mount Marty College is the development of the total individual. This includes intellectual competence, professional and personal skills, and a composite of moral, spiritual, and social values. Service to humanity not only reflects the strong Benedictine values of the College, but also promotes a strong work ethic and personal development in each student.

Students are attracted to the outstanding programs and reputation of Mount Marty as well as its hospitable size. Regardless of their area of study, teaching faculty members (not graduate students) facilitate each and every class. This allows students the luxury of learning firsthand from seasoned professionals while developing the social skills and etiquette required for their field.

The Yankton campus includes housing for students, dining facilities, a bookstore, and recreation facilities. Entertainment on campus may include theater events, guest speakers, art exhibits, and much more. Other services available at the College include free tutoring, professional career counseling, health services, 24-hour computer access, and religious services at Bishop Marty Chapel. Part of the NAIA Great Plains Athletic Conference, Mount Marty College is also host to intercollegiate athletics, including men's and women's basketball, cross-country, and track and field; women's volleyball and softball; and men's soccer and baseball.

Mount Marty College is accredited by the Commission on Institutions of Higher Education of the North Central Association of Colleges and Schools (30 North LaSalle Street, Suite 2400, Chicago, Illinois 60602-2504; telephone: 312-263-0456). Other accrediting groups have endorsed specific programs at the College.

Location

Mount Marty College is located on the bluffs of the Missouri River in Yankton, South Dakota (population 15,000). A thriving community, Yankton offers a variety of work and cultural activities and is home to one of the best-developed river recreation areas in South Dakota. Yankton is located within 2 hours of Sioux Falls, South Dakota, and Omaha, Nebraska, and within an hour of Sioux City, Iowa. The main highways into Yankton include U.S. Highway 81 and South Dakota Highway 50 via Interstates 90 and 29.

Majors and Degrees

Mount Marty College offers a Bachelor of Arts in accounting, athletic training, biology, business administration, chemistry, computer science, criminal justice, elementary education, English, environmental science, history, math, music, nutrition and food science, psychology, recreation management, religious studies, secondary education, selected studies, and special education.

Bachelor of Science degrees are awarded in medical technology, nursing, radiologic technology, and selected studies.

Associate of Arts degrees are offered in accounting, business administration, criminal justice, religious studies, and selected studies.

Minors include accounting, art, biology, business administration, chemistry, computer science, criminal justice, English, environmental science, French, history, math, music, nutrition and food science, philosophy, physical education/recreation, political science, psychology, religious studies, sociology, Spanish, and speech and theater.

Preprofessional degrees are offered in a variety of health disciplines.

Academic Program

Mount Marty College operates throughout the calendar year with the usual nine-month academic year and summer sessions held May through August. The academic year includes a fall semester that commences in September and ends in December, a spring semester that commences in January and ends in May, and four summer sessions held in May, June, July, and August. The curriculum is scheduled in such a manner that a full-time student with an average work load may graduate with a bachelor's degree in four years.

Degree programs are enhanced with internships, extracurricular activities, outreach programs, clinical assignments, professional and industry visits, and first-hand experience.

The Master of Arts in Pastoral Ministries is conducted primarily through distance learning delivered via the Internet. Other programs at Mount Marty use bulletin boards and chat rooms to share information and provide feedback.

Academic Facilities

Mount Marty's 24-hour computer access, convenient library hours, and study areas offer students ample opportunity to further their studies. A tutoring program provides assistance through peers and instructors to keep students on track in the classroom. Well-equipped laboratories with professional-level instruments also assist students in developing career skills in line with the industry.

Costs

Mount Marty College offers a tuition freeze for full-time students. The tuition freeze guarantees that tuition will not be increased during the entire degree process as long as a student maintains full-time status and attends consecutive semesters. For 2000–01, a full-time student could expect their tuition of $9710 to remain constant for all four years of college. Required fees for 2000–01 are $924 per year, and room and board costs are $4272 (costs are subject to change). Other expenses may include books, transportation, and supplies.

Part-time tuition is $168 per credit for students taking 1 to 8 credits and $405 per credit for students taking 9 to 11 credits.

Financial Aid

Mount Marty College offers institutional and federal aid to more than 90 percent of its students. In fact, the College was named as one of America's Best 100 College Buys and as offering America's Best College Scholarships by Institutional Research & Evaluation, Inc. of Gainesville, Georgia. Mount Marty offers a vast array of scholarship and other aid opportunities to students. Awards ranging from several hundred dollars to full tuition are awarded as a result of interviews conducted during Scholarship Days. Other scholarships are awarded prior to and after Scholarship Days based on high academic achievement and athletic and musical talent.

Faculty

With campuses in Yankton, Watertown, and Sioux Falls, Mount Marty College employs 38 full-time and 96 part-time instructors. All courses are taught by faculty members. The faculty-student ratio is 1:11.

Student Government

The Student Government Association at Mount Marty is composed of executive officers, student senate, and committees. The purpose of this association is to promote student activities and to advance the welfare of all students. Student government activities include Family Weekend, Homecoming, dances, live entertainment, and intramural activities. All full-time students are voting members of the SGA.

Admission Requirements

Admission to Mount Marty College is open to students of all faiths, regardless of age, sex, race, national or ethnic origin, sexual orientation, veteran status, or physical ability. The admissions process is ongoing, and applicants are accepted based on academic record, experiences, and potential for growth. Applications for admission are available at the Mount Marty Web site listed below or by calling the Admissions Office. Students may visit the campus at any time by contacting the Admissions Office.

Application and Information

To be considered for enrollment, students must complete an application for admission and provide high school transcripts and official ACT or SAT I scores. A nonrefundable fee of $35 is required before students may register for classes. Transfer students should provide transcripts from their previous college as well as their high school transcripts.

For more information regarding admissions, students should contact:

Admissions Office
Dean for Enrollment Management
Mount Marty College
1105 West 8th Street
Yankton, South Dakota 57078
Telephone: 605-668-1545
        800-658-4552 (toll-free)
Fax: 605-668-1607
E-mail: admit@mtmc.edu
World Wide Web: http://www.mtmc.edu

Students enjoy warm weather in front of Bede Hall, the first campus structure at Mount Marty College.

MOUNT MARY COLLEGE
MILWAUKEE, WISCONSIN

The College

Mount Mary College, Wisconsin's oldest college for women, was founded at Prairie du Chien on the Mississippi River in 1913 and moved to Milwaukee in 1929. Mount Mary is sponsored by the School Sisters of Notre Dame, traditionally recognized as excellent educators. More than 1,300 students from a variety of backgrounds attend Mount Mary. They represent more than thirteen states and many countries, although the majority of the students are from the Midwest.

Academic organizations span a wide spectrum of interests. Special and professional interests are served by affiliates of national societies. Music and drama groups present concerts and plays, while clubs attract students with common interests. Physical fitness and an interest in athletics are fostered through various activities, fitness programs, health and dance courses, and intramural and intercollegiate athletics. Mount Mary offers varsity soccer, tennis, and volleyball. Facilities include a gymnasium, an indoor swimming pool, and a fitness center. The College is situated on a beautiful 80-acre wooded campus, and there is a parkway for biking and jogging and for cross-country skiing during the winter.

In addition to the undergraduate programs, Mount Mary College offers graduate programs leading to a Master of Science degree in dietetics or occupational therapy and a Master of Arts degree in art therapy, education, or gerontology.

Location

Mount Mary College is located in a residential area of Milwaukee, only 15 minutes from downtown Milwaukee and less than 5 minutes from a popular shopping mall. Students can use public transportation to get to any location in the Milwaukee area. The city has a major symphony, well-respected dance and theater companies, a beautiful lakefront art museum, and a fine natural history museum. Numerous professional and college sports teams are centered in Milwaukee.

Majors and Degrees

Majors leading to the Bachelor of Arts or Bachelor of Science degree are offered in accounting; art; art therapy; behavioral science (courses in anthropology, psychology, and sociology); behavioral science/psychology; biology; business; business administration; business administration/international commerce; chemistry; communication; consumer science; dietetics; education (early childhood/elementary, elementary/middle, and middle/secondary); English; English/professional writing; fashion (concentrations in apparel design, merchandising, and patternmaking); French; graphic design; history; interior design; marketing; mathematics; music; occupational therapy; philosophy; preprofessional programs (dentistry, law, medicine, and veterinary studies); public relations; social work; Spanish; and theology.

Academic Program

Mount Mary College's curriculum is based on the institution's primary focus on integrating leadership skills into each student's educational focus. Students divide their studies into three areas of concentration: core courses, which provide the student with a broad base of knowledge from the liberal arts; major courses, which prepare the student for specific career training; and electives. The core curriculum consists of studies in five areas of the liberal arts: Synoptics requires 12 credit hours of study in the areas of theology and philosophy, including an introductory course entitled Search for Meaning, which is required for all students; Symbolics requires 8 credit hours of study in communication arts, speech, foreign language, and/or mathematics; Esthetics requires 12 credit hours of study in literature and the fine arts, including art, music, dance, and drama; Humanistics requires 12 credit hours of study in history and behavioral or social science; and Empirics requires 4 credit hours of study in biology, chemistry, physics, or geography. These core courses provide an introduction to major areas of knowledge and a foundation for continuing academic development.

To qualify for graduation, all baccalaureate degree students must complete a minimum of 128 credits with a grade point average of 2.0 or better. These credits must consist of 48 core credits, a minimum of 24 credits in the major (the number varies among majors), and enough credits in elective courses to complete the requirements. Each department specifies its own sequence requirements for the major and the GPA needed for graduation. Students apply for admission to a major department at the end of their freshman year. A student transferring to Mount Mary at the sophomore level or above must apply for admission to the department of her choice as well as to the College.

Students may receive credit through the College Board's Advanced Placement Program or College-Level Examination Program (CLEP). Many adult students can also be evaluated for life experience credits.

The Office of Non-Traditional and Graduate Programs offers students an opportunity to earn degrees in accounting (business courses are accelerated), art therapy, communication, English/professional writing, and graphic design. The office also offers accelerated degree programs in business administration, business administration/international commerce, and business/professional communication.

Off-Campus Arrangements

Mount Mary offers a number of off-campus study opportunities for which credit is awarded. The coordinated undergraduate program in dietetics offers students clinical experience through the College's affiliation with thirty local hospitals and healthcare facilities. The occupational therapy department provides internships through its nationwide ties with accredited hospitals. Student teaching is done under a cooperative program with Milwaukee-area public and private school systems. The behavioral science program and the social work program require students to have field experience in Milwaukee-area public and private social agencies. Internships are available in most other majors as well.

Study abroad may be arranged on an individual basis.

Academic Facilities

The Patrick and Beatrice Haggerty Library is dedicated to the information gathering, research, curricular support, and lifelong learning needs of the College community. The library's core collection includes more than 110,000 volumes and 800 current periodical titles along with significant collections of audiovisual and government document materials. As a member of the SWITCH library consortium, the Haggerty Library is electronically connected to extensive supplementary collections that are available to students at the push of a button. Spacious study space, private group study rooms, and copying and audiovisual equipment as well as a public computing cluster are available for students' use with the assistance of a trained, caring staff. A Web-based, online catalog and interactive library Web site provide services both on campus and off.

Costs

For the 1999–2000 academic year, tuition and fees were $12,270. Room and board averaged $4250 in 1999–2000. Books and supplies cost approximately $750 per year. Additional costs for personal expenses averaged $1200 per year.

Financial Aid

The College's Financial Aid Office develops a package of financial aid, on an individual basis, for every qualified student in need. More than 85 percent of Mount Mary's students receive some form of financial assistance. Students applying for aid must file the Free Application for Federal Student Aid. Numerous merit-based scholarships and grants are available for incoming freshmen as well as transfer students. For more information about these scholarships and grants, students should contact the Office of Admissions.

Faculty

All teaching is done by faculty members holding advanced degrees. No classes are taught by teaching assistants. With a student-teacher ratio of 14:1, each faculty member is able to participate in academic advising.

Student Government

Students are encouraged to participate in the governance of the College. Every Mount Mary College student is a member of the Student Government, which makes recommendations about College policies and other matters of importance to students and serves as a liaison to the Mount Mary College administration, faculty, and staff.

Student representatives have voting power on the following committees: the Academic and Student Affairs Committee of the Board of Trustees, the Curriculum Committee, the Strategic Planning Committee, the Enrollment and Marketing Committee, the Student Life Committee, the Diversity Committee, the Facilities Planning Committee, the Academic Calendar Committee, the Commencement Committee, and the Honors Program Committee. Students participate in many ad hoc committees and task forces, as well.

Admission Requirements

Candidates for admission are considered on the basis of academic preparation, scholarship, and evidence of the ability to do college work and benefit from it. Sixteen secondary school units are required; of these, 11 must be academic (3 in English; 2 in college-preparatory mathematics; 2 in science; and 4 in history, a foreign language, or social science) and 4 in electives. Students must also have a minimum grade point average of 2.3, rank in the upper half of their high school graduating class, and submit test scores on either the ACT or the SAT I. International students must take the Test of English as a Foreign Language (TOEFL).

Mount Mary does not discriminate against any individual because of race, color, age, national or ethnic origin, or handicap.

Application and Information

Early acceptance is available, and advanced placement is honored. Mount Mary College has a policy of rolling admission. An admission decision is sent as soon as all required materials have been received and reviewed. After notification of acceptance, students are required to forward a $100 tuition deposit.

For further information, students should contact:

Director of Enrollment
Mount Mary College
2900 North Menomonee River Parkway
Milwaukee, Wisconsin 53222-4597
Telephone: 414-256-1219
         800-321-6265 (toll-free long distance)
E-mail: admiss@mtmary.edu
World Wide Web: http://www.mtmary.edu

Mount Mary College is located on 80 spacious acres in a convenient Milwaukee neighborhood. Students will find a safe, secure environment in which to live and learn.

MOUNT MERCY COLLEGE
CEDAR RAPIDS, IOWA

The College

Mount Mercy College is distinguished by a unique blend of career preparation and liberal arts, as well as a strong emphasis on leadership and service. A Catholic, independent, coeducational four-year college, Mount Mercy is fully accredited by the North Central Association of Colleges and Schools.

Although the College offers a number of professional programs, its career preparation is not limited to those areas. Students majoring in English or history, for example, are just as likely to benefit from internships as are students in business or social work. There is a focus on workplace skills such as group process and presentations—competencies that help graduates begin their careers. However, Mount Mercy believes even more strongly in a firm liberal arts foundation of analysis, critical thinking, and communication—skills that help graduates adapt to a changing world and find long-term career success.

Through its Emerging Leaders and Campus Ministry programs, the College supports the concept of servant leadership. This tradition of service is a legacy of the Sisters of Mercy, who founded the College in 1928. The College welcomes students of all faiths.

Mount Mercy's high academic quality and its relatively moderate cost make it one of the best values in Iowa higher education. *U.S. News & World Report* ranks Mount Mercy in the top tier of Midwest regional liberal arts colleges. The College offers more than thirty major fields of study, including several interdisciplinary majors. In the College's Partnership program, professors are paired with freshman students to support their transition to college and to enhance the intellectual growth needed to assure academic success.

Student activities include more than thirty clubs and organizations, a student newspaper, a choir and pep band, and a pom squad and cheerleaders, along with such annual events as Hillfest and Spring Fling. Each May, commencement exercises are followed by a celebration for graduates and their families on Mount Mercy's hilltop. During the school year, many student activities—including Club Friday, a Friday afternoon gathering of students, faculty, and staff—take place in the Lundy Commons, which houses a game room, TV rooms, snack bar, conference rooms, student organization offices, the *Mount Mercy Times* office, lounge areas, and a bookstore.

Mount Mercy College is a member of the National Association of Intercollegiate Athletics (NAIA) and the Midwest Classic Conference. The College offers intercollegiate competition in men's basketball, baseball, cross-country, golf, soccer, and track and field. In women's sports, the College offers basketball, cross-country, golf, soccer, softball, track and field, and volleyball. These programs have combined for more than twenty conference championships and has sent teams and individuals to regional and national championship events. In addition, Mount Mercy student-athletes are annually recognized as NAIA academic all-Americans. Intramural activities include basketball, cross-country, flag football, golf, softball, and volleyball.

About 470 of Mount Mercy's 1,300 students live in campus housing. The residence halls offer a variety of living arrangements. The College's newest residence, which opened in fall 1999, houses 144 students in eight home-like, four-bedroom suites. A network of tunnels connects campus buildings; many students wear shorts all winter.

Location

Mount Mercy is just minutes from downtown Cedar Rapids' museums, malls, movie theaters, and restaurants and businesses offering internship and employment opportunities. The 40-acre, tree-lined campus is tucked into a residential neighborhood of well-kept homes, neat lawns, and good neighbors. Mount Mercy's hilltop, with its sweeping view of the city skyline, is said to be the highest point in Linn County. The city bus stops at the College's "front door," providing convenient in-town transportation. Cedar Rapids is served by six major airlines and is just a 4- or 5-hour drive from Chicago, Minneapolis–St. Paul, Omaha, and St. Louis. Mount Mercy's location in a thriving Midwestern city helps students explore career possibilities and, when they graduate, find promising opportunities. Both economically and culturally, Cedar Rapids offers an outstanding quality of life.

Majors and Degrees

Mount Mercy awards the Bachelor of Arts, Bachelor of Science, Bachelor of Business Administration, Bachelor of Applied Science, and Bachelor of Applied Arts degrees.

The Bachelor of Arts degree is awarded to graduates who major in art, biology, criminal justice studies, English, history, interdisciplinary majors (applied philosophy, international studies, and urban and community studies), mathematics, music, political science, psychology, public relations, religious studies, social work, sociology, and speech/drama.

The Bachelor of Science degree is awarded to graduates who major in biology, computer information systems, computer science, elementary education, mathematics, medical technology, and nursing. (Majors in biology and mathematics may elect either the Bachelor of Science or Bachelor of Arts degree.)

The Bachelor of Business Administration is awarded to graduates who major in accounting, management, marketing, and the prestructured business administration majors (criminal justice administration, English administration, health services administration, political science administration, psychology administration, sociology administration, and visual arts administration).

The following majors offer endorsements for secondary education: American history, art, biology, business, English, mathematics, multicategorical resource room, music, social science, speech/drama, and world history.

The Bachelor of Applied Science and Bachelor of Applied Arts degree programs are designed for technically trained students who wish to broaden their specialized background to include a liberal arts education. Degrees are awarded to graduates who major in accounting, art, biology, computer information systems, computer science, criminal justice studies, history, management, marketing, mathematics, music, political science, psychology, religious studies, sociology, and speech/drama.

Academic Program

Mount Mercy College requires 123 semester hours for graduation, with a cumulative grade point average of at least 2.0 (on a 4.0 scale). General education requirements include two courses in English, two in social sciences, and one each in fine arts, history, mathematics, multicultural studies, natural science, philosophy, religious studies, and speech. Students apply for admission to their major program in the spring of the sophomore year. The College gives credit for related experience based on portfolio presentations and for independent study arranged by the student and the instructor. Graduation requirements may vary according to the major field of study.

Special academic opportunities are offered to outstanding students through special honors sections of general education courses. Students graduating in the honors program receive special recognition at commencement.

Mount Mercy's academic year consists of fall and spring semesters, plus a winter term. This four-week term offers required courses as well as exploratory electives, allowing students to make more rapid progress toward their degrees. Two five-week summer sessions are also held.

Off-Campus Arrangements

Mount Mercy College has an exchange program with the University of Palacky in the Czech Republic. This program allows students to study abroad without any additional expense for tuition, room, and board.

Academic Facilities

The Busse Library provides an inviting study and research environment. Internet access opens other major libraries to students as well. Library services include computerized literature searches, bibliographic instruction, interlibrary loans, and other types of individual assistance in searching for information. The library houses the computer center; a computer classroom used for instruction in writing, accounting, and computer skills; a media center; individual study carrels; group study rooms; and a variety of other comfortable study areas.

All on-campus student rooms and faculty/staff offices are connected to a campus network. The College also has an ICN (Iowa Communications Network) fiber-optics classroom, making it possible for students in more than one location to take the same course, interacting with other students and with the instructor.

Costs

Full-time tuition for the 2000–01 academic year is $13,850, about at the midpoint among Iowa private colleges. Major fees are included in this figure. Room costs are $1870 in residence halls and $2395 in apartments. Two meal plans are offered: the nineteen-meal-per-week plan at $2730 and the fifteen-meal plan at $2550. Estimated annual costs for a resident student, including books, supplies, and personal expenses, are $21,714.

Financial Aid

Ninety-eight percent of Mount Mercy freshmen who apply receive some form of financial aid, including Mount Mercy scholarships or grants, federal or state grants, loans, on-campus employment, or a combination of these sources. The College awarded more than 100 Presidential Scholarships of up to $7500 for the 1999–2000 school year to high school seniors who had an ACT score of at least 26 and a high school grade point average of at least 3.5. Other awards are also made on the basis of ACT score and GPA. Each year, students who have been admitted to Mount Mercy and identified as Presidential Scholars are invited to campus to compete for the Holland Presidential Scholarship, a full-tuition award named for the first president of Mount Mercy. Three Holland Scholarships were awarded for the 1999–2000 school year. Students may also apply for Mount Mercy Trustees' Leadership Grants, awarded to entering freshmen and transfer students on the basis of their demonstrated leadership in school and community activities. In addition, scholarships are available to students with records of achievement in art, drama, and music and to those who are planning to major in social work. In 1999–2000, the College awarded more than $2.5 million in institutional scholarships and grants to qualified students.

Students who show financial need may be eligible for the Federal Pell Grant, the Iowa Tuition Grant, Federal Stafford Student Loan, and on-campus employment. Students in work-study positions typically earn from $1000 to $1500 a year.

To apply for Mount Mercy scholarships and grants, students must first be admitted to the College. Early application is advised. The priority deadline for filing the FAFSA (Free Application for Federal Student Aid) is March 1. Students should check other deadlines with their high school counselors or call the Mount Mercy financial aid office.

Faculty

Mount Mercy has 65 full-time faculty members, most of whom hold the terminal degree in their fields. Many have been recognized for their achievements: 2 have been Fulbright Fellows, several have received grants from the National Endowment for the Humanities and the National Endowment for the Arts, and many others have been recognized by their professional organizations. With an average class size of 12.5, Mount Mercy offers students the opportunity to know their teachers well and to learn from them in an informal, friendly, and supportive environment.

Student Government

The official voice of the student at Mount Mercy is the Student Government Association (SGA). Its officers serve on College committees, and SGA is represented at regular faculty meetings. An SGA petition to the faculty resulted in adding a fall break to the academic calendar. SGA is the body through which all other campus organizations are formed and funded.

Admission Requirements

Mount Mercy admits students whose academic preparation, abilities, interests, and personal qualities give promise of success in college. Applicants are considered on the basis of academic record, class rank, test scores, and recommendations. The applications of students with minimum qualifications are reviewed by an Admission Committee. To apply, students must submit an application for admission, a transcript of high school credits, scores from ACT or SAT examinations, and a $20 application fee. Transfer students must submit official transcripts from all colleges attended. Mount Mercy College has an agreement with several two-year colleges in Iowa through which degree graduates of these colleges may be admitted to Mount Mercy with junior standing.

Prospective students are encouraged to visit the campus and meet with a faculty member in their area of interest. Special campus visit days are scheduled each year, and individual appointments also may be made. Overnight accommodations in residence halls can be arranged.

Application and Information

Students who wish to be considered for Mount Mercy scholarships and grants should submit their applications for admission as early as possible after their junior year in high school. Admission decisions are made on a rolling basis, and the College notifies students of its decision within ten days of receiving the necessary forms.

Application forms and additional information may be obtained by contacting:

Office of Admission
Mount Mercy College
1330 Elmhurst Drive, NE
Cedar Rapids, Iowa 52402

Telephone: 319-368-6460
           319-363-5270
           800-248-4504 (toll-free)
E-mail: admission@mmc.mtmercy.edu
World Wide Web: http://www.mtmercy.edu

Students on the campus of Mount Mercy College.

MOUNT OLIVE COLLEGE
MOUNT OLIVE, NORTH CAROLINA

The College

Chartered in 1951, Mount Olive College is a private, four-year liberal arts-based institution dedicated to the total development of its students in an environment nurtured by Christian values. The College is affiliated with the Convention of Original Free Will Baptists.

Mount Olive College exists primarily for its students. Small classes, personal attention, and flexibility encourage the development of individual interests, talents, and abilities. Dedicated faculty members and staff help students grow personally, socially, spiritually, and intellectually into whole human beings through caring, mentor relationships.

Mount Olive College is committed to providing its students academic quality, a student focus, career preparation, a global perspective, affordable programs, Christian values, and a wholesome, safe environment.

More than 1,600 students are enrolled in academic programs at Mount Olive's five locations. This includes approximately 530 traditional students on the Mount Olive campus, of whom about 270 reside on campus and 260 commute. Another 150 nontraditional students attend degree-completion programs during evenings and on Saturdays; another 950 students are enrolled in traditional and nontraditional courses and programs at Mount Olive's academic centers in Goldsboro (at Seymour Johnson Air Force Base), New Bern, Wilmington, and Research Triangle Park, North Carolina.

In addition to academic programs, many students participate in a variety of extracurricular activities, providing additional academic, art, music, religious, social, and athletic opportunities for personal enrichment. Mount Olive College is a member of the Carolinas-Virginia Athletics Conference competing in NCAA Division II play with colleges comparable in demographics and philosophy. Men's intercollegiate sports include baseball, basketball, cross-country, golf, soccer, and tennis. Women compete in basketball, cross-country, soccer, softball, tennis, and volleyball.

The Lois K. Murphy Regional Center serves as the student center, with facilities for meetings, seminars, food service, recreation, special events, offices, and student services. In addition to the academic facilities listed below, the College has six residence halls for students, an administration building containing business offices and a bookstore, and two smaller office buildings for staff and faculty members. The College also owns two off-site facilities: a 100-acre camp in a rustic setting, used for retreats, picnics, outdoor education, and recreation, and a house in Morehead City used for seminars, retreats, conferences, and meetings.

Students, faculty members, and staff care for one another in a way that is not possible at larger institutions. Ultimately, Mount Olive College strives to enrich students with a philosophy and experience of higher learning, higher standards, and higher values.

Location

The campus at Mount Olive College is located in southern Wayne county on 123 beautiful acres in the town of Mount Olive, North Carolina. The College is geographically in the center of the Carolinas' coastal plains, approximately 60 miles southeast of Raleigh, the capital of North Carolina, and approximately 75 miles west of many of North Carolina's beautiful beaches. It is accessible from Interstates 95 and 40 and precisely located where U.S. 117 and Route 55 intersect. The College is also located in North Carolina's Global TransPark Zone, a consortium of government agencies and private industry designed to develop a thirteen-county region of eastern North Carolina into a center for international commerce. Mount Olive College also has programs in Goldsboro at Seymour Johnson Air Force Base, New Bern, and Wilmington—all strategically located to provide opportunities in higher education for traditional and nontraditional students in eastern North Carolina.

Majors and Degrees

Mount Olive College is accredited by the Commission on Colleges of the Southern Association of Colleges and Schools (1866 Southern Lane, Decatur, Georgia 30033-4097; telephone: 404-679-4501) to award the following degrees: Bachelor of Arts, Bachelor of Science, Bachelor of Applied Science, Associate in Arts, and Associate in Science.

The Bachelor of Arts degree is offered in art, biology, English, English communication, English with secondary school certification, fine arts, general studies, history, music, psychology, recreation and leisure studies, religion, and visual communication.

The Bachelor of Science degree is offered in art; biology; business administration with tracks in accounting, business management, computer information systems, industrial management, health science management, and management and organizational development; church ministries; criminal justice; fine arts; general studies; history; human resource development; human services counseling; middle grades education; music; psychology; recreation and leisure studies; religion; and visual communication.

Academic Program

The Mount Olive College curriculum comprises courses from the General Education Program, the student's major, and electives. The General Education Program is the core of the liberal arts program and consists of 44 semester hours in humanities, science and mathematics, and social sciences. A Freshman Seminar, teaching study habits and social skills to help new freshmen adjust to college life, is required and carries one semester hour of elective credit. Completion of a minimum of 126 semester hours, including general education requirements (GER) and degree program requirements as specified in the current catalog, are required for graduation and award of a bachelor's degree.

Off-Campus Arrangements

Mount Olive College's reach and support for students extends beyond the Mount Olive campus to four other campuses in eastern North Carolina. These academic learning centers are located at Seymour Johnson Air Force Base in Goldsboro and in New Bern, Research Triangle Park, and Wilmington, and offer courses and programs for traditional and nontraditional students. Policy and support for all of the College programs emanate from the Mount Olive campus.

Academic Facilities

The heart of Mount Olive College's academic facilities is Moye Library. Using the Library of Congress classification system, the library has more than 64,000 volumes and 29,000 other documents in microtext and receives approximately 3,000 periodicals in various formats. Since 1972, the library has been a selective U.S. government depository, with a collection of 50,000 items. Moye Library also houses the Free Will Baptist Historical Collection and provides interlibrary loan services and access to databases through its online Internet connection. The catalog is on line as well.

Other academic facilities include Henderson Building, the main academic building, housing classrooms and biology, chemistry, physics, and computer laboratories, offices, and a student lounge; Laughinghouse Hall, housing art and photography studios, a music suite, and offices; College Hall, housing classrooms, a gymnasium, racquetball courts, a weight room, locker rooms, trainer facilities, and offices; and Rodgers Chapel, appropriately located in the center of campus for religious services, lectures, and recitals. The College leases office and classroom facilities in New Bern, Research Triangle Park, and Wilmington and utilizes the education center at Seymour Johnson Air Force Base for programs at these locations.

Costs

Annual tuition and fees, including room and board, for the 2000–01 year are $9205 for resident students and $9195 for commuters. Room and board in a dormitory for a year are $4000. While the cost of books and incidentals varies among students, it is estimated at $1500.

Financial Aid

A wide range of financial aid package options are offered by Mount Olive College to provide every eligible and capable student the opportunity to attain a college education. Based on need, financial aid includes scholarships, grants, loans, and work-study opportunities.

Institutional scholarships are available to qualified students for excellence in academics, leadership, music, ministry, visual communication, fine arts, and athletics. Federal programs include Pell Grants, Supplemental Educational Opportunity Grants, Work-Study, Perkins Loans, Stafford Student Loans (subsidized and unsubsidized), PLUS loans, and Veterans Administration loans and grants. For North Carolina residents, the state makes funding available through Legislative Tuition Grants, Contractual Scholarship Funds, Student Incentive Grants, National Guard Tuition Assistance, Vocational Rehabilitation Grants, Services for the Blind, and Prospective Teacher Student Loans. The Convention of Original Free Will Baptists offers annual grants to Free Will Baptist students. All students in need of financial assistance should submit a Free Application for Federal Student Aid between January 1 and March 15 for the coming academic year.

Faculty

Mount Olive College's faculty members are committed to teaching at the undergraduate level. The full-time faculty numbers 40 and is augmented by 55 part-time instructors. Of the full-time faculty members, 60 percent hold doctoral degrees and 40 percent hold master's degrees. The student-faculty ratio is 14:1. Classes are small, averaging 18 students per class. A number of classes have fewer than 10 students. Most faculty members serve as student advisers and are accessible to students during posted office hours and at College events. Mount Olive's intimate campus setting encourages the development of wholesome relationships between students and instructors. Many faculty members live nearby and open their homes to students.

Student Government

The Student Government Association (SGA) at Mount Olive College exists to provide students with a forum to develop and promote student activities, enhance social life on campus, participate in the development and evaluation of educational programs, and interact with the College's administration concerning policies and issues. Students elect class officers. SGA is active and meets weekly, allowing students the opportunity to participate and have their individual and collective voice heard. SGA operates under the auspices of the dean of student development and has access to the academic dean and the president.

Admission Requirements

Mount Olive College seeks to admit students whose academic potential and personal abilities are compatible with the distinctive mission of the College. In making admission decisions, a student's overall high school record, achievement on the SAT I or ACT, and demonstrated desire to earn a degree are considered. A candidate must have earned a high school diploma or acceptable scores on the General Educational Development test. Transfer students are considered based on their overall performance at other colleges, seriousness of purpose, and recommendations. Students who have earned fewer than 24 semester hours must meet both freshman and transfer requirements. An interview may be required by the Admissions Office or requested by the candidate. All prospective students are invited and encouraged to visit the campus.

Application and Information

Application to Mount Olive College involves submitting a completed application with a recent photo and a nonrefundable $20 application fee; having an official high school transcript forwarded to the Admissions Office; and having SAT I or ACT scores sent to the Admissions Office. Transfer students must have official transcripts of all college work sent to the Admissions Office. An interview may be requested by the Admissions Office. The Admissions Office is open Monday through Thursday, from 8 a.m. to 6 p.m.; Friday, from 8 a.m. to 5 p.m.; and at other times by appointment. For additional information, an application, a catalog, an interview, or a campus tour, students should contact:

Director of Admissions
Mount Olive College
634 Henderson Street
Mount Olive, North Carolina 28365
Telephone: 919-658-2502 or 7164
          800-653-0854 (toll-free)
Fax: 919-658-7180

Students walk across the green in front of Moye Library at Mount Olive College.

MOUNT ST. CLARE COLLEGE
CLINTON, IOWA

The College

Mount St. Clare College is a four-year, Franciscan, coeducational liberal arts college that takes deep pride in its heritage and commitment to the Franciscan philosophical cornerstones of concern, compassion, respect, and service. The College was founded by the Sisters of St. Francis of Clinton, Iowa, in 1918 and is accredited by the North Central Association of Colleges and Schools. Ever faithful to its Franciscan traditions, this small college provides an educational environment that builds competence, character, and values within a high-quality liberal arts framework.

Enrollment in fall 1999 was 675 students, representing a 118 percent growth over the last eight years. This growth has earned the College the distinction of being one of the fastest-growing liberal arts colleges in Iowa. Mount St. Clare enjoys a diverse student body, with students from thirteen states and ten countries. Nearly 10 percent are minority students, and 4 percent are international. Approximately 74 percent are full-time, about one third live on campus, and 57 percent are women.

Students choose Mount St. Clare College for a number of reasons. Foremost among them is the personalized attention they receive from faculty, staff, and administration. With a low student-faculty ratio of 12:1, students are certain to interact more closely with professors and other students. At Mount St. Clare College, students are known by their names and are individually supported and encouraged.

An attractive feature of the College is the wide array of activities, athletics, events, and clubs available to students. The College fields teams in sixteen sports, including men's baseball, basketball, cross-country, golf, soccer, tennis, track, and wrestling and women's basketball, cheerleading, cross-country, soccer, softball, tennis, track, and volleyball. Mount St. Clare has a great concert choir, an active theater group, and a budding wind ensemble. The choir and the theater group present a fall play, a spring musical, and an annual madrigal Christmas dinner. Other organizations include honor societies, Student Senate, Black Student Union, Christian Fellowship Club, Circle K, Hispanic American Leadership Organization, International Club, Residence Hall Council, Student Ambassadors, cheerleaders, Student Iowa State Education Association, the *Clarion* (student newspaper), the yearbook, and the Varsity Club. Phi Beta Lambda, a business student association, has won many honors in state, regional, and national competitions. Some of these organizations reach out to the community through service projects. There are two new student groups: Prism, which promotes tolerance of all people, and the Green Thumb Organization, which advocates concern for the environment.

Many special events are scheduled during the year, including lectures, entertainment, pep rallies, dances, Saturday movies, and trips to nearby cities and attractions.

The College has a compact, safe, and secure campus. Five of the six buildings on campus, built in a corner section of a 100-acre area on a bluff, are interconnected, and the residence hall is a short walk away. In the residence hall, students find an appealing suite arrangement—two bedrooms with one bathroom. Regis Hall adjoins the administration building and is the site of another residence hall for students and the Mount St. Clare College Speech and Hearing Center. In the heart of the campus is the Durgin Educational Center, a multipurpose educational center for recreational, athletic, social, and academic use.

Location

Mount St. Clare College is located on a wooded bluff near the Mississippi River in Clinton, Iowa (population 28,000). Clinton was rated first in public safety in the 1997 rating guide, *Life in America's Small Cities*, published by Prometheus Books, Amherst, New York. Situated midway between Chicago and Des Moines, the city of Clinton is home to a minor league baseball team, a symphony orchestra, a preprofessional ballet company, summer stock theater, art shows, and other cultural events. Clinton is 45 minutes from the Quad Cities, 3 hours from Chicago, and 5 hours from Minneapolis. The quality of life in the city and on campus is typical of the wholesome lifestyle the Midwest is known for throughout the country.

Majors and Degrees

Mount St. Clare College awards Bachelor of Arts degrees in accounting, business administration, clinical cytotechnology, computer information systems, elementary education, English, health-care management, liberal arts, music education, preprofessional fields, secondary education, and social science; a Bachelor of Science in biology; a Bachelor of Applied Science; a Bachelor of General Studies; and an Associate of Arts degree.

The liberal arts program offers ten concentrations: environmental studies, fine arts, human behavior, humanities, journalism, literature, music, science, social science, and visual arts. The optional concentrations in business administration are communication, environmental studies, finance, health-care management, human resource management, and marketing. The social science program also has optional concentrations in human services and psychology, and the health-care management program, an optional concentration in long-term care. The accounting program has a professional/CPA track, a regular accounting track, and a choice of two optional concentrations in communication and environmental studies. Students in most majors can pursue a minor in accounting, athletic administration, business administration, computer information systems, journalism, liberal arts, marketing communications, music, psychology, and visual arts. A coaching authorization is also offered.

Academic Program

The basic philosophy of Mount St. Clare College is to develop caring and informed citizens who think critically, communicate well, and adapt creatively to change. The College imbues its teachings with the timeless messages of St. Francis and St. Clare, whose philosophies centered around living in peace with humankind and nature, service to others, and the core Christian values of love, respect, and compassion to all.

The curriculum in the first two years contains a set of courses to build competencies in writing, math, and computer skills and a general education core in six areas of study. These areas are values, speech and literature, general reasoning, social awareness, natural world, and aesthetic awareness.

Toward the end of the sophomore year, students choose their majors. To ensure that students choose the right courses, they are assigned a faculty adviser in their field of interest as early as their freshman year.

Several programs are available to enhance the academic curriculum. Academically gifted students may choose to participate in the Bonaventure Scholars program by earning extra credits in selected classes. Under a study-abroad program, students have the opportunity to study for one semester or a year at the Loyola University–Chicago's Rome Center of Liberal Arts in Rome, Italy. The Assisi-Perugia study-abroad program brings students to Italy for three to five weeks in the summer. A short summer course in environmental science takes students to a wildlife sanctuary in Minnesota.

Internships are available for students interested in gaining practical experience before they graduate. Many companies in the area welcome Mount St. Clare College students as interns during the year or in the summer.

The Bridges Program gives underprepared students the chance to achieve their potential for success in college.

Academic Facilities

The computer lab provides students with PC-compatible computers, laser printers, and multiple software applications. The library houses more than 78,000 volumes, more than 1,200 periodicals, and more than 3,000 nonprint materials and offers online access to virtually every college and university library in Iowa. In addition, students can access books from more than twenty-seven area libraries through QUAD LINC. Students have access to the Internet at the library and computer lab. The library has a Curriculum Resource Lab with Macintosh computers and curriculum materials for elementary education majors. A Macintosh lab is used for publications and visual arts courses and an advanced computer lab is available to teach networking hardware assembly for advanced computer projects.

The Career Service Office offers individualized career counseling, personality and vocational interest assessment, assistance with job placement, preparatory workshops for job interviews, and arrangements to attend job fairs.

The Durgin Educational Center is a multipurpose educational center for recreational, athletic, social, and academic use. The center also provides space for conferences, large gatherings, and special community programs. Its features include conference rooms with fiber-optic technology, an arena with two regulation-size basketball courts that have retractable seats with backs and armrests, a state-of-the-art fitness center, a four-lane perimeter track on the second level that overlooks the arena, and locker rooms, team rooms, a training room, and offices.

Costs

For 1999–2000, tuition was $12,580 per year. Room (semiprivate) was $1990 a year. Board, with the standard nineteen-meal plan, was $2360. There was an activity fee of $130 per year. Part-time tuition was $367 per credit hour. The College guarantees that students who start as freshmen, stay with one major, and make reasonable academic progress will graduate in four years or the fifth year is free.

Financial Aid

Mount St. Clare College believes in making a college education affordable for any qualified student. To this end, Mount St. Clare has developed an aggressive financial aid program designed to offer each student a financial aid package that best meets the student's needs. The Director of Financial Aid meets personally with each student every year to review his or her needs and discuss the financial aid package.

Mount St. Clare College utilizes institutional, federal, and state resources in its financial aid program. In February, the College holds an annual academic scholarship competition in twenty-two areas. Awards at the competition range from $1500 to full tuition. Other scholarships and grants are also available for both full-time and part-time and traditional and nontraditional students. These awards are renewable every year subject to the students' academic performance. Funds for athletic grants and work-study employment are also available.

Faculty

Mount St. Clare College faculty members honor teaching as their first priority. Faculty members take personal interest in their students. As advisers, they have opportunities to know the students better and keep track of their progress throughout the students' stay at the College. Mount St. Clare faculty members enrich their teaching by the practical experience they bring to the classroom. The College has 61 full-time and part-time faculty members. More than 55 percent of full-time faculty members hold doctorates or the highest degree in their field. The student-faculty ratio is 12:1.

Student Government

The Mount St. Clare College Student Association provides a means of expression for the student body and an opportunity to participate and share the responsibility for student life. All students automatically become members of the Student Association with the payment of their activity fee. The Student Senate is the representative body of the Student Association and directs student elections, social and cultural activities, and special events. The Student Senate is made up of 4 officers, 2 representatives from each class, and 1 representative each from nontraditional students, commuters, the Hispanic American Leadership Organization, and the Black Student Union. The officers and members are elected each spring. Meetings are held weekly and are open to all students.

Admission Requirements

Admission to Mount St. Clare College is open to persons of any age, sex, race, religious preference, national or ethnic origin, sexual orientation, veteran status, and physical ability. Admissions decisions are based on a comprehensive review of the applicant's academic record, work and/or community-related experiences, and evidence of potential for personal and academic growth at the College. Mount St. Clare encourages all applicants to visit the campus and to have a personal interview with an admissions counselor.

Application and Information

To apply as freshmen, students must submit a completed application form, high school transcripts, official ACT or SAT I scores, and a nonrefundable fee of $20. Transfer students must submit a completed application form and transcripts from each college or university attended. If a transfer student has fewer than 30 credits, the high school transcript is also required. Admissions decisions are made on a rolling basis. Notification of admission is made within ten days after receipt of all necessary forms, transcripts, and test scores. International students must submit TOEFL scores. For an application form or additional information, students should contact:

Waunita Sullivan
Director of Enrollment
Mount St. Clare College
400 North Bluff Boulevard
Clinton, Iowa 52732
Telephone: 319-242-4023
           800-242-4153 (toll-free)
Fax: 319-243-6102
E-mail: admissns@clare.edu
World Wide Web: http://www.clare.edu

Students on the Mount St. Clare College campus.

MOUNT SAINT MARY COLLEGE
NEWBURGH, NEW YORK

The College
Mount Saint Mary College is a private, four-year liberal arts college for men and women founded in 1960 by the Dominican Sisters of Newburgh.

The College has set the goal of preparing its students, within the environment of a small, independent, undergraduate college, to assume, by choice and preparation, their roles in an ever-changing cultural, intellectual, psychological, and social climate. According to the plan of its founders and the aims of the total college community, Mount Saint Mary College strives to produce alumni marked by intellectual acuity and professional competence who possess constructive attitudes toward the challenges of living in the world of their times. With its favorable student-faculty ratio of 16:1, the Mount provides an atmosphere that is warm and personal, and it also gives students an educational experience that will prove valuable throughout their lifetime. Mount Saint Mary College is a young, vibrant, growing school where group commitment is made to the individual student.

The current enrollment is about 2,000 men and women. Students at Mount Saint Mary College come to the campus with various backgrounds and educational objectives. They are able to express individual desires and find an avenue for special talents not only in the academic environment but also through participation in extracurricular activities. A wide variety of choices make it possible for all students to find activities that fit their own interests. Intercollegiate athletics programs include baseball, basketball, soccer, softball, swimming, tennis, and volleyball. The 47,000-square-foot Recreational Facility features two NCAA basketball/volleyball courts, a cardiovascular fitness center, a weight room, an aerobics/dance studio, a swimming pool, a raised running track, training rooms, study lounges, a TV lounge, a snack bar, a game room, and four classrooms. Social programs, such as dances and other intercollegiate events, are held frequently in conjunction with neighboring colleges and the Military Academy at West Point. Students and their guests attend such social activities as Oktoberfest and Siblings' Weekend. Traditional College events include Parents' Weekend, Freshman Investiture, and One Hundredth Night.

The Mount provides twenty-eight garden-apartment or townhouse-style residence halls, which include separate facilities for men and women as well as for freshmen and upperclass students. The halls are equipped with full kitchen facilities, lounges, and laundry facilities.

In addition to its undergraduate curricula, the Mount offers graduate programs leading to the Master of Science degree in elementary education, elementary/special education, secondary education, and special education; the Master of Business Administration; and the Master of Science in Nursing.

Location
Mount Saint Mary College is located in a residential section of Newburgh, New York, about 60 miles north of New York City and 15 minutes north of the United States Military Academy at West Point. The accessibility of New York City makes it possible for students to take advantage of a variety of cultural and social activities as well as the many attractions of the Mid-Hudson Valley. Recreational areas nearby provide facilities for skiing, boating, hiking, golfing, riding, and swimming. Shopping facilities are near the College. Many students are involved in some aspect of community service, often combining their academic interests with a community activity.

Majors and Degrees
Mount Saint Mary College awards Bachelor of Arts (B.A.) and Bachelor of Science (B.S.) degrees in such programs as accounting, biology, business management and administration, chemistry, communication arts/media studies, computer science, criminal justice, English, finance, Hispanic studies, history, history/political science, human services (counseling/client services, general concentrations, and social/community services), interdisciplinary studies, international studies, mathematics, medical technology, nursing, psychology, public relations, social science, and sociology. Certification programs are available in elementary, elementary/special, and secondary education. Preprofessional studies are available in dentistry, law, medicine, and veterinary medicine. The College offers a 3-2 physical therapy program with New York Medical College.

Academic Program
The Mount is dedicated to providing a diversity of programs to accommodate people with individual needs and specific objectives, while developing a total learning environment for all students. Each individualized program is geared to the complex and varied needs of each student seeking to become a whole person, ready for a rewarding career and ready to make full use of his or her leisure hours. A minimum of 120 credit hours is required for degrees granted by the Mount, including 90 credit hours in the liberal arts and sciences for the Bachelor of Arts degree and 60 credit hours in the liberal arts and sciences for the Bachelor of Science degree. A core curriculum of 39 credit hours is also required. Major requirements consist of 28 to 40 credit hours.

Advanced placement, credit for life experience, accelerated courses, and an honors program are available. Students are encouraged to take part in the Mount's study-abroad program. All students have the opportunity to gain practical experience within their major through cooperative education and internships.

Academic Facilities
Aquinas Hall, the main College building, has laptop-friendly smart classrooms with LCD projection and stereo sound systems; science, nursing, language, and state-of-the-art computer science laboratories; an art studio; administrative and faculty offices; the library; a theater; a multimedia digital production center; a video production studio; a photography lab; and the music department's facilities. The fully automated Curtain Memorial Library, a trilevel wing at the southern end of Aquinas Hall, houses 120,000 volumes plus subscriptions to 1,129 current journals and periodicals. The Media Center contains recordings, cassettes, filmstrips, and tapes, along with individual listening areas and carrels to augment innovative courses and independent study. Internet access is available to all students in the Academic Computing Lab and throughout campus via the Wireless Academic Network. The Curriculum Library has been designed to meet the many needs of education students, and the Bishop Dunn Memorial School, an elementary and junior high school on campus, provides a place where

education students can participate in observing and teaching. Individually guided instruction is conducted here, as well as a modified Montessori program and classes in special education. The on-campus Office of Academic Assessment and Developmental Instruction assists students in academic endeavors through tutorial services and skills development at no additional cost.

Costs

Tuition for the 1999–2000 academic year was $11,100 for most full-time students. Room and board costs were $5700, including a room and a full weekly meal plan. Additional fees total approximately $370 annually.

Financial Aid

About 80 percent of the College's students receive financial aid from one or more sources. Scholarships, grants, loans, and work-study programs constitute most awards. The College provides aid from all federal aid programs, such as the Federal Pell Grant, Federal Supplemental Educational Opportunity Grant, Federal Perkins Loan, Nursing Scholarship and/or Loan, and Federal Work-Study programs. New York State residents may be eligible for Tuition Assistance Program (TAP) awards. The Mount also offers its own scholarship and grant programs. On-campus jobs are plentiful. All students are encouraged to apply for financial aid. Application may be made by filing the Free Application for Federal Student Aid (FAFSA) and the Mount Saint Mary College Supplemental Form (New York State residents should file the TAP Form) by March 15. For further information about financial aid, students should contact the director of financial aid.

All students who apply for admission are eligible for consideration for half tuition Presidential Scholarships, Merit Grant Awards, and Mount Saint Mary College Scholarships.

Faculty

Mount Saint Mary College offers its students an environment that fosters close student-teacher interaction with the aid of a very committed faculty. The student-teacher ratio is 16:1, which allows for individualized advisement and instruction. The average class size is 25, and classes emphasize seminar and discussion-based learning.

Student Government

Students at Mount Saint Mary College participate in a very active system of student governance. Student representatives are members of every College committee. The Resident Living Council governs and represents the resident students of the College, while the Commuter Council focuses on the commuting population. Most student activities are generated by Student Government organizations, and the Student Government plays a leading role in the development of College policy; it is the main outlet for student participation in the College's decision-making process and in the planning of events. The Student Government manages its own student activities budget.

Admission Requirements

Mount Saint Mary College welcomes students whose potential for academic and social success is in keeping with the objectives of the College. Applicants are evaluated primarily on their past academic performance. SAT I scores and class rank are also considered. Transfer applicants should be in good academic standing at their previous college. Campus visits and interviews are strongly recommended.

Early admission to the College is available.

Application and Information

Students who wish to apply to the Mount should submit a completed application and a $25 application fee to the Admissions Office. Students should also make arrangements for their high school transcript and SAT I scores to be forwarded to the same office. Letters of recommendation, while not required, are strongly advised. Mount Saint Mary College operates on a rolling admission policy. Once a student's file is complete, he or she is usually notified of the admission decision within two to four weeks.

For further information, students should contact:

Director of Admissions
Mount Saint Mary College
330 Powell Avenue
Newburgh, New York 12550
Telephone: 914-569-3248
         888-YES-MSMC (toll-free)
E-mail: mtstmary@msmc.edu
World Wide Web: http://www.msmc.edu

Mount Saint Mary College, with the Hudson River in the background.

MOUNT ST. MARY'S COLLEGE
LOS ANGELES, CALIFORNIA

The College
Mount St. Mary's College in southern California is a college of two campuses with one mission: to educate women who want to make a difference in their professions, their communities, and their lives. Founded by the Sisters of St. Joseph of Carondelet in 1925, Mount St. Mary's is an independent, Catholic college with a special concern for the education of women. Every aspect of an MSMC education is characterized by concern for the individual student—her goals, her talents, and her development. The College offers a curriculum in which career preparation is firmly based in the liberal arts and sciences. The confidence and self-esteem resulting from a Mount education prepare women to reach their full potential in the fields of their choice.

For undergraduates, the College offers both the two-year Associate in Arts degree and four-year baccalaureate degrees. The Weekend College enables students who work full-time to earn associate or baccalaureate degrees in selected majors. Graduate programs are available in education, physical therapy, and religious studies. Men are admitted to the undergraduate music, nursing, and physical therapist assistant programs, to graduate programs, to the Weekend College, and to summer sessions.

MSMC's nationally recognized Women's Leadership Program provides students with a rare opportunity to learn leadership skills in theory and practice through individual courses or a minor in leadership. The program includes membership in the Public Leadership Education Network (PLEN) consortium and internships with community and business leaders.

Although small, Mount St. Mary's student body is remarkably diverse: 1,100 students represent forty-two states and forty-three countries. The ethnic diversity of the student body closely parallels that of southern California: 22 percent are white, 20 percent Asian, 7 percent black, 41 percent Hispanic, and 10 percent of other backgrounds. Freshmen in the baccalaureate programs have SAT I or ACT scores that place them in the top quarter of college-bound students nationwide. Approximately 60 percent are Catholic. About half of the students reside on campus. Over the past five years, all students who have requested residence and completed the necessary paperwork by May 1 have been accommodated.

Student life at Mount St. Mary's is diverse, stimulating, and fun. Clubs and organizations cover almost every area of interest. For students interested in exploring culture (their own and that of others), there are groups such as the Asian Club, the Hispanic Student Organization, and the African American Student Union. The musically talented may be interested in Mount Chorus or Mount Singers, while writers and journalists gravitate to the *Oracle*, MSMC's newspaper. Model United Nations attracts those fascinated by politics. Sororities, College-sponsored dances, ski trips, theater parties, and beach days are ways for students to relax and enjoy themselves.

Location
Mount St. Mary's is located on two beautiful campuses in Los Angeles, California, one of the most exciting cities in the United States. Traditional cultural opportunities such as theater and the symphony flourish alongside the art of other cultures. First-run movie theaters, sports events, great restaurants, beaches, winter sports in the mountains, and unparalleled shopping opportunities are all available when students want to relax. Los Angeles continues to grow economically, providing excellent internship, business, and employment opportunities.

Majors and Degrees
Mount St. Mary's confers the following baccalaureate degrees: the Bachelor of Arts with majors in American studies, art, biological sciences, business, chemistry, child development, English, French, gerontology, history, liberal studies (for elementary teaching credential students), mathematics (computer science emphasis), music, philosophy, political sciences, psychology, religious studies, social science, sociology, and Spanish; the Bachelor of Science with majors in biochemistry, biological sciences, chemistry, health sciences, and nursing; and the Bachelor of Music with a major in music. Elementary and secondary teaching credential programs are also available.

Mount St. Mary's offers the Associate in Arts degree with the following majors: business, early childhood education, human services, liberal arts, occupational therapy assistant studies, physical therapist assistant studies, and pre–health sciences.

Academic Program
MSMC's academic program is composed of two parts: the general studies program, which provides a broad background of knowledge and skills, and the academic major, which allows specialization in a particular area of study and supports career preparation. Baccalaureate students take approximately eighteen courses selected from the general studies program in areas such as analytical skills, arts and sciences, communications skills, foreign languages, and philosophy/religious studies. Requirements for the major differ from program to program. Most commonly, students take about twelve courses in the major, but some areas of study, such as nursing and physical therapy, require more. In total, baccalaureate students must complete 124 academic units; the last 30 before graduation must be taken at MSMC. Students pursuing a two-year Associate in Arts degree must complete 60 units of credit, the last 24 at MSMC. The College operates on the semester system with an optional summer session.

Since the general studies program is designed to provide flexibility, students may choose a double major or a major with a minor in a related field or opt to earn two baccalaureate degrees. Students can design a major with the approval of the academic dean. Credit for prior life experience can be earned by examination or by the submission of a portfolio documenting learning to the major department. Approximately 65 percent of each year's Associate in Arts students go on to baccalaureate study at MSMC or another college or university.

The honors program at MSMC provides special challenges for outstanding students, including honors courses in particular subjects, interdisciplinary honors theme courses, honors contracts, and a senior thesis option. All majors provide opportunities for internships and practical experience.

Off-Campus Arrangements
MSMC's agreements with other colleges and universities make it possible for students to travel across town, across country, or across the world to enrich their education. A formal arrangement with UCLA enables students to pursue an area of special interest through cross-registration. Mount St. Mary's College is affiliated with the American University in Washington, D.C., so that students can spend a semester in the nation's capital. Through the Carondelet College Exchange Program, students

can spend up to two semesters studying at one of MSMC's sister colleges: Avila College in Kansas City, Missouri; the College of St. Catherine in St. Paul, Minnesota; the College of Saint Rose in Albany, New York; or Fontbonne College in St. Louis, Missouri. MSMC also encourages study in other countries through the Junior Year Abroad program and special sister college arrangements with Nagoya Women's University and College Shin-Ai Kurume in Japan.

Academic Facilities

The Chalon and Doheny campuses have their own library and media centers. Together, these house more than 140,000 books and 800 periodicals and provide access to the vast collection of resources at UCLA through the Orion computer network. They also provide access to all the major database systems for full-text and bibliographic information. Computer facilities are located on both campuses. Students have access to ninety-eight PCs and twenty Macintoshes, which drive twenty-eight printers. All students are eligible for accounts on the College's mainframe computer. Generally, every student who wishes to use a computer can be accommodated without delay. Each campus features modern classroom buildings, science laboratories, and an auditorium that seats more than 400 people. The Jose Drudis-Biada Hall on the Chalon campus houses full studio facilities and an art gallery that features shows of contemporary artists.

Costs

The cost of tuition and fees for the 2000–01 school year is $17,615. Room and board average $7032 per year. The following amounts are approximate: $560 for books and supplies, $575 for transportation, and $1640 for personal expenses.

Financial Aid

Mount St. Mary's is committed to helping every qualified student afford an MSMC education. Funds are available through a variety of programs. Students with financial need may be eligible for grants from the federal government (Federal Pell Grants and Federal Supplemental Educational Opportunity Grants), from the state of California (Cal Grants A, B, and C), and from MSMC (Dean's Award, Travel Grants). A student with a strong academic record and/or special talents may apply for a merit-based scholarship; MSMC offers President's Scholarships (in amounts up to full tuition for four years), Future Teacher's Scholarships, Achievement Scholarships, Community Service Scholarships, Scholar Athlete awards, and Art and Music scholarships. A wide assortment of low-interest loans are available. Approximately 30 percent of full-time undergraduates participate in work-study programs.

Students applying for financial aid must fill out the FAFSA, which may be obtained from a high school counselor or Mount St. Mary's Office of Financial Aid. Financial aid is awarded on a rolling basis, with earlier applicants receiving priority consideration. Students interested in merit scholarships should apply for financial aid before March 2.

Faculty

At Mount St. Mary's, teaching is the faculty's number one priority. Although the professors have rich intellectual lives, publish in scholarly journals, and contribute to national organizations in their fields, they are teachers first and foremost. Students, including freshmen, are taught by senior faculty members in classes that have an average of 16 students. The student-faculty ratio of 12:1 means that faculty members get to know students personally. Faculty members serve as academic advisers, sponsors of organizations, and—at events like the faculty-student tennis tournament and College Olympics—team captains and coaches. The College has 74 full-time and 142 part-time faculty members. Excluding those in health services, 84 percent of the faculty hold earned doctorates.

Student Government

A priority of Mount St. Mary's College is to provide women with distinctive leadership opportunities. The Associated Student Body is the student governance organization. Its branches include Student Senate, whose members provide input into the College's decision-making process and serve on College committees, and Student Activities Council, which plans a rich calendar of social and cultural events for the College community. The Residence Hall Association is the governing body for the dormitories, which are largely self-regulating.

Admission Requirements

Mount St. Mary's welcomes students from all parts of the United States and the world. No preferential treatment is given to applicants from California or to the children of alumnae. For admission to the baccalaureate program, students need at least a B average for their high school work (which must include a minimum of 16 academic units) and commensurate SAT I or ACT scores. Test scores, high school grade point average (GPA), and rank in class are given most weight in the admission decision. Recommendations are optional. Mount St. Mary's encourages, but does not require, an on-campus interview. Students interested in the associate degree program must have a high school GPA of at least 2.2 and must submit SAT I or ACT scores.

Mount St. Mary's is delighted to accept applications from transfer students. To make the process easier, transfer students are admitted in both the fall and the spring semester with no minimum number of college units required.

Application and Information

Mount St. Mary's has a rolling admission policy. Students are informed of acceptance two weeks after their admission files have been completed, starting on January 2 for fall admission.

Further information may be obtained from:

Director of Admission
Mount St. Mary's College
12001 Chalon Road
Los Angeles, California 90049
Telephone: 310-954-4250
        800-999-9893 (toll-free)
World Wide Web: http://www.msmc.la.edu

The Chalon campus.

MOUNT SAINT MARY'S COLLEGE
EMMITSBURG, MARYLAND

The College

As the nation's second-oldest Catholic college, Mount Saint Mary's is blessed with a heritage that few can match. Founded in 1808, the Mount provided the Catholic Church with many of its early leaders in America, including Archbishop John Hughes, who began New York's St. Patrick's Cathedral, and his successor, John McCloskey, the first native-born American cardinal. Many other colleges and universities were founded by Mount graduates. Later alumni include a Supreme Court Justice, a president of Mexico, and the founder of Boys' Town. Today, the Most Rev. Harry J. Flynn, Archbishop of St. Paul/Minneapolis; Susan O'Malley, President of the Washington Wizards NBA team; and Matt McHugh, who served nine terms in the U.S. House of Representatives, are counted among the Mount's 12,000 alumni. Most students come from Maryland and other Mid-Atlantic states, but typically more than half of the U.S. states and ten to twenty additional countries are represented by the 1,400 undergraduates.

Current Mount students are well prepared to join their predecessors in service to "the Church, the Republic, and the Professions." The Core Curriculum, which has received national recognition, provides a strong grounding in the liberal arts, developing reading, writing, and critical thinking skills—attributes needed for success in any career path. Academic majors and minors add specialized knowledge. Outside of the classroom the Mount offers even more: a full range of extracurricular and cocurricular activities and the opportunity to build people skills in a residential college environment. Among the more than seventy-five clubs and special interest groups are student media (radio, TV, newspaper, yearbook, and literary magazine), a drama group, the campus ministry, and community service opportunities.

The Mount is one of the smallest colleges competing at the NCAA Division I level, which gives students many opportunities for participation on the eighteen varsity sports teams. Club sports and intramurals are also available, as are indoor and outdoor recreation facilities. Of particular note is the 105,000-square-foot Knott Athletic Recreation Convocation Complex, with courts for tennis, volleyball, basketball, and handball/racquetball; a swimming pool; an indoor track; and aerobics and weight rooms (both recently outfitted with new weight-training equipment).

Student residences include traditional dormitories, suites, apartments, and special interest housing. Students are guaranteed housing for all four years. The Student Union Building houses the dining hall, snack bar, and social gathering places, as well as the bookstore, mailroom, and offices.

In addition to the undergraduate college, the Mount includes one of the country's largest and most successful Catholic seminaries, other graduate programs in business and education, and the National Shrine Grotto of Lourdes.

Location

The 1,400-acre campus is in north-central Maryland, one hour west of Baltimore and slightly farther northwest of Washington, D.C. Historic Gettysburg, Pennsylvania, is 12 miles north, and Frederick, Maryland's second-largest city and an attractive shopping and entertainment destination, is 20 miles south. Emmitsburg is a town of 1,500, with a variety of restaurants and shops. Elizabeth Ann "Mother" Seton, America's first native-born saint, began her religious order and the country's first parochial school here, and both survive to this day. Nearby attractions include Ski Liberty, national and state parks (including Catoctin Mountain National Park, home of the Camp David presidential retreat), and golf courses. Horseback riding is also available in the area.

Majors and Degrees

Majors leading to Bachelor of Arts or Bachelor of Science degrees are offered in accounting, biochemistry, biology, business (concentrations in finance; international business, sports management, and economics; management; and marketing), chemistry, computer science, economics, elementary education, English, fine arts (concentrations in art, music, and theater), foreign languages (multilingual), French, German, history, international studies, mathematics, philosophy, political science, psychology, rhetoric and communication (concentrations in communications, creative writing, journalism, and professional and technical writing), secondary education (concentrations in English, social studies, and other areas), sociology (concentration in criminal justice), Spanish, and theology. Students may also design their own majors. A 3-2 program in nursing is available with Johns Hopkins University. Minors are offered in all major areas and in African-American studies, gender studies, Latin American studies, and non-Western studies. Predental, prelaw, and premedicine programs are offered.

Academic Program

The academic majors offer strong preparation for a variety of careers, but Mount students take one half of the 120 credit hours required for graduation in the Core Curriculum, a carefully integrated four-year sequence of courses in Western civilization, American and non-Western culture, philosophy and theology, foreign languages, mathematics, and the social and natural sciences. This program helps students gain a broader perspective and a better understanding of themselves and the world around them and fosters the development and strengthening of a rational value system. After core and major requirements, students complete their course work with electives. The Mount accepts Advanced Placement and CLEP credits.

Mount Saint Mary's yearlong Freshman Seminar is designed to build reading, writing, and critical thinking skills. Students are placed in seminar sections of about 18 students each, taught by their advisers. Students with outstanding high school records are invited into the Freshman Honors Program; sophomores enter the College Honors Program. The latter includes an interdisciplinary honors seminar for juniors and a special senior project in a student's major.

The Mount sponsors its own international study programs in Costa Rica, England, France, Germany, Ireland, and Italy, and affiliated programs make it possible to study in other countries. At home, the Mount offers an aggressive internship program and a variety of career-preparation services.

Academic Facilities

Classes are held in two major academic buildings—the Knott Academic Center and the Coad Science Building—and in several other smaller or multiple-use buildings. Most classrooms are small because most classes are small. The science lab facilities are newly renovated, and continuous improvements are being made to computing facilities. PC and Macintosh labs are available, and online research resources are abundant through Phillips Library or any networked computer. Internet access is free. The library contains more than 200,000 books, including a reference collection of 3,000 volumes, CD-ROMS, and electronic databases. More than 2,000 periodicals are available in print, microfilm, or electronic form. Online access provides additional possibilities worldwide. Many special events are held in the 550-seat Marion Burk Knott Auditorium.

Costs

Tuition and fees total $17,200 for 2000–01; room and board are $6860. Books, supplies, laundry, transportation, and personal expenses average about $1600 per year.

Financial Aid

Mount Saint Mary's offers financial assistance to qualified students in the form of scholarships, grants, loans, student employment, and special payment plans. Almost 90 percent of students attending the Mount receive some form of financial aid. Through its scholarship program and financial aid packages, the College attempts as much as possible to relieve the financial burden of attending college. The Mount participates in all major federal financial aid programs, including the Federal Pell Grant, Federal Perkins Loan, Federal Stafford Student Loan, and Federal Work-Study Programs. Federal PLUS loans may also be used.

The College awards a wide range of merit and merit-and-need scholarships. In 1999–2000, about 300 were awarded to entering freshmen (370 total) at an average of nearly $7300 per year. Three full-tuition Kuderer-Trustee Scholarships are awarded to qualified candidates on the basis of an essay exam competition. The full-tuition Marion Burk Knott Scholarships, usually one or two per year, are offered to qualified Catholic students residing in the Archdiocese of Baltimore. Mount Scholarships and Mount Merit Grants are offered to qualified students in amounts typically ranging from $5000 to $12,500 per year. Funston V. Collins and Bolivar–San Martin Scholarships and Grants-in-Aid are offered to qualified African-American and Hispanic-American students, respectively. All scholarships are renewable annually based on academic performance. In addition, as an NCAA Division I school, the Mount offers athletic scholarships to men and women in all intercollegiate sports.

The Free Application for Federal Student Aid (FAFSA) and the Financial Aid PROFILE must be submitted by March 15 and should be filed as soon after January 1 as possible.

Faculty

More than 90 full-time faculty members—85 percent with Ph.D. or equivalent degrees—bring the Mount curriculum to life. All faculty members personalize the educational experience by working with and getting to know each student. The student-faculty ratio is 16:1, and the average class size is 21. Every professor serves as an academic adviser. No graduate assistants teach class. Faculty members are committed to teaching, but many are also active researchers, and opportunities exist for students to become involved in research projects.

Student Government

The Student Government Association (SGA) provides funding for other student organizations and a conduit for student feedback to the Mount administration. The SGA President sits on the Mount Council, the College's governing body. The Campus Activities Board schedules dances, concerts, movies, bus trips, and other social events.

Admission Requirements

Candidates for admission to the College must be of good character and must show evidence that they have successfully completed a four-year college-preparatory program in high school. All students applying for admission should have a minimum of 16 academic units, including English, 4; social studies, 3; mathematics, 3; sciences, 3; and a foreign language, 2. Students must also present recommendations from a guidance counselor or a teacher in an academic course, as well as scores on the SAT I or ACT.

Application and Information

Students applying to the Mount should send test scores, high school transcripts, and recommendations to the Admissions Office along with a $35 application fee. Transfer students in good standing should forward both their college and high school transcripts. Information and forms are also available on the Mount's Web site, listed below.

For further information, students may contact:

Director of Admissions
Mount Saint Mary's College
Emmitsburg, Maryland 21727
Telephone: 301-447-5214
           800-448-4347 (toll-free)
E-mail: admissions@msmary.edu
World Wide Web: http://www.msmary.edu

Students in front of the Coad Science Building on the campus of Mount Saint Mary's College.

MOUNT SAINT VINCENT UNIVERSITY
HALIFAX, NOVA SCOTIA, CANADA

The University

Recognized as a leader in innovative education for women, Mount Saint Vincent University is a dynamic, challenging, and welcoming community. With about 4,000 students, most classes are small; professors take the time to get to know their students on an individual basis.

The Mount offers bachelor's degrees in liberal arts and sciences, as well as a range of professional programs, and master's degrees in child and youth study, education, human ecology, and women's studies. The University promotes academic excellence and a high degree of personalized education. A student-centered approach and a strong sense of community ensure that all students have an equal opportunity to develop leadership skills through participation in student government or societies, athletics, and volunteer activities. A commitment to accessibility through student-focused programs and policies has also earned the University a reputation for innovation. The University is a regional leader in distance learning and continuing education, offering more than 100 credit courses via various forms of technology, including courses leading to various programs at the certificate, bachelor's, and master's levels. Current distance enrollment exceeds 1,000 students.

The University is also a leader in cooperative education, with co-op programs available in applied human nutrition, business administration, information technology, public relations, and tourism and hospitality management. The campus is home to various resources that enrich academic and campus life, such as the Centre for Women in Business, the Nova Scotia Centre on Aging, the Institute for the Study of Women, the Catherine Wallace Centre for Women in Science, and the Nancy Rowell Jackman Chair in Women's Studies. The Mount's distinctive programs, emphasis on women, distance outreach, and co-op education attract students from across Canada, the United States, the Caribbean, Africa, and the Middle East.

The University has 242 residence rooms in twelve-story Assisi Hall and the Birches town houses. Residence spaces are available to both male and female students. Students have access to excellent on-campus recreation and fitness facilities and a wide range of intercollegiate sports. Support services include counseling, health services and physioclinic, a career resource centre, and study skills programs. An on-campus bookstore stocks textbooks, school supplies, and crested clothing.

The Mount offers graduate programs in child and youth study, education, human ecology, and women's studies; diplomas in business administration and information technology; and certificate programs in business administration, community residential services, gerontology, information technology, marketing, proficiency in French, and tourism and hospitality management.

The University offers the following master's programs: a Master of Education (nonthesis) in adult education, curriculum studies, educational foundations, educational psychology, elementary education, and literacy education; a Master of Arts in School Psychology; a research Master of Arts; a Master of Arts in child and youth study; a Master of Human Ecology; and a Master of Arts in women's studies. Program requirements are detailed in the University calendar or on the School's Web site listed below.

Location

The Mount is located in the City of Halifax, which is the capital of Nova Scotia and the largest urban centre in the province, with a population of 343,000. Halifax is a bustling centre of business, education, and culture and is a charming historic seaport. The University is just minutes from downtown on a beautiful hillside overlooking Bedford Basin, a narrow arm of the ocean. The treed campus, with its walking trails and duck ponds, offers a pleasant environment in which to study and relax. The campus is located on major bus routes and within easy access to shopping, entertainment, museums, theatres, and restaurants. Because the Mount is a partner in the Metro Halifax Universities Consortium, students have access to a wide range of opportunities at other Halifax universities.

Majors and Degrees

Mount Saint Vincent University offers bachelor's degrees in applied arts (child and youth study), applied arts (family studies and gerontology), applied arts (information technology), arts, business administration, education, public relations, science, science (applied human nutrition), and tourism and hospitality management.

Academic Programs

Undergraduate degrees combine core courses in a student's chosen program and electives, which students can take out of personal interest. Each degree has specific requirements for both. Students wishing to enroll in a Bachelor of Arts or Science program can choose from a 15-unit general studies program, a 15- or 20-unit Bachelor of Arts or Science with a major, or a 20-unit advanced major or honours degree. Professional programs include a 23-unit Bachelor of Applied Arts (child and youth study); 20-unit bachelor's degrees in applied arts (information technology), public relations, science (applied human nutrition), and tourism and hospitality management; and a two-year Bachelor of Education program. The Mount offers 12-unit diploma programs in business administration, information technology and computer studies, and tourism and hospitality management and 6-unit certificate programs in community residential services, gerontology, information technology, marketing, proficiency in French, and tourism and hospitality management.

Off-Campus Arrangements

The Mount has established student exchange programs with universities in Canada, the United States, and overseas. The deans' offices assist students who wish to take advantage of these opportunities. Current programs include the Nova Scotia/New England Student Exchange Program and the French and Spanish Year Abroad Program (in Québec, France, or Spain). Generally, students accepted on exchange programs pay Mount tuition and other fees and retain any Canadian financial aid they may have. Students must be eligible for student visas if required and are responsible for travel, living, and other personal costs, including health care.

Academic Facilities

The library shares the modern E. Margaret Fulton Communications Centre with Information Technology and Services and facilities for distance learning and continuing education. The

Mount is a member of the Novanet library consortium, which brings together the bibliographic library resources of nine Nova Scotia universities. Some highlights of the Mount's on-campus holdings include an English literature collection of 13,000 first and limited editions and a women's centenary collection. Students have access to a wide range of computing facilities, including a multimedia lab for education students and a sophisticated language lab for students studying modern languages.

Students can take more than 100 courses via distance, including courses leading to a certificate or diploma in business administration, a Certificate in Gerontology, a Certificate of Proficiency in French, and a Bachelor of Tourism and Hospitality Management.

Various resources and programs are available for students who have been out of the high school system for some time or are studying part-time.

Specialized resources include a modern reading centre for graduate education students, which offers diagnostic and tutoring programs, and the Child Study Centre, which is a training, research, and observation facility for child and youth study students. The Art Gallery is nationally known as a showcase for women and emerging regional artists.

Costs

For the 1999–2000 academic year, tuition fees for Canadian citizens and permanent residents taking a full-time course load were approximately $3915; Bachelor of Education students paid $3940. A differential fee of $2700 was charged to international students. Residence fees for 1998–99, including meal plans, ranged from $4590 to $5090. (Meal plans are mandatory except in the International/Mature Birch residence where the room-only fee was $2895.) Additional student union and medical fees total approximately $325 ($800 for international students). All figures are represented in Canadian dollars.

Financial Aid

Students entering directly from high school are eligible for scholarships from $1000 to $12,000 (no separate application required). The Mount offers many in-course awards as well as bursaries to students with demonstrated financial need. In addition, there are on-campus employment opportunities for students. Students may contact 902-457-6419 for scholarship information and 902-457-6351 for information on bursaries.

Faculty

Mount Saint Vincent University places a strong emphasis on teaching excellence, which, when combined with a focus on personalized education, ensures a positive, stimulating learning environment for students. The University has 363 full- and part-time faculty members and a student-faculty ratio of 12:1. Eighty percent of full-time faculty members have Ph.D.'s, and a high proportion (74 percent) of undergraduate classes are taught by tenured faculty members. Faculty members are also active in research; currently, 14 percent have received national research awards in the areas of science, medicine, social sciences, and the humanities. Sixty-two percent of full-time faculty members are women.

Student Government

The student union is composed of all full- and part-time students of the University. The governing body of the union is the student council, which is composed of elected and appointed representatives from various faculties as well as student senators and Board of Governors representatives. The executive consists of the president and five vice presidents (executive, academic, external, internal, and finance). The student council represents the interests of students to the University administration, faculty, and external organizations, including government. The student union is the publisher of the student newspaper. The variety store, pub, student lounge, games room, and the play centre for students' children are all managed by the student union.

Admission Requirements

There are special admission requirements depending on the program. In addition, application procedures vary depending on whether the applicant is coming directly from high school, has previous postsecondary study, or has been out of the high school system for a period of time. All of these are detailed in the academic calendar or on the Web site listed below.

Application and Information

Application deadlines for September entrance range from early March to mid-May, depending upon the program. All application dossiers must be complete (transcripts, supporting documents, and application fee) and received by the deadlines. For additional information about admissions, program information, or campus tours or to receive an application, students may contact:

Admissions Office
Mount Saint Vincent University
Halifax, Nova Scotia B3M 2J6
Canada
Telephone: 902-457-6128
Fax: 902-457-6498
E-mail: admissions@msvu.ca
World Wide Web: http://www.msvu.ca

Mount Saint Vincent University: a sense of community.

MOUNT UNION COLLEGE
ALLIANCE, OHIO

The College

Mount Union College was established in 1846 as a select school to meet the educational demands of a small community. Mount Union College offers a liberal arts education grounded in the Judeo-Christian tradition. The College affirms the importance of reason, open inquiry, living faith, and individual worth. Mount Union's mission is to prepare students for meaningful work, fulfilling lives, and responsible citizenship.

Mount Union is primarily a residential campus, and its residence halls mirror the variety of lifestyles and diversity of interests of the students. Students have the opportunity to select from large residence halls housing from 70 to 175, small houses, or fraternity houses. Upperclass students in good academic standing may be permitted to live off campus.

Student activities are an important complement to the academic program. From clubs allied with academic interests to those that are purely social, Mount Union has more than eighty student organizations in its cocurricular program, including chapters of four national sororities and five national fraternities. Nearly 85 percent of Mount Union students participate in the cocurricular program either on or off campus. There are facilities on campus for racquetball, volleyball, basketball, swimming, wrestling, tennis, track, and dance. The College also has a physical education complex, which includes the McPherson Wellness Center, the Peterson Field House, and the Timken Physical Education Building. Nearly 65 percent of Mount Union students participate in organized intramural or intercollegiate sports. Mount Union competes in twenty-one intercollegiate sports: baseball, basketball, cross-country, football, golf, indoor track, outdoor track, soccer, swimming, tennis, and wrestling for men and basketball, cross-country, golf, indoor track, outdoor track, soccer, softball, swimming, tennis, and volleyball for women.

Location

Mount Union College is located in Alliance, Ohio, a town of approximately 25,000 people. Alliance is situated 55 miles southeast of Cleveland, 75 miles northwest of Pittsburgh, 35 miles southeast of Akron, 40 miles west of Youngstown, and 15 miles northeast of Canton.

Majors and Degrees

The Bachelor of Arts is offered in accounting, American studies, art, business administration, communications studies, early childhood education, economics, education, English, French, German, history, international business, Japanese, mass media, media computing, music, non-Western studies, philosophy, physical education and health, political science, psychology, religion, sociology, Spanish, sport management, sports medicine, theater, and writing.

The Bachelor of Science is offered in athletic training, biology, chemistry, computer science, exercise science, geology, information systems, mathematics, and physics and astronomy.

The Bachelor of Music is offered in applied music, and the Bachelor of Music Education is offered in elementary and secondary music teaching, music education, and music performance.

Preprofessional programs are available in dentistry, engineering, law, medicine, and the ministry.

Academic Program

The Mount Union education program is based on an academic year divided into two semesters of fifteen weeks each. The regular academic load is 12 to 18 semester hours per semester.

The Mount Union curriculum is designed with considerable flexibility to meet the needs of students who enter with widely varying educational backgrounds and objectives. The College has five basic educational plans: (1) a program geared toward specialization, with the student taking as many as sixteen courses in one department; (2) a program with a lesser degree of specialization, in which the student takes the minimum number of courses required for a major; (3) a program that permits concentration in interdepartmental areas, such as American studies, non-Western studies, or communications; (4) a preprofessional program that prepares students for entry into professional degree programs in dentistry, engineering, law, medicine, and the ministry; and (5) an interdisciplinary, individualized program, which students design in conjunction with a committee of faculty advisers to meet particular interests. While students have considerable latitude in determining their individual programs, the all-College comprehensive requirements ensure exposure to the fine arts, the humanities, the social sciences, the physical sciences, and mathematics. In addition, each student must complete a major requirement and a senior-year culminating experience.

Advanced placement, involving the awarding of credit or the waiving of certain prerequisites or requirements, is based on high school records, scores on College Board examinations or similar tests, scores and school reports on College Board Advanced Placement Program examinations, and tests devised and administered by departments within the College. Entering students are encouraged to take placement tests in applicable areas in order to begin course work at the proper level.

Academic Facilities

The library contains more than 250,000 volumes, receives about 925 periodicals, and provides seating for 350 persons. The computer center, housed in the library, is equipped with the latest in computer and communications technology. McMaster Hall houses a computer laboratory with forty personal computers and printers that are fully compatible with the IBM PC line. There is also an eighteen-station PC lab in East Hall, a twenty-station PC lab in the Hoover-Price Campus Center, and a twenty-station Macintosh lab in Chapman Hall. All residence halls are wired for computers and closed-circuit television. The Fine Arts Complex includes a 290-seat theater, an art gallery, a music library, an outdoor Greek theater, a large rehearsal hall, and a recital hall with a three-manual organ. The Eells Art Center contains classrooms, a printmaking area, a drawing and design studio, a kiln room, a sculpture and woodworking area, and a drama rehearsal hall. Wilson Hall and Tolerton and Hood Hall of Science house laboratory equipment for biology, chemistry, geology, mathematics, and physics. The X-ray laboratory is equipped with an X-ray diffractometer and a vacuum X-ray spectrograph. The Clarke Astronomical Observatory is located on campus, and a nearby private observatory is also used by the College. Students also use Rodman Observatory. The College has a 109-acre nature center, located 6 miles from campus, for biology, chemistry, and ecology studies.

Costs

For 2000–01, the cost of a year at Mount Union College is $20,110, including $14,720 for tuition, $830 for fees, $1820 for a room, and $2740 for board. This figure may vary slightly, depending upon the type of on-campus housing selected by the student. An additional $1000 should cover such expenses as books and transportation.

Financial Aid

Mount Union College believes that no student should fail to apply for admission to the College purely for financial reasons. Approximately 80 percent of students receive some financial assistance based on demonstrated need. The College also offers allocated institutional dollars to students as merit-based awards. In 1998-99, Mount Union students received financial aid in excess of $22 million. More than $6.1 million of that total was awarded in the form of College grants. An additional $3.4 million was given in the form of various scholarships.

Faculty

Mount Union employs 105 full-time and 60 part-time faculty members, 80 percent of whom hold a terminal degree. The student-faculty ratio is 16:1.

Student Government

Student government is a significant part of Mount Union's decision-making process. Students are represented on all major campus committees that discuss matters affecting student life, and they serve as representatives at meetings of the administration, faculty, and trustees.

Admission Requirements

Mount Union College does not discriminate on the basis of race, sex, religion, age, color, creed, national or ethnic origin, marital or parental status, or handicap in student admissions, financial aid, educational or athletic programs, or employment. Admission decisions are made with a view toward enrolling those students who are best qualified to participate intelligently and creatively in the total life of the academic community. The qualifications of each candidate are evaluated on the basis of academic background, class rank, references, a required essay, recommendations, and entrance examinations. Candidates who find it possible to visit the campus are encouraged to schedule an interview, although this is not a requirement. Applicants should have pursued a strong college-preparatory course in high school. All candidates are required to submit either SAT I or ACT scores. The Office of Admissions is located in Beeghly Hall and is open throughout the year from 8 a.m. until 4:30 p.m. on weekdays and from 8:30 a.m. until noon on Saturdays throughout the academic year.

Mount Union welcomes applications from students wishing to transfer from other institutions.

Application and Information

Admission decisions are made on a rolling basis throughout the year. The first admission decisions are made in October. A $1.50 application fee is required. The admission packet contains instructions, an application form, a secondary school transcript form, and a reference request form. Students can also apply on line via the College's Web site, listed below.

Applicants may obtain further information by contacting:

Director of Admissions
Mount Union College
1972 Clark Avenue
Alliance, Ohio 44601
Telephone: 330-823-2590 Ext. 2590
           800-334-6682 (toll-free)
E-mail: admissn@muc.edu
World Wide Web: http://www.muc.edu

Chapman Hall, built in 1864, serves as one of the main classroom buildings at Mount Union College.

MUHLENBERG COLLEGE
ALLENTOWN, PENNSYLVANIA

The College

Founded in 1848 and affiliated with the Lutheran Church, Muhlenberg College has the primary purpose of helping students develop those capacities of imaginative and critical thinking that make possible humane and responsible living within a free society. A secondary, but related, purpose is to provide students with excellent undergraduate preparation for socially useful and fulfilling occupations.

Muhlenberg students achieve the College's goals by assuming strong individual responsibility for intense involvement in vigorous academic work and for personal involvement within the College community. The more than 100 student organizations provide outlets for the diversified cultural, athletic, religious, social, leadership, and service interests of the students. The campus is primarily residential; more than 90 percent of the 1,950 students live on campus. A close sense of community develops naturally, one in which their diversified academic and personal interests enable students to contribute positively to the intellectual and personal growth of their peers.

Students are aided by an active Career Planning and Placement Service in relating academic and personal knowledge and skills to appropriate career goals and in obtaining positions upon graduation. More than one third of a typical graduating class proceeds immediately to graduate or professional school.

Location

Muhlenberg College is located in suburban west Allentown, an area made up primarily of attractive family homes and parks. The central area of Allentown, a city of approximately 104,000 people, is a 10-minute ride from the campus. The College is located 90 miles west of New York City and 60 miles north of Philadelphia.

Majors and Degrees

Muhlenberg offers the Bachelor of Arts (A.B.) degree in the following fields: accounting, American studies, art, business administration, classics, communications, dance, drama, economics, English, French, German, history, history/government, human resources administration, international studies, Latin, music, philosophy, philosophy/political thought, political economy, political science, psychology, religion, Russian studies, social science, sociology, and Spanish. The Bachelor of Science (B.S.) degree is offered in the following fields: biochemistry, biology, chemistry, computer science, environmental science, mathematics, natural sciences, and physics. Students may also design their own major.

In addition, students may receive certification to teach at the elementary and secondary levels. Other opportunities include a 4-4 guaranteed-admission program with MCP Hahnemann University School of Medicine; a 3-4 dental program with the University of Pennsylvania; a 3-2/4-2 combined program in engineering, offered in cooperation with Columbia University and Washington University; and a 3-2 combined program in forestry, offered in cooperation with Duke University.

Academic Program

The A.B. and B.S. programs emphasize breadth of study in the liberal arts as well as in-depth study of a particular academic major. All students must fulfill requirements in the humanities, social sciences, natural sciences, and physical education and must demonstrate proficiency in one foreign language. Strong achievement on Advanced Placement examinations may enable a student to receive advanced placement, possibly with credit. Scores of 4 or 5 earn automatic credit. Scores of 3 are evaluated by the appropriate department.

Students work closely with academic advisers to formulate programs well suited to their individual interests, abilities, needs, and goals. Generally, students are expected to declare their major at the end of the freshman year; however, many students later change their academic major with no difficulty. A double major is possible, and several fields are available as minor programs. These minor fields are accounting, anthropology, business administration, chemistry, computer science, economics, English, French, German, history, Latin, mathematics, music, philosophy, physics, political science, religion, sociology, Spanish, and women's studies. In addition, independent study and research are available. The College also enriches the freshman-year experience through more than thirty special-focus Freshman Seminars.

Off-Campus Arrangements

Study abroad is available through Muhlenberg's Semester-in-London Program, Netherlands Semester, or the International Student Exchange Program. In addition, the Lehigh Valley Association of Independent Colleges sponsors summer study-abroad options in England, France, Germany, Israel, and Spain. Credit for study-abroad programs sponsored by other institutions or by private agencies may also be transferred to Muhlenberg.

Students may participate in a variety of internships in local businesses, health-care facilities, schools, public agencies, theaters, broadcasting stations, and magazines. Government internships in Harrisburg, Pennsylvania, and Washington, D.C., and an Ethics and Public Affairs semester in Washington, D.C., are also available.

Students may enroll in courses offered at any of the five other member institutions of the Lehigh Valley Association of Independent Colleges: Lafayette College, Lehigh University, Cedar Crest College, Allentown College of St. Francis De Sales, and Moravian College.

Academic Facilities

Muhlenberg's library collection contains more than 200,000 volumes as well as numerous government documents, periodicals, and microforms. The $12-million Harry C. Trexler Library, a state-of-the-art library facility, opened in 1988. Students may also use library materials owned by the other institutions participating in the Lehigh Valley Association of Independent Colleges.

The Baker Center for the Arts was designed for Muhlenberg by the well-known architect Philip Johnson. It houses a modern theater complex, a recital hall, classrooms, art studios, and a fine arts gallery. The Trexler Performing Arts Pavilion opened in 2000 and provides dance performance and studio space, a new theater, a Black Box, and additional arts spaces.

Life science facilities include numerous laboratories, classrooms, two electron microscopes, an isolation room used for growing and studying viruses, and a museum of natural history. Facilities supporting students in the physical sciences include equipment for optics, electronics, and atomic, nuclear, and solid-state physics. Currently, there are sixty-five microcomputers and more than one hundred computer terminals linked to the College's network, and these are available for student use. The College uses a UNIX/Windows computer system with Novell software.

Costs

The comprehensive tuition fee for 2000–01 is $21,050. The room and board fee is $5650. The total cost for a resident student is $26,700.

Financial Aid

Muhlenberg College endeavors to make its educational opportunities available to all qualified students regardless of their financial circumstances. While most financial aid at Muhlenberg is based on financial need as demonstrated by the College Scholarship Service Financial Aid PROFILE, there is also a limited amount of merit aid available. Typically, about 65 percent of Muhlenberg's students qualify for and receive financial aid.

Faculty

The Muhlenberg faculty consists of 131 full-time and 82 part-time members, 87 percent of whom hold doctoral or terminal degrees. While many faculty members are distinguished for their scholarly research, teaching is the main emphasis of their work. Professors at all levels work closely with students both inside and outside of the classroom. Most department heads teach introductory courses.

Student Government

Muhlenberg students are expected to demonstrate a high level of responsibility with regard to their own governance and to participate extensively in internal decision making and communication processes throughout the campus. These responsibilities are coordinated by the Student Council, which transacts all business pertaining to the student body. This organization is in charge of a $250,000 student activities budget. In addition, 2 students serve as representatives to the Board of Directors, and students hold full voting privileges on many faculty committees.

Admission Requirements

The College selects students who give evidence of ability and scholastic achievement, seriousness of purpose, and the capacity to make constructive contributions to the College community. Approximately 55 percent of a typical freshman class ranked in the top fifth of their secondary school class. SAT I scores for entering freshmen average approximately 585 verbal and 590 math.

Submission of SAT I or ACT scores is optional. An on-campus interview is strongly recommended for all applicants and required for students who choose not to submit standardized test scores.

Application and Information

Students who wish to be considered for admission should submit a completed application form as early as possible during their senior year of secondary school and no later than February 15. Candidates receive notice of admission decisions in late March. Early decision and early admission plans and transfer admission are possible.

For further information, interested students should contact:

Christopher Hooker-Haring
Dean of Admission and Financial Aid
Muhlenberg College
Allentown, Pennsylvania 18104-5586

Telephone: 484-664-3200
E-mail: admissions@muhlenberg.edu
World Wide Web: http://www.muhlenberg.edu

The Bell Tower of the Haas College Center stands as the focal point of the Muhlenberg College campus.

NAROPA UNIVERSITY
Naropa College
BOULDER, COLORADO

The College

Naropa University is a private, nonsectarian, accredited liberal arts University providing a unique educational environment and a four-year undergraduate program in a wide range of majors. The undergraduate program at Naropa is referred to as Naropa College. The aim of education at Naropa College is to uncover wisdom, cultivate compassion, and develop the intellectual knowledge and skills necessary for effective action. Naropa's approach to learning is called "contemplative education," embodying the spirit of many contemplative traditions around the world and based in the practice of cultivating one's awareness of the present moment. Contemplative education teaches students to combine intellect with wisdom and encourages the desire to work for the benefit of others.

Naropa College grew out of an educational philosophy that dates back to Nalanda University, a major center of learning that was founded in India and that was presided over in the eleventh century by Naropa, a highly respected Buddhist scholar. Naropa College was originally founded in 1974 by the Tibetan meditation master and scholar Chögyam Trungpa. This Buddhist educational heritage has been the ongoing inspiration for the development of Naropa College.

Naropa's academic programs are rigorous. They are designed for students who are resourceful and willing to go beyond habitual patterns. The curriculum allows students to wholeheartedly train in a chosen field of study while engaged in a learning process that fosters precision, gentleness, spontaneity, and critical intellect.

Naropa College provides an atmosphere that is vital and dignified. The faculty members and student body at Naropa form a close-knit community, and this relationship between students and faculty members is a unique part of the educational experience. Drawn from more than thirty-five states and nearly twenty countries, students at Naropa represent a wide range of life experiences, backgrounds, and ages. Of the 986 degree-seeking students at Naropa, 397 are undergraduate students enrolled in Naropa College.

Naropa intends to provide limited student housing starting in fall 2000. The Office of Student Affairs also provides a variety of resources to assist students in finding the right living situation.

Accredited by the North Central Association of Colleges and Schools since 1986, Naropa offers a four-year undergraduate program through Naropa College, as well as M.A., M.F.A., and M.L.A. degrees through Naropa University.

Location

Naropa College is located in Boulder, Colorado, a town nestled at the base of the majestic Rocky Mountain foothills. The city of Boulder, a town of 100,000, is located 25 miles northwest of Denver and was rated by *Outdoor Magazine* in 1997 as one of the top ten places to live for health and recreation. It is home to many theater, dance, and music companies, as well as to the University of Colorado. Boulder has bike paths all over town, and Boulder public transportation provides a frequent and comprehensive bus schedule throughout the day.

Naropa's main campus and surrounding grounds include a Performing Arts Center, a meditation hall, the Allen Ginsberg Library and Computer Center, Naropa Gallery, a student lounge, a bookstore, and Naropa Café.

Majors and Degrees

Naropa offers nine undergraduate programs leading to a Bachelor of Arts (B.A.) degree: contemplative psychology, early childhood education, environmental studies, interarts studies, interdisciplinary studies, religious studies, traditional Eastern arts, visual arts, and writing and literature.

Contemplative psychology has two main components: a contemplative core and areas of concentration, which include Buddhist and Western psychology, expressive arts and well-being, psychology of health and healing, and transpersonal and humanistic psychology.

Early childhood education draws from the holistic and spiritual traditions of Montessori, Waldorf, and Shambhala. Graduates are preapproved by the state of Colorado for certification as preschool teachers, private kindergarten teachers, and directors of child-care centers.

Environmental studies applies ecocentric, holistic, and systems science perspectives to ecological and cultural systems. Students may minor in anthropology, ecology, ecopsychology, horticulture, and Native American studies.

Interarts studies provides an innovative environment in which students study composition, improvisation, and performance. Students are given the opportunity to study with leading innovators and artists, while concentrating in one of four areas: theater, dance therapy, dance/movement, and music.

Interdisciplinary studies does not require a minor, allowing students to develop a varied curriculum from the College's majors for a personally directed educational experience.

Religious studies offers a nonsectarian, scholarly, and critical examination of the major religions of the world (Buddhism, Hinduism, Christianity, Judaism, Islam, Native American traditions, and the religions of East Asia) as living traditions.

Traditional Eastern arts is the only degree program of its kind, offering training and study in the traditional arts of Tai-chi Chuan, aikido, and Yoga, combined with sitting meditation.

Visual arts provides a hands-on studio approach. Students study traditional and contemporary artistic techniques from many world cultures, with an emphasis on meditative disciplines, art history, and portfolio/gallery presentations.

The writing and literature program fosters an environment of original writing combined with scholarship, contemplative study, and sharp-minded criticism. The curriculum includes writing workshops, literature courses, and training in oral presentations of creative work.

Academic Program

Undergraduate students spend the first two years at Naropa College in the College Core Program, selecting courses from the following eight areas: contemplative practices, world wisdom traditions, cultural and historical studies, artistic processes, group and leadership skills, healing arts, communication arts, and complex systems. During this time, students receive support and advisement, while completing graduation requirements and exploring courses from all of Naropa's academic offerings. Upon completion of 60 credits or at the end of the sophomore year, students declare a major.

Students must complete a total of 120 semester credits to earn an undergraduate degree.

Off-Campus Arrangements

Naropa College's study-abroad program provides a thorough introduction to the living traditions of Nepal and Bali. In addition to lectures, field trips, and classes, students experience these diverse cultures directly through community gatherings and cultural events. To apply, a minimum grade point average of 2.5 is required of degree-seeking students, and financial aid is available. Undergraduate and graduate students from other colleges are invited to apply and may inquire about financial aid through their home institutions. Study-abroad programs are also open to the public.

Naropa has also introduced a new distance education option for select students who prefer the flexibility of online classes. Naropa Online offers a sample of Naropa's courses via the World Wide Web, using the latest in Internet technology. Naropa Online offers ample opportunity for interaction with faculty members and fellow students through the use of threaded discussions, chat rooms, journals, e-mail, and collaborative workspaces.

Costs

Undergraduate tuition for the 1999–2000 academic year was $410 per semester credit. In addition, there is a registration fee of $283.50 per semester.

Financial Aid

Naropa College makes every attempt to assist students who do not have the financial resources to accomplish their educational objectives. Naropa offers institutional grants and scholarships, as well as all types of federal student aid. Some financial aid for international students is also available. Approximately 70 percent of Naropa degree-seeking students receive financial assistance in the form of loans, student employment, scholarships, and grants.

Faculty

The Naropa College faculty is distinguished by a wealth of experience in the professional, artistic, and scholastic applications of their disciplines. They are committed to a heartfelt philosophy that brings out the individual insight and intelligence of each student. In addition to the outstanding core faculty, an international community of scholars and artists is consistently drawn to Naropa because of its strong vision and leadership in education. Classes range in size from 8 to 25 students, and Naropa's student-teacher ratio is 10:1.

Student Government

The Student Union of Naropa (SUN) was established in 1989. SUN allows students to participate effectively with faculty members and the administration to ensure that student concerns are addressed and to help shape school policy. Through the formation of student groups, SUN takes active steps to ensure an environment of dignity for all Naropa students.

Admission Requirements

Naropa College seeks students who have a strong appetite for learning and enjoy experiential education in an academic setting. The Admissions Committee considers inquisitiveness and engagement with the work, as well as previous academic achievement, when making admission decisions. A student's statement of interest, interview, and letters of recommendation play important roles in the admissions process. SAT I and ACT scores are not required.

Undergraduate students with fewer than 60 semester credits must apply to Naropa's College Core Program (the lower division). Students with at least 60 semester credits may apply directly to one of Naropa College's nine upper-division majors. A maximum of 60 semester credits are accepted for transfer. In addition, students who are currently enrolled in other institutions are invited to spend a semester or year at Naropa as visiting students.

Application and Information

A completed application for admission into Naropa College includes the following: a completed application form, a $35 application fee (waived for international students), a two- to four-page statement of interest, two letters of recommendation, high school transcripts for all applicants with fewer than 30 semester college credits, and official transcripts from all previous college-level study. Many departments require supplemental application materials and may require a telephone or on-site interview. Students applying as transfer students with more than 60 semester college credits apply directly to the department of their desired major.

Prospective students are strongly encouraged to visit the school. The Office of Admissions hosts an open house each semester, and guided campus tours are offered throughout the year.

Naropa uses a suggested deadline as the initial deadline for receiving completed applications. Any application received after the suggested deadline will be reviewed on a space available basis. The suggested deadline for the fall semester is February 15, and the suggested deadline for the spring semester is October 15. For additional information, prospective students should contact:

Admissions Office
Naropa College
2130 Arapahoe Avenue
Boulder, Colorado 80302-6697
Telephone: 303-546-3572
        800-772-6951 (toll-free outside Colorado)
Fax: 303-546-3583
E-mail: admissions@naropa.edu
World Wide Web: http://www.naropa.edu

A seminar group takes advantage of a fall day on the Naropa campus.

NATIONAL AMERICAN UNIVERSITY
RAPID CITY, SOUTH DAKOTA

The University

The mission of National American University (NAU) is to provide career education to students of diverse backgrounds, interests, and abilities. NAU is a private, multicampus institution of higher education committed to building a learning partnership with students by creating a challenging and effective educational environment. National American University offers educational programs that are responsive to the career interests and objectives of its students and to the needs of employers, government, and society.

The first campus of National American University (formerly called National College) was established in Rapid City, South Dakota, in 1941. The curriculum was focused on business administration. Since then, the curriculum has expanded to include a variety of high-demand career choices, such as athletic training, computers and information systems, occupational therapy assistant studies, paralegal studies, sport management, and veterinary technology. The name change from National College to National American University was a natural evolution in the development and growth of the institution. National American University is accredited by the North Central Association of Colleges and Schools.

Today, more than 800 students are enrolled at the Rapid City campus. The diverse student body consists of students from across the U.S. and around the world. National American University is about giving students the tools they need to pursue their dreams. Whether a student's career path leads to business administration or computer information systems, NAU prepares students to excel in today's competitive marketplace. Nearly every degree program requires an internship prior to graduation, and employment during college within a student's career choice is strongly encouraged and supported by faculty and staff members. Students also have the advantage of classes in their major during their freshman year.

Campus life revolves around student organizations, intramural sports, and varsity athletics. The National American University Mavericks are members of the National Association of Intercollegiate Athletics (NAIA) and the National Intercollegiate Rodeo Association (NIRA). Intercollegiate athletics include men's baseball, men's and women's rodeo, men's and women's soccer, women's softball, and women's volleyball.

Location

National American University is located in a Midwestern community with a population of about 60,000 residents. Rapid City is a retail hub for several Midwestern states. Rapid City's shops, entertainment facilities, and wide array of dining establishments offer a big-city feel without the crime, pollution, and overcrowding. A strong Rapid City economy provides many part-time employment opportunities for college students.

Just 20 minutes away lies one of the most popular tourist areas in the world—Mount Rushmore. Nestled in the majestic Black Hills, Rapid City offers everything from Rushmore Mall and the Dahl Fine Arts Center to wilderness activities such as mountain biking and snow skiing. Rapid City offers the social and cultural diversity that students desire.

In addition to the main campus in Rapid City, NAU has other branch campuses in the following locations: Albuquerque, New Mexico; the Mall of America, Bloomington, Minnesota; Brooklyn Center, Minnesota; Denver and Colorado Springs, Colorado; Sioux Falls, South Dakota; Kansas City, Missouri; and St. Paul, Minnesota. Extension Centers are located at Rio Rancho, New Mexico, and Ellsworth Air Force Base, South Dakota.

Majors and Degrees

At the Rapid City campus, bachelor's and/or associate degrees are offered in accounting, applied management, athletic training, business administration (with emphases in accounting, computer technology, e-commerce, financial management, international business, management, marketing, prelaw, ranch, and sport management), computer information systems, equine management, general education studies, management information systems, web developer/webmaster (Novell and Microsoft certifications), occupational therapy assistant studies, paralegal studies, and veterinary technology.

Similar programs can be found at the branch locations.

Academic Program

In order to obtain a Bachelor of Science degree, students are required to complete all capstone courses with a minimum grade of C, finish with a minimum 2.0 grade point average overall in the major core, and complete 187 quarter hours of credit, with the final 48 coming in residence at NAU.

National American University accepts credits earned through the College-Level Examination Program (CLEP), the Defense Activity for Non-Traditional Education Support (DANTES), and ACT PEP. NAU also has its own credit-by-examination program. Certification exams can be taken on site at the NAU Prometric Testing Centers at either the Rapid City or Sioux Falls campuses.

National American University offers a strong English as a second language (ESL) program for international students.

Selected Internet courses are available to students, allowing them to take classes from around the globe on line.

Academic Facilities

National American University's on-campus library provides students with up-to-date business and paralegal resources. The computer laboratory gives students a state-of-the-art study aid with computerized library search capabilities and Internet access.

Costs

Tuition for the 1999–2000 academic year was $8880 for full-time students (based on 16 credit hours per quarter). The residence hall charge was $1605, and board was $1935. All costs are per-year costs based upon three quarters.

Financial Aid

NAU understands that financing higher education is a concern, and the financial aid staff works with students on affordability options. The University provides assistance in the form of grants, scholarships, work-study, and low-interest loan programs through federal, state, and local sources. When students apply for federal student aid, the information reported is used in a formula established by the U.S. Congress that calculates Expected Family Contribution (EFC). This is an amount that students and their families are expected to contribute toward education. The EFC determines the student's eligibility for federal financial aid programs.

Merit-based academic and athletic scholarships are also available to qualified new and continuing students. In addition, many NAU students work part-time while attending the University.

Faculty

A 15:1 student-faculty ratio promotes individual attention in the classroom. Instructors are individuals with experience in their fields, providing real-world experience with textbook knowledge. Instructors also serve as academic advisers and student organization sponsors, providing invaluable interaction with students. Free tutoring is also available.

Student Government

The Student Senate provides funding for various campus student groups as well as school functions throughout the year.

Admission Requirements

It is recommended that applicants and their families visit National American University to become acquainted with the faculty, staff, and facilities of the University. A personal interview should be scheduled with a member of the admissions staff. The applicant is encouraged to contact the Director of Admissions in advance so that necessary arrangements can be made.

Graduation from high school is a requirement for regular admission to NAU for applicants who are seeking a diploma or degree. Those who have satisfied graduation requirements through the General Educational Development (GED) test are also eligible for regular admission.

If a student chooses not to attend full-time, a schedule may be arranged for one or more courses. Credits earned may be applied to degree or diploma programs.

A special student is one who is not enrolled in a diploma or degree program. Special students are not eligible for receipt of financial aid.

Students who have successfully completed course work at other accredited postsecondary institutions may apply for admission to NAU.

The international student admissions procedure requires that the student complete and submit an admission application along with a $45 application fee. International applicants must obtain official transcripts and diplomas, if earned, from all high schools and colleges attended (non-English documents must be accompanied by certified English translations). They must also present an official copy of one of the following: the Test of English as a Foreign Language (TOEFL) report with a minimum score of 500, an ESL Language Center score of 107 or above, or other comparable demonstration of English proficiency (students who have not yet taken the TOEFL or do not have an ESL proficiency are recommended to attend the ESL Center at the Rapid City campus or contact the respective branch campus for information on the ESL programs in their areas). International applicants must also provide a certified bank statement, an annual statement of earnings, and a letter of financial commitment that indicates the ability to meet financial obligations (students under contracted agreement or written verification of full sponsorship may be exempt from a portion of the above financial certification requirements). They must also provide proof of status with the Immigration and Naturalization Services if currently living in the United States.

National American University may be in contact with respective embassies in assisting students to maintain proper immigration status.

Application and Information

In order for students to apply for admission, an application for admission must be completed and mailed or personally delivered to the Director of Admissions. Application materials may be obtained and arrangements may be made for visiting the University through the Admissions Office. Students may also apply on line at the Web site listed below.

The application for admission must be submitted along with a $25 application fee. A letter of acceptance is mailed as soon as possible. If the applicant is not accepted, the application fee is refunded. Early application is encouraged, especially if campus housing (at the Rapid City location), financial aid, and/or part-time employment are desired.

For applications or more information, students should contact:

Director of Admissions
National American University
321 Kansas City Street
Rapid City, South Dakota 57701
Telephone: 605-394-4827
        800-843-8892 (toll-free)
World Wide Web: http://www.national.edu

National American University students enjoy a break between classes outside the Thomas Jefferson Library.

NATIONAL-LOUIS UNIVERSITY
EVANSTON, CHICAGO, ELGIN, WHEATON, AND WHEELING, ILLINOIS

The University

National-Louis University was founded in Chicago in 1886 as the National College of Education; its mission for the next ninety years was to prepare students for careers in teacher education. During the early 1970s, that mission was expanded to such nonteaching professions as management and business, allied health, human services, and arts and sciences, and in 1982, the School of Arts and Sciences was formed to encompass those programs. The institution expanded further in 1989 with the establishment of the College of Management and Business. Today, National-Louis University offers more than sixty academic programs across a wide range of disciplines. It awards bachelor's, master's, and doctoral degrees as well as the Specialist in Education degree.

The 7,500 students, of whom 3,500 are undergraduates, range from freshmen directly out of high school to employed adults who wish to focus their interests on education of high quality. Varied geographic, ethnic, and economic groups are represented in the student body.

The Office of Student Affairs provides programs and services for the intellectual and personal benefit of all students. These include counseling, health services, new student orientations, student programs, events and activities, student clubs and organizations, several honorary societies, a student newsletter, development programs, residence hall programs, special events, and career development and placement.

Location

The University's main campus is in Evanston, Illinois. Additional campuses are located in Chicago, Elgin, Wheaton, and Wheeling, Illinois; St. Louis, Missouri; Washington, D.C./McLean, Virginia; Tampa/Orlando, Florida; Milwaukee/Beloit, Wisconsin; Atlanta, Georgia; and Heidelberg, Germany. The Evanston campus is located immediately north of Chicago in a community rich in educational, cultural, and entertainment amenities and is easily accessible by public transportation. The Chicago campus is located in the heart of the city's Loop area. The Wheaton campus is located in the rapidly developing western suburbs, and the Wheeling campus is located in the vibrant northwest suburban area. The Elgin campus is located 40 miles west of Chicago. The out-of-state campuses are located in easily accessible areas near major cities.

Majors and Degrees

National-Louis University offers traditional undergraduate programs in the following areas: accounting, business administration (specializations in marketing and international business), computer information and systems management, early childhood education, elementary education, English, human services (areas include alcohol/substance abuse studies, gerontology, psychology, and social and behavioral studies), liberal arts studies (majors include anthropology, applied economics, biology, English, mathematics/quantitative studies, multicultural studies, psychology, psychology/human development, science, social science, theater arts, and theater/fine arts), mathematics/quantitative studies, medical technology, psychology, radiation therapy, respiratory care, and theater arts. All programs provide a strong foundation in the liberal arts.

Degree-completion undergraduate programs geared toward working adults are offered in the areas of applied behavioral sciences, health-care leadership, and management.

Academic Program

The Evanston, Chicago, and Wheaton campuses offer most of the programs in the liberal arts, human services, and education. The Chicago campus offers accounting, business administration, and computer information and systems management. Select programs are offered at other campuses.

Students who are interested in teacher education are initially admitted to the College of Arts and Sciences and apply for admission to the National College of Education after the completion of 50 quarter hours in general studies. The baccalaureate degree in early childhood education offers a concentration in psychology/human development, and elementary education concentrations include anthropology, art, biology, mathematics, mathematics/elementary, mathematics/middle school, psychology/human development, psychology/nonspecific, science, sociology, sociology/anthropology, and theater arts. The Chicago campus emphasizes a concentration in multicultural studies and prepares students specifically for teaching in an urban setting. The education programs are enriched by an on-campus preK–8 demonstration school on the Evanston campus.

National-Louis University's human services programs are designed to train professionals who wish to pursue counseling careers through direct-care, agency, community service, and/or administrative settings. The professional studies sequence begins in the junior year and includes practicums in clinical affiliates. Sequences include alcoholism/substance abuse studies, general studies, gerontology, psychology, and social and behavioral studies (nonclinical).

The Allied Health Department prepares students for initial entry into health professions as well as career advancement. The nationally accredited medical technology, respiratory care, and radiation therapy programs provide students with technical and clinical training and prepare them for board certification. Clinical affiliates include many of the fine hospitals in the Chicago area. The health-care leadership program is designed as a degree-completion program; students must possess a license or certificate in one or more of the allied health professions to qualify for admission.

Academic Facilities

The main campus in Evanston is located on a 4-acre site that includes classrooms, offices, a bookstore, the 155,000-volume University Library, the Baker Demonstration School, the Weinstein Center for the Performing Arts, and the Baker Residence Hall. The Chicago campus at 18 South Michigan Avenue occupies 5½ floors of a historic landmark office building. Facilities include classrooms, offices, developmental skills laboratories, and the Language Institute. The Wheaton campus is housed in the historic former DuPage County courthouse complex. Along with classrooms and offices, the Wheaton campus is the site for the Center for Learning, the Teacher Leadership Center, and the CAS Counseling Center. The Wheeling campus, located in a modern three-story office building in the northwest suburbs, is the location of the majority of the University's administrative offices as well as classroom facilities. Computer laboratories and interactive video classrooms are located on all five of the Chicago-area campuses. Branch libraries are located in Chicago, Wheaton, and Wheeling, and electronic library access is available at all other campuses. A full range of University services are available at every campus.

Costs

Annual full-time undergraduate tuition in 1998–99 at National-Louis University was $12,510. Room and board fees ranged from $5118 to $6984 annually. In addition, students should allow for books, laboratory fees, and transportation costs.

Financial Aid

Approximately 85 percent of the current freshman class receive financial aid from the following sources: scholarships, grants (including the Federal Pell Grant and the Federal Supplemental Education Opportunity Grant), loans (including Federal Perkins Loans), and campus employment (including Federal Work-Study). Merit-based awards are made to qualified students who rank in the top quarter of their high school class as well as to qualified transfer students. Financial aid packages are renewable yearly and may be adjusted in accordance with changes in need. Non-need scholarships are available to students who meet prescribed academic and professional criteria.

Faculty

Both the size of the school and the system of evaluation result in a very close relationship between students and faculty members. All members of the teaching faculty have at least a master's degree, and 65 percent have earned doctorates. Faculty members serve willingly as advisers to student organizations. In addition, they are asked regularly to contribute to student-formed committees. Department chairmen act as academic advisers to students concentrating in their fields.

Student Government

The Student Senate at National-Louis University is active in all areas of college life. Through the senate, student representatives hold seats on every policymaking council and committee on campus. The student voice is heard and respected by the administration. Just as there are voting faculty members in the student government, students also have a vote in the Faculty Association. The residence hall is run by students as well. The Baker Association of Resident Students forms the main judicial and legislative branch of residence hall government. An executive group with combined student-faculty memberships forms the other branch.

Admission Requirements

The admission process is designed to insure that students' needs are properly identified and matched to appropriate degree programs. The admission process seeks to consider individual students through a personalized review, which takes into account prior academic record, personal and professional achievement, and student goals and objectives. Many programs have specific admission requirements. Admission to the University does not guarantee students admission to the program of their choice. Applicants are not discriminated against on the grounds of age, sex, religion, race, or ethnic origin.

Application and Information

Prospective freshmen must submit an application, a $25 application fee, a high school transcript, and ACT or SAT I scores (if under 21 years of age). Transfer applicants must include records of all previous college work along with the application, the application fee, and proof of high school graduation (if entering with fewer than 15 quarter hours of transferable credit). Applicants to certain allied health and human services programs are required to submit two letters of recommendation. Personal interviews, though not required for regular admission, are strongly encouraged. All new undergraduates are required to complete a skills assessment prior to registration. In addition to an application, application fee, and official secondary and postsecondary transcripts with English translation and credentials evaluation, international students must show financial affidavits for all financial responsibilities.

National-Louis University operates on a system of rolling admission and accepts applications all year round. Applicants are usually notified of the admission decision within two weeks of submitting a completed application.

Inquiries should be addressed to:

Office of Enrollment Services
National-Louis University
2840 Sheridan Road
Evanston, Illinois 60201
Telephone: 800-443-5522 Ext. 5151 (toll-free)
E-mail: nluinfo@wheeling1.nl.edu

The Evanston campus.

NAZARETH COLLEGE OF ROCHESTER
ROCHESTER, NEW YORK

The College
Nazareth College is an independent, coeducational, liberal arts college that offers career programs solidly based in the liberal arts. Its suburban campus is located in Pittsford in western upstate New York, approximately 7 miles from the city of Rochester. Founded in 1924, the College has conferred more than 11,000 baccalaureate and master's degrees. Of the more than 2,900 men and women enrolled at Nazareth, 1,550 are undergraduates.

Eighteen buildings of traditional and contemporary design are conveniently situated on the College's 75-acre parklike campus. The Otto A. Shults Community Center, housing a 20,000-square-foot gymnasium, the student union, a multifaith religious center, a 25-meter swimming pool, the newly expanded fitness center, and student personnel offices, is the hub of on-campus student life. The resident students, constituting 61 percent of the undergraduate population, are housed in nine separate dormitories. As an alternative to traditional campus housing, foreign language majors may live in La Maison Française, which is maintained by the language department. The Casa Italiana and Casa Hispana serve as facilities for social, cultural, and academic programs reflecting Italian and Spanish heritages, respectively.

Intercollegiate and intramural athletics are fully represented in the areas of men's and women's basketball, lacrosse, soccer, swimming and diving, and tennis; women's field hockey and volleyball; and a variety of other NCAA-recognized sports programs.

Location
Rochester, a city of more than 300,000 people, is the third-largest city in New York State and the site of cultural, educational, and industrial centers. Located on the shore of Lake Ontario, the city is noted for the Eastman School of Music, the Strasenburg Planetarium, and the International Museum of Photography at the George Eastman House. Rochester is the world headquarters of Eastman Kodak and Bausch & Lomb and the site of a major Xerox facility. It is only 20 minutes from beautiful mountains, lakes, and recreational areas, where students can enjoy various outdoor activities, including skiing, hiking, water sports, and camping. The city supports professional sports teams in baseball, hockey, lacrosse, and soccer.

Majors and Degrees
Nazareth College awards Bachelor of Arts and Bachelor of Science degrees in accounting, American studies, applied music, art (studio), art education, art history, biochemistry, biology, business administration, business education, chemistry, economics, English, environmental science, fine arts, foreign languages (French, German, Italian, and Spanish), history, international studies, management science, mathematics, music, music education, music theory, music therapy, philosophy, physical therapy, political science, psychology, religious studies, social science, social work, sociology, speech pathology, and theater arts. A Bachelor of Music degree is also granted. A B.S. program is offered in nursing for registered nurses only. Preprofessional programs are available in dentistry, law, and medicine. Teacher certification (K–6 and 7–12) is offered with many majors. Certification in learning disabilities is available through an undergraduate program in special education. Certification for K–12 is offered in art education, music education, and speech pathology (communication sciences and disorders).

Academic Program
To qualify for a degree, a candidate must fulfill the core curriculum requirements of the College as well as those of the major department or area of concentration. The candidate must also earn a minimum of 120 semester credits and satisfy a comprehensive test requirement in the major field during the senior year.

Off-Campus Arrangements
Nazareth College offers Junior Year Abroad programs in affiliation with the Université de Haute Bretagne in Rennes, France; the Institute of Spanish Students in Valencia, Spain; and the Universita degli G. D'Annunzio in Pescara, Italy. Students need not be language majors to take advantage of this exceptional program. Language students taking German, may arrange to participate in approved international study programs through consultation with their advisers.

Nazareth College is a member of the Rochester Area Colleges, a consortium that includes Rochester Institute of Technology, the State University of New York College at Geneseo, and the University of Rochester, among others. Through this consortium, Nazareth College students can cross-register for credit in up to two courses per semester at any of the member institutions on a space-available basis.

Academic Facilities
Most of Nazareth's classrooms, laboratories, and studios are in Smyth Hall, the award-winning Arts Center, which houses art, music, and theater facilities as well as a 1,200-seat auditorium within its three wings. Recently expanded Carroll Hall houses speech pathology, physical therapy, counseling, and health services. Also recently expanded, Lorette Wilmot Library houses more than 278,200 volumes and has extensive resources in such areas as women's studies, education, minority issues, and religions in America. The library subscribes to approximately 2,010 periodicals and other serials. The building has seating for 450 students and includes a large number of individual carrels. The library also has a fine collection of lecture tapes and a growing collection of musical and spoken-word disks and tapes. The Rare Book Room is distinguished by special collections of works by Maurice Baring, Hilaire Belloc, Gilbert Keith Chesterton, and the Sitwells. The library is currently enlarging its resources and services in the nonprint media. In addition, the College's membership in the regional consortium and the Online Computer Library Center provides students with access to the resources of 1,300 other academic and research libraries.

Costs
Total costs for 2000–01 are estimated at $20,975. This includes $14,070 for tuition, $6470 for room and board, and $435 for the required fees. The total does not include books, personal expenses, or transportation (if applicable). All fees are subject to change; up-to-date information can be obtained from the Admissions Office.

Financial Aid

Nazareth College endeavors to meet financial need as demonstrated on the Free Application for Federal Student Aid (FAFSA). The FAFSA should be submitted by February 15 of the year in which the student intends to enroll. The CSS PROFILE is required of early decision applicants only and should be submitted by November 15. Financial assistance is available through grants, loans, employment, and scholarships. Sources of aid include the Federal Pell Grant, New York Tuition Assistance, Federal Perkins Loan, and Federal Work-Study programs; the New York State Higher Education Services Corporation; and Nazareth College merit scholarships and grants.

Faculty

The full-time faculty members in the various academic departments hold advanced degrees from more than 100 institutions throughout the United States and abroad. Nintey-six percent of the faculty members hold the highest degree offered in their field of study. The student-faculty ratio of approximately 13:1 and an average class size of 25 ensure that students receive the individual attention that only a small college can offer.

Student Government

The Undergraduate Association of Nazareth College is the vehicle through which students can express the need for and initiate change within the College community. It is also responsible for the disbursement of funds, generated from the undergraduate activities fee, to various activities and social/cultural clubs.

Admission Requirements

Nazareth College welcomes applicants of all ages and educational backgrounds. Students of any race, color, sex, or national or ethnic origin are admitted to all of the rights, privileges, programs, and activities generally accorded or made available to students at the College. Nazareth College does not discriminate on the basis of race, color, sex, or national or ethnic origin in the administration of its educational policies, scholarship and loan programs, and sports and other school-administered programs.

Recommended academic preparation includes courses in English, college-preparatory mathematics, social studies, a foreign language, and science. Although the Admissions Committee gives primary consideration to academic achievement and potential for collegiate success, it also considers talent in art, drama, or music and involvement in cocurricular activities. A personal interview, although not required, is recommended, as it allows the applicant to view the campus and facilities, talk with students and faculty members, and meet with an admissions counselor.

Nazareth College is pleased to consider applications from students in good standing at both two- and four-year colleges and universities. A GPA of 2.5 or better is expected. Transfer applicants who hold, or will hold prior to registration, the Associate in Arts (A.A.) or the Associate in Science (A.S.) degree from a fully accredited college may transfer a maximum of 60 semester hours of credit and enter with full junior status. Transfer applicants who hold, or will hold prior to registration, the Associate in Applied Science (A.A.S.) degree or the Associate of Occupational Studies (A.O.S.) degree from a fully accredited college or institute will have these credits evaluated on a course-by-course basis. Careful advisement on tailoring programs for holders of these degrees is offered by Nazareth College.

Application and Information

Regular decision applicants for the fall semester should submit the application form, transcripts, standardized test scores, an essay, recommendations, and a $40 application fee by March 1 (by November 15 for early decision). Notification begins February 1 for regular decision applicants and December 15 for early decision applicants.

For an application packet or information about a campus tour and interview, applicants should contact:

Dean of Admissions
Nazareth College
4245 East Avenue
Rochester, New York 14618-3790
Telephone: 716-389-2860
        800-462-3944 (toll-free in New York State)

NEUMANN COLLEGE
ASTON, PENNSYLVANIA

The College

Neumann College, a Catholic coeducational institution in the Franciscan tradition, recognizes the value of developing intellectual excellence, professional competence, and strong community life. As a college that balances the liberal arts with the professions, Neumann was founded to meet and expand the educational and professional horizons of men and women. With the addition of the Living and Learning Center, multimedia-capable residences, Neumann College is positioned to serve a more diverse geographic and demographic population.

Founded and sponsored by the Sisters of St. Francis of Philadelphia, the College is committed to a varied student body and welcomes students of all denominations. Current enrollment is 1,624.

The Life Center houses the Meagher Theatre, the Bruder Athletic Center, and the Crossroads Cafe dining facility by Sodexho-Marriott, Inc. Intercollegiate sports include women's basketball, cross-country, field hockey, lacrosse, soccer, softball, tennis, and volleyball and men's baseball, basketball, cross-country, golf, ice hockey, lacrosse, soccer, and tennis. Neumann College competes as a member of the National Collegiate Athletic Association (NCAA) Division III, the Pennsylvania Athletic Conference (PAC), and the Eastern Collegiate Athletic Conference (ECAC). Intramural sports are available to all members of the campus community.

The Living and Learning Center is designed to provide a state-of-the-art residential experience, with a focus on education within a real-world living environment. Technologically smart, the center connects students to both faculty members and friends via the Internet, which is available in every suite and apartment. The system provides full access to and knowledge of campus resources and activities, as well as activities and resources worldwide. The center also houses a separate computer lab, a fitness center, a reflection room, various study rooms with warming kitchens for group study or meetings, and a laundry.

The College provides a full range of services to students, including career placement, which averages above 95 percent in the student's field of interest; career and personal counseling; a tutoring program; and health services.

Neumann students are involved in a wide variety of campus and community activities. Major and special interest clubs are available for student participation. Clubs bring together students who share common interests and help foster new friendships.

At Neumann, the spiritual dimension of one's life is recognized as integral to total human development. The Ministry Team provides a pastoral presence on campus and promotes a sense of community. The entire College community is invited to serve the needs of the poor and neglected in society through various outreach programs, with special attention to the need for peace and justice in the world today.

Neumann is well positioned to respond to the academic and extracurricular needs of students who are of traditional or nontraditional age, commuters or residents, and full-time or part-time.

In addition to undergraduate programs, Neumann confers master's degrees in education, nursing, pastoral counseling, physical therapy, and sports management.

Location

Neumann, with a beautiful suburban campus in Aston, Delaware County, Pennsylvania, is a short distance from Philadelphia; Wilmington, Delaware; southern New Jersey; and Maryland. It is easily accessible from major arteries such as I-95, Route 476, Route 1, and the Pennsylvania Turnpike.

Majors and Degrees

Neumann offers strong academic majors leading to a Bachelor of Arts degree or a Bachelor of Science degree in accounting, biological science, business administration, communication arts, computer and information management, education, English, environmental studies, international business/international studies (dual degree), liberal arts, marketing, nursing, political science, psychology, and sport management. The education programs lead to teacher certification in Pennsylvania and reciprocating states, with secondary certification in biology/general science, English, or social studies. Preprofessional programs in law and medicine are also available. An accelerated evening program for adults using a 6-credit seminar format leads to an Associate of Arts, Bachelor of Arts, or Bachelor of Science degree in liberal studies.

Academic Program

The academic program at Neumann College is composed of a core curriculum (required of all students), a major area of study (chosen by each student), and a wide range of elective offerings. Students may also choose a minor area of study. The College's broad base of liberal arts offerings prepares students for the intellectual and social challenges that they will face in the employment marketplace and throughout their lives. The core is intended to provide basic knowledge of the liberal arts and sciences; develop verbal, written, and symbolic communication skills; and stimulate interest in a broad range of topics for the purpose of enhancing the individual's contributions to society, thereby enabling the individual to realize full human potential.

Classroom instruction is supplemented by cooperative education through which juniors and seniors can earn credit for working in a job related to their career interest. Fieldwork and student teaching are required of all education majors. Clinical practice for the nursing major occurs in a variety of health-care facilities in the tristate area.

The honors program is an opportunity for academically talented students to explore imaginative and innovative perspectives on learning. It is also an opportunity to stimulate and motivate students to expand their knowledge and interest and to strive for greater excellence. Moreover, it is a reward for prior perseverance and dedication as well as an obligation to utilize skills and abilities in service to others. Admission to the honors program is by invitation.

Neumann College has transfer articulation agreements with numerous colleges throughout the area.

Academic Facilities

The Child Development Center is a state-of-the-art, octagonal-shaped building, specifically designed to house an educational program for preschoolers. As a state-licensed day-care facility, it enrolls children of Neumann students, the faculty, and the community. The Child Development Center is part of the Division of Education and Human Services. Students enrolled in education courses use the center for observation, practical experience, and student teaching.

The Academic Computer Center is located on the ground floor of the College. The computers are viewed as tools to support all fields of study and all students and faculty members. Neumann College has installed a Local Area Network (LAN) that connects various computers and provides shared services such as printing, e-mail, and support for the instructional use of computers by providing for the sharing of files. Computers are available to all students. Both systems have CD-ROM drives. Software related to various academic disciplines are available. Access to the World Wide Web and the Internet is available.

The Learning Assistance Center is a service that enables students to meet Neumann's academic standards and successfully attain their personal educational goals.

The College library contains a balanced collection of more than 90,000 volumes and 700 periodical subscriptions. Private study rooms and conference rooms are available for both student and faculty use. In addition to traditional media services support, a full-color video studio and a graphics production area are available. Serving as a comprehensive resource for students, other holdings include Neumann's online catalog system, Francis, which is accessible via the World Wide Web; a video and film collection of more than 1,200 items; and nearly 10,000 sound recordings. The library is a member of the Tri-State College Library Cooperative, the Consortium for Health Information and Library Services, SEPCHE, and the Online College Library Computer, which provide additional convenient resources for students. The library subscribes to various online and CD-ROM computer research services.

Costs

Tuition for full-time students (12 to 18 credits per semester) in 2000–01 is $6875 per semester. There is a general fee of $285 per semester that covers library services, counseling and testing services, athletics, accident insurance, health services, special lectures, parking, the student government fee, and an I.D. card. Room and board are $3250 per semester.

Financial Aid

Typically, about 75 percent of Neumann students receive some form of financial aid—scholarships, grants, and student loans—for a total of almost $12 million. The College contributes approximately $4 million to the total.

Neumann offers a variety of renewable scholarships each year to entering full-time freshmen. Interested applicants should contact the Office of Admissions and Financial Aid as soon as possible to determine eligibility.

In addition to Neumann scholarships, funds are available through the Federal Pell Grant, Federal Supplemental Educational Opportunity Grant, and Federal Work-Study Programs. Many states provide grant money to attend Neumann (non-Pennsylvania residents should check with their state's higher education agency for details). Veterans Administration benefits can be received by qualified veterans or their dependents. Federal Stafford Student Loans and Federal PLUS Program loans are available and can be applied for through Neumann's preferred lender or any participating bank. Neumann also offers institutional need-based grants. All students requesting financial aid must complete the Free Application for Federal Student Aid (FAFSA) each year to determine eligibility. In order to expedite processing, the FAFSA must be submitted by March 15 for the following school year. Financial aid funds are renewable annually based on need as determined by the FAFSA results.

Faculty

Neumann students describe faculty members as sincere, hard working, determined, and energetic. Faculty members view themselves, first and foremost, as teachers and are proud partners in their students' journeys toward self-discovery. Each student has a faculty adviser who assists in arranging a program designed to meet the student's educational goals; many faculty members serve as moderators of student clubs. The student-faculty ratio is 13:1.

Student Government

The Student Government Association (SGA) is the representative body for all students. Its function is to implement the aims and purposes of the College, foster cooperation in interstudent relationships, assist the College in being responsive to the needs of the student body, and encourage personal responsibility for an intelligent system of student self-government. Through the Student Activities Board, social functions are planned throughout the year. Students serve on various College committees, including Student Affairs Committee of the Board, Academic Advising Committee, Honors Program Committee, Registration/Orientation Task Force, and Student Judicial Board. For full-time students, a Student Government Association fee of $35 per semester is required.

Admission Requirements

Neumann has a rolling admission policy and accepts applications throughout the year. Applicants are considered on the basis of high school record, SAT or ACT scores, recommendations, class rank, and other indicators of potential to succeed in college-level studies. Applications for admission are reviewed without regard to sex, race, creed, color, national origin, age, sexual orientation, pregnancy, military status, religion, or disability. Applicants should be graduates of an accredited high school (or present equivalent credentials) and have a minimum of 16 units of high school course work distributed as follows: 4 in English, 2 to 3 in science, 2 in mathematics, 2 in social studies, 2 in foreign language, and 4 in electives. Students intending to pursue a major in biology or clinical laboratory science must have at least 1 year of high school biology and chemistry, and high school physics is also highly recommended.

Neumann participates in the Advanced Placement (AP) Program and the College-Level Examination Program (CLEP). Students with superior ability and a sound academic background may begin College studies at the end of the junior year in high school.

An interview and tour of the campus are highly recommended for all prospective students and parents. Tours will be scheduled at the convenience of the interested student.

Application and Information

Applicants for freshman admission are requested to have SAT or ACT scores and high school transcripts sent to the Office of Admissions and Financial Aid. A nonrefundable $35 application fee should accompany the completed application.

Neumann College welcomes applications from students who have attended or are currently attending either two-year or four-year regionally accredited institutions of higher learning.

For further information, students should contact:

Scott Bogard, Executive Director
Office of Admissions and Financial Aid
Neumann College
One Neumann Drive
Aston, Pennsylvania 19014-1298
Telephone: 610-558-5616
        800-9NEUMAN (toll-free)
E-mail: neumann@neumann.edu

NEWBERRY COLLEGE
NEWBERRY, SOUTH CAROLINA

The College
A private undergraduate liberal arts institution established in 1856, Newberry College is affiliated with the Evangelical Lutheran Church in America. With a mission focused on educating the whole person, Newberry epitomizes the small-college amenities of personal attention, easy rapport between students and faculty, and a supportive environment for academic, personal, and social development.

Newberry College's student body is made up of about 750 men and women from twenty-four states and several countries. About 48 percent are women and 52 percent are men. Seventy percent of the students live in College residence halls; others live off campus or commute from home.

Students participate in a variety of College-sponsored activities, including five national fraternities and four national sororities; eight music-related organizations; three campus publications; musical theater and drama productions; intramural sports; ethnic, political, and religious organizations; honor, service, and leadership societies; the Newberry College Student Government Association (student government); the Newberry College Student Ambassadors; and special interest groups.

The Newberry College Indians maintain a full schedule of NCAA Division II intercollegiate athletic competition in men's baseball, basketball, cross-country, football, golf, soccer, and tennis and women's basketball, cross-country, golf, soccer, tennis, softball, and volleyball.

The College's buildings represent a pleasant combination of antebellum and contemporary architecture. Four buildings around the quadrangle make up the Newberry College Historic District and are listed on the National Register of Historic Places. Wiles Chapel, which contains the College Theatre, exemplifies modern Gothic architecture with some influence from the Prairie school. The physical education and athletic complex, including the 1,600-seat Eleazer Arena, was completed in 1982. The Casey Student Center, which adjoins the athletic complex on the northern edge of the campus, serves as the location for the Student Affairs Office, Career Services Center, College Bookstore, and Presidential Dining Room.

Location
Listed as one of the best 100 small towns in the United States in which to live, Newberry is situated in the gently rolling hills of the South Carolina Piedmont, with average winter temperatures ranging from highs of 56 to 63 degrees. Newberry is home to approximately 10,000 permanent residents. The city was founded in 1794 and is replete with historically significant homes and buildings. It is easily accessible via three exits on Interstate 26 and lies at the juncture of U.S. 76 and South Carolina 34 and 121. Newberry's closest metropolitan neighbor is Columbia, the state capital and its largest city, which is approximately 40 miles southeast. The Greenville/Spartanburg metropolitan area is 1 hour northwest of Newberry. Other points of interest within easy driving distance are Myrtle Beach and the Grand Strand (3 hours); Charleston (2½ hours); Hilton Head (3½ hours); Charlotte, North Carolina (1½ hours); the Great Smoky Mountains (2 hours); and Atlanta, Georgia (3½ hours).

Majors and Degrees
The Bachelor of Science (B.S.) degree is awarded in accounting, arts management, biology, business administration, chemistry, elementary education, mathematics, mathematics/computer science, physical education (including athletic training, leisure services, sports management, and teacher certification), special education/learning disabilities, and veterinary technology.

The Bachelor of Arts (B.A.) degree is awarded in art, communications, economics, English, foreign languages (French, German, and Spanish), history, international government and commerce, music (including applied music, music literature, and music theory), political science, psychology, religion and philosophy, sociology, and theater/speech communications.

The Bachelor of Music (B.M.) degree is awarded in music performance. The Bachelor of Music Education (B.M.E.) degree is awarded in choral music and instrumental music in teacher certification.

Preprofessional programs are offered in dentistry, environmental sciences, forestry, law, medicine, nursing, pharmacy, and theology. Nondegree programs of study are available in Chinese, community service, military science, physics, and professional writing and editing.

Newberry offers 3-2 dual-degree programs in engineering with Clemson University and in forestry with Duke University. Special dual-degree programs in a number of health-related professions are available with the Medical University of South Carolina.

Academic Program
A student must satisfactorily complete a minimum of 126 semester hours of course work with a minimum cumulative grade point average of 2.0 (on a 4.0 scale) to be eligible for a Newberry bachelor's degree. A core curriculum of 43–50 semester-hours is required of all students regardless of their declared major(s) and includes course work in the following disciplines: history and social sciences, humanities, natural sciences, English, foreign language, mathematics, religion, speech, physical education, and College Life, a freshman experience course. In addition, students must also fulfill three fine arts and lecture requirements per semester. The Summerland Honors Community program, a four-year interdisciplinary core program, is offered to gifted students.

Students may receive advanced-placement and college credit by participating in the Advanced Placement (AP) Program, the International Baccalaureate (I.B.) Program, or the College-Level Examination Program (CLEP). Students should consult the latest edition of the Newberry College catalog or contact the Office of Admissions for exact requirements.

The College operates on the two-semester calendar, consisting of a fall semester and a spring semester, each lasting sixteen weeks. The fall semester begins in late August and ends in mid-December; the spring semester begins in early January and ends in early May, with a one-week spring break in March. The College's summer session consists of two 5-week terms. During the fall and spring semesters, the normal class load ranges from 15 to 19 hours; for the summer session, two courses per term is normal.

Off-Campus Arrangements
Newberry's international studies program for sophomores and juniors gives qualified students the opportunity to study for a summer, a semester, or a full academic year in selected international colleges and universities as part of Newberry's regular academic program. Although this program is open to students in all majors, some proficiency in the language spoken in the host country is required.

Academic Facilities

Langford Communications Center contains state-of-the-art equipment and resources for the student of radio and television communications. As an Internet node with its own World Wide Web site, the College can extend free in-room dialing access for students using the Internet. Another modern building is dedicated to the study of music. The recently refurbished Wessels Library contains nearly 100,000 books, sound and video recordings, CD-ROMs, and online electronic resources. Complete facilities for the use of audiovisual materials are provided. The library also subscribes to more than 450 magazines, newspapers, and scholarly journals. The College Archives are also displayed in the library. In addition to Wessels, students may use a smaller library that is housed in the Music Department in the Alumni Music Center.

Costs

In 1999–2000, tuition and fees were $13,952 and room and board were $3959. The total cost for a residential student was $17,911. The College estimated annual personal expenses (including books, supplies, automobile registration, and other costs) to be $2200. Once they are accepted for admission, students are requested to submit a $200 deposit, which is refundable through May 1 for fall semester admission and December 1 for spring semester admission.

Financial Aid

More than 90 percent of students at Newberry receive some form of financial assistance. Student aid counselors are available to work with students and families to design financial aid packages that make a Newberry education affordable. Assistance is available in the form of scholarships, loans, and campus employment based on need or merit. Newberry College awards more than 200 endowed scholarships, including the prestigious Founders and Presidential Scholarship awards. Music, theater, and athletic scholarships are also available for men and women. Residents of South Carolina usually qualify for a South Carolina Tuition Grant. Communing members of a Lutheran church may receive a variety of tuition and scholarship grants from the Lutheran Scholarship Program. To apply for student aid, students should complete the Free Application for Federal Student Aid (FAFSA), which is available from high school counselors or from the Newberry student aid office.

Faculty

The student-faculty ratio is 12:1. Classes are small, and the easy interchange of ideas is a constant stimulus to both student and teacher. Seventy-four percent of the full-time faculty members have earned doctorates or terminal degrees. No classes are taught by graduate students.

Student Government

The Newberry College Student Government Association (NCSGA) is composed of students elected to the Newberry Student Senate. Through its committee assignments, it assists in the formulation and implementation of College policies. The NCSGA officers are selected through campuswide elections, and senators and other representatives are elected by the various campus constituencies.

Admission Requirements

In determining the admission status of all applicants to Newberry College, the following factors are taken into consideration: SAT I or ACT, grade point average on academic courses, predicted first-semester college grade point average, high school rank, type of course work pursued, cocurricular activities, relationship(s) to Newberry College alumni, and other relevant factors such as part-time employment.

Students whose profiles fall below acceptable standards may be referred to the Admissions Committee. This committee, composed of members of the College faculty and administration, carefully deliberates before determining admission status. Upon review, applicants may be regularly admitted, admitted with a reduced course load, have their applications held for additional grades or test scores, or be denied admission.

As soon as possible following the admissions decision, the applicant is notified by mail. Acceptance of the applicant is always contingent upon successful completion of course work in progress. Following high school graduation, an additional official final transcript bearing the date of graduation is required.

Application and Information

The College operates on a rolling admission basis, notifying most applicants of their status within three weeks after the application is complete. The application for admission, along with a $30 nonrefundable fee, should be accompanied by official high school and/or college transcripts, SAT I and/or ACT scores, letters of recommendation, and other supporting materials that may be required by the Director of Admissions.

Interviews can be scheduled through the Office of Admissions. Although walk-in visitors are welcome, a visitor's special needs and desires can best be met if he or she makes an appointment. Saturday morning visits are available by appointment only. In addition, the Office of Admissions hosts two open-house functions each year for the benefit of prospective students and parents.

Students are encouraged to apply for admission on the Internet and may do so at the World Wide Web address given below.

For additional information, students should contact:

Office of Admissions
Newberry College
2100 College Street
Newberry, South Carolina 29108
Telephone: 803-321-5127
          800-845-4955 (toll-free in the United States and Canada)
World Wide Web: http://www.newberry.edu

Newberry College's Holland Hall.

NEWBURY COLLEGE
BROOKLINE, MASSACHUSETTS

The College
Newbury College is a private coeducational college that offers a four-year bachelor's degree program in selected areas as well as a host of two-year associate degree programs. Nearly 800 men and women are currently enrolled as full-time day students, and the total College enrollment is near 2,600. Approximately 40 percent of the College's day students come from states other than Massachusetts. The College provides housing for men and women on campus. Residence halls differ in age and design, providing a variety of styles. Approximately 35 percent of the day students live in the College's residence halls.

Founded in 1962, Newbury College has grown and changed dramatically in the past thirty-five years. However, its educational philosophy remains the same: to prepare graduates to succeed in their chosen career. Newbury recently inaugurated Dr. Roy J. Nirschel, the second president in the history of the College. All of the College's regionally accredited academic programs feature hands-on training to sharpen job skills. The College is accredited by the New England Association of Schools and Colleges. The interior design program is accredited by the Foundation for Interior Design and Education Research (FIDER).

Newbury College has an active student body and offers more than twenty student clubs and organizations in which to join. Newbury is a member of NCAA Division III and offers a variety of intercollegiate sports.

Location
Situated only minutes from downtown Boston, Newbury College's Brookline campus encompasses 11 landscaped acres in a beautiful residential neighborhood with easy access to public transportation, first-run cinemas, and prestigious shopping centers.

Boston is the cultural, business, and education capital of New England. The city provides students with important educational resources and the opportunity to bring career goals into focus through internships and field trips. Just as important is the fact that Boston is the home of the world's largest and most diverse population of college students.

Majors and Degrees
Degrees are offered within the School of Arts, Science and Technology; the School of Business and Management; the School of Health Professions; and the Program in Culinary Arts. Bachelor of Science (B.S.) degrees within the School of Arts, Science and Technology include a Bachelor of Science in legal studies, with concentrations in criminal justice, paralegal studies, and a 3+3 program in prelaw. A Bachelor of Science degree is also offered in computer science. Bachelor's degrees within business management include concentrations in accounting, culinary management, general management, hospitality management, human resource management, international business management, marketing, and retail management. The School of Health Professions offers a B.S. in health-care management. An associate degree is offered within the Program in Culinary Arts. Newbury College also offers a host of associate degrees.

Newbury's Continuing Education Program offers both evening and weekend classes for adult learners at nine conveniently located classroom centers throughout eastern Massachusetts.

Academic Program
Working with an adviser, students plan their course of study around a prescribed major core. Program requirements establish a framework that includes intensive study in the major area where hands-on training is stressed as well as course work in general education. By fulfilling the general education requirements and selecting courses outside the major, students receive a well-rounded education. At least 121 credit hours, usually five courses per semester, are required for graduation in most bachelor degree programs. At least 60 credit hours are required for the associate degree.

Internships are an integral part of the academic programs and provide students with on-the-job experience in their chosen field.

The College observes a two-semester academic calendar, with first-semester examinations falling before the December holiday break. There is also a summer session.

Academic Facilities
The Newbury College Library, with its new $4-million, 16,000-square-foot addition, houses 31,825 volumes and subscribes to 1,010 periodicals. In 1998, the college also completed renovations to the college dining hall, student lounge, and the college bookstore, which is operated by Barnes & Noble bookstores. Special learning facilities include a staffed Academic Resource Center, a computer resource center, an in-house television and radio studio, a hospitality center equipped with state-of-the-art airline and hotel reservation systems, and seven fully equipped culinary arts kitchens.

Costs
For 2000–01, the total cost of a year in most programs at Newbury is estimated to be as follows: tuition, $13,050; room and board, $7350. There is an annual $550 comprehensive fee. Part-time day students and Continuing Education Students pay tuition based on per-credit hour.

Financial Aid
It is the College's hope that all qualified and motivated students have the opportunity to pursue a college degree. To this end, Newbury endeavors to meet the financial needs of all students who qualify for financial aid. In order to apply for financial aid, applicants are required to complete the FAFSA. If eligible for federal financial aid, this could be in the form of grants, scholarships, loans, or a work-study program. The College also offers merit-based scholarships, which are determined by a Scholarship Committee. These scholarships are based on academic history, leadership potential, school or community involvement, and SAT scores. These include Presidential, Distinguished, and Newbury Scholarships.

Faculty
Newbury has a total faculty of more than 507 members, 47 of whom are full-time. A low student-faculty ratio of 17:1 encourages student and faculty interaction. Faculty members are skilled professionals with years of experience and expertise

in their fields. They also serve as academic advisers, helping students explore career options outside of the classroom.

Student Government

The Student Government Association (SGA) at Newbury College has an elected president, vice president, treasurer, and secretary who represent the student body. Working with the administration and staff, representatives of the SGA help to plan activities and provide a means of communication within the College structure. The SGA has the responsibility of administering the calendar of school events, coordinating the expenditures of the activities budget, and planning the College activities program. All full-time students belong to the SGA.

Admission Requirements

The Committee on Admission considers each applicant on an individual basis. Requirements include a $50 application fee, official transcripts from all previous secondary and applicable college study, and two letters of recommendation; a college essay and SAT I scores are highly recommended. The TOEFL exam is required for all international applicants. Students must file the official Application for Admission, or they may apply over the Internet. (see Web site, below)

Application and Information

Application deadlines for freshmen applicants are as follows: early application deadline, December 1; and regular decision application deadline, March 15. Transfer applicants may apply on a rolling basis. In order to enroll in time for January admission, students must apply by November 1. If the application deadline has passed, students should contact the Office of Admission regarding space availability.

For more information, students should contact:

Office of Admission
Newbury College
129 Fisher Avenue
Brookline, Massachusetts 02445-5796
Telephone: 617-730-7007
          800-NEWBURY (toll-free)
E-mail: info@newbury.edu
World Wide Web: http://www.newbury.edu

Newbury's low student-faculty ratio supports its philosophy of student-centered education.

NEW COLLEGE OF CALIFORNIA
School of Humanities
SAN FRANCISCO, CALIFORNIA

The College and The School

Since its founding in 1971, New College of California has been a leader in the alternative education movement. The College is dedicated to providing an education integrated with social change. New College puts students at the center of the learning process and gives them significant opportunities to shape their education. The College fosters interdisciplinary learning and critical perspectives that place knowledge within social and historical contexts. It encourages a deeper understanding and appreciation of diversity, and emphasizes community-building and an activist orientation to empower students to work towards a just and humane world. Accredited by the Western Association of Schools and Colleges, New College offers two undergraduate programs: the Humanities B.A. program and the Weekend College B.A. degree-completion program. It also offers graduate studies leading to the M.A. or M.F.A. degrees. New College also has a Public Interest law school, a teaching credential program, and a science institute. New College's recently established campus in Santa Rosa, California, offers both B.A. and M.A. studies in culture, ecology, and sustainable community.

The School of Humanities at New College offers two undergraduate programs leading to the Bachelor of Arts degree. The weekday Humanities Program comprises a small academic community with approximately 200 part-time and full-time students. Through mentoring with a core faculty member, students are guided and their course of study is tailored to their needs. The program offers a four-year interdisciplinary curriculum with emphasis areas and a variety of learning options. The Weekend College is an accelerated degree completion program designed for self-motivated working adults. The curriculum includes interdisciplinary humanities seminars, journal work, and an undergraduate thesis.

The average age of students in the weekday Humanities Program is 26, with many transfer students in their twenties. Most students in the Weekend College are completing their degrees after having spent time in the workplace. They tend to be in their thirties, forties, and fifties. A majority of New College students come from California and the Western states; however, a significant number come from the East and Midwest as well as several European, Latin American, and Asian countries. Many New College students are committed to social change and hope to pursue public interest careers upon graduation.

Location

New College has two campuses located in San Francisco, one of the most diverse and progressive cities in the nation. San Francisco offers a mass transit system and a range of inexpensive cultural, political, and social activities. The Fell Street campus is located downtown in the Civic Center area. It is a short walk from the main branch of the public library, City Hall, museums, and theaters. The Valencia Street campus, which includes the undergraduate Humanities Building, is located in the vibrant Mission District, where students can find numerous bookstores, cafés, and shops.

Majors and Degrees

New College awards the Bachelor of Arts in humanities. Students in the Humanities Program may choose from the following emphasis areas: anthropology/sociology; cultural histories; ecological studies; education/youth in society; gender studies; Irish studies; jazz studies; Latin American studies; movement studies; poetics; politics and society; psychology; theater and performance; video and multimedia art; visual arts; and writing, literature, and publishing. The poetics program offers a B.A./M.A. option. Students may also opt to combine two or more of these emphases or to create their own, with the help of their faculty adviser. Weekend College students design their own emphasis or focus their work on interdisciplinary humanities.

Academic Program

The Humanities Program curriculum is a set of resources from which each student designs, with an adviser, a meaningful program of study. Each student's program emphasizes a breadth of knowledge in the humanities, as well as a refined level of skill and experience within a chosen emphasis area.

The Humanities curriculum is organized into three broad clusters, each with core courses that provide a foundation for the emphasis areas within that cluster: Arts, Music, and Literature; Community and Global Studies; and Cultural Studies. Students can construct their own emphasis area from courses offered by any of the clusters. Emphasis areas generally have one to three core courses of their own. Students can extend their studies through nontraditional forms of learning, including independent studies, tutorials, and practica. Students can also earn up to one year of college credit for previous life/work experience through the Prior Learning Program. All humanities students complete 24 units of Breadth Requirements (including a practicum and senior project) and at least 24 units in their emphasis area. A minimum of 120 units is required for graduation.

The Weekend College Program was developed to assist those who previously began college-level course work but, for various reasons, did not complete their degrees. Students entering the program with 75 transferable units may complete the Weekend College Program in one year (three semesters). Students entering the program with fewer than 75 units, but at least 45 units, may earn additional units for life experience through the Prior Learning Program and/or by taking the CLEP exams. It is also possible to complete the program in two trimesters by transferring a total of 90 college units, 12 of which must be upper-division units.

All Weekend College students participate in a seminar series one full weekend per month. Class topics vary each semester and may include literature, ecopsychology, gender studies, science and spirituality, and Asian studies. Through the undergraduate thesis, students have an opportunity to undertake a major independent research project in their area of academic emphasis or professional interest.

Off-Campus Arrangements

The Humanities Program requires each student to complete a 3-unit practicum in a community organization. The College maintains a file of practicum placements, which includes health, women's, Latino, environmental, peace, African-American, and labor groups, among others.

Academic Facilities

The Humanities Library collection is small but specialized. It includes material of interest to New College students and faculty, especially in the areas of literature and poetry, psychology, ethnic studies, and health studies. The library is a member of the Online Computer Library Center (OCLC), an international library database with more than 20 million book titles, periodicals, records, and videotapes, most of which can be borrowed through interlibrary loan. The Rod Holt Labor Library is an endowed library that has a collection of rare books and documents on labor history.

The Learning Center provides academic support services for the entire college. Students have access to IBM PCs and Macintosh computers for word processing, database management, Internet access, and other user needs. Tutorial services are also available.

The College's arts facilities include a fine arts and graphic arts studio, a desktop publishing lab, a video editing suite, a music practice room, and two theaters.

Costs

For 2000–01, full-time tuition for the weekday Humanities Program is $8750 per year or $4375 per semester; part-time tuition is $375 per unit. B.A. completion program tuition is $4375 per trimester for full-time enrollment or $375 per unit for part-time enrollment.

Financial Aid

Financial assistance is available to students who qualify. Nearly 75 percent of Humanities Program students receive some form of federal, state, or local financial aid, including Federal Pell Grants, Federal Supplemental Educational Opportunity Grants, Federal Perkins Loans, Federal Stafford Student Loans, Federal Work-Study awards, Cal Grants, and Marin Educational Opportunity Loans. The average award is approximately $5500. Students must submit the Free Application for Federal Student Aid (FAFSA) and an institutional form. The College Scholarship Service PROFILE and the California state form are required for some forms of aid. The priority deadline is March 1 for the following academic year. Forms are available from the Financial Aid Office by calling 415-437-3442.

Faculty

New College is dedicated to excellence in teaching. The ratio of students to faculty members in the Humanities Program is 10:1, one of the best in the country. In addition to teaching, each core faculty member spends a significant amount of time advising 15–20 students. New College faculty members have outstanding reputations in their field of expertise. Many have extensive ties to the community and experience in both practical and academic settings.

Student Government

New College encourages students to participate in shaping the direction of their community. Students have developed services, planned events, published a newsletter, and provided general advocacy work on behalf of students.

Admission Requirements

Admission to the Humanities Program is based on an "open admission" policy. The minimum requirement for financial aid is a high school diploma or an acceptable GED score. Because New College recognizes that many excellent students do not perform well in traditional academic environments, it does not base its admission policy on previous college or high school grades, and standardized admission tests (ACT or SAT I) are not required. Instead, prospective students are evaluated on their enthusiasm for learning and their potential to achieve in an alternative, student-centered environment. Students may transfer up to 90 units of academic credit from accredited colleges and universities.

Admission to the Weekend College is also decided on a case-by-case basis. The admission process is a dialogue between the candidate and admission counselor that results in the mutual assessment of the candidate's appropriateness for the program. Admission tests are not required.

Application and Information

Students must submit an admission application for the Humanities Program or Weekend College, official transcripts of all previous college work, an official high school transcript or GED score, and a $40 application fee. Each program also requires a personal statement. Admission decisions are made on a rolling basis.

For further information, students should contact:

New College Admissions
777 Valencia Street
San Francisco, California 94110
Telephone: 415-437-3460
          800-335-6262 (toll-free)
Fax: 415-437-3417
E-mail: admissions@ncgate.newcollege.edu
World Wide Web: http://www.newcollege.edu

NEW COLLEGE OF THE UNIVERSITY OF SOUTH FLORIDA
SARASOTA, FLORIDA

The College

New College offers serious students the opportunity to pursue rigorous academic study in an environment designed to promote depth in thinking, free exchange of ideas, and highly individualized interaction with faculty. Throughout the history of New College, four principles have defined the College's educational philosophy: each student is ultimately responsible for his or her education; the best education demands a joint search for knowledge by exciting teachers and able-minded students; students' progress should be based on demonstrated competence and real mastery rather than on the accumulation of credits and grades; and students should have, from the outset, opportunities to explore, in depth, areas of interest to them.

Study is focused in the liberal arts and sciences and is highly accelerated and independent. More than 50 percent of the College's graduates pursue graduate or professional study, gaining admission to Harvard, Yale, MIT, Brown, Georgetown Law Center, Berkeley, and other major graduate centers. Indeed, New College ranks among the top schools in the percentage of graduates earning Ph.D.'s. The top ten law schools nationally have each admitted New College graduates. New College students consistently score high on the GRE, LSAT, and other graduate exams.

The nationally recognized public liberal arts college of Florida, New College was established in 1960 by community leaders working in conjunction with nationally prominent leaders in education. Founded as a private institution, the College began with a devotion to the values implicit in a liberal arts education, dedicated to creating an innovative academic community of talented young scholars and outstanding faculty. Affiliation with the state of Florida in 1975 served to strengthen and perpetuate the idealistic vision of the College's founders. A public-private funding arrangement between USF and the New College Foundation enables the offering of a private honors college experience at public cost. The College's private endowment currently exceeds $26 million.

The College's population is 617, 37 percent men and 63 percent women; approximately 38 percent are out-of-state or overseas residents. First-year students must live on campus, but many continuing students choose to live on campus as well. The Pei residence halls were designed by the eminent architect of the same name. The 131-room, three-court complex is designed so students can't walk anywhere by moving in a straight line. Each room is distinctive, including individual entrances, private baths, central air-conditioning, and various combinations of large picture windows, sliding glass doors, and balconies. The new Dort and Goldstein dorms provide apartment-style housing with four single rooms, two bathrooms, and a common living room and kitchenette. A dining hall provides a full meal plan. The Counseling and Wellness Center offers basic health care and personal counseling as well as a variety of related services.

New College student life is informal. Activities are largely student initiated and include academic, artistic, religious, political, and recreational athletic pursuits. The College's 140-acre bayfront location on the Gulf of Mexico contains basketball, racquetball, and tennis courts; a multipurpose field; a running path; a volleyball pit; a 25-meter swimming pool; and a fitness center. Sailboats, sailboards, and canoes are available for use on Sarasota Bay.

Location

New College, situated on Sarasota Bay, serves as the northern gateway to Sarasota, a city of more than 50,000 located 50 miles south of Tampa on the west coast of Florida. The city is located within Sarasota County, which has a population of 275,000. Noted as a cultural and recreational center, Sarasota's professional theater, art, and music, as well as its beautiful public beaches, attract visitors and new residents from throughout the world. The climate is semitropical, consisting of long, warm autumns and springs and mild winters. Transportation from throughout the nation and within the city is readily accessible. Many major airlines serve Sarasota and within the city, buses link the campus to downtown, shopping malls, and parks and beaches. New College is in a residential neighborhood; mass transit is available, but the bicycle is a favored means of transportation among students.

Majors and Degrees

New College awards the Bachelor of Arts degree. Students work within three academic divisions: Humanities, Natural Sciences, and Social Sciences. Disciplines include anthropology, art history, biology, chemistry, classics, economics, fine arts, French, German, history, literature, mathematics, music, philosophy, physics, political science, psychology, religion, Russian, sociology, and Spanish.

Each area of concentration (major) at New College is an individualized program of study that a student designs in consultation with, and with the approval of, faculty. Areas of concentration are built around the above disciplines but can be interdisciplinary (for example, environmental studies or public policy).

Academic Program

The New College academic program aims to encourage academic excellence, creativity, and personal initiative and to provide essential tools for lifelong intellectual and personal growth. The College's distinctive curriculum, based on the academic contract, enables students, in close consultation with faculty, to develop programs of seminars, tutorials, independent research, and off-campus experiences that meet personal goals.

New College has no distribution requirements. Students receive detailed narrative evaluations of their work as well as satisfactory/unsatisfactory assessments. In order to graduate, students must satisfactorily complete seven contracts (one per semester), three independent study projects (one per year), a senior thesis or project, and an oral baccalaureate examination.

The College operates on a 4-1-4 calendar. In January, students undertake independent study projects, which they design and complete under faculty sponsorship.

Off-Campus Arrangements

Intellectual challenge cannot be confined to a campus. Internships, fieldwork, and independent research away from campus offer opportunities to gain new skills and test career interests. Exposure to other cultures provides new learning experiences, personal skills, and insights into one's own way of life. Because off-campus study can make a major contribution to an undergraduate education, New College facilitates such study through its flexible, individualized curriculum and special support services. In addition to helping students participate in programs offered by other institutions in the United States and abroad, the College has special student exchanges with the University of Newcastle (England) and the University of Glasgow. New College students have joined the School for International Training in a variety of countries, and students and faculty also regularly participate in the State University System of Florida programs in Florence, Italy, and London, England. Through a faculty exchange agreement with Oxford University, each year an Oxford professor visits the New College campus to offer lectures.

Academic Facilities

The Jane Bancroft Cook Library, a $6-million facility, has a capacity of 350,000 volumes. Trustees, faculty, students, and the New College Library Association have implemented an ambitious acquisition program to expand the current holdings of 259,000 volumes. The USF Tampa campus library gives students access to an additional collection of more than 1 million volumes. New College students have ready access to holdings throughout the State University System of Florida through the interlibrary loan program.

The Sudakoff Conference Center hosts visiting lecturers, meetings of campus and community organizations, and diverse special events. The Caples Fine Arts Complex includes the 264-seat Mildred Sainer Music & Arts Pavilion; the Lota Mundy Music Building, which houses eight practice rooms and the Benjamin and Barbara Slavin Electronic Music Studio; the Christianne Felsmann Fine Arts Building; the Betty Isermann fine arts gallery and studio; and the Sculpture and Ceramic Studio. Currently under construction are the $7.5-million R. V. Heiser Natural Sciences Complex (laboratories, classrooms, offices, and an auditorium) and the $2.5-million Rhoda and Jack Pritzker Marine Biology Research Center, which will have state-of-the-art culture rooms, laboratories, and aquarium facilities with water drawn from Sarasota Bay. Both facilities will be ready for occupancy in June 2000.

Science facilities include a computer center with local and remote systems, laboratories accessible around the clock (containing reserved space for students in advanced research), and two electron microscopes. A number of personal computers are maintained for student use.

Costs

For the 1999–2000 academic year, in-state tuition and fees were $2492, and out-of-state tuition and fees were $10,878. Room and board costs were $4663. The 1999–2000 tuition, fees, room, and board for Florida residents totaled $7155. For out-of-state students, the total was $15,541.

Financial Aid

The actual cost of providing this highly individualized honors college experience is far greater than the state funding appropriated for support of the College. The New College Foundation secures independent funding designed to provide the difference. Part of the endowment produces income used for scholarships.

Approximately 85 percent of the College's students receive some additional form of financial assistance, including scholarships from external programs and organizations. Need-based aid (grants, loans, and work-study awards) is distributed by the University of South Florida, and the New College Admissions Office awards scholarships. In addition, the University provides special scholarships to National Achievement Scholars, National Hispanic Scholars, and National Merit Scholars who designate New College as their first choice. To apply for financial aid, students should file the Free Application for Federal Student Aid (FAFSA). March 1 is the priority date for need-based financial aid. For scholarship consideration, March 1 is the deadline to complete the application for admission. No additional application is necessary.

Faculty

Ninety-eight percent of New College faculty members hold the Ph.D. They have come to New College from the finest universities nationally and abroad, drawn by an environment that emphasizes excellence in teaching and fosters a close-knit community of scholars. Faculty members sponsor individual students in the formulation of their academic programs, gradually moving toward a form of mentorship through which joint research is sometimes pursued. An 11:1 student-faculty ratio is a key factor in the College's individualized approach to education.

Student Government

Student input is a decisive factor in campus governance. Student representatives, elected by their peers, serve on most major policymaking committees and are voting participants in divisional and campuswide faculty meetings. The New College Student Alliance has authority over funding for recreation, social events, and student organizations.

Admission Requirements

New College seeks highly capable students eager to take responsibility for their own education. Cutoffs and quotas are not employed in admission decisions. The Admissions Committee reviews each candidate individually, assessing potential for success within, and contribution to, the College's special environment. Writing ability, depth of thought, and course selection are focal points of the committee's review. The majority of freshmen entering in fall 1999 ranked in the top tenth of their high school class. Eighty-two percent of the freshman SAT I takers scored 1200 or higher, and 66 percent of the ACT takers scored 27 or higher.

All prospective students may apply for entrance to the fall term. Only transfer candidates may apply for spring term admission. Candidates must submit a New College Application and fee, official transcript(s), SAT I or ACT scores, a counselor recommendation, an academic teacher recommendation, and an original graded analytical paper. Applicants are encouraged to augment their applications with evidence of maturity, self-discipline, and motivation for rigorous in-depth study. Thorough research into the College is recommended for all those with serious interest in applying. Campus tours, interviews, and class visits are welcomed and recommended for all candidates, if possible and practical.

Application and Information

Admission application materials and descriptive literature are available through the New College Office of Admissions. The College employs a rolling admission system. Candidates for the fall class are evaluated by the Admissions Committee from September through May 1; the class may be closed earlier if admission or enrollment goals have already been met. Notification of the admission decision occurs approximately four weeks after an application and all supporting credentials have been received.

Inquiries and application requests should be directed to:

Kathleen Killion
Director of Admissions
New College of the University of South Florida
5700 North Tamiami Trail
Sarasota, Florida 34243-2197

Telephone: 941-359-4269
Fax: 941-359-4435
E-mail: ncadmissions@sar.usf.edu
World Wide Web: http://www.newcollege.usf.edu

College Hall, former home of Charles Ringling and part of a National Historic District, houses New College classrooms and faculty offices.

NEW ENGLAND COLLEGE
HENNIKER, NEW HAMPSHIRE

The College

Founded in 1946, New England College is a young and vibrant college that values flexibility, educational innovation, and responsiveness to individual needs. The current enrollment is 700 undergraduates. Students come from all areas of the United States and twenty-six countries. This diversity fosters the multicultural view and global consciousness that are essential for educated men and women. The College is committed to providing an enriching liberal arts education that prepares men and women for lives of success and fulfillment. The College recognizes that this commitment carries with it the responsibility to provide instruction, resources, and support services of the highest quality within a nurturing environment. New England College is a community of people interested in students—people whose ability to care about students' growth and development may provide the vital spark for academic success.

The campus encompasses thirty-one buildings that represent a mix of modern facilities and restored New England–style structures up to 150 years old. The newest facility is the Nautilus Fitness Center, opened in January 1996. The Simon Center, a $2.5-million student center, opened in 1994. The College also has the Lee Clement Ice Arena. This regulation ice rink accommodates 1,000 spectators and is the home of the New England College Pilgrims. A covered bridge over the Contoocook River connects the residence halls with 26 acres of athletic fields. The environment is comfortable, informal, and friendly. The campus is characterized by a strong sense of community among the College's faculty, staff, and students and between the College and the townspeople.

Location

The campus is situated in an area of New Hampshire's great natural beauty. Henniker, a village of 3,800, is located on the Contoocook River in a mountainous area of this unspoiled state—yet just 90 miles from Boston and 15 miles from Concord, the capital city of New Hampshire. This exceptional location provides numerous opportunities for enjoying the outdoors. Alpine skiing is offered just a few miles away, and Nordic ski trails are available on campus. At the same time, shopping, restaurants, and cultural events of Manchester, the state's largest city, and Concord are just a short drive from the College. This setting truly gives students the best of both worlds.

Majors and Degrees

New England College balances two vital educational roles: a fundamental liberal arts education and career preparation. The College awards the Bachelor of Arts degree for the completion of major requirements. Students in education may also satisfy requirements for teacher certification at the elementary and secondary school levels in approximately forty-five states. Majors at New England College include art, biology, business administration, communication, creative writing, criminal justice, education, English and comparative literature, environmental science, health sciences, history, kinesiology, philosophy, physical education, political science, psychology, sociology, special education, sport and recreation management, theater, and women's studies. Concentrations in these majors allow special preparation in advertising and promotion, art history, computer technology, exercise physiology, finance/accounting, management, marketing, new media, photojournalism, photography, pre–physical therapy, print and electronic media, public relations, and small business entrepreneurship.

An individually designed major enables students to develop a course of study tailored to their own interests, goals, and needs. Internships are available in most majors as well. Examples of recent internships are a marketing study for Velcro International and psychology majors working with at-risk adolescents. Students may also choose to fulfill the requirements of a minor program in order to have a greater opportunity for career focus. In addition, course work is offered in arts and sciences, chemistry, foreign languages, humanities, and physics.

Academic Program

The New England College Honors Program is nonexclusionary and is open to all students. The fundamental philosophy of the honors program is that all students are capable of earning honors by doing additional work at a higher intellectual level, and all students at New England College are encouraged to do so. Electing honors in a course increases the course credit by one hour; for example, a regular 3-hour course becomes a 4-hour honors course. Also, honors courses carry additional quality points. Students who complete a minimum of eight honors courses are eligible to receive an Honors Diploma and are designated as Honors Graduates on their transcript.

The Academic Advising and Support Center is open to all students. It helps students improve their learning and studying efficiency through tutoring, writing support, computer/word processing instruction, academic counseling, and programs for study-skills improvement. It offers a wide range of services to students who need additional support but choose to study in a mainstream academic program. The Academic Advising and Support Center is run by full-time faculty and staffed with professional tutors.

Candidates for graduation are required to successfully complete at least 120 academic credits and at least 43 credits in approved courses meeting the general education requirements. Students may apply for credit on the basis of results from general exams administered by the CLEP, GCE "A" Levels, and the International Baccalaureate. Students who take College Board Advanced Placement tests and earn scores of 3, 4, or 5 will be granted up to 8 credits, depending on the exam and score. Placement and course equivalencies are determined by the appropriate discipline.

The fall semester begins the first week of September and ends about the third week of December. The spring semester begins in mid-January and ends in early May. There are two 6-week summer sessions beginning in May.

Off-Campus Arrangements

The College encourages students to see themselves as citizens of the world and to understand and appreciate other cultures. The best way to do that is to experience another culture firsthand by spending a semester or year abroad. Students may study at Regent's College in the heart of London, at the American University in Paris, or at the College's branch in Israel. Under the New England/Quebec Student Exchange Program, eligible full-time students may spend one or two semesters during their sophomore or junior years at one of eighteen participating Quebec institutions.

New England College is a member of the New Hampshire College and University Council, which includes ten private and three state institutions. Through this cooperative effort, students can enroll and study at other member colleges and receive full credit toward degree requirements.

Academic Facilities

The H. Raymond Danforth Library holds more than 104,000 volumes and more than 650 periodical subscriptions. In addition, the library holds 36,000 microforms, 2,000 audiovisual materials, and 3,200 separate government documents.

Students utilize a number of computing resources. The College provided access to the Internet in 1995. State-of-the-art IBM PCs, Macintosh PCs, laser printers, flat-bed and slide scanners, and color printers are available for student use.

Costs

For the 2000–01 academic year, tuition is $18,382. Room is $3268 for double occupancy; board is $3270 (nineteen-meal plan). Personal expenses, including books and supplies, clothing, laundry, travel, and recreation, vary among students but average $1200–$2000 per academic year. Other fees total $504.

Financial Aid

Approximately 72 percent of the students at New England College receive some form of need-based financial assistance. Determination of the amount depends on the level of a student's financial need. Loans and part-time on-campus employment are also available. An average financial aid package received by a New England College student for the current year is $15,014. The College also provides non-need-based merit scholarships that range from $1500 to $5000 per year. All are renewable and will be granted in addition to any need-based aid. Information on these plans is available from the Office of Financial Aid. To ensure that all required materials reach the College before available funds are assigned, students are urged to apply for financial aid when applying for admission. The priority date for receipt of financial aid forms is March 1.

Faculty

Of the 51 full-time faculty members, 75 percent hold terminal degrees in their field. All faculty place their professional emphasis on teaching, while maintaining strong academic credentials through research, publication, and community service. The quality of the College's faculty, coupled with a 12:1 student-faculty ratio, ensures a student-oriented educational approach. Classes average 16 students, further enhancing the opportunities for individual attention.

Student Government

New England College has a strong student government association. This organization represents the students and acts as a liaison among the students, faculty, and administration. The student government has its own budget in excess of $95,000, used for clubs, organizations, and student activities.

Admission Requirements

Freshman applicants must have a secondary school diploma or equivalent credentials and should have at least 14 high school units of college-preparatory work: 4 in English, 2 in math, 2 in science, 3 in social studies, and 3 in electives. Admission to New England College is dependent upon the applicant's academic preparation, personal qualifications, and potential for success at the college level. In the evaluation of these characteristics, the major criteria used are the applicant's four-year high school achievement record, high school class rank, and high school recommendations. Results from standardized tests are not required for admission but may be submitted. On-campus interviews are strongly recommended.

Application and Information

New England College has a rolling admission system, though an early-notification option does exist for students interested in receiving a decision prior to December 20. All candidates must submit a completed application form, the $30 nonrefundable application fee, a high school transcript (including senior grades and class rank when available), and recommendations by a high school teacher or guidance counselor. TOEFL scores are required for students graduating from a secondary school in which the language of instruction is not English. For students needing additional English language instruction, the College offers an English as a Second Language Transition Program. This program provides intensive ESL instruction with the opportunity to enroll in courses for graduation credit.

Application forms and additional information may be obtained by contacting:

Donald N. Parker
Dean of Admission
New England College
26 Bridge Street
Henniker, New Hampshire 03242-3297

Telephone: 800-521-7642 (toll-free)
Fax: 603-428-7230
E-mail: admis@nec1.nec.edu

Students relax in New England College's spectacular Simon Center.

NEW HAMPSHIRE COLLEGE
MANCHESTER, NEW HAMPSHIRE

The College

New Hampshire College, founded in 1932, is a private, accredited, nonprofit, coeducational, professional college. The College has a full-time day school enrollment of more than 1,300 students and a total enrollment of more than 7,000 in the undergraduate, graduate, and continuing education divisions.

The campus, on 280 wooded acres, is located along the Merrimack River in Manchester, New Hampshire. Campus facilities include twenty-four major buildings: classroom/administrative buildings, residence halls, a computer center, a library complex, a student center with dining facilities, and an athletic/recreational complex. The student body is varied in background and represents more than twenty-three states and thirty-eight countries.

Student organizations range from social clubs, such as fraternities and sororities, to career-related associations, such as the Accounting Association. Athletic facilities include an indoor 25-meter competition-size swimming pool, Nautilus equipment, one racquetball court, a dance studio, cardiovascular equipment, four outdoor lighted tennis courts, a soccer field, two baseball diamonds, numerous practice fields, and two indoor gymnasiums with six full basketball courts, providing areas for indoor tennis, broom hockey, and many other activities. The College supports an active athletic program, both intercollegiate and intramural, as an integral part of the educational process. At the intercollegiate level, teams are fielded in baseball, basketball, cross-country, golf, ice hockey, lacrosse, soccer, softball, tennis, and volleyball. New Hampshire College is a member of the National Collegiate Athletic Association (Division II), the Eastern College Athletic Conference, and, beginning in fall 2000, the Northeast Ten Collegic Conference. The modern, well-equipped Wellness Center provides short-term health care, health education, and counseling services for NHC students, and the buildings and facilities are accessible to the physically handicapped. A well-qualified student-services staff provides personal, career, and academic counseling; counselors are available on campus. Lifetime job placement service is available to all current students and to alumni.

New Hampshire College maintains Continuing Education centers in Laconia, Manchester, Nashua, Portsmouth, and Salem, New Hampshire; Brunswick, Maine; Roosevelt Roads, Puerto Rico; and Klang, Malaysia. Master of Business Administration and Master of Science programs are offered at the Manchester; Salem; Nashua; Portsmouth; Brunswick; Athens, Greece; Dubai; and Roosevelt Roads campuses through the Graduate School of Business.

Location

Manchester, New Hampshire, is the crossroads of northern New England. It is an hour's drive from the best skiing in the East, the beaches of New Hampshire and Maine, and the cultural activity of Boston. Manchester is home to some 100,000 residents and offers many social and cultural activities. New Hampshire College students are very much involved in the Manchester community. In 1998, Manchester was ranked by *Money* magazine as the most livable city in the East.

Majors and Degrees

New Hampshire College provides students with a solid educational foundation and professional training through programs in its three divisions: Business, Liberal Arts, and Hospitality Administration. Degree programs available within the Division of Business include accounting, advertising, business administration, business studies, computer information systems, economics, economics/finance, fashion merchandising, international business, management advisory services, marketing, retailing, sport management, and technical management. Degree programs offered by the Division of Liberal Arts include American studies, communication, English language and literature, humanities, political science, psychology, social science, and teacher education (concentrations in business, English, marketing, and social studies). Special programs are also available for prelaw and pre-M.B.A. Degree programs conferred by the Division of Hospitality Administration include culinary arts, hotel management, restaurant management, and tourism management. An Associate in Applied Science degree is offered in culinary arts.

An exciting nationally recognized program that the College offers is a three-year Bachelor of Science degree in business administration. This competency-based, technology-driven program allows select students to complete the equivalent of a four-year program in three years.

A Bachelor of Applied Science in Hospitality Administration (B.A.S.H.A.) is designed for students who have already earned an associate degree from an approved institution. The B.A.S.H.A. program allows students to complete a bachelor's degree in two years while they get firsthand experience with the hospitality industry.

Academic Program

Academic programs in the Divisions of Business and Hospitality Administration are career oriented and designed to combine professional preparation in business, education, and the liberal arts. All students are required to take courses in accounting, business administration, computer information systems, and liberal arts in addition to those courses required in their major field of study. Academic programs in the Division of Liberal Arts are built around an interdisciplinary two-semester course in the humanities. From this foundation, the core curriculum and all major course content radiate. The humanities sequence paves the way for the more in-depth study in the liberal arts core curriculum and in major course work. Each liberal arts program is flexible enough to allow students to select any one of a number of traditional business minors.

Off-Campus Arrangements

Cooperative education work experiences are available in all academic programs and range from 3 to 12 credits; all students have the option of participating in work experiences abroad. Selected students also have the opportunity to live and learn in England through arrangements with the University of North London; Leeuwarden, the Netherlands; and Sepang Institute of Technology in Malaysia.

Through the College's membership in the New Hampshire College and University Council, New Hampshire College students may take advantage of academic facilities and course offerings at the eleven other four-year colleges and universities in the consortium.

Academic Facilities

The Harry A. B. and Gertrude C. Shapiro Library has a networked computer center, a specialized career and placement area, student conference rooms, and a consistently expanding collection of bound volumes, microfilm, microfiche, and ultrafiche. Audio-visual facilities include a videotape recording studio, a 150-seat theater, an Internet-based radio station, a listening room, and a closed-circuit video network throughout the campus. The Computer Center is equipped with an NEC Powermate V166e computer and state-of-the-art equipment used in the most sophisticated corporate environments. All computers have Internet access. The system supports more than 250 direct-access computers on campus. The Academic Advising Center offers centralized academic advising to all students and coordinates support services free of charge. Academic support services include professional and peer tutoring and supplemental instruction labs.

Costs

The 2000–01 tuition for the undergraduate day school is $15,598. The Culinary Institute tuition is $15,098. Room and board costs are $6790. The student activity fee is $250 per year. Other expenses include books, supplies, and miscellaneous personal expenses.

Financial Aid

Approximately 75 percent of New Hampshire College's full-time day undergraduates receive financial assistance, ranging from $250 to full cost. The average financial aid package, including gift, loan, and employment assistance, exceeds $8000. The College participates in the Federal Pell Grant Program, the Federal Supplemental Educational Opportunity Grant Program, the Federal Perkins Loan Program, the Federal Work-Study Program, and the Federal Stafford Student Loan Program. The College requires that students submit the Free Application for Federal Student Aid (FAFSA). The College also encourages students to submit an early financial aid estimator by December 15, which is available from the Office of Admission. The aid program is designed to assist deserving students who, without assistance, would be unable to pursue or continue a program of study at New Hampshire College. Academic, leadership, and athletic scholarships are available for qualified students, and emphasis is also placed on demonstrated financial need. Academic performance and promise are also given consideration.

Faculty

New Hampshire College employs 99 full-time and 153 part-time faculty members collegewide. About 70 percent of the total faculty hold a terminal degree in their field. The student-to-faculty ratio is 18:1. Some faculty members serve as consultants in the Manchester business world, and many have had prior industry-related job experience. Most accounting personnel are registered CPAs. Graduate students do not serve as instructors.

Student Government

The Student Government Association is led by 26 students—including 5 officers—who represent all the students at the College. Their primary function is to represent the student body in campus affairs and to dispense student activity funds collected by the College. One student is appointed to the Board of Trustees, the governing body of the College. Students are also appointed to most other standing committees of the College, including the Financial Aid Advisory Committee, the Curriculum Advisory Committee, the Library Committee, and judiciary committees.

Admission Requirements

New Hampshire College seeks to attract students who are prepared to take full advantage of the academic and cocurricular opportunities offered. Applicants must have graduated from high school or secured a GED certificate before entering.

Application and Information

Applicants for the four- or two-year programs must submit a formal application for admission, an up-to-date high school transcript, a personal essay, and high school recommendations. SAT I or ACT scores are required of freshman applicants. Three-year bachelor's degree candidates, in addition to the above, are required to have an interview with the program director. Culinary students are not required to submit SAT I scores. Transfer students must also submit a supplemental transfer form and official transcripts from all schools previously attended. International students whose native language is other than English must prove proficiency in the English language through the TOEFL examination. Admission decisions are based on the quality of academic performance, but a campus visit and interview are strongly recommended for all candidates. The College operates on a rolling admission basis, and applicants can expect a decision within one month of the receipt of their credentials. Applicants may also apply as early action candidates by submitting their application prior to November 15. There is no application fee.

For further information about New Hampshire College, students should contact:

Office of Admission
New Hampshire College
2500 North River Road
Manchester, New Hampshire 03106-1045

Telephone: 603-645-9611
          800-NHC-4YOU (toll-free)
Fax: 603-645-9693
World Wide Web: http://www.nhc.edu

Students relaxing in front of New Hampshire College's Washington Hall, a 250-bed dormitory.

NEW JERSEY CITY UNIVERSITY
JERSEY CITY, NEW JERSEY

The University

There is much to discover at New Jersey City University (NJCU). This vital, 70-year-old liberal arts institution (formerly Jersey City State College) offers an incomparable educational experience at an affordable price.

At the heart of the University is a strong academic program that is recognized by a host of accrediting institutions. NJCU has an esteemed and caring faculty and extensive student support services. Twenty-five undergraduate degree programs are offered, as are graduate studies and teacher certification programs. NJCU provides unparalleled opportunity for academic and personal growth through such study options as its nationally recognized Cooperative Education Program, which enables undergraduates in all majors to earn income and academic credit while experiencing field study at one of hundreds of participating corporations, agencies, and organizations.

There is a sense of excitement on the 47-acre, tree-lined campus, which is located in the midst of one of the world's largest metropolitan areas. The University community is rich in diversity; people from many cultures come together and learn from each other. The student population includes high school graduates pursuing the four-year degree sequence, part-time and weekend students, nontraditional older students, and students seeking job retraining—all of whom are able to take advantage of the University's flexible class scheduling. While drawn primarily from northern New Jersey and the New York metropolitan area, students from fifteen other states, some as distant as California and Florida, and the Virgin Islands are enrolled. International students, who come to the University from more than fifty-one countries around the globe, enrich the multicultural nature of the campus.

The total undergraduate and graduate enrollment for full- and part-time students at the University is 10,000. An average class size of 19, smaller than that of most universities, enables students to work closely and directly with faculty members and classmates, encouraging intellectual exchange and fostering successful mentoring relationships.

The richness of university life at NJCU is seen in the extracurricular activities, services, and facilities that are available. Most student activities take place in the spacious, modern Michael B. Gilligan Student Union. Special features of the facility include quiet study lounges, a game room, a TV lounge, the University bookstore, a cafeteria, indoor parking, small and large meeting rooms, a private dining room, and a multipurpose room, which can accommodate banquets, special events, lectures, festivals, and fairs. The Gilligan Student Union is also home to the Student Government Organization, the student newspaper and radio station, and many clubs, organizations, fraternities, and sororities.

All students can participate in sports through the University's extensive varsity, intramural, and recreational athletic programs, which include baseball, basketball, cross-country, football, racquetball, soccer, softball, tennis, and volleyball. The University's Athletic and Fitness Center is a 72,000-square-foot state-of-the-art facility that houses a 25-yard, six-lane swimming pool; saunas; a 2,000-seat basketball/volleyball arena; an elevated jogging track; a fitness center and training facility; and three racquetball courts.

The Thomas M. Gerrity Athletic Complex, home to NJCU's outdoor sports and located a mile southwest of the main campus, is a 14-acre facility that features a 3,000-seat football stadium, an enclosed press box, and a natural grass surface. The University campus also houses six composition-surface outdoor tennis courts, which are home to the NJCU varsity tennis team and available to the University community.

Location

New Jersey City University is located in Jersey City, New Jersey, within minutes of New York City. While the University's location in the urban center of the Northeast affords students all the cultural and intellectual stimulation of the metropolitan area, the campus has retained a quiet atmosphere for study. The University's urban setting also makes travel to and from campus convenient, providing easy access by car, train, and bus. An international airport is located minutes away.

Majors and Degrees

Undergraduate programs at New Jersey City University lead to the Bachelor of Arts (B.A.), Bachelor of Science (B.S.), Bachelor of Fine Arts (B.F.A.), or Bachelor of Science in Nursing (B.S.N.) degrees.

NJCU's College of Arts and Sciences offers major programs leading to a bachelor's degree in art (B.A. or B.F.A.); biology (B.A. or B.S.), geoscience/geography (B.A. or B.S.), and physics (B.A. or B.S.); chemistry and computer science (B.S.); and economics, English, history, mathematics, media arts, music, philosophy, political science, psychology, sociology, and Spanish (B.A.). A B.S. in clinical laboratory sciences is offered jointly with the University of Medicine and Dentistry of New Jersey (UMDNJ).

The College of Education offers major programs leading to a Bachelor of Arts degree in early childhood education, elementary education, and special education. Also offered are undergraduate programs that lead to certification, such as New Jersey Department of Education certification in secondary education. The College of Professional Studies offers major programs leading to a Bachelor of Science degree in business administration, criminal justice/fire safety/security administration, and health sciences and a Bachelor of Science in Nursing (B.S.N.).

Academic Program

An institution committed to the liberal arts, New Jersey City University requires 12 credits of core courses that prepare students for the required 42 credits of general studies for all degree programs. Students select courses from each of six clusters: natural sciences, social sciences, fine and performing arts, humanities, communications, and the contemporary world. Students must also fulfill an all-University requirement of 12 credits in communications, mathematics, and computers. There are specific major requirements as well as electives in each degree program. In addition, students may use general electives to complete a minor or a second major, strengthen a major, or pursue areas of personal interest. In their junior and senior years of study, students have ample opportunity to engage in fieldwork in their major.

The University calendar is based on a two-semester system with two summer sessions.

Off-Campus Arrangements

NJCU, the premier cooperative education university in New Jersey, offers sophomores, juniors, and seniors in all academic areas the opportunity to study for a degree while working in salaried positions in related fields. NJCU's Cooperative Education Program works with more than 550 local and international employers.

Academic Facilities

The Forrest A. Irwin Library houses 250,000 books and monographs, subscribes to 1,579 periodicals and journals, receives approximately 5,000 selected U.S. government publications per year, and maintains a collection of official state of New Jersey publications. The library has a complete file of microfiche issued by the

Educational Research Information Center, a clearinghouse for research in all areas of education, and more than 500,000 fully indexed publications on microfilm. The library also maintains an online system catalog for academic reference. Irwin Library is currently undergoing a complete renovation. Upon reopening in September 1999, the library is now a state-of-the-art research facility, fully wired for Internet access.

NJCU's Electronic Learning Laboratory provides computer laboratory support services to students.

NJCU's Media Arts Center is a 16,000-square-foot facility that houses two full-color broadcast-quality television studios, a radio and audio production studio, a complete 16-mm production studio and processing laboratory, two large projection/seminar rooms, an animation laboratory, a graphic production studio, individual student editing space, and work rooms. The Media Arts Center is the home of the Black Maria Film Festival, a 19-year-old international showcase for alternative film and video.

The University's A. Harry Moore Center for Special Education is comprised of the A. Harry Moore Laboratory School, the A. Harry Moore Special Education Camp at Stokes State Park, and the University's Department of Special Education.

NJCU's Center for Public Policy and Urban Research designs and conducts basic and applied research on issues related to urban education, urban development, and public policy.

The University has established the Center for HIV Educational Studies and Training through funding from The Centers for Disease Control and Prevention (CDC). Under the aegis of the CDC, the University is participating in a two-year cooperative agreement, gathering formative research data and developing a pilot behavioral intervention plan.

NJCU's Asian Institute addresses economic, political, and cultural issues through conferences that bring together prominent scholars and business and civic leaders. The institute also sponsors exchange programs and funds special projects.

The Peter W. Rodino Institute of Criminal Justice at NJCU serves as a major avenue for the exchange of ideas between the community, criminal justice professionals, and the University. The institute sponsors conferences and seminars; provides technical assistance to local police, court, correctional, probation, parole, and juvenile justice agencies; conducts innovative research and demonstration projects; and assists in the development of student internships at criminal justice agencies.

The NJCU Women's Center offers a range of services to women, and presents programs on women's issues for NJCU and the community. The center provides a supportive atmosphere, informal counseling and referrals, and various education services.

NJCU's Medical, Counseling and Psychological Services Center provides medical care, counseling, and psychotherapy services.

The Career Development Center provides career counseling services and placement assistance to recent graduates.

NJCU's Early Childhood Learning Center provides educationally focused child care to foster the development of the children of students.

Costs

Undergraduate tuition and fees for the 1999–2000 academic year were $4357.50 for New Jersey residents and $7545 for nonresidents. Room and board in NJCU's Vodra Hall Dormitory, Cooperative Education Dormitory, or apartment complex were $5200.

Financial Aid

NJCU strives to offer students maximum opportunities for financial aid. Financial aid available for eligible students includes needs-based grants, merit-based Corporate Scholarships, Federal Perkins Loans, Federal Stafford Student Loans, and jobs provided under the Federal Work-Study Program. Applicants for aid must submit the Free Application for Federal Student Aid (FAFSA). Approximately 65 percent of NJCU full-time undergraduates receive financial aid.

Faculty

Seventy-one percent of NJCU's faculty members hold the highest degrees attainable in their fields. A student-faculty ratio of 19:1 supports the development of close mentoring relationships and fosters the academic, social, and cultural growth of undergraduates. This student-faculty ratio also enables NJCU professors to be very accessible to their students.

Student Government

NJCU's Student Government Organization (SGO) charters and regulates all student clubs and organizations funded by student activity fees, providing a necessary degree of leadership and coordination. The SGO is administered by the Student Council, which is composed of the Student Executive Committee and class representatives. Members of the SGO serve in the University Senate to represent the interests and concerns of students.

Admission Requirements

Admission to New Jersey City University is based on a student's projected ability to complete a degree program. All admission decisions are made without regard to race, religion, sex, age, handicap, or national origin. It is desirable that freshman applicants rank in the top half of their high school class and complete a college-preparatory program that includes 4 units of English, 3 units of mathematics, 2 units of social science, and 2 units of laboratory science. A student's combined SAT I score or ACT score is taken into account in determining acceptance in individual cases.

Highly qualified high school juniors may apply for early admission with a recommendation from their high school principals.

New Jersey residents who demonstrate financial need and do not meet traditional admissions requirements but have the academic potential and motivation to succeed in college may apply for admission through NJCU's Opportunity Scholarship Program (OSP). The University also accepts students who have been identified as learning disabled through its Project Mentor Program. Transfer applicants are required to have a minimum grade point average of 2.0. Students are accepted for transfer primarily into the sophomore and junior classes; a limited number are accepted with senior class standing.

Application and Information

Application for admission may be made by submitting a completed application, a $35 application fee, an official high school transcript, and SAT I or ACT scores. Transfer students must submit all college transcripts. Applications for the fall semester should be received by April 1; applications for the spring semester should be received by November 1. These dates are subject to change. Admission decisions are made on a rolling basis.

For additional information and application forms, students should contact:

Director of Admissions
New Jersey City University
2039 Kennedy Boulevard
Jersey City, New Jersey 07305
Telephone: 888-441-NJCU (toll-free)

The Hepburn Building's Gothic tower at New Jersey City University.

NEW JERSEY INSTITUTE OF TECHNOLOGY
UNIVERSITY HEIGHTS, NEWARK, NEW JERSEY

The University

Founded in 1881, NJIT is New Jersey's public, technological, research university, with a national reputation for excellence in instruction and research. NJIT has five schools: Newark College of Engineering (1919), the New Jersey School of Architecture (1975), the College of Science and Liberal Arts (1982), School of Management (1988), and the Albert Dorman Honors College (1994). The total enrollment is more than 8,200, of whom 5,265 are undergraduates. About 1,200 full-time students live in the four residence halls on campus. Many students live nearby in fraternity houses.

NJIT's programs in engineering, architecture, management, and the sciences are demanding, rewarding, and highly regarded by employers and graduate schools. These programs include significant research and public service components with the goal of providing an academic environment that fosters intellectual depth and breadth as well as social responsibility. Numerous collegiate guides, such as those published by *U.S. News & World Report* and *Money Magazine*, give NJIT consistently high rankings, and NJIT graduates are recruited by top employers and graduate and professional schools. NJIT has a computing-intensive campus, and computer technology pervades all aspects of university operations. From online registration and extensive computer labs to "wired" residence halls and required computer science courses, NJIT makes sure that graduates regard computing as an integral aspect of everyday life. *Yahoo! Internet Life* has ranked NJIT as America's most wired public university for 1998 and 1999.

Always known for the quality of its academics, NJIT has become a leader in interdisciplinary applied research. The university expends more than $40 million annually on research. Major funding is obtained from leading U.S. corporations, foundations, and government agencies, including the National Science Foundation, the New Jersey Commission on Science and Technology, the New Jersey Department of Transportation, the U.S. Department of Transportation, the U.S. Department of Environmental Protection, the New Jersey Department of Environmental Protection, and many others.

NJIT is the largest technological university in the New York metropolitan region. The university has state-of-the-art facilities, with more than 2 million square feet of space located on a 45-acre campus in Newark, a Technology and Engineering Center at the 125-acre campus in Mount Laurel that is shared with Burlington County College, and a solar observatory in Big Bear, California. With robust extension and distance education programs, NJIT's degree and nondegree programs are available throughout the state and the world.

NJIT's gymnasium complex includes a swimming pool, racquetball courts, specialized sports areas, a fitness center, an athletics field, and tennis courts. Men's varsity sports are baseball, basketball, bowling, cross-country, fencing, golf, judo, skiing, soccer, tennis, and volleyball. Intercollegiate sports for women are basketball, cross-country, fencing, golf, judo, skiing, softball, tennis, and volleyball. In 1997, NJIT athletics moved to NCAA Division II.

Location

NJIT is within walking distance of the Newark downtown area and nearby campuses of Rutgers University–Newark, Essex County College, the University of Medicine and Dentistry of New Jersey, and Seton Hall Law School, which, along with NJIT, are located in Newark's University Heights section. Students may take advantage of Newark's nationally ranked museum, library, and New Jersey Performing Arts Center (NJPAC) and may enjoy the city's burgeoning art scene. In addition, students have easy access to the vast cultural resources of the New York/New Jersey metropolitan area. NJIT is located only 20 minutes from both midtown and downtown Manhattan, and the city is easy to reach by bus, train, or car. A joint Rutgers/NJIT shuttle bus provides regular free commuting service to principal transportation centers.

Majors and Degrees

NJIT is a public research university that awards bachelor's degrees in applied mathematics; applied physics; architecture; biology; chemical engineering; chemistry; civil engineering; computer engineering; computer science; electrical engineering; engineering science (biomedical engineering, prelaw, preoptometry, premedicine, and predentistry); engineering technology (transfers only; concentrations in computers, construction/contracting, electrical, manufacturing, mechanical, and surveying); environmental science; geoscience engineering; history; industrial engineering; information systems; information technology (pending); management; mechanical engineering; professional and technical communication; science, technology, and society (interdisciplinary course work in humanities, social and natural sciences, and engineering or architecture); and statistics and actuarial science. Qualified students may major in two disciplines within NJIT. Students may also pursue a program combining bachelor's and master's degrees, which is normally completed in five years.

Academic Program

Academic programs that are designed to prepare professionals who can think critically and solve problems using information-age technology are available through NJIT's five colleges: Newark College of Engineering, which features a variety of engineering programs that are widely respected in business and government; New Jersey School of Architecture, which is a national leader in computer-aided design; College of Science and Liberal Arts, which offers a high-quality academic core, analytical leadership skills, one of the largest computer science departments, and a computational biology program; School of Management, which is designed to give students a firm grasp of the new technology-driven business world; and the Albert Dorman Honors College, which is among the nation's leading technology-oriented honors programs.

Students may pursue degrees in day and evening courses. Most day programs can be completed in four years of full-time study, and evening programs can be completed in eight years of part-time study. The Bachelor of Science degree in architecture is a four-year, full-time program that offers day and evening courses, while the Bachelor of Architecture degree requires five years of full-time study that is available only during the day. Students with associate degrees or the equivalent can earn a Bachelor of Science degree, notably in the engineering technology program. NJIT's engineering science degree permits students to design their own major in biomedical engineering, environmental science, or materials science.

New options include joint-degree programs with other schools. Administered by NJIT's Albert Dorman Honors College, the options include an accelerated B.S./M.D. or B.S./D.M.D. degree with the University of Medicine and Dentistry of New Jersey, a B.S./M.D. degree with St. George's University, a B.S./D.D.S. degree with the New York University College of Dentistry, a

B.S./O.D. degree with the SUNY College of Optometry, and a B.S./J.D. degree with the Rutgers University Law School.

Off-Campus Arrangements

NJIT cooperates with neighboring Rutgers University and Essex County College in cross-college enrollment programs. Nine degree programs are offered at NJIT's branch campus in Mt. Laurel, New Jersey. Undergraduate programs or courses are also offered in other regions of the state.

Academic Facilities

NJIT's extensive and powerful computing facilities support academic study, research, and administrative functions. Using fiber optics between buildings, a campuswide network connects more than 400 computing nodes that can be accessed from 2,000 on-campus and off-campus locations.

All full-time, first-time freshmen receive their own Pentium computer to use during their undergraduate years. Each computer package includes a hard disk drive, a floppy disk drive, a CD-ROM drive, a SVGA graphic card, a color VGA monitor, and an array of sophisticated software and equipment.

The university's Robert W. Van Houten Library along with a separate architecture library offer modern facilities for study, researching, and browsing. An electronic catalog provides local and remote access to its collection of approximately 150,000 books and 1,000 journal subscriptions. Access to journal literature on engineering, science, management, architecture, and other subject areas is provided by a variety of indexing and abstracting services. Electronic literature search is available on line and in CD-ROM formats. The library provides individualized reference services, instruction on the use of information resources, and orientation tours. In addition, students may supplement NJIT library resources by borrowing material from the Newark Public Library and the libraries of Rutgers University–Newark Campus, the University of Medicine and Dentistry, and the state colleges of New Jersey. Interlibrary loan arrangements with more distant institutions are also available.

Costs

For 1999–2000, the basic academic-year expenses for in-state, full-time undergraduate day students were $6480 for tuition and fees and approximately $950 for books and supplies. Out-of-state and international students paid $10,824 in tuition and fees. Room and board averaged $6772.

Financial Aid

Many NJIT students receive some sort of financial aid, which is awarded on the basis of financial need and academic record. Honors College scholars receive at least a one-half tuition scholarship award. Exceptionally well-prepared students may be eligible for additional scholarships and partial room grants. The Educational Opportunity Program (EOP) is available for educationally and financially disadvantaged students—regardless of their race, color, or creed—whose academic records may not adequately reflect their capabilities. EOP students are accepted at NJIT based on a special review of their potential for success. Most EOP students need financial aid and are eligible for state and federal assistance through funds at the university. Candidates for EOP must be New Jersey residents. Cooperative education at NJIT involves both academic credit and salary (an average of $27,000 to $32,000 for two professional experiences during 1999–2000) for professional job placements in business and industry related to the student's area of study. The placements alternate or are concurrent with course work and are available as an option for the bachelor's degree and for the joint B.S./M.S. Co-op Honors Program. Applications for financial aid should be submitted by March 15 for the fall semester. Information and applications may be obtained by writing to the Office of Financial Aid. Inquiries concerning the Honors College should be sent to its director.

Faculty

The university has a full-time faculty of 347 and an adjunct staff of 227. Ninety-eight percent of faculty members have the highest academic degree attainable in their field, are graduates of leading universities in the U.S. and abroad, and are engaged in specific research projects. The university highly values and each year recognizes teaching excellence with a special awards presentation. The student-faculty ratio is 14:1.

Student Government

NJIT's student affairs are presided over by a Student Senate, which administers a wide range of programs through the Activities Council, the Publications Council, Class Councils, the Interclub Council, the Honor Societies Council, and the Professional Societies Council. Students coordinate various events for an interesting and diversified social calendar and participate with faculty and administrators in formulating university policy.

Admission Requirements

All applicants for admission to programs leading to the bachelor's degree are required to complete 16 high school units in a college-preparatory program. This work must include 4 units of English and 2 units of laboratory science. Applicants for engineering, engineering science, or computer science are encouraged to take physics and chemistry as their laboratory sciences. Applicants for the program in architecture are encouraged to take biology and physics as their laboratory sciences. Mathematics requirements vary, depending on the bachelor's degree the applicant plans to pursue. Engineering, engineering science, computer science, statistics and actuarial science, applied chemistry, and architecture require 4 units of mathematics, including trigonometry. The SAT I or the ACT is required of all freshman applicants (the SAT I is preferred), and the SAT II: Subject Test in Mathematics (Level I or II) is required of applicants to the Honors College. Applicants in the top 30 percent of their class who have an SAT I mathematics score of at least 600 and a verbal score of 500 or better are usually considered for admission.

Transfer agreements exist with virtually every two-year college in the state.

NJIT does not discriminate on the basis of age, sex, sexual orientation, race, color, religion, national or ethnic origin, handicap, or veteran status in its educational programs, activities, or employment. NJIT's facilities are accessible to the disabled.

Application and Information

Applicants must submit a completed NJIT Undergraduate Admissions Form together with a nonrefundable application fee of $35 and an official transcript of secondary school work. Freshman applications should be received no later than April 1 for the fall semester and by December 1 for the spring semester. Transfer students should submit applications by June 1 for the fall semester and by November 1 for the spring semester. Applications may be submitted electronically via NJIT's World Wide Web home page. Notification of acceptance is on a rolling admission basis.

All application requests, catalog requests, and questions should be directed to:

University Admissions
New Jersey Institute of Technology
University Heights, Newark, New Jersey 07102-1982

Telephone: 973-596-3300
              800-925-NJIT (toll-free)
Fax: 973-596-3461
E-mail: admissions@njit.edu
World Wide Web: http://www.njit.edu

NEW MEXICO INSTITUTE OF MINING AND TECHNOLOGY
SOCORRO, NEW MEXICO

The Institute

The New Mexico Institute of Mining and Technology was founded in 1889 as the New Mexico School of Mines. The school's name was changed in 1951 to reflect a broadened curriculum that included the sciences and more fields of engineering. Referred to as New Mexico Tech by its students and faculty members, the university still celebrates its mining heritage with an annual 49ers Celebration.

New Mexico Tech is a research-oriented public university specializing in science and engineering. Tech students benefit from the low tuition of a public university and the personal attention characteristic of an expensive private college. A verdant, tree-filled campus with Southwestern-style architecture, a small-town setting, sunny weather, and spectacular views add to Tech's allure.

New Mexico Tech is accredited by the North Central Association of Colleges and Schools. All engineering programs are accredited by the Accreditation Board for Engineering and Technology, Inc.

Socorro and its surroundings are enjoyed by mountain bikers, runners, astronomers, hikers, campers, rock climbers, birders, geologists, rock hounds, photographers, and people who like the slower pace of small-town life. Tech's Performing Arts Series brings a variety of entertainment to campus each semester, and students can participate in the Music Program's vocal or instrumental performing groups, which present several public concerts and one musical production each year. Tech students also enjoy an active intramural sports program, a gymnasium with a weight room and sports equipment rentals, a Swim Center, and a championship 18-hole golf course.

Tech students participate in numerous clubs, from major-related ones, such as the Astronomy Club and the Institute of Electronic and Electrical Engineers student chapter; to clubs for specific groups, such as the Society of Women Engineers, Society of Hispanic Professional Engineers, and American Indian Science and Engineering Society; to interest-related groups, such as the Ski Club, Juggling Club, and the Children of the Sun skateboarding club.

Tech has eight residence halls and thirty-six student family housing units located on campus. Almost half of all students live on campus, although this is not required. Apartments, rental houses, and mobile homes are available in town for students who desire to live off campus. Rent and other costs of living are typically lower in Socorro than in most college towns.

The Campus Dining Room and Canteen Snack Bar, both located in the SUB, provide a variety of convenient and nutritious meals, all prepared fresh daily. On-campus residents are required to purchase a minimum meal plan of two meals per day Monday through Friday. Other meal plans are available to help students meet their schedules, including two meals per day on weekends. Students who require special dietary plans because of health or religious concerns are accommodated through a special menu developed with the student's and food service provider's input.

Student services provided by Tech include academic advising and tutoring, career placement services, short-term personal counseling, and programs for international students and students who are members of minority groups. An on-campus health clinic provides basic medical services. Special services for disabled students are available through the Counseling Office.

Location

Socorro (population 9,000) is located in the central Rio Grande valley, 76 miles south of Albuquerque and 194 miles north of El Paso. Air travelers can fly into Albuquerque's International Sunport and take a shuttle to Socorro. Commercial bus service is available from both Albuquerque and El Paso.

Majors and Degrees

New Mexico Tech offers Bachelor of Science degrees in basic sciences, biology, chemistry, computer science, earth science, environmental science, management and management of technology, mathematics, physics, psychology, and technical communication and in eight fields of engineering: chemical, electrical, engineering mechanics, environmental, general, materials, mineral, and petroleum.

Tech's Department of Earth and Environmental Sciences has the largest number of degree options: environmental science, geochemistry, geology, geophysics, and hydrology. The Computer Science, Electrical Engineering, and Physics Departments have the largest current enrollments, totaling 34 percent of all students.

Academic Program

Tech has a two-semester calendar with an eight-week summer session. All departments offer senior-level independent study courses. Engineering departments require yearlong senior design courses in which students work in teams.

Depending on the major, students must earn 130 to 139 credit hours to graduate. All students must satisfy general degree requirements, which include English, technical writing, humanities, social sciences, physics, chemistry, and mathematics. Engineering students must also satisfy a depth requirement in the humanities and social sciences. Most majors do not require a foreign language.

Academic Facilities

The library has 170,000 book and bound periodical volumes, 330,000 government documents, 17,650 maps, 43,000 nongovernment microforms, and several hundred computer files and compact discs. The electronic catalog and interlibrary loan service make a wide variety of books available.

The Tech Computer Center (TCC) operates a network of Sun, Linux, and Windows workstations. The TCC also has PC labs with Windows computers and an Apple lab with ten Macintosh systems. The campus network is connected to the National Science Foundation nationwide computer network, giving Tech access to thousands of other sites worldwide. All residence hall rooms are hardwired for Ethernet access.

The average Tech graduate accumulates seven months of work experience in research facilities located on campus. These facilities include the National Radio Astronomy Observatory, which operates its Very Large Array (VLA) radio telescope from its campus offices; Energetic Materials Research and Testing Center; Langmuir Laboratory for Atmospheric Research; Mount Erebus Volcanic Observatory; New Mexico Bureau of Mines and

Mineral Resources; New Mexico Geochronology Research Laboratory; New Mexico Tech Seismological Observatory; the Petroleum Recovery Research Center; and the IRIS/PASSCAL Instrument Center, which maintains more than 1,000 portable seismic instruments for use worldwide.

Costs

In 2000–01, resident undergraduate tuition is $1704 for the academic year. For undergraduates from out-of-state, it is $7030. Room costs range from about $760 to $1670 per semester, and board charges range from $412 to $1092 per semester, depending on the meal plan chosen.

Financial Aid

At New Mexico Tech, no student is denied the opportunity for a university education because of limited resources. Scholarships, grants, on-campus jobs, and educational loans are available through the Financial Aid Office. About 90 percent of Tech students receive financial aid.

Students are automatically considered for merit-based scholarships when they apply for admission to Tech. Students interested in receiving merit scholarships should apply as early as possible, since the scholarships with the highest dollar value have an application deadline of February 1. The deadline for most other undergraduate scholarships is March 1. The deadline for scholarships for transfer students is June 1.

New Mexico also offers Student Incentive Grants for residents. Residents of other states should check with their home states for information about similar grants.

Tech participates in the Federal Pell Grant, Federal Supplemental Educational Opportunity Grant (FSEOG), Federal Perkins Loan, and Federal PLUS loan programs. To apply for need-based federal financial aid, students must complete a Free Application for Federal Student Aid (FAFSA) and submit it to the appropriate agency before March 1.

Faculty

Nearly all (99 percent) of Tech's faculty members have a Ph.D. and conduct research. Yet, most classes are taught by full-time faculty members rather than graduate students. A remarkable 11:1 student-faculty ratio allows extensive interaction with professors in the classroom and laboratory. Most professors also live in Socorro and participate in Tech's social life along with their students. This extraordinary level of contact between faculty members and students promotes mentoring, which Tech alumni say is a key factor in their subsequent career successes.

Student Government

All full-time undergraduate students are members of Tech's Student Association. Any student may run for a seat on the Student Senate, the representative body that regulates student activities and organizations and provides funding for campus clubs and special events. Elections are held twice a year for one-year terms.

Admission Requirements

First-time students must have graduated from a regionally accredited high school with a 2.0 or higher grade point average or have passed the General Educational Development (GED) exam with a score of 50 or greater. They must also have successfully completed the following courses in high school: English, 4 units, with least 1 unit in composition at the junior or senior level; science, 2 units, with laboratories (from among biology, physics, chemistry, and earth science); mathematics, 3 units from among algebra I, algebra II, geometry, trigonometry, or higher mathematics; and social science, 3 units, including history. In addition, they must submit official ACT or SAT I scores. Tech's minimum requirement is an ACT composite score of 21 or a combined SAT I score of 970.

Transfer students must have completed the same high school courses required of first-time students. Transfer students must also submit college transcripts showing at least 30 credit hours and a cumulative GPA of 2.0 or higher and be in good academic standing and eligible to re-enroll at the last institution attended. New Mexico Tech accepts academic credits from accredited institutions of higher education. All credits are evaluated on a course-by-course basis. No credit earned at any institution while a student is on academic or disciplinary suspension is accepted. Actual course grades do not transfer.

Application and Information

First-time students must complete Tech's Application for Undergraduate Admission and Scholarship. They must also provide an official high school transcript and an official ACT Student Profile Report or an SAT College Report and pay a $15 application fee.

Transfer applicants must fulfill the requirements listed for first-time students and provide official transcripts from all colleges attended.

Application deadlines are August 1 for the fall semester, December 15 for the spring semester, and June 1 for the summer session.

Students should address inquiries to:

Melissa Jaramillo-Fleming
Director of Admission
New Mexico Institute of Mining and Technology
801 Leroy Place
Socorro, New Mexico 87801
Telephone: 505-835-5424
        800-428-TECH (8324) (toll-free)
Fax: 505-835-5989
E-mail: admission@admin.nmt.edu
World Wide Web: http://www.nmt.edu

NEW MEXICO STATE UNIVERSITY
LAS CRUCES, NEW MEXICO

The University

Founded in 1888 as Las Cruces College, New Mexico State University (NMSU) was designated the land-grant institution for New Mexico in 1889 and was renamed New Mexico College of Agriculture and Mechanic Arts. In 1960, the present name was adopted. NMSU has been accredited since 1926 by the North Central Association of Colleges and Schools as a degree-granting institution and now has 15,449 students from all fifty states and eighty-seven countries. In addition to its six undergraduate colleges, the University has a graduate college that offers fifty-one master's, four educational specialist, and twenty-four doctoral major areas. NMSU is ranked as one of eighty-eight top research universities in the nation by the Carnegie Foundation for the Advancement of Teaching.

University housing is available on campus in residence halls for men and women, family housing, and fraternity and sorority houses. The residence halls have space available for 2,800 single students, and housing assignments are made on a date-priority basis; half of the rooms are reserved for incoming freshmen. Students are encouraged to apply early for housing.

There are approximately 200 professional, social, academic, religious, and service groups on campus as well as an eighteen-hole golf course, lighted tennis courts, indoor and outdoor swimming pools, playing fields, and a track surfaced with rubberized asphalt. The activity center has dance rooms, weight-training equipment, an indoor track, and basketball, volleyball, and racquetball courts. NMSU has one of the best intramural programs in the country, offering more than fifty events. New Mexico State is a member of the NCAA Big West Conference. Men's teams compete in baseball, basketball, cross-country, football, golf, and tennis. Women's teams compete in basketball, cross-country, golf, softball, swimming, tennis, track, and volleyball.

Location

Las Cruces, the second-largest city in New Mexico, is a pleasant blend of its tricultural (Indian, Spanish, and Anglo) past and modern technology. The space shuttle *Columbia* landed at nearby White Sands Missile Range, just 45 miles from Old Mesilla, the stately Spanish plaza where the Gadsden Purchase was signed in 1853. The Organ Mountains are to the east, and the Rio Grande is to the west. Bordering the city are fertile farmlands. Only an hour and a half away are the ski resorts of Cloudcroft and Ruidoso. The largest cities on the border—El Paso, Texas, and Juárez, Mexico—are 40 minutes away.

Majors and Degrees

New Mexico State University's main campus offers undergraduate degrees through the Colleges of Agriculture and Home Economics, Arts and Sciences, Business Administration and Economics, Education, Engineering, and Health and Social Services. The following majors are offered, leading to the bachelor's degree: accounting; agricultural and extension education; agricultural biology; agricultural business and agricultural economics; agricultural engineering; agronomy; animal science; anthropology; art; athletic training education; biochemistry; biology; business computer systems; chemical engineering; chemistry; city and regional planning; civil engineering; clothing, textiles, and fashion merchandising; communication studies; communication disorders; community health; computer science; criminal justice; dance; early childhood education; economics; electrical/computer engineering; elementary education; engineering technology; English; environmental and occupational health; environmental science; family and child science; family and consumer sciences education; finance; fine arts; fishery science; food science and human nutrition; foreign languages; general agriculture; general business; geography; geological engineering; geology; government; history; horticulture; hotel, restaurant, and tourism management; individualized studies; industrial engineering; international business; journalism and mass communication; management; marketing; mathematics; mechanical engineering; microbiology; music; music education; nursing; philosophy; physics; psychology; range science; recreational areas management; secondary education (with endorsements in bilingual education, business education, foreign languages, general science, language arts, mathematics, physical education, social studies, and teaching English to speakers of other languages); social work; sociology; soil science; special education; studio art; surveying; theater arts; and wildlife science. Preprofessional programs are offered in chiropractic, dentistry, forestry, law, medicine, pharmacy, and veterinary medicine. Two-year associate degree programs are offered in arts, education paraprofessional studies, engineering technology, criminal justice, and prebusiness.

Academic Program

New Mexico State offers courses during two semesters and two 6-week summer sessions. NMSU awards both a designated and an undesignated associate degree following completion of 66 semester credits. The last 15–30 credits, depending on the requirements of the college in which the degree is pursued, must be completed at NMSU or one of its branches. To earn the bachelor's degree, students must meet the University's basic skill requirements in English and mathematics, successfully complete general education or constant courses as required in their particular college, complete 128–132 semester hours (including at least 55 in upper-division courses), and have a cumulative grade point average of 2.0 or higher. Students may receive credit for scores of 3, 4, or 5 on the Advanced Placement examinations of the College Board. A total of 30 credits may be obtained through the College-Level Examination Program general or subject examinations.

An honors program is available to entering freshmen with a minimum ACT composite score of 26. Continued participation is contingent on the maintenance of a minimum GPA of 3.3 in the freshman year and 3.5 in the sophomore, junior, and senior years. Students who attain higher overall GPAs and complete 18 credits of honors work are eligible to graduate with University Honors or with Distinction in University Honors.

Off-Campus Arrangements

NMSU's Cooperative Education Program had 657 students in 1998–99. Elements of the program include voluntary participation, three types of work-study schedules, and possible academic credit. In addition, through the National Student Exchange, students who qualify may study at any of 148 colleges and universities across the nation for credit while paying NMSU tuition.

Academic Facilities

Although New Mexico State's campus is one of the largest in the world (5,800 acres), the academic, administrative, and residence buildings are conveniently located close together. During the last ten years, more than fifteen buildings have been constructed, enlarged, or renovated. Each undergraduate college has a research division, and there are various specialized research institutes on campus, including the New Mexico Southwest Technology Development Institute and the Water Resources Institute. More than 1 million volumes and approximately 6,200 current periodicals are available in the two libraries, along with hundreds of thousands of government documents, maps, and archival materials. The library is open approximately 95 hours a week and provides a number of special services, including computerized literature searching and interlibrary loans.

Costs

Expenses for the 1999–2000 academic year (two semesters) were as follows: tuition, $2502 for New Mexico residents and $8166 for out-of-state residents; room and board, approximately $3975, depending on the housing and meal plan selected; and books and supplies, $634. Travel and personal expenses are additional. (All charges are subject to change.)

Financial Aid

The University has a broad financial aid program for students, including scholarships (academic need and non-need, activity, and athletic). Tuition scholarships are awarded on the basis of ACT scores and GPA; in-state recipients are granted a full waiver of tuition and fees, while out-of-state recipients are eligible to pay in-state tuition. Students wishing to apply for scholarships should complete the NMSU scholarship application form in the *Scholarship Guide*, available from the Financial Aid Office. All scholarship applicants must be admitted to the University before they can be given consideration and must meet a March 1 application deadline. NMSU participates in all federal programs, including the Federal Work-Study, Federal Perkins Loan, Federal Stafford Student Loan, Federal Pell Grant, and Federal Supplemental Educational Opportunity Grant programs, and in New Mexico state financial aid programs. Students may apply for these by completing the Free Application for Federal Student Aid (FAFSA) and must meet the March 1 deadline to be eligible. In the 1998–99 academic year, 77 percent of the enrolled students received aid. A wide variety of part-time jobs for students are available on campus; students should contact the Placement Office for further information.

Faculty

New Mexico State employs 652 full-time faculty members, 84 percent of whom hold doctoral degrees. The student-faculty ratio is about 18:1. There is generally no distinction between the graduate and undergraduate faculty members, many of whom are engaged in research projects. A faculty member from the department in which a student is majoring serves as the student's academic adviser. No major classes are taught by graduate students.

Student Government

There are six college councils that work closely with the dean of each college. The Associated Students of New Mexico State University is the student governing body and has an annual budget of approximately $700,000 (of which about $100,000 is for campus entertainment). The *Student Handbook* describes students' rights and responsibilities.

Admission Requirements

Prospective freshmen should apply during their senior year. Course work in high school must include 4 units in English, 2 of which must be in composition (1 of these must be at the junior/senior level); 3 units of mathematics, from algebra I, algebra II, geometry, trigonometry, or advanced math; 2 units of science beyond general science; and 1 unit of a foreign language or the fine arts. Students are eligible for regular admission if they graduate from a regionally accredited high school with the previously listed courses and meet one of the following conditions: (1) graduate with a cumulative GPA of 2.5 (on a 4.0 scale) or higher, or (2) graduate with an ACT composite score of 21 or higher, or (3) graduate with a GPA of at least 2.0 and an ACT composite score of at least 20. Once admitted, students will receive an invitation to one of the summer orientation/registration programs.

Transfer students must have a cumulative transfer grade point average of 2.0 (on a 4.0 scale) or higher. Transfer students who have not completed 30 credits must meet the freshman requirements. Official transcripts must be sent from each college or university attended. Transfer students who were suspended from the institution previously attended are not considered for admission until the terms of the suspension have been met.

Application and Information

The application and all required materials must be received by the Office of Admissions prior to registering for course work. New Mexico State has a rolling admission policy.

Inquiries should be addressed to:
Angela Mora-Riley
Director of Admissions, MSC 3A
Box 30001
New Mexico State University
Las Cruces, New Mexico 88003-8001
Telephone: 505-646-3121
        800-662-6678 (toll-free; for admissions only)
E-mail: admissions@nmsu.edu
World Wide Web: http://www.nmsu.edu

NEW SCHOOL BACHELOR OF ARTS
NEW SCHOOL UNIVERSITY
NEW YORK, NEW YORK

The University

New School University, formerly the New School for Social Research, was founded in 1919 by a small group of renowned American scholars and intellectuals, including John Dewey, Alvin Johnson, and Thorstein Veblen. They sought to develop a new kind of academic institution—a school of advanced adult education that would be free to address the real problems facing society in the twentieth century. Since 1944, the New School has offered adult students the opportunity to pursue course work in the liberal arts leading to the Bachelor of Arts degree. Established to meet the needs of students returning to college after World War II, the New School Bachelor of Arts Program allowed working adults to complete an undergraduate degree part-time or full-time during either the day or the evening. The approach was new but very much in keeping with the commitment of the New School to adult education and to the idea of learning as a lifelong endeavor.

The student body, numbering approximately 400, represents a particularly diverse group of individuals. While a significant number of students attend full-time, an even larger group attends on a part-time basis. The New York metropolitan area accounts for three quarters of the student body; international students and students from other states make up the remainder. Although the majority are in their twenties and thirties, students of all ages are present. Most students hold jobs while attending school and many have family responsibilities.

The New School has long been a home for leading artists, educators, and public figures. The New School was the first institution of higher learning to offer college-level courses in such "new" fields as psychoanalysis, taught by Freud's disciple, Sandor Ferenczi in 1926; African-American culture and history, taught by W. E. B. DuBois in 1948; and women's studies, offered by Gerda Lerner in 1962. It also was one of the first colleges or universities to offer instruction in art forms that flourished during the twentieth century, such as photography, film, jazz, and modern dance. Among the world-famous artists and performers who have taught at the New School are Martha Graham, Berenice Abbott, Aaron Copland, Frank Lloyd Wright, and Thomas Hart Benton. Today, many noted scholars and creative artists are among the hundreds of instructors who teach at the New School.

The New School, the founding division of New School University, offers graduate programs in media studies, teacher education, and creative writing in addition to the Bachelor of Arts Program.

The other academic divisions of New School University are the Graduate Faculty of Political and Social Science (founded in 1933 as the University in Exile), which grants M.A. and Ph.D. degrees; the Milano Graduate School of Management and Urban Policy, which awards the M.S. and Ph.D. degrees; Parsons School of Design, with programs in the fine arts and design on the undergraduate and graduate levels; Eugene Lang College, an undergraduate degree program for traditional-age students; the Mannes School of Music, with undergraduate and graduate programs in performance and theory (including both classical and jazz); and the Actors Studio School of Dramatic Arts, which offers an M.F.A. in acting, directing, and playwriting. In 1999–2000, the university served approximately 20,000 students (part-time and full-time) each semester.

Location

The New School is located in New York City's Greenwich Village, which historically has been a center for intellectual and artistic life. Over and above the resources of Greenwich Village, New York City offers virtually unlimited cultural, artistic, recreational, and intellectual resources.

Majors and Degrees

The New School offers the Bachelor of Arts degree in liberal arts. There are no majors, but formal concentrations are available in film, literature, psychology, and writing. Most students develop individualized concentrations in a wide variety of academic fields as well as in interdisciplinary areas. In addition, professional certificates are offered in the following fields: alcohol and substance abuse counseling, creative arts therapies, English language teaching, and film production.

Academic Program

Fully integrated with the curriculum of the New School, the Bachelor of Arts serves a broad range of adult students who are committed to learning in an environment that is flexible and intellectually challenging. While three quarters of the 120 credits applied toward the degree must be in liberal arts, students are encouraged to develop a program appropriate to their own needs. Choices are made from more than 1,000 courses offered each semester in the humanities, social and natural sciences, fine arts, performing arts, foreign languages, writing, communication, and business. In consultation with a faculty adviser, students plan a program of study that enables them to explore their intellectual and career objectives. The primary organizing principle is determined by the individual interests, talents, and goals of each student. Within this context, students may elect structured concentrations of course work in a particular field or may design their own course of study.

Credit may be awarded for prior learning based on a portfolio assessment process or standardized examinations such as CLEP.

Most classes are small, with 15 to 25 students, and are conducted through a combination of lecture and discussion. Classes are scheduled during a variety of times, allowing adults with work and family responsibilities to choose class times that are convenient for them. Classes are offered every weekday, beginning at 9 a.m. and continuing until 9:30 p.m., with the majority scheduled in the late afternoon and early evening. A few courses are offered on weekends as well. The New School operates on a semester system, with 15 week terms during the fall and spring and an intensive summer session that begins in early June and ends in July.

For students planning to go on to a graduate program at the university, the New School offers an accelerated B.A./M.A. program. Students may apply for B.A./M.A. status upon completion of 60 college credits and at least one semester of satisfactory work in the Bachelor of Arts Program. Students admitted to an accelerated degree program may apply up to 12 graduate credits toward the 120 undergraduate credits required to earn the B.A. degree. These same graduate credits apply toward completion of the graduate degree when the student matriculates in the designated master's program.

Accelerated B.A./M.A. programs are available in anthropology, economics, gender studies, historical studies, liberal studies, media studies, philosophy, political science, psychoanalytic studies, psychology, sociology, and urban policy analysis and management.

An accelerated B.A./M.S.T. program is available in teacher education on the secondary level.

Off-Campus Arrangements

In addition to traditional classes, the New School offers an alternative approach to adult education through DIAL (Distance Instruction for Adult Learners). Using asynchronous computer conferencing, students can participate in their classes any time and any place they have access to the Internet. All students matriculating in the Bachelor of Arts Program can include DIAL courses in their programs. Students living outside the New York area who meet special admissions requirements can take all of their courses through DIAL.

Qualified students are also able to participate in independent study, internships, and study-abroad programs.

Academic Facilities

The Bachelor of Arts Program is situated in the main academic center at 66 West 12th Street.

New School Bachelor of Arts students have full access to the Raymond Fogelman Library (New School/Graduate Faculty), the Adam and Sophie Gimble Design Library (New School/Parsons), the Cooper Union for the Advancement of Science and Art Library (Cooper Union), and the Elmer Bobst Library (New York University). Together, these libraries house approximately 3 million volumes that cover all the traditional liberal arts disciplines and the fine arts.

New School Bachelor of Arts students also have access to additional university facilities that include a University Computing Center with both Macintosh and IBM-compatible computers, laser printers, and software; a 500-seat auditorium; various galleries; extensive darkroom and filmmaking facilities; dance facilities; and studios for the fine arts as well as classrooms and faculty offices.

Costs

Tuition for the 2000–01 academic year is $558 per credit. Students pay a $100 registration fee each semester, and there is a student services fee of $8.

Financial Aid

B.A. degree candidates enrolled for 6 or more credits are eligible to apply for federal, state, and institutional aid. All applicants must file the Free Application for Federal Student Aid (FAFSA). The Title IV code for the New School is 002780. Students may begin the process of applying for financial aid prior to admission. Financial aid awards are made on a rolling basis after the applicant has been accepted into the program. Institutional aid is awarded on the basis of both need and merit. Financial aid is renewable each year as long as need continues and students maintain satisfactory academic standing.

Faculty

Instructors at the New School come from diverse fields within and outside the field of education. They all share one common motivation: teaching what they are most interested in and what they consider most valuable to know. In addition to academic scholars, many are working professionals who bring to the classroom the benefit of their experience. Writing workshops are taught by published authors, film production workshops by filmmakers, theater arts courses by actors and directors, and business courses by professionals with substantial business and corporate experience. The combination of interest and professional competence makes for a rich classroom experience.

Student advising is an essential feature of the Bachelor of Arts Program. A small number of instructors in the humanities and social sciences hold special appointments as core faculty members. These faculty members work closely with students in planning the students' academic programs and are available throughout the year for educational advising.

Student Government

Students are encouraged to participate in the governance of the program and the School in a number of ways. Student Advisory Committees serve at both the program and university levels. Students are invited to serve on many university committees, such as diversity, food services, library, and student life.

Admission Requirements

The New School welcomes applications from individuals who have the maturity necessary to be responsible for their own learning process and who can demonstrate their ability to work successfully in an intellectually rigorous and challenging environment. Most applicants have completed at least one year of study (30 credits) at an accredited college or university. Applicants who are 24 years old or older and have fewer than 30 transfer credits may apply for special admission. Applicants who live at a distance from the New School and plan to complete their course work through DIAL must have completed at least 60 credits at an accredited college or university prior to admission. All applicants must submit transcripts from each college previously attended; an application form, including an essay and statement of purpose; and a nonrefundable $30 application fee. An interview, either in person or by telephone if the applicant lives at a distance, is required of all applicants.

Application and Information

Application deadlines are August 1 for the fall semester and December 1 for the spring semester. Applications are reviewed as they are completed and applicants are informed of decisions shortly after the interview. A Bachelor of Arts Program brochure and the *New School Bulletin* will be sent upon request. Open houses are held approximately once a month.

For further information students may contact:

Office of Admissions
New School Bachelor of Arts Program
New School University
66 West 12th Street, Room 401
New York, New York 10011
Telephone: 212-229-5630
              800-862-5039 (toll-free)
E-mail: admissions@dialnsa.edu
World Wide Web: http://www.nsu.newschool.edu/ba/

NEW YORK INSTITUTE OF TECHNOLOGY
OLD WESTBURY, CENTRAL ISLIP, AND MANHATTAN CAMPUSES, NEW YORK

The College

New York Institute of Technology is an independent, nonsectarian, coeducational, and fully accredited college. Graduate and undergraduate curriculums prepare students for realistic goals in business and the professions. College-level courses are available for qualified high school students. Master's programs include business administration, communication arts, human relations, computer science, energy management, clinical nutrition, human resources management and labor relations, instructional technology, elementary education, environmental technology, and electrical engineering. Specialized courses, accelerated study, and noncredit and certificate programs are available for adults. Some courses are available in a distance learning format using fiber-optic laboratories.

NYIT's total enrollment is 10,221 men and women, of whom about 7,301 are undergraduates. Students who live or work in and around New York City find the Manhattan Campus conducive to academic life. The urban campus contains a full complement of offerings, is centrally located, and takes advantage of cultural resources. The 750-acre Dorothy Schure Old Westbury Campus in Nassau County, less than 25 miles east of New York City, is composed of former Gold Coast estates. A Student Activity Center provides facilities for dining, recreation, athletics, and social events. It adjoins a gymnasium/field house complex. The Central Islip Campus provides residence halls, a golf course, dining rooms, a Student Activities Center, a swimming pool, bowling alleys, and library and computer facilities in addition to the many graduate and undergraduate curriculums offered during day and evening hours. NYIT has six national honor societies in business, behavioral sciences, physics, technology, economics, and broadcasting. There are varsity sports for men and women. Baseball, basketball, cross-country, lacrosse, soccer, softball, track and field, and volleyball contests are scheduled at home and away. Intramural sports are available. NYIT has a full range of career-development, cooperative education services that assist students in obtaining vocational testing and advisement, employment upon graduation, or part-time employment while still in school. Specialized counseling services assist students with academic or social problems. The majority of students commute daily to all campuses. However, other living accommodations are available in addition to the residence halls at the Central Islip Campus. The College-Wide Cultural Committee sponsors programs and events, including concerts, dance performances, and lectures.

New York College of Osteopathic Medicine of NYIT, the first of its kind in New York State, is affiliated with several teaching hospitals. Students pursue the Doctor of Osteopathy (D.O.) degree and are prepared for internships and residencies in family practice or for advanced study in medical specialties. NYCOM's Academic Health Care Centers serve the medical needs of the NYIT community and the general public.

Location

The Long Island campuses take advantage of the special offerings of Nassau and Suffolk counties—Long Island Sound, Jones Beach, the many shopping malls, restaurants, summer resorts and motels, libraries, theaters, and proximity to Manhattan. Buses and the Long Island Rail Road serve Old Westbury and Central Islip; the Manhattan Campus is within walking distance of Columbus Circle and Lincoln Center and is easily reached by public transportation. Highlights of the city contribute to the educational experience.

Majors and Degrees

New York Institute of Technology offers Associate in Applied Science, Associate in Occupational Studies, Bachelor of Science, Bachelor of Arts, Bachelor of Fine Arts, Bachelor of Architecture (five years), Bachelor of Technology, and Bachelor of Professional Studies degrees. Majors and options are accounting, advertising, aerospace engineering, architectural technology, architecture, behavioral sciences, biology, biomedical engineering, biomedical engineering technology, business administration, chemistry, communication arts, community mental health, computer science, criminal justice, culinary arts, electrical and computer engineering, electrical engineering technology, elementary education, English, environmental technology, finance, fine arts/computer graphics, graphic design, hospitality management, human resources management, interdisciplinary studies, interior design, life sciences, management, management of information systems, marketing, mechanical engineering, mechanical technology, nursing, nutrition science, occupational therapy, physician assistant studies, physical therapy, political science, premedical and allied health professions, psychology, small business management and entrepreneurship, sociology, teacher and occupational education, and telecommunications management.

Students who qualify may enroll in a bachelor's degree/osteopathic medicine degree (B.S./D.O.) curriculum, reducing study time from eight years to seven. Combined-degree programs leading to the Bachelor of Fine Arts/Master of Arts in communication arts, a BS/JD degree in conjunction with Touro Law Center, and the Bachelor of Science in architectural technology/Master of Science in energy management are also available.

Academic Program

The academic year consists of two semesters. Summer sessions, accelerated courses, and intersession are also available. Undergraduate programs prepare students for careers in the professional and operational ranks of business and industry. Programs expose students to basic principles of specialized skills and encourage development of management and middle management leadership qualities. Humanities and social sciences courses extend throughout all programs of study, and each major includes a choice of electives.

Academic components are organized into areas of related curriculums, thereby providing opportunities for interdisciplinary study within and among the Schools of Allied Health and Life Sciences; Architecture and Design; Education; Engineering and Technology; Arts, Sciences and Communication; and Management.

Entering students who have not decided on a major are placed into the Interdisciplinary Studies Program to explore one or more study areas before choosing a concentration. Credits earned in the first semester apply toward the chosen major. Degree requirements vary according to program.

NYIT, in collaboration with the U.S. Air Force, offers the

AFROTC program on the Central Islip campus. ROTC scholarships are available for qualified applicants in four- and two-year programs.

Off-Campus Arrangements

Architecture students are involved in supervised community and professional projects, working with local citizens and practicing architects. A special externship program, open to qualified students, offers an opportunity to earn college credits while acquiring professional experience. Students majoring in communication arts are assigned to television and radio stations, media departments of various systems, and professional environments. In their senior year, fine arts students work for advertising and interior design firms. Culinary arts students participate in the operation of two outstanding dining and catering facilities on the Old Westbury and Central Islip campuses. Field placements are available for students in behavioral sciences. NYIT cooperates with other colleges in student-exchange plans for course work and library use.

Academic Facilities

Modern technological equipment supports the variety of career offerings. Laboratories serve natural science disciplines in chemistry, physics, and biology, as well as engineering and technology curricula in mechanical, electrical, and computer areas. Communication students use full-color equipment that simulates commercial broadcasting stations. NYIT's News Bureau produces "LI News Tonight," a nightly local news show, aired on five cable television systems. Radio stations WNYT and WTNY are student operated and offer valuable experience in broadcasting. There are architectural studios, a library, display areas, and classrooms supporting the only professional five-year Bachelor of Architecture program in the Nassau-Suffolk County region. The Office of Technology Based Learning Systems has a network of computers for instruction, research, and administrative data processing. Microcomputers and Internet are available for student and faculty member access. Specialized computer graphics facilities are available for students showing research aptitude in this area. Computer-aided design (CAD) and other applications of computers in architecture are served by a laboratory facility. Wisser Memorial Library in Old Westbury serves all campuses. The ultramodern (electronic library with videodisc and CD-ROM reference tools and workstations) three-story facility provides space for student research and study, as well as a library research skills classroom.

Costs

Basic tuition and fees for the 1999–2000 academic year were $11,990 or $13,610 (depending on the major) for full-time undergraduates. Room and board figures vary. Tuition and laboratory and special fees are listed in all NYIT publications, along with refund policies.

Financial Aid

NYIT offers a variety of financial aid to qualified students who might otherwise be unable to attend college. The program draws from NYIT funds and from state and federal funds, and it offers scholarships, grants-in-aid, loans, and employment. Awards recognize scholastic achievement, financial need, character and promise, competence in a particular field, or distinctive contribution to the college or community. NYIT is a member of the College Scholarship Service and requests all aid applicants to file the Free Application for Federal Student Aid (FAFSA). Forms can be obtained from NYIT or a high school guidance office. Service-to-school grants-in-aid recognize demonstrated ability in athletics as well as academic achievement.

The Honor and Challenge Scholarship recognizes high school achievers if they have at least a B average and either a minimum combined SAT I score of 1180 or a minimum composite ACT score of 27. This award is based on ability and is not related to financial need. Transfer scholarships are available for graduates from accredited two- and four-year colleges. Awards are based on cumulative quality grade point averages. Students should contact the director of financial aid in Old Westbury for all details.

Faculty

The resident faculty is a distinguished one, holding professorial ranks and various professional credentials. A generous salary schedule and a wholesome governance structure have attracted a talented faculty whose members respond to the contemporary needs of NYIT and its student body. Students' college life is enriched by the presence on campus of professionals to whom they can turn for motivation and guidance as well as instruction.

Student Government

Full-time day students are automatically members of the student government association at each campus. Each government charters student organizations and controls funds granted by the college. Students participate in selection of officers and representatives. Student-elected representatives deal with faculty and administration on various issues.

Admission Requirements

Admission is based on educational preparation and the personal ability necessary for academic success. Evidence of character and maturity is regarded as essential. Applicants must have a high school diploma or the equivalent. Each applicant receives individual consideration through a comprehensive evaluation of previous records, the recommendation of a principal or guidance counselor, SAT I or ACT scores, and aptitude and motivation for success in a specific program. Some programs, such as B.S./D.O., occupational therapy, physical therapy, and nursing, have special requirements, such as interviews and letters of recommendation. Transfer students (including those from junior colleges) are considered for admission under the same general procedure. Official transcripts should be forwarded to the Office of Admissions. Transfer credit may be given for courses completed at accredited institutions acceptable to NYIT standards.

Application and Information

A nonrefundable fee of $50 is required with the completed application. An online application is available at the World Wide Web address listed below. Students are admitted on a rolling basis (with the exception of selected Allied Health Programs), and the Committee on Admissions notifies applicants by mail, usually within a month after all proper credentials have been received. To arrange for an interview and a tour of any campus or to receive additional information, students should contact:

Director of Admissions
New York Institute of Technology
P.O. Box 8000
Old Westbury, New York 11568-8000
Telephone: 516-686-7520 (Old Westbury)
           800-345-NYIT (toll-free)
           212-261-1508 (Manhattan)
           516-348-3200 (Central Islip)
           800-873-NYIT (toll-free)
E-mail: admissions@nyit.edu
World Wide Web: http://www.nyit.edu

NEW YORK SCHOOL OF INTERIOR DESIGN
NEW YORK, NEW YORK

The School

The New York School of Interior Design (NYSID) is an independent, coeducational, nonprofit college accredited by NASAD. It was established in 1916 by architect Sherrill Whiton and chartered by the Board of Regents of the University of the State of New York in 1924. Throughout its history, the School has devoted all of its resources to a single field of study—interior design—and has played a significant role in the development of the interior design profession. Enrollment is approximately 700.

NYSID continually updates its curriculum to reflect the many changes taking place in interior design. Today's students learn not only the colors and materials appropriate to period residential interiors, but also how to design hospitals and restaurants and offices with barrier-free access. Whether learning the importance of historic preservation or the latest programs in computer-aided design, NYSID students learn a wide range of skills and techniques taught by faculty members who work in the field. The area's professional design studios, art and antique shops, showrooms, and museums are all an exciting part of the college's "campus."

The atmosphere of the college is cosmopolitan, not only because of its excellent location but also because it attracts students from all areas of the United States and abroad. International students make up approximately 10 percent of the student population. Students also transfer from other colleges in order to obtain a more professional, career-directed education.

Because of its select faculty and established reputation, the School continues to maintain a close relationship with the interior design industry. This provides an excellent means for students to develop associations that offer opportunities to move into the profession after completing their degree program at NYSID. As part of the mission statement of the New York School of Interior Design, founder Sherrill Whiton wrote: "The value in studying the decorative arts is not limited to its contribution toward creative effort or to the development of the imagination. A greater benefit is the cultural information that is acquired in the process. The roots of these arts entwine themselves around nearly all branches of human thought and activity, and an understanding of them will aid greatly in the development of one's ability to analyze, reason and judge human affairs."

In addition to the three major programs in interior design listed below, NYSID also offers a postprofessional Master of Fine Arts (M.F.A.) degree in interior design.

Location

The New York School of Interior Design is located on Manhattan's upper East Side, where many of the major interior design studios are located. Many of the world's most important museums, galleries, and showrooms are close by, most within walking distance. The city is world-renowned for its cultural activities, architecture, historic districts, and cosmopolitan urban experience. The college can be reached easily by bus, subway, train, and car.

Majors and Degrees

The New York School of Interior Design offers three major programs in interior design: a four-year Bachelor of Fine Arts (B.F.A.) degree accredited by FIDER, a two-year Associate in Applied Science (A.A.S.) degree, and a 24-credit nondegree Basic Interior Design Program.

Academic Program

The New York School of Interior Design is a single-major college. It devotes all of its resources to providing a comprehensive education in interior design, and the carefully organized curriculum is constantly evaluated by professionals in the field. The various academic programs compose an integrated curriculum covering interior design concepts; history of art, architecture, interiors, and furniture; technical and communication skills, materials and methods, philosophy and theory; and professional design procedures and design problem solving.

The Basic Interior Design Program consists of a 24-credit required sequence of basic courses in which all students enroll. These courses provide a general, cultural, and professional introduction to the field of interior design. Although completion of the Basic Interior Design Program may be the major goal for some, for most students it serves as the foundation for matriculation into the degree programs.

The A.A.S. degree program provides the minimum educational requirement to become a certified interior designer in New York State. The 66-credit program includes professional, design, and liberal arts courses.

The 132-credit Bachelor of Fine Arts degree program provides the education that, with practical experience, enables the graduate to take qualifying exams for interior design certification in many states and to join national and local professional associations. Studies focus on the development of a broad array of technical skills, conceptual analysis, creative problem solving, and relevant cultural developments. Students are required to take liberal arts courses in art and architectural history in addition to varied design courses.

The program planning is flexible and permits students, at various points in their college career, to take courses on a part-time basis during the day or evening and on Saturday. The School maintains an active job placement service. Students may be placed in a wide variety of positions that reflect the full spectrum of job opportunities in the interior design profession.

Academic Facilities

The School is located at 170 East 70th Street in a five-level Beaux Arts–style building constructed in 1901 and designed by C. P. Gilbert. It has two lecture halls; sixteen classrooms; a large atelier where students can work between and after classes; two galleries to feature exhibitions of special interest; a computer-aided design lab; a new lighting design lab; and a library containing a comprehensive collection of books, journals, periodicals, trade and auction catalogs, and other publications devoted to interior design and related fine arts. An adjacent building houses student services and administrative offices.

Costs

Tuition for 2000–01 is $500 per credit, plus a $70 registration/technology fee each semester. There are additional costs for supplies and textbooks, depending on the courses for which a student registers. Typical full-time expenses for the first year (exclusive of room and board, which the college does not provide, and personal expenses) are as follows: tuition, $16,000 (16 credits per semester); registration fees, $140; and supplies and textbooks, $1000.

Financial Aid

The New York School of Interior Design is concerned about students with limited financial resources and makes every attempt to provide assistance. Several institutional scholarships are available for students who meet the criteria. Students are encouraged to apply for the New York State Tuition Assistance Program (TAP—for New York State residents only), the Federal Pell Grant, and Federal Education Loans. In addition, because of the college's location and its close relationship with the interior design industry, its job placement counselor is very effective in helping students find part-time employment.

Faculty

The college's programs are supported by an excellent and dedicated faculty of 95. In addition to teaching, faculty members have active professional careers in interior design, architecture, lighting design, fine arts, furniture and fabric design, history, psychology, decorative arts, law, and appraising.

Student Government

The college has a student government and an active student chapter of the American Society of Interior Designers (ASID). ASID organizes lectures, tours, workshops, and other events throughout the school year, providing an inside view of the interior design industry.

Admission Requirements

All applicants must submit an application, an official secondary school transcript, SAT I or ACT scores, and two letters of recommendation. Applicants to degree programs must meet the visual requirements by providing a portfolio or sketchbook described in the catalog; transfer students must also submit college transcripts.

Interviews are recommended for all applicants.

International applicants should contact the college's International Student Adviser for assistance in applying.

Application and Information

Admission decisions are made on a rolling basis; it is recommended that applications be submitted at least eight weeks prior to the start of the first semester for which the student applies. Applicants are notified of the Admission Committee's decision by mail shortly after all required documents have been received and visual requirements fulfilled.

Inquiries and applications should be directed to:

Director of Admissions
New York School of Interior Design
170 East 70th Street
New York, New York 10021-5110
Telephone: 212-472-1500 Ext. 204
              800-336-9743 (toll-free)
Fax: 212-472-1867
E-mail: admissions@nysid.edu
World Wide Web: http://www.nysid.edu

Home of the New York School of Interior Design, a landmark building at 170 East 70th Street, New York City.

NEW YORK UNIVERSITY
NEW YORK, NEW YORK

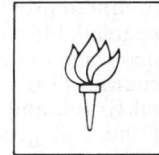

The University

New York University (NYU) was founded in 1831 by Albert Gallatin, Secretary of the Treasury under Thomas Jefferson; he believed that the place for a university was not in "the seclusion of cloistered halls but in the throbbing heart of a great city." NYU draws top students from every state and more than 120 countries. The distinguished academic atmosphere attracts the teachers, and the teachers and the atmosphere together attract the students who are capable of benefiting from both. Within three years of graduation, 80 percent of NYU's students go on to postbaccalaureate work. Of those who apply for admission to medical school, 85 percent are accepted, placing NYU well above the national average. The faculty includes world-famous scholars, researchers, and artists, among them Nobel laureates, winners of the Pulitzer Prize, and members of the National Science Foundation. NYU is a member of the prestigious Association of American Universities. A study sponsored by the National Science Foundation placed NYU among the top four universities in the country in the number of "leading intellectuals" on the faculty. Full professors teach on both the graduate and undergraduate levels. Seven undergraduate divisions provide extensive offerings in a wide range of subjects: more than 2,500 courses in 160 major fields are available to NYU's full-time undergraduates. The average class size is under 30, and the faculty-student ratio is 1:13—benefits generally associated with a much smaller institution.

NYU's residence hall program is an important aspect of the total educational experience. Approximately 7,600 undergraduate students live in fifteen University residence halls. All freshmen who request housing on their admission application and meet all deadlines are guaranteed housing accommodations during all their years of undergraduate study. All residence halls are located on or within close walking distance of Washington Square, the focal point of the campus. Freshmen are not required to live on campus, and many students live in private apartments off campus.

The traditions of campus life—more than 250 clubs, eleven fraternities and eleven sororities, and athletics and other activities—are very much a part of the University. Students have the opportunity to write for six campus newspapers and twelve journals and magazines and to work with the University's own radio stations, WNYU-AM and WNYU-FM. The Jerome S. Coles Sports and Recreation Center serves the recreational needs of all students, provides the setting for a full intramural sports program, and is home to NYU's nineteen intercollegiate teams. NYU and eight other private, urban research universities have formed a varsity league, the University Athletic Association. The athletic program includes men's basketball, fencing, golf, soccer, swimming and diving, tennis, track and cross-country, volleyball, and wrestling and women's basketball, cross-country, fencing, soccer, swimming and diving, tennis, track, and volleyball.

Location

NYU's undergraduate center is located in historic Greenwich Village, which is virtually an extension of the University. Greenwich Village, traditionally a community of artists and intellectuals, is famous for its contributions to the fine arts, literature, and drama and for its small-scale, European style of living. NYU's campus is within minutes of off-Broadway drama and dance, boutiques, art galleries, coffeehouses, restaurants, clubs, bookstores, record stores, Little Italy, Chinatown, and world-renowned museums and libraries. Intellectual stimulation abounds.

Through course work and through outside activities, students can enjoy all of the advantages of New York City. As an international center of finance, culture, and communications, New York City offers unmatched educational, internship, and social opportunities. NYU's campus is perhaps one campus in America that could not be mistaken for any other.

Majors and Degrees

The College of Arts and Science awards B.A. and B.S. degrees in Africana studies; ancient studies; anthropology; anthropology-linguistics; Arabic; archaeology; art history; Asian/Pacific/American studies; astronomy; biochemistry; biology; chemistry; Chinese; classical civilization and Hellenic studies; classics; classics-anthropology; classics (fine arts); comparative literature; computer science; computer science and mathematics; creative writing; dramatic literature, theater history, and the cinema; earth and environmental science; East Asian languages (Chinese/Japanese/Korean); East Asian studies; economics; economics and computer science; economics and mathematics; education; engineering (chemical, civil, computer, electrical, environmental, mechanical, and engineering physics); English; English and American literature; European studies; fine arts; French and linguistics; French language and literature; German and linguistics; Germanic languages and literature; Greek; Hebrew language and literature; Hellenic studies; history; Italian and linguistics; Italian language and literature; Japanese; Jewish history and civilization; journalism and mass communications; Korean; language and mind; Latin; Latin American literature; Latin American studies; Latin and Greek; law and society; linguistics; literature in translation; Luso-Brazilian language and literature; mathematics; mathematics and computer science; medieval and Renaissance studies; metropolitan studies; Middle Eastern civilization; Middle Eastern languages; Middle Eastern studies; music; neural science; peace and global policy; Persian; philosophy; physics; politics; Portuguese language and literature; psychology; public policy; religious studies; Romance languages; Russian; Russian and Slavic studies; social work; sociology; Spanish and linguistics; Spanish language and literature; Turkish; urban design and architecture studies; West European studies; and women's studies. Preprofessional programs are available in dentistry, law, medicine, optometry, and podiatry. A B.S./B.E. program in engineering, a seven-year B.A./D.D.S. program, and an eight-year B.A./M.D. program are available.

Stern School of Business awards the B.S. degree in accounting, actuarial science, economics, finance, general business, information systems, international business, management, marketing, operations research, and statistics. An accelerated B.S./M.P.A. program and a five-year B.S./M.S. program in statistics and operations research are available.

The School of Education awards the B.S. degree in arts professions (with majors in studio art and educational theater), communications (with majors in communication studies and in graphic communications management and technology), education (with majors in early childhood and elementary education; secondary education with a teaching specialization in English, foreign language, mathematics, science, or social studies; and special education), health and nursing (with majors in nursing; nutrition and food studies; speech-language pathology and audiology for teachers of speech and hearing handicapped; and applied psychological studies, for transfer students only), and music (with majors in music business, music technology, music education, music performance, music theory and composition, and voice).

Tisch School of the Arts awards the B.F.A. degree in animation, cinema studies (film history, theory, and criticism), dance, drama (acting, musical theater, directing, and technical management), dramatic writing, film production, photography, radio production, and television production. The School of Social Work awards the B.S. degree in social work. The Gallatin School of Individualized Study awards the B.A. degree. The School of Continuing and Professional Studies offers a two-year liberal arts (general studies) program leading to the Associate in Arts degree, the B.S. degree in sports management and leisure studies, the B.S. degree in hotel and tourism management, and the B.A. degree for adults.

Academic Program

Requirements for graduation vary among departments and schools. A liberal arts core curriculum is an integral part of all areas of concentration. The baccalaureate degree requires completion of at least 128 credits. The University calendar is organized on the traditional semester system, including two 6-week summer sessions. Some divisions offer part-time programs during the day and evening and on weekends.

Off-Campus Arrangements

Through its seven undergraduate colleges, the University administers a number of programs abroad, including those at NYU sites in Paris, Madrid, Florence, London, Buenos Aires, and Prague. Exchange programs with several historically black colleges and universities from around the world are also offered.

Academic Facilities

NYU's Bobst Library, one of the largest open-stack research libraries in the world, has more than 40 miles of open stacks housing some 2.5 million volumes. Among the collections in Bobst are the Avery R. Fisher Center for Music and Media, the Microfilm Center, and the largest official depository of United Nations records and publications outside of the UN itself. Bobst is one of seven NYU libraries. La Maison Française, the Deutsches Haus, the Alexander Onassis Center for Hellenic Studies, the Lewis L. and Loretta Brennen Glucksman Ireland House, the Hagop Kervorkian Center for Near Eastern Studies, the Casa Italiana, and the King Juan Carlos I of Spain Center broaden the range of international programs on campus. The Grey Art Gallery and Study Center, the University's fine arts museum, presents six or seven innovative exhibitions each year that encompass all aspects of the visual arts.

Costs

For 2000–01, tuition and fees cost $24,336, and room and board cost $9226. Books and supplies cost about $450, and personal expenses total between $500 and $1000.

Financial Aid

Financial aid at NYU comes from many sources. All students are encouraged to apply for financial assistance or one of NYU's innovative financing plans. Seventy-seven percent of NYU's undergraduates receive financial assistance. Each year more than 1,700 entering freshmen are awarded scholarships based on academic promise and/or financial need. The University may offer a package of aid that includes scholarships or grants, loans, or work-study programs. NYU requires the submission of the Free Application for Federal Student Aid (FAFSA). The deadline for filing this financial aid form is February 15 for the fall semester and November 1 for the spring semester.

Faculty

NYU employs 3,507 faculty members (1,465 full-time and 2,042 part-time). Ninety-nine percent have the doctoral degree. The faculty-student ratio is 1:13. The faculty devotes equal time to teaching and research. All faculty members keep office hours, and each student meets regularly with a faculty adviser. Seventy percent of the faculty reside on campus. Faculty honors include 134 Guggenheim Fellowships, 3 Nobel and Crafoord prizes, 10 MacArthur Foundation Awards, 3 Pulitzer Prizes, 7 Lasker Awards, 16 elected to the National Academy of Sciences, and numerous Tony, Obie, and Academy awards.

Student Government

Each of NYU's schools and colleges has a student council, organized by its respective students, that represents those students. The University Senate, the major policymaking body for all matters relating to academic concerns not delegated to the separate schools and colleges, has 20 student members.

Admission Requirements

Admission is highly selective. The Committee on Admissions carefully considers each student's high school record, recommendations from guidance counselors and teachers, and scores on standardized tests (the SAT I or ACT). NYU actively seeks students who have a variety of interests, talents, and goals and looks for a diversity of social and economic backgrounds. Consideration is also given to participation in meaningful school, community, and work activities. Portfolios, creative materials, or auditions are required for some majors. Sound preparation, however, should include 4 years of English (with a heavy emphasis on writing), 3 or 4 years of social studies, 3 or 4 years of mathematics, 2 or 3 years of foreign languages, and 2 or 3 years of laboratory sciences. Special consideration is given for honors or Advanced Placement courses. Applicants to the premedical, predental, and pre-engineering programs typically have 1 unit each from at least two of the major sciences—physics, chemistry, and biology. It is recommended that applicants submit three SAT II Subject Test scores: English writing and two other examinations. Applicants to the B.A./M.D. program must submit scores from the SAT II Subject Tests.

Application and Information

For entrance in the fall term, the application for admission—including all supporting credentials—must be received by November 15 (early decision freshman candidates), January 15 (freshmen), or March 1 (transfer students). For entrance in the spring term, the application materials must be received by December 1 for both freshman and transfer candidates. For entrance in the summer, the application materials should be received by April 15 for both freshman and transfer candidates. Applications for admission received after these dates are considered only if space remains. Official notification of fall admission is made on April 1 and on a rolling basis thereafter. A campus tour or an appointment for an information session can be arranged by calling 212-998-4524.

Office of Undergraduate Admissions
New York University
22 Washington Square North
New York, New York 10011
Telephone: 212-998-4500
World Wide Web: http://www.nyu.edu/ugadmissions/

NIAGARA UNIVERSITY
NIAGARA UNIVERSITY, NEW YORK

The University

Niagara University (NU), founded in 1856, is a private, independent university rooted in a Catholic and Vincentian tradition. The suburban 160-acre campus combines the old and new; both ivy-covered buildings and modern architectural structures are among its twenty-seven buildings. DeVeaux, a 50-acre satellite campus, is located a mile from the main campus. The DeVeaux Campus provides Niagara students with additional theater and athletic facilities. The University is easily accessible from every major city in the eastern and midwestern United States via the New York State Thruway, Buffalo International Airport, and rail and bus service.

There are 2,357 undergraduate and 583 graduate students enrolled at Niagara. Of the total enrollment, approximately 58 percent live on campus. A large percentage of students take advantage of the more than seventy extracurricular and cocurricular activities offered. Volunteer work in the community is popular among the students and enhances community relations. Students work with the Association for Retarded Children, Big Brothers/Big Sisters, Maranatha (a shelter for homeless men), and the Skating Association for the Blind and Handicapped. University teams compete on the Division I level and are members of the NCAA, the Eastern College Athletic Conference, and the Metro Atlantic Athletic Conference. Intercollegiate sports include baseball, basketball, cross-country, golf, ice hockey, lacrosse, soccer, softball, swimming and diving, tennis, and volleyball. Club sports include hockey, lacrosse, martial arts, and rugby. The Kiernan Center offers a variety of sports and recreational facilities, including a multipurpose gymnasium, a swimming and diving pool, an indoor track, racquetball courts, free-weight and Nautilus rooms, and aerobics rooms. There are several outdoor athletic fields and basketball and tennis courts.

Special student services include the Health Center, which provides inpatient and outpatient care during the day; the Learning Center, which provides free tutoring services; and the Career Development Office, which offers professional and career counseling. Other services include counseling, orientation, academic planning, career planning, and job placement.

Niagara University houses approximately 1,200 students in five residence halls and a grouping of four small cottages. Both coed and single-gender accommodations are available.

The University offers graduate studies in business, counseling, criminal justice, and education.

Location

Niagara University is situated on Monteagle Ridge overlooking the gorge of the Niagara River, which connects the two Great Lakes of Erie and Ontario. Niagara's suburban campus setting is just a few miles from the world-famous Niagara Falls. Millions of visitors view the scenic majesty of the Falls every year. NU is located 30 minutes from Buffalo, which offers a variety of cultural events, sports, and entertainment opportunities. Toronto, Canada's largest metropolitan area, is just 90 minutes north of Niagara's campus and offers an even wider variety of experiences for NU students. The University is only 10 minutes from the Niagara Falls International Convention Center, which is the site of a wide range of cultural and entertainment activities during the year.

Majors and Degrees

The College of Arts and Sciences offers the Bachelor of Arts degree in chemistry, communication studies, English, French, history, international studies, life sciences, mathematics, philosophy, political science, psychology, religious studies, social sciences, sociology, and Spanish. The Bachelor of Science degree is awarded in biochemistry, biology (concentration in biotechnology), chemistry, computer and information sciences, criminal justice and criminology, mathematics, and social work. This division also offers the Bachelor of Fine Arts degree in theater studies. Preprofessional courses are offered in dentistry, law, and medicine. Pre-engineering is offered as a two-year A.S. degree transfer program. An Associate of Arts degree is available in liberal arts. In addition, Niagara offers an environmental studies concentration to supplement a degree in biology, chemistry, or political science. Enrichment courses in fine arts and languages are also available.

The College of Business Administration grants a B.B.A. degree in accounting and a B.S. degree in commerce with concentrations in economics, general business, human resources, management, marketing, and transportation. An A.A.S. degree can also be earned in business. Through various innovative programs and courses, such as the cooperative education programs and the small-business institute, students have the opportunity to gain valuable work-related experience.

The College of Education offers programs leading to the bachelor's degree and New York State teacher certification in the following areas: biology, chemistry, English, French, mathematics, social studies, and Spanish for grades N–6 (elementary) and 7–12 (secondary). Business education is offered only at the secondary level. A fourteen-week student teaching experience usually occurs during the senior year. Niagara also offers a middle-level extension program. This program enables certification in elementary education to be extended to include grades 7, 8, and 9 and in the secondary level to include grades 5 and 6. This optional program includes additional course work. The College of Education also offers a Bachelor of Arts (B.A.) degree in inclusion education, which leads to two certifications—one in elementary education (grades Pre-K–6) and the other in special education (grades Pre-K–12).

The Institute of Travel, Hotel, and Restaurant Administration (ITHRA) provides a career-oriented curriculum leading to a B.S. degree in either travel/tourism or hotel/restaurant management. NU offered the world's first bachelor's degree in tourism when it was founded in 1968. ITHRA's hotel and restaurant program, the second oldest in New York State, has the distinction of being the seventh program nationally to be accredited by the Accreditation Commission for Programs in Hospitality Administration by the Council of Hotel, Restaurant, and Institutional Education. The Institute introduces students to a comprehensive body of knowledge about the hotel, restaurant, tourism, and recreational areas and applies this knowledge to current industry challenges. The Institute requires that its students accumulate 800 hours of industry-related experience. These and other practical experiences offer ITHRA students the knowledge necessary to advance in the field. Students work with industry leaders in classroom projects, join academic clubs and professional organizations, and participate in special field trips to trade shows and conventions and specially designed study-abroad experiences, making NU a national leader in the area.

For students who are undecided about which major to choose, Niagara University offers an Academic Exploration Program (AEP). AEP provides a structured opportunity for students to participate in a thorough, organized process of selecting a major that meets their academic talents and career goals.

Academic Program

Niagara University's curricula enable students to pursue their academic preferences and to complete courses that lead to proficiency in other academic areas. Courses that have been considered upper-division courses are available to all students. This provides students with the opportunity to avoid introductory and survey courses and permits motivated students to take advantage of more challenging courses early in their collegiate career. The honors program provides special academic opportunities that stimulate, encourage, and challenge participants. In addition, an accelerated three-year degree program is offered to qualified students.

Students pursuing a bachelor's degree must complete a total of 40 or 42 course units (120 or 126 hours) to meet graduation requirements. Niagara grants credit for successful scores on the Advanced Placement tests, College-Level Examination Program tests, and College Proficiency Examinations.

Internships, research, independent study, and cooperative education are available in many academic programs. An Army ROTC program is also offered.

The University operates on a two-semester plan (fall and spring). A comprehensive summer session offers a diversity of courses.

NU is fully accredited by the Middle States Association of Colleges and Schools. Its programs in the respective areas are accredited by the National Council for Accreditation of Teacher Education, the Council on Social Work Education, and the American Chemical Society. The travel, hotel, and restaurant administration program is accredited by the Commission for Programs in Hospitality Administration.

Off-Campus Arrangements

For those students who wish to study abroad, NU offers semester and summer programs in England, France, Spain, and Switzerland. Upon request, programs may be offered in other countries. Niagara is also affiliated with Western New York Consortium. Through this program, students may take courses at other colleges and universities and apply the credits to NU graduation requirements.

Academic Facilities

The University's open-stack library includes 311,849 volumes and 4,278, which includes print and full-text electronic subscriptions. The library is housed in a modern facility that includes seating for 500 people, including individual study carrels. The library is affiliated with the Online Computer Library Center (OCLC) network.

The prize-winning Dunleavy Hall, outstanding both educationally and architecturally, includes a behavioral science laboratory, a computerized lecture hall, and TV production rooms. The University's facilities also include the Computer Center; DePaul Hall of Science; St. Vincent's Hall; the Kiernan Center, NU's athletic and recreation center; the Leary Theatre; the Castellani Art Museum; Bailo Hall, which houses the Office of Admissions; and the Dwyer Arena, a dual-rink ice hockey complex.

Costs

Tuition for 2000–01 is $14,000. Room and board (with a choice of meal plans) cost an additional $6660 per year. Fees are estimated at $560 per year. Niagara estimates that an additional $1000 per year is adequate for books, laundry, and other essentials, exclusive of travel to and from home.

Financial Aid

Ninety-seven percent of the incoming students who enrolled at NU received a financial aid package. They receive assistance in the form of merit scholarships, loans, grants, or campus employment. Students seeking financial aid should file the Free Application for Federal Student Aid (FAFSA). New York State residents should also file a Tuition Assistance Program (TAP) application.

Faculty

Niagara University has a dedicated, accessible faculty who genuinely cares about the academic and personal growth of their students. Their commitment to teaching is their primary concern. A student-faculty ratio of 16:1 and an average class size of 22 allow personal attention and classroom interaction.

Student Government

The Student Government represents all parts of the student body equally. It coordinates and legislates all student activities, serving as both liaison to and a participating member of the University as a whole. In addition, students serve on all major departmental committees and on the University Senate, which is the major advisory committee to the president and Board of Trustees.

Admission Requirements

The University welcomes men and women who have demonstrated aptitude and academic achievement at the high school level. Either SAT I or ACT test scores are required. International students are required to submit the results of their TOEFL examination. Interviews are recommended. Transfer students are accepted in any semester. (Transfer credit is evaluated individually by the dean of each division.) Students who complete high school in less than four years are eligible for early admission. Students may also apply under an early decision program. Economically and educationally disadvantaged students from New York State are eligible to apply for admission through the Higher Educational Opportunity Program (HEOP).

Application and Information

Niagara operates on a rolling admission basis and adheres to the College Board Candidates Reply Date. A visit to the campus is encouraged, and overnight accommodations in a residence hall are available.

Information on all aspects of the University can be obtained by contacting the Admissions Office.

Mike Konopski
Director of Admissions
639 Bailo Hall
Niagara University
Niagara University, New York 14109-2011
Telephone: 716-286-8700
          800-462-2111 (toll-free)
Fax: 716-286-8710
E-mail: admissions@niagara.edu
World Wide Web: http://www.niagara.edu

The main campus of Niagara University.

NICHOLS COLLEGE
DUDLEY, MASSACHUSETTS

The College

Nichols College is committed to providing the best practically oriented business education in New England. The College transforms students into competent, assertive business professionals who respond to challenges, are eager for responsibility, and stand ready to rise in the world of commerce.

The College traces its roots back to 1815 when industrialist Amasa Nichols founded Nichols Academy. In 1931, the school became Nichols Junior College, a two-year business college for men. The institution grew into a four-year college in 1958, offering the Bachelor of Science in Business Administration degree. In 1970, the College became coeducational, and, in 1971, it received authority to grant the Master of Business Administration along with degrees in public administration and the liberal arts. Nichols is accredited by the New England Association of Schools and Colleges and follows the curriculum guidelines of AACSB–The International Association for Management Education.

Three quarters of the 700 students live on campus; 80 percent come from communities within a 250-mile radius of the College. Students not living with their families are required to reside on campus in one of eleven residence halls. Kuppenheimer Hall, which consists of eleven 2-bedroom, 4-person suites, opened in 1998. In 1997, the field house, dining hall, and snack bar were renovated, and a new telecommunications system was installed. In keeping with the College's commitment to upgrading its physical facilities, a new residence hall, Remillard Hall, and a performance gym open in fall 2000. Students are allowed to keep automobiles on campus.

Nichols offers an extensive program of varsity and intramural sports. The College fields thirteen intercollegiate teams: seven for men (baseball, basketball, football, ice hockey, lacrosse, soccer, and tennis) and six for women (basketball, field hockey, lacrosse, soccer, softball, and tennis). Golf is offered as a coed sport. Nichols College has a nine-hole, 5,100-yard golf course adjacent to the campus.

Student organizations and extracurricular activities contribute to the social calendar. There are several honor societies on campus, media clubs (newspaper, yearbook, and radio station), academic clubs (accounting, finance, marketing, and economics), club sports (skiing, men's and women's rugby, women's volleyball, cheerleading, and racquetball), and a lettermen's club. The student government association oversees all student organizations. Nichols also has chapters of the American Marketing Association, the Society for the Advancement of Management, and BACCHUS on campus.

The Freshman Professional Development program is a yearlong project designed to help freshmen adapt to college life. It acquaints students with the College's facilities, programs, and personnel. Seminars and workshops help develop study skills, easing the transition between high school and college.

Location

Nichols College is located in Dudley, Massachusetts, 20 minutes south of Worcester and an hour from Boston, Providence, and Hartford. The atmosphere is peaceful, and the rural landscape offers the best of all seasons. Major cultural and enrichment centers are easily accessible.

Majors and Degrees

The College offers the Bachelor of Science in Business Administration (B.S.B.A.) and the Bachelor of Arts (B.A.) degrees. Business concentrations include accounting, economics, finance, general business, management, management information systems, marketing, and sport management. Liberal arts majors include English, history, human resource management, mathematics, psychology, and teacher-preparation programs (pending evaluation by the Massachusetts Department of Education) for middle and secondary school educators. The continuing education division offers certificate, associate, and bachelor's degree programs.

Academic Program

The first semester begins in early September and continues through late December. The second semester runs from mid-January to mid-May. A minimum of 122 credits is required to earn a bachelor's degree. During the first two years, students follow a program of core courses made up of foundation studies in a variety of subjects. More extensive study in the student's chosen major is reserved for the junior and senior years. The Nichols PC Plan requires each student to own a personal computer, ensuring that students are fluent in key software programs by the time they graduate. Students may obtain advanced standing in several ways: through successful scores on the College-Level Examination Program (CLEP) or the Advanced Placement (AP) Program tests, through transfer of credit earned at other accredited colleges and universities, for military service school experience, and from the Defense Activity for Non-Traditional Education Support (DANTES) program. The Office of the Registrar provides information on these programs.

Off-Campus Arrangements

Nichols College offers academic credit for internships with local businesses; a Washington, D.C., internship program with the Washington Center; and a semester-abroad program in cooperation with Regent's College in London, England, and other colleges and universities throughout the world.

Academic Facilities

Conant Library contains the College's main collection of 60,000 volumes, 450 periodicals, and 8,000 microfilms. There are three auditoriums for film and group presentations. Personal computers linked to the Internet are strategically located throughout the library for use by students. Laboratory assistance is available daily in a variety of subject areas. The Academic Resource Center, also housed in Conant Library, assists and challenges all students in developing skills necessary for successful independent learning.

Costs

Tuition for 2000–01 is $15,200; room and board charges are $6640 to $7810. Additional fees total $450. Students should anticipate spending $500 per year for books and supplies. In addition, each student is required to have a personal computer. The College makes arrangements for the system, which includes the notebook computer, software, and accessories; the cost of the full system is included in tuition. Resident students are required to pay a $100 security deposit. Medical insurance is required for students not covered by family health insurance plans.

Financial Aid

Nichols College offers a wide variety of institutional, state, and federal financial aid in the form of scholarships, grants, loans, and work-study awards. The Free Application for Federal Student Aid is required to determine eligibility for aid. No supplemental forms are required. Financing plans are also available. The priority deadline for financial aid is March 1.

Faculty

The College is proud of its faculty members, 76 percent of whom have earned the doctorate or the highest appropriate degree in their fields. Moreover, members of the business faculty bring to the classroom years of on-the-job experience in business and industry, providing both theoretical and practical aspects of a balanced education. The focus of the Nichols faculty is teaching. The average class size is 23. The faculty-student ratio is 1:18. Each Nichols student is assigned a faculty adviser to meet with on a regular basis. Faculty members also serve as advisers to clubs and organizations and are an integral part of the extracurricular activities.

Student Government

The Nichols Student Government Association has jurisdiction over social activities on campus, clubs and student associations, student conduct, and residence life. Members of the administration and student government work together closely and hold meetings regularly.

Admission Requirements

Nichols College offers admission without regard to color, race, creed, national origin, age, religion, veteran status, or disability and follows the guidelines for records established by the Family Educational Rights and Privacy Act (1974). Nichols does not discriminate with respect to "educational" decisions, including but not limited to, those bearing on admissions. Applicants are required to submit an official high school transcript, SAT I/ACT scores, an essay, and a letter of recommendation. Interviews are strongly encouraged and, in some cases, required. Each applicant is judged on his or her potential for a successful college experience. The application fee is $25. In 1999, admission was offered to 88 percent of the students who applied, 33 percent of whom enrolled in September. Nichols College is approved by the Massachusetts Board of Regents of Higher Education for the training of eligible veterans.

An applicant should have the following units of work in high school to be considered for admission: English, 4 units; mathematics, 3 units for the business and public administration programs and 2 units for liberal arts programs; social science, 2 units; laboratory science, 2 units; and academic electives, 5 units. Liberal arts candidates who present 2 units of a modern foreign language from high school are exempted from the liberal arts foreign language requirement on the college level. Admission to degree candidacy requires that the applicant either be a high school graduate or have a high school equivalency diploma. Early admission (at the end of the junior year) may be arranged with the written approval of the student's high school.

Application and Information

The College has a rolling admission policy. The applicant is responsible for having official high school records, official college or university transcripts, and test scores sent to the Admissions Office.

For application forms or for other information, students should contact:

Dean of Admissions
Nichols College
Dudley, Massachusetts 01571-5000
Telephone: 508-943-2055
              800-470-3379 (toll-free)
Fax: 508-943-9885
E-mail: admissions@nichols.edu
World Wide Web: http://www.nichols.edu

Students relax outside Conrad Hall.

NORTH CAROLINA AGRICULTURAL AND TECHNICAL STATE UNIVERSITY
GREENSBORO, NORTH CAROLINA

The University

North Carolina Agricultural and Technical State University was founded in 1891 as one of two land-grant institutions in the state. Originally, it was established to provide postsecondary education and training for black students. Today, the University is a comprehensive institution of higher education with an integrated faculty and student body, and it has been designated a constituent institution of the University of North Carolina, offering degrees at the baccalaureate, master's, and doctoral degree levels. Located on a 191-acre campus, the University has ninety-one buildings, including six men's and nine women's dormitories. Of a total undergraduate population of 6,367, 3,126 students are men and 3,241 are women.

North Carolina Agricultural and Technical State University provides outstanding academic programs through five undergraduate schools, two colleges, and a graduate school.

The mission of the University is to provide an intellectual setting in which students may find a sense of belonging, responsibility, and achievement that prepares them for roles of leadership and service in the communities where they will live and work. In this sense, the University serves as a laboratory for the development of excellence in teaching, research, and public service. As a result, A&T today stands as an example of well-directed higher education for all students.

Student life at the University is active and purposeful. The broad objective of the program provided by Student Development Services is to aid students in attaining the attitudes, understandings, insights, and skills that enable them to be socially competent. The program places special emphasis on campus relationships and experiences that complement formal instruction. Some of the services that are available are counseling, housing, health, and placement services. There is a University Student Union, and there are special services for international and minority students, veterans, and handicapped students. The University also provides a well-balanced program of activities to foster the moral, spiritual, cultural, and physical development of its students.

Location

Greensboro, North Carolina, is 300 miles south of Washington, D.C., and 349 miles north of Atlanta. It is readily accessible by air, bus, and automobile. The city offers a variety of cultural and recreational activities and facilities. These include sports events, concerts, bowling, boating, fishing, tennis, golf, and other popular forms of recreation. There are major shopping centers, churches, theaters, and medical facilities near the University. The heavy concentration of factories, service industries, government agencies, and shopping centers provides many job opportunities for students who desire part-time employment.

Majors and Degrees

North Carolina Agricultural and Technical State University grants the following degrees: Bachelor of Arts, Bachelor of Science, Bachelor of Fine Arts, Bachelor of Science in Nursing, and Bachelor of Social Work.

The School of Agriculture and Environmental and Allied Sciences offers programs in agricultural and biosystems engineering, agricultural economics, agricultural economics (agricultural business), agricultural education, agricultural education (agricultural extension), agricultural science–earth and environmental science (earth and environmental science, landscape horticulture design, plant science, soil science), agricultural science–natural resources (plant science), animal science, animal science (animal industry), child development, child development–early education and family studies B–K (teaching), family and consumer science (fashion merchandising and design), family and consumer science education, food and nutritional sciences, laboratory animal science, and landscape architecture.

In the College of Arts and Sciences, programs are available in applied mathematics, biology, biology–secondary education, broadcast news, broadcast production, chemistry, chemistry–secondary education, engineering physics, English, English–secondary education, French, French–Romance languages and literatures, French–secondary education, history, history–secondary education, mathematics, mathematics–secondary education, music education, music–general, music–performance, physics, physics–secondary education, political science, print journalism, professional theater, psychology, public relations, sociology, social work, Spanish–Romance languages and literatures, Spanish–secondary education, speech, speech (speech pathology/audiology), visual arts–art education, and visual arts–design.

The School of Business and Economics offers programs in accounting, business education, business education (administrative systems, vocational business education, vocational business education–data processing), economics, finance, management, management (management information systems), marketing, and transportation.

In the School of Education, programs are available in elementary education, health and physical education (fitness/wellness management), health and physical education (teaching), recreation administration, and special education.

In the College of Engineering, programs are offered in architectural engineering, chemical engineering, civil engineering, computer science, electrical engineering, industrial engineering, and mechanical engineering.

The School of Nursing grants the Bachelor of Science in Nursing (B.S.N.) degree.

The School of Technology has programs in construction management, electronics technology, graphic communication systems, manufacturing systems, occupational safety and health, technology education, and vocational industrial education.

Academic Program

Students must complete a minimum of 124 semester hours to earn a bachelor's degree; the exact number varies with the program. Students are also required to demonstrate competence in English and mathematics.

As complements to the academic programs, the University's Army and Air Force ROTC programs and cooperative education program provide excellent opportunities for students to enrich their educational experiences. The ROTC programs are designed to prepare college graduates for military service careers. The cooperative education program provides an opportunity for qualified students to alternate periods of study on campus and meaningful employment off campus in private industrial or business firms or government agencies.

Academic Facilities

The University library has current holdings that include 449,766 book volumes and bound periodicals and 4,004 serial subscriptions. As a selected depository in North Carolina for U.S. government documents, the library contains a collection of more than 240,000 official publications. Among the library's other holdings are an outstanding collection of films, audiovisuals, and 958,271 microforms; archives; and special collections in black studies and teacher-education materials. A chemistry collection is located in the Chemistry Department in Hines Hall. Special services are provided through formal and informal instruction on how to use the library, online computer searches of literature, interlibrary loans, and photocopying facilities.

The University's educational support centers are the Learning Assistance Center, the Audiovisual Center, the Closed Circuit Television Facility, a 1,000-watt student-operated educational radio station, the Computer Center, the Reading Center, the Language Laboratory, and the Center for Manpower Research and Training. The H. Clinton Taylor Art Gallery and the African Heritage Center are two exceptional art museums on campus. Throughout the year, these museums have on display a number of special exhibits of sculpture, paintings, graphics, and other media.

Costs

In 1999–2000, tuition and fees for North Carolina residents were $1909 per year; for nonresidents of the state, they were $9179. Board and lodging for the academic year were $4010.

Financial Aid

Through the student financial aid program, the University makes every effort to ensure that no qualified student is denied the opportunity to attend because of a lack of funds. Students who demonstrate financial need and have the potential to achieve academic success at the University may obtain assistance to meet their expenses in accordance with the funds available. Financial aid is awarded without regard to race, religion, color, national origin, or sex. The University provides financial aid for students from four basic sources: grants, scholarships, loans, and employment. To apply for aid, students must submit the Free Application for Federal Student Aid (FAFSA). The priority filing deadline is March 15 for fall semester. North Carolina residents may call 800-443-0835 (toll-free).

Faculty

The University's teaching faculty consists of 600 highly qualified members, of whom 65 percent hold the doctoral degree or the first professional degree in their discipline. Faculty members are recruited from many areas and backgrounds, thereby bringing together a diverse cadre of academic professionals from many nations.

Student Government

The Student Government Association (SGA), composed of senators elected from the student body, is primarily a policy-recommending group and represents the views and concerns of the students. The president of SGA reports directly to the vice-chancellor for student affairs. In addition, each student organization is represented by a senator, and these senators sit on the Faculty Senate.

Admission Requirements

Applicants for undergraduate admission are considered individually and in accordance with criteria that are applied flexibly to ensure that applicants with unusual qualifications are not denied admission. However, admission for out-of-state freshman students is competitive due to an 18 percent out-of-state enrollment cap. Students who are applying for admission as freshmen are expected to have completed a college-preparatory program in high school and taken the SAT I or the ACT. General requirements include graduation from an accredited high school with 16 units of credit, with no more than 4 units in vocational subjects and with at least 2 units in physical education; a satisfactory score on the SAT I or ACT; and a respectable GPA and/or class rank. The General Educational Development (GED) test score results or a high school equivalency certificate from the state department of education may be submitted in lieu of the high school transcript for applicants receiving equivalency before January 1988.

North Carolina A&T State University welcomes applications from graduates of accredited community, technical, and junior colleges and from students who wish to transfer from other senior colleges.

Application and Information

The suggested application deadline for students who expect to live on campus is February 1; for commuting students, it is June 1. Applications are processed upon the receipt of the completed application form with the application fee of $35, official transcripts, and SAT I or ACT scores. Out-of-state admission is limited; therefore applications for admission should be filed by February 1.

To arrange an interview or a visit to the campus, students should contact:

Office of Admissions
B. C. Webb Hall
North Carolina Agricultural and Technical State University
Greensboro, North Carolina 27411

Telephone: 336-334-7946 or 7947
                800-443-8964 (toll-free in North Carolina)
World Wide Web: http://www.ncat.edu

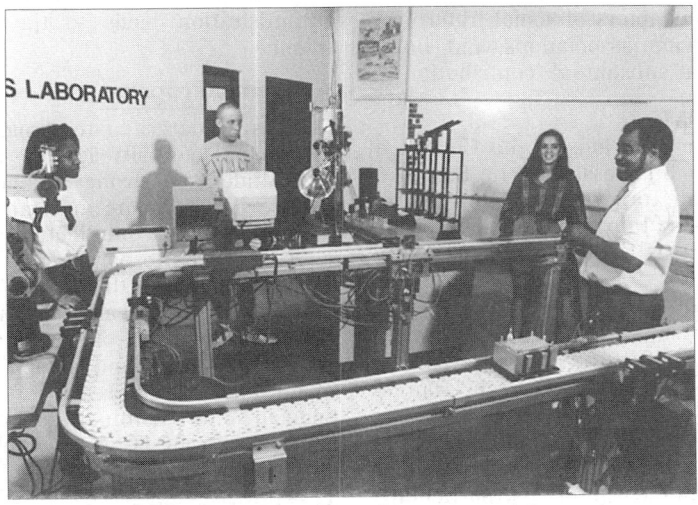

A professor and students in the chemical engineering lab.

NORTH CAROLINA CENTRAL UNIVERSITY
DURHAM, NORTH CAROLINA

The University

North Carolina Central University (NCCU) is a comprehensive public university, a constituent institution of the sixteen-campus University of North Carolina System. NCCU was founded in 1910 by Dr. James Edward Shepard, a pharmacist and political leader. In 1925, the institution became America's first state-supported liberal arts college for black people. Today, NCCU enrolls 5,580 students in undergraduate, graduate, and professional programs. Predominantly black (13 percent of the students are Caucasian), NCCU enrolls slightly more than 2 women to every 1 man. The average age of full-time undergraduate students is 23 years. Only 11 percent of the student body is from outside the state of North Carolina, the percentage that prevails at almost every one of the sixteen state institutions. Approximately 50 of these students are from outside the United States. About 40 percent of the students are from Durham County and five contiguous counties, and most of these are commuting students. On-campus housing is available for approximately 2,000 students.

NCCU's slogan is "Truth and service," and over the years the University's alumni have taken leadership roles in political life and the law. The current mayors of Atlanta and Durham hold NCCU degrees, as does the speaker of the North Carolina House of Representatives. NCCU graduates have served as district attorneys in the federal and state courts and as judges of state appellate courts, including a state supreme court. Other NCCU graduates are outstanding teachers at all levels of academic life, lawyers of national reputation, corporate vice presidents and executives, and school and university administrators.

NCCU is a member of the Central Intercollegiate Athletic Association and fields teams in football; men's and women's basketball, cross-country, tennis, and track; and women's softball and volleyball. NCCU has strong student ensembles in choral music, band music, and jazz, and NCCU's dramatic arts department is among America's strongest in terms of student productions. The University has chapters of social fraternities and sororities, as well as service associations and honor societies, all of which make a substantial contribution to campus life.

In addition to the undergraduate programs of the College of Arts and Sciences, the School of Business, and the School of Education, NCCU offers graduate programs in those three schools and its School of Library and Information Sciences. The first professional law degree, a Juris Doctor, is offered by the NCCU School of Law.

Location

Durham is at the center of North Carolina's Research Triangle, which incorporates three major research universities in addition to NCCU, as well as three senior liberal arts colleges, two private junior colleges, and two state-funded technical community colleges. Several major corporations, particularly electronics and pharmaceutical operations, have large facilities in the Research Triangle area, whose total population is approximately 500,000. Durham itself is called the City of Medicine, with a quarter of the population employed in the field of health care.

Majors and Degrees

NCCU offers the following degrees and their respective majors: the Bachelor of Arts in art (general), art education, dramatic arts, dramatic arts (secondary education), early childhood education, economics, elementary education, English, English (concentrations in media journalism and secondary education), fine arts, French, French (secondary education), history, history (secondary education), middle grades education, music, music education, political science, political science (concentrations in criminal justice and public administration), psychology, social sciences, sociology, Spanish, Spanish (secondary education), theater arts education (K–12), and visual communications; the Bachelor of Business Administration in accounting, banking and finance, business administration, computer information systems, economics, management, and marketing; the Bachelor of Music in jazz and sacred music; the Bachelor of Science in actuarial science, biology, biology (secondary education), chemistry, chemistry (secondary education), community health education, computer science, geography, health education, mathematics, mathematics (secondary education), physical education, physics, physics (secondary education), and recreation administration; the Bachelor of Science in Commerce in business education (secondary basic) and business education (secondary comprehensive); the Bachelor of Science in Human Sciences in clothing and textiles, foods and nutrition, general home economics, and secondary education; and the Bachelor of Science in Nursing.

NCCU has a cooperative arrangement with Georgia Institute of Technology and Duke University that enables a student, over a period of approximately five years, to earn a bachelor's degree in physics from NCCU and a bachelor's degree in engineering from Georgia Tech.

There are organized preprofessional programs in dentistry, law, and medicine. The English department offers a substantial curriculum in media journalism as an alternative route to the Bachelor of Arts degree in English. A concentration in public administration leads to the bachelor's degree in political science.

Academic Program

NCCU's undergraduate program is designed to stimulate intellectual curiosity and the habit of disciplined learning, to give students a strong background in both general Western culture and African-American culture, and to equip students with marketable intellectual and professional skills. Credit hours required to earn a degree may range between 124 and 149, depending on the student's choice of major or concentration and desire to earn teaching certification. A core curriculum, the General College Studies program, includes specific courses in English and history, a senior seminar in the student's major, and a structured menu of electives in other disciplines. Special honors seminars are open to qualified freshmen and sophomores. ROTC is available by cooperative arrangement with neighboring institutions.

Academic Facilities

NCCU's James E. Shepard Memorial Library has a collection of some 600,000 volumes, not including serials, microforms, manuscripts, or graphics, audio, film, or video materials. A Learning Resources Center provides technical assistance and support for academic programs, including the production of audiovisual materials. The University's academic facilities include 147 classrooms and 143 laboratories.

Costs

In 1999–2000, the cost, including tuition, for in-state students residing in a dormitory was $5555; out-of-state students residing in a dormitory paid $12,825. In-state students not residing in a dormitory paid $2079.50; out-of-state students not residing in a dormitory paid $9349.50. Costs are subject to change by the state legislature.

Financial Aid

NCCU's financial aid program has the primary purpose of providing aid to students who would not otherwise be able to attend the University. Typically, students receiving financial aid hold federal grants (Federal Pell Grant or Federal Supplemental Educational Opportunity Grant), federal loans, and Federal Work-Study assignments. A significant number of scholarships, some need-based, are available from institutional and private resources. On-campus employment, primarily through the Federal Work-Study Program, is typically available to approximately 350 students. The primary instrument for application for undergraduate financial aid is the Family Financial Statement of American College Testing, available from NCCU or from high school counseling and guidance offices. Forms should be completed and returned, with NCCU identified as a recipient of information, as soon as possible after January 1. Awards to new students are typically made after March 31 for the ensuing fall semester.

Faculty

NCCU's teaching faculty members number approximately 414, of whom about 289 are full-time teachers. (Specific numbers vary from semester to semester.) Of the full-time faculty members, 65 percent hold a doctorate. An additional 6 percent hold degrees considered to be the terminal degree in their discipline or specialty. Departments and schools offering undergraduate programs assign all of their faculty members to teach undergraduate courses, and very limited use is made of graduate students as teaching assistants. (A number of part-time teachers, most of whom have completed all course requirements for their doctorate, are doctoral candidates at neighboring research universities.)

Student Government

Undergraduate students elect class representatives to the Student Congress and the president and vice president of the Student Government Association. Also elected by student vote are Miss NCCU and officers of the four undergraduate classes. The Student Government Association recommends policies and regulations governing student life to the vice chancellor for student affairs. From the vice chancellor the recommendations go to the chancellor and the institutional Board of Trustees, to which the general authority to set regulations and policies affecting student life and discipline has been delegated by the Board of Governors of the University of North Carolina System. The president of the Student Government Association is a voting member of the Board of Trustees. The Student Government Association has substantial authority in managing the expenditure of student activity fees collected from undergraduates.

Admission Requirements

Applicants for entry as freshmen must provide evidence (a complete transcript) of graduation from an approved or accredited high school and a satisfactory score on the SAT I or ACT. Students who graduated from high school after spring 1990 must present in their high school transcripts 4 course units in English, emphasizing grammar, composition, and literature; 3 course units in mathematics, including algebra I, algebra II, and geometry or a higher-level mathematics course for which algebra II is a prerequisite; 3 course units in science, including at least 1 unit in a life or biological science, at least 1 unit in a physical science, and at least one laboratory course in science; and 2 course units in social studies, including 1 unit in U.S. history. Two units of the same foreign language are recommended, and students are encouraged to take a math class and a foreign language class during the senior year. NCCU and other North Carolina state universities are required to limit out-of-state freshman enrollment. In practice, out-of-state students admitted have higher SAT I scores and higher class standing. Transfer students in good standing with their previous college or university are encouraged to apply.

Application and Information

Students should submit applications for the fall semester by July 1 (March 1 for out-of-state students and for students seeking on-campus housing or financial aid) and for the semester beginning in January by November 1. Earlier application with partial transcripts is encouraged, but final admission is deferred until full transcripts are received. Application forms and additional information are available from:

Director of Undergraduate Admissions
North Carolina Central University
P.O. Box 19717
Durham, North Carolina 27707
Telephone: 877-667-7533
Fax: 919-530-7625
E-mail: ebridges@wpo.nccu.edu
World Wide Web: http://www.nccu.edu

NORTH CAROLINA WESLEYAN COLLEGE
ROCKY MOUNT, NORTH CAROLINA

The College

North Carolina Wesleyan College, situated on a private and picturesque campus of 200 acres, provides students from twenty-two states and nine countries with the personal attention of a small campus. The College enrolls 800 full-time traditional students at the Rocky Mount campus and 1,100 part-time adult students at extension sites in Raleigh, Goldsboro, and Durham.

The College promises attention to the individual and considers commitment to work and service as integral to a meaningful life. Students explore questions of ethics, values, and integrity through the integration of academic and cocurricular experiences in a personalized learning environment. Students are encouraged to act on their interests through involvement with a wide range of campus activities, including the Campus Activities Board, educational clubs, honorary societies, academic and professional organizations, fraternities, sororities, the student newspaper, the College yearbook, the Tar River Orchestra, the Wesleyan College Choir, and the Gospel Choir.

The well-planned campus includes four north campus and two south campus residence halls. Housing options include freshman and upperclass residence halls and suites. Halls are air conditioned and equipped with Internet ports, voice mail, cable television access, exercise rooms, and computer rooms. There is also an off-campus housing option. A recreational facility that includes an aerobics room is available to all students. Renovations to the recreation center are planned for 2001. Approximately 60 percent of students live on campus. Athletic facilities include intramural fields, a softball field, and a tennis complex. The soccer and baseball fields rank among the best in the South. The College is a member of the Dixie Intercollegiate Athletic Conference and Division III of the NCAA. The ten NCAA Division III teams are men's baseball, basketball, golf, and soccer, women's basketball, soccer, softball, and volleyball, and men's and women's tennis. Intramural and club sports include badminton, basketball, beach volleyball, billiards, cheerleading, 5-kilometer run, flag football, indoor volleyball, lacrosse, soccer, softball, table tennis, tennis, and turkey trot.

A registered nurse and a counselor hold convenient office hours in the College Wellness Center. The Student Services Center offers a freshman pre-major advising program designed to help students develop academic and personal goals through study skills development, course selection, academic self-monitoring, and the assessment of career objectives. The Center integrates career planning, experiential education/internships, and peer tutoring. Other services include a student referral program, graduate school entrance assistance, and a comprehensive career library. In addition, Tutor's Crossing, also located in the Center, provides a variety of academic support services, including help with writing and mathematics, assignments in specific courses, and use of several computers.

Location

The Wesleyan campus, located in Rocky Mount, North Carolina, on Highway 301, is in the coastal plain region of the state. Rocky Mount has a population of 58,000 and was recognized as an All-American City in 1969 and 1999. It is the entrepreneurial center of eastern North Carolina, with many recreational, cultural, and health services in the area. (Nash Health Care Systems and Community Hospital are only 10 minutes from campus.)

Rocky Mount's location permits easy access to other interesting areas. North Carolina's favorite beaches are approximately 100 miles away; Richmond, Virginia, 110 miles; Washington, D.C., 200 miles; and Raleigh, North Carolina, just 55 miles. Rocky Mount is easily accessible by Interstate 95 or North Carolina Highway 64. Amtrak provides daily rail service to the city, and Greyhound Trailways bus lines can also be used. Air transportation is convenient through USAir flights to and from the Rocky Mount–Wilson Airport.

Majors and Degrees

Wesleyan offers the Bachelor of Arts degree in biology, chemistry, English, environmental science, history, justice studies, mathematics, political science, psychology, religious studies, sociology, and theater. The Bachelor of Science degree is available in accounting, biology, business administration, chemistry, computer information systems, elementary education, food service and hotel management, mathematics, middle grades education, exercise science, and premedicine.

Minor areas of study are available in biology, business administration, chemistry, computer information systems, criminal justice, English, history, journalism, justice studies, mathematics, philosophy, psychology, religion, secondary education, sociology, theater, and visual arts.

Academic Program

Wesleyan operates on a 4-1-4 academic calendar. The January term offers students unique opportunities to travel abroad and take courses outside of their normal core curriculum. The fall and spring terms are each 15 weeks in length, with a recommended 15- to 16-semester-hour course load. Courses are also offered during two summer sessions.

The academic curriculum provides both focus and flexibility for the individual student. All students complete a general education core curriculum distributed across all four years of their studies. The core emphasizes the development of vital skills (reading, writing, critical thinking, quantitative reasoning, speaking, and listening). In addition, each student selects one of twenty-two majors. Within a major, students, in close cooperation with their academic adviser, can select specific courses to orient their program of study more precisely toward future needs or goals. The traditional classroom approach is complemented by an emphasis on nonclassroom activities. Special projects, internships, and cooperative education give students the opportunity to gain practical, working knowledge that will relate directly to the major.

Any student entering Wesleyan may receive credit through the College-Level Examination Program (CLEP), the Advanced Placement Program, and the International Baccalaureate Diploma program.

Academic Facilities

The focal point and academic center of campus is formed by the Braswell Administration Building, Pearsall Classroom Building, and Gravely Science Building. These three buildings are connected and house administrative offices, faculty offices, classrooms, science laboratories, the Student Services Center, Tutor's Crossing, and the computer laboratory. A greenhouse facility is available for student studies. The latest addition to campus is a 1,200-seat Performing Arts Center, where students enjoy art, music, and theater. The computer lab is available for both instruction and general student use. The workstations in the computer lab and student workstations available in the library are networked and offer a wide range of software packages, including Microsoft Office Professional. Additional computers are available in the residence halls. Wesleyan is established as an Internet host system, allowing access to the more than 30 million Internet users and systems worldwide. Access to the Internet and the World Wide Web is available throughout campus.

The Pearsall Library is a multipurpose facility for research and for class and casual reading. The library contains 75,000 volumes and subscribes to 500 current periodicals and journals. All holdings are listed in the online catalog. There is in-house traditional and CD-ROM indexing supplemented by the online access to more than 400 remote databases. The College is a selected depository for federal and state documents. The library includes a computer laboratory and provides access to the campus network and to the Internet.

Costs
Tuition in 2000–01 for both in-state and out-of-state students is $8332 per academic year. Room and board are $5612 per year, and student fees are $904, for an annual total of $14,848. Personal expenses, book costs, and transportation expenses vary according to individual need.

Financial Aid
Every effort is made to ensure that any student admitted to North Carolina Wesleyan College who demonstrates financial need will receive assistance commensurate with that need. Approximately 85 percent of students receive some type of financial assistance in the form of presidential and endowed scholarships, honors scholarships, federal loans, state loans, or College or Federal Work-Study. The College participates in all federal grant and loan programs as well as North Carolina grant programs. Students are encouraged to submit the Free Application for Federal Student Aid (FAFSA) by March 1 to receive top priority in the award process.

Faculty
A student-teacher ratio of 15:1 and an average class size of 18 make close relationships possible in all areas of campus life. Currently, the faculty numbers 47 full-time and 13 part-time members; 75 percent hold earned doctoral degrees. An additional 100 part-time faculty members serve the adult programs.

Student Government
Every student is automatically a member of the Student Government Association, which makes many of the major decisions affecting student life on campus. The council has student representation on the Wesleyan board of trustees.

Admission Requirements
Each applicant to Wesleyan is individually reviewed in an attempt to determine if he or she will succeed in, and benefit from, Wesleyan's particular programs. Candidates for admission are required to be graduates of an accredited secondary school and have completed a minimum of 16 high school units. Secondary school courses strongly recommended for admission include 4 units of English, 2 units in social studies, 2 units of a foreign language, 3 units of mathematics (algebra I, algebra II, and geometry), and 2 units of a laboratory science. The GED is normally recognized. The applicant's completed courses, grades, and standardized test results (SAT I or ACT) are considered. Campus visits are highly recommended, and two letters of recommendation are encouraged. NC Wesleyan is an equal opportunity institution and is approved for veterans.

Applicants wishing to transfer from another college or university should present a cumulative GPA of at least 2.0 (C) in order to qualify for regular transfer acceptance. All transfer applicants must be eligible to return to the institution they last attended, or at least one full regular term must elapse before they can be considered for admission. Wesleyan has articulation agreements with twenty-six colleges.

Application and Information
North Carolina Wesleyan College follows a program of rolling admission, and applicants are notified of admission decisions soon after their files are complete. After July 15, applications are accepted on a space-available basis. A $25 nonrefundable application fee is required, and files are not considered complete until appropriate transcripts, SAT I or ACT scores, and academic information are received.

Office of Admissions
North Carolina Wesleyan College
3400 North Wesleyan Boulevard
Rocky Mount, North Carolina 27804
Telephone: 252-985-5200
           800-488-6292 (toll-free)
Fax: 252-985-5295
E-mail: adm@ncwc.edu
World Wide Web: http://www.ncwc.edu

The entrance to North Carolina Wesleyan College.

NORTH CENTRAL COLLEGE
NAPERVILLE, ILLINOIS

The College

Founded in 1861, North Central College has a distinctive heritage as a comprehensive college that educates students in both the liberal arts and sciences and in preprofessional fields.

A private, United Methodist–affiliated institution, the College has long been recognized for academic excellence, with its educational philosophy of incorporating leadership, ethics, and values into academic and cocurricular activities. North Central's 2,545 students include traditional-age undergraduate, part-time, and graduate students. Master's degree programs are offered in business administration, computer science, education, information systems, leadership studies, and liberal studies. Twenty-five states are represented (89 percent of the student body are Illinois residents), 11 percent of full-time students are from minority populations, and 75 percent of freshmen live in one of nine residence halls. Twenty-three other countries are represented. Kaufman Dining Hall serves the entire campus.

Cocurricular programs parallel many academic majors and include the nationally acclaimed Students in Free Enterprise, Cardinals in Action (a community service organization), campus radio station WONC, Mock Trial, Model United Nations, and forensics. North Central student athletes compete in nineteen NCAA Division III intercollegiate varsity sports within the College Conference of Illinois and Wisconsin. The varsity sports include baseball, basketball, cross-country, football, golf, soccer, swimming, tennis, track and field, and wrestling for men. Women participate in basketball, cross-country, golf, soccer, softball, swimming, tennis, track and field, and volleyball. Students have many options for social activities: programmed events through the College Union Activities Board, residence life activities, an active intramural program, and travel to both downtown Naperville and Chicago. Student services include centers for academic advising, counseling, writing, foreign language, and career development.

Location

Naperville, a city of more than 122,000 people and the tenth fastest growing city in the nation, is situated in the middle of a center of technological research and development. Chicago, the nation's third-largest metropolitan area, is 29 miles to the east. The cultural, sporting, and social events in that city are easily accessible by commuter trains that stop frequently just two blocks from campus. Students find Naperville safe, friendly, and a great place to relax.

The Illinois Research and Development Corridor, which is bounded on the east by Argonne National Laboratory and on the west by Fermi National Accelerator Laboratory, offers North Central students numerous internships and a wealth of job and research opportunities.

Majors and Degrees

North Central College awards the Bachelor of Arts (B.A.) degree in accounting, art, arts and letters, athletic training, biology, broadcasting, business (management, management information systems, and marketing), chemistry, classics, computer science, creative writing, economics, education (elementary and secondary), English, English literature, finance, French, German, health and physical education, history, humanities, international business, international studies, Japanese, journalism, mathematics, music, organizational communication, philosophy, physics, political science, psychology, religious studies, science, sociology and anthropology, Spanish, and speech communications/theater. The Bachelor of Science (B.S.) degree is awarded in accounting, biochemistry, biology, business (management, management information systems, and marketing), chemistry, computer science, economics, finance, international business, mathematics, and psychology.

Preprofessional programs are offered in dentistry, law, medical technology, medicine, physical therapy, and veterinary medicine. A 3-2 engineering program is offered in cooperation with Marquette University, the University of Minnesota, the University of Illinois at Urbana-Champaign, and Washington University in St. Louis. Both 2-2 and 3-2 programs in nursing are available in cooperation with Rush University in Chicago. Students may also design other majors that bridge two or more areas of study.

Academic Program

North Central provides a comprehensive education with the goal of preparing students to live free, ethically responsible, and intellectually rewarding lives. Each student must complete a minimum of 120 credit hours, including all general education requirements and an approved major. CLEP, AP, and IB exams are considered for college credit and/or advanced course placement.

The academic year comprises three 10½-week terms and a monthlong Interim Term between Thanksgiving and the beginning of the new calendar year. Students usually take three courses during each term, while the Interim Term is used for independent study, taking courses, travel, research, work, or simply relaxation. The College actively supports internships as part of career preparation, and the College Scholars Honors Program is open to select students.

Off-Campus Arrangements

The Student-in-Residence-on-Leave (SIROL) program gives North Central students the opportunity to pursue a special program at another accredited college or university while remaining officially enrolled at the College. Numerous study-abroad programs, including the Washington Semester at American University and Drew University's United Nations Semester in New York, are examples of SIROL programs. Other off-campus programs include research at the Gulf Coast Research Laboratory in Ocean Springs, Mississippi, and in Roatan, Honduras; study field trips to the deserts of the Southwest; study-abroad programs to Costa Rica and London; and the distinctive Richter Independent Study Fellowship Program, which provides funds of up to $5000 for a single specialized project. Richter Independent Study projects have included travel and research on every continent. North Central also sponsors a student and faculty exchange program with Hirosaki Gakuin College in Japan.

Academic Facilities

North Central's 56-acre campus, in the heart of the historic district of Naperville, has more than twenty major buildings. Facilities range from the restored 1906 Carnegie Library building and the 1870 Old Main to the modern Larrance Academic Center and Cardinal Stadium. Pfeiffer Hall, with its 1,050-seat auditorium, is the cultural center for both the campus and the community. Oesterle Library provides access to more than 22 million volumes in forty-five college and university libraries in Illinois.

WONC (89.1 FM), the College's 1,500-watt radio station, is one of the most powerful student-staffed stations in the Midwest. With two fully operational state-of-the-art studios, a stereo console, an Associated Press Newsdesk Wireservice, and computerized music programming, the station is one of the most modern educational facilities in the region. WONC has won sixteen national Marconi Awards in past years. No other radio station has won more. All students, faculty members, and staff members have access to a voice, video, and data network installed in 1995, including full Internet access from their residence halls, classrooms, computer laboratories, and offices. In the sciences, students can use a scintillation counter; a nuclear magnetic resonance spectrometer; gas and liquid chromatographs; ultraviolet, visible, and infrared spectrophotometers; a pulsed nitrogen laser; and an environmental chamber to pursue laboratory research. Recently, the College raised funds to complete a $2-million challenge to purchase and create an endowment for scientific equipment, supported by a $500,000 commitment from the Kresge Foundation. North Central also has state-of-the-art language and market research laboratories.

Costs

For 2000–01, tuition at North Central College is $15,975. Room and board are $5472. Resident students pay a $195 technology fee. The student activity fee is $120 and estimated additional expenses are $425 for books and supplies. Students should also budget personal expenses and transportation costs.

Financial Aid

The Offices of Admission and Financial Aid believe that no student should be excluded from attending North Central College for financial reasons. Scholarships, loans, grants, and work-study assistance are awarded on the basis of demonstrated financial need and the academic record. Students are required to submit the Free Application for Federal Student Aid (FAFSA). Funds are also available through the Illinois State Monetary Award Program (for Illinois residents only), the Federal Pell Grant Program, Federal Supplemental Educational Opportunity Grant, and the Federal Stafford Student Loan Program. The College awarded $9 million from institutional sources for 1999–2000. A large portion of those funds was allocated through the academic-based Presidential Scholarship Program. Awards range from $3000 to $15,500, renewable annually. Students may also audition for scholarships in theater, forensics, and vocal and instrumental music and submit art portfolios.

Faculty

Members of the North Central faculty, 86 percent of whom hold the Ph.D. or another terminal degree, are first—and foremost—teachers. A student-faculty ratio of 14:1 and an average class size of 17 students ensure opportunities for a stimulating exchange of ideas. All faculty members also serve as academic advisers to provide guidance and counseling for students. Students get to know their professors on a personal basis, and the list of independent study projects is extensive. Faculty members teach both undergraduate and graduate courses.

Student Government

All undergraduates are members of the Student Association, which is governed by its elected officers. The Student Association is a vital and influential force in campus activities, and it takes an active role in the development and implementation of policies concerning student life on campus. Representatives of the student body have a voice on faculty, trustee, and administrative committees, while the College Union Activities Board plans social and service events.

Admission Requirements

New students are accepted individually on the basis of their overall academic preparation, character, and potential for success at North Central College. Graduation from an accredited secondary school is a basic requirement for admission. Other criteria used in the selection of prospective students are the high school academic record, personal recommendations of high school counselors, ACT or SAT I scores, and involvement in extracurricular activities. Members of the North Central freshman class of 1999–2000 scored an average of 25 on the ACT and ranked in the 77th percentile of their high school graduating class. North Central does not discriminate on the basis of sex, race, ethnic background, age, or physical handicap.

Application and Information

North Central College operates on a rolling admission basis, which allows students to apply at any time during or after their senior year in high school. Applicants receive notification within two weeks after the College receives all documentation. Early application is recommended to ensure availability of campus housing. The application must be accompanied by a $25 fee, an official high school transcript, and official reports of ACT or SAT I scores from the testing agency. For additional information or application forms, students should contact:

Office of Admission
North Central College
30 North Brainard Street
P.O. Box 3065
Naperville, Illinois 60566-7065
Telephone: 630-637-5800
        800-411-1861 (toll-free)
Fax: 630-637-5819
E-mail: ncadm@noctrl.edu
World Wide Web: http://www.northcentralcollege.edu

Historic Old Main, built in 1870 and renovated in 1998, houses the Offices of Admission, Financial Aid, and the Registrar.

NORTHEASTERN UNIVERSITY
BOSTON, MASSACHUSETTS

The University

Located at the center of Boston's thriving educational and cultural life, Northeastern University is dedicated to excellence in research and scholarship and is committed to responding to individual and community educational needs. Since its founding in 1898, Northeastern has pioneered a wide range of educational programs and services for students of all ages. The University is an internationally recognized leader in cooperative education—a unique approach to undergraduate education that joins the challenges of traditional classroom instruction on campus with the adventure of learning in a variety of paid professional employment situations in industry, government, or public service organizations. Each year students graduate from Northeastern with a solid sense of themselves and their relationship to the community as well as a valuable head start on their careers. The current undergraduate enrollment is 12,872 full-time and 6,493 part-time students.

Location

Northeastern University is located in Boston's Back Bay area, known for its many cultural and educational institutions. Symphony Hall (home of the Boston Symphony Orchestra), Horticultural Hall (home of the Massachusetts Horticultural Society), the New England Conservatory of Music, the Museum of Fine Arts, and the Isabella Stewart Gardner Museum are all nearby. The Fenway area, with its beautiful rose garden, bicycle and jogging paths, and Fenway Park (home of the Boston Red Sox), is just a few blocks away. The campus comprises thirty-seven buildings in an area of 60 acres. Northeastern provides a wide range of on-campus housing that accommodates 5,000 students from around the world.

Majors and Degrees

Bouvé College of Health Sciences awards a Bachelor of Science in athletic training, cardiopulmonary sciences (with concentrations in exercise physiology and respiratory therapy), medical laboratory science, nursing, pharmacy, physical therapy, speech pathology and audiology, and toxicology. The College also offers a six-year Pharm.D. program and a six-year physical therapy program leading to a master's degree in physical therapy. The College of Arts and Sciences awards a Bachelor of Arts or Bachelor of Science in African-American studies, anthropology, art (including a concentration in architecture), behavioral neuroscience, biology, biomedical physics, chemistry, communication studies, early childhood education, economics, English, environmental geology, environmental studies, geology, history, human services, international affairs, journalism, linguistics, mathematics, media arts and design, modern languages, multimedia studies, music (including a concentration in the music industry), philosophy, physics, political science (concentration in law and legal issues), psychology, sociology, and theater. A B.S. degree is awarded in American Sign Language–English interpreting, applied physics, and biochemistry. Study-abroad opportunities are also available. The College of Business Administration awards the Bachelor of Science in Business Administration with concentrations in accounting, entrepreneurship and new-venture management, finance and insurance, human resources management, international business, management, management information systems, marketing, and supply-chain management. A Bachelor of Science in international business is also offered. The College of Computer Science awards the Bachelor of Arts or Bachelor of Science in computer science and the Bachelor of Science in information science. The College of Criminal Justice awards a Bachelor of Science in Criminal Justice. Students may concentrate in criminology and corrections, legal studies, and policing and security. The College of Engineering offers the Bachelor of Science in chemical, civil and environmental, computer, electrical (including options in computer and power systems engineering), industrial, mechanical, and unspecified-general engineering. The College also offers part-time evening programs leading to the Bachelor of Science degree in civil, electrical, and mechanical engineering. In addition, the College offers joint B.S./M.S. degree programs in electrical engineering, industrial engineering, and mechanical engineering.

The School of Engineering Technology offers full-time day and part-time programs leading to the Bachelor of Science in Engineering Technology (B.S.E.T.) degree and part-time engineering programs leading to Associate in Engineering (A.E.) and Associate in Science (A.S.) degrees. Programs in computer technology, electrical engineering technology, and mechanical engineering technology are available in a full-time day cooperative curriculum leading to the B.S.E.T. degree. The Lowell Institute School, the School of Engineering Technology's part-time evening division, offers pretechnology preparatory courses and degree programs leading to the A.E. degree in electrical, environmental, and mechanical engineering technologies and computer technology. In the part-time division, the B.S.E.T. degree may be earned in computer technology and electrical, manufacturing, mechanical, and mechanical-manufacturing engineering technology. The Associate in Science degree is offered in telecommunications through the School of Engineering Technology's part-time division.

University College offers part-time day and evening programs leading to B.S., B.A., B.S.B.A., B.S.N., B.S.H.S., and A.S. degrees and certificates in business administration, criminal justice and security, health professions and sciences, and liberal arts. Radiologic technology programs are offered full-time in the day and part-time in the evening. The School of General Studies offers an integrated, flexible, full-time curriculum that leads directly to enrollment as a sophomore in the University.

Academic Program

A University-wide honors program gives students opportunities to participate in enriched educational experiences, such as honors equivalents of required academic courses and interdisciplinary colloquia. These experiences are designed to help students expand special interests and develop an understanding of new fields. Honors students are selected on the basis of demonstrated ability and academic promise.

The Cooperative Education Program enables students to gain practical experience in the workplace while helping to finance their education. The program is both national and international in scope. Alternate quarters of work and study (after a traditional freshman year) constitute a five-year program leading to a bachelor's degree. A four-year co-op option is available to engineering, business, and computer science students, and a four-year non–co-op schedule is available in the College of Arts and Sciences.

Credit may be awarded through the Advanced Placement program. CLEP examinations are accepted for credit only in the undergraduate evening programs.

The Ujima Scholars Program is an academic support program designed to assist students of color who have demonstrated an ability to succeed in college but need additional academic assistance, particularly during their first year. Such students must enroll in a credit-offering reading and study skills course, attend tutorial sessions and group meetings, complete profile assessments, and participate in career/vocational workshops, individual counseling, and academic advising and scheduling sessions. Every student enrolled in Ujima has a full-time counselor, and the student's academic activities are monitored throughout his or her time at Northeastern. NUPRIME, a program designed to aid African-Americans, Hispanic-Americans, and Native Americans, is offered through the College of Engineering.

The Department of Military Science (Army ROTC) offers a program of instruction leading to a commission as a second lieutenant in the active Army, Army Reserve, or Army National Guard. The Naval ROTC Nurse Program and Air Force ROTC are also available. Scholarship opportunities are available.

Support services for students with disabilities include orientation, special registration, counseling, housing, textbooks on tape, modified testing, readers, interpreters, notetakers, auxiliary aids, adaptive physical education, physical and speech therapy, sign-language classes, and scribes. Students with disabilities should contact the Disabilities Resource Center as early as possible before the start of the quarter. The numbers are 617-373-2675 and 617-373-2730 for TTY.

Degree programs have been specifically designed for adults who wish to further their education on a part-time basis. All formal courses of study leading to degrees in the Lowell Institute School and University College are approved by the undergraduate faculties concerned and are governed by the same qualitative and quantitative standards as the regular day curricula. Courses are scheduled in the day and evening at the Boston campus, the suburban campuses in Burlington and Dedham, the downtown Boston campus, and six other locations near Boston. Nondegree programs are offered by the Center for Continuing Education.

Academic Facilities

University libraries contain more than 893,000 volumes; 2 million microforms; 168,800 documents; 8,600 serial titles; 21,800 audio, video, and computer software titles; and thirty-four CD-ROM optical laser databases. The library's Media Center provides a language lab and audio, video, satellite downlink, and microcomputer facilities. Library services incorporate online, electronic, and media technologies that are associated with information resources, including an online catalog and circulation system, an information gateway, and a seventeen-station CD-ROM network. The catalog and gateway are also accessible through the campus academic computing network. From many study carrels in the library, students with a laptop can also directly access the campus computing network.

Costs

For 1999–2000, freshman tuition was $18,675. Other freshman-year expenses were books and supplies, about $600, and other fees, about $192. Upperclass tuition was $15,560. Room costs were $950 to $2325 per quarter; board per quarter costs were $1375 for nineteen meals a week.

Financial Aid

The University operates a substantial aid program designed to make attendance at Northeastern feasible for all qualified students. By coordinating the resources of the University and various public and private scholarship programs, the Office of Student Financial Services was able to provide more than $100 million to more than 8,630 students last year. Approximately 76 percent of the freshman class received financial assistance from University-based sources, and another 5 percent received aid through the Federal Stafford Student Loan Program. In addition, the University's cooperative plan enables students to earn income that offsets a portion of their college expenses after their freshman year. Financial aid is based on need and academic promise and may consist of a grant, a loan, part-time employment, or any combination of these three. To apply, students must file a Free Application for Federal Student Aid (FAFSA) and a PROFILE form with the College Scholarship Service by February 15. Students who are accepted by March 2 have priority in receiving funds.

Faculty

The University has 751 full-time faculty members and a staff of academic counselors in each college who work closely with students to assist them in developing programs suited to their interests and abilities.

Student Government

The Student Government Association, a group of students from the various colleges, is the official liaison between undergraduate students and the administration. Providing advice and opinions on a wide variety of issues, the association strives to improve the quality of life at Northeastern.

Admission Requirements

Each candidate should have completed a secondary school program that is as challenging as his or her ability permits. Courses in English, a foreign language, mathematics, laboratory science, and history are recommended. Of particular importance are continuity and proficiency in subjects critical to the proposed area of study at the University, as well as a wise choice of electives. The quality and scope of the student's secondary school record are of primary importance. Candidates are required to take the SAT I or the ACT.

Application and Information

Under Northeastern's rolling admission plan, candidates may apply and be accepted at the point in their secondary school careers where there is sufficient evidence that they can profit from University study. Applications completed by March 1 will secure a decision in time for the April 15 Candidates Reply Date (applies to fall quarter freshman applicants only). Junior-year and deferred admissions are available, and students who have successfully completed study at other accredited institutions are eligible for advanced standing. Freshmen may enroll in all programs in September and, depending on the availability of courses, in January, April, and June. Transfer students in most programs may apply for entrance at the beginning of each quarter. Personal interviews are recommended but not required. Campus tours and group information sessions are held daily, and open house programs are scheduled throughout the year.

For more information, students should contact:

Office of Undergraduate Admissions
Northeastern University
360 Huntington Avenue
Boston, Massachusetts 02115
Telephone: 617-373-2200 (voice)
           617-373-3100 (TTY)
E-mail: undergrad-admissions@neu.edu

NORTHERN ARIZONA UNIVERSITY
FLAGSTAFF, ARIZONA

The University

Northern Arizona University is a fully accredited, state-supported, four-year institution with 13,329 full-time students on its main campus. Since 1899, the University has made a major commitment to undergraduate education, and its goal has been to preserve a friendly campus atmosphere and close student-faculty relationships through classroom teaching of the highest quality and faculty guidance for each student.

The University is composed of the Colleges of Arts and Science, Business Administration, Ecosystem Science and Management, Engineering and Technology, Health Professions, and Social and Behavioral Sciences; the Schools of Communication, Fine Arts, Hotel and Restaurant Management, and Performing Arts; and the Center of Excellence in Education. Undergraduate, master's, and doctoral degrees are offered in more than 150 major areas and in a number of interdisciplinary and preprofessional curricula. A graduate degree is available in physical therapy.

Eleven advisement centers assist the University in realizing its strong commitment to one-on-one advising, and regular office hours are maintained by faculty members. An average class size of 26 is another example of the institution's attention to high-quality education.

Nonacademic facilities include seven buildings listed on the National Register of Historic Places. In addition, there are three student unions, a student health center, an Olympic-size swimming and diving complex, a 16,230-seat multiuse wooden dome, and a multipurpose recreational facility.

As a residential campus, NAU provides an atmosphere of friendship and community. Fifty-three percent of the undergraduate students live in the 21 residence halls and 346 family housing apartments located on the campus. Of the 11,790 full-time undergraduates enrolled in the 1999 fall semester, 4,990 were men and 6,800 were women.

Northern Arizona University is an Equal Opportunity/Affirmative Action institution.

Location

Northern Arizona University's 730-acre mountain campus is located in Flagstaff, a community with 58,000 residents. Flagstaff is located at an elevation of 7,000 feet, just south of the 12,600-foot-high San Francisco Peaks, a major winter-sports center. The University is at the junction of Interstate Highways 40 (U.S. 66) and 17, less than a 3-hour drive from Phoenix and about a 5-hour drive from Tucson, Arizona; Albuquerque, New Mexico; and Las Vegas, Nevada. The city is served by Amtrak, Greyhound buses, and a commercial airline. The campus is surrounded by scenic beauty and natural wonders, such as the Grand Canyon and a student favorite, Oak Creek Canyon. The varied northern land of mountains, gorges, forests, and lakes provides the University with natural classrooms and laboratories for research as well as recreation.

Majors and Degrees

Northern Arizona University offers baccalaureate degrees in approximately ninety major areas, embracing most of the recognized fields in the arts and sciences and a number of interdisciplinary majors. NAU also offers a number of special programs, including arts management, criminal justice, dental hygiene, forestry, hotel and restaurant management, and parks and recreation management.

Academic Program

A four-year baccalaureate degree program at Northern Arizona University requires the successful completion of 120 semester hours of course work, including 35 hours of liberal studies courses. The liberal studies program consists of foundation studies and studies in various disciplines designed to assist students in cultivating their abilities to recognize significant problems and to define, analyze, and defend solutions in a variety of contexts. Major-field requirements vary from 35 to 73 semester hours. Students may combine a major field with one or more 18-hour minors, take two majors or an extended major of 63 to 65 hours in a field of their interest, or select the merged major programs.

NAU has a long-established honors program designed to challenge the talented student. This leads to graduation with honors, and honor students may elect to take the special degree of Bachelor of Arts: Honors. The program provides special courses and seminars and offers superior students opportunities for independent study and research.

A three-year bachelor's degree program is available in forty-six majors. The program offers intellectual and academic challenges for well-prepared and motivated students, allowing them to take the fast track to graduation and graduate programs.

Off-Campus Arrangements

NAU actively cooperates in the work and research programs of several major scientific institutions that are located close to its campus. These include the Lowell Observatory; the U.S. Naval Observatory's Flagstaff station; various facilities of the U.S. Geological Survey, including its space-oriented Astrogeology Center; the U.S. Forest Service Rocky Mountain and Range Experiment station; and the Museum of Northern Arizona and its multidisciplinary Colton Research Center. The specialized libraries, laboratories, and other facilities of these institutions are available to qualified students at the University. NAU sponsors a marine biology camp in Mexico on the Gulf of California, as well as scientific field trips to many of the distinctive natural areas of northern Arizona, including an annual geological study tour through the nearby Grand Canyon.

The Northern Arizona University Centers in London, England; Tübingen, Germany; Granada, Spain; Montpellier, France; and Shanghai and Beijing, China, offer students an opportunity for exciting enrichment programs for one or two semesters in Europe or Asia. Students may also study for one semester in Cuernavaca, Mexico. Through field trips, students explore the history, literature, and culture of these regions. All students except freshmen may enroll.

Through the National Student Exchange program, NAU students have an opportunity to broaden their educational horizons by attending a college or university in another state for one semester or one year while paying tuition and fees at NAU. There are more than 150 participating institutions nationwide from which students may choose.

Academic Facilities

NAU's facilities for education and research are extensive. The University library contains more than 1.6 million volumes, 6,253 current periodical titles, a media center, and a number of special research collections of original documents relating to the history, economy, and culture of Arizona and the Southwest. The library recently completed an expansion from 83,000 to

203,000 square feet. The facility now has an online public access catalog and a book capacity of 2 million volumes.

Well-equipped general and specialized laboratories serve students in the basic sciences and health professions. Specially designed studios, workrooms, theaters, auditoriums, and an art gallery are available to students in the creative arts. Closed-circuit television hookups, student-paced audiovisual systems, language laboratories, an observatory, and a major computer center are used regularly by students for both learning and research. The Bilby Research Center augments NAU's research facilities.

NAU makes extensive use of the spectacular Colorado Plateau country surrounding its campus as a natural laboratory for anthropology, biology, ecology, geology, geophysics, paleontology, and other sciences. Prehistoric Indian ruins and the living cultures of the Navajo, Hopi, and many other Indian peoples of the Southwest provide rich resources for students of archaeology, ethnology, and linguistics. The University also maintains a 4,000-acre research forest for forestry students. The area's 7,000-foot elevation and unusually clear, dry air have made it a major center for astronomy and the atmospheric sciences.

Costs

For 1999–2000, the charges for an academic year of two semesters for an in-state student were tuition and fees, $2262, and average board and room, $3802. Books and supplies averaged $730. The total cost for Arizona residents was $6804 per academic year. The out-of-state tuition fee was $8378, for an academic-year cost of $12,910. This does not include travel or personal expenses, which vary for each student. (All costs are subject to change by the Arizona Board of Regents.)

Financial Aid

Northern Arizona University maintains an extensive program of financial assistance to aid students in pursuing their educational goals. The amount of financial aid awarded to a student is based upon the student's need level, as computed from the Free Application for Federal Student Aid (FAFSA). However, some scholarships are awarded on the basis of a student's demonstration of academic excellence and/or participation in various University activities.

In the 1999–2000 academic year, more than $70 million was available for loans, scholarships, grants, veterans' benefits, and work-study programs. About 60 percent of the students at NAU receive some form of financial aid.

Along with grants, loans, and scholarships, on- and off-campus employment is available to help students meet financial obligations. More than 4,500 NAU students are currently employed in a wide variety of jobs on the campus.

Faculty

NAU's faculty is made up of outstanding and dedicated professionals. More than 85 percent of the 690 full-time and 632 part-time faculty members hold doctoral degrees. Many are nationally distinguished scientists and scholars. The student-faculty ratio is 17:1, with more than 85 percent of the classes taught by faculty members rather than graduate assistants.

Student Government

Each student who enters NAU is a member of the Associated Students of Northern Arizona University (ASNAU), which represents the students' interests in all matters that affect them.

Besides ASNAU, other student governing groups are the Associated Women Students, Association of University Residence Halls, Panhellenic Council, and Inter-Fraternity Council. About 50 percent of the students belong to one or more of the 192 student groups and organizations.

Admission Requirements

Applicants for admission must complete both general aptitude and basic competence requirements. Conditional admission for non-Arizona residents is granted on a space-available basis. Participation in some form of assistance program may be required for those admitted conditionally.

For unconditional admission, the general aptitude requirements for new freshmen are any one of the following: a cumulative GPA of 3.0 or better (on a 4.0 scale), a class rank in the upper quarter, a minimum ACT composite score of 22 (24 for non-Arizona residents), or a minimum combined SAT I score of 1040 (1100 for nonresidents). For conditional admission, the requirements are a cumulative GPA between 2.5 and 2.99 or a class rank at least in the upper half with test scores below the previously stated minimums. The GPA to meet the general aptitude requirement for admission is calculated using only the sixteen required core courses. Transfers with fewer than 12 transferable academic semester credits must meet the same standards as new freshmen. If 12 or more semester credits have been earned, the cumulative GPA must be at least 2.0 for unconditional or conditional admission for Arizona residents. Non-Arizona residents must have a cumulative GPA of at least 2.5 for unconditional admission or between 2.0 and 2.49 for conditional admission.

Basic competency requirements must be met by all freshmen and transfer students, either through high school course work and/or transferable higher education courses. Generally, one 3-hour college course equals one year of high school study. Core course requirements include 4 years of English, 4 years of mathematics, 3 years of laboratory science, 2 years of social science, 2 years of foreign language, and 1 year of fine art. There are specific course requirements within these areas, and some requirements may be met by achieving minimum scores on standardized tests. Students should contact the Admissions Office for more information.

March 1 is the priority deadline for the summer and fall semesters; December 1 is for the spring semester. Applications and supporting documents received after these dates are processed on a space-available basis.

Application and Information

The NAU information booklet, which includes an application for admission and information about financial aid, housing, and academic programs, may be obtained by contacting:

Admissions Office
Box 4084
Northern Arizona University
Flagstaff, Arizona 86011-4084

Telephone: 888-MORE-NAU (toll-free)
E-mail: undergraduate.admissions@nau.edu

A friendly residential campus and the four-season climate of Flagstaff, Arizona, attract about 12,000 undergraduate students each year to Northern Arizona University.

NORTHERN KENTUCKY UNIVERSITY
HIGHLAND HEIGHTS, KENTUCKY

The University

Northern Kentucky University (NKU) was founded in 1968 and is the newest of Kentucky's eight state universities. The atmosphere of the campus is futuristic, emphasizing a high-quality education by supporting the liberal arts. Twelve major buildings are of modern, contemporary architectural design and are set on 300 acres of rolling countryside. NKU has an enrollment of approximately 12,000 students from thirty states and forty-nine countries and is accredited by the Southern Association of Colleges and Schools. The Salmon P. Chase College of Law is accredited by both the American Bar Association and the Association of American Law Schools.

There are more than eighty student organizations. NKU competes in the NCAA Division II Great Lakes Valley Conference. Intercollegiate sports are offered for men and women in basketball, cross-country, soccer, and tennis; for men in baseball and golf; and for women in fast-pitch softball and volleyball. Intramural activities are archery, badminton, basketball, canoeing, flag football, innertube water polo, racquetball, soccer, softball, track and field, volleyball, water basketball, and water volleyball.

Location

NKU is located in the largest metropolitan area of any state university in Kentucky. It is located at the junction of U.S. Highway 27 and Interstates 275 and 471 in Highland Heights, Kentucky, 8 miles southeast of Cincinnati, Ohio. NKU is only 60 miles from Dayton, 79 miles from Lexington, 93 miles from Louisville, and 114 miles from Indianapolis. While the immediate surroundings are suburban, NKU is part of the metropolitan area of greater Cincinnati.

Majors and Degrees

Northern Kentucky University awards the Bachelor of Arts, Bachelor of Fine Arts, Bachelor of Music, Bachelor of Science, Bachelor of Science in Nursing, and Bachelor of Social Work degrees. NKU also offers preprofessional programs, secondary education teacher certification, and the Associate of Applied Science degree.

The B.A. and B.S. degrees are offered in accounting, anthropology, applied sociology–anthropology, biological sciences, business education, chemistry, computer science, economics, electronics engineering technology, elementary education, English, environmental science, finance, French, geography, geology, graphic design, history, industrial and labor relations, industrial education, industrial technology construction, industrial technology manufacturing, information systems, international studies, journalism, justice studies, management, manufacturing engineering technology, marketing, mathematics, mental health–human services, middle grades education, organizational studies, philosophy, physical education, physics, political science, psychology, public administration, radio-TV, recreation-fitness, sociology, Spanish, special education, speech, studio arts, and theater.

The B.F.A. degree is granted in art and in theater arts. The B.Mus. degree is offered in music. The B.S.N. degree is offered in the nursing major and the B.S.W. degree in the social work major.

Preprofessional programs are available in dentistry, engineering, forestry, law, medicine, optometry, pharmacy, physical therapy, veterinary medicine, and wildlife management. In addition, the University offers majors, minors, and areas of discipline for secondary education teacher certification.

The University also awards the A.A.S. degree in aviation administration, construction technology, human services, industrial education, industrial production technology, industrial supervision, law enforcement, nursing, piano pedagogy, prebusiness studies, radiologic technology, respiratory care, and technology.

Academic Program

NKU operates on a semester calendar. To receive a bachelor's degree, students must complete a minimum of 128 credit hours. At least 64 credit hours are required for the associate degree.

The University offers a variety of career planning and placement, internship, independent study, work-study, and cooperative education programs. There is also an Advising, Counseling, and Testing Center available. Other programs include an honors program, a program that allows for the dual enrollment of high school students, a program where students can combine their career interests in the liberal arts and engineering fields, and University 101, an orientation program for freshmen.

NKU recognizes credit earned through the Advanced Placement Program and the general, subject, and institutional tests of the College-Level Examination Program. A maximum of 45 credit hours may be applied toward the bachelor's degree from the AP and CLEP examinations. The International Baccalaureate Program allows students to earn credit in science, mathematics, psychology, and languages.

Off-Campus Arrangements

A variety of study-abroad opportunities are available to NKU students through membership in several consortia and through NKU exchange agreements with international universities.

Study in Australia, Canada, England, Ireland, New Zealand, Scotland, and South Africa is possible in a wide range of courses and programs available through NKU's membership in the Cooperative Center for Study Abroad (CCSA), which is headquartered at NKU.

The Kentucky Institute for International Studies (KIIS) offers students academic language programs in Austria, China, Ecuador, France, Germany, Greece, Italy, Mexico, and Spain. The NKU International Programs office has expanded its own international offerings to include student and faculty exchanges in Aarhus, Denmark; Gifu, Japan; Glasgow, Scotland; Munich, Germany; and Leon, Spain.

Academic Facilities

Among the academic facilities at NKU are an anthropology museum, a biology museum, and a geology exhibit at Landrum Hall. The University also has nursing, respiratory care, and radiologic technology laboratories and an art gallery with rotating exhibits. The W. Frank Steely Library at NKU contains 218,734 book titles and maintains 1,526 periodical subscriptions. Computer laboratories offer students opportunities to learn a variety of software programs.

Costs

Tuition and fees for 1999–2000 were $2460 for Kentucky residents and $6500 for out-of-state students. Room costs were between $1700 and $3575 a year; board costs averaged $1700 a year. The cost of books and supplies amounted to about $300, and miscellaneous expenses were $400.

Financial Aid

Last year, 51 percent of undergraduates received some form of financial assistance. To receive financial aid, applicants must complete the Free Application for Federal Student Aid (FAFSA). Academic, athletic, music-drama, and art scholarships and scholarships for members of minority groups are available at Northern Kentucky University.

The application deadline for all academic scholarships is February 1. There is no deadline for the University's financial aid application; however, students who wish to receive institutional aid must apply by April 1 for priority consideration. Applicants are notified of acceptance on a rolling basis.

Faculty

More than 82 percent of the faculty members at NKU hold a doctoral degree or the terminal degree in their field. Classes are small, with a student-faculty ratio of 16:1. All classes are taught by faculty members; no classes are taught by graduate assistants.

Student Government

Student Government (SG) is the elected student assembly at Northern Kentucky University. It is the official student voice on campus and represents the student viewpoint on University committees. All SG meetings are open, and students are encouraged to attend.

Admission Requirements

Incoming freshmen must submit an application for admission, arrange for the official ACT score report to be sent, and request that the high school send an official transcript and precollege curriculum verification. Students must meet precollege curriculum requirements for Kentucky: 20 course units with at least 4 in English; 3 in mathematics, including algebra I, algebra II, and geometry; 2 in science, including biology and either chemistry or physics; and 2 in social sciences, including U.S. history and world civilization. Out-of-state applicants must also meet the Kentucky precollege curriculum requirements, with the exception of the world civilization requirement.

Application and Information

There is a $25 fee that may be waived for applicants with demonstrated need. The fall semester early action and scholarship deadline is February 1; the priority application deadline is May 1. The priority application deadline for the nursing program is January 31. The deadline for the radiologic technology program is February 15. The priority application deadline for the respiratory care program is April 15.

For more information, students should contact:

Office of Admissions
Northern Kentucky University
Highland Heights, Kentucky 41099
Telephone: 606-572-5220
            800-637-9948 (toll-free)
E-mail: admitnku@nku.edu
World Wide Web: http://www.nku.edu

Northern Kentucky University's modern campus is set in Highland Heights, just minutes from downtown Cincinnati.

NORTH GEORGIA COLLEGE & STATE UNIVERSITY
The Military College of Georgia
DAHLONEGA, GEORGIA

The College

Following the Civil War, the abandoned U.S. Mint property was given to the state of Georgia for educational purposes; thus, what is now North Georgia College & State University was born. Originally named North Georgia Agricultural College, the institution was established in 1873 as a land-grant school of agriculture and mechanical arts, particularly mining engineering. As area gold resources were depleted and agricultural education was assumed by the University of Georgia, the mission of the institution evolved into one emphasizing arts and sciences. The school was renamed North Georgia College in summer 1929 and North Georgia College & State University (NGCSU) in fall 1996. NGCSU is a member of the University System of Georgia.

North Georgia College & State University's first class of students requested that military training be a part of the curriculum. Today, approximately 20 percent of the student body choose to be in NGCSU's nationally prominent ROTC program, which is administered by the U.S. Army. NGCSU is the senior military college of Georgia and is one of the only four military colleges in the nation. In fact, NGCSU is the only public, coeducational, liberal arts, military school in the country. NGCSU is unique in that it serves as a military college for its Corps of Cadets and as a liberal arts academic institution for all its students. Among the institution's many distinctions are its firsts for women: NGCSU was first public college in Georgia to award a degree to a woman, the first to grant athletic scholarships to women, and the first military college in the nation to accept women in the Corps of Cadets. Women have been fully qualified members of the Corps of Cadets since 1973.

NGCSU's incoming freshmen routinely post the highest average SAT I scores and highest graduation rates of all senior colleges in the University System of Georgia. Total enrollment is approximately 3,430 students (3,150 undergraduate and 280 graduate). Sixty percent of the students commute, and 65 percent of the total student population is female. Approximately 85 percent of the student body is of traditional student age (18–22 years old). More than 90 percent of the students are Georgia residents. The Corps of Cadets comprises approximately 20 percent of the student body and 40 percent of the resident population. All male resident students are required to be members of the Corps of Cadets. Although military service is not required after graduation, students who participate in the Corps may advance to a commission in the active Army or U.S. Army Reserve. Membership in the Corps is optional for women and commuter students.

North Georgia College & State University offers varied programs of study leading to degrees at the associate, bachelor's, and master's level. At the undergraduate level, degrees offered include the Bachelor of Arts (A.B.), Associate of Science in Nursing (A.S.N.), Bachelor of Science (B.S.), Bachelor of Business Administration (B.B.A.), and Bachelor of Science in Nursing (B.S.N.) Master's degree programs in community counseling, education, nursing, physical therapy, and public administration are available. An Educational Specialist Degree in teacher leadership is also available. The preprofessional programs have reputations as being among the finest in the area. The largest number of students is enrolled in education, business, and criminal justice programs. Dual-degree programs in cooperation with the Georgia Institute of Technology and Clemson University prepare students for careers in engineering, computer science, and business.

North Georgia College & State University emphasizes a liberal arts curriculum while providing outstanding leadership training through the Corps of Cadets and active involvement in extracurricular groups. With more than sixty student clubs and organizations to choose from, participation in campus extracurricular activities is encouraged for both resident and commuting students. Students may choose to participate in activities such as student government, military organizations, student publications, music ensembles, honor societies, religious organizations, special interest groups, intramural sports, and Greek life. Four national sororities, four national fraternities, and two local fraternities exist on campus. Varsity sports include baseball, basketball, cross-country, soccer, and tennis for men and basketball, cross-country, soccer, softball, and tennis for women. NGCSU competes in the Georgia Athletic Conference and the National Association for Intercollegiate Athletics.

Location

North Georgia is located in Dahlonega, Georgia, a 1-hour drive north of Atlanta and 90 minutes from Hartsfield International Airport. The city of Dahlonega (population 3,500) is nestled in the foothills of the Blue Ridge Mountains and is a popular tourist site. The institution's main campus covers 120 acres, with twenty-one major buildings. Price Memorial Hall, whose majestic steeple is covered with Dahlonega gold, is a nationally registered historic site. Additionally, the campus' location provides easy access to numerous recreational opportunities, such as the Appalachian Trail, white-water rafting, camping grounds, fishing, Lake Lanier (site of the 1996 Olympic rowing events), snow skiing, and metropolitan Atlanta.

Majors and Degrees

The Associate in Nursing degree is offered. The Bachelor of Arts is offered in art, English, French, history, music, political science, and Spanish. The Bachelor of Business Administration is offered in accounting, finance, management and marketing. The Bachelor of Science is offered in art, art marketing, biology, chemistry, computer information systems, computer science, criminal justice, early childhood education, mathematics, middle grades education, physical education, physics, political science, psychology, social science, sociology, and special education. The Bachelor of Science, with teacher certification for secondary education, is offered in art, biology, chemistry, English, French, health and physical education, mathematics, music, music education with National Association certification, physics, social science, sociology, and Spanish. The Bachelor of Science in Nursing is offered. Preprofessional programs are available in dental hygiene, dentistry, forestry, health information management, law, medical technology, medicine, occupational therapy, pharmacy, physical therapy, physician assistant studies, respiratory therapy, and veterinary medicine. Dual-degree (3+2) programs in computer science, engineering, and industrial management provide students with a strong liberal arts background before they complete academic course work at the Georgia Institute of Technology or Clemson University. Upon completion of the academic program, bachelor's degrees from both North Georgia College & State University and the cooperating institution are awarded. Qualified students seeking a Bachelor of Engineering degree may participate in the Regents Engineering Transfer (2+2) program, which enables students to transfer to the Georgia Institute of Technology upon completion of the pre-engineering curriculum at NGCSU.

Academic Program

North Georgia requires all students to complete core curriculum requirements. The core curriculum consists of 9 semester hours of English and mathematics; 4 semester hours institutionally required (ethics, speech, philosophy); 6 semester hours of humanities/fine arts; 11 semester hours of science, mathematics, and technology; 12 semester hours of social science; and 18 semester hours related to the major. The minimum requirement for a degree is 120 semester hours, including 12 hours of military science for members of the Corps of Cadets. All students must complete an additional 3 semester hours of physical education. The state of Georgia requires all graduates to meet U.S. and Georgia history and U.S. and Georgia Constitution requirements. These are met upon completion of the core curriculum. All students must also pass the Regents' Test of Reading and Writing before graduating.

Participation in the Honors Program is limited to 20 freshman each year. In addition to completing approximately 20 hours of the required honors-only course work, honors students participate in numerous on- and off-campus enrichment programs, such as field trips and faculty mentoring opportunities. Completion of a senior research paper is required of all Honors Program participants.

Academic Facilities

The campus library houses 115,000 volumes and 500,000 microfiche records and is connected to all state library facilities via the GALILEO computer network. Newly renovated laboratory facilities provide access to state-of-the-art research facilities and modern equipment. Five student computer laboratories that house 175 computers are available for student use. All residence hall rooms are wired and networked for free access to e-mail and Internet services.

Costs

Tuition for the 1999–2000 school year was $1808 for in-state residents and $7232 for out-of-state residents. Room and board (twenty-one meals) were $3428, and mandatory fees were $402. Books are estimated to cost $700 per year. Personal expenses vary from $1500 to $2500. All costs are subject to change at the end of any semester.

Financial Aid

Of those students who apply for financial assistance, more than 80 percent receive financial aid. Aid is available through a combination of scholarships, grants, loans, and campus employment. Among the federal funds available are grants, student loans, Federal Work-Study, and ROTC scholarships. Georgia residents who participate in the Corps of Cadets receive $750 per semester, provided they maintain a cumulative average of 2.0. Nonresidents who participate in the Corps of Cadets may have their out-of-state tuition waived if they maintain a cumulative average of 2.0.

Faculty

Because of NGCSU's emphasis on the liberal arts curriculum, a focus on teaching is maintained. None of the undergraduate classes are taught by teaching assistants. Most faculty members share in the responsibility of advising students. Furthermore, the low student-faculty ratio of 21:1 provides ample opportunity for students to interact with their professors. The faculty consists of 170 teaching faculty members, and an additional 21 faculty members have primarily administrative responsibilities. Seventy percent of the faculty members hold a doctorate. Twenty part-time faculty members will be employed in the 2000–01 school year.

Student Government

The North Georgia College & State University Student Government Association (SGA) has been chosen as the top association in the University System of Georgia for eight of the past ten years. The SGA is composed of elected representatives from each class on campus and executive officers from the student body at large. It is the umbrella student organization of all other student groups on campus. As the coordinating body of various student activities, organizations, and class elections, the SGA is the medium for communication between the administration/faculty and the student body. Among the responsibilities of the SGA is the preparation of a budget recommending the allocation of student activity fees.

Admission Requirements

For regular admission, the applicant must meet the following requirements: be 16 years old on or before the registration date, be of good moral character, be a graduate of an accredited high school or a high school that is approved by the College, complete the approved pre-college curriculum of that high school, and meet minimum score requirements on either the SAT I or ACT. The approved pre-college curriculum requires 4 years of English, 4 years of mathematics (2 algebra, 1 geometry, and 1 advanced math), 3 years of science (at least 2 from biology, chemistry, or physics), 3 years of social science (including American and world history and government/economics), and 2 years of the same foreign language. In addition, the applicant must have a 2.0 high school grade point average in required subjects, a minimum 480 verbal SAT I score (21 ACT/English) and 440 mathematics SAT I score (19 ACT/math) and a predicated freshman average grade of 2.0 for regular admission. International students must have a minimum score of 550 on the TOEFL. A certificate of immunization against communicable diseases must be completed prior to admission. Transfer students must have a cumulative average of 2.0 or better and be in good academic standing with the institution from which they are transferring.

Students who wish to apply for the nursing program must file a separate application for undergraduate admission to NGCSU and the Nursing Department. Completion of the Associate of Science in Nursing degree or its equivalent is required prior to acceptance into the Bachelor of Science in Nursing program. Those who wish to apply for the teacher education program must file a separate application to the Education Department in addition to the application for undergraduate admission.

Completed applications must be returned to the Office of Undergraduate Admission at least twenty days prior to the beginning of the semester for which the application is made, along with high school transcripts, SAT I/ACT scores, properly completed health documents, and a nonrefundable $25 application fee. Students applying for transfer admission must have transcripts sent directly to the Office of Undergraduate Admission from the registrar's office of all other institutions attended. Admission is on a rolling basis.

North Georgia College & State University admits qualified applicants without regard to race, color, ethnic origin, religion, gender, age, or handicap.

Application and Information

Director of Admissions
North Georgia College & State University
Dahlonega, Georgia 30597
Telephone: 706-864-1800
          800-498-9581 (toll-free)
Fax: 706-864-1478
E-mail: admissions@ngcsu.edu
World Wide Web: http://www.ngcsu.edu

Price Memorial was the early home of the U.S. Mint in the 1840s. Following the Civil War, the federal government gave the abandoned property to Georgia for educational purposes; thus, the site became the first building on the North Georgia College & State University campus.

NORTH PARK UNIVERSITY
CHICAGO, ILLINOIS

The University

North Park University began its tradition of academic excellence in 1891 and traces its roots to first-generation Swedish Americans. Formerly North Park College, the institution changed its name to North Park University in 1997 to more accurately and inclusively describe academic programs, especially to graduate and international students. North Park University was from the beginning, and continues to be, affiliated with and generously supported by the Evangelical Covenant Church. It is a Christian university committed to relating faith in Jesus Christ to the aims of higher education. North Park believes that liberal arts education should prepare students for a rich, morally responsible life and equip them with those intellectual and social skills necessary to succeed in any vocation or pursuit.

To serve this end, North Park has created a program of general education that introduces students, usually as first- and second-year students, to a broad selection of academic subjects. Within these disciplines, students learn how to reason, examine values, and communicate—skills as important as the knowledge gained in these courses. Within the general education curriculum, breadth of understanding and versatility of response are the underlying objectives. When combined with advanced study in a major program, this foundation of courses prepares students to adapt to a society continually changing, nowhere more so than in the workplace.

North Park students are involved in and committed to a wealth of cocurricular activities that develop them personally, morally, and socially. North Park's Outreach Ministries program attracts students from around the country; more than 400 North Park students volunteer in one of the twenty-three programs on a weekly basis. Music, theater, and student government as well as athletics and religious involvement play an important role in the daily life of the students, who are challenged to examine their values, define their potential, and maximize their personal growth. North Park University is a member of the NCAA Division III and the College Conference of Illinois and Wisconsin (CCIW); men and women participate in national and regional competition in Division III. Competition in intramural sports is open to the entire campus community.

At the graduate level, the University offers a Master of Arts in Education (M.A.Ed.), a Master of Science (M.S.) with a major in nursing, an advanced nurse practitioner degree program and a geriatic nurse practitioner degree program, a Master of Business Administration (M.B.A.), a Master of Management (M.M.), and a Master of Arts in Community Development (M.A.C.D.); joint graduate degree programs between the business and nursing departments; and seminary degrees, including Christian education, divinity, and theological studies.

Location

Located in a pleasant residential neighborhood on the northwest side of Chicago, North Park's 30-acre campus has small-town flavor and warmth, yet its intimate environment is within one of the largest and most exciting metropolitan areas of the world. Chicago offers a multitude of cultural, recreational, and service opportunities—everything from the Art Institute of Chicago and the Chicago Symphony Orchestra to the Chicago Cubs and Bulls to the homeless shelter of Jesus People, U.S.A. The North Park campus hosts regular appearances by professional musicians. The impact of the city on the University's education program is significant. Several hundred student internship sites have been identified in the city. Easily accessed by public transportation, city life is available on demand.

Majors and Degrees

North Park University offers the Bachelor of Arts with major concentrations in accounting, anthropology, art (advertising and design, studio art), biblical and theological studies, biology, business administration, chemistry, communication arts (communications studies, speech education, theater and performance), economics, education (art K–12, early childhood, elementary, music K–12, physical education, secondary), English (literature and writing), exercise science, finance, foreign languages (French, Spanish, and Swedish), history, international affairs, international business, marketing, mathematics, medical technology, music (instrumental and voice), music education, nursing, occupational therapy, philosophy, physical education, physics, politics and government, psychology, sociology, sports medicine, and youth ministry.

The Bachelor of Science is offered with major concentrations in accounting, biology, business administration, chemistry, mathematics, medical technology, nursing, and physics. The Bachelor of Music is offered with major concentrations in instrumental music and voice.

GOAL, a degree completion program for adults, offers accelerated B.A. degrees in organizational management and human development. Classes meet in the evening and on weekends.

Preprofessional programs are offered in dentistry, law, medicine, occupational therapy, pharmaceutical science, physical therapy, and veterinary medicine. North Park participates in a 3-2 engineering program whereby a student receives a baccalaureate degree from North Park and an engineering degree from one of four participating universities.

Academic Program

North Park is committed to the development of the whole person. The curriculum, consisting of general education, major, and elective courses, has been shaped to provide graduates with skills and values that are fundamental to success in life. The general education curriculum focuses on the disciplines of English, biblical and theological studies, foreign language, fine arts, history, natural science, social science, Western civilization and culture, non-Western perspectives, mathematics, and health and physical education.

North Park operates on a calendar consisting of two 16-week semesters and a ten-day interim between the winter and spring terms. Students are considered full-time if they are enrolled in a minimum of 12 semester hours. To graduate, a student must complete 120 semester hours with an overall grade point average of 2.0 or better. There are also requirements for the major and the minor.

North Park recognizes high school graduates who have completed college-level courses in high school and have taken the Advanced Placement tests of the College Board. Students who have completed their junior year in high school, rank in the upper fourth of their class, have been enrolled in a college-preparatory curriculum, and show an aptitude test score that ranks at or above the mean score at the University may apply for early admission.

North Park seeks and attracts students of superior high school backgrounds and academic aptitude. A scholars program is offered to qualified first-year students and continues throughout their academic career. The North Park Scholars Program and the North Park Dean's Leadership Program provide such students with enriching curricular and cocurricular supplements to their undergraduate experiences.

Off-Campus Arrangements

North Park students may participate in a number of off-campus programs. The American Studies Program of the Council for Christian Colleges and Universities provides work-study opportunities in Washington, D.C. Other coalition programs are available in Hollywood (for film studies) and in Costa Rica (for Latin American studies), Egypt, and Russia. North Park also provides study-abroad programs in Israel, Korea, Mexico, and Scandinavia.

Academic Facilities

Library services at North Park support and extend the academic instruction of the University. Students have immediate access to more than 215,000 bound volumes, 1,500 titles on microform, 1,000 periodical subscriptions, and 5,000 records and tapes. In addition, North Park students have access to the resources of Northeastern Illinois University and all sixteen of the LIBRAS Colleges in the Chicago area. In addition to computer classrooms, North Park offers a full Computer Center and two student labs with nearly sixty Apple Macintosh and IBM-compatible microcomputers available. The Center for Africana Studies, Center for Korean Studies, Center for Latino Studies, Center for Middle Eastern Studies, Center for Scandinavian Studies, and Archives for the Swedish American Historical Society are research centers located on campus that can be utilized by students.

Costs

Tuition and fees for the 2000–01 academic year are $16,910. Room and board are $5480 for full-time students. Books and supplies are estimated at $600 but vary according to each student.

Financial Aid

At North Park, it is desired that no qualified student be prevented from obtaining a college education because of financial inability. In the 1999–2000 academic year, 90 percent of North Park students received some form of financial assistance. The University offers comprehensive academic merit scholarships for those students who demonstrate high academic performance.

Upon submission of the Free Application for Federal Student Aid (FAFSA), North Park awards financial assistance to eligible applicants through a combination of scholarships, grants, loans, and work-study. A student must be admitted to the University before financial aid is awarded.

Faculty

One of the most vital characteristics determining the quality of an institution is its faculty. The North Park faculty is committed to relating the values and understandings of Christian faith to the academic fields it represents. Nearly 80 percent of North Park's 70 full-time faculty members have earned doctorates or terminal degrees for their profession in the arts, sciences, and professional disciplines. Coming from a variety of denominational and educational backgrounds, faculty members share a commitment to North Park's goals as a Christian liberal arts university and are highly regarded in their scholarly fields.

Student Government

The North Park University Student Association represents the student body in all areas of University life. Its elected and appointed members work in cooperation with the administration and the faculty in shaping both academic and other areas of student life.

The association operates through three main branches: the Student Senate, a legislative body of elected representatives; the Executive, whose function is to recommend and execute policy as well as to coordinate the activities of the association; and the Judiciary, which renders interpretations of the Student Association constitution. The association encourages campus dialogue via four student publications and sponsors cultural and social events via the Student Senate, a late-night café, various departments (including Academic Affairs, Urban Outreach, Campus Ministries, Social Awareness, and Social Events), and eight special interest student organizations (including associations for African-American, Asian, Latin American, Middle Eastern, and Scandinavian students).

Admission Requirements

North Park is looking for young men and women who seek a future in a vibrant interpretation of the liberal arts, who seek a sense of vocation in leadership and servanthood in a global society, and who long to grow in knowledge and faith. North Park gives consideration to students who have demonstrated their readiness for college by presenting superior or above-average high school records and satisfactory SAT I or ACT scores. The University also considers evidence of serious purpose, the character and health of the applicant, and participation in extracurricular activities as demonstrated through the application, essay, and personal reference. An interview is recommended but not required. North Park University admits students regardless of race, creed, sex, national or ethnic origin, or disability.

North Park welcomes applications from transfer students. The student seeking transfer admission must have a cumulative grade point average of at least 2.0 from an accredited institution.

Application and Information

Admission decisions are made on a rolling basis, with a first priority deadline of December 15 and a second priority deadline of March 15.

To be considered for admission, students need to submit the following: a North Park University application, high school or college transcripts, ACT or SAT I test scores, a personal essay, and a personal reference.

Students are strongly encouraged to visit the campus. Those interested in more detailed information are invited to contact:

John M. Baworowsky, Vice President of Admission
   and Financial Aid
North Park University
3225 West Foster Avenue
Chicago, Illinois 60625-4895
Telephone: 773-244-5500
        800-888-6728 (toll-free)

NORTHWESTERN COLLEGE
ORANGE CITY, IOWA

The College
A Christian liberal arts college with about 1,200 students, Northwestern College emphasizes the development of the whole person—mind, body, and spirit—in a caring environment. The College promotes an integration of faith, learning, and living that prepares students for lives of service to God and to others. Affiliated with the Reformed Church in America, Northwestern was established in 1882. Students come from thirty states and seventeen countries, though 60 percent come from Iowa. Nearly all live in on-campus residence halls or apartments.

In addition to an academic program of high quality, Northwestern provides a full schedule of student-planned activities. Study breaks range from raft races and coffeehouses to airband contests and ski trips. The Rowenhorst Student Center is a popular gathering place. It is equipped with an art gallery, movie theater, bookstore, game room, the Career Development Center, a large-screen TV, snack bar, and lounge area. The adjoining DeWitt Physical Fitness Center offers facilities for individual and intramural sports such as racquetball, volleyball, tennis, jogging, basketball, and archery. The Bultman Center for Health, Physical Education, and Intercollegiate Athletics, opened in 1995, provides state-of-the-art facilities for the athletics, physical education, and health services departments. Students dine in the spacious DeWitt Center, which was dedicated in 1993. Opportunities for campus involvement abound, including more than forty clubs that cater to a wide range of interests. Northwestern's music groups include the A Cappella Choir, Symphonic Band, Jazz Band, Heritage Singers, Symphonette, Percussion Ensemble, and Women's Choir. An active theater program includes several productions as well as the Drama Ministries Ensemble and the annual children's play. Students have the chance to make a difference on campus by joining a group, from Orientation Committee and Ambassadors to International Club and Student Ministry Team.

The Northwestern sports tradition is one of winning. Competing in the NAIA, the football team has twice captured the Division II national championship. In the last twenty years, more than 100 Northwestern men and women athletes have been named all-Americans or Scholar-Athletes. Men's teams include baseball, basketball, cross-country, football, golf, soccer, tennis, track, and wrestling. Women's teams include basketball, cross-country, golf, soccer, softball, tennis, track, and volleyball.

Spiritual life on campus encompasses much more than the required chapel three days a week. An active Bible study and discipleship group program, retreats, and opportunities for Christian service help students learn and demonstrate what it means to follow Christ.

Location
Northwestern College is located in Orange City, a growing community of 5,000 in northwest Iowa. Named in the 1870s after the Dutch royal house, Orange City continues to have a strong Old World flavor, with Dutch architecture and a popular Tulip Festival in May. In the midst of a prosperous agricultural region, the town has a diversified base of significant light industry. A close relationship between the College and the town gives students an added sense of belonging and opportunities to become involved in community activities. Orange City is 45 minutes from Sioux City, Iowa, and 75 minutes from Sioux Falls, South Dakota.

Majors and Degrees
Bachelor of Arts degrees are offered in thirty majors: accounting, art, biology, business administration (with options in agribusiness, finance, general, information systems, management, and marketing), business education, chemistry, Christian education, communication studies, computer science, economics, elementary education, English, environmental science, exercise science, health professions, health sciences, history, humanities, mathematics, medical technology, music, philosophy, physical education, political science, psychology, religion, social work, sociology, Spanish, theater, theater/speech, and writing/rhetoric. Students may choose to take two majors or a major with one or two minors. Devising their own major is another option. An Associate of Arts degree is offered in office management. Teacher certification is available for elementary or secondary education, reading, coaching, early childhood education, middle school education, and mental disabilities and learning disabilities. Career concentrations teach entry-level skills in the following specific fields: agribusiness, athletic training, Christian education, Christian theater ministries, computer science, criminal justice, fitness management, mission service, recreation, and youth ministry. The twenty preprofessional programs are in agriculture, art therapy, chiropractic, church music, dentistry, engineering, graphic design, law, medicine, mortuary science, music performance, music therapy, nursing, occupational therapy, optometry, pharmacy, physical therapy, professional studio art, and veterinary medicine.

Academic Program
The Northwestern College academic program is based on the liberal arts tradition and a Christian perspective. All teaching and learning is approached from a biblical standpoint. By gaining a Christian view of any field of study, Northwestern's students are prepared to be effective thinkers willing to live their faith in today's world. Broad exposure to the natural sciences, religion, humanities, fine arts, and social sciences helps students to answer life's most important questions and prepares them for today's and tomorrow's careers.

The honors program allows scholastically talented students to take interdisciplinary honors seminars, participate in honors research projects, and substitute more advanced courses for general studies requirements or major/minor requirements. Outstanding students may also apply for the Junior Scholars Program, in which they receive a stipend to work on an educational project or pursue research with a faculty scholar. Independent Study and Honors Research courses are available.

The academic calendar at Northwestern College consists of two 16-week semesters. Students take a maximum of four primary courses at a time to allow for in-depth study in each class. To graduate, students must earn at least 124 credit hours, pass 44 to 57 hours of required general studies courses, and meet academic major and GPA requirements.

Off-Campus Arrangements
Qualified juniors and seniors may spend a semester or a full year in off-campus study for academic credit. Domestic programs include the Chicago Metropolitan Center, the Los Angeles Film Studies Center, and the American Studies Program in Washington, D.C., all of which offer internships and courses. Northwestern College also participates in the Au Sable Institute of Environmental Studies in Michigan's northern

peninsula. Spanish majors are required to study abroad for at least one semester. This may be done in San José, Costa Rica, through the Latin American Studies Program, or in Spain or Mexico. Studying in China, Russia, the Netherlands, countries in the Middle East, or nine other nations for a semester is also an option. In addition, on-campus courses may be combined with service project work in countries such as Ecuador, Taiwan, and Ireland. Every spring and summer break, Northwestern students volunteer to help others through domestic and international Christian service projects. More than 150 students are involved each year.

Academic Facilities

Eighty percent of Northwestern's classrooms have been built or renovated since 1986. These include the main academic building, Van Peursem Hall, as well as the Bultman Center for Health, Physical Education, and Intercollegiate Athletics; the DEMCO Business/Economics Center; and the Kresge Education Center. The award-winning Christ Chapel/Performing Arts Center and DeWitt Music Hall was dedicated in 1988. It has excellent acoustics, seats 1,000 for chapel and cultural events, and houses music classrooms, rehearsal space, and faculty offices. A 45-stop, four-manual concert quality pipe organ is available for student use in the chapel. Ramaker Library, with more than 200,000 entries, is equipped with a computer search and circulation system, CD-ROM databases, microfiche, scholarly journals, and periodicals. All residence hall rooms and all campus buildings are wired to a fiber-optic computer network that offers access to the Internet and more than eighty software packages. The Learning Resource Center is home base for this network and also houses a high-performance computing lab and an extensive collection of audiovisual equipment. Radio and TV studios for the campus radio station and the local cable TV station are located in Van Peursem Hall. The Bushmer Art Center has eight teaching studios and intaglio printmaking equipment. The Playhouse seats 165 for theater productions and has a turntable stage, a digital sound system, an extensive costume collection, and computerized lighting.

Costs

For the 2000–01 academic year, estimated costs are $13,000 for tuition and fees and $3650 for room and board. Northwestern College estimates that an additional $400 a year is needed for books and supplies.

Financial Aid

Northwestern participates in all major federal and state assistance programs. About 99 percent of students receive some type of financial assistance, ranging from scholarships and grants to loans and campus employment. Many non-need-based awards are available, including Norman Vincent Peale Scholarships, Departmental Major Scholarships, Academic Honor Scholarships, and Activity Awards for students who excel in athletics, music, theater, art, or journalism.

Students seeking financial aid are asked to submit the Free Application for Federal Student Aid (FAFSA) as soon as possible after January 1. Early application is recommended. The deadline for financial aid application is April 15. Accepted students are offered a financial aid package approximately four weeks after applying for aid.

Faculty

Of the 66 full-time faculty members, approximately 90 percent hold doctorates or terminal degrees in their field. Since the College has a student-faculty ratio of 16:1, students receive individualized attention from professors. Each faculty member serves as an academic adviser, assisting with course scheduling and providing guidance and encouragement. While teaching is their main priority, faculty members are also involved in research and often are assisted in these projects by students.

Student Government

Student-elected representatives serve on the Student Government Association (SGA), working to improve campus life and maintain a good spirit and morale among students. SGA members also serve on faculty committees.

At Northwestern College there is a balance between freedom and responsibility, allowing personal choices under biblical guidelines. Students are not permitted to have alcoholic beverages or to be intoxicated while on campus, and illegal drugs are not allowed. Smoking is not allowed in campus buildings.

Admission Requirements

Each applicant is considered on the basis of probable success at Northwestern College, as indicated primarily by high school grades, rank in class, and test scores. Requirements for admission include a high school diploma or the equivalent. A class rank in the upper half and ACT composite scores above the 50th percentile are preferable. SAT I scores are accepted. The following high school units are recommended: 4 years of English, 3 years of social sciences, 3 years of mathematics, 2 years of natural sciences, and 2 years of foreign language. Applicants who do not meet these standards are given consideration by the Admissions Committee upon review of transcripts, recommendations, seriousness of purpose, and extent of deficiencies. Northwestern College grants up to 24 hours of credit toward a degree on the basis of test performance in the College-Level Examination Program. Students who wish to be considered for advanced placement on the basis of college-level courses taken in high school must present Advanced Placement examination scores from the College Board. Because qualities of character are important at Northwestern College, a personal interview and campus visit are recommended.

Application and Information

Students interested in attending Northwestern College are encouraged to submit an application early in their senior year of high school. Applicants must complete and return to the Northwestern College Office of Admissions an application for admission along with a nonrefundable $25 application fee. A current high school transcript and a transcript from every college previously attended must be submitted. Also required are SAT I or ACT test results and a counselor's recommendation. The deadline for all application materials is August 15. Students are notified of the College's decision one to two weeks after receipt of the complete application. A $100 deposit is required within twenty-one days after acceptance. The deposit is refundable until May 1.

For more information, students should contact:

Ron De Jong
Dean of Admissions
Northwestern College
101 College Lane
Orange City, Iowa 51041
Telephone: 712-737-7130
              800-747-4757 (toll-free)
Fax: 712-737-7164
E-mail: admissions@nwciowa.edu
World Wide Web: http://www.nwciowa.edu

NORTHWEST NAZARENE UNIVERSITY
NAMPA, IDAHO

The University

Northwest Nazarene University (NNU) is a Christian liberal arts university committed to the education of the whole person, a dynamic process that engages students in both the pursuit of academic excellence and an exploration of Christian faith. The essential mission of the University is the development of a Christ-centered scholar.

The desire to provide a Christian-inspired education led the founders of NNU, under the leadership of Eugene Emerson, to organize a secondary school in 1913. In 1915, the first student was graduated from the high school. The first four degrees were conferred upon a class of 4 graduates in 1917.

The early years of the University laid a strong spiritual and academic foundation upon which steady growth and development have taken place. Master's degrees are available in school counseling, administration, curriculum and instruction, ministry, business administration, and social work. The University has received distinction through professional and national accreditation in several areas: education (NCATE), music (NASM), and social work (CSWE). A regionally acknowledged strength is the Division of Mathematics and Natural Science, which has maintained a 90 percent placement rate for premedical students.

The 100-acre campus provides a residential campus environment for more than 70 percent of the students in seven residence halls and two apartment complexes. The campus is a melting pot for many backgrounds and interests. Living and learning together are people from twenty-nine religious denominations, varied ethnic backgrounds, twenty-three states, and twelve countries. The University's 1,100 students take part in numerous extracurricular activities on campus, including six intercollegiate sports for men and six for women, intramural sports, campus theatrical productions, a strong debate team, large and small choral ensembles, various instrumental ensembles that include concert and jazz bands, student clubs, sponsored social ministries, and honors activities.

The Montgomery fieldhouse, with its 3,500-seat gymnasium and Olympic-size pool, is an outstanding facility and has hosted the NAIA Division II National Men's Basketball Tournament.

Location

Northwest Nazarene University is located in Nampa, Idaho (population 50,000), one of the fastest-growing cities in Idaho. Nampa is part of the Boise Valley area, which provides both urban and rural advantages. The Boise Valley area, as the home of NNU, the state capital, Albertson College, and Boise State University, is able to offer Northwest Nazarene students a diversity of cultural opportunities that are not available at most small private universities.

The Boise Valley area supports a symphony orchestra, several regional chamber music groups, an excellent community theater, and theatrical productions such as *Shakespeare in the Park* and touring productions. It is also the home of Ballet Idaho. The Boise Valley area strongly supports the arts.

The area is nationally known for its skiing, hunting, and fishing and its rodeo competitions. Backpacking, white-water rafting, waterskiing, and tennis at a world-class resort are all available within a few hours' drive. During winter term, a student's physical education course could be skiing at Bogus Basin, a nationally known ski area.

The University and the Boise Valley area are able to provide a small-university environment that is within minutes of both city life and a relaxed horseback ride in the country.

Majors and Degrees

Northwest Nazarene University offers the Bachelor of Arts (B.A.) and the Bachelor of Science (B.S.) degrees. Majors for a bachelor's degree are accounting, art, art education, biology (B.S. and B.A.), biology education, business administration, chemistry, chemistry education, computer science, elementary education, engineering (3-2 program: three years at NNU, two at a cooperating institution), engineering physics, English, English education, history, history education, international studies, kinesiology, kinesiology education, liberal studies, mass communications, mathematics, mathematics and natural science, mathematics education, music (applied, church music, general music, music education, and music theory), philosophy, physical science education, physics (B.S. and B.A.), political science, practical studies (pre–dental, prelaw, premedical, premedical technology, pre–optometry, prephysical therapy, and pre–veterinary), psychology, public communication, recreation and leisure studies, religion, religious studies, social science education, social service ministries, social work, and special ministries (religious education, compassionate ministries, and music). A four-year B.S. degree in nursing was added in fall 1999, along with a B.A. in computer graphics. Two-year preprofessional transfer programs include prepharmacy and pre–dental hygiene.

Academic Program

NNU is committed to providing its students with an acquaintanceship with the major fields of knowledge, an effective foundation in and a working grasp of one field, a balanced development of their own powers, and an encouragement to Christian commitment. Every student is required to take a basic core of courses in the liberal arts in addition to a major program of study. The core curriculum includes biblical literature, English, history, and theology. A minimum of 124 semester credits is required for a Bachelor of Arts or Bachelor of Science degree. Advanced credit is possible for transfer students. It is also possible to earn credit by examination, to receive credit for Advanced Placement programs taken in secondary school, and to receive credit for military experience. The academic year is divided into two semesters plus two summer school sessions.

A U.S. Army ROTC program is available at the University.

Academic Facilities

The John E. Riley Library at NNU has more than 125,000 volumes of books and periodicals. In addition, the Library of American Civilization, consisting of 19,500 volumes of microfiche, is available. The Riley Library participates in the Washington Library Network, making an additional 1.3 million titles available. The Wiley Learning Center houses classrooms, offices, and the Educational Media Center. These facilities include computer labs and classrooms, classrooms equipped with the latest in high-tech media equipment, large- and small-group video viewing rooms, audio and video recording, and education labs. The entire campus is computer networked. Three labs equipped with Pentium II computers, plus mini-labs in every dorm, offer more than 200 networked computers for student use. Every dorm room has campus network and Internet access. The Study Skills Center provides general study-skills development, reading instruction, mathematics instruction, course-related tutoring, and individualized learning activities in such areas as spelling improvement and general editing improvement, vocabulary building, speed reading, analytical reading, and preprofessional achievement test preparation. Also available are chemistry, biology, and physics laboratories.

The Brandt Fine Arts/Convocation Center opened in the fall of 1997, complete with a 1,300-seat auditorium and two art galleries. The music and art departments have state-of-the-art music and computer graphics labs.

Costs

Tuition and fees for the 2000–01 academic year are $13,500; annual room and board charges are $4020. Book costs and personal expenses vary, depending on individual needs. The cost of weekly private music lessons is $100, or two lessons per week may be taken for $145.

Financial Aid

Northwest Nazarene University awarded more than $12 million in financial assistance through government and University programs in 1999–2000. More than 90 percent of full-time students received financial aid in the form of grants, scholarships, allowances, loans, and work-study positions. Freshmen judged to have need in 1998–99 received an average award of $9259, meeting 75 percent of their need. NNU participates in various federal programs, including the Federal Pell Grant, Federal Supplemental Educational Opportunity Grant, Federal Perkins Loan, Federal Work-Study, and Federal Stafford Student Loan programs.

Scholarships are awarded in three main categories: academic achievement scholarships, activity scholarships, and departmental scholarships. Academic scholarships range from Honor Scholarships of $1200 and $600 to President's scholarships of $7800. These are renewable for up to four academic years as long as a stipulated grade point average is maintained. Activity scholarships are awarded in the areas of art, athletics, music, speech/debate/drama, and student government publications and may be renewed for subsequent years. Departmental scholarships are awarded to deserving students after the freshman year.

To be considered for scholarships or financial aid, applicants must apply for admission and submit the Free Application for Federal Student Aid (FAFSA).

Faculty

There are 90 full-time faculty members and 40 part-time members constituting the graduate and undergraduate faculties. Graduate students do not serve as undergraduate instructors. The full-time faculty members have counseling and advising roles and are in residence. Of the full-time faculty members, 87 percent are full-time teachers and 12 percent have other assignments. More than 60 percent have earned doctorates.

Student Government

All students enrolled at NNU are members of the Associated Students of Northwest Nazarene University, which is divided into three branches: administrative (Executive Council), legislative, and judicial. These three sectors of student government set budgets; plan student concerts, recreational and social activities, and service projects; coordinate joint efforts with the University administration; and provide mechanisms for the review of student grievances. In addition, the student government appoints student representatives to membership on faculty committees and councils.

All aspects of life at NNU are viewed within the context of its mission statement ("the development of Christian character within the philosophy and framework of genuine scholarship"). Thus, each student is aware that behavioral and value issues spring from this special environment of Christian scholars. The traditions and practices of the sponsoring denomination, the Church of the Nazarene, shape the particular interpretation given to the community's lifestyle (for example, a stance against the use and abuse of chemical substances, including tobacco). A desire to develop within each student a personal commitment to Christ and the development of life for Christian growth, ministry, and service characterize student government and its constituent parts.

Admission Requirements

Northwest Nazarene University admits students of any race, color, and national and ethnic origin to all the rights, privileges, programs, and activities generally accorded or made available to students at the University. Three factors are noted in considering an application for admission: educational ability, character, and state of health. Students are also expected to be sympathetic to the University's religious orientation and life-style requirements. There are no required high school courses for admission, but the following provide an excellent preparation for university work: 4 years of English, 3 years of history/social sciences, 3 years of mathematics, 3 years of science, and 2 years of a foreign language. Regular admission is normally granted to graduates of an accredited high school who have earned a cumulative 2.5 or above (on a 4.0 scale) and to transfer students from an accredited university who have achieved the cumulative grade point average required for classification. Persons who do not meet the requirements for admission with regular standing are normally considered for admission with provisional status and registered in a restricted program.

Application and Information

A candidate for freshman admission should complete the application and return it with the $20 application fee, request that a transcript of all high school work be sent directly to the NNU Office of Enrollment Services, give the recommendation forms to the designated persons, and take the ACT.

Transfer students should submit the application form and fee and should request that a transcript of all college or university work be sent to the Office of Enrollment Services.

Application forms for admission and more detailed brochures are available from the Office of Admission and Financial Aid.

Office of Enrollment Services
Northwest Nazarene University
623 Holly Street
Nampa, Idaho 83686

Telephone: 208-467-8496
877-NNU-4YOU (toll-free)
E-mail: admissions@nnu.edu
World Wide Web: http://www.nnu.edu

On the campus of Northwest Nazarene University.

NORTHWOOD UNIVERSITY
MIDLAND, MICHIGAN; CEDAR HILL, TEXAS; AND
WEST PALM BEACH, FLORIDA

The University

Northwood University was founded in 1959 by Dr. Arthur E. Turner and Dr. R. Gary Stauffer, who had decided that the liberal arts approach to business did not really expose students to the wealth of opportunities the world of work had to offer. Established originally in Alma, Michigan, the school moved to Midland in 1961. The Texas campus was opened in 1966. Other expansions include the Florida campus in West Palm Beach and the Northwood University Margaret Chase Smith Library Center in Skowhegan, Maine.

Northwood University also coordinates a nontraditional program, University College, headquartered at the Midland, Michigan campus; extension centers are located on all three campuses and in Carlsbad, New Mexico; Chicago, Illinois; Fort Worth, Texas; Detroit, Flint, and Lansing, Michigan; Tampa, Florida; Indianapolis, Indiana; Louisville, Kentucky; New Orleans, Louisiana; and Selfridge ANG Base, Michigan. University College is dedicated to providing nontraditional options for earning management degrees for students who are balancing work schedules, family responsibilities, community involvement, and educational goals.

Executive and full-time M.B.A. programs are offered at the University through the Richard DeVos Graduate School of Management, which adds to a series of bachelor and associate degree programs that offer an exceptionally wide array of free-market-based degrees in management and entrepreneurship.

In terms of facilities, the Michigan campus is the most fully developed. The 268-acre campus is heavily wooded, and all of the buildings were designed by Alden B. Dow. About 60 percent of the students live on campus. Important activities on campus include the student government, advertising club, ski club, Free Enterprise Group, radio station, fraternities, sororities, service clubs, intramural sports, and the drama club.

The Michigan campus has a well-developed athletic program, headquartered in the Bennett Sports Center. Outstanding teams are fielded every year in men's varsity baseball, basketball, football, golf, lacrosse, tennis, and track and field. Women's varsity teams include basketball, soccer, softball, tennis, track and field, and volleyball. The Sports Center has a six-lane pool; facilities for basketball, dance, and indoor tennis; and a state-of-the-art fitness center that features Nautilus weight machines. Northwood's Michigan campus is a member of the National Collegiate Athletic Association (NCAA, Division II), and the Florida and Texas campuses are members of the National Association of Intercollegiate Athletics (NAIA).

The Texas campus is located near the Dallas–Fort Worth metroplex. Students participate in intercollegiate baseball, cross-country, the Student Senate, newspaper and yearbook, Auto Club, DECA, field trips, and the annual ribfest and chili cook-off.

Current facilities on the Florida campus comprise more than 26,000 square feet of classroom, office, and library space and include a 38,000-square-foot multipurpose building. On-campus housing for students is also available.

Even though Northwood's campuses are in different locations, with students coming from more than forty states and many countries, all have one goal in common: the preservation and promotion of the American free enterprise work ethic. Students come to Northwood to develop entry-level skills for management positions in business and industry.

Location

Midland, a professional town, is the site of the world headquarters of Dow Chemical U.S.A. It has 2,600 acres of parks and forests, the impressive Center for the Arts, the Chippewa Nature Center, and the Dow Gardens. The famous Michigan North Country begins in Midland County, and students have easy access to skiing, camping, hiking, fishing, and hunting. A large number of students work in the surrounding area.

The campus in Cedar Hill is located in the cedar-covered hills and valleys south of Dallas. Students work and have access to activities and facilities in Dallas and Fort Worth, including football games, shopping, and symphony concerts.

The Florida campus is located in the rapidly developing area of West Palm Beach. Numerous cultural and recreational facilities are available.

Majors and Degrees

Northwood University offers programs leading to the Associate of Arts degree in accounting; advertising; automotive aftermarket management; automotive marketing; banking and finance; business management; computer science/management; fashion marketing and merchandising; health-care management; hotel, restaurant, and resort management; international business; and rapid text entry. Not all degree programs are offered at all campuses and extension centers.

Qualified graduates of an associate degree program may enter directly into the Bachelor of Business Administration program, which is available at all campuses and at the extension centers. This degree program offers majors in accounting; automotive aftermarket management; banking and finance/management; computer information management; health-care management; hotel, restaurant, and resort management; international business; management; management/automotive marketing; management/computer science; management/economics; management information systems; management/marketing; and verbatim systems.

Academic Program

Northwood University's programs have been designed to prepare men and women for specific career goals. The courses for the major (approximately 30 percent of the total requirements) are reinforced by classes in general business (30 percent) and the humanities (40 percent). Associate degree candidates are required to complete 90 term hours with a minimum GPA of 2.0. Bachelor's degree candidates must complete 180 term hours with a minimum GPA of 2.0.

Northwood's terms last ten weeks. The fall term runs from September through November, the winter term from December through February, and the spring term from March through May. In addition, the college offers three 3-week summer sessions.

Northwood believes strongly in the free enterprise system and, accordingly, has designed its curriculum to reflect this belief. All students must satisfactorily complete core courses in accounting, business law, economics, management, and marketing. No matter what the ultimate career goal of a student may be, he or she will have acquired a set of basic skills as preparation for the productive world of work. This academic program, however, does not prohibit students from appreciating the arts. Northwood strongly promotes the interrelationship between the business and art worlds by providing on- and off-campus voluntary programs.

Employers of Northwood University graduates constantly stress their need to have employee candidates who demonstrate experiences, attitudes, and leadership abilities beyond those provided in the classroom and those reflected on the academic transcript. The EXCEL program goes beyond the curriculum to enhance the employability of Northwood University graduates and provide valuable experiences and dimensions beyond the classroom. Through EXCEL, students participate in valuable, documentable activities, resulting in a Student Development Transcript that is issued along with the academic transcript. Students document a minimum of five extracurricular activities per year; honors and awards are reflected on this transcript as well. The Student Development Transcript has no bearing on meeting degree requirements reflected through the academic transcript, but the EXCEL program provides opportunities to expand and document students' Northwood University education well beyond the classroom requirements and to enrich students' lives and prospects for employment.

Off-Campus Arrangements

In keeping with its interest in the world marketplace, Northwood University offers its students an optional opportunity each fall to participate in the Term-in-Europe program. Formal classes are supplemented by student tours, industry and cultural visits, and opportunities to meet with students and industry leaders from host countries such as the Czech Republic, France, Germany, Greece, Italy, and the Netherlands.

Academic Facilities

The Strosacker Library contains 47,000 volumes, receives 410 periodicals, and has an especially strong reference division on business management. The Griswold Communications Center has full-color videotape capability and a closed-circuit television-monitor system. The National Auto Dealers Association Center is equipped with a twenty-five-room hotel, classrooms, and a conference center. All students receive training in business computer application and IBM PC–compatible computers. Additional facilities are available on the Texas and Florida campuses.

Costs

The 1999–2000 costs for the Michigan campus for both in-state and out-of-state students attending full-time were $11,325 for tuition and fees, $2178 for a room, and $3030 for meals. Students spent about $825 per year for books. Costs vary slightly on each campus.

Financial Aid

Students should file the Free Application for Federal Student Aid (FAFSA). Available aid includes Federal Pell Grants, Federal Supplemental Educational Opportunity Grants, state and institutional grants and scholarships, Federal Stafford Student Loans, loans for parents, and Federal Work-Study awards. Approximately 70 percent of students receive some type of financial aid.

Faculty

The faculty members at Northwood not only have academic credentials (90 percent have earned an advanced degree) but also bring to the classroom a wealth of business experience. These professionals are hired from business and industry to impart not only the theoretical concepts but also the practical, real-world aspects of a discipline. Faculty members are not engaged in research; their primary duty is in the classroom. In addition, each member is involved in at least one extracurricular activity with students. The student-faculty ratio is approximately 26:1.

Student Government

In keeping with Northwood University's philosophy of training future management leaders, the student government has these responsibilities: to provide for the formulation and expression of student attitudes and opinions, to represent the student body in discussions with the faculty members and administration, to provide student activities, to appropriate and disburse funds, and to investigate and resolve complaints from faculty members, students, and the administration.

Admission Requirements

Northwood is fully committed to maintaining diversity among its student population. Young adults from a variety of social, geographic, and economic backgrounds have begun their careers at Northwood. Interested students should design their high school program to include 4 years of English, 3 years of mathematics, accounting, and typing. Candidates must submit a complete high school transcript, and ACT or SAT I scores are required. Personal interviews are recommended.

Application and Information

There is no deadline for submitting applications for freshman-year admission. Transfer students are admitted year-round.

For more information, students should contact the appropriate location:

Director of Admissions
Northwood University
3225 Cook Road
Midland, Michigan 48640
Telephone: 517-837-4273
 800-457-7878 (toll-free)
World Wide Web: http://www.northwood.edu

Director of Admissions
Northwood University, Florida Campus
2600 North Military Trail
West Palm Beach, Florida 33409
Telephone: 561-478-5500
 800-458-8325 (toll-free)

Director of Admissions
Northwood University, Texas Campus
1114 West FM 1382
P.O. Box 58
Cedar Hill, Texas 75104
Telephone: 214-291-1541
 800-927-9663 (toll-free)

Director of Admissions
University College
3225 Cook Road
Midland, Michigan 48640
Telephone: 517-837-4411
 800-445-5873 (toll-free)

Students in Northwood's interactive classrooms in Florida and Michigan listen to author Clive Chajet talk about his book *Image by Design*.

NORWICH UNIVERSITY
NORTHFIELD, VERMONT

The University

Norwich University is unique among institutions of higher education. No other university combines a military tradition of nearly two centuries, a broad range of traditional undergraduate degree programs, and five of the more innovative low-residency and nonresidency programs in higher education.

Students on the Northfield campus may enroll in the Corps of Cadets and follow a disciplined military regime or join civilian students who lead a more traditional collegiate lifestyle. Both groups are coeducational and attend classes and participate in sports and other activities together. There are approximately 1,600 students enrolled on the Northfield campus. In keeping with its mission, the University provides opportunities for all students to develop leadership skills and a strong commitment to community services.

Founded in 1819 by Alden Partridge, Norwich University was the first private military college in the United States. Here the idea of the citizen soldier developed, a guiding philosophy that later became the impetus for the creation of the Reserve Officer Training Corps (ROTC). It was the first private school to offer engineering and, in 1974, the first school to offer military training to women, preceding the armed service academies by two years.

Norwich students have come from forty-eight states and twenty-nine countries. The University's minority enrollment is consistently the largest representation by percentage of any Vermont college or university.

In addition, 1,000 adult students are served by a number of programs on the Vermont College campus in Montpelier. Both undergraduate and graduate degrees are offered in brief or no residency models on a campus that is dedicated to the adult learner. Current offerings on the Vermont College campus include the Adult Degree Program, a low-residency bachelor's degree; New College; the Graduate Program, a nonresidency graduate degree; and the M.F.A. degrees in writing and children's writing, Master of Arts in art therapy, and M.F.A. in visual art low-residency graduate degrees.

Norwich has the only professional five-year Master of Architecture program in northern New England. Full accreditation by the National Architectural Accrediting Board (NAAB) was granted in 1996.

Location

Norwich University is located in the heart of the Green Mountains of Vermont—one of the nation's most beautiful natural areas. The 1,125-acre campus comprises both valley and mountainside and is located in the village of Northfield, a community of about 4,200. Norwich may be reached from Exit 5 off I-89 and is less than an hour's drive from the Burlington International Airport.

The Vermont College campus in Montpelier, the state capital, is only 12 miles from Northfield.

Majors and Degrees

The University offers students more than thirty academic majors from which to choose. The Bachelor of Arts degree is awarded in communications; criminal justice; English; history; international studies; peace, war, and diplomacy studies; political science; and psychology. The Bachelor of Science degree is awarded in accounting, biochemistry, biology, biomedical technology, chemistry, civil engineering, communications, computer information systems, computer science, economics, electrical engineering, environmental science, geology, management, mathematics, mechanical engineering, physical education, physics, and sports medicine.

Academic Program

To qualify for the baccalaureate degree, students must have a final cumulative quality point average of at least 2.0. Teacher licensure candidates reserve the eighth semester for sixteen weeks of student teaching. Individual departmental requirements are outlined in the Norwich catalog. Approximately 25 percent of entering freshmen have undeclared majors.

For military cadets, eight semesters of Army, Air Force, or Naval ROTC are required. Prior to the start of the junior year, a cadet may elect to contract with his or her ROTC program of study for consideration for a commission upon graduation as a second lieutenant in the Army, Air Force, or Marine Corps or as an ensign in the Navy. A cadet not wishing to contract for a commission has no military obligation upon completion of the required four years of ROTC courses.

Norwich students entering their junior year may enroll in the nation's first college-based Peace Corps Preparatory Program. Participants in the program take specialized courses designed to prepare them for assignments in Third World countries, perform voluntary community service during the school year, and spend six weeks in a foreign country, during the summer between their junior and senior years, with an established service agency. The curriculum is an acceptable alternative to the Military College requirement for junior and senior year ROTC participation for those students not seeking an officer's commission.

Academic Facilities

Centrally located on each campus is a reference library. The two libraries combined contain 340,000 volumes, and each provides interlibrary loan service, a microfilm library, and a professional library staff to assist the researcher. The centralized computing platform consists of four DEC Alpha platforms and several servers. The University library system is supported by a DEC MicroVAX 3100. The University supports DEC's UNIX operating system, Microsoft Windows, and Windows NT. Accessible to students on both campuses are a total of 150 computer terminals. Two modern language laboratories equipped with more than 10,000 tapes are available for students of French, Spanish, and German. In 1997, construction was completed on a $15-million math, science, and engineering building. This fully equipped and modern complex houses all mathematics, science, and electrical, civil, environmental, and mechanical engineering programs.

Costs

For 2000–01, tuition and fees are $15,450 for all undergraduate degree programs. The cost of room and board is $5890. Books and supplies average $300 per semester.

Financial Aid

All applicants for financial aid must submit both the CSS PROFILE form and the Free Application for Federal Student Aid (FAFSA). Financial awards are made on the basis of need, but academic and extracurricular activities are taken into consideration. Most awards consist of an aid package of University scholarships, work-study programs, federal grants, and student loans.

Winners of three- and four-year Army, Air Force, and Naval ROTC scholarships are strongly encouraged to consider the Norwich program. ROTC scholarship winners attending Norwich University receive full scholarships for room and board as long as they maintain scholarship status each year. ROTC students receive an annual uniform allowance, and students who are working toward a commission through advanced ROTC receive a monthly subsistence allowance during the school year. Eligible students may also apply for three- and two-year Air Force, Army, and Naval ROTC scholarships while attending Norwich. For further ROTC scholarship information, students should write to the Admissions Office.

Norwich offers academic scholarships to students who have demonstrated outstanding academic achievements. These scholarships are offered to students who are placed in the top 10 or 20 percent of their high school class. The Norwich Academic Honor Scholarship is automatically awarded to students who are in the top 10 percent of their high school class. This scholarship pays half of the tuition for four years. The Norwich Academic Merit Scholarship is awarded to students who are in the top 20 percent of their high school class. This scholarship pays one third of the tuition for four years. Students whose high schools do not rank should contact the Admissions Office. Students who receive an ROTC scholarship receive the Norwich University ROTC Scholarship incentives in lieu of any other scholarships.

Faculty

The student-faculty ratio at the University is approximately 13:1. Faculty members are full-time instructors with advanced degrees; 80 percent hold a doctorate. Small classes help promote close student-faculty relationships, and each student is assigned a faculty adviser from his or her major department.

Student Government

The Norwich University Corps of Cadets is, in effect, a self-governing student organization. The corps is organized as a regiment and is commanded by cadet officers and noncommissioned officers under the supervision of the commandant of cadets.

The Student Government Association for civilian students has the opportunity to set the tone for creativity and leadership. Members, chosen on the basis of a campuswide election, are encouraged to participate in all campus issues, as this provides the major channel for change.

Admission Requirements

Admission is based upon a review of the applicant's academic record, recommendations, extracurricular activities, and leadership potential. Submission of either SAT or ACT scores is required.

Application and Information

There is no deadline for applications. The University uses a rolling admission system; an admission decision is announced as soon as all of an applicant's materials have been received, processed, and reviewed.

Dean of Enrollment Management
Norwich University
158 Harmon Drive
Northfield, Vermont 05663

Telephone: 800-468-NORWICH (6679) (toll-free)
E-mail: nuadm@norwich.edu
World Wide Web: http://www.norwich.edu

Norwich University's Kreitzberg Library is the pride of the Northfield campus.

NOTRE DAME COLLEGE
MANCHESTER, NEW HAMPSHIRE

The College

Notre Dame College is a coeducational, Catholic, liberal arts college that was founded by the Sisters of Holy Cross in 1950. The College community is made up of people of various religious beliefs, but Christian values provide the foundation for the College's daily activities and overall mission. The current undergraduate enrollment is 750 women and men. Students can be members of student government, Amnesty International, Outing Club, Habitat for Humanity, student newspaper, Student Activities Union, Drama Club, Campus Ministry Council, and intramurals. They also may participate in coed crew and men's and women's basketball, soccer, and softball intercollegiate teams as well as other clubs and associations.

The College is committed to the spiritual, intellectual, and moral values of the Christian tradition. This includes a profound respect for life that comes from the belief that all of existence is a gift of God. A concerted effort is made to demonstrate to students the relevance of Christian values to higher learning and personal development and to provide for all students, Catholic and non-Catholic, an atmosphere conducive to the individual development of religious beliefs, learning, and personal growth. Students are urged to develop a sense of responsibility, independence in both thought and expression, an appreciation for the relevance of tradition in developing adaptive skills for tomorrow's world, and an understanding that human wholeness involves the nurturing of the intellectual, spiritual, emotional, and physical self.

Notre Dame College's residence houses are designed to provide comfortable learning and living accommodations. Seven former private residences provide a homelike atmosphere that helps foster the personal development expected from on-campus living. Other residences provide a comfortable atmosphere for medium-sized groups.

Undergraduate studies are offered within the three academic divisions of education, humanities, and sciences. Notre Dame College offers the Master of Education degree in the following areas of specialization: curriculum and instruction (K–12), elementary or secondary teaching certification with or without general special education certification, emotional and behavioral disorders/general special education (K–12), integrated studies, learning and language disabilities/general special education (K–12), school counseling, and teaching English as a second language. Certification in general special education is also offered. An accelerated Master of Education degree program is offered in curriculum and instruction. The College also offers Master of Arts degrees in counseling psychology and theology, a Master in Physical Therapy (M.P.T.), and a Master in Physician Assistant Studies (M.P.A.S.).

Notre Dame is a member of the American Council on Education, Association of American Colleges, College Entrance Examination Board, Federation of Holy Cross Colleges, National Association of Independent Colleges and Universities, National Catholic Educational Association, New Hampshire College and University Council, and American Association for Higher Education. The College is accredited by the New England Association of Schools and Colleges, and its teacher training program is certified by the State Board of Education of New Hampshire and the Council for Teacher Education.

Location

The College is situated in Manchester, New Hampshire's largest city. The campus is in the city's attractive, residential north end, noted for its elegant old Victorian mansions and quiet, broad tree-lined streets. Manchester is located on the Merrimack River, which once provided waterpower for the largest textile mill in the world. Manchester grew quickly and it is no longer dependent on one industry; smaller but diversified businesses have been drawn to the area in the past forty years. Located at the junction of several major highways and connected by bus and airplane with all parts of the country, Manchester has become the distribution, service, and trade center of northern New England. With a population of more than 100,000, the city also supports a number of cultural institutions, and four colleges are situated within its boundaries. In addition to being located in a historic and flourishing area of New Hampshire, Notre Dame College is an hour from Boston, the White Mountains, and the seacoast.

Majors and Degrees

Notre Dame College offers the Bachelor of Arts degree in art history, biology, child development, English, fine arts, general science, graphic design and illustration, history, interdisciplinary studies, justice administration, management, paralegal studies, prelaw, psychology, theology, and writing and publishing. The teacher preparation program prepares students for certification in art education, early childhood education, and elementary education/general special education as well as secondary certification in biology, English, general science, and social studies. Bachelor of Science degrees are offered in biology, exercise science, pre–physician assistant studies, and pre–physical therapy.

The Associate in Arts degree is offered in child development and in general studies.

Academic Program

A liberal arts education at Notre Dame balances the arts and sciences and is designed to provide students with an enlightened perspective from which to view the world, a bountiful resource from which to draw a means of improving the quality of life, and a basis for continuing education. The liberal arts curriculum is the thread that weaves a pattern into a total learning experience. Students begin to learn how to acquire and use knowledge to attain career goals as well as to fulfill personal ambitions. Students with a broad liberal arts background develop a concern for contemporary issues, gain a greater awareness of personal values, and learn to respect their fellow students within the educational environment. Although degree requirements vary according to the program, bachelor's degree candidates must earn a minimum of 123 credit hours, and associate degree candidates must earn a minimum of 60 credit hours. Students in both degree programs must have a minimum GPA of 2.0 to graduate.

The College offers all its students a personalized educational atmosphere. The small classes, individual instruction, and faculty interest help to fulfill individual and academic needs. The educational experience at Notre Dame is further enhanced by the College's tradition as a Catholic institution.

Off-Campus Arrangements

Fieldwork and internship opportunities have been incorporated into many of the disciplines at Notre Dame to help students acquire a working knowledge of their areas of study. The College highly values practical field experiences that help its students bridge the gap between the theory of the classroom and the reality of actual professional situations.

As a member of the New Hampshire College and University Council (NHCUC), a consortium of twelve colleges organized in 1966 for the purpose of interinstitutional cooperation, Notre Dame College offers its undergraduates opportunities to enroll for single courses or for an entire semester at other consortium colleges without paying additional tuition.

Academic Facilities

Holy Cross Hall houses classrooms, science laboratories, and art and music studios as well as the computer center and faculty offices. The Carol Rines Center for Health Sciences and the Arts houses the graduate programs in counseling, physician assistant studies, and physical therapy. The Paul Harvey Library is located nearby and houses 55,000 volumes, 6,800 audiovisual items, 700 periodical titles, study carrels, and the Learning Enrichment Center. Through the College's membership in NHCUC, Notre Dame students have access to the libraries of all member institutions and may borrow directly or order materials. The Counseling and Development Center houses the career services, placement, and counseling offices.

Costs

Tuition and fees at Notre Dame College for 1999–2000 were $14,098, and room and board were $5713, which brought the annual charge for a full-time resident student to $19,811 (not including fees).

Financial Aid

The primary purpose of the financial aid program at Notre Dame College is to assist those students who, without aid, would be unable to pursue their education. The College utilizes a need analysis system approved by the Department of Education to select aid recipients. Primary emphasis is placed on demonstrated financial need—the difference between the cost of attending college and what students and their families are able to pay. In order to apply for financial aid at Notre Dame College, all full-time students should file the Free Application for Federal Student Aid (FAFSA) and a Notre Dame Financial Aid Application. The College has a priority date of March 15 for all new students. However, all applications reviewed after this date are evaluated and awards are given based on the funds available at that time. Students must apply for financial aid each year. Those in good standing, with continuing need, may expect financial aid to be renewed each year. Notre Dame College awards funds through a number of federal programs and also has its own institutional scholarship, grant, and work program. In addition to offering need-based aid, Notre Dame College offers awards through a merit scholarship program.

Faculty

The faculty consists of 66 full-time and 81 part-time lay and religious men and women. The undergraduate student-faculty ratio is 16:1.

Student Government

Participation in student leadership is encouraged. The Student Senate represents the undergraduate student body. It consists of three major divisions: the Student Activities Union, Officer's Council, and Issue's Board. By representing and governing the student body, the Student Senate oversees many facets of campus life. In addition, students are selected to serve on key administrative committees and task forces at the College, including three of the five committees of the Board of Trustees.

Admission Requirements

Notre Dame College strives to admit a freshman class composed of students from as diverse economic, social, and regional backgrounds as possible. No discrimination is practiced in the admission of students on the basis of race, color, religion, national origin, age, sex, or handicap. The Office of Admissions treats each applicant as an individual and evaluates the student's academic preparation and college potential accordingly. The requirements for admission consideration are an official transcript (with seal or guidance counselor's signature and current date) of high school grades or an equivalency certificate. A personal interview is strongly recommended although not required. The submission of scores on the SAT I of the College Board or on the ACT of American College Testing, Inc., is required. Art majors are required to submit a portfolio of their work.

Transfer students who have earned an associate degree from an accredited two-year college or who have completed at least one semester's work at another institution may apply for the fall or spring term. Full credit and junior status are granted to holders of A.A. or A.S. degrees. Transfer students with a two-year degree must have attained a cumulative grade point average of at least 2.0 to be considered for admission.

Application and Information

Students should apply as early as possible in the year preceding desired entrance. A nonrefundable fee of $35 should accompany the application. After completing and mailing the application to the Office of Admissions at Notre Dame College, applicants to the freshman class should request that their high school send official transcripts. Transfer students should have official transcripts from all colleges attended sent to the College in order to have a credit evaluation completed by the registrar. A letter of recommendation from the high school guidance counselor, teacher, or principal or the appropriate college official should also be requested, and a written essay is required.

Students may obtain information and application materials by contacting:

Office of Admissions
Notre Dame College
2321 Elm Street
Manchester, New Hampshire 03104
Telephone: 603-669-4298
        800-754-0405 (toll-free)

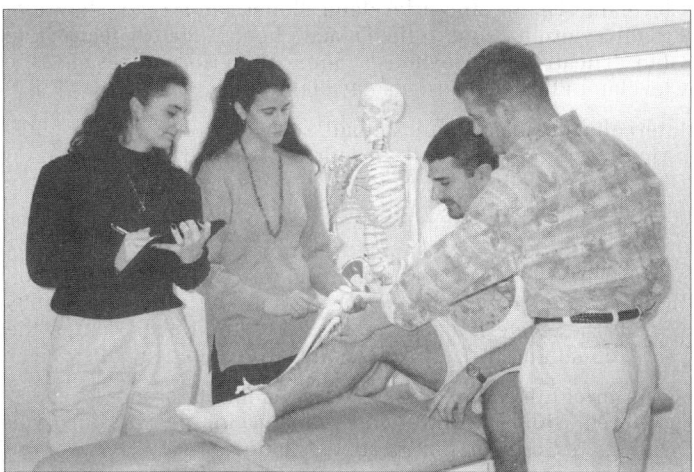

Students in the first year of the professional phase of the College's physical therapy program.

NOTRE DAME COLLEGE OF OHIO
SOUTH EUCLID, OHIO

The College

Notre Dame College of Ohio was established in 1922 by the Sisters of Notre Dame of Cleveland. The College exists today largely because of the spirit of the foundress of the Notre Dame order, St. Julie Billiart, the eighteenth-century pioneer in the education of women, especially those of moderate financial means. The College believes that truly progressive education selectively blends traditional values with new ideas that represent real growth. Within the scope of a career-oriented liberal arts education, women can grow to meet the challenges of the present and the future. The College is accredited by the North Central Association of Colleges and Schools and the American Dietetic Association. It is registered for the awarding of State Teachers' Certificates by the State of Ohio Department of Education. The paralegal studies program is approved by the American Bar Association.

A variety of clubs and activities enrich the educational experiences of the College's 650 students. Student clubs include chapters of the American Chemical Society and the American Institute of Biological Sciences. The Masquers promotes talent in the performing arts and provides entertainment for the College community and general public. Campus publications include the monthly *Notre Dame News* and *PIVOT*, the literary magazine. A committee of faculty members and students schedules and coordinates lectures, plays, performances, and concerts. Most on-campus events are free, and students may purchase tickets at reduced rates for off-campus programs such as performances of the world-famous Cleveland Orchestra, the Cleveland Opera, the Cleveland Ballet, and road shows of Broadway productions at the Palace Theatre, State Theatre, and Ohio Theatre at Playhouse Square. Performances at the Cleveland Playhouse are also available.

Intercollegiate basketball, softball, soccer, cross-country, tennis, swimming, and volleyball are offered. Notre Dame College of Ohio is a member of the National Association of Intercollegiate Athletics and competes in the Mid-Ohio Conference.

The beautiful 53-acre wooded campus provides the perfect setting for the Clara Fritzsche Library; the Administration Building, housing all of the classrooms and offices; Connelly Center, the cafeteria and student center; the Keller Center, the recreational and fitness facility; and two residence halls.

A Master of Education degree, designed for classroom teachers, is offered with concentrations available in special education, reading, and critical and creative thinking.

Location

The College is located in South Euclid, 25 minutes from downtown Cleveland. The area combines the excitement and cultural wealth of a major urban and educational center with the relaxed atmosphere of a suburban setting. University Circle in Cleveland, a 500-acre complex containing an unusual blend of cultural, educational, medical, religious, and social service institutions, is easily accessible from the College.

Situated on the shores of Lake Erie, Cleveland is the home of the Rock-and-Roll Hall of Fame, professional sports, and the Flats entertainment district. The Cleveland Metroparks offer a variety of activities and recreational opportunities. Snowy winters provide abundant opportunities for skiing and tobogganing, and popular ski areas are located a short distance from the city.

Majors and Degrees

The College awards the Bachelor of Arts degree in accounting; communication; education, including early childhood (PK–3), middle childhood (4–9), and secondary education; English; history/political science; information systems; management; marketing; psychology; Spanish; and theology. The Bachelor of Science is awarded in biology, chemistry, dietetics, mathematics, and nutrition science. A student can also design her own major that leads to a Bachelor of Arts or Bachelor of Science degree by combining two or three academic areas, such as graphic design, human resource management, and public relations.

Certification programs are offered in business, environmental technology, and paralegal studies. Teacher certification is available in elementary school education, kindergarten, prekindergarten, and secondary education (grades 7–12).

The Associate in Arts degree is awarded at the completion of two-year programs in business management, environmental technology, and pastoral ministry.

The Center for Pastoral Theology and Ministry grants a two-year catechetical diploma and the Bachelor of Arts degree.

Academic Program

All students pursue a career-oriented liberal arts education. For the bachelor's degree, students must earn 128 semester hours of credit, with a minimum cumulative grade point average of 2.0. From 30 to 45 semester hours of credit are required in the major field of study.

Through a cooperative education program, students may receive up to 6 semester hours of credit for paid or volunteer work experience related to their academic field of study.

Advanced placement credit is awarded to students who have demonstrated the ability to pursue course work beyond the level of entering freshmen, as indicated by their scores on the Advanced Placement (AP) or College-Level Examination Program (CLEP) tests of the College Board. College credit is given on the basis of a decision made jointly by the academic dean and the department involved.

Academic Facilities

The Clara Fritzsche Library, housing the modern Media Center, has a capacity for 100,000 volumes. The state-of-the-art Science Research Center houses $1 million in sophisticated instrumentation and computers that allow students to work side-by-side with faculty members on research projects. Undergraduates learn to operate such equipment as a Fourier-transform infrared spectrometer, Fourier-transform nuclear magnetic resonance spectrometer, and gas chromatograph/mass spectrometer, allowing science majors to develop independence and confidence in laboratory practices.

The $1-million Dwyer Learning Center is the computer hub of campus, with forty-eight computer stations for student use. The center includes an electronic classroom, areas for peer tutoring, a writing lab, and curriculum-specific software in science, math, history, and foreign languages.

The Center for Professional Development offers resources for teachers on the topics of cooperative learning and teaching to multiple intelligences. The center also offers seminars and workshops throughout the year.

Costs

For the 2000–01 academic year, tuition charges are $13,686. Room and board costs are $5416 for double occupancy. Part-time tuition is $346 per hour. Student fees are $200.

Financial Aid

A comprehensive financial assistance program of approximately $2.2 million assists nearly 90 percent of all full-time students. One hundred percent of the 1998–99 freshman class received some type of financial assistance.

Students applying for aid must submit the Free Application for Federal Student Aid (FAFSA). Forms are available from the College's Office of Student Financial Assistance.

Faculty

The faculty has 37 full-time and 64 part-time members; 65 percent of full-time faculty members have doctoral/terminal/first-professional degrees. This faculty of 101 is augmented by several highly qualified instructors in special areas. Faculty members hold advanced degrees from more than thirty universities in the United States, Canada, and Europe.

Student Government

The Undergraduate Student Senate and the Resident Association Board are the active student governing bodies. In addition, students have representation on various College committees.

Admission Requirements

In fulfilling its mission, Notre Dame College of Ohio seeks to attract women of diverse religious, racial, and economic backgrounds. Candidates for admission as first-time, full-time freshmen are reviewed on an individual basis, and decisions are based on a broad range of criteria. The most important consideration is the candidate's high school performance, as demonstrated by her overall grade average, class rank, grade trends, and level of courses completed. Aptitude for verbal and mathematical reasoning, as measured by performance on standardized tests, is also considered. In addition, counselor and teacher recommendations are reviewed.

Notre Dame College of Ohio requires at least 16 units of high school credit in academic subjects as a prerequisite for matriculation in the College. The distribution of these subject areas and the units are as follows: English, 4; mathematics, 3 (to include algebra I, geometry, and algebra II); science, 3 (with laboratory experience); social studies, 3; foreign language, 2 (from the same language); and fine arts, 1. Applicants should generally rank in the upper half of their high school graduating class and have a minimum average of C+. Either ACT or SAT I scores are accepted.

Students wishing to transfer from other regionally accredited colleges and universities are admitted to advanced standing upon presentation of satisfactory evidence of scholarship and character.

Special consideration may be granted to an applicant whose academic preparation is not consistent with the requirements stated above.

Notre Dame College of Ohio strongly recommends that prospective students schedule an appointment to visit the campus and talk with an admissions counselor. Open houses throughout the year also give prospective students the chance to visit the campus.

Application and Information

The College maintains a rolling admission policy. To apply, students should submit the completed application for undergraduate admission, an official transcript of their high school record that includes class rank, results of the ACT or SAT I, a letter of recommendation, and a nonrefundable $30 application fee to:

Office of Admissions
Notre Dame College of Ohio
4545 College Road
South Euclid, Ohio 44121
Telephone: 216-381-1680 Ext. 355
        800-NDC-1680 Ext. 355 (toll-free)
Fax: 216-381-3802
E-mail: admissions@ndc.edu
World Wide Web: http://www.ndc.edu

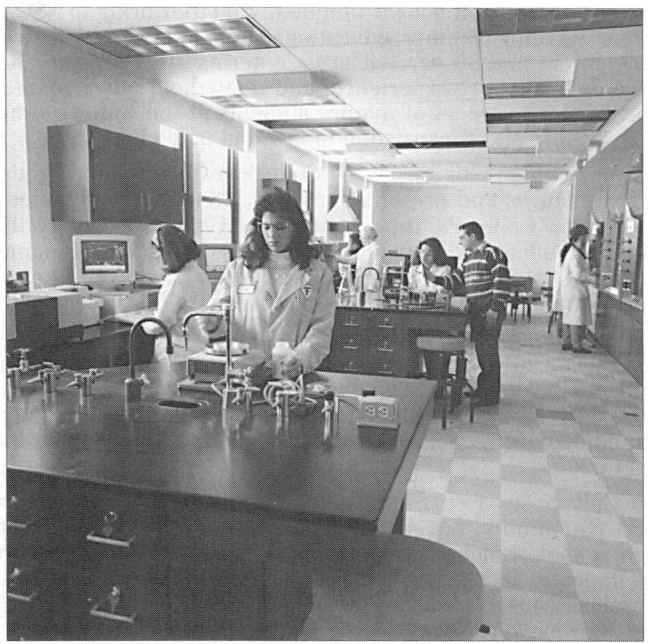

The Science Research Center allows undergraduate students to conduct research with faculty members.

NOVA SCOTIA COLLEGE OF ART AND DESIGN
HALIFAX, NOVA SCOTIA, CANADA

The College

Nova Scotia College of Art and Design (NSCAD) is the only art college in Canada that offers undergraduate and graduate degree programs in fields that include communication design, crafts, digital design, environmental planning, and studio and media arts. A bachelor's degree in art education is offered in cooperation with Mount Saint Vincent University, also located in Halifax. NSCAD was founded in 1887 as the Victoria School of Art and Design, only two blocks from its present residence on the Halifax waterfront. Today, the College occupies more than 160,000 square feet in eleven buildings that are joined by a complex network of walkways and are surrounded by spectacular views of the Atlantic Ocean. The College is located in a downtown core that includes the recently refurbished Neptune Theatre, the Costume Studies Department of Dalhousie University, and the Electropolis sound and production facilities. A number of independent galleries are also nearby.

Enrollment at the College currently averages between 750 and 775 students, and there are about 80 full-time and part-time faculty members. The College is a full member of the Association of Universities and Colleges of Canada.

Graduate degrees offered by the College include the Master of Fine Arts in crafts, design, and fine and media arts and the Master of Arts in art education.

The NSCAD student body is unique in that they bring to NSCAD a rare breadth of other educational and career experiences. Between 30 and 35 percent of its entering students have had previous university experience, and many hold other degrees. The previous careers of mature students at the College range from mining and construction to law and medicine.

Extracurricular activities at the College revolve around visiting artists lectures and presentations and attending weekly openings at the College's Anna Leonowens Gallery, a gallery that features student and traveling exhibitions. The gallery is named for one of the founders of the College, Anna Leonowens, known more famously worldwide as the governess portrayed in the *King and I*.

Dalhousie University, Saint Mary's University, and Mount Saint Vincent University, all located in Halifax, offer further opportunities for viewing traveling art exhibitions and have featured exhibitions of the work of Robert Frank and Romare Beardon, among others.

The College strives to establish innovative connections with the local community. NSCAD design students have worked with high school students from the local black community in the development of a home page for a project called the African Presence. This project has enabled worldwide access through the Internet to Nova Scotia black history. Environmental planning students have researched the potential for hemp pulp production in Nova Scotia. Ceramics students and a visiting Chinese ceramist studied centuries-old Chinese pottery shards at Fort Louisbourg, an early French military settlement in Nova Scotia. The projects undertaken by students indicate a mature and engaged social consciousness that creatively responds to social issues. The craft division has continued to energize the NSCAD community with the Hungry Bowls Project: each fall, prior to the Christmas break, ceramics students individually produce unique bowls, which are then filled with gourmet soups and sold. The proceeds from the Hungry Bowls Project are donated to family shelters in Halifax.

Location

The College and five other universities are located in Halifax, which is easily accessible by plane or car. Frequent direct flights are available from the Halifax International Airport to Newark, Boston, Toronto, Montreal, Calgary, London, and Reykjavík (Iceland). The airport is located about 20 miles from Halifax and is readily accessible by airport shuttle or taxi. Halifax is the capital city of Nova Scotia. Therefore, the College enjoys a proximity to government and other provincial facilities, a number of banking and business institutions, and numerous hotels and restaurants. Halifax may be reached overland by car from either Maine or Quebec or by car and passenger ferry from Bar Harbor, Maine. The distance from the ferry landing in Yarmouth to Halifax is about 4 hours by car.

Recreation facilities are readily available to students through the local universities and through city facilities. Camping and hiking are popular pastimes immediately available even within the city limits of Dartmouth—Halifax's sister city across the harbor. Many students and faculty members live in Dartmouth and travel each day to Halifax via a 10-minute ferry ride. A metro bus system is also available.

Majors and Degrees

The College offers four undergraduate degrees, which include a number of majors. The Bachelor of Fine Arts degree offers majors in ceramics, fine arts, jewelry design, media arts, photography, and textiles. The Bachelor of Design (honours) is offered in communication design, digital communication design, and environmental planning. The Bachelor of Design (nonhonours) is offered in environmental design. The Bachelor of Arts in Visual Arts degree is offered with a major in art history. Minor programs are available in art history, digital media, drawing, environmental design, geography (in cooperation with Saint Mary's University), and graphic design.

Academic Program

The College offers a two-semester Foundation Program that introduces the practices, principles, approaches, and issues of art, craft, and design. Students entering degree programs begin their studies by completing the Foundation Program. Studio courses combine theory and practice in the learning environment of the studio. NSCAD students must complete a required number of studio credits. Credits in liberal arts and science courses are also required and provide, through research and writing, contexts for students to engage their critical thinking skills. These courses range from Medieval art history to feminist art criticism to semiotic theory. The College offers year-round study and hosts visiting students from institutions in both the U.S. and Canada who are continuing their degree studies during the summer semester.

The College invites many guests to the campus throughout the year. These include artists, designers, performers, and lecturers in various fields. Often, visiting artists and designers spend a week in residence exploring ideas in the various disciplines of art and design, showing and discussing their work during evening lectures open to the public, and working with students and faculty members in the College studios.

Off-Campus Arrangements

About 8 percent of NSCAD students participate in off-campus and exchange programs. Exchange agreements have been initiated with more than fifty institutions, from Australia to

China to the Czech Republic. NSCAD is also a member of the Association of Independent Colleges of Art and Design, which allows students access to many U.S. institutions. Returning students confirm that the College's facilities are equal to any they find at host exchange institutions. The off-campus study option allows students to pursue self-directed projects, practicums, and internships throughout the world. Practicum examples range from design work at firms in Paris and Rome to exhibition design at the Smithsonian.

Academic Facilities

The Anna Leonowens Gallery hosts and presents work related to the activities that take place within the College. The gallery also hosts related events, such as artist lectures, video screenings, performances, and panel discussions. All activities are open to the public, and many residents of the local community regularly attend Monday night openings. The gallery hosts approximately 130 exhibitions per year, and 17,000 visitors attend annually. The gallery sponsors a 6-credit curatorial internship program for students registered at the College.

The College Library has a collection of more than 30,000 books and periodicals. A major feature of the library is the Non-Print Collection, which has more than 125,000 slides as well as videotapes and audiotapes. The Non-Print Collection also houses the Regional Film Collection of the National Film Board of Canada. The library is a partner in the Nova Scotia university library consortium (NOVANET), which facilitates the sharing of library collections. Through a shared computer system, more than 2 million items are made available to students and faculty members at the College. Additional library services include access to CD-ROM indexes and Internet search stations.

Costs

Tuition costs for 1999–2000 were Can$3986.10 for two semesters. International students, including those from the U.S., paid Can$7389 for two semesters. International students are also required to purchase health insurance; in 1999–2000, the cost was Can$480 for one calendar year. Room and board costs ranged from Can$3400 to Can$4000. Books and supplies are estimated to cost about Can$1900 for two semesters.

Financial Aid

Some students finance a portion of their university costs through the Canada Student Loan Program. American students are similarly encouraged to access federal or state guaranteed loans if they are unable to meet their educational costs through independent resources. International students must be able to document the amount and source of their funds before they are issued a permit to study by Canada Immigration. The College offers limited financial aid to Canadian students. A number of merit scholarships are available to students who demonstrate academic and visual excellence in their work at the College.

Faculty

The College has 42 full-time faculty members and from 45 to 50 part-time instructors, depending on the semester. The faculty members—both full-time and part-time—are practicing artists, designers, and scholars who continue their professional activities in conjunction with their teaching responsibilities. Therefore, students simultaneously experience practice and teaching.

Student Government

The Student Union of the Nova Scotia College of Art and Design (SUNSCAD) Council is made up of three bodies: the Executive, the Departmental Representatives, and the Constituency Group Representatives. The Executive is responsible for the operation of the union and represents the union on the Board of Governors, the Alumni Association, the Faculty Union, the Students' Union of Nova Scotia, and the Canadian Federation of Students. Departmental Representatives provide liaison between the union and each College department and promote effective communication between the groups.

Admission Requirements

The Nova Scotia College of Art and Design bases its admission policies on evidence of reasonable maturity in the prospective student, the student's interest in working within the College's programs, and the student's ability to benefit from the offerings of the College. The College offers full-time programs during each of three semesters, which begin in September, January, and May. Successful applicants may begin a program of study in either the September or January semester. Students may continue their studies at the College during the summer semester.

Applicants may submit application materials at any time of the year, but reviews of complete applications take place twice yearly in April/May and October. Early application is urged for all semesters, and applicants are advised to submit complete applications well before the final deadlines. No application is reviewed until it is complete. To complete the application, an applicant must submit the application forms, a brief admissions essay, transcripts of all secondary and/or postsecondary studies, and a portfolio, instructions for which may be obtained from the Admissions Office. All inquiries and requests for application forms should be forwarded to the Coordinator of Admissions. Applicants are welcome to visit the College to discuss admission requirements, programs, and facilities. The College hosts information sessions and portfolio previews for Foundation Program applicants and other interested individuals, such as parents, guardians, and teachers. These sessions are held twice yearly on a Saturday in October and March and enable individuals to tour the College facilities, discuss visual submissions with members of the Admissions Committee, and explore program offerings with College faculty members and students.

Advanced standing may be granted to students who are able to display by portfolio review and/or transcript that they have met the expected outcomes of the Foundation Program and can transfer at least one full year of art- and/or design-related study from a previous university-level program or college-level program determined to be transferable to the College's degree programs.

Application and Information

Applications and program information may be obtained from:
 The Office of Student and Academic Services
 Nova Scotia College of Art and Design
 5163 Duke Street
 Halifax, Nova Scotia B3J 3J6
 Canada
 Telephone: 902-494-8129
 Fax: 902-425-2987
 E-mail: tbailey@nscad.ns.ca
 World Wide Web: http://www.nscad.ns.ca

Nova Scotia College of Art and Design is situated in the downtown core of Halifax.

NOVA SOUTHEASTERN UNIVERSITY
FORT LAUDERDALE, FLORIDA

The University

Nova Southeastern University is the largest independent or non-tax-supported university in the state of Florida. Based upon annual expenditures, it is among the 100 largest independent colleges and universities in this country. Nova Southeastern University is an independent, nonsectarian, nonprofit, and racially nondiscriminatory university. It is accredited by the Southern Association of Colleges and Schools.

Unusual among institutions of higher education, NSU is a university for all ages: the University School for children, numerous undergraduate and graduate degree programs in a variety of fields, and nondegree continuing education programs are all available at Nova Southeastern. The traditional population in the undergraduate program is approximately 1,200 students. Since its beginning, the University has been distinguished by its uncommon programs, which provide alternative choices in forms of education, and by its research, which is aimed at finding solutions to problems of immediate concern to mankind. With students from Florida, forty-nine other states, and thirty-three other countries, NSU is a university of national scope.

Student activities include twenty faculty-sponsored clubs; events sponsored by the student government; intercollegiate sports such as baseball, basketball, cross-country, golf, soccer, softball, tennis, and volleyball; an International Student Club; a newspaper; a radio station; intramurals; four national fraternities and two national sororities; and eighteen sport clubs.

Location

The main campus of Nova Southeastern University is located on a 232-acre site in Fort Lauderdale, West Broward County, Florida. Broward County is a principal coastal area in south Florida and a rapidly growing community for business, industrial, electronics, and computer opportunities. The climate is subtropical and has an average year-round temperature of 75 degrees. The University is surrounded by natural areas for such outdoor activities as sailing, fishing, golf, tennis, and swimming. With tourism as a major industry, Fort Lauderdale provides the best in shopping, dining, and cultural offerings, which include concerts, opera, ballet, museums, and theater.

Majors and Degrees

Nova Southeastern University offers B.S. degrees in accounting; administrative studies; business administration; computer information systems; computer science; education (early childhood, elementary, and exceptional); environmental science/studies; hospitality management; legal assisting; legal studies (prelaw); life sciences (premedical); middle school science education; ocean studies; psychology; science and the business environment; science and the law; and sport and wellness studies. The B.A. degree is offered in humanities. The life sciences program may lead to Health Professions Division programs in dentistry, occupational therapy, optometry, osteopathy, pharmacy, physician's assistant studies, and physical therapy. Also offered are a number of certificate programs as well as a variety of credit and noncredit courses, workshops, and institutes.

NSU offers a dual admission program for a select number of highly motivated, qualified students interested in pursuing both undergraduate and graduate studies in business, computer sciences, dentistry, dispute resolution, education, family therapy, law, mental health counseling, occupational therapy, oceanography, optometry, osteopathic medicine, pharmacy, physical therapy, psychology, or speech-language pathology. A dual admission program is also available to the physician assistant major. Students who successfully meet all program requirements will have a seat reserved for them in one of the specified NSU graduate or professional schools.

Academic Program

The undergraduate program for Nova Southeastern's daytime population combines a core curriculum with a set of majors designed to prepare students for work in graduate school or a professional career. The general education program assumes that the most appropriate learning experience is intensive and focused on issues, thinking skills, and communication and computation, rather than focused simply on disciplinary content. General education courses, therefore, are interdisciplinary in their approach to content and integrate lectures, student-based discussions, films, speakers, and research and field experiences into the curriculum. Through a small, intimate classroom setting, NSU's program provides a cooperative form of learning in which students are encouraged to help each other achieve competence while they receive close personal attention and support from individual instructors. The legal studies and other programs may lead to enrollment in the NSU Law School.

The academic year is divided into six terms of eight weeks each, permitting students to be enrolled for up to 9 credits of time-intensive course work per term. Each course of study leads to the Bachelor of Science or Bachelor of Arts degree.

Other Nova Southeastern University programs are organized for the adult working population. Courses are offered in the evenings and on weekends at the main campus, as well as at off-campus locations convenient to students. Although course content is designed to satisfy traditional educational requirements, courses are scheduled to meet the needs of employed students and are taught by utilizing a blend of University professors and knowledgeable practicing professionals. Most students are employed and have passed the traditional age of undergraduates; many have families. Credits may be awarded for prior learning experiences after a student's application for such credit has been approved by a faculty committee. Additional credit may be earned through PEP and CLEP general and subject examinations. Credit toward a degree may also be transferred from regionally accredited institutions.

Academic Facilities

Students enrolled in academic programs at Nova Southeastern University have numerous academic facilities available to them. Microcomputer laboratories provide courses and programs in applied microcomputer technology. The University Computing Center provides data processing facilities and services to meet the instructional, research, and administrative needs of the University and is available to qualified students for computer-oriented course work. Other facilities within the University include the Biofeedback Laboratory, the University School (prekindergarten through grade 12), the Family Center, the Learning Technology Laboratory, the Law School, the Oceanography Center, the Health Professions Division, the Center for

Psychological Studies, and the Einstein Library. Construction begins in early spring 2000 on a new high-tech, state-of-the-art academic center.

Costs

Tuition for undergraduate students at Nova Southeastern University varies according to the academic program. For the 2000–01 academic year, tuition for the full-time day program is $12,200. Textbooks cost approximately $500 per year, and on-campus housing is approximately $3700 for the year. Meal plan costs are approximately $2600 per academic year.

Financial Aid

Nova Southeastern University offers a comprehensive program of financial aid to assist students in meeting their educational expenses. Financial aid is available to help cover direct educational costs, such as tuition, fees, books, and supplies, as well as indirect costs, such as food, clothing, and transportation. The following forms of financial aid are available to qualified undergraduate students: Federal Pell Grants, Federal Supplemental Educational Opportunity Grants, Florida Student Assistance Grants, Florida Academic Scholars Fund awards, Florida Tuition Vouchers, Federal Stafford Student Loans, Federal Perkins Loans, Federal PLUS loans, Federal Work-Study awards, and Florida College Career Work Experience Program awards. In addition, many academic scholarships are available. Deferred-payment plans and veterans' benefits are also offered.

Applicants for financial aid are required to submit the Free Application for Federal Student Aid (FAFSA) in order to be considered for all campus-based aid programs. Students who apply before April 1 are given priority consideration for funds; however, applications are accepted all year.

Faculty

The undergraduate faculty at Nova Southeastern University is full-time and resident. In addition, faculty members are drawn from qualified professionals in the community, as well as from other centers and programs within the University. Most of the faculty members have backgrounds in professional, industrial, managerial, civic, educational, or other private and public sectors of the community. For example, lawyers and judges teach criminal justice courses; accountants, personnel managers, and others teach in their respective fields; and principals and teacher curriculum specialists teach education courses. All faculty members are dedicated to the philosophy that contemporary higher education combines theory and practice and that the education of working professionals and adult students requires the active participation of both the student and the instructor.

Student Government

All Nova Southeastern University students benefit from the services of the Student Government Association (SGA). The SGA has proved to be an influential organization in campus affairs; it instills a sense of community in the student body. Students in the undergraduate programs enjoy the same rights and services as all other Nova Southeastern University students, including use of University study and recreational facilities, access to all support services, and participation in student affairs.

Admission Requirements

Admission requirements vary according to the program. A counseling session is recommended. Freshman applicants must submit official high school transcripts and SAT I or ACT scores.

Transfer applicants must submit official college transcripts. Each student's record is evaluated individually to determine the number of transferable credits. There is a maximum of 90 transferable credits, and students must complete 30 semester hours at Nova Southeastern University.

Application and Information

The application should be submitted with a nonrefundable $25 application fee. There is no closing date for applications for the fall term. Applicants are notified of the admission decision on a rolling basis. Deferred admission is available.

For further information, prospective applicants are invited to contact:

Office of Undergraduate Admissions
Nova Southeastern University
3301 College Avenue
Fort Lauderdale, Florida 33314
Telephone: 954-262-8001
         954-262-8002 (for adult programs)
         800-338-4723 Ext. 8001 (toll-free)
E-mail: ncsinfo@polaris.nova.edu
World Wide Web: http://www.undergrad.nova.edu

Students enjoy a break between classes as they talk with professors and fellow classmates.

OAKLAND UNIVERSITY
ROCHESTER, MICHIGAN

The University

Pioneering the Future is the best way to describe the excitement building at Oakland University (OU) today. The comprehensive campus is in its 41st year and continues to increase its programs, facilities, resources, and enrollment. Oakland University was created in 1957 when the late Alfred G. and Matilda R. Wilson donated their 1,500-acre estate and $2 million to Michigan State University to begin a new college in Oakland County. Named Michigan State University–Oakland, the new campus enrolled its first students in 1959. In 1963 its name was changed to Oakland University, and in 1970 the Michigan legislature recognized the maturity and state of the University by granting it autonomy. From its beginning, the University has flourished, emphasizing academic quality and concentrating on providing its students with a broad liberal arts education by a nationally recognized faculty.

Dedicated to preparing learners for the twenty-first-century workplace and society, the university today is organized into the College of Arts and Sciences and the Schools of Business Administration, Education and Human Services, Engineering and Computer Science, Health Sciences, and Nursing. Oakland offers undergraduate programs in more than seventy areas, with master's and doctoral programs in fifty-four areas. OU also features an active Honors College for students looking for a more challenging academic experience. Oakland was rated twenty-fourth in academic reputation among the 123 top Midwestern regional colleges and universities for 1998 by *U.S. News & World Report*.

Enrollment at Oakland University continues to set new records, reaching 14,664 students in 1999–2000. Oakland retains the best features of a small-campus setting even as the University grows and changes to meet enrollment demands.

Oakland is committed to preparing students for a rapidly changing work environment. The University has major institutes and centers in eye research, wellness, biochemistry technology, and international studies. Students use multimedia applications and interactive learning to reach their potential. Through innovative, technology-enriched delivery of educational services, Oakland University is preparing a community of learners for the opportunities of today and tomorrow.

OU is home to approximately 1,100 students who live on campus in six residence halls and a 48-unit apartment complex. All rooms are equipped with phones with voice mail and cable TV. Cars are allowed for all class levels.

Oakland University has ninety-five recognized student organizations, including thirty-six academically oriented organizations and fifteen Greek letter organizations.

In 1999, OU's athletic programs moved from Division II to Division I competition. OU joined the Mid-Continent Conference and competes in six men's sports and eight women's sports.

Oakland's cultural enterprises attract more than 500,000 visitors to campus each year. Students can enjoy events offered through OU's Meadow Brook Theatre, Meadow Brook Art Gallery, and Meadow Brook Hall. Meadow Brook Music Festival stages a variety of summer concerts.

Location

Oakland University's 1,441-acre campus is conveniently located in suburban Rochester, Michigan. The University's location in Oakland County offers many cultural and recreational opportunities, such as the Palace of Auburn Hills and the Pontiac Silverdome. Oakland County, the fastest-growing county in the state, plans to add about 40,000 new jobs within the next two years, which will mean more opportunities for Oakland's students and graduates.

Majors and Degrees

The College of Arts and Sciences offers bachelor's degrees in anthropology, applied statistics, art history, biochemistry, biology, chemistry, communication arts, East Asian studies/China, East Asian studies/Japan, economics, English, environmental health, French, general studies, German/German studies, history, international studies, journalism, Latin American languages/civilization, Latin American studies, linguistics, mathematics, medical physics, modern languages, music, music education, performing arts (music, theater, and dance), philosophy, physics, political science, predentistry, prelaw, premedicine, preoptometry, psychology, public administration and public policy, Russian language/civilization, Slavic studies, sociology, South Asian studies/India, and Spanish. The School of Business Administration offers bachelor's degrees in accounting, economics, finance, general management, human resource management, management information systems, and marketing. The School of Engineering and Computer Science offers bachelor's degrees in computer engineering, computer science, electrical engineering, engineering chemistry, engineering physics, mechanical engineering, and systems engineering. The School of Health Sciences offers bachelor's degrees in industrial health and safety, medical laboratory sciences, medical physics, physical therapy, and radiation therapy. The School of Education and Human Services offers bachelor's degrees in elementary education, human resource development, and secondary education with certification in biology, chemistry, English, French, German, history, mathematics, music, physics, and Spanish. The School of Nursing offers a bachelor's degree in nursing.

Academic Program

While each school has its own sequence requirements, all students must satisfy the following requirements: 32 credits in general education, writing proficiency, and one course in ethnic diversity. Students must also have a cumulative grade point average of at least 2.0 in courses taken at Oakland University. In certain programs, additional GPA requirements must be met. Finally, students must successfully complete 32 credits in courses at the 300 level or above. Students at Oakland have the unique opportunity to conduct research at the undergraduate level.

Off-Campus Arrangements

Oakland prepares students for the twenty-first-century workplace by offering meaningful challenges and experiences. Oakland is one of four Michigan colleges participating in the federally funded Americorps program, patterned after the Peace Corps.

At Oakland, students have opportunities to gain paid work experience. Many students work in internships and cooperative job placements in government, business, and industry throughout southeastern Michigan.

Oakland also offers study-abroad opportunities in England, France, Italy, Japan, and Vienna.

Academic Facilities

To accommodate ongoing growth, several capital improvements are underway at Oakland. A new science and engineering complex, an Honors College, and a $31-million recreation and athletic center have opened recently. A new business administration building is scheduled to open in 2000.

Oakland University's Kresge Library includes a 1.7-million piece collection of books, microforms, and periodicals. The library also houses private study rooms, a major computer lab, and an interlibrary database so students can access materials at other libraries.

Computer labs are located in various campus buildings, offering current software and applications, high-quality printers, and advanced computer graphics.

Costs

Tuition for the 1999–2000 academic year was $118.70 per credit hour for freshmen and sophomores, $130.55 per credit hour for juniors and seniors, and $349.65 per credit hour for out-of-state students. A typical full-time semester schedule consists of 12 to 16 credit hours. The 1999–2000 room and board cost was $4715. Books and supplies average $475.

Financial Aid

Oakland offers two programs of assistance to students: scholarships based on academic achievement and financial aid based on need. Students must submit the Supplemental Application for Scholarships and Financial Aid for consideration.

Faculty

Oakland's faculty members encourage curiosity, foster critical thinking, and help students develop skills that allow them to analyze an increasingly complex world. Of the University's 371 faculty members, 90 percent hold a doctoral degree in a specialized field of study from many of the nation's finest research institutions. Virtually all courses (99 percent) are taught by faculty members. The student-to-faculty ratio is 18:1. Small classes contribute to Oakland's student-focused learning environment.

Student Government

Oakland's student government, University Student Congress, is an elected, campuswide governmental body that serves students' needs. In addition to its administrative duties, University Student Congress provides funding for the Student Activities Funding Board, which allocates money to recognized student organizations, and for the Student Program Board, a student committee responsible for programming films, lectures, concerts, and other recreational activities. The elected student leaders also lobby on behalf of students at the state and national level.

Admission Requirements

Freshman applicants should have completed a high school college-preparatory program and have a B average or better. The ACT is required. Transfer students must be in good academic standing at the time of transfer and have at least a 2.5 GPA. For both freshman and transfer applicants, required grade point averages vary for certain programs.

Application and Information

For more information, students should contact:

Office of Admissions
101 North Foundation Hall
Oakland University
Rochester, Michigan 48309-4475
Telephone: 248-370-3360
                800-OAK-UNIV (toll-free)
E-mail: applynow@oakland.edu
World Wide Web: http://www.oakland.edu

Students enjoy a break between classes at the newly renovated food court at the Oakland Center.

OBERLIN COLLEGE
OBERLIN, OHIO

The College

Oberlin College, founded in 1833, is an independent, coeducational, liberal arts college dedicated to recruiting students from diverse backgrounds. Oberlin comprises two divisions: the College of Arts and Sciences, with roughly 2,350 students, and the Conservatory of Music, with about 550 students. Students in both divisions share one campus; they also share residence and dining halls as part of one academic community. Many students take courses in both divisions. Oberlin awards the Bachelor of Arts and the Bachelor of Music degrees. In Oberlin's unique double-degree program, students pursue the B.A. and the B.Mus. degrees in a unified, five-year program. Selected master's degrees are offered in the Conservatory.

Oberlin was the first college in the country to admit women, and one of the first to admit African Americans. By 1900 nearly half of all the black college graduates in the country—128 to be exact—had graduated from Oberlin. This core of Oberlin-educated men and women formed the first black professional class in the country.

Today, Oberlin's progressive history lives on in the idealism and conviction of its students. Students are united by a commitment to social justice and a willingness to confront social issues that many would prefer to ignore. As the *New York Times* noted in an article marking Oberlin's 150th anniversary, "In its century and a half, while Harvard worried about the classics and Yale about God, Oberlin worried about the state of America and the world beyond."

Oberlin seeks a diverse and promising student body. Recognizing that diversity broadens perspectives, Oberlin is dedicated to recruiting a culturally, economically, geographically, and racially diverse group of students. Interaction with others of widely different backgrounds and experiences fosters the effective and concerned participation in the larger society so characteristic of Oberlin graduates. Among primarily undergraduate institutions, Oberlin ranks first for the number of graduates who go on to earn Ph.D. degrees. Its alumni, who include three Nobel laureates, are leaders in law, scientific and scholarly research, medicine, the arts, theology, communications, business, and government.

Oberlin has several special academic programs. During the four-week Winter Term, students create independent projects (group or individual) that can be pursued on- or off-campus. These projects may have an academic or career focus and need not be connected to a student's major. Oberlin's Experimental College, a student-run program, offers courses for limited academic credit taught by Oberlin students, townspeople, administrators, and faculty members.

While Oberlin offers a small-town atmosphere, there is never a lack of something to do. More than 400 concerts and recitals take place on campus annually, from ticketed events like the Cleveland Orchestra to free student and faculty recitals. Each year the Conservatory stages two operas, and the theater and dance program presents several productions. Numerous lectures and readings feature guests prominent in a variety of disciplines.

Location

Oberlin College is an integral part of the city of Oberlin, a town of about 8,000 residents located 35 miles southwest of Cleveland. The town is primarily residential, with tree-lined streets and fine old clapboard houses. The College is located in the center of town, close to the business district, and virtually everything a student needs is within walking or biking distance.

Majors and Degrees

Oberlin offers the Bachelor of Arts degree (awarded by the College of Arts and Sciences), and the Bachelor of Music degree (awarded by the Conservatory of Music). Oberlin also offers a unique "double-degree" program, a five-year course of study leading to the B.A. and B.Mus. degrees. Students wishing to enter the double-degree program must be accepted by both the College of Arts and Sciences and the Conservatory of Music.

The B.A. is awarded in African-American studies, anthropology, archaeological studies, art (history and studio), biology, biopsychology, chemistry, classics (Greek, Latin, and classical civilization), comparative literature, computer science, creative writing, dance, East Asian studies, economics, English, environmental studies, French, geology, German, history, Jewish studies, Latin American studies, law and society, mathematics, music, neuroscience, philosophy, physics, politics, psychology, religion, Russian, Russian studies, sociology, Spanish, theater, Third World studies, 3/2 engineering, and women's studies. In addition, many students pursue interdisciplinary individual majors.

The B.Mus. is awarded in composition, electronic and computer music, historical performance, jazz studies (performance or composition), music education, music history, and performance (baroque cello/viola da gamba, baroque flute, baroque oboe, baroque violin, bassoon, clarinet, classical guitar, double bass, flute, harp, harpsichord, horn, lute, oboe, organ, percussion, piano, recorder, saxophone, trombone, trumpet, tuba, viola, violin, violoncello, and voice). A major in music theory is only offered as part of a double major.

The Conservatory of Music also offers combined 5-year B.Mus. and M.Mus. degrees in opera theater, conducting, and music education and teaching as well as an M.Mus. in historical performance and a four-semester Artist Diploma.

Academic Program

To receive the B.A. or the B.Mus. degree, students must complete a major; nine credit hours in each of Oberlin's three divisions: humanities, natural sciences, and social sciences; and three Winter Term projects. Students must also demonstrate quantitative proficiency and writing proficiency. For the B.A., 112 credit hours are required for graduation; for the B.Mus. 124 hours are required. The recommended semester course load is 14 credit hours for students in the College of Arts and Sciences and 15 or 16 credit hours for students in the Conservatory of Music.

Academic Facilities

Oberlin's five libraries contain more than 1.75 million items, including 1.1 million catalogued volumes— an unusually large collection for a college of Oberlin's size. Other features include an online catalog, connections to several networks, and access to numerous online and CD-ROM databases. The College's Allen Memorial Art Museum is considered one of the top college or university art museums in the nation. Seventeenth-century Dutch and Flemish painting, European art of the late nineteenth and twentieth centuries, and contemporary art are especially well-represented among the more than 14,000 objects spanning the range of art history in the museum.

The Conservatory of music contains 153 practice rooms—all with windows—and houses 168 Steinway grand pianos and 18 uprights. The Conservatory also has two concert halls, numerous instrument collections, state-of-the-art electronic music studios, and recording facilities.

Oberlin's Irvin E. Houck Computing Center provides more than 125 Macintosh and IBM-compatible computers for student use in several locations on campus. The Center's Digital Equipment Corporation VAX 6000-410 mainframe computer provides access to the Internet and is accessible to students through 50 terminals and microcomputers in several academic buildings, as well as via modem from all residence hall rooms. In about half of the residence hall rooms, students have direct access to the Internet from their personal computers. Computer accounts are available to all students at no charge.

Costs

Tuition for the 2000–01 academic year is $25,180. Double-room and board fees are an additional $6365. The student activity fee is $175.

Financial Aid

In an average year, Oberlin commits more than $15 million, more than one-fifth of the College budget, to financial aid. The Office of Financial Aid works to develop financial aid packages that meet the demonstrated financial need of all regularly admitted students who comply with the filing deadlines. Oberlin's policy is to award financial aid packages with larger proportions of grant aid to those incoming students who show great academic promise or who can contribute to the College's diversity.

To apply for assistance, students must submit the Financial Aid PROFILE of the College Scholarship Service and the Free Application for Federal Student Aid (FAFSA).

Faculty

Of Oberlin's 339 faculty members, 253 teach in the College of Arts and Sciences and 86 teach in the Conservatory of Music. They are eminently qualified for their positions with more than 95 percent having earned doctoral or terminal degrees in their field, many from the world's finest graduate institutions. The faculty-student ratio is 12:1 in the College and 8:1 in the Conservatory.

Student Government

By serving on Oberlin's Student Senate and in other ways, Oberlin College students have the opportunity to influence College policy on academic and student-life issues. Student representatives sit on nearly every faculty committee, and allocation of the student activity fee is determined by a committee composed solely of students.

Admission Requirements

Admission to both the College of Arts and Sciences and the Conservatory of Music is highly selective. Candidates for admission must submit the results of the SAT I or ACT. The College also recommends that three SAT II Subject Tests be taken. For the class of 2000, the median SAT I scores were 670 verbal and 640 math. Of those students who attend high schools that rank their students, 59 percent were in the top tenth of their high school class and 79 percent were in the top fifth. For admission to the Conservatory of Music, the most important factor is the performance audition, or in the case of composition and electronic and computer music applicants, the compositions, tapes, and supporting materials submitted.

Application and Information

For more information or to request an application students should write to:

Office of Admissions, College of Arts and Sciences
Oberlin College
Oberlin, Ohio 44074

Telephone: 440-775-8411
             800-622-OBIE (toll-free)
E-mail: college.admissions@oberlin.edu

Office of Admissions, Conservatory of Music
Oberlin College
Oberlin, Ohio 44074

Telephone: 440-775-8413
E-mail: conservatory.admissions@oberlin.edu
World Wide Web: http://www.oberlin.edu

OGLETHORPE UNIVERSITY
ATLANTA, GEORGIA

The University

Standing as a landmark in north Atlanta since the beginning of this century, Oglethorpe University is located on 118 acres of unquestionable beauty. Only 10 miles from the heart of downtown Atlanta, the campus, with its classic neo-Gothic architecture, maintains an Old World charm. The current undergraduate enrollment is about 1,230 men and women. Approximately two thirds of the full-time students live on campus in the seven residence halls. The ethnic and religious backgrounds of the student body are diverse; students come to Oglethorpe from thirty-two states and about thirty countries.

Numerous activities are offered on campus, such as concerts, exhibits, and social affairs. The University has a student center, six tennis courts, a Reslite track, a swimming pool, an intramural field, and a field house with seating for 2,000. There is an extensive intramural program. Intercollegiate sports are offered for men in baseball, basketball, cross-country, golf, soccer, tennis, and track and field and for women in basketball, cross-country, golf, soccer, tennis, track and field, and volleyball.

There are many avenues for development of leadership potential, including a new Urban Leadership Certificate Program. Omicron Delta Kappa, a national leadership organization, recognizes outstanding leadership on campus. Alpha Phi Omega, a national service fraternity that is open to both men and women, is one of Oglethorpe's largest organizations; its purpose is to serve the school, the community, and the nation. Alpha Phi Omega emphasizes service, friendship, and leadership as qualifications for membership. Students also have excellent opportunities to develop their extracurricular interests. More than fifty clubs and organizations are open to students, including fraternities and sororities, honor societies, academic societies, and special interest groups. One of the distinctive features of Oglethorpe is the interest and support the University gives to such activities. This is in keeping with the goals of the institution, which are to stimulate personal as well as intellectual growth and development.

Location

Oglethorpe maintains a good rapport with the surrounding neighborhood. Students enjoy the many benefits of being on a small suburban campus near a large metropolitan cultural center. Metropolitan Atlanta's population is more than 3 million, and the community offers all the entertainment advantages of a large city, including professional athletics, concerts by well-known artists, movie theaters, and restaurants. Cultural centers and recreational facilities are easily accessible, and good transportation is available.

Majors and Degrees

Oglethorpe University confers the Bachelor of Arts (B.A.) and Bachelor of Science (B.S.) degrees. Majors leading to the B.A. are offered in American studies, art, business administration and behavioral science, communications, economics, education (early childhood, middle grades, and secondary), English, French, history, individually planned major, international studies, philosophy, political studies, psychology, sociology, sociology–social work, and Spanish. Majors leading to the B.S. are accounting, biology, business administration, business administration and computer science, chemistry, economics, mathematics, mathematics/computer science, and physics. Preprofessional programs are offered in dentistry, law, medicine, optometry, and pharmacy. Dual-degree programs are offered in art in conjunction with Atlanta College of Art and in engineering in cooperation with Georgia Institute of Technology, Auburn University, the University of Southern California, and the University of Florida.

Academic Program

Each new student is assigned a faculty adviser, who is responsible for assisting the student with academic and many other matters. Close relationships between students and teachers are the heart of Oglethorpe's educational approach. Fresh Focus, a seminar for freshmen, provides a way for new students to get to know each other and to explore academic programs, career interests, and academic resources.

The program for undergraduates is viewed as a process of personal and intellectual development. The liberal arts and sciences provide the forum for increasing competence in reading, writing, speaking, reasoning, and the fundamental fields of knowledge, the arts and sciences. A core curriculum constitutes about 25 percent of each student's requirements. The core encourages students to reflect upon and discuss matters fundamental to understanding who they are and what they ought to be. This includes how they understand themselves as individuals and as members of society, how the study of the past informs a sense of who they are as human beings, and the ways in which the practice of science informs them on the physical and biological processes influencing human nature. Readings are based on primary sources rather than textbooks. Outstanding internship opportunities are available to students; sites include CNN, the Centers for Disease Control and Prevention, major accounting firms and corporations, and state government.

Off-Campus Arrangements

Study-abroad programs in Europe, Moscow, South America, Mexico, and Asia award academic credit. The University also offers excellent internship programs with various scientific, government, and business organizations. Students may earn a maximum of 15 semester hours of credit through these programs.

Academic Facilities

The Philip Weltner Library was dedicated in 1992. The 56,000-square-foot facility houses an art museum, a 24-hour study area, and a viewing room with state-of-the-art equipment. Current library holdings include more than 150,000 book holdings, an extensive collection of movies on videodisc, the *New York Times* on microfilm, and more than 800 periodicals. Oglethorpe participates in a library sharing program with several other colleges and universities in the Atlanta area. Several computer laboratories are available for student use. Through GALILEO, students have online access to any college library in Georgia.

Costs

The comprehensive fee for 2000–01 is about $24,810. This fee includes $18,150 for tuition, $5560 for room and board, and a student activity fee of $100. An additional $1800 should be sufficient for books, supplies, and personal expenses.

Financial Aid

The University offers aid from various federal programs, including the Federal Perkins Loan, Federal PLUS loan, Federal Pell Grant, Federal Supplemental Educational Opportunity Grant, and Federal Work-Study programs. Applications for these funds should be received by March 1. The James Edward Oglethorpe Award for freshmen is a full tuition, room, and board program. The University also offers the Oglethorpe Scholar Awards for outstanding students. These scholarships, which award up to $12,000 per year, are based on scholastic performance, participation in activities, qualities of leadership and citizenship, and potential for success. Institutional need-based awards and campus employment are other possibilities. Annual renewal of awards is based on a student's cumulative average and participation in activities. Approximately 85 percent of the University's students receive some type of assistance.

Faculty

Oglethorpe has an outstanding faculty; 96 percent of the members hold doctoral or other terminal degrees, many from the finest graduate schools in the country. The student-faculty ratio is 13:1, and no graduate assistants serve as undergraduate instructors. Although Oglethorpe is primarily a teaching institution, several faculty members are engaged in various research projects. Faculty members, however, are selected on the basis of their ability to teach and their interest in student development. Professors are available for student counseling and generally take an active role in campus activities.

Student Government

Undergraduate life at Oglethorpe University is, in a large sense, that of a democratic community; student government is mainly self-government. The Oglethorpe Student Association, consisting of a president, a vice president, a secretary and treasurer, a parliamentarian, and the presidents of the four classes, is the organization that guides and governs student life.

Admission Requirements

Throughout its history, Oglethorpe has welcomed students from all sections of the country as well as from abroad. Admission to the University is selective. It is the policy of the Admission Committee to accept those students who present the strongest evidence of purpose, maturity, scholastic ability, and potential for success. In making these judgments, the committee considers the applicant's high school program and grades, high school rank if available, SAT I or ACT scores, a personal essay, and the recommendations of counselors and teachers. Students entering Oglethorpe should have completed a minimum of 15 academic units, including 4 units of English, 2 of mathematics, 2 of science, and 2 of social studies; 2 units of language are recommended.

The SAT I range of the middle 50 percent of accepted applicants in 1998 was 1130–1320. The median ACT composite was 27. Candidates for regular decision admission may submit their applications at any time, although the University accepts applicants after March 1 only as space is available. Regular decision applicants receive admission decision letters on or about February 1, and afterward on a rolling basis. Early decision applicants must apply by November 30, and they are notified of the admission decision on or about December 15. Priority decision candidates must apply by December 30 and are notified of the decision on or by January 15. Transfer applicants and students applying for joint enrollment are welcome.

Application and Information

Additional information about Oglethorpe may be obtained by contacting:

Director of Admission
Oglethorpe University
4484 Peachtree Road, NE
Atlanta, Georgia 30319
Telephone: 404-364-8307
 404-261-1441 Ext. 8307
E-mail: admission@oglethorpe.edu
World Wide Web: http://www.oglethorpe.edu

Oglethorpe's history, dating back to 1835, is reflected in its architecture.

OHIO DOMINICAN COLLEGE
COLUMBUS, OHIO

The College

Ohio Dominican College, a private, Catholic liberal arts college, was founded in 1911 as the College of Saint Mary of the Springs. The name was changed in 1968 to reflect the new coeducational composition of the student body. Ohio Dominican offers a fully accredited, high-quality, career-oriented education in a distinctive setting. The campus covers 62 beautifully wooded acres, and its architectural style mixes the charm of older buildings with the technology of contemporary buildings.

Nearly 2,000 students attend Ohio Dominican's day and weekend college programs. Students come from across the nation and from more than thirty countries, creating an enriching cultural experience on campus. One third of the students live in the two spacious and modern residence halls.

Ohio Dominican is one of only a small number of small colleges in the nation to offer its students "an invitation to tomorrow," preparation for life and work in the twenty-first century. The focus is on the learner, not the teacher, and the competencies students will need at work and at home. State-of-the-art technology in a student-center environment opens the door to learning collaboration among students, with instructors, and in combination with resources across the globe through the Internet.

A full calendar of academic, cultural, and social events is provided for student enjoyment. The student newspaper, Circle K, Black Student Union, Campus Ministry, College Choir, cheerleaders, American International Membership, and Theatrical Society are just a few of the many organizations students can join. The College offers a full range of sports opportunities. Ohio Dominican is a member of the Mid-Ohio Conference of the NAIA. The College offers intercollegiate basketball, softball, soccer, tennis, and volleyball for women and baseball, basketball, soccer, and tennis for men. Men's volleyball is played as a club sport. Intramural programs include basketball, bowling, golf, skiing, tennis, and volleyball.

Ohio Dominican's Counseling and Career Information Center helps students plan for careers and provides valuable resources for finding jobs after graduation. The College provides the computer system SIGI+ for student use in considering career options.

Location

Ohio Dominican is located in a residential section of Columbus, just minutes from downtown. The capital of the state of Ohio, Columbus is one of the fastest-growing cities in the nation and offers a wide variety of cultural opportunities, such as theater, the Columbus Museum of Art, the Ohio Historical Society, Ballet Met, and the world's largest state fair. In addition, students may choose from many internship options in this center of business and industry. Located less than 5 minutes from Port Columbus Airport, Ohio Dominican is also easily accessible from Columbus's major highways.

Majors and Degrees

Ohio Dominican confers bachelor's degrees in accounting, art, biology, business administration, chemistry, communication arts, computer science, criminal justice, cross-disciplinary studies, economics, early childhood education, English language and literature, history, information systems, international business, intervention specialist, library and information systems, mathematics, middle childhood education, philosophy, political science, political science with environmental issues concentration, psychology, public relations, school library media services, social science, social work, sociology, Spanish, teaching English to speakers of other languages, theology, and visual communication.

Associate degrees are offered in chemistry, cross-disciplinary studies, gerontology, legal studies, liberal studies, library services, and theology.

Students may receive secondary teaching certification in many subject areas and special teaching certification in the visual arts or in educational media.

Preprofessional programs in dentistry, law, and medicine are also available.

Academic Program

Ohio Dominican College combines the ideals of a liberal arts education with the best possible preparation for a career. The nationally acclaimed Humanities Program is part of every student's academic study at Ohio Dominican. This combination of courses is designed to help students think critically and communicate more clearly and persuasively. In addition to the liberal arts courses required for graduation, students are encouraged to participate in internship and study-abroad programs. These provide enriching off-campus experiences that can be very beneficial to future career plans. A minimum of 124 semester credits is required for graduation with a bachelor's degree from Ohio Dominican.

The honors program provides students with the opportunity to graduate with distinction through a combination of seminars, honors-designated course work, and senior research projects.

The academic calendar consists of two 16-week semesters; the year begins in early September and ends in early May. Summer courses are also offered.

Students come from all over the world to Ohio Dominican for its associate and bachelor's degree programs, special short-term study programs (such as the Pre-MBA Program), and intensive English language training. The English as a second language (ESL) program has been an integral part of the campus community for more than twenty-five years. Courses in it are offered year-round. New international students take part in special orientation programming.

Academic Facilities

Academic excellence is the result of an outstanding faculty working with students in modern facilities. Ohio Dominican provides exceptional facilities to support the high quality of a student's education. The Spangler Learning Center houses the Spangler Library, the Multimedia Center, the Academic Center, and the Computing Services Department. Spangler Library houses 154,000 volumes, as well as thirteen CD-ROMs and several online databases. The Multimedia Center houses scanners, laminators, letter makers, and many more multimedia technologies. The Science Center provides a superior facility for teaching and hands-on experience using the latest technology and equipment. The Academic Center offers students a wide variety of academic assistance opportunities, including workshops and individual tutoring. Computing Services is responsible for the campus network, including Microsoft Professional Office, full Internet access, e-mail, and other software packages. Along with Computing Services, the Spangler Learning Center houses two state-of-the-art computer classrooms, each of which includes twenty-five networked computer stations. In addition, there are more than fifty networked computer terminals available to students throughout the building.

Costs

Tuition at Ohio Dominican is modest in comparison with other private colleges. Tuition for the 1999–2000 academic year was $10,250. Room and board were $5070, and books and supplies averaged $650.

Financial Aid

Ohio Dominican is committed to making a high-quality education affordable. More than 85 percent of Ohio Dominican's full-time students receive some form of financial assistance. In addition to need-based aid, students may receive academic and athletics scholarships solely on the basis of ability. Ohio residents are eligible for the Ohio Student Choice Grant as well. Aid based on financial need may include funds from the Federal Pell Grant, Ohio Instructional Grant, Federal Supplemental Educational Opportunity Grant, Ohio Dominican College Grant, Federal Work-Study, Federal Perkins Loan, and Federal Stafford Student Loan programs. To be considered for any form of aid, a student must complete the Free Application for Federal Student Aid (FAFSA) provided by the College Scholarship Service.

Faculty

Fifty-four full-time and 61 part-time professors compose Ohio Dominican's faculty. The student-faculty ratio is 16:1. About 80 percent of the full-time faculty members hold a terminal degree or a doctorate, and no courses are taught by teaching assistants. Ohio Dominican is committed to high-quality teaching. Sabbaticals ensure that teaching faculty members remain experts in their academic field. The faculty members believe that the personal attention they give to their students is a valuable benefit of study at Ohio Dominican College.

Student Government

Student leadership and involvement are fostered through the College Council. In this organization, students, faculty members, and administrators join together to make the decisions that have an impact on student life at Ohio Dominican. Each spring, campuswide elections determine who will be on this council to represent the student classes and organizations. Students are also elected to sit on various governing committees of the College. These committees include the Admissions, Student Affairs, Budget, Athletic Advisory, and Planning committees. Ohio Dominican believes in the importance of the students' involvement in all aspects of their college life.

Admission Requirements

To be considered for admission to Ohio Dominican College, students must complete an application for admission, for which there is no fee. A high school transcript, ACT or SAT I scores, and an interview (for in-state applicants) are required.

A significant number of students transfer to Ohio Dominican each year. Along with official transcripts from all colleges previously attended, transfer students must submit a high school transcript if they have completed fewer than 30 semester credits of college work.

Students may be considered for admission following the completion of their junior year of high school.

The campus visit is an important part of the application process. Students are encouraged to tour the campus, meet with faculty members and students, talk to coaches, and visit classes, in addition to meeting with an admission counselor.

International applicants must submit the International Student Application Form, the Declaration and Certification of Finances form with supporting documentation, transcripts or certified true copies of original transcripts for all academic preparation beyond age 15, and a $25 application fee. No TOEFL score is required for admission to the ESL program; students are placed in it upon arrival through testing.

Application and Information

Ohio Dominican uses a rolling admission process whereby students are notified of the admission decision as soon as their application is complete.

For additional information, students should contact:

Director of Admissions
Ohio Dominican College
1216 Sunbury Road
Columbus, Ohio 43219-2099
Telephone: 614-251-4500
          800-955-OHIO (toll-free)
E-mail: admissions@odc.edu
World Wide Web: http://www.odc.edu

Commencement ceremonies at Ohio Dominican College.

OHIO NORTHERN UNIVERSITY
ADA, OHIO

The University

Founded in 1871, Ohio Northern University offers a dynamic learning environment, with its four undergraduate colleges, the College of Law, and a combination of professional and liberal arts programs. The University is related to the United Methodist Church and is committed to promoting spiritual as well as intellectual values. With a student population of more than 3,000, ONU is small enough to provide a personalized atmosphere but large enough to attract students with many different educational goals. Students attending Ohio Northern are presented with many opportunities to explore a wide range of activities—academic, social, spiritual, and physical.

Residence hall living is considered to be an integral part of the educational program, and the residence halls' professional staff, facilities, and programs contribute to students' personal development. The residence halls serve as key places for study sessions and student activities. There are ten residence halls on campus. The dining hall is located in the student union. There are also eight national fraternities and four national sororities, as well as thirty-two honorary societies that recognize scholastic achievement or service.

The University is a member of the Ohio Athletic Conference and fields intercollegiate teams in men's baseball, basketball, cross-country, football, golf, indoor and outdoor track, soccer, swimming and diving, tennis, and wrestling and in women's basketball, cross-country, fast-pitch softball, golf, indoor and outdoor track, soccer, swimming and diving, tennis, and volleyball.

Location

Surrounding the campus is the town of Ada, a small, quiet, friendly community of 5,000 residents. Located in northwestern Ohio, Ohio Northern and Ada are easily accessible by major highways. Students have convenient access to Columbus, Dayton, and Toledo while enjoying the hospitality and comfort of Ada's hometown atmosphere.

Majors and Degrees

Ohio Northern University offers the degrees of Doctor of Pharmacy (Pharm.D.), Bachelor of Arts, Bachelor of Fine Arts, Bachelor of Music, and Bachelor of Science. Majors are offered in accounting, art (graphic design and studio arts), athletic training, biochemistry, biology, chemistry, civil engineering, communication arts (broadcasting and electronic media, musical theater, professional and organizational communication, public relations, and theater), computer engineering, computer science, criminal justice, early childhood education, electrical engineering, English creative writing, English language arts, English literature, English professional writing, environmental studies, French, health education, history, international business and economics, international studies, journalism, management, mathematics, mathematics/statistics, mechanical engineering, medical technology, medicinal chemistry, middle childhood education, molecular biology, music, music composition, music education, music performance, music with elective studies in business, pharmacy, philosophy, philosophy/religion, physical education, physics, political science, psychology, religion, social studies, sociology, Spanish, sport management, technology, and wellness.

Special programs are available in predentistry, prelaw, premedicine, pre–occupational therapy, pre–physical therapy, pre–physician's assistant studies, preseminary, and pre–veterinary medicine. Interdisciplinary degree programs are available in arts/engineering and arts/pharmacy. Additional programs are offered in athletics coaching, athletics training, driver's education, and reading validation. Teacher licensure programs are offered at the early childhood, middle childhood, and adolescent levels in thirty-two program areas.

Academic Program

In the College of Arts and Sciences, the first two years of study are usually devoted to a program of general education. Work in a major is usually taken at the advanced level during the junior and senior years. To graduate with a Bachelor of Arts, Bachelor of Fine Arts, or Bachelor of Science degree, students are required to complete a minimum of 182 quarter hours, which includes appropriate general education courses, completion of an appropriate major, and an accumulative grade point average of at least 2.0. To graduate with a Bachelor of Music degree, students are required to complete a minimum of 182 quarter hours for the concentration in music performance or the concentration in music education. To fulfill the minimum residence requirements, all students must spend the last three quarters of their program in residence and complete 45 quarter hours with at least 90 quality points in courses elected mainly from junior- and senior-level courses. The Bachelor of Science in medical technology has different requirements.

In the College of Business Administration, the first two years of study are devoted to general education courses plus introductory courses in several of the business disciplines. To graduate, a student must satisfactorily complete a minimum of 182 quarter hours of appropriate course work for the specific major(s) and maintain at least a 2.0 grade point average. Students in all three majors are encouraged to participate in an internship program in either the junior or senior year.

The College of Engineering offers degrees in civil engineering, computer engineering, electrical engineering, and mechanical engineering. The courses for the first academic year are essentially the same for each degree program, offering students an easy track to move from one program to another if they are initially uncertain which disciplines they prefer to study. Students are required to maintain a minimum cumulative grade point average of 2.0 as well as a minimum GPA of 2.0 computed for all engineering, math, and science courses. An optional five-year co-op program is available for students in each engineering program provided they maintain a minimum 2.5 GPA. A minor in computer science and options in environmental studies and business administration are available to engineering students provided they maintain at least a 2.5 GPA.

The College of Pharmacy offers the six-year Doctor of Pharmacy program, and admission may be granted to students directly out of their high school programs. After three years of course work in the physical sciences, social sciences, humanities, and professional areas, students spend two years studying the practice of pharmacy through a patient-care-oriented curriculum that utilizes body system and disease-based modules as well as modules with an administrative and practice-based focus. The last year is experiential and takes place in a variety of clinical settings throughout the country. The College also offers a nontraditional Doctor of Pharmacy program for pharmacists holding the B.S. degree. The didactic portion of this curriculum is Internet based. Resident students have available a strong undergraduate research program and may pursue minors or dual majors in biochemistry and medicinal chemistry.

The University offers a special prelaw program, which guarantees Ohio Northern graduates admission to the Pettit College of Law if they complete the specially designed program with a grade point average of at least 3.2 in any of ONU's undergraduate colleges.

Off-Campus Arrangements

Many majors may take part in study-abroad programs developed in consultation with faculty members. Field experiences and internships are available in most majors. Externships are required of all pharmacy majors and place students in retail and clinical experiences. Teacher licensure requires one quarter of primary or secondary classroom teaching experience under the supervision of practicing teachers. All of these off-campus learning experiences carry credit.

Academic Facilities

ONU's Heterick Memorial Library and the Taggart Law Library provide information resources and services to support course offerings and foster independent study. In addition to books and periodicals, the library houses microforms, CD-ROM services, state and federal documents, records, audiotapes, videocassette tapes, films, filmstrips, and slides. Facilities include individual study carrels, study rooms, microform reading and printing equipment, copy services, audiovisual equipment, personal computers, and access to the University's computer network. An online catalog system, compact disc indexing, and abstract services are readily available in the library and through the campus computer network.

The Freed Center for the Performing Arts features a 550-seat theater/concert hall, a 120-seat studio theater, and television and radio production facilities. WONB-FM is the commercial-free 3,000-watt voice of ONU. The facility accommodates the entire Communication Arts Department in state-of-the-art style.

In support of the administrative computing requirements of the campus, the University provides a heterogeneous environment of computer equipment, primarily an Aviion 8500, integrated via local area networks attached to a campuswide fiber-optic backbone. The campus network is connected to the Ohio Academic Resources Network (OARnet). OARnet provides the University with contact to other research and academic institutions around the world.

An IBM RISC System/6000, located in the Biggs Engineering Building, runs the AIX (UNIX) operating system. This computer provides Internet services to the campus as well as general access to the UNIX environment. Each college has a local area network linked to the campus network that provides both DOS and Apple file services.

Costs

Charges for the 1999–2000 year were $25,680 for tuition, room, and board for the Colleges of Arts and Sciences and Business Administration, $28,260 for the College of Pharmacy, and $27,090 for the College of Engineering. The cost of books and supplies was approximately $600 per year.

Financial Aid

Ohio Northern University makes every effort to ensure that no qualified applicant is denied admission because of inability to pay the total cost. More than 90 percent of the student body receive some type of financial assistance. To be considered for financial assistance, the student should submit the FAFSA and the ONU financial aid application to the University along with the admission application. Both merit and need-based aid are available to students.

Faculty

Students are served by 161 full-time and 58 part-time faculty members whose full responsibilities are to the undergraduate students. The primary interest of the faculty is teaching, although research as an adjunct to good teaching is pursued by many faculty members in order to maintain current professional awareness. Most of the faculty members live near the campus and participate in some area of cocurricular student activities. Emphasis is placed on careful advising of students in academic and personal matters. The student-faculty ratio is 13:1.

Student Government

The Student Senate provides self-government in many areas of student life and seeks to further ideals of character and service to the University. Officers of the Student Senate are elected by the students, and the group meets on a weekly basis. The Student Senate serves as the official representative group of the student body to the University administration and agencies in matters pertaining to the student body.

Admission Requirements

High school students applying for admission to the University should present an official transcript indicating at least 16 total units, including work in the academic areas indicated by each college, as follows: College of Arts and Sciences, 12 units—4 in English, 2 in mathematics (algebra and geometry), and 6 in history, social studies, language, or natural science or any combination thereof; College of Business Administration, 13 units—4 in English, 3 in mathematics (including algebra and geometry), and 6 in history, social studies, language, or natural sciences; College of Engineering, 10 units—4 in English, 4 in mathematics (algebra I and II, geometry, and at least ½ unit in trigonometry or its equivalent), and 2 in science (1 in physics and preferably 1 in chemistry); and College of Pharmacy, 11 units—4 in English, 4 in mathematics (algebra I and II, geometry, and trigonometry or precalculus), and 3 in science (including biology, chemistry, and physics).

Applicants are also required to submit scores on the ACT of American College Testing. (Scores on the SAT I of the College Board may be substituted for the ACT.) An interview on campus is recommended.

Application and Information

Completed applications should be sent along with a $30 nonrefundable application fee. It is recommended that students apply for admission at the end of their junior year in high school or early in the senior year. The University operates on the rolling admission plan, and applications are processed immediately upon receipt of all necessary information. Requests for catalogs, application forms, or additional information should be directed to:

Dean of Admissions
Ohio Northern University
Ada, Ohio 45810

Telephone: 419-772-2260
Fax: 419-772-2313
E-mail: admissions-ug@onu.edu
World Wide Web: http://www.onu.edu

Freed Center for the Performing Arts.

OHIO UNIVERSITY
ATHENS, OHIO

The University

Chartered in 1804, Ohio University symbolizes America's early commitment to higher education. Its historic campus provides a setting matched by only a handful of other universities in the country. Students choose Ohio University mainly because of its academic strength, but the beautiful setting and college-town atmosphere are also factors in their decision. About 19,241 students (16,332 at the undergraduate level and 2,909 at the graduate level) study at Ohio University, and visitors frequently comment that it does not seem as large as they expected it would.

Ohio University is a residential campus. Forty-two percent of its undergraduates live in residence halls; however, most upperclass students live off-campus within walking or biking distance. On-campus living emphasizes student interaction. Eighty-five percent of the students are Ohio residents, while 8 percent are from out of state, and 7 percent are international students from approximately 100 countries.

Because the University is located in a small town, most extracurricular activities take place on campus. More than 335 student organizations are registered with the University, and each student tends to get involved in at least one group. About 36 percent of the students take part in intramural sports, and University-sponsored plays, art exhibits, and recitals are quite popular. Sororities and fraternities are the choice of about 15 percent of the student body. There are four dining halls as well as a snack bar and convenience store.

Campus recreational facilities include an indoor Olympic-size pool, an ice rink, a fitness center, lighted intramural fields, indoor and outdoor tennis courts, a nine-hole golf course, and a jogging/bicycling path that partially encircles the campus. A $26-million student recreation center opened in 1996.

Location

Ohio University is the central focus of Athens, Ohio, a city of about 21,000, located approximately 75 miles southeast of Columbus, the state capital. Athens is a classic college town; the community and the University mesh together so well that it is difficult to figure out where the campus ends and the city begins.

Athens' location in the foothills of the Appalachian Mountains provides endless recreational opportunities at nearby state parks, forests, and lakes for those who enjoy the outdoors.

Majors and Degrees

Ohio University awards the degrees of Bachelor of Arts or Bachelor of Science in African-American studies, airway science, biological sciences, chemistry, classical languages, communication, computer science, economics, education, engineering (chemical, civil, computer science, electrical, industrial and systems, and mechanical), English, environmental and plant biology, environmental studies, geography, geological sciences, health science, hearing and speech science, history, human and consumer sciences, industrial technology, international studies, journalism, linguistics, mathematics, modern languages, nursing, philosophy, physics, political science, psychology, social work, sociology, and sports sciences.

The Bachelor of Business Administration is offered in accounting, finance, management systems, and marketing. The Bachelor of Fine Arts degree is awarded in art, dance, theater, and visual communication. The Bachelor of Music degree is offered through the School of Music.

Minors are offered in nearly all academic areas.

Academic Program

All undergraduate students at Ohio University must complete a core curriculum structured in three tiers. Tier One consists of English composition and mathematics competency-based courses as well as a junior-level English course. Tier Two is made up of 30 quarter hours of work selected from five areas: applied sciences, social sciences, natural sciences, humanities, and Third World cultures. Taken during the senior year, Tier Three is a synthesis course that combines learning from different disciplines. All bachelor's degree programs at Ohio University require 192 quarter hours for graduation.

The Honors Tutorial College, the University's excellent honors program, gives students the chance to learn in tutorial settings. The program is limited to 40 freshmen each year, and many honors students earn their degree in three years.

Both Army and Air Force ROTC programs are offered.

Academic Facilities

The Vernon R. Alden Library, centrally located on the Ohio University campus, contains more than 2.1 million bound volumes, three computer labs, and several special collections, including archives, a children's collection, and government documents, and subscribes to 15,032 periodicals.

Computer labs can be found in most academic buildings, and the University has recently renovated its main campus computer center. Computers were placed in all freshman residence hall rooms in fall 1999. By the end of fall quarter 2000, all residence hall rooms will be equipped with computers and printers. The College of Business completed an $8-million renovation in 1995.

Presentations by guest speakers sponsored through the Kennedy Lecture Series and dozens of other events during the year take place in the newly renovated 2,500-seat Templeton-Blackburn Memorial Auditorium. The University's theater facilities were completely renovated in 1991, and well-equipped radio and television stations support the top-notch journalism and telecommunication programs.

Costs

In 1999–2000, tuition and fees for Ohio residents were $4800 for the year; nonresident tuition was $10,284. Room rates per quarter for a single were $1105; a double, $899; a triple, $742; and a quad, $840. Per-quarter board costs were $929 for twenty meals per week, $870 for fourteen meals per week, and $631 for seven meals per week. Books and supplies were estimated at $260 for each quarter.

Financial Aid

Ohio University awards financial aid from federally funded and state-funded programs as well as from privately funded sources. All types of aid fall within two categories: need-based and merit-based assistance. Awards are made based on demonstration of financial need, special merit, or both. Seventy-two percent of Ohio University's undergraduate students receive some form of financial assistance.

The University requires all students applying for need-based assistance to complete the Free Application for Federal Student Aid (FAFSA).

Freshman scholarships range in value from $750 to full tuition. Scholarships for upperclass students are offered as well. Generally, upperclass students with a grade point average of at least 3.4 are eligible to apply for scholarship assistance.

Faculty

Ohio University employs 887 full-time faculty members, 93 percent of whom have earned a Ph.D. or a terminal degree. Ninety-two percent of courses at the undergraduate level are taught by a faculty member; the remainder are led by graduate assistant instructors. Most faculty members conduct research and stay active in their field. They also serve undergraduates as advisers to aid in course selection and to offer career assistance.

Student Government

The student body of Ohio University tends to be both active and forward-thinking. Student government exists on many levels, from each residence hall up to the campuswide student senate. During the last decade, the student government and the University's administration have enjoyed a very positive working relationship.

Admission Requirements

Admission to Ohio University is selective. Freshman applicants are required to submit a completed application, academic transcripts, and scores from either the ACT or the SAT. In determining a student's eligibility for acceptance, the Office of Admissions considers class rank, strength of curriculum, grade point average, and ACT or SAT scores. Applicants have the option of providing more information through a written essay. Admission interviews are not part of the application process, and no preference is given to in-state students. Some programs of study enforce greater admission selectivity.

Ohio University is committed to providing special consideration for students from historically underrepresented groups and students with special talents or abilities.

Transfer applicants must have earned at least 20 semester credit hours, or 30 quarter credit hours, with a minimum grade point average of 2.5 from an accredited institution to be eligible to transfer. Some programs are more selective and require additional credit hours earned and/or a higher minimum grade point average.

Application and Information

The deadline for admission to the fall term for freshman applicants is February 1; for transfer students entering in the fall, it is May 15. Some programs reserve the right to close admission before the deadline.

Admission decisions are made on a rolling basis beginning in October and continue until all applications received by the deadline have been processed. All applicants, including those who apply electronically, are notified of admission status within four weeks after receipt of all application materials.

Inquiries should be made to:

Office of Admissions
Ohio University
Chubb Hall 120
Athens, Ohio 45701-2979
Telephone: 740-593-4100
Fax: 740-593-0560
E-mail: uadmiss1@ohiou.edu
World Wide Web: http://www.ohiou.edu/

OHIO WESLEYAN UNIVERSITY
DELAWARE, OHIO

The University

An unusual synthesis of liberal arts learning and preprofessional preparation has set Ohio Wesleyan University apart. It is one of the country's five independent four-year colleges to rank among the top twenty in both the number of graduates earning Ph.D.'s and the number who are U.S. business leaders. Founded by the United Methodist Church in 1842, the University is strongly committed to developing the service ethic in students, to fusing theory with its practical applications, and to confronting specific issues of long-range public importance.

Undergraduate enrollment is about 1,850 men and women. Students come to Ohio Wesleyan from forty-two states and fifty-eight countries, and most reside on the attractive 200-acre campus. OWU ranks sixth in the nation (among schools in its class) in the proportion of students with international origins. Housing options include six large residence halls with special interest corridors; a number of smaller special interest units, such as the Tree House and the Peace and Justice House; and eleven fraternity houses. The five sorority houses are nonresidential.

There is a wide range of cocurricular activities. Students initiate discussion groups, service projects, and intramural athletics. Other activities include a fully independent student newspaper; cultural- and ethnic-interest groups such as the Student Union on Black Awareness and the Christian Fellowship; crisis intervention work; the College Republicans and Young Democrats; and prelaw and premed clubs. In the course of a year, students may enjoy more than 100 concerts, plays, dance programs, films, exhibits, and timely speakers. The Theatre and Dance Department stages five major productions and much additional studio work each year, while the Music Department sponsors seven large groups and other small ensembles. An impressive $12-million Campus Center is the hub of cocurricular life on campus.

There are twenty-one varsity athletic teams—ten for men, ten for women, and a coed sailing team. The teams that often have national ranking in NCAA Division III are the men's teams in baseball, golf, lacrosse, soccer, and tennis and the women's cross-country, field hockey, soccer, swimming, and track teams. OWU captured the 1998 NCAA Division III national men's soccer title. In recent years, individual all-Americans have been named in these sports and in football and men's cross-country and track. Intramural programs are extensive, and all students have access to racquet sports, swimming, and weight-lifting facilities in the modern Branch Rickey Physical Education Center. Off-campus opportunities for backpacking, boating, camping, golf, skiing, and swimming are abundant.

Location

Delaware combines the small-town pace and maple-lined streets of the county seat (population 23,000) with easy access to the state capital, Columbus, the sixteenth-largest city in America. Thirty minutes south of the campus, Columbus provides rich internship opportunities, international research centers, fine dining and shopping, and cultural events that complement campus life. Delaware, founded in 1808, retains a stately, post-Colonial charm in many of its sections. Because the campus is in the town, students find a degree of solitude but not a sense of isolation. About half of the faculty members live a short walk from the campus.

Majors and Degrees

Ohio Wesleyan offers the Bachelor of Arts degree in accounting, astronomy, biological sciences (botany, microbiology, and zoology), chemistry, computer science, economics (including accounting, international business, and management), education (elementary and secondary licensing in seventeen areas), English literature and writing, environmental science, fine arts, French, geography, geology, German, history, humanities-classics, journalism and broadcast journalism, mathematics, music (applied or history/literature), neuroscience, philosophy, physical education, physics, politics and government, psychology, religion, sociology/anthropology, Spanish, and theater and dance. Fifteen interdisciplinary majors include black studies, East Asian studies, environmental studies, international studies, urban studies, and women's studies as well as prelaw and premedicine. Students may also design majors in topical, period, or regional studies.

Two professional degrees are awarded: the Bachelor of Fine Arts in art history, arts education, pre–art therapy, and studio art and the Bachelor of Music in music education, performance, and pre–music therapy. Combined-degree (generally 3-2) programs are offered in engineering, medical technologies, optometry, and physical therapy.

Academic Program

Ohio Wesleyan provides opportunities for students to acquire not only depth in a major area but also knowledge about their cultural past through the insight provided by a broad curriculum. At Ohio Wesleyan, education is placed in a context of values, and students are encouraged to develop the intellectual skills of effective communication, independent and logical thought, and creative problem solving. To these ends, students are required to demonstrate competence in English composition and a foreign language (often through placement testing) and to complete distributional study in the natural and social sciences, the humanities, and the arts. With few exceptions, the major requires the completion of eight to fifteen courses; double majors and minors are recommended. Completion of thirty-four courses is required for graduation.

Advanced placement is available with or without credit. Under the four-year honors program, freshmen may be named Merit Scholars and work individually with faculty mentors on research, directed readings, or original creative work. Upperclass students are also encouraged to participate in independent study. Phi Beta Kappa is one of more than twenty scholastic honorary societies with chapters on campus.

The objectives of an Ohio Wesleyan education are crystallized in the distinctive Sagan National Colloquium, a program focused annually on one issue of compelling public importance, such as Decoding Gender: Rules, Roles and Identity. Through weekly speakers and semester-long seminars, the colloquium stimulates campuswide dialogue and encourages students to integrate knowledge from many different disciplines and apply what is studied to life. Participants should discover not only what they think about the issue but also why they think as they do, as well as how to make important decisions based on their beliefs.

Off-Campus Arrangements

Full-semester internships and apprenticeships, as well as programs of advanced research, are actively developed through most departments. Many are approved by the Great Lakes Colleges Association (GLCA), a highly regarded academic consortium of twelve independent institutions. Programs include the Philadelphia Urban Semester, the GLCA Arts Program in New York, and the Oak Ridge National Laboratory Science Semester. Other cooperative arrangements include the Newberry Library Program, Wesleyan in Washington, and the Drew University United Nations Semester. Research is done locally at the U.S. Department of Agriculture (USDA) Laboratories in Delaware, the nearby Columbus Zoo, and several other sites.

Ohio Wesleyan has been long committed to education for a global society. Consequently, the curriculum has an international perspective, a significant portion of the student body is drawn from other countries, and a wide variety of opportunities are offered overseas. Individual work may be arranged elsewhere, but formal programs are offered in more than twenty countries. These include Ohio Wesleyan's affiliation with the University of Salamanca in Salamanca, Spain, and its program in Strasbourg, France, as well as programs in Africa, China, Colombia, England, India/Nepal, Japan, Russia, and Scotland.

Academic Facilities

The University is engaged in a dynamic fund-raising effort, raising more than $85 million to date for renovations, new buildings, computers, and a state-of-the-art phone system. The Beeghly Library houses 490,000 volumes, one of the largest collections in the country for a private university of Ohio Wesleyan's size. The library's federal documents depository is among the nation's oldest and largest, providing an additional 200,000 reference publications. Beeghly also offers the Online Computer Library Center's most advanced cataloging system. The collection is enhanced by OHIOLINK and CONSORT membership.

The comprehensive academic computing system is accessible to all students 24 hours per day, and all residence hall rooms are wired for network access. There are two main computers: an Alpha 2100 (running the VMS operating system) and an Alpha 3000 (running the UNIX operating system). There are also more than 125 microcomputers in six laboratories across campus as well as a Sun Laboratory with networked Sun SPARC workstations for student use.

Two modern science buildings house an unusually wide variety of state-of-the-art instrumentation, including a scanning electron microscope in Stewart Hall and scanning and transmission electron microscopes, which are co-owned by the USDA Labs. The University has a state-of-the-art Geographic Information Systems Computer Laboratory. Perkins Observatory houses a 32-inch reflector telescope and two smaller instruments. Two University wilderness preserves cover a total of 100 acres. Other special facilities are the multistage Chappelear Drama Center, built in 1972; the recently renovated Sanborn Hall, home to the Music Department; and Gray Chapel/Auditorium, acoustically one of the region's preeminent concert halls. Gray Chapel houses one of the three Klais concert organs in the United States.

Costs

The general fee for 2000–01 is $28,490. This amount covers tuition ($21,880), room ($3330), and board ($3280). Books and personal expenses average $1100. Nominal fees are charged for some studio art courses, off-campus study, private music lessons for students who are not majoring in music, and student teaching.

Financial Aid

Nearly all freshmen who demonstrate need have been awarded an aid package. Packages include grant, loan, and employment assistance from Ohio Wesleyan and the standard federal and state programs (such as the Federal Pell Grant, Federal Stafford Student Loan, Federal Perkins Loan, and Federal Work-Study programs). More than two thirds of the student body receive some form of need-based aid, and another quarter receive merit- or non-need-based aid. More than 75 percent of all aid is provided by grants and scholarships. On the average, students on financial aid at Ohio Wesleyan receive more scholarship and grant assistance, and rely less on loan support, than do students at most other institutions.

Several merit scholarship programs worth as much as $20,940 per year, private loan programs, and flexible payment plans are available without regard to financial need. This year, more than 132 enrolling freshmen received merit awards.

Faculty

The full-time faculty numbers 126, providing a student-faculty ratio of approximately 13:1. All of the full-time faculty members hold the highest degree in their field. Although committed first to teaching and advising, most faculty members maintain active research programs and publish important articles and books. Some members of the faculty are practicing artists whose contributions include the creation and exhibition of original works of art and theater.

Student Government

Students have a significant voice in the government of campus life. The Wesleyan Council on Student Affairs, more than two thirds of whose members are students, formulates basic policy. Students also sit on judicial boards and nine faculty committees and are represented at all meetings of the Board of Trustees.

Admission Requirements

The admission process is competitive. Each application is carefully studied on an individual basis. Although the applicant's academic record is most important, followed closely by teacher and counselor evaluations and SAT I or ACT scores, many other factors are considered, such as evidence of creativity, community service, and leadership. A sixteen-course preparatory program is required. Four units of English and 3 each of mathematics, social studies, science, and foreign language are recommended, but variations of this program are considered. SAT II Subject Tests are not required but may qualify students for advanced placement. Candidates for the B.Mus. degree must audition (tapes are accepted). Early action, early decision, and transfer admission are offered. Campus interviews are strongly recommended but not required. In 1998, approximately 2,060 applications were received; about 1,750 of the applicants gained admission.

Application and Information

Students are urged to complete the application process as early as possible in the senior year of secondary school, especially if they are applying for financial aid. Once complete credentials (application, transcript, recommendations, and SAT I or ACT scores) are received, decisions are made on a rolling basis after January 1. The student's response is required by May 1. The deadline for early action and early decision application is December 1; notification is given within two weeks. After April 1, students are admitted on a space-available, rolling admission basis.

For further information, students should contact:

Office of Admission
Ohio Wesleyan University
Delaware, Ohio 43015

Telephone: 800-922-8953 (toll-free)
Fax: 740-368-3314
E-mail: owuadmit@cc.owu.edu
World Wide Web: http://www.owu.edu

The Hamilton-Williams Campus Center is a magnificent meeting place for the campus community.

OKLAHOMA BAPTIST UNIVERSITY
SHAWNEE, OKLAHOMA

The University

OBU is a distinctively Christian university that emphasizes academic excellence from a liberal arts tradition, equipping leaders committed to serving humanity around the world. Founded in 1910, the University has grown to include five schools and colleges, with a national reputation for quality.

OBU's unique Unified Studies core curriculum is the backbone for a well-rounded liberal arts education. Throughout its existence, the University has maintained an emphasis on high-quality teaching. OBU has highly regarded programs in teacher education, business, ministry training, nursing, premedicine, music, and telecommunication, as well as several other fields. Last fall, *U.S. News & World Report* named OBU one of the top liberal arts colleges in the western United States, the "Best Value," and the "Most Efficient" liberal arts college in the western U.S. A recent national study conducted by Franklin and Marshall College ranked OBU in the top 10 in its category in the number of graduates who have earned doctorates in professional fields of study. OBU has been named to the Templeton Honor Roll for character-building colleges and universities six times. Honors for efficiency, character, quality, and outstanding students make OBU worth a closer look.

The University had an enrollment of 2,098 in fall 1999. Two thirds of the students came from Oklahoma, while the remainder came from thirty-six other states and thirty-eight other countries. More than 80 percent of OBU's students are Baptist. Off-campus courses in Christian studies, offered at twenty-nine locations, serve more than 300 students.

OBU has a growing international program, with a variety of study-abroad options. The University is a leader among Christian colleges in mission and service involvement. Each summer, more than 250 students, faculty members, and staff serve in projects around the world. In addition, more than 300 students are involved in local service projects each year.

With approximately 1,200 students living on the campus, called Bison Hill, OBU maintains a residential environment that includes a variety of on-campus concerts, activities, and varsity and intramural athletic events. There are eleven local social clubs for men and women, active student government and Baptist Collegiate Ministries programs, and more than sixty other academic and special interest organizations on campus.

OBU's Laura Scales Cafeteria and food court offers twenty meals per week. On-campus housing includes three dormitory facilities and two apartment complexes for women students, and one dormitory and two apartment complexes for men students. There are four facilities for married students.

In addition to its baccalaureate programs, OBU offers a master's degree program in marriage and family therapy. A total of 25 graduate students were enrolled in the program during fall 1999.

Nationally competitive in athletics, OBU has compiled eleven top-five finishes in the 1990s. Varsity programs are offered in men's and women's basketball, cross country, indoor and outdoor track and field, and tennis and in men's baseball and women's softball.

Location

OBU is located on the northwest edge of Shawnee, less than 2 miles south of Interstate 40. A growing suburban city, Shawnee has a population of approximately 26,000. Shawnee is 35 miles east of Oklahoma City and 90 miles southwest of Tulsa. The local community offers a variety of recreational, employment, and entertainment opportunities. A regional hub for east central Oklahoma, Shawnee offers a shopping mall, national chain restaurants, and a collection of local businesses and eateries that lend a small-town flavor to an area with urban conveniences. Major industries in the area, including Mobil and TDK, afford students internship opportunities throughout the year. OBU students work in the community through more than a dozen local service programs. Students can take advantage of local events and businesses or be in the major metropolitan area of Oklahoma City in less than 45 minutes. The city offers a collection of dining, theater, concert, sports, shopping, and museum options.

Majors and Degrees

OBU offers nine degree programs through five schools and colleges: the College of Arts and Sciences, the Joe L. Ingram School of Christian Service, the School of Nursing, the Paul Dickinson School of Business, and the Warren M. Angell College of Fine Arts.

The nine baccalaureate degree programs include Bachelor of Arts (B.A.), Bachelor of Humanities (B.H.), Bachelor of Science (B.S.), Bachelor of Science in Education (B.S.E.), Bachelor of Business Administration (B.B.A.), Bachelor of Music (B.M.), Bachelor of Music Education (B.M.E.), Bachelor of Fine Arts (B.F.A.), and Bachelor of Musical Arts (B.M.A.).

OBU's seventy-four fields of study include accounting, applied ministry (children's emphasis), applied ministry (church administration emphasis), applied ministry (educational emphasis), applied ministry (missions), applied ministry (pastoral emphasis), applied ministry (youth emphasis), art, art education (K–12), biology, chemistry, child-care administration, Christian studies, church music, computer information systems, computer science (data management emphasis), computer science (interdisciplinary emphasis), early childhood education, elementary education, English, English education (secondary), exercise and sports science (pre–physical therapy emphasis), exercise and sports science (sports medicine emphasis), family development, family psychology, finance, French, French education (K–12), German, German education (K–12), health and physical education (K–12), health-care administration, history, interdisciplinary, instrumental: wind, string, percussion (instrumental certificate, K–12), international business, interpersonal and public communication, journalism, management, marketing, marriage and family therapy, mathematics, multilingual communication, music, natural science, nursing, organ, organ performance, philosophy, physics, piano, piano performance, political science, psychology, public relations, recreational administration, religion (Bible emphasis), religion (departmental), secondary business education, secondary mathematics education, secondary science education, secondary social sciences education, secondary speech and drama education, social work, sociology, Spanish, Spanish education (K–12), special education (K–12), telecommunication, theater, theory and composition, studio art, voice (vocal certificate, K–12), and voice performance.

Preprofessional study programs are offered for law, medicine, pharmacy, dentistry, and theological studies.

Academic Program

OBU's academic program is known for its unique Unified Studies core curriculum. The Unified Studies concept, first developed by the faculty in 1970, allows students to integrate their course work across varied academic disciplines. The Unified Studies approach is designed to strengthen the student's liberal arts education.

In addition to the core curriculum, students complete a degree core and at least 40 hours in an area of concentration. A total of 128 credit hours is required for completion of a bachelor's degree. Students must pass an English Proficiency Examination and demonstrate microcomputer literacy before graduating.

OBU operates on a 4-1-4 calendar, with a four-week January term offered between fall and spring semesters. Two 4-week summer terms are also available.

The University's Honors Program exists to offer outstanding, highly motivated students an enhancement of the regular curriculum. Students with a high school GPA of 3.5 or higher and ACT scores of 29 or higher or recentered SAT I scores of 1300 and above are encouraged to apply for the Honors Program. Admission is offered to a limited number of entering freshmen. Honors Program students take several designated honors courses and complete two of three "capstone" experiences: a service project, travel and study abroad, or a thesis.

Students may earn up to 32 credit hours through Advanced Standing examinations, College Level Examination Program subject examinations, International Baccalaureate, or CEEB Advanced Placement examinations.

Off-Campus Arrangements

Students are encouraged to pursue international study opportunities during their college experience. OBU participates in an exchange relationship with Xinjiang University in Urumqi, China. Through the program, OBU students study and teach English as a second language at the Chinese university each summer. OBU also participates in a yearlong exchange program with Seinan Gakuin University in Fukuoka, Japan, for students pursuing Asian studies. OBU students also attend Hong Kong Baptist University.

OBU faculty members teach several study-abroad courses during each January term. The courses are taught in England, Europe, Russia, Chile, Brazil, Guyana, and the Pacific Rim.

OBU–Global Options Inc., a nonprofit organization with main offices on the OBU campus, conducts ongoing business and educational programs in Moscow, Russia, and Belo Horizonte, Brazil. OBU is a member of Cooperative Services International, a consortium of Baptist colleges and universities that promotes international study and service opportunities.

Academic Facilities

The Mabee Learning Center, OBU's library, contains more than 300,000 volumes, accessed through a computerized catalog system. The collection includes books, periodicals, microforms, music scores, audio cassettes, compact discs, films, videos and laser discs, CD-ROM materials, and online services.

Several academic facilities have been constructed within the past decade, including the W.P. Wood Science Building, Sarkeys Telecommunication Center, and the Bailey Business Center. Raley Chapel houses outstanding facilities for vocal, piano, organ, and instrumental studies. OBU is the only university in the state with a permanent student-operated planetarium on campus.

The University offers six computer laboratories, which contain approximately 150 computers.

Costs

Tuition and fees in 2000–01 are $9440 for the fall and spring semesters (16 hours per term). Total cost for tuition, fees, room and board is estimated at $12,850, depending on the type of room and board plan the student selects.

Financial Aid

The Office of Student Financial Services helps students in financial planning and locating financial assistance. Merit-based and need-based scholarships range from $500 to full tuition. Athletic and activity scholarships are also available. The University participates in federal and state financial aid programs. The priority deadline for applications for financial assistance is March 1. To apply for aid, institutional, IRS, and FAFSA forms are required. A completed application for admission must be on file before financial assistance applications are considered. Interest-free installment payment plans are also available.

Faculty

All OBU courses are taught by faculty members. The University's long-standing emphasis on teaching has helped it shape a full-time faculty of 119 individuals committed to teaching excellence. Almost 80 percent of OBU's full-time faculty members hold earned doctorates. OBU's 14:1 student-faculty ratio allows faculty members to develop personal relationships with their students, enhancing the liberal arts experience.

Student Government

OBU's Student Government Association takes an active role in addressing campus and community issues. Students enrolled for 6 or more hours are members of the SGA. By serving on University committees and reporting to the OBU Board of Trustees, the SGA fulfills its role as the voice of the student body.

Admission Requirements

Admission to the University is moderately competitive. Students are considered for regular admission to OBU based on these requirements: an ACT composite of at least 20 or recentered SAT I score of at least 950 and a high school GPA of at least 2.5 or class rank in the upper half.

Applicants who do not meet the criteria stated above may be admitted only by action of the Admissions Committee. International students desiring admission are required to forward results of their qualifying examination, including the TOEFL.

The University recommends a college-preparatory high school curriculum that includes 4 years of English; at least 3 years each of mathematics, natural sciences, and social sciences; and 2 years of foreign language study.

The 418 freshmen in fall 1999 had an average high school GPA of 3.67, an average ACT score of 24, and an average SAT I score of 1160.

Application and Information

OBU's rolling admissions policy has a March 15 regular admission deadline. Students, especially those pursuing academic merit-based scholarships or need-based financial aid, are encouraged to apply before February 1 in their senior year. The nonrefundable application fee is $25.

The Admissions Office is open weekdays from 8 a.m. to 5 p.m. The office is also open on selected Saturday mornings during the fall and spring. Special Saturday campus preview days are offered in October, November, and March. For more information, a campus tour, or application forms, students should contact:

Office of Admission
Oklahoma Baptist University
500 West University
Shawnee, Oklahoma 74804
Telephone: 405-878-2033
          800-654-3285 (toll-free)
E-mail: admissions@mail.okbu.edu
World Wide Web: http://www.okbu.edu

John Wesley Raley Chapel at Oklahoma Baptist University.

OKLAHOMA CITY UNIVERSITY
OKLAHOMA CITY, OKLAHOMA

The University

Oklahoma City University (OCU) takes pride in its dual role as the city's university and as the university for the United Methodist Church in Oklahoma. Located in the geographic center of Oklahoma's capital city, OCU provides a wide variety of educational, social, and cultural opportunities for the campus community. OCU has more than 4,300 full- and part-time students who represent forty-seven states and sixty-four other countries. With a ninety-six-year tradition of church-related service and academic excellence, OCU continues to be a vital and growing institution.

Oklahoma City University is accredited by the North Central Association of Colleges and Secondary Schools and approved by the University Senate of the United Methodist Church, the National Association of Schools of Music, the American Bar Association, the Association of Collegiate Business Schools and Programs, the Supreme Court of the State of Oklahoma, and the Oklahoma State Board of Education. The Kramer School of Nursing is approved by the Oklahoma Board of Nursing and is accredited by the National League for Nursing Accrediting Commission.

The Prior Learning and University Studies (PLUS) program is an alternate undergraduate program for adult learners in which credit is accepted for life experience. In addition to its undergraduate programs, OCU offers the M.A. degree in religion; the M.S. in accounting and computer science; the Master of Business Administration, Criminal Justice Administration, Education, Liberal Arts, Music, Performing Arts, and Religious Education; and the J.D. degree.

All single full-time undergraduates under the age of 22 must live on campus unless they are living with their parents or legal guardian. There are five residence halls on campus. The Cokesbury Court apartment complex includes options of one-, two-, and four-bedroom apartments, with a swimming pool and Jacuzzi, as well as parking and laundry facilities. Both environments are excellent for living and learning. Students living in residence halls are required to participate in one of the University board plans. Students are encouraged to participate in activities both on and off campus. There are more than thirty-five social and academic organizations, intramural sports, dramatics, student publications, music ensembles, dance companies, and a wide range of cultural enrichment events available to all OCU students. The University is a member of the National Association of Intercollegiate Athletics (NAIA) and sponsors ten competitive sports programs. The tradition of OCU's sports programs is known nationwide.

Location

Oklahoma City offers a wide variety of cultural, civic, religious, entertainment, and sports events in a unique setting of modern facilities and Southwestern hospitality. With more than 1 million people in the metropolitan area, the city is a dynamic location offering a wide range of opportunities. From the State Capitol and the center of Oklahoma's political and governmental activity to the cultural offerings of the Oklahoma City Philharmonic, Lyric Theatre, and Ballet Oklahoma to the attractions of the National Cowboy Hall of Fame, the Firefighters' Museum, the Oklahoma City Zoo and Omniplex and professional baseball and hockey, Oklahoma City stands as a vibrant metropolitan center of the Southwest. OCU students are involved in city life through internships in governmental and social agencies and extracurricular activities that involve the city's many resources and facilities. The many opportunities and activities available in this growing metropolitan area add another dimension to the high quality of education available at Oklahoma City University.

Oklahoma City is linked by interstate highways to other major cities in the region, and the city's Will Rogers International Airport, one of the busiest in the region, provides coast-to-coast jet service and international flights to Europe, Asia, and South America. The campus is located near the center of Oklahoma City. While close to the business community, the State Capitol, and all the conveniences of a major city, the OCU campus environment is quiet, sheltered, and natural.

Majors and Degrees

The Bachelor of Arts degree is offered in the following subject areas: Asian studies, biology, business, chemistry, criminal justice, education, English, French, German, German/Russian or Russian/German, history, history/political science, humanities, mass communications, math, music, philosophy, philosophy/religion, political science, professional sociology, psychology, religion, religion/philosophy, Spanish, speech communication, studio art, and theater. The Bachelor of Science degree is offered in the following subject areas: biochemistry, biology, biophysics, business, chemistry, computer science, criminal justice, dance management, education, entertainment business, history, history/American studies, history/political science, math, music business, physics, political science, professional sociology, psychology, science, and technical theater. The Bachelor of Fine Arts degree includes programs in graphic design and studio art. The Bachelor of Science in Business is offered in the following subjects: accounting, business administration, economics, finance, information systems management, international business, management, and marketing. The Bachelor of Music is available in applied piano pedagogy and composition, with elective studies in business administration, guitar, musical theater, orchestral instrument, organ, piano, and voice. Other degrees include the Bachelor of Music Education, instrumental and vocal; the Bachelor of Performing Arts in dance; and the Bachelor of Nursing.

Academic Program

All undergraduate degree programs require a minimum of 124 semester hours, including the Foundation Curriculum, which represents general education requirements that must be fulfilled by all undergraduate students. OCU believes that the experience of value-conscious education makes a difference. The curriculum has been specially designed to place a premium on teaching students how to learn rather than merely what to learn. As an integral part of the Foundation Curriculum, the University has established an Honors Program designed to meet the special interests and needs of intellectually gifted students. Honors sections of Foundation Curriculum courses feature limited enrollment with greater emphasis placed on the seminar format and interdisciplinary design. All honors classes are weighted an additional .25 grade point higher than regular classes. Upon completion of 25 hours of honors courses with a 3.5 cumulative University GPA, an honors student receives special recognition at graduation and a special designation on his or her diploma.

OCU operates on a two-semester calendar.

Off-Campus Arrangements

Departments offering international study include German, biology, and sociology and the Meinders School of Business. The Washington Semester Program, at American University, provides students with the opportunity to conduct an intensive inquiry into the institutions and policymaking processes of their chosen fields. OCU also sponsors overseas trips for performing arts majors.

OCU offers programs that identify and match students to study-abroad/internship opportunities in England, Germany, and Argentina. Relationships exist with the University of Göttingen, Germany; Edge Hill College, England; Voronezh State University, Russia; Safe University, Bulgaria; and Tianjin Normal University, People's Republic of China. In the past, OCU students have studied in England, Mexico, France, Republic of China, Japan, Germany, Russia, Ecuador, Chile, and Italy. OCU is a member of the Council on International Education.

Academic Facilities

During the past eighteen years, seven academic classroom facilities have been constructed. The Loeffler Math and Science Building, Jones Administration Building, Gold Star Building, and the Margaret E. Petree School of Music and Performing Arts have all had major renovations in the last seven years. The research center for the campus, the Dulaney-Browne Library, has more than 306,844 items, including books, videos, cassettes, bound periodicals, microfiche and microfilm periodicals, periodical CD-ROMs, government documents, and more than 900 current periodical subscriptions. The C. Q. Smith Student Faculty Center (SFC), where the snack bar and Marriot Food service are located, is a hub of activity. Also in the SFC are the University Book Store and Placement Office. Campus religious life functions around the Bishop Angie Smith Chapel, an award-winning architectural structure.

Costs

The typical expenses for one term include tuition ($4940 for undergraduates taking 12 to 16 hours), room and board ($2265 for a double room and eighteen meals per week), $100 in fees, and an estimated cost of $750 for books.

Financial Aid

The University is committed to making the utmost effort to assist students who are seeking an education at OCU. The Financial Aid Office assists any admissible student in working out a financial aid package to help meet basic education expenses. In granting aid, the student's demonstrated financial need is considered, together with academic potential and personal qualities. Academic ability and other talents may be recognized through non-need-based scholarships.

To be considered for any kind of financial assistance, a student must first complete the application procedure for admission to the University. The student should then file the FAFSA and designate Oklahoma City University to receive a copy. The FAFSA may be obtained from high school guidance offices, the Financial Aid Office, or the Undergraduate Admissions Office. The suggested priority deadline for scholarships and financial aid is March 1.

Faculty

OCU has 168 full-time and 184 part-time faculty members. Of the full-time faculty members, 71 percent hold doctorates or terminal degrees in their fields. The student-faculty ratio at OCU is 14:1. No classes are taught by graduate assistants or teacher assistants.

Student Government

Each student at Oklahoma City University is a member of the OCU Student Association. The Student Senate is composed of 20 students who are elected by their peers. Each class is represented in the Senate, and at-large seats are held by graduate and law students. The Student Senate is funded through fees assessed to each student and sponsors social, cultural, and recreational events both on and off campus. Senate members meet regularly with the University administration to ensure that communication lines remain open. They also serve as voting members of many University committees. OCU is recognized as an institution that provides many outstanding leadership opportunities.

Admission Requirements

All incoming freshmen must take either the ACT or the SAT I; the results are used in admission determination, student evaluations, counseling, and awarding scholarships. OCU's SAT code number is 6543; the ACT code number is 3416. Students must meet two of the following three criteria to be considered admittable: a minimum score of 20 on the ACT or 930 on the SAT I, a minimum cumulative GPA of 2.5, and a class rank in the upper half.

Transfer students must have a minimum GPA of 2.0 from an accredited college or university to be considered for admission to the University. Transfer students who have earned fewer than 26 college hours are required to provide the Admissions Office with their high school transcripts and test scores.

Application and Information

Entering freshmen must submit an application for admission, accompanied by a $20 nonrefundable fee, to the Undergraduate Admissions Office as soon as possible before the term in which the student plans to enroll. An official high school transcript or GED certificate should also be submitted; the student's high school counselor or principal must send an official copy of the transcript. An official final high school transcript with graduation date posted must be received prior to the start of classes.

Transfer applicants must submit an application for admission, along with a $20 nonrefundable fee, to the Undergraduate Admissions Office; an official transcript from each institution attended is also required. Students should request that the proper official send an official transcript directly to the Undergraduate Admissions Office. A high school transcript is required for transfer students who have earned fewer than 26 hours of college credit.

For answers to questions or for an application, students should write or call:

Undergraduate Admissions Office
Oklahoma City University
2501 North Blackwelder
Oklahoma City, Oklahoma 73106
Telephone: 405-521-5050
           800-633-7242 (toll-free)
E-mail: uadmissions@frodo.okcu.edu
World Wide Web: http://www.okcu.edu/

The Gold Star Building on the campus of Oklahoma City University.

OLIVET NAZARENE UNIVERSITY
KANKAKEE, ILLINOIS

The University

Olivet Nazarene University (ONU) is a Christian liberal arts university with a strong emphasis on both academic excellence and Christ-centered living. ONU offers one of the finest liberal arts educations in the Midwest, world-class facilities for learning and entertainment, and an atmosphere that promotes the fun, relationship building, and spiritual growth that goes hand-in-hand with the Christian way of life.

Olivet's high retention, graduation, and employment/placement rates demonstrate the University's commitment to the student's success. The faculty, staff, and administration are dedicated to teaching, encouraging, and mentoring each student as a whole person—academically, socially, and spiritually.

With 2,500 total students (1,800 undergraduates), Olivet offers an ideal student population for a private institution, maintaining good diversity without sacrificing personalized attention. Just over half of the student body comes from the Nazarene denomination, while the remainder come from some thirty other denominations. A majority of U.S. states are represented, as are close to twenty countries.

The campus offers a championship-caliber athletic department (eighteen intercollegiate sports in all) and a large intramural sports program. Music and drama groups involve hundreds of students, and many clubs are organized for a wide variety of interests. Olivet students are also heavily involved in more than a dozen ministry groups, small-group Bible studies, and weekly student-led services.

The University is completing a major capital campaign. The dining hall recently underwent a major renovation, a new Admissions Welcome Center and campus entrance have been constructed, dormitories are receiving updates each summer, and a new academic building was begun in spring 2000.

Location

The University is located 50 minutes south of downtown Chicago in the village of Bourbonnais, a secure community within the greater Kankakee area. The area includes a wide variety of shopping (including a major mall), restaurants, entertainment, and natural recreation areas centered around the Kankakee River. Olivet students enjoy many of these activities near the University and often make the quick trip north to sample the limitless offerings of Chicago and its surroundings.

In addition to recreation, students find numerous opportunities for employment and internships in the Kankakee area (ranked as one of the top locations in the nation for small businesses) and the vast professional resources of Chicago. Students, faculty members, and staff members also find themselves working side by side in local and regional ministry projects. Olivet students are recognized professionally and ministerially as a valuable commodity by area businesses, churches, and parachurch organizations.

Majors and Degrees

Olivet confers Bachelor of Arts (B.A.) and/or Bachelor of Science (B.S.) degrees in the following fields of study (includes all majors, minors, and concentrations): accounting, art, art history, athletic training, biblical literature, biblical studies, biochemistry, biology, broadcasting, business administration, chemistry, Christian education, church music, clinical laboratory science, commercial graphics, computer information systems, computer science, counseling, cross-cultural ministries, dietetics, drawing, early childhood education, earth and space science, economics and finance, elementary education, engineering (electrical), engineering (mechanical), English, environmental science, family and consumer sciences, fashion merchandising, film studies, finance, French, general studies, geochemistry, geoengineering, geology, Greek, history, housing and environmental design, international business, journalism, literature, management, marketing, mathematics, music education, music performance, nursing, nutrition, personnel psychology, philosophy and religion, physical education, physical science, physics, political science, predentistry, prelaw, premedicine, prepharmacy, pre–physical therapy, preveterinary medicine, psychology, public policy, religion, religious studies, Romance languages, secondary education, social justice, social science, social work, sociology, Spanish, special education, speech communication, theater, writing, youth ministry, and zoology.

Academic Program

Olivet seeks to offer an "Education with a Christian Purpose." The University believes this commitment to Christ mandates nothing less than the highest quality academic programs. Olivet's liberal arts curriculum requires that students complete 53 to 61 hours of general education courses. With the addition of major and minor programs of study, students must complete a minimum of 128 credit hours to obtain a bachelor's degree. Credit may be earned through AP and CLEP tests. Students may also participate in ROTC.

Olivet operates on a two-semester schedule, from August to May. Two summer sessions are also available.

Off-Campus Arrangements

Olivet students are encouraged to participate in the various off-campus study programs offered each semester. Foreign locations include Beijing, China; San José, Costa Rica; Cairo, Egypt; Oxford, England; Irian Jaya, Indonesia; Moscow, Nizhni Novgorod, and St. Petersburg, Russia; and Sighisoara, Transylvania (Romania). Domestic opportunities include the American Studies Program in Washington, D.C.; the Los Angeles Film Studies Program in Burbank, California; and the AuSable Institute (environmental science) in northern Michigan. Costs are usually comparable to a semester at Olivet, and credit is given for these programs.

In addition, many Olivet students participate in ministerial and educational short-term trips available during the Christmas, spring, and summer breaks.

Academic Facilities

Olivet's $75-million campus offers leading-edge academic facilities. These include excellent natural science, engineering, and nursing laboratories; "smart" classrooms in the biology, nursing, and education departments; and an observatory. It is one of only a handful of small college campuses in the nation to have a planetarium. Each department uses the top software in its field. Nine campus computer labs are available for student use, and two network ports in each dorm room give students access to e-mail, the Internet, and classroom applications 24 hours a day.

Benner Library and Resource Center provides unlimited access to any material a student needs, either on-site from its 160,000 volumes, 1,000 periodicals, government documents, and CD-ROMs or through the interlibrary loan system.

Costs

Tuition (12 to 18 credit hours per semester), fees, room, and board for the 1999–2000 school year were $16,924. Of that total, tuition was $11,528, room and board were $4696, and fees were $700.

Financial Aid

More than 85 percent of Olivet students receive some form of financial aid each year. Merit and need-based scholarships range from $500 to full tuition. The University also participates in all federal and state financial aid programs. The priority deadline for filing the Free Application for Federal Student Aid (FAFSA) is March 1. To apply for aid, students must fill out the FAFSA as well as Olivet's application for financial aid. The student must be an accepted applicant before a financial aid package can be put together. Olivet offers a monthly installment plan in addition to the traditional three-payment plan.

Faculty

Olivet's 100 full-time faculty members are the key to excellence in and out of the classroom. Teaching is a ministry for these dedicated Christian individuals, and Olivet's 17:1 student-faculty ratio gives them an opportunity to teach, mentor, and encourage students on a personal level. To that end, the faculty is heavily involved in campus life, whether sponsoring social organizations or participating in talent shows.

Within the traditional liberal arts curriculum, 75 percent of Olivet's faculty members have terminal degrees. Including the more practical programs of study, such as nursing and family and consumer sciences, the total is a strong 68 percent.

Student Government

The Associated Student Council is the student government organization on campus. Its Executive Council consists of a President, Vice President of Finance, Vice President of Spiritual Life, Vice President of Social Affairs, Vice President of Women's Residential Life, Vice President of Men's Residential Life, Vice President of Office Management, the *Glimmerglass* (student newspaper) editor, and the *Aurora* (yearbook) editor. They work alongside the University's administrative team to ensure the health and promotion of campus activities and organizations.

Admission Requirements

Admission to the University is minimally difficult. Students are considered for admission on the basis of their high school GPA, ACT or SAT I scores, and personal recommendations. An ACT score is required for placement in courses. For international students, TOEFL results are an additional factor in the admission decision. Students with low test scores and GPAs may be admitted on a provisional basis. A campus visit and interview are strongly recommended for all prospective students.

Application and Information

Admission is on a rolling basis. Students may apply at Olivet's home page on the World Wide Web or in print. The application process includes the written (or electronic) application, high school transcripts, two letters of recommendation, ACT or SAT I scores, and health form. There is no application fee, but a $30 room deposit places the student on the list for housing.

For more information or to arrange a campus visit, students should contact:

Office of Admissions
Olivet Nazarene University
P.O. Box 592
Kankakee, Illinois 60901
Telephone: 815-939-5203
            800-648-1463 (toll-free)
E-mail: admissions@olivet.edu
World Wide Web: http://www.olivet.edu

Olivet students enjoy championship-caliber athletic programs.

OREGON STATE UNIVERSITY
CORVALLIS, OREGON

OREGON STATE UNIVERSITY

The University

Exceptional students, an outstanding faculty, and a challenging curriculum combine to make Oregon State University (OSU) a nationally and internationally recognized comprehensive university.

OSU is the only Oregon university to earn the Carnegie Research I designation for commitment to education and research. Widely recognized research programs add to the quality of teaching by bringing new knowledge into the classroom and by encouraging undergraduate students to work with faculty members on research projects in many fields. About 600 top students are in the University Honors College, which offers interaction with top professors and a small-college atmosphere in the midst of a major university.

The University's 16,000 students come from every state and from more than ninety countries to pursue a wide choice of undergraduate programs that prepare them for careers and leadership positions in business and industry, government, engineering and computer-related fields, science, teaching, natural resources, pharmacy, and other professions. Employers recognize the value of an OSU degree, and more of them recruit at Oregon State University each year than at any other school in the state.

OSU is committed to offering students the resources they need to be successful in their education. In 1997, Oregon State was named the leading institution in the U.S. and Canada for electronic services to students. In presenting the award, the American Productivity and Quality Center recognized OSU for innovative programs, including bringing Internet access to every residence hall room on campus. OSU has earned the distinction of being named one of "America's 100 Most Wired Colleges" by *Yahoo! Internet Life* (May 1999).

Students also benefit from more than 300 cocurricular activities on campus. These include student government, student media, theater and music, intramural and club sports, and numerous social, academic, cultural, and professional clubs and organizations. In addition, Dixon Recreation Center offers opportunities for swimming and diving, weight training, aerobic exercise, and recreational sports on campus. A campus child-care facility offers educationally oriented day-care programs for children of students and faculty and staff members.

OSU offers a wide range of housing and dining options, including special program residence halls, cooperative houses, student family housing, and fraternity and sorority housing. Many apartments and houses are available within biking or walking distance of OSU for students who choose to live off campus. There are more than fifteen restaurants on campus, and many more are nearby.

Graduate degrees are offered through the Colleges of Agricultural Sciences, Business, Engineering, Forestry, Health and Human Performance, Home Economics and Education, Liberal Arts, Oceanography, Pharmacy, Science, and Veterinary Medicine.

Location

The OSU main campus is in Corvallis, which is consistently ranked as one of the safest university communities on the West Coast. With about 50,000 residents, Corvallis offers a friendly, university-oriented atmosphere. Miles of bike lanes and free city bus service make it easy for students to get around town. Within a couple hours of Corvallis are the Oregon Coast; the Cascade Mountains, with skiing, hiking, camping, and snowboarding; and Portland, Oregon's largest city.

Majors and Degrees

Oregon State is a comprehensive university, with more than 200 academic programs. Undergraduate degrees are offered through the Colleges of Agricultural Sciences, Business, Engineering, Forestry, Health and Human Performance, Home Economics and Education, Liberal Arts, Pharmacy, and Science.

Students in any undergraduate major can strengthen their transcripts by earning an Honors Degree or an International Degree. The University offers twenty-eight programs to prepare students for professional studies in the health sciences, it has a strong prelaw program, and it prepares teachers for higher-than-usual starting salaries through a combined undergraduate and graduate program.

Academic Program

All undergraduate students at Oregon State complete the Baccalaureate Core, which helps develop skills and knowledge in writing, critical thinking, cultural diversity, the arts, science, literature, lifelong fitness, and global awareness, ensuring that as graduates they will be well prepared for life as well as a career.

Many students take advantage of OSU's first-year experience program, called Odyssey, which offers opportunities for new students to interact with faculty members and other students throughout the year, thus easing the transition to college life. The year begins with a five-day "connect" orientation that features small group meetings between faculty members and students, a barbecue, outdoor movies, open houses, and more.

Undergraduate research is an important component of many academic programs, and more than 2,000 OSU undergraduates participate with faculty members and graduate students on research projects each year.

OSU has more majors, minors, and special programs than any other college in Oregon and offers a University Exploratory Studies Program for students who want to try various options before choosing a major field.

Learning and resource centers around campus help OSU students deal with problems and develop the skills they will need in college and beyond. The Center for Writing and Learning, the Mathematics Learning Center, and departmental resource centers assist students in preparing for assignments in specific areas, while the African American, Hispanic American, Asian American, and Native American education offices, along with the Educational Opportunities Program, help ensure that specific groups of students have successful college careers. University Counseling and Psychological Services offers learning resource materials and professional assistance to help students deal with problems, both in and out of the classroom. Career Services assists students in locating internships and in finding jobs when they graduate.

Oregon State uses the quarter system for its academic year. Most majors require between 180 and 192 credit hours for a bachelor's degree.

Off-Campus Arrangements

Through International Degree and international internship programs, OSU students can create study, work, or research opportunities almost anywhere in the world. In addition, Oregon State students are currently involved in study-abroad programs at forty-six universities in seventeen other countries. Programs, which range from a term to a full year, are in Australia, Canada, China, Denmark, Ecuador, England, France, Germany, Hungary, Italy, Japan, Korea, Mexico, New Zealand, Norway, Russia, Spain, and Thailand.

OSU also participates in the National Student Exchange Program, allowing students to spend up to a year at one of more than 160 colleges and universities in the U.S. and its possessions while paying in-state tuition and fees.

Academic Facilities

A $47-million expansion project over the past two years has made OSU's Valley Library a state-of-the-art facility that offers modern electronic services and unique special collections as well as traditional library services to students and the community. The OSU library is the first academic library to be named "Library of the Year" by *Library Journal* (1999). Library holdings include more than 2.5 million books, periodicals, and government documents on paper or microform. A reciprocal agreement makes more than 5 million additional volumes in the Oregon University System available to OSU students and faculty members. OSU's special collections include the papers and memorabilia of Linus Pauling, the only winner of two unshared Nobel prizes, and the Atomic Energy Collection. The Valley Library is an official depository for U.S. government and state of Oregon publications.

Students at OSU have access to more than 2,200 computers at labs around campus, including some that are available 24 hours per day. In addition, all rooms in campus residence facilities are wired for high-speed access to the Internet. All students have Internet and e-mail accounts.

Facilities also include the Northwest's only stereographic classroom, which shows scientific principles in 3-D format; a fully equipped multimedia classroom; and modern laboratories, including an undergraduate biology lab that allows students to explore a wide range of studies, from analysis of DNA molecules to the nature of cancer cells. Special research facilities include OSU's Mark O. Hatfield Marine Science Center, the Forest Research Laboratory, and the Radiation Center.

Costs

In-state undergraduate tuition and fees were $3549 for the 1999–2000 academic year, while nonresident charges were $12,313. The average cost for a residence hall double room and meal plan was approximately $5394, while the room and board cost in University-owned cooperatives averaged $3000. Students who live in a fraternity or sorority house pay about the same for housing and meals as those students who live in residence halls.

Financial Aid

OSU offers the full range of scholarships, grants, work-study, and loans from federal, state, and University sources. Every effort is made to offer students the best package possible. To qualify, students must have applied for admission and must submit the Free Application for Federal Student Aid (FAFSA), listing OSU as one of their top six choices. Some students help meet educational expenses with one of the many part-time jobs available on or near campus. For financial aid information, interested students should contact the Office of Financial Aid, 218 Kerr Administration Building, Corvallis, Oregon 97331 (telephone: 541-737-2241, World Wide Web: http://osu.orst.edu/admin/finaid/).

Through the OSU Scholars Program, the University offers a variety of scholarships for new students who have strong academic records. Scholarships range from $500 to $6000 annually for up to four years. In addition, most OSU colleges offer scholarships to new students, and the financial aid office has a number of University-wide scholarships.

Faculty

Undergraduate education is a priority at OSU, and nationally prominent scholars and scientists regularly teach undergraduate courses at all levels. Students receive individual attention and the chance to know their professors both in and out of the classroom. Faculty members consistently receive awards for teaching and research, and many of them are nationally and internationally renowned. The more than $100 million in external research funds received annually by OSU faculty members exceeds that of all other Oregon public universities combined. With more than 1,300 teaching faculty members, OSU has a student-faculty ratio of 16:1.

Student Government

The Associated Students of Oregon State University (ASOSU) plays a major role in making policy and regulating activities for students and in governing the University through student participation on more than fifty University-wide committees. In recent years, ASOSU has become more involved with local, state, and national issues that affect the welfare of students.

Admission Requirements

A minimum 3.0 high school GPA (on a 4.0 scale) guarantees freshman admission to OSU when all subject requirements are met. Applicants who do not meet the GPA requirement may be considered based on a combination of high school GPA and SAT I or ACT scores that predict success at OSU. High school subject requirements are 4 years of English, 3 years each of mathematics and social studies, and 2 years each of science and a foreign language. Students who do not meet the subject requirements may be considered for admission by earning a 1410 total score on three SAT II Subject Tests or by successfully completing course work to make up specific deficiencies. The alternatives must by completed by the time of high school graduation.

Transfer admission requires successful completion of at least 36 graded, transferable credits (24 semester credits) from accredited U.S. institutions, with a minimum GPA of 2.25. Grades of C- or better are required in college-level writing and mathematics. Students with less than 36 transferable credits are considered for admission on the basis of their high school records.

Application and Information

An *OSU Viewbook*, with an application form and information on specific academic programs, housing, financial aid, scholarships, and activities are sent to students upon request. Additional information and an online application are on the OSU World Wide Web site (listed below).

Prospective students are encouraged to visit OSU to determine for themselves whether the University meets their needs. A visit, including a campus tour and an opportunity to talk to faculty members in the student's area of interest, can be arranged by calling the Office of Admission and Orientation (listed below).

For an application or to request more information, students should write or call:

Office of Admission and Orientation
150 Kerr Administration Building
Oregon State University
Corvallis, Oregon 97331-2106
Telephone: 800-291-4192 (toll-free)
Fax: 541-737-2482
E-mail: osuadmit@orst.edu
World Wide Web: http://osu.orst.edu

OTIS COLLEGE OF ART AND DESIGN
LOS ANGELES, CALIFORNIA

The College
Throughout the twentieth century, Otis College of Art and Design has evolved as a trend-setting leader in art and design education. In 1918, Harrison Gray Otis, founder and editor of the *Los Angeles Times,* bequeathed his estate, located near Westlake Park, to establish Los Angeles' first art school, Otis Art Institute. After the passing of the California tax initiative Proposition 103, much of the county's funding for art was lost, and Otis was not excluded. In 1979, Otis merged with the New School for Social Research in New York and became part of a three-school consortium with the Parsons School of Design in New York and in Paris. As the Los Angeles school began to look to the future, it became apparent that the best way to meet its educational goals was to become an independent, nonprofit college with its own sources of funding and financial support. In 1992, Otis College of Art and Design was reborn with the election of its first independent boards of governors and trustees. That same year, the College began to look for new facilities that would better accommodate the needs of students and enhance its educational goals. The Goldsmith campus in Los Angeles' Westchester district has been designed as the realization of the dreams of Otis' working faculty members and dedicated administrators. Otis is an artist's art school, where the spaces are designed specifically for the activities that happen in them and include the newest and most advanced facilities and equipment.

Approximately 750 students from thirty states and twenty countries are enrolled in the B.F.A. and M.F.A. programs, with an additional 1,000 students participating in evening and weekend courses offered through the Continuing Education Division. Otis also offers a two-year, studio-based Master of Fine Arts degree. Otis is accredited by the Western Association of Schools and Colleges (WASC) and the National Association of Schools of Art and Design (NASAD).

The College's commitment to exposing students to the professional art community includes programs ranging from internships to visiting artists. The curriculum also includes opportunities to study abroad and experiences in local artist studios. The small class sizes and the diversity of the student body allow the student to create a communal learning environment. Otis alumni include such historically recognized artists as Philip Guston, Robert Irwin, and John Baldesarri. Famous alumni include costume designer Edith Head, as well as Paul Soldner, Billy Al Bengston, Kent Twitchell, Alison Saar, and Lita Albuquerque.

Location
Otis College of Art and Design is located on the west side of Los Angeles on a 5-acre campus in the heart of southern California's technical film, digital imaging, and toy design industries. The nearby communities of Venice and Santa Monica are home to many of Los Angeles' most important fine art studios and galleries. Otis is an "artist's art school," where the spaces resemble artist lofts with high ceilings, open spaces, and exposed structural supports.

Majors and Degrees
Otis offers programs leading to the Bachelor of Fine Arts degree in digital media design, environmental arts, fashion design, graphic design, illustration, painting, photography, printmaking, sculpture/new genres, toy design, and video.

Academic Program
The Foundation Year helps new students to master a broad spectrum of studio skills and gives a comprehensive introduction to the liberal arts and sciences. A Foundation Honors Course is an additional challenge for qualified students in English and art history. The primary goal of both the Fine Art and Design departments is to prepare students in each major for a professional career. While intensive studio classes form the core of the Otis experience, courses in the liberal arts and sciences, art history, and criticism ensure that students acquire the broad-based education the College feels is necessary for a successful life. Other special features include professional internships in the fine arts and design and a written thesis component for most seniors.

Off-Campus Arrangements
The Mobility Program at Otis College of Art and Design allows students to study for one semester at another art college during their junior year. Otis participates in a mobility program with the Association of Independent Colleges of Art and Design (AICAD). Participating colleges include premier AICAD art colleges in the United States as well as selected colleges in Europe and Canada. Application procedures and deadlines are available through the Office of Student Development.

Academic Facilities
Large, well-lighted, multiuse studios support the interdisciplinary nature of the programs at Otis. The facilities include a fully equipped ceramics studio with multi-kiln firing capabilities, full foundry and casting facilities, a photographic darkroom with extensive color and black-and-white processing capabilities, fully equipped printmaking studios, a video production laboratory, both photography and video studios, a fine-books press room, a woodworking studio, and a metalworking shop.

The Millard Sheets Library houses more than 25,000 volumes as well as periodicals, films, videotapes, 75,000 slides, and a growing collection of videos and CD-ROMs. Its large collection of artist-made books is renowned and contains an inventory of artists' files that include show invitations, catalogs, and brochures.

The Otis Gallery is well-known for its year-round program of exhibitions in contemporary art and design. In the past few years, the Gallery has shown Jean-Michel Basquiat, Luca Buvoli, Karen Carson, Kim Dingle, Terry Fox, Coco Fusco, Larry Johnson, Lorna Simpson, Jessica Stockholder, and Emerson Woelffer. The Bolsky Gallery is located next to the main gallery and is designed to highlight student works in a professional exhibition environment.

The Computer Center consists of an Open Access/Media Lab and three computer classrooms. More than 130 Power Macintosh computers are available for student use, as well as flat-bed color scanners, tabloid laser printers, and Internet-Access workstations. Students use the latest software, including the Adobe Suite, Director, and 3-D Studio MAX. The American Film Institute and Otis share access to a Windows-NT lab consisting of fourteen NT workstations.

The School of Fashion is located in the heart of Los Angeles' garment districts at the CaliforniaMart. This state-of-the-art facility is 18,000 square feet of work rooms, drawing rooms, and classroom space dedicated to the advanced study of the art of fashion design. This access to industry professionals gives Otis students a unique resource and valuable practical experience.

Costs
Tuition and fees for academic year 1999–2000 were $18,400. Housing and cost of living and other incidental personal

expenses vary depending upon individual circumstances. These costs are estimated to run from $2000 to $5670 per year. Costs are subject to increase for the 2000–01 academic year. Students should call the Office of Admissions for information on updated costs.

Financial Aid

Otis is proud to award more than $2.5 million in scholarships to its students. In addition, aid from other sources, such as the state and federal governments, provides aid monies to more than 75 percent of the student body.

Students must complete the Free Application for Federal Student Aid (FAFSA) and the Otis Financial Aid Application. Applicants for fall admission are encouraged to file on or before the February 15 priority deadline; applicants for January admission should submit all forms before December 1. California residents are encouraged to file the Cal Grant GPA Verification Form and FAFSA before the strict February 15 deadline. The FAFSA and Supplemental Application may be submitted after these priority dates, but aid will be awarded on a first-come, first-served basis according to availability. All aid is based on artistic and academic merit and a student's financial eligibility as determined by the United States Department of Education.

Faculty

The Otis faculty comprises practicing artists and designers who have chosen to enrich their professional experience by sharing their expertise with new generations of artists and designers. There are currently 23 full-time and more than 220 part-time faculty members.

Student Government

The Otis Student Government (OSG) comprises students from every department of study in the college. The OSG plays an active role in student life and produces a wide variety of student-oriented lectures and events.

Admission Requirements

A high school diploma or its equivalent is required of all students applying to the Bachelor of Fine Arts program. A good academic record can weigh heavily in the application process. Students must also submit a portfolio of twelve to twenty pieces of original artwork. While slides are preferable, flat work will be accepted. Half of the portfolio should consist of drawings from observation, including a self-portrait. The remaining pieces should reflect the student's interests and strengths and may be in any medium, regardless of their intended major. The application is reviewed by a committee and all portions of the application are weighed equally.

Application and Information

Applicants must complete the Otis Application for Admission and attach the nonrefundable $50 application fee. Supporting documents may be sent separate from the application itself. High school transcripts should be sent unless the student has received a bachelor's degree. Students with previous college experience should have transcripts from each institution forwarded as well. Applicants currently in high school must submit either SAT I or ACT scores. Letters of recommendation are encouraged, but are not required. Additional requirements include a portfolio and an essay describing the student's decision to become an artist or designer.

The priority deadline for applying to Otis College of Art and Design is February 15. Otis maintains a rolling admission policy.

Students are encouraged to visit the Otis campus. For more information about Otis or to schedule an appointment, students should contact:

The Office of Admissions
Otis College of Art and Design
9045 Lincoln Boulevard
Los Angeles, California 90045-9785
Telephone: 310-665-6820 (Los Angeles residents)
800-527-6847 (toll-free)
E-mail: otisart@otisart.edu
World Wide Web: http://www.otisart.edu

Otis College of Art and Design is now located on the west side of Los Angeles on a 5-acre campus.

OTTERBEIN COLLEGE
WESTERVILLE, OHIO

The College

Otterbein College, a private, coeducational institution affiliated with the United Methodist Church, blends the traditional and contemporary and continues to pride itself on offering a broad-based liberal arts education. Its 1,786 full-time and 1,210 part-time students come from all over the United States and several countries, but the majority, including 441 graduate students, are from Ohio. Founded in 1847 with only two buildings on 8 acres of land, Otterbein has since grown to twenty-seven buildings on 140 acres in the heart of historic Westerville, Ohio, a suburb of Columbus.

The College offers a wide range of extracurricular activities. They include theater productions, vocal and instrumental ensembles, religious programming activities, the weekly student newspaper, the campus radio station (WOBN), the Otterbein-Westerville television station (WOCC), and intramural and intercollegiate athletics. Otterbein men and women compete in the Ohio Athletic Conference, NCAA Division III. There are eight varsity sports for men and eight for women. The Rike Physical Education–Recreation Center is the home for men's and women's athletics and physical education facilities and includes racquetball and tennis courts, an indoor track, a weight room, and seating for 3,000. Six local fraternities and six local sororities attract approximately 35 percent of Otterbein's students. Roush Hall, a multipurpose, handicapped-accessible building, houses academic departments, multimedia classrooms, contemporary conference rooms, a gallery, and a computer center.

A Master of Science in Nursing program is now offered for students who have completed a four-year baccalaureate program.

A Master of Arts in Teaching (M.A.T.) degree program is available to qualified liberal arts graduates to prepare for teacher certification in elementary education or secondary education—biology (life science), computer science, English, and mathematics. A Master of Arts in Education (M.A.E.) degree program is available to certified teachers. Majors are offered in curriculum and instruction, reading, and teacher leadership and supervision. Otterbein also offers an M.B.A. program.

Location

Otterbein is located in Westerville, Ohio, 20 minutes from downtown Columbus, one of the fastest-growing cities in the Midwest and Northeast. The College's proximity to Columbus means more than access to entertainment and recreation; as a thriving business center, the city provides many internship opportunities for students that often lead to full-time employment after graduation. The College is located near Interstates 70 and 71 and is easily accessible from Port Columbus International Airport.

Majors and Degrees

The Bachelor of Arts degree is offered in accounting, broadcasting, business administration, business/organizational communication, chemistry, computer science, dance, economics, English, equine science, French, health education, history, international studies, journalism, life science, mathematics, music, philosophy, physical education, physics, political science, psychology, public relations, religion, secondary education, sociology, Spanish, speech communication, sports medicine, sports wellness and management, theater, and visual arts. The Bachelor of Science degree is offered in accounting, business administration, chemistry, computer science, equine science, life science, mathematics, physics, psychology, and sports medicine. The Bachelor of Fine Arts is offered in theater with concentrations in acting-directing and design-technical programs. The Bachelor of Music Education prepares students for teaching careers in music. The Bachelor of Science in Education is awarded in early childhood education and middle childhood education. The Bachelor of Science in Nursing degree is also offered. In fall 1999, Otterbein began offering a Bachelor of Music for students interested in performance careers.

Preprofessional programs are offered in dentistry, law, medicine, optometry, and veterinary medicine.

A dual degree in engineering is offered in conjunction with Washington University in St. Louis and Case Western Reserve University in Cleveland.

Minors are offered in accounting, athletic training, black studies, broadcasting, business, chemistry, coaching, computer science, dance, economics, English, equestrian studies, French, geology, health sciences, history, mathematics, music, philosophy, physical education, physics, political science, psychology, public relations, religion, sociology, Spanish, speech communication, visual arts, and women's studies.

Academic Program

Otterbein College offers a program of liberal arts education in the Christian tradition. The College encourages serious dialogue so that students will develop to serve within the community. The fulfillment of this purpose requires students to read well, write well, think clearly, and identify ideas; know how to discuss, listen, and seek data; and have the abilities of synthesis and creativity.

Graduation with a bachelor's degree from the College requires successful completion of 180 quarter hours, of which 50 quarter hours are in core requirements offered under the title of Integrative Studies in Human Nature. The College's quarter calendar lends itself to the wide variety of internships and other off-campus educational opportunities offered by the College. The academic year begins in mid-September and ends in early June.

Through other academic opportunities, students may design an individualized major as well as receive advanced placement by examination and credit through CLEP examinations in some academic areas.

Off-Campus Arrangements

A variety of off-campus programs are available, including foreign language study in Dijon, France. Semester at Sea, a shipboard-campus program offered in cooperation with the University of Pittsburgh, enables students to take a variety of liberal arts courses while cruising. Study opportunities also exist with the Washington Semester Plan, operated through the American University in Washington, D.C., and with the Philadelphia Center. The Roehampton Exchange, located in the Wimbledon area of London, England, consists of a federation of four institutions, providing the student with many cultural opportunities.

Academic Facilities

Roush Hall houses state-of-the-art computer labs, classrooms, a multimedia room, a two-story art gallery, and faculty and administrative offices. The Courtright Memorial Library houses 188,100 volumes and 1,015 periodical subscriptions, and has an outstanding modern learning-resource center that includes the studios of the Otterbein-Westerville television station, WOCC. The McFadden-Schear Science Hall has modern laboratories and classrooms and a renovated planetarium and observatory. Cowan Hall houses modern facilities for speech and theater, including WOBN-FM, the campus radio station. The Battelle Fine Arts Center is the home for programs in music, art, and dance and also houses an electronic music laboratory. Historic Towers Hall, a campus landmark since 1870, houses classrooms, faculty offices, and updated math and computer science labs.

Costs

For 2000–2001, Otterbein's tuition and fees are $16,911. Room and board cost $5289 per year. Books and supplies amount to approximately $400–$600 per year.

Financial Aid

Otterbein offers a wide variety of scholarships and grants, including Presidential Scholar Awards, Otterbein Scholar Awards, Endowed Scholarships, Alumni Scholarships, Federal Pell Grants, Ohio Instructional Grants, and Ammons-Thomas minority scholarships. In addition, Federal Perkins Loans, Federal Stafford Student Loans, and United Methodist Student Loans are available. To be considered for need-based College financial aid, students must file the Free Application for Federal Student Aid (FAFSA). Otterbein's financial aid policy is to attempt to meet 100 percent of the demonstrated financial need for each admitted student who files financial aid forms by April 1.

Approximately 95 percent of Otterbein's students receive some form of financial aid. In addition to its need-based awards, the College offers scholarships to students on the basis of academic ability and proven talent.

Faculty

Otterbein has a faculty of 138 full-time and 65 part-time members (giving a student-faculty ratio of 13:1). Eighty-six percent of the full-time faculty members hold a doctorate or appropriate terminal degree. Faculty members are actively involved in campus governance, committees, and activities. The extensive sabbatical plan at Otterbein helps ensure that the faculty members constantly update and improve their classroom teaching.

Student Government

Otterbein's nationally acclaimed governance program gives students a voting voice along with faculty and administrators on all campus policymaking and decision-making bodies. Students are elected to the College Senate, to all governance committees, and to the College's Board of Trustees.

Admission Requirements

To be considered for admission to Otterbein College, students must complete and sign an admission application, submit an official copy of their high school transcript, and provide the College with their scores on either the ACT or SAT I. Applicants should have a solid high school academic record with at least 16 college-preparatory units. Otterbein does not discriminate on the basis of sex, race, gender, sexual orientation, age, political affiliation, national origin, or disabling condition in the admission of students, educational policies, financial aid and scholarships, housing, athletics, employment, and other activities. Inquiries regarding compliance with federal nondiscrimination regulations may be directed to the chairperson of the Affirmative Action Committee, the vice president for academic affairs, or the vice president for business affairs.

Students can gain a fuller understanding of student life at Otterbein by spending a day on campus. Prospective students are welcome to visit classes, eat in the Campus Center, and talk informally with Otterbein students and should simply notify the Office of Admission in advance so arrangements can be made.

Application and Information

Students are urged to begin the application process early in their senior year of high school. Applicants are notified of their admission status as soon as their application file is completed.

For further information, students should contact:

Office of Admission
Otterbein College
Westerville, Ohio 43081
Telephone: 614-823-1500
              800-488-8144 (toll-free)
E-mail: uotterb@otterbein.edu

Students on the campus of Otterbein College.

OUR LADY OF THE LAKE UNIVERSITY OF SAN ANTONIO
SAN ANTONIO, TEXAS

The University

Our Lady of the Lake University, founded in 1895 by the Congregation of Divine Providence (http://www.ollusa.edu/CDP), is a coed liberal arts institution enrolling approximately 3,600 students in ninety-eight undergraduate, graduate, doctoral, and professional programs in the College of Arts and Sciences, the School of Business, the School of Education and Clinical Studies, and the Worden School of Social Service. The Lake's combination of historic Gothic buildings and modern facilities is the setting for innovative academic programs. The Congregation of Divine Providence's majestic Sacred Heart Conventual Chapel on campus has undergone preservation. The Lake is proud of its emphasis on service to others, its tradition of academic excellence, and its personal, student-centered atmosphere.

The University's student body ranges from recent high school graduates to older adults who have returned to college. The University offers Weekend College programs in San Antonio, Dallas, and Houston. A majority of the students are from Texas, but twenty-seven states and seventeen other countries are represented on campus. The average age of new freshmen is 18. About 53 percent of the University's students are Hispanic, 9 percent are African American, and 1 percent are international. Seven residence halls are available, with space for 465 students.

The Campus Activities Office sponsors events throughout the year. Students are encouraged to join campus organizations to foster a well-rounded education by developing leadership skills through out-of-the-classroom involvement. Our Lady of the Lake University has four types of organizations to meet the needs of students: special interest groups, academic organizations, honor societies, and chartered organizations.

Campus Ministry serves the entire University. The distinctive task of Campus Ministry is to call the total institution to spread the Gospel and to preserve and enrich its religious traditions. Campus Ministry offers opportunities to live out the commitment and mission of the Church through daily Eucharist, paraliturgical services, retreats, and renewal experiences. It sponsors various programs, including the Christian Association for Reaching Everyone (CARE), the Awakening Retreat Program, Peer Ministry, chapel choir, Spirit Retreat Team, and liturgy involvement (lectors, eucharistic ministers, greeters). Students and faculty and staff members have opportunities for spiritual direction, pastoral counseling, and faith enrichment on campus.

Intramural sports include basketball, football, racquetball, soccer, softball, tennis, and volleyball. Campus athletic facilities include playing fields, tennis courts, sand volleyball courts, an outdoor track with Fit-Trail equipment, indoor and outdoor temperature-controlled swimming pools and basketball courts, and the University Wellness and Activities Center, which houses a gymnasium, aerobics room, weight room, racquetball courts, computer lab, lounge/study areas, and other facilities.

Location

The Lake's 72-acre campus is located in a residential area 3 miles west of downtown San Antonio, the nation's eighth-largest city. City bus routes link the campus to downtown. With a mix of Mexican, Spanish, German, and other heritages, San Antonio is known for Fiesta, the rodeo, the Spanish missions (including the Alamo), the beautiful RiverWalk, a Mexican market, world-class museums, the 1999 NBA World Champion San Antonio Spurs basketball team, a professional hockey team, an annual arts festival, the third-largest zoo in the United States, a symphony orchestra, and a sunny climate. San Antonio is less than 3 hours by car from the Gulf Coast and from Mexico and a short drive to the state capital.

Majors and Degrees

The Bachelor of Arts degree is offered in American studies, art, biology, chemistry, communication and learning disorders (speech pathology), communication arts, drama, English, fine arts, history, human resource development, human sciences, liberal studies (includes elementary education), management, mathematics, natural sciences (including a core in environmental science), philosophy, political science, psychology, religious studies, social studies, sociology, and Spanish. The Bachelor of Science is awarded in computer information systems, early childhood education, electronic commerce, generic special education, and reading education. The Bachelor of Social Work is offered in social work. The Bachelor of Business Administration is offered in accounting, computer information systems, electronic commerce, and management (with concentrations in general, human resources, and marketing). The Bachelor of Applied Studies is available in chemistry, communication arts, English, fine arts, human sciences, liberal studies, management, mathematics, natural sciences (including a core in environmental science), philosophy, social studies, and Spanish. The applied studies degree is available for students who have 18–30 hours of credit in a technological specialization from transfer courses, life or work experience, or credit by examination. Students pursuing careers as secondary school teachers major in their first teaching field and minor in a second teaching field. Students pursuing careers as elementary school teachers select a concentration in an academic specialization, with supporting courses required for teacher certification. Teaching certificates are available in bilingual education, early childhood education, elementary education, exercise and sports science, secondary education, and special education. Prelaw, premedical, and prenursing programs are offered. Interdisciplinary majors are available in eleven fields.

Academic Program

Requirements for a bachelor's degree at The Lake include a minimum of 128 semester hours, 36 of which must be on the advanced level, a cumulative grade point average of at least 2.0, an average of at least 2.0 on all work taken at the University, a minimum of 32 semester hours in residence, and computer literacy requirements specified by the major or area of concentration. General education requirements are listed in the University bulletin. Applicants may have their prior learning experiences evaluated for credit according to methods approved by the University and the Council for the Assessment of Experiential Learning. The Lake offers computer-assisted learning, internships, practice in professional fields, and independent study. Army or Air Force ROTC courses are available.

Academic Facilities

The Electronic Commerce Lab and Technical Center, the Grossman Computer Instructional Laboratory, the Sueltenfuss Science/Math Computer Laboratory, the English Computer Laboratory, and the computer resource room in the main library contain terminals, microcomputers, and printers. A computer lab is also located in the University Wellness and Activities Center. E-mail is offered to all students. The St. Florence Library contains most of the University library system's holdings, including ERIC microfiche, a Texana collection, and several rare book collections. Other libraries include the Media Services Center, the Worden School of Social Service Library, and the Old Spanish Missions Historical Research Library. The new 49,000-square-foot Sueltenfuss Library, which will include a computer lab and a 24-hour study room, opened in early 2000.

Modern laboratory facilities are available in general chemistry, general biology, bacteriology, physiology, organic chemistry, analytical chemistry, and physics. The Science Research

Laboratory, which opened in August 1998, is designed to enable undergraduate science majors to perform research projects under the supervision of two new research faculty members —one each in biology and chemistry. The lab contains a wide variety of new instruments and allows students to leave projects set up, as the lab is not used for teaching classes. Communication arts students have access to a fully equipped small-format video studio. The Decision Theater, a simulated boardroom arena with one-way observation galleries, is used to teach decision making and problem solving.

As part of its research and student practicum facilities, the University maintains the Harry Jersig Center for communication and learning disorders; the Community Counseling Service for marriage, family, and individual counseling; the St. Martin Hall Demonstration Elementary School; the Child Development Center for training and studying developmental learning; the International Center; the Center for Women in Church and Society; and the Center for Social Service Research.

Costs

Full-time (12–19 semester hours) undergraduate tuition for 2000–01 is $5854 per semester. Part-time undergraduate tuition is $380 per credit hour, with a general fee of $59 per semester plus a $4 per credit hour technology fee per semester. The same tuition rate applies to in-state and out-of-state students. University housing costs vary, but average $2484 per year in 2000–01. All students who reside in University housing must participate in one of three board plans ($825, $925, or $1025 plus tax per semester).

Financial Aid

Most of The Lake's dependent undergraduate students receive some form of financial assistance. The University awards scholarships and academic grants on the basis of the student's composite score on the ACT or combined score on the SAT I and high school or college grade point averages. Freshmen and transfer students accepted for admission are automatically considered for awards.

Students can apply for additional financial assistance. Federal and state grant and loan programs are available. Work awards are available through the federally funded Federal Work-Study Program, and the Lake's Campus Employment Program. To be considered for financial aid, students must complete the Free Application for Federal Student Aid (FAFSA). On the FAFSA, students should list Our Lady of the Lake University, code number 003598. The Lake will receive the FAFSA data electronically and will then calculate a financial aid award. Financial aid applicants must be accepted for admission to the University before the award can be issued. More documentation may be needed for government programs. All financial aid is awarded on a first-come, first-served basis.

Faculty

The Lake has 128 full-time and 141 part-time faculty members. Sixty-nine percent of the full-time faculty members hold a doctoral or other terminal degree. The student-faculty ratio is 13:1. Faculty members advise sophomores, juniors, and seniors; serve as sponsors of student clubs and organizations; participate in intramural sports programs; and are available to students in person and via e-mail.

Student Government

The Student Government Association (SGA) provides a forum for students to examine issues affecting the welfare of students and to propose solutions for positive change. It provides students an opportunity to stay involved in campus issues and activities and to build leadership skills. SGA consists of a 7-member executive board, which oversees two legislative branches: the Senate, with elected student representatives from each academic class and each school of the University, and the House of Representatives, with representatives of each recognized student organization.

The president of the Student Government Association is the student representative to the University's Board of Trustees. Students and faculty members share faculty-student policymaking and advisory committees. Students are represented on University planning councils and search committees for administrative positions.

Admission Requirements

The Lake seeks a diverse student body and offers equal educational opportunity to all students regardless of race, color, creed, sex, age, national or ethnic origin, or disability. Entering freshmen must give the following evidence of academic preparation and aptitude: graduation from an accredited high school with 16 units of credit, including 4 in English, 3 in social science, 2 in mathematics, 2 in a laboratory science, and 2 in a foreign language (or 2 additional units in English, math, social science, or natural science), or successful completion of the GED test or successful completion of college-level work at another accredited postsecondary institution; or a satisfactory combination of scores on the SAT I or ACT and the high school grade point average. No preference is given to in-state students or to children of alumni.

Application and Information

Prospective students should send a completed application form, a nonrefundable $25 application fee, and SAT I or ACT scores to the Admissions & Advisement Center. Entering freshmen must submit a transcript of high school credits (this may be done as early as the completion of the junior year) or evidence of successful completion of the GED test. Transfer students must submit an official transcript from each institution attended. Transfer students with fewer than 30 transferable college credit hours must also submit scores on the SAT I or ACT and an official high school transcript if the college/university transcript does not indicate high school credits. All credentials must be received ten working days prior to registration for any term.

Admission decisions are made within two weeks of receiving completed application forms and all required documents. A $100 advance tuition deposit reserves the student's place in the entering class and the residence halls for resident students. The students must complete and return the housing application to the Office of Residence Life as soon as possible. Commuter students receive $100 credit toward their first semester enrollment.

To arrange a campus visit and tour, students should call the Admissions & Advisement Center.

Inquiries and application materials should be directed to:

Admissions & Advisement Center
Our Lady of the Lake University
411 Southwest 24th Street
San Antonio, Texas 78207-4689

Telephone: 210-434-6711 Ext. 314
           800-436-OLLU (toll-free)
E-mail: admission@lake.ollusa.edu
World Wide Web: http://www.ollusa.edu

Our Lady of the Lake University, located in beautiful San Antonio, the nation's eighth-largest city with a small-town atmosphere.

PACE UNIVERSITY
NEW YORK CITY AND PLEASANTVILLE, NEW YORK

The University

Pace University was founded in 1906 by two brothers, Homer and Charles Pace. The vision they had in 1906 is reflected in Pace's motto: "Opportunitas." Pace provides a remarkable array of learning, living, and working opportunities to all students. More than 100 majors and 3,000 courses of study are offered in the following five undergraduate schools: the Dyson College of Arts and Sciences, the Lubin School of Business, the School of Computer Science and Information Systems, the School of Education, and the Lienhard School of Nursing.

There are many activities and clubs to choose from, including the Black Students Organization, the Chinese Club, the Caribbean Students Association, student government associations, fraternities, sororities, two campus newspapers, two literary magazines, two yearbooks, two campus radio stations, and intercollegiate baseball, basketball, cross-country running, equestrian sports, football, lacrosse, soccer (women's), softball, tennis, and volleyball.

In 1999–2000, approximately 9,070 undergraduate students were enrolled at Pace. The student body is diversified, with students coming from across the United States and from more than sixty-five countries.

Location

Pace offers a variety of campus and living opportunities. Each campus is different. From the New York City campus, Wall Street and the South Street Seaport are a short walk, and Lincoln Center, the theater district, the Metropolitan Museum, and other world-famous centers of the arts are just a few minutes away by subway. On the Pleasantville campus, the residence halls and town houses are adjacent to an environmental center, riding stables, and a variety of recreational facilities. Briarcliff, just down the road from Pleasantville, offers on-campus camaraderie with an off-campus feeling. The campus is surrounded by towns and villages that have gifted resident artisans, local musical and theatrical groups, and museums. It is also easily accessible by car, bus, and railroad commuter service and is within easy reach of the resort and ski areas of the Catskills, Berkshires, and Poconos.

Students can live and take courses at either the Pleasantville or New York City campus; a minibus connects both campuses and is available at no charge to students. Residence facilities on both campuses feature Internet connectivity, voice mail, and cable TV access.

Majors and Degrees

Pace University in New York City grants the Bachelor of Business Administration degree with majors in business economics; finance; general accounting; general business; information systems, international management; management; management with a concentration in business, hotel, human resources, or operations management; management science with a minor in mathematics; marketing; and public accounting (CPA preparation). Four-year combined B.B.A./M.B.A. and B.B.A./M.S. (pending approval from New York State Department of Education) programs in public accounting are offered for qualified students. The Bachelor of Arts degree is granted in art history, computer science, computer science with a minor in education, dramatic arts, economics, economics with a minor in education, elementary education, English, English with a minor in education, French with a minor in education, history, history with a minor in education, human relations, language culture and world trade, liberal studies, mathematics, modern languages and cultures, political science, political science with a minor in education, psychology, social science, social science with a minor in education, sociology/anthropology, sociology/anthropology with a minor in education, Spanish with a minor in education, speech arts with a minor in education, speech communication, and speech pathology. B.A. degrees are also awarded in the teaching of speech and hearing handicapped and the teaching of speech and hearing handicapped/bilingual track with a minor in education. The Bachelor of Science degree is offered in biology, biology with a minor in education, business education, chemistry, chemistry with an minor in education, computer science, early childhood development, elementary education, information systems, mathematics (with an applied concentration or minor), nursing (upper division), office information systems, and a program in the allied health area. Pace recently added the physician assistant studies program in cooperation with Lenox Hill Hospital and is applying for provisional accreditation from the Commission on Accreditation of Allied Health Education Programs (CAAHEP) during the 1999–2000 academic year. Programs leading to the B.A./M.B.A. or B.S./M.B.A. are available. B.A. and B.S. students may minor in secondary education. The Bachelor of Fine Arts degree is also offered in theater. The Associate in Arts degree is granted in general arts and sciences. The Associate in Science is offered in early childhood development, general science, and office technology. The Associate in Applied Science is offered in accounting, banking, and general business.

Pace University in Pleasantville/Briarcliff confers the B.A. in art with an education minor, art history, biological sciences, computer science, computer science with a minor in education, economics, elementary education, elementary education/special education, history, history with a minor in education, human relations, human services, journalism, liberal studies, literature and communications, literature and communications with an education minor, mathematics, modern languages and cultures with an education minor, political science, political science with a minor in education, psychology, social science, and social science with an education minor. The B.S. degree is granted in art, art with an education minor, biochemistry, biology, biology with an education minor, chemistry, chemistry with an education minor, computer science, criminal justice, elementary education, elementary education/special education, information systems, mathematics (with an applied concentration or education minor), medical technology, nursing, physics, physics with an education minor, science, and science with an education minor. B.A./M.B.A., B.S./M.B.A., and B.A./M.P.A. combined-degree programs are also offered. B.A. and B.S. students may minor in secondary education. The B.B.A. is offered with majors in finance, general accounting, international management, management information systems, marketing, and public accounting. Four-year combined B.B.A./M.B.A. and B.B.A./M.S. (pending approval from New York State Department of Education) programs are offered in public accounting (CPA preparation). The following degree programs are also available: the A.A. in design, fine arts, and general arts and sciences; and the A.A.S. with majors in accounting and general business.

Pace University offers two 5-year engineering programs in cooperation with Manhattan College and with Rensselaer Polytechnic Institute; the student spends the first three years at Pace and the last two in the engineering program at Manhattan or Rensselaer. One program leads to a B.S. degree from Pace in science with a concentration in physics and a B.S. degree from Manhattan in electrical engineering; the other leads to a B.S. degree from Pace in chemistry and a B.C.E. in chemical engineering from Manhattan or a B.S. degree from Pace and a B.S. in engineering from Rensselaer.

Academic Program

The pattern of study at Pace University emphasizes the breadth of the core curriculum and involves taking prerequisites in the first two years and major courses plus electives in the junior and senior years. Selective academic programs in the University are preparatory to professional training in dentistry, law, medicine, and veterinary science.

The University honors program is designed to foster the intellectual life of outstanding students by enabling them to take greater responsibility and initiative in their academic work. Honors advisers assist students through individual advising. The Open Curriculum privilege permits an honors program member to choose courses in arts and sciences with a greater degree of freedom. The Independent Study Program encourages qualified students to undertake research and study to a depth beyond the normal course requirements. Pace participates in the Advanced Placement Program of the College Board.

The Cooperative Education Program offers qualified students the opportunity to gain experience in their field while earning a four-year degree. Students can choose full-time, part-time, or summer schedules, working in an area directly related to their major course of study. It is recommended that admission to the program take place during the first year at the University.

Academic Facilities

All campuses have the laboratories, classrooms, computer and data processing equipment, and other facilities necessary to carry on excellent programs at the undergraduate level. The New York City campus library has 388,548 volumes and the Pleasantville/Briarcliff campus libraries has 192,279 volumes; the White Plains campus library currently has 102,933 volumes.

Costs

Tuition for 1999–2000 was $15,130 per year, a room was $4720 per year, and board was $1800 per year. Additional fees were $500, and books and supplies averaged $700.

Financial Aid

Financial aid is available through scholarships, institutional grants-in-aid, athletic scholarships, Federal Pell Grants, Federal Supplemental Educational Opportunity Grants, Federal Perkins Loans, Federal Stafford Student Loans, New York State Tuition Assistance Program awards (as well as awards from other states' incentive grant programs), Federal Work-Study awards, federal nursing scholarships and loans, and Law Enforcement Education Program awards. Further information on these programs may be obtained by contacting the Office of Financial Aid at the appropriate campus.

Faculty

The undergraduate faculty at Pace is an outstanding teaching faculty, and senior members, including department heads, teach freshman and sophomore students as well as upper-division classes. Approximately 95 percent of the full-time faculty members hold a doctoral degree; many act as professional consultants to other educational institutions or in business and government. Many adjunct faculty members pursue professional careers while teaching their specialty.

Student Government

The Day Student Government Association is a major instrument for self-government on all campuses. At the New York City campus, there is also an Evening Student Council. The University Senate, which operates on behalf of the entire institution, is composed of representatives from the student body, faculty, alumni, and administration of all campuses. The senate plays an active role in the formulation of University policy.

Admission Requirements

A minimum of 16 units from an accredited secondary school, or the equivalent, is required. Academic subjects in high school should be distributed as follows: 4 units of English; 2 units of college-preparatory mathematics (3–4 units of mathematics are recommended for computer science and business majors); 2 units of modern languages; 7 academic units with at least one 3-unit group and one 2-unit group in mathematics, science, history, social studies, or foreign languages; and 3 units of electives in either academic or nonacademic subjects. Applicants for the mathematics, science, and nursing programs are required to have 2 units of laboratory science. All applicants are required to take the SAT I or ACT examination and have the results forwarded to the University.

Application and Information

Requests for application forms and information for both the Pleasantville and New York City campuses should be addressed to the Student Information Center at the following address.

Student Information Center
Pace University
1 Pace Plaza
New York City, New York 10038
Telephone: 800-874-7223 Ext. UPGI
Fax: 212-346-1821
E-mail: infoctr@pace.edu
World Wide Web: http://www.pace.edu

PACIFIC LUTHERAN UNIVERSITY
TACOMA, WASHINGTON

The University

Three characteristics make prospective students enthusiastic about Pacific Lutheran University (PLU). The first is academic distinction, documented nationally in *U.S. News & World Report* and *Peterson's Competitive Colleges*. The second is the personality of the University community, which makes a difference in determining the type of student, professor, or employee who chooses to become associated with PLU. Each knows that the University's objectives reflect Christian principles and ideals, a willingness to help and serve, and a sensitivity to the welfare, happiness, and personal integrity of others. The third most alluring feature of the University is its geographic location, which is one of the most beautiful natural environments in the country.

Founded in 1890 by Scandinavian Lutheran pioneers, PLU retains pride in its heritage while seeking diversity to stimulate exchange and broaden understanding. A private university owned by the Evangelical Lutheran Church in America, PLU offers many opportunities for expressing and deepening Christian faith. At the same time, many forms of self-expression enrich a campus devoted to the development of knowledgeable, thoughtful, responsible, and dedicated citizens.

The University's 3,600 students represent thirty-seven states and twenty-five countries. Multiethnic and international students represent about 16 percent of the campus population.

About two thirds of the full-time students reside in twelve housing units. The eleven coed units are divided into male-female floors or wings with common lounges and service facilities. The four-story University Center enhances social and cultural activities with its multipurpose facilities, dining halls, games room, student media offices, bookstore, coffee shop, and the CAVE, a student-operated coffeehouse. Both the community and the University are served by the Scandinavian Cultural Center, housed in the lower level of the University Center.

Some fifty special interest, service, religious, and professional organizations are active on campus. Both participants and audiences have the opportunity to enjoy a variety of visual and performing arts, provided by both campus and professional groups. Personal expression is emphasized in debate, the student newspaper, campus television and radio, the yearbook, and the National Public Radio affiliate, KPLU-FM.

The athletic-recreation complex, available for everyone's use, has an indoor swimming pool; two gymnasiums; a field house with an artificial turf surface; an outdoor sand volleyball court; lighted tennis courts; a nine-hole golf course; racquetball and squash courts; a fitness center featuring free weights, weight machines, fitness machines, aerobics areas, and an indoor running track; outdoor athletics fields; and other outdoor recreation facilities. Women compete in eight varsity and two club sports. The women's soccer team has won the national team championship in three of the last eight years, the football team has won three national championships since 1980, and several other sports are nationally ranked. Men compete in ten varsity and five club sports, with many of those programs nationally ranked. PLU men's and women's athletic teams have won the conference All-Sports trophy for the last ten years. A strong intramural program, in which more than 60 percent of the students participate, emphasizes the University's encouragement of lifetime fitness of body, as well as of mind and spirit.

The Division of Graduate Studies awards the following degrees: Master of Arts in Education, Master of Arts in Social Sciences, Master of Business Administration, and Master of Science in Nursing. Master of Arts in Education specialties are educational administration, elementary or secondary classroom teaching, initial teaching certificate, reading, and special education. Master of Arts in Social Sciences offers the only regional accredited program in marriage and family therapy.

Location

Pacific Lutheran is located 6 miles south of downtown Tacoma, Washington, in a suburban environment. The beautiful and tranquil natural setting of mountains, water, and forests is complemented by the Seattle-Tacoma metropolitan area, long rated among the country's most desirable places to live. There are museums, galleries, excellent restaurants, shopping areas, parks, zoos, and aquariums, as well as a wealth of cultural and entertainment offerings. The PLU campus is a community cultural, intellectual, and recreational center in itself, with a variety of activities for campus and community involvement scheduled throughout the year.

Majors and Degrees

Pacific Lutheran University awards the following undergraduate degrees: Bachelor of Arts, Bachelor of Science, Bachelor of Arts in Education, Bachelor of Business Administration, Bachelor of Fine Arts, Bachelor of Music, Bachelor of Music Education, Bachelor of Musical Arts, Bachelor of Science in Nursing, Bachelor of Arts in Recreation, Bachelor of Arts in Physical Education, and Bachelor of Science in Physical Education. B.A. majors are anthropology, art, biology, chemistry, Chinese studies, classics, communication arts (print/broadcast journalism, critical communication studies, public relations, and theater), computer science, economics, English, French, geosciences, German, history, mathematics, music, Norwegian, philosophy, physical education, physics, political science, psychology, religion, Scandinavian area studies, social work, sociology, Spanish, and women's studies. B.S. majors are available in applied physics, biology, chemistry, computer engineering, computer science, engineering science, geosciences, mathematics, and psychology. There are Bachelor of Arts in Education degree concentrations in eighteen major subject areas. The Bachelor of Business Administration degree may be earned with concentrations in entrepreneurship and new venture management, financial resources management, human resource management, international business, marketing resource management, operations and information technology, and professional accounting. Bachelor of Fine Arts majors are available in art or communication arts (broadcasting, communication, and theater). Bachelor of Music majors are organ, piano, theory and composition, and vocal or instrumental performance.

Preprofessional preparation is offered in dentistry, law, medical technology, medicine, optometry, pharmacy, physical therapy, theological studies, and veterinary medicine.

International programs encourage students to expand their understanding of humanity's global condition in a changing world. They include the global studies program, with clusters on Asia, the Third World, Europe, Scandinavia, development and modernization, and global resources and trade, and with thematic modules in international affairs and international trade; a complementary global studies major; a Scandinavian area studies program; Chinese studies; and the program of the Intensive English Language Institute.

Academic Program

PLU operates on a 4-1-4 calendar, with two 14-week semesters bridged by a 4-week January term. Three 4-week summer sessions are often used by full-time students to accelerate their college careers.

All degree-seeking students, regardless of major, may choose one of two core curriculums. Core I (distributive core) requires nine courses in each of the following areas: arts and literature, natural sciences and mathematics, philosophy, religious studies, and social sciences. Core II (integrated studies program) requires completion of seven interdisciplinary classes that explore the theme "The Dynamics of Change." The nationally regarded core emphasizes the interrelationships among all fields of knowledge.

Most courses provide 4 semester hours of credit, with 128 semester hours required for graduation. The January term provides a variety of traditional and nontraditional courses, on and off campus, across the country and around the world.

Off-Campus Arrangements

During the January term particularly, students have the opportunity to participate in study tours of other countries. In recent years, such tours have been made to Africa, Australia, Central America, Cuba, Europe, the Middle East, the People's Republic of China, and Scandinavia. In addition, the Study Abroad Program makes available many PLU-sponsored opportunities for semester or yearlong studies in twenty countries, including Denmark, England, Germany, Mexico, Norway, the People's Republic of China, the Republic of China, Spain, and Sweden. Additional U.S. and study-abroad opportunities are sponsored periodically by campus departments and organizations, primarily during the January term.

Academic Facilities

The PLU campus reflects a dignified union of traditional and modern architecture in a magnificent evergreen setting. The critically acclaimed Mary Baker Russell Music Center is just one of the many outstanding facilities available to undergraduates. Excellent facilities now complement the outstanding programs in most academic disciplines.

Costs

Tuition and fees for 2000–2001 are $16,800, room is $2600, and standard board fees are $2700. The total costs for a student living on campus vary, although average costs, including books, supplies, and personal expenses, are approximately $24,000.

Financial Aid

The Free Application for Federal Student Aid (FAFSA) is used to determine a student's financial need for the awarding of scholarships, grants, and loans. More than $42 million in financial aid is distributed annually to nearly 95 percent of PLU students. The average financial aid package totals more than $14,000. Most awards are made in midspring for the following academic year. Students may find employment on or off campus with the assistance of the Office of Financial Aid and Student Employment.

Faculty

There are 237 full-time faculty members. Among them are alumni of many of the most prestigious educational institutions in the world. Eighty-two percent hold doctoral degrees, and they all teach. Most are at PLU because teaching is their top personal and professional priority.

Student Government

The Associated Students of Pacific Lutheran University is the recognized voice of all students, who are represented by 4 executive officers and 17 senators. Students are represented on most University committees, and student officers sit as advisory members on the Board of Regents.

Admission Requirements

Candidates for admission are encouraged to apply as early during their senior year of secondary school as possible. Early action students, upon acceptance, get first assistance in housing and registration. Selection factors include the high school grade average, class rank, transcript pattern, test scores, essay, and recommendations. PLU admits students without regard to race, color, sex, religion, national or ethnic origin, or disabling condition. Accepted students receive individual class-registration counseling during the summer preceding their freshman enrollment to help launch their collegiate career on a solid footing.

Application and Information

Application for admission may be made by submitting a PLU application, which is available from the Admissions Office; a $35 nonrefundable fee; transcripts of high school credits at least through the junior year as well as those of any college course work; SAT I or ACT test scores; a completed essay form; and one recommendation from a qualified person, such as a principal, a teacher, a counselor, or a pastor. Applicants seeking financial aid must submit the FAFSA to the Federal Processing Agent by January 31 for maximum consideration.

Office of Admissions
Pacific Lutheran University
Tacoma, Washington 98447
Telephone: 800-274-6758 (toll-free)
Fax: 253-536-5136
World Wide Web: http://www.plu.edu

Members of the PLU crew team compete annually at the Head of the Charles Regatta in Boston, Massachusetts.

PACIFIC UNIVERSITY
FOREST GROVE, OREGON

The University

Pacific University is a private, fully accredited four-year liberal arts university that encompasses an undergraduate College of Arts and Sciences and six graduate programs: five in the health professions and one in teacher education. Founded in 1849 by Congregational pioneers, Pacific is still a frontier institution, proud of its tradition in liberal arts and sciences and innovative in its programs for the rapidly changing health-care professions.

Pacific's 1,800 students come from all over the United States and twenty-eight countries, creating a diverse and dynamic student body. Students are taught by the University's 147 full-time faculty members, each of whom is chosen for his or her distinctive devotion to teaching and an emphasis on individual mentoring.

The College of Arts and Sciences is noted for its exceptionally personalized approach to education which is grounded in a philosophy of service. It is recognized for outstanding programs in the natural sciences, business, psychology, world languages, and the humanities.

Pacific's select group of graduate health profession programs includes the Pacific Northwest's only college of optometry as well as schools of physical therapy, occupational therapy, clinical and counseling psychology, and physician's assistant studies. In addition, a school of education offers undergraduate and master's-level programs leading to teacher licensure.

The lively and vigorous campus springs from the college's residential nature (freshmen and sophomores under 21 are required to live in one of the University's coed residence facilities). Students who choose to live off-campus may live in the University-owned housing units or other nearby apartment complexes. On campus, the University Center is a hub of activity that houses the campus bookstore, the dining commons, a new lounge, student government offices, Macintosh and IBM lab facilities, the campus radio station, and the newspaper office. The Associated Students of Pacific University (ASPU) provides funding to twenty-seven student interest groups ranging from the Outback program to the Hawaiian Club to the Politics and Law Forum. The Pacific Outback program provides a multitude of outdoor activities for interested students, such as kayaking, hiking, cross-country and downhill skiing trips, camping, and outings to Portland-area events.

In athletics, Pacific is a member of the Northwest Conference of Independent Colleges and the NCAA Division III. Men's intercollegiate sports are baseball, basketball, cross-country, golf, soccer, tennis, track, and wrestling. Women compete in basketball, cross-country, golf, soccer, softball, tennis, track, and volleyball. Pacific athletes train and compete in the Pacific Athletic Center, which includes a gymnasium; a multipurpose field house; racquetball, handball, and squash courts; saunas; a dance studio; a weight room; and a complete sports medicine training facility.

Location

Situated in the northwest corner of Oregon between metropolitan Portland and the Pacific Ocean, the University is located in Forest Grove (population 16,000). The 60-acre oak-covered campus is surrounded by green countryside and the foothills of the Coast Range, beyond which is the 300-mile stretch of Oregon coast. Opportunities abound in Oregon for hiking, skiing, camping, fishing, beach combing, and bicycling. The climate is temperate throughout the year with winter rainfall tapering off to a pleasant spring and sunny summer.

Majors and Degrees

Major programs leading to the B.A. or B.S. degree are offered through the College of Arts and Sciences in anthropology/sociology, applied science, art, biology, business administration (with an emphasis in accounting, finance, management, or marketing), chemistry (with an emphasis in biological chemistry, chemical physics, or environmental chemistry), Chinese studies, computer science, coordinated studies in humanities, creative writing, economics, education and learning, environmental biology, exercise science (with an emphasis in sports medicine or human performance), French studies, German studies, history, international studies, Japanese studies, literature, mathematics, media arts (with an emphasis in film production, film studies, integrated media, journalism, or video production), modern languages (with an emphasis in Chinese, French, German, Japanese, or Spanish), music (with an emphasis in education or performance), philosophy (with a bioethics emphasis), physics, political science, psychology, social work, sociology, Spanish, and theater. The B.M. degree is offered in music. Secondary education certification is available in art, biology, English, French, German, health education (combined endorsement only), integrated science, Japanese, mathematics, music, reading (combined endorsement only), social studies (secondary education students only), and Spanish.

Pacific offers five programs in the health professions that require undergraduate study. These include optometry (O.D.), professional psychology (M.A., M.S., and Psy.D.), physical therapy (M.S., D.P.T. anticipated for fall 2000), occupational therapy (M.O.T.), and a physician's assistant studies program (M.S.). Programs in teacher education include the fifth-year M.A.T., M.A.T. Flex, M.Ed., and the M.Ed. in Visual Function and Learning (in conjunction with the optometry program). Physical therapy students must complete three years of undergraduate prerequisite work before being admitted into the program. Optometry students spend three years in undergraduate prerequisite work before being admitted into the four-year doctoral graduate program. Occupational therapy students spend three years in undergraduate prerequisite work and 2 ½ years in the master's program. The physician's assistant studies master's program is a twenty-seven-month consecutive program.

Pacific offers 3-2 programs in computer science, electrical engineering, and environmental science through a cooperative program with the nearby Oregon Graduate Institute. At the completion of the program, the student receives both a bachelor's degree from Pacific and a master's degree in their specialty from Oregon Graduate Institute.

Academic Program

Pacific provides an excellent education in the liberal arts and sciences. The undergraduate core curriculum emphasizes writing, reasoning, and communication skills with attention given to cross-cultural education and work in the natural sciences and the fine arts. All freshmen participate in a semester-long first-year seminar program designed to introduce students to college-level writing and research expectations. Pacific has a long tradition of ethical concern that is reflected in its undergraduate courses and its many opportunities for service both on-campus and within the broader community. As a small college, Pacific maintains small classes that ensure close contact among students and faculty.

Special programs in the College of Arts and Sciences include the Honors Program for advanced and individual study, the Peace and Conflict Studies Program, as well as a minor in feminist studies.

Basic requirements for the B.A. or B.S. degree are 124 semester hours of credit, completion of a major, and completion of the core requirements in the College of Arts and Sciences. The year is divided into two semesters with a three-week winter term between the two semesters. Students typically take 15 credit hours during each semester and three credit hours during the winter term.

Pacific grants credit for both subject and general CLEP examinations. Each department or school at Pacific University determines whether or not a specific examination may substitute for a specific course. Students who score 4 or better on the Advanced Placement examinations of the College Board are given advanced placement and credit toward graduation. Pacific recognizes the International Baccalaureate program as providing college-level work. Six semester credits will be awarded for each higher examination passed at a score of 5 or higher.

Off-Campus Arrangements

Pacific offers study-abroad programs with thirty-three schools in fifteen countries, including Austria, China, Denmark, Ecuador, France, Germany, Hungary, Italy, Japan, Korea, Mexico, Netherlands, Spain, Thailand, and Wales. Foreign language and international studies majors are required to spend at least one semester studying abroad and may use financial aid toward their foreign study. Pacific also emphasizes internships, which are regularly arranged for students in business, communications, political science, psychology, sociology, and other fields. The internships, which may be arranged for periods lasting from fourteen weeks to an entire academic year, offer the opportunity to become thoroughly acquainted with professional work and often lead to employment upon graduation.

Academic Facilities

The 60-acre campus, a picturesque setting with green lawns and tall shade trees, has eighteen major buildings. Historic Marsh Hall, which was originally constructed in 1893 and completely refurbished in 1977, holds classrooms, professors' offices, and administration facilities. Old College Hall, built in 1850, was the first permanent structure of Pacific University. This building contains museum galleries, historic exhibits, and the campus chapel. The Douglas C. Strain Science Center and the Taylor-Meade Performing Arts Center were additions to campus in 1993. Students live in one of three residence halls or in the Vandervelden apartments. All on-campus rooms are connected to the campus computer network linked to the Internet. The Harvey W. Scott Library has 133,329 bound volumes, documents, periodicals, microfilm, microfiche, and musical recordings and scores. Pacific is part of OCLC (On-Line Computer Library Center), which allows students access to libraries all over the nation. Also available are a foreign language laboratory, a study-skills center, a rare books room, and various audiovisual services.

Costs

Tuition and fees for the 2000–01 school year are $17,804. Room and board are estimated at $4855 for a double room and a nineteen-meal-per-week plan. Books and supplies are estimated at approximately $700.

Financial Aid

Financial assistance at Pacific is awarded on the basis of demonstrated need, academic merit, and talent. The Free Application for Federal Student Aid (FAFSA) is used in evaluating need. Prospective students are encouraged to apply for financial assistance by submitting the FAFSA to the federal processor as soon after January 1 as possible. Pacific provides financial assistance through grants, scholarships, loans, and part-time employment.

Faculty

Pacific's outstanding faculty members provide the foundation for the University's academic program. A student-faculty ratio of 12:1 allows for personal attention by the professors. Pacific's faculty is made up of 147 dedicated educators, of whom 96 percent hold terminal degrees in their field. As professionals, they uphold the University's standard of academic excellence. Pacific does not use graduate or teaching assistants in any course.

Student Government

Participatory government at Pacific enables students to help shape the campus community in which they live and work. Students are encouraged to voice their opinions and to pursue new ideas that not only further personal growth but also the overall growth and development of the University. The official student government body manages activity funds, reviews and supports student issues, and coordinates student participation within the system.

Admission Requirements

Pacific University is selective in considering new students. Primary consideration is given to a candidate's academic preparation and potential for successful study at the college level, as assessed by evaluating the student's transcripts of college-preparatory work, counselor and teacher recommendations, personal essay, SAT I or ACT scores, and other student-submitted information (such as teacher recommendations). Transfer students must submit high school records and test scores if they have completed less than 30 semester hours, plus official transcripts from any institution previously attended.

Application and Information

Students may apply early and may be notified early through the modified rolling admissions plan. The regular priority deadline for admission is February 15.

For additional information, interested students should contact:
Director of Undergraduate Admissions
Pacific University
2043 College Way
Forest Grove, Oregon 97116
Telephone: 503-359-2218
           800-677-6712 (toll-free)
E-mail: admissions@pacificu.edu

PAIER COLLEGE OF ART, INC.
HAMDEN, CONNECTICUT

The College

Paier College of Art, Inc., founded in 1946 as Paier School of Applied Arts, has educated artists in advertising, illustration, design, interior design, photography, and graphics, as well as in other applied art fields. Upon receiving a charter in 1982, the College expanded its commitment to provide as wide a range of art education as possible while maintaining its focus on preparing its students for professional careers in the arts. At Paier a professional art education occurs in the context of the education of the individual as a whole. The College maintains close relations with the professional art community as well as with the community at large. Instructors and full-time faculty members are all active professionals in their fields and provide an invaluable resource in terms of professional experience and expertise. The curriculum combines career skills with a background in the liberal arts. This approach to instruction—with its expectations of study in the fine arts through drawing, painting, composition, and computer skills, and in the mastery of procedures of the specialized field and development of portfolios geared to the workplace—has attracted students seeking rigorous preparation and has resulted in graduates of Paier College of Art finding rewarding careers in the professional world.

Students participate in semiannual shows and sales sponsored by the Student Association. These shows provide the student with exposure and reviews from the community at large, peers, and professionals in the field. Paier College of Art is approved by the Connecticut Board of Governors for Higher Education and accredited by the Accrediting Commission for Career Schools and Colleges of Technology and is a member of the International Council of Design Schools.

The current undergraduate enrollment is 276 men and women. The College provides no on-campus living arrangements. Private houses and apartments near the campus offer accommodations for both men and women. A list of rooms may be obtained from the admission office. Also, dormitories are available at nearby Albertus Magnus College.

Location

Paier College of Art is located on the edge of New Haven. Public transportation provides students with easy access to other area colleges and universities. New Haven and the surrounding communities contain many centers of art display and activity. The Yale Gallery, the Peabody Museum, and the Mellon Center for British Art are examples of the art collections available locally. The Greater New Haven area supports many galleries, theaters, and dance and musical organizations. New Haven also supports a variety of shopping facilities, hotels, and restaurants. The rolling, picturesque Connecticut countryside is only a short distance away and is complemented by the fine beaches that dot the length of New England's coastline. All of New England, rich in the tradition of early America and alive with the creative energy of a well-educated population, surrounds the Paier student with countless opportunities for cultural experiences. Students are also within easy reach of New York, Hartford, and Boston.

Majors and Degrees

Paier College of Art offers programs of study leading to the Bachelor of Fine Arts (B.F.A.) degree in the following studio majors: fine arts, graphic design, illustration, and interior design. An Associate of Fine Arts (A.F.A.) degree is available in photography. Paier College also offers programs of study leading to a diploma in fine arts, graphic design, illustration, interior design, and photography. Certificate programs are offered in graphic production, interior design, portrait and figure painting, and sharp focus/trompe l'oeil painting. Students completing certificate programs may apply the credits earned toward a Bachelor of Fine Arts degree or diploma in their field.

Academic Program

Degree and diploma candidates begin with a foundation year of required study. A progressive, contemporary philosophy is shared with a respect for classical tradition and structured discipline. The foundation year of study reflects this philosophy and is and has been directed and staffed by outstanding practitioners since the school's inception a half century ago. Classes are mixed, with candidates for degree, diploma, and certificate programs working together. The same degree of professionalism is demanded of and shown to all students regardless of their program of study. The B.F.A. requires 130 semester hours of study, of which 88 must be in studio work and 42 must be in the humanities and sciences. The diploma requires 104 semester hours, of which 92 must be in studio work and 12 must be in the humanities and sciences. The A.F.A. in photography requires 43 semester hours of studio work and 21 semester hours in the humanities and sciences. The diploma in photography requires 43 semester hours of studio work and 9 semester hours in the humanities and sciences. Certificate programs require from 28 to 32 semester hours of study, consisting almost entirely of studio work.

Paier College of Art operates on the semester academic calendar. Spring and fall semesters are supplemented by a summer session.

Academic Facilities

The campus is situated at the corner of Circular and Gorham Avenues. Administration activities, including admissions, personnel matters, consideration and disbursement of financial aid, maintenance of student records, and general administration, are conducted at 20 Gorham Avenue. Instructional activities in classrooms, studios, and laboratories designed for the College's purposes are conducted in four buildings that include the library, the auditorium, the computer lab, and exhibition spaces. The library contains 15,000 volumes, subscribes to 77 periodicals, houses a picture reference file of more than 250,000 images, and has a slide library containing more than 65,000 slides. In addition to extensive holdings in the field of the arts, the library contains a well-balanced collection of volumes in the humanities, social sciences, and physical sciences.

Costs

Tuition for 2000–01 is $10,900 per year for full-time degree students and $9100 per year for full-time diploma students. Part-time tuition is $350 per semester hour. Fees and supplies vary by program of study.

Financial Aid

Paier College of Art has a program of financial aid for those who are eligible that includes the Federal Pell Grant, Federal

Supplemental Educational Opportunity Grant, and Connecticut Independent College Student Grant. Loans may be obtained through the following programs: Federal Perkins Loan, Federal Stafford Student Loans, Universal Education Loans, and Federal PLUS. Further information may be obtained from the Office of Financial Aid at Paier College of Art.

Faculty

Faculty members at Paier College of Art are all professionals in their fields. As such, their level of expertise in preparing students to enter their chosen profession is invaluable. There are 43 faculty members, including both full-time and part-time practicing professionals. The student-faculty ratio is 6:1.

Student Government

Every member of the College student body is encouraged to participate in the Student Association, which is a vital and influential force in campus activities. The officers of the Student Association act as a liaison between the students and the College administration. Activities include socials, exhibitions of student and faculty work, field trips to major exhibits in Boston and New York, and cultural presentations.

Admission Requirements

Paier College of Art maintains a rolling admission system in which decisions are made throughout the year. Students may apply for full-time or part-time program status or for full-time or part-time nonmatriculated status. All high school and college transcripts, scores on either the SAT I or the ACT (for BFA students only), and two letter of recommendation are required. A nonrefundable application fee of $25 must accompany the completed application materials. An interview is required and is a vital part of the application process. A portfolio of recent artwork should be presented at the interview. Students with earned credit from other colleges may be admitted with advanced standing.

Application and Information

Application forms and additional information are available by contacting:

Office of Admissions
Paier College of Art, Inc.
20 Gorham Avenue
Hamden, Connecticut 06514

Telephone: 203-287-3031
Fax: 203-287-3021
E-mail: info@paierart.com
World Wide Web: http://www.paierart.com

Students interact with 3-D sculptures.

PAINE COLLEGE
AUGUSTA, GEORGIA

The College

Paine College is private, four-year, coeducational, and residential. Established in 1882 by the United Methodist Church and the Christian Methodist Episcopal (C.M.E.) Church, Paine offers a broad-based educational program in the liberal arts. Historically black in enrollment, Paine is one of the forty-one colleges and universities associated with the United Negro College Fund.

The mission of Paine College is to provide a high-quality liberal arts education that emphasizes ethical and spiritual values, social responsibility, and personal development. Paine is committed to timeless standards of instructional quality within a curriculum that responds to the needs of its students. Paine's excellent academic environment, its small size, and competent, caring faculty form the matrix of an extraordinarily nurturing experience.

Paine's attractive 55-acre campus provides a thriving yet relaxed social center for college life. Central to the campus setting is a beautiful tree-lined quadrangle, with Haygood-Holsey Hall, the administration building, and the Gilbert-Lambuth Memorial Chapel as its anchors. There are 915 students enrolled at Paine. Sixty percent of the students live on campus in six residence halls. Represented among the more than forty clubs and organizations are eight fraternities and sororities. Planned recreational activities are usually held at the Peters Campus Center or the Randall A. Carter Gymnasium. The chapel is the setting for assemblies, formal convocations, religious services, and commencement exercises.

Paine competes in the Southern Intercollegiate Athletic Conference (SIAC), which is affiliated with the National Collegiate Athletic Association (NCAA) Division II. Athletic programs include men's and women's basketball, cross-country, and track; women's softball and volleyball; and men's baseball.

Location

Located in Augusta, Georgia, Paine is situated in the heart of the state's second-largest metropolitan area. Augusta is located 150 miles east of Atlanta on the west bank of the Savannah River. The riverbank is a hub of activity, including the $4-million Riverwalk—a complex of shops, restaurants, and entertainment spots. Augusta is known internationally as the host city for the Masters Golf Tournament, which draws spectators from around the world. The city has two major malls and numerous shopping centers. The Augusta–Richmond County Civic Center and the Bell Auditorium offer a variety of entertainment, including national performers and cultural events. Public transportation is available to all parts of the city. Augusta is easily accessible by car or air.

Majors and Degrees

Paine College offers thirteen majors leading to the Bachelor of Science or Bachelor of Arts degree. The College's major areas of study are biology, business administration, chemistry, early childhood education, English, history, mass communications, mathematics, middle grades education, music education, psychology, religion and philosophy, and sociology. Concentrations or emphases include computer science, criminology, information systems, and secondary education. Many majors may be selected as minors, or students may choose from several areas designated as minors only, including art, economics, French, music, physical education, physics, and political science.

Academic Program

A challenging academic program offers numerous opportunities for development and preparation for a diverse and flexible future. Paine's comprehensive curriculum is continually enhanced to challenge and stretch the mind of every student. While the curriculum is grounded in the liberal arts, the College recognizes the changing career patterns its graduates will face in the twenty-first century and offers expanded opportunities in new technologies. The curriculum is designed to provide opportunities for sound physical, intellectual, moral, social, and spiritual growth under Christian influences.

The academic year is divided into fall and spring semesters. There is also a summer session. Credit for courses is recorded in semester hours, with a minimum of 124 hours required for graduation. The 61-hour general education requirement includes courses in English, fine arts, physical education, mathematics, natural sciences, social sciences, philosophy, religion, and a foreign language. A core of at least 34 hours is required for each major.

Special programs include ROTC, an honors program, cooperative education, and a preprofessional sciences program that prepares students for graduate and professional study in medicine, dentistry, pharmacy, and veterinary medicine. The preprofessional sciences program also offers students early acceptance to the Medical College of Georgia in nursing and eleven allied health fields. In addition to the health sciences programs, Paine offers a strong program in teacher education, which has been cited by the state of Georgia as a model. Teacher education has a 100 percent placement record, and the demand for graduates has surpassed the number of students in the program. The College has received several grants to support the growth of the teacher-education program.

Enhancement courses and the Tutorial and Enrichment Center supplement the academic program. The College is accredited by the Southern Association of Colleges and Schools.

Academic Facilities

Paine College's academic buildings include Haygood-Holsey Hall, Mary Helm Hall, Warren A. Candler Building, Walker Science Building, and the Gilbert-Lambuth Annex. The Collins-Callaway Library is a state-of-the-art library and learning resources center. The two-story, 30,000-square-foot facility is equipped to house more than 125,000 volumes. In the learning resources center, students have access to more than 150 microcomputers and more than 500 computer programs.

Costs

Tuition and fees for the 1999–2000 academic year totaled $7068. Room and board charges were $3286. Fees are $460. An optional meal plan is available for commuter students. Tuition and fees are subject to change annually.

Financial Aid

It is Paine College policy to provide every eligible student with the maximum amount of financial aid available. In fact, 90 percent of Paine College students receive some form of financial assistance. Paine College offers scholarships, grants, loans, and part-time employment, from various funding sources, to assist eligible students in meeting their educational expenses. The largest amount of support comes from the federal government through Federal Pell Grant, Federal Perkins Loan, Federal Supplemental Educational Opportunity Grant, Federal Work-Study, Federal Stafford Student Loan, and Federal PLUS Programs.

A student's eligibility for federal financial aid is determined by the information the applicant and his or her family provide on the Paine College Application for Financial Assistance and the College Scholarship Service Financial Aid PROFILE. Paine College recommends that every student complete and submit the necessary financial aid forms as soon as possible. The priority deadline for applications is April 15.

Faculty

Paine College has 65 full-time and 11 part-time faculty members. A student-teacher ratio of 12:1 enables Paine's talented and energetic faculty to provide the kind of individualized attention for which the College is known. Approximately 50 percent of Paine's faculty have earned doctorates. All faculty members have advanced degrees.

Student Government

Once enrolled, students automatically become members of the Student Government Association (SGA). The SGA is the chief agent between the students and the faculty. Paine College believes that student input is important. The president of the SGA is a member of the College's Board of Trustees, and a student government representative serves on the Committee on Strategic Planning.

Admission Requirements

Students are admitted on the basis of scholastic achievement, academic potential, seriousness of educational purpose, and leadership. To that end, Paine is committed to giving all who qualify an opportunity to learn and grow. New freshmen are expected to have at least a 2.0 average on a 4.0 scale in 16 units of college-preparatory courses from a school accredited by a state or regional accrediting agency. The courses must include English (4 units), mathematics (2 units), social sciences (2 units, including 1 in history), natural science (2 units), and electives (6 units). An early admission program is available to students of superior ability and maturity who have completed the eleventh grade.

Application and Information

Candidates for admission must submit a Paine College Application for Admission, the $10 application fee, SAT I or ACT scores, an autobiographical essay, a reference or letter of recommendation, and a high school transcript or passing scores on the GED test. Application deadlines are August 1 for the fall semester, December 1 for the spring semester, and June 1 for the summer session.

For an admission and financial aid packet, students should contact:

Office of Admissions and Financial Aid
Paine College
1235 Fifteenth Street
Augusta, Georgia 30901-3182
Telephone: 706-821-8320
              800-476-7703 (toll-free)
World Wide Web: http://www.paine.edu

Paine College's small setting and strong academic program promote an atmosphere for intellectual growth and discovery.

PALM BEACH ATLANTIC COLLEGE
WEST PALM BEACH, FLORIDA

The College

Palm Beach Atlantic College (PBA) was founded in 1968 by concerned Palm Beach County residents who felt the need for a distinctive institution of higher learning that would stress not only academic quality but also character development and spiritual maturity. Chartered as a Christian liberal arts college, Palm Beach Atlantic offers a high-quality education for students of all faiths. In 1972, the College was accredited by the Southern Association of Colleges and Schools to award bachelor's degrees.

By 1999, PBA had grown to serve nearly 2,200 students in a variety of traditional and nontraditional programs. Five master's degree programs also are offered: Master of Business Administration, Master of Science in Human Resource Development, Master of Education in elementary education, Master of Science in counseling psychology, and Master of Arts in ministry.

For both undergraduate and graduate students, Palm Beach Atlantic seeks to promote intellectual, moral, and spiritual growth. The undergraduate may opt for a variety of ways to get involved in college life, including service and leadership organizations, intercollegiate and intramural sports, fine arts, religious groups, and professionally oriented organizations such as Kappa Delta Epsilon and Phi Beta Lambda. In 2000, the College will break ground on several new building projects as part of its comprehensive campus growth plan. The DeSantis Chapel will provide exciting opportunities for multiple weekly chapels on the PBA campus. All students attend weekly chapel services. A residence hall with parking garage will supplement current housing and offer convenient access to the College's educational and cultural programs.

Location

Palm Beach Atlantic College occupies nearly 25 acres in the heart of West Palm Beach on the Intracoastal Waterway across from Palm Beach, approximately 1 mile from the Atlantic Ocean. Palm Beach County provides a broad spectrum of cultural activities in music, theater, and fine arts. The downtown area of West Palm Beach and its shopping and service opportunities are virtually at the College's doorstep.

Majors and Degrees

The Bachelor of Arts is offered in art; art education (K–12); biblical studies; Christian leadership; Christian social ministry; communication; elementary education, with specializations in middle grades English and middle grades social sciences; English; history; ministry; music; musical theater; philosophy and religion; political science; religious studies; secondary education, with specializations in drama (6–12), English (6–12), social science/history (6–12), and social science/political science (6–12); and theater arts (dance). A Bachelor of General Studies is also available.

The Bachelor of Music degree is offered in church music, instrument performance, keyboard performance, music composition, music education, and voice performance.

The Bachelor of Science is offered in applied finance and accounting; athletic training; biology; computer information systems; elementary education, with specializations in pre-K primary, middle grades general sciences, middle grades mathematics, specific learning disabilities (K–12), and varying exceptionalities certification; international business; management; marine biology; marketing; mathematics; organizational management; psychology; and secondary education, with specializations in biology (6–12), mathematics (6–12), and physical education (6–12).

Minors are offered in accounting, art, athletic training, biblical studies, biology, business administration, chemistry, Christian leadership, Christian social ministry, communication, communication/performance studies, computer information systems, computer science, dance, English, history, marketing, mathematics, ministry to the child, missions, music, musical theater, oceanography, philosophy, physical education, political science, psychology, public relations, religion, sociology, Spanish, theater arts, and youth ministry.

Preprofessional programs are offered in legal studies and health.

Academic Program

A minimum of 120 semester hours of academic work with a minimum overall grade point average of 2.0 is required for graduation. The student must complete a major of 30 or more semester hours and a minor of 15 or more hours. Double majors are possible. The major and minor are usually declared by the midpoint of the sophomore year, although changes after this time may be allowed.

Culture is the unifying force in the general education program that is required of all degree programs. The Unified Studies program is designed to give students a "wide-angle lens" on the world with an interdisciplinary focus on four areas: Faith and Culture, Communication and Culture, History and Culture, and Science and Culture. The program is a collaborative effort among faculty, not only from within the department of instruction but also from related areas. Guest lectures and team-teaching are integral components, and students shape their own experiences by becoming participating, active learners.

College-Level Examination Program (CLEP) and Advanced Placement (AP) test credits are accepted, and advanced standing is granted to qualified students. Opportunities are available for independent and directed study.

The academic year is divided into two semesters, one running from September through December, the second from January through April. A six-week summer term is offered as well.

Off-Campus Arrangements

Several courses during the May and summer terms include opportunities for study abroad that carry academic credit. Semester-abroad programs are also available.

Academic Facilities

The Blomeyer Library contains more than 130,000 volumes. Every residence hall room contains a computer, printer, and high-speed Internet connection via PalmNET, the campuswide fiber-optic system. The Greene Complex for Sports and Recreation, which opened in 1998, houses a 2,500-seat arena/convocation center, classrooms, and training facilities. In 2000, the College will break ground on several new building projects as part of its comprehensive campus growth plan. Vera

Lee Rinker Hall, which will house the School of Music and Fine Arts, is the first building slated for construction in the proposed fine arts quadrangle, to include buildings for theater, communications, and the visual arts as well as a performance hall.

Costs

The tuition, room, and board costs make PBA an affordable institution in comparison with other colleges across the country. The cost for a full-time student attending Palm Beach Atlantic College during the 2000–01 school year is $11,500 per year (12–18 hours). Room and board costs are approximately $4950 per year. Expenses for books, personal items, and travel should be considered when estimating the total cost of attending the College.

Financial Aid

More than 90 percent of the students at PBA receive some type of financial aid. Each student should submit the Free Application for Federal Student Aid (FAFSA). Students may be eligible for federal and state grants, federal loans, and work-study programs as well as institutional grants and scholarships from the following four categories: academics, Christian experience, talent, and the Theodore R. and Vivian M. Johnson Foundation.

Faculty

The College has an outstanding faculty of 171 full- and part-time members who are dedicated to Christian education. Approximately 70 percent hold earned doctorates, and individualized attention results from the favorable student-faculty ratio of 18:1. The College's family atmosphere allows for a great deal of student-faculty interaction in and out of the classroom. No graduate assistants teach at PBA.

Student Government

An active Student Government Association represents student opinion and plans student activities at the College. Students are represented on most faculty committees and are active in setting the direction of the College.

Admission Requirements

High school graduates are required to submit an application with a personal essay, one academic and one character recommendation, official transcripts indicating at least a 2.5 grade point average in college-preparatory studies, and a minimum score of 960 on the SAT I (combined) or 20 on the ACT (composite). Each element of the application file is important; special consideration may be given to students who do not meet all requirements but exhibit academic potential. International students must also demonstrate English proficiency on the Test of English as a Foreign Language (TOEFL).

Transfer students must be eligible to return to their previous college or must have been out of school for at least one semester. One academic and one character recommendation are required in addition to official transcripts indicating a grade point average of 2.0 or better in previous college work.

Application and Information

Both freshmen and transfer students are admitted in either semester. Admission decisions are made on a rolling basis as admission materials are submitted to the College. On-campus interviews are recommended.

Applications are accepted throughout the year, but students who wish to live in residence halls on campus are encouraged to apply early because of housing capacity limitations. Candidates must submit an official College application to the Admissions Office along with a $25 nonrefundable application fee and the required materials (transcript, test scores, and recommendations).

For materials and additional information, students should contact:

Admissions Office
Palm Beach Atlantic College
P.O. Box 24708
West Palm Beach, Florida 33416-4708
Telephone: 561-803-2100
   888-GO-TO-PBA (toll-free)
E-mail: admit@pbac.edu
World Wide Web: http://www.pbac.edu

Palm Beach Atlantic College offers the best of both worlds: the diversity of an urban setting coupled with the recreational activities and stunning vistas of Florida's waterways.

PAUL SMITH'S COLLEGE
PAUL SMITHS, NEW YORK

The College
Paul Smith's College was named for an entrepreneur whose famous resort on Lower St. Regis Lake was synonymous with Adirondack hospitality. Many of the rich and famous of the late nineteenth and early twentieth centuries gathered at the resort to enjoy the mountain wilderness and the comfortable accommodations provided by Paul Smith and his wife, Lydia. Vast land holdings, acquired over the years, were passed on to Smith's son Phelps, who, upon his death in 1937, bequeathed the bulk of the estate to the establishment of a college in his father's name. Paul Smith's College was chartered as a college of the arts and sciences; however, in the tradition of Paul Smith, who believed in "learning by doing," the school provides students with the opportunity to gain practical experience in a chosen field, while obtaining the academic background necessary for a well-rounded education. Today, the College-owned Hotel Saranac, in nearby Saranac Lake, provides students of hotel and restaurant management, culinary arts, and travel and tourism with experience in many aspects of the hospitality industry. Furthermore, the immense expanse of woodlands, lakes, and streams surrounding the campus offers students of forestry, ecology and environmental technology, and environmental studies a large-scale laboratory in which to practice. The combination of "hands-on" and classroom learning that Paul Smith's prescribes has attracted students from twenty-eight states and nine other countries to the campus.

Student activities are an important part of life at Paul Smith's. Popular organizations include the Forestry Club, Adirondack Experience Club, Travel Club, American Junior Culinary Federation, yearbook, campus radio station, and Emergency Wilderness Response Team.

For those interested in athletics, Paul Smith's has a swimming pool, basketball courts, a fitness center with Universal and free weights, an archery and rifle range, a padded aerobics room, a rock-climbing wall, and a multiple-use court for badminton, volleyball, and other indoor sports. Outside, the College has tennis courts, sand volleyball courts, and miles of wooded trails for the cross-country runner or mountain biking enthusiast. Paul Smith's participates at the intercollegiate level in men's and women's Alpine skiing, basketball, soccer, and woodsmen's competitions and men's ice hockey.

Paul Smith's College of Arts and Sciences is approved and chartered by the Regents of the University of the State of New York and the Commissioner of Education of New York State. The College is accredited by the Commission on Higher Education of the Middle States Association of Colleges and Schools. Paul Smith's is accredited additionally by the Society of American Foresters (forest recreation and forest technician); the Technology Accreditation Commission of the Accreditation Board for Engineering and Technology (surveying technology); and the American Culinary Federation Educational Institute Accrediting Commission (culinary arts).

Location
The College is located in the midst of approximately 14,200 acres of College-owned forests and lakes on the shore of Lower St. Regis Lake in the Adirondack Mountains of northern New York State. Students have access to 23 miles of navigable water for boating and fishing, while nearby forests and mountains provide sites for hiking, climbing, and more. The campus is located 22 miles from Lake Placid, site of the 1932 and 1980 Winter Olympics. Students go there to shop or to watch athletes train in luge, bobsled, ski jumping, and other winter sports. Whiteface Mountain, Big Tupper Ski Area, and Titus Mountain provide skiing venues for the beginner as well as the expert.

Majors and Degrees
Paul Smith's College awards Bachelor of Science (B.S.), Bachelor of Professional Studies (B.P.S.), Associate in Science (A.S.), Associate in Arts (A.A.), and Associate in Applied Science (A.A.S.) degrees.

Bachelor's degree programs of study include culinary arts and service management (B.P.S.); hotel, resort and tourism management (B.S.); and natural resources (with a concentration in either environmental science or management and policy) (B.S.). Associate degree programs of study include business administration, culinary arts, ecology and environmental technology, environmental studies, forest recreation, forest technology, hotel and restaurant management, liberal arts, outdoor recreation, preprofessional forestry, surveying technology, tourism and travel, and urban tree management. Paul Smith's also offers a one-year certificate program in baking.

Academic Program
Students in the baccalaureate program in natural resources have the option of pursuing either an environmental science or a management and policy concentration. In the environmental science concentration, courses address the basic scientific questions associated with natural resource management. Students use scientific exploration to better understand human impact on the environment and provide the scientific base for rational decision making. In the management and policy concentration, students gain an understanding of the policy implications of protected areas of management and models of land-use management that provide for optimum human activity while maintaining ecosystem viability.

The Bachelor of Science degree in hotel, resort and tourism management prepares students for professional positions in the hospitality and tourism industries, with an understanding and appreciation of the interdependent dynamics of hospitality and tourism industries in the global service economy. This program prepares students as professionals concerned with the management and development of hospitality industry operations. At the same time, the program makes them aware of the economic and environmental implications of a burgeoning travel and resort industry and the growing interest in the "greening of the industry."

The Bachelor of Professional Studies program in culinary arts and service management develops a student's ability to research, understand, analyze, and manage contemporary restaurant and food service operations. This program is founded on the premise that the hospitality industry—encompassing hotel operations, food service, and tourism—will continue to evolve as the need increases for managers of facilities who can produce high-quality food, embrace and effectively utilize computer technology, and employ personnel management strategies consistent with the twenty-first century.

Information on the associate degree programs can be found in *Peterson's Guide to Two-Year Colleges*.

Off-Campus Arrangements

Cooperative work experiences for credit are required in the following programs: baking, culinary arts, hotel and restaurant management, surveying technology, tourism and travel, and urban tree management. Students in these programs have the opportunity to practice what they have learned at locations throughout the country.

Academic Facilities

Thousands of acres of College-owned lands and waterways in the Adirondack Mountains provide the natural laboratories for students in the forestry and environmental programs. The ninety-two-room Hotel Saranac, with its restaurants, banquet and catering facilities, lounge, and gift shop, offers occupational experience for hotel and restaurant management, culinary arts, and tourism and travel students. Located in the College's more traditional classroom buildings are state-of-the-art laboratories for chemistry, biology, physics, computers, graphic arts, photography, mechanical drawing, and culinary arts. The Forestry Division's resources are augmented by a permanent Lane sawmill complex, a mechanical skidder, recreational campsites, and a sugar bush. Paul Smith's library houses 56,000 volumes, 430 periodicals, a computer lab, audiovisual equipment, and four study rooms. Paul Smith's also provides for its students a Student Health Center, 24-hour campus security, a job placement and college transfer office, personal counseling, and campus ministry.

Costs

For each of the fall and spring terms in 2000–01, tuition is $6370, board is $1395, and housing is $1395. Summer sessions are required for some programs, and the costs vary by program. Additional fees to cover lab charges, student activities, and other costs vary from $155 to $575 per semester, depending on the program. The cost of books and supplies is estimated at $250 to $500 per semester.

Financial Aid

Federal programs available at the College include the Federal Pell Grant, Federal Supplemental Educational Opportunity Grant (FSEOG), Federal Stafford Student Loan, Federal Perkins Loan, and Federal Work-Study programs. The Federal Work-Study awards provide work for more than 70 percent of the student body, and more than 80 percent of the students receive some form of financial aid. The Financial Aid Office encourages students to apply for aid with the Free Application for Federal Student Aid (FAFSA) by the end of January to be processed by March 15. A financial aid brochure is available. State programs processed through the College include New York State Tuition Assistance Program (TAP), Vermont State Assistance Program, and Rhode Island Educational Assistance Program. College scholarship programs include the Presidential Scholarship, a non-need-based scholarship awarded to outstanding first-year students; the Paul Smith's Scholarship, which has been established to defray costs for prospective students who demonstrate financial need and academic ability; Vocational Scholarships for students who have been recommended by their vocational high school programs; Alumni "Pass it On" Scholarships for students recommended by Paul Smith's College graduates; special Achievement Awards for leadership in athletics; and the Adirondack Scholarship, which is offered to eligible prospective students who have graduated from a high school located within the Adirondack Park.

Faculty

Paul Smith's College faculty is composed of 85 full-time and 10 part-time members. Most faculty members live on or near the campus and participate in all phases of academic life. The student-faculty ratio is approximately 14:1.

Student Government

The Student Government is primarily responsible for the sponsorship and funding of a variety of campuswide activities, such as freshman orientation, concerts, dances, talent nights, and weekly movies.

Admission Requirements

Admission requirements vary by program. Each candidate is evaluated individually based on the requirements of the program applied for. Emphasis for the forestry and environmental programs is on math and science skills. Emphasis for the culinary arts, hospitality, and liberal arts programs is on communication and math skills. Incoming freshmen must complete one of the associate degree programs before applying for a bachelor's degree program. Students wishing to transfer into a bachelor's degree program must have completed at least 45 credit hours to apply and 60 credit hours to enroll and have a minimum overall GPA of 2.0. Assuming all course prerequisites have been fulfilled, admissions decisions are based on academic performance, extracurricular activities, and a personal interview.

Application and Information

Applicants for either the associate or bachelor's degree programs must submit a formal application for admission, a $25 application fee, SAT I and/or ACT scores, and an official high school transcript. For incoming freshmen, recommendations, a personal interview, and an essay are all highly recommended but not required. Transfer students interested in a bachelor's degree program must submit an official copy of their college transcript, three letters of recommendation, and an essay. International students are required to submit scores from the TOEFL examination. Because the College operates on a continuing admissions system, applicants are urged to apply as early as possible. Prospective students normally receive a decision within three to five weeks of receipt of all application materials.

For more information, students should contact:

Douglas Zander
Vice President for Enrollment Management
Paul Smith's College
Paul Smiths, New York 12970
Telephone: 518-327-6227
          800-421-2605 (toll-free)
          (Monday through Friday, 8 a.m. to 5 p.m.)
Fax: 518-327-6016
World Wide Web: http://www.paulsmiths.edu

Students learning in Paul Smith's outdoor classroom.

PEACE COLLEGE
RALEIGH, NORTH CAROLINA

The College
Peace College is a baccalaureate college of arts and sciences that challenges women to an adventure of intellectual and personal discovery, preparing women for graduate and lifelong learning, for meaningful careers, and for ethical lives of purpose, leadership, and service. The institution was founded in 1857 and named for founding benefactor William Peace, an elder of the First Presbyterian Church of Raleigh.

The main campus setting is in a 15-acre grove of native oaks. Attractive brick and wrought-iron fencing extends around the campus. Facilities include five air-conditioned residence halls, an athletic field, six all-weather tennis courts, and an indoor swimming pool.

Location
Peace College is located at 15 East Peace Street in historic downtown Raleigh, North Carolina. The State Capitol, Legislative Building, State Library, North Carolina Symphony, Exploris (a global learning center), and several museums (art, history, and natural sciences) lie within a few blocks of the campus. Also, Raleigh is one of the cities that comprise North Carolina's Research Triangle Park. Such a location provides many opportunities for personal enrichment and professional development.

Majors and Degrees
Bachelor of Arts degrees are offered in biology, business administration, communication, English, human resources, leadership studies, liberal studies, music performance, psychology, Spanish, and visual communication. The following associate degrees are also available: the A.A. with a choice of twenty concentrations, the A.S. in allied health fields, and the A.F.A. in music. The teaching licensure option is available through a partnership with Meredith College.

Academic Program
The B.A. degree requires a minimum of 125 semester hours, and the associate degrees require a minimum of 63 hours for graduation. All degree programs require a strong general education component. Requirements include 19 hours of "Essential Skills" (developing written, oral, computing, mathematical, and analytical competencies) and 24 hours of "Essential Knowledge" courses (liberal arts and sciences). In addition to the hours required for each major, all B.A. programs have a third category of "Advanced Skills and Knowledge," including a required internship related to the major; a senior seminar course, "Ethics in the Modern World;" and 9 hours of additional general education courses chosen to complement the declared major. A liberal number of electives and Peace College's participation in a consortium of local colleges and universities provide students with an opportunity to build desired credentials by taking double majors, concentrations, and minors. Honors, independent study, research, and special topics courses are available, as are career exploration internships for lower-division students. There are no off-campus credit programs except international programs. Peace College supports a variety of international programs through its Ragland endowment. An ROTC program is available through the local consortium, Cooperating Raleigh Colleges (CRC).

Academic Facilities
The Finch Library contains a total of 51,788 titles, including 8,366 volumes of 390 periodicals and 950 recordings, videotapes, and computer disks. The library also provides electronic and interlibrary loan access to collections of other colleges and research universities in Raleigh, the Research Triangle, and the state. The library also subscribes to online database resources to meet the information needs of students and faculty members.

All academic facilities are networked and provided with Internet service. Computer laboratories, the library, and the student publications area are equipped with Pentium-based platforms. Macintosh laboratories are also available in the biology, music, and visual communication departments. Student laboratories in the chemistry, general biology, and molecular and cellular biology departments are available. A recital hall in the music building, the Leggett Theater, and a dance studio are available for students in the fine arts department. Beginning in fall 2000, a new classroom and faculty office building will be in use, making $500,000 of instructional technology available to students and faculty members. The new academic building features an 84-seat amphitheater/lecture hall for campus and public events, a communication media laboratory, a psychology/anthropology laboratory, a psychology observation room, a business/human resources laboratory, and an additional computer laboratory for student use.

Costs
For 2000–01, tuition and fees for full-time study total $4964 per semester. The charge for part-time study is $300 per credit hour. Room and board are $2500 per semester.

Financial Aid
Students and/or their families are expected to pay for educational expenses, to the extent that it is possible. However, it is the goal of Peace College that no student will be denied the opportunity to attend because of financial need. Accordingly, the College administers a generous program of financial aid, including Federal Work-Study opportunities, Federal Pell Grants, Federal Supplemental Educational Opportunity Grants, and North Carolina State Contractual Scholarship Grants. The College administers loans under the Federal Family Education Loan Program. Academic, talent, and outstanding citizenship scholarships are also available for all eligible students, including transfer students.

To apply for financial aid, students must submit a completed FAFSA, either to the processor or to the College, for electronic processing. Applicants must demonstrate financial need and show evidence of academic promise or academic achievement to receive assistance from federally funded programs. Students may also apply for Peace College scholarships by completing an application form that is available from the Financial Aid Office. North Carolina residents are eligible for the North Carolina Legislative Tuition Grant (NCLTG), which is currently valued at $875 per semester. The NCLTG is awarded to students who have resided in North Carolina for a minimum of twelve months prior to enrolling, who meet state residency requirements, and who complete and submit to the Financial Aid Office an application for the grant. Out-of-state students receive a comparable grant that is funded through the College.

Faculty

There are 37 full-time faculty members who teach 80 percent of all courses. Approximately 31 part-time faculty members teach courses for curricular enrichment and when a full load for a new full-time member does not exist. Because Peace is an undergraduate institution that focuses on excellent teaching, all classes, including laboratories, are taught by its regular faculty. Although faculty members are expected to sustain a scholarly interest, the most important factor in all evaluations for promotion, tenure, and merit pay is the quality of teaching. The role of faculty members is to teach, supervise student research and internships, and advise students. Faculty members are also expected to show support of the extracurricular activities of their students. Some faculty members have some release time when serving as division chairs or program coordinators, but the substantial majority of their workload is instruction-related, not administrative. All Peace faculty members have advanced degrees (except those who teach an occasional physical education activity class, such as skiing or scuba diving). About 74 percent of the full-time faculty members hold terminal degrees in their disciplines. It is the policy of Peace College to maintain a student-faculty ratio of less than 14:1.

Student Government

The Student Government Association at Peace College is an organization of student leaders, both elected and appointed, who create an avenue of change in which the individual concerns and opinions of the student body are represented. The Student Government Association meets on a biweekly basis, and meetings are open to all students.

There are 39 voting members representing various campus constituencies. The purposes of the association are to cooperate with the administration and faculty in enforcing regulations concerning academic matters, health, public safety, maintenance of buildings and grounds, and publicity; to make recommendations to the administration and/or faculty concerning areas outside student control; and to cooperate with the administration in setting and maintaining creditable standards of living in all phases of college life.

The powers of the association are to consult with the administration in formulating and enforcing legislation and regulation in all areas concerning student life; to formulate policies regarding activities that are under student control; to control use of funds of the association; and to supervise the election of students to all offices and positions of honor in various student organizations.

The governance of student conduct is based upon the honor system, in which all individuals associated with the community have a responsibility for establishing, maintaining, and fostering an understanding and appreciation for academic as well as conduct standards and values.

Admission Requirements

Peace College recruits and admits women who will benefit from the College's various academic programs and who will contribute to the life of the Peace College community. The College encourages women with varied talents and interests representative of all social, economic, ethnic, and racial backgrounds to apply.

Applications are reviewed individually. Decisions are based on the following credentials: course selection, grade point average in academic courses (see minimum required courses, below), SAT I or ACT scores, rank in class, and recommendations.

Further consideration is given to an applicant's personal qualifications, potential for success, and ability to add to the social, cultural, and spiritual environment for which Peace College is known. The major criteria for admission are the strength of the high school courses taken and the grades in the academic courses. Each applicant's grade point average is refigured using only the grades in academic courses.

To meet the minimum academic requirements, applicants must complete 4 units of English; 3 units of mathematics (algebra I, algebra II, and geometry); 2 to 3 units of science; 2 units of social science, and 2 units of the same foreign language. Students are encouraged to take additional courses in math and science when possible.

Application and Information

Admissions decisions are made on a rolling basis. The Admissions Committee begins reviewing applications in September for the following fall. Applications received after April 1 for the fall semester and after November 1 for the spring semester are reviewed on a space-available basis.

The College requires each freshman applicant to submit an application, a nonrefundable $25 fee, SAT I or ACT scores (senior year scores are preferred), and an official high school transcript of all courses taken in high school. Transfer applicants must also submit official transcripts from all colleges attended.

Application forms and additional information may be obtained by contacting:

Admissions Office
Peace College
15 East Peace Street
Raleigh, North Carolina 27604
Telephone: 919-508-2000
        800-PEACE-47 (toll-free)
Fax: 919-508-2506
World Wide Web: http://www.peace.edu (complete inquiry card on line)

Peace College's Main Building is the centerpiece of a picturesque 15-acre campus in the heart of downtown Raleigh, North Carolina.

PEIRCE COLLEGE
PHILADELPHIA, PENNSYLVANIA

The College

Peirce College is a four-year, nonprofit, independent, coeducational college that was founded in 1865. Peirce's mission is to provide leading-edge business, career, and technical education to a diverse student community in an academic environment that supports the professional excellence of faculty members, staff members, alumni, and the business community. Peirce is committed to the philosophy that education should be practical and useful and that each student's ambitions are important.

The urban campus, located in Center City Philadelphia, has a seven-story academic building and an adjacent structure used for offices and student support functions. Housed in a separate facility, the Student/Faculty Center gives students space for meetings and informal gatherings. Faculty members have offices in this facility.

Degree programs are also offered throughout the greater Philadelphia area at employer sites and community-based locations.

In the fall 1999 term, Peirce College set an all-time enrollment record with 2,691 degree-seeking students. The student body is primarily composed of adult learners. International students represent 2 percent of the total student population. All students live off campus.

Peirce College is accredited by the Commission on Higher Education of the Middle States Association of Colleges and Schools and the Pennsylvania Department of Education to award associate and bachelor's degrees. The business administration associate degree program is accredited by the Association of Collegiate Business Schools and Programs (ACBSP). Peirce is approved by the Veterans Administration for education benefits obtainable under the G.I. Bill. The Paralegal Studies Program is approved by the American Bar Association.

Location

The College is located in the center of Philadelphia, one half block from the Avenue of the Arts. All of the distinctive business, educational, historical, and cultural features of one of the nation's largest and most diversified metropolitan areas are available to Peirce students. All sections of the city and suburban areas are easily accessible to the College community by public transportation.

In addition, the classes that are held at corporate sites and community locations throughout the greater Philadelphia region literally bring the convenience and accessibility of a Peirce education to the students' doorsteps.

Majors and Degrees

Students may earn an associate or bachelor's degree in business administration, with concentrations available in seven fields: accounting; general business administration; health-care management; hospitality management, travel and tourism; international business; legal, medical, and administrative office technologies; and marketing. Associate and bachelor's degrees are offered in information technology, with concentrations in business information systems, networking, and technology management. Paralegal Studies is available in associate and bachelor's degree programs. An associate degree program in general studies is also offered.

Academic Program

Peirce focuses on business and career oriented programs that give students a firm foundation in general education. All degree programs include training in information technology. Peirce maintains strong business community relationships and continually upgrades courses to reflect hiring trends. In all degree programs, students must take general education core courses in English/communications, humanities, social science, and math or science. Word processing is an integral component of the office technology concentrations. Supervised cooperative education is available in all programs except general studies. Most of the bachelor's degree programs include a capstone course in the last term of the program.

A minimum of 60 credits is required for associate degrees and 120 credits for bachelor's degrees. Certificates of proficiency require 27 to 30 credits.

Students may enroll in programs in the day and evening format over the fall, spring, and summer terms of each academic year; in an accelerated evening or weekend format; in a Friday-only format; and through the Peirce Cluster Program.

The Continuing Education Department offers noncredit programs, including computer software skill workshops, healthcare training, and business skills instruction, during the day, evening, and weekend.

Academic Facilities

Classrooms and laboratories are designed and equipped for up-to-date teaching and learning techniques. Peirce College and its facilities are handicap accessible.

Peirce College has several networked classrooms that include state-of-the-art equipment that reflects what is currently used in the workplace. A comprehensive package of instructional and tutorial software can be accessed through the network. In addition, a dedicated technology lab serves the developmental education needs of Peirce students.

The Peirce College library provides services to students and faculty members. The library staff offers formal and informal training in library use, Internet search techniques, and the retrieval of information in traditional and electronic formats. The library contains a comprehensive collection of 35,000 volumes, periodicals, microforms, and databases; Internet access supplements the collections. The library provides guidance to Internet searching and sites in the library portion of the College's Web page. A 5,000-volume law library and online WESTLAW and LEXIS-NEXIS databases support the paralegal and other programs with federal, regional, and local resources citing case and statutory law. A member of ACCESS PA and the Tri-State College Library Cooperative (TCLC), the Peirce library actively promotes resource sharing, interlibrary loans, and access to information beyond the facility. The library can arrange for Peirce students to borrow materials from other TCLC institutions.

The Center for Academic Excellence provides counseling, tutoring, and academic advising and offers a comfortable atmosphere for students to study and receive support and encouragement. The Perkins Center is federally funded through the Carl D. Perkins Act and provides the following services: career information, English as a second language (ESL) and

Limited English Proficiency (LEP), tutoring developmental classes, and a computer learning center.

Costs

In 1999–2000, tuition and fees were $266 per credit hour for day and evening students. Books and supplies averaged approximately $80 per course. Costs are subject to change.

Financial Aid

About 90 percent of the College's students received approximately $7 million in financial aid. Financial assistance includes scholarships, grants, loans, and on-campus employment. Peirce College participates in most federal and state aid programs. Scholarships and grants from College sources are available for both new and returning students. Applicants for aid must submit the Free Application for Federal Student Aid (FAFSA). The priority filing date is February 15.

Faculty

Peirce College has 30 full-time and 323 adjunct faculty members with broad and diverse professional backgrounds. Most of the faculty members have advanced degrees and many are practitioners in their fields. Attorneys, certified public accountants, psychologists, market analysts, computer experts, health-care professionals, business managers, and other professionals are among the teaching staff at Peirce. Small class sizes ensure that faculty members are readily available to offer professional advice to individual students. Faculty members also serve as career and academic advisers.

Admission Requirements

It is the policy of Peirce College to offer admission to applicants without regard to sex, sexual orientation, ancestry, age, race, creed, color, national origin, or an individual's handicap. Admission is based on the student's academic record, work experience, personal qualifications, and aptitude for the program selected. Requirements include a high school diploma or general equivalency diploma and a high school transcript and significant work experience. SAT scores are not required, but are recommended. Admission interviews are strongly recommended. The Center for Enrollment Services provides a one-stop shop for all enrollment needs. Up to 30 semester credit hours for an associate degree and 60 semester credit hours for a bachelor's degree (in which a grade of C or better is earned) may be accepted for transfer credit. A skills assessment test is required for all new students. International students must submit proof of English ability, usually by means of the TOEFL. Alternative methods are available for students to attain academic credit for prior learning, usually documented through portfolio assessment, credit by examination, and the College-Level Examination Program (CLEP).

Application and Information

Applications, transcripts, and testing results should be forwarded to the Center for Enrollment Services. Applicants are notified of the admission decision shortly after they have taken the skills assessment and all necessary credentials have been received and reviewed.

>   Center for Enrollment Services
>   Peirce College
>   1420 Pine Street
>   Philadelphia, Pennsylvania 19102-4699
>   Telephone: 215-545-6400 Ext. 9217
>   888-GO-PEIRCE (467-3472, toll-free)
>   Fax: 215-546-5996
>   E-mail: info@peirce.edu
>   World Wide Web: http://www.peirce.edu

Peirce College is conveniently located in the heart of Center City Philadelphia, adjacent to the exciting Avenue of the Arts.

PENNSYLVANIA COLLEGE OF TECHNOLOGY
An Affiliate of Pennsylvania State University
WILLIAMSPORT, PENNSYLVANIA

The College

Pennsylvania College of Technology (Penn College) is an affiliate of the Pennsylvania State University (Penn State). It is a unique institution offering bachelor's and associate degrees and specialized educational opportunities focused on applied technology. Penn College is an integral part of the Penn State system, offering students the opportunity to combine a hands-on technical education with theory and management practice.

As Pennsylvania's premier technical college, Penn College also holds a national reputation for the high quality and diversity of its traditional and advanced technology majors. Partnerships with industry leaders, including Toyota, Ford, Mack Trucks, Caterpillar, and others, provide students unique opportunities to build school-to-work relations that can lead to advancement in their future careers.

Graduate surveys indicate a placement success rate that exceeds 90 percent annually. Among the keys to graduate success is Penn College's emphasis on small classes, personal attention, and hands-on experience using the latest technology.

In fall 1999, a total of 5,389 students attended Penn College. Full-time enrollment was 4,294; part-time, enrollment was 1,095. Another 1,528 students took part in the extensive noncredit and continuing education program, which includes customized business and industry courses offered through Penn College's Technology Transfer Center.

Location

Penn College's ultramodern campus is located in beautiful north-central Pennsylvania. The main campus is in Williamsport.

Besides the main campus, Penn College also offers classes at four other locations: the Advanced Automotive Technology Center, Wahoo Drive Industrial Park in Williamsport; the Aviation Center at the Williamsport–Lycoming County Airport in Montoursville; the Earth Science Center, 12 miles south of Williamsport in Allenwood; and the North Campus in Wellsboro.

Majors and Degrees

Unique Bachelor of Science (B.S.) degrees focus on the applied technology in growing career fields. Majors include accounting; applied health studies; applied human services; automotive technology management; aviation maintenance technology; business administration; civil engineering technology; computer-aided product and systems design; computer information technology (analysis and design concentration or data communication and networking concentration); construction management; culinary arts; dental hygiene; electronics engineering technology; graphic design; heating, ventilation, and air conditioning (HVAC) technology; nursing; physician assistant studies; plastics and polymer engineering technology; printing and publishing technology; technical and professional communication; technology management; and welding and fabrication engineering technology.

Associate degrees (A.A.S., A.A.A., A.A., or A.S.) are offered in accounting; advertising art; architectural technology; auto body technology; automated manufacturing technology; automotive engineering technology; automotive service management; automotive technology (including programs that emphasize Ford and Toyota training); aviation technology; avionics technology; baking and pastry arts; banking; biology; broadcast communications; building construction technology; building construction technology/masonry emphasis; business management; business management/travel and tourism emphasis; civil engineering technology; computer-aided drafting; computer information systems (with emphasis in business programming, computer science, microcomputer applications development, or microcomputer specialist studies); culinary arts technology; dental hygiene; diesel technology; diesel technology/Mack emphasis; dietary manager technology; early childhood education; electrical technology; electronics technology (with emphasis in biomedical electronics, communications/fiber optics, computer-automation maintenance, electronics engineering technology, industrial laser/optics, or industrial process control); environmental technology; floral design/interior plantscape; food and hospitality management; forest technology; general studies; health arts (with emphasis in cardiovascular technology, emergency medical services, general studies, paramedic studies, or practical nursing); heating, ventilation, and air conditioning (HVAC) technology; heavy construction equipment technology; heavy construction equipment technology/CAT emphasis; human services; individual studies; industrial maintenance technology; landscape/nursery technology; legal assistant (paralegal) studies; mass communications; nursing; occupational therapy assisting; office information systems; office technology (with emphasis in executive or medical studies); physical fitness specialist studies; physical sciences; plastics and polymer technology; pre-engineering; printing and publishing production; radiography; surveying technology; toolmaking technology; and welding technology.

Certificate programs are offered in auto body technician studies, automotive service technician studies, aviation maintenance technician studies, cabinetmaking and millwork, computer applications technology, construction carpentry, diesel technician studies, electrical occupations, heavy construction equipment technician studies, machinist general studies, plumbing, practical nursing, and welding.

Academic Program

Penn College awards associate and bachelor degrees that are designed to prepare students for employment or to serve as the basis for additional education. Associate degree programs require a minimum of 60 credits. The A.A.A. programs offer students the opportunity to gain the technical and professional skills needed for employment (or to articulate with a number of bachelor degree majors) and to prepare for transfer to a four-year college. The A.A. and A.S. degree programs are designed to parallel the first two years of a liberal arts education at a four-year college. Credits can usually be transferred toward the first two years of a bachelor's degree program. Bachelor degrees build upon the foundation of associate degrees and emphasize practical applications. Certificate programs are not primarily designed for transfer but, in certain cases, can be used to transfer to some colleges. Certificate programs vary in length but do not exceed two years of course work. A feature of these programs is the elective. Students have the option of selecting elective courses to broaden the basic academic work required in order to enrich their educational experience.

Off-Campus Arrangements

Penn College students earn academic credit for real work experience if they choose to participate in cooperative education (co-op). Many majors require internships. Penn College co-op students have worked throughout Pennsylvania as well as in eighteen other states, the District of Columbia, Canada, and Puerto Rico.

Academic Facilities

The hands-on experience offered at Penn College creates a need for a variety of special academic facilities that house sophisticated equipment. Penn College students enjoy access to an advanced computer network and campus computer labs. Penn College's average of one computer for every 6 students (1:6) is three times higher than the national average (1:18).

Besides extensive, accessible computer labs, the main campus has an architectural studio, an automated manufacturing center, an automotive repair center, a broadcast studio, a building trades center, a campus guest house, computer-aided drafting labs, a dental hygiene clinic, a fine dining restaurant, a machine shop, modern science laboratories, a plastics manufacturing center, a printing and publishing facility, and a welding shop.

Off-campus sites include one of the nation's finest aviation and avionics instructional facilities, located at the local airport, and an earth science center, located on 180 acres of wooded land, that features greenhouses, a working sawmill, a diesel center, and a heavy equipment training site.

The library on the main campus is open every day during the academic semesters and offers an impressive selection of print and electronic resources. Services available include a professional reference staff, online and CD-ROM computer database searches, and interlibrary loans and reserves.

Costs

Tuition and related fees are based on a per-credit-hour charge. Annual tuition and fees (not including housing, food and living expenses or lab fees, books, tools, uniforms or supplies required in a specific program of study) for 1999–2000 were approximately $7300 for in-state students ($236.20 per credit hour) and $8600 for out-of-state students ($278.80 per credit hour). The exact amount students pay depends upon the specific courses and number of credits taken each semester. Students may also participate in meal plans offered by the College dining facility.

Students residing in the Village at Penn College or Campus View Apartments (on-campus housing) paid $1590 per semester in spring 2000. The Village and the Campus View Apartments are College-supervised, alcohol-free, drug-free, and noise-controlled residence halls that offer two-bedroom units designed to house 4 students. The cost of living includes utilities, basic cable, basic phone, computer access, voice mail, garbage removal, and building and grounds maintenance. Residents may also purchase a College meal plan. Nonresident students may also purchase meal plans, which are accepted in dining facilities, including the cafeteria, a bistro-style restaurant, a gourmet restaurant, a convenience store, and a coffeehouse.

Financial Aid

Approximately 4 out of 5 Penn College students receive financial assistance totaling $29 million. Types of aid available include Federal Pell Grants, Pennsylvania Higher Education Assistance Agency grants, Federal Supplemental Educational Opportunity Grants, Federal Work-Study awards, Federal Stafford Student Loans, Federal PLUS loans, veterans' benefits, Bureau of Vocational Rehabilitation benefits, and emergency loans. A deferred-payment plan allows students to spread their tuition cost over two payments each semester.

Penn College is currently expanding its scholarship offerings. Penn College offers academic and technical scholarships to qualified students. Selections for all scholarships are made according to the process and eligibility criteria. Detailed information on scholarships can be obtained from either the Financial Aid Office or the Office of Admissions.

Faculty

Penn College's 401 faculty members (243 full-time and 158 part-time) provide the kind of individual attention students need to be successful in the classroom and in the workplace. Faculty members are both educated and experienced in their field. Each year Penn College recognizes excellence among the faculty members through distinguished faculty award programs.

Small class sizes (with a current student-faculty ratio of 19:1) provide individual faculty attention and promote student success. In addition, advisory committees of faculty members and business and industry leaders representing fields related to the College's programs of study work together to ensure that programs meet current workplace needs.

Student Government

The Student Government Association (SGA) and the Wildcat Events Board (WEB) represent the student body in matters related to College policy and activities. All enrolled students are members of SGA and WEB. Active participation offers the opportunity to develop leadership skills while contributing to the well-being of the College and the student body. In addition, more than sixty student organizations offer opportunities for organized campus activity.

Admission Requirements

Penn College offers educational opportunities to anyone who has the interest, desire, and ability to pursue advanced study. Due to the wide variety of program offerings, admission criteria varies according to program offering. At a minimum, applicants must have a high school diploma or its equivalent. Some programs are restricted to people who meet certain academic skills and prerequisites, have attained levels of academic achievement, and have earned an acceptable score on the SAT I. Questions regarding the admission standards for specific programs should be directed to the Office of Admissions.

To ensure that applicants have the entry-level skills needed for success in College programs, all students are required to take placement examinations, which are used to assess skills in math, English, and reading. The College provides opportunities for students to develop the basic skills necessary for enrollment in associate degree and certificate programs when the placement tests indicate that such help is needed. International students whose native language is not English are required to take the TOEFL, submit an affidavit of support, and comply with test regulations of the Immigration and Naturalization Service, along with meeting all other admission requirements.

Penn College offers opportunities for students to transfer course credit earned at other institutions, college credit earned before high school graduation, service credit, DANTES credit, and credit earned through the College-Level Examination Program (CLEP).

The College offers equal opportunity for admission without regard to age, race, color, creed, sex, national origin, handicap, veteran status, or political affiliation.

Application and Information

College catalogs, viewbooks, financial aid information, and other informative brochures, along with applications for admission, are available from the Office of Admissions. The College invites prospective students and their families to contact the Office of Admissions to arrange a personal interview or campus tour.

All inquiries should be addressed to:
Office of Admissions
Pennsylvania College of Technology
One College Avenue
Williamsport, Pennsylvania 17701-5799
Telephone: 570-327-4761
          800-367-9222 (toll-free)
E-mail: cschuman@pct.edu
World Wide Web: http://www.pct.edu

PENNSYLVANIA STATE UNIVERSITY ABINGTON COLLEGE
ABINGTON, PENNSYLVANIA

The College

Penn State Abington offers the resources of one of the nation's premier teaching and research universities combined with a small-college atmosphere in a suburban setting. The mission of Penn State Abington is to provide high-quality teaching in a wide array of programs in the arts, humanities, and sciences. Ten 4-year baccalaureate degree programs and two 2-year associate degree programs are offered, as are the first two years of most baccalaureate degrees that can be completed at other Penn State locations.

Penn State Abington was established in 1950 when Abby A. Sutherland, principal and owner of the elite Ogontz School for Girls, gave the campus and facilities to the Pennsylvania State University. The campus is located on a picturesque 45 acres in a northern suburb of Philadelphia.

The campus currently has 3,296 undergraduate students attending classes in its modern academic buildings and labs. Penn State Abington does not have residence halls; however, private housing is available minutes from the campus.

Penn State Abington participates in a variety of varsity sports and is a member of several local athletic conferences, including the Commonwealth Campus Athletic Conference, the Eastern Pennsylvanian Collegiate Conference, and the Philadelphia Association of Intercollegiate Athletics for Women. Varsity sports include softball and volleyball for women, baseball and golf for men, and basketball, soccer, and tennis for both men and women. The intramural athletic program includes badminton, basketball, flag football, softball, street hockey, tennis, volleyball, and weight lifting. Opportunities also exist to participate in noncompetitive programs, such as aerobics, dance, and fitness.

Location

At Penn State Abington, students benefit from a convenient location less than a half mile from Route 611. The community of Abington is about 15 miles north of Center City Philadelphia and 4 miles south of the Willow Grove exit of the Pennsylvania Turnpike. The campus is easily accessible by car, public transportation, and the Penn State Abington shuttle.

Majors and Degrees

Penn State Abington offers the Bachelor of Arts degree in administration of justice; American studies; English; history; integrative arts; letters, arts, and sciences; and psychological and social sciences. The Bachelor of Science degree is offered in administration of justice, business, information sciences and technology, psychological and social sciences, and science. The Associate in Arts is awarded in one major: letters, arts, and sciences. The Associate in Science is offered in business administration.

Penn State Abington also gives students the opportunity to complete the first two years of most of the more than 160 University degrees before changing location to the University Park Campus; Penn State Erie, the Behrend College; Penn State Harrisburg, the Capitol College; or any other Penn State location where students can complete their degrees.

Academic Program

Each baccalaureate program has two components: at least 46 credits in general education and at least 78 credits in specific requirements for the major. Students must complete a minimum of 124 credits to earn a bachelor's degree; the exact number depends on the program. Associate degrees require a minimum of 60 credits. All baccalaureate degrees offered at Penn State Abington require an overall grade point average of at least 2.0 and a grade of C or better in upper-level courses in the major. An honors program and the Schreyer Honors College program are available to students who demonstrate exceptional promise.

Several majors serve as excellent preparation for law or medical school. Special prelaw and premed advisers assist students in planning their programs. The Division of Undergraduate Studies enables those who have not yet decided on an academic major to explore several areas of study before selecting a specific program.

The fall and spring semesters are each fifteen weeks in length. Registration and advising take place before the first week of classes, and the final examinations are given after the last week. There are also two summer sessions of six weeks each. The campus provides a comprehensive orientation program, which includes individual academic and career advising and is popular with students and their parents.

Penn State Abington wants students to succeed, not only in getting a degree but also in having a rich, fulfilling future. The campus provides many avenues to help students achieve their goals, including honors studies through the Schreyer Honors College program or the Penn State Abington Honors program; research projects with faculty members at the forefront of their fields; independent study; internships through the Career Development Center; cooperative (co-op) education through the College of Engineering; the Educational Opportunity Program, which offers a strong program of academic support and personal counseling; and Army ROTC.

When students enroll at Penn State Abington, they are assigned an academic adviser who assists them with scheduling, interpreting degree requirements, and matching their interests and abilities to their career goals. In addition, professional advisers are available in the Division of Undergraduate Studies. The Career Development Center staff is committed to helping students in all stages of their career planning—from choosing a major to gaining an internship to interviewing for jobs.

Academic Facilities

The Penn State Abington Computer Center houses both IBM and Macintosh computers, which can access the IBM mainframe system at the University Park Campus, the Library Information Access System (LIAS), and the Internet. AutoCAD workstations for graphic design are also available. The computer center has evening and weekend hours to accommodate student schedules. Additional Macintosh computers are accessible in the Computer-Assisted Learning Center, where students can familiarize themselves with computer applications in an informal environment. The Penn State Abington Learning Center offers free professional and peer tutoring to all students who want to improve their skills in math, sciences, English composition, and many other subject areas. At Penn State Abington, students have access to an extensive library system. The Penn State University Libraries comprise a vast collection of more than 3.5 million books, periodicals, and other documents available either on site or through interlibrary loan. The College is linked electronically to every library in the University Libraries system through the computerized LIAS.

Costs

For the 1999–2000 academic year, tuition for an in-state student for one year was $6058 full-time or $243 per credit part-time. An out-of-state student's tuition for one year was $9418 full-time or $393 per credit part-time. Mandatory computer fees and student activity fees ranged from $43 to $127 per semester, depending on the number of credits scheduled. Other costs were a nonrefundable $50 application fee, a nonrefundable $150 enrollment fee, and a $50 general deposit.

Financial Aid

Student financial aid awards are based on an analysis of the student's financial need. Students should file the Free Application for Federal Student Aid (FAFSA) by February 15 of their senior year of high school. Students are encouraged to seek grant assistance from their home state. Financial aid applications are available from high school counselors and financial aid offices at colleges and other institutions. These forms and the application for admission are the only forms that incoming freshmen need to complete to be considered for federal, state, and University aid. Aid includes Federal Pell Grants, Federal Work-Study Program awards, Federal Perkins Loans, Federal Supplemental Educational Opportunity Grants, Federal Stafford Student Loans, and Penn State awards and scholarships. Students at Penn State Abington receive nearly $3.2 million in scholarships and grants each year. Many of the campus-based scholarships have been created through the generosity of alumni, corporations, faculty members, staff members, and friends who try to help students who demonstrate academic merit or financial need.

Faculty

The faculty members at Penn State Abington are well known in their fields of research. They take great pride in the honors they have received for their teaching excellence, and they pass their knowledge and enthusiasm on to their students in the classroom. Because Penn State Abington is a small, close-knit campus, students have the advantage of a one-on-one relationship with their professors on both a teaching and an advising level. Penn State Abington has 215 faculty members, of whom 95 are full-time; 82 percent have terminal degrees.

Student Government

Penn State Abington offers a wide variety of student organizations that involve leadership, community service, ethnicity, and social events. The Student Government Association is the official representative of the student body. In addition to representing students to the administration and faculty, the Student Government Association charters all student organizations and allocates funds to support and promote student activities. The association also appoints student representatives to serve on all key administrative and faculty committees and the appropriate adjudicatory boards.

Admission Requirements

As part of the Pennsylvania State University, in compliance with federal and state laws, Penn State Abington is committed to the policy that all persons shall have equal access to admission without regard to race, religion, sex, national origin, ancestry, color, sexual orientation, handicap, age, or status as a disabled or Vietnam veteran. Each applicant is evaluated on the basis of his or her high school record and the results of the SAT I. The high school grade point average, when combined with the SAT I score, produces an evaluation index, and students are admitted on the basis of this index.

Application and Information

Students interested in freshman admission to Penn State Abington may obtain an admission application form from any Penn State campus or by writing to Penn State Abington. Application forms are available in late summer. The recommended deadline for submitting an application is November 30. Applicants admitted to Penn State Abington are notified approximately four to six weeks after the application and credentials are received. The student must make certain that the Educational Testing Service forwards the SAT I scores to the Undergraduate Admissions Office, Pennsylvania State University, University Park, Pennsylvania 16802.

This description is available in alternative media upon request.

Students interested in scheduling a campus tour of Penn State Abington should call 215-881-7500. For an application form or additional information, interested students should contact:

Admissions Office
Pennsylvania State University Abington College
1600 Woodland Road
Abington, Pennsylvania 19001-3990

Telephone: 215-881-7600
Fax: 215-881-7317
World Wide Web: http://www.abington.psu.edu/

Penn State's mascot is the Nittany Lion.

PENNSYLVANIA STATE UNIVERSITY ALTOONA COLLEGE
ALTOONA, PENNSYLVANIA

The College

Penn State Altoona's goal is to be one of the best small public, undergraduate, residential colleges in the United States. The College seeks to enhance student development and to provide for a continually improving student-centered learning community.

Penn State Altoona offers a world-class team of faculty members, small classes, and excellent support systems that enable students to reach their fullest potential. The small-campus environment allows for a comprehensive learning experience while combining the high standards of a major research university. Penn State Altoona is one of twenty-three campuses making up the Pennsylvania State University System. It has the second-largest enrollment of the twenty-three campuses, with the University Park campus placing first, and is a full-service residential campus located 42 miles from the 40,000-student research campus at University Park. The College offers nine baccalaureate degree (four-year) programs, nine associate degree (two-year) programs, and course work for more than 160 Penn State majors.

The Altoona Undergraduate Center opened in 1939 with 119 students and 9 faculty members. In 1947, the Altoona Campus Advisory Board purchased the former Ivyside Amusement Park grounds and converted park buildings for school use, and the campus moved to its present location.

Fall 1999 enrollment reached an estimated 3,600 students, of whom more than 3,100 were in-state residents and more than 400 were out-of-state. Enrollment also included students from twenty other countries, including Brazil, Ghana, Malaysia, and Thailand. This year, Penn State Altoona has 128 students named to the honors program. Penn State Altoona also welcomed 102 new students who are members of minority groups, bringing its estimated total to more than 300 students. The campus provides four residence halls, all coed, including Cedar Hall, a brand-new facility providing 320 student living spaces. Oak Hall, Spruce Hall, and Maple Hall each provide an additional 600 student living spaces. Ample off-campus housing is available.

The Penn State Altoona intercollegiate athletics program (NCAA Division III) includes nine varsity sports teams: five for women and four for men. Intercollegiate teams are men's and women's basketball (fall/spring), women's volleyball (fall), men's baseball (spring), women's softball (spring), men's and women's tennis (fall/spring), and men's and women's swimming (fall). The Intramural and Recreational Sports Program at Penn Altoona is one of the best and most competitive in the Penn State system.

Location

Altoona is located in Blair County at the foothills of the Allegheny Mountains. The lush forests and fields make up 63 percent of Blair County, which has a total population of more than 130,000. Altoona is the county's largest city, with a population of 51,000. The new I-99/Route 220 corridor runs north and south and links the area with I-80 and the Pennsylvania Turnpike. Altoona is less than 2 hours from such metropolitan areas as Pittsburgh and Harrisburg. Larger cities, such as Philadelphia, Baltimore, and Washington, D.C., are less than 5 hours from Altoona.

The city's main thoroughfare, Plank Road, provides a wealth of shopping and dining activities. Logan Valley Mall is a regional two-story mall.

Majors and Degrees

Penn State Altoona offers associate (two-year) degrees in business administration; criminal justice; electrical engineering technology; human development and family studies; information science and technology; letters, arts and science; mechanical engineering technology; nursing; and science. Four-year degrees include the Bachelor of Arts and Bachelor of Science in criminal justice; the Bachelor of Science in electromechanical engineering technology; the Bachelor of Arts in English; the Bachelor of Arts in environmental studies; the Bachelor of Science in human development and family studies; the Bachelor of Arts in integrative arts; the Bachelor of Arts in letters, arts and science; the Bachelor of Science in nursing; and the Bachelor of Science in business. Additional academic programs include the third year of elementary education study and two years of course work for more than 160 Penn State majors.

Academic Program

Each baccalaureate program has two components: at least 46 credits in general education and at least 78 credits in specific requirements for the major. Students must complete a minimum of 124 semester hours to earn a bachelor's degree; the exact number depends on the program. Associate degrees require a minimum of 60 semester hours. All Penn State Altoona majors require an overall grade point average of at least 2.0 and a grade of C or better in all courses designated by the major as a C-registered course. An honors program and the University Scholars Program are available to students who show exceptional promise. ROTC participants may receive scholarships or upon graduation request entry into the U.S. Army Reserve or Army National Guard.

The fall and spring semesters are each fifteen weeks in length. Registration and advising take place before the first week of classes, and the final examinations are given after the last week. There are also three summer sessions, one 4-week intersession and two 6-week consecutive sessions. The Division of Undergraduate Studies provides a summer preregistration and counseling service for all entering freshmen and their parents.

Academic Facilities

Penn State Altoona's more than twenty buildings are centered around a reflecting pond in Altoona, Pennsylvania. The 125-acre complex includes four residence halls, a student union, an athletic complex, a computer center, a library, a state-of-the-art science and engineering building, a theater, art and music studios, and an advanced technology center.

Costs

Educational costs at Penn State Altoona vary depending on whether the student is a resident of Pennsylvania and whether he or she lives off campus or in a residence hall. The 1999–2000 tuition and fees at Penn State Altoona for Pennsylvania residents were $3151 per semester. For out-of-state students, tuition and fees were $4842 per semester. Costs for residence hall living varied depending on the hall. Per semester costs included Oak

Hall at $1140, Maple Hall at $1140, Spruce Hall at $1350, and Cedar Hall at $1460. Meal plan costs ranged from $1105 to $1380 per semester.

Financial Aid

Federal grant eligibility is based on financial need, and amounts vary for each student. Federal grants available include the Federal Pell Grant and Federal Supplemental Educational Opportunity Grant. Federal Work-Study eligibility is based on financial need. Students work when not in class. Money is earned as the student works.

The state grant program is administered by the student's state agency. The state agency notifies students directly if they are eligible for a state grant. Pennsylvania residents are considered for a Pennsylvania Higher Education Assistance Agency (PHEAA) Grant. Non-Pennsylvania residents should contact their state grant agency to determine if their state has a reciprocal agreement with Pennsylvania schools.

Each year, students receive private donor and campus scholarships and awards. A scholarship committee selects appropriate students to receive the scholarships or awards. Penn State Altoona acknowledges academic excellence and achievement. Criteria have been established to emphasize excellence in scholarship, with leadership and citizenship also considered for some awards. Campus faculty and staff members nominate recipients. The campuswide effort to select the outstanding student for each award underscores the campus mission of providing students with opportunities to increase their knowledge and individual growth in analyzing, creating, and communicating.

Faculty

The College has 118 full-time and 145 part-time faculty members during the academic year. The student-faculty ratio is approximately 28:1. In addition to having faculty members advise students, the College provides professional advising, counseling, and referral services.

Student Government

The Student Government Association (SGA) is the governing body for students on campus. The SGA is responsible for recognizing and chartering all organizations and clubs and for appropriating initial funds to them. Officers for the SGA are elected in the spring semester and serve for one academic year. Freshman senators are elected the third week of the fall semester and serve through the following spring term. The Penn State Altoona Student Government Association is a member of the Penn State Commonwealth Campus Student Government, a University-wide organization whose membership includes SGA presidents and representatives of Penn State campuses. Local representatives attend conferences and workshops to develop, coordinate, and improve the programs of the University; train and maintain student leaders at each campus; and improve the lines of communication among all Penn State locations.

Admission Requirements

Each student is unique. Penn State does not have a cut-off on grades or standardized test scores. Approximately two thirds of the evaluation is based on high school grades and one third on standardized test scores. Freshman student admission decisions are made on the basis of several factors, including final grades (in all subject areas, for years nine, ten, and eleven of high school), weighted average or class rank for students who have taken AP/Honors courses, required Carnegie (high school) units, and standardized test scores (SAT I or ACT).

As part of the Pennsylvania State University, in compliance with federal and state laws, Penn State Altoona is committed to the policy that all persons shall have equal access to admission without regard to race, religion, sex, national origin, ancestry, color, sexual orientation, handicap, age, or status as a disabled or Vietnam veteran. Each applicant is evaluated on the basis of his or her high school record and the results of the SAT I or ACT. The high school grade point average, when combined with the SAT I or ACT score, produces an evaluation index, and students are admitted on the basis of that index.

Application and Information

Penn State has a rolling admissions process. There are no deadlines for applying to Penn State. However, students should apply before November 30 of their senior year for best availability of housing and academic programs. Once the application is complete (high school transcripts, SAT I or ACT scores, and application fee), students are notified in six to eight weeks by mail. The first offer of admission is sent out the beginning of November.

Students interested in transferring to Penn State Altoona should note that on every Friday, a counselor meets with students and can help them with admission to Penn State Altoona. Students should bring a working copy of a college transcript, a Penn State Altoona application (if they have any questions), and any other information that may be of importance. Penn State Altoona gives students an admissions check sheet and instructions to complete the application process at the time of their visit.

For further information, students should contact:

Office of Admissions
Pennsylvania State University Altoona College
3000 Ivyside Drive
Altoona, Pennsylvania 16601
Telephone: 814-949-5466
            800-848-9843 (toll-free)
Fax: 814-949-5564
E-mail: aaadmit@psu.edu

The entrance to the campus of Penn State Altoona.

PENNSYLVANIA STATE UNIVERSITY AT ERIE, THE BEHREND COLLEGE
ERIE, PENNSYLVANIA

The College

Penn State Erie, The Behrend College, is committed to providing the best possible education in the disciplines of business, engineering, engineering technology, the humanities, science, and social science. A Penn State degree completed at Penn State Behrend combines the high standards of a major research university with the personal attention of a liberal arts college. The College offers twenty-six 4-year baccalaureate degree programs and six 2-year associate degree programs.

Penn State Behrend was established in 1948 on the estate of and in memory of Ernst Behrend, founder of the Hammermill Paper Company. The campus is magnificent, with 730 hilltop acres overlooking Lake Erie and Presque Isle State Park. The park has many miles of sandy beaches, with some of the most beautiful sunsets in the world. Penn State Behrend's campus has extensive woodlands, deep gorges, beautiful streams, and vineyards and features cross-country skiing, fitness trails, and lighted tennis courts.

Nearly 3,700 students attend classes in modern academic buildings and labs. Eight residence halls for freshmen and sophomores and student apartments for juniors and seniors house 1,500 students. On-campus housing is not guaranteed, but assistance is offered in securing accommodations off campus.

Penn State Behrend participates in seventeen varsity sports and is an NCAA Division III member. Varsity sports include men's baseball, basketball, cross-country, golf, soccer, swimming, tennis, track and field, and water polo and women's basketball, cross-country, golf, soccer, softball, swimming, tennis, track and field, and volleyball. More than 60 percent of Penn State Behrend's students participate in a comprehensive intramural program as part of a team from their residence hall floor, fraternity or sorority, or as part of a student club. A new athletics/recreation center, featuring a swimming pool, a gymnasium, exercise facilities, and classrooms, opens in 2000.

Location

Penn State Behrend students benefit from the College's ideal location near I-90, just east of I-79, in a suburb of Erie, Pennsylvania. The population of the area is 300,000, and there is plenty to do. The College bus provides transportation to a large shopping mall, movie theaters, and a sports complex featuring indoor tennis and soccer, which are only 10 minutes away. A ski resort is only 25 minutes from campus. Public transportation leaves campus every half hour to other points throughout the Erie area, including dozens of movie theaters, ethnic restaurants, theaters, a Philharmonic, museums, and a zoo. A convention center in downtown Erie features Broadway plays and top-name performers in rock, classical, and country music. Pittsburgh, Cleveland, and Buffalo are each only 2 hours away. Knowledge Park at Penn State Erie is a research and development area situated on Penn State Behrend's campus that is designed to enable knowledge-based organizations to locate closer to and take fuller advantage of the College's intellectual and physical resources.

Majors and Degrees

Penn State Behrend confers the Bachelor of Arts degree in communication, economics, English, general arts and sciences, history, political science, psychology, and science. The Bachelor of Science degree is offered in accounting; biology; business economics; business, liberal arts, and sciences; chemistry; computer engineering; electrical engineering; electrical engineering technology; finance; management; management information systems; marketing; marketing and international business; mathematics; mechanical engineering; mechanical engineering technology; physics; plastics engineering technology; and psychology.

The Associate in Arts is awarded in one major—letters, arts, and sciences. The Associate in Science is offered in business, and the Associate in Engineering is offered in electrical engineering technology, manufacturing technology, mechanical engineering technology, and plastics engineering technology.

Academic Program

Each baccalaureate program has two components: at least 46 credits in general education and at least 78 credits in specific requirements for the major. Students must complete a minimum of 124 semester hours to earn a bachelor's degree; the exact number depends on the program. Associate degrees require a minimum of 60 semester hours. All Penn State Behrend majors require an overall grade point average of at least 2.0 and a grade of C or better in all upper-level courses in the major. An honors program and the Schreyer Scholars Program are available to students who show exceptional promise.

Several majors serve as excellent preparation for law or medical school. Special prelaw and premed advisers assist students in planning their programs. The Division of Undergraduate Studies enables those who have not yet decided on an academic major to explore several areas of study before selecting a specific program.

The fall and spring semesters are each fifteen weeks in length. Registration and advising take place before the first week of classes, and the final examinations are given after the last week. There also are two summer sessions of three and eight weeks. The Division of Undergraduate Studies provides a summer preregistration and counseling service for all entering freshmen and their parents.

Academic Facilities

Penn State's mix of contemporary and traditional buildings, including a 100,000-square-foot library–academic building and a complex of laboratory buildings, contains classrooms, laboratories, a theater, the General Electric Foundation Computer Center, state-of-the-art language labs, and student activity facilities. While the Penn State Behrend library has a collection of 93,000 volumes and 788 periodicals, students attending the College also have computerized access to the entire Penn State library system, with its 2 million bound volumes, 16,000 periodicals, and 1 million government documents. Publications ordered from the system arrive on campus within days of their selection.

Costs

Educational costs at Penn State Behrend vary depending on whether the student is a resident of Pennsylvania, whether enrollment is in the upper or lower division, and whether he or she lives off campus or in a residence hall. The 1999–2000 tuition and fees at Penn State Behrend for Pennsylvania residents (lower division) were $6436 for the academic year. For out-of-state students, the tuition and fees were $12,110 for the academic year. For some majors, there is an additional $225 surcharge. On-campus rooms are a fixed cost, but board and all other costs are variable and fluctuate according to each student's spending habits. In 1999–2000 these variable costs were approximately $4698 for room and board, $620 for books and supplies, and $1200 to $2400 for personal expenses, including clothing, laundry, travel, and miscellaneous items. Other costs were a nonrefundable $50 application fee, a nonrefundable $100 enrollment fee, a $100 general deposit, and a $100 housing deposit for students living in on-campus residences.

Financial Aid

More than 75 percent of the students at Penn State Behrend receive some form of financial aid. Awards are based on an analysis of the student's financial need. Students should file the Free Application for Federal Student Aid (FAFSA) by February 15 of their senior year of high school. Students are encouraged to seek grant assistance from their home state. Financial aid applications are available from high school counselors and financial aid offices at colleges and other institutions. These forms and the application for admission are the only forms that incoming freshmen need to complete to be considered for federal, state, and University aid. Aid includes Federal Pell Grants, Pennsylvania Higher Education Assistance Agency Grants, Federal Work-Study Program awards, Federal Perkins Loans, Federal Supplemental Educational Opportunity Grants, Federal Stafford Student Loans, and Penn State awards and scholarships.

Faculty

A first-rate faculty is at the heart of the Penn State Behrend experience. Of the 175 faculty members who teach both graduate and undergraduate students, almost all have earned the terminal degree in their major field. There are no teaching assistants, and part-time teaching is very limited. The faculty members are distinguished scholars and superb teachers. They are extensively involved in research and publishing, but they are also caring people with a record of excellence in advising students. Professors and students know each other. Such close relationships have many educational and career advantages.

Student Government

The Student Government Association is the official representative of the student body at Penn State Behrend. In addition to representing students to the administration and faculty, the Student Government Association charters all student organizations and allocates funds to support and promote student activities. The association also appoints student representatives to serve on all key administrative and faculty committees and the appropriate adjudicatory boards.

Admission Requirements

As part of the Pennsylvania State University, in compliance with federal and state laws, Penn State Behrend is committed to the policy that all persons shall have equal access to admission without regard to race, religion, sex, national origin, ancestry, color, sexual orientation, handicap, age, or status as a disabled or Vietnam veteran. Each applicant is evaluated on the basis of his or her high school record and the results of the SAT I. The high school grade point average, when combined with the SAT I score, produces an evaluation index, and students are admitted on the basis of that index.

Application and Information

Students interested in freshman admission to Penn State Behrend may obtain an admission application form from any Penn State campus, by writing to Penn State Behrend, or through the World Wide Web (listed below). Application forms are available in late summer. The recommended deadline for submitting an application is November 30. Applicants admitted to Penn State Behrend are notified approximately four to six weeks after the application and credentials are received. The student must make certain that the Educational Testing Service forwards the SAT I scores to the Undergraduate Admissions Office, Pennsylvania State University, University Park, Pennsylvania 16802.

This description is available in alternative media upon request.

For application forms, more information, or a campus visit, interested students should contact:

Office of Admissions
Penn State Erie, The Behrend College
Station Road
Erie, Pennsylvania 16563-0105

Telephone: 814-898-6100
E-mail: behrend.admissions@psu.edu
World Wide Web: http://www.pserie.psu.edu

The library at Penn State Behrend features access to all of the holdings in the Penn State system.

PEPPERDINE UNIVERSITY
Seaver College
MALIBU, CALIFORNIA

The University and The College

Pepperdine University is committed to providing education of high academic quality with particular attention to Christian values.

Seaver College is the liberal arts college of the University. Fifty percent of Seaver's 2,800 students come from California, 44 percent from the other forty-nine states, and 10 percent from other countries. The 1999–2000 freshman class had a median high school GPA of 3.7. Housing is guaranteed for the first two years. Students who live on campus may live in the twenty-two residence houses, the "Towers" Hall, or in University apartments.

A wide range of student organizations and activities are available, including social, honor, service, spiritual, professional, divisional, and special interest clubs; a campus radio station; a weekly student newspaper; and a television studio. Pepperdine participates in intercollegiate sports, including baseball, basketball, cross-country, golf, tennis, volleyball, and water polo for men and basketball, cross-country, golf, soccer, swimming, tennis, and volleyball for women. The University is a member of the West Coast Conference, the NCAA, and the Southern California Women's Intercollegiate Athletic Conference. Both men's and women's teams compete in Division I and have been very successful in regional and national competitions. Sports facilities include a 3,500-seat gymnasium, an Olympic-size swimming pool, a tennis pavilion and sixteen additional tennis courts, an intramural field, a baseball diamond, stables and riding rings, and a 2,000-seat baseball stadium.

The Master of Arts degree is offered at Seaver College in American studies, communication, history, and religion; the Master of Science degree is offered in ministry. The J.D. degree is offered by the School of Law and the master's degree is offered at the School of Public Policy; both schools are located on the Malibu campus. The Graduate School of Education and Psychology and the George L. Graziadio School of Business and Management offer graduate degrees at five locations in the Los Angeles area.

Location

Nestled in the Santa Monica Mountains and overlooking the Pacific Ocean, yet less than an hour from Los Angeles, Seaver's campus offers both the serenity of a tranquil setting and the advantages of proximity to a major metropolitan area. Malibu has a movie theater, excellent restaurants, and two small shopping centers complete with banking facilities and a variety of shops and services. The winding seashore, the rugged beauty of Malibu Canyon, and the clean air provide an environment conducive to study, while the moderate climate permits year-round outdoor recreation. In addition to making use of the physical education facilities on campus, students can enjoy swimming, surfing, horseback riding, fishing, boating, and other activities in the vicinity. As an international center for trade, recreation, culture, industry, and education, Los Angeles provides students with a wide range of opportunities.

Majors and Degrees

Seaver College awards the Bachelor of Arts in advertising, art, biology, chemistry, communication, credential program, economics, English, French, German, history, humanities, international studies, journalism, liberal arts, music, philosophy, political science, psychology, public relations, religion, sociology, Spanish, speech communication, telecommunication, and theater. The Bachelor of Science is awarded in accounting, biology, business administration, chemistry, computer science/mathematics, international business, mathematics, natural science (engineering 3-2), nutritional science, physical education, and sports medicine.

Academic Program

The academic programs at Seaver College provide students with a liberal arts education in a Christian atmosphere and relate it to the dynamic qualities of life in the twentieth century. Students must complete 128 units for the B.A. or B.S. degree, including 64 units in general education requirements and 40 or more in upper-division studies. Major requirements may be fulfilled through three basic arrangements. Students who specialize in a discipline must complete at least 24 units of upper-division work in one discipline. Students may choose an interdisciplinary major, entailing at least 40 units of upper-division work, with courses ranging broadly across disciplinary lines within a division and on occasion crossing divisional lines, in one of the following fields of study: communication, English, humanities, international studies, liberal arts, or religion. Alternatively, students may initiate a contract major by presenting an application for specific upper-division courses to the dean of Seaver College.

The College functions on a semester plan, and the regular academic year consists of two semesters, from late August to April. In addition to the regular academic year, summer sessions run from late April to early August.

At Seaver, instruction and study are adapted both to students' abilities and to the nature of the course content, instead of utilizing only the traditional lecture method. Programs involve several types of learning experiences: seminars, integrated lectures, individual study, fieldwork, and laboratories. The Dean's List of undergraduate students in the top 10 percent of the class with a grade point index not lower than 3.5 is published each semester. Other honors include cum laude for students graduating with a scholastic level of at least 3.5, magna cum laude for 3.7, and summa cum laude for 3.9.

Off-Campus Arrangements

Seaver offers students the opportunity to study abroad in Heidelberg, Germany; London, England; and Florence, Italy; a new program in Latin America is located in San Jose, Costa Rica, during the fall semester and continues in Buenos Aires, Argentina, during the spring semester. The academic program emphasizes European or Latin American history and culture. Serious study and the daily experiences of living in another country give students a special depth of understanding of other people and their cultures. Classes are taught in English by Seaver faculty members. A four-day class schedule permits extensive weekend travel throughout Europe and Latin America. Seaver also offers summer language programs in Spain and France, an archaeological dig in Israel, and study tours in the Far East, Asia, and Russia. Sports medicine majors have the opportunity to pursue studies in Canberra, Australia, and a Mediterranean Biblical Studies Tour allows students to visit significant biblical sites.

The Heidelberg program has space for approximately 50 students at Moore Haus, located near the city's famous castle. Classes are held in modern facilities in downtown Heidelberg, and students have full access to a 20,000-volume library of books in English at the nearby Amerika Haus. The London program has space for approximately 40 students at 56 Prince's Gate in the Knightsbridge area. In addition to living quarters, the facility includes classrooms, a library, a computer room, offices, and a student center. The Florence program accommodates approximately 55 students. Students reside in a University-owned Florentine Villa and residential complex with classrooms, a library, a microcomputer facility, and recreational facilities. The Latin American program houses approximately 40 students who live in apartment hotels (Apartotel Cristina in San Jose and Residencias Universitarias Master II in Buenos Aires).

Academic Facilities

The Payson Library houses a collection of approximately 475,000 volumes. Students have access to an additional 227,000 volumes at the law school. Reading rooms and periodical and stack space facilitate use of library materials. The 300-seat George Elkins Auditorium is used for public presentations and lectures. Six academic complexes contain seminar and lecture rooms, art studios, a museum, communication facilities, workshops, science and computer laboratories, minitheaters, a recital hall, and administrative offices. There is also a theater arts and music complex.

Costs

Charges for the 1999–2000 academic year were $23,000 for tuition, $7010 for room and board, and $70 for the student government fee.

Financial Aid

Approximately 75 percent of Seaver's students receive some form of financial assistance through scholarships, loans, grants, work-study programs, or jobs within the University or community. To be eligible for financial assistance from institutional resources, an undergraduate student must be enrolled in at least 12 units. An applicant must be admitted to the University before being awarded assistance, but the financial assistance application may be submitted with an admission application. To ensure full consideration, the Pepperdine financial assistance application should be submitted by February 15 for the fall semester, October 15 for the winter semester, and March 15 for the summer semester. Students are also responsible for applying for the California State Scholarship (California residents only) and Federal Pell Grant by submitting the Free Application for Federal Student Aid (FAFSA) in addition to Pepperdine's one-page financial assistance form, which is included in the application for admission.

Faculty

Seaver College's faculty includes 315 men and women of high academic distinction, 100 percent of whom hold an earned doctorate or the terminal degree in their field. The teaching faculty of Seaver College is committed primarily to the instruction of undergraduate students. The student-faculty ratio of 13:1 allows ample individual assistance through classroom instruction and counseling. Upon enrollment, each student is assigned an academic adviser from among the faculty members. A qualified counseling staff is also available to serve personal and professional academic needs.

Student Government

The Student Government Association (SGA) is composed of student leaders and works in coordination with the Campus Life Office in establishing activities and maintaining school policies. SGA coordinates on-campus movies, sightseeing trips, guest performances, dances, and speakers and serves as the voice of the students to the Seaver administration.

Admission Requirements

Applicants are admitted on the basis of their academic record; SAT I or ACT scores; SAT II Subject Test scores, if available; and personal information and references. Admission decisions are made without regard to race, religion, sex, or national background. Students who have completed at least 30 transferable semester units with a minimum grade point average of 2.7 will be considered for admission as transfer students. Students who apply with fewer than 30 units will be classified as freshmen with transfer units. To ensure full consideration, students should apply by January 15 for the fall semester, October 15 for the winter semester, and March 15 for the summer semester. Decision letter dates are announced in the current application form.

Application and Information

For the bulletin or application forms, students should contact:

Paul A. Long
Dean of Admission and Enrollment Management
Seaver College
Pepperdine University
Malibu, California 90263-4392
Telephone: 310-456-4392

The 830-acre Malibu campus of Pepperdine University, Seaver College, overlooks the Pacific Ocean, 35 miles west of Los Angeles, California.

PERU STATE COLLEGE
PERU, NEBRASKA

The College

Peru State College offers a high-quality education at a minimum personal cost to the student. Students receive substantial personal attention with a 16:1 student-teacher ratio and thrive in a supportive learning environment designed for students with diverse abilities.

Peru State College was founded in 1867 as Nebraska's first college. It operates as a public state-assisted institution that offers Bachelor of Arts, Bachelor of Science, and Bachelor of Technology degrees in the principal areas of teacher education, business, humanities, and science and technology as well as numerous preprofessional programs and a Master of Science in Education. The College is accredited by the North Central Association of Colleges and Schools and the National Council for Accreditation of Teacher Education.

Nearly 600 of Peru State's full-time students live in the eight residence halls on campus. Residence life options include single-sex halls as well as coed buildings and married student housing.

Students enjoy high-quality campus facilities, and an active social life is available on campus. The College offers more than thirty social and academic clubs, a fine arts theater, Benford Recital Hall, a coffeehouse, the Student Center, and an activities center/natatorium. Many students participate in the fifteen intramural sports offered. The Peru State Bobcats field NAIA teams in women's basketball, softball, and volleyball and in men's baseball, basketball, and football. The football program competes in the Central States Football League. All other sports teams are members of the Midlands Collegiate Athletic Conference.

Location

Peru State College, a prominent feature of the historic town of Peru, Nebraska, overlooks the Missouri River Valley. "The Campus of a Thousand Oaks" offers students the rural beauty of southeastern Nebraska only 65 miles from the state's two largest cities, Omaha and Lincoln. International airlines, passenger trains, bus service, and major highways provide convenient transportation for travelers to the area.

Peru State students enjoy four distinct seasons, from the red-gold blaze of autumn to lush green fields in spring. Many students enjoy hiking, mountain biking, camping, hunting, and fishing at nearby Indian Cave State Park.

Movie theaters and a variety of fast-food restaurants in nearby Auburn and Nebraska City provide students with additional entertainment opportunities.

Majors and Degrees

Peru State College awards the Bachelor of Arts and/or Bachelor of Science degrees in art; business, with options in accounting, management, management information systems, and marketing; computer science, with options in technical and business applications; education, with endorsements in art, biology, business, chemistry, computer science, English, history, language arts, mathematics, physical science, psychology, sociology, and special education; elementary education, with endorsements in early childhood education, middle school education, preschool handicapped, and special education; physical education, with an option in sports management and teaching endorsements in athletic coaching, physical education (K–6), and physical education (7–12); English; mathematics; music, with options in music performance and music marketing and teaching endorsements in elementary vocal music education (K–6) and vocal/instrumental music education (7–12); natural science, with options in biological science, natural science, nuclear technology, physical science, and wildlife ecology; psychology/sociology, with options in criminal justice, psychology, psychology-sociology, and sociology; and social science, with an option in history. The College also offers Bachelor of Technology degrees in distribution, management, and supervision.

Minors are available in computer science and music.

Academic Program

Peru State College provides a strong liberal arts education designed to produce graduates who are literate critical thinkers with the social and technological skills needed to apply their knowledge effectively as they pursue their social and civic roles in a complex and changing world.

The academic year at Peru State College is divided into two 15-week semesters (fall and spring) with two optional 5-week summer sessions. Students who are seeking a Bachelor of Arts or Bachelor of Science degree must earn a minimum of 125 semester credit hours, at least 40 of which are upper-division 300- and 400-level courses. All bachelor's degree candidates must complete the general studies program, which is designed to provide students with a solid foundation in the liberal arts; a major (or for teacher education candidates, one field endorsement or two subject endorsements); and elective courses that support their educational objectives.

A minimum cumulative grade point average (GPA) of 2.5 is required for all teacher education degrees. A minimum cumulative GPA of 2.0 is required for all other degrees and for all courses used to fulfill requirements in an academic major. In addition, no grade lower than a D+ (or C for transfer credits) may be used to fulfill requirements in an academic major. A maximum of 66 semester credit hours may be transferred from a two-year institution toward requirements for a bachelor's degree program. A minimum of 30 semester credit hours must be earned from Peru State College; 24 of the last 30 semester credit hours must be earned in residence unless earned from another Nebraska state college or from a college with an official cooperative agreement with Peru State College.

An Honors program is offered to challenge academically gifted students. Honors courses are designed to stimulate critical thinking through an interactive seminar structure.

Students who are seeking a Bachelor of Technology degree from Peru State College must first complete a technical associate degree or its equivalent from a regionally accredited institution. The Bachelor of Technology program requires a minimum of 125 semester credit hours, at least 20 of which are at the 300 level or higher. A minimum of 59 semester credit hours must be earned at an accredited institution of higher education, and 30 semester credit hours must be earned through Peru State College. A maximum of 66 semester credit hours may be transferred into the program from the technical associate degree program. A minimum cumulative GPA of 2.0 is required for all courses earned at Peru State College.

Students may earn credit toward degree programs through several standardized examination programs including the College-Level Examination Program (CLEP), the Proficiency Examination Program (PEP), and Defense Activity for Non-Traditional Education Support (DANTES). Credits earned through examination are considered transfer credits.

Off-Campus Arrangements

Career Services offers students individualized career planning assistance. A resource library, Cooperative Education Internship information, computer technology and equipment, employment directories and search magazines, and major newspapers are available to students. Open and closed credential files are maintained for students and alumni. Individual assistance is provided in such areas as career counseling, designing an internship experience, job search correspondence, interviewing, and negotiating job offers. The staff assists students in developing resumes, cover letters, and job search skills, and provides help in using electronic job search information. The resource library contains information on graduate schools, scholarships, career choices, job openings, and company/employee literature via computer programs.

Cooperative Education Internships are encouraged for students in every academic area. Students earn credit hours and gain applied work experience through field internships with outside organizations. The Cooperative Education Internship Program provides students with the opportunity to explore their chosen field of work and to gain valuable work experience while earning academic credit in their major or area of career interest. The maximum number of hours allowed for graduation is 12. To facilitate a beneficial work experience for students, the cooperative education staff, faculty members, and the respective division chairs approve each placement. Each internship is monitored by the cooperative education staff.

Academic Facilities

The Peru State College Library offers students access to several online databases and research utilities in addition to 105,615 bound volumes, 46,554 titles on microfilm, 7,070 audiovisual materials, and more than 1,500 print and full-text, online periodical subscriptions. Students have free access to the Internet from computer labs throughout the campus, including labs in each residence hall.

The Benford Recital Hall and the Art Gallery provide outlets for vocal, instrumental, and fine art presentations. Wheeler Activity Center houses an indoor running track as well as tennis, basketball, and volleyball courts; a weight room; and an Olympic-size swimming pool. The 15,000-square-foot Regional Technology Center in nearby Nebraska City offers distance learning opportunities via satellite in addition to computer labs and classrooms.

Costs

Tuition, fees, room, and board for a Nebraska resident for the 1999–2000 school year total approximately $5965 (based on 30 semester credit hours, a semiprivate room, and a fifteen-meal plan). Additional expenses for books, supplies, and travel are estimated at $1100.

Financial Aid

Currently, more than 85 percent of Peru State's full-time students are receiving financial aid. The College tries to meet the financial needs of all qualified students through a combination of federal, state, and institutional funds. In addition, merit-based scholarships are awarded for academic achievement, leadership, and demonstrated ability in the areas of art, drama, instrumental music, vocal music, and athletics. Nonresident scholarships are also available to qualified candidates.

All students should file the Free Application for Federal Student Aid (FAFSA) to be considered for the Federal Pell Grant, Federal Work-Study, Federal Supplemental Educational Opportunity Grant, Federal Perkins Loan, and Federal Family Education Loan programs.

Faculty

Peru State's student-faculty ratio of 16:1 ensures students personal interaction and an individualized education from 50 full-time and 50 part-time faculty members who are committed to undergraduate teaching and academic advising. Approximately 50 percent of full-time faculty members hold the highest degree in their field.

Student Government

The 23-member Student Senate, which consists of delegates elected from each class, is actively involved in decisions regarding the College's academic calendar, programs, and civic and cultural activities. The Campus Activities Board organizes hundreds of social, cultural, and recreational activities on campus each year.

Admission Requirements

Peru State College offers open admission to the state's residents who hold a Nebraska high school diploma or GED and who have not previously attended college. Admission is also granted to qualified transfer students, non-Nebraska residents, international students, and personal enrichment students. High school students may apply for admission as early as the first semester of their senior year, and all applicants should submit materials at least one month prior to the beginning of the semester they wish to be admitted.

Articulation agreements with twelve community colleges and technical schools provide efficient transfer of credits for students who wish to apply their Associate of Art, Associate of Science, or Associate of Applied Science degrees toward a bachelor's degree program at Peru State. Transfer students may apply for admission during their last year of attendance at another college or university.

Application and Information

Freshman applicants should submit a completed application for admission; a $10 application fee; an official high school transcript that lists cumulative grade point average, class rank, and graduation date; official ACT or SAT I score reports sent from the testing organization; and a Peru State College Medical/Immunization Form.

Transfer applicants should submit a completed application for admission, a $10 application fee, official transcripts from every postsecondary institution attended or enrolled in, official high school transcript (if applicant has completed fewer than 30 transferable semester credits), a Transfer Student Report, and a Peru State College Medical/Immunization Form.

To receive application forms, a College catalog, or any additional information, students should contact:

Office of Admissions
Peru State College
P.O. Box 10
Peru, Nebraska 68421
Telephone: 402-872-2221
           800-742-4412 (toll-free)
E-mail: admissions@bobcat.peru.edu
World Wide Web: http://www.peru.edu

PFEIFFER UNIVERSITY
MISENHEIMER, NORTH CAROLINA

The University
Pfeiffer University traces its history back to 1885. Over the decades, high academic standards, curriculum flexibility, a concern for the individual student, financial assistance to students with need, and emphasis on Christian life have been trademarks of the institution. Attractive Georgian buildings plus a modern gymnasium and swimming pool complex offer a pleasant setting. Activities and social life center on the student entertainment series, choirs and instrumental groups, drama, publications, an active (voluntary) religious-life program, student clubs, and intramural and intercollegiate athletics. Pfeiffer fields varsity teams for men in baseball, basketball, golf, lacrosse, soccer, cross-country, and tennis and for women in basketball, cross-country, golf, lacrosse, soccer, softball, swimming, tennis, and volleyball.

The current undergraduate enrollment is 963 men and women, who come from twenty-seven states and seventeen countries. Students who want a friendly, small-college community, a close student-faculty relationship, and both traditional and innovative educational approaches will enjoy Pfeiffer. The University is accredited by the Southern Association of Colleges and Schools, and individual programs are approved by the National Association of Schools of Music and the North Carolina State Board of Education.

Location
Misenheimer, North Carolina, is a small community on U.S. Highway 52 near its intersection with N.C. Highway 49, about 12 miles from Albemarle. Salisbury, 16 miles away, and Charlotte, 35 miles away, provide entertainment, shopping, restaurants, and transportation. Many students work with area schools, churches, and social-service agencies in volunteer projects.

Majors and Degrees
The Bachelor of Science degree is awarded in accounting, biology, business administration, chemistry, chemistry-business, computer information systems, economics, environmental science, golf facility management, mathematics, and sports medicine. The Bachelor of Arts degree is awarded in American culture, arts administration, Christian education, Christian education–music, communications, criminal justice, early childhood education, English, history, human services, intermediate education, music, physical education, psychology, religion, social studies, sociology, special education, sports management, and youth ministry.

Secondary education certification is offered through major programs in English, mathematics, music, physical education, and social studies.

Prelaw and premedical tracks are available for students completing appropriate related majors.

Dual-degree programs in engineering are offered in cooperation with Auburn University.

Pfeiffer also has an urban campus in Charlotte, North Carolina, which provides for the needs of the adult learner. Bachelor's degree-completion programs in eight business and social science fields are offered to those holding an associate (two-year) degree or the equivalent.

Academic Program
The academic program follows a core-concept approach, with courses required in English, mathematics, history or political science, a laboratory science, fine arts, social sciences, and religion. Students must complete 124 semester hours (120 nonactivity hours and 4 activity hours) and 60 cultural units. Cultural units are earned through attending lectures, concerts, and other University events. Faculty members use a variety of teaching methods, including lectures, seminars, discussions, case studies, field trips, and laboratory projects. Honors programs and independent studies are offered.

Off-Campus Arrangements
Supervised internships and fieldwork for academic credit are available in the social sciences, criminal justice, Christian education, elementary education, physical education, sports medicine, and sports management.

Academic Facilities
The University's exceptionally well equipped science laboratories are open 24 hours a day, seven days a week, as are the computer labs. The library houses an open-stack collection of more than 115,000 volumes. Other resources include more than 9,000 microforms, 2,200 recordings, a complete microfilm edition of the *New York Times,* and a special collection of North Carolina and Methodist historical materials. The periodical room subscribes to more than 700 journals and magazines. Sports-related instruction is conducted in the Merner Center for Health and Physical Education. The computer center houses a modern system used in many classes, and terminals are available at several locations on campus. Pfeiffer students can access NC Live, a database consisting of thousands of electronic academic journals.

Costs
For the 2000–01 academic year, the basic cost for dormitory students (tuition, fixed fees, room, and board) is $15,940; for day students, the cost is $11,380. There are additional costs for private music lessons (if applicable) and for books and supplies. Other expenditures for travel, entertainment, laundry, and incidentals vary according to individual needs.

Financial Aid
More than 90 percent of the University's students receive financial aid, and awards valued at more than $5-million were made in 1998–99. The financial aid program includes competitive academic scholarships, athletic scholarships for men and women, work-study awards, federal and state grants, and Perkins Loans. A student who enters Pfeiffer without an academic scholarship may earn one later through the University's innovative Incentive Scholarship System. The same program also enables Pfeiffer students with good grades and already holding a scholarship to increase the amount of their award. Applications for financial aid should be filed by May 1 but are considered as long as funds are available. A number of jobs are available on campus. Notification of awards is generally made in the spring. Applicants for a loan, grant-in-aid, or work-study award must file the Free Application for Federal Student Aid (FAFSA) with the Federal Student Aid Program (P.O. Box 4005, Iowa City, Iowa 52243).

Faculty
The University has 51 full-time and 4 part-time faculty members, ensuring a favorable student-faculty ratio and many small classes. Sixty-four percent of faculty members hold the doctorate or an equivalent terminal degree, and all science

laboratory instructors hold the Ph.D. Each student has a faculty adviser. Three fourths of the faculty members live on campus or within 5 miles. Faculty teams participate in several intramural sports.

Student Government

The Pfeiffer Student Government Association (SGA) is the most active campus organization, and its president sits on the University's Board of Trustees. The SGA operates the student judicial system, makes recommendations to the administration on residence hall policies, and assists the University in fund-raising functions and student recruitment. Students often sit on faculty committees.

Admission Requirements

Candidates for admission should be high school graduates. Although most applicants rank in the upper half of their class, every applicant is given careful consideration. A normal college-preparatory course sequence is recommended; however, many who have not followed this sequence are able to do successful work at Pfeiffer. All candidates must demonstrate proficiency in English. SAT I or ACT scores must be submitted. The minimum acceptable scores are determined on an individual basis in conjunction with evaluation of other application materials. The University seeks evidence of natural ability and motivation, as demonstrated by high school performance and participation in extracurricular activities. Students from all geographic areas and all racial and ethnic groups are encouraged to apply.

A limited number of high school students who have completed the junior year are accepted into an early admissions program. Candidates for a music major must audition for the music faculty. Veterans are granted special admission status in recognition of their maturity, age, and service experience. A liberal plan has been established with many two- and four-year institutions for the transferring of credits to Pfeiffer.

Admissions counselors visit Florida, Georgia, Kentucky, Maryland, New Jersey, New York, North Carolina, Ohio, Pennsylvania, South Carolina, Tennessee, Virginia, and the New England area. An on-campus interview is strongly recommended. The University Admissions Office will arrange to meet prospective students at nearby Charlotte (air, bus, and train terminals) or Salisbury (bus and train terminals).

Application and Information

Admission application forms are available upon request. Applications should be filed after the end of the junior year in high school. The notification of the admission decision is mailed within ten days of receipt of all materials. Requests for a brochure, the University catalog, application forms, and financial aid information should be addressed to the Director of Admissions.

Director of Admissions
Pfeiffer University
Misenheimer, North Carolina 28109
Telephone: 704-463-1360 Ext. 2060
           800-338-2060 (toll-free)
E-mail: admiss@pfeiffer.edu
World Wide Web: http://www.pfeiffer.edu

A view of the main campus at Pfeiffer University.

PHILADELPHIA UNIVERSITY
PHILADELPHIA, PENNSYLVANIA

The University

Philadelphia University (formerly Philadelphia College of Textiles and Science) is a private university for men and women with high motivation and academic ability. Founded in 1884 to educate professionals for the textile industry, the University has evolved into a diverse, professionally oriented institution with programs in architecture, design, business, fashion, the sciences, and health care, in addition to textile engineering and design. The University's enrollment of approximately 2,200 undergraduates represents a diverse group of talented students from forty-one states and forty-one countries. With an average class size of 18 and a 12:1 student-faculty ratio, students receive the personal attention so important to social and professional growth.

Through a unique blend of liberal and specialized education, the University prepares students to become competent professionals in today's complex, interdependent global society. Recognized as a premier professional college, Philadelphia University has established a phenomenal record of career success for its graduates. The University maintains that success through extensive networking with prospective employees (bringing company recruiters to campus and facilitating nearly 400 student interviews last year), innovative programs that meet emerging needs in the marketplace, and extensive career-planning support for students. More than 22,000 resumes for 2,200 positions were distributed on behalf of students and alumni to 1,200 employers. It all adds up to a placement rate that is consistently more than 90 percent.

Philadelphia University believes the college experience of every student should extend well beyond the classroom. The Student Life program at Philadelphia University seeks to build bridges between the classroom (curricular) and out-of-class (cocurricular) experiences to create a dynamic learning community for students. Twelve varsity teams compose the intercollegiate athletics program. The men's soccer team competes in NCAA Division I, while the men's baseball, basketball, golf, and tennis teams and the women's basketball, field hockey, lacrosse, soccer, softball, tennis, and volleyball teams participate at the Division II level. An extensive intramural sports program is available to all students. Students are actively engaged in campus life, whether it be through one of the nationally ranked athletic teams, events sponsored by SGA and the Program Board, a wide array of community service opportunities, an extensive intramural program, or participation in the more than thirty student clubs and organizations.

More than 1,100 students live on campus in residence halls, apartments, and town houses. Within each of the residential areas live professional and paraprofessional staff who assist students with daily concerns and who program activities to enhance residential living.

The University holds accreditation from the Middle States Association of Colleges and Schools, the National Architectural Accrediting Board (NAAB), the Foundation for Interior Design Education and Research (FIDER), the American Chemical Society (ACS), and the Commission for Accreditation of Allied Health Education Programs (CAAHEP).

Location

The University's sprawling, 100-acre campus is adjacent to Fairmount Park, the largest urban park system in the country. Students enjoy the best of both worlds—a beautiful campus with tree-lined walkways, spacious lawns, and classical architecture, and easy access to Philadelphia (just minutes away) for entertainment, cultural events, great night spots, and more than 300 years of American history.

Philadelphia also serves as a "living lab" where students frequently interact with area professionals for class projects, internships, co-ops, and off-campus jobs.

Majors and Degrees

Philadelphia University offers the Bachelor of Science in thirty-one areas: accounting, architecture, architectural studies, biochemistry, biology, biopsychology, business and science, chemistry, chemistry/applied science, computer science, environmental science, fashion/apparel management, fashion design, fashion merchandising, finance, graphic design communication, human resource management, industrial design, interior design, international business, management, management information systems, marketing, physician assistant studies, premedicine, psychology, small business/retailing, textile design, textile engineering, textile management/marketing, and textile technology. The University also offers several five-year B.S./M.B.A. joint programs. The five-year architecture program leads to a Bachelor of Architecture (B.Arch.). For students wishing to keep their options open, a "Freshman Choice" option offers an introduction to college courses in preparation for entering a specific major in the sophomore year.

Academic Program

The University's commitment to quality professional education is realized in a curriculum that combines a solid foundation in liberal studies with career preparation. The curricula are designed to enhance students' ability and desire to learn; to ensure them an understanding of the ideas, traditions, and values of their own and other cultures; and to prepare them to apply the concepts and techniques of both general and specialized learning to their lives as citizens with productive careers. Degree requirements include successful completion of 121 to 138 credits (depending upon the major chosen), successful completion of both major and general education programs, and the satisfactory completion of at least 60 credits in residence at the University. All students have the option to participate in the University's Co-op Program, through which they earn both academic credit and a salary.

As a rule, the University grants credit to students who obtain satisfactory grades in subject examinations developed by the Advanced Placement Program, the College-Level Examination Program, and the Proficiency Examination Program. Students may, by invitation, participate in the Honors Program, which offers a number of courses expressly for honors students.

The University's academic calendar consists of two semesters and two summer sessions.

Off-Campus Arrangements

The University has a dynamic Study Abroad Program that includes a formal affiliation with the University of Rome, Italy.

Students at the Philadelphia University, Center for Study Abroad study in areas such as architecture, fashion merchandising, fashion design, and apparel.

Studying abroad is an exciting way for students to see the world, experience other cultures, and learn about their field of study. Architecture students, for example, can travel to England to see firsthand the work of Christopher Wren; fashion design students can study in London, Paris, or Italy; and international business students can explore global trade in Spain or other overseas locations.

Cooperative education or fieldwork experiences are also available. Study-abroad options include Austria, Australia, England, France, Germany, Ireland, Italy, Japan, Mexico, Scotland, and Spain. The University's Co-op office has affiliations with such organizations as Walt Disney World, L. L. Bean, Isdaner and Co., Mellon Bank, Burlington Industries, J. Crew, and Liz Claiborne.

Academic Facilities

Many major labs and studios enable students to gain practical experience in art, design, textiles, apparel manufacturing, foreign language study, the sciences, computer technologies, and physician assistant studies. The University's Paul J. Gutman Library is a state-of-the-art information center. Through the contemporary information system, students can search the library's collections, as well as major indexes and full-text journals, from on or off campus. An international computer network links Philadelphia University to the resources of more than 14,000 libraries world-wide. With more than 400 study spaces and nine group study rooms, the library provides an ideal environment for reading and research. The Architecture and Design Center houses studio space, a photo lab, and computer-aided design labs. The Paley Design Center houses an extensive collection of textile artifacts and hosts changing exhibits in its galleries.

The computer labs are updated on an ongoing basis as technology changes. They are currently equipped primarily with Pentium computers running at speeds of up to 600 Mhz. The University is fully networked with a 100-megabyte fast Ethernet network that provides students with access to resources such as the Internet and e-mail from on or off campus.

Costs

The University's 1999–2000 cost for regular tuition was $14,692. Room was $3202, and board was $3374.

Financial Aid

In 1999–2000, Philadelphia University's total financial aid program amounted to just over $27 million; about $9.5 million came from the University itself and the remainder came from federal, state, and private sources. While 89 percent of the University's students receive direct institutional scholarship assistance, 94 percent receive some form of aid each year (e.g., other scholarships, loans, and job opportunities). The University attempts to meet the remainder of the financial need with University, state, and federal grants, scholarships, and loans. Candidates for aid should complete the Free Application for Federal Student Aid by April 15. The University offers a wide range of institutional scholarships and grants to incoming students each year. Award amounts will vary according to the quality of each student's academic record. The University's scholarship program is available to all prospective students (freshmen and transfer students). Scholarships are awarded regardless of financial need. Students and parents are strongly encouraged to call the admissions or financial aid offices for further information.

Faculty

Primarily a teaching institution, the University encourages close connections between faculty members and students. Classes are intentionally kept small and faculty members make a practice of being available to students outside the classroom. Often, students can partner with faculty members to pursue joint research interests and gain career experience. The University's faculty is a diverse group of professionals who hold not only strong academic credentials, but also frequently possess impressive work experience. They are frequently sought out as consultants in their fields.

Student Government

The Student Government Association (SGA) is an independent, self-governing student group. In addition to the basic responsibility of protecting students' rights, SGA recommends students to University-wide committees, addresses student grievances, and sponsors campuswide events. The Programming Board is the major programming organization on campus. Its primary responsibility is to provide a wide variety of cultural, scholastic, social, educational, and recreational programs.

Admission Requirements

The University evaluates applicants on the basis of their high school record (including GPA and quality of courses taken), scores on either the SAT I or the ACT, and extracurricular activities. Normally, 14 units of secondary school preparation are required for admission. Three units of mathematics (including algebra II) are required for admission. Students who wish to enter a science curriculum are strongly encouraged to take four units of mathematics. The University actively recruits qualified transfer students, who represent approximately one fifth of the incoming class each fall. The University also has a large international student population. These students must score at least 170 (computer-based) on the TOEFL in order to be considered for admission.

Application and Information

The University maintains a rolling admission plan. Applications are reviewed and decisions are made soon after an application, academic credentials, and standardized test scores are received. Students are encouraged to submit applications early in the senior year; applications received after March 1 are considered on a space-available basis. All applicants are encouraged to come to campus for an interview with a member of the professional admission staff.

Laurie C. Grover
Director of Admissions
Philadelphia University
School House Lane and Henry Avenue
Philadelphia, Pennsylvania 19144
Telephone: 215-951-2800
            800-951-7287 (toll-free)
Fax: 215-951-2907
E-mail: admissions@philau.edu
World Wide Web: http://www.philau.edu

PIEDMONT COLLEGE
DEMOREST, GEORGIA

The College

With more than 1,700 students and an 11:1 student-faculty ratio, Piedmont College offers personal instruction in a scholarly, tradition-rich environment. Fully accredited by the Southern Association of Colleges and Schools, Piedmont is a private liberal arts college offering bachelor's degrees in twenty-three areas and master's degrees in early childhood education, emotional/behavior disorders, secondary education, and public administration.

Students from across the country and around the world bring a diversity of backgrounds and beliefs to Piedmont College, which is associated with the Congregational Christian Churches. The small classes and sense of a cohesive college community that Piedmont offers help students develop their full potential and acquire the skills needed for successful professional careers.

Piedmont is a residential college and encourages students to live in the on-campus residence halls available for men and women. Clubs and organizations on campus allow students to be involved in many areas of interest, including Alpha Chi honor society, anthropology, art, music and chorale, commerce, history, karate, student newspaper, literary society, math and physics, Psi Chi honor society, psychology, science, education, government, world culture, religion, and the yearbook. In addition, the College offers a Lyceum series that serves to enrich the student body and community through lectures and performances. The Piedmont Honors College allows a select group of students to pursue their studies in a seminar setting with a designated professor assigned to each discipline.

Piedmont College is a member of the National Association of Intercollegiate Athletics (NAIA) Division I and a provisional member of the National Collegiate Athletic Association (NCAA) Division III. Intercollegiate sports include men's and women's basketball and soccer, men's baseball, women's fast-pitch softball, and women's volleyball. There is also a variety of intramural and club teams. A new athletic center housing a gymnasium, a fitness center, and training rooms opens in spring 2000.

Piedmont offers graduate programs for students seeking a master's degree in public administration or education (initial or advanced certification). Degrees are offered in early childhood education and in secondary education, with specialty areas that include English, math, science, social science, and Spanish.

Location

Founded in 1897, Piedmont College gets its name from the rolling foothills of the Appalachian Mountains in north Georgia, one of the most scenic areas of the United States. The nearby Chattahoochee National Forest is ideal for every type of outdoor activity, including white-water canoeing and rafting, birding, hiking, and camping. The Appalachian Trail, which extends all the way to Maine, begins nearby, although trails for the less adventurous feature numerous waterfalls and green glens filled with wildflowers. The mountain streams are full of trout, and nearby lakes offer plenty of outdoor recreation. Water-skiers find Lake Burton or Lake Lanier just 20 minutes away, and snow skiing in the mountains of North Carolina is just 2 hours away.

The College itself is located on about 100 wooded acres overlooking Demorest Lake in the small town of Demorest. The region is rich with the history of the Native Americans who first occupied the area and the gold prospectors who later opened the area to early settlers. Each of these heritages can be seen in the traditional crafts that are still produced by local artisans.

Piedmont is rural, but it is not remote. Atlanta, with its diverse cultural and recreational attractions, is an easy 1½-hour drive from the campus. Frequent student outings include trips to the internationally acclaimed Atlanta Symphony, live theater, and the Atlanta Zoological Park, as well as organized trips to see professional baseball, football, and basketball games.

Majors and Degrees

Piedmont's curriculum is grounded in a strong core of liberal arts courses, leading to the Bachelor of Arts degree, the Bachelor of Science degree, or the Bachelor of Science in Nursing degree.

The Bachelor of Arts degree is offered with majors in art, art education, business administration, early childhood education, English, environmental studies, history, interdisciplinary studies, mass communication, middle grades education, music, music education, philosophy/religion, psychology, sociology, Spanish, special education/mental retardation, and theater arts.

The Bachelor of Science degree is offered with majors in biology, chemistry, exercise physiology, mathematics, and mathematics/computer science.

Minors or concentrations include all the disciplines in which majors are offered in addition to accounting, anthropology, coaching, computer information systems, economics, French, philosophy, physical education, physical science, political science, quantitative method teaching, religion, and teaching. In addition, courses of study may be followed to meet requirements for entry into a number of professional programs such as dentistry, law, medicine, nursing, pharmacy, and veterinary medicine, among others.

Academic Program

The regular academic year is divided into two semesters, each approximately sixteen weeks long. Summer classes are held in two sessions. Students can be admitted at the beginning of any semester. For the best orientation to college life and the planned sequence of courses, it is recommended that freshmen enter college at the beginning of the fall semester. The normal study load is five courses or 15 semester hours per semester. Students who wish to take more than 19 semester hours must have a cumulative grade point average of at least 3.0. A student may take no more than 22 hours during any semester. A student must complete at least 121–124 semester credit hours to be a candidate for graduation.

Academic Facilities

Piedmont College's main academic building, Daniel Hall, houses classrooms, faculty and administrative offices, academic support, and Jenkins Auditorium, which contains a theater and a lounge area. Daniel Hall is also home to the Daniel School of Nursing and Health Sciences. Adjacent to Daniel Hall is Stewart Hall, which is Piedmont's new math, science, and technology center. Completed in 2000, this building houses all chemistry, physics, biology, and earth science labs and state-of-the-art computer modeling facilities. The College's new 38,000-square-foot library features an automated online system, conference and meeting rooms, study carrels, a computer center, a distance learning classroom (audiovisual), an educational curriculum center, and an archives room. Currently, the library's holdings include eighty commercial online services; 100,000 books, serial backfiles, and government documents accessible through the library's catalog; 365 titles on microform; 305 audiovisual materials; and 460 serials.

The College Chapel houses classrooms, music practice facilities, and the faculty offices of the music department. There are also studio art facilities and a new Martens Botanical Center with labs and classrooms. A new athletic center, completed in spring 2000, includes a new gymnasium, a fitness center, classrooms, and meeting facilities.

Costs

Undergraduate tuition for the 2000–01 academic year is $9500. Room and board charges vary according to the type of meal plan students choose and the dorm in which they live and can range from $4400 to $4700 per academic year. The state of Georgia provides Tuition Equalization Grants and HOPE Scholarships to legal residents who enroll at Piedmont College. Students should keep in mind the additional cost of books, supplies, travel, and personal expenses.

Financial Aid

The College makes every effort to assist students with financial need through scholarships, grants, loans, and work-aid programs. Approximately 95 percent of Piedmont College students receive some form of financial assistance. Piedmont also offers renewable merit-based scholarships to qualified entering students.

Faculty

All members of the Piedmont faculty provide students with the personal attention and encouragement they need to succeed. Eighty-six percent of the full-time teaching faculty members hold Ph.D.'s or the highest degrees in their fields.

Student Government

The Student Government Association (SGA) has general responsibility for and supervision of all student organizations and extracurricular activities. All students enrolled at Piedmont belong to the SGA.

Admission Requirements

Piedmont College welcomes students who demonstrate preparation for and the ability to perform college work satisfactorily. Applicants must have completed a four-year high school course of not fewer than 21 units or have earned a GED certificate. Other criteria for admission are the high school record of the applicant and the results of the SAT I of the College Board and/or ACT Assessment scores. Each applicant's complete record is carefully reviewed to arrive at an admission decision. Character and personality qualifications, references, and an interview are also considered. Admission to Piedmont College does not depend upon any one criterion.

A limited number of applicants may be admitted on conditional standing. These students must successfully complete all course work in order to return the following semester.

Application and Information

Applicants must submit a completed application form, a $20 application fee, official transcripts of all high school and/or college credit, and SAT I or ACT scores. An applicant is notified as soon as the Admissions Committee has reached a decision. The acceptance of a student is based upon satisfactory completion of any pertinent work in progress. Piedmont College must receive notification of successful completion of such work before acceptance is final.

Prospective students and their parents are encouraged to visit the campus at any time. Campus visits may be arranged through the Admissions Office.

For more information, students should contact:

Director of Admissions
Piedmont College
P.O. Box 10
Demorest, Georgia 30535
Telephone: 706-776-0103
          800-277-7020 (toll-free)
E-mail: cbrown@piedmont.edu
World Wide Web: http://www.piedmont.edu

Piedmont College in northeast Georgia was founded in 1897.

PINE MANOR COLLEGE
CHESTNUT HILL, MASSACHUSETTS

The College
Founded in 1911, Pine Manor is a four-year liberal arts college dedicated to educating women for inclusive leadership and social responsibility in their workplaces, communities, and families. Originally located in Wellesley, Massachusetts, the College moved to Chestnut Hill in 1965. On its 60-acre wooded campus are thirty-three buildings, with interactive teaching facilities in each classroom building. A new campus center opened in 1998. Students enrolled represent twenty-six states and nineteen countries. More than 90 percent of the B.A. graduates enter professional careers; graduate school placements are above the national average. Pine Manor is accredited by the New England Association of Schools and Colleges.

Among the major activities and organizations are the Student Government Association, newspaper, yearbook, Drama Club, WPMC radio, Campus Activities Board, ALANA (African, Latina, Asian, Native American, and All), literary magazine, and psychology club. Varsity sports include basketball, cross-country, golf, soccer, softball, tennis, and volleyball, while instruction is available in lifetime fitness activities and other areas of physical education. Members of the Performing Arts Department and their students present musical, dramatic, and dance performances throughout the year. The Visual Arts Department sponsors professional and student exhibits throughout the year in the Hess Gallery.

There are three village complexes on campus, each including five residence units and a commons. All first-year students are encouraged to live on campus, and housing is guaranteed for students for four years. Housing is also available to all adult learners who wish to reside on campus. Meals are served in the dining center.

Location
Pine Manor College is 5 miles from the cultural and intellectual facilities of Boston. Some of these include the fifty-three colleges and universities in the area, Boston Symphony, Boston Opera Company, Boston Ballet Company, Museum of Fine Arts, Museum of Science, and many fine professional and university theaters. Cape Cod and the New England ski areas are also easily accessible. Public transportation is within walking distance of the campus. In addition, an evening shuttle is provided by the College for transportation from the campus to the subway and the local shopping area.

Majors and Degrees
Pine Manor College offers a four-year liberal arts program leading to the Bachelor of Arts (B.A.) degree and a two-year program leading to an Associate in Arts (A.A.) or Associate in Science (A.S.) degree. Majors and concentrations for the B.A. degree are offered in biology, business administration, communication, English, history and culture, psychology, social and political systems, and visual arts. Students majoring in psychology may elect to pursue teacher certification in grades K-3 or 1-6. Secondary certification is available in English. Concentrations in the A.A. program include art history, biology, child study, drama, English, history and political science, liberal studies, management, psychology, and visual arts. The A.S. degree is offered in health sciences. Individualized and interdisciplinary majors may be arranged by the student in consultation with her adviser. Certificate programs are also available.

Academic Program
For the B.A. degree, students must complete thirty-two full-semester courses, or 132 semester credit hours. To receive the A.A. or A.S. degree, students must successfully complete sixteen full-semester courses or 64 semester credit hours. Core curriculum requirements create a solid academic foundation for students by framing the major requirements with courses from the following: humanities, social sciences, natural and behavioral sciences, fine and performing arts, mathematics, and English composition.

An outcomes-based general education program, with portfolio assessment, is a College requirement. Faculty members emphasize collaborative, active learning techniques.

A four-year leadership program compliments the portfolio program. This program assists students in exploring inclusive and socially responsible leadership.

Adult learners may apply CLEP, transfer credits, or credits for prior learning toward their degrees and may take courses part-time or full-time. Certificate programs are offered in business communications and marketing.

The English Language Institute at Pine Manor is a coed program designed for men and women whose native language is not English. Noncredit instruction in English is offered at the elementary and intermediate levels on a year-round basis. Sessions begin every two weeks, and last anywhere from two to fifty weeks, depending on the individual needs of each student.

Off-Campus Arrangements
Study-abroad options are available throughout the world. Pine Manor College students may also take part in the Washington Semester program for juniors sponsored by the American University in Washington, D.C.; the Washington Center; and the Semester at Sea program.

Pine Manor College participates in a program of cross-registration with Babson College and Boston College.

Career-exploration internships in the Boston area for academic credit are part of all degree programs. All students participate in an internship during their senior year. In addition, students may engage in an exploratory internship prior to their senior year, which enables underclass students to examine the many career alternatives available and helps undecided students select a major closely aligned with their interests and abilities. Students may choose from more than 1,000 established sites.

Academic Facilities
The Ferry Administration Building accommodates most of the administrative offices and student services; Haldan Hall contains modern classrooms, faculty offices, and language laboratories; the recently renovated Dane Science Center has classrooms, laboratories for science courses, and computer laboratories; and Ellsworth Hall, the performing arts center, has a theater, classrooms, computer facilities, and listening and practice rooms. The Abercrombie Fine Arts Wing has studios for sculpture, printmaking, painting, design, and photography, as well as design-related computer equipment. The gymnasium includes basketball, tennis, volleyball, and badminton courts; a dance and exercise studio; and a fitness room with multistation exercise equipment. Other athletic facilities include cross-

country running/skiing trails, an outdoor fitness circuit, and the Hedley soccer/lacrosse field. The Annenberg Library and Communications Center houses the library, Learning Resource Center, Cherry Computer Center, radio and TV production studios, Hess Art Gallery, lecture halls, seminar rooms, and music-listening areas.

Costs

For 2000–01, tuition is $11,894. A room is $3725, board is $3725, and the orientation fee for freshman students is $100. Private music lessons and student parking facilities are available for an extra charge.

Financial Aid

The College's financial aid resources include Pine Manor grants, merit grants, Federal Work-Study jobs, Federal Stafford Student Loans, Federal Supplemental Educational Opportunity Grants, Federal Pell Grants, and state scholarships.

Pine Manor participates in the College Scholarship Service of the College Board. A copy of the Free Application for Federal Student Aid (FAFSA) and Financial Aid PROFILE must be on file with the College Scholarship Service by May 1. A copy of the Pine Manor application for financial aid must also be on file in the College's Financial Aid Office by May 1.

Faculty

Teaching is the number one priority of Pine Manor's faculty members. Eighty percent of Pine Manor's full-time professors hold terminal degrees. Part-time faculty members are professional practitioners in their fields of expertise. The low student-to-faculty ratio of 9:1 allows faculty members to take an active part in every phase of College life.

Student Government

Students participate in decision making at Pine Manor through both the Student Government Association. In addition, student representatives sit on the Curriculum Committee, Library Committee, Speakers and Programs Committee, and the Academic Ethics Council.

Admission Requirements

Students are selected on the basis of an evaluation of their secondary school performance, SAT I or ACT scores, program of studies, school recommendations, and personal essay. While an interview is not required for admission, it is strongly recommended. SAT I scores are not required of international students; TOEFL scores, however, are required. Applicants are expected to have 16 academic credits, distributed among the following: English, social studies, mathematics, science, and foreign languages. Transfer students must submit transcripts of previous college courses completed. Accepted students may choose to enroll on a part-time basis.

The College will consider applications from juniors in secondary school who have fulfilled the admission requirements (or who will have fulfilled them by September of the year they wish to enter).

Application and Information

All applications are handled on a rolling admission basis.

The College uses the College Board's Candidates Reply Date of May 1.

For further information, students should contact:
Dean of Admissions
Pine Manor College
400 Heath Street
Chestnut Hill, Massachusetts 02467
Telephone: 617-731-7104
          800-PMC-1357 (toll-free)
Fax: 617-731-7199

The Annenberg Library and Communications Center.

PITZER COLLEGE
CLAREMONT, CALIFORNIA

The College

Pitzer is a nationally recognized independent, residential liberal arts and sciences college. The College's emphasis on interdisciplinary studies, intercultural understanding, and concern with social responsibility and the ethical implications of knowledge and action sets it apart from most of the other colleges in the country. The College believes that students should take an active part in formulating their individualized plans of study, bringing a spirit of inquiry and adventure to the process of planning. Because there are fewer required specific general education courses, Pitzer gives its students more freedom to choose the courses they want to take.

Pitzer offers the best of both worlds: membership in a small, closely knit academic community and access to the resources of a midsize university through Pitzer's partnership in the Claremont Colleges. The Claremont Colleges are a consortium of five distinct undergraduate colleges (Pitzer, Claremont McKenna, Harvey Mudd, Pomona, and Scripps) and two graduate institutions, the Claremont Graduate University and the Keck Institute for Applied Biological Sciences. Each school has its own academic focus and personality but all share major facilities, such as the main library, bookstore, campus security, health services, counseling center, ethnic study centers, and chaplains' offices. The total enrollment of all of the colleges is about 6,000 students. Students at Pitzer may enroll in courses offered by the other colleges and may consult with professors on all of the adjoining campuses.

The College was established in 1963. Historically, Pitzer was the Claremont College that focused on the behavioral and social sciences. Through the years, the curricular emphasis has expanded to include the arts, humanities, and sciences. Majors with the largest enrollments include anthropology, art, biology, economics, English, environmental studies, history, organizational studies, political studies, psychology, and sociology.

The 1999 freshman class of 246 students represented twenty-eight different states and seven other countries. About half of the first-year students came from California.

Pitzer has had a deep commitment to welcoming members of underrepresented groups since its founding. In 1999, members of underrepresented groups made up 30 percent of the total student body, including 10 percent Asian American and Pacific Islander, 14 percent Chicano/Latino, 5 percent African American, and 1 percent Native American.

Residential life plays a significant role in the student's educational experience. Each of the three residence halls establishes its own Hall Council annually to serve as a forum for addressing and meeting the needs of the community. Pitzer students have a long tradition of arranging their living communities based on common interests. All rooms are wired for Internet access, television, and phone service.

Opportunities abound at Pitzer and within the other Claremont Colleges for students to participate in a wide variety of sports, clubs, community service programs, and social activities. Pitzer joins Pomona College to field NCAA Division III teams in baseball, basketball, cross-country, football, golf, soccer, softball, swimming and diving, tennis, track and field, volleyball, and water polo. Badminton, cycling, fencing, lacrosse, and rugby are offered as intramural sports. Currently, more than seventy-five student organizations allow students to get involved in a wide variety of activities.

Location

Pitzer is located in the city of Claremont (population 35,000) at the base of the San Gabriel Mountains, about 35 miles east of Los Angeles and 78 miles west of Palm Springs. Pitzer is within short driving distances of rock climbing at Joshua Tree National Park; the Getty, Norton Simon, and other Los Angeles County museums; skiing; and the beaches of southern California.

Majors and Degrees

Pitzer grants the Bachelor of Arts degree in forty fields of study. Concentrations are available in American studies; anthropology; art; Asian-American studies; Asian studies; biology; black studies; chemistry; Chicano studies; classics; economics; English and world literature; environmental studies; European studies; French; gender and feminist studies; history; human biology; international and intercultural studies; Latin American and Caribbean studies; linguistics; management engineering; mathematical economics; mathematics; media studies; music; organizational studies; philosophy; physics; political economy; political studies; psychobiology; psychology; religious studies; science and management; science, technology and society; sociology; Spanish; theater; and Third World studies.

Academic Program

To earn the Bachelor of Arts degree, students are required to complete thirty-two courses, about one third of which are in a field of concentration. Students work with faculty advisers to organize a curriculum that meets the educational objectives of the College: breadth of knowledge, understanding in depth, written expression, interdisciplinary and intercultural exploration, and social responsibility and the ethical implications of knowledge and action. Specific course requirements depend upon the student's academic interests. Certain concentrations require a senior thesis.

The system of cross-registration at the Claremont Colleges provides Pitzer students with the opportunity to take advantage of the wide range of courses available at each of the other colleges. Advanced students may also enroll in certain courses at the Claremont Graduate University.

The College observes an early semester calendar; classes begin in early September and end in mid-May. There is a study break near the middle of each semester and another break between semesters from mid-December through mid-January.

Off-Campus Arrangements

About 65 percent of students participate in study-abroad programs at more than 100 sites throughout the world. Pitzer administers eight of its own language and culture programs in China, Ecuador, Italy (Parma and Modena), Nepal, Turkey, Venezuela, Wales, and Zimbabwe.

The College also offers an innovative program in the city of Ontario, California. This program is modeled in part on the study sites abroad and emphasizes community involvement. The program features homestays with local families, internships with a wide range of city and nongovernmental agencies, and a program center in the community that serves as a base for classes and community service projects.

Academic Facilities

The central services of the Claremont Colleges include the Honnold-Mudd Library, which houses more than 1.4 million volumes, more than 4,000 periodicals, and nearly ninety newspaper subscriptions. Other shared facilities include theaters, music halls, music and dance studios, the Keck Joint Science Center, and a counseling/health center.

Specialized facilities at Pitzer include a television studio, film editing rooms, art galleries, social science laboratories, an arboretum, a reading library, and several computing facilities, including a computer center that is open 24 hours.

Costs

Expenses for 1999–2000 were as follows: tuition and fees, $24,096; room and board, $6240; and books and personal expenses, $1750. Travel expenses vary. Costs are subject to change for 2000–01.

Financial Aid

Fifty-four percent of Pitzer's students receive aid in the forms of grants, loans, and work-study. To apply for aid, students must complete the Free Application for Federal Student Aid (FAFSA) and the Financial Aid PROFILE. California residents should also apply for California state grants. Students must reapply for aid each spring.

Faculty

Ninety-nine percent of Pitzer's faculty members hold a Ph.D. degree or the terminal degree in their field of expertise. Graduate students do not teach classes. The student-faculty ratio is 12:1, and faculty members are readily available for academic advising. Most faculty members are conversant with at least one other field of study in addition to the area of their degrees and may teach in more than one area.

Student Government

Pitzer's governmental structure is distinctive among American colleges. Instead of the traditional student government that restricts student participation to limited areas, students are represented on all of the standing committees of the College, including those that deal with the most vital and sensitive issues of the College community. Though it demands a serious commitment of time and energy from those who choose to participate, it offers interested students an active educational experience and the opportunity to make a genuine impact on the life of the College and its students, faculty, and staff.

Admission Requirements

Pitzer has developed a highly personalized admission process. Each applicant is considered on the basis of his or her own strengths. In general, the College seeks students who have performed well in high school, who have shown a significant amount of involvement in activities outside of the classroom, who are motivated to learn, and who are interested in the opportunity to take an active role in planning their education in a liberal arts framework. The selection process is designed to help achieve a diverse and energetic entering class. Selection is based on high school transcripts, recommendations, SAT I or ACT scores, a personal essay, academic interests, extracurricular activities, and special talents. Applicants are encouraged to visit the campus and arrange for an interview.

Application and Information

Students must submit their applications for admission by February 1. In addition, they should supply ACT or SAT I scores, an official transcript of grades, two recommendations, and the application fee of $40. The Common Application is accepted. If submitting the Common Application, students should include a paragraph explaining why they have chosen to apply to Pitzer.

For further information, students should contact:

Office of Admission
Pitzer College
1050 North Mills Avenue
Claremont, California 91711-6101

Telephone: 909-621-8129
              800-PITZER1 (800-748-9371, toll-free)
Fax: 909-621-8770
E-mail: admission@pitzer.edu
World Wide Web: http://www.pitzer.edu

Students on the campus of Pitzer College.

PLATTSBURGH STATE UNIVERSITY OF NEW YORK

PLATTSBURGH, NEW YORK

The University

Plattsburgh State University (PSU) is a comprehensive, coeducational, public institution within the State University of New York (SUNY). The college is guided by four principal themes: a commitment to professional preparation of students achieved through a strong liberal arts foundation, a dedication to the highest-quality teaching and scholarship, a belief in the values of service and civic responsibility, and a celebration of the college's remarkable location in the Champlain Valley. These themes are embodied in a spirit of academic freedom, intellectual inquiry, and an appreciation of diversity. They prevail inside and outside the classroom. They are supported by an outstanding faculty and staff. The college recognizes a responsibility to serve the people of New York State and the surrounding region. Students are encouraged to participate in a host of local and national programs that engender civic responsibility, and the college provides scholarships for community service. The college concentrates on undergraduate education. More than thirty academic departments offer a variety of programs and courses in the liberal arts and professional studies to approximately 5,400 students. Underlying all courses of study is a belief that liberal education and professional preparation constitute complementary rather than conflicting goals. PSU also offers a selection of graduate degrees (M.A., M.S., M.S.T., and C.A.S.). More than 600 students are enrolled in the graduate programs, which address regional needs, including support of school systems and sustaining economic development. The campus atmosphere at PSU is strongly residential, with twelve residence halls located on an easy-to-walk campus. All dorm rooms are wired for computer access as well as for telephone and cable television. About ninety student clubs are supported by the college and an active Student Association. Fraternities and sororities comprise about 6 percent of the student population. Both club and intramural sports complement the many recreational opportunities that can be found in the region. Montreal, Lake Placid, and Burlington, Vermont, are popular student destinations within an hour's drive of the campus. Intercollegiate athletics are offered at the NCAA Division III level, with nine men's teams and ten women's teams.

Location

Plattsburgh State University is located in upstate New York's scenic Champlain Valley. The campus is situated in a small city that is on the shore of Lake Champlain, near the Adirondack Mountains and the Green Mountains of Vermont. It is accessible by interstate, rail, and air (with a small airport nearby and three larger airports in Montreal and Burlington). Shopping malls, multiplex movie theaters, restaurants, and hotels are all located within a few miles of the campus. The region is rich in history and recreational opportunities.

Majors and Degrees

Plattsburgh State University offers nearly sixty undergraduate degree programs (B.A., B.S., B.F.A., B.S.Ed.) in liberal arts and science, professional studies, and business. Education, communication, psychology, accounting, nursing, art, environmental science, criminal justice, journalism, hotel-restaurant-tourism management, and biology (including premedicine) are popular majors. Approximately forty minor programs complement the curriculum. These include gerontology, graphic design, athletic coaching, health-care management, and recreation.

Academic Program

Plattsburgh State University's programs provide students with the intellectual and experiential preparation they need to become successful professionals after graduation or after continued study in a graduate or professional school. Values of service, civic responsibility, and leadership are embraced both in and out of the classroom. Academic programs help students to develop as thoughtful human beings, encouraging them to achieve something beyond the mere acquisition of knowledge. A large selection of internships provides students with hands-on learning. Liberal Arts and Science, Professional Studies, and the School of Business and Economics comprise the College's principal divisions. A general education program provides a broad-based foundation of study. Prelaw and premedicine advisement are available. Baccalaureate degree programs require 120 credits for graduation. Learning Communities (courses clustered around a theme) are open to freshmen, and a special Adirondack Experience program creates opportunities for outdoor learning. A high level of student-faculty interaction enhances the academic experience. Classes average 25 students, and all are taught by faculty members, not by graduate teaching assistants. An active Honors Program offers a full range of courses and provides students with small seminars, tutorials, mentoring, and advanced projects. The college also hosts twenty-three honor societies. Classes at PSU are taught on a fall-spring calendar, with two summer terms available. The college accepts transfer credit from accredited institutions and awards nontraditional credit based on acceptable scores on the College-Level Examination Program (CLEP), Advanced Placement (AP), and the New York State College Proficiency Examination (CPE).

Off-Campus Arrangements

Plattsburgh State University participates in the National Student Exchange as well as a large SUNY network of some 300 study-abroad programs, a number of which are hosted by the College. Programs carry credit and are offered year-round.

Academic Facilities

The college's facilities are well supported by up-to-date technology, including multimedia and computer-based smart classrooms. The Feinberg Library and the computing environment at Plattsburgh offer a host of sophisticated services, including electronic databases, high-speed Internet access, e-mail, specialized software, instruction in information and computer literacy, document delivery, and a strong book and periodical collection. The library houses more than 300,000 volumes and subscribes to over 1,400 periodicals. The Division of Library and Information Services assists students and faculty members in their information and teaching needs, including a computer help desk, walk-in and electronic reference services, residence hall support, and microcomputer labs. All residence hall rooms are wired for fast (Ethernet) access to campus computing, the Internet, and World Wide Web.

Costs

Plattsburgh's state-subsidized costs help make it an exceptional value. In 2000–01, annual billed costs for full-time tuition, fees, meals, and housing for New York State residents total $9101. Nonresidents' billed costs total $14,001.

Financial Aid

Plattsburgh offers a variety of aid programs to students, including college-sponsored scholarships. Merit scholarships are awarded based on the credentials established in the regular admission process. Many renewable merit-based scholarships and other awards are available, including $2500 study grants for international and out-of-state students living on campus. To apply for need-based aid, students must file the Free Application for Federal Student Aid (FAFSA), covering eligibility for the Federal Pell Grant, Federal Supplemental Educational Opportunity Grant (FSEOG), Federal Work-Study Program, Federal Perkins Loan, Federal Nursing Loan, Federal Direct Loan, and need-based scholarships. New York State residents must file a separate Express Tuition Assistance Program (ETA) application in addition to the FAFSA. Part-time employment (on and off campus) is available.

Faculty

PSU's outstanding faculty members view themselves as teachers/scholars and teachers/artists. About 85 percent of the full-time faculty members hold a doctoral degree, and a number are recognized nationally and internationally on the merits of their scholarship, the importance of their published works, and the honors they have received. Faculty members regularly involve students in their research; this has led to a growing number of projects in which students are listed jointly with faculty members on publications, as participants in exhibitions and performances, or as presenters at conferences.

Student Government

The Student Association (SA) is a self-governing body that promotes the educational and general welfare of students. It acts as a unifying factor for the student voice and formulates, in conjunction with the faculty and administration, policies and procedures concerning overall aspects of college life. The SA sponsors many clubs and provides transportation, legal, financial, and recreational services for students.

Admission Requirements

Admission to Plattsburgh State University is competitive and is based primarily on a review of academic credentials. The entire student profile, however, is considered in admission review. Strength of program and grades are the most important considerations. Freshman applicants should have a college-preparatory program of study in high school with a minimum average of 83 (B) in academic subjects. The SAT I or the ACT is required. An SAT I score of 1000 or better or an ACT score of 22 or better is recommended. Secondary review factors include activities, awards, the essay (required), and personal interview (optional). Students holding a high school equivalency diploma are required to submit a high school transcript and SAT I or ACT scores along with their proof of high school equivalency. Transfer applicants are required to submit official transcripts from all colleges they have attended previously, with no more than one semester of course work undocumented at the time of application. A cumulative grade point average is calculated based on all course work. Students with GPAs of at least 2.0 are considered for admission; however, a higher GPA may be required in certain programs. Transfers with fewer than two full-time semesters of college course work completed at the time of application are required to submit a high school transcript along with SAT I or ACT scores. Plattsburgh State University maintains an affirmative action policy and embraces the goal of increasing ethnic diversity on campus; therefore, PSU encourages applicants to identify their ethnicity at the time of application. Applicants who are not residents of New York State are at no disadvantage in the admissions process.

Application and Information

Fall freshman applicants should apply before December 1 of their senior year in high school. Students requesting early decision need to apply by November 1. Spring applicants (freshman and transfer) should apply by November 1. Transfer applicants for fall should apply after they have completed the previous fall semester so that no more than one semester (spring) is undocumented at the time of admission review.

For an application or to request information, students should contact:

Admissions
Plattsburgh State University
101 Broad Street
Plattsburgh, New York 12901
Telephone: 518-564-2040
        888-673-0012 (toll-free)
E-mail: admissions@plattsburgh.edu
World Wide Web: http://www.plattsburgh.edu

Plattsburgh State students benefit from close contact with an outstanding faculty.

PLYMOUTH STATE COLLEGE OF THE UNIVERSITY SYSTEM OF NEW HAMPSHIRE

PLYMOUTH, NEW HAMPSHIRE

The College

Plymouth State College (PSC) is a coeducational, residential college with an enrollment of approximately 3,500 full-time undergraduate students and 1,000 part-time and graduate students. Plymouth State was founded in 1871 and over the years has expanded to 170 acres and forty-six buildings. PSC preserves the brick-and-ivy look of its New England small-college heritage while integrating state-of-the-art technology and facilities into an attractive, contemporary campus design.

Plymouth's proud history has created a strong architectural identity, and successful renovations are part of a new, dynamic, and modern campus. Superb facilities have recently been added. The impressive physical facilities include living accommodations, which range from traditional residence halls to student apartments that are set in a wooded, landscaped section of the campus. All residences are wired for the Internet and cable television.

The new student union, located in the center of the campus, is called the Hartman Union Building or, more popularly, the HUB. It houses a snack bar and café, the College bookstore, fitness and aerobics rooms, a gymnasium, a multipurpose room, administrative offices, and offices for student government, media, and activities. Nearly 2,500 meetings, receptions, programs, and conferences are held there annually.

Plymouth's athletic facilities and fields, supporting eighteen intercollegiate teams as well as numerous state and regional athletic contests, have long been recognized as being among the best in Division III New England.

Students come to Plymouth State College for its caring academic community and friendly campus, the Main Street New England setting, and easy access to New Hampshire's great outdoors.

Student publications include *The Clock*, the weekly newspaper; *The Continuum*, the literary magazine; and *The Conning Tower*, the yearbook. An FM radio station, WPCR, regularly has 40 on-air disc jockeys and provides an eclectic range of musical programming seven days a week. Hundreds of activities and programs are sponsored each semester by Programming Activities in a College Environment (PACE) and other student organizations.

In addition to its undergraduate degrees, PSC offers the M.B.A., the M.Ed., and the Certificate in Advanced Graduate Studies.

Location

With the White Mountains to the north, the Lakes Region to the south, and the Pemigewasset River bordering the town to the east, Plymouth, New Hampshire, is home to some of the country's most spectacular wilderness. Plymouth State College students step outside every morning into a natural landscape that provides four seasons of recreational and educational adventure. Here, the outdoors offer a natural laboratory, a classroom, and a playground. Students in the arts and sciences sketch, describe, and study the area's distinctive seasonal landscapes. Meteorology students forecast the local weather and work in the surrounding areas on grant projects involving wind energy and climate changes. Geology students hike local trails and track the glacial migration of the last Ice Age. Archaeological field schools dig the land and dive the waters to discover lost pieces of America's heritage. During their free time, students cycle the area's back roads and highways; jog wooded paths; ski the slopes at Tenney, Cannon, Loon, Waterville Valley, and a number of other mountains; and snowshoe and hike dozens of trails within a short drive. Neighboring Rumney is famous for rock climbing. The Pemigewasset and Baker Rivers provide white water to kayakers and canoeists. The lakes—Little Squam, Big Squam, Newfound, and Winnipesaukee—are popular for sailing, flat-water paddling, water skiing, even scuba diving. The campus is nestled in the town of Plymouth, which has been ranked seventh in *The 100 Best Small Towns in America*. Plymouth is less than 2 hours' drive from Boston on Interstate 93. Two hours to the east is Portland, Maine; 2 hours northwest is Burlington, Vermont; and 3½ hours north is Montreal, Canada.

Majors and Degrees

Plymouth State College offers the B.A., B.F.A., B.S., and A.A. degrees in forty-seven undergraduate majors, with several options within each major. Some of these majors include accounting, anthropology/sociology, applied computer science, applied economics, art, athletic training, biology, chemistry, childhood studies, communications, community and regional planning, English, environmental biology, French, general studies, geography, health education, history, humanities, information technology, interdisciplinary studies, management, marketing, mathematics, medieval studies, meteorology, music, outdoor recreation, philosophy, physical education, political science, psychology, public management, public service, social work, Spanish, and theater arts. Within these majors are fifteen state-approved and NCATE-accredited teacher certification programs. Individualized and interdisciplinary majors may be arranged in consultation with a College adviser.

Academic Program

Education in the liberal arts and sciences and in several professional fields is provided through associate and baccalaureate degree programs. The Plymouth State College curriculum provides the student with expertise in at least one area of knowledge and a broad background concerning the nature of humanity, the universe, and cultures of the world. If students are uncertain of the specific field of study they should follow, Plymouth allows them to consider a variety of programs in the first year of college while progressing toward a degree. In addition, a degree in interdisciplinary studies allows a student to concentrate in two or three areas. A wide variety of minors are also available, giving students an opportunity to study outside their chosen major and enhance their academic experience in other fields of interest.

Plymouth students usually enroll in five courses per semester. The school year consists of two 16-week semesters, a one-month optional January term (Winterim), and two optional summer sessions. In addition to the major courses, study in the humanities, social science, and mathematics and natural science is required.

Credit is granted for successful scores on Advanced Placement and CLEP examinations. Honors courses and independent study are also offered to Plymouth students.

Off-Campus Arrangements

Students are encouraged to broaden their academic experience by studying for a semester or a year as part of a national or international exchange program. Through its affiliation with the University System of New Hampshire and as a member of the New Hampshire College & University Council, Plymouth State College offers students an opportunity for in-residence study at other colleges within the state. In cooperation with the Universities of New Hampshire and Vermont, Plymouth State offers travel/study programs in Seville, Spain; Dijon and Nice, France; Salzburg, Austria; and Cuernavaca, Mexico. Plymouth also has exchange programs with Bishop's University in Lennoxville, Quebec, and with Bretton Hall College in Yorkshire, England.

Academic Facilities

The College's renovated and expanded Lamson Library provides more than 250,000 printed volumes, 500,000 microform and audiovisual items, online facilities for database searches, a public-access catalog of its holdings, and an automated circulation system. The restored Draper & Maynard Building houses three floors of visual art studio space and the Karl Drerup Art Gallery. The Silver Culture Arts Center is home to the performing arts, with a 665-seat main stage theater, a 174-seat recital hall, and a multipurpose black box studio theater as well as classrooms and practice facilities for music, theater, and dance students. Plans are under way to renovate Boyd Hall, which is home to the natural science department and a planetarium that offers monthly programs to the public.

Older buildings on campus reflect Plymouth's historical importance to the region. The College has five sites that are listed on the New Hampshire Heritage Trail. Its landmark, Rounds Hall, is home to the education department and contains a bell in its clock tower that was cast by apprentices of Paul Revere. Poet Robert Frost taught education and psychology at Frost Cottage from 1911 to 1912. Holmes's Rock marks the site of Holmes Plymouth Academy, established in 1808, which was the first training school for teachers in New Hampshire. Holmes House now houses the College's residential life offices. The recently renovated Silver Cultural Arts Center showcases three performance spaces and the College's department of music and theater. It also hosts world-class performers year round in Plymouth and was formerly a stop on the Underground Railroad. The beautifully restored Draper & Maynard Building is home to the art department and the department of health, physical education, and recreation.

The most recent addition to the campus is the expanded and renovated Herbert H. Lamson Library, which has 750,000 units of print, microform, and electronic resources and was built to serve generations of students to come well into the twenty-first century.

Costs

For New Hampshire residents, tuition in 1999–2000 was $3830; for out-of-state students, it was $9140. Typical room and board costs for 1999–2000 were $5030 for both New Hampshire residents and out-of-state students. Required fees totaled $1202.

Financial Aid

Nearly three fourths of Plymouth's students receive some financial assistance from federal, state, College, or other sources. Scholarships, grants, loans, and work-study jobs are available for qualified students. Many students work at part-time jobs on campus and in or near Plymouth. Applicants for financial aid should file the Free Application for Federal Student Aid (FAFSA) with the College Scholarship Service by March 1.

Faculty

The resident faculty totals 170 men and women who share a commitment to teaching and preparing students for careers in their field. Eighty-nine percent of the faculty members hold a doctoral or other terminal degree in their field. Faculty members are also active in their respective fields—attending conferences; presenting papers, workshops, and seminars; working as consultants; participating in exhibits; performing in concerts; and writing books and articles. The student-faculty ratio is 17:1. Each student has a faculty member as an adviser.

Student Government

The Student Senate provides a structure through which social, cultural, and recreational activities are organized and financed. Senators are elected to represent all four classes, residence halls, fraternities, sororities, nontraditional students, off-campus students, and graduate students.

Admission Requirements

A student is considered well prepared if the high school program has included English and literature, social sciences, natural sciences, foreign language, and three years of mathematics. Auditions are required for music majors, but no portfolio is required for art majors. Official transcripts and SAT I or ACT scores are required.

Plymouth welcomes applications from transfer candidates with proven academic ability. Transfer applicants must submit official transcripts from each college attended previously.

Application and Information

Applications are accepted for the fall or the spring semester. Application deadlines are April 1 for the fall semester and January 1 for the spring semester. Plymouth uses a system of rolling admissions, and students are notified of the admission decision after all materials have been received and evaluated. Applications received after the deadlines are considered on a space-available basis only.

For more information about Plymouth State College, students should contact:

Admission Office
MSC #52
Plymouth State College
17 High Street
Plymouth, New Hampshire 03264-1595
Telephone: 603-535-2237
                 800-842-6900 (toll-free)
Fax: 603-535-2714
E-mail: pscadmit@mail.plymouth.edu
World Wide Web: http://www.plymouth.edu

The campus at Plymouth State College.

POINT PARK COLLEGE
PITTSBURGH, PENNSYLVANIA

The College

Point Park College, founded in 1960, has undergone a vigorous development and is accredited by the Middle States Association of Colleges and Schools. Enrollment has grown to 2,300, and the number of majors available now totals more than thirty, including a Master of Arts degree program in journalism and mass communications, an international M.B.A., and an accelerated M.B.A.

Characterized by a willingness to innovate, the College has been active since its inception in establishing internship possibilities with the many resources for career preparation in Pittsburgh. In addition to those for the performing arts, internship programs have been developed with local broadcasting stations, area hospitals, and the management and technical training programs of such corporate giants as USX and PPG Industries. The College's numerous activities are designed to meet the needs of a diversified student body, representing more than forty-two states and thirty-nine countries. Clubs associated with specific majors, fraternities, sororities, the Point Park College Singers, and the Student Activities Center are a few of the organizations that students may join. Intramural sports include basketball, billiards, body building, flag football, Ping-Pong, soccer, street hockey, tennis, volleyball, and weight lifting. The men's intercollegiate basketball and baseball teams are perennially included in the National Association of Intercollegiate Athletics (NAIA) national rankings and district and national playoffs. Point Park also has men's intercollegiate cross-country and soccer teams (NAIA). The women's basketball, cross-country, softball, and volleyball teams add another strong tradition to the Point Park College sports program. The College's teams compete in the American Mideast Conference (AMC).

Location

Metropolitan Pittsburgh has a population of more than 2 million. In the Golden Triangle, gleaming office towers loom high above landscaped plazas, fountains, and a 36-acre park fronting on Pittsburgh's three rivers. More than 100 major corporations have their headquarters in the city, making it the fifth-largest corporate center in the nation. Through its prominence as a corporate hub, a home for high-tech industries, and a major production center for steel, the city provides a vast array of career opportunities, as well as a distinctive population mix. Pittsburgh continues to be named one of the most livable cities in the United States in *Rand McNally Places Rated Almanac*.

Through the philanthropic efforts of such financial entrepreneurs as Carnegie and Frick, Pittsburgh has had a long tradition as a cultural center. The city has an excellent symphony and ballet, and the Pittsburgh Opera gives performances regularly. Legitimate theater, ethnic festivals, and top nightclub attractions fill out the entertainment spectrum. In addition, the nation's first educational TV station, WQED, provides a wealth of stimulating offerings. Three Rivers Stadium and the Civic Arena, with its retractable dome, are sites of professional sporting events and frequent entertainment spectacles and are within walking distance of the College. A short bus ride away is the Oakland Civic Center, the location of several renowned museums. Close to Point Park's campus are the YMCA and YWCA, where a nominal fee entitles students to the use of extensive and varied facilities the year round.

Majors and Degrees

The Bachelor of Arts degree is offered in advertising/public relations, applied arts, applied history, behavioral sciences, broadcasting, children's theater, dance, early childhood education, elementary education, English, general studies, international studies, journalism, legal studies, marketing communications, mass communications, political science, psychology, secondary education, and theater arts. The Bachelor of Fine Arts degree is conferred in dance, film and video production (in conjunction with Pittsburgh Filmmakers), and theater arts. The Bachelor of Science degree is conferred in accounting, biological sciences, business management, civil engineering technology, criminal justice, electrical engineering technology, environmental health science and protection, general studies, health services, human resources management, information technology, management services, mathematics/secondary education, mechanical engineering technology, public administration, specialized professional studies–funeral service, and systems process control engineering technology.

Preparation for teachers in secondary education is a cooperative effort of the Department of Education and the department of the student's major subject. Programs in predental, prelaw, and premedical studies are arranged within suitable majors.

Academic Program

Point Park is an innovative institution. Its philosophy is one of meeting and adapting to individual requirements within the framework of a sound humanistic education. This commitment is reflected in programs that, while providing for the expansion of mind and spirit that the liberal arts alone can give, places strong emphasis on developing career skills. Thus, all degree programs, with the exception of the B.F.A. programs, include a core curriculum requirement of 42 credit hours. The core curriculum includes choices in the humanities as well as in the social, behavioral, and natural sciences. Aside from completing the prerequisites for major offerings, students may elect to fulfill their core requirements on a schedule of their own choosing. At the same time, the student's introduction to specific career preparation can begin the first semester. Indeed, this is typical for students majoring in computer science, dance, engineering technology, film production, journalism and communications, and theater arts. In order to encourage student experimentation, the College permits eight courses from the core curriculum to be taken under a pass/fail option.

With the approval of their guidance offices, high school students may take courses at Point Park for full college credit. The College grants advanced standing on the basis of the College Board's Advanced Placement tests, the CLEP examinations, and educational experiences in the armed forces. In addition, the College has long-standing experience in meeting the needs of transfer students.

The academic calendar consists of two semesters and a summer schedule offering two 6-week sessions and one 12-week session. This year-round utilization of facilities, combined with the College's extensive evening and Saturday programs, provides students with maximum flexibility in planning their schedules.

Off-Campus Arrangements

Point Park's membership in the Pittsburgh Council on Higher Education gives students the chance to cross-register at any of nine area institutions, including the University of Pittsburgh and Carnegie Mellon University.

Point Park College gives students the opportunity to earn a number of credits at various off-campus sites.

Academic Facilities

The Library Center of Point Park College, a joint operation with the Carnegie Library of Pittsburgh, opened in downtown Pittsburgh in May 1997. The Library Center houses the Point

Park College Library and the Carnegie Library of Pittsburgh's Downtown and Business Information Center. Students have access to a 110,000-volume collection, 600 current periodicals and newspapers, and 100 computer terminals and are able to access online databases, CD-ROM, e-mail, and the Internet. This is the first collaborative effort between a private institution and a public library. A science and journalism laboratory complex, on-campus radio and television studios, ownership of the newspaper and magazine, an on-campus laboratory school, on-campus dance studios, two computer terminal rooms, a CADD lab, and other facilities and programs contribute to the College's philosophy of carefully balancing theory with practical experience. The College's location in the heart of Pittsburgh's business district opens numerous opportunities for practical learning. Point Park owns and operates the Point Park College Playhouse, which shows fifteen dance and theater performances per year.

Costs

For 1999–2000, tuition and fees for full-time study totaled $6227 per semester. The charge for part-time study was $327 per credit hour. Room and board were $2667 per term for double occupancy. The majority of rooms are for double occupancy with private bath and phone.

Financial Aid

Point Park makes a sincere effort to ensure that each student who desires to attend is able to do so. Accordingly, the College administers a generous program of financial aid, including Federal Work-Study awards and Point Park, Federal Pell, and Federal Supplemental Educational Opportunity grants. The College administers loans under the Federal Perkins Loan Program and the Federal Stafford Student Loan Program. Academic, talent, and athletic scholarships are also available for all students, including transfer students.

Applicants for financial aid must demonstrate financial need and show evidence of academic promise or achievement. To apply, students must submit a completed College application form. All students must submit applications for federal, state, and Point Park financial aid through the Pennsylvania Higher Education Assistance Agency (PHEAA).

Faculty

Full- and part-time faculty members provide undergraduate instruction at an average faculty-student ratio of 1:15. Forty-four percent of full-time faculty members in the academic disciplines hold doctoral degrees. Faculty members in the performing arts and practical disciplines are involved in their professions outside of the College as well as in the classroom. The top priority among this faculty group is the instruction of undergraduate students rather than specialized research and publication. Students are advised throughout their college career by a designated faculty member in their major area.

Student Government

The United Student Government actively participates in the affairs of the College. The Student Affairs Committee acts in conjunction with the dean of students to coordinate social programs on the campus as well as to provide input for College policy.

Admission Requirements

Point Park College is very much concerned with the needs and interests of its students. This concern is extended not only to matriculated students but also to prospective students. For this reason, the admissions staff pursues a policy that is individualized, personal, and humanistic. Each student is viewed in terms of his or her own personal and academic potential. Recommendations from guidance counselors and teachers and an interview, while not required, are considered, along with motivational factors and relative maturity, in conjunction with the traditional objective criteria, such as class rank, high school record, and standardized test scores. All candidates are required to take either the SAT I or the ACT.

Application and Information

Applications for the fall semester are taken on a rolling basis; however, students are urged to apply early in their senior year of secondary school. Early application is particularly important for students desiring residence hall accommodations and financial aid. Applications from freshman and transfer candidates are also considered for the spring semester and should be filed by December 15. The College requires each freshman applicant to submit an application, a nonrefundable $20 fee, SAT I or ACT scores, and an official high school transcript. Transfer applicants must also submit official transcripts from all colleges and postsecondary schools attended.

Application forms and additional information may be obtained by writing to:

Office of Admission
Point Park College
201 Wood Street
Pittsburgh, Pennsylvania 15222-1984

Telephone: 412-392-3430
800-321-0129 (toll-free)
Fax: 412-392-3902
E-mail: enroll@ppc.edu
World Wide Web: http://www.ppc.edu

Point Park students enjoy the many social and sporting activities that Pittsburgh has to offer.

POLYTECHNIC UNIVERSITY
BROOKLYN AND FARMINGDALE, NEW YORK

The University

Long recognized as a leading technological university and research center, Polytechnic University—formerly Polytechnic Institute of New York—offers fourteen majors leading to degrees in engineering, computer science, information management, and the arts and sciences. Polytechnic's two campuses have an undergraduate student body of 1,600. A student-faculty ratio of 14:1 enables students to work closely in the classroom and in research labs with the members of an internationally renowned faculty. Located at Polytechnic are a variety of research centers where students and faculty members are involved in exciting and innovative fields of study, including telecommunications, digital systems, and microwaves.

The Brooklyn campus dates from 1854. The Long Island campus opened as a graduate center in 1961 and added undergraduate programs in 1974. Its smaller enrollment and suburban atmosphere make it very different from the urban Brooklyn campus.

Polytechnic University offers a wide variety of student activities. The Student Council, a school newspaper and magazine, and a photography club are just a few of the options available. A number of academic organizations, many with national affiliations, host programs, lectures, and discussion groups for students majoring in the various disciplines. Athletics—from basketball to volleyball—are popular and widely available at Polytechnic on both intercollegiate and intramural levels.

Polytechnic is an active part of the communities in which its campuses are located. Although it emphasizes science and engineering, the University has long recognized the importance of tempering technology with humanistic understanding.

Location

The two campuses of Polytechnic University are located in downtown Brooklyn and in Farmingdale, Long Island. Both the Brooklyn and the Long Island campuses are within easy reach of the world's greatest concentration of cultural, educational, entertainment, and sports activities. The Metropolitan New York area has exciting theaters, museums, historic sites, architectural wonders, and famous stores and shops. Long Island is a paradise for boating, fishing, swimming, and other water sports. All of these attractions are readily accessible via public transportation and a network of modern highways.

Majors and Degrees

Polytechnic University offers the Bachelor of Science degree. Major areas of undergraduate study on the Brooklyn campus include chemical, civil, computer, electrical, and mechanical engineering; biomedical sciences; chemistry; computer science; environmental science; humanities; journalism/technical writing; mathematics; physics; and social science. Preprofessional programs in medicine and law are also available.

On Polytechnic's Long Island campus in Farmingdale, four-year undergraduate programs are offered in chemical, civil, computer, electrical, and mechanical engineering; computer science; and information management.

A major in civil engineering, with a concentration in environmental engineering, and a major in mechanical engineering, with a concentration in aeronautical engineering, are available on both campuses.

Academic Program

While requirements vary according to the major, students must complete an average of 128 credits with an average of at least 2.0 (on a 4.0 scale) to earn the Bachelor of Science degree. Science and engineering students begin fundamental courses in their specialties during their second year and concentrate on advanced courses in their last two years.

Off-Campus Arrangements

Polytechnic offers an optional five-year cooperative education program that combines alternate periods of study on campus and work experience. Through this program, students spend up to nineteen months with a corporation or a government agency in a salaried position. Students are placed by Polytechnic in a job related to their studies.

Academic Facilities

The Bern Dibner Library of Science and Technology houses one of the finest collections of technical and scientific literature in the metropolitan area. Well known for research, Polytechnic sponsors a number of important research centers that typically involve multidisciplinary teams of Polytechnic faculty members, research staff, and students. Included among these centers are the Center for Applied Large-Scale Computing, the Transportation Training and Research Center, the Institute for Imaging Sciences, the internationally recognized Microwave Research Institute, and the Polymer Research Institute, the oldest academic center of polymer investigation in the United States. In 1983, the University was designated a Center for Advanced Technology in Telecommunications in New York State. This has been renamed the Center for Research and Strategic Initiatives.

MetroTech, a joint undertaking of Polytechnic University and the city of New York, has redeveloped an area of downtown Brooklyn into a technology office and research park, surrounding a 5-acre landscaped commons/campus. By making available more than 2 million square feet of low-cost commercial space as well as a Polytechnic technology and science library and a telecommunications training and research center, MetroTech links the capacity and facilities of a major technological teaching and research institution with the needs of technology users in New York.

Costs

Tuition for 1998–99 was $19,530. Estimates of other expenses are $600 for fees, $500 for books, $1200 for personal expenses, and $5100 for room and board.

Financial Aid

Scholarships and loans are the principal sources of financial aid for full-time undergraduates. Federal sources of funds include Federal Pell Grants, Federal Supplemental Educational Opportunity Grants, Federal Stafford Student Loans, Federal Perkins Loans, and Federal Work-Study Program awards. New York State residents may be eligible for assistance under the New York State Tuition Assistance Program. In addition to the usual financial aid programs, Polytechnic offers a large number of scholarships, including several full-cost, four-year scholarships. Approximately 90 percent of all undergraduates at the University receive some financial aid. Opportunities for student employment are good.

The average scholarship offer for 1998–99 was more than $7800, while the average financial aid package was more than $17,000.

Students desiring financial assistance should submit the Free Application for Federal Student Aid, preferably by March 1. For more detailed information about financial aid, students should contact the Office of Financial Aid at Polytechnic.

Faculty

Polytechnic has 176 full-time faculty members, about 95 percent of whom have doctoral degrees. Most of the faculty members teach both graduate and undergraduate courses. The University's faculty is world renowned for the research and scholarly publications of its members. Several are members of the National Academy of Engineering and many are frequent recipients of both national and international awards for excellence. Recent examples include the Institute of Electrical and Electronics Engineers Educational Medal for Excellence, the President's Medal of Sciences, and the prestigious Humboldt Award. The American Society for Engineering Education recently ranked the graduate electrical engineering faculty, many of whom also teach on the undergraduate level, among the top ten in the nation for scholarly activity.

Student Government

The Student Councils are important forces on both campuses. They direct the activities of the undergraduate student body and speak for student interests. As the administrating agencies for student fees, the councils allocate money to student organizations, publications, and activities. Student representatives serve on many faculty and administrative committees dealing with all phases of academic and student life.

Admission Requirements

Admission to Polytechnic is competitive. Candidates must submit a formal application for admission, secondary school transcript, two academic recommendations, and standardized test scores (SAT I or ACT). The Committee on Admissions evaluates each applicant on an individual basis regardless of financial need and seeks students who rank in the top 25 percent of their graduating class, have taken three to four years of college-preparatory math and science, have achieved a grade point average of B+ or higher, and have scored a minimum of 590 on the mathematics section of the SAT I.

Students whose first language is not English are advised to submit scores on the Test of English as a Foreign Language (TOEFL). This test must be taken by all international applicants whose native language is not English regardless of whether or not their previous education was conducted in English. Students can also meet the language requirement by completing the Berlitz on Campus intensive language program. Polytechnic University is a host school for the Berlitz program.

Advanced placement is awarded to students whose scores on the Advanced Placement tests indicate proficiency in a given subject.

Application and Information

A completed application form, $40 application fee, and supporting documents are required for evaluation of prospective students. Applications should be submitted as early as possible, preferably by February 1 for admission in the fall, and December 1 for admission in the spring. Admission decisions are made on a rolling basis. The deadline for early admission is at the end of the applicant's junior year in high school. Early Action candidates for freshman admission who submit their applications by November 1 will receive an admission decision by December 1. Students participating in Early Action are not obliged to attend Polytechnic University.

For application forms and additional information, students should contact one of the offices below.

Office of Undergraduate Admissions
Polytechnic University
6 MetroTech Center
Brooklyn, New York 11201
Telephone: 718-260-3100
E-mail: admitme@poly.edu

Office of Admissions
Long Island Campus
Polytechnic University
Route 110
Farmingdale, New York 11735
Telephone: 516-755-4200
E-mail: admitme@poly.edu

Polytechnic's state-of-the-art Bern Dibner Library of Science and Technology and Center for Advanced Technology in Telecommunications.

POMONA COLLEGE
CLAREMONT, CALIFORNIA

The College

An undergraduate residential college of 1,400 students, Pomona College is consistently recognized as one of the nation's finest colleges of the liberal arts and sciences. Pomona has been coeducational since its founding in 1887, and today it enrolls a student body whose diversity and talents are unmatched by those of similar institutions.

With complete devotion to undergraduate education and a student-faculty ratio of 9:1, the College enables students to interact closely with faculty members. As both researchers and teachers, Pomona's faculty provide students the opportunity to participate in research in almost every academic discipline, an experience rarely available at most large institutions.

Pomona's substantial endowment guarantees students access to resources and facilities rarely found at a college of this size. The endowment also supports a need-blind admissions program as well as a financial aid commitment to meeting each student's demonstrated need.

Pomona College is the founding member of the Claremont Colleges, five undergraduate colleges and a graduate school that together constitute a major academic community of 5,000 students. Pomona students benefit from the additional resources of the consortium and share the academic and social opportunities available at a university without sacrificing the individual focus of a small college.

More than 95 percent of Pomona's students live on campus in the College's twelve dormitories. The campus is a center of social activities, including several film series, lectures and discussions, and student and professional music and theater productions, as well as a variety of more informal social events. Nineteen varsity and twelve club athletic teams compete intercollegiately, while intramural sports involve more than two thirds of the student body. The Liliore Green Rains Center for Sport and Recreation houses two gymnasiums, complete weight and training facilities, and six racquetball and squash courts. The facility is complemented by an all-weather track and field, fourteen lighted tennis courts, a 50-meter swimming pool that opened in 1993, and renovated baseball, football, and soccer fields. The new Smith Campus Center features a 200-seat movie theater, student organization offices and lounges, meeting rooms, the college store, the career development office, the multicultural center, game rooms, a snack bar, and dining facilities.

Location

A residential community near the foothills of the San Gabriel Mountains, Claremont offers a quiet environment and easy accessibility. The Pomona campus and the center of town are readily traveled on foot or by bicycle. Thirty-five miles to the west of Claremont lies Los Angeles, the commercial and cultural capital of the western United States. Students can take full advantage of one of the world's greatest cities, as well as of all of southern California's cultural, educational, and recreational opportunities.

Majors and Degrees

Pomona College grants the Bachelor of Arts degree in the fields of American studies, anthropology, art and art history, Asian studies, biology, Black studies, chemistry, Chinese, classics, computer science, economics, English, foreign languages, foreign literatures, French, geology, German, German studies, history, international relations, Japanese, linguistics, mathematics, media studies, molecular biology, music, neuroscience, philosophy, physics (astronomy option), politics, PPE (philosophy, politics, and economics), psychology, religious studies, Russian, sociology, Spanish, STS (science, technology, and society), theater/dance, and women's studies. Pomona sponsors 3-2 programs in engineering with the California Institute of Technology in Pasadena and with Washington University in St. Louis, Missouri. Students may also pursue independent study or design their own concentrations. Programs complementing the forty concentrations available include Chicano studies and public policy analysis.

Academic Program

To receive the Bachelor of Arts degree, Pomona College students take thirty-two courses. In 1994, the faculty developed and adopted an innovative general education program unique among college and university programs. The program is built around the development of perception, analysis, and communication skills in ten key areas: reading literature critically; using and understanding the scientific method; using and understanding formal reasoning; understanding and analyzing data; analyzing creative art critically; performing or producing creative art; exploring and understanding human behavior; exploring and understanding a historical culture; comparing and contrasting contemporary cultures; and thinking critically about values and rationality.

In addition to fulfilling the general education requirements, students must demonstrate proficiency in a foreign language and take writing-intensive and speaking-intensive classes. All freshmen enroll in Critical Inquiry, a writing-intensive, discussion-oriented seminar with enrollment limited to 15.

More than two thirds of the College's classes enroll fewer than 20 students; the average class size is 14 students. The seminar format promotes discussion and encourages students to challenge themselves, one another, and the faculty members and allows a variety of viewpoints to enhance the learning process. Pomona College offers 600 classes annually, and students can also choose from more than 2,500 classes offered at the Claremont Colleges.

Credits may be awarded for Advanced Placement work and college-level courses taken in high school. The Claremont Colleges are on a semester calendar that begins in early September and ends in mid-May.

Off-Campus Arrangements

Pomona College encourages students to broaden their educational experiences with several programs that go beyond the traditional classroom setting. The Oldenborg Center for Modern Languages and International Relations is a dormitory for language study and the setting of the international relations colloquia. Almost half of the College's students study abroad, choosing from thirty-nine programs in thirty-five locations in twenty-two countries. Pomona students take internships in Washington, D.C., and participate in exchange programs with Colby, Smith, Spelman, and Swarthmore colleges.

A number of programs provide students practical experience while they are still undergraduates. The Office of Career Development arranges internships with more than 100 organizations in the Los Angeles area. The Claremont Colleges Liberal Arts Clinics allow students to use their knowledge and experience in solving immediate, real-world problems presented by industries and governments.

Academic Facilities

Pomona College students have access to facilities that are among the finest at any small liberal arts college. Seaver Science Center houses state-of-the-art laboratory equipment available for use by undergraduates. Brackett Observatory has two telescopes—one 12-inch and one 22-inch; the College operates a 40-inch telescope with the Jet Propulsion Laboratory at Table Mountain Observatory in the San Gabriel Mountains. With two microcomputer labs on campus, students have access to the College's DEC VAX Alpha 4000-710 for unrestricted academic use. A teaching theater complex opened in 1990 and contains an auditorium seating 350, a 100-seat experimental "black box" theater, two studios, and costume and set shops.

In addition to the wealth of resources available at Pomona, students can take advantage of the facilities of the Claremont Colleges. These include a jointly held library system with holdings of more than 1.8 million volumes, two art galleries (Montgomery Gallery is at Pomona), a major bookstore, and a 2,500-seat performance hall.

Costs

Expenses for full-paying students in 2000–01 are tuition, $23,910; room and board, $8170; fees, $260; and books and personal expenses, approximately $1800.

Financial Aid

Pomona College guarantees to fund the full financial need of every enrolling student and admits students without regard to their ability to pay. The College awards aid on the basis of demonstrated financial need. More than 50 percent of the students receive some form of aid, which includes a combination of grants, loans, and part-time employment.

Faculty

All faculty members above the rank of lecturer hold a doctoral degree except in fields where a doctorate is not customary. As an undergraduate college, at Pomona all courses are taught by professors. The student-faculty ratio of less than 9:1 and the average class size of 14 ensure that students can work closely with their professors. The first priority of the faculty is to teach, but the College also recognizes that scholarship plays an essential role in the teaching process. In recent years, Pomona faculty have received grants in support of their research from such agencies as the National Science Foundation, the National Institutes of Health, the National Endowment for the Humanities, the Howard Hughes Medical Institute, and the Pew Charitable Trusts, and they publish annually more than 250 articles and reviews, many of which are coauthored by students.

Student Government

Officers of the Associated Students of Pomona College coordinate student activities and administer the affairs and properties of the Associated Students. Since most matters that affect the College are of concern to both faculty members and students, students also sit as voting members of policy-forming committees. Each residence hall is self-governing.

Admission Requirements

Admission to Pomona College is highly selective, based on a thorough review of each candidate's application materials. The Office of Admissions admits a freshman class whose members represent a broad range of interests, viewpoints, talents, and backgrounds. At Pomona, a diverse student body is considered an educational asset.

The primary criterion for admission is academic achievement. Eighty percent of the freshmen admitted in 1999 were in the top 10 percent of their high school graduating class; their combined median SAT I scores exceeded 1400.

Beyond academic achievement, Pomona seeks students who are aware of a broader world around them—locally, nationally, and internationally—students who have demonstrated a sense of responsibility and commitment to a larger community. The College enrolls students who have shown leadership or special talents in the sciences, communications, the arts, music, theater, athletics, government, or community service.

Early admission, deferred entrance, and transfer admission are available. Freshman candidates may apply under early decision or regular decision programs. The College admits first-year students for entrance in the fall semester only. Transfer students may also apply for midyear admission.

Students are strongly encouraged to visit the campus and arrange for an interview before applying. Information sessions and tours are offered daily and require no appointment. Freshman candidates outside of southern California who cannot visit Pomona may request an interview with an alumni volunteer.

Application and Information

Students applying to Pomona College are expected to furnish transcripts of all their academic work in high school and college; a school recommendation; two teacher references; and either ACT or SAT I and SAT II results. If students choose to take the SAT I, they must also take SAT II Subject Tests in writing and in two other subjects of their choice. Interviews are strongly recommended but not required. All application materials must be received by November 15 for early decision I applicants, by December 28 for early decision II applicants, or by January 1 for regular decision applicants. The transfer application deadline is March 15 for fall admission and November 1 for midyear admission.

For further information, students should contact:

Office of Admissions
Pomona College
333 North College Way
Claremont, California 91711-6312
Telephone: 909-621-8134
E-mail: admissions@pomona.edu
World Wide Web: http://www.pomona.edu

Carnegie Building, Pomona College.

PRAIRIE VIEW A&M UNIVERSITY
PRAIRIE VIEW, TEXAS

The University

The modern mission of Prairie View A&M University was most recently redefined by the people of Texas by an amendment to the state's constitution in 1984. Through that amendment, Prairie View A&M University joined the University of Texas at Austin and Texas A&M University as the state's only constitutionally designated "institutions of the first class." In support of that designation, in 1985, the Board of Regents of the Texas A&M University System expressed its intention that Prairie View A&M University become "an institution nationally recognized in its areas of education and research." Prairie View A&M University is a land-grant institution by federal statute. It is also a statewide special-purpose institution by state statute.

While striving to maintain excellent instruction and a strong curriculum, the University nurtures students' academic development and intellectual curiosity by providing a stimulating physical and cultural environment. As a special-purpose university, Prairie View A&M develops special programming to identify and assist talented students who may otherwise be overlooked. The University believes it can and should help students understand some of the possibilities of the mind and spirit so that they may be productive citizens and lead fulfilling lives.

The enrollment at Prairie View exceeds 6,000 students, fairly evenly divided between men and women. Approximately 83 percent of the students are state residents. Students from other countries account for 7 percent of the total enrollment. Approximately 55 percent of the student body are between the ages of 18 and 24. On-campus housing consists of four residence halls and twenty-nine apartment buildings that collectively accommodate 3,370 students. Each residence hall room is equipped with direct-line telephone and cable television services. A limited number of units with a microwave and freezer/refrigerator combination are available for rent. The apartment buildings consist of suites with two or four private bedroom units, a community living room, and a kitchenette. A limited number (about 30 percent) of the apartments have full kitchens. All housing facilities have accommodations (per ADA requirements) for the physically challenged.

Student life programs are aimed at giving students an opportunity to achieve their educational and career goals without neglecting the support, encouragement, and sense of community that foster a feeling of belonging. The student development staff is committed to enriching the University environment so that students can establish personal value systems and refine interpersonal skills in support of their lifetime aims and objectives. Student organizations include sororities, fraternities, honor societies, the band, the choir, religious groups, special interest clubs, drama (Charles Gilpin Players), the forensic team, and social clubs. Students also have the opportunity to enhance their leadership skills. The University Marching and Symphonic Bands and the Percussion Ensemble develop students' musical talents. The Prairie View Panthers varsity sports teams for men and women compete in the Southwestern Athletic Conference and in NCAA baseball, basketball, bowling, football, golf, softball, tennis, track, and volleyball. Active intramural sports and recreational programs are provided.

Location

The main campus of Prairie View A&M University is situated on a 1,440-acre site in Waller County, approximately 45 miles northwest of Houston. It is accessible by major highways; bus service is available from Houston, Austin, and Dallas. Bush Intercontinental Airport and Hobby Airport provide air transportation. The University's location offers the advantages of a pleasant, semirural environment with convenient access to the excitement of a major American city. The city of Prairie View provides an opportunity to observe government at close range. There are a variety of restaurants, shopping facilities, rodeo events, and ethnic festivals as well as access to lakes for water sports and facilities for horseback riding in the area.

Majors and Degrees

The University offers the following undergraduate degrees: Bachelor of Architecture, Bachelor of Arts, Bachelor of Arts in Social Work, Bachelor of Business Administration, Bachelor of Music, and Bachelor of Science. Undergraduate degree majors include accounting, accounting and information systems, agricultural engineering, agriculture, applied music, architecture, biology, chemical engineering, chemistry, civil engineering, communications, computer-aided drafting and design, computer engineering technology, computer science, criminal justice, dietetics, drama, electrical engineering, electrical engineering technology, English, family and community services, finance, health, history, human development and the family, human performance, human science, industrial technology, interdisciplinary studies, management, marketing, mathematics, mechanical engineering, mechanical engineering technology, merchandising and design, music, nursing, physics, political science, psychology, social work, sociology, and Spanish. Coordinate degrees are offered in biology, business, chemistry, education, engineering, human sciences, and sociology.

Academic Program

The requirements for a bachelor's degree at Prairie View A&M University ensure that graduates have a well-rounded educational experience. Students must complete the University core course requirements in addition to the specific course and semester hour requirements for the degree program selected. The University requires a minimum of 120 semester hours and at least a 2.0 cumulative grade point average for graduation. Specializations are offered within the major areas of study in some degree programs. Advanced Placement examinations are available, and the University awards credit for successful scores. Highly motivated students are rewarded with an opportunity to challenge themselves academically through the accelerated courses offered by the University Scholars Program. Military science programs include Army ROTC and Naval ROTC. Cooperative education programs are available in some departments. Support services, tutoring, assessment testing, career exploration, precollege programs, international-student advising, undecided-major advising, multicultural programs, crisis counseling, and placement counseling are offered through the Offices of Career Services, Cooperative Education, School Relations, and Developmental Studies; the Center for Academic Support; the Academic Advising Center, the Academy for Collegiate Excellence and Student Success (ACCESS); and University College.

The academic calendar is based on the semester system. In addition, four-week and eight-week summer terms are offered. The normal course load ranges from 12 semester hours to 18 semester hours during the regular academic year and from 6 to 7 semester hours during the summer terms.

Academic Facilities

Modern facilities include well-equipped classrooms and laboratories. Specially designed studios, theaters, and auditoriums are available for the visual and performing arts. The most modern facilities include a new science building, a multimedia foreign language laboratory, an engineering technology building, a chemical engineering building, and the John B. Coleman Library, which features state-of-the-art equipment, an expanded Learning Resources Center, and a laboratory for computer-assisted instruction. The library contains 300,000 volumes, 363,788 microforms, and several special collections. More than 1,900 periodicals and other serials are currently received by the library. Nursing students who have fulfilled their foundation course work complete five semesters in the College of Nursing facility, located in the heart of the Houston medical complex. Other campus facilities include the Academic Computing Center and studios for Prairie View's radio station (KPVU) and cable television operations.

Costs

For 1999–2000, students who are Texas residents paid $36 per semester hour but not less than $120 per academic semester. Out-of-state students paid $249 per semester hour. On-campus residence hall and university village room rates vary according to the accommodations selected. All students who reside in University residence halls are required to participate in the University food service plan; students have the option of five, seven, ten, fourteen, or twenty-one cafeteria-style meals per week. The approximate total cost of room and board was $4000 per academic year. Annual costs of books and supplies vary according to major and class load but typically average $600. Additional fees vary, but the minimum full-time charge was $1182 per semester for a student enrolled for 15 semester hours.

Financial Aid

Prairie View A&M University administers a wide range of programs to help students meet the cost of attending the University. Various factors are considered in determining who qualifies for financial aid. Programs available to provide financial support include academic and need-based scholarships, state and federal loans and grants, and student employment. Students are required to complete a need analysis to determine their extent of need and eligibility for aid. Approximately 78 percent of the students at Prairie View receive some form of financial assistance. For more information, students should contact the Office of Student Financial Services at 936-857-2424.

Faculty

The University's faculty consists of 329 full-time faculty members, 47 percent of whom have earned doctoral degrees.

Student Government

All members of the student body are members of the Student Government Association (SGA). The SGA is the official voice through which students' opinions may be expressed. Its elected student members provide effective representation and responsible participation in the overall policy-making and decision-making processes of the University. While the SGA promotes academic excellence and quality education, its student members have the opportunity to obtain valuable leadership and management experience. The SGA also recommends students to serve on various committees and advisory boards of the University.

Admission Requirements

Admission to Prairie View A&M University is open to qualified individuals regardless of race, color, sex, creed, age, national origin, or educationally unrelated handicap. To apply for admission, students must provide a completed application and a $25 application fee, a certified high school transcript or a GED certificate (high school equivalency diploma), and SAT or ACT scores. In addition to the admission application, transfer applicants must submit transcripts from previous colleges attended and the confidential questionnaire. International students must also submit an Affidavit of Financial Support and Test of English as a Foreign Language (TOEFL) scores, along with supporting documents. Applicants should note that the Texas State Education Code requires that all students "... who enter Texas public institutions of higher education in the fall of 1989 and thereafter must be tested for reading, writing, and mathematics skills." This includes all "... full-time and part-time students enrolled in a certificate or degree program..." Transfer students must provide Texas Academic Skills Program (TASP) scores or proof of exemption or take the test. Students who plan to enroll must take the TASP test before enrolling in any college-level courses.

Application and Information

Office of Undergraduate Admissions/Recruitment
Prairie View A&M University
P.O. Box 3089
Prairie View, Texas 77446
Telephone: 936-857-2626
Fax: 936-857-2699
E-mail: admissions@pvamu.edu
recruitment@pvamu.edu
World Wide Web: http://www.pvamu.edu

The Wilhelmina Fitzgerald Delco building.

PRATT INSTITUTE
BROOKLYN, NEW YORK

The Institute

Founded in 1887 on its present site in Brooklyn by industrialist and philanthropist Charles Pratt, the Institute educated on nonbaccalaureate levels for its first half-century. As the educational preparation necessary for various professions expanded, Pratt Institute moved with the times. It granted its first baccalaureate degree in 1938 and started its first graduate program in 1950. Pratt continues to add programs at all educational levels, including undergraduate and graduate programs in art history and graduate programs in art education and design management. Although the characteristics and educational requirements of the professions for which Pratt prepares people have changed over the course of a century, the Institute has succeeded in pursuing its abiding purpose—to blend theoretical learning with professional and humanistic development.

In educating more than four generations of students to be creative, technically skilled, and adaptable professionals as well as responsible citizens, Pratt has gained a national and international reputation that attracts undergraduate and graduate students from more than forty-six states, the District of Columbia, Puerto Rico, the Virgin Islands, and seventy countries. The total Institute enrollment is 4,121; 2,697 are undergraduates. Unlike the typical American college student, most of those who choose Pratt already have career objectives, and most are somewhat older than the typical student in a liberal arts college.

A short bus or subway ride from the museum, gallery, and design centers of both Manhattan and Brooklyn, Pratt Institute has twenty-four buildings of differing architectural styles spread about a 25-acre campus. Eighteen of the buildings house studios, classrooms, laboratories, administrative offices, auditoria, sports facilities, food services, and student centers. Six buildings are student residences, including the seventeen-floor Willoughby Residence Hall, which houses 850 students in apartments with kitchens. On-campus housing is available for all students who request it, and there are adequate parking facilities for residents and commuters. Student services include career planning and placement, counseling, and student development. The more than sixty student organizations include fraternities and sororities, honorary societies, professional societies, and clubs.

Location

Pratt Institute is located in the Clinton Hill section of Brooklyn and offers some of its courses at the Pratt Manhattan Center, about ½ hour away by subway. A campus so close to the heart of New York City, a world center for most of the fields in which Pratt students major, offers exceptional opportunities. The chance to obtain professional experience and expertise is an invaluable resource, as are the many cultural and recreational attractions. Pratt has a parklike campus in an urban neighborhood of Victorian buildings set in the midst of one of the most vibrant cities in the world.

Majors and Degrees

Pratt Institute offers the Bachelor of Architecture, Bachelor of Fine Arts, Bachelor of Industrial Design, Bachelor of Professional Studies, Bachelor of Science, and Associate of Occupational Studies degrees. The Bachelor of Architecture degree program is a five-year program.

For the Bachelor of Fine Arts degree, a candidate may choose to major in art and design education, art history, communications design (advertising, graphic design, illustration), computer graphics, fashion design, fashion merchandising and management, film/video, fine arts (ceramics, drawing, jewelry, painting, printmaking, sculpture), industrial design, interior design, photography, or writing for publication, performance, and media. In the Bachelor of Professional Studies degree program, the major is in construction management. Students seeking the Bachelor of Science degree can major in construction management or information systems. The two-year Associate of Occupational Studies degree is offered in graphic design, illustration, and digital design and interactive media.

Students may also earn combined bachelor's/master's degrees. Programs include the B.F.A./M.S. in art history; B.Arch./M.S. in architecture; B.Arch./M.S. in urban design; and B.Arch./M.S. in city and regional planning.

Academic Program

Educating professionals for productive careers in artistic and technical fields has been the mission of Pratt Institute since it assembled its first group of students in 1887. Within the structure of that professional education, Pratt students are encouraged to acquire the diverse knowledge that is necessary for them to succeed in their chosen fields. In addition to the professional studies, the curriculum in each of Pratt's schools includes a broad range of liberal arts courses. Students from all schools take these courses together and have the opportunity to examine the interrelationships of art, science, technology, and human need.

At the time of graduation, students in the associate degree programs have completed 66 credit hours of course work. In the bachelor's programs, credit-hour requirements range from 132 to 135 credits, depending on the particular program. For the Bachelor of Architecture degree, 175 credits are required. With an additional 27 or 49 credits of study, students in the School of Architecture can choose a combined B.Arch./M.S. in urban design or a combined B.Arch./M.S. in city and regional planning degree program.

Pratt's academic calendar consists of two semesters plus a winter term that allows students to choose alternative courses or various options usually not offered during the fall or spring semester. A number of summer sessions are offered.

Off-Campus Arrangements

Pratt Institute offers credit for a wide variety of off-campus study programs. The Internship Program offers qualified students challenging on-the-job experience related to their major fields of interest; this extension of the classroom and laboratory into the professional world adds a practical dimension to periods of on-campus study.

International programs, available during all academic sessions, have included art and design offerings in the cities of Copenhagen and Rome and in the countries of England, France, and Mexico. Architecture programs have been held in Venice, Italy, and in England, Finland, and Japan. New programs are developed regularly in these and other countries.

Academic Facilities

Founded as the first free library in Brooklyn, the Pratt Institute Library now has 208,174 bound volumes, 540 periodical and newspaper subscriptions, 66,000 slides, 190,000 pictures, and 50,000 microforms. Through the use of their ID cards, Pratt students also have access to numerous college libraries in the metropolitan area. The Multi-Media Center has been developed to facilitate and improve the educational communication process by providing materials in multimedia formats to support and enrich the Institute's curricula. These include slides, ¾-inch videotapes, 16-mm films, audiocassettes, and other formats appropriate for group use.

Extensive studio and state-of-the-art computer lab facilities are provided for all Pratt students. In the School of Art and Design, these include studio, shop, and technical facilities for work in all media, from the traditional to the most experimental. Graphics labs include color Macintosh IIs, Macintosh SEs, Cubicomps, Targa TIPS PCs with digitizer tablets, ALIAS labs, and a Quantel graphics system. Within the School of Architecture, students benefit not only from the design studios but also from the collective research facilities of the Institute. The School of Architecture uses SKOK CAD, Sun, and IRIS workstations. The School of Liberal Arts and Sciences maintains laboratory facilities for all science courses. Apple, AT&T, IBM, LSI-11, and TI microcomputers; a Burroughs batch-processing system; and an HP 100 computer are available to students in all majors. Pratt also has a DEC VAX 6210 minicomputer for Institute-wide integration of computer graphics and computer-aided design capabilities as well as AT&T 386 PCs and an extensive telecommunications laboratory. Gallery space, both on campus and at Pratt Manhattan, is extensive, showing the work of students, alumni, faculty members, staff members, and other well-known artists, architects, and designers. The Pratt Institute Center for Community and Environmental Development functions as a laboratory for the study of planning and advocacy issues in real-world situations.

Costs

Tuition for the 1999–2000 academic year was $18,612. Room charges were $4562 per academic year. A meal plan was available and cost about $3200 per year. The activities and registration fees totaled $550, and there was a separate telecommunication fee of $350. The estimated cost of books and supplies was $2000 per academic year. Students should allow an additional $2000 for transportation and personal expenses.

Financial Aid

Pratt Institute offers a large number of grants, scholarships, loans, and awards on the basis of academic achievement, financial need, or both. More than 75 percent of Pratt students receive aid in one or more of these forms. Through funds from the federal and state governments, contributions from Pratt alumni, and industry scholarships, Pratt is able to maintain an effective aid program in a time of escalating costs. Pratt attempts to ensure that no student is prevented by lack of funds from completing his or her education.

Faculty

The faculty at Pratt Institute is exceptional in that a large number of practicing professionals augment the regular full-time faculty. There are 95 full-time and 532 part-time faculty members; there are no graduate teaching assistants. In small classes and studios, students have easy access to professors whose natural environment is the design studio, the architectural office, or the industrial research department.

Student Government

The Student Government Association (SGA) maintains primary responsibility for all student interests and involvement at Pratt. The SGA structure includes the Executive Committee, Senate, Finance Committee, Buildings and Grounds Committee, Academic and Administrative Affairs Committee, and Program Board. Student representatives serve on the Board of Trustees and on its various committees. All undergraduate students are encouraged to become involved in the SGA, whose main functions are allocating and administering funds collected through the student activities fee, scheduling student activities, and representing the student viewpoint to the rest of the Pratt community.

Admission Requirements

Pratt Institute attracts and enrolls highly motivated and talented students from diverse backgrounds. Applications are welcome from all qualified students, regardless of age, sex, race, color, religion, national origin, or handicap. Admission standards at Pratt are high. One of the major components for admission consideration in art, design, or architecture is the evaluation of a student's portfolio by means of an interview, attendance at a Portfolio Day, or through the submission of work samples on slides.

The admission committee bases its decisions on careful reviews of all credentials submitted by applicants in relation to the requirements of the program to which students seek admission. The SAT I or ACT and a strong college-preparatory background are required of all applicants. In certain cases an extraordinary talent may offset a low grade or a test score.

Application and Information

Pratt has two admissions deadlines: January 1 and February 1. To receive full consideration, students are encouraged to submit applications by February 1 for anticipated entrance in the fall semester and by October 15 for anticipated entrance in the spring semester. All applicants must submit transcripts from high schools and any college attended and letters of recommendation. Additional professional requirements are requested by each department.

For more information about Pratt Institute, students should contact:

Office of Admissions
Pratt Institute
200 Willoughby Avenue
Brooklyn, New York 11205
Telephone: 718-636-3669
              800-331-0834 (toll-free)
E-mail: admissions@pratt.edu
World Wide Web: http://www.pratt.edu

PRESBYTERIAN COLLEGE
CLINTON, SOUTH CAROLINA

The College

Founded in 1880, Presbyterian College (PC) is a fully accredited, private four-year college of liberal arts and sciences. The College is widely known for its excellent academic program and congenial, friendly atmosphere. Twenty-six states and six countries are represented in the student body of 1,119 men and women. PC is associated with the Presbyterian Church USA, and approximately 33 percent of the students are members of the Presbyterian Church. The College welcomes students of all faiths.

Extracurricular activities are an extensive and vital part of the development of all students. There are intercollegiate athletic teams for men in baseball, basketball, cross-country, football, golf, soccer, and tennis and for women in basketball, cross-country, soccer, softball, tennis, and volleyball. The College also offers team handball as a club sport for men and women. An extensive intramural program provides exercise and entertainment in a variety of sports for both men and women. The Student Union Board provides a series of concerts, comedians, films, and special events. Students may also participate in a variety of fine arts, Greek, honorary, political, preprofessional, and religious organizations. More than 60 percent of PC students volunteer for community service. The College sponsors thirty-eight service projects, including tutoring, adult literacy, Big Brother/Big Sister, Habitat for Humanity, and Special Olympics.

The 240-acre campus has twenty-six major buildings of classical Jeffersonian architecture. These buildings are grouped around three plazas. Facilities include a 1,200-seat auditorium, 342-seat recital hall, modern science center, library, art gallery, drama theater, four men's and five women's dormitories, six major classroom buildings, dining hall, infirmary, student center, gymnasium, six-house fraternity court, Panhellenic house, and a 31-acre intramural park.

Students may keep automobiles on campus. Eighty-seven percent of students live in a college residence hall. All single students are required to live on campus. Housing within the community is available for married students. All residence halls will be wired for Internet access.

Location

Clinton, population 10,000, is located in the heart of the South Carolina piedmont. Interstates 26 and 385 meet outside of Clinton and provide easy access from the metropolitan areas of Greenville, Spartanburg, and Columbia. It is a short drive from Clinton to the ski slopes of western North Carolina and to the coast of South Carolina, as well as to professional athletic events in Charlotte, North Carolina.

Majors and Degrees

Presbyterian College offers the Bachelor of Arts and the Bachelor of Science degrees, with majors in accounting, art, biology, business administration, chemistry, Christian education, computer science, early childhood education, economics, elementary education, English, fine arts, French, German, history, mathematics, modern foreign languages, music, music education, physics, political science, psychology, religion, religion-philosophy, social studies, sociology, Spanish, special education, theater arts, and visual arts. Students may minor in African–American studies, athletic coaching, Christian youth work, international studies, journalism, media studies, physical education, secondary education certification, and in each of the major areas. Preprofessional programs are offered in Army ROTC, dentistry, law, medicine, ministry, pharmacy, and veterinary medicine.

The College offers dual-degree programs in engineering with Auburn, Clemson, Mercer, and Vanderbilt Universities. A dual-degree program in forestry and environmental science is available with Duke University. With the Presbyterian School of Christian Education, students may receive a dual degree in Christian education.

Academic Program

All Presbyterian College students gain a comprehension of the liberal arts through a general education in English, fine arts, history, mathematics, modern foreign language, physical education, religion, science, and social science. To graduate, students must complete the required general education courses, fulfill the requirements of a major, attend forty cultural enrichment events, and pass 122 semester hours with a minimum cumulative average of 2.0.

The College operates on a semester system. The fall semester extends from late August to mid-December, and the spring semester runs from mid-January through early May. Classes meet Monday through Friday. An optional May fleximester enables students to travel and study with other PC students and staff. Two five-week summer sessions also are offered.

Directed study, honors seminars, honors research, internships, and independent research are offered through academic departments.

Students may earn credit by submitting scores from the College Board's Advanced Placement subject examinations. CLEP credit is granted for successful scores on the subject exams only. Sophomore status will be conferred upon students with an International Baccalaureate Diploma who have earned grades of 5 or better on the three higher-level subject tests. Students without a diploma may also be offered credit in areas in which test grades of 5 or better have been earned.

An Army ROTC program is available.

Off-Campus Arrangements

Presbyterian College offers a variety of programs for students who are interested in spending a semester, summer, or academic year studying abroad. The College is associated with fifty programs in Austria, China, England, France, Finland, Honduras, Ireland, Italy, Japan, Korea, Mexico, the Netherlands, New Zealand, Scotland, Spain, and Wales and the continent of Australia. Students also may study for a semester in Washington, D.C. All credits that are earned through these programs count toward graduation from Presbyterian College. Other study-abroad programs may be developed by the student and his or her adviser to ensure credit toward graduation.

Special courses are available for students during PC's optional May fleximester. These for-credit courses provide students off-campus educational experiences in Africa and Australia and such areas as the Caribbean, Galapagos Islands, and Southwestern United States.

Students have the opportunity to participate in a summer program at Oxford University's Corpus Christi College in England. This three-week course includes studies of two subjects in addition to travel and field trips in England.

Presbyterian College is affiliated with the Gulf Coast Research Laboratory and Duke University's marine research center. Students may enroll in marine science courses during the academic year or summer.

Academic Facilities

Harrington-Peachtree Hall, PC's new mathematics and social science building, opened in 1996. The building contains psychology labs, classrooms with state-of-the-art audiovisual technology, and a computer lab. The Harper Center houses an art gallery and black box theater. Other academic facilities include Richardson Science Hall, Neville Hall for the humanities, and Jacobs Hall for economics and military science. Thomason Library contains 165,000 volumes, provides extensive reference sources, and features a media learning center. Computer facilities are available in all major academic buildings, with more than 100 computer terminals available for students. Through the College, all students may have free access to the Internet.

Costs

For the 2000–01 school year, the cost of tuition is $15,870. Fees are $1462. Room is $2314 and board $2586 with the fifteen-meal plan. The cost of books, supplies, travel, and personal expenses is estimated at an additional $2500 per year.

Financial Aid

Presbyterian College endeavors to meet the financial need of all accepted students through scholarships, grants, loans, work-study, or a combination of these. The College may award academic, athletic, leadership, and music grants-in-aid to students with superior talent or achievement. Approximately 75 percent of the students receive some financial assistance each year. The Free Application for Federal Student Aid (FAFSA) and an institutional form are required of all financial aid applicants. For priority consideration, all financial aid information should be submitted by March 15 of a student's senior year. For further information, students should contact the Financial Aid Office at the College.

Faculty

Presbyterian College has a full-time faculty of 77 members. Ninety percent of the faculty members hold doctoral or terminal degrees in their field. The student-faculty ratio is 12:1. Students and instructors work closely together in both learning and counseling situations. All faculty members teach lower-division and freshman classes as well as upper-division courses. No graduate students serve as instructors at PC. Each student has an assigned faculty adviser for assistance in course selection and personal counseling.

Student Government

All Presbyterian College students are members of the Student Government Association and are encouraged to fully participate in campus government. The Student Council is composed of an executive council, the class representatives, and the organizational representatives. The duly elected Student Council regulates the affairs of the student body, oversees the Student Union Board and student publications, and approves Judicial Council membership.

The Judicial Council enforces the College's Honor Code and Code of Conduct. All students pledge to enforce the honor system and to not lie, steal, cheat, or plagiarize. The honor system fosters a great deal of trust among students and faculty members. Professors may give unproctored exams; students may leave possessions unattended; and students may reschedule exams.

Representatives from the student body serve on administrative, faculty, and trustee committees.

Admission Requirements

Presbyterian College normally requires for entrance the completion of a four-year high school course of study including 4 units of English, 3 units of math, and 2 or more units each of foreign language, history, laboratory science, and social science.

Admission is very selective. Once a student applies, the admissions committee carefully reviews the application, essay, high school transcript, recommendation from a high school official, and scores from the SAT I or the ACT. The College admits students based on the applicant's academic and personal qualifications. An interview is not required, but interested students are encouraged to visit the campus. An early decision plan is available. Presbyterian College strives to recruit a diverse student body. The College does not discriminate against applicants or students on the basis of handicap, national origin, race, religion, or sex.

Transfer students must submit an application, essay, college and high school transcripts, board scores, and clearance forms. To be considered for admission, a transfer student must have a minimum overall C average in college work.

Application and Information

The application fee is $30 and is nonrefundable. Students may submit applications at any time during their senior year. If students wish to be considered for academic scholarships, they must apply before December 15 of their senior year.

Presbyterian College uses a rolling admissions process. Applicants are notified of the admission committee's decision shortly after the College receives the necessary credentials.

Students may apply electronically from the College's Web site.

For further information, please contact:

Richard Dana Paul
Vice President for Enrollment and Dean of Admissions
Presbyterian College
503 South Broad Street
Clinton, South Carolina 29325
Telephone: 864-833-8230
          800-476-7272 (toll-free)
Fax: 864-833-8481
E-mail: admissions@presby.edu
World Wide Web: http://www.presby.edu

The fountain plaza behind Neville Hall at dusk.

PRESCOTT COLLEGE
Resident Degree Program
PRESCOTT, ARIZONA

The College

Prescott College, an independent four-year liberal arts college, is committed to offering a personalized educational experience. Using nontraditional methods, Prescott College delivers a classical liberal arts education that focuses on communication, critical thinking, and problem solving. The educational philosophy stresses experiential learning and self-direction within an interdisciplinary curriculum. Respected for its environmental focus, Prescott College continually strives to expand and share its environmental mission by encouraging students to examine the relationship between human societies and the natural world.

Prescott College was established in 1966. Currently, there are two distinct programs: the Resident Degree Program (RDP) and the Adult Degree Programs (ADP). This information focuses on the Resident Degree Program. The 1998–99 RDP enrollment was 500 students.

Location

Located a mile above sea level in the forested mountains of central Arizona, Prescott has a moderate climate with four distinct seasons. Described by *Arizona Highways* magazine as "Everybody's Hometown," the community of Prescott is known for its fine quality of life, friendly atmosphere, and small-town charm. Because it has a growing spirit, the community strives to balance the needs of an environmentally conscious life-style with an expanding economy. Many of the College's students participate in municipal sports leagues. The town offers facilities for racquetball, tennis, swimming, and horseback riding. Forests and wilderness areas are easily accessible for out-of-doors activities, and hiking, backpacking, and mountain climbing are popular with students. Fine arts interest many, and many people are active in such artistic endeavors as photography, music, weaving, and dance. Prescott is, in fact, the home of a lively and growing artistic community. The Mountain Artists Guild and the Prescott Fine Arts Association make a substantial cultural impact. The Phoenix Symphony, visiting ballet and opera companies, and numerous art shows also provide regular programs.

Majors and Degrees

The Prescott College Resident Degree Program offers the Bachelor of Arts degree in a variety of individually student-designed areas. Under the general headings of adventure education, arts and letters, environmental studies, and integrative studies, students design competence-based graduation plans in such topics as agroecology, conservation, counseling, cultural studies, ecological design, ecopsychology, education, environmental education, experiential education, field ecology, fine arts, holistic health, human development, human ecology, literature, natural history, outdoor adventure education, peace studies, philosophy, photography, psychology, religion, social and political studies, wilderness leadership, and writing.

Academic Program

The College has created an innovative approach to higher education. It offers small classes, extensive field work, a close community atmosphere, a student-faculty ratio of 10:1, and the opportunity for students to design their own educational path. The philosophy of experiential education emphasizes the concept that learning is a lifelong process that helps students gain competence, creativity, and self-direction. In cooperation with an outstanding faculty, students are able to work in such special interdisciplinary fields as cultural and regional studies, ecopsychology, education, environmental education and interpretation, human ecology, outdoor adventure education, social and political studies, and wilderness leadership.

Academic Facilities

The Prescott College Library has a collection of more than 21,000 volumes, 100 microforms, 950 audiocassettes and videocassettes, and 250 periodical titles, all of which relate specifically to the College's program offerings. The library is computer networked with all of the regional libraries in the area, including two other college libraries and the public libraries. If students are not able to locate necessary information from any of these sources, the College librarian borrows books through the interlibrary loan system. Because the College places great emphasis on student services, the faculty and staff work diligently to assist each student in finding all information necessary for his or her pursuit of knowledge.

The Computer Lab, which houses twenty-nine computers (both Macintosh and IBM compatibles), is an important resource for Prescott College students. It is staffed full-time by a competent team of computer professionals and College work-study students. There are laser printers available, and students have access to the Internet for research and e-mail.

Because the Southwest itself serves the College as a classroom, Prescott owns white-water rafts, kayaks, sea kayaks, cross-country skis, rock-climbing gear, camping equipment, and other equipment that is important for the exploration and understanding of the southwestern United States and Mexico.

Three off-campus field sites complement the Prescott facilities: the Rim Institute, Wolfberry Farm, and the Kino Bay Center. The Rim Institute is located on 24 forested acres in the Mogollon Rim area of the Tonto National Forest at an elevation of 6,300 feet. The College utilizes the Rim Institute to provide a viable, sustainable curriculum dedicated to the themes of personal growth, spiritual renewal, and planetary healing by incorporating the arts, human development, and environmental education.

About 15 miles north of Prescott is Wolfberry Farm, 30 acres of land the College has acquired to develop a farm dedicated to education, demonstration, and research in agroecology. Wolfberry Farm serves as the outdoor classroom for the summer program in agroecology and as a place where students can carry out independent studies and senior projects.

The Kino Bay Center is located in Kino Bay, Mexico, on the Sea of Cortez. This field station is used by a variety of classes, such as Coastal and Cultural Ecology of Kino Bay, A Sense of Place, Field Methods for Intertidal Ecology, and Marine Conservation. It also serves as a launching point for sea kayaking courses and as a meeting place for many Mexican and American researchers.

Costs

Tuition for new and returning RDP students for 2000–2001 is $12,844.

Financial Aid

The types of financial aid available are Federal Pell Grants, Prescott College grants, Federal Perkins Loans, Arizona State Student Incentive Grants, Federal Supplemental Educational Opportunity Grants, work-study programs, Federal Stafford Student Loans, the Arizona Voucher Program, campus employment, and scholarships. More than 65 percent of the students at Prescott College receive financial aid.

Prescott College uses the Free Application for Federal Student Aid (FAFSA) to determine a student's financial need. Students wishing to apply for aid for the fall term should complete the financial aid form by April 15 for priority funding. Aid is awarded on a first-come, first-served basis until all available funds are used. FAFSA forms take four to six weeks to process, so students should submit them early, even if their plans are indefinite.

Faculty

The faculty members of Prescott College are devoted solely to the instruction of students. They are not burdened by the traditional "publish or perish" mandate faced by most educators but direct their energy toward being innovative instructors, positive role models, mentors, advisers, and friends. The faculty members are committed to the special educational mission of Prescott College. They thoroughly enjoy teaching, participating in College social activities, and working with individual students to help them comprehend challenging material.

Approximately 60 percent of the 40 full-time RDP faculty members hold doctorates or terminal degrees. The College recognizes the importance of individualized attention and small classes; the student-faculty ratio is 10:1, and the average class size is 10 students.

Student Government

Students participate in all levels of governance at Prescott College. Currently, 1 student is a full voting member of the Board of Trustees. Students are also represented on hiring committees. The Student Union is composed of all full-time students, each of whom has a vote.

Admission Requirements

In evaluating an applicant, the Admissions Committee seeks evidence of preparation for college-level academic work, a strong sense of community, and a desire to become a self-directed learner. The Admissions Committee looks for the ability to plan and make decisions and commitments and carry them out effectively. The applicant's essays, letters of recommendation, and transcripts are the strongest determining factors in the admission decision. Visits to the College and personal interviews are strongly recommended, and, in some cases, they are required. Students who consider applying to Prescott College should first attempt to gain a thorough understanding of the College's educational philosophy and practices. Once this information has been obtained, they can then determine whether or not Prescott College is suited to their individual educational goals and expectations.

Prescott College has created a special learning environment that requires motivation, maturity, and a desire to be actively involved in learning. Through the admission process, the Admissions Committee attempts to determine if a student will succeed in this kind of setting.

Application and Information

The Resident Degree Program operates on a regular admissions system. The Admissions Office strongly encourages applicants to submit all required application materials by the priority due date. Complete files are then reviewed by the Admissions Committee, and admissions decisions are communicated by the notification date. Files that are received or completed after the priority due date will still be considered on a rolling basis.

Once students are offered admission to an incoming class, they must submit a tuition deposit prior to the reply date to give evidence of intention to enroll and to reserve a space in that class. Tuition deposits are nonrefundable; applicants are advised to submit them only after determining that they are ready to commit to Prescott College. Tuition deposits received after the reply date are accepted on a first-come, first-served basis until the class has filled. Students whose deposits are received after the class is filled are placed on a wait list.

Applications for fall should be received by February 1; for spring, the priority filing date is September 1. The notification date for fall is March 15, for spring, October 15. The reply dates (deposit due dates) for fall and spring are, respectively, May 1 and November 1. Applications that are received or completed after the priority due date will still be considered. These applications will be reviewed after those that were received and completed by the priority due date.

For more information, students should contact:
Resident Degree Program–Admissions
Prescott College
220-P Grove Avenue
Prescott, Arizona 86301
Telephone: 800-628-6364 (toll-free)
E-mail: rdpadmissions@prescott.edu
World Wide Web: http://www.prescott.edu

Prescott College students active in experiential education in a Southwestern classroom.

PRINCETON UNIVERSITY
PRINCETON, NEW JERSEY

The University

Founded in 1746 as the College of New Jersey, Princeton University has its roots deep in America's past. The country's fourth-oldest university, it enjoys a tradition that is unusually rich in scholastic excellence and national service. More delegates to the Constitutional Convention in 1787 were graduates of Princeton than of any other American or British university, and, in the years following that date, the University has produced some eighty senators and two presidents of the United States.

The University owns more than 2,000 acres of land, of which 200 constitute the main campus. A wealth of architectural styles are displayed, ranging from the oldest Colonial buildings to the predominantly Gothic dormitories to modern structures by such eminent architects as Minoru Yamasaki, Edward Larrabee Barnes, Lew Davis, I. M. Pei, and Robert Venturi.

The total enrollment is about 6,300, of whom 4,600 men and women are undergraduates. In the three most recent entering classes, the ratio of men to women was about 52:48. Students at Princeton come from all fifty states, Puerto Rico, the Virgin Islands, Guam, and more than seventy countries. They come from a wide variety of ethnic and socioeconomic backgrounds. The University sponsors Third World, International, and Women's centers, which are open to all students. Interaction among students of different backgrounds is an important part of a Princeton education.

There are currently more than 200 student clubs and organizations, including a radio station, a daily newspaper, assorted publications, and numerous cultural, ethnic, political, religious, and service organizations. The largest student organization on campus is the Student Volunteers Council, with approximately 2,000 students participating. Performing arts facilities include Richardson Auditorium, McCarter Theatre (home to a professional company and performing arts center, as well as Princeton's famed Triangle Club), and 185 Nassau Street, which is home to an auditorium and studios for a variety of the fine and performing arts.

Princeton has two gymnasiums. Jadwin Gym provides 250,000 square feet of indoor space for basketball, track, wrestling, fencing, squash, and tennis, in addition to large practice areas for outdoor field sports. Dillon Gym has facilities for swimming, diving, gymnastics, dance, weight training, and volleyball, plus additional space for basketball, wrestling, fencing, and squash. Other sports facilities include Princeton Stadium (multiuse), 1952 Stadium for lacrosse and field hockey, William Weaver Memorial Stadium for track and field, the DeNunzio Pool swimming and diving complex, Baker Rink for hockey and skating, Lake Carnegie's Olympic-quality racing course for crew and sailing, thirty-seven outdoor tennis courts, an eighteen-hole golf course, and numerous playing fields.

The University guarantees housing for all undergraduates. All freshmen and sophomores live and dine in five residential colleges. A small number of juniors and seniors live and eat in the residential colleges; but most live in the upperclass dorms, and more than half dine in the nonresidential independent eating clubs. The Center for Jewish Life offers a kosher dining facility open to all students and sponsors a wide array of social, educational, and religious programs.

Location

The town of Princeton, adjoining the University campus, has a population of 30,000. New York and Philadelphia are easily accessible by public transportation, and there are hourly departures throughout most of the day. The University regularly subsidizes and otherwise facilitates students' attendance at cultural, sports, and social events in both cities. Boston and Washington, D.C., are near enough for weekend visits by trains that stop in Princeton.

Majors and Degrees

Princeton University awards a Bachelor of Arts (A.B.) degree in anthropology, architecture, art and archaeology, astrophysical sciences, chemistry, classics, comparative literature, computer science, East Asian studies, ecology and evolutionary biology, economics, English, geosciences, Germanic languages and literatures, history, mathematics, molecular biology, music, Near Eastern studies, philosophy, physics, politics, psychology, religion, Romance languages and literatures, Slavic languages and literatures, and sociology. An A.B. degree in public and international affairs is offered through the Woodrow Wilson School of Public and International Affairs. In addition, Princeton offers courses in twenty-four interdepartmental programs, many of which award a certificate of study. These programs include African-American studies, creative writing, environmental studies, musical performance, theater and dance, visual arts, and women's studies.

The Bachelor of Science in Engineering (B.S.E.) degree is awarded in chemical engineering, civil engineering, computer science, electrical engineering, mechanical and aerospace engineering, and operations research and financial engineering. Interdepartmental and topical programs are offered in areas such as engineering biology, engineering physics, geological engineering, materials science and engineering, and robotics and intelligent systems.

Academic Program

Princeton endeavors to provide a broad education with emphasis in a particular field of study. Consequently, A.B. students are required to fulfill distribution, foreign language, and writing requirements, and every A.B. student is required to complete a total of thirty courses with at least eight in his or her concentration. In addition, students are expected to do independent research, which takes the form of junior papers and a senior thesis under the guidance of a departmental adviser.

The School of Engineering and Applied Science requires thirty-six courses for graduation, and at least seven of these must be liberal arts electives. While specific prerequisites and requirements within each department may vary, all emphasize independent work during the junior and senior years.

Freshmen with scores of 4 or 5 on the Advanced Placement tests given by the College Board or scores of 6 or 7 on the International Baccalaureate Higher Level exams may, with the approval of the appropriate department, be granted advanced placement/standing.

Academic Facilities

The Princeton University library system consists of the Harvey S. Firestone Memorial Library, one of the country's major university libraries, which houses the largest portion of Princeton's collection, and eighteen special libraries, including fifteen academic department collections. Firestone Library's open-stack collections include more than 5 million books, records, and 3 million microforms. There are reading spaces for 2,000, study carrels for 500, and a number of offices and conference rooms.

The Engineering Quadrangle, home of the School of Engineering and Applied Science, contains numerous laboratories and classrooms, a library, a machine shop, a convocation room, more than 125 faculty offices and graduate-study spaces, and an energy-research facility.

The Art Museum has an extensive permanent collection that ranges from artifacts of the ancient world to paintings and sculpture of the Renaissance, modern Europe, and America.

Princeton's computing resources include a large IBM mainframe, a general use UNIX system, specialized workstations, and various microcomputers. TigerNet, a broad-based communications system, connects the dormitories with other campus buildings and with global information services.

Costs

The basic 2000–01 academic-year expenses for all students are $25,430 for tuition and fees and $7206 for room and board.

Financial Aid

Admission decisions are need-blind. Princeton provides assistance to meet the full demonstrated financial need of all admitted students. Once admitted with aid, a student receives assistance for succeeding undergraduate years, as long as the family continues to demonstrate need and the student makes normal progress toward a degree. Financial aid packages generally consist of a combination of the University scholarship and federal assistance in the form of a grant, work-study opportunities, and a low-interest loan.

Approximately 75 percent of the student body receives financial aid from outside sources and/or the University each year; about 43 percent receive some form of financial aid from the University.

Faculty

One of Princeton's outstanding assets is its faculty. A single faculty teaches both undergraduate and graduate students, all of whom have close contact with scholars of national and international reputation. The current student-faculty ratio is 6:1.

Student Government

The Undergraduate Student Government (USG) is the undergraduate representative body that advocates students' interests to other groups. Other purposes of the USG include the exercise of leadership in undergraduate activities and the running of services for members of the University community.

Admission Requirements

Princeton does not require a specific set of secondary school courses for admission. It does, however, strongly recommend the following as a basic preparation for study at the University: 4 years each of English (including continued practice in writing), mathematics, and a single foreign language; 2 years each of laboratory science and history (including that of the United States and another country or area); some study of art or music; and, if possible, a second foreign language.

All candidates must submit the results of the SAT I and SAT II in three different subject areas of their own choice. (Candidates whose only other college choices require the ACT may substitute ACT results for the SAT I.) Students interested in pursuing a B.S.E. degree are expected to take SAT II Subject Tests in either Physics or Chemistry and in either Level I or Level II Mathematics.

Interviews on campus are not required but are available to those who wish them. Depending upon demand, interviews may be held with individuals or small groups. Applicants are encouraged to have an interview in their home area with a member of one of Princeton's Alumni Schools Committees.

Application and Information

Students should apply to Princeton on an application form provided by the University. Those wishing to apply through the early decision program should submit materials by November 1; they are notified of the admission decision in early December. The deadline for regular decision application is January 2, and notification is in early April.

Requests for additional information and application forms should be addressed to:

Admission Office
Princeton University
P.O. Box 430
Princeton, New Jersey 08544-0430
Telephone: 609-258-3060

Blair Hall, with its distinctive arch, is a landmark building at Princeton University.

PROVIDENCE COLLEGE
PROVIDENCE, RHODE ISLAND

The College

Conducted under the auspices of the Order of Preachers of the Province of St. Joseph, commonly known as the Dominicans, Providence College (PC) was established in 1917. Originally a college for men, it became coeducational in 1971. The College's full-time undergraduate enrollment is nearly 3,700 students. Approximately 1,800 students live in nine residential halls, and an additional 900 upperclass students are housed in one of the five College apartment complexes. The remainder of the students live in apartments directly off campus or commute from home. At the graduate level, the College offers M.A., M.S., M.Ed., M.B.A., and Ph.D. degree programs.

The modern Slavin Center, as the nucleus of student social, cultural, and recreational activity, provides numerous facilities; they include lounges, a newly renovated dining facility, club offices, an ATM machine, a bookstore/gift shop, the Office of Student Services, and offices for the Student Congress, the Board of Programmers, student publications, the Counseling and Placement Center, and the chaplain.

The Peterson Recreation Center is the site of intramural athletic activities on campus, in which more than 80 percent of the students participate. The center has five convertible basketball, tennis, and volleyball courts; a 220-yard track; three racquetball courts; and a 25-meter pool. Providence College has a fine tradition of competition in intercollegiate athletics, and it continues to play an active role through its membership in the NCAA, RIRW, ECAC, Hockey East Conference, and Big East Conference. Additional on-campus sports facilities include Alumni Hall, Schneider Arena, and three large fields and recreational areas.

Location

The College is situated on a 105-acre campus in the city of Providence, Rhode Island. It has the advantages of an atmosphere far removed from the traffic and commerce of the metropolitan area but is also conveniently located near the many cultural attractions of a city that is not only the capital of a historic state but the center of a variety of institutions of higher learning. Providence College has an established relationship with the Tony Award–winning Trinity Square Repertory Company, located in downtown Providence. Trinity provides special discount rates for students for the full spectrum of its programs. The Providence Performing Arts Center, originally a movie palace, has been restored to its former baroque splendor and now serves as the site of symphony concerts, opera, ballet, and road shows of Broadway musicals. In addition, the Providence Civic Center attracts well-known performers and rock groups, trade shows, and sports events. The center is also the home court of the Friars, PC's basketball team.

Majors and Degrees

Providence College offers the B.A. degree with major programs of study in American studies, art and art history, biology, business economics, chemistry, economics, education (elementary, secondary, and special), English, history, humanities, mathematics, modern languages, music/music education (K–12), philosophy, political science, psychology, public and community service studies, social science, social work, sociology, theater arts, and theology. The B.S. degree is offered with major programs of study in accountancy, applied physics, biochemistry, biology, chemistry, computer science, engineering (3-2 program), environmental studies, finance, health policy and management, management, and marketing. The College also offers a 4+1 B.A./B.S./M.B.A. program for qualified students.

Academic Program

The primary objective of Providence College is to further the intellectual development of its students through the disciplines of the sciences and the humanities. The liberal education provided by the College gives students the chance to increase their ability to formulate their thoughts and communicate them to others, evaluate their varied experiences, and achieve insight into the past, present, and future of civilization. The College is concerned about preparing students to become intelligent, productive, and responsible citizens in a democratic society. To this end, it endeavors not only to develop the students' capacity for disciplined thinking and critical exactness but also to give them opportunities for healthy physical development and a wide range of activities that foster a sense of social responsibility. The College's programs are also designed to help students discover their particular aptitude and prepare them to undertake specialized studies leading to careers.

Students are required to complete a total of 116 credit hours in the core curriculum, in a selected major, and in electives. The core curriculum is built around a broad range of disciplines, and 20 semester hours are allotted to study of the development of Western civilization, 6 to social science, 6 to philosophy, 6 to religion, 6 to natural science, 3 to mathematics, and 3 to the fine arts. Special academic programs offered to enhance the educational experience and allow for a variety of interests, including double majors, individualized programs, nondepartmental courses, liberal arts honors, preprofessional medical and legal programs, the Early Identification Program (offered to Rhode Island residents in cooperation with Brown University Medical School), and Army ROTC.

The College participates in the Advanced Placement Program administered by the College Board. Students who demonstrate superior performance (a score of 4 or 5) on any of the Advanced Placement examinations are considered for advanced placement and standing in the area of study in which they qualify.

PC operates on a two-semester calendar. Fall-semester classes begin in early September and spring-semester classes begin in mid-January.

Off-Campus Arrangements

For more than twenty-five years, Providence College has encouraged qualified students to consider the advantages of study abroad. Committed to offering students a comprehensive opportunity for a truly liberal education, the Providence-In-Europe Office extends an invitation to all interested first-year and sophomore students to explore the possibilities for enriching their undergraduate education through a sojourn abroad. Providence College is one of the few institutions to have study-abroad arrangements with both Oxford University and Cambridge University in England. Students may also choose from the University of Glasgow in Scotland; Trinity College and University College in Dublin and National University of Ireland in Galway, Ireland; and the University of Salamanca in Spain. In addition, the College offers a direct exchange program with Kansai-Gaidai University in Japan. Providence-In-Europe may be able to make other opportunities available for study abroad when the PC-sponsored programs are not suited to individual academic needs. In recent years, PC students have studied abroad in Rome, Florence, Salzburg, Madrid, Cannes, Paris, London, and Sydney.

Academic Facilities

The Phillips Memorial Library, which has received two national architectural awards for its design, is the center of intellectual activity at the College. The library has current holdings of

282,573 volumes in open stacks and seating accommodations for 750 students. Phillips Library also houses various faculty offices, reading and rare book rooms, archives, the Department of English, and the Office of Academic Services. The library is a member of the Consortium of Rhode Island Academic and Research Libraries, through which the resources of most of the libraries in the state are accessible to Providence College students. Located in Accino Hall and Koffler Hall are the College's academic microcomputer laboratories, which serve the computer instruction and research needs of faculty members and students. The College's state-of-the-art science laboratories, computer workstations, and research facilities are located in the Albertus Magnus-Hickey Science Complex. The Feinstein Academic Center is a newly renovated academic facility that is the home of the Feinstein Institute for Public Service Program, the Liberal Arts Honors Program, and the Center for Teaching Excellence. The auditorium of Harkins Hall, now called the Blackfriars Theatre, has been totally renovated to provide versatile seating and staging for the performing arts.

Costs

The total costs for the 2000–01 academic year are tuition, $18,440; room, $3785; and board, $3840 (19-meal plan) or $3510 (15-meal plan); Books, travel, and personal supplies are estimated to cost $1500.

Financial Aid

Providence College's financial aid is distributed on the basis of demonstrated need and the student's ability to benefit from the educational opportunity the assistance offers. To apply for financial aid, candidates must submit both a College Scholarship Service PROFILE application and the Free Application for Federal Student Aid (FAFSA) by February 1. Upon final determination of students' need, the Office of Financial Aid constructs aid packages consisting of work, loan, and grant assistance in accordance with federal regulations, the availability of funds, and institutional policy as approved by the College's Financial Aid Advisory Committee. Sources of financial aid include Federal Work-Study awards, Federal Perkins Loans, Federal Pell Grants, Federal Supplemental Educational Opportunity Grants (FSEOG), Providence College grants-in-aid, Providence College Achievement Scholarships, and Merit Scholarships.

Faculty

The faculty consists of 248 full-time and 18 visiting and adjunct professors, approximately 11 percent of whom are Dominican fathers. The majority of PC instructors teach both undergraduate- and graduate-level courses; no graduate students or student assistants teach at either level. About 90 percent of the faculty members hold doctorates or terminal degrees. All professors devote their time primarily to teaching and advising undergraduates; all students are assigned a faculty adviser in their major area. The student-faculty ratio is 14:1.

Student Government

The Student Congress represents the students in its emphasis upon life-styles and student prerogatives. Its officers are elected annually by the entire student community, and representatives are elected by each class. The Student Congress has created the Providence College Bill of Rights, the most significant of its legislative actions. Student representatives are appointed annually by the Student Congress to all standing committees of the College. The Student Congress has primary responsibility for the allocation of $125,500 in student activity funds to support most student-run organizations.

Admission Requirements

The admission committee gives recognition to students with various talents, backgrounds, and geographic origins. Admission decisions are made without regard to race, color, sex, handicap, age, or national or ethnic origin. An estimate of the applicant's character and accomplishments by his or her college adviser in secondary school and an official transcript of the secondary school record should be sent to the College no later than January 15. The secondary school transcript should consist of courses of a substantially college-preparatory nature. Although individual cases may vary, the College recommends that a student complete 4 years of English, at least 3 years of mathematics, 3 of foreign language, at least 2 of laboratory sciences, and 2 of social sciences. Four additional units may be taken in any subjects that meet the secondary school's requirements for graduation. Applicants whose collegiate major would require the inclusion of college-level mathematics are advised to have 4 units of mathematics. Applicants are encouraged to submit letters of recommendation and evaluation from their secondary school teachers, especially from English teachers. Letters of recommendation from people who know the applicant personally and who have been involved in his or her scholastic development are most valuable. Applicants are also required to submit their official scores on the College Board's Scholastic Assessment Test (SAT I). In addition, the admission committee recommends the submission of SAT II: Subject Test scores on the Writing Test and on two other tests of the applicant's choice (preferably in subject areas that will be studied in college). In lieu of SAT I scores, applicants may submit scores on the ACT Assessment of American College Testing. Information concerning these tests may be obtained from a high school guidance office; the College Board, Box 592, Princeton, New Jersey 08541, or P.O. Box 1025, Berkeley, California 94720; or American College Testing, P.O. Box 168, Iowa City, Iowa 52240.

Application and Information

The deadlines for receiving applications for the September term are January 15 for regular applicants and March 15 for transfer students. Early action applicants must file an application by November 1. The deadlines for receiving applications for the January term are November 1 for regular applicants and December 1 for transfer students.

Further information may be obtained by contacting:

Office of Admission
Providence College
549 River Avenue
Providence, Rhode Island 02918-0001
Telephone: 401-865-2535
           800-721-6444 (toll-free)
Fax: 401-865-2826
E-mail: pcadmiss@providence.edu
World Wide Web: http://www.providence.edu

Harkins Hall, the administration building at Providence College.

PURCHASE COLLEGE, STATE UNIVERSITY OF NEW YORK
PURCHASE, NEW YORK

The College

Purchase College is a public coeducational college that serves both residential and commuter students. It has an enrollment of 3,500. Founded in 1967, Purchase College is one of the first institutions of higher learning to fuse the educational goals and traditions of a university and an arts conservatory by combining the visual and performing arts and liberal arts and sciences on one campus. The combination of conservatory and liberal arts reflects the College's conviction that the artist and the scholar are both vital to an enlightened democratic society.

Representing a broad range of age groups and geographic, ethnic, and socioeconomic backgrounds, Purchase College students are characterized by individualism and creativity. The emphasis on individualized study—through tutorials, independent study, and the required senior project—encourages students to assume significant responsibility for their education. The intersection of the arts and liberal arts and sciences fosters an appreciation in students of the contribution of both scholarly and artistic achievement to a humane culture.

Although Purchase College is the youngest of the SUNY system's sixty-four campuses, it has rapidly emerged and is increasingly recognized as a distinguished, imaginative, and dynamic institution for the study of the liberal arts and sciences and the visual and performing arts and for its service to the region and the state.

Purchase is primarily a full-time undergraduate institution, but in fulfilling its role as a public institution, Purchase College welcomes the opportunity to promote lifelong learning for students of all ages, backgrounds, and incomes and to serve the community and the state that sustain it. As part of its mission to meet the needs of a diverse constituency, Purchase's Division of Continuing Education offers many credit and noncredit courses, certificate programs, and part-time degree programs.

In addition to its baccalaureate degrees, Purchase College offers the M.F.A. in music, in theater arts/stage design, and in visual arts and an M.A. in art history.

Location

The Purchase campus, built on the 500-acre former Strathglass estate, combines the advantages of a semirural setting with proximity to the educational and cultural opportunities of New York City and Westchester County. As the only senior public institution in Westchester, Purchase College is a cultural resource for the entire community. Approximately 200,000 people visit the campus each year to take advantage of its many programs and activities, such as the President's Leadership Forum, the Purchase College Westchester School Partnership, exhibits at the Neuberger Museum, and the Performing Arts Center.

Majors and Degrees

Purchase College offers professional and conservatory training programs that lead to a B.F.A. degree in acting, dance, film, music, stage design/technology, and visual arts.

Purchase College's liberal arts and sciences programs lead to the B.A. and B.S. The College offers a full range of disciplines through its three divisions: Humanities (art history, creative writing, drama studies, history, journalism, language and culture, literature, and philosophy), Natural Sciences (biology, chemistry, environmental science, mathematics, mathematics/computer science, and psychology), and Social Sciences (anthropology, business economics, political science, social science and arts, and sociology). Students may also study premedicine or prelaw. There are growing interdisciplinary programs in media studies, dramatic writing, and arts management.

Academic Program

Purchase College operates on a semester calendar. Students normally take 16 credits per semester so they can meet the minimum requirement of 120 hours for a bachelor's degree as well as the SUNY-mandated general education requirements.

Purchase has the only conservatory training programs for the arts within the State University of New York System. Professional training is provided by practicing professionals. Proximity to New York City gives access to these professionals and their respective art worlds. Purchase graduates benefit from the network of contacts developed during the undergraduate years, and placement in professional jobs begins at an early stage, often before graduation. For example, some students occasionally interrupt their study program to work with a professional dance company or with a professional filmmaker.

Students in the liberal arts and sciences declare their major concentration by the junior year, electing intensive course work that builds toward their senior project. This project represents a culmination of their four years at Purchase and can take the form of a research paper, presentation, or original expression of thought and research (e.g., poem, artwork, multimedia presentation). Senior projects in natural sciences are often published or copublished with a faculty member.

For many Purchase students, internships in agencies, businesses, and corporations are also an important part of their educational experience and often lead to full-time employment.

Academic Facilities

The College's extraordinary facilities include the first building in the United States designed exclusively for the study and performance of dance; a large science research center; the Performing Arts Center, containing four theaters; the Neuberger Museum, which has an outstanding collection of modern American art; an exceptionally well equipped physical education building; an increasing number of multimedia and computer classrooms; and a 160,000-square-foot visual arts building.

Costs

For 1999–2000, tuition for undergraduate in-state residents was $3400 for the academic year, $8300 for nonresidents. Total room and board (dormitory double room and full meal plan) fees were $5404. Books and supplies were estimated at $1025. There is also an applied music fee of $1600 per year for music majors. This fee does not apply to studio composition or production majors. Costs are subject to change for 2000–01.

Financial Aid

Purchase College participates in all federal and state need-based aid programs. Seventy-nine percent of students receive financial aid. Students who apply for aid by June 1 generally receive packages covering their full need.

Both merit and need-based scholarships for the arts and academics are available to qualified students.

Faculty

The Purchase College faculty is distinguished by depth of specialized knowledge as well as broad interdisciplinary interests, scholarly and professional activity, and dedication to undergraduate teaching. The liberal arts and sciences faculty includes prominent scholars in a variety of fields. More than 90 percent hold doctorates from prestigious schools and have won Guggenheim, Fulbright, NEH, and NEA awards, among others. The visual and performance arts faculty consists of leading teachers and practicing professionals in dance, film, music, theater, and visual arts.

Student Government

The Student Union, a campuswide organization, is made up of students elected by their peers. The union is responsible for campus activities, sends representatives to faculty and administrative councils, and administers its own budget of approximately $240,000.

Admission Requirements

Applicants are considered by the Board of Admissions on an individual basis without regard to race, religion, geographic origin, or handicap. Major factors for admission consideration in the liberal arts and sciences programs are the high school and the academic records, including rank in class, subjects studied, proficiency in English, test scores (SAT I or ACT), and recommendations. A rolling admission system is used at Purchase College, with selective deadlines in some programs.

In the visual and performing arts, students must show proof of talent by means of an audition, interview, or portfolio review in addition to a review of their academic credentials. Entrance to these programs is very competitive. Therefore, the filing of an early application is encouraged for both freshmen and transfers. Typically, auditions of conservatory candidates are completed by mid-April.

Application and Information

Students are urged to visit the campus for information sessions. For further information, students should contact:

Betsy Immergut
Director of Admissions
Purchase College,
    State University of New York
735 Anderson Hill Road
Purchase, New York 10577-1400

Telephone: 914-251-6300
Fax: 914-251-6314
E-mail: admissn@purchase.edu
World Wide Web: http://www.purchase.edu

A reason to cheer—graduation day at Purchase College.

QUEENS COLLEGE OF THE CITY UNIVERSITY OF NEW YORK

FLUSHING, NEW YORK

The College

Queens College opened in 1937 with 400 students and a staff of 40 on a 76-acre landscaped campus in Flushing, New York. Today, Queens, with more than 14,000 undergraduates, is one of the largest of the four-year colleges in the nineteen-college City University of New York (CUNY) system, which was founded in 1961. Like the other CUNY colleges, Queens is a commuter school. Most Queens College students live in one of New York City's five boroughs or in Nassau, Suffolk, or Westchester County. Funded by the state of New York, Queens College serves all the people of New York State. The College is built on a hill and has thirty buildings. Seven of the original stucco and tile buildings still stand, contributing to the pleasantly eclectic style of the campus.

In 1949 a chapter of Phi Beta Kappa was authorized, and in January 1950 the Sigma chapter was installed at the College; in 1968 Queens College became a member of Sigma Xi, the national science honor society. The American Association of University Women includes Queens College in its list of approved colleges for membership.

As a state-funded municipal college, Queens College is particularly aware of its mission in the broader community. Its services include Community Classroom, a program that takes students into the community as volunteers, combining public service with academic discipline; continuing education courses and lectures; Student Union facilities and programs; exhibits in the Art Center and the gallery in Kiely Hall; and plays, concerts, dance recitals, and other cultural and educational programs, presented in Colden Auditorium and the Queens College Theatre. The Upward Bound Program, a special federally funded precollege program, provides disadvantaged tenth- and eleventh-grade students with the basic skills and motivation necessary for success in postsecondary education. It involves a full-time summer program and a follow-up program during the regular school year.

College facilities and cultural opportunities that are open to the public, as well as to students and staff, for enjoyment and participation are the Queens College Choral Society; the Queens College Orchestral Society, a symphony orchestra that performs major works each season in Colden Auditorium; the Queens College Speech and Hearing Center, whose services include diagnostic speech, language, and hearing evaluations and speech and language therapy; the Center for Preparatory Studies in Music, which provides music training to students of all ages; and athletic facilities that include a summer day camp program for children.

Location

Queens College is located in the New York City borough of Queens, a residential area close to major highways and bus transportation. The area is midway between the Long Island suburbs and the many cultural and recreational facilities of Manhattan.

Majors and Degrees

The Bachelor of Arts degree is awarded in accounting, American studies, anthropology, art, art history, biology, chemistry, communication sciences and disorders, comparative literature, computer science, dietetics, drama and theater, earth and environmental studies, East Asian studies, economics, education (early childhood and elementary and secondary), English, film studies, French, geology, German, Greek, Hebrew, history, home economics, Italian, Jewish studies, labor studies, Latin, Latin American area studies, linguistics, mathematics, media studies, music, philosophy, physical education, physics, political science and government, psychology, Russian, sociology, Spanish, theater-dance, and urban studies. The Bachelor of Arts program in secondary school teaching includes the following subject areas: art, biology, chemistry, earth sciences, English, French, German, home economics, Latin, mathematics, music, physics, social studies, and Spanish. The College also awards the Bachelor of Arts in interdisciplinary studies, an individualized Bachelor of Arts program, the Bachelor of Fine Arts in art, the Bachelor of Music (through the Aaron Copland School of Music) in instrumental or vocal performance studies, and the Bachelor of Science in physical education.

The Departments of Chemistry, Philosophy, Physics, and Political Science and the Aaron Copland School of Music offer qualified undergraduates the opportunity to take combined master's and bachelor's degree programs.

Special interdisciplinary programs include Africana studies, American studies, Byzantine and modern Greek studies, Honors in Mathematical and Natural Sciences, Honors in the Humanities, Business and Liberal Arts Studies, Journalism, Irish studies, Italian-American studies, Puerto Rican studies, and religious studies. Special programs and advisement are also available in accounting, pre-engineering, prelaw, and the pre-health professions.

Academic Program

Queens College's original curriculum was planned by its first president, Dr. Paul Klapper, according to the liberal arts model of the University of Chicago, encouraging the development of the whole person through a required sampling of the humanities, social sciences, sciences, languages, and the arts; a more intensive preparation in a single subject; and freedom of choice in a third group of courses. The College provides a liberal arts education of the highest caliber to New Yorkers from many ethnic, social, and economic backgrounds. A distinguished faculty, a comprehensive curriculum, and an impressive record of achievement by its graduates contribute to the College's increasing stature as one of the finest undergraduate institutions in the country. The wide range of majors and interdisciplinary studies, combined with the award-winning Freshman Year Initiative Program, encourages students to explore their interests and abilities to the fullest. The four-year bachelor's degree programs require the completion of 120 credits.

The Business and Liberal Arts Studies program is designed for those who want to study the theory and practice of business in a liberal arts context. Internships are sponsored by participating corporations.

The B.A./M.D. program with the SUNY Health Sciences Center and the B.A./D.D.S. program with Columbia University are new offerings available for students interested in the health science professions.

Honors in the Humanities, designed for students of demonstrated high academic achievement, includes a special, challenging curriculum based on the Great Books. Its facilities provide a quiet place for scholarly work and original research.

Honors in Mathematical and Natural Sciences is a program intended for students who have demonstrated exceptional ability in mathematics and science at the high school level and plan to continue in those studies at Queens.

The Adult Collegiate Education program, offered for students 25 years of age or older, includes the option of obtaining college credit for life achievement.

Academic Facilities

Among the many centers where research and creativity are joined in the pursuit of knowledge are the 2,200-seat Colden Center for the Performing Arts, which includes the Queens College Theatre, designed especially for the staging of experimental student productions; the Aaron Copland School of Music facility, which includes thirty-five practice rooms and the 500-seat Lefrak recital hall; the Institute for Low-Temperature Physics; the Center for Byzantine and Modern Greek Studies; the Asian-American Center; the Center for the Improvement of Education in the Middle Grades, which has a program in experimental education at the Louis Armstrong School (I.S. 227); the Speech and Hearing Center, which investigates communication handicaps and provides clinical experience for students of speech and hearing therapy; the Center for Jewish Studies; the Calandra Italian-American Institute; and the Taft Institute for Government. The former country estate of Marshall Field III at Caumsett State Park houses the Queens College Center for Environmental Teaching and Research. At this 1,800-acre site, which has dormitories and classrooms, students study coastal geology, botany, wetland ecology, landscape painting and drawing, and post-Columbian archaeology.

The Benjamin Rosenthal Library, a center for study and research on campus, has more than 700,000 volumes.

Costs

For New York State residents, undergraduate tuition for 1999–2000 was $1600 per semester (full-time) or $135 per credit (part-time). For out-of-state and international students, undergraduate tuition was $3400 per semester (full-time) or $285 per credit (part-time). There is a student activity fee of approximately $90 per semester for full-time undergraduate students and $61 per semester for part-time undergraduate students.

Financial Aid

More than 50 percent of Queens College students receive need-based financial aid. The aid may include state and federal loans and grants, Tuition Assistance Program awards, Regents Scholarships, Federal Stafford Student Loans, Federal Pell Grants, State Aid for Native Americans, and Federal Work-Study awards.

The Queens College Scholars Program offers a variety of merit-based scholarships to full-time freshmen, with awards ranging from $2000 to $5000 per year. In 1999, more than 80 members of the class of 2003 received these awards. Selection is competitive, and scholarships are awarded on the basis of the high school record, test scores (SAT I and SAT II Subject Tests), writing ability, letters of recommendation, and extracurricular activities. Scholarships are renewable with continued high academic achievement. Applicants who rank in or near the top 10 percent of their class and have a rigorous academic program, excellent grades, and minimum combined SAT I scores of 1250 are encouraged to apply. The application deadline is February 1.

Faculty

More than 90 percent of the full-time members of the Queens College faculty have doctorates. Faculty members have received support and recognition for their work from major foundations and international agencies. Among the awards given to faculty members are two of the thirty-nine Rockefeller Foundation Fellowships in the Humanities, granted nationwide; several American Council of Learned Societies grants; four National Endowment for the Humanities fellowships; and a Guggenheim Fellowship. Among the more widely known faculty members are Barry Commoner, Director of the Center for the Biology of Natural Systems; Luc Montagnier, Professor of Biology and codiscoverer of the HIV virus; Thea Musgrave, Professor of Music and composer; Dennis Sullivan, Einstein Professor of Mathematics; and Yevgeny Yevtushenko, Professor of European Languages and poet.

Student Government

Through the Student Association, students at Queens are able to run many services and activities that influence the daily operations of the College. Its elected officers and senators poll students regularly about relevant topics and sponsor such services as free legal advice, a typing center, apartment and tutor referral, and voter registration. In addition, students constitute one third of the College's Academic Senate.

Admission Requirements

Queens College seeks to admit freshmen who have completed a strong college-preparatory program in high school with at least a B+ average. Admission is based on a variety of factors, including the applicant's high school grades, academic program, and SAT I or ACT scores. Successful candidates will have chosen a well-rounded program of study that includes academic course work in math (3 years), English (4 years), science (2 years), social studies (4 years), and foreign language (3 years).

The Search for Education, Elevation & Knowledge Program (SEEK) offers academic support, counseling, and financial assistance to motivated students who would not otherwise qualify for admission. The SEEK Program has its own admissions criteria, including financial need.

For earliest consideration, students should apply by January 1 for fall admission and by October 15 for spring admission.

Application and Information

The staff of the Undergraduate Office of Admissions is available to answer questions and give more information. To make an appointment for a tour or to meet with an admissions counselor, students should contact:

Undergraduate Office of Admissions
Kiely Hall, Room 217
Queens College of the City University of New York
65-30 Kissena Boulevard
Flushing, New York 11367
Telephone: 718-997-5600
World Wide Web: http://www.qc.edu

QUEEN'S UNIVERSITY
KINGSTON, ONTARIO, CANADA

The University

Founded in 1841 by Royal Charter of Queen Victoria and named in honour of that monarch, Queen's University is the most exclusive university in Canada. Established as a Presbyterian seminary, Queen's has grown in a century and a half into an institution that offers undergraduate, graduate, and professional degrees in fifteen faculties, schools, and colleges and draws its faculty members and students from across Canada and throughout the world.

Queen's is recognized as a leader in postsecondary education. It was the first Canadian university to establish a scholarly journal, the *Queen's Quarterly*. Queen's was the first Canadian university to offer graduate programs and correspondence study and to establish programs in more than a dozen academic areas, including business and commerce, engineering physics, art conservation, policy studies, and industrial relations.

Queen's is host to fourteen federal and provincial research centres of excellence and the home of twenty-three research groups and institutes, including Canada's Cancer Clinical Trials Group and the Sudbury Neutrino Observatory. The University receives more than $70 million in research grants and contracts annually from federal and provincial governments and businesses, primarily in the fields of medicine, engineering, science, and social science.

National magazine polls of high school counsellors, academic administrators, and CEOs of major Canadian corporations consistently rank Queen's first in terms of its reputation for the quality of its programs, for its reputation for educating Canada's leaders of tomorrow, and for having the highest admission standards in the country.

Queen's students come from every Canadian province and more than seventy countries around the world. More than 13,000 students enrol annually, including 2,000 graduate students, medical residents, and interns. Another 3,000 students enrol in part-time and distance education programs. Undergraduate and professional enrolment is limited to approximately 11,000, and entrance requirements are the highest of all Canadian universities.

Queen's has the oldest student association in Canada, the Alma Mater Society (AMS). The AMS oversees more than 200 student clubs, including the Debating Union, the Queen's Project on International Development, and CFRC-FM Radio. Apart from the Marconi companies, Queen's CFRC has the longest continuous history in radio of any institution in the world. When President Franklin Delano Roosevelt received his honourary degree from Queen's University in 1938 and used the occasion to make an important foreign policy speech, CFRC carried a feed to every radio network in North America.

Athletics and extracurricular activities are a long-standing tradition at Queen's. With forty-one interuniversity teams, Queen's is tied with Harvard University for having the largest varsity sports program in North America. Queen's athletes are internationally competitive, having won Olympic, Commonwealth, and World University Games medals. Queen's sailing is the most competitive Canadian team competing in the U.S. circuit. A team member won the U.S. College Singlehanded Championship in 1997 and earned Academic All-American status. The Queen's women's rowing team won the Club 8 Race at the 1997 Head of the Charles Regatta. In the past four years, Queen's varsity teams have won twenty-three provincial and national titles.

Location

Queen's main campus is situated in the city of Kingston, Ontario, on the northeastern shore of Lake Ontario. It is halfway between Canada's two largest cities, Toronto and Montreal; a 2-hour drive from the nation's capital of Ottawa; and 90 miles north of Syracuse, New York. Founded in 1673, Kingston is one of Canada's oldest settlements and was the first capital of Canada. Kingston was originally settled by Europeans for its military value, and its strategic location and intellectual resources have made it home to international businesses such as Alcan, Bombardier, Bosal, Celanese, and DuPont. More than 1 million tourists visit the city annually to explore the museums and historic sites and enjoy the offerings of theatre troupes, classical concert groups, the Kingston Symphony, and art galleries and studios. Kingston is also a mecca for sailors, with some of the best freshwater sailing in the world. In 1976, the city hosted the sailing events of the XXI Olympiad.

Queen's also maintains a campus in the United Kingdom. Queen's International Study Centre (ISC) at Herstmonceux, East Sussex, is a modern educational facility housed within the walls of the fifteenth-century Herstmonceux Castle. The campus of the ISC is in a sheltered valley of gardens, walks, and groves in East Sussex, approximately 60 miles south of London.

Majors and Degrees

The Bachelor of Arts degree is offered in applied economics; art history; biology; Canadian studies; chemistry; classical studies; classics; Commonwealth studies; computing and information science; developmental studies; drama; economics; English; environmental studies; film; French studies; geography; geological sciences; German; German studies; Greek; history; Italian; Jewish studies; language and linguistics; Latin; mathematics; mediaeval studies; modern literature; music; philosophy; physics; political studies; psychology; religious studies; sociology; Spanish; Spanish and Latin American studies; stage and screen studies; statistics; and women's studies.

The Bachelor of Science degree is offered in astrophysics, biochemistry, biology, chemical physics, chemistry, cognitive science, computing and information science, environmental science, geography, geological sciences, geological sciences with physics, life sciences, mathematical physics, mathematics, physics, psychology, respiratory therapy, software design, statistics, and x-ray technology.

The Bachelor of Science in Engineering degree is offered with the following specializations: chemical, civil, computer, electrical, geological, mechanical, mining, and engineering physics as well as two programs (engineering chemistry and mathematics and engineering) unique among Canadian universities. Five programs offer course patterns that lead to careers in environmental engineering.

The Bachelor of Commerce degree is offered with the following specializations: accounting, finance, industrial and human relations, international business, management information systems, marketing, operations, and quantitative methods.

Queen's offers a Bachelor of Education, a Bachelor of Fine Art, a Bachelor of Music, a Bachelor of Nursing Science, a Bachelor of Physical and Health Education, and a Bachelor of Rehabilitation Therapy, with specializations in occupational therapy and physical therapy. Professional degrees are available in business administration, law, and medicine.

Academic Program

The academic year runs from September through April and is divided into two 12-week terms. Spring and summer sessions are offered from May through August. Most undergraduate programs are of four years' duration.

Off-Campus Arrangements

Queen's International Study Centre at Herstmonceux, East Sussex, United Kingdom, offers students the opportunity to work toward their academic and professional goals with other university students from around the world. The ISC offers a number of programs, including the Canadian University Study Abroad Program (first-year and upper-year options), Visiting Upper Year Students Program, ESL Plus, and a spring term program. Programs permit students to choose from a series of courses that focus on the culture, history, and economics of Europe. The limited enrolment of the ISC helps create an enriched academic environment both inside and outside the classroom. Field studies are integrated into most courses to take advantage of the natural, historical, and cultural riches of Britain and Europe. In a typical term, art history students visit galleries, monuments, and buildings in and around London, and history students visit local sites of interest, such as Bath and Chichester. Major excursions to Brussels or Paris permit interdisciplinary visits to museums, embassies, international organizations, and agencies important to understanding the politics, economics, history, and culture of Europe. Regular excursions from the ISC to London also allow students to experience this major world capital both as students and as tourists. In addition to the established opportunities for participation in national and international exchanges, students may also arrange their own study-abroad term at any university in the world.

Queen's University also offers students the opportunity to participate in many exchange programs, including those in countries such as Australia, England, France, Germany, Scotland, and Sweden.

Academic Facilities

The Queen's Libraries, including the recently completed $42-million Stauffer Library, the Douglas Engineering and Science Library, four departmental libraries, and the faculty libraries of education, health sciences, and law, hold more than 5 million items, including books, journals, pamphlets, newspapers, audio-visual materials, and collections of microfilms, maps, aerial photographs, slides, and prints. The Queen's Libraries also provide access to hundreds of electronic resources and databases. The University Archives houses material of national, provincial, and regional significance. The Reading Room can accommodate laptop computers, allowing students to access materials relating to Canadian public affairs, business, literature, art, Kingston and the area, and the University itself.

The $56-million Biosciences Complex is home to the Biology Department, the School of Environmental Studies, three chemical engineering labs working on fermentation and bioremediation, the Kingston Technology Exchange Centre, a Molecular Evolution Laboratory, and a state-of-the-art Phytotron, including six research-quality greenhouses and twenty-five plant growth chambers.

Queen's 5,000-acre biology station at Lake Opinicon is the largest research station of its kind in Canada. The station is internationally recognized for studies in freshwater biology. The Agnes Etherington Art Centre on Queen's campus is one of Canada's most attractive art galleries, the third largest among provincial galleries in Ontario, and Kingston's only art museum. Queen's Information Technology Services helps students and staff members to connect electronically with people and information across campus and around the world. All Queen's students, whether they live in residence (where all 3,100 rooms have high-speed Ethernet connections) or off campus, have access to the Internet, unlimited e-mail, and personal space on the World Wide Web. Many professors now post lectures and other course materials on Web pages.

Costs

Queen's University is a publicly supported institution. There are significant financial advantages for American students who choose to attend Canada's most prestigious university. The fees charged to international students are very competitive when compared to those of programs of equivalent stature in the U.S. All fees are in U.S. dollars. Tuition fees for American and international students in the 1999–2000 academic year were $7104 for arts and science students and $11,587 for engineering students. Room and board fees for students in on-campus residences were approximately $4414, regardless of citizenship. Health insurance, books, transportation, entertainment, and personal expenses are not included in the above fees.

Financial Aid

After one year of study at Queen's, all students, regardless of citizenship, are eligible for all upper-year student awards and scholarships. U.S. students who qualify for the Federal Stafford Student Loan program may apply such funds to Queen's University fees. Queen's has been authorized by the U.S. Department of Education to administer Stafford Loans. Any student with Canadian citizenship, regardless of residency, is eligible for all entrance scholarships.

Faculty

Queen's faculty is drawn from leading institutions around the world. More than half of the teaching faculty members hold graduate degrees from universities outside of Canada, and nearly one third of the teaching faculty holds graduate degrees from U.S. colleges and universities, including Harvard, Princeton, MIT, Berkeley, and Cornell. More than 850 full-time faculty members are assisted by highly qualified adjunct faculty and staff members.

Student Government

The Alma Mater Society, the oldest student association in Canada, is the elected governing body of all Queen's students, except those in the School of Graduate Studies and Research, who elect their own Graduate Student Society. Students participate in all levels of decision making, with nearly one quarter of the seventy spaces on the University Senate devoted to elected students. The Board of Trustees also counts student representatives within its ranks.

Admission Requirements

Individual consideration is given to all candidates from an American school system. Students graduating from a university-preparatory program are considered for admission after providing midyear grade 12 marks (or final grade 12 marks if already graduated), SAT I scores (minimum combined score of 1200 and minimum scores of 580 verbal and 520 math), rank in class (if available), and a school profile. For programs in which mathematics is a requirement, four (preferably five) full-year credit courses in mathematics are required. For programs in which biology, physics, and/or chemistry are required, one (preferably two) full-credit courses in each are required. Advanced Placement (AP) courses in prerequisite subjects are highly recommended whenever possible. AP courses are considered excellent preparation for university courses. However, these courses do not carry degree credit.

Accommodation for first-year students is guaranteed in Queen's on-campus residences, provided the deadline for accepting the offer of admission is met.

Application and Information

Applications for full- or part-time studies must be submitted through the Ontario Universities' Application Centre (OUAC), Box 1328, Guelph, Ontario N1H 7P4, Canada; telephone: 519-823-1940. Online applications are available at http://www.ouac.on.ca.

For additional information, students should contact:

Admission Services
Queen's University
110 Alfred Street
Kingston, Ontario K7L 3N6
Canada
Telephone: 613-533-2218
Fax: 613-533-6810
E-mail: admissn@post.queensu.ca
World Wide Web: http://www.queensu.ca

QUINCY UNIVERSITY
QUINCY, ILLINOIS

The University
Quincy University is a private Roman Catholic university of the liberal arts and sciences. It was founded in 1860 by the Franciscan Friars, who have influenced the world by caring about people as people and urging them to fulfill their potential. This spirit is still maintained at Quincy University today. The University prides itself on its personal approach to learning. Small classes, a dedicated faculty, close faculty-student relationships, and a comfortable atmosphere on campus all create an environment conducive to personal growth and development. The University offers courses on both its 52-acre main campus and the 23-acre North Campus, ten blocks away. Shuttle bus service moves students between these campuses regularly.

The 1,100 students come from diverse social and economic backgrounds. Although the majority are from the Midwest, thirty-six states and sixteen countries are represented in the student body. Quincy University is a residential campus with more than 70 percent of the students living on campus. Campus housing options are varied and include single-sex and coed residence halls, apartments, and houses. Numerous campus organizations offer unlimited opportunities for students to participate in both University and community activities. A National Public Radio station, music performance groups, publications, honor and service societies, a lecture series, and concerts are a few of the many extracurricular opportunities available to students. Eighty percent of the students participate in intramural sports. Quincy University also maintains membership in the NCAA and the Great Lakes Valley Conference. Intercollegiate sports for men are baseball, basketball, cross-country, football, golf, soccer, tennis, track, and volleyball. Women's intercollegiate sports are basketball, cross-country, soccer, softball, tennis, track, and volleyball.

Career planning and placement counseling is available to students throughout their academic career. Quincy University has an outstanding placement record; more than 96 percent of graduates are placed in jobs or graduate schools within 180 days of graduation. Individual assistance with academic planning, study skills, and tutorial work, as well as personal and vocational counseling, is provided free of charge.

At the graduate level, Quincy University offers programs of study leading to the M.B.A. and M.S.Ed. degrees.

Location
The University is located in a residential section of Quincy, a city of 50,000 people, situated on the bluffs of the Mississippi River. It is within easy traveling time of St. Louis (2 hours), Kansas City (4 hours), and Chicago (4½ hours). Good highways and bus, train, and air service make the area easily accessible from any part of the nation. Quincy has a rich and distinguished tradition in the arts. It is noted for its fine architecture and extensive park system.

Majors and Degrees
Quincy University awards the Bachelor of Arts (B.A.), Bachelor of Fine Arts (B.F.A.), Bachelor of Science (B.S.), and Bachelor of Social Work (B.S.W.) degrees. Programs of study include accounting, art, art education, arts management, athletic training, biology, biological sciences, biological sciences education, business administration, chemistry, clinical laboratory science, computer information systems, computer science, criminal justice, elementary education, English, English education, environmental studies, finance, history, history education, humanities (interdisciplinary), management, marketing, mathematics, mathematics education, media and communication, music, music/business (interdisciplinary), music education, nursing, philosophy, physical education, political science, psychology, social work, sociology, special education–learning disabilities, sports management, theology, and theology/pastoral ministry. A Bachelor of Science in Nursing (B.S.N.) is available through a cooperative program with Blessing-Riemann College of Nursing.

Minors are available in most programs, including women's and gender studies; concentrations are offered in physics and reading. A certificate program in business and a coaching specialty in physical education are also available.

Preprofessional programs include dentistry, engineering, law, medicine, physical therapy, and veterinary medicine.

Academic Program
The academic program at Quincy University is based on the belief that liberal arts is the most functional and exciting tradition in education. The curriculum is designed to provide students with the fundamentals of a liberal arts education and at the same time prepare them for a rewarding professional and personal life. The flexible curriculum design allows for double majors or major-minor combinations, student-designed majors, and interdepartmental majors. An honors program, independent studies, special-topics courses, independent research, practicums, and internships are also available to meet the special needs of students.

To be eligible for a baccalaureate degree, a student must complete a minimum of 124 semester hours of university courses with at least a C average. The degree program requires 43 semester hours in general education and "tools" courses, 30–33 hours in a major, and at least 36 hours each in distributed electives and upper-level course work.

Quincy University accepts credit earned through the Advanced Placement Program, the College-Level Examination Program, challenge examinations, and, in some cases, academically related experience.

Off-Campus Arrangements
Arrangements are made with area schools, health facilities, businesses, and industries for such credit-bearing activities as student teaching, clinical training, internships, and practicums. The University also promotes the Early Exploratory Internship Program to its first- and second-year students, allowing them to gain preprofessional experience with area businesses and agencies. Study abroad is possible through many options, with the academic credit for this study preplanned and integrated into the degree program.

Academic Facilities
The Brenner Library, considered one of the top three private-college libraries in the state of Illinois, houses more than 234,000 volumes and 155,000 microtext items and subscribes to more than 650 periodicals. Among the outstanding holdings are a rare book collection, the 75,000-volume Bonaventure Collec-

tion of early Christian and medieval history and theology, and the 4,000-volume Fraborese Collection on Spanish-American history. Through the University's membership in the Online Computer Library Center, Quincy University students have access to millions of books in libraries throughout the Midwest and the nation. The library is also equipped with a computerized reference service.

A modern academic complex located at North Campus houses laboratories for chemistry, physics, biology, and psychology as well as lecture halls and faculty offices. Six computer labs and more than 180 workstations are available for student use. Students also have unlimited access to personal computers, including Pentiums, various networks, Internet, and UNIX. Additional special facilities are a radio station; a fully equipped television studio; the Ameritech Center for Communication, a state-of-the-art computer writing lab and classroom; and an environmental studies field station.

Costs

The costs for the 2000–01 academic year are $14,300 for tuition (12–18 credit hours), $400 for the student activity/computer fee, $2850 for room (double occupancy), and $1930 for board.

Financial Aid

More than 95 percent of the students at Quincy University receive some form of financial assistance. The University participates in the Federal Pell Grant, Federal Supplemental Educational Opportunity Grant (FSEOG), Federal Perkins Loan, Federal Work-Study (FWS), and Federal Stafford Student Loan programs. Illinois State Grants are available for qualified Illinois residents. Quincy University awards academic scholarships ranging from $500 to full tuition. Need-based grants are also available. Students who wish to apply for aid must complete the Free Application for Federal Student Aid (FAFSA) as well as the brief QU Application for Financial Aid. Notification of financial aid awards is made on a rolling basis. Early application is recommended, and priority is given to students who apply before February 15. Transfer applicants are required to submit a transcript from each college or university attended.

Faculty

The Quincy University faculty is composed of 101 professionals, highly qualified in their respective fields. Although many are engaged in research, teaching is the top priority at Quincy University. The University's favorable student-faculty ratio of 12:1 and its experienced faculty members, many of whom have had actual work experience in their field, bring an added dimension to the classroom. Eighty-five percent of the faculty members have the highest degree possible in their field.

Student Government

Students participate in University governance through representation on most University committees, including the Academic Affairs Committee, Athletic Advisory Committee, Student Life Committee, and University Judicial Board. The Student Senate provides for effective student participation in all aspects of University life.

Admission Requirements

Quincy University encourages applications from students who are serious about enrolling in a coeducational university of the liberal arts and sciences and who have demonstrated through their previous academic work an ability to profit from and contribute to the University. Each applicant for admission is evaluated individually. Primary consideration is given to the student's previous academic record. Quincy University recommends that prospective students take a strong college-preparatory program in high school. The Office of Admissions evaluates the prospective freshman's high school record in the following areas: number of academic courses taken, level of difficulty of courses attempted, type of high school attended, grade point average, standardized test scores, class rank, and extracurricular activities. All freshmen are required to submit SAT I or ACT scores.

Transfer students who have earned fewer than 24 semester hours must submit a high school transcript in addition to their college transcripts and should have maintained an overall grade point average of at least 2.0 (C) during their collegiate years. Transfer students may enter at three times during the year: August, January, or June.

International students must submit a transcript from each secondary and collegiate institution they have attended. All non-English transcripts must be translated into English before submission to the Office of Admissions. All international students must also submit TOEFL scores or demonstrate proficiency in the English language.

Application and Information

All students seeking admission are encouraged to apply early. Applications are evaluated after all required application materials have been received. Notification of admission decisions is made on a rolling basis.

Parents, students, and student groups are always welcome to visit the University. The Office of Admissions welcomes visitors from 8 a.m. to 5 p.m., Monday through Friday. Saturday visitors are welcome by appointment. If possible, campus visits should be scheduled during the academic year, when classes are in session. Accepted students may stay overnight in residence halls during the academic year.

For more information about the University's 140-year tradition of excellence, students should contact:

Director of Admissions
Quincy University
1800 College Avenue
Quincy, Illinois 62301-2699
Telephone: 217-228-5210
        800-688-HAWK (4295) (toll-free)
E-mail: admissions@quincy.edu
World Wide Web: http://www.quincy.edu

Brenner Library, one of the premier independent school libraries in the state of Illinois.

Peterson's Guide to Four-Year Colleges 2001   www.petersons.com

QUINNIPIAC UNIVERSITY
HAMDEN, CONNECTICUT

The College

Quinnipiac offers four-year and graduate-level degree programs leading to careers in health sciences, business, mass communications, natural sciences, education, liberal arts, and law. A curriculum that combines career skills with a globally oriented liberal arts background prepares graduates for the future, whether they start their careers right after commencement or opt to pursue advanced study.

Quinnipiac is coeducational and nonsectarian and currently enrolls 4,018 full-time undergraduates, 842 full-time graduates, and 1,187 part-time students in its undergraduate, graduate, professional, and continuing education programs. Less than 35 percent of the students are residents of Connecticut; the rest represent all regions of the United States and many other countries. The emphasis at Quinnipiac is on community. Students, faculty, and staff interact both in and out of the classroom and office. Quinnipiac is big enough to sustain a wide variety of people and programs but small enough to keep students from getting lost in the shuffle. Life on campus emphasizes students' personal, as well as academic, growth. The approximately sixty student organizations and extracurricular activities, including intramural and intercollegiate (NCAA Division I) athletics, give students a chance to exercise their talents, their muscles, and their leadership skills. The University has a student newspaper and an FM radio station (WQAQ) and intercollegiate teams in men's baseball, basketball, cross-country, golf, ice hockey, lacrosse, soccer, tennis, and track and in women's basketball, cross-country, field hockey, ice hockey, lacrosse, soccer, softball, tennis, track, and volleyball.

Quinnipiac's 250-acre main campus has forty-six buildings. In addition to the academic facilities described in the section on the next page, the University has twenty-five residence halls of different styles, all with functional furnishings and decor. The residence halls house 2,775 men and women, about 70 percent of the undergraduate population. All students have in-room access to e-mail and Netscape. The Carl Hansen Student Center—containing recreational facilities, meeting rooms, and offices for student organizations—is adjacent to Alumni Hall, a large multipurpose auditorium used for theater productions, concerts, lectures, films, and various University and community events. Facilities for athletic and fitness activities are found in and around the gymnasium and physical education building. The gymnasium seats 1,500 and includes two regulation-size basketball courts. Also available are a steam room, a sauna, and a 24,000-square-foot recreation/fitness center with a large free-weight room, exercise machine center, aerobic studios, basketball, volleyball, and tennis courts, and an indoor track. There are also lighted tennis courts, playing fields, and miles of scenic routes for running and biking.

Quinnipiac offers a full range of services to assist students in achieving personal and career goals. Individual career counseling is supplemented by a computerized guidance system that lets students enter information about their interests and skills and receive a printout with current data on professions, jobs, and graduate schools. Quinnipiac also has an active career and internship placement office that serves as a liaison between the corporate community and students, new graduates, and alumni.

Graduate programs lead to the Master of Science degree in advanced and neurorehabilitation and orthopedic physical therapy, journalism, and molecular and cell biology; the Master of Health Science in medical lab sciences, pathologist assistant studies, and physician assistant studies; the Master of Science in Nursing in nurse practitioner studies; the Master of Health Administration; the Master of Business Administration; and the Master of Arts in Teaching. In the Quinnipiac University School of Law, an on-campus $22-million facility houses the School of Law and its library. The School offers full-time and part-time programs leading to a J.D. degree or J.D./M.B.A. or J.D./M.H.A. degrees in combination with the School of Business.

Location

Situated at the foot of Sleeping Giant Mountain in the New Haven suburb of Hamden, Quinnipiac provides the best of the country and the city. The University is only 10 minutes from New Haven, 30 minutes from Hartford (the state capital), and less than 2 hours from New York City and Boston. The woodlands, fields, rivers, and wetlands that surround the campus offer opportunities for hiking, picnicking, fishing, ice-skating, and cross-country skiing as well as nature study. Bordering the campus is Sleeping Giant State Park, which also provides a range of recreational activities. In addition to adjacent towns such as Cheshire, Wallingford, and North Haven, a short trip by car or bus puts students in New Haven, where they can visit the acclaimed Yale Center for British Art, attend a performance at the Schubert or Long Wharf Theater, marvel at the dinosaurs in the Peabody Museum of Natural History, or dine in fine restaurants. Quinnipiac's New England location also makes it convenient to enjoy a day in the surf or on the slopes. The beaches on Long Island Sound are easy to reach, and major ski resorts are only an hour's drive from campus.

Majors and Degrees

The School of Health Sciences grants bachelor's degrees in biochemistry, biology (with premedical options in chiropractic, dentistry, medicine, podiatry, and veterinary medicine), chemistry, diagnostic imaging, medical laboratory sciences, medical technology, microbiology/biotechnology, nursing, occupational therapy, physical therapy (5½-year entry-level master's), physician assistant studies (6-year freshman entry-level master's), respiratory care, and veterinary technology.

In the School of Business, bachelor's degree programs are offered in accounting, advertising, computer information systems, finance, health administration, international business, management (areas of concentration: human resource management, production and operations management, and strategic and entrepreneurial management), and marketing (with concentrations available in international marketing, marketing communications, and marketing management). The School also offers a five-year combined-degree program in which students may be awarded both the B.S. degree in business and the M.B.A. or M.H.A. degree.

The College of Liberal Arts offers bachelor's degree programs in computer science, criminal justice, English, gerontology, history, legal studies (paralegal), liberal studies, mathematics, political science, psychology (with concentrations in child development and in human services), social services, sociology, and Spanish. Students can also design their own majors. Certification for teaching elementary, intermediate, and secondary education is offered through a five-year program, resulting in a Master of Arts in Teaching. A bachelor's degree program in psychobiology is interdisciplinary in nature. Students can also continue their study in graduate programs in business, law, or journalism. The School of Communications offers undergraduate majors in communications and public relations, and graduate programs in journalism, and E-Media for writing and design in the journalistic community.

Academic Program

All degree programs at Quinnipiac University are offered through one of the five academic schools. The academic year consists of two 15-week fall and spring semesters and two summer sessions. All baccalaureate candidates are required to complete the Core Curriculum, which consists of up to 50 of the 120 semester hours of credit generally needed for graduation at the bachelor's degree level. The Core Curriculum promotes the achievement of college-level competence in English, mathematics, and such specialized areas as foreign language or computer science. It requires study in the artistic tradition, behavioral and social sciences, humanities, physical and biological sciences, and economic and managerial fields.

Advanced placement, credit, or both are given for appropriate scores on Advanced Placement tests and CLEP general and subject examinations as well as for International Baccalaureate higher-level subjects.

Off-Campus Arrangements

Students in any of the four undergraduate schools can get hands-on experience in their field through off-campus internships. The University is affiliated with outstanding health and scientific institutions—such as Children's Hospital (Boston), Yale–New Haven Hospital, Hartford Hospital, Gaylord Rehabilitation Hospital (Wallingford), and the University of Connecticut Health Center—throughout the state and the nation. Opportunities for internships also exist in industry, large and small businesses, and social and governmental agencies. Academic credit is available for internships and affiliations, which are often part of degree requirements.

Academic Facilities

Academic life focuses on the Bernhard Library building, which recently underwent a $12-million renovation. The library is automated with CD-ROM access and Internet capability. This air-conditioned structure houses the library, with its extensive collections of books, periodicals, government documents, films, tapes, and microforms, and the audiovisual department. Modern classrooms and laboratories are located in Tator Hall, which also contains the Computer Center. The Computer Center supports a Digital Equipment Alpha 2100 server that runs DigitalUnix and several Dell NT servers. Four classrooms and a teaching lab house 160 Dell workstations, and the Multimedia Lab in the Center for Mass Communications includes twelve Apple Macintosh G3 multimedia workstations. Classrooms in the School of Business have data network connections at each student seat. All dormitory rooms have access to the campus data network. Freshmen in the School of Business are required to purchase a laptop computer. The center is open to all students 16 hours a day, including weekends. The Academic Center houses classrooms, laboratories, and an auditorium lecture hall. The Echlin Health Sciences Center houses physical and occupational therapy, nursing, and related fields of study. Buckman Center is where many of the science labs are located, including those for chemistry, medical laboratory sciences, respiratory care, and veterinary technology. A clinical skills lab, for use by nursing students and the physician assistant program, simulates a critical care hospital center. Also in the center is the Buckman Theatre, which holds plays, concerts, and lectures. The Lender School of Business Center has local area network classrooms, satellite capabilities, and the Ed McMahon Center for Mass Communications, containing state-of-the-art TV and radio broadcast studios, print journalism and desktop publishing laboratories, and a news technology center.

Costs

The basic 2000–01 cost is $25,950, of which tuition and fees are $17,000 and room and board are, on average, $8170. Other expenses (typically $1000 per year) include books, laboratory and course fees associated with specific courses, and travel costs.

Financial Aid

Quinnipiac designs financial aid packages to include grants and scholarships that do not have to be repaid, self-help financial aid programs such as federal and University-based work study, and loans. Quinnipiac uses a supplementary College form and the Free Application for Federal Student Aid (FAFSA) to determine need. Transfer students are eligible for the same need-based financial aid consideration as first-time freshmen. Quinnipiac also offers a number of renewable scholarships to new, full-time freshmen that are awarded partly or entirely on the basis of academic merit.

Faculty

The faculty is characterized by its teaching competence and outstanding academic qualifications. Of the 245 full-time faculty members, 70 percent have earned a Ph.D. or the appropriate terminal degree in their field. The faculty also includes a number of part-time teachers who are practicing professionals and experts in their fields. Classes are taught by these scholars and professionals and not by student instructors, and a low student-faculty ratio promotes close associations among faculty and students.

Student Government

The Student Government is the student legislative body of Quinnipiac. It represents student opinion, promotes student welfare, supervises student organizations, appropriates funds for student groups, and provides voting student representation on the Judicial Board, the College Senate, and the Board of Trustees.

Admission Requirements

Quinnipiac seeks students from a broad range of backgrounds. Candidates are evaluated on the basis of a completed application, as described below. Interviews are not always required, but visits to campus are strongly encouraged. Transfer students are welcome. Quinnipiac sponsors four open house programs during the year.

Application and Information

Quinnipiac has a rolling admission policy for its undergraduate programs but recommends that freshman applicants submit their application materials by February 15 and that students applying to the physical and occupational therapy and physician assistant studies programs submit their applications by December 31. Applications can be filed at any time beginning in the senior year of high school. Selection decisions are made as soon as applications are completed. For most programs, a completed application consists of a Quinnipiac application form, a transcript of completed high school courses (including grades for the first quarter of the senior year), a score report for either the SAT I or ACT, a personal statement (essay), and the application fee ($45 for new freshmen as well as transfers). Transfer students are expected to forward a transcript of college course work undertaken. Quinnipiac subscribes to the May 1 Candidates Reply Date Agreement. For information regarding full-time undergraduate study, students should contact:

   Office of Undergraduate Admissions
   Quinnipiac University
   Hamden, Connecticut 06518-1940
   Telephone: 203-281-8600
          203-582-8600 (after July 1, 2000)
          800-462-1944 (toll-free)
   Fax: 203-281-8906
          203-582-8906 (after July 1, 2000)
   E-mail: admissions@quinnipiac.edu
   World Wide Web: http://www.quinnipiac.edu

For information regarding part-time study:

   Office of Part-time Admissions
   Quinnipiac University
   Hamden, Connecticut 06518-1940
   Telephone: 203-281-8612
          203-582-8612 (after 7/1/00)
   World Wide Web: http://www.quinnipiac.edu

RADFORD UNIVERSITY
RADFORD, VIRGINIA

The University

Radford University is a comprehensive, residential university committed to individualized instruction in medium-size classes, high academic standards, and excellence in teaching. Established in 1910, Radford's enrollment has grown to about 9,000, of whom 85 percent are undergraduates. The state-supported University offers 112 undergraduate and more than forty-five graduate program options through the College of Arts and Sciences, the College of Business and Economics, the College of Education and Human Development, the College of Visual and Performing Arts, the Waldron College of Health and Human Services, and the College of Graduate and Extended Studies.

At the graduate level, Radford University awards M.S., M.A., M.B.A., M.F.A., and Ed.S. degrees.

Fifteen residence halls, housing from 120 to 950 students each, offer a variety of options to the 3,100 students who live on campus. All residence halls are in suite arrangements, with two rooms sharing one bathroom. Freshmen are required to live on campus and can choose one of several learning/residential communities. Most off-campus students reside in rental housing within four to five blocks of the campus. Members of the student body come from all over Virginia as well as from forty-five other states and forty-three countries. Radford provides many opportunities for students to participate in exchange and study-abroad programs.

Radford University offers guest speakers; theater productions; concerts; films; social fraternities and sororities; student publications; radio and television; intramural sports; and other cultural, social, and leisure opportunities. In all, there are more than 200 clubs and organizations on campus. Heth Student Center has lounge, recreation, study, and meeting areas. Dalton Hall, the student services building, houses the food court, dining hall, bookstore, and post office. The Dedmon Center, a $10.8-million sports and recreation complex, provides complete sports and fitness facilities. Radford University's teams participate in twenty intercollegiate sports and are members of NCAA Division I.

Location

Radford, a city of 16,200 people, is located approximately 36 miles southwest of Roanoke in the Blue Ridge Mountains in scenic western Virginia. The Blue Ridge Parkway, Appalachian Trail, New River, and Claytor Lake, which has more than 100 miles of shoreline, offer many outdoor activities in a region noted for its natural beauty. Students can ski, hike, canoe, bicycle, and enjoy other seasonal activities.

The local community offers opportunities for dining, socializing, shopping, and off-campus living. The University's campus is near I-81 and is located about 45 minutes from the Roanoke airport.

Majors and Degrees

Radford University awards B.A., B.S., B.F.A., B.M., B.B.A., and B.G.S. degrees in the areas of accounting, administrative systems, anthropology, art, biology, chemistry, communication sciences and disorders, computer science, criminal justice, dance, economics, English, fashion, finance, foods and nutrition, foreign languages (French, German, Spanish), geography, geology, history, human development, information systems, interdisciplinary studies (education), interior design, leisure services, liberal studies, management, marketing, mathematics and statistics, media studies, medical technology, music, music therapy, nursing, philosophy and religious studies, physical education, physical science, political science, psychology, social science, social work, sociology, speech communication, and theater.

Academic Program

To be eligible for an undergraduate degree, students must complete at least 120 semester hours of college-level academic work, including 50 semester hours of general education courses. Honors courses are available to students enrolled in the Highlander Scholars Program and to any qualified student. The Office of New Student Programs coordinates several programs designed to ease the transition from high school to college. The University 100 class and Success Starts Here are programs that help first-year students become active and successful college students. Quest, Radford's summer orientation program, allows incoming students to acclimate themselves with the campus, receive advising, register for classes, and make friends before coming to school in the fall. An Army ROTC program is also available to interested and qualified students.

The University year consists of two semesters, August to December (fall) and January to May (spring), and summer sessions.

Academic Facilities

The McConnell Library offers students access to textual material, periodicals, and information recorded on film, microfilm, records, compact audio discs, and tapes. Services include interlibrary loans and computer-assisted bibliographical searches.

New academic facilities include the International Education Building and Waldron Hall. Completed in 1998, the International Educational Building houses the English Language Institute, International Programs Office, Foreign Languages Media Center, and the Business Assistance Center. Academic departments include geography, history, and foreign languages and literatures. The building features a large room with multimedia capabilities and a state-of-the-art Geographic Information Systems (GIS) lab. Completed in fall 2000, Waldron Hall serves as the new home for the Waldron College of Health and Human Services. Academic divisions include the Schools of Nursing, Social Work, and Allied Health. An onsite interdisciplinary clinic, in which teams of students and faculty members assess the health status of people who are uninsured, underinsured, or are at risk for health problems, provides students with hands-on experience in their chosen fields.

Costs

The basic expenses for the 1999–2000 academic year (August–May) were $2888 for tuition and fees for in-state undergraduate students ($8642 for out-of-state students), $4770 for room and board, and an average of $650 for books and supplies.

Financial Aid

The University provides financial aid awards, based on demonstrated financial need, and scholarships, based on leadership, character, and academic achievement. Financial aid at Radford University is provided through loans, work-study awards, and grants from the federal and state governments and from private funds established through the Radford University Foundation. In addition, some departments have special fellowship funds for undergraduates. Students seeking financial aid should submit the Free Application for Federal Student Aid (FAFSA) to Federal Student Aid Programs by March 1. Transfer students who have attended summer school or who transfer for the spring semester must also request a completed Financial Aid Transcript from colleges and universities previously attended, even if financial aid was not received.

Faculty

Eighty-two percent of Radford University's faculty members hold terminal degrees in their fields of study. The faculty represents forty-five states and eleven countries. With a student-faculty ratio of 16:1, Radford is committed to interaction between faculty members and students both in and out of the classroom. In addition to their primary responsibilities of teaching and advising students, faculty members are engaged in research, publication, and other professional activities. Only 4.2 percent of Radford's undergraduate classes are taught by graduate instructors.

Student Government

Radford University's Student Government Association enables students to participate in the administration of their own affairs and provides representation on the students' behalf. Every undergraduate student is automatically a member of the Student Government Association. The chief divisions of the association are the executive council, cabinet, senate, house of representatives, off-campus student council, graduate student council, class representatives council, black student affairs council, international student affairs council, and diversity promotions council.

Admission Requirements

Admission to Radford University is based on a review of each applicant's academic qualifications. The University admits students whose ability, preparation, and character indicate potential for success in the programs of study offered. Admission is not based on race, sex, handicap, age, veteran status, national origin, religious or political affiliation, or sexual preference. Applicants for admission are considered on the basis of high school records (course of study, grade average, and rank in class), SAT I or ACT scores, and evidence of interest and motivation. Students are considered for admission when they have completed 21 units of college-preparatory work. Most successful applicants have taken 4 units of English, 3 units of mathematics (algebra I and II and geometry), 2 units of foreign language, 3 units of lab science, and 2 units of social science (including American history). Students planning to major in nursing should complete units in both biology and chemistry. Interviews are not generally required, but are certainly encouraged. Students who wish to visit the campus are encouraged to phone or write for an appointment between 8 a.m. and 5 p.m., Monday through Friday, or between 9 a.m. and noon on Saturday, during the academic year. Tours of the campus are conducted at 10 a.m., noon, and 2 p.m., Monday through Friday, and at 10 a.m., 11 a.m., and noon on most Saturdays during the academic year.

Application and Information

A complete application consists of an official application form returned with a nonrefundable application fee, an official transcript of high school work completed, and official SAT I or ACT results. Students wishing to transfer to Radford University from an accredited college or university should send an application form and official transcripts of work attempted at all colleges attended. Applications for fall admission should be received by April 1. Applications received after that date are reviewed on a space-available basis.

For more information, students should contact:

Office of Admissions
Radford University
Radford, Virginia 24142-6903
Telephone: 540-831-5371
            540-831-5128 (V/TDD)
            800-890-4265 (toll-free)
Fax: 540-831-5038
E-mail: ruadmiss@runet.edu
World Wide Web: http://www.radford.edu

Whitt Hall at Radford University.

RAMAPO COLLEGE OF NEW JERSEY
MAHWAH, NEW JERSEY

The College

Ramapo College of New Jersey has been recognized by the State General Assembly as New Jersey's "public liberal arts college." Offering a diverse student body the educational ambience associated with liberal arts colleges, Ramapo has fulfilled its promise as one of the more distinguished institutions of moderate size. In recognition of Ramapo College of New Jersey's strong commitment to character-building programs, The John Templeton Foundation, which publishes a reference guide for students, families, and high schools, named Ramapo to its Honor Roll for 2000–01. The Honor Roll program recognizes and promotes colleges and universities that emphasize character building as an integral part of the college experience.

Today, Ramapo is a coeducational college of liberal arts and professional studies that offers degree programs in the traditional arts and sciences, in interdisciplinary studies such as environmental science and law and society, and in the professions of business administration, education, nursing, and social work. The student body reflects the diversity of the regions served by the College, including more than fifteen states and fifty countries. This diversity, the talents of the faculty, the expectations the College has of its students, and the proximity of the College to some of the world's major multinational organizations give Ramapo an edge in meeting its objective of preparing students of all ages for an increasingly interdependent and multicultural world. For these reasons, Ramapo is called "the college of choice for a global education."

Ramapo College takes pride in four distinctive features that enhance each student's education: (1) concern for student development in and out of the classroom; (2) an exemplary faculty committed to a curricular emphasis on the international and multicultural dimensions of all fields of study; (3) an interdisciplinary orientation in its philosophy and programs; and (4) a collaborative association with local corporations, communities, and educational institutions in the development of experiential educational opportunities and other new ventures both nationally and globally.

The current undergraduate enrollment is about 4,700 men and women. During the academic year, the campus is alive with exciting cultural events, such as music festivals, plays, art exhibits, and film and lecture series. The Student Center, with recreation rooms, lounges, and club offices, is the hub of on-campus activity. Students take an active part in planning the calendar of events for the College community. The campus contains attractive residential units housing approximately 1,500 students. A 250-bed residence hall/dining facility, currently under construction, is scheduled to open in fall 2000. A sports complex has twelve lighted tennis courts; baseball, soccer, and softball fields; and a track. The gym is equipped with a full-size basketball court, an Olympic-size indoor pool, and a fitness center. At Ramapo, sports facilities are available for all students, not just the varsity athletes, who participate in fourteen intercollegiate sports in the most challenging NCAA Division III conference in the country. The College offers a rewarding blend of academic, social, and cultural experiences in the students' daily routine.

In addition to bachelor's degrees, the College offers the Master of Arts in Liberal Studies, the Master of Business Administration, and the Master of Science in Educational Technology.

Location

Ramapo College's barrier-free campus, more than 300 acres in size, is located in the foothills of the Ramapo Mountains in Mahwah, New Jersey, just 25 miles from New York City and all of its cultural advantages.

Majors and Degrees

Ramapo College offers programs of study leading to the Bachelor of Arts degree in accounting, American studies, communication arts, contemporary arts, economics, environmental studies, fine arts, history, international business, international studies, law and society, literature, political science, psychology, social science, and sociology. The Bachelor of Science degree is awarded in accounting, biology, business administration (including finance, management, and marketing), chemistry, computer science, environmental science, information systems, mathematics, physics, and psychology. The Bachelor of Social Work and Bachelor of Science in Nursing degrees are also offered.

Ramapo has offered state-approved teacher education programs to train and certify teachers for the past twenty-five years. Students seeking teacher certification take a sequence of professional education courses in the following subjects relating to elementary, middle school, junior high, and senior high curricula: art, business, communications, elementary education, English, health, mathematics, psychology, science, social studies, and speech arts and dramatics.

Academic Program

Each course at Ramapo is offered through one of five academic units, called schools. These units are relatively small groupings of faculty, organized around individual themes considered to be important and useful areas of study.

The five schools offer major programs and recommend students for degrees. These are the Schools of Administration/Business, American/International Studies, Contemporary Arts, Social Science/Human Services, and Theoretical/Applied Science. Each student is associated with one of these schools while at Ramapo. This association brings the student in contact with others who have the same or similar academic interests and provides the student with easy access to academic advisement and to most of the courses needed to satisfy degree requirements.

Academic Facilities

The campus houses a complex of award-winning academic buildings; state-of-the-art computer centers, telecommunications centers with satellite uplink and downlink capability, and TV centers; a four-story science building with modern facilities; an administration building; and the newly completed Angelica and Russ Berrie Center for Performing and Visual Arts. The College library is housed in a four-story building adjacent to the classroom buildings. The book collection contains approximately 135,000 volumes. In addition, the library has a collection of slides, films, records, cassettes, multimedia kits, and simulation games and maintains a collection of United States, New Jersey, and Bergen County government documents. It also contains all issues of *The New York Times* since it was first published in 1851.

Costs

Full-time tuition and fees in 1999–2000 were $5180 for New Jersey residents and $8046 for out-of-state students. The combined cost of tuition and fees was $156 per credit for New Jersey residents and $245 for out-of-state students. Other charges, depending upon circumstances, include $6600 per year for room and board and a parking fee of $55 per year for commuting students. Books and supplies cost about $700 per year.

Financial Aid

Most financial aid is awarded on the basis of a student's financial need. To qualify for aid at Ramapo, students must complete the Free Application for Federal Student Aid (FAFSA). A student should apply for financial aid prior to May 1 to receive preferential consideration. Federal Perkins Loans, Federal Pell Grants, and Federal Work-Study Program funds are vital parts of the College financial aid program. New Jersey residents should also apply for a state-supported tuition-aid grant. In addition, Ramapo College offers scholarships for high-achieving incoming freshmen students. These awards include tuition and fees, housing, or both. Merit awards are offered for eight semesters as long as the student maintains the required grade point average. New student applicants are automatically considered for these scholarships. Continuing students not receiving an initial scholarship award may apply for additional merit awards based on their academic achievement at the College.

Faculty

Ramapo College has 286 full- and part-time faculty members. Most have been at the College for a number of years and have played a significant role in shaping the College and building strong academic programs. Faculty members have been recruited principally for their effectiveness as teachers of undergraduate students. The College believes it has a distinguished faculty in this regard. Of the full-time faculty members teaching academic courses, 94 percent have a doctoral or equivalent final degree. Their graduate research training—from Ivy League institutions, from the great state universities of the nation, and from some universities abroad—as well as their professional experience—indicate that faculty members possess high quality and diverse experience in the subject matter of their courses.

Student Government

There is an active student government. Each spring, students are elected to this body. The group meets on a weekly basis to discuss any issues that it feels affect the welfare of the student body. Executive officers of the student government meet regularly with the College president and participate actively on committees of the Board of Trustees. Each year students elect a student trustee and student trustee alternate. A member of the Faculty Assembly is designated as liaison to the group so students and others are aware of issues being discussed by the faculty. The president of the Student Government Association makes presentations to both the Faculty Assembly and the trustees at their regular meetings. Students also participate actively in the governance of the College's schools as members of the unit councils. It is here that students have the greatest opportunity to influence decisions on personnel and academic programs.

Admission Requirements

High school seniors generally are expected to have completed a minimum of 16 academic units, distributed as follows: 4 units of English, 2 units of social studies, 3 units of mathematics (including algebra, algebra II, and geometry), 2 units of laboratory science, and 5 units of academic electives. A minimum of 2 years of a foreign language is recommended. In addition, students applying from high school must take the SAT I or the ACT and have their test scores sent to Ramapo. If a prospective applicant has not been graduated from high school but holds a general equivalency diploma, an official copy of the scores of the tests taken for this diploma must be submitted to the admissions office.

Admission of candidates is made on the basis of the academic record, a school counselor's evaluation, evidence of motivation, community and school contributions, and SAT I or ACT scores. Rank in the top one third of the student's secondary school class is expected. Transfer students are also admitted. Deferred admission is possible.

Immediate Decision Day, Ramapo College of New Jersey's antidote to the stress of the college selection and application process, is an opportunity to apply and receive a notice of acceptance in just one day. On the appointed day, high school seniors submit their applications and supporting materials, have an admissions interview, and receive an acceptance notice, all on the same day and before the start of the new year. In addition, students who are eligible for a scholarship are offered one at that time.

On the day of their visit, students and their families receive information about the College, tour the campus (including the residence halls), attend a class, and then have lunch in the student dining hall. They also meet individually with an admissions officer. At the end of the day, students receive the College's decision regarding their application. Immediate Decision Days are scheduled in October, November, and December.

The College hosts open house programs during the fall and spring that give students and their families the opportunity to learn about academic programs, admissions, and financial aid; to meet faculty and staff members and students; and to tour the campus. Students are encouraged to visit during these special events. Weekday tours of the campus are available as well and personal interviews are available during the Immediate Decision Days in the fall. Interested students should contact the Office of Admissions at 201-684-7300 or 7301 or visit Ramapo's Web site for further details about campus visits.

Application and Information

Students may enter in September or January. Freshmen are encouraged to apply during the fall of their senior year. Applications for the freshman year are accepted until March 15. Applications from transfer students are accepted until May 1. Applying for admission as a matriculating (degree-seeking) student involves completing an application, having the high school and college (if a transfer student) forward transcripts, and sending a $45 nonrefundable fee to the admissions office. Students may obtain the forms and instructions by visiting or contacting the admissions office. Admission decisions are made on a rolling basis. The College Board Candidates Reply Date of May 1 is used for confirming an offer of admission.

For a catalog, application forms, and additional information, including current costs, students should contact:

Director of Admissions
Ramapo College of New Jersey
505 Ramapo Valley Road
Mahwah, New Jersey 07430
Telephone: 201-684-7300 or 7301
E-mail: admissions@ramapo.edu
World Wide Web: http://www.ramapo.edu

The new Russ and Angelica Berrie Center for the Performing and Visual Arts on the campus of Ramapo College of New Jersey.

RANDOLPH–MACON COLLEGE
ASHLAND, VIRGINIA

The College

Randolph-Macon is an independent liberal arts college for men and women founded in 1830. With 1,145 students, the College has deliberately maintained a limited enrollment so that it can give its students the opportunity for dialogue and more personal relationships that only a midsize college can provide. Randolph-Macon is fully accredited by the Southern Association of Colleges and Schools and is historically affiliated with the United Methodist Church.

Students come mostly from Virginia and nearby mid-Atlantic states, but usually about thirty-five states, the District of Columbia, and fourteen countries are represented in the student body. There is diversity among the students, and an atmosphere of informality and friendliness is evident. Students indicate that they are attracted to the College primarily because of its size, the quality of its academic program, and its supportive, unpretentious atmosphere.

The campus, situated on 110 wooded acres in the town of Ashland, is both convenient and spacious. Most students reside in dormitories, fraternity houses, sorority houses, new townhouse apartments, and special interest houses. The Frank E. Brown Campus Center provides centralized facilities for a wide variety of student activities, including student government and the literary staffs, and also houses the bookstore, photography laboratory, game room, post office, and snack bar. Other noteworthy facilities include the McGraw-Page Library, the spacious Estes Dining Hall, the Crenshaw Gymnasium, the Center for Counseling and Career Planning, the Keeble Observatory with its 12-inch reflecting telescope, and several historic buildings, including the beautifully renovated Washington-Franklin Hall. The new 73,000-square-foot Brock Sports and Recreation Center contains a field house for basketball, volleyball, badminton, and other activities; a six-lane, 25-yard pool; three racquetball courts; one squash court; a 4,000-square-foot fitness room; an indoor track; an aerobics room; a climbing wall; and a sauna and locker room for students and faculty members. A new performing arts center is planned.

Location

Ashland, the home of Randolph-Macon for more than a century, is a pleasant residential town with a population of 6,000. Two shopping centers three blocks from campus offer a variety of stores. Daily Amtrak service is available just one block from the edge of campus. Ashland is 15 miles north of Richmond, the capital of Virginia, and 90 miles south of Washington, D.C. This proximity allows access to excellent facilities, such as the Smithsonian Institution, the Library of Congress, the Virginia Museum of Fine Arts, the Virginia State Library, and other educational resources. Shuttle service to downtown Richmond is available. These nearby cities are also popular sites for the College's fast-growing internship program. Midway between the Atlantic Ocean and the Blue Ridge Mountains, the College also provides students with diverse recreational opportunities.

Majors and Degrees

The B.A. and B.S. degrees are offered in the following fields: accounting, art history, arts management, biology, chemistry, classical studies (Greek and Latin), computer science, drama, economics, economics-business, English, environmental studies, French, German, Greek, history, international relations, international studies, Latin, mathematics, music, philosophy, physics, political science, psychology, religious studies, sociology, Spanish, studio art, and women's studies. In addition, students may formally select a minor field from the above areas. Additional minors are offered in Asian studies, black studies, astrophysics, elementary and secondary education, ehtics, Irish studies, journalism, and speech communication.

The College offers preprofessional studies for such fields as business, dentistry, law, medicine, the ministry, and teaching, as well as preparation for graduate school in other major fields of study. A state-approved teacher education program leads to certification for teaching both in elementary and secondary schools. Dual-degree programs in engineering and forestry enable students to spend the first three years at Randolph-Macon and the final two years at a recognized college of engineering or forestry. In addition, students who follow a prescribed course of study at Randolph-Macon can obtain a master's degree in accounting at Virginia Commonwealth University in one year instead of the usual two years.

Academic Program

The College offers a liberal arts curriculum that is designed to allow students considerable freedom in planning their own program, while assuring them that they will acquire not only the breadth of knowledge traditionally emphasized in a liberal education but also a sound foundation in a particular field. There is a flexible system of collegiate requirements in English, mathematics, a foreign language, and physical education. In addition, all students take courses in literature, the natural sciences, the social sciences, the fine arts, philosophy or religion, history, computer literacy, and oral communication.

The academic calendar is on the 4-1-4 plan, featuring a one-course term in January. During the January term, students may take special-topic courses, traditional and interdisciplinary courses, and travel-study courses in the United States and abroad, or they may participate in off-campus internships and field-study programs. Internships and other field-study experiences enable students to test classroom theory in practical situations. Internships are offered in Richmond, Washington, D.C., New York City (at the United Nations), and other locations both domestic and abroad. Independent study and senior project options are also available.

Off-Campus Arrangements

International study opportunities are offered through Randolph-Macon programs in France, Spain, England, Japan, Germany, Ireland, Italy, Korea, Mexico, Brazil, and Greece. Study abroad in other locations can be arranged through other institutions. The College is a member of a consortium composed of seven private colleges in Virginia. Students may apply to spend a term at one of the other participating institutions, taking advantage of special programs or courses offered at these colleges. The other colleges in the consortium are Washington and Lee, Hampden-Sydney, Mary Baldwin, Hollins, Sweet Briar, and Randolph-Macon Woman's College.

Academic Facilities

The multimillion-dollar Copley Science Center houses classrooms, study rooms, research and teaching laboratory facilities, and an expanded computer center featuring a DEC VAX super minicomputer and several SUN Workstations. In addition, a personal computer center and microcomputers in other campus locations provide students with access to more than 200 computers for various word processing and programming needs. The modern McGraw-Page Library, the College's main library and principal research center, currently contains 171,531 volumes and subscribes to 1,039 periodicals. Open stacks are maintained except in the special collections. The library also provides an audiovisual center, a personal computer lab, and space for 100,000 additional volumes.

Costs

College fees for 2000–01 total $23,255. This includes tuition, fees, and room and board. Approximately $600 will pay for a student's books for a year if he or she buys them new. Transportation and personal expenses of up to $900 should also be anticipated. Members of fraternities and sororities must pay initiation fees as well as monthly dues.

Financial Aid

The College administers a diversified program of scholarships, grants, loans, student employment, and other forms of aid. Financial aid comes from a variety of sources, including federal (Federal Pell Grants, Federal Supplemental Educational Opportunity Grants, Federal Perkins Loans, and Federal Work-Study awards), state, College, and private funds. Academic scholarships (Randolph-Macon College Scholarships) are offered to outstanding students, and additional grants and scholarships are awarded on the basis of exceptional achievement and special talents. However, most financial aid is awarded on the basis of demonstrated need. Applicants should file the Free Application for Federal Student Aid no later than February 1. Virginia residents attending Randolph-Macon are eligible to receive the Virginia Tuition Assistance Grant (TAG), which amounts to $2700 in 1999–2000. The College mails TAG applications to all Virginia residents who have been admitted. Most on-campus job opportunities are reserved for students in the Federal Work-Study program; however, a limited number of student assistantships are available through the various academic departments and other College offices. The Financial Aid Office also provides a student referral service for part-time jobs with employers within walking distance of the College. Inquiries regarding financial aid should be addressed to the director of financial aid.

Faculty

As an undergraduate institution, Randolph-Macon offers students full access to its teaching faculty. Ninety percent of the faculty members have earned the doctorate or highest appropriate degree in their field. The student-faculty ratio is 11:1. Almost all professors teach classes at all levels. Thus, a freshman is as likely as a senior to encounter the most distinguished and experienced members of the faculty.

Student Government

At Randolph-Macon the principal governing and coordinating agency for students is the Student Government Association (SGA). It represents student interests on College committees that deal with the curriculum, academic policies, orientation, and college life. In addition, the SGA charters and allocates funds for student organizations and activities. Together with the Committee on Assemblies and Special Events, SGA plans and sponsors social, cultural, and educational events throughout the year for the entire College community.

Admission Requirements

The Admissions Committee places primary emphasis on the applicant's secondary school record, scores on the SAT I or the ACT, the secondary school counselor's recommendation, personal characteristics, and evidence of leadership and involvement in extracurricular activities. The submission of SAT II: Subject Test scores for Writing, Mathematics, and a foreign language, although not required, is suggested.

In administration of its admission policies, educational policies, financial aid programs, athletics, and other College-administered programs and policies, Randolph-Macon College does not discriminate on the basis of race, color, religion, national or ethnic origin, handicap, or sex.

Applications should be received by March 1. Applications received after that date are considered as long as space is available. Students who have applied by March 1 are informed of the admission decision no later than April 1. The College also offers a first choice, early decision plan through which well-qualified applicants may apply for early notification of acceptance. Students may now apply online via the Internet.

Application and Information

For more information, prospective students should contact:

Dean of Admissions
Randolph-Macon College
P.O. Box 5005
Ashland, Virginia 23005-5005
Telephone: 804-752-7305
               800-888-1762 (toll-free)
E-mail: admiss_office@rmc.edu
World Wide Web: http://www.rmc.edu

Randolph-Macon's 110-acre campus has been planned to complement the educational program and enhance student life.

RANDOLPH–MACON WOMAN'S COLLEGE
LYNCHBURG, VIRGINIA

The College
Randolph-Macon Woman's College (R-MWC) was the first women's college to be accredited by the Southern Association of Colleges and Schools and the first southern women's college to be granted a Phi Beta Kappa charter. Academic excellence through the liberal arts and an emphasis on individual learning continue to be Randolph-Macon's top priorities. The College's enduring commitment to women's education has fostered strong programs in career development and in alumnae networking.

The current enrollment is about 700 women. Students come from more than forty states and twenty-eight countries. Surveys show that many choose R-MWC for its academic reputation and for its warm, friendly atmosphere. There are six residence halls on the 100-acre campus, housing 90 percent of the students. The College's location near the Blue Ridge Mountains provides ample recreational opportunities, and proximity to neighboring men's colleges and major universities enhances the social life on and off campus. Most students are involved in at least one of the many clubs or organizations and activities, which include campus publications, Chorale and Songshine, the Dance Group, political organizations, language clubs, theater, religious and volunteer organizations, an outdoor club, and a nationally ranked riding program. Intercollegiate sports include basketball, field hockey, lacrosse, riding, soccer, softball, swimming, tennis, and volleyball. Rugby is a club sport. Courses are also offered in a variety of activities and sports, including aerobics, fitness walking, golf, kickboxing, weight training, and yoga.

To supplement the academic program and student activities, the College brings noted speakers, performers, and artists to the campus, including Boston Globe columnist Ellen Goodman, architect scholar Vincent Scully, photographer Sally Mann, and the former president of the Philippines, Corazon Aquino. In addition, various concerts, plays, films, and exhibitions are presented throughout the year.

Location
R-MWC is located in a beautiful residential area of Lynchburg, a city of 70,000 people in the foothills of the Blue Ridge Mountains. Shopping areas are convenient to the campus, and public transportation is readily available. Lynchburg is within easy driving distance of Washington, D.C., and Richmond, Virginia.

Majors and Degrees
Randolph-Macon Woman's College offers programs of study leading to the Bachelor of Arts (A.B.) degree in twenty-three fields: art (history, museum studies, and studio), biology, chemistry, classics (archaeology, classical civilization, and classical languages), communication, dance, economics, English (creative writing and literature), French, German studies, history, international relations, mathematics, music (history, performance, and theory), philosophy, physics, politics, psychology, religion, Russian studies, sociology-anthropology, Spanish, and theater. A Bachelor of Science (B.S.) degree may be elected by students majoring in biology, chemistry, mathematics, or physics. The double major is a popular option, and there is also the opportunity to devise a special major such as comparative literature, environmental studies, or mathematical biology. In addition, there is the education program, which offers courses that meet the requirements for primary and secondary education certification. Travel/study opportunities and visiting scholar programs augment the international curriculum.

Every student has the option of selecting up to two concentrations in addition to her major. Concentrations are offered in all of the major fields as well as the interdisciplinary areas of American arts, Asian studies, British history and literature, the classical tradition, French civilization, French for commerce, human movement, human services, journalism, Renaissance studies, symbol and myth, and women's studies. Students declare majors and concentrations in the spring of the sophomore year.

R-MWC has cooperative 3-2 programs in nursing with Johns Hopkins University and a program in public health administration with the University of Rochester.

Academic Program
R-MWC's academic program offers the student both flexibility and choice. Through consultation with her faculty adviser, each student develops a four-year plan to integrate academic interests with career planning, leadership, and volunteer activities. The academic requirements encourage students to pursue a well-rounded curriculum in the liberal arts. A student selects courses from at least four different departments during each of her first two semesters at the College. At least 124 semester hours of credit are required for both the A.B. and B.S. degrees, including a minimum of 24 hours and no more than 62 hours in the major field.

The College operates on a traditional semester system, with self-scheduled exams given before the December vacation and at the end of the second semester in May. Most classes meet either two or three times a week. R-MWC provides maximum opportunity for independent study and research.

The collegewide Writing Program includes formal evaluation of student writing skills in all courses at the end of every semester. There are elective courses in intermediate composition and in academic writing as well as writing-intensive sections across the curriculum. First-year students may be granted exemption from the English composition degree requirement on the basis of their entering record (usually Advanced Placement examination scores).

Sixty-five percent of R-MWC graduates continue their studies beyond the undergraduate level within five years of graduation. Special advisers at the College counsel students who are preparing for medical, veterinary, or law school or other specialized graduate study. Research is encouraged in the various areas of academic concentration, and in the senior year students may pursue honors work involving the presentation and defense of a thesis under the supervision of a faculty member. Sixty-seven percent of all seniors had their education broadened through internships or special summer experiences for academic credit.

Off-Campus Arrangements
Internships provide an exciting opportunity for students to gain valuable work experience in area hospitals, veterinary clinics, schools, law firms, industries, courts, social service agencies, and radio and television stations. The College maintains a listing of nearly 1,000 internship opportunities through which students may earn up to 6 hours of credit toward the Randolph-Macon degree.

More than one fourth of the juniors study abroad. Approximately 30 juniors majoring in all fields participate in the College's Junior Year Abroad program at the University of Reading, England. In addition, students have studied recently in Argentina, Australia, the Czech Republic, France, Japan, Russia, Scotland, and Spain. Other students participate in programs sponsored by other colleges. Students of the classics may spend a summer working at an archaeological dig in Carthage, Tunisia.

Programs in this country include the Washington Semester at American University. Randolph-Macon participates in the seven-college consortium of colleges in Virginia, along with Hampden-Sydney College, Hollins College, Mary Baldwin College, Randolph-Macon College (in Ashland, Virginia), Sweet Briar College, and Washington and Lee University. The local Tri-College Consortium of R-MWC, Lynchburg College, and Sweet Briar College increases the diversity of courses open to students.

The College's spring semester American Culture Program offers a rigorous, interdisciplinary immersion into the study of American culture both on campus and at key locations in Virginia and across the nation. The program capitalizes on the College's central location in historic Virginia as well as its own outstanding Maier Museum of Art's collection of American art. This one-semester program is open to students from Randolph-Macon Woman's College as well as to undergraduate students, both men and women, from other institutions.

Academic Facilities

The Lipscomb Library contains 168,000 volumes, 860 current periodical titles, and periodical back files on microform. The Martin Science Building has been completely renovated to incorporate state-of-the-art laboratory design and instrumentation, enhanced facilities for student-faculty research, and multimedia instructional centers. Equipment and resources readily available for student use include an FT-NMR and computer-driven IR and UV spectrometers, exceptional herbarium and fossil collections, a greenhouse, and nature preserves. The Winfree Observatory houses a 14-inch pier-mounted telescope equipped with a computer-operated CCD camera for variable star research to support instruction in physics and astronomy. The Ethyl Science and Mathematics Resource Center in Martin offers a networked computer cluster with specific software for science and math applications and library, study, and lounge facilities. A satellite telecommunications program with the University of Virginia has been established to broaden learning opportunities.

Language laboratories, art studios, a communications media center, and a theater-auditorium are located in the Leggett Building. The College's Maier Museum of Art houses an outstanding collection of nineteenth- and twentieth-century American paintings and is one of only two such museums in the country. Presser Hall, the music building, includes a concert auditorium, studios, listening rooms, and practice rooms. The Learning Resources Center and the Writing Lab offer academic support and tutorial services related to study skills, word processing, and the writing program.

Macintosh and PC-compatible classrooms in Main Hall support general word processing, spreadsheet, and database applications; software tailored for various academic disciplines, including music, theater design, psychology, and the sciences; and Internet access. These facilities are available for individual student projects as well as classroom instruction and assignments. Campuswide networking, including student-room access, was completed in 1995. The College's World Wide Web site offers general information and frequent updates of campus activities.

Costs

The 2000–01 comprehensive fee for room, board, and tuition is $24,460. The College recommends a budget of $1000 for books, supplies, fees, and personal expenses, excluding travel costs.

Financial Aid

R-MWC administers almost $10 million in aid each year through a comprehensive program of financial assistance, which includes merit-based scholarships, need-based grants, low-interest student loans, and campus employment. All students are encouraged to apply for financial aid, even those who assume that they are ineligible for assistance due to family income level. Merit scholarships, which range from $4000 per year to full tuition, are renewable for four years. The student's application for admission serves as her application for all merit scholarships, with the exception of the full-tuition Gottwald Scholarship. More than 95 percent of R-MWC students receive financial assistance of some kind. The average need-based financial aid package is $15,000. To apply for need-based aid, students are encouraged to submit the Free Application for Federal Student Aid (FAFSA) by March 1. International students are eligible for merit scholarships, which range from $4000 to $10,000 per year.

Faculty

Approximately 96 percent of the full-time teaching faculty members hold a Ph.D. degree or terminal degree; about half of the faculty members are women. The faculty-student ratio of 1:9 encourages individual rapport between faculty members and students and contributes to the close community that typifies Randolph-Macon. Faculty members are dedicated primarily to teaching, with secondary emphasis on research and publication.

Student Government

The honor system is a vital part of college life at R-MWC and allows students to live and study in an atmosphere of integrity and trust. Each student is a member of the Student Government, which voices student opinion, oversees student activities, and makes policy through the elected representatives. Students serve on almost all College committees.

Admission Requirements

A minimum of 16 academic high school units is recommended and should be distributed as follows: 4 units of English, 3 units of mathematics, 3–4 units of a foreign language, 2 units of laboratory science, 2 units of social studies, and sufficient electives from these areas to make up the recommended total. Because of the flexible nature of the College's curriculum, favorable consideration may be given to students whose high school preparation departs from the recommendations outlined above. Each applicant must have maintained a good academic record and must submit scores on the SAT I or ACT. SAT II: Subject Tests are recommended for placement. R-MWC readily accepts the Common Application. An online application is available on the College's Web site.

Application and Information

Early decision candidates should apply by November 15 of the senior year in secondary school and will receive notification from the College about December 15. Candidates for general admission must apply by March 1 in order to receive preferential consideration; they will receive notification at the time their files are complete, beginning in late January. A $25 application fee must accompany the application for admission, but this fee may be waived in cases of hardship at the request of the student and the recommendation of her high school counselor. R-MWC also participates in the College Board test fee waiver program.

For more information, students should contact:

Director of Admissions
Randolph-Macon Woman's College
2500 Rivermont Avenue
Lynchburg, Virginia 24503
Telephone: 804-947-8100
           800-745-7692 (toll-free)
E-mail: admissions@rmwc.edu
World Wide Web: http://www.rmwc.edu

REED COLLEGE
PORTLAND, OREGON

The College
For its 1,300 students and 125 faculty members, Reed College is foremost an intellectual community. Since its founding in 1909, Reed has attracted students with a high degree of self-discipline and a genuine enthusiasm for academic work and intellectual challenge. Reed attracts a geographically diversified student body: four fifths of Reed's students come from outside the Northwest, with more than 20 percent from the Northeast and 5 percent from outside the United States.

Campus social opportunities are open to all, with no closed clubs or organizations and no sororities or fraternities. Community life is full of activity and variety, with more than fifty student organizations. Club sports are competitive in a number of areas, but Reed is a college where varsity sports have always been viewed with skepticism. Fitness and development of lifelong skills take precedence over competition.

Location
Reed's 100-acre wooded campus is located in a quiet, suburban setting with easy access to downtown Portland. The nearby ocean and mountains of the Pacific Northwest provide a balance to the social and cultural offerings of the greater Portland metropolitan area.

Majors and Degrees
Reed awards the Bachelor of Arts degree in a wide variety of fields, based on work in traditional departments or in interdisciplinary combinations. Students may select from the following: American studies, anthropology, art, biochemistry and molecular biology, biology, chemistry, chemistry-physics, Chinese, classics, classics-religion, dance-theater, economics, English literature, French literature, German literature, history, history-literature, international and comparative policy studies, linguistics, literature-philosophy, literature-theater, mathematics, mathematics-economics, mathematics-physics, music, philosophy, philosophy-mathematics, philosophy-religion, physics, political science, psychology, religion, Russian literature, sociology, Spanish literature, and theater.

Students may design interdisciplinary majors. The approval of special programs that link two or more disciplines is reviewed by the student's adviser and the departments concerned.

Reed offers several combined 3-2 programs, which allow the student to earn both a bachelor's degree from Reed and a professional degree from the cooperating institution. Science programs and institutions include applied physics and electronic science (Oregon Graduate Institute); engineering (California Institute of Technology, Columbia University, Rensselaer Polytechnic Institute, and Washington University); and forestry and environmental sciences (Duke University). The College also has combined programs in fine arts (Pacific Northwest College of Art) and in business (University of Oregon).

Academic Program
Hallmarks of academic life at Reed include the demanding, small group conference method of teaching and its reliance on active student participation, a de-emphasis of grades, a yearlong interdisciplinary humanities program, and an integrated academic program that balances the breadth of traditional course content and distribution requirements with flexibility in designing an in-depth senior thesis. Learning and the development of skills in preparation for a life of learning take precedence over the mere memorization of facts. In addition to fulfilling the requirements for the major, taking the humanities course, and writing the senior thesis, students must satisfy a distributional requirement, consisting of two core classes from each of the following academic divisions: literature, philosophy, and the arts; history, social sciences, and psychology; the natural sciences; and math, foreign language, logic, and linguistics.

Off-Campus Arrangements
Reed participates in domestic exchange programs with Howard University in Washington, D.C., and with Sarah Lawrence College in New York. Individual students may arrange independent study plans in consultation with appropriate faculty members, the director for off-campus studies, and the registrar. Reed provides study-abroad opportunities for students, including institutional exchanges with the University of East Anglia, Université de Rennes II, Capital Normal University in Beijing, Hebrew University of Jerusalem, and Tübingen University. Additional study programs include the Russian language studies program in Moscow or St. Petersburg, the Reed Munich program at the University of Munich, the University of Costa Rica program in San José, the Budapest semester in mathematics in Hungary, and the classical studies program in Rome.

Academic Facilities
Students have access to Reed's substantial library collection (450,000 volumes, 1,600 periodicals, and 300,000 government documents) by searching the online catalog in the library or from any computer on the campus network. Through its participation in PORTALS (Portland Area Library System), Reed provides online access to other library catalogs and databases. Students may borrow materials directly from academic libraries in the Portland area, and they have access to collections worldwide through interlibrary loan. A recent $7-million addition to the Reed library accommodates a first-rate art gallery, a language lab, and a music listening facility. The Reed library is open 18 hours most days (24 hours a day during examinations).

Computer technology is highly developed at Reed and widely used for instruction, research, and communication by all members of the College community. A state-of-the-art campus network links all residence halls, classrooms, laboratories, offices, and the library to one another and to the global Internet. A recent $14.5-million science facility project enabled Reed to construct one of the best undergraduate chemistry facilities in the nation, to make major improvements to the biology/physics complex, and to completely renovate the psychology complex. Reed's research nuclear reactor (the only reactor in the country that is staffed primarily by undergraduates) and radiochemistry lab is actively used for student research, instruction, and training. For those interested in the arts, the campus houses studio art and performing arts facilities, twenty instrumental practice rooms, a computer music laboratory, a recording system, and an 800-seat auditorium. Other popular facilities include a radio station and a modern sports center.

Costs
Tuition and fees for 2000–01 are $25,020 and room and board are $6820. The cost of books and incidental expenses averages $1500, bringing the yearly total cost to approximately $33,340.

Financial Aid
Nearly half of Reed students receive financial assistance from the College. A full need-based financial aid program makes Reed accessible to students from a wide range of economic backgrounds. The College guarantees to meet the full demonstrated need of all continuing students in good academic standing and who file their financial aid applications on time. In addition, during their first two semesters, approximately 50

percent of the freshmen and transfer students receive financial assistance equal to their demonstrated need. Admission decisions are separate from financial aid procedures, and students are admitted regardless of ability to pay. Reed's own funds are the primary source of grants to students. The College budgeted more than $8.9 million for this purpose in 1999–2000, with individual awards ranging from $930 to $26,590. Reed also administers federal grants and a variety of other awards. Perkins Loans and other federally subsidized loans are available, along with campus employment and work-study programs. The size of a financial aid award is based upon analysis of the student's need. The financial aid program includes grants, loans, and work opportunities.

Faculty

All classes at Reed are taught by professors, 85 percent of whom hold the highest degree in their field. Reed students point to the opportunity to work closely with faculty members as one of the great benefits of a Reed education. Reed faculty members point to the opportunity to work with students who are serious scholars as one of the great benefits of teaching at Reed. Faculty members commit themselves primarily to teaching, with scholarly and scientific research furthering this primary goal; they view students as partners in learning, often serving as coauthors and coinvestigators on professional papers and research projects. This close association is due, in large part, to a 11:1 student-faculty ratio, and the one-on-one relationship between thesis adviser (a professor) and student during the senior year.

Student Government

The Student Senate is the central body in student governance. The Senate consists of the student body president, vice president, and 8 student representatives, all elected by the students. Its two primary functions are to allocate student body funds and to represent student interests and concerns to the faculty, administration, and the Board of Trustees. The Senate distributes approximately $80,000 each semester to the many student organizations on campus. As agreed under the community constitution, students participate fully in discussions and decisions on a wide variety of issues. The Student Committee on Academic Policy and Planning participates in debate about the curriculum at Reed; many other committees, from the Library Board to the Reactor Committee, have substantial student input. The Senate and student body president make all student appointments to such committees.

Admission Requirements

Reed welcomes applications from freshman and transfer candidates who are genuinely committed to the pursuit of a liberal arts education and a rigorous academic program. Those applicants are admitted who, in the view of the Committee on Admission, are most likely to become successful members of and contribute significantly to the Reed community. The College is committed to maintaining a student body distinguished by its intellectual passion, yet diversified in its range of backgrounds, interests, and talents.

Admission decisions are based on many integrated factors, but academic accomplishments and talents are given the greatest weight in the selection process. A strong secondary school preparation, including honors and advanced courses where available, will improve a student's chances for admission. Such a program usually would include 4 years of English, at least 3 years of a foreign or classical language, 3 to 4 years of mathematics, 3 to 4 years of science, and 3 to 4 years of history or social studies. Given the wide variation in high school programs and quality, however, there are no fixed requirements for secondary school courses. Applicants are expected to have obtained a secondary school diploma prior to enrollment, although exceptions are occasionally made. There are no "cutoff points" for high school or college grades or for examination scores.

Reed recognizes the qualities of character—in particular, motivation, intellectual curiosity, individual responsibility, and social consciousness—as important considerations in the selection process, beyond a demonstrated commitment to academic excellence. Thus, the Committee on Admission looks for students whose accomplishments and interests in various fields of endeavor will contribute to the overall liveliness of the Reed community. Personal interviews, either on campus or off campus, are not a requirement in the admission process but are strongly recommended whenever possible. Applications for early decision should be submitted by November 15 (Option I) or January 2 (Option II); regular freshman admission by January 15; and transfer candidates by November 15 (spring semester) or March 1 (fall semester).

Application and Information

The Office of Admission is open Monday through Friday, from 8:30 a.m. until 5 p.m. (Pacific time) all year, except for major holidays. For further information or to arrange a campus tour, overnight stay, information session, or interview, students should call or write:

Office of Admission
Reed College
3203 Southeast Woodstock Boulevard
Portland, Oregon 97202-8199

Telephone: 503-777-7511
           800-547-4750 (toll-free)
Fax: 503-777-7553
E-mail: admission@reed.edu
World Wide Web: http://www.reed.edu

Reed College—where students enjoy their individuality as much as they do their academics.

Peterson's Guide to Four-Year Colleges 2001   www.petersons.com   2315

REGENTS COLLEGE
ALBANY, NEW YORK

The College

A recognized leader in the field of nontraditional college education for more than twenty-five years, Regents College has enabled more than 83,000 individuals—primarily working adults—to earn accredited associate and baccalaureate degrees in liberal arts, business, nursing, and technology. Believing that what individuals know is more important than where or how they learned it, Regents College pioneered the process of knowledge evaluation and assessment. The College has no residency requirement, and its programs are available worldwide. Most Regents College students are returning to college to complete an education begun elsewhere. The College accepts the broadest possible array of prior college-level credit in transfer, including classroom and distance courses from accredited colleges, proficiency examinations, and accredited on-the-job or military training. Regents College faculty members, drawn from other colleges and universities, design the curriculum and determine how credit can be earned. Professional academic advisers help students design individualized study plans using college courses, examinations, and other sources of credit to complete their degree requirements. Students work at their own pace while maintaining full-time work schedules and family and civic responsibilities.

Regents College is accredited by the Commission on Higher Education of the Middle States Association of Colleges and Schools. The Commission on Higher Education is an institutional accrediting agency recognized by the U.S. Department of Education and the Council for Higher Education Accreditation (CHEA). The associate and baccalaureate programs in nursing at Regents College are accredited by the National League for Nursing Accrediting Commission (NLNAC). The Bachelor of Science degrees in nuclear engineering technology and electronics engineering technology are accredited by the Technology Accreditation Commission (TAC) of the Accreditation Board for Engineering and Technology, Inc. (ABET). The NLNAC and TAC of ABET are specialized accrediting agencies recognized by the U.S. Department of Education. All academic programs are registered (i.e., approved) by the New York State Education Department. Regents College Examinations are recognized by the American Council on Education (ACE), Center for Adult Learning and Educational Credentials, for the award of college-level credit. Regents College examinations in nursing are the only nursing exams that are approved by ACE.

Regents College has approximately 17,000 students currently enrolled. Approximately 5,000 graduate each year, many going directly on to graduate school. Students live in every state in the United States and many other countries. The average student age is 40, but some are as "young" as 80. More than 81 percent are working adults employed full-time. Nearly 23 percent of currently enrolled students belong to groups historically underserved by higher education.

Location

Regents College is located wherever students seek degrees. Because its program is totally portable, the College moves with students whenever and wherever they move. The administrative offices of Regents College are located in Albany, the capital of New York State, and once a year the College holds a formal commencement ceremony to recognize all who have completed degree programs that year. Proud of their accomplishments, many students travel great distances to participate.

Majors and Degrees

The College offers thirty associate and baccalaureate degrees in its liberal arts, business, nursing, and technology programs as well as a Master of Arts degree in liberal studies and a Master of Science degree in nursing.

The most flexible degrees are those in the liberal arts program. The College offers 60-credit associate degrees that articulate with the baccalaureate degrees. At the baccalaureate level, a student may earn either a Bachelor of Arts or a Bachelor of Science degree in liberal studies or in a concentration. Concentrations include area studies, chemistry, communication, economics, geography, geology, history, literature in English, mathematics, music, philosophy, physics, political science, psychology, sociology, and world language and literature. The baccalaureate degrees require 120 semester hours of credit, at least 30 of which must be upper level. There are arts and sciences requirements in general education, written English, humanities, and quantitative reasoning. The baccalaureate degree also requires that students demonstrate depth of knowledge in two separate disciplines through the accumulation of 12 credits (3 at the upper level) in each. For those completing a concentration, the concentration will satisfy one of the depth requirements. There are no time limits on the transfer of credit earned in the past.

In the business program, the College offers two 60-credit associate degree programs—an Associate in Applied Science in administrative/management studies designed to meet the needs of those with military backgrounds and an Associate in Science in business that articulates with the baccalaureate degrees. The B.S. degrees require 120 credits and are offered in the fields of accounting (general or NYS CPA track), finance, general business, international business, management information systems, management of human resources, marketing, and operations management. In addition to required arts and sciences courses, students must complete a written English requirement and examinations or course work in macroeconomics, microeconomics, mathematics at the level of precalculus or higher, and statistics. Required core business courses at the baccalaureate level include introduction to accounting I and II, introduction to business law, computers, principles of management, principles of marketing, financial management, production/operations management, business policy, ethics, and organizational behavior. For credit applied to the business component, there is a twenty-year time limit on transfer credit.

The undergraduate nursing program offers two associate degrees in nursing—an Associate in Science and an Associate in Applied Science—and a Bachelor of Science in Nursing. An associate degree program is divided into two components: general education (30 semester hours) and nursing (36 semester hours). The general education component is very flexible so that adult students may build the degree to meet their interests and needs. It includes requirements in anatomy, physiology, microbiology, life span developmental psychology, and sociology. Students can meet these requirements through classroom or distance courses from regionally accredited colleges or through proficiency examinations. The nursing component comprises six written Regents College Examinations and one performance examination. In the baccalaureate program, students may elect to complete a minor in biology, psychology, sociology, or human resource management. Baccalaureate students complete a 69-credit general education component that includes requirements in written English, humanities, anatomy, physiology, microbiology, psychology, sociology, and statistics. The 51-credit nursing component of the baccalaureate program comprises six written Regents College Examinations and four performance examinations. To test the clinical competencies of its nursing students, Regents College pioneered the creation of rigorous performance examinations. College courses in nursing and nursing examinations must have been completed within five years of enrollment.

Regents College nursing degree programs are specifically designed to serve individuals with significant background or experience in clinically oriented health-care disciplines. Therefore, admission to the programs is open to registered nurses, licensed practical/vocational nurses, paramedics, emergency medical technicians, military service corpsmen, individuals who hold degrees in clinically oriented health-care fields in which they have had the opportunity to provide direct patient care (i.e., physicians, respiratory therapists, chiropractors, and physicians' assistants), or individuals who have completed 50 percent or more of the clinical nursing courses in registered nursing education programs. Exceptions may be made for individuals who do not meet these qualifications but who can document significant clinical background.

In its technology program, the College offers the Associate in Occupational Studies in aviation (60 credits), the Associate in Applied Science in aviation studies (60 credits), and the Associate in Applied Science in technical studies with specialty (60 credits), all designed to meet the needs of those with military backgrounds. In addition, the College offers Associate in Science degrees in computer software (60 credits), electronics technology (64 credits), nuclear technology (60 credits), and technology with specialty (60 credits), which articulate with the relevant baccalaureate degrees. On the baccalaureate level, the College offers degrees in computer information systems (120 credits), computer technology (124 credits), electronics engineering technology (124 credits), nuclear engineering technology (124 credits), and technology with specialty (120 credits). Of the total, 60 credits must be earned in the arts and sciences and must include examinations or course work in written English, humanities, social sciences/history, natural sciences, and mathematics, depending on the degree selected. Each degree also has core requirements in the technology component. Time limits apply to some credit applied toward the technology component.

Academic Program

Regents College has demanding academic requirements, but its programs are self-paced and highly flexible. Most students bring prior college credit with them when they enroll. Upon enrollment, students receive an initial evaluation of all prior college-level learning, which includes credit for regionally accredited college course work earned in the classroom or by distance study such as correspondence, video, or computer courses. Students also transfer credit earned through proficiency examinations such as Regents College Examinations, the College-Level Examination Program (CLEP) Subject Examinations, the Graduate Record Examinations (GRE) Subject Tests, and DANTES Subject Standardized Tests. Other credit sources include military and corporate training evaluated by the American Council on Education as college-level and certain certificate and licensure programs.

Thousands of people take and pass Regents College Examinations every year, using the results to obtain credit or advanced placement at colleges and universities, to apply credit toward Regents College degree requirements, and for other purposes. Examinations are available in the arts and sciences, business, education, and nursing. Several carry upper-level credit.

Upon enrollment, students work with professional academic advisers by phone, mail, and e-mail to plan how they will complete their degree programs. They use not only the sources listed above, but also performance examinations, portfolio assessments, and special assessments. The Regents College/Peterson's Web site at http://www.lifelonglearning.com offers free access to DistanceLearn, a searchable database of more than 10,500 college-level courses and proficiency examinations available at a distance that can be used by enrolled students to fulfill Regents College degree requirements. The courses listed on DistanceLearn are available in several different delivery systems, including Internet, video, computer, and traditional print-based correspondence format. Students in the nursing programs may also contact nurse educators for advice and guidance about preparing for the clinical performance examinations.

Off-Campus Arrangements

To facilitate the academic work of their employees, some employers enter into agreements with Regents College to form study and advisement groups. The College also assists businesses that wish to have their training evaluated for college-level credit by the American Council on Education or New York State Board of Regents National Program on Noncollegiate Sponsored Instruction (National PONSI). In addition, the College has formed collaborations with some community colleges to help students to continue using the community college facilities while pursuing baccalaureate degrees.

Academic Facilities

Regents College, as an assessment institution, does not offer classes on-site. The College helps students to locate appropriate credit sources either in their local community or through distance providers and, through Regents College Examinations, offers opportunities to earn college-level credit that is applicable toward Regents College degrees and accepted by nearly 1,000 other colleges and universities as well.

Costs

Regents College charges a $685 (associate degree programs) or $800 (baccalaureate degree programs) fee for enrollment (which covers initial evaluation of a student's existing academic records and advisement and program planning services for one year), a $325 (associate degree programs) or $350 (baccalaureate degree programs) student service annual fee for each year after the first that covers the ongoing evaluation of academic records submitted by a student and academic and program planning services for an additional twelve months, and a $410 (associate degree programs) or $440 (baccalaureate degree programs) fee for a final evaluation and verification of all academic records prior to program completion and graduation. Different fees and fee structures apply to military students and to the RN-MSN and graduate programs. Detailed fee schedules are available in hard copy and on the College's Web site. Additional costs depend on the amount of credit students need to earn and what credit sources they choose. Proficiency examinations are typically the least expensive mode of earning credit. Students should also figure in costs for books, travel (if necessary), and communication with the College.

Financial Aid

Some financial aid is available, particularly the College's own President's Scholarships and aid connected with Veterans Affairs benefits. The College participates in a variety of loan programs. Because of the nontraditional nature of Regents College, students seeking financial aid should contact the Regents College Financial Aid Office before enrolling (e-mail: finaid@regents.edu).

Faculty

The 360 faculty members of Regents College are drawn from many colleges and universities in New York and other states and from various industries and health-care facilities. Faculty members establish and monitor academic policies and standards; determine degree requirements, including the ways in which credit can be earned; develop the content for all examinations; review the records of students to verify their degree completion; and recommend degree conferral to the Board of Trustees.

Admission Requirements

Regents College has open admissions except in the nursing program, which is open primarily to individuals with significant background or experience in clinically oriented health-care disciplines.

Application and Information

Students may apply at any time during the year. For information, prospective students should contact:
Regents College
7 Columbia Circle
Albany, New York 12203-5159
Telephone: 518-464-8500
              888-647-2388 (toll-free)
E-mail: rcinfo@regents.edu
World Wide Web: http://www.regents.edu

REGIS COLLEGE
WESTON, MASSACHUSETTS

The College
Regis College, a leading Catholic liberal arts and sciences college, is committed to the education of women. Rooted in a strong tradition of academic excellence, Regis College was founded in 1927 by the Sisters of St. Joseph. The College offers challenging academic programs, professional internships, opportunities for developing leadership talents, and a social environment conducive to acquiring friendships that will last a lifetime. The focus of Regis College is on the development of the whole person, enabling students to become educated in all aspects of human behavior: intellectual, spiritual, occupational, social, physical, and emotional. Students engage in a partnership of learning with the faculty while exploring the sciences, the arts, and professional programs. The Regis College academic experience challenges students to discover their power to influence society, the world, and their future as they examine issues from individual, societal, and global perspectives.

While many of the College's 889 undergraduates and 242 graduate students are New England residents, other students are from several different states, Puerto Rico, and twelve countries—Albania, Brazil, Ghana, Honduras, Indonesia, Japan, Northern Ireland, Oman, Poland, Russia, Saudi Arabia, and Venezuela. Campus-based housing is guaranteed for all students. The multicultural student body offers a diversity that is shared and celebrated on the Regis College campus through programs and activities.

Twelve percent of the members of recent graduating classes have chosen to pursue graduate studies immediately. Among the career and employment fields recent graduates have entered are business (including banking, marketing, and sales), communications, counseling, graphic design, law, medical research, social work, and teaching.

A vital part of the Regis College experience is student involvement in activities outside the classroom. Cocurricular programs are offered for leadership development in more than forty campus organizations. A variety of campus activities gives students the opportunity to explore their interests, make new acquaintances, and serve the community. Students with interests in specific areas may develop their talents and skills by becoming involved in such organizations as the Glee Club, AHANA, Drama Society, the Model U.N., and student government. Students who want to enhance their literary, drawing, and photographic skills can contribute to the College publications, *Hemetera*, the literary magazine, and *Mount Regis*, the College yearbook. Regis students are engaged in a wide range of service activities through the Regis College Service Learning Project and volunteer activities through the Campus Ministry Program.

Regis College has a modern athletic/recreation facility, which accommodates intercollegiate athletics, intramural activities, and physical and health education classes. This campus facility features a six-lane swimming pool; a sauna and Jacuzzi; an area that can be used interchangeably for two indoor tennis courts, a regulation basketball court, and volleyball and badminton courts; a training room; athletics offices; a dance studio; squash courts; and a state-of-the-art fitness center. Outdoor sports facilities include four tennis courts and an athletic field. Students at Regis College compete on an intercollegiate NCAA Division III level in basketball, crew, cross-country, field hockey, soccer, softball, swimming and diving, tennis, track and field, and volleyball, as well as in an intramural sports program.

In addition to the undergraduate degrees listed, Regis College offers the Master of Arts in Teaching and the Master of Science degree in nursing.

The College has four modern dormitories: Angela Hall, Domitilla Hall, Maria Hall, and College Hall. Alumnae Hall, the student union building, houses the residents' dining room, the commuters' café, the Tower Tavern, a campus radio station, the bookstore, numerous offices, and three multipurpose lounge areas for College meetings and lectures.

Location
Weston, Massachusetts, ideally located just 12 miles west of Boston, is a suburban town of 10,900 residents that has retained its New England charm. The campus is an 18-minute drive from downtown Boston and other towns such as Lexington, Concord, and Cambridge that have an abundance of cultural and historic sites. Regis operates its own hourly shuttle service, which provides quick and easy access to Boston and to the colleges in Regis's cross-registration program.

Majors and Degrees
Regis College grants a Bachelor of Arts degree in the following subjects: art, biochemistry, biology, chemistry, classics, communication, economics, education, English, French, German, history, management, mathematics, political science, psychology, sociology, social work, Spanish, and theater. In addition, a student may decide to complete an interdepartmental major or an individually designed major.

Regis College offers 3-2 dual-degree programs in a variety of technical areas in cooperation with Worcester Polytechnic Institute. The College also offers preprofessional preparation in communications; computer science; graphic arts; legal studies; management studies; early childhood, elementary, and secondary teacher certification; and social work.

Academic Program
Completion of thirty-eight courses is required to earn the bachelor's degree. All bachelor's degree programs include an eleven-course liberal arts core curriculum, an academic major of concentrated study, and elective courses chosen according to the student's interests. The eleven-course core curriculum consists of courses in the following areas: natural sciences, social sciences, English composition, foreign language, religious studies, and humanities. To fulfill departmental requirements, students must complete from nine to twelve courses in their major field of study. For graduation with Departmental Honors, students are required to complete a two-course sequence of independent study culminating in a written thesis, which must be orally defended, and to maintain averages of at least 3.0 overall and 3.3 in their major field.

Off-Campus Arrangements
Regis College participates in a cross-registration program with Babson College, Bentley College, and Boston College. Students may also study abroad in programs in many countries, including England, France, Germany, Greece, Ireland, Italy, Japan, and Spain. The Washington Semester, sponsored by the

American University in Washington, D.C., provides students with an intensive program involving course work, research, seminars, and internships in government offices. The internship program and the Regis College Career Office provide Regis College students with professional experience in numerous agencies throughout the Boston area, across the U.S., and abroad.

Academic Facilities

The Regis Library's collection now stands at 131,749 volumes and 890 periodicals and serials. The library has a spacious reading room, extensive open stacks, private study carrels for concentrated research, seminar rooms for small classes and group study, and microfilm and microcard readers. Because of the College's proximity to Boston and its membership in the WEBnet Consortium, students also have access to many other libraries, including those of Babson, Bentley, and Pine Manor Colleges. Cardinal O'Connell Hall has modern laboratory and lecture halls for biology, chemistry, physics, and psychology courses. The Fine Arts Center contains an art history lecture hall, classrooms for the study of music, graphic and fine art studios, the 650-seat Elinor Welch Casey Theatre, and the Carney Art Gallery, in which artwork by faculty members, alumnae, and local artists is displayed. College Hall, the academic nucleus, houses most classrooms, a photography laboratory, an academic achievement center, and extensive computer laboratories.

Costs

For 1999–2000, tuition for all students was $16,860, and room and board fees totaled $7870.

Financial Aid

Regis College endeavors to meet the need of every student through its financial aid program. Regis sponsors financial aid through federally funded grants, loans, and work-study awards and also provides scholarships from College operating funds. To apply for any scholarship or financial aid program, applicants should submit the Free Application for Federal Student Aid and the CSS Financial Aid PROFILE form. All financial aid applicants are also required to forward a complete copy of their parents' federal income tax return. Students who request scholarships or other financial aid through Regis College are informed of the College's financial aid award decision between March 1 and April 30. Seventy-five percent of all Regis students receive scholarships and financial assistance through federal and College funds.

Regis College offers merit scholarships for first-year and transfer students in recognition of academic performance, community service, and leadership abilities. There are several levels of merit scholarships at the College: Presidential Scholar, $9000 per year; Dean's Scholar, $6000 per year; Tower Scholar, $3000 per year; and Alumnae Sponsor Award, $2000 per year. These scholarships are awarded on a competitive basis. Information regarding the specifications for each of the merit scholarships can be obtained by contacting the Office of Admission.

Faculty

The Regis College faculty consists of 67 full-time members and 68 part-time members; all hold advanced degrees. In addition to carrying out research and publishing within their individual fields, faculty members at Regis possess a highly developed commitment to teaching. Each student has a faculty adviser to assist with course selection. A student-faculty ratio of 10:1 enables each student to receive personal attention, support, and academic advice.

Student Government

The Student Government is composed of elected representatives who administer the budget for all clubs and organizations. The representatives are involved with educational policy, social events, elections, and student publications.

Admission Requirements

Applicants for admission as first-year students are expected to complete a college-preparatory program at an accredited secondary school. The preparation for entrance should include 4 years of English, 2 years of foreign language, 3 years of mathematics, 2 years of laboratory science, 2 years of social science, and three or four electives. Consideration is given to applicants whose educational background varies from this profile. The Admissions Committee places primary emphasis on the secondary school record (courses selected, grades received, and rank in class), two teacher recommendations, involvement in extracurricular activities, and SAT I or ACT scores. International students must submit the results of the Test of English as a Foreign Language (TOEFL) and a Declaration of Finance form. Interviews are not required but are strongly encouraged. The Admissions Committee does not discriminate against applicants on the basis of race, color, religion, national origin, or handicap; in fact, Regis welcomes diversity among students. The Admissions Committee considers applicants for early admission, rolling admission, delayed admission, and advanced placement. The College grants credit and advanced placement for scores of 3 or better on the Advanced Placement examinations sponsored by the College Board.

Transfer applicants for the fall or spring semester should be in good academic standing at the institution previously attended, have a quality point average of at least 2.0 on the Regis College scale, and not be on academic or disciplinary probation at the former institution. A maximum of twenty college-level courses will be considered for transfer.

Application and Information

An applicant for admission registers by completing the application form, available upon request from the Admissions Office, and returning it with the $30 application fee. Regis College operates on a rolling admission basis; students will hear from the Admissions Office regarding their status within one month of receipt of completed applications. Students are encouraged to visit the campus for interviews and guided tours. For more information and an application for admission, students should contact:

Director of Admission
Regis College
235 Wellesley Street
Weston, Massachusetts 02493
Telephone: 781-768-7100
              800-456-1820 (toll-free)
E-mail: admission@regiscollege.edu
World Wide Web: http://www.regiscollege.edu

REGIS UNIVERSITY
DENVER, COLORADO

The University

In 1540, when Ignatius Loyola founded the Society of Jesus (Jesuits)—a community of companions and scholars resolved to serve their fellow men—a guiding principle of the Society was that it would meet the needs of its age and would "form leaders who would carry forth into their personal and professional lives a mission of service to others." For four centuries, the Jesuit fathers have been perfecting an educational tradition of academic excellence, values-centered education, and service to the community.

Regis University has continued the Jesuit tradition since 1877, when a band of Jesuit missionaries from Naples, Italy, carved out a college on the edge of the desert in New Mexico and named it Las Vegas College. In 1884, Bishop Joseph P. Machebeuf of the Diocese of Denver, eager to have a respected school for boys in Colorado, persuaded the Jesuits to relocate their New Mexico college to Morrison, Colorado, where it was renamed the College of the Sacred Heart. In 1888, when the Morrison site proved too remote, Dominic Pantanella, S.J., the college's first president, moved the college to its present location in northwest Denver, where it also included an associated Jesuit high school.

Recognizing the need for educating men and women together, the college became a coeducational institution in 1968. In 1979, because of the expanding needs of high school and college education, Regis Jesuit High School and Regis College became independent institutions.

In 1977, Regis College began to offer specific programs to adult learners through classes at Fort Carson and Peterson Field and in temporary facilities at St. Mary's High School in Colorado Springs. This beginning led to the development of the School for Professional Studies. In 1988, the nursing program from Loretto Heights was transferred to Regis to set the groundwork for the School for Health Care Professions. In 1991, Regis College became Regis University.

Regis University is one of twenty-eight Jesuit colleges and universities in the United States. The most recent *U.S. News & World Report* places Regis as one of the Tier One Western Colleges and Universities.

In 1992 and again in 1995, Regis was fortunate to benefit from the vision of Clare Boothe Luce, who left the bulk of her estate, $70 million, to create the largest private philanthropic endowment ever established to aid women in science. Funds from the foundation added 2 Clare Boothe Luce Professors to the distinguished faculty at Regis. In addition, 3 Regis faculty members have been chosen as Fulbright Scholars in the past four years.

Regis University is accredited by the North Central Association of Colleges and Schools. The Health Information Management Program in the School for Health Care Professions is accredited by the Commission on Accreditation of Allied Health Education Programs. The Nursing Program in the School for Health Care Professions is accredited by the National League for Nursing Accrediting Commission. The Physical Therapy Program is accredited by the Commission on Accreditation of the American Physical Therapy Association. The University is approved by the Colorado and Wyoming State Departments of Education for preparing students for state teacher's licensure in early childhood, elementary, middle, and secondary levels and in special education and English as a second language. These accreditations and authorizations ensure a student complete professional recognition of the degree he or she receives from Regis University and its acceptability when applying for admission to graduate schools. In addition to the above affiliations, the University is represented in numerous professional and academic societies through individual memberships held by its faculty members and administrators.

Regis University is composed of three separate academic areas—Regis College, the School for Professional Studies, and the School for Health Care Professions. Regis College offers a full range of undergraduate programs in the liberal arts, sciences, business, and education and a Master of Arts in whole-learning education. The School for Professional Studies serves more than 9,000 adult students in undergraduate, graduate, and certificate programs at seven campuses across Colorado and Nevada and through distance (video) learning, guided independent study, and on-site corporate education. Undergraduate students may choose from many majors in multiple learning formats, including accounting, business administration, communication, communications and media technology, computer information systems, computer science, human resource management, organizational development, and many more. The undergraduate distance learning (video) degree serves students across the country. Graduate students may choose from six graduate degrees in many different learning formats: M.B.A.—Master of Business Administration (in classroom-based and distance learning formats), M.A.C.L.—Master of Arts in Community Leadership (combining classroom-based and guided independent study), M.L.S.—Master of Arts in Liberal Studies (guided independent study), M.N.M.—Master of Nonprofit Management, M.S.C.I.S.—Master of Science in Computer Information Systems, and M.S.M.—Master of Science in Management. The new external M.B.A. degree, in alliance with Bisk Publishing Company, is pioneering a graduate business degree with multimedia resources, including computer software, video presentations, and audiocassette lectures. Regis University's Corporate Education Services bridges organizational training needs and the University's comprehensive resources, including credit, certificate, and noncredit courses. The School for Health Care Professions includes the undergraduate program in nursing, with the Traditional Nursing Option; the Accelerated Nursing Option; the RN to B.S.N. (Bachelor of Science in Nursing) Degree Completion Option, which is taught on campus and on site at area hospitals; the Health Care Administration Program; the Health Information Management Program; and the Medical Imaging Management Program. The school also offers graduate programs in nursing and physical therapy.

Location

The Regis campus comprises fourteen buildings situated on 90 acres that are located a few miles north of downtown Denver in a pleasant residential neighborhood. Denver, the "mile-high city," is the hub of Colorado's cultural, economic, and recreational life. The beautiful Rocky Mountain foothills are less than a half hour from campus. For skiers, it is less than a 2-hour drive from the residence halls to the slopes of Vail. As Colorado's state capital, Denver offers students diverse resources with extensive opportunities for on-the-job experiences. The city has major-league baseball, basketball, football, and hockey teams. With more than 2 million people living in the metropolitan area, Denver is one of America's fastest-growing metropolitan regions. Denver offers the pleasures of four distinct and spectacular seasons, with 300 days of sunshine a year.

Majors and Degrees

Regis College offers bachelor's degrees in five divisions of study. The Division of Business offers majors in business administration, economics, finance, international business, marketing, management, management information systems, and accounting/M.B.A. The Humanities Division offers majors in communications arts, English, French, political economy, Spanish, and visual arts. Majors in the Division of Natural Sciences include biochemistry, biology, chemistry, computer information systems, computer science, engineering (3-2 program), environmental studies/human ecology, health information management, mathematics, predentistry, premedicine, and pre–physical therapy. Bachelor's degrees are also offered in philosophy and religious studies. The Division of Social Sciences offers the following degree programs: criminal justice, education, history, political science, prelaw, psychology, and sociology. In addition, a Bachelor of Science in Nursing is offered to undergraduates.

Academic Program

Regis is part of a 450-year-old Jesuit tradition that provides a value-centered liberal arts education. A Jesuit education is known for excellence, service to others, and career preparation within the context of a liberal arts education. All students at Regis experience a liberal arts education through the core curriculum. This education is designed to prepare students for life as well as a career. The core curriculum requires students to reflect on the purposes of human existence, to understand the roots of modern culture, to come to grips with philosophical and religious perspectives, and to think critically. These courses enrich perceptions, challenge assumptions, and broaden vision.

A total of 128 semester hours is required for a bachelor's degree. Regis chooses a select group of students for its honors program each year and offers a comprehensive schedule of undergraduate courses in the Summer School Program. The University's Center for Service Learning actively involves students in community service projects. Internships and study abroad are options offered through the University's Experiential Education Department.

Academic Facilities

Regis is committed to providing state-of-the-art facilities. The University offers students 24-hour access to personal computers, online services, and research tools in common lab facilities. In addition, labs are located in the residence halls and in specific departments. All students are offered full access to an e-mail account on the Internet.

The University has four libraries, housing more than 280,000 volumes, 2,100 periodical subscriptions, 600 CD-ROMs, 110,000 microforms, and an 85,000-slide art history collection. Its CARL online catalog is a comprehensive index to the collections and provides 140 databases and document delivery options. The main library, which includes media services, has been completely renovated and expanded to become one of the first libraries in the country to provide network ports at every place that a student studies for ease of access to the Internet and the Regis databases.

The Coors Life Directions Center, constructed in 1987, houses the Offices of Career Services and Personal Counseling as well as the Fitness Program and the Health Center.

Costs

Undergraduate tuition in Regis College for the 1999–2000 academic year was $16,500. Room and board for the academic year cost $6700.

Financial Aid

In an effort to keep its high-quality Jesuit education affordable, Regis is committed to helping as many students as possible by continuing to increase scholarships and University grant funds. The student financial aid program invests more than $11 million in undergraduates. More than 81 percent of full-time Regis College students receive some financial assistance. Scholarships and grants are awarded on the bases of need, academic achievement, and leadership. The University participates in all federal and Colorado-supported programs. The Free Application for Federal Student Aid (FAFSA) or Renewal Application must be filed.

Faculty

Regis College has 60 full-time faculty members; 92 percent hold terminal degrees. Fifteen percent of faculty members are Jesuits, and Regis has no graduate students/teaching assistants on staff. The College has a 16:1 student-faculty ratio. Professional staff, Jesuit priests, and religious live and teach on the Regis campus. These committed adults are available for both academic and personal direction for Regis students. In addition, each undergraduate has an individual faculty adviser who assists students in their academic choices.

Student Government

The Student Government at Regis is led by the Executive Board. The board is supported by the Senate, which comprises class representatives, members-at-large, and various activities representatives. The student leaders serve on University committees, plan entertainment, help determine student policy, and oversee the more than thirty student organizations.

Admission Requirements

Regis College actively recruits students for equal opportunity and nondiscrimination in the consideration of eligibility. In 1998, the average ACT composite score for incoming freshmen was 24. Admission is determined by a student's high school record, including grades, test scores, personal abilities, and leadership qualities.

Requirements for freshman admission include high school graduation or its equivalency and evidence of college-level competency, as shown in high school courses, grades, ACT or SAT I test scores, a personal essay, and recommendations. Freshmen should present a minimum of 15 academic units. Successful candidates must have a satisfactory high school or college record in order to be admitted.

Application and Information

Completed applications for admission should be submitted to the Director of Admissions. Applications may be submitted any time after the beginning of the senior year. The Office of Admissions usually notifies each applicant regarding the decision within eight weeks after the completed application and supporting documents have been received by the Office of Admissions. All requests for information or application forms should be addressed to:

Director of Admissions
Regis College Office of Admissions, A-12
Regis University
3333 Regis Boulevard
Denver, Colorado 80221-1099

Telephone: 303-458-4900
Fax: 303-964-5534
E-mail: regisadm.@regis.edu
World Wide Web: http://www.regis.edu/

The Regis campus, which comprises fourteen buildings situated on 90 acres, is located in a pleasant residential neighborhood a few miles north of Denver.

RENSSELAER POLYTECHNIC INSTITUTE
TROY, NEW YORK

The Institute

The oldest technological university in the English-speaking world, Rensselaer Polytechnic Institute was founded in 1824 "for the purpose of instructing persons in the application of science to the common purposes of life." Still pursuing that original mission, Rensselaer has become one of the world's premier research universities.

More than 100 programs and 1,000 courses lead to bachelor's, master's, and doctoral degrees. Undergraduates pursue their studies in the Schools of Architecture, Engineering, Humanities and Social Sciences, Management and Technology, and Science and in the interdisciplinary program in information technology (IT).

Rensselaer's long tradition of cross-disciplinary, real-world, industry-oriented research and education is clearly reflected in cross-school programs, such as product design and innovation, and unusual degree offerings, such as bioinformatics and molecular biology; electronic media, arts, and communication; and information technology. Rensselaer's unique B.S. degree program in information technology requires students to choose an area in which they wish to apply IT from thirty-six second disciplines that are taught by experts from across the University.

Work in Rensselaer's thirteen major interdisciplinary research centers has achieved international recognition in such fields as microelectronics, simulation-based engineering, advanced computing, and composite materials. Strong and deep ties to a broad range of firms, from large multinational corporations to fast-growing entrepreneurial ventures, help ensure the relevance of educational and research initiatives and offer rich co-op, internship, and employment opportunities for students.

Rensselaer's 4,800 undergraduate and 1,800 graduate students are a bright, ambitious, and technologically savvy group who come from all fifty states, the District of Columbia, Puerto Rico, the Virgin Islands, and seventy-eight other countries.

A wide variety of nonacademic activities, virtually all of which are run by the students, are available. There are thirty fraternities and six sororities, a weekly newspaper, a progressive 10,000-watt FM stereo station, dramatics groups, musical ensembles, and more than 170 clubs, special interest groups, professional societies, sports, and organizations. More than 5,000 students participate in eighteen intramural sports. Varsity sports include a Division I men's ice hockey team and twenty-two Division III men's and women's teams in thirteen sports. Recreational facilities include an indoor track, all-weather track and field facilities, handball and squash courts, weight rooms, several indoor tennis courts, and two swimming pools. The Student Union, Chapel and Cultural Center, and Houston Field House bring many forms of entertainment and nationally known performing groups and lecturers to campus.

Location

Rensselaer is located in the heart of New York's Capital District. The region, which includes the cities of Albany, Schenectady, and Troy and their suburbs, has a combined population of approximately 870,000 and is an important business, government, industrial, and academic hub. There are 40,000 college students at fourteen colleges and universities in the immediate area.

Overlooking the city of Troy and the historic Hudson River, Rensselaer's 260-acre campus blends a cluster of classical-style, ivy-covered brick buildings dating from the turn of the century with more recently constructed facilities, like the Center for Industrial Innovation. A program of extensive renovation has equipped the campus with ultramodern teaching facilities while preserving the traditional elegance of its historic buildings. Rensselaer retains the quiet and natural beauty of a parklike setting while offering many conveniences of a city campus.

Students enjoy easy access to Boston (3 hours away), New York City (2½ hours away), and Montreal (4 hours away). The Adirondacks, the Berkshires, and the Catskills, all within an hour of Troy, offer hundreds of areas for camping, hiking, and skiing. Many student clubs take full advantage of these natural resources.

Majors and Degrees

The Bachelor of Science is offered in aeronautical engineering; applied physics; biochemistry and biophysics; bioinformatics and molecular biology; biology; biomedical engineering; building sciences; chemical engineering; chemistry; civil engineering; communication; computer and systems engineering; computer science; economics; electrical engineering; electric power engineering; electronic media, arts, and communication; engineering physics; engineering science; environmental engineering; environmental science; geology; hydrogeology; industrial and management engineering; information technology; interdisciplinary science; management; materials engineering; mathematics; mechanical engineering; nuclear engineering; philosophy; physics; psychology; and science, technology, and society.

Professionally accredited degree programs are offered in the fields of architecture and engineering. Architecture students may earn the Bachelor of Architecture after five years or the Master of Architecture after six. A five-year professional engineering curriculum can be accelerated to allow completion of both the Bachelor of Science and Master of Engineering degrees in four years. Rensselaer's professional program in engineering is one of the first of its type in the nation.

Seven-year accelerated programs for students pursuing health or science professions are offered by Rensselaer in conjunction with other universities. Accelerated dental students earn a B.S. degree in biology and a D.M.D. (with the University of Pennsylvania School of Dental Medicine). Accelerated physician-scientist students earn a B.S. degree in biology and an M.D. (with Albany Medical College). Accelerated podiatric students earn a B.S. degree in biology and a D.P.D. (with Temple University). Accelerated law programs allow management or science, technology, and society majors to earn a B.S. degree from Rensselaer and a J.D. from Albany Law School in six years. Other programs allow students to earn a B.S. in three years, a B.S./M.S. in four or five years, or a B.S./M.B.A. in a total of five years.

Undergraduates at forty-four liberal arts colleges may transfer to Rensselaer and earn a B.A. from the first college and a B.S. or a master's degree from Rensselaer.

Academic Program

Rensselaer leads the nation in educational reform with its award-winning, studio-based interactive approach to teaching. Although there are still lectures, more and more classes involve lively discussion, team problem solving, and faculty mentoring as opposed to instructing. In the past two years, faculty members have also renewed the curriculum, replacing the traditional five or six 3-credit-course model with a "4x4" curriculum of four 4-credit-hour courses. All first-year students are required to have a laptop computer that meets Rensselaer's specifications.

While each school has its own sequence requirements, the following minimums apply to all students: 124 credit hours and a

1.8 quality point average in total courses; 24 credit hours in physical, life, and engineering sciences; 24 in humanities and social sciences; 30 in a selected discipline; and 24 in electives.

Students are strongly encouraged to learn outside of the classroom with independent projects, faculty research, study abroad, and cooperative education. The Undergraduate Research Program offers hands-on experience to students in hundreds of areas. Any full-time undergraduate can participate for credit or pay during the academic year or the summer. Co-op assignments give students the opportunity to add practical experience to their academic study. The study-work schedule is such that students graduate in the class with which they matriculated. Air Force, Army, and Naval/Marine ROTC programs are available on an elective basis.

Off-Campus Arrangements

Rensselaer has formal exchange programs with Williams College in Massachusetts and Harvey Mudd College in California, as well as study-abroad programs in Australia, China, Denmark, England, France, Germany, India, Italy, Japan, Spain, Switzerland, and Turkey. Cooperative programs with 15 two- and four-year institutions in the area allow Rensselaer students to take courses for credit and at no additional cost. More than 200 Rensselaer students use this cross-registration program each year. Rensselaer has transfer agreements with more than ninety institutions, including the 107 campuses of the California state community college system.

Academic Facilities

Studio classrooms and laboratories across campus capitalize on the latest educational technologies. With more than 600 networked computer workstations in classrooms and dormitories and specialized systems, like the visualization laboratory for high-performance computing, Rensselaer is at the forefront among colleges in computing capacity. Students are encouraged to participate in extensive research projects supported by excellent facilities, such as the Center for Industrial Innovation, Fresh Water Institute, Center for Integrated Electronics, and Lighting Research Center. All state-of-the-art teaching and research facilities, including an advanced computer center, are available to undergraduate students.

Costs

Tuition for 2000–01 is $23,525. Fees are $700. Room and board costs average $7750. Books and miscellaneous personal expenses are about $1400. A required laptop costs about $2500.

Financial Aid

Nearly all freshmen who have financial need are offered assistance under a comprehensive program of scholarships, loans, and part-time employment that provides annual assistance ranging from $100 up to full tuition, room, and board. Available federal funds include student loans, Federal Work-Study Program awards, and ROTC scholarships.

Faculty

Rensselaer's internationally recognized studio-style classes, faculty-undergraduate research opportunities, and academic advising make professors highly accessible, both inside and outside of the classroom. While graduate students assist in some laboratory and recitation sessions, it is Rensselaer's policy to have professors teach undergraduate courses. Excellence in teaching is encouraged and rewarded. Rensselaer's full-time faculty numbers about 350; all hold a doctorate or the highest degree in their field.

Student Government

Rensselaer's student government, a vital and influential force, takes major responsibility for campus life. Administering a budget of $6.5 million, elected student leaders oversee 170 student clubs, sports, and organizations and are currently heading a $9-million building revitalization project.

Admission Requirements

Campus visits are strongly encouraged, but interviews are not required. Requirements are 4 years of English, 4 years of science including physics and chemistry, and 4 years of mathematics (algebra through precalculus). The SAT I or ACT is required. Architecture applicants must submit a portfolio. Applicants for accelerated programs are required to take the SAT I and the SAT II Subject Tests in Mathematics (level I, level IC, level II, or level IIC), Writing, and Physics, Chemistry, or Biology, or they may take the ACT. The TOEFL is required of students for whom English is a second language. Applicants must demonstrate above-average promise of academic success. Academic achievement and secondary school recommendations are of primary importance; test scores are significant as they relate to the record of achievement. The closing date for September admission is January 1 of the student's senior year. January admission is offered to a limited number of freshman and transfer students.

Rensselaer admits qualified students without regard to race, color, sexual orientation, national or ethnic origin, religion, gender, age, or disability.

Application and Information

Dean of Undergraduate Admissions
Rensselaer Polytechnic Institute
Troy, New York 12180
Telephone: 518-276-6216
Fax: 518-276-4072
E-mail: admissions@rpi.edu
World Wide Web: http://admissions.rpi.edu

Many of Rensselaer's turn-of-the-century buildings house ultramodern classrooms and laboratories.

RHODES COLLEGE
MEMPHIS, TENNESSEE

The College

Rhodes College brings together, in one of the nation's premier liberal arts colleges, three major purposes of learning that are seldom found at a single institution: intellectual growth that is fostered by intensive interaction between students and faculty members, preparation for professional life that is supported by a unique internship program that draws on the city's resources, and a development of values that is part of a diverse student body that adheres to a student-run honor code.

Rhodes College is a private, coeducational college of liberal arts and sciences, founded in 1848 in Clarksville, Tennessee. The College moved to Memphis in 1925. The College is affiliated with the Presbyterian Church (U.S.A.). *U.S. News & World Report* and the *Fiske Guide to Colleges* recently named Rhodes as one of the "best buys" among the nation's leading institutions. Rhodes is one of only forty schools listed in Loren Pope's *Colleges That Change Lives* and is also ranked among the top 100 colleges and universities in America in *Choosing the Right College: The Whole Truth About America's Top 100 Schools*.

Rhodes' 1,510 students represent thirty-one states and seventeen countries. About 70 percent of them live on campus in fourteen ivy-covered residence halls. Freshmen and sophomores are required to live on campus. Campus unity and activities were greatly enhanced in 1998 with the completion of the $22.5 million Bryan Campus Life Center, a multiuse campus-gathering and recreational facility for students and faculty and staff members. Residents and commuters alike enjoy the rich mix of extracurricular activities, from the internationally touring Rhodes Singers to the award-winning Mock Trial teams (second in the nation in 1999) to an active Black Student Association. Students are active in community service and numerous projects that help those in need. Rhodes sponsors more than eighty activities, clubs, and organizations—including six national fraternities and seven national sororities. More than 250 events each year are sponsored by the College or these student organizations, including films, dances, lectures, art exhibits, service projects, concerts, and theater. There are several campus publications, a weekly newspaper, a literary journal, the yearbook, and student home pages on the World Wide Web.

Rhodes is a member of Division III of the NCAA, and men's basketball, football, and soccer and women's tennis teams all have gone to national playoffs in recent years. More than 25 percent of the student body competes in varsity sports: baseball, basketball, cross-country, football, golf, soccer, swimming, tennis, and indoor and outdoor track for men and basketball, cross-country, field hockey, golf, soccer, softball, swimming, tennis, indoor and outdoor track, and volleyball for women. About 75 percent participate in the intramural and club sports programs, which include basketball, equitation, lacrosse, rugby, softball, tae kwon do, and volleyball.

In addition to the undergraduate degrees listed below, Rhodes awards the Master of Science degree in accounting.

Location

Cited as one of America's most beautiful campuses, Rhodes' 100 acres are situated in an attractive residential section of midtown Memphis, just minutes from downtown and within walking distance of the Memphis Zoo and the Memphis Brooks Museum of Art. Memphis is America's fifteenth-largest city and the region's medical and business hub. The city offers many internships, research opportunities, and potential jobs. Sixty percent of students take part in local and international internships by the time they graduate. The birthplace of the blues and the home of international companies, including Federal Express and International Paper, Memphis is a city of arts and culture, with ten local theaters, twelve museums and art galleries, three ballet companies, visiting Broadway shows, a symphony, and an opera company. Hundreds of restaurants, professional sports events, and good shopping facilities round out the entertainment package.

Majors and Degrees

Rhodes grants the Bachelor of Arts or Bachelor of Science degree in thirty-four departmental and interdisciplinary areas: anthropology/sociology, art, biology, business administration, business administration–computer science, business administration–international studies, business administration–mathematics, chemistry, economics, economics–business administration, economics–international studies, economics–mathematics, English, French, German, Greek and Roman studies, history, international studies, international studies–foreign languages, international studies–history, international studies–political science, Latin American cultural studies, mathematics, mathematics–computer science, music, philosophy, physics, political science, psychology, religious studies, Russian/Soviet cultural studies, Spanish, theater, and urban studies. Students may design their own interdisciplinary majors.

Academic Program

Rhodes students are required to take a representative group of courses from four major areas: humanities, social sciences, natural sciences, and fine arts. Students must fulfill the basic humanities requirement by taking a four-term, 12-credit-hour interdisciplinary course, Search for Values in the Light of Western History and Religion, or by taking four courses in religious studies and philosophy. The College requires one term of writing as well as one term of a foreign language at the intermediate level, but either can be waived by demonstrated proficiency. Students must successfully complete 112 credit hours to graduate and must have a GPA of at least 2.0. The academic year is divided into two semesters of fourteen weeks each, with an additional week for exams.

The College's high academic reputation is reflected in the fact that 97 percent of Rhodes graduates either secured jobs or were accepted into graduate school. In 1998, the acceptance rate of students who applied and were accepted into medical schools was 94 percent. More than 95 percent were accepted into master's and Ph.D. programs, and 100 percent of those who applied to schools of law, business, and divinity were accepted.

Rhodes' strong career-counseling program provides advisers in law, business, international business, finance, museum careers, psychological and social services, medicine, accounting, church professions, foreign service, music, and teaching. Advisers not only counsel their students but in many cases help them find summer internships and permanent positions in their fields. The College provides a fully staffed career development and placement office. Students may gain additional knowledge and experience through independent research, internships, and honors programs.

Off-Campus Arrangements

Rhodes offers many off-campus credit-earning programs. Among them are a semester in Europe focusing on literature, religion, art, history, and drama and a summer British Studies Program in Oxford. Rhodes also has an exchange program in Germany with the Eberhard Karls University of Tübingen, in Japan with the Kansai University of Foreign Study, in France with the University of Poitiers, and in the Commonwealth of Independent States (CIS) with a consortium of universities. Through the Institute of European Studies, Rhodes also offers programs in scores of countries in Europe, Central and South America, South Africa, and Asia. The Oak Ridge Science Semester, a summer marine sciences program at the Gulf Coast Research Laboratory, and the Washington

Semester program in Washington, D.C., are also popular. Rhodes also offers all-expenses-paid summer internships abroad.

Academic Facilities

Many first-time visitors to Rhodes say, "This is what a great liberal arts college should look like." The stone and slate buildings on campus are constructed in collegiate Gothic style, and thirteen of them are listed on the National Register of Historic Places. The Burrow Library contains more than 250,000 bound volumes; 64,000 microform items; more than 8,500 records, tapes, and videos; and more than 1,200 periodicals. Departmental libraries, an online card catalog, an expansive microfiche file in the social sciences, Dialog (a computerized library retrieval system), and a citywide library consortium put more than 1.6 million volumes at the fingertips of Rhodes students.

Excellent science facilities include physics laboratories equipped for sophisticated solar-emissions research and biology and chemistry laboratories with an electron microscope, a cell culture lab, and a nuclear magnetic resonance instrument. The College's dual-platform computer network includes file, print, and e-mail servers and more than 200 microcomputers available primarily for student use. Rhodes is listed as one of the top 100 most wired college campuses by *Yahoo! Internet Life* magazine. The mathematics/computer science and physics departments are equipped with labs containing high-powered Sun Ultra workstations. Rhodes' campus network is connected to the worldwide Internet, with all residence hall rooms having an Ethernet connection for each resident. More information is available at http://www.rhodes.edu.

Costs

Tuition at Rhodes for 1999–2000 was $18,561, and room and board fees were $5454. There is a $158 student activity fee. Estimated expenses for books and supplies are $750. Transportation and personal expenses are additional.

Financial Aid

Rhodes invests considerable funds in need-based assistance to help make it possible for students who are admitted to the College to attend. The average need-based award for 1999–2000 was more than $16,000. A large number of merit-based scholarships are also available, ranging from $500 to full tuition, fees, room, and board. Students interested in financial aid must fill out the Free Application for Federal Student Aid (FAFSA) and the CSS PROFILE. Those interested in merit-based scholarships must submit the application for admission by January 15. Students nominated for scholarships covering full tuition, fees, room, and board must also apply by January 15. Notification of need-based financial aid awards occurs between April 1 and April 15.

Faculty

The College's 160 faculty members (122 full-time) are first and foremost teachers, but they also engage in research and creative activities, often working with students on scholarly projects. The student-faculty ratio is 12:1, and the average class size is 17. Ninety-nine percent of full-time tenured or tenure-track faculty members hold the Ph.D. or other terminal degree.

Student Government

Students govern their lives on campus through the Student Government Association, the Honor Council, and the Social Regulations Council and through their participation on the Board of Trustees and various College committees. The honor system prevails at Rhodes; professors regularly leave the room when tests are administered. Students are even on their honor in the cafeteria.

Admission Requirements

Rhodes considers a number of criteria in the selection of its students: academic achievements, writing ability, letters of recommendation, standardized test scores, and extracurricular activities. The middle 50 percent of the freshman class who entered in fall 1998 had a combined score (recentered) ranging from 1210 to 1370 and a composite ACT score ranging from 26 to 30, and 75 percent were in the top 20 percent of their high school class. Of the 448 freshmen, 42 were presidents of their class or student government, and 47 were valedictorians or salutatorians. The College enthusiastically seeks geographic and racial diversity for its student body.

Applicants should have 16 or more high school academic units, with 4 of the units in English, 3 in mathematics (2 in algebra and 1 in geometry or the equivalent), 2 in the same foreign language, 2 years of laboratory science, and 2 years of history or social science. Either the SAT I or ACT is required. In addition to submitting the same application supporting documents as all other students, home-schooled students must submit the results of two SAT II Subject Tests from areas other than English or mathematics. Rhodes offers early decision, early admission, and deferred admission. Advanced placement credit is normally given for scores of 4 or 5 on the Advanced Placement tests and 5, 6, or 7 on International Baccalaureate Diploma higher-level exams. An interview is not required but is strongly recommended for scholarship candidates. Appointments may be scheduled from 9 a.m. to 4 p.m., Monday through Friday, and on Saturday morning by special arrangement during the academic year. If they give notice, visitors may spend the night in a residence hall between Sunday and Thursday as well as attend classes and meet with faculty members and students during the week.

Application and Information

Priority is given to applications received by February 1 (January 15 for those applying for competitive scholarships). Students are notified of the admission decision by February 1. Early decision candidates must file by November 1 for decision notification by December 1 or by December 1 for decision by February 1. Accompanying the application must be a $40 fee, an official high school transcript, results of the SAT I or the ACT exam, a counselor's report, and a teacher's recommendation. For further information, students may contact:

David J. Wottle
Dean of Admissions and Financial Aid
Rhodes College
2000 North Parkway
Memphis, Tennessee 38112-1690

Telephone: 901-843-3700
              800-844-3969 (toll-free)
E-mail: adminfo@rhodes.edu
World Wide Web: http://www.admissions.rhodes.edu

Rhodes College has one of the most spectacular college campuses in America. Thirteen buildings have been named to the National Register of Historic Places for representing "one of the finest and most harmonious groupings of collegiate Gothic architecture in the nation."

RICE UNIVERSITY
HOUSTON, TEXAS

The University

Dedicated to the advancement of letters, science, and art, William Marsh Rice University offers undergraduate and graduate degrees in architecture, engineering, humanities, music, social sciences, and natural sciences. The faculty-student ratio is 1:5 and the median class size is 12 students. Undergraduates choose from more than fifty different majors and find research opportunities in more than thirty interdisciplinary research centers on campus.

Of the more than 4,000 students currently enrolled, 2,700 are undergraduates. The student body hails from all fifty states and thirty-two other countries. Thirty-four percent are members of minority groups. More than 70 percent of the entering freshmen ranked in the top 5 percent of their high school class.

Perhaps the most distinctive feature of Rice's campus life is the residential college system. All new students are randomly assigned to one of eight residential colleges. The colleges serve not only as residence halls but also as primary centers for dining, studying, playing, networking, and developing leadership skills. The residential colleges facilitate a high degree of student-faculty interaction. A faculty master and his or her family live in a house adjacent to the college. The masters and two resident associates (faculty or staff members who live in the college) assist students in various ways, from enriching intellectual life to participating in cultural and service activities to cheering on intramural teams. Approximately 20 other professors per college are nonresident associates, eating lunch in the college, serving as academic advisers, and participating in a myriad of extracurricular activities organized by the students.

Rice undergraduates pursue the highest levels of athletic competition through NCAA Division I-A sports and through club sports. As members of the Western Athletic Conference, Rice athletes compete in baseball, basketball, cross-country, football, golf, swimming, tennis, and track and field. Club sports include badminton, crew, cricket, cycling, fencing, lacrosse, karate, rugby, sailing, shooting, soccer, Ultimate Frisbee, and volleyball.

Location

The fourth-largest city in the nation, Houston is a vibrant center for the arts and culture. The downtown Theater District, only 5 miles from the Rice campus, is host to permanent companies in ballet, opera, symphony, and theater. Just 3 blocks from campus is the Museum District, which is composed of eleven museums that feature outstanding collections and exhibitions of art, nature, science, medicine, and history. The district also encompasses Hermann Park, home to the Houston Zoo, an amphitheater, a public golf course, and a Japanese garden. The Texas Medical Center, the world's largest medical center, is adjacent to Hermann Park and across the street from Rice. The campus itself covers 300 acres, shaded by almost 4,000 trees and bordered by a 3-mile jogging trail. Rice is located on the edge of one of Houston's most beautiful residential areas and in one of the safest sections of the city.

Majors and Degrees

Students interested in architecture choose between the four-year B.A. program and the six-year Bachelor of Architecture (B.Arch.) degree. Those who have been admitted to the B.Arch. program spend their fifth year in a working preceptorship with an architectural firm, returning to Rice to complete a final year of architectural study for the degree. Among the approved preceptorships are Pei Cobb Freed & Partners, Cesar Pelli & Associates, Michael Graves, and Renzo Piano Building Shop.

The George R. Brown School of Engineering offers, through nine departments, majors in bioengineering, chemical engineering, civil engineering, computational and applied mathematics, computer science, electrical and computer engineering, mechanical engineering, materials science, and statistics. Environmental science is available as a double major with another science or engineering field. These programs lead to either the B.A. or the B.S. degree.

Through the School of Humanities, students may declare majors in art and art history, classics, English, French studies, German and Slavic studies, Hispanic studies, history, kinesiology, linguistics, philosophy, and religious studies. Interdisciplinary majors are available in ancient Mediterranean civilizations, Asian studies, medieval studies, and the study of women and gender.

Music students may opt for either a B.A. or a Bachelor of Music (B.Mus.) degree in composition, music history, music theory, or performance. Students who pass the qualifying examination may elect an honors program that leads to the simultaneous awarding of the B.Mus. and the Master of Music (M.Mus.) degrees after five years of study, the final two years of which are devoted to the student's particular specialization.

The Wiess School of Natural Sciences awards the B.A. degree in the fields of biochemistry and cell biology, chemistry, ecology and evolutionary biology, geology and geophysics, mathematics, and physics. Space physics and astronomy are concentrations offered through the physics major.

The School of Social Sciences offers majors in anthropology, economics, mathematical economic analysis, political science, psychology, and sociology.

Several interdepartmental majors are offered. The policy studies major includes six areas of specialization, ranging from environmental policy to international affairs, and a research project. The cognitive sciences degree provides a multidisciplinary study of the mind, and managerial studies is composed of course work in accounting, economics, political science, psychology, and statistics.

Students may pursue programs at Rice that satisfy the requirements for admission to graduate schools of business, dentistry, diplomacy, finance, health science, law, and medicine.

Academic Program

Because it believes that undergraduates should become acquainted with areas of study outside their specialization, Rice has implemented a set of distribution requirements. There is no core curriculum; rather, all students choose courses within the schools of humanities, natural sciences, and social sciences that they wish to take in order to fulfill the distribution requirements. The flexibility of the curriculum allows students the option of completing double or triple majors, interdepartmental majors, or area majors. Students are assisted in these choices by faculty advisers, who begin working with students as early as freshman orientation.

Classroom learning is enhanced by additional experiences. Each year, the number of internship opportunities posted by the Career Services Center exceeds the number of students looking for internships. In addition, a large number of undergraduates are conducting primary research. In 1999, 16 undergraduates earned graduate fellowships from the National Science Foundation.

Rice observes a two-semester calendar, and students enroll in an average of five courses per semester.

Off-Campus Arrangements

Recognizing the importance of a global perspective, Rice encourages students to enrich their academic experience with a summer, semester, or year of study abroad. The Office of International Education and faculty members assist students in identifying the best programs for their individual interests and needs. Rice-sponsored programs are administered by the University and faculty members in Hispanic and classical studies, art and art history, and architecture. These programs send students to Chile, Spain, France, and Greece. Rice-affiliated programs allow students to study on every continent. Direct exchange programs allow Rice students to change places with German, British, or Japanese students. In the United States, Rice sponsors an exchange program with Swarthmore College in Pennsylvania and American University in Washington, D.C. Financial assistance is available for study-abroad and exchange programs.

Academic Facilities

The Fondren Library is accessible to students 24 hours a day and is a charter member of JSTOR, an electronic archive of important journals. The library contains more than 2 million volumes, 2.6 million microforms, and 14,000 current periodicals. The library's holdings include extensive special collections, such as those in art and music and the NASA archive. Students have on-site and remote access to the library's online catalog, indexes, and full-text reference sources and direct access to the stacks, which are lined with private study carrels. Powerbooks and Macintosh and UNIX workstations are located throughout the building.

Rice students have access to some of the best computing facilities in the country. Owlnet is Rice's educational computing system, which includes computing tools on the UNIX, Macintosh, and PC computing platforms. All undergraduates are eligible for an Owlnet account, which gives them access to e-mail, word processing, spreadsheets, statistical and graphics software, and many other packages. Owlnet computing labs are located across the campus, including one in each residential college. Each residential college room is equipped with one network connection port for every student resident.

The Rice Media Center, which specializes in contemporary filmmaking and photography, is popular on campus. The Rice University Gallery functions principally as an extension of the teaching activities of the art and art history department and sponsors major exhibits regularly. Hamman Hall provides theater space for the student drama group. The Alice Pratt Brown Hall houses the Shepherd School of Music and provides concert facilities for the Shepherd School of Music series and for the Houston Friends of Music, the city's major sponsor of world-renowned chamber music ensembles. In addition, the University has extensive science and engineering laboratories, language laboratories, art studios, spacious architectural laboratories, and the Gardiner Symonds Teaching Laboratory, which facilitates interactive teaching through innovative architecture and computer technology.

Costs

Tuition at Rice is substantially less than that at comparable universities—$15,950 for the academic year 2000-01. The average cost, including tuition, room and board ($6850), fees ($450), books and supplies ($600), and personal expenses ($1400), totals $25,250. Rice guarantees that tuition increases between the freshman and senior years will not exceed inflation, as measured by the Consumer Price Index. As a result, families of Rice students are secure in the knowledge that tuition costs over four years will not exceed their expectations.

Financial Aid

Rice offers need- and merit-based financial aid. To determine financial need, Rice requires the Rice University Financial Aid Form, the Free Application for Federal Student Aid (FAFSA), and a copy of the family's tax return. If need exists, Rice meets 100 percent of demonstrated need with a combination of grants, loans, and campus employment. The University also provides merit awards. All applicants are automatically considered regardless of financial status. Rice has been recognized consistently by *U.S. News & World Report*, *Time*, and *Money* magazine as one of the best values in higher education.

Faculty

Rice has a distinguished faculty that is devoted to teaching and research. In addition to the $40 million of sponsored research projects that are currently under way, one third of the faculty members edit or serve on editorial boards of scholarly research journals. Rice professors bring this excitement of discovery to the classroom. Ninety-six percent of undergraduate courses are taught by faculty members rather than graduate students. Professors regularly interact with undergraduates in the classroom, as members of the residential colleges, and as academic advisers.

Student Government

All undergraduates are members of the Rice Student Association, which is governed through a Student Senate. Every student is also a member of one of eight residential colleges, each of which has its own government and judicial system. Rice also has an honor system, which is administered by an elected student Honor Council. All written examinations and assignments are conducted under the honor code.

Admission Requirements

The Admission Committee seeks students of keen intellect who will benefit from the Rice experience. Rice strives to create a rich learning environment in which all students will meet individuals whose life experiences differ significantly from their own. The Admission Committee evaluates course selection, grades, recommendations, personal qualities, essays, and standardized testing. All applicants are required to submit scores from the SAT I or the ACT and three subject tests from the SAT II. Interviews are optional.

Application and Information

Three application plans are available for freshmen. Early decision is binding; students apply by November 1 and are notified by December 15. Interim and regular decision are not binding; for interim, students apply by December 1 and are notified by February 10. Regular decision candidates apply by January 2 and are notified by April 1. Students who have completed two full semesters of college work may apply as transfers by November 1 for midyear (January) enrollment or by April 1 for fall-term (August) enrollment. There is a $35 application fee.

Director of Admission-MS 17
Rice University
P.O. Box 1892
Houston, Texas 77251-1892
Telephone: 713-348-RICE
              800-527-OWLS (toll-free)
World Wide Web: http://www.rice.edu

Lovett Hall, with its trademark Sallyport, is the oldest building on the Rice campus.

THE RICHARD STOCKTON COLLEGE OF NEW JERSEY
POMONA, NEW JERSEY

The College

The Richard Stockton College of New Jersey is an undergraduate college of arts, sciences, and professional studies within the New Jersey System of Higher Education. Named for Richard Stockton, one of the New Jersey signers of the Declaration of Independence, the College was authorized by the passage of the state's 1968 bond referendum for higher education and accepted its charter class in 1971.

More than 6,000 students are enrolled at the College, which provides distinctive traditional and alternative approaches to education. Stockton seeks to develop the analytic and creative capabilities of its students by encouraging them to undertake individually planned courses of study that promote self-reliance and an acceptance of and responsiveness to change.

The College's campus provides an excellent natural setting for a wide range of outdoor recreational activities, including sailing, canoeing, hiking, jogging, and fishing. Students, faculty, and staff take part together in an extensive intramural and club sports program that includes aikido, crew, flag football, golf, soccer, softball, street hockey, swimming, and volleyball. At the intercollegiate level, the College fields teams in men's baseball, basketball, lacrosse, and soccer; women's basketball, crew, soccer, softball, and volleyball; and men's and women's cross-country and track and field. In addition, the College has a gymnasium with fitness facilities, an Olympic-size indoor swimming pool, racquetball courts, weight rooms, and outdoor recreational facilities.

College Center I provides a focal point for social, recreational, cultural, and leisure activities. More than eighty clubs and organizations have their offices in the center: social clubs, such as the Film Committee, Concert Committee, and Performing Arts Committee; service clubs, including the Social Work Club, Speech and Hearing Association, and Unified Black Students' Society; special interest clubs, such as the Accounting and Finance Society, Dance Club, and Photography Club; and independent organizations, including the Jewish Student Union, New Life Christian Fellowship, and thirteen sororities and fraternities. Participation in cocurricular activities can be documented through the College's student development program, ULTRA (Undergraduate Learning, Training, and Awareness), and issuance of a Cocurricular Transcript to students.

College Center II, which is connected to the main academic complex, is a living-room-type facility and features a cafeteria for on-campus students, a wide-screen television, a game room, lounge areas, and several conference rooms.

The Residential Life Center provides a curricular/cocurricular facility within the dormitory area. With its large and small meeting rooms, convenience store, and microcomputer room, the center permits the expansion of activities programs for both organized and informal student groups.

The Lakeside Center is located in the Housing I garden apartment area. The facility contains a convenience store, an outdoor concert area, a snack bar/pizza facility, a microcomputer lab, a multipurpose room for large programs, and a small meeting room for student groups.

On-campus housing for more than 2,000 students is available in the Housing I garden apartments, the Housing II and III residence halls, and the Housing IV complex, which opened in fall 1999. All types of units are fully furnished and air conditioned and are within easy walking distance of the College's main academic complex.

The College is accredited by the Commission on Higher Education of the Middle States Association of Colleges and Schools. As a college of the New Jersey System of Higher Education, Stockton offers programs that are approved by the State Board of Higher Education. The Environmental Health Program is accredited by the National Environmental Health Science and Protection Accreditation Council; the Social Work Program has been accredited by the Council on Social Work Education; the teacher education sequence has been approved by the New Jersey Department of Education and the National Association of State Directors of Teacher Education and Certification; the Nursing Program has been accredited by the National League for Nursing and is approved by the New Jersey Board of Nursing; and the Chemistry Program has been accredited by the American Chemical Society.

In addition to its bachelor's degrees, the College offers several graduate programs: a Master of Physical Therapy, a Master of Business Studies (concentrations in accounting, marketing, and management), a Master of Occupational Therapy, a Master of Instructional Technology; a Master of Nursing (speciality for adult health practitioner); and a Master of Arts in Holocaust and Genocide Studies.

Location

Stockton College is located in Pomona, New Jersey, and can be reached from Exit 44 South on the Garden State Parkway and Exit 12 of the Atlantic City Expressway. By car, the campus is approximately 1 hour from Philadelphia and 2½ hours from New York City.

The campus, which has lakes, forests, and hiking trails, is supplemented by nearby Brigantine Wildlife Refuge and the Bass River, Penn, and Wharton state forests. The active program of concerts, art exhibitions, lectures, recreation, and sports on campus is complemented by the nearby resort seashore. Within a 15-minute drive, students will find fishing, boating, swimming, and theatrical productions as well as the famous Atlantic City Boardwalk.

Majors and Degrees

The Bachelor of Arts degree is offered in applied physics, biology, business studies (corporate and public accounting, finance, international business, management, and marketing), chemistry, communication, criminal justice, economics, environmental studies and geology, historical studies, information and computer sciences, liberal studies, literature and language, marine science, mathematics, philosophy and religion, political science, psychology, sociology and anthropology, and studies in the arts. The Bachelor of Science degree is offered in applied physics, biochemistry/molecular biology, biology, business studies (accounting, finance, international business, management, and marketing), chemistry, environmental studies and geology, information and computer sciences, marine science, mathematics, predentistry, pre-engineering, premedicine, preveterinary medicine, psychology, public health, social work, and speech pathology and audiology. The degree of Bachelor of Science in Nursing is offered to upper-division students.

The College has seven-year dual-degree programs with the University of Medicine and Dentistry of New Jersey, the Robert Wood Johnson Medical School, the Pennsylvania College of Podiatric Medicine, and the New York College of Podiatric Medicine, which guarantee Stockton students admission to medical and/or dental school. Students participating in the programs earn a Bachelor of Science degree from Stockton and an M.D. degree from the appropriate medical school. Stockton also has an articulation program with Cornell University for veterinary medicine as well as five-year dual-degree programs with New Jersey Institute of Technology and Rutgers, The State University of New Jersey, for students interested in engineering. Students participating in the programs earn a Bachelor of Science degree in chemistry, physics, or math from Stockton and a Bachelor of Science degree in engineering from NJIT or Rutgers.

In addition, Stockton provides preparation for teacher certification in subject areas and elementary and other education programs.

Academic Program

To earn a baccalaureate degree at Stockton, a student must satisfactorily complete a minimum of 128 semester credits. Degree programs include a combination of general studies and program (major field) studies. The Bachelor of Arts student must earn a total of 64 credits in general studies; the Bachelor of Science student must earn 48. General studies courses are broad cross-disciplinary courses designed to introduce students to all major areas of the curriculum and to the broadly applicable intellectual skills necessary for success in college. Students must select some courses from each major curricular area. The only specifically required courses within general studies are the basic studies courses (up to three), from which students may be exempted on the basis of diagnostic testing. The Bachelor of Arts student must earn a total of 64 credits in program studies; the Bachelor of Science student must earn 80. Program studies (major field) requirements are carefully structured and emphasize sequences of specific courses.

Students at Stockton have special opportunities to influence what and how they learn by participating in the major decisions that shape their academic lives. The main avenue of participation is the preceptorial system, which enables students to work, on a personalized basis, with an assigned faculty-staff preceptor in the planning and evaluation of individualized courses of study and in the exploration of various career alternatives. Stockton's academic programs emphasize curricular organization and methods of instruction that promote independent learning and research, cross-disciplinary study, problem solving, and decision making through analysis and synthesis.

Off-Campus Arrangements

Off-campus educational experiences for college credits are a central feature of most of the degree programs at Stockton. Internships, research projects, and field studies allow students to apply the principles and methods they have learned in their formal training. Opportunities for foreign study are also available.

The Washington, D.C., Internship Program gives Stockton students the opportunity to gain professional working experience. Stockton sends more students to the program than any other college or university outside the Washington area.

Coordination of off-campus internship programs is provided by the academic divisional offices; coordination of foreign study is provided by the coordinator of international education.

Academic Facilities

Situated on an attractive, heavily wooded 1,600-acre campus, Stockton's award-winning academic complex has been planned to serve as a living-learning center; academic, recreational, and living spaces are mixed to promote interaction among all faculty, students, and staff. The facilities, all constructed since 1971, include several large classroom-office buildings, a library, a lecture hall/auditorium, and a 550-seat Performing Arts Center. Currently under construction, the Multipurpose Recreational Center will include a gymnasium/field house, an outdoor NCAA track, field-event venues, and four playing fields for soccer and lacrosse.

The library contains more than 300,000 volumes, more than 2,600 current periodical subscriptions, 280,000 government documents, more than 19,000 reels of microfilm, and about 68,000 other units of microtext. The media collection includes films, slides, videotapes and audiotapes, compact discs, and phonographs. The library also houses a special collection on the New Jersey Pine Barrens and is a depository for federal, state, and Atlantic City documents.

Costs

Costs for the 1999–2000 academic year were as follows: tuition and fees, based on 32 credits—$4400 for in-state students and $6432 for out-of-state students; on-campus housing—$3360; and board—$2050 for a nineteen-meal plan. Books, supplies, transportation, and personal items are extra. All costs are subject to change.

Financial Aid

Financial aid is available in the form of scholarships, grants, loans, and jobs. Aid is awarded both on a competitive (merit) basis and according to need. Students seeking financial aid should file the Free Application for Federal Student Aid (FAFSA) by March 1. This form is used by the College in evaluating all applications for financial aid.

Faculty

Stockton's faculty numbers 193 full-time and 112 part-time and adjunct members. They represent excellent and highly diversified academic backgrounds and training, with 95 percent holding a terminal degree in their field. Faculty members work closely with students through the College's preceptorial system and share with students and staff the initiative and responsibility for the College's social, recreational, athletics, and cultural programs and activities. This arrangement supports the exceptional rapport and communication that exist among students and faculty members.

Student Government

The Stockton College Student Senate consists of 25 student members. The advisory council is made up of 1 faculty member and 2 staff members. Student senators hold office for one year, and elections are held every spring. Among its other duties, the Student Senate reviews and makes recommendations on budgets of funded student organizations and acts as the official representative of the student body.

Admission Requirements

Stockton operates a continuous admission program. Students may apply for admission to the fall or spring term and are notified of the admission decision as soon as their application file has been completed. Applicants must submit ACT or SAT I scores. Admission is selective.

Stockton offers early acceptance programs for high school students in their junior year. Veterans and people who have been away from formal education for some time are also invited to apply for admission on an individual basis. Stockton makes no distinction between part- and full-time students in offering admission.

Stockton has a program that permits the admission on an individual basis of a limited number of students from educationally and financially disadvantaged backgrounds. Students who desire to explore this opportunity at the College should write expressing their interest in this program.

Transfer students are encouraged to apply for admission to either the fall or the spring semester.

Application and Information

For more information or application forms, students should contact:

Dean of Enrollment Management
The Richard Stockton College of New Jersey
P.O. Box 195
Pomona, New Jersey 08240-0195
Telephone: 609-652-4261
Fax: 609-748-5541
E-mail: admissions@stockton.edu
World Wide Web: http://www.stockton.edu

RICHMOND, THE AMERICAN INTERNATIONAL UNIVERSITY IN LONDON
LONDON, ENGLAND

The University

Richmond, The American International University in London, prepares men and women to serve with purpose and generosity in an interdependent and multicultural world. Richmond offers a strong academic program with many choices of fields of study, an exceptional faculty, superb campus life, and fellow students from all over the world. In the United States, Richmond is accredited by the Commission on Higher Education of the Middle States Association of Colleges and Schools, a regional accrediting body recognized by the U.S. Department of Education. Richmond is accredited in the United Kingdom by the Open University and holds related degree validation. The University's undergraduate and graduate degrees are designated by the United Kingdom's Department of Education and Employment. The University is a comprehensive American liberal arts and professional university. In addition to the undergraduate degree programs described below, Richmond offers a Master of Arts in art history, a Master of Business Administration (M.B.A.), and a Master of Science in systems engineering and management.

Freshmen and sophomores study and live at the Richmond campus, 7 miles from central London. Junior and senior years are spent at the Kensington campus in one of London's most beautiful residential and historic districts. As part of their four-year B.A. degree program, students may spend a semester or a year studying at one of the University's international study centers in Italy and Japan. Richmond currently enrolls 1,200 students from more than eighty countries. Approximately 33 percent of the degree students are from Europe and the United Kingdom, 23 percent are from Pacific Rim countries, and 16 percent are from the Middle East. Nine percent of the student body represent the continent of Africa, and 4 percent are from Latin America. The remaining 15 percent are from North America. About 175 study-abroad U.S. students are enrolled for a semester or a year at the University.

Small classes, averaging 18 students, enable students to receive personal attention from professors in a supportive environment. The curriculum and academic advising system are structured to enable students to choose courses that provide broad knowledge, relevant skills, and an understanding of the world's many cultures and nations.

Richmond students supplement academic programs with activities that complement and balance the classroom experience. Many extracurricular and cocurricular programs are available to students, including Student Council, sports, and debate, drama, computer, Hellenic, Pan-African, and business clubs. There is also a University Honor Society.

Location

The upper campus is located in the heart of London's Borough of Kensington, which has fine museums, libraries, theatres, concert halls, historic buildings, and well-known cultural and educational resources. The University takes full advantage of London's cultural and social resources through selected academic courses, work experience placements with multinational corporations, and special visits to museums, art galleries, theatres, and concert halls.

The lower campus in the London suburb of Richmond offers a variety of entertainment, shopping, cultural, and recreational opportunities. Only yards from the University campus is Richmond Park, more than 2,200 acres of rolling hills and lush woodland, where one can ride horses, jog, or simply relax. The journey from Richmond into Central London takes about 30 minutes.

Majors and Degrees

Richmond operates its academic program on the American system. The University offers the four-year Bachelor of Arts (B.A.) degree in seventeen majors, with a further choice of twenty-seven minors, as well as the two-year Associate of Arts (A.A.) degree. A joint engineering program, offered with George Washington University in the United States, leads to the Bachelor of Science (B.S.) degree. Majors offered by the University are anthropology/sociology, art history, business administration, communications, computing (graphic design/information engineering/information systems), economics, engineering (jointly with George Washington University), environmental studies, history, international business, international relations, literature, mathematical sciences, political science, psychology, studio art, systems engineering and management, and theatre arts.

Academic Program

In order to graduate with a B.A., students must earn a minimum of 120 credits. Usually, this means taking a full load for four years, or eight semesters. Within these 120 credits, students must complete all course requirements for their majors. Students must also meet the University's Language Proficiency and General Education requirements. In addition, valuable work experience for credit is offered through the International Internship and Career Apprenticeship programs. Recent placements have been at the International Herald Tribune, General Electric, The House of Commons, CNN, the United Nations, Lloyds Bank, the Museum of London, and Sony Music Corporation.

Credit is also awarded for Advanced Placement tests (6 credits for each subject grade of 3, 4, or 5); a grade of A, B, or C on the "A" Level exams is awarded 9 credits (6 for D or E). Credit is also awarded for the International Baccalaureate, the Baccalauréat de l'Enseignement du Second Degré (France), the Abitur/Reifzuegnis (Germany), the Diploma di Maturità (Italy), and the School Leaving Diploma (Denmark, Finland, Norway, and Sweden).

The fall semester begins in late August and ends in mid-December. The spring semester begins in early January and runs through mid-May. Two sessions of summer school run from mid-May to mid-June and mid-June to mid-July.

Off-Campus Arrangements

Students may complement their studies in London with a semester, year, or summer at one of two international study centers. The centers, each offering intensive study of the language and culture of the country, are in Florence, Italy, and Shizuoka, Japan. The Florence Study Center emphasizes studio and fine arts. The Shizuoka Center is ideally situated to introduce students to the complexities of modern Japan through courses on the Japanese economic system and mode of business organization. Special attention is given to the rapid development in the Pacific Rim.

Academic Facilities

Information technology is integrated into the curriculum in ways that are natural to the discipline under study. Supporting this are six student computer laboratories with 300 PCs and Macintosh computers, which connect to the Internet and are networked for student, faculty, and administrative use.

Richmond's libraries support the courses taught at each campus. Students may use either campus library. The libraries house 60,000 volumes and add approximately 4,000 new titles each year. In addition, the libraries have subscriptions to approximately 300 periodicals. Computers are available in both libraries for CD-ROM data searches and access to online databases through the network. Richmond students also make frequent use of the libraries in London.

Costs

Tuition for the 2000–01 academic year is $14,230. Room and board will be $8460. Mandatory insurance and activity fees total $1080. Personal expenses, books and supplies, clothing, recreation, and travel costs also need to be factored in.

Financial Aid

Forty to fifty new academic achievement scholarships averaging $2500 are awarded annually to students of high academic ability who also demonstrate financial need. Financial aid for U.S. citizens includes Federal Stafford Student Loans and Federal PLUS loans. All U.S. citizens must file the Free Application for Federal Student Aid (FAFSA) to qualify. Students should contact the admissions office for details regarding application procedures for scholarships and financial aid.

Faculty

The student-faculty ratio of 12:1 enables optimum interaction and individualized instructional assistance. The 100 faculty members (45 full-time, 55 part-time) have professional degrees from top European and American universities such as Harvard, Yale, the University of Michigan, Cambridge, Oxford, the London School of Economics, the Sorbonne, and the University of Bonn.

Student Government

Student Council is a student-elected and student-run organization. The council provides an opportunity for students to get directly involved with University governance and community life. Student Council organizes social events and student activities and provides a forum for students' concerns.

Admission Requirements

Applicants are admitted on the basis of academic performance, references, intended major, and career interests. The required autobiographical essay is of paramount importance. Applicants to Richmond have usually completed a total of twelve years of primary and secondary school with a minimum grade of C+ (2.5 out of 4.0) in the American high school grading system, or its equivalent. British system students should have attained a minimum of five GCSE passes (grades of A, B, or C) in acceptable academic subjects, one of which must be mathematics or science. Equivalent qualifications gained under other educational systems are also considered for the purpose of admission.

Students must submit a completed application form, an autobiographical essay, transcripts of all secondary and postsecondary school work, two letters of recommendation, and SAT I or ACT scores (applies only to students graduating from the American education system). The ATP code for Richmond is 0823L. The ACT code is 5244. Evidence of proficiency in the English language is required from students whose first language is not English or who did not attend English-speaking schools. Standardized test scores, such as the TOEFL or the ALIGU, or completion of recognized examinations, such as GCSE, Pitman, RSA, or lower Cambridge, are considered in assessing students' language capability.

Richmond admits students on a rolling basis, and applicants are encouraged to submit their application at the earliest opportunity. All documents in languages other than English must be accompanied by official translations. Applicants are usually notified of a decision within two to three weeks.

Application and Information

An application for admission and further information may be obtained by contacting the appropriate admissions office.

Applicants residing in the United States should contact:
Director of U.S. Admissions
U.S. Office of Admissions
Richmond, The American International University
   in London
19 Bay State Road
Boston, Massachusetts 02215
Telephone: 617-954-9942
Fax: 617-236-4703
E-mail: us_admissions@richmond.ac.uk
World Wide Web: http://www.richmond.ac.uk

Applicants residing in all other countries should contact:
Director of Admissions
Office of Admissions
Richmond, The American International University
   in London
Queens Road, Richmond
Surrey TW10 6JP
England
Telephone: 44-20-8332-9000
Fax: 44-20-8332-1596
E-mail: enroll@richmond.ac.uk
World Wide Web: http://www.richmond.ac.uk

The Richmond Hill campus is situated near the River Thames in one of London's most attractive and secure areas. The impressive neo-Gothic structure was constructed in 1843.

RIDER UNIVERSITY
LAWRENCEVILLE, NEW JERSEY

The University

Founded in 1865, Rider University is an independent, coeducational, nonsectarian institution accredited by the Middle States Association of Colleges and Schools. Rider has two campuses, one in Lawrenceville, New Jersey, and one in Princeton, New Jersey.

Rider's four academic units include the College of Business Administration; the College of Liberal Arts, Education, and Sciences; the College of Continuing Studies; and Westminster Choir College, located in Princeton, New Jersey.

More than 95 percent of Rider's full-time faculty members hold a doctorate or other appropriate advanced degree. Primarily a teaching institution, Rider University selects instructors who are committed to imparting the knowledge and skills of a particular discipline. Full professors teach at all levels. There are no teaching assistants in the classrooms or laboratories.

Rider University is located on a 353-acre campus that contains large open areas and thirty-eight modern buildings constructed within the past twenty-five years. Approximately 70 percent of the 2,900 undergraduates live in University residence halls or in fraternities or sororities on the campus. Entering students and returning students are guaranteed housing on the campus provided that they meet the stated deadlines for submission of housing applications and deposits.

Rider participates in NCAA Division I in all of its intercollegiate sports. Women's sports are basketball, cross-country, field hockey, soccer, softball, swimming, tennis, track and field, and volleyball. Men's sports are basketball, cross-country, baseball, golf, soccer, swimming, tennis, track and field, and wrestling.

Location

Rider University is located in the suburban community of Lawrenceville, New Jersey, midway between Princeton and Trenton, New Jersey. It is approximately 35 miles northeast of Philadelphia and 65 miles southwest of New York City. The location combines the advantages of accessibility to the cultural and recreational facilities of major urban areas and to the peaceful surroundings of a suburban community.

Majors and Degrees

The College of Business Administration awards the Bachelor of Science in Business Administration (B.S.B.A.) degree in accounting, actuarial science, advertising, business administration, computer information systems, economics, finance, global business, human resource management, management and organizational behavior, and marketing. The program is accredited by AACSB–The International Association for Management Education.

The College of Liberal Arts, Education, and Sciences (CLAES) awards the Bachelor of Arts (B.A.) degree in elementary education and secondary education and the Bachelor of Science (B.S.) degree in business education. Rider's education programs are recognized by the National Council for the Accreditation of Teacher Education (NCATE).

The CLAES also awards the B.A. degree in American studies, communications, economics, English, fine arts, French, German, history, journalism, mathematics, philosophy, physics, political science, psychology, Russian, sociology, and Spanish. It offers the B.S. degree in biochemistry, biology, biopsychology, chemistry, environmental science, geosciences, and marine science.

Preprofessional programs are available in allied health, dentistry, law, and medicine. Three out of four of Rider's premed graduates who apply to medical schools are accepted to medical school.

Preparation for career success goes beyond the classroom at Rider. The Office of Career Placement and the Career Development Program help students prepare for their future with career counseling, resume writing, job search workshops, video interview sessions, and individualized counseling. Internships, on-campus recruiting by a wide variety of international, national, and regional companies, and an off-campus referral service helped more than 94 percent of Rider's graduates to successfully find employment or pursue advanced degree programs.

Academic Program

Rider University operates on the semester system. Each College requires a minimum of 120 semester hours of credit for graduation; the last 30 semester hours of credit must be earned at Rider University. The College of Business Administration requires that a student earn at least 45 semester hours, including the last 30, at Rider University.

The Baccalaureate Honors Program is available to students in all programs. To be considered for the program, incoming freshmen must be in the top 10 percent of their high school class and have a combined SAT I score of 1150 or higher. Students currently enrolled in the University and transfer students must have at least a 3.25 cumulative grade point average. All applicants are interviewed by the Baccalaureate Honors Program Committee.

Rider University recognizes the Advanced Placement (AP) Program and offers credit and placement for scores of 3, 4, or 5 on most AP tests. Credit is awarded for the College-Level Examination Program (CLEP) tests provided that the minimum required score is obtained. The minimum score varies according to the specific area covered by the examination.

Off-Campus Arrangements

Rider University offers semester-long and academic-year programs in Austria, England, France, Israel, Puerto Rico, and Spain. It offers a six-week summer program in Japan.

Academic Facilities

The Franklin F. Moore Library contains 353,000 volumes, arranged in open stacks, and more than 1,500 periodicals and technical journals, magazines, and business services. The library is automated and has a computerized catalog and circulation system. To complement its on-campus holdings, the library offers online database searches of holdings of other libraries.

Students have direct access to a fiber-optic campus network linking approximately 300 terminals located in the Computer Center, Library, and academic buildings. Students may use computing laboratories with multimedia workstations and comprehensive software libraries. Local area networks connect to the campus network to help students develop class projects and presentations. Digital VAX computer clusters in the central Computer Center provide students with network access, extensive software offerings, and compilation resources. E-mail, bulletin boards, Internet access, and other campus computer services are available via the University network.

Other academic facilities include well-equipped science laboratories for biochemistry, biology, biopsychology, chemistry, environmental science, geology, physics, and psychology and two 400-seat theaters.

Costs

The total annual tuition charge for new students who begin their studies in 2000–01 is $17,180. Mandatory fees include a student activity fee of $140 and a one-time orientation fee of $155. Room (standard 2 to a room) and board charges total $7080 for the academic year. It is estimated that books and supplies, personal expenses, and transportation average $1900.

Financial Aid

Most financial aid is based upon demonstrated financial need. Students and their parents are required to file the Free Application for Federal Student Aid (FAFSA) prior to March 1 to be considered for financial assistance administered by Rider University. The University maintains a need-blind admission policy and attempts to meet the full financial need of all eligible applicants. Entering students are eligible for consideration for Federal Pell Grants, Federal Supplemental Educational Opportunity Grants, Federal Work-Study awards, Federal Perkins Loans, New Jersey Tuition Aid Grants, New Jersey Distinguished Scholar Scholarships, and Rider University grants, Trustee Scholarships, Alumni Scholarships, and other forms of institutional aid. Rider University offers six merit-based scholarship programs for qualified applicants. These scholarships, the Presidential, Diversity, Provost, Dean's, Founders, and Transfer scholarships, are for up to $12,000 and are renewable for up to four years of study if the student maintains the minimum grade point average specified by the Scholarship Committee. Rider also offers two full-tuition actors scholarships.

Faculty

There are 226 full-time and 187 part-time faculty members. Ninety-five percent of the faculty hold a doctorate or terminal degree in their field. The same faculty teaches both graduate and undergraduate courses; graduate assistants do not teach classes at Rider University. The student-faculty ratio is approximately 13:1. Faculty members serve on student affairs committees and as faculty advisers to all student organizations.

Student Government

There is an active Student Government Association (SGA) on the campus. The SGA sponsors concerts, lectures, plays, and other events. All social rules and regulations are made, enforced, and adjudicated by students. Each class, each residence hall, the Interfraternity Council, the Panhellenic Society, and commuting students are represented in the Student Government Association.

Admission Requirements

Students applying for admission to Rider University are expected to have completed a minimum of 16 acceptable college-preparatory units of study by the end of their senior year in high school. These 16 units must include 4 in English, and the other 12 units should be selected from traditional academic areas, including history, mathematics, science, social studies, foreign languages, and literature. Business or vocational courses completed in high school are not considered college-preparatory units. Students applying for admission to programs in premedicine, predentistry, science, business, and mathematics are expected to have completed 3 years of mathematics (algebra I, algebra II, and geometry). Students are required to submit official SAT I results in support of their application. Most successful applicants rank in the upper half of their high school senior class.

Rider University seeks a diverse student body and encourages applications from students from varied ethnic, economic, and geographic backgrounds. Campus interviews are strongly recommended but not required for most candidates. There is an active Student Ambassador Program on campus, which consists of faculty-recommended student volunteers from each major area. These student ambassadors host prospective students individually, taking them to class and to lunch and seeing that they meet faculty members and other students. This allows the prospective student to experience life at Rider University for a day.

Application and Information

Rider University works on a rolling admissions basis, but it encourages applications for the fall semester to be submitted by February 15 if the student wishes to obtain housing on the campus. Applications for the spring semester should be submitted by December 15. An early action option is available. Students must submit all necessary documentation by November 15 and are notified of an admissions decision by December 15. The application fee of $35 should be included with the application. Students are notified of the admission decision in approximately 3 to 4 weeks, in accordance with the rolling admission policy. Transfer applicants receive the same priority for admission, housing, and financial aid as freshman applicants.

Interested students are encouraged to contact:

Director of Admissions
Rider University
2083 Lawrenceville Road
Lawrenceville, New Jersey 08648-3099
Telephone: 609-896-5042
          800-257-9026 (toll-free)
E-mail: admissions@rider.edu
World Wide Web: http://www.rider.edu

Centennial Lake and Franklin F. Moore Library.

RIPON COLLEGE
RIPON, WISCONSIN

The College
One key reason why students choose Ripon College from among the more than 3,500 colleges and universities in the country is that Ripon offers an intensely personal undergraduate education. Since 1851, Ripon has provided a personal liberal arts education that makes a remarkable difference in the lives of students. *U.S. News & World Report* recently ranked Ripon in a fifth-place tie among those national liberal arts colleges that offer "high quality education at a reasonable cost."

Companies look for college graduates who can adapt to change and who can write, use modern technology with confidence, communicate, and make a contribution to a team. These are the skills that a Ripon education offers students.

Ripon's curricular emphasis focuses on Communicating Plus. This program aims to assist students in the development of superior written and oral communication, critical-thinking, and problem-solving skills.

Ripon is a residential college; 90 percent of students live on campus, and because students remain on campus after classes have ended, learning occurs around the clock. All students are encouraged to participate in Ripon's numerous extracurricular activities, including the campus radio station and the Student Senate.

Ripon College is fully accredited by the North Central Association of Colleges and Schools.

Location
Ripon College is situated on 250 tree-lined, rolling acres adjacent to downtown Ripon, Wisconsin, a charming turn-of-the-century community of 7,500 people. Ripon is a short drive from Green Bay, Madison, and Milwaukee. A variety of year-round recreational activities are available in Ripon and in Green Lake, a city just 6 miles from the campus.

Majors and Degrees
The Bachelor of Arts is offered in thirty majors: anthropology, art, biology, business management, chemistry, chemistry-biology, computer science, economics, educational studies, English, environmental studies, foreign languages, French, German, global studies, history, Latin American studies, mathematics, music, philosophy, physical education, physics, politics and government, psychobiology, psychology, religion, sociology-anthropology, Spanish, speech communications, and theater. Self-designed majors and preprofessional programs are also available. Minors are available in most of the departments listed above and in leadership studies and women's studies. In addition, the educational studies department offers certification programs in elementary education, music, physical education, and secondary education.

Under a special program for engineers, a student may study for three years at Ripon and two at an engineering school, receiving a bachelor's degree from each institution. Ripon has formal cooperative engineering programs with Washington University in St. Louis and Rensselaer Polytechnic Institute. A student who desires to go into forestry may study for three years at Ripon and two years at Duke University, receiving both a bachelor's degree and a master's degree. In addition, Ripon College and Rush-Presbyterian-St. Luke's Medical Center in Chicago offer a cooperative program in nursing and allied health sciences in which students spend their first two years at Ripon and then transfer to Rush for their final two years.

Academic Program
Since its founding, Ripon has been a liberal arts college. Students have the opportunity to study all fields of human knowledge, including the social sciences, the natural sciences, the humanities, and the fine arts. While other colleges have become increasingly specialized, Ripon has remained steadfast in its belief that the liberal arts are the key for a life of both personal and professional success. Ripon operates on a schedule of two 15-week semesters and an optional 3-week "Maymester."

Off-Campus Arrangements
Ripon's off-campus studies program sends students to such places as Costa Rica, England, France, Germany, Italy, Japan, and Spain to study for a semester. In addition, students can select programs within the U.S., such as the Oak Ridge Laboratory Semester in Tennessee, the Newberry Library Seminar in the Humanities in Chicago, urban studies and urban teaching in Chicago, and study at the Wilderness Field Station for Biology in Minnesota.

Academic Facilities
Ripon's campus combines the best of both historic and modern architecture. The College's three original buildings, constructed between 1851 and 1867, are still used for offices and classes. The Farr Hall of Science, which recently received a $4.4-million renovation and addition, holds a planetarium, a greenhouse, ample laboratory space, and state-of-the-art equipment. On the west side of campus, the C. J. Rodman Center for the Arts and the J. M. Storzer Physical Education Center house a recital hall, a theater, an art gallery, a sculpture garden, a multipurpose gymnasium, a pool, racquetball courts, free-weight and Nautilus rooms, and aerobics rooms. Adjacent to the Storzer Center is the Ceresco Prairie Conservancy, 3½ miles of recreational trails and 130 acres of restored native habitat. Ripon's student center, Harwood Memorial Union, holds a lecture hall, the Pub, a game room, the radio station, and student organization offices.

Costs
The costs for 2000–01 are as follows: tuition, $18,000; room and board, $4400; and fees, books, and miscellaneous personal expenses, $1000.

Financial Aid
Ninety percent of Ripon students receive financial assistance that meets 100 percent of their financial need. The average financial aid award equals 71 percent of a student's total costs. Ripon's extensive scholarship program is designed to recognize and reward applicants for their talents and abilities. Currently, seventeen types of scholarships that range from $2000 to full tuition annually are available.

Faculty
Ripon College's student-faculty ratio is 10:1, and the average class size is 11. Ninety percent of the full-time faculty members

have earned the highest degree in their fields, and, as a result of their hard work, Ripon has received ten National Science Foundation Grants since 1992 and six Fulbright Fellowships since 1989.

Student Government

The Student Senate, composed of representatives of all resident groups and campus organizations, is the main governing body and administers a budget of more than $100,000 for student organizations and activities. It is an active and influential means of bringing student opinion to bear on College affairs.

Admission Requirements

Important factors considered in the admission process include graduation from an accredited secondary school (or GED equivalent), the secondary school transcript, and results of standardized tests (SAT or ACT).

Application and Information

Prospective students who value a challenging liberal arts and sciences education in a small, caring community are invited to visit the campus, sit in on Ripon classes, and see firsthand how Ripon students and professors interact with one another.

Students who wish to apply to Ripon College should submit a completed application form, a secondary school transcript, results of standardized tests, and the $25 application fee. Ripon College application forms are available from the admission office and at the College's Web site (address below). Ripon participates in the Common Application Plan and accepts photocopies of the Common Application in place of the Ripon College application form. Common Application forms are available in many secondary school guidance offices. Ripon also accepts applications that are made through the CollegeNet program (http://apply.review.com).

Candidates for fall term consideration are encouraged to apply early. Notification of fall term admission occurs within two weeks of the completion of the student's application. Students applying for spring term consideration should submit applications by December 15. Notification occurs shortly thereafter.

For further information, students should contact:

Dean of Admission
Ripon College
300 Seward Street
P.O. Box 248
Ripon, Wisconsin 54971-0248
Telephone: 800-94-RIPON (toll-free)
E-mail: adminfo@ripon.edu
World Wide Web: http://www.ripon.edu

Ripon College students and their families celebrate commencement on the lawn of Harwood Memorial Union.

RIVIER COLLEGE
NASHUA, NEW HAMPSHIRE

The College

Rivier College, a private, Catholic liberal arts college founded in 1933, has gained a reputation for academic excellence in more than sixty programs. The College has adapted to changing needs by developing liberal arts/career-oriented programs designed to prepare graduates in many fields.

The undergraduate programs in the School of Undergraduate Studies enroll approximately 1,550 students, including 700 full-time day students. This results in an 18:1 student-faculty ratio, small classes, and the opportunity for students to become active members of the academic and social community. Rivier is growing, but it remains a small college, where an outstanding teaching faculty offers support and encouragement to its students.

Most full-time undergraduate day students are between 18 and 22 years old. The majority are residents of New England, although other states are represented, including New York, New Jersey, Florida, Texas, and Virginia. International students represent countries in Africa, Asia, Europe, the Middle East, and South America. Students who live on campus reside in three modern residence halls. Most rooms are doubles. In addition, there are more than 300 commuting students in the undergraduate day division. The Dion Center houses the dining room, the commuter lounge, the mail room, a bookstore, student development offices, and meeting rooms. Students are permitted to have cars on campus.

Orientation sessions for new students are sponsored by the Office of Student Development. Assistance is offered throughout the year in academic and personal counseling. A full-time chaplain and Campus Ministry team coordinate spiritual activities. A comprehensive career development service helps students prepare for employment after graduation. Students' health needs are met by a physician and a registered nurse. The Office of Student Development, the Student Government Association, and more than twenty-five student clubs and organizations provide an exciting calendar of social, cultural, and recreational activities, including dances, live entertainment, films, and sports events. Rivier offers a wide range of team and individual sports, including NCAA Division III men's baseball, basketball, cross-country, soccer, and volleyball and women's basketball, cross-country, softball, soccer, and volleyball. Intramural sports and fitness activities include tennis, volleyball, floor hockey, weight training, aerobics, self-defense, and skiing (downhill and cross-country). The College and student organizations frequently organize outings, including trips to Boston for shopping, dining, museums, concerts, or theater productions. Students also enjoy a variety of performances by the Rivier Theater Company.

Location

Nashua (population 84,000) is located in southern New Hampshire. The city of Boston lies within easy access 40 miles to the south. Local access to public transportation provides for easy travel to and from campus. Recreational activities abound year-round at nearby lakes and ski areas, in the White Mountains to the north, and at the seacoast, just an hour's drive to the east.

Majors and Degrees

Rivier College awards the Bachelor of Arts, the Bachelor of Fine Arts, and the Bachelor of Science degrees in the following areas of concentration: art (art education, drawing and painting, graphic design, illustration, photography and digital imaging, and studio art), athletic training, biology and biology education, business (accounting, administration, information systems, and management), chemistry, chemistry education, communications (broadcast/print journalism, desktop publishing, and public relations), computer science, education (early childhood/special, elementary/special, and secondary), English, English education, exercise physiology, history, human development, law and government, liberal studies, mathematics, mathematics education, modern languages (French, modern-language education, and Spanish), nursing, psychology, social science education, and sociology. Associate degrees are offered in art, business (accounting, business administration, and information management), computer science, early childhood education, liberal arts, and nursing. Preprofessional programs are offered in dentistry, law, medicine, physical therapy, and veterinary medicine.

Academic Program

Rivier College takes special pride in its curriculum, which offers both liberal arts and professional studies in order to prepare students for a fast-changing, highly technological society. The curriculum is broad-based, with emphasis on preparing students for challenging and rewarding careers and furthering their personal growth. Core curriculum requirements may vary slightly, depending on the degree to be obtained, but generally include courses in the areas of English, mathematics and/or natural sciences, modern language and literature, philosophy, religious studies, social science, and Western civilization. No fewer than ten courses must be taken in the major field. Electives may be chosen according to the student's interests. For the bachelor's degree, a minimum of 120 credits with a grade point average of at least 2.0 is required. For the associate degree, the student must complete a minimum of 60 credits with a grade point average of at least 2.0.

All departments encourage qualified students to pursue internships in their field of study during their junior or senior year. Education specialists student teach in local schools. Nursing majors complete clinical rotations in health-care facilities throughout southern New Hampshire and Boston. Law and government majors may work in a law office, business, legal-assistance agency, or government agency. Sociology and psychology majors work with local social service agencies. English and communications majors work in public relations, broadcasting, or corporate communications positions. Art majors work in advertising or graphic design or at local galleries. Career programs include the ABA-accredited B.A. in legal studies program and the associate and bachelor's degree programs in nursing.

Honors awards include placement on the dean's list, membership in Kappa Gamma Pi, listing in *Who's Who Among Students in American Universities and Colleges,* listing in *The National Dean's List,* and degrees with honors. Academically talented students may also apply to the four-year Honors Program.

The college year is divided into two 15-week semesters, with first-semester examinations held before Christmas recess. Students usually take five courses each semester. Academic credit may be granted to incoming freshmen on the basis of scores on Advanced Placement tests and CLEP examinations. Students may also "challenge" courses and receive credit by special examination.

Off-Campus Arrangements

Through Rivier College's membership in the New Hampshire College and University Council, a twelve-member consortium of senior colleges, Rivier students may register for courses at any of the member colleges and receive transfer credits.

Academic Facilities

Academic facilities include Memorial Hall, housing fourteen classrooms, faculty offices, a lecture hall, a Macintosh Electronic Imaging Lab, and art department facilities that include an art gallery, slide library, and studios. Other academic facilities include fully equipped science laboratories; the Education Center, which houses an eight-classroom Early Childhood Center, preschool and observation rooms, and an Educational Resource Center; and the Campus Computer Center, which houses microcomputer laboratories featuring Apple and IBM workstations with a full range of cutting-edge software and Internet and e-mail access, a data processing lab, and a time-sharing lab. Other campus facilities include the Regina Library, housing more than 128,000 holdings, a law library, and a micromedia center; the Writing Center, staffed by professional writing consultants as well as student tutors; the Muldoon Health and Fitness Center; soccer and softball fields; and the newly completed 26,000-square-foot addition to Sylvia Trottier Hall, which houses health science laboratories and classrooms.

Costs

Tuition and fees for the academic year 1999–2000 were $13,950; room and board, $5690; and books and supplies, approximately $700. Students should expect to pay a $100 activities fee and a $25 registration fee each semester.

Financial Aid

Financial aid is awarded on the basis of the financial need of the student and family. Approximately 80 percent of Rivier's students receive financial aid from the College or from government or private sources. Federal aid includes Federal Pell Grants, Federal Supplemental Educational Opportunity Grants, Federal Perkins Loans, Federal Stafford Student Loans, the Federal PLUS loan program, and the Federal Work-Study Program. To be considered for financial aid a student must file the Free Application for Federal Student Aid (FAFSA) with the federal government as soon as possible after January 1 for the coming year. FAFSA results should be on file with the College Financial Aid Office prior to March 1 for the following academic year. Each applicant is assessed individually to determine the best combination of grant, work, scholarship, and loan amounts to meet the need of the student. The College awards several merit-based scholarships and grants ranging in value from $1000 to full tuition. For more information students should contact the Director of Financial Aid.

Faculty

The College employs 80 full-time faculty members. The full-time student–faculty ratio is 13:1. Part-time instructors in specialized areas are working professionals who bring current knowledge and expertise in their field to their classes. All classes are taught by faculty members, and department chairs serve as academic advisers to students in their major programs.

Student Government

Every full-time day student automatically becomes a member of the Student Government Association (SGA) upon registration and payment of the student activity fee. The main goals of the SGA are to stimulate active participation in all College functions, to establish and maintain effective channels of communication among members of the College community and the community at large, and to foster a mutual trust, encourage a spirit of cooperation, and initiate new endeavors. The SGA also supervises student clubs and organizations and oversees their finances. The SGA Executive Board serves as the channel of communication through which the views of the students on institutional policies reach the College administration.

Admission Requirements

Applicants for admission should ordinarily have completed, in an accredited high school, a minimum of 16 academic units, including 4 in English, 2 in a modern foreign language, 3 in mathematics, 2 in social science, 2 in science, and 3 in electives. (In some cases, the language requirement may be waived.) The most successful candidates are in the upper half of their class, with at least a B average. Combined SAT I scores average 950–1000. A personal interview is strongly recommended but not required.

Rivier welcomes applications from qualified transfer candidates from accredited institutions, as well as applications from international students. Transfer students must forward transcripts of all previous college work and a high school transcript. International students must fulfill the requirements for general admission, but they may be required to submit TOEFL (Test of English as a Foreign Language) scores. Deferred admission may be granted to students who wish to postpone entrance for up to one year, provided that they have not been enrolled full-time at some other postsecondary institution.

Application and Information

Applications must be accompanied by a nonrefundable $25 application fee, SAT I scores, one letter of recommendation, and a high school transcript. The School of Undergraduate Studies employs a system of rolling admission that allows qualified students to be admitted approximately one month after their application is completed. Transfers should apply by June 1 for fall admission and by December 1 for spring admission. Those applying for financial aid should observe the March 1 deadline. Prospective art majors must submit a portfolio of their work. Interviews are arranged through the Admissions Office.

More specific information and application forms can be obtained by contacting:

Director of Undergraduate Admissions
Rivier College
420 Main Street
Nashua, New Hampshire 03060

Telephone: 603-897-8507
           800-44-RIVIER (toll-free)
Fax: 603-891-1799
E-mail: rivadmit@rivier.edu
World Wide Web: http://www.rivier.edu

Memorial Hall, principal classroom building at Rivier College.

ROBERT MORRIS COLLEGE
CHICAGO, BENSENVILLE, NAPERVILLE, OAK LAWN, ORLAND PARK, AND SPRINGFIELD, ILLINOIS

The College

Robert Morris College (RMC) is a private, not-for-profit, independent college dedicated to providing intensive career education and general education opportunities. Professional diplomas, associate degrees, the Bachelor of Business Administration degree, and the Bachelor of Applied Science degree in graphic design are awarded. The College is accredited by the North Central Association of Colleges and Schools (NCA, 30 North LaSalle Street, Chicago, Illinois 60602; telephone: 312-263-0456). Its history dates back to 1913 and the Moser School, a Chicago-based school that became a part of Robert Morris College in 1975. The College now provides students with a choice of six locations: Chicago, Bensenville, Naperville, Oak Lawn, Orland Park, and Springfield, Illinois.

Robert Morris College offers programs via the School of Business Administration, the School of Health Studies, the School of Computer Studies, and the Institute of Art and Design. The College recognizes the diversity among its student body and its requirements for options to fit students' individual needs and circumstances and offers choices that include three levels of academic achievement: the Bachelor of Business Administration and the Bachelor of Applied Science degree in graphic design in three years, an associate degree in fifteen months, and a professional diploma in ten months. RMC's unique five-quarter system divides long-term objectives into short-term goals. As students complete each academic level, they have the opportunity to continue to the next academic level or to enter the career of their choice. This allows students to evaluate their educational objective as they progress, without losing credit or time.

The student body of 5,400 is a cross-cultural, ethnic, and racial mix representative of the communities served.

Each student at the College is the center of a small team revolving around his or her chosen career major. Program directors, instructors, and placement specialists provide personalized services to assist the student in successfully achieving educational and career goals. The records of the College's students and graduates are the best indicators of what a prospective student can expect. Seventy-two percent of Robert Morris College students graduate from the programs they begin, compared to significantly lower percentages at other private and public colleges and universities.

The Placement Department, which has offices at each of the College's campuses, continuously cultivates employment opportunities for RMC graduates with representatives in the business, allied health, art, and computer industries. Last year, 9 out of 10 RMC graduates who requested job placement assistance successfully secured employment in their chosen fields.

Robert Morris College is a member of the National Association of Intercollegiate Athletics (NAIA) and the Chicagoland Collegiate Athletic Conference (CCAC), Division II. The College offers men's and women's basketball and cross-country. It also offers men's baseball and women's soccer, softball, and volleyball.

Location

Located in the heart of Chicago's bustling cultural and financial districts, the College's main campus is minutes from all that Chicago offers, including the Chicago Board of Trade, Merchandise Mart, Art Institute, Field Museum, lakefront, sports arenas, theaters, and all forms of public transportation. The Chicago campus is located at 401 South State Street and is readily accessible from all parts of the city and suburbs by bus lines and trains. Parking is available in the immediate vicinity. Robert Morris Center is across the street from the renowned Harold Washington Public Library.

The Bensenville Center, opened in September 1999 to better serve the residents of DuPage County and to meet the demands of employers in the area. A curriculum is offered via the School of Computer Studies. The Oak Lawn Center, the newest suburban location, which opened in September 1999, serves students in a community where there is a high demand for educational services but students may have a difficult time getting to other Robert Morris College locations. A curriculum is offered via the School of Business Administration. The Springfield Campus is located at 3101 Montvale Drive (Montvale Drive and Wabash Avenue), just east of White Oaks Mall. The College is accessible by bus, and ample parking is also available. The Orland Park Campus is located at 43 Orland Square, adjacent to the Orland Square Mall. The campus is situated approximately 30 miles southwest of Chicago and is accessible via public transportation and Interstate 80 and 55, which run parallel on the south and north end of the campus, respectively. Known as the "golf center of the world," Orland Park is also becoming a corporate center of the southwest Chicago suburbs, offering students ample opportunity for professional growth through externships and employment. The Naperville Campus is located at 1804 Centre Point Circle and was opened to better serve students as well as the employers along the East-West High Tech Corridor. The campus is located in the heart of rapid technological development and close to a wide range of employers. All locations provide students with access to the unlimited variety of business services that Chicago, Bensenville, Naperville, Oak Lawn, Orland Park, and Springfield have to offer and enhance the students' understanding of the world of work and the employment process.

Majors and Degrees

The Bachelor of Business Administration degree at Robert Morris College offers concentrations in accounting, computer networking, health-care management, and management. The Bachelor of Applied Science degree program offers concentrations in graphic arts and media arts. RMC also awards associate degrees in accounting; administrative assistant studies; business administration; CAD/drafting; computer network specialist studies; computer programming; computer systems specialist studies; graphic arts; legal office assistant/paralegal studies; legal secretary studies; media arts; medical assisting; travel, hospitality, and tourism; and Web design. More than twenty-six transfer agreements have been established between RMC and community colleges, allowing students who have earned associate degrees elsewhere to complete their bachelor's degrees at RMC by transferring in as a junior. RMC awards more associate degrees to members of minority groups than any other private college in the country. RMC is also recognized as a Hispanic Serving Institution by the Hispanic Association of Colleges and Universities (HACU) and is the only baccalaureate degree-granting institution in Illinois with this distinction. RMC is also the fourteenth-largest granter of bachelor's degrees in business administration to Hispanics in the country, according to the July 1999 edition of *Black Issues in Higher Education*.

Professional diplomas can be earned in all the above areas, with the exception of computer programming and Web design.

Degrees vary among campuses.

Academic Program

The College's academic calendar consists of five quarters, each of which is ten weeks long. The program of study is designed so that students can complete their course work and enter their careers in the shortest time possible. The calendar enables students to earn a professional diploma in ten months, an associate degree in fifteen months, and a Bachelor of Business Administration or Bachelor of Applied Science degree in graphic design in three years. The College requires its students to comply with dress and attendance policies as part of their career training.

By concentrating on the specialized subjects related to the student's chosen career field, the College's professional diploma curriculums provide students with the skills and knowledge necessary to enter the job market. Each major consists of courses prescribed by the College to lead to this objective. A professional diploma requires 64 quarter hours of credit, with core requirements dependent on the student's major.

An associate degree requires at least 100 quarter hours of credit with a minimum of 39 hours of credit in general education in the areas of communications, humanities, math and science, and social and behavioral science. A minimum of 52 quarter hours of credit is required in career courses, and the remaining hours are electives split between general education and career courses. All credits earned toward a professional diploma can be applied toward meeting associate and bachelor's degree requirements.

The bachelor's degree requires a minimum of 180 quarter hours of credit. A minimum of 78 hours of credit are required in general education courses, and 104 hours are required in major course work.

Off-Campus Arrangements

The College has well-established cooperative education programs for all majors in Chicago. Major area corporations and professional offices are among participating co-op employers. Robert Morris College offers students the opportunity to study abroad at the Institute of European Studies in Vienna, Austria, and at Regent's College in London, England.

Academic Facilities

General purpose classrooms, specialized laboratories, and study, practice, and leisure lounges are among the facilities the College provides at each campus. The technology-based library has online capability that connects the College's five campuses. Multimedia CD-ROMs, as well as online access to the Internet, offer students advanced research capabilities. Sizable collections of reference and resource volumes, as well as periodical subscriptions and vertical file information, are available in addition to numerous computer and audio resources and a job search center.

Costs

Robert Morris College has one of the lowest tuition rates of any baccalaureate degree–granting private college in the state. Tuition for 1999–2000 was $3650 per quarter. Book and supply costs vary by major from $200 to $300 per quarter.

Financial Aid

Robert Morris College participates in the following federal and state financial aid programs: the Federal Pell Grant, Illinois Monetary Award (SSIG/IMA), Federal Supplemental Educational Opportunity Grant (FSEOG), Federal Stafford Student Loan, Federal Perkins Loan, Federal PLUS Loan, and Federal Work-Study (FWS) programs. In addition, the College awards institutional Support-a-Student grants on the basis of need, scholarship, residence, academic major, or a combination of these factors. All students must complete a financial planning interview with their admissions counselor, and all are urged to complete the Free Application for Federal Student Aid (FAFSA). Approximately 85 percent of the student body receive some financial assistance. In the 1998–99 academic year, the College awarded more than $8 million in institutional aid.

Faculty

The faculty members at Robert Morris College are selected on the basis of their academic credentials, career experiences in their field and dedication to giving special attention to every student. All faculty members possess a master's degree in their chosen field, and many possess a Ph.D. in their area of specialization. In addition to teaching courses, faculty members promote the progress of their students through the individualized academic, employment, and personal development counseling they provide.

Student Government

Robert Morris College has no formal student government. Student representatives serve on committees that make recommendations about campus issues. Student organizations and activities are available.

Admission Requirements

The individualized admissions process consists of the evaluation of the student's high school transcript or GED test scores by the Admissions Review Board and an interview with an admissions counselor.

The College offers a tuition-free College Prep program to applicants whose high school records indicate a need for strengthening communications and study skills before beginning career programs. College Prep concentrates students' efforts on study skills, grammar, word usage, oral communication, basic math skills, time management, and personal development through counseling regarding attitudes and attendance. Upon successful completion of College Prep, applicants may enter professional diploma or degree programs.

Robert Morris College admits students of any race, color, sex, or national origin or with any handicap and grants them all the rights and privileges accorded to RMC students. It does not discriminate on any of these bases in administration of its admissions or educational policies, loan programs, placement service, housing, or other College-administered programs.

Application and Information

Applications can be obtained by contacting the Admissions Office at any of the College's campuses. The completed application and the $20 application fee should be sent to the Admissions Office. The College operates on a rolling admissions basis, and students can enroll during any one of the five times offered during the year. For further information, prospective students should contact:

Admissions Office
Robert Morris College
401 South State Street
Chicago, Illinois 60605
Telephone: 312-935-6835
       800-225-1520 (toll-free)

Admissions Office
Robert Morris College
1000 Tower Lane
Bensenville, Illinois 60106
Telephone: 800-789-8735 (toll-free)

Admissions Office
Robert Morris College
1804 Centre Point Circle
Naperville, Illinois 60563
Telephone: 630-577-8700
       800-789-8735 (toll-free)

Admissions Office
Robert Morris College
9400 Southwest Highway
Oak Lawn, Illinois 60453
Telephone: 708-226-3800
       800-880-9373 (toll-free)

Admissions Office
Robert Morris College
45 Orland Square
Orland Park, Illinois 60462
Telephone: 708-226-3850
       800-880-9373 (toll-free)

Admissions Office
Robert Morris College
3101 Montvale Drive
Springfield, Illinois 62704
Telephone: 217-795-2500
       800-445-7271 (toll-free)

ROBERT MORRIS COLLEGE
PITTSBURGH AND MOON TOWNSHIP, PENNSYLVANIA

The College
Robert Morris College offers both traditional and innovative educational opportunities in programs that prepare graduates for careers in business, communications, teaching, and health-related fields. In addition, Robert Morris provides an unusual choice of environments with a center in Pittsburgh for commuting students and a spacious residential suburban campus in Moon Township, 17 miles northwest of Pittsburgh.

Founded in 1921, the College has a total undergraduate enrollment of 2,616 full-time and 1,216 part-time students, with a graduate student enrollment of 921. Robert Morris is a private, independent institution accredited by the Middle States Association of Colleges and Schools and the Joint Review Committee on Radiologic Technology Education of the American Medical Association and approved by the Department of Education of the Commonwealth of Pennsylvania.

In addition to its undergraduate degree programs, Robert Morris College offers graduate degree programs in ten areas. These include the Master of Business Administration and a Master of Science degree in accounting, business education, communications and information systems, finance, information systems management, instructional leadership, marketing, sport management, and taxation. In addition, students can earn a Doctor of Science degree in information systems and communication.

The College strives to provide an environment in which the members of the College community are committed to scholarship, diversity of opinion, and open communication that encourages intellectual, social, personal, and professional growth. Internships provide students with opportunities for practical experience in business, government, health, and education to enhance their classroom learning.

The College competes in NCAA Division I and is a member of the Northeast Conference, offering intercollegiate sports in men's and women's basketball, cross-country, indoor and outdoor track, soccer, and tennis; women's crew, softball, and volleyball; and men's golf. Men's and women's bowling, men's hockey, and men's volleyball are intercollegiate club sports. The College also fields a Division I-AA football program.

Location
The 230-acre Moon Township Campus is 17 miles northwest of Pittsburgh near the Pittsburgh International Airport. Located within the area of the nation's eleventh-largest concentration of Fortune 500 corporate headquarters, the Pittsburgh Center provides an eight-level classroom and library facility and a four-level student services and administrative complex.

Majors and Degrees
Robert Morris College grants degrees at the undergraduate, graduate, and doctoral levels. Students can earn the Bachelor of Science in Business Administration degree with majors in accounting, aviation management, economics, finance, finance/economics, health services management, hospitality management, human resource management, logistics management, long-term health-care management, marketing, nursing and managed-care administration, operations management/decision sciences, sport management, and tourism management. The Bachelor of Arts degree is offered in applied mathematics, communication, economics, English, secondary education (teacher certification in communication, English, and social studies), and social science. Students may also earn a Bachelor of Science degree in applied mathematics, economics, elementary education, engineering (logistics and software), hospitality administration, information sciences, information systems management, secondary education (teacher certification in applied mathematics and business education), social science, and tourism administration.

Academic Program
Robert Morris is on a two-semester schedule with various summer sessions. A total of 126 credits are required for the bachelor's degree. Internship or co-op credits of 3 to 12 hours may be used toward degree requirements. The College participates in a cross-registration program with nine local colleges through the Pittsburgh Council on Higher Education consortium.

Academic Facilities
The Learning Resource Center provides a variety of learning facilities, including a traditional library with 129,761 bound volumes, 345,436 items on microfilm and microfiche, and 908 current periodical subscriptions. The collection includes an extensive tax library and specializes in business information and materials made available to the professional and business community of the city.

The Academic Media Center, with full production facilities, provides students with opportunities to collaborate on projects in all areas of media, including television production, audio production, and photography.

Robert Morris College provides students with the opportunity for individualized study facilitated by audio and video tapes, films, and slides. The office administration and business education faculty utilize a competency-based curriculum and the independent progress methodology to teach office skills in a microcomputer classroom. There are 350 personal computers available for student use in laboratories and throughout the campus.

Costs
Annual tuition for the 1999–2000 year was $8460, based on a 30-credit, two-semester schedule at $282 per credit hour; room and board fees were $6062. Resident facilities are available only at the Moon Township Campus. Books average $800. College fees are approximately $480 for all students. Campus activities fees are approximately $530 for full-time students.

Financial Aid
The College has a comprehensive financial aid program that includes scholarships, grants, loans, and work-study programs. There are both need-based and achievement-based awards available. The Robert Morris Merit and Honors Scholarship Awards are offered to freshman applicants who demonstrate high academic achievement and leadership qualities. Other endowed scholarships and grants are available to transfer and continuing students. All applicants must complete the admis-

sions application, the Free Application for Federal Student Aid, and the grant forms from their own state.

Faculty

The College has 278 full- and part-time faculty members. The average class size is 19. Students may take advantage of the expertise offered by the faculty in academic advisement and counseling.

Student Government

The Student Government Association represents all student organizations, including fraternities and sororities, and members participate in the planning of all social and cultural student activities.

Admission Requirements

Robert Morris encourages students from other states to apply; the specialized business and communications programs, especially in the fields of accounting and sport management, attract students from many areas of the country. Primary consideration is given to the applicant's performance in secondary school and scores on the SAT I or ACT.

Transfer students who have earned credits from another regionally accredited institution are evaluated for admission on the basis of their college performance.

Interviews are not required for admission except for students interested in the engineering and elementary education programs. Students are encouraged to visit an enrollment manager either at the Moon Township campus or the Pittsburgh Center.

Robert Morris College is committed to a policy of nondiscrimination on the basis of race, sex, color, religion, national origin, or handicap.

Application and Information

Students are encouraged to submit applications in the fall of their senior year of high school. Official transcripts and counselor recommendations should accompany the application; there is a $30 application processing fee.

Robert Morris uses a rolling admission system; students are considered for acceptance as soon as all application materials have been received and evaluated.

For additional information and application materials, students should contact:

Office of Enrollment Services
Robert Morris College
881 Narrows Run Road
Moon Township, Pennsylvania 15108
Telephone: 412-262-8206
         800-762-0097 (toll-free)
World Wide Web: http://www.robert-morris.edu

Robert Morris College's state-of-the-art student center.

ROBERTS WESLEYAN COLLEGE
ROCHESTER, NEW YORK

The College

Roberts Wesleyan College (RWC) was founded in 1866 as the first Free Methodist academic institution in North America. Since then, the institution has continually adapted its programs to meet the current academic, professional, and personal needs of its students. The integration of broad-based intellectual thought with the Judeo-Christian heritage is and always has been the motivation for Roberts Wesleyan's existence. The College fosters wholesome principles by setting standards for student life, requiring regular chapel attendance (three times per week), and maintaining a perspective rich in values within the classroom.

The current enrollment is 944 women and 461 men. Although students come primarily from New York State, twenty-five other states and seventeen other countries are represented. The majority of students are between 18 and 25 years of age, but there is a growing population of married and older students. The campus is primarily residential, while approximately 30 percent of the students commute.

RWC offers a broad selection of student activities. Student leaders plan a calendar of numerous events each year, including social, cultural, and religious programs. The College's suburban Rochester location also allows students to take advantage of cultural and academic opportunities within the community. The College's intramural program complements the intercollegiate sports program. There are four varsity sports for men: basketball, cross-country, soccer, and track and field; there are five varsity sports for women: basketball, cross-country, soccer, track and field, and volleyball. Students may take advantage of the beautiful Voller Athletic Center, which includes a pool, four basketball courts, an indoor track, racquetball courts, a weight room, saunas, a student center, a snack bar, and a bookstore. The Career Planning and Placement Office provides numerous services for students. Other College services available to students include academic advisement, counseling, and assistance from the Learning Center.

The College is a member of the Middle States Association of Colleges and Schools, the Association of Colleges and Universities of the State of New York, Rochester Area Colleges, the Association of Free Methodist Educational Institutions, the Council of Independent Colleges and Universities, and the Coalition for Christian Colleges and Universities. The programs in accounting, art, business, music, nursing, and social work are professionally accredited. The Art Department is accredited by the National Association of Schools of Art and Design. The Music Department is an accredited member of the National Association of Schools of Music. The Division of Nursing is accredited by the National League for Nursing Accrediting Commission, and the Social Work Department is accredited by the Council on Social Work Education. The Division of Business Administration and Accounting was recently accredited by the Association of Collegiate Business Schools and Programs.

In addition to its undergraduate programs, Roberts Wesleyan offers the Master of Education, the Master of Social Work, and Master of Science in Management degrees. Northeastern Seminary at Roberts Wesleyan College offers the M.Div., M.A. in Theological Studies, and M.Div./M.S.W.

Location

Roberts Wesleyan College is located 8 miles southwest of Rochester, New York, in the suburb of North Chili. Rochester, a city of more than 250,000, is a thriving cultural and corporate area. Eastman School of Music, the Rochester Philharmonic Orchestra, and several of America's leading corporations, such as Eastman Kodak, Xerox, and Bausch & Lomb, make their home there.

The College continues to develop a strong relationship with the community, and the resulting internships and opportunities for practical work are particularly advantageous for Roberts Wesleyan students. Current students and graduates enjoy the extensive employment opportunities that result from Rochester's healthy economy. Lake Ontario, Niagara Falls, Watkins Glen, Letchworth Park, and the Finger Lakes are all nearby.

Majors and Degrees

The Associate of Science degree is offered in natural science and physical science. The Bachelor of Arts degree may be obtained in art, biology, chemistry, communication, comprehensive science, comprehensive social studies, contemporary ministries, English, fine arts, history, humanities, mathematics, music, physics, psychology, religion/philosophy, and sociology. The Bachelor of Science degree is offered in accounting, art, art education, biochemistry, biology (including a concentration in medical technology), business administration, chemistry, computer science, criminal justice, elementary education, mathematics, music–applied pedagogy (piano and voice), music education, nursing, organizational management, physics, and social work.

A 3-2 program in engineering is offered in cooperation with Clarkson University, Rensselaer Polytechnic Institute, and Rochester Institute of Technology. The program leads to a B.S. in mathematics, chemistry, or physics from RWC and a B.S. in engineering from Clarkson, Rensselaer, or Rochester Institute of Technology.

Secondary teaching certification may be earned in biochemistry, biology, English, mathematics, physics, and social studies. Preprofessional programs include dentistry, law, medicine, pharmacy, and veterinary medicine.

Academic Program

The two central objectives of the academic program are to provide a broad-based education and to offer courses of study that encourage career-oriented specialization. Approximately 45 semester hours of core courses are required of each baccalaureate degree candidate. These liberal arts survey courses introduce four main fields of knowledge: biological science, physical science, and mathematics; history and the behavioral sciences; language, literature, and the fine arts; and biblical studies and philosophy. A total of 124 semester hours is required for graduation with a baccalaureate degree, including a minimum of 30 to 67 semester hours within the student's major discipline.

Several academic programs at Roberts Wesleyan include internships or practical work experiences. Independent study and cross-cultural study opportunities are also available. Students may receive credit through the Advanced Placement Program, Regents College Examinations, or College-Level Examination Program. The Learning Center provides assistance for students possessing exceptional skills or a deficiency in any particular area.

The College calendar consists of two 15-week semesters scheduled from September to December and from January to May. Two 3-week summer sessions are held following the second semester.

Off-Campus Arrangements

Various off-campus opportunities exist for which credit is awarded. These include the Appalachian Semester in Kentucky, Focus on the Family Institute in Colorado, EDUVenture in Irian Jaya, and a semester or full year of study at Richmond College in London, England. Under the direction of an RWC professor, students may also participate in a short-term exchange study program with Osaka Christian College and Seminary in Osaka,

Japan. Opportunities for off-campus experiences also exist for Roberts students through the Coalition for Christian Colleges and Universities. These include the American Studies Program, Latin American Studies Program, Los Angeles Film Studies Center, Middle East Studies Program, Russian Studies Program, and Oxford Summer School. The January Experience Program offers transcultural and enrichment courses in this country or abroad. In addition, through RWC's membership in the Rochester Area Colleges consortium, RWC students may cross-register to take courses at any of the other member institutions.

Academic Facilities

The Sprague Library, with 250 student stations, occupies a modern, air-conditioned building and holds more than 108,000 volumes, 877 periodicals, and more than 150,000 microforms, as well as recordings, filmstrips, and slides. Also included in the library are the Learning Center, the Audio-Visual Center, the Historical Room, and the Rare Books Room. Through its participation in the Rochester Regional Research Library Council, the library provides access to extensive interlibrary loan resources. Well-equipped science laboratories, a lecture auditorium, and computer laboratories connected to the campus network are included in the Merlin G. Smith Science Center. Other facilities are the music studios, practice rooms, and recital auditorium of Cox Hall, the educational curriculum laboratory in Carpenter Hall, and the new Cultural Life Center.

Costs

For the 2000–01 academic year, tuition for full-time study is $13,690. Costs vary if a student's course load is fewer than 12 or more than 16 hours. Additional fees are charged for music and laboratory courses. Room and board are $4758. Book costs and personal expenses vary, depending on individual needs.

Financial Aid

Roberts Wesleyan College offers a complete financial aid program, consisting of grants, scholarships, loans, and employment. Filing the Free Application for Federal Student Aid (FAFSA) is a prerequisite for determining eligibility for most financial aid programs. Sources of aid include Federal Pell Grants, Federal Supplemental Educational Opportunity Grants, Federal Perkins Loans, and Federal Stafford Student Loans; New York State Tuition Assistance Program awards; and institutional resources. Numerous on-campus employment opportunities are available. Institutional aid is also available in recognition of academic, athletic, artistic, and musical achievement. More than 90 percent of the student body receives financial aid each year.

Faculty

The primary concern of the faculty at RWC is to provide an educational experience of high quality. Forty-five percent of the professors hold the doctoral or terminal degree, and all are well respected within their specific discipline. The 73 full-time and 56 part-time faculty members are committed to Christian higher education and are genuinely interested in each student's development. A 14:1 student-faculty ratio allows for much individualized attention, and most professors go well beyond their tasks of teaching and advising to participate in campus activities.

Student Government

All students belong to the Student Association and have the freedom to express their opinions to the staff, faculty, and administration. There are also elected senators and officers, under the direction of the Student Services Office, who act as liaisons between the student body and the administration in areas concerning academics and student activities.

Admission Requirements

Because the type of student a college enrolls significantly determines the personality of the institution, Roberts Wesleyan looks for students who will contribute to the College's environment of friendliness and genuine caring. It seeks students whose personal lives are characterized by honesty, integrity, and devotion to high moral and ethical standards. Admission consideration is given to applicants who rank in the upper three fifths of their graduating class and have earned a minimum of 12 academic units of high school credit, with no fewer than 4 units in English, 2 units in algebra (or 1 in algebra and 1 in geometry), and 1 unit in biology, chemistry, or physics. Three years each of social studies, a foreign language, and science are strongly recommended. Further preparation in mathematics and science is required of applicants who wish to enter degree programs in nursing, mathematics, or science. Scores on the SAT I or ACT and a formal recommendation are required. Special talents are considered an asset for applicants but are not required. An on-campus admission interview is strongly recommended. In admitting students, the College does not discriminate on the basis of race, age, color, sex, handicap, creed, or national or ethnic origin. Children of alumni and staff are considered for admission on the same basis as all other applicants.

Transfer students must fulfill the same admission requirements as beginning students and must also have transcripts forwarded to the College from all the institutions they have attended. Credit is usually accepted for any course in which a grade of C or above has been earned if the course parallels to some degree a course given at RWC or if the course fits into the student's total program.

Application and Information

Applicants should submit an application form, the $35 application fee, a completed recommendation form, SAT I or ACT scores, and transcripts from all schools previously attended. Art students should prepare a portfolio for review by the art faculty, and music students should schedule an audition with the music department. Students are encouraged to submit an application prior to the February 1 deadline. Admission decisions are made on a rolling basis, and students are notified of the admission decision as soon as all of their credentials have been received and evaluated.

For additional information and application forms, students should contact:

Linda E. Kurtz
Director of Admissions
Roberts Wesleyan College
2301 Westside Drive
Rochester, New York 14624-1997

Telephone: 716-594-6400
800-777-4RWC (toll-free)
E-mail: admissions@roberts.edu
World Wide Web: http://www.roberts.edu

Roberts Wesleyan students enjoy a sunny walk across campus.

ROCHESTER INSTITUTE OF TECHNOLOGY
ROCHESTER, NEW YORK

The Institute

Rochester Institute of Technology (RIT) was founded in 1829 and has always had a strong orientation toward professional and technological career training. The more than 9,000 full-time undergraduates currently enrolled come from fifty states and eighty countries; 35 percent are women. Many graduates move directly into the careers for which their RIT education has prepared them. A variety of graduate degree programs are offered, including the nation's first and only Ph.D. program in imaging science.

In 1968, RIT moved to its present 1,300-acre campus in a suburban location. Cars are permitted, and many students commute from nearby areas. Unmarried freshmen not living with relatives are required to live in the residence halls or in fraternity or sorority houses and to participate in the board plan. A number of on-campus apartments are available for upperclass students. Besides the social fraternities and sororities, there are professional and honorary societies. A complete program of intercollegiate and intramural sports is offered, as are complementary activities for those with special interests.

Location

The greater Rochester area—the city and its immediate suburbs—has a population of about 700,000. Per capita income is among the highest for metropolitan centers in the nation. The area's many internationally known industries employ a high proportion of scientists, technologists, and skilled workers. Rochester is the world center of photography, the largest producer of optical goods in the United States, and among the leaders in graphic arts and reproduction and in production of electronic equipment and precision instruments. Rochester's industries have always been closely associated with RIT's programs and progress.

Majors and Degrees

The College of Applied Science and Technology offers the Bachelor of Science in computer science, environmental management, food management, food marketing, hotel/resort management, information technology, nutrition management, packaging science, safety technology, software engineering, and travel management. It also grants the Bachelor of Science in civil, computer, electrical, manufacturing, mechanical, and telecommunications engineering technology.

The College of Business offers the B.S. in accounting, finance, information systems, international business, management, marketing, and photographic marketing management. An accelerated B.S./M.B.A. option is available to outstanding students.

The Kate Gleason College of Engineering grants the B.S. in computer, electrical, industrial, mechanical, mechanical/aerospace, mechanical/automotive, microelectronic, and software engineering. An undeclared engineering program is available for undecided freshmen. Accelerated B.S./M.S. programs are also offered.

The College of Imaging Arts and Sciences offers the B.F.A. in advertising photography; ceramics and ceramic sculpture; film, video and animation; fine art photography; fine arts; glass; graphic design; illustration; industrial design; interior design; medical illustration; metalcrafts and jewelry; new media design; photojournalism; and woodworking and furniture design. The College also offers the B.S. in biomedical photographic communications, imaging and photographic technology, imaging systems management, new media publishing, newspaper operations management, printing, and printing and applied computer science.

The College of Liberal Arts confers the B.S. in criminal justice, economics, professional and technical communication, psychology, and social work. The Career Decision Program is a one-year program option for undecided students.

The College of Science offers the B.S. in applied mathematics, applied statistics, biology, biochemistry, biomedical computing, biotechnology, chemistry, computational mathematics, environmental science, imaging science, medical technology, nuclear medicine technology, physician assistant studies, physics, polymer chemistry, and ultrasound.

The National Technical Institute for the Deaf, which has the only program of its kind in this country, provides certificate, diploma, and degree curricula for the hearing-impaired.

Academic Program

Students entering RIT enroll directly in the college and academic program of their choice; specialization is spread over the duration of their study. Approximately one third of the program of each professional curriculum consists of general education courses in the humanities, sciences, and social sciences.

An integral part of the degree requirements in the Colleges of Business, Engineering, and Science and in the Departments of Computer Science, Information Technology, Engineering Technology, Hospitality and Service Management, and Printing Management and Sciences is the cooperative education program. In this program, the student alternates quarters of study with quarters of paid work experience in business or industry during the upper-division years. This is not only invaluable experience but also a way of meeting the expenses of these years. The cooperative program is offered as an option in several other academic departments. Field experience is integrated with academic programs in the areas of criminal justice and social work.

A number of RIT's programs are unusual baccalaureate degree offerings. Among these are the programs of the School for American Crafts; programs in biotechnology, imaging science, international business, microelectronic engineering, nuclear medicine technology, packaging, photography, physician assistant studies, printing, software engineering, and telecommunications; and the programs of the National Technical Institute for the Deaf.

Air Force and Army ROTC programs are available on campus. A Naval ROTC program is offered jointly with the University of Rochester.

Off-Campus Arrangements

The School for American Crafts, in cooperation with the Scandinavian Seminars, offers a junior year abroad with full credit in the field of crafts. An off-campus program at Sheffield University in England is available to business students. RIT maintains an exchange agreement with Japan's Kanazawa Institute of Technology. Many additional opportunities for off-campus study abroad are provided through a partnership with Syracuse University.

Academic Facilities

Wallace Memorial Library is a true multimedia learning center. Its collections are exceptionally extensive in the areas of the arts, education for the deaf, photography, and printing. A $9.2-million library expansion project was completed in 1992.

RIT's modern campus provides maximum laboratory space for undergraduates to pursue their individual projects. The Institute's Center for Microelectronic and Computer Engineering and the Carlson Center for Imaging Science are recognized as the finest facilities of their kind in the United States. A $22-million Center for Integrated Manufacturing Studies opened in 1996, and a new addition to the College of Science opened in 1998. New facilities housing the Departments of Computer Science, Information Technology, and Engineering Technology opened in 1999.

Costs

For 1999–2000, tuition for the normal academic year (three academic quarters) was $17,328. Students on the cooperative education plan pay tuition only for the quarters they are at RIT. Fees, including the activities and health fees, were $309 for the academic year. Room and board (twenty meals per week) cost $6942.

Financial Aid

Approximately 70 percent of the full-time undergraduates receive some form of financial aid: Institute scholarships; regional, alumni, or industry-supported scholarships; and state and federal government grants. A variety of loans and part-time work positions are also available. The FAFSA must be submitted by March 15. Giving full recognition to scholarship apart from financial need, RIT awards a number of academic scholarships based on grades, test scores, and activities. Freshmen applying by February 1 and transfers applying as juniors by February 15 are considered for these scholarships.

Faculty

There are 605 full-time faculty members, 486 part-time faculty members, and an administrative and supporting staff of more than 900. Approximately 80 percent of the faculty have earned a Ph.D. or the terminal degree in their field.

Student Government

The Student Government is the representative body for students. It works with RIT administration, faculty, and staff to communicate the needs and desires of the student body and to communicate the decisions of the administration to the students. Fraternity and sorority, off-campus, hearing-impaired, and minority students elect special representative bodies.

All full-time and part-time undergraduate and graduate students are members of the Student Government when they pay the student activities fee.

Admission Requirements

The general requirements for freshman entrance are graduation from high school (a high school equivalency diploma is considered), high school grades that give evidence of the ability to complete college work successfully, satisfactory scores on the SAT I or ACT, and the presentation of proper credit for any prerequisite courses indicated in the current undergraduate catalog. A very important factor for admission is the record of academic achievement in high school (or in another college in the case of transfer students). Transfer students are placed at the highest level possible at which success is predicted. The results of standardized tests, while important, are supplementary. Students applying for programs in the fine and applied arts must submit a portfolio of original artwork.

Rochester Institute of Technology admits qualified men and women of any race, color, national or ethnic origin, religion, or marital status. RIT does not discriminate on the basis of handicap in the recruitment or admission of students or in the operation of any of its programs or activities, as specified by federal laws and regulations.

Application and Information

An application, a nonrefundable processing fee of $40 (payable to Rochester Institute of Technology), official transcripts of all high school or college records, and (for prospective freshmen) SAT I or ACT scores should be forwarded to RIT. Freshman applicants for entry in the fall quarter who provide all required materials by March 1 receive admission notification by March 15. Prospective freshmen who apply after March 1 and all transfer students are notified of the admission decision by mail on a rolling basis four to six weeks after their application is complete. RIT also offers an early decision plan, whereby prospective freshmen must have their completed application with all supporting credentials on file in the Admissions Office by December 15 to receive notification by January 15.

For application forms, students should contact:

Director of Admissions
Rochester Institute of Technology
60 Lomb Memorial Drive
Rochester, New York 14623-5604
Telephone: 716-475-6631
Fax: 716-475-7424
E-mail: admissions@rit.edu
World Wide Web: http://www.rit.edu

An aerial view of the campus.

ROCKFORD COLLEGE
ROCKFORD, ILLINOIS

The College
Rockford College, founded in 1847, is a fully accredited, private, independent, coeducational institution. The College offers undergraduate programs in more than forty fields of study and graduate programs in business and education. Academic programs are based on a foundation of learning in the liberal arts and sciences. The College emphasizes excellence in teaching and has a strong commitment to scholarly activity, creative expression, and community service. In 1998, Rockford College was named by *Barron's* as best buy in college education, one of only thirteen in Illinois and 280 in the nation. It is also one of only ten colleges and universities in Illinois with a Phi Beta Kappa chapter.

Currently, 1,400 students attend the College, of whom more than 800 are full-time. Students come from more than twenty-five states and twenty countries. Residential students can choose from a variety of living arrangements. Rockford College strongly believes that campus life is vital to a well-rounded college education. Intramural programs, community service activities, departmental clubs, and honorary academic societies present opportunities for developing friendships and sharpening leadership skills. The Student Affairs Division provides career services, international student support services, recreational programming, and health and counseling services.

Approximately 25 percent of all full-time students participate in the intercollegiate athletic program. The Rockford College Regents are a member of the NCAA Division III and compete in the Northern Illinois and Iowa Conference (NIIC). Women compete in basketball, soccer, softball, tennis, and volleyball. Men compete in baseball, basketball, football, golf, soccer, and tennis.

Location
Rockford, the second-largest city in Illinois, is only 75 miles from both Chicago and Milwaukee and is easily accessible by car, bus, and plane. The College is located on a 130-acre wooded campus. The city of Rockford offers students all the advantages of a thriving community: off-campus entertainment includes more than 500 restaurants, concerts and attractions at the MetroCentre, the New American Theater, the Rockford Dance Company, numerous malls and shopping centers, museums, riverside events, and an award-winning park district. Students benefit from volunteer, internship, and employment opportunities in the community. A student's involvement with the community is a chance for unlimited experiences that enhance and complement his or her Rockford College education.

Majors and Degrees
The Bachelor of Arts degree is awarded in accounting, anthropology/sociology, art (with concentrations in ceramics, drawing, painting, photography, printmaking, and sculpture), art history, biology, business administration (with tracks in management and marketing), chemistry, classics, computer science (management information systems), criminal justice (program in anthropology/sociology), economics (with tracks in finance, international economics, and public policy), education/child development, English, French, German, history, Latin, mathematics, music history and literature, philosophy, physical education (with tracks in athletic training, business, science, and teaching), political science, psychology, science and mathematics, social sciences, Spanish, theater arts, and urban studies.

The Bachelor of Fine Arts degree is awarded in art (with concentrations in ceramics, drawing, painting, photography, printmaking, and sculpture) and performing arts (musical theater performance).

The Bachelor of Science degree is awarded in accounting, anthropology/sociology, biochemistry, biology, business administration (with tracks in management and marketing), chemistry, computer science (management information systems), economics (with tracks in finance, international economics, and public policy), education/child development, English, history, mathematics, physical education (with tracks in business, science, and teaching), political science, pre–social work (program in anthropology/sociology), psychology, science and mathematics, social sciences, and urban studies.

A four-year NLNAC-accredited Bachelor of Science in Nursing program is offered. A B.S.N. completion program designed specifically for registered nurses is also available.

Preprofessional programs are carefully designed to meet the needs of students who plan to pursue careers in dentistry, engineering (3-2 program), health professions (optometry and physical therapy), law, medicine, pharmacy, and veterinary medicine.

In addition to the majors/programs/degrees listed above, Rockford College also offers minors in the following areas of study: British studies, communication, dance, Greek, human development, military science, peace and conflict studies, physics, and religious studies.

Academic Program
Education at Rockford College is intended to be both broad-based and preparatory. The liberal arts curriculum allows for a choice of course work with emphasis on a major. To earn a degree from Rockford College, students must complete at least 124 credit hours. Courses are offered by semester; there are two semesters per year. Summer courses are also available. The Honors Program in Liberal Arts offers extensive study in the humanities, a challenging core curriculum, and rigorous distribution requirements. Entrance to this program is limited and available by application only. The Forum Series offers exposure to great scholars, artists, and ideas. Special features of the College's academic program include Phi Beta Kappa and other scholastic honor societies, public policy forums, the Archaeological Institute of America, faculty seminars, art exhibitions, independent study, academic internships, and an extensive study-abroad program. A freshman seminar program is required for new students.

Off-Campus Arrangements
Rockford College gives its students an opportunity to study for a semester or a year at Regent's College in London, England, for approximately the same cost as attending the Illinois campus. Regent's College, a residential campus located in Regent's Park, offers a wide variety of courses, including academic internships, in a fully accredited program. The campus is conveniently located close to the museums, galleries, theaters, and other attractions. Residence at Regent's College makes travel possible throughout Britain and on the Continent.

Rockford College also participates in programs that allow students to study in France, Germany, Spain, and other countries.

In the United States, Rockford students may participate in the Washington and United Nations semesters.

Academic Facilities

Among the major academic buildings on the Rockford College campus is the Howard Colman Library, which houses 170,000 volumes and more than 800 periodical subscriptions. CD-ROM computers provide easy access to library holdings and national indexes; the availability of resources is enhanced by the interlibrary loan system. Private study carrels are provided. Starr Science Building houses the major science facilities, which include physics laboratories, chemistry teaching and research laboratories with a fully equipped instrumentation lab, biology and psychology teaching and research laboratories, and nursing laboratories. It also houses the student computer lab, language lab, and a nursing student computer lab. Programs in fine and performing arts are housed in Clark Arts Center, which has a 570-seat theater with computerized lighting and sound equipment; an experimental theater; an art gallery; a sculpture garden; studios for lithography/printmaking, drawing, painting, sculpting, and ceramics; a darkroom; and facilities for dance and music. Seaver Physical Education Building is the campus sports complex. It includes locker rooms, a pool, a basketball court, a free-weight room, a fitness center, training room, and classrooms. Dayton Hall houses the Learning Resources Center, which offers free tutoring. Scarborough Hall houses classrooms, faculty member offices, and the writing center.

Costs

Costs for the 2000–01 academic year are $16,800 for tuition and $3300 for a double room. Several board plans are available, starting at $2130. Books are estimated to cost $800 per year. Miscellaneous expenses, including transportation, vary with individual needs but total approximately $2000 per year.

Financial Aid

Approximately 95 percent of students receive financial aid. A student may be considered for financial assistance if he or she is taking at least 6 credit hours per semester. Merit-based awards, including several full-tuition scholarships, are available to full-time students. Need-based awards are determined by the results of the Free Application for Federal Student Aid (FAFSA). These awards include Rockford College grants and institutional loans as well as federal and state funds. Students are encouraged to file for financial aid by June 1. Rockford College attempts to meet 100 percent of a student's need. Rockford College students who attend Regent's College are eligible for the above awards.

Faculty

The student-faculty ratio at Rockford College is 14:1. The full-time faculty is composed of more than 80 men and women with outstanding academic backgrounds and varied international experience. Seventy percent hold terminal degrees in their respective fields. Some departments enlist part-time faculty members from the Rockford and Chicago professional communities to augment their programs. An extensive faculty development program helps ensure that the faculty members constantly update and improve their classroom teaching. Faculty members are involved in the lives of their students by serving as academic advisers, club and organization advisers, coaches, and mentors. A freshman advising program matches incoming freshmen with full-time faculty members who serve as advisers and mentors.

Student Government

The Rockford College Student Government serves its constituency in all areas of campus life. Students serve on College committees, judge their peers in student court, uphold the campus honor code, monitor campus media, and are consulted regarding changes in College policy. The Entertainment Council is responsible for organizing campus activities, including concerts, lectures, dances, and other social events.

Admission Requirements

Admission to Rockford College is based upon the applicant's potential for success as determined by prior academic preparation and personal achievement and is subject to satisfactory completion of academic work currently in progress. Students may apply upon completion of their junior year of high school. Admission is based on high school GPA, ACT or SAT test results, and class rank. Applicants must meet the following three criteria: a 2.5 CGPA on a 4.0 scale, placement in the top 50 percent of their class, an ACT score of 18 or higher, or an SAT score of 840 or higher. Applicants must provide official copies of these documents. Transfer applicants with more than 12 hours of college course work are evaluated on the cumulative GPA of all college course work attempted and must provide official transcripts from all colleges attended.

All applicants must submit an application and a nonrefundable $35 application fee. The fee is waived for students who visit the campus. On-campus interviews and personal statements are highly encouraged. Recommendations may be requested.

International students are welcome to apply; they should contact the Director of International Student Admission for specific application information. A TOEFL score of at least 550 is required of international applicants.

Students wishing to pursue a Rockford College degree are expected to have completed a college-preparatory program of 15 units at an accredited secondary school. A proper foundation for success at Rockford includes 4 years of English and at least three of the following four areas: 2 years of mathematics (algebra and geometry), 1 year of history, 1 year of foreign language, and 1 year of laboratory science. Freshmen who intend to pursue a Bachelor of Science in Nursing degree should take both biology and chemistry at the high school level.

Application and Information

Rockford College uses a rolling admission policy. Students can expect to be notified of decisions within two weeks of receipt of the completed application and all necessary documents.

For further information, students should contact:

Office of Admission
Rockford College
5050 East State Street
Rockford, Illinois 61108-2393
Telephone: 815-226-4050
    800-892-2984 (toll-free in the U.S. and Canada)
E-mail: admission@rockford.edu
World Wide Web: http://www.rockford.edu

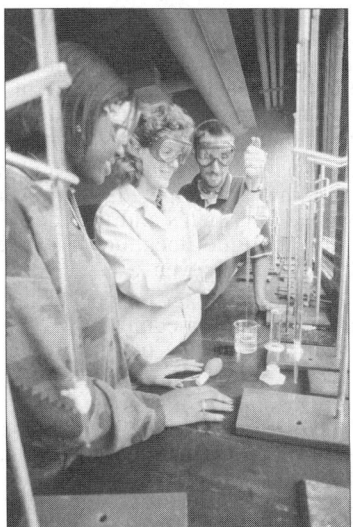

The Rockford College faculty's dedication to teaching and small class size result in a high-quality liberal arts education.

ROCKHURST UNIVERSITY
KANSAS CITY, MISSOURI

The University

Rockhurst University believes in experience-based learning. The goal is to help students confront the challenges they will encounter in the real world by using the wide range of resources available in Kansas City as a learning laboratory. Through activities such as professional internships, research projects, and community service work throughout the city, students learn by doing. This approach to education helps students clarify their professional interests as well as acquire a deeper sense of confidence in themselves, their skills, and their life choices.

The intellectual community of 2,000 undergraduate students encourages students to find their own capacity for original thinking and to approach new challenges as questioning, open-minded thinkers. This ability is one of the great gifts of a Jesuit education. Rockhurst is one of the most intimate, manageable, and affordable of the nation's twenty-eight Jesuit colleges and universities. It has been consistently ranked as one of the top five "Best Buys" in the Midwest by *U.S. News & World Report*.

Rockhurst enjoys an excellent reputation that translates into outstanding employment opportunities for graduates. About 1 in 10 graduates are presidents, chief executive officers, top leaders for not-for-profit organizations, or owners of their own companies.

Activities outside of class are a critical component of the Rockhurst experience. Rockhurst freshmen begin their college careers doing community service through the Finucane Service Project during orientation; seniors complete their education by participating in the Van Ackeren Service Project. In addition, many students spend spring break on a service project.

Classroom work is linked to service and extracurricular achievement. A few examples: one organizational behavior class studied a social service agency and eventually became the agency's consulting team; students have received National Science Foundation grants for undergraduate research; 2 students have been the only undergraduate presenters at the 7,000-person American Political Science Association convention; and students take leading roles in developing the campus master plan and the University's strategic plan.

Rockhurst recognizes that campus life involves more than academics and cocurricular activities. The Town House Village student residence complex provides an apartment-style residence experience for juniors and seniors. About half of Rockhurst's students live on the 35-acre main campus, located just a few blocks south of the famed Country Club Plaza.

Men's and women's basketball and soccer and women's volleyball teams have regularly participated in NCAA national tournaments. Men's baseball and men's and women's tennis, golf, and cross-country teams continue Rockhurst's strong athletic traditions at the NCAA Division II level.

Students can also take advantage of the Rockhurst network in Kansas City's thriving business community. The Career Center offers the Cooperative Education program, placing students in full-time jobs for a semester, where they earn both pay and credit.

Rockhurst also provides opportunities for learning after students receive a bachelor's degree. Master of Occupational Therapy, Master of Physical Therapy, Master of Integrated Humanities and Education, Master in Communicative Sciences and Disorders, and traditional and executive Master of Business Administration degrees are offered.

Rockhurst's emphasis on values and lifelong learning leads students to new definitions of success. The process of being a successful person has been mastered by many famous "Rocks," as Rockhurst alumni are known. From space scientists to entrepreneurs to founders of a clinic for crack babies to college presidents, famous "Rocks" are found in nearly every state, making a difference in their fields and in their communities.

Location

The 35-acre Rockhurst campus is right in the cultural heart of thriving Kansas City. Rustic stone classroom buildings surrounded by beautiful, shaded walkways provide the perfect atmosphere for study and relaxation. The campus is a short stroll from Kansas City's brightest cultural attractions, including the Nelson-Atkins Museum of Art and the Country Club Plaza. All of the metropolitan area's attractions, such as the Truman Sports Complex (home to the Chiefs and Royals), Crown Center, and jazz and rock concert halls, are easily accessible.

Majors and Degrees

Rockhurst University offers Bachelor of Arts, Bachelor of Science, Bachelor of Science in Business Administration, Bachelor of Professional Studies, and Bachelor of Science in Nursing degrees. Programs and majors in the College of Arts and Sciences include biology, business communication, chemistry, communication, communication sciences and disorders, computer information systems, computer science, cytotechnology, education, English, French, global studies, history, mathematics, medical technology, philosophy, physics, political science, psychology, sociology, Spanish, theater arts, and theology. The School of Management awards degrees in accounting, economics, finance/economics, human resources/industrial relations, management, marketing, and personnel/human resources. The Research College of Nursing offers a degree in nursing. The School of Professional Studies offers degrees in accounting, business, computer technology, organizational communication, organizational leadership, and paralegal studies.

Preprofessional programs are available in dentistry, engineering, law, medicine, optometry, osteopathic medicine, pharmacy, physician assistant studies, and veterinary medicine (including the PreMed Scholars program). Areas of study include human service administration, engineering science, and economics education.

Academic Program

Depending upon their intended major, beginning students are advised in the College of Arts and Sciences, the School of Management, or the Research College of Nursing. Students eventually declare a major in one of these three schools. The Research College of Nursing provides an accelerated program for students with degrees in other fields. The School of Professional Studies offers opportunities for working adults to complete the bachelor's degree through part-time study. The University has an excellent honors program. A minimum of 128 credit hours is required for graduation; there are specific requirements for each degree area.

The University's six-year bachelor's degree/master's degree programs in occupational therapy and physical therapy respond to the growing need for health-care professionals. Students entering Rockhurst as freshmen may pursue a program that leads to a bachelor's degree in a related field after four years and a master's degree in occupational therapy or physical therapy after an additional two years.

The Cooperative Education Program enables students to earn college credit while gaining valuable work experience in major companies. Cooperative education provides students with an opportunity to match academic learning with workplace experience, testing career choices and potential employers. By alternating semesters of study and work, students can complete course work in four years (including summers) and have a year's experience in real-world jobs. Many co-op students are offered permanent positions with firms for which they have worked in the program.

2348 www.petersons.com Peterson's Guide to Four-Year Colleges 2001

Off-Campus Arrangements

The Study-Away Program coordinates course work in nine European cities: Madrid, Spain; Rome and Florence, Italy; Aix-en-Provence, Avignon, and Toulon, France; and Richmond, Surrey, and Kensington, England. In addition, scholarships have funded dozens of students on study trips to Russia, and a study in Mexico program is offered every summer in Xalapa, Mexico. Rockhurst students regularly find internships in government and in the nonprofit and private sectors through the Washington Center, in the nation's capital. Special scholarships have also provided internships in Congress for Rockhurst students. Students may also take courses at other local institutions, such as the Kansas City Art Institute and the Conservatory of Music of the University of Missouri at Kansas City, through an exchange program.

Academic Facilities

The Greenlease Library houses more than 100,000 volumes and is a repository for a variety of government documents, including the *Federal Register*, Congressional reports, Supreme Court decisions, and presidential papers. Rockhurst students also have access to the renowned Linda Hall Science Library, which is just a few blocks from campus. The University offers excellent computing, physical therapy, and science facilities. Accredited by the American Chemical Society, Rockhurst has the most current chemistry instrumentation available. The Richardson Science Center houses science programs.

Costs

In 1999–2000, the cost of tuition was $12,500; room and board costs averaged $4920.

Financial Aid

Rockhurst University arranges significant financial aid packages, which include scholarships, grants, loans, and part-time jobs, for eligible students. Nearly half of the entering freshman class receives partial to full scholarship awards based on academic, leadership, service, and athletic achievements. Federal, state, Rockhurst University, and research grants are available. Low-interest student loans include the Federal Stafford Student and Federal Perkins loans; Federal PLUS loans are available for parents. The Federal Work-Study Program provides campus jobs. The Career Center helps students find part-time jobs throughout the Kansas City area. A monthly payment plan allows students to pay all or part of their fees in installments without interest. Students must file a Financial Aid Form to be considered for financial assistance. The Guaranteed Tuition Program offers a cushion against tuition increases.

Faculty

Rockhurst's outstanding faculty of 96 full-time and 72 part-time professors, including 16 Jesuits, staff day classes. Approximately 70 percent of full-time faculty members hold Ph.D.'s or the terminal degree in their field. All classes and labs, including those on the freshman level, are taught by professors or instructors, not teaching assistants. Faculty members also act as academic advisers to students. Rockhurst's student-faculty ratio of 15:1 ensures close interaction between students, from freshmen to seniors, and faculty members.

Student Government

All full-time students can participate in the Student Senate. Students elect senate representatives and officers annually. The Student Activities Board, also elected, organizes social activities and allocates student activity fees. Resident students elect Residence Hall Councils to plan activities and help administer the residence halls. Students may also serve on tripartite committees that include students, faculty members, and administrators. These committees advise the President and others on policy issues. The Interfraternity Council provides leadership for the fraternities and sororities on campus.

Admission Requirements

Applicants must submit scores on the SAT I or ACT examination. Sixteen units of college-preparatory work are required, and an interview is recommended.

Application and Information

The University employs a rolling admission policy, with a priority application deadline of December 15. There is a $20 application fee.

For further information, students should contact:
Mark S. Kopenski
Vice President for Enrollment
Rockhurst University
1100 Rockhurst Road
Kansas City, Missouri 64110-2561

Telephone: 816-501-4100
               800-842-6776 (toll-free)
Fax: 816-501-4241
E-mail: admission@rockhurst.edu
World Wide Web: http://www.rockhurst.edu

Rockhurst University students can get the personal attention, academic challenge, and Jesuit emphasis on values that bring out their best.

ROCKY MOUNTAIN COLLEGE
BILLINGS, MONTANA

The College

Situated in Billings, the "Magic City" of Montana, Rocky Mountain College captures for its students the best of the rugged West and urban opportunities. With a heritage that predates statehood, Rocky Mountain College is Montana's oldest institution of higher learning. Rocky is a private, church-related, liberal arts college, and its mission and vision draw from the past to stretch to the future. The College is moving forward to ensure that students are educated for the twenty-first century.

Rocky students grow from the nurturing they receive to become leaders in government, industry, medicine, arts, and sciences. Students work alongside faculty members in classes that average 15–20 students and enjoy a 14:1 student-faculty ratio. This enables Rocky faculty members to mentor students both in and out of the classroom. The College is a "diverse community of learners working together to better understand who we are and how we live recognizing the importance of the liberal arts as the foundation of all learning."

As a college founded in the Christian tradition, Rocky seeks to understand that tradition in a open and nonsectarian way. Rocky's ties to the United Methodist Church; Presbyterian Churches, U.S.A.; and United Church of Christ uphold the importance of one's own beliefs with respect for others' beliefs. Students are welcomed from all walks of life and come from thirty-eight states and thirteen other countries.

Rocky Mountain College prepares students, both in and out of the classroom, to act responsibly as members of an academically, socially, economically, ecologically, and spiritually interconnected world. Numerous extracurricular activities ranging from sports to the arts are available through the Fortin Education Center, student activities programming, the outdoor recreation program, and residence halls. Three coeducational residence halls, Anderson, Widenhouse, and Jorgensen, provide an excellent learning and living environment.

The Fortin Education Center, in addition to academic facilities, is the athletic and recreation center of campus. NAIA Division II men's and women's basketball and women's volleyball are hosted in Fortin's two gymnasiums. In addition, Rocky supports a football team, men's and women's ski teams, and men's and women's golf. Fortin's outdoor recreational program leads backpacking, kayaking, and rock and ice climbing trips and many more outdoor opportunities. Also in Fortin lies an indoor running track, a free weight room, a swimming pool, a cardiovascular center, and racquetball and squash courts.

Rocky Mountain College prides itself not only on its recreational opportunities, but more importantly on the placement of its graduates in the workforce and graduate and professional schools. Throughout the 1990s, that placement within four months of graduation stood at 96 percent. In 1996, Rocky Mountain College was selected by *U.S. News & World Report* as one of the top ten values in the West for liberal arts colleges.

Location

Billings, a city of 100,000, is an ideal place to live and learn. Billings provides cultural, retail, recreational, and outdoor opportunities associated with larger cities and still offers a distinct Western atmosphere and small-town friendliness. The Yellowstone River, the Rimrocks, the Pryor Mountains, and the Beartooth Mountains are backyard to Billings and Rocky Mountain College. The 60-acre campus is located in a residential area of northwest Billings. This safe, secure environment allows students to focus on their college experiences.

Majors and Degrees

Rocky Mountain College offers programs of study leading to the B.A. or B.S. in art, aviation (aviation management and professional pilot studies), biology, chemistry, computer science, earth and environmental science (environmental biology, environmental chemistry, environmental geology, environmental science, and geology), economics and business administration (accountancy, accounting, agribusiness, business management, economics, and management information systems), education (elementary, K–12, and secondary), English, equestrian studies (equine business, equine writing and publications, equitation and training, and riding instructor studies), history, history and political science, international studies, mathematics, music performance, natural science and mathematics, philosophy and religious thought, physical education and health (athletic training, education K–12, exercise science, and nonteaching), physician assistant studies, psychology, sociology and anthropology, and theater arts (performance and technical theater).

Preprofessional programs can be tailored to meet students' needs and are available in dentistry, law, medicine, ministry, optometry, pharmacy, physical therapy, physician assistant studies, and veterinary. Upon completion, students are qualified to seek admission to graduate or professional schools.

A 3-2 engineering program can be designed to fit students' needs, and a 3-2 occupational therapy program, in conjunction with Washington University (St. Louis), is available.

Academic Program

Rocky Mountain College, from its distinct heritage as a liberal arts school and a polytechnic institute, emphasizes a strong core curriculum and the liberal arts and preprofessional and job-oriented options. Through excellent academic and internship opportunities, the College produces graduates who are not only in demand in the marketplace, but who are also sought after in graduate and professional schools.

The core curriculum, or general education requirements, ensures that students have writing, math, and speaking skills; are exposed to the humanities, fine arts, and social and natural sciences; and recognize the relationship between academic fields. Within the major field of study, students work closely with a faculty adviser to maximize their educational experience and obtain their degree. Traditional course work is augmented by field practica, cooperative education, internships, seminars, independent study, and study abroad.

Off-Campus Arrangements

Rocky Mountain College seeks to understand the history and environment of its region as a bridge to understanding the history and environment of the larger world. To this end, there are diverse opportunities for off-campus study and study abroad. Ranging from a spring break mission trip to study of the ecosystem of Yellowstone National Park to study at one of the U.S. National Laboratories, unique experiences are available for individual pursuit. International opportunities include archaeological digs in Bethsaida, Israel; study at Regents College in London; and many other study-abroad programs coordinated by the international student adviser.

Academic Facilities

Rocky Mountain College combines the history of student-constructed sandstone buildings with an aggressive building and renovation plan. The Bair Family Student Center, completed in 1997, provides students with modern recreation, dining, student services, and educational facilities, including state-of-the-art computer access. The library, completed in 1999, is Rocky's Educational Resource Center for the future. The Bair Science Center houses modern science classrooms and laboratories. Fortin Education Center, in addition to sports and recreation, offers a wide array of academic services. Fortin houses classrooms, computer laboratories, the Fortin Auditorium, clinical facilities for the physician assistant studies program, Services for Academic Success, and the student health services suite. Tyler, Alden, and Tech Halls are historic buildings on campus and have faculty offices, classrooms, and laboratories.

Costs

Rocky Mountain College, rated by *U.S. News & World Report* as one of the top ten values in West, is a very affordable private college. Costs for the 2000–01 academic year are tuition and fees, $12,243, and room and board, $4150. The estimated annual cost for books and supplies is $600; personal expenses and travel are approximately $1200. Since Rocky Mountain College is a private college, there is no difference in cost for out-of-state students.

Financial Aid

About 80 percent of entering students receive some form of assistance, whether from Rocky Mountain College or external sources. Rocky Mountain College provides more than $2 million to students each year in the form of scholarships, grants, and work-study. External sources include Federal Pell Grants, Federal Supplemental Educational Opportunity Grants, Federal Work-Study, Federal Stafford Loans, Federal Perkins Loans, Federal PLUS Loans, and scholarships and grants that students earn on their own.

Students seeking financial aid must complete the applications for admission and financial aid and the Free Application for Financial Aid (FAFSA). Students must be accepted for admission before any financial aid is awarded.

Faculty

Rocky's 50 full-time faculty members place their highest priority on teaching. Students never have a graduate assistant or teaching assistant for a professor. Seventy-eight percent of Rocky faculty members have a doctorate or other terminal degree in their field. The regular faculty is augmented by educators from industry.

Student Government

The Associated Students of Rocky Mountain College (ASRMC) is an essential and active group on campus. All Rocky students are members, and elected board members serve as representatives. They are the governing body representing students in all aspects of the College.

ASRMC and the student activities programmer combine efforts to provide educational and entertainment opportunities for the entire Rocky community. Such opportunities have included world-famous entertainers and lecturers and a myriad of social events.

Students are essential in making decisions that affect Rocky Mountain College. Rocky students serve on all committees of the College, including faculty and administrative searches, Board of Trustees committees, and committees of faculty and staff members.

Admission Requirements

Rocky Mountain College actively seeks freshman and transfer students who demonstrate academic ability and are seriously interested in total development of character, intellect, and leadership skills. The College admits qualified students, on a rolling basis, of any race, gender, handicap, or national or ethnic origin. The College's commitment to all students can be found through the Services for Academic Success program and the American Indian Student Advisor.

Students seeking freshman admission must submit the application for admission, a $25 application fee, official secondary school transcripts, and results of either the ACT or SAT I. Students seeking transfer admission must submit official college transcripts in addition to the above. An on-campus interview is recommended for all students. When the admissions file is complete, it is reviewed on an individual basis. Each applicant is considered on the basis of his/her potential success at Rocky Mountain College. Freshmen entering Rocky Mountain College have had an average ACT composite score of 22, a SAT I combined score of 1030, and a high school grade point average of 3.2.

Application and Information

Rocky Mountain College operates a rolling admission process, and students are notified immediately of an admissions decision. Admissions files are reviewed until the class is filled. Requests for additional information and application material should be addressed to:

Admissions Office
Rocky Mountain College
1511 Poly Drive
Billings, Montana 59101-1796
Telephone: 406-657-1026
        800-87-ROCKY (toll-free)
Fax: 406-259-9751
E-mail: admissions@rocky.edu
World Wide Web: http://www.rocky.edu

Rocky Mountain students walking to class in front of Losekamp Hall, one of many historic sandstone buildings on campus.

ROGER WILLIAMS UNIVERSITY
BRISTOL, RHODE ISLAND

The University

Founded in 1956, Roger Williams University is an independent, coeducational university of liberal arts and sciences and selected professional programs accredited by the New England Association of Schools and Colleges. The University enrolls approximately 2,100 full-time day students (and 1,700 part-time students) in more than forty undergraduate majors instructed by a full-time faculty of 120 in a residential campus setting. The Ralph R. Papitto School of Law, the first and only law school in Rhode Island, offers the Juris Doctor and enrolls approximately 500 students. The University's average class size of 20 and its strong teaching orientation ensure personalized instruction.

The main campus, overlooking Mt. Hope Bay in Bristol, opened in 1969 and features modern academic and recreational facilities, including the waterfront Center for Economic and Environmental Development; the 150,000-square-foot School of Law and Law Library; an $8-million Main Library; the award-winning Architecture Building and Architecture Library; the Performing Arts Center; and the Thomas J. Paolino Recreation Center, offering students a weight room, a fully equipped exercise room, and three courts for basketball, volleyball, and tennis, surrounded by a jogging track.

Outdoor recreational facilities include softball and baseball diamonds, three rugby/lacrosse/soccer fields, six tennis courts (four lighted), and a jogging track. Roger Williams University teams compete in Division III of the National Collegiate Athletic Association (NCAA), the Eastern College Athletic Conference (ECAC), and the Commonwealth Coast Conference (CCC). The University sponsors seventeen varsity sports for men and women as well as clubs in men's rugby, coed crew, and coed track and field. In addition, an extensive program of intramural and recreational activities is offered all year long, with drop-in recreational activities available to the student body.

A variety of residence complexes located on the main campus offer students a choice of coeducational or single-sex residential living in modern facilities directly on Mt. Hope Bay. The Bayside Courts offers town-house-style accommodations overlooking the water. There is also an apartment complex, managed by the University, two miles from campus. Residential units include 24-hour quiet areas for study and some specialized living/learning units by major.

The Student Union complex includes a dining hall, snack bar, coffeehouse, game room, and bookstore. All students residing on campus are required to participate in the board plan, with the exception of those students residing in the apartment complexes. Students with special dietary needs may establish individual meal plans.

The University sponsors many athletic, social, cultural, and academic activities, and students may choose from a variety of structured and informal activities, including the Alive! Arts Series, Main Season theater and dance productions, Penny Arcade Film Series, visiting speakers forum, and lectures by visiting speakers, novelists, and poets. The student radio station, WQRI, provides opportunities to gain broadcasting experience. Students gain journalism and publishing experience working on the yearbook, newspaper, and literary magazine. Additional opportunities include participation in campus and community choruses, service projects both on and off campus through the Feinstein Enriching America Program and the Community Service Association, numerous student clubs and organizations, and student government. Also of note are Alpha Chi (a national honor society), numerous departmental honor societies, continuing education opportunities, and a strong Career Services department.

Location

The University is ideally situated within walking distance of Bristol, a historic seacoast town with a small-town, residential character. Newport and Providence, Rhode Island, with their restored buildings, shops, museums, theaters, and numerous cultural, educational, and recreational attractions, are within a half-hour drive of campus; downtown Boston is approximately 1 hour away by car or bus; and New York City is a 3½-hour drive away. A bus stop is located directly in front of the campus.

Majors and Degrees

At the undergraduate level, the University awards the Bachelor of Science, Bachelor of Arts, Bachelor of Fine Arts, and Bachelor of Architecture. Academic programs are offered through two colleges and five schools that combine traditional liberal arts education with professional studies. Professional programs are offered through the School of Architecture, Art, and Historic Preservation; the Gabelli School of Business; the School of Engineering; and the School of Justice Studies. Liberal arts majors are offered through the Feinstein College of Arts and Sciences. Continuing education is available through the University College.

All students complete an interdisciplinary core curriculum, a major, and a liberal arts concentration. Students select their majors and/or minors from the following disciplines: accounting, American studies, architecture, art and architectural history, biology, business management, chemistry, computer information systems, computer science, construction management, creative writing, criminal justice, dance performance, elementary and secondary education, engineering, English literature, environmental engineering, environmental science, financial services, foreign languages, general business, heritage resource studies, historic preservation, history, industrial technology, international business, marine biology, marketing, mathematics, paralegal studies, philosophy, political science, psychology, public administration, social and health services, social science, theater, undeclared major (architecture, engineering, and liberal arts), and visual arts studies (graphic design, painting, and sculpture). Other programs include prelaw, premedicine, pre–veterinary science, and a 3+3 program (a combination bachelor's/Juris Doctor degree). Students can also study English as a second language.

Academic Program

The fall semester begins in September and ends in December; the spring semester begins in late January and ends in May. During the month of January, students may participate in special on- and off-campus intersession programs, including opportunities for travel and service. Similar opportunities are offered during the summer. Undergraduate day and evening classes are available in Bristol, and evening classes only are available at the University's Metropolitan Center for Education and Law in Providence. The University Honors Program is offered by invitation to high school students who have demonstrated academic excellence.

Off-Campus Arrangements

Honors, cooperative education, internships, study-abroad, and community service programs (Feinstein Enriching America) enhance undergraduate studies. University career planning counselors work one-on-one with students and alumni, providing career development guidance, assessment, employment search skills, and placement assistance. Students can participate in study abroad in Italy, England, and other sites.

Academic Facilities

Two undergraduate libraries (Main and Architecture) with a total of more than 165,000 volumes are open 92 hours a week to students, faculty members, and community residents. The 50,000-square-foot main library houses 1,000 periodical titles, seating and quiet study/reading areas for 425 students, computerized databases, an online catalog, and 200 carrels wired for data. The main library also houses special collections and the University archives. A computerized system allows students to utilize library services of five additional Rhode Island institutions.

Students have access to academic computer labs that are operated seven days a week and are staffed to assist students with software issues and aid in the use of peripherals, such as plotters, scanners, and color printers.

All students have individual e-mail accounts, and all resident students have individual Internet access in their dormitories. Also, space for student Web pages is available.

The Center for Economic and Environmental Development, housing science and mathematics departments, features a wet-laboratory with flowing seawater, research space, and modern physics, chemistry, and biology laboratories. The renovated engineering building supports modern lab facilities equipped for computing; construction; drafting; electronics; surveying; soil, fluid, and materials mechanics; and digital and environmental systems. Graphics rooms, art and sculpting studios, an art gallery, photography labs, a theater, a dance studio, rehearsal rooms, and scene and costume shops support fine arts studies. The award-winning School of Architecture, Art, and Historic Preservation building includes design studios, review and seminar rooms, a library, a photography studio and darkroom, a model shop, computer labs, and an exhibition gallery.

Costs

Tuition at the Bristol campus was $16,560 for 12 to 17 credit hours ($18,960 for architecture majors) for the 1999–2000 academic year. Room and board charges for on-campus housing (double occupancy) were $8215 annually.

Financial Aid

Roger Williams University offers merit scholarships, which are awarded regardless of financial need, to recognize students with superior academic achievement. Merit scholarship recipients are determined by high school or prior college record, grade point average (GPA), and SAT I scores. These scholarships are renewable yearly, provided that recipients maintain a designated GPA while enrolled full-time at the University. There is no separate application(s) for these scholarships. Each applicant's record is examined to determine eligibility as part of the routine admissions process.

The vast majority of the funds and programs administered by the Office of Student Financial Aid and Financial Planning at Roger Williams University require the demonstration of financial need as an essential consideration. Those not based on a need determination include Federal Stafford Loan, PLUS loans, alternative loan programs, and various outside/external scholarships (where selection is made by the donor or organization). With few exceptions, all other programs require that need be evaluated and determined by the Office of Student Financial Aid and Financial Planning.

The University requires the submission of the Free Application for Federal Student Aid (FAFSA). Only freshmen are required to file the PROFILE application. The Roger Williams University Title IV code number is 003410. The form must be received by the processor no later than March 1 to be considered for maximum available aid.

Faculty

The University's undergraduate program employs 120 full-time faculty members. Teaching is central to the undergraduate mission of the University, as is academic advisement. The University does not utilize teaching assistants, and all faculty members devote much time working with students both in and outside of the classroom. The University faculty members also reflect distinguished scholarship and research.

Student Government

Leadership opportunities are available to students through the Student Government Association. Students may serve in elected positions on the Student Senate, which carries out the executive and legislative functions of the association.

Admission Requirements

The University encourages applications from motivated students who have completed college-preparatory courses. In determining admissibility, the Office of Admissions considers the applicant's intended major, high school courses and grades, GPA, SAT I scores, an essay, recommendation, and additional information (such as auditions or a portfolio). Early decision is available for students who designate Roger Williams University as their first choice. The University requires submission of SAT I or ACT scores. The University codes for submitting these scores are 3729 for the SAT I and 3814 for the ACT.

Application and Information

Applicants may submit applications and transcripts after September 1 for the following fall. The deadline for early decision is December 1. The architecture program deadline is February 1. A nonrefundable application fee of $35 must accompany the application.

Application forms and admission information may be obtained by contacting:

Office of Admissions
Roger Williams University
One Old Ferry Road
Bristol, Rhode Island 02809-2921
Telephone: 401-254-3500
        800-458-7144 (toll-free outside Rhode Island)
E-mail: admit@alpha.rwu.edu
World Wide Web: http://www.rwu.edu

Roger Williams University is located on 140 scenic acres overlooking Mt. Hope Bay.

ROLLINS COLLEGE
WINTER PARK, FLORIDA

The College
Founded in 1885, Rollins College is Florida's oldest postsecondary institution. It is coeducational, nondenominational, and independently supported by income from tuition, gifts, and investments. Primarily a four-year undergraduate liberal arts college, Rollins offers graduate study in the Crummer Graduate School of Business and graduate studies in counseling, education, human resources, and liberal studies. The undergraduate student body numbers approximately 1,480 and is international in scope. Most states of the Union, the District of Columbia, and approximately forty countries are represented.

The 67-acre campus is beautifully landscaped, and its buildings emphasize a traditional Spanish-Mediterranean architecture. The College is completing a five-year, $100 million comprehensive campaign to secure funds for financial aid, endowed faculty chairs, programming, and facilities, including the newly opened $8-million Cornell Campus Center and the Olin Electronic Research and Information Center, made possible by a $2.5 million grant from the F. W. Olin Foundation.

Location
Winter Park is considered one of the nation's most beautiful residential communities. The town is adjacent to Orlando, the nation's fastest growing metropolitan area and an important center of business, science, and technology. Located 50 miles from the Atlantic Ocean and 90 miles from the Gulf of Mexico, the Rollins campus is bounded by Lake Virginia to the east and south.

Majors and Degrees
Rollins College confers the Bachelor of Arts degree in the following major areas: anthropology, art, biology, chemistry, classical studies, computer science, economics, elementary education, English, environmental studies, European studies, French, history, international business, international relations, Latin American and Caribbean affairs, mathematical sciences, music, philosophy, physics, politics, pre-engineering, psychology, religious studies, sociology, Spanish, and theater arts. Minors are also offered in African and African-American studies, Archaeology, Australian studies, business administration, communications, dance, German, Jewish studies, Russian, women's studies, and writing. Course sequences can be arranged in predentistry, prelaw, premedicine, and preveterinary studies. Dual-degree (3-2) programs are available in pre-engineering in cooperation with Auburn University, Case Western Reserve University, Columbia University, and Washington University; in pre-environmental management and preforestry with Duke University; and in business management with the Crummer Graduate School of Business.

Academic Program
The Rollins faculty has adopted a curriculum based upon a liberal arts pattern from the freshman year to graduation, designed to ensure that broadly educated graduates will be well prepared in a field of concentration. The student must complete the general education requirements, which are divided into three main areas: skills, cognitive courses, and affective courses. Self-designed majors are available to students who desire concentrations in more than one major field. The Honors Degree Program allows selected academically superior students to enter Rollins with full sophomore status and graduate with a special Honors B.A. degree in as few as three years by satisfying stringent criteria. All freshmen participate in the Rollins Conference, a fall term seminar program taught by faculty members who also serve as the students' academic advisers. The Rollins Advantage Program (RAP) is an option for students who want to get an early start on graduate school and career planning.

The academic calendar consists of a fifteen-week fall semester and a fifteen-week spring semester.

Credit is awarded for appropriate Advanced Placement examination and CLEP scores, dual enrollment programs, and for achievement in the International Baccalaureate Program.

Off-Campus Arrangements
For approximately the same tuition and fees that they pay at Rollins, students may spend their fall semester at the University of Sydney in Australia, their fall or spring semester at the Tandem School in Madrid, Spain, or their spring semester in London, England. In addition to traditional semester-long programs, Rollins offers dozens of study-abroad opportunities at various times of the year—from Hong Kong, to Rome, to Costa Rica, to Ghana.

Academic Facilities
The College's academic facilities include the Knowles Memorial Chapel/Annie Russell Theatre complex, which through the years has become the traditional landmark of the College, and the Olin Library, which features reader stations, computer terminals, study areas, and faculty research offices. Other major academic facilities include the Bush Science Center, the Cornell Fine Arts Center, the Cornell Hall for the Social Sciences, the Johnson Center for Psychology, and the Olin Electronic Research and Information Center.

Costs
The basic academic-year expenses for 2000–01 are $22,206 for tuition and fees and $7000 for room and board for a total of $29,868.

Financial Aid
Rollins seeks to help qualified students attend college regardless of their ability to meet the expenses. Funds are provided by Rollins College as well as by federal and state sources. Student aid consists of scholarships, grants, loans, and employment opportunities. Most students receiving aid are given a package consisting of two or three of these forms of aid. Aid is awarded on the basis of proven financial need and academic achievement. To apply for aid, a student must file the Free Application for Federal Student Aid and the Rollins College Undergraduate Financial Aid Application.

A number of renewable academic merit scholarships are available to entering freshmen, including Alonzo Rollins and Presidential Scholarships for overall academic excellence (up to $12,000 annually) and Donald Cram Scholarships for majors in mathematics and physical sciences ($5000 annually). In addition, Centennial Award of $3000 per year are awarded to students with strong academic records who have demonstrated a significant contribution to school or community. All applicants are considered for these scholarships, and financial need is not a criterion. Scholarships are also awarded for artistic and athletic talent. More information may be obtained from the Offices of Admission and Financial Aid.

Due to the high number of student aid applicants and the limitation of funds, it is important that application for admission to the College be made no later than February 15 and preferably in the fall of the senior year of secondary school. Details and regulations regarding student aid are found in the College's *General Catalogue*.

Faculty

Ninety-two percent of the members of Rollins' teaching faculty hold doctoral degrees or the highest degree available in their field from distinguished universities in this country and abroad. The student-faculty ratio is 12:1. Students receive instruction from full-time faculty members, who also serve as academic advisers.

Student Government

The Student Government Association consists of a student senate elected from across the campus and an executive committee. The SGA is composed of executive, legislative, and judicial branches, each designed to provide a series of checks and balances in the administrative process. The SGA affords students participation in the decision-making process of college life and represents student opinion to the trustees, administration, alumni, faculty, and staff. It provides an avenue for student expression, social interaction, cultural awareness, and student services and publications.

Admission Requirements

Admission is competitive; approximately 2,000 applications are received annually for a freshman class of 415 and a transfer class of 65. More than 80 percent of the members of each entering freshman class rank in the top two fifths of their high school graduating class. The middle 50 percent of College Board SAT I combined verbal and math scores range from 1080 to 1250 and the middle 50 percent of ACT composite scores range from 23 to 27. Emphasis is placed on the student's high school record, including class standing; counselor's recommendation; the results of either the SAT I or ACT; and extracurricular involvement.

Application and Information

Candidates are encouraged to apply in the fall of their senior year. Applications should be submitted no later than February 15 of the senior year. Students are notified of a decision by April 1. The Candidates' Reply Date is May 1. Two early decision dates are available for 2000–01: applications must be received by November 15 for Round I applicants and by January 15 for Round II applicants. Candidates for early decision are notified by December 15 and February 1, respectively. A deposit of $500 ($300 tuition/$200 housing) is due and payable upon notification of acceptance.

Early admission candidates may be considered for entrance prior to secondary school graduation, usually for entrance following their junior year.

Application forms and additional information may be obtained by writing or calling:

Office of Admission
Rollins College
1000 Holt Avenue-2720
Winter Park, Florida 32789-4499
Telephone: 407-646-2161
Fax: 407-646-1502
E-mail: admission@rollins.edu

The new Cornell Campus Center features comfortable gathering places, state-of-the-art technology, outstanding dining options, and spectacular programming and meeting locations.

ROOSEVELT UNIVERSITY
CHICAGO AND SCHAUMBURG, ILLINOIS

The University

Roosevelt University was founded in 1945 to provide opportunities for learning and teaching in conditions of freedom and equality. Since 1947, the home of Roosevelt's Chicago Campus has been the famous Auditorium Building overlooking Grant Park and Lake Michigan. The University has restored to their original splendor various areas of this National Historic Landmark building. The Schaumburg Campus was established in 1978 and has become the largest and most comprehensive university in the northwest suburban area.

The University seeks to develop individuals who will be dedicated to the essential themes of a democratic society, who possess an understanding of human history and the basic ideas of the humanities and sciences, and who will accept their responsibilities as citizens of a vital nation and a changing world.

Involvement in the metropolitan experience is an integral part of the academic curriculum. The University is committed to serving the developing needs of Chicago as well as suburban communities. The Schaumburg Campus offers more than sixty undergraduate and graduate degree programs and enrolls 2,900 students.

Roosevelt serves nearly 7,000 undergraduate and graduate students in the Colleges of Arts and Sciences, Business Administration, and Education; College of the Performing Arts; and University College (adult degrees).

Roosevelt schedules classes days, evenings, and weekends so that students may work while attending school. Approximately 85 percent of Roosevelt's students are residents of the greater Chicago metropolitan area; the other 15 percent represent more than twenty states and sixty-three countries. The seventeen-story Herman Crown Center provides housing for 300 students.

Roosevelt University is accredited by the North Central Association of Colleges and Schools, and its programs are accredited by the American Chemical Society, the Illinois State Examining Board for Teacher Education, the National Association of Schools of Music, and the National Council for Accreditation of Teacher Education.

Location

Roosevelt University's Chicago Campus is conveniently located on Michigan Avenue in the heart of Chicago's cultural and political center, within easy commuting distance by car or public transportation. Students can take advantage of the many events and activities in the city. The Schaumburg Campus is located 30 miles northwest of downtown Chicago in Schaumburg, near O'Hare International Airport and numerous corporate headquarters.

Majors and Degrees

The Bachelor of Arts degree is awarded in African-American studies, American studies, art history, biology, broadcast journalism, chemistry, computer science, economics, English, history, integrated marketing communications/advertising, international studies, journalism, mathematical sciences, metropolitan studies, music, philosophy, political science, psychology, public relations, social science, sociology, Spanish, and theater arts. The Bachelor of Science degree is awarded in actuarial science, allied health (medical technology and nuclear medicine technology), biology, chemistry, computing and information science, electronics engineering technology, environmental studies, hospitality and tourism management, mathematical science, psychology, and telecommunications. The Bachelor of Fine Arts is awarded in music theater. The Bachelor of Science in Business Administration is awarded in accounting, economics, finance, hospitality and tourism management, human resource management, management, and marketing. The Bachelor of Music degree is awarded in classical guitar, composition (traditional and electronic), jazz studies (performance and composition), music business, music education (including jazz studies), music history, music theory, performance (all instruments, orchestral/band, and voice), and piano pedagogy. The Bachelor of General Studies degree (for adults) is awarded with concentrations in administrative studies, business communications, computer science, history, hospitality and tourism management, languages, liberal arts, literature, metropolitan studies, organizational communications, political science, professional administration, professional studies–insurance industry, psychology, sociology, telecommunications, and women's studies. The Bachelor of Arts in Education degree is awarded in early childhood and elementary education. A sequence for secondary education certification is available in business-teacher education, English, general science, history, mathematics, social studies, and Spanish.

Academic Program

The requirements for the B.A., B.A.E., and B.S. degrees are completion of a minimum of 120 semester hours with at least a 2.0 average (2.5 in education), a major of no fewer than 24 semester hours, and at least 60 semester hours of work at the advanced level. The requirements for the Bachelor of Science in Business Administration degree are completion of a minimum of 120 semester hours, a major of no fewer than 18 semester hours, at least 54 semester hours in business administration, and at least 57 semester hours in arts and sciences. The requirements for the Bachelor of Music degree are completion of at least 120 semester hours with an average of 2.0 or better (2.3 in music education); participation in orchestra, band, chorus, or other related ensembles; completion of at least 27 semester hours of liberal arts courses; and a senior recital, thesis, or public performance of one original composition. The Bachelor of General Studies is a special degree program for adults (25 or over), and degree requirements vary according to the individual student's program.

Roosevelt University awards credit for successful completion of many CLEP examinations, as well as for satisfactory scores on Advanced Placement tests.

Roosevelt University has a special cooperative arrangement with the School of the Art Institute of Chicago, in which Roosevelt students can apply courses taken in their major at the Art Institute to their Roosevelt degree.

A special support program is available for learning-disabled students.

Academic Facilities

The collections of the main library exceed 350,000 volumes, including 63,000 microforms. The Music Library houses an additional 40,000 books, 12,000 sound recordings, and 10,000 pieces of sheet music and is furnished with audio equipment for individual listening. Roosevelt's students also have access to more than 25 million additional volumes through the University's membership in the Chicago Academic Library Council and the Illinois Library Network. Materials in libraries all over the country can be located quickly by means of the University's Online Computer Library Center (OCLC) computer terminals.

The University has IBM microcomputer laboratories, science laboratories, classrooms, and seminar rooms. Other University academic facilities include a language laboratory; a reading laboratory; Mildred Fagen Theatre of Art History, which has extensive collections of art slides; and a suite of thirty-five modern music practice rooms. Each year, music students and faculty members present more than 100 recitals and concerts in Rudolph Ganz Memorial Hall. Operatic and theatrical productions are staged in O'Malley Workshop Theatre.

The Schaumburg Campus is a 135,000-square-foot facility with sixty-one classrooms, an electronic library serving all research needs, computer classrooms, computer labs, and biology and research chemistry labs.

Costs

Tuition for the 1999–2000 academic year was $402 per semester hour or $12,060 (for 30 hours) per year. Room and board costs for the school year were $5850.

Financial Aid

Scholarships are awarded to entering freshmen and transfer students on the basis of academic ability. They range from partial to three quarters of tuition, and many are renewable up to the completion of the bachelor's degree program. The University also has a limited number of Music Performance Awards, which are available through Chicago Musical College. Talent awards are also available for theater majors.

Roosevelt's policy is to provide maximum financial assistance for students who demonstrate financial need. Students must submit the Free Application for Federal Student Aid (FAFSA). The priority deadline for applying for University financial aid is April 1 prior to the academic year for which aid is requested.

Faculty

The faculty includes 530 members, 175 of whom teach full-time. Although many faculty members conduct serious research and have numerous publications to their credit, they are primarily dedicated to classroom instruction. The student-faculty ratio is 14:1, and the average faculty age is 45. Most faculty members serve as academic advisers and participate in University affairs through the Faculty Senate, the Board of Trustees, and the major University committees.

Student Government

The student body has its own Student Senate, composed of students from the various colleges. Students also serve as voting members of the Faculty Senate and most major University committees and departmental groups.

Admission Requirements

Admission to Roosevelt University is an individual determination, based on the student's academic ability as demonstrated by grades, class rank, and test scores. Freshman applicants may submit either ACT or SAT I scores. Preference is given to applicants in the upper half of their class, with at least 16 units of high school work, a cumulative average of 2.0 or higher, and a minimum ACT composite score of 20 or SAT I scores of at least 520 verbal and 440 mathematics.

Roosevelt's Early Action Plan (REAP) enables high school seniors who qualify for admission by December 15 to receive advance notification of assessment and advising, financial aid and scholarship estimates, housing information, and registration opportunities.

Roosevelt Scholars is an honors experience that blends academic rigor with opportunities for developing metropolitan leadership abilities. Major scholarship support is available, along with mentoring relationships with Chicago's corporate, political, and social leaders.

High school students may also attend Roosevelt University during the summer between their junior and senior years as well as evenings and weekends during the senior year. Only one fourth of the regular tuition is charged for University attendance concurrent with high school attendance. Regular freshman admission requirements must be met in order for students to attend.

Transfer students must have at least a 2.0 cumulative average (on a 4.0 scale).

All admitted, degree-seeking undergraduate students, including all transfers and adult students, are required to take the Roosevelt University Assessment (RUA) test.

Application and Information

To complete the admission process, the student must submit an application, a high school transcript (or GED test scores), official college transcript(s), either the ACT or other standardized test scores, and the nonrefundable $25 application fee. Admission decisions may be expected approximately two weeks after receipt of all necessary records.

For additional information, students should contact:

Office of Admission
Roosevelt University
Chicago Campus
430 South Michigan Avenue
Chicago, Illinois 60605
Telephone: 312-341-3515

Office of Admission
Roosevelt University
Schaumburg Campus
1400 North Roosevelt Boulevard
Schaumburg, Illinois 60173
Telephone: 847-619-8600
World Wide Web: http://www.roosevelt.edu

ROSEMONT COLLEGE
ROSEMONT, PENNSYLVANIA

The College

Founded in 1921, Rosemont College is a residential liberal arts college for undergraduate women. In addition, it offers a nonresidence undergraduate Accelerated Degree Program for both women and men. The College also provides coeducational graduate degrees and professional studies programs. The M.A., M.Ed., and an accelerated M.S. in management are offered. Founded in the Catholic tradition, Rosemont welcomes individuals of all backgrounds and beliefs. A strong academic program and a commitment to women's education and achievement have long been hallmarks of a Rosemont education. With an enrollment of more than 500 women, Rosemont is a friendly and personal community that both supports and challenges students. Rosemont endeavors to prepare women to be active and responsible members of society.

For eleven years, Rosemont College has been ranked by *U.S. News & World Report* as one of the top regional liberal arts colleges. Rosemont has also been selected for the *John Templeton Foundation's Honor Roll for Character-Building Colleges*, one of only 134 such colleges nationwide. Moreover, Rosemont is listed among *Barron's Best Buys in College Education*.

Life at Rosemont is characterized by attention to the development of the personal, social, moral, cultural, and intellectual strengths that help women meet the challenges of modern life. Rosemont urges women to assess individual strengths and interests to develop the competence and determination necessary to achieve success. The close community atmosphere of the College lends to the development of the individual. For example, the 8:1 student-faculty ratio provides individual attention both in and out of the classroom and promotes lively discussion and conversation.

Rosemont College firmly believes in the liberal arts education. A solid foundation in a variety of different fields of study provides the Rosemont student with an all-encompassing background to create a well-rounded individual.

In addition to a rigorous academic environment, Rosemont participates in NCAA Division III varsity teams of basketball, field hockey, softball, tennis, lacrosse, and volleyball.

Location

Rosemont's 56-acre campus is located in the town of Rosemont, a suburban historic community with many shops, movie theaters, restaurants, and bookstores. The city of Philadelphia is 11 miles east of Rosemont and just a 20-minute train ride from the campus. Rosemont's proximity to Philadelphia provides students with a vast array of cultural and social opportunities, such as the Philadelphia Museum of Art, the Philadelphia Orchestra, the Pennsylvania Ballet, and various professional sports events, including Phillies, Flyers, and Eagles games. Within the Philadelphia area there are approximately eighty other colleges and universities. Rosemont is ideally located for recreational activities; it is only a short distance from both the Pocono mountains and the New Jersey shore.

Majors and Degrees

Rosemont College awards the Bachelor of Arts, the Bachelor of Fine Arts, and the Bachelor of Science degrees. Majors are offered in the following fields: accounting, biochemistry, biology, business, chemistry, economics, English, French, German, history, history of art, international business, mathematics, philosophy, political science, psychology, religious studies, sociology, Spanish, studio art, and women's studies. Interdisciplinary majors are offered in American studies, environmental studies, humanities, Italian studies, and social science. Prelaw and premedical programs and teacher certification for elementary, secondary, art, early childhood, and special education areas are available. Minors are available in most majors in addition to computer science and theater. Students may also choose to pursue a double major or create their own cross-disciplinary individualized major. Other special programs include a dual-degree program in chemical engineering and a transfer nursing program with nearby Villanova University and a cooperative program in information systems and technology with Drexel University.

In addition, Rosemont offers a five-year B.A./M.A. in English and publishing and a five-year B.A./M.A. in counseling psychology.

Academic Program

To earn a Rosemont degree, each candidate must complete 117 credits (120 credits for the B.F.A. and the B.S. in business). In addition to the requirements of a major concentration, all students must complete the general requirements. The general requirements, or core curriculum, focus on the fields of study closely associated with traditional liberal arts and sciences curricula: writing, literature, foreign language, philosophy, religious studies, history, mathematics, natural science, social science, and art. During their senior year, all students must successfully complete a comprehensive exam exhibiting competency in their declared major.

At the end of the freshman year, students exhibiting exceptional independence in their work and interest in serious academic pursuits are nominated by a faculty member to participate in a Special Academic Program, which substitutes for the general core curriculum requirements. Rosemont also has an Honors Society, which, in addition to its academic focus, fosters involvement in both cultural and community service activities.

Rosemont College offers a joint admissions medical program with Medical College of Pennsylvania/Hahnemann University (MCPHU); this assures a Rosemont freshman of early acceptance into its medical school. This program is highly selective, and a December 31 deadline applies.

For students interested in a French and business major, Rosemont offers specialized courses in business French to prepare students for the examination of the Chambre de Commerce et d'Industrie de Paris. The Certificat Pratique de Français Commercial et Économique is awarded to students who successfully complete this exam.

Rosemont offers programs granting certification in the following teaching areas: early childhood education/elementary education, elementary education, secondary education, art education, and special education with a concentration in hearing impaired.

Rosemont freshmen participate in a comprehensive advising program called Freshman Colloquia. These colloquia are special vehicles for beginning and deepening a relationship with Rosemont. It is an improved system of advising that reaches beyond mere counseling in course selection.

Off-Campus Arrangements

Through academic exchange programs that expand course offerings, students may take courses at neighboring Villanova University, Eastern College, and Cabrini College. The Art Institutes International Exchange Program, which allows studio art candidates to apply for admission into the commercial art program offered at any one of the eight Art Institute International Schools located in Philadelphia, Pittsburgh, Fort Lauderdale, Denver, Atlanta, Houston, Seattle, and Dallas, is also available.

Rosemont students may participate in any of a variety of study-abroad programs. These programs give students the opportunity to combine travel with academic and cultural study. Students receive full credit at Rosemont for course work successfully completed on an approved program. Rosemont, in cooperation with Villanova University, sponsors its own summer study-abroad program to Siena, Italy. This program focuses on course work in studio art, Italian Renaissance art history, and Italian language and literature.

There are many opportunities for full semester internships in various fields of study. Each candidate must be academically qualified and meet the approval of the appropriate faculty member. Fieldwork and practica, as well as summer internships, are also available.

Academic Facilities

The Gertrude Kistler Memorial Library creates a conducive setting for study and research. The library was the first academic building erected on the campus and was renovated in 1998. It houses more than 154,500 volumes, approximately 670 current periodicals, and numerous electronic indexes and databases as well as access to the Internet. The online catalog, the Rosemont Electronic Learning and Library System (TRELLIS), is the basic index to the library's collections. TRELLIS includes a number of computerized periodical indexes and encyclopedias and provides access to the Internet's World Wide Web.

The renovated science building is composed of the Dorothy McKenna Brown Science Building and the McShain Performing Arts Center. The Brown Science Building provides laboratory facilities and lecture rooms for the natural sciences. State-of-the-art equipment includes a phase microscope with video camera and color-TV monitor, physiographs, spectrophotometers, and an environment chamber. The building also houses a microcomputer center complete with PC Windows and Macintosh computers. The McShain Performing Arts Center is a 413-seat auditorium used for special forums, theatrical performances, and ceremonies.

The Conwell Learning Center offers academic support, learning supplementation, and enrichment for all students. The center is also a fully equipped language laboratory with an extensive library containing videotapes and audiotapes, CD-ROMs, and software. Tutoring is offered in writing, reading, study skills, and math as well as other subjects across the curriculum. A variety of academic workshops are also presented. Students may schedule weekly tutoring appointments or drop in.

Costs

For 2000–01, costs for full-time students include tuition, $14,020; room and board, $7030; and general fees, $800.

Financial Aid

More than 70 percent of all Rosemont students receive some form of financial aid. Financial aid includes scholarships, grants, loans, and work-study awards. Most financial packages are a combination of various forms of aid. To apply for aid, students are required to submit the Free Application for Federal Student Aid (FAFSA) by March 1.

Faculty

The faculty is one of Rosemont's most important assets. The members are dedicated individuals who believe the student must be engaged to learn; therefore, all classes at Rosemont are small, which lends to the discussion or seminar format. Ninety percent of the faculty members hold the Ph.D or the highest degree in their field.

Student Government

The student government at Rosemont coordinates the ongoing governing processes to be responsive to the needs and opinions of students, to stimulate change as needed, to provide a range of programs and activities, and to represent students to the College as a whole.

Admission Requirements

Rosemont College seeks to enroll women interested in the liberal arts and who have the capacity and the desire to pursue a rigorous academic program. Students are considered without regard to race, religion, disability, or ethnic or national origin. A candidate for admission must present a satisfactory record of scholastic ability and personal integrity from an accredited high school as well as acceptable scores on the SAT I. Applicants' records are reviewed by the Admissions Committee. The student must have an official copy of her high school transcript sent to Rosemont's Office of Admissions. An applicant's secondary school preparation should include sixteen college-preparatory courses. For admission to the traditional college program, all applicants are advised to include in their high school program a minimum of 4 units of English, 2 units of foreign language, 2 units of social studies, 2 units of college-preparatory math, and 2 units of laboratory science. Prospective business majors must present additional units of college-preparatory math. Applicants are expected to carry a full academic program during their senior year of high school.

Two recommendations are required in support of the student's application. The applicant should ask her guidance counselor and a teacher to submit recommendations on her behalf, and forward them to Rosemont's Office of Admissions. All applicants are required to submit results of the SAT I. The applicant may obtain the registration form for the test from her school or by writing to the College Board, Box 592, Princeton, NJ 08540. The code for Rosemont College is 2763. Puerto Rican students may submit scores from the Prueba de Aptitud Académica (PAA) in place of the SAT I. Students may also submit ACT scores. The code for Rosemont College is 3676. More information can be obtained by writing to ACT Registration–81, Box 414, Iowa City, IA 53343-0414. A personal interview with a member of the admissions staff is strongly recommended as an important part of the application process. Students who are seriously considering Rosemont should visit the campus to enhance their understanding of the academic and social atmosphere. Prospective students are also encouraged to make arrangements to visit classes, meet Rosemont students, and whenever possible, stay overnight. Arrangements can be made by calling the Office of Admissions.

Application and Information

Applications are accepted on a rolling basis. Those interested in scholarships should apply no later than February 1. To arrange for an interview and a tour, or to receive additional information, students should contact:

Sandra L. Zerby
Dean of Enrollment Management
Rosemont College
1400 Montgomery Avenue
Rosemont, Pennsylvania 19010-1699
Telephone: 610-526-2966
        800-331-0708 (toll-free)
E-mail: admissions@rosemont.edu
World Wide Web: http://www.rosemont.edu

Rosemont College—linking strong traditions with the future.

ROWAN UNIVERSITY
GLASSBORO, NEW JERSEY

The University

Rowan University is a selective New Jersey public institution that offers thirty-four undergraduate majors, plus graduate degrees and certificates. The 200-acre campus hosts approximately 6,200 undergraduates in Glassboro, New Jersey, just 17 miles from Philadelphia and central to the major urban areas of the East Coast, including New York City and Washington, D.C. Sixty-five percent of the full-time undergraduate students live on campus.

The University, established in 1923 for teacher training and later known as Glassboro State College, made philanthropic history with the 1992 Rowan $100-million donation. The University consists of six academic colleges—Business, Communication, Engineering, Fine and Performing Arts, Liberal Arts and Sciences, and Education.

The University is the home of the Glassboro Center for the Arts. The Wilson Music Building is the site of operas, plays, recitals, dance programs, and the Celebrity Concert Series each year. Varsity, intramural, and lifelong sports activities are also an important part of campus life.

Location

The University's main campus is located in the southern New Jersey town of Glassboro. It was because of the University's convenient location, halfway between New York and Washington, D.C., that it was chosen as the site of the historic conference in 1967 between President Johnson and Soviet Premier Kosygin. The town of Glassboro has been named "Summit City" because of that historic Hollybush Summit Conference. Facilities for all forms of surface and air transportation, including Philadelphia International Airport, are within minutes of the campus.

Just 20 minutes away from the main campus, Rowan University Camden Campus serves the urban community with emphasis on nontraditional students in three degree programs, plus ESL studies and other services.

Majors and Degrees

The Bachelor of Arts degree is offered in art (areas of specialization in art education and fine arts), collaborative education, communication (areas of specialization in communication studies, journalism and creative writing, public relations/advertising, and radio/TV/film), economics, elementary/early childhood education, English, geography, health and exercise science, history, law/justice, liberal studies (American studies and math/science options), mathematics, music, political science, psychology, sociology, Spanish, special education, and theater. The Bachelor of Fine Arts degree is awarded in art (areas of specialization in ceramics, drawing, illustration/graphic design, jewelry/metalry, painting, photography, printmaking, and sculpture). The Bachelor of Music degree is awarded in jazz studies, music education, performance, and theory and composition. The Bachelor of Science degree is awarded in accounting, biology, business administration (areas of specialization in finance, management, management information systems, and marketing), chemistry, computer science, engineering (majors in chemical, civil, electrical, and mechanical), mathematics, physical sciences, and physics.

Academic Program

Most degree programs include a 60-semester-hour general education requirement. Some degree programs require fewer semester hours. Students select their general education courses from the following areas of study: communications, science and mathematics, social and behavioral sciences, history, humanities and languages, and fine arts. In addition, most academic departments offering undergraduate majors have specified some general education courses that must be taken by students majoring in that academic area. Each degree program includes individual major requirements and free electives. A minimum of 30 semester hours is required in a major program, but many departments require more.

Students are encouraged to use free electives to establish a second major, a concentration, or a minor; strengthen their major program; or pursue personal interests.

Internships are available to juniors and seniors in most major programs. The University offers work-study opportunities through the academic departments and academic field experiences.

The University calendar is based on the two-semester system with a summer session.

Off-Campus Arrangements

Rowan University offers a variety of travel/study programs in which students may participate for a year, a semester, or shorter periods of time. Among these are programs in Australia, the Commonwealth of Independent States, Denmark, England, France, Germany, Scotland, Spain, and Wales.

Academic Facilities

A library opened in 1995, the largest in southern New Jersey. It contains more than 300,000 volumes and more than 75,000 microforms and subscribes to 2,000 periodicals. Media resources include multipurpose listening booths, a microform room with reader-printer equipment, and photocopying machines.

Costs

In 1999–2000, tuition and fees were $4921 for New Jersey residents and $8671 for out-of-state students based on flat-rate tuition for full-time undergraduates taking 24 to 36 semester hours per year. Room and board costs for 1999–2000 were $5666, based on housing in a double room and declining balance meal account. Apartment-style housing is available on campus for 944 students in any one of the three University-owned complexes. There are different dining options available to suit the needs of each student.

Financial Aid

In 1999–2000, about 70 percent of all full-time undergraduate students received some form of financial aid. Federal aid is available in the form of Federal Direct Student Loans, Federal Pell Grants, Federal Supplemental Educational Opportunity Grants, and Federal Work-Study awards. State aid includes Garden State Scholarships, Educational Opportunity Fund awards, and Tuition Aid Grants. Students should submit a Free

Application for Federal Student Aid (FAFSA) and the Student Aid Report (SAR) by March 31 to be evaluated for the earliest consideration.

Faculty

Rowan University has 364 full-time faculty members. The faculty members' regularly scheduled office hours and participation in virtually all areas of campus governance and operations ensure that they have continual interaction with students. Part-time faculty members, including business leaders, industry representatives, and practicing professionals, provide valuable links with the community and offer knowledge of practical experiences to Rowan University students. The student-faculty ratio is approximately 15:1. All courses are taught by professors, not graduate assistants.

Student Government

The Student Government Association (SGA) is composed entirely of students chosen through campuswide elections. In 1999–2000, student officers administered a budget of more than $600,000, derived from student activity fees and receipts. All students who have paid student activity fees are members of the SGA. Free legal advice, personal property insurance, and a tenants' association are some of the SGA's projects. The SGA oversees more than 150 chartered clubs on campus and sponsors intercollegiate athletics, social events, and service activities.

The University administration wholly supports the concept of student rights and student participation in all areas of campus governance.

Admission Requirements

Admission to Rowan University is based on a student's projected ability to complete a degree program, without regard to age, sex, race, color, creed, or national origin. SAT I scores and high school transcripts are required of all freshman applicants.

Applicants are also expected to have completed a minimum of 16 college-preparatory units: 4 units of English, 3 units of college-preparatory mathematics, 2 units of laboratory science, 2 units of social studies, and 5 units representing additional work in at least two of the following areas: history, languages (a minimum of two years), mathematics, and sciences. Exceptions to standards may be made in some individual cases. Highly qualified high school juniors may apply for early admission if they have a recommendation from their high school guidance counselor. Freshmen entering in 1999 ranked in the top quarter of their high school classes and attained an average combined SAT I score of 1140.

Admission for transfer students is competitive and offered on a space-available basis. Minimum grade point averages required for admission vary; for most programs, a 2.5 cumulative average is needed. If fewer than 24 college credits have been earned, a transfer applicant must meet freshman admission requirements and send a high school transcript and SAT I scores to Rowan University.

Application and Information

The University application, a $50 application fee, a high school or college transcript, and SAT I results should be forwarded to the Admissions Office. The application deadline for freshman and transfer applicants is March 15, except for transfer applicants to the elementary education program who must apply by February 15. The freshman enrollment deposit must be received by May 1. Students must also submit SAT II: Writing Test scores prior to enrollment. Campus visits are recommended.

For additional information and application forms, students should contact:

Marvin G. Sills
Director of Admissions
Rowan University
Glassboro, New Jersey 08028
Telephone: 856-256-4200
                800-447-1165 (toll-free)
World Wide Web: http://www.rowan.edu

Bunce Hall is at the head of the University Green, where the commencement ceremony is held each year.

RUSSELL SAGE COLLEGE
TROY, NEW YORK

The College
More than eighty years ago, Margaret Olivia Slocum Sage founded Russell Sage College as a "practical arts" college for women preparing for employment. It was an inspired innovation then that finds new relevance today, as women of all ages—recent high school graduates and adult learners—pursue new interests and vocations. Easy access to the resources of the Capital District of New York State gives the College great advantages in providing interesting internships. With business and industry, state and local government offices, social service and health agencies, and a large number of other colleges and universities nearby, resources are almost limitless. The unusual urban campus environment has formal courtyards and walled gardens, pools, and flowering shrubs. Beautiful Victorian-era buildings contrast with modern structures; together they make up the academic and residential facilities. Russell Sage College is one of the Sage Colleges, which comprise Russell Sage College, Sage Junior College of Albany, Sage Evening College, and Sage Graduate School.

The majority of the 1,000 women enrolled are from the Northeast and Middle Atlantic States.

Extracurricular activities include the newspaper and literary magazine, the choral group, drama and dance production groups, NCAA intercollegiate sports (basketball, soccer, softball, tennis, and volleyball), intramural and club sports, service clubs, the Student Government, professional and honorary societies, and religious groups. Social activities are numerous because of the presence of fifteen colleges and universities in the tri-cities area.

Location
Russell Sage is located along the Hudson River in historic Troy, New York, a city of 57,000. Albany, the capital of New York State, is 10 minutes away. The cities of Albany, Schenectady, and Troy constitute a metropolitan area of more than 500,000. Troy is located near the hub of air, bus, rail, and superhighway transportation and is 3 hours from Boston, New York City, and Montreal.

Majors and Degrees
The Bachelor of Science degree is offered in athletic training, biochemistry, business administration, chemistry, computer information systems, computer network administration, computer science, criminal justice, elementary education (N–6), nursing, nutrition, and occupational therapy.

The Bachelor of Arts degree is offered in biology, biopsychology, communications, creative arts in therapy, English, history, mathematics, political science, psychology, psychology/human services, sociology, sociology/human services, Spanish, and theater.

Interdisciplinary programs are offered in computer information systems (B.S.), and international studies (B.A. or B.S.). Other interdisciplinary majors may be designed by students and a faculty adviser.

Accelerated undergraduate/graduate programs include a five-year Russell Sage option leading to a B.S./M.S. in elementary education and special education, a B.A. or B.S./Master of Public Administration, or a B.A. or B.S./Master of Business Administration; a five-year program leading to a B.A. in math from Russell Sage and a B.S. in engineering from Rensselaer Polytechnic Institute; a six-year program leading to a B.A. or B.S. from Russell Sage College and a law degree (J.D.) from Albany Law School; a combined B.S./M.S. degree in physical therapy; and a combined B.S./M.S. degree in occupational therapy.

Minors are available in many disciplines.

Academic Program
The general education requirement of 39 credit hours provides all students with a background in three main areas: foundations of knowledge; analytic, quantitative, and communication skills; and values and consequences.

Russell Sage College operates on a two-semester calendar. Students take a full course load during the fall and spring semesters.

The academic program is enhanced by a four-year student development program called the Sage Strategies for Success. This distinctive six-part plan is designed to give students preparation and confidence for attaining professional success.

Off-Campus Arrangements
Russell Sage College is a member of a consortium of fifteen educational institutions known as the Hudson-Mohawk Association of Colleges and Universities. A course that is not offered at Russell Sage may be taken by full-time students through cross-registration with other consortium members at no additional cost. The following institutions are the other consortium members: Albany College of Pharmacy, Albany Law School, Albany Medical College, College of St. Rose, Empire State College, Hartwick College, Hudson Valley Community College, Sage Junior College of Albany (one of the Sage Colleges), Maria College, Rensselaer Polytechnic Institute, Schenectady County Community College, Siena College, Skidmore College, University at Albany, and Union College. Russell Sage College also has a consortial exchange relationship with Mills College in California, Mount Vernon College in Washington, D.C., and Bennett College in North Carolina.

Russell Sage College sponsors several international study programs and is affiliated with other colleges for programs in France and Germany. Internships are arranged in Seville, Spain, and London, England, for qualified students.

Academic Facilities
The library contains more than 300,000 volumes and currently receives nearly 1,500 periodicals, indexes, and newspapers. Through the consortium and the Capital District Library Council, fifty area libraries are brought together for rapid sharing of resources through interlibrary loans.

The Schacht Fine Arts Center, with an auditorium seating capacity of 1,400, is used for a wide variety of cultural programs. The Meader Little Theatre, with seating for 225, is flexible in design, adaptable to theater-in-the-round, thrust, or conventional productions.

The Robison Athletic and Recreation Center has two gymnasiums, a weight-training room, and a human performance laboratory. The center has a multipurpose room, which is used for activities ranging from aerobics classes to formal dinners. A swimming pool, bowling lanes, an outdoor playing field, and tennis courts are adjacent to the Robison Center.

The Academic Computer Center links terminals to mainframe computers at Rensselaer Polytechnic Institute and University at Albany, State University of New York. In addition, a microcomputer facility and a separate computer center on the Albany Campus are available for student use. Through Sage College's own network, all students have access to the Internet in their residence hall rooms. The Science Hall offers several laboratories with state-of-the-art equipment, including a gas/liquid chromatograph, a bomb calorimeter, an expanded-scale pH meter, a mercury analyzer, a portable vacuum line, a spectrophotometer, an atomic absorption spectrophotometer, a nuclear magnetic resonance spectrometer, and an infrared spectrophotometer.

Costs

Tuition for 2000–01 is $15,920. Room and board are $6038 (based on a fourteen-meal plan). The comprehensive fee is $300 and the technology fee for resident students is $300. Books and supplies are estimated at $700; personal expenses and transportation are estimated at $850. The approximate total cost for a full-time resident student is $23,258.

Financial Aid

Ninety percent of the students receive some kind of aid from the College; approximately half of Sage students augment their college funds by working on campus. Russell Sage is committed to providing financial assistance to enable students to meet educational expenses at the College. A wide variety of scholarships, grants, loans, and employment opportunities are available. The Free Application for Federal Student Aid (FAFSA) is required for financial aid consideration by the College. Transfer students must also submit financial aid transcripts from institutions previously attended. The preferred application date for new students applying for financial aid is March 1. Some assistance may be available on a limited basis after this date.

Faculty

The College has more than 166 full-time faculty members. Most hold an earned doctorate or the highest academic degree in their field. The student-faculty ratio of 12:1 enables faculty members to give personal attention to students' academic and career interests.

Student Government

Student Government at Sage is active in communicating the students' voice to all constituencies. Both the Student Senate and Executive Board of Student Government oversee issues relating to campus life. Community Council, composed of representatives of the students, faculty, and administration, is the major legislative group that reviews and establishes policies on matters presented to it by College constituencies.

Admission Requirements

Requirements for admission are 16 units of academic work at an approved four-year secondary school in English, foreign language, social studies, science, and mathematics. Some majors, such as physical therapy, occupational therapy, and nursing, require specific course preparation. Students should contact the Office of Admissions for details. An applicant who is ranked in the top 20 percent of her secondary school class may or may not elect to submit SAT or ACT scores for consideration. Other requirements include an official high school transcript, a writing sample in the form of an essay or a graded paper, a letter of recommendation from the student's guidance counselor, a letter of recommendation from one of the student's teachers, and a $30 nonrefundable application fee.

Application and Information

Regular first-year applicants are encouraged to apply early in their senior year and are reviewed on a rolling basis. Students applying for early decision must submit applications by December 1. Transfer applications are processed on a rolling basis except for those of students applying to the occupational and physical therapy programs, who must submit credentials by February 1.

Director of Admissions
Russell Sage College
45 Ferry Street
Troy, New York 12180
Telephone: 518-244-2217
            888-VERY-SAGE (toll-free)
E-mail: rscadm@sage.edu
World Wide Web: http://www.sage.edu

On the campus of Russell Sage College.

SACRED HEART UNIVERSITY
FAIRFIELD, CONNECTICUT

The University

Sacred Heart University, established in 1963, is a coeducational independent institution of higher learning in the Catholic intellectual tradition whose primary objective is to prepare men and women to live in and make their contributions to the human community. The University aims to assist in the development of people who are knowledgeable of self, rooted in faith, educated in mind, compassionate in heart, responsive to social and civic obligations, and able to respond to an ever-changing world. Sacred Heart University is committed to combining education for life with preparation for professional excellence.

A five-year Strategic Plan provides a road map for the University as it strives to meet the needs of today's students. The Plan calls for the construction of new facilities as well as the implementation of new academic, athletic, and social programs. Seven new residence halls have opened in the last four years. A $17-million health and recreation complex opened in 1997.

The current undergraduate enrollment includes approximately 2,400 full-time students. Extracurricular activities include fraternities, sororities, student government, the student newspaper, the student yearbook, a student radio station, academic clubs in almost every area of study, the debate club, the International Club, La Hispanidad, and intramural sports programs. Sacred Heart University offers men's and women's competition in NCAA Division I baseball, basketball, bowling, crew, cross-country, equestrian, fencing, field hockey, football, golf, ice hockey, lacrosse, soccer, softball, swimming, tennis, track and field (indoor and outdoor), volleyball, and wrestling.

Sacred Heart University is committed to providing students with extensive services to complement their education. The University Learning Center offers tutoring and assistance in basic study skills.

In addition to its bachelor's degree programs, the University offers seven graduate degree programs: Master of Arts in Religious Studies (M.A.R.S.), Master of Arts in Teaching (M.A.T.), Master of Business Administration (M.B.A.), Master of Science in Nursing (M.S.N.), Master of Science in chemistry, Master of Science in computer science, Master of Science in physical therapy, and Master of Science in occupational therapy.

Location

Ideally located in Fairfield County in southwestern Connecticut, Sacred Heart University is 1 hour northeast of New York City, 2½ hours southwest of Boston, and 1 hour southwest of Hartford. More than half of the 56-acre campus is surrounded by a thirty-six-hole golf course.

Opportunities for internships and co-op programs are extensive due to the number of corporate headquarters located throughout Fairfield County. Sacred Heart University's neighbors include the world headquarters for General Electric and *Golf Digest/Tennis* magazine as well as the Discovery Museum of Science and Industry.

Majors and Degrees

Sacred Heart University offers Bachelor of Arts and Bachelor of Science degrees. Programs of study in allied health include human movement and sports science/athletic training, nursing, occupational therapy, and physical therapy. The occupational therapy program and the physical therapy program are six-year B.S./M.S. programs. In the arts and sciences, the following areas of study are available: art, biology, chemistry, communications/media studies, criminal justice, education, English, environmental science, French (minor only), global studies, history, Italian (minor only), mathematics, music (minor only), philosophy, political science, psychology, religious studies, social work, sociology, Spanish, theater studies, and women's studies (minor only). In business, the University offers accounting, business administration, computer science, economics, finance, international business, paralegal studies/legal administration, and sports management (minor only).

Preprofessional programs are available in dentistry, law, medicine, optometry, pharmacy, podiatry, and veterinary medicine.

Special programs include cooperative education; educational certification programs in elementary, middle school, and secondary education; English as a second language; the Honors Program; internships; legislative internships; and study abroad.

Academic Program

A strong liberal arts core forms the basis for all curricula. Academic course work is divided into four colleges—the College of Arts and Sciences, the College of Business, the College of Education and Health Professions, and the University College. The academic year consists of two 15-week semesters. Both day and evening courses are available.

Candidates for the bachelor's degree must complete at least 120 credits, with a minimum of 30 credits taken at the University. The baccalaureate curriculum is made up of five components: the required core (18 credits), the elective core (30–32 credits), the B.A./B.S. requirements (6–8 credits), the major field (30–58 credits), and electives (4–36 credits).

Off-Campus Arrangements

Through the Internship Program, students combine employment in business, industry, government, or social service agencies with classroom work and receive academic credit for learning derived from the work experience. Cooperative education opportunities are also offered within various departments, such as accounting, communications/media studies, criminal justice, political science, psychology, social work, and sociology. Through a summer internship program, students may be employed in an area related to their major and their career goals.

Academic Facilities

The University's library contains more than 164,000 volumes, 716 periodical titles, and 110,000 nonprint items such as videotapes, audiocassettes, phonodiscs, microforms, filmstrips, and slide sets. It also provides on-line database searching services. The Art Department includes studios for painting, design, drawing, and illustration. Science facilities include four biology labs, a climate-controlled greenhouse, a microbiology preparation lab, and six chemistry labs. The modern foreign language laboratory is state-of-the-art. The campus also houses an 850-seat theater, an art gallery, and a professional radio station.

Sacred Heart University is in the fifth year of its Student Mobile Computing Program. Full-time students receive an IBM ThinkPad computer. The campus has been transformed into a fully networked environment. The mission of the University calls people to combine education for life with preparation for professional excellence. Sacred Heart University believes that computer literacy is a necessary component of that preparation. Therefore, the University is committed to a system in which students can carry the laptop to class, to the library, and to their residence hall.

Costs

Costs for 1999–2000 were $13,972 for full-time undergraduate tuition, $6870 for room and board, and $832 per year for a laptop computer. The cost of books is estimated to be $400 per year.

Financial Aid

Sacred Heart University maintains a strong commitment to provide higher education to as many students as possible by making available scholarships, grants, loans, and part-time employment. Financial aid packages are developed by combining Sacred Heart University's own resources with a variety of federal and state financial aid programs. Eighty-five percent of all students receive some form of financial aid.

Any undergraduate or graduate student who is enrolled in the University on at least a part-time basis (6 credit hours per semester) is eligible for consideration. Emphasis is placed on students who are enrolled in a full-time degree program; part-time awards are limited. Applicants for aid must submit the Free Application for Federal Student Aid (FAFSA) and the PROFILE to the College Scholarship Service on or before March 1.

The University offers several sources of financial aid, including academic scholarships, Connecticut Stafford Loans, Federal Perkins Loans, and Federal Supplemental Educational Opportunity Grants. A Family Allowance is available when 2 or more members of the same family attend the University. Deferred-payment plans and endowed scholarships are also awarded. Employment within the University is awarded under the terms of the Federal Work-Study Program. The Office of Career Development maintains a list of part-time jobs in the local area. Further information can be obtained from the director of student financial assistance.

Faculty

The student-faculty ratio is 17:1. There are 392 faculty members, 130 of whom are full-time. Eighty-two percent have terminal degrees in their field, and 44 percent have tenure. Many faculty members are involved in research, writing, or production, yet their primary focus is on teaching. Close communication between students and faculty members is encouraged. All students are assigned faculty advisers within their major field.

Student Government

Students play a major role in planning and decision making. Student Government representatives and class officers are concerned with improving the University and working for the needs of their classmates. In addition to sponsoring many functions, the Student Government serves as a liaison between the administration/staff and the student body.

Admission Requirements

Sacred Heart University is small enough to work with each student individually throughout the admissions process. The University is committed to enrolling a diverse, highly qualified, and well-motivated student body. Candidates for admission must demonstrate their ability to perform academically and contribute significantly to the life of the University. High school seniors should submit an official high school transcript, SAT I or ACT scores, two letters of recommendation, and a completed application. Transfer students should submit an official transcript from all previously attended colleges, a high school transcript, and two letters of recommendation as well as a completed application.

Application and Information

Full-time students may enroll in either the fall or the spring semester. All applicants must submit a completed application, all necessary credentials, and an application fee of $45. Applications for the Early Decision Program must be received by October 1 for an October 15 notification date or December 1 for a December 15 notification date. Applications for Priority Admissions must be received by March 1 for an April 1 notification date. All other applications are considered on a rolling admission basis; candidates are notified of the admission decision as soon as all credentials have been received and reviewed.

Inquiries or application materials should be sent to:

Dean of Undergraduate Admissions
Sacred Heart University
5151 Park Avenue
Fairfield, Connecticut 06432-1000
Telephone: 203-371-7880
E-mail: guastelk@sacredheart.edu
World Wide web: http://www.sacredheart.edu

ST. AMBROSE UNIVERSITY
DAVENPORT, IOWA

The University

St. Ambrose offers all the resources needed for a successful college experience as well as a successful future. The student body of 2,900 (57 percent women, 43 percent men) consists of people differing in age and background. Students are encouraged to acquire intellectual awareness for lifelong self-education. St. Ambrose has been providing education of high quality for more than 100 years. Founded in 1882, the University was named for St. Ambrose, the fourth-century saint and bishop of Milan, who was a doctor, scholar, author, orator, and teacher. Classes first met in two rooms of a diocesan school. Today the campus covers nearly fifteen square blocks. There are twenty-six buildings, including historic Ambrose Hall. Extracurricular learning opportunities are available through a student newspaper, a campus radio station, cable TV facilities, athletic programs for men and women, honor societies, professional clubs, and other organizations. A special Student Mentor Program, under the direction of the senior academic vice president, enables students to meet with their faculty advisers at least three times each semester to discuss any aspect of their academic or personal lives. A Student Government Advisory Committee also helps freshmen and transfer students to make the transition to St. Ambrose. Developmental and remedial services and comprehensive counseling are available at no cost through the Academic Skills (Support) Center. Multicultural advisers are available as is a coordinator for international and minority students. A variety of on-campus housing is offered for men and women, including single and double accommodations, single-gender residence halls, a coed apartment complex, town houses, and campus houses.

At the graduate level, the University offers master's degrees in accountancy, business, criminal justice, occupational therapy, orthodics, pastoral studies, physical therapy, social work, and special education.

St. Ambrose has eighteen varsity sports for men and women in a widely varied athletic program. In addition, the intramural sports and recreation programs are an integral part of the St. Ambrose liberal arts tradition. Activities are centered around the multipurpose PE Center. Recreational facilities include a gymnasium, racquetball courts, a tennis court, an indoor track, weightlifting rooms, and a swimming pool. St. Ambrose, a member of the National Association of Intercollegiate Athletics (NAIA), sponsors men's teams in baseball, basketball, cross-country, football, golf, soccer, tennis, track, and volleyball and women's teams in basketball, cross-country, dance, golf, soccer, softball, tennis, track, and volleyball.

St. Ambrose is a nonprofit educational institution that admits academically qualified students of any race, color, age, sex, religion, or national origin, without regard to any physical handicap, to all the rights, privileges, programs, and activities generally available to students at the University. It does not discriminate on the basis of race, color, sex, religion, national origin, or physical handicap in administration of any of its educational policies or programs, including admissions, financial aid, and athletics. It is also an equal opportunity employer. The school is authorized under federal law to enroll nonimmigrant alien students.

Location

Davenport, which has a population of 100,000, is the largest municipality in the Iowa-Illinois Quad Cities (population 320,000), which are situated on either side of the Mississippi River. The area is easily reached by eight major highways, and the Quad City Metropolitan Airport in Moline is 15 minutes away from the campus. The area offers a host of river activities as well as a riverside jazz festival of international fame and the world-renowned Bix 7 road race. There are scores of parks and athletic and recreational facilities, as well as numerous museums, galleries, theater groups, and musical organizations. The Quad-City Symphony Orchestra features world-famous artists in concert. The symphony, the twelfth oldest in the United States, offers college students special season-ticket prices and encourages musically inclined students to audition. The Quad City Arts Council offers cultural events of unusual variety through its affiliate artist programs, many of which take place on the St. Ambrose University campus.

Majors and Degrees

Programs are offered leading to the degrees of Bachelor of Arts, Bachelor of Science, Bachelor of Science in Industrial Engineering, Bachelor of Music, Bachelor of Music Education, Bachelor of Arts in Special Studies, and Bachelor of Elected Studies. Undergraduate programs include accounting, art, athletic training, biology, business administration, chemistry, communication, computer communications, computer science, criminal justice, economics, education (early childhood, elementary, and secondary), engineering (industrial engineering or engineering physics), English, environmental management, history, languages, management science and statistics (operations research), mathematics, mathematics education, music, music education, natural science, networking administration, nursing, philosophy, physical education, physical therapy, physics, political science, psychology, public administration, special education, speech and theater, sports medicine, special studies (an individually designed major), and theology.

Academic Program

St. Ambrose is committed to combining the liberal arts with career preparation. The liberal arts component in each student's program consists of courses in six major divisions: arts, languages and literature, natural sciences, philosophy and theology, physical education, and social sciences and/or economics. Students are required to study history and literature. Individual courses are chosen by the student in consultation with an academic adviser. Students working toward a bachelor's degree in special studies may develop their own major with the help of a faculty adviser, with the approval of the Board of Studies.

Courses are scheduled for morning, afternoon, and evening. St. Ambrose has a two-semester calendar. Fall semester examinations are taken before the Christmas break. A special term has been added between semesters for cultural tours of Europe, South America, the Mideast, and Asia, and students also take advantage of summer sessions.

To be eligible for graduation, students must maintain an average grade of at least C (2.0) and must complete a minimum of 120 semester credits (usually forty courses) in the Bachelor of Arts, Bachelor of Science (but 135 semester credits for the Bachelor of Science in Industrial Engineering degree program), Bachelor of Arts in Special Studies, and Bachelor of Elected Studies degree programs or 136 semester credits in the Bachelor of Music and Bachelor of Music Education degree programs. The English written-communication requirement may be waived for students who demonstrate competence on an examination given through the College-Level Examination

Program (CLEP). Credit is given for the CLEP general examination in English with essay. The foreign language/intercultural-understanding requirement may be waived for students who have completed 1 unit of a foreign language in high school or at the college level. Students must demonstrate competence in public oral communication and in mathematics. Credit for nonclassroom learning is awarded through CLEP or through assessment by individual departments of the University.

Off-Campus Arrangements

Through the International Studies Program, St. Ambrose students may spend a year abroad while earning up to 44 credits. A cooperative education program (University-sponsored experiential learning opportunities) and internships are available in most departments, including business administration, communication, criminal justice, economics, education, industrial engineering, occupational therapy, physical therapy, political science, psychology, and sociology.

Academic Facilities

O'Keefe Library and Learning Center has more than 160,000 volumes and includes a full range of audiovisual equipment, materials, and services that help to increase the scope of independent study. The Galvin Fine Arts and Communications Center houses the Departments of Art, Communication, Music, and Speech and Theater. It includes the Allaert Auditorium, a 1,200-seat facility that can be subdivided into five sections, and the Catich Gallery of calligraphic art and stained glass works. The Physical Education Center, which seats up to 2,200 people, serves multiple academic purposes and provides space for classrooms and offices, recreational activities, physical conditioning, and athletic competition.

Costs

The 2000–01 tuition for undergraduates is $13,890 per year (other fees are included in this cost). The 860 resident students living on campus in a dormitory have room and board expenses of $5100 per year (based on double occupancy and a nineteen-meal-per-week plan and including a medical fee).

Financial Aid

Federal, state, and University financial aid programs, scholarships, loans, grants, work-study and cooperative programs, and University employment opportunities are available. Federal programs include the Federal Pell Grant, Federal Supplemental Educational Opportunity Grant, Federal Work-Study, and Federal Perkins Loan programs. State programs are the Iowa Scholarship, Iowa PLUS Loan, and Iowa Tuition Grant programs. The priority deadline for financial aid applications is March 15 for the next fall semester. In addition to submitting an application for admission, applicants for financial aid must submit the Free Application for Federal Student Aid (FAFSA). This form is available in the offices of high school counselors or in the St. Ambrose University Financial Aid Office, or on line at http://fafsa.ed.gov/.

Faculty

The faculty of St. Ambrose University is composed of 147 full-time and 98 part-time members who are dedicated primarily to teaching. About 85 percent of the full-time faculty members hold a terminal degree, and all teach in their primary area of expertise. No classes are taught by graduate assistants. Each faculty member advises from 10 to 50 students and considers this responsibility to be as important as teaching.

Student Government

All registered students are members of the St. Ambrose Student Government Association (SGA). Organized in 1925, the SGA served as one of the prototypes of such organizations among American colleges. Members conduct and coordinate all student activities at the University, including student elections and cultural, social, educational, and special events. Students are represented on virtually every committee of the University. The SGA is also involved in community activities.

Admission Requirements

Admission to St. Ambrose is selective. Students who satisfy at least two of the following three requirements are encouraged to apply: a minimum 2.5 cumulative GPA, an ACT composite score of 20 or above or an SAT I combined score of 950 or higher, and/or ranking in the upper half of their graduating class. Prospective students must take the ACT or SAT I before being admitted. Test scores, class rank, and grade point average are very important in the selection process. Placement tests in reading, math, and writing are required of all students upon admission.

St. Ambrose encourages applications from students who have postponed their education for various reasons, such as work or family responsibilities, as well as from students directly out of high school, transfer students, and international students. St. Ambrose also has a program for students with learning disabilities. More information is available from the Admissions Office. All applicants are considered individually. Early acceptance, early decision, and deferred entrance are possible, and many students enter with advanced standing. Applicants are strongly encouraged to visit the campus.

Application and Information

The completed application for admission, high school transcripts or equivalent credentials, and test scores should be sent to the Director of Admissions. Students also may apply on line at http://www.sau.edu/administration/newstudent/admitform.htm.

For more information or to arrange a campus visit, students should contact:

Meg Flaherty
Director of Admissions
St. Ambrose University
518 West Locust Street
Davenport, Iowa 52805

Telephone: 319-333-6300
               800-383-2627 (toll-free)
E-mail: mflahery@sau.edu
World Wide Web: http://www.sau.edu

Ambrose Hall, which is on the National Register of Historic Places.

ST. ANDREWS PRESBYTERIAN COLLEGE
LAURINBURG, NORTH CAROLINA

The College
A small private college, St. Andrews is affiliated with the Presbyterian Church (U.S.A.) and welcomes students of all beliefs who are seeking a strong, relevant, and broad liberal arts education grounded in such hands-on, practical experience as internships and study-abroad programs. It is this blending of theory and practice that attracts the 700 students (55 percent women and 45 percent men) and that has allowed graduates to succeed through the changing times since the College was founded in 1958 with the merging of two older institutions with histories dating back to 1896.

St. Andrews students come from across the United States and from thirty countries and pursue active community involvement to the same extent as their academic studies. St. Andrews students experience diversity and develop tolerance. They explore responsible living on a global scale, are encouraged to develop individual responsibility, and are challenged to expect the best of themselves and to contribute their best to the world.

St. Andrews is committed to providing the full range of programs and services necessary to help students successfully make the transition from college to the world of work. Between 20 and 25 percent of graduates go on for graduate or professional degrees. Ninety-five percent of graduates are either employed or continuing their education within six months of graduation.

More than 90 percent of students reside on the award-winning, barrier-free 640-acre campus, which is located on two shores of Lake Ansley C. Moore and joined by a causewalk. The College has eight residence halls, including a residence hall designed especially for students with physical challenges, where 24-hour care is available on a limited basis.

Among its twenty majors, St. Andrews offers two distinctive programs of study, both among the first in the nation and both pilot programs for others: therapeutic riding and international business.

St. Andrews' top-ranked equestrian team has won many titles on both the IHSA and the ANRC circuits. St. Andrews also participates in thirteen NCAA Division II sports, including men's and women's basketball, cross-country, equestrian sports, and soccer; women's softball and volleyball; and men's baseball and lacrosse.

The Physical Education Center houses a multipurpose gymnasium seating 1,400, a swimming pool, racquetball courts, a sports medicine lab, weight rooms, and a smaller additional gym. Outdoor athletic facilities include an all-weather track, a baseball field, and lacrosse, soccer, and softball fields. In addition, the 640-acre campus surrounding a 70-acre lake is a wonderful recreational resource for walkers, joggers, and bikers who, due to the mild climate, may enjoy these and other outdoor activities nearly year-round.

Location
Laurinburg, North Carolina, is a town of 17,500 located in the south-central Sandhills section of the state, near the resort communities of Pinehurst and Southern Pines. St. Andrews' location is also within driving distance of the Smoky Mountains of western North Carolina and the relatively unpopulated Atlantic beaches of the Carolinas. Within a 2-hour drive are Charlotte, Raleigh, and Durham; the Research Triangle Park; and Columbia, South Carolina.

Majors and Degrees
St. Andrews College grants Bachelor of Arts, Bachelor of Fine Arts, and Bachelor of Science degrees, with majors in Asian studies, biology, business administration, chemistry, communications and theater arts, creative writing, education, English, exercise science, history, international business, liberal arts, mathematics, philosophy, politics, psychology, religious studies, therapeutic riding, and visual arts. The College also offers preprofessional programs in dentistry, law, medicine, physical therapy, theology, and veterinary medicine. A 3-2 program in engineering is offered in conjunction with North Carolina State University. A prelaw certificate program is also offered.

Academic Program
In addition to the twenty majors listed above, St. Andrews students have the opportunity to work closely with their advisers to design a liberal arts thematic major that best fits their academic and career goals. All students take SAGE (St. Andrews General Education), which has been designed not only to impart the essential skills of critical thinking, reading, and writing but also to explore centuries of human accomplishment and to formulate action-based values from their studies. All students are advised by faculty members concerning course selection and postgraduation plans. A total of 120 credits is required for the baccalaureate degree.

Off-Campus Arrangements
All students are strongly encouraged to seek out and to participate in internships and other practical, hands-on experiences. St. Andrews' internship program is very strong, with more than 80 students per year participating in for-credit internships at businesses, social service agencies, stables, museums, laboratories, industries, and other locations. St. Andrews also offers a special long-term internship at the Washington Center in Washington, D.C., with agencies such as the U.S. State Department and the Smithsonian Institution. More than 50 percent of students complete internships during their time at St. Andrews. The College's demi-semester calendar makes it easy for students to participate in these internships as well as to study abroad. St. Andrews offers yearlong study-abroad programs in coordination with Hannan University in Korea and Kansai Gadai University in Japan. The College is also a cooperating member of the Central College Consortium, which sponsors semester-long and yearlong study programs in Austria, England, the Netherlands, Spain, and Wales. In addition, the College places students in the Aix-en-Provence language/cultural studies program and has collaborative relationships with Mansfield College, Oxford (England), and with the University of St. Andrews, Scotland.

Programs are also established with Brunnenburg Castle in the Tyrolian Alps of northern Italy; Capital Normal University in Beijing, China; and the Universidad de Cuenca in Cuenca, Ecuador. St. Andrews students have also recently traveled to Vietnam, Greece, Zimbabwe, Mexico, Switzerland, and India, with new destinations added each year as student and faculty interests demand.

Academic Facilities

The College library houses more than 130,000 volumes and is online to several databases. Internet and World Wide Web capabilities are also readily available. The main science laboratory—covering 20,000 square feet—has won awards for its "open concept" design in which students of all sciences work side by side to foster scientific inquiry and cross-exploration. The laboratory is open outside of class time nearly 24 hours per day. Sophisticated scientific instrumentation is also available, including electron microscopes, chromatographs, a sterile culture laboratory, spectrophotometers, a vertebrate museum, an herbarium, an animal research facility, and a greenhouse.

St. Andrews has an Electronic Fine Arts Center, with graphics computers, color printers, and electronic music editing and creation capabilities.

Seven networked campus laboratories with e-mail and Internet connections are located on the academic and residential sides of the campus and are open 24 hours per day.

St. Andrews is the site of the most recent Electronic Commerce Research Center (ECRC), offering expert training to professionals throughout the region.

Education facilities include the John P. Daughtrey Resource Center, which serves as an education materials library, a software preview site, a materials construction laboratory, and a meeting place for education students and their professors.

The Singing Wood Farm annex is the home of St. Andrews' equestrian program, which has consistently placed riders in IHSA and ANRC regional and national championships, in which they have earned IHSA and ANRC national and reserve titles. The 17-acre facility features a 200-foot by 300-foot lighted outdoor arena, another nonlighted outdoor ring, a hitchcock pen, an outside hunter course, and miles of riding trails.

Costs

St. Andrews' tuition and fees are $14,015 per academic year in 2000–01. The complete cost of tuition and room and board in campus residence halls is $19,315.

Financial Aid

The financial aid program combines merit-based assistance with traditional need-based assistance. Nearly 80 percent of all St. Andrews students receive some type of financial assistance. The College administers traditional federal and state programs, including the Federal Pell Grant, Federal Stafford Student Loan, Federal Perkins Loan, and Federal PLUS Loan, as well as the North Carolina Legislative Tuition Grant for North Carolina students. Campus employment is available. To apply for assistance, students must complete a Free Application for Federal Student Aid (FAFSA).

Faculty

The College currently has a teaching faculty of 46 full-time members. Eighty-four percent have their earned doctorate, and 89 percent hold a terminal degree in their field. All faculty members advise students. St. Andrews faculty members have a broad range of experience in all areas and are committed to teaching and to ensuring that St. Andrews students make the most of their educational experience. The student-faculty ratio is 12:1.

Student Government

Since St. Andrews seeks to develop action-based values in its students, the involvement of students is welcomed and encouraged through such channels as Student Government and thirty-three other active organizations and committees.

Admission Requirements

St. Andrews is selective in admission. Application and notification are rolling. All students must complete 16 units of high school study, including 12 units in English, mathematics, history, natural science, social science, and foreign language. High school grade point average, class rank, ACT or SAT I scores, writing samples, personal interviews, and recommendations are considered in determining the applicant's potential to succeed at St. Andrews. Applicants from nontraditional high schools are encouraged to apply.

Transfer students are evaluated with regard to the college-level work they have completed in addition to the standard criteria for admission. A minimum of 32 hours must be completed in residence, including the major requirements.

Application and Information

For more information, students should contact:

Dean of Admissions and Student Financial Planning
St. Andrews College
1700 Dogwood Mile
Laurinburg, North Carolina 28352
Telephone: 800-763-0198 (toll-free)
Fax: 910-277-5087
E-mail: admissions@sapc.edu
World Wide Web: http://www.sapc.edu

The Katherine McKay Belk Tower reflected in the lake at the center of the St. Andrews campus, Laurinburg, North Carolina.

SAINT ANSELM COLLEGE
MANCHESTER, NEW HAMPSHIRE

The College

Founded in 1889 by the Order of Saint Benedict, Saint Anselm is the third-oldest Catholic college in New England. From its beginning, Saint Anselm has been, and desires to remain, a small college. With an enrollment of 1,899 (837 men and 1,062 women), the school continues to adhere to this decision not only because it wishes to accept only those students it can efficiently prepare for their life's work but also because it wishes to retain the family spirit that is characteristic of a Benedictine institution.

All students at Saint Anselm pursue specialized major courses of study in such areas as liberal arts, business, the sciences, nursing, and preprofessional preparation. The College's primary goal, however, is to provide educational opportunities that will endow students with a well-rounded, creative, and open-minded spirit. Saint Anselm prides itself on the ability to regard each student as a special individual with important personal goals.

Surrounded by the natural beauty of a scenic New Hampshire landscape, the campus blends both traditional and modern buildings to form a picturesque and striking academic setting. The College has students from twenty-nine states and nine countries. Approximately 80 percent of the students live on campus in traditional dormitories and modern apartments. There are more than sixty clubs and other organizations to satisfy students' diverse interests. Among these are the Abbey Players (theater group), a debate group, choral groups, a music society, a jazz band, a center for volunteers, a premed society, a prelaw society, an economics club, an outing club, and a local chapter of the Knights of Columbus. Intercollegiate sports are offered for men in baseball, basketball, cross-country, football, golf, hockey, lacrosse, skiing, soccer, and tennis and for women in basketball, cross-country, lacrosse, skiing, soccer, softball, tennis, and volleyball. Intramural sports are basketball, ice hockey, indoor and outdoor soccer, racquetball, softball, tennis, touch football, and volleyball. There are club sports for men and women in both rugby and crew.

The John Maurus Carr Activities Center provides students with a multipurpose recreational facility that includes racquetball courts and a comprehensive fitness center. The Davison Hall dining commons, available throughout the day, is a beautiful, spacious addition to campus life. Other facilities include the Cushing Student Center, which houses academic and career counseling facilities, student organizations, health services, and the Academic Resource Center, and Stoutenburgh Gymnasium, home of Saint Anselm varsity athletics.

Location

Located on the outskirts of Manchester, the largest city in New Hampshire, Saint Anselm College offers the benefits of a primarily residential community in a suburban setting. The city has excellent restaurants, shopping malls, and movie theaters. Public transportation from the campus to the city is provided on an hourly basis.

Southern New Hampshire is an excellent setting for students who seek an active college lifestyle. For example, within less than an hour's drive are some of the finest mountains in America, the Atlantic Ocean at Hampton, and the many cultural and recreational resources of the vibrant city of Boston.

Majors and Degrees

Saint Anselm College awards the Bachelor of Arts degree in accounting, biochemistry, biology, business, chemistry, classics, computer science, computer science with business, computer science with mathematics, criminal justice, economics, English, environmental science, financial economics, fine arts, French, history, liberal studies in the great books, mathematics, mathematics with economics, natural science, philosophy, politics, psychology, sociology, Spanish, and theology. It also offers a program leading to the Bachelor of Science in Nursing (B.S.N.) degree.

The College offers preprofessional programs in dentistry, education (secondary), law, medicine, and theology.

A 3-2 program in engineering is available in cooperation with the University of Notre Dame, Catholic University of America, Manhattan College, and the University of Massachusetts Lowell.

Academic Program

Saint Anselm College provides students with a strong liberal arts background to complement their major area of study. Students generally take from ten to fifteen courses in their major, while the liberal arts core courses and a wide range of electives make up the remainder of the forty courses required for graduation. Honors Program participants distinguish themselves by taking additional courses in order to graduate with honors.

All Saint Anselm students participate in the College's nationally recognized humanities program during their freshman and sophomore years. This challenging program, entitled "Portraits of Human Greatness," is centered on lectures and small-group seminars that explore Western civilization.

Saint Anselm College participates in the Advanced Placement Program of the College Board. Students who receive a score of 3 or better on the Advanced Placement examinations may obtain advanced placement and credit in the pertinent subject matter. Applicants who have completed examinations under the College-Level Examination Program may receive advanced placement and credit if the scores they receive are acceptable.

Off-Campus Arrangements

Most departments throughout the College offer a number of internship experiences related to the major fields of study. The internship program helps students to combine the theoretical experience gained in the classroom with a practical application to a specific area of study. Internships are generally taken in the junior or senior year. They are available either in Manchester, New York City, or in Washington, D.C., through American University.

The College also offers several study-abroad programs and provides students with access to others. These programs can be integrated into most majors and give students excellent opportunities to learn a foreign language and to study other cultures and civilizations.

Academic Facilities

The spacious, wooded 460-acre campus has forty-six buildings. The six most recent facilities reflect the College's continued commitment to adapt to the needs of its students. Poisson Computer Science Center houses more than 200 microcomputers and a specially equipped computer classroom, as well as general-purpose classrooms and faculty offices. The Charles A. Dana Center houses a 700-seat theater and serves as the home of the humanities program. The Geisel Library, which holds 210,000 bound volumes and 56,491 microform titles and maintains a collection of 1,795 periodical titles, provides an excellent research base for Saint Anselm students and faculty. A major expansion and reconstruction project to enlarge the library to meet the expanding needs of the College community has been completed as well as a $10-million expansion and renovation of the Goulet Science Center.

Costs

Tuition for the 2000–01 school year has been set at $18,350, and room and board charges are $7000, for a total of $25,350. Books and other miscellaneous fees cost approximately $1200.

Financial Aid

Saint Anselm College offers financial aid through various federal and private programs. Assistance is awarded as a supplement to the reasonable financial sacrifice that the College expects will be made by the interested student and his or her parents. Eighty-five percent of Saint Anselm's students are receiving some form of financial assistance to help defray the cost of their education. Financial aid packages consist of scholarships, grants, loans, and work opportunities. Merit awards (Presidential Scholarships) are awarded to outstanding students.

Two forms are required in applying for aid. The student must submit the Financial Aid PROFILE and the Free Application for Federal Student Aid (FAFSA) to the College Scholarship Service by March 15.

Faculty

The College's faculty consists of 112 full-time and 58 part-time members. Ninety-two percent of the faculty have earned doctorates or the appropriate terminal degrees in their fields. With a student-teacher ratio of 15:1, close interaction is possible between students and professors. In addition to their teaching responsibilities, faculty members serve as advisers to students enrolled in their department. No classes are taught by graduate students.

Student Government

Student government means students organizing themselves for a common purpose. At Saint Anselm, student government exists as the Student Senate, the Campus Activities Board, and the Class Councils. The aim of student government is to complement the essential aim of a college education: scholarship. Student government organizes and unifies social, intellectual, and cultural activities so that they become an important part of liberal education. Student government helps students develop such qualities as initiative, cooperation, and leadership.

Admission Requirements

In selecting a freshman class, the admission committee considers each candidate personally and thoroughly. The committee evaluates each student's high school record, scores on the SAT I, letters of recommendation, and written essay (part of the application). Of greatest importance is the student's high school transcript, in terms of both the quality of courses taken and the grades earned.

Transfer and international students are welcome to apply. The same general admission procedures are required, along with at least a C average in all transferable courses and, for international students, a satisfactory score on the TOEFL.

Application and Information

The College follows a rolling admission policy, with a priority date of March 1. The Admissions Office is open from 8:30 a.m. to 4:30 p.m. on weekdays and, during the fall and winter, from 9 a.m. to 1 p.m. on Saturday. The College strongly recommends that students visit the campus and have an interview in order to discover the many benefits of Saint Anselm.

For more information, students should contact:

Director of Admissions
Saint Anselm College
100 Saint Anselm Drive
Manchester, New Hampshire 03102
Telephone: 603-641-7500
                888-426-7356 (toll-free)
Fax: 603-641-7550
E-mail: admissions@anselm.edu

Saint Anselm College Alumni Hall.

ST. BONAVENTURE UNIVERSITY
ST. BONAVENTURE, NEW YORK

The University

St. Bonaventure University provides a traditional Franciscan liberal arts education with individual attention from professors, a beautiful residential setting, and a friendly, close-knit atmosphere. Of the 2,850 students enrolled, 2,200 are undergraduates. More than 75 percent of the undergraduates are full-time residents. Complementing St. Bonaventure's traditions are innovative degree programs, computerized career placement aids, comprehensive student life activities, and modern academic facilities. Among major campus events during the academic year are concerts and coffeehouse acts, indoor and outdoor intramural and recreational programs, current and classic film offerings, and dramatic and musical plays. Aspiring writers and broadcasters from all academic majors will find challenging and plentiful opportunities working with one of the four University media: WSBU-FM, the campus radio station currently ranked fifth in the nation; the *Bona Venture*, the award-winning weekly newspaper; the *Bonadieu*, the yearbook; and the *Laurel*, the nation's oldest student literary publication, which marked its 100th anniversary in 1999. Other organizations on campus include academic fraternities, academic honor societies, a variety of club and intramural sports, and arts organizations that include choral, instrumental, dance, and drama ensembles. The Thomas Merton Ministry Center is open 24 hours a day and aims to foster a community of friendship and mutual service. Many students take the opportunity to serve as Bona Buddies to area children or senior citizens; help with The Warming House, the oldest student-run soup kitchen in the nation; or volunteer in other service organizations. Volunteer opportunities expanded in 1999–2000 with the opening of St. Bonaventure's Franciscan Center for Social Concern, which offers immersion experiences and service opportunities with the poor.

St. Bonaventure University students enjoy three athletic facilities, the Reilly Center, housing a sports arena and swimming pool; a fitness center, housing indoor tennis courts, racquetball courts, a volleyball court, a squash court, a multistation Universal Gym, free weights and Nautilus machines, an exercise room, and Lifecycles; and the recently renovated Butler Gym, which offers a basketball court and an indoor track. Also available are outdoor tennis and basketball courts, a nine-hole golf course, and a nearby ski resort and ice rink. NCAA Division I athletics for men are baseball, basketball, cross-country, golf, soccer, swimming, and tennis. Division I competition for women includes basketball, cross-country, lacrosse, soccer, softball, swimming, and tennis.

In addition to its undergraduate programs, St. Bonaventure offers the Master of Arts degree in English, Franciscan studies, history, psychology, teaching, and theology. A Master of Science is offered in professional leadership, while a Master of Science in Education program includes advanced teacher education, counselor education, educational administration, supervision and curriculum, reading, and special education. A Master of Business Administration degree program is also available with concentrations in accounting/finance, general business, international business, and management/marketing. Certification programs in business, education, and Franciscan and theological studies are also offered.

Location

St. Bonaventure is located on Route 417 between Olean, a city of approximately 20,000 residents, and Allegany, a village with about 2,000 residents. Shops, restaurants, and theaters are all within walking distance. The campus is spread over 500 acres in a valley surrounded by the Allegheny Hills. The Bona Bus connects the campus with Olean and Allegany, carrying students to and from the area attractions. The region around St. Bonaventure provides a beautiful setting for many outdoor activities. A ski resort, ice-rink, and snow-tubing resort attract students, and nearby Allegany State Park offers excellent facilities for swimming, boating, and hiking. St. Bonaventure is accessible by car, bus, and commercial air transportation, with airports in Olean, Buffalo, and Rochester, New York, and nearby Bradford, Pennsylvania.

Majors and Degrees

St. Bonaventure University grants the Bachelor of Arts degree with majors in classical languages, English, history, interdisciplinary studies, journalism and mass communication, modern languages (French and Spanish), philosophy, political science, psychology, social sciences, sociology, and visual arts. The Bachelor of Science is granted with majors in biochemistry, biology, chemistry, computer science, economics, elementary education, environmental science, interdisciplinary studies, mathematics, physical education, physics, and psychology. The Bachelor of Business Administration is granted with majors in accounting, finance, interdisciplinary studies, management sciences, and marketing. Popular five-year programs are also available in business, English, physics, and psychology.

Academic Program

St. Bonaventure's core curriculum, completed by all students in all majors, is Clare College, which is based on an interdisciplinary approach to learning grounded in the vision of St. Francis and St. Bonaventure. Composed of 49 credits, it begins with "The Intellectual Journey" and continues through courses in composition and critical thinking, reasoning, and various core areas, followed by a capstone University forum.

A candidate for a bachelor's degree must complete at least 120 credit hours, with a cumulative index of 2.0 or better in the major field and the overall program. A pass/fail grade option, available to all upperclass students, may be elected for one course per semester, but not for courses in a student's major field.

Advanced credit is granted for grades of C or better on either the College Proficiency Examination or the College-Level Examination Program tests. Advanced placement is granted on the basis of scores obtained on the College Board's Advanced Placement examinations.

Men and women may also elect to participate in the University's Army ROTC program, which earned the MacArthur Award as best small unit in the nation in 1998.

Off-Campus Arrangements

More than twenty-five semester-long international study programs are available, including St. Bonaventure-sponsored study in Spain, Ireland, and Australia, to students in good academic standing in their junior year. A business immersion program is also available to students, including an affiliation with the University of Southern Europe in Monaco. For further information, students should contact the Office of International Studies. Fieldwork or internships are available in several major programs.

Academic Facilities

The library houses more than 250,000 volumes and includes a trilevel resource center with a curriculum center, the University archives, and an audiovisual area. An automated online card catalog greatly improves research capabilities.

DeLaRoche Hall houses equipment for instruction and research in a variety of fields, including chemistry, geology, mathematics, microbiology, physics, and psychology. Research facilities include an atomic absorption spectrophotometer, a tissue-culture laboratory, a greenhouse, a radioactivity laboratory, equipment for research in the growth of microorganisms, and an extensive mammal collection.

The John J. Murphy Professional Building provides the most up-to-date equipment for the School of Business and the School of Journalism and Mass Communication. The Bob Koop Broadcast Journalism Laboratory, dedicated in fall 1998, features a television studio with an anchor desk, one digital editing bay, and three videotape editing bays, while the building also houses offices, classrooms, and a 432-seat auditorium. A fiber-optic network connects microcomputers in academic and administrative areas. There are seven labs for student use containing more than 100 DOS and Macintosh systems. St. Bonaventure students also have access to the Internet via every residence hall.

An annex to Plassmann Hall houses computer-adaptable education classrooms, seminar rooms, and offices for the education faculty. An observatory allows students access to three compact telescopes, two 8-inch Celestron telescopes, and one 11-inch Schmidt-Cassegrain telescope, along with a heated classroom.

The Regina A. Quick Center for the Arts provides acoustically designed classroom space for music courses and painting and drawing studios for students enrolled in visual arts classes. The center, completed in 1995, is a state-of-the-art facility that also includes a MIDI (musical instrument digital interface) lab, three climate-controlled galleries, a 325-seat theater, and an atrium that is often used for poetry readings and impromptu musical performances.

In 1999, St. Bonaventure completed the most comprehensive renovation project in its history, comprising $5 million in renovations to its residence halls and academic facilities. An additional $2 million will fund new apartment housing for 96 students.

Costs

For 2000–01, the annual costs are $14,510 for tuition and $630 for fees. Room and board costs average $5790 per year.

Financial Aid

Students who qualify for financial aid normally receive a package consisting of a combination of scholarships, grants, loans, and work-study awards. Athletic grants-in-aid are available for men in baseball, basketball, golf, soccer, swimming, and tennis and for women in basketball, lacrosse, soccer, softball, swimming, and tennis. Music scholarships are also available. Students must file the Free Application for Federal Student Aid (FAFSA) in order to be considered for financial assistance. For more complete details, a student should contact the Director of Financial Aid at the University.

Faculty

Like the student body, the 147 faculty members at St. Bonaventure come from a wide range of geographic, ethnic, and religious backgrounds. Eighty-five percent of the faculty members hold the terminal degree in their field. Friars, many of whom teach, add to the unique atmosphere of St. Bonaventure.

Student Government

Life at St. Bonaventure is centered on the residence halls, and the foundation of student government begins in the dormitories with the Residence Hall Councils. The councils, composed of elected residents, determine the norms by which the residents are guided in their daily lives. The Student Congress, whose members are elected from the student body, serves as the general student-governing unit, and its members serve on every major University board and committee.

Admission Requirements

St. Bonaventure University welcomes applications for admission from all serious candidates from a variety of backgrounds. St. Bonaventure University provides equal opportunity without regard to race, creed, color, gender, age, national or ethnic origin, marital status, veteran status, or disability in admission, employment, and in all of its educational programs and activities. Applicants must show evidence of academic achievement to be selected for admission. The criteria used in making admission decisions, in order of importance, are quality of the high school curriculum, grade point average in college-preparatory courses, SAT I or ACT (preferred) scores, class rank, recommendations from high school teacher and counselors, and extracurricular activities. Students may submit the traditional paper application or apply on line through the University's Web site (listed below).

Application and Information

For more information about St. Bonaventure University, prospective students should contact:

Director of Admissions
St. Bonaventure University
P.O. Box D
St. Bonaventure, New York 14778
Telephone: 716-375-2400
　　　　　800-462-5050 (toll-free)
E-mail: admissions@sbu.edu
World Wide Web: http://www.sbu.edu

Built in 1928 and renovated in 1999, Devereux Hall is an example of the beautiful Florentine architecture found at St. Bonaventure University.

ST. EDWARD'S UNIVERSITY
AUSTIN, TEXAS

The University

St. Edward's is a private liberal arts university with a commitment to challenge its diverse student population within a small college environment. The University's Catholic heritage promotes academic excellence and personal dedication to teaching and learning. St. Edward's seeks to enable individuals not only to be independent and productive but also to have the competence and conviction to use their skills to confront the critical issues of society.

The student body, which numbers more than 3,600, represents more than thirty states and fifty-five countries; 55 percent are women. More than 700 students are currently seeking graduate degrees in the fields of business administration and human services.

The 180-acre hilltop campus offers a variety of educational and recreational facilities. The Main Building, which has been named a Texas Historic Landmark for its architectural significance, is the center of campus life and houses several classrooms, faculty offices, Student Financial Aid Services, and the Office of Admission. St. Edward's architecture clearly reflects the evolution of its history. The campus maintains a comfortable balance of modern and traditional buildings, including four residence halls, student apartments (available to upperclass students), the Scarborough-Phillips Library, the Ragsdale Campus Center, the Mary Moody Northen Theatre, and the Recreation and Convocation Center, which houses an indoor/outdoor swimming pool, two basketball and volleyball courts, racquetball/handball courts, and a weight room. Students have access to exercise and computer facilities in the residence halls. On-campus housing is offered to all students, and freshmen are required to live in the residence halls unless they are living with their parents.

St. Edward's is a member of the NCAA Division II. Men compete in baseball, basketball, golf, soccer, and tennis. Women compete in basketball, soccer, softball, tennis, and volleyball.

An essential part of the academic experience at St. Edward's involves participation in the services provided by the Office of Career Planning and Experiential Learning (CPEL). Freshmen begin their college experience by planning for life after graduation. CPEL combines focused career exploration, exposure to employment and internship opportunities, and ongoing workshops designed to prepare seniors for graduate school and employment.

Location

Located on the banks of the Colorado River in the hill country of central Texas, Austin is the state capital and one of the educational and political centers of the South. As the fifth-largest city in the state, Austin provides exciting cultural and recreational opportunities for the growing population of just over 600,000 residents. Local theaters, galleries, and museums exhibit the talents of Austin's gifted artists, and nationally recognized musicians fill the popular night spots along Austin's most talked about avenue, Sixth Street.

Outdoor activities include boating, skiing, swimming, and windsurfing on area rivers and lakes. Biking, camping, and hiking throughout the city's 200 parks are enjoyed by St. Edward's students almost year-round.

Majors and Degrees

The University confers the degrees of Bachelor of Arts, Bachelor of Business Administration, and Bachelor of Science. Under the School of Behavioral and Social Sciences, undergraduate majors are offered in criminal justice, history, international studies, political science, psychology, social work, and sociology. Under the School of Business Administration, majors are offered in accounting, business administration and management, and economics. The School of Natural Sciences offers majors in biochemistry, biology, chemistry, computer information science, computer science, and mathematics. Under the School of Humanities, majors are offered in art, communication, English literature, English writing, liberal studies, philosophy, photocommunications, religious studies, Spanish, Spanish and international business, and theater arts. The School of Education offers majors in kinesiology, language arts, social science, and Spanish bilingual teacher education to students seeking elementary or secondary teacher certification. Many students choose to pursue a preprofessional program in conjunction with their established major. St. Edward's offers preprofessional programs in dentistry, engineering, law, medicine, and physical therapy.

Academic Program

All students share an intensive general education requirement of 57 credit hours spanning all four years. The requirements are split into three areas: foundational skills (English writing, college math, computational skills, oral communication, and foreign language), cultural foundations (six courses including American Dilemma, Rise of the West, and Contemporary World Issues), and foundation for values and decisions (five courses including Ethics and Science in Perspective). The general education curriculum culminates with Capstone, a writing course in which students are required to investigate a controversial issue, analyze it, and propose a resolution to it, both orally and in a major paper. The reasoning and communication skills and the understanding of society that these general studies develop are reinforced in each student's in-depth study of a major discipline.

Graduation is based on the successful completion of 120 semester hours of study. St. Edward's observes a two-semester academic calendar, and a flexible summer course schedule offers day and evening classes.

Academic Facilities

St. Edward's academic facilities include the Scarborough-Phillips Library, the Moody Hall classroom building (housing the Instructional Technology Center, the Learning Assistance Center, the IBM Computer Classroom, the Advising Center, and the Computer Center), the Fine Arts Building (housing state-of-the-art photo-processing labs and studios), and Fleck Hall (housing classrooms and labs for the natural sciences).

Costs

The 2000–01 fees for full-time undergraduate students are tuition, $11,896, and room and board, $4850 to $6992 (depending on choice of residence hall and meal plan).

Financial Aid

St. Edward's is committed to meeting the financial needs of every accepted student. The University administers several financial aid programs funded by federal, institutional, and state resources. These programs help students meet college expenses through grants, scholarships, low-interest loans, and work-study programs. To qualify for financial aid, accepted students should submit, through the College Scholarship Service, the Free Application for Federal Student Aid (FAFSA). All students are automatically reviewed for academic scholarships when they apply for admission. The priority deadline for application for the fall semester is March 1.

Faculty

The majority of the full-time faculty hold doctoral degrees. The student-faculty ratio is 15:1. All entering students are paired with faculty advisers who assist them in planning degree programs and who provide academic counseling throughout the students' college careers.

Student Government

Student Government, composed of elected student officers, has campuswide representation. It meets biweekly in a general assembly to plan and direct activities that involve the entire St. Edward's community. In addition, the president of the organization acts as the voice of the student body and regularly attends Board of Trustees meetings.

Admission Requirements

Students who apply for admission to St. Edward's are evaluated individually on the basis of their academic performance in high school, rank in class, SAT I or ACT scores, and level of high school curriculum. To be considered for admission, qualified applicants should rank in the top half of their class and have test scores at or above the national average for college-bound students.

Application and Information

St. Edward's University employs a rolling admission policy. The Admission Committee makes decisions on applications shortly after a student's file becomes complete. A completed file consists of an application, a $30 nonrefundable application fee, SAT I or ACT scores, and official high school transcripts.

All admission credentials should be mailed to:

Office of Admission
St. Edward's University
3001 South Congress
Austin, Texas 78704
Telephone: 512-448-8500
           800-555-0164 (toll-free)
Fax: 512-464-8877
E-mail: seu.admit@admin.stedwards.edu
World Wide Web: http://www.stedwards.edu

The Main Building, designated a Texas Historic Landmark in 1973, is the center of the St. Edward's community.

ST. FRANCIS COLLEGE
BROOKLYN HEIGHTS, NEW YORK

The College

Small, urban, friendly, and caring, St. Francis College was established in 1884 by the Franciscan Brothers of Brooklyn. Today St. Francis is an independent Catholic, Franciscan coeducational college that confers degrees in the arts and sciences and preprofessional disciplines. It is chartered by the Board of Regents of the University of the State of New York and accredited by the Middle States Association of Colleges and Schools. Throughout its long history, the College has offered an education of high quality that reflects its willingness to adapt to a constantly changing society and at the same time retain its tradition of liberal education.

St. Francis has an average enrollment of 2,100 students, most of whom come from the Greater New York metropolitan area. The College also takes pride in its sizable international student population; almost eighty nations are represented. Young men and women from a variety of backgrounds feel at home and fit in at St. Francis. It is easy to make friends in the warm, trusting atmosphere that characterizes this college community.

St. Francis has a full range of extracurricular activities and publications as well as twenty-nine clubs and four fraternities and sororities. Major activities include student government, the yearbook, the campus newspaper, the literary magazine, and professional societies such as the St. Thomas More Pre-Law Society. Athletics are a high priority at St. Francis, and the College is a member of the Northeast Conference and NCAA Division I. St. Francis sponsors eighteen varsity sports, which include championship men's baseball, basketball, and soccer teams; women's basketball, softball, and volleyball teams; and men's and women's cross-country, indoor/outdoor track, swimming, tennis, and water polo teams. In addition, there is an extensive intramural program that includes basketball, billiards, softball, and volleyball.

Location

The College is located in Brooklyn Heights, a National Historic District and one of New York's most charming and desirable neighborhoods for living, working, or attending school. Borough Hall, the Supreme Court building, art galleries, theaters, restaurants, and shops are all nearby. Because of its location, St. Francis also offers all the advantages of New York City. Wall Street, Madison Avenue, and the museums, galleries, theaters, concert halls, and avant-garde clubs of Manhattan are a short subway ride away. Opportunities abound for students to gain firsthand experience in the business and professional world as well as exposure to significant cultural events.

Majors and Degrees

St. Francis College offers the degrees of Bachelor of Arts (B.A.), Bachelor of Science (B.S.), Associate in Applied Science (A.A.S.), Associate in Science (A.S.), and Associate in Arts (A.A.).

Majors leading to the B.A. degree include communications, economics, English, history, international cultural studies, philosophy, political science, psychology, social studies, and sociology. Majors leading to the B.S. include accounting, accounting and business practice, aviation administration, aviation business studies, biology, biomedical science, chemistry, criminal justice, health-care management, health promotion, health services administration, management, mathematics, medical technology, physician assistant, physical education, and special studies. The A.A.S. can be earned in business administration and criminal justice, the A.S. in electronic data processing, and the A.A. in liberal arts. Teacher training programs in primary and secondary education are also available.

St. Francis offers several special opportunities for students to receive certification in various health-care fields. In conjunction with the State University of New York (SUNY) Health Science Center at Brooklyn, programs leading to B.S. degrees in the fields of occupational and physical therapy, physician assistant studies, and diagnostic medical imaging are offered. After completing two years of academic study at St. Francis College, the student commences clinical training at the Health Science Center. The baccalaureate degree is awarded by the SUNY Health Science Center at Brooklyn.

In cooperative efforts with the New York College of Podiatric Medicine and the New York University (NYU) College of Dentistry, the Biology Department has accelerated biomedical science programs that enable highly qualified students to complete a science-studies curriculum in three years and then make application to the New York College of Podiatric Medicine or the New York University College of Dentistry.

The program in medical technology prepares the student for acceptance into one of the clinical facilities with which St. Francis has an affiliation, either Catholic Medical Center or Methodist Hospital. Upon completion of clinical training, the student receives a B.S. in medical technology from St. Francis College and a certificate of program completion from the respective School of Medical Technology attended. The student is also awarded a Board of Health permit as a laboratory technologist and is eligible to sit for certification examinations.

Two programs in physician assistant studies and radiologic sciences are offered jointly with the Catholic Medical Center of Brooklyn and Queens. After completing two years of academic study at St. Francis College, the student commences clinical training at Catholic Medical Center. The baccalaureate degree is awarded by St. Francis College.

Academic Program

Each candidate for a bachelor's degree must complete a total of 128 credit hours and achieve a cumulative index of at least 2.0. In keeping with its liberal arts framework, the College requires all students to take a core curriculum of 42 credit hours in the humanities, social sciences, and natural sciences. For each major, each department specifies a number of required courses to give depth, unity, and direction to the course of study. After meeting these College and departmental requirements, students may select the remainder of their courses to suit their own needs and special interests. To enhance its degree programs, the College offers minors in a wide variety of subject areas.

St. Francis has an ongoing commitment to increased academic quality and program excellence. The thriving honors program, which has small seminars and personal faculty mentors, has grown by 300 percent in the last two years. Students in the program participate in the annual conference of the National Collegiate Honors Council. Air Force and Army ROTC programs are also available on a cross-registration basis.

The Franciscan tradition at St. Francis provides the basis for an atmosphere of personal integrity. Each student is treated as an individual and as an important part of the St. Francis College community. Student development is encouraged on all levels: academically, socially, and spiritually. Each student is given every opportunity to achieve personal and career success.

Off-Campus Arrangements

Independent study, both at the College and abroad, is tailored to specific student interests. Students have studied language, culture, and economics at the Catholic University in Paris, the London School of Economics, the University of Madrid, and the

University of Mexico. Recent internships have included placement at the New York City Mayor's office, at the United Nations, and with major television networks.

Regularly scheduled trips abroad are an exciting part of study at St. Francis. Several times a year, usually during school breaks, students have the opportunity to tour international cities, escorted by a faculty member. College credit can be earned as part of these trips for the course Nations of the Modern World. Recent excursions have been to China, England, France, Greece, Italy, Japan, Russia, and Spain. The College also sponsors summer semester study at the University of Galway and offers a junior-year-abroad program and other opportunities for international study.

Academic Facilities

The campus consists of five interconnected buildings. Facilities include the McGarry Library, which houses approximately 130,000 volumes. The library has access to more than 570 periodicals, via either the Internet or current subscription, and has an automated CD-ROM book catalog and periodical indexes. McArdle Student Center, which includes a cafeteria, two lounges, and a game room, provides modern and attractive spaces for relaxing, dining, and conversation. The gym has recently been renovated, and a state-of-the-art fitness center has been added. A television production studio and an Olympic-size swimming pool are also available.

Personal computers, laser printers, and color scanners are available for student use at many locations throughout the campus. All computers are state-of-the-art and are equipped with Pentium processors. They provide access to the Internet, the College's local area network, and the complete line of Microsoft Office software. The McGarry Library features a twenty-five-workstation computer research center. The College operates three electronic classrooms that are fully equipped for courses that require each student to use a personal computer. Technology is being utilized in every academic area; for example, a model high-technology education center provides a "classroom of the future" for education majors. For additional information, students can visit the College's Web site, which is listed below.

Costs

Cited by *U.S. News & World Report*, St. Francis is ranked among the highest-rated regional liberal arts colleges in the country for students incurring the least amount of debt. In addition, it is the least expensive private college in New York State, with tuition and fees only slightly higher than those of state-supported colleges and universities. The 1999–2000 academic year tuition for a typical full-time freshman was approximately $8250. Per credit hour, tuition was $285, and additional fees averaged $160.

Financial Aid

More than 80 percent of the students at St. Francis receive some form of financial aid. A comprehensive financial aid program enables the College to offer eligible students financial aid packages that consist of combinations of scholarships, grants, loans, and student employment. A typical student receives more than $7000 in scholarships, grants, and government support. Financial assistance is available from the TAP, Federal Pell Grant, and Federal Supplemental Educational Opportunity Grant Programs. Merit scholarships provided by the College can enhance government funds, and range from $1500 to full tuition. Students seeking assistance for the academic year must file the appropriate College forms by February 15 in order for their financial aid to be processed.

Faculty

All classes are taught by fully qualified, experienced professors, not teaching assistants. The student-faculty ratio is 20:1. The faculty is primarily a teaching faculty, committed to excellence in the classroom. Many St. Francis professors are also actively involved in business, the arts, or science in New York City. Thus, they are capable of personally bridging the gap between the theoretical knowledge gained in the classroom and the wealth of practical career-related experience the city offers. Currently, there are 65 full-time and 111 part-time faculty members.

Student Government

The student government coordinates activities of the student body. It acts as a sounding board for student desires and interests and as a vehicle for the expression of these desires and interests. It participates actively in all efforts to make a better St. Francis.

Admission Requirements

The College admits individuals without regard to race, color, religion, national or ethnic origin, or gender. All applicants must be graduates of an approved secondary school and must have achieved satisfactory standing in their class. Applicants must also furnish a letter of recommendation from their high school principal or guidance counselor. It is required that applicants take the Scholastic Assessment Test (SAT I). An interview with the director of admissions or admission officer is strongly recommended.

The College is more interested in applicants' potential to succeed in college than in any pattern of scores and grades. When a student's preparation differs from that required in New York State, his or her record is studied for evidence of unusual aptitude, especially in the fields that are prerequisites to the curriculum the applicant wishes to pursue.

Application and Information

While applications are accepted on a rolling basis, those received before April 1 receive priority of consideration. More information about St. Francis College is available from the Office of Admissions.

Office of Admissions
St. Francis College
180 Remsen Street
Brooklyn Heights, New York 11201

Telephone: 718-489-5200
E-mail: admissions@stfranciscollege.edu
World Wide Web: http://www.stfranciscollege.edu

St. Francis College students working in one of the many computer laboratories.

SAINT FRANCIS COLLEGE
LORETTO, PENNSYLVANIA

The College

Saint Francis College is a small, coeducational, liberal arts college. The College was founded in 1847 and conducted under the tradition of the Franciscan Friars of the Third Order Regular. The College is concerned with the development of each student for the world of today. For more than 150 years, the College's philosophy of education and student life has continued to emphasize two values: instruction of high quality and respect for the student as an individual. The College believes that a liberal arts education, encompassing a major field of study, is the soundest kind of preparation a student can have for a productive life. The College is accredited by the Middle States Association of Colleges and Schools. The social work program is accredited by the Council on Social Work Education, and the programs in teacher education have been approved by the Pennsylvania State Department of Education. The physician assistant science program is accredited by the Committee on Allied Health Education and Accreditation on behalf of the American Medical Association. The nursing program has full approval by the Pennsylvania State Board of Nurse Examiners and is fully accredited by the National League for Nursing Accrediting Commission (NLNAC).

Students at Saint Francis College can find a number of outlets for their talents, interests, and abilities. Departmental clubs; volunteer organizations; social, business, and service fraternities; social sororities; and a service sorority are part of campus life. Athletics have played a major role in the College's history, and the athletics program offers nineteen NCAA Division I sports for men and women as well as intramural sports. The Student Activities Organization sponsors an impressive program of lectures, films, and concerts. The Southern Alleghenies Museum of Art, separately chartered, is located on the campus as well.

The full-time undergraduate enrollment is 526 men and 741 women; the College as a whole enrolls 1,913 students. Saint Francis College offers Associate of Science degrees in business administration, real estate, and religious education. On the graduate level, Saint Francis grants a Master of Arts degree in industrial relations, with concentrations in labor relations or personnel administration. The College also offers the Master of Business Administration, Master of Medical Science in physician assistant science, Master of Science in Occupational Therapy, and Master of Science in Physical Therapy degrees. A Master of Education degree and a Master of Arts in Pastoral Ministry degree are available through the Office of Continuing Education.

Location

Saint Francis College is situated on 600 acres in the heart of the Allegheny Mountains. The campus is located in the borough of Loretto, which has a population of approximately 1,400. The campus is 6 miles from the county seat of Ebensburg, which has a population of 4,000. The cities of Johnstown and Altoona are within 25 miles of Loretto and have populations of 35,000 and 55,000, respectively. The College is a 90-minute drive east of Pittsburgh.

Majors and Degrees

Saint Francis College grants the Bachelor of Arts degree and offers majors in American studies, biology, computer science, criminal justice, engineering (3-2 program), English, English/communications, history, mathematics, philosophy, political science, psychology, public administration/government service, religious studies, and sociology. The Bachelor of Science degree is also granted, with majors in accounting, biology, chemistry, computer science, criminal justice, economics and finance, elementary education/special education, environmental management (3-2 program), information systems, management, marketing, mathematics, medical technology, nursing, occupational therapy (five-year master's), physical therapy (six-year master's), physician assistant science (five-year master's), podiatric science, psychology, public administration/government service, social work, and sociology.

Areas of preprofessional study include dentistry, engineering (3-2 program), law, medicine, optometry, and veterinary medicine. Areas of concentration within majors include anthropology, communications, computer science, criminal justice, environmental politics, environmental science, international studies, marine and environmental education specialties, marine biology, political communications, public management, public relations, and systems/languages. The College also grants secondary education certification in the areas of biology, chemistry, English, general science, mathematics, and social studies. A 3-2 cooperative program with Duke University in forestry and environmental management and a 4-1 bachelor's/master's degree program in human resource management/industrial relations are also offered.

It is possible for students to major in one area and minor in another or to have a double major. A self-designed major program is available as well. The College offers an honors program to challenge intellectually ambitious students from all disciplines. While pursuing their major field of study, students enroll in the full four-year curriculum, which allow in-depth, creative study in a variety of subject areas.

A continuing education program provides credit and noncredit courses on campus as well as in the communities surrounding Loretto. The Office of Continuing Education offers Associate of Science degrees in business administration, real estate, and religious education and Bachelor of Science degrees in accounting and management.

Academic Program

The program of study leading to a bachelor's degree is usually completed in eight semesters. To qualify for graduation, a student must follow a program of study, approved by the Vice President for Academic Affairs, that totals at least 128 credits distributed among liberal arts courses, major requirements, collateral requirements, and general electives. All students, regardless of major, are required to complete the College's general education program of 58 credits.

The academic calendar is divided into two semesters and three summer sessions.

Electronic capabilities at Saint Francis College enable students to access library holdings and communicate with professors, fellow students, and the world through the use of personal computers via electronic mail and the Internet. Every classroom and residence hall room is wired for Internet access. The College has several classrooms equipped with state-of-the-art equipment that allows videoconferencing.

Off-Campus Arrangements

Students at Saint Francis College may, with permission of the College's administration, spend their junior year of study abroad or may earn credit for participation in summer programs conducted in Canada, France, Germany, Spain, and other countries by accredited American colleges and universities.

A number of departments offer students the opportunity for off-campus study. For some majors, such as nursing, physician assistant science, education, medical technology, and social work, off-campus study is required; in all other majors, an internship is available as an elective. Such an internship can be a meaningful experience and can significantly enhance a student's career preparation.

Academic Facilities

The six-story Pasquerilla Library contains more than 176,000 volumes, 582 periodicals, and a substantial microfilm collection. Other features of the library are typing areas, seminar rooms, reading rooms, microfilm reading rooms, and a collection of study items and educational materials for elementary and secondary education majors. Special features of the library include a PC laboratory with printers, an automated card catalog, periodical search systems, and a satellite hookup.

Scotus and Padua halls contain modern classroom facilities, language laboratories, two computer laboratories, a recording studio for radio and television, and lecture facilities (halls and an amphitheater). Sullivan Science Hall contains twelve well-equipped biology, chemistry, and physics laboratories, a fully equipped electronic classroom, a greenhouse for botanical research, an examining room for use in the physician assistant science program, a nursing instructional center, and other facilities.

Costs

For 2000–01, tuition is $15,808 and room and board are $6770, for a total of $22,578.

Financial Aid

Approximately 87 percent of the Saint Francis College student body receive financial aid. In addition to participating in federal and state need-based student aid programs, Saint Francis College offers its own substantial grant program and a generous scholarship program that is based on SAT I or ACT scores, high school average, and class rank. Academic awards amount to as much as $10,000 per year.

Faculty

Faculty members are chosen for their knowledge of subject matter, as well as for their ability to communicate. Of the teaching faculty at Saint Francis College, 73 percent hold a doctorate or the highest degree attainable in their specific field of expertise. No graduate students teach classes at Saint Francis College.

Student Government

The Student Government Association's Steering Committee involves students who are interested in self-government. Students also serve on a number of committees in the Faculty Senate. The Student Government offices are located in the John F. Kennedy Student Center, which also houses a 600-seat auditorium, a campus bookstore and post office, a study lounge, a cafeteria, and the College dispensary.

Admission Requirements

The admission committee considers applicants and renders decisions on the basis of the secondary school record, the recommendation of the secondary school principal or counselor, and the results of the SAT I or ACT. Applicants should have a minimum of 16 academic units and are strongly encouraged to visit the College campus for an admission interview and tour. Interviews and campus tours are available Monday through Friday throughout the year and select Saturday mornings while classes are in session.

Transfer students must submit a formal transfer application and a college clearance form in addition to official transcripts from each high school and college previously attended. Transfer students receive an advanced standing evaluation after an offer of admission has been made.

Saint Francis College, an equal opportunity/affirmative action employer, complies with applicable federal and state laws regarding nondiscrimination and affirmative action, including Title IX of the Educational Amendments of 1972), Titles VI and VII of the Civil Rights Act of 1964), and Section 504 of the Rehabilitation Act of 1973). Saint Francis College is committed to a policy of nondiscrimination and equal opportunity for all persons, regardless of race, gender, color, religion, national origin or ancestry, age, marital status, disability, or Vietnam-era veteran status, in employment, education programs and activities, and admissions. Inquiries or complaints may be addressed to the College's Director of Human Resources/Affirmative Action/Title IX Coordinator, Saint Francis College, Loretto, Pennsylvania 15940; telephone: 814-472-3264. For other College information, students should call 814-472-3000.

Application and Information

The College operates under a rolling admission policy. An early decision option is available to those students who have designated Saint Francis College to be their first-choice college. The application for admission and all supporting materials must be received by November 15. The application deadline for the physical therapy and physician assistant programs is January 15. For further information about Saint Francis College, students should contact:

Evan Lipp
Dean for Enrollment Management
Saint Francis College
P.O. Box 600
Loretto, Pennsylvania 15940
Telephone: 814-472-3100
           800-342-5732 (toll-free)
E-mail: admissions@sfcpa.edu
World Wide Web: http://www.sfcpa.edu

After four years of planning, research, and design, Saint Francis College recently dedicated Christian Hall.

ST. FRANCIS XAVIER UNIVERSITY
ANTIGONISH, NOVA SCOTIA, CANADA

The University

Set in the breathtaking hills of Nova Scotia on a picturesque campus, St. Francis Xavier University (StFX) was founded in 1853. The University is renowned for its tradition of academic excellence, community service, loyal alumni, and strong athletics. StFX prides itself on a personalized learning experience, international outreach, and an innovative teaching and research environment.

StFX is ranked among the top universities in Canada with respect to its undergraduate programs, postgraduate scholarships, and research grants. Primarily an undergraduate university, StFX provides liberal arts, science, and applied studies programs to 4,000 students. Among its unique areas of study are Celtic studies, Catholic studies, jazz studies, and aquatic resources.

Sixty-seven percent of the students are from Nova Scotia, with the remainder from every province in Canada, the United States, and around the world.

The unique WebFX program combines state-of-the-art technology with innovative teaching techniques and positions StFX as a leader in the world-connected learning community of the twenty-first century. StFX also is consistently a leader in receiving approvals from the country's premier granting agency, the National Sciences and Engineering Research Council (NSERC). In recent years, StFX has received the most student scholarships per capita of any university in Canada.

A hallmark of StFX is its service to the community. The Antigonish Movement, a self-help program for farmers and fisheries workers, was pioneered early in this century. It provided the foundation for the establishment of the University's Extension Department in 1928. This was augmented in 1959 by the establishment of the world-renowned Coady International Institute, which annually attracts more than 50 Third World leaders to its social development programs. The training on campus and through overseas programs empowers people of developing countries to reach their potential through economic and social action.

While maintaining a strong Catholic tradition, StFX welcomes students and faculty and staff members of all denominations. One hundred years ago, in 1897, degrees were granted to 4 women, making StFX the first coeducational Catholic institution in North America. Today, 55 percent of the students are women.

Location

St. Francis Xavier University is located in the dynamic coastal town of Antigonish, in the Canadian province of Nova Scotia. Known as the Highland Heart of Nova Scotia, Antigonish is a two-hour drive from the capital city, Halifax. The town is a service hub for 15,000 residents of surrounding areas with a full range of modern facilities, including a hospital, banks, a shopping mall, and numerous restaurants and food outlets. Vibrant Main Street is home to many shops, services, and entertainment venues. The cultural diversity of the area, lived by the descendants of the Mi'kmaq, Acadian, Scottish, Black, and Dutch settlers, is reflected in most aspects of the community. The area is surrounded by picturesque beaches, highlands, hiking trails, and a wildlife sanctuary within walking distance. Antigonish, home to many artists, is a popular tourist attraction with the renowned Highland Games, Theatre Antigonish, lobster and salmon suppers, and the area's natural, unspoiled beauty.

Majors and Degrees

The Bachelor of Arts degree with major is offered in aquatic resources; Catholic studies; Celtic studies; economics; English; French; history; mathematics, statistics, and computer science; music; philosophy; political science; psychology; religious studies; sociology/anthropology; and women's studies.

For the Bachelor of Business Administration, students may choose the general degree; the degree with aquatic resources; the major in accounting, economics, enterprise development, finance, information systems, management, or marketing; honours in accounting, enterprise development, finance, management or marketing; or joint honours in business administration and economics.

The Bachelor of Information Systems is a major program designed to prepare graduates as systems analysts, applications programmers, and information systems specialists.

The Bachelor of Arts in human kinetics studies human movement from an arts (humanities/social sciences) perspective. It prepares students for careers in coaching, health and fitness, or sports-related media and for further studies in education, sport history, sport philosophy, sport psychology, or sport sociology.

The Bachelor of Arts in music is an advanced major or honours degree program in classical music or the advanced major or honours degree program in jazz performance. The Bachelor of Music in jazz studies combines composition, arranging, and performance. The Diploma in jazz studies is designed for students who wish to enter the field of commercial music.

The Bachelor of Education is a professional degree program that prepares graduates to enter the school system as teachers at either the elementary or the secondary level.

The Bachelor of Science with major is offered in aquatic resources; biology; chemistry; geology; mathematics, statistics, and computer science; and physics. The advanced major, joint advanced major, honours, or joint honours programs are available in the above subjects, economics, and psychology but not aquatic resources.

The Bachelor of Science in human kinetics focuses on the scientific study of human movement and prepares students for careers in the health and fitness sector; studies at the graduate level in biomechanics, motor control, or exercise physiology; and admission to programs such as education, physiotherapy, athletic/exercise therapy, or medicine.

The Bachelor of Science in human nutrition program is offered with a concentration in foods and/or nutrition. Graduates may qualify for entrance to the Dietitians of Canada dietetic internship programs.

The Bachelor of Science in Nursing focuses on a unique health profession that is both an art and a science. Nursing is the professional practice of caring. The emphasis of the program is on understanding the personal, family, group, and community dimensions of health and illness by blending biological and social sciences, humanities, and professional nursing courses.

The Bachelor of Engineering program consists of a two-year diploma at StFX, which is followed by two years of study at DalTech, Dalhousie University in Halifax, or a comparable university. A student entering the second year of the diploma must choose one of the following engineering disciplines: biological, chemical, civil, computer, electrical, environmental, industrial, mechanical, metallurgical, or mining engineering.

In association with DalTech, Dalhousie University, StFX offers the first two years of a minimum of four calendar years of study in architecture leading to a Bachelor of Environmental Design Studies degree.

Academic Program

All bachelor's degrees, except the two-year Bachelor of Education, are four years. The Diploma in engineering and the Diploma in jazz are two-year programs. In the four-year programs, students declare a major only in the second half of the second year, thus permitting students to sample a broad selection of courses. Over the next two years, students pursue courses in their major and minor subjects in greater depth. Where available, students may choose the advanced major or honours program during the second year of study. Many courses have a service learning component in which students have the opportunity to become involved in community-based issues and projects, thus making their classroom learning more relevant.

The academic year is from September to April. Because of the condensed year, students have four months (May to August) for employment, study, or travel. StFX has an intersession (May–June) and a summer session (July–August); each lasts six weeks.

StFX ranks third in students who complete their degrees in the primarily undergraduate universities in Canada.

Off-Campus Arrangements

StFX has exchange agreements with more than twenty-five colleges and universities in the United States, Mexico, and England for the junior year abroad. Students have also studied at universities in Russia, Scotland, Lesotho, and Israel. Students on an exchange pay tuition to StFX; room and board are paid at the host institution.

Academic Facilities

StFX consists of thirty buildings on 100 acres of land with fifteen residences. The campus has state-of-the-art classrooms, labs, offices, dining halls, playing fields, gyms, a swimming pool, an ice rink, a theatre, an auditorium, and chapels. The Angus L. Macdonald Library has more than 800,000 books, periodicals, newspapers, and government documents. It houses one of the largest collections of Scottish and Gaelic materials in North America. NOVANET allows students access to library holdings at most universities and colleges in the province. The campuswide WebFX technology systems allow all students and the faculty access to world-class software and systems that are designed to enhance teaching and learning. All residence rooms have access to telephone and cable television at no additional cost, and each student is also given a telephone voice-mailbox account. Rooms are also wired for computer access.

Costs

In 1999–2000 undergraduate tuition was $4160 for students from Canada. Students from other countries paid $7160. The Students' Union fee was $123 for all full-time students. Room and board varied depending on the type of room and meal plan chosen, but were approximately $5000. Books cost up to $1000.

Financial Aid

Scholarships range from $1000 to $5000 per year. Entrance scholarships are awarded on the basis of academic performance in high school; usually students in the top 5 percent of their graduating class are considered. Students compete for in-course scholarships each year, with awards given to students who rank in the top 10 percent of their class.

Twenty percent of all students at StFX receive some form of assistance from the University. In addition, about one quarter of students find part-time work on campus. Many other students work in the town. A number of University bursaries are available, as well as a short-term emergency loan program.

Faculty

StFX has close to 200 full-time faculty members and 30 part-time faculty members. With a student-faculty ratio of 17:1, students receive personalized attention both inside and outside of the classroom. All new students are either assigned a faculty adviser or meet with the faculty of their departments prior to registration. Eighty-four percent of first-year classes are taught by tenured or tenure-track professors, and 90 percent of full-time faculty members have their Ph.D. degree. Most faculty members are actively engaged in primary research, and students have many opportunities to become involved.

Student Government

The St. Francis Xavier University Students' Union is the official representative organization of the students. There are more than forty clubs and societies, along with regular organized social activities such as concerts, dances, and intramural sports. The union employs nearly forty students on a part-time basis. The activities of the executive are overseen by the Students' Council, which is made up of elected student representatives from the residences and off-campus constituencies.

Admission Requirements

Students are admitted upon the completion of Nova Scotia Grade XII or the equivalent. The minimum requirements are a combined average of B or the equivalent in Grade XI and Grade XII, to include English each year and credit for five university-preparatory courses in each of Grade XI and Grade XII.

Students from the United States must have completed sixteen academic subjects, with at least four English courses to be considered. Students from a British system of education must have a General Certificate of Education at the ordinary level, including English and four other academic subjects, with no mark below a C or equivalent. Other students are considered on an individual basis.

Application and Information

StFX begins to process applications in January for September admission and employs a rolling admissions policy. However, since many programs have a limited enrollment, students are encouraged to apply as early in the new year as possible.

All applications are considered on an individual basis by using the quality of the high school record, recommendations, and any other information submitted. An audition, performed in person or submitted on a tape, is required for any music program.

Students may obtain an application from their high school guidance counsellor, the StFX Web site, or the address listed below. Applicants must request transcripts from high schools and any postsecondary schools attended. Students from the United States must submit ACT or SAT I results. Students for whom English is a second language are required to achieve a TOEFL score of at least 550 and a TWE score of at least 4. StFX may admit and grant advanced standing to a student who has attended another college or university.

StFX recognizes that some individuals have physical or learning disabilities. To assist individuals with disabilities, the University offers the services of a contact person. For further information, students should call 902-867-2281.

Students are encouraged to visit during the academic year. If visits are planned in advance, students may attend classes, meet with professors, talk with the admissions or high school liaison officer, visit a residence, and have a meal on campus. If students have to travel a long distance, complimentary accommodations on campus can be reserved when available.

For information on admissions or to schedule a campus visit, students should contact:

High School Liaison Office
St. Francis Xavier University
P.O. Box 5000
Antigonish, Nova Scotia B2G 2W5
Canada
Telephone: 902-867-2445
          877-867-7839 (toll-free in Canada or the U.S.)
Fax: 902-867-2329
E-mail: visit@stfx.ca
World Wide Web: http://www.stfx.ca

ST. JOHN FISHER COLLEGE
ROCHESTER, NEW YORK

The College

Founded in 1948 by Basilian fathers, St. John Fisher College is dedicated to serving the individual needs of its students. Originally a Catholic college for men, Fisher is now an independent, coeducational college with 58 percent women and 50 percent resident students. The College offers undergraduate programs in business, the humanities, nursing, social sciences, and sciences and is accredited by the Middle States Association of Colleges and Schools. The College offers eleven graduate programs through the School of Adult and Graduate Education (SAGE).

Fisher offers a full range of extracurricular activities designed to cater to the diverse interests of the 1,600 full-time and 500 part-time undergraduate students. Such activities include a student newspaper, a touring glee club, a campus radio station, a complete intramural program, and almost forty student organizations. In addition, the Student Activities Board sponsors appearances by on-campus lecturers and entertainers, often taking advantage of the FishBowl, the new student union.

Fisher is a member of NCAA Division III, ECAC, and the Empire Eight. Men's intercollegiate sports are baseball, basketball, cross-country, football, golf, soccer, and tennis. Women's intercollegiate sports are basketball, cross-country, lacrosse, soccer, softball, tennis, and volleyball. Club sports include bowling, rugby, skiing, and tae kwon do. The Student Life Center, which is the hub of the athletics activities, includes an indoor track; courts for basketball, racquetball, squash, tennis, and volleyball; and a sauna, a whirlpool, a lounge, an exercise area, and game rooms. Last fall, the College installed an all-weather synthetic playing field to allow for all-season and nighttime play. A 2,100-seat stadium with bleacher seating and a press box was also added to the athletic complex.

St. John Fisher offers courses leading to the Master of Business Administration.

Location

Located on 136 park-like acres, Fisher offers a balance of city activity and suburban tranquility. Just 10 minutes from the Fisher campus, Rochester, the "World's Image Center," offers many cultural attractions, including the Eastman Theater, the Rochester Philharmonic Orchestra, the International Museum of Photography at George Eastman House, the Rochester Museum and Science Center, and the Strasenburgh Planetarium. Home to a number of Fortune 500 companies, such as Eastman Kodak Company, Xerox Corporation, and Bausch and Lomb, the city of Rochester offers Fisher students opportunities for internships and employment after graduation.

Majors and Degrees

St. John Fisher College offers courses leading to the Bachelor of Arts and Bachelor of Science degrees. Undergraduate majors are offered in accounting, anthropology, biology, chemistry, communication/journalism, computer science, economics, elementary education, English, French, German, history, interdisciplinary studies, Italian, management, mathematics, math/science/technology education, nursing, philosophy, physics, political science, psychology, religious studies, sociology, Spanish, special education, and sport studies. The areas of concentration available in the management major include finance, general business management, human resources management, and marketing.

Fisher offers a 4+1 B.S. in management/M.B.A.; a 4+1 B.S. in accounting/M.B.A.; a fast track to the M.S. in international accounting through an undergraduate degree in anthropology, history, international studies, or political science; a 4+1 B.S./M.S. in elementary education/reading; and R.N./B.S./M.S. in nursing; and a B.S./M.S. in nursing. The College also offers a cooperative 3+4 program with the Pennsylvania College of Optometry and a cooperative engineering program with the University of Detroit Mercy, Clarkson University, Manhattan College, Columbia University, and SUNY at Buffalo.

Independent research is available for students majoring in the fields of anthropology, biology, chemistry, communication/journalism, computer science, education, English, history, languages, management, mathematics, philosophy, physics, political science, and psychology. Sixty percent of students participate in internships.

Academic Program

The bachelor's degree is conferred upon those who complete a minimum of 120 semester hours of credit with a cumulative GPA of at least 2.0. Thirty hours of credit and half of the requirements for the major must be earned at St. John Fisher College. Graduates of the accounting program are eligible to sit for the CPA and CMA examinations.

The College is on a semester system. Three summer sessions are offered as well.

Off-Campus Arrangements

Fisher offers a multitude of special programs designed to complement its academic programs. Students in various disciplines can take advantage of an internship program, Albany and Washington semesters, and cross-registration with fourteen member colleges of the Rochester Area College Consortium.

Academic Facilities

The College is in the midst of a $12-million building project designed to upgrade and enhance the academic and athletic facilities on campus. Classrooms have been modernized and outfitted with state-of-the-art media facilities. Laboratory space has been upgraded with "state-of-the-market" educational technology. An academic gateway, complete with a cyber café and a learning resource center, is being built in summer 2000. Last year, the residence halls were renovated, giving all students access to the Internet and cable television.

Lavery Library houses 200,350 volumes and approximately 28,000 records, tapes, and CDs; subscribes to 1,330 periodicals; and features group-study areas, the Bill Givens Multimedia Center, and many special collections. The library is open beyond regular academic hours for the convenience of students.

Costs

Tuition and fees for 1999–2000 were $13,990. Room and board were $6000 with a fourteen-meal plan and a room in one of Fisher's residence halls. Other room and board options are available.

Financial Aid

Committed to helping students meet the cost of their education, Fisher works to assess each individual's financial need. Financial aid is provided through scholarships, grants, loans, and work-study arrangements and is awarded by Fisher, the state, and the federal government. In 1999–2000, the average financial aid package for Fisher students was $11,900.

St. John Fisher College offers a generous academic scholarship program that is based on high school average, class rank, and

SAT I or ACT results. Students eligible for academic scholarships are automatically notified by the Office of Admissions. Minimum scholarship award amounts are $2500.

Three years ago, the College introduced the Service Scholars program. This program is designed to recognize and reward high school seniors who demonstrate an ongoing interest in serving the needs of others through a commitment to community service. Scholarship awards equal one third of the total yearly cost of tuition, fees, room, and board for four years. In 1999, for the second time, this program was recognized by the John Templeton Foundation as an exemplary program—one of only sixty such programs in the country.

In fall 1998, the College announced the creation of the Fannie and Sam Constantino First Generation Scholarship Program, designed to provide financial assistance to students who are the first in their families to attend a post-secondary institution—much like the pioneer classes of St. John Fisher College. Recipients receive annual scholarships ranging from $3500 to one third of the total yearly cost of Fisher's tuition, fees, room, and board for four years.

Faculty

Fisher's 228 full- and part-time faculty members are dedicated to helping students, both in and out of the classroom, as they strive to achieve their goals. Eighty-one percent of full-time faculty members hold doctoral or terminal degrees. The student-teacher ratio of 16:1 offers a personal approach to education; 75 percent of the classes have fewer than 30 students. Fisher's Student Development Center and an outstanding faculty share responsibility for academic advising, helping students to explore the twenty-six majors that are available to them.

Student Government

Student leadership skills are developed through the Student Government Association, which is responsible for the social, cultural, and judicial areas of student life. Resident students elect a Resident Student Association, while commuting students elect a Commuter Council to represent them in planning special activities.

Admission Requirements

Admission to St. John Fisher College is based primarily on the following areas of consideration: high school record, scores on standardized tests (SAT I/ACT), extracurricular activities, and the high school's evaluation of the candidate. Interviews are also considered and strongly encouraged.

A candidate for admission to the freshman class must be a graduate of an approved secondary school and present a minimum of 16 units of college-preparatory course work in English, foreign languages, mathematics, and natural and social sciences. An applicant should present a secondary school average of 84 percent or above in these academic subjects. Students who do not meet these qualifications may apply if they are above the college-recommending level of their secondary school and can demonstrate the potential to successfully complete a bachelor's degree program.

Fisher welcomes qualified transfer students from two- and four-year colleges for both the fall and spring terms. To be considered for admission, transfer students must have a cumulative grade point average of 2.0 or better. If the student has obtained an A.A., A.S., or A.A.S. degree, 60 to 66 credit hours are transferred. Transfer applicants should consult the Undergraduate Bulletin for details.

The College has various special admission programs, including early decision, abbreviated procedures for veterans and other military personnel, deferred admissions, and admission for nondegree and part-time study.

The College offers the New York State Higher Education Opportunity Program (NYS HEOP) for students who need special academic and financial assistance. The program provides academic support services, counseling, and financial aid for qualified students to help them achieve academic success.

Fisher grants college credit for satisfactory grades on the Advanced Placement test, the New York College Proficiency Examination, and the College-Level Examination Program. Only students who receive a 3 or better in all AP subjects and a 4 or better on the AP science and language exams are granted advanced placement credit.

Application and Information

Applications are accepted on a rolling basis. Early decision applications are due December 1. A personal interview is not ordinarily required for admission; however, all applicants are encouraged to visit the College. Interviews are available on weekdays from 8:30 a.m. to 4:30 p.m. and on specified Saturdays from 9 a.m. to noon.

For additional information or an application, students should contact:

Office of Undergraduate Admissions
St. John Fisher College
3690 East Avenue
Rochester, New York 14618
Telephone: 716-385-8064
        800-444-4640 (toll-free)
E-mail: admissions@sjfc.edu

On the campus, with Kearney Tower rising in the background.

ST. JOHN'S COLLEGE
ANNAPOLIS, MARYLAND, AND SANTA FE, NEW MEXICO

The College

St. John's College maintains two widely separated campuses, one in Annapolis, Maryland, and another in Santa Fe, New Mexico. Each has its own admissions and financial aid offices. A common curriculum, however, enables students and faculty members to move from one campus to the other. Both campuses are cohesive intellectual communities in which students are eagerly responsive to one another. Students also pursue interests in such activities as publications, dance, dramatics, photography, art, wilderness exploration, and sailing. The social climate is informal and lively, and students enjoy many celebrations each year. Facilities are available for almost any intramural sport; most students participate. There is a bookstore on each campus. In fall 1998, opening enrollment at the Annapolis campus was 452 men and women; the opening enrollment was 435 students at the Santa Fe campus.

The students on both campuses are outstanding, yet they fit no pattern. Though their backgrounds are varied geographically, academically, and otherwise, they are, most typically, young people who habitually read books and value good conversation. Their commitment to ideas and their enthusiasm for the St. John's program are well illustrated by the fact that about one third of them on each campus have transferred to St. John's as freshmen after a year or more of college elsewhere.

Location

St. John's is the third-oldest college in the United States. It has been located since 1696 in the Colonial seaport city of Annapolis, the capital of Maryland, 30 miles from Washington, D.C. In 1964, a second campus was opened at the foot of the mountains surrounding Santa Fe, a cultural center and the capital of New Mexico. The campuses are alike in curriculum and methods, but their settings and moods are as different as sailing on the Chesapeake Bay and skiing in the Sangre de Cristo Mountains, as Georgian and Spanish Colonial architecture. St. John's students participate in a number of activities of benefit to their communities at large.

Majors and Degrees

St. John's College is committed to liberal education in the most traditional and yet radical way. It accomplishes this through direct engagement with the books in which the greatest minds of Western civilization have expressed themselves and through translation, mathematical demonstration, musical analysis, and laboratory experimentation. Whether in Annapolis or in Santa Fe, all St. John's students follow the same course of study leading to the B.A. degree. One of the purposes of this program is to emphasize the unity of knowledge; thus the faculty is not divided into departments and there are no majors.

Academic Program

The academic program is a unified, cohesive whole; instruction takes the form of annual sequences of related seminars, tutorials, and laboratories, in each of which the books that form the core of the curriculum are the basis of study and discussion. To ensure that the intellectual life of the College extends beyond the classroom and that students bring a common frame of reference to the continuing discussion, this academic program is required of everyone, but no two students are expected to approach any subject in the same way or to reach the same conclusions about it. A central purpose of the St. John's program is to give students both the opportunity and the obligation to think for themselves. The books at the heart of the program serve to foster that thinking. They not only illuminate the enduring questions of human existence but also have great relevance to contemporary problems. They can change minds, move hearts, and touch spirits. They help all students to arrive independently at rational opinions and conclusions of their own. From this common curriculum, about 35 percent of the students in each class go on to graduate and professional study in a wide range of fields.

There are two semesters a year. All classes are small discussion groups and range in size from between 12 and 16 students in tutorials to between 18 and 20 in seminars and laboratories. Final examinations are oral and individual. Students are not routinely informed of their grades. Instead, a student's tutors, as members of the faculty are called, evaluate the student's intellectual performance twice a year in his or her presence and with his or her help. St. John's students are participants in their own education. Annual essays and shorter papers, prepared by students without recourse to secondary sources, are based directly on the books of the program.

Seminars are devoted to reading works of the greatest minds and engaging in thoughtful discussion about them. The first-year seminar focuses on Greek authors; the second on the works of the Roman, medieval, and early Renaissance periods; the third on books of the seventeenth and eighteenth centuries; and the fourth on writings from the nineteenth and twentieth centuries. The seminar consists almost exclusively of student conversation. The aim of the discussions is to ascertain not how things were but how things are. Everyone's opinion must be heard and must also be supported by argument and evidence. The role of the tutors is not to give information or to produce the "right" interpretation; it is to guide the discussion, to aid in defining the issues, and to help the students to understand the authors, the issues, and themselves. If tutors do take a definite stand and enter the argument, they are expected to defend their positions just as students do. Reason is the only recognized authority.

Preceptorials replace seminars for eight weeks of the junior and senior years. In the preceptorial, students and tutors gather in groups of 8 or 9 to discuss, with more leisure than the pace and discipline of the seminar permit, books or topics of particular interest to them.

In the language tutorial, Greek is studied in the first two years and French in the last two. By translating works written in Greek and French into English and comparing those languages with each other as well as with English, the student gains an appreciation of all three and learns something of the nature of language in general.

The language of number and figure does not require a special aptitude. Rather, mathematics is an integral and necessary part of comprehending the world. The mathematics tutorial seeks to effect an understanding of the fundamental nature and intention of mathematics. Throughout the four years, the student is in contact not only with the pure science of mathematics but also with the foundations of mathematical physics and astronomy. The blackboard becomes an arena of logical struggle, which brings the imagination constantly into play.

The music tutorial aims at understanding music through study of musical theory and analysis of significant works. Students investigate rhythm, the diatonic system, the ratios of musical intervals, melody, counterpoint, and harmony.

In the modern world, the liberal arts are practiced at their best and fullest in the laboratory. This practice puts into serious question the common distinction between the "natural sciences" and the "humanities." The laboratory is a part of the program in all years but the second. It weaves together the main themes of physics, biology, and chemistry with careful scrutiny of the interplay of hypothesis, theory, and observed fact.

On Friday evenings, the College community assembles for a formal lecture or concert by a tutor or visitor. It is the only time the students are lectured to. Afterward, interested students and faculty members engage the speaker or performer in questions and discussion.

Academic Facilities

The library on each campus—about 100,000 volumes in Annapolis, nearly 60,000 in Santa Fe—emphasizes material appropriate to the nature of the academic program, supplemented by a more general collection and by a variety of special collections. Recordings and representative periodicals and newspapers are included. Academic facilities on each campus also include the resources and equipment necessary for study and experimentation in physics, chemistry, and biology (including a planetarium in Annapolis); for audition and performance of music; for display and studio work in art, photography, and other crafts; and for drama productions.

Costs

For 1999–2000, annual tuition and fees total $23,290 in Annapolis and $22,000 in Santa Fe. Room and board are $6360 in Annapolis and $6386 in Santa Fe. Books and supplies range in cost from $200 to $275. Personal expenses depend on the student's habits and tastes.

Financial Aid

The criterion for financial assistance is need. On both campuses the application for financial aid is the CSS PROFILE supplemented by the Free Application for Federal Student Aid (FAFSA) and an institutional aid application. More than half of all St. John's students receive aid, usually in a combination of grant, loan, and employment. Federal Perkins Loans, Federal Pell Grants, Federal Supplemental Educational Opportunity Grants, Federal Work-Study employment, and College grants and jobs are available.

Faculty

The faculty-student ratio is 1:8 on each campus. Faculty members all hold the same rank. Their intellectual range and vitality come from teaching throughout the curriculum. This breadth and tension and the fact that St. John's is an intellectual community in which all teach and all learn are distinctive characteristics of the St. John's faculty.

Student Government

Inside the classroom and out, the dignity of the students as adults is respected. On both campuses, student government is part of the general College pattern. A Delegate Council and Student Committee on Instruction work with the faculty and administrators on matters of mutual concern.

Admission Requirements

Criteria for admission to either campus are intellectual and academic, though any accomplishment showing initiative and drive may strengthen an application. The written application consists of a series of reflective essays. The academic record and recommendations are considered supplements to it. SAT I or ACT scores are optional but may prove helpful. There are no minimums for grades or test scores; both may be made irrelevant by what the candidate writes. On each campus, applicants are judged on their own merits. Each year a small percentage enter directly from the eleventh grade. Although interviews are not required except in special cases, interested students are urged to visit either campus for several days to sit in on seminars and tutorials.

Application and Information

Students may be admitted to either campus for the fall term or, if they are prepared to continue their studies through the following summer, in January. Application must be made to one campus or the other, not to both. Early application is advisable. Each campus seeks to complete its class by mid-May. All applications for admission and financial aid are acted on as soon as they are complete, and the candidate is notified of the decision within two weeks.

In response to inquiries, the College sends a catalog, information on financial aid, an application form, and forms for the school report and for recommendations. Students should contact:

John Christensen
Director of Admissions
St. John's College
Annapolis, Maryland 21404

Larry Clendenin
Director of Admissions
St. John's College
Santa Fe, New Mexico 87501

ST. JOHN'S UNIVERSITY
JAMAICA, STATEN ISLAND, AND EASTERN LONG ISLAND, NEW YORK, AND ROME, ITALY

The University

Since its inception 130 years ago, St. John's University has excelled at preparing young people for personal and professional success. Founded by the Vincentian Fathers in 1870, the University has flourished since its early years as a one-building campus in downtown Brooklyn. Today, St. John's is one of America's leading Catholic universities.

St. John's occupies four handsome sites: a tree-lined, 96-acre residential campus in Jamaica, Queens; a charming, 16.5-acre residential campus in Grymes Hill, Staten Island; a 175-acre Eastern Long Island campus in Oakdale, New York; and a campus in Rome, Italy. Chartered by the State Education Department of New York, St. John's is accredited by the Middle States Association of Colleges and Schools. Its varied programs are accredited by such organizations as AACSB–The International Association for Management Education, the American Association for Accreditation of Laboratory Animal Care, the American Bar Association, the American Chemical Society, the American Council on Pharmaceutical Education, the American Library Association, the American Psychological Association, the American Speech-Language-Hearing Association, and the Association of American Law Schools.

St. John's enrolls more than 14,000 undergraduates, yet its low 19:1 student-faculty ratio ensures personal attention in the classroom. Many of the University's 130,000 alumni hold top-level positions in government, industry, and the private sector. The Queens campus comprises St. John's College of Liberal Arts and Sciences, the College of Business Administration, the School of Education and Human Services, the College of Pharmacy and Allied Health Professions, the College of Professional Studies, the School of Law, and the Metropolitan College. The Staten Island campus includes St. John's College of Liberal Arts and Sciences, the College of Business Administration, the School of Education and Human Services, and the College of Professional Studies. The Rome, Italy, campus offers an M.A. in government and politics and an M.B.A. program.

Location

The Queens campus is located in a residential neighborhood that is just off the Grand Central Parkway. The Staten Island campus, on a hill that overlooks New York Harbor, is a few miles from the Verrazano Narrows Bridge. By car, these two campuses are 50 minutes at most from the many attractions of midtown Manhattan. The Eastern Long Island campus is on Suffolk County's south shore. The Rome campus is located at the Pontificio Oratorio San Pietro, off Via Aurelia on Via Santa Maria Mediatrice.

Majors and Degrees

St. John's offers more than 100 academic majors in its six acclaimed undergraduate colleges. At the Queens campus, St. John's College of Liberal Arts and Sciences offers programs leading to the B.A. in American studies, anthropology, economics, English, environmental studies, French, government and politics, history, Italian, mathematics, philosophy, psychology, public administration and public service, sociology, Spanish, speech (general and public address), speech pathology and audiology, and theology.

The Bachelor of Fine Arts is available in art (painting, printmaking, and sculpture), creative photography, graphic design, and illustration. The Bachelor of Science is available in biology, chemistry, environmental studies, mathematical physics, mathematics, physical science, and physics. St. John's College also offers a five-year B.A./M.A. program in English, government and politics, history, mathematics, sociology, Spanish, and theology. Students may also choose five-year B.S./M.S. programs in biology and chemistry, a B.A./J.D. or B.S./J.D. degree that combines any undergraduate degree with a law degree from St. John's School of Law, a B.S./D.D.S. degree that combines an undergraduate biology degree with a Doctor of Dental Surgery degree from Columbia University's School of Dental and Oral Medicine, and a B.S./O.D. degree that combines an undergraduate degree in biology with a Doctor of Optometry degree from SUNY College of Optometry. Bachelor's degree students in St. John's College are eligible for the pre-M.B.A. program. The Institute of Asian Studies, under the auspices of St. John's College, offers a B.A. in Asian studies and a five-year B.A./M.A. in East Asian studies. The College of Business Administration offers programs leading to the B.S. in accounting, economics, finance, management, and marketing. A five-year B.S./M.S. in accounting is also available. In the School of Education and Human Services, programs lead to the Bachelor of Science in Education (B.S.Ed.), including education; elementary education; elementary education coupled with bilingual-bicultural, junior high, or special education; and teaching of the speech and hearing handicapped. Also offered are the B.S. in human services and the B.S.Ed./M.S. in education. The School of Education and Human Services also offers a secondary education degree program in cooperation with St. John's College of Liberal Arts and Sciences. The College of Pharmacy and Allied Health Professions grants the Doctor of Pharmacy (Pharm.D., six years), the Bachelor of Science in cytotechnology, and the Bachelor of Science in Medical Technology. There is a five-year B.S./M.S. degree program in toxicology, as well as programs of study leading to the B.S. in pathologist assistant studies, physician assistant studies, and toxicology. Programs in the College of Professional Studies lead to the B.S. in administrative studies, communication arts, computer science, criminal justice, funeral service administration, health-care administration, hospitality management, journalism, microcomputer systems, paralegal studies, real estate management, safety and corporate security, sports management, telecommunications, and television and film production. The B.A. is available with majors in literature and speech and in social science. Also offered are five-year B.S./M.A. programs in communication arts/government and politics, communication arts/sociology, criminal justice/government and politics, criminal justice/sociology, health-care administration/government and politics, health-care administration/sociology, journalism/government and politics, and paralegal studies/sociology.

Preprofessional programs include dentistry, engineering, law, medicine, osteopathy, social work, veterinary medicine, and other health-related fields. A combined B.A./J.D. or B.S./J.D. degree program is available with any undergraduate major.

In addition, the College of Professional Studies offers an A.A. degree in liberal arts, as well as A.S. degrees in business (accounting and general business), criminal justice, electronic data processing, microcomputer technology, paralegal studies, paraprofessional school service, and telecommunications. Certificate programs are available in business administration, computer science, health-care administration, international criminal justice, paralegal studies, sports management, and telecommunications. Most programs are also offered on evenings and weekends.

At the Staten Island campus, St. John's College of Liberal Arts and Sciences offers programs leading to the B.A. or B.S. in English, government and politics, history, mathematics, psychology, social studies, sociology, and speech (general). St. John's College also offers B.A. degrees in economics, philosophy, and theology, as well as a B.S. in computer science and speech-language pathology and audiology. Students may choose a five-year B.A./M.A. program in government and politics. Also available are a B.A./J.D. or B.S./J.D. degree that combines any undergraduate degree with a law degree from St. John's School of Law. Students pursuing a liberal arts degree may pursue a preprofessional concentration in business. The A.A. in liberal arts is also available.

The College of Business Administration at Staten Island offers programs of study leading to the B.S. in accounting, economics, finance, management, and marketing. Also offered is a five-year B.S./M.S. in accounting. In the School of Education and Human Services, students may pursue programs of study leading to the B.S. in elementary education and special education. In addition, the School of Education offers a secondary education degree program in cooperation with St. John's College of Liberal Arts and Sciences.

The Staten Island campus also offers a number of degree and certificate programs through the College of Professional Studies. Programs of study lead to the B.S. in communication arts, computer science, criminal justice, funeral service administration, health-care administration, hospitality management, paralegal studies, real estate management, safety and corporate security, sports management, telecommunication, television and film production, and transportation and logistics. There is a combined B.A./J.D. or B.S./J.D. program. Also available are A.S. degree programs in business (accounting and general business), criminal justice, paralegal studies, and telecommunications. Preprofessional programs include dentistry, engineering, law, medicine, osteopathy, social work, veterinary medicine, and other health-related fields.

Academic Program

To graduate, students in St. John's College of Liberal Arts and Sciences are expected to complete a minimum of 126 semester hours for the B.A., 126 semester hours for the B.S., or 144 semester hours for the B.F.A. The School of Education and Human Services requires completion of 126 to 139 semester hours.

The College of Professional Studies requires completion of 126 to 127 semester hours for the B.S. and B.A. degrees. Students in the College of Business Administration must complete 130 to 134 semester hours. In the College of Pharmacy and Allied Health Professions, students in the six-year pharmacy program are expected to complete a minimum of 201 semester hours. The B.S. program in cytotechnology requires 128 semester hours. For the physician assistant studies program, 134 semester hours must be completed; 133 semester hours in the toxicology or pathologist assistant studies program; and 132 semester hours in the medical technology program.

Students in associate degree programs are required to complete 60–63 semester hours. All students are expected to fulfill core requirements for their college, along with completing their major sequence and free-elective groupings.

Academic Facilities

The St. John's University Libraries comprise three major research libraries on two campuses. Their collections total more than 1.7 million volumes of books, periodicals, microfilm, microfiche, and audiovisual materials.

The Queens campus is home to the Main Library and the Law School Library. St. Augustine Hall houses the Main Library, including a selective depository for United States government documents. The Main Library also includes the Governor Hugh L. Carey Collection, the William M. Fischer Lawn Tennis Library, the Asian Collection, the Health Education Resource Center, an Instructional Materials Center that contains curriculum materials for grades pre-K through 12, and a Media Center.

On the Staten Island campus, the Loretto Memorial Library includes a collection of literary masterpieces, a record collection of music and poetry readings, a language laboratory, and an audiovisual department.

Both campuses feature state-of-the art computer laboratories, with approximately 400 microcomputers available for student use. There are more than 100 high-tech classrooms and advanced laboratories for research in biology, chemistry, physics, pharmacy, and allied health. The Queens campus also has a special laboratory that is specifically for students taking language majors.

On the Queens campus, a new residential village offers students the best in on-campus living, including fully wired rooms, 24-hour security, a fitness center, club space, and a spacious dining hall. On Staten Island, students can choose comfortable, apartment-style residences that are adjacent to the campus.

Costs

In the 1999–2000 academic year, tuition for a full-time student (12 to 18 credits per semester) was $13,990 per academic year. Tuition may vary by program and class year. Mandatory fees totaled $430. St. John's offers a Fixed Rate Tuition Option for students who want to lock in at a set cost for all four years. Room and board were $8550.

Financial Aid

During the 1998–99 academic year, more than 13,500 students at St. John's received some form of financial assistance. The University provided in excess of $148 million in aid through scholarships, loans, grants, and work-study programs. At St. John's, financial aid is awarded primarily on the basis of financial need. Students are encouraged to file the Free Application for Federal Student Aid (FAFSA) as their major financial aid application no later than February 1.

Faculty

Professors at St. John's enjoy international recognition for their scholarship and commitment to teaching. There are 1,111 faculty members (561 full-time, 550 part-time); 89 percent of full-time faculty members hold doctoral or other terminal degrees in their fields.

Student Government

At St. John's, the Student Government represents and serves the student body through effective and responsible leadership. It also functions as a liaison between students and the administration and the faculty. Student Government funds and coordinates the more than 180 student organizations and clubs on both the Queens and Staten Island campuses.

Admission Requirements

Admission to St. John's is determined by the applicant's previous academic performance, satisfactory achievement on appropriate standardized tests, recommendations, and other factors that suggest academic potential and personal motivation.

A minimum of 16 academic units earned at an accredited secondary institution or an appropriate score on the GED test is required. The units should include 6 electives, of which at least 3 must be in academic subjects; 4 in English; 2 in mathematics (elementary algebra, plane geometry, or tenth-year mathematics); 2 in foreign language; 1 in history; and 1 in science. These requirements may vary, depending on the program.

Application and Information

Students may apply by submitting an official high school transcript, official scores on the SAT I or ACT, and a completed and signed application for admission. Transfer students are encouraged to apply and form a large contingent of the undergraduate population. St. John's advises transfer students to have all records of previous high school and college work forwarded to the Office of Admission. On-campus interviews are conducted through the Office of Admission. Students may apply anytime under St. John's rolling admission policy; this is true for all but the pharmacy degree programs, which have a February 1 deadline. For further information, students should contact:

Office of Admission
St. John's University
8000 Utopia Parkway
Jamaica, New York 11439
Telephone: 718-990-2000
           888-9STJOHNS (toll-free)
Fax: 718-990-2096

Office of Admission
St. John's University
300 Howard Avenue
Staten Island, New York 10301
Telephone: 718-390-4500
           888-9STJOHNS (toll-free)
Fax: 718-390-4298
E-mail: admissions@stjohns.edu
World Wide Web: http://www.stjohns.edu

SAINT JOSEPH COLLEGE
WEST HARTFORD, CONNECTICUT

The College

For more than sixty years, Saint Joseph College has been combining excellence in liberal arts with professional education for women. Founded in 1932 by the Sisters of Mercy, the original women's college has expanded to include a coeducational graduate school and an innovative weekend baccalaureate program for men and women. In partnership with each other, these units of the College offer a diverse student population unmatched opportunities to excel—intellectually, socially, and ethically.

There are 1,185 undergraduates in the Women's College, where faculty members and students have high mutual expectations and strive to maximize each person's potential. The College is a community that promotes the growth of the whole person in a caring environment that encourages strong ethical values, personal integrity, and a sense of responsibility to the needs of society. Women lead every organization, from the Business Society and Student Government to Campus Ministry and Intercultural Affairs. They edit the journals; lead the choirs, dance, and drama groups; and captain every athletic team. Students also serve with faculty members and administrators on all major committees, from strategic planning to Web site development to the Administrative Council—a small group of top advisers to the President. In just five years since the state-of-the-art athletic center was constructed, the College has become competitive in seven NCAA Division III sports: basketball, cross-country, softball, soccer, swimming/diving, tennis, and volleyball. The athletic center features a six-lane pool, gymnasium, suspended jogging track, dance studio, and fitness center.

Saint Joseph College has thirteen Georgian brick buildings, including four residence halls, which are arranged around two tree-lined quadrangles on an 84-acre campus. Approximately 50 percent of the full-time Women's College students live on campus. Special student services include career planning, alumnae mentors, internship placement, counseling, health services, academic advisement, and a campus ministry team. Most recently, the College constructed the new Carol Autorino Center for the Arts and Humanities to establish the arts and humanities as an integral part of the student psyche. The center, with its separate east and west wings, celebrates and articulates the College's rich liberal arts tradition.

Saint Joseph College alumnae have considerable impact on the welfare of their communities. They are leaders in many fields, including aerospace research, business, medicine, education, social work, environmental science, law, and politics. Recent graduates enjoy successful careers in business, industry, government, nonprofit organizations, education, health care, human services, and the arts.

Saint Joseph College is accredited by the New England Association of Schools and Colleges. The chemistry program is approved by the American Chemical Society and the social work program, by the Council on Social Work Education. The Coordinated Undergraduate Program in Dietetics is accredited by the American Dietetic Association. The nursing program is accredited by the National League for Nursing Accrediting Commission.

Location

The College is located in suburban West Hartford, 4 miles from the state capital and the city of Hartford's arts and entertainment district. Among the nearby attractions are the Hartford Civic Center and Coliseum; Bushnell Memorial Hall, where the latest Broadway musicals are performed; and the Wadsworth Atheneum, the oldest public art gallery in the United States. Hartford is a cosmopolitan city with diverse ethnic flavors. It is also the home of the Tony Award–winning Hartford Stage Company; the Hartford Symphony Orchestra; the Connecticut Opera Company and the Hartford Ballet; the Meadows Music Theatre, which features indoor and outdoor concerts; and several shopping venues, coffee bars, and restaurants.

Majors and Degrees

Saint Joseph College has always enjoyed a strong academic reputation based on a combination of liberal arts and professional majors. The College awards the B.A. or B.S. in American studies, art history, biology, biology/chemistry, business administration: accounting and management, chemistry, child study, dietetics, economics, English, environmental science, family studies, foods and nutrition, French, history, history/political science, home economics education, humanities, international studies, mathematics, mathematics/computer science, mathematics/economics, natural sciences, nursing, philosophy, political science, psychology, religious studies, social science and history, social work, sociology, Spanish, and special education.

Teaching certification is offered in five areas: early childhood education, elementary education, middle school education, secondary education, and special education.

Research, clinical, and work placements are factored into all majors as an important component of each student's program. For instance, nursing majors begin their clinical training early in the sophomore year.

Academic Program

Each student must complete a minimum of 120 credits to obtain a baccalaureate degree, and 53 of those credits should be distributed among the general education/liberal arts courses at the College. Specifically, students must take courses in the humanities, social sciences, natural sciences, mathematics, religious studies, and physical education. The study of a foreign language is recommended. An academic adviser assists each student in planning her program of study.

An honors program is available. The Academic Resources Center provides tutoring and other academic support services. Students may design their own major or may develop an interdisciplinary major or minor around a particular theme or problem related to their special talents, personal interests, or career goals. An exciting component of most majors at Saint Joseph College is the internship. These supervised field placements provide on-the-job experience, introduce students to various career opportunities, and produce significant employment contacts. Students earn credit for internships at a variety of sites, including the state capital, the Bushnell Theatre, Aetna, Legislative Office, the Connecticut Department of Economic Development, WVIT-TV, Connecticut Children's Medical Center, and the Science Center of Connecticut.

Off-Campus Arrangements

Students at Saint Joseph College may take courses at cooperating institutions through the Hartford Consortium for Higher Education. This is a special arrangement among Hartford-area colleges—Saint Joseph College, Rensselaer at Hartford, Trinity College, Saint Thomas Seminary, and the University of Hartford—through which students are able to take courses not offered at their home institution. No additional tuition is charged, and all credits are transferable.

Students at Saint Joseph College may study abroad during their junior year, a winter recess, or a summer session. Certain majors have specific international-study recommendations and opportunities, and the student is assisted by the Director of International Study in planning for an international-study experience. Cultural exchange programs with institutions in Japan, England, and Denmark are also available.

Academic Facilities

The Pope Pius XII Library has a collection of more than 134,000 volumes, including computer databases, periodicals, microforms, audiovisuals, an OPAC, and a Web page. A collection of materials used in elementary and secondary education is featured in the Curriculum Materials Center.

The College has two laboratory schools. The renowned School for Young Children is located one block from campus. It is a preschool and kindergarten that provides child study majors with training and experience. The Gengras Center is located on campus. It is a community resource serving children and young adults (ages 3–21). It provides for special education needs and also helps to prepare special education teachers.

The College's primary technology centers are located in McDonough Hall. World Wide Web and e-mail services are available. Each student is assigned a user ID to access the Internet.

The College Network Center houses four classrooms, a computer laboratory, a faculty development laboratory, a lounge, space for the site of a future learning center, and the information technology staff's offices. Additional facilities and services include a media center that provides production materials, expertise, and equipment for making and using a number of media instructional aids; state-of-the-art science and nursing labs; the Academic Resources Center, which provides professional and peer tutoring; music and dance facilities; and an art study gallery that exhibits changing selections from the more than 500 prints and several hundred paintings that are part of the College's art collection.

Costs

The tuition and fees for freshmen entering in 1999 were $15,900. Room and board cost $6610. The cost per credit for part-time students was $405.

Financial Aid

A highly effective program of financial aid demonstrates Saint Joseph College's strong commitment to helping students obtain a high-quality private college education. In 1999–2000, 87 percent of the College's full-time undergraduate students received some form of financial aid, including student need- and merit-based grants and scholarships, loans, and work-study.

Faculty

Saint Joseph College's faculty consists of 74 full-time faculty members and 4 librarians. Of the total faculty, 75 percent are women. Of the full-time faculty, 85 percent have a doctorate or another terminal degree in their field. Small classes benefit both students and professors. The faculty-student ratio is 1:11. The faculty and all members of the College community promote the welfare of students and help them attain the objectives set forth by the College's mission. Faculty members also participate in many extracurricular activities, including sports, campus ministry, and community service; direct students in independent study; involve students in scholarly research; and act as mentors before and after graduation.

Student Government

The Student Government Association works for effective communication among students, faculty members, and administrators. Students are encouraged to voice their opinions and concerns to the association for consideration and action. In addition, student representatives sit as voting members with faculty members and administrators on major College-wide committees. The Student Government Association encourages the development of leadership skills and provides funds annually for several of its members to attend leadership workshops.

Admission Requirements

Saint Joseph College seeks women who are willing to accept the challenge of an excellent academic program while pursuing the interests and goals that will shape their future lives. Applications are encouraged from interested students of every race, age, and religious affiliation. In accordance with Section 504 of the Rehabilitation Act of 1973, which prohibits discrimination on the basis of disability, and the Americans with Disabilities Act of 1990, Saint Joseph College is committed to the goal of achieving equal educational opportunities and full participation for people with disabilities in higher education. Candidates for freshman admission should complete a four-year course of study in a regionally accredited secondary school. The program should include 16 academic units in college-preparatory courses distributed among the areas of English, mathematics, natural sciences, social studies, and foreign languages. Applicants are required to submit scores of the SAT I or ACT tests. A personal interview is a highly recommended part of the admission procedure, since it offers a mutual opportunity for the student and College personnel to discuss educational and professional goals. The Committee on Admissions operates on the principle that a student's ability, motivation, and maturity should be determined by a careful individual review of all the applicant's credentials, including the academic record, standardized test scores, and guidance counselor's evaluation. Special consideration may be given to some applicants whose preparation varies from the recommended pattern but whose record gives evidence of genuine intellectual ability and interest. International students should contact the director of admissions for further information. Saint Joseph College admits qualified students for transfer in both fall and spring semesters.

Application and Information

The Committee on Admissions recommends that application for freshman admission be made early in the first semester of the senior year in secondary school. All applications must be completed by May 1. Candidates for financial aid should complete the admission procedure by February 15. A nonrefundable $35 fee must be sent to the director of admissions with the application.

Transfer applicants for the spring semester must apply by December 1; applicants for the fall semester, by July 1. However, transfer candidates who wish to apply for financial aid must complete the admission procedure by June 1.

For further information about undergraduate programs, students should contact:

Kelly Getman Crowley
Director of Admissions
Saint Joseph College
1678 Asylum Avenue
West Hartford, Connecticut 06117
Telephone: 860-231-5216
           800-285-6565 (toll-free)
Fax: 860-233-5695
E-mail: admissions@sjc.edu
World Wide Web: http://www.sjc.edu

Students at Saint Joseph College.

SAINT JOSEPH'S COLLEGE
RENSSELAER, INDIANA

The College

Saint Joseph's College was founded in 1891 by the Missionaries of the Precious Blood (C.PP.S.) and issued its first diplomas in 1896. In 1968, the College admitted women for the first time. Students enrolled at the College have various backgrounds and come from twenty-seven states and seven countries. At the graduate level, Saint Joseph's offers a Master of Arts in Music degree, with a concentration in church music and liturgy (summers only). The College is affiliated with the Roman Catholic Church.

The center of academic activity at the College is the Rev. Charles Banet Core Education Center, dedicated in 1995. The Banet Center includes state-of-the-art multimedia classrooms, computer and science laboratories, and forty-five faculty offices.

The hub of all campus social activities can best be visualized as three concentric circles encompassing the residential complex, the athletic complex, and Halleck Student Center. The Student Center includes a dining facility, the College Store, a 300-seat ballroom, student government offices, a counseling and career service center, campus life offices, a commuting-student lounge, and the Marching Puma Band headquarters and office, as well as a licensed private club and an after-hours snack bar known as the Halleck Center Bistro (HUB).

The College fosters opportunities for students to become actively involved in self-government. Thirty-three academic and social clubs serve the out-of-class needs of students to make a difference in their collegiate world. Volunteer groups, which complement academic areas of study, also are popular with current students. An active social calendar is in force throughout the year and includes major weekend celebrations, such as Homecoming, Li'l Sibs Weekend, "I Hate Winter" Weekend, "Little 500" Go-Kart Race, and Parents' Weekend. In addition, the Office of Student Activities sponsors several trips each semester to cultural, sporting, and recreational events in Indianapolis and Chicago. Students also actively participate in a 10-watt radio station, WPUM (90.5 FM), and a 42 channel TV/FM cable system in which students develop programs and events for three channels.

The *Pumas* are members of the Great Lakes Valley Conference and are Division II members of the NCAA. The teams compete in a complete program of intercollegiate men's baseball, basketball, cross-country, football, golf, soccer, tennis, and track; women compete in basketball, cross-country, golf, soccer, softball, tennis, track, and volleyball. An active intramural sports program encourages students to keep fit and enjoy competition among the various residence halls in their leisure time.

The residence hall program promotes a close living/learning community and has seniors, juniors, sophomores, and freshmen living on each floor. Students learn from peers and pass on valuable traditions of school spirit, active participation, and academic integrity.

Location

Saint Joseph's College lies just south of Rensselaer's city limits and is within walking distance of the town. Rensselaer has a population of 5,500. It is 90 minutes southeast of Chicago, 90 minutes northwest of Indianapolis, and 40 minutes northwest of Lafayette.

Majors and Degrees

Saint Joseph's College confers the Bachelor of Arts and Bachelor of Science degrees in accounting, accounting–finance, accounting–information systems, biology, biology-chemistry, chemistry, communications and theater arts, computer science, criminal justice, economics, economics–finance, elementary education, English, English/creative writing, environmental science, finance, finance–information systems, history, human services, international business, international studies, management, management/marketing/information systems, marketing, mass communications, mathematics, mathematics-computer, mathematics-physics, medical technology, music, music–business administration, philosophy, physical education, political science, psychology, religion/philosophy, and sociology.

Preprofessional programs are offered in dentistry, engineering, law, medicine, optometry, physical therapy, and veterinary science.

Five-year engineering programs are available in aeronautical, chemical, civil, electrical, industrial, mechanical, and metallurgical engineering in cooperation with any accredited engineering college or university.

The College also offers a designer major, wherein qualified students can create individualized programs of study.

Associate degrees are offered in a number of areas, including early childhood education and business–computer science.

Academic Program

The general education requirements of the College are incorporated in a single four-year sequence common to all students and totaling 45 credit hours. This core curriculum comprises extensive reading, writing, and discussion as well as lectures and other presentations focusing on the different aspects of the human condition in relation to various academic areas, including philosophy, history, science, and religion.

In addition to completing these 45 hours, a student must earn a minimum of 36 semester hours in a major and 18 semester hours in a minor. A minimum of 120 semester hours is required for graduation.

Saint Joseph's is an "electronic campus," where students can use a personal computer to access software and library holdings and to communicate with professors, fellow students, and the world via electronic mail, the Internet, and the World Wide Web.

The College operates on a 4-4-1 academic calendar.

Off-Campus Arrangements

There are two types of programs available for students who wish to spend a semester or year abroad. An affiliation with Central University of Iowa allows students to study in Austria, England, France, Germany, Mexico, the Netherlands, Spain, and Wales. Also, students can attend Harlaxton College in England through an affiliation with the University of Evansville.

The College provides off-campus internship opportunities in all degree programs.

The Washington Semester program offers students the chance to live and learn in the nation's capital. On-the-job experience, through various private businesses, associations, government agencies, nonprofit organizations, and the U.S. Congress, is combined with academic study in Washington, D.C.

Academic Facilities

The College library holds 163,587 books and bound periodicals and currently receives 559 periodicals. Microfilm material and an extensive audio library are available for student use.

A collection of more than 33,000 maps is separately housed in the earth science department. The biology laboratories provide equipment for courses in fundamental zoology and botany, microtechnique embryology, histology, comparative vertebrate anatomy, human anatomy, and physiology. There are also laboratories for general inorganic and organic chemistry, biochemistry, and quantitative and qualitative analysis. Geology laboratories serve the fields of physical geology, mineralogy, petrology, paleontology, subsurface geology, stratigraphy, and economic geology.

Various computer facilities give students the opportunity to train in both scientific and commercial data processing fields and to participate in computer-assisted instruction. Videotape facilities help students gain experience in television production and direction through an on-campus cable TV station, and the campus radio station, WPUM-FM, provides training in broadcasting.

Costs

The costs per year for 2000–01 are tuition, $14,920; room and board, $5380; and fees, $160.

Financial Aid

Financial aid is available in a variety of forms, including scholarships, grants, loans, and campus employment. More than 90 percent of the student body receives financial aid.

All candidates for financial aid must be accepted by the College and submit the Free Application for Federal Student Aid (FAFSA).

Academic merit scholarships are awarded in amounts varying from $3000 to full tuition, room, and board, based on academic record and talents. Performance Scholarships in band, choir, and drama and athletic scholarships are also available. Other scholarships are awarded on the basis of need, and the financial aid program also includes nationally funded grants, guaranteed loans, and Federal Work-Study awards.

Faculty

The full-time-equivalent faculty numbers 63. Eighty percent hold terminal degrees. Most classes range in size from 15 to 25 students. No classes are taught by graduate students.

Student Government

All full-time students are members of the Student Government Association and are governed by its constitution and bylaws. These students elect four officers of the Student Association, including a president who holds a seat on the College's Board of Trustees and appoints students to faculty and administrative committees. These officers, the four class presidents, and elected residence hall and commuting student representatives compose the Student Senate. This group provides a channel of communication among students on the one hand and with faculty members and administrators on the other. Acting in concert, the Student Association officers and the Student Senate serve to propose policies and implement procedures to better the quality of life on the campus.

Admission Requirements

Candidates for freshman standing are selected from applicants who present the following academic credentials: a certificate of graduation from an approved high school; a minimum of 15 units, 10 of which must be in academic areas and completed with a minimum C average; and SAT I or ACT scores, all to be forwarded to the Office of Admissions.

In addition to fulfilling these requirements, a transfer student must be eligible to continue in the institution from which he or she wishes to transfer, be entitled to honorable separation from the institution last attended, and present a minimum 2.0 (C) cumulative index for all completed work.

An early admission policy is followed for exceptionally well qualified students who have not graduated from high school.

Campus tours, conducted by Saint Joseph's students, are highly recommended.

Application and Information

An application form must be filled out completely by the applicant and must be sent to the College along with a $25 nonrefundable fee. Priority is given to applications received by March 1. Official transcripts of credits from all high schools and colleges previously attended must be mailed directly from the schools to the Office of Admissions at Saint Joseph's. Evidence of good health and proper immunization must be provided on an official medical certificate form supplied by the College after an application has been approved.

For further information, students should contact:

Office of Admissions
Saint Joseph's College
P.O. Box 890
Rensselaer, Indiana 47978
Telephone: 219-866-6170
         800-447-8781 (toll-free)
Fax: 219-866-6122
E-mail: admissions@saintjoe.edu
World Wide Web: http://www.saintjoe.edu

Saint Joseph's College Chapel.

SAINT JOSEPH'S COLLEGE
STANDISH, MAINE

The College
Saint Joseph's College of Maine, the only Catholic college in Maine, offers a liberal arts education to men and women of all ages and faiths. Founded in 1912 and sponsored by the Sisters of Mercy, the College's mission focuses on the intellectual, spiritual, and social growth of its students within a values-centered environment. Special emphasis on internships and career-oriented majors, such as communications and nursing, complement the traditional curriculum.

The sustained growth in student population has led to the opening of a new residence hall, Carmel Hall, which houses 90 students. The Harold Alfond Student Center opened in summer 1999. It houses a swimming pool, basketball courts, an elevated jogging track, a rock-climbing wall, weight rooms, and a dance/aerobics studio. Future construction plans include two residence halls.

Full-time undergraduate enrollment averages 800 students annually. Overall student enrollment in the traditional undergraduate program numbers 1,300, with a student-faculty ratio of 16:1. Sixty percent of the students are women; 40 percent are men. The geographical distribution shows twelve states and three countries represented, with most students coming from the Northeast. More than 80 percent of full-time students live on campus. The nine residence halls include a choice of single-sex, coed, and substance-free housing options. Off-campus housing is readily available in the local area.

Saint Joseph's College of Maine looks to its students to take an active role in campus leadership. Opportunities to get involved in student government, athletics, cultural, and social organizations are numerous. The College has a close-knit family atmosphere that permeates campus life. Social life revolves around clubs and organizations and the many events held in the Chalet and the Alfond Center.

Intercollegiate athletic competition for both men and women is actively sponsored by the College. Teams compete in baseball, basketball, cross-country, field hockey, golf, soccer, softball, and volleyball. Recreational facilities include tennis courts, a private sandy beach on Sebago Lake, a skating pond, and cross-country running and ski trails as well as the Alfond Center.

Location
The 331-acre campus is located on the shore of Sebago Lake and offers students a rural setting 3 miles from the town of Windham, 16 miles from Portland, and 125 miles from Boston. The Sebago Lake region, one of Maine's most beautiful spots, is also well known as one of the state's premier four-season recreational areas. The Greater Portland community has many cultural, artistic, social, and recreational facilities and events. Portland is served by six airlines and two major bus companies.

Majors and Degrees
Saint Joseph's College of Maine grants the Bachelor of Arts, Bachelor of Science, and Bachelor of Science in Nursing (B.S.N.) degrees.

Undergraduate majors include business administration with concentrations in accounting, advertising, banking, finance, international business, management, and marketing; liberal arts with concentrations in biology, communications (with concentrations in advertising/public relations, broadcast journalism, and print journalism), English, environmental science, history, human development, mathematics, natural science, philosophy, psychology, religious studies, and sociology (with concentrations in criminal justice and social work); nursing; preprofessional studies in dentistry, law, medicine, and veterinary medicine; radiologic technology; and teacher education with majors in elementary education, physical education, and secondary education with certification in biology, English, history, mathematics, and natural science.

Academic Program
The College follows a traditional two-semester calendar, running from late August to mid-May. The Continuing and Professional Studies Program operates summer sessions for its students. Candidates for a bachelor's degree must earn 128 semester hours and 256 quality points. An honors program for selected students is in place. General education requirements for all students include courses in English, fine arts, foreign language, history, mathematics, philosophy, religion, and science. Credit by examination is available through CLEP, ACT-PEP, DANTES, and Advanced Placement examinations with scores of 4 or higher.

An Army ROTC program is also available.

The College's nationally known Continuing and Professional Studies Program, formerly called Distance Education, enrolls more than 4,000 students from the United States and around the world. Students earn their degrees through both independent, self-directed study and on-campus summer sessions. Continuing and Professional Studies, designed primarily for working adults, offers degrees at the associate, bachelor's, and master's levels.

Off-Campus Arrangements
The College has a commitment to service learning and emphasizes hands-on experience for all its students. Internships and work experience are a vital part of each student's curriculum. Education majors begin observation and teaching in their first year; nursing majors begin clinical training in their sophomore year; communications majors begin studio work as early as their first year; and business administration majors work for companies locally. Other components of service learning, including a senior seminar, help students relate their academic study to the working world.

An Outdoor Leadership program gives students an opportunity to hone their camping and hiking skills in a recreational environment.

For students who seek an international program, the College participates in both ISEP, the International Student Exchange Program, through the local area consortium, and the Nova Scotia Exchange Program. With ISEP, students may study for up to one year in one of fifty countries worldwide. As part of the Nova Scotia Exchange Program, students may select one of several universities located in the Canadian maritime province.

Saint Joseph's also participates in an exchange program with the Irish College for the Humanities in Tralee, County Kerry, Ireland. Other off-campus opportunities include a semester of study at Drew University, located near New York City; American University in Washington, D.C.; and Agnes Scott College, near Atlanta.

Academic Facilities
The Margaret H. Heffernan Center (1983) complements the distinguished original estate buildings and the other campus

facilities that were added when the College moved to its present location in 1956. Located in the Heffernan Center are the library/learning center, an auditorium, the chapel, and a large foyer for social gatherings. Mercy Hall, the main academic building, houses classrooms, science laboratories, the computer center, and faculty offices. The communications department and the College's radio station are housed in Saint Joseph's Hall. All student residence hall rooms are networked to accommodate e-mail and Internet access, cable television, and free local-area telephone calls.

Costs

For 2000–01, tuition for the regular campus-based programs is $13,920, room and board are $6250, and general fees are approximately $495, for a total of $20,665. Students usually budget between $800 and $1000 for books, travel, and miscellaneous expenses.

Financial Aid

The College granted aid to more than 90 percent of the most recent first-year class in the form of grants, scholarships, work-study awards, and loans. Saint Joseph's participates in the Federal Work-Study program and assists students from College funds and through the Federal Pell Grant and Federal Supplemental Educational Opportunity Grant programs. Most of the students who receive aid work on the campus and acquire Federal Stafford Student Loans. Scholarships are awarded on the basis of financial need, outstanding scholastic achievement, leadership skills, community service, and other talents.

Students who apply for aid must file the Free Application for Federal Student Aid (FAFSA) and the College's one-page application. Preference is given to those whose aid applications are on file in the Financial Aid office by March 1. Financial aid status does not affect admission decisions.

Faculty

A special feature of Saint Joseph's College of Maine is the care and concern given by the faculty members and administration to each student in every aspect of his or her collegiate life. The faculty is an outstanding group of professional educators; 95 percent have an earned doctorate or another appropriate terminal degree. The student-faculty ratio is 16:1. The faculty adviser system is particularly strong, and members of the faculty are very accessible to their advisees.

Student Government

The Student Government Association has an active voice in campus affairs, and it manages a large budget funded by student activity fees. A full slate of officers is elected annually. Students are also represented in College committees and on all standing committees of the Faculty Senate.

Admission Requirements

Applicants to the first-year class are admitted on the strength of their secondary school curriculum, class rank, grade point average, and SAT I or ACT scores in relation to their intended major. Ninety-nine percent of last year's freshman class had at least a 2.0 grade point average in high school, 75 percent ranked in the top half of their class, and their median SAT I verbal and mathematics scores were in line with the national averages. Counselor recommendations are required. Campus interviews are strongly recommended, and most prospective first-year students visit the College.

Transfer students, a valuable addition to the student body, may be admitted in either the fall or spring semester.

Application and Information

Students are encouraged to call the Office of Admissions in advance to schedule campus visits and interviews. Saint Joseph's sponsors small-scale visitation days throughout the year. In fall and early winter, Saint Joseph's offers an innovative one-day program, Application Day, that allows students to apply, learn about the College, and receive a decision on admission. Saint Joseph's College of Maine has a rolling admission policy, and students are notified of admission decisions beginning December 1. There is no deadline for applying, but early application is recommended; the freshman class is usually filled by June 1.

For information about the Continuing and Professional Studies Program, students should contact the Dean, Continuing and Professional Studies Program, at the address listed below. To obtain the College viewbook, a fact sheet, and information on each campus-based academic program, prospective students should contact the Office of Admission.

Office of Admission
Saint Joseph's College of Maine
278 Whites Bridge Road
Standish, Maine 04084-5263
Telephone: 207-893-7746
800-338-7057 (toll-free)

Students in front of the Heffernan Center.

ST. JOSEPH'S COLLEGE
BROOKLYN AND PATCHOGUE, NEW YORK

The College

St. Joseph's College, founded in 1916, is a private, coeducational institution specializing in the liberal arts and preprofessional programs. The College maintains separate campuses in Brooklyn and Patchogue, New York, and enrolls a total of 4,294 students in its School of Arts and Sciences and School of Adult and Professional Education.

The College seeks to create a free atmosphere in which students and faculty together can investigate the major areas of human knowledge as the basis for a more effective participation in today's world. In support of this philosophy, the College pursues a number of specific objectives, including providing an atmosphere for open dialogue, individual attention, and innovative teaching; inspiring in students a spirit of inquiry and the joy of learning as an ongoing part of their lives; and preparing students for their lifework by providing the necessary professional and preprofessional training.

While neither campus maintains residence halls, St. Joseph's College offers numerous extracurricular and cocurricular activities designed to help its students grow personally as well as academically. Each campus offers more than twenty clubs and activities, including intercollegiate basketball, women's softball, and volleyball. The Patchogue campus also offers men's soccer, a women's swim team, and a coed equestrian team. The social life is maintained through these clubs, which sponsor numerous dances, barbecues, intramural sports, screenings of current films, and vacation trips each year. Since all students live in the vicinity of their respective campuses, they often organize informal social events among themselves.

The ultramodern, 48,250-square-foot John A. Danzi Athletic Center houses a competition-sized basketball court, an elevated jogging and walking track, seating for 1,500 spectators, a 25-yard pool, and an aerobic and fitness center.

Location

The Brooklyn campus in the historic Clinton Hill section of Brooklyn is easily accessible by public transit lines and automobile. The convenient location, where undergraduates can enjoy the freedom of campus life while profiting from the many cultural advantages of the New York City area, attracts students from every part of the metropolitan region. The College is in the center of one of the nation's most diversified academic communities, with six colleges and universities within a 2-mile radius. St. Joseph's offers its students easy access to the other colleges and such cultural facilities as the Brooklyn Academy of Music, the Brooklyn Public Library, and the Brooklyn Museum.

The Patchogue campus, located on the beautiful south shore of Long Island, is easily accessible to its students from both Nassau and Suffolk Counties. Situated on the western rim of the Great Patchogue Lake, the 28-acre campus features comfortable classrooms and administrative and student facilities, surrounded by athletic fields and spacious lawns. The College and its students have established close ties with the neighboring communities and with the Village of Patchogue itself.

Majors and Degrees

The Brooklyn campus offers four-year programs leading to B.A. and B.S. degrees, with majors in accounting, biology, business administration, chemistry, child study (a sequence in special education is optional), English, history, human relations, mathematics, psychology, social science (including economics, political science, and sociology), Spanish, and speech communication. Certificate programs are available in criminology/criminal justice, gerontology, information technology applications, leadership and supervision, management, and marketing, advertising, and public relations.

Through a partnership between St. Joseph's College and Polytechnic University, students at St. Joseph's now have the opportunity to earn a bachelor's degree in the field of their choice and a master's degree in computer science in a combined B.A./B.S. plus M.S. program. The bachelor's degree is issued from St. Joseph's, and the master's degree is issued from Polytechnic University.

The Brooklyn campus also offers an accelerated biomedical program in cooperation with the New York College of Podiatric Medicine. After two years at St. Joseph's, students spend four years at the NYCPM. At the end of the six years, students receive a B.S. in biology as well as the D.P.M. from NYCPM.

The Patchogue campus offers four-year programs leading to the B.A. degree, with majors in child study (including special education), English, history, human relations, mathematics, psychology, social sciences, and speech communication. The B.S. degree is available in accounting, biology, business administration, mathematics, mathematics/computers, and recreation. Certificate programs, which are registered with the New York State Education Department, are offered in applied sociology, criminology/criminal justice, gerontology, human resources, information technology applications, leadership and supervision, management, and marketing, advertising, and public relations.

Both campuses offer preprofessional programs in law, teaching, and numerous health fields, including dentistry, medicine, and optometry.

The School of Adult and Professional Education at each campus is designed especially for adults with nontraditional academic backgrounds or with professional training and experience. Bachelor of Science degrees are offered in community health, general studies, health administration, organizational management, and nursing.

Academic Program

The School of Arts and Sciences at each campus operates on the semester system, and there are limited course offerings during the summer and in January. Since students are expected to attain breadth and balance in their academic studies, a core curriculum is an integral part of the 128 credits required for graduation. However, a wide range of choices to satisfy the core curriculum requirements allows students to tailor their academic program in accordance with their personal and professional needs.

The College recognizes the Advanced Placement (AP) Program and offers credit and placement for scores of 3, 4, or 5 on the AP test. In each case, the score is reviewed by the registrar and/or department chairperson to determine credit and placement. Depending on the specific area covered by a College-Level Examination Program (CLEP) test, credit may be granted.

The School of Adult and Professional Education on each campus operates on numerous schedules. Courses are offered during the day, evenings, and/or weekends to best meet the needs of working students who are pursuing a degree. Some courses meet for a semester, some in six- or twelve-week sessions. An extensive summer program is offered.

Academic Facilities

The Brooklyn campus is composed of seven buildings. The Dillon Child Study Center, a laboratory preschool enrolling approximately a hundred 3-, 4-, and 5-year-olds, is used by child study students as a teaching and observation resource. McEntegart Hall, a modern five-level structure, houses the 122,563-volume library, audiovisual resource center, curriculum library, archives, and computer labs. Other academic facilities include fully equipped biology, chemistry, computer, physics, and psychology research laboratories.

At the Patchogue campus, the main building houses administrative and faculty offices; laboratories for biology, chemistry, physics, and psychology; the computer center; art and music studios; the Local History Center; and the Office of Counseling. A library building, with a capacity of 120,000 volumes, houses a curriculum library, seminar rooms, administrative offices, and two classrooms. The Clare Rose Playhouse, situated on the northeast corner of the campus, is an educational and cultural learning facility where students and local communities can explore the various aspects of theater from production to performance.

The College has constructed a high-speed fiber-optic intracampus network that connects all offices, institutional facilities, computer laboratories, and libraries on the Brooklyn and Patchogue campuses. Direct Internet access is available to all students and faculty and staff members through the College's server. The integrated online library system enables students to locate and check out books at either campus and also provides links to online databases and other electronic information sources.

Costs

In Brooklyn, the annual full-time undergraduate tuition for 2000–01 is $9030. Nonmatriculated or part-time students are charged $290 per credit. In Patchogue, the annual full-time undergraduate tuition for 2000–01 is $9290. Nonmatriculated or part-time students are charged $300 per credit. Mandatory fees are $322.

Financial Aid

Scholarships and grants-in-aid are available at St. Joseph's College. Students wishing to apply for either form of assistance must file the Free Application for Federal Student Aid (FAFSA), an institutional aid form, and a state aid form. After a student has been accepted to the College and all financial aid forms are properly processed, the Financial Aid Office will prepare packages of aid that usually consist of federal, state, and College funds. St. Joseph's is fully approved for veterans. Campus work-study programs are also available.

Faculty

The College's 16:1 student-faculty ratio ensures very close relationships between students and their professors. Faculty members serve as academic advisers, are active on student affairs committees, and act as moderators to student organizations.

Student Government

Student government on each campus is active in many facets of academic and student life and organizes social events such as mixers, film festivals, lectures, and off-campus trips.

Admission Requirements

St. Joseph's College seeks a diverse student body and welcomes applications from high school students, transfer students, and others who may have a nontraditional academic background. The College offers programs to serve all of these groups.

Students who wish to enter as freshmen are expected to have completed at least 18 units of college-preparatory work by the end of their senior year. This should include the following distribution: 4 years of English, 2 years of foreign language, 3 years of mathematics, 2 years of science, and 4 years of social studies. Applicants interested in accounting, allied health fields, biology, business administration, chemistry, or mathematics should have more extensive backgrounds in mathematics and science. The College will also consider students who have received a general equivalency diploma.

The School of Arts and Sciences requires the submission of official results from the SAT I.

St. Joseph's College will accept a block transfer of credits from students holding an A.A. or A.S. degree in certain majors from an accredited junior or community college. All other transfers are considered on an individual basis.

The Division of General Studies has more flexible admission requirements, reflecting its enrollment of adults with nontraditional academic backgrounds and work experience.

Application and Information

Admission is offered on a rolling basis. Applications and supporting documents should be submitted to the appropriate address below, along with a nonrefundable application fee of $25. Each application is reviewed very carefully, and a decision is usually sent within one month after receiving all necessary credentials. Students can access the school's Web site at the address listed below.

Director of Admissions
St. Joseph's College
245 Clinton Avenue
Brooklyn, New York 11205
Telephone: 718-636-6868

Director of Admissions
St. Joseph's College
155 West Roe Boulevard
Patchogue, New York 11772
Telephone: 631-447-3219
World Wide Web: http://www.sjcny.edu

Both campuses of St. Joseph's College provide up-to-date science, computer, and psychology laboratories.

SAINT JOSEPH'S UNIVERSITY
PHILADELPHIA, PENNSYLVANIA

The University

Saint Joseph's University, a nationally recognized, Catholic, Jesuit university, is distinguished by its personal size, comprehensive academic opportunities, respected teaching faculty, and highly successful students and alumni. The full-time undergraduate enrollment is approximately 3,000 students. A variety of part-time programs, as well as graduate studies in the arts and sciences and in business, provide continued education for the remainder of the University population.

The University requires that students pursue a broad core program of liberal arts studies together with a major field of concentration, which should be chosen by the sophomore year. Through this required core, Saint Joseph's aims to foster the development of actively concerned individuals who are intellectually and spiritually prepared to contribute to society. Saint Joseph's graduates enjoy success in many fields, including medicine, law, business, and education.

During Saint Joseph's rich history, curricular development has kept pace with the changing needs of each generation of students. The University's computer facilities have been expanded to include 250 computers that are available for student use, three computer classrooms, and several residence halls connected to a campuswide network. McShain Hall, a state-of-the-art Residence/Conference Center, has computer linkups to the Library Resource Center and the Science Center, houses 288 undergraduates, and provides full accessibility to handicapped residents. Freshman students may live in one of three high-rise residence halls. Returning students may choose from among the high rises, Victorian-style homes, apartments, and a new townhouse complex (juniors and seniors only). Housing is available for four years, but it is not guaranteed.

The Student Sports and Recreational Complex has an eight-lane, 25-meter swimming pool, racquetball courts, tennis courts, an indoor walking and running surface, and an aerobic fitness and training center. A $5-million chapel was dedicated in 1992.

Saint Joseph's has remained dedicated to its founding principle: that a liberal education teaches disciplined reasoning, effective communication, and love of learning. The University strives for excellence and balance in its academic programs, within the framework of the Jesuit tradition of service to others. The outcome of this centuries-old Jesuit heritage is a lasting sense of authentic community life. This community spirit distinguishes and enlivens Saint Joseph's and is most remembered by the students who come through the University.

Location

The University's 65-acre campus, situated on Philadelphia's western border, offers suburban charm within minutes of the nation's fifth-largest city. More than thirty colleges and universities are located in the Greater Philadelphia area, providing students with many educational and social options. Culturally, Philadelphia is a campus on its own. Hundreds of museums, libraries, theaters, and historic landmarks present students with opportunities to learn outside the classroom.

Majors and Degrees

Saint Joseph's offers full-time baccalaureate degree programs in thirty-two major fields of study and numerous specialty programs, which are administered by two separate colleges.

The College of Arts and Sciences awards the Bachelor of Arts degree in economics, English, fine and performing arts, French, French studies, German, history, international relations, philosophy, political science, Spanish, and theology and the Bachelor of Science degree in biology, chemistry, computer science, criminal justice, elementary education, environmental science, interdisciplinary health services, labor studies, mathematics, physics, psychology, and sociology.

The Erivan K. Haub School of Business awards the Bachelor of Science degree in accounting, finance, food marketing, information systems, international marketing, management, marketing, and public administration.

Four 5-year B.S./M.S. programs are offered in criminal justice, elementary education, international marketing, and psychology. The University also offers special academic programs in aerospace studies (Air Force ROTC); allied health (diagnostic imaging, laboratory sciences, nursing, occupational therapy, and physical therapy); American, European, gender, Latin American, medieval, Renaissance, and Russian and East Central European studies; and teacher certification at the elementary and secondary levels. Preprofessional study is available in most major fields. Classics is available as a minor program.

Academic Program

At Saint Joseph's University, the aim of providing the student with the qualities of a liberally educated individual is pursued through a threefold plan encompassing 120 academic credits. The major concentration (30–45 credits) is intended to provide students with depth in a given field in order to prepare them for effective work in that field or for graduate study. The general education requirement (60 credits) is intended to ensure that students have mastered basic skills necessary for further work, have been exposed to the main divisions of learning, and have been introduced to several new fields of study. Languages and literature, mathematics, natural sciences, history, social sciences, philosophy, and theology are among the areas of study included in the general education requirement. Free electives (15–30 credits) are intended to provide flexibility by encouraging students to pursue studies in areas they have found interesting, to test their interest in an unexplored area, or to deepen their knowledge in the major field.

A competitive honors program is available for qualified students, as are independent and interdisciplinary study options. A new honors suite on campus provides a place for students to have meetings, study, and relax.

Off-Campus Arrangements

Saint Joseph's offers to an increasing number of students the opportunity to study abroad and directly sponsors programs each year in London, England; Strasbourg, France; Marburg, Germany; Galway and Cork, Ireland; Tokyo, Japan; Mexico City, Mexico; and Madrid, Spain. International Study Tours have been made to Africa, Australia, Brazil, Canada, Greece, Ireland, Italy, Japan, Scotland, and Spain.

Saint Joseph's participates annually in the Jesuit Student Exchange. Through this option, undergraduates may plan a semester at most of the twenty-seven other Jesuit colleges and universities in the United States. Other students may take advantage of an arrangement with the Washington Center for Learning Alternatives, which allows for a one-semester internship in the nation's capital.

Fieldwork experiences are required in several majors, and the University's location provides for internship opportunities to support virtually all other disciplines. The Career Services

Center has a full-time internship coordinator and provides opportunities for on-campus interviews. The Alumni Mentor Alliance matches students with alumni in their fields of interest to gain real-world perspectives.

Academic Facilities

The facilities at Saint Joseph's are a blend of the old and the new. Barbelin/Lonergan Hall, which houses most of the University's administrative offices, is a fine example of collegiate Gothic architecture. Its spired carillon tower rises above the campus and is easily the most recognizable landmark at Saint Joseph's. Mandeville Hall, a state-of-the-art international academic center, opened in fall 1998. Home of the Haub School of Business, Mandeville offers distance learning technology and unique learning environments. The Drexel Library has a collection of 335,000 volumes, 1,850 current periodical subscriptions, and 750,000 microforms.

Costs

For the 2000–01 academic year, tuition in the College of Arts and Sciences for social science and humanities majors is $19,410, and for majors in the physical sciences and computer science, it is $19,680. Tuition in the Erivan K. Haub School of Business totals $19,940. Room fees range from $4800 to $5550 per year, and board fees cost $2920 per year.

Financial Aid

The program of financial aid is intended to provide assistance to students who could not otherwise afford to attend a private liberal arts university. The University offers opportunities for academic and athletic scholarships, grants, loans, and employment, either singly or in combination. To ensure the best opportunity for receipt of merit scholarships, students should apply by the December 1 priority date. Other grants are available through state and federal agencies. Students should submit the Free Application for Federal Student Aid (FAFSA) by March 1 of their senior year of high school. The Financial Aid Committee at the University assumes that all students interested in receiving aid will apply for state and federal grants.

Faculty

At Saint Joseph's, undergraduate teaching is the primary responsibility of every faculty member. A student-faculty ratio of 15:1 and an average class size of 25 offer excellent opportunities for student-faculty member exchange, both inside and outside the classroom. Approximately 90 percent of the 160 full-time faculty members hold a doctorate or terminal degree in their field.

Student Government

The University recognizes the need for students to participate in the governance of academic and social affairs, not only because of its concern that students have the educational experience but, more important, because it also believes that students have a vital contribution to make to the enterprise. Therefore, students may become active in the University Council and its standing committees, the Student Government Association (SGA), the Student Union Board, and student advisory groups in each academic department.

All undergraduates are members of the SGA, which provides the opportunity for direct and substantive participation in matters of the University community and student self-government. Financially supported by student fees, the SGA represents its student constituents to the general school community, initiates programs through its committees and boards, coordinates the activities of the many student organizations and interest groups, and develops cultural and social programs.

Admission Requirements

Candidates for admission to the freshman class are ordinarily expected to complete a secondary school program with a minimum of four academic subjects each year. Candidates must submit evidence of academic achievement in a college-preparatory program, which should emphasize study in English, mathematics, foreign languages (classical or modern), science, history, and social studies. Typical successful candidates have had a secondary school background that included the following units: English, 4 units; foreign languages, 2 units; history and social studies, 3 units; mathematics, 3 units (4 units for students interested in the natural sciences or math); and science, 2 units. Applicants are required to submit scores on the SAT I or the ACT.

Application and Information

A completed application form may be submitted with the $40 application fee at any time after the student's junior year. The University adheres to a rolling admissions policy, with decisions being made approximately six weeks after the applicant's file becomes complete. Students are encouraged to apply early in their senior year. The student should also see that the required test scores, a high school transcript, and one letter of recommendation are sent to the Admissions Office. This transcript should normally include grades from ninth grade through the first marking period of twelfth grade.

Susan P. Kassab
Director of Admission
Saint Joseph's University
5600 City Avenue
Philadelphia, Pennsylvania 19131-1395
Telephone: 610-660-1300
  888-BE-A-HAWK (toll-free)
Fax: 610-660-1314
E-mail: admi@sju.edu
World Wide Web: http://www.sju.edu

Mandeville Hall, Saint Joseph's new international academic center and home of the Haub School of Business.

ST. LAWRENCE UNIVERSITY
CANTON, NEW YORK

The University

St. Lawrence University invites students to learn new ways of seeing the world, voicing ideas, and connecting with others. Graduates have the tools with which to think clearly, express themselves persuasively, and step into the world community with an understanding of their responsibility to all people and to the planet.

Founded in 1856, St. Lawrence is the oldest continuously coeducational degree-granting institution of higher learning in New York State. Initially established as a theology school for the Universalist Church, it quickly evolved into the liberal arts college that it is today. St. Lawrence is a private, nonsectarian university of approximately 1,950 undergraduate men and women, with a small graduate program in education. St. Lawrence is known for its residential/academic First-Year Program, its international study opportunities and area studies programs, its students' strong interest in the environment and the outdoors, and its friendliness.

St. Lawrence students are self-starters. The self-designed major is popular, intramural sports leagues are always full, and more than 100 student organizations serve broad interests from communication to community service and creativity to social action. The University routinely hosts well-known speakers, and concerts, plays, and films are regulars on the weekly events calendar.

St. Lawrence students have historically placed high value on athletic activity, and a large number participate in varsity, intramural, or club sports. The thirty-two varsity men's and women's teams compete at the Division III level of the NCAA, with the exception of men's and women's ice hockey, which compete in Division I. Recreational facilities include cross-country ski and running trails, a complete Nautilus facility, indoor and outdoor tennis courts, a gymnasium/field house complex, a pool, a skating rink, an equestrian center, and a golf course. A nine-lane all-weather track, an artificial turf practice field, and a new performance field for football and lacrosse, as well as six new squash courts and a new softball field, were completed for competition in 1999. Expansion and renovation of other athletic facilities are under way.

Residential life is an important aspect of the St. Lawrence experience. The University's innovative and highly regarded First-Year Program creates communities where groups of approximately 50 first-year students live and learn together. In the upperclass years, students can choose from traditional dormitories, Greek chapter houses, and suites and theme cottages that focus on student interests such as low-impact living and community service. St. Lawrence sponsors a full range of student services, from counseling to career planning.

Location

St. Lawrence is situated on a 1,000-acre campus on the edge of the village of Canton, New York (population 6,400), the seat of St. Lawrence County. Canton, with its Victorian homes, tree-lined streets, village green, and small shops, is typical of college towns throughout the Northeast. Students and residents often mix in stores, at athletic events, and in community projects. Ottawa, Canada's capital, is 90 minutes to the north, while Lake Placid, one of America's hiking and skiing meccas, is 90 minutes to the southeast.

Majors and Degrees

St. Lawrence offers the Bachelor of Arts and Bachelor of Science degrees; students can choose from thirty-three majors and have the option of picking one of thirty-two minors. Combined five-year programs with other institutions are in place in engineering and management, and specialized advising is offered in preparation for postgraduate work in dentistry, law, medicine, and veterinary medicine.

Academic Program

St. Lawrence's foremost mission is to provide its students with a liberal arts education. The core curriculum includes requirements in six areas and concentrated work in a major field of the student's choosing. Before graduating, students are expected to show competence in writing. Close faculty-student interaction is a hallmark of a St. Lawrence education, and every semester many students engage in independent or honors projects, often working with professors on joint research projects that lead to publication in leading scholarly journals.

Off-Campus Arrangements

More than one third of St. Lawrence students study in one of the University's international programs during their collegiate careers. St. Lawrence operates programs in Australia, Austria, Canada, Costa Rica, Denmark, England, France, India, Japan, Kenya, Russia, and Spain. In addition, the University's membership in the International Student Exchange Program permits students to choose from more than 100 countries in which to study. St. Lawrence also operates programs at two other campuses in the U.S.: Fisk University in Nashville, Tennessee, and American University in Washington, D.C.

Academic Facilities

Owen D. Young Library and Launders Science Library contain more than half a million volumes as well as electronic resources and ample space for reading and research. Griffiths Arts Center is home to the University's music, speech, and theater and fine arts programs, as well as two theaters and an art gallery in which selections from St. Lawrence's 7,000-piece collection are frequently shown. A unified science complex houses the Departments of Biology, Chemistry, Physics, Mathematics, Psychology, and Geology and is connected via a covered hallway to the science library and computing center. Richardson Hall, St. Lawrence's oldest building and on the National Register of Historic Places, is home to the English and religious studies departments. Other departments can be found in various buildings, which are clustered on one part of the campus so as not to be a long walk apart.

Costs

The comprehensive fee for 2000–01 is $31,430, including tuition, fees, and average room and board. Students should allow approximately $1450 for books and personal expenses.

Financial Aid

St. Lawrence awards both merit scholarships and need-based financial aid. More than 81 percent of the University's students receive some form of financial assistance, including scholarships, grants, student loans, and campus jobs. St. Lawrence is committed to assisting as many students as possible and will recognize academic and personal achievement in making financial aid decisions. To apply for need-based financial aid, students must file the Free Application for Federal Student Aid (FAFSA) between January 1 and February 15 and request that the results be sent directly to St. Lawrence. Submission of the Financial Aid PROFILE form is encouraged; completion of the St. Lawrence supplemental form is an acceptable alternative to the PROFILE.

Faculty

The 182 members of St. Lawrence's faculty are teachers and scholars. While teaching is their primary responsibility, they are also active researchers, artists, performers, and regular contributors in their academic disciplines. Faculty members teach all courses at St. Lawrence; no undergraduate courses are taught by graduate students. Active teaching assistant and tutoring programs, involving qualified upperclass students, are closely supervised by faculty members. The student-faculty ratio is about 11:1. Faculty members hold regular office hours, serve as academic advisers to students, and frequently take part in extracurricular activities on campus.

Student Government

The Thelomathesian Society, comprising all students on campus, is governed by a senate of elected representatives. The senate parcels out funds in support of student activities and provides two student delegates to the University's Board of Trustees.

Admission Requirements

St. Lawrence seeks students who can be successful in a demanding academic program and who can contribute to the quality of life of the community. The University is committed to enrolling students who represent the widest possible diversity of economic, social, ethnic, and geographic backgrounds. Academic preparation is, of course, important, but demonstrated ability in the creative arts, athletics, or social service is also a measure of a student's potential to benefit St. Lawrence. Scores on the SAT I or ACT are required for admission. A campus visit is strongly encouraged, and interviews may be scheduled on campus or off campus in certain areas.

Although there is no set distribution of high school courses, successful applicants typically show strong preparation in the humanities, the social sciences, mathematics, and the natural sciences. Honors work and Advanced Placement are opportunities for applicants to demonstrate intellectual maturity and curiosity, qualities highly valued in the admission process.

Application and Information

Application materials may be requested directly from the University or students may use the Common Application. The application processing fee is $50. Regular decision applications should be submitted by February 15, with notification by late March. Students who decide that St. Lawrence is their first choice may apply under one of the early decision deadlines: November 15 or January 15. In each case, notification is one month after the deadline. Transfer candidates should submit applications no later than November 1 for the spring semester or April 1 for the fall semester.

To request an application or for more information, students should contact:

Office of Admissions and Financial Aid
St. Lawrence University
Canton, New York 13617
Telephone: 315-229-5261
               800-285-1856 (toll-free)
World Wide Web: http://www.stlawu.edu

SAINT LEO UNIVERSITY
SAINT LEO, FLORIDA

The University

Saint Leo University is a four-year, private, coeducational university affiliated with the Catholic Church. Founded in 1889 by the Order of Saint Benedict, Saint Leo has grown to an enrollment of 1,500 full- and part-time students on the main campus and 7,000 students in extension programs located on eleven military bases stretching from Virginia to Key West. The student body represents thirty-four states and twenty-seven countries: 60 percent are from Florida, 21 percent are from the Northeast, 6 percent are from the Midwest, and 6 percent are international students. Of the students on the main campus, approximately 500 live on campus in the seven residence halls.

Students can participate in the nationally recognized honors program and the more than forty different clubs and organizations on campus, including national fraternities and sororities.

Saint Leo competes in NCAA Division II sports for men in baseball, basketball, cross-country, golf, soccer, and tennis and for women in basketball, cross-country, golf, soccer, softball, tennis, and volleyball. Students can also participate in a variety of intramurals as well as sailing. On the campus there are lighted racquetball and tennis courts; soccer, baseball, and softball fields; a weight room; and an outdoor swimming pool. A 154-acre lake and an eighteen-hole golf course are adjacent to the campus. The University also hosts a variety of events that are open to the University community and residents of the surrounding area. There are art exhibits and choral concerts. In addition, the Student Government Union and various campus organizations sponsor movies, lectures, dances, and special events throughout the academic year.

Saint Leo is committed to giving its students an education that prepares them for the future. The goal of the University is to develop the whole person, both academically and personally, through the Catholic tradition.

Saint Leo University is accredited by the Commission on Colleges of the Southern Association of Colleges and Schools to award the associate and bachelor's degrees. Saint Leo University's program in social work is accredited by the Commission on Accreditation of the Council on Social Work Education (B.S.W. level). Saint Leo University has Teacher Education Program approval by the state of Florida Department of Education.

In addition to associate and bachelor's degrees, Saint Leo University offers a Master of Business Administration (M.B.A.) degree and a Master of Education (M.Ed.) degree. A master's degree in psychology will be added in 2001.

Location

Saint Leo is located 25 miles north of Tampa and 60 miles west of Orlando. The campus occupies 170 acres of rolling hills and wooded grounds. The rural setting is conducive to academic success, but the University is located near enough to metropolitan areas to give the students the advantage of a number of social and professional options.

Majors and Degrees

Saint Leo University offers nearly forty traditional majors, preprofessional programs, specializations, and career-oriented studies. Degrees offered are the Bachelor of Arts, Bachelor of Science, and Bachelor of Social Work.

The School of Business offers majors in accounting; business administration, with specializations in management, marketing, hospitality and tourism, and international business; computer information systems; health-care administration; human resource administration; and sport management. The School of Arts and Sciences offers majors in biology, English, environmental science, history, international studies, medical technology, political science, psychology, and religion. The School of Education and Social Services offers majors in criminology, elementary and secondary education, health services management, and social work. Preprofessional programs in dentistry, law, medicine, and veterinary science are also offered.

Academic Program

Candidates for the bachelor's degree gain a broad exposure to the liberal arts through the completion of the University's general education requirements. General education at Saint Leo consists of fifteen courses in English, fine arts, religious studies and philosophy, science and math, social science, humanities, and computer science. General education courses form a basic foundation for all majors. General education is usually completed during the freshman and sophomore years.

Most students at Saint Leo earn the 122 credits needed for their bachelor's degree through a four-year program of study. All major programs require a minimum grade point average of 2.0 (C) for graduation. Saint Leo has an academic skills program to assist first-year students in their adjustment to University life. Included in this program are freshman studies, tutoring, and advising. All first-year students at Saint Leo are assigned faculty advisers who act as mentors from the first day that the student arrives on campus through the time when the student selects a major.

Students have the opportunity to receive credit through examination. Students who demonstrate course mastery for any course listed in the catalog may earn up to 40 hours of credit through examination. Information about credit by examination is available through the Records Office.

Off-Campus Arrangements

Saint Leo University is committed to helping students expand their horizons with study-abroad programs. Saint Leo currently has partnerships with schools in Rome, Italy; Paris, France; Leysin and Engelberg, Switzerland; London, England; and Ecuador. The University continues to add new programs and partnerships in order to provide students with a wide variety of experiences.

Academic Facilities

The Daniel A. Cannon Library contains 136,398 volumes and 743 current periodical and newspaper subscriptions, microforms, and a variety of media software. Also located in the library are the Hugh Culverhouse Computer Lab and an audiovisual lab that are available for student use. There is a biology lab on campus for research. Crawford Hall and the Julia Deal Lewis Hall of Science provide general classrooms.

Costs

For the 1999–2000 school year, tuition was $11,450, room and board costs were $6050, and the student activity fee was $200.

There was also a one-time orientation fee of $200. Estimated miscellaneous costs for the year totaled $1800.

Financial Aid

Financial aid is available in the form of scholarships, grants, and loans that are both federally funded and given through the University. Financial aid is allocated on the basis of need, as determined by the federal government from the financial information provided on the Free Application for Federal Student Aid (FAFSA). On-campus jobs are available for students, with priority given to students with demonstrated financial need.

Faculty

There are a total of 117 faculty members, 50 full-time and 67 part-time. Most courses are taught by full-time faculty members. In some cases, part-time faculty specialists are employed to provide students with real-world experience in their classes. Seventy-eight percent of all full-time faculty members hold a doctorate. The student-faculty ratio is 15:1.

Student Government

A significant contribution to the University comes from the activities initiated by the Student Government Union (SGU). The SGU is an annually elected body organized and conducted in accordance with democratic procedures. This organization strives to foster leadership and loyalty among the students, to formulate recommendations for student life, and to recognize all extracurricular activities.

Admission Requirements

All candidates for admission should be, or expect to be, graduates of secondary schools accredited by a regional or state accrediting agency. Applicants should show successful progress toward graduation with a minimum of 16 academic units of course work: 4 units of English, 3 units of mathematics (algebra I and II and geometry), 3 units of social studies, 2 units of science, and 4 units of electives. All applicants are required to take the SAT I or the ACT examination. A letter of recommendation from the student's guidance counselor is also required. The preferred candidate is a student with a C+ or better average grade and a combined score of at least 1010 on the SAT I or 22 on the ACT. The records of students who do not meet these criteria are also reviewed by the Admissions Committee and considered for the Learning Enhancement for Academic Progress (LEAP) program.

Once the applicant has sent in the application with the $35 application fee, admission essay, high school transcripts, and letter of recommendation, the file is reviewed and a decision is rendered. Notification is on a rolling basis. The application deadline is thirty days prior to registration, but all applicants are encouraged to apply early.

Transfer and international students are also encouraged to apply. The same general admission procedures are required, along with at least a C average for all college work (for transfer students) and a score of at least 550 on the TOEFL (for international students).

Campus visits and interviews are recommended but not required. The Office of Admission schedules appointments Monday through Friday from 9 a.m. to 4 p.m. and on select Saturdays at 9:30 a.m. or 11 a.m.

Application and Information

Additional information and application forms can be obtained by contacting the Office of Admission.

Dr. Susan Hallenbeck
Director of Undergraduate Admission
Office of Admission—MC2008
Saint Leo University
P.O. Box 6665
Saint Leo, Florida 33574-6665
Telephone: 352-588-8283
　　　　　800-334-5532 (toll-free)
Fax: 352-588-8257
E-mail: admissions@saintleo.edu

The Saint Leo University campus.

ST. LOUIS COLLEGE OF PHARMACY
ST. LOUIS, MISSOURI

The College
St. Louis College of Pharmacy is an independent, private, nondenominational, coeducational institution that was established in 1864. The College is continuing to improve the campus with recent additions of a new library, new student center, and new computer laboratory. This modernization provides faculty members and students with some of the finest facilities to be found in any college of pharmacy in the nation. The residence hall adjacent to the main academic building accommodates 132 students and has a spacious, comfortable lounge and a cafeteria. Upper-level students may elect to live in Rabe Hall, a fifty-seven-unit apartment building. It contains studio, one-bedroom, and two-bedroom units.

The total enrollment for 1999–2000 was 562 women and 292 men. The students of the College maintain chapters of the Academy of Students in Pharmacy, the student National Association of Retail Druggists (NARD), and the Student National Pharmaceutical Association. These chapters conduct programs of professional and general interest that are directed toward the development of higher standards in pharmacy. The College recognizes six national professional fraternal organizations. These groups provide social activities in addition to their professional functions. All six groups are governed by an Interfraternity Council. A national honor pharmaceutical society, Rho Chi, was installed at the College in 1955 and is open to fourth- through sixth-year students who are both academically and professionally outstanding.

The College offers a master's program in pharmacy administration and managed care pharmacy and a certificate in managed care pharmacy.

The Master of Science (M.S.) degree in pharmacy administration is offered as a part-time graduate program and provides upper-level management electives for fourth- through sixth-year students.

Extracurricular activities include the College band; chorus; theater and musical programs; dances; movies; lecture programs; the student newspaper, the *Pharmakon;* and the student yearbook, the *Prescripto*. Student ambassadors act as hosts at College functions.

St. Louis College of Pharmacy offers an athletic program for both varsity and intramural sports. As of August 1993, the College became a member of NAIA Division III in men's basketball and women's volleyball. The student center has an indoor running track as well as excellent facilities for weight training, aerobics, and body conditioning.

Location
Known for generations as the Gateway to the West, St. Louis is a center for cultural, educational, and industrial activities. It has many fine museums, a symphony orchestra, theaters, professional sports, historic landmarks, zoological and botanical gardens, and one of the nation's foremost medical centers. A number of these outstanding attractions are within a 2-mile radius of the College. St. Louis College of Pharmacy is located in the Washington University medical complex of St. Louis, one block from Forest Park and two blocks from Barnes Hospital.

Majors and Degrees
The College offers both a five-year program leading to a Bachelor of Science (B.S.) in pharmacy degree and a six-year program leading to the Doctor of Pharmacy (Pharm.D.) degree.

Academic Program
All students entering the College follow the same curriculum for the first four years. In the fifth year, they exercise their option to complete the five-year B.S. curriculum during the remaining year or to follow the Pharm.D. track, which requires one additional year after completion of the B.S. curriculum. Candidates for the degree of Bachelor of Science in pharmacy must complete a prescribed five-year curriculum. The program includes intensive courses in biology, chemistry, mathematics, and physics, as well as electives. Courses in literature, humanities, and social and behavioral sciences constitute 20 percent of the curriculum. An in-hospital clinical pharmacy program gives students the opportunity to apply nearly all facets of their education. This enables students to develop communicative and professional interactions with other health-care practitioners and with patients. The six-year Pharm.D. program comprises specialized didactic courses and includes a calendar year of clinical study.

Off-Campus Arrangements
The St. Louis College of Pharmacy offers clinical training in cooperation with the Washington University and Saint Louis University schools of medicine and in other facilities that include the Jewish, St. Louis Children's, St. John's Mercy, and St. Louis State hospitals. Additional hospital, institutional, and community settings provide supervised experience during the externship program, which is completed by all students during the tenth semester of study.

Academic Facilities
The O. J. Cloughly Alumni Library, located adjacent to the main academic building, is an integral supplement to the instructional program and contains a continually increasing number of volumes in the field of pharmacy, its allied sciences, and the liberal arts. It receives the leading pharmaceutical and scientific periodicals, journals, bulletins, and reports. The library is open throughout the day and most evenings and weekends under the administration of a professional librarian. The main academic building contains classrooms, lecture halls, laboratories, research laboratories, and faculty offices. Whelpley Hall, the newest building on campus, contains a 300-seat auditorium in addition to small- and medium-size classrooms and faculty offices.

Costs
For 2000–01, tuition fees for students in the first and second years are $13,250; tuition fees for those in the third through fifth years are $13,750; and tuition fees for those in the sixth year of the Pharm.D. program are $15,750. Laboratory fees are included in tuition costs. Room and board costs are $5375 for the academic year. Additional costs, including books, vary each year but average approximately $300 per semester.

Financial Aid
The awarding of financial aid is based on need and on the aid available. The College participates in all applicable federal

financial aid programs. Scholarships, grants, loans, and ample part-time employment are offered to help qualified students pay part of their college expenses. Financial aid may be funded by the federal or state government, the College, benefactors and friends of the College, or other sponsoring organizations or agencies. The College also offers scholarships based on academic merit regardless of financial need.

Students planning to attend the College in the fall semester should submit the Free Application for Federal Student Aid (FAFSA) and the College Financial Aids Certification and Draft Registration Compliance forms as early as possible during the previous spring semester. The College begins awarding financial aid as soon as federal programs are funded by Congress, usually in April or May, and continues to make awards on applications submitted later until the federal allocation of funds is exhausted. Further information on student financial aid may be obtained from the College's Financial Aid Office.

Faculty

A competent faculty teaches and counsels students at the College throughout their course of study. A favorable (1:13) faculty-student ratio ensures that there are no anonymous students. No classes are taught by graduate students. Fifty-three of the 63 campus-based faculty members hold a doctoral degree. Approximately 75 registered pharmacists serve as adjunct instructors in the externship-clerkship program.

Student Government

The Student Council represents the interests of all students. It is composed of representatives elected by the various classes and is supervised by a faculty adviser and the dean of students. The council budgets and supervises the expenditure of funds provided by the student activities fee and sponsors numerous student activities and social events.

Admission Requirements

All students applying for admission must present evidence of the satisfactory completion of a four-year course of study in, and graduation from, a high school approved by a recognized accrediting body. A transcript of the high school record, including class standing, should be sent by the high school directly to the director of admissions. The high school course of study should include 4 units of English, 2 units of algebra, 1 unit of geometry, and at least 2 units of biology, chemistry, or physics. The College requires that the ACT examination be completed.

Transfer students must present transcripts of their high school and college records. Such records must demonstrate satisfactory academic status.

Advanced credit may be earned through Advanced Placement examinations or CLEP subject examinations. Further details are available from the Office of Admissions.

Application and Information

The College uses a system of rolling admission for freshman applicants. Students may apply at any time but should recognize that applications are no longer considered after the freshman class has been filled. Applicants are notified of an admission decision as soon as all of their materials have been received and reviewed.

The application deadline for transfer students is February 1. However, due to the large number of transfer applications in recent years, transfer students are encouraged to apply well in advance of this date. Admission decisions are announced beginning in the early spring.

For application forms or additional information, students should contact:

Director of Admissions
St. Louis College of Pharmacy
4588 Parkview Place
St. Louis, Missouri 63110

Telephone: 314-367-8700
               800-278-5267 (toll-free)
E-mail: pbryant@stlcop.edu
World Wide Web: http://www.stlcop.edu

SAINT MARTIN'S COLLEGE
LACEY, WASHINGTON

The College

Students choose Saint Martin's College for its intimate approach to academic excellence. Founded in 1895 by the Catholic Order of Saint Benedict, Saint Martin's College is the only Benedictine-Catholic college in the western United States. The educational curriculum and student life programs are influenced by the Benedictine values of hospitality, graciousness, and tolerance. Saint Martin's believes in the inherent value and worth of the individual and seeks to develop and nurture each student's unique gifts and talents to his or her full potential.

Students can anticipate lively class discussions and tolerance for their opinions, whether or not others agree with them. At a teaching institution like Saint Martin's College, the hallmark of a good professor is that his or her students are learning. An emphasis on critical thinking and thoughtful expression is a part of developing graduates recognized for their competency and work ethic.

More than 100 years since its inception, Saint Martin's enjoys the distinction of having one of the most successful placement rates in the state of Washington. The placement rate of students accepted to graduate school or finding employment within their field of study within six months of graduation has exceeded 93 percent for the past thirteen years.

Saint Martin's Institute of Pacific Rim Studies offers academic and cultural programs, opportunities for students to study abroad, an English as a second language (ESL) program, and a Semester-in-Residence Program, as well as summer cultural programs.

In addition to preparing undergraduate students for today's world, Saint Martin's offers the following graduate degrees: Master of Business Administration, Master of Arts in Counseling Psychology, Master of Education, Master of Engineering Management, and Master in Teaching.

In a college where the students number approximately 1,000 it is easy to become involved in the educational process and campus community. In addition to Saint Martin's main campus in Lacey, Washington, two extension learning centers are located at the Fort Lewis Army Installation and McChord Air Force Base in Tacoma, Washington. Most students are from the Pacific Northwest, although twenty-one other states and nine countries are currently represented. Another 18 percent describe themselves as minority students. Two distinguishing characteristics of Saint Martin's students are their friendliness and their active involvement in the campus community.

Student life offerings are varied and easy to participate in. Students can choose to participate in social clubs, interest groups, cultural events, intramural sports, and student government, as well as sororities and fraternities. Many students choose to participate in organizations that compliment their field of study. NCAA Division II intercollegiate athletic offerings for men include baseball, basketball, cross-country, golf, and track. NCAA Division II athletic offerings for women include basketball, cross-country, fast-pitch, golf, track, and volleyball.

Residence life is a valuable aspect of the student's educational experience. Thirty-one percent of Saint Martin's full-time undergraduate students make their home in the coed residence halls. Safety and respect for one's neighbor are two constants in residence life. The safety of Saint Martin's students is a top priority for security personnel and the campus community alike. Security personnel are available 24 hours a day, seven days a week. Upon request, security also offers a personal escort to and from any campus location. Cars are permitted for all students, and registered vehicles may park on campus at no charge.

Location

Saint Martin's College is located in Lacey, Washington, just minutes from the state capital of Olympia (population 37,000). The 380-acre wooded campus provides a peaceful and contemplative environment for students to focus on academic endeavors and career preparation.

Though the serenity of the campus would leave one to believe otherwise, it is easily accessible from I-5. Commercial train and bus stops are only 10 minutes away, and the SeaTac International Airport is only a 45-minute drive away.

Opportunities for outdoor activities are ample. The Pacific Ocean waters of Puget Sound are only a 15-minute drive from campus. The Cascade Mountain Range is 1 hour to the east, and the Olympics are 1 hour to the west. Students can enjoy beachcombing, mountain biking, camping, rock climbing, fishing, hiking, kayaking, mountain climbing, and snow and water skiing, all within an hour's drive of campus.

The nearby downtown Olympia area provides an eclectic mix of coffee shops, restaurants, gift shops, theaters, and entertainment. People-watching opportunities abound, especially in the spring months at the local Farmer's Market.

Majors and Degrees

Saint Martin's College offers Bachelor of Arts and Bachelor of Science degrees in the following academic majors: accounting, biology, business administration (with areas of concentration in accounting, economics, finance, information systems management, management, and marketing), chemistry, civil engineering, community service, computer science, criminal justice, elementary education, English, history, humanities, mathematics, mechanical engineering, music, political science, psychology, religious studies, secondary education, social sciences, sociology and cultural anthropology, special education, and theater arts. Preprofessional programs are offered in dentistry, law, medicine, pharmacy, and physical therapy.

Academic Program

The academic program at Saint Martin's College is founded upon the belief that all academic preparation and professional development benefit from a grounding in the liberal arts. The curriculum allows double majors, independent studies, special-topic courses, practica, and internships designed to meet special student interests.

The College operates on a semester academic calendar, with fall semester beginning late in August and continuing through mid-December. Spring semester begins in mid-January and continues through mid-May. Three summer sessions are offered between mid-May and early August.

Academic Facilities

Saint Martin's College has completed a library fund-raising campaign of $10 million. Groundbreaking was held in September 1999, and projected building dedication is scheduled for January 2001. Current holdings are supplemented by online automation for interlibrary loan.

The Saint Martin's Computer Resource Center is available for use by all students. Both Macintosh and IBM-compatible computers are available for use. Internet access and e-mail are provided at no charge to students.

Costs

Tuition and fees for 2000–01 are $14,750. Room and board costs (based upon double occupancy) are $4768 annually. Travel and personal expenses vary. Books and supplies are estimated at $618 per year.

Financial Aid

Saint Martin's College recognizes that financing a college education is an important factor in selecting a college. The selection of a particular college is also dependent upon the quality of education available for the tuition dollar. Saint Martin's has one of the lowest tuition costs of any independent college in the state of Washington. In 1999–2000, the College distributed $12.2 million in financial aid, of which $2.1 million were institutional funds.

Saint Martin's College participates fully in all federal and state programs, including work-study, loan, and grant programs. Institutional scholarships and grants are awarded for academic achievement, community service, athletic participation, and demonstrated leadership. Some of the more distinctive scholarship programs at Saint Martin's are the Saint Benedict Award ($1000 to $4000), for students who have demonstrated involvement in community service and volunteer work; Returning Reward ($1000 to $4000), which encourages student retention by providing a "forgivable" loan during a student's freshman and sophomore years that is forgiven upon graduation from Saint Martin's; and a Valedictorian Scholarship (separate application required), which covers full tuition costs for four years. Academic scholarships range from $2000 to $6000 for freshmen (based upon grade point average and SAT I or ACT scores) and $1500 to $3000 for transfer students (based upon college or university grade point average). Athletic talent awards range between $500 and full tuition and are determined by recommendations from Saint Martin's coaching staff.

Students applying for financial aid should complete the Free Application for Federal Student Aid (FAFSA). Students must be accepted by Saint Martin's before a financial award can be processed. No separate application is required for institutional financial aid. Students are encouraged to mail the FAFSA by February 15 in order to meet the priority deadline of March 1.

Faculty

Saint Martin's College has 55 full-time and 13 part-time faculty members. Sixty-seven percent hold a Ph.D. or the terminal degree in their fields. All classes and lab sessions are taught by faculty members; graduate assistants do not teach classes. Faculty members are selected for their ability to teach, and classes are kept small so professors can know students not only by name but by personal interest, academic ability, and individual potential. SMC maintains a 12:1 student-faculty ratio. Class size ranges between 4 and 47, with an average of 15 to 25.

Student Government

The Associated Students of Saint Martin's College (ASSMC) sponsors campuswide programming events and serves as a liaison between students and the administration. The ASSMC includes the executive council, student senate, and club representatives. The ASSMC also supervises club activities and allocates student activity fees.

Admission Requirements

Saint Martin's College seeks to admit students who are comfortable with academic rigor, anticipate academic success, and look to become active members of the campus community. While admission to Saint Martin's is based primarily upon demonstrated academic ability, ACT or SAT I test scores and a personal essay are also required for consideration. A strong academic background including 4 years of English, 3 years of math, 2 years of science, and 2 years of social studies is preferred. Two years of foreign language is recommended. Extracurricular activities, leadership positions, and community involvement are looked upon favorably.

Freshman applicants should submit a completed Freshman Application for Admission, ACT or SAT I scores, an official high school transcript, and a personal essay. Upon graduation, a final official transcript must be submitted. Running-start students should also submit an official college transcript.

Transfer applicants should submit a completed Transfer Application for Admission, official transcripts from all colleges attended, and a personal essay.

Application and Information

Applications are accepted on a rolling basis, with priority deadlines of March 1 for the fall semester and November 1 for the spring semester. All students are encouraged to apply early, and high school seniors should aim to have applications submitted by late November. Students can expect to be notified within one week of the receipt of their completed application.

Additional information or application materials may be obtained by contacting:

Office of Admissions
Saint Martin's College
5300 Pacific Avenue, SE
Lacey, Washington 98503-1297
Telephone: 360-438-4311
          800-368-8803 (toll-free)
Fax: 360-459-4124
E-mail: admissions@stmartin.edu
World Wide Web: http://www.stmartin.edu

Old Main at Saint Martin's College houses classrooms and administrative offices.

SAINT MARY-OF-THE-WOODS COLLEGE
SAINT MARY-OF-THE-WOODS, INDIANA

The College

Saint Mary-of-the-Woods College is the nation's oldest Catholic liberal arts college for women. The College offers the rich and diverse traditions of academic excellence and dedication to educating women personally and professionally. It also offers an excellent international network of alumnae for career and community networking. Enrollment in the College's resident, commuter, and distance-learning (WED) programs is about 1,200.

Through an exceptional educational plan, Saint Mary-of-the-Woods College combines the liberal arts philosophy with important interrelated elements, so as to teach not only how to earn a living but also how to live. Critical thinking, strong communication skills, problem-solving skills, self-awareness, and an understanding of the world are emphasized. Integration of all these elements enables The Woods graduate to approach challenges from a multiple perspective—aesthetically, philosophically, scientifically, and spiritually.

The 67-acre wooded campus provides a lush rural setting for the Italian Renaissance buildings, with their formal gardens and expansive lawns, as well as ample space for cycling, jogging, and other outdoor activities. The campus has a fitness trail, a gymnasium, an indoor swimming pool, and a lake. Adjacent to the campus is the 200-acre complex of buildings owned by the Sisters of Providence.

Saint Mary-of-the-Woods College is accredited by the North Central Association of Colleges and Schools and is approved for teacher training by the Indiana Department of Education. Programs in various departments are certified. The College is a member of the Women's College Coalition, the National Small College Athletic Association, and the Council for Advancement and Support of Education.

In addition to its undergraduate degree programs, the College offers Master of Arts degree programs in art therapy, earth literacy, music therapy, and pastoral theology.

Location

Saint Mary-of-the-Woods College is located in west-central Indiana, 4 miles northwest of Terre Haute. The campus is convenient to other large metropolitan areas as well—Chicago is 190 miles north, St. Louis is 160 miles west, Cincinnati is 175 miles southeast, and Indianapolis is 72 miles east.

Majors and Degrees

Saint Mary-of-the-Woods College awards undergraduates Bachelor of Arts and Bachelor of Science degrees and Associate in Arts and Associate in Science degrees, as well as several certifications. Majors are available in accounting, accounting information systems, art, art education, art therapy, biology, business administration, computer information systems, digital media communications, education (early childhood [prekindergarten], kindergarten–primary [K–3], elementary [1–6, 7–8], and all grades [K–12] with special education, music, and visual arts), English, equine studies, French, general business, gerontology, history, humanities, human services, intercultural studies, journalism, management, marketing, mathematics, medical technology, music, music education, music therapy, paralegal studies, preprofessional studies, professional writing, psychology, social science, Spanish, and theology. Minors without majors include chemistry, creative writing, environmental sciences, philosophy, political science, public relations/advertising, sociology, speech communication and theater for secondary education, and theater. Occasionally, the College allows students to design their own major.

Academic Program

The College's traditional, on-campus undergraduates follow a general education core curriculum combined with work in the major. Professional experiences, leadership opportunities, and a comprehensive advising program are additional features, and spiritual and personal integrity are emphasized. Through a consortium agreement with neighboring colleges, students have the opportunity to broaden their classroom experience or focus on a specific aspect of their major by taking classes at Indiana State University or Rose-Hulman Institute of Technology. The College operates on a two-semester schedule.

The Woods offers a prelaw program, and predentistry, premedicine, and pre–veterinary science are available through the science preprofessional major.

Always a pioneer in the education of women, the College has a Women's External Degree Program that allows a student to pursue a fully accredited college degree through a guided, independent study format. Students receive Bachelor of Arts and Bachelor of Science degrees in twenty-eight majors and Associate in Arts and Associate in Science degrees in five majors. After the required two days of residency on campus, students work one-on-one with faculty members and develop their own course of study during daylong on-campus seminars each semester. The program offers flexible scheduling and financial aid.

Through the Career Development Center, students have access to a computer-based system designed to help them explore career options. An internship program allows them to receive valuable on-the-job experience in local businesses and professional institutions.

A distinctive program on campus is the Mari Hulman George School of Equine Studies. The emphasis is on equine science and management. The program prepares individuals for careers in equine-related science and medicine, stable management, horse-farm ownership, and writing for horse-industry publications.

Academic Facilities

The buildings that house the College's classrooms, dormitories, dining halls, music hall, and auxiliary buildings all have a distinctive beauty and history. The Cecilian Auditorium in the Conservatory of Music was built in 1913, as was Guerin Hall, which houses the office of the president and other administrative offices. Le Fer Hall, the main dormitory for resident students, was built in 1921.

The library, built in 1965, currently holds a collection of more than 150,000 volumes, and computer terminals link it to a centralized database and to the catalog listings at nearby Indiana State University and Rose-Hulman Institute of Technology. The Science Hall, built in 1969, is a modern building with classrooms, laboratories, art studios, and the student art gallery.

The Woods Day Care Center is one of only 700 on-site day-care facilities in the entire country. It provides child care and preschool activities for the children of faculty members and students and practical experience for psychology and education majors. The single-parent program is offered for women with young children.

Costs

Annual tuition and fees for Saint Mary-of-the-Woods College are $14,880 in 2000–01. Room and board are $5540. Books cost approximately $400 per semester.

Financial Aid

Saint Mary-of-the-Woods College supports a financial aid program to assist students with scholarships, grants, loans, and employment. It is the general policy to award financial assistance first of all in response to financial need but also in recognition of superior academic ability and artistic talent. Financial need is determined through the Free Application for Federal Student Aid (FAFSA). Approximately 90 percent of The Woods' students receive some type of financial aid.

Faculty

The College has more than 55 full- and part-time faculty members, whose duties are to teach, to do research, and to publish. One obvious advantage to a college the size of Saint Mary-of-the-Woods is the favorable ratio of faculty members to students. The small classes reflect the overall student-faculty ratio of 12:1. The attentive and knowledgeable faculty members do much to enhance student activities and to make College traditions meaningful.

Student Government

The primary forum on campus for student concerns and activities is the Student Senate. The senate acts as a liaison between the student body and the College Council by preparing and presenting legislation.

Admission Requirements

Students seeking admission to Saint Mary-of-the-Woods College should provide evidence of a broad range of academic abilities. The average test scores for entering first-year students are 22 on the ACT and 980 on the SAT; their cumulative grade point average is typically about 3.2. The Woods encourages a college-preparatory curriculum in high school and requires 4 years of English, 3 years of math (algebra I and II and geometry), 3 years of laboratory science, 3 years of social studies, and 2 years of a foreign language. For regular admission, students must have at least 750 on the SAT I or 15 on the ACT as well as a 2.0 or higher high school GPA.

Application and Information

Applications should be sent to the Office of Admission, accompanied by a nonrefundable $30 application fee, the high school transcript, SAT I or ACT scores, and a letter of recommendation. Transfer students must send transcripts from all colleges and universities attended.

Applications are accepted on a rolling admission basis. Once all materials are received, decisions are announced and the student receives a formal letter of acceptance.

For further information, students are encouraged to contact:

Office of Admission
Saint Mary-of-the-Woods College
Saint Mary-of-the-Woods, Indiana 47876
Telephone: 812-535-5106
        800-926-SMWC (toll-free)
E-mail: smwcadm@smwc.edu
World Wide Web: http://www.smwc.edu

Woods students enjoy classes and campus life in the lush setting.

SAINT MARY'S COLLEGE
NOTRE DAME, INDIANA

The College

One of the oldest Catholic colleges for women in the United States, Saint Mary's College was founded and continues to be sponsored by the Sisters of the Holy Cross in 1844. The College has long been recognized as a pioneer in exploring with integrity and imagination the roles of women in society. Today, Saint Mary's enjoys a national reputation for academic excellence and vitality of campus life.

With more than 1,500 students from fifty-one states and territories and thirteen countries, Saint Mary's brings together women from a wide range of geographical areas, social backgrounds, and educational experiences. International and minority students comprise 8 percent of the student body.

Saint Mary's College's liberal arts emphasis enhances a comprehensive curriculum. Strong programs in the humanities and sciences are complemented by professional programs in business administration, education, nursing, and social work; majors in the fine and performing arts; and courses of preprofessional study that prepare students for law school, medical school, or advanced study in other health professions.

Small classes (median size: 16) and a low student-faculty ratio (12:1) encourage student participation in class discussions, collaboration with faculty members, and preparation for real-world challenges. The College enjoys a unique exchange program with the University of Notre Dame.

Approximately 80 percent of Saint Mary's students live on campus in four residence halls, each with its own distinctive character. Upperclass students may live off-campus. Residence halls offer a full calendar of activities, from twice-yearly dances to discussions with professors. The College has a college center, a dining hall, and a clubhouse for extracurricular activities. Most residence halls have chapels, and the Church of Loretto is on campus.

As an NCAA Division III school and a member of the Michigan Intercollegiate Athletic Association, Saint Mary's sponsors varsity teams in basketball, cross-country, golf, soccer, softball, swimming and diving, tennis, track and field, and volleyball. Club sports, cosponsored with Notre Dame, include equestrian, gymnastics, sailing, skiing, and synchronized swimming. In addition, Saint Mary's offers many intramural sports.

The College's Angela Athletic Facility contains multipurpose courts for tennis, volleyball, and basketball; a training and fitness center; and racquetball courts. The campus has an indoor swimming pool, outdoor tennis courts, athletic fields, a track, and a driving range for golf.

Location

Saint Mary's 275-acre campus, set alongside the Saint Joseph River, has great natural beauty. However, the College, located just across the street from the University of Notre Dame, just north of the city of South Bend, and just 90 miles from Chicago, is at the hub of much activity. Students from Saint Mary's and Notre Dame form a dynamic intercollegiate community. South Bend provides sites for internships and practicums and opportunities for volunteer service.

Majors and Degrees

Saint Mary's College offers programs leading to the Bachelor of Arts, Bachelor of Science, Bachelor of Fine Arts, Bachelor of Business Administration, and Bachelor of Music degrees.

For a Bachelor of Arts degree, students may choose majors in art, biology, chemistry, communication, economics, elementary education, English literature, English writing, French, history, humanistic studies, mathematics, music, philosophy, political science, psychology, religious studies, social work, sociology, Spanish, statistics and actuarial mathematics, and theater.

A Bachelor of Science degree may be obtained in biology, chemistry, computational mathematics, cytotechnology, mathematics, medical technology, nursing, and statistics and actuarial mathematics.

The Bachelor of Music degree program, which is a member of the National Association of Schools of Music, offers concentrations in applied music and music education. For talented art students, Saint Mary's offers a Bachelor of Fine Arts degree.

The Bachelor of Business Administration degree program offers a major in business administration (with concentrations in accounting, finance, international business, management, and marketing) and a major in management information systems.

Superior students who are candidates for either a Bachelor of Arts or a Bachelor of Science degree may design a program of study outside of the traditional department structure.

For women interested in engineering fields, a five-year dual-degree program offered in cooperation with the University of Notre Dame leads to a bachelor's degree from Saint Mary's College and a Bachelor of Science in Engineering degree from Notre Dame.

Saint Mary's education department, accredited by the National Council for Accreditation of Teacher Education, offers certification in elementary and secondary education.

In addition, the College offers a large number of minors in a variety of fields, including American studies, information science, justice studies, Latin American studies, urban studies, and women's studies.

Academic Program

Graduation from Saint Mary's College requires successful completion of at least 128 semester hours of credit with a minimum quality point average of 2.0. Every student must also complete a comprehensive examination in her major, which may take the form of a thesis, a research or creative project, or a written or oral examination, depending on the discipline. All students must demonstrate writing proficiency by satisfactorily completing a writing-intensive "W" course, usually in the first year, and an advanced portfolio of writings in the major discipline, usually as seniors.

Students spend approximately one third of their time in general education courses in humanities, fine arts, foreign language, natural and social sciences, theology, and philosophy. Remaining course hours are devoted to their major and electives or minors. The College assists those students interested in pursuing independent study or research and internships.

Off-Campus Arrangements

Through Saint Mary's international study programs, students can study with Irish students at the National University of Ireland Maynooth, just outside Dublin. They can absorb Italian art and culture on Saint Mary's campus in the center of Rome, or experience Southeast Asia and the Far East with the India-based Semester Around the World Program.

Students can spend a month during the summer based in London, earning credit hours while also traveling to several other European countries.

Saint Mary's students may also enroll in Spanish language programs of the Center for Cross-Cultural Study in Seville, Spain.

Through a cooperative program with the University of Notre Dame, Saint Mary's students may study in Australia, Austria, France, Japan, Mexico, and Toledo, Spain, as well as Jerusalem.

A student majoring in political science has the opportunity to spend a semester at the American University in Washington, D.C. Saint Mary's also participates in student and faculty member exchange programs with the University of Notre Dame and members of the Northern Indiana Consortium for Education.

Academic Facilities

Students have abundant access to computers, the campus network, and the World Wide Web. Residence halls and classrooms are wired for network access. Computer labs for students are located in several campus buildings, and an expanding set of services and support is available. Many faculty members make use of information technology for teaching and research.

The modern Cushwa-Leighton Library houses a fine collection of 201,000 volumes and subscribes to 758 periodicals. It includes offices, study areas, an after-hours study lounge, a media center, computer facilities, the College archives, and a rare book room.

In addition to extensive biology, chemistry, and physics lab facilities, laboratories for psychology research and for foreign language study and practice are available to students. Art studios, music practice rooms, the O'Laughlin Auditorium, and Moreau's Little Theatre provide ample space for arts creation, practice, and performance.

The professionally staffed Early Childhood Development Center on campus provides education and psychology majors with an unusual opportunity to work with young children. Other facilities include the Madeleva classroom building, Science Hall, Havican nursing facility, and Moreau Art Galleries.

Costs

The approximate expenses for the 1999–2000 academic year were tuition and fees, $17,240; room and board, $5962 (double occupancy); and miscellaneous expenses (books, transportation, and living costs), $2225.

Financial Aid

The College strives to make a Saint Mary's education available for every student by offering eligible students financial aid packages that may include grants, scholarships, work-study, and loans. Competitive scholarships, awarded solely on merit, as well as those determined by a combination of financial need and academic achievement are available. Last year, nearly 76 percent of Saint Mary's students received more than $16.8 million in financial assistance, $6.6 million from the College alone.

All applicants for financial assistance must complete the Financial Aid PROFILE and the Free Application for Federal Student Aid (FAFSA) each year that they desire assistance. Applications for assistance must be received at the processing center by March 1 to be given priority consideration. Decisions concerning financial aid are made as soon as possible after a student has been accepted.

Faculty

Saint Mary's has 127 full-time and 68 part-time faculty members. About 97 percent of the faculty members hold earned doctorates or other terminal degrees; of these, most teach freshmen as well as upper-division students. Faculty members work with students in all phases of college life, including academic counseling.

Student Government

Students are active at every level of campus governance and share in community decision making. There are voting representatives on the president's two highest advisory boards, the Student Affairs Council and the Academic Affairs Council. A student is a voting member of the College Board of Trustees. Student government sponsors many extracurricular and cocurricular activities.

Admission Requirements

Applicants for admission to Saint Mary's College should be graduates of an accredited high school and should ordinarily have completed a four-year program of 16 or more academic units. They must include 4 units of English, 3 units of college-preparatory mathematics, 2 units of one foreign language, 2 units of social science, and 2 units of laboratory science. The remaining units should be in college-preparatory courses. An applicant's credentials should include an academic transcript showing current rank and senior-year subjects, a counselor/administrator recommendation, SAT I or ACT scores, and an essay.

Home-schooled students are encouraged to apply for admission and should contact the Admission Office for details.

An interview with an admission officer is recommended. Saint Mary's encourages students to visit the campus. The Admission Office can make arrangements for students who wish to attend classes or stay overnight.

Superior students who have studied for advanced placement may begin sophomore-level courses in their freshman year. Mature, well-qualified students who wish to enter college after three years of high school may apply for early admission. Saint Mary's College also grants deferred admission upon request to candidates who are accepted in the normal competition.

Application and Information

Saint Mary's has two application and notification programs: early decision and modified rolling admission. Highly qualified students who have selected Saint Mary's as their first choice for admission may apply under the early decision program. The application deadline is November 15, and the notification date is December 15. Students who apply for regular admission and whose application files are complete on or before December 1 are notified of the admission decision in mid-January. Candidates are encouraged to apply by the end of their junior year of high school or in the fall of their senior year. Applications are accepted, however, as long as space is available.

Interested students are encouraged to contact:

Director of Admission
Saint Mary's College
Notre Dame, Indiana 46556-5001
Telephone: 219-284-4587
Fax: 219-284-4841
E-mail: admission@saintmarys.edu
World Wide Web: http://www.saintmarys.edu

SAINT MARY'S COLLEGE
ORCHARD LAKE, MICHIGAN

The College
Founded in 1885, Saint Mary's College is in its second century of service to higher education. Saint Mary's College is a member of the Orchard Lake Schools, which were founded by Polish immigrants to educate native clergy sensitive to their particular ethnic concerns. From these beginnings, Saint Mary's College has evolved into a modern, coeducational, liberal arts college dedicated to the ideals of integrating a liberal arts education with Catholic faith and educating men and women for service to society and the Church.

The College today is a community of 396 students and 50 faculty members learning and growing together. Small classes and individualized instruction contribute to an educational environment that produces successful students and graduates who will be responsible citizens and leaders. Saint Mary's College is accredited by the North Central Association of Colleges and Schools.

The 120-acre lakeside campus is beautifully landscaped and shaded and includes eighteen contemporary buildings. Residence halls offer single or double rooms.

The Orchard Lake campus provides a broad range of extracurricular activities and organizations for student life, including dramatic theater and a student newspaper; fraternities and sororities; intramural programs; and intercollegiate sports, including men's baseball, basketball, and soccer and women's soccer.

Location
Saint Mary's College is located in Orchard Lake, Michigan, a suburb situated in the beautiful Bloomfield Hills region, approximately 20 miles northwest of Detroit. The College enjoys easy access to Detroit Metropolitan Airport, which is served by all major airlines. The College is also located near suburban shopping centers, theaters, and communities offering concerts and a variety of cultural events.

Majors and Degrees
Saint Mary's College offers the Bachelor of Arts degree in business administration, communication arts, community service/public administration, English, organizational management, philosophy, Polish studies, psychology, sociology, and theology.

Bachelor of Science degrees are offered in biology, chemistry, computer information science, environmental science, and radiologic technology.

Additional offerings include teacher education and preprofessional programs in law and medicine.

Academic Program
Saint Mary's is committed to providing a strong liberal arts curriculum integrated with career preparation. A total of 120 credit hours is required for graduation. The core curriculum includes 60 credit hours of general education courses in the humanities, natural sciences, and social sciences. To complete the degree requirements, the student selects at least one major of at least 36 credit hours plus a minor of 18 to 24 credit hours.

The College operates on the semester system with two sessions per year plus an optional spring term. The fall term runs from early September through December, the winter term from January through mid-May, and the spring term from May through July.

Off-Campus Arrangements
Saint Mary's College students can take advantage of the College's membership in the Detroit Area Consortium of Catholic Colleges to take elective or specialized courses. The consortium includes Madonna University, Marygrove College, Sacred Heart Major Seminary, and the University of Detroit Mercy.

Academic Facilities
Saint Mary's Alumni Memorial Library houses 70,000 volumes with access provided to consortium libraries. The library receives more than 400 periodicals and newspapers and houses specialized holdings in theology, philosophy, and Polish language and culture, in addition to well-developed holdings in sociology, psychology, literature, history, and political science. Of unusual interest is the library's Polish language collection, one of the largest in the United States at more than 8,000 volumes. Saint Mary's also maintains a Learning Resource Center and a computer laboratory open to students.

In cooperation with the Pope John Paul II Center located on the Orchard Lake campus, Saint Mary's College participates in the preservation and dissemination of information about the papacy of John Paul II.

Costs
Tuition and fees for the 2000–01 academic year are $7740. Room and board (double occupancy and twenty-one meals per week) are $5000. Cumulative expenses for an academic year, including books, supplies, and incidental needs, are $13,340. A $200 dormitory deposit is required before arrival and reserves a student's place in a dormitory.

Financial Aid
Saint Mary's College is committed to assisting students with demonstrated financial need. The College provides generous assistance in the form of grants, scholarships, loans, and employment in conjunction with the federal and state governments and the private sector.

Faculty
At Saint Mary's College, the 19 full-time and 34 part-time faculty members emphasize teaching and individualized attention to students. They serve as academic advisers and mentors, assisting students in selecting their academic programs and planning for careers after graduation. Faculty members also serve as advisers to all student clubs and organizations.

Student Government
The Student Senate is the representative body for Saint Mary's College students. It fosters regular exchanges among students, faculty, and administrators and offers students the opportunity to play a significant role in all aspects of their education. Standing committees of the Student Senate assist student government in carrying out its mission of service, and ad hoc committees cre-

ated to enlist talent for special projects offer all students the opportunity to get involved in many facets of college life.

Admission Requirements

Admission to Saint Mary's College is open to all students who meet the enrollment criteria. Applicants must have graduated from an accredited high school (or must present an equivalent credential) with a minimum 2.5 GPA (on a 4.0 scale). Standardized test scores must also be submitted. Applicants who do not meet these criteria, but demonstrate their potential in other ways, may be considered for admission on a conditional basis.

Students interested in transferring to Saint Mary's from another college must submit an application, along with high school and college transcripts.

Application and Information

Applications for admission should be submitted to the Office of Admissions with a $25 application fee. The College uses a rolling admission system, and students are notified of the admission decision as soon as all application materials have been received and evaluated.

Application forms or additional materials may be requested by contacting:

Office of Admissions
Saint Mary's College
Orchard Lake, Michigan 48324-9908
Telephone: 248-683-1757
World Wide Web: http://www.stmarys-orchardlake.edu

Saint Mary's College campus.

SAINT MARY'S COLLEGE OF CALIFORNIA

MORAGA, CALIFORNIA

The College

Saint Mary's College, now in its second century of providing education in the liberal arts, the sciences, business administration, and economics, is one of the oldest colleges in the West. Founded in San Francisco in 1863, it survived the earthquake in 1906 and moved to the current campus in Moraga in 1928. The Christian Brothers, the largest order of Catholic religious devoted exclusively to teaching, assumed direction and ownership of the College in 1868 and have guided its destiny since.

By design, Saint Mary's has always been a small college. Today, the total undergraduate enrollment stands at about 2,200, and enrollment in the freshman class is limited to approximately 550 to maintain the close contact among the students, faculty, staff, and Christian Brothers that is a hallmark of the institution. Along with academic excellence, this personal feeling both inside the classroom and out is what draws students to Saint Mary's.

Since Saint Mary's is a residential college, there is a very strong on-campus life. The student government, clubs, and dorms sponsor parties, movie and comedy nights, dances, and dinners. There are a variety of clubs on campus, ranging from the Science, English, and Pre-Law clubs to the Black Student Union and MEChA to the Committee of Lectures, Arts, and Music to College Republicans and Young Democrats to Students for Peace and Justice to the Chess Club to the Women's Issues Group. Students may also participate in campus ministry; singing groups; *The Collegian,* the campus fortnightly newspaper; and KSMC, the campus radio station. Intercollegiate athletic teams include men's and women's basketball, cross-country, soccer, and tennis; men's baseball, football, and golf; and women's crew, lacrosse, softball, and volleyball. All teams compete at the NCAA Division I level. Club sports are available in men's and women's lacrosse and men's ice hockey, rugby, volleyball, and water polo.

Saint Mary's College is a member of the West Coast Conference (WCC), a Division I National Collegiate Athletic Association (NCAA) conference. In addition to intercollegiate sports, there are numerous intramural leagues for both men and women in the following sports: basketball, flag football, indoor soccer, softball, Ultimate Frisbee, volleyball, and others as announced during the academic year.

The red tile roofs and white stucco walls of the Spanish architectural style of the College's buildings blend with the rolling green hills to create a campus of almost indescribable beauty. The 420-acre campus, only 50 acres of which are covered by buildings, provides both the quiet necessary for academic pursuits and the space for athletics or hiking in the hills. More than half of the students live on campus in residence halls or town houses (apartment-type housing). There are also many off-campus housing facilities available in the nearby suburban communities of Orinda, Moraga, and Lafayette.

Location

Nestled in the rolling hills of the Moraga Valley, 20 miles east of San Francisco, the Saint Mary's campus has the dual benefits of a pastoral setting and proximity to a major metropolitan center. San Francisco and its rich cultural and social offerings are a half hour away by car or easily accessible by public transportation.

Majors and Degrees

The School of Liberal Arts at Saint Mary's College offers the Bachelor of Arts degree in the following departmental areas: anthropology; art; classical languages; communication; economics; English and drama; French; health, physical education, and recreation; history; integral program (Great Books); international area studies; liberal and civic studies; mathematics; performing arts; philosophy; politics; religious studies; sociology; and Spanish. Interdisciplinary majors are also available, as are alternative-plan majors in American studies, cross-cultural studies, European studies, and Latin American studies. Bachelor of Science degrees are offered in biology, chemistry, computer science, mathematics, nursing, physics, and psychology through the following departmental areas: biology, chemistry, engineering (a 3+2 cooperative program with the University of Southern California, Boston University, and Washington University in St. Louis, Missouri), health science, mathematics/computer science, nursing (a cooperative program with Samuel Merritt College in Oakland), physics, preprofessional curricula (dentistry, medicine, occupational therapy, pharmacy, and physical therapy), and psychology.

The School of Economics and Business Administration offers the Bachelor of Science in accounting, business administration, and economics. An honors program in financial management is also available.

Academic Program

Saint Mary's College attempts to provide for both the academic and career needs of its students in all programs as far as that is compatible with the spirit of the liberal arts. Its goal is that most difficult liberation—liberation of mind. The favorable student-faculty ratio of 14:1 is conducive to the kind of dialogue necessary for intellectual, spiritual, and social growth among all members of the academic community.

The College's 4-1-4 calendar provides a framework for this faculty member-student interaction. During the fall and spring terms, students attend required seminars on the great books of the Western world and complete the specific core of study required by each of the major programs. Courses for the January Term vary from year to year and reflect the diversity of the Saint Mary's faculty. Besides providing an opportunity for students to focus all their energy on a single subject during one month, the January Term offers them the possibility of participating in various experimental courses, off-campus field study, travel courses in other countries, and special independent study projects.

To earn the bachelor's degree, students are required to complete at least thirty-six courses. Students must complete successfully both the general College requirements and the requirements of their major program.

Off-Campus Arrangements

Saint Mary's students are able to participate in study-abroad programs in Argentina, Australia, Belgium, China, England, France, Germany, Greece, Ireland, Italy, Mexico, Peru, Scotland, South Africa, and Spain. Internships in Sacramento and Washington, D.C., are available for government majors. Students who wish to spend part or all of their junior year away from campus are able to receive academic credit directly from

Saint Mary's College and to retain California State Grants. In addition, the College regularly conducts travel courses during the January Term.

Academic Facilities

Saint Albert Hall Library contains more than 190,000 volumes, receives 1,110 current periodical titles, and stocks newspapers, pamphlets, recordings, and audiovisual and microform materials. A new 60,000-square-foot state-of-the-art science center is currently under construction. The J. C. Gatehouse building is scheduled to open in fall 2000. The chemistry and physics collection is housed in Galileo Hall. Ferroggiaro Center houses LeFevre Theatre, the home of Saint Mary's drama and musical productions, which have been acclaimed throughout Contra Costa County and the greater Bay Area. The Hearst Art Gallery organizes four art exhibitions during each academic year. The shows cover a broad range of the visual arts, including painting, sculpture, crafts, graphics, and film. The gallery also maintains all of the College's extensive art collection, which is displayed in various places around the campus and occasionally highlighted in the gallery.

Costs

Tuition for full-time study for 2000–01 (including the January Term) is $18,120. Room and board (nineteen meals per week) are $7555. Required fees are $118. Town-house apartments with full living and kitchen facilities are available at $4500 per year.

Financial Aid

Seventy-one percent of the undergraduates at Saint Mary's College receive significant financial aid from a variety of sources. To apply for aid, applicants must file the Free Application for Federal Student Aid (FAFSA), which is distributed to high schools and colleges by the College Scholarship Service. Applicants who are residents of California and wish to apply for Cal Grants A and/or B must fill out the G.P.A. Verification Form in conjunction with the FAFSA. The financial aid deadline is March 2. Federal Pell Grants, Federal Supplemental Educational Opportunity Grants, Federal Perkins Loans, and Federal Stafford Student Loans are often part of an applicant's financial aid package.

Faculty

The undergraduate faculty at Saint Mary's consists of 153 full-time and 92 part-time members. Ninety-one percent hold Ph.D. degrees; but, regardless of the degree or professional status, the primary emphasis of the faculty is teaching. Department chairpersons and senior faculty members teach at least one freshman seminar or introductory major course each term. The Christian Brothers constitute one fifth of the faculty; the others are lay men and women. The student-faculty ratio is 14:1.

Student Government

The Associated Students of Saint Mary's College (ASSMC) is the governing body for all undergraduate students. The ASSMC president is an ad hoc member of the board of trustees, and the body as a whole administers significant funds to thirty-two clubs and organizations.

Admission Requirements

The chief qualities sought in a candidate for undergraduate admission are intellectual aptitude (as demonstrated by at least 16 units of college-preparatory courses completed with a minimum B average), seriousness of purpose, and moral integrity. The secondary school record is considered the most reliable measure of potential college ability. Scores on the SAT I of the College Board or on American College Testing's ACT and extracurricular accomplishments may strengthen an application insofar as they indicate special talents, maturity, and perseverance.

Application and Information

Applications must include SAT I or ACT scores, a completed secondary school recommendation form, and all academic transcripts. Applicants whose files are complete by November 30 receive early notification of the admission decision. The deadline for all other freshman applicants is February 1. The deadline for transfer applicants is July 1. Admission decisions for such applicants are made on a rolling admission basis, and students are notified of the admission decision as soon as all of their materials have been received and evaluated. Transfer students may apply for fall-term admission until July 1.

For additional information, a catalog, or an application form, students should contact:

Dorothy K. Benjamin
Director of Admissions
Saint Mary's College of California
P.O. Box 4800
Moraga, California 94575-4800
Telephone: 925-631-4224
Fax: 925-376-7193
E-mail: smcadmit@stmarys-ca.edu
World Wide Web: http://www.stmarys-ca.edu

The chapel of Saint Mary's College stands at the center of the 420-acre Moraga Valley campus.

ST. MARY'S COLLEGE OF MARYLAND
ST. MARY'S CITY, MARYLAND

The College

St. Mary's is a public, state-supported, coeducational college dedicated to providing an excellent liberal arts education. There are 644 men and 846 women enrolled full-time, and 1,082 of these students live on campus. Part-time enrollment is 177 students. St. Mary's combines the educational and personal advantages of a small private college with the affordability of a public institution. Active learning and the development of critical thinking are encouraged in the discussion-oriented format made possible by modest class size. Student leadership in academic, cultural, and social spheres is aided by the community atmosphere; opportunities are greater than at larger schools, and involvement is easier.

The College recently received a sizable building grant, which was used for the construction of town house–style residence halls, the renovation of existing dorms, and the construction of a library. A new science building was recently completed. The renovation of the campus center, Charles Hall, was completed in March 2000, and the expansion of the athletic facilities is about to begin.

The campus covers 275 acres, including riverfront, open space, and woodland. Among the waterfront facilities are a boat house, ocean kayaks, sailboards, and a fleet of sailboats. Other facilities include an Olympic-size indoor pool, lighted tennis courts, and an outdoor track. The College's teams compete in NCAA Division III. Varsity sports for men are baseball, basketball, lacrosse, sailing, soccer, swimming, and tennis; for women, basketball, field hockey, lacrosse, sailing, soccer, swimming, tennis, and volleyball.

The College is accredited by the Middle States Association of Colleges and Schools and the National Association of Schools of Music.

Location

St. Mary's College of Maryland is situated in one of the most beautiful settings in the United States. It is tidewater country, still inhabited by people who make their living from the land and water. Rivermen take oysters and crabs from the Potomac and Patuxent rivers and the Chesapeake Bay; wild swans, ducks, and Canada geese winter in the creeks of St. Mary's County. The Patuxent River Naval Air Station, the county's largest employer, is a naval aircraft testing site, attracting many firms that supply technical support to the Navy and sponsor internships. It is an environment that is alive, providing fresh air and space. It is also convenient to the nation's capital, just 68 miles away.

Majors and Degrees

St. Mary's College offers the Bachelor of Arts degree in anthropology/sociology, art, biology, chemistry, computer science, dramatic arts, economics, English, foreign languages (French, German, and Spanish), history, human studies, mathematics, music, natural science, philosophy, physics, political science, psychology, public policy, religious studies, and student-designed majors. Also available are elementary and secondary teacher education programs leading to certification in Maryland. Preprofessional sequences in dentistry, law, medicine, and veterinary medicine are available.

Academic Program

The course of study at the College provides both diversity and depth, leading to a broad understanding of the liberal arts and a specific competence in at least one major field. All students must complete requirements for one of the majors cited above and the general education requirements. The general education requirements are designed to develop skills in communication and analysis, acquaint students with the heritage of Western civilization, confront students with the forces and insights that are shaping the modern world, and promote the capacity for integration and synthesis of knowledge.

History students can take advantage of the College's location on the site of colonial St. Mary's City, Maryland's first state capital. Many experts consider this area to contain the most abundant and earliest undisturbed artifacts of any American seventeenth-century town.

St. Mary's College offers several courses in aquatic biology as an option within the major program in biology. The College's location on the St. Mary's River, a tributary of the Potomac near the mouth of the Chesapeake Bay, is ideal for the study of estuarine ecology.

A strong music program provides advanced training in composition and piano performance and the impetus for a jazz ensemble, a percussion ensemble, a choir, a chamber vocal group, and a chamber orchestra for classical performances.

Students may receive credit for high scores on the Advanced Placement Program examinations. Independent study for credit is possible in every major, allowing students to investigate subjects not covered in normal course offerings. Also available is the opportunity for students to design their own majors.

Off-Campus Arrangements

An internship program for academic credit is available for junior- and senior-level students. Students find in these semester-long internships a way to test their career interests. In recent years, St. Mary's interns have worked in state and federal government offices and laboratories, in the news media, in museums and art galleries, in commercial organizations, and in positions abroad. In a number of cases, internships have led either to full-time employment after graduation or to graduate or professional study.

A semester or year of study abroad at the Centre for Medieval and Renaissance Studies at Oxford is available for qualified St. Mary's students. In addition, St. Mary's has an exchange program with Johns Hopkins University and offers qualified students a year's study at Fudan University in Shanghai, China, and at the University of Heidelberg in Germany. St. Mary's also participates in the National Student Exchange Program with other colleges throughout the United States.

Academic Facilities

The College's laboratories are equipped for course work in biology, chemistry, physics, and psychology. There are eight computer laboratories on campus, including 24-hour labs in three of the residence halls. The College provides student accounts that include free e-mail and Internet access as well as access to the most up-to-date word processing and spreadsheet applications from anywhere on campus. St. Mary's also provides

Macintosh laboratories on campus for students who are completing technical art or photography projects. In the foreign language and music computer lab, PCs are equipped with specialized programs and equipment for these two disciplines. The biology and chemistry departments use Hewlett-Packard Kayak workstations, and physics primarily uses Macintosh G3s. All residence hall rooms and town houses are wired with high-speed cable modems that allow students free Internet access and e-mail from their own computers. These modems access the College's server.

The College library, which has a special research collection of early Maryland history, houses communication facilities with audiovisual aids and audio/video recording capability. Interlibrary loan and online database search services provide access to excellent resources at no cost to students. An expansion of the library, doubling its size, was completed in 1989.

The Montgomery Fine Arts Center includes facilities for performance in music and theater. It also contains an art gallery and facilities for the Division of Arts and Letters.

Students have access to a staffed writing clinic, which provides assistance in writing and researching papers.

Costs

Annual costs for 2000–01 include tuition and fees of $7360 for Maryland residents and $12,200 for nonresidents. Residence hall rooms are available for about $3425 per year, and board is provided for a cost ranging between $2700 and $2900 per year. Books and supplies are estimated at $800 per year. Semester charges for tuition, room, board, and other fees are payable at or prior to registration in the fall and in the spring.

Financial Aid

The Office of Financial Aid provides advice and assistance to students in need of financial aid and joins other College offices in awarding scholarships and loans and in offering part-time employment under the work-study program. Several full scholarships are awarded to Maryland residents on a merit basis, and other scholarships, loans, and grants for students are awarded on the basis of ability and need as determined by the federal government's Free Application for Federal Student Aid, which should be filed no later than March 1.

Faculty

Faculty appointments and promotions are made on the basis of commitment to undergraduate teaching, an interest in new approaches to education, and academic and scholarly achievement. The faculty members have experience in a wide range of activities, including government, business, research, environmental studies, civil rights, the theater, musical performance, and writing. In recent years, 14 faculty members have been awarded Fulbright grants for study abroad. Ninety-eight percent of the faculty members hold a doctorate or other terminal degree in their field. A student-faculty ratio of approximately 13:1, the relatively small size of the College, and the informal atmosphere encourage close and personal relationships between students and faculty. Faculty members serve as academic advisers and also provide much informal counseling and individual attention to students' academic and personal development outside of the formal structure.

Student Government

Student government is the center of many activities and sponsors a variety of social and cultural events, including campus movies, speakers, dances, concerts, and excursions to cultural centers such as Washington, D.C. Opportunities exist for students to serve as voting members on various faculty committees.

Admission Requirements

Applicants for freshman admission are urged to apply before January 15. Strong high school preparation usually includes 4 units of English, 3 units of social science (including U.S. history), 3 units of laboratory science (exclusive of ninth-grade general courses in science), 3 units of mathematics, and 2 units of foreign language. Upon entrance, the student should have obtained a high school diploma with a minimum of 20 units or should present evidence of equivalent achievement (e.g., a passing score on the high school equivalency examination administered by the student's state department of education). The applicant must present scores on the SAT I and/or the ACT examination, which should be taken by the fall of the senior year. It may also be in the interest of individuals who know English as a second language to take the TOEFL. St. Mary's College is interested in evidence of talent and mature ability as demonstrated in a variety of ways by each student. Although admission is based primarily on the high school record and standardized test scores, recommendations and the essay on the application are also very important.

Transfer applicants with at least 24 semester hours of credit will be evaluated on the basis of their college transcripts. Students who have earned fewer than 24 semester hours of credit must submit their high school records and SAT I scores.

The College may grant credit toward a degree for satisfactory performance on the College Board's Advanced Placement tests or appropriate CLEP tests, for work completed in correspondence courses or at other two- or four-year colleges, or through DANTES.

St. Mary's College of Maryland does not discriminate for reasons of race, religion, ethnic origin, sex, or marital status in the admission of students. The College is in compliance with federal regulations prohibiting discrimination on the basis of age, conditions of handicap, or status as a veteran. The College complies with Title IX of the Education Amendments of 1972.

Application and Information

An application form, financial aid information, and other materials are available by contacting:

Director of Admission
St. Mary's College of Maryland
18952 East Fisher Road
St. Mary's City, Maryland 20686
Telephone: 301-862-0292
              800-492-7181 (toll-free)
Fax: 301-862-0906
E-mail: admissions@honors.smcm.edu

A waterfront location and a lengthy sailing season provide recreational opportunities at St. Mary's College of Maryland.

Peterson's Guide to Four-Year Colleges 2001   www.petersons.com   **2415**

SAINT MARY'S UNIVERSITY
HALIFAX, NOVA SCOTIA, CANADA

The University

Saint Mary's offers a unique university experience. Graduates describe it best when they talk about the spirit of the Saint Mary's community and school pride, the quality of the programs, and the individual attention received. In national surveys of primarily undergraduate universities in Canada, Saint Mary's has ranked in the top five in the categories of highest quality, leaders of tomorrow, best overall, and most innovative. Saint Mary's University is one of the oldest universities in Canada and is now in one of its most exciting periods in history. The Frank H. Sobey, Faculty of Commerce, the largest and leading business school in Atlantic Canada, offers a Ph.D. program in management. The Sobey Building is a state-of-the-art facility that recently opened and rivals the best instructional facilities in North America. The Faculty of Commerce also offers M.B.A., executive, and professional programs. Graduate programs are offered in applied psychology, astronomy, Atlantic Canada studies, business administration, criminology, history, international development studies, philosophy, and women's studies.

In addition to the leading business school, Saint Mary's has the largest arts faculty in Nova Scotia, with a diverse range of programs and a science faculty with some of the most respected professors who actively engage their students in research projects.

There are more than 7,500 full- and part-time students at Saint Mary's, and more than 1,000 of them live on campus in one of the many different living options. All buildings on campus, including the residences, are connected by pedways or tunnels. There is a cafeteria, coffee shop, grocery minimart, laundromat, and hairdresser on campus.

The Saint Mary's pride comes from several regional and national championships captured by the Huskies' varsity sports programs. All full-time Saint Mary's students receive membership to the Tower, a fully equipped sports, fitness, and recreational facility. There are also a wide variety of student organizations and societies on campus that reflect the diversity of students contributing to the Saint Mary's community.

Location

Saint Mary's is located on one city block in Halifax, Nova Scotia, Atlantic Canada's leading educational, business, and cultural centre. Located on Canada's eastern seaboard, Halifax offers all the convenience and excitement of a big city, with a small-town atmosphere. Halifax is a safe and clean city with all the amenities close to the Saint Mary's campus. Saint Mary's is surrounded by tree-lined streets in Halifax's historic South End and only minutes from downtown shopping areas, banks, restaurants, cinemas, and Point Pleasant Park, a natural forest park on the edge of the ocean. Halifax enjoys four distinct seasons with moderate weather all year round.

Majors and Degrees

The Faculty of Commerce offers majors in accounting, computing and information systems, computing science and business administration, criminology, economics, finance, general business studies, global business management, human resource management and industrial relations, management, marketing, and small business and entrepreneurship. The Faculty of Arts offers programs in anthropology, criminology, economics, English, geography, history, Irish studies, mathematics, modern languages and classics, philosophy, political science, psychology, religious studies, and sociology, as well as interdisciplinary studies in Asian studies, Atlantic Canada studies, Chinese studies, criminology, image studies, international development studies, linguistics, Japanese studies, and women's studies. The Faculty of Science offers programs in astronomy and physics, astrophysics, biology, chemistry, computing science and business administration, engineering, environmental studies, geology, geology/geography, geology/commerce, mathematics and computing science, physics, and psychology. Preprofessional programs are available in architecture, dentistry, law, medicine, occupational therapy, optometry, theology, and veterinary medicine. There are year-round language, cultural, and orientation programs for non-English-speaking students, as well as a certificate program in teaching English as a second language. Co-op education options are available in many programs.

Academic Program

In the Faculty of Arts, Commerce, and Science, the normal course load in an academic session for full-time undergraduates is five courses per semester. Undergraduate students registered in fewer than three courses are considered to be part-time. The academic year consists of fall and winter semesters that are four months in length, in addition to two summer sessions beginning in May and July. Program requirements are specific to the degree and are detailed in the academic calendar or on the University's Web site listed below.

Off-Campus Arrangements

Saint Mary's believes that exposure to other cultures in the national and international communities is an important part of a university education. Saint Mary's has exchange programs in Bermuda, China, France, Great Britain, Japan, Mexico, Norway, Quebec, and the United States. There is also the co-op education option, which provides students with the opportunity to gain hands-on related experience in their academic field by alternating academic course work and work terms.

Academic Facilities

Saint Mary's Patrick Power Library has extensive collections of general books and serials, reference materials, rare books, microforms, annual reports, government documents, and the University archives. The Library belongs to NOVANET, a computerized system that provides access to the collections of eight Nova Scotia universities' libraries and to national and international computer information systems. Saint Mary's students can access a wide range of computing facilities. Each student has free 24-hour access to the Internet and personal e-mail accounts. There are more than 1,000 computer workstations on campus and twelve general access computer labs on the high-speed Ethernet backbone available for many applications, including Internet access. Several departments also have their own labs for specialized applications. Several classrooms have multimedia presentation equipment (overhead projector, VCR, and networked PC). The Sobey Building has 1,000 Internet ports and seven innovative labs. The Internet is in every classroom, multimedia is in twenty-five classrooms, and advanced multimedia is in six classrooms.

Costs

For the 1999–2000 academic year, tuition fees for a full-time course load were approximately $4010 for Canadian citizens and permanent residents and $7650 for non-Canadian students.

Residence costs, including meal plans, ranged from $4090 to $5440 for the academic year. There are various room and meal plan options to choose from. The student association fee was $108.50, and students can expect to spend about $800 on textbooks, course materials, and supplies for the academic year. Medical insurance for the year was $97 for Canadian students and $264 for non-Canadian students.

Financial Aid

Saint Mary's offers more than 850 entrance scholarships each year, valued at between $500 and $3000 to high school students with high academic standing. The Presidential Scholarships, valued at $6000 (renewable for a total of $24,000 over four years) are awarded to high school students. Santamarian Scholarships, valued at $3000, are renewable for a total of $12,000 over four years. Students who are highly ranked in their graduating class are considered. Canadian students who are ranked number one in their graduating class are considered and must provide a resume and letters of recommendation from their school. Class rank, tests, and letters of recommendation are important in the selection of entrance scholarship recipients. Students can apply for a number of scholarships and bursaries. For more information on scholarships available to both Canadian and international students, students should visit the University's Web site.

Faculty

Saint Mary's has the highest number, per capita, of faculty members with Ph.D.'s in Canada. The faculty placed second in the country in receiving the most awards and research grants. There are 370 full- and part-time faculty members. The student-faculty ratio is 19:1. The faculty is a teaching and research faculty, and all teach at both the graduate and undergraduate levels.

Student Government

The Saint Mary's University Student Association (SMUSA) is the official representative organization of the students at Saint Mary's. SMUSA is dedicated to representing the interests of students and fostering an understanding and fellowship among all sectors of the University. SMUSA has voting representation on the University's Senate and Board of Governors.

SMUSA provides many services and activities for students, including a health plan, Huskies Patrol (a drive home service), game rooms, an information desk, Frosh Week, Grad Week, Winter Fest, Charter Day, student handbook, yearbook, the Gorsebrook Lounge, student societies, and more. *The Journal* is the weekly student newspaper, and CFSM is the campus radio station.

Admission Requirements

In order to be considered for admission to Saint Mary's undergraduate programs, students must have completed high school with an average (in five subjects) of 65 percent and no mark below 60 percent. Required subjects include English for all programs and other faculty-specific requirements. Students whose first language is not English and who have not attended an English language secondary school must have successfully completed one of the standardized English language proficiency tests. Students are admitted on the basis of their academic record. An interview is not required. Transcripts and test results must be sent with the application. Qualified students from around the world are admitted each year. The University has streamlined its procedures to permit the transfer of qualified students from other recognized institutions. Detailed information on admission as a mature student (22 years of age or older), transfer student, or graduate student can be found on the University's Web site or by calling the Admissions Office (902-420-5415).

Application and Information

The application deadline for Saint Mary's University for Canadian applicants is July 1 for the September admission and November 1 for the January admission. International applications for September admission must be received by April 1, and for the January admission, August 1. Late applications are considered on an individual basis. Students are notified within two to three weeks after receipt of all required documents (application, transcripts, and appropriate test results). Applications can be found on the University's Web site. University tours can be arranged.

Students with inquiries or a request for application materials should contact:
Director of Admissions
Saint Mary's University
Halifax, Nova Scotia B3H 3C3
Canada
Telephone: 902-420-5415
Fax: 902-496-8100
E-mail: admissions@stmarys.ca
adult.international@stmarys.ca (international e-mail)
World Wide Web: http://www.stmarys.ca

Aerial view of the campus of Saint Mary's University.

SAINT MARY'S UNIVERSITY OF MINNESOTA
WINONA, MINNESOTA

The University

Founded in 1912 by Bishop Patrick Heffron, Saint Mary's University of Minnesota (SMU) was originally an academy and junior college for young men in Minnesota's Diocese of Winona. In 1925, it became a four-year liberal arts college. The De La Salle Christian Brothers, an international Catholic teaching order founded in France by Saint John Baptist de La Salle, purchased Saint Mary's College from the Diocese of Winona in 1933.

Saint Mary's University, as a Lasallian Catholic institution, traces its origins to a priest and educational innovator of seventeenth-century France, Saint John Baptist de La Salle. Born in 1651, de La Salle began a new system of Christian schools in which teachers assist parents in the educational, ethical, and religious formation of their children. To continue his vision, John Baptist de La Salle founded the Institute of the Brothers of the Christian Schools (better known today as the De La Salle Christian Brothers). Today, SMU remains true to its Lasallian heritage by meeting the needs of people of the times. The University continues to carry out this integral aspect and integrates educational excellence in the traditional liberal arts and sciences by attending to the individual needs of each person. The curriculum embraces a diverse mix of the arts and sciences, the most current technology, general education, and major studies while dealing with sociological, physical, and spiritual needs of students. This has been a hallmark of the University's success and a critical dimension that seems most appropriate in these ever-changing, conflicted times.

Today, Saint Mary's enrolls more than 1,400 undergraduates every year on the Winona campus. Additional sites are located in the Twin Cities metropolitan area and Rochester, Minnesota. In 1994, a campus in Nairobi, Kenya, was established, offering a bachelor's degree in education and a master's degree in African studies. Graduate studies are available on all campuses.

The Winona campus offers graduate degree programs in the following areas: Master of Arts in arts administration, Master of Arts in instruction, Master of Arts in international business, Master of Arts in pastoral ministries, Master of Arts in philanthropy and development, Master of Education in teaching and learning, and Master of Science in resource analysis.

Location

Located in the scenic bluffs of the Mississippi River Valley, students have the opportunity to hike and ski along 15 kilometers of cross-country trails, study by a stream, or collect research for a biology project, all of which can be done on 400 acres of campus. Historic Winona is a safe environment for students and provides a quaint atmosphere of small-town friendliness. Winona is located 30 miles from La Crosse, Wisconsin; 40 miles from Rochester, Minnesota; and 110 miles from Minneapolis, Minnesota.

Majors and Degrees

Saint Mary's University grants the Bachelor of Arts degree in the following majors: accounting, art (art studio), art (graphic design), biology, biology (cytotechnology), biology (medical technology), biology (nuclear medicine technology), biology (pre–physical therapy), chemistry, computer science, criminal justice, electronic publishing, elementary education, English (education), English (literature), English (writing and publishing), environmental biology, French, history, human services, international business, management, marketing, mathematics, mathematics (education), music business, music (classroom instrumental), music (classroom vocal), music performance, music recording and technology, pastoral and youth ministries, philosophy, physical science (education-chemistry), physical science (education-physics), physics (biophysics), physics (chemical physics), physics (engineering), political science, predentistry, pre-engineering, prelaw, premedicine, pre-optometry, pre–physical therapy, preprofessional studies, pretheology, pre–veterinary science, psychology, public administration, public relations, social science, social science (education), sociology, Spanish, theater (education), theater speech (education), and theology.

Academic Program

Interdisciplinary, general, and major courses are required for all graduates of Saint Mary's University. To be classified as full-time students, undergraduates must carry at least 12 credit hours per semester. To earn the Saint Mary's University Bachelor of Arts degree at the Winona campus, a candidate must fulfill 122 credit hours, maintain a grade point average of at least 2.0 in the major field, complete 45 credit hours in courses numbered 300 and above, and complete the general education program (interdisciplinary and general course work).

Interdisciplinary studies are 20 credit hours that focus on the theme Freedom and Responsibility: A Christian Approach to Understanding the Human Condition. This program helps students acquire and refine the knowledge and skills needed to describe, evaluate, and respond appropriately to humanity's current condition, both as a society and as individuals. In addition to completing the interdisciplinary and general education programs, students must complete the writing and mathematics requirements and two sport activity, lifestyle, and/or dance classes.

The Lasallian Honors Program of the Hendrickson Institute for Ethical Leadership promotes personal growth and prepares students for professional or graduate school. In conjunction with the Lasallian philosophy, the honors program is open to all SMU students who enjoy the liberal arts, challenge, discipline, and distinction.

Off-Campus Arrangements

Off-campus programs are available for second-semester sophomores, juniors, or seniors in good academic standing. Eligibility requirements and information about the application process, which may vary between programs, are on file in the Study Abroad Programs Office.

International Semester: Florence, Italy, is based in Fiesole, which overlooks central Florence. The program offers courses in art, architecture, business, history, language and culture, politics, and theology and fulfills general education requirements. All students participate in the class International Perspectives: Italy, which incorporates field trips to cities such as Assisi, Pisa, Siena, and Rome. Accommodations for students are in a hotel villa during the semester.

International Semester: London, England, is a twelve-week program that offers Saint Mary's University courses in art, theater, literature, theology, history, and culture, which fulfill various general education requirements. All students participate in the course International Perspectives: United Kingdom, which incorporates field trips to various locations in the United Kingdom. Students live in apartments or flats during their stay in London.

International Semester: Mexico is designed for juniors majoring in human services and criminal justice. It is adaptable to other majors on an individual basis. The program is located at LaSalle University in Mexico City. Classes range from Spanish and Mexican history to cross-cultural field experience. Travel throughout the country is also included during the semester. Students are housed with local families in Mexico City during their stay.

Student teaching abroad is available in private, international, English-speaking schools throughout the world.

Through the Washington Center Internship Program, students can work and earn college credit in their chosen academic field in the heart of the nation's capital, Washington, D.C. Internships are arranged in government or private nonprofit organizations. The Washington Center offers optional, low-cost housing for the semester.

Academic Facilities

The Winona Campus has embarked on a rigorous building campaign to update and equip the University to move easily into the twenty-first century. Technology updates have been implemented in the science laboratories and renovated classrooms across campus. The state-of-the-art Performance Center allows students to perform on a Broadway-size stage. A library addition has been created with an alternative study environment. The Hendrickson Center contains a leadership institute and the computer center, which houses the latest technology. The De La Salle Language Institute provides English language studies and cultural activities for international students.

Costs

Tuition, room, and board, including fees, average $18,975 for the 2000–01 school year. Extra fees include an activity fee, a laundry fee, and a technology fee, which entitles students to cable television in their residence hall and unlimited Internet access.

Financial Aid

The primary purpose of the financial aid program of Saint Mary's University is to provide assistance to students with financial need who would otherwise be unable to receive an undergraduate education at the college.

Faculty

Saint Mary's has 97 full-time and 40 part-time faculty members. Eighty percent of the faculty members hold the highest degree in their field. The student-faculty ratio is 12:1.

Student Government

Student government at Saint Mary's University offers a wide range of leadership opportunities for all students. The Student Senate is the representative voice of the student body and is responsible for communicating concerns of the student community to the administration. The senate oversees and distributes money to student groups, capital improvements, and hall funds. An executive board is elected each spring, and senators from each class and living area are elected each fall. A House of Representatives is composed of one member of each student organization.

The Student Activities Committee (SAC) is the Student Senate committee that is responsible for planning, organizing, and facilitating activities that are social, cultural, recreational, and educational in nature for the entire SMU community.

Admission Requirements

The pattern of high school college-preparatory courses and performance, while not the sole criterion for acceptance, is of primary importance. Rank in class, a personal essay, test scores, activities, and school recommendations all provide additional data used in the evaluation of a student's academic potential for university success.

The University processes admission applications throughout the year for fall or winter semester entrance. In addition to an application for admission, high school transcripts, ACT or SAT I test scores, and a personal essay are required to begin the admission process. Once materials are received, the vice president for admission evaluates the student's file.

Generally, Saint Mary's accepts students on the basis of six semesters of high school work, expecting that the quality of achievement will be consistent throughout the senior year. Some students, however, are asked to submit seventh- and/or eighth-semester transcripts before a final decision is reached. All incoming freshmen must send a final high school transcript certifying their graduation to the vice president for admission.

A student applying for freshman admission is expected to have completed certain units of high school course work. A unit represents a year's study of a subject. A well-rounded high school academic program might include the following: 4 units of English, 3 units of mathematics, 2 units of social studies, 2 units of natural science, and 7 units of academic electives (such as foreign language and additional units of math or science).

Application and Information

Rolling admission is offered for the application process; however, Saint Mary's University applies a priority deadline of May 1 for financial aid and housing. All applications should be sent to:
Admission Office
Saint Mary's University of Minnesota
700 Terrace Heights #2
Winona, Minnesota 55987
Telephone: 507-457-1700
          800-635-5987 (toll-free)
Fax: 507-457-1722
World Wide Web: http://www.smumn.edu/admission/app/html

Saint Mary's University, nestled in the bluffs of the Mississippi River Valley.

ST. MARY'S UNIVERSITY OF SAN ANTONIO
SAN ANTONIO, TEXAS

The University

St. Mary's University is a private, coeducational institution administered by the Society of Mary (Marianists), a teaching order of Catholic priests and brothers. St. Mary's offers small classes and personalized instruction while integrating a value-centered core curriculum into each student's degree plan. Encompassing course work in the arts, humanities, social sciences, natural sciences, and quantitative disciplines, the core helps develop creativity, analytical skills, and an understanding of the human condition. A St. Mary's education challenges students to academic excellence and personal integrity, preparing them for success in their careers and their lives. Founded in 1852 on the banks of the San Antonio River, the University maintains a 135-acre campus in a residential area of northwest San Antonio. Modern and historic buildings combine to provide students with state-of-the-art learning facilities and comfortable living areas. In fall 1999, St. Mary's enrolled 762 students in the Graduate School, 760 students in the School of Law, and 2,543 undergraduates in the Schools of Business and Administration; Humanities and Social Sciences; and Science, Engineering and Technology. Women make up 58 percent of the undergraduate population, which includes students from more than twenty states and thirty-four countries. Active student organizations include sororities and fraternities, the Student Government Association, a campus newspaper, honor societies, ethnic and cultural organizations, scientific clubs, and the International Student Association. There is an active Campus Ministry.

Beyond the undergraduate level, St. Mary's offers the Master of Arts degree in communication studies, counseling, economics, educational school leadership, English language and literature, history, international relations, justice administration, pastoral administration, political science, psychology, reading, and theology; the Master of Science in computer information systems, engineering (electrical and industrial), psychology, public administration, and systems administration; the Master of Business Administration with concentrations in accounting, computer systems management, finance, international business, and management; the Doctor of Philosophy in counseling; and the Doctor of Jurisprudence.

St. Mary's is accredited by the Southern Association of Colleges and Schools, the Association of Texas Colleges and Universities, the Texas Education Agency, and the Accreditation Board for Engineering and Technology, Inc., and holds membership in the American Association of University Women, the National Catholic Educational Association, the Association of American Colleges, the American Council on Education, and the Association of American Law Schools. It is an associate member of the National Association of Schools of Music. The School of Business and Administration is accredited by the AACSB–The International Association for Management Education.

St. Mary's University is an equal opportunity institution and an Affirmative Action employer.

Location

Although it has grown to become America's ninth-largest city, San Antonio has retained its friendliness and charm amid the bustle of urban life. Located in southern Texas just 150 miles from Mexico, the city is blessed by the cultural diversity of its 1 million people. San Antonio's attractions include its five historic Spanish missions, three art museums, the Fiesta Texas theme park, Sea World of Texas, and the beautiful Paseo del Rio—a collection of quaint shops, restaurants, and outdoor cafés along the San Antonio River. The Alamo city is also home to eleven colleges and universities, the South Texas Medical Center's eight hospitals, five military bases, a symphony orchestra, an opera company, a burgeoning art community, and numerous cultural festivals. The VIA Transit System provides St. Mary's students with access to all parts of San Antonio.

Majors and Degrees

A Bachelor of Arts degree is offered in biochemistry, biology, chemistry, computer information systems, computer science/application systems, earth sciences, economics, English, English communication arts, exercise and sport science, French, history, international relations, mathematics, multinational organizational studies, music, philosophy, physics, political science, psychology, public justice, sociology, Spanish, speech communication, and theology. Approved teacher preparation in elementary or secondary education also leads to a Bachelor of Arts degree.

A Bachelor of Science degree is offered in applied physics, biochemistry, biology, chemistry, computer engineering, computer science, earth sciences, electrical engineering, engineering science, geology, industrial engineering, mathematics, physics, software engineering, and computer applications.

A Bachelor of Business Administration degree is offered in accounting, corporate finance, entrepreneurial studies, financial services/risk management, general business, human resource management, information systems management, international business, and marketing.

Preprofessional preparation is offered in dentistry, engineering, law, medical technology, medicine, optometry, pharmacy, and physical therapy. Students may also obtain Texas elementary and secondary teacher certification or earn a commission through the Army ROTC program.

Academic Program

For the Bachelor of Arts degree, 128 hours of prescribed courses and electives must be completed. Requirements include English, natural science, mathematics, computer science, social science, theology, philosophy, foreign language, public speaking, and fine arts. Forty-five hours of study in residence are required, 12 of which should be in the major. Students seeking a Bachelor of Science degree are required to complete the same residence and core requirements as those for the Bachelor of Arts program, plus additional hours in their field of study. The Bachelor of Business Administration requires completion of 129 hours (132 hours for accounting); 45 hours must be completed in residence, and 12 of these must be in the major. Requirements include philosophy, English, social science, mathematics, natural science, economics, accounting, speech, fine arts, and theology. In addition to a liberal arts core of 66 hours, requirements for the Bachelor of Business Administration include 36 hours of a common body of business knowledge and 18–24 hours of upper-division course work in the major.

The University operates on a semester calendar. Advanced placement and/or credit may be granted to students who have scored 3 or higher on the appropriate College Board Advanced Placement examination. Up to 30 credit hours may be granted through the general examinations of the College-Level Examination Program (CLEP) or specific University-administered departmental exams.

Admission into an honors program is available for freshmen demonstrating high ability.

Off-Campus Arrangements

St. Mary's conducts a European Semester each year, the Washington Semester in cooperation with American University, a spring semester in Mexico, and a summer program in Innsbruck, Austria (the Innsbruck program is limited to business and law students).

Academic Facilities

The Academic and Law Libraries house approximately 700,000 catalogued items, 175,000 U.S. government documents, the curriculum collection for teacher education, and an extensive collection of audiovisual aids. The Learning Resources Center contains fully equipped studios for audio, video, photographic, and graphic arts production. The Sarita Kenedy East Law Library, one of the premier legal research centers of the Southwest, houses 245,000 volumes, and the Center for Legal and Social Justice provides a location for pro bono community service. St. Mary's has state-of-the-art laboratories for physics, engineering, biology, and geology that house equipment for X-ray diffraction and laser research, a metallurgical microscope, and a 150-keV accelerator. Computing facilities support Windows 95 clients on Windows NT servers and Novell servers at roughly 350 PC and Macintosh workstations campuswide. Students can run word processing, desktop publishing, spreadsheet, database, and mathematics application software packages and, through the Internet, can access computer sites throughout the world. Student e-mail accounts are available.

Costs

For full-time students, tuition for 1999–2000 was $11,500 per year and total mandatory fees were $380. The average room and board costs were $4500 per year.

Financial Aid

More than 80 percent of all St. Mary's students receive financial aid funds. A number of academic, music, and athletic scholarships are awarded on a non-need basis. All other financial aid awards are based solely on financial need, as determined by an analysis of the Free Application for Federal Student Aid (FAFSA). Presidential Scholarships may be awarded to incoming freshmen who are in the top 10 percent of their high school class and have an ACT composite score of at least 26 or an SAT I combined score of at least 1150. All students who have applied by March 1 are considered for scholarships. Students should mail the FAFSA by February 1 so that the processed document is on file in the Office of Financial Assistance by April 1, the financial assistance priority deadline.

St. Mary's undergraduates may qualify for the federally sponsored Federal Pell Grant, Federal Supplemental Educational Opportunity Grant, Federal Perkins Loan, Federal PLUS loan, Federal Stafford Student Loan, and Federal Work-Study programs. At the state level, students can apply for the Tuition Equalization Grant, State Incentive Grant, College Access Loan, and Texas College Work-Study programs. In addition, students may qualify for the St. Mary's University grants and scholarships.

Faculty

St. Mary's student-faculty ratio of 17:1 and average class size of 21 enable the faculty to provide students with instruction and advisement in a personalized setting. Faculty members take an active interest in students outside the classroom, with many serving as club moderators. Their concern for the individual student is matched by their professional accomplishment—92 percent of the full-time faculty members have earned the Ph.D. or the highest degree in their field. No courses are taught by graduate assistants.

Student Government

The University has increasingly allowed students to administer certain funds and to be represented on, or to advise, bodies governing all student and some University activities. The Student Government Association president sits on the Student Development Council, and students are represented on all University standing committees dealing with student personnel service areas (athletic, rules and discipline, religious activities, student financial aid, and publications). The bylaws of the Board of Trustees provide for representatives of the Student Government Association to sit on the committees of the board. Students are represented in some departmental staff meetings and sit on committees that prepare budgets and administer funds collected from the student activity fee.

Admission Requirements

For admission, students must have graduated from an accredited high school with 16 academic units, consisting of 4 in English, 3 in mathematics (including algebra II and geometry), 3 in social science, 3 in natural science, 2 in foreign language, and 1 additional academic unit. Applicants for engineering, biology, physics, chemistry, or mathematics must also have credits in solid geometry, trigonometry, and analysis. All freshman applicants are required to submit a high school transcript and to take either the ACT or SAT I. The General Educational Development (GED) test may serve as the high school transcript, provided that the total score is 45 or above and no area has a score lower than 40. International students must follow the same application process and must also submit a TOEFL score. A minimum score of 550 is required for admission. An intensive summer English program is available for applicants who meet all other admission requirements but score in the 440–547 range on the TOEFL. Transfer students must have a 2.0 average on a 4.0 scale and be in good academic standing at their former college to be considered for admission. Transcripts must be submitted from every college previously attended. Transfer students who have completed fewer than 30 hours of college work must also submit high school transcripts and ACT or SAT I scores. Each application is considered in its entirety.

Application and Information

The application deadline is two weeks prior to registration; however, applicants interested in scholarship consideration must apply by March 1 of the year they intend to enroll. Students applying for financial aid and/or residence hall space on campus are strongly urged to submit all necessary forms and information prior to April 1. When all records are on file, the Admissions Committee will notify the student of its decision.

For application forms and more information, students should contact:

Director of Admissions
St. Mary's University of San Antonio
One Camino Santa Maria
San Antonio, Texas 78228-8503
Telephone: 210-436-3126
           800-FOR-STMU (toll-free)
Fax: 210-431-6742
E-mail: uadm@stmarytx.edu
World Wide Web: http://www.stmarytx.edu

Students find small classes, excellent teaching, and personal attention at St. Mary's.

SAINT MICHAEL'S COLLEGE

WINOOSKI PARK
COLCHESTER, VERMONT

The College

Founded in 1904 by the Society of Saint Edmund, Saint Michael's has developed into an independent college in the Catholic tradition. It is the mission of Saint Michael's to contribute through higher education to the development of human culture and enhancement of the human person in the light of the Catholic faith. While Saint Michael's conducts five graduate programs and several international programs, its mission focuses on traditional undergraduate students, their learning in a liberal arts mode, and their individual personal development.

The current enrollment of 1,800 full-time undergraduate students live on a 440-acre residential hilltop campus with excellent academic and athletic facilities. With 80 percent of students coming from outside of Vermont, almost 95 percent reside on campus for all four years, contributing to a very strong sense of community and an active campus life both on weekends and during the week. A strong tradition of community service is manifested among student activities.

Campus organizations meet a variety of interests and range from the weekly campus newspaper to service organizations and the Wilderness Program. A recreational sports program is offered for all students. There are twenty-one varsity sports for men and women, including a women's ice hockey team that will play its first season in 2000–01. Most sports are played on the Division II level of the NCAA in the Northeast 10 Conference. The Jeremiah & Katherine Tarrant Recreation Center, a 67,000-square-foot addition to the existing Vincent C. Ross Sports Center, contains four indoor courts that can be used for tennis, volleyball, or basketball. The facility has a ⅛ mile indoor track, three racquetball courts, and a squash court. Strength training, cardiovascular training, and aerobics are also popular features of the facility, as is a rock-climbing wall.

Location

Although located in the Winooski Park section of Colchester, Saint Michael's is really considered to be part of the Burlington area and is only 3 miles from downtown. Burlington is the state's largest city and is home to four other colleges, including the University of Vermont. The presence of 12,000 college students contributes to Burlington's vibrancy and cultural richness. Situated on the shores of Lake Champlain, Burlington has a natural beauty that attracts many. The Adirondacks to the west and the Green Mountains to the east of the campus serve as constant reminders of the great recreational opportunities available nearby, including the best skiing in the East. Saint Michael's students take full advantage of all the cultural, social, and recreational opportunities available to them in the Burlington region.

The area is accessed by rail, air, and bus transportation on a daily basis. The Burlington International Airport, served by several airlines, is just 3 miles from campus.

Majors and Degrees

Saint Michael's College offers bachelor's degrees in the following areas: accounting, American studies, biochemistry, biology, business administration, chemistry, classics, computer science, economics, elementary education, engineering, English, environmental science, fine arts (art, drama, and music), French, history, journalism, mathematics, philosophy, physical science, physics, political science, psychology, religious studies, sociology, and Spanish. In addition, advising programs for predentistry, prelaw, premedicine, and pre–veterinary studies are available. Secondary school licensure is also available in several subject areas.

A special 3+2 engineering program is offered in conjunction with Clarkson University (Potsdam, New York) and University of Vermont (Burlington, Vermont) for students interested in combining a liberal arts background with engineering. A 4+1 M.B.A. program is offered in conjunction with Clarkson University. An English as a second language program is available for international students. Saint Michael's also offers minors in several subject areas.

Academic Program

Saint Michael's academic year consists of two semesters and two summer sessions. The College's focus is on undergraduate instruction, and its small classes generally support this primary emphasis. All students must complete the liberal studies requirements, which include course work in the following areas: religious studies, philosophy, social sciences, organization studies, natural and mathematical sciences, humanities, and artistic experience. Students must also demonstrate writing and foreign language proficiency. In addition to fulfilling these requirements, students must complete the degree requirements for any of the majors listed above or for an approved combination of those majors.

Off-Campus Arrangements

Many students enhance their academic work with an internship related to their career goals and major. Internships are available both locally and in other selected areas around the country. Sites have included scientific research laboratories, brokerage houses, hospitals, schools, newspapers, and accounting firms.

Study-abroad programs are available to students in most majors. Programs and locations are selected by the student in consultation with the Director of Study Abroad.

An exchange program with Xavier University (New Orleans, Louisiana) gives students an opportunity to experience another region of the country and a different institution for a semester or a year.

Academic Facilities

The Jeremiah Durick Library holds more than 170,500 volumes, 25,000 microfilm units, 1,390 periodical subscriptions, and more than 20,000 items such as tapes and filmstrips. Students in all majors are able to take short courses in word processing and have access to more than 200 computers connected to the College's campuswide information technology network. This network provides access to PC applications, including Microsoft Office, the World Wide Web, e-mail, and the College library. Computer hookups are available in all residence hall rooms.

Cheray Science Hall has facilities for the study of biochemistry, biology, chemistry, environmental science, and physics. Generous grants in recent years have provided state-of-the-art research equipment that is always available to undergraduates.

Saint Edmund's Hall, an impressive academic complex, includes journalism labs, psychology labs, computer facilities, and language labs, in addition to traditional classroom and lecture hall space.

Costs

For 2000–01, tuition and fees are $18,782, a standard room is $4508, and a standard meal plan is $2745. A reduced meal plan is available to those who desire one, and town-house–style housing is available to most upperclass students at an additional charge. Some science, journalism, language, and art courses require laboratory fees. Book, personal, and travel expenses vary according to course selection and individual needs.

Financial Aid

Financial aid at Saint Michael's is awarded primarily on the basis of financial need, as computed according to the FAFSA. In addition to need-based aid, the College offers a limited number of tuition scholarships based upon achievement in high school and on standardized college entrance examinations. The deadline for financial aid applications is March 15 for fall semester enrollment.

Faculty

The undergraduate faculty at Saint Michael's consists of 132 full-time and 63 part-time professors. Eighty-three percent of the faculty members have the doctoral or terminal degree in their field, and many have been recipients of grants, awards, and honors in recent years. While undergraduate instruction is the focus of the College, faculty members are encouraged to remain abreast of developments in their field through research and publication, often facilitated through sabbaticals. The faculty-student ratio is 1:13.

Student Government

The Student Association (SA), an active and important part of campus life, is an elected body of students that authorizes and funds most other student activities and organizations. Representatives from the SA sit on many campuswide committees, including the Curriculum Committee and various committees of the Board of Trustees.

Admission Requirements

Successful applicants to Saint Michael's typically rank in the top 25 percent of their high school class and have a strong college-preparatory background. Students should have completed 16 units of courses in English, foreign language, mathematics, science, and social science. Candidates must also submit SAT I scores. (The range of SAT I scores for typical students at Saint Michael's is 1020 to 1180.) In addition, students should submit a counselor recommendation and any teacher recommendations they choose. An interview is not required but is strongly recommended. Alumni interviews are available in some locations. Transfer applicants must submit transcripts of all college work along with the appropriate catalog in addition to the information required of first-year applicants.

Application and Information

The application deadline for early notification I is November 15. The early notification II deadline is December 15. The regular application deadline is February 1. Candidates for the fall semester are notified of their admission decision on or before April 1. A limited number of students may be admitted to the spring semester and should have their applications in by November 1. The College adheres to the Candidates Reply Date of May 1 for the fall semester.

For further information, students should contact:

Office of Admissions
Saint Michael's College
One Winooski Park
Colchester, Vermont 05439

Telephone: 800-762-8000 (toll-free)
Fax: 802-654-2591
E-mail: admission@smcvt.edu
World Wide Web: http://www.smcvt.edu

Students enjoy walking to and from class on a warm afternoon, with Saint Edmund's Hall in the background.

ST. NORBERT COLLEGE
DE PERE, WISCONSIN

The College

Father Bernard Pennings, a Norbertine priest, founded St. Norbert College (SNC) in 1898 as a Catholic men's college. Women were admitted in the early 1950s; today's coed enrollment is about 2,000 men and women. More than 80 percent of the students are between 18 and 22 years old. Students from twenty-six states and thirty countries attend St. Norbert; more than half of the student body come from distances of more than 100 miles. Seventy-one percent of the students graduated from public schools. The geographic diversity and the balance of students from both public and private high schools ensure variety in the student body.

About eighty student activities and organizations—academic honor societies, independent social organizations, academic clubs, local and national fraternities and sororities, and special-interest activities—await the St. Norbert student. The student who wants to write for a newspaper, get involved in television news or sportscasting, work for political candidates, or gain other leadership experiences will find them at St. Norbert. Students who like physical activities should know that St. Norbert maintains membership in the Midwest Conference for men and women, offers NCAA Division III teams in nineteen sports, and is a member of the Northern Collegiate Hockey Association. Successful men's and women's teams have acquired forty-five conference championships since St. Norbert joined the Midwest Conference in 1983–84. An extensive intramural program complements the activities program and helps guarantee that St. Norbert will never be a suitcase college.

An innovative Career Services Office provides four years of service to help students toward a lifetime of productive, satisfying employment. Counseling, aptitude and interest assessments, career shadowing, career exploration workshops, resume writing workshops, on-campus recruitment interviews, and job-search strategies are among the services available. St. Norbert pioneered the Career Network, in which professionals—many of whom are alumni of the College—conduct interviews with St. Norbert students. The students learn about their chosen profession from people in the field and develop leads to future employment. On- and off-campus internships also complement classroom learning and ease the transition to the professional world. The goal is to achieve near-perfect placement for St. Norbert graduates. Twenty-seven percent of a typical graduating class attends graduate or professional schools. Ninety-five percent of new graduates seeking employment or graduate school admission are successful.

The religious heritage of the College is important to every member of the College community. The on-campus parish is well attended. A student-elected Campus Ministry Council sponsors a wide variety of activities for those who seek to serve the less fortunate. Parish members work with the poor, the elderly, the sick, disadvantaged children, and those for whom the English language is a bewildering barrier. Students volunteer in the local community and also help in the inner-city areas of Chicago; Jackson, Mississippi; Minneapolis; and Washington, D.C.

Location

The St. Norbert campus—about 86 acres—is located on the banks of the Fox River in De Pere, Wisconsin, just minutes south of Green Bay, a metropolitan area of about 250,000 people and home to the world-famous Green Bay Packers football team. Wisconsin's oldest community, today De Pere is a charming blend of old and new. The community of 20,000 has recently redeveloped its business district, which is just minutes from the campus. Motels of the major chains are within a few miles, and Door County, Wisconsin's favorite vacation spot, is less than an hour away. Greater Green Bay serves St. Norbert students as an internship laboratory. Students are found in financial, industrial, and retail organizations and as reporters and writers at newspapers and television stations.

Majors and Degrees

St. Norbert offers programs leading to the Bachelor of Arts, Bachelor of Science, Bachelor of Music, and Bachelor of Business Administration degrees. The Bachelor of Arts can be earned in art; communication, media, and theater; economics; education; English; graphic communication; history; international economics; international studies; mathematics; modern foreign languages (French, German, and Spanish); music education; philosophy; political science; psychology; religious studies; and sociology.

Bachelor of Science degrees are conferred in biology, chemistry, computer information systems, computer science, environmental policy, environmental science, geology, mathematics/computer science, medical technology, natural sciences, and physics. In addition, a Bachelor of Science in natural sciences is awarded to students bound for professional schools (dentistry, medicine, and veterinary medicine). The Bachelor of Music is awarded in applied music. The Bachelor of Business Administration degree is offered to majors in accounting, business administration, and international business and language area studies.

Academic Program

Degrees are awarded upon the successful completion of thirty-two courses (128 semester hours) that include an approved major sequence, course work in general education, and either an academic minor or electives. Academic majors can be begun as early as the first semester of the freshman year. Early selection of a major is encouraged but not required in most majors.

The General Education Program spans nine areas. The goal is to educate students broadly, regardless of major. Competence in writing and quantitative skills is required of all graduates. Other areas include study of philosophy, religion, the sciences, fine arts, American heritage, foreign heritage, and social science areas, e.g., sociology and psychology. The academic minor option provides flexibility for students planning graduate or professional study or those who seek career-related course work prior to entering the job market. An Honors Program offers unusual challenge in areas of general education to those of superior ability, and an honors degree is awarded to those who successfully complete the program.

The accounting program is accredited by the Wisconsin Accounting Examination Board, and SNC is a member of the American Assembly of Collegiate Schools of Business. The education programs lead to certification at elementary and secondary levels. A nursery school option is included in the elementary program. Student teaching can be completed in the greater Green Bay area or in Australia, Belize, England, Kenya, New Zealand, Scotland, Ireland, the Virgin Islands, and Wales. A program leading to certification for K–12 teaching in music is available.

Army ROTC is available at St. Norbert through a collaborative program with the University of Wisconsin–Oshkosh. Several SNC students are recipients of full Army ROTC scholarships each year. Among the College's alumni are 9 Army generals who completed ROTC at the College.

Off-Campus Arrangements

Students in varied majors can spend a summer, a semester, or a year abroad. Students completing liberal arts majors are encouraged to spend at least a semester abroad. A foreign study component is a part of majors in French, Spanish, and German and both the international business program and the international studies major. All approved foreign study carries regular academic credit. St. Norbert scholarship assistance and other financial aid can assist participation. Study-abroad opportunities include a Third World science field trip; exchange programs in Australia, France, Japan, Germany, the Philippines, Spain, and Ukraine; student teaching in Europe, Africa, Australia, and Latin America; and other study sites throughout Europe, in South America, and in Egypt. Programs from the International Center help students, faculty members, and others discover new and exciting ways to explore and broaden their global horizons. St. Norbert's international curriculum, taught by a faculty committed to global learning, prepares students to live in a global society. To give students the international experience St. Norbert considers vital to today's graduates is a key component of the College's educational mission. The Washington Semester is available through American University.

Academic Facilities

The John Minahan Science Hall houses the science programs and thirty-eight laboratories, including the Center for Adaptive Education. Austin E. Cofrin Hall houses the business administration, computer science, mathematics, and economics programs. It also contains computing resources for the campus, which include minicomputers and 200 microcomputers. The Todd Wehr Library's open concept provides easy access to the College's 182,455 books, periodicals, and manuscripts. The College's archives are located in the library. The College's art collection can be viewed throughout the campus. The F. K. Bemis International Center provides students with increased opportunities to prepare for careers with greater international emphasis. It is also a culture and language resource to K–12 schools and Wisconsin businesses. The expansions in the past six years include the $3.4-million renovation and expansion of the Abbot Pennings Hall of Fine Arts; the $3.1-million renovation of Main Hall; the construction of the $6-million Austin E. Cofrin Hall; and the $9.2-million F. K. Bemis International Center. The $6.6-million Ray Van Den Heuvel Family Campus Center opens in September 2000. A $4 million expansion of the art facilities will be completed in 2001. Global links via multifaceted telecommunications technology, including compressed video, two-way interactive video, and satellite downlinks bring world news to student residence halls, classrooms, and conference and seminar rooms. Computer labs are available for student use at no charge.

Costs

For 1999–2000, tuition and required fees for full-time students totaled $15,800. Room costs averaged $2740 per year, and the average meal plan for full-time students was $2420 per year.

Financial Aid

Students share in more than $21 million of financial aid each year, including scholarships and grants, campus jobs, and educational loans. SNC awards $9 million of its own scholarships and grants annually. Awards are based on need and merit. No-need scholarships available for freshmen include the Trustees Distinguished Scholarship (special consideration for National Merit and National Achievement commended students, semifinalists, and winners), the Presidential Scholarship, and the John F. Kennedy Scholarship.

Wisconsin residents who show need can qualify for assistance provided by the state through the Wisconsin Tuition Grant Program, which pays up to $2172 of tuition each year. Students also utilize Federal Pell Grants and Federal Stafford Student Loans. The College participates in the Federal Supplemental Educational Opportunity Grant, Federal Perkins Loan, and Federal Work-Study programs. Each year, nearly 1,300 SNC students are employed on campus. The typical job involves about 10 hours of work per week and produces about $1600. A number of students are hired through the College's own $1.7-million-per-year employment program. Qualified students, regardless of financial need, fill positions.

Need-based awards are made on the basis of the Free Application for Federal Student Aid (FAFSA) and the St. Norbert College institutional application for financial aid. Freshman applicants should submit these forms by March of their senior year of high school.

Faculty

The St. Norbert faculty is composed of 170 men and women, 126 of whom are full-time. Ninety-two percent of the full-time faculty members hold the doctoral or other terminal degree in their field. The faculty-student ratio is approximately 1:14. Faculty members work closely with students in their major area of study, help students prepare for graduate school, and work with those who seek independent study and research opportunities. Faculty members also work with Career Services in its professional practice program.

Student Government

Students with an interest in College government have varied political options. The Student Government Association is active and involved. The College Activities Board is student-run and determines programming throughout the academic year. The Residence Hall Association governs and conducts programs for the 87 percent of students who live in campus housing. The needs of off-campus students are met by the Commuter Student Association and the Office of Student Life. Students serve on many College committees and on the National Alumni Board.

Admission Requirements

The student's high school record is the single most important element in the admission decision. Students who have taken an academic or college-preparatory program are considered best qualified. Nearly 80 percent of the freshman class ranked in the top two fifths of their high school senior class. The average composite ACT score is 24. Students with superior scores and grades may enroll in the honors program.

The College seeks a diversified student body. Because St. Norbert is residential in nature, great emphasis in admission decisions is placed on how a student used his or her spare time during the high school years. The College seeks students who have participated in, or are interested in participating in, a variety of athletic, social, cultural, and intellectual activities. Transfer students are encouraged to apply. The minimum acceptable GPA for transfers is 2.5 (C+) on a 4.0 scale.

Application and Information

Early applications for the freshman class are encouraged in order for students to benefit from the College's practice of registering students and assigning them housing in the order in which they enroll. Notification of the admission decision is made on a rolling basis beginning September 1. A $300 deposit is required to confirm enrollment. Deposits received for the fall semester are refundable until May 1. For more information about St. Norbert, students should contact:

Dean of Admission
St. Norbert College
100 Grant Street
De Pere, Wisconsin 54115
Telephone: 920-403-3005
          800-236-4878 (toll-free)
World Wide Web: http://www.snc.edu

SAINT PETER'S COLLEGE
JERSEY CITY, NEW JERSEY

The College

Chartered in 1872, Saint Peter's College (SPC) is an independent, coeducational, liberal arts college in the Jesuit tradition. The College has more than thirty-five academic programs that are firmly grounded in the liberal arts, and all students must complete a core curriculum requirement. SPC's main campus has an undergraduate enrollment of 2,461 full-time day students and also offers evening and Saturday sessions to undergraduate and graduate adult learners. The College's branch campus in Englewood Cliffs enrolls another 890 undergraduate and 539 graduate adult students. Both campuses offer associate, baccalaureate, and graduate degree programs, as well as certificate programs. Master's degrees are awarded in accountancy; education, with specializations in administration and supervision, computer science/data processing, reading, science and technology education, and teaching; nursing; and business administration, with concentrations in finance, international business, management, management information systems, and marketing.

Diversity enhances the learning environment at SPC. Fifty-five percent of the College's full-time student body belongs to minority groups; 1 percent are international students. While SPC is a Catholic college, it is not narrowly sectarian, and only 68 percent of the current student body is Catholic.

The College is accredited by the Middle States Association of Colleges and Schools. Individual programs are accredited by the National League for Nursing, the National Association of State Directors of Teacher Education and Certification, and the American Chemical Society.

True to the Jesuit tradition of academic excellence and personal care, the College places great emphasis on each student's personal, intellectual, and career development. Small classes, a caring faculty, and numerous support services combine to create an atmosphere conducive to growth, learning, and creativity. Active Career Development and Cooperative Education offices are open to all students regardless of class year. Personal counseling is provided by staff professionals in the Counseling Center while the Campus Ministry Office offers spiritual programs and retreats. Peer tutoring, offered through the Center for the Advancement of Language and Learning (CALL), is available in all subjects.

SPC is a 15-acre urban campus situated in a residential neighborhood surrounding Kennedy Boulevard. At the center of campus are residence facilities: Whelan Hall, the first traditional residence hall, opened in 1993, housing 164 freshmen; Saint Peter Hall, opened in 1994, housing 88 undergraduate students; and several one- and two-bedroom garden-style apartments, with private baths and kitchens are available. The newest residence facility, Millennium Hall, opened in fall 1999 and houses 148 students. Forty percent of the freshman class live on campus.

McIntyre Lounge offers students a place to grab a bite to eat and meet with friends, take a study break and watch television, or listen to WSPC, the College radio station. Student Affairs offers more than forty student organizations, including the Student Senate; academic, service, ethnic, and social clubs; and student publications such as the newspaper, yearbook, and literary magazine. Students are strongly encouraged to become involved.

SPC Peacocks and Peahens participate in intercollegiate athletics at the NCAA Division I level in all sports except football, which is Division I-AA. A member of the prestigious Metro-Atlantic Athletic Conference, the College sponsors twenty intercollegiate teams, including baseball, bowling, cross-country, football, golf, soccer, softball, swimming and diving, tennis, track, and women's volleyball. The College is probably best known for its basketball teams, which consistently win regular season titles and advance to postseason tournaments. SPC also hosts an extensive intramural sports program. The Yanitelli Recreational Life Center offers a competition-size swimming and diving facility; a fitness room; tennis, squash, basketball, and racquetball courts; an indoor track; and weight-training and multipurpose rooms.

Location

The College is easily accessible by all major forms of transportation. From Journal Square, midtown Manhattan is only a 20-minute ride on the PATH subway system; the World Trade Center is only a 12-minute ride. A shuttle van is provided to and from the PATH station in the evenings. Newark International Airport is 20 minutes away by car, and Amtrak trains and Greyhound buses leave from Penn Station in Newark and New York City, the Erie-Lackawanna Railroad Terminal in Hoboken, and Grand Central Station in New York City. SPC is also easily accessible from the New Jersey Turnpike and other major highways. The College's proximity to New York City provides students with a myriad of cultural, educational, recreational, and employment opportunities.

Majors and Degrees

Saint Peter's College offers baccalaureate degrees in accountancy, American studies, art history, biological chemistry, biology, business management, chemistry, classical civilizations, classical languages, communications, computer science, computer science/CIS, computer science/MIS, criminal justice, economics, education, English literature, fine arts, health-care management*, history, humanities*, international business and trade, marketing management, mathematical economics, mathematics, modern languages and literature, natural science, nursing (RN required)*, philosophy, physics, political science, psychology, social sciences*, sociology, Spanish, theology, urban studies, and visual arts. Five-year bachelor's degree programs in cytotechnology, medical technology, and toxicology are offered in affiliation with the University of Medicine and Dentistry of New Jersey. Associate degrees are offered in banking*, business management, finance, humanities, information systems, international business and trade, marketing management, public policy*, and social sciences. (*Evening-division only.)

Academic Program

All students complete a core curriculum requirement consisting of at least 69 credits, distributed as follows: 3 credits each of composition and fine arts; 6 credits each of literature, a modern language, history, social sciences, philosophy, and theology; 6 to 8 credits of mathematics; 9 credits of natural science; and 12 credits of core electives (including one course in ethical values). The remainder of the academic program is devoted to the major field of specialization. Students must earn 129 credits to graduate. Most courses carry 3 credits, and some are very unique, such as Art in the City, which enables students to visit museums and study art in New York City. Students may pursue a double major by completing requirements for two separate majors or may design a composite major in consultation with the appropriate academic dean. Minors are available in twenty-nine areas of concentration. Nine certificate programs are also offered. Undergraduate day courses are offered on a semester calendar, evening and Saturday courses on a trimester basis. Day and evening summer sessions are available on both campuses.

A four-year honors program provides academically talented students an opportunity to do extensive scholarly research and participate in small seminars that emphasize class discussion. Selected students are invited to join this program and, upon successful completion, are awarded degrees *in cursu honorum*. The Army ROTC program, which leads to a commission as second lieutenant in either the U.S. Army Reserve or the Regular Army, is offered in affiliation with Seton Hall University in South Orange, New Jersey. The Air Force ROTC program is conducted in affiliation with New Jersey Institute of Technology in Newark, New Jersey. Academic credit is applicable toward graduation. The College recognizes the Advanced Placement (AP) Program and generally offers credit for scores of 3 or better. Credit is awarded through the College-Level Examination Program (CLEP) tests, provided that the minimum required score is obtained.

Off-Campus Arrangements

Supervised, off-campus cooperative education opportunities and internships are available in all fields. Students in SPC's nationally ranked Cooperative Education Program may earn a maximum of 9 academic credits and up to $10,000. Up to 15 credits are awarded through the Washington Center Program in Washington, D.C., which provides experience working in the nation's capital in a wide range of internship positions. Study abroad is arranged through the International Student Exchange Program, which conducts programs in more than sixty universities in Europe, Asia, Africa, and Latin America.

Academic Facilities

The O'Toole Library in Jersey City houses approximately 350,000 volumes and 2,000 periodical subscriptions on four floors. An additional 20,000 volumes are housed in the Englewood Cliffs campus library. The libraries are fully automated, with access to the catalog and numerous databases via the World Wide Web at http://www.spc.edu/library. Twenty-two CD-ROM titles are also available. Gannon Hall houses several well-equipped laboratories for the natural sciences, including state-of-the-art multimedia classrooms; it is currently undergoing renovations and will reopen in fall 2000. The College's computers are linked to worldwide computer networks such as the Internet and Usenet. All students have free access to these networks upon registration. An academic computing center with an open-door policy includes a DEC VAX 4000, two DEC PDP 11/44s, three UNIX servers, 486 DXs, and Pentium computers. All systems are equipped with online capabilities and networked through DECServers to allow access from any terminal on either campus. PCs are also located in the Center for the Advancement of Language and Learning (CALL), the O'Toole Library, and the residence halls at the Jersey City campus.

Costs

Annual tuition costs for 1999–2000 (based on 30 credits) were $490 per credit or $14,520 for full-time study. Student fees were $456. Housing costs (2 students per room) in 1999–2000 were $3380 for Saint Peter Hall or $3550 for Whelan Hall. The cost of the GOLD nineteen-meal-per-week plan was $2550. Personal expenses, books, supplies, and transportation expenses are estimated to be $3450 for the commuter student and $1800 for the resident student.

Financial Aid

Saint Peter's College admits students regardless of financial status. Eighty-seven percent of SPC students receive financial assistance, and the average package is $14,410 for commuting students and $15,340 for resident students. The only form required is the Free Application for Federal Student Aid (FAFSA). It is recommended that students file the FAFSA by April 15 for fullest consideration of all federal, state, and institutional sources available.

Federal sources include Federal Pell Grants, Federal Supplemental Educational Opportunity Grants (FSEOG), the Federal Work-Study Program (FWS), Federal Stafford Student Loans, and Parent Loans for Undergraduate Students (PLUS). New Jersey state sources include Tuition Aid Grants (TAG) and the Educational Opportunity Fund (EOF). All applications for admission are reviewed for academic scholarships, incentive awards, athletic scholarships, and residential and need-based grants. Students should call the Office of Student Financial Aid (201-915-9308 or 9309) for more information.

Faculty

There are 114 full-time faculty members at the College. Eighty-three percent have doctorates. Graduate students/assistants do not teach courses. The student-faculty ratio is 14:1, and the average class size is 22 students.

Student Government

The Student Senate consists of an elected executive committee and 5 elected student senators from each class. The objectives of the Student Senate are to coordinate student activities, provide effective means of communication between the student body and the College administration, and strive to maintain and further the spirit and ideals of Saint Peter's College.

Admission Requirements

Admission to Saint Peter's College is based upon a student's demonstrated academic performance, academic preparation, and potential for success in college-level study. Each application is reviewed on an individual basis, and SAT I scores, class rank, high school record, personal statement, letters of recommendation, part-time employment, leadership positions, athletics/extracurricular activities, and community service are all considered. Interviews are required for scholarship candidates and are strongly recommended for all other applicants. Students are expected to have a solid preparation for college. Saint Peter's requires a minimum of 16 units of high school academic courses for admission: 4 units in English, 2 units in history, 2 units in a modern language, 3 units of college-preparatory mathematics, and 2 units of science (including at least 1 unit of a laboratory science). In addition to these 13 basic units, students must have completed at least 3 more units in any combination of the subject areas listed above. (One unit is the equivalent of one year of study in a high school subject.)

Application and Information

Students are encouraged to submit their applications in the fall of their senior year of high school. Admission is given on a rolling basis. Students who wish to be considered for an academic scholarship must apply by March 1. When a student's completed application and records are on file, they will be reviewed by the committee. Students are ordinarily notified of the admission decision within two weeks of receipt of the complete admission file, which must include the completed application form, including a personal statement, a high school transcript with official SAT I scores, recommendations, and a $30 application fee ($40 for transfer students). Transfer students must submit official copies of all college transcripts and their application fee by December 1 for admission to the spring semester and before August 1 for admission to the fall semester.

To complete their admission file, international students should submit the results of the Test of English as a Foreign Language (TOEFL) or the equivalent, all official documents of education, and an affidavit of financial support as well as the completed application form, including a personal statement, and $40 application fee. International students are encouraged to apply before March 1 for the fall term and before October 1 for the spring term.

For more information, students should contact:

Office of Admissions
Saint Peter's College
2641 Kennedy Boulevard
Jersey City, New Jersey 07306-5944
Telephone: 201-915-9213
   888-SPC-9933 (toll-free)
Fax: 201-432-5860
E-mail: admissions@spcvxa.spc.edu
World Wide Web: http://www.spc.edu

ST. THOMAS AQUINAS COLLEGE
SPARKILL, NEW YORK

The College
St. Thomas Aquinas College was founded in 1952 as a three-year teacher-training college with 30 students. Today, the College offers thirty majors and has a student body of 2,200. Much growth and development has taken place over the College's brief history. The College offers a Master of Science in Education with concentrations in elementary, reading, secondary, and special education, as well as postgraduate certificate programs. The College also offers a trimester weekend Master of Business Administration (M.B.A.) program with concentrations in marketing, management, and finance.

The College's most dramatic growth has occurred to meet the challenges of the twenty-first century. Capital improvements were made and new facilities added, so that the main campus now consists of sixteen buildings on 43 acres. The suburban campus includes two residential complexes: Aquinas Village, which consists of self-contained town-house units that house 132 students; and the McNelis Commons, which consists of town-house residential units that house 293 students and a common dining hall and laundry building. Approximately 35 percent of the College's full-time student population resides on campus.

Extracurricular activities are provided through some twenty-five different organizations, including the dramatic group (Laetare Players), a student-run radio station (WSTK), and the student-edited campus newspaper and yearbook. The College has excellent sports facilities, and several of its athletic teams have competed in national championships. The College fields NCAA Division II teams in coed cross-country and golf; women's basketball, soccer, softball, and volleyball; and men's baseball, basketball, and soccer. Intramural athletics are also available.

The College has a campus ministry and health, housing, placement, and counseling services.

Location
The College is located in Sparkill, a hamlet in southern Rockland County, New York, 16 miles north of New York City and adjacent to Bergen County, New Jersey. Rockland County, a sprawling, rural area of about 300,000 people, is rich in Revolutionary War history and convenient to the vast cultural and educational resources of New York City. Major arteries connect Sparkill to the tristate metropolitan area.

Majors and Degrees
St. Thomas Aquinas College awards Bachelor of Arts (B.A.), Bachelor of Science (B.S.), Bachelor of Science in Education (B.S.Ed.), Associate in Arts (A.A.), and Associate in Science (A.S.) degrees as well as certificates. Majors under the B.A. are art, art education (K-12 New York State certification), art therapy, communication arts, English, English education (7-12 New York State certification), graphic design, history, philosophy/religious studies, Romance languages, Spanish, and Spanish education (7-12 New York State certification). Majors under the B.S. are accounting, biology, business administration, criminal justice, finance, liberal arts and sciences, marketing, mathematics, mathematics education (7-12 New York State certification), medical technology, natural sciences (7-12 New York State certification in biology, chemistry, and physics), psychology, recreation and leisure, social sciences, and social sciences education (7-12 New York State certification). Majors under the B.S.Ed. are elementary education and special education. The A.A. is offered in humanities and social sciences, and the A.S. in business administration.

A 3-2 dual-degree program in engineering is offered in cooperation with George Washington University and Manhattan College. Students spend the first three years at St. Thomas Aquinas College in general liberal arts and mathematics study and the final two years in engineering study at GWU in Washington, D.C., or Manhattan, in New York. At the completion of the program, students are awarded a B.S. degree in mathematics from St. Thomas and a B.S. degree in engineering from GWU or Manhattan.

Similarly, in addition to a handful of other programs, students may obtain a B.S. in biology in three years and then move on to New York Medical College and obtain an M.S. in physical therapy in two years.

The following specializations may be taken within the framework of certain majors: actuarial science; computer information science; early childhood education; education of emotionally disturbed children, children with learning disabilities, and socially maladjusted children; management information systems; organizational psychology/management relations; prelaw; premedicine; prenursing; and prepharmacy.

Academic Program
The College maintains an academic flexibility and is committed to responding to the needs of individual students. The College strives to develop students who are not only generally educated but also possess advanced knowledge in specialized areas, are prepared for further study, and have the background to undertake fulfilling careers. To earn a bachelor's degree, students must complete a total of 120 semester hours, including a minimum of 51 credits in a core curriculum; complete all requirements for the specific major; and complete the final 30 hours at St. Thomas. The College awards up to 30 credits for life experience and up to 30 credits for achievement on College-Level Examination Program (CLEP) or New York State College Proficiency Examination (CPE) tests. The College operates on a semester calendar (trimester on the M.B.A. level). Students may enroll in classes in the fall, winter (a one-month session), spring, and summer (three separate sessions). Classes are scheduled during the day and evening, and students are permitted considerable academic flexibility in planning their programs.

Students can pursue independent study and internships, and many majors require a field practicum. The College maintains an active Academic Skills Center as a resource for developmental skills, and students are encouraged to meet regularly with faculty advisers for academic guidance and career direction.

Several unusual programs supplement the traditional academic areas. The College has a widely recognized program for college-age learning-disabled students called the STAC Exchange (at an additional cost). In addition, students may participate in Air Force ROTC programs through cooperative cross-enrollment with Manhattan College. The College also participates in the New York State Higher Education Opportunity Program for economically and academically disadvantaged students and provides an Honors Program for exceptionally qualified students.

Off-Campus Arrangements

The College offers a campus interchange program involving three other fully accredited colleges (Barry University in Miami Shores, Florida; Dominican College of San Rafael in San Rafael, California; and Aquinas College in Grand Rapids, Michigan) through which a student may attend a semester at one of the participating colleges during the junior year.

The College offers courses at local businesses and industries and an associate degree program at West Point for eligible students at the United States Military Academy and Stewart Army Subpost. The College also maintains articulation agreements with Long Island University's College of Pharmacy and Health Sciences, New York Chiropractic College, and New York College of Podiatric Medicine.

A Study Abroad Program is offered through the College, providing students with the opportunity to study at colleges and universities in such places as Rome, Italy; Budapest, Hungary; Nova Scotia, Canada; London, England; or Dublin, Ireland. Several other locations are available.

Academic Facilities

The Lougheed Library, a federal depository library, is located in Spellman Hall and houses 100,000 volumes, more than 600 periodicals, a comprehensive collection of microforms, several special collections, and the Communications Center, which has extensive audiovisual equipment, including a videotaping system. Spellman Hall has classrooms, a language laboratory, and science facilities that include engineering and physics laboratories. Aquinas Hall houses the recreation-teaching facilities and the Pre-School Center. Maguire Hall contains classrooms, art studios, photography labs, seminar rooms, the broadcasting studio, and large lecture halls. Marian Hall houses classrooms, a computer laboratory, a television studio, and administrative/faculty offices. All student services are housed in the Joseph F. Romano Student-Alumni Center.

Costs

For 1999–2000, the tuition for full-time study (12 to 16 credits per semester) was $11,200. Room and board at the College Commons cost $7125. Certain studio, laboratory, and computer courses carry fees.

Financial Aid

The College is committed to providing competent but needy students with the resources necessary to continue their education. Students who lack adequate financial resources should submit the Financial Aid Form to the College Scholarship Service and to the College. Financial aid is usually granted in a package of awards. Financial aid programs include Presidential Grants, special scholarships, athletic grants, Federal Pell Grants, Federal Supplemental Educational Opportunity Grants, New York State Tuition Assistance Program (TAP) grants, Federal Perkins Loans, Federal Stafford Student Loans, Federal PLUS loans, and Federal Work-Study Program awards.

In 1999–2000, 75 percent of the student body received financial aid. Athletic grants-in-aid are awarded to full-time students (men and women) in recognition of demonstrated athletic ability, academic achievement, and financial need.

Faculty

The faculty has 75 full-time and 55 part-time members; 75 percent have earned doctorates. The student-faculty ratio is 18:1. All faculty members participate in the academic advising of students and serve on College committees. Many serve as advisers to extracurricular activities.

Student Government

The Student Government consists of elected members who officially represent the student body, are responsible for planning and implementing student-originated programs, and coordinate and oversee all extracurricular organizations. Through its various offices, students play a vital part in offering consultation on new policies, planning social and cultural events, managing student funds, and operating the judicial system. In addition, the All-College Forum, composed of elected students, faculty members, alumni, administrators, and trustees, meets regularly to discuss policies, procedures, long-range plans, and any problems affecting the College.

Admission Requirements

All applicants must have successfully completed an approved secondary school program or the equivalent, including 4 years in English, 2 in college-preparatory mathematics, at least 2 in science, 1 in a single foreign language, and at least 1 in American history. Applicants whose high school background varies from the recommended pattern are considered if they demonstrate interest and ability. Freshman applicants must submit the application for admission, high school transcripts, SAT I scores, and their guidance counselor's recommendation. Transfer students must submit the application and official transcripts of all previous college work. All students are encouraged to visit the campus for an interview. An academic evaluation is prepared for every matriculant. The College does not discriminate against students, faculty members, staff members, or other beneficiaries on the basis of race, color, national origin, gender, age, disability, marital or veteran status, or religious affiliation in admission to or in the provision of its programs and services. The Director of Human Resources is the Section 504 coordinator, the Title IX coordinator, and the Age Act coordinator (Marian Hall 216, 914-398-4038).

Application and Information

Candidates should submit completed application forms to the Admissions and Financial Aid Office and must request that their official transcripts be sent to the Admissions Office from their school. Students are notified of the admission decision on a rolling basis upon receipt of all the necessary credentials.

For more information or an application, students should call or write to:

Admissions and Financial Aid Office
St. Thomas Aquinas College
125 Route 340
Sparkill, New York 10976-1050
Telephone: 800-999-STAC (toll-free)
World Wide Web: http://www.stac.edu

STAC's McNelis Commons residence complex.

ST. THOMAS UNIVERSITY
MIAMI, FLORIDA

The University

Founded in 1961 by the Augustinian Order of Villanova, Pennsylvania, at the invitation of the late Most Reverend Coleman F. Carroll, the Archbishop of Miami, St. Thomas University has grown from an institution with an initial enrollment of 45 students to become one of Florida's most comprehensive Catholic coeducational universities, with more than 2,500 students in all programs of study. Founded originally as Biscayne College, the institution achieved university status in 1984 and changed its name to St. Thomas University. The University is sponsored by the Archdiocese of Miami and is accredited by the Southern Association of Colleges and Schools. At present, the undergraduate student population represents twenty-eight states, the District of Columbia, Puerto Rico, the Virgin Islands, and sixty-five countries. Fifty-six percent of the undergraduates are women; 30 percent of the undergraduates reside on campus. The Graduate School offers the Master of Business Administration (M.B.A.); Master of Science (M.S.) in guidance and counseling, management, marriage and family therapy, mental health counseling, and sports administration; Master of Accounting (M.Acc.); and Master of Arts (M.A.) in pastoral ministry. The Ambassador Nicholas H. Morley Law Center was established in 1984 with a charter class of 160 students. St. Thomas University School of Law offers the Juris Doctor degree (J.D.) and is the only accredited Catholic law school south of Georgetown University's law school in Washington, D.C.

The University is located in northwest Miami on a 140-acre campus with fifteen major buildings. The Student Center contains a student lounge, a bookstore, the rathskeller, and other facilities. Adjacent to the University's two dormitories are the dining hall and the University Inn. Sports facilities include six tennis courts, a recreational swimming pool, two basketball courts, four baseball fields, a soccer field, and two football fields. As a member of the NAIA, St. Thomas supports men's varsity teams in baseball, golf, soccer, and tennis and women's varsity teams in fast-pitch softball, golf, soccer, tennis, and volleyball. The University offers a full range of cultural, governmental, and social activities, including publications and clubs. The Office of Campus Ministry provides liturgical celebrations in the University chapel and sponsors social justice and community service activities.

Location

Located midway between Fort Lauderdale and downtown Miami, the University is near numerous cultural and recreational facilities. The area's subtropical climate allows students to enjoy the nearby Atlantic Ocean beaches and many other natural attractions, such as the Florida Keys, Everglades National Park, and state and county parks, throughout the year. A short drive from campus are Key Biscayne, Bal Harbour, Miami Beach, Fort Lauderdale, and other cities of Florida's Gold Coast. The city of Miami and surrounding Dade County, known as the "Gateway to South America," house an international banking and trade center and offer a truly cosmopolitan atmosphere.

Majors and Degrees

St. Thomas University awards the Bachelor of Arts (B.A.) or Bachelor of Business Administration (B.B.A) degree through day and evening programs in twenty-six major fields of study: accounting, biology, business management, chemistry, communication arts, computer information systems, computer science, criminal justice, elementary education, English, finance, history, hospitality management, human services, international business, international management, liberal studies, marketing, political science/public administration, psychology, religious studies, secondary education, sociology, sports administration, and travel/tourism management. St. Thomas also offers a minor in environmental studies; preprofessional programs, which include dentistry, law, medicine, and veterinary studies; and courses in French, humanities, Italian, philosophy, and South Florida regional studies.

Academic Program

The University's academic calendar consists of two 15-week semesters, beginning in early September and in mid-January, along with two 6-week summer sessions. There are also three 1-week minimesters: one in January, one in May, and one in August.

To receive a bachelor's degree, students must complete at least 120 semester credits with a minimum grade point average of 2.0 overall and an average of at least 2.25 in their academic major; 30 of the last 36 semester credit hours must be earned and at least half of a student's academic major courses must be taken at St. Thomas University. All students must fulfill the general core education requirements of 57 semester credits, which include courses in English, humanities/foreign language, history, social science, mathematics/physical science, philosophy, and religious studies. An honors program is offered to qualified students to provide them with an interesting, stimulating, alternative way of fulfilling some or all of the University's general education requirements. The normal full-time academic load is 15 semester credit hours, but the load may range between 12 and 18 credit hours per semester. To graduate, all students must take an area of concentration or an academic major. A student may enter as an exploratory student but, with the assistance of a faculty adviser or a division chairperson, must declare his or her academic major by the second semester of the sophomore year.

Special academic features at the University include the Academic Support Center, Institute for Pastoral Ministries, summer school, and study abroad.

Off-Campus Arrangements

Internships are offered in nearly every academic major. A cooperative education program is also available. In addition, qualified students may participate in the Semester Abroad Program in Spain (El Escorial) and in Study Abroad for Earth (SAFE) in Italy.

Academic Facilities

The 50,000-square-foot library houses a 145,000-volume book collection, 850 periodicals, a reference room, a technical processing area, a convocation hall that seats 600 people, four seminar rooms for small classes and group study, and a Media Center with two screening rooms, a video studio, and an audiovisual laboratory with individually wired carrels. Kennedy Hall, the University's main academic center, includes administrative offices, classrooms, science laboratories, the Academic Support Center, the chapel, and the Computer Lab.

Costs

Tuition for the 1999–2000 academic year is $12,000 ($400 per undergraduate semester credit hour), room and board costs are $4200, and fees are $560 per year. Insurance, which is mandatory for all resident students, is estimated at $500 for the year. These costs do not include books, supplies, travel, and personal expenses and are subject to change.

Financial Aid

The University has established a financial aid program to assist as many students as possible. University scholarships and grants, along with federally funded scholarships, grants, loans, and work-study awards, are allocated in a financial aid package according to a student's financial need. Currently, about 85 percent of the University's students receive financial aid. Of all financial aid recipients, 65 percent receive University scholarships and grants. To be eligible for any scholarship or financial aid program, an applicant should complete the University's financial aid application and file a Free Application for Federal Student Aid (FAFSA) with the Department of Education. The filing deadline for University financial aid funds is April 1. Applicants should indicate affirmatively on the FAFSA that their information may be forwarded from the U.S. Department of Education in order to be considered for any state grants for which they may be eligible. The application deadline for need-based state financial aid programs is April 1.

Florida applicants who have resided in Florida for the prior twelve consecutive months are eligible to be awarded a Florida Resident Access Grant to attend a private four-year college or university in Florida. The funds for the Florida Resident Grant Program are dependent upon yearly appropriations from the Florida legislature. These funds are outright grants and are not based on financial need.

Faculty

The St. Thomas University faculty is a teaching faculty that is dedicated to furthering the academic and personal growth of students. The undergraduate student-faculty ratio is 15:1. Faculty-student interaction is a hallmark of the University because classes are small and because members of the faculty are available outside the classroom. Faculty members also participate in the academic advisement program to give students individual academic guidance, and they serve as advisers to student clubs and organizations.

Student Government

The Undergraduate Student Government Association, of which all full-time undergraduates are members, provides students with the opportunity to become involved in representative government. This democratic body is governed by elected student officers who serve on the Administrative Council and by representatives from each class who compose the Student Assembly. The association also assists in planning a varied program of social and cultural activities. In addition, students are represented on key committees throughout the University community. The Resident Council, consisting of representatives from each of the four dormitories, voices the concerns of residential students and is involved in the planning and implementation of University policies regarding residential life.

Admission Requirements

St. Thomas University seeks academically prepared students who are eager to improve themselves intellectually and socially within the University community. The Admissions Committee evaluates applicants individually in light of personal accomplishments, motivation, and the academic major selected. The committee places primary emphasis on the secondary school record, SAT I or ACT scores, a personal interview, a recommended 250- to 300-word personal essay, and a teacher's or guidance counselor's recommendation. Interviews are not required but are recommended. The committee does not discriminate against applicants on the basis of race, sex, religion, or national origin; in fact, the University welcomes diversity. Applicants for most divisions must have earned 16 units from an accredited high school in a college-preparatory program that included 4 years of English, 2 years of mathematics, 2 years of social studies, 1 year of science, 1 year of a foreign language or computer elective, and six electives; applicants for the Division of Science must have earned 17 units, including 3 years of mathematics (including trigonometry) and 3 years of science, but they need have only four electives. All international applicants for either freshman or transfer entrance must also submit letters of financial guarantee.

The University offers early acceptance, deferred admission, dual enrollment, and early decision. It also gives credit and advanced placement for scores of 3 or better on the Advanced Placement examinations of the College Board. Credit is also awarded for successful scores on both the general and subject tests of the College Board's College-Level Examination Program.

Transfer applicants should be in good academic standing with a GPA of at least 2.0 and not be on disciplinary or academic probation at their former college. The University will grant junior-year status to any admitted transfer student graduating from a Florida community college with an Associate of Arts degree. Transfer applicants must submit official transcripts from each of their previous colleges.

Application and Information

To facilitate the admission and financial aid processes, students should submit applications during the fall or winter of their senior year in high school and have all supporting material forwarded directly to the University's Undergraduate Admissions Office. Application for entrance as a resident student for the fall semester should be filed by May 15; for entrance as a commuting student, by August 1. Application for the spring semester should be made by December 15. The University operates with a policy of rolling admissions; beginning December 15, applicants for the fall semester are notified of the admission decision within a three-week period provided that all appropriate information has been received. The University adheres to the College Board's Candidates Reply Date of May 1 and does not require a tuition deposit or a room reservation deposit until May 1 in order to allow students ample opportunity to select the college or university of their choice. Dormitory space, however, is limited and is assigned in the order that room reservation deposits are received.

For further information, students should contact:

Office of Admissions
St. Thomas University
16400 Northwest 32nd Avenue
Miami, Florida 33054
Telephone: 305-628-6546
                800-367-9006 (toll-free in Florida)
                800-367-9010 (toll-free outside Florida)
E-mail: signup@stu.edu
World Wide Web: http://www.stu.edu

SAINT XAVIER UNIVERSITY
CHICAGO, ILLINOIS

The University

Saint Xavier University is Chicago's oldest Catholic university and one of the first institutions of higher learning in Illinois. Founded in 1846 and chartered in 1847 by the Sisters of Mercy, Saint Xavier continues its commitment to the pursuit of academic excellence within the context of respect, caring, and justice. The members of the University community affirm the rich tradition of Catholic higher education in America—one marked by spiritual development and intellectual vigor.

As a coeducational private Catholic university, Saint Xavier offers a solid liberal arts core and outstanding professional programs. The University serves a diverse student population of more than 4,000. Although most students are from the Chicago area and other parts of Illinois, various states and countries are also represented. Located in the southwest corner of one of the world's busiest, most exciting cities, Saint Xavier University is within easy driving distance for a majority of commuting students. Some students prefer to live on campus to enjoy the convenience of being only steps away from classes, the library, and the computer center. There are two coed residence halls, and a new athletic and convocation center opened in November 1999.

At Saint Xavier University, students are challenged to critically examine values that recognize individual dignity and worth and promote personal growth, professional integrity, and multicultural experiences. More than thirty clubs and organizations sponsor projects, dances, picnics, and lectures, so there are always activities going on outside of class. These clubs and organizations offer students social, cultural, professional, and athletic opportunities beyond the curriculum. As a member of the National Association of Intercollegiate Athletics, SXU's varsity athletic programs include intercollegiate basketball, baseball, football, and soccer for men and intercollegiate basketball, cross-country, soccer, softball, and volleyball for women. A variety of intramural programs are available to all students.

At the graduate level, master's degrees are offered in business, counseling psychology, education, English, finance, health administration, management, nursing, public health, and speech-language pathology.

Location

Saint Xavier University is located on the city's southwest side, on 103rd Street and Central Park, between Pulaski Road and Kedzie Avenue. The campus is easily accessible by public transportation, major expressways, and through streets, including I-94, I-294, I-57, and Cicero Avenue. SXU is adjacent to the suburbs of Evergreen Park and Oak Lawn and is 15 miles from the heart of Chicago's Loop, only 8 miles from Midway Airport, and 35 miles from O'Hare International Airport.

Majors and Degrees

Saint Xavier University shares in the rich tradition of Catholic liberal arts higher education while offering flexibility in course scheduling and diversity of degrees available. Saint Xavier University offers programs leading to a bachelor's degree in accounting, art, biology, botany, business administration, chemistry, communications, computer science, computer studies, criminal justice, education, English, history, international business, international studies, mathematics, mathematics education, music, natural science, nursing, philosophy, political science, psychology, religious studies, social science, sociology, Spanish, and speech-language pathology. Preprofessional programs include dentistry, law, medicine, optometry, pharmacy, podiatry, and veterinary medicine.

Minors are offered in most of the fields listed above as well as in anthropology, Catholic studies, pastoral ministry, physical education, speech communication, theater, women's studies, and writing.

Adult College is a specialized program offering majors in accounting, business administration, computer studies, English, industrial/organizational psychology, liberal studies, psychology, religious studies, RN completion, and sociology.

Academic Program

Saint Xavier University's core curriculum expresses the University's commitment to the values of a liberal education designed to be both foundational and exploratory. The curriculum develops the student's critical skills of writing, speaking, reading, and thinking as well as an understanding of the methods, approaches, and thought processes of the liberal arts disciplines. The core includes courses in natural science, mathematics, social sciences, history, literature, religious studies, philosophy, writing, and speech.

For graduation, a student must earn at least 120 semester hours, including completion of the University's specified curricular components. Transfer students must complete at least 30 semester hours and one third of the requirement in their major area at the University, including clinical or practicum experience in programs requiring such a component.

Academic Facilities

The academic facilities of the University's main campus include classrooms, labs, a library, an athletic and convocation center, an auditorium, conference center, residence halls, and clinical facilities.

The University's computer equipment consists of twelve computer labs. The University is connected to the Internet. Incoming students have the option of attending a workshop on computer literacy and word processing. Tutoring can be scheduled for assistance on several software packages.

The Byrne Memorial Library at Saint Xavier University houses more than 164,000 volumes and an extensive microfiche and microfilm collection. With membership in three consortia, ILCSO, LIBRAS, and ILLINET-ONLINE, students have access to the collections of more than 800 academic, public, and special libraries.

Saint Xavier University's interactive learning program uses the technology of live color compressed-video television, which has two-way full-motion video and audio capabilities to link SXU students with any of the nine other colleges and universities involved in this alternative learning program. Participants have the opportunity to speak with their instructor without ever leaving their designated sites.

Costs

Basic tuition for the 2000–01 academic year is $480 per credit hour. Room and board charges are $5744.

Financial Aid

Saint Xavier University's extensive financial aid program assists more than 80 percent of the student body. The Financial Aid Office participates in and coordinates aid from federal, state, University, and private sources. These funds help eligible students meet the cost of higher education. The University also offers academic and athletic scholarships to eligible students. Transfer students, new freshmen, and continuing studies students may be eligible for a "no-need" scholarship based on proven academic excellence. Any student interested in applying for aid must complete a Free Application for Federal Student Aid, which is used for federal, state, and Saint Xavier University aid programs. Students must file their financial aid application by March 1 to receive maximum consideration.

Faculty

Saint Xavier's student-faculty ratio allows students accessibility to faculty members, who offer personal attention and act as both teacher and adviser. The University has 149 full-time faculty members, 82 percent of whom have terminal degrees. Nearly 80 percent of all classes are taught by full-time faculty members.

Student Government

Members of the Student Activities Board (SAB) apply and interview for paid positions in the following areas: finance, interclub council, intramurals, programming, and public relations. SAB offers students a wide variety of programs, such as dances, entertainment events, films, lectures, intramural sports, and parties. The University holds an election to choose the 8-member board who will serve as advisers on student life issues.

Admission Requirements

During the admission process, consideration is given to previous academic work, recommendations from counselors and teachers, and scores on the ACT or SAT I, as well as the student's ability and desire to do college work. The Admissions Committee is interested in the quality of a student's work and the kind of courses taken in high school. Candidates should have a minimum of 16 units in English, math, natural and social sciences, foreign language, and academic electives. Applicants must submit an application for admission along with high school transcripts and test scores. Admission counselors are available to guide students through the application process.

Transfer students may be admitted to SXU if they present evidence of at least a 2.5 GPA in all college-level course work. For further information, students should contact the Office of Admission. All transfer credit is subject to validation by the academic departments. SXU will accept a maximum of 70 semester hours from a community college and 90 semester hours from a four-year college/university. Saint Xavier also has a number of transfer articulation agreements with area community colleges and is a participant in the Illinois Articulation Initiative.

Application and Information

Application forms for admission are available from the Office of Admission. Freshman applicants should submit an application for admission, ACT or SAT I scores, and high school transcripts in addition to a nonrefundable $25 fee. Transfer applicants are required to submit an admission application and a transcript from each institution where college-level work has been completed.

Office of Admission
Saint Xavier University
3700 West 103rd Street
Chicago, Illinois 60655

Telephone: 773-298-3050
           800-GO 2 XAVU (toll-free)
Fax: 773-298-3076
E-mail: admissions@sxu.edu
World Wide Web: http://www.sxu.edu

Saint Xavier University.

SALEM COLLEGE
WINSTON-SALEM, NORTH CAROLINA

The College

Since its founding in 1772, Salem College has been committed to preparing young women for productive lives and careers, increasing and adjusting its programs to educate women for roles in a continuously changing society. Of special interest to the 900 women at Salem today are the services of the Career Planning and Placement Office, which aids students in formulating career goals.

Students are encouraged to take advantage of the broad selection of extracurricular activities on campus, including intercollegiate and intramural athletics, publications, performing groups in the arts, academic organizations related to specific subjects, and social organizations.

The Center for Student Life and Fitness provides space for athletic, fitness, and recreational activities in the gymnasium and 25-meter competition indoor swimming pool. The Salem Commons is a four-level student center with lounges for dances and large social gatherings, meeting rooms, a dance studio, and performance space.

Location

The College's 57-acre campus is located in the nationally recognized Old Salem restoration area of Winston-Salem, only a 10-minute walk from the downtown area. Winston-Salem (population 150,000) is a recognized cultural center of the Southeast.

Winston-Salem is served by major airlines at Piedmont Triad International Airport near Greensboro and at Smith Reynolds Airport in Winston-Salem.

Majors and Degrees

The B.A., B.S., and B.M. degrees are conferred with majors in accounting, American studies, art history, arts management, biology, business administration, chemistry, communication, economics, English, French, German, history, interior design, international business, international relations, mathematics, medical technology, music, music performance, philosophy, physician's assistant program, psychology, religion, sociology, Spanish, and studio art.

A careful selection of courses provides a foundation for a wide variety of professional careers, including business, communication, computer science, law, library work, medicine, and social service. Students may earn teacher certification in elementary education, secondary school subjects, and learning disabilities.

Salem also offers a 3-2 program in engineering in cooperation with Duke University and Vanderbilt University.

Academic Program

Each degree program includes certain basic distribution requirements, the completion of a major, and a varying number of elective courses. The distribution requirements offer considerable latitude in the planning of individual programs. Independent study, planned jointly by students and faculty members, is encouraged. Minors in twenty-three areas and a special program in computer science may be taken in addition to a major to enhance and expand a student's academic experience. All students participate in the unique Salem Signature Program, a series of leadership/personal development courses. As part of the Salem Signature, each student completes 30 hours of community service and an internship in her field of interest before graduating.

Salem offers a four-year College Honors Program for exceptional students who wish to pursue more advanced academic studies.

Salem's 4-1-4 calendar gives students opportunities for preprofessional internships, in-depth courses, and independent studies during the January term, either on campus or abroad, at other colleges, or at any location appropriate to the student's special project or research.

Off-Campus Arrangements

A full-time student may register at Wake Forest University for any course unavailable at Salem. Salem is affiliated with the Bowman Gray School of Medicine and Forsyth Memorial Hospital for professional training in medical technology and the physician's assistant program.

Salem offers a variety of options for study abroad. The College also participates in the American University Washington Semester and the Drew University United Nations Semester.

Salem students have the opportunity to work closely with social and health agencies, public schools, the police department, business firms, and churches in Winston-Salem.

Academic Facilities

The Dale H. Gramley Library contains 121,783 volumes, 1,860 current periodicals, 227,102 microcards and microfilms, and a shared online catalog with access to more than 600,000 circulating items. The Fine Arts Center houses a large auditorium, a smaller recital hall, a workshop theater, extensive gallery space, music teaching rooms, practice rooms, a library, four listening rooms, classrooms, a rehearsal-lecture hall, and large art studios. The four-story Science Building has modern, fully equipped classrooms and laboratories for the teaching of biology, chemistry, physics, mathematics, and computer science; a computer lab; and a library containing current science publications and reference volumes.

Costs

The comprehensive fee in 2000–01 for traditional-age students who reside on campus is $21,970 (traditional-age students must reside on campus unless they reside with family in the immediate vicinity). Tuition is $13,730 and room and board cost $8240. Books and supplies are estimated at $400 to $500 per year. The student government fee of approximately $215 covers class dues, the yearbook, other student publications, and organizational dues. Students enrolled in the Adult Degree Program pay $720 per course.

Financial Aid

The College makes every effort to assist as many qualified students as funds will permit. Approximately 70 percent of students receive assistance through scholarships, loans, employment, and grants-in-aid. The Free Application for Federal Student Aid and the Salem College application form are required.

Salem participates in the Federal Perkins Loan Program, the Federal Pell Grant Program, and the Federal Work-Study

Program. The Federal Stafford Student Loan Program is also available. Competitive scholarships based on general academic excellence, as well as on talent in music, are available for freshmen. Special application must be made for these Honor Awards.

Faculty

The Salem faculty numbers 86. Approximately 90 percent of the full-time faculty members hold Ph.D.'s or the equivalent. The emphasis at Salem is on teaching, and full professors teach freshmen and upperclass students. The student-faculty ratio is 14:1.

Student Government

The primary goals of the Student Government Association are to build a spirit of community and unity among students and to set and maintain standards for achievement and behavior in keeping with Salem's honor tradition. Regulations governing student life are made by the students, with the approval of the Faculty Advisory Board. Students serve as consultants or voting members of faculty committees and the Board of Trustees.

Admission Requirements

Salem welcomes applicants whose school records give evidence of academic ability, personal integrity, and a desire for continuing growth and achievement. Students from all social, religious, geographical, racial, and ethnic backgrounds are encouraged to apply. The Admissions Committee recommends 16 academic units (4 in English, 3 in mathematics: 2 in algebra and 1 in geometry, 2 to 4 in foreign languages, 2 in history, 3 in science, and 4 academic electives), scores on the SAT I or ACT, and two recommendations. Applications are evaluated on the basis of individual merit; the selection of courses, grade point average, test scores, and recommendations receive major emphasis, and participation in extracurricular and community activities is also noted. Auditions are required of all prospective music majors. Interviews are recommended.

Application and Information

All students are urged to submit their applications in the fall of the year preceding proposed college entrance. The evaluation of applications is done on a rolling basis, beginning in the fall. The College reserves the right to defer a decision on an applicant until after the receipt of first-semester grades from her senior year in secondary school and senior-year SAT I or ACT scores. There is no deadline for transfer applicants, but it is suggested that their credentials be submitted by March 1. The College subscribes to the College Board's Candidates Reply Date of May 1.

Arrangements for an interview, a campus tour, or class visits may be made through the Admissions Office. An application form, a College catalog, and other informational brochures may be obtained by writing to:

Dean of Admissions
Salem College
Winston-Salem, North Carolina 27108
Telephone: 336-721-2621
E-mail: admissions@salem.edu
World Wide Web: http://www.salem.edu

Back campus courtyard.

SALEM-TEIKYO UNIVERSITY
SALEM, WEST VIRGINIA

The University

Salem-Teikyo University (S-TU) is a private, fully accredited institution in a partnership with Teikyo University of Tokyo, Japan, that grants associate, bachelor's, and master's degrees. Founded in 1888 as Salem Academy, it was established as a college by state charter in 1889. Since its founding, when most of the students were residents of the town of Salem, the University has concerned itself with providing education of high quality to meet the practical needs of the community. Its mission today is "to educate a world citizen who acquires wide knowledge without prejudice and makes decisions with an international point of view."

The University offers extensive programs in the liberal arts, humanities, and sciences, as well as unique programs in Japanese studies (with emphasis on international business or humanities), aviation, equine careers and industry management, international business, golf industry management, and youth and human services management. Master's degrees are offered in molecular biology/biotechnology and education (specializations in Appalachian folklife, curriculum and instruction, elementary education, equine education, mathematics, physical education and health, and technology). The University's management studies department has additional accreditation through the Association of Collegiate Business Schools and Programs, and its equine program is endorsed by the British Horse Society.

While lectures and labs are the basis for the academic program, activities outside the classroom also contribute to a Salem-Teikyo education. Students interact with classmates from more than twenty nations and most U.S. states. The student body of about 700 is one third West Virginian, one third other American, and one third international.

The Office of Student Affairs is concerned with the quality of life and education outside the classroom. Numerous programs and services are offered that expose students to new ideas and interests drawn from cultures all over the world.

The Student Administration publishes the yearbook (*Dirigo*) and the campus newspaper (*Green and White*) and operates a campus radio station. Several social fraternities and sororities provide additional campus activities.

The Salem-Teikyo University Tigers compete in men's and women's basketball, soccer, swimming, tennis, water polo, and equestrian events; men's baseball and golf; and women's softball and volleyball. As members of the NCAA Division II and the West Virginia Intercollegiate Athletic Conference, S-TU teams have received high ranking, and players have gained all-conference and all-American honors. S-TU's nationally ranked men's basketball team participated in national NCAA Division II competition in 1997 and 1999, reaching the Final Four in 1997.

To meet the varied interests of S-TU students, an increased emphasis has been placed on lifetime sports such as tennis, swimming, and golf. A wide variety of team competition is also available through intramural and club sports.

Orientation, counseling, health service programs, and student support services are included in services offered to students. Housing is provided in on-campus residence halls.

Location

The campus of Salem-Teikyo University is composed of approximately 300 acres of land in the foothills of scenic north-central West Virginia. The West Virginia countryside and nearby parks and recreational facilities offer ideal sites for rock climbing, camping, backpacking, canoeing, kayaking, rafting, and skiing.

The campus is accessible by major highway and is within a few hours of the Washington, D.C., and Pittsburgh, Pennsylvania, airports.

Majors and Degrees

Bachelor's degrees are offered in the following majors: athletic training, aviation (specializations in aviation management and pilot training), biology, business administration (specializations in accounting, international business, and management), communication (specializations in broadcasting/telecommunications and speech communication), criminal justice, education (elementary and secondary), English studies (English as a second language), environmental science, equine careers and industry management, golf industry management, information technology, Japanese studies (specializations in humanities and international business), liberal studies, mathematics and computer science (specialization in either field), molecular biology/biotechnology, public/community health, sport management, and youth and human services management. Associate degrees are offered in communication, English studies, and liberal studies.

Academic Program

Salem-Teikyo University emphasizes a strong liberal arts core curriculum. The liberal arts serve as an introduction to the world of ideas and knowledge and to the many complexities of human experience on every continent. The liberal arts core, combined with courses that build communication skills, fosters the students' analytical abilities and helps them to reach well-informed conclusions and to succeed in a rapidly changing world.

Salem-Teikyo University follows a modular (block) curriculum, which consists of twelve 18-class-day modules. Students can enter the University at any time and attend classes for a full twelve-month period if they so desire. The modular system allows students to focus their talent, energy, and creativity on one course at a time.

An important supplement to the Salem-Teikyo curriculum is the Office of Experiential Education and Career Services, which provides students with a four-year counseling and guidance program as well as assistance with preparing for career planning and placement. Counselors provide assistance in developing career paths to students who already have definite goals, and they also assist students in deciding on a major. The center also offers a series of seminars and workshops on career areas in order to acquaint students with various career possibilities.

Salem recognizes Advanced Placement tests and the College-Level Examination Program of the College Board.

Off-Campus Arrangements

Salem-Teikyo University offers students several opportunities to study off campus. There are study-abroad options in Japan and Germany; a minor in European studies is possible through the program in Germany. There are also many domestic and international internships available to students from a wide variety of majors.

Academic Facilities

The University's campus contains approximately twenty-five buildings, including a 77,000-square-foot equestrian center, located 6 miles from the campus on a 140-acre farm. The nucleus of the campus is the Valley of Learning, which holds the five main buildings of the University: Benedum Library, Carlson Hall of Science, T. Edward Davis Building, Randolph Campus Center, and the Brewster All Faiths Chapel. Other facilities include the Barker Equestrian Center and the World Citizen Center. All campus buildings, including residence halls, are linked to a fiber-optic network that allows Internet access. About fifty Internet-accessible terminals are placed throughout the campus for all students to use. The library has 200,000 volumes. Also located on the campus are the Jennings Randolph Center for Public Service and Fort New Salem, an authentic re-creation of a late-eighteenth-century frontier settlement, which serves as a center for the preservation and teaching of outdoor museum services.

Costs

Tuition, fees, room, and board for the 1999–2000 year were $17,263 for a normal academic credit load of 24 to 36 hours taken over a period of eight months. Tuition, room, and board for international students, who usually take more courses per year, vary by national currency.

Financial Aid

American students who have demonstrated high academic achievement are eligible for scholarships. The University attempts to meet 100 percent of the demonstrated financial need of all eligible applicants for aid through a program of scholarships, grants, loans, and part-time employment. The amount of aid is determined through the Free Application for Federal Student Aid (FAFSA). Students should apply as soon as possible after January 1 in order to meet appropriate federal and state deadlines.

Faculty

Faculty members are the cornerstone of S-TU's educational program. Although other members of the University community contribute to an S-TU education, faculty members are the prime movers. They hold degrees from some of the finest institutions in the country: Princeton, Amherst, Yale, William and Mary, Duke, Duquesne, Cornell, and West Virginia. Nearly 80 percent of S-TU faculty members hold doctorate degrees.

In addition to having impressive academic credentials, S-TU faculty members are supportive and eager to be of help. With a 14:1 student-faculty ratio in the average module, there is plenty of time for meeting individual needs inside and outside the classroom.

Student Government

The students of S-TU, through their elected officers and organization representatives to the Student Administration, are self-governing. While major University policy decisions must have the approval of the Administrative Cabinet and the Board of Trustees, the Student Administration recommends policies affecting all phases of student life.

Admission Requirements

S-TU welcomes and gives individual consideration to all applicants for admission. Each student is evaluated on his or her standardized test scores, cumulative grade point average, academic units, letters of recommendation, and motivation to live and learn in an international environment.

Transfer and international students are welcome. Any student who is in good academic and social standing at an accredited college is eligible for transfer to S-TU.

One of the best ways to learn about S-TU is to visit the campus. By contacting the Office of Admissions, prospective students can arrange to tour the campus, stay in a residence hall, meet professors and current students, attend classes, and talk with faculty and coaches.

Application and Information

An application for admission should be filed with the Admissions Office as soon as possible before the beginning of the module in which the student wishes to enroll; the University operates on a rolling admission basis. High school transcripts and ACT or SAT I scores should be included with the application form. Transfer students should include transcripts from all institutions that they have attended and should list all course work they are currently taking or are planning to take in the immediate future. Prospective students are notified of the University's admissions decision as soon as all credentials are on file.

For more information, students should contact:

Admissions Office
Salem-Teikyo University
P.O. Box 500
Salem, West Virginia 26426-0500
Telephone: 304-782-5336
        800-283-4562 (toll-free nationwide)
E-mail: admissions@stunix.salem-teikyo.wvnet.edu
World Wide Web: http://www.salem-teikyo.wvnet.edu

Salem-Teikyo University: an international community of students and educators.

SALISBURY STATE UNIVERSITY
SALISBURY, MARYLAND

The University

Salisbury State University (SSU) is gaining a growing national reputation for excellence in undergraduate teaching and learning. In its most recent review of public institutions, *Kiplinger's Personal Finance Magazine* ranked SSU among the top 10 percent nationally; *U.S. News & World Report* included SSU among its top 10 public regional universities in the North; and *Princeton Review* ranked SSU among the nation's 331 best campuses, both public and private.

The key to Salisbury State's success is the significance placed on the relationship between students and professors. Some 5,500 undergraduates are taught by 394 professors on a campus of 130 acres. A cross-campus walk takes 5 minutes. In this close-knit community, students give the faculty high marks for accessibility in the classroom and out. Full professors serve as undergraduate advisers. They often teach freshman courses and routinely lead students on trips and retreats, from exploring the Chesapeake Bay to touring Europe and beyond. Their professional concern for educating the whole student has had measurable results: according to the latest figures, Salisbury State freshmen have the highest graduation rates for colleges and universities in the University System of Maryland.

Salisbury State students come from thirty-two states, the District of Columbia, Puerto Rico, the U.S. Virgin Islands, and twenty-nine other countries. Some 43 percent are from Maryland's western shore, which contains the Metropolitan Baltimore-Washington corridor. Twenty percent are from outside the state. Thirty-seven percent of the full-time students live on campus in ten residence halls. Two International Houses allow students from other countries to study and socialize together in a residential environment.

All students, resident and commuter, are expected to contribute to University life. Many of the University's ninety student organizations and clubs find a home in the Guerrieri University Center. Approximately 50 percent of the student body participate in a thirty-seven-sport intramural program. SSU is a member of NCAA Division III for intercollegiate athletics. Women's sports are basketball, cross-country, field hockey, lacrosse, soccer, softball, swimming, tennis, track and field, and volleyball. Men's sports are baseball, basketball, cross-country, football, lacrosse, soccer, swimming, tennis, and track and field. SSU was recently national champion in men's lacrosse.

The University has two art galleries; supports an International Film Series, several distinguished lecture series, and artist-in-residence programs; maintains WSCL-FM, a national public radio affiliate, and WSUR, a student-run cable radio station; offers performing arts disciplines in music, theater, and dance; and serves as home to the Salisbury Symphony. Beyond the campus are the scenic Eastern Shore, the pleasures of Ocean City, Maryland (a nearby popular beach resort), the activities of an energetic Outdoor Club, and University-sponsored bus trips to theaters and museums in New York and Washington, D.C. Faculty members also lead trips abroad during winter and summer terms.

Graduate degrees offered by Salisbury State are the Master of Business Administration, the Master of Science in nursing, the Master of Science in applied health physiology, the Master of Education, the Master of Arts in Teaching, the Master of Education in public school administration, and the Master of Arts in English and history.

Location

With a population of some 80,000, metropolitan Salisbury is the cultural and economic hub of Delmarva (containing portions of Delaware, Maryland, and Virginia), a historically and ecologically rich peninsula located between the Atlantic Ocean and Chesapeake Bay. The city is ½ hour west of the white beaches of Assateague and Ocean City, Maryland; approximately 2 hours from Baltimore, Washington, D.C., Wilmington, and Norfolk; and 4½ hours from New York City.

Majors and Degrees

Three undergraduate degrees are offered in addition to the Bachelor of Arts and Bachelor of Science: the Bachelor of Arts in Social Work (B.A.S.W.), the Bachelor of Science in Nursing (B.S.N.), and the Bachelor of Fine Arts (B.F.A.) in art. B.A. degrees are awarded in art, communication arts, economics, English, French, history, liberal studies, music, philosophy, political science, psychology, sociology, and Spanish. Bachelor of Science degrees are awarded in accounting, biology, business administration, chemistry, computer science, electrical engineering, elementary education, environmental health science, environmental marine science, geography and regional planning, liberal studies, management information systems, mathematics, medical technology, nursing, physical education, physics, physics/microelectronics, and respiratory therapy. From business to social work, the University's academic departments have earned both national recognition and accreditation.

At Salisbury State, majors are designed to educate the whole student. No false distinctions are made between the liberal arts and the professions. While gaining a liberal education, for example, students in preprofessional programs prepare for careers in dentistry, law, medicine, optometry, pharmacy, physical therapy, podiatry, and veterinary science. Certification programs train educators for both elementary and secondary teaching. Dual-degree programs with the University of Maryland Eastern Shore enable students to earn two bachelor's degrees in four years in social work/sociology and biology/environmental marine science. Both the graduate and the undergraduate programs of its business school are nationally accredited by AACSB–The International Association for Management Education. Other national accreditations are in chemistry, allied health, social work, clinical laboratory science, nursing, and athletic training and through the Middle States Association of Colleges and Schools.

Academic Program

Four schools administer the University's thirty undergraduate majors. All four are endowed, a rarity among public institutions in Maryland. They are the Franklin P. Perdue School of Business, the Samuel W. and Marilyn C. Seidel School of Education and Professional Studies, the Charles R. and Martha N. Fulton School of Liberal Arts, and the Richard A. Henson School of Science and Technology. These recent endowments have enriched the scholastic climate of the campus, providing expanded scholarships, resources, and opportunities for students.

University planning encourages interdisciplinary study. All students, whatever their major, must take 45 credits within three disciplines: the humanities, the social sciences, and the mathematical and general sciences. Nine credits must be taken in English composition and literature. All course syllabi, from science to music to business, require written assignments in analysis/criticism, research, or creative writing.

Academic advising with faculty members and counselors is a must. Exceptional orientation programs for students and their parents help freshmen make a successful transition from home to college. For example, SSU offers a freshman orientation-in-the-wilderness experience, which won the Maryland Association for Higher Education Distinguished Program Award. Other orientation options include community service.

Learning is not regimented. Incoming students may earn credit through Advanced Placement and departmental challenge

2438 www.petersons.com Peterson's Guide to Four-Year Colleges 2001

examinations and the College-Level Examination Program (CLEP) for nontraditional educational experiences. Popular with students are internship programs, available in all four schools. Internships have included work abroad, legislative service in both Washington, D.C., and Annapolis, and media experience in fields ranging from fine arts to television. Students who relish intellectual challenge are invited to join the Honors Program housed in the Thomas E. Bellavance Honors Center. Travel and semester-abroad programs are increasingly popular. For example, Salisbury State students were recently studying simultaneously in Asia, Europe, and South America.

Academic Facilities

Blackwell Library, which has a number of computers available for research and nearly a quarter of a million books and bound periodicals, is the main research center. In addition to an online catalog, library users have access to many other databases, including FirstSearch and the World Wide Web. Seven labs with more than 210 IBM and Macintosh personal computers are part of the campus Novell network, which connects students to various software applications, e-mail, and the Internet. Resident students also have network connections for the Internet and e-mail available in their rooms. Three theaters, including the acoustically lauded Holloway Hall Auditorium, are homes to the performing arts. Salisbury State is the only institution in the University System of Maryland with an endowed theater program. The Edward H. Nabb Research Center for Delmarva History and Culture is earning a national reputation for historical research of the Middle Atlantic area. The Communications Center has fully-equipped television and recording studios. Fulton Hall, a $17-million classroom building, includes a state-of-the-art electronic music studio, a music library, a custom-designed black box theater, a full complement of rehearsal halls, and extensive studio and darkroom facilities.

Costs

Maryland residents paid undergraduate tuition and fees of $4156 for the academic year 1999–2000. Tuition for out-of-state undergraduates was $8550. Students living on campus paid approximately $5590 for room and board; the figure varies, depending on the residence hall.

Financial Aid

Financial assistance is available to students through loans, grants, scholarships, and on-campus and off-campus employment. The University participates in the Federal Perkins Loan, Federal Pell Grant, Federal Supplemental Educational Opportunity Grant, and Federal Work-Study programs. Numerous other forms of financial aid are available on the state and local levels. These awards are based exclusively on demonstrated financial need. All students who wish to apply for financial assistance are required to complete the Free Application for Federal Student Aid (FAFSA) by February 15. Complete details are available through the University's Office of Admissions and Financial Aid.

Through the University's Work Experience Program, which has a budget in excess of $2 million and provides employment for one quarter of the student body, students may be assigned to jobs related to their academic interest. They can earn a minimum of $1500 to $2000 per academic year by working 10 to 15 hours a week. About ninety non-need academic scholarships are available to incoming freshmen and are awarded on the basis of high school performance and SAT I scores. The application for admission to the University is the initial step in applying for these scholarships.

Faculty

The faculty at Salisbury State is highly respected. They have won national teaching, research, and leadership awards. More than three quarters of the faculty, many of them National Endowment for the Humanities and Fulbright professors, have the Ph.D. or other highest degree in their field. Professors not only publish but donate countless hours to community service, thus teaching by deed as well as word. The student-professor ratio is 18:1, but smaller classes are not unusual.

Student Government

All full-time students are members of the tripartite student government. The Student Organization for Activity Planning (SOAP) schedules campus entertainment and events; the Appropriations Board budgets student activities fees; the Student Government Association (SGA) is an elected body that oversees both. Each residence hall has its own governing body. The Union of African-American Students promotes better understanding and relationships between all racial groups and minorities. The University Forum, attended by all members of the campus community—students, faculty members, and administrators—meets regularly to discuss issues affecting the University.

Admission Requirements

The University seeks to admit students whose academic qualifications give promise of success in college. Race, religion, and ethnic background are not factors in the admission process. Most successful candidates for admission will have earned above-average high school grades in a strong academic program and a score above the national average on the SAT I or ACT. In addition to the high school record, test scores, and essay, recommendations of the high school principal and guidance counselors are considered. Interviews are not required, but applicants are encouraged to discuss programs and procedures for housing and financial aid with the admissions/financial aid office staff.

Transfer students must have earned at least 24 semester hours at an accredited community college or four-year college or university and have a minimum 2.0 average (on a 4.0 scale). For transfer students who have attempted fewer than 24 hours at another institution, the University's admission policy for entering freshmen applies.

Application and Information

Applications are accepted beginning September 1 for the spring and fall semesters. Applications received by January 1 for the spring semester and by February 1 for the fall semester are given the fullest attention. The University reserves the right, however, to close admissions when the projected enrollment is met.

For further information, students should contact:

Office of Admissions
1101 Camden Avenue
Salisbury State University
Salisbury, Maryland 21801-6862

Telephone: 888-543-0148 (toll-free)
410-543-6161
Fax: 410-546-6016
E-mail: admissions@ssu.edu
World Wide Web: http://www.ssu.edu

The $22-million Commons building houses the campus post office, the bookstore, meeting rooms, and dining areas that feature nine separate food stations.

SALVE REGINA UNIVERSITY
NEWPORT, RHODE ISLAND

The University

Salve Regina is a private, coeducational university of distinction that offers a comprehensive undergraduate program in the arts and sciences. The University is accredited by the New England Association of Schools and Colleges, and the Salve Regina campus is composed of a number of historic Newport estates that were built at the turn of the century against the backdrop of the Atlantic Ocean in the world-famous resort city of Newport. Chartered in 1934 by the state of Rhode Island and founded in 1947 by the Religious Sisters of Mercy, Salve Regina has positioned itself for academic excellence in the new millennium.

Today, more than 1,700 undergraduate and 600 graduate students from forty-six states and twenty-six other countries are enrolled in twenty-nine undergraduate majors and sixteen graduate programs, including a Ph.D. in humanities. Nearly 14,000 alumni have distinguished themselves in public service as health-care professionals and community leaders.

On-campus residence is an integral component of the Salve Regina educational experience—a living and learning environment that is like no other. Most of the University's residence halls are buildings of historical significance.

The University offers a wide spectrum of extracurricular activities, including student government, honor societies, art, theater and music programs, community outreach activities, and a full athletics program. A member of the Eastern Collegiate Athletic Conference and the Commonwealth Coast Conference, Salve Regina offers twenty varsity sports at the Division III level for men and women, including baseball, equestrian, field hockey, football, golf, sailing, softball, and track and field and men's and women's basketball, cross-country, ice hockey, lacrosse, soccer, and tennis. The new 69,000-square-foot recreation center will meet the athletic and recreational needs of Salve Regina students and faculty and staff members. The Student Activities Program draws inspiration from the University's mission of service to others, and it includes many service clubs and organizations. Through the Feinstein Enriching America Program, students participate in an array of community enrichment projects and activities that broaden their classroom education. Students serve as volunteers and interns at local hospitals, schools, museums, libraries, human service agencies, and other institutions. The campus is also home to the Pell Center for International Relations and Public Policy, where international dialogue is enhanced in an effort to achieve world peace.

Location

With the good fortune to be located in the historic city of Newport, Rhode Island, Salve Regina has a unique campus situated in a recognized National Historic District, with a landscape befitting a national park. Against the backdrop of the Atlantic Ocean and Newport's famous Cliff Walk, the University campus contains twenty historic and significant buildings constructed at or near the turn of the century. These former "summer cottages" and estate buildings have been adapted by Salve Regina for academic, administrative, and residential uses. They have been augmented by the construction of modern residence halls and academic buildings that fit in with the historic flavor and distinctive landscape of the campus, which includes century-old shade trees imported from Europe and the Far East and beautifully sculpted gardens. Nearby Newport's world-famous harbor and beautifully preserved architecture reflect its colonial seaport heritage, yet the city maintains a modern resort personality. Cobbled streets and brick sidewalks in downtown Newport, just a short walk from the Salve Regina campus, connect historic homes to the city's museums, art galleries, quaint shops, world-class restaurants, and recreational areas. Just minutes from campus students will find beautiful beaches, nature trails, and the famous 10-mile Ocean Drive, ideal for hiking and biking. Newport is centrally located less than a 90-minute drive from Boston, 45 minutes from Providence, and 3½ hours from New York. Train and air connections are available less than an hour from the Salve Regina campus, and a University shuttle provides regular transportation between the campus and the surrounding community.

Majors and Degrees

The University offers a selection of undergraduate degrees, including Associate of Arts (A.A.), Associate of Science (A.S.), Bachelor of Arts (B.A.), Bachelor of Science (B.S.), and Bachelor of Arts and Science (B.A.S.). Academic programs include accounting, administration of justice, American studies, anthropology, art, biology, ceramics, chemistry, communication media, cultural and historic preservation, cytotechnology, early childhood education, economics, elementary education, English, environmental science, finance, French, global studies (economics), graphic design, history, human resource management, information systems science, journalism, judicial administration, liberal studies, literature, management, marketing, mathematics, medical technology, microbiology, music, nursing, painting, philosophy, photography, politics, prelaw, premedicine, professional writing, psychology, religious studies, secondary education, social work, sociology, Spanish, special education, and theater. Five-year programs offer students the opportunity to complete both a bachelor's and a master's degree within five academic years. Five-year combined degrees are offered in accounting, administration of justice, biomedical technology and management, business administration, human resource management, and international relations.

Academic Program

Students receiving an associate degree must complete a minimum of 64 semester hours. A bachelor's degree requires a minimum of 128 semester hours. Departments may require additional semester hours of course work in particular concentrations. General education requirements comprise approximately 40 percent of course work leading to a degree. Usually completed by the end of the sophomore year, the general education course work provides a foundation in economics or geography, English, history or politics, logic, mathematics, modern foreign language, philosophy, religious studies, science, social sciences, and the visual and performing arts. The undergraduate program operates on a two-semester calendar, with fall classes beginning in September and ending in December and spring classes beginning in mid-January and running through mid-May.

Off-Campus Arrangements

Salve Regina has built strong relationships with public and private agencies and businesses that provide numerous internship opportunities for students as well as expanded professional activities that enhance academic programs. Students in accounting, administration of justice, information systems science, management, medical technology, nursing, and social work all benefit from hands-on experience at professional agencies and organizations. Internships in all fields can be pursued both on and off campus to augment classroom learning with experience in a professional setting. Students seeking internships for academic credit must receive approval from the appropriate department chair and the academic vice president. Salve Regina also offers students the opportunity to study abroad as a way of increasing global awareness. Programs are available in Mexico and Italy, among other locations. The University also encourages full-year and summer study-abroad programs in affiliation with other institutions.

Academic Facilities

With a modern library serving as a hub of University academic activity, Salve Regina combines modern facilities with historic structures in its academic setting. The McKillop Library, in fact, was designed to reflect the architectural lines of nearby turn-of-the-century buildings, but its functional interior includes state-of-the-art information technology that provides educational resources to meet any research needs. Students and faculty members have direct access to an array of international research databases and other online tools from workstations throughout the building, and the library's circulation and internal procedures are fully automated. Salve Regina's academic facilities are informed by tradition and architectural history, with a number of nineteenth-century estate buildings serving as classrooms, visual and performing arts studio spaces, and faculty offices. Other academic facilities have been built to accommodate the specialized requirements of science laboratories, computer laboratories, and lecture halls for large audiences.

Costs

Tuition and fees for the 2000–01 academic year are $17,550. Room and board cost approximately $7750, depending on specific campus housing and dining arrangements.

Financial Aid

Salve Regina University is strongly committed to helping students obtain a private education. Approximately 70 percent of Salve Regina students receive financial aid through a combination of scholarships, loans, grants, and work-study employment. The University requires the Free Application for Federal Student Aid (FAFSA) and the College Scholarship Service PROFILE. A Salve Regina Financial Aid Institutional Form must also be submitted. These forms must be filed no later than March 1.

Faculty

During the 1998–99 academic year, there were 197 faculty members. Approximately 58 percent of the full-time faculty members are tenured. Approximately 70 percent have earned a doctoral or terminal degree. Faculty members are committed to excellence in teaching and to the development of the academic potential of each student.

Student Government

Students have the opportunity to offer input into University activities and policies by participating in Student Government and the Activities Funding Board. In addition, students serve as elected class officers.

Admission Requirements

The qualifications of each applicant are evaluated by a committee on admission, which focuses on academic ability, intellectual curiosity, strength of character, motivation, and promise for personal growth and development. The committee reviews applicants without regard to age, race, sex, creed, national or ethnic origin, or handicap. While secondary school preparation varies, the University strongly recommends that students accomplish the following 16 units: 4 in English, 3 in mathematics, 2 in laboratory science, 2 in foreign language, 1 in history, and 4 in electives. Salve Regina follows a rolling admissions policy but has a priority deadline of March 1. Transfer students should follow the procedure for regular application to the University. Applicants to the Nursing Program will also be evaluated by a Nursing Review Committee. Students with superior academic credentials may be considered for a number of academic scholarship programs provided by the University.

Application and Information

Candidates for admission must furnish evidence of completion or anticipated completion of a level of education equivalent to four years of high school or submit results of the GED test. All candidates must furnish a completed application with a nonrefundable fee of $25 (unless a waiver is obtained from the dean of admissions), an official transcript of high school work and class rank, results of the SAT I or ACT, and two letters of recommendation. Early decision candidates should file an application before November 15, and notification of acceptance under this plan will be sent by December 15.

Applications for admission and further information may be obtained by contacting:

Admissions Office
Salve Regina University
100 Ochre Point Avenue
Newport, Rhode Island 02840-4192
Telephone: 401-847-6650 Ext. 2908
        888-GO-SALVE (toll-free)
Fax: 401-848-2823
E-mail: sruadmis@salve.edu
World Wide Web: http://www.salve.edu

Ochre Court is one of many historic buildings on campus that make the learning environment at Salve Regina like no other.

SAMFORD UNIVERSITY
BIRMINGHAM, ALABAMA

The University

Samford University is a private, liberal arts university with high academic standards. The University's academic reputation is due to well-prepared, accessible faculty members who take time to know and interact with students. Samford, which has some 4,500 students, offers a wide range of extracurricular activities diverse enough to satisfy the social, cultural, physical, and spiritual needs of all of its students. A lively Greek system; an honors program; men's and women's intramural and varsity athletics, including seventeen NCAA Division I sports; music and drama groups; an award-winning debate program; and other interest groups bond the students and the faculty members into a community of friends and scholars. Students come from forty-three states and thirty countries. A large number of students live on campus, enhancing the sense of school spirit and involvement. Students enjoy modern recreational facilities, including a concert hall, a theater, an indoor pool, racquetball and tennis courts, and an indoor track. Comfortable housing, including modern apartment-style units and fraternity/sorority residence facilities, is available.

Samford University has ranked in the top sixty of the nation's more than 500 regional universities, as published by *U.S. News & World Report*; ranked in *Money* magazine's top 100 "Best College Buys"; and has been selected for *Peterson's Competitive Colleges* in each of the past five years. The Templeton Foundation has rated Samford one of the nation's 100 best "character-building" colleges and universities.

Special student services include an active and successful Career Development Center, which offers guidance in career exploration as well as ample opportunities for placement interviews. Co-op programs add work experience and business contacts to the rewards of achievement and income for the participants. The co-op program is an excellent source of financial assistance that complements the significant scholarship and federal aid programs available to Samford students.

In addition to its extensive undergraduate program, Samford University grants the following graduate degrees: Doctor of Ministry, Doctor of Juridical Science, Doctor of Pharmacy, Educational Specialist, Juris Doctor, Master of Accountancy, Master of Business Administration, Master of Divinity, Master of Laws, Master of Science in environmental management, Master of Music, Master of Music Education, Master of Science in Education, Master of Science in nursing, and Master of Theological Studies.

Location

Samford's wooded 200-acre campus, with its Georgian architecture, is one of the most beautiful in the nation. Located in the picturesque, mountainous area of Shades Valley, the campus is less than 6 miles from the heart of Birmingham, Alabama's largest city and the state's industrial, business, and cultural center. Birmingham was an Olympic Soccer site in 1996 and annually hosts the Bruno's Classic Professional Golf Association Seniors Tournament and other major sports events. The city attracts national entertainment acts to its Civic Center, historic Alabama Theater, and Oak Mountain Outdoor Amphitheater. Gulf Coast beaches to the south and ski slopes to the north can be reached within 4½ hours by car. The world's largest space and rocket museum, located in Huntsville, Alabama, is also only a short drive away. Alabama's abundant freshwater lakes and rivers are sites for enjoyable outings. The South's largest shopping center, the Riverchase Galleria, is only 7 miles from the Samford campus. The Samford student enjoys the best of two worlds: a suburban setting for study, contemplation, and social enjoyment and easy access to the varied offerings of a metropolitan area.

Majors and Degrees

The Howard College of Arts and Sciences offers the Bachelor of Arts (B.A.) degree in the following majors: art, communication, congregational studies, English, French, geography, German, graphic design, history, human resources development, interior design, language and world trade, language arts, philosophy, political science, psychology, public administration, religion, sociology, Spanish, speech communication, and theater. The Bachelor of Science (B.S.) degree majors are biblical studies, biology, chemistry, computer science, engineering physics, environmental science and geographic information systems, forestry, marine science, mathematics, natural and theoretical sciences, and physics.

The School of Business awards the Bachelor of Science in Business Administration, with an opportunity for study in either accounting or management.

The Orlean Bullard Beeson School of Education and Professional Studies awards the Bachelor of Science in Education in early childhood education, elementary education, home economics education, physical education, and social studies; the B.S. is awarded in art education, athletic training, church recreation, counseling foundations, exercise science, fitness management, general science, human development and family studies, language arts, nutrition and dietetics, physical education, social studies, and sports medicine.

The School of Music confers the Bachelor of Science in Music in church music, instrumental music, music education, organ, piano, theory and composition, and voice.

The Ida V. Moffett School of Nursing offers the Associate of Science and the Bachelor of Science in Nursing degrees.

The Degree with Honors is available to students whose academic achievement is remarkable.

Academic Program

In order to graduate, students must complete a minimum of 128 semester credits with an average grade of C. The core curriculum consists of the following six courses: Cultural Perspectives I and II, Communication Arts I and II, Biblical Perspectives, and Concepts of Fitness and Health. The curriculum is designed to address ideas and issues that cross the usual disciplinary boundaries and to help students actively engage in learning rather than simply memorizing notes for an exam. The core is also designed to promote a global perspective, recognizing the influence and achievement of many cultures.

In addition, students complete several education courses designed to prepare them for work in a major field and/or to help them experience the sciences, the social sciences, the humanities, and the fine arts.

At least 40 credits must be earned in junior- and senior-level courses. The last 32 credits must be earned at Samford University. Between the end of the sophomore year and graduation, undergraduate students (including transfer students) must pass a writing proficiency test.

Off-Campus Arrangements

A semester-abroad program, headquartered in Samford's Daniel House Study Centre in London, England, offers opportunities to develop a broad worldview.

Academic Facilities

The Harwell Goodwin Davis Library furnishes the facilities and materials necessary for reference, research, and independent study. Its reading areas with individual carrels provide ideal working conditions for Samford students. The open-stack system allows students easy access to a collection of more than 853,240 volumes of books, periodicals, microfilm and microfiche, records, and tape. The library annually adds 7,000 volumes and 2,600 government documents. The library's Multimedia Collection houses the Religious Education Curriculum Laboratory and provides audiovisual aids and hardware, computers, and computer software. A staff of professional librarians guides students in the use of the fully equipped library. The Alabama Baptist Historical Commission's collection of Baptist church records and other important historical materials is located in the library and is maintained by the Special Collection Department. Historical documents are also preserved through an active microfilming program. The Samford library system includes the L. R. Jordan Nursing Library; the Cordell Hull Law Library, which has more than 232,850 volumes; the Education Curriculum Laboratory; and the Music Library, which has more than 8,000 CDs, records, scores, and audiocassettes. University library holdings are accessed through a state-of-the-art library system. Other libraries in the Birmingham area cooperate with Samford on a reciprocal basis.

Costs

The cost of attending Samford is significantly lower than that of many institutions of comparable size and commitment to quality. The basic charge for 1999–2000, including tuition ($10,300), room, and board, was $14,860. The typical student spends about $500 per year for books and supplies.

Financial Aid

At Samford University, a student's educational costs are frequently offset by scholarship and other financial assistance programs, which annually total more than $30 million. Applications for financial assistance are provided as students apply for admission. Awards are usually made by June. Most aid is need-based and is awarded according to the needs analysis report provided by the College Scholarship Service or American College Testing. In addition, non-need-based scholarship awards, usually based on academic merit, range from $500 to full tuition.

Faculty

Samford's faculty consists of 246 full-time and 216 part-time members who have earned academic degrees from universities throughout the world. All classes are taught by members of the faculty; the faculty-student ratio is 1:14. Faculty members serve as academic advisers and also serve on many University committees, including the Admissions, Scholarship, and Honors Committees.

Student Government

The Student Government Association (SGA) provides an excellent opportunity for students to participate in and influence governance. The SGA has autonomy in many programs, activities, and budgetary decisions; through the Student Senate, proposals related to improvement of campus life are sent to the University administration for consideration. The largest SGA organization is the Student Entertainment Board. Through its committees a variety of activities are provided, including concerts, lectures, dances, and outdoor recreation. The largest student-run activity is Step Sing, an annual variety show involving several hundred students that fills the 2,700-seat concert hall for three consecutive nights. Students are also involved in disciplining students who do not live up to University values. Alcohol is not permitted on campus, and regular visitation by persons of the opposite sex in residence hall rooms is not allowed.

Admission Requirements

Samford University seeks to enroll students capable of success in a challenging academic environment. Every applicant is evaluated individually on the basis of academic preparedness and potential, as well as personal fit with the mission and purpose of the University. The Admission Committee considers factors such as the strength of the high school curriculum, grade point average, standardized test scores, and recommendations. The freshman class that entered in 1999 possessed an ACT composite middle 50 percent range of 23 to 27; the SAT I middle 50 percent range was 1040 to 1233. The average high school grade point average of the entering class was 3.6. These statistics continue to demonstrate the competitive environment of Samford. International students must also demonstrate proficiency on the Test of English as a Foreign Language (TOEFL). Transfer students should have completed at least 24 semester hours or 36 quarter hours and maintained at least a 2.5 cumulative grade point average. Early admission is available to high school juniors who present an outstanding academic record and the recommendations of their parents and principal. Credit can be earned through CLEP and Advanced Placement tests. One school recommendation and an essay are required of every applicant. A campus visit is recommended.

Application and Information

Applications are received and processed on a monthly rolling basis. Applications are accepted until the class is filled. Notification is given on a rolling basis.

Application inquiries should be addressed to:

Phil Kimrey
Dean of Admission and Financial Aid
Samford University
Birmingham, Alabama 35229

Telephone: 205-726-3673
            800-888-7218 (toll-free)
E-mail: admission@samford.edu
World Wide Web: http://www.samford.edu

The Harwell G. Davis Library on the campus of Samford University.

SAN FRANCISCO ART INSTITUTE
SAN FRANCISCO, CALIFORNIA

The Institute

At 127 years, the San Francisco Art Institute encompasses one of the oldest and most prestigious colleges of art in the United States. Among its alumni and faculty are many of the country's leading artists. Committed to fine arts education, the Institute provides both undergraduate (B.F.A.) and graduate (M.F.A.) degree programs that are fully accredited by the Western Association of Schools and Colleges and by the National Association of Schools of Art and Design. The Art Institute is affiliated with the University of California. The current undergraduate enrollment is 499 men and women.

Complementing the curriculum and exhibitions programs of the Art Institute are a continuing series of lectures by visiting artists and critics, regular film screenings, poetry readings, concerts, performances, and other special events.

Location

The San Francisco Art Institute is located on the bayward slope of San Francisco's Russian Hill, within easy walking distance of historic North Beach and Chinatown. Extensive systems of public transportation link the Institute to the rest of the city and nearby communities.

The San Francisco Bay region is the country's sixth-largest metropolitan area and is home to an exciting art scene that includes museums, galleries, and alternative spaces for performance and other work. The area also offers a wealth of cultural and educational resources—opera, dance, legitimate and experimental theater, symphony orchestras and new music, cinema, and libraries. Favored by a climate that is mild year-round, San Francisco is among the world's most livable cities. Physically beautiful, with its hills, bay views, bridges, eclectic architecture, and fine light, the city is home to some 700,000 people representing at least thirty distinct ethnic groups and a wide variety of lifestyles and human concerns.

Majors and Degrees

The San Francisco Art Institute offers the Bachelor of Fine Arts degree in drawing, filmmaking, painting, performance/video, photography, printmaking, and sculpture/ceramic sculpture. Students may major in more than one discipline or pursue an interdisciplinary curriculum.

Academic Program

To earn the B.F.A. degree, students must complete a total of 120 semester units in studio art, art history, and the humanities. The curriculum emphasizes studio work, which represents approximately two thirds of the degree requirements in each major. Courses in art history and the humanities are designed to support and complement students' studio work. Normally, a full-time undergraduate program consists of 15 semester units, with at least one class in the declared major. The academic year consists of two 15-week semesters; two 6-week sessions are offered each summer.

Academic Facilities

In filmmaking, there are complete facilities for shooting Super-8 and 16-mm film, silent or with synchronized sound; two studios for lighting and staging; complete editing facilities for both Super-8 and 16-mm film, including workprint and interlock projectors; two large-scale animation stands with compound tables, pantograph, and over/under lighting (one stand with a tracking camera mount and rotoscope capability); two pin-registration optical printers for direct copying, enlarging, reducing, step-printing, color control, and special effects; a sound-mixing and recording studio; a four-channel, ¼-inch-tape editing room with mixing, rerecording, and matrix pin-patch facilities; and a portable synthesizer. Check-out equipment includes cameras, tripods, recorders, digital cassettes, microphones, tape-editing decks, a high-speed camera, a matte box, a titler, and transducers. Five flatbed editing tables are available: a Super-8 four-plate, a Super-8/16-mm six-plate Kem, a 16-mm six-plate Showcron, a 16-mm six-plate Moviola, and a 16-mm eight-plate Kem.

Painting facilities include four large painting studios with racks, an area for spray painting, and two spacious drawing studios. Supplies are available at a substantial discount through the school store. For third- and fourth-year students who participate in the honors studio program, there are semiprivate studios on campus. A painting/sculpture slide room is available for lectures and demonstrations. A secure storage area has spaces for approximately 600 canvases.

Photography facilities include a laboratory with eighteen private darkrooms and a group laboratory accommodating up to 10 students. There are two rooms facilitating 8 x 10 and 5 x 7 negatives and a mural room for projecting both black-and-white and color. Seventeen of the private darkrooms accommodate from 35mm to 4 x 5 negatives. Color facilities include a 42-inch Hope color processor, three Omega D-5's, six Saunders 4 x 5 color enlargers, and two Cibachrome processors. Students enrolled in large format photo classes are provided with viewcameras and tripods. A nonsilver darkroom includes a UV box and light table and an enlarger with processes covering blacktype, Van Dyke, and gum bichromate; some dry chemistry is provided. A copy camera room for making slides of work and matte-cutting facilities are also available.

Printmaking facilities include three Brand presses and an offset press for lithography and an acid-bath sink, transfer of air, and two Brand presses for etching. The Printmaking Department's darkroom serves the photographic needs of the area.

Sculpture facilities include areas for work in plaster, wood, and metal and an area for work in fiberglass, plastic, stone, and cement. The ceramic sculpture studio is equipped for low-fire clay bodies and glazes. There are facilities for slip casting, making ceramic decals, china painting, throwing, building, airbrushing, and spraying. Equipment includes a 30-cubic-foot gas kiln, a small gas test kiln, three large electric kilns, and two small electric test kilns.

A large, versatile studio is available for use by performance/video majors seven days and seven evenings per week. In this studio, students can work out pieces with or without the aid of a technician, who is available to help with the operation of video and audio equipment. The department has ¾-inch facilities, including two portable setups and two ¾-inch editing systems. A number of Video-8 systems have recently been added to the department. The addition of a computer arts facility gives students access to state-of-the-art visual technology.

Audiovisual facilities, located in the Institute's 250-seat lecture hall, provide students with an area for viewing slides, projecting films, listening to audiotapes, and viewing video works. The department's intermedia workshop enables students to work privately or in small groups.

An invaluable resource for students is the Anne Bremer Memorial Library, with its general collection of more than

27,000 volumes; special collections of rare books, artists' books, international exhibition catalogs, and Institute archives; and subscriptions to more than 200 periodicals. The library's Media Department houses more than 30,000 slides; audiotapes of poetry readings, experimental music, and visiting artists' lectures; artists' videotapes; and the Louis B. Mayer film collection. Viewing and listening facilities are available to all students.

Exhibition spaces at the Art Institute include the Emanuel Walter and Atholl McBean galleries, with a continuous, year-round program of contemporary exhibitions, and the Diego Rivera Gallery, reserved for the exhibition of student work. In addition, there is an outdoor amphitheater for performances and special events.

In fall 1995, the Institute established a Digital Media Center for fine art digital imaging. The DMC is a Macintosh-based facility with applications/software appropriate to support art-making in all fine art disciplines currently offered through the Institute's curriculum. This facility encompasses CD-ROM, multimedia, sound, and Internet access, as well as specific applications for printmaking, photography, painting and drawing, sculpture, film and video, and other genres.

Costs

For the 1999–2000 academic year, expenses for undergraduate students were $19,300 for full-time tuition, $1400 for supplies and books, about $1300 for personal expenses, and $315 for municipal transportation. Housing for a single student costs about $6000 for the year, and meals cost an estimated $2000. All students live off campus in private apartments or studios, and the Institute recommends several local residence clubs for temporary or long-term room and board, in which new students may reserve space before their arrival. The Institute also maintains a roommate referral service and housing bulletin boards.

Financial Aid

The San Francisco Art Institute administers four categories of aid: scholarships, loans, grants, and work-study opportunities. In addition to making awards solely on the basis of demonstrated financial need, the Institute has established the Merit Scholarship Competition, which each spring awards merit-based scholarships to students admitted for undergraduate study beginning in the subsequent fall semester.

Application for all types of financial aid administered by the Institute requires a completed application for admission and the Free Application for Federal Student Aid (FAFSA). The FAFSA should be forwarded to the appropriate processing center. Students who apply by April 1 receive priority consideration for available financial aid funds. All applications for merit-based aid must be completed by this date.

Approximately 75 percent of the Institute's students receive some form of financial aid. In addition to applying for aid through the Federal Pell Grant Program, students should write to their state department of education for information about state grant and loan programs. Additional information is available from the Institute's Financial Aid Office.

Faculty

The studio faculty is composed of 64 professional artists, all of whom have exhibited widely and are recognized in their respective media of expression. An additional 12 faculty members teach courses in letters and science and in art history. The current student-faculty ratio is slightly less than 12:1, conducive to close interaction between students and the faculty members with whom they choose to work. The Institute is committed to a personalized system of learning that emphasizes freedom and experimentation.

Student Government

The Student Senate is a forum for discussion and action concerning all matters of interest to students. Three Student Senate members are elected to the Institute's Board of Trustees and participate in all its governing committees. Also under the jurisdiction of the Student Senate are the exhibitions program of the Diego Rivera Gallery, student publications, and various social functions.

Admission Requirements

All applicants are required to submit a portfolio of ten to fifteen slides of original artwork. Official transcripts from all secondary and postsecondary institutions, SAT I or ACT scores, a statement of purpose, an application form, one letter of recommendation, and a $50 nonrefundable application fee are also required.

The most important element in the application is the portfolio. Academic grades and test scores are taken into consideration as well. Personal interviews and letters of recommendation may be required in some cases.

Admission decisions are made on an individual basis, taking into account artistic achievement, personal maturity, and dedication to fine art, as well as academic background.

Application and Information

All applicants must file a completed application form, letter of recommendation, portfolio, and transcripts with the Office of Admissions. The Institute has a rolling admission policy; applicants are notified of the admission decision as soon as their file has been reviewed. For preferential consideration in the proposed major, applications should be received by April 1 for admission in the next fall semester and by October 1 for admission in the subsequent spring semester. International students are encouraged to apply.

Application forms, a current college bulletin, and additional information may be obtained by contacting:

Office of Admissions
San Francisco Art Institute
800 Chestnut Street
San Francisco, California 94133

Telephone: 800-345-SFAI (toll-free)
E-mail: admissions@sfai.edu
World Wide Web: http://www.sfai.edu

A student in one of the Art Institute's painting studios.

SANTA CLARA UNIVERSITY
SANTA CLARA, CALIFORNIA

The University

Located in the heart of California's Silicon Valley, Santa Clara University (SCU) offers a rigorous undergraduate curriculum in the arts and sciences, business, and engineering. It has nationally recognized graduate and professional schools in business, law, engineering, pastoral ministries, and counseling psychology and education.

The 7,700-student Jesuit university has a 150-year tradition of educating the whole person for a life of service and leadership. There are approximately 4,500 undergraduate students, most full-time, 2,200 mostly part-time graduate students, and 1,000 mostly full-time law students. This diverse community of scholars, characterized by small classes and a values-oriented curriculum, is dedicated to educating students for competence, conscience, and compassion.

The University has three schools that offer undergraduate programs: the College of Arts and Sciences, the Leavey School of Business, and the School of Engineering. Graduate programs are offered by the engineering and business schools, the School of Law, and the divisions of Pastoral Studies and Counseling Psychology and Education.

SCU, founded in 1851 by the Society of Jesus, is California's oldest institution of higher learning. It was established on the site of the Mission Santa Clara de Asis, the eighth of the original twenty-one California missions. In 1928, the high school division was separated from the University and became Bellarmine College Preparatory, a private boys' high school. For 110 years, SCU was an all-male school. In 1961, the University admitted women students, making it the first coeducational Catholic university in California. SCU celebrates its sesquicentennial in the 2000–01 school year with three national conferences and other community events.

The new Pat Malley Fitness and Recreation Center is open seven days a week and provides free use of forty-four cardiovascular machines, saunas in locker rooms, three full basketball courts, a 2,100-square-foot multipurpose room, and indoor and outdoor lounge areas. The facility also has new offices for expanded SCU recreation and wellness programs for students and faculty and staff members. The recreation programs include five interscholastic club sports and seven coeducational intramural programs. Brono scholar-athletes distinguish themselves in seventeen intercollegiate sports. In 1999, five SCU teams competed in NCAA postseason tournaments, with the men's and women's soccer teams reaching the national semifinals. The school colors are Santa Clara red and white.

The University sponsors a wide variety of clubs and organizations to provide for academic and cultural enrichment, increased community involvement, and forums for special interest groups on campus. Among those offered are the Community Action Program, MeCha/El Frente, Black Student Union, and Asian/Pacific Union. Other special interests are served by the Campus Ministry and the student-run Multicultural Center.

SCU prides itself on its diversity. In fall 1999, the University enrolled 4,477 undergraduates and 3,191 graduate students, with male-female ratios at 46:54 undergraduate and 56:44 graduate. In the same term, 39 percent of undergraduates and 41 percent of graduate students were members of minority groups. Two thirds of SCU undergraduate students are from California; the others are from thirty-seven states and fourteen other countries.

SCU alumni live in all fifty states, although most—nearly 60 percent—live in the Bay Area, where many of them are leaders in business, law, engineering, academia, and public service. The University endowment reached $424 million in 2000.

Location

The 104-acre campus is located on El Camino Real in Santa Clara, near the southern end of San Francisco Bay. At the campus center is the Mission Church, restored in 1928 and surrounded by the roses and palm and olive trees of the historic Mission Gardens. It is located less than two miles from the San Jose Airport and five miles from downtown San Jose, the nation's eleventh-largest city. San Francisco is 45 miles away, conveniently reached by a CalTrain station that stops next to the campus. The campus is a half-hour drive from Pacific Ocean beaches and about a four hours' drive from Yosemite National Park and the ski resorts of the Sierra Nevada.

Majors and Degrees

The College of Arts and Sciences offers B.A. degrees in ancient studies, art history, chemistry, classical studies, communication, English, French and francophone studies, Greek, history, individual studies, Italian studies, Latin, Latin/Greek, liberal studies, music, philosophy, religious studies, Spanish studies, studio art, and theater arts (theater and dance) and B.S. degrees in anthropology, biology, chemistry, combined sciences, computer science/mathematics, economics, engineering physics, mathematics, physics, political science, psychology, and sociology. The Leavey School of Business offers the B.S. in Commerce degree in accounting, economics, finance, management, marketing, operations and management information systems, and organizational analysis. The School of Engineering offers the B.S. degree in civil engineering, computer engineering, electrical engineering, engineering, and mechanical engineering.

Academic Program

SCU underscores its commitment to education with a strong undergraduate core curriculum. Opportunities for learning and personal development can be found in a wide variety of courses, interdisciplinary institutes, internships, an honors program, Army ROTC, undergraduate thesis projects and in the University's Office of Student Leadership. Also, students work with the Markkula Center for Applied Ethics in values education in local schools.

SCU's commitment to learning is expressed in the fact that 92 percent of freshmen advance to the sophomore year and 81 percent graduate, among the highest percentages in the country. Undergraduate classes are small, averaging 27 students, with an overall faculty/student ratio of 13:1.

The academic year is divided into three 11-week terms. Students generally take four courses per quarter. Classes begin in late September and end in mid-June. Approximately 1,000 students participate in a limited summer school program.

Requirements for a degree vary according to the major program, but all degree candidates must spend at least one full year of study on the campus after achieving junior status.

Off-Campus Arrangements

Approximately 200 SCU students choose to study abroad during their junior year, often at other Jesuit universities in Europe, Latin America, Asia, and Australia, for which academic credit is given. Students may also earn full academic credit for spending a semester in Washington, D.C., in internship programs.

In the 13-year-old Eastside Project, SCU students combine community service with the course work in a wide range of disciplines. Students can choose to work at a variety of nonprofit organizations that have established partnerships with SCU, including homeless shelters, multilingual/ESL educational programs, convalescent hospitals, immigrant service centers, and even a parish-based theater company. Each year, approximately 1,300 SCU students participate in the program in seventy-five different Eastside Project courses. Law school students volunteer legal aid for indigent clients through the Eastside Law Center.

Academic Facilities

The fifty-four buildings on campus include thirteen residence halls, two libraries, a student center, and extensive athletic facilities. In 2000, the University completed a $68-million construction program, including two new science laboratory and classroom buildings, a performing arts center for music and dance, new arts and sciences and communications classrooms, state-of-the-art television production facilities, a recreation and fitness center, an upperclass residence complex, and a new parking structure.

The main library, Orradre Library, has 695,105 volumes, plus computer laboratories. The library's card catalog is accessible via computer. There are also 544,232 government documents and 735,257 microform units. Computer and telecommunications technology is an integral part of the life and learning at SCU. All residence hall rooms and approximately 90 percent of classrooms are connected to high-speed Internet access and campus e-mail; in addition, students use 695 computers in twenty-three computer laboratories.

The new John B. Drahmann Undergraduate Advising and Learning Resource Center consolidates several historically separate programs into a single operation that seeks to promote the goal of student learning. Among its aims are connecting academic advising support and learning resources more effectively and efficiently; providing for more direct faculty involvement in key student learning areas, such as new student programs; and helping to promote the faculty-student interaction essential to a community of scholars by supporting residential learning communities and the peer educator program. The Drahmann Center provides academic advising in all undergraduate programs and also provides tutoring, learning resources, fellowship information, a disabilities resources program, and orientation programs for new students. In conjunction with the new Center for Multicultural Learning, the Drahmann Center also undertakes outreach to historically underserved students to ensure that they are connected to resources that will support their academic success.

Costs

The basic expenses for undergraduate students for the 2000–01 academic year are as follows: tuition, $20,337; room and board, $8034; and books and personal expenses, $2548.

Financial Aid

SCU administers four categories of financial aid: scholarships, loans, grants, and work-study awards. Seventy-one percent of the student body receives some type of financial assistance. Awards are made on the basis of financial need and academic record. Students should contact the Financial Aid Office regarding application deadlines in order to receive full consideration for available funds. Students must also apply for the California State Grant program (Cal Grant A, B), when applicable, and for the Federal Pell Grant. Other supplementary aid opportunities are available through the Federal Perkins Loan, Ford Federal Direct Student Loan, and Federal PLUS loan programs and through Army ROTC. Further information may be obtained from the Financial Aid Office.

Faculty

The faculty at SCU is composed of Jesuit priests and lay teachers. Ninety-two percent of the full-time faculty members hold doctoral degrees. At SCU, there are no teaching assistants; all classes are taught by the professors of the University.

Student Government

The Associated Students for Santa Clara University (ASSCU) is the official organization for student government. Every student is automatically a member of ASSCU and participates through his or her elected representative in making policies that affect student life on campus. Student participation in University decision making is possible through student representation on the Board of Governors and other administration advisory committees.

Admission Requirements

Admission decisions for freshman applicants are based on the following criteria: the high school record, SAT I or ACT scores, secondary school recommendation, and personal qualifications. A four-year curriculum of solid college-preparatory courses and a B average (3.0) or better are essential. An applicant's high school record should include 16 college-preparatory courses as follows: 4 units of English, 3 of foreign language, 2 of algebra, 1 of geometry, 1 of history, 1 of laboratory science, and 4 in additional yearlong courses chosen from among these areas of study. Additional work in math and science is required for some programs. Transfer students applying after completing 30 semester or 45 quarter units of college work are not required to submit SAT I scores, but all transfer students must submit a high school transcript. Although interviews are available, they are not required. Counseling appointments and campus tours should be scheduled in advance.

Application and Information

Applications for freshman admission must be submitted by January 15 for the fall quarter. Transfer candidates must submit applications by May 15 for the fall term, by October 15 for the winter term, and by January 15 for the spring term. Full consideration for admission cannot be guaranteed on applications completed after the deadlines.

Application forms and additional information may be obtained by contacting:

Deans of Admissions
Santa Clara University
Santa Clara, California 95053

Telephone: 408-554-4700
Fax: 408-554-5255
E-mail: ugadmissions@scu.edu
World Wide Web: http://www.scu.edu

The Mission Garden area of campus at SCU.

SARAH LAWRENCE COLLEGE
BRONXVILLE, NEW YORK

The College

Sarah Lawrence College is a model for individualized education among leading liberal arts colleges. It offers an innovative program of study that encourages students to take intellectual risks and explore highly challenging topics as they take an active role in the planning and pursuit of their education.

The College's forty-six buildings are set on a 40-acre campus reminiscent of a rural English village. There are 1,178 undergraduates and 317 graduate students. Approximately 60 students attend the Center for Continuing Education, a flexible, supportive program for returning adult students. The College draws its students from across the country and around the world. Ninety percent live on campus. Sarah Lawrence has an active campus, offering opportunities for involvement in clubs, student organizations, dramatic productions, literary societies, student publications, student government, and intramural athletics. There are no sororities or fraternities.

The College is accredited by the Middle States Association of Colleges and Schools and approved by the New York State Education Department.

On the graduate level, the College offers programs in women's history, human genetics, health advocacy, art of teaching, child development, dance, theater, and writing.

Location

Sarah Lawrence is located in southern Westchester County, 15 miles north of midtown Manhattan. Main roads and the railroad make it possible to reach the city in 30 minutes, enabling students to take advantage of a wide range of social and cultural riches as well as internship possibilities. Students obtain internships in the arts, business, communications, law, medicine, publishing, social services, and the theater.

Majors and Degree

Sarah Lawrence grants the Bachelor of Arts degree to undergraduate students. The academic program is divided into four divisions: history and the social sciences, consisting of anthropology, economics, history, political science, psychology, public policy, science technology and society, and sociology; humanities, consisting of art history, Asian studies, film history, languages, literature, music history, philosophy, and religion; natural sciences and mathematics, consisting of biology, chemistry, geology, mathematics, and physics; and creative and performing arts, consisting of dance, music, theater, writing, and visual arts (ceramic sculpture, drawing, filmmaking, painting, photography, printmaking, and sculpture). There are no required courses, but students are expected to work in at least three of the four divisions.

Academic Program

Each student works with his or her faculty adviser, called a don, in the Oxford and Cambridge tradition, to plan a course of study. Most courses consist of two parts: the seminar, limited to 15 students, and the conference, a private, biweekly meeting with the seminar professor. In conference, students create individual projects that extend the material assigned in the seminar and connect it to their academic and career goals. In the performing arts—dance, music, and theater—students participate in several components that together constitute a full course. While transcripts of official grades are available for graduate school, written evaluations that more clearly define strengths, weaknesses, and progress are provided to each student.

The College operates on the semester system, with terms beginning in early September and late January.

Off-Campus Arrangements

Sarah Lawrence College sponsors academic programs in Paris, Oxford, and Florence, as well as a program in cooperation with the British American Drama Academy in London. Students may also combine on-campus study with off-campus fieldwork and do so at a variety of places, including art museums, theaters, and hospitals and with various orchestras, dance companies, publications, social action programs, government agencies, and businesses.

Academic Facilities

The College's facilities include classrooms, laboratories, and computer centers; a college-wide academic network to which all students' rooms are fully wired; a T-1 connection to the Internet; a library with 288,000 volumes and 1,135 periodicals, which is linked by computer to more than 6,000 other libraries; the Performing Arts Center, consisting of four theaters, a dance studio, and a concert hall; a music building, including a music library; a new Sports Center with a competition pool, basketball and squash courts, a fitness center, an aerobics room, and a rowing tank; a laboratory preschool; a science center; the Center for Continuing Education; and a newly refurbished and expanded student social space, the Ruth Leff Siegel Center.

Costs

Tuition for the 1999–2000 academic year was $24,810. The costs of a room and the average meal plan were $7991. The College fee was $446.

Financial Aid

All applicants with financial need are considered for Sarah Lawrence College aid programs and all federal campus-based programs. About 60 percent of the students receive financial aid. The awarding of institutional funds is based solely upon a determination of the student's financial need. Students are expected to apply for financial aid from the Federal Pell Grant Program and from their state scholarship and grant programs. Students must submit the Financial Aid PROFILE and the Free Application for Federal Student Aid (FAFSA) by February 1.

Faculty

Sarah Lawrence's student-faculty ratio is 6:1, one of the lowest in the country. Students work closely with an exceptional faculty of respected scholars, writers, artists, scientists, historians, and social scientists. Each faculty member is a committed teacher who attaches great importance to individual work with students. Ninety-one percent of Sarah Lawrence's faculty members in the sciences, social sciences, and the humanities hold a Ph.D. or terminal degree. Faculty members in the arts have achieved demonstrable excellence in the fields of music, dance, theater, the visual arts, and writing.

Student Government

The Sarah Lawrence College student body is self-governed by the Student Senate and the Student Life Committee. The

Student Senate is the principal policymaking and legislative body for matters concerning student affairs.

Admission Requirements

Sarah Lawrence College accepts freshman and transfer applicants for both the fall and spring semesters. The College recognizes that intelligence and creative power can be expressed in many different ways and is willing to look at both traditional and nontraditional criteria in assessing applicants. The completion of 16 units of secondary school work or the equivalent is the standard academic requirement for freshman admission. The College does not specify these units but recommends the usual distribution of rigorous college-preparatory courses.

High school seniors who consider Sarah Lawrence their first-choice college and who wish to be informed of an admission decision early in their senior year may apply as early decision candidates. The Admission Committee will also consider as early admission applicants those students with very strong academic qualifications and personal maturity who have completed three years of high school.

The College welcomes transfer applications from students who have completed at least one full year of college and from students who expect, in qualifying for the Bachelor of Arts degree, to spend at least two consecutive years at Sarah Lawrence College. (Students with less than one full year of credits who have matriculated at another college may apply for freshman admission with possible advanced standing.) Approximately 45 transfers matriculate each year from a wide range of postsecondary institutions.

Sophomores, juniors, and seniors enrolled at other institutions may apply to the Sarah Lawrence Guest Year Program for one semester or a complete year of full-time study at the College. Guests attend Sarah Lawrence to concentrate in a particular discipline not offered at their home institution, to work with respected master teachers one-on-one in conferences, and to take advantage of the facilities of New York City in conjunction with rigorous academic study. Students who have not matriculated elsewhere but wish to enroll in one or two specific courses for credit may apply as special students.

Scores on the SAT I or on three SAT II Subject Tests or on the ACT are required from all freshman applicants. The Test of English as a Foreign Language (TOEFL) must be taken by students who speak English as a second language. A personal interview on campus or with a local alumna/alumnus is strongly recommended for all applicants.

Sarah Lawrence College admits students regardless of race, color, sex, sexual orientation, handicap, or national origin and thereafter accords them all the rights and privileges generally made available to students at the College. The College is strongly committed to basing judgments about individuals upon their qualifications and abilities and to protecting individual rights of privacy, association, belief, and expression.

Application and Information

Students interested in attending Sarah Lawrence College should request application materials from the Office of Admission. The application deadline for freshmen for the fall semester is February 1. The notification date is early April, and the reply date is May 1. The College has two early decision programs. The fall early decision deadline is November 15, and notification is made on December 15. The winter early decision deadline is January 1, and notification is made on February 15.

The preferred filing date for transfer applicants for fall semester is April 1. Applications for transfer students are accepted and admission decisions are rendered on a rolling basis. The notification date is May 1, and the reply date is June 1. Applications for spring semester are accepted on a rolling basis. The preferred filing date is December 1. Application forms and additional information may be obtained by contacting:

Office of Admission
Sarah Lawrence College
Bronxville, New York 10708
Telephone: 914-395-2510
          800-888-2858 (toll-free)
E-mail: slcadmit@slc.edu
World Wide Web: http://www.slc.edu

Students relax on Westland's lawn.

SAVANNAH COLLEGE OF ART AND DESIGN
SAVANNAH, GEORGIA

The College

The Savannah College of Art and Design (SCAD), a private coeducational college, is open to both resident and nonresident students. Its philosophy is based on the premise that talent in the visual arts is best nurtured through an education focused on the individual, an education providing that individual with an intellectual diversity that enriches, a learning experience that challenges, and an environment that is creatively centered. The College's mission is to prepare talented students for careers in the visual and performing arts, design, building arts, and the history of art and architecture by emphasizing individual attention in a positively oriented environment. A uniquely balanced curriculum has attracted students from every state and from more than seventy-five countries to the school, making it the largest art and design college in the United States; its current enrollment is approximately 4,500 students.

Attractive residence hall accommodations, with meal plans, are provided for students who wish to reside in the College area. While students are not required to live in College housing, the camaraderie and intellectual stimulation enjoyed are usually considered highlights of the College experience. Space is available on a first-come, first-served basis. Furnishings (including drafting tables) and utilities are covered by the dormitory housing fee, which is payable in advance for the entire academic year. Early reservations are strongly recommended.

Competing as a Division III–level member of the NCAA, the College offers the following intercollegiate sports for both men and women: basketball, crew, equestrian, golf, soccer, and tennis; for women only, softball and volleyball; and for men only, baseball. Cheerleading, sailing, and cross-country are offered as club sports. A seasonal intramural program is also available, and students are encouraged to maintain a healthy lifestyle.

In addition to baccalaureate degrees, the College awards the Master of Fine Arts (M.F.A.) degree, the Master of Arts (M.A.) degree, and the Master of Architecture (M.Arch.) degree.

The College is accredited by the Commission on Colleges of the Southern Association of Colleges and Schools (1866 Southern Lane, Decatur, Georgia 30033-4097; telephone: 404-679-4500) to award bachelor's and master's degrees. The Bachelor of Architecture (B.Arch.) is also accredited by the National Architectural Accrediting Board (NAAB). Among its distinctions, the College has been cited with an Honor Award by the National Trust for Historic Preservation for its adaptive reuse of more than forty historic buildings to create a unique urban campus.

Location

The College is situated in the center of Savannah, Georgia's oldest city, only minutes from the Atlantic Ocean. Savannah has one of the nation's largest urban Historic Landmark Districts and provides a stimulating environment for the visually oriented student of art and design. Students majoring in historic preservation, architectural history, and architecture find the city to be a living laboratory. Savannah's mild climate and proximity to the ocean allow for many outdoor activities. Pleasant weather prevails, with normal mean temperatures ranging from 81 degrees in July to 51 degrees in December. Savannah has a cultural diversity that is outstanding among Southern cities. A symphony orchestra, several theater companies, more than twenty-five museums, the nation's second-largest St. Patrick's Day celebration, and many ethnic and arts festivals make Savannah both a cultural and a visual delight. Restaurants, movie theaters, clubs, and shops are easily accessible by foot, bike, or bus. Charleston, Jacksonville, Atlanta, and coastal islands such as Hilton Head are within driving distance and are pleasant to visit for a day or a weekend.

Majors and Degrees

The Savannah College of Art and Design grants the Bachelor of Fine Arts (B.F.A.) degree in architectural history, art history, computer art, fashion, fibers, furniture design, graphic design, historic preservation, illustration, interior design, media and performing arts, metals and jewelry, painting, photography, product design, sequential art, and video/film. The College also awards a five-year Bachelor of Architecture degree. Minors are offered in eleven areas of concentration, including architectural history, art history, decorative arts, drawing, electronic design, media and performing arts, museum studies, printmaking, sculpture, sound design, and writing.

Academic Program

The College operates on the quarter system. Fall, winter, and spring sessions extend from mid-September through May. Summer sessions in Savannah run from mid-June through mid-August. The College also offers a two-week summer session in New York and three-week sessions abroad through the off-campus program. Students may accumulate credits during all sessions.

The uniquely balanced curriculum prepares students for careers and offers them a well-rounded liberal arts general education, the traditional components of a fine arts education, the opportunity to acquire contemporary high-tech skills complemented by state-of-the-art facilities, and a comprehensive curriculum that encourages double majors and multidisciplinary explorations. The total course of study for a B.F.A. degree consists of 180 quarter credit hours (thirty-six courses). Of these, a student takes 35–50 hours in the foundation studio program, 55–65 hours in general education/liberal arts, 60–70 hours in the major area of study, and 10–20 hours of electives. The B.Arch. degree requires 225 hours, which include 35 foundation hours, 60 hours in general education/liberal arts, 95 hours in the major program, and 35 hours of electives. Independent study programs are also available to students wishing to pursue a highly specialized area of study. To enhance the academic programs, the College offers seminars, lectures, and workshops by distinguished artists, scholars, and other professionals during the academic year at no charge. Study trips to major centers of artistic activity are made each quarter and provide further opportunities for enrichment. The College offers supportive academic counseling, with special programs for first-year students and tutors for all students available at no charge. The Writing Assistance Center offers consultative assistance to students at all levels of the writing process.

Academic Facilities

The urban campus is made up of historically significant structures of elegant style and proportion located in the heart of Savannah's Historic Landmark District. Well-equipped studios and classrooms with state-of-the-art facilities are available in each area of concentration: for computer art, an Intranet of Power Macintosh, Intergraph, and Silicon Graphics workstations; for fashion, computer-aided design and Nedgraphics design and pattern technology; for fibers, traditional floor looms, a Jacquard loom, and looms for computer-aided woven design; for graphic design, multiple computer labs and production equipment; for metals and jewelry, casting and finishing rooms and other studios; for painting, spacious, well-lit studio areas and individual studios; for photography, a digital imaging computer lab and multiple darkrooms; for product design, electronic design studios connected to a client/network server configured with a diverse range of software, including Autocad, Catia, Microstation, Adobe Photoshop, 3D Studio Max, SurfCAM, and Alias; for sequential art, computers for computer coloring classes; and for video/film, a Super Panther dolly, a steadicam, a variety of editing suites, a chromakey/bluescreen studio, a sound stage, a 24-track Mozart audio production suite, scriptwriting lab, and a large concentration of AVID equipment. The facility that houses architecture, historic preservation, furniture design, and interior design offers several computer-aided design (CAD) labs, metals conservation and paint analysis labs, a photography studio, a woodshop, a model shop, and other studios. Trustees Theater, a 28,000-square-foot Art Moderne–style building, operates as a venue for media and performing arts. The College library contains more than 60,000 volumes, 295,000 slides, 893 serials, 1,850 videotapes, and 2,553 microform units, providing support to the academic majors of art history and architectural history, as well as other major programs. A number of on-campus galleries exhibit student and faculty work as well as that of nationally recognized artists. The campus supports thirty-five computer labs, including homework, Internet, and major-specific labs.

Costs

Undergraduate tuition for the 2000–01 academic year is $16,200. This includes all fees, but not the cost of books and art materials. The housing fee for the academic year (three quarters) is $4200, which includes a $500 nonrefundable deposit. A meal plan for the 2000–01 academic year costs $2550. The College's restaurants serve three meals per day, which may be purchased individually. Students also may prepare their own meals in some student housing facilities.

Financial Aid

Approximately 73 percent of the College's students receive financial assistance. The Savannah College of Art and Design has a number of financial aid programs, which may consist of scholarships, grants, loans, or any combination of these, from federal (including the Federal Direct Loan Program), state, and College sources. Application may be made at any time during the academic year; however, early application is advised. Students may also help finance educational expenses through the Federal Work-Study Program and the College's Student Placement Service. Many employment opportunities exist in the Savannah area, and the College refers interested students to appropriate part-time or freelance jobs when they are available. A detailed listing of the financial aid programs may be obtained from the financial aid office.

Faculty

A large and distinguished international faculty consists of professors with diverse backgrounds, both professionally and educationally. The College maintains a low student/faculty ratio (approximately 17:1), with classes taught by caring, dedicated faculty members who hold terminal degrees or other outstanding credentials in their fields. Individual attention is emphasized, and all faculty members adhere to the belief that it is the teacher's responsibility to help and encourage the student during class time as well as in individual conferences.

Student Government

The United Student Forum is composed of representatives from various leadership groups on campus. The Inter-Club Council consists of delegates from the more than forty officially recognized student organizations. Campus events such as concerts, film screenings, dances, and other entertainment as well as cultural, recreational, and social programs are planned and produced by the Student Activities Council.

Admission Requirements

The Savannah College of Art and Design is committed to the pursuit of excellence and welcomes applicants who have the same high standards. New students may enter in the fall, winter, spring, or summer quarter. Applicants must submit the following: the College's admission application form, nonrefundable application fee, SAT I or ACT scores, official transcripts from each high school or college attended, and three letters of recommendation. A portfolio and interview are encouraged but are not required. Preference is given to students with a GPA of 3.0 or above. A minimum SAT math score of 540 or ACT math score of 23 is required for acceptance into the architecture program. Prospective students should possess exceptional aptitude for the visual arts.

A student may be admitted at the end of his or her junior year in high school (omitting the senior year) or on a part-time basis during the senior year if he or she has a GPA of 3.5 (B+) or higher through the eleventh grade, if the SAT I or ACT scores are above the national average, and if the student's counselor or teacher recommends early admission.

Freshman-, sophomore-, junior-, and senior-level transfer students are accepted. Students must complete in residence the final 45 hours of any degree earned at the College.

International students currently make up 12 percent of the student population. International applicants must submit scores on the Test of English as a Foreign Language (TOEFL). Preference is given to applicants with a score of 500 or above. Art history applicants must have a minimum score of 550. SAT I or ACT scores are not required for international applicants. International students must present proof of having adequate funds for one year.

Exceptions to the general rules on admission may be made for students of unusual motivation and ability. The Savannah College of Art and Design does not discriminate on the basis of race, color, national or ethnic origin, religion, age, sex, handicap, or marital status in administering its educational policies, admission policies, scholarship and loan programs, athletics, and other institutionally administered programs or activities generally made available to students at the College.

Application and Information

Applicants are encouraged to apply as early as possible. The nonrefundable application fee is $50. Admission decisions are made on a rolling basis.

For further information on the Savannah College of Art and Design, students should contact:

Director of Undergraduate Enrollment
Admissions Department
Savannah College of Art and Design
342 Bull Street
P.O. Box 3146
Savannah, Georgia 31402-3146
Telephone: 912-525-5100
        800-869-SCAD (toll-free)
Fax: 912-525-5983
E-mail: admissions@scad.edu
World Wide Web: http://www.scad.edu

Poetter Hall, SCAD's flagship building in Savannah's Historic District.

SAVANNAH STATE UNIVERSITY
SAVANNAH, GEORGIA

The University

Savannah State University is a senior coeducational unit of the University System of Georgia. The University is committed to serving students who are well prepared academically. Its programs are designed to provide opportunities for students to improve themselves, attain career objectives, and compete effectively in the job market. The University comprises three colleges: the College of Business Administration, the College of Liberal Arts and Social Sciences, and the College of Sciences and Technology. In addition to its undergraduate programs, the University offers three master's degrees: the Master of Public Administration, the Master of Social Work, and the Master of Urban Studies. All degree programs at Savannah State University are accredited by the Southern Association of Colleges and Schools. The programs in civil, electronics, and mechanical engineering technology are accredited by the Accreditation Board for Engineering and Technology and the social work programs by the Council on Social Work Education.

Most of the 2,560 undergraduate students enrolled at Savannah State University are Georgia residents, although eighteen states and seventeen other countries are represented. Students can participate in numerous social and academic organizations as well as in intercollegiate and intramural sports. Savannah State athletes compete in baseball, basketball, cross-country, football, tennis, track, and volleyball. On-campus housing is available.

Through the University's Army and Naval ROTC programs, students can prepare for commissioned service as regular officers in the Army, Navy, or Marine Corps while earning their degrees. The Army and Naval ROTC programs constitute academic minors in military science and naval science, respectively.

Location

The University is located in the Hostess City of the South, beautiful, historic Savannah, Georgia. The campus is a 10-minute drive from the Atlantic Ocean and the sandy beaches of Tybee Island. Students at Savannah State enjoy the best of two worlds—the cultural advantages of a metropolitan city and the sun and surf of the ocean and boating, fishing, and waterskiing on the many area rivers. The city also offers excellent golfing and tennis facilities.

Savannah offers exciting scientific resources like the Skidaway Marine Science Complex and the Savannah Science Museum. Culturally, the city offers the Savannah Symphony Orchestra, ballet and theater groups, the Telfair Museum of Arts and Sciences, the King-Tisdell Black Heritage Museum, and special celebrations and festivals such as Night in Old Savannah.

Savannah has a population of approximately 250,000 and is famous for its Low Country cuisine, scenic boat tours, specialty shops, and riverfront activities. The international airport and extensive railway system make Savannah easily accessible to all of the Southeast and the nation.

Majors and Degrees

Savannah State University provides innovative instruction of high quality through the College of Business Administration, the College of Liberal Arts and Social Sciences, and the College of Sciences and Technology.

The College of Business Administration offers programs that lead to the Bachelor of Business Administration in accounting, computer information systems, international business management, management, and marketing.

The College of Liberal Arts and Social Sciences grants the Bachelor of Arts degree in African and African-American studies, English language and literature, history, mass communication, and music and the Bachelor of Science degree in criminal justice, political science, recreation and parks administration, and sociology. The College also offers a Bachelor of Social Work degree. Minor areas include African and African-American studies, art, criminal justice, English language and literature, French, gerontology, history, mass communication, political science, psychology, recreation and park administration, religious and philosophical studies, sociology, Spanish, and theater.

The College of Sciences and Technology offers the Bachelor of Science degree in biology (premedicine or preprofessional), chemical engineering technology, chemistry, civil engineering technology, computer science technology, electronics engineering technology, environmental studies, marine sciences, mathematics, and mechanical engineering technology.

Academic Program

The core curriculum of the University System of Georgia is the foundation upon which all degree programs are built. All candidates for a baccalaureate degree must complete a minimum of 125 semester hours, including health, physical education, and orientation; maintain a scholastic average of C or better; and satisfactorily complete the minimum requirements of the core curriculum and of the specific degree programs. Students must also satisfactorily complete the University System of Georgia Language Skills Examination and the major comprehensive examinations as prescribed by their specific schools.

The University offers four-year Naval ROTC programs and two-year and three-year Army ROTC programs through either a scholarship or a regular University program. Graduates receive a commission as a second lieutenant in the U.S. Marine Corps, as an ensign in the U.S. Navy, or as a second lieutenant in the U.S. Army.

The University operates on the semester system, with each semester extending over a period of fifteen weeks. Normally, the baccalaureate degree is earned in eight semesters. A full course load is considered to be 12 hours, with the maximum load being 19 hours.

Savannah State may grant credit for satisfactory scores on selected tests of the College-Level Examination Program (CLEP), for satisfactory completion of appropriate courses and tests offered through DANTES (formerly the United States Armed Forces Institute), for work completed at military service schools, and for military experience as recommended by the Commission on Accreditation of Service Experiences of the American Council on Education. Such credits may not exceed more than one fourth of the work counted toward a degree. Advanced Placement scores are accepted from the College Board.

Off-Campus Arrangements

The Continuing Education Center in Savannah provides opportunities to a wide cross-section of members of the community who could not otherwise get to classes on the campus.

The cooperative education program provides an off-campus option that enables students to receive on-the-job training while earning money for their tuition. The University will arrange and approve assignments with cooperating companies and agencies, and supervision is provided by representatives of the University as well as the employers.

In addition to offering instruction on campus, Savannah State University is authorized to offer correspondence courses at the college level. Such courses have become recognized sources of public education, reflecting a sense of obligation to those who cannot undertake resident instruction and to those who do not require resident instruction for personal growth and enrichment.

Academic Facilities

Gordon Library, a modern library with excellent facilities and a well-prepared staff, serves the University and the community. It houses more than 182,000 cataloged volumes, approximately 900 periodicals, more than 558,000 microfilms, and 25,000 bound periodicals. Approximately 8,000 volumes are added yearly to keep the collection up-to-date. There is an extensive collection of materials about African Americans. The library, which is the cultural and intellectual center of the University, can house 290,000 volumes. The building has many conference and individual study areas, an audiovisual department, two Distant Learning Centers, a Curriculum Materials Center, open stacks, classrooms, and typing facilities. The library is easily distinguishable from the other buildings on campus because of its distinctive circular shape.

Other campus facilities include the School of Business building and the Marine Biology Wet Laboratory.

Costs

In 1999–2000, tuition and fees for students living on campus were $3220 per semester for Georgia residents and $5932 per semester for non-Georgia residents. The above costs included the matriculation fee, health fee, student activity fee, athletics fee, room, board, and laundry. Books cost approximately $200 per semester.

Financial Aid

Almost 87 percent of all Savannah State University students receive financial aid through federal and state grants, including Pell Grants, Supplemental Educational Opportunity Grants, Georgia Incentive Grants, Perkins Loans, College Work-Study Program awards, and work opportunities provided by the University. Students requesting financial aid are required to submit the Free Application for Federal Student Aid (FAFSA), the University's own institutional financial aid form, and their parents' 1040 federal income tax form.

Faculty

Savannah State University has a full-time faculty of 137 members, with nearly 70 percent of them holding an earned doctorate. The full-time student-faculty ratio is 15:1.

Student Government

The Student Government Association serves the needs of the students; its members are elected by the student body. This organization is set up with executive, legislative, and judicial branches, and it is influential in campus affairs. The Student Government Association is the chief student organization on campus. It helps to govern the student body as well as to plan social events for the academic year. Students also serve on all major University committees.

Admission Requirements

Factors considered in assessing a student's readiness for admission to Savannah State University include the high school grade point average and curriculum, test scores, previous college work, and other qualifications. Each applicant for admission to the freshman class is required to take the SAT I or the ACT. Completion of the College Preparatory Curriculum (CPC) is required. Transfers must have maintained a minimum 2.0 grade point average.

Application and Information

Application can be made anytime following completion of the junior year of high school. Students are notified of the admission decision soon after receipt of the completed application and supporting documents.

Office of Admissions
Savannah State University
P.O. Box 20209
Savannah, Georgia 31404
Telephone: 912-356-2181
        800-788-0478 (toll-free)
Fax: 912-356-2256

SCHILLER INTERNATIONAL UNIVERSITY
DUNEDIN, FLORIDA

The University

Schiller International University (SIU) was founded in 1964. Although originally intended for American students, the University soon attracted men and women from other nations and is now an international, coeducational four-year institution with eight locations in six countries and alumni from more than 130 countries. SIU prepares students for careers in business and management, multinational organizations, government agencies, academic institutions, and the social services as well as for further study. Through enrollment in both practical and theoretical courses and through discussions with instructors and classmates with multicultural backgrounds, students gain firsthand knowledge of business and cultural relations among the peoples of the world. In addition, SIU students have the unique opportunity to transfer between SIU campuses, without losing any credits, while continuing their chosen program of study. The language of instruction at all campuses is English. The current enrollment is 1,755 students.

SIU students are housed in University residence halls, with selected host families, or in private rooms or apartments. On-campus residence is required at the Engelberg campus. Residence hall accommodations are also available at the London and Florida campuses and in Heidelberg, Strasbourg, and Leysin. At all campuses not requiring on-campus residence, or in the event that all residence halls are full, trained staff assist students in securing housing in the private market or with families.

SIU offers the Master of Arts degree in international hotel and tourism management and in international relations and diplomacy with an optional specialization in international business or European studies; the Master of Business Administration degree in international business and in international hotel and tourism management; and the Master of International Management in international business.

Schiller International University is an accredited member of the Accrediting Council for Independent Colleges and Schools, which is recognized by the United States Department of Education as a national institutional accrediting agency. SIU degrees correspond to the American system of university education and are authorized at the European campuses by the Delaware State Board of Education and at the Florida campus by the Florida State Board of Independent Colleges and Universities.

Location

Schiller International University has campuses in Dunedin, Florida; central London, England; Paris and Strasbourg, France; Heidelberg, Germany; Madrid, Spain; and Engelberg and Leysin, Switzerland. More detail about each campus location is offered below.

SIU–Florida (residential)—the main campus is in the city of Dunedin on the Gulf of Mexico, one of America's most beautiful coastal regions, near the Tampa–St. Petersburg metropolitan area. The campus facilities, a large former hotel and three additional buildings, face directly on the beach and include a large auditorium and swimming pool. The English Language Institute–Florida is on campus.

SIU–London—Waterloo (central London–residential) is in the magnificent Royal Waterloo House, centrally located near the Waterloo Bridge and the South Bank cultural center.

SIU–Paris (nonresidential) is centrally located in a modern building on the left bank of the Seine in the exciting Montparnasse area, with easy access to all of Paris.

SIU–Strasbourg (residential) occupies the Château de Pourtalès in Robertsau at the northern edge of the city. The Château offers classroom, dormitory, and dining facilities (two restaurants and a Salon de Thé) and access to the European Community's Parliament Building and Court of Justice in Strasbourg.

SIU–Heidelberg (residential) is located next to the Law School of the University of Heidelberg in the center of town. The Graduate Center and student residence are located just across the Neckar River in the beautiful Palais Friedrich.

SIU–Madrid (nonresidential) is located in a modern building in the Arguelles, one of the city's most attractive districts.

SIU–Engelberg (Switzerland-residential) is located in SIU's Hotel Europe, a large, well-known hotel of long tradition, and in the lovely Hotel Bellevue, both in the heart of the Swiss Alps, not far from Lucerne.

American College of Switzerland (residential) is a campus of SIU located above the eastern end of Lake Geneva in the French-speaking portion of Switzerland, near Geneva and the French and Italian borders. (A separate catalog is available.)

Majors and Degrees

Schiller International University offers the Bachelor of International Business Administration (B.B.A. in international business) degree, with concentrations in banking, financial management, management, and marketing. Schiller also offers the Bachelor of Business Administration degree in international hotel and tourism management, with concentrations in hotel management and tourism management.

The Bachelor of Arts (B.A.) degree is offered in interdepartmental studies, international economics, international relations and diplomacy, and psychology.

The Bachelor of Science (B.S.) degree is offered in economics and international business administration.

The associate degree in business administration (A.S.) is offered with an optional concentration in computer system management.

Schiller also offers the associate degree in business administration (A.S.) in international hotel and tourism management, with concentrations in hotel management and tourism management.

Associate of Science (A.S.) degrees are offered in pre-engineering, premedicine, and pre–veterinary medicine.

Associate of Arts (A.A.) degrees are offered in general studies, with a concentration in art and design.

Diplomas are available in hotel operational management and Swiss hotel management. The hotel operational management diploma requires two semesters of on-campus study and a six-month internship.

Certificates (awarded after completion of a one-year program) are offered in hotel operations.

Academic Program

The academic emphasis at Schiller International University is on international business, international relations and diplomacy, international hotel and tourism management, and languages.

The Collegium Palatinum, a division of the University, offers intensive language programs in German, French, and Spanish and in English as a foreign language (EFL) at the Language Institutes located on various campuses. EFL courses are offered at all SIU campuses. Regular University courses in German, French, Spanish, and English are also offered, although not all languages are available at every campus.

An associate degree program requires 62 credits; a bachelor's degree program requires 124 credits. An average grade of C (2.0) or higher is required for all programs. Each credit reflects 15 academic hours of classroom work; typical courses earn 3–4 credits.

Classes run during two 15-week semesters and a 7-week summer session in a manner similar to that at most universities in the United States.

Academic Facilities

Each campus includes classrooms, computer facilities, a library, and a student lounge. The University library holdings are about 92,000 volumes. In addition, students also have access to extensive external libraries for original research.

Costs

For 2000–01, tuition and required fees at the Florida campus are $6780 per semester; room and board are $2750 per semester. Costs at the European campuses are $7280 per semester for tuition and required fees and $3600 per semester for room and board. Full room and board are available in London and Engelberg only; room without board is available in Heidelberg. (The American College of Switzerland campus has a separate schedule of fees. Students are encouraged to see that school's statistical profile information at the front of this volume.)

Financial Aid

SIU grants two kinds of financial aid: academic scholarships (for 200 students) and University service (work-study) grants. Total aid will not exceed one half of the tuition. Students are encouraged to seek assistance through private or government loan and scholarship programs before applying to the University. Eligible students may apply for a Federal Stafford Student Loan (U.S. citizens only) or a Canada Student Loan (Canadian citizens only). Applications for financial aid must be received by March 31 for the following academic year.

Faculty

The faculty consists of more than 280 men and women who are academically qualified and experienced in their fields. Extensive student-faculty interaction is encouraged; the faculty-student ratio is about 1:18.

Student Government

Each campus has an elected Student Council that acts as a liaison between the students and the administration and is involved in many areas of academic and social life.

Admission Requirements

Applicants must have completed the secondary level of education in a government-recognized educational system, generally of twelve years' duration, or have the equivalent of five GCE-O-level examinations (British school system). Students who have not completed the equivalent of high school studies or five GCE-O-level examinations may be eligible to apply for special University-preparatory programs.

All nonnative English speakers must take the SIU–English Placement Test when first enrolling. Those whose English language proficiency is not adequate for University-level studies will be required to take additional English language courses.

Application and Information

Applications are handled individually and without regard to race, sex, religion, national or ethnic origin, or country of citizenship. Because SIU operates on a rolling admissions system, applicants are advised of their admission status soon after all application materials (a completed application form and official transcripts of all secondary-level education and, for transfer applicants, all college-level study) and the $35 application fee have been received. For application forms or further information, students should contact the appropriate campus below.

Admissions Office
Royal Waterloo House
Schiller International University
51-55 Waterloo Road
London, SE1 8TX
England
Telephone: 71 928 8484
Fax: 71 620 1226

Admissions Office
Schiller International University
453 Edgewater Drive
Dunedin, Florida 34698-4964
Telephone: 727-736-5082
        800-336-4133 (toll-free within the U.S. only)
Fax: 727-734-0359
E-mail: admissions@schiller.edu
World Wide Web: http://www.schiller.edu/

The Dunedin, Florida, campus of Schiller International University.

SCHOOL OF THE ART INSTITUTE OF CHICAGO
CHICAGO, ILLINOIS

The School

Founded in 1866 as the Chicago Academy of Design, the School of the Art Institute of Chicago has been in continuous operation since then. The Michigan Avenue Museum building was originally constructed for the 1892 Columbian Exposition; in 1895, the Museum and the School acquired the structure. Expansion has continued through the years, and currently School facilities number five buildings. In 1997, the School purchased a 190-bed residence hall; in fall 2000, another 467-bed residence hall opens. The School now enrolls 1,612 full- and part-time undergraduate students representing forty-nine states and forty countries. Students are granted free entrance to the Art Institute of Chicago.

The School believes in facilitating the artist's imaginative depth and reach and seeks to promote the climate and base from which students can explore many artistic directions through a variety of media. No single aesthetic or style dominates the curriculum, the faculty, or the work of students. Every member of the faculty and staff and every student influences the School and helps determine its present and future directions.

The School offers a broad spectrum of services to accommodate its diverse population, including an international student office, multicultural affairs office, health and counseling services, and a learning center (offering one-on-one tutoring as well as support services for students with learning disabilities). Students may also take advantage of cooperative education opportunities throughout Chicago and the nation with individual artists, museums and galleries, multimedia firms, film and video production houses, interior architecture firms, fashion designers, and community service organizations. In addition, the Career Development Center recognizes the varied opportunities for employment in art-related fields and offers students assistance in developing skills, such as writing grants; preparing portfolios, artist statements, and teaching philosophies; exploring exhibition possibilities; and understanding the legal aspects of entrepreneurship. The center also maintains listings of many local and national positions, including freelance, part-time, and full-time employment.

There are currently fifteen student groups on campus, ranging from the Chinese Cultural Association to the Photography Club. The School also has an award-winning monthly student newspaper, *F Magazine,* and recently introduced a television station.

Location

The School of the Art Institute of Chicago is located in the heart of downtown Chicago, the nation's third-largest city and home to the nation's second-largest art scene, including museums, more than 150 galleries, alternative spaces, and organizations supporting the arts. Students have a wide variety of cultural and recreational resources from which to choose: ballet, opera, theater, orchestra halls, cinemas, libraries, architecture, blues and jazz clubs, parks, ethnic restaurants, and street festivals. An extensive public transportation system allows students access to citywide events and to outlying communities.

Majors and Degrees

The School of the Art Institute of Chicago offers a four-year program leading to the Bachelor of Fine Arts degree, working in one or any combination of the following studio areas: art and technology, art education, ceramics, fashion design, fiber, filmmaking, interior architecture, painting and drawing, performance, photography, printmaking, sculpture, sound, video, and visual communication. The School also offers a Bachelor of Interior Architecture program, intended for students who plan to become registered professional interior designers. In addition, the School offers Illinois teacher certification (K–12) in art education, a Bachelor of Fine Arts degree with emphasis in art history, and a Bachelor of Arts in visual and critical studies.

Academic Program

Completion of 132 hours is required for the B.F.A. degree, approximately two thirds being in studio areas and one third in academic course work. All entering students who have completed fewer than 18 semester hours of college-level studio art must enroll in the First Year Program. Students in the First Year Program take two-, three-, and four-dimensional (performance, video, film, electronics, and kinetics) studio courses and art history and elective course work and attend colloquium presentations that feature visiting artists and various School department heads. Majors are not required, and students develop their own areas of concentration with faculty and staff guidance. Courses are graded on a pass/fail basis.

Off-Campus Arrangements

Students attending the School of the Art Institute of Chicago can choose from a wide variety of off-campus programs. The Mobility program allows students to attend partner schools within the United States and Canada and includes the New York Studio semester. The School also maintains semester exchange agreements with more than twenty schools in Europe, Asia, and South America. The Off-Campus Programs office works closely with students to help them develop their individual programs. The School's faculty members also lead two- or three-week study trips during each summer and winter interim. In the past, groups have gone to China, England, France, Ireland, Italy, and South Africa.

Academic Facilities

The School of the Art Institute of Chicago's campus encompasses six buildings in downtown Chicago. There are fully equipped studios for each area of concentration, and the School's policy allows 24-hour access to facilities. In 1995, a 40,000-square-foot permanent exhibition space was added.

The painting and drawing department has many well-lit studios, individual space for select undergraduate and graduate students, and space for critiques. There are classes in particular disciplines, such as figure painting and drawing and materials and techniques, as well as classes that encourage freely creative activity. Facilities in the sculpture department include a complete wood shop, a welding shop, a bronze and aluminum foundry, a plaster room, and an outdoor exhibition space. A well-equipped metals shop allows for forging, forming, joining, and casting of nonferrous metals. The printmaking department has five etching presses, six stone lithography presses, a Heidelberg Kord and Chief offset press, a process camera, a large-format camera, a professional photomechanical darkroom, bookbinding equipment, a Macintosh computer lab, and a Novajet printer.

The art and technology department supports several computer labs, including Macintosh-based labs and Silicon Graphics facilities equipped with ten Maya systems; in addition, an input-output room supports printing and scanning. All labs are networked together and are connected to the Internet via a high-speed link. The department also maintains a high-end video editing room, a multimedia authoring suite, an electronics construction shop, a microcontroller development and programming area, a kinetics shop, a fully equipped neon studio, a holography studio, dedicated installation space, and MIDI and digital sound systems. The video department currently has a full range of video tools, ranging from a unique hand-built image processor to the latest industrial equipment. Editing systems support Hi-8, ¾-inch, S-VHS, and Beta SP, and there are AVID and MEDIA 100 digital editing suites. Equipment available to students includes Hi-8 and digital cameras, projectors, switchers, light kits, and microphones.

The filmmaking department facilities include a sixty-seat theater, a 25-foot shooting set, work studios for 3-D and 2-D animation, and a professional interlock sound suite. Equipment for students includes sync and nonsync cameras, sound equipment, optical printers, a wet lab for image processing, and an animation stand and camera. The photography department has three large printing labs, an alternative process darkroom, fourteen individual color exposing rooms, three mural printing rooms, 30 inch by 50 inch processors for color negative and positive printing, a computer classroom with thirteen stations, a computer peripheral with flatbed and a variety of film scanners, a 4 by 5 film recorder, various inkjet printers, and a 36-inch Novajet inkjet printer. Equipment checkout privileges give students access to photography equipment, supplies, and chemicals.

The ceramics department facilities include three clay mixers, an extruder, a slab roller, complete mold making and casting facilities, and several styles of wheels. Bulk materials (clay, slip, and glazes) are provided, and diverse firing options in various kiln styles include high- and low-fire oxidation and reduction, soda, and raku. The visual communication department facilities include a state-of-the-art computer lab with color scanners, a copy stand, and spacious studios. Fashion design students study design and construction in a spacious facility with industrial-grade equipment and a dedicated staff. The department houses a Fashion Resource Center with a collection of worldwide designer garments and a research library with rare books, videotapes, and international publications. The fiber and material studies department has thirty-two looms, a large area for hand construction, a computer lab with five stations, a computer loom, and a kitchen with industrial-sized washers and dryers used for the setting of dyes.

The John M. Flaxman Library collections include approximately 60,000 volumes on art and the liberal arts and sciences, 360 periodical subscriptions, and films, videos, audiotapes, CDs, microforms, and picture files. The Joan Flasch Artists' Book Collection contains more than 3,000 artists' books along with a research collection of exhibition catalogs and other related material. Students may also utilize the research collections of the Art Institute of Chicago's Ryerson and Burnham Libraries, one of the oldest, largest, and finest art museum libraries in the country. Its noncirculating, closed-stack collections include more than 300,000 volumes and 2,225 periodicals, constituting an invaluable resource for students of the history of art and architecture. The MacLean Visual Resource Center maintains a noncirculating collection of more than 500,000 slides.

The Video Data Bank houses more than 1,800 titles by and about contemporary artists, including experimental tapes spanning the history of video as an art form. The Film Center is a theater, research center, and archive, screening more than 500 films per year. The Poetry Center at the School provides a forum for public reading by local, national, and international poets and writers.

The School's exhibition spaces include the Betty Rymer Gallery, which highlights work from departments and presents special exhibitions, and Gallery 2, with exhibition space, a performance space, and a space designed for site-specific installations. In addition, Gallery X and the Lounge Gallery, sponsored by the Student Union Galleries, provide exhibition space for currently enrolled students.

Costs

Tuition for the 1999–2000 academic year was $19,140 for full-time undergraduate students (15 credit hours per semester) and $638 per credit hour. Students choosing to live in student housing facilities paid between $6540 and $7320 per academic year for a single room or $6070 per academic year for double occupancy. Unlike most schools, the School does not charge a lab or activities fee in addition to tuition. At present, the estimated costs for books and supplies, room and board, travel, and personal expenses are between $12,000 and $13,000 per academic year, depending on individual need.

Financial Aid

The School makes every effort to assist students who need help in financing their education. Through an extensive financial aid program, $13.2 million in gift aid funding from private, institutional, state, and federal sources is distributed annually. In addition to scholarships and grants, the School grants merit scholarships and offers an extensive college work-study program. To apply for financial aid, students should complete the Free Application for Federal Student Aid (FAFSA), available from the Financial Aid Office. To receive priority consideration, students should submit completed forms to the Financial Aid Office no later than March 15. All awards are made on a first-come, first-served basis to students in good standing who demonstrate need.

Faculty

Faculty members are selected for their effectiveness and dedication as teachers and for their professional activity and commitment as artists, designers, and scholars. There are currently 347 full- and part-time faculty members, among them 10 Guggenheim recipients and numerous NEA and NEH grant recipients. Each year, more than 100 well-known visiting artists, including poets and political activists, as well as visual artists, present workshops and provide individual student critiques.

Student Government

Student government officers are elected each spring, and their mission is to promote student interests and concerns to the broader School community. Student government representatives attend faculty department heads meetings and space-planning meetings and often sit on search committees for new faculty members. Open student government meetings are held weekly.

Admission Requirements

The School maintains a selective admission policy, favoring students who demonstrate an interest in producing work and exploring the possibilities of the visual arts in a professional setting. High school graduates, recipients of a high school equivalency certificate, and college transfer students are invited to apply. To be considered for the B.F.A. program, applicants are required to submit the admissions application; a nonrefundable application fee of $45; a portfolio of fifteen to twenty slides or original pieces showing a full range of the applicant's work; a statement of purpose; transcript(s) from high school(s) or an official copy of the high school equivalency certificate; transcripts from any college previously attended; one letter of recommendation; and, for all applicants who do not have two full years of college credit, SAT I or ACT scores and TOEFL scores for international students. Applicants with more than 18 semester hours of studio transfer credit must submit thirty slides of their art work, representing their current interest and educational experience. In addition to the above, the portfolio of Bachelor of Interior Architecture applicants should demonstrate understanding of and sensitivity to the built environment, including drawings from direct observation and a selection of plans, sections, and elevations.

Application and Information

Students may apply to the School by using the Immediate Decision Option (IDO) or the traditional admission procedure. The Immediate Decision Option allows those students who bring the required application materials listed above to visit the School on a designated day and have an admissions decision made on the end of that day. IDO applicants are encouraged to bring actual work with them rather than slides. During an IDO day, students tour the School facility, meet with currently enrolled students, and attend financial aid and career presentations.

Those students applying through the traditional admission procedure have their portfolio and academic credentials reviewed and evaluated by the Admissions Committee. Students are admitted on a rolling basis and are informed of the committee's decision by mail. Students who anticipate a need for financial assistance are urged to complete applications for admission and financial aid by March 1 in order to receive priority consideration. Application forms and additional information are available from:

Office of Admissions
School of the Art Institute of Chicago
37 South Wabash
Chicago, Illinois 60603
Telephone: 312-899-5219
    800-232-7242 (toll-free)
E-mail: admiss@artic.edu
World Wide Web: http://www.artic.edu/saic/saichome.html

SCHOOL OF THE MUSEUM OF FINE ARTS
BOSTON, MASSACHUSETTS

The School

The School of the Museum of Fine Arts (SMFA) offers students the opportunity to design their own individualized course of study and to tailor a program that best suits their needs and goals. A division of the Museum of Fine Arts and affiliated with Tufts University, the SMFA offers a diverse curriculum with a full range of studio and academic resources. A large faculty of working artists and an intimate student-faculty ratio of 10:1 provide each student extensive opportunities for individual consultation and dialogue.

Similar to an artists' colony, the SMFA's focus is on creative investigation, risk-taking, and the exploration of individual vision. For artists working in the new millennium, individual vision may take many forms: private acts of object-making, performance, collaboration, electronic imaging, or computer networking.

In order to educate individuals who will become working artists of significance in local and global culture, the SMFA embraces a wide range of media and perspectives in the production of artwork. Similarly, the School makes available a number of different programs to accommodate the varied backgrounds and experiences of the individuals who attend.

The School's extensive interdisciplinary studio curriculum is developed continually in order to incorporate new media and new approaches, concepts, and theories. A rapidly changing and culturally diverse art world is further introduced through the School's dynamic exhibition and visiting artists programs.

Since the studio curriculum is entirely elective, the School requires only that students determine which faculty member, classroom, peer, and community resources are important for their development, and then pursue their work.

Students are free to work in a single medium or move across media, combining them according to their interests and inclinations. In this way, each student shapes a focus. Students may work in painting and video, in electronic imaging and stained glass, or in printmaking, film, and drawing—the combinations are endless, as are the results.

Student Services has a knowledgeable staff that is available to assist students in finding living accommodations and to answer questions. Limited residence hall housing is available at neighboring Simmons College (for women) and the Boston Conservatory (for men). The office also provides a comprehensive guide to housing in the city and listings of local realtors, studio contacts, and currently available apartments and roommates.

In addition to its undergraduate degree and diploma programs, the SMFA offers a postbaccalaureate certificate as well as a Master of Arts in Teaching and Master of Fine Arts in affiliation with Tufts University.

Location

Boston is home to many educational and cultural institutions. The SMFA is a vital member of the art community, presenting a dynamic schedule of exhibitions, lectures, and panel discussions throughout the year. A variety of social events and activities are also presented, including frequent trips to New York City. An extensive public transportation system includes subways, buses, and commuter trains.

Majors and Degrees

The School of the Museum of Fine Arts offers the following programs: the All-Studio Diploma, the Fifth Year Certificate, and the Post-Baccalaureate Certificate. In affiliation with Tufts University, it offers the following degree programs: B.F.A., B.F.A. in art education, and five-year combined B.A./B.S. and B.F.A. The School offers courses in the following areas: art of Africa, artists' books and multiples, ceramics, computer arts, drawing, electronic arts, film and animation, glass, graphic design and illustration, metalsmithing, painting, papermaking, performance, photography, printmaking, sculpture, video, and visual and critical studies.

Academic Program

Students design their own programs of study, with advice from teachers and members of the administration. The only limitations on this elective system in studio art are the prerequisites stipulated for some courses. The School recommends basic courses for students who need foundation work in any studio area.

Teaching methods range from structured classes, requiring regular attendance, to individual instruction for work done independently outside the School, with periodic visits by the teacher.

Students' studio art work is evaluated at the end of every semester by a review board made up of teachers and students; the student being reviewed participates in this evaluation. Letter grades are not given for studio courses. Students advance on an individual basis. In some cases, extra credits are granted for exceptional accomplishments, permitting a student to graduate in less than the usual four years. Academic courses are graded in the traditional manner.

The School's degree programs, offered in affiliation with Tufts University, are variations on the diploma curriculum. Students in the degree programs take courses in studio art at the School and courses in academic areas of study at Tufts.

To earn a diploma, students must accumulate 120 studio credits. B.F.A. programs require a range of eighteen to twenty-four academic courses (depending on the program) and 90 semester-hour credits in studio art.

The SMFA also offers selective cross-registration with MIT and a dual-degree program with Wheaton College. The School is also a member of the Pro Arts Consortium, which allows students to take classes on a space-available basis at Berklee College of Music, the Boston Architectural Center, Emerson College, the Boston Conservatory, and Massachusetts College of Art.

Academic Facilities

The School is a division of the Museum of Fine Arts. Students and faculty members have special privileges of access to the museum's curatorial departments and library. The School also has its own library. The Exhibition Committee plans a program of shows covering work accomplished during the entire academic year. Work by students in each area of the School is represented on a rotating basis in the lobby, corridor, and student galleries.

Costs

For 1999–2000, the full-year tuition for a diploma program was $16,950 plus $620 in general fees. Tuition for degree program students in any one semester varies individually with the ratio of academic to studio courses taken in that semester.

Financial Aid

Financial aid is awarded on the basis of demonstrated financial need; approximately 50 percent of the undergraduates apply for financial aid and more than 80 percent of them receive it. Merit scholarships range from advanced standing to full tuition scholarships. Students are eligible to apply for Federal Pell Grants, Federal Supplemental Educational Opportunity Grants, Federal Work-Study Program awards, Federal Stafford Student Loans, and SMFA Scholarships, which range from $200 to full tuition. The priority deadline for receipt of completed application forms is February 15. Students should contact the Financial Aid Office to request the necessary forms.

Faculty

All of the faculty members teaching studio courses are practicing professional artists who have regional, national, and international reputations in their fields. There are 50 full-time and 93 part-time faculty members. Selected members of the undergraduate faculty also work with graduate students. The student-faculty ratio is approximately 10:1.

Student Government

The standing committees of the School, made up of administrative staff members, students, and faculty members, meet regularly to review the School's goals, curriculum, and problems. Proposals voted on and approved by the School's Executive Committee become part of the School's program. Each student, teacher, or member of the administration has an equal opportunity to join committees.

Admission Requirements

The Admissions Committee endeavors to select for entrance those applicants who appear highly motivated and best suited by apparent creative potential and background to benefit from the professional education offered by the School.

Diploma evaluation criteria is based primarily on the strength of the applicant's portfolio. Degree program evaluation criteria consists of a review of the applicant's portfolio as well as the strength of his or her academic records. At the discretion of the committee, certain applicants may be invited to attend a six-week summer session before a final decision on acceptance is made. The School strongly recommends that prospective students arrange to tour the School or have an interview before a formal application is filed. Qualified secondary school students in their junior year are encouraged to apply at that time for early acceptance for the term beginning in the September following their senior year. Because of the special structure of the School, the status of transfer students differs from that at other schools. Transfer students are placed at a studio level that the Admissions Committee deems appropriate, based on their portfolio presentation. Academic courses are transferable up to a limit of eight courses for the B.F.A. and B.F.A. in art education programs and twelve courses for the combined B.F.A. with B.A./B.S. program.

Application and Information

Applicants should arrange for all of the following to be delivered to the School: transcripts from the secondary school and any institution of higher education attended, official SAT I or ACT scores, an application form and the $35 nonrefundable application fee, and a portfolio. The portfolio of work must be sent to the School to be reviewed by the Admissions Committee. The School intentionally does not designate any specific composition or number of pieces for the portfolio (a minimum of fifteen to twenty pieces is recommended). It should be made up of what the applicant—rather than an art teacher, counselor, or relative—feels will best show a potential for development in visual art. Freehand drawing is often useful for the portfolio, but work in any technique may be submitted. A wide variety of techniques is not in itself considered a virtue. Original work is preferred.

The admission's deadline is on a rolling basis for the diploma program. Portfolios received from September to May are reviewed within ten days, and diploma applicants are notified of the Admissions Committee's decision by mail within three weeks. Portfolios received from June through August are reviewed on a weekly basis. Students may be accepted to the diploma program for the second semester beginning in January. The regular procedure is followed, and all application materials should be delivered to the School by December 15. The deadlines for application to B.F.A. or B.F.A. in art education programs is February 1 for first-time freshmen and March 1 for transfer students for spring admission; the deadlines for spring admission are October 1 for first-time freshmen and November 15 for transfer students. The deadline for application to the combined B.A./B.S. and B.F.A. programs is January 1 for first-time freshmen and March 1 for transfer students for fall admission, and for spring admission, November 15 for both first-time freshmen and transfer students. Applicants to the degree programs will be notified of the Committee's decision by April 1 for fall admission and December 1 for spring admission.

Applications from international students are welcome.

Applicants from countries other than the United States should offer documentary evidence of financial resources sufficient to satisfy all educational and living expenses for one year of study at the School. Applicants whose native language is not English should also submit scores on the Test of English as a Foreign Language (TOEFL).

For further information, students should contact:

Admissions Office
School of the Museum of Fine Arts
230 The Fenway
Boston, Massachusetts 02115

Telephone: 617-369-3626
               800-643-6078 (toll-free)
E-mail: admissions@smfa.edu
World Wide Web: http://www.smfa.edu

The Review Board system, in which students are awarded credit based on a review of new and evolving artwork by a panel of faculty members and students, is a hallmark of the SMFA education.

SCHOOL OF VISUAL ARTS
NEW YORK, NEW YORK

The School

Founded in 1947, the School of Visual Arts (SVA) has grown steadily and is today the largest undergraduate college of art in the country, with a full-time enrollment of 2,800 men and women. It is located in midtown Manhattan in five buildings within walking distance of each other. Visitors are most often impressed by the energetic atmosphere and the students' dedication to work.

While SVA currently enrolls degree candidates from more than forty states and twenty-three countries, 65 percent of the students at SVA are from the tristate metropolitan region.

At the graduate level, the School of Visual Arts offers Master of Fine Arts (M.F.A.) degrees in computer art, design, fine arts, illustration, and photography.

Location

Because the college is well-positioned in the heart of New York City, students have an opportunity to become acquainted with one of America's largest and most vibrant cities, the art and design capital of the world. Unlimited opportunities exist for constant involvement in the arts. Furthermore, the School of Visual Arts was conceived as a New York City institution from the beginning. The energy, the spirit, and the desire to be the best that characterize New York—embodied in SVA's renowned professional faculty—constantly challenge and inspire the students. The unparalleled leadership and accomplishment of the city's arts and design communities demand excellence, and the School of Visual Arts prepares students to compete successfully in this environment. Eighty-seven percent of the young women and men who graduate from SVA are working in their field within one year.

Majors and Degrees

SVA offers Bachelor of Fine Arts (B.F.A.) degrees in animation, computer art, film and video (live action, screenwriting, and videotape), fine arts (drawing, painting, printmaking, and sculpture), graphic design and advertising, illustration and cartooning, interior design (corporate, residential, restaurant, and retail), and photography.

Academic Program

The curriculum has been designed to prepare students to graduate as working professionals in the arts. Consequently, the four-year curriculum is designed to allow students greater freedom of choice in electives and requirements with each succeeding year. The first year of the program, a foundation year, ensures the mastery of basic skills in the chosen discipline, as well as in writing and art history. After the first year, students choose their own area of concentration and, under the guidance of the academic advisers and faculty members, pursue their own individual goals.

The B.F.A. degree programs require the completion of 120 credits, including 72 studio credits, at least 12 in art history, 6 in electives, and 30 in liberal arts. An English as a second language (ESL) program is offered in the summer term. A specially designed foundation program for high school students is offered for college credit on Saturdays in the fall and spring terms and in an intensive three-week format during the summer.

SVA's academic year is composed of two semesters that run from September to December and from January to May. The summer session begins in June.

Off-Campus Arrangements

The School of Visual Arts offers summer painting programs in Barcelona, Spain and an archaeological tour of Greece.

Academic Facilities

The Film/Video and Animation Department has two fully equipped animation studios, one Stop Motion Control Studio, one 16–35mm Master Oxberry stand, one 16mm Jr. Oxberry stand, five pencil test facilities, one Motion Control Pencil test stand, two motion control tables, and a Digital Compositing Ink and Paint System.

Film offers students the hands-on opportunity to learn by providing sixty Bolex cameras, fifteen Arriflex S camera packages, and twelve Arriflex BL camera packages. Thesis students reserve six Arriflex SR camera packages along with a variety of support accessories, including videotapes and Zeiss super-speed lenses. In addition, the department houses a large inventory of lighting and grip equipment. Sound equipment for film consists of Sony D-10 Pro II DAT recorders, ten Nagra recorders, Fostex digital time code recorders, a sound transfer facility, and a large collection of microphones and mixers. Film editing facilities include nineteen flatbed Steenbeck suites.

Students can access a film library that houses a combination of more than 1,500 titles (feature films, shorts, past student work, animations, and instructional titles) from a variety of film, video, DVD, laser, and tape formats. A ninety-seat film theater is available for cinema studies classes to screen classic and international films and to provide students a forum for screening their work.

Video offers its students VX1000 digital video cameras, PD-100 and EZ-1 digital video cameras, and more than forty combination Hi-8 cameras (including TR-700 Hi-8s, TR-715, TR-910 and 940 camera packages, two EV-300s, two 325s, two 537s, and one VX3 Hi-8).

Postproduction facilities include a state-of-the-art AVID center housing ten Meridian nonlinear workstations, a new Pro Tools work facility complete with twenty-four mix workstations, dub rooms, a telecine room, nine offline rooms, and one Beta online/AVID studio.

In the Fine Arts Department, fourth-year students have their own studio spaces. Printmaking studios are fully equipped for etching, intaglio, lithography (stone and offset), and serigraphy. A copy camera is available for those working in silk-screen processes. The sculpture studio has a foundry and facilities for welding, woodworking, stone carving, and ceramics.

Graphic design and advertising students use the Digital Imaging Center, which features leading technology in a number of areas. The center houses 140 Power Macintosh G3 computers with Zip drives, Jazz drives, and CD-ROM burners. There are three slide and nine flatbed scanners as well as ten 8½ x 11 to 11 x 17 color printers and an array of black and white and color copiers (8½ x 11 to 18 x 24). Software includes Adobe Illustrator, Adobe Photoshop, Quark Xpress, MacroMedia Director, and other print media applications.

SVA's Computer Art Department continues to feature the finest and most powerful digital tools available today. Currently there are fifty SGI, thirty Intergraph, and more than 200 Apple Macintosh computers in fifteen instructional labs and DV editing facilities. The department features the latest software applications, including Alias Wavefront Maya, AVID SoftImage, Discreet Logic Flint, 3D Studio Max, Adobe AfterEffects, Adobe Photoshop, MacroMedia Director, and Quark Xpress.

Computer art majors can choose to concentrate their studies in the fields of computer animation, interactive media, or dynamic media. From the freshman to the senior year, B.F.A. computer art students work with accomplished professionals and leading artists in the widely diverse fields the new digital media have created over the past ten years.

The Photography Department has exclusive computer facilities where students work with state-of-the-art equipment to produce digital imaging. It also has available seven major shooting studios, fifty large-format view cameras, fifty studio strobe units, and all accessories. The nine darkrooms hold ninety-two Omega D5 enlargers, offer printing facilities for color and black-and-white film from 35mm to 8 x 10, and include one 30-inch and one-16 inch Kronite RA-4 color-print processor and one 20-inch cibachrome processor.

The Interior Design Program employs a curriculum that integrates state-of-the-art technology with the traditions of drawing and drafting. Classes are held in a studio environment, where students use AutoCAD, Form Z, RenderZone, and 3D Studio Max software. Output options include a large-format ink-jet Epson Stylus 1520 printer and a Hewlett-Packard Design Jet 650C plotter.

SVA's library has 64,500 volumes, 95,000 art slides, and a picture collection of 230,000 pieces. Seventy percent of the library's holdings are related to art.

The college has five galleries and the Visual Arts Museum, a professional gallery housed within the main complex of buildings. In addition, the School has a gallery at 137 Wooster Street, in the heart of SoHo, exclusively for student exhibitions.

Costs

Tuition for the 1999–2000 academic year was $15,000. SVA offers dormitory space, accommodating 600 students, at costs that ranged from $5900 to $7860 per academic year. Other annual costs vary greatly, but it is estimated that books and art supplies cost $1435; transportation, $735; and personal expenses, $1815.

Financial Aid

The School of Visual Arts offers scholarships and other financial aid based upon need and merit. Approximately 75 percent of students receive some form of aid. The School of Visual Arts uses federal, state, and institutional guidelines to determine student need. The Office of Student Financial Services is able to provide more information on need-based assistance.

Each year SVA sets aside more than $1 million for Silas H. Rhodes Merit Scholarships, awarded annually to outstanding students accepted into the B.F.A. programs beginning in the fall semester of each year. The deadline for freshman applications for the scholarship competition is February 1, 2001; the transfer deadline is March 15, 2001. Students may contact the Office of Admissions for applications and further information.

Faculty

Since the School of Visual Arts brings working professionals to its facility, the faculty of 800 members is composed of practicing artists, filmmakers, designers, and photographers who teach part-time. The 90 full-time faculty members are also active in their professions. As a result of this policy of using working professionals to teach, the School has been able to attract to the faculty some of the most prominent artists in New York. The liberal arts faculty has 82 members, 40 percent of whom have completed their Ph.D. The ratio of full-time-equivalent students to full-time-equivalent faculty is 13:1.

Student Government

The student body is governed by the Visual Arts Student Association, whose members are elected annually. The student government administers the student activities budget, which funds extracurricular activities, student galleries, lectures, film showings, theater presentations, and readings. In addition, representatives of the student government meet with the president on a biweekly basis to discuss relevant plans and activities. The Student Rules of Conduct are similar to those of other colleges and are designed to ensure that each student has the maximum opportunity to develop as a working professional artist without unnecessary interference.

Admission Requirements

The School of Visual Arts enrolls new students for both fall and spring semesters. The college maintains a moderately difficult admissions policy for those students who demonstrate a strong commitment to producing work and exploring and defining opportunities specific to their strengths and interests in the visual arts in the context of a professional art and design college. Generally, a 2.5 minimum grade point average (GPA) is expected, except in the film/video, animation, and computer art programs, where the minimum GPA is 3.0. Students with strong portfolios whose traditional skills are weaker than the minimum GPAs may be given, depending on circumstances, special assistance to bring those skills up to college level. Special programs can be designed within the normal curriculum to address, for example, learning disabilities and benefit students' personal and professional growth.

In making its decisions, the Committee on Admission considers information and materials that all applicants are required to submit. All students must send the completed application, the high school and/or college transcript, a 250–500-word statement of intent, and SAT I or ACT scores. A portfolio of work is required of applicants to all programs with the exception of the film/video department—a two-part descriptive essay is required of film/video majors. All applicants must have a personal interview. The interview is waived, however, for students living more than 200 miles from the campus.

For academic year 1999–2000, the School of Visual Arts received more than 3,000 undergraduate applications.

Application and Information

Since the college accepts students for admission to the majority of its departments on a rolling admission basis, it is suggested that prospective students apply as early as possible. Applicants to the Film/Video, Animation, and Computer Art Departments should note that applications must be completed and submitted no later than March 15, 2001. Transfer students from other schools may be accepted for either the fall or spring semester.

For application forms and catalogs, students should contact:

Rick Longo
Director of Admissions
School of Visual Arts
209 East 23rd Street
New York, New York 10010

Telephone: 212-592-2100
Fax: 212-592-2116
E-mail: admissions@adm.schoolofvisualarts.edu
World Wide Web: http://www.schoolofvisualarts.edu

Located in the heart of New York City, the School of Visual Arts provides students unlimited opportunities for involvement in the art and design capital of the world.

SCHREINER COLLEGE
KERRVILLE, TEXAS

The College

Schreiner is a four-year independent coeducational liberal arts college related by covenant to the Presbyterian Church (U.S.A.). Founded in 1917 by Capt. Charles Schreiner, a Texas rancher, banker, merchant, and philanthropist, the College has a colorful history, rich with Texas heritage and traditions. The College has grown in size and offerings to meet the needs of its constituents. The current enrollment is about 800 students, representing many states and several nations.

The College has four residence halls, a new $6-million student activity center, and a student center complete with cafeteria, student lounge, game room, and snack bar. A separate building houses the Office of Student Affairs, which includes career services, housing, student activities, and the campus minister.

Intercollegiate and intramural athletic programs are available for both men and women. NCAA Division III intercollegiate team sports are baseball, basketball, soccer, and tennis for men and basketball, soccer, softball, tennis, and volleyball for women. Intramural programs include basketball, billiards, flag football, Ping-Pong, racquetball, soccer, softball, swimming, and tennis. The sports complex comprises a field house; an outdoor pavilion; tennis, racquetball, and handball courts; a weight room; a training room; a golf driving range and putting green; soccer and softball fields; and a ¼-mile track. The Schreiner Mountaineers compete in the American Southwest Conference.

A variety of social, political, religious, and service clubs exist to encourage student participation and meet personal interests. Student publications, such as *The Mountaineer*, a newspaper, and *The Muse*, an annual literary magazine, provide a showcase for the artistic and journalistic efforts of students, staff, and faculty.

A master's degree in education is also offered.

Location

The College is located in Kerrville, Texas, a growing resort community of more than 22,000 people. Located just 50 miles northwest of San Antonio, the eighth-largest city in the United States, the area offers the best of country and city living. Kerrville is in the heart of the Texas Hill Country, best known for its expansive outdoor activities, such as camping, hiking, hunting, and fishing, and a variety of other sports, such as golf, tennis, swimming, and waterskiing. The rustic charm of the area's rolling hills, clear waters, and open spaces provides a pleasing and healthy atmosphere conducive to study and learning.

Majors and Degrees

A Bachelor of Arts degree is awarded in biochemistry, biology, chemistry, computer studies, creative arts, English, exercise science, finance, general studies, graphic design, history, humanities, legal studies, marketing, mathematics, music, philosophy, psychology, and religion. A Bachelor of Business Administration degree is available; concentrations within the business administration major are accounting, computer studies, finance, management, and marketing. A Bachelor of General Studies degree is also offered. A 3-2 program in engineering results in an engineering degree from a large state university and a general studies degree from Schreiner College. The Associate of Arts degree is awarded in liberal arts. A one-year certificate program in vocational nursing is offered. Students may also choose to pursue four-year preprofessional programs in dentistry, engineering, law, medicine, pharmacy, and religion. Teacher certification (elementary and secondary) is offered in art, biology, English, exercise science, history, and mathematics.

Academic Program

The Bachelor of Arts and Bachelor of Business Administration degrees require completion of 120 hours, of which 64 are in basic course work and 56 are in advanced study. Students in all four-year programs of study are required to complete a basic curriculum that gives them a broad background. This consists of courses in English, mathematics, science, foreign language, computer science, health and physical education, social science, philosophy, and religion or logic.

The Schreiner Honors Program exists for qualified high academic achievers. It is a multifaceted program for aggressive learners.

The College operates on a 4-1-4 calendar.

Advanced placement is granted to students who earn a score of at least 3 on the College Board Advanced Placement examinations. Credit is also granted for successful scores on individual departmental challenge examinations and/or for scores at the 90th percentile or better on the ACT or SAT I.

Off-Campus Arrangements

A variety of business internships are available through the Bachelor of Business Administration and Bachelor of Arts programs. This work experience enables students to apply theory learned in the classroom to practical situations. Off-campus study experiences are available in other countries, as well as in the continental United States.

Academic Facilities

The spacious 175-acre campus has twenty buildings. There are four classroom buildings, with fully equipped science, computer, and nursing laboratories and office space.

A renovated $5.5-million library facility houses audiovisual equipment, nearly 100,000 bound volumes, 700 periodical subscriptions, study and conference rooms, the College bookstore, and a post office. A new $6.5-million campus activity center will serve as the focal point for student development and activity.

Costs

Tuition and fees for the academic year 2000–01 are estimated at $11,740. Room and board costs are $6796.

Financial Aid

Federal, state, and institutional aid programs are available for students who demonstrate need. Nearly 70 percent of Schreiner's students receive some form of need-based aid. On-campus work-study jobs and low-interest loans are two examples of self-help aid available on a need basis. Non-need aid, such as scholarships and grants, is awarded to students who demonstrate leadership skills, high academic achievement, or proficiency in athletics.

The College hosts an annual on-campus scholarship program called Schreiner Scholars; the scholarships range from $3000 to full tuition. Students should submit an application by January 11 to be considered for this scholarship.

To ensure consideration for adequate financial aid, students should submit an application to the College by the April 15 priority deadline.

Faculty

The 1:17 faculty-student ratio allows for personal interaction between the faculty and students both inside and outside the classroom. All students are assigned a faculty adviser who gives them career and academic counseling. More than 75 percent of the full-time faculty members have earned doctorates in their teaching field, and all have advanced degrees. Some full-time faculty members reside on campus.

Student Government

Students are encouraged to take a leadership role in many of the social and business affairs of the College. Through active participation in the Student Senate, students also serve on standing and ad hoc committees involving the governance of the College. In addition, students may serve on Residence Hall Councils.

Admission Requirements

Candidates for admission are selected on the basis of their personal and academic merit. Specific requirements include ACT or SAT I scores, the application and a $20 nonrefundable application fee, and an official high school transcript. Personal interviews are not always required as part of the admissions process, but most students regard a campus visit and interview as a valuable experience. Arrangements for a campus visit should be made through the Admission Office.

Application and Information

The recommended application deadline is May 1. However, the College uses a rolling admissions procedure, and applications may be submitted at any time. An admission decision is given as soon as all of an applicant's materials have been received and evaluated.

Students may request an application form and additional information from:

Dean of Admission and Financial Aid
Schreiner College
Kerrville, Texas 78028

Telephone: 830-896-5411
              800-343-4919 (toll-free)
Fax: 830-792-7226
E-mail: admissions@schreiner.edu
World Wide Web: http://www.schreiner.edu

Aerial view of Schreiner College.

SCRIPPS COLLEGE
CLAREMONT, CALIFORNIA

The College

Since its founding in 1926 as one of the few institutions in the West dedicated to educating women for professional careers as well as personal intellectual growth, Scripps College has championed the qualities of mind and spirit described by its founder, newspaper entrepreneur and philanthropist Ellen Browning Scripps. Scripps remains a women's college because it believes that having women at the core of its concerns provides the very best environment for intellectually ambitious women to learn from a distinguished teaching faculty and from each other. Scripps emphasizes a challenging core curriculum based on interdisciplinary humanistic studies, combined with rigorous training in the disciplines, and sees this as the best possible foundation for any goals a woman may pursue.

Scripps aspires to be a diverse community committed to the principles of free inquiry and free expression based on mutual respect. The College chooses to remain a largely residential college of fewer than 1,000 students, a scale that encourages women to participate actively in their community and to develop a sense of both personal ethics and social responsibility. Scripps cherishes its campus of uncommon beauty, a tribute to the founder's vision that the College's architecture and landscape should reflect and influence taste and judgment.

As full participants in the Claremont Colleges consortium, Scripps students are members of a small university community where they may enjoy academic and other educational opportunities throughout the coordinating colleges and the graduate school. As residents of southern California, Scripps women may explore varied cultural, ethnic, and geographical resources.

Scripps students have the opportunity to participate in a variety of activities on campus, or they may choose to get involved in any of more than 200 five-college clubs, ten NCAA Division III sports teams, intramural and club sports teams, coffeehouses, and a multitude of five-college and Scripps campus events. In March 2000, Scripps dedicated the Elizabeth Hubert Malott Commons, which houses a large centralized dining facility, the student-run Motley Coffeehouse, a newly expanded Career Planning & Resource Center, a student activities office, the College mailroom, a student store, and a banquet facility that highlights a variety of speakers across many disciplines. In August 2000, a new residence hall opens, adding to the beauty of the campus.

Scripps emphasizes high aspirations, high achievement, and personal integrity in all pursuits, and it expects students, faculty members, staff, and alumnae to contribute to Scripps and to their own communities throughout their professional, social, and civic lives. Scripps believes that this form of challenging and individualized education will best prepare women for lives of confidence, courage, and hope.

Location

Listed on the National Register of Historic Places, Scripps is located in Claremont, California, a college town of 35,000 people. It is 40 miles east of Los Angeles and 20 miles east of Pasadena. The mountains, beaches, and deserts of southern California are easily accessible by car. The climate is cool and dry in the winter, warming in the late spring.

Majors and Degrees

Scripps College awards the Bachelor of Arts degree in accounting, American studies, anthropology, art history, Asian-American studies, Asian studies, biology, biology/chemistry, black studies, chemistry, Chicano studies, Chinese, classics, computer science, dance, economics, engineering, English, environmental studies, European studies, foreign languages and literature, French studies, geology, German literature/civilization, Hispanic studies, history, human biology, international relations, Italian literature/civilization, Japanese, Jewish studies, Latin American studies, legal studies, linguistics, mathematical economics, mathematics, media studies, music, organizational studies, philosophy, physics, politics and international relations, psychology, religious studies, Russian, science and management, science/technology and society, sociology, Spanish literature/civilization, studio art, theater, and women's studies.

Scripps also cooperates in a dual bachelor's degree program in engineering with a large number of institutions, including Boston University, Columbia University, Rensselaer Polytechnic Institute, USC, and Washington University. Other 3-2 programs offering a bachelor's and a master's degree are available with the Claremont Graduate University in American politics, business administration, economics, international studies, philosophy, public policy studies, and religious studies.

Academic Program

To graduate with a Bachelor of Arts degree from Scripps, students must successfully complete a minimum of thirty-two courses. Course work is divided into three parts: core curriculum requirements, major concentration course work, and elective or minor concentration course work. Core curriculum requirements provide a solid academic frame, while electives allow students significant flexibility in studying courses from the social sciences, humanities, fine arts, natural sciences, and mathematics.

Scripps operates on a semester calendar, beginning in early September and ending in mid-May.

Off-Campus Arrangements

Local off-campus opportunities include internships with career professionals in a variety of fields: journalism, law, business, communications, medicine, and the arts. Examples of internship sites are the Getty Museum, the Walt Disney Company, Merrill Lynch, Warner Bros., The Minority Advertising Program, and INROADS. Students may also participate in political internships in Washington, D.C., and Sacramento, California, or in other internships in museums, biological field stations, and public policy organizations such as the United Nations.

Approximately 50 percent of Scripps students supplement their education and life experience by studying abroad or participating in domestic off-campus study programs. Students can select from more than fifty international options each year, including France, Germany, Ecuador, Zimbabwe, Greece, Nepal, China, and Japan. Students may also opt for domestic programs; going on exchange to Caltech, Haverford, Spelman, or Colby College; or combining classes in Washington, D.C., with an internship.

Academic Facilities

The Claremont Colleges library system holds more than 2 million volumes. The Denison Library at Scripps houses an impressive humanities and fine art collection and is renowned for its special and rare books. A cross-linked computer system affords access to off-campus libraries, including the University of California system.

The Millard Sheets Art Center, a $4-million facility that opened in 1994, provides studio space for painting, drawing, printmaking, and ceramics and contains a state-of-the-art computer art and design laboratory and photography studio. The W. M. Keck Joint Science Center, a national model of undergraduate science facilities that opened in 1992, offers students of biology, chemistry, and physics top-grade facilities, research opportunities, and a biological field station. The Clark Humanities

Museum and Ruth Chandler Williamson Art Gallery exhibit the work of professionals and students.

The Scripps Computer Facility, a well-equipped microcomputer laboratory, houses both Macintosh and IBM computers as well as dot matrix and laser printers. Scripps has opened a Multimedia Learning Center for faculty use in teaching and a Modern Language Laboratory/Technical Teaching Classroom. Six "smart classrooms," each equipped with a new Macintosh G3 computer, an overhead projector, a laser disc player, and a VCR, are also available for instructional purposes. Users have access to a six-college network as well as the Internet. The Science Center and the Art Center have their own computer labs. The libraries and music studio also have computer facilities. All student rooms have access to the Scripps network and the Internet; all offer direct Ethernet access. Every residence hall offers a computer with Pentium multimedia systems for student use.

Costs

For the 2000–01 academic year, tuition and fees are $22,600, room and board are $7800, and books and incidentals are approximately $1650.

Financial Aid

It is the goal of Scripps College to attract the best students, regardless of their ability to pay. Approximately 60 percent of Scripps students receive financial aid, usually in a combination of grants and scholarships, loans, and part-time student employment. Awards are based on the financial need of the student. The College also supports the James E. Scripps Scholarship Program, which provides merit scholarships to students with outstanding records of achievement.

Faculty

With a student-faculty ratio of 11:1, the College is dedicated to a personalized education. Faculty members remain active in their fields, while making teaching Scripps students their first priority. Classes are taught by professors, not by graduate students. Of the full-time ongoing faculty members, 96 percent hold terminal degrees in their field; 52 percent are women; 100 percent participate in the faculty/student advising program.

Student Government

One of the most important aspects of life at Scripps is the governance system. Students participate in the curricular and policymaking functions of the College. The College Council is composed of student body officers elected each spring and is chaired by the president of the student body. Each of the seven residence halls is self-governing, and students serve on a variety of Board of Trustees committees. The College has a serious commitment to the concept of shared responsibility for governance among students, the faculty, and administrators.

Admission Requirements

Scripps College seeks energetic and intellectually curious students who are interested in pursuing a challenging liberal arts curriculum. In addition to high levels of academic and personal achievement, Scripps values demonstrated leadership, initiative, integrity, and creativity.

The Admission Committee gives careful consideration to every aspect of a student's application. Particular attention is given to the quality of an applicant's academic preparation. A recommended course of study consists of five academic subjects in each year of high school including 4 years of English, 4 years of mathematics, 3 years of social studies, 3 years of laboratory science (biology, chemistry, or physics), and either 3 years of a foreign language or 2 years each of two different languages. Applicants are encouraged to select Honors, Advanced Placement, or International Baccalaureate courses whenever available.

Application and Information

Students applying to Scripps College are expected to submit transcripts of all academic work in high school and college, a counselor recommendation, two teacher recommendations from teachers in different academic subject areas, a graded writing assignment, and SAT I or ACT results, along with the application and essay. Students are encouraged to take SAT II Subject Tests. The deadlines for application are November 1 or January 1 for early decision, November 1 for the James E. Scripps Scholars Program, and February 1 for regular decision.

Further information is available from:

Office of Admission
Scripps College
1030 Columbia Avenue
Claremont, California 91711-3948
Telephone: 909-621-8149
         800-770-1333 (toll-free)
Fax: 909-607-7508
E-mail: admission@scrippscollege.edu
World Wide Web: http://www.scrippscollege.edu

Students relax amid the tree-lined terraces and Mediterranean buildings of the Scripps College campus.

SEATTLE PACIFIC UNIVERSITY
SEATTLE, WASHINGTON

The University

Seattle Pacific University (SPU) is a flourishing Christian university of the arts, sciences, and professions serving nearly 3,400 students. Founded in 1891 by the Free Methodist Church of North America, it is recognized for both academic excellence and public service. SPU has been designated one of "America's Best Colleges" by *U.S. News & World Report* and has been acknowledged as one of the country's character-building institutions.

Seattle Pacific is fully accredited by the Washington State Board of Education and the Northwest Association of Schools and Colleges. Its programs are accredited by the National Council for Accreditation of Teacher Education at both the graduate and undergraduate levels, the Washington State Board of Education, the American Dietetic Association Council on Education, the Washington State Nursing Care Quality Assurance Commission, the National League for Nursing Accrediting Commission at both the undergraduate and graduate levels, and the Engineering Accreditation Commission of the Accreditation Board for Engineering and Technology, Inc. SPU is also a member of the Association of American Colleges, the American Association of Colleges for Teacher Education, the National Association of Schools of Music, the AACSB–The International Association for Management Education, and the Association for Continuing Higher Education. A charter member of the Christian College Consortium and the Coalition of Christian Colleges and Universities, Seattle Pacific meets the requirements of the Commission on Christian Education of the Free Methodist Church and those of other denominations for the collegiate preparation of ministers.

Students come to SPU from forty states and thirty-nine countries, representing more than fifty different Christian denominations. More than half of Seattle Pacific's undergraduate students live on campus in six residence halls and several apartment complexes. All Seattle Pacific residence halls have been wired to allow students dedicated online connections to e-mail, the Internet, and the campus computer network.

Seattle Pacific's intercollegiate athletic program fields NCAA Division II teams in men's and women's basketball, crew, cross-country, and track and field; men's soccer; and women's gymnastics and volleyball. All students have access to sixty-five intramural sports as well as extramurals, special events, and health and fitness activities.

The University's unique leadership program encourages students to cultivate their individual talents by putting them to work in student government, ministries, performing groups, publications, clubs, and organizations.

In addition to its bachelor's degrees, SPU awards M.A., M.B.A., M.Ed., M.S., MATESOL, M.S.N., Ed.D., and Ph.D. degrees.

Location

Seattle Pacific's beautiful 35-acre, tree-lined city campus lies in a residential area just 7 minutes from downtown Seattle, the business and cultural heart of the Pacific Northwest. A gateway to Canada and the Pacific Rim, Seattle offers easy access to a wide variety of outdoor recreation such as sailing, skiing, hiking, and camping. The city also offers world-class fine arts, including opera, theater, symphony, and ballet. Seattle Pacific takes advantage of its urban setting by providing hundreds of internship and service experiences in the city's hospitals, schools, businesses, and churches.

Majors and Degrees

An array of academic options in the arts, sciences, and professions allows Seattle Pacific students to specialize in one discipline while exploring many others. The University awards B.A. and B.S. degrees and offers more than fifty-six undergraduate majors.

The College of Arts and Sciences offers the following undergraduate majors: art; biochemistry; biology; chemistry; classics; communication; computer science; educational ministry/Christian education; electrical engineering; engineering and applied science; English; European studies (French, German, Latin, Russian, and Spanish); exercise science; family and consumer sciences; fine and applied arts education; food and nutritional sciences; general studies; history; language arts education; Latin American studies; mathematics; mathematics education; music; music education; philosophy; physical education; physics; political science; psychology; religious studies; science education; social science education; sociology; textiles, clothing, and interiors; and theater. Student-designed majors are also available.

The School of Business and Economics offers undergraduate majors in accounting, business administration, and economics. The School of Education offers elementary certification in any major of the University, secondary certification in sixteen majors, and a major in special education. The School of Health Sciences offers an undergraduate nursing degree. Preprofessional programs are available in dentistry, law, medicine, optometry, and physical therapy.

Academic Program

Seattle Pacific's academic disciplines set high standards for students. Undergraduate students are taught not by graduate assistants but by experienced professors recognized locally and nationally for the quality of their scholarship. Small classes mean students actively participate in their own education, gaining the confidence to achieve their goals. In addition, SPU's clear Christian commitment gives depth and perspective to classroom learning, balancing knowledge with values.

The Common Curriculum, which includes seven required courses spread out over four years, is at the heart of an undergraduate liberal arts education at Seattle Pacific. Only 5 percent of four-year institutions in the United States, most of them very small and homogenous, offer such a curriculum. Until now, no comprehensive university in an urban setting with an equal mix of residential and commuter students requires participation in common learning over four years.

SPU students begin in the first quarter of their freshman year with University Seminar, an intensive exploration of a special interdisciplinary topic. The maximum 20 students enrolled in each course form a "cohort" and attend other freshman classes in the Common Curriculum together, with their University Seminar professor serving as their academic adviser. In their freshman, sophomore, and junior years, students participate in two parallel sequences of required courses that address key human questions from the perspective of various disciplines and the foundations of Christian faith. Cumulative and developmental in nature, these classes are designed to support and enhance students' learning in the majors.

Off-Campus Arrangements

Seattle Pacific students have many opportunities to enhance their education with off-campus study. The Pacific Northwest itself provides a living laboratory for academic pursuits in all disciplines. SPU's own campuses on Whidbey Island and Blakely Island are ideal for research and field study in areas such as marine biology and environmental science.

Each year, approximately 30 Seattle Pacific students study and travel in Europe for eleven weeks. During quarter and summer breaks, students have the opportunity to join Seattle Pacific Reachout International (SPRINT) teams that travel to countries like Northern Ireland, Russia, Nicaragua, Uganda, and Romania for a short-term mission experience.

The University maintains exchange agreements with institutions in Kenya, Japan, and Korea. Students may also apply to take one or two quarters of study at one of the twelve other Christian College Consortium campuses, or they may enroll in one of three programs sponsored by the Council for Christian Colleges and Universities: American Studies in Washington, D.C.; Latin American Studies in Costa Rica; and Film Studies in Los Angeles.

Academic Facilities

At the heart of the Seattle Pacific campus is the library, completed in 1994. This spacious, 62,000-square-foot, four-level facility serves as the center for academic endeavors outside the classroom. It provides learning resource services, the latest technology, space for study and research, and approximately 150,000 volumes arranged on open shelves for easy access. The library collection is accessible online in the library and through the campus computer network via its automated catalog. The library's Technology and Learning Center offers media production, satellite downlink, duplication services, and the management of a multimedia library.

Among the other educational facilities at SPU is the Otto M. Miller Science Learning Center, which features alternative energy systems, a fully equipped electrical engineering laboratory, and a ½-acre multidisciplinary laboratory. The University's flexible-forestage performing arts facility, E. E. Bach Theatre, is one of the city's finest, and the recent renovation of Royal Brougham Pavilion produced one of the premier sports and recreation arenas in the Puget Sound area.

Costs

Tuition for the 2000–01 academic year is $15,381; annual room and board are $5895 (based on 2 people in a room, full-meal plan). Individualized meal plans are available. Book costs and personal expenses vary, depending on personal needs.

Financial Aid

Need-based financial aid is available in the form of scholarships, grants, loans, and employment. To be considered for maximum aid, students must submit the Free Application for Federal Student Aid (FAFSA) as soon as possible after January 1 and be admitted to the University by March 1. SPU participates in various federal aid programs, including the Federal Pell Grant, Federal Supplemental Educational Opportunity Grant, Federal Perkins Loan, Federal Work-Study, and Federal Stafford Student Loan programs. The University annually awards more than $25 million in aid to students.

Merit-based University scholarships are given annually to students who exhibit academic excellence and exemplify the ideals of the institution. Merit scholarships are available in amounts ranging from $1500 to $10,000. The Division of Fine Arts offers renewable scholarships (up to $3000) regardless of major. The Athletic Department awards scholarship aid to top Christian athletes.

Faculty

The full-time faculty at Seattle Pacific is composed of 156 dedicated scholars who are committed to the highest academic standards. Eighty-five percent of SPU's full-time faculty members hold the Ph.D. or an equivalent terminal degree. Seattle Pacific professors are experts in their fields: they publish, speak, and conduct research throughout the world. Their first priority, however, is teaching. SPU faculty members also make themselves available to students outside the classroom and act as models of compassionate, educated Christians.

Student Government

All full-time students are members of the Associated Students of Seattle Pacific (ASSP). Each spring, students elect 7 ASSP executive officers along with representatives to the ASSP Senate, the student governing body. ASSP provides services to students in the areas of campus activities, campus ministries, leadership development, and student publications.

Admission Requirements

Admission to Seattle Pacific is offered on the basis of academic credentials and personal qualifications. SPU selects those students who will benefit most from a Christian university education. Factors in the admission decision include high school or college grades, academic and personal recommendations, the application essays, and scores on the SAT I or the ACT. An applicant is also evaluated in terms of leadership potential, church and community activities, special talents, and personal responsibility. Prospective students are encouraged to visit the campus at any time.

Application and Information

Prospective students may write to the Seattle Pacific Office of Undergraduate Admissions to request application materials. High school students should request these materials early in the senior year. While applications for Autumn Quarter are accepted until June 1, prospective students must be admitted by March 1 in order to be considered for scholarships and the best financial aid, housing, and course registration opportunities.

Applications are reviewed in the order they are received in the Office of Undergraduate Admissions. Beginning December 1, decisions regarding admission are made on a rolling basis after all application materials have been received. If an interview is required, students are contacted by telephone.

For further details, students should contact:
Kenneth Cornell
Director of Undergraduate Admissions
Seattle Pacific University
Seattle, Washington 98119
Telephone: 206-281-2021
        800-366-3344 (toll-free)
E-mail: admissions@spu.edu
World Wide Web: http://www.spu.edu/

SEATTLE UNIVERSITY
SEATTLE, WASHINGTON

The University

Seattle University (SU) provides an ideal environment for motivated students interested in self-reliance, awareness of different cultures, social justice, and the fulfillment that comes from making a difference. Its location in the center of one of the nation's most diverse and progressive cities attracts a varied student body, faculty, and staff. Its urban setting promotes the development of leadership skills and independence and provides a variety of opportunities for students to apply what they learn through internships, clinical experiences, and volunteer work. It is an environment that allows students to "connect the mind to what matters."

As a Jesuit institution, Seattle University is part of a network of twenty-eight colleges and universities and forty-three high schools noted for academic strength across the United States. Academic offerings are designed to provide leadership opportunities, develop global awareness, and enable graduates to serve society through a demanding liberal arts and sciences foundation. In the Jesuit educational tradition, students are taught how to think, not what to think. Professional undergraduate offerings include highly respected Schools of Business, Nursing, and Science and Engineering and career-oriented liberal arts programs such as communications, creative writing, criminal justice, and journalism. The University's Schools of Education, Law, and Theology and Ministry offer graduate-level opportunities.

Seattle University is noted for its focus on the individual through small, faculty-taught classes and excellent service. The result is mirrored by graduates who lead fulfilling and economically successful lives. SU leads the Pacific Northwest in producing Truman and Wilson scholars.

The fall quarter has a freshman class of 650, and 50 percent are from outside Washington State. The 3,200 undergraduate students represent forty-four states and sixty-two nations. Approximately 12 percent are international students. The ethnic breakdown for the fall 1999 freshman class is 61 percent white, 29 percent Asian American, and 10 percent African American, Latino, and American Indian.

The residential campus has undergone $120 million in recent improvements. Although it is in the center of Seattle, the campus has been designated by Washington State as an Official Backyard Sanctuary for its distinctive landscaping and environmentally conscious practices.

There is a wide variety of on-campus housing that accommodates 1,500 students, including a new apartment complex, and 85 percent of freshmen live on campus. There is a two-year on-campus residence requirement.

Seattle University has more than seventy extracurricular clubs and organizations and has five varsity teams for men (basketball, cross-country, soccer, swimming, and tennis) and five for women (basketball, soccer, softball, swimming, and volleyball). SU is joining NCAA Division II. The student life program includes sixty extracurricular clubs and organizations, including the Hawaiian Club, crew, Associated Students of African Descent, Hiyu Coulee Hiking Club, Beta Alpha Psi (national accounting honorary), and other professional honoraries and clubs.

The Connolly Athletic Center serves as the major facility for varsity and intramural athletics and recreation. It features two swimming pools, two full-size gymnasiums, and locker room saunas. A 6-acre complex provides fields for outdoor sports.

Seattle University receives the highest professional accreditation from the Accreditation Board for Engineering and Technology, Inc.; the AACSB–The International Association for Management Education; the American Bar Association; the American Chemical Society; the Association of Theological Schools; the Commission on Accreditation of Allied Health Education Programs; the National Council for Accreditation of Teacher Education; the National League for Nursing Accrediting Commission; and the Northwest Association of Schools and Colleges.

Location

Seattle University is located on First Hill in a port city of unsurpassed natural beauty. As the Pacific Northwest's largest city (and the fourteenth-largest metropolitan area in the U.S.), Seattle is a scenic and cultural center in a setting that includes breathtaking mountain views of the Cascades to the east and the Olympics to the west; skiing is within 60 minutes of campus. In addition to being situated along Puget Sound, Seattle also contains Lakes Union and Washington; both provide a wide variety of recreational opportunities. Seattle's residents love the outdoors, and areas for hiking, backpacking, and climbing are minutes from campus. Biking is also popular and special trails for cycling and running are located throughout the city.

Seattle's sights and sounds, rich ethnic diversity, celebrated restaurants, first–run entertainment, major-league athletics, theater, opera, and ballet are within walking distance and enhance campus life.

Majors and Degrees

Seattle University offers the following undergraduate degrees: Bachelor of Arts, Bachelor of Science, Bachelor of Science in Nursing, and the Bachelor of Arts in Business Administration.

The University offers programs in six major academic units. The Albers School of Business and Economics awards degrees in accounting, business economics, e-commerce, finance, general business, international business, management, marketing, operations management, and risk management. The College of Arts and Sciences grants degrees in art, communication studies, criminal justice, drama, ecological studies, economics, English, fine arts, foreign languages, history, humanities, international studies, journalism, liberal studies, philosophy, political science, psychology, public administration, sociology, and theology and religious studies. The School of Nursing offers a Bachelor of Science in Nursing degree. The School of Science and Engineering offers degree programs in biochemistry, biology, chemistry, civil engineering, computer engineering, computer science, diagnostic ultrasound, electrical engineering, environmental engineering, general science, manufacturing and mechanical engineering, mathematics, mechanical engineering, medical technology, and physics. In addition to a program in addiction studies, preprofessional programs include dentistry, law, medicine, optometry, and veterinary medicine.

Academic Program

The Core Curriculum is known for its strength and has several distinguishing characteristics in keeping with the Jesuit tradition: it provides an integrated freshman year; it gives order and sequence to student learning; it provides experience in the methods and content of the range of liberal arts, sciences, philosophy, and theology; it calls for active learning in all classes for practice in writing and thinking, and for an awareness of values; and it fosters a global perspective and a sense of social and personal responsibility.

Seattle University also offers a special two-year honors program. This seminar-oriented study of the humanities provides intensive work in philosophy, theology, literature, history, art, and science. The honors program fulfills all core requirements and does not increase the number of quarters required to complete a degree. Admission requires a separate application and is based upon course selection, individual course performance, an essay, an interview, and letters of recommendation.

SU operates on a quarter calendar. The fall quarter begins in mid-September; the winter quarter in early January; the spring quarter in late March; and the summer quarter in mid-June. Undergraduates typically take 15 hours each during the fall, winter, and spring quarters.

Off-Campus Arrangements

SU offers three international study programs—a program for accounting majors in Italy, French in France, Latin American studies in Mexico and two reciprocal exchange programs with the University of Graz in Austria and Sophia University in Japan. These are open to all students in all majors and emphasize appreciation of the language and culture. This is accomplished through the total immersion concept. Other programs include Campus Ministry missions in Nicaragua and Belize and Albers School of Business and Economics tours in Mexico, Italy, Hong Kong, and Vietnam. Seattle University maintains the only Calcutta Club in which students volunteer annually on behalf of Mother Teresa's ministry. Additional study-abroad programs in other nations, in conjunction with other colleges' overseas programs, are also offered. Arrangements are made through SU's Study Abroad Office.

Academic Facilities

The University is located on 45 acres in the First Hill neighborhood in the center of Seattle. There are twenty-eight buildings recently enhanced by $60 million in additions, renovations, and new construction.

Costs

In 1999–2000, tuition was $16,110; room and meals were $5868. The estimate for books, fees, and personal expenses was an additional $3973. Travel costs varied among students. Costs are subject to change.

Financial Aid

Seattle University awarded $3.1 million in its own financial aid to fall 1998 freshmen, including 191 scholarships ranging from $5000 to $11,000. Seventy-nine percent of freshmen received University aid. Students are required to apply for financial aid by February 1 as awards are made early each spring for the following fall quarter. Applications that are received after this deadline will be evaluated in order received for any remaining aid. Students must submit the Free Application for Federal Student Aid (FAFSA) and be accepted for admission to be considered for financial assistance. There are also a number of scholarships for freshmen that are awarded on the basis of academic achievement, extracurricular involvement, and community service. Similar transfer scholarships are determined primarily on the basis of course selection and cumulative grade point average.

Faculty

There are 425 faculty members; 89 percent of full-time faculty members possess doctoral or terminal degrees. Like the University, the mission of faculty members who choose Seattle University is teaching. Most classes average 20; the faculty-student ratio is 1:14. All classes are taught by faculty members.

The involvement of faculty members extends beyond the classroom. Faculty members are available to provide extra assistance, to help students with their research, and to assist in the arranging of internships. Faculty advisers provide guidance, direction, and encouragement throughout the year. New students are assigned faculty advisers according to major prior to registration.

Student Government

All undergraduates belong to the Associated Students of Seattle University (ASSU). This is the central student organization on campus. ASSU is organized around an elected president, an executive vice president, and an activities vice president. In addition, a 12-member representative council oversees every facet of the student body and is responsible for policymaking. Its primary responsibility is to provide a diverse activities program to meet the needs of SU's diverse student body. In addition, ASSU communicates student needs to the administration and faculty. ASSU oversees eighty-five clubs and organizations.

Admission Requirements

Freshman applicants are required to have a college-preparatory program, including 4 years of English, 3 years of social studies/history, 3 years of mathematics, 2 years of laboratory science, and 2 years of a foreign language. ACT or SAT scores, two recommendations, and an essay are also required. The middle 50 percent of freshman GPAs are between 3.1 and 3.8 on a 4.0 scale. The average score on the ACT is between 22 and 26, and the average SAT I scores are between 510 and 620 (verbal) and 510 and 610 (math). Seattle University accepts the Common Application, the Uniform Application, Peterson's Universal Application, the Catholic College Admissions Association Application, and its own admission application.

Essays or personal statements are required for admission and are carefully considered during application review.

College credit is awarded to those who have successfully completed Advanced Placement or International Baccalaureate examinations. Minimum scores can be obtained by contacting the Office of the Registrar.

Application and Information

Applications can be obtained by contacting the Office of Undergraduate Admission. Secondary school students who have completed at least six semesters are encouraged to apply by January of their senior year. Transfer students must submit official transcripts from all postsecondary institutions attended, regardless of whether course work was completed. For fall admission, freshmen should complete the process by February 1 to receive consideration for scholarships and other Seattle University financial aid; the recommended financial aid/admissions deadline for transfers is March 1. Please note that applications will usually be accepted after these dates but funds for financial aid may no longer be available. Campus visits can be scheduled Monday through Friday and most Saturdays. Guests can attend a class, meet with a faculty adviser, participate in a campus tour, and speak individually with representatives from admissions and financial aid.

For additional information students should contact:

Michael K. McKeon, Dean
Admissions Office
Seattle University
900 Broadway
Seattle, Washington 98122-4340
Telephone: 206-296-5800
  800-542-0833 (toll-free in Washington State)
  800-426-7123 (toll-free from all other states)
E-mail: admissions@seattleu.edu
World Wide Web: http://www.seattleu.edu

SETON HALL UNIVERSITY
SOUTH ORANGE, NEW JERSEY

The University

Seton Hall University was founded in 1856 by James Roosevelt Bayley, the first Catholic bishop of Newark, who named the college after his aunt, St. Elizabeth Ann Seton, the founder of the first American community of the Sisters of Charity. The institution was established as the first diocesan college in the United States and was organized into a university in 1950. It continues to operate under the auspices of the Roman Catholic Diocese of Newark. While Seton Hall is a Catholic university, it is not narrowly sectarian and welcomes students of all denominations. The University emphasizes Judeo-Christian intellectual traditions and values. The current undergraduate enrollment is about 4,700 men and women.

The University is composed of nine schools: the College of Arts and Sciences, the W. Paul Stillman School of Business, the College of Education and Human Services, the College of Nursing, the School of Diplomacy and International Relations, Immaculate Conception Seminary and School of Theology, University College, and the School of Graduate Medical Education, all on the South Orange campus, and the School of Law in Newark. The School of Law in Newark, which opened in 1951, is the only law school in the state operated by a private university. In addition to its regular three-year program, it has an evening program for students who cannot matriculate during the day. It also offers the only law school summer session in New Jersey. It is the largest law school in New Jersey and the twenty-first largest in the nation. In addition to its undergraduate curriculum, the University also offers selected graduate programs in business, education, nursing, science, and theology leading to master's and doctoral degrees. The University is accredited by the Middle States Association of Colleges and Schools, and its professional schools are accredited by appropriate accrediting bodies. The College of Education and Human Services is accredited by the National Council for Accreditation of Teacher Education and is approved by the State Department of Education in New Jersey under standards of the National Association of State Directors of Teacher Education and Certification. The W. Paul Stillman School of Business is accredited by the AACSB–The International Association for Management Education. The College of Nursing is accredited by the New Jersey State Board of Nursing and the National League for Nursing Accrediting Commission.

The University has a 58-acre campus. The coeducational residence halls and University-operated apartments house approximately 2,100 students. A seminary complex consists of classrooms for the School of Theology and residential facilities for graduate seminarians and faculty members. There are numerous student activities, including a student newspaper and yearbook; radio, drama, and choral groups; a nationally ranked debate team; musical theater; a pep band; the Black Students Union; the International Students Organization; community service organizations; the Puerto Rican Institute; and fraternities and sororities. There is also an active campus ministry for people of all faiths. Varsity teams are available for men in baseball, basketball, cross-country, golf, indoor and outdoor track, soccer, swimming, tennis, and wrestling. Varsity teams for women are available in basketball, cross-country, indoor and outdoor track, soccer, softball, swimming, tennis, and volleyball. There are also intramural sports. Athletic facilities include fields and tennis courts. Walsh Auditorium-Gymnasium has a main arena seating 2,000 spectators and classrooms for physical education and houses the University's 2,400-watt FM radio station. The recreation center is equipped with a 25-meter pool, a track, a long-jump pit, locker rooms, racquetball courts, offices, multipurpose rooms, a field house, and batting cages. Student services include personal and career counseling, aptitude testing, health services, career services, and special services. The campus is handicapped accessible.

Location

The suburban village of South Orange, New Jersey, is 14 miles from New York City. All the cultural and entertainment resources of New York City are easily accessible by bus, train, or car. All types of recreational activities are found within a radius of 100 miles of South Orange in resort areas and state parks. The northern New Jersey location—the site of an extensive pharmaceutical, chemical, and financial center—provides many learning and employment opportunities and internships for students.

Majors and Degrees

The College of Arts and Sciences offers the B.A. in African-American studies, anthropology, art, Asian studies, classical studies, communication, criminal justice, economics, English, French, history, Italian, liberal studies, modern languages, music, philosophy, political science, psychology, religious studies, social and behavioral sciences, social work, sociology, and Spanish. It offers the B.S. in biology, chemistry, computer science, mathematics, and physics. The W. Paul Stillman School of Business offers the B.S. in accounting, economics, finance, management, management information systems, marketing, and sports management and the B.A. in business administration. The College of Education and Human Services offers the B.S. in elementary, secondary, and special education. Teacher certification programs are available. The School of Diplomacy and International Relations offers the B.S. in international relations. The College of Nursing offers the Bachelor of Science in Nursing (B.S.N.).

Preprofessional programs are available in dentistry, law, medicine, and optometry. Engineering is offered jointly with the New Jersey Institute of Technology and Stevens Institute of Technology. Six-year physical therapy and physician's assistant programs are offered jointly with the University of Medicine and Dentistry of New Jersey (B.S./M.S.). A six-year occupational therapy program (B.A./M.S.) is also available. A dual-admission seven-year law program is offered jointly with the Seton Hall School of Law.

Academic Program

The University uses a semester calendar. It also offers day and evening summer sessions.

The College of Arts and Sciences is the largest division of the University. To earn the B.A. or B.S., students must complete at least 130 credits and maintain a minimum grade point average of 2.0 in the major field.

The program in the W. Paul Stillman School of Business is founded upon a background of liberal arts courses. Studies in the first two years provide the economic, quantitative, behavioral, and scientific foundations of business and society in general. Business core courses in finance, management, and marketing are taken in the last two years. To earn the B.S., students must complete at least 128 credits.

The program in the College of Education and Human Services prepares students for certification to teach in elementary and secondary schools in twenty-nine states. All education students major or take background courses in the liberal arts. Emphasis is on integration of the study of education with other academic disciplines and active participation in school situations to stimulate the intellectual, humanistic, and creative potential of the future teacher. To earn the B.S., students must complete 126–131 credits and maintain a 2.5 grade point average.

The program in the College of Nursing combines study in the liberal arts with professional education in nursing to prepare nurses for careers in a variety of health-care settings. Clinical experience is provided in hospitals, public health agencies, schools, nursing homes, industrial organizations, and other community agencies. Graduates of the program are eligible to sit for the examination for licensure as a registered nurse. To earn the B.S.N., students must complete at least 130 credits.

The School of Diplomacy and International Relations is affiliated with the United Nations Association and offers a Bachelor of Science degree in international relations. This program emphasizes ethnopolitical studies or world cultures and development of management and leadership skills, as well as a high degree of competency in a second language. Requirements of the program include study abroad and hands-on global-based computer technology. To earn the B.S., students must earn 130 credits.

The University offers internships in many programs, cooperative education programs through the W. Paul Stillman School of Business and the College of Arts and Sciences, and independent study programs. A four-year honors program is available in the College of Arts and Sciences for outstanding students. Credit is generally given for scores of 4 or higher on Advanced Placement tests or for successful scores on selected CLEP general and subject examinations. A maximum of 30 semester hours of credit by examination may be counted toward a degree.

The University offers an Army ROTC program on campus. An Air Force ROTC program is available through the New Jersey Institute of Technology.

Off-Campus Arrangements

The University offers study-abroad programs in the People's Republic of China, Japan, Korea, the Dominican Republic, and Puerto Rico. Through the International Student Exchange Program, students may study at any of 101 universities in thirty-five countries for one academic year. Students have several opportunities for cooperative learning and internships in the metropolitan area. Many co-op positions are with Fortune 500 companies, while others are with leading government, cultural, charitable, and scientific organizations. A semester in Washington, D.C., is also available for students to obtain internships and to take classes at exchange universities.

Academic Facilities

The University's library is a twenty-first-century research center with a computerized card catalog, four electronic multimedia rooms, ten CD-ROM information search and retrieval stations, 200 computer workstations for students, and nearly 1 million holdings. The Humanities Building contains classrooms and offices, a TV studio, two classroom amphitheaters, language and journalism laboratories, and the University Museum. In McNulty Hall science building, there are well-equipped laboratories for biology, chemistry, and physics. The Art Center (a registered National Historic Landmark) houses an art gallery, studios, classrooms, and offices of the Department of Art and Music. The College of Nursing has multipurpose and audiovisual laboratories. Kozlowski Hall, completed in 1997, contains modern lecture halls, computer rooms, faculty offices, and conference rooms for several of the University's academic programs, including the School of Business, the College of Education and Human Services, and the Psychology Department. There are also microcomputer laboratories in several locations on campus, and a large University-operated mainframe computer is located in the Computer Center. The University also has various centers and research institutes.

Costs

For the 1999–2000 academic year, tuition was $516 per credit, and fees were $940 (which includes the mobile computing fee) per semester. The charge for a room was $5240 per year. Board charges ranged from $981 to $1545 per semester, depending upon the meal plan chosen.

Financial Aid

The University offers federal, state, and institutional aid. Most aid is based on need, but many scholarships are based on outstanding scholastic ability and achievement. Athletic grants are also available. Currently, about 80 percent of the students receive financial aid; 26 percent work part-time on campus. All applicants for aid are required to file the Free Application for Federal Student Aid (FAFSA) by April 1 for fall entry and by October 1 for spring entry.

Faculty

The University has 343 full-time and 390 part-time faculty members. More than two thirds of the full-time faculty members have a doctoral degree. The ratio of full-time students to full-time faculty members is 14:1. Faculty members serve as advisers to students in their department.

Student Government

The Student Government Association is a bicameral body of students with the responsibility of representing their fellow students and providing programs of interest to the campus community. Students are elected to seats on the University Senate, which deals with all legislative matters pertinent to the University. In addition, the Resident Student Association represents the interests of resident students, and the Commuter Council represents the interests of commuter students.

Admission Requirements

Applicants are selected on the basis of their school achievement record, SAT I or ACT scores, and teacher and counselor recommendations. Students must graduate from an accredited high school or have passing scores on the GED test. Sixteen high school units are required: 4 in English, 3 in mathematics, 2 in social studies, 2 in foreign language, 1 in laboratory science, and 4 in approved academic electives. Special admission policies exist for students who have been out of high school for an extended period of time.

Transfer applicants must have a minimum 2.5 grade point average (a minimum 2.75 GPA for programs in science, business, math, and computer science) and must be in good standing at the last institution attended. Credit is usually given for grades of 2.0 or higher in University-equivalent courses taken at approved institutions; a maximum of 100 semester hours of transferable credit are allowed toward a bachelor's degree.

Application and Information

Freshman candidates must supply high school transcripts, SAT I or ACT scores, and a $45 application fee. Teacher and/or counselor recommendations, an essay, and an interview are optional. Transfer applicants must also submit transcripts from all colleges and universities attended. The application fee may be waived for applicants with financial need. The University uses rolling admission. Admission decisions are announced on a rolling basis starting December 1. The preferred application deadlines are March 1 for freshman admission and June 1 for transfers.

Alyssa McCloud
Acting Director of Admissions
Seton Hall University
400 South Orange Avenue
South Orange, New Jersey 07079-2680
Telephone: 800-THE-HALL (toll-free)
E-mail: thehall@shu.edu
World Wide Web: http://www.shu.edu

SETON HILL COLLEGE
GREENSBURG, PENNSYLVANIA

The College

In 1918, the Sisters of Charity founded Seton Hill College to help women open new doors through the power of education. Since that time, Seton Hill has been recognized as a leader in liberal arts education. Today, Seton Hill College is ranked by *U.S. News & World Report* as a top-tier institution for its academic reputation among northern liberal arts colleges.

Seton Hill College, a liberal arts college focused on women, is situated in the Laurel Highlands, an area of southwestern Pennsylvania known for its beautiful scenery and wealth of outdoor activities such as skiing, cycling, hiking, and whitewater rafting. Recreational opportunities include on-campus lectures, theater productions, a fitness center, and aerobics classes, as well as College-sponsored trips to Pittsburgh for cultural and sports events.

Seton Hill has varsity teams in basketball, cross-country, equestrian competition, golf, soccer, softball, tennis, and volleyball, plus a variety of intramural teams.

At the graduate level, Seton Hill grants the Master of Arts degree in art therapy, counseling psychology, elementary education, special education, and writing popular fiction, and a Master of Science in management.

Location

Seton Hill College's beautiful 200-acre campus is located in Greensburg, Pennsylvania. As a private college, Seton Hill is able to maintain a safe, secure environment that allows students to concentrate on academics.

Seton Hill is easily accessible by car, train, or plane. Just 35 miles east of Pittsburgh, Greensburg enjoys all the advantages of a large city while maintaining a small-town atmosphere. The seat of Westmoreland County, Greensburg is home to the Westmoreland Museum of Art, the Westmoreland Symphony Orchestra, two large malls, several shopping centers, and a hospital.

Majors and Degrees

The College grants the Bachelor of Arts, Bachelor of Fine Arts, Bachelor of Science, Bachelor of Music, and Bachelor of Social Work degrees.

Women and men choose from the following programs: accounting; art, including art and technology, art education, art history, art therapy, graphic design, studio art, and visual arts management; biology; business administration, including finance; chemistry, including biochemistry; communication; computer science; dietetics; economics; education, including early childhood, elementary, secondary, and special education; English, including creative writing, journalism, and literature; family and consumer sciences, including child care and food service management; family and consumer science education; family studies; French; history; international studies; management, including allied health, entrepreneurial studies, human resources, information management, international organization management, and marketing; mathematics, including actuary science and a 3+2 engineering program; medical technology; music, including music education, performance, and sacred music; music theater; a 2+2 nursing program; physician assistant studies; physics; political science; psychology; religious studies/theology; social work; sociology; Spanish; theater, including music theater, technical theater, theater arts, theater education, theater management, and theater performance; and women's studies.

The College offers preprofessional preparation for dentistry, law, medicine, occupational therapy, optometry, physical therapy, physician assistant studies, podiatry, and veterinary medicine.

Academic Program

Seton Hill offers five divisions, with the opportunity to self-design a major, all enhanced by the College's award-winning core curriculum. Special programs are available for students who are undecided about their major.

The Seton Hill College Honors Program is available for students who have distinguished themselves academically in high school.

Students hoping to one day own a business may be interested in Seton Hill College's National Education Center for Women in Business. The center is the first organization of its kind in the United States to offer courses in business ownership and entrepreneurial activities to students in any major.

Off-Campus Arrangements

Seton Hill College recognizes that important learning experiences occur in nonacademic settings. For this reason, the College offers a variety of internships, fieldwork experiences, and cooperative education opportunities. The Office of Career Development and College faculty members assist students in finding an off-campus placement where practical experience related to the major and valuable job contacts for the future may be gained.

In addition, students may opt to spend a semester or year studying abroad.

Academic Facilities

At the center of the Seton Hill campus is Reeves Hall, housing a theater, art gallery, and spacious library that serves as the College's information center. In the library, access to information is made easy through an automated catalog and CD-ROM databases. In addition, students have access to six Pentium labs, a Power Mac lab, a multimedia lab, a Silicon Graphics lab, and clusters of computers in all residence halls. All students receive an Internet account for e-mail, navigating the Web, and conducting research. The on-campus Cyber Castle combines high technology with entertainment for all students.

In order to provide the maximum benefits possible, Seton Hill's nineteen academic and residence facilities have been specially designed with students' convenience in mind.

Costs

For the 2000–01 academic year, tuition for the full-time student is $15,225. Room and board fees are $5200. Books and personal expenses amount to an additional $1000–$2000 per year.

Financial Aid

Seton Hill College's Financial Aid Office works with each student to develop an aid package from the wide variety of scholarships, grants, loans, and work-study programs available.

Seton Hill offers Presidential Scholarships valued annually from $3800 to $7600, which are automatically awarded to students who rank in the top 10 percent, 20 percent, or 30 percent of their high school class and meet the admission criteria. In addition, art, music, theater, biology, chemistry, math, and athletic scholarships and the prestigious Bayer Science Scholarships are awarded based on merit.

Faculty

With a student-faculty ratio of 13:1, Seton Hill faculty members can explore the needs of each student and offer individual attention. The low student-faculty ratio allows each student to become personally acquainted with the instructor. In addition, Seton Hill faculty members understand the importance of being accessible to their students.

The Seton Hill faculty consists of 45 full-time professors, 72 percent of whom have doctoral or terminal degrees.

Student Government

Through the Seton Hill Government Association, students participate in the government of the College and enjoy voting representation on a number of faculty committees. Each residence hall floor is represented by a senator who acts as a liaison between the student senate and the student body. Participation in student government is a valuable experience that develops leadership skills and a working understanding of government.

In addition, the student government helps to sponsor numerous on-campus political, cultural, and social events. Off-campus activities include trips to Pittsburgh, New York City, and Washington, D.C.

Admission Requirements

Acceptance to the College is based on the successful completion of a college-preparatory curriculum in high school. Applicants must have completed at least 15 secondary school academic units. These units must include 4 units of English, 2 units of college-preparatory mathematics, 2 units of social science, 2 units of the same foreign language, 1 unit of laboratory science, and 4 academic electives.

Students who wish to transfer credits to Seton Hill College from another college or university must present their transcripts for evaluation on a course-by-course basis. A transfer student will receive a credit evaluation after the student has been admitted to the College.

Application and Information

Seton Hill College has a rolling admissions policy. Decisions of the Admissions Committee are rendered shortly after all application materials have been submitted.

The first-time freshman applicant should submit a completed application form, a $30 nonrefundable application fee, an official secondary school transcript that includes the applicant's rank and cumulative grade point average, and official score reports from either the SAT I or ACT.

For more information, students should contact:

Kathleen H. Berard
Director of Admissions
Seton Hill College
Seton Hill Drive
Greensburg, Pennsylvania 15601-1599
Telephone: 724-838-4255
   800-826-6234 (toll-free)
Fax: 724-830-1294
E-mail: admit@setonhill.edu
World Wide Web: http://www.setonhill.edu

The newly renovated Administration Building is a picturesque focal point on the Seton Hill campus.

SHAWNEE STATE UNIVERSITY
PORTSMOUTH, OHIO

The College

Shawnee State University (SSU), with 3,613 students, is Ohio's newest state university. Previously a community college, Shawnee State became the state's thirteenth university in 1986.

Although most students come from Ohio and contiguous states, Shawnee State encourages applications from other states and countries. Shawnee State is committed to the special educational value that is provided by a residential campus community. The University holds the belief that students who live on campus gain valuable life experience and form many lasting friendships. For that reason, freshmen and sophomores who are single, under the age of 23, and live outside of a 50-mile radius of the University are required to live in campus housing and participate in a meal plan.

To help new students through their first year on campus, Shawnee State's Student Success Center offers advising and scheduling of classes, counseling, and referral services to various support offices on campus.

The University's small-campus environment provides many opportunities for involvement and leadership in out-of-class activities, including Student Government Association, the student newspaper, athletics, various clubs and organizations, and fraternities and sororities. The James A. Rhodes Athletic Center, which houses a junior Olympic-size pool, racquetball courts, tennis courts, a Nautilus room and free weights, fitness machines, a whirlpool, and saunas, is also open to Shawnee State students.

Location

Shawnee State's 50-acre campus is situated between the Ohio River and downtown Portsmouth, Ohio. A city of 23,000 people, Portsmouth provides the conveniences of life in a small town. With proximity to the larger cities of Columbus and Cincinnati, Ohio, and Huntington, West Virginia, SSU also offers the benefits of those metropolitan areas. Outdoor recreational opportunities are available at Shawnee State Park, which is located only a few miles from campus. This state facility provides nature trails and opportunities for hiking, boating, fishing, and golfing.

Majors and Degrees

Shawnee State University offers both baccalaureate and associate degrees. Bachelor of Arts (B.A.) programs include English/humanities; English/humanities, with an option in education licensure; history; social sciences, with integrated social studies licensure; and social sciences, with options in education licensure and legal assisting (2+2). Bachelor of Fine Arts (B.F.A.) degrees are offered with majors in ceramics, drawing, painting, and studio arts with a multi-age visual arts licensure. Majors offered for the Bachelor of Science (B.S.) degree include accounting; biology; biology, with an option in premedicine; business administration; business administration, with options in health management, management information systems, and legal assisting (2+2); chemistry; chemistry, with an option in premedicine; computer engineering technology; education, with licensure in early childhood, middle childhood, and intervention; environmental engineering technology; mathematical sciences; medical laboratory science; natural science; natural science, with options in applied mathematics, applied mathematics/education licensure, biology, biology/education licensure, biology/environmental science, chemistry, chemistry/education licensure, and chemistry/environmental science; occupational therapy; plastics engineering technology; and sports studies, with options in athletic training and sports management.

Associate of Applied Business degree programs include accounting, business information systems, business management, legal assisting, and office administration. Associate of Applied Science degree programs are offered in computer-aided drafting and design, dental hygiene, electromechanical engineering technology, instrumentation and control, medical laboratory studies, nursing, occupational therapy assistant studies, physical therapist assistant studies, plastics engineering technology, radiologic technology, and respiratory therapy. Associate of Arts degree programs include arts/humanities (with options in art, communications, English, and music) and social science. The Associate of Science degree is offered in mathematics and sciences.

Academic Program

Recognizing the importance of knowledge, values, and cultural enrichment, Shawnee State University is committed to providing an undergraduate education that fosters competence in oral and written communication, scientific and quantitative reasoning, and critical analysis/logical thinking. In addition to the course requirements in the academic major, all baccalaureate programs require the General Education Program (GEP), a combination of required and elective courses that contribute to the skills and knowledge characteristic of university graduates. All students also take Senior Seminar, which involves the research and writing of a major paper and an oral presentation of findings. Baccalaureate degree programs require a minimum of 186 quarter hours, including 48 credit hours in the General Education Program. Associate degrees generally require 90 quarter hours.

Off-Campus Arrangements

Some Shawnee State University students have participated in short-term exchange programs with Nizhny Novgorod State University in Russia; and in cultural exchange programs with Zittau, Germany, and Orizaba, Mexico, sister cities of Portsmouth, Ohio, and with Universitat Jaume I in Castelló, Spain. Other off-campus opportunities include internships that are available through the Office of Career Services.

Academic Facilities

Shawnee State University is situated on a modern campus, with five major building projects completed since 1991. Among the newest buildings is the library, which houses more than 122,000 bound volumes and 1,000 periodical subscriptions, and provides 700 study stations and ten group study rooms. The Advanced Technology Center provides classrooms and computer laboratories for engineering technology students and houses a planetarium that features Digistar II, a computer that runs software of the heavens and the center of the earth.

Opened in 1995, the Vern Riffe Center for the Arts includes a 1,150-seat theater designed by George C. Izenour, a recital hall, a virtual-reality audio room, and art galleries. This state-of-the-art center also houses classrooms and studios for subjects that range from graphic studies and electronic graphics to printing, lithography, intaglio, painting, and sculpture.

Costs

Tuition and fees for Ohio residents in 2000–01 are $3162, and room and board are approximately $4780. Out-of-state tuition is

$5565. Students from Boyd, Greenup, Lewis, and Mason Counties in Kentucky and Wayne and Cabell Counties in West Virginia qualify for a district tuition, which is $4071 in 2000–01. Approximately $600 should be anticipated for books. To further ensure affordability, Shawnee State provides budget payment plans for tuition, room, and board.

Financial Aid

More than 80 percent of Shawnee students receive some form of financial aid, including more than 100 scholarships, grants, college work-study, and student loans. To apply for financial aid, students must file the Free Application for Federal Student Aid (FAFSA). Approximately $1 million in scholarship money is earmarked each year.

Faculty

While applied research and community service are respected and valued, Shawnee State University is first and foremost a teaching institution. All classes are taught by full-time or part-time faculty members, and all full-time faculty members serve as academic advisers. Classes are small, with a faculty-student ratio of 1:16. Fifty percent of full-time faculty members hold doctoral degrees.

Student Government

The Shawnee State University Student Government Association is composed of 25 students who are elected by the student body. The Student Government Association is the parent organization of the University's student clubs and organizations and provides an avenue to students to be represented on various university committees.

In addition to representation on the Student Government Association, 2 students, appointed by the Governor of Ohio, serve on the Shawnee State University Board of Trustees.

Admission Requirements

Admission to Shawnee State University is open and rolling. Applicants must be high school graduates or recipients of the GED. To be accepted without condition, applicants must file an application for admission and arrange for an official final transcript to be sent directly from the high school to Shawnee State. Transfer students must have official transcripts forwarded from all other colleges and universities previously attended.

The programs in health science are selective in admission and limited in enrollment. These may require specific academic preparation in high school and minimum high school GPA and ACT scores; some require specific volunteer experiences. All have deadlines by which all requirements must be met to be considered for program admission. There is a $15 application fee for health sciences programs.

Application and Information

The Office of Admission is open from 8 a.m. to 5 p.m. on weekdays. Saturday appointments are available. For further information about Shawnee State University, academic programs, and visitation days or to schedule a campus visit and tour, students should contact:

Office of Admission
Shawnee State University
940 Second Street
Portsmouth, Ohio 45662
Telephone: 740-355-2221
              800-959-2SSU (toll-free)
Fax: 740-355-2111
E-mail: admsn@shawnee.edu
World Wide Web: http://www.shawnee.edu/

The courtyard in front of Massie Hall.

SHENANDOAH UNIVERSITY
WINCHESTER, VIRGINIA

The University

Shenandoah University was founded at Dayton, Virginia, in 1875. Although the institution was established to provide "classical" and music studies, by 1877 an unusual blend of educational opportunities had been formulated that included arts, sciences, music, medical arts, and business management. These programs, on a much more sophisticated basis, are found at Shenandoah today. In 1960, Shenandoah moved to a 62-acre campus in Winchester, Virginia. The main campus is now approximately 100 acres with eighteen buildings, including six residence halls. Of these six facilities for boarding students, one is for women and five are coeducational. There are five additional buildings at off-campus locations. Shenandoah's historical relationship with the United Methodist Church does not place sectarian obligations on any student.

Shenandoah's students have the distinct advantage of being on a small campus near large metropolitan cultural centers. Such student organizations as academic fraternities, service and honor organizations, and various departmental clubs provide opportunities for leadership and recreation. Students come to Shenandoah because they want an educational experience of superior quality and believe that the facilities of a small campus, with a relaxed and personal atmosphere, are the most conducive to achieving this experience. Fifty-eight percent of the 2,269 students are from Virginia; the remaining 42 percent represent thirty-nine states and twenty-six countries.

Graduate study is also available at Shenandoah. Degrees offered include the Master of Business Administration; the Master of Music in church music, composition, conducting, dance accompanying, pedagogy, performance, or piano accompanying; the Master of Fine Arts in dance choreography and performance; the Master of Music Therapy; the Master of Music Education; the Master of Science in Arts Administration; the Master of Science in Computers in Education; the Master of Science in Education; the Master of Science in Nursing; the Master of Science in Occupational Therapy; the Master of Physical Therapy; and three doctoral programs: the Doctor of Pharmacy, the Doctor of Pharmacy (nontraditional), and the Doctor of Musical Arts. Graduate certificates are offered in church music, health-care management, information systems and computer technology, public management, and TESOL. Further information about graduate study may be obtained by writing to the Director of Admissions.

Shenandoah University is accredited by the Commission on Colleges of the Southern Association of Colleges and Schools (1866 Southern Lane, Decatur, GA 30033-4097; telephone: 404-679-4501) to award associate, bachelor's, and master's degrees and is a candidate for accreditation to award the doctoral degree. Shenandoah holds membership in a number of professional organizations, including the National Association of Schools of Music, the National League for Nursing, the National Association of Music Therapy, the American Physical Therapy Association, and the American Occupational Therapy Association.

Location

The Shenandoah campus, adjacent to Interstate 81, is located 72 miles west of Washington, D.C., in the historic Shenandoah Valley of Virginia. The University is located on the southeast edge of the city of Winchester, Virginia. Winchester/Frederick County, rich in history, is a vigorous community of approximately 70,000 people. The region has a moderate, healthful climate; cultural groups; park and recreation areas; resorts; fishing; hunting; winter sports; modern retail centers; and major medical facilities.

Majors and Degrees

Shenandoah University offers ten undergraduate degrees: the Bachelor of Accountancy, the Bachelor of Arts, the Bachelor of Business Administration, the Bachelor of Fine Arts, the Bachelor of International Business, the Bachelor of Management, the Bachelor of Music, the Bachelor of Music Therapy, the Bachelor of Science, the Associate in Science, and several certificate programs. Programs of study available include accountancy, administration of justice, American studies, arts management (dance, music, and theater), arts studies, biology, business administration (accounting, banking and finance, information systems and computer technology, international business, management, and marketing), business studies, chemistry, Christian leadership, church music, commercial music, composition, dance, dance education, elementary/middle school education, English, environmental studies, health-care management, history, information systems and computer technology, international business, jazz studies, kinesiology (physical education and health, sports medicine–athletic training, sports medicine–exercise science, and sports medicine–preprofessional), management, mass communications, mathematics, music, music education, music theater, music therapy, nursing (both two- and four-year degree programs), pedagogy (guitar or piano), performance (opera and pedagogy), piano accompanying, piano pedagogy, psychology, public administration/political science, public management, purchasing management, religion, respiratory care (both two- and four-year degree programs), secondary education, sociology, Spanish interpreting, teaching English to speakers of other languages, theater (acting, costume design, directing, and scenic and lighting design), theater for youth, and university studies. Selected programs of study may result in double majors for students who wish to concentrate on more than one area of study. Preprofessional programs are available in certain disciplines on the Shenandoah campus.

Academic Program

Shenandoah's academic calendar is divided into fall and spring semesters, and summer terms, ranging in length from two to eleven weeks, are also available. Shenandoah has an excellent conservatory of music, dance, and theater, with 499 undergraduate music students and more than thirty performing ensembles. Many academic programs at Shenandoah are flexible enough to allow the student to develop an individualized educational program. Each academic division (arts and sciences, business, the conservatory, and health professions) offers diversified programs, with specific courses required by the various accreditation agencies. Credit is available through the tests of the College-Level Examination Program (CLEP), Proficiency Examination Program (PEP), and Advanced Placement (AP) Program and through various departmental challenge examinations. Honorably discharged veterans of the U.S. armed forces may be allowed credit for certain physical education courses as well as for academic work completed in service schools where equivalence has been recommended by *The Guide to the Evaluation of Educational Experiences in the Armed Services*.

Off-Campus Arrangements

Clinical practice, internships, and student-teaching opportunities are arranged with local businesses, hospitals, clinics, nursing homes, mental-health-care centers, and elementary, middle, and secondary schools in the Winchester area. Students are given the opportunity to enrich their educational experience through travel and study-abroad programs.

Academic Facilities

A large number of support facilities and programs supplement the various academic offerings at Shenandoah. The Alson H. Smith, Jr. Library serves as the nucleus of the learning experience. It contains 114,822 volumes, 124,695 microforms, 16,891 records and CDs, and 15,000 music scores and subscribes to 1,163 periodicals. The media center contains both visual and audio materials and equipment, preview and listening rooms, computer workstations, educational television viewing facilities, and forty study carrels. The Ohrstrom-Bryant Theatre building, which houses the Glaize Studio Theatre, provides an excellent atmosphere for the major performing arts programs in music, theater, and dance. The facilities for the program in church music are enriched by an elaborate Möller tracker-action organ, housed in the Goodson Chapel–Recital Hall. The commercial music program is enriched by the recording studio, which is a fully equipped twenty-four-track professional recording facility.

Laboratories in the Gregory Building serve instructional needs for courses in acoustics, biology, chemistry, computer science, environmental studies, modern languages, and physics. The Environmental Studies Laboratory includes an attached greenhouse used for teaching, growing specimens for lab studies, and student research projects. The Shingleton Building has practice areas for varsity sports, a basketball court with spectator seating, two dance studios, a fitness room, and classroom facilities. The Dorothy Ewing Dance Studio provides additional dance facilities. The floor measures 35 by 60 feet, and the 12-foot ceiling allows ample room for lifts and leaps. The Harry F. Byrd Jr. School of Business is housed in Henkel Hall. This facility contains a 200-seat lecture hall, a gallery, classrooms, seminar rooms, offices, a boardroom, and laboratories equipped with various computers. The John Kerr Building, located in historic downtown Winchester, is the home of Shenandoah's Conservatory Arts Academy. A modern, 55,000-square-foot Health Professions Building, located on the Winchester Medical Center campus approximately 2 miles from the main campus, houses the School of Pharmacy and the nursing and respiratory care programs. The facility contains an in-depth pharmacy library and drug information center, a computer lab with ninety-five workstations, multimedia classrooms, research laboratories, and a computer-equipped dispensing laboratory. Interactive video and computer laboratories simulate clinical practice realities. The occupational and physical therapy programs are housed in the Cork Street Center, formerly the Winchester Medical Center. State-of-the-art equipment is utilized in the Center for Clinical Research and the Clinical Skills Laboratory. A Compaq-Pentium–based academic computing network is available on site for student and faculty use.

The Shenandoah University Network (SUnet) structure provides a high-speed fiber backbone that supports an IBM AS/400 administration system and numerous networked Windows and Macintosh workstations. The campus has four IBM-platform labs and a Macintosh-platform lab for general use. The IBM labs are equipped with a total of 130 Compaq-Pentium multimedia computers and HP laser printers and support, among other software packages, Microsoft Windows, Word, Excel, SPSS, Pascal, PowerPoint, and Access. The Macintosh lab is equipped with eighteen Macintosh computers and supports Microsoft Word, Works, Excel, PowerPoint, and other special packages. The campus has Internet access. All workstations in the labs have full Internet and e-mail access, and all Shenandoah University students have Internet and e-mail accounts. The campus is also equipped with e-mail stations. Remote access is available for faculty, staff, and student use. The University supports state-of-the-art computer technology, and the goal of the campus computing office is to give students easy access to available information technology in order to facilitate students' scholarly goals and objectives.

Costs

The 1999–2000 comprehensive annual fee (two semesters) for resident full-time undergraduate students was $21,000, which included tuition and room and board. The comprehensive annual tuition (two semesters) for commuting (day) full-time undergraduate students was $15,700. Undergraduate part-time tuition was $490 per credit hour. Private applied music lessons for music students cost an additional $500 per year for major study (1 hour per week) and $250 per year for minor study (1 half hour per week). Such incidentals as transportation, personal expenses, and laundry vary in cost; textbook costs, however, can be estimated at $750 per year. There is no difference in the cost of tuition and fees for out-of-state students. The Board of Trustees reserves the right to alter charges at any time.

Financial Aid

Shenandoah makes every effort to assist students in finding resources to finance their education. Approximately 91 percent of the University's students receive some type of financial aid. Shenandoah annually awards more than $18 million in aid to students in the form of grants, loans, scholarships, and employment on the campus. Previous financial aid packages have averaged approximately $11,200 per student per year. To qualify for scholarships and financial aid, students must submit the Free Application for Federal Student Aid (FAFSA). Aid is awarded on a first-come, first-served basis, as funds are available. A student must be accepted for admission to a degree program before a financial aid decision is made. Specific information regarding financial aid should be requested from the Director of Financial Aid.

Faculty

Shenandoah has 154 full-time faculty members and 136 part-time faculty members; 137 faculty members (112 full-time and 25 part-time) hold a Ph.D. or other terminal degree. The faculty-student ratio is approximately 1:8. The small size of the student body encourages excellent communication and rapport among students and faculty members. Members of the faculty advise students and plan activities that concern the student body as a whole. Shenandoah faculty members have a strong commitment to teaching and counseling students.

Student Government

The Student Government Association (SGA) is the main student organization on campus. In addition to promoting activities of varied interest, the SGA provides a means of communication and understanding among students, faculty members, and administrators. Students are encouraged to participate in the governing of Shenandoah and are represented on all faculty and administrative committees.

Admission Requirements

Shenandoah seeks a diverse student body through the individualized admission processing of each applicant under a rolling admission program. Applicants are evaluated on the basis of their high school record and SAT I or ACT scores. Students applying for degree programs in music, dance, or theater must successfully complete an audition. Shenandoah does not discriminate on the basis of sex, race, color, religion, national or ethnic origin, age, or physical disability. Although interviews are not required, students are encouraged to visit the campus.

Application and Information

To apply, a student must submit an application with a $30 nonrefundable application fee, SAT I or ACT scores, and an official high school transcript. Transfer students must submit an official college transcript for all postsecondary course work in addition to meeting the freshman score and transcript requirements. Applicants are notified of the admission decision after receipt of all credentials. An application form, financial aid information, and other materials may be obtained by contacting:

Director of Admissions
Shenandoah University
1460 University Drive
Winchester, Virginia 22601
Telephone: 540-665-4581
        800-432-2266 (toll-free)
Fax: 540-665-4627
E-mail: admit@su.edu

SHEPHERD COLLEGE
SHEPHERDSTOWN, WEST VIRGINIA

The College

Shepherd College, founded in 1871, is a very competitive, four-year, state-supported institution offering seventy fields of study in the liberal arts and sciences, business, and teacher education. Shepherd is the fastest-growing institution in West Virginia. There are 4,600 students on the 323-acre campus; 60 percent come from West Virginia, and the remaining 40 percent represent forty other states and twenty-one countries.

The College prides itself on its friendly and helpful atmosphere and the individual contact the students receive as a result of small classes. On campus there are fifty organizations, ranging from national fraternities and sororities to community service groups, from professional organizations to student government. Students are encouraged to join and interact with all of the groups that interest them.

Shepherd College also offers both men's and women's intercollegiate sports. The men's program consists of baseball, basketball, cross-country, football, golf, soccer, and tennis. The women's sports program consists of basketball, cheerleading, cross-country, soccer, softball, tennis, and volleyball. Men and women compete in the NCAA Division II program. A club lacrosse program is available for both men and women. For students not interested in playing intercollegiate sports, an extensive intramural and recreation program is also available.

Students are housed on campus in twelve residence halls. Seven offer suite arrangements with 4 students sharing two bedrooms, a living room, and bath. Five buildings house students in traditional 2-student dorm rooms. All buildings are coeducational.

Location

Shepherd College is located in historic Shepherdstown (founded in 1730), a small community on the banks of the Potomac River with a population of approximately 5,000. Shepherdstown is the oldest town in West Virginia and the site of the launching of the first successful steamboat in 1787 by James Rumsey. Shepherdstown hosted the Syrian-Israeli Peace Talks in January 2000. Other historic landmarks, located within 8 miles of campus, include the Antietam National Battlefield Park, Harpers Ferry National Historical Park, and the Chesapeake and Ohio Canal Historical Park and Trail. The area is rural, and hunting, fishing, horseback riding, waterskiing, and snow skiing are available for recreation. Communication and cooperation between the community and the College are very good, and many cultural events are sponsored jointly.

The College is a 10-minute drive from Martinsburg, West Virginia; 15 minutes from Charles Town and Harpers Ferry, West Virginia; 25 minutes from Hagerstown and Frederick, Maryland; and 90 minutes from Washington, D.C., and Baltimore, Maryland.

Majors and Degrees

Shepherd College offers the Bachelor of Arts, Bachelor of Fine Arts, and Bachelor of Science degrees in accounting, art and art education (graphic design, painting, photography, and printmaking), athletic training, biochemistry, biology, broadcasting, business administration, business education, chemistry, communications, computer mathematics, computer programming and information systems, early childhood education, economics, elementary education, English, environmental chemistry, environmental studies, family and consumer sciences, general science, health education, history, library science, literature, management, marketing, mathematics, music and music education (pedagogy, performance, and theory/composition), nursing, physical education, physics, political science, psychology, recreation and leisure services (commercial and hospitality, sport communications, sport fitness, sport management, and therapeutic recreation), social work, sociology, and theater.

Shepherd College offers the Associate of Arts, Associate of Applied Science, and Associate of Science degrees in accounting, banking, business administration, business information technology, culinary arts, electronics technology, engineering (2 + 2 program), fashion merchandising, fire service and safety technology, general studies, graphic design, marketing, nursing, office technology, photography, and studio art.

Preprofessional programs are available in the fields of dentistry, law, medicine, pharmacy, theology, and veterinary science.

Academic Program

All candidates for the baccalaureate degree must complete a minimum of 128 semester hours of course work with a minimum 2.0 overall average and a minimum 2.0 average in their major. Students in teacher education must have a minimum 2.5 average in their elementary education or secondary education field. The 128 semester hours include a general studies core, consisting of 19 hours in the humanities, 11 hours in science and mathematics, 15 hours in social sciences, and 2 hours in physical education. To earn the associate degree, students must complete 64 to 73 semester hours, depending on the program of study.

Student internships and practicums are required or recommended in the following areas of study: communications, education, fashion merchandising, graphic design, hotel-motel and restaurant management, library science, nursing, photography, psychology, recreation and leisure services, and social work. Biology and chemistry majors may utilize such nearby research facilities as the U.S. Fish and Wildlife Service National Education Training Center, the National Cancer Research Center at Fort Dietrick, the National Fisheries Center at Leetown, and the Appalachian Fruit Research Center at Bardane for their directed research projects. The Washington Gateway and Washington Semester programs provide formal internships in Washington, D.C. Co-op programs may be arranged in most major fields.

Academic Facilities

Academic facilities on the Shepherd College campus include an open-stack library with a collection of 392,694 materials; six academic buildings housing classrooms and laboratories; a Creative Arts Center housing the departments of art, music, and theater; and a comprehensive health, physical education, and athletic complex, which opened in 1989. The nearby libraries, museums, and cultural and research centers of the Washington, D.C., metropolitan area are also available for research and study.

Costs

For 1999–2000, tuition and fees were $2430 per year for West Virginia residents and $5754 per year for out-of-state students. Average room and board charges are $4112 per year. Books and supplies are about $1000 a year. Additional expenses vary, depending on a student's personal tastes, but are estimated to be between $40 and $80 per week.

Financial Aid

The College offers financial aid through the Federal Pell Grant, Federal Supplemental Educational Opportunity Grant, Federal Perkins Loan, Federal Stafford Student Loan, and Federal Work-Study programs. Federally insured student loans (arranged in cooperation with the student's local bank) are also available. The College offers academic, athletic, and talent scholarships based on merit.

Faculty

Of the College's 120 full-time faculty members, 65 percent have earned doctorates; all other faculty members have completed advanced work beyond the master's level, and many are doctoral candidates. All teaching is done by faculty members. The student-faculty ratio is 19:1. Faculty members serve as advisers to students in their respective disciplines, and they work with and participate in extracurricular organizations and activities on campus.

Student Government

The Shepherd College Student Government Association (SGA) consists of a policy-making body, the Executive Council, composed of the student body president and the cabinet, and an advisory and regulatory body, the Senate, composed of student representatives. Also affiliated with the SGA are 3 students who are elected to serve on the Student Affairs Committee, the central decision-making body on the campus concerned with student-life policies. The SGA sanctions student organizations and activities and controls the student activity fees and their disbursement among the various units of the College. Student representatives are members of all policy-making and program committees on campus.

Admission Requirements

Applicants must be graduates of accredited high schools and have at least 21 academic units of high school credit. Shepherd College requires that the 21 units be in the following areas: English, 4 units (years); mathematics, 3 units (algebra I and II and geometry); science, 3 units (biology, chemistry, and physics); social studies, 3 units (including American history); foreign language, 2 units; physical education, 2 units; and electives, at least 4 units (in such areas as music, art, drama, and computer science).

Applicants wishing full consideration for admission should have about a B average in high school, and they should have SAT I combined scores of about 1100 or ACT composite scores of about 21. Students are encouraged to take honors or advanced-placement courses in high school. College credit is given for most Advanced Placement test scores of 4 and 5 and in some cases for scores of 3. Written recommendations from high school guidance counselors are highly recommended for all freshman applicants. Admission interviews are not required, but campus visits are strongly advised.

Transfer students should have a minimum cumulative grade point average of 2.5 and a recommendation from the dean of students at their previous institution. Shepherd College does not admit transfer students who are on academic probation or suspension at any other institution. Transfer students majoring in any area of education must submit either SAT I or ACT scores for admission to the teacher education program.

Application and Information

The priority deadline for applications for the fall term is February 1, for the spring term it is November 1, and for the summer term it is February 1. Applications are accepted until June 15 if space remains in some academic programs. A separate departmental application must be filed along with the College application for entrance to the engineering and nursing programs (for fall term only). Art applicants must submit a portfolio, and music majors must audition for admission to the program. Teacher education majors must take and pass the PPST examination before enrollment in any Education Department courses. Early action applicants are notified of their admission status after December 15 of their senior year in high school. Students applying for regular admission are notified of their admission status on April 1. A nonrefundable enrollment deposit is due May 1, in compliance with the National Association for College Admission Counseling (NACAC) guidelines. Students are strongly encouraged to call the admissions office to schedule an admissions interview and a tour of campus.

For information about admission and programs, prospective students should contact:

Office of Admissions
Shepherd College
Shepherdstown, West Virginia 25443-1569

Telephone: 304-876-5212 or 5213
　　　　　　800-344-5231 (toll-free)
Fax: 304-876-5165
E-mail: kwolf@shepherd.edu
World Wide Web: http://www.shepherd.edu

McMurran Hall, built in 1859, houses the Office of Admissions.

SHIMER COLLEGE
WAUKEGAN, ILLINOIS

The College

Shimer College, a distinctive four-year liberal arts institution, is one of a handful of schools with an integrated curriculum based upon the reading of original source materials, sometimes called great books. Shimer's classes are small (fewer than 12 students) and utilize the process of discussion and shared inquiry. It is the mission of the College to teach people how—not what—to think and to develop the skills of clear expression and analytical reasoning.

The College believes that education is more than the mere transmittal of knowledge or the imparting of vocational skills. Specifically, Shimer is dedicated to the following principles: that the educational process must be intellectually stimulating and challenging; that the classroom should foster clarity in thought, speech, and writing; that a liberal arts education facilitates the formation of enlightened attitudes, concerns, and values; that the College exists to nurture the critical and creative abilities inherent in each student; and that students must develop skills that will enable them to succeed in whatever profession they choose.

Shimer College was founded in 1853 to provide higher education in pioneer Illinois. In 1950, Shimer adopted the Hutchins Plan, the great books curriculum and the Socratic colloquium format for class discussion. Shimer College flourished academically, and it was evaluated and acclaimed by social scientists and experts in the field of education as one of the U.S. campuses with an ideal intellectual climate.

Shimer provides an education for life by promoting the classical aim of education—freedom—through an exploration of the relationships among all branches of knowledge. The College is dedicated to the concept of integrative studies, the interweaving of clusters of knowledge. Further, the College is dedicated to the goal of developing its students either intensively in their field of study or practically through the Internship Program.

Shimer College maintains more than 140 years of history, tradition, academic excellence, and the highest ideal of the liberal arts education, which is the insistence that education is a process and a lifelong pursuit.

Location

Shimer is located in Waukegan, Illinois, a small urban community of 70,000 people that is located midway between Chicago and Milwaukee, on the shores of Lake Michigan and in the midst of the Lake County vacationland. Shimer is easily accessible from O'Hare International Airport by bus or from Chicago and Milwaukee by commuter train or car.

Majors and Degrees

Shimer students may earn a Bachelor of Arts (B.A.) degree in general studies, the humanities, natural sciences, or social sciences or a Bachelor of Science (B.S.) degree in the natural sciences or social sciences. By taking concentration courses within their area of study, students can develop competence in a special subject area.

Academic Program

The initial contact a student has with a subject of study is through the writings of the original great thinkers in the humanities, social sciences, and natural sciences. These works have been the basis of formal education for centuries and have been studied by the great scholars of all periods. Students are asked to place these works in their historical context and then to consider their relevance to contemporary life and thought.

The Shimer College core curriculum consists of a series of four courses each in humanities, social science, natural science, and integrative studies. All students must complete the 85 semester hours of courses before graduation, although transfer credits and placement examinations may suffice for actual course completion. The student then must pass a Basic Studies Comprehensive Examination. In addition to the Core, students take area studies, advanced general courses, advanced integrative studies, courses in their own concentration, tutorials, field internships, and electives. An Area Comprehensive Examination and a Senior Thesis complete the requirements for graduation.

For either the B.A. or B.S. degree, 125 credit hours are required. These hours are as follows for the B.A.: 30 in basic studies, 30 in area studies, 25 in integrative studies, and 40 in the concentration and electives.

Teaching is accomplished by shared inquiry. The discussion method used, often called the Socratic method, has an ancient precedent described in the writings of Plato in the fourth century B.C. Students gain the sound habits of thinking and of learning to ask the right questions. The method encourages students to become actively involved in their own education. The excitement of genuine dialogue generates self-knowledge and shared insight. Shimer classes are small to facilitate discussion and shared inquiry for all present.

Shimer College expects clear writing to be one of the skills imparted to students who earn a degree. The development and mastery of a competent prose style are emphasized in a semester writing week, the semester paper, the Basic Studies and Area Comprehensive Exams, and the senior thesis.

The academic calendar consists of an autumn semester, from early September through December, and a spring semester, from early February through May. Summer courses are offered on a limited basis.

The Early Entrant Program is available for students who have not completed high school. They take part in the same academic program as regularly admitted students.

Off-Campus Arrangements

Shimer College has an established Overseas Program. Since 1964, it has usually been held in Oxford, England. Shimer is also affiliated with the Partnership for Service Learning, which allows students to study in any of ten countries. Other off-campus arrangements, such as the Internship Program, can be made according to individual student needs.

Shimer offers a Weekend Program for working adults. This program began in 1982 and addresses the needs of adults with outside commitments and responsibilities. Seven weekends of intensive study constitute a semester; a student can complete a degree in four years or even less with transfer credits. Currently, students at the Weekend College range from 23 to 60 years of age.

Academic Facilities

The Shimer College library is housed in the Waukegan Public Library, a short walk from the College. The Shimer collection includes 35,000 volumes. The Waukegan library houses 200,000 volumes.

Costs

The comprehensive cost of tuition and fees in 1999–2000 was $14,180. Room costs were $1950, and board costs varied since students may use kitchens in their rooms.

Financial Aid

More than 90 percent of the students at Shimer receive some financial assistance in the form of scholarships, grants, loans, or College work-study jobs.

Faculty

Shimer has 16 full-time faculty members; 63 percent hold doctoral degrees. The student-instructor ratio is 8:1.

Student Government

Since 1977, Shimer College has been governed within the institution by the faculty members and students working together within a structure of committees, administration, and a working body of the whole, known as the Assembly. The uniqueness of Shimer College has made such a working relationship the heart of the College. Faculty members are regularly expected to participate in the administrative life of the College. Students are represented on every major committee except the Academic Standing Committee and sit as voting members on the Board of Trustees. In its attempts to attain the goal of being a working democracy, Shimer College enables its students to participate in the democratic process at a direct level that is not possible nationally. By participating in the Assembly, where faculty members and students are "one person, one vote," students learn the pros and cons of participatory, democratic self-governance. The College feels that this is an important learning process, one that is in line with its goal of graduating well-rounded and independent-thinking individuals.

Admission Requirements

The aim of Shimer College is to select students who will benefit from and contribute to the intellectual community. Each applicant is considered as an individual. Motivation, intellectual curiosity, and the commitment to a rigorous and integrative educational program are important qualifications.

Students should submit an application (part of the Shimer catalog), application essays or a writing portfolio, and all high school or college transcripts. ACT, SAT, or PSAT scores should be sent if the student has taken these tests. Students must arrange for an interview and send letters of recommendation (waived for weekend students who interview). Results of personal contacts with College personnel, letters of recommendation, and writing samples are the most important items in a student's admissions packet. Applicants who do not have strong academic records or standardized test scores should plan to submit additional materials in support of their application. Since each applicant is considered on an individual basis, some requirements may be waived under special circumstances. Homeschoolers and students from alternative schools of all types are encouraged to apply.

Application and Information

Shimer admissions decisions are made on a rolling basis. As soon as all necessary application materials have been received, a decision is made and the candidate is notified. Students are advised to apply as early as possible to secure maximum financial aid.

For more information, students should contact:

Office of Admissions
Shimer College
P.O. Box 500
Waukegan, Illinois 60070-0500
Telephone: 847-623-8400
              800-215-7173 (toll-free)
E-mail: admiss@shimer.edu
World Wide Web: http://www.shimer.edu

A student discusses a point in a Social Science 2 class.

SHIPPENSBURG UNIVERSITY OF PENNSYLVANIA
SHIPPENSBURG, PENNSYLVANIA

The University

Shippensburg University, founded in 1871, is a comprehensive public institution in south-central Pennsylvania enrolling more than 5,700 undergraduate students and approximately 1,000 graduate students. Of the undergraduates, 54 percent are women and 46 percent are men. The University is divided into the College of Arts and Sciences, the College of Education and Human Services, the John L. Grove College of Business, and the School of Graduate Studies. There is also a Division of Special Academic Programs, which includes the Division of Undeclared Majors.

Shippensburg University is a member of Pennsylvania's State System of Higher Education and is accredited by the Middle States Association of Colleges and Schools. Other accreditation is by the AACSB–The International Association for Management Education, the American Chemical Society, the Council on Social Work Education, the Council for the Accreditation of Counseling and Related Educational Programs, the International Association of Counseling Services, and the National Council for the Accreditation of Teachers. Shippensburg University is a member of the Council of Graduate Schools.

Graduate degrees conferred are the Master of Arts, Master of Education, Master of Science, and Master of Public Administration. Programs are as follows: Master of Science in administration of justice, biology, communication studies, computer science, counseling, geoenvironmental studies, information systems, mathematics, and psychology; Master of Arts in English and history; Master of Public Administration in public administration; and Master of Education in biology, counseling, educational administration, elementary education, English, mathematics, reading, and special education. The School of Graduate Studies also offers post-master's degree curricula leading to various types of education certification, including supervisory certification, and is one of twenty-three national sites for a post-graduate academic training program in Reading Recovery.

More than 200 student clubs, organizations, and activity groups, resulting in nearly 600 leadership opportunities, are available. Organizations include academic clubs, community service groups, special interest organizations, media organizations, musical groups, performing arts troupes, and twenty-four national or local fraternities and sororities.

Student activities are complemented by programs that bring nationally and internationally known figures to campus. Coretta Scott King, widow of Dr. Martin Luther King Jr.; U.S. Supreme Court Justice Harry A. Blackmun; Nobel Peace Prize recipient Archbishop Desmond Tutu; Rev. Jesse Jackson; actor Danny Glover; author and poet Maya Angelou; former Secretary of Defense Dick Cheney; author Kurt Vonnegut Jr.; former U.N. Ambassador Jeane Kirkpatrick; and Elizabeth Dole have all appeared on campus.

Each of the eight residence halls is equipped with lounges, exercise rooms, music practice rooms, study rooms, and computer connections to the online library catalog system. Each residence hall room has one cable television and two direct computer network connections. Most residence hall rooms are double occupancy; some single rooms are available. Seavers Apartments houses six students in each unit. Student safety is emphasized through controlled access to the residence halls, trained supervisory personnel, and a keycard entry system.

The University offers a variety of athletic facilities for both intercollegiate and intramural sports. These include a 2,768-seat field house, an 8,000-seat stadium, a gymnasium, fourteen outdoor tennis courts, indoor and outdoor tracks, two indoor swimming pools, squash and handball courts, a physical fitness center, a rehabilitation center, and sand volleyball courts. The University is a member of the Pennsylvania State Athletic Conference and NCAA Division II. Men's intercollegiate sports include baseball, basketball, cross-country, football, soccer, swimming, track and field, and wrestling. Women's intercollegiate sports include basketball, cross-country, field hockey, lacrosse, soccer, softball, swimming, tennis, track and field, and volleyball. Intramural team sports include basketball, soccer, softball, street hockey, Ultimate Frisbee, and volleyball. Intramural individual sports include billiards, cross-country, racquetball, swimming, table tennis, and wrestling. There are twelve sports clubs that include men's and women's rugby and ice hockey.

Etter Health Center provides 24-hour access to medical services. The eight-bed infirmary is staffed by a team of physicians and nurses. Chambersburg Hospital is only 20 minutes from campus.

Students have access to comprehensive counseling services on request in academic, career, psychological, social, personal growth, and religious areas. The Career Development Center offers career counseling, workshops in resume preparation, job interview techniques, and job search assistance.

Location

Shippensburg University is on 200 acres overlooking its namesake community, a borough of approximately 6,700 people in the Cumberland Valley. The University is about 50 minutes southwest of Harrisburg, 2 hours from both Baltimore and Washington, D.C., and 3 hours from Philadelphia. The campus is within easy walking distance of the center of town.

Majors and Degrees

Undergraduate degrees conferred are the Bachelor of Arts (B.A.), Bachelor of Science (B.S.), Bachelor of Science in Business Administration (B.S.B.A.), and Bachelor of Science in Education (B.S.Ed.). The College of Arts and Sciences awards the B.A. degree in art; communication/journalism (print media, public relations, electronic media); English (secondary education certification); French (secondary education certification); history; interdisciplinary arts; mathematics (computer science); physics; political science; psychology; sociology; Spanish (secondary education certification); speech communications (African-American communication, applied communication, rhetoric/communication theory, women's communication); and urban studies. The B.S. degree is awarded in applied physics; biology (ecology and environmental, environmental education, health professions, medical technology, secondary education certification); chemistry (biochemistry, health professions, medical technology, secondary education certification); computer science (information systems, scientific programming, systems programming); geoenvironmental studies; geography (cartography–spatial analysis, land use, regional development and tourism); mathematics (actuarial, applied, computer science, secondary education certification); medical technology; and public administration (labor relations). The B.S.Ed. degree is awarded in communication arts, CSS/geography, CSS/history, CSS/political science, CSS/sociology, earth and space science, and physics.

The John L. Grove College of Business awards the B.S.B.A. degree in accounting, business information systems, decision science, economics, finance, information technology for business education, management (general management, human resource management, international management), and marketing; the B.S.Ed. degree in CSS/economics; and the B.A. degree in economics.

The College of Education and Human Services awards the B.S. degree in criminal justice (corrections, juvenile justice, law enforcement); the B.A. degree in social work; and the B.S.Ed. degree in elementary education (biology, chemistry, environmental education, mathematics, multicultural education, sociology, TESOL).

Preprofessional preparation is available for admission to schools of chiropractic, dentistry, engineering, law, medicine, optometry, pharmacy, physical therapy, podiatry, and veterinary medicine.

Academic Program

The University is on the semester system with a fall semester beginning in late August and a spring semester beginning in mid-January. Three terms, one of three weeks and two of five weeks, comprise the summer program.

The general education program, which comprises one half of the credits required for graduation, is the core of the undergraduate curriculum. It includes courses to develop competence in writing, speaking, mathematics, and reading. The program ensures exposure to history; language and numbers; literary, artistic, and cultural traditions; laboratory science; biological and physical sciences; political, economic, and geographic sciences; and social and behavioral sciences. Ample elective opportunities are available.

Academic options include an honors program, independent study and research, internships, field experience (mandatory in such areas as teacher education, social work, and medical technology), the Marine Science Consortium Program at Wallops Island, a 3+2 engineering program with several major schools of engineering, and Army ROTC.

Academic Facilities

Ezra Lehman Memorial Library has a computerized library system that includes access to full-text journal articles and electronic indexes to journal literature. The library also provides access to the Internet and many CD-ROM databases. The library's collection of more than 440,000 items includes books, journals, government documents, maps, and audiovisual material. The library participates in several consortia that have reciprocal borrowing privileges for students.

Student instruction is supported by multiple computer systems for student e-mail and computer network connections to the Internet. Several hundred terminals or personal computers for student use are available in residence halls, the library, academic buildings, microcomputer labs, and the Information and Computing Technologies Center. Students with their own computers also have access to the systems. All students can use the systems 24 hours a day and have unlimited computer time at no additional expense. The University also has its own campuswide information system available on and off campus.

Costs

For Pennsylvania residents, the cost per semester in 1999–2000 included tuition of $1734; housing, $1201; food service, $805; educational services fee, $173; student activities fee, $80; student union fee, $102; health services fee, $64; and recreation center fee, $20. Nonresidents paid tuition of $4412 per semester; the remaining fees were the same.

Financial Aid

The University's extensive financial aid program helps students who deserve a college education but who cannot afford to pay the full cost themselves. Shippensburg offers a wide range of aid in the form of grants, scholarships, loans, and campus employment. Most aid is awarded as a package consisting of all types for which the applicant is qualified. Nearly 70 percent of undergraduates receive some form of financial assistance.

Faculty

The University has 333 full-time faculty members. The undergraduate student-faculty ratio is 20:1. Approximately 88 percent of the full-time instructional faculty members hold a doctorate or other terminal degree in their field. Each student has a faculty adviser.

Student Government

Shippensburg has a strong Student Association, built around a Student Senate, standing committees, and an Activities Program Board, which provides a highly diversified program of student activities. Students also sit on many policymaking administration-faculty committees and administer their own budget for the Student Association.

Admission Requirements

Shippensburg University, in compliance with federal and state laws and university policy, provides equal educational, employment, and economic opportunities for all people without regard to race, color, gender, age, ethnicity, national origin, religion, sexual orientation, or marital, veteran, or disability status. A student's potential for success is judged by the high school average, rank in class, aptitude test scores (SAT I or ACT), and recommendations. The high school record is generally considered the most important factor. A college-preparatory program, consisting of 4 units of English, at least 3 units of math, 3 units in the sciences, 2 units of social studies, and 2 units in the same foreign language, is strongly recommended. A campus interview and visit are encouraged. Transfer students in good standing are welcome.

Application and Information

To be considered for admission, a student should submit the application form with a $30 application fee. The high school transcript, recommendations, and aptitude test results should be sent by the high school. Transfer students must submit college transcripts. The Admissions Office operates on a rolling basis.

Students can obtain application materials and information by contacting:

Dean of Admissions
Shippensburg University of Pennsylvania
Shippensburg, Pennsylvania 17257
Telephone: 717-477-1231
           800-822-8028 (toll-free)
Fax: 717-477-4016
E-mail: admiss@ship.edu
World Wide Web: http://www.ship.edu

The 200-acre Shippensburg University campus is located 40 miles southwest of Harrisburg, Pennsylvania.

SHORTER COLLEGE
ROME, GEORGIA

The College

Since 1873, Shorter College has been combining academic excellence with caring Christian commitment. The College was established through the generosity of a Baptist layman, Alfred Shorter, and the vision of his pastor. They led a group of northwestern Georgia Baptists in founding the school, originally named Cherokee Baptist Female College. The name was changed to Shorter Female College in 1878 and to Shorter College in 1923. The College became coeducational in 1951. Shorter's enrollment of 1,849 includes students in both traditional semester programs and in innovative continuous programs for working adults. Approximately 850 of these students are located on our main campus in Rome, Georgia. Semester students come from all parts of the United States and from other countries around the world. Over the past ten years, approximately 78 percent of Shorter graduates who applied to medical schools have been accepted. Affiliated with the Georgia Baptist Convention, the College carries forth its Christian heritage by holding weekly chapel services. Each year the campus is visited by noted Christian leaders, scholars, and outstanding musical performers. The campus minister works with the director of religious activities to provide a wide range of opportunities for spiritual growth. The largest religious organization on campus is the Baptist Student Union (BSU), which includes Christians of many denominations. Student publications include a newspaper, a yearbook, and a literary magazine. Highly skilled music and drama groups include the Shorter Chorale, the Shorter Classic, the Shorter Mixed Chorus, the Shorter Players, the Opera Workshop, and the Wind Ensemble. The Shorter Chorale was selected to represent the United States in choral festivals held in Yugoslavia, France, and Austria and represented the College in St. Petersburg, Russia. Shorter has also been the home of numerous National Metropolitan Opera Audition winners and finalists. The College has two local fraternities and three local sororities, as well as chapters of two national music fraternities and honor societies for majors in biology, English, music, religion, social sciences, and theater. Shorter College is a member of the Georgia Intercollegiate Athletic Conference of the NAIA. Varsity teams compete in men's baseball, basketball, cross-country, golf, and tennis and in women's basketball, cross-country, golf, and tennis.

Location

The College is situated on 150 acres atop Shorter Hill, in Rome, Georgia (area population 85,000). Rome is located just 65 miles northwest of Atlanta and 65 miles south of Chattanooga, Tennessee, and cultural opportunities abound. In the city of Rome there are the Symphony Orchestra, Rome Little Theatre, Rome Area Council for the Arts events, popular concerts and attractions at the Roman Forum, and the 334,859-volume modern city library. The College sponsors numerous events, including faculty, alumni, student, and guest musical recitals; four guest-lecture series; speech festivals and recitals; drama and opera productions; art exhibits; and athletic events.

Majors and Degrees

Shorter College offers eight degrees: the Bachelor of Arts, the Bachelor of Science, the Bachelor of Business Administration, the Bachelor of Science in Education, the Bachelor of Fine Arts, the Bachelor of Music, the Bachelor of Music Education, and the Bachelor of Church Music. The Bachelor of Arts is offered in art, communication arts (with concentrations in electronic media, journalism, and speech communication), economics, English, French, history and political science, liberal arts, mathematics, music, psychology, public relations, religion, sociology, and Spanish. The Bachelor of Science is offered biology, Christian ministry, economics, environmental science/conservation biology, general studies, mathematics, mathematics education, psychology, recreation management (with concentrations in church recreation, public recreation, and therapeutic recreation), and sociology. The Bachelor of Business Administration is offered in accounting (CPA track) and business administration. The Bachelor of Science in Education is offered in early childhood education (K–4) and middle grades (4–8). Programs leading to certification in secondary school teaching are available in English, general science, history, mathematics, and social science. Certification is also offered in music for grades K–12. The Bachelor of Fine Arts is offered in art, musical theater, and theater. The Bachelor of Music is offered in organ performance, piano pedagogy, piano performance, and voice performance. Preprofessional programs are available in allied health, dentistry, law, medicine, pharmacy, physical therapy, physician's assistant studies, and veterinary medicine. Courses are also available in German, health and physical education, and interdisciplinary studies.

Academic Program

Shorter is accredited by the Southern Association of Colleges and Schools and the National Association of Schools of Music, and strives to provide an academic environment of high quality. Teacher programs are approved by the Georgia Professional Standards Commission. Small classes (freshman lecture courses average 23 students) taught by dedicated and highly qualified professors (86 percent of freshman lecture courses are taught by full-time faculty, 26 percent by full professors) ensure that each student receives an education that is both challenging and personally rewarding. For any degree, a candidate must have earned a minimum of 126 semester hours; some degrees require a greater number of hours. As part of the orientation program at the beginning of the fall semester, each new student is assigned to one of several small orientation groups that assist the student in adjusting to college life; the student is also assigned to an academic adviser who assists in the selection and scheduling of courses. Early registration sessions are available in the summer. Freshman advisers are specially trained faculty and staff members. The academic calendar is divided into two semesters from September to May, with two "mini" sessions offered during the summer. On-campus evening classes are available in selected disciplines. Shorter offers an honors program that spans all four years and provides students with learning opportunities not generally available to undergraduates.

Off-Campus Arrangements

The College conducts a program of extension courses in off-campus locations. A selection of courses is offered in the late afternoon and evening hours in nearby cities. Shorter's School of Professional Programs offers general education and degree-completion programs, specifically designed for working adults, on campus and in Lawrenceville and Marietta, Georgia. Classes meet one evening or weekend per week, year-round, with a required weekly study group.

MAYTERM is the four-week period immediately following the end of the second semester in May. It is designed as a study-abroad program, in which students earn 9 semester hours of credit through travel, study, and classroom experiences. Students are housed in student residences or college dormitories, and the cost of most meals is usually included. The most likely location is the British Isles, but other sites are possible. Shorter College faculty members accompany the students and teach the courses that are offered. In cooperation with the

American Institute for Foreign Study, Shorter is able to offer students the opportunity to study in London, England, at Richmond College. Since Richmond College is accredited by one of the recognized regional accrediting bodies in the United States, credits earned for a summer, a semester, or a year of study are readily transferable back to Shorter. MAYTERM is offered every other year. On alternate years, Shorter offers the China Educational Exchange, a four-week study-abroad program to Zhengzhou University in Henan Province, People's Republic of China. An agreement with Hong Kong Baptist University allows 1 student per year to study at that university. Studies in other countries can be arranged on an individual basis through the Office of International Programs.

Academic Facilities

Livingston Library, dedicated in 1976 as a memorial to Ray Livingston, houses more than 126,000 books, 612 periodicals, 6,475 microform materials, 8,669 musical scores, and 10,788 audio/video items. The library also contains conference rooms (for both individual and group study), projection rooms, a graphics preparation room, computer terminals, typewriters, and music listening facilities for student use. The Alice Allgood Cooper Fine Arts Building and the Randall H. Minor Fine Arts Building are connected to form an outstanding fine arts complex, providing up-to-date facilities for the Departments of Music, Communication Arts, and Art. The Cooper Building contains classrooms, music faculty offices, the art department's drawing and painting studio, and Brookes Chapel, the meeting place for convocations, concerts, recitals, and lectures. A renovated home adjacent to the campus houses expanded art facilities. The Minor Building contains classrooms, twenty-five music practice rooms (with a baby grand piano in each), a choral rehearsal room, a dance studio, faculty offices, photography facilities, a theater, a desktop publishing lab, a radio studio, and an art gallery. Rome Hall was named in honor of the citizens of Rome in appreciation of their generous support of the College. It contains classrooms, science laboratories (including the Stergus Collection of Internal Organs, one of the most complete pathology collections in the United States), faculty offices, lounges, and the Robert T. Connor exhibit of some 150 African and North American animals and skins. Alumni Hall houses the educational materials center and faculty offices. Construction of a $3.76-million gymnasium/athletics complex, the Winthrop-King Centre, was completed in 1994. Construction of a new $3-million Student Union was completed in 1998. A computer lab (with twenty-five terminals) is available for student use. Computer labs for business (twenty terminals) and communication arts (nine terminals) are also available. Smaller computer labs are available for art, music, and recreation. All residence halls have computer and Internet access.

Costs

Tuition for 2000–01 is $9350. Room and board cost $4900, fees are $120, and books and supplies are estimated at $700.

Financial Aid

Shorter College offers aid through each of the five federal programs: the Federal Pell Grant, Federal Supplemental Educational Opportunity Grant, Federal Work-Study, Federal Perkins Loan, and Federal Stafford Student Loan. Full-time students who are Georgia residents are eligible to receive the Georgia Tuition Equalization Grant and may be eligible to receive the HOPE Scholarship. Scholarships are offered for achievement in academics, music, art, theater, humanities, and athletics. Awards range from $500 to full tuition. Academic scholarships are renewable each year, provided the student maintains at least the required grade point average. Special grants and scholarships are available to students who plan to enter church-related vocations, who are members of churches in the Georgia Baptist Convention, or who are dependents of employees of a Southern Baptist church, institution, or agency. Small grants are also awarded to students recommended directly by alumni and when 2 or more students from the same family are enrolled at Shorter. Shorter does not award institutional aid toward room and board costs. One hundred percent of all full-time Shorter students receive some financial aid.

Faculty

The Shorter College faculty is composed of 65 full-time, highly qualified professors, of whom two thirds hold doctoral degrees. The College also employs 168 part-time faculty members, most of whom teach in the working adult program. A favorable student-teacher ratio of 13:1 in traditional programs ensures that each student receives individual attention.

Student Government

One of Shorter's truly distinctive features is that students may participate in a wide variety of significant extracurricular activities, each of which affords a chance to develop social and leadership skills that prepare a student to win in a competitive world. The Student Government Association (SGA) is the official voice of the students. Through SGA's Executive Council, Senate, judicial boards, and special committees, students are directly involved in the life of the College.

Admission Requirements

Students are admitted into the freshman class based on their academic grade point average and SAT I or ACT scores. A review of the student's goals and their compatibility with the purpose of the College are also determining factors. The College requires 4 years of English, 4 years of mathematics (including 2 years of algebra), 3 years of history/social science, 3 years of science, and 2 units of foreign language. In addition to the general requirements for admission to the College, students majoring in music must meet the following requirements: each student must perform in an audition of approximately 10 minutes in his or her major medium, and each student must take a series of music placement tests. Students must successfully fulfill these requirements prior to the beginning of classes in August of their freshman year, since the music curriculum requires at least four years for completion. An audition is also required for students majoring in theater, and an art portfolio review is required for students majoring in art. High school students who have completed their junior year, have an outstanding academic record, and have completed the units outlined above may be considered for early admission. High school seniors entering their senior year may be admitted on a joint enrollment basis. Such students should have above-average grades and SAT I or ACT scores. Transfer and international students are also welcome to apply. A minimum paper-based TOEFL score of 500 or a computer-based score of 173 is required for international students. Credit for college work below a C cannot be transferred. Homeschooled students should contact the Office of Admissions directly for requirements.

Application and Information

Shorter accepts students on a rolling basis. Campus visits are highly recommended through a personal campus tour or one of four Open Houses.

Director of Admissions
Shorter College
315 Shorter Avenue
Rome, Georgia 30165-4298
Telephone: 706-233-7319
        800-868-6980 Ext. 7319 (toll-free)
Fax: 706-233-7224
E-mail: admissions@shorter.edu
World Wide Web: http://www.shorter.edu

SIENA COLLEGE
LOUDONVILLE, NEW YORK

The College

Siena College is a four-year, coeducational, independent liberal arts college with a Franciscan and Catholic tradition. It is a community of 2,600 full-time students that offers undergraduate degrees in the arts, business, and science. Student-focused professors are at the heart of a supportive learning community that prepares students for careers, for an active role in their communities, and for the real world. Founded by the Franciscan Friars in 1937, Siena provides a personal, values-oriented education one student at a time. It welcomes all races and creeds and prides itself on the care and concern for the intellectual, personal, and social growth of all students that is the Franciscan trademark.

About 1,800 students live on campus in three housing options—traditional dormitories, suites for 4 or 6 students, and town-house units for 7 or 8. When Siena students are not in class or in their residences, they have plenty to do. More than sixty teams, clubs, and committees are active each year. The Franciscan Center for Service and Advocacy places more than 300 students each week in some volunteer activity, including Big Brothers and Big Sisters, Habitat for Humanity, soup kitchens, and teaching in religious education programs. More than 75 percent of the student body is involved in some type of athletic program, from eighteen intercollegiate sports to club teams to intramurals. Siena also provides numerous student support services, including counseling, tutoring, health services, peer counseling, and a career center. Popular activities include the student theater company, the student newspaper, the radio station, the yearbook, the Karate Club, the Black and Latin Student Union, and the Model United Nations.

Siena provides additional learning and cultural experiences outside of its academic programs to both its students and the wider community. Examples of these efforts include the Martin Luther King Jr. Lecture Series, the Niebuhr Institute of Religion and Culture, the Jewish-Christian Institute, and the Women and Minorities Studies Committee, which plan programs to include the public on topics of current interest. The Greyfriar Living Literature Series (which features guest writers) and the Alternative Film Series are free to the public.

Siena has developed a number of cooperative and special programs. Among them are a premed program with Albany Medical College; a five-year M.B.A. program with Clarkson University; a seven-year accelerated predental program with Boston University; a 3-2 engineering program in cooperation with Clarkson University, Catholic University, Rensselaer Polytechnic Institute, Manhattan College, SUNY Binghamton, and Western New England College; and the Washington Semester at American University.

In addition to its bachelor's degrees and certificate programs, Siena also offers a Master of Business Administration (M.B.A.) with an emphasis in accounting. Freshman accounting majors at Siena may study in a five-year, two-degree program that combines the Bachelor of Business Administration with the M.B.A.

Location

Siena's 155-acre campus is located in Loudonville, a suburban community 2 miles north of the New York State capital of Albany. With eighteen colleges in the area, there is a wide variety of activities on weekends. Regional theater, performances by major concert artists, and professional sports events compete with the activities on the campuses. Within 50 miles are the Adirondacks, the Berkshires, and the Catskills, providing outdoor recreation throughout the year. New York City and Boston are less than 3 hours away. With all of the professional, cultural, and recreational opportunities the Capital Region offers, many Siena graduates choose to begin their careers there.

Majors and Degrees

The College offers the Bachelor of Business Administration degree in accounting; the Bachelor of Arts in American studies, classics, economics, English, environmental studies, French, history, mathematics, philosophy, political science, psychology, religious studies, social work, sociology, and Spanish; and the Bachelor of Science in biology, chemistry, computer science, economics, finance, marketing and management, mathematics, and physics. Certificate programs are available in computer science; environmental studies; health studies; international studies, foreign language, and business; peace studies; secondary education; and theater arts.

Academic Program

A strong humanities core forms the basis for all curricula. Course work is structured within the School of Business, School of Humanities and Social Science, and School of Science. All students take courses within a broad core requirement: 30 hours in the humanities and social sciences (including a 6-credit freshman foundations course), 9 hours in mathematics and science (with 3 of these in a natural science), and 3 hours in fine arts. Students must also maintain a minimum cumulative index of 2.0 and earn at least a C in every major field concentration course. Within the major, students must take a minimum of 30 credits, with no more than 39 credits counting toward the degree requirements. A total of 120 hours is required to qualify for a bachelor's degree.

Students may get credit for prior work by taking standardized college proficiency exams with the approval of the head of the department in the discipline to be examined. A total of 18 credits may be obtained this way. Siena offers honors courses in English and history. Many departments have seminars to cover current topics in the field. ROTC affiliation is available at Siena in a U.S. Army unit, and an Air Force ROTC unit is available at a nearby college through cross-registration.

Siena's academic year is two semesters. There are two summer sessions offered.

Off-Campus Arrangements

Siena students are encouraged to spend a semester or a year abroad. Five programs are directly affiliated with the College: Siena at Regent's College, London; the Siena in London Internship Experience; the Siena semester at the Centre d'Etudes Franco-Americain de Management in Lyon, France; the Center for Cross-Cultural Studies in Seville, Spain; and Australearn at various locations in Australia. In addition, programs are available for all majors everywhere on the globe. International study is typically pursued during the junior year.

Locally, hundreds of internships are available through government, business, and nonprofit organizations on a two- or three-day-a-week basis, enabling students to continue with their course work at the same time. Many students are offered jobs by their internship organization upon graduation.

In addition, through the Hudson Mohawk Association of Colleges and Universities (which comprises the eighteen colleges in the area), cross-registration is possible at such institutions as Union College, Skidmore College, Rensselaer Polytechnic Institute, and the University at Albany.

Academic Facilities

The most recent addition to the Siena campus is the J. Spencer and Patricia Standish Library. The mission of the Standish Library is to provide service and access to educational material and information to support the curricular and research needs of the students and faculty members. The library collection of more than 285,000 volumes consists of books, journals, microforms, compact discs, videocassettes, and a growing number of electronic information sources. More than 6,000 volumes are added annually, and 1,600 serial subscriptions are currently maintained, with electronic access to thousands of additional journals.

All academic and residential buildings are interconnected with a high-speed Ethernet network connected via fiber optics. This network backbone runs at 10 and 100 Mbps. Every student residence space includes a 10 Mbps connection point to access the College's network and the Internet. The network includes more than 2,500 ports. The computer facilities are accessible 24 hours a day, seven days a week. Numerous computers are available throughout the campus for student use.

Kiernan Hall, opened in 1987, supplements the facilities of Siena Hall, the College's main classroom building, and Roger Bacon Hall, the science center. Numbers Place, home to the mathematics and computer science departments, opened in 1992.

Marcelle Athletic Complex features a natatorium, a field house with an elevated running track, racquetball and squash courts, an aerobics/dance studio, and an area with exercise and other weight-training equipment.

Costs

Tuition at Siena remains reasonable, helping the College to provide an education of fine quality at moderate cost. For 2000–01, tuition is $14,330; room, $3965; and board, $2480. There are lab fees for accounting, natural sciences, languages, and some fine arts and psychology courses. Miscellaneous fees may account for about $470 per year.

Financial Aid

Siena has nearly doubled its College scholarship aid in the last five years. Awards are based on need, academic ability, personal qualities, and community involvement. Federal programs that Siena students may qualify for include Federal Pell Grants, Federal Supplemental Educational Opportunity Grants, Federal Perkins Loans, Federal Stafford Student Loans, and Federal PLUS loans. Residents of New York State may receive Tuition Assistance Program and Aid for Part-time Study awards. Financial need is determined by the Free Application for Federal Student Aid and, where applicable, the state version of the supplemental Financial Aid Form. Aid is usually awarded in a package combining scholarships or grants, loans, and a job. Students remaining in good academic standing will find aid renewed.

Faculty

Siena's faculty is committed to teaching, and student concerns and development are at the heart of the curriculum. Eighty-three percent of the 154 full-time faculty members have terminal degrees. The student-faculty ratio of 14:1 helps to develop interaction with students, as does the fact that Siena professors even teach labs. Students are assigned a faculty adviser to help in the planning of their course of study.

Student Government

The Student Senate directs student involvement in academic and social life and interprets students' attitudes, opinions, and rights for the faculty and administration. It charters all student organizations and provides funds for many through fees collected by the College. The governing board is made up of officers and representatives of all four classes and of the commuting students. Elections are held in April for the following year, except for freshmen, who are elected in September.

Admission Requirements

Siena seeks bright, articulate young people who will blossom in the caring atmosphere that the College provides. The College is reaching out to more diverse geographical and ethnic groups. Academic standards are demanding without being threatening. Seventy percent of incoming freshmen have combined SAT I scores ranging from 1050 to 1200. School, grades, recommendations, and an interview all affect the final decision. Students seeking degrees in the science or business division should be well versed in mathematics. Those interested in American studies, English, history, or philosophy will find a working knowledge of a foreign language helpful.

Application and Information

The preferred deadline for the submission of a regular application is March 1 of a student's senior year in high school. Decisions are sent starting in mid-March. Siena also offers an early decision and an early action program. Early applications should be submitted before December 1. Candidates will be notified by January 1. Presidential scholar candidates must apply by January 15.

Transfer students must apply by December 1 for the spring semester or by June 1 for the fall semester. Generally, transfers are expected to have a cumulative average of at least 2.5. A minimum of 30 semester hours and half of the credits for the major must be earned at Siena. A maximum of 66 credits may be transferred from accredited two-year institutions. Credit will be given only for courses that are similar in content, level, and scope to those at Siena.

For more information, students should contact:

Admissions Office
Siena College
515 Loudon Road
Loudonville, New York 12211
Telephone: 518-783-2423
         888-AT-SIENA (toll-free)

SIENA HEIGHTS UNIVERSITY
ADRIAN, MICHIGAN

The University

Siena Heights University (SHU) was founded in 1919 by the Adrian Dominican Congregation as a Catholic liberal arts college. The name Siena honors Saint Catherine of Siena, a fourteenth-century Italian Dominican who dedicated her life to a quest for truth and social responsibility. Similarly, the mission of the University—to help students become more competent, purposeful, and ethical through a teaching and learning environment that respects the dignity of all—grows out of the philosophy of life exemplified in Saint Catherine of Siena.

Throughout its history, Siena Heights University has built a proud tradition of innovative response to challenging social needs. Originally a university for women who intended to become teachers, Siena broadened its offerings over the years and by the 1950s was recognized as one of the nation's ten best liberal arts colleges for women.

Today Siena Heights University continues its long tradition of integrating liberal arts and career education. A student's total development as an intellectually, socially, and spiritually responsible human being is the basis of Siena Heights University's education philosophy. The University provides an education that will help students create meaning in their lives and inspire others by their aspirations and achievements.

The mission of Siena Heights University is to assist students to become more competent, purposeful, and ethical through a teaching and learning environment that respects the dignity of all. The University therefore provides an educational process that challenges individuals to identify, to refine, and to achieve their personal goals. Through this process, Siena Heights University expects to engage each of its students in the development of a personal philosophy of life.

The University is accredited by the North Central Association of Colleges and Schools, the Department of Education of the state of Michigan, and the National Association of Schools of Art and Design and is organized into six departments: Art; Business and Management; Computing, Mathematics and the Sciences; Human Services; Humanities; and Performing Arts and Education.

More than 1,100 students (55 percent women, 45 percent men) study at Siena Heights University. Siena Heights students hail from twenty-eight states and eight countries.

Siena Heights University houses 380 students on campus. Hundreds of students live off campus within walking or biking distance. Students also commute from surrounding cities.

The University's Career Planning and Placement Center provides students with excellent placement services. Supported by state-of-the-art technology, the University has a 98 percent placement rate among its students within six months of graduation.

The Fieldhouse, home to the Saints' athletics programs, has five basketball courts, four volleyball courts, two indoor tennis courts, a 200-meter running track, and a training room. Outdoor facilities on campus include a soccer field, baseball fields, two tennis courts, a sand volleyball court, and a new softball complex.

Siena Heights University is proud of the accomplishments of its student athletes both in intercollegiate competition and in the classroom. The Saints have won three straight Wolverine-Hoosier Athletic Conference (WHAC) All-Sports competitions. Since 1985, Siena Heights athletic teams have won several conference, district, and regional championships, making SHU one of the finest athletic programs of its size in the nation.

The Saints have produced 62 NAIA All-Americans and 48 All-American Scholar-Athletes over the past two decades. The men's basketball team has advanced to the NAIA National Championship Tournament six times in the past eight years, and the 1997 team went 30-7 and was the national runner-up. In 1995, the men's baseball team became only the third NAIA institution in the state of Michigan to qualify for the NAIA World Series, and the women's soccer team has competed in three NAIA national championship tournaments in its twelve-year history.

More than thirty-five student clubs and organizations are available on the campus. They range from national social organizations to choirs, from Student Senate to intramural sports, and from international student organizations to various honor societies.

In addition to associate and bachelor's degree programs, Siena Heights offers later afternoon and evening graduate courses that lead to the Master of Arts degree.

Location

Siena Heights University is located in Adrian (population 22,000), which serves as the hub of the Lenawee County area. The campus is 75 miles from the Detroit metropolitan area, 30 miles from Ann Arbor, and 30 miles from Toledo, Ohio.

Majors and Degrees

Siena offers Associate of Art, Associate of Science, Bachelor of Arts, Bachelor of Fine Arts, Bachelor of Science, and Bachelor of Applied Science degrees.

The majors offered are accounting; art (ceramics, drawing, graphics, metalsmithing, painting, photography, printmaking, sculpture, watercolor); biology (premedical studies); business (business administration, hospitality management, management, marketing, retailing, retail merchandising); business education; chemistry; child development; computer and information systems; criminal justice; English (children's literature, communications, creative writing, English general); general studies; history; human services (gerontology, social work); humanities; language arts; mathematics (pre-actuarial studies); Montessori education; music (music business, electronic music synthesis, music general, music education); natural science; prelaw studies; philosophy; preprofessional science (dentistry, pharmacy, engineering, veterinary science); psychology; religious studies; social science; Spanish; teacher certification (nondegree program); theater/speech communications; and special majors such as contracted major, inverted major, and tri-major.

Academic Program

The academic calendar consists of two semesters; a summer session is available. In a typical baccalaureate program, 120 credit hours are required.

Off-Campus Arrangements

There are internships in all majors. The cooperative education program allows freshmen and sophomores to test potential career fields, while giving upperclass students on-the-job training. The foreign study program sends students to Florence, Italy; Paris, France; and Mexico.

Academic Facilities

The University Library currently holds 140,000 volumes, with the capacity to expand to 160,000. Resources include books, bound periodicals, microfilm, audiovisual materials, and a paperback collection. Features include a computerized card catalog, which makes materials easier to locate; automated circulation and book reserve functions; an expanded version of the academic index INFOTRAC to assist in retrieving recent periodical citations by subject; and Internet access.

Dominican Hall, a $5-million multipurpose facility that opened in 1994, is the newest addition to the campus. The building houses a 150-seat lecture/recital hall, a conference center, a classroom floor, and a state-of-the-art computer facility that occupies the entire third floor.

Costs

For academic year 2000–01, basic expenses are $12,400 for tuition and fees and $4626 for room and board, for a total of $17,026. There are no additional fees for out-of-state students. The average cost for books and supplies is approximately $200 per semester.

Financial Aid

Siena Heights University is committed to making an education affordable for every accepted student. Some form of financial assistance is given to nearly 86 percent of the University's full-time students. Need-based grants, loans, and work-study programs are available through the federal and state governments and the University itself. Siena Heights University also offers various academic scholarships. These awards are made on the basis of academic and leadership excellence, not necessarily because of need.

Students applying for financial aid should file the Free Application for Federal Student Aid (FAFSA) and have the results sent to Siena Heights. Applications are processed on a first-come, first-served basis only after a student has been accepted to the University.

Faculty

Siena Heights University employs more than 130 faculty members. Of the 65 full-time faculty members, more than 50 percent hold a doctorate or other terminal degree. Faculty members conduct recognized research and serve as advisers to aid in course selection and to offer career assistance.

Student Government

The Student Senate is involved with many topical issues touching all areas of University life. Students may serve in University government as elected senators or as volunteers on Student Senate committees. The Student Senate is open to all students of Siena Heights University.

Admission Requirements

Siena Heights admits students who are academically qualified, capable, enthusiastic, motivated, ready to be challenged, and ready to achieve. Admission decisions are based on high school academic performance, ACT or SAT I scores, extracurricular activities, leadership potential, class rank, and personal recommendations. The typical profile of a regularly admitted freshman reflects a minimum cumulative grade point average of 2.3 on a 4.0 scale and a minimum composite ACT score of 17. Provisional admission is available to students who show academic potential.

Application and Information

Admission decisions are made on a rolling basis, and applicants are notified of an admission status within one week after receipt of all application materials. Tours and general information sessions are available Monday through Saturday; annual Campus Visit Days are also scheduled.

For further information, students should contact:

Office of Admissions
Siena Heights University
1247 East Siena Heights Drive
Adrian, Michigan 49221-1796
Telephone: 517-264-7180
          800-521-0009 (toll-free)
Fax: 517-264-7745
E-mail: admissions@sienahts.edu
World Wide Web: http://www.sienahts.edu

Dominican Hall on the campus of Siena Heights University.

SIERRA NEVADA COLLEGE
INCLINE VILLAGE, NEVADA

The College

When the famous American author Mark Twain first viewed Lake Tahoe, he remarked: "I thought it surely must be the fairest sight the whole earth affords." Nestled at 6,700 feet above sea level and surrounded by spectacular scenery, Sierra Nevada College (SNC), an independent, nonprofit, coeducational four-year institution, offers a strong liberal arts curriculum with career-oriented majors. Sierra Nevada takes great pride in its excellent faculty, small classes, and friendly and active campus life.

On October 2, 1969, Governor Paul Laxalt dedicated Sierra Nevada College, which had opened its doors a few weeks earlier with a handful of dedicated students and faculty members. Within four years, the College had achieved candidate status for accreditation with the Northwest Association of Schools and Colleges. Early academic programs included alternative energy, liberal arts, creative arts, and business. Since that time, the College has added several additional programs and campus facilities have tripled.

In May 1995, ground was broken for an 18-acre campus addition, increasing the campus size to 38 acres. The construction of the first two buildings, a student residence life facility and a dining/classroom facility, is completed. Additional buildings to be added are a learning resource center, a student union, three other residence life facilities, specialized academic buildings, a fine arts center, a performing arts center, and administration offices. The new additions will put the College on the cutting edge of collegiate facilities.

On-campus housing is available for freshmen in Campbell-Friedman Residence Hall; residents enjoy in-room cable television, personal bathrooms, laundry facilities, large and comfortable study lounges, and a comprehensive meal plan. Housing for upperclass students is available in Prim-Schultz Hall, a three-story residence hall that accommodates 104 students. There are eighteen single rooms on the third floor, and double rooms are available on the first and second floors. All rooms come equipped with a private bath; the building is located adjacent to Campbell-Friedman Hall.

The Sierra Nevada College men's and women's ski teams compete in the northern California division of the United States Collegiate Ski Association. Teams have been the National Collegiate Ski Champions in both men's and women's Alpine Combined Team categories for the past nine years. SNC also offers a coed soccer team that currently competes against local soccer clubs in the Reno/Tahoe area. Local sports leagues available to SNC students include volleyball, softball, indoor soccer, and basketball. The College equestrian team trains at a facility in Carson City and competes at the intercollegiate level. Also, the snowboard team competes with distinction at the national level.

Location

Sierra Nevada College is located approximately 2 miles from the shore of Lake Tahoe, at an elevation of 6,300 feet above sea level. The elevation of the Tahoe Basin ranges from lake level, 6,225 feet, to nearly 11,000 feet at the summit of Mount Rose, directly above the campus. The lake is located 98 miles northeast of Sacramento, California, and 35 miles southwest of Reno, Nevada.

According to the Chamber of Commerce, the chances of sunshine are at least 80 percent in any season. This statistic is borne out by meteorological observations on campus. High altitude and low humidity make both high and low temperature extremes quite comfortable. In keeping with the location and the climate, more than twenty Alpine and Nordic ski areas, mountain biking, backpacking, hiking, rock climbing, parasailing, windsurfing, beach volleyball, and horseback riding are all available within an hour of the campus.

Majors and Degrees

Sierra Nevada offers the following: Bachelor of Science in business administration (with a concentration in hotel, restaurant, and resort management), computer science, ecology, environmental science and entrepreneurship, psychology, and ski business and resort management; Bachelor of Science or Bachelor of Arts in humanities, with concentrations in English/literature, history, and psychology; Bachelor of Arts in art, biology, and international studies; and the Bachelor of Science in Nursing.

Academic Program

Sierra Nevada offers a semester calendar as well as summer sessions for credit. Students have an interactive, participatory learning experience. The bachelor's degree, which requires 120 credits, is based on a liberal arts foundation with career-oriented majors. Programs are also available that lead to elementary and secondary teaching credentials.

Academic Facilities

The College buildings encompass approximately 60,000 square feet. Major educational facilities include a library, science laboratories, art studios, music practice rooms and a recording studio, a theater and dance studio, and the MacLean Observatory atop Mount Rose. Most classrooms are equipped with audiovisual equipment. Facilities are open to full- and part-time students, but a lab fee may be required when expendable materials are used.

Costs

Estimated annual costs for 2000–01 are fixed tuition (30 credit units), $12,000; fees (lab, etc.), $300; housing (on-campus), $3000 (double-occupancy) or $4500 (single-occupancy); food, $2510; books and supplies, $500; health insurance, $300; technology fee, $630; and personal expenses, $750.

Financial Aid

Financial aid is designed to help eligible students pay for their education. A number of factors determine a student's eligibility for aid. These factors are age, marital status, financial resources, and, in most cases, the financial status of the supporting parent(s). Eligibility for financial aid is determined by entering these factors into a formula analyzed by the federal government. In many cases, it is necessary for students and parents to submit copies of their income tax returns.

Sierra Nevada College participates in a variety of government and private programs that offer financial assistance to students who demonstrate need. Usually this assistance does not cover all educational costs; however, it can cover 60 to 80 percent of the costs.

Applicants should be aware that because of the processing required, the financial aid application must be completed and mailed at least two months before the start of the school semester. Otherwise, the award will not be ready in time to defray registration, housing, and other costs. Students wishing to apply for aid should contact the College; a package of information will be sent immediately.

Faculty

At Sierra Nevada College, the student-faculty ratio is 15:1, with highly qualified faculty members who know students on a first-name basis. Classes are not taught by graduate or teachers' assistants. Professors are mentors, advisers, teammates, and even friends. Students work with them because they want to, not because they have to. Faculty members are always available to provide extra help when needed.

Student Government

The Associated Students of Sierra Nevada College (ASSNC) is the official governing body for students. Officers consist of a president, vice president, secretary/treasurer, and 6 department representatives. All College students are invited to attend ASSNC meetings, which are customarily held on a weekly basis at the SNC Student Center. ASSNC sponsors a variety of activities each semester, including dances with live music, lunchtime and evening barbecues, beach parties, movie nights, weekend biking, hiking, ski trips, college nights in town, and special holiday events.

Admission Requirements

An applicant to a degree program must be a high school graduate or have achieved an average score of 50 on the GED or a passing score on a similar test, such as the California High School Proficiency Examination; SAT I or ACT scores are required. International students must submit results of the Test of English as a Foreign Language (TOEFL) or the Michigan Test of English Language Proficiency and a statement from a home country bank indicating that funds are available to cover educational and living expenses. Immigration forms will be issued when one full semester's tuition has been received by the College.

Application and Information

Sierra Nevada College evaluates applicants on a rolling basis, which means that an application will be reviewed as soon as the file is complete. Candidates are notified of the Admissions Committee's decision as soon as possible. Applications for admission from transfer students are accepted for any semester, provided the program applied to has not reached its maximum enrollment.

For additional information and application materials, prospective students should contact the Admissions Office at:

Sierra Nevada College
800 College Drive
P.O. Box 4269
Incline Village, Nevada 89450
Telephone: 775-831-1314
              800-332-8666 (toll-free)

Students and faculty members participate in fall orientation.

SIMMONS COLLEGE
BOSTON, MASSACHUSETTS

The College

Simmons College was founded in 1899 by John Simmons, a Boston businessman, who believed that women were entitled to an education that would prepare them to assume meaningful careers. Since it opened its doors in 1902, Simmons has provided a combination of liberal arts education and professional preparation that has enabled women to succeed in achieving their personal and professional goals. This educational concept is as valid—or even more so—for students today as it was at its inception. In every program, students receive the benefits of a broad-based liberal arts education strengthened by direct experience in their area of concentration, gained through an internship or independent study. Simmons students graduate with a strong sense of direction and confidence in their abilities.

Simmons is located in Boston, in the midst of museums, hospitals, and other colleges and universities. The College has two campuses: the Academic Campus and the Residence Campus. The Academic Campus includes the Main College Building, which houses a dining and commons area, classrooms, lounges, administrative and faculty offices, functional rooms, the bookstore, the Student Activities Center, the Trustman Art Gallery, an art studio, and music practice rooms; the Park Science Center; and the library. The Residence Campus is located two blocks away from the Academic Campus. Here, nine dormitories (two are handicapped-accessible), differing in age, size, and atmosphere, surround a landscaped quadrangle. Bartol Hall, the central dining room, is also located here, as are the Health Center, an activities center, and a Sports Center. Approximately 85 percent of the freshmen reside on campus.

There are 1,148 women enrolled as full-time undergraduates and 249 women enrolled as part-time undergraduates. Simmons students come from many parts of the United States as well as from many other countries. Generally, students come to Simmons to receive an education that stresses both liberal arts study and professional preparation. They are interested in furthering their leadership skills and enjoy taking responsibility for their lives. The College's Boston location is also a major attraction.

A variety of clubs and activities are available for students, including academic clubs, student government, cultural and special interest groups, and music and drama clubs. There are ten varsity sports: basketball, crew, cross-country, field hockey, sailing, soccer, swimming and diving, tennis, track, and volleyball.

At the graduate level, Simmons College offers the following degree programs, which are open to both men and women: the M.A. in children's literature, English, French, liberal studies, and Spanish; the M.S. in communications management, education (several programs), health-care administration, library and information science, nursing (adult nurse practitioner/occupational health practitioner program), and physical therapy; the Master of Social Work; the Master of Philosophy in English; the M.A.T.; the M.A.T.E.S.L.; the Master of Business Administration; the Doctor of Arts in library and information science; and the Doctor of Philosophy in social work.

Location

Simmons College's Boston location is ideal for educational, cultural, and social pursuits. The College is located next door to the Gardner Museum and the Museum of Fine Arts. Symphony Hall and the theater district are only a short distance away. There are approximately twenty-four colleges and universities within a 3-mile radius of the campus. Simmons is also located in the midst of a major medical area of the city.

Majors and Degrees

Simmons College grants the Bachelor of Arts degree in accounting, advertising, African-American studies, art, art administration, communications, East Asian studies, economics, education, English, finance, French, global management, graphic design, history, human services, international management, international relations, management, marketing, music, philosophy, political science, psychology, public relations, public relations and market communications, retail management, sociology, Spanish, and women's studies. The Bachelor of Science degree is granted in biochemistry, biology, chemistry, chemistry management, computer science, dietetics, environmental science, management information systems, mathematics, nursing, nutrition, physical therapy, and psychobiology.

Simmons College offers a dual-degree program in chemistry and pharmacy in cooperation with the Massachusetts College of Pharmacy and Allied Health Sciences.

Students interested in preprofessional programs as preparation for entry into schools of dentistry, medicine, and veterinary medicine meet with the premedical adviser to plan suitable academic programs. Students considering applying to law school meet with the prelaw adviser to plan a preprofessional program.

Academic Program

Simmons College seeks to provide its students with a liberal arts education in combination with professional study. The approach to education is flexible, and the curriculum allows each student to develop a program suited to her individual interests and career goals. Students must complete a minimum of 128 semester hours before being graduated. To fulfill the requirements of the basic plan of study, students must demonstrate competence in math and foreign language, complete background courses in the liberal arts and sciences, complete the courses required for the selected major, participate in independent study, and round out their program with appropriate electives. The liberal arts and sciences requirement constitutes 40 semester hours of course work, and the major requires 20 to 40 semester hours, depending on the program. The independent learning requirement constitutes a minimum of 8 and a maximum of 16 semester hours. Independent study is an important component of the Simmons educational program, as it emphasizes student initiative and planning and enables the student to acquire direct professional experience. The requirement may be fulfilled through internships, fieldwork, independent study, and an integrative seminar.

Students have the option of selecting interdepartmental programs or double majors. In addition, the OPEN program allows students to design their own program of study, combining courses from several fields. Students have a variety of ways to combine undergraduate studies with master's programs in the Simmons College graduate programs and professional schools, including programs in physical therapy, nutrition, nursing, and library science.

Off-Campus Arrangements

Students may arrange to take courses at the New England Conservatory of Music, Emmanuel College, Hebrew College, the Massachusetts College of Pharmacy and Allied Health Sciences, Wheelock College, and Wentworth Institute of Technology. One or two semesters of the sophomore or junior year may be spent in the Domestic Exchange Program at Mills College, Spelman College, or Fisk University. Juniors are eligible to apply for the Washington Semester at American University in Washington, D.C. Students interested in international study may elect to spend one semester or one year at the Simmons program in Cordoba, Spain; at a European university; in the Simmons Summer Study in Spain; or other approved study-abroad programs.

Simmons College also offers a study-abroad opportunity called Short Term Programs. Short Term courses are four-week courses that take place at the end of the spring semester in various countries. The courses vary in discipline and content; for example, studies in local culture, language, or science are available. The Short Term courses are considered spring semester courses and can be taken as part of a student's regular spring semester course load or as additional credits for the semester.

Academic Facilities

The Simmons library system includes nine major components, with holdings totaling more than 270,000 volumes. There are rapidly expanding media collections and more than 2,000 current periodical subscriptions. The libraries provide an online catalog and Internet access to journal citations. The library staff offers in-depth reference service, instructional programs, and interlibrary loans. Through the College's membership in the Fenway Library Consortium, students may also use the libraries of thirteen area institutions.

The Media Center, located on the first floor of the Beatley Library, has a video studio and editing facility as well as a media lab for the production of slide tape presentations and graphics materials. There are also microcomputer classrooms and a laboratory, offering access to Macintosh and DOS/Windows machines.

In addition to administrative and faculty offices, the Main College Building houses lecture and conference rooms, a language laboratory, art and music studios, the Trustman Art Gallery, the Career Resource Center, the Career Planning and Counseling Center, and the Career Service and Placement Office.

The Park Science Center houses more than fifty laboratories and classrooms, environmental rooms, and special research facilities, including observation rooms for psychological testing, individual laboratories, food science kitchens, and physical therapy laboratories. The center also contains a variety of research instruments, including a computer-supported SCAT system.

Costs

Tuition and fees for the 2000–01 academic year are $20,890; room and board charges are $8410. Total costs, not including books, supplies, and personal expenses, are $29,300.

Financial Aid

Simmons makes its educational opportunities available to as many capable, promising students as possible. Applications for financial aid are welcome from students who cannot meet their college expenses without assistance. Approximately 69 percent of Simmons students receive financial aid. Financial aid packages offered by the College consist of federal, state, and institutional grants, loans, and work opportunities. To apply for financial aid, students must complete two forms: the Simmons financial aid application and the Free Application for Federal Student Aid (FAFSA). Freshmen are encouraged to mail the FAFSA by January 15, using estimated information if necessary, in order to meet the priority deadline of February 1. The deadline for transfers is April 1.

Faculty

The College's 10:1 student-faculty ratio ensures a strong tie between students and faculty members. The Simmons College faculty consists of 115 full-time members, more than half of whom are women; 68 percent hold doctoral or other appropriate terminal degrees.

Student Government

The Student Government Association (SGA), composed of all full-time undergraduates and elected officers, seeks to further the interests of the student body by working closely with the faculty and administration of the College. The SGA also coordinates the policies and activities of various student organizations and allocates the student activities funds. Each class elects class officers.

Every academic department at Simmons has an organization known as a liaison, which is composed of students interested in concentrating in that department as well as students who have already chosen it as an area of concentration. Liaisons participate in evaluations of departments and promote educational and social activities for students, faculty members, and staff members.

Admission Requirements

The students at Simmons represent a variety of religious, racial, and economic backgrounds and have many different educational and extracurricular interests. It is the responsibility of the Committee on Admission to maintain this diversity. To do this, the committee has established admission policies that focus on the special qualities and achievements of each applicant.

Evaluated in the application process are the student's performance in high school, scores on the SAT I or ACT, recommendations, and application essay. If English is not a student's native language, the TOEFL is also required. An interview, although not required, is strongly recommended, as it gives the committee a better perspective on the applicant's abilities and interests and at the same time gives the student the opportunity to see the campus and meet with faculty members and students.

Applications are welcome from transfer students, as the College feels they bring an important perspective to the Simmons community. Transfer applicants should submit an official high school transcript, SAT I or ACT scores, official records of any college work, a dean's report from their current institution, and recommendations. If English is not a student's native language, the TOEFL is required in lieu of the SAT I or ACT. Interviews are highly recommended.

Application and Information

To apply, students should submit the Simmons application or the Common Application, along with the $35 fee and all supporting credentials. There are two early decision deadlines: November 15 (notification by December 15) and January 1 (notification by February 1). The deadline for freshman applicants is February 1. Transfer students are evaluated on a rolling basis; the preferred filing date for applications is April 1. Students applying for the semester beginning in January should apply by December 1.

Students are encouraged to visit the College in order to have a campus tour, meet the faculty, attend a class, or have an interview. The Office of Admission should be contacted for further information.

Office of Admission
Simmons College
300 The Fenway
Boston, Massachusetts 02115
Telephone: 617-521-2051
   800-345-8468 (toll-free)
Fax: 617-521-3190
World Wide Web: http://www.simmons.edu

SIMON'S ROCK COLLEGE OF BARD
GREAT BARRINGTON, MASSACHUSETTS

The College

Simon's Rock College of Bard is the nation's only four-year college of liberal arts and sciences devoted solely to the acceleration and enrichment of younger scholars. The average age of an entering freshman is 16. Most candidates for admission enter after the tenth or eleventh grade of secondary school.

Simon's Rock challenges the traditional assumption that students must be 18 before they can be asked to seriously develop their intelligence, imagination, and self-discipline. Students at Simon's Rock pursue an academic program that enables them to fulfill their potential at an age when their interest, energy, and curiosity are at a peak. The College provides an academic and social structure for a distinctive peer group. Sixteen- and 17-year-old freshmen are the norm at Simon's Rock, not the exception.

The College was founded in 1964 by Elizabeth Blodgett Hall, former headmistress of Concord Academy, and first admitted students in 1966. Since its inception, Simon's Rock has based its program on a set of assumptions that thirty-six years of experience have proved to be valid: that highly motivated students of high school age are fully capable of engaging in college work, that they are best able to develop in a small-college environment, that serving these students well requires a faculty committed to distinction in teaching and scholarship as well as active participation in the students' social and moral development, that a coherent general education in the liberal arts and sciences should be the foundation for such students, and that an early college founded on these assumptions should serve as a model for reform in American education.

In 1979, Simon's Rock became a part of Bard College, located 50 miles away at Annandale-on-Hudson, New York.

Location

The College is built on 275 rolling and wooded acres 1½ miles west of Great Barrington, a town of 8,500, in the Berkshire Hills of western Massachusetts. Boston and New York City are 140 miles away; Albany and Springfield are 40 miles away. The Berkshires' natural beauty and wide variety of cultural attractions make the area an unusually attractive place in which to live. Many artists, writers, and craftsmen live nearby; several contribute to the College's cultural and artistic programs. The countryside provides excellent terrain for hiking, bicycling, cross-country and Alpine skiing, canoeing, and climbing. The Tanglewood Music Festival, Jacob's Pillow Dance Festival, and numerous summer theaters are located in nearby towns. Great Barrington itself is a thriving business community with a variety of schools and service agencies in which Simon's Rock students work and volunteer.

Majors and Degrees

Simon's Rock offers programs leading to the A.A. and B.A. degrees in the liberal arts and sciences. Students may complete their B.A. studies with a concentration in most traditional disciplines such as biology, creative writing, humanities, mathematics, or choose one of several interdisciplinary concentrations such as gender studies, intellectual history, or Latin American studies. There is also a joint B.A. program with Bard College that allows students to take advanced courses and work closely with faculty members at both colleges in completing their degree requirements.

Academic Program

The academic program at Simon's Rock combines a substantial and coherent required core curriculum in the liberal arts and sciences with electives and extensive opportunities for students to pursue their own interests through advanced courses and independent study. The program is designed to engage students in the life of the mind by making them aware of their cultural heritage, introducing them to the spectrum of thought in the arts and sciences, and empowering them to satisfy their curiosity by thinking and learning independently.

Because Simon's Rock students begin college earlier than their peers, the College is particularly conscious of its responsibility to ensure that all students develop the skills and knowledge expected of an educated person. Consequently, during their first two years at Simon's Rock, all students are required to complete a core curriculum that comprises approximately half of their total academic load. The core curriculum includes a writing and thinking workshop (which new students attend during the week before the regular semester begins); first-year, sophomore, and cultural perspectives seminars and requirements in the arts, mathematics, natural science, and foreign language. The College also requires that students participate in a recreational athletics program and attend a series of health lectures.

All new students are assigned a faculty adviser, who meets with them weekly during their first semester and regularly throughout the rest of their career at Simon's Rock. Classes are small, faculty members are accessible, and the opportunities for students to pursue diverse interests are extensive.

The curriculum of the first two years at Simon's Rock leads to the A.A. in liberal arts. Students who successfully complete the A.A. requirements may continue at Simon's Rock for a B.A. or transfer to Bard College or another college or university to complete their baccalaureate degree. About one third of each class remains to complete a B.A. at Simon's Rock in one of thirty-four interdisciplinary concentrations; two thirds choose to transfer. The transfer record of Simon's Rock A.A. graduates is excellent.

Students wishing to stay at Simon's Rock for a B.A. must apply for admission to a major through a process called Moderation. At a formal conference, a faculty Moderation Committee and the student review the student's accomplishments and together plan the remainder of the student's education program. Students suggest and are advised of junior- and senior-year opportunities. These traditionally include advanced seminars, independent study involvement in faculty research projects, specialized tutorials, internships, courses at Bard, and a possible semester or full year of study abroad.

The senior thesis is the focus of each B.A. student's final year. A thesis project carries 8 credits and is expected to take a full academic year to complete. Drawing on the skills in analysis and synthesis acquired during the previous three years, students devote themselves wholeheartedly to the project and to learning, which has been personally defined and developed. Recent theses have taken many forms: critical studies in literature, sociological research, musical compositions, creative fiction, translations, scientific experiments, mathematical problem solving, artistic exhibitions and performances, and various combinations of these forms.

The regular academic program is supplemented by extensive cocurricular offerings, including annual poetry, fiction, concert, humanities, women's studies, and lecture series.

Off-Campus Arrangements

Juniors pursue a variety of study-abroad programs and options. In recent years, students have conducted extended campus field study projects in Ecuador, England, Honduras, Kenya, and Nepal. Through the School of International Training, Simon's Rock students have also participated in study programs at universities in England, India, Morocco, Nepal, and Israel. Others have studied at Oxford University in England, the University of Stirling in Scotland, Trinity College in Dublin, University of the Bosphorus in Turkey, and the University of Berlin in Germany. Students have also spent semesters away at a variety of colleges and universities throughout the United States and have participated in educational programs sponsored by the Washington Center for Learning Alternatives, the School for Field Studies, Global Roots, and the Semester at Sea program. Students have also earned credit for internship projects in journalism, government, business, and environmental policy.

Academic Facilities

Every student, faculty member, and staff member at Simon's Rock can establish a free personal Internet account. The newest building, the 16,000-square-foot Fisher Science and Academic Center was completed in January 1998. The center houses the College's biology, chemistry, ecology, and physics laboratories; research labs for faculty members and students; classrooms and tutorial rooms; a 60-seat lecture center; and faculty offices. There is also a public-access computer lab with Macintosh computers, and the library has several CD-ROM workstations and terminals dedicated to accessing the Internet. The mathematics department has a lab of IBM-clone computers and a NeXT cube workstation. The Arts Center incorporates a 200-seat theater; studios for painting, graphics, sculpture, photography, and ceramics; multimedia graphics workstations and scanning equipment; and an art gallery. The Liebowitz Arts and Humanities Building includes a dance studio and gallery, as well as classrooms, offices, and a slide library. A music hall, a recording studio, and music practice rooms are also available to students in the arts. The campus library houses 68,000 volumes and collections of recordings and periodicals, a listening room, and a language laboratory. Simon's Rock students also have access to the Bard College library. An interlibrary loan system provides access to other college and university collections. A 53,000-square-foot athletic complex with squash courts, a basketball court, an elevated track, and a swimming pool was completed in 1999.

Costs

For 2000–01, tuition is $21,740, room and board are $6700, and the student services fee is $2610, for a total of $31,050. The student services fee reflects the exceptional emphasis Simon's Rock, as an early college, places on student services. The fee provides funds for athletics programs, activities, health services, academic counseling, residence supervision, and security. For first-year students, there is also an orientation fee.

Financial Aid

Parents seeking consideration for financial aid should so indicate on the admission application. Simon's Rock promptly sends all the necessary forms and instructions. Upon completion of the Financial Aid PROFILE and the Free Application for Federal Student Aid (FAFSA), candidates are considered for all forms of financial aid available through Simon's Rock. Notification of awards is made as soon as possible after the decision regarding admission. Awards generally consist of several forms of government assistance combined with scholarships and campus employment opportunities.

Faculty

The College has 33 full-time faculty members, 87 percent of whom hold either an earned doctorate or an equivalent terminal degree in their field. Simon's Rock supplements this full-time faculty with visiting scholars, regular adjunct faculty members in music and studio arts, and part-time faculty members in other areas as needed. Faculty members are distinguished not only by their excellence in teaching and advising but also by their sensitivity to the particular developmental needs of the College's younger students.

Student Government

Students at Simon's Rock participate in the decision making and governance of the community through elected and appointed positions on House Councils, the Community Council, the Judicial Committee, and the Harassment Committee. Student representatives also serve on the College's Policy and Program and the Standards and Procedures faculty committees. The social life of the College is characterized by respect for individual rights and a strong sense of community.

Admission Requirements

Simon's Rock seeks students for early entrance who demonstrate the intellectual ability, motivation, and self-discipline to pursue college studies at a high school age. The admission staff recognizes its special responsibility to work closely with each prospective student and his or her parents to ensure that the decision to enter Simon's Rock is the right one. For this reason, a personal interview is required of each applicant. In addition to the interview, the College requires submission of written essays, two letters of recommendation, an official high school transcript, standardized test scores (PSAT, SAT I, ACT, or P-ACT), and a parent's statement. International students are required to submit TOEFL scores.

Application and Information

Candidates should submit their materials by June 30 for fall admission or by December 1 for January admission. Applications received after these dates are considered if spaces are available. The application fee is $40.

To schedule an interview or request further information, students should contact:

Dean of Admission
Simon's Rock College of Bard
84 Alford Road
Great Barrington, Massachusetts 01230-9702
Telephone: 413-528-7312
          800-235-7186 (toll-free)
Fax: 413-528-7334
E-mail: admit@simons-rock.edu
World Wide Web: http://www.simons-rock.edu

In the laboratory.

SIMPSON COLLEGE
INDIANOLA, IOWA

The College
Simpson College was founded in 1860. The institution was named Simpson College to honor Bishop Matthew Simpson (1811–1884), one of the best-known and most influential religious leaders of his day. The College is coeducational; although it is affiliated with the United Methodist Church, it is nonsectarian in spirit and accepts students without regard to race, color, creed, national origin, religion, sex, age, or disability.

For more than a century, Simpson has played a vital role in the educational, cultural, intellectual, political, and religious life of the nation. The College has thirty-two buildings on 73 acres of beautiful campus and enrolls 1,900 students.

Extracurricular activities at Simpson are designed to supplement and reinforce the academic program and contribute toward a total learning experience. Students may participate in student government, publications, music, theater, and social groups. Simpson competes in eighteen intercollegiate sports and has an extensive intramural program for both men and women. Men's and women's athletics at Simpson are governed by the NCAA. Simpson also has chapters of three national fraternities, one local fraternity, and four national sororities.

Location
Simpson is located in the city of Indianola, a residential community of 12,000 people. Indianola is 12 miles south of Des Moines, Iowa's capital city; 12 miles east of Interstate 35; and 15 miles south of Interstates 80 and 235. The Des Moines International Airport is 20 minutes from campus. Five miles south of Indianola is Lake Ahquabi State Park, where swimming and other recreational facilities can be found. Every summer, Indianola is the home of the National Hot Air Balloon Classic and of the Des Moines Metropolitan Summer Opera Festival. The location of the residential campus provides the best of both metropolitan and suburban activities.

Majors and Degrees
Simpson College grants Bachelor of Arts and Bachelor of Music degrees in major and career programs, including accounting, art, biochemistry, biology, chemistry, computer information systems, computer science, corporate communication, criminal justice, economics, education, English, environmental science, French, German, history, international management, international relations, journalism and mass communication, management, mathematics, music, music education, music performance, philosophy, physical education, political science, psychology, religion, rhetoric and speech communication, sociology, Spanish, sports administration, and theater arts.

Simpson offers preprofessional programs in dentistry, engineering, law, medical technology, medicine, nursing, optometry, physical therapy, theology, and veterinary medicine.

Academic Program
Simpson operates on a 4-4-1 academic calendar. The first semester starts in late August and ends in mid-December; the second semester starts in mid-January and ends in late April. A three-week session takes place during the month of May. During this period, students have the opportunity to take one class that focuses on a single subject, to study abroad, or to participate in a field experience or internship.

New students are assigned faculty advisers who aid them in constructing academically sound majors. Students must participate in one May Term class or program for each year of full-time study or its equivalent at Simpson College. All students must complete the requirements of the Cornerstone Studies in liberal arts and competencies in foreign language, math, and writing. To earn the Bachelor of Arts degree, students may take no more than 42 hours in the major department, excluding May Term programs, and 84 hours in the division of the major, including May Term programs. Also, at least 128 semester hours of course work must be accumulated with a grade point average of C (2.0) or better.

For a Bachelor of Music degree, the same requirements apply, except that 84 hours must be earned in the major, excluding May Terms, and the candidate is limited to 12 additional hours in the division of fine arts. Also, at least 132 hours of course work must be completed with a cumulative grade point average of C (2.0) or better.

Off-Campus Arrangements
A variety of programs are offered for off-campus study. During the fall semester in alternate years, students have the opportunity to study in London with the Simpson Semester in London program. In addition, during the spring semester in alternate years, qualified students have the opportunity to participate in the Simpson German Semester in Schorndorf, Germany, or in the Simpson Spanish Semester in Managua, Nicaragua. During the May Term and an optional summer session in June, qualified students may study in Mérida in the Yucatán Peninsula. The students live with Mexican families, which helps to maximize acquisition of language skills. Students also may study in Paris and other cities in France for a semester or year. The Simpson May Term in France is offered every other year.

Simpson is an affiliate of the American Institute for Foreign Study, which provides access to carefully planned semester or academic-year study programs in Austria, Britain, China, France, Germany, Italy, and Spain. International travel programs are offered on a regular basis during the May Term as well.

The Washington Semester, offered in conjunction with the American University in Washington, D.C., permits a qualified student to study the political process in the nation's capital. Also available is the United Nations Semester with Drew University in Madison, New Jersey. Students undertake a course of study at Drew and at the United Nations in New York City. With both programs, students maintain enrollment at Simpson. In addition, the Washington Center Internships and Symposia Program consists of semester-long, full-time, supervised work experiences in the nation's capital, supplemented by weekly academic seminars.

Academic Facilities
The George Washington Carver Science Center provides state-of-the-art research facilities, computer labs, and classrooms. The computer labs contain Macintosh and IBM-compatible microcomputers. For academic computing, Simpson has an Alpha 2100 computer and a campuswide Ethernet fiber-optic network.

The Henry H. and Thomas H. McNeill Hall houses classrooms for management, accounting, economics, and communication studies. In addition, the hall houses a seminar room and the Pioneer Hi-Bred International Conference Center.

The Amy Robertson Music Center houses the music department and contains the Sven and Mildred Lekberg Recital Hall, ten studios, twenty-two practice rooms, a music computer lab, and the band rehearsal room. A new wing, completed in 1997, includes a choral rehearsal room, a classroom, and studios.

Dunn Library, a contemporary learning resource center, contains more than 142,200 volumes, 600 current periodicals, sound recordings, cassette tapes, and microfilm materials. Additional materials for research can be obtained through a national computer-based interlibrary loan network. The library also provides audiovisual equipment and services to the campus.

The A. H. and Theo Blank Performing Arts Center accommodates Simpson's well-known programs in theater arts and opera and includes the magnificent 500-seat Pote Theatre, with both proscenium and hydraulically controlled thrust stages; a studio theater; the Barborka Gallery; technical facilities and shops; and classrooms.

Wallace Hall reopened in 1996 after a complete internal renovation. Named to the National Register of Historic Places in 1991, Wallace Hall contains facilities for education, psychology, sociology, applied social science, and a biofeedback/psychology laboratory.

Costs

Tuition and fees for 2000–01 are $15,150, a room is $2395, and board is $2645. These figures do not include books, music fees, or personal expenses.

Financial Aid

Simpson College seeks to make it financially possible for qualified students to experience the advantages of a college education. Generous gifts from alumni, trustees, and friends of the College, in addition to state and federal programs of student aid, make this opportunity possible. Simpson offers financial aid on both a need and non-need basis. Need is determined by filing the Free Application for Federal Student Aid.

Financial aid granted on a non-need basis includes academic scholarships, which are awarded on the basis of prior academic records, and talent scholarships, which are available in theater, music, and art. The talent scholarships are determined by audition/portfolio.

Faculty

Seventy-eight percent of Simpson's 80 full-time faculty members have earned their terminal degrees. At Simpson, faculty members serve as academic advisers as well as teachers and often attend College plays, operas, and athletic events, reinforcing their sincere interest in students. The student-faculty ratio of 14:1 (for full-time students) provides for individualized help and an education of high quality.

Student Government

Student involvement in College governance is an integral part of the organization of the College. Students annually elect a president and vice president of the Student Government. The members of each housing unit and the off-campus students elect representatives to the Student Senate, chaired by the vice president of Student Government. The Student Senate appoints student members to all College committees in which students hold membership. The senate also appoints 4 students-at-large who attend plenary sessions of the Board of Trustees as members on the Student Affairs Committee. Six students, nominated by Student Government and confirmed by the faculty, serve as representatives at faculty meetings, which are open to all members of the academic community.

Admission Requirements

Admission to Simpson College is selective and competitive. A strong academic record is essential. Applications are acted upon by an admissions committee, which is elected by the faculty and represents the five academic divisions of the College. These faculty members consider the college-preparatory courses taken, the grades received in those courses, rank in class, and standardized test scores (ACT and/or SAT I), including test subscores. A short time after all required credentials are received, the application is reviewed by the faculty admissions committee. Transfer applicants are accepted on the basis of successful completion of academic work at an accredited college or university. In addition, transfer applicants are required to submit official high school transcripts and ACT/SAT I results.

Application and Information

Simpson's rolling admission policy allows flexibility; however, early application is recommended. Transfer and foreign students are welcome. Students are strongly encouraged to visit the campus.

For additional information or to obtain application materials, students should contact:

Office of Admissions
Simpson College
701 North "C" Street
Indianola, Iowa 50125
Telephone: 515-961-1624
            800-362-2454 (toll-free)
E-mail: admiss@simpson.edu
World Wide Web: http://www.simpson.edu

The renovation and expansion of the George Washington Carver Science Center have provided Simpson students with state-of-the-art labs and research facilities.

SKIDMORE COLLEGE
SARATOGA SPRINGS, NEW YORK

The College

Skidmore College is an independent liberal arts college of 2,175 men and women. Founded as the Skidmore School of Arts in 1911, it became Skidmore College in 1922. In addition to being accredited by the Middle States Association of Colleges and Schools, the College has a chapter of Phi Beta Kappa and has program accreditation with the Council on Social Work Education and the National Association of Schools of Art and Design.

Throughout its history, Skidmore has steadily reflected a spirit of innovation and imagination in response to need. In the 1960s, the College decided to build an entirely new campus; in 1971, to become a coeducational college; in 1983, to completely revise its curriculum; and in 1993, to install a graduate program leading to the Master of Arts in Liberal Studies degree. Skidmore has welcomed change, seeing in it the opportunity to serve the needs and realize the potential of its students. By expanding its programs, the College has broadened its educational mission to reflect the evolving opportunities and challenges of a global society.

Students enjoy a full schedule of cultural, intellectual, and social activities, including lectures, art exhibits, concerts, opera, dance, and theater. There are more than eighty student organizations, such as a weekly newspaper, an FM stereo radio station, a TV station, an art and literary journal, a journal of social science and philosophy opinion, and the student-directed art gallery. There are no fraternities or sororities. A strong intercollegiate sports program for men and women includes baseball, basketball, field hockey, golf, ice hockey, lacrosse, rowing, soccer, softball, swimming, tennis, riding, and volleyball. The College has a vigorous intramural program and supports team activities of club status as well.

The modern campus of Skidmore College includes fifty buildings. A new library and science center have recently been completed, and the sports and recreation complex includes a pool, racquet-sport courts, basketball courts, a small stadium with artificial turf field and a 400-meter all-weather track, three dance studios, a weight room, a fitness center, and other recreational and competitive sport facilities. The new $11-million Tang Teaching Museum and Art Gallery opens in fall 2000.

Location

Set on 800 acres on the outskirts of Saratoga Springs, New York, the College offers students the advantage of a rural campus setting and the convenience of location in a historic city of 30,000 residents. Saratoga Springs has long been famous as a resort and as a horse-racing and cultural center. The city is located 30 miles north of Albany, the capital of New York State, and is cosmopolitan in character. Skidmore is within an hour of major ski areas, state parks, large lakes, and mountainous regions of eastern New York, Vermont, and western Massachusetts. During the summer, groups such as the New York City Ballet and the Philadelphia Orchestra are in residence at the Saratoga Performing Arts Center.

Bus service is available from Saratoga Springs to New York City, Montreal, Boston, and other major cities. There are daily trains to and from New York City and Montreal. Rental cars are available at the Albany International Airport, which is served by major airlines. The College is located near Exit 15 of I-87 (the Northway).

Majors and Degrees

Skidmore College grants a Bachelor of Arts degree in the following liberal arts subjects: American studies, anthropology, biology, chemistry, classical studies, computer science, economics, English, foreign languages and literatures (French, German, and Spanish), geology, government, history, history of art, mathematics, music, philosophy, physics, psychology, religion, and sociology. The Bachelor of Science degree is granted in areas of a more professional nature, including business, dance, education, exercise science, social work, studio art, and theater. There are thirty-three interdepartmental majors. Self-determined majors, double majors, and minors are also available.

The College offers 3-2 programs with the Thayer School of Engineering at Dartmouth College and with Clarkson University. Also available is a 4-1 M.B.A. program offered with the School of Management at Clarkson, a 3-2 M.B.A. program offered through Rensselaer Polytechnic Institute, and a 4-1 Master of Arts in Teaching program with Union College. Through a cooperative program with the Cardozo Law School, Skidmore students may obtain a bachelor's degree and a law degree in six years. In addition, Skidmore has certification programs in teaching and social work and preprofessional programs in law and medicine.

Academic Program

Skidmore College is known for its unusual blend of courses in the traditional liberal arts with opportunities in preprofessional disciplines. It is also recognized for its liberal studies core curriculum in which students are required to take at least two interdisciplinary courses. Additional core requirements include two courses in science, two in the social sciences, two in the arts, zero to four in a foreign language (depending on competence), and one in non-Western culture. All students choose a major at the end of their sophomore year from among sixty options, some of which include interdepartmental concentrations, self-determined majors, and minors.

The College operates on a two-semester system with opportunities for internships directly following the end of the second semester in May. Students normally carry four or five courses during each semester.

The College offers a six-week residential academic summer program (PASS) enabling high school students to take two courses for college credit.

University Without Walls (UWW) is the nontraditional, nonresidential baccalaureate degree program of Skidmore College. Students admitted to the program work individually with a faculty adviser to define the specific content of their degree programs. Skidmore UWW also encourages and helps the student to identify and use nontraditional means to acquire the requisite knowledge, including independent and self-directed study, as well as experiences gained in paid volunteer work. A similarly designed Master of Arts in Liberal Studies program was implemented in 1993.

Off-Campus Arrangements

Skidmore's membership in the Hudson-Mohawk Association of Colleges and Universities enables students to cross-register at any of fourteen other colleges and universities in the area. The Washington Semester, conducted through American University in Washington, D.C., offers an intensive workshop experience through course work, seminars, research projects, and internships with government committees. Skidmore's Study Abroad program enables students to study in England, France, Spain, and India. Skidmore is also affiliated with other study-abroad programs, facilitating study for a semester or a year in many locations in Asia, Australia, Europe, and Latin America.

Arrangements for student internships are made through academic departments or through the Office of Career Planning and Field Experience Programs. Internships are available in such diverse fields as government, social work, the arts (dance, theater, and museum work), business, scientific research, and medicine.

Academic Facilities

Scribner Library, housing approximately 500,000 volumes, has been designated a depository for U.S. government documents. Students have access to forty libraries in the region through the College's membership in an area council. Skidmore also participates in the Lockheed/Dialog system for information search and retrieval. Dana Science Center has laboratories and sophisticated equipment for the biology, chemistry, physics, and geology departments. The Filene Music Building contains a large recital hall, practice and listening rooms, and a music library. Other special facilities include a language laboratory in Bolton Hall; the Art Building, with studio space, numerous kilns, and ceramics, weaving, and jewelry-making studios; the Skidmore Theatre; and dance studios. Students have access to a computer center served by a cluster of nine SunSPARC-2 workstations. In 2000–01, Skidmore will open an $11-million art museum at the center of its campus.

Costs

Tuition in 1999–2000 for all students was $24,000. Students living in dormitories paid a room and board fee of $6950. Additional fees were $250.

Financial Aid

Skidmore awards financial aid based on demonstrated need. The Free Application for Federal Student Aid (FAFSA), a copy of the federal income tax form, and the CSS PROFILE must be filed each year. The application date is January 15 for entering freshmen. The College hosts an annual Filene Music Scholarship Competition to award four $32,000 ($8000 per year) scholarships on the basis of musical ability without regard to financial need. Five $10,000 merit scholarships in math and science are also awarded annually. Detailed information concerning scholarships, grants, loans, and/or work awards can be obtained through the Office of Student Aid and Family Finance.

Faculty

Skidmore College has 189 full-time teaching faculty members and 10 part-time members, including those with special appointments. More than 90 percent of the liberal arts faculty members have doctoral degrees. The ratio of students to full-time faculty is about 11:1, and the average class size is 16. Although actively engaged in research and publication in their individual fields, the Skidmore faculty members regard teaching as their primary commitment. All students have faculty advisers who assist them in selecting courses and in designing individual academic programs.

Student Government

Students at Skidmore play an active role in College governance. Through the Student Government Association (SGA) and by membership on a number of major College committees, they participate in all phases of academic and social life. The SGA operates under the authority granted by the Board of Trustees and is dedicated to the principles of democratic self-government and responsible citizenship. Within the association, elected faculty members and student representatives serve on the All-College Council, the Academic Integrity Board, and the Social Integrity Board. The broad concerns of the SGA include educational policy, elections, social and student events, freshman orientation, student publications, and student clubs and organizations.

Admission Requirements

Applicants for admission to the freshman class are expected to complete a secondary school program with a minimum of 16 college-preparatory credits. The Admissions Committee is also pleased to consider applications from qualified high school juniors who plan to accelerate and enter college early. Typical preparation for entrance includes 4 years of English, 3 years of a foreign language, 3 years of mathematics, 3 years of social studies, and 2 years of laboratory science. Among the required credentials are a secondary school transcript, a report from the school guidance counselor, and assessments from 2 teachers. Skidmore also requires applicants to take the SAT I or ACT examination and recommends that three SAT II Subject Tests, including the Writing Test and one in foreign language, be taken. A campus interview is strongly recommended.

Through the Higher Education Opportunity Program (HEOP), Skidmore enrolls talented, energetic, and motivated students from New York State who would otherwise be unable to attend college under traditional admission requirements because of academic and financial circumstances.

Application and Information

An applicant for admission registers by completing Skidmore's application form or the Common Application and returning it with a $50 fee. All information should reach the Admissions Office by January 15. Applications from early decision candidates may be submitted by December 1 for the Round I early decision plan or by January 15 for the Round II early decision plan. Transfer candidates are urged to apply by April 1 for the next fall term and by November 15 for the next spring term. Interested students are strongly urged to visit the campus for interviews and guided tours.

Mary Lou W. Bates
Director of Admissions
Skidmore College
Saratoga Springs, New York 12866
Telephone: 800-867-6007 (toll-free)
  518-580-5570
E-mail: admissions@skidmore.edu

Aerial view of the Skidmore College campus.

SLIPPERY ROCK UNIVERSITY OF PENNSYLVANIA
SLIPPERY ROCK, PENNSYLVANIA

The University
In 1889, the citizens of the borough of Slippery Rock founded the college and gave it the town's picturesque name. In 1983, the school became Slippery Rock University of Pennsylvania, a state-owned, multipurpose institution. The academic divisions of the University are the Colleges of Arts and Sciences, Education, Health and Human Services, and Information Science and Business Administration, and Graduate Studies and Research. While most of the University's 7,000 students are Pennsylvania residents, approximately 5 percent are from other states and about 3 percent are international students from more than seventy countries. Residence halls are popular, with close to half of the student population living on campus. Freshmen are required to live in University residence halls. Approximately 30 percent of the students live in off-campus fraternity and sorority houses, private residence halls, and houses and apartments, and some students commute from neighboring cities and towns.

Students can participate in more than 160 social, honorary, and special interest clubs. Intercollegiate and intramural sports for both men and women are popular and played in the University's spacious indoor and outdoor facilities. Concerts, plays, lectures, blockbuster movies, and other cultural activities fill the University calendar to create an active tone in a congenial setting.

Counseling and tutorial services are available to all students, and professionals are available to provide services for students with disabilities. A unique do-it-yourself career laboratory allows students to clarify interests and research job opportunities. An effective placement service provides assistance to students in their search for employment after graduation. Ninety percent of graduates find employment in their respective fields or attend graduate or professional schools.

Location
Located in western Pennsylvania, the University is easily accessible. Two major interstate highways, I-79 and I-80, intersect within 7 miles of the University. Pittsburgh, one of the country's largest cities and a setting for major cultural and sporting events, is less than an hour's drive south. Erie, Pennsylvania, is located 75 miles north, and Youngstown, Ohio, is just 35 miles west. The University is located in a town of about 3,000 that is in the middle of a population center of about 120,000.

Majors and Degrees
The Bachelor of Arts degree is offered in anthropology, art, biology, chemistry, communication, dance, economics, English, environmental geoscience, French, geography, history, mathematics, music, philosophy, physics, political science, psychology, sociology, Spanish, and theater. The Bachelor of Fine Arts degree is offered in art and the Bachelor of Music degree is offered in music.

The Bachelor of Science degree is offered in applied science, biology, chemistry, computer science, economics, English, environmental science, geography, information systems, information technology, mathematics, parks and recreation, physical education: exercise science, physics, public administration, psychology, safety and environmental management, social work, special education: community programs for Americans with disabilities, and sport management. The Bachelor of Science in Nursing degree program is available to registered nurses who have received their basic training at hospitals or similar institutions. The Bachelor of Science in Business Administration degree is offered in accounting, economics, finance, human resource management, international business, management, and marketing.

The Bachelor of Science in Education degree is offered in elementary education; environmental education; physical education; health; music; secondary education in English, French, Spanish, social studies; and special education.

The University also sponsors special degree programs. A dual-degree program in engineering is offered with Pennsylvania State University. The program involves three years of pre-engineering course work at Slippery Rock and two years of engineering study at Penn State. Students in this three-two program are awarded Bachelor of Science degrees from both institutions. Students can participate also in a "3 Plus 3" program between the University and Widener College of Law: three years of undergraduate preparation at the University plus three years of law school leads to the awarding of baccalaureate and law degrees. Students can also enroll in several baccalaureate degree programs that precede the University's Doctor of Physical Therapy program. Students must apply for admission to the professional curriculum in physical therapy after four years of undergraduate preparation.

Academic Program
Two semesters make up the regular University calendar; the first semester ends before Christmas break. The summer term is divided into two 5-week sessions, a three-week session, and a seven-week evening session. A minimum of 128 hours, 42 to 55 of which are in the core liberal studies curriculum, and a minimum grade point average of 2.0 are required for graduation.

To assist eligible students who are underprepared for college, the University sponsors the University Enrichment Semester. Students who are admitted under this program enter in the fall semester and are given the necessary support services to provide them with the best opportunities for success.

Through a continuing education program, the University offers credit and noncredit courses and workshops at on- and off-campus sites.

Interested students may participate in the Army Reserve Officers' Training Corps program on campus. Completion of the ROTC program can result in a student's commissioning as an officer in the U.S. Army Reserve or National Guard upon graduation.

Off-Campus Arrangements
Domestic or international internships are recommended in most academic disciplines. Students in teacher education programs are required to take a semester of student teaching in their senior year. Student teaching experiences occur in many of the surrounding school districts and, in addition, the University offers student teaching experiences in Ireland, Mexico, and Las Vegas. Students interested in marine sciences have the opportunity to participate in summer school sessions

at Wallops Island Marine Science Center in Virginia and to utilize the instructional facilities at nearby Lake Arthur and the Jennings Environmental Education Center. The University's extensive and expanding international studies program offers educational opportunities for students in twenty-eight programs in nineteen countries: Austria, Bulgaria, Canada, China, England, France, Germany, Hungary, Ireland, Japan, Korea, Mexico, Poland, Russia, Slovakia, Scotland, Spain, Trinidad, and Wales. Scholarships are available for students who want to study abroad for a year, a semester, or a summer.

Academic Facilities

The University's library houses more than 850,000 volumes, subscribes to numerous journals and periodicals, maintains an extensive instructional materials center, and operates a media services center. Vincent Science Hall has numerous laboratories for the programs in the natural sciences as well as a planetarium, a greenhouse, and an aquarium. The University also operates laboratories for the behavioral sciences and a laboratory school for instruction in special education. A large theater and radio and television studios are used by theater and communication majors. Swope Music Hall provides modern facilities for music and music therapy majors. Student computer labs are strategically located in many classroom buildings. Through the University's computing services, every residence hall room is connected with all classroom buildings, the library, and—via the Internet—to the world.

Costs

Tuition for academic year 1999–2000 at Slippery Rock University was $3618 for Pennsylvania residents and $9046 for out-of-state students. Room and board was $3800 for the year, special fees were $900, and books and supplies were estimated at $700. In addition, students should budget approximately $1,300 a year for miscellaneous expenses such as travel and personal items.

Financial Aid

About 80 percent of the University's students receive some form of financial aid. Slippery Rock participates in five college-based federal aid programs: the Federal Perkins Loan, Federal Stafford Student Loan, Federal PLUS, Federal Work-Study, and Federal Supplemental Educational Opportunity Grant programs. Federal Pell Grants are also available. Pennsylvania students may be eligible for Pennsylvania Higher Education Assistance Agency (PHEAA) grants and scholarships. Competitive University scholarships are also available. Job opportunities are available on-campus and also in businesses in the surrounding area. Students interested in financial aid should contact the office of financial aid.

Faculty

Sixty-eight percent of the University's 400 faculty members have earned doctoral degrees, and many are nationally known in their professions. Teaching is the prime responsibility of the University faculty. It is the faculty member, not a graduate teaching assistant, who students see in the classroom. To better serve students' interests, each faculty member also acts as an academic adviser to students. Many faculty members are involved in University activities and professional faculty-student relations are common reflecting the friendly, personal character of the University.

Student Government

The Student Government Association (SGA), composed of elected student representatives from each class, is the primary student governing body at Slippery Rock University. The SGA regulates co-curricular activities, promotes spirit and unity, encourages student participation in University activities, and serves as an advocate for student interests. Students are active on all major University committees and on the Council of Trustees, one of the University's governing boards.

Admission Requirements

Students from all economic, geographical, cultural, and religious backgrounds are welcome at Slippery Rock University. The University encourages applications from students who have graduated from high school in the top three-fifths of their class with a strong academic program and at least a C+ average. The University also considers students who have earned the high school equivalency diploma. Transfer students with a minimum cumulative grade point average of approximately 2.3 from an accredited or non-accredited college who are in good academic standing at the last school attended are also eligible for admission. Students who demonstrate their expertise in specific areas through testing may receive college credit and elect to substitute certain required courses through the Advanced Placement Program and the College-Level Examination Program. The University offers an early admission program for outstanding high school seniors. Students who plan to major in dance, music, music education, or music therapy are required to audition with the dance/music department prior to admission.

Application and Information

Students seeking admission must complete an application for admission form, submit a high school transcript, and have their scores from either the ACT or SAT I college entrance examinations sent to the University. In addition to filing the application form, transfer students must submit transcripts of all previous college work. The recommended deadline for applying for admission is May 1, but applications are accepted on a limited basis after that date. Personal interviews and a campus visit are highly recommended.

To get an application for admission, for additional information on admission or any other aspect of the University, contact:

Director of Admission
Slippery Rock University
Slippery Rock, Pennsylvania 16057-1326
Telephone: 724-738-2015
        800-SRU-9111 (toll-free)
E-mail: apply@sru.edu
World Wide Web: http://www.sru.edu/

SMITH COLLEGE
NORTHAMPTON, MASSACHUSETTS

The College

Smith College was founded in 1871 as a liberal arts college for women and rapidly became one of the first such institutions to match the standards and facilities of the best colleges of the day. Today, with 2,560 undergraduates on campus, Smith is the largest privately endowed college for women in the country. Graduate degrees (master's, Ph.D.) are offered in a number of departments and in the Smith College School for Social Work. Currently, all fifty states and sixty countries are represented in the Smith student body. Approximately 80 percent of the members of each entering class were in the top fifth of their high school class; most chose Smith because of the excellence of its faculty and curriculum. Although most Smith students are between the ages of 18 and 22, Smith's Ada Comstock Scholars Program enables older women whose educations have been interrupted and who meet the College's admission standards to pursue an A.B. degree or one of several graduate degrees.

Smith's house system is unusual and highly regarded. Each of the College's thirty-three houses is home to between 15 and 100 women. Most houses have their own kitchens, dining rooms, living rooms, and study areas, and each building has a charm and character of its own. The house system stresses individual freedom, group autonomy, and mutual respect. Optional facilities, such as a cooperative house, a French house, and townhouse apartments, are available. Smith offers a wide variety of extracurricular possibilities, ranging from service organizations to musical groups and from student publications to fourteen intercollegiate sports teams. The already varied cultural and social opportunities—lectures, workshops, dance and theatrical performances, art exhibits, concerts, and social events—are increased by participation in Five Colleges, Inc., a consortium that opens to Smith students classes and activities at Amherst, Hampshire, and Mount Holyoke colleges and at the University of Massachusetts. Smith's athletic facilities include two gymnasia, six squash courts, a 75-foot six-lane swimming pool with 1- and 3-meter diving boards, weight-training rooms, a human performance laboratory, and an indoor track and tennis facility, which houses four tennis courts and a 200-meter track and accommodates all field events. Outside are 30 acres of athletic fields, a 400-meter track, a 5,000-meter cross-country course, and twelve lighted tennis courts. Smith also has indoor and outdoor Olympic-size riding rings and a forty-two-unit stable.

Location

Northampton, a cosmopolitan city with a population of more than 30,000, is in the Connecticut River valley of western Massachusetts. It is 93 miles west of Boston and 156 miles northeast of New York City. There are many shops and restaurants within walking distance of the campus and within the service area of a free Five College bus system. Buses run frequently to Boston and New York. Many students are involved in local organizations, and some intern in local city or county offices. Others participate on an extracurricular level in nonprofit agencies, day-care centers, or similar institutions.

Majors and Degrees

Smith College awards the Bachelor of Arts (A.B.) degree. Areas of major concentration include Afro-American studies, American studies, ancient studies, anthropology (anthropology, sociology and anthropology), art, astronomy, biochemistry, biological sciences, chemistry, classical languages and literatures (Greek, Latin, the classics, classical studies), comparative literature, computer science, dance, economics, education and child study, English language and literature, French language and literature (French language and literature, French studies), geology, German studies (German culture studies, German literature studies), government, history, Italian language and literature, Latin American studies, mathematics, medieval studies, music, philosophy, physics, psychology, religion and biblical literature, Russian language and literature (Russian literature, Russian civilization), sociology (sociology, sociology and anthropology), Spanish and Portuguese (Peninsular Spanish literature, Latin American literature, Portuguese-Brazilian studies), theater, and women's studies. Smith College recently announced a new program leading to a Bachelor of Science (B.S.) degree in engineering. Interdepartmental majors and minors are offered in a variety of fields.

Academic Program

The academic year is divided into two semesters, the first ending before winter recess. Interterm courses, some for credit, are offered during January. Smith believes in the goals of a liberal arts education. Students have great freedom to design their own courses of study; the only requirement outside a student's field of concentration is one writing-intensive course. One hundred twenty-eight credits of academic work are required, with the normal course load consisting of 16 credits in each of eight semesters. There are no specific distribution requirements, but 64 credits must be taken outside the major field of study. If a student's educational needs cannot be met within any of the existing majors, she may design and undertake an interdepartmental major, subject to the approval of the Subcommittee on Honors and Independent Programs. A student may also complete the requirements of two departmental majors or of one departmental major and another departmental minor.

Through credit earned on Advanced Placement or International Baccalaureate Diploma examinations and by independent work and summer study, some students may be able to accelerate and complete degree requirements in six or seven semesters. The Departmental Honors Program enables a student with a strong academic background to study a particular topic in depth or undertake research in the field of her major. Through the Smith Scholars Program, some undergraduates can spend one or two years on projects they design, freed in varying degrees from normal College requirements.

Off-Campus Arrangements

Smith students may take academic courses and participate in social and cultural activities at any of the institutions participating in the Five College consortium, described above. Smith students may also spend a year at another member institution of the Twelve College Exchange Program (Amherst, Bowdoin, Connecticut, Dartmouth, Mount Holyoke, Trinity, Vassar, Wellesley, Wesleyan, Wheaton, and Williams) or spend a year at one of several historically black colleges in the South. Some students participate in the Jean Picker Semester-in-Washington Program in public policy, a fall internship program in Washington, D.C., sponsored by the College's Department of Government. The American Studies Program offers an internship at the Smithsonian Institution.

Smith offers Junior Year Abroad programs in Florence, Geneva, Hamburg, and Paris. Students may apply to affiliated programs in South India, Spain, Japan, and China, and some may study at the Intercollegiate Center for Classical Studies in Rome. Smith students may also participate in other programs arranged independently or by the College. Students eligible for financial aid are able to take that aid with them to any approved program.

Academic Facilities

The Smith College Library is the largest undergraduate library of any liberal arts college in this country. Its 1.3 million holdings are housed in the centrally located William Allan Neilson Library and in the libraries of the fine arts, performing arts, and science centers. The Neilson Library also houses a rare book room, the Nonprint Resource Center, the College archives, and the Sophia Smith Collection, a women's history archive. Since 1965, science, performing arts, and fine arts facilities have opened. The Clark Science Center is a five-building complex that accommodates the 26 percent of students who major in the sciences. The facilities include general laboratories, a molecular genetics facility, classrooms, a rooftop astronomy observatory, animal care facilities, scanning and transmission electron microscopes, an analytic ultracentrifuge, and a high-field nuclear magnetic resonance spectrometer. Academic computer facilities include more than 550 networked Windows and Macintosh computers in public labs, classrooms, the libraries, and the foreign language center. All buildings and student residences are networked to the academic UNIX systems, Novell file servers, and the Internet via a campus-wide fiber-optic network. These resources are available for student use without charge. Smith also has a digital design studio, seven electronic classrooms, and a cluster of DEC VAX and Sun minicomputers that are used for statistical analysis and electronic communication over the Internet. The Bass Science Building houses the psychology department, the scientific computing center, and Young Library, one of the largest undergraduate science libraries in the country. The Bass laboratories provide numerous facilities for research in neuroscience. The Mendenhall Center for the Performing Arts contains an experimental theater and a traditional theater, dance studios, and television and audio recording rooms. Sage Hall, the music building, includes an electronic music studio, a small recital hall, dozens of practice rooms, and a 750-seat concert hall. The Smith College Museum of Art houses one of the finest teaching collections in the country, and Hillyer Hall contains eleven art studios as well as printmaking, darkroom, and sculpture facilities. Smith's Center for Foreign Languages and Cultures maintains a multimedia laboratory and classroom housing a network of student workstations with integrated and interactive computer, audio, and video components.

Costs

Tuition for 1999–2000 was $22,440. The room and board charge for regular dormitories was $7820. Optional health insurance is estimated at $840; the activity fee was approximately $182; and books, supplies, and personal expenses are estimated at $1500.

Financial Aid

Approximately 56 percent of all Smith students receive some form of financial assistance from grants, loans, and/or campus jobs. Aid is awarded on the basis of need, as determined by the College. Each applicant must submit the Free Application for Federal Student Aid (FAFSA), the PROFILE form from the College Scholarship Service, Smith's Application for Financial Aid, and a copy of her family's most recent federal income tax return. For all traditional-age admitted students, Smith will make every effort to fully meet documented need. The first portion of an aid award is an offer of a loan and campus employment; the remaining need is covered by grants from federal, state, and/or College funds.

Faculty

The teaching of undergraduate women is the priority of the Smith faculty. There are approximately 265 faculty members; most have earned a doctoral degree and are well known in their professional field. Close ties between undergraduates and their teachers are forged through small classes (more than 50 percent have 15 or fewer students) and generous access to faculty members during and outside of regular office hours.

Student Government

Smith students assume much of the responsibility for their personal, social, and academic life at the College through the Student Government Association, which gives students representation on major College-policy committees and regulates the functioning of the house system.

Admission Requirements

Smith seeks students whose motivation, academic preparation, and diversity of interests will enable them to profit from and contribute to the varied possibilities of a liberal arts college. Smith is interested in the woman behind the record and the scores. However, as a highly competitive college, Smith gives primary consideration to the academic record of each candidate for admission. Strong high school programs usually have a basis of 4 years of English, at least 3 years in one foreign language or 2 years in each of two languages, 3 years of mathematics, 3 years of science, and 2 years of history. It is hoped that areas of special interest will have been pursued in depth. Students should submit ACT or SAT I scores. SAT II Subject Tests, especially the Writing Test, are strongly recommended but not required. An on-campus interview and tour are strongly recommended. Either an on-campus interview or an interview with a local alumna can be arranged by calling the Office of Admission. A first-choice early decision plan is available.

Applications are also welcomed from students who wish to transfer from other college-level institutions or who wish to enter the Visiting Students Program or the Ada Comstock Scholars Program. Smith admits students of any race, color, creed, handicap, or national or ethnic origin.

Application and Information

A student interested in applying to Smith has three options: fall early decision, winter early decision, or regular decision. Applicants for fall early decision should apply by November 15 and receive a decision by December 15. Applicants for winter early decision should apply by January 1 and receive a decision in early February. Regular decision applicants should submit the Part I Application by January 15; all other parts of the application are due by February 1. These candidates receive their admission decision by early April. Transfer applicants for January admission should apply by November 15 and receive an admission decision by mid-December. The preferred deadline for September transfer admission is February 1, with notification in early April. Applications will be accepted until June 1, with decisions being made on a rolling basis. Students applying to the Visiting Students Program should have a completed application in by July 1 and will receive notification on a rolling basis.

For more information about Smith College, students should contact:

Director of Admission
Smith College
Northampton, Massachusetts 01063

Telephone: 413-585-2500
Fax: 413-585-2527
E-mail: admission@smith.edu
World Wide Web: http://www.smith.edu

Smith offers small classes and individual instruction.

SOUTHEASTERN UNIVERSITY
WASHINGTON, D.C.

The University

Southeastern University is a dynamic, small, business-oriented international university with campuses in London and Washington, D.C., with a declared mission as an academic innovator. The roots of the University reach back to 1879, when the Young Men's Christian Association (YMCA) organized business and liberal arts courses for residents of Washington, D.C. The University is chartered by an act of the Congress of the United States, is accredited by the Commission on Higher Education of the Middle States Association of Colleges and Schools, and is a full member of the prestigious Consortium of Universities of the Washington Metropolitan Area.

Although half of the students enrolled at the Washington campus are international (representing from forty to forty-five countries at any one time), traditionally, most students are adult workers who hold full- or part-time jobs. Some students come to the University directly from high school, while others—frequently, those who obtain jobs with the federal government and move to Washington—transfer credits previously earned from institutions of higher education.

The University has emerged in recent years as an intellectual, cultural, and economic force in the southwest quadrant of the city and as a leader in the attempt to organize Washington's institutions of higher education on behalf of businesses and economic development throughout the Potomac region.

The University offers Associate of Science, Bachelor of Science, and a wide variety of master's degrees. Graduate specialties include accounting, business administration, computer information systems, computer science, finance, government management, government program management, health services administration, information systems management, legal studies, marketing, and taxation. Many teachers in the D.C. Public School system take an exciting master's degree program that is offered in a compressed format as a result of a partnership between the University and the Washington Teachers Union. Southeastern offers a wide range of other instructional and in-service courses for D.C. teachers.

Over the past century, many of the city's leading professional practitioners have graduated from Southeastern. Also, the University has sponsored a widely commended and highly successful College Access Program for local high school graduates. Enrollment has tripled over the past several years, and more than 900 students currently enroll in Southeastern's Washington campus programs each quadmester—quarter terms with full semester credits.

Southeastern University partners or joint ventures with a number of the most advanced professional associations and private industries on the Eastern Seaboard. These dynamic partnerships arise from the role played by the University's president, Dr. Charlene Drew Jarvis, a longtime District of Columbia Councilmember and distinguished expert on urban economic and community development.

The University partners with the Greater Washington Society of Certified Public Accountants, providing a wide range of programs jointly through the Washington School of Accountancy. CPAs from throughout the country may obtain a master's degree while satisfying their annual state continuing education requirements; courses have been specially designed with the working professional in mind.

The University also partners with several prominent private and public organizations to sponsor the new, multimillion-dollar D.C. Link and Learn, a state-of-the-art high-technology center that provides Washingtonians and others with all levels of training, including the most advanced, in emerging fields of technology that are significant to the advancement of the Potomac region. The University's associate degree programs in computer and information science are headquartered at D.C. Link and Learn, which is located across from the main campus.

The University cosponsors a Small Business Development Subcenter with nearby Friendship House. The subcenter, an affiliate of the federally funded Howard University Small Business Center, offers training and counseling throughout the year to many entrepreneurs and small-business owners. Southeastern is a partner and sponsor of Techworld Public Charter School, cosponsors the Certified Nurses Aide Program with Rosario Adult Charter School and Medlantic Hospital, and partners with groups such as the Marshall Heights Community Development Organization, the Potomac Regional Educational Partnership, and the Community Business Partnership of the Greater Washington Board of Trade.

In addition, the University's Student Government Association sponsors an active social and cultural program; prominent national and local leaders speak at colloquia, and access is facilitated to national institutions located on the Mall—"America's front yard"—just two blocks from the site of the main campus. A professional academic advising staff is available full-time, and there is a very active Student Services Office as well. Active student groups include Omega Psi Phi fraternity, Phi Chi Theta, the Chinese Students Association, and a variety of other political and social organizations.

Location

The University's main office is located in an attractive contemporary building close to the Maine Avenue waterfront in the redeveloped southwest section of Washington, D.C. The University is close to such well-known cultural institutions as the Arena Stage and L'Enfant Plaza and to the United States Capitol, the Supreme Court, the Smithsonian Institution, the Library of Congress, and many other significant political and aesthetic foci of American life. The proximity of most of Washington's federal agencies makes Southeastern especially convenient for many federal employees and others who live and work in Washington.

Majors and Degrees

Southeastern University awards the Associate of Science degree in business management (accounting, finance, and legal studies), computer information systems, computer science, government management, and health services administration.

The Bachelor of Science degree is granted in accounting, banking, business management, computer information systems, computer science, financial management, general studies, government management, health services administration, and marketing.

Academic Program

The Associate of Science degree normally requires two years of study and 60 credit hours, of which at least 30 credit hours must be earned at the University.

The B.S. degree requires the completion of a minimum of 120 credit hours. At least 60 credit hours must be earned at the University. Baccalaureate candidates are required to complete 60 credit hours of general education course requirements; the remaining 60 credit hours consist of major courses or supplementary business courses.

A maximum of 30 credit hours may be awarded to undergraduates who earn successful scores on College-Level Examination

Program tests. Students may also seek credit by examination, and up to 25 percent of the total credit hours needed to complete the degree may be awarded for life/work experience in the undergraduate program. Southeastern University also recognizes the credit recommendations given in the *Guide to Evaluation of Educational Experience in the Armed Services*, published by the American Council on Education. Southeastern University also has a cooperative education program through which a student can earn up to 12 credit hours while working.

Southeastern University operates on a quadmester system, meaning that the academic year consists of four semesters per year. This is not a quarter system. Students receive full semester credits for each course. The four quadmesters—winter, spring, summer, and fall—begin, respectively, in early January, early April, late June, and late September. Under the quadmester system, students can conveniently take up to one third more courses during an academic year, flexibility in scheduling becomes greater, international students find it easier to meet immigration requirements, slightly expanded class sessions provide innovative teaching approaches, and transfer students can enroll during any term. Undergraduate courses are taught on weekdays during day and evening hours as well as on weekends.

The English as a Second Language Program at Southeastern University is used by many international students in order to prepare themselves for successful academic endeavors at an American college. The program offers an intensive course that leads to a certificate in English communication skills and American cultural studies. Upon completion of the program, a student is prepared for admission to the undergraduate program of Southeastern University or to another college.

Academic Facilities

The University's facilities include an impressive library with audiovisual materials, several computerized classrooms, a computer center (equipped with the latest-model hardware and software), and many other innovations.

Costs

Undergraduate tuition for 2000–01 is $200 per credit hour. Tuition and fees for two semesters are $5150, and tuition and fees for three semesters are $7725. A full-time undergraduate taking 12 credit hours per term for four terms pays $10,300 in tuition and fees for the academic year. Book costs are estimated at $1000 per year, but the University is committed to working with students in order to facilitate their academic progress.

Financial Aid

Southeastern University participates in federally funded and subsidized student financial aid programs. Most financial aid awards are based on need, and eligible students are usually awarded a combination of grants and loans in a financial package. Federal Work-Study Program awards are available, as are a number of academic scholarships. Financial aid applications may be submitted at any time during the year, although the bulk of funds is committed to students who enter in the fall term. Grants constitute 40 percent of the financial aid awards, and 65 percent of the student body receives aid. A large and helpful staff is available to assist and guide each student through the financial aid process.

Faculty

There are 12 full-time and 77 part-time faculty members. Full-time faculty members are drawn from a national search process; they publish, teach, and perform community service in Washington. Part-time faculty members are outstanding professionals selected specifically for their special background and position; essentially all part-time faculty members are employed full-time in their disciplines and teach on the weekends or at night. Virtually every full-time faculty member holds a doctorate, as do most part-time members. The student-faculty ratio is 15:1. Faculty members act as academic and career advisers and are involved in many student organizations.

Student Government

The Student Government Association (SGA) works to promote and provide an organized program of student activities. The SGA is involved in developing new activities and organizations. Through the SGA and the representation of that body on the University's Board of Trustees, students have an active voice in University administration.

Admission Requirements

All entering students are required to take the University placement test (English and mathematics). Although SAT I or ACT scores are recommended, there is no minimum score requirement, nor are these tests mandated for students who desire to enter the University. Test scores are used for placement purposes only. International students, however, are required to submit TOEFL scores for determination of English proficiency; all courses are taught in English. Students who do not meet language or other standards and who do not qualify as degree candidates may be enrolled in either the English as a Foreign Language Program or in the widely acclaimed Developmental Studies Program. Then, when they achieve language or academic proficiency, they are automatically admitted into the regular program.

In addition, there are a number of programs the University offers for degree and nondegree students who are seeking job promotion and professional development. The University also partners with prominent businesses in the Washington area in an effort to place every graduate and those students who need ongoing job placement.

Application and Information

Southeastern University is a highly respected institution in Washington, D.C. To accommodate student interest, therefore, the University maintains a rolling admission plan. Applicants are notified of admissions decisions four to six weeks after receipt of all required documents. A nonrefundable $45 application fee is required of all applicants. Admission is granted to incoming students for any of the fours terms during the year.

For more information, students should contact:

Admissions Office
Southeastern University
501 I Street, SW
Washington, D.C. 20024
Telephone: 202-COLLEGE
World Wide Web: http://www.seu.edu

SOUTHERN CALIFORNIA INSTITUTE OF ARCHITECTURE
LOS ANGELES, CALIFORNIA

The Institute

The Southern California Institute of Architecture (SCI-Arc) has established an international reputation with its approach to design education. Because SCI-Arc offers one of the few privately funded architecture programs in the world, it responds rapidly to the needs and interests of architectural change. After almost twenty years at its original site on Berkeley Street in Santa Monica, SCI-Arc moved to new quarters at 5454 Beethoven Street in Los Angeles in 1992. The former factory and office building provides double the previously available square footage as well as numerous other student facilities.

SCI-Arc began in 1972 when a small group of faculty members and students, feeling the restrictions of a larger institution, leased a 20,000-square-foot industrial building in Santa Monica, California. In its early years, the school developed and structured its programs and policies in accordance with its own academic philosophy rather than requirements dictated by a larger university system. During the first fifteen years, under its founding director, Raymond Kappe, the institution received accreditation by the National Architectural Accrediting Board for both its Bachelor of Architecture and its Master of Architecture programs. In 1995, SCI-Arc was granted accreditation from the Western Association of Schools and Colleges.

From 1987 to 1998, Michael Rotondi and an Academic Advisory Committee developed a curriculum based on instructors and students working together to extend the boundaries set by existing theories, practices, and values of the discipline. Since 1998, when Neil M. Denari assumed the directorship, the school has actively engaged in extending its institutional boundaries. The globalization of media and language, combined with business, entertainment, and the shifting borders of territories, point to a need to teach with a greater degree of awareness of the environment than ever before. The Institute gives its graduates the necessary tools not simply to cope with the unfurling complexity of the contemporary city but to create new strategies for practice.

Location

Located in west Los Angeles, California, SCI-Arc is 3 miles from the Pacific Ocean and is close to museums, theaters, galleries, architecturally significant buildings, and cultural events of the city. L.A.'s volatile environment has nurtured SCI-Arc's flexible and experimental approach. Students study architecture and urbanism in the world's most sprawling and intense horizontal laboratory.

Majors and Degrees

The Bachelor of Architecture degree is awarded upon successful completion of a five-year program.

Academic Program

SCI-Arc's undergraduate program provides students with the education necessary to practice architecture at the highest level in a way that tests the limits of the discipline. In keeping with the formative values of the school, architecture is seen as a creative discipline, a process of research and experimentation that is based on enduring principles, as well as an extended cultural practice that operates in the production of ideas and forms. From construction technology, interior environments, and engineering to infrastructure and landscape architecture, housing and urbanism to information technology, architecture is examined as a characteristic form of cultural representation and a mode of spatial inquiry and production.

The undergraduate core program is built around an integral core curriculum of the architecture studio, the visual studies and object-making sequence, and interdisciplinary seminars in the arts, sciences, and humanities and leads to upper-division courses in professional practice and technology, advanced imaging and representation, architectural history and theory, vertical (elective) studios, and a final studio or thesis. Central to the program is the idea of architecture as a process of pure and applied research. Consequently, undergraduate students at SCI-Arc have various opportunities to engage in empirical research and practice as assistants or fellows with faculty members through the Architecture and Research Program and the City Practice Research Center.

Philosophically, the course of study is based on values that span from the pragmatic to the poetic. Technical precision and exactitude, combined with conceptual and perceptual knowledge, are seen as the foundation of an architectural education. Over the course of five years, students develop a knowledge of material and spatial organizations and acquire the skills necessary for working in physical and digital environments that unfold as a series of linear and nonlinear trajectories and flows. The curriculum constantly evolves and responds to the context of existing and emerging regional and global cultures.

Candidates for the Bachelor of Architecture degree must complete 186 credit units.

SCI-Arc offers two Summer Studios to accommodate nonmatriculating (degree-seeking) students. The first program, Making and Meaning; the Foundation Program in Architecture, is an intensive five-week summer program that develops essential architectural skills and sensitivities. Started in 1988, the program is open to students at all levels who wish to learn more about the changing nature of the physical environment as well as the history, theory, and practice of architecture. Participants in past summers have ranged in age from 16 to 56 and come from South and Central America, Europe, and Asia as well as the United States. The program is centered in the studio and complemented by visual studies laboratories, seminars in critical theory, field trips, films, and readings. Parallel to these activities is the preparation of a portfolio.

The second program, L.A./L.A. (Los Angeles/Latin America), is a six-week program that uses Los Angeles as a laboratory to explore the changing boundaries of the Americas and architectural education. The design studio becomes a forum in which students from North America, Central America, South America, the Caribbean, and Europe exchange their narratives, histories, and identities through images and words. Their interchanges establish a foundation for a global culture driven by cross-cultural communication and interdisciplinary contact.

Off-Campus Arrangements

SCI-Arc encourages educational experiences that expose the student to new cultures and bring the student into direct contact with the great architecture of the past. In addition to formal exchange programs with the Royal Melbourne Institute of Technology in Australia, the Bartlett School in London, and the Shibaura Institute of Technology in Tokyo, SCI-Arc students and faculty members have arranged their own study tours and academic exchanges in Austria, China, Egypt, Mexico, the Netherlands, Russia, and Turkey.

Academic Facilities

Facilities for the school are housed in a transformed industrial building located in west Los Angeles. The facility includes studios, lecture and seminar rooms, woodshop, metal fabrication shop, media center, library, computer labs, darkroom, gallery, administrative offices, and a cafe.

Costs

Tuition for the 1999–2000 school year was $8013 per semester. There were an additional $25 academic fee and a $10 student fee per term. The average cost for sharing an apartment (there are no residence halls) was $300–$500 a month. The cost of food, art supplies, and incidentals ranged from $1000 to $1500 a month.

Financial Aid

Admission to SCI-Arc is determined without regard to a student's ability to pay the full cost of his or her education. The school's financial aid policy is designed to maximize the assistance to all admitted students who demonstrate financial need. All students who wish to apply for financial aid must complete a Financial Aid Packet from the Financial Aid Office.

Financial aid is available for undergraduate students who are U.S. citizens in the form of Federal Pell Grants, Federal Supplemental Educational Opportunity Grants, Federal Stafford Student Loans, and Federal PLUS loans. The Federal Work-Study Program, sponsored by the federal government, provides subsidized part-time employment opportunities for those who qualify.

In addition, SCI-Arc has a limited scholarship program. Scholarships are awarded on the basis of merit and need.

Faculty

The SCI-Arc faculty includes among its approximately 80 members some of the leading practitioners of the discipline of architecture. Since its founding, SCI-Arc has attracted practicing architects who are committed to the lively and exacting interchange between teaching and practice. With one of the few independent architecture programs in the world, the school continuously develops its curriculum in response to change and challenges in the discipline. SCI-Arc's faculty members represent a wide range of contemporary approaches to design, history, and urban theory. Among its faculty members are some of the leading practitioners of the discipline of architecture, as well as renowned theorists, critics, and historians. These Los Angeles-based practitioners have devoted their careers to investigating how broad aesthetic, social, and cultural concerns can be integrated into an overall understanding of the built and natural environments. Faculty members teach at both the undergraduate and graduate levels. Those who offer advanced elective studios, where undergraduate and graduate students work together, represent a wide range of design methodologies.

All design studios and seminar classes are taught by faculty members. The ratio of students to faculty is 15:1 in all studios, encouraging a close working relationship. The design studio instructors work on a one-to-one basis with students.

Student Government

The Student Council is an active body with primary responsibility for representing the students. As the council has described its role, "Our belief in the importance of how you become an architect is further reflected at SCI-Arc by the students' unique part in this institution. The students' critical role in developing goals and guiding SCI-Arc is a hallmark of this educational community. The process constantly reminds us that every individual at SCI-Arc, student or instructor, cares passionately about architecture."

Admission Requirements

The Southern California Institute of Architecture seeks applicants who demonstrate interest, ability, and academic achievement that reveal potential for the study of architecture.

Students who have completed high school are eligible for admission to the first professional degree program. One year of college-level work is recommended, and admission preference is given to students who have a balanced education in the arts, sciences, and humanities. Preparation in the visual arts is required; it may include drawing, sculpture, graphics, photography, or video.

Application and Information

Completed applications are due May 1 for fall entrance into the undergraduate program and October 1 for spring entrance. An interview is preferred. Late applications may be considered, but the applicant should be aware that enrollment is generally filled early; available spaces are limited for students applying for admission beyond the first-year, first-semester program.

Inquiries and requests for application forms and a catalog should be addressed to:

Director of Admissions
Southern California Institute of Architecture
5454 Beethoven Street
Los Angeles, California 90066
Telephone: 310-574-1123 Ext. 320
Fax: 310-574-3801
E-mail: admissions@sciarc.edu
World Wide Web: http://www.sciarc.edu

SOUTHERN CONNECTICUT STATE UNIVERSITY
NEW HAVEN, CONNECTICUT

The University

Founded in 1893, Southern Connecticut State University is located on a 168-acre campus in New Haven, a city renowned for its academic and cultural advantages. During its long history, Southern has grown in diversity and excellence. Today, Southern offers bachelor's and master's degrees and sixth-year diplomas in more than 150 areas of study, providing its students with a challenging variety of academic, professional, and personal opportunities. Southern is part of the Connecticut State University System.

Southern comprises seven academic schools: Arts and Sciences; Business; Education; Communication, Information, and Library Sciences; Health and Human Services, which includes programs in nursing, public health, recreation and leisure studies, and social work; Graduate Studies; and Extended Learning. For highly motivated students, Southern offers a number of honors programs, including the Honors College. Enrolling the most able and motivated members of the undergraduate student body, the Honors College is a four-year alternative program that features team-taught interdisciplinary courses and symposia and requires the writing of a thesis. Tutorial support for students in need of special academic assistance is provided through the Office of Student Supportive Services.

The student body represents the full spectrum of ethnic and socioeconomic groups. Although most students come from Connecticut, Southern students also represent more than thirty states and forty countries. There are approximately 12,000 students enrolled, about 8,000 of whom are undergraduates. Of the 5,500 full-time undergraduates, 2,000 live on campus in twelve modern residence halls and town houses. The rest live at home or in off-campus housing in the Southern neighborhood.

The focal point of student life on campus is the University Student Center, which houses the student newspaper and radio station, a modern cafeteria, two game rooms, a TV lounge, a copy center, and other campus facilities. The University also supports more than seventy campus clubs and organizations, ranging from academic and career groups, such as the marketing club and the literary magazine, to religious, theatrical, and political clubs. Besides giving students a chance to meet others with similar interests and concerns, these groups sponsor a long list of extracurricular activities, including film festivals, concerts, dances, and art exhibits. Southern's intramural and intercollegiate sports programs provide year-round activities for seasoned athletes and eager amateurs alike. Intramural and club sports include badminton, basketball, cheerleading, golf, ice hockey, lacrosse, rugby, soccer, tennis, triathlon, touch football, volleyball, and weight lifting. The Owls, members of the New England Collegiate Conference and the National Collegiate Athletic Association, compete in numerous Division II programs for men and women. Men's programs are offered in baseball, basketball, cross-country, football, gymnastics, soccer, swimming, and indoor and outdoor track. Southern ranks among the top ten colleges and universities in NCAA Division II individual titles won. In addition, the Owls have won nine NCAA team titles, six in soccer and three in gymnastics. Southern offers intercollegiate programs for women in basketball, cross-country, field hockey, gymnastics, soccer, softball, swimming, indoor and outdoor track, and volleyball. All of Southern's athletes have access to outstanding facilities in Moore Fieldhouse, Pelz Gymnasium, and the Jess Dow Field outdoor sports complex.

Location

New Haven, Connecticut, is a sophisticated city of 130,000 people on picturesque Long Island Sound. New Haven has recently been selected as a winner in the All-American City competition and rated by *Money* magazine as the fourth-best medium Northeast metro area. Rich in history and tradition, New Haven is a classic college town; about 35,000 students are enrolled in its half-dozen fine universities and colleges. Just 75 miles from New York City and 3 hours from Boston, New Haven is an integral part of the economic, cultural, and social life of the Northeast. In addition to movies, restaurants, and concerts, students enjoy world-famous theaters—like the Yale Repertory, the Shubert, and Long Wharf—art and natural history museums, and a whole range of sports and seaside activities.

Majors and Degrees

Southern offers the Bachelor of Arts and the Bachelor of Science degrees. The Bachelor of Arts degree is awarded in art history, biology, chemistry, communication, earth science, economics, English, French, geography, German, history, Italian, journalism, liberal studies, mathematics, philosophy, physics, political science, psychology, sociology, Spanish, studio art, and theater. The Bachelor of Science degree is awarded in accounting, art education, biochemistry, biology, business economics, chemistry, computer science, corporate communication, early childhood education, earth science, elementary education, exercise science (including athletic training, human performance, and physical education), finance, French, geography, German, history, Italian, journalism, liberal studies, library-information service, management, marketing, mathematics, music, nursing, physics, political science, psychology, public health, recreation and leisure studies, school health, social work, sociology, Spanish, special education, and studio art. Certification in secondary education is available in biology, chemistry, earth science, English, foreign languages, general science, geography, history, mathematics, physics, political science, social science, and sociology/anthropology. Southern also offers preprofessional study in dentistry, engineering, law, medicine, and veterinary science.

Academic Program

The University operates on a two-semester calendar. The fall semester usually begins the first week in September and ends before Christmas. The spring semester, which includes a one-week spring recess in March, runs from the third week of January to the middle of May. Southern also offers two 5-week sessions during the summer and a three-week intersession program each January.

Throughout its history, Southern has held fast to the conviction that the best education stresses the liberal arts and sciences. To ensure all students a chance to acquire such an education, Southern has designed a strong yet flexible program that underscores the basics while encouraging individual choice and self-expression. All baccalaureate degree candidates are required to complete a minimum of 122 hours of credit. Majors consist of at least 30 prescribed hours of credit in one specific, approved field. Degree candidates must also fulfill the All-University Requirements, a common core of courses ranging from 41 to 54 credits in liberal studies. In addition, candidates for the B.A. degree must meet a foreign language requirement and select 28 credits of electives from areas of interest. Candidates for the B.S. degree must also satisfy the foreign language requirement and meet certain distribution requirements. Some of the professional B.S. degree programs enable students to develop a minor or a concentration in addition to the major. Students in these programs are allowed a minimum of 12 credits in electives.

Off-Campus Arrangements

Southern's growing list of internships enables its students to use the city as a laboratory for learning. For Southern's social work students, New Haven's urban environment adds immediacy and relevance to their classroom study. Similarly, students enrolled in Southern's B.S. degree program in nursing acquire firsthand clinical experience at Yale–New Haven Hospital and the Hospital of Saint Raphael (and can complete course work at area hospitals through a distance learning program taught on video), while journalism students pound the keyboards in city newsrooms and cover late-breaking news at local TV stations.

Academic Facilities

The University's thirty-building campus provides students with a full range of learning facilities. The Hilton C. Buley Library maintains 470,000 bound volumes and 5,700 periodical subscriptions. There are also 23,000 microfilm reels, 677,000 microfiche pieces, and 287,000 government documents. The lower level of the library is the site of a modern Macintosh lab, where students have access to thirty-four Macintosh SE terminals with laser printers and dot-matrix printers. The library also houses the Learning Resources Center, which features an education curriculum laboratory, a growing collection of audiotapes and videotapes, and the equipment necessary for individual viewing and study. The newest academic building on campus is Manson Van B. Jennings Hall, the University's $13.1-million science center. Jennings Hall contains sixty-six laboratories, a large amphitheater, classrooms, and the University's Academic Computer Center, which houses more than 100 computer workstations for student and faculty research. Other campus facilities include a journalism lab with a satellite dish that picks up wire-service stories, a modern television studio in Ralph Earl Hall of Fine Arts, and the John Lyman Center for the Performing Arts, which contains a 1,650-seat theater for major productions and the Robert Kendall Drama Lab for experimental theater.

Costs

Annual tuition and fees for 1999–2000 for Connecticut residents were $4029. Tuition and fees for out-of-state residents were $9707. On-campus room and board fees for the year totaled $5934. Books, supplies, and personal expenses averaged $2000 a year. All costs are subject to change without notice. Students should check with the Financial Aid Office for the most current information.

Financial Aid

The Financial Aid Office coordinates a number of programs. These programs, which include grants and scholarships, long-term low-interest loans, and part-time student employment, are based on the demonstrated financial need of students and their families. The University offers the Federal Perkins Loan, the Federal Pell Grant, the Federal Supplemental Educational Opportunity Grant, the Federal Stafford Student Loan, the Federal PLUS loan, and the Federal Work-Study Program. Southern also provides assistance through alumni scholarships. More than 40 percent of Southern's undergraduates receive some form of financial aid. Students interested in applying for assistance must complete the Free Application for Federal Student Aid (FAFSA) and send it to the central processor so that it is received by April 15. The Financial Aid Office also requires students to submit additional forms, including a University financial aid application. All required forms have deadlines and are available at the Financial Aid Office.

Faculty

Like its student body, Southern's faculty represents a wide range of backgrounds, interests, and scholarly achievements. Faculty members have a deep commitment to teaching and a serious dedication to writing and research. More than 50 percent of the 700 full- and part-time faculty members hold Ph.D.'s from major colleges and universities around the world. All courses at the University are taught by faculty members, many of whom also serve as academic advisers. In addition, the University offers counseling services to help students with academic, personal, and career decisions. The student-faculty ratio is 15:1.

Student Government

The Student Government is the voice of the undergraduate student body on the Southern campus. Consisting of 24 voting members who meet eight times each semester, the Student Government provides a means through which individual students working together can influence a wide range of areas, from funding issues to academic policy. Student Government members also serve with faculty members and administrators on a number of key University committees. Resident students govern themselves through their own residence hall councils and, collectively, through the Inter-Residence Council.

Admission Requirements

Southern's admission policy is selective. The University considers each student on an individual basis, giving special consideration to personal accomplishments and motivation. Southern seeks a student body that reflects a wide range of cultural values and backgrounds; no applicant is accepted or rejected because of race, color, gender, sexual orientation, age, disability, religion, or national origin. Candidates must be high school graduates or have received an equivalency diploma. Their secondary school program should include at least 13 academic units of college-preparatory work, including 4 years of English, 3 years of mathematics, 2 years of foreign language, 2 years of science (including 1 year of laboratory science), and 2 years of social sciences (including U.S. history). Other factors include the student's general high school record, rank in class (preferably in the upper half of the high school graduating class), and competitive SAT I scores.

Application and Information

Candidates for admission should apply by May of their senior year in high school. The Admissions Office mails its first notice of acceptance on December 1, and early applicants have priority for housing and financial aid. Applicants must submit previous academic records, including a complete transcript of high school grades and rank in class; an admission application; a $40 nonrefundable fee; a written recommendation from the high school principal, a teacher, or a guidance counselor; and an official copy of the SAT I report. To request application forms and further information, students should contact:

Sharon Brennan
Director of Admissions and Enrollment Management
Admissions House
Southern Connecticut State University
131 Farnham Avenue
New Haven, Connecticut 06515-1355
Telephone: 203-392-SCSU
          888-500-SCSU (toll-free)
World Wide Web: http://www.Southernct.edu

Southern's "Serie Metafisica XVIII" (1983), an outdoor sculpture by Herk Van Tongeren, provides the ideal setting for study in the sunshine.

SOUTHERN ILLINOIS UNIVERSITY CARBONDALE
CARBONDALE, ILLINOIS

The University

Southern Illinois University Carbondale (SIUC), chartered in 1869, is a comprehensive state-supported institution with nationally and internationally recognized instructional, research, and service programs.

SIUC is fully accredited by the North Central Association of Colleges and Schools.

SIUC offers more than 200 undergraduate majors, specializations, and minors; sixty master's degree programs; twenty-eight doctoral programs; and professional degrees in law and medicine. SIUC is a multicampus university and includes the SIUC School of Medicine at Springfield and a branch campus in Nakajo, Japan.

During the 1999–2000 academic year, SIUC's enrollment reached 17,829 undergraduate students, 3,762 graduate students, and 674 professional students. The average age of undergraduates who live on campus is 20; the average age of all undergraduates is 24.

Six percent of SIUC's enrolled students are international students. Of U.S. students, 14 percent are African American, .5 percent are Native American, 2 percent are Asian or Pacific Islander, and 2 percent are Hispanic. Of all SIUC students, 94 percent are from the U.S.

Students who are ready to start college but not ready to commit to a specific major can enroll in SIUC's Pre-Major Program. Premajor advisers and career counselors help premajor students plan their education and careers.

SIUC faculty members, staff members, and alumni help students arrange internships, cooperative education programs, and work-study programs.

Thirty percent of SIUC undergraduates live on campus. SIUC has three on-campus residential areas for single students. Each area includes a cafeteria, a post office, laundry facilities, and computer labs.

SIUC residence hall dining services provide nineteen meals per week with no limit on quantity at each meal. Optional meal plans are available. Meal hours are long enough to accommodate most schedules, but students with conflicts can arrange for take-out lunches or late plates. Dining services provide a variety of menus and a full-time dietitian to help students who have special dietary needs.

Off-campus housing includes many types of privately owned units, including residence halls, apartments, and houses; many are within easy walking distance of the campus.

SIUC intercollegiate sports teams compete at the NCAA Division I level (football is Division I-AA). Conference affiliations include the Missouri Valley and Gateway Conferences. Intercollegiate sports teams include men's and women's basketball, cross-country, diving, golf, swimming, tennis, and track and field; men's baseball and football; and women's softball and volleyball.

The campus holds various playfields, several tennis courts, and a campus lake with a beach and a boat dock. SIUC's Student Recreation Center houses an Olympic-size pool; indoor tracks; handball/racquetball and squash courts; a climbing wall; weight rooms; and basketball, volleyball, and tennis courts.

The Student Center contains a bookstore, several restaurants, and facilities for bowling and billiards. It is headquarters for SIUC's 450 student organizations and the student government office. On-campus events throughout the year include concerts, plays, festivals, guest speakers, and musicals.

Location

Carbondale is 6 hours south of Chicago, 2 hours southeast of St. Louis, and 3 hours north of Nashville. Four large recreational lakes, the two great rivers (the Mississippi and the Ohio), and the spectacular 270,000-acre Shawnee National Forest are within minutes of the campus. The mid-South climate is ideal for year-round outdoor activities.

Carbondale is a small city of 27,000 people that supports one large enclosed mall, several mini-malls, theaters, and restaurants. *Life in America's Small Cities* rated Carbondale the best small city in which to live in Illinois. Carbondale is among the ten cities in the U.S. with the lowest cost of living. Students frequent the shops and restaurants that line Illinois and Grand Avenues.

Majors and Degrees

The University offers associate in applied science degree programs at the College of Applied Sciences and Arts in aviation flight, aviation maintenance, dental technology, office systems and specialties, physical therapist assistant studies, and respiratory therapy technology.

The College of Applied Sciences and Arts offers bachelor's degree programs in advanced technical studies, architectural studies, automotive technology, aviation management, aviation technologies, dental hygiene, electronics management, fire science management, health-care management, information systems technologies, interior design, mortuary science and funeral service, physician assistant studies, and radiologic sciences.

The College of Agriculture offers bachelor's degree programs in agribusiness economics, animal science, food and nutrition, forestry, general agriculture, and plant and soil science. Minors include equine studies.

The College of Business and Administration offers bachelor's degree programs in accounting, business and administration, business economics, finance, management, and marketing.

The College of Education offers bachelor's degree programs in clothing and textiles, early childhood education, elementary education, health education, physical education, recreation, rehabilitation services, secondary education, social studies, social work, special education, and workforce education and development. Teacher preparation is available in art, biological sciences, English, French, German, history, mathematics, music, and Spanish. Minors are available in aquatics, athletic training, child and family services, and coaching.

The College of Engineering offers bachelor's degree programs in civil engineering, electrical engineering, mechanical engineering, mining engineering, engineering technology, and industrial technology.

The College of Liberal Arts offers bachelor's degrees in administration of justice, anthropology, art, classics, design, economics, English, foreign language and international trade, French, geography, German, history, linguistics, mathematics, music, paralegal studies, philosophy, political science, prelaw, psychology, Russian, sociology, Spanish, speech communication, theater, and university studies. Minors include African studies, Asian studies, Black American studies, Chinese, classical civilization, East Asian civilizations, Greek, Japanese, Latin, museum studies, and world literature.

The College of Mass Communication and Media Arts offers bachelor's degrees in cinema and photography, journalism, and radio-television.

The College of Science offers bachelor's degree programs in biological sciences, chemistry, computer science, geology, mathematics, microbiology, physics, physiology, plant biology, zoology, and preprofessional programs in dentistry, medicine, nursing, optometry, osteopathy, pharmacy, physical therapy, physician assistant studies, podiatry, and veterinary medicine.

An interdisciplinary minor is offered in environmental studies.

Academic Program

Each bachelor's degree candidate must earn a minimum of 120 semester hours of credit, including at least 60 at a senior-level institution and the last 30 at SIUC. Each student must maintain at least a C average in all course work at SIUC. Each student must fulfill the University core curriculum (41 semester hours) and the specific requirements of their degree programs. SIUC awards credit through qualifying extension and correspondence programs, military experience, the High School Advanced Placement Program, the College-Level Examination Program (CLEP), SIUC's proficiency examination program, and work experience.

SIUC offers honors course work and special recognition for students who demonstrate exceptional academic achievement. The Air Force and Army offer ROTC programs at SIUC.

The fall 2000 semester is from August 21 through December 15. The spring 2001 semester is from January 16 through May 12. Summer 2001 intersession is from June 11 through August 4. Students may begin most undergraduate programs in the fall, spring, or summer.

Off-Campus Arrangements

SIUC offers opportunities for undergraduate study in more than forty-four countries. SIUC students can fulfill University and major requirements while overseas. Many study-abroad courses are taught in English as well as in other languages.

SIUC offers students the opportunity to complete correspondence-type course work through its Individualized Learning Program.

SIUC offers Bachelor of Science degree programs at thirty-five military bases throughout the United States.

SIUC belongs to the Southern Illinois Collegiate Common Market and the Southwestern Illinois Higher Education Consortium and participates in a statewide initiative to use distance-learning technology to offer courses electronically at off-campus sites.

Academic Facilities

In addition to the 2.4 million volumes, 3.1 million microfilms, and 12,500 periodicals currently available in Morris Library, students and faculty members have access to 30,000 records, tapes, and CDs; 2,400 CD-ROMs; and forty-two online bibliographic services.

SIUC students have access to several computer learning centers that are equipped, in all, with more than 500 microcomputers.

Other facilities where students learn and practice include the Southern Illinois Airport; outdoor laboratories; the student-run *Daily Egyptian* newspaper, WSIU TV, WSIU FM, art and natural history museums, a literary magazine, McCleod Theater, a vivarium, the plant biology greenhouses, the University Farms, and the Touch of Nature Environmental Center.

Costs

Estimated 2000–01 tuition and fee charges for the academic year (fall and spring) for students enrolled in 15 or more semester hours are $4150 for Illinois residents and $7200 for out-of-state residents, including international students. Room and board are $4376. All costs are subject to change. The cost of books and school supplies varies among programs. The average cost is $600 per academic year. Some courses require that students purchase special materials.

All students need funds for such things as clothing, shampoo, movies, postage stamps, and transportation to and from home. Depending on a student's lifestyle and spending habits, such expenses can range from $2000 to $3000 per academic year.

Financial Aid

More than $137 million in financial aid was distributed to 20,173 SIUC students in fiscal year 1999 through federal, state, and institutionally funded financial aid programs.

To apply for financial aid at SIUC, students should complete a Free Application for Federal Student Aid (FAFSA). Applications that are filed before April 1 receive priority consideration for campus-based aid. The FAFSA can be completed electronically at the U.S. Department of Education's Web site (http://www.fafsa.ed.gov). When completing the FAFSA, students should list Southern Illinois University Carbondale (Federal School Code 001758) as a school of choice.

SIUC has one of the largest student employment programs in the country, with approximately 8,000 students employed each year in nearly a hundred job classifications.

SIUC offers competitive scholarships based on talent and academic achievement.

Faculty

Faculty members are dedicated to excellence in teaching and to their advancement of knowledge in a wide variety of disciplines and professions. Many faculty members are well-known both nationally and internationally for their varied research contributions. The undergraduate student-faculty ratio is 18:1. There are 241 full-time professors, 286 full-time associate professors, 274 full-time assistant professors, and 117 full-time instructors and lecturers. The total number of faculty members is 1,105.

Teaching assistants at SIUC are graduate students who assist faculty members in teaching. While some teach introductory undergraduate classes, others provide support to faculty members by assisting in laboratories, monitoring tests, and helping students.

Student Government

The undergraduate student government consists of a president, vice president, and chief of staff. Under the vice president, there are 38 senators: 2 senators per college, 2 per on-campus residential area, and 5 each on the east and west campuses. Under the chief of staff are 12 commissioners who represent the undergraduate student body on various University and city political bodies. The student government meets twice weekly and writes and passes legislation on University policies, funding, student organizations, and other matters that affect the students and the University.

Admission Requirements

Freshman applicants whose ACT or SAT score is at or above the 50th percentile or whose ACT or SAT score is at or above the 33rd percentile and whose class rank is in the upper half are admitted. Admission standards are subject to change. Freshman applicants must meet course pattern requirements: 4 years of English, 3 years of mathematics, 3 years of laboratory science, 3 years of social science, and 2 years of electives.

Transfer applicants must have an overall grade point average of at least 2.0 on a 4.0 scale, based on work attempted at all institutions and calculated by SIUC grading policies. Transfer applicants must also be eligible to continue at the last institution attended.

Some programs have higher admission requirements or require additional screening for admission. Undergraduates can apply on line (http://salukinet.siu.edu/admit/).

Application and Information

Admission is granted on a rolling basis. Some programs begin in fall only, and other programs reach enrollment capacity and close admission. For more information, students should contact:

New Student Admissions
Southern Illinois University Carbondale
Carbondale, Illinois 62901-4710

Telephone: 618-536-4405
Fax: 618-453-3250
E-mail: admrec@siu.edu
World Wide Web: http://www.siu.edu/siuc/

SOUTHERN METHODIST UNIVERSITY
DALLAS, TEXAS

The University

Southern Methodist University (SMU) recognizes that students preparing for life and leadership in the twenty-first century must be educated to meet the challenges of a changing world, intellectually equipped for lifelong learning, and prepared for specific careers. SMU provides this breadth of education through a comprehensive curriculum with a strong foundation in the humanities and sciences. Classroom learning is enhanced by opportunities for mentoring relationships, internships, leadership development, research experience, international study, and community service.

Founded in 1911 by what today is the United Methodist Church, SMU welcomes students of every religion, race, color, ethnic origin, and economic status. SMU students come from every state in the Union and from more than sixty countries. The total University enrollment is 10,038; 5,620 are undergraduates. The undergraduate male-female ratio is usually 1:1.

Breadth and diversity also characterize extracurricular activities. SMU offers nearly 150 student activities and organizations to help students build upon existing interests, establish new ones, and develop leadership skills.

The major groups sponsoring campuswide programs are the Student Senate, Student Foundation, Program Council, the Inter-Fraternity Council, and Panhellenic. SMU also has a large number of scholarship honoraries, including chapters of Mortar Board, Golden Key, and Phi Beta Kappa.

The University is a member of the National Collegiate Athletic Association and participates in the Western Athletic Conference Division I-A. Teams compete in basketball, cross-country, football, golf, soccer, swimming/diving, tennis, track, and women's volleyball.

SMU operates twelve residence halls in addition to apartments for single or married students. More than half of all residence hall rooms have been renovated since 1996, and plans exist to phase in renovations of all remaining spaces. First-year students are required to live in the residence halls unless they live with their parents or a spouse. Applications for housing should be submitted at the earliest possible date after receipt of an acceptance from the Office of Admission.

Location

Located 5 miles north of downtown Dallas, SMU offers the tranquility of a suburban campus and a pleasant year-round Sun Belt climate. Its location in the eighth-largest city in the United States also offers countless opportunities for internships, additional learning experiences, and future employment, since Dallas is a major national center in business, industry, finance, medicine, high technology, fashion, transportation, advertising, and filmmaking.

Majors and Degrees

To provide in-depth knowledge of specific fields, SMU offers more than seventy degrees through its four undergraduate schools. Dedman College, the school of humanities and sciences, offers a Bachelor of Arts (B.A.) degree with a major in any department of the College and a Bachelor of Science (B.S.) degree with a major in mathematics, a natural science, or selected social sciences. In addition, the College offers two part-time multidisciplinary evening degrees: the Bachelor of Humanities (B.Hum.) and the Bachelor of Social Science (B.Soc.Sci.). The Edwin L. Cox School of Business awards the Bachelor of Business Administration (B.B.A.) degree. The Meadows School of the Arts awards the Bachelor of Fine Arts (B.F.A.) in art, art history, dance, and theater; the Bachelor of Arts (B.A.) in advertising, art history, cinema, journalism, music, public relations, and television/radio; and the Bachelor of Music (B.M.) degrees. The School of Engineering and Applied Science offers a Bachelor of Arts (B.A.) degree in computer science and a Bachelor of Science (B.S.) degree in these eight fields: computer engineering, computer science, electrical engineering, (with biomedical engineering option), environmental engineering, environmental science, management science, mechanical engineering, and telecommunications.

Academic Program

All first-year students enter Dedman College of Humanities and Sciences, which provides the general education curriculum, which is designed to help students develop the skills of analysis and expression, the ability to explore ethical issues, and a broad understanding of the world. The general education curriculum includes courses in such categories as cultural formations, perspectives, human diversity, and information technology. Students who know their career interest can select courses in their planned major while in Dedman College and can transfer to one of the other colleges after two or four semesters. Students majoring in the humanities, mathematics, the natural sciences, and the social or behavioral sciences remain in Dedman College. Requirements for graduation vary according to the major program.

SMU grants both credit and advanced placement for satisfactory completion of Advanced Placement courses in high school. Credit of 3 to 6 semester hours is given for each course in which a score of 4 or 5 was earned on the Advanced Placement examinations of the College Board. Three to 6 hours of credit can be granted for AP math. Twelve to 14 hours of credit can be granted for foreign languages with a score of 4 or 5. In addition, SMU gives credit for departmental examinations in some of its own departments. Credit is also awarded for scores of 5, 6, or 7 on higher level exams in transferable subjects for the International Baccalaureate. A maximum of 32 credits can be awarded. Credit is not awarded for subsidiary level exams.

The academic year at SMU is composed basically of two semesters, plus an optional summer session that comprises two 5-week terms. A May term is also available.

Off-Campus Arrangements

Study-abroad programs are available in Great Britain, France, Spain, Austria, Denmark, Italy, Japan, Mexico, Russia, Australia, Beijing, and Southeast Asia.

Academic Facilities

A new fund-raising campaign provides resources for academic initiatives, including the construction of several new buildings. Among them are the Dedman Life Sciences Building, a new engineering facility, the Blanton Student Services Building, and an addition to the Fondren Library Center.

The libraries of the University contain more than 3 million volumes. Fondren Library, the largest of the four principal libraries, contains a catalog of all holdings and major works of a general nature. Other collections are located in the Science Information Center, the Underwood Law Library, the Bridwell Library (a component of Perkins School of Theology), Hamon Arts Library, DeGolyer Library, and the Business Information Center.

Southern Methodist University has laboratories and equipment for classes in accounting, anthropology, art, biology, chemistry, computer science, foreign languages, geology, health and physical education, journalism, management sciences, physics, psychology, statistics, theater, and computer, electrical, and mechanical engineering. The biology, chemistry, geology, and physics laboratories are in the Fondren Science Building. Specialized laboratories include the Dallas Seismological Observatory and the electron microscopy laboratory. The Institute for the Study of Earth and Man, established for the study of present and past human environments, houses specialized laboratories for archaeology, ethnology, geology, and physical anthropology. The institute is located in Heroy Science Hall on the SMU campus.

The University owns numerous original works of art, which are distributed throughout the campus. On view in the Meadows Museum are important collections of Spanish paintings, including major examples by Juan de Borgoña, Velázquez, Zurbarán, Ribera, Murillo, and Goya and a representative selection of nineteenth- and twentieth-century artists, including Picasso, Juan Gris, and Miró.

Costs

The comprehensive cost for full-time undergraduate students for the 1999–2000 academic year was $25,411. This amount included tuition and fees totaling $18,510, a room charge of $3881, and a board charge of $3020.

Financial Aid

Seventy percent of all SMU undergraduates receive some type of financial aid. The University assists all qualified students who cannot afford the cost of an SMU education. Financial aid decisions are based on academic performance and financial need. The SMU financial aid program includes University, state, and federal scholarships; grants; loans; and part-time jobs. Students interested in financial aid who are accepted for admission at SMU must file the Free Application for Federal Student Aid (FAFSA). Students must apply for merit-based scholarships by January 15. It is highly recommended that students apply for need-based assistance by February 1 to receive primary consideration for aid.

Faculty

Classes are generally small, providing an opportunity for students to interact with faculty members. Most undergraduate classes (74 percent) are taught by regular, full-time faculty members. The number of full-time faculty members is 502.

Student Government

The SMU Student Senate is a comprehensive governing body that initiates and facilitates action on student affairs. Legislation is drafted and implemented within the University setting. The complex organizational structure consists of 4 student body officers, 40 senators, and ten committees. Meetings are held weekly.

Admission Requirements

The Office of Admission bases selection of applicants on several criteria: the high school program and the grades received, SAT I or ACT scores, recommendations, an essay, and any other information about the student that is available. Applicants should have a good record in a college-preparatory program and are expected to complete a minimum of 4 years of English; 3 of mathematics, including algebra I and II and plane geometry; 3 of a natural science (2 of these being a lab science); 3 of social studies; and 2 of a foreign language. However, SMU is concerned with more than statistics about students; in the consideration of an applicant, a value is placed on personal accomplishment, and an attempt is made to get to know the person behind the scores and the grades. Testing needs to be completed as soon as possible in the senior year.

As a privately endowed institution, SMU has no limits on enrollment based solely on geography, and it makes no distinctions in tuition, fees, or other costs based on the home state of the student. The University is open to applicants without regard to race, color, ethnic or national origin, creed, or gender.

Application and Information

Students should apply soon after completing the junior year of high school. SMU processes applications for the fall semester under three plans. For early action, the application deadline is November 1, the notification date is December 30, and the student reply date is May 1. For regular decision, the application deadline is January 15, the notification date is March 15, and the student reply date is May 1. All applications received and completed after January 15 and before April 1 are reviewed on a rolling admission basis; notification begins after April 1. Students who wish to apply for admission to the University may obtain an application by contacting:

Division of Enrollment Services
Southern Methodist University
Box 750181
Dallas, Texas 75275-0181
Telephone: 214-SMU-2058
           800-323-0672 (toll-free)
E-mail: enroll_serv@mail.smu.edu

Dallas Hall is the landmark building of SMU, reflecting the neo-Georgian architecture of the campus.

SOUTHERN OREGON UNIVERSITY
ASHLAND, OREGON

The University

Southern Oregon University, founded in 1869, is a public institution with a private-college feel. The University provides its 5,341 undergraduate students with a well-rounded liberal arts and sciences education with opportunities for hands-on experience.

Students are attracted to the University because of its size, beautiful mountainous location, excellent academic programs, dynamic cultural environment, and diverse student body. The institution offers bachelor's degrees in thirty-seven majors, forty-six minors, and seventeen preprofessional programs. One of the few universities in the U.S. to offer an Accelerated Baccalaureate Degree Program, Southern offers motivated, goal-oriented students an opportunity to complete a bachelor's degree in three years. The University emphasizes undergraduate education but also offers master's degrees in arts and letters, elementary education, secondary education, environmental education, management, science, and social science.

The size of the campus allows for a personalized education. The average class size of 25 students encourages discussion and interaction among students and faculty members. Courses are taught by faculty members rather than graduate teaching assistants. Faculty members are easily accessible to students and provide opportunities for research, internships, practicums, and other educational experiences beyond the classroom. Seventy-eight percent of the student body is from Oregon. Twenty-two percent of the student population is out-of-state. Student members of minority groups comprise 8.3 percent of the student body and there are approximately 150 international students from more than thirty-two countries.

SOU offers an impressive variety of extracurricular activities, clubs, and organizations. The University's newspaper; literary publication; honor societies; social issue groups; social clubs; and religious, preprofessional, international, and academic organizations provide students with opportunities for involvement. Extreme sports, including sky diving, bungee jumping, rock climbing, kayaking, and mountain bike racing are very popular. More than 40 percent of the student body participates in intramural sports and many compete in intercollegiate club sports, including skiing (Northern California Intercollegiate Conference), soccer, swimming, tennis, water polo, rugby, shotokan, baseball, softball, and men's tennis. The University is a member of NAIA. Women's varsity sports include basketball, cross-country, tennis, track and field, and volleyball. Women's junior varsity sports include soccer and softball. Men's varsity sports include basketball, cross-country, football, track and field, and wrestling.

The campus is a culturally dynamic, stimulating environment. Annual music concerts bring world-class musicians and performers to the campus. The theater department has two seasons and performs before capacity crowds. Music groups include the chamber choir, chamber ensemble, instrumental jazz ensemble, symphonic wind ensemble, vocal jazz, vocal jazz annex, Rogue Valley symphony, and opera workshop. Five art galleries feature the work of students; faculty members; and locally, nationally, and internationally acclaimed artists, and the International Writer Series attracts recognized writers, poets, and novelists from around the world.

Approximately 25 percent of the student body lives in one of thirteen residence halls or in the newly constructed family housing units. Freshmen are required to live on campus. The majority of students living off campus live in the immediate surrounding area. The Residence Life Program won the School of the Year award for three years in the Pacific region for excellence in the quality of life provided. The track; the football field; volleyball, basketball, and tennis courts; climbing walls; a large swimming pool; dance studios; and the student fitness center are all nearby. The Cascade Food Court is open from 7 a.m. to 10 p.m. and offers a variety of food choices for every range of tastes.

The University's Student ACCESS Center houses student support services, including counseling services, academic advising, career advising, disabled student services, a learning center, testing center, and tutorial programs.

Location

Ashland is known for its beautiful forested setting and commitment to the arts. Home of the Oregon Shakespeare Festival, the town of 19,000 draws 385,000 visitors each year to enjoy the lively downtown, exquisite Lithia Park, and abundant theater, music events, and other cultural happenings. The Ashland area has five fairs, thirteen festivals, twenty-five art galleries, and twenty-four museums. The town itself has 60 lodging facilities and 80 restaurants. Colorful flags and banners announcing events create a festive environment and the many boutiques, cafes, coffee shops, movie theaters, and bookstores create an ideal environment for college students. Mt. Ashland and the Siskiyou mountains serve as the town's backdrop and offer downhill skiing, cross-country skiing, hiking, and mountain biking. The Cascade Mountains, Rogue and Klamath Rivers, Crater Lake National Park, and numerous lakes are an easy drive and offer world-class white water, camping, hiking, sailing, kayaking, and rock climbing.

Majors and Degrees

The University is organized into four schools: Arts and Letters; Business; Sciences; and Social Science, Education, Health, and Physical Education. Bachelor of Arts and Bachelor of Science (B.A. and B.S.) degrees are available in the following majors: anthropology, art, arts and letters, biology, business administration† (accounting; hotel, restaurant, and resort management; management; marketing), business–chemistry*, business–mathematics*, business–music*, business–physics*, chemistry, communication† (human communication, journalism, or mass media), computer science†, criminology, economics†, English, environmental studies*, geography†, geology, health and physical education, history, interdisciplinary studies, international studies*, language and culture, mathematics†, mathematics–computer science*, music, nursing (with Oregon Health Sciences University), physics, political science†, psychology, science*, social science*, sociology, Spanish†, and theater arts. Bachelor of Fine Arts (B.F.A.) degrees are available in art and theater. (An * indicates interdisciplinary programs; majors with a † offer the Accelerated Degree option.) Preprofessional programs include agriculture, chiropractic medicine, dental hygiene, dentistry, engineering, law, medical technology, medicine, nursing, occupational therapy, optometry, pharmacy, physical therapy, physician's assistant studies, podiatry, range management and conservation, theology, and veterinary medicine.

Minors include Africa–Middle East history; American history; anthropology; applied multimedia studies; art; art history; Asian history; biology; British literature; business administration; chemistry; computer science; creative writing; criminology; economics; education; European history; French; geography; geology; German; history of women and minorities; hotel, restaurant, and resort management; human communication; interdisciplinary ethics; international peace studies; journalism; language and writing; Latin American history; mass media studies; mathematics; military science; music; Native American studies; philosophy; photography; physics; political science; printmaking; psychology; remote sensing; sociology; Spanish; studio art; theater arts; U.S. literature; video production; and women's studies.

Academic Program

Students are required to complete general education requirements in addition to the major requirements. The general education requirements provide students with effective communication, critical judgement, and research skills and cultivate an awareness of the social, artistic, cultural, and scientific traditions of civilization. The required freshman colloquium provides a solid foundation in the areas of reading, writing, communication, and critical thinking. Class size is limited to 25 students and the Colloquium professor also serves as an adviser. Students in a four-year bachelor's program must have a minimum of 180 quarter credits to graduate. Students admitted to the selective Accelerated Baccalaureate Degree Program complete between 135 and 150 quarter credits to graduate.

Off-Campus Arrangements

Southern Oregon University offers a wide variety of study-abroad and overseas internship opportunities. The University also participates in National Student Exchange, which allows students to attend any of 140 colleges and universities nationwide and pay resident tuition. The University is a member of the Western Undergraduate Exchange and offers selected programs to residents of Alaska, Arizona, Colorado, Hawaii, Idaho, Montana, Nevada, New Mexico, North Dakota, South Dakota, Utah, Washington, and Wyoming at 150 percent of the cost of in-state tuition and fees.

Academic Facilities

The library is open 78 hours a week each term and contains 280,000 volumes in the general collection. The University is a member of Orbis, a unified library catalog that provides students with access to 5 million books, sound recordings, films, video tapes, and more.

Students have extensive access to computers and software on SOU's campus. The Computing Services Center lab is open more than 81 hours a week and houses 170 Windows PCs and forty-one PowerMacs that are free for student use. A new multimedia lab and computer labs in departments across campus offer additional resources. The residence halls also have three computer labs, and most rooms are wired for computer access. Students also have e-mail accounts and access to the Internet free of charge.

Jefferson Public Radio, one of the nation's largest public radio stations, and award-winning Rogue Valley Community Television offer students important opportunities to work as producers, editors, directors, and equipment operators.

Costs

Resident tuition and fees for the 2000–01 academic year are $3234. Nonresident and international student tuition and fees are $10,191. Tuition and fees for participants in the Western Undergraduate Exchange are $4500. Room and board costs, including a double room and the middle meal plan, are $4821.

Financial Aid

Financial aid is available in the form of grants, loans, and/or work-study. Sixty-five percent of freshmen who enrolled in fall 1999 received some form of financial aid. Students must file the Free Application for Federal Student Aid (FAFSA) to qualify. To be considered for financial aid at Southern Oregon University, students must have applied to the University for admission and have indicated the institution as one of their first six choices on the FAFSA. Students should mail the FAFSA by February 1 to receive maximum consideration for fall. The University offers merit and diversity scholarships to new freshmen and transfer students. Additional scholarships are available through departments and the Office of Financial Aid. For more information, students should contact the Financial Aid Office at 541-552-6161. For those seeking employment, the Student Employment Office lists the work-study and regular jobs available on and off campus.

Faculty

Every class and lab is taught by faculty members; 93 percent have a Ph.D. or the highest degree in their field. There are 187 full-time faculty members. The primary emphasis of the faculty is on teaching and advising undergraduate students. Faculty members frequently include undergraduates in research projects and many students have coauthored papers and made joint presentations at national conferences. The student-to-faculty ratio of 18:1 enables faculty members to get to know their student advisees on a first-name basis, help individualize their academic programs, and meet their interests and needs. Every student is assigned an adviser when they declare a major.

Student Government

The Associated Students' governing body implements policies, makes budget recommendations, and participates in the allocation of more than $1.4 million each year to various clubs and organizations. They also work with the Oregon Student Lobby on issues important in higher education. Elected, appointed, and volunteer positions offer students valuable leadership experience and the opportunity to contribute significantly to the institution and its governance.

Admission Requirements

Applicants for freshman admission must have achieved a 2.75 cumulative high school GPA or a minimum combined score of 1010 on the SAT I, or an ACT composite score of 21. In addition, applicants must have completed the following high school course requirements: 4 years of English, 3 years of mathematics (including geometry, algebra I, and algebra II), 3 years of social science, 2 years of science (1 of which must have a lab), and 2 years of one foreign language. Students transferring from an accredited college or university must earn 36 quarter credits of transfer-level credit with a minimum 2.25 GPA and meet the language requirement (if a high school graduate of 1997 or later). Transfer applicants with fewer than 36 quarter credits must also meet the freshman admission requirements. Applicants to the selective Accelerated Baccalaureate Degree Program must have a 3.4 minimum high school GPA, a combined score of 1150 on the SAT I (with a minimum score of 500 on the verbal and math sections), or an ACT score of 25 (with a minimum score of 22 on the math and English sections). They must also meet the freshman subject requirements.

Application and Information

Applicants must submit an application with a $50 nonrefundable application fee and official transcripts from each high school and/or university or college attended. Freshmen must submit official SAT I or ACT scores. Students may apply after September 1 for the following academic year. Admission is rolling, but the priority deadline for the fall is June 1.

A campus visit is encouraged. Tours are offered Monday through Friday at 10 a.m. and 2 p.m. at the Office of Admissions. Overnight stays in the residence halls are possible Monday through Thursday. For a tour or more information, students should write or call:

Southern Oregon University
Office of Admissions
1250 Siskiyou Boulevard
Ashland, Oregon 97520
Telephone: 541-552-6411
    800-482-7672 (toll-free in Oregon and
               area codes 916, 707, and 530)
E-mail: admissions@sou.edu
World Wide Web: http://www.sou.edu

SOUTHERN POLYTECHNIC STATE UNIVERSITY
MARIETTA, GEORGIA

The University

Southern Polytechnic State University (SPSU), a residential university located in Marietta, Georgia, offers bachelor's and master's degrees. Long recognized for its engineering technology and science-related programs, the University has steadily expanded its offerings to include arts and sciences, management, and the only nationally accredited Bachelor of Architecture degree in the University System of Georgia.

Southern Polytechnic enrolls 3,800 students from thirty-nine states and eighty-five countries who attend day and evening classes. An active international student association represents 350 students. Student life includes about fifty professional, student government, student media, and Greek organizations, as well as recreational and intramural sports such as softball, flag football, swimming, and golf. Students compete in the National Association of Intercollegiate Athletics in basketball, baseball, and tennis.

The University offers the Bachelor of Architecture degree; the Bachelor of Science degree in fifteen majors, ranging from civil engineering technology to manufacturing to physics; and the Bachelor of Arts degree in five majors. The Master of Science degree is offered in computer science, construction, engineering technology (electrical concentration), information technology, management, quality assurance, software engineering, and technical and professional communications.

Founded in 1948 as a school that offered two-year programs as part of Georgia Tech, Southern Polytechnic was named as a senior college in 1970. It became independent of Georgia Tech in 1980 and began offering master's degrees in 1986. It was named Southern Polytechnic State University in July 1996.

Fitness and wellness facilities feature tennis, basketball, and racquetball courts; baseball, soccer, and flag football fields; jogging tracks; and swimming and aerobics facilities.

Location

Located in one of the fastest-growing areas of the state, Southern Polytechnic is about 20 minutes from downtown Atlanta in Marietta, Georgia. The Cobb County campus sits on 232 acres of wooded property, 90 acres of which are developed.

Majors and Degrees

The Bachelor of Science degree is offered in apparel/textile engineering technology, civil engineering technology, computer engineering technology, computer science, construction, electrical engineering technology, industrial distribution, industrial engineering technology, management, manufacturing, mathematics, mechanical engineering technology, physics, surveying and mapping, technical and professional communications, and telecommunications.

The Bachelor of Arts is offered in computer science, management, mathematics, physics, and technical and professional communications.

The University also offers a nationally accredited Bachelor of Architecture, a five-year professional architecture program.

Academic Program

Southern Polytechnic State University in Marietta is a campus of the University System of Georgia. It is a teaching institution dedicated to excellence in the promotion of the intellectual, technological, and economic enhancement of the state, region, and nation.

The academic year consists of two semesters and a summer term.

Academic advising is mandatory and is available in the academic department in which the major has been declared. Special advising is provided in the professional areas of engineering, law, and medicine, and career counseling is available through the Office of Career Services.

Academic Facilities

Several centers of excellence bring recognition to the University, including the W. Clair Harris Apparel and Textile Center. The University is the site of Georgia's only NASA Teacher Resource Center, which provides K–12 teachers with instructional materials. It also serves as the headquarters of the Georgia Youth Science and Technology Centers, which boosts interest in science and technology among elementary and middle school teachers and students across the state. The University's Center for Quality Excellence helps organizations implement total quality management.

Costs

Undergraduate Georgia residents attended the University at a cost of $2150 for tuition for the 1999–2000 academic year. The cost of books was approximately $750, and the cost of a room was approximately $2000. Out-of-state students paid an additional tuition fee of $5500 per year.

Financial Aid

During the 1998–99 academic year, approximately 90 percent of the University's students received in excess of $10.5 million in student aid funds through the University and through federal student aid sources. Financial assistance includes loans, scholarships, part-time employment, and such federal programs as the Pell Grant, the Supplemental Educational Opportunity Grant, the Work-Study Program, and the Perkins Loan.

Freshmen who are residents of Georgia may be eligible for the Georgia HOPE scholarship if they have graduated from an eligible Georgia high school and have filed the U.S. Department of Education Free Application for Federal Student Aid (FAFSA).

Applications for financial aid are accepted at any time, but those received by March 15 for the following year are given priority. SPSU uses the FAFSA to determine financial need.

Faculty

The primary mission of Southern Polytechnic is to be a teaching institution, and the faculty's primary interests lie in this area. Areas in which faculty members excel are commitment to teaching and remaining up-to-date in their respective fields through research and consulting. Faculty members have been recruited from a variety of educational institutions throughout the United States.

Student Government

The Student Government Association (SGA) at Southern Polytechnic has traditionally played an important role in student life. Each spring, campuswide elections are held to elect the president, vice president, secretary/treasurer, and the 10-member Student Council. The student government represents the student body on important campus issues, is involved in campus projects, and has members assigned to various committees of the institution. The Student Government Association, through its various committees and projects, provides an excellent leadership opportunity for interested students.

Admission Requirements

Students who are considering Southern Polytechnic should have completed the following college-preparatory courses: English (4 years), mathematics (3 years), science (3 years), social science (3 years), and foreign language (2 years), plus two additional academic credits. Freshman applicants must submit official SAT I or ACT scores and high school transcripts with a minimum GPA of 2.0 on a 4.0 scale.

Transfer applicants who have fewer than 30 transferable semester hours must have a minimum college GPA of 2.0 and must meet the freshman admission requirements. Students with 30 or more transferable semester hours must have a minimum GPA of 2.0.

Application and Information

Applications for admission are accepted as early as one year prior to the anticipated date of enrollment. A nonrefundable application fee is charged. For an application form and more information, students should contact:

Office of Admissions
Southern Polytechnic State University
1100 South Marietta Parkway
Marietta, Georgia 30060
Telephone: 770-528-7281
              800-635-3204 (toll-free)
E-mail: admissions@spsu.edu
World Wide Web: http://www.spsu.edu

SOUTHERN VERMONT COLLEGE
BENNINGTON, VERMONT

The College

Southern Vermont College's philosophy begins with a deep belief in the potential of every individual. The College is committed to offering a career-oriented liberal arts education to a student body from diverse academic backgrounds. The College places an emphasis on serving students who have yet to fulfill their potential, ensuring accessibility to those with extra needs, financial and academic, who are serious about bettering their lives through higher education.

Southern Vermont College is located on a 371-acre campus at the base of Mount Anthony. The main College building, the former Everett mansion, is of English-Norman architecture and is patterned after mansions of the fourteenth century. The expansive twenty-seven-room building has been converted into classrooms, administrative offices, and the library. The five coed residence halls offer housing for all freshmen and other students who wish to live on campus. The nearly 600 students can major in any of the bachelor's and associate degree programs listed below. A student-faculty ratio of 11:1 and small classes allow for maximum interaction. Special academic options include an honors program, internships, and independent studies. Unique opportunities for study abroad also exist. Southern Vermont College is accredited by the New England Association of Schools and Colleges.

Southern Vermont College has intercollegiate sports with teams competing at the NCAA Division III level. The College is also a member of the Great Northeast Athletic Conference (GNAC). Intercollegiate programs include men's and women's basketball, cross-country, and soccer, as well as men's baseball and women's softball. Beginning in 2000–01, women's volleyball will be offered as a club-level sport, with its inclusion in Division III intercollegiate programs beginning in 2001–02. Many students participate in the numerous clubs, intramural sports, student government activities, publications, and theater programs available.

Location

Bennington, an historic New England town with a population of 19,000, is located in the heart of the Green Mountains tucked away in the southwest corner of the state. Bennington borders both New York and Massachusetts, and is a 1-hour drive from Albany and 3½ hours from Boston and New York City. The College is central to both prime ski country and the performing arts. Ten major ski resorts, along with the performing arts centers of Tanglewood, Saratoga, and Williamstown, are within 2 hours. Opportunities for hiking, cross-country skiing, and mountain biking are right outside one's campus room door.

Majors and Degrees

Southern Vermont College offers the baccalaureate degree with concentrations in accounting, business administration, child development, communications, creative writing and literature, criminal justice, English, environmental studies, hospitality/resort management, human services, liberal arts, liberal arts/management, nursing, prelaw, and psychology. Associate degree programs are offered in accounting, business, child development, criminal justice, environmental studies, hospitality/resort management, human services, liberal arts, liberal arts leading to secondary education licensure, and nursing.

Academic Program

The academic programs at Southern Vermont College challenge students to think independently and creatively. The College uses active learning to foster student growth with strong academic preparation and experiential learning. Virtually every academic program requires or recommends a practicum or internship experience. Southern Vermont College specializes in the development of management skills in some of the baccalaureate degree programs. The "management core," which consists of six to eight courses, is designed to provide graduates with the expertise to assume entry-level and midlevel management positions. In addition, students may design an individualized major with the help of faculty advisers. Baccalaureate degree candidates must successfully complete 120 semester hours of credit in the selected program of study; those studying for the associate degree must complete 60 semester hours of credit.

Common to all academic programs is the completion of the Liberal Arts General Core Curriculum. Included in the 42-hour general core requirements for the baccalaureate degree are courses in composition, communication, computers, economics, mathematics, professional ethics, environmental issues, and history or government as well as courses from each of the following three clusters: natural sciences, social sciences, and humanities. For the associate degree, the general core requirements include courses in composition, computers, and mathematics as well as courses from each of the following three clusters: natural sciences, social sciences, and humanities.

In order to identify initial skill levels, all incoming students are tested in math and English. Students needing extra help may receive free tutoring through the College tutorial office and writing center. Each semester students meet with their faculty advisers to select a group of courses from their major field, the general core, the minor concentration, and/or electives.

Credit is transferred from all accredited colleges and universities. Transfer credits are applied to fulfill degree requirements if the grade earned was C or better. Students may transfer up to 45 credits for the associate degree and up to 90 credits for the bachelor's degree (but no more than 66 credits of 100- and 200-level courses). Through the College's Life Experience Program, credits may be awarded for life and work experience.

The Learning Disabilities Program at Southern Vermont College offers a highly supportive environment for students with special educational needs. Students who participate in the program are offered a wide range of support services tailored to their individual needs.

The academic year consists of fall and spring semesters and a variety of summer sessions that last from four to twelve weeks.

Academic Facilities

The library contains more than 26,000 volumes of reading and research material and 1,500 periodicals, newspapers, and government documents that have been carefully selected to support the academic programs. The College laboratory provides the necessary facilities and support equipment for the study of the natural sciences. The computer center, which is located next to the residence halls, is accessible 24 hours a day.

Costs

Tuition for the 2000–01 academic year is $10,990. Room and board charges are $5680 for the academic year. There are no mandatory fees, but certain optional fees may apply. Students should budget approximately $1200 for books and supplies for the year.

Financial Aid

Southern Vermont College is committed to meeting the demonstrated financial needs of motivated students who are unable to meet college costs with their own or their families' earnings, savings, or assets. In order to be considered for aid, a student must file the Free Application for Federal Student Aid (FAFSA) and the Southern Vermont College Financial Aid Application. The College participates in a variety of federal, state, and local financial aid programs, including the Federal Pell Grant, Federal Supplemental Opportunity Educational Grant, and Federal Work-Study programs; various student loan programs; state grant programs; and the Southern Vermont College Opportunity Grant program. Of first-year students, 88 percent receive some form of financial aid. The average financial aid package is nearly $12,000, with an average gift-based award of $7700. Students are encouraged to research state, community, and private organizations for additional funding sources.

Faculty

The 21 full-time and 40 part-time faculty members at Southern Vermont College enrich classes through the personal association with each student. Knowing a student academically as well as on a personal level outside the classroom is just one of the reasons for the College's extraordinary retention rate. The current student-faculty ratio is 15:1.

Student Government

The College's philosophy is aimed at providing each student with the opportunity to cultivate civic awareness and to develop responsible attitudes through involvement at all levels of institutional policy discussion and decision making. Central to this process is the Student Association, which coordinates the activities of the student body.

Admission Requirements

Applicants are evaluated not only on the basis of their academic performance, but also on potential for achievement in college. While test scores, grades, and rank in class all play an important part in the selection of the freshman class, other factors, such as recommendations, extracurricular activities, and the essay, are also important in gauging a student's potential. Southern Vermont College also has a program for the learning disabled. Students who are interested in the Disabilities Program should contact the Disabilities Coordinator for more information.

Application and Information

Southern Vermont College follows a rolling admission policy. To be considered for admission, students must submit a completed application form with a $30 fee; scores on the ACT, the SAT I, or the Southern Vermont College Placement Tests; an official transcript from their high school and any colleges previously attended; at least two recommendations from teachers, guidance counselors, employers, or civic officials; and a 300-word essay. While a tour and interview are not required at Southern Vermont College, students are encouraged to visit the campus and meet with an admissions counselor.

For more information about Southern Vermont College, students should contact:

Admissions Office
Southern Vermont College
982 Mansion Road
Bennington, Vermont 05201
Telephone: 800-378-2782 (toll-free)
E-mail: admis@svc.edu
World Wide Web: http://www.svc.edu

The Everett mansion houses the main administrative offices, classrooms, and the library at Southern Vermont College.

SOUTHWEST MISSOURI STATE UNIVERSITY
SPRINGFIELD, MISSOURI

The University

A short walk across the tree-covered Springfield campus of Southwest Missouri State University (SMSU) reveals high-tech classroom buildings, nationally acclaimed residence halls, and comfortable, quiet places to visit with friends and professors. Energetic students and friendly faculty members attest to the spirit and vitality of this major university.

More than 16,800 students, 54 percent women and 46 percent men, have come to SMSU from throughout Missouri, forty-nine other states, and more than seventy countries. Full-time students represent 85 percent of the total enrollment. Of the eight colleges within the University, the College of Business Administration enrolls the largest number of students, followed by the College of Health and Human Services, the College of Arts and Letters, the College of Education, the College of Natural and Applied Sciences, and the College of Humanities and Public Affairs.

The University's primary focus is on undergraduate education, and more than 80 percent of the students are seeking undergraduate degrees. Experienced faculty members teach courses at all levels. SMSU also offers graduate programs leading to a master's degree in thirty-seven fields as well as the Specialist in Education degree.

In 1995, SMSU was granted a statewide mission in public affairs by the Missouri legislature. Through this mission the University is committed to preparing students for success not only in their chosen career fields but also in their lifelong careers as citizens and leaders. This is accomplished through the curriculum, optional service-learning courses, special lectures and forums, and other opportunities to develop a greater understanding of the issues facing society. The John Templeton Foundation has named SMSU to its Honor Roll for Character-Building Colleges, a designation that recognizes colleges and universities that emphasize character building as an integral part of the college experience.

The University has more than 250 student organizations, including social, service, religious, political, and departmental organizations. There is an extensive intramural and recreational sports program. SMSU is a member of NCAA Division I and participates in men's intercollegiate baseball, basketball, cross-country, football (Division I-AA), golf, indoor and outdoor track, soccer, swimming, and tennis. NCAA Division I women's sports include basketball, cross-country, field hockey, golf, softball, swimming, tennis, track and field, and volleyball.

The University is accredited by the North Central Association of Colleges and Schools and has additional accreditation by the AACSB–The International Association for Management Education; the National Association of Schools of Music; the National League for Nursing Accrediting Commission; the American Chemical Society; the Council on Social Work Education; the Computing Sciences Accreditation Board; the National Recreation and Park Association; the American Association for Leisure and Recreation; the American Home Economics Association; the National Athletic Trainers Association; the American Speech, Language, and Hearing Association; the National Council on Education for the Deaf; and the American Dietetics Association.

Location

Springfield, a city of 150,000, is Missouri's third-largest city and one of the fastest growing in the country. Located in Ozark Mountain country, one of the most popular entertainment, vacation, and resort areas in the nation, Springfield is within an hour's drive of several major lakes (Table Rock, Taneycomo, Stockton, Pomme de Terre, and Bull Shoals). SMSU students may take advantage of the cultural and career opportunities of the metropolitan area surrounding the University and still enjoy many outdoor recreational activities in the Ozarks.

Majors and Degrees

SMSU offers more than 140 programs of study in forty-two academic departments. Preprofessional programs in many fields are also available. The academic departments are accountancy; agriculture; antiquities; art and design; biology; biomedical sciences; chemistry; communication sciences and disorders; communications and mass media; computer information systems; computer science; consumer and family studies; defense and strategic studies; early childhood, elementary, and middle school education; economics; English; finance and general business; geography, geology, and planning; gerontology; health, physical education, and recreation; history; library science; management; marketing and quantitative analysis; mathematics; military science; modern and classical languages; music; nursing; philosophy; physics, astronomy, and materials science; political science; psychology; reading and special education; religious studies; secondary education, foundations, and educational technology; social work; sociology and anthropology; sports medicine and athletic training; technology; and theater and dance. Individualized majors are available through the University College.

Academic Program

A fall semester and a spring semester constitute the academic year; a summer session is also offered. All students take a base of 43 to 54 semester hours of general education courses in English, mathematics, speech, physical well-being, American studies, the natural world, culture and society, and self-understanding. A bachelor's degree requires 125 semester hours. Each degree program has specific course requirements and may require certain minimum grade point averages.

In addition to the traditional classroom experiences, SMSU offers one of the largest cooperative education programs in the Midwest, Army ROTC, practicums and internships, interactive video courses, and special-topics courses. A highly successful Honors College has attracted significant numbers of high-achieving students.

Students may receive credit by examination for selected subjects through the Advanced Placement (AP) Program, the International Baccalaureate (IB) Program, and the College-Level Examination Program (CLEP), as well as through departmental examinations.

Off-Campus Arrangements

SMSU is a member of the International Student Exchange Program (ISEP) and the National Student Exchange (NSE). A semester-abroad program, based in London, is offered to SMSU students for credit. Students may also take a great variety of short-term study tours for credit. In the past, these tours have visited China, England, Russia, and Spain.

Field studies are a required part of many academic programs. Students may take marine biology courses during the summer at the Gulf Coast Research Laboratory in Mississippi. Students in anthropology and antiquities can participate in archaeological research projects. Students majoring in recreation, social work, consumer and family studies, and many other academic programs participate in supervised internships or practicums. Geology students have a variety of field opportunities, including those offered at a permanent base camp in Colorado.

Academic Facilities

SMSU libraries, in Meyer Library and two branches, have more than 1.5 million items, including more than 640,000 cataloged items and approximately 4,800 periodicals. Meyer Library is a depository for federal and state government publications and has a map collection, a large reference collection, textbooks, curriculum guides, special learning materials, a curriculum library with a collection of children's literature, extensive back files of journals and newspapers, a variety of compact disc indexes, the online catalog and circulation systems, a Macintosh computer lab, and equipment adapted for students with disabilities. Meyer Library is open more than 100 hours per week.

Students in the sciences have access to 13-inch and 16-inch telescopes, an electron microscope, a thin-film polymer laboratory, a molecular beam epitaxy laboratory, and other well-equipped laboratories. Computer science and computer information systems students have the opportunity to work on the state-of-the-art, full-scale computer systems as well as minicomputer and microcomputer systems. Students may link to mainframe systems (IBM ES 9000 and several IBM RS 6000 units) with personal computers via modem. Each residence hall has computer facilities, and Hammons House and New Hall have a computer in each living unit.

The Public Affairs Classroom Building, the University's $20.25-million classroom facility, houses twenty-one classrooms, seven laboratories, seven seminar rooms, 161 offices, and the College of Humanities and Public Affairs. Glass Hall is home for more than 3,100 business majors and is recognized as an outstanding teaching facility. Laboratories, studio facilities, and practice rooms are available for science, music, and art students. There are also excellent facilities for theater and dance. The University Childcare Center and Greenwood Laboratory School provide facilities for students in education, psychology, and other courses that require interaction with and observation of children. The University also has various research and service centers, such as the Sports Medicine Clinic, the Speech and Hearing Clinic, the Center for Gerontological Studies, the Center for Business Research and Development, the Archaeological Research Center, and the Center for Ozark Studies.

Costs

Fees are assessed based upon the number of hours for which a student enrolls. Most undergraduate students take 14–16 credit hours per semester. The fee for the 2000–01 school year for 15 credit hours is $1782 per semester for Missouri residents and $3372 for non-Missouri residents. The average cost per semester for textbooks is $250–$325. Fees are subject to change by the University Board of Governors.

The University offers nine options for on-campus living. The average cost of room and board is $3846 per year. The University estimates annual personal expenses (exclusive of automobile-related expenses) to be $2200.

Financial Aid

Financial aid at SMSU consists of outstanding scholarship programs, Federal Pell Grants, Federal Stafford Student Loans, work-study programs, Federal Perkins Loans, Federal Supplemental Educational Opportunity Grants, Federal Parent Loans for Undergraduate Students, Missouri Student Grants, and SMSU short-term loans. Grants and other aid are provided for selected student athletes, and a student employment service is available for students seeking part-time work either on or off campus. SMSU is also a sponsoring institution of the National Merit Scholarship program. March 31 is the priority date for scholarship and financial aid application. Contact the Financial Aid Office for information about scholarships that have earlier application deadlines.

A financial aid and scholarship booklet may be obtained by writing to the Student Financial Aid Office. The Free Application for Federal Student Aid (FAFSA) is the preferred application form; however, other financial aid assessment forms may be used.

Faculty

There are nearly 700 full-time faculty members; more than 80 percent hold doctorates or terminal degrees in their fields of study. Faculty members work closely with students as academic advisers in their area of specialization.

Student Government

The Student Government Association, the representative body of the student community, is composed of students who work toward problem solving, campus improvements, and meeting the needs of the SMSU student body. The association is organized into executive, legislative, and judicial branches.

Admission Requirements

For freshman applicants, requirements are based upon a combination of high school class rank or GPA and ACT composite scores. Students will automatically qualify if they have a selection index (sum of class rank percentile and ACT percentile) of 100 or higher. These requirements are for the fall 2000 semester. In addition, students must meet the 16-unit core curriculum requirement. Transfer students must have at least a 2.0 (C) average in courses that are accepted in transfer to SMSU. International students must present evidence of an above-average record and are encouraged to write to the Office of International Student Services for specific admission information.

The application deadline for the University is three weeks prior to the start of each semester. Students are encouraged to apply early to receive preference in housing and registration.

Application and Information

For more information about undergraduate programs and admission to Southwest Missouri State University, students should contact:

Office of Admissions
Southwest Missouri State University
901 South National
Springfield, Missouri 65804
Telephone: 417-836-5517
           800-492-7900 (toll-free)
           800-836-4770 (TDD)
E-mail: smsuinfo@mail.smsu.edu
World Wide Web: http://www.smsu.edu

A view of Carrington Hall—the SMSU administration building.

SOUTHWEST TEXAS STATE UNIVERSITY
SAN MARCOS, TEXAS

The University

Southwest Texas State University (SWT) is a comprehensive public university committed to providing an intellectually stimulating and socially diverse climate for its graduate and undergraduate students. Serving approximately 22,000 students, SWT is the sixth-largest public university in the state.

Chartered in 1899, SWT's original mission was to prepare Texas public school teachers. It became renowned for carrying out this mission, but today it does far more. The school has grown to become a multipurpose university offering programs in the Colleges of Applied Arts, Business, Fine Arts and Communication, Health Professions, Education, Liberal Arts, and Science and in the Graduate School.

Beyond the classroom, SWT promotes self-enrichment and intellectual vigor in a number of affordable ways. Performances in theater, opera, and film, as well as a full range of musical concerts provide students with an assortment of cultural arts events to attend. Other University-sponsored student activities include intramural and club sports; peer mentoring; various bands, including marching, symphonic, and jazz; the student media; a Greek system; and a variety of outdoor recreational activities. The $26.5-million LBJ Student Center is the focal point of most campus activity and also houses SWT's student support offices.

Varsity athletics are also an important component of student life at SWT. Competing at the Division I-AA level in football only, SWT fields Division I-A teams in the following men's sports: baseball, basketball, cross-country, golf, and track and field. Division I-A women's sports include basketball, cross-country, golf, soccer, softball, tennis, track and field, and volleyball. A member of the NCAA's Southland Conference, SWT has seen a number of its athletes compete on both the national and international levels.

Since living on campus is required for most freshmen and sophomores, SWT students can choose from twenty residence halls (thirteen coed) on campus. For students seeking a complete living-learning experience, SWT offers the Residential College—the first of its kind at a Texas public university. Residential College students enroll in the same core courses as other students and interact more directly with faculty members who live in two of the three Residential College halls. An application is required for the Residential College.

SWT is proud of its most famous alumnus, Lyndon Baines Johnson, the thirty-sixth president of the United States. LBJ remains the only U.S. president to have graduated from a Texas college.

Location

Located at the edge of the Texas Hill Country, San Marcos is a small community (population 38,000) situated between two of the most exciting metropolitan areas in the country. The city of Austin, which is the capital of Texas, is 30 miles north of SWT. San Antonio, the nation's ninth-largest city, lies just 45 miles south of San Marcos. SWT's 423-acre hilltop campus is located on the banks of the crystal-clear San Marcos River.

Majors and Degrees

SWT offers a full range of specialized programs that include 109 major areas of study.

Majors include accounting, advertising, agricultural business, animal science, anthropology, aquatic biology, art, athletic training, bilingual education, biology, botany, broadcasting, cartography and photogrammetry, chemistry, clinical lab science, communication design, communication disorders, computer information systems, computer science, construction technology, corrections, criminal justice, dance, early childhood education, economics, elementary education, engineering technology, English, exercise and sports science, family and child development, family and consumer sciences, fashion merchandising/clothing/textiles, finance, French, general agriculture, general physiology, geography, German, health and fitness management, health and wellness promotion, health-care administration, health education, health information management, history, horticultural science, industrial technology, interior design, international studies (Asian, European, international relations, inter-American, jazz studies, Middle Eastern and African, Russian/East European), law enforcement, management, manufacturing technology, marine biology, marketing, mass communication, mathematics, microbiology, music education, music performance, musical theater, nutrition and foods, occupational education, philosophy, physical and applied geography, physics, political science, print journalism, psychology, public administration, public relations, radiation therapy, recreational administration, resource and environmental studies, respiratory care, social work, sociology, sound recording technology, Spanish, special education, speech communication, studio art, theater, urban/regional planning, visual communication technology, wildlife biology, and zoology.

SWT offers 3+2 engineering programs with Texas A&M and with the University of Texas at Austin and a 3+4 dental program with the University of Texas Health Science Center at San Antonio.

Academic Program

SWT operates on a two-semester calendar system with the fall semester beginning in late August and the spring semester in mid-January. SWT also offers two 5-week summer sessions. Students may earn college credit hours through the University's credit-by-examination program (AP, CLEP, and departmental exams). The Honors Program offers interdisciplinary courses as part of a five-course requirement, which includes the honors thesis, for graduation in the program. Class size is limited to 17 students. Air Force and Army ROTC programs are also offered. At SWT, all students are required to complete a 52- to 55-hour general studies curriculum that serves as the common foundation for all majors. The requirement for a bachelor's degree is the successful completion of approximately 128 to 136 semester hours, depending on the degree plan.

Off-Campus Arrangements

SWT offers its students the opportunity to participate in study-abroad programs in England, France, Germany, Japan, Mexico, Spain, and Sweden. It also offers student teaching in England, Mexico, and New Zealand. Internships are available in Belgium, England, France, Germany, and Spain. To encourage study abroad, SWT awards international scholarships to students on the basis of academic merit and financial need. SWT also has teacher/student exchange agreements with twenty-nine universities around the world. SWT also participates in the National Student Exchange Program, which allows students to enroll for courses and earn credit at participating colleges and universities across the U.S.

Academic Facilities

The Alkek Library contains more than 1.2 million bound volumes, more than 482,000 microform titles, and 26,000 title units in audiovisual software. In addition, the library receives more than

5,500 periodical and serial titles. The library contains the finest collection of original manuscripts, artwork, and photography of artists in the Southwest. Special collection materials found in the Southwestern Writer's Collection include the *Texas Monthly* archives. The Student Learning Assistance Lab (SLAC) provides a drop-in learning lab and tutorial referral service and is located on the fourth floor of the Alkek Library. One of the many campus computer labs is also conveniently located in the library.

Special research facilities include the Edwards Aquifer Research and Data Center, Polymer Research Group, Molecular Genetics Research Group, Intergraph Lab, and archaeology and physical anthropology labs.

Costs

The estimated 2000–01 cost of tuition and fees for full-time students (14 hours) who are Texas residents is $3200. Tuition and fees for nonresidents total $9200. On-campus room and board rates average about $5150 per academic year. The annual costs of books and supplies typically average $750 but may vary according to major. These rates are subject to change.

Financial Aid

Financial aid is provided in the form of grants, loans, work-study, and scholarships. Students should apply early for financial aid. The priority deadline for returning the Free Application for Federal Student Aid (FAFSA) form for the fall semester is April 1. To ensure an early response, students should apply as soon as possible after January 1. For an application or other financial aid materials, students should write to the Office of Student Financial Aid, 601 University Drive, San Marcos, Texas 78666-4602.

Scholarships are awarded on a competitive basis and are available at SWT for qualified new and continuing students. They range from $500 to $5000, with a variety of criteria, including academic achievement, proposed major, hometown, economic need, and athletic and performance-based talent.

SWT's premier scholarship is the Mitte Foundation Scholarship Program. Each year, 25 entering freshmen are selected as Mitte Scholars and are awarded a $5000 renewable scholarship. To be considered, a prospective freshman must be a Commended Student, a Semifinalist, or a Finalist in the National Merit Competition; a valedictorian or salutatorian of his/her graduating class; or ranked in the top 5 percent of his/her graduating class. The scholarship application is available through the Offices of Admission and Student Financial Aid. The deadline for returning the scholarship application for the fall semester is February 1.

Faculty

At SWT, the faculty members place a premium on effective and personalized undergraduate teaching. The majority of SWT's 950 faculty members hold the terminal degree in their major field of study, and many participate in the University-sponsored student mentorship program. The average class size is 37 students, and the student-teacher ratio is 21:1. Ninety-seven percent of SWT's undergraduate classes are taught by professors.

Student Government

Students are afforded considerable opportunity for involvement and leadership at SWT. The Associated Student Government (ASG), composed of elected student members, serves as the representative voice of the student body. ASG works to improve student services and programs and to maintain a high-quality education. Students living on campus may participate in the Residence Hall Association (RHA), which consists of representatives who are elected from each of SWT's twenty halls.

Admission Requirements

Admission decisions for freshman applicants are based on the completion of required high school courses, high school ranking, and SAT I or ACT test scores: for students in the top 10 percent of their class, no minimum test score is required; students in the first quarter need an SAT I test score of 920 or ACT test score of 20; second quarter, 1010 or 22; third quarter, 1180 or 26; and fourth quarter, 1270 or 29. Required high school courses are 4 units of college-preparatory English, 3 units of math (algebra I and II, geometry), 3 units each of science (2 lab sciences) and social studies (world history or world geography, 1 unit; U.S. history, 1 unit; civics/government, 1/2 unit; economics, 1/2 unit), and 2 units of the same foreign language. In fall 1999, 50 percent of SWT's new freshmen were ranked in the top quarter of their graduation class, and 94 percent were ranked in the top half of their class.

Transfer admission decisions are based upon academic proficiency, as demonstrated by a student's grade point average (GPA) in all transferable college credit hours. For students who have fewer than 30 hours of transferable credit, the entrance requirements are a minimum GPA of 2.0 and meeting or exceeding SWT's freshman admission criteria. Students who hold more than 30 hours of transferable credit must have earned a minimum GPA of 2.25 on all college work.

Application and Information

To apply for freshman admission (0 to 29 hours completed), students must submit the Texas Common Application (sections A to E), an official high school transcript verifying class rank, an SAT I or ACT test score, a $25 application fee, and one essay of their choosing from section E of the Texas Common Application. Transfer applicants (30 hours or more) must submit the Texas Common Application for Transfer Students, official college transcripts from all previously attended institutions, and a $25 application fee. Deadlines for freshman and transfer candidates are as follows: fall semester, July 1; spring semester, December 1; summer semester I, May 1; and summer semester II, June 15. Fall semester applicants whose files are complete are notified of their admission decision on a rolling basis beginning October 15.

The undergraduate admission application and catalog are available on line at the SWT home page. For additional information, students may also contact SWT at any of the following addresses:

Office of Admission
Southwest Texas State University
429 North Guadalupe
San Marcos, Texas 78666-5709
Telephone: 512-245-2340
E-mail: admissions@swt.edu
World Wide Web: http://www.swt.edu

Centrally located between Austin and San Antonio, SWT's hilltop campus is situated on the edge of the Texas Hill Country. Just beyond the University's perimeter is the spring-fed San Marcos River.

SPELMAN COLLEGE
ATLANTA, GEORGIA

The College
Spelman, a private, independent, historically black, four-year liberal arts college for women, was founded in 1881. The campus has grown from 9 acres of drill ground and five frame barracks used for federal troops after the Civil War to 32 acres and twenty-four buildings. As an integral part of the Atlanta University Center, Spelman benefits from proximity to and cooperation with the other member institutions, but it maintains its own identity nonetheless, thus offering outstanding opportunities for the education of women for leadership roles.

A focal point of campus activity for the 1,879 women enrolled is the Manley College Center, which houses the dining hall, a food court, faculty and student lounges, student government offices, and some administrative offices. There is a varied program of student and professional cultural activities on the campus. Many of the extracurricular activities are planned and sponsored by the Student Government Association. Others are presented by departmental honor societies and clubs, excellent dance groups, and both jazz and classical instrumental ensembles. The strong tradition in fine arts at Spelman gives students maximum cultural exposure through the renowned Spelman Glee Club, the Spelman-Morehouse Chorus, and the Spelman-Morehouse Players. Health and physical education facilities include a gymnasium, tennis courts, a swimming pool, bowling lanes, dance studios, and a weight room.

Student thought is expressed through several publications: *Reflections*, the yearbook; *Spotlight*, the newspaper; and *Focus*, the literary magazine. Religious life and services form an important part of campus life. Opportunities to experience fellowship in a meaningful fashion, special convocations, and counseling are provided.

Location
Spelman College is located in Atlanta, "The Gateway to the South," a city that is rapidly becoming one of the most dynamic and vital urban areas in the country. Proximity to other colleges and universities in the area provides additional educational, social, and cultural opportunities. Spelman College is one of six institutions that constitute the Atlanta University Center (AUC) consortium.

The city is one of the most exciting learning laboratories imaginable. Here, women can observe politics at work and can meet some of the world's leaders. As an urban center with crucial social problems, Atlanta challenges students to become involved in community programs. An extensive community services program coordinates the placement of students in community agencies.

Majors and Degrees
Spelman offers the Bachelor of Arts and the Bachelor of Science degrees. Majors are offered in art, biochemistry, biology, chemistry, child development, comparative women's studies, computer science, drama and dance, economics, engineering (through participating schools), English, French, history, mathematics, music, philosophy, physics, political science, psychology, sociology/anthropology, and Spanish. An independent major option is also available. Special minors are available in dance, international studies, management and organization, teacher certification, women's studies, and writing. Premedical and prelaw sequences are offered.

Spelman participates in a dual-degree engineering program through which students may combine three years of liberal arts courses at Spelman with two years of engineering studies at Georgia Institute of Technology, California Institute of Technology, Dartmouth College, University of Florida, Columbia University, Rochester Institute of Technology, Boston University, Rensselaer Polytechnic Institute, Auburn University, North Carolina A&T, and the University of Alabama in Huntsville. Students receive a bachelor's degree from each institution upon completing the program.

Academic Program
Spelman operates on a two-semester academic calendar. Through its core curriculum, the College introduces students to the principal branches of learning—languages and literature, natural sciences, mathematics, social sciences, fine arts, and humanities. All students are enrolled in courses designed to develop effective writing and reading skills and logical and imaginative thinking. An honors program is offered to academically outstanding students.

Credit-hour requirements vary with the major area. The core curriculum requirement includes a two-semester interdisciplinary survey course, the African Diaspora in the World, English composition, foreign language, health and physical education, history, literature, and mathematics. A minimum of 4 credits is also required in each of the following areas: fine arts, humanities, natural sciences, and social sciences.

Off-Campus Arrangements
Under the AUC consortium, four undergraduate colleges, one graduate and professional university, and one graduate theological seminary share facilities, resources, and activities. Through cross-registration, Spelman students may elect to take such courses as business administration, mass communication, and social welfare at the other undergraduate institutions.

Academic Facilities
Spelman's science building contains modern laboratory equipment and comfortable classrooms and includes a laboratory. The Fine Arts Building houses a small, up-to-date proscenium theater, music and art studios, and practice rooms. A language laboratory and an educational media center are also available. Spelman students are entitled to use the facilities of the Robert Woodruff Library of the Atlanta University Center, which has 500,000 volumes and a microfilm depository. Two living-learning centers house conference rooms and residence hall facilities. They provide space for work outside of the classroom. The College's newest building is the Camille Olivia Hanks Cosby Academic Center, which was completed in 1996.

Costs
Tuition costs in 1999–2000 were $9260 per year; room and board were $6730 per year. Fees were $1455 for students living on campus and $1675 for students living off campus. Additional costs included transportation, $950; books, $750; and personal expenses, $1550. These costs are subject to change for 1999–2000. Total costs for students living on campus were $20,695; for students living off campus, total costs were $13,965.

Financial Aid

The College makes every effort to assist students with financial need through scholarships, grants, loans, and work-study programs. The amount of aid is determined by need as indicated by the Free Application for Federal Student Aid (FAFSA). Although the Spelman Financial Aid Application deadline is April 1, applicants are advised to begin the process much earlier. Financial aid funds are limited and are awarded on a first-come, first-served basis. Spelman cannot meet the full documented need of every student who applies for financial aid. Those students whose financial aid files are complete by March 1 receive priority processing and consideration.

The Spelman scholarship program is meant to encourage academic excellence and to recognize outstanding achievement. Scholarships are awarded to entering first-year and continuing students on a competitive basis. Consideration is given to academic and personal achievement as evidenced by academic records, standardized test scores, leadership, special talent, character, community service, and, in some cases, financial need. Interested students must submit the Spelman College Application for Admission to be considered for Spelman scholarships. Additional application materials are required for the Spelman Presidential Scholarship, the Women in Science and Engineering (WISE) Program Scholarship, and the Bonner Scholar Program.

Faculty

Spelman's full-time faculty numbers 138 members. More than 85 percent hold doctoral or other terminal degrees. The low student-faculty ratio (14:1) permits individualized instruction and small classes.

Student Government

Every student is a member of the Student Government Association (SGA). The SGA, with the approval of the administration, sets policies that govern student life. Meetings of the association are announced and held regularly, and all students are urged to attend.

Admission Requirements

Applicants for first-year admission are selected on the basis of their high school records, SAT I or ACT scores, recommendations, and personal information submitted in the application for admission. First-year students are admitted for the fall term only.

A limited number of spaces are available each term for transfer students. Applicants for transfer admission are selected based upon their complete academic records, recommendations, personal information submitted in the application for admission, and whether space is available in requested academic majors. Applicants who have achieved the equivalent of senior status are not considered.

The College selects qualified women candidates without regard to race; color; national, ethnic, or regional origin; physical challenge; or religious preference. The College seeks to admit students whose credentials give evidence of potential for academic success at Spelman and who demonstrate personal characteristics of high motivation, purpose, and integrity. Interviews are not required. Prospective applicants may request individual information sessions or tours through the Office of Admissions and Orientation Services.

Application and Information

Completed first-year applications for admission under the Early Action Plan must be postmarked and mailed by November 15 of the senior year. Notification of the admission decision is made by January 1. Completed regular first-year applications must be postmarked and mailed by February 1 of the senior year. Notification of the admission decision is made by April 1.

Completed transfer applications for the fall term must be postmarked and mailed by February 1. Notification of the admission decision is made by April 1. Completed transfer applications for the spring term must be postmarked and mailed by November 1. Notification of the admission decision is made by December 1.

For application forms and additional information, interested students should contact:

Office of Admissions and Orientation Services
Box 277
Spelman College
Atlanta, Georgia 30314
Telephone: 404-681-3643 Ext. 2188
              800-982-2411 (toll-free)
E-mail: admiss@spelman.edu
World Wide Web: http://www.spelman.edu

Sisters Chapel at Spelman College.

SPRING ARBOR COLLEGE
SPRING ARBOR, MICHIGAN

The College

Spring Arbor College is a coeducational, evangelical Christian college founded in 1873 by leaders of the Free Methodist Church. From its beginnings as a private academy with elementary and secondary grades, the College evolved into an institution of higher learning, achieving four-year status in 1963. Spring Arbor is accredited by the North Central Association of Colleges and Schools and offers a solid academic program within a small and supportive Christian community. Although the College is affiliated with the Free Methodist Church, it is nonsectarian, and more than twenty other denominations are represented in its student body.

Spring Arbor is a community of students distinguished by their serious study of the liberal arts, their total commitment to Jesus Christ as the perspective for learning, and their participation in the affairs of the contemporary world. Because Spring Arbor is a Christian college dedicated to the academic, social, and spiritual growth of its students, community chapel services and courses in biblical studies are required, and students are expected to govern their lives in harmony with College expectations and regulations. The use of alcoholic beverages, nonprescribed drugs, and tobacco is prohibited.

Spring Arbor takes seriously its responsibility to keep the religious life of the campus active and relevant to personal spiritual growth. In addition to required chapel, there are small-group Bible studies, Christian concerts, and seminars with a spiritual emphasis. Other extracurricular activities include special interest clubs, vocal and instrumental music ensembles, the campus newspaper, the yearbook, and the radio station (WSAE-FM and KTGG-AM). A variety of cultural events are provided through the Cultural Life Series. Opportunities are available for students to become involved in community outreach and service programs, such as a crisis pregnancy center, the Red Cross, a nursing home fellowship program, Special Olympics, and a prison ministry.

Spring Arbor's extensive athletics program and excellent facilities provide opportunities for leisure as well as competitive recreation. Men compete in varsity baseball, basketball, cross-country running, golf, soccer, tennis, and track. Women compete in varsity basketball, cross-country running, soccer, softball, tennis, track, and volleyball. Intramural teams are organized in basketball, flag football, floor hockey, Ping-Pong, soccer, softball, tennis, volleyball, and water polo. Other recreational activities include bicycling, hiking, and swimming.

About 88 percent of the 1,025 students come from Michigan, and others represent twenty-seven states and seven other countries. Three residence halls, four apartment buildings, and nine houses provide housing for single students, and thirty-four apartments are available for married students.

Location

Spring Arbor's 70-acre campus is located in south-central Michigan, 7 miles west of Jackson, a community of 37,000. Spring Arbor is within an hour's drive of Ann Arbor, Lansing, and Battle Creek.

Majors and Degrees

Spring Arbor College offers the Associate of Arts degree in arts and sciences and the Bachelor of Arts degree in accounting, art, biochemistry, biology, business administration, chemistry, Christian ministries, clinical sociology, communication (concentrations in advertising/public relations, broadcasting, drama/film, drama/speech, film production, professional writing, and speech), computer science, contemporary music ministries, economics/business, education (certification in early childhood, elementary, and secondary education), English, English/speech, exercise and sport science, history, language arts, management information systems, mathematics, music, philosophy, philosophy/religion, physics/mathematics, psychology, social studies, social work, sociology, and Spanish. Courses are also offered in economics, English as a second language, French, geography, global studies, Greek, political science, and urban studies. An Associate of Piano Pedagogy degree is also available. Preprofessional programs are offered in dentistry, law, medicine, and physical therapy.

Academic Program

A liberal arts education exposes the student to many academic areas that enrich and enhance study in the major field. To provide this broad foundation, the College requires each student to take courses from each of the five academic divisions (fine arts, humanities, natural science, philosophy/religion, and social science), to demonstrate competence in oral and written communication, and to take a physical education course. The Christian perspective in the liberal arts is emphasized throughout the curriculum but particularly in four interdisciplinary, issue-oriented core courses required of all students. All students must also participate in a three-week cross-cultural experience.

Off-Campus Arrangements

A number of off-campus opportunities are available for students at Spring Arbor College. The Environmental Semester at Au Sable Trails Institute of Environmental Studies in northern Michigan is valuable for students interested in biology, natural resource management, and recreation. Through the Coalition for Christian Colleges, Spring Arbor students can participate in an academic seminar program in the American Studies Program in Washington, D.C. The Wesleyan Urban Coalition and the Urban Life Center provide programs enabling students to live in downtown Chicago, take courses on urban issues and ministries, and work in a Christian ministry or with a social service, educational, or community agency. Individual off-campus practicums or independent studies may also be arranged.

Academic Facilities

Excellent facilities are provided in most areas. The campus buildings include a modern, well-equipped science center; a physical education center housing an Olympic-style pool, an indoor track, and basketball, volleyball, and tennis courts; and a library containing 90,854 volumes, 1,413 periodicals, and 4,420 audio and video tapes, CDs, and records.

Costs

Tuition for the 2000–01 academic year is $12,200. The cost for room is $2060, and the cost for board is $2520.

Financial Aid

Spring Arbor College is aware of the financial commitment that the costs of a college education demand. The College's program of aid is designed to supplement students' resources to meet the costs of education. More than 90 percent of all students at Spring Arbor receive financial aid through a variety of aid programs, including scholarships, grants, loans, and employment. The College participates in the Federal Work-Study

Program and assists students in applying for aid through the Federal Pell Grant, Federal Supplemental Educational Opportunity Grant, Federal Perkins Loan, and the Federal Stafford Student Loan programs. Residents of Michigan may be eligible for the Michigan Tuition Grant or the State Competitive Scholarship.

Students seeking financial aid are required to submit a copy of the Free Application for Federal Student Aid. Aid is awarded on the basis of financial eligibility and outstanding scholastic or athletic achievement; students whose application and financial aid files are complete by February 28 receive preference.

Faculty

Members of the faculty at Spring Arbor College are both well-trained scholars and concerned human beings, dedicated to academic excellence and involved in the lives of their students. Coming from many backgrounds and representing a variety of academic disciplines, they share a Christian concern for students that reveals itself in the time and dedication they give to them. The student-faculty ratio is 16:1, and approximately 50 percent of the full-time faculty members hold an earned doctorate.

Student Government

Student government provides many opportunities for men and women to assume leadership roles. Through the Student Association, elected officers and representatives work to enhance campus life academically, socially, and spiritually. The Student Association President represents students on the President's Cabinet.

Admission Requirements

Applications are welcome from students who have an academic background that indicates a potential for a successful college experience and who can contribute to the Christian ideals of the College. While the potential for academic success is a primary consideration, a student's goals, the recommendations he or she submits, and the College's ability to serve the student are considered as well. For freshmen, an ACT composite score of at least 20 and a minimum grade point average of 2.6 are recommended; transfer students should have a cumulative GPA of 2.0 or higher in order to be considered for admission.

Applications are accepted from any student without regard to race, color, national origin, creed, sex, age, or handicap. The student's signature on the application form is an indication of his or her acceptance of Spring Arbor's requirements concerning the academic program and student life.

Application and Information

Spring Arbor requires students to submit an application form and a $15 application fee, an official transcript of high school grades, and ACT or SAT I scores. Transfer students should also submit transcripts from all colleges attended.

Applications are accepted throughout the year. Both freshmen and transfer students may enter in the fall semester (September–December), Spring A semester (January), or Spring B semester (February–May). There is a rolling admission policy. For application and financial aid forms or more information, students should contact:

Office of Admissions
Spring Arbor College
Spring Arbor, Michigan 49283
Telephone: 800-968-0011 (admissions office, toll-free)
E-mail: admissions@admin.arbor.edu
World Wide Web: http://www.arbor.edu

At Spring Arbor College, students actively pursue academics and faith.

SPRINGFIELD COLLEGE
SPRINGFIELD, MASSACHUSETTS

The College

Originally founded as a school for training students for service in the YMCA, Springfield College is in its second century of preparing talented young men and women for careers in the human-helping professions. Just a few years after opening its doors to the first eighteen students in 1885, Springfield College could boast an international reputation as a pioneer in teaching and scholarship related to physical education, wellness, and the training of YMCA executives. Today, with a coed undergraduate and graduate body of 3,946, Springfield College is proud of its reputation in these fields and throughout the human helping professions. Springfield's 28,000 alumni work in almost sixty nations. Alumni have served in various capacities, such as a university president in China, initiators of the Olympic movement in Eastern European countries, and educational leaders in Central and South America. Wherever they work or live, Springfield alumni become vital links in a human chain that leads to impressive achievements.

Participation in cocurricular activities forms an integral part of the Springfield College experience. Clubs range from drama, music, dance, and publications to professional interest groups and community service organizations. More than 90 percent of the traditional undergraduate student body turns out for participation in an extensive intramural sports program, and more than 30 percent participate in intercollegiate athletics. Women's sports include basketball, cross-country, field hockey, gymnastics, lacrosse, soccer, softball, swimming, tennis, track, and volleyball. Men participate in baseball, basketball, cross-country, football, golf, gymnastics, lacrosse, soccer, swimming, tennis, track, volleyball, and wrestling.

On-campus housing is guaranteed for four years, and students have the option of living in either a coeducational or a single-sex dormitory. After the junior year, students may elect to live in off-campus housing.

Location

Springfield College is located along Lake Massasoit in Springfield, Massachusetts, the fourth-largest city in New England, with a population of approximately 150,000. Springfield and the surrounding area offer a variety of social and cultural experiences.

The George Walter Vincent Smith Art Museum, the Springfield Science Museum, the Connecticut Valley Historical Museum, and the Museum of Fine Art surround the Quadrangle in the heart of downtown Springfield. Also located in the downtown area are the Springfield Symphony Hall and CityStage, which features off-Broadway plays, musicals, and dance performances. The city is also the site of the Basketball Hall of Fame and the Springfield Civic Center, which is home to the American Hockey League's Springfield Falcons and which is the host of the annual Tip-Off Classic, the official start of the college basketball season.

Nearby cities offer additional resources and opportunities. Holyoke is home to Holyoke Mall at Ingleside, which provides three floors of stores and restaurants. West Springfield hosts one of New England's most popular annual events, The Big E, which features agricultural exhibits and carnival rides and games. Within a 45-minute drive north is Northampton, with its trendy shops, coffeehouses, health-food stores, galleries, theater productions, nightclubs, and restaurants. The nearby Berkshire Mountains offer hiking, skiing, mountain biking, and other outdoor activities. Boston and New York can be reached by car in only 2 and 3 hours, respectively.

Majors and Degrees

Springfield College offers the Bachelor of Science or Bachelor of Arts degree in the following programs: applied exercise science, art, art therapy, athletic training, biochemical technology, biology, business management, chemistry/biology, communications/sports journalism, computer and information sciences, computer graphics, disabled sports and movement studies, early childhood and elementary education, emergency medical services management, English, environmental science, gerontology, health services administration, health studies, history, human services and administration, mathematics, medical informatics, medical technology/laboratory science, movement and sports studies, outdoor recreation management, physical education teacher preparation, physician assistant studies, political science, psychology, recreation management, rehabilitation services, secondary education, sociology, special needs education, sports biology, sports management, and therapeutic recreation services. Physical therapy is offered as an entry-level 5½-year program culminating in a Master of Science degree. A limited number of seniors can enter the five-year graduate-level occupational therapy program.

Academic Program

Humanics, the philosophy that has inspired Springfield College from its beginning, calls for educating the whole person—spirit, mind, and body. Undergraduate education at Springfield College is designed to promote an understanding of how these different aspects of ourselves work together in preparation for a life of leadership in service to others. In the classroom, the humanics approach translates to a careful balance of theory and practice—the daily application of an education that connects people to people.

The College has a two-semester academic calendar. In order to successfully complete the Springfield College experience, students are required to accumulate a minimum of 130 credits toward graduation. These credits comprise major requirements, elective courses, and the All-College Requirements (which include studies in English, philosophy, social science, health, history, math, and natural science). Qualified students may also earn credit through the Advanced Placement Program and the College-Level Examination Program administered by the College Board.

Off-Campus Arrangements

Following the theory that the community is the best laboratory, Springfield College maintains a strong relationship with businesses and human service agencies in Springfield and the surrounding area. Its fieldwork component is among the most extensive and challenging offered by institutions of higher learning. Fieldwork sites includes the Basketball Hall of Fame, the American Hockey League, the *Boston Globe*, YMCAs, the American Heart Association, MassMutual, Children's Hospital, the Hilton Head Crowne Plaza, the Reebok Health and Fitness Center, Baystate Medical Center Cardiac Rehabilitation, and parks and recreation departments.

In addition, Springfield College offers a cooperative education program to provide work experience that enhances the student's field of study. This work-learn opportunity also provides students with income to assist in financing their education. Each student averages 15–20 hours per week of work that complements academic study. The program is open to all full-time sophomore, junior, senior, and graduate students.

Study-abroad programs are available for students who wish to supplement their education with studies in another country. Closer to home, students may enroll in courses offered at some of the other colleges, public and private, in the Springfield area.

Academic Facilities

Babson Library serves as the College's major resource center, holding more than 650,000 microforms, 170,000 books, 2,200 videos, 670 periodical subscriptions, 25,000 bound periodical volumes, and an archives collection. Babson maintains complete files of the Education Resources Information Center (ERIC), Human Relations Area Files, and the Physical Education and Recreation Dissertation and Theses collections. Students have Web access to virtually all of the library's research indexes and databases. The library also houses the Information and Technology Center, which features teaching classrooms, a training/multimedia classroom, and an open computer lab.

Among the College's additional academic facilities are the language laboratory and the Allied Health Sciences Center, with its human anatomy lab, performance assessment lab, exercise physiology/biomechanics lab, academic computer station, and isokinetic muscle-testing device.

The Physical Education Complex combines the Art Linkletter Natatorium; Blake Arena, with seating for 2,000; Keith Locker Room and Training Facility; and Winston Paul Academic Center, which includes two teaching gymnasiums and handball/racquetball courts. Other athletic facilities include Benedum Field (with new Astroturf), eight tennis courts, two baseball diamonds, one softball diamond, an eight-lane outdoor track, a weight room, and an indoor jogging track. The Wellness Center offers fitness testing and assessment, computerized check-in and tracking, exercise prescription, and personal training. The College's Strength and Conditioning Center is equipped with a wide selection of free weights and is designed specifically as a classroom/laboratory.

The multipurpose 300-seat Fuller Performing Arts Center features a proscenium theater for performances and a lecture hall for classes and symposia. The 20,000-square-foot Visual Arts Center provides studio work space and serves as a public exhibition center for students and regional artists.

The College's 52-acre East Campus, located a mile from the main campus, comprises a forest ecosystem with camping facilities, a picnic grove, and 2 miles of shoreline on Lake Massasoit. East Campus affords an ideal working laboratory and training ground for students in a variety of academic programs. The Springfield College Child Development Center is also located at East Campus. Licensed by the Massachusetts Office for Children and accredited by the National Association for the Education of Young Children, it provides an exceptional and convenient facility for teacher-supervised fieldwork for students concentrating in early childhood education, physical education teacher preparation, or psychology.

Springfield offers on-campus opportunities for students to gain valuable experience by helping to provide coverage of collegiate sports scores and other sport information on the World Wide Web. These electronic media opportunities enable students to develop practical management and technological skills that are particularly beneficial for students in the sport management and sports journalism fields.

Costs

For the academic year 2000–01, tuition costs $17,100, required fees total $200, room is $3285, and board costs $2750. The cost for books and personal expenses varies, depending upon the individual student and course of study.

Financial Aid

Students who feel they do not have sufficient funds to pay for the total cost of their education are encouraged to apply for financial aid in the form of grants, loans, and student employment. All financial aid offered by Springfield College is based on need, intellectual promise, leadership, and character. Students who submit the Free Application for Federal Student Aid (FAFSA) and the College Scholarship Service Financial Aid PROFILE by the following dates are given full consideration for aid: January 30 for early decision candidates, March 15 for first-year students, and May 1 for transfer students. Students not eligible for financial aid may still be considered for institutional employment.

Faculty

A committed group of 330 faculty members allows for a student-teacher ratio of 12:1. The small size of classes enables students to develop both personal and academic relationships with their professors, most of whom hold doctorates or other terminal degrees appropriate to their field. Springfield's small-college environment attracts and holds highly dedicated faculty members who share a commitment to students' whole development.

Student Government

Student government at Springfield College is best characterized as government by and for the students. The Student Association and the Board of Governors are responsible for the planning and implementation of student programs. The Beveridge Student Center houses the offices of both of these organizations, and its operation is supervised by students under the guidance of the director of student activities.

Admission Requirements

In keeping with its humanics philosophy, Springfield College evaluates applicants on the basis of academic and personal factors. Students interested in applying to Springfield under either the early decision or regular admissions program must submit the following items to the admissions office: an application, the high school transcript, one personal reference, and SAT I scores. A personal interview is also required. Transfer students must also submit a transcript and a dean's report from each college attended. Just as the admissions staff is interested in getting to know each applicant, applicants are encouraged to get to know Springfield College. Contact with the admissions staff, alumni, and current students is encouraged and facilitated. Personal interviews, campus tours, and open-house programs provide candidates with an opportunity to visit the College and experience campus life.

Application and Information

Springfield College's rolling admissions program allows applicants to go into review with the Admissions Committee immediately upon completion of the application process. The deadline for submission of applications for the first-year class is April 1; however, students applying for the programs in physical therapy and athletic training must submit an application prior to December 1. Students applying for the physician assistant program must submit an application prior to January 1. Transfer students must file an application before August 1.

Application forms and further information may be obtained by contacting:
Office of Admissions
Springfield College
263 Alden Street
Box M
Springfield, Massachusetts 01109
Telephone: 413-748-3136
  800-343-1257 (toll-free)
E-mail: admissions@spfldcol.edu
World Wide Web: http://www.spfldcol.edu (online application available)

On the campus of Springfield College.

STANFORD UNIVERSITY
STANFORD, CALIFORNIA

The University

The Leland Stanford Junior University, referred to today simply as Stanford University, was founded in 1885 by Senator and Mrs. Leland Stanford, who devoted their entire fortune and their estate to its establishment in memory of their only child, Leland Jr., who died at an age when many young men and women are planning a college education. Leland Stanford, a distinguished businessman, governor of California, and U.S. Senator, patterned the University after the great European universities. He set a pattern for students to receive a broad liberal education, as well as a practical one, that was remarkable for its time—one that would cultivate the imagination and develop character.

Although the University has grown and changed in many ways over the years, it is very much a product of its physical setting and of its early educational goals of practicality, humanism, and excellence. In terms of enrollment, Stanford is a medium-sized university, but its campus consists of more than 8,180 acres. Frederick Olmsted, the designer of New York's Central Park and America's foremost landscape architect of his day, was commissioned to locate the original central campus, indicate the layout and general character of the buildings, and plan the grounds. These original buildings with buff sandstone walls, red-tiled roofs, and long sandstone arcades still constitute the center of the campus today. Over the years, newer structures have been built to blend with the original architecture.

There are 14,219 students enrolled at the University; 6,594 are undergraduates. Undergraduate students come to Stanford from every state in the Union and about sixty other countries. Although they represent widely differing backgrounds and interests, the great majority have displayed energy, intellectual curiosity, and commitment to their education both in and out of the classroom. All freshmen are required to live on campus. The undergraduate housing system includes eighty residential facilities, including academic, cross-cultural, Greek and language theme and focus houses; self-managed houses; apartments; suites; and traditional dormitories. Most students choose to live on campus all four years. Stanford supports a strong program of education in the residential setting to supplement students' classroom programs. Some faculty and staff members live in the residences; others come for meals and serve as guest speakers.

The scope of extracurricular activities reflects the diversity of backgrounds, interests, abilities, and experiences of the student body, and more than 500 organized student groups are available. These include a wide variety of academic, political, religious, social, and ethnic associations. In addition, students actively participate in music, drama, and journalism projects. The University's extensive athletic facilities include an 85,500-seat stadium, a 7,391-seat pavilion, a championship golf course, a fourteen-court tennis complex, and a three-pool swimming complex. Stanford fields men's varsity teams in baseball, basketball, crew, cross-country, fencing, football, golf, gymnastics, sailing, soccer, swimming and diving, tennis, track and field, volleyball, water polo, and wrestling. Women's varsity teams are fielded in basketball, crew, cross-country, fencing, field hockey, golf, gymnastics, lacrosse, sailing, soccer, softball, swimming and diving, synchronized swimming, tennis, track and field, volleyball, and water polo. Twenty additional club sports are available, and extensive intramural programs are also offered.

The University provides many student services, including academic advising, a health center, counseling and psychological services, and career development.

Location

Stanford is adjacent to the suburban communities of Palo Alto and Menlo Park, 30 miles south of San Francisco. Extensive cultural opportunities are available in the area. The famed Monterey peninsula is 75 miles to the south; Sierra Nevada, where there is skiing in the winter, and Yosemite National Park are each 4 hours away.

Majors and Degrees

Stanford University awards the Bachelor of Arts (A.B.) or Bachelor of Science (B.S.) degrees in the following fields: African and Afro-American studies, American studies, anthropology, art, Asian languages (Chinese, Japanese), biological sciences, chemistry, classics (Greek, Latin), communication, comparative literature, comparative studies in race and ethnicity (Asian-American studies, Chicano studies, Native American studies), computer science, drama, earth sciences (earth systems, geological and environmental sciences, geophysics, petroleum engineering), East Asian studies, economics, engineering (chemical; civil and environmental; computer systems; electrical; general; industrial; materials science; mechanical; product design; science, technology, and society), English, feminist studies, French, German studies, history, human biology, international relations, Italian, Latin American studies, linguistics, mathematical and computational science, mathematics, modern thought and literature, music, philosophy, physics, political science, psychology, public policy, religious studies, Slavic languages and literatures, sociology, Spanish and Portuguese, symbolic systems, urban studies, and individually designed majors.

Academic Program

Stanford provides the means for undergraduates to acquire a liberal education—one that broadens their knowledge and awareness in each of the major areas of human knowledge, significantly deepens it in one or two, and prepares them for a lifetime of continual learning. The curriculum allows considerable flexibility. Individually designed majors, double majors that combine bachelor's and master's degrees, tutorials, and honors programs are all available for qualified students. A special emphasis is placed on encouraging close faculty and student interaction in the first two years through Stanford Introductory Studies, which includes freshman seminars. Students may declare a major at any time but must do so by the end of the sophomore year. Freshmen are assigned to general advisers upon entering; when they declare a major, they are assigned to an adviser from the faculty of the major department or program. To earn the A.B. or B.S. degree, students must complete 180 units; fulfill writing, general education, and foreign language requirements; and complete the requirements of at least one major department or program. All students take a three-quarter "Introduction to the Humanities" sequence as well as three courses (with at least one in each of the areas) in the humanities and social sciences. A requirement in natural sciences, applied science and technology, and mathematics may be fulfilled by three certified courses in these areas (no more than two in the same area) or by completing a three-course science, mathematics, and engineering core. One certified course in at least two of the three areas of world cultures, American cultures, and gender studies is also required. Stanford's commitment to a broad liberal arts education is expressed through the yearlong course requirement "Introduction to the Humanities." The courses build an intellectual foundation in the study of human thought, values, beliefs, creativity, and culture. They also enhance students' skills in analysis, reasoning, argumentation, and oral and written expression. Students may select from a variety of courses that share these common goals. At least 45 units (including the last 18) must be completed at Stanford. With certain limited exceptions, no more than 90 quarter units of credit for work done elsewhere may be counted toward the bachelor's degree at Stanford.

Entering students may be allowed up to 45 units of credit on the basis of successful scores on the College Board's Advanced Placement tests or the International Baccalaureate examinations.

Off-Campus Arrangements

Stanford has overseas study programs in Argentina, Chile, England, France, Germany, Italy, Japan, Mexico, and Russia. Students may attend these centers for a three-, six-, or nine-month period, obtaining full academic credit. The teaching staff at each center consists of regular Stanford professors and resident academic staff members of the host country. Stanford also provides a special opportunity for students to study classics in Rome, Italy, through a consortium arrangement with other universities. Approximately 25 percent of Stanford's students participate in overseas programs.

Stanford students also have the opportunity to study in the nation's capital under the Stanford-in-Washington program. In addition, Stanford offers exchange programs with Dartmouth College, Howard University, Morehouse College, and Spelman College.

Academic Facilities

Stanford's library collection consists of more than 7 million books and journals, 100 million archival and manuscript documents, and thousands of other materials spread among the main Green Library, the Meyer Undergraduate Library, and more than twenty-five branch and department libraries. The undergraduate library serves as the hub of undergraduate resources and contains study carrels, classrooms, listening rooms, and a well-equipped language library with tapes and texts for nearly 100 languages. The Green Library houses the library system's central collections and also holds maps, microtexts, newspapers, government documents, rare books, and special collections, including writings of such notables as Sir Isaac Newton, Martin Luther, William Butler Yeats, and John Steinbeck. An added benefit for researchers is the cooperative link between Stanford's libraries and the University of California at Berkeley's library system.

Stanford's facilities are outstanding and include well-equipped classrooms, laboratories, computer facilities, and research centers. Among the University's many distinguished facilities are the John C. Blume Earthquake Engineering Center; the Remote Sensing Laboratory; the Environmental and Water Quality Laboratory; the Stanford Linear Accelerator Center; the Hoover Institution on War, Revolution, and Peace; the Center for Economic Policy Research; and the Institute for International Studies. In addition, the Jasper Ridge Biological Preserve constitutes a natural laboratory for biology and ecology students, and the Hopkins Marine Station in Pacific Grove, California, offers students an excellent opportunity to study marine biology in a natural habitat.

Costs

Tuition for the 2000–01 year is $24,441. Room and board costs are $8030. The cost of books is estimated at $1020 per year. Personal expenses are estimated at $1545 per year.

Financial Aid

Approximately 70 percent of the students at Stanford receive some kind of external or internal financial aid. Admission is need blind except for international students. Need-based aid at Stanford is budgeted at more than $40 million annually. Awards range in value depending on need and are renewable for each of the four undergraduate years on the basis of continuing need. Home value is capped at three times the annual parent income before home equity is determined in financial need calculations. There are also opportunities for students and their parents to secure long-term loans to help defray college costs. To apply for aid, applicants should complete the Free Application for Federal Student Aid (FAFSA) and the College Scholarship Service PROFILE. All financial aid applicants are expected to apply for Federal Pell Grants. California residents applying for financial aid must apply for Cal Grants, which require the FAFSA and the high school grade point average certification.

Forty percent of students work on campus during the academic year, and opportunities for off-campus part-time employment are numerous.

Faculty

Stanford has 1,595 faculty members who have attained professorial rank, plus well over 500 other teaching personnel, including lecturers and graduate teaching assistants. A high proportion of the full-time professors are involved in undergraduate teaching and advising. Stanford's current community of scholars includes 15 Nobel laureates, 3 Pulitzer Prize winners, 1 winner of the Congressional Medal of Honor, 22 MacArthur Fellows, 19 recipients of the National Medal of Science, 3 National Medal of Technology recipients, 212 members of the American Academy of Arts and Sciences, 117 members of the National Academy of Sciences, 75 National Academy of Engineering members, 26 members of the National Academy of Education, 40 American Philosophical Society members, 6 Wolf Foundation Prize for Mathematics winners, 4 winners of the Koret Foundation Prize, and 2 Presidential Medal of Freedom winners. The student-faculty ratio is 7.3:1. All faculty members keep regular office hours, and students are encouraged to develop contacts with the faculty in and out of the classroom for advice and guidance.

Student Government

The Associated Students of Stanford University (ASSU) includes all registered students and serves as a forum for the expression of student opinion through its executive and legislative branches. The ASSU plans and executes numerous programs and activities. Students have many opportunities to become actively involved on councils, committees, and panels that offer interaction with professors and staff. Many of the concrete and philosophical changes that have taken place at the University are attributable to student initiative, input, and interaction.

Admission Requirements

Admission is highly competitive, with more than 17,900 applications received for the 1999–2000 entering class of 1,610 students. The University seeks an able and diverse student body, and no single criterion determines admission. Students are evaluated individually on the basis of their academic record, test scores, nonacademic achievements, and personal qualities. Because opportunities vary tremendously, students are judged on how well they have used the resources available to them. Every candidate for undergraduate admission must submit SAT I or ACT scores. College Board SAT II Subject Test scores are strongly recommended; Writing and Math IIC tests are preferred; any additional tests should be in the student's strongest subject areas. Transfer students, entering either the sophomore or the junior class, are admitted annually in the fall quarter only. The University does not use any racial, religious, ethnic, geographic, or sex-related quotas in admissions.

Application and Information

Application forms and other information about Stanford may be obtained from the Office of Admission. Bulletins giving detailed course descriptions and University policies can be purchased through the Stanford Bookstore (telephone: 800-533-2670, ext. 398). Applications for the freshman class must be postmarked by December 15. Regular review applicants will be notified around April 1. Stanford also offers an early decision option, with a deadline of November 1. Early decision applicants are notified approximately six weeks after the deadline. The deadline for the completion of transfer applications for autumn-quarter admission is March 15.

Office of Undergraduate Admission
Room 2321
Old Union
Stanford University
Stanford, California 94305-3005
Telephone: 650-723-2091
Fax: 650-725-2846
World Wide Web: http://www.stanford.edu

STATE UNIVERSITY OF NEW YORK AT ALBANY
ALBANY, NEW YORK

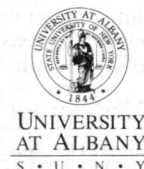

The University

A University Center of the State University of New York (SUNY), the State University of New York at Albany offers a broad spectrum of academic programs for undergraduate and graduate students while fulfilling the missions of research and service. More than 16,000 students, including 11,000 undergraduates, are enrolled in the University's eight schools and colleges: arts and sciences, business, education, criminal justice, public affairs, information science and policy, social welfare, and public health.

Albany is distinguished by the high quality of its academic programs, many of which are consistently ranked among the best in the nation. These include atmospheric science, management information systems, criminal justice, public administration and policy, social welfare, psychology, and sociology. More than 900 faculty members jointly offer Albany's graduate and undergraduate programs, thus giving all students access to leading researchers in an environment that emphasizes active learning, inquiry, and discovery. Throughout their undergraduate education, students are encouraged to pursue the intellectual goals of breadth and coherence while acquiring the skills of critical inquiry and public responsibility.

Freshmen are invited to participate in Project Renaissance, a distinctive general education program. Project Renaissance offers an integrated introduction to the University through a yearlong 12-credit interdisciplinary course that is team taught by several faculty members. The course includes inquiry projects, which grow out of students' community action work and require them to behave as researchers, inquiring into the meaning of events that surround them. Thus, students learn how the larger issues of research are often tied to everyday life and how systematic inquiry helps address these questions. Project Renaissance courses are unified by the theme of "Human Identity and Technology." Students create a true living-learning community by also sharing a residence hall.

Since the University is located in New York State's capital, Albany students have access to a wide range of internship opportunities, including a full-semester, 15-credit internship with the New York State Legislature.

Albany's Presidential Scholars Program considers only the top students admitted to the freshman class. The fourfold increase in the number of Presidential Scholars since the program was established in 1993 attests to the outstanding quality of incoming freshman classes. Presidential Scholars must have a high school average of at least 91 and outstanding standardized test scores. Frederick Douglass Scholars, selected from Presidential Scholars, have demonstrated high academic achievement and are from underrepresented groups. Presidential Scholars, Frederick Douglass Scholars, and students who complete a semester or more at Albany with an average of 3.5 or higher are invited to enter the General Education Honors Program. Honors programs are also available in the following majors and departments: anthropology, atmospheric science, biology, economics, English, geography, history, Italian, Judaic studies, mathematics, philosophy, physics, political science, psychology, rhetoric and communication, Russian, Spanish, and sociology.

About 40 percent of Albany graduates go directly on to graduate or professional school. More than 80 percent of the qualified medical school applicants educated at Albany are accepted, while more than 70 percent of law school applicants from Albany are accepted. Albany's graduation rate is 20 points higher than the national average. A network of more than 100,000 Albany alumni throughout the nation and the world provide an important link to business, education, law, medicine, and state, national, and international government as well as other related fields.

Five residential quadrangles uptown and one quad downtown house 6,000 Albany students. Most residential facilities are organized in suite arrangements, and each resident student has access to an individual phone line and voice mail, cable television hookup, and a high-speed Ethernet connection to the Internet via ResNet. There are fifteen special-interest housing options.

Campus life is sustained by the activities of the nearly 200 University-recognized social and professional clubs, which offer numerous opportunities for leadership development. The University, now competing at the NCAA Division II level in the New England Collegiate Conference, moved to Division I in the 1999–2000 academic year. Men's varsity sports are baseball, basketball, cross-country, football, indoor track, lacrosse, outdoor track, and soccer. Women's varsity sports are basketball, cross-country, field hockey, golf, indoor track, lacrosse, outdoor track, soccer, softball, tennis, and volleyball. In addition, Albany offers a wide range of intramural opportunities, and more than 5,000 Albany students participate in intramural sports each year. The Recreation and Convocation Center (RACC) offers students the latest in sports facilities, including three full basketball courts, racquetball and squash courts, a main arena with an indoor track, and a fitness center with Nautilus equipment. The RACC's 4,800-seat arena is also used for concerts and other events.

Location

Albany, the hub of the lively Capital Region, offers students a host of internship and work opportunities in government, finance, education, business, and the arts as well as the cultural and social environment of a major city. The climate is milder than elsewhere in upstate New York and New England, with stunning natural beauty. Albany's historic Hudson Valley location is convenient to recreation areas in Vermont's Green Mountains, the Berkshires of Massachusetts, the Catskills, and the Adirondacks, site of two Winter Olympics. Boston, Hartford, New York City, Montreal, and Philadelphia are also within a convenient distance. Two major interstates, I-87 and I-90, serve the campus, and airline, train, and bus terminals are just minutes away.

Majors and Degrees

Undergraduates may choose from 100 degree programs. SUNY at Albany offers the bachelor's degree in accounting, actuarial and mathematical sciences, Africana studies, anthropology, art, atmospheric science, biology, business administration, chemistry, Chinese studies, computer science, computer science and applied mathematics, criminal justice, earth science, economics, English, French, geography, geology, Greek and Roman civilization, history, information science, Italian, Judaic studies, Latin, Latin American and Caribbean studies, linguistics, mathematics, medical technology, music, philosophy, physics, political science, psychology, public affairs, Puerto Rican studies, rhetoric and communication, Russian, Russian and East European studies, social studies, social welfare, sociology, Spanish, theater, and women's studies. Interdisciplinary majors are offered in art history, Asian studies, biochemistry and molecular biology, East Asian studies, human biology, Japanese studies, medieval and Renaissance studies, Mediterranean archaeology, and religious studies. Student-designed interdisciplinary majors are available with the guidance of a faculty member. Secondary school teacher education programs for grades 7–12 are offered in biology, chemistry, earth science, English, French, mathematics, physics, Russian, social studies, and Spanish.

Academic Program

To earn the bachelor's degree, a student must complete a minimum of 120 credits (including general education requirements), satisfy major requirements, and complete a minor or a second major. Students are admitted to the University as open majors and are encouraged to use their general education requirements to explore a variety of disciplinary interests. General education requirements specify that students complete 6 credits of approved course work in each of three categories: humanities and the arts, natural sciences, and social sciences. In addition, students must satisfactorily complete two writing-intensive courses, a 3-credit course in cultural and historical perspectives, and a 3-credit course in human diversity.

Students may elect a double major or create their own interdisciplinary major if no existing program suits their particular interests. Prehealth, predental, and prelaw preparation is available through selected course work with any of the major programs. Special advisement for these programs is also available. Admission to most programs occurs at the end of the student's sophomore year.

The University also offers many combined bachelor's/master's degree programs that allow students to complete the requirements of both degrees at an accelerated pace. A host of combined degree options is available, including the option of combining a bachelor's degree in an area of the liberal arts and sciences with the M.B.A. degree. Albany's 3-3 program with Albany Law School allows students to earn a bachelor's degree and a law degree in a total of six years rather than seven. Students apply for this program as freshmen. The 3-2 engineering program allows Albany students to study physics on the Albany campus for three years and then complete an engineering degree through Clarkson University, Rensselaer Polytechnic Institute, SUNY at Binghamton, or SUNY at New Paltz.

Albany also offers three special admissions programs for prehealth students: the Early Assurance of Admission to Albany Medical College; the Joint Seven-Year Biology/Optometry Program, in conjunction with the SUNY College of Optometry in New York City; and a seven-year dental program with Boston University's Goldman School of Dental Medicine.

Off-Campus Arrangements

For juniors and seniors, Albany offers study-abroad programs in Brazil, China, Costa Rica, Denmark, France, Germany, Great Britain, Hungary, Israel, Japan, the Netherlands, Russia, Singapore, and Spain. Albany students may also participate in any of the more than 300 study-abroad programs offered through the State University of New York.

The University also offers summer archaeological dig programs, performance experiences in music and theater, and opportunities for independent study and projects.

The school's location in New York State's capital has created exciting career-preparation opportunities for students. A wide range of other internships is available, including those in agencies, accounting firms, a major medical facility, local and national television stations, and various corporations. In addition, students may also participate in an internship through the Washington Center or elect the Washington Semester at American University in Washington, D.C. They can also earn academic credit while performing approved volunteer work through the Community and Public Service Program.

Academic Facilities

SUNY at Albany's main campus, designed by the noted architect Edward Durrell Stone, is a unique architectural structure. Its thirteen academic buildings rest on a common "Academic Podium" of classrooms, laboratories, and offices. The University also has a large computing center, a nuclear-particle accelerator, and the largest fine arts museum in the SUNY system.

The University Library on the main campus and the Graduate Library for Public Affairs and Policy on the downtown campus house more than 1.8 million volumes and more than 9,000 periodical titles. A third library facility is under construction on the main campus.

Costs

For 1999–2000, the annual undergraduate tuition for New York State residents was $3400; tuition for out-of-state students was $8300. Mandatory fees totaled $900. Room cost $3595 and board cost $1876.

Financial Aid

Merit scholarships are available to Presidential Scholars and other exceptional students. The Office of Financial Aid administers all undergraduate financial assistance, including Federal Work-Study Program employment, Federal Perkins Loans, Federal Supplemental Educational Opportunity Grants, New York Equality of Opportunity Grants, Alumni Scholarships, Federal Pell Grants, Federal Stafford Student Loans, New York Tuition Assistance Program awards, and New York Regents Scholarships. General part-time employment is available both on and off the campus. Aid awarded to students through the Office of Financial Aid is based on demonstrated financial need as determined by the Free Application for Federal Student Aid (FAFSA).

Faculty

At SUNY at Albany, the faculty is fully engaged in teaching undergraduates. There are 585 full-time faculty members, 99 percent of whom have earned a Ph.D. Undergraduates have the opportunity to conduct supervised research with Albany faculty members, who are known for their expertise in a wide variety of fields. The University is also the home of the New York State Writers Institute, headed by Pulitzer Prize–winning author William Kennedy. The Institute affords students access to lectures and readings by acclaimed authors and poets. Residential quads include a faculty member in residence. The student-faculty ratio is 18:1.

Student Government

Students are represented on the University Senate and its committees and have their own governing organization, the Student Association (SA). The Central Council, the SA's legislative body, deals with internal policy and administers about $1 million from student activity fees.

Admission Requirements

Applicants are evaluated on the basis of their three-year high school average, class ranking, and SAT I and/or ACT scores. Students should generally have grades of at least B+ and rank within the top quarter of their class in order to be competitive. All applicants must complete a minimum of 18 credits in high school, including 2 units of academic mathematics, 1 unit of which must be in elementary algebra. The University also actively seeks transfer students; competition for admission varies, depending on the program sought. Generally, a minimum 2.5 cumulative average is required. (Applicants for the Schools of Business, Criminal Justice, and Social Welfare are expected to achieve a cumulative average above 3.0.) The University also welcomes applications from educationally and financially disadvantaged students (Educational Opportunity Program), multicultural students, and international students. Recommendations are not required but are welcome, especially when they will help the University to assess the validity of the credentials being reviewed. Interviews are generally not required. The Admissions Office conducts information sessions, and student-led tours are available daily when classes are in session.

Application and Information

Students may apply for fall, spring, or summer admission. SUNY Common Application forms are available in New York State high schools and all SUNY two- and four-year colleges. To receive full consideration, students should apply by February 15 for the fall term and by November 15 for the spring. Transfer students are encouraged to apply as early as possible and no later than June 15 for fall admission and December 15 for spring admission. Notification is on a rolling basis.

For further information, students should contact:

Director of Admissions
State University of New York at Albany
1400 Washington Avenue
Albany, New York 12222
Telephone: 518-442-5435
E-mail: ugadmit@safnet.albany.edu
World Wide Web: http://www.albany.edu/

STATE UNIVERSITY OF NEW YORK AT BINGHAMTON

BINGHAMTON, NEW YORK

The University

Founded in 1946, the school that has become Binghamton University enrolls 9,872 undergraduates and 2,692 graduate students. Binghamton includes Harpur College of Arts and Sciences, the School of Management, the Decker School of Nursing, the School of Education and Human Development, and the Watson School of Engineering and Applied Science. Together, these five schools provide an extremely high-quality, affordable education for students from New York State, more than forty other states, and at least seventy-five other nations. Strong graduate programs provide an excellent research base upon which undergraduate instruction is built. Several dozen academic majors provide students with richness of choice. In Harpur College, almost one fifth of the undergraduates pursue more than one major, and many also select a minor field of study. Such combinations enable students to choose new directions, combine career paths with avocations, and deepen their knowledge of related fields. All academic programs are accredited by the State of New York, by the Middle States Association of Colleges and Schools, and by several professional associations. A complete list of accreditations may be found in the University Bulletin.

Binghamton is proud of its traditions of excellence and diversity. Almost one third of the undergraduates are persons of color, and many students come from homes where members speak languages other than English. Many parents were educated in other nations, and students bring to campus a wealth of traditions to share with friends and classmates. The curriculum at Binghamton includes an international focus. Students may choose an International Studies Certificate, study abroad at more than 260 locations, and pursue languages, area studies, and innovative programs such as Languages Across the Curriculum, Science Across the Curriculum, and Writing Across the Curriculum. Graduates often comment that the strength of their Binghamton education is epitomized by strong writing and critical-thinking skills. Students are pleased by the accessibility of faculty members and by their interest in students, which results in productive partnerships.

More than 9,870 undergraduates enrolled in fall 1999, including 2,053 freshmen and 726 transfers. Typically, more than 90 percent of the freshmen return as sophomores. Around 70 percent graduate in four years, and about 80 percent take five years. More than half of the graduates of Harpur College go to graduate or professional school immediately or within a few years of completing their bachelor's degrees. Graduates of the programs in engineering, accounting, nursing, human development, computer science, and management typically go first to work, then later go to graduate school.

A very distinctive feature at Binghamton is residential life. Residence halls are clustered into colleges and communities, each with a dining center, recreation space, hall and community student government, theater companies, study lounges, and special interest housing floors. The traditional ceremonies and celebrations, including such whimsically titled events as Newing Navy, Hinman Hysteria, and Mutant Mania, bring students together to compete for prizes, socialize, and cheer each other on. Housing is guaranteed for all four years for entering freshmen. Some buildings have 2-person rooms along corridors; others have suites featuring two or three bedrooms designed for 2 students each, with a common living area and bathroom. The dining centers in each community are complemented by other facilities, including a Kosher kitchen, vending machines, and snack bars.

More than 170 student organizations help students develop new skills, meet new friends, and express commitments. They are as varied as culture, language, religion, and service to others. Participation in sports; managing the campus radio and television stations and the campus bus system and ambulance service; student government; and many other activities bring growth and enjoyment. Binghamton's intercollegiate athletics program, featuring nine sports for women and ten for men, is moving from the NCAA Division II to Division I in 2001. There are also many intercollegiate sports clubs and myriad intramural sports, such as inner-tube water polo, floor hockey, volleyball, and co-rec football.

Students who come to Binghamton expect a high-quality education at a very affordable cost. They expect openness and a generosity of spirit between students and faculty members. There is a great deal of mutual help among students as they compete against the standard of a class rather than against each other.

Location

Binghamton University is located on a very green 828-acre campus with an adjoining nature preserve. The campus is in a suburban area, just 10 minutes from the small city of Binghamton, on gently sloping, wooded land with large lawns. The Binghamton Regional Airport is less than 10 miles from campus, and the bus companies downtown are within 10 minutes by cab. Syracuse is 72 miles to the north, and Scranton, Pennsylvania, is equidistant to the south. Ithaca is within an hour's drive of campus.

Majors and Degrees

The areas of study are accounting; Africana studies; anthropology; Arabic; art; art history; biochemistry; biological sciences; chemistry; cinema; classical studies; comparative literature; computer engineering; computer science; economics; electrical engineering; English; environmental studies; French; geography; geological sciences; German; Hebrew; history; human development; industrial and systems engineering; Innovational Projects Board individualized majors; Italian; Judaic studies; Latin American and Caribbean area studies; management; mathematical sciences; mechanical engineering; medieval studies; music; philosophy; philosophy, politics, and law; physics; political science; psychobiology; psychology; sociology; Spanish; and theater.

Academic Program

All students participate in the General Education core curriculum while also selecting a major and elective courses from the school to which they are admitted. Students enter one of the five schools mentioned above, though they may take some courses offered by the other four schools, as appropriate.

There are honors programs for several undergraduate schools, and a campuswide honors program is soon to be implemented. Binghamton students are eligible for more than eighteen honor societies, including Phi Beta Kappa, Tau Beta Pi, and Golden Key. More than 80 percent of all freshmen bring Advanced

Placement credit, credit earned through Project Advance or the International Baccalaureate program, or credit from other colleges or universities.

Off-Campus Arrangements

In addition to more than 260 study-abroad options offered by Binghamton and other State University of New York campuses, there are hundreds of credit-bearing internships in the community sponsored jointly by the University and local agencies, businesses, and health providers. Binghamton participates in the National Student Exchange, which allows its students to spend a semester or year elsewhere, and students from other universities enroll at Binghamton.

Academic Facilities

Nearly 100 buildings grace the Binghamton campus. More than $150 million in expansion or renovation, including expansion of the University Union and construction of a new residence hall, is under way, as is design work for a new field house and engineering building. There are extensive, excellent library and computing facilities, and the Anderson Center for the Performing Arts brings world-renowned artists to one of the most acoustically outstanding theaters in the country. The new Academic Complex is home to three professional schools and enrollment services. The Center for Academic Excellence is a campus-sponsored tutorial center available to students. The Educational Opportunity Program offers its students additional sources of help: the Campos/Robeson Tutorial Center and counselors in the Michael V. Boyd EOP Center. Other buildings include excellent science labs, two gymnasiums, and a fine arts museum.

Costs

In 1999–2000, in-state tuition, fees, and room and board costs totaled $9932. Out-of-state tuition cost $4900 more.

Financial Aid

About 65 percent of all undergraduates have need-based aid. A number of merit scholarships are also awarded. Financial aid is not provided for international undergraduate students. Binghamton students graduate with among the lowest loan indebtedness of any university students in the United States.

Faculty

Almost 800 full- and part-time faculty members teach students in classes that average 29. The student-faculty ratio is 17:1. More than 95 percent of the faculty members have the doctorate or appropriate terminal degree in their field. Faculty members conduct research and teach, and students are routinely able to participate in research, sometimes coauthoring publications.

Student Government

The Student Association is the campuswide elected group of student representatives who allocate student activity funds to, and help oversee, 170 student organizations. In addition, each residential community has student governance comprising elected hall officers. Extensive participatory democracy is a mark of the Binghamton experience.

Admission Requirements

Admission is highly selective. Students are admitted to one of the five schools. Watson students choose engineering or computer science. Typically, more than 16,000 freshmen apply for about 1,900 places, and about 40 percent are offered admission. SAT I or ACT scores are required, as are an essay and other supplementary information. The average freshman GPA is 92, the mean SAT I score is 1201, and the middle 50 percent of freshmen have SAT scores between 1100 and 1330. Transfer students are admitted based on the strength of previous college work. A 3.2 (on a 4.0 scale) is the mean GPA of all admitted transfers, but the range varies by school and with personal circumstances, including evidence of maturity and growth. The application fee is $30.

Application and Information

Freshman applications for fall's nonbinding Early Action program must be submitted by November 1. Other applications are received until mid-February. Transfer applications are received until spaces for programs fill. While the programs in management, accounting, and computer science are among the most selective and students should apply as early as possible, limits of certain state and federal financial aid funds make it important for all transfers to apply as early as possible. Some freshman and transfer students are also admitted for the spring semester, and applications should be in by November 1. Freshmen must submit the Supplementary Admissions Form (SAF). All transfers are either required or strongly encouraged to submit the SAF as well.

Office of Undergraduate Admissions
Binghamton University
P.O. Box 6001
Binghamton, New York 13902-6001
Telephone: 607-777-2171
E-mail: admit@binghamton.edu
World Wide Web: http://www.binghamton.edu

Binghamton's scenic campus.

STATE UNIVERSITY OF NEW YORK AT BUFFALO

BUFFALO, NEW YORK

The University

The University at Buffalo (UB) is a multifaceted public university where undergraduate education is enriched and intensified by its close association with graduate programs and cutting-edge research. With more than 100 bachelor's degree programs and more than seventy undergraduate minors, 112 master's and 98 doctoral degree programs, and more than 3,000 courses, UB offers more academic choices than any other public university in New York and New England. In addition to twenty-nine departments in the College of Arts and Sciences, UB has schools of architecture, dental medicine, education (graduate, with a provisional teacher certification program for undergraduates), engineering, health-related professions (which offers a new professional doctoral degree in physical therapy), information studies, law, management, medicine, nursing, pharmacy, and social work.

Because UB is a research-intensive university, undergraduates study and work with faculty members who are leaders in their fields in academic and research facilities that support work at the most advanced levels of knowledge. This environment involves students in the discovery process and encourages them to develop the kind of critical thinking required in the creation of new knowledge. UB undergraduates have an opportunity to combine elements from several fields of knowledge or to design their own bachelor's degree programs.

UB's Honors Program now enrolls more than 750 students with SAT I scores ranging from 1300 to 1600. UB awards more merit-based scholarships than any other public university in New York State. In 2000, the combined total of Honors and Academic Excellence Scholarships for new students is $1.3 million. Graduates of UB's Honors Program have won Fulbright, Marshall, Guggenheim, and other distinguished awards. In addition, a significant amount in athletic grants-in-aid is awarded to student athletes recruited to participate in UB's NCAA Division I intercollegiate athletics programs.

As a large university with approximately 24,000 students, of whom some 14,000 are daytime undergraduates, the University at Buffalo can sustain a rich and varied student life. The University has energetic men's and women's sports programs at both the intramural and NCAA Division I levels, extensive recreational and entertainment facilities, more than 250 student organizations that range from newspaper and magazine publishing to Ultimate Frisbee and the Community Action Corps, and a busy calendar of general interest lectures, concerts, and films.

The University at Buffalo has two campuses. Its North Campus, the seat of most of the undergraduate academic programs, occupies 2 square miles of fields and woods in suburban Amherst. It is one of the most modern university campuses in the nation. More than 5 million square feet of academic space, laboratories, libraries, residence halls, and recreation facilities have been built there since 1972. An expanded Student Union, a Center for the Arts, an athletics stadium, and a Natural Sciences Complex were completed between 1993 and 1995. The University's commitment to adding apartment-style living space has resulted in three new apartment complexes on or adjacent to campus—more than 850 units. Flickinger Court, Hadley Village, and South Lake Village apartments opened in 1998, 1999, and 2000, and more are planned for the future. A new mathematics building will be completed in 2001.

The South Campus, 3 miles away in the residential northeast corner of Buffalo, is largely devoted to the health sciences and architecture. Buffalo's rapid transit line connects that campus with the city center and the waterfront. The South Campus also has residence halls for undergraduates. Many students who live off campus find rooms and apartments in the surrounding area.

Location

Buffalo is a Great Lakes city on an international border with a metropolitan area population of more than 1 million. It is a city of friendly neighborhoods with big-city recreation for all tastes: professional sports teams, the Buffalo Philharmonic Orchestra, the renowned twentieth-century art collection in the Albright-Knox Art Gallery, and a lively club scene. It also has a dramatic setting on Lake Erie and the Niagara River. Buffalo has abundant outdoor recreation in all four seasons. Skiing, hiking, camping, Lake Erie beaches, and the natural wonder of Niagara Falls are all nearby.

Majors and Degrees

UB is organized into one college and seven schools that serve undergraduates. The College of Arts and Sciences offers academic majors in African-American studies, American studies, anthropology, art, art history, biological sciences, chemistry, classics, communication, computational physics, computer science, dance, economics, English, fine arts, geography, geological sciences, history, linguistics, mathematics, mathematics-economics, mathematics-physics, media study, modern languages and literatures (French, German, Italian, and Spanish), music, music performance, music theater, philosophy, physics, political science, psychology, sociology, speech and hearing science, studio art, theater, and women's studies. An interdisciplinary degree program in the social sciences, with concentrations in cognitive science, environmental studies, health and human services, international studies, legal studies, and urban and public policy studies, is offered. The School of Architecture and Planning offers majors in architecture and environmental design. The School of Engineering and Applied Sciences offers academic majors in engineering physics and in aerospace, chemical, civil, computer, electrical, environmental, industrial, and mechanical engineering. The School of Health Related Professions offers academic majors in exercise science, medical technology, nuclear medicine technology, and occupational therapy. Physical therapy is offered as an advanced degree program; undergraduates major in exercise science. The School of Management offers a major in business administration, with concentrations in accounting, financial analysis, human resources management, internal auditing, international business, management information systems, and marketing. The School of Medicine and Biomedical Sciences offers academic majors in biochemistry and biophysics. The School of Nursing offers an academic major in nursing. The School of Pharmacy offers academic majors in biochemical pharmacology, medicinal chemistry, and pharmaceutics and a six-year Pharm.D. pharmacy program. UB also offers an undergraduate certification program for secondary education. UB has more than a dozen combined-degree programs (B.A./M.A. and B.S./M.B.A., for example) that can be completed in five years. Students whose objectives cannot be met through existing programs can formulate their own degree programs through double-degree or double-, joint-, or special-major options and an extensive minors program.

Academic Program

Candidates for a baccalaureate degree are required to complete a minimum of 120 semester hours, 30 of which must be completed in residence, and earn a minimum grade point average of 2.0. Students have great flexibility in planning their academic programs. All students must fulfill a University general education requirement. They must also complete an academic major, which is selected, with the advice of an academic adviser, usually by the end of the sophomore year. Students also have ample opportunity for independent study under departmental or faculty auspices. Placement and credit are granted on the basis of Advanced Placement or College-Level Examination Program scores. The academic year has two semesters, one beginning in late August, the other in late January. An extensive summer session is also offered.

Off-Campus Arrangements

Full-time undergraduates may cross-register for a maximum of two courses per term at other colleges in western New York. Many students take advantage of study-abroad programs. UB administers more than sixty overseas programs in twenty-five countries for full academic years or fall, spring, or summer sessions. Students who wish to study abroad in locations not offered by UB may take advantage of nearly 300 programs offered by other colleges in the SUNY system.

Academic Facilities

The University at Buffalo's academic library collections are the largest in the SUNY System; in addition to more than 3.2 million bound volumes, they include 23,000 serials and periodicals, 5 million microforms, specialized holdings including one of the world's largest collection of James Joyce manuscripts and collateral material, and a renowned collection of twentieth-century poetry in manuscript. All the library holdings are digitally cataloged on a system accessible from campus terminals and student computers on and off campus. More than 170 state-of-the-art computer workstations are in public sites in UB's ten libraries.

The University's varied computational facilities, including three supercomputer configurations at the Center for Computational Research, can support learning, instruction, and research on any scale. Undergraduates are exposed to the latest in educational technology innovation at every level of the University, from free, unlimited e-mail and Internet use and Web-based course materials to online "chat" with math tutors. For everyday use, the UB has more than 100 public and departmental labs with more than 1,800 workstations for students. Many labs are available 24 hours a day, seven days a week. All students receive free UB IT accounts, which provide access to the Internet and to UB services. Residence halls and University apartments are all wired with high-speed (Ethernet) data connections. According to *Yahoo! Internet Life* magazine, UB is one of the top fifty "wired" campuses in the country.

Costs

In 1999–2000, tuition for New York State residents was $3400 and for out-of-state residents, $8300. For all students, fees were $1255, and room and board were $6004. Students should expect additional expenses for books and supplies, transportation, and personal expenses. (This is an annual budget.)

Financial Aid

The University at Buffalo participates in all New York State and federal financial aid programs, including the Tuition Assistance Program (available only to New York State residents) and the Federal Pell Grant, Federal Work-Study, Federal Direct Student Loan, and Federal Perkins Loan programs. Interested students must complete the Free Application for Federal Student Aid in early March for fall semester entry. All inquiries concerning financial aid should be addressed to the Office of Financial Aid, Hayes C, State University of New York at Buffalo.

Faculty

Of the 1,869 faculty members, 98 percent hold the doctorate or another appropriate terminal degree. A large number have published books or scholarly articles. Many have held major national or international fellowships; conducted research funded by government agencies or national foundations; served as consultants to business, education, and government; or otherwise demonstrated professional expertise. More than 100 faculty members have won the SUNY Chancellor's Award for Excellence in Teaching. This is the largest number of recipients on any one of the SUNY campuses.

Student Government

All daytime undergraduate students are members of the Student Association and are entitled to participate in its activities. The Student Association is involved at every level of student life, from freshman orientation to commencement. By their membership on many University-wide policy committees, representatives of the association are given a legitimate, permanent voice in the policies and direction of the University.

Admission Requirements

Applicants are required to submit their high school record and the results of the SAT I or ACT. Applicants should plan to take the SAT I or ACT no later than November. Application review and notification begins in mid-December and continues until the freshman class is filled. Most freshmen are admitted to the College of Arts and Sciences and make application to the major of their choice during the sophomore year. However, architecture, art, engineering, management, and music offer departmental admission to freshman applicants.

Admission is competitive. Most successful students at the University have come to it with a strong level of academic preparation in basic academic areas. In recent years, nearly 85 percent of accepted freshmen had high school averages of 85 or higher, and about 70 percent had combined SAT I scores of 1100 or higher.

The Individualized Admission Program provides an opportunity for enrollment in the freshman class to a limited number of students who demonstrate academic potential through means other than the quantitative scholastic measures described above. Creative talent in architecture, art, music, theater, or writing; athletics; special academic achievement; demonstrated leadership; community service; and personal circumstances are examples of areas that students may cite and support with evidence in requesting consideration under this program. Students who may qualify for this program will be sent a supplementary admission form.

Transfer applicants must have completed a minimum of 24 semester hours at a regionally accredited college prior to application. Students with fewer than 24 semester hours are evaluated on the basis of their college and high school credentials in combination with standardized test score results. Admission of transfer students is based on the quality of previous academic performance and space availability. All students presenting a minimum grade point average of 2.0 (calculated according to UB grading policy) will be considered for admission to the College of Arts and Sciences. Admission to an academic department may occur concurrently with University admission if the applicant has fulfilled prerequisite requirements. These requirements include completed courses, but may also comprise essay, portfolio, exam, or audition requirements. Some departments have significantly higher GPA standards and early deadlines for application.

Application and Information

Applications are available in New York State high schools or by contacting:

Office of Admissions
15 Capen Hall
State University of New York at Buffalo
Buffalo, New York 14260-1660

Office of Admissions
State University of New York at Buffalo
125 Park Avenue, 15th Floor
New York, New York 10017-5529

Telephone: 716-645-6900 (Buffalo)
212-808-8116 (New York City)
888-UB-ADMIT (toll-free)
E-mail: ub-admissions@admissions.buffalo.edu
World Wide Web: http://www.buffalo.edu

STATE UNIVERSITY OF NEW YORK AT BUFFALO
School of Engineering and Applied Sciences
BUFFALO, NEW YORK

The University

The State University of New York at Buffalo, founded in 1846 as the University of Buffalo, is today the largest single unit and most comprehensive undergraduate and graduate center of the State University, enrolling about 25,000 students (about 18,375 attending full-time). There are 1,900 undergraduate students in the School of Engineering and Applied Sciences. The merger in 1962 with the State University System signaled a period of dramatic development. The University offers ninety-three undergraduate, 112 master's, ninety-eight doctoral, and six professional programs.

The School of Engineering and Applied Sciences is located on the North Campus, a 1,200-acre site in Amherst, New York. This campus has modern residence halls that accommodate more than 4,000 students. The University also maintains five residence halls on the South Campus for more than 1,000 students. Shuttle-bus transportation, scheduled to meet student needs, makes it possible to meet dining hall, classroom, and social commitments. Students seeking housing should write to University Residence Halls, Spaulding Quad Room 106, Ellicott Complex, Buffalo, New York 14261, or telephone the Housing Office at 716-645-2171 e-mail: (residence-halls@acsu.buffalo.edu).

Within the University, the Career Planning and Placement Office provides assistance to students seeking temporary and permanent employment as well as educational placement.

Location

Buffalo, located along Lake Erie and the Niagara River, is New York State's second-largest city and the dynamic capital of its expanding Niagara Frontier. Metropolitan Buffalo has nearly 1.5 million inhabitants. It ranks eighth nationally in expenditures for research and supports more than 100 private, industrial, and institutional laboratories. The city's rapidly expanding cultural facilities include the world-famous Albright-Knox Art Gallery, the Buffalo Philharmonic Orchestra, the State University of New York at Buffalo's programs of performing arts, the Studio Arena Theater, and numerous historical and science museums. Recreational facilities are available in and around the metropolitan area for both summer (swimming, boating, and fishing) and winter (skating, sleighing, and skiing) sports. A major sports stadium and an auditorium house the spectator events. There are several city parks for picnics and outings, including a zoological park and a children's zoo. Niagara Falls, the major scenic attraction in the area, is within a half-hour drive of downtown Buffalo. The network of highways in and around the city makes all areas easily accessible to the University, which is situated in a residential area at the Buffalo city limits.

Majors and Degrees

The School of Engineering and Applied Sciences offers six undergraduate engineering programs that are accredited by the Engineering Accreditation Commission of the Accreditation Board for Engineering and Technology and lead to a B.S. degree in the following areas: aerospace engineering, chemical engineering, civil engineering, electrical engineering, industrial engineering, and mechanical engineering. A B.S. degree in engineering physics is offered in cooperation with the Department of Physics, and B.S. degrees in computer and environmental engineering are also offered.

Academic Program

To graduate, a student is required to complete 128 semester hours. In all engineering programs, students normally complete 64 semester hours by the end of their sophomore year. Included in the 64 semester hours is a required core curriculum that all Bachelor of Science candidates are expected to take during the first two years. Usually in the sophomore year, students specialize in an area by selecting a major and fulfilling departmental requirements in their field of interest. Each engineering area varies in the required number of technical courses. Students should consult the program or department office for the most recent information.

Upon admission, each entering student meets with an adviser whose functions are to aid the student in identifying educational goals, to provide information concerning academic programs and procedures, and to help the student plan a program by selecting courses commensurate with his or her background, interests, and vocational goals. The adviser also helps the student to identify and explore any problem areas and, when necessary, refers the student to services on or off campus. A student is assigned a faculty adviser in their intended engineering major.

Students may study for the B.S. degree in civil, electrical, and mechanical engineering by taking courses offered in the Millard Fillmore College evening program. This program is designed for students who must maintain full-time employment yet have a desire to further their education.

Qualified students may plan a combined course of study in which the first three years in one of the sciences are taken at a participating college and the last two years in engineering are taken at the State University of New York at Buffalo. If the student is recommended and space is available, he or she is admitted to the State University of New York at Buffalo at the end of the junior year. The student receives a bachelor's degree from the participating college and the Bachelor of Science degree in a field of engineering from the State University of New York at Buffalo.

Buffalo enjoys a wealth of industrial resources, and opportunities to gain practical experience exist with leading companies throughout New York State and the nation. Internships and a cooperative education program are available through each department. Summer positions are available, following the junior year, through the Engineering Career Institute.

Classes for fall semester 2000 begin on August 28 and end on December 8. The last day of exams is December 18. Classes for spring semester 2001 begin on January 16 and end on April 30. The last day of exams is May 10.

Academic Facilities

Ten libraries, with holdings of more than 2.6 million volumes and approximately 23,000 current journal subscriptions, are strategically located across both campuses in areas that permit maximum accessibility. Among the noteworthy special collections are the government documents collection, microfilm collections of parliamentary debates and international documents and newspapers, U.S. Atomic Energy Commission and NASA reports and publications, and the Human Relations Area Files. The Poetry/Rare Books Library is the home of the James Joyce Collection and a world-renowned collection of modern poetry and first editions. Computerized bibliographic-search equipment facilitates the preparation of bibliographies on a variety of topics.

The University Computing Center and SEAS Computer Services provide computing facilities for faculty members, students, and researchers. The center, located on the North Campus, features an IBM 3090, a UNIX cluster, and a Sun cluster. Several engineering graphics laboratories of networked Sun Workstations support image processing and graphics for computer-aided design (CAD) and modeling. The School of Engineering also operates its own UNIX cluster. Work sites, open to all students, are available at many locations; they house terminals, IBM PCs, Macintosh computers, and Sun Workstations and are staffed by consultants ready to provide assistance.

Costs

The total budget for New York State residents for the 2000–01 academic year is approximately $12,000, which includes $3400 for tuition, $1254 for fees, and $5800 for room and board. The balance of the budget estimate is reserved for books and supplies, personal expenses, and transportation. Out-of-state tuition is $8300.

Financial Aid

The University at Buffalo participates in all New York State and federal financial aid programs, including the Tuition Assistance Program (available only to New York State residents) and the Federal Pell Grant, Federal Work-Study, Federal Stafford Student Loan, and Federal Perkins Loan programs. Interested students must complete the Free Application for Federal Student Aid in early March. All inquiries concerning financial aid should be addressed to the Office of Financial Aid, Hayes C, State University of New York at Buffalo. Prospective University students should not wait for an admission decision before applying for financial aid. Further information is available in all New York State high schools and may also be obtained by calling the Office of Financial Aid at 716-829-3724.

Faculty

The faculty in Engineering and Applied Sciences consists of about 100 members who are responsible for both undergraduate and graduate education. Most of them hold doctorates in their area of expertise. A large number have written textbooks and scholarly articles, are active in research, and serve as consultants to business, education, and government. Only faculty members teach undergraduate engineering courses, and almost all faculty members are involved in undergraduate instruction.

Student Government

All regularly enrolled daytime undergraduate students are members of the Student Association and are entitled to participate in its activities. The Student Association is involved at every level of student life from freshman orientation to commencement. By their membership on many University-wide policy committees, representatives of the association are given a legitimate, permanent voice in the policies and direction of the State University of New York at Buffalo. The School of Engineering and Applied Sciences also has its own student government association.

Admission Requirements

Candidates for admission applying from secondary schools must meet the minimum requirements of the University. For engineering applicants, high school preparation should include 4 years of mathematics; chemistry and physics are also recommended. Applicants are required to submit their high school records and the results of the SAT I or ACT. These tests should be taken no later than December for September admission.

Transfer applicants must have completed a minimum of 24 semester hours of work at a regionally accredited college prior to enrollment. Students with fewer than 24 semester hours are evaluated on the basis of their college and high school credentials. Admission of transfer students is based on the quality of previous academic performance and space availability.

Application and Information

Students are urged to submit their applications as early as possible. All applications for admission to the fall term (first semester) that are received by the Processing Center before January 5 will receive full and equal consideration for admission in September. Applications received after January 5 will be considered on a space-available basis. Applications for admission to the spring term (second semester) should be completed before December 1.

Tours of the School of Engineering and Applied Sciences are available by appointment most Fridays at 9:30 a.m. or by arrangement. Students should contact the School at 716-645-2774 for further information. The e-mail address is meryan@eng.buffalo.edu for those who prefer to use it.

Application forms are available in all New York State high schools. For additional information about either freshman studies or the transfer program, students should address requests to:

Office of Admissions
15 Capen Hall
State University of New York at Buffalo
Box 601660
Buffalo, New York 14260-1660

Telephone: 716-645-6900
E-mail: meryan@eng.buffalo.edu
World Wide Web: http://www.buffalo.edu

STATE UNIVERSITY OF NEW YORK AT FARMINGDALE
College of Technology
FARMINGDALE, NEW YORK

The College

Located within the high-technology corridor of Long Island, the State University of New York at Farmingdale College of Technology serves local business and industry with graduates of its broad range of programs in the technologies and applied sciences. The College was founded in 1912 as the New York State School of Agriculture to serve a largely agrarian community. Today, in addition to traditional programs in business, health sciences, and liberal arts, the College offers distinct baccalaureate degree and associate degree programs in the technologies and applied sciences that support the economic growth and development of the region.

Students participate in on-campus activities throughout the year, including films, concerts, theater productions, lectures, art exhibitions, and all-College theme weekends; there are also opportunities to become involved in the campus radio station. Dozens of clubs and organizations respond to a variety of interests, ranging from skydiving to philosophy. Intercollegiate competition for men is sponsored in baseball, basketball, cross-country, golf, indoor and outdoor track, lacrosse, and soccer. Women's intercollegiate sports are basketball, cross-country, soccer, softball, track, and volleyball. An extensive intramural program is also available. While the Farmingdale student body numbers more than 5,000, more than 22,000 people utilize the campus each year, attending workshops, seminars, summer sessions, sports events, the Festival of the Arts, and the circus.

Five residence halls feature lounges, study rooms, recreation rooms, and laundry facilities. The Cohen Infirmary is equipped and staffed for both inpatient and outpatient care. The Student Union houses a theater, gymnasium, weight room, and billiards room. The Career Development Center offers career counseling, career-planning seminars, job interviews, resume writing, job placement for the disabled, and opportunities for permanent, part-time, and summer jobs. A reference library of occupational and educational information is open daily. Counseling and support services include academic, financial aid, career, psychological, and residence-life counseling.

Recent reports show that Farmingdale graduates experience a high job placement and transfer rate. Of those employed, 90 percent are working in the area in which they were prepared at Farmingdale. Fifty-five percent of the respondents in last year's graduating class transferred to public and private colleges and universities throughout the nation.

Location

The picturesque 380-acre Farmingdale campus is located 1 mile north of the village of Farmingdale on Melville Road. Just off Route 110 and midway between the Southern State Parkway and Long Island Expressway, Farmingdale is on the border between Nassau and Suffolk counties. New York City is 45 minutes away by car, and some of the world's best beaches (including Jones Beach and Fire Island) are minutes away to the south of the campus.

Majors and Degrees

The College presently offers the Bachelor of Science degree in aeronautical science-professional pilot, applied mathematics, automotive management technology, aviation administration, computer (engineering) technology, construction (engineering) management technology, electrical engineering technology, facility management technology, management of technology, manufacturing engineering technology, and security systems. The Bachelor of Technology degree is offered in visual communications.

The College parallel associate degree programs include advertising art and design, apprentice training, automotive engineering technology, automotive technology, business administration, computer information systems, computer science, computer systems technology: business programming and systems, construction/architectural engineering technology, criminal justice, dental hygiene, electrical engineering technology, food and nutrition, liberal arts and sciences, mechanical engineering technology, medical laboratory technology, nursing, and ornamental horticulture. In addition, the College offers many certificate programs along with a one-year college preparatory program and the one- or two-semester undeclared major program.

Academic Program

The curricula are organized into four schools: Arts and Sciences, Business, Engineering Technologies, and Health Sciences and Human Services. Graduation credit requirements vary from program to program. Students must maintain a minimum GPA of 2.0.

To address the needs of working adults, many courses are offered in the evenings and on weekends. A diverse array of credit-free courses in computer software applications and professional development topics are sponsored by the Continuing Education Department. The College maintains partnerships with major employers of the region to provide ongoing workforce development programs for employees, either at their workplace or the campus. The education and training needs of small business are also an ongoing priority of the College and are often served by customized courses that are designed to address special needs.

The College also provides learning opportunities for older adults through its Institute for Learning in Retirement and Auditing Seniors Program.

Transfer opportunities for degree recipients include a number of articulation and Joint Admissions agreements designed to accommodate incoming transfers at the junior-year level as well as Farmingdale graduating seniors.

The Educational Opportunity Center (EOC) of Long Island, based at the Farmingdale campus, is designed to provide a tuition-free, nondegree education for economically and educationally disadvantaged persons. Farmingdale's Educational Opportunity Program (EOP) provides tutorial assistance, developmental courses in mathematics and reading, special work in study skills, and intensive counseling for students who meet the program's economic and educational criteria.

The College calendar consists of a fall and spring semester and a three-part summer session.

SUNY Farmingdale is fully accredited by the Middle States Association of Colleges and Schools. All programs are approved by the New York State Department of Education. All applicable programs are registered with and accredited by the requisite professional accrediting bodies.

Academic Facilities

The Greenley Library has a collection of more than 131,000 volumes and 106,000 pamphlets, periodicals, and other materials. Tutoring services in all disciplines taught at the College are available as are evaluations to detect learning disabilities and assess problems in reading, writing, and mathematics. Computer facilities include a multinode DEC cluster computer system, numerous online video monitor terminals, hundreds of microcomputers, and a computer graphics center. An on-campus Child Care Center provides child care for the children of students, faculty members, and alumni. The 19,000-square-foot Aviation Educational Center at Republic Airport provides classrooms, teaching laboratories (including aircraft and engine labs), a flight simulation laboratory, flight operations and briefing, and an aircraft maintenance hangar as well as offices for faculty members. The fleet includes sixteen aircraft, including low-noise, fuel-efficient aircraft. New Media Design is the student in-house advertising agency, which produces professional-quality work on a pro bono basis for various organizations, such as the American Heart Association, United Cerebral Palsy, Long Island Aquarium, and Hi-Hello Child Care. The Technology Transfer and Utilization Center provides students opportunities to work on state-of-the-art manufacturing processes in order to assist small- and medium-sized companies in making decisions. Equipment includes full industrial scale systems in the areas of laser cutting, thermal spray coating, rapid prototyping, vision-guided robots for automated assembly, CNC machining, DCC/CMM, CAD/CAM, and cellular manufacturing systems. The Center for Rehabilitation Technology and Research has received seed money to research and develop technologies that will aid in the improvement of the general health and well-being of the country's estimated 1.5 million geriatric institutional patients and more than 30 million home-care patients, including the frail elderly and the disabled. A consortium is working to ease suffering and create jobs. A relief cushion developed for use in wheelchairs to decrease the incidence of decubiti (skin ulcers) has passed through its clinical trials. The design and development of a pediatric wheelchair is also underway. The Ornamental Horticulture Teaching Gardens provide a living laboratory for students and faculty members as well as a place of beauty for all. The 8-acre gardens include a rose garden, a fragrant English perennial garden, water gardens, a walled ghost garden, and an exotic tropical garden. The Security Systems Laboratories include four specialized teaching and research labs in access control, closed-circuit television, computer forensics, and intrusion detection. The Advanced Manufacturing and Applied Engineering Incubator at SUNY Farmingdale provides space, ready access to consulting help, and a supply of part-time, highly motivated workers to a maximum of six start-up companies. Other academic facilities include a modern physical education facility, health-care facilities, abundant state-of-the-art technical equipment, modern classrooms, and many laboratories for engineering, biology, chemistry, and physics.

Costs

For 1999–2000, annual costs for full-time attendance at Farmingdale for New York State residents were tuition, $3200 (plus nominal fees); room and board, $6114; and books and supplies, approximately $600. Tuition for out-of-state students was $8300 per year. (Tuition and fees are subject to change.)

Financial Aid

Almost 70 percent of Farmingdale's students receive some kind of financial aid. Farmingdale participates in the Federal Pell Grant, Federal Supplemental Educational Opportunity Grant (FSEOG), Federal Work-Study, Federal Perkins Loan, Federal PLUS loan, Federal Stafford Student Loan, and Federal Unsubsidized Stafford Loans programs. The College also participates in New York State's Tuition Assistance Program (TAP), Regents Award for Children of Deceased Police Officers or Firefighters, Scholarship for Children of Deceased or Disabled Veterans, and U.S. Bureau of Indian Affairs Aid to Native Americans as well as other state grant and scholarship programs. Students are encouraged to apply for private scholarships from the Farmingdale College Foundation, Farmingdale Alumni Association, and other organizations and companies. Emergency loans are available from the Student Government Association and Alumni Association. Approximately $8 million is awarded annually through these programs.

To apply for financial aid, students must file the Free Application for Federal Student Aid as early as possible. In addition, April 1 is the preferred and recommended filing date for the College's financial aid application.

Faculty

There is a distinguished full-time faculty, consisting of 170 members, who possess both the highest credentials and industrial experience. Most faculty members in the College's curricula are still actively involved with business and industry, thereby constantly exposing their students to the most contemporary practices in their respective fields of study. In addition, the College is recognized and commended for its small class size and accessible faculty members by students and alumni responding to annual surveys.

Student Government

The Student Government Association has authority over all student organizations and elects officers on an annual basis. Sixteen senators and 7 executive board members compose the governing board, which acts in matters promoting the interests of the College and its students.

Admission Requirements

Applicants to the baccalaureate and associate degree programs must have graduated from high school or hold a high school equivalency diploma. Students apply and are accepted to a specific curriculum. Admission requirements vary according to the program selected. The SAT I or ACT is required. Decisions are based primarily on grades earned in academic courses, including the specific high school prerequisite courses of each curriculum. The review process takes into account the applicant's individual overall background, including available data such as test scores, rank in class, and teacher/counselor recommendations. A personal interview is not required but may be beneficial to the candidate. Applicants with subject deficiencies may make up work prior to registration. When necessary, remedial programs are recommended.

A limited number of high school seniors are admitted to Farmingdale under an early admission program.

Applicants for admission to baccalaureate programs may apply as freshmen or transfer students.

Application and Information

Farmingdale operates on a rolling admission system, admitting students on a first-come, first-served basis. Applicants are encouraged to submit applications as early as possible. Applicants to the associate degree programs in dental hygiene and nursing are urged to submit their application materials by January 15.

Candidates must submit the State University of New York Application Form, available in all New York State high school guidance offices and college transfer offices as well as online at the College's Web site.

Requests for further information should be addressed to:
Admissions Office
State University of New York at Farmingdale
2350 Broad Hollow Road, Route 110
Farmingdale, New York 11735-9695
Telephone: 631-420-2200
877-4-FARMINGDALE (toll-free)
World Wide Web: http://www.farmingdale.edu

STATE UNIVERSITY OF NEW YORK AT OSWEGO
OSWEGO, NEW YORK

The University

Founded in 1861, Oswego State is well into its second century of meeting the needs of today's students. Although its origins were in teacher education, the curriculum expanded in 1962 to include the arts and sciences and professional studies.

Today, Oswego is a comprehensive college with an excellent academic reputation and commitment to undergraduate education. A wide array of liberal arts and career-oriented programs are offered through the College of Arts and Sciences as well as through the School of Business and the School of Education.

Located on 696 acres on the southern shore of Lake Ontario, the spacious tree-lined campus consists of forty-five buildings. Eleven residence halls offer on-campus housing opportunities to all degree-seeking students.

The campus is alive with more than 120 extracurricular organizations covering a wide range of social, academic, cultural, and intellectual interests. Theater, art, film, music, and dance events crowd the campus cultural calendar. Oswego State also offers a full slate of intercollegiate and intramural sports for men and women. Approximately 2,850 men and 3,200 women are currently enrolled as full-time undergraduates.

Traditionally, Oswego receives among the largest number of applications of any similar-size college in the northeast. It is accredited by the Middle States Association of Colleges and Schools and has been recognized by a number of authoritative guides as a college with outstanding academic opportunities and high academic standards.

During the last several years, Oswego State has been cited in *Barron's Guide to the Best, Most Popular and Most Exciting Colleges*, *Kiplinger's Personal Finance Magazine*, and *U.S. News & World Report*'s *Best Colleges Guide*.

Location

With a population of approximately 20,000, the city of Oswego is a medium-sized upstate New York community. It is the country's oldest freshwater port and one of the leading ports on the Great Lakes/St. Lawrence Seaway. The city and its surrounding area are well known for all kinds of summer and winter recreation, including camping, boating, sailing, fishing, tennis, golf, and, in the winter months, ice-skating, cross-country skiing, and sledding. It is at the heart of the booming sports fishing industry, and tourism is on the upswing. The campus is conveniently located 35 miles northwest of Syracuse and 65 miles east of Rochester. Frequent bus service to Syracuse is available, along with connecting service throughout the Northeast by bus, train, and plane.

Majors and Degrees

Oswego State awards the Bachelor of Arts, Bachelor of Science, and Bachelor of Fine Arts degrees for programs through its College of Arts and Sciences, School of Business, and School of Education.

Through the College of Arts and Sciences students can earn a baccalaureate in American studies, anthropology, art, biology, broadcasting, chemistry, cognitive science, communication studies, computer science, earth science, economics, English, French, geochemistry, geology, German, graphic design, history, human development, information science, journalism, linguistics, math economics applied, mathematics, mathematics applied, meteorology, music, philosophy, philosophy-psychology, physics, political science, psychology, public justice, public relations, sociology, Spanish, theater, women's studies, and zoology.

The School of Business offers Bachelor of Science degree programs in accounting, accounting management, business administration, finance, human resource management, management science, and marketing.

In addition, a five-year combined B.S. in accounting and M.B.A. in management is offered.

The School of Education offers Bachelor of Science degree programs in elementary education, industrial training and development, secondary education, technology education, technology management, vocational-technical education, and wellness management.

Special programs offered by Oswego include zoo technology, resulting in a bachelor's degree in zoology at Oswego and an associate degree in zoo technology from Santa Fe Community College (Florida); 3+2 engineering programs leading to a bachelor's degree from Oswego in chemistry or physics and a B.S. in engineering from the cooperating colleges (Case Western Reserve, Clarkson, or SUNY Binghamton); 2+2 programs leading to a B.S. in cytotechnology, medical technology, respiratory care, or cardiovascular perfusion from SUNY Upstate Medical University (formerly SUNY Health Science Center) in Syracuse; a 2+3 program leading to a B.S./M.P.S. in physical therapy from SUNY Upstate Medical University; and a 3+4 pre-optometry program leading to a B.S. in chemistry from Oswego and an O.D. in optometry from SUNY College of Optometry.

Academic Program

Because interest in obtaining marketable skills continues to increase, Oswego State University offers students a broad range of courses in the liberal arts and in preprofessional and professional studies.

In addition to core courses within a major, all students must satisfy general education requirements designed to strengthen basic writing and analytical proficiency, give students awareness of their cultural heritage, and provide them with a level of literacy in the social and behavioral sciences, natural sciences, and humanities.

By completing these general education requirements during their first two years of study, Oswego students are able to select a major with a sense of confidence and purpose. However, students who are certain of their academic interest may begin working on their major program in the first year.

Upon arrival on campus, students are assigned an adviser from either their major area or the college's Student Advisement Center. Advisers assist students who have not declared a major; help students with their academic, personal, and career concerns; and collaborate in the scheduling of courses needed for graduation.

Students may consider applying for the Honors Program in Liberal Studies, which provides a challenging academic experience for high achievers regardless of major. Students also have the option of receiving credit through proficiency CLEP and Advanced Placement (AP) examinations.

Off-Campus Arrangements

Opportunities exist for students to broaden their knowledge of other countries by participating in one of the more than eighty overseas academic programs offered by the State University of New York. Programs are offered throughout the world, and costs are held as close as possible to the cost of an average semester on the Oswego campus. Through cooperative arrangements, Oswego participates in semester programs in Albany and Washington.

Internships and other field experiences are available for students from all disciplines through the Experience Based Education Office. Each year more than 800 Oswego students participate in internships on the Oswego campus, in the local area, and throughout the Northeast and beyond.

Academic Facilities

The Penfield library houses a collection of more than 2.7 million items, including 450,000 bound volumes, more than 1.8 million microforms, 180,000 government documents, and 42,000 nonprint media items. In addition, the library subscribes to more than 1,400 different journals and magazines and 22 newspapers. The library's listening area has more than 8,000 recordings, audiocassettes, and CDs, ranging from rock to classical. Additional facilities include an online catalog, periodical indexes and full-text databases on CD-ROM, a 24-hour study room, study carrels, and a microcomputer laboratory utilized for word processing, Internet access, and classroom applications.

Campuswide computer facilities for student use include a myriad of SUN Servers and desktop workstations. There are several hundred PC, Macintosh, and Sun workstations available in seven computer laboratories across campus, with three located in the residence halls. E-mail access, as well as other application and file services, is made available to students through the Instructional Computing Center (ICC). All academic and residence hall buildings are on a campuswide network through the use of ATM technology. The campus is connected to the Internet via five T1 (1.5 Mbps) lines, and an upgrade to a T-3 (45 Mbps) Internet connection is currently being developed. Approximately 200 high-speed dial-up lines are available for student access.

Adjacent to campus, the college maintains Rice Creek Field Station, including the 26-acre Rice Pond surrounded by 400 acres of natural habitat. The facility contains two lab/classrooms, a lecture room, and exhibit areas with an indoor viewing gallery providing a unique view of the creek and pond. Both college classes and community education programs are regularly held at the Field Station, which ranks among the five most extensively used facilities of its kind in the country. The State University Research Center at Oswego supplements Rice Creek opportunities through its participation in various research projects.

Located in Tyler Hall, Oswego's fine arts center, are two art galleries that feature annual traveling exhibitions, locally produced theme exhibitions, and the best work of students and faculty members. Waterman Theatre, also located in Tyler Hall, is cited as one of the fifty best theaters built in the United States since 1960.

WRVO, the college's 24,000-watt stereo public radio station, and two television studios are located in the Lanigan Hall Learning Resource Center. In addition, a student-run TV station, radio station, and two college newspaper offices are located in the Media Center in the Hewitt Union.

Costs

Tuition for 1999–2000 was $1700 per semester for New York State residents and $4150 per semester for nonresidents. Room and board charges were approximately $3080 per semester for entering students, depending on the meal plan selected. Oswego guarantees that a student's initial first-year costs for room and board will be frozen for up to four consecutive years. Books and supplies cost approximately $300 per semester, depending on the student's choice of major program. Although many activities on campus are free of charge, students will need to budget for personal expenses.

Financial Aid

Financial assistance, granted according to student need, consists of grants, loans, and part-time employment. Students interested in financial aid must file a Free Application for Federal Student Aid. New York State residents also need to file a TAP application for the state's Tuition Assistance Program. Priority is given to those applications on file by April 1 for the fall term and November 15 for the spring term.

Faculty

Oswego's faculty, consisting of 307 full-time educators, is dedicated to teaching undergraduate students. With 75 percent holding doctoral degrees from many of the finest institutions in the country, students can be assured of the opportunity for an outstanding undergraduate education. The faculty-student ratio is approximately 1:19. While the Oswego faculty is first and foremost dedicated to teaching, faculty members are actively engaged in research, publication, and public service.

Student Government

Students at Oswego are represented by the Student Association, which has as its aim the efficient and intelligent governance of a democratic student body. The functions of the Student Association are divided among various committees that allocate funds to student organizations, intercollegiate and intramural athletics, the student newspaper, the yearbook, and the student literary magazine, along with various campus social, cultural, and intellectual activities.

Admission Requirements

Admission to Oswego is competitive, with high school average, academic program, and standardized test scores being the most important criteria for applicants. Special talents such as artistic, musical, athletic, and creative writing skills are also considered. The Committee on Admissions accepts results on either the ACT or the SAT I. Although not required, a campus admissions visit is encouraged.

Transfer students in good standing are encouraged to apply for admission through a specific program. Transfer admission to many programs is restricted and quite selective.

Application and Information

Application forms are available from New York State high school guidance offices and college transfer offices. Oswego evaluates applications as they are completed and as space remains available. Those applications completed by January 15 for the fall term or October 15 for the spring term are assured of equal consideration. Applications received after those dates will be considered as space remains available.

Prospective students and their parents are encouraged to visit the campus to participate in a student-guided tour and speak with an admissions counselor. Interested candidates should call the Office of Admissions at least one or two weeks in advance to schedule a visit.

For further information, students should contact:

Office of Admissions
Oswego State University
Oswego, New York 13126

Telephone: 315-341-2250
Fax: 315-341-3260
E-mail: admiss@oswego.oswego.edu
World Wide Web: http://www.oswego.edu

Oswego State University is located on 696 acres on the southern shore of Lake Ontario.

STATE UNIVERSITY OF NEW YORK AT STONY BROOK

STONY BROOK, LONG ISLAND, NEW YORK

The University

The State University of New York at Stony Brook was founded in 1956. In the forty-four years since its founding, the University has grown tremendously and is now recognized as one of the nation's leading centers of learning and scholarship, fulfilling the mandate given by the State Board of Regents in 1960 to become a university that would "stand with the finest in the country."

Stony Brook is at the forefront of integrating research and education at the undergraduate level; it was recently selected by the National Science Foundation as one of only ten universities in the nation to receive a special recognition for this based on educational vision, a significant record of accomplishments, and leadership in the field of higher education. In fact, a recent study, *The Rise of American Research Universities,* ranks Stony Brook second in the nation among all public research universities, and it is one of only eighty-eight public and private colleges and universities nationwide to be classified a Research I institute by the Carnegie Foundation. With seventy academic departments, Stony Brook is among the top twenty-five institutions funded by the National Science Foundation, and external support for research has grown to an annual sum of more than $125 million.

Stony Brook enrolls 19,128 full- and part-time students—12,692 undergraduates and 6,436 graduate and professional students. Students hail from all fifty states and fifty-four other countries. Nearly 16,000 students are enrolled full-time. More than half of Stony Brook's undergraduates live in campus residence halls, which are organized as small residential colleges in order to foster social, intellectual, and cultural interaction.

The Stony Brook Seawolves' nineteen varsity teams compete in NCAA Division I and include men's lacrosse, baseball, and football; women's golf and volleyball; and men's and women's basketball, cross-country, soccer, swimming, tennis, and indoor and outdoor track and field. Athletic facilities are extensive and include the Indoor Sports Complex, which seats up to 5,000, as well as several outdoor athletic fields, tennis courts, bicycle and jogging paths, handball courts, and a track.

Location

Situated on 1,100 wooded acres, Stony Brook is located midway between New York City and the resort area of the Hamptons on Long Island's East End, a setting rich in both natural and architectural beauty. Students find large wooded areas on and around campus, sandy beaches are a comfortable bicycle ride away, a working harbor and tourist area are nearby, and a historic community that was once home to George Washington's Revolutionary War spy ring is within walking distance.

Majors and Degrees

Stony Brook has exceptional strength in the sciences, mathematics, humanities, fine arts, social sciences, engineering, and health professions, with the University as a whole and many of its programs individually ranked among the top fifty nationwide by *The Gourman Report* in 1998. Major academic units of the University include the College of Arts and Sciences, the College of Engineering and Applied Sciences, the W. Averell Harriman School for Management and Policy, the Marine Sciences Research Center, and the Health Sciences Center, which is made up of the Schools of Medicine, Health Technology and Management, Dental Medicine, Nursing, and Social Welfare.

The University offers undergraduate majors leading to Bachelor of Arts (B.A.), Bachelor of Science (B.S.), and Bachelor of Engineering (B.E.) degrees in Africana studies, anthropology, applied mathematics and statistics, art history and criticism, astronomy and planetary sciences, atmospheric and oceanic sciences, biochemistry, biology, business management, chemistry, cinema and cultural studies, clinical laboratory sciences, comparative literature, computer engineering, computer science, cytotechnology, earth and space sciences, economics, electrical engineering, engineering chemistry, engineering science, English, French, geology, German, history, humanities, information systems, Italian, linguistics, mathematics, mechanical engineering, multidisciplinary studies, music, nursing, occupational therapy, philosophy, physician's assistant studies, physics, political science, psychology, religious studies, respiratory care, Russian, social sciences, social work, sociology, Spanish, studio art, theater arts, and women's studies. The University also offers nearly sixty minors.

Students may earn New York State provisional certification for secondary school teaching in biology, chemistry, earth science, English, French, German, Italian, mathematics, physics, Russian, social studies, Spanish, and K–12 in teaching English as a second language.

Dual bachelor's/master's degree programs are available in all of the engineering departments, applied mathematics and statistics, geological oceanography, health sciences/physical therapy, mathematics secondary teacher preparation, nursing, and political science/public affairs.

Academic Program

Innovative learning communities at Stony Brook provide a small-college environment along with all the advantages of a major research university for groups of students with shared interests. These learning communities include Women in Science and Engineering for women interested in mathematics, science, and engineering; Freshman Learning Communities for premedical students and for those interested in the humanities and social sciences; Living/Learning Centers, where students with common interests live and learn together; Federated Learning Communities, where students study a subject from the perspective of multiple disciplines with the benefit of a faculty "master learner"; and the Honors College for high-achieving students.

Stony Brook accepts up to 30 credits by examination toward the bachelor's degree, through such means as AP, CLEP, CPE, higher-level International Baccalaureate subjects, and Stony Brook's own Challenge Program.

Students need a minimum of 120 credits for the B.A. or B.S. degree and 128 credits for the B.E. degree; 39 of these credits must be earned at the upper-division level. All students must satisfy general education requirements and maintain at least a 2.0 cumulative grade point average. Grading is traditional; a pass/no-credit option is available for some elective courses.

Stony Brook's academic year starts in early September and ends in mid-May, with the exception of some Health Sciences Center programs that begin in June or July.

Off-Campus Arrangements

Students have the opportunity to enrich their education by pursuing their academic interests in an overseas location for a summer, semester, or academic year. Stony Brook sponsors programs in England, France, Germany, Italy, Japan, Korea,

Madagascar, and Spain; students may also participate in programs sponsored by the State University of New York system in Western Europe, the Middle East, the Far East, Canada, and Latin America.

Statewide and national exchanges enable students to study for up to a year at one of more than fifty colleges and universities in New York and eight institutions elsewhere in the United States.

Opportunities also exist for students to earn academic credit and gain valuable experience while participating in internships and field research. Placements include government agencies and laboratories, hospitals and clinics, businesses and industries, and legal and social agencies on Long Island and in New York City, Albany, and Washington, D.C.

Academic Facilities

Stony Brook's major academic facilities include the Frank Melville, Jr. Memorial Library, one of the nation's largest academic libraries, with holdings of more than 1.9 million volumes and 3 million publications in microformat; the University Teaching Hospital, which is ranked among the top fifteen in the nation; and the five-theater Staller Center for the Arts. The nation's largest Asian-American Center and the Center for Molecular Medicine and Life Sciences are currently under construction and are due for completion in spring 2000. Stony Brook is also home to a myriad of centers, laboratories, and institutes. Some of these include the Institute for Theoretical Physics, Institute for Mathematical Sciences, Institute for Pattern Recognition, Institute for Terrestrial and Planetary Atmospheres, Center for High Pressure Geophysics, Center for Biotechnology, Howard Hughes Medical Institute, and Center for Regional Policy Studies.

Costs

For 2000–01, the annual tuition and fees for New York State residents are $3975. Nonresident tuition and fees are $8875. Room and board costs are $6230. Books and supplies are estimated at $750.

Financial Aid

The Office of Financial Aid and Student Employment administers several federal and state programs, including the Federal Perkins Loan, Federal Supplemental Educational Opportunity Grant, Federal Work-Study Program, New York State Higher Education Tuition Assistance Program (TAP), and Federal Stafford Student Loan. To apply for these programs, a student must complete the Free Application for Federal Student Aid (FAFSA). The FAFSA is available at all high schools and colleges. The University's scholarship program includes a selected number of scholarships awarded to students based on meritorious academic performance.

Faculty

Stony Brook's faculty members are intellectual leaders in their disciplines and include a Nobel laureate, a Pulitzer Prize winner, 4 MacArthur Fellows, a Fields prize winner, recipients of the national Medal of Technology and the Benjamin Franklin Medal, 14 members of the National Academy of Sciences, 11 members of the American Academy of Arts and Sciences, and 3 members of the National Academy of Engineering. They are also dedicated teachers and include 73 recipients of the Chancellor's Awards for Excellence in Teaching.

With 1,737 faculty members, the faculty-student ratio is about 1:18. All of Stony Brook's full-time faculty members hold either doctoral or terminal degrees in their fields, and more than 90 percent are engaged in active research that leads to publication. In fact, Stony Brook's faculty is ranked second in the nation in articles published in prestigious journals.

Student Government

Undergraduates are represented by Polity, the student government, whose members are elected by the students. Student representatives help shape University policy and advise fellow students as members of the University Senate and other organizations. Polity administers an annual budget of more than $1 million, which it uses to sponsor more than 100 student interest clubs and organizations. Varied student interests are represented by groups as diverse as the Pre-Med Society, the Commuter Student Association, Stony Brook at Law, the Cycling Club, the Committee on Cinematic Arts (COCA), the Chess Masters, the Science Fiction Forum, and several cultural clubs that include the Caribbean Students Organization, Asian Students' Alliance, Club India, African Student Union, and Latin American Student Organization.

Admission Requirements

Stony Brook is a selective institution and evaluates applicants on an individual basis. There is no automatic cutoff in the admission process, either in grade point average, rank, or test scores. The Admissions Committee seeks to enroll the strongest and most diverse class possible. Stony Brook welcomes applications from those with special talent or exceptional ability in a particular area.

Freshman admission is based primarily upon the strength and breadth of the student's academic preparatory program, grade point average, and standardized test scores. Additional criteria include class rank, extracurricular activities, and letters of recommendation, if requested. The University accepts a limited number of high school students for early admission.

Students who have attended college or university after graduating from high school are eligible to apply as transfers. Transfer applicants are expected to have performed well in a strong academic program. Transfer students applying to the upper-division programs in the Health Sciences Center must have completed at least 57 credits in liberal arts and sciences and some specific course requirements. If fewer than 24 credits were earned, the student's high school record will be requested for review.

Application and Information

Students are encouraged to submit applications for admission by July 10 for fall admission and by December 20 for spring admission. The deadline for filing early decision applications for fall admission is November 1; students receive notification of the early decision by December 15. Although interviews are not mandatory, they are recommended as a useful part of the application process.

Admission counselors are available to meet with prospective students and their families by appointment throughout the year. Campus tours with knowledgeable student guides are also available throughout the year; interested students should call ahead for a schedule.

To request an application form, schedule an interview, sign up for a campus tour, or obtain additional information, students should contact:

Office of Undergraduate Admissions
State University of New York
   at Stony Brook
Stony Brook, New York 11794-1901
Telephone: 516-632-6868
          516-632-6859 (TDD)
Fax: 516-632-9898
World Wide Web: http://www.sunysb.edu/admissions/

STATE UNIVERSITY OF NEW YORK COLLEGE AT BROCKPORT
BROCKPORT, NEW YORK

The College

SUNY Brockport cherishes its rise to prominence in higher education. Founded in 1835 as the Brockport Collegiate Institute, it became a normal school for teachers in 1867. The comprehensive college of arts and sciences found at Brockport today represents a 133-year tradition of providing education of the highest quality. Student success is the College's highest priority. It is committed to serving the citizens of New York, including the large, diverse student population, whose varying interests and needs reflect the complex challenges of contemporary society. Most of its 6,719 undergraduate students come from New York State, 11 percent represent minorities, and 1 percent are international students. There are more than 2,200 students living in various types of campus residence halls, including coed and special option housing for freshmen and transfers. The rest live in private accommodations off campus or commute from their homes. Freshman applicants are guaranteed College housing; there are no triples. Students living on campus are required to sign a housing agreement for the full academic year (September through May).

The College mall stretches from the traditional Hartwell Hall classroom and office building to the contemporary high-rise residence halls, centering on Seymour College Union. The student government recognizes and supports more than eighty separate activities, special interest clubs, intercollegiate athletic teams, and intramural and recreational events. The Tuttle Physical Education Complex has six gymnasiums, two Olympic-size swimming pools, an ice rink, two weight rooms, a gymnastics gym, a 9,500-seat stadium, an eight-lane all-weather track, and volleyball, handball, racquetball and squash, and new tennis courts. Intercollegiate sports for men are baseball, basketball, cross-country, football, ice hockey, indoor and outdoor track and field, lacrosse (beginning in fall 2000), soccer, swimming, and wrestling. Varsity sports for women are basketball, cross-country, field hockey, golf, gymnastics, indoor and outdoor track and field, lacrosse, soccer, softball, swimming, tennis, and volleyball. SUNY Brockport competes at the NCAA Division III level.

SUNY Brockport also offers a Weekend College option as well as a range of courses at the MetroCenter, a satellite facility located in Rochester, and at more than fifteen other sites in the region.

The College awards the Master of Arts degree in seven areas, the Master of Science in six areas, the Master of Fine Arts in two areas, the Master of Public Administration, the Master of Science in Education, the Master of Social Work, and several Certificates of Advanced Study.

Location

Brockport, a village of some 9,800 residents, lies along the banks of the historic Erie Canal, 16 miles west of Rochester, 60 miles east of Buffalo, and 15 minutes from Lake Ontario. Stores, churches, cinemas, and restaurants are within easy walking distance of the campus. Nearby Rochester is an All-American city and has been judged one of the ten best cities for living in the United States. It has a nationally known Philharmonic Orchestra, outstanding museums, an ultramodern planetarium, and professional baseball, soccer, and hockey teams.

Majors and Degrees

The College offers both the B.A. and B.S. in African and African American studies, anthropology, art (studio), biological sciences, chemistry, communication, computational science, computer science, dance, earth sciences, English, environmental science, French, geology, health science, history, interdisciplinary arts for children, journalism, mathematics, meteorology, philosophy, physical education, physics, political science, psychology, sociology, Spanish, theater, and water resources; the B.A. in international business and economics and international studies; the B.F.A. in studio art and dance; the B.S. in accounting, business administration, criminal justice, medical technology, recreation and leisure studies, and social work; and the B.S.N. in nursing.

Teacher certification programs are offered in elementary education; secondary education in the areas of biology and general science, chemistry and general science, earth science and general science, English, French, mathematics, physics and general science, social studies, and Spanish; and K–12 education in health education and physical education. Students preparing for a teaching career complete both an academic major and an appropriate teacher preparation program.

The College offers a 3-2 engineering program combining three years of liberal arts at SUNY Brockport and two years of engineering at Case Western Reserve University, Clarkson University, SUNY at Binghamton, SUNY at Buffalo, or Syracuse University. The program results in a B.A. or B.S. in chemistry, computer science, mathematics, or physics from Brockport and a degree in engineering from Binghamton, Buffalo, Case Western Reserve, Clarkson, or Syracuse. Brockport offers undergraduates one of the best opportunities available to do research with their major professor as a result of the strength of the sciences program at the College.

Academic Program

SUNY Brockport's educational programs strengthen, develop, and enrich the intellectual and social abilities of its students, who must complete a minimum of 120 credits in an approved program with a minimum earned academic average of 2.0 (C). Included in the 120 credits are an academic major program and a general education program of courses in composition and quantitative skills, computer literacy, contemporary issues, fine arts, humanities, natural sciences and mathematics, perspectives on women, and social sciences. Freshmen are required to take an Academic Planning Seminar (APS), which introduces them to the academic rigors and opportunities of college life and assists them in planning an individual program of study that relates to their academic, personal, and career goals. APS is taught in small groups by professors who also advise the students.

SUNY Brockport has a number of special programs: Delta College offers an emphasis on experiential learning, an interdisciplinary program core, and a time-shortened or time-variable option; the 3-1-3 program is a time- and cost-saving program for area high school seniors to earn up to 30 college credits through high school Advanced Placement courses and college courses taken on the SUNY Brockport campus; a bilingual-multicultural concentration results in a Spanish major and provisional elementary-teacher certification for students who wish to become bilingual-program teachers; an interdisciplinary program minor in international studies has been designed to highlight the international aspects of students' primary fields of interest; and an interdisciplinary program in women's studies emphasizes the past, present, and future contributions of women to society. Army ROTC is available on campus for all interested students and can provide substantial scholarship funds.

SUNY Brockport awards transfer credit for course work done at other regionally accredited colleges and universities prior to matriculation. Students may earn credit by examination, AP or CLEP, for courses offered by the College. Freshmen with outstanding high school academic records may enroll in the honors program, which includes an honors version of APS and a parallel honors general education program.

For the 2000–01 academic year, fall semester classes begin August 28, semester examinations end December 16, spring semester classes begin January 22, and semester examinations end May 12.

Off-Campus Arrangements

SUNY Brockport's study-abroad program is the largest in SUNY. Opportunities exist to study in numerous academic fields in Australia, Latin America, Europe, Asia (including Vietnam), and Africa. The Political Science Semester in Washington, D.C., allows intensive study and internship in government and politics in the nation's capital. A cooperative education program, internships, and community service options are offered through the Office of Career Services and several academic departments. SUNY Brockport is a member of the Rochester Area Colleges consortium. With the approval of their major adviser, SUNY Brockport students may take courses not offered by the College at one of the participating institutions.

Academic Facilities

SUNY Brockport's sixty-six buildings, structures, and athletic playing fields occupy about one quarter of the 435-acre campus, which is located at the edge of the village of Brockport. Along the College mall are classroom buildings, lecture halls, seminar rooms, and the Smith-Lennon Science Center (undergoing a complete renovation). North of the mall is the Tower Fine Arts Center, home of the art, foreign languages, and theater departments, with a 400-seat theater, two art galleries, studios, rehearsal halls, practice rooms, listening laboratories, and classrooms fully equipped for sculpture, ceramics, photography, jewelry making, painting, set design, and stagecraft. South of the mall is the open-stack Drake Library, with its online catalog and a collection of more than 530,000 bound volumes, 2,000 periodicals and serials, and more than 2 million microfilm items; it is also a depository for U.S. and New York State government documents. On the east, historic Hartwell Hall houses the Departments of Business Administration, English, Health Science, and Philosophy, as well as the Department of Dance, with its new performance theater, studios, and labs. The Rakov Center for Student Services combines a number of student services under one roof: Admissions, Advisement Services, the Bursar, Career Services, Educational Opportunity Program, Financial Aid, Registration and Records, and Student Employment.

Costs

For 1999–2000, the annual tuition for New York State residents was $3400 for undergraduates. Tuition for out-of-state students was $8300. Room and board cost $5410 per year. Fees totaled $614 per year, including a $145 student government activity fee, a $25 College fee, a $150 athletic fee, a $150 health fee, and a $144 technology fee. The cost of books was estimated at $700, personal expenses at $946.

Financial Aid

Approximately 83 percent of SUNY Brockport's students receive some form of financial aid. The College participates in the Federal Pell Grant, Federal Supplemental Educational Opportunity Grant, Federal Direct Student Loan, Federal Perkins Loan, Nursing Loans, and Federal Work-Study programs. New York State residents may qualify for Tuition Assistance Program awards and other state programs. The Office of Financial Aid assists students in identifying applicable programs, has an extensive student aid resource center, and prepares estimated financial aid packages for all newly accepted students prior to the payment of any advance fees. The Student Employment Office arranges part-time work for students on and off the campus. Numerous campus-controlled scholarships are available, including twenty-five Alumni Association Awards. More than 250 academic merit scholarships are available to incoming freshmen and transfer students, ranging from $614 to almost $10,000 per year. Minimum qualifications for freshmen include SAT scores of 1100 (ACT score of at least 24) and an 88 or higher high school average. Transfer students must have a transfer GPA of at least 3.6 and enter with junior status. These scholarships are renewable for those students meeting specified academic criteria. The Free Application for Federal Student Aid (FAFSA) is required of all aid applicants.

Faculty

Of the 300 full-time faculty members, 90 percent hold the highest professional degree in their field. Faculty members are active in both teaching and research. All lectures are given by faculty members; the student-faculty ratio is 19:1.

Student Government

The president, vice president, and 7 of the 13 members of the Board of Directors of the Brockport Student Government (BSG) are chosen in campuswide elections. The vice president chairs the board, and the other 5 members are nominated by major student-activity areas. BSG administers an annual budget of nearly $975,000. Students also serve on numerous other boards, councils, and academic-department organizations.

Admission Requirements

Students applying for freshman admission are evaluated on the basis of their three-year high school average, class rank, and ACT or SAT I scores. All applicants must have earned a minimum of 18 academic units in English, mathematics, science, social studies, and foreign language courses. Admission is selective; 55 percent of freshman applicants were accepted for fall 1999. The mean high school average of 85 enrolled freshmen for fall 1999 was 85, with a mean SAT I combined verbal and math score of 1035. The ACT mean composite score was 21.

Special admission programs, including the Educational Opportunity Program, Transition Program, and Exceptional Talent Admission, are also offered. Interviews are not required, but a visit to the campus and a meeting with an admission representative or faculty member are strongly encouraged. A supplemental information form is recommended from all applicants. Admission to SUNY Brockport is granted without regard to race, ethnicity, religion, gender, sexual orientation, national origin, age, disability, marital status, or status as a Vietnam-era or disabled veteran.

SUNY Brockport encourages the application of transfer students who have earned the associate degree (A.A., A.S., or A.A.S.) with a minimum GPA of 2.25. Enrollment quotas and prerequisites may restrict admission to some majors (accounting, business administration, criminal justice, international business and economics, nursing, physical education and sport, and social work) and teacher certification programs. Accepted applicants receive 60–64 transfer credits and junior status with completion of the associate degree.

Application and Information

Students may apply for fall or spring on a rolling admission basis. Accepted applicants may also attend summer sessions. Application forms are available from the Admissions Office or from guidance offices in all New York State high schools and all SUNY two-year and four-year colleges. Students should apply by January 15 for the fall semester and by December 1 for the spring semester.

Director of Admissions
State University of New York College at Brockport
350 New Campus Drive
Brockport, New York 14420-2915
Telephone: 716-395-2751
           800-382-8447 (toll-free)
E-mail: admit@brockport.edu
World Wide Web: http://www.brockport.edu

STATE UNIVERSITY OF NEW YORK COLLEGE AT BUFFALO

BUFFALO, NEW YORK

The College

Buffalo State is the largest college within the State University of New York (SUNY) System and offers academically excellent programs at the bachelor's, master's, and certificate of advanced study levels. The College takes special pride in having all of its courses taught by well-prepared faculty members rather than by teaching assistants. With seventy-six majors and forty-nine minors, students can virtually design their own degree program. Sixteen degree programs and seven minors are available entirely through evening and weekend study.

Of a total enrollment of 11,162 students, 9,252 are undergraduates. Most come from New York State; 15 percent are students from historically underrepresented groups. A variety of living/learning options are provided in on-campus housing, including the newly renovated Moore complex, which offers apartment-style housing for students with children. Off-campus housing opportunities are readily available in the surrounding residential neighborhoods.

The College professional staff complements the academic staff by providing a range of services to its diverse student body. These services include academic advisement for students who have not yet chosen a major, tutoring in the Academic Skills Center, personal counseling in the nationally accredited College Counseling Center, career assistance in the Career Development Center, medical and dental health care in the Weigel Health Center, and 24-hour protection by University Police officers.

The Sports Arena, which houses Buffalo's only college ice hockey rink, is home court to the NCAA Division III Bengals and Lady Bengals basketball teams. Buffalo State also offers varsity men's and women's teams in cross-country, indoor track, soccer, swimming and diving, and track and field. Men's varsity sports include football and ice hockey, and women's varsity teams include lacrosse, softball, tennis, and volleyball. In addition to varsity teams, the student government sponsors club teams for baseball, bowling, men's and women's rugby, skiing, and water polo.

Buffalo State is one of four educational institutions in New York State and the only SUNY institution to be accredited by the National Council for Accreditation of Teacher Education. The College also is accredited by the Council on Social Work Education; Accreditation Commission for Programs in Hospitality Administration; Accrediting Board for Engineering and Technology; American Chemical Society (approval); American Dietetic Association; American Speech-Language-Hearing Association; New York State Board of Regents; International Association of Counseling Services; Middle States Association of Colleges and Schools; National Association of Industrial Technology; and National Academy of Early Childhood Programs.

Location

Buffalo State is the only SUNY college located in a metropolitan area. The College is situated in the Elmwood Museum District adjacent to the 365-acre Delaware Park, which features the world-famous Albright-Knox Art Gallery, the Buffalo and Erie County Historical Society, Hoyt Lake, tennis courts, playing fields, and the Buffalo Zoo. The neighborhood includes many trendy restaurants and cafés. This location affords Buffalo State students and faculty members special advantages—ample work/study opportunities, an open invitation to cultural events, and plenty of social/recreational activities—all conveniently accessible by public transportation.

Located on Lake Erie, Buffalo provides easy access to sailing and other water sports. Western New York also has many opportunities for hiking, camping, climbing, and skiing.

Buffalo is New York State's second-largest city, with an area population of about 1 million. "The City of Good Neighbors" is a center for business and regional government, a focal point for the visual and performing arts, and home to some of the nation's most avid sports fans, who enjoy professional home teams in football, soccer, ice hockey, roller hockey, lacrosse, and baseball.

The city, in the heart of the Niagara frontier, is minutes from Niagara Falls and less than 2 hours from Toronto.

Majors and Degrees

The Bachelor of Arts degree is available with majors in anthropology, art, art history, the arts, biology, broadcasting, chemistry, communication, economics, English, French (language and literature), geography, geology, history, humanities, journalism, mathematics, music, philosophy, physics, political science, psychology, public communication (public relations and advertising), sociology, Spanish (language and literature), and theater.

The Bachelor of Science degree is awarded in the following programs: art education, biology (7–12), business and distributive education, business education, business studies, chemistry (7–12), computer information systems, criminal justice, design, dietetics, earth science (7–12), earth sciences, economics, elementary education plus early secondary education certification (in English, math, science, social studies, French, and Spanish), English (7–12), fashion and textile technology, forensic chemistry, French (7–12), general studies, health/wellness, hospitality administration, industrial technology, mathematics, mathematics (7–12), physics, physics (7–12), psychology, social studies education (5–12), social work, sociology, Spanish (7–12), speech language pathology, technology education, urban-regional analysis and planning, and vocational technical education.

The Bachelor of Fine Arts is awarded in design, painting, photography, printmaking, and sculpture.

The Bachelor of Science in Education is awarded in exceptional education.

The Bachelor of Technology is awarded in engineering technology: mechanical, electrical (power and machines), and electrical (electronics).

Forty-nine minors are available. Some of these are attached to the majors listed above, including anthropology, biology, chemistry, computer information systems, criminal justice, design, English, exceptional education, French, history, mathematics, physics, political science, psychology, sociology, and Spanish. Interdisciplinary or special interest minors include African and African-American studies, aging, art history, art therapy, astronomy, Canadian studies, coaching, creative studies, dance, deviance, environmental science, exceptionality, fashion design, geography, geology, German, interior design, Italian, management economics, medieval studies, meteorology, music, planning, Polish/Russian/East European studies, public administration, quality, religious studies, safety studies, social welfare, speech, theater, urban studies, women's studies, and writing.

The College also offers a special advisement program for prelaw students and for pre–health professions students preparing for graduate study in dentistry, medicine, veterinary science, and related areas.

Academic Program

All Buffalo State students must complete a minimum of 123 credit hours to qualify for a bachelor's degree. Through the careful arrangement of general education courses and electives, the College provides a general framework for understanding the human experience and an intellectual context from which to evaluate personal and social values while, at the same time, for building a foundation for a career.

Buffalo State offers an All-College Honors Program as well as honors sequences in seventeen majors.

The College operates on a semester basis, with a three-week intersemester term in January. A summer program of three 4-week sessions is also offered.

Off-Campus Arrangements

Internships, independent study projects, clinical practice, workshops, exchange opportunities with 148 other U.S. colleges and universities and more than 300 institutions around the world, credit for experiential learning, and the ability to cross-register or complete degrees at other schools through 3+2 arrangements provide flexibility to broaden intellectual horizons, offer nonconventional educational opportunities tailored to individual interests and career goals, and encourage students to work on their own as they probe issues of particular interest to them.

Academic Facilities

The 115-acre campus of thirty-eight buildings is equipped for academic achievement, beginning with such facilities as Butler Library and its 475,560 volumes (including bound periodicals), 910,297 microforms, 21,116 audiovisual items, 2,858 periodical subscriptions, and 133 CD-ROMs as well as a user-friendly online catalog. Students may choose from more than 500 personal computers with fifty instructional programs. Every student has a personal computer account with e-mail and Internet access 24 hours a day. The Creative Studies Special Collection has the largest creativity library in the world. Other special collections include videos and scripts of *Homicide: Life on the Street* and *St. Elsewhere* by Buffalo State alumnus Tom Fontana and scripts for *Murphy Brown* and *Love and War* by alumna Diane English.

The Whitworth Ferguson Planetarium has a year-round calendar of shows; a fully equipped television studio is a resource for broadcasting students; the Upton Gallery features student and faculty artwork; and a 100-seat black box theater graces the renovated Theater Arts Building. The 856-seat auditorium in stately Rockwell Hall houses the Performing Arts Center, while the Burchfield-Penney Art Center, accredited by the American Association of Museums, houses the world's largest collection of works by watercolorist Charles E. Burchfield.

The 40-foot research vessel *Aquarius* and other boats in the College fleet are used by undergraduate students performing important environmental research on Lake Erie.

Costs

For academic year 1999–2000, full-time tuition for in-state students was $3400 and fees were $395. For room and board, residential students paid an additional $5070 (including a $1900 allotment for meals). Out-of-state students paid $8695 per year in tuition and fees. Part-time state residents paid $153.85 per credit (including fees), and nonresidents paid $362.85 per credit (including fees). Books, supplies, and personal expenses are estimated at $2120 per year. Costs are subject to change.

Financial Aid

Seventy percent of Buffalo State undergraduates receive financial assistance through grants, scholarships, loans, and campus jobs averaging $5738.

The Financial Aid Office is very successful in helping students find ways and means of financing their college educations. The office oversees distribution of more than $30 million in federal and state grants, loans, and jobs annually.

For information on financial aid, students should contact the Director of Financial Aid at the address below or 716-878-4901 (telephone) or 716-878-4903 (fax). The recommended filing date for submission of aid applications for summer, fall, and spring semesters is March 15. Applications accepted after March 15 are processed on a first-come, first-served basis, with awards subject to availability of funds.

Faculty

The greatest resource for students is the faculty. The Middle States Association of Colleges and Schools has called Buffalo State's faculty "a major source of excellence." Nineteen faculty members are recipients of the SUNY Chancellor's Award for Excellence in Teaching.

Buffalo State's faculty consists of 391 full-time and 279 part-time members. Ninety-three percent of the faculty members have earned doctorates or terminal degrees in their fields. Classes are small, with nearly 90 percent having fewer than 40 students; most classes for majors have 12–25 students. Faculty-student interaction is enhanced by faculty members who maintain frequent office hours and focus on teaching and mentoring students. Buffalo State averages just 19 students for each faculty member.

Student Government

United Students Government (USG) represents the interests of all students and encourages their active participation in educational, recreational, cultural, and social programs and activities. USG also provides a variety of services that range from a resume service to a dental clinic. All programs and services are funded through the mandatory student activity fee.

Admission Requirements

Admission decisions are based on a variety of factors, including high school grades, rank in class, strength of program, scores on standardized examinations (SAT I or ACT), and high school recommendations. Satisfactory results of the state high school equivalency diploma program are also acceptable.

Buffalo State also accepts a limited number of students who would not normally be admitted if academic criteria were the sole basis for decision.

For transfer students with more than 30 credits, a minimum grade point average of 2.0 out of 4.0 is necessary for acceptance, although some programs require a higher grade point average.

Application and Information

Candidates must complete the State University of New York application, available in high school guidance offices, college transfer offices, and the Buffalo State Admissions Office. Decisions are made on a rolling basis beginning in mid-September for spring applicants and in mid-December for fall applicants. Processing of applications continues until new student enrollment goals have been met. On-campus interviews are encouraged. Students who seek additional information may contact:

Director of Admissions
Buffalo State
1300 Elmwood Avenue
Buffalo, New York 14222-1095

Telephone: 716-878-4017
Fax: 716-878-6100
E-mail: admissio@buffalostate.edu
World Wide Web: http://www.buffalostate.edu

STATE UNIVERSITY OF NEW YORK COLLEGE AT FREDONIA

FREDONIA, NEW YORK

The College

Founded as an academy in 1826, the College has a student body that reflects the great diversity of cultures in New York State. A public, coeducational institution, Fredonia has emerged as a highly respected liberal arts institution with recognized programs in accounting, business, education, communications, science, social sciences, and the fine and performing arts. The College maintains a traditional small-college atmosphere, and students enjoy a variety of cultural and social activities. A high percentage of students participate actively in athletics and intramural sports.

The 230-acre campus has twenty-nine buildings. A modern field house provides facilities for ice hockey and indoor track and includes a large gymnasium to complement a second facility, which contains a fitness center, a dance studio, gymnasia, and handball courts. The thirteen residence halls house 2,300 students and offer accommodations to suit a variety of lifestyles, including traditional, coed, independent, and apartment-style dorms. On-campus housing is guaranteed for all undergraduates. The undergraduate enrollment at Fredonia is 4,727.

Location

The village of Fredonia has a population of 11,000 and is located 45 miles south of Buffalo near Lake Erie. The village has preserved its traditional small-town atmosphere. Tree-lined streets lead to a spacious downtown common surrounded by outstanding examples of nineteenth-century village architecture. Fredonia, essentially residential in nature, is surrounded by orchards and vineyards leading south to the Allegheny foothills. To the north lie the city of Dunkirk and Lake Erie. Summer and winter recreational facilities abound. The College benefits from its relative proximity to the cities of Buffalo, Niagara Falls, and Toronto.

Majors and Degrees

The College at Fredonia offers the Bachelor of Arts (B.A.) degree with majors in applied music, art, earth science, economics, English, French, history, philosophy, political science, psychology, sociology, Spanish, and theater. A Bachelor of Fine Arts (B.F.A.) degree is awarded in acting, art, media arts, musical theater, and production design. The Bachelor of Music (Mus.B.) degree is available with majors in composition, music education, and performance. The Bachelor of Science (B.S.) degree is awarded with majors in accounting, biochemistry, biology, business administration, chemistry, communication, computer and information sciences, geochemistry, geology, geophysics, health services administration, industrial management, mathematics, mathematics-physics, medical technology, music therapy, physics, recombinant gene technology, social work, and sound recording technology. A Bachelor of Science in Education (B.S.Ed.) degree is offered with majors in elementary education and speech and hearing handicapped education. Secondary certification is available in biology, chemistry, earth science, English, French, mathematics, physics, social studies, and Spanish.

The Interdisciplinary Studies degree gives students the opportunity to design an individualized interdisciplinary major with guidance from experienced faculty members. Students in these programs work toward a Bachelor of Arts or Bachelor of Science degree. The Interdisciplinary Studies option also offers model majors or minors in such areas as American studies, arts administration, criminal justice, dance, electronic publication, environmental sciences, geographic information systems, gerontology, legal studies, music business, scientific computation and modeling, and women's studies.

The College is affiliated in a cooperative (3-2) engineering program with the following institutions: Alfred University, Case Western Reserve, Clarkson, Columbia, Cornell, Louisiana Tech, Ohio State, Rensselaer Polytechnic Institute, Rochester Institute of Technology, SUNY at Binghamton, SUNY at Buffalo, Syracuse, and Tri-State University. A cooperative agricultural program has been developed with Cornell. In addition, a special education major is available with SUNY College at Buffalo. The Department of Business Administration offers an accelerated M.B.A. program, including a 3-2 program with SUNY at Binghamton and SUNY at Buffalo and a 4-1 program with Clarkson and the University of Pittsburgh.

Academic Program

The bachelor's degree requires 120 credit hours, including a general education component, and there are opportunities for double majors, minors, and/or concentrations. The College offers an honors program for academically talented students. Up to 30 credits may be awarded through CLEP and Advanced Placement examinations.

Fredonia operates on a semester system with the fall term beginning in early September and ending in mid-December. The spring term begins the third week of January and continues into May. A summer program of two 5-week sessions is available.

Graduation rates of entering freshmen at Fredonia are among the highest in the nation. To ensure continued success, the College has implemented "Fredonia in 4," a program for first-time freshmen that stipulates that the College pledges to adhere to a commonly understood agreement to provide the necessary courses and academic advising that guarantee that students finish in four years.

Off-Campus Arrangements

Fredonia students may participate in State University of New York overseas programs throughout the world. These programs provide educational opportunities in virtually every discipline. The College offers internships in courts and government agencies as well as in the areas of public relations, psychology, journalism, television production, radio, business, and the health sciences. Fredonia participates in the Washington Semester Program and in the Visiting Student Program, which enables students to study for a semester or a year at one of more than fifty participating colleges and universities. Credit is awarded on the basis of an academic contract.

Academic Facilities

Reed Library contains 402,298 bound volumes and 1,043,000 titles on microform, plus 1,960 professional and academic journals. There is seating for 1,054 students, including open study carrels. Open-stack privileges are available to all students, and separate areas are provided for special collections, a microtext room, and a music section consisting of 26,249 audio and video materials and 30,000 scores.

The College provides students and faculty members with extensive computing facilities. Campus computing facilities are used for instruction, research, and administrative projects by faculty members, students, and the staff. All students at Fredonia are assigned an access code and password that allow them to interact with the College mainframe and various servers located throughout the campus. Students have access both on and off campus to the World Wide Web. The Computing Center, various faculty and staff members, and some departments host workshops and seminars to assist new and intermediate users in gaining new skills. Workshop and seminar topics include time-sharing, networking, word processing, statistical packages, database creation, microcomputers, navigation of the World Wide Web, home pages, and e-mail. Personal computers for student use are located in all academic buildings and various residence halls. Students living in residence halls have instant Internet connectivity in their rooms via an Ethernet connection to a T-100 line.

The Rockefeller Arts Center provides outstanding facilities for concert and theatrical productions and houses an art gallery, art studios, and classrooms.

Costs

Tuition and fees for 1999–2000 were $4125 per year for state residents and $9025 for nonresidents. Students living in College residence halls paid an additional fee of $3150 for room and $2050 for board. (Tuition costs are subject to change for 2000–01.)

Financial Aid

In 1999–2000, 77 percent of Fredonia's students received financial assistance. The average award, consisting of grants, scholarships, loans, and campus jobs, was $5480. Students who are interested in applying for aid must complete the Free Application for Federal Student Aid (FAFSA) by March 15. Sources of aid include Federal Pell Grants, Federal Supplemental Educational Opportunity Grants, Tuition Assistance Program awards, Educational Opportunity Grants, Federal Perkins Loans, New York State Stafford Student Loans, Federal Work-Study Program awards, on- and off-campus jobs, and Fredonia College Scholarships, including a freshman merit scholarship program.

Faculty

Fredonia's faculty consists of 226 full-time and 154 part-time instructional staff members. Ninety percent of the faculty have earned doctorates or a terminal degree in their field. All professors have weekly office hours, during which they are available to students. Faculty members are involved in instruction, research, publication, and academic advising. The small size of classes contributes to excellent faculty-student interaction.

Student Government

All students are members of the Student Association, which functions through elected officers and elected senators from the various College groups and organizations. Student representatives are voting members of the Faculty Council and are represented on most committees of the College. The Student Association provides funding for all chartered campus organizations and clubs.

Admission Requirements

Admission to Fredonia is competitive. Particular attention is given to the quality of the academic program and the high school average. Other factors considered in the admissions process are the results of the SAT I or ACT, recommendations, rank in class, and extracurricular activities. Applicants should have completed at least 16 academic units of preparation. Those seeking admissions to math or science-related majors should include 4 units each of mathematics and science; those seeking admission to programs in business administration and accounting should include 4 units of college-preparatory mathematics. An audition is required for admission to programs in music, acting, musical theater, and production design. A portfolio is required for admission to an art major. A campus visit is recommended, but a personal interview is not required.

Application and Information

New York State residents may obtain application material from their high school guidance offices or any SUNY campus. Nonresidents should contact the Office of Admissions. An electronic application is available. Notification is made on a rolling basis, and the College subscribes to the Candidates Reply Date of May 1. Applicants may seek admission through the Early Decision Program. A deposit of $100 is required to reserve a space in the entering class. Students interested in visiting the campus may obtain a visiting schedule and an appointment by calling the number below.

For further information, contact:

Office of Admissions
Fenner House
State University of New York College at Fredonia
Fredonia, New York 14063
Telephone: 716-673-3251
          800-252-1212 (toll-free)
E-mail: admissionsinq@fredonia.edu
World Wide Web: http://www.fredonia.edu

Campus view, including Reed Library and Houghton Hall, two of many campus facilities designed by I. M. Pei.

STATE UNIVERSITY OF NEW YORK COLLEGE AT GENESEO
GENESEO, NEW YORK

The College

Geneseo was established more than 125 years ago as the Geneseo Normal School by James and William Wadsworth, whose descendants still live in the village their family founded in the late 1700s. The traditions and collegiate history of the area are in large part responsible for the atmosphere at Geneseo, which is embodied by brick sidewalks, shady maples, and flourishing ivy. People make Geneseo what it is, but the location and distinctive surroundings are a big part of the Geneseo experience. A residential campus of 5,300 students, it is a distinctive college of the State University of New York (SUNY), having joined SUNY in 1948.

Geneseo offers a broad range of liberal arts and sciences programs and other professional programs at the undergraduate level. In addition, Geneseo's curriculum balances its strong liberal arts core with specialized study in a variety of majors and minors. The College offers approximately forty-five academic majors. A faculty-student ratio of 1:19 provides opportunities for classroom instruction where people can relate to one another on a personal level and challenge each other to think critically and creatively about important ideas. At Geneseo, class sizes are small and intimate; 25 students comprise the average class, and 80 percent of classrooms hold fewer than forty chairs.

Geneseo offers an extensive program of intramural, intercollegiate, and recreational athletics. The College competes on the Division III level in men's basketball, cross-country, hockey, lacrosse, soccer, swimming, and track and women's basketball, cross-country, field hockey, lacrosse, soccer, softball, swimming, and track. In addition, about twenty-five intramural teams and fifteen club sports are available.

Two thirds of Geneseo students reside in the fourteen residence halls on campus. In addition, the College has two central dining facilities. There are also a large student activities center and an extensive physical education complex, which includes a state-of-the-art workout center, an Olympic-style swimming pool, and acres of playing fields.

Location

The village of Geneseo has 7,000 residents and is located in the Finger Lakes region of western New York. The College is small and delightfully personal and sits on a hillside overlooking the valley. Downtown Geneseo, which is listed in the National Register of Historic Places and is one of only nine communities in the nation to be named a Preservation District, reminds visitors of a quaint New England village, with its small shops, wide sidewalks, and colorful awnings. In many ways, Geneseo combines the best of two worlds; it is close to two major cities, Rochester and Buffalo, yet it also offers the scenic beauty and recreational opportunities of the Finger Lakes region.

Majors and Degrees

Baccalaureate degrees are offered in accounting, American studies, anthropology, applied physics, art history, art studio, biochemistry, biology, biophysics, black studies, chemistry, communication, comparative literature, computer science, economics, elementary education, English, French, geochemistry, geography, geology, geophysics, history, international relations, management, mathematics, music, philosophy, physics, political science, pre-engineering, psychology, secondary education, special education, sociology, Spanish, speech pathology, theater, and theater and English.

Academic Program

A Geneseo education stresses skills that are important in the pursuit of an interesting life and that are valuable to success in the world of work. This education seeks to develop in students an understanding of the world's diverse societies and cultures, a comprehension of the nature of science and mathematics, a capacity to think critically and constructively, and an ability to express ideas clearly. A Geneseo education promotes the understanding of moral, social, and political options for individuals.

Completion of 120 academic credits, with a minimum of 45 credits beyond the introductory level, is required for graduation. All students must complete a general education core of classes that includes course work in the natural sciences, fine arts, social sciences, critical reasoning, humanities, and non-Western traditions.

A maximum of 30 credit hours may be awarded for achievement on college-level examinations, such as the Advanced Placement examinations (AP) and the College-Level Examination Program (CLEP). Each academic department at Geneseo determines the minimum test score required for academic credit for AP courses; 3 general elective credits are guaranteed with a score of 3 or higher. CLEP credit is awarded based on achievement of specified minimum scores.

Off-Campus Arrangements

The College believes that education for life includes preparation for a career, and internships can be among the best ways to experience the world of work while testing some of the ideas students have explored in the classroom. Student interns—nearly 300 each year—earn academic credit while working on special projects, conducting research, and preparing reports. Popular sites for internships include law offices, radio and television stations, government agencies, medical centers, and corporate offices of major business firms such as Kodak and Xerox.

Academic Facilities

A recent report by the Middle States Association of Colleges and Schools rated Geneseo's Milne Library as an outstanding facility for study and research. The library houses a collection of 1,303,187 books, microtexts, and other documents and subscribes to 3,117 periodicals. The library provides open stacks for easy access to materials and comfortable seating for 1,000 students. Books & Bytes, a small café located in the Milne Library, is available to students throughout the day and evening. In addition, the College's Fraser Library houses special collections and the School of Business library.

Three comprehensive computer systems and numerous microcomputer labs are available for student use. Microcomputer facilities are located in most buildings on campus and in every residence hall. In addition, through "ResNet," students have full Internet access from their residence halls to the World Wide Web and e-mail.

Three theaters, two dance studios, and many art galleries host a variety of student, faculty, and invited stage productions and exhibits. There are also a lecture and communication center, a planetarium, two science complexes, and a nuclear accelerator laboratory.

Costs

For a New York State resident, full-time tuition is $3400 per year for 2000–01; annual fees are $796. Out-of-state students pay $8300 per year for tuition. Residential students pay $4590 per year for room and board. A cost of $137 is charged per credit hour for part-time, in-state students ($347 per credit hour for out-of-state residents). Costs are subject to change without notice.

Financial Aid

Approximately 75 percent of Geneseo students receive some form of financial aid. To apply, students must complete the Free Application for Federal Student Aid (FAFSA) and the New York State Tuition Assistance Program (TAP) application. The Financial Aid Office encourages students to apply for aid by February 15 for fall semester consideration. For further information, students should contact the Financial Aid Office at 716-245-5731. If students are both economically and financially disadvantaged, they may qualify for admission through the Educational Opportunity Program (EOP); interested students should contact the EOP Office at 716-245-5725 for additional information.

Faculty

Outstanding teaching means more than lecturing. At Geneseo, faculty members play a highly active role in learning; they guide students in the process of discovery and understanding. Geneseo professors come from the nation's top universities. They are scholars who have published widely and are respected by their peers. They come to Geneseo to teach, and because they do that so well, they create a community where there is respect for ideas, where everyone's opinion is valued, and where special bonds are formed between people. Faculty members, not graduate students, teach all courses at Geneseo, regardless of whether it is an introductory course for freshmen or an advanced course for seniors.

Ninety percent of the 249 full-time faculty members hold terminal degrees, and many are nationally recognized experts in their field. They are known as teachers as well as scholars and mentors. Fifty-two Geneseo professors have received the highly competitive SUNY Chancellor's Award for Excellence in Teaching, and 13 have been named SUNY Distinguished Teaching Professors.

Student Government

Student clubs and organizations serve virtually every social, recreational, educational, political, and religious interest. The Student Association supports more than 180 groups through fees that are collected from all students. Every spring, Geneseo students elect seven of their fellow students to the offices on the Student Association's Central Council. As the executive body of the Student Association, Central Council both supervises and coordinates the many services, activities, and organizations that are funded with the students' mandatory student fees.

Admission Requirements

Admission to Geneseo is very competitive. Decisions are based primarily on students' high school academic records and the results of one college entrance examination (SAT I or ACT). Strong academic programs (especially honors-level courses) that represent four years of math, science, foreign language, social studies, and English are preferred. In addition, students are asked to supply information about extracurricular accomplishments, to write an essay, and to submit letters of recommendation.

Geneseo encourages applications from high school students, transfers from other colleges and universities, and international students. Students can apply to Geneseo by using the *SUNY Application Viewbook*, which is available at all New York State high schools and community colleges. Geneseo encourages candidates to apply by December 1, and all admission decisions are announced on March 15. An early decision deadline of November 15 is available for students who list Geneseo as their first choice. While prospective students are encouraged to visit the campus, interviews are not a requirement of the admission process.

Application and Information

To arrange for a visit to the campus, request additional information, or ask for an application, students should contact:

Office of Admissions
SUNY Geneseo
1 College Circle
Geneseo, New York 14454
Telephone: 716-245-5571
Fax: 716-245-5550
World Wide Web: http://www.geneseo.edu

The campus of the State University of New York College at Geneseo.

STATE UNIVERSITY OF NEW YORK COLLEGE AT OLD WESTBURY
OLD WESTBURY, NEW YORK

The College

Founded in 1965, the State University of New York (SUNY), College at Old Westbury offers an invigorating atmosphere dedicated to academic excellence and the development of leadership qualities in its students. The buildings cluster among the stately trees of the former F. Ambrose Clark estate, leaving most of the 605 acres of woodland and rolling meadows untouched and environmentally sound. Approximately 3,400 students representing seventeen countries comprise the diverse student body. Eight hundred live on campus, while the others commute from all parts of Long Island and New York City's five boroughs. About half the students come to the College with some prior experience, most often at one of the three neighboring two-year colleges. SUNY College at Old Westbury is considered to be "in the vanguard of the future" because the ethnic and gender mix of the student population reflects the demographics predicted for the next century.

The faculty members at the College are internationally educated and acclaimed. Seven are Distinguished Teaching Professors, the highest honor granted to State University of New York faculty members, and two are Distinguished Service Professors.

Old Westbury offers a fine program of intercollegiate and recreational athletics. The varsity program competes on the NCAA Division III level in men's baseball, basketball, cross-country, soccer, tennis, and volleyball and women's basketball, cross-country, softball, and volleyball. The Physical Education and Recreation Center, opened in 1981, includes three basketball courts, two handball courts, two squash courts, two racquetball courts, a 25-yard swimming-diving pool, and a weight-training room. There are also outdoor facilities for tennis, handball/paddleball, baseball, softball, and soccer. The gently rolling hills of the 605-acre campus also provide tranquility and space for jogging, walking, cycling, and picnics.

Campus facilities include nine residence halls. Dormitory suites each accommodate 6 students in two double and two single rooms. Housing is assigned on a first-come, first-served basis.

Beautiful, new facilities are scheduled for construction over the next two years. A new student union building and a new 200-bed residence hall will become operational during the early part of 2001. Additional residence halls are also scheduled for occupation later in the year.

Location

Located in the village of Old Westbury on Long Island's historic North Shore, the College offers a peaceful learning environment. Although the oak- and evergreen-studded campus offers unsurpassed opportunities for cycling and exploring nature, the College is just 22 miles from midtown Manhattan's urban resources and a 20-minute drive from Jones Beach. This ideal location allows students to benefit from fieldwork and research opportunities in the major cultural, merchandising, and financial centers of New York City as well as in Long Island communities rich in history, arts and crafts, music, and theater. The campus is a few minutes' ride from movie theaters, shopping malls, banks, sports arenas, and concert halls.

Majors and Degrees

SUNY/Old Westbury offers baccalaureate degrees in accounting; American studies; biological sciences; business and management; chemistry; comparative humanities, language, and literature; computer science; criminology; electronic media; finance; health and society; industrial and labor relations; management information systems; marketing; mathematics; media and communications; philosophy and religion; politics, economics, and society; psychology; sociology; Spanish language, Hispanic literature, and culture; teacher education (bilingual, elementary, secondary, and special); and visual arts.

Academic Program

The goal of the College is to educate students to achieve their potential and exceed their goals. Although students are expected to focus on a major program of study, the College believes it is equally important for them to acquire a broad base of general knowledge and to develop strong analytical and creative skills.

Completion of 120 to 128 academic credits with a minimum of 45 credits beyond the introductory/survey level is required for graduation. All students must demonstrate proficiency in mathematics and English reading and writing skills.

A general education program provides students with a broad multidisciplinary liberal arts education that serves as an intellectual foundation for further education, career preparation, and participation in our increasingly complex society. All students must take a writing/reasoning skills cluster (group of related courses), as well as four additional clusters selected from such areas as science; U.S. society, history, and culture; international and cross-cultural studies; foreign languages; creativity and the arts; and modes of enlightenment.

The College-Level Examination Program (CLEP) allows students to earn credits by passing a single exam. Students may also earn credits for life experience. Under the Accreditation for Experiential Learning program, the College assesses this learning and translates some if not all of its value into conventional college-level academic credit. In addition to the regular academic program, the College provides an array of support programs and facilities, such as personal and career counseling, academic advisement, orientation, tutoring, learning centers, computer and science laboratories, studios, and practice rooms.

Off-Campus Arrangements

Because the College believes that education is reinforced and enhanced by varied experiences, students are offered the opportunity to earn credits outside of the traditional classroom setting. Many academic departments recommend that their students participate in internships or field research. The chance to study abroad is also available to Old Westbury students via international exchange agreements and SUNY travel-abroad programs.

Academic Facilities

Modern facilities with state-of-the-art equipment are available to students at the College. The Natural Science Building, which opened in 1985, adds essential scientific laboratories, classrooms, a lecture hall, and a greenhouse to the picturesque, $100-million campus.

The Library/Media Center provides students with a collection of more than 376,000 bound volumes and microfilm periodicals and has a variety of study and reading facilities that accommodate about 800 people. Students have audiovisual equipment at their fingertips in the Media Center, as well as language labs so they can hear subject languages spoken.

Many classes are held in the Academic Village, which is surrounded by nine residence halls, and in the Campus Center, where the dining hall, Campus Café, and library are also located. The Rathskeller, Women's Center, student newspaper, Café 9, Student Health Center, and student activities offices occupy premises in the Academic Village.

The entire campus community enjoys two fine theaters. The Maguire Theatre, with a seating capacity of 400, perfect sightlines, and fine acoustics, stages student productions and hosts prominent theater companies and guest performers. The Duane L. Jones Recital Hall, a 330-seat amphitheater, is ideal for concerts, lectures, and informal performances.

The College also has the Amelie A. Wallace Gallery, a unique triple-tier art gallery, which features rotating exhibitions of sculpture, paintings, and other art by students, faculty members, and outside artists.

Costs

For a New York State resident, full-time tuition is $3400 per year for 2000–01, plus an annual College/student government/intercollegiate athletics/Health Service fee of $331. Residential students pay $5903 for room and board combined (double room, nineteen meals). Out-of-state students pay $8300 per year in tuition. Part-time students who are state residents pay $137 per credit; nonresident part-time students pay $346 per credit. (Costs are subject to change without notice.)

Financial Aid

Old Westbury participates in federal, state, and local financial aid programs that help make higher education available. The services and resources in the Office of Financial Aid are available to all students. Financial aid advisers help students apply for financial aid and develop financial aid awards tailored to meet college-related expenses. Debt management counseling and college work-study placement/job services are also provided. The forms and instructions needed for applying for financial aid are sent automatically to all prospective students who apply for admission. The Office of Financial Aid, at 516-876-3222, can supply further information.

Faculty

Of the 113 full-time faculty members at Old Westbury, 85 percent have earned their doctorates or other terminal degrees. The College is proud to have on its faculty 6 Distinguished Teaching Professors and 3 Distinguished Service Professors selected by the SUNY chancellor for special recognition among the 16,000 professors in the State University of New York System. In addition, many of Old Westbury's faculty members have been internationally acclaimed for high achievement in their disciplines, receiving awards, fellowships, and grants for work in the visual arts and for original scientific research. A member of Old Westbury's Biological Sciences faculty was selected as 1991 New York State Professor of the Year by the Council for the Advancement and Support of Education (CASE).

Students may choose a faculty member in their major for academic advisement. The student-faculty ratio is 22:1, and the College's professors take a high degree of interest in students as individuals; small classes allow them to pay attention to specific student needs.

Student Government

The students at Old Westbury have formed forty clubs and organizations (including an AM radio station), which are funded through the Student Government Association fee. Fraternities and sororities—nationally affiliated and local—attract members on campus. Students are invited and encouraged to serve in various aspects of campus life, creating an inclusive academic learning environment.

Admission Requirements

The College seeks students who possess solid academic credentials (Regent's level). Admission to the College is based on a number of factors. A high school average of at least 80 or a minimum combined SAT I score of 1000 or a composite ACT score of at least 22 and motivation to learn are essential criteria. Qualified candidates are encouraged to apply for admission.

Old Westbury welcomes inquiries from high school students, transfers from other colleges and universities, international students, and adults interested in beginning or resuming their education. Prospective students are encouraged to visit the campus and schedule an interview with an admissions counselor. Although there is no specific deadline for applications, students should apply early to secure appropriate courses, financial aid, and housing (if needed). Due to the popularity of campus living, students are advised to apply early to ensure eligibility for housing.

Application and Information

A map and specific directions to the College are available from the enrollment services office, located in Campus Center, Room I-202.

To arrange a visit, make an appointment with a counselor, or request an application or additional information, students should contact:

Office of Enrollment Services
State University of New York
  College at Old Westbury
P.O. Box 307
Old Westbury, New York 11568-0307
Telephone: 516-876-3073

Students at SUNY College at Old Westbury take a breather between classes in front of the Natural Science Building (right). The Library/Media Center is in the background.

STATE UNIVERSITY OF NEW YORK COLLEGE AT ONEONTA
ONEONTA, NEW YORK

The College

A comprehensive college of arts and sciences in the SUNY system, the College at Oneonta strives to develop students to their full potential both academically and personally. The John Templeton Foundation named the College at Oneonta to its 1997–98 and 1998–99 *Honor Roll of Character-Building Colleges*, the only SUNY institution to be so named. Emphasizing excellence in classroom instruction, Oneonta's curriculum includes courses that broaden students' understanding of the human experience; sharpen writing, reasoning, and analytical skills; and offer in-depth, career-focused work in a broad range of major fields. With the largest library collection in its sector of SUNY, excellent computer facilities, and strong advisement and support programs, Oneonta provides students a solid academic foundation for careers or graduate study. Varied residence life programs and outstanding volunteer service and internship arrangements offer students vast opportunities for personal development. The College's Center for Social Responsibility and Community, established through a $500,000 Kellogg Foundation grant, actively develops and coordinates community service opportunities for students. Career planning and placement services assist students in preparing for careers and securing employment after graduation. A recent survey of graduates indicated that more than 80 percent were employed or enrolled in graduate study within six months.

Established as a state normal school in 1889, Oneonta was a founding college of the SUNY system in 1948. The College, ranked in 1996, 1997, and 1998 as one of *Money* magazine's 100 best buys in American higher education, is accredited by the Middle States Association of Colleges and Schools; its programs in home economics are accredited by the American Home Economics Association, and its programs in chemistry are accredited by the American Chemical Society. The 250-acre campus has more than forty buildings. Off-campus facilities include the 672-acre Biological Field Station and research area on Otsego Lake and a History and Museum Studies graduate program in nearby Cooperstown.

Though more than 90 percent of Oneonta students are state residents, the College attracts many out-of-state and international students. The College's 5,000 undergraduates represent a medley of cultures, backgrounds, ages, and experiences. Approximately half of Oneonta's students live in the sixteen on-campus residence halls, which have full-time professional directors and staffs of resident advisers. Residence life options include special interest areas. Residence halls are wired for telephone, cable television, and computer hook-ups. With keyed entry to residence halls, a campuswide emergency phone system, and other security measures, Oneonta has been cited as the safest campus setting in New York State for colleges of 5,000 or more students and the ninth-safest in the country. The Counseling, Health, and Wellness Center furnishes on-campus health care and confidential counseling. Two dining halls, snack bars, and a convenience store offer various dining options from early morning to late evening. Off-campus apartments and rooms are available in the community. A regular bus service, funded through activity fees, is provided free of additional charge.

More than seventy student organizations provide extracurricular cultural, social, athletic, and intellectual activities. A gymnasium, fitness center, and new Alumni Field House provide recreational facilities. Eight varsity men's teams and nine women's teams compete in Division III intercollegiate sports, with the Division I men's soccer team recognized nationally. Nearby state parks, ski resorts, museums, and theaters enhance on-campus recreational and cultural opportunities.

Location

Located in the scenic, historic Susquehanna Valley in the western foothills of the Catskills, Oneonta (population 15,000) is midway between Albany and Binghamton on Interstate 88. A convenient 3-hour drive from the New York City area and accessible from anywhere in the state, the city provides an exceptional setting for college life. Downtown Oneonta, a short walk from campus, offers many restaurants and shops. The campus bus service provides transportation to and from downtown businesses, malls, and recreational facilities. Students are heavily involved in volunteer service and employment in the Oneonta community.

Majors and Degrees

The SUNY College at Oneonta offers a wide range of undergraduate programs leading to Bachelor of Arts and Bachelor of Science degrees. In the Division of Behavioral and Applied Science, majors are offered in accounting; adulthood and aging studies; business economics; child and family studies; dietetics; economics; elementary education, with an optional early childhood annotation; food service and restaurant administration; human ecology, with options in child development and family studies, consumer studies, general human ecology, and fashion merchandising and design; home economics education; international studies; psychology; secondary education in business; and sociology, with options in general sociology and preprofessional sociology.

In the Division of Humanities and Fine Arts, majors are offered in art history; art studio; English; French; interdisciplinary studies; mass communication; music; music industry; philosophy; secondary education in English, French, or Spanish; Spanish; speech communication; studio art; and theater.

In the Division of Science and Social Science, majors are offered in anthropology; biology, with options in biotechnology, ecological science, general biology, and human biology; Africana and Latino studies; chemistry; computer science; earth science; environmental sciences, with options in biology, earth science, general environmental sciences, and planning; geography, with options in cartography, general geography, and urban and regional planning; geology; history; mathematics; meteorology; physics; political science; secondary education in biology, earth science, mathematics, and social science; statistics; and water resources.

Preprofessional programs prepare students for advanced study in dentistry, law, medicine, and veterinary science.

Oneonta offers a variety of programs in conjunction with other institutions: 3 + 2 dual majors in management, accounting, and business economics; a 4 + 1 M.B.A. program; cooperative programs in engineering; 3 + 1 programs in advertising and communications, advertising design, fashion buying and merchandising, and fashion design; programs in nursing and physical therapy; programs in pre-environmental science and forestry; and a program in hospitality management.

Academic Program

Oneonta's academic program has three primary components: a general education requirement, specialized in-depth study in a major, and free electives. The combination helps students understand a plurality of perspectives, enables them to clarify their thought processes, and enhances their abilities to communicate effectively. The 36-hour general education requirement includes courses in perspectives on nature and mathematics, on society and human behavior, on human value and expression and integrative perspectives, as well as courses that develop thinking, problem-solving, and communication skills.

In their major, students complete 30–60 hours of course work on their way to the 122 hours required for graduation. Transfer applications are encouraged, and students may transfer up to 66 credits from two-year colleges or 77 credits from four-year institutions. Degree credits may be earned through proficiency examinations, course challenges, and assessment of prior learning. Students must declare a major by their junior year. A strong academic advisement program provides assistance in choosing curriculums and planning the academic year, which is divided into two 15-week semesters with optional summer sessions.

The Oneonta Scholars Program is designed for students with demonstrated high academic ability, a desire to succeed, and a willingness to seek out new challenges and experiences. The program offers scholars all the benefits of an enriched undergraduate experience while emphasizing flexibility and choice.

Off-Campus Arrangements

Oneonta offers many opportunities to earn degree credits while studying abroad and to gain valuable employment experience through internships. The SUNY Study Abroad Program enables students to study throughout the world in nearly 100 programs. Oneonta offers programs with the University of Würzburg in Germany, intersession programs in Europe, semester or academic-year programs in Ireland and England, direct exchange programs with Seinan Gakuin University in Japan, fall semester programs in India, and summer programs in Israel. Credit-bearing internships are available through many academic departments and agencies. The Center for Social Responsibility and Community provides opportunities for noncredit community service, often in a field related to the student's major.

Academic Facilities

An exceptional library, excellent computer equipment, and several specialized facilities provide outstanding academic resources for students. The Milne Library houses more than 500,000 volumes of print material, offers an online catalog and computers with access to specialized CD-ROMs and the Internet, and provides study space for 900 students. The College's twenty computer labs, nine of which are open seven days a week, provide more than 400 computers. Students have free access to a powerful campuswide network and the Internet, with connections available in all academic buildings and in residence halls. Unique computer facilities include the nationally recognized Chemistry and Physics Multimedia Lab, the Computer Art Lab, and the Geographic Information Systems Lab. A new "smart classroom" enables faculty members to incorporate multimedia presentations into their classes. Recently upgraded television, music, and video production equipment enables the campus to broadcast live events and the students to produce videos. The hands-on Science Discovery Center and the observatory and planetarium offer unique resources. Academic support services provide individualized self-instructional programs, tutorials, and skill-building classes.

Costs

Tuition for 1999–2000 was $3400 per year for state residents and $8300 for nonresidents. Fees were $753. Room and board were $5456. Annual expenses for books, supplies, and personal expenses vary.

Financial Aid

Approximately 80 percent of Oneonta's full-time undergraduate students receive financial aid through federal, state, and local programs, including the Federal Pell Grant Program, Federal Supplemental Educational Opportunity Grants, Federal Perkins Loans, Federal Family Educational Loan Program, Federal Work-Study Program, on-campus part-time employment, and College scholarships. To be eligible for financial assistance, students must submit the Free Application for Federal Student Aid to the College as early as possible. Through a concerted effort to expand scholarship opportunities, the College now offers more than 120 scholarship awards. Information about scholarships is available through the Admissions or Financial Aid Offices.

Faculty

Oneonta's 260 instructional faculty members, nearly all of whom hold doctoral degrees, are responsible for the development and implementation of the undergraduate programs. While many undertake research, their primary focus is on instruction, advisement, and counseling. A genuine sense of concern for the individual student's intellectual and personal development is the hallmark of Oneonta's faculty.

Student Government

Oneonta's Student Association, of which all registered students are members, is managed through democratically elected executive, legislative, and judicial branches. The Student Senate, composed of representatives of residence halls and off-campus residents, administers the student activity budget, which funds the campus organizations, athletics, entertainment activities, bus service, campus radio station, and student newspaper. Students are represented on the College Council, Alumni Association, College Senate, and many College-wide committees.

Admission Requirements

The College is strongly committed to academic excellence and the development of students to their full potential. Oneonta receives many more applications than there are available spaces, so admission is competitive. Applicants are evaluated on academic records, including their program of studies and results of standardized tests (ACT or SAT I), and on personal experiences, achievements, and talents. Each fall, the College enrolls some 1,000 freshmen and 700 transfer students. Approximately 250 additional students enter in the spring. The College welcomes applications from all candidates, including out-of-state and international students.

On-campus interviews, tours, and information sessions are available but not required. Oneonta offers early decision, admission through the Educational Opportunity Program, and admission to qualified high school students who graduate early. Freshman candidates should present a solid college-preparatory academic program, with at least 8 units of mathematics, science, and foreign language in addition to required social science and English courses. Accepted candidates generally rank in the top third of their class and have above-average test scores. Transfer students must present a minimum GPA of 2.0 (C), though most accepted transfer students have GPAs of 2.5 or better.

Application and Information

The College at Oneonta uses the standard SUNY application, available in most New York State high school guidance offices or from the College's Admissions Office. Applications are accepted year-round and are evaluated on a rolling basis. For fall semester admission, freshman applicants should submit all materials by February 1; transfer applicants should submit materials by June 1. For more information, students should contact:

Director of Admissions
State University of New York College at Oneonta
Oneonta, New York 13820
Telephone: 607-436-2524
           800-SUNY-123 (toll-free)
Fax: 607-436-3074
E-mail: admissions@oneonta.edu
World Wide Web: http://www.oneonta.edu

STATE UNIVERSITY OF NEW YORK COLLEGE AT POTSDAM

POTSDAM, NEW YORK

The College

SUNY Potsdam was established in 1816 as the St. Lawrence Academy and, consequently, has the longest history of any SUNY school. Although SUNY Potsdam continues its tradition of teacher preparation, the liberal arts are at the core of the curriculum. With the recent state approval of a $48-million master plan over the next ten to fifteen years, Potsdam is looking forward to the rejuvenation and diversification of its facilities.

The undergraduate enrollment is about 3,600 men and women. Students come from throughout New York State, and the College's student body represents the greatest geographical diversity of any four-year college in the SUNY System. There are about 100 extracurricular groups and activities, including fraternities and sororities, student government, yearbook and newspaper staffs, a literary magazine, a broadcast FM radio station, and musical and performing arts groups. Approximately 75 percent of the students participate in intramural sports, and there are nine women's and seven men's varsity sports teams. Roughly two thirds of all students live on campus; freshmen and sophomores are required to do so. Student services are offered through an academic advising center, the Career Planning Office, a counseling center, the Student Health Service (consisting of a health clinic and laboratory on campus), tutoring services, the Educational Opportunity Program, and the Orientation Program. The 240-acre campus is in the village of Potsdam and is a short walk from the downtown area.

Location

Potsdam is a small Victorian village built in the 1800s on the banks of the Raquette River, about 30 miles south of the Canadian border at Massena, New York, and Cornwall, Ontario, Canada. In addition to the 10,000 permanent residents of the village, about 8,000 students are enrolled at Clarkson University and SUNY Potsdam, which are both located in Potsdam. Potsdam's downtown area has been recently restored and is registered as a National Historic District.

Majors and Degrees

The School of Arts and Sciences awards the B.A. in anthropology, archeological studies, art history, art studio (including painting, photography, pottery, printmaking, and sculpture), biology, business economics, chemistry, community health (B.S.), computer and information sciences, criminal justice, dance, drama, economics, employment relations, English (with concentration in literature or writing), French, geology, history (with concentration in American or European history), interdisciplinary natural science, mathematics, philosophy, physics, political science, psychology, sociology, Spanish, and speech communication. There is also a student-initiated interdepartmental major, as well as a B.S. in business economics jointly registered with neighboring SUNY Canton. The School of Education offers programs in elementary education and secondary education. The Crane School of Music grants the Bachelor of Arts in music and the Bachelor of Music in musical studies, music business, music composition, music education, and performance. Undergraduate concentrations are available in jazz and commercial music, music and business, piano pedagogy, recording arts, and special education.

Academic Program

To qualify for a Bachelor of Arts degree from SUNY Potsdam, students must complete 120 academic hours, plus four physical education activities. The Freshman Experience comprises a minimum of 10 credit hours of course work in quantitative and verbal areas. The quantitative requirement includes a course emphasizing analytical and reasoning capabilities or one stressing problem-solving skills. The verbal requirement includes one course examining writing and critical-thinking skills and another course involving speaking, reasoning, and research skills. Students are required to complete an additional minimum of 30 credit hours of course work emphasizing the following: aesthetic expression, cross-cultural perspectives, historical investigation, philosophical inquiry, social analysis, and scientific inquiry. Students must fulfill a major requirement of at least 30 credit hours; any student majoring in teacher education is also required to complete a second major in an academic area. Writing and speaking skills are also fostered through additional course work. Approximately 44 credit hours may be taken in free electives. In the Crane School of Music, students working toward the Bachelor of Music degree must complete a minimum of 124 to 128 credit hours, of which approximately 80 credits are in the major. Crane students are required to complete an additional 40 credits of nonmusic study in the liberal arts.

Off-Campus Arrangements

SUNY Potsdam offers several study-abroad programs for academic credit in Grenoble, France; Potsdam, Germany; Lincoln, Liverpool, and Birmingham, England; Rockhamton, Australia; and Puebla, Mexico. Potsdam students may also choose to participate in any of more than 250 other study-abroad programs offered throughout the SUNY System. SUNY Potsdam is a member of the National Student Exchange Program, a consortium of eighty-three public colleges and universities throughout the United States, through which Potsdam students may study at any of the colleges for either a semester or a full year without transferring. Potsdam is also a member of the Associated Colleges of the St. Lawrence Valley. Membership in this consortium makes it possible for Potsdam students to cross-register for courses at three other colleges in the area: St. Lawrence University, Clarkson University, and SUNY College of Technology at Canton. In addition, internships are available in many disciplines. These internships enable students to gain both academic credit and practical experience. Students can also take advantage of the Career Experience Program, which enables them to arrange for a work experience away from the College during a semester. Both Army and Air Force ROTC programs are available to Potsdam students through Clarkson University.

Academic Facilities

Crumb Library, which seats up to 600 people, is located in the center of the academic quadrangle. It is open 96 hours per week and houses more than 1.03 million items, including 398,202 bound volumes, 604 microforms and other nonbook materials, 55,000 federal and state documents, and 1,300 active periodicals. The library's online catalog and an array of specialized equipment, such as copiers, microfilm reader-printers, audiovisual equipment, CD-ROM search stations, and aids for physically challenged users, provide access to materials in various formats. The professional staff is dedicated to helping students find and use information sources of all kinds.

The Crane Music Library maintains the most extensive music collection in northern New York State. The collection includes 16,000 books, 24,000 music scores, 16,000 sound recordings, and tapes of performances at Crane dating back to the late 1940s. The library's audio facilities include ten listening rooms and twenty-nine listening carrels. Also located in the library are computers and printers for patron use.

SUNY Potsdam offers its students and faculty members a robust computing environment to support their academic work. In addition to its campus mainframe cluster (DEC Alpha 2100), Potsdam has more than 375 personal computers located in student computing centers around the campus. These centers include the Levitt Memorial Computing Center, a general-use facility, a number of computer classrooms, a student word processing center, and a microcomputer laboratory for educators. All of these personal computers, in addition to those owned by students and faculty members, are tied into centralized computing facilities via a campuswide network. These facilities provide electronic mail, conferencing, and Internet access for electronic communication between students and faculty members and other colleges. The purchase of personal computers is strongly recommended at Potsdam because of their increased use in course work and research. Each room is equipped with a port for each occupant to access the Internet. The campus supports an Apple Macintosh computer purchase program. Workshops and individual assistance in the use of personal computers are available for students.

The Art Department has studios for pottery, sculpture, printmaking, design, drawing, and photography, as well as two galleries for displaying exhibits. The College Theatre, which seats 825, is equipped for drama and music productions. The Dance Department has a large dance studio, as well as a combination studio and performance space. Dancers also perform in the Snell Music Theater. The Foreign Language Department has a language laboratory with an electronic thirty-six-station Tandberg system. The Anthropology Department maintains a lab, study collections of archaeological materials, and equipment for surveying and excavation. For biology, chemistry, physics, and geology, there are fifteen conventional labs, two multistation research labs, a radiation lab, and a planetarium.

Costs

For New York State residents, undergraduate tuition for 1999–2000 was $3400, mandatory fees were $675, room and board averaged $5710 (depending upon the size of room and meal plan chosen), books and supplies were approximately $800, and personal and travel expenses were estimated at $1500, for a total cost of about $12,085. Out-of-state students paid an additional $4900 for tuition.

Financial Aid

Aid is available through the Federal Pell Grant, Federal Work-Study, Federal Supplemental Educational Opportunity Grant, and Federal Perkins Loan programs. Tuition Assistance Program (TAP) awards are also available for eligible New York State residents. Students may apply for Federal Direct Student Loans and Federal Direct PLUS loans through the College. Various SUNY Potsdam scholarships are available for qualified incoming freshmen and transfer students through Potsdam's endowment fund and the Empire State Minority Honors Scholarship Fund. Students not eligible for Federal Work-Study funds can find jobs on campus.

Approximately $20 million in financial aid was disbursed to SUNY Potsdam students in 1998–99, and 84 percent of the qualified undergraduates received some form of financial assistance. The Free Application for Federal Student Aid (FAFSA) is required. There is no filing deadline.

Faculty

The full-time teaching faculty has 196 members, and there are 92 part-time faculty members. Seventy-two percent of the faculty members hold doctorates or terminal degrees in their discipline. Senior faculty members regularly teach beginning courses, as well as more advanced courses, and are available to help students outside of class. The student-faculty ratio is 11:1 in the Crane School of Music and 16:1 in all other areas. Many faculty members are engaged in research that involves students, and most participate in a variety of academic assignments outside the classroom. Students are assigned a general faculty adviser as freshmen and an adviser in their discipline when they declare a major. The absence of teaching assistants makes the faculty members truly committed to teaching and to their students.

Student Government

The Student Government Association (SGA) is composed of all undergraduate students enrolled at the College. Students elect their own representatives to organizations that are vital to the out-of-class life of students. All activities, clubs, and organizations are chartered and recognized by the SGA. The student activity fee to support these activities is administered by the SGA and totals nearly $300,000. Students are voting members of all faculty governance committees and assist in reviewing and initiating changes in academic policies of the College. Similarly, residence halls and other agencies have student governing bodies that shape their policies.

Admission Requirements

SUNY Potsdam is selective in its admission standards. Students are evaluated on their academic ability, chosen curriculum, extracurricular activities, and performance on standardized tests. Interviews are strongly encouraged and are conducted by the professional staff. They are offered each weekday throughout the year. Admission to the Crane School of Music requires an audition as well, and the submission of a portfolio is recommended for admission in art. Competition for admission is especially keen for the Crane School of Music. Students may tour the campus, visit classes, interview with faculty members and staff, and attend special programs presented by the College. Admission staff members also visit high schools and attend college information sessions.

Application and Information

Application forms are available in New York State schools and community colleges and from Potsdam's Office of Admission. Because the major in music is a limited-enrollment program, students applying for admission to this major must so indicate at the time of application; an audition is required. It is suggested that all applications be filed by March 1. Decisions are made on a rolling basis, and the student reply date is May 1 or within thirty days of acceptance.

Students who wish to request additional information should contact:

Director of Admission
State University of New York
　College at Potsdam
44 Pierrepont Avenue
Potsdam, New York 13676

Telephone: 315-267-2180
E-mail: admissions@potsdam.edu
World Wide Web: http://www.potsdam.edu

STATE UNIVERSITY OF NEW YORK COLLEGE OF AGRICULTURE AND TECHNOLOGY AT COBLESKILL

COBLESKILL, NEW YORK

The College

Founded in 1911, SUNY Cobleskill is a fully accredited, residential college of the State University of New York. More than 2,200 men and women are enrolled in one of forty associate degree programs or the upper-division Bachelor of Technology degree program in agriculture. The College offers five strong program areas, including agriculture and natural resources; business and computer technologies; culinary arts, hospitality and tourism; early childhood; liberal arts and sciences; and undeclared/exploratory studies. Courses in the applied sciences and technologies are supported by a strong liberal arts and sciences program.

Diversity is the key to the Cobleskill Quality Experience. While more than half of the students are 18 to 19 years of age, fifteen percent are older than 25 and nearly half are women. Approximately ten percent are students of color or from other countries. The student body is both ethnically and culturally diverse.

Facilities on campus include an art gallery, a theater, downhill ski trails and a lodge, and outstanding physical education facilities. An on-campus child care center provides child care for the children of students, faculty members, and alumni.

SUNY Cobleskill has an outstanding 98 percent placement/transfer rate. More than two thirds of students transfer after graduation. To assist students with the transfer process, the College has negotiated articulation arrangements with a wide range of four-year public and private colleges and universities throughout the nation. Of those employed, 95 percent are working in the area in which they are prepared.

With more than forty active student organizations, there is always something to do at SUNY Cobleskill. Some of the most popular groups include Ag Business Club, Ag Engineering Club, American Animal Producers Club, American Culinary Chapter, Black and Latino Alliance, College Activities Team, College Choir, College Chorus, Community Service Club, Dairy Cattle Club, Delta Psi Omega, Early Childhood Association, Equestrian Team, Fish and Wildlife Club, Hillel, International Club, Jazz Ensemble, Landscape Contractors of America, Latin-American Student Organization, Little Theater, Orange Key Society, Outing Club, Phi Theta Kappa, Photography Club, Plant Science Club, Post-Secondary Agricultural Students Club, Ski Club, Soil and Water Conservation Club, Student Fine Foods Club, Student Government, Student Horsemen's Association, Student Medical Response Team, Voice '98 Yearbook, and Xpressions of Kolor.

SUNY Cobleskill offers one of the largest varsity athletic programs of any two-year college in the Northeast. Intercollegiate competition for men is sponsored in baseball, basketball, cross-country, golf, lacrosse, soccer, swimming and diving, tennis, track and field, and wrestling. Women's intercollegiate sports include basketball, cross-country, golf, soccer, softball, swimming and diving, tennis, track and field, and volleyball. An extensive intramural program is available. Physical education classes stress lifetime sports such as archery, bowling, golf, skiing, swimming, and tennis.

More than two thirds of the student body live in on-campus student housing. Ten residence halls feature lounges, study rooms equipped with computers, recreation rooms, laundry facilities, and more than a dozen different lifestyle preferences. Each room has a phone/voice mail system and connections to cable television and a state-of-the-art computer network. The Beard Wellness Center is equipped and staffed for both inpatient and outpatient care. A special residence hall is offered to upper-class students enrolled in the Bachelor of Technology degree program or students who have independent status. This mature students' living community emphasizes a strong academic focus and independent lifestyle. Special amenities such as room refrigerator/microwave units, single or double room options, flexible guest policies, meal plan flexibility, conference space, a computer lab, and a kitchen area for floor or individual meals are all part of this special option. The hall is open for all vacation and recess periods, August through May.

Location

SUNY Cobleskill is located in the village of Cobleskill, set in scenic and historic Schoharie County. The county, with a population of 30,000, offers the rare combination of rural quality of life and proximity to metropolitan areas. State and private parks, streams, lakes, mountain trails and ski areas provide a full range of outdoor activities. North of the county lies the great Mohawk Valley and the Adirondacks; to the south and west stretch the Catskills.

Schoharie County is abundant in cultural, recreational, historic and tourist attractions, including Minekill State Park, the Old Stone Fort, the Iroquois Indian Museum, and the internationally known Howe Caverns and Secret Caverns.

The village of Cobleskill is a small, friendly college town with 5,300 residents. Convenient shopping, entertainment, fast food restaurants, fine dining, a movie theater and health services are located near the College. Cobleskill is located midway between Oneonta and Albany, about 160 miles northwest of New York City. The village is less than an hour's drive from the Albany-Schenectady-Troy area.

Majors and Degrees

SUNY Cobleskill offers more than forty academic programs leading to the Bachelor of Technology, Associate in Arts, Associate in Science, Associate in Applied Science, and Associate in Occupational Studies degrees and certificates.

Upper-division baccalaureate degrees are offered in agricultural business (agricultural communications, agri-enterprise, food distribution and marketing, and information technology management), agricultural equipment technology, animal science (aquaculture, dairy, equine, histotechnology, livestock, and wildlife management), and plant science (agronomy, environmental studies, floriculture, landscape contracting and nursery management, and turfgrass and recreation and sports area management).

Associate degrees are offered in accounting, agricultural business, agricultural engineering, agricultural science, agricultural industrial equipment, agricultural power machinery technology (John Deere agricultural technology), agronomy, animal science, beef and livestock studies, biological technology, business administration (international business), chemical technology, child and family services, computer information systems (microcomputer support specialist, programming), computer science (math/science, programming), culinary arts, dairy production and management, diesel technology, early childhood (child care), environmental studies, equine studies, fisheries and wildlife technology, floriculture, hotel technology, humanities (communications, graphic design technology), institutional foods, landscape development, mathematics, medical career transfer programs, medical laboratory technology, nursery management, pre–environmental science and forestry, recreation sports area management, restaurant management, science, social science (Native American studies, physical education, psychology), telecommunications management, thoroughbred management, travel and resort marketing, turf and grounds care equipment (John Deere lawn and grounds care), and turfgrass management.

Academic Program

The College offers one-year certificate programs in commercial cooking and childcare, a 1+1 forest technology transfer program, and an undeclared/exploratory studies program. SUNY Cobleskill also offers an Honors Program, which gives motivated students an opportunity to work individually and collectively with faculty members at an advanced level.

Bachelor of Technology students are required to complete a 15-credit-hour off-campus internship to obtain real-world work experience in their fields of expertise.

Academic Facilities

Fifty-seven facilities are located on the 750-acre campus. Cobleskill's facilities include modern classrooms and laboratories, a multimedia learning resources center, state-of-the-art computing networks, and modern food preparation kitchens and a student-operated restaurant. The 500-acre agricultural campus includes an arboretum, a fish hatchery, fourteen greenhouses, agricultural engineering laboratories, and a working farm.

Costs

For 2000–01, annual costs for full-time attendance at Cobleskill for New York State residents are tuition, $3200; room and board, $5920; fees, $867; and books and supplies, $700. Annual tuition for out-of-state residents (including international students) is $5000. Tuition and fees are subject to change.

Financial Aid

Cobleskill awards more than $8 million in need-based financial aid to approximately 80 percent of its student body. The College offers a comprehensive financial aid program that includes both federal and state programs. Federal programs include Federal Pell Grants, Federal College Work-Study, Federal Perkins Loans, PLUS Loans, Federal Stafford Subsidized and Unsubsidized Loans, and U.S. Bureau of Indian Affairs Aid to Native Americans. State programs include New York State's Tuition Assistance Program (TAP), the Regents Award for Children of Deceased Police Officers or Firefighters, Scholarship for Children of Deceased or Disabled Veterans, and Aid to Native Americans. The College also offers a number of scholarships sponsored by the Cobleskill College Foundation and the Cobleskill Alumni Association. Emergency loans are available from the College's Faculty Student Association and the Financial Aid Office.

To apply for financial aid, students must file the Free Application for Federal Student Aid (FAFSA). The FAFSA should be filed as early as possible. March 10 is the preferred filing date for the College's financial aid application. New York State residents should also submit the Tuition Assistance Program application. Applications are available at all New York State high school guidance offices and college transfer offices or by request from the Office of Financial Aid.

Faculty

The College has 118 full-time faculty members who combine to provide a 18:1 student-faculty ratio. A significant number of Cobleskill faculty members come to the classroom from business, industry, and service professions. They bring to their students the benefit of their work and personal experiences. Cobleskill students work side by side in small classes with faculty members who are world-renowned lecturers, authors, and award winners.

Student Government

The Student Government Association (SGA) provides significant leadership opportunities for a wide cross section of the College student body. The SGA supports the activities of more than forty student organizations and serves as the student voice in areas affecting College policy. Officers are elected on an annual basis.

Admission Requirements

Applicants to associate degree programs must have graduated from high school or hold a high school equivalency diploma and meet individual program course requirements. Applicants to the Bachelor of Technology program must have earned an associate degree or a minimum of 60 credits with a 2.0 or higher cumulative grade point average and meet individual program course requirements. Transfer students should submit official high school and college transcripts. Admission decisions are based primarily on the student's academic record. A personal interview, while not required, is recommended. Students are expected, as part of the admissions process, to visit campus during one of the College's Saturday Campus Visitation Day programs. A limited number of high school seniors are admitted to Cobleskill under the early admission program. The College admits students on a first-come, first-served basis.

Application and Information

To apply for admission, students must submit a completed State University of New York application for admission to the SUNY Application Processing Center with a $30 nonrefundable application fee. Applications are available at all New York State high school guidance offices and college transfer offices or by request from the Office of Admissions.

For further information, students should contact:

Director of Admissions
SUNY Cobleskill
Cobleskill, New York 12043

Telephone: 518-255-5525
　　　　　　800-295-8988 (toll-free)
Fax: 518-255-6769
E-mail: admissions@cobleskill.edu
World Wide Web: http://www.cobleskill.edu

SUNY Cobleskill's scenic campus is an ideal place for students to study and learn together.

STATE UNIVERSITY OF NEW YORK COLLEGE OF ENVIRONMENTAL SCIENCE AND FORESTRY

SYRACUSE, NEW YORK

The College

Since it was founded in 1911 as the New York State College of Forestry, the College of Environmental Science and Forestry (ESF) has expanded both its role in education and its physical boundaries. The College has extended its initial emphasis on forestry to include professional education in landscape architecture and engineering in addition to distinguished programs in the biological and physical sciences. Throughout its history, the College has focused on the environmental issues of the time in each of its three mission areas—instruction, research, and public service. The College is dedicated to educating future scientists and managers who, through specialized skills, will be able to use a holistic approach to solving the environmental and resource problems facing society.

A leader in its field, ESF is one of seven specialized colleges in the State University of New York System. The College currently supports undergraduate and graduate degree programs in several disciplinary areas and in its broad program in environmental science. (Undergraduate programs are described in the Majors and Degrees section below.) Graduate programs lead to the Master of Science (M.S.), Master of Landscape Architecture (M.L.A.), Master of Professional Studies (M.P.S.), and Doctor of Philosophy (Ph.D.) degrees. ESF's research program has attracted a worldwide clientele, and support currently amounts to $5.5 million a year.

ESF's main campus is located on 12 acres adjacent to Syracuse University and the SUNY Health Science Center at Syracuse in an urban residential setting. There are 1,197 undergraduates enrolled (32 percent are women); the College's traditional affiliation with Syracuse University offers ESF students the opportunity for academic diversity and depth, as well as participation in cultural events, honorary societies, social fraternities and sororities, and professional and academic organizations.

Location

Syracuse, a metropolitan area of nearly 464,000 people, is a leader in the manufacture of china, air-conditioning equipment, medical diagnostic equipment, drugs, automotive parts, and lighting equipment. It offers many cultural, recreational, and educational opportunities, including a symphony orchestra, museums, live theater, and historic points of interest. Syracuse is one of the few cities in the nation situated at the crossing point of two superhighways. The driving time to Syracuse from New York City, Philadelphia, Boston, Toronto, and Montreal is about 5 hours; from Buffalo and Albany, about 3 hours. The city is served by a modern international airport and major bus and rail lines.

Majors and Degrees

The College of Environmental Science and Forestry offers three undergraduate degrees: the Bachelor of Science (B.S.), the Bachelor of Landscape Architecture (B.L.A.), and the Associate in Applied Science (A.A.S.). The B.S. degree is awarded in chemistry, construction management and wood products engineering, environmental and forest biology, environmental resources and forest engineering, environmental studies, forest resources management, and paper science and engineering. A dual option in forest resources management and environmental and forest biology is also offered, as are a number of options and concentrations within specific curricula. The B.L.A. degree, which requires an additional year of study, is awarded in landscape architecture. The A.A.S. is awarded in forest technology at the campus in Wanakena.

Academic Program

Specialized study options within the environmental and forest biology program include plant physiology, entomology, environmental microbiology, fish and wildlife biology and management, forest pathology and mycology, pest management, plant physiology, plant science, environmental interpretation, and zoology. A five-week period of summer field study, usually taken at ESF's Cranberry Lake Biological Station after the junior year, is required as part of the program. Options for specialization within the chemistry program include biochemistry and natural products chemistry, environmental chemistry, and natural and synthetic polymer chemistry. Within the construction management and wood products engineering curriculum, options are available in construction management and engineering or wood science. The forest resources management curriculum offers concentrations in forestry, water resources management, recreation resources management, urban and community forestry, and forest-based business and a minor in management in conjunction with Syracuse University. The program requires participation in a seven-week period of summer field study, usually taken at ESF's Wanakena campus, prior to the junior year. Environmental studies offers specialization in environmental communication and information, land use planning, policy and management, information and technology, and biological science applications. Work in the first semester of the fifth year of the landscape architecture curriculum requires participation in off-campus independent study. A new undeclared option has been added for freshmen.

Academic Facilities

Specialized facilities and equipment include electron microscopes, plant-growth chambers, air-conditioned greenhouses, an animal environmental simulation chamber, a bioacoustical laboratory, a radioisotope laboratory, a computer center, nuclear magnetic resonance spectrometers, gas chromatography apparatus, a mass spectrometer, ultracentrifuges, and X-ray and infrared spectrophotometers. The photogrammetric and geodetic facilities of the environmental resources and forest engineering department are among the most extensive available in the United States. The paper science and engineering laboratory has a semicommercial paper mill with accessory equipment. The construction management and wood products engineering faculty has a complete strength-of-materials laboratory, a pilot-scale plywood laboratory, and a machining laboratory. The landscape architecture faculty has a one-of-a-kind environmental simulation laboratory with a visual simulator. The greenhouses and forest insectary are used to produce plant and insect materials for the classroom and laboratory. Extensive collections are available, including wood samples from all over the world, botanical materials, insects, birds, mammals, and fishes. A new six-story chemistry facility with thirty-six laboratories opened in 1997.

The F. Franklin Moon Library contains 106,000 cataloged items. More than 1,846 journals and their corresponding indexes are currently received. The library also provides comprehensive abstract and indexing services relevant to the College's programs. These facilities and services are supplemented by the collections of Syracuse University and the SUNY Health Science Center at Syracuse, both of which are within easy walking distance.

ESF's regional campuses in Tully, Warrensburg, Cranberry Lake, Newcomb, and Wanakena have a great diversity of forest sites that are used as outdoor teaching laboratories and for intensive research. ESF also operates several field stations to support its instruction, research, and public service programs.

Costs

Estimated costs for the 2000–01 academic year include resident tuition and fees of $3737 and out-of-state tuition and fees of $8637. Room and board, which are provided for ESF students by Syracuse University, are $8310. Books, personal expenses, and travel are estimated at $1350.

Financial Aid

A wide variety of financial aid is available for ESF students, and more than 80 percent of the students receive some type of support. The forms of financial aid include grants and scholarships, low-interest student loans, and student employment programs. All students are encouraged to apply for financial aid by completing the Free Application for Federal Student Aid (FAFSA).

Faculty

The members of the faculty at ESF are highly trained and are dedicated to the College's teaching, research, and public-service missions. There are 119 regular faculty members, 12 research associates, and 46 adjunct members. Many are nationally and internationally recognized for their expertise in specialized fields. Nearly all regular faculty members serve full-time, and most hold twelve-month appointments. Just over 80 percent are tenured, and more than half are full professors, of whom 93 percent have earned doctorates. There is no distinction between the undergraduate and graduate faculty. Faculty members teach at both levels, and no courses are taught by teaching assistants. Faculty members serve as advisers to students and student groups and encourage excellence in scholarship and research. The student-faculty ratio is about 25:1.

Student Government

The College has a representative Undergraduate Student Association, and student representatives also participate in a counterpart association at Syracuse University. The ESF student government body organizes and presents student social activities, and its representatives attend College administrative meetings, communicate students' concerns and ideas to the administration, and serve as a conduit of information back to the student body. A formal set of student rules and regulations has been established. In addition, ESF students are obligated to abide by Syracuse University's general rules and regulations.

Admission Requirements

Students interested in the academic programs offered at ESF have four enrollment options: Early Decision, Regular Freshman Entry, Guarantee Transfer Admissions, and Transfer Admissions.

The Early Decision option is for candidates who have thoroughly researched all of the college opportunities and have decided that if offered admission, they would definitely attend ESF. Early Decision candidates must have their application completed by November 15 and are notified by December 15. Those candidates accepted under this option have the opportunity of a preliminary financial aid package by January 20. Students not admitted under this option are considered for Regular Freshman Entry.

Regular Freshman Entry is for applicants who want to enroll immediately following high school. These candidates should demonstrate strong academic performance in a college-preparatory program with emphasis on mathematics and science preparation. Freshman candidates must apply to their intended programs of study.

Guarantee Transfer Admissions (GTA) candidates apply to ESF as high school seniors but are offered admission to either their sophomore or junior year. Students who plan to attend another college prior to transferring to ESF select this option to ensure a place at ESF for their chosen entry date. This option may be offered to students who do not meet the freshman admissions criteria. Those who are accepted for admission receive a letter of acceptance for their sophomore or junior year of college, contingent upon the successful completion of all the prerequisite courses required for the curriculum they have selected. The prerequisite courses are outlined and described in an enclosure with the student's acceptance letter.

Students not applying or not accepted under these programs are considered for admission to ESF on the basis of their previous college course work, overall academic aptitude, and interest in the College's programs. Consideration is given to both the quality and the appropriateness of each student's prior academic experience. Students spend one or two years at any college of their choice. The College, working in cooperation with other four-year and two-year colleges in New York, Alabama, Connecticut, Maryland, Massachusetts, New Jersey, Pennsylvania, and Rhode Island, has developed Cooperative Transfer Programs. In addition, since many ESF students have been previously enrolled at Syracuse University, the two institutions have an articulated program through which students can move from Syracuse University to ESF after the sophomore year with no loss of credits. All admission acceptances are conditional upon satisfactory completion of course work in progress.

Application and Information

Students may apply for fall or spring admission. Admission decisions are made on a rolling basis until the class is filled. Decisions for the fall semester are made beginning on or about January 15, and decisions for the spring semester are made beginning on or about October 15. Application forms are available for New York State residents at New York State high schools and at all SUNY two- and four-year colleges. Out-of-state students should request an application form directly from the Office of Undergraduate Admissions at ESF. Requests for more information should be directed to:

Office of Undergraduate Admissions
106 Bray Hall
State University of New York College
   of Environmental Science and Forestry
1 Forestry Drive
Syracuse, New York 13210-2779
Telephone: 315-470-6600
         800-777-7373 (toll-free)
Fax: 315-470-6933
E-mail: esfinfo@esf.edu
World Wide Web: http://www.esf.edu

STATE UNIVERSITY OF NEW YORK INSTITUTE OF TECHNOLOGY AT UTICA/ROME

UTICA, NEW YORK

The Institute

The State University of New York Institute of Technology was originally established in 1966 as the State University Upper Division College at Utica/Rome by the State University of New York Board of Trustees for the purpose of providing upper-level and graduate-level education in the sciences and technologies. As an upper-division college located in central New York State's Mohawk Valley region, the Institute serves as an upper-level extension for two-year institutions throughout New York State. As the only designated upper-division college offering comprehensive studies in the sixty-four-campus system of the State University of New York, the Institute continues to provide professional, technical, and liberal arts programs to meet the needs of the state's two-year-college graduates. Graduate programs in accountancy, adult nurse practitioner studies, advanced technology, applied sociology, business management, computer science, family nurse practitioner studies, health services administration, information design and technology, nursing administration, and telecommunications are also offered. The Institute currently enrolls 2,041 undergraduate and 366 graduate students on both a full-time and part-time basis. The male-female ratio is approximately 1:1. Ten percent of the student population are from minority groups; 1 percent are international students.

In addition to its academic facilities, the Institute provides student services through the Residence Life, Career Services, and Counseling Center Offices. Townhouse-style residence halls provide on-campus housing to 584 students. The Campus Center provides health, physical education, and recreation facilities, as well as a dining hall and student services offices. In addition to providing a wide variety of intramural sports for students, the Institute of Technology competes intercollegiately in men's and women's basketball, bowling, and soccer; men's baseball, golf, and lacrosse; and women's softball and volleyball.

Location

The SUNY Institute of Technology is located in Utica, New York. The city of Utica, which has a population of 70,000, is situated in the geographic center of New York State, approximately 220 miles from New York City and 190 miles from Buffalo on the New York State Thruway. Utica, a cultural and recreational center for this area of New York State, has a variety of recreational and educational opportunities. Museums, theaters, restaurants, and professional sports events are available either within walking distance of the campus or a short bus ride away. As the natural gateway to the Adirondack Mountains, Utica provides its residents with access to hiking, boating, skiing, and other outdoor activities. Served by buses, Amtrak, and airlines, the city is easily reached from locations throughout the eastern United States.

Majors and Degrees

The SUNY Institute of Technology awards the following baccalaureate degrees: Bachelor of Professional Studies (B.P.S.), Bachelor of Technology (B.Tech.), Bachelor of Science (B.S.), Bachelor of Arts (B.A.), and Bachelor of Business Administration (B.B.A.). Academic majors include accounting, applied mathematics, business/public management, civil engineering technology, computer information systems, computer and information science, computer engineering technology, electrical engineering technology, finance, general studies, health information management, health services management, industrial engineering technology, mechanical engineering technology, nursing, photonics, professional and technical communication, psychology, sociology, and telecommunications. A number of options and concentrations within specific curricula are also available, as well as minors in accounting; anthropology; computer science; economics; finance; gerontology; health services management; manufacturing/quality assurance technology; mathematics; physics; professional and technical communication; psychology; science, technology, and society; and sociology.

Academic Program

The mission of the SUNY Institute of Technology is to provide professionally oriented education at the upper-division level in a variety of academic areas. The course of study is built on the foundations laid by two-year associate-level programs and is designed specifically to meet the needs of graduates of two-year community colleges, colleges of technology, junior colleges, or professional schools. The academic year is divided into two semesters and runs from September through May. Summer and winterim sessions are also available.

Baccalaureate degree requirements vary among curricula but usually consist of a 60-semester-hour combination of specific major courses and liberal arts studies. Specializations and other options exist within the Schools of Arts and Sciences, Information Systems and Engineering Technology, and Management. Specializations are developed through the use of electives and individual advisement.

Off-Campus Arrangements

Internship and cooperative education experiences are integral to effective career planning and job search strategies. These experiences can influence career plans by providing an opportunity for occupational exploration, developing marketable career-related skills and characteristics, and establishing a network of contacts that can provide relevant and timely information critical to the career decision-making process. In addition employers are increasingly using internships and cooperative education programs as a training opportunity leading to full-time permanent employment. All students, regardless of major, are encouraged to consider gaining experience in their chosen field that complements classroom learning. For additional information, students should contact their academic department and the Office of Career Services.

Academic Facilities

The Institute's academic facilities are located on its scenic 800-acre campus just north of the city of Utica and are easily accessible by municipal bus service. The campus consists of three building complexes, a facilities building, and residence halls. Kunsela Hall, named for the Institute's first president, contains the library, administrative offices, and classrooms and laboratories for the telecommunications, electrical engineering technology, and computer science curricula. Donovan Hall, the academic complex, houses classrooms, faculty offices, and laboratory facilities for all other curricula, including business, industrial engineering technology, mechanical engineering technology, health services management, nursing, and arts and sciences. A comprehensive student center contains a gymnasium, a swimming pool, recreational facilities, a cafeteria, a bookstore, student services offices, and meeting rooms for clubs, special activities, and student government.

Library resources include 161,260 bound volumes, 23,251 microforms, and an extensive collection of professional journals, newspapers, and other national publications. In addition, the library is a federal depository for government documents, selecting 14 percent of available items for a total collection of approximately 56,000 documents. The library also provides 14 full-text databases and 16 databases in FirstSearch; all workstations have Internet access. In addition, the library will be moving to a new state-of-the art facility in spring 2001.

Costs

Costs for the 1999–2000 academic year included state resident tuition and fees of $3949 and out-of-state tuition and fees of $8849. Room and board costs were $5300, and personal expenses, books, supplies, and travel cost approximately $2345. The total expenses were about $12,490 for New York State residents and $17,390 for out-of-state students. Costs may be subject to change.

Financial Aid

A wide variety of financial aid is available to students at the Institute. All financial aid is awarded on the basis of need, as determined by an assessment of the Free Application for Federal Student Aid. At present, approximately 85 percent of the students receive financial assistance. The forms of financial aid available include Tuition Assistance Program awards (for New York State residents only), Federal Supplemental Educational Opportunity Grants, Federal Pell Grants, Federal Work-Study Program employment, Federal Perkins Loans, federal Nursing Student Loans, Federal Direct Student Loans, a variety of state-sponsored loans, and a broad range of private scholarships and grants. Students with a GPA of 3.25 or better are automatically considered for transfer merit scholarships at the time of their application. A number of transfer scholarships, based on previous academic performance, are available to students who have demonstrated exceptional scholastic ability at their two-year college.

Faculty

The faculty members at the Institute of Technology have been assembled with the professionally oriented emphasis of the school's curricula in mind. Previous professional work experience in their teaching area and excellent academic credentials are standard requirements for faculty members, and there is a faculty commitment to teaching, academic orientation and advisement, individualized instruction, cooperative faculty-student efforts in research projects, and concern for the student as an individual. Outside the classroom, the 90 full-time faculty members and a variety of adjunct resource people are actively involved in the overall social and academic life of the college community. Such participation has been important in fostering a personalized atmosphere at the Institute of Technology. The student-faculty ratio is 19:1.

Student Government

All full-time undergraduates are members of the Utica/Rome Student Association (URSA). The primary functions of URSA are to develop and monitor the student-activity-fee budget, to approve and oversee all student organizations, to debate issues of concern to students and take action as needed, and to develop programs of interest to all Institute of Technology students. URSA consists of a 7-person executive committee and 11 senators. Students are encouraged to take an active role in the governance process, and many opportunities for involvement, in addition to those listed above, are available for interested students.

Admission Requirements

The requirements for admission to the State University of New York Institute of Technology are dictated by the upper-division nature of the institution and include the following criteria: all students must have earned an associate degree or generally completed 56 semester hours (or the equivalent) of lower-division college credit prior to entry, and students should be in good academic standing at their time of departure from the lower-division institution(s). Credit hours to be transferred into the selected program at the Institute of Technology must result in at least an overall 2.0 cumulative index. Specific requirements vary by program. Most programs are competitive, requiring a minimum GPA of 2.5 for guaranteed admission. Students with a GPA between 2.0 and 2.5 will be considered on an individual basis. Prospective students are encouraged to contact the admissions office at the SUNY Institute of Technology for additional information.

Students with a cumulative GPA of at least 3.25 are automatically considered for merit and residential scholarships; no separate application is required.

Application and Information

Applications are accepted on a rolling admissions basis. Prospective students are urged to apply early.

Students who wish to apply to the Institute should obtain a copy of the State University of New York application booklet from a two-year college, a local high school, or the admission office at the Institute of Technology. In addition, students may apply on line through the college's Web site. Applicants should note that they need not supply the high school information requested in the application when they are applying to the Institute of Technology. Application forms for international students may also be obtained through the admissions office.

The SUNY Institute of Technology adheres to the principle that all persons should have equal opportunity and access to its educational facilities without regard to race, creed, sex, or national origin.

Official transcripts from all colleges previously attended should be sent to the director of admissions at the address below. All communications and requests for additional information should also be directed to:

Director of Admissions
State University of New York
    Institute of Technology at Utica/Rome
P.O. Box 3050
Utica, New York 13504-3050
Telephone: 315-792-7500
        800-SUNYTECH (toll-free)
Fax: 315-792-7837
E-mail: admissions@sunyit.edu
World Wide Web: http://www.sunyit.edu

Town-house-style residence halls afford students the opportunity to live and learn in a convenient, safe, and comfortable environment.

STATE UNIVERSITY OF NEW YORK MARITIME COLLEGE
FORT SCHUYLER, THROGGS NECK, NEW YORK

The College

Founded in 1874, the State University of New York Maritime College is the oldest U.S. Coast Guard–approved nautical college in the United States. At Maritime College, cadets earn bachelor's degrees in various fields of engineering, science, business, and humanities while concurrently preparing for the U.S. Merchant Marine officer's license of third mate or third assistant engineer.

An important part of all Maritime College curricula is the annual Summer Sea Term aboard the 565-foot training ship, *Empire State VI*, the best-equipped training ship in the United States. The Summer Sea Terms also provide a leadership laboratory in which cadets assume responsibility for the operation of the ship under the supervision of licensed officers and staff. The *Empire State VI* normally calls on three European ports on each cruise. During the regular academic year, cadets also have the opportunities for training in inland waterways aboard the College's 110-foot tugboat, barge, and a 174-foot coastal training tanker; ashore, the cadets also have the opportunity to train at the most advanced center for marine simulation in the nation—the Maritime College Center for Simulated Maritime Operations.

Maritime College has recently been designated as a regional maritime college. Because of this designation, students from Connecticut, New Jersey, Delaware, Pennsylvania, Maryland, and Virginia pay New York State tuition rates of $3400 per year.

Under a special, federally funded program, out-of-state students may pay New York state tuition if they qualify for the Student Incentive Program (SIP) and agree to serve in the U.S. Naval Reserve/Merchant Marine Reserve. All participants in SIP, whether in-state or out-of-state students, also receive an incentive of $3000 a year during their undergraduate years.

Maritime College fields sixteen varsity sports, four intercollegiate club sports, and sixteen intramurals and is nationally known for its sailing and crew teams. The College ranks nationally in sailing and crew. The men's crew team finished in first place on the East Coast for the 1994 season.

Maritime College has as its primary mission the preparation of men and women for the full spectrum of professional careers in the maritime industry, including the U.S. Merchant Marine. Its graduates receive a well-rounded education that enables them to pursue career options in industry, government service, or at sea as civilian officers of merchant ships, research ships, and other U.S. vessels. In addition, commissioning options exist for those seeking careers as officers in the U.S. Navy, Marine Corps, Coast Guard, or Air Force or in the National Oceanographic and Atmospheric Administration (NOAA). Maritime College is the only college that hosts a Naval ROTC program in the greater New York metropolitan area.

Location

The scenic 56-acre campus is located at historic Fort Schuyler on the Throggs Neck peninsula, where the East River meets Long Island Sound. The College campus has a small New England town flavor to it, although it is only 50 minutes by express bus from Rockefeller Center in Manhattan. The peninsula offers panoramic views of the East River and Long Island Sound with impressive sights of coastal Connecticut, the North Shore of Long Island, and the Manhattan skyline off in the distance.

The College's extensive waterfront property contains a refurbished pier (where the training ship, tugboat, barge, and coastal training tanker are docked) as well as a waterfront activities center/boat house, which is home for its fleet of 420s, Lasers, FJ's, and offshore racing yachts.

Majors and Degrees

The College offers the Bachelor of Engineering degree in marine engineering (with mechanical, electrical, and conventional power options) and naval architecture. It offers the Bachelor of Science degree in business administration/marine transportation, engineering (facilities, marine electrical and electronic systems, and marine operations), humanities concentration, and marine environmental science (with a meteorology and oceanography concentration). All degree programs are combined with preparation for the professional license as a U.S. Merchant Marine Officer. There is also a two-year associate degree in marine technology/small vessel operations that offers a 200-ton U.S. Coast Guard license.

Academic Program

Curricula lead to the Bachelor of Science or Bachelor of Engineering degree with licensure as a third officer (mate or engineer) for the Merchant Marine. The license, issued by the Coast Guard, opens up the full spectrum of shoreside maritime industry-related jobs and civilian sea-going employment (merchant ships, offshore drilling and mineral resource recovery, research ships, etc.). Graduates are qualified to sail on oceangoing vessels, on inland waterways, on the Great Lakes, and on coastal waters, which includes tug and barge operations.

Business administration/marine transportation students complete a strong traditional core curriculum in business administration, with minor concentrations in management, international business, transportation management, and marine operations. This program is integrated into a deck-license training program in which cadets study all aspects of navigation, ship handling, and nautical rules of the road. Graduates are qualified to sail as merchant marine officers or to work ashore in the various aspects of the maritime industry, including ship chartering, ship brokerage, the import/export business, port management, and transportation management.

The College also offers outstanding programs in engineering and naval architecture. Marine engineering prepares Maritime College graduates with a broad understanding of the energy and power industries. This program is offered with a third-assistant engineer's license. Engine-license candidates get the experience of operating a live power plant aboard the training ship, a powerful combination of design engineering and hands-on technology. Naval architecture, offered with deck or engine license, teaches the design of ships and sea-based structures, with specialty concentrations in the study and design of commercial ships, small craft, naval vessels, and offshore structures. Two new B.S. degree programs in engineering (marine operations and marine electrical and electronic systems) are offered with a deck license.

Other degrees offered at Maritime College include marine environmental science, offered with a deck license option; a humanities study area concentration, available with deck- or engine-license preparation; and the associate degree in marine technology/small vessel operations, which is offered with a 200-ton license.

Academic Facilities

Fort Schuyler, built in the 1850s, houses the Business Administration/Marine Transportation Department, a government depository library, a maritime museum, and the new $1.5 million Center for Simulation and Marine Operations, which contains a state-of-the-art full bridge simulator, a liquid cargo simulator, an electronic navigation simulator, two Automatic Radar Plotting Aid (ARPA) equipped radar simulators, and two Global Maritime Distress and Safety System (GMDSS) simulators. The fort is flanked by modern dining halls, residence halls, lecture halls, recreational facilities, and well equipped science and engineering laboratories. The Science and Engineering Building contains a diesel simulator, a towing tank, and a CAD/CAM laboratory, as well as advanced electrical and mechanical engineering labs. The Stephen B. Luce Library has more than 80,000 volumes and subscribes to more than 350 periodicals. The collection is accessed through an online catalog. Full-text CD-ROM databases and online searches are available on six PC workstations in the library.

Costs

For 1999–2000, costs were as follows: for in-state and out-of-state students who participated in SIP, tuition was $3400 per year. Under the new Regional Maritime College status, students from Connecticut, New Jersey, Delaware, Pennsylvania, Maryland, and Virginia pay New York State tuition rates. For other out-of-state students who did not participate in SIP and for international students, tuition was $8300 per year. Fees averaged $1065. Room and board, including the two-month Summer Sea Term, were $7100 per year. Uniforms cost $1800 (first year only). Books and supplies average $800 per year. Students should budget $1500 per year for personal expenses.

Financial Aid

Maritime College cadets have access to two special forms of aid. Cadets who are selected for the federal Student Incentive Program (SIP) receive $3000 per year. They must be U.S. citizens, physically qualified for the merchant marine license, and must not have reached their 25th birthday at the start of the program. Out-of-state students who are selected to participate in SIP pay in-state tuition fees. Full-tuition scholarships are also available through Navy ROTC. Four-year NROTC scholarship winners are also offered free room and board at the College. In addition to scholarships, Navy ROTC offers the College Program, which provides an allowance of $100 per month during the last two years of college study. Participants in the College Program may reapply for the Navy ROTC scholarship after enrollment. A variety of privately funded scholarships are available to students at the College, including a number of Admiral's Scholarships, which cover the full cost of New York State tuition. There are no military obligations attached to the Admiral's and other privately funded scholarships.

The Maritime Academy Reserve Training Program (MARTP) is a Coast Guard Commissioning Program that provides generous compensation to select Maritime College cadets at the beginning of their sophomore year.

New York State residents who are in great need financially and who have not been able to achieve up to their academic potential because of factors beyond their control may apply for assistance through the Educational Opportunity Program when they apply for admission.

In addition to these forms of aid, students may apply for need-based aid, including Federal Pell Grants, TAP grants, Federal Perkins Loans, Federal Stafford Student Loans, and Federal Work-Study awards. The Free Application for Federal Student Aid (FAFSA) is required to apply for need-based financial aid.

Faculty

Maritime College prides itself on the teaching capabilities of its faculty. Small classes and an interested faculty make for a stimulating and supportive learning environment. The faculty members involved with license preparation course work have the appropriate United States Coast Guard licenses and professional credentials. Faculty members teaching in traditional academic disciplines possess appropriate credentials, with 35 holding the doctoral or other terminal degree in their field. A student-faculty ratio of 16:1 is maintained. Many faculty members are involved with consulting work, most commonly with the maritime industry, which gives them important exposure to current problems and practices as well as contacts for student projects.

Student Government

The College has an active student government association, which administers the student activities fee that supports College-wide activities, clubs and organizations, and a diverse athletic program. Students are also represented on various faculty committees.

Admission Requirements

Admission is competitive and is based strictly on the applicant's abilities. Political nomination is not required. Decisions are based on strength of academic preparation; grades, rank in class, and test scores; outside activities and achievements; and trends in performance. Transfer students are welcome. Math through at least intermediate algebra and trigonometry and a year of either chemistry or physics are required. All students who are attracted to a Maritime education are encouraged to apply. Those who may not be competitive or are not adequately prepared for admission are given counseling on ways to prepare for later admission.

Application and Information

Applications (the SUNY Common Application for Admission form and College forms), catalogs, and additional information are available from the Office of Admissions. Prospective students are encouraged to schedule an interview and a cadet-guided tour (arranged with the admissions office), preferably from September to early May. Students may apply on line through the College's Web page.

Office of Admissions
State University of New York Maritime College
Fort Schuyler
Throggs Neck, New York 10465
Telephone: 718-409-7220
         800-654-1874 (toll-free in New York State)
         800-642-1874 (toll-free in the Northeast)
Fax: 718-409-7465
E-mail: admissions@sunymaritime.edu
World Wide Web: http://www.sunymaritime.edu

Maritime College—a degree and more!

STATE UNIVERSITY OF WEST GEORGIA
CARROLLTON, GEORGIA

The University

A coeducational, residential institution, the State University of West Georgia (UWG) is a charter member of the University System of Georgia. From its beginnings in 1908 as the Fourth District Agricultural and Mechanical School, West Georgia has grown into a leading comprehensive regional university that enrolled 8,665 students in fall 1999 from most counties in Georgia, thirty-seven other states, and sixty-nine other countries. About 65 percent of enrolled students are women, and 24 percent belong to minority groups. Today, UWG offers ten undergraduate degrees in more than fifty majors through four colleges—the College of Arts and Sciences, the Richards College of Business, the College of Education, and the newly created Honors College, the only college of its kind in Georgia. In addition, two new bachelor's degrees will be offered in fall 2000. The Graduate School offers nine graduate degrees in more than thirty major fields and has one of the highest percentages of students enrolled in graduate classes in the University System. The University is also the home of the Advanced Academy of Georgia, one of the nation's fewer than ten residential programs for gifted high school juniors and seniors.

UWG takes its motto of Educational Excellence in a Personal Environment seriously. Faculty members teach their own courses and take a personal interest in students. Undergraduates receive access to technology and research opportunities that are not usually available at other schools. Freshmen live on campus in one of eleven residence halls and can join a learning community of students who live in the same hall, share classes, and often earn higher grades as a result. Extracurricular activities are sponsored through more then ninety student organizations, which cover academics, professional and honor groups, politics, religion, service, recreation and sports, social fraternities and sororities, and a debate team that finished second in the nation in 1999. The athletics program, one of the most varied among college-division schools, fields men's intercollegiate teams in baseball, basketball, cross-country, football, and tennis and women's teams in basketball, cross-country, softball, tennis, and volleyball—all affiliated with Division II of the NCAA.

The State University of West Georgia is accredited by the Commission on Colleges of the Southern Association of Colleges and Schools (SACS) to award bachelor's, master's, and education specialist's degrees. The Board of Regents has recently approved a Doctor of Education in school improvement degree (to be offered starting in June 2000), which is being reviewed by SACS for accreditation. All programs preparing teachers through the master's level are accredited by the National Council for Accreditation of Teacher Education, and the Georgia Professional Standards Commission approves UWG to recommend candidates for education certificates. The Georgia State Department of Education offers full recognition and accreditation as well. The undergraduate and graduate College of Business programs are accredited by the AACSB–The International Association for Management Education. Only 7 percent of business schools across the nation—and only twelve other institutions in Georgia—hold this accreditation. Both the Bachelor and Master of Professional Accounting programs are accredited separately by the AACSB–The International Association for Management Education. The University's Department of Chemistry is accredited by the American Chemical Society, and the Department of Psychology by the Consortium for Diversified Psychology Programs. The Master of Public Administration degree program is accredited by the National Association of Schools of Public Affairs and Administration. Other programs are accredited by the National League for Nursing Accrediting Commission and the National Association of Schools of Music. All art programs are accredited by the National Association of Schools of Art and Design.

Location

Fifty miles west of Atlanta, the campus extends over 400 wooded acres, and its picturesque blend of pre–Civil War and late-twentieth-century architecture complements the similar style of surrounding Carrollton, Georgia. Together, Carrollton and Atlanta offer endless opportunities for entertainment, cultural enrichment, and professional work experiences. Downtown Carrollton features small family-run businesses that lend an air of Southern hospitality to shopping, and the city also offers dining that ranges from Southern to international cuisine, movies, dancing, theatrical productions, and other cultural activities.

Majors and Degrees

UWG offers ten baccalaureate degrees in more than fifty major fields of study. Those degrees are as follows: Bachelor of Arts in anthropology, art, biology, chemistry, English, French, geography, history, international economic affairs, mass communications, mathematics, philosophy, political science, psychology, sociology, Spanish, and theater arts; Bachelor of Business Administration in accounting, administrative systems, business information systems, economics, finance, management, marketing, and real estate; Bachelor of Fine Arts in art and art education; Bachelor of Music in composition, music education, music with studies in business, performance, performance with emphasis in jazz studies, and performance with emphasis in piano pedagogy; Bachelor of Science in biology, computer science, criminal justice, economics, geography, geology, mathematics, physics, political science, and sociology; Bachelor of Science in Chemistry; Bachelor of Science in Earth Science; Bachelor of Science in Education in business education, early childhood education, middle grades education, physical education, secondary science education, secondary social science education, special education in mental retardation, and special education in speech-language pathology; Bachelor of Science in Nursing; and Bachelor of Science in Recreation. The Bachelor of Science in Environmental Science and the Bachelor of Science in Environmental Studies will be offered beginning in fall 2000. Preprofessional programs are available in chemistry, dental hygiene, dentistry, forestry, law, medicine, pharmacy, physical therapy, physician's assistant studies, and veterinary studies. A dual-degree program in engineering is offered with Georgia Institute of Technology, Auburn University, and Mercer University.

Academic Program

In fall 1998, UWG, as part of the University System of Georgia, changed from the quarter system to the semester system. The new academic year consists of two 15-week semesters that begin in August and January, a three-week miniterm in May, and summer semesters of about four or eight weeks.

During the freshman and sophomore years, students complete the core curriculum, 60 semester hours of general education courses designed by the faculty to provide a foundation for all degree programs. Included in the core are courses in written and oral communication, mathematics, natural science, technology, social science, and the humanities and fine arts as well as courses designed to lead to one's chosen major. Undergraduates have nationally acclaimed access to research opportunities, and instruction is enhanced by faculty member research that is supported by more than $2 million in grants.

Off-Campus Arrangements

Off-campus classes are offered in Newnan, Georgia, at the University's Newnan Center and in Dalton, Georgia, through the cooperative External Degree Program with Dalton College. Courses are offered to students at remote locations through the Distance Education Program, which conducts classes both on line and through two-way live videoconferencing. Some degrees may be earned by attending only evening and weekend classes through UWG's Evening/Weekend University. Study-abroad programs for credit are offered in art (Bayeux, Paris, and London), economics and finance (Atlanta, New York, and London), French language and civilization (Tours, Paris, and Nice), music (Germany), and Spanish language and culture (Cuernavaca). Students may also participate in multidisciplinary programs in London, Paris, and St. Petersburg.

Academic Facilities

The new $19.5-million Technology-Enhanced Learning Center will be completed by fall 2000. The three-building facility, which occupies more than 1 acre, will include laboratories, lecture halls, classrooms, and offices. About 2,600 computer network connections will make it possible for students to access the Internet from virtually anywhere in the complex, including stairwells. The building will be one of the first on the East Coast to feature SmartPanel audiovisual control systems in classrooms, and each classroom will also be equipped with a VCR, a computer, a projector, a SmartBoard, and a ceiling-mount screen. Studio laboratories for chemistry, computing, and engineering will allow students to work at both computers and tabletop labs during class and share computer access with the professor and classmates.

The Irvine Sullivan Ingram Library is one of the most modern library facilities in Georgia. It contains seminar and conference rooms, individual study carrels, and the Annie Belle Weaver Special Collections Room and offers video players, microform readers, photocopiers, and networked printers to assist students and faculty members with study and research. Ingram Library houses 355,522 bound volumes and 1,040,266 physical units of microform as well as 19,828 maps and charts and 27,398 volumes/pieces of special-collection material. It has subscriptions to 1,372 magazines and newspapers in paper format and provides access to more than 3,000 additional titles electronically. Ingram Library is the Seventh Congressional District selective depository for 220,531 U.S. government publications. It also participates in the University System of Georgia's state-of-the-art information system, Georgia Library Learning Online (GALILEO), an Internet-based complex of databases that include full-text articles, complete subject and browsing indexing, and Internet resources. Local resources, GALILEO, and the new Georgia Interconnected Libraries (GIL) project provide students with complete access to local, state, regional, and international library collections.

The Townsend Center for the Performing Arts is available for performances of theatrical and musical events by both students and community groups. The center also presents a number of special performances and concerts, including appearances by local, regional, and national entertainers and personalities. It features a 455-seat main-stage area, a 155-seat experimental theater, rehearsal rooms, dressing rooms, and a set design center.

Costs

Based on a 12-hour or more on-campus semester, tuition and fees for the 1999–2000 school year were $1125 for Georgia residents and $3837 for nonresidents. Room charges were $1013 per semester, and board cost $890 per semester. Books totaled approximately $300 per semester, and other expenses totaled about $400 per semester. Fees and charges are due on the day of registration. Graduation fees were $12. Part-time students are charged tuition and fees on a prorated basis.

Financial Aid

All applicants interested in federal and state financial aid programs must submit a Free Application for Federal Student Aid (FAFSA) and any required documents regarding their own and their family's financial resources. In order to receive financial aid at the State University of West Georgia, students must be in good academic standing or they must be accepted for admission. The state of Georgia provides the HOPE Scholarship to eligible students who are Georgia residents. In addition, UWG offers outstanding students a wide variety of academic and performing arts scholarships. Some academic scholarships are available to students regardless of their major, and others are for students majoring in particular fields. Still others are designed to encourage students from a specific county or minority group to attend the University. Work programs that are open to students include the Federal Work-Study Program, student assistantships, internships, and cooperative work situations.

Faculty

UWG has 332 full-time faculty members, 81 percent of whom hold the terminal degree in their associated field. The student-to-faculty ratio is approximately 19:1.

Student Government

The Student Government Association deals with matters of student affairs, sets forth general principles of governance of the student body, and approves mandatory student fees. Any enrolled undergraduate or graduate student is eligible to participate in student government.

Admission Requirements

To ensure admission as a freshman, it is desirable for applicants to have combined SAT I scores in the range of 800 to 900 or an ACT composite score of 18 to 20 as well as a high school grade point average in academic courses of 2.0 or higher. In addition, all applicants should complete the College Preparatory Curriculum (CPC) according to standards approved by the University System of Georgia. Transfer students are considered for admission on the basis of their previous college records and such additional information as is pertinent to their academic abilities.

Application and Information

Every applicant must submit a formal application to the Admissions Office along with a $15 nonrefundable application fee. The deadline for making application for any semester is twenty calendar days before that semester begins. However, entering freshmen are encouraged to complete application procedures during the first half of the senior year in high school. For further information, students should contact:

Director of Admissions
State University of West Georgia
Carrollton, Georgia 30118
Telephone: 770-836-6416
E-mail: admiss@westga.edu
World Wide Web: http://www.westga.edu

Classes at the State University of West Georgia are small and dynamic, and faculty members take a personal interest in students.

STEPHENS COLLEGE
COLUMBIA, MISSOURI

The College

Stephens College, founded in 1833 as the nation's second-oldest women's college, is the only four-year college for women in Missouri. Stephens is ranked in the top tier of Midwestern liberal arts colleges in *U.S. News & World Report* and has repeatedly been selected to the *Princeton Review*'s list of the best colleges in the country. Students from around the globe enrich Stephens with their varied talents, interests, and backgrounds. Students at this national liberal arts college enjoy a spacious 200-acre campus located in the heart of Columbia and adjacent to the University of Missouri and Columbia College. Stephens students may choose to join one of twelve honorary societies on campus, including Psi Chi, Alpha Epsilon Rho, and Mortar Board, or become involved in student government. Leadership experience is emphasized in all aspects of life at Stephens. Stephens' residence halls provide much of the focus for campus activity. The Searcy House Plan offers a living/learning environment in the humanities to a select group of freshmen each year. Since it began in the 1960s as an experiment funded by the Ford Foundation, the Searcy program has served as a model for similar living/learning communities in colleges and universities across the nation. Fashioned after Searcy, the Prunty Science House Plan is also available to Stephens freshmen who wish to explore the fields of math, science, and technology.

In addition to undergraduate degrees, Stephens offers Master's degrees.

Location

Stephens College is located in Columbia, Missouri. Situated halfway between Kansas City and St. Louis, Columbia is the cultural, medical, and business center of mid-Missouri. Often called "College Town, USA," Columbia is also the home of Columbia College and the University of Missouri. Stephens students have easy access to Columbia's shopping, dining, and entertainment offerings.

Majors and Degrees

Stephens College awards the Associate in Arts, Bachelor of Arts, Bachelor of Fine Arts, and Bachelor of Science. Majors include accounting; biology and health sciences; business administration; creative writing; dance; early childhood education; elementary education; English; environmental biology; environmental communication; equestrian business management; fashion design and product development; fashion marketing and management; health sciences; international studies; law, philosophy, and rhetoric; liberal studies; marketing: public relations and advertising; mass communication (broadcast media, communication studies, journalism, or public relations); mathematical sciences; psychology; social sciences: history; social sciences: political science; student-initiated majors; and theater arts. The B.F.A. program includes professional-level work in the fine or performing arts plus a strong component in liberal studies.

Academic Program

The B.A. degree is generally completed in four years. Students pursue depth of study in an academic area, breadth in liberal arts study, and elective course work with guidance from faculty advisers. Academic departments require relevant internships and often provide opportunities for research projects in field settings.

Stephens has introduced many innovative educational concepts into its programs. A three-year baccalaureate option permits greater flexibility in academic programming. Stephens emphasizes personalized teaching and development of the individual. Small classes are offered, and most departments offer tutorial projects and readings.

Students in the bachelor's degree programs, either B.A., B.F.A., or B.S., must complete the residence requirement of seven semesters. Students must demonstrate the ability to write proper English or pass two courses in English composition, and must complete at least twelve courses at an advanced level (including five in the major). All degree candidates take eight courses selected from seven areas: natural sciences, social and behavioral sciences, languages and literature, fine arts, history, humanities/religion/philosophy, and mathematics and analytical reasoning. In addition, all degree candidates complete one upper-level general education requirement in each of the following areas: cross-cultural studies, interdisciplinary studies, and moral and ethical issues.

Degree requirements for the Bachelor of Arts include completion of ten to fifteen courses in a department. Students also may elect to design an interdisciplinary student-initiated major.

Degree requirements for the Bachelor of Fine Arts include completion of as many as twenty-six courses in a B.F.A. major, which is the maximum number allowed in a B.F.A. major within a forty-course degree program. The B.F.A. is completed in three years and two summers.

The Bachelor of Science degree program requires completion of fifteen to seventeen courses, including a senior requirement and at least five courses at or above the 300 level. B.S. candidates may elect additional courses in the major department, but no more than twenty courses may count toward a forty-course degree program.

Through Stephens College School of Graduate and Continuing Education, nontraditional students throughout the country have the opportunity to complete a self-paced liberal arts program that builds on past learning. Most of Stephens' programs, including courses of study leading to the B.A. degree, are open to Stephens College School of Graduate and Continuing Education students. In addition, the School of Graduate and Continuing Education has programs in business administration; education; English; health care and a second area; health information administration (the first accredited external degree program in medical record administration in the country); health science and a second area; law, philosophy, and rhetoric; psychology; and student-initiated majors. In addition, Stephens offers graduate degrees in business and education.

Off-Campus Arrangements

Stephens sponsors summer seminars in several countries, including China, France, Italy, and Japan, as extensions of courses that are regularly offered at the College. Summer-study programs include drama and musical theater at Lake Okoboji, Spirit Lake, Iowa. Stephens also offers full-year study opportunities in Cambridge, England.

Many other study opportunities are available through global partnerships with other universities.

Academic Facilities

The Hugh Stephens Resources Library contains more than 125,000 volumes. The library is the central building of a quadrangle that includes the Helis Communication Center and the Patricia Barry Television Studio. The E. S. Pillsbury Science Center houses science and mathematics classrooms and laboratories, and the Ellis Learning Laboratories provide modern equipment for individual and group study of foreign languages. Other working laboratories include the experimental arena-type Warehouse Theatre, the Johnson Plant Laboratory, and the Audrey Webb Child Study Center, which has an enrollment of approximately 100 children in preschool through third grade.

Costs

For 2000–01, tuition is $15,770, and a double room and board are $5870. Costs for room and board are subject to change. Additional costs for books, supplies, and personal expenses range between $750 and $1000. The enrollment deposit is $100.

Financial Aid

More than 80 percent of the student body receive some form of assistance through scholarships, grants, loans, or employment. Stephens participates in the Federal Pell Grant, Federal Supplemental Educational Opportunity Grant, Federal Perkins Loan, Federal Stafford Student Loan, and Federal Work-Study programs. Missouri residents are encouraged to apply for aid under the Missouri Student Grant Program. The Free Application for Federal Student Aid (FAFSA) is required for financial aid consideration. Applications for financial aid should be received by March 15. Stephens also offers a financial aid estimate service.

Faculty

Stephens has a professional and supporting staff of 101. Instructors are drawn from a variety of backgrounds. The 60 full-time-equivalent members of the faculty obtained their most advanced degrees from universities, institutes, and conservatories around the world. Though most faculty members have come to college teaching via the recognized route of graduate study and scholarship, some have prepared for teaching through work experience, particularly those in applied and performing arts with careers as actors, dancers, musicians, and artists. The faculty is primarily a teaching faculty, and many of the instructors include students in independent scholarly research. Men and women join the Stephens faculty with a commitment to individualized education. They are actively engaged in academic advising and tutorial relationships and frequently spend many more hours working with students outside the classroom than in formal teaching situations. The student-faculty ratio is 10:1.

Student Government

Each student is a member of the Student Government Association (SGA). Working in the SGA provides women with experience in planning and administering cultural, social, and recreational activities and in dealing with academic, residential, and community concerns. The association has executive and legislative powers to govern student activities and to develop and maintain group-living standards. Students also serve as voting members of established faculty committees and in advisory capacities to committees of the Board of Trustees. Stephens has been nationally recognized for the many leadership opportunities it provides for students.

Admission Requirements

Applicants are considered by the Dean of Enrollment Services and the Admission Committee on an individual basis without regard to race, religion, geographic origin, or handicap. Major factors for admission consideration are the high school attended, recommendations, and the academic record, including rank in class, subjects studied, grade point average, proficiency in English, and test scores (SAT I and ACT).

Application and Information

Candidates for admission should submit the application with the $25 application fee and arrange to have transcripts and recommendations mailed to the Office of Admission. Upon receipt of the application, any additional material is mailed to the student. Qualified students are accepted on a rolling admission basis upon receipt of all necessary credentials.

Office of Admission
Campus Box 2121
Stephens College
Columbia, Missouri 65215
Telephone: 573-876-7207
 800-876-7207 (toll-free)
Fax: 573-876-7237
E-mail: apply@sc.stephens.edu
World Wide Web: http://www.stephens.edu

On the Stephens College campus.

STERLING COLLEGE
CRAFTSBURY COMMON, VERMONT

The College

Sterling was founded in 1958 as a boys' preparatory school, with much of its educational philosophy rooted in the precepts of the Gordonstoun School in Scotland. Founded in 1934 by Kurt Hahn, the German-born educator, his four compelling educational pillars—academics, physical challenge, craftsmanship, and service to others—found solid footing in this Northeast Kingdom community.

During the 1970s, Sterling launched the Academic Short-Course in Outdoor Leadership, a twenty-one-day program for students. This brought hundreds of young people to Sterling over the next four years for an intense learning experience with one of the most effective of teachers—the Vermont winter.

Granted higher education status in 1978, Sterling awarded its first Associate of Arts degree in resource management in 1982 and became Sterling College in 1984. Accreditation by the New England Association of Schools and Colleges was granted in 1987. In 1997, the College received approval for an accredited Bachelor of Arts degree program. With a projected enrollment of 120 students, Sterling remains one of the smallest coeducational colleges in the country.

The majority of Sterling College students arrive from the northeast United States, with the greater number coming from New England. Annually, there is a representation of students from the Midwest, California, and the Northwest. International students are welcome at Sterling, with the greatest number coming from Japan. Two thirds of Sterling's student body are recent graduates of traditional public and private high school education. The remaining third have been home schooled, attended high school in an alternative setting, or took a few years to travel and work before attending college. The average age of the Sterling College student is 19.

Location

Sterling College's campus is very much a part of life in Craftsbury Common, a community of classic New England beauty that sits on a ridgetop overlooking the forested sweep of northern Vermont's hills and mountains. The College's white clapboard buildings blend in with those of the neighbors around the Common, where baseball games are played on spring afternoons and the town gathers for concerts from the bandstand on summer evenings.

For Sterling students, the setting is no mere scenic backdrop. Students engage it—from local craftspeople and other community members to the rivers, woods, and mountains all around—as part of a living laboratory for Sterling's approach to learning.

Craftsbury Common was first settled in 1789, and the local economy has always been based on forestry, farming, and education. The town of Craftsbury has its own school system, three churches, two public libraries, a volunteer fire department, and numerous small businesses.

Northern Vermont is also the home of many creative artists, among them writers, musicians, and visual and film artists. Most notable among regional events are the productions presented by the Bread and Puppet Theater, the Vermont Reggae Festival, and the summer concerts by the Craftsbury Chamber Players.

Craftsbury is surrounded by a variety of rich resources for outdoor sports. Northern Vermont is gifted with dozens of beautiful rivers, lakes, and streams, as well as mountains for hiking, several nearby Alpine ski resorts, and hundreds of kilometers of cross-country skiing trails.

Locally, the Craftsbury Sports Center is an important training and competition facility for world-class Nordic skiers, scullers, and runners as well as mountain bikers and soccer players.

Majors and Degrees

During the two-year associate degree program, Sterling guides each student through a trio of linked experiences: academic studies that examine humankind's relationship with the environment; hands-on skills development in the realms of agriculture, forestry, wildlife, and outdoor leadership; and a program of outdoor challenge activities that can include backcountry travel, rock climbing, white-water canoeing, winter expeditions, hiking, and cross-country skiing.

Students in their second year of study alternate between on-campus studies and an off-campus internship. The internship builds on and brings alive their classroom experiences. Together, the internship and every other aspect of the associate degree program allow students to learn from the natural environment and the world around them.

Associate degree students may develop a concentration by earning at least 10 on-campus credits in a particular area and completing an internship in their area of concentration. Thus, a student could have a forestry, agriculture, environmental management, or wildlife concentration by choosing appropriate courses over the two years at Sterling.

Building on the skills and knowledge developed during the associate degree program, bachelor's degree candidates focus their final two years of study on making a difference in the world. Graduates earn a Bachelor of Arts degree and select a concentration in outdoor education and leadership, sustainable agriculture, or wildlands ecology and management.

The bachelor's degree program offers many options, including an in-depth independent study, community service projects, a Colorado Field Semester, and exchange semesters with colleges in the United States and overseas. The culmination of the Sterling experience is the Senior Project—an integrated learning experience in which students tackle a real problem in their area of concentration.

Academic Program

The Sterling College curriculum combines the following important elements: academic study to provide a theoretical foundation for both applied work and further study, laboratory and fieldwork exercises to develop specific skills, practical experience to foster a responsible work ethic, and stress/challenge activities to enhance self-confidence and the ability to work effectively in groups.

Core courses required of all first-year students carry 21½ credits. Elective courses must be selected to meet the required 30-credit minimum. The second-year core curriculum carries 23 credits, including a 6-credit off-campus internship. Second-year students must choose elective courses to earn at least 60 credits by the end of their second year of study. The third-year core curriculum carries 11½ credits. Third-year students may also choose up to 5½ credits of on-campus electives and concentration requirements and earn approximately 15 credits in off-campus programs approved by the College and related to their concentration. The fourth-year curriculum carries 25 credits, including 6 credits of requirements specific to concentrations and a major senior project within that concentration. Fourth-year students also choose electives to meet graduation distribution requirements.

Candidates for the Bachelor of Arts degree must first earn their Associate of Arts degree or transfer in equivalent credits from other programs. Candidates for the B.A. degree must earn a minimum of 120 credits. B.A. students must also pass required courses within their chosen concentration. The outdoor education and leadership concentration includes requirements that can be met during the off-campus Colorado Field Semester. Students in other concentrations earn additional credits related to their concentration through individually designed off-campus semesters, often at cooperating colleges and universities.

All students living on campus participate in a noncredit work program that involves chores in the kitchen, farm, and dorms. The work program seeks to provide Sterling College students with opportunities to contribute positively to the maintenance, appearance, and sustainability of the College campus and community.

Academic Facilities

The on-campus facilities include twelve residential, administrative, and classroom buildings, including a woodshop, a darkroom, and a 15,000-volume library. Outdoor teaching facilities include a managed woodlot, a challenge course, an organic garden, and a working livestock farm. Sterling also has arrangements with a number of northern Vermont landowners, farmers, and businesses to provide students with work and "lab" experiences.

Costs

Total costs for room, board, and tuition for the 1999–2000 academic year were $18,900. There was an additional fee of $125 to cover student activities and a refundable room deposit. Additional curriculum and on-campus living expenses normally do not exceed $750. Some field courses include additional lab fees.

The overall cost of tuition for the 1999–2000 academic year was reduced by $660 for each student residing on campus. This is the result of Sterling's participation in the National Work College Consortium that provides matching funds to assist in reducing college costs. Students earned this reduction through campus employment and service to the local community.

Financial Aid

Sterling College makes every effort to ensure that financial concerns do not stand in the way of applicants. The combination of funds from federal assistance programs, Sterling's scholarship funds, and a student's personal resources work effectively to meet costs. More than half of the College's students receive financial assistance. Sterling College uses the Free Application for Federal Student Aid (FAFSA) to determine a student's financial need in order to measure the student's ability to pay.

Applicants may qualify for up to five federal aid programs: Pell Grants, Work-Study, Supplemental Educational Opportunity Grants, Stafford Student Loans, and PLUS loans. Sterling Grants are awarded as part of an assistance package that reflects the commitment of the College to help meet educational expenses.

Faculty

Sterling's faculty is composed of 22 individuals (7 full-time and 15 adjunct) and is a surprisingly diverse group with a broad range of teaching styles. They are united by an affinity for small-town life, a strong interest in relating human experience to natural resources, and a determination to work with students as whole people.

Student Government

The Student Life Committee serves as a forum to bring up community issues, discuss College policy, and coordinate extracurricular events and entertainment. Representatives are elected by each residence, and the meetings are always open to anyone who wants to attend. Committee members are responsible for organizing and running the weekly Community Meeting.

Admission Requirements

Sterling's programs are designed for men and women 17 years of age and older who are academically prepared for college studies, eager to embrace the demands of Sterling, and able to participate in all physical aspects of the curriculum. Sterling College applicants typically include high school graduates who are searching for challenge, close ties with faculty members, and a way to unite their love for the outdoors with their college education; college students who are eager to vary their traditionally structured college years with a learning program that is based on blending academics with a variety of challenges and hands-on learning experiences; and men and women between 20 and 30 years old who may have spent time in the workforce or the armed forces.

Previous academic records play an important part in admissions decisions, but equally important are academic potential, level of maturity, life experience, and readiness to commit to the Sterling program. Students admitted to Sterling must show the receipt of either a high school diploma or an equivalency diploma. In the case of home-schooled students, a portfolio of educational and life experiences may be submitted in lieu of a diploma or equivalency.

The Sterling College Admissions Committee evaluates the candidate using the following elements: a completed application with required essays; transcripts of high school and college grades, with SAT scores when available; character recommendations from 3 adults, two of whom should be a teacher; and a campus visit, which is always recommended and sometimes required.

Application and Information

Sterling College operates on a rolling admissions basis; applications are accepted throughout the year. Transfer applicants are encouraged to speak directly with the admission office regarding credit transfer and other related issues.

An application can be obtained by contacting:

Office of Admission
Sterling College
Craftsbury Common, Vermont 05827

Telephone: 800-648-3591 (toll-free)
Fax: 802-586-2596
E-mail: admissions@sterlingcollege.edu
World Wide Web: http://www.sterlingcollege.edu

Sterling College students and faculty members gather for a team-building activity.

STETSON UNIVERSITY
DELAND, FLORIDA

The University

Stetson University, with its curriculum breadth, small classes, many nationally recognized programs, and commitment to values and social responsibility, offers students an educational experience that is unique in the Southeast. At Florida's first private university, Stetson students encounter the "feel" of a small college—close interaction with professors who teach all undergraduates, concern for the individual, and opportunities to learn and test leadership skills and to form lifelong friendships. Stetson's university-class curriculum offers students a broad foundation of knowledge in the context of contemporary issues and needs.

Stetson is committed to undergraduate education that is enriched by selected high-quality graduate programs. The College of Arts and Sciences, the School of Business Administration, and the School of Music are located on the DeLand campus. The College of Law has its own campus in St. Petersburg. Master's degrees are awarded in accounting, business administration, counseling, education, and English on the DeLand campus; the College of Law awards the Juris Doctorate and the Master of Laws.

Stetson's diverse campus community enables students to see the world from many points of view. The University's 2,064 undergraduates are from thirty-three states and numerous other countries. The student population is 57 percent women and 43 percent men. Ten percent are members of minority groups, and 77 percent of students are Florida residents. The most prestigious accrediting groups recognize Stetson's quality, including the Southern Association of Colleges and Schools, the American Association of Colleges and Schools of Business, the American Bar Association, the National Association of Schools of Music, the Association of Collegiate Business Schools and Programs, the National Council for Accreditation of Teacher Education, the National Athletic Training Association, and the American Chemical Society. The College of Arts and Sciences was awarded the first private-university Phi Beta Kappa chapter in Florida.

Campus living is important at Stetson. Sharing experiences, having fun, learning to live in a community, and taking responsibility for shaping residence hall life are part of the self-discovery process that makes Stetson so rewarding. Seventy percent of all Stetson students choose to live in on-campus housing; all single undergraduate students who are younger than 21 and who do not reside with immediate family are expected to live on campus. Stetson is a caring community that encourages students to make a difference, both on campus and in their future lives. Stetson students are known for their volunteerism and social responsibility. Through the Hollis Leadership Program, the Program in Religion and Ethics, and a range of campus organizations, most students participate in volunteer projects such as recycling, building housing for the disadvantaged, and tutoring at-risk high school students. The School of Music enriches the cultural life of the campus. Performances are given in Elizabeth Hall Auditorium by the all-student Stetson Symphonic Orchestra, choir, and band, and faculty members and students give recitals. Musical theater presentations are also performed. The Duncan Gallery of Art exhibits both professional and student work. Stover Theatre regularly hosts student drama productions. Stetson's athletic membership in NCAA Division I provides a wide range of intercollegiate sports for both spectators and participants. Junior varsity opportunities and an extensive intramural program offer team and individual sports competition. A $9.5-million campus expansion program to increase learning and recreational opportunities for students has been completed and includes the Hollis Center, a recreation and wellness center adjacent to the present outdoor pool and Carlton Student Union; the addition of a 13,400-square-foot wing to the duPont-Ball Library and renovations that have significantly increased its technological capabilities; a new tennis center; and expanded classroom and lab space for allied health programs in the Sport and Exercise Science Department. The heart of the campus is the Carlton Student Union, which has dining facilities; offices for student organizations, the student newspaper, and Residential Life staff; the student lounge and a night club; the Stetson Bookstore; and the post office. Several meal plan options are available in The Commons cafeteria and The Hat Rack sandwich shop. Behind the Student Union are Student Health Services and the Counseling Center.

Location

Stetson's hometown, DeLand, is a charming central Florida city of 30,000 with unique shops, unusual restaurants, and many cultural and recreational opportunities. Because of its location in central Florida, the University is less than an hour away from Daytona Beach and Orlando. The nearby St. Johns River and numerous lakes offer water sports opportunities. The cooperative relationship between Stetson and the city of DeLand enhances the student experience. Students learn citizenship firsthand through internships with Volusia County Government and help shape the area's economy by conducting marketing surveys and preparing business development plans for the Mainstreet DeLand Association.

Academic Program

Stetson students participate in a wide range of educational experiences. They can research the habits of pygmy rattlesnakes at a national wildlife preserve minutes from campus, develop software programs for an international firm, or develop a marketing plan for a classical music ensemble. These diverse opportunities flow from the University's breadth of curriculum. Bachelor of Arts degrees are offered in American studies, art, biology, communication studies, computer information systems, computer science, digital arts, economics, elementary education, English, English–secondary education, environmental science, French, geography, German, history, humanities, international business, Latin American studies, mathematics, music (liberal arts), philosophy, political science, psychology, religious studies, Russian studies, social science and social science–education, sociology, Spanish, sport and exercise science (sport administration), and theater arts. Bachelor of Business Administration degrees are offered in accounting, computer information systems, economics, finance, general business administration, international business, management, and marketing. Bachelor of Music degree programs are available in digital arts, guitar, piano/organ, theory and composition, and voice. Bachelor of Music Education degrees are offered in instrumental/general studies, and vocal/general studies. Bachelor of Science degrees are offered in biochemistry, biology, chemistry, computer information systems, computer science, economics, elementary education, environmental science, geography, mathematics, molecular biology, physics, political science, psychology, sociology, and sport and exercise science (athletic training, exercise science, or movement therapy). Students' choices are further broadened by other multidisciplinary programs such as Africana studies, applied ethics, the Family Business Center, health-care issues, the Hollis Leadership Development Program, journalism, urban studies, and women and gender studies and by strong preprofessional and cooperative programs in dentistry, engineering, forestry, law, medicine, and veterinary medicine. DeLand campus students who meet rigorous academic requirements are guaranteed admission to the College of Law on a regular or accelerated schedule. The Discovery Program assists undecided students in choosing a major. The University Experience Program quickly integrates newcomers into the campus community. Degree sequences "in honors" are offered through the Honors Program in arts, science, music, and business. A growing Army ROTC program provides scholarship assistance for students interested in careers with the nation's armed forces. A developing Africana Studies program focuses on the development and spread of the heritage of Sub-Saharan Africa. Stetson's year-round academic calendar includes 15-week fall and spring terms and an 8-week summer term. Degrees are conferred at the end of each academic term. Most undergraduate degrees require completion of 120 semester hours of work that are distributed among core requirements, the major field, and electives. Students must maintain a C average or better.

Off-Campus Arrangements

Through programs such as Russian Studies, Latin American Studies, International Studies, the Washington Semester, and the Summer Business Program, Stetson students prepare to succeed in the global marketplace. With the Institute for Christian Ethics, these programs bring to Stetson political and cultural leaders from around the world, including scientist and conservationist Jane Goodall, former president Jimmy Carter, South African Archbishop Desmond Tutu, Nobel Peace Laureate Elie Wiesel, and journalist and author Bill Moyers, to lecture and meet informally with students. During the Washington Seminar, students intern in the nation's capital and at the United Nations. Stetson students can study for a semester or a full year at universities in Avignon, France; Freiburg, Germany; Madrid, Spain; Nottingham, England; Guanajuato, Mexico; Hong Kong, China; and Moscow, Russia. Through a linkage program with the American Graduate School of International Management, Stetson students can earn a master's degree in international management in just one year. Stetson also has relationships with institutions in the Republic of Korea and Latin America.

Academic Facilities

Stetson's campus is a charming mix of historical and contemporary buildings among green lawns, palms, and oaks. The heart of the campus is in the Stetson University National Historic District, while the five-floor, state-of-the-art Lynn Business Center houses the School of Business Administration. The duPont-Ball Library, which includes the new North Wing, provides students access to more than 26 million cataloging records in libraries worldwide through its advanced computer retrieval system. The Gillespie Museum of Minerals boasts the largest private mineral collection outside the Smithsonian Institution. Edmunds Activity Center, a 5,000-seat gymnasium-field house, hosts intercollegiate athletic events, contemporary concerts, and special events such as commencement. Other facilities include Sage Hall Science Center, which houses highly advanced equipment and individual research areas; computer labs with Internet access for student use in each school; and Presser Hall, home of the School of Music, which has a variety of individual and ensemble practice halls.

Costs

Tuition and fees (two semesters) for all students in 2000–01 are $18,385. Room and board average $6070 for the academic year.

Financial Aid

Financial aid needs have no bearing on the admission process. To reward outstanding academic achievement and special talents and to assure access for qualified students, Stetson made nearly $10.8 million available from University funds in 1999–2000. Assistance is offered through academic merit and music talent scholarships, athletic grants-in-aid, a monthly payment plan, and low- and no-interest loans. Stetson participates in federal and state need-based programs. Help from other external sources, such as line of credit programs, also is available. The amount of aid awarded to students is determined by an analysis of their financial need through the Free Application for Federal Student Aid (FAFSA). Financial aid forms should be submitted as soon as possible after January 1 and before March 1 of the year in which admitted students plan to enter Stetson. Stetson encourages families to utilize the financial aid estimator as early as the summer prior to the student's senior year.

Faculty

Stetson's 174 faculty members have many individual interests, but they are united by their desire to help undergraduates achieve a broad understanding of the world in which they will live and work. Ninety-six percent of full-time faculty members hold Ph.D.'s or equivalent degrees. Seminar-size classes and personal attention from professors are hallmarks of an education at Stetson. The low student-faculty ratio of 12 to 1 means that classes are small enough for personal interaction. Professors are accessible, and high-quality advising is a faculty priority. In satisfaction surveys, Stetson students rate class size, faculty quality, and student-faculty member interaction very high.

Student Government

Stetson emphasizes individual growth and the development of leadership skills. Students participate directly in forming campus-wide policy through such groups as the Student Government Association and the Council for Student Activities. The Student Strategic Planning Council advises the president on policy and long-range planning issues. More than 100 student organizations encourage diverse interests. Included are service and special interest organizations; seventeen scholastic and honorary societies, including Phi Beta Kappa; and twelve national sororities and fraternities.

Admission Requirements

All new students at Stetson have completed a college-preparatory program, and most rank in the top 30 percent of their high school class. High school preparation should include 4 years of English, 3 of mathematics and laboratory science, and 2 years of foreign language and social sciences, plus college-preparatory electives. Admission to Stetson is based on academic course selection, grade achievement, involvement in school and community, leadership potential, and achievement on standardized tests. Prospective music students are required to audition. Transfer students must be in good standing at their former institution and must have achieved a cumulative grade point average of at least 2.6 on a 4.0 scale. Early admission is offered to promising high school juniors who have completed their required course work. A student may earn credit and advanced standing through the Advanced Placement Program, the International Baccalaureate, and department exams.

Application and Information

The application priority deadline for the fall semester is March 15; for spring, January 1; and for summer, May 1. Regular decision candidates for fall admission receive notification by April 1. Under an early notification policy, candidates with the strongest credentials will be notified after December 1, as soon as their applications are processed. An early decision option is for exceptionally qualified students who are certain Stetson is their first choice. Candidates should apply before November 1. Early start students can improve English, mathematics, reading, and study skills in a special summer session. A complimentary loan video on Stetson University is available through VIDEC INC. To receive a copy, students should call 800-255-0384. For more information, students can contact:

Office of Admissions
Stetson University
421 North Woodland Boulevard, Unit 8378
DeLand, Florida 32720-3771
Telephone: 904-822-7100
               800-688-0101 (toll-free)
Fax: 904-822-7112
E-mail: admissions@stetson.edu
World Wide Web: http://www.stetson.edu

STEVENS INSTITUTE OF TECHNOLOGY
HOBOKEN, NEW JERSEY

The Institute

Founded in 1870, Stevens Institute of Technology's mission is to educate and inspire students to acquire the knowledge needed to lead in the creation, application, and management of technology and to excel in solving problems in any profession. Approximately 130 years later, Stevens upholds its purpose and has become a leader in technology.

Twenty-first-century careers will be increasingly rooted in ever-changing technologies, and Stevens undergraduates have a strong and versatile background in business, engineering, the applied sciences, computer science, management, and the humanities. A broad-based education is the cornerstone, intertwined with hands-on experience in research and with industry.

Stevens holds general accreditation in engineering and specialized accreditation in all engineering disciplines from the Accreditation Board for Engineering and Technology, Inc., as well as general accreditation from the Middle States Association of Colleges and Schools. It is also included in the first group of colleges to receive accreditation in computer science from the Computer Science Accreditation Board, and the chemistry program is accredited by the American Chemical Society.

The Institute encompasses three schools: the Schaefer School of Engineering, the School of Applied Sciences and Liberal Arts, and the Howe School of Technology Management. Bachelor's degrees are awarded in various areas within applied science, business, computer science, engineering, and the humanities.

Master's and doctoral degrees are also awarded in a multitude of areas within the applied sciences, computer and information sciences/systems, engineering, and management.

Stevens has long-standing ties with industry leaders, including Arthur Andersen, AT&T, Bell Atlantic, Becton Dickinson, Exxon, Johnson & Johnson, Lockheed Martin, Lucent, and Merck, among others.

Overlooking the Hudson River and New York City from Castle Point in Hoboken, New Jersey, the 55-acre Stevens campus encompasses more than thirty buildings, including classroom, residence, departmental, administrative, and research facilities. Approximately 80 percent of all undergraduate students live on campus, and they originate from more than thirty states and international countries.

There are more than ninety student activities and organizations, including *The State*, the weekly campus newspaper; *The Link*, the yearbook; WCRR, the radio station; the Glee Club; brass and jazz ensembles; the Drama Society; ethnic and religious organizations; and national honor and professional societies. Nine national fraternities and three sororities have chapters on campus, and most maintain houses where members live. Approximately 35 percent of the 1,550 undergraduates join a fraternity or sorority. The state-of-the-art Charles V. Schaefer, Jr. '36 Athletic and Recreation Center houses a swimming pool and jacuzzi, basketball courts, racquetball courts, and a fitness room with Stairmasters and Universal weight equipment. Other facilities include Walker Gym, Davis Field, and four tennis courts. Varsity sports are men's baseball, basketball, cross-country, fencing, indoor/outdoor track and field, lacrosse, soccer, tennis, and volleyball and women's basketball, cross-country, fencing, indoor/outdoor track and field, soccer, swimming, tennis, and volleyball. Students may also play a club sport or intramurals.

Location

The city of Hoboken is contemporary with a small-town aura. Due to its waterfront location, the quaint mile-square city, with its charming old brownstones and dozens of shops and restaurants, welcomes a diversity of new residents and is the focus of an urban renaissance. A project is under way to turn the waterfront's old ferry slips and empty piers into a $500-million complex of housing units, office space for high-tech businesses, parks, marina and hotel facilities, and biking/jogging paths.

Located on a high bank of the Hudson River, the parklike Stevens campus, with red brick buildings and old maple and elm trees, is just minutes from Manhattan, and students take advantage of the many educational, cultural, and social opportunities available in New York City as well.

Majors and Degrees

Stevens Institute of Technology awards the degrees of Bachelor of Engineering (B.E.), Bachelor of Science (B.S.), and Bachelor of Arts (B.A.). Majors in engineering include chemical, civil, computer, electrical, environmental, materials, and mechanical engineering; and engineering management. Science majors include chemical biology, chemistry, mathematical sciences, and applied physics. Computer science features a selection of concentrated courses in computer theory and applications, database management, and management information systems. The business program enables students to create a comprehensive business plan and to concentrate in an area such as e-commerce. Humanities specialties are English and American literature, history, and philosophy. There are preprofessional programs in medicine and dentistry (seven years) and law (five years); there are accelerated scholars programs in these three areas as well.

Academic Program

The undergraduate division is concerned with the intellectual enrichment and education of the student as a whole person in preparation for a satisfying, productive, and successful future in a technological world. Computer fluency and usage are essential; therefore, all entering students are required to have a personal computer. The learning process is fulfilled by having students solve real-world problems, undertake internship projects, and participate in simulations and faculty research investigations. The rigorous education in technical, scientific, and management subjects is carefully balanced by eight humanities courses (for technology students) and six physical education courses. In the typical baccalaureate program, 156 credit hours are earned. The academic calendar consists of two semesters and a summer session.

Stevens offers a number of special programs. The Stevens Scholars Program for truly talented students provides the challenge of accelerated course work as well as the opportunity to earn the master's degree in addition to the bachelor's degree within four years at no additional cost. The Personalized Self-Paced Instruction program (PSI) provides an alternative to the conventional lecture-recitation method of instruction, enabling students to work with self-instruction materials at their own pace in selective courses. The Lore-El Center for Women offers a variety of mentoring and networking programs. The Stevens Technical Enrichment Program (STEP), a precollege and in-college program, broadens the access of minority and economically disadvantaged students to careers in technology.

Undergraduate Projects in Technology and Medicine (UPTAM), conducted in cooperation with the University of Medicine and Dentistry of New Jersey and other area medical facilities, is a summer program for selected students interested in medical engineering or biomedical sciences. The Cooperative Education Program is available for any undergraduate wanting to alternate semesters of classroom study with semesters of paid, professional work experience over a five-year period. The Academic Support Center also offers academic tutoring and other resources.

Off-Campus Arrangements

Through the International Scholars Program, students can spend their junior year abroad at the University of Dundee in Scotland.

Academic Facilities

As one of the Top 100 Most Wired Colleges, the environment of Stevens is highly computer intensive. More than 2,100 systems are distributed throughout the campus, and each of the 1,550 undergraduates must own a personal computer. Notebooks lead in popularity as a way to enable students to plug into their residence hall rooms, networked SMART classrooms, and even Café on the Hudson, the cyber coffee café. The computer center has a multitude of high-capacity UNIX servers and various workstations and personal computers. Department labs for student use are distributed throughout campus, and T1 lines connect the campus network to the Internet. All residence halls and academic buildings are wired to gigabit networking to enable additional resources for networked notebook access as well as for delivery of additional distance learning instruction. Among the specialized laboratory facilities used for academic and research functions are Davidson Laboratory, a center for the study of marine hydrodynamics and coastal engineering; the Keck Geoenvironmental Laboratory; the Nicoll Environmental Laboratory; the Advanced Telecommunications Institute; the Design and Manufacturing Institute; the Highly Filled Materials Institute; the Plasma and Surface Physics Laboratory; the High Sensitivity Laser Spectroscopy Laboratory; the Clean Air Vehicle Center; the Robotics Laboratory; the Center for Improved Engineering and Science Education; the Center for Product Lifecycle Management; the Noise and Vibration Control Lab; the Optical Communications Lab; the Polymer Processing Institute; the Technology Ventures Incubator; and the Schacht Management Lab. Stevens is also an institutional member of the New Jersey Space Grant Consortium and the Hazardous Substance Management Research Consortium. The Samuel C. Williams Library has been recognized as one of the top twenty providing just-in-time delivery and access to 30 million volumes. The DeBaun Auditorium, a New York metro area cultural and educational facility, provides the technology infrastructure for distance learning programs, teleconferencing, and, like other campus facilities, Internet and intranet connections.

Costs

Tuition for the 1999–2000 year was $20,890. The cost of room and board was $7460. Other estimated costs include $700 for books and supplies, $750 for personal/miscellaneous expenses, and $500 for first-year fees.

Financial Aid

Stevens offers a variety of both need- and merit-based institutional aid programs in addition to all federal and New Jersey state assistance. (New Jersey programs are for state residents only.) Merit scholarships range from $1000 to full tuition annually and are renewable for up to four years. Specific grade point averages are required for renewal. Need-based grants range from approximately $100 to $12,000 annually and are renewable for four years based on financial eligibility.

All incoming students should submit the Free Application for Federal Student Aid (FAFSA) no later than February 15.

Matriculated students electing to extend their undergraduate course of study to five years (a total of ten semesters) will not be charged tuition during their fifth year as long as arrangements are made during their first semester of enrollment at Stevens.

Faculty

The full-time faculty is composed of 120 men and women, 95 percent of whom hold doctoral degrees. Most faculty members are engaged in specific research projects. Special faculty and research staffs number an additional 110 people. The student-faculty ratio is approximately 9:1.

Student Government

The Undergraduate Student Government Association (SGA) directs and funds all student clubs and activities. Other governing bodies include the Student Review Board and the Commuter, Ethnic Student, Co-op Student, Interfraternity, Interdormitory, Panhellenic, and Athletic Councils. The Stevens Honor System, in existence since 1907, is directed by the Honor Board, a group of students elected by their peers to investigate any students violating this pledge.

Admission Requirements

Admission is very selective. Each year, about 60 percent of the applicants are accepted, and 35 percent enroll. Strength in mathematics and science is essential. The high school record should include English (4 years); standard college-preparatory mathematics (4 years), including algebra, geometry, trigonometry, and precalculus/calculus; chemistry (1 year); and physics (1 year). Applicants are required to submit scores on the SAT I or ACT. SAT II Subject Tests in mathematics, science, and English are highly recommended. Extracurricular activities, leadership positions, and other nonacademic factors are considered of major importance in the admission decision. Recommendations and a personal statement are optional. An interview is required for all students who live within a 250-mile radius. Eighty percent of entering freshmen graduated in the top 20 percent of their high school class, earned an average SAT I score of 620 on the verbal portion and 680 on the math portion, and earned an average 3.8 GPA.

Advanced placement credit is given to students who have taken Advanced Placement (AP) courses in high school and have earned a 3 or more in math–calculus AB or BC, a 4 or more on the College Board's AP exams in biology, chemistry, economics, English, government and politics, history, physics, and psychology.

Stevens Institute of Technology does not discriminate against any person because of race, creed, color, national origin, sex, age, marital status, handicap, liability for service in the armed forces, or status as a disabled or Vietnam-era veteran.

Application and Information

Applications may be submitted after completion of the junior year of high school. The application deadline is February 1. Early decision and early admission programs are available. The deadline is November 15. Transfer students should apply by July 1 for the fall semester and December 1 for the spring semester. All decisions are made on a rolling basis once a student's file is complete. All students must apply either by using the traditional paper application or electronically via the admissions Web page. Students with requests for further information should contact:

Office of Undergraduate Admissions
Stevens Institute of Technology
Castle Point on the Hudson
Hoboken, New Jersey 07030
Telephone: 800-458-5323 (toll-free)
          201-216-5194
Fax: 201-216-8348
E-mail: admissions@stevens-tech.edu
World Wide Web: http://www.stevens-tech.edu

STONEHILL COLLEGE
EASTON, MASSACHUSETTS

The College

Stonehill is a competitive, coeducational, Catholic college located just south of Boston. Established in 1948 by the Congregation of Holy Cross (founders of the University of Notre Dame, Indiana), Stonehill continues the rich Holy Cross tradition of a rigorous liberal education. As a comprehensive undergraduate college of 2,100 students, Stonehill offers thirty-one major programs in the liberal arts, natural sciences, and business. The College's programs, through an involved and engaging faculty and a commitment to hands-on learning, aim to foster effective communication, critical-thinking, and problem-solving skills in all students.

Stonehill provides its students with a powerful environment for learning where students are safe, known, and valued. The College has a beautiful campus, an enviable location, and state-of-the-art facilities. Stonehill fields varsity teams (NCAA Division II) in eighteen sports, in addition to a vibrant intercollegiate club and intramural sports program. More than 80 percent of the students live in first-rate on-campus housing and take advantage of the wide range of social and cultural activities offered on campus or in nearby Boston. Housing is guaranteed for four years.

In addition to the undergraduate programs listed below, the College offers a Master of Science in Accountancy degree.

Location

Just 20 miles south of Boston, Stonehill is located in the town of Easton (population 22,659). Featuring stunning Georgian-style architecture, the College's twenty-seven main buildings are set among a beautifully landscaped 375-acre campus of ponds, rolling fields, and wooded glens. The beaches of Cape Cod and the mansions and history of Newport and Providence, Rhode Island, are within 45 minutes of the campus, as are major concert (the Tweeter Center for Performing Arts) and sports (Foxboro Stadium) venues. The most popular off-campus destination is Boston. Students from more than sixty area colleges and universities converge on Boston to experience its museums, art galleries, theaters, sporting events, and other exciting nightlife offerings. During the week, Stonehill students enhance their academic experience through internships with the city's plethora of high-tech, medical, and financial institutions.

Students may bring a car to the campus; however, the College provides a van service that connects to Boston's subway system. Stonehill's student government and campus ministry organizations also have vans that students can reserve for trips to sporting events, concerts, skiing, and other events.

Majors and Degrees

The College offers Bachelor of Arts degrees in American studies, chemistry, communication, criminal justice, economics, education studies (early childhood, elementary and secondary), English, fine arts, foreign languages, health-care administration, history, international studies, managerial economics, mathematics, multidisciplinary studies, philosophy, political science, psychology, public administration, religious studies, and sociology. Bachelor of Science degrees are offered in biology, chemistry, computer engineering, computer science, math–computer science, and medical technology. Bachelor of Science in Business Administration degrees are offered in accounting, finance, management, and marketing.

Preprofessional programs are offered in dentistry, education, law, medicine, and veterinary medicine. Students interested in the field of education can receive early childhood, elementary, and secondary school teacher certification. Students may also design their own majors by combining various departmental courses into a comprehensive multidisciplinary program.

Academic Program

Stonehill's primary mission is to provide a challenging program of academic studies in the liberal arts tradition that engages students in a lifelong quest for intellectual excellence and dedication to service. All students receive a strong foundation in the liberal arts in addition to expertise in one or more fields. The fourteen liberal arts courses in the core curriculum are designed to help students understand their culture, find and analyze information, develop critical-thinking skills, and become effective communicators. Developing writing proficiency is a central objective of the core curriculum and is emphasized in all classes.

Interaction with faculty members and academic advisers is a vital part of a Stonehill education. At freshman orientation, each student is assigned an academic adviser. Students who declare a major are assigned a faculty mentor from within their major; students who do not declare a major receive assistance from an adviser who specializes in helping undecided students. Advisers help students choose their major, approve course selections, and give advice on study-abroad, internship, and graduate school opportunities.

Students are encouraged to explore various fields of interest in their first two years, but they must choose a major by the middle of their junior year. They take five courses a semester and must complete forty courses to receive a bachelor's degree.

Off-Campus Arrangements

In addition to the tremendous on-campus opportunities at Stonehill, the College offers an abundance of domestic and international programs to enhance a student's learning experience. One of the most exciting opportunities at Stonehill is internships, which are offered in every major. Internships give students hands-on experience in their chosen field, help them focus their career objectives, and afford them opportunities to network with professionals.

Within the United States, students have the opportunity to participate in internship programs in Boston; Providence, Rhode Island; Washington, D.C.; and Orlando, Florida. Stonehill participates in the Washington Center in Washington, D.C., and the Marine Studies Consortium in Boston. Students can also choose to take classes at eight nearby colleges through a specially designed consortium to which Stonehill belongs.

Stonehill students have the option of interning or studying in virtually any country. The College administers a study-abroad program in Dublin, Ireland, and has exchange programs with the University of Nice in France, as well as with the universities in Quebec, Canada. Students can also earn a full semester of credit participating in a full-time international internship in cities like Dublin, London, Brussels, Paris, Montreal, and Madrid. Examples of domestic and international internship sites include Fleet Bank, PriceWaterhouseCoopers, Gillette, Massachusetts General Hospital, Fidelity Investments, Reebok International, Eli Lilly Pharmaceuticals, and the *Boston Globe*.

Academic Facilities

Stonehill's outstanding facilities include state-of-the-art technologies incorporated into architecturally stunning buildings. Students have access to the Internet and the College's intranet from virtually any building on campus, including their rooms in the residence halls. The newest addition to Stonehill's impressive array of Georgian-influenced buildings is the MacPhaidin Library, which opened in 1998. The library provides access to the Internet, College intranet, electronic journals, multimedia computer clusters, and an extensive collection of texts, novels, and publications. The Joseph W. Martin, Jr. Institute for Law and Society is a regional center for education, research, and public service. It houses an archival research library, the Center for Regional and Policy Analysis, and the Stonehill Educational Project. Housed in the institute are the papers of former Speaker of the U.S. House of Representatives Joseph Martin and Templeton Award winner Michael Novak. The Lockary Computer Center supports Windows-based computers and provides students with access to the College's computer network.

Costs

For the 2000–01 academic year, Stonehill's tuition for full-time students is $16,680. Room and board charges are $8166. These figures do not include a comprehensive fee of $640, health insurance (optional), books, supplies, or travel and personal expenses.

Financial Aid

Financial aid is awarded on the basis of financial need and academic performance, as well as for merit only. Financial aid is packaged in a combination of scholarships, grants, loans, and/or campus employment. Stonehill uses the Federal Methodology to determine student eligibility for federal and state government funds. The information is obtained from the student's Free Application for Federal Student Aid (FAFSA). An Institutional Methodology (used by most private colleges and universities) is used to assess a student's eligibility for College awards. The College Scholarship Service's PROFILE form is the vehicle used to determine a family's "Expected Family Contribution," which is subtracted from Stonehill's total educational costs to determine a family's level of financial need. In addition to scholarships that are awarded on the basis of need or a combination of merit and need, there are also scholarships available on a non-need basis, which are awarded as a result of a student's academic performance. Special forms are not required, as all applicants are considered for non-need-based merit scholarships.

Faculty

Stonehill's faculty is committed to teaching, advising, and working closely with students. At Stonehill, every professor is not only directly engaged with students in class, but is also involved beyond the classroom as well. Many students are involved in faculty members' research, which sometimes leads to joint publications and/or presentations at professional conferences. The faculty-student ratio is 1:12; classes are small enough to ensure that students receive the individual attention they need. At Stonehill, there are no teaching assistants, and the majority of the faculty members hold terminal degrees in their respective fields.

Student Government

The Student Government Association (SGA) is the most influential student organization on campus, and its goal is to improve the quality of student life at Stonehill. SGA members participate in academic and strategic planning, sit with the Board of Trustees, plan and organize campus social and cultural events, and help ensure that Stonehill remains a vibrant and fun community. In addition to SGA, students can get involved in more than sixty-five clubs and organizations, ranging from volunteer groups to political activism, to recreational clubs. Stonehill offers something for all of its students.

Admission Requirements

With approximately 5,100 applicants for 510 freshman places, admission to Stonehill is selective. The College actively seeks an academically strong, geographically, culturally, and ethnically diverse student body. In the admissions process, all information on each applicant is carefully considered, but academic performance in high school is given the greatest weight. The Admissions Committee evaluates the depth and strength of each applicant's course selection and the consistency of their grades. Competitive students should have completed a strong academic program from among their high school's most challenging offerings. Students must submit scores from either the SAT I or ACT, which should be taken no later than January of the senior year. The committee also evaluates extracurricular activities, work, volunteer and community activities, recommendations, and writing samples. In 1999, 31 percent of the incoming freshmen were in the top 10 percent of their class, and 77 percent were in the top 25 percent of their class. The College awards credit for strong scores on Advanced Placement, CLEP, and higher-level International Baccalaureate exams.

Application and Information

Stonehill uses the Common Application as its primary application for freshman, transfer, and international students. The application, along with the $50 application fee, should be given to the high school guidance counselor, who forwards it to Stonehill with transcripts, recommendations, and other supporting documents. The deadline under the freshman Regular Decision process for September admission is February 1, and for January admission, it is November 1. Applicants for September admission are notified between March 15 and March 31; applicants for January admission are notified no later than December 31. The deadline for freshman students applying through the Early Decision process is November 1. Early Decision notifications are sent on December 31. The transfer student application deadlines are April 1 for September admission and November 1 for January admission. Stonehill does not conduct individual interviews as part of the freshman admission process, but serious candidates are strongly encouraged to attend a Group Information Session and campus tour. Group Information Sessions and campus tours are offered on a regular basis throughout the year. Students should telephone the Admissions Office to schedule a session and tour. For further information or application forms, students should contact:

Dean of Admissions and Enrollment
Stonehill College
320 Washington Street
Easton, Massachusetts 02357-5610

Telephone: 508-565-1373
Fax: 508-565-1545
E-mail: webmaster@stonehill.edu
World Wide Web: http://www.stonehill.edu

The Martin Institute for Law and Society is a regional center for education, research, and policy analysis.

SULLIVAN COLLEGE
LOUISVILLE, KENTUCKY

The College

In 1962, A. O. Sullivan, a postsecondary educator since 1926, and his son, A. R. Sullivan, decided to form a higher education institution founded on the highest ideals and standards to prepare students for successful careers. Since that time, the College has earned a reputation as one of the leading career institutions in the nation. Accredited by the Commission on Colleges of the Southern Association of Colleges and Schools, Sullivan offers master's, baccalaureate, associate, and diploma programs. Since achieving Level III accreditation in December 1996 and baccalaureate accreditation in January 1992, Sullivan has grown to become both Kentucky's newest four-year college and its largest independent college or university. The College also has a branch in Lexington, Kentucky, and an extension at Fort Knox, Kentucky.

With a current enrollment of more than 3,000 men and women, Sullivan is a nationally recognized leader in career training. For students with special physical needs, the College is equipped with special parking facilities, ramped entrances, elevator services, and handicapped-accessible rest-room facilities.

At Sullivan, students gain not only a valuable education but access to a variety of helpful services. All Sullivan graduates have access to the Graduate Employment Service, which provides lifetime, nationwide assistance and boasts a 99 percent graduate employment rate. In order for students to get hands-on experience in their chosen field from the very first day, the College also offers a special "inverted curriculum" in which students take skills courses in their particular field first and general education courses later in their course of study. To whet the student's appetite, the College's award-winning National Center for Hospitality Studies provides delicious meals at the Culinary Food Service Center on campus.

The Dean of Students coordinates a variety of activities in conjunction with the Assistant Dean of Students, such as academic advisement; clubs and organizations, including Phi Beta Lambda, Student Government Association, the Baptist Student Union, Summit Club, Travel Club; and clubs related to several academic disciplines. Annual events that bring excitement to the College are the cruise down the Ohio River on the Belle of Louisville Riverboat, the Spring Jam Festival, the annual summer picnic, and special camping and ski trips. Available to students under 21 are spacious apartments near campus furnished with modern furniture.

Sullivan students have won the NSCAA National Bowling Championships for both men and women in recent years.

In addition to undergraduate degrees, Sullivan College also offers the Master of Business Administration degree.

Location

Only minutes from downtown Louisville, Kentucky, Sullivan is conveniently located within a block of one of Louisville's major interstate highways. Students can enjoy the metropolitan environment of Louisville by attending the symphony, ballet, opera, art museums, theaters, the Museum of History and Science with its IMAX theater, the Louisville Zoo, the Louisville Slugger Museum, historic sites, quaint restaurants, multiple shopping centers, or a professional ice hockey game. With the flowering of spring comes the thundering excitement of the Kentucky Derby. For nature lovers, the Ohio River as well as nearby lakes and parks provide leisurely activities after a day of studies.

Majors and Degrees

Sullivan College confers the Bachelor of Science degree in business administration (with options in accounting, computer science, management, and marketing), the Bachelor of Science degree in hospitality management, and the Bachelor of Science degree in paralegal studies. The Associate of Science degree is offered in baking and pastry arts, business administration (with options in accounting, business management, and marketing and sales management), computer science (with options in computer programming, Internet/Intranet programming, and PC support specialist studies), culinary arts, hotel/restaurant management, office administration (with options in executive secretary studies, legal secretary studies, medical office management, and office administration specialist studies), paralegal studies, professional catering, and travel and tourism. Sullivan also offers business administration, child-care management, legal nurse consultant studies, office administration, professional baker studies, professional cook studies, professional nanny studies, and travel and tourism diplomas as well as Microsoft certificate programs in MCSE and MCSD.

Academic Program

All Sullivan students study practical courses designed to build a foundation for their careers. Just the opposite of most colleges and universities, Sullivan students begin by concentrating specifically on their areas of interest; then, their general and advanced education courses are taken within the final few months, or quarters, of the degree program. The College operates on a quarter-hour system of four 11-week sessions, which allows baccalaureate students to finish their degrees in as little as thirty-six months. Credits are awarded on a credit-hour basis. Day classes are offered every day of the week except Friday. "Plus Friday" is a free day when students may utilize the facilities and equipment for individual study and practice and faculty members are available to give students special assistance.

To qualify for graduation in the Bachelor of Science program, students must complete a minimum of 180 credit hours. In addition, all students must attain a minimum cumulative grade point average of 2.0 on a 4.0 scale. The curriculum includes 60 credit hours of core business requirements, 28 credit hours of business support requirements, 16 credit hours of classes in the student's option, 48 hours of general studies, and 60 hours of electives.

Sullivan College offers a number of courses and programs on line, with nearly 40 databases available through its participation in the Kentucky Commonwealth Virtual University. This exciting method of delivery is rapidly becoming very popular with Sullivan's busy student population. To learn more about this option, students should consult the College's Web site (address below).

Students may earn credit for certain requirements by taking the College-Level Examination Program (CLEP) subject examinations. Students may also receive credit for courses by taking the College bypass examinations.

Academic Facilities

Sullivan College's multimillion-dollar complex is climate-controlled and houses a variety of training equipment. From the state-of-the-art AS-400 and numerous personal computer labs utilizing the latest in software packages to the World Span computerized travel reservation system, Sullivan students have outstanding technology right at their fingertips. A new, multimillion-dollar, state-of-the-art Sullivan College Library opened in January 1999. The library contains a diversity of current reference and circulating materials as well as a high-speed computer network that provides access to the Sullivan College virtual library's (http://www.sullivan.edu/library) latest full-text and full-image electronic databases, such as ABI/Inform and LEXIS-NEXIS. Sullivan College also has resource sharing agreements with six other area libraries.

Costs

Expenses for the 2000–01 academic year range from $10,080 to $10,950 for tuition and $170 to $300 for first-quarter books. Housing costs $2970, the general fee is $350, and there is a $60 fee for parking. An additional comprehensive fee is applied for some hospitality programs.

Financial Aid

Students attending Sullivan have access to numerous federal and state financial aid programs, such as all Title IV programs as well as Job Training Partnership Act (JTPA) funds. Many loans, grants, work-study programs, academic scholarships, and private scholarships are also available. As directed by the Department of Education, federal funds are allotted to the lowest-income families first, but funds are also available for middle- and upper-income families.

Faculty

Sullivan's 70 faculty members share years of education and experience with their students. Faculty members are available daily for student assistance. With an 18:1 student-faculty ratio, the faculty can provide students with the academic guidance that they deserve.

Student Government

The Student Government Association is responsible for coordinating most student activities and social affairs. Officers serve for a term of two quarters. In addition, representatives and alternates are elected from each class to serve for one quarter. The Student Government Association offers an excellent opportunity for involvement in the very heart of most student social events and fosters cooperation among the student body, administration, and the faculty of Sullivan College.

Admission Requirements

To be considered for admission to Sullivan College, a student is required to demonstrate the appropriate aptitude and background for his or her anticipated field of study by successful completion of an entrance test and/or submission of ACT or SAT I test scores. Students also must have a high school diploma or its equivalent, such as a General Educational Development (GED) certificate. Sullivan has a rolling admissions policy; those who apply first are accepted first. The College individually interviews and advises each person seeking admission either at the College or at the student's home. Students from other regions of the United States and international students may complete the application by mail. A College preview video is available for review if a visit is impossible prior to entry. New classes normally begin the first week of January, April, July, and October of each year.

Application and Information

Students considering applying to the College are strongly encouraged to visit the campus. Included in a weekday visit are an interview with an admissions officer, a tour of the campus, an opportunity to observe classes, and discussions with professors and students. A Sullivan representative assists out-of-town visitors in finding accommodations. Approximately six open houses per year allow prospective students and their families an opportunity to visit the campus and participate in campus activities.

For more information and application materials, prospective students should contact the appropriate campus:

Director of Admissions
Sullivan College
P.O. Box 33-308
Louisville, Kentucky 40232-9735
Telephone: 502-456-6505
        800-844-1354 (toll-free)
World Wide Web: http://www.sullivan.edu

Director of Admissions
Sullivan College, Lexington
2659 Regency Road
Lexington, Kentucky 40503
Telephone: 606-276-4357
        800-467-6281 (toll-free)

Director of Admissions
Sullivan College, Ft. Knox
P.O. Box 998
Fort Knox, Kentucky 40121
Telephone: 502-942-8500
        800-562-6713 (toll-free)

Greek revival–style architecture and picturesque grounds characterize Sullivan College.

SUSQUEHANNA UNIVERSITY
SELINSGROVE, PENNSYLVANIA

The University

Susquehanna is a comprehensive, residential undergraduate university. Its three schools (the School of Arts, Humanities, and Communications; the Sigmund Weis School of Business; and the School of Natural and Social Sciences) offer a combination of professional programs and a broad-based educational experience. Susquehanna's enrollment of approximately 1,650 men and women, its small classes, and the dedication of its faculty members to undergraduate students enhance its responsive character. Susquehanna is affiliated with the Evangelical Lutheran Church in America, but since its founding in 1858, the University has welcomed students, faculty, and staff members from all racial, ethnic, and religious backgrounds.

As a residential university, Susquehanna believes extracurricular activities should be an integral part of each student's experience. There are twenty-two intercollegiate sports teams as well as an extensive intramural program, numerous academic clubs, one of the most powerful student-run radio stations in Pennsylvania, a host of musical activities, and many other organizations, ranging from the Marketing Club to the Student Association for Cultural Awareness. Approximately 80 percent of the students are in residence, living in seven residence halls, three apartment-style units, several academic or volunteer student project suites and houses, a scholars' house, four fraternity houses, and four sorority houses.

Location

Selinsgrove is a town of about 6,000 inhabitants. It is 50 miles north of Harrisburg, the state capital, and is situated on the scenic Susquehanna River. The town is approximately 200 miles from New York City, Philadelphia, Pittsburgh, Baltimore, and Washington. Located on U.S. Routes 11 and 15 and near I-80, the area is readily accessible, and public transportation is available. Cultural, dining, recreational, and shopping opportunities abound. Susquehanna has close ties with the community, where a number of students serve internships and where many take part in the University's extensive, award-winning volunteer program. Susquehanna is one of three universities in the area.

Majors and Degrees

Susquehanna University offers the Bachelor of Science degree, with majors in biochemistry, biology, chemistry, education, environmental science, and physics, and the Bachelor of Arts degree, with majors in art, art history, chemistry, communications and theater arts, computer science, economics, English, environmental science, French, German, history, information systems, international studies, mathematics, music, philosophy, physics, political science, psychology, religion, sociology, and Spanish. The Bachelor of Music is offered in church music, music education, and performance. The Bachelor of Science in Business is offered in accounting, in business administration (with emphasis in finance, global or human resource management, information systems, or marketing), and in economics. There are also a number of program options with interdisciplinary and self-designed majors.

Two dual-degree programs are available: 3-2 programs in engineering with Pennsylvania State University and the 3-2 program in forestry or environmental management with Duke University. A 2+2 program in allied health is offered with Thomas Jefferson University.

Academic Program

Susquehanna's core curriculum, which provides the breadth of knowledge needed for graduate school or a career, includes traditional, contemporary, and anticipatory components. The traditional courses offer exposure to the humanities, social sciences, and natural sciences; contemporary courses help students understand relationships among individuals, organizations, and the natural world; and anticipatory courses, including futures courses, attempt to anticipate how history, contemporary trends, and choices may affect the future. Susquehanna's core curriculum also has an extensive personal development sequence, which includes the nation's first required course on career planning.

Susquehanna offers a competitive four-year interdisciplinary honors program affiliated with the National Collegiate Honors Council. Preprofessional studies may be pursued in law, medicine and allied health fields, and the ministry. Teaching certification is offered at the elementary and secondary levels in all the usual subjects. Teachers are certified for grades K–12 in music and modern foreign languages (French, German, and Spanish). Nearly fifty academic minors, including programs in film, Jewish studies, journalism, and writing, are available. Army ROTC is available under a cross-enrollment program with Bucknell University.

Off-Campus Arrangements

Susquehanna students may participate in a variety of off-campus programs, including the Washington Center in the nation's capital, the Washington Semester of American University, the United Nations Semester of Drew University, the Appalachian Semester of Union College in Kentucky, and the Philadelphia Center Program. Each semester, the University approves numerous off-campus departmental internships, some of which are in other countries. Students are encouraged to study abroad, and Susquehanna is a participating member of the Institute of European Studies. The University is a coordinating institution with Senshu University in Japan and offers a semester in London for juniors majoring in business. Susquehanna-designed focus programs complement special groups of courses with travel to the country being studied. Recent trips included Australia, Ecuador, Martinique, and South Africa. All of these programs carry academic credit.

Academic Facilities

Susquehanna is an undergraduate university. All facilities and equipment are for the exclusive use of undergraduate students. The Blough-Weis Library houses Susquehanna's language lab, music and sound media, and the Film Institute. The library collection numbers about 386,000 volumes and other items, including microforms and records. About 2,400 periodicals are received, and 350 individual study spaces are maintained. Fisher Science Hall provides facilities for all the sciences, including experimental psychology. General classrooms are in Steele and Bogar Halls. Heilman Hall is the home of the Department of Music. Seibert Hall houses the University Computer Center. A new technology center, opened in fall 1999, provides the business and communications programs with multimedia computer labs, video studios, offices, and conference, presentation, and seminar rooms. The Charles B.

Degenstein Campus Center houses the Lore A. Degenstein Art Gallery and a state-of-the-art 450-seat teaching theater.

Costs

Tuition and fees for 2000–01 are $20,440. Room and board costs are $5770. A student's personal expenses, including books, travel, and other costs, are estimated at $1200 to $1600 per year.

Financial Aid

The primary purpose of financial aid is to permit attendance at Susquehanna University by full-time students whose personal and family resources are not sufficient to meet the costs. The amount of financial aid is based on need, not on family income alone. The extent of need is determined annually by information provided on the PROFILE and the Free Application for Federal Student Aid (FAFSA). About 95 percent of all students currently receive financial assistance that ranges from $1000 to full need. The average amount received is more than $16,000 per recipient, and the total aid budget exceeds $20 million. Aid is provided in packages that may include grants, scholarships, loans, and jobs. The various state and federal assistance programs are also taken into consideration when aid packages are created. In addition, Susquehanna offers academic and music scholarships, which are awarded on a competitive basis without regard to financial need.

Faculty

Susquehanna's teaching faculty helps students develop their views of themselves and of the world and plays a part in preparing them for life after college. The faculty-student ratio is 1:14, and 92 percent of the 108 full-time faculty members hold an earned doctorate. Most faculty members serve as student advisers, and full-time counseling services are also available. There are no graduate assistants at Susquehanna.

Student Government

The Student Government Association provides a representative student organization to assure students of a voice in University governance. The Student Senate, the legislative branch, provides a forum for student opinion, deals with issues of concern to the entire student body, and seeks solutions to campus problems. The senate is responsible for the allocation of funds collected through the student activity fee and is the body that designates student representatives for University committees and the Board of Directors, of which 2 students are voting members.

Admission Requirements

Susquehanna admits students without regard to race, color, religion, national or ethnic origin, age, sex, or handicap. Students who gain admission are those whom the Admissions Committee deems able to profit from and contribute to the Susquehanna experience. Graduation from an accredited secondary school or a high school equivalency certificate is required. Experience has shown that the best preparation includes at least 4 years of English, 4 years of mathematics, 3 years of social science, 2 or 3 years of one foreign language, 2 or 3 years of laboratory science, and 3 or more units of electives. In evaluating a candidate, the committee considers academic performance, major interests, test scores, recommendations, extracurricular activities, and demonstrated interest in the University. In addition to the application and secondary school records, the candidate must submit scores on either the SAT I or the ACT, unless he or she chooses the writing option. An applicant with a cumulative ranking in the top 20 percent of the high school class may submit two graded writing samples instead of standardized test scores. Although SAT II Subject Tests are not required for admission to Susquehanna, it is strongly recommended that the candidate take the Writing Test and one other test of his or her choice. Subject Test scores assist in placement as well as admission decisions. Applications for early decision are encouraged, and deferred admission is available. Interviews are strongly suggested for early decision and transfer candidates, although all candidates are encouraged to arrange a visit to the campus. Applicants to the Bachelor of Music program and to the Bachelor of Arts program in music must audition. Applicants to the Bachelor of Arts in writing program must also submit a portfolio. Transfer candidates can be considered for either semester, and the University recognizes the Advanced Placement and CLEP programs of the College Board and the International Baccalaureate program.

Application and Information

Application materials and introductory and departmental information may be obtained by contacting the Office of Admissions. Transfer candidates should contact the Office of Admissions to obtain appropriate materials and details relating to the transfer process. All interview appointments should be made two weeks in advance to allow time for faculty contact and the scheduling of student-conducted tours. The priority application deadline is March 1 (for early decision, December 15). The University adheres to the Candidates Reply Date of May 1 and is pleased to accept photocopies of the Common Application or applications submitted on line via Susquehanna's Web site.

Office of Admissions
Susquehanna University
514 University Avenue
Selinsgrove, Pennsylvania 17870-1040
Telephone: 570-372-4260
            800-326-9672 (toll-free)
Fax: 570-372-2722
E-mail: suadmiss@susqu.edu
World Wide Web: http://www.susqu.edu

Graceful Seibert Hall at Susquehanna University.

SWARTHMORE COLLEGE
SWARTHMORE, PENNSYLVANIA

The College

Swarthmore, regularly ranked among the top three liberal arts colleges in the country, is well known as an academic powerhouse.

But, while intellectual, Swarthmore is also alive with passions. It is peopled by students and professors who are both brilliant and adventurous, thinkers who live vigorously. Everyone spends a good bit of time in classes and at the library; most people spend a great deal more time engaged in philosophy debates with friends at dinner, working in soup kitchens, doing soccer drills, partying, playing music, tutoring children, and walking in the woods. The trick is to fit it all into a 24-hour day.

There is, after all, lots to do. Twenty-four sports teams compete in Division III. There are 150 student organizations, including the African American, Asian American, and Latino student organizations; music ensembles; the Outing Club; the student newspaper; the radio station; the yearbook; a lesbian/bisexual/gay group; religious organizations; a wide range of community service programs; and several political organizations. Students are welcome to start new groups with support from the activities fund. All campus events are free as part of Swarthmore's commitment to equality of opportunity.

Swarthmore is rooted in the ideals of its Quaker founders: social action, pacifism, and respect for the "inner light" of each person. Professors and administrators encourage students to follow their own stars. There are even funds to support student-run projects. Professors pitch in on student projects with expertise and elbow grease, and students take responsibility for helping each other. As a result, Swarthmoreans can take tremendous personal and intellectual risks in safety—and grow enormously in the process.

Almost all of the College's 1,500 students live on campus in residence halls ranging from tiny Woolman (originally a private Victorian house) to the Elizabethan-style Worth to nearly new Mertz. Most dorms are coed, but single-sex housing is available too. Everyone eats together in a central dining hall, so ideas and friendships spread rapidly around the campus.

Swarthmore actively welcomes and knits together people of widely diverse backgrounds. Students come from fifty states and sixty other countries, and the College's policy of admitting students without regard to financial need means that students' economic and social circumstances vary widely too.

Location

Swarthmore's campus is a 330-acre arboretum whose beauty defies description. A gorgeous 50-acre carpet of emerald lawn at the center of the campus invites reading, studying, playing, and napping outdoors in fall and spring. The wooded creek, with an amphitheater terraced into its hillside, makes a wonderful refuge for walks, conversations, and contemplation.

At the same time, all the excitement, history, and culture of downtown Philadelphia is less than half an hour away by the train that leaves from the foot of the campus. Philadelphia's many and diverse restaurants are renowned, and a walk around the city offers a primer in the history of architecture since 1600. Music, dance, and theater events are plentiful each week.

Majors and Degrees

Swarthmore offers undergraduate education only, with programs leading to a B.A. or B.S. degree in art history/art, Asian studies, astronomy, biology, black studies, chemistry, classics, cognitive science, computer science, economics, engineering, English literature, environmental studies, Francophone studies, German studies, history, interpretation theory, Latin American studies, linguistics, literature, mathematics, medieval studies, modern languages and literatures, music and dance, peace and conflict studies, philosophy, physics, political science, psychology, public policy, religion, sociology and anthropology, special major, statistics, theater studies, and women's studies. Students can also design an interdepartmental special major.

Swarthmore's strong engineering program is one of the few in the country that offers students a chance to acquire both a top-notch engineering education and an extraordinary liberal arts background.

Academic Program

Swarthmore's Honors Program (which is almost impossible to explain on paper, although it is fairly simple in practice) offers a rare opportunity to do graduate-style work as an undergraduate.

Students choose to follow either the Course or Honors Program starting in their junior year. Course students continue to take an average of four classes each semester, generally selecting courses from among a number of departments. The Course Program offers the chance to investigate a wide range of disciplines.

Honors students, on the other hand, take just four "preparations" over the course of their junior and senior years—three in the major and one in a minor. Like graduate seminars, these involve a tremendous amount of individual study and a collegial relationship with professors. The preparations may take the form of seminars, independent reading, thesis work, or other projects designed by the student and the department.

Perhaps the most striking feature of Honors is that final examinations are given by "external examiners"—distinguished faculty members from other colleges—rather than by the professors with whom the student has been working.

Off-Campus Arrangements

Swarthmore actively encourages students to study abroad as an excellent way to enrich study in any field and to discover broad perspectives.

In recent years, Swarthmore students have completed international study programs in Australia, Brazil, Cameroon, Chile, China, Colombia, Ecuador, Egypt, England, France, Germany, Ghana, Greece, Hungary, India, Ireland, Italy, Japan, Kenya, Mexico, Nepal, Nigeria, Russia, Scotland, Spain, Sri Lanka, Sweden, Taiwan, and Thailand.

A special Office for Foreign Study offers support and guidance, and financial aid is normally applicable to international study.

Students can also spend a semester at Tufts University, Rice University, Pomona College, Mills College, Middlebury College, and Harvey Mudd College, with which Swarthmore has exchange arrangements. And of course, while at Swarthmore, it's possible to take courses at nearby Haverford College, Bryn Mawr College, and the University of Pennsylvania.

Academic Facilities

There are 1 million books and 6,000 periodical subscriptions housed in McCabe Library and the Cornell Science Library. Also on campus are a computer center; an observatory; engineering and science laboratories; a greenhouse; a music building with a 420-seat concert hall and eleven practice rooms; a new theater complex with a flexible stage/seating arena; and large, light-washed dance and art studios.

A wonderful, airy student center, built inside the Gothic shell of a stone-and-stained-glass theater, is a splendid spot to meet friends and professors over a snack any time of year.

Costs

For 2000–01, fees are $33,004, which includes tuition of $24,950. Room is $4004, board is $3800, and the activities fee is $250. Additional costs families should consider when budgeting include books, supplies, and travel.

Financial Aid

The College is committed to a long-standing policy of admitting students without regard to financial need. As a result, a very high percentage—more than half—of Swarthmore students receive substantial financial aid. The average award, including work, loan, and grant, equaled $23,040 last year.

Faculty

There are just 8 students per professor at Swarthmore. All professors dedicate their time and attention exclusively to teaching undergraduates. There are no teaching assistants, so students work directly with the most expert minds on the campus.

Student Government

The 20-member Student Council is elected by the student body to represent student opinion to faculty and administration and encourage discussion of important community issues. The Council's Budget Committee controls and allocates the multi-thousand dollar student fund, and its Appointment Committee places students on committees of administration and faculty, alumni/alumnae committees, and the board of managers.

Admission Requirements

Admission to Swarthmore is highly competitive. A strong academic record is essential; in addition, the College looks for far-ranging interests and abilities, especially an interest in social action and service. Swarthmore encourages all students to visit the campus and, if possible, to have an interview on campus or close to where they live.

Applications must include SAT I or ACT scores; scores in three SAT II Subject Tests, one of which must be the writing test; a high school transcript; a brief personal essay on a meaningful interest or activity; and a longer essay on a topic specified by the College. Swarthmore is also interested in hearing about applicants' reading, research, work, and travel experience, both in school and out.

Application and Information

The deadline for fall early decision is November 15 and for winter early decision, January 1. The deadline for regular decision is also January 1. April 1 is the date for fall transfer applications. For more information or an application, students should write or call:

Admissions Office
Swarthmore College
500 College Avenue
Swarthmore, Pennsylvania 19081-1390
Telephone: 610-328-8300
        800-667-3110 (toll-free)
E-mail: admissions@swarthmore.edu

Tree-lined Magill Walk, Swarthmore College.

SWEET BRIAR COLLEGE
SWEET BRIAR, VIRGINIA

The College
Sweet Briar College, the first women's college to establish a prelaw chapter of Phi Alpha Delta Law Fraternity, is consistently ranked as one of the top colleges for women in the nation. Its academic reputation, beautiful location, and attention to the individual attract smart, confident women who want to excel. The College's focus on women allows students, in full partnership with the faculty, to fulfill their promise as scholars and develop exceptional leadership skills. A four-year career planning program capitalizes on the international network of successful Sweet Briar alumnae for worldwide career opportunities and postgraduate education.

Students work one-on-one with faculty members and visiting scholars and engage in meaningful research. Classes are small, averaging 12 students. The four-year Honors Program is nationally recognized for its innovative partnering of interdisciplinary academic and cocurricular programs. The College has a wide geographic, ethnic, and socioeconomic representation. About 600 women from more than forty states and twenty countries are enrolled at Sweet Briar's Virginia campus; another 100 students are enrolled in Sweet Briar's coed Junior Year in France and Junior Year in Spain.

Social, recreational, and cocurricular events are coordinated with neighboring colleges. Students participate in and assist in planning an extensive program of concerts, films, and dance and theater productions, as well as workshops and master classes by visiting scholars and performers. Students play an active role in campus organizations, including honor societies, community service groups, student newspaper, drama and dance clubs, radio club, and singing groups. Varsity athletes compete in NCAA Division III field hockey, lacrosse, riding, soccer, swimming, tennis, and volleyball. Club sports include fencing, riding, and softball.

Location
Sweet Briar's 3,300-acre campus in the foothills of the Blue Ridge Mountains is crisscrossed with hiking, biking, and riding trails through woodlands and dells and around small lakes that provide spectacular outdoor recreational activities. The on-campus riding center, one of the largest and best-designed college facilities in the country, attracts both competitive and recreational riders. The College is centrally located on the outskirts of Lynchburg, Virginia, southwest of Washington, D.C., and Charlottesville. Students also enjoy activities in nearby Roanoke and Richmond.

Majors and Degrees
Sweet Briar awards the Bachelor of Arts or Bachelor of Science degree in thirty-seven majors: anthropology, art (history or studio), biochemistry–molecular biology, biology, chemistry, classical civilization, computer science, dance, economics, economics–computer science, English, English and creative writing, environmental science, French/French studies, German/German studies, government, Greek, history, international affairs, Italian studies, Latin, mathematical physics, mathematics, mathematics–computer science, mathematics-economics, modern languages, music, philosophy, physics, pre-engineering studies, psychology, religion, sociology, Spanish/business, Spanish/Hispanic studies, and theater. Special programs focus on archaeology, arts management, business management, environmental studies, European civilization, film studies, international studies, musical theater, public administration, and women and gender studies. Students may design an interdisciplinary major focused on a topic of special interest or may construct individualized majors. Although there is no major in education, students are able to meet certification requirements for early childhood, elementary, and secondary teaching.

Academic Program
Sweet Briar's academic program supports its mission to prepare women to be active, responsible members of a world community by integrating the liberal arts and sciences with opportunities for internships, campus and community leadership, and career planning. Students complete courses in English, literature or the arts, science, foreign language, non-Western studies, social sciences, humanities, and physical education. Independent studies, available at all levels, and seminars are included in most majors, and a culminating senior course or exercise is required in all majors. General honors that may be awarded with the degree are cum laude, magna cum laude, or summa cum laude. Sweet Briar has a chapter of Phi Beta Kappa and offers an honors program that provides an opportunity to take special tutorials and seminars and to do a yearlong research project culminating in an honors thesis on an original topic. The Honors Degree may be awarded with honors, high honors, or highest honors.

Sweet Briar's two-semester calendar allows students to participate in intensive courses, independent research projects, or internships on campus or throughout the world.

Off-Campus Arrangements
More than a third of Sweet Briar's junior class studies abroad. The Sweet Briar Junior Year in France, the first program in Paris for American students, is considered the most academically rigorous program available today. Students from 258 colleges and universities have participated in the coed program, now in its fifty-first year. The Junior Year in Spain in Seville is modeled on the success of the Junior Year in France program. The College has special relationships with Oxford University, the University of London (Royal Holloway), the University of St. Andrews in Scotland, and the University of Urbino in Italy. Students also study abroad in Australia, Austria, China, Germany, and Japan. Students may participate in a tri-college exchange or seven-college exchange at several coeducational or single-sex colleges in the mid-Atlantic region. Arrangements for off-campus study also include an Environmental Junior Year, the Washington Semester at American University, and summer programs at St. Anne's College, Oxford, in Münster, Germany, and in Rome, Italy.

Academic Facilities
Sweet Briar has excellent library resources of more than 240,000 volumes, as well as more than 1,800 journal subscriptions, 350,000 microforms, more than 6,000 audiovisual materials, and special libraries in art, music, and the sciences. Some of the most notable special holdings include Virginia Woolf, T. E. Lawrence, George Meredith, W. H. Auden, and a rare collection of twentieth-century Chinese works. The libraries provide easy access to more than 50 million bibliographic records on line. A fiber-optic backbone allows high-speed Ethernet communica-

tion among all academic and administrative buildings, as well as in residence hall rooms, with more than 1,000 terminal and network connections campuswide. Access to the global Internet is achieved through T-1 connections, which allow students, faculty, and administrators to exchange e-mail; access bulletin boards, Web pages, and library information; and exchange files with any of thousands of computers around the world. Three computer labs with Macintosh and Pentium computers are open free of charge 24 hours a day. The student-to-computer ratio is 6:1. Students studying science use state-of-the-art equipment that enhances faculty-student collaborative research. Biology equipment includes a scanning electron microscope with digital imaging system, equipment for plant and animal tissue culture, DNA sequencing equipment, and advanced video production facilities; chemistry students have access to a nuclear magnetic resonance spectrometer (NMR), a diode array UV/Vis spectrometer, a Fourier transform-infrared spectrometer (FT-IR), a modular LASER laboratory, a gas chromatograph/mass spectrograph (GC/MS), a high-pressure liquid chromatograph (HPLC), and a differential scanning calorimeter (DSC); mathematics facilities include a calculus computer lab with advanced Pentium computer systems; and physics equipment includes a scanning tunneling microscope, an X-ray crystallography system, and holographic instrumentation. The Academic Resource Center provides assistance to students in writing, reading, study skills, time management, stress management, and peer tutoring. The Babcock Fine Arts Center includes individual practice rooms, an electronic piano lab, art studios, a photography lab, and computer graphics facilities.

Costs

For 2000–01, tuition is $17,174 and room and board are $7016. Books, supplies, and fees cost about $750. Personal expenses average $750. All students may have cars.

Financial Aid

A family's financial circumstances do not limit a student's choices at Sweet Briar because of the College's generous financial aid program. About 60 percent of students receive need-based aid, including grants, loans, and work-study awards. Academic merit awards are available, including the Founders', Commonwealth, Prothro, Betty Bean Black, and Sweet Briar scholarships. Other academic, merit, and leadership awards are also available.

Faculty

Sweet Briar's faculty is actively engaged in teaching, research, publication, and other forms of creative activity. Of the 69 full-time faculty members, 97 percent hold doctorates or the terminal degree in their field. About one half are women. The student-faculty ratio is about 7:1.

Student Government

All students are members of the Student Government Association and play a critical role in the administration of the College. A strong honor system builds trust and mutual respect in a genuinely warm community focused on individual maturity and commitment. Students serve on virtually every committee with faculty members and administrators.

Admission Requirements

The Committee on Admissions requires a minimum of 4 units in English, 3 in mathematics (including algebra I and II and geometry), 3 of social studies (including 2 in history, 1 of them U.S. history), 2 sequential years of foreign language, and 3 of science, as well as additional units in these subjects to total 16. Most candidates have 20 such academic units. Additional units may be earned in other subjects but will not count as academic units. Special attention is given to the difficulty of the applicant's curriculum, her class rank, and the school attended; scores on the SAT I or on the ACT are required. The College strongly recommends that students take SAT II Subject Tests and suggests the areas of English (preferably the Writing Test), mathematics, and foreign language. An interview at the College is strongly recommended but not required. Candidates who are unable to visit the campus are urged to meet with staff members, to talk with alumnae in their home towns, or to request the Sweet Briar video.

Application and Information

Scholarship candidates should apply by January 15, and regular candidates should apply by February 15 of the senior year. Early decision applications are due by December 1 of the senior year, and notifications are sent December 15; the reservation deposit is due January 15. Transfer applications for the sophomore and junior classes are due by July 1. A completed application includes a transcript of the candidate's school work, scores on the required tests, recommendations from the guidance counselor and a teacher, and essays written by the candidate. Sweet Briar also accepts the Common Application (with an additional essay required) and the CollegeLink application. All materials should be sent to the address given below; information may be requested from the same office.

Director of Admissions
Sweet Briar College
Sweet Briar, Virginia 24595

Telephone: 804-381-6142
              800-381-6142 (toll-free)
Fax: 804-381-6152
E-mail: admissions@sbc.edu
World Wide Web: http://www.sbc.edu

SYRACUSE UNIVERSITY
SYRACUSE, NEW YORK

The University

Syracuse University, founded in 1870, is an independent, privately endowed university with an international reputation. Students attend from all over the United States and from more than ninety other countries. There are 14,500 students enrolled; 10,000 are undergraduates. Approximately 70 percent of the students live in University housing, which includes modern residence halls, apartments, and fraternity and sorority houses. The 200-acre campus features a main grassy quadrangle surrounded by academic buildings, with residential facilities nearby. The campus is situated on a hill overlooking the downtown area of Syracuse. Social life is centered on the campus, and there are innumerable recreational, athletic, and academic activities. The 50,000-seat Carrier Dome is the site of concerts, sports events, and commencement. The residence halls are wired for direct connections from student rooms to the campus computer network.

Location

The city of Syracuse (metropolitan area population of 500,000) is the business, educational, and cultural hub of central New York. The city offers professional theater and opera, as well as visiting artists and performers. Highlights of the downtown area include the Everson Museum of Art, the impressive Civic Center, and the Armory Square shopping area. Central New York has many lakes, parks, mountains, and outstanding recreational opportunities.

Majors and Degrees

Syracuse University awards A.B., B.S., B.Arch., B.I.D., B.Mus., and B.F.A. degrees.

The School of Architecture offers a five-year baccalaureate program leading to the first professional degree of B.Arch.

Majors in the College of Arts and Sciences are African-American studies, American studies, anthropology, biochemistry, biology, chemistry, classical civilization, classics, comparative literature, earth sciences, economics, English and textual studies, European literature, fine arts, French, geography, German, history, history of architecture, honors studies, international relations, Italian, Latin, Latino-American studies, linguistic studies, mathematics, medieval and Renaissance studies, modern foreign languages, philosophy, physics, policy studies, political philosophy, political science, psychology, religion, Russian, Russian studies, sociology, Spanish, and women's studies.

The School of Education offers majors in art education, communication sciences and disorders, elementary education (inclusive with special education), health and exercise science, music education, physical education, secondary education, and special education (inclusive with elementary education).

The College of Engineering and Computer Science majors include aerospace, chemical, civil, computer, electrical, environmental, and mechanical engineering; bioengineering; computer science; engineering physics; and systems and information science.

The College for Human Development majors include child and family studies, consumer studies, environmental design (interiors), fashion design, hospitality and food service management, nutrition/dietetics, nutrition science, retailing, selected studies, and textile design.

The School of Information Studies offers a four-year baccalaureate program in information management and technology.

The School of Management majors include accounting, entrepreneurship and emerging enterprises, finance, general studies in management, marketing management, and supply chain management.

The College of Nursing offers a four-year baccalaureate program in nursing.

The Newhouse School of Public Communications majors are in the following areas: advertising, broadcast journalism, graphic arts, magazine, newspaper, photography, public relations, and television/radio/film.

The School of Social Work offers a four-year baccalaureate program in social work.

The College of Visual and Performing Arts majors include art, drama, music, and speech communication. Art majors offered are advertising design, art education, art photography, art video, ceramics, communications design, computer graphics, fiber arts, film, history of art, illustration, industrial design, interior design, metalsmithing, painting, printmaking, sculpture, and surface pattern design. Drama majors include design/technical theater, drama, and musical theater. Music majors include music composition, music education, music industry, organ, percussion, piano, string instruments, voice, and wind instruments. Speech majors include speech communication.

Academic Program

The University operates on a two-semester calendar with two 6-week summer sessions. Students generally take five 3-credit-hour courses each semester. A minimum of 120 credit hours is required for graduation. Special programs include dual, combined, and accelerated enrollment; selected studies; internships; an honors program; ROTC; and preprofessional advising for students going on to study dentistry, law, medicine, or veterinary science.

Off-Campus Arrangements

Through the University's Division of International Programs Abroad, students may study in Australia, Belgium, Chile, China, Czech Republic, France, Germany, Hungary, Ireland, Israel, Italy, Japan, Poland, Russia, Spain, United Kingdom, and Zimbabwe.

Academic Facilities

The academic buildings at Syracuse University span the century, with fifteen listed in the National Register of Historic Places and others representative of some of the most modern and technologically sophisticated architecture in the country. The Ernest Stevenson Bird Library houses approximately 3 million volumes; 16,000 periodicals/serials and CD-ROMs; 3.7 million microforms; rare books; and archives. The University has computer facilities with laboratories and a data communications network that links computers to hundreds of terminals. The Newhouse Communications Center has some of the finest facilities available for journalism and telecommunications. The Center for Science and Technology is a state-of-the-art facility uniting research and academic programs in computer science and technology. It also houses the CASE Center for research in computer applications and software engineering. The high-tech Melvin A. Eggers Hall offers superior facilities for the University's social science programs.

Costs

Tuition for 2000–01 is $20,380, room and board are $8414, and fees are $446. These costs do not include books, supplies, personal expenses, and travel.

Financial Aid

About 80 percent of all entering freshmen and transfers receive some form of financial aid. By filing the Free Application for Federal Student Aid (FAFSA), students are automatically considered for all financial aid programs administered by Syracuse University, including federal financial aid, Syracuse University grants, and Federal Work-Study awards. Merit scholarships are available to both freshmen and transfer students, based solely on their academic record. Syracuse University evaluates candidates for admission without respect to financial need. Information on financial aid policies, procedures, and deadlines can be obtained from the Office of Admissions and Financial Aid.

Faculty

The majority of faculty members hold the highest degree in their professional field. There are 805 full-time faculty members, including recognized experts in their fields who teach at both the graduate and undergraduate levels.

Student Government

The Syracuse University Student Association works to protect students' rights and offers services through its three branches—the executive, the legislative, and the judicial.

Admission Requirements

Syracuse University seeks a diverse student body from all social, cultural, and educational backgrounds. Each candidate is evaluated individually, based on the requirements of the college of the University to which he or she has applied. Emphasis is placed on students' high school performance, standardized test scores (SAT I or ACT), an essay, recommendations, extracurricular activities, and portfolios or auditions when required. Special admission requirements for some programs are described in the *Undergraduate Application for Admission*. Transfer students are evaluated individually, since requirements vary by college.

Syracuse University is an Equal Opportunity/Affirmative Action institution and does not discriminate on the basis of race, creed, color, gender, national origin, religion, marital status, age, disability, or sexual orientation.

Application and Information

Regular decision applicants for the fall semester should submit the application form, transcripts, standardized test scores, essay, and recommendations and fulfill any special admission requirements by January 15 (postmarked). Notification takes place in early March.

Early decision applicants must meet a deadline of November 15 (postmarked). Notification takes place in late December.

Detailed information and application forms may be obtained by contacting:

Office of Admissions and Financial Aid
201 Tolley Administration Building
Syracuse University
Syracuse, New York 13244

Telephone: 315-443-3611
E-mail: orange@syr.edu
World Wide Web: http://www.syracuse.edu

The main quadrangle reflects the architectural span of the century, from the 50,000-seat Carrier Dome (left) to the classic Hendricks Chapel (center) and Crouse College spires (right).

TALLADEGA COLLEGE
TALLADEGA, ALABAMA

The College

Talladega College is a private, four-year liberal arts college founded in 1867 by former slaves Thomas Tarrant and William Savery. Tarrant and Savery met in Mobile, Alabama, with a group of newly freed men in 1865. The commitment and pledge written from this meeting, "we regard the education of our children and youth as vital to the preservation of our liberties, and true religion as the foundation of all real virtue, and shall use our utmost endeavors to promote these blessings in our common country," was the beginning of Tarrant's and Savery's ambition to provide a school for the children of former slaves. With the help of the American Missionary Association and General Wager Swayne of the Freedman's Bureau, they were able to purchase a three-story brick high school building and 34 acres. This building was built by slave labor and was originally used to educate young white men.

Talladega College provides a culturally extensive education in a nurturing environment. The beautiful tree-lined campus comprises forty-two buildings and 135 acres that sit in the heart of a fertile valley in the foothills of the Blue Ridge Mountains. Swayne Hall, the College's oldest building, is a national historic landmark. DeForest Chapel is used for religious services and convocations. Callanan Union Building is the center of recreational activities. It houses a swimming pool, a gymnasium, a bookstore, a student lounge, a weight room, and a snack bar and offers after-hours recreational activities. Silsby Athletic Field, which is about 15 acres in size, is an enclosed field used for touch football, baseball, softball, and track. Four outdoor tennis courts provide additional recreational amenities. The Golf Driving Range is open to the public and serves as a practice tee for the Talladega College golf team. Talladega hosts the Annual Golf Invitational Tournament for four-year colleges and universities. The women's and men's Tornado basketball teams compete in the Southern States Conference (SSC) of the National Association of Intercollegiate Athletics (NAIA).

Extracurricular activities are consistently planned by the Student Government Association and the Office of Student Activities. Eight fraternities and sororities and several social, civic, professional, and academic organizations operate on campus. Students are exposed to a variety of outstanding artists and scientists and political, business, and civic leaders throughout the year.

Location

Talladega College is located in the historic district of Talladega, Alabama. Talladega is about 50 miles east of Birmingham, 25 miles south of Anniston, 85 miles north of Montgomery, and 115 miles west of Atlanta, Georgia. The city is also home to the International Motorsports Hall of Fame Museum and the Talladega Superspeedway, which hosts the Winston Select 500, the International Race of Champions, and ARCA's Mountain Dew 500k.

Majors and Degrees

The Bachelor of Arts degree is awarded in various majors by the Divisions of Administration and Business, Natural Sciences and Mathematics, Social and Professional Studies, and Humanities. Majors offered are biology, business administration (accounting, economics, or management emphasis), chemistry, computer science, English, finance and banking, history, marketing, mathematics, music education (N–12), music performance (piano or voice emphasis), physics, psychology, public administration, secondary education, social work, and sociology. Programs are also provided for students with career interests in computational sciences, languages and literature, pre-engineering and pre–allied health, and prelegal and pre-medical-professional studies.

A dual-degree program is offered for students who wish to pursue careers in allied health, computer engineering, engineering, geology, marine science, nursing, pharmacy, and veterinary medicine. Students may remain at Talladega College to receive a degree in one of the sciences or transfer to a cooperating professional institution after two or three years to complete the professional phase of the program. Upon completion of the transfer program, an undergraduate degree from Talladega College and a professional degree, certificate, or diploma is awarded from the professional school.

Academic Program

Talladega is a college where fostering leadership is a tradition. Since its founding, it has sought to instill in its graduates the values of morality, intellectual excellence, and hard work. Peterson's has identified Talladega as one of approximately 200 colleges and universities in the United States that offers an outstanding undergraduate program in science and mathematics. The College seeks to nurture the whole person through close, personal relations between faculty members and students and by providing experiences that develop a strong personal value system. Talladega College believes that an essential part of leadership is skill in communications. Thus, it places special emphasis on the ability to listen and to read critically, to write and to speak with clarity, and to think analytically and strategically. The College is also mindful that it is part of a larger universe of nations, cultures, races, and religions and seeks to instill an understanding and appreciation of those differences through its curriculum and multicultural faculty. The College maintains its tradition of preparing students thoroughly—not only for the world of work but also for advanced graduate education. According to the National Science Foundation, Talladega ranks second in the United States in producing Black graduates who receive terminal degrees. Talladega College prepares students to be well-rounded individuals who are articulate, view the world with an international perspective, possess confidence in themselves and ethical moral values, and are able to serve their community.

The academic year is divided into fall and spring semesters. During the summer, many students participate in internship programs, some of which are recorded on the official transcript. Course credit is earned in semester hours. Credit-hour requirements vary with the major area.

Course work is divided into two phases: the General Division and the Major Division. In the General Division, students are acquainted with the various fields of knowledge and acquire foundational skills needed for further course work. The Major Division permits the student to give in-depth study to the field of interest and professional plans.

Incoming students take examinations for course-level placement. Students showing exceptional skills in mathematics or communications may be exempted from one or both semesters of the regular first-year courses. The innovative Student Support Program is designed to enhance academic success through skill development and individualized tutoring in academic areas.

Several programs expand career opportunities and allow students to enhance basic major programs. Among these programs are cooperative education, Army Reserve Officers' Training Corps, the Career Opportunities in Research Education and Training Program of the National Institute of Mental Health, Kennon Investment Group, Black Executive Exchange Program, Project Reachout: Family Life Center, the Ronald E. McNair Post-Baccalaureate Achievement Program, the Minority Biomedical Research Support Program, and the MARC Honors Undergraduate Research Training Program. Talladega College is one of two colleges in the state of Alabama that has a human cadaver for anatomy instruction. The College is accredited by the Southern Association of Colleges and Schools.

Academic Facilities

Academic buildings include Andrews Hall, Callanan Union Building, Goodnow Fine Arts Center, Silsby Science Hall, Swayne Hall, and Drewry Hall. Savery Library houses the Science Drop-In Center, and the Computer Assisted Instruction/ Curriculum Learning Laboratories, and the Amistad murals. DeForest Chapel also contains classrooms for studies in humanities.

Costs

There is no out-of-state fee for attending Talladega College. Tuition and fees for each semester are $2974.50. Room, board, telephone, and cable total $1549.50 per semester. Off-campus yearly costs (tuition and fees) total $5949, and on-campus yearly costs (room, board, tuition, and fees) total $9048.

Financial Aid

The financing of a college education may well be one of the largest investments students and their families will make in a lifetime. Through a comprehensive financial aid program administered and coordinated by the Office of Student Financial Aid, Talladega College is committed to assisting all students who demonstrate financial need and have a strong desire for education.

In order to be considered for financial aid, candidates must complete the Free Application for Federal Student Aid (FAFSA). This application must be filed with the director of financial aid. Four types of financial assistance are available: scholarships, grants, part-time employment, and loans.

Faculty

Talladega College has 40 full-time instructors and 6 adjunct instructors. Students receive personal attention at Talladega College from instructors and College staff. The student-teacher ratio is 13:1. Sixty-two percent of the full-time faculty have terminal degrees. Talladega College attracts faculty members who are at the top of their field and who have a special blend of dedication and teaching commitment to students.

Student Government

Each student enrolled at the College is a member of the Student Government Association. The governing body is patterned after the national government with a Senate, House of Representatives, Executive Cabinet, and class officers. SGA meetings are held monthly. The SGA President meets weekly with the Office of Student Affairs to discuss concerns of the student body. The SGA sponsors an annual spring carnival.

Admission Requirements

Talladega College welcomes students of all races, creeds, and national origins. SAT I or ACT scores are required, as is a high school diploma. Students for whom English is not the first language should submit Test of English as a Foreign Language (TOEFL) scores. College-preparatory courses should include 3 years of math and 3 years of science. Some foreign language is recommended. Talladega also requests one letter of recommendation and a personal essay.

Transfer students are required to have a minimum GPA of 2.35 and to submit high school and college transcripts.

Application and Information

Application for admission should be made as soon as possible before the beginning of the school year. The College uses the rolling admission plan and therefore can accept students until registration for the semester.

Applications are available from the Office of Admissions, to which all applications and inquiries should be addressed.

Office of Admissions
Talladega College
627 West Battle Street
Talladega, Alabama 35160

Telephone: 205-761-6416
           800-762-2468 (toll-free in Alabama)
           800-633-2440 (toll-free outside Alabama)
World Wide Web: http://www.talladega.edu

Swayne Hall, listed on the National Register of Historic Places, contains classrooms, a Hearing and Vision Laboratory, and a Writing Laboratory.

TAYLOR UNIVERSITY
UPLAND, INDIANA

The University

Founded in 1846, Taylor University was named for the missionary statesman Bishop William Taylor and is one of America's oldest evangelical Christian liberal arts colleges. The University offers residential living in an environment conducive to Christian growth. There is a strong community of faith, where the love of God becomes real intellectually as well as spiritually. As a Christian college, Taylor recognizes that all truth has its source in God. The quest for truth begins with this conviction and relates to all aspects of education. Academic pursuits are intensive and demand imagination, dedication, and integrity from students and faculty members alike. The students value the "whole person" educational adventure for which Taylor is well-known. The University prepares young people for meaningful careers and educates them for effective Christian living.

Student activities, which are coordinated by the Student Activities Council, are noted for their excellence and large number. Intercollegiate athletics are offered in eight sports for men and seven for women. There is also an outstanding intramural program. Cocurricular activities include student publications, musical organizations, a University radio station, a TV studio, clubs in nearly every field, and various cultural events. Numerous ministry opportunities are also available. Student services include a counseling center, a career-development program, and a student-orientation program, which carries credit.

The current enrollment on the Upland campus is more than 1,875; more than 400 students are on the Fort Wayne campus. Eighty-one percent live in residence halls. Approximately 65 percent of Taylor's students are from out of state.

Location

Taylor University has two locations. Taylor University's Upland campus covers 250 acres and is located 65 miles north of Indianapolis and 45 miles south of Fort Wayne. Taylor University's Fort Wayne campus is located on 32 acres in a historic residential neighborhood of Indiana's second-largest city.

Majors and Degrees

Baccalaureate majors are offered in the following areas: accounting, art, biblical literature, biology (one concentration area), biology science education, business administration, chemistry (two concentration areas), chemistry–environmental science, Christian education, communication arts education, communication studies, computer engineering, computer graphic arts, computer science (five concentration areas), economics, elementary education, engineering physics, English (nonteaching major with two concentration areas), English education, environmental biology, French, history, individual goal-oriented studies, international business, international studies (eight concentration areas), mass communication, mathematics, mathematics–environmental science, math science education, music (five concentration areas), music education, natural science (one concentration area), philosophy, physical education (six concentration areas), physics (one concentration area), physics–environmental science, physics science education, political science, psychology, science-biology, science-chemistry, science-math, science-physics, social studies, social work, sociology (four concentration areas), Spanish, sport management, theater arts, and wellness. Preprofessional programs include engineering, law, medical technology, medicine, and theology. Associate of Arts degrees are offered in business administration, early childhood education, liberal arts, and management information systems. Certificates may be earned in the areas of coaching, missions, religious studies, and youth ministry.

Academic Program

Taylor University offers programs leading to the Bachelor of Arts degree, Bachelor of Science degree, Bachelor of Music degree, Associate of Arts degree, and preprofessional training. Each student selects a major and meets the requirements for the chosen course of study. In addition, every student meets general requirements and may select from electives to complete his or her studies. A foreign language is required of students pursuing the Bachelor of Arts degree. The Bachelor of Arts and Bachelor of Music degrees may by augmented with education, environmental science, and/or systems analysis. Most Bachelor of Science degree programs are only available when combined with education, environmental science, and/or systems analysis. Only one degree is awarded for each major. A minimum of 128 hours is required for a baccalaureate degree. The Associate of Arts degree requires a minimum of 64 hours, including 30 hours of general education.

Several special programs are available. Students of high ability are eligible to apply for admission to the honors program. Normally, a beginning freshman who wishes to enter this program should have earned at least a 3.7 high school average, ranked in the top 10 percent of his or her class, and had a combined SAT I score of at least 1300. Students may also apply to enter the honors program at any time during their freshman or sophomore year. Students with clearly defined personal or professional goals may—with the help of an adviser—design an individualized, goal-oriented major from the existing curriculum in lieu of one of the traditional majors.

The purpose of the Science Research Training Program (SRTP) is to provide students with undergraduate research projects in various disciplines that promote scientific presentations and publications leading to partnership projects with the national research community and future graduate study. The SRTP encourages scholarly research and crossover interactions between various disciplines and promotes publication in select professional journals by Taylor University faculty members and students. Taylor has research contracts with the National Aeronautics and Space Administration (NASA), National Science Foundation (NSF), Office of Naval Research (ONR), Air Force, and the Council on Undergraduate Research and is a member of the Indiana Space Grant Consortium.

The University awards credit for acceptable scores on Advanced Placement, CLEP, college proficiency examinations, and International Baccalaureate programs. Students may use a limited number of these credits to complete their college degree in 3 to 3½ years.

The University operates on a 4-1-4 academic calendar. A January interterm that lasts 3½ weeks features experimental and conventional courses. In addition, two summer sessions are offered for a total of nine weeks.

Off-Campus Arrangements

Opportunities for travel and course study are regularly available for students who wish to accompany professors going to Asia, Europe, Israel, Greece, Albania, Latin America, Ireland, India, Zimbabwe, and the Bahamas. Taylor University is affiliated with AuSable Institute of Environmental Studies in Mancelona, Michigan, where students may take summer courses for credit. Taylor is also affiliated with the Christian Center for Urban Studies (CCUS) located in Chicago. Through its affiliation with the Coalition of Christian Colleges and Universities, Taylor provides an opportunity for students to study in the following areas: American Studies Program, Washington, D.C.; Latin

American Studies Program, San Jose, Costa Rica; Summer Institute of Journalism; Middle East Studies Program, Cairo, Egypt; the Russian Studies Program, Moscow, St. Petersburg, and Nizhni Novgorod; China Studies Program, Beijing; Oxford Honors Program, Keble College of the University of Oxford; or the Los Angeles Film Studies Center. In addition, students may spend one semester on the campus of another coalition college without formally transferring. Taylor maintains an affiliation with Jerusalem University College in Israel. Taylor has also established exchange programs with Lithuania Christian College and the Royal Institute of Technology in Stockholm. There is a consortium agreement between Hong Kong Baptist University and Taylor University providing fall and spring semester study opportunities. There is an exchange program with Daystar University in Nairobi, Kenya, through the Christian College Consortium. Taylor students participate in study during January interterm at the Heart Institute in Lake Wales, Florida, and at Oak Ridge Institute for Science and Education in Oak Ridge, Tennessee.

Academic Facilities

Taylor operates an extensive computing network utilizing Windows NT, Windows 95–98, and Digital's Open/VMS running on a series of Intel-based servers and DEC's Alpha hardware platform. Each residence hall on the Upland campus has been wired so that the Taylor network and Internet access is available from each student's room. In addition, extensive networking to all academic and administrative buildings provides full network access from virtually all offices on both campuses. General-purpose and specialized computer labs are available throughout both campuses. Taylor maintains a high-speed connection to the Internet and operates its own external Web server to disseminate information regarding the University. In addition to the Internet, there is an active and expanding Intranet system that presents Web-based information throughout the institution. Taylor also has moved to a leading-edge voice/video/data network implementing a high-speed connection between the two campuses that includes an integrated voice system as well as videoconferencing facilities used by faculty members, students, and staff members.

Professional quality radio and TV production facilities are enhanced by 3-chip cameras and a postproduction editing suite with ¾-time-code editing. The science center, which contains laboratories, a greenhouse, and the computing center, serves students majoring in biology, chemistry, computer science, mathematics, and physics. The liberal arts building houses an Educational Technology Center. The University library has 192,000 volumes, 700 current periodicals, and sixteen newspapers and houses the Learning Support Center. In addition, Taylor's library belongs to national networks and features an online catalog for electronic searching for all private colleges and universities in Indiana. Taylor also provides online access to thousands of databases, including major library holdings around the world. The music center has a recital hall, practice rooms, and a band rehearsal room. The state-of-the-art Randall Center for Environmental Studies, which sits on the edge of Taylor's 65-acre arboretum, houses fully equipped spatial analysis and biotic analysis labs used for classroom instruction and individual research projects.

Costs

Tuition and fees for 2000–01 are $15,820. Room and board are $4740 a year. The cost for books is approximately $600, and incidental expenses are estimated at $1400.

Financial Aid

Scholarships, grants, loans, work-study, and church matching grants are available for students who need assistance in meeting college expenses. Merit scholarships are available to incoming freshmen. In addition, nearly 600 employment opportunities are available through the University. Nearly 79 percent of Taylor's students receive some form of financial aid.

Faculty

The faculty consists of 132 full-time and 31 part-time professors; 72 percent have earned a terminal degree. Faculty members are academically recognized, personally committed to the authority of Scripture, and available to and involved with students. The student-faculty ratio is 16:1.

Student Government

The Taylor Student Organization (TSO) has several branches: the president, the Student Senate, the Student Activities Council, the Student Services Council, the Multi Cultural Cabinet, the Interclass Council, the Finance Committee, the Press Services Board, and Leadership Services.

Admission Requirements

Applicants to Taylor should have studied 4 years of high school English, 3 to 4 years of college-preparatory mathematics, 3 to 4 years of laboratory science, and 2 years of social sciences. Two years of a foreign language are strongly recommended. In addition, applicants should have graduated from an accredited secondary school in the upper 40 percent of their class, have at least a B average, and present satisfactory standardized test scores (ACT or SAT I). Past freshman classes have averaged a 3.6 GPA with test scores of 1200 SAT I and 26 ACT. Recommendations from a guidance counselor and the student's pastor and a commitment to adhere to Taylor's Life Together Covenant are also required. International applicants must present satisfactory SAT I scores or achieve five General Certificate of Education (GCE) 0 levels of grade C or above.

Application and Information

All application materials (including interview) should be received in the Admissions Office by January 15. Students whose applications are received by this priority date are notified of an admission decision by February 15. However, applicants who demonstrate exceptional academic ability or qualify for reserved positions in select areas and meet all admissions requirements may be offered admission on a rolling basis throughout the fall. Therefore, candidates are strongly encouraged to apply as early as possible following the completion of their junior year. All students must complete an official campus visit or a personal interview by January 15.

For further information, students should contact:
Director of Admissions
Taylor University
236 West Reade Avenue
Upland, Indiana 46989-1001
Telephone: 765-998-5134
        800-882-3456 (toll-free)
E-mail: admissions_u@tayloru.edu
World Wide Web: http://www.tayloru.edu

The Taylor tradition: scholarship, leadership, and Christian commitment.

TEIKYO POST UNIVERSITY
WATERBURY, CONNECTICUT

The University

Founded in 1890, Teikyo Post University is a globally focused, private, coeducational, residential institution. The University is accredited by the New England Association of Schools and Colleges. In 1990, the former Post College became affiliated with the Teikyo University Group, which resulted in a name change and a dramatically enlarged mission and scope. Teikyo Post University's mission centers around four fundamental themes: globalization, restructuring the economy around information and knowledge, technology, and collaboration.

As a small, private university, Teikyo Post has the time and resources to take a personal interest in every student. The University is dedicated to providing a cohesive global environment in which more than 1,200 students from the United States and thirty countries learn to become knowledgeable participants in the global marketplace. While participating in a close and caring University community, students learn to appreciate attitudes and cultures through classes, course offerings, activities, and one-on-one relationships with faculty members and peers. Approximately half of Teikyo Post University's students live on campus in one of the five residence halls. Twenty percent of the student body are international students.

The 70-acre campus is a safe, comfortable, and pleasant environment for learning. The Leever Student Center houses a dining facility, student service offices, and a student lounge. The Teikyo Post student activities calendar is filled with options and opportunities. Local civic, religious, and professional organizations bring forums, seminars, lectures, exhibits, shows, and other events to the University. Clubs and activities abound, and day trips are often scheduled to New York City and Boston.

Teikyo Post students participate in a year-round schedule of intercollegiate and intramural athletic activities. The Teikyo Post University Eagles are members of the National Collegiate Athletic Association (NCAA) Division II and the New England Collegiate Conference (NECC). Men's intercollegiate sports teams include baseball, basketball, cross-country, and soccer. Women's athletics include basketball, cross-country, soccer, softball, and volleyball. The University also sponsors an active, coeducational equestrian team. Intramural sports are diverse, ranging from softball and volleyball to basketball and flag football. Students enjoy the facilities of the Drubner Conference and Fitness Center, including a gymnasium, a swimming pool, tennis and racquetball courts, a fitness club, and weight training rooms. The Drubner Conference and Fitness Center also houses the campus bookstore.

Location

Located midway between New York City and Boston, Teikyo Post University's 70-acre campus in the hills outside suburban Waterbury, Connecticut, offers a variety of opportunities for social, cultural, and recreational activities.

Majors and Degrees

Teikyo Post offers four undergraduate degrees: the Bachelor of Arts, the Bachelor of Science, the Associate in Arts, and the Associate in Science.

The Division of Business Administration offers the Bachelor of Science degree with majors in accounting, criminal justice, equine management, integrated business, international business, legal assistant studies, management, management information systems, and marketing. The Associate in Science degree is offered with majors in accounting, equine studies, general business management, legal assistant studies, management, and marketing. The School of Arts and Sciences offers the Bachelor of Science in environmental science and general studies and the Bachelor of Arts with majors in English, environmental studies, history, psychology, and sociology; the Associate in Arts in liberal arts; and the Associate in Science with majors in early childhood education, equine studies, and general studies. Advising in course selection for a prelaw concentration is also available.

Academic Program

To receive an associate degree from Teikyo Post, students must complete a minimum of 60 credit hours. For the bachelor's degree, students must complete a minimum of 120 credit hours.

As an institution offering both four-year and two-year programs, Teikyo Post provides associate degree students with three options upon graduation: pursue a career in their field of study, remain at the University in the Bachelor of Science or Bachelor of Arts degree program, or transfer to another four-year college or university.

All programs offer opportunities for internships and cooperative education. For students seeking additional academic challenges, the Teikyo Post University Honors Program offers the opportunity to pursue independent research and special projects under the guidance of a faculty member.

The University has a two-semester calendar.

Off-Campus Arrangements

Teikyo Post University, as a member of the Teikyo University Group, offers several study-abroad programs for interested students, including a semester abroad in either Berlin, Germany, Cracow, Poland, or Maastricht, the Netherlands; or a summer-study program in Tokyo, Japan. The equine management program offers a study-abroad option in England. Through these programs, students have an opportunity to broaden their perspective and experience. Courses taken abroad are accepted for degree credit at Teikyo Post University.

To qualify for study abroad, a student must have a cumulative grade point average of 2.0 or better at the time of attendance.

Academic Facilities

All classroom buildings are equipped with the facilities necessary for the applied arts and sciences, business, and liberal arts curricula. The Academic Computer Center houses microcomputers to serve all components of the academic curriculum. The Center is open to all students who use the facility for course assignments, simulations, and special projects. The Harold Leever Center for Learning Alternatives provides learning systems structured to meet the needs of individual students. A media-equipped Programmed Auto Learning Systems Laboratory (PALS Lab) is an integral part of this program. The PALS Lab is a unique, self-paced, and widely diverse facility giving instructional support to the center's program by providing supplementary and review materials through the use of audiovisual software, media equipment, and innovative use of computer-assisted instruction. The Traurig Library and

Learning Resource Center has a capacity of more then 45,000 volumes and a growing media collection. As a government document depository, the library houses an extensive government publications collection. University-wide Internet access is available. Students majoring in the equine area use several nearby facilities.

Costs

For 1999–2000, full-time resident students paid a comprehensive fee of $19,300, covering tuition, most fees, and room and board. For commuting students, this comprehensive fee was $13,125 per year. Equine and laboratory fees, the $40 application fee, and an estimated $500 per year for books and supplies were not included in this basic comprehensive fee.

Financial Aid

Teikyo Post offers financial assistance through the Federal Work-Study, Federal Supplemental Educational Opportunity Grant, Federal Stafford Student Loan, and Federal Perkins Loan programs. Aid is awarded upon evidence of financial need, as determined by the Free Application for Federal Student Aid (FAFSA). In addition, the University has its own scholarship and grant-in-aid programs, both academic and athletic, and participates in all state programs that are applicable. In order to apply for financial assistance, a student must apply for admission and be accepted to Teikyo Post and then submit the FAFSA. An institutional application for financial aid must also be submitted. A student may apply for the Federal Pell Grant by submitting the application directly to the federal government or by submitting the FAFSA.

Faculty

The Teikyo Post faculty has 24 full-time and many part-time members, the majority of whom hold advanced degrees in their respective fields. Faculty members focus on instruction and are involved in all facets of student life. All full-time faculty members serve as academic advisers and maintain weekly office hours for student consultation. The student-faculty ratio is 15:1.

Student Government

Students actively participate in the operation of the University. The Student Government Association (SGA) is the official vehicle for student expression at Teikyo Post University. SGA formulates major recommendations regarding student life on campus, oversees all student organizations, and provides funding for all active clubs. The Student Activities Committee plays an active role in programming and calendar planning. Students are represented on many of the University's standing committees.

Admission Requirements

Teikyo Post University seeks students who will benefit from the University's multicultural atmosphere and welcomes applications from individuals interested in pursuing academic studies. A decision with respect to a candidate's admission is made by the Admissions Committee and is based upon careful evaluation of the student's qualifications. A student who wishes to be considered for admission should provide Teikyo Post with an official copy of the secondary school transcript, a written recommendation from a counselor or teacher, and SAT I or ACT scores. If the candidate holds an equivalency diploma (GED), a copy must be submitted in lieu of a secondary school transcript. International students must submit a minimum TOEFL score of 500 in addition to the requirements listed above. Teikyo Post offers English as a second language to those students who do not meet the minimum TOEFL score requirement. If possible, an interview with an admissions counselor is strongly recommended.

Students interested in transferring to Teikyo Post must submit transcripts from all colleges previously attended. A GPA of at least 2.0 (on a 4.0 scale) is required. Credit may be awarded for grades of C or better. Teikyo Post University accepts a maximum of 90 credits toward the baccalaureate degree and a maximum of 30 credits toward an associate degree.

Application and Information

Students should send an application for admission, accompanied by a nonrefundable application fee of $40. Teikyo Post University accommodates candidates by processing applications on a rolling basis. It is advantageous to file an application as early as possible. This allows the Admissions Committee to give an application the attention it deserves and enables the applicant to prepare for college life. An application is reviewed when all the necessary credentials have been received. Applications are available online at the e-mail address listed below.

Further information may be obtained by contacting:

Office of Admission
Teikyo Post University
800 Country Club Road
P.O. Box 2540
Waterbury, Connecticut 06723-2540
Telephone 203-596-4520
              800-345-2562 (toll-free)
Fax: 203-756-5810
E-mail: tpuadmis@teikyopost.edu
World Wide Web: http://www.teikyopost.edu

The Teikyo Post University campus is lovely year-round.

TEMPLE UNIVERSITY
PHILADELPHIA, PENNSYLVANIA

The University

Students come to Temple University to build their futures. Temple, a state-related institution, is located in Philadelphia. Its reputation for excellence in teaching and research, however, stretches around the world. Temple offers 125 undergraduate, 130 master's, and sixty-five doctoral and professional programs of study on five regional campuses as well as international campuses in Rome and Tokyo. Studies are guided by an excellent faculty whose members include winners of prestigious research and teaching awards.

Temple's Philadelphia-area campuses include the 100-acre main campus, located 2 miles from the city's center. This is where nine of the eleven undergraduate schools and colleges are headquartered. It is also home to performance spaces for theater, music, dance, and film; a large indoor-outdoor athletic complex; the Liacouras Center; and the Learning Center. The Liacouras Center, a recreation, entertainment, and convocation center featuring space for sports, cultural, and educational events, was completed in 1997. In 1999 it was joined by The Learning Center, a four-story hub of computer labs, lounges, smart classrooms, and distance learning sites linking students to educational resources on Temple's campuses, across the country, and around the world.

Temple University-Ambler is Temple's 187-acre suburban home; all undergraduate programs can be started there and fifteen can be taken there in their entirety. Ambler features its own science labs, library and computing center, bookstore, fitness center, pool, and athletic courts, all in a spacious natural setting of woodlands, meadows, formal gardens, and greenhouses. These amenities are integral to the programs in landscape architecture and horticulture, which reside at Ambler. Temple's other local campuses include Tyler, just outside Philadelphia, home to the Tyler School of Art, and the Health Sciences Center, where the College of Allied Health Professions, Temple University Hospital, Temple University School of Medicine, and Temple Dental School are located.

Temple's campuses offer lots to do. On the main campus the calendar is crammed with theater, dance, and music performances as well as movies, guest speakers, and the activities of more than 100 clubs and groups. Sports are available on the individual, intramural, and intercollegiate levels. About 3,000 Temple students live on campus, mostly on the main campus, but at Ambler and Tyler too. Accommodations on the main campus include high-rise residence halls and apartments, and students can choose among coed or single-sex floors. Wellness floors, where residents pledge to follow a healthy lifestyle, have proven very popular.

Location

Philadelphia enhances the Temple experience in many ways. The cultural, commercial, and intellectual life of America's fifth-largest city touches every academic program, providing real-world reference points to sharpen and focus classroom learning. Aside from enhancing education, the region offers a wealth of activities, from the nightlife of Penn's Landing to the enthusiasm of the sports complex in South Philadelphia to the quieter pleasures of the renowned Philadelphia Museum of Art. To keep active, students can ski down a Pocono mountain or wade into the Jersey surf, both within an easy drive of Temple's campuses.

Majors and Degrees

The College of Allied Health Professions (an upper-division college that requires two years of preprofessional study as a prerequisite for admission) offers the Bachelor of Science in communication sciences, health information management, nursing, and occupational therapy.

The Fox School of Business and Management offers the Bachelor of Business Administration in accounting, actuarial science, business administration, business law, computer information sciences, economics, finance, human resource management, international business administration, management, marketing, real estate, risk management and insurance, and statistics.

The School of Communications and Theater offers the Bachelor of Arts in broadcasting-telecommunications and mass media; communications and theater; film and media arts; journalism, public relations, and advertising; and theater.

The College of Education offers the Bachelor of Science in career and technical education in business education, distributive education, industrial arts education, and industrial education; early childhood education and elementary education; secondary education in English/communications, foreign languages, mathematics, science, and social studies.

The College of Engineering offers the Bachelor of Science in Engineering in civil engineering, electrical engineering, and mechanical engineering. The Bachelor of Science is offered in civil engineering/construction technology, electrical engineering technology, environmental engineering technology, general engineering technology, and mechanical engineering technology.

The College of Liberal Arts offers the Bachelor of Arts in African American studies, American studies, anthropology, Asian studies, classics, criminal justice, economics, English, French, geography, German, Hebrew, history, Italian, linguistics, philosophy, political science, Portuguese, psychology, religion, Russian, sociology, Spanish, urban studies, and women's studies.

The Esther Boyer College of Music offers the Bachelor of Music in composition, jazz and commercial music, music history, music therapy, performance (specific instrument or voice), and theory; the Bachelor of Music Education is offered in music education.

The College of Science and Technology offers the Bachelor of Science in biology, chemistry, computer and information sciences, environmental studies, geology, mathematical economics, mathematics, and physics.

The School of Social Administration offers the Bachelor of Social Work degree as well as degrees in health studies.

The School of Tourism and Hospitality Management offers the Bachelor of Science in sport and recreation management and in tourism and hospitality management.

The Tyler School of Art offers the Bachelor of Fine Arts with concentrations in ceramics/glass, fibers, graphic design, metalsmithing, painting, photography, printmaking, and sculpture.

The Architecture Program confers the Bachelor of Architecture and the Bachelor of Science in architecture.

The Department of Landscape Architecture and Horticulture offers two-year Associate of Science degree programs in horticulture and landscape design. Bachelor of Science degree programs are also available in horticulture and landscape architecture.

Academic Program

Temple provides an excellent and affordable education which not only prepares the student for the specific demands of a career, but also enhances understanding of the world and ability to continue learning throughout life.

All students are required to complete the core curriculum, a cross-section of liberal arts courses that form the intellectual foundation of a Temple education. Many first-year students take advantage of Learning Communities—groups of 20 to 30 participants who pursue common studies under the direction of a faculty team. They spend a semester together, taking a few common courses, participating in faculty-led discussion groups, studying together, and taking field trips related to their studies. The Academic Resource Center (ARC) is a home for the many students who have not declared a major and for students interested in graduate or professional programs in health fields. Academically qualified students may seek extra intellectual challenge through the Honors Program, taking about a quarter of their course work in the program's smaller, more demanding classes. The TempleMed Scholars Program offers exceptional students provisional admission to Temple University School of Medicine at the same time they are admitted as undergraduates, contingent on their academic performance in college.

Recognizing that academic credentials are complemented by work experience, Temple has an active Career Development Services office. Career Development Services arranges cooperative education assignments, schedules on-campus interviews with employers and graduate schools, offers employment skills workshops, provides career and graduate school advisement, and maintains a network of thousands of successful Temple alumni.

Off-Campus Arrangements

Temple offers many ways for students to combine travel with study. On the Rome campus, students can take courses in architecture, business, liberal arts, and visual arts, while Temple University Japan, in Tokyo, instructs Japanese and American students in the Japanese language and Asian studies. The Temple Overseas study-abroad program enables students to spend a summer in Paris studying French literature and civilization, in London examining British mass media, or in Ghana learning about West African civilization. The University also participates in exchange programs with the University of Puerto Rico, the University of Hamburg (Germany), the Institut Franco-Americain de Management (Paris), and others.

Academic Facilities

Learning requires information, lots of it, and Temple has it both on shelves and on line. The Samuel Paley Library, the centerpiece of the University library system, contains 1.8 million volumes and 11,000 periodicals, including the Blockson Collection of African-American History and the archives of the *Philadelphia Bulletin.* There are also smaller libraries for individual schools and colleges, departments, and campuses, bringing the total volumes in circulation at Temple to 2.1 million. The University also has fifty-six computer laboratories with the addition of the Learning Center, a four-story facility of classrooms, lounges, and computer laboratories.

Costs

Tuition and fees for the 1999–2000 academic year were $6622 for Pennsylvania residents and $11,740 for out-of-state residents. Room and board for the academic year were $6000.

Financial Aid

Scholarships, grants, loans, and work-study programs are available; 2 out of every 3 Temple students receive financial aid. Four-year academic merit scholarships for talented entering freshman range from $2000 to full tuition. Students need only apply for admission to be eligible for these scholarships. Applicants for need-based aid must file the Free Application for Federal Student Aid (FAFSA). Transfer students must file a financial aid transcript, even if they have received no aid from their previous school.

Faculty

At Temple, faculty members are valued not only for their ability to pursue knowledge, but also to share that knowledge with students. Full-time faculty members teach many introductory courses, and often act as academic advisers; from their first semester students can expect to have contact with the people at the forefront of their fields, winners of prestigious teaching and research awards such as the Lindback, the Golden Apple, the Sowell, the Fulbright, the Guggenheim, the Carnegie, and the National Endowment.

In addition to being superlative teachers and researchers, Temple faculty members are also known for their practical experience. For example, a marketing class may be led by a successful entrepreneur, or music lessons given by a member of the Philadelphia Orchestra. Marine biologists, newspaper editors, published authors, practicing architects, and health-care professionals all bring their expertise to the classroom to enhance students' education.

Student Government

Students may participate in governing Temple on a departmental, collegial, or University level. Temple Student Government advocates students' views to faculty members and the administration regarding University policies and programs through its members' participation in various University committees, both on a voting and nonvoting basis.

Application Requirements

Admissions decisions are based on evidence that applicants have the necessary qualifications for successful work at Temple. An applicant should be a graduate of an accredited secondary school or hold an equivalent diploma earned by completion of the General Educational Development (GED) test. Applicants should also have completed the following distribution of high school credits: 4 years of English, 2 years of mathematics, 2 years of the same foreign language, 1 year of history, 1 year of a laboratory science, and 6 additional academic credits in mathematics, science, history, or a foreign language. Scores on the SAT I or ACT are required. The Tyler School of Art, the Department of Dance, and the Esther Boyer College of Music have additional requirements. The University offers an early admission program for academically qualified high school juniors. Transfer students must submit official copies of high school and college transcripts.

Application and Information

A completed file should contain an application form accompanied by a nonrefundable $35 fee, a secondary school transcript (sent by the student's school), and SAT I or ACT scores. The University has a rolling admission policy; applicants will be notified of the admission decision as soon as possible after all credentials have been received and reviewed.

For additional information, students may contact:

Office of Undergraduate Admissions
Temple University (041-09)
Philadelphia, Pennsylvania 19122-1803
Telephone: 215-204-7200
          888-340-2222 (toll-free)
E-mail: tuadm@vm.temple.edu
World Wide Web: http://www.temple.edu

TENNESSEE STATE UNIVERSITY
NASHVILLE, TENNESSEE

The University

Tennessee State University (founded in 1912) is a multiracial, urban, land-grant university that fulfills its mission of providing education, research, and public service for residents of central Tennessee through myriad academic, cultural, research, service, and professional activities. Students can pursue degrees during the day or in evening courses. The Center for Extended Education and Public Service offers a wide variety of off-campus credit programs, contract credit classes with local employers, noncredit courses, and seminars to serve the expanding educational needs of local business and the professional community. The University also offers graduate programs and is dedicated to providing all students with a strong academic background. The Graduate School offers programs leading to the master's, Educational Specialist, and doctoral degrees. (Information on graduate programs is available from Graduate Admissions at the address given at the end of this description.) It is hoped that students will take full advantage of the University's offerings, use the experiences to serve themselves and society, and continue the institution's tradition of excellence.

The 8,836 students (7,277 undergraduates) currently enrolled at Tennessee State University come from a variety of cultural backgrounds and geographical areas. Although there are seven dormitories (four for women, three for men), a large percentage of students live off campus. Easily accessible public transportation facilitates the commute to either campus. Extracurricular activities include Greek fraternities and sororities, academic societies, drama and dance groups, a concert choir, and marching, jazz, and concert bands. The University has competitive intercollegiate athletic programs in football as well as men's and women's basketball, cross-country, golf, track, and tennis. There are women's programs in softball and volleyball. Intramural sports are also offered. An athletic and convocation complex seats 10,000 for basketball games and assemblies; it also contains a 220-yard indoor track, dance studios, racquetball courts, and a 35-meter swimming pool. The football team won the Ohio Valley Conference Championships in 1998.

Special student services are offered through such resources as a counseling center, reading center, health service center, and career placement center. Tennessee State University is in the midst of a $112-million capital improvement project. The capital project includes seven new buildings and a completely landscaped campus with courtyards, plazas, and a state-of-the-art utility tunnel. The three-story campus center houses student services facilities, including offices for student organizations, admissions and records, and financial aid, and a bookstore and additional recreational facilities.

Location

Nashville is the state capital and the second-largest city in Tennessee. More than 600,000 people live in this thriving center of government, business, industry, and education. Known internationally as "Music City USA," it is the hub of the nation's country music industry. The entertainment and cultural scene does not stop there, however. A performing arts center offers an active schedule of Broadway plays, community theater, films, and performances by professional dance troupes, the Nashville Symphony, and a variety of vocal and instrumental musicians. Nashville also has three professional sports teams. Night spots and restaurants cater to a variety of cultural and ethnic tastes. Nashville's 6,000 acres of public parks and recreational facilities allow for the pursuit of many sports and leisure activities. As the city's only public four-year institution, Tennessee State University occupies an important place in Nashville. Its Main Campus is located in a residential area of the city, providing students with the atmosphere of a neighborly community. The Avon Williams Campus is located in the heart of downtown Nashville, within walking distance of the capitol and the central business district. TSU students and graduates are involved in a wide variety of academic and employment activities throughout the city.

Majors and Degrees

The College of Arts and Sciences offers majors in Africana studies, art, biological sciences, chemistry, computer science, criminal justice, English, foreign languages (French and Spanish), history, mathematics, music, physics, political science, social work, sociology, and speech communications and theater. The College also offers an interdisciplinary degree with concentrations in the humanities, the sciences, and the social sciences. Teacher certification in art, biological sciences, chemistry, elementary education, English, foreign languages, history, mathematics, music, political science, and speech communications and theater is also available. The College awards both the Bachelor of Arts and the Bachelor of Science degrees.

The College of Business offers majors in accounting, business administration, business information systems, and economics and finance and grants the Bachelor of Business Administration degree.

The College of Education certifies students in elementary, special, and secondary education and awards the Bachelor of Science degree to students majoring in health, physical, and recreational education. The Bachelor of Arts degree is also awarded to students who major in psychology.

The College of Engineering and Technology offers Bachelor of Science degree programs in aeronautical and industrial technology, architectural engineering, civil engineering, electrical engineering, and mechanical engineering.

The School of Nursing grants the two-year Associate of Science and four-year Bachelor of Science degrees in nursing. The School of Allied Health Professions offers an Associate of Applied Science degree in dental hygiene and a Bachelor of Science degree to students who major in dental hygiene, health-care administration and planning, medical records administration, medical technology, occupational therapy, respiratory therapy, or speech pathology and audiology. The School of Agriculture and Home Economics offers undergraduate programs leading to the Bachelor of Science degree in agricultural sciences, early childhood education, family and consumer sciences, and hotel and restaurant administration. The Department of Agricultural Sciences offers a bachelor's degree in agricultural sciences with options in agribusiness, agricultural education, agricultural statistics, agronomy, animal science and pre–veterinary medicine, food technology, ornamental horticulture, and resource economics. The Department of Family and Consumer Sciences offers bachelor's degrees in early childhood education and family and consumer sciences, with options in child development and family relationships, clothing and textiles, design, fashion merchandising, foods and nutrition, and food service management. The Department of Hotel and Restaurant Administration offers a curriculum that prepares graduates for career management positions in the hotel, restaurant, and tourism industries.

Academic Program

Tennessee State University operates on a semester calendar and conducts two sessions during the summer. A minimum of 130 credit hours and a 2.0 or higher cumulative GPA are required for graduation. Individual departments may have additional requirements. An honors program, independent study, cooperative education, teacher certification, and the Air Force ROTC program are available. Early admission and advanced standing are offered to qualified students, and credit is given for satisfactory scores on the College-Level Examination Program tests.

The University honors program is designed to provide the challenge and opportunity for the academically superior student to achieve academic excellence. Honors courses require a higher level of achievement than those in the regular curriculum and are restricted to students in the honors program and to those with a B average who are recommended by an adviser or a teacher. Other courses from the regular curriculum may be taken for honors credit.

Off-Campus Arrangements

So that students can receive the practical training necessary for some professions, Tennessee State University has affiliations with several public and private institutions and agencies. The opportunities include a joint-degree program in allied health with Meharry Medical College, clinical training for nursing students through contractual arrangements with local hospitals, student teaching programs with the Metropolitan-Davidson County Public Schools, and field training programs with government agencies for students in social welfare and criminal justice. Students who participate in these programs earn credit toward their degree. The College of Arts and Sciences offers a dual degree in chemistry and pharmacy with Howard University and a dual degree in biology and medicine with Meharry Medical College, as well as co-op and internship experiences.

Academic Facilities

Tennessee State University has two campuses, the Main Campus and the Avon Williams Campus. The Main Campus, located on 450 acres, consists of sixty-five buildings, farmlands, and pastures. The Tennessee State University libraries house 463,621 volumes, 1,272 current periodical subscriptions, 78,185 bound periodicals, 754,955 microfiche, and 14,748 microfilm reels. A CD-ROM LAN serves both libraries with eleven CD databases; additional CD-ROM databases and Dialog services are also available. The Avon Williams Campus is housed in a large, modern building containing a library, a cafeteria, and ample meeting rooms. Parking facilities are adjacent to the building. A full curriculum is offered at this campus during evening hours.

A Learning Resource Center provides multimedia support for both campuses. Students pursuing programs in agriculture, engineering, biological sciences, chemistry, physics, dental hygiene, and nursing have access to fully equipped laboratories. Students also have access to advanced computer equipment and software.

Costs

Costs fall into four areas—maintenance, tuition, room and board, and special fees. In 1999–2000, the maintenance fee for in-state students was $1010 (12 hours). Board plans ranged from $250 to $755 per semester, and room rental costs ranged from $710 to $1350 per semester. The average total cost for a full-time, in-state undergraduate was $3021 per semester ($6042 per year). Out-of-state undergraduates paid tuition of $5147 per semester (including maintenance and special fees) in addition to room and board. Out-of-state students paid an average tuition of $11,158 per year. Average expenses for books, supplies, and personal items were $700 per semester ($1400 per year) for most students.

Financial Aid

The University has a strong commitment to assist students seeking financial aid. The types of aid available include grants, scholarships, loans, and employment. The University participates in the Federal Pell Grant, FSEOG, Federal Perkins Loan, Federal Stafford Student Loan, Federal PLUS loan, Federal Work-Study, and Tennessee Student Assistance Grant programs. Presidential Scholarships, Academic Work Scholarships, University Scholarships, Departmental Scholarships, and several private scholarship programs are also available. The minimum financial aid award is about $200, the average is about $4500, and the maximum is about $10,000. Approximately 80 percent of freshmen receive some type of financial assistance. Students who have a high school GPA of 3.0 or above (on a 4.0 scale) and an ACT score of 21 or above may apply for scholarships.

Prospective students must file the Free Application for Federal Student Aid by April 1 in order to be considered for financial aid. Students are also required to submit a processed Student Aid Report to the Financial Aid Office. All students are urged to apply early.

Faculty

Tennessee State University has a 308-member full-time faculty and a part-time faculty of 170, some of whom teach at both the undergraduate and graduate levels. Eighty percent of the faculty members hold doctoral degrees. The student-faculty ratio is 17:1. Some faculty members, particularly in the areas of agriculture, biological sciences, history, and psychology, are actively involved in research. Faculty members serve as advisers for students majoring in their discipline, and some also serve as advisers for student organizations.

Student Government

The Student Government Association consists of a president, a vice president, class officers, representatives-at-large, and organization representatives, all elected by student vote. The association operates under a formal constitution and is recognized by University administrators as the official voice of students.

Admission Requirements

In-state residents must pass the High School Proficiency Exam and have a high school GPA of 2.25 or better, an ACT score of at least 19, or a minimum SAT I score of 900. Out-of-state residents must have a GPA of 2.5 or better, an ACT score of at least 19, or an SAT I score of at least 900. In addition, students must pass fourteen State Board of Regents high school unit requirements. Scores on the TOEFL are required of international students.

Transfer applicants must submit a transcript from every college attended and must present a minimum grade point average of 2.0. Transfer students usually receive credit for grades of 2.0 and higher in Tennessee State University-equivalent courses taken at approved institutions. At least 30 hours must be completed in residence at Tennessee State University.

Application and Information

Applications should be received by August 1; the fee is $15. Late applications are accepted. Additional information is available from:

Office of Admissions and Records
Tennessee State University
3500 John A. Merritt Boulevard
P.O. Box 9609
Nashville, Tennessee 37209-1561
Telephone: 615-963-5101
World Wide Web: http://www.tnstate.edu

TENNESSEE TECHNOLOGICAL UNIVERSITY
COOKEVILLE, TENNESSEE

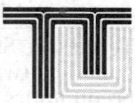

The University

Tennessee Technological University has no typical students, for the present student body is diverse, representing many different backgrounds and groups. Although most students come from Tennessee and the bordering states, there are students from thirty-eight states and twenty-four other countries. The current enrollment consists of 8,554 men and women. Tech students are characterized as friendly and mentally alert; they are confident about their future and concerned about their education. They want to be—among other things—doctors, lawyers, sales representatives, teachers, engineers, and scientists. They want to be useful to society and successful in their chosen fields.

The Graduate School offers programs leading to a master's degree in biology, chemistry, education, engineering, English, and mathematics. In addition, the Education Specialist degree is awarded in the College of Education and the Doctor of Philosophy in the College of Engineering. The M.B.A. degree is also available. Admission to graduate study at Tennessee Tech is on a merit basis and is limited to applicants whose previous study is of sufficient quality and scope to indicate promise of high success as a graduate student. Interested students should write to the dean of the Graduate School for specific information.

Location

Tennessee Tech is located in Cookeville, Tennessee, on the Eastern Highland Rim. The city of Cookeville, with a metropolitan population of about 25,000, offers a cordial welcome to Tennessee Tech students. Churches, theaters, banks, and shopping facilities are easily accessible from the campus, and students are welcome to share in the civic and cultural events of the community.

Situated in one of the most picturesque sections of the southeastern United States, the area abounds in the scenic beauty of hills, lakes, and waterfalls. Several state parks are within a short driving distance. An elevation of 1,140 feet provides a favorable climate the year round.

The Tennessee Tech campus is located on Interstate 40, Highway 111, and Highway 70 North. Modern highways radiate in all directions, and Greyhound Bus Lines furnishes convenient transportation from any point in Tennessee and the Southeast. Nashville is only 1¼ hours away by interstate highway; Knoxville is less than 2 hours away. Major airline service is available from Nashville, Knoxville, and Chattanooga. The White County Regional Airport, located near the campus, provides service for private planes.

Majors and Degrees

Tennessee Technological University offers the Bachelor of Science degree in accounting, agribusiness management, agricultural engineering technology, agricultural environmental agriscience, agriculture education, agronomy and soils, animal science, art education, biochemistry, biology, business management (management information systems, personnel and labor relations, and production and operations management), chemical engineering, chemistry, civil and environmental engineering, computer engineering, computer science (information and systems emphasis and software and scientific applications), early childhood education, economics (through the College of Business or the College of Arts and Sciences), electrical engineering, elementary education, finance, health and physical education, history, human ecology (child and family science, with concentrations in the child and the family; child care services; consumer homemaking education; foods, nutrition, and dietetics, with concentrations in dietetics and food service administration; and merchandising, with concentrations in fashion and design), horticulture, industrial engineering, industrial technology, journalism, marketing, mathematics, mechanical engineering, music education, music therapy, nursery and landscape management, nursing, physics (applied and traditional), political science, psychology, secondary education (biology, chemistry, communications, earth and space science, English, French, German, history, mathematics, physics, professional communications, social science, Spanish, and speech), sociology, special education, and wildlife and fisheries science. Tennessee Tech also offers the Bachelor of Arts in English, foreign language (French, German, and Spanish), and history; the Bachelor of Science in world cultures and business; and the Bachelor of Fine Arts in fine arts.

Strong preprofessional programs in medicine, dental hygiene, dentistry, health information management, medical technology, optometry, pharmacy, and physical therapy are offered through the College of Arts and Sciences. The College of Agriculture offers pre–veterinary medicine and preforestry.

Academic Program

Tennessee Tech continues to demonstrate that values are relevant, that humanity's accumulated knowledge is useful, and that broad, general study can be combined effectively with either specialized preparation for a profession or intensive pursuit of a discipline.

The general requirements for a baccalaureate degree include a major as outlined under the curriculum chosen, a first minor of 18 semester hours, and a second minor of 12 semester hours; a minimum of 132 semester hours, including 36 of junior and senior rank, in approved courses; and a minimum general grade point average of 2.0 (C) and a minimum general average of 2.0 in the courses offered in the major subject. Special course requirements in the humanities and sciences differ according to the degree sought.

The University offers an Army ROTC program on campus. Air Force ROTC is offered in affiliation with Tennessee State University in Nashville.

Off-Campus Arrangements

The voluntary cooperative education program integrates formal class work with practical off-campus experience in all fields. Campus studies and industrial or business assignments are alternated on an annual basis: the first, third, and fifth years involve eight semesters of resident academic study, and the second and fourth years are spent off campus in employment. This program gives students the opportunity early in their educational experience to become involved in work that directly relates to a chosen professional career. The cooperative program normally involves students after the completion of three semesters of academic work; however, upperclass students and transfer students may also apply.

Tennessee Tech is affiliated with the Gulf Coast Research Laboratory in Ocean Springs, Mississippi. This affiliation permits students to enroll in marine biology courses that otherwise would be unavailable so far inland.

Academic Facilities

The Tennessee Tech Library contains 282,875 bound volumes and 100,000 periodicals as well as more than a million microform items. The D. W. Mattson Computer Center houses three Digital Equipment Corporation VAX-11/785 computers, one VAX 8530, one VAX 8800, one VAX-11/750, and one MicroVAX II with a total of approximately 10 gigabytes of disk storage. The facilities of the center are available to any curriculum on campus. Excellent laboratories are furnished for modern languages and for each of the physical sciences. The Learning Resources Center provides students in the College of Education with the best in teaching materials, including microteaching facilities and closed-circuit television. The College of Business Administration houses the Fleetguard Cummins Computer Center and offers training in systems analysis and computer applications in business. The Research Resources Center in the College of Business Administration provides reference material and research support to faculty and students. The School of Human Ecology has a home management laboratory, an arts and crafts laboratory, and a nursery school. A 300-acre farm, including an agricultural pavilion, provides practical training for agriculture majors. Modern engineering laboratories support instruction and research within the Departments of Chemical, Civil, Electrical, Industrial, and Mechanical Engineering, Engineering Science, and Industrial Technology. There are individual practice rooms and auditoriums for the Department of Music, as well as special facilities for physical education, drama, and Army ROTC. The Appalachian Center for Crafts offers courses and experience in such craft areas as wood, clay, fibers, metals, and glass.

Costs

Tuition is free to Tennessee residents. For out-of-state students, 1999–2000 tuition was $255 per semester. Fees were $1095, room and board were $3484, books and supplies cost approximately $350, and the technology access fee was $100 per semester. The total costs were $3287 per semester or $6574 per year for Tennessee residents and $6574 per semester or $12,212 per year for out-of-state students. These costs are subject to change for 2000–01.

Financial Aid

Financial aid includes grants, scholarships, loans, and work-study opportunities. The University participates in the Federal Pell Grant, Federal Work-Study, Federal Perkins Loan, and Tennessee Student Assistance Corporation programs and also offers a variety of private agency scholarships. The minimum financial aid award is $75, the average is $2700, and the maximum is $7800. Of the full-time enrolled students, 75 percent receive some type of financial aid. Applicants for aid are required to file the Free Application for Federal Student Aid (FAFSA). The deadline for application is April 15; notification is on a rolling basis after May 1. Student employment opportunities are available. Financial aid brochures, application forms, and other relevant information may be obtained from the Office of Student Financial Aid.

Faculty

The student-faculty ratio is about 17:1. There are 362 full-time and 98 part-time faculty members, and more than 79 percent hold doctoral degrees from diverse institutions throughout the nation. The graduate faculty also serves at the undergraduate level. The faculty is reasonably active in research and public service, although most members are also active in academic advising, freshman orientation, and student organizations. Limited use is made of well-qualified part-time faculty members, and approximately 15 carefully selected graduate teaching assistants have direct teaching assignments.

Student Government

The Student Government Association (SGA) is composed of all regularly enrolled students at Tennessee Tech. Its purposes are to promote student participation in the affairs of the University, to serve as a channel for the expression of student opinion, to coordinate student activities on campus, to uphold the constitutional liberties and rights and promote the general welfare of all segments of the University community, and to encourage the development of student responsibility, character, leadership, scholarship, and citizenship. The student government organization is composed of the Executive Council, made up of the SGA executive officers and the President's Cabinet; the Student Senate; and the SGA Student Supreme Court. The SGA officers are elected by the entire student population, while members of the senate are elected by the students from the University's various colleges and schools. A weekly luncheon forum, open to every student, offers a lively interchange of ideas among administrators, faculty, and students. Every standing committee of the faculty includes student representatives.

Admission Requirements

Scores on the ACT are required for admission. Applicants must also present a high school transcript showing graduation, or the GED equivalent. Transfer students are welcome. To find out how many previously earned credits can be transferred, the transfer applicant should apply for admission to Tennessee Tech in the regular fashion and have an official transcript of previous college work mailed to the Admissions Office. The official evaluation should be received within two weeks. A student must have a high school academic average of at least 2.35 on a 4.0 scale or have an ACT composite score of 19.

A prefreshman summer program is offered in which high-achieving high school juniors can earn college credit and return to their high schools to graduate. Such students must have the approval of their high school principal and guidance counselor and must have completed 12 or more academic units with at least a B (3.2) average.

Application and Information

Transcripts and test scores must be submitted. The application fee is $15. Students are notified of the admission decision within a few days of the receipt of all materials.

For more information, students should contact:

James R. Rose
Assistant Vice President for Enrollment and Records
Tennessee Technological University
Cookeville, Tennessee 38505
Telephone: 931-372-3888
        800-255-8881 (toll-free)
World Wide Web: http://www.tntech.edu

On the campus of Tennessee Technological University.

TENNESSEE TECHNOLOGICAL UNIVERSITY
College of Engineering
COOKEVILLE, TENNESSEE

The University and The College

Tennessee Technological University has no typical students, for the present student body is diverse, representing many different backgrounds and groups. Although most students come from Tennessee and the bordering states, there are students from thirty-eight states and twenty-four other countries. The current enrollment consists of more than 8,500 men and women (more than 20 percent in engineering). Tech students are characterized as friendly and mentally alert; they are confident about their future and concerned about their education. They want to be—among other things—doctors, lawyers, sales representatives, teachers, engineers, and scientists. They want to be useful to society and successful in their chosen fields.

The undergraduate engineering curricula are accredited by the Engineering Accreditation Commission of the Accreditation Board for Engineering and Technology, Inc. (ABET). The industrial technology curriculum is accredited by the National Association of Industrial Technology (NAIT).

The Graduate School offers programs leading to a master's degree in biology, chemistry, education, engineering, English, and mathematics. In addition, the Education Specialist degree is awarded in the College of Education and the Doctor of Philosophy in the College of Engineering. The M.B.A. degree is also available. Admission to graduate study at Tennessee Tech is on a merit basis and is limited to applicants whose previous study is of sufficient quality and scope to indicate promise of high success as a graduate student. Interested students should write to the dean of the Graduate School for specific information.

Location

Tennessee Tech is located in Cookeville, Tennessee, on the Eastern Highland Rim. The city of Cookeville, with a metropolitan population of about 30,000, offers a cordial welcome to Tennessee Tech students. Churches, theaters, banks, and shopping facilities are easily accessible from the campus, and students are welcome to share in the civic and cultural events of the community.

Situated in one of the most picturesque sections of the southeastern United States, the area abounds in the scenic beauty of hills, lakes, and waterfalls. Several state parks are within a short driving distance. An elevation of 1,140 feet provides a favorable climate the year round.

The Tennessee Tech campus is located on Interstate 40, Highway 111, and Highway 70 North. Modern highways radiate in all directions, and Greyhound Bus Lines furnishes convenient transportation from any point in Tennessee and the Southeast. Nashville is a little more than an hour away by interstate highway; Knoxville is less than 2 hours away. Major airline service is available from Nashville, Knoxville, and Chattanooga. The Upper Cumberland Regional Airport, located near the campus, provides service for private planes.

Majors and Degrees

The College of Engineering includes seven programs with curricula leading to Bachelor of Science degrees in chemical engineering, civil engineering, computer engineering, electrical engineering, industrial engineering, mechanical engineering, and industrial technology.

Academic Program

The principal mission is to offer the strong academic program needed to prepare students to become educated members of society who can join the engineering profession and to provide the opportunity for students to prepare for graduate studies. The undergraduate program is structured to provide an education consisting of mathematics, basic sciences, engineering sciences, engineering design, humanities, and social sciences that is consistent with accreditation standards and national needs.

A uniform first-year curriculum (34 semester hours) is provided by the basic engineering program, allowing sufficient time for the student to select a field of specialization. Each department requires an additional 100 to 102 semester hours. Most of the hours are specified core courses that provide a structured, well-rounded background within the degree programs. Elective courses are also included in the programs to provide greater depth in areas of specialty.

The normal load in the engineering and industrial technology curricula is approximately 17 semester hours. Students may enroll for lighter loads or co-op, which results in an increase in the number of semesters necessary to complete the requirements for graduation.

The general requirements for the baccalaureate degree include the completion of the curriculum for the major subject chosen with a minimum general grade point average of 2.0 (C) and a minimum average of 2.0 (C) in the courses offered in the major subject. The programs for civil, computer, electrical, industrial, and mechanical engineering require each student to take the Fundamentals of Engineering Examination administered by the Tennessee State Board of Architecture and Engineering Examiners.

Off-Campus Arrangements

The voluntary cooperative education program integrates formal class work with practical off-campus experience in all fields. Campus studies and industrial or business assignments are alternated on an annual basis: the first, third, and fifth years involve eight semesters of resident academic study, and the second and fourth years are spent off campus in employment. An alternating semester work plan is also available. This program gives students the opportunity early in their educational experience to become involved in work that directly relates to a chosen professional career. The cooperative program normally involves students after the completion of three semesters of academic work; however, upperclass students and transfer students may also apply.

Academic Facilities

The Tennessee Tech Library contains 300,000 bound volumes and 100,000 periodicals as well as more than a million microform items. The computer center houses several computer systems manufactured by Digital Equipment Corporation. These systems include a VAX 7620, an AlphaServer 4100 5/466, and two AXP 3000-M600s. The center also has terminals, workstations, and microcomputers. A campuswide Ethernet local area network makes computing services available using fiber-optic media. Modern engineering laboratories support instruction and research within the Departments of Chemical, Civil, Electrical and Computer, Industrial, and Mechanical Engineering and Industrial Technology. In addition to the labs in the computer center, each engineering building has its own computer lab with state-of-the-art hardware and software. The University also has a student fitness center to encourage physical conditioning in addition to the daily mental training.

Costs

The total estimated 2000–01 costs are $9000 for Tennessee residents and $14,400 for out-of-state students. Out-of-state students must also pay tuition of $5400. Fees are $2590; room and board are $4170; and books, supplies, and other miscellaneous items are $2240.

Financial Aid

Financial aid includes grants, scholarships, loans, and work-study opportunities. The University participates in the Federal Pell Grant, Federal Work-Study, Federal Perkins Loan, and Tennessee Student Assistance Corporation programs and also offers a variety of private agency scholarships. The minimum financial aid award is $75 and the average is $2700. Of the full-time enrolled students, 75 percent receive some type of financial aid. Applicants for aid are required to file the Free Application for Federal Student Aid (FAFSA). The deadline for application is April 15; notification is on a rolling basis after May 1. Student employment opportunities are available. Financial aid brochures, application forms, and other relevant information may be obtained from the Office of Student Financial Aid.

In late February of each year, the College provides an opportunity for prospective students (high school and transfer) to compete in the Engineering Scholarship Awards Program by taking an examination. Based on the results of the exam, about $200,000 in scholarships are awarded to those with the top scores, including special minority scholarships. Numerous scholarships are also available to upperclass students through the departments and the College.

Faculty

The engineering student-faculty ratio is about 22:1. There are 70 full-time and 6 part-time engineering faculty members, and more than 90 percent hold doctoral degrees from diverse institutions throughout the nation. The graduate faculty also serves at the undergraduate level. The faculty is reasonably active in research and public service, although most members are also active in academic advising, freshman orientation, and student organizations. Limited use is made of well-qualified part-time faculty members, and a few carefully selected graduate teaching assistants have direct teaching assignments.

Student Government

The Student Government Association (SGA) is composed of all regularly enrolled students at Tennessee Tech. Its purposes are to promote student participation in the affairs of the University, to serve as a channel for the expression of student opinion, to coordinate student activities on campus, to uphold the constitutional liberties and rights and promote the general welfare of all segments of the University community, and to encourage the development of student responsibility, character, leadership, scholarship, and citizenship. The student government organization is composed of the Executive Council, made up of the SGA executive officers and the President's Cabinet; the Student Senate; and the SGA Student Supreme Court. The SGA officers are elected by the entire student population, while members of the senate are elected by the students from the University's various colleges and schools. A weekly luncheon forum, open to every student, offers a lively interchange of ideas among administrators, faculty, and students. Every standing committee of the faculty includes student representatives.

Admission Requirements

Scores on the ACT are required for admission. Applicants must also present a high school transcript showing graduation, or the GED equivalent. Transfer students are welcome. To find out how many previously earned credits can be transferred, the transfer applicant should apply for admission to Tennessee Tech in the regular fashion and have an official transcript of previous college work mailed to the Admissions Office. The official evaluation should be received within several weeks. In addition to meeting the requirements for admission to the University, students seeking admission to an engineering major must have at least a 2.35 high school average and both a composite score and a mathematics subtest score of at least 20 on the enhanced ACT. It is advisable for basic engineering students to complete 4 units of science and at least 3½ units of college-preparatory mathematics, including a study of trigonometric identities.

A prefreshman summer program is offered in which high-achieving high school juniors and sophomores are introduced to the world of engineering and related career opportunities. Such students must be in the upper 20 percent of their math/science classes and be recommended by their school faculty.

Application and Information

Transcripts and test scores must be submitted. The application fee is $15. Students are notified of the admission decision within a few days of the receipt of all materials.

For more information, students should contact:
Admissions Office
Tennessee Technological University
Cookeville, Tennessee 38505
Telephone: 931-372-3888
  800-255-8881 (toll-free)
World Wide Web: http://www.tntech.edu

On the campus of Tennessee Technological University.

TEXAS A&M UNIVERSITY AT GALVESTON
GALVESTON, TEXAS

The University

At Texas A&M University at Galveston (TAMUG), the ocean is our classroom. Ocean voyages, sailing in Galveston Bay, beachfront experiments, and independent study complement the rigorous classroom experience at the "island campus."

The by-the-sea campus environment complements the distinctive curricular offerings. The atmosphere fostered by the faculty, staff, and students emphasizes the intimate relationship between the University and the sea.

TAMUG is recognized nationally for academic excellence. The ocean-oriented academic programs are accredited regionally and professionally. The quality of instruction has consistently scored a high national ranking in the Gourman Report and by *U.S. News & World Report*, which not only ranks TAMUG among the best small liberal arts and sciences colleges west of the Mississippi River but also lists TAMUG as a "best buy." TAMUG engineering programs are ranked in the top fifty in the U.S. in this report.

A common trait of all TAMUG students is a desire to work and study in an ocean environment. Enrollment at TAMUG increased from 551 students in 1987 to more than 1,300 students in 2000. Students are from forty-nine different states and the District of Columbia. Science and engineering majors comprise 75 percent of the student body; 49 percent of the study body are women, and about 50 percent reported themselves in the top 20 percent of their high school classes. Fifty-seven percent plan to pursue a master's or Ph.D. degree, and about 65 percent receive some type of financial aid.

The Corps of Cadets at Texas A&M University at Galveston provides students with opportunities in the U.S. Navy, the U.S. Coast Guard, and the American Merchant Marine. The campus houses the Texas Maritime Academy, which is one of five seacoast maritime academies in the U.S. that prepares graduates for licensing as officers aboard U.S. flag ships.

Outdoor facilities include tennis, basketball, and sand volleyball courts; a swimming pool; intramural athletic fields; and a fleet of small sail and power boats.

Location

The island location of the campus on Galveston Bay and near the open ocean is in symmetry with the ocean-oriented academic programs offered at TAMUG. The Mitchell Campus, situated on the Galveston harbor and close to the confluence of the Galveston and Houston ship channels, has immediate access to the ocean and to estuarine areas, including Galveston Bay. The Port of Galveston and the Port of Houston are nearby, as are many Gulf Coast industries.

Campus life is enhanced by the cultural and social activities in Galveston. Galveston Island was once the financial center of the South. Today, the city has become a major tourist center with a strong representation of marine and maritime interests. College dances have been held in the Ashton Villa Ballroom (a restored 1859 mansion), in the Garten Verein (a restored octagonal dancing pavilion in Kempner Park), and aboard the *Elissa* and the *Colonel*.

The Grand 1894 Opera House, the Lone Star Amphitheater, and other local theaters allow TAMUG students involvement in theater events. The new Moody Gardens Conference Center contains the Southwest's finest 3-D MAX theater, a discovery museum, and a unique tropical garden pyramid biome. The city has several historical districts, museums, and musical groups, including the Galveston Symphony Orchestra and the Galveston Beach Band.

Majors and Degrees

TAMUG offers ocean-oriented four-year courses of study, with excellent programs in business, oceanographic/physical sciences, biological sciences, engineering, and transportation. Degrees are awarded by Texas A&M University.

Academic Program

Computer science and technical writing courses are taught across curricula, regardless of a student's major field. In every course each semester, formally administered questionnaires invite students to appraise the effectiveness of teaching. Several unique courses have been developed in response to the University's marine orientation. For instance, "Literature of the Sea" examines the sea through the work of great authors. "Introduction to Marine Sciences" introduces students to a number of disciplines through lectures, seminars, and industry contacts. The geography course taught aboard the summer cruise emphasizes the ports being visited.

The Texas Maritime Academy provides an opportunity for students to learn how to operate and maintain an oceangoing vessel. In addition to classroom and field training during the regular school year, students sail aboard a training vessel during three summer cruises to gain practical experience in seamanship, navigation, and operations.

The Naval Reserve Officer Training Corps (NROTC) Program offers men and women an opportunity to qualify for a commission in the Navy while attending TAMUG. All NROTC students are required to participate in the U.S. Maritime Service Corps of Cadets and may qualify for licensing as a Third Mate or Third Assistant Engineer. Any student may join the NROTC Program either as a National Scholarship winner or as a nonsubsidized college program student. A similar program, the Marine Academy Reserve Training Program (MARTP), provides maritime students the opportunity to participate in the U.S. Coast Guard Reserve and earn a commission upon graduation.

Off-Campus Arrangements

Each summer, the *Texas Clipper II* (with its complement of about 240 cadets and faculty and staff members) sails to exotic ports of call. Cruises are varied to include Northern Europe, the Caribbean, the Mediterranean, and the United States. At the conclusion of the program, cadets are tested to become licensed officers in the U.S. Merchant Marine and may seek employment in the exciting field of marine transportation as a licensed Third Mate or Third Assistant Engineer.

The Summer School at Sea program allows entering freshmen to take their first college credits at sea during the summer cruise of the *Texas Clipper II*. This program is open to students who have just completed high school. These students, known as prep cadets, have the opportunity to experience the cruise without actually entering the Corps as a part of their curriculum.

Students in science programs may have the opportunity to study in Belize, where TAMUG researchers conduct an ongoing coral reef study. Biospeleology students may travel to Mexico to study the biology of cave organisms.

Academic Facilities

Housed at the Mitchell Campus are a fleet of vessels, ranging from the 48-foot *Roamin' Empire* to the 394-foot training ship *Texas Clipper II*,, to smaller power and sail boats. These floating classrooms and laboratories perform a variety of educational services. On board these vessels, students learn seamanship, research techniques, and the practical application of theory.

The Mitchell Campus includes three dormitories, classroom and laboratory buildings, the Jack K. Williams Library, and the Mary Moody Northen Student Center. The physical education facility houses weight training, aerobic, and racquetball facilities as well as classrooms and a gymnasium.

The Jack K. Williams Library has 27,000 square feet of space, with seating for 200 people. An online public access catalog and a computerized card catalog system allow students to access the library from any computer terminal and many personal computers on campus.

Texas A&M University at Galveston is computer intensive. The Learning Resource Center in the library provides microcomputers and computer terminals for student use.

The campus provides a state-of-the-art ship-handling simulator for training maritime students. This new training capability complements the real-world radar and diesel simulation training that has been available at TAMUG for several years.

In addition to being a floating campus during summer cruises, the 394-foot training ship *Texas Clipper II* provides classroom, meeting, and training space during the school year.

Costs

Texas residents pay an estimated $3400 per semester for room, board, tuition, and fees for an average load of 15 credit hours. Tuition is $40 per semester credit hour for Texas residents and $251 per semester credit hour for nonresidents. Members of the U.S. Maritime Service Corps of Cadets pay $50 per semester credit hour regardless of state residency.

Financial Aid

Approximately 65 percent of all full-time students receive some type of financial aid in the form of scholarships, grants, loans, work-study, or any combination of these. In addition, students in the Corps of Cadets may qualify for student incentive payments of $3000 per year. All applicants for federal or state financial aid are required to file the Free Application for Federal Student Aid (FAFSA).

Faculty

Eighty-two percent of TAMUG's faculty members hold doctoral degrees or the equivalent. The student-faculty ratio is 12:1. Faculty and staff members participate in student-sponsored social events, athletic competitions, and cultural events. In addition, frequent field trips, weekend training, research exercises, and ocean voyages give students and faculty members a close association rarely found at the university level of education.

Student Government

A Student Senate, with members elected from each class, represents the students and provides a student forum for interaction with the University administration. Campus clubs include the Caving Club, Dive Club, Student Life Organization, Propeller Club, Sail Club, Surf Club, Endangered Species Club, Volleyball Club, engineering societies, Women's Maritime Association, and Drama Club, which produces two plays annually.

Admission Requirements

For admission information, students should contact the Student Relations Office at the address below or by telephoning 1-87-SeaAggie (toll-free). Applicants must have a high school counselor or registrar forward an official transcript to the Office of Admissions and Records. Scores on either the SAT (code 6835) or ACT (code 6592) should be forwarded to Texas A&M University at Galveston.

Application and Information

To obtain an enrollment packet or to schedule a campus visit, students should contact:

Student Relations Office
Texas A&M University at Galveston
P.O. Box 1675
Galveston, Texas 77553-1675
Telephone: 87-SEA-AGGIE (toll-free)
E-mail: seaaggie@tamug.tamu.edu
World Wide Web: http://www.tamug.tamu.edu

Texas A&M University at Galveston marine biology students intern at Sea World of San Antonio during the Christmas break.

TEXAS CHRISTIAN UNIVERSITY
FORT WORTH, TEXAS

The University

Texas Christian University (TCU) is a major teaching and research institution with the student-centered atmosphere typical of small colleges. The University encourages personal growth and leadership in both academic and extracurricular activities. Founded on the cattle frontier in 1873, TCU is an independent, self-governing institution related to the Christian Church (Disciples of Christ); however, student participation in religious activity is voluntary. TCU is a member of leading educational organizations that require the highest standards of program, faculty, facilities, and resources. Phi Beta Kappa, Sigma Xi, and Mortar Board have active chapters on campus. Research-oriented Ph.D. programs are offered in chemistry, divinity, English, history, physics, and psychology.

TCU enrolls about 6,000 full-time undergraduate men and women. Facilities and services include sixteen residence halls that house about 3,000 students (each room has two telephone, cable, and Internet connection lines), three cafeterias, a sub sandwich shop, a coffee bar, a student center, a campus store and post office, a forty-two-bed health center with 3 full-time physicians, a professional counseling center, a multidenominational campus ministry, a recreation center that includes two large gymnasiums, two sand volleyball courts, ten handball courts, a swimming and diving pool, and thirty-one tennis courts. The University competes in NCAA Division I. It sponsors intramural and extramural sports programs. Frequent musical and theatrical events are also offered. Students publish an award-winning newspaper and magazine and operate an FM radio station. Most students participate in at least one of the 209 campus organizations.

Location

TCU is 4 miles southwest of downtown Fort Worth, which is 30 miles west of Dallas. The campus is spread comfortably over 237 landscaped acres in a residential neighborhood.

Fort Worth has retained a traditional Southwestern friendliness while growing into a city of more than 465,000. Its winters are mild; its air is clean. Nearly 5,000 wooded acres in more than a hundred parks (two of which begin four blocks from TCU's campus) and a dozen nearby lakes invite outdoor activity. Thirty miles of interstate connect the downtowns of Fort Worth and more urban Dallas, the hubs of a metropolitan area of 2.5 million people that offers an immense variety of recreational, cultural, professional, spiritual, and service opportunities. Both cities have nationally known museums and professional symphonies, operas, theaters, ballets, and choruses. Twenty institutions of higher learning are located in the area. There are professional football, baseball, soccer, basketball, hockey, and rodeo events.

Majors and Degrees

Programs lead to fourteen bachelor's degrees in more than eighty major areas: advertising/public relations; allied-health professions (athletic training, pre-occupational therapy*, pre-physical therapy*, and pre-physician's assistant studies*); art (art history; art education; studio, with concentrations in ceramics, painting, photography, and sculpture); astronomy; ballet; biology; broadcast journalism; business (with concentrations in accounting, electronic business, finance, management, and marketing, all of which are available with an international emphasis); chemistry; communication sciences and disorders (speech-language-pathology and habilitation of the deaf); computer science; computer information science; criminal justice; design, merchandising, and textiles (fashion merchandising, fashion promotion, interior design, and interior merchandising); dietetics; economics; education (with majors in education of elementary students, education of exceptional students, education of young children, and mathematics; science education and certification in elementary, secondary, and all-level; and endorsements in early childhood and English as a second language); engineering (electrical and mechanical); English; environmental sciences; environmental earth resources; food management; foreign languages; general studies; geology; graphic design; health and fitness; history; international communications (with emphases in advertising/public relations and news); journalism (news-editorial and broadcast journalism); Latin-American studies; liberal studies; lighting for visual presentation (minor); mathematics; modern dance; modern languages and literature (majors in French and Spanish and minors in German, Japanese, and Russian); movement science; music (performance, piano pedagogy, theory/composition, music history; church music, and music education); neuroscience; nursing; nutrition; philosophy; physical education; physics; political science (with an emphasis in international relations); pre-health professions (pre-dentistry, pre-medicine, pre-optometry, pre-podiatry, and pre-veterinary); pre-law; psychology; radio-TV-film (production, criticism, and industry); ranch management (certification); religion; Reserve Officers' Training Corps (ROTC) (aerospace studies (Air Force) or military science (Army)); social work; sociology; Spanish; Spanish with concentration on teaching; speech communication (communication in human relations, and communication studies); sports and recreation; theater (performance, production, and theater and television); women's studies (minor). Programs that are indicated by * are those programs that are begun at TCU and completed elsewhere.

Preprofessional programs are available in dentistry, law, and medicine. A 3-2 program leading to the M.B.A. is also available. There is a certificate program in ranch management; other certificate programs are available through the Office of Extended Education.

Academic Program

TCU specializes in a liberal arts education that strives to expose students to the world around them. Within the University requirements generally completed during the first two years, students have wide choices in the humanities, natural sciences, social sciences, fine arts, religion, and physical education. Emphasis is placed on writing skills and critical and evaluative thinking.

Departmental requirements vary according to the degree sought. Generally, the B.A. is built on a major of 24 hours and a minor of 18; the B.S. and most other bachelor's degrees are usually built on heavier concentrations in a single field and/or studies related to that area. Some degree programs are highly structured and specify most courses that are not part of the core curriculum; in others, students are expected to choose from broad options (with faculty and/or departmental approval) to meet individual goals. Faculty advisers assist in course selections. Degree candidates must complete, with an average of C or better, a minimum of 124 to 132 semester hours of work, the number of hours depending on the degree sought. Students may elect the pass/no credit grading system, although not usually on courses in their major field.

The Center for Academic Services provides full-time advisers for students who choose to postpone the choice of a major. During the first four semesters of study, such students can satisfy University requirements while investigating potential majors. The Writing Center, also provided by the Center for Academic Services, is available to all students and faculty members who wish to refine or improve their writing skills. Individual consultation and group workshops are conducted by a full-time professional writing staff.

The honors program challenges students to pursue high intellectual goals. It joins interdisciplinary colloquia and independent research with dedicated faculty and motivated students in all fields of study.

Army and Air Force ROTC programs operate on campus.

Off-Campus Arrangements

The TCU London Center offers fall, spring, and summer courses in a variety of disciplines. Study-abroad experiences are also available in twenty-eight other countries, including Germany, Hungary, Japan, Mexico, Spain, and the United Kingdom. In addition, annual summer-study tours abroad, with faculty-led seminars, are conducted in a variety of fields, such as language, art, and international business.

Most TCU programs include internships, practicums, or other field experiences with organizations in the Fort Worth–Dallas area. Such local off-campus learning experience is required of all students in nursing, medical technology, and education.

Academic Facilities

The library houses nearly 1.8 million volumes and has special collections in music, theology, government documents, and rare books; more than 9,000 serials and periodicals are received. The science research center has excellent equipment for graduate and undergraduate studies. Computer labs are available for student use. Of two concert halls, one is rated among the country's best acoustically; the ballet building has spacious studios. There are buildings for speech and hearing pathology, special education, nursing, design/merchandising, physical education, and visual arts and communication. The design of Charles Tandy Hall is similar to a modern business center; it is equipped with a "trading room" with stock market quote machines and news wire services, presentation rooms with videotape equipment, "board rooms," a staffed computer resource center, and classrooms with computers at each desk to provide an optimal learning environment. The M. J. Neeley School of Business is home to the Center for American Enterprise and the Educational Investment Fund. Music and theater students enjoy the new Walsh Center for Performing Arts, which includes a performance hall, a theater, a piano wing, and two large rehearsal rooms.

Costs

For 2000–01, tuition is $390 per semester hour, or $11,700 for 30 hours. The general University fee is $1425 per academic year. The cost of residence hall quarters averages $2990 per academic year. Board fees, which average $1300 per academic year, cover the cost of most meals in campus cafeterias or snack bars. Books and supplies average $700 a year. Thus, annual costs for resident students are about $18,115, plus personal expenses of at least $1000.

Financial Aid

Approximately 66 percent of undergraduate students receive aid. Academic scholarships are based on the student's SAT I or ACT scores, rank in class, and overall application. Awards range from $1000 to full tuition and include the Chancellor, Dean's, Faculty, and TCU scholarships. National Merit Finalists who name TCU as their first choice receive a basic scholarship of $4000 and may be eligible for higher awards. Students with demonstrated financial need are eligible for federal-, state-, and University-funded awards, which include grants loans, and work-study programs.

Faculty

The 355 full-time faculty members hold their highest degrees from 125 different institutions; more than 94 percent have the Ph.D. or other appropriate terminal degree. The University has kept classes comparatively small, and less than 4 percent of all classes have more than 50 students; most instructors have an open-door policy for students, and all instructors post regular office hours. Some departments enlist part-time faculty members from the Fort Worth–Dallas professional community to augment their programs.

Student Government

The House of Student Representatives, composed of elected members, serves as the basis for student government. Its officers and programming council direct a varied program of entertainment, speakers, films, and social and cultural events. The Student House makes many of its own policies within broad University guidelines. Residence halls form student councils to recommend policies and to provide activities for the hall. Students are voting members of all University-wide committees that recommend policy changes.

Admission Requirements

TCU evaluates applications by using broad criteria. Emphasis is placed on both test scores and on individual character. While academic credentials are most important, TCU also looks for talent, leadership potential, and personal determination to make a difference. Admitted students show above-average academic ability. Applicants are expected to have completed a college-preparatory curriculum during high school. A campus visit and interview are recommended before a decision is reached; admitted students are required to take part in an orientation session on campus before enrolling officially at TCU. Qualified students are admitted without regard to race, color, creed, age, sex, or ethnic or national origin, in accordance with Title IX and other government regulations.

Application and Information

Information about application deadlines and notification dates may be obtained from:

Sandra Ware
Dean of Admissions
TCU Box 297013
Texas Christian University
2800 South University Drive
Fort Worth, Texas 76129
Telephone: 817-257-7490
 800-TCU-3764 (toll-free)
Fax: 817-257-7268
E-mail: frogmail@tcu.edu
World Wide Web: http://www.tcu.edu

The M. J. Neeley School of Business prepares students for successful careers.

TEXAS LUTHERAN UNIVERSITY
SEGUIN, TEXAS

The University

Texas Lutheran University is a fully accredited coeducational liberal arts college supported by the Evangelical Lutheran Church in America. Texas Lutheran traces its roots back to 1891, when the first Evangelical Lutheran Synod of Texas founded a college in Brenham. The University moved to Seguin in 1912. The Seguin campus has grown from an original 15 acres to its present 196 acres.

Approximately 5 percent of the University's 1,562 students come from outside the state of Texas. Lutherans constitute 31 percent of the student body. Students may participate in more than forty campus organizations, including nine academic honor societies, nine local social sororities and fraternities, various student volunteer groups, the Concert Band, the Concert Choir, the Chapel Choir, a newspaper, a yearbook, the Black Student Union, and the Mexican-American Student Association. There are fourteen intramural sports. Intercollegiate sports are baseball, basketball, football, golf, soccer, and tennis for men and basketball, cross-country, golf, soccer, softball, tennis, and volleyball for women.

The 20,000-square-foot Hein Dining Hall was dedicated in 1993. With four separate dining/meeting areas, this facility serves as the gathering place for students during meal time, as well as the site for Language Tables, faculty lunches, special event meals, and other college functions. The Alumni Student Center, totally refurbished in 1995, is the center of activity and has a large snack bar, enclosed game room, three computer labs, a "great lounge," the University bookstore, the post office, student government office, student publication office, multipurpose room for student organizations, a counseling center, and office space.

Location

Seguin, a city of 23,000 people, is 35 miles east of San Antonio. This proximity makes it easy for students to take advantage of that historic city's cultural, social, and artistic attractions. Facilities for such outdoor sports as fishing, waterskiing, scuba diving, rafting, and sailing are readily available on the rivers and lakes of the surrounding Texas hill country. In addition, the sun, sand, and surf of the Texas Gulf Coast are only a 2-hour drive away.

Majors and Degrees

Texas Lutheran University grants the Bachelor of Arts (B.A.) and Bachelor of Science (B.S.) degrees. Bachelor of Arts degrees are offered in biology, business administration, chemistry, communication studies, computer science, computer systems management, economics, English studies, German, history, kinesiology, mathematics, multidisciplinary studies, music, philosophy, physics, political science, psychology, social work, Spanish, theater, theology, and visual arts. Bachelor of Science degrees are available in biology, chemistry, and mathematics. A collateral major is offered in international studies. Concentrations are also available in certain majors: accounting, applied music, athletic training, environmental biology, exercise science, finance, international business, management, marketing, molecular biology, music history/literature, public history, and sport and fitness management. Twenty-two minors are also offered. A Bachelor of Business Administration (B.B.A.) degree is offered in accounting as a concurrent with the B.A. for professional concentration in accounting.

Professional preparation is offered in education and sports medicine.

Preprofessional preparation is available in dentistry, law, medicine, nursing, occupational therapy, pharmacy, physical therapy, theology, and veterinary science. A 3-2 engineering program is also available.

Academic Program

The academic program at Texas Lutheran University is designed to provide an education in the liberal arts that makes life more exciting and satisfying. TLU students pursue a broad and general education while following programs of study that prepare them for employment directly after graduation or for further academic work at graduate or specialized professional schools.

Texas Lutheran uses a 4-4 academic calendar. The fall semester of four months begins in late August, and final examinations are completed before the Christmas vacation begins. The spring semester of four months starts in mid-January and ends in May.

Special academic programs offered include international studies, the Scholars program, independent study, off-campus semester programs, Mexican-American studies, the International Student Exchange Program, the Center for Women's Studies, and the KROST Life Enrichment Program. The KROST Symposium annually brings scholars, journalists, and government officials to campus to discuss issues of relevance and importance to the community at large. Emphasis is placed on the TLU Internship Program. These valuable career experiences, in conjunction with the efforts of the Career Services Center, have resulted in 95 percent of the alumni being placed in graduate school or professional careers within six months of graduation.

To graduate with a bachelor's degree, students must complete a minimum of 124 semester hours with a cumulative grade point average of at least 2.0. Each student attending TLU is required to complete a general education curriculum in addition to a major area of study.

Off-Campus Arrangements

Students may participate in a variety of off-campus programs, all of which carry academic credit. The Washington Semester Program allows students to enroll in a 12-semester-hour curriculum at the American University in Washington, D.C. The curriculum involves research, seminars, and lectures and is open to juniors and seniors who have taken a basic course in American government. In the German Semester Program, TLU offers students the opportunity to study at one of four German universities. The Puebla program is an intensive Spanish language program offered in conjunction with the English/Spanish Training Center in Puebla, Mexico. Students receive credit hours for language study and Mexican culture and history. Additional study-abroad opportunities are available through the International Student Exchange Program. This exchange brings students from various countries to Texas Lutheran as well as placing TLU students in universities across the globe.

Academic Facilities

The O. G. Beck College Center houses administrative and math faculty offices, a classroom, and meeting rooms. The Jesse H. Jones Physical Education Complex incorporates a 2,200-seat gym, fitness center, auxiliary activity center, faculty offices, a classroom, handball/racquetball courts, and an eight-lane heated aquatic center. The Blumberg Memorial Library houses more than 260,000 items of library materials and subscribes to 720 journal titles. The Yolanda Schuech Fine Arts Center is a multipurpose facility that includes a little theater, recital hall, music studios, band hall, art labs, and art gallery. Chapel of the Abiding Presence, Weinert Memorial is the campus worship center, seating 500 and containing a tracker-action Schlicker organ. Moody Science Building provides classrooms, laboratories, and student research space. In 1995, an additional 10,000-square-foot KROST Center was added to include seminar rooms, classrooms, student labs, offices, and equipment for the KROST fitness tests. The 1,100-seat John and Katie Jackson auditorium is the sight for student productions, fine art presentations, and major lectures and serves as home for the Mid-Texas Symphony. A building immediately adjacent to the campus has been converted into the psychology building with classroom space, numerous experimentation labs, a lounge, and study space. Langner and Weeber Halls contain various size and style classrooms and professor offices.

Costs

For 2000–01, the comprehensive fee is $16,690, which includes room, board, tuition, phone service, and the activities fee. Health insurance and refrigerators are available to students at additional cost. Parking fees are $25 per year. Private music lessons (one lesson per week) cost $350 per semester. Most students spend about $2400 for books, entertainment, travel, clothing, and other expenses.

Financial Aid

More than 90 percent of the students at Texas Lutheran University receive some type of need-based or merit-based financial support. In 1999–2000, more than $12.5 million in financial aid was given to TLU students; the average financial aid package was $9975. Campus employment and work-study awards are readily available. A variety of merit and competitive scholarships are also offered.

Faculty

In 1999–2000, Texas Lutheran employed 83 full-time and 57 part-time faculty members; 72 percent of the faculty members have doctorates or terminal degrees in their fields. The student-faculty ratio is 13:1, which allows the students' names to be known, their faces recognized, and their futures brought into focus with the professors' supportive guidance.

Student Government

All full-time students are members of the Student Government Association, a comprehensive student government structure. The president and vice president of the student body, together with a representative Student Government Association, work with the faculty and staff in achieving University goals and in providing an open forum for student opinion and action. Students appointed by the student-body president represent student opinion on most faculty committees that are concerned with academic matters as well as with certain aspects of the cocurricular program.

Admission Requirements

Each candidate is considered individually by the Admissions Committee, which evaluates the student's probable success at TLU based on courses taken in secondary school, test scores (either ACT or SAT I), grade point average, essay, and activities. Although not required, a personal interview is recommended. Seventy percent of the freshmen rank in the top half of their high school graduating class. Fifty-four percent of the freshmen have a minimum SAT I verbal score of 500, and 52 percent have a minimum SAT I math score of 500. Sixty-five percent of the freshmen have a minimum ACT score of 21.

Transfer applicants must submit a transcript from each college previously attended and may be asked to submit their high school records. A minimum 2.25 grade point average on previous college work is required for admission consideration.

Application and Information

A completed application form, SAT I or ACT scores, and an official transcript are required for admission. Admission decisions are announced on a rolling basis.

For current deadlines and more information about TLU, students should contact:

Norm Jones
Vice President for Enrollment Services
Texas Lutheran University
1000 West Court Street
Seguin, Texas 78155
Telephone: 830-372-8050
           800-771-8521 (toll-free)
E-mail: admissions@txlutheran.edu
World Wide Web: http://www.txlutheran.edu

A view across the center of the campus as seen from the front doors of Blumberg Memorial Library.

TEXAS TECH UNIVERSITY
LUBBOCK, TEXAS

The University

Texas Tech University, founded in 1923, is a residential state university with a population of 25,000 students. Students come from all fifty states and ninety-nine other countries. Students at Texas Tech have the opportunity to study in more than 300 graduate and undergraduate degree programs.

The University is built around eight colleges: Agricultural Sciences and Natural Resources, Architecture, Arts and Sciences, Business Administration, Education, Engineering, Honors, and Human Sciences. A law school, which often has the highest number of students passing the bar exam in Texas, is conveniently located on the main campus. Students also find the Texas Tech University Health Sciences Center, with its Schools of Medicine, Nursing, Pharmacy and Allied Health.

In 1996, the Board of Regents chose Texas Senator John T. Montford to serve as the University's first chancellor and to oversee its $300-million capital campaign. Presently, the campaign goal is expected to be met earlier than anticipated.

Excellence at Texas Tech is evidenced in the success of its alumni. NASA astronauts, U.S. Cabinet members, Metropolitan Opera soloists, Pulitzer Prize winners, and heads of international corporations received their education at Texas Tech.

Texas Tech is a leader in academic programs focusing on student interaction. Undergraduate students at Texas Tech work side by side with top researchers in pioneering studies with the U.S. Department of Agriculture as well as with the state's textile and cotton industries. Student researchers are also working to improve alternative fuel capabilities for the nation's leading automakers, and their wind engineering research is creating shelters to withstand the nation's most deadly tornadoes.

A new addition to the University is the Institute for Environmental and Human Health, which provides graduate and undergraduate education in environmental science, toxicology, and environmental health.

The M.D./M.B.A. Joint Degree Program attracts students whose knowledge and expertise will further shape the health-care delivery system into one that balances patient care and business management.

Students also find a strong commitment to the arts. The University offers the only interdisciplinary fine arts doctoral program in the country. Graduates are well-rounded professionals in the arts workforce as college professors, theater center directors, museum directors, and symphony managers.

While academic excellence is the top priority at Texas Tech, the campus is also the cultural center for students and community members. The University sponsors a full season of theater productions, professional speakers, performers, and art exhibits.

The University is a member of the Big XII Conference for intercollegiate athletics. Men participate in football, basketball, tennis, track and field, golf, and baseball. Women participate in basketball, track and field, golf, tennis, volleyball, soccer, and softball. There are twenty-two available intercollegiate club sports, including lacrosse, polo, swimming, rugby, and wrestling.

Location

The 1,839-acre campus is located in Lubbock, a west Texas city of 200,000 people. Within a few hours' drive, students find snow skiing in the mountains of New Mexico and hiking in the Texas hill country or the vast canyons of Palo Duro and Big Bend. Temperatures are mild in the winter and warm in the summer, with an average of 267 days of sunshine each year.

Majors and Degrees

Texas Tech University, through the College of Agricultural Science and Natural Resources, offers programs in agribusiness, agricultural communications, agricultural economics, agricultural education, agronomy, animal production, animal science, crop and soil sciences, entomology, environmental conservation, food technology, horticulture, landscape architecture, pre–veterinary medicine, range management, and wildlife and fisheries management. The College of Architecture offers programs in architectural design, delineation, design–business administration, history and historic preservation, structures, structures–civil engineering, and urban design. The College of Arts and Sciences offers programs in advertising, aerospace studies, anthropology, art (studio), art education, art history, Asian Pacific Rim studies, atmospheric science, biochemistry, biology, botany, broadcast journalism, cell and molecular biology, chemistry, classics, communication studies, community and urban studies, comparative literature, creative writing, dance, design communications, economics, English, environmental studies, ethnic studies, exercise and sport sciences, French, geography, geology, geophysics, geosciences, German, health, history, international economics, international studies, Italian, Japanese, journalism, Latin, Latin American area studies, liberal arts, linguistics, literature, mathematics, microbiology, military science, music composition, music education, music history and literature, music performance, music theory, philosophy, photocommunications, physics, political science, pre–clinical laboratory science, pre–communication disorders, predentistry, prelaw, premedicine, prenursing, pre–occupational therapy, preoptometry, prepharmacy, pre–physical therapy, psychology, public relations, recreation and leisure services, Russian language and area studies, social work, sociology, Spanish, statistics, technical communication, telecommunications, theater arts, and zoology. The College of Business Administration offers programs in accounting, agricultural economics–business, business economics, finance, finance–real estate, international emphasis, management, management information systems, marketing, and petroleum land management. The College of Education offers certification programs in elementary and secondary education. The College of Engineering offers programs in chemical engineering, civil engineering, computer science, electrical engineering, engineering physics, engineering technology, environmental engineering, industrial engineering, mechanical engineering, and petroleum engineering. The College of Human Sciences offers programs in early childhood education, interior design, merchandising, restaurant/hotel/institutional management, and substance abuse studies.

Academic Program

Texas Tech's undergraduate curriculum provides a broad range of courses in more than 150 majors. The Honors College has expanded to include studies and, in some cases, outstanding research for students in all disciplines. Recently, students at Texas Tech have seen an increase in competitive scholarships. In 1999, students at Texas Tech ranked first in receiving the prestigious Barry M. Goldwater Scholarship and second in receiving grants from the Howard Hughes Medical Institute. Both scholarships provide financial support for research in medicine, biology, science education, engineering, and mathematics.

Off-Campus Arrangements

Texas Tech University operates a 400-acre south Texas center at Junction, where summer classes and May intersessions are held, and the Lubbock Lake Landmark Historical Park excavation site, where Texas Tech researchers have documented a 12,000-year record of continuous human habitation. In addition, numerous international study opportunities are available for college credit in most countries around the world.

Academic Facilities

The University Library is one of only two regional depositories in the state for U.S. government documents. An online catalog, easily accessed from off-campus sites, links the University Library to the Southwest Collection archival library, the Law Library, and the Architecture Library.

The library also houses the Advanced Technology Learning Center, a multiroom lab with a wide variety of computers and programs available to students for daily use. Other computer facilities are located in each college and residence halls throughout the campus.

Costs

The average cost for 30 undergraduate credit hours, including books and nine-month room and board, is $8345 for Texas residents. Residents of Arkansas, New Mexico, and Oklahoma who live in counties bordering Texas pay in-state tuition. Residents of New Mexico and Oklahoma not living in a bordering county pay an additional $900. Students from other states pay an additional $6480. It is important to note that students who receive a $1000 scholarship from Texas Tech are exempt from out-of-state fees. Costs are estimated and subject to change.

Financial Aid

A variety of financial aid is offered in the form of scholarships, grants, and loans. Competitive scholarships are awarded on academic merit, SAT or ACT scores, and class rank. More than 300 Presidential Endowed Scholarships are awarded to students each year. Need-based assistance is also available in the form of scholarships, government and private loans, grants, and work-study. Students' need for assistance is determined from the Free Application for Federal Student Aid (FAFSA). For a guide to scholarships and deadlines, students should contact the Office of Financial Aid (telephone: 806-742-3681).

Faculty

Full-time faculty members number 830. Part-time faculty members and teaching assistants number 806. Among the faculty members are distinguished professionals serving as visiting and adjunct professors. Faculty members' research has gained international attention and has been published in leading academic journals. The University's average student-faculty ratio is 18:1.

Student Government

The Texas Tech Student Government Association includes a Student Senate, two vice presidents, and a student body president. Elected members serve as official student representatives and act as liaisons to the Lubbock community and the University administration. In addition, a freshman council of first-year students works to address issues relating to the freshman experience.

Admission Requirements

Admission criteria for all students are designed to ensure academic success. For freshmen, admission is based primarily on test scores and class rank. Additional factors such as leadership experience, extracurricular activities, community or volunteer service, talents, and special honors and achievements are considered.

Students in the top 10 percent of their graduating class are guaranteed admission to the University. For ensured admission, students who rank in the first quarter of their class must score at least 1140 on the SAT I or 25 on the ACT. Students who rank in the second quarter must score at least 1230 on the SAT I or 28 on the ACT. Those in the lower half must score at least 1270 on the SAT I or 29 on the ACT. Applicants not meeting the ensured admission criteria are reviewed. Students who are not admitted with a favorable review may be accepted in the Provisional Program. Provisionally admitted students must attend Texas Tech or a community college during the summer after high school graduation. Before enrollment at Texas Tech in the fall, the student must complete a prescribed number of college hours and earn a specific minimum grade point average.

Admission requirements for transfer students differ depending on the number of college hours a student has earned. Transfer students who have completed 24 or more hours from an accredited institution with at least a 2.25 grade point average are admitted to Texas Tech. Students who have completed 12 to 23 hours and earned at least a 2.5 grade point average are also admitted to the University. Students with less than 12 transfer hours must meet the requirements for freshman admission. All students must be eligible to return to the institution from which they are transferring.

The University admits all students who hold scholarships awarded by an official Texas Tech University scholarship committee.

Application and Information

All students should submit the State of Texas Common Application, a high school transcript, SAT I or ACT test scores, and the $25 application fee.

Requests for applications and other information should be directed to:

Office of Admissions and School Relations
Texas Tech University
Box 45005
Lubbock, Texas 79409-5005

Telephone: 806-742-1480
Fax: 806-742-0980
E-mail: nsr@ttu.edu
World Wide Web: http://www.texastech.edu

Students receive support and encouragement to achieve academic and personal goals at Texas Tech University.

TEXAS WOMAN'S UNIVERSITY
DENTON, TEXAS

The University

Texas Woman's University (TWU) is a comprehensive public university, primarily for women, offering bachelor's, master's, and doctoral degree programs. A teaching and research institution, TWU emphasizes the liberal arts and specialized or professional studies. With a total enrollment of almost 8,600 students (fall 1999), TWU is the nation's largest university primarily for women; the current undergraduate enrollment is 4,744 women and 339 men. The University welcomes all qualified students.

Established in 1901 by the Texas Legislature, Texas Woman's University is organized into three major academic divisions: the University General Divisions, the Institute of Health Sciences, and the Graduate School. Included in the University General Divisions are the College of Arts and Sciences, College of Education and Human Ecology, and School of Library and Information Studies. The Institute of Health Sciences includes the College of Health Sciences, College of Nursing, School of Occupational Therapy, and School of Physical Therapy. The Graduate School coordinates advanced degree programs across the University.

Old Main, the University's first building, still stands amid high-rise buildings and other modern facilities that distinguish the beautiful 270-acre wooded campus in Denton. Residence halls, recreational facilities, the conference center, the library, and classroom buildings are conveniently located throughout the campus. Special campus landmarks include the statue of the Pioneer Woman and the historic Little Chapel-in-the-Woods.

Location

TWU's main campus is in Denton, Texas (population 76,000), just 35 miles north of Dallas and Fort Worth—the nation's ninth-largest urban center. Clinical centers, offering upper-level and graduate studies in the health sciences, are located in Dallas, near Parkland and Presbyterian hospitals, and in Houston, in the Texas Medical Center.

Majors and Degrees

Undergraduate programs lead to the Bachelor of Arts, Bachelor of Business Administration, Bachelor of Fine Arts, Bachelor of Science, and Bachelor of Social Work degrees. Baccalaureate degrees are offered in art history, biology (with a concentration in human biology), business administration (with concentrations in accounting, management, marketing, and office records administration), chemistry, child development, communication science, community health, computer science, consumer sciences, criminal justice, dance, dental hygiene, design (with concentrations in advertising, fashion illustrating, and medical illustration), dietetics, drama, economics, English, food and nutrition, family studies, fashion design, fashion merchandising, government (with concentrations in government service and paralegal studies), history, kinesiology, library science, mass communications, mathematics, medical technology, music (with concentrations in applied music, music pedagogy, and music therapy), nursing, nutrition, pre-dental science, prelaw, premedicine, pre–occupational therapy, pre–physical therapy, psychology, social work, sociology, studio art (with concentrations in ceramics, fabrics and printed textiles, jewelry and metalsmithing, painting, photography, and sculpture), and teacher preparation for elementary, reading and bilingual, secondary, and special education.

Academic Program

TWU is accredited by the Commission on Colleges of the Southern Association of Colleges and Schools to award bachelor's, master's, and doctoral degrees. Various programs are also accredited by appropriate state, regional, and national agencies. The University emphasizes the importance of a liberal arts education and specialized or professional study, especially in the health sciences. The University has one of the lowest computer-to-student ratios (1:13) in north Texas and one of the lowest in the state.

The University's requirement for all bachelor's degrees comprises the successful completion of a minimum of 139 credit hours, including at least 42 semester credit hours of core curriculum requirements, plus additional hours specified for each degree. The University calendar consists of two semesters of approximately four months each, one minimester, two summer terms of five weeks each, and one summer session of ten weeks. Most degree programs are designed to allow students who carry a normal course load to complete degree requirements in eight semesters.

Any full- or part-time student who has not earned at least 3 semester credit hours prior to fall 1989 must be tested for reading, writing, and mathematics skills under the Texas Academic Skills Program (TASP). No student may graduate from a baccalaureate degree program without passing all sections of the examination, unless she or he meets specific requirements for exemption. (That exemption does not apply to students entering teacher education.)

Off-Campus Arrangements

Programs in each of the University's colleges and schools include clinical and practicum experiences that give students access to outstanding facilities of major health-care, business, and other institutions located in major metropolitan centers. Programs are offered annually to provide study-travel opportunities in the United States and abroad. A diverse cooperative education program integrates classroom study with planned and supervised work experience in educational activities outside the formal classroom.

Academic Facilities

University library holdings include 725,786 volumes, 8,474 current periodical and serial publications, 1,488,084 microforms, and 86,175 audiovisual materials to support all major areas of study at TWU. Special resources include the Woman's Collection, the largest depository in the South and Southwest of research materials about women. Other materials include a rare book collection, as well as a departmental children's library in the School of Library and Information Studies. Students have access to fifty-four state university libraries through TexShare. The Dallas Center maintains a special collection for students in the health sciences. Students at the Houston Center have access to more than 268,523 volumes in the Houston Academy of Medicine–Texas Medical Center Library.

Numerous classroom and laboratory buildings, including an undergraduate science laboratory building, are conveniently located on the Denton campus to meet specific needs of the individual components of the University. Special facilities on the Denton campus include competitive honors and international programs with special housing facilities; Margo Jones Performance Hall, a theater, an auditorium, and four dance studios; television studios; numerous art and music studios and practice rooms; science laboratories; a computer center and computer center learning laboratory; a writing laboratory; woodworking, weaving, and other laboratory facilities for programs related to therapy; the Institute for Women's Health; and the Institute for Mental and Physical Development. Clinics are provided for speech and hearing, dental hygiene, occupational therapy, and reading. A nursery school and a child-care center serve as laboratories for students majoring in child-development programs. Also included are tennis courts, a golf course, an indoor track, indoor and outdoor pools, a Wellness Center and fitness room, and other facilities that support programs in physical education and human movement. Most residence hall rooms are linked to the campus computer network.

The Dallas Center includes a campus in the Parkland Memorial Hospital complex and a campus adjacent to Presbyterian Hospital of Dallas. The Houston Center is located in the heart of the Texas Medical Center. Both centers offer outstanding instructional facilities, including excellent library holdings, clinical learning resources, simulation and research laboratories, laboratories for occupational and physical therapy, and anatomy laboratories. The Dallas and Houston Centers also have renovated nursing skills laboratories, and the Houston Center has research laboratories in biochemistry and nutrition.

Costs

The average cost for in-state resident students in 1999–2000 for one semester of 15 semester hours was $1250 plus course fees and $250 for books and supplies. For out-of-state residents, the average cost of tuition for 15 semester hours was $4465. Residence hall rates, meals, and personal expenses vary. All rates are subject to change. Scholarship programs for honors students, class valedictorians from Texas, freshmen, transfer students, and international students are available.

Financial Aid

More than 50 percent of TWU's students receive financial aid in the form of scholarships, grants, loans, or on-campus employment. In addition to offering numerous scholarships and grants funded by the state and by friends of the University, TWU participates in many federally funded programs. Federal Pell Grants, Federal Supplemental Educational Opportunity Grants, Federal Perkins Loans, nursing student loans, and Federal Work-Study Program awards are available. Suggested filing dates for financial aid applicants are April 1 for the fall and spring terms and March 1 for summer sessions. Applications for academic scholarships for both the fall and spring semesters should be made by March 15.

Faculty

A faculty of approximately 500 guides the academic program at TWU and gives careful attention to student needs. Faculty members hold the doctoral degree or another terminal or graduate degree in their field.

Student Government

All students are members of the United Student Association, which enables them to participate in a wide variety of activities. Students work with the faculty and administrators to develop University policies and programs of special interest and concern to the student body. Students also serve on various University committees. Leadership development is a special focus.

Admission Requirements

First-time freshman applicants are assured admission to Texas Woman's University if they have graduated from a regionally accredited high school in Texas within the last two years and have a class ranking that places them in the top 25 percent of their high school graduating class. Regular admission to the University is based on graduation from an accredited high school; applicants must have obtained a grade point average of at least 2.0 on a 4.0 scale. They must also submit satisfactory test scores: at least 910 on the SAT I or 19 on the ACT. In addition, applicants must have completed 22 secondary school units. Transfer students must submit an official transcript from each college previously attended. They must have obtained a GPA of 2.0 or higher on a 4.0 scale when transferring to the University.

Application and Information

Applicants should submit a completed application for admission and their official transcripts to the Office of Admissions. The fall and spring deadlines are June 30 and December 1, respectively. There is a $30 application fee for all new students.

Additional information about the University and its programs is available from:

Office of Admissions
Texas Woman's University
P.O. Box 425589
Denton, Texas 76204-5589
Telephone: 940-898-3047
World Wide Web: http://www.twu.edu

Traditional and nontraditional students from all backgrounds and all walks of life share their experiences at Texas Woman's University, the nation's largest university primarily for women.

THIEL COLLEGE
GREENVILLE, PENNSYLVANIA

The College

Thiel College was founded in 1866 as one of the first coeducational institutions of higher education in the United States. Located in Greenville, Pennsylvania, in the northwestern corner of the commonwealth, Thiel has become known for the quality of its educational offerings and its blending of liberal arts cutting-edge technology and experiential learning through extensive cooperative education and internship opportunities.

Affiliated with the Evangelical Lutheran Church in America, the College enrolls just over 1,000 women and men. Most students come from Pennsylvania, Ohio, and the Middle Atlantic States. Nine percent of the students are members of minority groups, and 5 percent are from seventeen other countries.

Thiel has been ranked in the "top tier" of northern liberal arts colleges by *U.S. News & World Report*, and its sciences and mathematics programs are rated "among the 200 best in the United States" by *Peterson's Guide to the Sciences*.

Social life at Thiel is based on involvement as part of a holistic approach to education. Students are encouraged to participate in activities and sports programs that are of interest to them. Cocurricular activities and sports programs are viewed as an important complement to the academic life of the College community and to the individual.

Thiel College competes in the Presidents' Athletic Conference and the NCAA Division III. The athletic team nicknames are Tomcats and Lady Cats. Intercollegiate sports include basketball, cheerleading, cross-country, golf, soccer, tennis, and track and field; men's baseball, football, and wrestling; and women's softball and volleyball. Intramural competition is available in a variety of sports for men and women. Outstanding fitness and recreation includes downhill and cross-country skiing, hiking, boating, hunting, and fishing.

Fraternities and sororities add to the mix of college organizations, but student life includes all students whether they are Greeks or non-Greeks. The fraternities include Alpha Chi Rho, Delta Sigma Phi, Kappa Sigma, Phi Theta Phi, and Sigma Phi Epsilon. The sororities include Alpha Xi Delta, Chi Omega, Sigma Kappa, and Zeta Tau Alpha.

Students are normally expected to reside in one of the College's residence halls. Three halls are reserved for entering students: Sawhill and Hodge Halls are men's residence halls and Florence West Hall is a residence for women. Additional options include Harter, Livingston, Bane, and Stewart Halls, which complete the traditional residence hall options.

Thiel offers its students two dining choices: the Livingston Hall dining room and the Alternative, Thiel's snack bar.

The College Counseling Center is located in the Howard Miller Student Center, Thiel's student union, and is affiliated with the Sharon Regional Health System. Counseling services are available on a variety of topics. The Thiel College Pastor can also provide pastoral assistance and spiritual guidance.

Location

Thiel College is located in Greenville, a small town of about 7,000 people in the northwestern corner of the commonwealth. The 135-acre campus is an attractive combination of wooded walkways and academic, residential, and recreational use facilities.

Students find ample shopping, dining, and entertainment options in the Greenville area. Thiel College and Greenville have a mutually supportive relationship.

Because of their proximity, the Cleveland, Pittsburgh, Erie, and Youngstown metro areas are used by Thiel students and faculty members for additional cultural, shopping, and recreational experiences.

Majors and Degrees

Thiel College awards the Associate of Arts, the Bachelor of Arts, and the Bachelor of Science in Nursing degrees. Bachelor's degrees are awarded in accounting, actuarial studies, animation/multimedia, art, bioforestry, biology, biology/conservation, business administration, business communication, chemistry, communication, computer science, criminal justice, cytotechnology, English, environmental science, French, gerontology, history, international business, management information science, mathematics, medical illustration, medical technology, mortuary science, nursing (B.S.N.), parish education, philosophy, physics, political science, psychology, religion, sociology, Spanish, speech and hearing science, and exploratory (undeclared major). Preprofessional programs are offered in the areas of dentistry, engineering 3-2, law, medicine, ministry, pharmacy, physical therapy, and veterinary medicine. Teacher certification is available in elementary education and secondary education.

Thiel awards Associate of Arts degrees in general studies, accounting, and management information science.

Academic Program

Thiel College provides students with a liberal arts education that increases general and special knowledge of the world, promotes creative and critical thinking, and strengthens communication skills. Each of the majors and degree programs combines liberal arts instruction and values with cutting-edge technology and hands-on learning through internships and co-ops.

The Bachelor of Arts degree programs and the Bachelor of Science in Nursing degree program require a minimum of 124 credits for graduation. The Associate of Arts degree programs require a minimum of 64 credits for graduation. All majors must complete liberal arts integrative requirements as well as core and elective courses.

Advanced Placement (AP) and CLEP examination scores are welcome from students entering Thiel. Courses taken at other colleges while students are still in high school will be accepted for consideration provided that the grade earned is a C or better (on a 4.0 scale).

The Honors Program is offered to outstanding students and provides students with the opportunity to develop special projects, interests, and activities; to meet with visiting artists, scholars, and public figures; and to work closely with professors and other members of the College community.

Thiel College follows a two-semester system. Classes typically start near Labor Day in August or September and end in mid-December. Second-term classes begin in mid-January and continue through mid-May. Summer session classes are also offered.

Off-Campus Arrangements

Students at Thiel are encouraged to broaden their horizons, to take advantage of off-campus learning experiences, and to integrate a world community approach to their studies.

Cooperative learning (co-op) experiences are available to students in industry, government agencies, and educational institutions and with nonprofit and charitable organizations. The co-op enhances professional development through planned supervised work experiences.

The Haller Enterprise Institute at Thiel is an innovative concept that encourages students to pursue their business ideas while they continue their education. The Institute is a support system through which students with entrepreneurial ideas can receive advice, training, and encouragement in starting their own businesses.

Additional options for students include Thiel's Center for Women's Leadership; junior year study-abroad programs in the country or countries of the student's choice; the Semester in Washington program, which focuses on ethical issues and public affairs; the United Nations Semester; the Washington Semester, open to any major; the Appalachian Semester; Argonne National Laboratories Semester; EWHA Woman's University Semester in Seoul, Korea; the Drew University Art Semester; and the Saltillo Experience in Mexico.

A cooperative degree program with the Art Institute of Pittsburgh allows Thiel students to earn a baccalaureate degree in art with commercial art emphasis. Thiel College and the Pittsburgh Institute of Mortuary Science offer a cooperative program leading to a Bachelor of Arts degree in business administration and a diploma in funeral directing/embalming.

Academic Facilities

Thiel College is set on a parklike 135-acre campus. Greenville Hall, the oldest building at the College, was constructed in 1872 and houses classrooms as well as offices for humanities faculty members. The Beeghly-Rissel Gymnasia house the basketball, wrestling, and volleyball arenas; a fitness center; weight-lifting center; team locker rooms; and coaches' offices. Roth Memorial Hall is home to administrative offices and the auditorium for the Thiel Players, the college theater company.

Langenheim Memorial Library houses study carrels for 600 students and contains a computer center for instruction or Internet access. The library collection includes 151,000 books, 213,000 government documents, 921 periodicals, and more than 22,000 microfiche/microfilm items.

The Academic Center/Science Hall is an integrated five-level complex, which includes classrooms, laboratories, art studios, a rooftop greenhouse, specialized teaching facilities, faculty offices, lecture halls, and computer centers.

The William Passavant Memorial Center, a multiuse conference and convocation center, contains a 2,000-seat auditorium, which is also home to the Greenville Symphony.

The Brucker Great Blue Heron Sanctuary and the East Acres complex provide natural outdoor laboratories for wildlife and biological observation and environmental and geological study.

Costs

Tuition for the 2000–01 year is $10,732. Room and board charges are $5674. Books, fees, and personal expenses average an additional $1200–$1500 per year.

Financial Aid

Thiel College participates in all federal financial aid programs. Students are encouraged to check with state agencies as well as with local, community, civic, industrial, and church-related groups for additional funding sources.

Students are encouraged to file the Free Application for Federal Student Aid (FAFSA) as early as possible after January 1 of their senior year. Award notifications are mailed beginning in late January and continue until funding is exhausted. Admission decisions are non-need-based.

Thiel College awards its institutional funds after consideration of academic achievement, special talents and skills, and financial need. Thiel maintains an extensive grant, loan, scholarship, and college work program. In 2000–01, $5.4 million will be awarded to students from institutional resources, and 96 percent of students will receive funding through a combination of federal, state, local, and Thiel resources.

Faculty

Fifty-five full-time faculty members and 30 adjunct/part-time faculty members are responsible for instruction. Most faculty members serve as advisers to students, and 75 percent hold advanced degrees. Faculty members are very involved in the life of the Thiel community and work with students on campus media, theater, music, student government, special interest clubs, and organizations and with fraternities and sororities. No graduate students or teaching assistants/fellows are employed by Thiel College. The student-faculty ratio is 12:1.

Student Government

Students have many options for involvement and governance at Thiel. Elections are held each spring to elect a collegewide Student Government Association. In addition, each class elects its own officers. The Student Government Association works with the administration on matters of concern and supervises the various clubs, organizations, and student activities at the College. The Greeks are served as well by Panhellenic and intrafraternity advisory boards.

Admission Requirements

Thiel College seeks students who are interested in taking an active part in their education. The College is committed to diversity and, as part of its world view, encourages international applicants and transfer students to complete degree studies at Thiel.

Applicants to Thiel directly from high school are expected to have completed or be nearing completion of a college-prep curriculum that is strong in English, social sciences, mathematics, natural and laboratory sciences, a second language, and academic electives. Applicants should have a minimum of 16 academic units. Average SAT I scores are 950; average ACT scores are 22. Most applicants have earned a B average (on a 4.0 scale) and are in the top two fifths of their high school class. The Admissions Committee considers special talents and encourages students to submit an essay as well as letters of recommendation. Interviews prior to application are highly recommended.

Application and Information

Thiel begins to consider applicants in late September each year for the following fall. Decisions are made on a rolling basis, and applicants are notified within ten days of the completion of an application packet. Applications should be received no later than August 1 for the fall term and December 1 for the spring term.

For inquiries and requests for information, students should contact:

Thiel College Admissions Office
75 College Avenue
Greenville, Pennsylvania 16125
Telephone: 724-589-2345
            800-248-4435 (toll-free)
Fax: 724-589-2013
E-mail: admissio@thiel.edu

THOMAS EDISON STATE COLLEGE
TRENTON, NEW JERSEY

The College

Thomas Edison State College provides adults with access to some of the best choices in higher education. Cited as "one of the brighter stars of higher learning" by the *New York Times* and identified by *Forbes* magazine as one of the top twenty colleges and universities in the nation in the use of technology to create learning opportunities for adults, Thomas Edison State College provides high-quality higher education to adults wherever they live and work. Founded in 1972, Thomas Edison State College enables adult learners to complete associate, baccalaureate, and master's degrees through distance learning and the assessment of knowledge they already have.

The College's convenient programs are designed to help learners pursue their educational goals while attending to the challenges and priorities of adult life. Accredited by the Commission on Institutions of Higher Education of the Middle States Association of Colleges and Schools, Thomas Edison State College offers a distinguished academic program for the self-motivated adult learner. The College has more than 15,000 alumni worldwide.

Academic advisement is provided to enrolled students by the College's Advisement Center, which assists students in integrating their learning style, background, and educational goals with the credit-earning methods and programs available. Students can access advisement through telephone and in-person appointments through the Advisement Phone Center, and they have 24-hour-a-day access through fax and e-mail.

In addition to the undergraduate programs described below, the College offers an online Master of Science in Management (M.S.M.) degree, which has two brief residency requirements. The M.S.M. degree serves employed adults who have had professional experience in the management field. The degree is designed to have broad appeal for those not served by conventional programs. The program integrates the theory and practice of management as it applies to diverse organizations, educational institutions, and nonprofit agencies. The emphasis is on theory and practice in the management of organizations. A specialized track in project management is also offered within the M.S.M. degree. In addition, the College has received approval to develop a Master of Arts in Professional Studies degree. This degree will enable learners to study and apply the liberal arts to their professional lives.

Location

Thomas Edison State College is located in Trenton, New Jersey.

Majors and Degrees

Thomas Edison State College offers fourteen associate, baccalaureate, and master's degree programs in more than 100 major areas of study. Degrees offered include Associate in Applied Science, Associate in Applied Science in Radiologic Technology, Associate in Science in Management, Associate in Science in Applied Science and Technology, Associate in Arts, Associate in Science in Natural Science and Mathematics, Associate in Science in Public and Social Services, Bachelor of Arts, Bachelor of Science in Applied Science and Technology, Bachelor of Science in Business Administration, Bachelor of Science in Health Sciences (a joint-degree program with the University of Medicine and Dentistry of New Jersey (UMDNJ) School of Health Related Professions (SHRP)), Bachelor of Science in Human Services, and Bachelor of Science in Nursing. The College's prospectus contains a list of the more than 100 major areas of study available within these degrees. To obtain a prospectus, students should call 609-984-1150 or e-mail info@tesc.edu.

Academic Program

At Thomas Edison State College, students have the opportunity to earn degrees through traditional and nontraditional methods. These methods take into consideration personal needs and interests while ensuring both breadth and depth of knowledge within the degree program. Thomas Edison State College offers one of the most highly regarded, comprehensive distance learning programs in the United States. Students at Thomas Edison State College can use several convenient methods of meeting degree requirements, depending upon their individual learning styles and preferences. Guided Study, On-Line Computer Classroom®, Contract Learning, examinations, portfolio assessment, corporate or military education, telecourses, approved correspondence courses, and credits earned at other colleges can be combined in a number of ways to earn credits toward an undergraduate degree.

Each undergraduate degree requires work in general education, a major area of study, and elective subjects. Students are encouraged to familiarize themselves with the requirements of their chosen degree and work in conjunction with one of the College's knowledgeable program advisers to develop a program plan that best meets their individual needs, goals, and interests.

Thomas Edison State College's Military Degree Completion Program (MDCP) serves military personnel worldwide. The MDCP was developed to accommodate the special needs of military personnel whose location, relocation, and time constraints make traditional college attendance difficult, if not impossible. The program allows students to engage in a degree program wherever they may be stationed. The program allows maximum credit for military training and education.

In addition, the College has a very unique program designed specifically for community college students. The program, called Degree Pathways, allows community college students or graduates to complete a baccalaureate degree at home, in the workplace, or at their local two-year college.

Degree Pathways lets students at community colleges make a smooth transition directly into a Thomas Edison State College baccalaureate program. The Degree Pathways program allows students to transfer up to 80 credits from a community college toward the 120 credits needed for a bachelor's degree.

The New Jersey Pathways Program is a partnership between Thomas Edison State College and New Jersey's county and community colleges developed to help students make a seamless transition by providing coordinated support in admissions, academic programming, advisement, registration, and the sharing of technologies.

Once students have completed their first year at a community college or a minimum of 30 credits, they are eligible for the Degree Pathways program. Students may continue to take classes and use technologies available at their community college as they move toward completing their associate degree as well as taking additional credits toward the 80-credit limit while meeting credit requirements toward a baccalaureate degree.

In addition, students are able to take distance learning courses through Thomas Edison State College, and they may earn credit for what they already know through testing, portfolio assessment, and other methods of earning credit available through the College.

Thomas Edison State College also provides services for individuals not seeking a degree. These are credit-earning options for nondegree students, credit banking, and credit for licenses and certificate.

Credit-earning options for nondegree students benefit individuals who would like to earn credits through examinations, portfolio assessment, and Thomas Edison State College courses. They may do so by paying the appropriate fee for these programs. An application to Thomas Edison State College is not required to take advantage of these credit-earning options.

Credit Banking is for students who wish to document college-level learning gained through military experience, professional licenses, college proficiency examinations, college-level corporate training programs, or American Council on Education (ACE) recommendations. Thomas Edison State College offers a Credit Banking service for individuals who wish to consolidate college-level work into a Thomas Edison State College transcript. Credits transcripted under the Credit Banking program may or may not apply to a degree program at Thomas Edison State College.

Thomas Edison State College grants credit for current professional licenses or certificates that have been approved for credit by the College's Academic Council. Students who have earned one of the licenses or certificates approved for credit must submit notarized copies of the license or certificate and a current renewal card, if appropriate, to receive credit. A list of licenses and certificates approved for credit can be found in the College's prospectus.

Academic Facilities

Distance education courses are provided through several venues, including guided study at home or work, the On-Line Computer Classroom®, and Contract Learning, a one-to-one learning experience with individual faculty members. Interactive television classrooms with satellite downlinks and cable access also are also utilized. The College's distance learning program is administered through its Center for Distance & Independent Adult Learning (DIAL).

Costs

Because the College uses efficient distance learning technologies, Thomas Edison State College's tuition and fees are among the most affordable in the nation. Undergraduate students may choose one of two payment plans: a comprehensive fee paid annually, which includes enrollment, technology services, courses, testing, and portfolio assessment; or the per-service fee, which enables students to pay for services as they use them. A complete listing of tuition and fees is included in the College's information packet, available by calling 609-984-1150 or via e-mail at info@tesc.edu.

Financial Aid

Thomas Edison State College participates in a number of federal and state aid programs. Eligible students may receive Federal Pell Grants or federal education loans, such as the Federal Stafford Loan (subsidized and unsubsidized), for courses offered by the College. Eligible New Jersey residents may also tap a variety of state grant and loan programs. Students may use state aid to meet all or part of their College costs, provided they are taking at least 12 credits per semester.

Thomas Edison State College financing plans through First Union Bank offer students the option of spreading payment of fees over a number of years, if necessary. Students may borrow as little as $1000 or as much as $15,000. The financing plans offer a competitive interest rate and no prepayment penalty. The approval process for the financing plans takes only 48 hours after an application is submitted.

Students interested in using financial assistance, including student loans, should file an application and submit all required documentation by the following priority deadlines: fall applicants, June 30; winter applicants, October 30; and summer applicants, February 27. Once a student's financial aid file is complete, a letter is sent to the student indicating what aid has been awarded. Students are urged to file the Free Application for Federal Student Aid (FAFSA) and submit the required documents well before the application and registration deadlines.

Detailed information about the financial aid process can be found in the financial aid packet, which is available from the Office of Financial Aid and Veterans' Services. To receive this information, students should call 609-984-1150 or e-mail finaid@tesc.edu.

Faculty

There are more than 500 consulting faculty members at Thomas Edison State College. Drawn from other highly regarded colleges and universities, consulting faculty members provide many services to Thomas Edison State College, including assessment of knowledge adults already have, mentoring, and other special assignments.

Admission Requirements

Adults seeking an associate, bachelor's, or master's degree who are high school graduates are eligible to become Thomas Edison State College students. There are no tests required for admission to Thomas Edison State College. Because Thomas Edison State College delivers high-quality education directly to students wherever they live or work, students can complete degree requirements at their convenience without travel to Thomas Edison State College's campus. There are no on-campus residency requirements. A computer is not required to complete an undergraduate degree. A computer is only required to take On-Line Computer Classroom® courses. Once a student is enrolled in a specific degree program, an evaluator determines the number of credits the student has already earned and fits those into the degree program requirements. Orientation is not required at Thomas Edison State College.

Application and Information

Students may apply to Thomas Edison State College any day of the year by mail or fax or through the College's Web site. The Office of Admissions assists potential applicants in determining whether Thomas Edison State College suits their particular academic goals. For more information, students should contact:

Director of Admissions
Thomas Edison State College
101 West State Street
Trenton, New Jersey 08608-1176
Telephone: 609-984-1150
          888-442-8372 (toll-free)
Fax: 609-984-8447
E-mail: admissions@tesc.edu
World Wide Web: http://www.tesc.edu

THOMAS JEFFERSON UNIVERSITY
College of Health Professions
PHILADELPHIA, PENNSYLVANIA

The University and The College

Thomas Jefferson University is one of the oldest and largest academic health centers in the United States. The University comprises Jefferson Medical College, one of the largest private medical schools in the country; the College of Graduate Studies, for advanced study in the basic medical sciences; and the College of Health Professions. The University shares its campus with the Thomas Jefferson University Hospital, one of the nation's premier health-care facilities, and is a member of Jefferson Health System, a regional, integrated health-care delivery system. The College of Health Professions provides innovative academic programs for a highly qualified, culturally diverse student population. An integral component of the College is the generation of new health-care knowledge through scholarship and applied, collaborative, and interdisciplinary research.

The student body is heterogeneous, with the majority of students coming from the Middle Atlantic states. Twenty-five percent are members of minority groups. The current undergraduate enrollment in the College of Health Professions is 662 women and 145 men. Student activities include lectures, musical programs, social mixers, and intramural sports. Professional counseling services are available for all students who need assistance in resolving academic, vocational, and personal concerns.

Dormitory space is available in the James R. Martin Residence Hall. Additional on-campus housing is available in Orlowitz Residence Hall, a modern twenty-story apartment building, and Barringer Hall, a ten-story apartment building. Information about other housing facilities in the community may be obtained from the Housing Office. Food services are available on campus.

Master of Science degrees are offered in nursing, occupational therapy, and laboratory sciences. Additional master's degrees will soon be available.

Location

The University is located in downtown Philadelphia, within walking distance of many places of cultural interest, including theaters, museums, art galleries, and historic sites. Many intercollegiate and professional athletic events take place nearby. Convenient bus, rail, and subway lines offer transportation to a variety of interesting attractions. The nearby New Jersey shore and Pennsylvania mountains offer year-round recreational opportunities, and New York City and Washington, D.C., are just a few hours away.

Majors and Degrees

The College of Health Professions is an upper-division college (junior and senior years only) that provides undergraduate education in the health-related professions. Approximately two years of college credit are required for admission; students enter at the junior-year level. Baccalaureate degree programs are offered in biotechnology, cytogenetic technology, cytotechnology, diagnostic imaging (radiography/ultrasound/computed tomography/magnetic resonance imaging, nuclear medicine technology, and cardiovascular technology), medical technology, nursing, and occupational therapy. The College offers a three-year combined Bachelor of Science and Master of Science degree program in physical therapy, also beginning in the junior year.

Advanced placement/postbaccalaureate certificate programs are available in biotechnology, computed tomography, cytogenetic technology, cytotechnology, diagnostic medical sonography, magnetic resonance imaging, medical technology, nuclear medicine technology, and nursing for credentialed professionals in these areas who wish to pursue the Bachelor of Science degree in their field.

In addition, the College houses the Department of General Studies, which offers general courses in arts, humanities, and sciences as well as associate degrees and certificate programs.

Academic Program

The biotechnology program is designed to educate students for health care–related laboratory careers in the development of products using biologic and engineering principles. Through a combination of classroom and laboratory experience, students are prepared to work with DNA, molecular modeling, and related areas.

Cytogenetic technology is a specialized medical laboratory field whose practitioners study and identify normal and abnormal chromosomes. Using a microscope, students analyze and photograph cultured specimens of bone marrow, peripheral blood, solid tissue, and amniotic fluid and interpret chromosome karyotypes.

In the cytotechnology program, students learn the specific microscopy skills necessary to study slides for evidence of normality or disease. The interpretation of microscopic findings, as well as of clinical information, is facilitated by study of normal body functions and disease processes. Electron microscopy, cytogenetics, and the preparation and study of tissues add to the student's educational background and realm of possibilities for further study, research, or teaching.

The program in diagnostic imaging prepares students to function competently in the expanding and multifaceted role of diagnostic imager, thereby meeting the challenges of the present and the future in health care and society. Recent trends and advances in the delivery of health care indicate that the diagnostic imaging curriculum must provide the student with expanded opportunities to develop skills in more than one imaging modality. Of equal importance is the need for the graduate to understand the relationships of each of the imaging specialties to the overall pattern of patient care. Graduates of the Multicompetency Program (radiography and a choice of ultrasound, computed tomography, nuclear medicine technology, or magnetic resonance imaging) are eligible to take the examinations of the American Registry of Radiologic Technologists and American Registry of Diagnostic Medical Sonographers. Students who pass these examinations receive national certification.

The cardiovascular technology program prepares students to assist physicians in detecting, diagnosing, and treating patients with heart and vascular disease. Echocardiography is the focus for the first year, and students may choose either cardiac catheterization or peripheral vascular studies for the second year.

The medical technology curriculum provides a thorough background in the physical and biological sciences, culminating in the application of research, theory, and principles to the performance of clinical laboratory procedures. Intensified theoretical science preparation in automation and computer technology is provided in the junior year. The senior year prepares the student for a high level of proficiency in the clinical laboratory, with emphasis on laboratory technique, professional practice, quality control, and administrative functions. The curriculum provides a firm foundation for teaching, supervisory functions, or graduate study.

The baccalaureate nursing program prepares men and women to become effective professional nurses with the background necessary to be responsible, self-directed practitioners of nursing. This educational program is designed to provide students with the knowledge and clinical skills necessary to plan, implement, and evaluate nursing care for individuals, families, and communities. Emphasis is placed on health promotion, prevention and control of disease and disability, and rehabilitation. Both day and evening programs are available.

The program in occupational therapy provides students with an understanding of the development of human occupation and the application of purposeful activity to facilitate a client's achievement of good health. Emphasis is placed on a bio-psycho-social approach to health care that concentrates on an individual's ability to perform daily-living activities, including self-care, work, and leisure. Course work is supplemented by six to nine months of supervised fieldwork. The program gives students the foundation necessary to successfully complete the national certification examination after graduation and to develop skills in the areas of clinical practice, teaching, administration, or research.

The physical therapy program emphasizes course work in the physical and biological sciences and physical therapy theory and practice. The curriculum integrates lecture and laboratory classwork related to clinical skills with carefully supervised clinical practice. The program prepares graduates to meet the challenging responsibilities of diagnostic evaluation, treatment implementation, and ongoing assessment. It also provides a firm foundation in the areas of administration, research, consultation, planning, and education, as well as in clinical practice.

Academic Facilities

The Edison Building houses various College of Health Professions administrative and departmental offices, classrooms, laboratories, and the College's Learning Resource Center, which includes a computer laboratory. Jefferson Alumni Hall, a basic medical science/student commons building, houses the College of Graduate Studies, basic science departments, classrooms, and research laboratories. The Scott Building houses University administrative offices and the University library. Clinical experience is acquired at Thomas Jefferson University Hospital or at more than 1,500 clinical affiliate sites.

Costs

Tuition for 1999–2000 was $16,785 for full-time students. Housing costs were $2250 for a double room and about $450 to $1000 per month for a one- to three-bedroom apartment. Meal plans are not offered. Fees for the advanced placement/postcertificate programs vary with each student according to the number and type of credits completed on campus.

Financial Aid

Aid includes Federal Pell Grants, Federal Perkins Loans, Federal Work-Study program awards, Air Force ROTC scholarships, Nursing Scholarships, Nursing Loans, state grants or scholarships, and state-guaranteed loans. About 76 percent of the current students receive financial assistance. To apply for aid, students must submit the Free Application for Federal Student Aid (FAFSA) as well as a Thomas Jefferson University application. Completed applications must be received by the Financial Aid Office not later than May 1.

Faculty

The College of Health Professions has 45 full-time and more than 100 part-time faculty members; most of the part-time faculty members serve in clinical teaching positions. The student-faculty ratio for the entire college is 9:1.

Student Government

Students are free to express their views on issues of institutional policy and on matters of student interest. Active membership on faculty and administrative committees enables students to participate in the formulation and application of University and College policy.

Admission Requirements

Admission for high school students is available through the Plan A College Education (PACE) Program based on a student's academic record, scores on the SAT, recommendations, an interview, extracurricular activities, and possible work experience. Students admitted through PACE attend another college for at least two years to complete prerequisite courses. Approximately two years of college-level course work (39–65 semester credits, depending on the program) are required for transfer admission. For a list of specific prerequisite courses and application deadlines for each program, prospective students should contact the Office of Admissions.

The College of Health Professions offers an equal opportunity for admission to all candidates who meet the admission requirements, without regard to race, color, national and ethnic origin, age, religion, sex, sexual orientation, disability, or veteran status.

Interviews are recommended after all credentials have been received. The nonrefundable application fee is $45.

Application and Information

Admission and financial aid application forms and further information can be obtained by contacting:

Director of Admissions
College of Health Professions
Thomas Jefferson University
Edison Building, Suite 1610
130 South 9th Street
Philadelphia, Pennsylvania 19107-5233
Telephone: 215-503-8890
        800-JEFF-CHP (toll-free)
World Wide Web: http://www.tju.edu/chp

The Scott Building.

THOMAS MORE COLLEGE
CRESTVIEW HILLS, KENTUCKY

The College

Thomas More College is a small, private, Catholic liberal arts college affiliated with the Diocese of Covington, Kentucky. Thomas More College fulfills its liberal arts commitment by maintaining an atmosphere and curriculum that give students the opportunity to grow academically, spiritually, and professionally.

Of the diverse student population of 1,550, 840 attend classes full-time; 155 are resident students. The student body is drawn primarily from the states of Kentucky, Ohio, and Indiana, but many other states and a number of countries are also represented. Students who choose to live on campus reside in one of three townhouse-style residence halls. The new Holbrook Student Center was completed in fall 1999.

The students' college experience is enhanced through their participation in many academic, social, and sports organizations. Intercollegiate athletics are governed by NCAA Division III. Thomas More College competes in men's baseball, basketball, cross-country, football, golf, soccer, and tennis and women's basketball, cross-country, fast-pitch softball, golf, soccer, tennis, and volleyball. Intramural sports offered include, among others, coed flag football, basketball, and volleyball.

Location

Thomas More College is located 10 minutes south of Cincinnati, Ohio, in Crestview Hills, Kentucky. The campus is convenient to major highways. The Greater Cincinnati International Airport is just 10 minutes away. All students are permitted to have cars on campus.

The Greater Cincinnati area offers a wide array of cultural and sporting events. Local attractions include the Broadway Series, the Cincinnati Pops, the Riverbend Music Center, and the Cincinnati Reds and Bengals. Numerous shopping areas and restaurants are also available.

Majors and Degrees

Thomas More College offers bachelor's degrees in accounting, art, biology, business administration, chemistry, computer information systems, criminal justice, drama, economics, education, English, history, international studies, mathematics, medical technology, nursing, philosophy, physics, psychology, sociology, speech communication, and theology.

Preprofessional programs are available in dentistry, law, medicine, occupational therapy, optometry, pharmacy, physical therapy, and veterinary science. There is a 3-2 program in engineering.

The Associate of Arts degree is available in accounting, art, art history, biology, business administration, chemistry, computer information systems, criminal justice, drama, economics, English, exercise science, French, gerontology, history, international studies, math, philosophy, physics, political science, prelegal studies, psychology, sociology, Spanish, speech communication, and theology.

Academic Program

To earn the Bachelor of Arts, Bachelor of Science, or Bachelor of Science in Nursing degree, a student must complete 128 credit hours, including 61 credit hours in liberal arts courses. The Associate of Arts degree requires the completion of 64 credit hours, including a liberal arts component.

The academic calendar is composed of a fall and a spring semester and two summer sessions. The Office of Continuing Education offers a full schedule of evening and Saturday classes.

The Cooperative Education program enables students to gain hands-on professional experience in their field of interest. All students are eligible for this program after the completion of their freshman year. Cooperative Air Force and Army ROTC programs are available in conjunction with nearby universities.

Off-Campus Arrangements

Thirteen area colleges, including Thomas More College, form the Greater Cincinnati Consortium of Colleges and Universities through which all students at the local member colleges may take courses not available at their home institution. Thomas More encourages full-time students to take advantage of this opportunity for curriculum enrichment through cross-registration. In addition, students who wish to spend a year abroad as part of their undergraduate education have a number of possibilities open to them.

Academic Facilities

The library has a collection of more than 130,000 volumes of books, periodicals, and audiovisual materials, and as a selective depository it houses more than 12,000 volumes of U.S. government documents. In addition, the library's membership in the Greater Cincinnati Library Consortium gives Thomas More students access to more than 10.6 million books and more than 50,000 periodicals held by forty-four other libraries in the region.

Thomas More's computer facilities include a PC classroom and three labs containing Pentium 350 PCs for student use. Student computers are also available in some academic departments and in the library. All PCs are connected to a campuswide Novell network, with access to e-mail, the Internet, and an on-campus Intranet server. There is a laser printer in each lab and a color laser and scanner in the PC lab in the main computer center. Software includes Microsoft Windows 98, Office 97 and Visual Studio; Adobe PageMaker and Illustrator; MicroFocus COBOL; and additional software used for departmental instruction.

Students in the science programs receive hands-on experience through the use of the advanced biology, chemistry, and physics laboratories. The facilities include an environmental chamber, an aquatic research station, research and measurement labs, a synthesis lab, a light-sensitive project room, and a machine and electronics shop.

The nursing and sociology departments have excellent working relationships with nearby hospitals and social service agencies.

Costs

The 1999–2000 annual costs for Thomas More College were $12,300 for tuition and $3556 for room (double-occupancy) and board (minimum debit card deposit of $800 per semester). There is a differential fee of $30 per semester hour for all nursing courses. The Student Government fee is $40 per semester and the computer fee is $100 per semester for full-time students. The cost of books is estimated at $400 per year.

Financial Aid

Thomas More College assists approximately 90 percent of its full-time students in meeting college costs. Awards are determined on a rolling basis, with priority consideration given to applications filed by March 1. Financial aid awards are based on economic need, merit, scholastic achievement, and extracurricular activities. The filing of the Free Application for Federal Student Aid (FAFSA) and the Thomas More College Application for Financial Aid and Scholarship is required before any awards are determined. Other Thomas More College awards may require additional applications.

An extensive Federal Work-Study program is in place, and there are excellent opportunities for outside employment in the immediate area.

Faculty

The faculty is committed to the ideals of a Catholic liberal arts education with the main focus on teaching. The faculty has 174 members, of whom 30 percent hold tenure and 62 percent hold doctoral or other terminal degrees. Faculty members serve as academic advisers to students in their disciplines. The student-faculty ratio is 12:1.

Student Government

The purpose of the Student Government Association is to serve as the official representative organization of the Thomas More College student body; to serve as the liaison between the student body and the faculty, administration, and Board of Trustees; to promote student projects and activities and improve the quality of student life; to assist the Dean of Students in supervising student organizations and student activities on campus; to protect the rights of the individual; and to preserve the general welfare of the student body of Thomas More College.

Admission Requirements

The admission criteria are as follows: an applicant should have a high school grade point average (based on college-preparatory courses) of 80 percent or better; a high school rank in the top half of the graduating class; and a minimum composite score of 20 on the ACT Assessment, with a minimum of 20 in English, or a minimum combined score of 1010 on the SAT I, with a minimum of 530 on the verbal portion. If the applicant does not meet all the admission criteria, the file is forwarded to the Admissions Committee for individual consideration.

Transfer students with 24 or more semester hours of transferable credit and an overall grade point average of at least 2.0 on a 4.0 scale are automatically accepted. Transfer students with fewer than 24 transferable hours must meet the general admission criteria.

The applicant must provide a completed application with a nonrefundable $25 fee, high school transcripts, college transcripts (if applicable), and ACT or SAT I score reports. Telephone calls are welcome if there are any questions.

Application and Information

Thomas More College operates under a rolling admission policy, with a final application deadline of August 15. Admission decisions are usually made within two weeks of receiving all application materials. Students can apply online at the Website listed below.

For further information or to schedule a campus visit, students should contact:

Robert A. McDermott
Director of Admissions
Thomas More College
333 Thomas More Parkway
Crestview Hills, Kentucky 41017
Telephone: 606-344-3332
　　　　　　800-825-4557 (toll-free)
E-mail: robert.mcdermott@thomasmore.edu
World Wide Web: http://www.thomasmore.edu

Residence life on the Thomas More College campus.

THOMAS MORE COLLEGE OF LIBERAL ARTS
MERRIMACK, NEW HAMPSHIRE

The College

The Thomas More College of Liberal Arts embodies a fresh approach to the study of Western thought and letters. Established in 1978 by Catholic laymen, this private college embraces the Greco-Roman tradition as it has been transformed by the Judeo-Christian experience. The intellectual and cultural tradition is not viewed as the relic of ancient world views; rather, the Western tradition is understood as a living legacy that enables conversation with the great minds and hearts of the past.

The course of studies at the Thomas More College emphasizes a return to the sources—the great poetic, philosophic, political, and theological works of the West. Students read seminal works not for the acquisition of information or skills but for the love of learning. Learning reawakens the imagination through wide-ranging studies that invite the student to reexamine the human condition and its relation to the natural and the divine orders. This reexamination of sources results in a felicity of both written and spoken expression.

The study of Western culture proceeds at Thomas More in an atmosphere of community and includes lectures and seminars with the faculty as well as major independent research projects in the junior and senior years. Central to the community is the fact that all students take 6 credit hours of course work together each semester for all four years. By experiencing the form of the whole curriculum, students grow in appreciation of the perennial wisdom, its cultural forms, and symbolic orders. They come to understand Western culture as a gift whose stewardship will dictate man's future.

The College currently enrolls 70 full-time students from twenty-seven states, Canada, and Greece. Nearly all students live on campus. Men and women occupy separate quarters; intervisitation is not allowed. A residential growth of 200 is anticipated. With this modest size, it is possible to develop and sustain deep and genuine friendships among the student body and faculty.

All campus life is understood as a natural extension of the academic program, as a continuation of the conversation begun in the classroom. It includes such activities as public lectures, a film series, coffeehouses, day trips, dramatic readings, celebrations of feast days and holidays, and intramural sports.

Students find easy access to Cambridge and Boston. The surrounding mountains make skiing and hiking convenient, and the 17-mile-long seacoast offers additional recreational options. Across the road from the campus, the Merrimack athletic facility provides all students with a complete athletic complex.

More than 60 percent of the graduates have gone on to pursue graduate study, not only in their undergraduate majors but also in theology, psychology, classics, history, liturgical music, education, counseling, business, law, medicine, languages, and urban and environmental planning.

Location

The location of the Thomas More College in southern New Hampshire, just 45 minutes north of Boston and on the southern edge of the residential community of Merrimack, enables students to know their American heritage in the state whose motto is "Live free or die." Built on a seventeenth-century land grant from the king, the renovated old farmhouse and barn retain for the campus the character of a Colonial New England farm. The second-largest city in the state, with a population of 80,000, the city of Nashua is just south of the campus. Although Nashua is a high-tech area, it maintains a symphony and choral society.

Majors and Degrees

The Cowan Program in Liberal Arts offers programs leading to the Bachelor of Arts degree in biology, literature, philosophy, and political science. No major is declared until the end of the sophomore year. Though limited in number, the disciplines that are offered as majors are chosen because they are modes of knowing the whole of reality—through literary representation, through philosophy, through science, and through political life. Students also find these majors to be excellent preparation for careers in unrelated fields.

Academic Program

The Cowan Program of Liberal Arts is structured around a renewed understanding of learning. By submitting to the 6-credit-hour humanities course required for all eight semesters, every student reads more than 100 unabridged great books of Western civilization. However, the core should not be understood as a Catholic great books program. Books are representative of the living community in and about which they were written. The sequence of the humanities core is in accord with the cultural development of the West: the ancient world (two semesters), the Early and High Middle Ages (two semesters), the Renaissance and Reformation, early modern studies, American studies, and the late and postmodern era. In addition to the 48 credit hours of humanities, every student takes 12 hours of writing workshop. Students must study Latin or Greek for two years. Six hours of mathematics and 6 of biology are required.

Twenty-four hours of study in one's major are required. The junior project is a special study required of all majors, wherein a great writer's works are mastered for an oral exam. The senior project consists of independent research and original work on a thesis within one's discipline, culminating in a formal address. All seniors must pass a 7-hour comprehensive exam in their discipline. A total of 120 credit hours is required for graduation.

Off-Campus Arrangements

The Rome Program is a key part of the curriculum. All second-semester sophomores and transfer students who have 45 or more hours of accepted credit continue to pursue the core curriculum and fulfill other requirements in Rome for one semester. Thomas More faculty members teach the sequential core courses and upper-division courses; adjunct professors teach theology and 3 credit hours in the history of art and architecture. The residence in Rome was designed by Borromini and is located in Trastevere, a medieval district of Rome. Day trips outside of Rome are regularly arranged, as is a general audience with the Pope. The cost for full-time students is remarkably low, and financial aid is available. Many students travel afterward for part of the summer.

Academic Facilities

Dedicated in 1990, Louis Bancel Warren Library has 30,000 volumes, as well as conference rooms, a large classroom, and a ballroom.

Costs

For 1999–2000, the cost of tuition for a full-time student was $9200, and room and board were $7000. In-state and out-of-state costs were the same.

Financial Aid

The Thomas More College of Liberal Arts tries to meet the demonstrated need of all its students. The great majority of the student body receives financial aid in the form of grants, loans, work-study, and scholarships. The College requires the Free Application for Federal Student Aid (FAFSA).

Faculty

The faculty of the Thomas More College of Liberal Arts is a teaching faculty. One hundred percent of the full-time faculty hold the terminal degree or the Oxford degree. There are no teaching assistants; all major professors teach freshman and sophomore courses. Each faculty member views teaching as an all-encompassing vocation, and this commitment is part of the reason that the graduates have enjoyed such remarkable success in pursuing advanced degrees. The faculty as a whole shares a common vision of liberal education.

Student Government

Given its small size, the Thomas More College of Liberal Arts has seen no need as yet for a formal representative student organization. However, a Social Council has assumed responsibility for the cocurricular activities that were formerly planned by College administrators. The Council has arranged for competitions in some games and sports, for Saturday day trips, for Wednesday evening transportation to the mall, and for weekend social events. There is also time each semester for the scheduling of informal dances, for dramatic readings of humanities assignments, and for the traditional academic pastimes of satirical gibes at the intellectual life itself. A student liaison reports directly to the President of the College.

Admission Requirements

The College selects both incoming freshmen and transfer students primarily on the basis of their desire to submit to a complete and unified liberal arts education. The experience of the Admissions Committee is that there is a self-selection process that maintains the quality of accepted students. Though required, standardized test scores do not determine admissibility. Rank in class and the difficulty of the course work attempted are more important factors. The Office of Admissions attempts to ascertain a student's degree of confidence and motivation through recommendations, an interview, and the essay on the application form. Applicants should have at least the following college-preparatory units: English, 4; mathematics, 3; foreign language, 2; social science, 2; and laboratory science, 2. An exception to any one of these required units can be made by the committee whenever the course work has provided an adequate challenge and when the student's overall preparedness is deemed sufficiently strong. Transfer students are welcome, and credits are evaluated after admission.

Application and Information

Students must submit a completed application form, a transcript showing seven semesters of high school work, two academic letters of recommendation, scores on either the SAT I or ACT, and an application fee of $25. Transfer students must submit transcripts from all previously attended colleges. There is a rolling admission policy maintained through August 31. Early decision is available. Visits to the campus are strongly recommended. Arrangements should be made with the Office of Admissions.

For additional information, students are encouraged to contact:

Dr. Kristen S. Kelly, Director of Admissions
Thomas More College of Liberal Arts
Six Manchester Street
Merrimack, New Hampshire 03054
Telephone: 603-880-8308
Fax: 603-880-9280
E-mail: thomaemorae@earthlink.com
World Wide Web: http://www.thomasmorecollege.edu

Sophomores study in Rome for their spring semester.

TIFFIN UNIVERSITY
TIFFIN, OHIO

The University

Tiffin University, established in 1888, is an independent, coeducational institution with no religious affiliation. The University is accredited by the Commission on Institutions of Higher Education of the North Central Association of Colleges and Schools.

The programs of emphasis at Tiffin University are accounting, forensic psychology, hospitality management, law enforcement, and liberal studies, which draw students from all over Ohio, eighteen states, and twenty countries.

Tiffin University also grants the Master of Business Administration degree.

Tiffin University provides a variety of living arrangements for students interested in on-campus housing. These students enjoy both the traditional residence-hall environment as well as small-group living on Tiffin's 103-acre campus. Living options include coed and single-sex residence halls and fraternity and sorority houses. All of the units are in proximity to the academic buildings, recreational and laundry facilities, and the dining hall. Students residing in University housing are required to participate in the University board plan, which offers three options in dining.

There are two sororities and two fraternities on campus. The Delta Beta Chapters of the Alpha Iota sorority and the Phi Theta Pi fraternity are international groups concerned with commerce and business. The Sigma Delta Sigma sorority and Sigma Omega Sigma fraternity sponsor a variety of events for the University community. There are also two honor societies on campus. Other student organizations include the student government, the International Student Association, the Black United Students, the Intervarsity Christian Fellowship Club, the school newspaper, and departmental clubs.

Tiffin University is a member of the NCAA, the NAIA, the American Mid-Eastern Conference, and the Mid-States Football Association. The University offers intercollegiate athletics for men in baseball, basketball, cross-country, football, golf, soccer, and tennis. Women's varsity athletics include basketball, cross-country, soccer, softball, tennis, and volleyball. The University also sponsors coed intramural sports events. The Gillmor Student Center houses a basketball gymnasium, an activities room, offices, and a bookstore. Student services include career and placement counseling, academic tutoring, and personal counseling. Construction has begun on a 78-acre multifield athletic complex.

Location

Tiffin University is located on Ohio Route 53 in Tiffin, which is 50 miles south of Toledo, 90 miles southwest of Cleveland, and 90 miles north of Columbus. The city of Tiffin, with a population of approximately 22,000, is the center of an area rich in college tradition. Within a 70-mile radius are located fourteen private colleges and universities, two state universities and several two-year branch campuses, and community colleges. Tiffin is located on the green banks of the Sandusky River in north-central Ohio, and offers residents and visitors a variety of fine restaurants, shopping, a museum, historic sites, and numerous recreational opportunities. Tiffin is the home of the historic Ritz Theatre, which offers a wide selection of cultural events throughout the year.

Majors and Degrees

Tiffin University grants the Bachelor of Arts degree, the Bachelor of Business Administration degree, the Bachelor of Criminal Justice degree, the Associate of Business Administration degree, and the Associate of Science in Business Technology degree.

The Bachelor of Arts degree is granted in liberal studies in the humanities and in liberal studies in the social sciences.

Majors in the business administration program are accounting, administrative management, finance, hospitality management (hotel/motel, restaurant/food service, and travel/tourism), information systems, international studies (accounting and finance, hospitality management, and marketing), management (human resource management, international business, managerial studies, operations management, and sports management), and marketing.

The Bachelor of Criminal Justice degree is granted in corrections, forensic psychology, and law enforcement.

The Associate of Business Administration degree is granted in accounting, business administration, computer programming, and hospitality management.

The Associate of Science in Business Technology degree is granted in law enforcement.

Academic Program

Tiffin University operates on a semester system. Students must complete at least 130 semester hours with a minimum grade point average of 2.0 to earn a bachelor's degree. Students work with academic advisers to organize a schedule that meets the requirements of the University.

The Sworn Internship Program for law enforcement majors is unequaled anywhere. After two years, a student can be appointed by a police department as a reserve officer, complete the Police Academy training, and participate in two internships in his or her senior year as a sworn officer. The Sworn Internship Program is designed to provide professionally trained and field-proven candidates for employment. Tiffin University juniors are appointed by selected police agencies to serve as reserve officers. These students must then complete the basic training for which they receive college credit.

The hospitality management curriculum includes such specialized topics as front-office operations, housekeeping and property management, restaurant operations, hotel sales and marketing, managerial accounting, law of innkeeping and food service, and tourism. Students also have internship opportunities available to them at such places as Disney World, Marriott hotels, and Holiday Inns. Students also receive hands-on experience at the historic Pioneer Mill restaurant in Tiffin.

Along with their regular course work, students must also participate in Tiffin University's cocurricular program. This program provides students with the opportunity to develop an interest in such areas as health and personal fitness, recreation, the arts, and community service. Students are required to participate in 26 clock hours (2 units) of cocurricular activity to graduate.

Off-Campus Arrangements

Tiffin University has established a junior-year study-abroad semester in cooperation with Regents College in London, England.

Regents College draws upon the academic traditions and resources of both Great Britain and the United States. Its university-level programs are taught by teachers from both countries and are accredited in the United States.

Tiffin University's agreement with Regents College permits students to study overseas and receive academic credit for course work taken at Regents. The credit received at Regents College is transferred directly to Tiffin University.

Academic Facilities

Tiffin University's campus is small, and the academic buildings are within a short walking distance of the residence halls.

The focal point of the Tiffin campus is the classroom building, which was built in 1884 and is now listed on the National Register of Historic Places. The classroom building houses classrooms, faculty and administrative offices, a computer center, and graduate offices. The computer center has sixty IBM-compatible PCs available for student use.

The Richard C. Pfeiffer Library has 255 subscriptions to magazines and newspapers, 27,500 books, 32,000 microfiche units, and several other computers for online searching. The library is a member of OhioLink and Online Computer Library Center (OCLC). The Pfeiffer Library also has classrooms in the lower level. Construction of a classroom building and residence hall was completed in fall 1994, and a library expansion was completed in early 1996, doubling the size of the facility.

Costs

For 2000–01, tuition is approximately $11,130, and average room and board charges are approximately $5050, for a total of $16,180. Books and supplies are approximately $800. Travel costs vary.

Financial Aid

Seventy percent of all students at Tiffin University receive some type of financial aid. The average award is $8200. Aid is available in the form of scholarships, grants and loans given by the University, and state and federal loans. A complete Free Application for Federal Student Aid (FAFSA) is required for financial aid consideration. Some scholarships and grants require special applications, tests, or recommendations from counselors, teachers, and coaches. Additional information can be obtained from the Financial Aid Office.

Faculty

The Tiffin University faculty is composed of 70 dedicated individuals serving in either a full-time or adjunct capacity. Of the full-time faculty, 77 percent hold doctorates or the highest certification in their field. Many faculty members are involved in the business community in either a research or consulting capacity. Members of the faculty also serve as officers in regional and national academic organizations. Faculty members are accessible to students and show genuine interest in their academic and personal concerns.

Student Government

Tiffin University's student government is one of the most active organizations on campus. It is responsible for planning, organizing, and executing social, cultural, and educational programs and activities. With representatives from all facets of the student body, along with 5 officers, the group serves as a voice for student concerns and needs. The student government fosters a sense of community among faculty, administrators, and students. In addition, the group offers students the opportunity to obtain and utilize valuable leadership skills necessary for today's business world.

Admission Requirements

Individuals wishing to further their education are invited to apply to Tiffin. Even though admission policies are liberal, applicants must be graduates of secondary schools and must meet specific entrance requirements. Applications may be submitted anytime after students complete their junior year in high school. It is recommended that a student's high school transcript show credit for at least the following: 4 units of English, 3 units of mathematics, 2 units of science, and 2 units of social studies, as well as 3 units of electives from academic or commercial subjects and 2 other units of electives.

Applicants are considered for admission according to their potential to benefit from instruction at Tiffin University. Students with less than a 2.0 grade point average in their high school career may be admitted through the Learning Assistance Program.

Application and Information

Students must submit a completed application to Tiffin University's admission office. In addition to the application, they should supply ACT or SAT scores, an official transcript of grades, and a $20 application fee.

For further information, students should contact:

Office of Admission
Tiffin University
155 Miami Street
Tiffin, Ohio 44883
Telephone: 419-447-6443
              800-968-OHIO (toll-free)
Fax: 419-443-5006
E-mail: admiss@tiffin.edu
World Wide Web: http://www.tiffin.edu

Franks Hall is the latest addition, along with a residence hall and a library expansion, to Tiffin University's growing campus.

TOCCOA FALLS COLLEGE
TOCCOA FALLS, GEORGIA

The College
Toccoa Falls College, founded in 1907, is a four-year, private, coeducational, interdenominational Christian college, offering both Bible and liberal arts courses in an intensely Christian environment. It is known as one of the finest Christian colleges in the nation. As a private Christian college, it occupies a strategic position in meeting the needs of today's world. Through the eight schools of study, Toccoa Falls College prepares men and women for vocational and professional Christian ministries around the world. Today, almost 1,000 students from forty-nine states and twenty-five other countries study at Toccoa Falls College. Toccoa Falls College is about students—committed students who are serious about their ministry to people. A committed administration, faculty, and staff meet the spiritual, cultural, educational, and social needs of the students at Toccoa. The College is also committed to maintaining the highest standards of scholarship. Toccoa Falls College is expanding. With the steady growth of its student population, new buildings have been added and others renovated. Recent completion of a new World Missions Center has greatly enhanced campus facilities. This spacious facility houses the School of World Missions. Toccoa Falls College has a commitment to remain faithful to the challenge of preparing men and women for leadership and for the proclamation of the Christian message around the world. The College is accredited by the Accrediting Association of Bible Colleges and the Commission on Colleges of the Southern Association of Colleges and Schools. It holds teacher education approval by the Professional Standards Commission of the state of Georgia and membership in the National Association of Schools of Music. For the fall 1999 semester, the College enrolled 945 students from forty-nine states, Puerto Rico, and twenty-five countries; students represent more than thirty evangelical denominations. Toccoa Falls College's modular-formatted School of Graduate Studies offers a terminal M.Min. degree in three concentrations: Christian education, intercultural studies, and pastoral ministries. Each weekend the social calendar has something to offer—from parties, student government, and formal banquets to hayrides, musical performances, and athletic events. Varsity intercollegiate sports include men's baseball, basketball, cheerleading, and soccer and women's teams in basketball, cheerleading, soccer, and volleyball. The College also offers a full range of intramural sports, with men's, women's, coed, faculty, and staff teams participating. On-campus housing for single students includes men's dormitories, women's dormitories, cottages, and terrace dormitories. Married students live in apartments or the College's mobile community. All students, excluding those with special health needs, are placed into the housing of their choice, in the order by date the housing deposit is received. Thirty-five percent of the students live off campus. Dining facilities include a full-service dining hall, a snack shop, and a campus restaurant.

Location
Toccoa Falls College's 1,100-acre campus, complete with a 186-foot waterfall and remarkable location, gives students immediate access to lakes, rivers, mountains, and state parks that invite such diversions as waterskiing, boating, river-rafting, repelling, rock climbing, caving, hiking, fishing, golf, camping, and picnicking. Georgia's mild Southern climate permits many months of open-air fun. The city of Toccoa offers a wide variety of choices for dining, entertainment, and employment. Just a short drive away is Georgia's most exciting city, Atlanta—the home of the 1996 summer Olympics. Atlanta offers a full range of cultural enrichments, including entertainment opportunities with restaurants, parks, professional athletics, shopping, and various other historic charms of the state's capital. Whatever one's pleasure, big city advantages or small town hospitality, one will find the perfect solution at Toccoa Falls College.

Majors and Degrees
Toccoa Falls College confers the Bachelor of Science and Bachelor of Arts degrees in the following twenty-three major programs: biblical languages, biblical studies, broadcasting, business administration, Christian education, counseling skills, cross-cultural studies (with a medical professions option), early childhood education, English, family ministries, interpersonal and organizational communication, journalism and print media, middle grades education (with concentrations in language arts, mathematics, science, social science, music), missiology, music (emphases in church music, composition, performance), music education (choral, instrumental), pastoral ministries, philosophy and religion, psychology, secondary education: English, secondary education: history, and youth ministries. The College also confers the Associate of Arts degree in general studies. A one- or two-year certificate CLIMB program in biblical studies is also available.

Academic Program
The College operates under the semester calendar and offers one winterim session and two summer sessions. Prior to graduation, students must earn a minimum of 66 credit hours, with satisfactory completion of at least two semesters of field experience in student ministry for the associate degree. A minimum of 124 credit hours and satisfactory completion of at least four semesters of field experience in student ministry is required for the bachelor's degree. Each bachelor's degree student must earn a minimum of 30 credit hours in Bible and theology. Other requirements are needed for specific majors and degree programs. Core courses are required. Single, double, and individually designed majors give students flexibility in planning their futures. Students may also minor in one or more of thirty-nine programs. Students have the opportunity to participate in internship experiences, study-travel, and overseas study.

Academic Facilities
Academic life centers around the Seby Jones Library, which currently houses a total of more than 103,800 holdings, including books, bound volumes, scores, vertical files, audiovisuals, and microfiche, with 299 periodical subscriptions in paper format and thousands of full-text journals available on line. This building also houses a full-service Media Center and curriculum labs for teacher education. Other resources include the Interlibrary Loan Service, GALILEO (Georgia's statewide resource-sharing project), and direct access to the Internet; all give students access to resources throughout Georgia and the southeastern United States. Other academic facilities include the WRAF 100,000-watt FM radio station–flagship station of the Toccoa Falls College radio network; the Toccoa Falls College computer lab; the Julian A. Bandy Music Building, housing practice rooms and the music library containing curriculum, music scores, and sound recordings; the Recital Hall; the Clary Science Building, including the chemistry and biology labs; the Woerner World Missions Building; and the White Memorial Photo Lab, complete with photo labs and curriculum labs for Christian education materials. The College is currently raising funds for a new chapel/performance arts center that is being built, along with many other campus additions and renovations.

Costs
Tuition for 2000–01 full-time students (12 or more semester hours) is $8888. Resident costs, including room, meals, and health fees, are $4012. Other estimated typical miscellaneous costs, includ-

ing fees and books, are $665. Lab fees for music, computer, science, photography, and other courses range from $25 to $100 per course. Personal expenses for transportation, recreation, and miscellaneous needs vary with the individual student.

Financial Aid

Toccoa Falls College seeks to assist every qualified student who demonstrates financial need with one or more of the following types of aid: grants, loans, scholarships, work-study programs, and employment on or off campus. Funds come from federal, state, private, and school resources. Currently, 85 percent of Toccoa Falls College students receive some type of aid, with the average award covering 70 percent of tuition, room, and meals. All students must complete and submit the FAFSA, as well as the Toccoa Falls College Financial Aid Information Form to apply for specific programs. All awards, other than academic honor scholarships, music scholarships, and leadership scholarships, are awarded on the basis of financial need. To receive priority consideration on all forms, applications must be submitted by March 1 for the fall term and October 15 for the spring term. Toccoa Falls College raises funds for its financial aid program through an ongoing, aggressive capital fund campaign managed through the Office of Advancement/Development.

Faculty

Toccoa Falls College has 67 faculty members: 49 full-time and 18 part-time. All courses are taught by degree-holding faculty members, not student aid teachers. Instructors for the School of Graduate Studies consist of professors from the undergraduate division and high-quality adjunct teaching faculty members. Fifty-three percent of full-time teaching faculty members have earned a doctorate degree or the highest degree in their field. Many faculty members have published books, have written for major magazines, have served on national organizations or memberships, or are featured guest speakers or lecturers. All are actively involved in the interests of the students and serve as faculty advisers to assist in the course selection and academic counseling needs of the students. The student-faculty ratio is 17:1.

Student Government

The Student Association is made up of all students currently enrolled at Toccoa Falls College. Full-time students are voting members and part-time students are associate members. Student Government is the legislative and governing organization of the Student Association. The Executive Committee of the Student Government is elected by the voting members of the Student Association. The purpose of Student Government is to serve the Student Association, promote unity and spiritual growth, and control the budget of the Student Association funds. The Student Government plays a vital role in the communication between faculty members, staff, and students and represents the needs of students to various official administrative committees. Many of the social events, activities, and spiritual meetings planned throughout the year are a direct ministry of the Student Government Association.

Admission Requirements

In selecting students for admission, Toccoa Falls College seeks evidence of Christian commitment and character and the capacity and desire to learn. Students interested in the evangelical Christian perspective and curriculum at Toccoa Falls College and who demonstrate a commitment to the philosophy of education are eligible for consideration for admission. Although the promise of academic success and the personal Christian testimony of the applicant are of primary consideration, the aspirations of the applicant and the personal recommendations are also considered in the admissions decision. Transfer and international students are welcome. In addition, Toccoa Falls College has the following spiritual requirements: students must have accepted the Lord Jesus Christ as Savior at least six months prior to enrollment, have evidence of good Christian character (information from written personal testimony and three character references, one from the student's pastor), have abstained from the use of tobacco, alcohol, and illegal drugs prior to enrollment, have regular attendance in an evangelical church, and be in agreement with or accept the College's doctrinal statement and policies as printed in the current catalog and handbook. All qualified new students should have completed all high school graduation requirements or have a GED certificate to be considered for normal admission status. Transfer students with a GPA of 2.0 or better are granted admission with advanced standing if they have completed acceptable academic work at other accredited institutions (12 semester hours or the equivalent).

Along with the $20 application fee and completed application form, all applicants must submit three personal recommendations, an official and complete high school transcript, and ACT or SAT I test scores (SAT I is preferred for placement purposes). All new freshman, transfer, international, transient, joint/early admit, and special student applicants from both in and out of state are considered on an equal basis. Campus visits and personal interviews are highly encouraged. Toccoa Falls College reserves the right to further examine an applicant by psychological, achievement, and aptitude tests or by personal interview. Toccoa Falls College admits qualified students without regard to race, age, creed, color, gender, physical handicap, or national or ethnic origin.

Application and Information

Qualified students are encouraged to apply as early as possible during their final year of high school. Toccoa Falls College admits qualified students who have completed all application materials and have been accepted by the Admissions Committee for enrollment in all semesters on a rolling basis. Applicants are notified of their admission status by mail and by phone approximately one week after all admissions materials have been received.

For further information and application materials, students should contact:

Toccoa Falls College
Office of Admissions
Toccoa Falls, Georgia 30598
Telephone: 706-886-6831
           800-868-3257 (toll-free)
Fax: 706-282-6012
E-mail: admissions@toccoafalls.edu
World Wide Web: http://www.toccoafalls.edu

The Toccoa Falls College campus has a beautiful 186-foot waterfall.

TOURO COLLEGE
NEW YORK, NEW YORK

The College

Touro College is a Jewish-sponsored independent institution of higher and professional education, founded by Dr. Bernard Lander. The College was established primarily to enrich the Jewish heritage and to serve the larger American community. Touro College derives its name from Judah and Isaac Touro, leaders of colonial America who represented the ideals upon which the College bases its mission. Touro was chartered by New York State in 1970. In 1971, the College opened with an entering class of 35 male liberal arts and sciences students. Between 1971 and 1986, the College showed substantial growth. A women's division was added to the College of Liberal Arts and Sciences, and the Schools of General Studies, Law, Health Sciences, and Graduate Jewish Studies were subsequently organized. Since 1986, the College has added the School of Career and Applied Studies, the Graduate School of Education and Psychology, the School for Lifelong Education, and the International School of Business. Through its various schools and divisions, Touro offers many study-abroad opportunities in countries such as Israel, Russia, and India. Touro is accredited by the Commission on Higher Education of the Middle States Association of Colleges and Schools. The College holds an absolute charter from the Regents of the State of New York.

The College now enrolls close to 9,000 students. The student body reflects the diversity of New York City. The ages of Touro students range from 17 to 70. Touro College effectively serves a broad range of students with varying interests, including traditional-age high school graduates, young adults who found it necessary to enter the job market immediately upon leaving high school and are now able to carry the responsibilities of both work and school, and older students who are achieving lifelong dreams of obtaining a higher education. Others are preparing for career changes. There is a healthy population of international students and recent immigrants at Touro College.

Many services and support systems are available to Touro College students. The advisement and counseling staff assists students in selecting courses and a program of study to satisfy their educational goals. Comprehensive Learning Resource Centers are found in each of the College's major locations. Effective one-on-one tutoring in a variety of subjects is available free of charge to any Touro College student seeking academic support. There is an outstanding English for speakers of other languages (ESL) faculty and demonstrated success in working with nonnative English speakers. The Career Planning and Placement Office assists students in finding full- and part-time employment opportunities.

Location

Touro College has campuses in Manhattan, Brooklyn, and Queens in New York City. The College prides itself on its accessibility to New York City residents. In addition, there are locations in Bay Shore, Long Island; Huntington, Long Island; and San Francisco, California, which house the Schools of Health Sciences, Law, and Osteopathy, respectively. Touro also operates a number of programs overseas.

Majors and Degrees

Touro College offers certificate, associate, bachelor's, master's, and professional degrees.

The following major is available in the Associate of Arts degree program: liberal arts and science. The following majors are available in the Associate in Science degree program: business management and administration, desktop publishing, finance, human services, and management. The following Associate in Applied Science degree programs are available: accounting, finance, human services, information systems and data communications, management, marketing, occupational therapy assistant studies, office technology, and physical therapist assistant studies. The following Associate in Occupational Studies degree programs are available: accounting, finance, human services, information technology and data communications, management, marketing, and office technology.

Certificate programs are available in the following areas: accounting, biomedical equipment technician studies, business management, data processing, desktop publishing, electronic document processing, medical coding and billing, microcomputer software support technician studies, networking, office management, and programming.

A good number of the Touro College associate degree graduates continue their studies at Touro to obtain a baccalaureate degree, which is offered in the following areas: accounting, biology, business management and administration, chemistry, computer science, economics, elementary education (N–6), finance, Hebrew language and literature, history, human services, interdisciplinary arts and science, interdisciplinary science, Judaic studies, liberal arts and sciences, literature "English," management, mathematics, philosophy, political science, psychology, special education, social science, sociology, and speech and communication.

Academic Program

Touro College provides courses of study that prepare students for their eventual academic and professional goals. The Associate in Arts and Associate in Science degrees prepare students to matriculate in bachelor-level studies. The certificate, Associate in Applied Science, and Associate in Occupational Studies programs provide students with practical skills to prepare them for immediate entry into a career. Touro College operates on a semester calendar with summer sessions.

Academic Facilities

Library services are available at all major locations. Each location contains full computer facilities with full Internet access. Science laboratories are available for all related courses.

Costs

Tuition costs are based on a per-credit charge of $390 or a flat rate of $4625 for up to 18 credits per semester. The College maintains no student housing facilities.

Financial Aid

Touro College makes every effort to assist students in making their education possible. Applications for financial aid must be completed once every academic year. Financial aid counselors are available to assist students in completing their applications, the Free Application for Federal Student Aid, and the New York State Higher Education Services Corporation Tuition Assistance

Program application. A typical financial aid package consists of a combination of federal and state grants and student loans.

Faculty

There are 307 full-time and 532 part-time faculty members.

Student Government

There is a Student Government Association at every major location. All students are encouraged to join and actively participate.

Admission Requirements

Touro College admits students who demonstrate the competence, motivation, energy, and maturity to pursue a degree program while meeting life's complex responsibilities. The standard used in measuring these qualities is present motivation rather than past performance. Though a high school diploma or the equivalent is generally required for admission into an associate degree program at Touro, the College recognizes that the knowledge skills and ability that are expected of entering college students may be acquired through a variety of nontraditional learning experiences.

Application and Information

Applications for admission are accepted on an ongoing basis for the next available semester.

Information can be obtained through:
Office of Admissions
Touro College
27-33 West 23rd Street
New York, New York 10010
Telephone: 212-463-0400 Ext. 500

TOWSON UNIVERSITY
TOWSON, MARYLAND

The University

Founded in 1866, Towson University (TU) is a regional comprehensive university that offers degree programs in the liberal arts and sciences and preprofessional and professional areas of study. The University's beautiful 328-acre campus is located in the suburban community of Towson, Maryland, just 7 miles north of downtown Baltimore. Towson offers bachelor's degrees in fifty-two fields of study and master's degrees in twenty-seven. The University emphasizes excellence in teaching and continued scholarly growth by faculty members. Towson is nationally recognized for its excellent programs in business, communications, computer information systems, fine arts, health professions, teacher education, and women's studies.

Towson University is composed of eight colleges: the College of Business and Economics, the College of Education, the College of Fine Arts and Communication, the College of Health Professions, the College of Liberal Arts, the College of Science and Mathematics, the College of Graduate Education and Research, and the College of Extended Programs.

The University enrolls more than 16,000 full- and part-time students, including more than 500 international students from ninety countries. More than 13,000 TU students are undergraduates, and about 15 percent of the student body are members of minority groups. More than 3,300 students (almost 65 percent of the freshman class) live on campus at TU. There are twelve residence halls, including modern high-rise towers, apartment complexes, and two- and three-story traditional buildings. Student life on campus offers exciting academic, social, cultural, and athletic opportunities. There are more than 100 student clubs and campus organizations, including fraternities, sororities, and social and professional clubs. The University Union is a popular gathering place, housing the campus bookstore, the post office, dining facilities, ATM machines, a recreation/bowling center, and more. The University's health center, counseling center, academic advising center, and career center are also available to students.

Towson University is a Division I member of the National Collegiate Athletic Association (NCAA) and fields teams in eleven men's and twelve women's sports. The Tigers compete in the America East Conference in twenty-one sports, the East Atlantic Gymnastics League, and the Patriot League for football. The University's 24-acre sports complex includes Minnegan Stadium, where the Tiger football, track, field hockey, and lacrosse teams play, and the Towson Center, which seats more than 5,000 spectators. TU's athletic facilities include an NCAA-regulation swimming pool, three gymnasiums, two weight training rooms, a sand volleyball court, twenty-three tennis courts, a fitness center, six racquetball courts, and six squash courts. Towson also offers intramural sports with leagues for men and women.

Location

Towson is located in Baltimore County, in the suburban community of Towson. The campus is 10 minutes from Towson Town Center, the region's largest upscale shopping mall, and within walking distance of restaurants, bookstores, movie theaters, and libraries. The University is 20 minutes from the cultural and educational resources of downtown Baltimore, home of the National Aquarium, the Maryland Science Center, Oriole Park at Camden Yards, the Walters Art Gallery, and Federal Hill. Towson is also centrally located in the mid-Atlantic region, convenient to the Atlantic beaches; the Appalachian Mountains; Washington, D.C.; Philadelphia; and New York City.

Majors and Degrees

The Bachelor of Arts or Bachelor of Science degree is offered in accounting; art; art education; athletic training; biology; business administration; chemistry; communication studies; computer information systems; computer science; cultural studies; dance performance and education; early childhood education; economics; electronic media and film; elementary education; English; environmental science and studies; exercise science; family studies; French; geography and environmental planning; geosciences; German; gerontology; health science; health-care management; history; interdisciplinary studies; international studies; law and American civilization; mass communication; mathematics; metropolitan studies; molecular biology, biochemistry, and bioinformatics; music; music education; nursing; occupational therapy; philosophy; physical education; physics; political science; psychology; secondary education; social science; sociology/anthropology; Spanish; special education; speech-language pathology and audiology; sport management; sport studies; theater; and women's studies. The Bachelor of Fine Arts degree is offered in dance.

Academic Program

The University follows the semester system with spring and fall semesters, an optional January minimester, three 5-week summer sessions, and one 7-week summer session.

The University's first and most important goal is to provide a sound liberal arts and sciences education for all students. To fulfill this goal, the University provides a core program of General Education (GenEd) requirements to provide a basic introduction to all concepts of the arts and sciences. To be awarded a bachelor's degree, students must satisfactorily complete a minimum of 120 hours of college credit and attain a grade of C (2.0) or higher in their major and a cumulative average of at least 2.0. In addition to fulfilling the requirements of the major program, all students must complete up to 46 hours in General Education course requirements, including a basic composition course and an advanced composition writing course. A program of academic advising is an essential part of the University's entire mission.

Students who qualify are invited to participate in the Honors College. Honors College courses offer students opportunities for research, course work, and mentoring in a wide range of academic disciplines. Honors College students receive priority scheduling and can apply for honors scholarships. Extracurricular seminars and programs are offered as well.

Towson University offers more than 900 courses during the spring and fall semesters and the summer sessions. Students can attend full-time or part-time during the day, in the evening, and on Saturday.

Off-Campus Arrangements

The University offers opportunities for study in more than forty countries in Asia, Australia, Canada, Central and South America, Europe, and the Middle East. More than 180 students from a variety of disciplines participate in study-abroad and exchange programs each year.

TU's Internship Program offers students opportunities to earn college credit, gain work experience, network, and explore career choices. Each year, Towson places more than 700 students in internships around the country.

Academic Facilities

The Albert S. Cook Library, located near the center of campus, contains more than 575,000 books, more than 2,000 periodicals, and a variety of other media, including microforms, audiocassettes and videocassettes, CD-ROMs, and online databases. The library's online catalog system gives Towson students access to the collections of all eleven University System of Maryland campuses. Web resources on MdUSA provide a virtual library with indexing, abstracting, and full-text articles. The Center for the Arts houses the departments of art, dance, music, and theater arts; a 346-seat main stage theater; a 520-seat concert hall; and two art galleries. Van Bokkelen Hall, which houses the Department of Communication Sciences and Disorders and the Department of Mass Communication and Communication Studies, contains modern communication equipment and a clinic that offers services to people with hearing and speech disorders. Smith Hall, home to the science departments, contains modern laboratory facilities and a planetarium. Historic Stephens Hall houses the College of Business and Economics and the 700-seat Stephens Hall Auditorium. The University's Media Center is the location of the student-run television station (WMJF-TV), the campus radio stations, and the Department of Electronic Media and Film.

Costs

Anticipated 2000–01 tuition and fees are $2355 per semester for Maryland residents and $5570 per semester for out-of-state students. The estimated cost for room and board is approximately $2950 per semester.

Financial Aid

Approximately 65 percent of Towson University students receive financial aid. Aid for eligible students who have financial need may come from programs funded by federal, state, and university sources. In addition, Towson University offers academic and non-need-based scholarships to qualified students.

Faculty

Towson offers many opportunities for close student-faculty contact and promotes a supportive environment designed to meet the professional and personal goals of students. A student-faculty ratio of 16:1 and small classes, which average 25 to 30 students, allow students to interact closely with their professors.

Eighty-seven percent of the full-time faculty members have earned the highest degree of academic preparation in their fields of specialization from some of the finest colleges and universities in the world. Many of the 521 full-time instructors are recognized nationally and internationally for published works and honors they have received.

Student Government

The Student Government Association (SGA) officially represents all students on campus. The SGA plans, organizes, and directs student organizations and programs on campus and works with the faculty and administration in certain areas of University governance.

Admission Requirements

Applicants with college-preparatory course experience are considered for admission on the basis of the cumulative academic high school grade point average, SAT I or ACT scores, recommendations from appropriate high school officials, and other evidence of the ability to do college-level work. All matriculating freshmen are evaluated for placement in reading, writing, and mathematics. To be considered for transfer admission, an applicant must have completed at least 30 transferable semester hours of college-level work with a corresponding minimum 2.25 cumulative grade point average. Priority admission is reserved for transfer students who have earned at least 56 transferable credits with a minimum 2.0 cumulative GPA. Transfer applicants must submit transcripts from all colleges previously attended. The basic skills of transfer students who have fewer than 30 transferable credits are also assessed to determine any deficiencies. International applicants whose native language is not English are required to submit an official report of Test of English as a Foreign Language (TOEFL) scores. A minimum score of 500 is required on the paper-based TOEFL; 173 is required on the computer-based TOEFL. Admission to Towson University is selective. Sixty-nine percent of the applicants for fall 1999 were offered admission. The SAT I range for the middle 50 percentile of all admitted students was 500 to 590 for both verbal and math. The mean GPA for the same group was 3.21.

Application and Information

Towson renders admission decisions to qualified candidates on a continuous (rolling admissions) basis. Applicants should submit all appropriate application materials and required academic credentials by May 1 for fall admission and by December 1 for spring admission. Priority admission is granted beginning October 1 to those freshman applicants whose secondary school record indicates an overall 3.0 or above average in academic courses from grades 9–11 and whose combined SAT I score is at least 1100.

It is the responsibility of each applicant to make certain that all required forms and credentials (test scores, transcripts, and recommendations) are forwarded to the Admissions Office in accordance with the established deadlines. Incomplete applications or those improperly filled out are subject to cancellation. A nonrefundable $35 application fee or authorized fee-deferment form is required at the time the application is filed. Application forms are available by calling or writing to the Admissions Office.

Admissions Office
Towson University
8000 York Road
Towson, Maryland 21252-0001

Telephone: 410-830-2113
          888-4TOWSON (toll-free)
World Wide Web: http://www.towson.edu

Stephens Hall at Towson University.

TRANSYLVANIA UNIVERSITY
LEXINGTON, KENTUCKY

The University

Transylvania, a small, private liberal arts college of about 1,075 men and women, is consistently ranked among the best of its kind in the nation. The name—from the Latin that means across the woods—refers to the heavily forested Transylvania settlement in which the University was founded in 1780. Transylvania was the first college west of the Allegheny Mountains and the sixteenth in the nation. The University established the first schools of medicine and law in what was then the West and educated the doctors, lawyers, ministers, political leaders, and others who helped shape the young nation. Transylvania also founded the first college literary magazine in the West, *The Transylvanian*, still published by students today. Transylvania's link with early Lexington is symbolized by its administration building, Old Morrison, a registered National Historic Landmark and the central feature on the official seal of the city of Lexington.

After more than 220 years of academic excellence, Transylvania continues as a pioneer in higher education, preparing future leaders in business, government, education, the sciences, and the arts. Students work closely with professors in small classes, many with fewer than 10 students. The student body represents twenty-eight states and eleven countries. A high percentage of graduates attend selective medical, law, and other professional programs.

Transylvania offers more than fifty cocurricular activities, and most students participate in several of these. The Lampas Circle of the national leadership honorary society Omicron Delta Kappa recognizes students for academic excellence and campus leadership. The athletics program includes seven varsity sports for men, eight for women, and more than a dozen intramural sports. Transylvania also has four national sororities and four national fraternities.

Location

Transylvania is located in Lexington, Kentucky, a city of 242,000 and a growing center of commerce, culture, research, and education. Known as the horse capital of the world, Lexington is surrounded by the rolling green pastures of the famous Bluegrass region of central Kentucky. The area is also home to nearly 30,000 college students. Transylvania's parklike campus is just a 5-minute walk from downtown, with easy access to restaurants, shops, and entertainment. The proximity to downtown is also an advantage for students who want convenient part-time jobs and internship opportunities in law offices, accounting firms, hospitals, and other organizations. Transylvania offers its students a shuttle service between the modern Transylvania library and the University of Kentucky libraries every day, and the Lexington Public Library is a few blocks from the campus. Lexington is served by major airlines, and Louisville and Cincinnati are only 80 miles away.

Majors and Degrees

The Bachelor of Arts degree is awarded in the following majors: accounting, art, biology, business administration (specializations in finance; hotel, restaurant, and tourism administration; management; and marketing), chemistry, computer science, drama, economics, education, English, exercise science, French, history, mathematics, music, philosophy, physical education, physics, political science, psychology, religion, sociology, sociology/anthropology, and Spanish. Individually designed majors also may be arranged. Minors are available in most majors and in anthropology; classical studies; communication; European studies; German; hotel, restaurant, and tourism administration; international affairs; multicultural studies; and women's studies. Advising and undergraduate preparation are provided for dentistry, engineering, law, medicine, ministry, pharmacy, physical therapy, and veterinary medicine. A cooperative program in engineering allows students to earn a B.A. in physics or liberal studies from Transylvania in three years and a B.S. in engineering from the University of Kentucky, Vanderbilt University, or Washington University in two years. A cooperative program in accounting allows students to earn a B.A. in accounting from Transylvania in four years and an M.S. in accounting from the University of Kentucky in one year; graduates qualify to take the CPA exam.

Academic Program

The academic year is based on a 4-4-1 academic calendar, with two 14-week terms (fall and winter) and a one-month May term. The fall term begins in early September and ends in mid-December. The winter term begins in mid-January and ends in late April. During the May term, students may participate in a variety of programs on or off campus. Students normally take four courses in each of the fall and winter terms and one course in the May term. Thirty-six courses are required to graduate. Freshmen participate in a two-term program called Foundations of the Liberal Arts, which features small-group discussions with a faculty leader; lectures, films, concerts, and other presentations; and a tutorial program in basic communication, critical thinking, and study skills. Special study-skills clinics and workshops are offered on an optional basis. Students must complete requirements designed to ensure broad familiarity with the major areas of learning and human endeavor in the humanities and fine arts, social sciences, natural sciences and mathematics, logic, and languages.

Transylvania grants credit for scores of 4 or 5 on the Advanced Placement examinations of the College Board and at least 5 on the International Baccalaureate program. Detailed information may be obtained from the Office of the Registrar.

Off-Campus Arrangements

Experiencing diverse cultures through international study is a vital part of a Transylvania education. It is common for Transylvania students to study abroad for a summer, a term, or a year. A program at Regent's College, London, allows students to study there for the same cost and course credit as a semester at Transylvania. Scholarships are available for both semester-long and summer study abroad. Summer study programs, including those in Austria, Brazil, China, Costa Rica, Ecuador, France, Germany, Italy, Japan, Mexico, and Spain, are available through Transylvania's affiliation with the Kentucky Institute for International Studies. Transylvania also cooperates with the English-Speaking Union to offer advanced students scholarships for summer study at Cambridge and Oxford Universities. Students may participate in seminars or internships in Washington, D.C., through the Washington Center. Internships with congressional offices, Kentucky state government, city government, and local firms are easily arranged. Participation in Reserve Officers' Training Corps (Air Force and Army ROTC) is offered in cooperation with the University of Kentucky.

Academic Facilities

Two new Georgian-style buildings combine elegance with high-tech facilities to offer the latest advances in teaching and learning. The Cowgill Center for Business, Economics, and Education includes a multimedia classroom where professors from any discipline can use a large display screen to show the entire class information from one of the twenty-five networked student computers or from a TV, video, CD-ROM, or satellite. A specialized area for education majors includes a laboratory classroom for teacher training. The new Lucille C. Little Theater, used for faculty- and student-directed productions and drama classes, is a technically innovative facility that includes computerized lighting and sound, flexible staging options, and movable seating.

The Frances Carrick Thomas/J. Douglas Gay, Jr. Library offers sophisticated computerized databases, which are invaluable for research and can be accessed from any computer connected to Transylvania's server, including PCs in dorm rooms. The Mitchell Fine Arts Center provides music program facilities, including practice rooms, a recital hall, and an auditorium. It also houses the Career Development Center, which provides free interest testing and helps students research careers, improve job search skills, arrange internships and part-time jobs, and apply to graduate schools. Mitchell also houses a teaching laboratory for the hotel, restaurant, and tourism administration program. A newly acquired building is dedicated to art classes, studios, and a student gallery. Other modern facilities include the L. A. Brown Science Center and the Haupt Humanities Building. Construction of a new four-level athletic and recreation center begins in summer 2000. About 80 percent of students live on campus in six residence halls—two for men, one for women, and three for men and women. These include apartment-style living for upperclass students and suite-style rooms. All rooms are airconditioned and completely furnished and offer private telephone service with voice mail, access to cable television and Transylvania's computer network, ample lounge and study areas, computer labs, and recreational facilities. The dining hall is in the women's residence hall. The William T. Young Campus Center offers a competition-size indoor pool, a gymnasium, a fitness center, and other facilities.

Costs

Transylvania charges an annual tuition that covers fall, winter, and May terms for a normal full-time schedule of courses. Special instruction fees are charged in addition for certain designated courses, such as applied music. For 2000–01, tuition is $14,700, the room and board (double occupancy) cost is $5530, and the general fee is $570.

Financial Aid

Transylvania is committed to providing financial aid to students and their families. Four types of financial assistance are available: scholarships, which are based on academic performance, leadership, and citizenship, and grants, loans, and campus work, which are based on financial need. About 90 percent of Transylvania students receive some form of financial assistance and many receive more than one type of aid. Outstanding entering freshmen may qualify for one of twenty-five William T. Young Scholarships—each worth more than $55,000 over four years—which cover tuition and fees. Submission of Transylvania's Application for Admission and Scholarships by the appropriate deadline is all that is necessary to be considered for all scholarships at Transylvania. Students who are interested in need-based aid must file the Free Application for Federal Student Aid (FAFSA).

Faculty

Transylvania's relatively small size and low student-faculty ratio of 13:1 allow for close, personal attention in teaching and advising. Ninety-six percent of full-time faculty members hold a doctorate or the highest degree in their field and have come to Transylvania from a variety of graduate and professional schools. Many faculty members are recognized for their scholarship and professional activities, but their central concern is teaching and advising students. Transylvania's commitment to outstanding teaching is reflected in its nationally recognized Bingham Program for Excellence in Teaching. The program seeks to attract and retain gifted teachers through an evaluation process and financial incentives.

Student Government

Students at Transylvania have a high degree of access to the administration and governing board of the University. The Student Government Association serves as a representative government, and students also hold positions on standing committees of the faculty and the Board of Trustees.

Admission Requirements

Each applicant is considered individually on the basis of academic records, SAT I scores and/or ACT scores, activities, interests, essays, and recommendations. Admission is also offered to transfer students, international students (through the SAT I, ACT, or Test of English as a Foreign Language), and nontraditional students. High school students who graduate at the end of their junior year may also be considered for admission.

Transylvania enrolled 308 new students for the 1999–2000 academic year. The middle 50 percent composite ACT score for the freshman class was 24 to 29; the middle 50 percent combined SAT I score was 1100 to 1290. Sixty percent were in the top 10 percent of their high school class.

Application and Information

Submission of a Transylvania Application for Admission and Scholarships is all that is necessary to be considered for admission and most merit scholarships at Transylvania. Application deadlines vary with particular scholarships and types of financial aid.

The priority admission and scholarships deadline is December 1 for applicants who wish to learn of their acceptance by January 1 and who want to be considered for all Transylvania scholarships. February 1 is the general admission and scholarships deadline for applicants who wish to be considered for all Transylvania scholarships except the William T. Young and Pioneer scholarships. Applicants who apply after the December 1 priority deadline and by February 1 are considered for admission and scholarships on a rolling basis. Applicants who apply after February 1 are considered on a space-available basis. The deadline for applications for the winter term, which begins in January, is December 5. The same deadlines apply to electronic applications, which may be submitted on the Internet at the Web address listed below.

Students considering Transylvania are urged to visit the campus. High school seniors are encouraged to stay overnight in a dorm with a student admissions assistant. Weekday visits may include a customized campus tour and an opportunity to attend classes; talk with professors, students, and admissions and financial aid counselors; and enjoy meals on campus. Visits should be arranged with the Office of Admissions, preferably one to two weeks in advance. Open houses are held in the fall and winter, and a visit day for high school juniors is held in the spring.

For more information and application materials, students should contact:

Office of Admissions
Transylvania University
300 North Broadway
Lexington, Kentucky 40508-1797
Telephone: 859-233-8242
           800-872-6798 (toll-free)
E-mail: admissions@mail.transy.edu
World Wide Web: http://www.transy.edu

Small class sizes at Transylvania give professors and students the opportunity to work closely together, and many are directly involved in student research projects.

TRENT UNIVERSITY
PETERBOROUGH, ONTARIO, CANADA

The University

With 3,800 full-time students, Trent is recognized as one of Canada's outstanding small universities. It offers extensive personal attention from professors and academic advisers, an emphasis on small-group teaching, a vibrant international community, and strong liberal arts and science programs. At Trent, students find a friendly, welcoming, and safe environment with a strong sense of community.

Trent University was formally created as an independent university with full degree-granting powers by the Ontario Legislature in 1963. It is a member of the Association of Universities and Colleges of Canada and the Association of Commonwealth Universities. Trent graduates have received prestigious graduate scholarships and have assumed leadership roles in both the public and private sectors.

The University has chosen to remain small and concentrate on undergraduate studies while gradually expanding its interdisciplinary graduate programs. More than 75 percent of first- and second-year classes have fewer than 25 students. In Trent's graduate programs—anthropology, watershed ecosystems, Canadian heritage and development studies, methodologies for the study of Western history and culture, and applications of modeling in the natural and social sciences—there are presently about 150 students.

Trent's 1,400-acre Symons campus, situated on the banks of the Otonabee River amid forests, lakes, and gently rolling hills, features award-winning modern architecture. On this campus, 3 miles north of Peterborough's downtown core, are located the administrative offices, library, athletic facilities, Science Complex, Environmental Sciences Centre, and three of the five residential colleges. The other two colleges, in residential areas of Peterborough, are housed in Victorian buildings with stained glass windows and hardwood floors. A shuttle bus makes the 10- to 20-minute trip between the Symons campus and the downtown colleges throughout the day.

The colleges combine residential and teaching space, allowing students to live and learn in a friendly, close-knit environment. All colleges have common areas, a dining hall, study and recreation areas, and laundry facilities, as well as academic, social, and athletic activities. Resident dons act as advisers to students. All international students who apply by April 1 are guaranteed a room in residence.

Trent provides students with the support services they need to succeed, from finding a part-time job or seeing a doctor to coping with family or personal relationships. For international students, Trent's International Program Office offers counselling in areas such as health insurance, immigration information, and academic programs. To ease the transition to university, the Office also publishes the *International Students Handbook* and organizes a three-day orientation camp in September.

After the camp, all new students take part in Introductory Seminar Week. Trent does not believe in initiating or hazing; "Intro Week" provides social activities and an opportunity for students to choose their courses. Academic departments give introductory lectures to provide a better understanding of course content and workload, and each student is assigned an academic adviser.

With a variety of clubs, facilities, and organizations such as music, student radio, and international groups, Trent offers diverse ways to spend time outside the classroom. Athletic facilities include a 25-metre pool, a gymnasium, squash courts, a floodlit playing field, tennis courts, a rowing course, and cross-country trails for skiing, running, and biking. The University hosts the largest timed rowing regatta in Canada each fall and a triathlon each March.

Location

Trent's Symons campus lies 3 miles north of downtown Peterborough, a city of 70,000 that blends small-town friendliness with big-city cultural life. Peterborough is close to many lakes, beaches, conservation areas, and hiking and ski trails. Peterborough is only a 90-minute drive from Toronto, Canada's largest city; 3½ hours from Ottawa, the national capital; and a day's drive from New York City.

Peterborough has a variety of restaurants, shops, art galleries, cinemas, museums, and a performing arts centre. Trent students, faculty members, and staff members are active in community activities, such as the Peterborough Symphony, theatre groups, and choirs.

Majors and Degrees

The majority of Trent students pursue honours degrees, the normal prerequisite for graduate studies.

Honours and General Bachelor of Arts degrees are available in ancient history and classics, anthropology, Canadian studies, comparative development studies, computer studies, cultural studies, economics, English, environmental and resource studies, environmental chemistry, environmental physics, geography, history, international studies, modern languages (French, German, and Spanish), Native studies, philosophy, political studies, psychology, sociology, and women's studies.

There are Honours or General Bachelor of Science degrees in anthropology, biochemistry, biology, chemical physics, chemistry, computer studies, economics, environmental and resource studies, environmental physics, geography, mathematics, physics, and psychology.

Trent also offers an Honours Bachelor of Administrative Studies.

Students may use the Special Emphasis option to create an integrating theme to govern their choice of courses if their academic needs cannot be met by any of the existing majors.

In the concurrent teacher education program, cosponsored by Queen's University in Kingston, Trent students graduate with a Bachelor of Arts or a Bachelor of Science from Trent and a Bachelor of Education from Queen's.

In affiliation with Sir Sandford Fleming College, Peterborough's community college, Trent offers degree programs in geographical information systems, museum studies, and nursing.

The University also offers diplomas in the following programs: Canadian studies, Native management and economic development, and Native studies.

Academic Program

The academic year consists of two sessions. The fall/winter session has two 12-week terms, September to December and January to April. The summer session runs from May to August and is made up of twelve-, eight- and six-week terms. September is the only entry point for full-time studies.

Four-year honours degrees require successful completion of 57 to 60 course credits. Three-year general degrees consist of 30 course credits. All degrees require completion of University and program requirements. Three course credits are equivalent to 6 semester hours.

The Academic Skills Centre offers assistance in writing, reading, and study techniques. It also offers tutoring in mathematics and French and additional help for students for whom English is a second language. The Special Needs Office assists students with physical, sensory, or learning disabilities.

Off-Campus Arrangements

Trent encourages students to spend a year of study outside Canada. Students in any academic program may apply to study in countries such as Finland, Israel, Japan, Korea, Poland, Russia, South Africa, Spain, the United Kingdom, and the United States. Year-abroad programs in France, Germany, and Mexico are available for language students. The Comparative Development Studies programs in Ecuador and Ghana and the Native Studies program in Thailand combine academic courses with work-placement experience. Students receive full credit for all courses successfully completed while abroad.

Academic Facilities

The bright and spacious Bata Library is electronically connected to the two in-town college libraries and the Peterborough Public Library. An extensive interlibrary loan network enables students to borrow material from all parts of North America.

Two hundred fifty computers are available for general student use in the computer centre, library, classrooms, residences, and labs. They provide access to the Internet, World Wide Web, Gopher, e-mail, and library catalogues.

Costs

For the 1999–2000 academic year, tuition fees, including ancillary fees, for Canadian citizens and permanent residents were Can$4585.91 and Can$11,119 for international students. A single room in residence (including three meals a day, seven days a week) cost Can$4200–Can$6200 for both Canadian and international students.

Financial Aid

All students are considered for entrance scholarships when admitted. Exceptional students are invited to apply for the Board of Governor's Scholarship and the two Champlain Scholarships, prestigious renewable scholarships. Upperclass students are automatically considered for in-course scholarships.

Bursary funds, to primarily assist in emergency situations, are available. There are scholarships and bursaries specifically for international students. International students also are allowed to work on campus.

Faculty

Much of the teaching at Trent takes place in seminars and labs that provide an interactive learning environment. Because these are generally led by professors rather than teaching assistants, students have ample opportunity to get to know their instructors.

Among primarily undergraduate institutions in Canada, according to the 1998 *Maclean's* magazine annual ranking, Trent has the highest proportion of faculty members who have received national awards, as well as research grants from Canadian government funding agencies.

Student Government

There is active involvement in student politics through such groups as the Trent Central Student Association and the five residential College Cabinets. Students have a voice in the administrative affairs of the University through membership in the University Senate and the Board of Governors.

Admission Requirements

For Ontario residents, an Ontario Secondary School Diploma (OSSD), including a minimum of 6 Ontario Academic Credits (OACs), is required. For Quebec residents, completion of Year I of a CEGEP program or its equivalent is required. Other Canadian residents are required to have a Grade 12 diploma.

Advanced credit is granted for select Advanced Placement programs with examination grades of 4 or better.

For students from the United States, a high school diploma, a minimum of a B average, and a reference from a high school teacher or counsellor are required. An overall SAT I score of at least 1100 is preferred.

General Certificate of Education requirements include passes in at least five subjects, two at the advanced level with grades of C or better, or passes in four subjects, three at the advanced level with grades of C or better. Two advanced supplementary courses may be substituted for one advanced-level course. Advanced credit may be granted for A levels with a grade of C or better.

International Baccalaureate requires a minimum 28 points. Advanced credit may be granted for higher-level subjects with a score of 4 or higher.

Students who believe that their marks do not accurately reflect their ability to succeed at university may send supporting documentation, such as references from teachers or guidance counsellors, to the Registrar's Office.

The language of instruction at Trent is English. All students must be proficient at speaking, reading, writing, and understanding English. Candidates from areas where English is not the language of instruction must provide evidence of language proficiency. Trent accepts results from a variety of tests. The more commonly used services and minimum required scores are as follows: Test of English as a Foreign Language (TOEFL), 550; Michigan English Language Assessment Battery (MELAB), 85; International English Language Testing System (IELTS), 6.5. Results from Canadian university English language testing services are also accepted. International students who meet all criteria for admission except the language requirements may be admitted to Trent's *English for University* program for one or two semesters. Upon successful completion of this program, students would continue regular degree programs.

Application and Information

Applications for admission for the 2001–02 academic year must be received by the Office of the Registrar no later than June 1, 2001. The deadline to apply for residence is also June 1, 2001. Early application is encouraged. Complete applications should include official transcripts, language test scores (if needed), and notarized translation of material not in English. For information on admission and programs and for application forms, students should contact:

Office of the Registrar
Trent University
Peterborough, Ontario K9J 7B8
Canada

E-mail: tip@trentu.ca
World Wide Web: http://www.trentu.ca

One of the residential colleges at Trent University.

TREVECCA NAZARENE UNIVERSITY
NASHVILLE, TENNESSEE

The University

Trevecca Nazarene University is a private, coeducational, four-year accredited liberal arts university. Founded in 1901 and affiliated with the Church of the Nazarene, its academic programs are based on Christian values that promote scholarship, critical thinking, and meaningful worship for students in preparation for lives of leadership and service to the church, the community, and the world. More than 1,600 students from thirty-six states and six countries are enrolled at Trevecca. They represent eighteen different denominations. Students who are members of minority groups make up 12 percent of the population. Trevecca places distinct emphasis on its community, with 78 percent of the student body living on campus. Trevecca is situated atop one of the only hills in the lively city of Nashville, with a view of beautiful Music City, USA. Campus life reflects the vibrancy of Nashville. A variety of extracurricular clubs and ministry opportunities are available. Student government, the campus newspaper and yearbook, special interest and discussion groups, theater productions, and two radio stations provide additional opportunities for involvement.

The University is a member of the NAIA Division I and participates in the highly competitive TranSouth Athletic Conference. Men compete in baseball, basketball, golf, and soccer, while women compete in basketball, golf, soccer, softball, and volleyball. An excellent intramural program includes basketball, football, indoor soccer, and volleyball. In addition, tennis tournaments, racquetball tournaments, golf tournaments, swimming, and aerobics are available. Athletic facilities include a gymnasium, tennis courts, racquetball courts, a 25-meter indoor pool, a state-of-the-art wellness center, a walking track, and a baseball diamond.

Location

Trevecca is located on a beautiful 68-acre campus in the middle of Tennessee. It is 10 minutes from the award-winning Nashville International Airport. The cities of Knoxville, Memphis, and Chattanooga are no more than 3 hours away. The Cumberland River, Old Hickory Lake, and the Great Smoky Mountains provide nearby beauty and opportunities for leisure. The city of Nashville is a center for internship and service opportunities.

Majors and Degrees

Trevecca offers fifty-one baccalaureate and six associate degrees through eight academic departments and five divisions. Undergraduate majors include accounting, allied health, biology, broadcast technology, business administration, chemistry, communication studies, computer information systems, criminology, dramatic arts, economics, education, English, general science, history, marketing, mathematics, music, music business, physical education, physics, political science, psychology, religion, social and behavioral sciences, social science, speech, sports and exercise science, and sports management.

Trevecca also offers nine preprofessional programs: dentistry, engineering, law, medicine, nursing, pharmacy, physical therapy, physician assistant studies, and veterinary science.

Academic Program

Trevecca's academic degrees are conferred upon successful completion of a major, at least one minor, and 59 (or an appropriate variation) credit hours of general education courses to meet the 128-credit-hour requirement for graduation. These general education core courses have been selected to provide broad liberal arts training as a foundation for students majoring in any field.

The University's academic year consists of two semesters (fall and spring) and several summer sessions. Orientation of new students is prior to each semester, with a special summer orientation program for first-time college freshmen.

Career internship elective courses are offered for credit to upperclass students. The student is in a professional setting in his or her field under contract supervision for one semester. Two career internships are recommended prior to graduation.

Academic Facilities

Trevecca recently opened a new state-of-the-art library and technology center, which will house more than 325,000 items from traditional and electronic sources. Academic computer labs include thirteen fully networked labs, which provide full Internet and LAN access. All undergraduate residence halls provide complete Internet and LAN connection capabilities, including a minilab and laser printer in each building. Also located on campus are a fine arts center, a sports center, a hall of science, and an education center.

Costs

Tuition for 2000–01 is $10,517. Room and board total $4670. The estimated cost of books is $800, travel costs about $960, and personal expenses are estimated at $1400.

Financial Aid

The purpose of the student aid program at Trevecca is to provide financial assistance to qualified students who, without such aid, would be unable to attend. Tuition, room, and board costs are consistently lower than the average cost of attending most private four-year colleges and universities.

Nearly $9 million is made available through institutional merit scholarships and need-based aid, federal and state grants, loans, and on-campus employment programs. Approximately 91 percent of students receive financial aid, with an average annual award per recipient of $13,000. The deadline to apply for institutional aid is March 15 for the following fall semester.

Students at Trevecca can divide charges into three equal payments during the semester or, through special arrangement, spread payment over ten months.

Faculty

Trevecca is a teaching-oriented institution whose mission is to prepare graduates of all degree programs to develop a depth of understanding in their major field and to prepare them for a career or graduate school following graduation. Faculty members must have a clear commitment to academic excellence and Christian values. There are 83 full-time teaching faculty members, of whom 67 percent hold earned doctorates. All faculty members serve as student advisers. The student-faculty ratio is 13:1.

Student Government

The Student Government Assembly (SGA) is composed of elected representatives of the associated student body of

Trevecca Nazarene University. It is self-governing and controls its own budget. Its purpose is to promote the best interests of all students. The SGA serves as a liaison between the faculty, the administration, and student groups. It plans programs and activities for the school year. Student representatives serve on all University committees and are nominated by the SGA. Each year, the SGA assists in the sponsorship of the Staley Lecture Series, which features outstanding Christian leaders.

Admission Requirements

As a private Christian university, Trevecca is open to any qualified student without regard to race, color, sex, age, creed, national or ethnic origin, or physical disability. Transfer and international students and students who are members of minority groups are welcome and encouraged to apply.

Trevecca is selective in its admission policy. A freshman applicant is admitted provided one of the following conditions is met: they must have a high school grade point average of 2.5 or above on a 4.0 scale, an ACT composite score of 18 or above, or an SAT I combined score of 860 or above. If none of the admission requirements is met, a freshman applicant who has an ACT composite score of 15 to 17 or an SAT I combined score of 720 to 850 and a minimum high school grade point average of 2.0 on a 4.0 scale is granted admission on academic restriction.

For the best preparation for college, Trevecca recommends that secondary school credits include 4 units of English, 2 units of mathematics, 2 units of foreign language, 2 units of social science, and 1 unit of natural science. SAT I scores (code 1809) are acceptable, although ACT scores (code 4016) are preferred. Transfer applicants should request that an official transcript be forwarded directly to Trevecca from each college or university previously attended. Trevecca provides all applicants with an official evaluation of their transfer credit.

Application and Information

Trevecca has a rolling admission policy: applications are reviewed and acted upon as they are received. The Office of Enrollment Services is open from 8 a.m. to 5 p.m. on weekdays. For more information, to arrange a campus visit, or to request a catalog and application, students should contact:

Enrollment Management
Trevecca Nazarene University
333 Murfreesboro Road
Nashville, Tennessee 37210

Telephone: 615-248-1320
               888-210-4TNU (toll-free in the U.S.)
Fax: 615-248-7406
E-mail: admissions_und@trevecca.edu
World Wide Web: http://www.trevecca.edu

Built in 1984, Jernigan Student Center houses the student dining room, a bookstore, a post office, student government and class offices, a snack shop, and several classrooms.

TRINITY CHRISTIAN COLLEGE
PALOS HEIGHTS, ILLINOIS

The College

Since the beginning of this century there has existed in the metropolitan Chicago area a system of private Christian elementary and secondary schools established by people who believe that education may not be divided into religious and secular components, but that all learning must be oriented toward a Christian view of life and the world. These schools are part of a network of more than 425 schools in North America known as Christian Schools International.

In 1952 a group of ten area business and professional people committed to that kind of education began to study the feasibility of establishing a two-year junior college. In April 1956, they drafted a constitution and incorporated as the Trinity Christian College Association. A board of trustees was elected to oversee the establishment and operation of a college, and in 1959 Navajo Hills Golf Course in Palos Heights, Illinois, was purchased to serve as a campus. The former clubhouse and pro shop were remodeled, and the college opened for classes that fall. The first class of 37 students was taught by 5 full-time faculty members. The program consisted of two years of liberal arts courses leading to a certificate for transfer to a senior college.

The college experienced steady growth in facilities, faculty, and programs throughout the 1960s, and in 1966 the board began to plan for expansion to become a four-year, degree-granting liberal arts college. A third year of studies was introduced in the fall of 1969 and a fourth in 1970. The first baccalaureate degrees were awarded in May 1971.

As an emerging four-year liberal arts college, the nature and scope of the institution have changed with the times. While maintaining a theoretical approach to the disciplines, undergirded with a strong core curriculum of philosophy, history, English, and theology, the College has enhanced its offerings to provide students with a broad base of programs in professional areas, such as business, education, and nursing, in addition to the traditional liberal arts.

Today, the student body of more than 700 is taught by a faculty that includes more than 40 full-time and 40 part-time instructors. More than 75 percent of the faculty members have terminal degrees in their disciplines. They also remain committed to the principles of Christian education espoused by the College's founders in 1959. Although members of the student body come from predominantly Reformed and Presbyterian church backgrounds, there is also a welcome diversity of traditions represented, such as Baptist, Lutheran, Methodist, and Roman Catholic.

Location

Trinity Christian College is located in Palos Heights, Illinois, which is a southwest suburb of Chicago. It takes only 30 minutes to drive to the heart of Chicago, and public transportation is only two blocks from the campus. The 50-acre campus is nestled among the thousands of acres of forest preserves that provide numerous outdoor activities. Palos Heights, home to 12,000 people, offers a small-town atmosphere yet it is ideally located just outside of Chicago. Trinity Christian's location provides a protected learning environment and allows the student to explore the possibilities of a metropolitan city.

Majors and Degrees

Trinity Christian College grants Bachelor of Arts, Bachelor of Science, and Bachelor of Science in Nursing degrees. Majors include accounting, art, biology, business, business communication, business education, chemistry, church education, communication arts, computer science, elementary and secondary education, English, history, information systems, mathematics, music, nursing, philosophy, physical education, psychology, science education, sociology, Spanish, special education, theology, and transportation. Preprofessional programs in dentistry, law, medicine, physical therapy and allied health services, and seminary are also available.

Academic Program

The specific courses that make up an individual student's degree program are a unique selection depending upon that person's educational interests and needs. In consultation with a faculty adviser, each student is encouraged to choose those courses that best meet his or her educational and vocational goals. A well-educated person must have knowledge and understanding that includes more than specialization, and true meaning can be grasped only when knowledge is seen in the context of a coherent whole. A minimum of 125 total semester hours of credit is required for each of the twenty-five majors.

Off-Campus Arrangements

Trinity requires each student to complete a field education course in at least one major program. The objective of the field education program is to introduce each student to a professional application of the chosen major to a work situation off campus in the metropolitan area. While remaining a Trinity student, the student has an opportunity to relate academic learning to its concrete use in an actual setting similar to the work situation he or she will face upon graduation. This experience also gives the opportunity to test the Christian cultural perspective gained at Trinity against the direction and spirit of contemporary society at a time when students are still able to discuss questions and problems with professors.

Field experience can be taken a variety of ways, depending on the major program. For example, nursing students work in different areas in hospitals, education students teach in area schools, and business majors consult with local businesses. The number of semester hours of credit earned is determined by the student's adviser, with a general guideline of 40 clock hours of experience for each credit. Students may earn no more than 12 semester hours total for field education or an internship. If the placement agency offers to pay compensation, it is permissible for students to accept wages for their work.

There is also the opportunity for a full semester of work and living off campus through Trinity's Chicago Metropolitan Studies program. In cooperation with other colleges who send students to the program, students may engage in a personally designed and planned full-time program of research, seminar work, and supervised professional work placement. This field opportunity may be applied for by all students regardless of major, because the work placement is designed to meet the interests and academic needs of a variety of people.

Trinity Christian is also a member of the Coalition for Christian Colleges and Universities, which is an association of more than ninety Christ-centered institutions of higher education. The coalition offers students programs in Hollywood, California; San Jose, Costa Rica; Cairo, Egypt; Nizhni Novgorod, Russia; and Washington, D.C.

Other off-campus programs offered by Trinity Christian College are the Semester in Spain program, a Spanish language program in Seville, Spain. A program in business is also offered in the Netherlands.

Costs

Trinity Christian College's tuition and fees are $13,240 for the academic year 2000–01. The complete cost, including room, board, and tuition, is $18,430.

Financial Aid

Ninety-two percent of Trinity Christian students receive financial aid to help them meet the costs of their education. Eligible students may receive scholarships, grants, work opportunities, educational loans, or any combination of these.

Trinity Christian College has many college scholarships. Included are merit-based scholarships awarded for honor students, leadership scholarships awarded for participation in extracurricular activities, and special scholarships. All entering students are automatically considered for honors scholarships when their applications are reviewed. Trinity also offers two founders' scholarships for each entering freshman class. The award is full tuition for four years. Students with a minimum 3.8 GPA and a minimum composite score of 30 on the ACT may apply for the founders' scholarship program. To apply for any type of need-based federal or state financial aid to attend Trinity Christian College, students must submit the Free Application for Federal Student Aid (FAFSA) and the Trinity Christian College Financial Aid Form. Information, help, and all forms are available directly from the admissions office.

Faculty

Trinity Christian College has 41 full-time faculty members. Sixty-eight percent have earned doctorates, and 75 percent hold a terminal degree in their field of teaching. All faculty members teach classes and advise students. The average class size is fewer than 25 students. Small class size allows students to receive individual attention and spiritual experience at Trinity Christian College. The faculty-student ratio is 1:12.

Admission Requirements

To gain admission to Trinity Christian, applicants must demonstrate academic potential. An official high school transcript is required, along with scores from either the SAT I or the ACT. Transfer students must provide official transcripts from every college attended. Students transferring with fewer than 24 hours of credit will be required to submit high school transcripts as well. Students who have earned associate degrees from an accredited community college can be accepted into Trinity as juniors.

Application and Information

For more information, students should contact:

Admissions Office
Trinity Christian College
6601 West College Drive
Palos Heights, Illinois 60463
Telephone: 800-748-0085 (toll-free)
E-mail: admissions@trnty.edu
World Wide Web: http://www.trnty.edu

The Jennie Huizenga Memorial Library in the center of campus.

TRINITY COLLEGE
HARTFORD, CONNECTICUT

The College

Since its founding in 1823, Trinity has provided an undergraduate education of uncommon quality. Widely acknowledged as one of the top liberal arts colleges in the country, Trinity was recently honored by a panel of national education editors for its "bold and innovative ideas" to advance the cause of higher education and ensure greater access.

In its commitment to the rigorous pursuit of the liberal arts and to instruction that is personal and conversational, Trinity is an ideal college. At the same time, Trinity is in close touch with the world beyond its campus. In that respect and in terms of the outstanding opportunities Trinity's capital city location offers students, a Trinity education is indeed a real education.

While remaining faithful to the classic liberal arts tradition, Trinity offers a distinctive educational experience that prepares students for the challenges and opportunities of the twenty-first century. Building on its traditional strengths in arts and humanities and exceptional offerings in science and engineering, Trinity engages students in a conversation with the world through its study-abroad programs, interdisciplinary programs whose multiple perspectives prepare students for a future of unprecedented change, state-of-the-art electronic facilities to support Trinity's pioneering use of information technology in classrooms, and innovative, rigorous new programs that draw on the rich cultural, educational, and professional assets of Hartford. The heart of a Trinity education, however, remains the personal encounter between professor and student, the intellectual partnership that discovers a world of ideas and ignites a passion for learning.

Trinity's students come from forty-six states and twenty-nine countries. The College believes that a diverse community makes learning flourish. Trinity's undergraduate enrollment of nearly 2,000 students is about equally composed of men and women. More than 90 percent of undergraduates live on campus in College housing. Trinity is engaged in a campus revitalization program that will preserve its impressive Gothic buildings as it also develops a campus for the new millennium.

Trinity offers a rich array of extracurricular activities—films, plays, concerts, musical theater, sports, academic symposia, and visits by nationally and internationally known writers, speakers, and performers. Participation is an important word on campus, and Trinity students have abundant opportunities to lead and to be involved in numerous student clubs; special interest groups; theater, dance, and music groups; debate; academic programs; campus cinema; Trinity's radio station; and many student publications, including *The TrinColl Journal*, the nation's first weekly multimedia Webzine. With 19 acres of playing fields, Trinity also offers an extensive athletic program. More than half of the student body participates on twenty-nine men's and women's varsity teams (Division III) and in ten intramural sports. The Ferris Athletic Center features a new swimming pool, a fully equipped fitness center, crew tanks, eight international-size squash courts, basketball courts, and an indoor track.

Location

Situated on a beautiful 100-acre campus in the center of Hartford, the capital of Connecticut, Trinity offers the best of both worlds—a supportive and active campus community located in a city that provides students with myriad opportunities for internships, community service, and cultural exploration. Hartford's businesses, governmental agencies, cultural organizations, and nonprofit institutions offer Trinity students hundreds of opportunities to explore future careers through the College's extensive internship program. Hartford is also host to a number of cultural institutions, including the Wadsworth Atheneum (the oldest public art museum in the nation), the Mark Twain House, the Harriet Beecher Stowe Center, the Connecticut Opera, the Hartford Ballet, the Hartford Symphony, the Hartford Stage, and a number of smaller theaters and clubs that provide a cultural stew of dance, theater, and music. The shopping districts of Hartford and the surrounding suburbs are nearby. The impressive Connecticut coast is easily accessible, and Boston and New York are each about 2 hours from campus.

Majors and Degrees

The College offers a Bachelor of Arts degree and, in select majors and at the student's request, a Bachelor of Science degree. Majors offered include American studies; anthropology; art history; biochemistry; biology; chemistry; classical civilization; classics; comparative literature; computer science; economics; engineering; English; history; international studies; Jewish studies; mathematics; modern languages: Chinese, French, German, Italian, Japanese, Russian, and Spanish; music, neuroscience; philosophy; physics; political science; psychology; public policy studies; religion; sociology; studio arts; theater and dance; and women's studies. Trinity offers two coordinate majors: the computer coordinate major and the educational studies coordinate major. Interdisciplinary majors may also be individually constructed. Trinity also offers a five-year program in engineering and computer science, which leads to a bachelor's degree from Trinity and a master's degree from Rensselaer Polytechnic Institute through Rensselaer at Hartford.

Academic Program

Featuring more than 750 courses per year, Trinity's curriculum provides a framework within which students may explore the many dimensions of an undergraduate education and, at the same time, offers each student flexibility to experiment, to deepen old interests and develop new ones, and to acquire specialized training in a major field. Students must demonstrate proficiency in writing and mathematics and fulfill a five-part distribution requirement that comprises at least one course in each of the following categories: arts, humanities, natural sciences, numerical and symbolic reasoning, and social sciences.

Off-Campus Arrangements

Nearly 50 percent of Trinity students study abroad for a semester or a year at Trinity's Rome Campus, at Trinity in Spain, or in other approved study programs in more than forty countries on five continents. In 1999, a Trinity-in-San Francisco campus was opened, and the first of several future Trinity-connected global learning sites opened in Cape Town, South Africa. This was followed by new sites in Trinidad and Nepal. Through the theater and dance department, Trinity offers the Trinity/LaMaMa Performing Arts Program in New York City and the Trinity/LaMaMa Abroad Program, two extraordinary programs that provide intensive study in theater, dance, and performance.

Academic Facilities

The Trinity Library houses more than 1 million volumes, making it one of the most comprehensive and largest small-college libraries in the nation. Designed to meet the needs of undergraduates and a faculty of serious scholars, the library also has a wealth of electronic resources, including an online catalog linked with Wesleyan University and Connecticut College. The library is home to the Watkinson Library, a research and archival library of rare books, manuscripts, and special collections. In 1997, Trinity launched a $95-million campus renewal program; the library will be renovated and expanded to incorporate the computing center to create a state-of-the-art learning resource center.

Fully networked for more than five years, Trinity offers students extensive computer resources, including software programs, e-mail, and Internet access. Students who own computers may plug into their dorm rooms, and the Mathematics, Computing, and Engineering Center offers virtually around-the-clock access to personal computers plus consultants to answer almost any question.

Costs

Costs for the 2000–01 academic year are $24,660 for tuition, $4310 for room, $2850 for board, and $780 for fees.

Financial Aid

The College meets 100 percent of the need of all students who are offered admission and show financial need. While need status is occasionally a factor, the vast majority of admissions decisions are made on a need-blind basis. Students must file the Free Application for Federal Student Aid (FAFSA) as well as the Financial Aid PROFILE of the College Scholarship Service. Admissions applications are due by January 15; FAFSA and PROFILE applications are due by February 1. Students are notified of admission and aid decisions by the first week of April. Normally, need is met with a financial aid package that includes grant assistance, work-study, and federal student loans. Federal funds for which accepted students are eligible include Pell Grants, Federal Supplemental Educational Opportunity Grants (FSEOG), Perkins Loans, Stafford Loans, and PLUS Loans. Most students who demonstrate need are granted an on-campus job as part of their financial aid package. Approximately 50 percent of all students have a job; about 40 percent of all students have employment based on need. The ratio of grant assistance to loans and work-study aid is sometimes affected by the academic strength of the student's record. Trinity continues to expand its aid budget to keep pace with the College's goal to increase the socioeconomic and ethnic diversity on campus. Forty-seven percent of the students receive financial aid, and the average award was $22,495 in 1999–2000.

Faculty

The distinctive strength of a Trinity education has always been the close interaction between students and a faculty of devoted teacher-scholars. A student-faculty ratio of 10:1 enables supportive yet challenging educational experiences that establish a foundation for lifetime learning and enables students to pursue academic interests with passion. Nearly 30 percent of recent graduating classes collaborated with faculty members in conducting research; many students have made joint presentations at international, national, or local symposia or have published jointly prepared papers. All courses are taught by Trinity faculty members and not by graduate assistants.

While the first calling of Trinity's professors is teaching, they are actively publishing scholars of national and international distinction. History professor Joan Hedrick, for example, won the Pulitzer Prize for her biography of Harriet Beecher Stowe. Other notable professors include internationally recognized urban studies expert Janice Perlman (founder of the Mega Cities Project, currently headquartered at Trinity), Obie-award-winning dramatist Robbie McCauley, prize-winning writers Michelle Cliff and Fred Pfeil (English), distinguished historian Samuel Kassow, biomedical engineering authority Joseph Bronzino, and Sharon Herzberger, a nationally known expert on family violence. Trinity professors pride themselves on their accessibility and keen interest in helping students.

Student Government

Trinity fosters the growth of future leaders by providing students with many opportunities to exercise and test their leadership skills. The Student Government Association (SGA), for example, provides students a strong voice in social, cultural, and—through membership on faculty committees—academic matters. Composed of elected class representatives, the SGA constantly seeks the expertise and insights of all interested students, and its committees offer enterprising students many chances to participate and to develop leadership skills.

Admission Requirements

Trinity seeks an ethnically and geographically diverse group of highly motivated students who have completed a rigorous course of study in secondary school and have demonstrated energy, talent, and leadership in a variety of extracurricular activities. Trinity has no specific GPA minimums or test-score cutoffs. The College is highly selective, and its candidates typically have an A– high school average and combined SAT I scores in the mid-1200s. At least 16 academic units of college-preparatory course work are recommended, including a minimum of 4 years of English, 2 years of foreign language, 2 years of laboratory science, 2 years of algebra, 1 year of geometry, and 2 years of history. Last year, more than 5,000 men and women from all over the nation and world applied for admission to the College, which enrolls an entering class of around 500 students. Transfer students with a 3.0 GPA in a strong course of study at another accredited college or university are considered for admission to the sophomore or junior classes.

Admissions officers review each application individually; decisions are based on each candidate's academic record (course of study and GPA), recommendations from secondary school teachers and counselors, test scores, personal strengths, talents, activities, and application essay.

Application and Information

Students must submit completed applications to the Admissions Office. Application deadlines are November 15 for early decision I applicants (with notification by December 15), February 1 for early decision II applicants (with notification by February 28), and January 15 for regular decision applicants (with notification by April 1). Transfer applicants must submit applications by April 1 for admission in the following fall semester (with notification by early June) and by November 15 for admission in the following spring semester (with notification by early January). Students may download an electronic Common Application from the Web address below.

Inquiries should be made to:

Larry Dow
Dean of Admissions and Financial Aid
Admissions Office
Trinity College
Hartford, Connecticut 06106-3100
Telephone: 860-297-2180
Fax: 860-297-2287
E-mail: admissions.office@trincoll.edu
World Wide Web: http://www.trincoll.edu/~admissio/commonapp/

The Long Walk at Trinity College.

TRINITY COLLEGE
WASHINGTON, D.C.

The College

Trinity College is one of the nation's first Catholic women's colleges. Founded in 1897 by the Sisters of Notre Dame de Namur, Trinity's commitment always has been to provide an excellent, value-centered education to women in a personalized atmosphere. Today, Trinity offers the best of all possible worlds—a tradition of academic excellence; a high-quality liberal arts program and a prestigious faculty; unlimited internship and career opportunities; and an exciting location in Washington, D.C. Our commitment to excellence has earned Trinity top ratings in *U.S. News & World Report*'s guides to "America's Best Colleges" and "America's Best College Values."

Trinity enrolls more than 1,500 full-time and part-time undergraduate and graduate students. The student body represents thirty-two states and fifteen countries. Sixty percent of the full-time students reside on campus.

Trinity's Honor Agreement is a vital part of the College's academic and social environment. The Honor Agreement expresses a way of life rooted in personal integrity and founded on mutual respect and cooperation. Each student signs the agreement that states her understanding and acceptance of the responsibility that is hers as a member of Trinity College.

Trinity offers NCAA Division III sports competition in crew, field hockey, lacrosse, soccer, tennis, and track and is also a member of the Atlantic Women's College Conference.

Location

Trinity College is located 2½ miles north of the Capitol on a 26-acre wooded campus that combines the serenity and beauty of a suburban setting with close proximity to the heart of urban Washington. Metro, Washington's bus and subway system, provides easy access to the city, its suburbs, Union Station, and National Airport.

The nation's capital offers a variety of cultural, educational, and social resources for an excellent education. Opportunities range from those in politics and government to those at the John F. Kennedy Center for the Performing Arts, the National Symphony, the Environmental Protection Agency, the Smithsonian Institution, and many museums and galleries. In addition to being the political hub of the United States, the Washington area, with eleven universities and colleges, is also a center for higher education.

Within miles of Washington are the tourist and recreational facilities of four states. Skiing is available in the mountains of West Virginia, Virginia, Maryland, and Pennsylvania. The Chesapeake Bay offers some of the finest sailing on the East Coast. The historic sites of Gettysburg, Jamestown, Williamsburg, Fredericksburg, Yorktown, and Mount Vernon are also within a few hours' drive.

Majors and Degrees

The College of Arts and Sciences and the School of Professional Studies grant undergraduate degrees, including the Bachelor of Arts (B.A.) and the Bachelor of Science (B.S.). Majors are offered under the Division of Arts and Humanities, the Division of Math and Natural Sciences, the Division of Social Sciences, and the School of Professional Studies.

Each division offers selected majors with professional focus areas in corporate affairs, culture, public policy, science, and teacher preparation. The Division of Arts and Humanities offers majors in art, English, history, and language and cultural studies. A student in the Division of Math and Natural Sciences may major in biochemistry, biology, chemistry, environmental science, or math. The Division of Social Sciences offers majors in economics, human relations, international studies, political science, psychology, and sociology. The School of Professional Studies offers majors in business administration, communications, and education. A special five-year program is available in which students complete an undergraduate degree in the liberal arts and earn a Master of Arts in Teaching. Trinity also offers courses in French, music, philosophy, physics, sociology, Spanish, theology, and women's studies.

Academic Program

The Trinity Foundation for Leadership Curriculum is an innovative interdisciplinary program designed to provide women with the knowledge, skills, and values to meet the challenges and opportunities of the twenty-first century. Trinity's curriculum and major programs offer a contemporary approach to education by combining the liberal arts with practical experience and a professional focus. Internships and selected career-related courses are available within the curriculum. Advising and career development programs assist in integrating academic studies with personal career goals. The Career and Academic Support Center provides personal, academic, and career counseling. The on-campus Writing and Math Centers provide students with additional resources for strengthening individual skills in these areas.

Trinity is one of only ten Catholic colleges and universities in the country with an active Phi Beta Kappa chapter, the oldest honor society in the nation.

Off-Campus Arrangements

Trinity is a member of the Consortium of Universities of the Washington Metropolitan Area, a cooperative arrangement among the major institutions of higher learning in and around the District of Columbia. Trinity students have the opportunity to take courses at the following member institutions: American University, Catholic University of America, Gallaudet University, George Mason University, Georgetown University, George Washington University, Howard University, Marymount University, the University of Maryland, and the University of the District of Columbia. Similarly, students from all consortium institutions may attend classes at Trinity.

Trinity's location in the nation's capital affords students unparalleled internship opportunities. Internships may be arranged through major programs or through the Trinity College/PLEN Public Policy Semester Program. Special programs also include the Trinity Center for Women in Public Policy and a partnership with Executive Women in Government. Internships offer students an opportunity to explore career options and to gain valuable experience in their chosen field. Credits may be earned for the completion of internships that are approved for credit by the College.

Students in every major may apply for the Trinity Mentor Program. This program provides opportunities for students to acquire resume writing and interviewing skills, attend career panels, and be matched with an alumna mentor who acts as a guide for students in making the transition from college to career.

The College also offers qualified students the opportunity to study abroad in approved programs around the globe. Programs in Australia, Costa Rica, France, Japan, Mexico, Poland, Russia, and Spain are only a few from which students may choose.

Academic Facilities

The Trinity library houses a collection of more than 180,000 volumes in support of the liberal arts curriculum and is a member of the Washington Region Library Consortium. Science, computer, and language laboratories are located on campus, as are art studios and a darkroom for photography students. The music department has practice rooms for student use.

Costs

Tuition with double-room occupancy and board for full-time weekday undergraduate students was $20,375 in 1999–2000. Tuition for nonresident students was $13,875. Tuition for students earning a Trinity degree through the Weekend College is $400 per credit hour.

Financial Aid

Financial aid is available in the form of scholarships, grants, loans, and student employment both on and off campus. About 80 percent of the students receive some form of financial assistance. Applicants must submit the Free Application for Federal Student Aid (FAFSA) and should request that an analysis be sent to Trinity. The Trinity College code in Section H of the FAFSA is 001460.

Faculty

There are 91 faculty members, 51 of whom are full-time. Ninety-five percent of the full-time faculty members hold doctoral degrees or the professional equivalent. Frequent interaction between students and faculty members is encouraged and made possible by the size of the College community and the advantageous faculty-student ratio of 1:8.

Student Government

The Student Association carries on an eighty-year tradition of responsible student participation in College governance and academic and social affairs. Through its three branches, the Student Association represents students and their concerns to the entire College community. It coordinates student activities and supervises the organization and functioning of all committees and organizations of the association. Primarily through its judicial branch, the Association takes responsibility for upholding the Honor Agreement.

Admission Requirements

Trinity College seeks women who have demonstrated academic achievement and promise as well as those who would bring varied talents, interests, and backgrounds to the student body. The Trinity College Admissions Committee reviews each application individually on a rolling decision basis. Candidates are encouraged to complete a four-year secondary school program, including a total of 16 credits in English, foreign languages, history, mathematics, science, and social science. Application evaluation is based on the student's academic record, letters of recommendation, writing samples, SAT I or ACT scores, personal interview, involvement in activities, and other submitted materials.

Advanced Placement course work may be considered for credit and advanced standing. Early entrance is available for mature and well-qualified students who wish to enter Trinity after their junior year of high school. Early entrance candidates are required to have an interview with a member of the Admissions Committee. Transfer students are encouraged to apply, and credit is given for all course work with the grade of C or higher from an accredited college or university. The Trinity College code for the SAT I is 5796 and for the ACT, 0696. All international students for whom English is not the first language are required to submit TOEFL scores.

Candidates are invited to arrange a personal interview with an Enrollment Counselor, tour the campus, attend class, and stay overnight on campus with a Trinity student. The Office of Admissions is open by appointment from 9 a.m. to 6 p.m., Monday through Friday, and each Saturday from 9 a.m. to 2 p.m. Experience Trinity overnight events are scheduled throughout the year.

Application and Information

Trinity College offers admission to qualified students in both the fall and spring. The application process is under a rolling policy and a decision is rendered once the student submits a completed application with all supporting documents. Students applying for scholarships are asked to submit applications to Trinity by December 15. Candidates for financial aid are asked to submit the FAFSA by March 1.

For additional information and applications, students should contact:

Director of Undergraduate Admissions
Trinity College
125 Michigan Avenue, NE
Washington, D.C. 20017-1094
Telephone: 202-884-9400
          800-492-6882 (toll-free)
Fax: 202-884-9403
World Wide Web: http://www.trinitydc.edu

The Capitol is located 2½ miles south of Trinity College.

TRINITY COLLEGE OF VERMONT
BURLINGTON, VERMONT

The College

Trinity College of Vermont is celebrating its seventy-fifth year as an independent institution dedicated to leading and directing change, building healthy communities, and promoting social justice. It is Vermont's only women's residential college and welcomes adult women and men, too, in its day, evening and weekend classes. Founded by the Sisters of Mercy, the College's legacy of academic excellence and Catholic traditions continues.

Trinity provides a stimulating academic and social environment, grounded in the liberal arts and sciences, that enables students to excel in their chosen fields and assume leadership roles. The College values the personalized faculty-student contact, individualized counseling, and sense of community that are a part of each student's campus experience because of the College's small size. This feature ensures that, along with a top-notch education, everyone is provided with the skills, training, and personal attention that are needed to make a difference in the workplace of the twenty-first century.

The College offers undergraduates a choice of eight majors. Internships, job shadowing, community service projects, and other off-campus opportunities are strongly encouraged to give students real-life learning experiences and invaluable hands-on preparation for future professions. Volunteer opportunities, intercollegiate athletics, campus ministry, and dozens of extracurricular clubs and organizations contribute to the richness of the Trinity College education. Students may choose to study abroad or take advantage of cross-registration and other special program arrangements with nearby University of Vermont, St. Michael's College, Champlain College, and the Community College of Vermont.

Past graduates who have gone on to excel in their professions and have been accepted into leading graduate schools around the country are a testament to the dedication, time, and energy Trinity devotes to offering the best career development and job placement services.

In addition to its undergraduate programs, the College also offers master's degree programs in education (M.Ed.), community mental health (M.S.), and management (M.S.) as well as a one-year postbaccalaureate premedical program.

Location

Trinity's beautifully landscaped, tree-lined campus is within walking distance of downtown Burlington, Vermont, a city known for its academic vibrancy, enduring beauty, and civic and cultural vitality. Nestled between the Green Mountains and the Adirondacks on the shores of Lake Champlain, Burlington has earned a national reputation as one of the best United States cities to live in. With a metropolitan area population of 122,000, Burlington is the largest city in the state. More than 20,000 students attend the six colleges in the area. It is rich in culture and offers diversions of all kinds: concerts, plays, sports events, museums, first-run movies, lectures, music and drama series, and excellent restaurants of many different ethnic persuasions.

Burlington is less than an hour's drive from great ski areas and only 95 miles from Montreal, 255 miles from Boston, and 290 miles from New York City. Daily bus and train and excellent air services are available.

Majors and Degrees

Trinity College awards the Bachelor of Arts (B.A.) degree in biology, education (teacher training programs in early childhood, elementary, secondary, and special education), human services, liberal studies, psychology, social work, and sociology/criminal justice. The Bachelor of Science (B.S.) degree is granted in biology and business management. A special-studies degree (B.A. or B.S.) is also available. Student-designed special-studies majors are available (recent examples are arts management, gerontology, and governmental studies). Associate degrees in accounting, business administration, human services, and liberal studies are available.

Academic Program

Trinity operates on a two-semester calendar and a flexible summer-session schedule. The first year is designed to give students maximum flexibility in their choice of concentration. To graduate, a student must complete 120 semester hours of credit, including 39 semester hours in the general education program, and achieve a minimum cumulative GPA of 2.0.

Programs providing professional preparation include social work, which is accredited nationally by the Council on Social Work Education, and teacher education, which is approved for certification by the State Board of Education in Vermont and by thirty other states. Trinity has affiliations with AMA-approved hospitals in Allentown, Pennsylvania; Burlington, Vermont; and Staunton, Virginia, for the fourth- or fifth-year clinical laboratory science program. Thirty additional hospitals accept applications from Trinity students.

Academic Facilities

The Farrell Family Library houses nearly 80,000 books, microfiche, and periodicals and can obtain through interlibrary loan any book or reference that is not in its collection. Trinity students may also use the libraries of the University of Vermont, St. Michael's College, and Champlain College.

The newly renovated Delehanty Hall (the main academic classroom building) houses both multipurpose and specialized instructional classrooms, including six fully equipped laboratories for teaching biology, chemistry, physics, and environmental science. The Learning Resource Center provides access to software and technology in many academic areas, including the Internet and other research databases, as well as direct instruction and tutoring in reading, writing, mathematics, and study skills. The Language Laboratory is available for multimedia presentations in language instruction, and the Language Immersion Center further enhances the study of language and culture with a satellite connection for news and social broadcasts from other countries. The Social Science Research Center facilitates conducting interviews and experiments and collecting and analyzing data. The Teacher Education Center offers a state-of-the-art teaching environment for education students.

The Child Care Center, located on campus, provides a practicum experience for students majoring in early childhood education. Also available is a writing center in which students may obtain diagnostic and one-on-one instructional assistance.

Costs

Tuition for 2000–01 is $14,040. Room and board costs average $6763. Student fees are approximately $500. All costs are subject to change.

Financial Aid

The Trinity McAuley Grant offers numerous need-based financial aid grants. In addition, there are a number of other need- and non-need-based financial aid programs to assist in making Trinity affordable, such as the Federal Pell Grant, Federal Supplemental Educational Opportunity Grant (FSEOG), Federal Stafford Student Loan, and work-study programs. To be considered for federal, state, and need-based institutional financial aid (grants, loans, and work), students must complete the Free Application for Federal Student Aid (FAFSA). The Title IV School Code for Trinity College of Vermont is 003695. Students must reapply for need-based aid each academic year. For more information about financial aid and financing options, students are encouraged to contact the Office of Student and Financial Services at 802-846-7170.

Faculty

Trinity's full- and part-time faculty consists of 85 members; more than 90 percent of the full-time faculty members hold the Ph.D. or other terminal degrees. Small classes benefit both students and teachers: the faculty-student ratio is 1:14. Faculty members serve as academic advisers, helping the student to devise a coherent, educationally sound degree completion plan. No classes are taught by graduate teaching assistants.

Student Government

Students govern themselves through the Student Association of Trinity. Every matriculating student at the College is a member of the association and elects representatives to the Student Senate. Through the standing committees, the students schedule and regulate campus social activities, make semiannual evaluations of all campus clubs and organizations, and administer the Student Senate and Student Activities funds.

Admission Requirements

To qualify for admission to Trinity College, a traditional student must be a graduate of an accredited secondary school or have a certificate of equivalency. All candidates are required to take the SAT I or the ACT. Applicants to the adult education PACE Program should contact the Admissions Office for specific admissions requirements.

It is recommended that applicants complete 4 years of English, 3 years of mathematics (including algebra and geometry), 2 years of a foreign language, 2 years of social sciences, and 2 years of a science, including a year of a laboratory science. A student may apply for advanced placement and/or college credit by taking the College Board's Advanced Placement exams in May. Credit toward graduation may be granted to those students who achieve a grade of 3 or higher. In special cases, students may petition to take College-Level Examination Program (CLEP) tests, which are arranged and supervised by the Educational Testing Service of Princeton, New Jersey. It is left to the discretion of the chairperson of the appropriate department at Trinity to determine whether a student is entitled to college credit for successfully passing these exams.

Transfer applicants should have a grade point average of at least 2.0. To earn a bachelor's degree, transfer students are required to complete at least 30 of their last 45 credits of course work at Trinity College of Vermont.

Trinity encourages international students to apply and welcomes people of all races, national origins, and religions.

Application and Information

Candidates for admission should complete an application form and return it to the Admissions Office at Trinity College of Vermont. All candidates should arrange to have their high school transcript and SAT I or ACT scores sent to the Admissions Office. A $40 application fee is required. Applicants are notified of an admission decision on a rolling basis. Although there is not an application deadline, interested students are urged to apply early in their senior year.

Transfer applicants must submit a high school transcript and transcripts from colleges previously attended. Students are encouraged to forward college catalogs from all institutions previously attended for reference in evaluation of completed credits. Trinity accepts college-level credit from regionally accredited institutions. A maximum of 64 credits may be transferred from two-year colleges and 90 credits from four-year institutions. Trinity has continuous admission of transfer students until places are filled for both the fall and spring semesters.

For further information, students should contact:

Admissions
Trinity College of Vermont
208 Colchester Avenue
Burlington, Vermont 05401
Telephone: 888-277-5975 (toll-free)
World Wide Web: http://www.trinityvt.edu

TRINITY UNIVERSITY
SAN ANTONIO, TEXAS

The University
Founded in 1869 when three small colleges merged in Tehuacana, Texas, Trinity University is an independent, privately supported, liberal arts and sciences university related by covenant to the Presbyterian Church. After a move to Waxahachie, Texas, in 1902, Trinity accepted an invitation from the San Antonio Chamber of Commerce to relocate to the Alamo City. Trinity moved to its present skyline location in 1952. Throughout its history, Trinity University has been guided by a commitment to excellence in undergraduate education.

Today Trinity is a nationally recognized institution characterized by a demanding curriculum, distinguished faculty members, exceptionally bright and diverse students, and a campus that is among the most modern and beautiful in the country. Though the size, character, and quality of the institution overall most closely resemble the nation's elite liberal arts colleges, Trinity University offers a unique curriculum that combines traditional liberal arts and sciences with the practical expertise to meet the challenges of the twenty-first century. The breadth of professional and preprofessional programs Trinity offers within the liberal arts and sciences context is rare in a school of this size and character. Conversely, Trinity is unique among comprehensive institutions in that it focuses its extraordinary resources almost wholly on undergraduates and provides an unusually large number of undergraduate research opportunities, even at the freshman and sophomore levels.

Students intensify their educational experience through interaction with diverse and talented students, rich cultural experiences, exposure to world leaders and newsmakers, and close contact with a distinguished faculty.

The William H. Bell Athletic Center provides a variety of athletic and recreational options. Trinity fields eighteen varsity teams, nine for men and nine for women, who compete in NCAA Division III and in the Southern Collegiate Athletic Conference. Nearly 70 percent of the student body participates in the popular intramural program.

Several endowed lecture series annually bring to campus such noted figures as General Colin Powell, news anchor Peter Jennings, author Philip Roth, and former prime minister Margaret Thatcher.

Trinity University is able to offer an exceptional educational experience, in part, due to its $580-million endowment. The endowment sustains Trinity's margin of excellence and subsidizes more than a third of the cost of a Trinity education.

U.S. News & World Report has ranked Trinity University the top comprehensive university in the West for the last nine years, and *Money* magazine included Trinity in its ten "best buys" among America's most selective colleges and universities.

Location
As the nation's eighth-largest city, San Antonio offers a wealth of social, recreational, and cultural possibilities. The skyline campus is located midway between San Antonio International Airport and downtown—a 10-minute drive to either location. In addition to the famed River Walk and historic missions, San Antonio boasts such attractions as Sea World and Fiesta Texas. The Texas hill country, with its scenic parks, lakes, and rivers, is within an easy drive, and Gulf Coast beaches and Mexico are just a few hours away. A symphony, numerous galleries, several excellent museums, and theaters expand the cultural options. Professional sports fans may enjoy the San Antonio Spurs basketball team and the Iguanas hockey team. Public transportation is readily accessible.

Majors and Degrees
Trinity offers majors in anthropology, art, art history, biochemistry, biochemistry and molecular biology, biology, business administration, chemistry, Chinese, classical studies, communication, computer science, drama, economics, engineering science, English, French, geosciences, German, Greek, history, international studies, Latin, mathematics, music, philosophy, physics, political science, psychology, religion, Russian, sociology, Spanish, speech, and urban studies.

Preprofessional programs are offered in health professions and law. Five-year programs in education and accounting lead to the bachelor's and master's degrees.

Interdisciplinary minors are offered in American intercultural studies, cognitive science, communication management, comparative literature, environmental studies, linguistics, medieval and Renaissance studies, and women's studies.

Academic Program
The academic program is rooted in the liberal arts and sciences tradition and further enhanced with select professional and preprofessional programs. Paramount among the skills it teaches is the ability to think creatively and critically and to express such thinking effectively both orally and in writing. The curriculum is flexible, intended to provide connections among the disciplines. All students participate in the Common Curriculum. This includes the interdisciplinary First Year Seminar and the writing workshop, courses in foreign language, computer and mathematical skills, health and fitness for students who have not satisfied Trinity's required levels of high school achievement in these areas, and courses grouped under the theme of Six Fundamental Understandings. These include The Intellectual Heritage of Western Culture, World Cultures, The Role of Values, The World Through Science, The Human Social Context, and The Aesthetic Experience and Artistic Creativity. Most students complete the Common Curriculum in two years. A major is declared at the end of the sophomore year.

To receive an undergraduate degree from Trinity University, students must successfully complete at least 124 semester hours (129 semester hours for a B.S. in engineering science; 132 hours for a B.M. in choral or instrumental music; and 141 hours for a B.M. in performance or composition), with 60 hours outside the major.

Additional programs include an honors program, study abroad, and physical education. All students, regardless of major, may participate in intercollegiate debate, musical ensembles, and drama productions.

Trinity observes a two-semester calendar, and first-semester exams fall before the Christmas break.

Off-Campus Arrangements
A wide choice of Trinity-approved programs allows for a semester or year abroad in almost any country. Trinity is an affiliate of the Institute of European Studies/Institute of Asian

Studies, a coordinating institution for Denmark International Studies, a member of the Intercollegiate Center for Classical Studies (Rome), and a member of the Council on International Education Exchange. Trinity also maintains close relationships with a number of other programs and universities. Trinity most directly sponsors programs as a member of the Associated Colleges of the South, with locations in Budapest and Costa Rica.

Academic Facilities

Trinity's Maddux Library, with more than 800,000 volumes and vast resources in microform, is one of the largest private undergraduate libraries in the nation. An annual acquisitions budget of $1 million ensures that status. Science facilities are spacious, modern, and well-equipped with sophisticated instrumentation. The Richardson Communications Center has electronic editing suites, control rooms, and remote and cable television news feed and production services. It also houses KRTU, the campus radio station. The Ruth Taylor Fine Arts complex houses studios, three theaters, and a concert hall as well as facilities for set design, production, and costuming. Electronic classrooms utilize the latest in computer technology to enhance the learning process and take advantage of the Internet resources. The computing center supports workstations throughout campus, and individual connections to the campus network and the Internet in each residence hall room further facilitate information access and mastery.

Costs

Tuition for the 2000–01 academic year is $15,660. Room and board (light eater plan) are $6700.

Financial Aid

More than 71 percent of Trinity students receive need-based financial aid or merit scholarships. The average need-based award is $15,745. Students receiving need-based assistance must submit a financial aid application each year. Awards are renewable, provided students make satisfactory progress toward their degree and family financial circumstances continue to indicate need. Need-based packages include a variety of federal, state, and Trinity grants, loans, and work-study. Academic scholarships are based solely on academic achievement.

Faculty

The Trinity faculty members, 99 percent of whom hold doctoral degrees, are internationally recognized, working scholars who share a dual commitment to undergraduate teaching and research. There are no teaching assistants at Trinity University. All classes are taught by professors. The student-faculty ratio of 11:1 ensures small classes, and close personal contact with professors is a significant and treasured component of the Trinity experience. Of the 220 full-time faculty members, 19 hold endowed Distinguished Professorships. The faculty adviser program pairs each student with a professor adviser.

Student Government

All full-time undergraduate students are members of the Association of Student Representatives, which is governed by a Student Senate elected by the student body. The University encourages students to hold seats on administrative committees in order to represent the student body there as well. The Student Court and the appellate University Court deal with infractions of campus rules and regulations.

Admission Requirements

Trinity University looks for gifted, motivated young people with skills, talents, and leadership qualities who are eager to develop their talents and contribute to the Trinity community. The Admissions Committee reviews both standard information and character traits. High school achievement encompasses not only grades, but also content and difficulty of courses taken. Applicants are expected to have completed upon high school graduation: 4 years of English; 3 or more years of college-preparatory mathematics, including trigonometry or precalculus; 3 years of social studies; 3 years of science; and 2 years of foreign language. A campus visit is strongly recommended.

The students accepted for the 1999 entering class had a mean SAT I score of 1271 and an average ACT composite score of 27.7. Their average high school GPA was 3.7.

Trinity does not discriminate on the basis of sex, race, ethnic background, age, or physical disability.

Application and Information

Deadline for early decision is November 15, with notification by December 15. Deadline for early action is December 15, with notification by February 1. Regular admission deadline is February 1, with notification by April 1. Transfer students must apply by April 15, for notification by June 1. A $30 fee must accompany all applications, and all required tests must be completed by the application deadline.

For more information, students should contact:

Office of Admissions
715 Stadium Drive
San Antonio, Texas 78212-7200
Telephone: 210-999-7207
        800-TRINITY (toll-free outside San Antonio)
E-mail: admissions@trinity.edu
World Wide Web: http://www.trinity.edu

Trinity's famed skyline campus overlooks the San Antonio skyline.

TRI-STATE UNIVERSITY
ANGOLA, INDIANA

The University

Tri-State University is a small, private, undergraduate, independent university. The University offers undergraduate programs in engineering (50 percent of students), business (20 percent of students), teacher education (10 percent of students), science and mathematics/computer science (10 percent of students), and psychology and criminal justice (10 percent of students).

Small class size, individual attention, caring faculty members, relevant academic programs, and an active Career Services Office contribute to the success of Tri-State's graduates. Within six months after graduation, 95 percent of Tri-State's May 1999 engineering, computer science, and business graduates were employed full-time in major-related positions. More than 90 percent of all Tri-State's May 1999 graduates were in major-related positions within six months after graduation.

Since its founding in 1884 as Tri-State Normal College, the emphasis has always been on career-oriented higher education. Tri-State's graduates have been known in industry and business as being "job ready." Teacher education graduates bring Tri-State's reputation for caring and concern (as well as expertise in their content areas) to their classrooms in elementary, middle, and high schools.

Tri-State's current undergraduate enrollment is about 1,200 men and women. About half of the students live on campus; freshmen are required to live in the residence halls. Coed and single-sex housing is available in double-occupancy rooms. The greatest number of students come from Indiana, Michigan, and Ohio. About 10 percent come from the Middle Atlantic and New England states, and approximately 10 percent come from other countries. The 400-acre campus has seventeen conveniently located buildings and a golf course. All students, including freshmen, are allowed to have automobiles.

Informality, friendliness, seriousness, and determination are the qualities characteristic of campus life. There are eight national social fraternities and four sororities (three local and one national); approximately 25 percent of the men and 15 percent of the women join after their freshman year. Students support strong intramural and intercollegiate sports programs. Men's intercollegiate sports are baseball, basketball, football, golf, soccer, swimming, tennis, track (including cross-country and indoor and outdoor track), and volleyball. Women's sports include basketball, golf, soccer, softball, swimming, tennis, track (including cross-country and indoor and outdoor track), and volleyball. For two decades, Tri-State has excelled in competitive basketball, golf, and track. The student senate, honor societies, professional organizations, campus newspaper, FM radio station, yearbook staff, and drama club are some of the possible activities.

Tri-State University is accredited by the Commission on Institutions of Higher Education of the North Central Association of Colleges and Schools (telephone: 312-263-0456; Web site: http://www.ncacihe.org) and is authorized by the state of Indiana to confer degrees. Its programs in chemical, civil, electrical, and mechanical engineering are accredited by the Engineering Accreditation Commission of the Accreditation Board for Engineering and Technology. The two-year program in drafting and design technology is accredited by the Technology Accreditation Commission of the Accreditation Board for Engineering and Technology. The department of education is accredited by the Indiana Professional Standards Board.

Location

Angola, Indiana, a town of about 9,000 people, is located in the scenic lake resort region of northeastern Indiana, about halfway between Chicago, Illinois, and Cleveland, Ohio. Pokagon State Park provides year-round recreational opportunities and is just 5 miles from campus. The security of a small-town environment provides pleasant surroundings day-to-day. Fort Wayne, Indiana, is a 45-minute drive via I-69. The resources and attractions of large metropolitan areas such as Chicago, Detroit, Cleveland, and Indianapolis are within a 3-hour drive via interstate highways.

Majors and Degrees

The School of Engineering and Sciences awards the following degrees in engineering: Bachelor of Science degrees in chemical, civil, electrical, and mechanical engineering; computer-aided drafting and design; and engineering administration. In the sciences, Bachelor of Science degrees are awarded in the following majors: biology, chemistry, computer science, environmental science, mathematics, physical science, and premedicine. Associate degrees are awarded in computer technology, construction management technology, drafting and design technology, manufacturing technology, and science.

The Ketner School of Business and Education awards the following bachelor's degrees in business: Bachelor of Science in Business Administration in accounting, business/arts and science, management, management information systems, and marketing; Bachelor of Science degrees in golf management and industrial management; and a Bachelor of Applied Management. In education, Bachelor of Science degrees are awarded in elementary education, physical education, and secondary education. In the social sciences and humanities, Bachelor of Arts degrees are awarded in communication, psychology, and social sciences; Bachelor of Science degrees are awarded in criminal justice and sports and recreation. Associate degrees are awarded in accounting, arts, business administration, and criminal justice.

Academic Program

Tri-State University graduates can take their places in industry, business, and education and perform in responsible positions with ability and competence. Graduation requirements for a bachelor's degree include a cumulative grade point average of not less than 2.0 (on a 4.0 scale) and the completion of 128–132 semester hours, depending upon the major.

Tri-State's engineering programs concentrate on providing a fundamental, application-oriented engineering education. In addition to concentrating in a specialized area, students are required to successfully complete courses in communication skills, sociohumanistic studies, and analysis and design.

The University's business programs include a broad range of hands-on practical experiences that acquaint the student with the practices, procedures, and problems of the contemporary business professional. Guest lecturers are frequent visitors to the campus, and field trips are considered vital to the total educational experience.

Tri-State University offers programs flexible enough to fill the needs of many individuals having diverse objectives. By careful selection of the major electives, a student can complete a preprofessional program in medicine, dentistry, medical technology, veterinary medicine, law, social work, and other professions that normally require specific undergraduate preparation. The programs in elementary and secondary education are characterized by the multitude of educational experiences in area school systems, commencing in the freshman year and continuing through student teaching. Science, mathematics, engineering, and computer science students have opportunities to participate in projects with direct application in area industries.

Off-Campus Arrangements

Co-op and internship opportunities are available in both of the University's schools. Semesters of classroom study are alternated with professional work experience, giving students the opportunity to integrate theory with practice and gain a competitive edge in the job market. The length of a co-op program depends upon the student's class status when entering the program. Work/study schedules require from three to six semesters on work assignments. During the semesters worked, students are paid directly by the employer.

Academic Facilities

The Ford Memorial Library contains a book collection of approximately 150,000 volumes, a reference collection, and 600 current periodicals and newspapers. It also offers several special services, including PALNI, a computer network of twenty-six college and university libraries; several CD-ROM newsline and educational research databases; and an educational and media resource center. Special collections include curriculum materials for elementary education and technical publications issued by NASA, AGARD, and NATO.

Fawick Hall of Engineering reopened on December 1, 1997, after a year-long $5-million complete interior demolition to load-bearing walls and then full reconstruction to house the University's Departments of Chemical Engineering, Civil and Environmental Engineering, Electrical and Computer Engineering, Mechanical and Aerospace Engineering, and Technology. Because of the University's commitment to quality undergraduate education, Tri-State's students use sophisticated equipment such as a scanning electron microscope in their cast metals laboratories and in projects related to industrial consulting. Each department has a computer lab with pertinent software for their students.

The John G. Best Hall of Science houses the Mathematics and Computer Science, Science, and Education Departments and the University's Computer Center. Tri-State's campus buildings are connected with a fiber-optic backbone LAN, and the residence halls are each wired for Internet access. There are approximately 200 networked Pentium computers across the campus for student academic computing as well as access to e-mail and the Internet. The Science Department equipment includes an atomic absorption spectrophotometer, a gas chromatograph–mass spectrograph, and a high performance liquid chromatograph. Students work with science faculty members on projects related to the ecological concerns of the surrounding lake areas. In addition, cross-disciplinary projects are encouraged with engineering departments.

Costs

Tuition for the academic year (two semesters) in 2000–01 is $13,450. In addition, there is a $250 technology fee. Room and board for the academic year (two semesters) are $4950. Students enrolled in engineering courses pay a surcharge of $65 per semester credit hour. Most entering freshmen are not enrolled in engineering courses. During their entire degree program, engineering majors enroll in about 60 semester hours of engineering courses.

Financial Aid

Financial aid may be awarded in the form of scholarships, grants, loans, or employment. Any of these aids or any combination may be necessary to supplement family and student resources to meet basic educational expenses.

Tri-State requires the use of the Free Application for Federal Student Aid (FAFSA) and recommends its submission by March 1. Admitted students who qualify for academic merit awards must complete the TSU Application for Scholarship form.

Faculty

Tri-State University has a full-time faculty of 57 members, most of whom have doctoral degrees and/or are registered professional engineers. The central mission of the faculty members is teaching. The student-faculty ratio is 14:1.

Student Government

The student senate is organized for the purpose of promoting and coordinating campus activities for students. Representatives elected from campus organizations form the senate, which sponsors social activities and campus projects and aids in formulating policies for student organizations.

Admission Requirements

Graduation from an approved high school or equivalent preparation is required for admission. Tri-State gives careful consideration to the caliber of the academic records. Selection is made without regard to race, religion, or color. The University requires that applicants for admission arrange to take American College Testing's examination (ACT) or the SAT prior to approval for admission.

Admission requirements for engineering include 4 years of English, 1 year of chemistry, 1 year of physics, 1 year of social studies, 2 years of algebra, 1 year of geometry, and ½ year of trigonometry. Preparatory courses are available for students who have not completed all the high school subjects normally required for admission.

Students who wish to enroll in business must have completed 4 years of English, 2 years of algebra, and 1 year of social studies.

All other applicants must have the following high school credits: 4 years of English, 2 years of mathematics (3 years for computer science majors), 2 years of science, and 2 years of social studies.

Tri-State's associate degree programs require 3 years of English, 2 years of algebra, and 1 year of social studies for entry into the computer technology program and 3 years of English, 1 year of algebra, and 1 year of geometry for drafting and design technology.

Graduates of preprofessional or college-parallel programs at approved community or junior colleges are eligible for transfer into Tri-State's baccalaureate programs. Qualified graduates of these programs may be granted junior standing upon transfer. In general, credit may be allowed for subjects equivalent to those in the program at Tri-State University provided that the student earned a C or better in the course.

Application and Information

Tri-State University operates on a semester schedule. Admission decisions are made on a rolling basis. Applicants are notified of their status within three weeks after the application and high school record have been received. Transfer students must also submit an official copy of their college transcript(s).

Interested students and their parents are encouraged to visit the campus. Arrangements can be made by writing or calling the Office of Admission.

For additional information, students should call or write:

Office of Admission
Tri-State University
1 University Avenue
Angola, Indiana 46703-1764
Telephone: 219-665-4132
        800-347-4TSU (toll-free within continental U.S.)
E-mail: admit@alpha.tristate.edu
World Wide Web: http://www.tristate.edu

TROY STATE UNIVERSITY
TROY, ALABAMA

The University

Troy State University was founded in 1887 as a Troy State Normal School. The name was changed to Troy State Teachers College in 1929, to Troy State College in 1957, and to Troy State University in 1967, when it was granted university status. Founded as a teacher-training institution more than 100 years ago, the University now offers arts and sciences, business and commerce, education, fine arts, health and human services, journalism and communications, applied science, and preprofessional programs. The University System operates four campuses in Alabama and more than fifty sites on military bases in twelve states and eight other countries. The availability of programs on these branch campuses may vary.

Students come from throughout the United States and several other countries. The total University enrollment is more than 17,000. There are 5,000 undergraduates enrolled at the main campus in Troy. Approximately half live on campus in men's, women's, or coeducational residence halls or in sorority or fraternity housing. Noncommuting students who are under 19 at the time of registration are required to live in University housing for one academic year. All students who live in the residence halls must choose from one of four meal plans. The Adams University Center provides areas for student services, dining, recreation, and quiet study. The University post office, store, and recreation room offer additional services. The offices of Placement, Student Activities, Student Government, the Union Board, *The Palladium* (yearbook), and the Interfraternity and Panhellenic Councils are all located in the University Center, and a performing arts theater, food court, and fitness center have recently been added.

The Ralph Wyatt Adams Administration Building contains the business office and University College in addition to the offices of enrollment management, financial aid, University records, public affairs, alumni affairs, development, institutional research and planning, student affairs, financial affairs, academic affairs, and the chancellor of The TSU System. Students may conduct most of their collegiate business within this one building.

Students participate in the Sound of the South Marching Band, Collegiate Singers, weekly newspaper, yearbook, radio and television stations, University Dancers, debate and forensics, musical theater productions, pageants, foreign language clubs, religious organizations, intramural sports, service clubs, honor societies, ethnic and political organizations, Trojan Ambassadors, social fraternities and sororities, and special interest clubs. A championship golf course is located on campus. The natatorium building houses an Olympic-size swimming pool, a sauna, a weight room, and a gymnasium. Lighted tennis and handball courts, a 17,000-seat football stadium, a 3,000-seat gymnasium, a baseball complex, a modern field house, intramural fields, an outdoor pool, sand volleyball courts, a state-of-the-art track, and a press box with VIP seating are among the athletic facilities. Troy State University is affiliated with the NCAA and fields fourteen intercollegiate sports. The Trojans play at the Division I-AA level in football and at the Division I-A level in all other sports.

Location

The University's beautifully landscaped 577-acre campus is situated in a residential area of Troy. The city offers numerous cultural resources. The State Theater, home of the Alabama Shakespeare Festival, is less than an hour's drive from the campus. Rivers, lakes, streams, and farmland surround Troy. Birmingham, Atlanta, and Mobile are a few hours away and the Gulf of Mexico is only 2 hours away.

Majors and Degrees

Troy State University awards a Bachelor of Arts (B.A.) or a Bachelor of Science (B.S.) degree in accounting, art, art history, athletic training, biology, broadcast journalism, business administration, chemistry, collaborative K–6 education, computer science, criminal justice, dramatic arts, economics, English, environmental science, finance, general science, geomatics, health education, history, journalism, management, marine biology, marketing, mathematics, medical technology, music education, nursing, physical education, physical science, political science, psychology, rehabilitation, secondary education, social work, sociology, speech communication, and sports and fitness management. Preprofessional concentrations are available in agriculture, dentistry, engineering, forestry, law, medicine, optometry, pharmacy, physical therapy, and veterinary medicine.

Academic Program

The general studies curriculum, consisting of 60 semester hours, is required of all students pursuing a bachelor's degree. It provides work in English grammar and composition, biology, algebra or general mathematics, music, literature, and visual arts. In addition to this, the student must select one series of courses in U.S. history or history of Western civilization; three courses chosen from anthropology, economics, ethics, geography, mythology, philosophy, political science, psychology, religion, or sociology; one course in earth or physical science; one course in microcomputing; and one course in speech in order to complete the general studies requirements. Ten hours in a foreign language will satisfy an elective portion of the general studies requirements.

Most degrees require 120 semester hours, 60 of which consist of major and/or minor courses. Double majors are available in various combinations. Besides meeting the requirements of a specific degree program, the student may choose courses from the general curriculum to satisfy elective requirements. Proficiency in English and mathematics is emphasized. The B.A. is awarded to students who enroll in at least 12 semester hours of a foreign language (French, German, Spanish, or Latin); other students are awarded the B.S. The average course load per term is 15 semester hours, or five classes carrying 3 semester hours of credit each. Students are encouraged to enroll in general studies and major courses simultaneously.

Academic Facilities

The University Library contains 247,761 volumes, more than 500 maps, 500,000 units of microtext, 47,000 government documents, and subscriptions to 1,500 periodicals and more than seventy newspapers. The library is part of an ultramodern Educational Resources Center, designed for comprehensive study and research, and includes a complete audiovisual facility. The Hall School of Journalism within this center features a 100,000-watt FM radio station affiliated with National Public Radio and a cablevision-affiliated television studio. The

Office of Communications Services includes a photography laboratory and studios, a printing and quick copy facility, and a graphics design studio.

Smith Hall Auditorium has a complete theater facility that is used for plays, pageants, ceremonies, and commencement exercises. It also provides a facility for students enrolled in the Department of Speech and Theatre. John Maloy Long Hall contains an acoustically perfect recording studio for the symphonic and concert bands and the collegiate and madrigal singers. McCartha Hall, housing the School of Education, contains a reading laboratory and an all-purpose lecture hall. The computer center is located in Bibb Graves Hall, along with offices and classrooms for the Sorrell College of Business and the Department of History and Social Sciences. The Center for Business and Economic Services, an office for research and information, is also located in Bibb Graves Hall. McCall and Sorrell halls contain laboratories and classrooms for science and mathematics. Smith Hall houses classrooms, offices, and lecture halls for the Department of English and studios for the Department of Music. *The Alabama Literary Review* operates from offices in Smith Hall. The Writing Center, staffed by permanent faculty members and student tutors, provides free services for students who are having difficulty with writing assignments. A similar facility, the Mathematics and Natural Science Laboratory, is designed to foster proficiency in those areas. A Fine Arts Center contains classrooms, studios, galleries, and a complete library to meet the needs of art, art history, and foreign language students.

Costs

Approximate annual full-time student expenses for the 1999–2000 academic year for fall through spring were as follows: in-state tuition, $2350, out-of-state tuition, $4700; on-campus housing (room rent), $2000; meal plan, $2200; and books and expenses, $500. The Trojan Incentive Plan is a cost-saving measure for students and parents in which the student pays for two academic years of on-campus housing and receives two academic years of on-campus housing free. The actual savings is approximately $4000.

Financial Aid

The University encourages all students to apply for admission regardless of their financial status. Scholarships, grants, loans, and work-study awards are given on the basis of priority and need analysis. For each academic year, beginning in September, the priority deadline is May 1. Approximately 70 percent of the current students are receiving financial assistance.

The University has an extensive scholarship program, which is based upon academic achievement and demonstration of leadership or particular talents. The following Troy State University Academic and Leadership Scholarships are awarded: Scholar's Award, a four-year full tuition, room, and board award; Chancellor's Award, a four-year full tuition award; and Leadership Award, for varied amounts. Other scholarships include athletic grants-in-aid and departmental and organizational awards.

Faculty

Individualized instruction and friendly student-teacher rapport are the keynotes of education at Troy State University. Even tenured full professors teach introductory-level courses. The number of courses taught by graduate teaching assistants is kept at a minimum. The visiting professor program has featured such dignitaries as Dr. Edward Teller, the nuclear physicist; Patrick Buchanan, syndicated columnist and former Presidential candidate; and Cyril Northcote Parkinson, the author of *Parkinson's Law*.

Student Government

The University's Student Government Association (SGA) consists of the president, vice president, secretary, and clerk who are elected by the student body to one-year terms. Senators are elected from each residence hall and from commuter seats. Senators may be chosen to serve on committees concerning academic affairs, publications, public relations, the Union Board, the Judicial Board, and curriculum revision. The SGA president is the only student member of the University's Board of Trustees.

Admission Requirements

Admission is based on the grade point average in high school or in previous college work, along with acceptable ACT or SAT I scores. Students are given placement examinations in mathematics and English before registering for classes in their first term of enrollment. Transfer students with fewer than 20 semester hours of college work are treated as beginning freshmen. Visits to the campus are recommended but are not required. Upon tentative acceptance of the application, the applicant is required to attend Pre-College Orientation, which takes place during the summer before the fall term. Similar shorter sessions are presented prior to each term. A student may enroll for any term, fall through summer. Prospective students are encouraged to visit the admissions office and make application well in advance of the term in which they wish to enroll.

Application and Information

There is no application deadline, but high school seniors are encouraged to apply as soon as possible during their senior year; housing assignments are made in the early spring. The application fee is $20.

Admissions Office
134 Adams Administration Building
Troy State University
Troy, Alabama 36082
Telephone: 334-670-3179
    800-551-9716 (toll-free)
World Wide Web: http://www.troyst.edu

TULANE UNIVERSITY
NEW ORLEANS, LOUISIANA

Tulane

The University

Tulane University in New Orleans is known nationally and internationally for its teaching and research. At Tulane a student can get an international education in a European city without leaving America. One of a handful of national independent universities in the South, Tulane was founded in 1834 as the Medical College of Louisiana and reorganized as Tulane in 1884. The University is comprehensive by nature, with more than 11,000 students enrolled in eleven schools and colleges ranging from the liberal arts and sciences through a full spectrum of professional schools: law, medicine, business, engineering, architecture, social work, and public health and tropical medicine. Tulane's 5,366 full-time undergraduates choose from sixty majors in colleges of liberal arts and sciences, engineering, architecture, and business and may opt for joint-degree programs in Tulane's professional schools to earn undergraduate and graduate degrees in a shorter period of time. Tulane's distinctive arrangement of undergraduate schools gives every student the personal attention and teaching excellence of a small college while providing the interdisciplinary opportunities and research resources of a university that *U.S. News and World Report* ranks in the nation's top quartile. The average class size is 22. Senior faculty members are in the classroom at all levels, and the 12:1 student-teacher ratio ensures individual attention.

On its residential campus about 4 miles from downtown New Orleans, Tulane requires housing for freshmen. Students may choose from several special interest floors in the residence halls, with areas for honors students, those interested in international and urban affairs, and women science majors, among others. Students participate in more than 200 campus organizations. About 1 student in 3 joins a fraternity or sorority; 2 in 3 play intramural or intercollegiate club sports, and more than 500 participate in Tulane's community volunteer organization. Tulane fields sixteen NCAA Division I sports, competing in the newly formed Conference USA.

More than 80 percent of Tulane students plan to go on eventually to graduate or professional school. Shortly after graduation, 10 percent enter medical school, 16 percent law school, 32 percent other graduate study, and just over one third accept jobs. Tulane students are among the country's most likely to be selected for several prestigious fellowships, including the Fulbright, Marshall, Rhodes, Truman, and Watson scholarships, that support postgraduate study.

Location

The University is in a historic New Orleans residential area next to renowned Audubon Park, which offers 440 acres of recreational facilities. While the 110-acre campus maintains a traditional collegiate atmosphere with Gothic stone and red brick amid blooming azaleas and lawns that are green year-round, new buildings are going up at the rate of one a year. Recent additions have included a state-of-the-art student recreation center, a center for engineering and biotechnology, a law school building, and a fine arts complex, with a new residence hall and a new science facility under construction. The only remaining streetcar line in the country clatters by the campus, connecting students with downtown New Orleans. Tulane students find enrichment through entertainment, education, and community service.

Majors and Degrees

The B.A., B.S., B.F.A., B.S.E, and B/M.Arch. degrees are offered. Programs are for four years with the exception of the five-year architecture program. Students interested in business spend two years in the liberal arts and sciences before enrolling in the A. B. Freeman School of Business in the junior year. Students may major in sixty departmental and interdisciplinary areas, including accounting; American studies; anthropology; architecture; art and biology; art history; art studio; Asian studies; biological chemistry; biomedical engineering; business; cell and molecular biology; chemical engineering; chemistry; civil engineering; classical studies; cognitive studies; communication; computer engineering; computer science; earth sciences; ecology, evolution, and organismal biology; economics; electrical engineering; engineering science; English; environmental engineering; environmental studies; exercise science; finance; French; geology; German; Greek; history; international relations; Italian; Jewish studies; Latin; Latin American studies; linguistics; management; marketing; mathematical economics; mathematics; mechanical engineering; medieval studies; music history or theory; music performance or composition; philosophy; physics; political economy; political science; Portuguese; psychology; religious traditions of the West; Russian; Russian studies; sociology; Spanish; theater; and women's studies. Talented students may also design their own majors, and those who meet requirements may begin professional study in law, medicine, or other professional schools in the senior year, reducing by a year the time spent earning undergraduate and graduate degrees.

Academic Program

Most freshmen enroll in one of five undergraduate colleges profiled below. Tulane has a two-semester calendar, with first-semester exams held before the holiday break. Faculty advisers assist in course selection and in planning major requirements.

The Paul Tulane College (for men) and Sophie Newcomb College (for women) offer programs leading to the B.A., B.S., and B.F.A. degrees. In Tulane's coordinate college structure, men and women attend classes together, Newcomb and Tulane share a faculty and a curriculum, and most residence halls are coeducational. The two-college model, however, gives men and women the opportunities for student government leadership, the personalized advising, and the sense of belonging that comes from affiliation with their own colleges. The liberal arts and sciences curriculum has proficiency requirements in English, a foreign language, and mathematics. Each student must also complete courses distributed across the disciplines—humanities and fine arts, social sciences, and sciences—in a nine-course requirement that gives each student a common basis of knowledge. Proficiency in writing is also required.

The School of Engineering emphasizes design, research, and laboratory experimentation for its Bachelor of Science degree programs in biomedical, chemical, civil, computer, electrical, environmental, and mechanical engineering as well as computer science. The modern laboratories in the engineering complex, including the $12-million Boggs Center for Energy and Biotechnology, support courses and studies in subjects as varied as robotics, environmental clean-up, the design of artificial joints, laser fabrication, and drug purification.

The School of Architecture takes advantage of its location in New Orleans, a fascinating living architecture laboratory, where about 300 students are enrolled in the five-year Bachelor/Master of Architecture program. Students graduate fully prepared to become licensed architects with no further study. The faculty members, nationally known for their scholarship and art as well as their teaching, often involve students in real-world architectural concerns.

The A. B. Freeman School of Business offers majors in accounting, business, finance, management, and marketing, leading to the Bachelor of Science in Management degree. The curriculum emphasizes ethics, entrepreneurship, international business, leadership, and communication skills as well as the major areas.

The Honors Program, with approximately 600 academically outstanding students, emphasizes small seminars during the first three college years and a research-based honors thesis the senior year. More than 100 students choose honors floors in the residence halls. The English as a Second Language/Bachelor of General Studies program, offered through University College, is specifically designed for international students who are academically qualified for Tulane but must improve their skills in English.

Off-Campus Arrangements

With more than 900 students from more than 100 countries at Tulane, undergraduates don't have to go abroad for an international experience. But many of them choose to take advantage of one of the University's programs for a summer, a semester, or a year of study abroad. Each year, approximately 100 academically talented Tulane students participate in the Tulane/Newcomb Junior Year Abroad (JYA) program, attending universities in France, Germany, Great Britain (including Scotland and Wales), Ireland, Israel, Italy, and Spain. Most scholarships and loans may be applied to JYA costs. Others opt for internships in New Orleans or Washington or places as far afield as London and Cambridge, England.

Academic Facilities

Tulane's library system is ranked among the nation's top 100 research collections. University library holdings total more than 2 million volumes, with several special research collections among the best in America: the William Ransom Hogan Jazz Archive; the Newcomb College Center for Research on Women; the Amistad Research Center, with its collection of primary source materials on the history of America's ethnic minorities, race relations, and civil rights. Other research facilities include the Roger Thayer Stone Center for Latin American Studies and the Murphy Institute for Political Economy. The Newcomb Gallery exhibits a wide range of art work, including shows by students and faculty members. State-of-the-art computing facilities include dozens of public terminals and a fiber-optic network connecting all campus buildings to the Internet.

Costs

In 1999–2000, the cost for a year at Tulane is $30,894. Of this amount, tuition and fees are $24,194 and room and board are $6700 for a typical double room and an all-you-can-eat twenty-three-meal plan (cost may vary for upperclass students).

Financial Aid

The University operates a comprehensive aid program; more than half of the students receive some form of financial aid. The average financial aid package (through scholarships, federal grants, loans, and work-study jobs) was about $20,000 for 1998–99. Need, determined by family financial information on the Free Application for Federal Student Aid and the PROFILE from the College Scholarship Service, establishes the appropriate amount of assistance. Merit, based on academic record, determines the proportion of Tulane-funded scholarships in the aid package. The University offers assistance to applicants who demonstrate financial need, and 90 percent of freshmen offered aid had their full need met. If financial need continues and the student has an acceptable academic record, aid extends through the normal period of undergraduate study. Notification of the financial aid award follows admission notification. Deans' Honor Scholarships are offered each year to approximately 100 freshmen and cover tuition for the undergraduate career; other merit scholarships, including those for middle-income students, are also available. Tulane also gives at least thirty National Merit Scholarships to National Merit Finalists who have named Tulane as their first-choice college. Tulane offers creative financing options for families that do not qualify for traditional aid but need assistance in meeting costs.

Faculty

The small, personal settings of Tulane classes give students immediate contact with their professors. Some of Tulane's most seasoned faculty members teach introductory and lower-level courses. About 98 percent of the 676 faculty members hold the highest academic degrees in their field, and there are broad opportunities for students, from the freshman year to graduation, to work closely with the faculty on research. Endowed chairs bring distinguished visiting lecturers to the campus every semester. Students have access to faculty members and counselors in the Career Services Center, the Newcomb College Center for Research on Women, and the Educational Resources and Counseling Center as well as in their own colleges and departments.

Student Government

Open communication between elected student representatives and the University's administrators makes Tulane responsive to students' needs. All students are members of the Associated Student Body of Tulane University and participate in University-wide elections. They can hold office and serve on a variety of student-faculty administrative committees. Students are also members of student government associations in each University college or division and can participate on a class level within those divisions.

Admission Requirements

Tulane seeks students who have proven academic capabilities combined with talents or achievements that would enrich the quality of life on campus. All applicants are considered without regard to race, sex, color, religion, sexual orientation, national origin, or physical handicap. Secondary school preparation consisting of 16 or more academic units is expected. In general, quality of achievement is more important than the number of units completed. Applicants to the School of Architecture are encouraged to submit evidence of creative interests with their application. Official SAT I or ACT scores are required. Three SAT II: Subject Tests are strongly recommended for course placement and are required of home-schooled applicants. Interviews are not required, but applicants are encouraged to visit the campus. The admission office is open year-round, except on holidays, from 8:30 a.m. to 5 p.m. central time, Monday through Friday.

Application and Information

Regualr decision applications should be submitted by January 15 for admission to the fall semester; admission notification is made no later than April 1, with a May 1 deposit deadline. Deans' Honor Scholarship applicants must apply by November 1 and are notified by February 20. Early decision/early application candidates should have all credentials on file by November 1 for notification by December 15. The application fee is $45.

Richard Whiteside
Vice President for Enrollment Management
   and Institutional Research
Tulane University
210 Gibson Hall
6823 St. Charles Avenue
New Orleans, Louisiana 70118-5680
Telephone: 504-865-5731
          800-873-9283 (toll-free)
Fax: 504-862-8715
E-mail: undergrad.admission@tulane.edu
World Wide Web: http://www.tulane.edu/Admission

TUSCULUM COLLEGE
GREENEVILLE, TENNESSEE

The College

Founded in 1794, Tusculum is one of the most innovative institutions in the nation. Not only is Tusculum the oldest college in Tennessee and the twenty-eighth oldest college in the country, it is the oldest coeducational institution affiliated with the Presbyterian Church (U.S.A.). Tusculum is one of the few colleges in the nation to offer students the opportunity to take one course at a time; this is called the focused calendar. The result is an accelerated academic schedule that encourages mastery and retention of subject matter over memorization. It also allows close daily interaction with instructors and classmates, building a community of learning through strong personal bonds. The calendar is an integral part of the College's civic arts mission: to build character and active citizenship through education.

Facilities on the wooded, 140-acre campus comprise nineteen buildings, eight of which are listed on the National Register of Historic Places. A new multipurpose facility, known as the Alpine Arena and the Niswonger commons, has recently been completed. The complex contains a gymnasium, training facilities, classrooms, and offices. The College's residence halls are single-sex and are within easy access of the classrooms, gymnasium, pool, student union, and tennis courts. Tusculum is a member of Division II of the NCAA. It fields teams in the following varsity sports: men's baseball and football, women's softball and volleyball, and men's and women's basketball, cheerleading, cross-country, golf, soccer, and tennis. Many other intramural sports, student organizations, and social events are sponsored by the College.

Location

Located in Greeneville, Tennessee, Tusculum is surrounded by mountains and beautiful rivers, streams, and lakes. The Great Smoky Mountains National Park and Cherokee National Forest are both within an hour's drive. It is an ideal area for many recreational activities, including hiking, camping, backpacking, white-water rafting, fishing, hunting, and skiing.

The city of Greeneville has been listed as number 38 in *The 100 Best Small Towns in America*. Greeneville, combined with Greene County, has a population of approximately 65,000. The region is rich in the history of east Tennessee, going back to pre–Revolutionary War times. With an elevation of about 1,500 feet, Greeneville has a moderate climate with four distinct seasons. In addition to providing recreational activities, the surrounding mountains offer cooling breezes in the summer and protective barriers from large snow storms in winter, although two or three light snows a year are not uncommon. Knoxville and the Tri-Cities—Kingsport, Johnson City, and Bristol—are all within an hour's drive, offering a wide variety of entertainment, shopping, and cultural activities. Off-campus employment opportunities are readily available within the Greeneville community.

Majors and Degrees

Tusculum College awards the Bachelor of Arts degree in athletic training, biology, computer information systems, computer science, education (early childhood, elementary, middle school, secondary, and special education), English, English/mass media, environmental science, history, management (accounting, general management, small business organization, and sports management), mathematics, museum studies, physical education, psychology, and visual arts.

Special programs are offered in medical technology, predentistry, prelaw, premedicine, pre-optometry, pre-pharmacy, and pre-veterinary studies. Teacher certification/licensure is awarded for secondary education in biology, science, English, history, and history with psychology. Teacher certification/licensure is also awarded for K–12 in physical education and visual arts. Students can choose to major in chemistry, journalism, music, political science, or religion in addition to any of the preceding areas of study.

Academic Program

Students generally complete course requirements for the baccalaureate degree in four calendar years. The College divides the academic year into two semesters. Each semester consists of four courses or blocks, where the students study the same subject for approximately 3½ weeks straight. When one course ends, students get a four-day break before the next one begins. Each course is worth 4 semester hours, resulting in 32 semester hours per year. A minimum of 128 credit hours is required for graduation. Within the 128 hours, students fulfill requirements not only in their chosen major but also in the College's core curriculum, called the Commons. The Commons is a combination of interdisciplinary courses and disciplinary courses in writing, mathematics, history, and environmental science. Tusculum also prepares students for a professional and productive life by guaranteeing graduates the skills necessary to succeed in life. These skills are reflected in the fourteen Competencies that are a critical component of all Tusculum's courses and an integral part of the graduation requirements.

The focused calendar, Commons courses, and Competencies enable students to experience the world for themselves and not just in a textbook. They also allow Tusculum graduates to become positive role models for the next generation. Upon arrival at Tusculum, students are assigned an academic adviser who serves as a mentor throughout their stay.

Students have the option of pursuing internships in conjunction with almost every major. They can also pursue an independent study project. Tusculum requires all students to complete a Service Learning Project before graduation. Credit is granted to students for AP exams and CLEP tests.

Off-Campus Arrangements

Tusculum College offers a 3-1 medical technology major. For the first three years the student must satisfy the fundamental course requirements. The program is completed in the fourth year by attending an approved hospital for clinical study and fieldwork. Tusculum also offers students the opportunity to study abroad in such places as Costa Rica, England, Mexico, Scotland, and Spain.

Academic Facilities

The Albert Columbus Tate Library, built in 1910 and a National Historic Site, houses more than 185,000 books and microform texts; 600 periodical titles, records, films, audiotapes, and videotapes; ERIC and Infotrac computerized databases; and Internet capability.

The College is also the site for the President Andrew Johnson Museum and Library, which houses the collection of the seventeenth president's private and family papers, donated to the College by Margaret Johnson Patterson Bartlett, Johnson's great-granddaughter. The library also holds the Charles C. Coffin Rare Book Collection, the original Tusculum College library, which is the largest extant library dating before 1807 in the Southeast. Named after an early president of the College, it contains books from the collections of Thomas Jefferson, Jonathan Edwards, John Hopkins, and the Mathers, with imprints back to the fifteenth century. The library is also a valuable resource for scholars interested in frontier education in the late eighteenth and early nineteenth centuries.

Costs

Tuition and fees for the 1999–2000 academic year were $12,500, and room and board cost $4100. Textbooks and supplies average $225 per semester. Personal expenses and travel costs vary with the individual student.

Financial Aid

Tusculum College offers a wide range of financial aid programs, and approximately 90 percent of all students receive some type of assistance. The forms of aid available include grants, loans, work-study, and scholarships. The Federal Pell Grant, Federal Supplemental Educational Opportunity Grant, and Tennessee Student Assistance Award are nonrepayable and funded by federal and state programs. Loans offered by Tusculum are repayable either by the student or parents and include the Federal Perkins Loan, Federal Stafford Student Loan, and Federal Parent Loan for Undergraduate Students (FPLUS). Most grants and loans are awarded on the basis of need, while most scholarships are awarded on a non-need, merit basis to students with exceptional academic or athletic talents. All applicants interested in receiving financial aid should check the appropriate box on the admission application, and a financial aid application packet will be sent; the student should return the appropriate materials to the College as soon as possible to be considered for all available programs. Priority is given to applications processed before April 1.

Faculty

The student-faculty ratio is 12:1. More than 80 percent of the full-time faculty members hold the Ph.D. or appropriate terminal degree. The primary responsibilities of the faculty are teaching and academic advising. Because of the focused calendar, the relationships between faculty members and students are strong and involved.

Student Government

As an institution dedicated to preparing people for effective participation in a democratic society, Tusculum offers many avenues for authentic deliberation, collaboration, and decision making. A set of committees composed of students, faculty members, and staff members, all voting members, oversees the academic and student life functions of the College. In addition to this participation in general campus governance, the Student Government Association is constituted entirely of students and serves to provide a democratic means for distributing student activity and organization funds and as a forum for presenting student concerns to faculty and administration.

Admission Requirements

Candidates for admission to Tusculum College must have graduated from an approved or accredited secondary school or have a general equivalency diploma. The College expects students to demonstrate their preparedness for college with a minimum 2.0 GPA in academic core courses. Students must have at least twelve academic core courses, including English, math (algebra I or higher), science, and social studies. Students must also have taken the SAT or the ACT. The curriculum at Tusculum places strong emphasis on writing, analytical reading, and critical analysis. A demonstration of personal commitment and motivation is also taken into consideration. Although a personal interview is not required for admission, prospective students are encouraged to visit the Tusculum campus.

Application and Information

Tusculum College has a rolling admission policy. Applicants are reviewed for admission once the application is completed. No application fee is required. Interviews and campus tours are available through the Admissions Office.

For additional information, students should contact:

Admissions Office
Tusculum College
P.O. Box 5097
Greeneville, Tennessee 37743
Telephone: 423-636-7312
               800-729-0256 (toll-free)
E-mail: admissions@tusculum.edu

The main entrance to Tusculum College and the Annie Hogan Byrd Fine Arts Building.

TUSKEGEE UNIVERSITY
TUSKEGEE, ALABAMA

The University

Tuskegee University is an international, independent, and nonprofit institution of higher learning that has a special and unique relationship with the state of Alabama. With distinctive strengths in the sciences, engineering, and other professions, the University's basic mission is to provide educational programs of exceptional quality that promote the development of liberally prepared and professionally oriented people.

Undergraduate instruction at Tuskegee is organized under five colleges: Agricultural, Environmental, and Natural Sciences; Business, Organization, and Management; Engineering, Architecture and Physical Sciences; Liberal Arts and Education; and Veterinary Medicine, Nursing, and Allied Health. Undergraduate courses are offered leading to the Bachelor of Architecture, Bachelor of Arts, and Bachelor of Science degrees.

Graduate instruction leading to the master's degree is offered in four of the five major areas: Agricultural, Environmental, and Natural Sciences; Engineering, Architecture, and Physical Sciences; Liberal Arts and Education; and Veterinary Medicine, Nursing, and Allied Health. This instruction is coordinated by the Dean of Graduate Programs and graduate faculty members, who include deans and faculty representatives from the areas offering graduate work.

The University also offers Master of Science degrees in agricultural economics, animal and poultry sciences, biology, chemistry, electrical engineering, environmental sciences, food and nutritional sciences, general science education, mechanical engineering, tropical animal health, and veterinary medicine.

A Master of Education degree is offered in general science education.

The curricula for the five major academic areas lead to bachelor's degrees in thirty-eight areas, master's degrees in twelve areas, the Doctor of Veterinary Medicine, and the Ph.D. in Materials Science and Engineering.

In addition to the challenges of the classroom, the Tuskegee Experience includes a range of extracurricular activities. Varsity and intramural sports are available to both men and women. The musically inclined can take advantage of the University Choir, Concert Band, Marching Band, and other musical ensembles. Students are initiated into social and service fraternities and sororities and a number of academic honor societies. Religious Enrichment Week is a highlight of the Tuskegee Chapel program, which also features weekly Sunday morning services. The Tuskegee University Honda Campus All-Star Challenge Team is the first to reign as national champions for two consecutive years (1993–94). There are organizations and activities to fit everyone's interests and needs—and new organizations and activities are being launched continuously.

After their first year of study at Tuskegee, all students are encouraged to register with the University's Career Development and Placement Center. In recent years, the Career Development Center has recorded more than 600 annual recruitment visits to the campus—officials from industries across the nation exploring employment opportunities with Tuskegee students.

Location

The town of Tuskegee, a community of more than 15,000 people, is approximately 40 miles east of Montgomery, Alabama, the state capital, and 120 miles south of Atlanta, Georgia. Travelers may fly to Montgomery's Regional Airport and drive to Tuskegee via Interstate 85 north or fly to Atlanta and drive to Tuskegee via Interstate 85 south. Montgomery's Regional Airport is served by Delta and Northwest Airlink.

Churches of all major denominations, a library, and a museum contribute to the cultural atmosphere of the town. Motels and hotels are located in the area. The town also has various fraternal, civic, and veteran's organizations.

Majors and Degrees

Tuskegee University offers Bachelor of Architecture, Bachelor of Arts, and Bachelor of Science degrees in accounting, aerospace science engineering, animal and poultry sciences, architecture, biology, business administration, chemical engineering, chemistry, computer science, construction science and management, early childhood education, economics, electrical engineering, elementary education, English, environmental sciences, finance, forest resources, general dietetics, general science education, history, hospitality management, language arts education, management science, marketing, mathematics, mathematics education, mechanical engineering, medical technology, nursing, occupational therapy, physical education, physics, plant and soil sciences, political science, predentistry, premedicine, psychology, social work, sociology, and veterinary medicine.

Academic Program

Tuskegee University's academic year comprises two semesters and one 8-week summer term. In addition to required courses in each academic major, all programs include elective and required courses in the liberal arts. Summer enrichment programs are available in engineering, computer science, veterinary medicine, and the natural sciences.

The requirements for a bachelor's degree vary, from 124 semester hours in some liberal arts programs to 139 semester hours in engineering.

The University is accredited by the Southern Association of Colleges and Schools, while some programs have additional national and specialized accreditation by the appropriate professional associations. These programs include architecture, chemistry, dietetics, engineering, medical technology, nursing, occupational therapy, social work, and veterinary medicine.

Off-Campus Arrangements

Many students elect to participate in cooperative education opportunities that have been available since 1963. Co-op students alternate semesters of study on campus with off-campus work assignments in industry. In addition to the significant financial compensation they receive, co-op students have a decided advantage in the pursuit of permanent employment because of the work experience they gain.

Students who elect not to take advantage of the cooperative education program may register for summer internships and gain work experience with several different companies and in several different professional environments during their course of study.

Academic Facilities

The University library system consists of the main library (Hollis Burke Frissell) and some departmental libraries. The collections in all libraries number approximately 308,007 volumes. Through purchased and gift subscriptions, 1,200 periodicals and 28 international and domestic newspapers are received regularly. The library has been a federal depository since 1907 and has a collection of more than 15,000 select government documents. In addition, the Washington Collection and Archives, consisting of manuscripts, books, rare books, photographs, and other artifacts by and about Africa and African Americans, contains more than 100,000 items and constitutes one of the few very strong collections of its kind in existence.

Well-equipped research and instructional laboratories are available to support academic programs. Computer laboratories are available for general use across the campus, including some residence halls.

Costs

Tuition is $9928 for the 2000–01 academic year. Room and board are $5328. Costs for any year are subject to change.

Financial Aid

Tuskegee University subscribes to the philosophy that all academically capable high school graduates should be given an opportunity to pursue a postsecondary education. Consequently, every effort is made to assist needy and qualified students through the University's financial aid programs. The amount of aid granted is determined by the availability of funds, the extent of a student's need, and academic performance. Most awards are given for one academic year and are divided equally between the two semesters. Students seeking financial aid must file the Free Application for Federal Student Aid (FAFSA). This form can be obtained from the Financial Aid Office at Tuskegee University.

Faculty

The student-faculty ratio of 12:1 permits individualized instruction and small classes. The normal teaching load is 12 credit hours, but professors also spend time advising students, doing research and committee work, and undertaking administrative duties. The University's faculty consists of 317 members, and approximately 70 percent hold doctoral degrees.

Student Government

The Student Government Association (SGA) is the official governing body and representative voice of all students at Tuskegee University. SGA officers are elected by a vote of the student body. All enrolled students are members. The student voice is also heard and represented at Tuskegee through the Student Senate.

Admission Requirements

Tuskegee University welcomes applications for the fall and spring semesters and the summer term. Applicants for admission must be graduates of an accredited high school and must present acceptable high school records and SAT I or ACT scores. Students who receive their education through home schooling are also considered for admission. Although personal interviews are not required, students and parents are encouraged to visit the campus during the admission process.

Application and Information

Students seeking admission to Tuskegee University for the fall semester, which starts in August, should apply by March 15. Those seeking admission for the spring semester, which starts in January, should apply by October 15. Those seeking admission for the summer term should apply by April 1. Tuskegee University does, however, have a rolling admission policy and considers students for admission throughout the year. Early application is always advisable.

For further information, students should contact:

Director of Admissions
Old Administration Building
Tuskegee University
Tuskegee, Alabama 36088
Telephone: 334-727-8500
           800-622-6531 (toll-free)
E-mail: admi@acd.tusk.edu
World Wide Web: http://www.tusk.edu

The clock on White Hall at Tuskegee University.

UNION COLLEGE
BARBOURVILLE, KENTUCKY

The College

Union College is a small, spirited, independent liberal arts college in the Appalachian Mountain range. The College, affiliated with the United Methodist Church, was founded in 1879, a time when simple survival, not higher education, was the top priority of most of the country. However, for the citizens of Barbourville, a town of 450 people and three brick buildings, establishing a college for their children was essential. The name they chose reflected the unity of purpose they felt; they believed education was the path to leadership.

Union's 331 men and 301 women full-time undergraduates and 289 graduate students represent twenty-three states and several countries. The College's academic program fulfills the goal of a liberal arts education. It also provides students with the skills necessary to compete in a diverse job market. The undergraduate liberal arts curriculum makes available a body of knowledge drawn from the applied sciences, humanities, natural sciences, and social sciences. Majors and areas of study in preprofessional, technical, and skills-oriented fields enhance postgraduate employment opportunities.

Union's 100-acre campus is on the edge of the beautiful Appalachian Mountains in southeastern Kentucky. The newest of the College's twenty buildings is a student apartment building. The College is also renovating one of its oldest buildings, creating a state-of-the-art academic center. Approximately 38 percent of the students live in three dormitories on campus. Dozens of student organizations offer many opportunities for participation in a wide range of extracurricular activities. Union's full-time campus minister organizes various religious activities, including weekly voluntary chapel services and monthly convocations.

Intercollegiate sports include basketball, diving, golf, mountain biking, soccer, and swimming for men and women; softball and volleyball for women; and baseball and football for men. Intramural sports vary according to student request. The College recently completed a new softball field and refurbished the baseball, soccer, and football fields.

Location

Just 17 miles east of Interstate 75, the town of Barbourville sits in the Appalachian Mountains and is surrounded by four state parks filled with waterfalls, lakes, and streams. The campus itself includes more than 100 gently rolling acres that are covered in overhanging elms, mountain laurel, and Georgian architecture. The famous Wilderness Road spans the east side of the campus, and Cumberland Gap National Historic Park is just 30 miles away. The air is clean and fresh, and the people are friendly and down to earth.

Majors and Degrees

Union College offers the Bachelor of Arts, the Bachelor of Science, and the Bachelor of Music degrees. Majors are available in accounting, biology, business administration, chemistry, Christian education, church music, communication, criminal justice, drama, education (business, elementary, middle grades, physical, secondary, and special), English, health, history, history and political science, mathematics, music, music/business, philosophy/religion, physics, psychology, religion, sociology, and sports management.

In addition to programs in the pure disciplines of biology, chemistry, mathematics, and physics and their education counterparts, Union has programs in place for professional and health science careers. These programs combine the advantages of the small private college and those of the large university and include dentistry, engineering, medical technology, medicine, optometry, pharmacy, physical therapy, and veterinary medicine. Some of the programs have cooperative agreements; some are based on competition, while others give preference to Union students.

Academic Program

Union College helps students make learning connections. Students are given opportunities for practical applications through an academically rigorous liberal arts curriculum. Upon admission to the College, students begin a process whereby career counselors and academic advisers help them articulate career goals, select academic courses of study appropriate to those goals, and achieve suitable placement upon completion of their studies.

The College operates on a two-semester calendar, with a May interim session and two summer terms. Students must successfully complete a total of 128 semester hours to earn a bachelor's degree, including 43 semester hours of required core classes from the four major divisions of study. To earn an associate degree, students must successfully complete 64 semester hours.

Off-Campus Arrangements

Union College is a cooperating member of the Kentucky Institute of International Studies (KIIS). The College joins with a number of other Kentucky colleges and universities to provide summer study opportunities in ten different locations. The programs in France, Spain, Mexico, Germany, Austria, Italy, and Ecuador are open to all Union College students, who may earn credits toward their degree at Union.

Academic Facilities

The Weeks-Townsend Memorial Library contains more than 120,000 books, periodicals, government documents, media materials, and online reference and full-text databases. Library functions, including the public catalog access (OPAC), circulation, and reserves, are fully automated through the Sirsi Unicorn Collection Management System. The twenty-one-seat computer lab is the center of campus access to the Internet, including e-mail and the World Wide Web. The College also has a variety of computers accessible to students. The library and Centennial computer labs each contain twenty-one workstations and a laser printer connected to the campus network. A third lab, the Hensley lab, provides the same type of access with fifteen computers. The labs are open a variety of hours each week to support the academic programs and provide student access to the campus network.

The Academic Resource Center (ARC) provides free services to Union College students in several academic support areas. Individual tutoring is available in a variety of subject areas in both upper- and lower-division classes. Students may work with a tutor to review for classes, refresh study skills, or prepare for professional examinations such as GMAT, LSAT, MCAT, GRE, and NTE. Each semester, courses that have been deemed academically challenging are selected for supplemental instruction (SI). Students attend group study sessions, which are held a minimum of three times a week, with a student leader who has already excelled in that particular course. The SI leaders model good study strategies and encourage collaborative learning.

Costs

Tuition for the 1999–2000 academic year was $10,590, and room and board were $3450, for a total of $14,040. Books were estimated at $500 per year. Personal expenses were estimated at $500 per year, depending upon the individual.

Financial Aid

In 1998–99, 89 percent of Union's undergraduate students received financial assistance. Students wishing to be considered for aid must file the Free Application for Federal Student Aid (FAFSA) by March 15. The Federal Pell Grant, Federal Supplemental Educational Opportunity Grant, and Federal Work-Study programs are sources of aid. Kentucky residents may apply for the Kentucky State Tuition Grant.

Faculty

Union's faculty members are intensely committed to the adventure of learning as well as the greater adventure of life. One faculty member had the adventure of a lifetime on a trek in the Amazon, and another is one of today's foremost authorities on one of the richer cultures in America, Appalachia. The faculty-student ratio is 1:13.

Student Government

Union College Community Government provides an opportunity to examine and seek solutions for quality-of-life issues of the campus. The Campus Activities Board seeks to design, sponsor, and produce a broad range of activities on campus. The Commuter Council seeks to examine the needs and interests of nonresidential students and to provide programs to meet those needs.

Admission Requirements

To be considered for admission, a student must submit a completed application, a $20 application fee, ACT or SAT I scores, and official high school transcripts. The following high school academic units are required: 4 in English, 3 in mathematics, 2 in social studies, and 2 in science. Foreign language study is recommended but not required. Applicants must have maintained a minimum average of C in their secondary school work. References and student activities are also considered.

Transfer students must submit a completed application, a $20 application fee, and official transcripts from any college or university previously attended. Official high school transcripts are required if the student is transferring fewer than 31 semester hours. Transfer students must be eligible to return to the institution last attended and may be admitted to Union in any semester or summer session.

At Union, the doors are open to anyone who wants a more fulfilling life, regardless of race, color, sex, disability, or national or ethnic origin.

Application and Information

Application forms may be obtained by writing to the Admission Office. Applications are processed on a rolling admission basis. Students must present ACT or SAT I scores and official high school transcripts. Upon acceptance, students must complete the health form provided by the College.

Additional information may be obtained by contacting:

Admission Office
Union College
310 College Street
Barbourville, Kentucky 40906
Telephone: 606-546-4151 Ext. 1657
 800-489-8646 (toll-free)
E-mail: enroll@unionky.edu
World Wide Web: http://www.unionky.edu

At Union College, students can take advantage of the mountain location.

UNION COLLEGE
LINCOLN, NEBRASKA

The College

Union College, established in 1891, is a Christian liberal arts institution offering four-year postsecondary degrees and a limited number of two-year degrees. Graduate programs in education and nursing are offered on campus through cooperating institutions.

Union's population exhibits a diverse international flavor. Students bring varied experiences and backgrounds from throughout the United States and forty other countries. The student body of approximately 900 makes the College small enough for each student to receive individual attention and to form lifelong friendships.

Union is renowned for its graduates in humanitarian service. Each year for more than ninety years, an average of 20 students and alumni have begun international humanitarian, medical, and educational services.

A multimillion-dollar capital campaign of renovations and additional campus facilities is nearly complete. Residence halls, new classrooms, and laboratory and performance centers are included in the proposed facilities and renovations. Union's percentage of alumni contribution is among the highest in the nation and allows for these major campus improvements.

The Career Center offers a resource center to assist students in making career decisions, writing resumes and cover letters, conducting job searches, perfecting interview techniques, and arranging career shadowing and internships.

Location

Union is perched on the highest point in Lincoln, the capital of Nebraska. The 110-year-old campus features more than 100 species of trees in a beautiful parklike setting. The 50 surrounding acres of property are a part of the statewide arboretum system. The College is a mix of ivy-covered neo-Greco brick buildings, brick walkways, and modern academic and student service structures. Near the campus are connections to more than 70 miles of scenic biking and walking trails within the city.

Lincoln is among the most rapidly growing medium-sized cities in the United States. It is small enough to have a sense of community yet large enough to have its own culture. The historic downtown Haymarket district offers shopping, bistros, galleries, boutiques, and ethnic restaurants. The downtown contains galleries, museums, playhouses, state and federal offices, gardens, fountains, banking centers, the Lied Center for the Performing Arts, one of two sprawling Lincoln campuses of the University of Nebraska, and the Devany Sports Complex.

Majors and Degrees

Union College offers majors, emphases, and minors (* denotes minor) in academic disciplines leading to the following seven degrees: Bachelor of Arts, Bachelor of Science, Bachelor of Science in Nursing, Bachelor of Technology, Bachelor of Social Work, Bachelor of Music, and Bachelor of Arts in Theology. Union offers programs of study in art (graphic design and studio art), behavioral science (psychology, social work, and sociology*), biology (biology and marine biology), business (accounting, administration, finance, institutional development, international business, international studies, management, marketing, science, small-business management, and theology), chemistry (biochemistry, chemistry, and general chemistry), communication (communication, drama*, journalism, and public relations), computer science (computer information systems and computer science), education (elementary and secondary), English (English literature/drama, speaking, and writing), general studies, health and human performance (business/sport management and fitness/cardiac rehabilitation), health science (clinical laboratory medical technology, nursing, and physician assistant studies), history, mathematics (mathematics and statistics), modern language (French, German, and Spanish), music education (instrumental, keyboard, and vocal), music performance (conducting, instrumental, keyboard, and vocal), physics, religion (missions and evangelism, pastoral care, religion, theology, and youth ministry*), and social science*.

Preprofessional programs are offered in architecture, dental assisting, dental hygiene, dentistry, dietetics, engineering, law, medical records, medicine, occupational therapy, optometry, osteopathy, pharmacy, physical therapy, public health, radiologic technology, respiratory therapy, speech-language pathology and audiology, and veterinary medicine.

National Council for the Accreditation of Teacher Education (NCATE)–approved teaching degrees and endorsements are offered in art, biology, business, chemistry, computer science, English, history, language arts, mathematics, music, physical education, physics, religious education, and social science. A limited number of technical degrees are also available.

Union offers Associate of Arts and Associate in Science degrees in accounting, art, business administration, computer information systems, engineering, graphic design, health science, music pedagogy, and office management (for which some courses are taken at affiliated local colleges).

Academic Program

Baccalaureate degrees are awarded after students complete requirements in general education, the major field of study, contextual requirements, and electives that total a minimum of 128 semester hours. At least 40 of these 128 semester hours must be in courses numbered at the 300 level or above. Thirty semester hours and at least half of the 300-level or above hours must be in the major. A minimum of 56 semester hours must be completed in four-year colleges or universities. Three writing-designated (WR) courses are required after satisfactory completion of ENGL 111 and ENGL 112. A minimum grade point average (GPA) of 2.0 in all course work attempted at Union College and all transferred credits is required. (Students should consult the Academic Bulletin for further details.)

Union Scholars, the College's honors program, offers an enriched academic experience and annual scholarship awards. In addition to traditional liberal arts education, Union offers practical experiences such as internships, career counseling, and study abroad.

Entering students with less than 24 semester hours of credit must complete UCC 101 College Success during their first semester at Union. This class assists the student in formulating a personalized college plan, selecting a satisfying career, and establishing a life mission.

The Teaching Learning Center offers such services as instruction, bypass strategies, note takers, and tutors for students with learning differences such as dyslexia.

Four levels of English as a second language (ESL) offer beginning conversation to university-level preparation. Students with TOEFL scores between 450 and 549 may take select university-level courses. Dual-enrollment tuition rates vary based on the number of ESL and non-ESL courses taken. All levels offer reduced tuition. Four hours of ESL classes may count toward a degree. The TOEFL is required of all nonnative English speakers upon arrival. Completion of the ESL program occurs when the student is able to score at least 550 on the TOEFL.

Academic Facilities

The Engel Hall fine arts complex houses both visual and musical arts programs. The Everett Dick Building includes the divisions of humanities, business and computer science, human development, and religion. Microcomputer labs use cutting-edge software and hardware and provide access to the Internet and advanced business, art, and desktop publishing programs. Jorgensen Hall houses engineering, chemistry, biology, and mathematics. Science students use an in-house HP 5890 capillary gas chromatography unit and other advanced analytical equipment. The Ella Johnson Crandall Memorial Library has more than 130,000 volumes of print and nonprint media. In addition to physician assistant studies, nursing, health, and exercise science classrooms, offices, and labs, the Larson Lifestyle Center houses an Olympic-size pool, weight rooms, a Jacuzzi, tennis courts, and sand volleyball courts. Classroom buildings contain PC and scientific/health science laboratories.

Each residence hall room's computer terminal provides free access to the Internet, WordPerfect, Quattro Pro, library card catalogs, e-mail, and more.

Costs

Annual estimated expenses for 2000–01 total $15,540 (tuition, $10,940; room, $2150; estimated cafeteria expenses, $1500; miscellaneous expenses, $250; and textbooks, $700). Tuition is based on 12 to 17.5 credit hours.

Financial Aid

Union College tailors financial aid packages to fit individual student needs. Proceeds from more than $5.8 million in endowments (117 endowed scholarship funds), federal and institutional scholarships, student loans, grants, and work-study programs are available to qualified students. On- and off-campus employment may also defray costs and provide career experience. Grants and loans are available from federal and state agencies.

If students finish a four-year degree at Union and later decide to change careers, they may come back to the school to complete another degree, tuition free. (Interested students should consult the Academic Bulletin for details.)

Students apply for financial aid by completing the Free Application for Federal Student Aid (FAFSA), which is available at any local college, many libraries, the Internet, and high school guidance counselors' offices.

Faculty

The Union College faculty includes 55 full-time faculty members and additional part-time faculty members. Forty-four percent of the full-time faculty members hold terminal degrees.

In addition to being qualified professionals, Union's professors are Christian role models who portray their values through their actions and speech. They are committed to the art of teaching and to caring for each student. Professors, not graduate assistants, teach classes and supervise labs.

Student Government

Students participate in college government through elected positions in the Associated Student Body (ASB). Students are also members of most campus committees. Regularly scheduled town hall assemblies are held to allow students direct interaction with administrators. In addition to the ASB, other recognized campus clubs and organizations meet regularly.

Admission Requirements

Specific admission requirements include at least a 2.5 GPA (applicants with a GPA of between 2.0 and 2.5 are accepted into the Academic Success and Advising Program (A.S.A.P.) only), an ACT score for entering freshmen, three references, high school transcripts (if applicable), home school transcripts (if applicable), and transcripts from other colleges (if applicable). Special assistance and admission is available to students with certified learning differences (interested students should see the Teaching Learning Center in the college bulletin for details).

Union College does not discriminate on the basis of race, religion, disability, age, or gender and is affiliated with the Adventist Church.

Application and Information

Applications may be submitted year-round. Notification of acceptance occurs approximately two weeks after all requirements are met. Prospective applicants should contact:

Office of Admissions
Union College
3800 South 48th Street
Lincoln, Nebraska 68506

Telephone: 402-486-2504 (outside North America)
800-228-4600 (toll-free inside North America)
Fax: 402-486-2566
World Wide Web: http://www.ucollege.edu

The Everett Dick Administration Building is one of six classroom buildings at Union College.

UNION COLLEGE
SCHENECTADY, NEW YORK

The College
Union College is an independent, primarily undergraduate, residential college for men and women of high academic promise and strong personal motivation. Founded in 1795, it was the first college chartered by the Regents of the state of New York and is one of the oldest nondenominational colleges in the country. The first college in America with a unified campus plan, Union was the first liberal arts college to offer engineering (in 1845). It has more than 19,000 alumni and an endowment of approximately $272 million. The College seeks a geographically and socially diverse student body; at this time, the 2,000 undergraduates represent thirty-seven states and twenty-two countries. Approximately 35 percent of each graduating class continues directly on to graduate or professional school, and Union has earned an excellent reputation for the placement of its graduates in medical, law, and business schools.

Union believes that a student's life outside the classroom is a vital part of his or her total education and therefore encourages a variety of student-funded organizations—approximately ninety-five at last count—and a rich cultural and social life. Union also offers an extensive program of intercollegiate, intramural, club, and recreational sports. Highlights among the athletic facilities are the Alumni Gymnasium with an eight-lane swimming/diving pool and squash and racquetball courts; a 3,000-seat ice rink; an Astroturf field; and an all-weather track. In addition, a $7-million Campus Center provides space for social and community activities and services for the entire campus. Dining facilities, a pub, an auditorium, a radio station, and multiple student activities spaces are important parts of the building. The Yulman Theatre greatly enhances the arts program at the College, and the historic Nott Memorial has been renovated into a discussion and display center for students and alumni.

About 80 percent of all students live on campus and have a variety of housing options, including residence halls, apartments, co-ops, theme houses, and fraternities and sororities.

Location
Union is located on 100 acres of land on a hill overlooking the small upstate New York city of Schenectady, founded in 1661 by the Dutch. The city is at the northwestern limit of a larger metropolitan area based on Albany, the capital of New York, 15 miles away. The metropolitan area has a population of more than 800,000, including more than 35,000 college and university students in more than a dozen public and private institutions. Schenectady is 3 hours from New York City and Boston and 4 hours from Montreal. Wilderness camping, white-water canoeing, skiing, and cross-country ski touring are all readily available to the Union student, as the Catskills, Adirondacks, Green Mountains, and Massachusetts Berkshires are within an hour and a half of the campus. A great number of volunteer opportunities are available within the Schenectady community.

Majors and Degrees
Union College offers the Bachelor of Arts degree in anthropology, art (art history, music, theater arts, and visual arts), classics, economics, English, history, modern languages, philosophy, political science, and sociology. The Bachelor of Science degree is awarded in biochemistry, biological sciences, chemistry, civil engineering, computer science, computer systems engineering, electrical engineering, geology, mathematics, mechanical engineering, physics, and psychology. Formal interdepartmental work is offered in Africana studies, American studies, computer information systems, East Asian studies, industrial economics, Latin American studies, managerial economics, Russian and Eastern European studies, and women's studies. Transdisciplinary studies, individually designed majors, and concentrations within departments are also available. Students may also declare a minor in any of twenty-five disciplines. An Educational Studies Program enables students to be certified to teach at the secondary level. In addition, Union offers programs that lead to a B.A. degree from Union and a law degree from Albany Law School (six-year accelerated law and public policy program) or to a B.S. and M.S. from Union and an M.D. from Albany Medical College (eight-year leadership in medicine program). Union also offers a variety of two-degree programs that permit a student to receive both a general bachelor's degree and an engineering degree. Other two-degree programs lead to a Bachelor of Science in an engineering field and a Master of Science in engineering or industrial administration or to a B.A. or B.S. and a Master of Business Administration.

Academic Program
As a college committed to the liberal arts ideal, Union prepares students for roles as useful, informed citizens and leaders as well as jobholders. Degree requirements include successful completion of thirty-six courses in all programs except engineering, which may require up to forty; successful completion of the requirements in the major and the general education program; and, normally, two years in residence at the College. Students are encouraged to strive for a breadth of learning that will complement the expertise acquired through studies in the major. A general education program is in effect, which enables students to develop a better understanding of the Western heritage as evidenced in history and reflected in literature and other expressions of Western culture. This program incorporates the previously existing Freshman Preceptorial and ensures exposure to important areas of knowledge, including science, mathematics, and social science. It also offers strong incentives to study other cultures. Independent study is encouraged. To foster initiative in educational programs and individual academic exploration, Union established an Internal Education Foundation. Using a portion of annual tuition revenues, the foundation makes grants for special projects to students, faculty members, and administrators. Through this and other means, the College vigorously promotes undergraduate research. Students who pass examinations taken under the College Board's Advanced Placement Program with a score of 4 or higher (except in mathematics, for which a score of 3 is acceptable) are typically given college course credit and are exempted from any requirement to take the equivalent college courses. Union's calendar consists of three 10-week terms, in which the student takes three courses. The academic year begins in early September and ends in early June.

Off-Campus Arrangements
As a member of the Hudson-Mohawk Association of Colleges and Universities, Union participates in programs of cross-registration that enable students to take courses at fourteen consortium colleges and universities in the capital area. Reserve Officers' Training Corps (ROTC) programs of the Army, Navy, and Air Force are available through this consortium. Union offers a wide range of formal resident-study programs in international countries. Currently, terms of study abroad are available in Austria, Barbados, Brazil, China, England, Fiji, France, Germany, Greece, Israel, Italy, Japan, Kenya, Mexico, and Spain, and a term of marine studies in Bermuda, Woods Hole, and Newfoundland is also offered. In addition, Union offers a summer trimester program in which students examine the national health programs of England, Holland, and Hungary; eleven formal exchange programs: full-year exchanges in Germany, Japan, Switzerland, and Wales and one-term exchanges in Barbados, Belgium, Bulgaria, China, the Czech Republic, India, and Korea; and political science internships in the New York State legislature and in Washington, D.C.

Academic Facilities

The recently completed F.W. Olin Center is a high-technology classroom and laboratory building, which contains a multimedia auditorium, collaborative computer classrooms, and a 20-inch remote-controlled telescope. Available for student use in the Science and Engineering Complex are such research tools as two electron microscopes, a nuclear magnetic resonance spectrometer, a two-2MeV tandem Pelletron accelerator, X-ray diffraction equipment, and a Fourier transform infrared spectrometer.

The Humanities Building houses a language laboratory with dial-access audio equipment, and the Arts Center has been extensively renovated. Housed in the Stanley G. Peschel Center for Computer Science and Information Systems, Union's central computer facility consists of several multiuser servers on a campuswide fiber-optic-based network. Included in the network are UNIX, Windows NT, and Apple Macintosh servers. The center also hosts the College's main Web server and its library automation system. Also connected to the network are more than 1,100 College-owned personal computers and workstations. There are more than twenty electronic classrooms, which are used to enhance the integration of technology and academic studies through the use of the Internet and multimedia materials. Each residence hall room is wired with one Ethernet network connection per resident, providing access to the College's computing resources and the Internet and World Wide Web. Personal computer laboratories with Windows, Apple Macintosh, and UNIX workstations are available for student use. Departmental computer labs provide access to specialized computing needs. Access to the Internet, personal Web page space, and e-mail is provided for all Union students and faculty and staff members. Scanners, digital cameras, and other equipment are also available for student use.

A major renovation and expansion of Schaffer Library was completed in 1998. The library houses more than 280,000 titles and approximately 5,300 current serials, together with a periodicals reading room, faculty studies, and more than 500 individual study spaces. The library is operated on the open-stack plan and provides interlibrary loans and duplication services, microfilm and microfiche readers, photocopy and duplicating machines, electronic document delivery, CD-ROM workstations, public-use computer terminals connected to the campus computer center, and online bibliographic retrieval and computer-assisted reference services. A professional librarian is on duty at all times during library hours.

Costs

Charges for 2000–01 include tuition, $24,750; average room and board, $6639; and an activities fee, $213.

Financial Aid

In 1999–2000, Union's total financial aid program amounted to approximately $26.8 million; about $17.6 million came from the College itself and the rest from federal, state, and private sources. While 57 percent of Union's students receive direct institutional scholarship assistance, 64 percent receive some form of aid each year (e.g., other scholarships, guaranteed loans, and job opportunities). Most students awarded financial aid from the College receive a package consisting of at least $3825 in self-help (loan and/or job). The amount of self-help varies with need but, in most cases, does not exceed $6900. The remainder of the financial need is met with College, state, and federal scholarships and grants. Candidates for aid should complete the Free Application for Federal Student Aid (FAFSA) and the College Scholarship Service's PROFILE form and mail them directly to the appropriate agencies by February 1. Aid is based upon need and is intended to recognize superior academic performance and personal credentials, as well as to help those who could not attend Union without the financial assistance of the College.

Faculty

Union is a teaching college. Its 189 full-time faculty members were chosen with specific reference to their capabilities as teachers. Excluding the library staff, 96 percent of the faculty members hold the doctorate, and faculty salaries are above the national averages for colleges of comparable size. Union does not determine the functions of faculty members on the basis of rank; full professors often teach introductory courses. Class size generally is small; many upper-level courses function as seminars.

Student Government

Students have full voting rights on the two councils that recommend educational policy and student life policy to the president. Students also have seats in groups that advise the president on such matters as budgetary planning and long-range needs.

Admission Requirements

The College considers four factors in evaluating each application: the secondary school record, including rank in class and the quality of courses taken; the recommendations of secondary school teachers; the personal qualities and extracurricular record of the applicant; and scores on the tests given by the College Board (SAT I) or ACT. Students are required to submit one of the following: the SAT I or three SAT II Subject Tests (Writing, Mathematics, and Science are required for the eight-year leadership in medicine program and preferred for engineering and science program candidates; all other students should submit scores on the Writing Test and two others) or the ACT. Those interested in accelerated programs must submit the SAT I and three SAT II Subject Tests. Normally, 16 units of secondary school preparation are required for admission. These should include credits in certain fundamental subjects, such as English, a foreign language, mathematics, social studies, and science. It is strongly recommended that students visit Union for an admission interview and a student-guided tour. Alumni interviews may be arranged for students by calling the Admissions Office.

Application and Information

Early decision candidates have two options. The application deadline for Option I is November 15, with notification by December 15. Option II has a January 15 deadline and February 1 notification. All supporting credentials are due November 15 for Option I and January 15 for Option II. Applications for regular admission should be filed by February 1, with the exception of the accelerated programs. Applications to the eight-year leadership in medicine program must be filed no later than December 15 and applications for the six-year law and public policy and the five-year B.A./B.S. and Master of Business Administration programs must be filed no later than January 1. Those deferred under early decision and all regular applicants are given a final decision by early April. Union adheres to the Candidates Reply Date of May 1.

Vice President of Admissions
Stanley R. Becker Hall
Union College
Schenectady, New York 12308
Telephone: 518-388-6112
               888-843-6688 (toll-free)
Fax: 518-388-6986
E-mail: admissions@union.edu
World Wide Web: http://www.union.edu

The sixteen-sided Nott Memorial is Union College's centerpiece.

UNITED STATES AIR FORCE ACADEMY
COLORADO SPRINGS, COLORADO

The Academy
Established in 1954, the Air Force Academy prepares and motivates cadets for careers as Air Force officers. The Academy stresses character development, military training, and physical fitness as well as academics, emphasizing leadership in all areas.

The total enrollment is 4,000; about 1,200 fourth class (freshman) students enter each year. The composition of the student body mirrors that of the Air Force officer corps: about 15 percent women and 16 percent minorities. Students come from all fifty states and several other countries. Their common bond is the desire to be military officers. All cadets must live in on-campus dormitories and wear uniforms.

The Academy is accredited by the North Central Association of Colleges and Schools. Its engineering programs are approved by the Engineering Accreditation Commission of the Accreditation Board for Engineering and Technology, and its computer courses are approved by the Computing Sciences Accreditation Board. The chemistry and biochemistry majors fulfill the requirements of the Commission on Professional Training of the American Chemical Society.

All cadets must participate in intramural, club, or intercollegiate athletics every semester. The intramural sports include basketball, cross-country, flag football, flickerball, racquetball, rugby, soccer, softball, team handball, tennis, ultimate frisbee, volleyball, wallyball, water polo, and men's boxing. The intercollegiate teams compete in Division I of the NCAA regionally and nationally. The men's teams include baseball, basketball, cross-country, fencing, football, golf, gymnastics, ice hockey, lacrosse, riflery, soccer, swimming, tennis, track, water polo, and wrestling. The women's teams include basketball, cross-country, fencing, gymnastics, riflery, soccer, swimming, tennis, track, and volleyball. Cadets may also choose from more than eighty extracurricular activities, which include professional organizations, mission support, competitive and recreational clubs, sports groups, and hobby clubs.

Qualified Academy graduates may enter flight training upon graduation, and approximately 75 percent of the students in each graduating class pursue graduate education at other institutions within ten years of their graduation. Each year, numerous Academy graduates receive graduate scholarships and fellowships, such as the Marshall, Rhodes, National Science Foundation, National Collegiate Athletic Association, and Guggenheim awards.

Location
The Academy campus sits in the foothills of the Rampart Range of the Rocky Mountains in a setting of natural beauty. Built on a mesa at 7,000 feet, it is one of Colorado's top tourist attractions. The Cadet Chapel, with its seventeen aluminum spires towering 150 feet into the air, highlights the contemporary architecture of the buildings in the cadet area. The space-age effect reflects the Academy's mission of preparing cadets to become officers and leaders in the Air Force of the future. The Academy borders the northern edge of Colorado Springs, which lies at the foot of the famous 14,100-foot Pikes Peak. Colorado Springs has a metropolitan population of more than 300,000. Denver, the state's capital, has a population of almost 2 million in its greater metropolitan area and is located 55 miles north of the Academy. In addition to the social, sports, and cultural activities available in these cities, cadets enjoy skiing, hunting, horseback riding, white-water rafting, and other activities in the Colorado Rocky Mountains and nearby resorts.

Majors and Degrees
Graduates of the four-year service academy receive the Bachelor of Science degree and a commission as a second lieutenant in the Air Force. The B.S. is granted in thirty-one majors: aeronautical engineering; astronautical engineering; basic sciences; behavioral sciences; biology; chemistry; civil engineering; computer engineering; computer science; economics; electrical engineering; engineering mechanics; engineering sciences; English; environmental engineering; foreign area studies; general engineering; geography; history; humanities; legal studies; management; mathematical sciences; mechanical engineering; meteorology; military doctrine, operations, and strategy; operations research; physics; political science; social sciences; and space operations. The Academy also offers minors in computer science, foreign languages, mathematics, military operations and strategy, and philosophy.

Academic Program
A class enters the Academy during the last week in June or the first week in July. Incoming cadets undergo a strenuous six-week summer training program that tests both their mental and physical abilities. Upperclass cadets conduct basic cadet training; commissioned officers serve as advisers. Basic cadets who complete this program are accepted into the Cadet Wing as fourth-class cadets. The academic year starts in early August and continues through May. During the first two years, cadets concentrate on core courses in engineering, humanities, science, and social science. During the last two years, they specialize in an academic major.

The required core courses prepare cadets for a broad scope of activity as Air Force officers. The core curriculum embraces courses in academic subjects, leadership and military training, and physical education and athletics. In addition, cadets complete the requirements for any of the thirty-one academic majors. To be eligible for graduation, cadets must also demonstrate an aptitude for commissioned service and leadership, demonstrate character consistent with professional military service, maintain a minimum cumulative grade point average and core grade point average of 2.0, and complete a minimum of 148 credit hours. The curriculum includes many elective courses.

All students must begin as freshmen; however, cadets who have taken some of the core course material prior to entry into the Academy may receive transfer or validation credit for this work. They may then substitute other courses for those granted transfer credit. Cadets who maintain the required grade point average may take advanced study classes.

The Academy aviation program familiarizes all cadets with operational activities of the Air Force. Optional courses provide instruction in soaring, parachuting, navigation, and basic flying. Those who take these courses may fulfill the requirements for Federal Aviation Administration pilot or glider certificates. Cadets who qualify and are selected for pilot or navigator training may enter Air Education and Training Command flight programs following graduation from the Academy.

Diversified summer programs in aviation and military training prepare cadets for officer responsibilities in the Air Force. Cadets may select their programs from several optional assignments at the Air Force Academy and other military installations.

Off-Campus Arrangements

Selected cadets may exchange visits with cadets from the Military Academy, Naval Academy, Coast Guard Academy, or one of fifteen international Air Force academies. The exchange program varies from one to two weeks for most of the international programs to a semester for the other U.S. service academies and the French and German Air Force academies.

Academic Facilities

The Air Force Academy's excellent facilities support the academic, military, and athletics programs. Most classrooms accommodate small class sessions of 12 to 20 students. Several classes and assemblies meet in larger lecture halls. Well-equipped laboratories supplement classroom instruction. Cadets conduct experiments using the Aeronautics Laboratory's wind tunnels, shock tubes, and rocket engines. A local network connects every dorm room, faculty and staff office, classroom, and laboratory at the Academy, and all entering cadets purchase a microcomputer for academic and personal use. The Academy planetarium is a multimedia education and research facility used for cadet instruction in astronomy and navigation. The Academy library, with more than 600,000 volumes, supports all educational programs and maintains a collection of historical materials concerning aeronautics.

Costs

There are no tuition charges; the cost, including room, board, and medical and dental care, is borne entirely by the U.S. government. In addition, cadets receive a monthly salary to pay for supplies, clothing, and personal expenses. Careful management of the money covers obligations, with only a small amount remaining for personal use. Prior to admission, appointees deposit $2500 to help defray the initial cost of uniforms and supplies.

Financial Aid

All cadets are on full scholarship at the Air Force Academy, as described above.

Faculty

The Academy's faculty is composed of Air Force officers and civilian professors. A few officers from other branches of the U.S. Armed Forces and from allied nations and distinguished civilian visiting professors supplement the faculty. There are no graduate student instructors. Faculty members must have a master's degree, and many have earned doctorates. Their educational backgrounds represent many outstanding colleges and universities in the United States, as well as some international institutions of higher education. Faculty members sponsor, coach, and referee extracurricular activities and athletics; adopt squadrons and attend their special events; and provide academic, career, and personal counseling.

Student Government

The Air Force Academy trains cadets for future leadership by allowing them to hold positions of responsibility in the Cadet Wing, the organization to which all cadets are assigned. The wing is under the operational supervision of first-class cadets (seniors). They hold cadet officer rank and command the wing and the subordinate units of groups, squadrons, flights, and elements. Through this organization, the upperclass cadets are responsible for military training of the underclasses, the honor education and honor system, character development, and ethics and human relations programs.

Admission Requirements

Each year, young men and women who are U.S. citizens may be appointed from all states and territories of the nation. Citizens of other countries are admitted in limited numbers. Applicants must be at least 17 and not yet 23 years of age on July 1 of the year in which they desire to be admitted. They must be unmarried, have no dependents, and have good moral character and physical health.

Applicants must receive an official nomination. Members of Congress make the majority of the nominations for residents of their states and districts. Senators and representatives nominate young men and women who have excelled academically in high school, have demonstrated leadership potential through school activities, are physically fit, are respected by associates, and want to pursue military careers. Applicants need not know their member of Congress personally. Students may be eligible in nomination categories other than congressional. They should ask their high school counselor or Air Force Admissions Liaison Officer about other categories available and apply for all nominations for which they are eligible.

To enter the Academy upon graduation from high school, students should apply as soon as possible after January 31 of their junior year. If successful in receiving a nomination, they must take a physical fitness test, a medical exam, and either the SAT I or the ACT.

Application and Information

High school juniors may obtain application forms by writing to the address below. Applicants should study the instructions included in the application package and follow the proper application procedures. The package also includes sample letters for requesting nominations. Air Force Admissions Liaison Officers, located in all states, assist students and counselors with the application and testing requirements. The Academy catalog lists the Liaison Officer Commanders in each state.

HQ USAFA/RRS
2304 Cadet Drive, Suite 200
USAF Academy, Colorado 80840-5025
Telephone: 719-333-2520
              800-443-9266 (toll-free)
World Wide Web: http://www.usafa.edu/rr/

The Cadet Color Guard is the centerpiece of a Cadet Parade.

UNITED STATES COAST GUARD ACADEMY
NEW LONDON, CONNECTICUT

The Academy

Founded in 1876, the United States Coast Guard Academy has a proud tradition as one of the finest and most selective colleges in America. The smallest of the five federal service academies, the Coast Guard provides a four-year Bachelor of Science program with a full scholarship for each individual. Unlike the other federal service academies, however, there are no congressional appointments.

The mission of the United States Coast Guard Academy goes well beyond academics: "To graduate young men and women with sound bodies, stout hearts, and alert minds, with a liking for the sea and its lore, with that high sense of honor, loyalty, and obedience which goes with trained initiative and leadership; well grounded in seamanship, the sciences, and amenities, and strong in the resolve to be worthy of the traditions of commissioned officers in the United States Coast Guard in the service of their country and humanity."

Students come to the Academy to be challenged academically, physically, and professionally. By providing excellent academic programs, a structured military regimen, and competitive athletics, the Academy graduates competent and professional military officers to serve the country. The Academy's four primary objectives are to provide by precept and example an environment that encourages a high sense of honor, loyalty, and obedience; to provide a sound undergraduate education in a field of interest to the Coast Guard; to provide a living laboratory for leadership education; and to provide training that enables graduates to assume their immediate duties as junior officers afloat.

After successfully completing the Academy program, each graduate receives a Bachelor of Science degree in one of eight majors and a commission as an Ensign in the U.S. Coast Guard. Each graduate is required to serve a minimum of five years of active duty upon graduation.

Admission to the Academy is based on nationwide competition. An average of 290 students enter the Academy each year out of approximately 5,500 applicants. Midyear students are not accepted. The student body, known as the Corps of Cadets, consists of approximately 850 cadets made up of approximately 30 percent women and 20 percent members of minority groups, plus international students representing various countries.

The Academy experience goes far beyond an ordinary classroom curriculum. Freshman year begins in July, seven weeks prior to the academic school year. The first seven weeks, known as "Swab Summer," are an invigorating period of physical, military, and leadership training. The last week is spent sailing aboard America's only active duty square rigger, Barque *Eagle*— America's Tall Ship.

Summer is devoted to professional and military training except for three weeks of vacation. Cadets spend five weeks of their sophomore summer sailing on board the training ship *Eagle*, three weeks at a Coast Guard unit, either ashore or afloat, and two weeks sailing small boats. Junior summer involves one week of leadership training, three weeks training the incoming freshmen, one week of specialized shipboard training, one week qualifying in rifle and pistol, and two weeks of aviation training. In preparation for shipboard life after graduation, seniors spend ten weeks aboard a Coast Guard cutter learning the roles they will be responsible for as junior officers. In addition, academic internships are available on Capitol Hill, Washington, D.C., and in Coast Guard specialty fields such as mechanical and civil engineering.

The athletic facilities include two pools, four basketball courts, two gyms, baseball and softball fields, football/soccer stadium, indoor and outdoor track, five racquetball courts, volleyball courts, eight outdoor and two indoor tennis courts, rifle/pistol range, a fully equipped Rowing Center, and a Seamanship-Sailing Center. The waterfront facilities are among the finest in the nation. Athletic participation in at least two of the three seasons at the intramural, club, or intercollegiate level is mandatory. Academy intercollegiate sports for men (m) and women (w) include baseball (m), basketball (m,w), crew (m,w), cross-country (m,w), football (m), indoor/outdoor track (m,w), pistol (m,w), rifle (m,w), sailing (m,w), soccer (m), softball (w), swimming/diving (m,w), tennis (m), volleyball (w), and wrestling (m). The Academy is a member of the National Collegiate Athletic Association (NCAA) Division III.

In addition to an extensive athletic program, there are various extracurricular activities. The music department has a variety of programs to offer, including the Regimental Band, CGA choir groups known as the Idlers and Icebreakers, Windjammer Drum and Bugle Corps, Bagpipe Band, Glee Club, Dixie Band, Protestant and Catholic choirs, a jazz band, a concert band, a pep band, an annual cadet musical, and various ensembles. The Academy's cadet yearbook staff produces the Academy's annual yearbook, *Tide Rips*. Various athletic clubs include hockey, marathon/road runner club, taekwondo/martial arts, water polo, lacrosse, bowling, women's soccer, women's tennis, men's volleyball, and the spirit team. Academy-sponsored clubs include outdoor sports (hiking/camping), paintball, scuba, snowboard, downhill skiing, dance, golf, fencing, international, and the Genesis Club. Additional extracurricular activities include the Political Affairs Association (PAA), Officer Christian Fellowship (OCF), American Society of Mechanical Engineering (ASME), Society of Women Engineering (SWE), Fellowship of Christian Athletes (FCA), Scoutmaster Council, Drill Team, and Big Brothers/Big Sisters.

Location

The campus is in New London, Connecticut, on the western shore of the Thames River. It has twenty-six buildings on 120 acres of land. Halfway between New York, New York, and Boston, Massachusetts, the Academy is easily accessible by plane, train, bus, or car.

Majors and Degrees

Each student graduates with a Bachelor of Science degree in one of the Academy's eight majors: civil engineering, electrical engineering, government, management, marine and environmental sciences, mechanical engineering, naval architecture and marine engineering, and operations research.

Academic Program

The Coast Guard Academy program is designed to provide a superb academic foundation in a military environment designed to produce future leaders of America. No one teaching method or forum is given precedence. Academic work is interactive and a joint effort of faculty members and students.

The Academy is fully accredited by the New England Association of Schools and Colleges (NEASC). Engineering majors are accredited by the Engineering Accreditation Commission of the Accreditation Board for Engineering and Technology (ABET). The core curriculum encompasses chemistry I and II; physics I and II; calculus I and II; introduction to engineering and design; introduction to electrical engineering; nautical science I, II, III, and IV; economics; American government; English composition and speech; criminal justice; maritime law enforcement; leaders in U.S. history; morals and ethics; literature of leadership; organizational behavior and leadership; oceanography; leadership and organizational development; and probability and statistics. Upon graduating, the student will have completed a minimum of 126 credit hours to earn a Bachelor of Science degree.

The typical Academy class size is small, resulting in an average instructor-student ratio of 1:8. Only a few of the lower-level classes are taught in large group/lecture format. Additional instruction and tutoring outside of the classroom is always available through a strong academic support program.

The Academy offers an Honors Program to combine a technical education with liberal arts and cultural awareness through a series of cultural events and seminars. The Honors Program can also lead to in-depth research projects and internships in Washington, D.C.

Upperclass students who have demonstrated a high level of academic performance may also take elective courses at Connecticut College in New London.

Academic Facilities

All academic buildings conveniently surround the living quarters and are well within walking distance. All students are required to live in CG Academy living quarters.

The Coast Guard Academy library houses 150,000 volumes, 600 periodicals, interlibrary loan/document deliver, and an Online Public Access Catalog (OPAC). The library provides a Cadet Writing Center for individual instruction in writing, reading, and comprehension.

Laboratories are maintained for physics, chemistry, computers, oceanography, electronics, navigation, and engineering experimentation and analysis. The Academy also has a Bridge/Combat Information Center simulator, a radar trainer, 65-foot training vessels, and the 295-foot sailing ship, *Eagle*.

Costs

There is no fee to apply. All candidates who are offered and accept an appointment to the Academy must pay an entrance fee of $3000. Other than this initial cost, there are no additional fees. Students receive a full four-year scholarship with a monthly stipend of about $600, which covers the cost of uniforms, textbooks, a brand new computer, and any other expenses. Each student receives a monthly allowance for personal expenses.

Upon graduating from the CG Academy, there is a five-year commitment to serve as a commissioned CG officer, the first two years of which are on a CG cutter.

Financial Aid

All cadets receive pay exceeding $7200 per year. Cadets' pay is not a wage or salary; it is money furnished by the government for uniforms, equipment, textbooks, and other expenses incidental to training. These funds cover all the cadets' expenses and are disbursed and expended only as directed by the Academy's superintendent. Each cadet receives a portion of his or her monthly stipend as an allowance for personal expenses. Any funds remaining in cadets' accounts are given to them upon graduation.

Faculty

The Academic Division consists of five departments under the direction and supervision of the Dean of Academics. These departments are completely staffed by Coast Guard officers and permanent professors, both civilian and military. Faculty members are invariably available for additional instruction as desired by the student. The amount of personal attention given to students by the faculty is one of the Academy's major strengths.

Each student is assigned an academic adviser to assist in choosing courses and to aid with any issues of concern.

Student Government

The students are known as cadets and organized as a regiment. This military organization of the student body is known as the Corps of Cadets. Within the regiment is a chain of command requiring compliance with military orders, rules, and regulations. Leadership and military discipline are required of each cadet.

The discipline of the Academy teaches how to respond to authority and how to be an effective leader by providing each person the opportunity to be a follower as well as a leader.

On a day-to-day basis, each cadet participates in routine regimental formations, watches, and military appearance inspections. Cadets' responsibility and authority increases as they advance through the four years, and individuals that excel are rewarded with special privileges and honors.

Admission Requirements

Competition is open to any young American across the country who meets the basic eligibility requirements. The U.S. Coast Guard Academy is unique from the other four federal service academies in that there is no congressional nomination involved. The individual must be a U.S. citizen (U.S. born or naturalized), unmarried, no dependents, 17–22 years of age (cannot be 23 prior to July 1 of the year of entrance into the Academy), a high school graduate, and have competed either the SAT I or ACT timed test. In addition, a medical exam must be passed.

Over the past four years, 90 percent of entering students have been in the top 25 percent of their high school class, and 62 percent in the top 10 percent of their high school class. Average SAT I scores in math were 652 and in verbal were 621. Average ACT scores in math were 28 and in English were 28.

Application and Information

Applications must be received by December 15 of the year prior to the year of entrance into the Academy. Upon acceptance of application, the Academy sends a packet of forms to be returned to the Academy no later than January 30. Students may apply on line at the Web site, listed below. Those accepted into the Academy receive appointments between November and April of each year. The Academy participates in an early action program allowing student who submit their entire packet of forms by November 1 a guaranteed notification of application results by December 15. Whether an applicant receives an appointment through the early action program or by meeting the standard deadlines, the student is required to notify the Academy of acceptance or decline by May 1 of the entering year.

A view book or CD-ROM and application may be obtained by contacting:

Director of Admissions
USCG Academy
31 Mohegan Avenue
New London, Connecticut 06320-8103
Telephone: 860-444-8501
          800-883-8724 (toll-free)
E-mail: admissions@cga.uscg.mil
World Wide Web: http://www.cga.edu

The United States Coast Guard Academy is located on the Thames River in New London, Connecticut.

UNITED STATES MERCHANT MARINE ACADEMY
KINGS POINT, NEW YORK

The Academy

The United States Merchant Marine Academy is a four-year, tuition-free federal service academy founded in 1943 to educate and train merchant marine officers, officers on active duty in the armed forces, and leaders in the maritime and intermodal transportation industry. It is an accredited, degree-granting college whose students are commissioned as ensigns in the Navy upon graduation. The Academy is one of the world's foremost institutions in the field of maritime education and is operated under the Maritime Administration of the Department of Transportation.

There are 950 men and women enrolled as midshipmen at the Academy. Their daily routine at Kings Point is very demanding. The academic day begins at 8 a.m. and concludes at 5 p.m. After classes, midshipmen are free to participate in recreational activities until dinnertime. After dinner, they are required to devote their time to study and academic preparation.

The extracurricular program is broad and varied. In addition to varsity athletics in eighteen intercollegiate sports, the Academy has an extensive intramural program that permits all students to enjoy physical activity and competition.

The nonathletic activities are also wide ranging and abundant, falling into as many categories as there are individual interests. Publications and the Debate Council, Glee Club, Regimental Band, Scuba-Diving Club, International Relations Club, and Broadcast Unit are but a few of the pursuits available to the midshipmen. Regimental and class dances and informal mixers provide the midshipmen with an interesting social program.

Midshipmen are granted liberty on weekends and leave at Thanksgiving, Christmas, and spring break as well as annual leave during July. Perhaps the most unusual and exciting part of the Academy curriculum is the Shipboard Training Program. Each midshipman, during half of the sophomore and half of the junior years, serves five months at sea aboard commercially operated American-flag merchant ships. This exceptional work-study program takes the midshipmen to many parts of the world and provides them with practical experience on several different types of vessels. It can be said that the world is their campus during their ten months of sea service.

Location

The Academy is located on 80.5 acres of land at Kings Point, on the North Shore of Long Island. Kings Point is a suburban residential community only 20 miles east of New York City, close to various cultural and recreational facilities.

Majors and Degrees

A graduate of the U.S. Merchant Marine Academy receives a Bachelor of Science degree, a merchant marine license as a third mate or third assistant engineer, and a commission as an ensign in the U.S. Naval Reserve. Six major programs are offered: marine transportation for the preparation of deck officers; ship's officer/deck (a marine transportation program enhanced with marine engineering studies); marine engineering for students interested in becoming engineering officers; marine engineering systems, which, in addition to leading to a license as a third assistant engineer, is accredited by the Accreditation Board for Engineering and Technology and includes a curriculum with greater depth in mathematics and a significant component of engineering design, as compared to the marine engineering curriculum; shipyard and engineering management; and Logistics and Intermodal Transportation, a marine transportation program focusing on logistics and intermodal systems management.

Academic Program

During the first trimester of the plebe (or freshman) year, all students take a common program of mathematics, science, English, and professional courses. This background enables midshipmen to determine intelligently the area of their special interest. After the second trimester, midshipmen select their major and from then on concentrate on a program aligned with their career choice. The professional majors each consist of required core courses in technical and general education areas as well as selected electives. The option program consists of six courses for marine transportation and marine engineering majors, who have a choice of taking a series of related elective courses in a specific area of concentration or any individual elective course for which they qualify. These courses include such specialized fields as nuclear engineering, management science, computer science, mathematics, chemistry, and naval architecture. By choosing to take the series of related courses, midshipmen can develop a proficiency in a subspecialty, supplementing their major field of study. Students in the dual-license and marine engineering systems majors are not offered the choice of electives because of the required course load in these programs. General education courses make up about one third of each of the professional curriculums, and all midshipmen are required to take naval science courses prescribed by the Department of the Navy.

Thus, the Academy provides a balanced program of theoretical and practical study designed to provide the undergraduate with technical competence, leadership skills, and the well-rounded general education so essential for responsible citizenship in contemporary society.

Exemption credit may be awarded for college-level work completed at an accredited college if the course is equivalent to a course offered at the Academy.

Academic Facilities

With the exception of Wiley Hall, the former residence of Walter P. Chrysler and now the Administration Building, all the buildings of the Academy have been constructed since 1942. The Inter-Faith Chapel was dedicated in 1961, a three-story library was completed in 1968, and an indoor swimming pool and an engineering and science wing have been added since 1972. A modernization of all other academic buildings was completed in 1982.

Costs

Tuition, room and board, and medical and dental care are provided by the U.S. government. Each midshipman also receives $600 per month while assigned aboard ship for training. Entering plebes are required to deposit approximately $5000 to defray the initial cost of lab fees, equipment, and a laptop computer.

Financial Aid

In effect, each midshipman receives a four-year scholarship from the U.S. government. Financial aid is also available.

Faculty

The Academy has 80 full-time faculty members and a student-faculty ratio of approximately 10:1. One third of the faculty are licensed deck or engineering officers. Most hold advanced degrees in an academic discipline: 90 percent of the total faculty hold master's degrees or higher; 50 percent have earned doctorates.

Student Government

The student body at the Academy is organized along military lines as a regiment, consisting of two battalions. Regimental life at the Academy is a form of student government and is an important part of the midshipman's total educational experience. The first classmen, or seniors, under the direction of the Commandant of Midshipmen, are responsible for exercising military command of the regiment and for administering the daily routine of the midshipmen. The military program is designed to develop leadership ability, self-discipline, and a sense of responsibility—attributes that are essential for effective citizenship as well as for a successful career as an officer.

Admission Requirements

Candidates for admission must be American citizens, between 17 and 25 years of age, and of good moral character. Candidates must be nominated by a U.S. representative or senator and must compete for vacancies allocated to their state in proportion to its representation in Congress. Candidates' competitive standing is determined by their College Board score, their high school academic record and extracurricular participation, and their overall leadership potential. All candidates must meet the physical requirements for appointment as a midshipman in the Naval Reserve.

Application and Information

Prospective candidates should write to the Admissions Office. They will be sent detailed information on the nomination procedure, required tests, application procedures, and specific requirements. It is advisable to apply for a nomination during the spring of the junior year in high school.

Further information may be obtained by contacting:

Director of Admissions
U.S. Merchant Marine Academy
Kings Point, New York 11024-1699

Telephone: 516-773-5391
           800-732-6267 (toll-free outside New York)

E-mail: admissions@usmma.edu

World Wide Web: http://www.usmma.edu

An aerial view of the 80.5-acre "sea campus" of the U.S. Merchant Marine Academy at Kings Point, Long Island, on the shores of Long Island Sound.

UNITED STATES MILITARY ACADEMY

WEST POINT, NEW YORK

The Academy

The United States Military Academy, the nation's oldest service academy, offers young men and women one of the most highly respected, quality education programs in the nation.

West Point advocates the "whole person" concept. The Military Academy has, since its founding in 1802, provided the broad college education demanded by the military profession while maintaining a degree of academic specialization comparable to that of civilian universities.

West Point's mission is to educate, train, and inspire the Corps of Cadets so that each graduate is a commissioned leader of character committed to the values of duty, honor, and country; professional growth throughout a career as an officer in the United States Army; and a lifetime of selfless service to the nation. The Military Academy provides its graduates with a solid foundation for intellectual and moral/ethical growth that is essential for successfully handling high-level responsibilities in national service.

When students enter West Point, they are also beginning a profession. Upon graduation, cadets are commissioned as second lieutenants in the U.S. Army and are normally required to serve on active duty for at least five years.

There are approximately 4,000 men and women enrolled at West Point. Cadets compete annually for Rhodes, Olmsted, Marshall, and Daedalian scholarships and for National Science Foundation, Truman, and Hertz graduate fellowships. West Pointers who remain in the Army are normally selected to attend civilian graduate schools in the United States or abroad between their fourth and tenth years of service.

The Academy develops the nation's future Army leaders by immersing cadets in programs of academic, military, and physical development. Each of these programs is rooted in principles of ethical-moral development, epitomized by the Academy motto, "Duty, Honor, Country." The Academy provides cadets with opportunities to observe and practice leadership and to develop vital intellectual and interpersonal skills through formal instruction. The honor code simply states: "A cadet will not lie, cheat, steal, or tolerate those who do." The code is a source of pride and mutual trust essential in the profession of arms.

In addition to academic and military education, cadets participate in athletic and extracurricular activities. Cadets have distinguished themselves in twenty-five intercollegiate varsity sports: baseball, basketball, cross-country, football, golf, gymnastics, hockey, indoor track, lacrosse, outdoor track, soccer, sprint football, swimming, tennis, and wrestling for men and basketball, cross-country, indoor track, outdoor track, rifle, soccer, softball, swimming, tennis, and volleyball for women.

West Point's modern academic facilities are matched by its athletic facilities. Michie Stadium, home of the Army football team, attracts crowds in excess of 39,000 during picturesque fall football weekends. In addition, ground was broken in June 2000 for the new Michie Sports Athletic Complex; it is scheduled to be completed in September 2002. Adjacent to the stadium is the Holleder Athletic Center, a multisport complex housing a hockey rink with seating for 2,746 and a basketball arena with a 5,043-seat capacity. The huge Arvin Cadet Physical Development Center is under major reconstruction and renovation. Temporary facilities are substituting for those affected by the project, which is anticipated to be completed in March 2005. West Point has a track stadium, a baseball stadium, an indoor tennis facility, and numerous athletic fields, outdoor tennis courts, and outdoor swimming facilities. Victor Constant Ski Slope is used for instructional and recreational skiing. A redesigned 18-hole golf course is also located on the Academy grounds.

There are more than 100 organized extracurricular activities, including mountaineering, hunting, fishing, scuba diving, archery, team handball, and orienteering clubs as well as clubs that compete on a national or intercollegiate level in crew, orienteering, power lifting, handball, rugby, sport parachuting, triathlon, horseback riding, sailing, judo, karate, bowling, and marathon running. There are academic clubs, including mathematics, language, and electronics clubs; the Cadet Fine Arts Forum; Model United Nations; and the Debate Council. The Student Conference on United States Affairs has met for more than thirty years.

Location

The military reservation, consisting of more than 16,000 acres, overlooks the Hudson River, 50 miles north of New York City.

Majors and Degrees

Cadets may choose an academic concentration from twenty-one majors and twenty-four fields of study. A cadet may study the American legal system; applied science and engineering; art, philosophy, and literature; basic sciences interdisciplinary; behavioral sciences; chemistry and life science; civil engineering; computer science; economics; electrical engineering; engineering management; environmental engineering; environmental science; foreign area studies (Latin American, Western Europe, Middle East, Eastern Europe, and East Asia); foreign languages (Arabic, Chinese, French, German, Portuguese, Russian, or Spanish or any two); geography; history; management; mathematical sciences; mechanical engineering; military art and science; nuclear engineering; operations research; physics; political science; social sciences; and systems engineering.

Academic Program

The academic program at the United States Military Academy provides cadets with a broad background in the arts and sciences and prepares them for future graduate study. The total curriculum is designed to develop essential character, competence, and intellectual ability in an officer. The core curriculum is the foundation of the academic program and provides a background in mathematics, physical science, engineering, humanities, behavioral science, and social science. The core curriculum, consisting of thirty-one courses, represents the essential broad base of knowledge necessary for success as a commissioned officer and supports the subsequent choice of an elected area of academic concentration. Courses are required in chemistry, computer science, economics, engineering design, engineering science, English, foreign languages, history, international relations, literature, mathematics, military history, military leadership, philosophy, physics, political science, psychology, and terrain analysis.

Classes at West Point are small, averaging 12 to 18 cadets per section. Cadets receive individual attention, and tutorial sessions are available upon request. Advanced and honors courses are available to cadets having exceptional ability.

All cadets study military science and receive classroom instruction in the principles of small-unit tactics and leadership during a two-week intersession between the first and second semesters. Concentrated summer field training provides each cadet with the opportunity to learn and practice individual military skills and to apply the principles of tactics and leadership studied in the classroom.

Off-Campus Arrangements

During the summer before their first (freshman) academic year, cadets are initiated into the Military Academy through a Cadet Basic Training program. Uniforms, room inspections, military drill, parades, and physical exercise become part of everyday life, and extensive demands are made upon new cadets to foster maturity, perseverance, and ability to succeed when challenged. During the summer following the first academic year, the entire class spends seven weeks at nearby Camp Buckner, where individual and small-unit training is conducted in infantry, artillery, rifle marksmanship, rappelling, military engineering, field communications, and survival. During their third summer, cadets participate in military specialty training and receive leadership experience in actual Army units. Specialty training options include northern warfare operations in Alaska; mountain warfare in Vermont; Airborne training at Fort Benning, Georgia; air assault training at Camp Smith, New York; sapper leader training at Fort Leonard Wood, Missouri; and survival, evasion, resistance, and escape training at the Air Force Academy in Colorado. Cadets also participate in Cadet Troop Leader Training, joining Regular Army units in Germany, Alaska, Hawaii, Korea, or other regions of the United States for practical experience as junior officers. Other cadets participate in the Drill Cadet Program, training the Army's new recruits in any of several U.S. basic training centers. Many cadets believe these experiences are the most valuable provided during their four years at the Academy. During their last summer, first class (senior) cadets are responsible for conducting both the Cadet Basic Training and the Third Class (sophomore) Cadet Field Training programs at West Point.

During the summers preceding both the junior and senior years, cadets select an academic, military, or physical development program that offers individual advanced development. Cadets may choose from more than 150 academic, military, or physical enrichment opportunities that normally involve about three weeks of active summer participation in educational experiences. For example, cadets participate in Operation Crossroads Africa, research work in technical laboratories throughout the United States, immersion language training in other countries, medical internships at Walter Reed Army Medical Center, and study at other civilian and military institutions.

Academic Facilities

West Point maintains some of the finest facilities and equipment in the world. There is a personal computer at every desk, and everyone is connected to a large array of powerful academic computing services at West Point, with unlimited access to the Internet. West Point has carefully crafted an electronic environment in which virtually every course offered has integrated computer use. This developmental "computer thread" fosters cadet use of personal computers in the barracks. Computer-aided math, design, and simulation; dynamic news sources; worldwide e-mail; spreadsheets; statistical analysis; database access; library bibliographic research; and electronic bulletin boards; document preparation, and printing, among other resources, all contribute to an academic environment rich with information resources and electronic media tools. Among the research facilities are general and physical chemistry laboratories and engineering, analog computer, digital computer, electromagnetic energy, electronics, physics, solid-state, hydraulic turbine, thermodynamics, fluid mechanics, nuclear science, free flight, rocket testing, land locomotion, and wind tunnel laboratories. The modern 600,000-volume library contains reading rooms, seminar rooms, and microfilm and audiovisual facilities.

Costs

The cost of the four-year West Point experience, including tuition, room, board, and medical and dental expenses, is paid by the U.S. government. Cadets, as members of the Army, receive an annual salary of approximately $7200, which helps to pay for uniforms, books, a personal computer, supplies, and incidental living expenses. A deposit of $2400 to $3000 is required to cover the initial uniform costs, a personal computer, and other incidental services (haircuts, laundry, etc.) during the first year.

Financial Aid

There are no financial aid programs because expenses are paid by the U.S. government. Scholarship awards may be used by candidates to offset the cost of the initial deposit.

Faculty

Most faculty members are Regular Army officers who hold advanced degrees from civilian colleges and universities; approximately 30 percent have earned doctorates. The teaching faculty numbers nearly 500 and includes civilian professors and several visiting professors from civilian academic institutions. Because many of the faculty members are Academy alumni and most are Army officers, the faculty has unusual rapport with the cadets. The student-faculty ratio is 8:1. Typical class size is 16.

Student Government

All cadets are strongly encouraged to serve in positions of student leadership and to seek responsibility as a means of enhancing their effectiveness as leaders. Cadets manage the social program, the Cadet Honor System, the intramural athletic program, and a wide range of extracurricular activities.

Admission Requirements

Admission is open to all unmarried U.S. citizens who are at least 17 and have not yet had their 23rd birthday on July 1 of the desired year of admission. They must have no legal responsibility to support a dependent (e.g., a child). West Point offers equal admission opportunities for all qualified applicants. Candidates for West Point must seek a nomination from a legal authority (usually a member of Congress), preferably in the spring of the junior year in high school. All candidates must take either the standardized timed ACT or the SAT. Applicants must also pass a Qualifying Medical Examination and a Physical Aptitude Examination.

The United States Military Academy has an Early Action Plan for well-qualified applicants who consider West Point their first choice among colleges of interest. Under the provisions of the Early Action Plan, those who complete an application file before the first Monday in December can be notified as to admission status in January. In addition, an applicant must notify West Point in writing by the third Monday in October to be considered under the Early Action Plan. Applicants under this plan need not have a nomination or the results from the medical examination to apply, but they must have both prior to admission.

Application and Information

Prospective candidates should write to Admissions, stating their interest in the Military Academy. Each applicant will be sent a Precandidate Questionnaire and prospectus, which outlines the West Point entrance requirements. All applicants are encouraged to start a candidate file at West Point at the end of their junior year or as soon thereafter as possible. This allows for early completion of all candidate file requirements.

Director of Admissions
United States Military Academy
606 Thayer Road
West Point, New York 10996-1797
Telephone: 845-938-4041
E-mail: admissions@www.usma.edu
World Wide Web: http://www.usma.edu/Admissions

Students examine soil properties during a civil engineering lab.

UNITY COLLEGE
UNITY, MAINE

The College

Unity College, a private, independent institution, was founded in 1965 by a group of local businessmen to provide educational opportunity for students demonstrating the desire and motivation to succeed. Key to Unity's continuing success has been the emphasis on the individual development of each student. Focusing on its strengths, the College has made a transition from being a traditional liberal arts college to being an institution committed to providing environmentally oriented education fused with the arts and humanities.

Unity College is young and unpretentious. Those accustomed to multimillion-dollar campus buildings will be surprised at how modest a college can be. Yet the Unity College campus fulfills its needs and, with its simplicity, complements the educational character of an environmentally aware institutional philosophy. The 500 men and women enrolled benefit from a close-knit community of faculty, staff, and students—all of whom share a love of the outdoors and a commitment to the personal development of each individual.

The College is situated on a 205-acre campus overlooking the village of Unity and nearby Lake Winnecook. One hundred acres have been designated a tree farm. In addition to twenty-one main classrooms, four residence halls, and administrative buildings, there are campus cottages that offer an alternative to traditional residence life. The College also owns a Wetlands Research Area, frontage on Lake Winnecook, and a 200-acre tree farm with sawmill in the nearby town of Plymouth. These facilities provide students with an opportunity for hands-on experience in addition to classroom and laboratory work.

Recreational facilities include a gymnasium; a weight room; outdoor basketball courts; nature trails; a ropes course; soccer, lacrosse, and softball fields; photography laboratories; and the Student Center.

Unity is a member of the Maine Association of Intercollegiate Athletics for Women, the National Small College Athletic Association, and the Northeast College Conference and competes with other member colleges in basketball (men), cross-country (men and women), soccer (men), and volleyball (women). The men and women of Unity's Woodsmen's team compete throughout New England and eastern Canada in events such as axe throwing, pulp throwing, and wood splitting. The women's soccer and basketball club teams as well as the men's lacrosse, ice hockey, and baseball club teams compete at other colleges. Unity also has a strong program of intramural athletics. Campus organizations include an outing club, a forest-fire-fighting crew, a kayaking club, and other social and educational organizations.

Location

The town of Unity, which has a population of 1,900, is located 18 miles east of Waterville and 40 miles south of Bangor and north of Augusta. The Penobscot Bay is 25 miles east of Unity. Primarily a rural, farming community, the town has little manufacturing or other industry. Community resources include a bank, a post office, a restaurant, a natural foods co-op, a pharmacy, a hardware store, markets, gas stations, hair stylists, and other small businesses.

Majors and Degrees

Unity College awards the following baccalaureate degrees: the Bachelor of Science in environmental science (concentrations in aquaculture, conservation law enforcement, ecology, environmental analysis, environmental biology, fisheries, forestry, urban and community forestry, and wildlife or self-designed), social science (concentrations in environmental education, environmental policy, and park management or self-designed), and wilderness-based outdoor recreation and the Bachelor of Arts in interdisciplinary studies, a self-designed program, and in environmental studies: humanities and the environment. The following associate degree programs are also offered: the Associate of Applied Science and the Associate of Arts in liberal studies.

Academic Program

The focus of the College is on environmental studies in a strong liberal arts context. The College holds the belief that, regardless of a student's career aspirations, liberal learning provides the intellectual flexibility for a successful life. Degree requirements for the B.S. and B.A. include 120 credit hours. Both baccalaureate programs include 40 credit hours of general education requirements. A.A.S. degrees involve 64 credit hours, 18 of which fulfill general education requirements. The A.A. and A.S. degree programs require 60 credit hours. A minimum grade point average of 2.0 must be maintained.

Internships, directed study, and independent study are options that are strongly encouraged. Unity College has a Cooperative Education Program, through which qualified students alternate study with work experience while earning academic credit.

The academic year consists of two 15-week semesters (early September to mid-December and late January to mid-May). In addition, special summer sessions and intersession programs are offered in some areas.

The program of the College's Learning Resource Center (LRC) is designed to ensure that every student who enrolls at Unity is given the opportunity to develop competence in reading, writing, mathematics, and academic survival skills. The LRC also offers academic tutoring, personal counseling, workshops, and courses designed to aid students in fulfilling their human potential. The LRC staff includes a learning disabilities specialist, who works with students who have specific diagnosed learning disabilities.

Students may earn up to 30 credit hours by achieving successful College-Level Examination Program (CLEP) scores in certain areas. By performing successfully on the Unity College Designed Examination for Placement (UCDEP), students who demonstrate advanced knowledge in particular subjects may bypass and receive credit for equivalent course work at Unity. In addition, a maximum of 60 course credits, satisfactorily completed at the level of C or better and equivalent to those offered by Unity College, are transferable from other colleges into a baccalaureate program. A maximum of 32 course credits are transferable into an A.A.S. program, a maximum of 30 credit hours into an A.A. program.

Academic Facilities

The College's modern library houses 46,000 volumes and 625 periodicals and serves the community as well as the campus.

While the woods, lakes, and fields surrounding the College often serve as outdoor laboratories, Unity also has traditional laboratories for biology, chemistry, wildlife, ecology, aquaculture, and other environmental sciences.

Costs

Tuition for the 2000–01 academic year is $12,330; this figure includes laboratory fees. Room and board are $5300. Students should anticipate spending an additional $1300 for books, personal expenses, and travel.

Financial Aid

In 1998–99, Unity College awarded almost $3.6 million in need-based assistance. Approximately 85 percent of all students received financial aid, and the average award package was approximately $5200, exclusive of loans. Types of aid include Federal Pell Grants, Federal Supplemental Educational Opportunity Grants, Federal Work-Study awards, state scholarships, and institutional scholarships. Federal Perkins funds are available. Eligibility for aid is determined through analysis of the Free Application for Federal Student Aid (FAFSA). A Unity College financial aid application, tax returns, and W-2s are also required. Financial aid forms are available from the Unity College Financial Aid Office.

Additional financial assistance in the form of academic and leadership scholarships and Federal Stafford Student Loans is available to qualified students. For further information, students should contact the Unity College Financial Aid Office at 207-948-3131 Ext. 235 or 201.

Faculty

The Unity College faculty consists of 36 full-time faculty members in addition to 15 adjunct members. The 15:1 student-faculty ratio and the small class sizes enable students to benefit from individual attention and guidance. Although teaching is their primary responsibility, Unity College faculty members are also respected researchers in their fields.

Student Government

Funded by the student activities fees, which total more than $30,000 per year, the Student Government is very active and has autonomy in the distribution of funds to campus clubs and organizations. The president of the Student Government sits as a full voting member on the Board of Trustees, and other members of Student Government and of the student body are active on many College committees.

Admission Requirements

A completed application form, a $25 application fee, an official high school transcript, and two letters of recommendation are the basic requirements for the admission process. The College bases admission decisions primarily on the student's academic preparation, motivation, and interest. All aspects of a student's performance are taken into consideration when making a decision. Students are encouraged to submit SAT I or ACT scores, although not required, and also may be required to come to campus for an interview.

Application and Information

Descriptive brochures and application forms are available from the Office of Admissions. When writing to the College, all interested students should indicate their preferred program of study and anticipated semester of entry. Entry to the College is possible in either September or January.

Although Unity does not have a specific application deadline, students should send their applications and transcripts as early as possible. Notification of the admission decision is made within one month of receipt of all required information.

Office of Admissions
Unity College
P.O. Box 532
Unity, Maine 04988-0532
Telephone: 207-948-3131
Fax: 207-948-6277
E-mail: admissions@unity.unity.edu
World Wide Web: http://www.unity.edu

A student at Unity College.

UNIVERSITÉ LAVAL
QUÉBEC CITY, QUÉBEC, CANADA

The University

The first French-speaking university in North America, Laval traces its origins to 1663 when Mgr. de Laval, the first Bishop of New France, founded Le Séminaire de Québec. In 1852, Queen Victoria granted Le Séminaire de Québec a Royal Charter, thus creating Université Laval.

Université Laval was, until 1920, the only French-speaking university in Canada. Through the years, it has contributed to the formation of the French-speaking intellectual elite of Québec and Canada, giving the country several Prime Ministers, artists, writers, and musicians. Considered a leading university since its founding, Laval is today a member of the "Group of Ten," which includes the ten top-ranked Canadian universities (in terms of research). The University's well-established reputation extends beyond Québec and Canada. Laval attracts students from more than 109 countries who enroll at Laval to obtain a diploma recognized throughout the world.

Université Laval offers some 350 programs to more than 32,000 students at both undergraduate and graduate levels. It is the only North American university to offer full programs in forestry and geomatics as well as agriculture and food sciences, with French as the language of instruction. Throughout Canada and the United States, Laval is particularly renowned for its teaching of French as a second language.

Laval is well known for its PEPS, a French acronym that refers to its Pavilion of Physical Education and Sports. The PEPS is considered one of the best-equipped university athletic centres in Canada. Some students even choose Laval for its PEPS. The PEPS is used for teaching physical education sciences, but all full-time students have free access to it. Its facilities include an Olympic-size swimming pool, an Olympic-size diving tower, an arena that houses two skating rinks, an interior track-and-field area, five gymnasiums, a tennis court, a football field, and more.

The Housing Service operates four residences, allowing 2,400 students to live on-campus. All residences are linked to the rest of the campus by underground walkways. Two of the four residences are coed. All rooms are single and the price includes cable television and a telephone with an automatic answering service. Cooking facilities are offered in every residence. Students who prefer to live off campus can easily find an apartment through the Off-Campus Housing Service.

Because Laval is a complete university, many services and attractions can be found on campus, including a Career and Placement Centre, a Financial Aid Service, a Medical Centre with a sports medicine division, a Psychology and Counselling Service, a Concert Hall, a theatre, a botanical garden, a few museums, a bookstore, a bank, a hairdresser, restaurants and fast-food counters, and more. International students may consult with the International Student Welcome Centre when they arrive on campus to learn more about the different services available.

Location

Choosing Laval is also choosing Québec City, the capital city of the province of Québec and the oldest city in North America. In this historic city, designated by the United Nations Educational, Scientific, and Cultural Organization (UNESCO) as part of the World's Heritage, one can still feel the soul of the French period. Old Québec's steep, winding, narrow streets give the city a European look and charm that makes it unique and unforgettable. Québec City is one of the most visited cities in North America.

Outside the strong walls of its eighteenth-century fortifications, Québec presents itself as a modern and dynamic city where one can find everything that makes life pleasant. Well known for its Winter Carnival, Québec offers a variety of cultural riches and activities throughout the year that suit many tastes, including numerous festivals, museums, movies, restaurants, theaters, art galleries, and more. The sports fan can ski, skate, play golf, and go swimming, rafting, or bicycling at locations within 30 minutes of downtown.

Université Laval's campus, straddling Sainte-Foy and Sillery, is one of the most striking in the province of Québec. It covers 1.2 square kilometers and includes almost thirty buildings, all linked by 10 kilometers of underground walkways. Université Laval also maintains a presence in Old Québec and the nearby downtown area, where its Faculty of Architecture, Planning and Visual Arts occupies a wing of the Petit Séminaire and part of the "La Fabrique" building.

Majors and Degrees

Laval offers some 350 programs at both undergraduate and graduate levels. Students may pursue a bachelor's degree in almost every field of study.

The Bachelor of Arts (B.A.) degree is offered in anthropology, archaeology, art history, classical studies, consumer studies, economics, English, English as a second language, English literature, French as a second language, French and Québec literature, geography, history, industrial relations, jazz and pop music, Jewish theology, linguistics, mass communication, music education, philosophy, political science, preschool and elementary teaching, professional teaching, psychology, Québec folklore, secondary teaching, sociology, Spanish, theater, and translation.

The Bachelor of Science (B.Sc.) degree is offered in actuarial science, biochemistry, biology, chemistry, geology, kinesiology, mathematics, microbiology, nursing, nutrition, occupational therapy, physical education, physical therapy, physics, secondary teaching, and statistics.

The Bachelor of Applied Science (B.Sc.A.) is offered in agricultural economics, agronomy, computer science, environmental and forest management, food sciences and technology, forest engineering, forestry sciences, geomatics sciences, and wood processing engineering.

The Bachelor of Engineering (B.Ing.) degree is offered in agricultural, chemical, civil, computer, electrical, food, geological, mechanical, metallurgical, mining and mineral, and physics engineering.

The University also offers a Bachelor of Architecture (B.Arch.), a Bachelor of Business Administration (B.A.A.), a Bachelor of Education (B.Ed.) in counselling and guidance, a Bachelor of Law (LL.B.), a Bachelor of Music (B.Mus.), a Bachelor of Pharmacy (B.Pharm.), a Bachelor of Social Work (B.Serv.Soc.), a Bachelor of Theology, (B.Th.), and a Bachelor of Visual Arts and Graphic Arts (B.A.V.).

The University offers a four-year program in dentistry (D.M.D.) and a five-year program in medicine (M.D.).

In most of these fields of study, Laval also offers diplomas (60 credits) or certificates (30 credits). It is also possible to obtain a 90-credit bachelor's degree by combining a diploma (major) with a certificate (minor) or combining three certificates.

Academic Program

The academic year is composed of two regular sessions (September through December and January through April) and one summer session, which is divided into two parts (May through June and July through August).

To meet the admission requirements, applicants must have completed a pre-university diploma totalling thirteen years of schooling. High school graduates who have completed a pre-university diploma totalling 12 years of schooling may be admitted to a preparatory-year program.

All degrees at Laval have specific requirements that students must meet in order to graduate. Teachers mix theory and practice with programs, including internships, in their regular curriculum. Laval has also adopted a Policy on Internationalisation according to which all programs must prepare students to face the globalisation of markets. To meet that policy, students are required to learn a second language.

Off-Campus Arrangements

Laval puts a special emphasis on establishing relations with universities and research centers inside and outside of Canada. It offers numerous exchange and study-abroad programs through partnering and institutional agreements with establishments on all continents. Moreover, Laval's membership in the "Group of Ten" allows Laval to offer its students specific exchange opportunities with other member universities. The Policy on Internationalisation also encourages and stimulates student participation in exchange programs.

In addition to regular programs, self-organised year-abroad projects are also possible for students who wish to make their own arrangements.

Academic credits may be earned for all of these programs.

Academic Facilities

The library offers nearly 2 million volumes, 44,700 periodical titles, 1.5 million audiovisual items (slides, microfiches, films, videos, discs, and aerial photographs), 120,000 maps, and 36,000 rare books. Students may use the Internet to borrow books from the University Library as well as from most university libraries around the world.

The Computing and Telecommunication Service provides services to the entire University community. Numerous computers are available for student use in every teaching pavilion, and all students owning a home computer can have free access to the Internet through the University network.

Costs

Full-time tuition fees range from Can$742.20 a session for Québec residents and French citizens to Can$1450.20 for Canadians and permanent residents of Canada. For international students, tuition ranges from Can$742.20 for students enrolled in French-related programs and students from countries that have signed an agreement with the Québec government to Can$4659 for other students. International students must also buy health insurance, which costs about Can$459. Housing on campus costs Can$196 a month. Travel expenses, books, food, clothes, and other personal expenses are not included in these figures.

Financial Aid

Several kinds of scholarship awards are offered to Laval students. Awards for academic merit are given by Université Laval as well as by external organisations. The Financial Aid Service issues a list of these awards each year. This list is also available on the Financial Aid Service's Web site (http://www.ulaval.ca/sbaf/). Laval also offers a Work-Study Program that allows students with financial needs to work on campus in fields related to their domain of study.

Faculty

The faculty is composed of more than 1,700 professors. Almost 85 percent hold a Ph.D., which is a particularly high percentage compared to other universities. In addition, some 700 assistant lecturers are hired every trimester.

Developing research is a strategic priority for Université Laval, and research is an important part of the mission of every faculty member and school. Nearly 1,100 professors receive research grants. They work in the 30 accredited research centres and institutes or in the almost 100 other research groups, centres, or laboratories. Université Laval is also very active on the international scene. It has set up eighteen projects involving developing countries with funding assistance from AUPELF-UREF, an international organisation of partly or entirely French-language universities.

Student Government

The partnership between the University management and its student population is of key importance; therefore, students participate in all levels of University government, be it consultative or governing. In addition, undergraduate students can join a University student union called CADEUL (Confédération des associations d'étudiantes et d'étudiants de l'Université Laval). Each Faculty and department also has one or more student associations. Many other clubs, groups, and associations exist that bring together students who share similar interests (social, ethnic, religious, and others).

Admission Requirements

A pre-university diploma totalling 13 years of schooling is the normal basis for admission. Graduates of secondary or high schools who have had a total of 12 years of schooling may be admitted to a preparatory-year program individually adjusted to allow them to complete different courses relevant to their intended area of study. In addition, all students must demonstrate proficiency in written and spoken French. Letters of recommendation and SAT I scores are not required. In some programs, applicants may be required to pass different tests (auditions, interviews, letters of intent, appreciation by simulation, or others). The Admission Guide provides full details on all admission requirements.

Application and Information

The admission deadline for the session beginning in September is March 1; for the January trimester, it is September 1 for students living outside of Canada and November 1 for students living in Canada; for the summer session, it is February 1 for students living outside of Canada and April 1 for students living in Canada. Late applications can be considered in programs in which places are still available. Application fees are Can$30. Application forms may be submitted through the Internet. All documents submitted with an application must be official and translated in French or in English.

For further information (in French) on programs and admission requirements or to obtain the Admission Guide and an application form, please write to:

Bureau d'information et de promotion
2435 Pavillon Jean-Charles-Bonenfant
Université Laval
Québec City, Québec G1K 7P4
Canada
Telephone: 418-656-2764
877-785-2825 (toll-free in Canada and the U.S.)
E-mail: info@vrd.ulaval.ca
World Wide Web: http://www.ulaval.ca

A modern university in the oldest city in North America.

UNIVERSITÉ SAINTE-ANNE
CHURCH POINT, NOVA SCOTIA, CANADA

The University

Université Sainte-Anne is the only French-language university in Nova Scotia. Founded in 1890, Université Sainte-Anne has since been providing high-quality university education to Acadians of the Maritimes, to French-speaking students from all Canadian provinces, and to English-speaking students from across Canada and abroad. The University has maintained a tradition of excellence in university education for more than a hundred years. It also plays an important role in the development of the Acadian community in Nova Scotia.

There are approximately 400 full-time equivalent students at Université Sainte-Anne. The majority of the student population is from Nova Scotia, with many also from Newfoundland. The University also attracts students from the rest of Canada, the United States (particularly Louisiana), and many other countries.

Location

Located on Canada's scenic Atlantic Coast, Nova Scotia is a politically stable, safe place to live and study. Université Sainte-Anne is located in the heart of French-speaking Nova Scotia. It is nestled in Church Point on the shores of picturesque Baie Sainte-Marie in southwestern Nova Scotia. Many different cultures compose the heartland of Nova Scotia, and the 10,000 Acadians who live along the coast are one of the oldest. Students who come to study at the University learn more than just a language. They discover a unique culture. Nova Scotia's Acadian culture is rich in music, literature, and traditional and performing arts.

Majors and Degrees

Université Sainte-Anne offers various programs leading to a degree in arts, business administration, education, and science. The general Bachelor of Arts and the Bachelor of Arts (Honors) degrees are offered with various majors in Acadian studies, Canadian studies, commerce, English, French, history, theatre, and Western civilization. The Bachelor of Business Administration is offered as a regular degree program and also as a co-op program. Students obtain a general degree that will prepare them to function effectively in different sectors of business and industry. The co-op program offers all the advantages of the regular program and also provides the student with three salaried work terms on the job market. The co-op program is based on a combination of work experience and classroom theory. The department also offers a two-year diploma in business administration.

Students have two options for the Bachelor of Science degree. They may choose to enroll in the first two years of a Bachelor of Science degree program and major in biology, chemistry, mathematics, or physics. Following their two years of study at Université Sainte-Anne, students can transfer to an honors program at another university. Transfer agreements exist with Acadia University, Université de Moncton, and other schools. They may also choose a three-year general Bachelor of Science degree program that is given at Université Sainte-Anne.

Students can also enroll in a pre-veterinary program. The University offers the two-year preparatory program for entry into the first year of the veterinary medicine program of the Atlantic Veterinary School in Prince Edward Island.

The Bachelor of Education (B.Ed.) degree program is a two-year program. Its focus is on the teaching of French as a first or a second language. A first bachelor's degree (general or honors) must be completed prior to entry into the B.Ed. program.

The University also offers French-immersion programs. Five-week sessions are offered in the spring and summer months, and a four-week immersion program for teachers is offered in July. Throughout the fall and winter terms, 100-day immersion programs are offered.

Academic Program

The academic year has two semesters, fall (September to December) and winter (January to April), and both spring and summer sessions. Some programs admit students in September only, while others can enroll students in either semester. Most programs take four years (eight semesters) to complete. The B.Ed. program takes two years (four semesters) to complete after receiving a first bachelor's degree.

Academic Facilities

The University has a library; a theater; an Acadian Centre, which contains many Acadian archives; and computer, science, and language labs. It also houses the Provincial Resource Centre for Acadian Schools: preschool, elementary, and secondary (CPRP). The Jodrey Centre for Small and Medium-sized Business is also located on campus.

Costs

Tuition costs for Canadian students for the 1999–2000 academic year were Can$1934 per semester for a normal five-course program; tuition for American and international students was Can$2810 per semester. The cost of residence was between Can$1130 and Can$1349 per semester, while meal plans varied from Can$1202 to Can$1245 per semester. Fees are subject to change.

Financial Aid

Université Sainte-Anne offers scholarships in many areas; a complete listing is found in the University Calendar. These scholarships are awarded on the basis of academic merit and may be available to international students after their first year of study.

Faculty

Université Sainte-Anne has a highly qualified faculty, which includes well-known researchers, creative writers, and artists. The faculty–undergraduate student ratio is about 1:15.

Student Government

There are several student groups at Université Sainte-Anne. The most important is the University's Student Council. It has voting representation on the University's senate and board of regents. It also owns and operates a student center, which houses a bar and games room. Students in business administration and in education also have their own student councils, which organize frequent activities of interest to students in those programs.

Admission Requirements

Applicants must have completed Nova Scotia grade 12 or its equivalent, with credits in five university preparatory subjects, including French and English. A minimum 60 percent average is required. Some programs require math and a 65 percent average. Complete information for specific provinces is available in the University Calendar and on the University's Web site.

Application and Information

The general deadline for application for September admission is March 25. To inquire or to request application materials, students should contact:

Admissions Office
Université Sainte-Anne
Pointe-de-l'Église, Nova Scotia B0W 1M0
Canada
Telephone: 902-769-2114 Ext.116
           888-3ÉTUDES (338-8337) (toll-free)
Fax: 902-769-2930
E-mail: admission@ustanne.ednet.ns.ca
World Wide Web: http://www.ustanne.ednet.ns.ca

At Université Sainte-Anne, students have the opportunity to work closely with highly qualified faculty members.

UNIVERSITY COLLEGE OF CAPE BRETON
SYDNEY, NOVA SCOTIA, CANADA

The University

University College of Cape Breton (UCCB), the first university college in Canada, was founded in 1974 through an amalgamation of a liberal arts junior college and an institute of technology. UCCB is unique in eastern Canada in that it offers a full range of undergraduate degrees and diploma and certificate programs in various areas of technology. UCCB is deeply committed to both the pursuit of academic scholarship and to serving its community, with the result that its programs and much of the research that is being carried out are community based or community oriented. UCCB is a Canadian leader in the development of cooperative education, which enables students to gain valuable work experience in addition to classroom study. Because of its philosophy of maximizing accessibility, it encourages applications from transfer students who have attended other universities and community colleges to integrate their prior learning experience into UCCB's program structures. UCCB's current enrolment is approximately 3,600 students, many from diverse backgrounds and cultures.

Built on its strong community economic development background, UCCB also offers a specialized M.B.A. program in community economic development.

Location

UCCB is located at 1250 Grand Lake Road in the Cape Breton Regional Municipality, the second-largest urban centre in Nova Scotia with a population of about 120,000. Popularly known as "Nova Scotia's Masterpiece," Cape Breton is one of the world's premier tourist destinations, an island of magnificent rugged scenery occupied by a unique blend of people who have maintained and developed a rich, vibrant, culture based on their Mi'kmaq, French, and Celtic traditions. The city is served by an airport located just minutes from UCCB, and a golf course is adjacent to the campus. Fortress Louisbourg National Historic Site and the Cape Breton Highlands National Park are nearby.

Majors and Degrees

In addition to the usual degrees in the arts, science, and business, UCCB has developed a unique Bachelor of Arts in Community Studies (B.A.C.S.) degree that emphasizes the development of problem-solving methodologies in both arts and science. The B.A.C.S. offers a number of majors, such as business, communications, leisure studies, and sport. The Bachelor of Technology degree enables students to major in a growing number of fields, such as chemical sciences, environmental technology, information technology, and manufacturing. Students wishing to earn a diploma in one of the technologies may use those credits toward a degree as well, which enables them to graduate with the combined benefits of practical hands-on learning and theoretical academic education. UCCB's Mi'kmaq Studies Program is the largest native studies program in eastern Canada.

Academic Program

Students may enroll in courses in September or January for either full-time or part-time studies, although the variety of courses available in January is less extensive than in September. Students may also enroll for part-time studies in May and July. All students are required to take courses in a core program in addition to departmental requirements for their particular degree or diploma.

Off-Campus Arrangements

UCCB offers many international exchange opportunities. Students may participate in these programs for one or two semesters at little or no additional tuition-related expenses beyond their UCCB fees. Credits earned in these programs are recognized by UCCB. In addition, many of UCCB's programs are cooperative, which provides salaried work experience for which academic credit is given, to supplement classroom study.

Academic Facilities

UCCB has a modern library containing about 300,000 volumes and 2,000 current periodicals. The library is linked electronically with all university libraries in Nova Scotia, so that books may be readily accessed from any of the twelve participating institutions. All UCCB students have access to a wide range of computing facilities, including free Internet accounts. Students living in the University's residence hall have telephones with voice-mail service in their rooms at no additional charge. The Beaton Institute is a regional archives and research centre for studies in Cape Breton history, politics, and culture. The Centre for International Studies operates a resource centre with materials on international relations, development, and human rights issues. The Boardmore Playhouse hosts an annual festival of one-act plays and many other theatrical and cultural productions. The Sullivan Fieldhouse is a world-class athletic facility, and there is an Olympic-size ice hockey arena.

Costs

For the 1999–2000 academic year, tuition fees for a full-time course load of 50 credits were approximately $6400 for non-Canadian students. The residence fee was $2200 (two semesters) and meal plans ranged from $1680 to $3030. There are other miscellaneous charges for course materials, books, and supplies that generally average $800. There is also a compulsory health insurance fee of $480 for international students during their first year in Nova Scotia.

Financial Aid

Non-Canadian students are eligible for scholarships offered by UCCB after their first year in attendance at the institution.

Faculty

UCCB's faculty members are recognized for excellence and innovation in University research, teaching, and service to the community. University policy is to keep classes as small as possible, which ensures close faculty-student interaction, and students are assured that they will receive personal attention from faculty members and deans at all times.

Student Government

The Student Union offers many services, including a health plan, a peer tutoring program, and student social facilities. It also funds a large number of clubs and organizations in addition to representing student interests at all levels of administration, from academic departments to the Board of Governors. In 1998–99, the President of the Student Union at UCCB was an international student.

Admission Requirements

UCCB actively seeks to increase the number of non-Canadian students in order to enrich the educational and cultural experience of all students and faculty members. All students who seek admission to UCCB must have completed the equivalent of Nova Scotia's high school diploma with five grade 12 university-preparatory courses and an average of at least 60 percent. Students from the United States must have completed a high school university program with 16 points, including four courses in English. SAT I or CEEB scores must be submitted. Students in the British system must have completed secondary school at the Ordinary level.

Application and Information

Further information may be obtained from UCCB's Web site listed below or by contacting the Admissions Office. International students are advised to submit their applications by May 1 for September admission. Applicants are urged to submit their applications and all supporting documentation well in advance of the published deadlines, particularly if they are seeking accommodation in the University residence. For students wishing to enter in January or May, application at least three months in advance is advised.

For additional information about admissions or academic programs, students should contact:

Admissions Office
University College of Cape Breton
P.O. Box 5300
Sydney, Nova Scotia B1P 6L2
Canada
Telephone: 902-563-1330
Fax: 902-563-1371
E-mail: registrar@uccb.ns.ca
World Wide Web: http://www.uccb.ns.ca

UNIVERSITY OF ADVANCING COMPUTER TECHNOLOGY
TEMPE, ARIZONA

The University

The University of Advancing Computer Technology (UACT) is a small, private technical university that offers unique bachelor's and master's degree programs in advancing computer technologies such as digital animation, interactive media, Web design, game design, application development, computer programming, Internet administration, network engineering, mechanical/industrial design, architectural/civil design, CAD, and interior design.

UACT was founded in 1983 and has grown from a small computer manufacturer and corporate training center to today's modern campus located in the Phoenix metropolitan area. The school has close ties to industry through its corporate training program and an industry advisory board. These industry leaders provide input into curriculum and insight into computer technologies needed in the workforce. This constant two-way communication between UACT and industry means that the University is on the leading edge of technology education and careers.

Classes are small, and students attend a full-time program in three 15-week semesters each year. Bachelor's degree programs are completed in less than three years and associate degrees in sixteen months. There are six available start dates annually.

Programs utilize a combination of learning methods that as designated as hyperlearning. Students are expected to attend lectures, participate in hands-on computer labs, and work on projects that emphasize teamwork and individual study. Emphasis is placed on problem-solving skills.

The newly constructed UACT campus is designed to enhance hyperlearning techniques as well as to develop the creative skills needed in the new technologies. There are drawing and art studios, digital media production studios, computer commons, a new technology laboratory to explore the latest in hardware and software, and an output lab with a variety of plotters and printers. The computer commons can be viewed through the UACT Web Cam at the address listed below.

The student body is composed of students from throughout the United States and the world. Students are a variety of ages, ranging from recent high school graduates to individuals working on their second career. Students live off campus in surrounding neighborhoods that are accessible by public transportation or bicycle as well as automobile. The University is close to major freeways and an international airport.

A Master of Science in technology degree program is offered, with a choice of two options: thesis option or capston project option.

Location

Arizona is a land of incredible beauty, contrast, and opportunity. The Grand Canyon, as well as snow-covered mountains and forest streams, is a short drive from the exquisite Sonoran Desert surrounding metropolitan Phoenix.

The Phoenix metropolitan area, which includes Tempe, is a cosmopolitan Southwestern center nestled in a beautiful desert valley. There are nearly 2 million people who live, work, and play in this modern financial and commercial hub. The weather is dry, the temperature is mild, and there are more than 300 days of sunshine a year.

The University is strategically located near the center of the Valley of the Sun, as the area is known. Students are minutes from the airport, Arizona State University, shops, restaurants and nightclubs, sports arenas, theaters, concert halls, and many culturally diverse activities. The school is within easy reach of Old Mexico, with its culture and beautiful beaches; Los Angeles and Disneyland; Las Vegas; and San Diego and Sea World. It's a short flight to skiing in Vail, Aspen, or Utah.

There are year-round outdoor activities such as hiking, camping, horseback riding, snow skiing, hunting, tennis, and golf. Numerous lakes are nearby for boating, swimming, fishing, and water skiing. It's a short drive to unspoiled Sonoran desert, rugged mountain forests, or the majestic Grand Canyon.

Brilliant sunsets and a relaxed Southwestern lifestyle provide an Old West charm that is world famous. Students can play tennis in shorts in November or study by the swimming pool in February.

Majors and Degrees

The College of Design offers programs leading to a Bachelor of Science in design, with program emphasis in architectural/civil design, interior design, or mechanical/industrial design; an Associate of Science in design, with program emphasis in CAD or interior design; and a diploma in CAD.

The College of Multimedia offers programs leading to a Bachelor of Arts in multimedia, with program emphasis in digital animation and production, game design, interactive media, or Web design. There is also an Associate of Arts in multimedia, with program emphasis in digital animation production, interactive media, or Web design.

The College of Software Engineering offers programs leading to a Bachelor of Science in software engineering, with program emphasis in application development, computer programming, Internet administration, or network engineering. There is an Associate of Science in software engineering, with program emphasis in application development, Internet administration, or network engineering.

Academic Program

The Bachelor of Science in design is a 120-week program that requires a minimum of 120 semester credits, 60 program core and area of emphasis credits, and 36 general studies credits. The Associate of Science in design is a sixty-week program that requires a minimum of 60 semester credits, 30 program core and area of emphasis credits, and 15 general studies credits. The Diploma in CAD is a forty-five-week program that requires a minimum of 45 semester credits and 30 program core and area of emphasis credits. The Bachelor of Arts in multimedia is a 120-week program that requires a minimum of 120 semester credits, 60 program core and area of emphasis credits, and 36 general studies credits. The Associate of Arts in multimedia is a sixty-week program that requires a minimum of 60 semester credits, 30 program core and area of emphasis credits, and 15 general studies credits. The Bachelor of Science in software engineering is a 120-week program that requires a minimum of 120 semester credits, 100.5 program core and area of emphasis credits, and 46 general studies credits. The Associate of Science in software engineering is a sixty-week program that requires a minimum of 60 semester credits, 30 program core and area of emphasis credits, and 15 general studies credits.

Academic Facilities
The UACT campus was completed in February 1998. The entire facility is designed for networked workstations connected by fiber-optic cable throughout the facility. There are a digital media theater, projection systems in the classrooms, a video production studio, artists' studios, electronic classrooms, a new technology laboratory, and a large computer commons area that looks out on the desert mountain landscape.

Costs
The registration fee for U.S. residents is $100 and $250 for non-resident U.S. residents. The 1999–2000 tuition was $308 per credit hour (not to exceed 15 credit hours) for resident and non-residents in undergraduate programs. Books average about $425–$450 each semester.

Financial Aid
The professionals in the UACT Financial Aid Department work closely with students to develop specific programs for obtaining funding for their education. The University of Advancing Computer Technology is approved for the training of veterans, and the University was among the first in the country to participate in the Direct Student Loan Program. For information about scholarships awarded through the University, students should contact the Admissions Department.

Faculty
There are approximately 50 full-time faculty members. Technical instructors have experience in industry and often utilize real-world examples in their classes. Faculty members are very student oriented and committed to helping students achieve their educational goals.

Student Government
There is no formal student government. Student feedback is achieved through meetings, surveys, a volunteer student mentor program, and other campus community-based informal groups.

Admission Requirements
University of Advancing Computer Technology programs are open to all persons who have a high school diploma or hold the educational equivalent and display a serious intent toward their education. Applicants under the age of 18 must have a legal guardian sign all admission agreements and a financial responsibility statement.

Prospective students must provide evidence of the required SAT I or ACT scores or complete a general skills (Wonderlic) test. Applicants also may be administered a personality profile that is used only for retention studies. An ACT minimum score of 21 meets the minimal requirement for admission in place of SAT I or Wonderlic scores. An SAT I minimum score of 500 in the verbal and 520 in the math or a combined minimum score of 1020 meets the minimal requirement for admission in place of ACT or Wonderlic scores. A general skills Wonderlic minimum test score meets the minimal requirement for admission in place of SAT I or ACT scores.

The minimum Wonderlic entrance requirement is 17 for the design and multimedia programs and 20 for the software engineering program. An applicant may retake the Wonderlic exam one time, normally after a one-week waiting period. At that time, the old test scores are discarded in favor of the more recent test scores. Meeting any of the above minimum test scores does not mean the applicant is automatically accepted for admission.

After meeting the minimum testing requirements for admission, applicants provide a written account of their goals, objectives, and serious intent toward education and discuss it with a school admissions representative. Motivation and employment potential of the student are evaluated by the school administration.

In addition to the standard admission requirements, non-U.S. citizens applying for admission to the University of Advancing Computer Technology must provide proof of English proficiency in one of the following ways: the Test of English as a Foreign Language (TOEFL) with a score of 500 or higher (Test of Written English must be included), successful completion of Level 108 from an ELS Center, completion of the ASPECT English Language Proficiency Level 5, or attendance for at least one year at a regionally accredited U.S. college or university and completion of English 101 and 102 (or equivalent) with grades of C or better. Proof of English proficiency is not required if English is the applicant's native language. International students are not required to provide test scores from ACT, SAT I, or Wonderlic exams if they are high school graduates from their country of origin. Official or unofficial transcripts must be submitted with an English translation and be evaluated for educational credentials (must show U.S. high school equivalent) by the Educational Credential Evaluators, Inc., P.O. Box 17499, Milwaukee, Wisconsin 53217-0499, U.S.A.

Application and Information
Applications are accepted throughout the year, and students may choose one of the six start dates throughout the year. Students may request an application from the address below.

UACT Admissions
2625 West Baseline Road
Tempe, Arizona 85283
Telephone: 602-383-UACT (8228)
 800-658-5744 (toll-free)
E-mail: admissions@uact.edu
World Wide Web: http://www.uact.edu

THE UNIVERSITY OF AKRON
AKRON, OHIO

The University

The University of Akron (UA) is a public, comprehensive research and teaching university offering degree programs from associate to doctorate levels. UA's nearly 23,300 students are drawn from Ohio, forty other states, and seventy other countries. UA's population, which includes students of various ages, races, and nationalities, reflects its strong commitment to diversity.

The University is accredited at the highest level as a comprehensive, doctoral-degree-granting institution by the North Central Association of Colleges and Schools. Its nine degree-granting colleges offer more than 200 undergraduate majors and areas of study, 100 master's degree programs and options, and eighteen doctoral degree programs. Its School of Law offers four law degree programs. UA's internationally recognized College of Polymer Science and Polymer Engineering offers the nation's largest academic polymers program. The University also excels in many other areas, including global business, biomedical engineering, organizational psychology, educational technology, marketing, dance, intellectual property law, and nursing.

The University of Akron campus, already one of the most modern in Ohio, has embarked on an ambitious venture to create "a new landscape for learning." With a $200-million investment, six new buildings and major expansions or renovations of fourteen other structures will be completed during the next five years. Among the new buildings will be a Student Recreation and Wellness Center and a Student Union. The campus will have 30 additional acres of green space as well. Recently, several residence halls were renovated to provide students with updated living spaces and direct access to the campuswide computer network. Kolbe Hall, an academic building, reopened in 1998 after extensive renovation and is now home to the School of Communication and WZIP-FM, one of the nation's top-rated student-operated campus radio stations.

UA's Division of Student Affairs provides new-student orientation, academic advising, counseling, testing, and career and placement services. Students have many opportunities for campus employment, internships, and cooperative education placements. UA has nearly 200 registered student organizations, including sixteen fraternities and seven sororities.

Culturally, the University is a rich resource, hosting concerts, performances, prominent speakers, and various special events. Its venues include the E. J. Thomas Performing Arts Hall, the Guzzetta Recital Hall, and the Paul A. Daum Theatre, where the talents of students in dance, theater, and music are showcased. The nationally acclaimed Ohio Ballet is in residence on campus.

Location

The University's attractive 170-acre campus, located in downtown Akron, is centrally situated in the Cleveland/Akron metropolitan area. Transportation, shopping, restaurants, and churches are all close by.

Akron is easily reached by car from major national east-west routes (Interstates 76, 90, and 80/the Ohio Turnpike) and north-south routes (Interstates 71 and 77). For airline passengers, limousine service is available from the Cleveland-Hopkins International Airport and from the Akron-Canton Airport.

Majors and Degrees

The Buchtel College of Arts and Sciences offers the Bachelor of Arts degree and the Bachelor of Science degree in biology, chemistry, geology, and statistics. The college offers the Bachelor of Arts degree in classical languages, classical civilization, economics, English, French, German, geography and planning, history, humanities, interdisciplinary anthropology, philosophy, political science, psychology, social science, social science–PPE Track (economics, philosophy, and political science), sociology, sociology/corrections, sociology/law enforcement, and Spanish. The college offers the Bachelor of Science degree in applied math, computer science, engineering geology, geography/cartography, geophysics, labor economics, mathematics, natural science, physics, political science/criminal justice, political science/public policy management, statistics/actuarial science, and statistics/statistical computer science.

A dual Bachelor of Science/Doctor of Medicine degree is offered as a joint program with the Buchtel College of Arts and Sciences and the Northeastern Ohio Universities College of Medicine.

The College of Engineering offers the Bachelor of Science degree in biomedical, chemical, civil, computer, electrical, mechanical, and mechanical polymer engineering and the Bachelor of Science in Engineering.

The College of Education offers the Bachelor of Arts in Education degree or the Bachelor of Science in Education degree in secondary education to those who qualify in one of the academic fields. The Bachelor of Science in Education degree is offered in elementary education, health and physical education, and special education. The College also offers the Bachelor of Science degree in technical education.

The College of Fine and Applied Arts offers the Bachelor of Arts degree in art history, business and organizational communication, child-life specialist, communication, communication/rhetoric, dance, family and child development, fashion merchandising (apparel, fiber arts tracks, and home furnishings), food science, interior design, mass media–communication, music, pre-kindergarten, social work, speech-language pathology and audiology, studio art, theater arts, and theater arts–musical theatre. The college offers the Bachelor of Fine Arts in art (ceramics, drawing, graphic design, metalsmithing, painting, photography, printmaking, and sculpture), dance, and dance–musical theatre. The college offers a Bachelor of Music in history and literature, jazz studies, music education, performance, and theory/composition. The college also offers a Bachelor of Science degree in dietetics and a Bachelor of Science degree in home economics education.

The College of Nursing offers the Bachelor of Science in Nursing. In addition, two special sequences allow licensed practical nurses and registered nurses to earn the Bachelor of Science in Nursing.

The Community and Technical College offers the Bachelor of Science degree in automated manufacturing engineering technology, electronic engineering technology, and mechanical engineering technology. The college also offers 24 two-year degree programs in the areas of allied health, arts, business technology, engineering and science technology, individualized study, and public service technology. Many programs are offered with a 2+2 option for continued study toward a bachelor's degree at UA.

Wayne College in Orrville, Ohio, offers Associate of Arts and Associate of Science degree programs, which fulfill the first two years of many UA bachelor's degree requirements for students intending to continue their education. The college has classes supporting some associate degree programs in UA's Community and Technical College and offers eight complete associate degree programs and seven one-year certificate programs.

The Reserve Officers' Training Corps (ROTC) program, one of the oldest in the country, offers two- and four-year programs in aerospace studies and military science, which lead to a commission in the U.S. Air Force, the U.S. Army, the Army Reserve, or the National Guard.

Academic Program

Freshman- and sophomore-level students complete prerequisite and general education requirements while in the University College before advancing to a degree-granting college.

Bachelor's degree candidates must complete from 128 to 144 credits with a minimum grade point average of 2.0 to 2.5, depending on the specific academic program. Associate degree candidates must complete from 64 to 74 credits, also depending on the program, with a minimum grade point average of 2.0.

To earn a degree from the University of Akron, transfer students must complete at least the last 32 credits in the baccalaureate or the last 16 credits in the associate degree program in residence at UA.

The University Honors Program offers curricular challenge and scholarship support to especially talented students from all undergraduate colleges. In consultation with faculty preceptors, students plan individual programs of liberal education and complete senior honors projects in their academic majors.

Academic Facilities

UA's library system includes the primary collection as well as specialized collections in the Science and Technology Library, the Law Library, the Psychology Archives, and the University Archives. UA belongs to OhioLINK, a consortium of Ohio college and universities that can provide access to 24 million items within 72 hours.

The Computer Center helps students make effective use of the latest technology. Computers are available to students throughout the campus.

UA has outstanding laboratories for basic and applied scientific research in various academic fields, including engineering, polymers, human motion analysis, and biomedical engineering.

Costs

The University offers a high-quality education at an affordable cost, with tuition rates among the lowest in Ohio. Typical 1999–2000 academic year tuition costs, with an average course load of 30 credits, were $4152 for Ohio residents and $10,352 for nonresidents. Room costs ranged from $2900 to $4060; meal plans cost from $1710 to $1850. All fees, tuition, room, and meal plan charges are subject to change.

Financial Aid

Thousands of University of Akron students receive more than $106 million yearly in financial aid through scholarships, grants, loans, and work-study opportunities. Applications are available from the Office of Student Financial Aid, Spicer Hall 119, The University of Akron, Akron, Ohio 44325-6211 or by calling 330-972-7052 or 800-621-5847 (toll-free).

Faculty

UA has a teaching faculty of 1,609 (including 765 full-time faculty members), 78 percent of whom hold a terminal degree in their field. The University recognizes the significant link between faculty research and classroom teaching and strives for a balance that serves students well. UA faculty members teach undergraduate and graduate courses, while graduate assistants teach some undergraduate classes. The university-wide student-faculty ratio is 19:1.

Student Government

Student government organizations include Associated Student Government, the Black Greek Council, the Interfraternity Council, the Panhellenic Council, and the Residence Hall Council. Two students serve on the University's Board of Trustees.

Admission Requirements

As a state-assisted university, UA is required by law to follow an open admissions policy. Freshmen are admitted on a "conditional/unconditional" basis. Unconditionally admitted students may enter directly into the academic program of their choice provided they meet specific academic standards. Conditionally admitted students may enroll in the University College or the Community and Technical College.

Admission procedures and requirements vary slightly for different types of students, but all applicants must submit SAT I or ACT scores and transcripts with their GPA.

Application and Information

Prospective students must send the application form, a $25 nonrefundable fee, high school transcripts for those under age 25, an official copy of college transcripts when appropriate, and ACT or SAT I test results for students under age 21. For application forms or information, students should contact:

Office of Admissions
The University of Akron
302 Buchtel Mall
Akron, Ohio 44325-2001
Telephone: 330-972-7077
              800-655-4884 (toll-free in Ohio)
Fax: 330-972-7022
E-mail: admissions@uakron.edu
World Wide Web: http://www.uakron.edu

The glass-walled Goodyear Polymer Center is a focal point for students walking across the University of Akron's Buchtel Common.

THE UNIVERSITY OF ALABAMA AT BIRMINGHAM

BIRMINGHAM, ALABAMA

The University

The University of Alabama at Birmingham (UAB) is a fully accredited, comprehensive, urban, research university and academic health center complex with an annual enrollment exceeding 16,000 students. In a short time, UAB has established outstanding programs through six liberal arts and professional schools, six health professional schools, and graduate programs serving all major units. As the University has grown, so have its contributions to the state, the nation, and the world. UAB is committed to education, research, and service programs of excellent quality and far-reaching scope. UAB is the only university in Alabama to earn top ranking (Research Universities I) in the Carnegie Foundation's classifications of American colleges and universities; selection is based on the amount of federal funds awarded for research and the number of doctoral degrees conferred. In such an environment, undergraduate students can pursue a wide array of research opportunities, gaining valuable experience that pays off later in graduate studies or career development.

As an autonomous campus of the University of Alabama System, the University of Alabama at Birmingham resides in the largest metropolitan area in the state and offers unique educational opportunities with day and evening classes. Both commuting and residential students learn in an environment supportive of the needs of the individual.

Part of the UAB experience is student life—a rich mix of academic organizations, honor clubs, social fraternities and sororities, volunteer groups, and activities ranging from sports to performing arts. With more than 200 campus organizations to keep students involved, UAB offers the chance to make lifelong friendships while assisting in the development of skills essential to leadership and teamwork. The South is the place for sports year-round, and UAB is no exception. The athletic program is a Division I member of the NCAA and a founding member of Conference USA, which includes twelve universities. UAB athletes participate in seventeen intercollegiate sports, including men's and women's basketball, golf, rifle, soccer, and tennis; men's baseball and football; and women's cross-country, track, softball, synchronized swimming, and volleyball. Intramural sports, aerobics, and outdoor recreation are also available. Student housing is limited and is available on a priority basis; early application is encouraged. For information about on-campus and off-campus housing, students should call 205-934-2092.

Location

Birmingham earned the name "The Magic City" during its first boom days. The expression still rings true as the metropolitan area continues to mirror UAB's phenomenal growth and reflects the many cultural opportunities available within the city. With a budget exceeding $900 million, UAB is the city's largest employer and the second largest in the state. Birmingham is easily reached by automobile from major national routes (Interstates 20, 59, and 65), and UAB is only minutes away from the Birmingham International Airport.

Majors and Degrees

UAB's degree programs offer strong career preparation. With fifty-seven majors from which to choose, UAB's broad curriculum allows students to explore new interests while receiving specialized training. Students may also integrate different areas of knowledge by choosing a minor in an additional field of study or by exploring the possibilities for developing an individually designed major.

The School of Arts and Humanities offers the Bachelor of Arts degree in art history, communication studies (concentrations in broadcasting, communication arts, journalism, mass communication, and public relations), English, French, German, music (concentration in music technology), philosophy, Spanish, studio art, and theater.

The School of Business offers the Bachelor of Science degree in accounting, economics (concentrations in economic analysis and policy and quantitative methods), finance (concentrations in financial management, investments and institutions, and real estate), industrial distribution, management (concentrations in general management, human resource management, management information systems, and operations management), and marketing.

The School of Education offers the Bachelor of Science degree in arts education, early childhood education, elementary education, health education, high school education, music education, physical education, and special education.

The School of Engineering offers the Bachelor of Science degree in civil engineering, electrical engineering, materials engineering, and mechanical engineering.

The School of Health Related Professions offers the Bachelor of Science degree in allied health sciences, cytotechnology, health information management, medical technology, nuclear medicine technology, radiologic sciences (concentrations in advanced imaging, radiation therapy, and radiographer studies), respiratory therapy, and surgical physician assistant studies.

The School of Natural Sciences and Mathematics offers the Bachelor of Science degree in biology, chemistry, computer and information sciences, mathematics, natural science, and physics.

The School of Nursing awards the Bachelor of Science degree. Students interested in pursuing the nursing degree and who meet the University's admission requirements are admitted to UAB as prenursing students. To be eligible for admission in good standing to the School of Nursing, students must successfully complete a prescribed set of courses with an acceptable grade point average.

The School of Social and Behavioral Sciences offers the Bachelor of Arts degree in anthropology, economics, history, international studies, political science, and sociology and the Bachelor of Science degree in criminal justice, psychology, and social work.

Academic Program

UAB's undergraduate instructional programs are broad based and designed to serve the needs of its diverse student body while providing a strong general education foundation. All programs of study leading to the baccalaureate degree have as an essential component a common Core Curriculum. The minimum total credit hours required for a baccalaureate degree are 128 semester hours with a cumulative grade point average of at least 2.0 (C) in all credit hours attempted. A student may obtain a certain number of semester hours of academic credit for knowledge acquired independently through Advanced

Placement (AP), International Baccalaureate (I.B.), College-Level Examination Program (CLEP), Credit by Examination (CBE), evaluation of noncollegiate-sponsored courses, armed services courses, and prior learning.

There are six academic terms during a calendar year. The fall, winter, spring, and summer terms each consist of approximately ten weeks of classes including final examinations. The other two terms are intensive terms, approximately three weeks in length, and are known as the September Miniterm and December Miniterm.

Academic Facilities

The UAB campus occupies more than 100 major buildings, more than 10 million gross square feet, and 70 square blocks near downtown Birmingham. The undergraduate area of campus is concentrated within a five-square-block area, however, giving students the convenience and togetherness that is so important to the college experience.

The Mervyn H. Sterne Library houses a collection of more than a million items selected to support teaching and research at UAB. In addition to books and subscriptions to more than 2,400 periodicals, the collection consists of microforms and other print and nonprint materials. Study areas and photocopying machines for the convenience of patrons are located throughout the library. The online catalog provides rapid access to the collection and to other major library collections in Alabama. The Educational Technology Services Department (ETS) includes dozens of microcomputers and is available to anyone with a valid UAB ID card. In addition to Sterne Library, the Lister Hill Library of the Health Sciences provides a comprehensive collection of materials for medical study and research.

In 1996, UAB unveiled the Alys Robinson Stephens Performing Arts Center, with concert halls and practice facilities that are state-of-the-art. This beautiful facility draws national and international performers, enhancing the strong cultural opportunities in Birmingham.

Costs

For the 1999–2000 academic year, tuition was $91 per semester hour for in-state students and $182 per semester hour for out-of-state students. Based on a typical load of 10 semester hours per term for the academic year (three terms), tuition and fees for Alabama residents totaled $3240 (including $2730 for tuition and $510 for required fees). A shared room ranged from $175 to $289 per month. A typical amount for books and supplies totaled $900.

Financial Aid

UAB's financial aid package (loans, employment, grants, and scholarships) enables students from all economic backgrounds to attend UAB. UAB offers a growing number of scholarships to provide support for eligible students attending UAB. Most scholarships have specific academic requirements and some have special conditions. Scholarship applications are available in the fall and have a February 1 deadline. Financial aid applications are available in early January for the following academic year, with a priority packaging deadline of May 1.

Faculty

UAB has 1,636 full-time faculty members, with 91 percent holding doctoral degrees. The student-faculty ratio is 18:1, with the vast majority of freshman- and sophomore-level courses taught by full-time faculty.

Student Government

In addition to eight student government associations, the Office of Student Life offers many student-run committees and programs that are open to all students. These committees provide entertainment through comedy, music, movies, lectures, and multicultural programming. Other opportunities to lead and serve include social fraternities and sororities, a student leadership program, an ambassador program, a volunteer program, a scholarship pageant, and three award-winning student publications.

Admission Requirements

UAB is an equal educational opportunity institution. The requirements for regular admission for entering freshmen include a high school GPA of at least 2.0 (on a 4.0 scale) in academic subjects and a minimum ACT score of 20 or SAT I score of 950. The UAB institutional code number for ACT is 0056; the code number for SAT is 1856. For tentative action, a transcript may be sent during the student's senior year in high school. A final transcript must be sent upon graduation.

Transfer students must have a cumulative GPA of at least 2.0 (on a 4.0 scale) after completing 24 semester hours (or 36 quarter hours) of college-level work. Students with previous college work must submit an official transcript from each institution attended and must be eligible to enroll at the last institution attended. UAB also encourages international students who have academic, linguistic, and financial capabilities to apply for admission. The code number for the Test of English as a Foreign Language (TOEFL) is 1856.

Application and Information

All students who wish to attend UAB must complete an application for admission and submit proof of immunization against measles. An application may be submitted as early as one year prior to admission. A completed application, a nonrefundable $25 application fee ($30 for international students), and all supporting documentation must be received by the Office of Undergraduate Admissions by the deadline for the term for which admission is requested. The application deadline for fall term 2000 is August 1, 2000. For an application and other information, students should contact:

UAB Undergraduate Admissions
Hill University Center, Room 260
The University of Alabama at Birmingham
1530 3rd Avenue, South
Birmingham, Alabama 35294-1150
Telephone: 205-934-8221
          800-421-8473 (toll-free)
E-mail: undergradadmit@uab.edu
World Wide Web: http://www.uab.edu

THE UNIVERSITY OF ALABAMA IN HUNTSVILLE

HUNTSVILLE, ALABAMA

The University

The University of Alabama in Huntsville (UAH) is a public, four-year, coeducational institution and is a member of the University of Alabama System. UAH was founded in 1950 as an extension center of the University of Alabama and became an autonomous campus in 1969. UAH has earned national recognition in engineering and the sciences, and its programs in the humanities, fine arts, social sciences, business, and nursing are outstanding. Students interact with some of the most productive researchers in their respective disciplines. Close ties with business, industry, and government give students real-world opportunities and experience. UAH is accredited by the Southern Association of Colleges and Schools' Commission on Colleges. In addition, UAH holds professional accreditation from the American Chemical Society; the Computing Sciences Accreditation Board; the Accreditation Board for Engineering and Technology, Inc.; the National League for Nursing Accrediting Commission; the National Association of Schools of Music; and AACSB–The International Association for Management Education.

The fall 1999 enrollment consisted of 5,639 undergraduate and 1,359 graduate students. The average age of undergraduate students is 25; 12 percent live on campus, 81 percent are from Alabama, 5 percent are from other countries, 51 percent are men, and 49 percent are women. UAH students represent forty-three states and seventy-four other countries. Of the total undergraduate enrollment, 22 percent are members of ethnic minority groups. The average ACT composite score for entering freshmen was 24; 39 percent were in the top 10 percent of their high school graduating class, and 79 percent had a high school GPA of 3.3 (on a 4.0 scale) or higher.

UAH has more than 120 student groups and organizations, including national fraternities and sororities, honor societies, special interest groups, religious organizations, the Student Government Association (SGA), the student-run newspaper, the student-run literary magazine, minority student organizations, international student organizations, the choir, the chorus, a film and lecture series, service organizations, professional interest groups, and intramural athletics. The University is a member of the NCAA Division II and the Gulf South Conference and competes in the following intercollegiate sports: men's baseball, basketball, cross-country, soccer, and tennis and women's basketball, cross-country, soccer, softball, tennis, and volleyball. In addition, UAH competes at the NCAA Division I level in men's ice hockey.

On-campus housing is available for undergraduate and graduate students. The Central Campus Residence Hall is a seven-story residence hall that offers private bedrooms, is located in the center of campus, and is connected to the University Center by an enclosed walkway. Student apartments in Southeast Housing are reserved for upperclassmen and graduate students. Private apartments are available for married students and students with children. Handicapped-accessible apartments are available. Meals are available in the University Center Cafeteria.

The Colleges of Administrative Science, Engineering, Liberal Arts, Nursing, and Science and the School of Graduate Studies administer the degree programs of the University. The School of Graduate Studies awards the master's degree in accounting, atmospheric science, biological science, chemical engineering, chemistry, civil engineering, computer engineering, computer science, electrical engineering, English, history, industrial and systems engineering, management, materials science, mathematics, mechanical engineering, nursing, operations research, physics, psychology, and public affairs. The Ph.D. degree is awarded in applied mathematics, atmospheric science, computer engineering, computer science, electrical engineering, industrial and systems engineering, materials science, mechanical engineering, optical science and engineering, and physics.

Location

The University of Alabama in Huntsville is located in the Tennessee River Valley of north-central Alabama, 100 miles north of Birmingham and 100 miles south of Nashville, Tennessee. Huntsville is home to more than fifty Fortune 500 companies that specialize in high technology, including aerospace engineering, rocket propulsion, computer technology, weapons systems, telecommunications, software engineering, information systems design, and engineering services. Most of these companies are located in one of the top ten research parks in the world, Cummings Research Park, which is adjacent to the UAH campus.

Majors and Degrees

The College of Administrative Science awards the Bachelor of Science in Business Administration (B.S.B.A.) degree in the fields of accounting, finance, management, management information systems, and marketing.

The College of Engineering awards the Bachelor of Science in Engineering (B.S.E.) degree in the following engineering disciplines: chemical, civil, computer, electrical, industrial and systems, mechanical, and optical.

The College of Nursing awards the Bachelor of Science in Nursing (B.S.N.) degree.

The Bachelor of Arts (B.A.) degree is awarded by the College of Liberal Arts in the fields of art, communication arts, education, English, foreign languages and international trade, French, German, history, music, philosophy, political science, psychology, Russian area studies, sociology, and Spanish.

In the College of Science, the Bachelor of Science (B.S.) degree is available in biological science, chemistry, computer science, mathematics, optical science, and physics. A Bachelor of Arts degree is available in biological science and mathematics.

Fifth-year certificates are available in accounting and education for individuals who already hold a bachelor's degree in another field. Undergraduate teacher certification programs are offered in the following areas: art education (N–12), elementary education (K–6), and music education (N–12) and in secondary/high school education (4–8 or 7–12), with majors in biology, chemistry, English, French, general science, German, history, language arts, mathematics, physics, social science, and Spanish.

Academic Program

The general education course work is designed to broaden intellectual awareness and enhance cultural literacy and analytical thinking. All undergraduates are required to complete course work in English composition, humanities and fine arts, history, social and behavioral sciences, natural and physical sciences, and mathematics. B.A., B.S., B.S.B.A., and B.S.N. degrees require the completion of at least 128 total semester hours; B.S.E. degrees in electrical and industrial and systems engineering require 129; the B.S.E. in chemical engineering, 134; B.S.E. degrees in civil and mechanical engineering, 133; the B.S.E. in optical engineering, 137; and the B.A. in music, 134. A variety of special academic programs and options are available, including academic remediation, accelerated degree completion, cooperative education, cross-registration with other institutions, distance learning, double majors, dual enrollment, English as a second language, an honors program, independent study, internships, and learning disabilities services. Credit is awarded for appropriate scores on CLEP and AP examinations. UAH offers Army ROTC at a participating institution off campus. Special services are available for handicapped students, including notetaking services, readers, tape recorders, tutors, interpreters for the hearing impaired, special transportation, special housing, adaptive equipment, and Braille services. The fall 2000 semester begins August 23 and ends December 14; spring semester 2001 begins January 8 and ends May 2. Two summer sessions are offered and begin May 14 and June 27, 2001.

Academic Facilities

The 376-acre campus is in northwest Huntsville. All academic buildings have been constructed since 1960 and exemplify modern functional design. The UAH library houses more than 400,000 books, serial backfiles, and government documents; more than 2,000 current serials; and more than 420,000 microforms. The UAH Art Gallery hosts art exhibits by local, regional, and national artists as well as by students and faculty members. More than 300 personal computers are available across the campus for student use. Computer labs, one of which is open 24 hours a day, are located in several buildings and are staffed to provide assistance. Access to the University fiber-optic network is available in all buildings, including the Central Campus Residence Hall. Internet access and e-mail are available to all students. UAH has a number of state-of-the-art research labs that are accessible to undergraduates.

Costs

In 1999–2000, tuition for undergraduate Alabama residents cost $3112 (15 credits each semester) for the academic year. Out-of-state students paid $6516 (15 credits each semester) for the academic year. Undergraduates can expect to spend approximately $720 on books and supplies for the academic year. Undergraduate students pay an estimated $2780 for room, $1300 for board, $900 for transportation, and $1200 for personal and miscellaneous expenses per year.

Financial Aid

UAH awards more than $20 million annually in need-based and non-need-based financial aid in the form of scholarships, grants, loans, and campus jobs. The following financial aid programs are available: Federal Stafford Student Loans (subsidized and unsubsidized), Federal PLUS Loans, Consolidation Loans, Federal Pell Grants, Federal Supplemental Educational Opportunity Grants (FSEOG), state scholarships and grants, private scholarships, and institutional scholarships. Non-need-based scholarships are available for athletics, ROTC, academic merit, creative and performing arts, special achievement, leadership skills, and minority status. Students should submit the Free Application for Federal Student Aid (FAFSA) and the UAH financial aid form before April 1 for priority consideration and no later than the final closing date of July 31. Award notifications are made on a rolling basis. The priority deadline for scholarship application is February 15.

Faculty

Of the 301 full-time instructional faculty members, 88 percent hold the Ph.D. or other terminal degree in their field. The student-faculty ratio is 14:1. Graduate students teach 13 percent of introductory undergraduate courses. The average introductory lecture class size is 18.

Student Government

The primary purpose of the Student Government Association is to help improve the educational environment and promote the welfare of students in all areas of University life. The SGA is responsible for developing and sponsoring programs that enrich the students' cultural, intellectual, and social life. An executive branch, a 15-member legislature, and a 5-member arbitration board are responsible for carrying out the official business of the organization. The SGA sponsors more than 110 clubs and organizations in addition to providing many student services, such as health insurance, special rates for community cultural events, and a student directory.

Admission Requirements

High school graduates may be admitted as regular freshmen based on acceptable high school achievement and standardized test scores (SAT I or ACT), which are considered together. A higher result in one area offsets a lower performance in the other. For example, a minimum high school GPA of 3.25 is required if the ACT composite score is 17 or below or the combined SAT I score is 840 or below. A high school GPA of 1.75 requires an ACT composite score of 24 or higher or a combined SAT I score of 1090 or higher. Applicants should present a minimum of 20 Carnegie high school units, including 4 units of English, 3 of social studies, 1 of algebra, 1 of geometry, 1 of biology (recommended), 1 of chemistry/physics (required by the Colleges of Engineering and Science and recommended by all other Colleges), 1 of algebra II/trigonometry (one each required by the College of Engineering and recommended by all other Colleges), and sufficient academic electives to meet the required 20 units. First-time freshmen and transfer students are admitted for every academic term. Transfer students with fewer than 18 hours of earned college credit are admitted based on high school transcripts, test scores, and college course work. Transfer students are required to submit transcripts of all university work and have at least a 2.0 average on all work attempted to qualify for regular admission.

Application and Information

Completed applications and a nonrefundable $20 application fee should be sent by August 15 for admission in the fall semester and by December 15 for admission in the spring semester. Admission notifications are sent on a rolling basis.

For an application form and more information, students should contact:

Office of Admissions
The University of Alabama in Huntsville
301 Sparkman Drive
Huntsville, Alabama 35899
Telephone: 256-890-6070
    800-UAH-CALL (toll-free)
Fax: 256-890-6073
E-mail: admitme@email.uah.edu
World Wide Web: http://www.uah.edu

UNIVERSITY OF ALASKA ANCHORAGE
ANCHORAGE, ALASKA

The University

The University of Alaska Anchorage (UAA) offers certificate, associate, baccalaureate, and master's degree programs and is accredited by the Commission on Colleges of the Northwest Association of Schools and Colleges. Since its creation, UAA has established a record of continuing growth and development in its academic, vocational, and public-service activities. The University has an attractive wooded campus. At the Anchorage campus, the student population currently numbers about 12,000. An additional 5,000 students attend extension campuses at Kodiak, Kenai, and Matanuska-Susitna; extension sites at Chugiak–Eagle River, Fort Richardson, Fort Wainwright, Fort Greeley, and Eielson Air Force Base; and the affiliated Prince William Sound Community College. The academic units on the Anchorage campus are the College of Arts and Sciences; College of Business and Public Policy; College of Health, Education, and Social Welfare; Community Technical College; and the School of Engineering. Central to the University's academic program is the goal of providing lifelong learning opportunities for students of all ages. Academic, vocational-technical, and personal enrichment opportunities are all found at UAA.

Research units located at UAA include the American Russian Center, the Center for Alcohol and Addiction Studies, the Center for Economic Education, the Center for Human Development, the Environment and Natural Resources Institute, the Institute for Circumpolar Health Studies, the Institute of Social and Economic Research, the Justice Center, the University of Alaska Center for Economic Development, and the University of Alaska Small Business Development Center. On the graduate level, the University offers a wide range of programs: the Master of Arts (M.A.) in English and interdisciplinary studies, the Master of Arts in Teaching (M.A.T.) in education and English; the Master of Business Administration (M.B.A.); the Master of Civil Engineering (M.C.E.); the Master of Education (M.Ed.) in adult education, counseling and guidance, educational leadership, master teacher, and special education; the Master of Fine Arts (M.F.A.) in creative writing and literary arts; the Master of Public Administration (M.P.A.); the Master of Science (M.S.) in arctic engineering, biological sciences, civil engineering, clinical psychology, engineering management, environmental quality engineering, environmental quality science, interdisciplinary studies, nursing science, science management, and vocational education; and the Master of Social Work (M.S.W.). All these programs are offered on the Anchorage campus.

Located in the Campus Center is a general information, message, and scheduling desk that is linked by computer terminals to other buildings on the campus. It also provides facilities for the student government and for the student newspaper. Activities are conducted in conference rooms and a variety of lounge areas. The Campus Center is equipped for full food service, and the staff can cater banquets for more than 400 people. The Pub serves a variety of food and has lighting and sound systems for lecturers, musicians, and other performers. The work of student artists is displayed in the Campus Center gallery, which also shows traveling exhibits. The University Sports Center provides facilities for badminton, basketball, calisthenics, dance, diving, gymnastics, handball, ice-skating, racquetball, squash, swimming, volleyball, and weight training. The Sports Center building has been designated specifically for individual, classroom, intramural, and intercollegiate use. Running, skiing, and bike trails are located immediately adjacent to the campus.

Location

The Anchorage campus is convenient to shopping, housing, and entertainment. It is served by a public transportation system, and many facilities are within walking distance. Surrounded by the spectacular scenery of snowcapped Alaskan peaks, UAA is only a short distance from fishing, hunting, and wilderness recreation. Summertime temperatures range between 60 and 70 degrees. Winters are less severe in Anchorage than in many other U.S. cities. Anchorage, a city of 250,000 people, is the chief business, professional, international transportation, and entertainment center for the state.

Majors and Degrees

The Bachelor of Arts (B.A.) degree is awarded in anthropology, art, biological sciences, computer science, economics, English, history, interdisciplinary studies, journalism and public communications, justice, languages, mathematics, music, political science, psychology, sociology, and theater. The Bachelor of Business Administration (B.B.A.) degree is offered in accounting, economics, finance, management, management information systems, and marketing. The Bachelor of Fine Arts (B.F.A.) degree is offered in art. The Bachelor of Music (B.M.) degree is offered in music (music education emphasis) and performance. The Bachelor of Science (B.S.) degree is offered in anthropology, biological sciences, chemistry, civil engineering, computer science, geomatics, interdisciplinary studies, mathematics, natural sciences, nursing science, psychology, sociology, and technology. The Bachelor of Social Work (B.S.W.) degree is offered in social work. The Bachelor of Human Services (B.H.S.) degree is offered in human services.

The Associate of Applied Science (A.A.S.) degree is awarded in accounting, air traffic control, architectural and engineering technology, automotive technology, aviation administration, aviation maintenance technology, business computer information systems, culinary arts, dental assisting, dental hygiene, diesel technology, early childhood development, electronics technology, fire service administration, geomatics, human services, medical assisting, medical laboratory technology, nursing, office management and technology, paramedical technology (limited availability), professional piloting, small business administration, and welding technology. The Associate of Arts (A.A.) degree is offered with a general studies program.

Certificate programs, designed to meet the needs of students who wish to attain a high level of proficiency in specific career areas, are offered in architectural drafting, automotive technology, aviation maintenance technology, civil engineering, dental assisting, diesel technology, early childhood development, electronics technology, mechanical and electrical drafting, office technology, paralegal studies, and structural drafting.

All of the baccalaureate degree, associate degree, and certificate programs listed above are offered on the Anchorage campus.

Academic Program

The goal of UAA is to provide programs of study and special interest courses that meet the student's need for personal enrichment, intellectual stimulation, career development, graduate school preparation, and continuing education. Students confer with their major adviser to construct a program suitable to their needs and interests.

UAA's fall semester begins in late August, the spring semester in January, and the summer session in May. An undergraduate student who registers for 12 or more credits is classified as full-time. The minimum number of credits that must be earned for a baccalaureate degree, including those accepted by transfer, is 120. A minimum of 60 semester credits is required to complete the Associate of Arts degree and most Associate of Applied Science degree programs. Completion requirements vary from one discipline to another. All degree and certificate programs offered by UAA require students to maintain a GPA of at least 2.0; some programs require a higher GPA.

Degree-seeking students with experience acquired outside the conventional college classroom have an opportunity to demonstrate college-level achievement. UAA grants advanced-placement credit for satisfactory performance (scores of 3 or higher) on the College Board Advanced Placement tests. UAA's credit-by-examination program rewards students who do well on College-Level Examination Program tests or challenge examinations, the latter of which are locally developed comprehensive exams covering specific subject areas. Through the University, credit is available by examinations and by alternative means for English 111 (Methods of Written Communication). Credit may be granted for military service. Details on eligibility, restrictions, and procedures are in the catalog.

Academic Facilities

The Consortium Library located on the Anchorage campus serves the academic clientele of the University and that of its nearby neighbor, Alaska Pacific University. The collections comprise more than a half million volumes of books, periodicals, and government documents. Special collections include materials on Alaska and the polar region, choral and symphonic music, and unpublished personal and organizational records relating to the social, cultural, and economic development of Alaska. In addition to CD online indexes on a LAN, the library offers computer-search services at cost, providing access to a large number of databases in a variety of subjects.

The Anchorage campus consists of twenty academic, administrative, and laboratory structures. These include specially equipped buildings for the arts, allied health science, business, and engineering. The Merrill Field Aviation Complex houses the aviation maintenance program. In Anchorage, courses are also taught at Elmendorf Air Force Base, Fort Richardson, and Chugiak–Eagle River.

Costs

In 1999–2000, an Alaska resident freshman carrying 12 undergraduate lower-division credits paid tuition of $900 per semester/session and mandatory student activity and technology fees. The nonresident undergraduate tuition was a minimum of $2808 for 12 lower-division credits. Housing in school-operated apartment-style dormitories was available for $1590 to $2150 per semester. Apartment complexes near UAA are also available; one-bedroom units cost $600–$900 per month. Food costs are additional, and extra funds are needed for student activity fees, textbooks, and miscellaneous expenses. There is a student health center with low-cost services for students who have paid the student activities fee.

Financial Aid

The Student Financial Aid Office assists students and prospective students in securing the funds needed to begin or continue studies at the University. The state and federal governments, the University, and many private organizations make available financial assistance in the form of grants, scholarships, loans, and employment opportunities for students who demonstrate the need for such assistance. Eligibility is determined by a careful assessment of each student's financial situation, taking into account the family's assets and income, the number of family members, and the estimated cost of attending college. The amount and type of award may vary depending upon state and federal guidelines, student need, and availability of funds. Applications for aid should be received by April 1 of the year the student plans to enroll. Further information, including information concerning scholarships, is available at the Student Financial Aid Office.

Faculty

A high percentage of UAA faculty members have doctoral degrees. Students find their introductory classes taught by highly qualified and experienced faculty members. Classes vary in size. Faculty members in the academic units assist students by providing academic advising and information on programs of study, degree requirements, and selection of majors.

Student Government

The Union of Students of the University of Alaska Anchorage (USUAA) is the sole official representative for students on campus. This body is duly recognized by the Board of Regents. USUAA administers funds for various student organizations, programs, and activities, such as movie tickets, concerts, dances, special events, lectures, legal services, the Club Council, the radio station, and the student newspaper.

Admission Requirements

The University of Alaska Anchorage maintains a policy of open enrollment, which means that any student who has completed an application for admission is accepted for general admission provided he or she has earned a high school diploma or the equivalent and has reached 18 years of age or is a member of a high school class that has graduated. No minimum grade point average in previous high school or college work is required for general admission, but official transcripts must be provided.

To qualify for baccalaureate degree admission, students must submit official SAT I or ACT results and official transcripts of all high school and college credits to Enrollment Services. These candidates must also have maintained a high school GPA of at least 2.5; a GPA of 2.0 or better is required for transfer applicants. Students wishing to take courses as non-degree-seeking students may register without applying for admission but must satisfy course prerequisites.

Application and Information

Prospective baccalaureate degree students must submit the application for admission and a nonrefundable $35 application fee. Recommended deadlines for receipt of the application and all supporting documents are May 1 for the fall semester, October 1 for the spring semester, and March 1 for the summer session.

Prospective associate degree and certificate students must submit the application for admission and a nonrefundable $35 application fee. Associate degree applications are reviewed on a rolling admission basis.

For more information concerning admission or the general curriculum, students should contact:

Cecile Mitchell
Director, Enrollment Services
Administration Building, Room 158
University of Alaska Anchorage
3211 Providence Drive
Anchorage, Alaska 99508
Telephone: 907-786-1480
World Wide Web: http://www.uaa.alaska.edu/

UNIVERSITY OF ALASKA FAIRBANKS
FAIRBANKS, ALASKA

The University

Founded in 1917, the University provides education, research, and service in the "last frontier." The Fairbanks campus, one of three in the statewide system of higher education, is the primary administrative and research center and has branches in Bethel, Dillingham, Kotzebue, and Nome, along with Rural Centers throughout the state.

The total University of Alaska Fairbanks (UAF) enrollment in the fall of 1998 was 8,235. Eighty-seven percent of the students come from Alaska; the 13 percent who make up the nonresident population represent forty-nine other states and thirty-eight countries. The nine residence halls on campus were recently renovated and are capable of lodging 1,279 students. The Student Apartment Complex has sixty furnished two-bedroom units reserved for sophomore and upperclass students. The Inupiat House, housing for rural students, holds 22 students. The University also manages 158 furnished apartments for students with families.

The large campus contains a core of academic buildings and residences, as well as miles of ski trails, two lakes, and an arboretum. Most of the University's research institutes, including the noted Geophysical Institute and the new International Arctic Research Center, are clustered on the West Ridge. The University's Agricultural Experiment Station farm is on campus, as are a Cooperative Fish and Wildlife Research Unit and various state and federal agencies and laboratories. The University awards graduate degrees in many of the same areas as the undergraduate studies, often in conjunction with one of its research institutes. A natural science facility, housing chemistry, physics, geology, and earth sciences, was completed in 1995.

Intercollegiate athletics include men's and women's basketball, cross-country running and skiing, and riflery and a women's volleyball team. The University sponsors an outstanding men's intercollegiate ice hockey team, which plays at the 4,665-seat Carlson Center. The UAF hockey team is a member of the Central Collegiate Hockey Association (CCHA). The Student Recreation Complex houses a variety of sports and physical activities facilities, including multipurpose areas for basketball, volleyball, badminton, tennis, calisthenics, dance, gymnastics, judo, and karate; a rifle and pistol range; courts for handball, racquetball, and squash; an elevated 200-meter, three-lane jogging track; a swimming pool; weight-training and modern fitness equipment areas; an ice arena for recreational skating and hockey; a special aerobics area; and a three-story climbing wall. The cheery and roomy student union, the William Ransom Wood Center, is the focus of various out-of-class activities for students and faculty members. The center houses meeting and exhibit rooms, lounges and television areas, the student government offices, campus information, a pub, a bowling alley, a games room, a cafeteria, a snack bar, an espresso bar, and a photography darkroom.

Location

The campus of the University of Alaska Fairbanks is situated on a ridge overlooking the valley of the Tanana River and the city of Fairbanks. Serving a population of more than 80,000 within the 7,561-square-mile North Star Borough, Fairbanks is a major trade center for outlying villages in Interior Alaska. The city is connected with the rest of the state and the lower forty-eight states by air and highway. Municipal bus service is available between downtown Fairbanks, the surrounding area, and the campus. Shuttle bus service is available around the UAF campus at no cost.

Fairbanks offers the sophistication of larger cities through such luxuries as first-run movies and fine restaurants while maintaining the atmosphere of smaller, more personal towns. Denali National Park and other vast wilderness areas are close at hand, and Anchorage is 350 miles south via the Parks Highway. Members of the Fairbanks community and the University join together in the University-Fairbanks Symphony Orchestra and in many other musical and theatrical enterprises.

Majors and Degrees

The University of Alaska Fairbanks awards certificates, A.A. and A.A.S. degrees, and B.A., B.S., B.T., B.B.A., B.Ed., B.M., and B.F.A. degrees in accounting, airframe studies, Alaska Native studies, anthropology, applied accounting, applied business, applied physics, apprenticeship technology, art, arts and sciences (leading to elementary education certification), aviation maintenance technology, aviation technology, biological sciences, business administration, chemistry, civil engineering, communication, community health, computer science, culinary arts, drafting technology, early childhood, earth science, economics, electrical engineering, English, Eskimo, fire science, fisheries, foreign languages, general science, geography (environmental studies), geological engineering, geology, ground vehicle maintenance technology, health technology, history, human service technology, Japanese studies, journalism, justice, linguistics, maintenance technology, mathematics, mechanical engineering, microcomputer support specialist studies, mining engineering, music, Native language education, natural resources management (including forestry), Northern studies, office management and technology, paralegal studies, petroleum engineering, philosophy, phlebotomy, physics, political science, powerplant studies, psychology, renewable resources, rural development, rural human services, Russian studies, social work, sociology, statistics, technology, theater, and wildlife biology.

Academic Program

The academic year is divided into two semesters; registration is in early September for the fall semester and in mid-January for the spring semester. Preregistration is available for returning students. In addition, there are three-week, six-week, and twelve-week summer sessions. UAF offers an early orientation for new students in the fall and spring semesters. The University is organized into four colleges and five professional schools: the College of Liberal Arts; the College of Science, Engineering and Mathematics; the College of Rural Alaska; the College of Natural Resource Development and Management; and the Schools of Agricultural and Land Resources Management, Education, Fisheries and Ocean Sciences, Management, and Mineral Engineering. A minimum of 120 semester credits must be completed for the four-year baccalaureate degree programs.

Students who receive scores of 3 or higher on the College Board's Advanced Placement tests may be awarded advanced-placement credit by the University. Currently enrolled students may challenge courses for credit by successfully completing College-Level Examination Program examinations or by completing locally prepared examinations. Requests for advanced-placement credit and credit by examination are coordinated through the Office of Admissions.

The honors program is designed for highly motivated undergraduate students who wish to acquire a superior understanding of the natural and social sciences, the arts, and the humanities. Prospective honors students need a minimum ACT composite score of 28 or a combined SAT I score of approximately 1270 with a minimum 3.6 high school GPA.

Off-Campus Arrangements

The University maintains exchange programs with McGill University in Canada and with universities in Australia, Denmark, Ecuador, England, Finland, Japan, Mexico, Norway, Russia, and Taiwan. The University also participates in the Northwest Interinstitutional Council for Study Abroad, providing students with an opportunity to enroll in liberal arts programs in Austria, England, France, Greece, Italy, and Spain. UAF is also a member of the National Student Exchange, participating with 150 colleges and universities.

Academic Facilities

The Fine Arts Complex features a 480-seat theater, a 1,072-seat concert hall, FM public radio (KUAC) and educational-television (PBS) studios, an art gallery, and the Elmer E. Rasmuson Library. The library collection contains more than 1.75 million volumes, including the prestigious Alaska and Polar Regions Collection. Electronic catalogs provide access to collections in 11,000 libraries nationwide.

Students have free use of the University's academic computing facilities (Aurora), which are accessible from Windows and Macintosh computer labs and by remote access. Various schools and colleges have their own special-purpose computer labs.

The University Museum attracts more than 100,000 visitors a year to Interior Alaska and is located on the UAF campus. The museum collects, preserves, and exhibits materials from Alaska and the North.

Costs

In 1999–2000, tuition and fees were $1364 per semester for full-time (12 credits) students. Nonresident students paid an additional $1908 for 12 credits of tuition each semester. Residents of Alaska, the Yukon Territory, and the Northwest Territories are exempt from the nonresident tuition fee. Students must live in Alaska for twelve months to qualify as residents. The approximate cost per semester for books and supplies is $500 and for personal items and recreation, $450. A double-occupancy residence hall room on campus cost $1175 per semester. Meals, which all residence hall occupants are required to purchase, cost approximately $1050 per semester. (These costs are subject to change.) Married student housing on campus is also available.

Financial Aid

About 70 percent of full-time UAF students received financial aid during the 1997–98 school year. The average amount of aid given was $3800 per student. A large portion of financial aid is derived from the Alaska State Student Loan Program, which is available only to students with one year or more of Alaska residence. Three kinds of aid are available: grants and scholarships (which need not be repaid), loans, and part-time employment. Students seeking financial assistance for the fall term should submit applications by March 15. Inquiries should be addressed to the Financial Aid Office, University of Alaska Fairbanks, P.O. Box 756560, Fairbanks, Alaska 99775-6560.

The Chancellor's Scholarship, a one-year tuition waiver, is available to entering freshmen with a minimum 3.0 GPA and 1150 SAT I combined score or 25 ACT composite score. To apply, students should submit an application for admission, a high school transcript, a tuition waiver application, and test scores for review. National Merit Finalists qualify for a four-year tuition waiver plus a $10,000 scholarship.

Faculty

Seventy percent of the 717 faculty members hold doctoral degrees, and many are actively engaged in research. In keeping with University policy, faculty members provide academic counseling for students. The combination of a student-faculty ratio of 15:1 and easy access to instructors for help outside of class produces a maximum educational benefit for students.

Student Government

The Associated Students of the University of Alaska Fairbanks (ASUAF) protects students' rights through its various governmental functions and also offers educational, social, recreational, and service activities. The school newspaper, *Sun Star*, is published weekly with the sponsorship of ASUAF, which also supports KSUA, the campus radio station; the international cinema and weekly movie series; and dances, concerts, and other entertainment. ASUAF publishes the results of its faculty evaluations and sends several student lobbyists to the Alaska state legislature in Juneau each spring. A student member sits on the Board of Regents of the University.

Admission Requirements

For admission to a baccalaureate program, applicants must be high school graduates with a cumulative grade point average of at least 2.0 and have earned a GPA of at least 2.5 in a high school core curriculum of 16 credits. Transfer students must also have a minimum grade point average of 2.0 in all previous college work. Applicants for a major in a scientific or technical field may be required to present a higher grade point average and to have completed specific background courses before being accepted into the major department. All entering freshmen are required to submit the results of either an ACT or SAT I examination prior to registration for placement in English and math courses.

Application and Information

The application deadlines are August 1 for the fall semester (April 1 for nonresident freshmen) and December 1 for the spring semester. Applications are processed after the deadlines only as long as space is available. Applicants are notified of the admission decision as soon as all application material has been received. Nonresident freshmen must pay a nonrefundable $100 enrollment deposit by June 1. Only accepted students are allowed to apply for campus housing. Students desiring campus housing should apply for admission as early as possible prior to the start of the semester to increase their chances of obtaining residence hall accommodations.

For further information, applicants should contact:

Office of Admissions
University of Alaska Fairbanks
P.O. Box 757480
Fairbanks, Alaska 99775-7480
Telephone: 907-474-7500
         800-478-1UAF (toll-free)
E-mail: fyapply@uaf.edu
World Wide Web: http://www.uaf.edu

The Plaza outside the classroom buildings at the University of Alaska Fairbanks. The flags represent the fifty states of the United States.

UNIVERSITY OF ALASKA SOUTHEAST
JUNEAU, KETCHIKAN, AND SITKA, ALASKA

The University

The University of Alaska Southeast (UAS) is a growing regional university with the main campus located in Juneau, the capital city of Alaska, and branch campuses located in Ketchikan and Sitka. All three campuses have a liberal arts emphasis and some vocational-technical opportunities. UAS is organized into one academic unit, with curriculum and policies established by a Dean of Faculty and the Faculty Council. The fall 1999 undergraduate enrollment for full-time students included 354 women and 296 men; enrollment for part-time students was 810 women and 562 men.

The Juneau campus also offers graduate programs leading to a Master of Business Administration, Master of Public Administration, Master of Arts in Teaching (emphases in elementary and secondary education), and Master of Education (emphases in early childhood education, elementary education, and secondary education).

The rich cultural environment of UAS offers student government activities, dances, concerts, clubs, art shows, lectures, a choir, a band, a symphony, and varied special events both on and off campus. Student activity fees support a variety of activities organized by the student government, including intramural sports (basketball, softball, and volleyball), dances, swimming (at discount rates), local racquet club use in Juneau, a climbing wall, and a variety of special interest clubs.

Southeast's abundant forests and beautiful waterways provide opportunities to enjoy kayaking, canoeing, camping, fishing, hiking, snowboarding, rock and ice climbing, scuba diving, and skiing. Few areas of the world can offer the wilderness access of Alaska, combined with the cosmopolitan flavor of its larger cities and the educational opportunities of UAS.

Location

Although small by "Lower 48" standards, Juneau, with a population of 30,000, is the largest community in southeast Alaska and the third-largest city in the state. Ketchikan is known as the "Gateway City" of Alaska, as it is the first port of entry for people entering Alaska by water. It is located on the west side of Revillagigedo Island on the Inside Passage, some 700 miles north of Seattle and 225 air miles southeast of Juneau. It is the fourth-largest city in Alaska, with a population of 15,000. Sitka, the former capital of Russian Alaska, is located on the west side of Baranof Island, 185 air miles northwest of Ketchikan and 95 air miles southwest of Juneau. Sitka has a population of 8,500.

The climate in all three cities is mild and wet, typical of a temperate rain forest. Juneau averages 56 inches of annual precipitation near the UAS campus and 99 inches downtown; Ketchikan averages 170 inches of annual precipitation; and Sitka averages 95 inches of annual precipitation.

Juneau, Ketchikan, and Sitka are accessible by air and water but not by road. Jet service from Seattle and Anchorage is offered daily. Those who bring cars must use the barge service from Seattle or the Alaska Marine Highway System, which operates large vessels that provide ferry service between Bellingham, Washington, and southeast Alaska throughout the year. The ferries provide a spectacular cruise on the scenically unsurpassed Inside Passage.

Majors and Degrees

The UAS Juneau campus offers the Bachelor of Liberal Arts with emphases areas in art, communication, general studies, government, literature, mathematics, and social science; Bachelor of Business Administration with emphases in accounting, business and government, and management; Bachelor of Science in biology or marine biology; Bachelor of Science in environmental science; Associate of Arts; Associate of Applied Science in apprenticeship technology, business administration, computer information and office systems support, construction technology, early childhood education, marine technology, paralegal studies, and power technology; and certificate programs in accounting, business information systems, construction technology, early childhood education, marine carpentry, power technology (with emphases in automotive, diesel/heavy duty, and diesel/marine), and welding technology.

The UAS Ketchikan campus awards the Associate of Arts; the Associate of Applied Science in apprenticeship technology, business administration, and computer information and office systems support; and certificates in accounting, business information systems, and welding. The UAS Sitka campus offers the Associate of Arts and Associate of Applied Science in apprenticeship technology, computer information and office systems support, environmental technology, and health information management and certificate programs in accounting, computer information and office systems support, law enforcement, and welding technology.

Academic Program

UAS operates on the semester system: semesters begin August 30 and January 10. A summer semester, which is divided into two sessions that begin in May and in June, is also offered. A minimum of 120 semester credits is required to complete a baccalaureate degree program, a minimum of 60 semester credits to complete an associate degree program, and a minimum of 30 semester credits to complete a certificate program. For all programs, students must maintain a minimum 2.0 grade point average; in some program core areas, the minimum GPA requirement is higher.

Advanced placement credit is given to high school students who achieve scores of 3 or higher on the College Board's Advanced Placement tests or scores above 600 on the SAT I verbal or 30 on the ACT English. Students who are currently enrolled may challenge courses for credit through either the College-Level Examination Program (CLEP) or University challenge examinations. Requests by students for advanced placement credit and credit by examination are coordinated through the Office of Records and Registration.

Academic Facilities

The main campus of UAS is located 11 miles from the city of Juneau on the shore of Auke Lake. It faces the Mendenhall Glacier, offering a spectacular view of the nearby forest, lake, mountains, and glacier. Within walking distance, on Auke Bay, is the Anderson Building, the location of the Juneau Center for Fisheries and Ocean Sciences. The Bill Ray Center is conveniently located in downtown Juneau near federal and state office buildings and the state capitol. A 5-acre complex on the downtown waterfront, the Marine-Technology Center serves as the base for the construction technology, marine technology, power technology, and welding programs as well as other vocational/technical programs.

All of the structures on the three UAS campuses have been built recently. The main buildings house classrooms, faculty offices, administrative offices, student centers, and the libraries. In Juneau, the William A. Egan Library contains more than 400,000 volumes. This award-winning facility offers seating for more than 200 users, the most current computer technology for access to information, and extended hours for student study. The learning center and media services are also housed in the Egan library, as is a modest collection of southeastern Alaskan native art, purchased with State of Alaska Art in Public Places funds. The library also houses the media classroom, which is the origination point for satellite-delivered, distance-education classes. The UAS Ketchikan library collection includes 45,000 volumes, and the UAS Sitka/Sheldon Jackson shared library includes 70,000 volumes. Each library also has collections of periodicals, newspapers, microform-equivalent volumes, audio records and cassettes, and state and federal documents. Access to the collections of other libraries within the cities and the university system is available through computer-based catalogs.

Students have ready access to computer resources. General-use microcomputer facilities are available in convenient locations at all three campuses. In addition, students have free access to the Digital VAX 8600 system at the Juneau campus and the VAX 8800s at the University of Alaska campuses in Anchorage and Fairbanks.

Costs

For 2000–01, an Alaska resident carrying 12 or more credit hours is considered a full-time student and pays tuition of $924 to $1044 per semester, depending on whether the courses taken are lower or upper division (100- and 200-level courses are $77 per credit hour; 300- and 400-level courses are $87 per credit hour). A resident is any person who has lived in Alaska for one year. Full-time nonresident students pay tuition of $2892 to $3012 per semester, depending on whether courses are lower or upper division. In most instances, students may establish residency in Alaska after one year. Students from the Yukon Territory and the Northwest Territories are exempt from the nonresident fees. UAS also participates in the Western Undergraduate Exchange (WUE) program for all degree programs. Students from Washington, California, and Arizona are also eligible for WUE tuition rates. WUE students pay from $1386 to $1506 per semester, depending on whether courses are lower or upper division. In addition, all students pay a mandatory $23 activity fee and a $5 per-credit-hour ($60 maximum) technology fee each semester.

On-campus housing is available on the Juneau campus. The cost per semester ranges from $1300 per person for a double occupancy bedroom in the new resident suites and $1500 for a private bedroom in apartment-style housing to approximately $3950 for family residency. Student housing is also available for students attending in Sitka, and off-campus housing options are available through the Student Service offices on all campuses. Meal plans are required for residents in suites, and may be purchased by students in apartments. The minimum meal plan costs $985 per semester.

Additional funds are needed for books, supplies, and personal expenses.

Financial Aid

UAS participates in the Federal Pell Grant, Federal Supplemental Educational Opportunity Grant, Federal Stafford Student Loan, and Federal Work-Study programs in addition to state student loan, family loan, and grant programs. Most aid is awarded on the basis of financial need. However, some scholarships are based on academic potential and performance. The deadline for merit-based UAS scholarships is rolling. To apply for need-based programs, students should request a financial aid packet from one of the campus financial aid offices.

Faculty

Classes are taught by a highly qualified and experienced faculty. The three UAS campuses have approximately 250 faculty and staff members. Classes vary in size but are typically much smaller than at larger institutions; the average class size is 15 students. The size of UAS contributes to a high degree of personal interaction between students and faculty members. In addition to their primary teaching responsibilities, some faculty members serve as advisers for upper-division undergraduate students as well as on advisory committees for graduate students.

Student Government

The student government plays an important role in the development of UAS policies and activities. Students serve on a number of important committees and participate in lobbying the state legislature on behalf of students' interests.

Admission Requirements

The University of Alaska Southeast has an open admissions policy. A student is qualified for admission as an undergraduate if he or she is a high school graduate with a minimum high school GPA of 2.0. Successful completion of the GED test is accepted as an equivalency of high school graduation. Submission of acceptable test scores from the ACT or the SAT I is requested. Specific admission requirements, which may vary for the different degree programs, are given in the University's academic catalog.

Application and Information

To apply, students must complete an application form and send it with the required $35 application processing fee to the Office of Admissions on the campus of intended enrollment. Official high school transcripts are required of all program applicants, as are official transcripts from all regionally accredited colleges and universities attended, if applicable. Admission is on a rolling basis; applications are processed in the order they are received. Applicants generally receive an initial response within two to three weeks.

For further information, application forms, or any other materials, prospective applicants should contact:

Greg Wagner
Student Resource Center
University of Alaska Southeast
11120 Glacier Highway
Juneau, Alaska 99801
Telephone: 907-465-6239
           877-465-4827 (toll-free)
Fax: 907-465-6365
E-mail: jyuas@uas.alaska.edu
World Wide Web: http://www.uas.alaska.edu (UAS)
           http://www.juneau.com (Juneau community)

UAS faculty members take advantage of on-campus "natural laboratories" for their teaching.

UNIVERSITY OF ARKANSAS
FAYETTEVILLE, ARKANSAS

The University

Established in 1871, the University of Arkansas (U of A) is the flagship campus of the University of Arkansas System. The University offers more than 200 undergraduate and graduate degrees in more than 150 fields of study in agricultural, food, and life sciences; human environmental sciences; arts and sciences; business; education; engineering; architecture; and law. The University is also recognized as the only comprehensive doctoral degree–granting institution in the state. Fayetteville's 420-acre campus is home to students from all counties in Arkansas, every state in the U.S., and more than one hundred countries throughout the world. The enrollment for the 1999–2000 school year was nearly 15,000 students (more than 11,500 in undergraduate programs) and included a diverse student population, with 811 international students representing 109 countries.

Convenient and safe on-campus housing is available. The Honors Halls are among the most popular on campus. Students accepted to these halls must have at least a 3.0 grade point average (GPA) and maintain a minimum 3.0 GPA while residing in these halls. There are also specialized floors for specific academic fields and 24-hour quiet floors for those who wish to avoid distractions.

There are more than 150 fields of study offered at the University; master's degrees are offered in eighty-six fields. The College of Education and Health Professions has recently added six degree programs, including a Master of Arts in Teaching and four Ph.D. programs. The School of Law offers a skilled and scholarly faculty of teaching and practicing lawyers. The National Center for Agricultural Law Research and Information has been praised for its research and publications and makes possible the law school's unique degree offering in agricultural law.

Location

The city of Fayetteville is a community of more than 55,000 people that was rated by *Money* magazine as one of the top ten most desirable places in the nation in which to live or work. Fayetteville is settled in the Ozark Mountains near lakes and rivers but accessible to major metropolitan amenities, making it an excellent place for a well-balanced college experience.

Majors and Degrees

The Dale Bumpers College of Agricultural, Food and Life Sciences offers more than twenty-five majors that give students the ability to improve agriculture and the family environment. The School of Architecture offers majors in architecture and landscape architecture. Named for Senator J. William Fulbright, the Fulbright College of Arts and Sciences is the largest of the U of A colleges, with seventeen departments offering majors in advertising and public relations, anthropology, architectural studies, art, art history, biochemistry, biology, botany, broadcast journalism, chemistry, classical studies, communication, computer science, criminal justice, drama, earth science, economics, English, French, geography, geology, German, history, journalism, magazine journalism, mathematics, microbiology, music, philosophy, physics, political science, psychology, social work, sociology, Spanish, and zoology. Preprofessional programs are offered in chiropractic, dental hygiene, dentistry, forestry, law, medical technology, medicine, nursing, occupational therapy, optometry, pharmacy, physical therapy, podiatry, theology, and veterinary medicine. There are also twenty-three programs leading to secondary education certification.

The Sam M. Walton College of Business Administration offers programs in accounting, administrative management, business economics, computer information systems (with a concentration in accounting), finance (banking, insurance, and real estate), financial management, general business, human resource management, industrial management, industrial marketing, international economics and business, marketing management, public administration, quantitative analysis, retail marketing, small business/entrepreneurship, and transportation. Preparing professionals for research, teaching, and service-oriented positions, the College of Education and Health Professions offers majors in art education (K–12), athletic training, business education, commercial recreation, elementary education, exercise science, health sciences, industrial education, kinesiology (K–12), music education (K–12), outdoor recreation, public recreation, secondary education, speech pathology–audiology, teaching the mildly handicapped, and therapeutic recreation as well as a Bachelor of Science in Nursing degree. The College of Engineering offers programs in biological and agricultural engineering, chemical engineering, civil engineering, computer systems engineering, electrical engineering, industrial engineering, and mechanical engineering.

Academic Program

The U of A operates on a traditional two-semester academic year schedule, with two regular summer sessions and some special concurrent summer sessions. Requirements for graduation include a minimum University-wide core along with core requirements in each college. The majority of undergraduate degree offerings follow a four-year plan requiring from 124 to 136 course hours for graduation; there are some exceptions to this requirement, such as the five-year, design-oriented architecture program, which requires 163 hours.

A course in English as a second language is offered in five 9-week sessions throughout the year. Classes focus on all language skills: grammar, reading, writing, and listening/speaking.

Off-Campus Arrangements

The University conducts extensive cooperative education programs through several colleges that offer off-campus opportunities for work or learning in other cities and countries.

Academic Facilities

The University library contains nearly 1.5 million volumes, 16,000 subscriptions to periodicals and journals, 2 million titles on microform, and more than 19,400 recordings. The University of Arkansas also provides computer labs with both IBM and Macintosh stations at locations across campus, some open around the clock. Recent renovations in the fine arts center provide stunning gallery and theater facilities. The state-of-the-art Bell Engineering Center is a recently built multimillion-dollar facility offering the optimum in computer capabilities and laboratory research. The Writing Center is a program offered to students to aid them in English grammar and style to further develop literacy skills and stimulate creativity. The Center of Excellence for Poultry Science is a new $22-million facility offering the finest training for poultry scientists in the U.S.

Costs

For the 1999–2000 school year, the full-time (15 hours) tuition rate for in-state students (Arkansas residents) was $1667 per semester; nonresidents paid $4159. Among those taking fewer hours, Arkansas residents paid $100 per credit hour, and nonresidents paid $278 per credit hour. Additional fees (for those enrolling in 6 hours or more) included a $56 student health fee, an $8 media fee, and a $15 student activity fee per semester. College miscellaneous fees, such as laboratory enhancement fees, ranged from $88 to $573. Students age 60 and older may have the fees waived for credit courses on a space-available basis. For international students, the annual nine-month academic year costs totaled $14,500 and included tuition, fees, housing, health insurance, books and supplies, equipment fees, and personal expenses. Summer living and full-time enrollment costs totaled $6900.

Financial Aid

Loans, grants, work-study, and scholarships are available to qualifying students. Any need-analysis form recognized by the U.S. Department of Education is acceptable to the Office of Student Financial Services. To receive priority consideration for scholarships, a student enrolling for the fall semester must submit an application by February 15. For other forms of financial aid (student loans, Federal Pell Grants, etc.), the priority application deadline is April 1. The fall scholarship deadline for international students is March 15. ACT or SAT scores are required for international scholarship consideration.

Faculty

The University has nearly 900 full-time faculty members, the majority of whom hold the highest degree in their field. There are also more than 600 part-time and graduate faculty members, as well as 2,000 staff members. For international students, an international student adviser and a fully staffed International Programs Office are available to assist with orientation sessions, immigration counseling, and activities programming.

Student Government

The University of Arkansas offers students the opportunity to participate in various forms of campus government. The Associated Student Government, the Off-Campus Student Government, Residents' Interhall Congress, the Interfraternity Council, and the Panhellenic Council are the main governing bodies that aid students in expressing their opinions or interests to the faculty, administration, and community.

Admission Requirements

Entering freshmen are advised to prepare for admission to the U of A while in high school by taking four years each of English and math and three years each of social studies, natural sciences, and electives such as foreign language and computer science. For the best possible chance of being admitted to the University of Arkansas, students should have a minimum average of a B (3.0) and try to score a minimum of 20 on the ACT or 960 on the SAT I. The ACT code for the U of A is 0144, and the SAT I code is 6866. Transfer students must have an overall GPA of at least 2.0 on all college course work attempted. Any transfer student with fewer than 24 hours must also meet the requirements for entering freshmen.

International students must have above-average secondary school records, and those who are not native speakers of English must submit a minimum TOEFL score of 550 (paper) or 213 (computer). The University of Arkansas offers qualified applicants conditional admission to the Spring International Language Center, with academic admission granted upon reaching a satisfactory English language level.

Application and Information

To enroll in the University, students must submit a completed Application for Undergraduate Admission and an application fee of $30. An online admission form can be found at the University's Web site listed below. The application deadline for the fall semester is August 15; the spring deadline is January 1. The student must also request that official transcripts be mailed to the Office of Admissions. A preliminary admission is provided for those high school seniors who have a transcript of six or seven semesters, but a final transcript is needed to certify high school graduation. ACT or SAT I scores no more than four years old must be submitted by all entering freshmen and transfer students with fewer than 24 transferable hours. These scores must be sent directly to the Office of Admissions from the testing agency.

International students must submit an application for admission with a $50 application fee. A financial statement, a TOEFL score, and official secondary and postsecondary academic recorded are also required. For the fall term, the application deadline is May 1; the summer term deadline is March 1; and the spring term deadline is October 1. International students can download the undergraduate application at www.uark.edu.

For further information, students should contact:

Ms. M. E. Lynes
Office of Admissions
200 Silas H. Hunt Hall
University of Arkansas
Fayetteville, Arkansas 72701
Telephone: 501-575-5346
　　　　　　800-377-UOFA (toll-free)
　　　　　　501-575-6246 (international)
Fax: 501-575-7515
E-mail: uafadmis@comp.uark.edu
　　　　uaiao@comp.uark.edu (international)
WWW: http://www.uark.edu/sis/apply/application.html

A friendly campus, the University of Arkansas offers a wide range of academic majors and campus activities for student involvement.

UNIVERSITY OF BALTIMORE
BALTIMORE, MARYLAND

The University

The University of Baltimore (UB) serves a unique role in the University System of Maryland. It is the state's only upper-division (transfer) and graduate institution, offering a diversity of bachelor's, master's, and first-professional degrees in liberal arts and business. UB operates a law school and a number of professionally oriented combined-degree programs with other Maryland colleges and universities. The University also offers a limited number of sophomore opportunities.

Founded in 1925, UB has a very clear mission: to provide flexible educational programs to professionally oriented students. Approximately 4,600 students study in the University's three schools—the Yale Gordon College of Liberal Arts, the Robert S. Merrick School of Business, and the School of Law. UB traditionally attracts students with strong career ambitions and provides them with the latest skills and techniques in their chosen fields.

UB students can choose from more than fifty active clubs and organizations, which range from the Student Government Association to discipline-specific clubs.

Location

The University of Baltimore is located in the cultural corridor of Baltimore, a thriving city with cultural, athletic, educational, and recreational opportunities that has received national recognition for its recent renaissance. The Meyerhoff Symphony Hall; the Lyric Opera House; Maryland Institute, College of Art; and the Baltimore Museum of Art are located within one mile of UB. Oriole Park at Camden Yards, PSINet (Ravens) Stadium, and Harborplace are approximately three miles south of campus. Annapolis, on the beautiful Chesapeake Bay, is a 45-minute drive away, and Washington, D.C., is a 1-hour commute from the University.

Majors and Degrees

Bachelor of Arts and Bachelor of Science degrees are offered in accounting, business administration, computer information systems, corporate communication, criminal justice, economics, English, entrepreneurship, finance, government and public policy, health systems management, history, human resource management, human services administration, interdisciplinary studies, international business, jurisprudence, management, marketing, and psychology. Specializations are offered in applied information technology; language; language, technology, and culture; literature; management information systems; professional writing and publishing; public history; and women's studies. A certificate is offered in computer information systems.

Academic Program

The University follows a semester system, with fall and spring semesters, a minimester session in January, and a summer session. The University offers several special degree programs that follow four 10-week sessions in an academic year. The University offers more than 600 courses during the fall, spring, and summer semesters. Students can attend full-time or part-time during the day or evening and on Saturdays.

A humanities-centered, interdisciplinary core curriculum is required of all undergraduate students. In these core courses, students examine the relationship between ethics and values while exploring business and public policy, and they trace major themes and ideas in philosophy and the arts. Throughout the core, students are assisted in refining their skills in critical thinking and oral and written communication. To be awarded a bachelor's degree, students must satisfactorily complete a minimum of 120 hours of college credit and have satisfactorily completed a specific curriculum with a grade point average of at least 2.0.

The University's Helen P. Denit honors program offers honors-level versions of the core curriculum courses. Students who transfer to UB with a grade point average of 3.5 or higher are invited to apply to the program. Other students may be nominated by a UB professor.

Off-Campus Arrangements

Several off-campus sites are available for students who desire to take courses closer to home. The University offers students opportunities to participate in professional internships, and students from certain majors may also participate in study-abroad opportunities.

Academic Facilities

Located on the corner of Mt. Royal and Charles Streets, the University of Baltimore offers a variety of campus facilities. The Academic Center houses many of the administration offices as well as classrooms, a fitness center, faculty offices, and the Dean's offices of the Yale Gordon College of Liberal Arts. Connected to the center is Charles Hall, which features the President's suite and a brand-new student lounge as well as business, registrar, and student affairs offices and classrooms. The Thumel Business Center houses the Merrick School of Business, with computer laboratories and state-of-the-art communication and computer-capable classrooms, and features a six-story atrium. UB's Langsdale Library compares favorably with those of its peer institutions in Maryland, both in breadth and quantity of holdings. It offers more than 300,000 volumes of books, periodicals, CD-ROM indexes, government documents, and audiovisual materials as well as several special collections. The Charles Royal Building is home to the School of Communications Design, and the Schaefer Center Building is the location for the School of Public Affairs. The John and Frances Angelos Law Center houses the library, classrooms, and administrative offices of the School of Law as well as Poe's Publick House, the University's dining complex.

Costs

Anticipated in-state full-time tuition for the 2000–01 academic year is $1771 per semester, plus fees. Part-time in-state tuition is $163 per credit, plus fees. Out-of-state full-time tuition is $5660 per semester, plus fees, and out-of-state part-time tuition is $472 per credit, plus fees. Tuition and fees are subject to change.

Financial Aid

Students at the University of Baltimore are eligible to participate in all regular federal financial aid programs, including the Pell Grant, the Supplemental Educational Opportunity Grant, the Perkins Loan, the Stafford Loan, the PLUS Loan, and the

Work-Study programs. Applications for federal aid programs should be submitted by April 1 for fall and November 1 for spring.

In addition, the University offers an extensive scholarship program for transfer students. Students who transfer with 56 or more credits and at least a 3.25 cumulative transfer GPA are eligible for a Dean's Scholarship (50 percent of full-time in-state tuition); students with a cumulative transfer of at least 3.5 and who are members of Phi Theta Kappa at their community college are eligible for a Phi Theta Kappa Scholarship (75 percent of full-time in-state tuition); and students with a cumulative transfer GPA of at least 3.5 are eligible for Wilson Scholarships (100 percent of full-time in-state tuition.) Scholarship recipients who are not residents of Maryland receive an additional $1500 above the amounts noted. The deadline for scholarship applications is March 1 for fall and November 1 for spring.

Faculty

With a student-faculty ratio of 16:1 and a personalized system of student advising, UB programs emphasize one-on-one interaction and individual attention for all students. The University of Baltimore employs 146 full-time and 124 part-time faculty members. Ninety-three percent of the full-time faculty members hold terminal degrees. All full-time faculty members teach at both the undergraduate and graduate levels and have responsibilities in research and public service. UB does not utilize graduate teaching assistants. Part-time faculty members are expert practitioners who are employed full-time in business, industry, and government.

Student Government

The Student Government Association is the representative body for all students at the University of Baltimore. The Senate oversees the allotment and expenditure of funds to undergraduate clubs and is responsible for staging the annual fall and spring block parties as well as the Merit Awards banquet.

Admission Requirements

The University of Baltimore is an upper-division university that offers the junior and senior years of undergraduate study leading to a Bachelor of Arts or Bachelor of Science degree. The University also admits a limited number of sophomores each academic year. Admission to a baccalaureate or certificate program is open to students who hold an associate's degree or who have at least 56 transferable credits with a GPA of at least 2.0, 42 transferable credits with a GPA of at least 2.3, or 24 transferable credits with at least a 2.5 GPA. Specific programs may have more restrictive admissions criteria. Applicants who are nonnative speakers of English must demonstrate a satisfactory level of English proficiency. A minimum score of 550 on the paper-based version or 213 on the computer-based version of the Test of English as a Foreign Language (TOEFL) is required of both degree and nondegree applicants regardless of citizenship or visa status. Applicants with international transcripts must arrange to have their academic records evaluated by a U.S. credential evaluation service.

Application and Information

The University of Baltimore has a rolling admissions policy, and applications are accepted until the last day of registration each semester, space permitting. However, the earlier an application and credentials are received, the earlier an admission decision can be made. It is recommended that students file an application by July 1 for the fall semester, November 1 for the spring semester, and April 1 for the summer session. A nonrefundable $20 application fee is required at time of application. An online application is available on the Web (http://www.acaff.usmh.usmd.edu/umsapp), or students may request an application by calling or writing the Admissions Office:

Admissions Office
University of Baltimore
1420 North Charles Street
Baltimore, Maryland 21201
Telephone: 410-837-4777
        877-ApplyUB (toll-free)
World Wide Web: http://www.ubalt.edu

On the campus of the University of Baltimore.

UNIVERSITY OF BRIDGEPORT
BRIDGEPORT, CONNECTICUT

The University

Founded in 1927, the University of Bridgeport is a private, nonsectarian, comprehensive, urban university located in Bridgeport, Connecticut. The University's 86-acre campus is situated on Long Island Sound. The University's Stamford center is located in Stamford, Connecticut, allowing for access from southern Fairfield County and Westchester County, New York. The University has a long-standing partnership with the local community to provide its residents with excellent educational opportunities that lead to degrees and career advancement.

The University's campus is composed of buildings of diverse architectural styles. The Bernhard Arts and Humanities Center is a cultural hub, and the Wheeler Recreation Center is a complete recreation and physical fitness facility. Residence halls are wired for individual computer hookups.

Although many of the students are Connecticut residents, the University has a student body that represents thirty-four states and ninety countries. The University is divided into the College of Graduate and Undergraduate Studies (CGUS) and the Division of Health Sciences. CGUS includes the School of Arts and Sciences, the School of Business, the School of Education and Human Resources, the School of General Studies, the School of Continuing Education, the School of Engineering and Design, and the College of Nations. The Division of Health Sciences includes the Fones School of Dental Hygiene, the College of Chiropractic, the College of Naturopathic Medicine, and the Nutrition Institute. Professional accreditations include those from the ABA, NASAD, ABET, CCE, and ADA. The School of Business is nationally and internationally accredited by the Association of Collegiate Business Schools and Programs (ACBSP).

Location

Bridgeport, a city of 148,000 people, is located in southwestern Connecticut. Bordered by the beautiful Long Island Sound, Bridgeport is 1 hour from New York City and 3 hours from Boston. The city is served by major bus and train systems and has a well-developed public transportation system for intracity travel. Perhaps the greatest value of the city to students is that it is the Fairfield County seat. The county is the home of many national and multinational corporations, providing students with many career opportunities. University faculty members also maintain close relationships with area corporations, school systems, and agencies.

Majors and Degrees

The School of Arts and Sciences offers the following degrees in its arts programs: the Bachelor of Fine Arts degree (B.F.A.) in graphic design and illustration; the Bachelor of Science degree (B.S.) and the Bachelor of Arts degree (B.A.) in biology and mathematics; the Bachelor of Music degree (B.Mus.) in jazz studies, music business, music education, and music performance; and the B.A. in literature and civilization, with concentrations in creative writing, English, history, philosophy, and psychology.

The College of Nations offers the B.A. in the following areas: international political economy and diplomacy; mass communications, with concentrations in advertising, communication studies, journalism, and public relations; social sciences, with concentrations in history, international studies, political science, psychology and sociology; and world religions.

The School of Education and Human Resources offers the B.S. in human services.

The School of General Studies offers the following degrees: the Associate of Arts (A.A.) degree in general studies, the Associate of Science (A.S.) degree in general studies, and the Bachelor of Elective Studies (B.E.S.) degree. Students can also earn the B.E.S. through participation in the IDEAL Program, an accelerated degree-completion program for adults.

The School of Business confers the A.A. degree in business administration, fashion merchandising and retailing, and legal assistant studies and the B.S. degree in accounting, business administration, business administration/legal administration, computer applications and information systems, fashion merchandising and retailing, finance, international business, management and industrial relations, and marketing.

The School of Engineering and Design confers the B.S. degree in computer engineering, computer science, industrial design, and interior design. The computer engineering program is nationally accredited by ABET.

Preprofessional programs in chiropractic, dentistry, medicine, naturopathic medicine, and veterinary medicine are available.

The Fones School of Dental Hygiene offers A.S. and B.S. degree options in dental hygiene.

The College of Chiropractic confers the Doctor of Chiropractic (D.C.) degree, including a 3+4 combined B.S. in biology/D.C. degree program in cooperation with the School of Engineering and Design.

The University also provides a foundation for students to become teachers. At the undergraduate level, students take 18 credits and minor in education while majoring in any relevant field. Students may then complete certification requirements through graduate study.

Academic Program

The University of Bridgeport operates on a two-semester calendar. A minimum of 120 credit hours is required for graduation, and the last 30 of those must be completed at the University. The University also provides one-on-one tutoring and group remedial work in the Academic Resource Center. This Center offers extensive advising, attention to developing essential academic skills, small classes, and the likelihood of increased academic achievement. Credit can be granted for subject area examinations of the College-Level Examination Program (CLEP) on which scores above the 50th percentile have been received. Credit is also granted for Advanced Placement examinations passed with the recommended score.

The University of Bridgeport offers an intensive English Language Institute on campus, designed to meet the needs of students whose native language is not English. The ELI program is open to all applicants regardless of initial proficiency in English. Students take a placement test and interview to determine the beginning level in the program.

Academic Facilities

The University's Wahlstrom Library contains approximately 270,000 bound volumes, including bound journals and indexes, and more than 1 million microforms. It subscribes to more than 1,700 periodicals and other serials. Online databases available from off campus via the library's Internet Web site include more than sixty databases in OCLC's FirstSearch, covering all subject areas; EBSCOhost's Academic Search FullTEXT Elite; Bell & Howell's ProQuest Direct ABI Inform Global; Alt-Health Watch; and MANTIS. Links are provided from the library's Web site to ERIC and PubMed. Additional online databases available throughout campus or in the library include LEXIS-NEXIS Academic Universe, STAT-USA, Financial Information Services Online (Moody's), Allied and Alternative Medicine, and the ACM Digital Library. An extension library is maintained at the Stamford campus, with more than 1,000 volumes, more than twenty periodicals, and extensive electronic access.

Costs

The standard tuition for the 1999–2000 academic year was $13,800; room and board costs were $6970. Additional fees may be required for some majors.

Financial Aid

The University's financial aid policies are intended to make it possible for students to attend the University who otherwise could not afford a private education. Financial assistance, consisting of grants, scholarships, loans, and employment, is based on the financial need of the student and his or her family. More than 85 percent of all students receive some form of financial assistance from the University and outside sources. Students who are interested in applying for financial aid must file the Free Application for Federal Student Aid (FAFSA). The University of Bridgeport also offers academic scholarships and grants to students on a competitive basis. These awards are renewable for four years based on satisfactory academic achievement and good standing in the University. Qualified students may be eligible to receive financial aid in addition to a scholarship or grant award. Athletic scholarships are also available.

Faculty

All courses at the University are taught by faculty members. More than 90 percent of the full-time faculty members hold doctoral degrees. Faculty members are selected and promoted on the basis of teaching effectiveness, professional performance, and contributions to the academic community. The student-faculty ratio is 12:1.

Faculty honors recipients include Fulbright scholars, National Science Foundation fellows, Ford fellows, National Endowment for the Humanities fellows, American Council for Learned Societies scholars, Phi Beta Kappa scholars, and Sigma Xi scholars.

Student Government

The Student Congress is the chief governing body for full-time students. Resident students are self-governed by means of their own hall community councils and collectively by the Residence Halls Association. The Commuters' Senate coordinates the activities of the commuting students. The Student Congress has jurisdiction over appointments to all committees at the University on which there is student representation. The Senate is the University legislative body and is composed of faculty members, administrators, and student representatives from each school/college.

Admission Requirements

Personal motivation and achievement, the secondary school record, and standardized test scores (SAT or ACT) are all considered in making admission decisions. Most students who are admitted are in the upper half of their high school graduating class.

All transfer students must have an overall cumulative grade point average of at least 2.0 (on a 4.0 scale) for most programs. However, the dental hygiene program, the School of Business, and the School of Engineering and Technology all recommend a GPA of 2.5 or higher. Information sessions, campus tours, and personal interviews may be scheduled by calling the Office of Admissions. All interested students are encouraged to visit the campus.

Application and Information

The University admits students for both the fall and the spring semesters on a rolling admission basis. The priority deadline for freshman applicants is April 1. The application must be completed and returned with a $25 fee. It is the student's responsibility to see that all of the necessary official transcripts and test scores are sent directly from the appropriate institutions to the University. Letters of recommendation are not required but may be submitted as supportive material. Additional requirements may be required by certain programs. Electronic applications are welcome through the University's Web site.

For more information, students should contact:

Office of Admissions
University of Bridgeport
126 Park Avenue
Bridgeport, Connecticut 06601
Telephone: 203-576-4552
        800-EXCEL-UB (toll-free)
Fax: 203-576-4941
E-mail: admit@bridgeport.edu
World Wide Web: http://www.bridgeport.edu

UNIVERSITY OF BRITISH COLUMBIA
VANCOUVER, BRITISH COLUMBIA, CANADA

The University

The University of British Columbia (UBC) is the third-largest university in Canada and is considered to be one of Canada's leading research universities. UBC was incorporated in 1908 and admitted its first students in 1915. The University's 1,000-acre campus atop a forested peninsula enjoys spectacular views of the Pacific Ocean, the Vancouver skyline, and the snowcapped peaks of the surrounding Coastal Mountains.

The University provides a wide range of bachelor's degree programs as well as graduate and professional programs through its twelve faculties and ten schools.

The number of students currently registered in degree programs is 35,505; 29,146 students are enrolled in undergraduate programs. A majority of students are from British Columbia and other provinces in Canada. More than 2,000 students are from the United States and 112 other countries. The University strives to be accessible to all members of society and provides support for students with special needs through the Disability Resource Centre, the Equity Office, the First Nations House of Learning, and the Women Students' Office. Through its International House, the University offers a full range of reception, advising, and social services to international students.

On-campus University residences provide spaces for more than 6,000 students in single-student coed housing and family housing units. The majority of students who live off campus commute to the University, which is well serviced by a reliable public transportation system. UBC's athletics and sport services administer one of Canada's most successful interuniversity athletic programs, and the Alma Mater Society maintains more than 200 clubs that cater to a wide variety of academic and social interests. Cultural activities are an important aspect of the University. Facilities include the Asian Centre, the new Chan Centre for the Performing Arts, the Museum of Anthropology, the Botanical Gardens, a conference centre, the aquatic centre, a fitness centre and gymnasium, tennis courts, and a sports stadium.

Location

The University of British Columbia is located a few miles from downtown Vancouver, Canada's third-largest city and one of its most important international business centres. Ideally located halfway between Europe and Asia, Vancouver is home to 2 million people from different ethnic backgrounds whose traditions contribute to the rich cultural life of the city. The city has its share of world-class art galleries, hotels, and restaurants and plays host to major sports, film, theatre, and music festivals throughout the year. The proximity of the mountains and miles of public beaches provides residents with an abundance of outdoor recreational opportunities year-round. Due to the moderating effects of warm Pacific currents, Vancouver winters are brief and mild; rain is common in the late fall and early spring.

Majors and Degrees

The Faculty of Agricultural Sciences offers a Bachelor of Science (B.Sc.) in agricultural economics, agriculture, agroecology, animal science, food science, global resource systems, plant science, and soil science. The Faculty also offers a Bachelor of Home Economics (B.H.E.).

The Faculty of Applied Sciences offers programs of study leading to the Bachelor of Applied Sciences (B.A.Sc.) in the following areas: bioresource and chemical engineering, civil engineering, electrical engineering, engineering physics, geological engineering, mechanical engineering, metals and materials engineering, and mining and mineral process engineering. The School of Nursing within the Faculty of Applied Science offers a four-year program of study leading to the B.S.N.

The Faculty of Arts offers undergraduate programs leading to the Bachelor of Arts (B.A.), Bachelor of Fine Arts (B.F.A.), Bachelor of Music (B.Mus.), and the Bachelor of Social Work (B.S.W.). The B.A. is offered in anthropology, archaeology, Asian studies, Canadian studies, classics, economics, English, ethnic studies, family science, film, French, geography, Germanic studies, Hispanic and Italian studies, history, international relations, linguistics, mathematics, music, philosophy, political science, psychology, religion and literature, religious studies, Romance studies and languages, Russian and Slavic languages and literatures, and sociology. The B.F.A. is offered in creative writing, fine arts, and theatre. The School of Music within the Faculty of Arts offers programs of study in performance and composition that lead to the B.Mus. as well as programs in musical scholarship and programs designed for prospective school teachers, both elementary and secondary.

The Faculty of Commerce and Business Administration offers undergraduate programs that lead to the Bachelor of Commerce (B.Comm.). The B.Comm. program consists of a year of study in either the Faculty of Arts or the Faculty of Science, followed by three years in the Faculty of Commerce and Business Administration. Options are available in accounting, commerce and economics, finance, general business management, industrial relations management, international business, management information systems, marketing, transportation and logistics, and urban land economics.

The Faculty of Dentistry offers a Bachelor of Dental Science (B.D.Sc.) in dental hygiene. Admission to the Doctor of Dental Medicine degree program requires completion of three academic years in the Faculty of Arts or the Faculty of Science at UBC or the equivalent.

The Faculty of Education offers initial teacher education leading to the Bachelor of Education (B.Ed.) in elementary teacher education, middle-years teacher education, and secondary teacher education. The latter provides a wide range of teaching concentrations, from arts and science to computer science and technology education. The School of Human Kinetics within the Faculty of Education offers a Bachelor of Human Kinetics (B.H.K.) in four courses of study: exercise science, health and fitness, leisure and sport management, and physical education.

The Faculty of Forestry offers the following four-year programs: a Bachelor of Science in Forestry (B.S.F.), with forest resources management and forest operations majors; a B.Sc. in natural resources conservation; a B.Sc. in wood products processing; and a B.Sc. (forestry) in forest science.

The Faculty of Law offers a Bachelor of Laws (LL.B.) upon successful completion of a three-year course that prepares students for admission to the practice of law. Admission to the Faculty of Law is competitive. To be eligible for selection, applicants must have obtained an undergraduate degree in an approved course of study or have successfully completed the first two years of an approved course of study at UBC (or another approved college or university) and be enrolled in the third year.

The Faculty of Medicine offers undergraduate programs of study that lead to the Doctor of Medicine (M.D.). Preference in the selection of candidates for admission to the Faculty of Medicine is currently given to well-qualified Canadian citizens and permanent residents residing in British Columbia. The Bachelor of Medical Laboratory Science (B.M.L.Sc.) offered by the Faculty of Medicine is granted upon the successful completion of a two-year program that consists of training in the theory and practice of medical laboratory science. A B.Sc. in occupational therapy and a B.Sc. in physical therapy are offered by the School of Rehabilitation Sciences within the Faculty of Medicine. Enrollment is limited, and primary consideration is given to residents of British Columbia.

The Faculty of Pharmaceutical Sciences offers courses that lead to the B.Sc. in pharmacy. For admission to the Faculty, students are required to complete the first year in the Faculty of Science with appropriate courses.

The Faculty of Science offers major and honours undergraduate programs that lead to the B.Sc. The B.Sc. can be earned in the following fields: aquacultural science, astronomy, atmospheric science, biochemistry, biology, chemistry, computer science, environmental sciences, general science, geography, geological sciences, geophysics, mathematics, microbiology, nutritional sciences, oceanography, pharmacology, physics, physiology, psychology, and statistics.

Academic Program

The academic year begins on the first day of September and ends on the last day of August. Winter Session consists of Term 1, from early September to late December, and Term 2, from early January to the end of April. Summer Session runs for two terms, May through August, but not all programs are offered during the Summer Session. In general, major or general programs require a minimum of 120 credits to obtain a bachelor's degree; honours programs may require 132 credits. Programs that allow for a cooperative education work term may take longer to complete. Co-op programs are available in the Faculties of Applied Sciences, Arts, Commerce and Business Administration, Forestry, and Science.

Off-Campus Arrangements

The University offers eighty-three exchange programs with universities in more than twenty-three countries and is a member of the Canadian Group of Ten Student Exchange Program and the Canadian University Study Abroad Programs. The Faculty of Commerce and Business Administration coordinates its own exchange programs through the Study Abroad and Exchange Office.

Academic Facilities

With nineteen branches, the University of British Columbia's library is one of the largest in Canada. The central libraries at UBC include the Walter C. Koerner Library (social sciences and humanities) and the Main Library (physical sciences and engineering). Students have access to free dial-in e-mail and direct access to the Internet. Most residences have access to the Internet over phone lines. A number of industry-related research centres and organizations are located on campus, including Tri-University Meson Facility (TRIUMF), one of the world's largest national accelerator facilities for research in subatomic physics.

Costs

UBC undergraduate program tuition fees for Canadian citizens and permanent residents for the 1999–2000 academic year were Can$76.50 per credit. Fees are higher in the Faculties of Dentistry, Law, and Medicine. A typical first-year course load of 30 credits cost Can$2295 plus applicable student fees. Tuition for a typical first-year course load for U.S. and international undergraduate students was Can$13,830. Room and board costs, plus other related living expenses for books, transportation, and health insurance, were approximately Can$9700 in 1999–2000.

Financial Aid

The University administers a number of merit-based awards for undergraduates, including major entrance scholarships for students who enter UBC from secondary school and the University's Undergraduate Scholarship Program, which recognizes students who achieve academic excellence. Students should contact UBC's Office of Awards and Financial Assistance for more information about application deadlines and for information about student loans and bursaries based on need.

Faculty

The University's full-time faculty members number 1,832, more than 97 percent of whom have earned a Ph.D. degree. UBC faculty members are regularly recognized with national awards for their outstanding teaching and achievement. UBC faculty innovations in teaching and learning have pioneered exceptional interdisciplinary first-year programs, such as Arts One and Arts Foundation and Science One and the Integrated Science option. Each of the faculties provides academic advising and mentoring programs to support undergraduate student achievement.

Student Government

Originally established in 1908, the Alma Mater Society (AMS) of UBC represents more than 30,000 students. The AMS is governed by a 45-member Student Council, which ensures student participation at all levels of student government, administers clubs, and lobbies the University and the provincial government on student-interest issues.

Admission Requirements

Admission to UBC is competitive and is based on a strong academic background. The minimum academic qualification for undergraduate admission is graduation from an accredited secondary school with an acceptable university preparatory curriculum and applicable program prerequisites. General admission for students following an American school system is based on four years of English and three years of math, with the admission average based on eight full-year academic courses: four from grade 11 and four from grade 12. There are also specific program requirements in math, chemistry, physics, and/or biology for students applying to science-based programs. First-year course credit is possible for students achieving a minimum grade of 5 on International Baccalaureate (I.B.) Arts courses and a minimum grade of 6 for I.B. Science courses. Students who achieve a final grade of 4 or better on Advanced Placement courses may receive credit for first-year UBC courses. SAT I scores are not required, but students are encouraged to submit them as they can be helpful in the evaluation process. UCB welcomes applications from well-qualified students at recognized universities and colleges who wish to transfer to UBC. Transfer students are expected to have completed the equivalent of 30 UBC credits before seeking admission to a second year at UBC. Applicants must complete an application for admission accompanied by a nonrefundable application fee. Early admission is possible for students with strong academic standing who are enrolled in their final year of secondary school. Students whose first language is not English are required to demonstrate competence prior to admission in English listening, reading, speaking, and writing skills using one of the standard English language proficiency tests.

Application and Information

Students are encouraged to apply to the University early to allow sufficient time for applications to be evaluated and processed. The deadline for undergraduate applications for September admission is April 30. Applications for Summer Session must be received by February 28. Application deadlines are earlier for some programs that may require a portfolio, audition, or manuscript. It is possible to apply directly to UBC via the Internet (http://www.admissions.ubc.ca).

Information Centre, Student Services
1874 East Mall, Brock Hall
University of British Columbia
Vancouver, British Columbia V6T 1Z1
Canada

For further information, Candian citizens and permanent residents should contact:
Telephone: 604-822-9836
Fax: 604-822-9858
E-mail: student.information@ubc.ca
World Wide Web: http://www.student-services.ubc.ca

For further information, U.S. and international students should contact:
Telephone: 604-822-8999
Fax: 604-822-9888
E-mail: international.reception@ubc.ca
World Wide Web: http://www.international.ubc.ca

UNIVERSITY OF CALIFORNIA, RIVERSIDE
RIVERSIDE, CALIFORNIA

The University

UC Riverside is one of nine general campuses of the University of California, one of the finest public universities in the world.

A major research institution, the University of California, Riverside (UCR), places significant emphasis on excellence in teaching. The student population is growing, but the campus remains relatively small and maintains a strong focus on undergraduate education. The campus is composed of the College of Humanities, Arts, and Social Sciences; the College of Natural and Agricultural Sciences; The Marlan and Rosemary Bourns College of Engineering; the School of Education; and The A. Gary Anderson Graduate School of Management.

Campus social and cultural life is very active. There are 180 student clubs, including twenty-one national fraternities and sororities and various multicultural, religious, academic, social, recreational, and community service interest groups. Several student newspapers serve the campus, as well as a campus radio station. This year, UCR begins competing in NCAA Division I athletics in the Big West Conference. The 80,000-square-foot Recreation Center offers extensive facilities, and about half of the students participate in intramural and recreational programs. Numerous recreational and cultural options for students include Wednesday "Nooner" bands; craft fairs; film series; extensive multicultural and special events; professional drama, music, and dance events as well as those offered by the UCR fine arts academic departments; speakers; and the residence unit activities.

The campus prides itself on personal attention and provides the individual support necessary for students to succeed. An extensive array of services includes academic support, career advising and placement, part-time job and internship placement, services for disabled and reentry/transfer students, health and personal counseling, multicultural programs, international services, and others.

Riverside enrolled 11,600 men and women in fall 1999. The 10,120 undergraduate students enrolled in seventy-three majors and forty-five minors. The 1,480 graduate students enrolled in thirty-seven Ph.D. programs, thirty-nine master's programs, and seven teaching and administrative credential programs. The incoming undergraduate class was about three quarters freshmen and one quarter transfer students from other two- and four-year colleges. Ninety-four percent of the undergraduate students are California residents. The ethnic mix of the student body was 38 percent Asian, 28 percent Caucasian, 19 percent Chicano/Latino, 5 percent African American, 1 percent Native American, and 2 percent of other ethnicities.

Twenty-five percent of UCR students live on campus in 1,800 residence hall spaces, 600 apartment spaces, and 268 family housing units. About 70 percent of incoming freshmen live in residence halls. All housing units have extensive services and social and cultural activities. Housing is readily available to new students, and rental rates are some of the most reasonable in California. Referral to ample off-campus housing is also available.

Location

UCR is set on 1,200 parklike acres and is located in the city of Riverside. The campus is approximately 60 miles east of Los Angeles and within an hour of Palm Springs, Big Bear Lake, mountain resorts, and the southern California beaches. Riverside, which has a population of approximately 250,000, is located in the rapidly expanding Inland Empire and offers numerous restaurants, shopping areas, theaters, museums, and performing groups.

Majors and Degrees

Undergraduate majors include African-American studies, anthropology, art history, art history/religious studies, art studio, Asian-American studies, Asian studies, biochemistry, biological studies, biology, biomedical sciences, botany and plant science, business administration, business economics, chemical engineering, chemistry, Chicano studies, Chinese, classical studies, comparative ancient civilizations, comparative literature, computer science, computer engineering, conservation biology, creative writing, dance, economics, economics/administrative studies, economics/law and society, electrical engineering, English, entomology, environmental engineering, environmental sciences, ethnic studies, French, geography, geology, geophysics, German, history, history/administrative studies, history/law and society, human development, humanities and social sciences interdisciplinary studies, language, Latin American studies, liberal studies, linguistics, mathematics, mechanical engineering, music, Native American studies, neurosciences, philosophy, philosophy/law and society, physics, political science, political science/administrative studies, political science/law and society, psychology, public service–political science, religious studies, Russian studies, social relations, sociology, sociology/administrative studies, sociology/law and society, Spanish, statistics, theater, and women's studies.

Academic Program

Degree programs are designed to expose students to both the breadth and depth of the University's curriculum by combining a wide distribution of courses with the opportunity to concentrate course work in a selected field or major. Riverside's University Honors Program is available to both freshmen and transfer students. The Biomedical Sciences Program offers successful students guaranteed admission to UCLA's medical school and the opportunity to earn the bachelor's and M.D. degrees in seven years instead of eight. The B.S. degree in business administration is one of only two such programs in the University of California. The engineering program has six major areas.

Classes at UCR are small, and there is easy access to faculty members. Two thirds have fewer than 25 students. The vast majority of incoming freshman students graduate in four years or less. Extensive undergraduate research and off-campus internship opportunities for academic credit are also available. Placement rates to medical, law, business, and doctoral programs are excellent.

Off-Campus Arrangements

Each year, about 30 UCR students participate in the Education Abroad Program, with opportunities available in more than thirty-five countries. Students may participate in the program at all levels, with the traditional year abroad taken as a junior. Substantial financial aid is available to bring this opportunity within the reach of qualified students who need financial help.

Academic Facilities

UCR's outstanding academic facilities include five libraries with 1.9 million volumes and more than 13,000 periodicals. Extensive computer access enhances student research.

Costs

Fees for 1999–2000 were $3937 for California residents, and room and board in the residence halls were $6900. Nonresidents are assessed tuition of $13,925 in addition to fees.

Financial Aid

More than half of the students enrolled on the Riverside campus receive some type of assistance in the form of grants, scholarships, fellowships, loans, or work-study support. Approximately $30 million is distributed to assist students. A full-need student can receive up to $13,000 in assistance, with a substantial portion provided in the form of grants.

Faculty

Riverside faculty members include many distinguished research scientists and scholars who have received numerous Guggenheim Fellowships. For the fifth straight year, UCR has led the nation in the number of researchers elected to the American Association for the Advancement of Science. Nine of UCR's professors were elected this year. As a research university, 98 percent of UCR's faculty members have doctorates and are active in ongoing research in their areas of specialty in addition to undergraduate and graduate instruction, which provides all students with cutting-edge instruction. The low student-faculty ratio assures students ample opportunity for interaction with professors.

Student Government

Associated Students of the University of California, Riverside (ASUCR), the student government organization, acts as the official student voice. All undergraduates are automatically members of ASUCR, and 20 students are elected to serve on the senate of the governing body. In both 1994–95 and 1995–96, a UC Riverside student represented all University of California students on the Board of Regents.

Admission Requirements

Eligibility for admission to Riverside is limited to graduates of California high schools who rank in the top 12.5 percent of their graduating class, graduates of out-of-state high schools who are highly qualified, and students with above-average academic records and the appropriate courses completed who wish to transfer from other colleges and universities. Freshman applicants must meet the eligibility requirements established for grade point average, performance on standardized college entrance examinations, and content of the student's secondary school courses. Minimum eligibility requirements are the same for all campuses of the University of California. Information on specific requirements and the application form may be obtained from high school or community college counselors or from UCR.

Application and Information

UCR accepts applications for all majors for fall quarter and for most majors during winter and spring. Applications for biochemistry, biological sciences, biology, biomedical sciences, chemistry, and majors in engineering are accepted for fall quarter only. The application priority filing period for the fall quarter is November 1 to 30. July 1 to 31 is the application priority filing period for winter quarter applicants, and October 1 to 31 for spring quarter applicants. Students are urged to submit their applications within the appropriate priority filing period to ensure full consideration for admission and scholarships. Campus tours and overnight HOST programs are also available.

Applicant inquiries should be directed to:

Office of Relations with Schools
1120 Hinderaker Hall
University of California
Riverside, California 92521-0219

Telephone: 909-787-4531
E-mail: discover@pop.ucr.edu
World Wide Web: http://www.students.ucr.edu

The Marlan and Rosemary Bourns College of Engineering.

UNIVERSITY OF CENTRAL ARKANSAS
CONWAY, ARKANSAS

The University

The University of Central Arkansas (UCA) strives to be Arkansas' best and most beautiful public university. Established in 1907, UCA has experienced significant growth and change in recent years. Long home to students from throughout Arkansas, UCA also enrolls students from about half of the other states and more recently has added a sizeable international population. The enrollment of 9,000 students is 60 percent women, 40 percent men, 25 percent nontraditional (age 25 and up), 15 percent minority, and 5 percent international. A 35 percent enrollment gain since the late 1980s has come in the face of rising admission standards. In addition to the enhanced academic environment, students benefit from more than $100 million in construction and improvement projects that have resulted in facilities and grounds praised for their beauty.

The most accessible campus in the state, UCA offers on-campus housing for more than 2,000 students. International students are housed in Minton Hall, where their special needs are accommodated. Students in the nationally acclaimed Honors College also enjoy unique housing in campus residence halls.

There are more than 100 fields of study offered at UCA, including master's degrees in twenty-five fields, and the Ph.D. in physical therapy and school psychology. Academic programs have consistently ranked high or highest in independent reviews. The University is accredited by the North Central Association of Colleges and Secondary Schools and the National Council for the Accreditation of Teacher Education as a bachelor's, master's, and specialist's degree–granting institution. The master's and baccalaureate degrees in business administration are accredited by the AACSB–The International Association for Management Education. The master's and baccalaureate degrees in nursing are accredited by the National League for Nursing Accrediting Commission. The baccalaureate programs in medical technology, radiography, respiratory therapy, and nuclear medicine technology are accredited in affiliated professional education programs by the Commission on Accreditation of Allied Health Education Programs of the American Medical Association. The baccalaureate program in occupational therapy is accredited by the American Occupational Therapy Association's Accreditation Council for Occupational Therapy Education. The master's degree program in speech-language pathology is accredited by the American Speech-Language-Hearing Association. Associate, baccalaureate, and master's degree programs in physical therapy are accredited by the Commission on Accreditation in Physical Therapy Education of the American Physical Therapy Association. The graduate dietetic internship program has been granted developmental accreditation status by the Commission on Accreditation for Dietetic Education of the American Dietetic Association. The University of Central Arkansas is an accredited institutional member of the National Association of Schools of Art and Design. The music program is accredited by the National Association of Schools of Music; the theater program is accredited by the National Association of Schools of Theatre. The master's degree program in school psychology is accredited by the National Association of School Psychology. Accreditation documentation is available in the President's Office. Students successfully completing a specified course of study in chemistry are certified by the American Chemical Society.

UCA's 262-acre campus has thirty-eight major buildings, including twelve residence halls, a fully computerized library, and a dozen academic buildings housing the six colleges—Business Administration, Education, Fine Arts and Communication, Health and Applied Sciences, Liberal Arts, and Natural Sciences and Mathematics. A new student center and physical therapy building have been completed, and a new activities center, communications building, conference center, and performance hall are under construction. UCA offers men's and women's intercollegiate athletics within the NCAA and competes in the Gulf South Conference, one of the strongest in Division II. Campus life is busy with Greek organizations, intramural athletics, student government, newspaper, yearbook, departmental and honor organizations, and an array of guest lectures, concerts, and special programs available on a regular basis.

UCA offers Associate of Arts, Associate of Applied Sciences, Associate of Sciences, Bachelor of Arts, Bachelor of Business Administration, Bachelor of Fine Arts, Bachelor of Music, Bachelor of Science, Bachelor of Science in Education, and Bachelor of Science in Nursing undergraduate degrees. At the graduate level, UCA offers Master of Arts, Master of Business Administration, Master of Music, Master of Music Education, Master of Science, Master of Science in Nursing, Educational Specialist, and Doctor of Philosophy in physical therapy degrees.

Location

UCA's campus is surrounded by residential areas in Conway, a thriving city of 40,000, just 30 minutes from Little Rock. Near the dividing line of two distinct geographic regions, the Delta and the Ozark mountains, the Conway area offers abundant outdoor recreational opportunities. One of the most desirable places to live in Arkansas, Conway is casual in atmosphere, yet bustling with college-related activity. The city is also the home of two other colleges, Hendrix and Central Baptist.

Majors and Degrees

Programs of study in the College of Business Administration include accounting, business administration, economics, finance, information systems, international trade, management, and marketing. Programs of study in the College of Education include advanced guidance counseling, advanced guidance supervision, business education, community service counseling, counseling psychology, early childhood education, early childhood and special education–mildly handicapped K–12, early childhood and special education–moderately and profoundly handicapped K–12, early childhood and special education–seriously emotionally disturbed K–12, educational leadership, elementary education, elementary education–gifted education emphasis, elementary school counseling, elementary school leadership, elementary–special education, industrial technology, library media and information technology, psychology, reading, school psychology, secondary school leadership, special education–mildly handicapped K–12, special education–moderately and profoundly handicapped K–12, special education–seriously emotionally disturbed K–12, student personnel services in higher education, technology education, and vocational–industrial education. Programs of study in the College of Fine Arts and Communication include art, journalism, mass communication, music, prearchitecture, pre–landscape architecture, speech, studio art, and theater. Programs of study in the College of Health and Applied Sciences include child-care management, family and consumer sciences–dietetics, family and consumer sciences–interior design, health education, health sciences, kinesiology, medical technology, nursing, occupational therapy, physical therapy, physical therapy assisting, radiography, respiratory therapy, and speech-language pathology. Programs of study in the College of Liberal Arts include English, French, geography, history, philosophy, prelaw, public administration, social studies, sociology, and Spanish. Programs of study in the College of Natural Sciences and Mathematics include biology, chemistry, computer science, general science, mathematics, physical science, physics, predentistry, pre–dental hygiene, pre-engineering, premedicine, preoptometry, prepharmacy, and pre–veterinary medicine.

Academic Program

UCA operates on a traditional two-semester academic year with two regular summer sessions and some concurrent summer sessions. Three-week intersessions are conducted for a limited number of courses in May and December. Courses are offered weekdays and evenings. In addition to their major and minor fields of study, students take courses in the general education curriculum as well as courses that satisfy specific degree requirements. The general education curriculum at UCA consists of a minimum of 9 hours of world cultural traditions, 8 hours of laboratory sciences, 6 hours each of composition and social sciences, and 3 hours each of oral communication, mathematics, fine arts, history/government, health studies, and humanities. The majority of the baccalaureate degree programs are four-year plans requiring 124 to 136 semester credit hours for graduation; there are some exceptions to this requirement, such as the programs in physical therapy and occupational therapy, which are rich in field experiences. English as a second language classes are offered through the Intensive English program on a year-round basis. These classes are coordinated by the Office of International Programs. In addition to department honors, the University has a University Honors College for outstanding students. A student chosen for this program fulfills certain general education requirements in specially designed classes that are interdisciplinary and limited in enrollment.

Off-Campus Arrangements

UCA offers several off-campus opportunities. Credit and noncredit classes are offered both on and off campus by the Division of Continuing Education. Opportunities for study abroad are available through the Office of International Programs. Several degree programs use electronic delivery systems to provide instruction to distance learning extension centers located throughout the state.

Academic Facilities

The thirty-eight major buildings, valued at $120 million, occupy a beautiful 262-acre campus. Torreyson Library is a government document depository with 25,000 volumes available. The library contains 380,000 volumes, 2,700 subscriptions to periodicals and journals, 83,000 titles on microform, and 4,000 sound recordings. All campus buildings are connected by a network of fiber-optic cables, which allows full participation by all academic departments and administrative offices in the modern campus computing facility. The University is connected to the Internet and a statewide educational computer network. Several computer labs containing a variety of platforms and popular software are available across the campus. The University Writing Center blends one-on-one tutorials with the latest in word processing; the Center for Academic Success is available to assist students in developing study skills; and departmental tutorial centers assist students in realizing their full potential in lower-division courses.

Costs

In 2000–01, the full-time tuition rate, including activity fees, is $1662 per semester for in-state students (Arkansas residents); nonresidents pay $3033 per semester. Among those taking fewer than 12 credit hours, Arkansas residents pay $138.50 per hour, and nonresidents pay $253 per hour. Room and board are $1645 per semester. The average cost of books is $300 per semester. Students 60 years of age and older attend UCA tuition-free.

Financial Aid

Anyone who needs financial assistance to attend UCA and is a citizen or permanent resident of the United States may apply for financial aid. Scholarships are available based on academic, fine arts, and athletic skills. UCA administers federal programs, including Federal Pell Grant, Federal Supplemental Educational Opportunity Grant, Federal Perkins Loan, Federal Stafford Student Loan, Federal PLUS, and Federal Work-Study. State programs, including Governor's Scholarship, Arkansas Academic Challenge Scholarship, Emergency Secondary Education Loan, and Arkansas Student Assistance Grant, are also available. Students must submit the Free Application for Federal Student Aid (FAFSA).

Faculty

UCA has 385 full-time teaching faculty members and 157 part-time faculty members. Most faculty members hold the highest degree in their fields. For international students, an international student adviser and a fully staffed Office of International Programs are available with orientation sessions, immigration counseling, and activities programming.

Student Government

Through various committees and organizations, particularly the Student Government Association, students have the opportunity to express their interests or opinions and to participate in the overall policymaking and decision-making processes of UCA.

Admission Requirements

Admission to the University of Central Arkansas is based on a number of factors, including high school GPA, ACT/SAT I scores, high school curriculum, and evidence of special abilities, talents, or achievements. Transfer students are required to have a cumulative GPA of at least 2.0 on all college work attempted.

International students must submit an application form, official transcripts of all secondary and university work (including English translation), a Confirmation of Financial Resources Form, and a nonrefundable application fee of $40 drawn from a U.S. bank or an international money order. In addition, any prospective international student whose first language is not English must present a minimum TOEFL score of 500.

Application and Information

Each applicant is required to submit a completed application for admission and show proof of immunization against measles and rubella. Entering freshmen must submit a high school transcript or GED test scores and ACT or SAT I test scores. Transfer students are required to send an official transcript of record from each institution of college rank attended. For further information or application forms, students should contact:

Office of Admissions
University of Central Arkansas
201 Donaghey Avenue
Conway, Arkansas 72035-0001
Telephone: 501-450-3128
           800-243-8245 (toll-free)
Fax: 501-450-5228
E-mail: admission@ecom.uca.edu

Office of International Programs
University of Central Arkansas
201 Donaghey Avenue
Conway, Arkansas 72035-0001
Telephone: 501-450-3445
Fax: 501-450-5095
E-mail: oip@ccl.uca.edu
World Wide Web: http://www.uca.edu/

UNIVERSITY OF CENTRAL FLORIDA
ORLANDO, FLORIDA

The University

The University of Central Florida is a comprehensive, metropolitan university with approximately 31,700 students. As one of the nation's fastest-growing universities, UCF enrolls a diverse student body representing forty-nine states and 114 countries. The University offers educational and research programs that complement a surging economy, with strong components in aerospace, banking, film, electronics, health, social sciences, and tourism. UCF's programs in communication and the fine arts help to meet the cultural and recreational needs of a growing metropolitan area. The University also offers many graduate programs leading to master's and doctoral degrees. UCF is accredited by the Commission on Colleges of the Southern Association of Colleges and Schools. In addition, a number of scientific, professional, and academic bodies confer accreditation in specific disciplines and groups of disciplines. In the College of Arts and Sciences, accreditation is conferred in chemistry by the American Chemical Society, in music by the National Association of Schools of Music, and in computer science by the Computing Sciences Accreditation Board. The programs of the College of Business Administration are accredited at the undergraduate and graduate levels by the American Assembly of Collegiate Schools of Business. In the College of Engineering, programs are accredited by the Engineering Accreditation Commission of the Accreditation Board for Engineering and Technology (ABET). Also, engineering technology programs in design, electronics, and operations engineering technology are accredited by the Technology Accreditation Commission of ABET. In the College of Health and Public Affairs, programs have been approved by the agencies indicated: health information management by the American Medical Record Association; medical records administration, medical technology, and radiologic technology, accredited by the Committee on Allied Health Education and Accreditation and the National Accrediting Agency for Clinical Laboratory Services; nursing, by the National League for Nursing Accrediting Commission and the Florida Board of Nursing; cardiopulmonary sciences, by the American Registry of Respiratory Therapists; speech pathology and audiology, by the American Speech-Language and Hearing Association; and social work, by the Council of Social Work Education. All teacher education programs are fully accredited by the Florida State Department of Education and by the National Council for Accreditation of Teacher Education.

UCF has established extensive partnerships with business and industry in the Central Florida area that provide students with exceptional research and learning experiences. These partnerships bring practical learning environments to UCF students through co-op and internship programs. Joint curriculum development strategies include BE2020, a widely modeled business curriculum incorporating classes taught by local business and industry executives.

The housing facilities on campus include traditional residence halls, apartment-style options, and Greek housing accommodating more than 2,200 students. Construction of new residential facilities that are designed as academic villages will begin this year and will accomodate 1,600 students. Several thousand students live in apartments located within walking distance of the campus. Approximately 400 students live in on-campus Greek housing.

Students participate in more than 250 organizations, including special interest clubs, multicultural associations, fraternities and sororities, honor societies, and academic and preprofessional organizations. The Offices of Student Life and Student Activities schedule a wide array of extracurricular programs, including concerts, movies, and guest speakers.

The University of Central Florida is a member of the NCAA and the Trans America Athletic Conference. All teams compete on the NCAA Division I level. UCF's men's teams compete in intercollegiate baseball, basketball, cross-country, football, golf, soccer, tennis, and track. Women's teams compete in basketball, cross-country, golf, soccer, tennis, track, and volleyball. Women's softball will be added in 2001. Intercollegiate coed club activities include championship cheerleading, crew, and waterskiing teams. The University intramural sports program offers disc golf, flag football, floor hockey, racquetball, soccer, softball, tennis, and volleyball.

Location

The University of Central Florida is located on 1,445 acres approximately 13 miles east of downtown Orlando. Branch campuses are located in Daytona Beach and Cocoa.

Majors and Degrees

The University awards the degrees of Bachelor of Arts, Bachelor of Fine Arts, Bachelor of Science, Bachelor of Science in Business Administration, Bachelor of Science in Aerospace Engineering, Bachelor of Science in Civil Engineering, Bachelor of Science in Computer Engineering, Bachelor of Science in Environmental Engineering, Bachelor of Science in Industrial Engineering, Bachelor of Science in Mechanical Engineering, Bachelor of Science in Engineering Technology, Bachelor of Science in Nursing, and Bachelor of Social Work. These degrees are available in the colleges listed below, with majors or areas of specialization as indicated.

The College of Arts and Sciences offers degrees in advertising, animation, anthropology, art, biological science, chemistry, communication, economics, English, film, foreign language combination, forensic science, French, history, humanities, journalism, liberal studies, mathematics, music, music education, philosophy, physics, political science, psychology, public relations, radio-television, social science (interdisciplinary), sociology, Spanish, speech, statistics, and theater. A preprofessional program in law is also offered.

The College of Business Administration offers degrees in accounting, economics, finance, general business administration, hospitality management, management, management information systems, and marketing.

The College of Education offers degrees in art education, early childhood education, elementary education, English language arts education, exceptional-child education, foreign language education, mathematics education, physical education, science education, social science education, and vocational education and industrial training.

The College of Engineering and Computer Science offers degrees in aerospace, civil, computer, electrical, environmental, industrial, and mechanical engineering and in computer science. The Bachelor of Science in Engineering Technology (B.S.E.T.) is awarded in computer, design, electronics, information systems, and operations engineering technology.

The College of Health and Public Affairs offers degrees in cardiopulmonary sciences, communicative disorders, criminal justice, health information management, health services administration, legal studies, medical laboratory sciences, molecular biology and microbiology, nursing, physical therapy (five-year master's program), public administration, radiologic sciences, and social work. Preprofessional programs are offered in chiropractic medicine, dentistry, medicine, optometry, pharmacy, podiatry, and veterinary medicine.

Academic Program

UCF provides for total education through a core curriculum of 36 hours of general education courses. In addition to fulfilling the general education requirement, each student must complete the necessary major and/or minor requirements to reach the minimum of 120 semester hours necessary for graduation.

Several special programs help students reach their academic and leadership potential. The UCF Honors College encourages students to achieve academic excellence through small classes and interactive symposiums. The innovative Leadership Enrichment and Academic Development (LEAD) Scholars Program fosters leadership and service commitment through a comprehensive student development program for freshmen. The Academic Exploration Program (AEP) helps entering freshmen define their career goals and develop an academic strategy to reach those goals. The University also offers an increasing number of Web-based courses and degree programs.

The University offers Air Force and Army ROTC programs.

Off-Campus Arrangements

A cooperative education program is offered, in which students alternate semesters of classroom study with equal periods of paid employment in government, industry, or business. The Department of Foreign Languages offers summer study programs in Canada, Eastern Europe, France, Germany, Italy, Poland, Spain, Sweden, and Russia. Courses are available in the subject areas of language (all levels), art, and civilization. UCF is also a participant in the National Student Exchange Consortium.

Academic Facilities

In addition to the academic programs offered on the main campus in Orlando, students can work toward a degree at campuses located in Daytona Beach, Cocoa, and South Orlando. Both the Daytona Beach and Cocoa campuses work cooperatively with local community colleges to provide all four years of course work in many academic areas. The library houses nearly 1.1 million volumes and subscribes to more than 7,000 periodicals and journals. In addition, students have access to an online computer catalog that provides information on the collections of the State University System libraries. An IBM 4341 and an IBM 4381 are located in the Computer Center, and an extensive online network of more than 500 computer terminals and a network of nearly 1,000 IBM PCs cover the campus. The Institute for Simulation and Training gives students the opportunity to pursue undergraduate research. The School of Optics allows faculty members and students to work directly with industrial personnel in conducting basic and applied research at the regional and national level. The Central Florida Research Park, located next to the UCF campus, houses more than seventy important high-technology firms and agencies. This proximity fosters relationships between industry and the University, which strengthens the academic programs at the University.

Costs

For Florida residents, the cost of tuition and fees in 1999–2000, based on a full-time course load, was $2297 for the year; for out-of-state residents, $9285. Room and board were $5429 per year, and costs for books and supplies were approximately $750.

Financial Aid

Financial aid is awarded according to each student's need in relation to college costs and may include grants, loans, scholarships, and/or part-time employment. The priority application deadline is March 15. Programs based on need include the Federal Perkins Loan, Federal Pell Grant, Florida Student Assistance Grant, Federal Work-Study, Florida College Career Work-Study Program, and Federal Stafford Student Loan. To qualify for these programs, students must complete the Free Application for Federal Student Aid. Approximately 66 percent of UCF students receive some form of financial aid.

Faculty

The University's faculty consists of more than 700 full-time members and 403 adjunct members. More than 80 percent of the full-time faculty members hold a doctoral degree. Undergraduate instruction is given by the full-time and adjunct faculty primarily; graduate students play a very minor role in undergraduate instruction. Students are assigned to faculty advisers in their area of specialization for assistance in academic matters. The student-faculty ratio is 16:1.

Student Government

UCF's Student Government Association, voted the best in Florida for three of the last four years, provides an opportunity for students to become involved at UCF. Every enrolled UCF student is a member of Student Government and is encouraged to voice his or her opinion through senate representatives. Student Government is divided into three branches—the elected executive branch, the elected legislative branch, and the appointed judicial branch. Student Government is responsible for allocation of all activity and services fees paid by students as part of their tuition. This money goes toward many student services, such as the on-campus Macintosh lab, homecoming activities, campus activities board, legal services, and funding for clubs and organizations. Admission is free to all events directly sponsored by the Student Government with activity and services fees.

Admission Requirements

A freshman applicant is a student with fewer than 12 hours of college course work after high school graduation. The most important criterion in the admissions decision for these applicants is the high school academic record: quality and level of difficulty of courses, grade point average, grade trends, consistency, and SAT I or ACT test scores. If the number of qualified applicants exceeds the number that the University is permitted to enroll, a waiting list is established. UCF operates on a rolling admissions basis. Students are generally notified of their admissions decision within two to four weeks after receipt of all supporting documents.

All applicants must have earned a minimum of 19 high school academic units (yearlong courses that are not remedial in nature). These include 4 units of English (3 must include substantial writing), 3 units of mathematics (at or above algebra I), 3 units of natural science (2 must include a laboratory), 3 units of social science, 2 units of one foreign language, and 4 units of academic electives. Grades in honors courses, International Baccalaureate, and Advanced Placement courses are given additional weight in the GPA computation. Students must meet the State University System minimum eligibility to be considered for admission.

Transfer applicants with fewer than 60 credit hours of college course work must submit high school transcripts, SAT I or ACT test scores, and college transcripts. Transfer students with more than 60 credit hours or who have earned an Associate of Arts or Associate of Science degree from a Florida public community college need only submit all college transcripts. A transfer credit summary evaluation is provided to students once they are accepted to the University.

Application and Information

Students are encouraged to apply several months in advance. Applications are accepted up to a year prior to the start of the term for which entry is desired. Priority application deadlines are May 15 for the fall semester, November 15 for the spring semester, and April 15 for the summer term.

Campus tours are given Monday through Friday at 10 a.m. and 2 p.m. (except holidays). Appointments are encouraged. For additional information, students should call Undergraduate Admissions at the number below, which also serves as a 24-hour application request line.

Office of Undergraduate Admissions
University of Central Florida
P.O. Box 160111
Orlando, Florida 32816-0111
Telephone: 407-823-3000
E-mail: admission@mail.ucf.edu
World Wide Web: http://www.ucf.edu

UNIVERSITY OF CHARLESTON
CHARLESTON, WEST VIRGINIA

The University

The University of Charleston strives to educate each student for a life of productive work, enlightened living, and community involvement. Therefore, the University takes very seriously its responsibility to provide students with the knowledge, abilities, and character necessary for them to have successful careers and to be active citizens.

Founded in 1888 and formerly known as Morris Harvey College, the University acquired its new name in 1979 when it began offering several graduate degrees. Today, 1,200 students representing twenty-nine states and twenty other countries enjoy the University's 40-acre riverfront campus overlooking the State Capitol Complex and the beautiful city of Charleston. Education at the University of Charleston focuses on learning and asks students to demonstrate what they have learned in order to earn the credits necessary for graduation. Demonstrable knowledge and skills in the areas of communication, critical thinking, citizenship, creative responsiveness, and ethical practice are integrated with knowledge and skills in a field of study. Future employers and graduate schools consistently recruit college graduates with these abilities. The University of Charleston has designed a program to help students master the knowledge and skills that are necessary for success.

Because the University believes that students learn from their involvement in community and campus activities, students are strongly encouraged to participate in one or more of the forty cocurricular organizations found at the University. There are academic clubs, publications, fraternities, sororities, religious organizations, intramural sports, honorary societies, drama, cheerleading, chorus and music ensembles, and many student leadership organizations. The University's Colleague program integrates student involvement, the academic curriculum, community service, and leadership. The Community Service Program provides opportunities for students to participate both on-campus and in the Charleston area. In addition, there are numerous civic, political, social, and charitable organizations easily accessible in the community.

The varsity sports program for men and women has become one of the University's most valuable assets. Men may participate in baseball, basketball, crew, golf, soccer, swimming, and tennis. Women may participate in basketball, crew, soccer, softball, swimming, tennis, and volleyball. The University's varsity athletic teams compete in Division II of the NCAA. In recent years, men's and women's teams have been contenders in the WVIAC tournaments, with some teams winning conference championships and attending national championship tournaments.

The University of Charleston is accredited by the North Central Association of Colleges and Schools; National Council for Accreditation of Teacher Education; National Athletic Trainers Association; Committee on Allied Health Education and Accreditation of the American Medical Association in cooperation with the Joint Review Committee on Education in Radiologic Technology; Committee on Allied Health Education and Accreditation of the American Medical Association in cooperation with the Joint Review Committee for Respiratory Therapy Education; Accreditation Association in Continuing Higher Education; and the National League for Nursing. The University holds a variety of professional recognitions, approvals, and memberships, including the AACSB–The International Association for Management Education.

Master's degrees are offered in Business Administration and Human Resources Management. The University also offers an Executive M.B.A. and a plus-one M.B.A. for full-time study one year beyond the bachelor's degree.

Location

Charleston, the state capital, is the cultural, social, political, and economic hub of West Virginia. Located in the Kanawha Valley, near the foothills of the Appalachian Mountains, it offers scenic tranquillity as well as the convenience and excitement of a modern city. With a metropolitan population of 250,000, Charleston has grown to be West Virginia's finest city. Accessibility to the city is quite easy via bus, car, plane, and train. A large civic center, historic sites, libraries, movie theaters, shopping malls, and a symphony orchestra are all highlights of the Charleston business district. The rapport between the University and the community is excellent, and many events are cosponsored annually. Downtown Charleston, just a 10-minute ride from the campus by campus shuttle or city bus, offers the kind of social and cultural opportunities that can be found only in a large city. In addition, fishing, hunting, horseback riding, waterskiing, snow skiing, and white-water rafting are just a few of the many recreational activities to be found within a short distance of the campus.

Majors and Degrees

The University of Charleston offers undergraduate degree programs through its various divisions: the Morris Harvey Division of Arts and Sciences, the Jones-Benedum Division of Business, and the Division of Health Sciences.

The Morris Harvey Division of Arts and Sciences offers the Bachelor of Arts degree with the following majors: art, art administration, education (elementary and secondary), English, general studies, history, interior design, mass communications, music, music administration, philosophy and religion, political science, psychology, and social science. The Bachelor of Science degree is offered with majors in biology, biology/chemistry (premedicine), chemistry, environmental science, general studies, mathematics, and physical education.

The Jones-Benedum Division of Business offers Bachelor of Science degree programs in accounting, business administration (with concentrations in finance, management, and marketing), computer information systems, and hospitality management. Associate of Science degree programs are offered in accounting, business administration, and computer information systems. Associate of Arts degree and certificate programs are offered in paralegal studies.

The Division of Health Sciences offers the Bachelor of Science degree in nursing, radiography, respiratory care, and sports medicine. Also offered is an Associate in Science degree program in nursing.

Academic Program

Candidates for a bachelor's degree from the University of Charleston are required to complete a minimum of 120 semester hours and have a cumulative grade point average of at least 2.0 on all college work attempted. This must include 30 hours in upper-division courses, a prescribed program of general education courses, and advanced work leading to a major in a department or a division. The minimum requirement for an associate degree is 60 semester hours and a cumulative grade point average of at least 2.0 on all college work attempted, including completion of a prescribed program of general education and specialized work in a department or in the liberal arts or the sciences.

Students may pursue directed independent study and internships in most majors. ROTC is offered to interested men and women. The Byrd Institute of Government Studies offers special opportunities to work with state and local governments.

The University follows a semester academic calendar and offers summer terms for students who wish to accelerate their college program.

Academic Facilities

A large number of support facilities and programs supplement the various academic offerings at the University of Charleston. The Schoenbaum Library serves as the center of the learning experience. Located in the Clay Center, it has a collection of 109,000 books, 130,800 titles on microfilm, 2,160 media items, and 500 serial and periodical titles selected to support the liberal arts and professional undergraduate and graduate curricula. In addition, numerous specialized collections, CD-ROM-based electronic indexes, and online electronic search services are at the students' disposal for specialized research and study.

The University has several computer labs for student and faculty use: the Cabot Apple Lab, IBM-PC combination classroom labs, an IBM-PC network lab, and an IBM-PC open lab. The Multi-Media Educational Technological (MET) Center offers a range of services that are available to the University community, including personal and group tutoring, audio and video tutorials, and software related to specific courses.

Riggleman Hall, the main college building, houses many classrooms, lecture halls, science laboratories, a greenhouse, a 976-seat auditorium and stage, educational and language laboratories, and the well-equipped Carleton Varney Department of Art and Design area.

Costs

For the academic year 2000–01, tuition costs $13,200, room (double occupancy) costs $1870, and board costs $2610 for a total of $17,680. This does not include the cost of books, insurance, or laboratory fees.

Financial Aid

The University of Charleston provides financial assistance that may include a combination of scholarships, grants, loans, and work-study. In 1999–2000, 90 percent of full-time students and 80 percent of part-time students received some form of financial aid. The average assistance level was more than $9000. Special academic scholarships and grants are awarded to outstanding full-time students. The University also offers grants to qualified athletes and to students who are involved in leadership, community service, or vocal music.

Faculty

The University has 65 full-time and 50 part-time undergraduate faculty members. Sixty-eight percent of full-time faculty members hold doctoral or other terminal degrees. At the University of Charleston, faculty members provide academic, career, and, in some cases, personal advice to students. These personal relationships are cultivated through a student-faculty ratio of 13:1.

Student Government

The Student Government Association is a policymaking body composed of students representing most campus organizations and student classes. Both the Student Government Association and the University believe that students should have the privilege, along with the faculty and administration, of participating in the governance of the University.

Admission Requirements

Admission to the University of Charleston is based on the academic records, potential for leadership and involvement, and personal qualities of the applicant. A qualified applicant's credentials must strongly suggest ability and motivation to succeed in higher education and in the University community. Candidates for admission must present a transcript of work from an accredited secondary school showing 16 academic units and grades indicating intellectual ability and promise. The pattern of courses must show purpose and continuity and furnish a background for the general education curriculum offered by the University. Since this curriculum emphasizes the fields of English, mathematics, natural science, and social science, the secondary school courses most acceptable would also emphasize these fields. Candidates are also required to submit scores on the ACT or SAT I. Students must have an above-average academic profile that includes a minimum 2.25 academic grade point average and a minimum ACT score of 18 or SAT I score of 850. Applicants for admission are considered on an individual basis without regard to race, religion, geographic origin, or handicap. Recommendations and a personal visit to campus, scheduled with the Admissions Office, are highly recommended.

Application and Information

For more information, interested students should contact:

Director of Admissions
University of Charleston
2300 MacCorkle Avenue, SE
Charleston, West Virginia 25304
Telephone: 304-357-4750
             800-995-GO UC
Fax: 304-357-4781
E-mail: admissions@uchaswv.edu
World Wide Web: http://www.uchaswv.edu/

The Clay Tower Building houses state-of-the-art science facilities and a library with lounges overlooking the river.

UNIVERSITY OF CHICAGO
CHICAGO, ILLINOIS

The University

With its Gothic quadrangles, dynamic faculty and student body, exciting research, and seminar-style classes that emphasize critical thinking and interdisciplinary scholarship, the University of Chicago stands as one of the world's great intellectual communities and centers of learning. Founded in 1891 by John D. Rockefeller who called it "the best investment I ever made," the University is private, nondenominational, and coeducational. Through the years, it has played a leading role in providing equal opportunity for women and minorities in higher education. The strength and distinction of its faculty is reflected in the more than 70 Nobel laureates who have been associated with Chicago, including 6 current faculty members. In addition to the undergraduate liberal arts college, the University of Chicago is composed of four graduate divisions, six graduate professional schools, the extensive library system, the Graham School of General Studies, the Laboratory Schools, and the University of Chicago Press. In more than a century of challenging existing educational traditions, Chicago has established new ones such as a coherent program of general education for undergraduates, the four-quarter system, and the "Chicago School" of thought in economics, sociology, and literary criticism.

The University of Chicago stands at the forefront of academic discovery. Some of the innovations and groundbreaking studies of Chicago scholars include Carbon-14 dating, REM sleep, urban sociology, classical literary criticism, the first controlled nuclear chain reaction, the F-scale for measuring tornado severity, pioneering scientific archaeology of the ancient Near East, the nation's first living-donor liver transplant, and discovery of two new dinosaurs in the last two years. Chicago undergraduates are often involved in academic exploration with graduate students and faculty members. In addition, they take graduate-level courses, travel and study abroad, and participate in internships in Chicago and beyond. Indeed, Chicago shows a dedication to the undergraduate college experience that is rare among research universities.

Currently enrolling 3,800 students, the undergraduate college is the largest division of the University of Chicago. Students come from all parts of the United States and thirty-four countries. Most undergraduates live on campus in the unique House System that includes graduate students and faculty members in housing that is guaranteed for all four years. Ninety percent of arts and sciences faculty members teach undergraduates. Eighty-eight percent of classes have fewer than 30 students, with most classes based in discussion and the free exchange of ideas and numbering fewer than 15. The student-faculty ratio is 4:1.

Students pursue every aspect of life–athletic, academic, social, cultural-enthusiastically and with a distinctly Chicago style. They are involved in more than 250 student organizations, including numerous groups for community service, academic interests, publications, cultural awareness, music, and theater. Some popular activities are University Theater, Model UN, Quiz Bowl, DOC Films, Jazz X-Tet, and the *Chicago Maroon* newspaper. A member of the Division III University Athletic Association, Chicago is a great place to play athletics, with nineteen varsity sports for men and women and more than 70 percent of the student body participating in intramural sports. In 2002, the new Gerald Ratner Athletics Center opens, providing new athletic facilities to the entire Chicago community.

Location

Located approximately 7 miles from the center of the city, the University of Chicago's dramatic Gothic buildings frame tree-shaded quadrangles and occupy a 203-acre campus. Recently, the campus was designated a botanic garden, and, with such architectural landmarks as Rockefeller Chapel and Frank Lloyd Wright's Robie House, it is listed on the National Register of Historic Places. The University's neighborhood, Hyde Park, is a residential community of 43,000 situated on the banks of Lake Michigan. Home to more than 60 percent of the faculty who walk or bike to campus, the neighborhood is often cited as a model of cosmopolitan and multiethnic city living. Other Chicago neighborhoods are accessible by commuter trains, University-operated express buses, and elevated trains. As the largest city in the Midwest and the third-largest in the nation, Chicago offers abundant cultural and entertainment opportunities, including the Lyric Opera, the Art Institute of Chicago, Comisky Park and Wrigley Field, the Field Museum of Natural History, Steppenwolf Theatre, and the city's myriad ethnic neighborhoods.

Majors and Degrees

The College of the University of Chicago grants Bachelor of Arts and Bachelor of Science degrees in fifty concentrations in the biological, physical, and social sciences, as well as in the humanities and interdisciplinary areas. A concentration may provide a comprehensive understanding of a well-defined field, such as anthropology or mathematics, or it may be an interdisciplinary program such as African and African-American studies, environmental studies, biological chemistry, or cinema and media studies. Joint B.A./M.A. and B.S./M.S. programs are offered in a number of disciplines. Degrees are awarded in the following majors: African and African-American studies; ancient studies; anthropology; art history; astronomy and astrophysics; biological chemistry; biological sciences; chemistry; cinema and media studies; classical studies; comparative literature; computer science; early Christian literature; East Asian languages and civilizations; economics; English Language and literature; environmental studies; fundamentals: issues and texts; gender studies; general studies in the humanities; geography; geophysical sciences; Germanic studies; history; history, philosophy, and social studies of science and medicine (HiPSS); international studies; Jewish studies; Latin American studies; law; letters and society; linguistics; mathematics; medieval studies; music; Near Eastern languages and civilizations; philosophy; physics; political science; psychology; public policy studies; religion and the humanities; religious studies; Romance languages and literatures; Russian and other Slavic languages and literatures; Russian civilization; sociology; South Asian languages and civilizations; South Asian studies; statistics; tutorial studies; and visual arts.

Academic Program

Chicago's undergraduate curriculum is designed to give students the opportunity to fully participate in the intellectual life of a world-renowned research university. The curriculum became famous in American higher education during the 1930s when it challenged the prevailing model of elective-based programs by introducing a coherent core of general education courses. These courses made it possible, then and now, for college students to share certain kinds of crucial intellectual experiences, to create a community of young scholars who can talk across disciplines, and to form habits of mind necessary for advanced study, for successful careers, and for a productive life. One third of the courses taken for graduation are modern descendants of that first revolutionary general education core. They include courses in social and natural sciences, humanities, mathematics, Western or non-Western civilization, and art or music. These small, faculty-taught courses, taken in the first two years, lead naturally to the next stages of the curriculum, which is equally divided between courses in the concentration and elective courses. The total program may also include research projects, honors projects, foreign travel and study, and internships. The eventual shape of the individual Chicago experience is determined by the student, in consultations with an academic adviser, departmental adviser, and faculty mentors.

Off-Campus Arrangements

Students in the College of the University of Chicago are encouraged to study abroad and can take part in programs in many countries. Programs range in length from a summer or a single academic quarter to a full academic year and include course work and other experiences that can be tailored to fit degree programs in any discipline, whether humanities, social sciences, or natural sciences. Most important, all programs provide the opportunity to live among people whose ways of living and thinking challenge students to look at their own lives with a fresh perspective.

These programs are sponsored by the University of Chicago, either alone or in cooperation with other universities and with two groups to which the University belongs: the Associated Colleges of the Midwest (ACM) and the Committee on Institutional Cooperation (CIC). For most programs, participants receive full credit for courses and are eligible for University of Chicago financial aid.

Academic Facilities

One of the strengths of the University of Chicago is that the campus maintains excellent academic facilities that serve the community as a whole. The University library system holds over 6 million volumes and 7 million manuscripts and archival materials. Regenstein Library for humanities and social sciences is one of the nation's largest academic libraries, and John Crerar Library is recognized as one of the best libraries in the country for research and teaching in the sciences, medicine, and technology. Joining Crerar Library to form a science quadrangle is the Kersten Physics Teaching Center, the most advanced facility in the U.S. for the teaching of undergraduate physics. Students in the College have access to all the University's special libraries, including the D'Angelo Law Library, Yerkes Observatory Library for astronomy and astrophysics (home of the world's largest refracting telescope), the Social Service Administration Library, and the Eckhart Library for mathematics and computer science.

Other facilities providing Chicago students with research and internship opportunities are the recently renovated Oriental Institute Museum, a showcase of the history, art, and archaeology of the ancient Near East; the Smart Museum, which houses a collection of more than 7,000 works of art, spanning five centuries of both Western and Eastern civilizations; the Enrico Fermi Institute, which has played a central role in nuclear physics and nuclear chemistry research, elementary particle physics, and astrophysics; Midway Studios, where art students enjoy studio space; and the University of Chicago Medical Center, which includes five major hospitals and 125 specialty outpatient clinics that work to advance biomedical innovation, serve the health needs of the community, and further the knowledge of medical students, physicians, and others dedicated to medicine.

Costs

Tuition for the 1999–2000 school year was $23,820, and room and board charges were $7835. Fees for other services, including health insurance, orientation, and activities, totaled $2900.

Financial Aid

Chicago is committed to helping students from all economic backgrounds attend the University and makes admissions decisions on a need-blind basis. Furthermore, the University meets 100 percent of students' demonstrated financial need. More than 65 percent of Chicago students receive some form of financial assistance. Students wishing to apply for financial aid should submit the University of Chicago financial aid application along with the Free Application for Federal Student Aid and the Financial Aid PROFILE of the College Scholarship Service. Merit scholarships are also available.

Faculty

The instructional faculty of the University of Chicago totals 1,841 and is composed of distinguished scholars and teachers. Faculty members typically teach both undergraduate and graduate courses, and senior professors often teach undergraduate general education courses. Because classes are small and discussion is the preferred mode of instruction, faculty members often become mentors and partners in inquiry with students.

Student Government

Student Government is composed of students in the College and other graduate and professional schools. Student government assists student organizations, sponsors events, and deals with the academic, social, and economic issues of University life. The Student Assembly, the legislative branch, is the only organization on campus that represents all students. Members of the Assembly are elected in the autumn quarter. Student Government also supports a number of committees that focus on issues ranging from student affairs to community relations to student services. The Inter-House Council serves as an advisory body for the House System and allocates money for Inter-House activities.

Admission Requirements

The Office of College Admissions doesn't have a rigid formula for the successful applicant and considers a candidate's entire application: academic and extracurricular records, essays, letters of recommendation, and SAT or ACT scores. A personal interview is encouraged because it provides prospective students with a chance to learn more about the College. The essay is an opportunity to show individuality, in addition to clear and effective writing ability.

Though no specific secondary school courses are prescribed, a standard college-preparatory program is recommended: 4 years of English, 3 to 4 years of math and laboratory sciences, 3 or more years of social sciences, and a foreign language. The University of Chicago does not employ numerical cut-offs when evaluating applications for admission. Of the 1,005 students in the Class of 2003, 78 percent graduated in the top 10 percent of their high school classes. The middle 50 percent of admitted students scored between 1310 and 1470 on the SAT or between 28 and 32 on the ACT.

Application and Information

The University of Chicago offers students two application plans. Early action is for candidates who seek an admission decision in mid-December and a provisional financial aid assessment by early January. Candidates must complete their applications by November 1 and may apply to other schools if they wish. Chicago's early action program is nonbinding; admitted students need not reply to the Office of Admissions until May 1. Regular notification is for candidates who prefer an admission and financial aid decision by early April. Candidates must complete their application by January 1 and must reply to the offer by May 1. Students who have completed one or two years of course work at another college are welcome to apply for transfer admission.

For further information students should contact:

Office of College Admissions
University of Chicago
1116 East 59th Street
Chicago, Illinois 60637
Telephone: 773-702-8650
E-mail: rhody@uchicago.edu
World Wide Web: http://www.uchicago.edu

UNIVERSITY OF CINCINNATI
CINCINNATI, OHIO

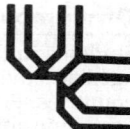

The University

The University of Cincinnati (UC), which traces its roots to 1819, is a multifaceted academic institution. The urban campus offers programs in applied science; business administration; design, architecture, art, and planning; education; engineering; liberal arts; nursing; performing arts; pharmacy; and social work. Many of its programs are nationally ranked. Its design programs are rated in the top five, the architecture program is rated in the top ten, the engineering program is ranked in the top ten, the Cincinnati Initiative for Teacher Education Program is a national leader, and the College-Conservatory of Music (CCM) is internationally renowned. Cincinnati has three two-year colleges that provide a general education, a high-quality technical education, and transfer programs that enable students to enroll successfully into bachelor programs at UC's main campus.

Both alumni and faculty members have made outstanding social contributions; UC is credited with the development of the first oral polio vaccine, the first antihistamine, the first electronic organ, the first steam fire engine and—more recently—performance of the first brain operation employing a YAG laser and the first inner-ear implant.

There are more than 34,000 students, of whom more than 27,000 are undergraduates. About 90 percent of the students are from Ohio, and 78 percent are graduates of public schools. Approximately 5,700 students make up the ethnic student population, while 1,552 international students are working toward undergraduate and graduate degrees. About 19 percent of baccalaureate freshman students ranked in the top tenth of their high school graduating class, and 54 percent ranked in the top third.

At UC, education is more than academics. The University believes that a significant part of a student's personal growth and development is learning to cooperate with others. Living on campus provides immediate access to academic and recreational facilities, helps a student establish meaningful social relationships, and promotes involvement in campus life. Residence halls accommodate 2,400 undergraduates, and there are 300 graduate family units. Each of the six halls is unique, with special features ranging from fireplaces and sun decks to computer facilities. Students can request coed or non-coed accommodation and arrange for such amenities as telephone voice mail, microwave ovens, and cable TV. Many students live in the surrounding neighborhoods of Clifton, which offer many apartment complexes, restaurants, and specialty shops as well as an active nightlife.

Student involvement is important at the University of Cincinnati. More than 275 student organizations are available, including 35 social fraternities and sororities and a broad variety of special interest groups. Bearcat basketball is played in the Shoemaker Center and UC football in the recently renovated Nippert Stadium. The University of Cincinnati competes at the NCAA Division I level, fielding varsity teams for men in football, basketball, baseball, cross-country, soccer, swimming and diving, and indoor/outdoor track and field and for women in basketball, volleyball, cross-country, soccer, tennis, golf, softball, and basketball. Athletic clubs provide opportunities for participation in ice hockey, lacrosse, rugby, sailing, skiing, and mountaineering. Students also enjoy free fitness facilities, including racquetball, track, swimming, and Nautilus weight lifting. Counseling services include STEPS (Steps Toward Educational Progress and Success), educational advising and orientation, career development and placement, and tutorial and referral services.

Location

Cincinnati was cited by *Places Rated Almanac* as the most livable city in the United States. The University of Cincinnati has made major contributions to the city's environment. The College-Conservatory of Music, for instance, provides more than 900 different entertainments each year, including concerts, Broadway musicals, ballet, drama, and opera. The cultural resources of the city complement those of the University. Jazz concerts, championship rodeos, the circus, rock concerts, and art exhibits all contribute to the rich atmosphere. Sports enthusiasts can watch the Reds or the Bengals or participate in a number of outdoor activities. Though Cincinnati offers all the amenities of a major city, it is within an hour's drive of several state parks.

Majors and Degrees

The University of Cincinnati offers a wide range of opportunities through forty certificate programs, eighty-six associate degree programs, and more than 200 bachelor's degree programs. The associate degree is offered through departments in the College of Applied Science, Clermont College, the College of Evening and Continuing Education, Raymond Walters College, and University College. A bachelor's degree is available through departments in the College of Allied Health Sciences; College of Applied Science; the McMicken College of Arts and Sciences; the College of Business Administration; the College-Conservatory of Music; the College of Design, Architecture, Art, and Planning; the College of Education; the College of Engineering; the College of Evening and Continuing Education; the College of Nursing; the College of Pharmacy; and the School of Social Work. Certificate programs are available through many colleges and vary from computer technology to historic preservation. More than twenty preprofessional programs are available, including those in education, law, medicine, nursing, and social work. The College of Pharmacy offers a Pharm.D. program.

Academic Program

The University of Cincinnati is unified in its basic academic values but highly diverse in its educational offerings. Credit hours required for graduation vary from college to college and from department to department; associate degree programs generally require at least 95 quarter credit hours and bachelor's degree programs generally require a minimum of 186 quarter credit hours.

Most of the colleges on campus participate in the University Honors Scholars Program. The honors program is highly flexible, broad in scope, and designed to provide students with the personal attention of a small college as well as the wide range of intellectual activity of a major university. ROTC programs are available in air science (Air Force ROTC) and military science (Army ROTC).

The academic calendar consists of three 10-week quarters and a summer session. The summer session offers three 3-week terms, each equivalent to a regular quarter; a ten-week term; and many shorter sessions, institutes, and workshops. The traditional academic year begins in late September and ends in early June.

Off-Campus Arrangements

Cooperative education, founded at the University in 1906, is one of the best programs in the country and serves as a model for colleges worldwide. This program integrates on-the-job experience with the student's academic program by alternating quarters of work in the student's field. More than 4,100 students from forty disciplines gain professional experience in more than 1,400 organizations in thirty-six states and eleven other countries.

Academic Facilities

The main campus sits on 392 acres and consists of 108 buildings, including state-of-the art facilities such as the Engineering Research Center, the Aronoff Center, the CCM Village, and the Vontz Center for Molecular Studies.

The University libraries contain more than 1.6 million books and more than 20,000 journal and serial publications. In addition to a modern central library featuring an online catalog system, the University library network includes a health sciences library, a law library, and nine college and department libraries. Media facilities and services include audiovisual equipment, photographic services, and a curriculum resource center.

Students in the College-Conservatory of Music, one of the premier music schools in the country, have several theaters on and off campus at their disposal.

As a major research institution, the University of Cincinnati offers many modern computer facilities and innovative applications. Eight PC labs house more than 150 personal computers for student use. A student access system for interactive computing is provided by VAX computers and by other terminal systems using the MVS operation. A number of electronic classrooms, which allow for a high degree of interaction between students and faculty members, are located throughout the University.

Costs

For 1999–2000, the central campus instructional and general fee was $4998 per year for Ohio residents and $12,879 per year for out-of-state students. For Clermont College, the instructional and general fee was $3096 per year for Ohio residents and $7566 for out-of-state students. The instructional and general fee for the College of Raymond Walters was $3573 for Ohio residents and $8997 for out-of-state students. Parking fees were included in the instructional and general fees of these two Colleges. On the main campus, room and board costs began at $6162 per year. The application fee is $30, and the matriculation fee is $50; both are nonrefundable. Books and supplies are estimated at $680 per year but may be greater for students in special programs. Costs for a 24-hour-parking decal begin at $51 per quarter. Students in the Professional Practice Program pay a $50 registration fee for the quarters they are working but pay one third less in annual student fees in their last two years.

Financial Aid

Financial aid is awarded on the basis of need through grants, loans, and work-study opportunities and/or on the basis of scholastic accomplishment through a variety of scholarships. Federal Pell Grants, Ohio Instructional Grants, and Federal Supplemental Educational Opportunity Grants are given to approximately 13,000 students each year. To apply for aid, students must file the Free Application for Federal Student Aid (FAFSA) after January 1. This form is available at the University's Student Financial Aid Office and at all colleges and high schools. Major loans are available through the Federal Perkins Loan, Federal Stafford Student Loan, and Federal PLUS loan programs. Short-term loans are provided by the University of Cincinnati for unexpected college-related expenses. The Federal Work-Study Program provides part-time work for students on the basis of financial need. The University awards scholarships for outstanding freshmen through a competition called the Cincinnatus Scholarship Competition. Each participant receives at least a $1500 renewable scholarship.

Faculty

The University of Cincinnati faculty consists of 2,621 full-time members and 2,386 part-time members. Approximately 72 percent have doctorates. Research and scholarship are emphasized but not to the exclusion of teaching and counseling. The ratio of undergraduate students to full-time faculty members is 13:1. The average class size is 18.

Student Government

Cabinet, senate, and executive branches make up the Student Government, which directs all student organizations and administers funds to student groups. Members of the Student Government serve on University committees and represent the student body at meetings of the Board of Trustees.

Admission Requirements

Freshman candidates may be admitted directly into baccalaureate programs. Each individual college has specific high school unit entrance requirements and class rank requirements. The minimum high school unit requirements for the baccalaureate colleges are 4 in English, 3 in mathematics, 2 in science, 2 in social science, 2 in foreign language, and 2 additional college-preparatory subjects in the aforementioned areas. An average letter grade of C must be earned across courses in these areas. ACT or SAT I scores must be submitted for consideration for admission to a baccalaureate college. The University of Cincinnati also operates several "open admission" colleges for students who wish to earn an associate degree or for students who wish to later gain access to a baccalaureate college after satisfying admission requirement deficiencies. Candidates for admission must be graduates of accredited high schools or, in the case of the "open admission" colleges, must possess a General Educational Development equivalency diploma.

Application and Information

To be assured of consideration, candidates for admission should submit an application between October 1 and January 15 of their senior year of high school. For highly competitive programs, it is recommended to apply by December 15. Notification is made on a rolling basis beginning November 1. Transfer applications generally are processed on the same basis as freshman applications. The UC Viewbook is available in many guidance libraries or upon request from the Office of Admissions.

University of Cincinnati
P.O. Box 210091
Cincinnati, Ohio 45221-0091

Telephone: 513-556-1100
Fax: 513-556-1105
E-mail: admissions@uc.edu
World Wide Web: http://www.uc.edu/www/admissions/home.html

A view of the University of Cincinnati's main campus.

UNIVERSITY OF COLORADO AT BOULDER
BOULDER, COLORADO

The University

The University of Colorado (CU) was founded in 1876, the same year that Colorado became the Centennial State. Today the University system, governed by a 9-member Board of Regents, includes the main campus at Boulder, campuses at Colorado Springs and Denver, and the Health Sciences Center in Denver. The University of Colorado is one of thirty-two public institutions belonging to the prestigious Association of American Universities (AAU) and the only member in the Rocky Mountain region. CU-Boulder ranked tenth among public research universities and third among rising research universities in the public sector in a study called "The Rise of American Research Universities: Elites and Challengers in the Postwar Era," published in 1997.

The Boulder campus, the largest in the CU system, offers more than 2,500 courses each semester in more than 150 areas of study. Outstanding academic departments and academic programs include astrophysical and planetary sciences, biochemistry, biology, chemistry, engineering, English, entrepreneurial business, geography, music, physics, psychology, and women studies. There are sixty-one academic programs available at the bachelor's level, forty-seven at the master's level, and forty-two at the doctoral level. Talented undergraduate students may participate in honors programs, the Undergraduate Research Opportunities Program, and several residential programs featuring small-class environments.

Total enrollment for fall 1999 at the Boulder campus was 28,373, including 22,660 undergraduate students. The student population comes from every state in the nation and eighty-eight countries. Approximately two thirds of the students come from Colorado. Many ethnic, religious, academic, and social backgrounds are represented, fostering the development of a multicultural community that enriches each student's educational experience.

Undergraduate students may apply to five colleges and two schools. The five colleges are Architecture and Planning, Arts and Sciences, Business and Administration, Engineering and Applied Science, and Music. The two schools are Journalism and Mass Communication and Education. Students are admitted to CU-Boulder's colleges directly from high school or as transfers from other institutions. Within the schools, students are admitted at the upper-division level.

CU-Boulder offers a wide variety of campus activities, from recreational opportunities to student clubs and organizations. Students may participate in student government; clubs and organizations; intramural, club, and intercollegiate sports; and fraternities and sororities. An extensive calendar of cultural events is available.

Location

CU-Boulder is located in a scenic valley at the foot of the Rocky Mountains, 1 mile above sea level. With a population of just over 96,000, Boulder is among the most dynamic, progressive, and attractive cities of its size in the United States. The Colorado state capital, Denver, is a 30-mile drive or bus ride (free for students) from Boulder. Boulder is surrounded by a greenbelt of more than 20,000 acres of open space. Much of the open space is crisscrossed by an extensive system of hiking, biking, and riding trails, as are the nearby mountains. Many CU-Boulder students enjoy skiing, hiking, backpacking, rock climbing, white-water rafting, or mountain biking. Recently, Boulder was ranked first by Norman Ford in *The 50 Healthiest Places to Live and Retire in the United States*. The October 1992 issue of *Sunset* magazine rated Boulder one of the five best college towns in the West.

CU-Boulder has been rated as one of the "most artistically successful campuses in the country" in *The Campus as a Work of Art* by Thomas Gaines. The 600-acre campus, in the heart of the city of Boulder, is distinguished by buildings featuring sandstone walls and dramatic red-tiled roofs.

Majors and Degrees

CU-Boulder offers the following undergraduate majors: accounting; aerospace engineering; American studies; anthropology; applied mathematics; architectural engineering; Asian studies; biochemistry; central and East European studies; chemical engineering; chemistry; Chinese; civil engineering; classics; communication; computer science; dance; distributed studies; economics; electrical and computer engineering; electrical engineering; engineering physics; English; environmental design–architecture; environmental design-design studies; environmental design-planning; environmental engineering; environmental, population, and organismic biology; environmental studies; ethnic studies; film studies; finance; fine arts–art history; fine arts–studio arts; French; geography; geology; Germanic studies; history; humanities; individually structured major; information systems; international affairs; Italian; Japanese; journalism-advertising; journalism–broadcast news; journalism–broadcast production management; journalism–media studies; kinesiology; Latin American studies; linguistics; management; marketing; mathematics; mechanical engineering; molecular, cellular, developmental biology; music; music–arts in music; music education; philosophy; physics; political science; predentistry sequence; premedicine sequence; pre–veterinary medicine sequence; psychology; religious studies; Russian studies; sociology; Spanish; speech, language, and hearing sciences; theater; and women's studies.

The following bachelor's degrees are offered: B.A., B.Envd., B.F.A., B.Mus., B.Mus.Ed., and B.S.

Academic Program

CU-Boulder operates on a two-semester academic calendar. The fall semester begins in late August and the spring semester begins in early January. Summer Session lasts ten weeks; courses meeting for shorter periods (1–4, 5, or 8 weeks) are scheduled during the ten-week session.

The mission of the University of Colorado at Boulder is to educate undergraduate and graduate students in the accumulated knowledge of humankind, discover new knowledge through research and creative work, and foster critical thought, artistic creativity, professional competence, and responsible citizenship. In addition, the University of Colorado at Boulder has introduced a Total Learning Environment initiative with a focus on providing a more enriching and relevant learning experience for students by supporting innovations in learning; being more responsive to students and other constituents; using technology to improve teaching, learning, research, and management; and enhancing the University's infrastructure. Depending on their degree program, students may be required to complete 120, 124, or 128 semester hours for graduation. CU-Boulder offers a very flexible curriculum. Students may graduate with more than one major and with two different degrees from different colleges. Minors also are offered in arts and sciences, business, and engineering. The College of Arts and Sciences, the College of Engineering and Applied Science, and the College of Music offer a four-year graduation guarantee, providing specific requirements are met. Concurrent bachelor's and master's degree programs are available in the following departments: East Languages and Literatures, Economics, German and Slavic Languages, Environmental Population and Organismic Biology, Business (accounting, finance, information systems), Linguistics, Psychology, and all engineering departments, including Aerospace, Architectural, Chemical, Civil, Computer Science, Electrical, Mechanical, and Telecommunications.

Off-Campus Arrangements

CU-Boulder sponsors more than 100 study-abroad programs to more than fifty countries. Programs are offered in Australia, Canada, Costa Rica, Denmark, Egypt, England, France, Germany, Hungary, Japan, and Mexico. More than 600 students participated in these programs in 1998–99, and 20 percent of 1998 graduates had studied abroad at some point during their undergraduate studies—an unusually high participation rate for a large public university.

Academic Facilities

The University library system consists of more than 2.9 million volumes, 5.9 million titles on microform, more than 25,000 periodical subscriptions, and more than 57,000 video and audio titles. The libraries system includes a main library and five branch libraries: Business, Earth Sciences, Engineering, Math-Physics, and Music. There is also a law library. Other facilities and resources aiding students in their studies include a planetarium and observatory, a natural history museum, extensive computing resources, a state-of-the-art foreign language technology center, a concert hall, and three theaters. A new Integrated Teaching and Learning Laboratory, unique in the world, provides hands-on, real-world experience to engineering undergraduates. This 34,400-square-foot engineering center has a unique inside-out design, movable and multipurpose laboratory environments, and small classrooms. Other new buildings include an earth sciences building, a rehearsal facility addition to the existing music building, a new humanities building, and a newly renovated cottage, home of the Women Studies Department.

Costs

For 1999–2000, annual expenses for undergraduate students who are Colorado residents totaled $13,200 ($3118 for tuition and fees as well as an estimated $695 for books and supplies, $5202 for room and board, and $4185 for transportation, medical, and personal expenses). Nonresident tuition and fees were $15,918.

Financial Aid

Slightly more than half of Boulder students receive some type of financial assistance, totaling more than $120 million in awards. Students receive aid in the form of grants, loans, work-study awards, and scholarships. Funding is provided from federal, state, University, and private sources. All applicants for financial aid are required to submit the Free Application for Federal Student Aid (FAFSA). Application forms are available from high school and community college counselors as well as from the CU-Boulder Office of Financial Aid. The priority processing deadline is April 1.

In 1993, CU-Boulder was among 105 institutions nationwide selected to participate in the Federal Direct Student Loan Program, allowing students to obtain loans directly from the Office of Financial Aid rather than from a private lender.

Faculty

Approximately 1,200 full-time instructional faculty members teach undergraduate and graduate courses. The faculty includes nationally and internationally recognized scholars with many academic honors and awards. Tom Cech, former professor of chemistry and biochemistry and now Director of the Howard Hughes Medical Institute, shared the 1989 Nobel Prize in chemistry with Sidney Altman of Yale University. Heading the list of the top ten research advances in 1995 was a new form of matter, created by CU-Boulder physicists Eric Cornell and Carl Wieman, named "Molecule of the Year." Seventeen faculty members belong to the prestigious National Academy of Sciences, 7 are members of the National Academy of Engineering, and 15 are included in the membership of the American Academy of Arts and Sciences.

Student Government

One of the most influential student governments in the nation, the University of Colorado Student Union (UCSU) administers an operating budget of more than $25 million. UCSU student leaders and volunteers, working with the University staff, make policy decisions concerning the operation of the University Memorial Center, Student Recreation Center, Wardenburg Student Health Center, cultural events, the campus radio station, and other programs. Student fees and student-generated revenue support all of these activities. The student government also takes an active role in advocating student concerns.

Admission Requirements

A number of factors are considered by the University in making admission decisions. Previous academic achievement, the rigor of courses taken, grades, college entrance test scores, a personal statement, and letters of recommendation are considered. Because CU-Boulder practices competitive admission, not all qualified applicants can be admitted. About one third of the freshman class typically ranks in the top 10 percent of their high school graduating class. In fall 1999, 58 percent of the freshman class were Colorado residents. The University seeks to enroll students from a wide range of ethnic, cultural, economic, geographic, and educational backgrounds. Applications are available in Colorado high school guidance offices, community college counseling centers, or from the CU-Boulder Office of Admissions.

Application and Information

Students are considered for admission for fall, spring, and summer terms. Each year, the Office of Admissions begins sending admissions notifications on October 1 (for spring) and November 1 (for summer and fall). Summer and fall application deadlines are February 15 for freshmen and April 1 for transfers. The spring application deadline for freshmen and transfers is October 1. After these dates, applications will be considered only if space is available. An online electronic application for admission is now available through the University's home page listed below.

For information and applications, students should contact:

Office of Admissions
Campus Box 30
University of Colorado at Boulder
Boulder, Colorado 80309-0030

Telephone: 303-492-6301 (for information)
               303-492-2456 (for applications)
               303-492-5998 (TTY)

World Wide Web: http://www.colorado.edu

The University of Colorado at Boulder is a major research and teaching university located in one of the most spectacular environments in the country, at the foot of the Rocky Mountains.

UNIVERSITY OF CONNECTICUT
STORRS, CONNECTICUT

The University

The University of Connecticut (UConn) is a premier public research university in the United States. Established in 1881 with a class of 12 students, UConn has grown into a nationally ranked university with more than 14,000 undergraduate students, 7,000 graduate and professional students, 1,500 faculty members, and 140,000 alumni. The University has been recognized in numerous college guides for its excellent academic programs, knowledgeable professors, and top-notch athletics. It has also been called a top value and a best buy.

UConn encompasses seventeen schools and colleges that offer eight undergraduate degrees in ninety-eight majors, twelve graduate degrees in eighty fields of study, and graduate professional programs in law, medicine, and dental medicine. The University consistently attracts and accepts some of the nation's most talented students. The University's faculty members are among the most impressive scholars in the U.S. and are recognized throughout the world as leaders in education, research, and scholarship. Ninety-one percent have a Ph.D. or the highest degree in their field.

The University's research activities advance knowledge in a range of academic disciplines. UConn stands among the country's leading institutions in the breadth and contribution of its research. The Carnegie Foundation classifies UConn as a Research I University; it is one of only two public universities in New England to hold this distinction. In terms of research funding, UConn is ranked in the top thirty-five public universities by the National Science Foundation.

The University library system maintains the largest publicly supported collection of research materials in Connecticut. The Homer Babbidge Library on the main campus in Storrs contains 2.1 million volumes and is among the top thirty major research libraries nationally in terms of total holdings and funding. UConn is home to the Roper Center for Public Opinion Research, the world's most comprehensive library of public opinion and survey data, and the Thomas Dodd Research Center, which maintains an international collection of historical manuscripts and archives, including an agreement between the African National Congress (ANC) and UConn to form a partnership to achieve and share with scholars material from the ANC's struggle for human rights in South Africa.

UConn's flagship campus is located on a beautiful 4,000-acre setting in Storrs, Connecticut. The University also offers the convenience and accessibility of campuses in Stamford, West Hartford, and Waterbury as well as the natural splendor of its Torrington and Avery Point facilities. The University's school of law is located in Hartford, while its schools of medicine and dental medicine are located at the University of Connecticut Health Center in Farmington. A graduate school of social work is in West Hartford. Through UCONN 2000, a landmark ten-year, $1-billion plan to renew, rebuild, and enhance UConn's campuses, the University is building and maintaining superior academic facilities throughout the state and creating state-of-the-art residential and recreational facilities at its main campus in Storrs.

The University of Connecticut maintains a strong tradition of student involvement. More than 250 clubs and organizations offer students access to everything from academic discussion groups to a vast assortment of intramural recreational programs offered in state-of-the-art facilities. UConn's athletic programs perennially rank among the best in the country. UConn offers twenty-two men's and women's varsity sports, most competing at the highest level. The Storrs campus also has student-run media, including radio station WHUS, *The Daily Campus* newspaper, and cable television station UCTV.

Location

The University is located in Storrs, Connecticut, midway between New York and Boston, each of which is about 1½ to 2½ hours away. The most used route to the University is exit 68 off I-84. The University's property to the east of the highway on the knoll where the campus begins includes pastures, hilltop cornfields, and picturesque barns, charming reminders of the area's agricultural origins of more than a century ago. Connecticut's capital city, Hartford, is only a half hour away. UConn is a cultural and recreational focal point in Connecticut.

Majors and Degrees

Undergraduates at the University of Connecticut may major in any of about ninety-eight different fields. The College of Liberal Arts and Sciences offers the Bachelor of Arts and Bachelor of Science degrees in approximately thirty-nine academic areas, ranging from anthropology to statistics and including coastal studies, ecology and evolutionary biology, and journalism. The College of Agriculture and Natural Resources offers the Bachelor of Science in ten special areas, including natural resources and environmental science. The School of Allied Health offers the Bachelor of Science in dietetics and medical laboratory sciences and the integrated Bachelor of Science/Master of Science in physical therapy. The School of Business Administration offers the Bachelor of Science in nine areas, including accounting, finance, and management information systems. The School of Education offers the five-year integrated bachelor's/master's teacher education program as well as the Bachelor of Arts and Bachelor of Science degrees in nine areas, included under sport, leisure, and exercise sciences. The School of Engineering offers the Bachelor of Science in Engineering degree and has programs in chemical, civil, computer engineering, computer science, electrical, materials, mechanical, and metallurgy and materials engineering; and management and engineering for manufacturing (in conjunction with the School of Business Administration). The School of Family Studies offers the Bachelor of Science with a major in human development and family relations. The School of Fine Arts offers the Bachelor of Fine Arts and Bachelor of Music degrees with majors in art, dramatic arts, music, and puppetry. The School of Nursing offers the Bachelor of Science in nursing. The School of Pharmacy offers a four-year Bachelor of Science program in pharmacy studies and a six-year Doctor of Pharmacy program.

The University offers an individualized major to meet the needs of students whose academic interests encompass two or more of the academic departments. The University also offers a Bachelor of General Studies degree program at the junior-senior level for nontraditional part-time students. A two-year associate degree is available through the Ratcliffe Hicks School of Agriculture.

Academic Program

Most bachelor's degree programs require the successful completion of 120 semester hours. The exceptions are nursing, which requires 131 semester hours; engineering, which requires 134; pharmacy studies, which requires 125, and the Doctor of Pharmacy, which requires 196; physical therapy (an integrated Bachelor of Science/Master of Science program), which requires 153; and education (an integrated bachelor's and master's degree program), which requires 150 semester hours. All programs require the completion of courses in eight core areas in addition to the work required for the major. The University follows a two-semester system. Shorter sessions are offered for summer study and during the intersession between the fall and spring semesters.

Entering freshmen at Storrs may be selected for admission to the Honors Scholar Program, a nationally competitive academic program for outstanding students. Admission to the program at a later time, but before the junior year, is open to students who have done exceptional work at the University.

A cooperative education program for students in most majors integrates classroom learning and work experience in business, industry, and public service. The University offers interdisciplinary majors in Latin American, Slavic, and East European language and area studies; urban and women's studies; environmental science; and mathematical actuarial science. Individualized majors are available in Judaic, Asian, European, Native American, medieval, and peace studies, as well as in public relations, international studies, and criminology. Intensive study of critical languages such as Arabic, Chinese, or Japanese is also offered. Army and Air Force ROTC programs are available.

Off-Campus Arrangements

The University grants credit for programs and courses taken abroad through programs sponsored by the University as well as other institutions and agencies in Argentina, Australia, Austria, Brazil, Canada, Chile, China, Costa Rica, Czech Republic, Denmark, Dominican Republic, England, France, Germany, Ghana, Hungary, Ireland, Israel, Italy, Japan, Mexico, the Netherlands, Poland, Portugal, Russia, Spain, Sweden, and Switzerland. The Semester-at-Sea Program is also offered. Since 1968, through the Urban Semester Program, the University has given students a special educational opportunity to live, learn, and work in Hartford, Connecticut. The University also participates in the National Student Exchange Program, which allows students to spend a year of study at another university.

Academic Facilities

The University's facilities are undergoing a huge transformation, thanks to a ten-year, $1-billion commitment from Connecticut's state legislature. Now in its fifth year, the program already has resulted in a completely renovated Student Recreational Facility, four multilevel buildings that comprise the South Campus residence halls, a 220,000-square-foot chemistry building, six additional student residence halls, more than forty classrooms that have been renovated, and the University's first parking garage. Construction is near completion on a new physics/biology building, and work has begun on a new School of Business Administration. The University's academic core has been transformed into a pedestrian campus. At least a dozen more buildings, including a huge addition to the Student Union, are scheduled for completion in the next three years. The Homer Babbidge Library at Storrs houses more than 2 million volumes, more than 3.1 million units of microtext, 603,790 government documents, and 7,867 current periodical subscriptions. It is one of the most technologically sophisticated research libraries in the United States. Specialized libraries in music and pharmacy are housed separately in those schools and raise the library systems total holdings to approximately 2.1 million volumes, including the regional campuses and law school. The art department has spacious, well-lighted studios and galleries. Other academic facilities provide specialized classroom and laboratory space for psychology, communication sciences, pathobiology, material sciences, physics, computer science, and human development and family relations, to name but a few. Computer facilities and laboratories are located in libraries, academic buildings, and residential facilities. There are 1,800 computers on campus in approximately ninety computer labs. The University also has an art museum, the William Benton Museum of Art, and the State Museum of Natural History. Theatrical, musical, and speaker programs take place in the Harriet S. Jorgensen Theatre, the Albert N. Jorgensen Auditorium, and the von der Mehden Recital Hall.

Costs

For students attending the Storrs campus, tuition and University and student fees are $5398 for state residents and $13,916 for out-of-state students in 2000–01. The average residence hall cost is $2894, and the seven-day University meal plan costs $2800. For students attending the University at a regional campus, in-state tuition and University and student fees total $4620 in 2000–01.

Financial Aid

Financial assistance in the form of grants, low-interest loans, and part-time employment is administered by the Student Financial Aid Office. All financial aid applications must be submitted by March 1 for both the fall and spring semesters. The assessment of need is based on the ability of the student's family to contribute, the amount of the student's savings for college, and other financial resources that may be available. To be considered for financial aid, all applicants must submit the Free Application for Federal Student Aid (FAFSA). Applicants for the Federal Stafford Student Loan must also file the FAFSA. The University awards a number of renewable merit-based scholarships to students with outstanding academic credentials, as well as to Finalists and Semifinalists in the National Merit Scholarship, National Achievement, and Hispanic Scholars programs.

Faculty

Nearly 91 percent of the University's 1,096 full-time faculty members hold a doctorate or another terminal degree in their field. The student-faculty ratio is 17:1. Faculty members at all levels teach undergraduate courses, including freshman courses. Faculty members engage in a wide variety of research, which in recent years has been sponsored by grants totaling about $110 million for the University and its Health Center schools.

Student Government

All undergraduates are members of the Undergraduate Student Government, the principal and officially recognized organization representing the undergraduate student body. The units of governance and service formed by this body reflect the major areas of interest and need among the students.

Admission Requirements

Applicants must be graduates of an approved secondary school and have completed at least 16 units of work. At least 15 of the secondary school units must consist of college-preparatory work, including 4 years of English, 2 years of a single foreign language (3 years strongly recommended), 3 years of mathematics (2 years of algebra and 1 year of geometry or the equivalent), 2 years of a laboratory science, and 2 years of social science, including at least 1 year of U.S. history. Several of the undergraduate schools and colleges of the University have additional course prerequisites for admission. Applicants should be in the upper range of their high school graduating class and must submit satisfactory scores on the SAT I or ACT. SAT II Subject Tests are not required for admission. The University is committed to ensuring access to higher education for students from minority groups. Transfer students are also encouraged to apply; their admission depends primarily upon the quality of the college record, the quantity and character of courses completed, and the intended field of study at the University. Advanced standing or course credit may be given to students on the basis of Advanced Placement examinations or through successful completion of regular University courses sponsored by the University at selected Connecticut secondary schools. Campus visits and interviews are encouraged although not required.

Application and Information

The application form, available from the University's Admissions Office or from the guidance offices of all Connecticut high schools, should be submitted early in the senior year of high school or no later than March 1 for freshmen; the application deadline for transfer students is May 1. For all students, the financial aid application deadline is March 1.

For more information, students should contact:

Office of Admissions
University of Connecticut
2131 Hillside Road, Box U-88
Storrs, Connecticut 06269-3088
Telephone: 860-486-3137 (freshmen and transfers)
860-486-4866 (campus tours)
E-mail: beahusky@uconnvm.uconn.edu
World Wide Web: http://www.uconn.edu/

UNIVERSITY OF DAYTON
DAYTON, OHIO

The University

Established in 1850 by the Marianists, the University of Dayton is among the nation's leading Catholic universities, committed to educating students as value-centered leaders in their chosen professions and in society. Currently, 10,200 students attend UD, including 6,400 full-time undergraduate students. Students attracted to the University, more than 95 percent of whom choose to be resident students, come from most states and many countries. The technology-enhanced learning and student computer initiative provides every student living in a UD residence with high-speed data access to learning resources and collaboration tools. Extensive programs of study are offered in the College of Arts and Sciences and in the Schools of Business Administration, Education and Allied Professions, Engineering, and Law.

The residential nature of the campus encourages active extracurricular involvement. More than 160 clubs and organizations exist on campus, including more than thirty service organizations, fifty-three professional clubs, twenty-three honorary societies, theatrical and musical performance groups, and fraternities and sororities. NCAA Division I intercollegiate athletics as well as intramural sports are also prevalent. Men's intercollegiate teams include baseball, basketball, football, golf, soccer, and tennis. Women's intercollegiate sports include basketball, crew, golf, indoor and outdoor track, soccer, softball, tennis, and volleyball. Cross-country is a coeducational intercollegiate sport. Club sports, such as crew, lacrosse, water polo, and rugby, are also popular. A variety of special events include everything from symposia and concerts to parents' weekends and a huge Christmas on Campus celebration every December 8.

The John F. Kennedy Memorial Union offers a variety of services for the University community, including numerous cultural, educational, social, and recreational activities. The facility includes a theater; an art gallery; a food court containing a pizzeria, bakery, grill, delicatessen, and candy counter; WDCR, a student-operated AM radio station; Flyer-TV, a student-run television station; bowling lanes and billiards; and the Commuter Lounge.

Location

The campus is located on a 110-acre hilltop, 2 miles from the city of Dayton. The Dayton metropolitan area is a healthy, growing community of approximately 951,000 people in southwestern Ohio. Top cultural, recreational, and entertainment programs are available during the year. Dayton has the highest concentration of scientists and engineers in the United States. Varied business, industrial, research, and educational enterprises provide students with extensive work opportunities related to their academic disciplines.

Majors and Degrees

The College of Arts and Sciences offers the Bachelor of Arts degree in American studies, chemistry, communication (electronic media, journalism, management, public relations, and theater), criminal justice studies, economics, English, fine arts, geology, history, international studies and human rights, languages (French, German, and Spanish), mathematics, music, philosophy, photography, political science, psychology, religious studies, sociology, theater, and visual arts (art education, art history, fine arts, photography, and visual communication design).

The Bachelor of Science is awarded in applied mathematical economics, biochemistry, biology, chemistry, computer information systems, computer science, environmental biology, environmental geology, geology, mathematics, physical science, physics, physics–computer science, predentistry, premedicine, and psychology.

The School of Business Administration offers the Bachelor of Science degree in accounting, economics, finance, international business, management, management information systems, and marketing.

The Bachelor of Science in Education is awarded in the ADA didactic program in dietetics, exercise science/fitness management, exercise science/fitness and nutrition, exercise science/pre–physical therapy, health information specialist studies, nutrition, physical education, and sport management through the Department of Health and Sport Science. Through the Department of Teacher Education, a Bachelor of Science degree is awarded in early childhood education, intervention specialist studies (special education), middle childhood education, and adolescence to young adult education. Students can also receive a validation in reading.

The School of Engineering awards the Bachelor of Chemical Engineering, Bachelor of Civil Engineering, Bachelor of Science in Computer Engineering, Bachelor of Electrical Engineering, and Bachelor of Mechanical Engineering. The School of Engineering also offers a Bachelor of Science in engineering technology, one of the few four-year programs available in the country, with programs in computer engineering technology, electronic engineering technology, industrial engineering technology, manufacturing engineering technology, and mechanical engineering technology.

The University also offers the Bachelor of Fine Arts (art, art education, photography, and visual communication design), Bachelor of Music (music composition, music education, music performance, and music therapy), and Bachelor of General Studies. Undeclared admission options are offered in the College of Arts and Sciences and the Schools of Business Administration, Education and Allied Professions, and Engineering. A prelaw program (including advising and assistance in course selection) is available to students in all degree programs.

Academic Program

The academic year consists of two semesters, with two 6-week sessions available during the summer. While graduation requirements vary according to academic majors, a minimum of 120 semester credit hours is required of all bachelor's degree programs. Students following four-year programs must successfully complete requirements in communication, English, mathematics, and philosophy and/or religious studies. Likewise, the University has instituted a program of study for all students that provides a general education in the humanities, arts, and social and natural sciences. This program develops students' abilities to integrate their knowledge and express themselves effectively.

The University scholars program provides special courses, seminars, and programming for students of proven ability and enthusiasm. An annual symposium allows students to interact with distinguished experts in their fields. Currently, more than 1,000 students are designated as University scholars. In addition, the honors program enrolls 160 of the nation's brightest students in its interdisciplinary, four-year curriculum. The program provides selected students with an opportunity to combine a solid liberal education with generously supported cutting-edge research.

Several opportunities also exist for students to integrate traditional academic majors with many progressive, innovative programs. These programs include study abroad, cooperative education and internship programs, the ability to earn the B.A. or B.S. degree with teacher certification, individually designed majors, and multidisciplinary programs.

Academic Facilities

The newest addition to the University is the Ryan C. Harris Learning-Teaching Center, which is technologically ahead of its time with a wireless network installed throughout the center. This high-tech, experimental learning space includes an adaptive computer lab to help students who have physical or learning disabilities and a meeting room with groupware capability—the latest technology available to facilitate effectiveness in decision making, brainstorming, and other group work. Dedicated in 1997, Joseph E. Keller Hall is the home for the School of Law. A 122,500-square-foot complex, this state-of-the-art facility provides law students the opportunity to learn through a comprehensive and technologically sophisticated environment. The $16.3-million Jesse Philips Center for the Humanities opened in fall 1993. Located in the heart of campus, the building's traditional stone and brick exterior encloses a modern facility for several departments responsible for UD's nationally famous general education program.

The Roesch Library, an eight-story facility with more than 1.3 million volumes, provides exceptional resources for research and scholarship. Recently renovated St. Joseph Hall, one of the University's most treasured academic buildings, houses five academic departments, as well as the Centers for International Studies, Women's Studies, and Family and Community Research. The Anderson Information Sciences Center, a $3.5-million complex donated to the University by NCR Corporation, contains state-of-the-art undergraduate computer laboratories and classrooms. Kettering Laboratories, location of the School of Engineering, also houses part of the University of Dayton Research Institute, currently performing $46 million annually in research. A multimillion-dollar renovation of the UD field house complex was completed in 1990, providing athletic offices, classrooms, and facilities. The $4.3-million Donoher Basketball Center, a 23,000-square-foot, NBA-level quality facility, opened in fall 1998.

Costs

Tuition, including the University fee, for 2000–01 is $8035 per semester. The cost of a double room in a residence hall is $1390 per semester. Private and University-owned accommodations are available off campus for upperclass students. Three types of meal plan contracts are available, ranging in cost from $1150 to $1300 per term. To cover weekend meals and other food expenses not covered by the meal plan, students may open a debit account, Flyer Express, which is accepted at most on-campus locations as well as at select vendors.

Financial Aid

Each year, more than 90 percent of first-year UD students receive financial aid. Assistance is available in the form of nonrepayable grants, educational loans, and part-time employment. A parent loan program and a University-sponsored payment plan are available. Students applying for federal, state, and University-sponsored financial aid must complete the Free Application for Federal Student Aid (FAFSA). Priority is given to students whose completed applications are received by the office of scholarships and financial aid by March 31.

In addition, UD has an extensive academic scholarship program. Scholarships are based on academic achievement, demonstrated leadership, and athletic and artistic talent. Students must complete the Application for Undergraduate Admission and Scholarship. Applications must be received on or before January 1. Due to the influx of applications for these awards, students are strongly encouraged to apply before the Christmas holiday. Athletic scholarships are available in men's intercollegiate basketball, baseball, soccer, golf, tennis, and cross-country, as well as women's intercollegiate basketball, volleyball, soccer, softball, golf, tennis, indoor/outdoor track, and cross-country. Athletic scholarship eligibility is determined by the Department of Intercollegiate Athletics. Music awards are available for both music majors and nonmajors who distinguish themselves as outstanding performers at their admission audition. Scholarships for musical or visual art talents are determined by the faculties of the appropriate academic departments.

A financial aid counselor is available to meet with interested students and their parents to review information pertaining to financial aid eligibility. High school seniors and their parents who are interested in receiving an estimate of financial aid eligibility are encouraged to request an appointment when scheduling a campus visit with the office of admission. Families should request and complete the Financial Need Estimator Form prior to their visit or bring along a copy of their completed FAFSA form so that their eligibility for aid can be discussed in detail.

Faculty

There are 386 full-time faculty members, of whom 92 percent hold the highest degree in their field. UD faculty members have been recognized for their excellence by several organizations, including General Motors Corporation, the National Institute of Education, and the National Endowment for the Humanities. Professors are actively engaged in research and scholarship, often involving undergraduate students, but their primary focus is teaching. Classes are generally small enough for close personal contact. Faculty members act as advisers to students and are frequently accessible in and out of the classroom.

Student Government

The Student Government Association (SGA) is an autonomous association that concerns itself with the academic, recreational, and cultural welfare of UD students. SGA support prompted the opening of UD's first student-owned and -operated convenience store. The organization's efforts were instrumental in creating the National Association for Students at Catholic Colleges and Universities, which addresses the specific concerns of Catholic campuses. SGA-sponsored activities include a speaker series, Little Siblings' Weekend, and the annual Dayton-to-Daytona trip.

Admission Requirements

The University of Dayton admits qualified students regardless of sex, race, color, creed, national or ethnic origin, age, or handicap. Students possessing the aptitude and motivation to succeed at UD are encouraged to apply for admission. Balanced consideration is given to all aspects of students' demonstrated preparation, including selection of college-preparatory courses, grade point average and grade pattern throughout high school, class rank, standardized test scores (SAT I or ACT), and record of leadership and service. A personal statement and guidance counselor recommendation are strongly recommended. In recent years, nearly 80 percent of entering students graduated in the top half of their high school class.

Applicants should present 16 core units from an accredited high school. The minimum core includes 4 units in English, 4 electives, 3 in math, 3 in social studies, and 2 in science. Some programs may require more extensive preparation in specific subject areas. Two units of a foreign language are required for admission to the College of Arts and Sciences. Students who plan to major in a natural science, mathematics, computer science, engineering, or business will find a strong mathematics background necessary.

Application and Information

The applicant must submit a completed UD Application for Undergraduate Admission, a satisfactory high school record, and results of the SAT I or ACT examination. The University operates on a rolling admission policy; however, there is a priority deadline of January 1. The first notifications of acceptance are mailed in October. Some academic programs close new student enrollment before others, so it is recommended that students apply as early as possible. The application fee is $30. The application fee is waived for students who submit the electronic application, which is available on UD's Web site listed below.

Director of Admission
University of Dayton
300 College Park Avenue
Dayton, Ohio 45469-1300
Telephone: 937-229-4411
              800-837-7433 (toll-free)
E-mail: admission@udayton.edu
World Wide Web: http://admission.udayton.edu/

UNIVERSITY OF DAYTON
School of Engineering
DAYTON, OHIO

The University

The University of Dayton was founded in 1850 and the School of Engineering in 1910. The total undergraduate enrollment in engineering and engineering technology is 1,264, of whom 999 are in the undergraduate engineering programs and 265 are in the engineering technology programs. States with the largest enrollments are New York, New Jersey, Pennsylvania, Indiana, Illinois, and Ohio. Twenty-nine countries are represented. The total University undergraduate enrollment is 6,458 full-time and 560 part-time students.

The University engages in intercollegiate competition in baseball, basketball, cross-country, football, golf, soccer, and tennis. Top-ranked basketball teams meet the University team in a modern arena that seats 13,450. The Kennedy Union is a center for social life.

Location

With its suburbs, Dayton has a metropolitan population of about 951,200. The area offers the recreational, cultural, social, and educational facilities that are usually found in communities of this size. It is within commuting distance of Cincinnati (60 minutes), and Indianapolis and Columbus are nearby.

Ohio ranks high among the states in the number of engineers and technologists who live within its boundaries, and Dayton ranks first among Ohio cities in the ratio of engineers and scientists to the total population. There is a heavy concentration of technology in the area, a favorable setting for a school of engineering and technology. Many engineering and engineering technology students either work part-time or serve summer internships in local industry.

Majors and Degrees

The School of Engineering offers four-year curricula leading to the degrees of Bachelor of Chemical Engineering, Bachelor of Civil Engineering, Bachelor of Electrical Engineering, Bachelor of Mechanical Engineering, Bachelor of Science in Computer Engineering, and Bachelor of Science in Engineering Technology. Engineering Technology curricula are offered in computer engineering technology, electronic engineering technology, industrial engineering technology, manufacturing engineering technology, and mechanical engineering technology.

Academic Program

The engineering program in each of the fields is designed to lead to a bachelor's degree in a four-year period. For the bachelor's degrees in engineering, the number of semester hours required varies from 133 to 137; for the Bachelor of Science in technology, from 130 to 132. For graduation, the cumulative grade point average must be 2.0 or higher. Each engineering program is flexible and permits additional minors in such areas as industrial, environmental, aerospace, and materials engineering, as well as mathematics, music, and languages. Students majoring in any engineering technology program may earn a minor in another engineering technology program by completing 12 approved semester hours of work in the second discipline. The Department of Mechanical and Aerospace Engineering offers the student the opportunity to pursue a concentration in aerospace engineering, and the Department of Electrical and Computer Engineering offers a concentration in computer engineering in addition to the Bachelor of Science in Computer Engineering.

As the first-year curriculum is the same for all branches of engineering, students may choose to wait until they have completed the first year before deciding on their special field. As an educational unit within a private university, the School places strong emphasis on the individualized faculty/student advising program that begins before the start of the student's formal course work at the University. The advising program is designed to ensure that each student will be challenged and will meet his or her educational objectives within the School's program by being paired with a faculty member. Advanced placement is granted to those students who qualify under certain Advanced Placement testing programs.

At the end of the junior year in engineering, students qualified for graduate study may arrange their senior year to include some courses for graduate credit.

Students may participate in the cooperative education, internship, and summer employment programs. These programs offer the student the opportunity to put classroom work into practical use while still in school, resulting in early career identification and greater motivation as well as providing a source of income.

Academic Facilities

The Eugene W. Kettering Engineering and Research Laboratories houses nearly all of the engineering, technology, and Research Institute activities. The six-floor structure is air conditioned and contains 88 laboratories, 3 computer classrooms, 11 classrooms, 115 faculty offices, and 8 seminar rooms in 211,000 square feet of space. All departments in the facility are directly connected with the facilities of the University computer center.

The University engages in approximately $40 million worth of research each year. Several research projects at the University of Dayton are attracting international attention.

Costs

Tuition and University fees for 2000–01 are $16,070 for two terms. The engineering surcharge is $535 per term. Room and board on campus are approximately $5080 for two terms. Books and supplies cost approximately $350 to $375 per term.

Financial Aid

The University of Dayton attempts to assist all qualified students in obtaining financial assistance to continue their education. The University has established a comprehensive program of student aid that includes loans, grants, scholarships, tuition reductions, and part-time employment. Approximately 90 percent of the students receive financial aid, primarily in the form of scholarships, grants, work-study, and loans. For a detailed description, interested students may write for a financial aid brochure.

Faculty

The School of Engineering has 64 full-time and 40 part-time faculty members, most of whom have doctoral degrees. Graduate assistants are employed in laboratory and research work, but classroom instruction is always conducted by regular faculty members. All faculty members serve as advisers to the students.

Student Government

The Student Government is the major vehicle for student opinion at the University of Dayton. Other student groups abound, including special interest clubs, service organizations, the Interfraternity Council, and the Panhellenic Council. There are twenty-one student organizations related to engineering and engineering technology.

Admission Requirements

Applicants for the first-year class must have graduated from a high school accredited by a regional accrediting association or by a state department of education. The following units are recommended for entrance into the engineering program: English, 4; algebra, 1; geometry, 1; trigonometry/algebra II, 1; math IV, 1; chemistry, 1; physics, 1; and foreign language, 2–4. For the engineering technology program, it is recommended that students have 4 units of English, 2 units of algebra, and 1 unit in another mathematics area.

To apply for entrance into the first-year class, candidates must submit a written application, a transcript of the high school record, and scores on the SAT I or ACT.

The School of Engineering welcomes transfer students from both community and senior colleges and works closely with many schools to facilitate transfers from pre-engineering programs. Students may complete the first two years of study in other accredited institutions and transfer to the University of Dayton with little or no loss of credit provided they follow a program similar to that prescribed by the University of Dayton School of Engineering.

Application and Information

Application forms may be obtained by contacting the admission office. Students can also submit the admission application electronically via the World Wide Web. Students may visit the University's admission page (http://admission.udayton.edu) or go directly to the application (https://admission.udayton.edu/application.asp). Applications are accepted throughout the year and reviewed on a rolling basis. Due to an increase in applications, some academic programs close new student enrollment early. The Office of Admission has implemented a priority application deadline of January 1. Students are encouraged to apply well in advance of the term in which they would like to enter the University.

For further information, students should contact:

Mr. Myron Achbach, Director of Admission
University of Dayton
300 College Park
Dayton, Ohio 45469-1300
Telephone: 937-229-4411
          800-837-7433 (toll-free)
Fax: 937-229-4729
E-mail: admission@udayton.edu
Dean
School of Engineering
University of Dayton
300 College Park
Dayton, Ohio 45469-0228
Telephone: 937-229-2736
E-mail: udsoe@engr.udayton.edu

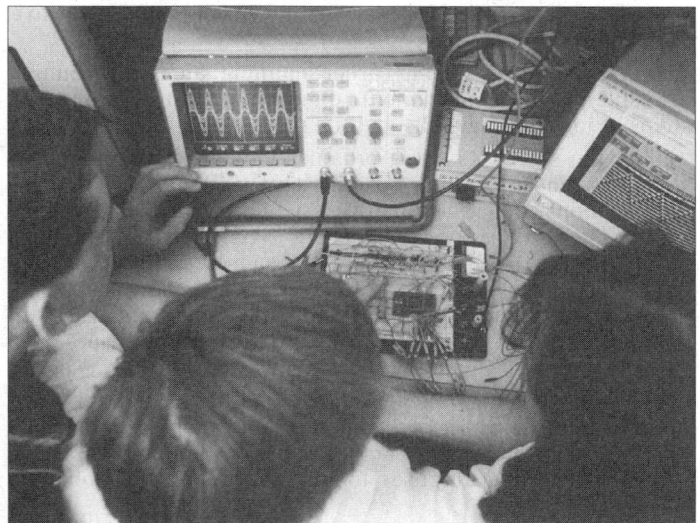

Students at the University of Dayton School of Engineering.

UNIVERSITY OF DETROIT MERCY
DETROIT, MICHIGAN

The University

University of Detroit Mercy (UDM) is the largest independent Catholic university in Michigan. It offers its students an education that is superior in scope and diversity and firmly rooted in the Jesuit and Mercy traditions of academic quality and community service. With an undergraduate enrollment of 4,000 students from thirty states and forty-five countries, the University combines academic excellence with a value-based, student-centered focus.

In addition to offering the baccalaureate majors, the University grants master's degrees in more than forty fields, as well as Ph.D. degrees in chemistry, clinical psychology, and engineering. The University also has its own law and dental schools. University of Detroit Mercy's current enrollment is approximately 6,200.

University services include career planning, an award-winning advising program, placement, diagnostic testing, and workshops in job-hunting skills and life planning.

Among the seventy student organizations are fraternities and sororities, most of them chapters of national Greek-letter organizations that recognize high achievement in specialized areas. The University competes in NCAA Division I men's baseball, basketball, cross-country, fencing, golf, soccer, and track. The women's varsity teams compete in basketball, cross-country, fencing, soccer, softball, tennis, and track. In addition, the University has an extensive intramural program for all students, including basketball, floor hockey, soccer, softball, and volleyball. Skiing clubs are also available.

Campus ministry assists and supports students in their spiritual growth and development. Campus ministry staff members serve students on both campuses for quiet prayer, reflection, and scheduled liturgy.

More than 800 students are currently housed in the University's seven residence halls on the McNichols campus. Limited on-campus facilities are available for married students.

Location

University of Detroit Mercy is located in Detroit and is surrounded by thousands of exciting sports, music and entertainment venues, museums and art galleries, and restaurants and pubs. UDM's urban location allows for faculty members and students to partner with leaders in the healthcare, business, and automotive industries. UDM is also just a short drive from Canada and another bustling metropolitan area, Windsor, Ontario. In addition, numerous parks and recreation areas are less than an hour's drive from the campus.

The University provides many services to the community through such facilities as its Dental Clinic, Urban Law Clinic, and Psychology Clinic, which offer training for students and are open to the public.

Majors and Degrees

The College of Liberal Arts awards bachelor's degrees in communication studies, economics, electronic critique, English, history, philosophy, political science, psychology, religious studies, sociology, and theater.

The College of Business Administration grants bachelor's degrees in accounting, business administration, and computer and information systems.

The College of Education and Human Services offers bachelor's degrees in addiction studies, criminal justice, human services, legal administration, social work, and teacher education (elementary education, secondary education, and special education). There are associate degree programs in addiction studies and legal assistant studies.

The College of Engineering and Science offers bachelor's degrees in chemical, civil, electrical, and mechanical engineering. The Bachelor of Science degree is awarded in biochemistry, biology, chemistry, computer science, and mathematics.

The College of Health Professions offers bachelor's degrees in health services, health services administration, and nursing.

The School of Dentistry offers an undergraduate program leading to a Bachelor of Science degree in dental hygiene.

Preprofessional programs are offered in dentistry, law, and medicine.

Academic Program

University of Detroit Mercy believes that all students benefit from a foundation in the liberal arts regardless of their choice of major. All students complete a core curriculum, consisting of courses designed to ensure that students receive, in addition to preprofessional training, a broad liberal education consistent with the mission of the University.

Degree programs in the College of Liberal Arts provide a balance of academic experience across a broad spectrum of programs. The award-winning Academic Exploration program helps undecided students clarify their academic and career goals.

The College of Business Administration offers a solid background in the liberal arts plus a breadth of business courses with specialization in a particular area of business. Instruction in ethics and the behavioral sciences and a knowledge of modern management concepts are stressed, contributing to the development of leadership skills.

Students in engineering programs in the College of Engineering and Science are encouraged to explore the humanities and social sciences. Students are advised to select one application area of in-depth study—automotive, environment, or manufacturing—to accompany their development in an engineering discipline. Three required terms of cooperative education provide full-time industrial experience. The professional and preprofessional programs in the sciences reflect the same value orientation found in all University programs, as well as the development of specialized areas of study.

The University has been in the forefront of cooperative education since 1911, when such a program was initiated along with the founding of the School of Engineering. Since then, the opportunity for cooperative education has been extended to all the undergraduate schools. Students are able to gain practical experience in a professional setting by alternating semesters of academic work and on-the-job training in business, industry, or government agencies. Students currently work in approximately 200 business, government, and community organizations in more than twenty states.

The Leadership Development Institute (LDI) coordinates student volunteer service learning opportunities in conjunction with classroom study. LDI also organizes community service projects and schedules workshops on goal setting, leadership skills, and civic responsibility.

The Urban Health Education Center (UHEC) promotes integrated learning experiences for students in the health, teacher education, and human services disciplines. Students benefit from the community-based, interpersonal clinical and practicum experiences as part of the learning process.

Off-Campus Arrangements

University of Detroit Mercy participates in a program of exchanges of students, faculty members, and certain resources with other member institutions of the Detroit Area Consortium of Catholic Colleges and Universities.

Academic Facilities

Each campus of the University has its own library. The libraries have a total collection of 797,582 volumes and approximately 11,000 audiovisual items, exclusive of a depository collection of U.S. government documents. Approximately 2,440 leading literary, scientific, and professional periodicals are received. In addition, as members of the Online Computer Library Center, a national computer network, the libraries have access to the collections of more than 15,000 member libraries with more than 27 million records.

The Ford Life Sciences Building houses biology laboratories and classrooms. The Smith Media Center houses facilities of the Communications Studies Department, as well as audiovisual services. The College of Engineering and Science has an advanced computer laboratory, an environmental center, and an automotive electronics laboratory. In addition, the world-renowned Polymer Institute for chemical and polymer research is located in the Engineering Building. The Health Professions, Education, and Human Services programs are primarily offered in Marian Hall on the Outer Drive campus. In 1997, a School of Dentistry building offering state-of-the-art classroom and clinical experience opened at the Outer Drive campus.

Costs

For 1999–2000, tuition for new students was $7050 per semester, and board and a double room cost $5110 per academic year. Books and supplies cost about $700.

Financial Aid

UDM's generous scholarship and financial aid packages make a private education affordable. More than 70 percent of UDM's students receive financial aid in combination packages of federal, state, and University scholarships, grants and loans, and part-time employment through the Federal Work-Study Program. The criteria used in granting aid are academic achievement (grade point average and standardized test scores) and financial need. Four-year, full-tuition scholarships are available to students with outstanding academic records and who demonstrate the ability to make an impact on the campus life at UDM. To apply for UDM scholarships and aid, students must complete an application for admission as well as submit the Free Application for Federal Student Aid (FAFSA).

Faculty

There are 323 faculty members teaching full-time at the University, 87 percent of whom have the terminal degree for their field and 71 percent of whom have the Ph.D. The faculty-student ratio is 1:15. Faculty advisory service is available for both academic and personal matters.

Student Government

The student governing body that represents all full-time students is the Student Senate, through which students and faculty members join in developing and coordinating the cocurricular activities of the University.

Admission Requirements

In making its selections, the Committee on Admissions considers academic performance in secondary school, the recommendations of the student's principal or guidance counselor, results on the ACT or SAT I, and the character, motivation, and leadership qualities demonstrated by the student in academic and extracurricular activities.

The freshman class that enrolled in September 1999 had the following characteristics: 3.3 grade point average and average test scores of 22 (composite) on the ACT. Fifty-seven percent of the incoming freshmen ranked in the top 25 percent of their high school graduating class.

University of Detroit Mercy is committed to the principle of equal opportunity for all, regardless of age, race, creed, national or ethnic origin, or handicap.

Application and Information

Further information on the University and on applying can be obtained by contacting the Admissions Office. A visit to the campus is advised.

Admissions Office
University of Detroit Mercy
4001 West McNichols Road
Detroit, Michigan 48221
Telephone: 313-993-1245
          800-635-5020 (toll-free)
E-mail: admissions@udmercy.edu
World Wide Web: http://www.udmercy.edu

A scenic tree-lined campus and a culturally diverse student body contribute to the enriching and stimulating educational environment at University of Detroit Mercy.

UNIVERSITY OF EVANSVILLE
EVANSVILLE, INDIANA

The University

The University of Evansville, established in 1854, is a private, coeducational university affiliated with the United Methodist Church. It offers a curriculum deeply entrenched in the traditional arts and sciences, while emphasizing skills essential to personal and professional success. Also inherent in the University of Evansville's educational mission is the enhancement of a student's view of the world. Students have the unique opportunity to experience study abroad at the University's own British campus, Harlaxton College, located in Grantham, England, or through a host of other international study opportunities made available to UE students.

EXCEL (Experiential and Collaborative Environment for Learning) is an innovative approach to the college learning and living experience. Through EXCEL, the University incorporates various programs designed to aid students in the transition from high school to college; to enhance their college community experience; to foster relationships with business, industry, and University alumni; and to utilize Internet technology in promoting UE graduates to potential employers.

The student body of 2,752 undergraduates is diverse; students come from fifty states and forty-three countries. Approximately 60 percent are Indiana residents. Students participate in more than 140 social and academic organizations and more than forty intercollegiate and intramural sports.

In addition to regional accreditation, the University has program accreditation with the American Bar Association, the Accreditation Board for Engineering and Technology, the American Chemical Society, the American Physical Therapy Association, the National Association of Schools of Music, the National Association for Music Therapy, the National Council for Accreditation of Teacher Education, and the National League for Nursing. Among the graduate degrees offered at the University is the Department of Physical Therapy's entry-level Master of Science degree in physical therapy.

Location

With a population of 136,000, Evansville, Indiana, is the third-largest city in the state. It is situated at the southwestern corner of Indiana on the banks of the Ohio River in proximity to Indianapolis, Indiana; St. Louis, Missouri; Nashville, Tennessee; and Louisville, Kentucky. The city has a variety of cultural outlets, such as museums, galleries, theaters, and orchestras, as well as numerous outdoor recreation adventures such as hiking in the nearby Hoosier National Forest, boating on the Ohio River, and snow skiing at Paoli Peaks, to name a few.

Students gain valuable real-world experience from cooperative relationships between the University and tri-state area businesses and industries via cooperative work programs, internships, and externships.

Majors and Degrees

Within the College of Arts and Sciences, degrees are awarded with majors in archaeology, athletic training, biochemistry, biology, chemistry, classical and biblical studies, creative writing, economics, English, English literature, environmental administration, environmental studies, exercise science, French, German, health and physical education, history, international studies, interpersonal communication, mass communication, mathematics, philosophy, physics, political science, psychobiology, psychology, religion, sociology, Spanish, and sports medicine. Preprofessional programs are available in dentistry, law, medicine, optometry, pharmacy, social work, theology, and veterinary science. Minors are offered in anthropology, criminal justice, geography, and women's studies.

The School of Business Administration confers the Bachelor of Science in Business Administration, with concentrations in finance, global studies, management, and marketing; the Bachelor of Science in Accounting; the Bachelor of Science in Economics; and the Bachelor of Science in Legal Studies.

The School of Education and Health Sciences confers the Bachelor of Science degree with majors in clinical special education, elementary education, physical education, and secondary education. Special education endorsements are available in education of the mildly disabled, seriously emotionally handicapped, and severely disabled. The School of Education participates in an Activity-Based Learning Experience program in elementary education, which enables students to take part in classroom experiences throughout their program. A Bachelor of Science degree in nursing, an entry-level master's degree, and an Associate of Science degree in physical therapist assistant studies are available, as is a certificate of specialization in gerontology.

The College of Engineering and Computer Science grants the Bachelor of Science degree in civil, computer, electrical, and mechanical engineering, as well as in computer science and engineering management. Degree programs in civil, computer, electrical, and mechanical engineering are accredited by the Engineering Accreditation Commission of the Accreditation Board for Engineering and Technology (ABET). A cooperative education program combining study with practical work experience is also available.

The Bachelor of Fine Arts is available in art, theater design and technology, and theater performance; the Bachelor of Music in music education, music performance, and music therapy; the Bachelor of Science in art, art and associated studies, graphic design, music, music management, theater, and theater management; and the Bachelor of Arts in art, art education, art history, music, and theater. The art and associated studies program is sound preparation for students seeking a graduate degree in art therapy.

Academic Program

Forty credit hours must be completed in general education for the bachelor's degree. General education is based on a world cultures theme. The requirement consists of a three-course sequence in world cultures; courses in humanities, fine arts, natural science, social science, mathematics, and foreign language; and a senior capstone course, all integrated into the theme. The University follows a semester calendar. Fall classes begin in late August, and the second semester begins in mid-January. Summer session course work is also offered.

Credit by examination may be granted to an incoming student who demonstrates a superior level of achievement in a particular subject. The University of Evansville participates in the College Board's Advanced Placement Program and College-Level Examination Program. For entering freshmen and transfer students, the University also conducts its own testing program during orientation through which a student may demonstrate proficiency or place out of course requirements.

Off-Campus Arrangements

Harlaxton College, the British campus of the University of Evansville, is located in Grantham, Lincolnshire, England—22 miles east of Nottingham and 110 miles north of London. Established by the University in 1971, Harlaxton College provides fully accredited course work in a variety of disciplines for 180 students each semester. This unusual study-abroad program offers students the opportunity to experience a culture different from their own while strengthening their understanding of our Western society. Study on the campus in England is open to all upperclass UE students and students from other colleges and universities who are currently in good academic standing. All financial assistance awarded at the Evansville campus may also be utilized at the Harlaxton campus.

Academic Facilities

The Bower-Suhrheinrich Library houses 263,627 bound books and journals; 1,380 current titles, including periodicals, newspapers, and government documents; 419,776 microforms; and 9,385 video and audio titles. A catalog of these holdings is accessible through a computerized database. The University also maintains a music listening library.

All University buildings, thirteen computer labs, and residence halls are connected with the Internet.

The Koch Center for Engineering and Sciences houses offices, classrooms, and laboratories for the College of Engineering and Computing Sciences as well as for the departments of biology, chemistry, mathematics, physics, and psychology.

The Krannert Hall of Fine Arts includes music listening and practice rooms, the Wheeler Concert Hall, an art exhibit gallery, studios, and art laboratories.

The University has an award-winning student-operated radio station with a Foreign Correspondent Program that is available through UE's Harlaxton College, located in Grantham, England. A TV production studio on campus also offers students hands-on experience.

Costs

Tuition for 2000–01 is $16,100; campus room and board are $5220. The required full-time registration and activity fees are $304, and the average cost of books and supplies is $700.

Financial Aid

The University's comprehensive financial aid program, through which 90 percent of the students receive assistance, consists of scholarships, grants, loans, and on-campus employment. UE participates in the Federal Pell Grant and Federal Work-Study programs. Federal Perkins Loans and Federal Stafford Student Loans are also available. Merit scholarships are also available and consist of Academic Departmental Scholarships, which are awarded by all academic departments to outstanding students displaying high academic achievement; the Leadership Activity Award for students who have been active in multiple school, church, or community organizations; the Multicultural Scholars Award for students of color; the Legacy Award for children or grandchildren of University of Evansville graduates; United Methodist Scholarships for students who are active in a United Methodist Church; and a Phi Theta Kappa Scholarship for transfer students who are members in good standing.

Students applying for aid must file the Free Application for Federal Student Aid (FAFSA) and the University's own financial aid form.

Faculty

Serious students require an excellent faculty, and the faculty of the University of Evansville is composed of 177 men and women who are outstanding in their respective fields of study. Eighty-four percent hold earned doctorates or other terminal degrees. Students are able to develop close personal relationships and to freely exchange ideas with faculty members because of the student-faculty ratio of 13:1 and because no classes are taught by graduate students.

Student Government

The Student Congress of the University is elected by the students and has representation on the President's Cabinet, the University Senate, and the University Judicial Board. The Student Association includes every enrolled student and, through its executive offices, is responsible for providing effective representative student government. The Student Activities Board is a student organization responsible for arranging social events for the campus community.

Admission Requirements

Factors considered in evaluating a student's readiness for admission to the University of Evansville include high school rank and strength of the curriculum, test scores, previous college work, and other qualifications. Recommendations from high school officials are also considered.

Each applicant for admission to the freshman class is required to take the SAT I or the ACT and must rank in the upper half of his or her high school class. A strong college-preparatory curriculum is necessary. Transfer students must have maintained a minimum 2.0 grade point average.

Application and Information

The University employs two selective deadline dates: an early notification deadline of December 1 and a regular decision deadline of February 1. Admission is on a rolling basis after February 1 as space in the freshman class is available. Transfer admission deadlines are on a rolling basis.

For additional information and application materials, students should contact:

Office of Admission
University of Evansville
1800 Lincoln Avenue
Evansville, Indiana 47722
Telephone: 812-479-2468
          800-423-8633 (toll-free)
E-mail: admission@evansville.edu
World Wide Web: http://www.evansville.edu

The University of Evansville's Olmsted Administration Hall.

THE UNIVERSITY OF FINDLAY
FINDLAY, OHIO

The University

The University of Findlay is a private coeducational institution with 4,000 full- and part-time students. Founded in 1882 by the Churches of God, General Conference, it emphasizes preparation for careers and professions in an educational program that blends liberal arts and career education. Students of many denominations attend Findlay, and religious participation is a matter of personal choice.

Bachelor of Arts degree programs are available in forty different majors. The Associate of Arts degree is awarded in nearly twenty areas. Master's degrees are offered in business administration, education, environmental management, and teaching English to speakers of other languages (TESOL).

The largest programs at Findlay are in natural sciences, business, and social sciences. Majors in the sciences include athletic training, equestrian studies (English, Western, and equine management), nuclear medicine, occupational therapy, physical therapy, physician assistant studies, and pre–veterinary medicine. Business degrees are founded in a three-year comprehensive core program with eight different majors, including an individualized major option.

Opportunities for internships and work-related experiences are available in most major fields through the Professional Experiences Program (PEP).

Most of Findlay's students come from Ohio and the surrounding states of Michigan, Indiana, and Pennsylvania. More than thirty other states are also represented. Because of the Intensive English Language Institute located on the campus, a significant number of international students are part of the total student body.

Resident students live in six modern residence halls. All students eat their meals in an attractive dining hall. Social life at Findlay centers on student organizations, fraternities, and sororities. Findlay has four officially recognized fraternities—Alpha Sigma Phi, Sigma Pi, Tau Kappa Epsilon, and Theta Chi—and two sororities. Each has its own house near campus. Organizations include department and special interest clubs, the newspaper, yearbook, musical groups, a radio station, Circle K, and Aristos Eklektos (honors).

Athletic programs are affiliated with NCAA Division II and the Great Lakes Intercollegiate Athletic Conference. Men's hockey, women's hockey, and men's volleyball are making a transition to Division I. Findlay offers thirteen intercollegiate sports for men: baseball, basketball, cross-country, football, golf, hockey, indoor track and field, outdoor track and field, soccer, swimming and diving, tennis, volleyball, and wrestling. It has eleven varsity sports for women: basketball, cross-country, golf, indoor track and field, outdoor track and field, soccer, softball, swimming and diving, tennis, track, and volleyball. Club sport teams include the equestrian, ice hockey, and water polo teams. Athletic scholarships are available.

Croy Physical Education Center has a 25-meter swimming pool, exercise areas, a gymnasium, offices, and classrooms. The Gardner Fitness Center is a state-of-the-art facility. The 130,000-square-foot Koehler Recreation and Fitness Complex opened in January 1999. It contains the Malcolm Athletic Center, with a six-lane, NCAA regulation track and four multipurpose courts; the Clauss Ice Arena; locker rooms; and offices for the athletic department.

Student services include career and placement counseling, a health center, academic tutoring and personal counseling, and study skills assistance through the Tri-S (Supporting Skills Services) Center.

Location

Findlay was voted the most livable micropolitan city in Ohio and scored among the top twelve in the United States. It is within easy driving distance of Toledo, Columbus, Detroit, and Fort Wayne. Interstate 75 and the Ohio Turnpike (Interstates 80 and 90) are major highways serving the area. Airports in Toledo, Columbus, and Detroit are convenient. The town of Findlay has 38,000 residents and is home to Marathon Oil Corporation and Cooper Tire and Rubber Company. The Findlay campus consists of more than 140 acres on several sites. A 70-acre campus-owned farm houses preveterinary and equine studies. A second 32-acre facility houses the English Hunt Seat Riding Program. Many opportunities exist for students who want business-related and social service agency experience. The University has established strong relationships with the community, which supports athletic and cultural events on the campus. Besides the full program of on-campus activities, off-campus trips to cultural and entertainment events are scheduled. The city of Findlay, which has an excellent business climate, offers part-time job opportunities, volunteer service organizations, and the chance to be involved with the larger civic community. Findlay's campus is attractive, safe, comfortable, and friendly.

Majors and Degrees

The Bachelor of Arts degree is awarded in the following majors: art; bilingual-multicultural education; communications (advertising emphasis); communications (broadcast journalism emphasis); communications (publications emphasis); communications (public relations emphasis); comprehensive religion, philosophy, and Christian education; comprehensive social science; criminal justice; English; English–speech education; history; Japanese; philosophy; political science; psychology; religion; social work; sociology; Spanish; Spanish bilingual-multicultural studies; Spanish-business; speech; speech-education; theater performance; theater production; technical writing; and writing.

Findlay has a dual-degree B.A./B.S.E. program with the engineering schools of Ohio Northern University, the University of Toledo, and Washington University in St. Louis. Minors are offered in gerontology, international business, international relations, and women's studies.

The Bachelor of Science degree is granted in accounting; athletic training; biology; business administration; comprehensive business education; computer science; economics; elementary education; environmental, safety, and occupational health management; equestrian studies (English and Western emphases); equine management; finance; hospitality management; marketing; mathematics; nature interpretation; nuclear medicine technology; occupational therapy; physical education; physical therapy; physician assistant studies; premedicine; prenursing; pre–veterinary medicine; science; systems analysis; and technology management.

The Associate of Arts degree is available in accounting, community social service, computer science, criminal justice (corrections or law enforcement emphasis), environmental and hazardous materials management, equestrian studies, financial management, general social studies, humanities, legal assisting, management information systems, nuclear medicine technology, office administration, religion, sales/retail management, small business/entrepreneurship, and technical communication.

Certificate programs are available in computer applications, environmental and hazardous materials management, gerontology, legal assisting, nuclear medicine technology, and the teaching of shorthand.

Academic Program

Findlay operates on the semester system. Students must complete at least 124 semester hours with a minimum overall grade point average of 2.0 to earn a bachelor's degree. General education requirements and competency requirements in English, reading, computer literacy, speech, and library use must be fulfilled. The Freshman Seminar introduces students to living and learning at Findlay and gives them the opportunity to work with the same teachers and student group in two related courses. The Foundations Program offers students the chance to develop those skills in writing, reading, and thinking needed for their success as college students. Study skills, time management, and academic advising are included. Students are selected for this program at the time of admission. The Honors Program provides additional challenge to those students who qualify on the basis of academic credentials. Study- and travel-abroad programs are offered by various departments. Credit and/or placement can be earned through Advanced Placement (AP) exams.

The Equestrian Program is a well-recognized program of its kind and serves approximately 200 students from throughout the United States and abroad. Majors in equine management and in English and Western riding are offered. The instruction, both in the classroom and on horseback, makes use of the expertise of recognized national equestrian champions. The pre–veterinary medicine program, using the farm facilities, offers the advantages of hands-on experience with livestock and an internship program in a distinctive curriculum. The pre–veterinary medicine program has a placement rate into veterinary schools that is much higher than the national average.

The Nuclear Medicine Institute provides the training necessary to qualify students for careers in nuclear medicine technology, a growing health-related career field.

Findlay's environmental science and hazardous materials management program is a bachelor's degree program that includes internships in the summer. Career opportunities for graduates in environmental sciences are excellent.

The Health Professions Program provides eleven majors, including athletic training, nuclear medicine, physical education (strength and conditioning or teaching emphasis), and recreational therapy. Occupational therapy, physical therapy, and physician assistant studies programs are in the final stages of development.

Academic Facilities

The focal point of the Findlay campus is Old Main, which houses classrooms, faculty and administrative offices, the Computer Center, facilities for various student activities, and Ritz Auditorium. Shafer Library is a member of a sixteen-university consortium that provides extensive resources to the student. The Gardner Fine Arts Pavilion, dedicated in 1994, houses the Mazza Collection of original art from children's books. The University has three networked computer labs in Old Main and one computer lab in Shafer Library. Other academic buildings include Frost Science Complex, with a greenhouse and the Newhard Planetarium, and Egner Fine Arts Center, which houses ceramics and art facilities, a 300-seat theater, and the student-operated radio station. A 101,000-square-foot athletic complex was completed in January 1999. This facility houses a six-lane indoor track, sand pits for long jump, a state-of-the-art timing system, and a wrestling room. Also under the same roof is an ice arena with a seating capacity of 1,200. Approximately 600 horses are stabled and trained at the Center for Equine Studies, which offers first-rate facilities that include barns and indoor and outdoor riding arenas.

Costs

Tuition for the 2000–01 academic year totals $15,830 for most programs, $18,650 for the equestrian programs, and $16,800 for the pre–veterinary medicine program. Room and board cost $5960. The estimated cost for transportation, books, and supplies is $1200.

Financial Aid

Eighty percent of Findlay students receive financial aid. Assistance is based on need as well as scholastic achievement. Factors used in determining aid are the Free Application for Federal Student Aid (FAFSA), grade point average, and ACT or SAT I results. Federal and state programs are used with institution grants and scholarships, including sibling grants. The FAFSA must be filed. Notification of aid awards is made on a rolling basis. Work-study jobs are available. Scholarships for high-achieving students and student athletes are offered.

Faculty

The 15:1 student-faculty ratio results in small classes—usually fewer than 30 students. Professors know their students, and every student has a faculty adviser.

Student Government

The Student Government Association (SGA) and the Campus Program Board are involved in planning and implementing student activities. SGA provides leadership experience for students and enhances cooperation between faculty, administration, and students. A representative from SGA sits on the Board of Trustees. The Campus Program Board plans activities for recreation and cultural enrichment, including free weekly movies and Homecoming and Family Weekend.

Admission Requirements

Applicants to Findlay should have a college-preparatory high school background, including 4 years of English, 2 to 3 years of mathematics, 2 to 3 years of social studies, and 2 years of sciences. A foreign language is recommended but not required. Results of the ACT or SAT I and high school transcripts should be submitted with the application for admission. Transfer students must be eligible to return to the institution last attended and must submit transcripts of all college work. Decisions are made on a rolling basis. Application deadlines are August 1 for fall semester and December 15 for spring semester. A campus visit is strongly recommended. Early admission and advanced standing programs are available. For students not meeting regular minimum admission requirements, Findlay has a Foundations Program, which provides skill building and academic support during the first semester of the freshman year. Findlay is an equal opportunity institution in admission and employment.

Application and Information

Application forms and other information may be obtained by contacting:

Office of Undergraduate Admissions
The University of Findlay
1000 North Main Street
Findlay, Ohio 45840
Telephone: 419-424-4732
              800-548-0932 (toll-free)
E-mail: admissions@findlay.edu
World Wide Web: http://www.findlay.edu

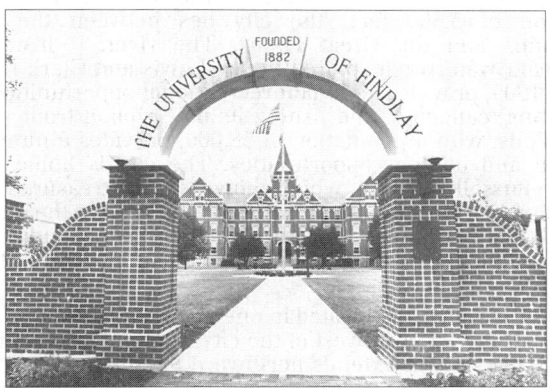

Old Main.

UNIVERSITY OF GREAT FALLS
GREAT FALLS, MONTANA

The University

Recognized as one of the "top 15 best educational buys in the West" in *Money* magazine's College Guide '97, the University of Great Falls (UGF) is a private, independent Catholic university sponsored by the Sisters of Providence within the jurisdiction of the Catholic Bishop of Great Falls–Billings. It is open to qualified men and women of every race and creed. Its academic programs are designed to educate students through curricula featuring liberal arts courses combined with career and professional preparation. The University of Great Falls's mission is to provide students with the opportunity to obtain a liberal arts education for lifelong learning and a successful career or profession. The faculty and staff of the University join with students in a cooperative and enthusiastic search for truth, meaning, and the analytical skills to resolve moral and ethical dilemmas, so that students may develop character, competence, and commitment. Although faculty members participate in applied research, the focus is on teaching. Because teaching students is the primary concern of faculty members, they combine traditional classroom instruction with education using multimedia computer technology and learning through experiences such as internships, field experiences, and community service.

The University was founded in 1932 by Bishop Edwin V. O'Hara to fill the need for an institution of higher education in Great Falls and the central Montana area. The present campus opened in 1960. The contemporary architectural design conveys a modern campus motif. Providence Tower, the main campus landmark, was constructed in 1964, and the McLaughlin Memorial Center, a spacious physical education and recreation facility, was added in 1965. The campus consists of more than a dozen modern buildings, including a classroom building, a library, the DiRocco-Peressini Science Center, a theater/music building, an art building, the Galerie Trinitas, the Trinitas Chapel, and the McLaughlin Recreation Center. The University of Great Falls has been accredited by the Northwest Association of Schools and Colleges since 1935.

In addition to its programs at the undergraduate level, the University also offers the Master of Human Services, the Master of Science in Counseling, the Master of Science in Counseling Psychology, the Master of Education, the Master of Arts in Teaching, the Master of Arts in Liberal Studies, the Master of Science in Criminal Justice Administration, and the Master of Information Systems degrees through the College of Graduate Studies.

Location

The city of Great Falls is located in north central Montana. Situated near the five waterfalls of the Missouri River at an elevation of 3,300 feet, the city lies between the Rocky Mountains and the Great Plains. The river, a historically significant waterway explored by the Lewis and Clark Expedition in 1805, provides abundant recreational opportunities such as boating, canoeing, and fishing its blue-ribbon trout waters. Great Falls, with a population of 58,000, provides a number of cultural and outdoor opportunities. The city is home to the Charlie Russell Museum, which showcases the treasured works of the famous western artist Charles M. Russell. On the museum grounds sits the Russell home and the artist's log studio. Great Falls exemplifies the Western heritage and ethos of the Big Sky Country of Montana.

Great Falls is centrally located in one of the nation's most scenic regions. About an hour west of the city lies the Rocky Mountain Front Range, which extends northward to one of the country's crown jewels, Glacier National Park. The majestic peaks of this area provide outdoor enthusiasts with hundreds of miles of trails and pristine lakes and streams. Four hours to the south of Great Falls is the nation's first national park, Yellowstone. In Yellowstone, abundant herds of bison and elk roam the vast spaces of the park. Many other species of wildlife call Yellowstone home, including the newly re-introduced wolf. For skiing enthusiasts, the Little Belt Mountains, an hour south of Great Falls, offer excellent downhill skiing at Showdown Ski Area and 17 miles of groomed cross-country trails at Silver Crest. In addition to skiing, the surrounding area provides extensive outdoor recreational activities including biking, hiking, camping, technical rock climbing, white-water rafting, archeological explorations, fishing, and hunting.

Majors and Degrees

At the undergraduate level, the University of Great Falls offers bachelor's degrees in twenty-six majors and associate degrees in ten majors. Through the integration of liberal arts and professional preparation, the University helps students prepare for lifelong learning and rewarding careers.

Academic Program

The University develops professional/career programs and continuing education courses designed to meet society's present and future needs, as well as traditional academic degrees in appropriate fields. As part of the undergraduate core curriculum, students acquire fundamental skills and experiences that facilitate comprehension, information processing, and communication within particular disciplines. Beyond the learning required for their chosen majors, students embark on a path of self-discovery and learn to apply meaning to the world around them from historical, contemporary, and future perspectives. All students are required to complete courses in philosophy, religion, history, social sciences, fine arts, literature, computer science, natural science, mathematics, communications, and composition.

The University offers students a foundation for actively implementing spiritual values and a variety of religious teachings, especially in the Catholic tradition, but it also serves students of all beliefs who wish to take advantage of its programs. Students are strongly encouraged to complement classroom learning with nonacademic learning in the areas of community service, wellness activities, and cultural arts.

Off-Campus Arrangements

The Distance Learning Program provides instruction to students throughout Montana, Wyoming, and Alberta, enabling them to complete ten specific bachelor's degrees from off-campus sites. Through distance learning, students in remote areas and those who are place-bound have access to educational opportunities. Distance learning students receive instruction through a variety of media technologies such as videotapes, audio on line, and compressed video.

Academic Facilities

The University library provides informational resources for students and faculty and staff members. The collection contains more than 72,000 books and 549 journal subscriptions. Services include reference, interlibrary loan through the Western Library Network, and online bibliographic search capabilities via Dialog. Research tools available on CD-ROM for student use are LaserCat, ERIC, and Social Science Index (full image). Online research tools for students include LEXIS-NEXIS. In addition, telefax service and word processors are available for student use. Special collections include the McDonald collection of business resources, the Bertsche collection of Montana history, and the Law Library. An audiovisual collection with videocassettes, records, audiocassettes, scores, and other media can be checked out or used in the library.

The main computer lab, located on the first floor of Emily Hall, houses more than forty personal computers, while other labs on campus house more than an additional twenty-five personal computers. These microcomputers are upgraded yearly and are available for use by all students. Students can access the Internet and e-mail through the UGFNET. The lab supports one of the most widely used Windows-based software suites, and printers are available.

The McLaughlin Recreation Center provides facilities for basketball, bowling, pocket billiards, swimming, weightlifting, and other activities. With seating for 357 people, the theater is used frequently by the campus and the community for classes, plays, recitals, and seminars.

Costs

Undergraduate tuition for the 1999–2000 school year was $255 per credit. Room and board for students living in University housing were approximately $1320 per year. Books and supplies were estimated to cost $600 per year.

Financial Aid

Approximately 90 percent of the University of Great Falls's students receive some form of student financial assistance. This assistance includes funding from the U.S. Department of Education, Department of Veterans Affairs, various state agencies, University-managed resources, and private donors. The University offers Federal Pell Grants, Federal Supplemental Educational Opportunity Grants, State Student Incentive Grants, Federal Perkins Loans, federal- and University-supported student employment, and Federal PLUS Loans. In addition, the University offers merit-based scholarships to new and continuing students. Information on need-based financial aid assistance programs is available from the Financial Aid Office. Scholarship information for new students is available from the Office of Admissions and Records. To be considered for financial aid and scholarships, students should submit applications by April 1.

The University of Great Falls requires the Free Application for Federal Student Financial Aid (FAFSA) form, available from a high school counselor or the University.

Faculty

The University of Great Falls features faculty members who possess personal philosophies compatible with a Catholic learning environment. These experienced teachers, of whom 65 percent possess terminal degrees, are not only highly competent in their academic fields, but are also persons of integrity to whom students can look to for example, inspiration, and information. Since a faculty member's influence is of paramount significance in education, ability and willingness to counsel students about classroom concerns are traits expected of each teacher.

Student Government

University of Great Falls's students are represented by the Associated Students of the University of Great Falls. The governing body is an elected Student Senate. The University student government was the first in Montana to eliminate the class structure in favor of giving greater representation to all students. One student is a full voting member of the Board of Trustees. Students are represented in each academic school and serve on the Curriculum Committee; the Admissions, Scholarships, and Financial Aid Committee; the Student Rights and Responsibilities Committee; and the Library Committee.

Admission Requirements

The University of Great Falls has an open admission policy and accepts applicants on a rolling admission basis. Applicants may apply for admission at any time; however, all applicants are strongly urged to apply at least one month prior to the first day of classes of the term for which they intend to enter the University. All required documents must be submitted before a student can be admitted and allowed to register for classes. It is particularly important that the UGF Placement Test be taken prior to registration and that all high school and college or university transcripts be sent to the Office of Admissions and Records in time to evaluate transfer credit and to prepare an academic advising file. The University also has an early admission program for students in high school. The University of Great Falls grants advanced standing credit for AP, CLEP, and ACE military programs.

Application and Information

The University of Great Falls has an open admission policy based on the philosophy that all high school graduates should have the opportunity to pursue a higher education degree. All students are encouraged to apply for admission. Their applications will be considered without regard to race, color, gender, age, religion, marital status, sexual orientation, financial status, physical or mental disabilities, and national origin. All required documents should be submitted to the Office of Admissions and Records. For additional information on the University of Great Falls and for an application packet, student should contact:

Office of Admissions and Records
University of Great Falls
1301 20th Street South
Great Falls, Montana 59405

Telephone: 406-791-5200
        800-856-9544 (toll-free in Colorado, Idaho, Montana, North Dakota, Oregon, South Dakota, Washington, Wyoming, Alberta, British Columbia, and Saskatchewan)
Fax: 406-791-5209
E-mail: adminrec@ugf.edu
World Wide Web: http://www.ugf.edu

The Trinitas Chapel on the campus of the University of Great Falls.

UNIVERSITY OF GUELPH
GUELPH, ONTARIO, CANADA

The University

The University of Guelph is ranked as the top comprehensive university in Canada by *Maclean's* magazine (Canada's national newsmagazine—equivalent to *Time* or *U.S. News & World Report*). This ranking reflects Guelph's distinctiveness as a high-quality, student-focused, residential college that is commited to innovative programs, dynamic student-faculty interaction, and an integration of learning and research. It offers a wide range of undergraduate and graduate programs in the arts, humanities, social sciences, and natural sciences. Building on these core disciplines, Guelph also has a strong commitment to interdisciplinary programs, to a selected range of professional and applied programs, and to agriculture and veterinary medicine as areas of special responsibility.

Established in 1964 when three century-old founding colleges joined with a new college of arts and science, the University of Guelph is a vital community of 13,500 students on a campus of historical and modern buildings and red brick walkways. By Canadian standards Guelph is of medium size, offering a wide range of academic programs while providing a safe, accommodating environment for learning. On-campus living is available for more than 4,600 students, with all new first-semester students guaranteed on-campus housing if they apply by the deadline.

Guelph features up-to-date athletic facilities that include a double arena with an Olympic-size ice surface, two pools, and a fieldhouse. Guelph offers thirty varsity sports teams and in recent years has fielded national and provincial championship football, hockey, and rugby teams.

With 80 percent of Guelph's undergraduate classes having fewer than 50 students, Guelph ensures a personal approach to learning with a 1:20 faculty-student ratio. Canada's first Office of First Year Studies assists new students with the transition for secondary school to university, which gives Guelph a more than 90 percent student retention and graduation rate, the highest among Canadian comprehensive universities.

The University of Guelph offers a Doctor of Veterinary Medicine degree as well as several diploma programs and more than seventy-five master's and doctoral degree programs. The Graduate Calendar is available on the Web at http://www.uoguelph.ca/GraduateStudies/calendar.

Location

Guelph is located in the southwestern Ontario region the *New York Times* calls "Canada's Technology Triangle," a locale known for its high-caliber educational institutions and its innovative companies. This city of almost 100,000 features internationally recognized folk, jazz, and writers' festivals as well as a new multipurpose performing arts center. Positioned within an hour's drive of Toronto, Canada's largest city and airline hub, Guelph offers the comfort of small-community living with the excitement of an international metropolis at its doorstep.

Majors and Degrees

The University of Guelph offers a number of undergraduate degree programs. Programs followed by * indicate co-op programs, which are not normally available to international students.

The University of Guelph offers Bachelor of Arts degrees in agricultural economics, anthropology, art history, classical languages, classical studies, computing and information science*, criminal justice and public policy, drama, economics*, English, European studies, French, geography, history, information systems and human behaviour, international development, management economics, mathematical economics, mathematics, music, philosophy, political science, psychology*, rural development sociology, sociology, Spanish, statistics, studio art, and women's studies.

Bachelor of Applied Science degrees are available in applied human nutrition, child studies*, family and social relations*, and gerontology*. Bachelor of Commerce degrees are available in agricultural business*, hotel and food administration*, housing and real estate management*, human resources management, management economics (industry and finance)*, marketing management*, public management, and tourism management.

Bachelor of Science degrees are available in animal biology, applied mathematics and statistics*, biomedical science, biochemistry*, biological science, biophysics*, chemical physics*, chemistry*, computing and information science*, earth surface science, ecology, environmental biology, food science*, human kinetics, marine and freshwater biology, mathematics, microbiology*, molecular biology and genetics, nutritional sciences, physical sciences, physics*, plant biology, psychology, statistics, theoretical physics, toxicology*, wildlife biology, and zoology.

Bachelor of Science, Agriculture degrees are available in agricultural economics, agroecosystem management, agronomy, animal science, and horticultural science. Bachelor of Science, Environmental Sciences degrees are available in earth and atmosphere science*, ecology*, environmental economics and policy*, environmental monitoring and analysis*, environmental protection*, environmetrics*, environmental geography*, and natural resources management*. Bachelor of Science, Engineering degrees are available in biological engineering*, engineering systems and computing*, environmental engineering*, and water resources engineering*. Bachelor of Science, Technology degrees are available in applied pharmaceutical chemistry* and physics and technology*. The University of Guelph also offers a Doctor of Veterinary Medicine degree and a Bachelor of Landscape Architecture degree as well as special first-year programs in Akademia and MPC^2.

Academic Program

The academic year is divided into three semesters: fall (September through December), winter (January through April), and summer (May through August), with the majority of students attending during the fall and winter semesters. Fall is the normal entry point for all students.

Four-year honors degrees require the completion of eight semesters. Three-year general degrees require the completion of six semesters. A typical full-time semester totals 2.5 credits.

Off-Campus Arrangements

An important part of Guelph's mission is to attract students from around the world and to develop a global perspective in its students. The campus attracts more than 500 international students from eighty-five countries and maintains sixty-five exchange programs with twenty countries. In addition, approximately 350 Guelph students study overseas each year in programs in Africa, Australia, Europe, and South and Central America.

More than thirty of the programs offered at the University of Guelph include co-op work semesters, with 90 percent of the students in these programs finding work. Guelph also offers more than 100 distance degree-credit courses to more than 6,500 Open Learning course registrants.

Academic Facilities

Guelph's two libraries are linked with libraries at two other universities in the region, providing students with access to

7.5 million items through a new state-of-the-art automated library system. Guelph's library holdings include Canada's largest collection of theatre archives, extensive Scottish study materials, and one of the best collections of postcolonial African literature in Canada.

A 30-acre research park adjacent to the campus is home to a growing number of research-intensive industries. Industry and government trust Guelph's faculty members to meet their research needs, offering approximately Can$80 million annually for research that ranges from workplace efficiency to developing better approaches to food packaging and marketing to ensuring the availability of clean water.

All students receive free Central Computing accounts, which allow access to the University's integrated electronic services from on or off campus. These services include e-mail, access to the World Wide Web, computer-assisted instruction, conferencing, and high-quality laser printing. All student residences are directly connected to the Internet via the campus high-speed network. Off-campus students have dial-up access to both free and chargeable modems.

The campus also features two art galleries, a Sculpture Park, and two performance stages. The 408-acre Arboretum has almost 5 miles of jogging trails and nature paths.

Costs

Full-time tuition for the 1999–2000 academic year ranged from Can$1897 to Can$2060 per semester for Canadian residents and from Can$4000 to Can$5750 per semester for international students. Mandatory fees totaled approximately Can$200 per semester, with slight variations according to each college. Student health/dental fees were Can$130 per semester. International students are obliged to purchase health-care coverage through the University. The cost for international students to attend Guelph for two semesters, including tuition and academic fees, housing, clothing, food, and books, totaled between Can$18,500 and Can$26,500.

Financial Aid

The University of Guelph is committed to ensuring that a university education remains an attainable goal. Since 1989, funding for student financial aid has increased 479 percent. In total, Can$10 million in annual student financial aid is given in the form of scholarships, awards, bursaries, and work-study opportunities. In 1999, close to 1,700 first-year students received awards totalling more than Can$2.5 million, and more than an additional Can$1 million was awarded to upper-year students. There are scholarships and bursaries specifically designed for international students, who are also allowed to work on campus.

Faculty

More than 97 percent of Guelph's 600 full-time professors hold the Ph.D. degree or its equivalent, and all strive to bring the excitement and process of research into the learning environment. More than 100 professors have been recognized for their excellence in teaching by external agencies, their peers, and students. No comparably sized faculty in the country has garnered more 3M awards, Canada's most prestigious university teaching honour. Guelph numbers 19 Fellows of the Royal Society of Canada among its researchers.

Student Government

Students are involved at all levels of University government, from the residence council to the Senate and the Board of Governors. The Central Student Association (CSA), which represents all undergraduate students, oversees more than fifty student clubs that range from political to recreational. In addition, there are more than fifty academic and other student-government organisations located on campus. Students also have access to a number of service groups on campus, which range from the Ontario Public Interest Research Group to a community radio station.

Admission Requirements

Ontario applicants must present the Ontario Secondary School Diploma (OSSD), with a minimum of 6 Ontario Academic Credits (OAC) and specific subject requirements for the degree program desired. OAC English 1 is required for all degree programs. For those outside the Ontario secondary school system, the secondary graduation certificate that would admit a student to a university in his or her home country is normally acceptable. Applicants must also satisfy the specific subject requirements for the program desired. Students admitted on the basis of having completed the International Baccalaureate (I.B.) are granted credit for higher-level courses with grades of 5 or better. Applicants who have completed Advanced Placement (AP) exams with a minimum grade of 4 are eligible to receive University credit to a maximum of 2 credits, which is subject to the discretion of the appropriate faculty. United States applicants are required to have a minimum grade point average of 3.0 and a combined SAT I score of 1100 or an ACT score of 23. Applicants should include specific subject requirements at the highest secondary school level offered.

Interested students should call Admission Services or should refer to the Undergraduate Calendar on the World Wide Web (http://www.uoguelph.ca/undergrad_calendar/) for application and document deadline dates and detailed admission information.

Application and Information

For additional information about admissions, academic programs, or University visits and tours, students should contact:

Admission Services
Office of Registrarial Services
Third Floor, University Centre
University of Guelph
Guelph, Ontario N1G 2W1
Canada

Telephone: 519-821-2130
Fax: 519-766-9481
E-mail: info@registrar.uoguelph.ca
World Wide Web: http://www.uoguelph.ca/liason

The University of Guelph's Johnston Hall Clocktower.

UNIVERSITY OF HARTFORD
WEST HARTFORD, CONNECTICUT

The University

The University of Hartford is a fully accredited, independent, nonsectarian institution. The University is composed of nine schools and colleges: the Colleges of Arts and Sciences, Engineering, and Education, Nursing, and Health Professions; Hillyer College; the Barney School of Business and Public Administration; the Hartford Art School; The Hartt School; S. I. Ward College of Technology; and Hartford College for Women.

The current full-time undergraduate enrollment is about 4,100 men and women. A wide range of interests, goals, and backgrounds is found among the students, who represent most of the states in the nation and fifty-four countries. There are about 100 organized student groups, including clubs devoted to special interests or to political, professional, religious, or civic activities. Intercollegiate (NCAA Division I) and intramural athletics, student publications, and AM and FM radio stations provide further opportunities for extracurricular involvement. In addition, The Hartt School, the Hartford Art School, and the University Players present a variety of concerts, exhibitions, and theatrical productions each year. Recreational and fitness needs of the University community as well as intramural and intercollegiate sports are served by a modern 130,000-square-foot Sports Center.

The University maintains a Career Development and Placement Center that provides vocational counseling and information on occupations, employers, testing, and graduate schools; serves as a reference and credential source; and provides an on-campus recruiting program for graduating students. The Division of University College addresses the needs of the part-time adult learner through courses, programs, and educational counseling. A trained counseling staff is available to assist part-time students in planning their education and resolving some of their special concerns and needs.

More than 64 percent of all full-time undergraduates reside on campus. The University offers a wide array of types of residence halls, from traditional dormitory-style to fully equipped town house–style apartments.

Location

The University maintains two campuses, which are located in the residential suburb of West Hartford. The area provides an environment conducive to the development of the student's cultural and intellectual pursuits. The many facilities include libraries, museums, theaters, the Hartford Civic Center and Coliseum, a symphony orchestra, several other colleges, modern shopping centers, fine restaurants, an international airport, surface transportation, and intercity highway systems.

Majors and Degrees

The Bachelor of Arts is offered with majors in art history, biology, chemistry, communication, criminal justice, drama, economics, English, foreign languages and literatures, history, interactive information technology, international studies, mathematics, music, philosophy, physics, political economy, politics and government, professional and technical writing, psychology, and sociology. A Bachelor of Arts in secondary education is offered in the College of Education, Nursing, and Health Professions, with majors in biology, chemistry, English, foreign languages and literatures (French, German, Italian, and Spanish), general science, history, mathematics, physics, and social studies. The Bachelor of Fine Arts is offered in actor theater training, ceramics, dance, design, drawing, experimental studio, illustration, music theater, painting, photography, printmaking, sculpture, and video.

The Bachelor of Music is offered at The Hartt School, with majors in applied music (guitar, orchestral instrument, organ, piano, and voice), composition, jazz studies, music education, music history, music management, music production and technology, opera, piano accompanying and ensemble, and theory. A five-year music education program is also offered, as are five-year double-major programs. Two interdisciplinary music programs are available: the Bachelor of Music with an emphasis in management, offered by The Hartt School in conjunction with the Barney School of Business and Public Administration, and the Bachelor of Science in Engineering with a music-acoustics major, offered by the College of Engineering.

The Bachelor of Science is awarded with majors in biology, chemistry, chemistry-biology, computer science, early childhood education, elementary education, health science, human services, mathematics, mathematics–management science, medical technology, nursing (for registered nurses only), occupational therapy, physics, radiologic technology, respiratory therapy, and special education, offering dual certification and covering emotional disabilities, learning disabilities, and mental retardation. Majors for the Bachelor of Science in Business Administration (B.S.B.A.) degree are accounting, economics and finance, entrepreneurial studies, finance and insurance, insurance, management, and marketing. A combined B.S. in health science and M.S. in physical therapy (B.S./M.S.T.) program is also available.

Additional B.S. programs, offered by the College of Engineering, include ABET-accredited B.S.E.E., B.S.M.E., and B.S.C.E. as well as B.S.Comp.E. and interdisciplinary B.S.E. options. The most popular B.S.E. options are acoustics/music, biomedical engineering, and environmental engineering. Ward College of Technology offers the Bachelor of Science in architectural engineering technology, audio engineering technology, chemical engineering technology, computer engineering technology, electronic engineering technology, and mechanical engineering technology as well as the Associate in Applied Science in electronic engineering technology (A.S.) and the Associate in Applied Science in computer engineering technology (A.S.). Also available is a fall-semester noncredit pretechnology program designed to prepare students for the degree program.

Hillyer College offers the Associate of Arts and provides the general education course work required to complete most of the University's baccalaureate programs. Particular emphasis is placed on the development of academic skills through small classes and close faculty-student interaction. Hartford College for Women offers four degree programs: Associate of Arts, Associate of Science in Legal Assistance, Bachelor of Arts in Women's Studies, and Bachelor of Science in Legal Assistance.

Academic Program

The University of Hartford enjoys a national reputation for the breadth and depth of its program. More than seventy undergraduate majors are offered through nine schools and colleges. Students are encouraged to sample a variety of academic areas and can enroll in courses in any of the colleges on campus. Those who have special interests can develop interdisciplinary majors that combine courses from the different schools within the University. Academic advisers are assigned to all students to help guide them in curriculum choices, career exploration, and the transition to University life. In order to help students learn more about how different academic disciplines approach related problems, the All-University Curriculum was developed. Each course is team taught from different fields of expertise, and topics are examined from the perspective of several academic disciplines. The University also has a special program to assist students who may be undecided about a major. A reading and writing center, where students on an individual basis are helped to increase their proficiency in writing, research, reading comprehension, and speed as well as study and test-taking skills, is available to the entire student body. Further help in math is given through the Math Tutoring Lab, which is staffed by full-time faculty members and math majors. Selected students are encouraged to participate in the Honors Program. Honors students have the opportunity to graduate with an Honors Degree.

Off-Campus Arrangements

Intercampus registration through the Hartford Consortium for Higher Education permits University of Hartford students to take certain courses at the School of the Hartford Ballet, Saint Joseph College, and Trinity College. Teaching and human services majors in the College of Education, Nursing, and Health Professions have opportunities for field and/or clinical experiences where applicable. A central cooperative education office is available to custom-tailor work experiences within many of the University's programs.

Academic Facilities

The eight colleges and schools are housed on the main campus. A recent addition is the Harry Jack Gray Center, which houses the enlarged William H. Mortensen Library; the Mildred P. Allen Memorial Library; the Museum of American Political Life; the Harry J. Gray Conference Center; the Joseloff Gallery; the University Bookstore; studios for art, radio, and television; and the Communication Department. The library has approximately 643,000 items, including books, musical scores, recordings, periodicals, journals, and microfilm units. Extensive resources are also available through the Hartford Consortium for Higher Education, the Hartford Library, and the Inter-Library-Loan systems.

Hartford College for Women's 13-acre wooded campus is listed on the National Register of Historic Places. The campus is a blend of traditional ivy-covered Georgian buildings and modern classroom and laboratory buildings.

The University of Hartford Computer Center houses the central computer systems and operates a high-performance campuswide network, which connects all student residential housing, all academic buildings on campus, and the University's remote locations. The University's network is connected via a high-speed telecommunication link to the Internet and the World Wide Web. The residential network gives each student resident his or her own Ethernet connection to the campus network and the Internet. The library is connected to the campus network and provides network access in study carrels and study rooms. The online systems of the library include the online catalog for book, audio, and video collections; CD-ROM databases; and certain Internet resources (e.g., 1,000 electronic journals). Ongoing improvements at the library include easy-to-use Web access for many of the library's online resources and electronic reserves. All of the University network resources may be accessed on campus at University facilities and off campus by using computers with modems.

Computing labs, used by all students of the University, are provided at six locations around the campus. The labs are equipped with microcomputers (PCs and Macintoshes), computer workstations, and terminals and are connected to the campus network and the Internet. Typical microcomputer software includes word processing, spreadsheet, database management, and graphics programs; HyperCard; programming languages; and Web browsers for accessing the Internet. Help is available from on-duty lab assistants. In addition to these computer labs, there are specialized computer facilities for instruction and learning. Some examples of these specialized facilities are the Gilman Center for Communication Technology for English and journalism instruction; Information Technology Center for MIS and quantitative methods; the Computer Assisted Learning Center; the Center for Computer and Electronic Music; the Computer Aided Design/Computer Aided Manufacturing Laboratory; the Sun Workstation Laboratory for Computer Science; and the Electronic Learning Laboratory (Instructional Media Services). Additional facilities and advanced equipment for the study of earth sciences are available at the nearby Talcott Mountain Science Center.

Costs

Tuition for incoming students is $18,626 for the 2000–01 academic year; student service fees, $1070; on-campus room costs, $4836; and board, $3004. A variety of on-campus housing accommodates about 3,500 students.

Financial Aid

The University's financial aid program totals approximately $52 million annually, including student loans. Scholarships, grants, loans, and work-study opportunities are provided through the federal government, private agencies, interested individuals, and University funds. University funds are disbursed based upon the college or school in which the student is enrolled, availability of funds, applicant pool, and competition for funds. About 85 percent of all full-time undergraduate students receive some type of assistance; the average amount is $12,900 per year. Partial-tuition scholarships are awarded to entering students who have demonstrated outstanding academic achievement.

Faculty

There are 625 full-time and adjunct faculty members. The undergraduate and graduate faculties are essentially the same group, and 78 percent of the members hold the terminal degree in their field. Academic and personal advisory service is readily available. Each new student is assigned to a faculty adviser during summer orientation.

Student Government

The student governing body that represents all full-time students is the Student Government Association, through which students and faculty join in developing and coordinating the cocurricular activities of the University. Students are also represented on all major administrative committees, including the Board of Regents.

Admission Requirements

The Committee on Admission considers the quality of the secondary school curriculum, academic performance in secondary school, recommendations of the secondary school principal or guidance counselor, ACT or SAT I results, evidence of a desire to succeed, and leadership qualities shown by academic and extracurricular activities. Auditions, portfolios, and other tests are required of music and art applicants.

Application and Information

The University employs a rolling admission policy. For further information, students should contact:

Richard A. Zeiser
Dean of Admission
University of Hartford
West Hartford, Connecticut 06117-0395
Telephone: 860-768-4296
          800-947-4303 (toll-free)
Fax: 860-768-4961
E-mail: admission@uhavax.hartford.edu
World Wide Web: http://www.hartford.edu

UNIVERSITY OF HOUSTON
HOUSTON, TEXAS

The University

The University of Houston (UH), a leading institution in the state-assisted system of higher education in Texas, stands on the forefront of education, research, and service. The largest and most comprehensive component of the University of Houston System, the UH main campus serves more than 32,000 students in fourteen colleges and a host of schools and programs offering more than 300 undergraduate, graduate, and special professional degrees.

UH conducts basic research in each academic department and operates more than forty research centers and institutes on campus. Through these facilities the University maintains creative partnerships with government and private industry, and the research conducted breaks new ground in such vital areas as superconductivity, space commercialization, chemical engineering, economics, and education. The Conrad N. Hilton College of Hotel and Restaurant Management attracts students from all over the country. The University's advanced professional programs include architecture, law, pharmacy, and optometry.

Sponsored research was at $45.5 million for fiscal year 1998. Considering its commitment to excellence, the University anticipates continued support and growth in the amount of grants and awards.

Outstanding faculty and facilities draw students from across the country and around the world. As a result, UH is characterized by a rich mix of cultural backgrounds in a student body that is 48 percent white, 17 percent Asian/Pacific Islander, 16 percent Hispanic, 12 percent African American, 7 percent international students who represent countries across the globe, and .5 percent Native American.

University of Houston public service and community activities, such as cultural offerings, clinical services, policy studies, and small-business initiatives, serve a diverse metropolitan population. Likewise, the resources of the Gulf Coast region complement and enrich the University's academic programs, providing students with professional expertise, practical experience, and career opportunities and allowing them to secure career-level jobs soon after graduation.

Location

Located just minutes away from downtown Houston on Interstate 45, UH is set on 548 acres of parks, fountains, plazas, sculptures, and recreational fields surrounding more than ninety modern facilities. This offers students a comfortable and well-equipped setting for academic pursuits and proximity to the resources of the nation's fourth-largest city. Gulf Coast beaches, Texas hill country, and piney woods are equally accessible from Houston, and a warm climate permits outdoor activity throughout the year.

Majors and Degrees

UH awards Bachelor of Arts and Bachelor of Science degrees with majors in accounting, accountancy, anthropology, applied music, architecture, art, art history, biochemical/biophysical sciences, biology, biomedical technology, chemical engineering, chemistry, civil engineering, civil technology, classical studies, communication disorders, computer drafting design, computer engineering technology, computer science, computer science–business, computer science–systems, construction management and technologies, consumer science and merchandising, creative writing, earth science, economics, education, electrical engineering, electrical technology, electrical technology–control systems, electrical technology–electrical power, English, entrepreneurship, environmental design, exercise science, finance, French, geology, geology-geophysics, German, graphic communications, health, history, hotel and restaurant management, human development and family studies, human nutrition and foods, industrial distribution, industrial engineering, industrial supervision, information systems technology, interdisciplinary studies, interior design, interpersonal communication, Italian studies, journalism, kinesiology, management, management information systems, manufacturing systems technology, marketing, mathematics, mathematics–applied analysis, mechanical and related technology, mechanical engineering, media policy/studies, media production, merchandising and industrial distribution, movement and sports studies, music, music composition, music theory, occupational technology and industrial studies, operations management, optometry, organizational/corporate communication, painting, pharmacy, philosophy, photography, physics, physics-geophysics, political science, preprofessional English studies, printmaking, psychology, Russian studies, sculpture, sociology, Spanish, sports administration, statistics and operations research, studio art, theater, and training/human resources.

Academic Program

UH offers an undergraduate curriculum that provides students with a broad base in the liberal arts complemented by in-depth studies in disciplines of their choice, affording students a foundation for lifelong learning. UH enrolls a substantial number of National Merit Scholars each year, and the quality of UH students is further reflected in the growing enrollment in the Honors College. Created to serve the intellectual needs of gifted undergraduates in more than 100 fields of study, the Honors College provides the careful guidance, flexibility, and personal instruction that nurture individual excellence. The Honors College offers all the advantages of a small college without sacrificing the wealth of resources and the rich diversity of a large university.

Off-Campus Arrangements

The College of Humanities, Fine Arts, and Communication and the College of Business Administration offer fall and spring semesters in London, during which students can earn 15 hours of credit. Courses are taught by UH professors, faculty members from other Texas universities, and the University of London faculty. The Department of Modern and Classical Languages sponsors two summer programs in Puebla, Mexico, and Madrid, Spain. The Department of French has a summer program in Bourges, France, and the College of Architecture sponsors two summer programs in Saintes and Paris, France. In addition, UH has a wide variety of courses and programs that are offered through distance education.

Academic Facilities

Libraries at UH provide abundant resources for research, with total collective holdings of more than 2 million volumes, 3.8 million microfilm units, 15,152 research journal subscriptions, and various other research materials. A computerized catalog system links all four UH System libraries and the specialized libraries in architecture, law, music, optometry, and pharmacy at UH. The University's computer-intensive environment enhances both teaching and research. A computer network links more than 4,000 workstations across campus, and UH is connected to several wide area networks providing access to more than 1,100 universities, research institutions, and corporations worldwide.

Costs

The estimated average total cost for the 1999–2000 school year was $7200 for Texas residents and $14,000 for nonresidents. This included average residence hall fees and meal plans. Costs are subject to change. Students should go to the University's Web site (listed below) for updated tuition information.

Financial Aid

Several types of student financial assistance are offered, including scholarships, which are generally based on measures of academic performance such as GPA, class rank, and SAT I or ACT scores, and need-based (as determined from the Free Application for Federal Student Aid) assistance, which includes loans, grants, and part-time employment. For applications and materials, students should write directly to: Office of Scholarships and Financial Aid, University of Houston, 4800 Calhoun Road, Houston, Texas 77204-2160.

Faculty

Ranked faculty members number more than 900. The number of lecturers, teaching fellows, and visiting and adjunct faculty members is also more than 900. Faculty members are published in the most prestigious journals, and their research garners national and international acclaim. Students also benefit from instruction at an urban institution where more than 1,000 business and community leaders bring their expertise and experience to the classroom.

Student Government

The Students' Association is the University's student government and official student representative organization. It works to improve the quality of education and campus life and participates in policymaking decisions. The association participates in student disciplinary cases and works to preserve student rights.

Admission Requirements

Freshmen should submit their high school transcript, including class rank and GPA plus SAT I or ACT test scores. Applicants should have taken 4 years of English and 3 years each of math and science in high school; 2 years of foreign language are recommended. Transfers should have 15 or more hours of college credit and a minimum GPA of 2.0 to 2.5. Some majors require a higher GPA. The TOEFL is required for international students.

Application and Information

Notifications of acceptance are based on a review of an applicant's complete file and continue on a rolling admission basis. An application fee of $40 is required. Students are urged to apply early. Deadlines are fall, May 17 for freshmen and June 1 for transfer students; spring, December 10; and summer, May 15.

Applicants are strongly encouraged to apply for admission using the Internet at the address listed below and are reminded to select the University of Houston as the receiving institution.

Requests for an application for admission, freshman and transfer scholarship applications, and information should be directed to:

Office of Admissions
University of Houston
4800 Calhoun Road
Houston, Texas 77204-2161

Telephone: 713-743-1010
E-mail: admissions@uh.edu
World Wide Web: http://www.uh.edu

Houston: The city and its university.

UNIVERSITY OF ILLINOIS AT CHICAGO
CHICAGO, ILLINOIS

The University

The University of Illinois at Chicago (UIC) is a comprehensive public university located in the heart of one of the nation's largest metropolitan areas. UIC is not only in the city of Chicago, it is of the city. Since its beginnings in the 1880s with the founding of schools that would eventually become the Colleges of Pharmacy and Medicine, UIC has been committed to Chicago. Today, with 25,000 students, UIC is the largest and most diverse university in the Chicago area. It is also very affordable. UIC is one of three campuses of the state's land-grant university, the University of Illinois. Its mission comprises three traditional elements—teaching, research, and public service—each of which is shaped by and relevant to its metropolitan setting. UIC offers students the chance to study with an outstanding faculty while taking advantage of the numerous cultural and social opportunities that the city has to offer. Through cooperative education programs, students have the opportunity to study with prominent business professionals, engineers, and architects, all leaders in their fields.

The campus covers 322 acres with 101 buildings, including some of Chicago's most prestigious facilities. These facilities include the nation's largest medical school; Hull House, the settlement house founded by Nobel laureate Jane Addams; and the Electronic Visualization Laboratory, a nationally known virtual reality facility.

With a culturally diverse and academically talented student body of approximately 25,000, UIC is the largest university in the Chicago area. In addition, UIC is one of only four Research I institutions in Illinois.

Location

Located just west of Chicago's Loop, UIC is located within a few miles of world-renowned museums, shops and restaurants, and sites that host athletic events and entertainment. The campus is a vital part of the educational, technological, and cultural fabric of the area. The city is a living text of American history, journalism, business, architecture, and performing arts. Subjects students study at UIC become more familiar and appreciated as their influence is seen reflected in the city.

Majors and Degrees

UIC offers bachelor's degrees in ninety-two areas. All undergraduate majors are organized into eight of the University's fourteen colleges. The degrees offered in the College of Architecture and the Arts are architectural studies, art education, art history, graphic design, industrial design, performing arts (music and theater), photography/film/electronic media, and studio arts (options in painting, printmaking, and sculpting).

The College of Business Administration offers majors in accounting, economics, finance, information and decision sciences, management, and marketing.

The College of Education offers a Bachelor of Arts (B.A.) degree in elementary education.

The College of Engineering offers degrees in bioengineering, chemical engineering, civil engineering, computer engineering, computer science, electrical engineering, engineering management, engineering physics, industrial engineering, and mechanical engineering.

The College of Health and Human Development Sciences offers majors in health information management, human nutrition and dietetics, kinesiology (including athletic training, exercise physiology, and physical education), and medical laboratory sciences.

The College of Liberal Arts and Sciences, the largest college at UIC, offers many majors, including those in African-American studies, anthropology, biochemistry, biological sciences, chemistry, classical civilization, classical languages and literatures, communication, criminal justice, earth and environmental sciences, economics, English (literature), English (writing), French, French business studies, geography, German, history, Italian, Latin American studies, mathematics, mathematics and computer science, philosophy, physics, Polish, political science, psychology, Russian, sociology, Spanish, Spanish (economics), and statistics and operations research. The College of Liberal Arts and Sciences also offers bachelor's degrees in many areas of secondary education. These areas include teaching of chemistry, teaching of English, teaching of French, teaching of German, teaching of history, teaching of mathematics, teaching of physics, teaching of Russian, and teaching of Spanish.

The College of Nursing offers the Bachelor of Science in Nursing (B.S.N.). The Jane Addams College of Social Work offers the Bachelor of Social Work (B.S.W.).

In addition to the majors listed, the College of Liberal Arts and Sciences offers preprofessional programs in predentistry, prelaw, premedicine, pre–occupational therapy, prepharmacy, pre–physical therapy, and pre–veterinary medicine.

Academic Program

While individual colleges and programs set degree requirements, all students who earn a bachelor's degree at UIC must earn a minimum of 120 semester hours of credit (some programs require additional hours). Each college establishes a core of general education requirements that a student must fulfill. Students must also fulfill residency requirements, usually by completing the last 30 semester hours of their degree at UIC.

UIC students may earn credit by examination through Advanced Placement or International Baccalaureate Programs prior to college admission and through satisfactory completion of certain CLEP exams. Academically talented students may participate in the UIC Honors College, a challenging program that offers special academic opportunities for students as well as mentorship, research, and scholarship assistance. Students may participate in Army, Navy, or Air Force ROTC. Many students choose to enhance their studies through study-abroad opportunities and cooperative-education and internship programs.

The fall semester runs from late August to early December; the spring semester begins in early January and ends in mid-May. There is an eight-week summer session in June and July.

Academic Facilities

The University Library consists of the Richard J. Daley Library (main library), the Architecture and Art Library, the Library of the Health Sciences, the Mathematics Collection, and the Science Library. The University Library features an online public access catalog, a collection of subject-based online databases, and a statewide circulation and resource sharing network, which provide access to UIC holdings and more than 31 million volumes held by the forty-five academic libraries in Illinois.

The Academic Computing and Communications Center supports the educational and research needs of the UIC community by providing a variety of computing resources. All registered students have access to both UNIX systems and personal computers. Fifteen microcomputer laboratories are available throughout the campus. All the labs are connected to the Internet and have access to a wide variety of software, including word processing, spreadsheets, and database management; graphics; statistical packages; programming languages; Web publishing; Web browsers; and remote log-in and file-transfer facilities.

The Writing Center at UIC provides free tutoring and consultation to students. Tutors are trained to help students from all academic disciplines with any aspect of their writing, including generating ideas; organizing, developing, and clarifying ideas; and revising.

The Language Laboratory provides audio materials for foreign-language students and students who need additional study in English. This service is intended to supplement regular classroom work as an integral part of the acquisition of language skills.

Costs

In academic year 1999–2000, full-time undergraduate students who were Illinois residents paid $4648 for tuition and fees. Nonresident undergraduates paid $10,924 for tuition and fees. The cost for tuition and fees can also vary depending on the number of hours taken and the program in which a student is enrolled. Campus housing costs vary depending on the choice of meal package and style of room. Average costs for the 1999–2000 year were $5800–$6700.

Financial Aid

The Office of Student Financial Aid administers the federal aid programs for UIC students. Students may qualify for local, state, and federal grants and loan programs as well as Federal Work-Study to help defray costs. Nearly 70 percent of UIC's undergraduate students receive financial aid that covers approximately 95 percent of their expenses. Many students are also eligible to receive institutional scholarships.

Faculty

There are more than 2,200 faculty members at UIC. More than 90 percent of the faculty members hold a Ph.D., and three fourths of UIC's tenured faculty members teach freshmen courses. In the last ten years, UIC faculty members have been awarded with more full-year fellowships from the National Endowment for the Humanities than any other university in Illinois during that period of time.

In addition, faculty members have gained international recognition for inventions and discoveries made at UIC. Virtual reality technology was invented at UIC. The CAVE, a virtual reality lab, is located on campus. Artificial skin to help burn victims was invented at UIC. Oil-eating microbes that clean up oil spills were created at UIC. The first kidney transplant in Illinois was performed at the UIC Medical Center.

UIC's overall class size is 30; the student-faculty ratio is 11:1.

Student Government

There are three forms of student governance at UIC. The Health Professional Student Council represents students primarily enrolled in the health sciences colleges and school. The Undergraduate Student Government represents undergraduate students. The Graduate Student Council represents graduate students at UIC.

Admission Requirements

Freshmen applicants must be at least 16 years of age, be a graduate of an accredited high school or submit satisfactory scores on the GED (250 minimum), and present a satisfactory combination of class rank and ACT or SAT scores plus an acceptable high school course pattern. For fall 2000 admission, minimum composite ACT scores combined with class rank are as follows: 16 with 84th percentile or above, 22 with 51st percentile or above, or 26 with 30th percentile or above. These numbers are higher in architecture and the arts, business, engineering, and kinesiology. Applicants below the 30th percentile are not eligible for admission. In 1998–99, the ACT scores of the middle 50 percent of the entering class ranged from 20 to 24. The average high school percentile rank was 76 percent. Transfer admissions are based on hours earned and grade point average and vary by UIC college.

Minimum standards are 24 semester hours of transferable credit and a cumulative grade point average of C+ (2.15 out of 4.0). Transcripts are evaluated on a course-by-course basis. Specific transfer guides are available.

Application and Information

The Office of Admissions and Records is open from 8:30 a.m. to 4:45 p.m., Monday through Friday. For further information, to arrange a campus tour, or to request an admissions packet, students should contact:

Office of Admissions and Records
University of Illinois at Chicago
Box 5220
Chicago, Illinois 60680-5220
Telephone: 312-996-4350
World Wide Web: http://www.uic.edu

The UIC campus is a vital part of the educational, technological, and cultural fabric of the metropolitan Chicago area.

UNIVERSITY OF INDIANAPOLIS
INDIANAPOLIS, INDIANA

The University

The University of Indianapolis is a private residential institution of higher learning. Established in 1902 and now an integral part of the educational and cultural life of Indianapolis, the University maintains a moderate size and a diverse student body, and it provides a comprehensive set of general, preprofessional, and professional programs, grounded in the liberal arts.

Students indicate that they choose the University because of its challenging, yet supportive, atmosphere and relatively small size, combined with the advantages of its location in the southern suburbs of a thriving state capital. As a result, there is a great sense of community and pride on the campus. The University helps students to determine and achieve their individual academic goals. The University of Indianapolis is currently engaged in a fund-raising campaign to facilitate the expansion of campus facilities and to increase funds for student scholarships. There is an enrollment of about 1,800 Day Division students, whose average age is 21. Of the Day Division students, about 20 percent represent minority groups and international students. There are students from fifty-seven countries and twenty states. Approximately 47 percent of the students live in on-campus housing.

In addition to the undergraduate division, the University is composed of the Graduate and Doctoral Division, including the nationally recognized Krannert School of Physical Therapy. The most popular programs in the undergraduate division include pre–physical therapy, accounting, business administration, law enforcement, nursing, education, premedical, pre–occupational therapy, and psychology. Social life is organized through the Campus Program Board Indianapolis Student Government and the Residence Hall Association, student organizations that plan weekly activities for all students. There are numerous social clubs and interest groups available for students who wish to become involved in extracurricular activities. Four residence halls house students; three house both men and women, and one is only for women. Students must be admitted on a full-time basis in order to be assigned housing. Varsity sports for men include baseball, basketball, cross-country, football, golf, soccer, swimming, tennis, track and field (indoor and outdoor), and wrestling. Varsity sports for women include basketball, cross-country, fast-pitch softball, golf, soccer, swimming, tennis, track and field (indoor and outdoor), and volleyball. There are eight intramural sports open to all students. The warmth and sensitivity of the faculty, staff, and students alike enable those who are a part of the campus to feel a sense of community.

Location

The University is located in the southern neighborhoods of Indianapolis, the nation's third-largest capital city. Indianapolis and the surrounding area constitute a metropolitan area of more than 1 million people. As a result, the city offers students valuable internship experiences as well as recreational and cultural opportunities too numerous to mention. The campus is extremely accessible, just a few blocks from two major interstate highways (I-65 and I-465). The campus is served by Metro bus, and Amtrak trains arrive daily at historic Union Station, just 10 minutes from the campus. Indianapolis International Airport is about 15 minutes away.

Majors and Degrees

The undergraduate programs are offered through the College of Arts and Sciences, the School of Business, the School of Nursing, the School of Education, and the Krannert School of Physical Therapy. The degrees awarded are the Associate in Arts, Associate in Science, Associate in Science in Nursing, Bachelor of Arts, Bachelor of Science, and Bachelor of Science in Nursing. Baccalaureate and preprofessional fields of study include accounting (CMA/CPA), anthropology, archeology, art, art therapy, athletic training, biology, business administration, chemistry, commercial art, communication studies, computer science, corporate communication, corrections, earth-space sciences, economics and finance, electrical engineering (dual degree), electronic media, elementary education, English, environmental management, environmental science, financial services, French, German, history, human biology, human resource management, information systems, international business, journalism, law enforcement, marketing, mathematics, mechanical engineering (dual degree), medical technology, music, music (contemporary practices), music performance, music theater, nursing, philosophy, physical education, physics, political science, predentistry, prelaw, premedicine, pre–occupational therapy, preoptometry, pre–physical therapy, pretheology, pre–veterinary science, production and operations management, psychology, public relations, religion, secondary education, social work, sociology, Spanish, speech communication, sports information, and theater. Teaching majors are offered in business education, English, French, mathematics, music (all grades), physical education (all grades), science (five primary areas), social studies (six primary areas), Spanish, speech communication and theater, and visual arts (all grades).

Associate degrees are awarded in business administration, chemistry, computer programming/ASI 400, corrections, industrial chemistry, financial services, information systems, law enforcement, legal assistant studies (paralegal), liberal arts, nursing, and physical therapist assistant studies.

Academic Program

The goal of the University is most accurately reflected in its motto, "Education for Service." Associate degrees require 62 semester hours of credit; baccalaureate degrees require 124 semester hours of credit. All students are required to complete the general education core curriculum, consisting of six courses for associate degree students and the equivalent of two years of full-time study for baccalaureate degree students. A complete testing program is in place that awards credit by examination through CLEP, PEP, DANTES, Advanced Placement examinations, University examinations, and other tests. In addition to credit, these may be for exemption or placement, depending upon the particular examination. The testing program is administered through the Office of the University Registrar.

Students are selected to participate in the honors program by invitation only, based upon their high school record. Students who complete three of five offered honors courses with a B– or higher and who satisfactorily complete a senior honors project receive the designation "Graduation with Distinction" at commencement. Through the Consortium for Urban Education, the University has a cross-registration program with six other area colleges. As a result, students may complete Army ROTC through Indiana University–Purdue University at Indianapolis.

The academic calendar is composed of two 15-week semesters (the last week is finals week), a three-week Spring Term beginning in April or May, and two 6-week summer sessions (with limited course offerings).

Off-Campus Arrangements

The University operates two fully accredited branch campuses in Cyprus in the eastern Mediterranean Sea and in Greece that offer students a unique exchange program. Other off-campus study opportunities take place during the Spring Term, including assorted overseas travel openings. The University has an Office of Career Services, which arranges off-campus internships related to one's field of study.

Academic Facilities

Krannert Memorial Library, which operates an online card catalog, houses more than 166,000 volumes, more than 1,000 periodicals, and more than 19,000 microfilm/microform/microfiche records. A full media center is available in the library. Lilly Hall, housing the sciences, nursing, and history, is a comprehensive, modern facility that includes the Noblitt Observatory with its powerful space telescope. Student microcomputer laboratories are available in nearly all of the academic buildings and in one residence hall. Students also have access to electronic mail, Internet, World Wide Web, FTP, and the campuswide information system from their rooms in the residence halls. Ransburg Auditorium, with seating for nearly 800, is the setting for many concerts, recitals, and theatrical productions. The $10-million Christel DeHaan Fine Arts Center features state-of-the-art music and art facilities, an art gallery, and a 450-seat, Viennese-style concert hall.

Martin Hall is the latest addition to the campus, housing state-of-the-art equipment for nursing, physical therapy, and occupational therapy classrooms and laboratories. The University of Indianapolis breaks ground in summer 2000 on a multimillion-dollar renovation of Schwitzer Student Center, which will add additional student organization offices, lounge areas, and dining service facilities.

Costs

Directly billed expenses for the 2000–01 academic year are $14,630 for tuition and $5225 for room and board. Nonbilled indirect expenses are estimated at $565 for books and supplies, an average of $450 for transportation, and $1080 for miscellaneous and personal expenses.

Financial Aid

All applicants for admission are eligible to apply for financial aid. Indiana residents should file the Free Application for Federal Student Aid (FAFSA) by March 1 to qualify for state of Indiana financial aid programs. All students should file the FAFSA along with the University of Indianapolis Application for Financial Aid by March 1 for priority consideration. For the 1999–2000 academic year, about 89 percent of the enrolled full-time students received more than $22 million from all sources.

Faculty

Of the Day Division classes, 69 percent are taught by full-time faculty members. All Day Division faculty members are assigned teaching (not research) duties, including many administrators and some professional staff personnel. Graduate students do not teach any undergraduate classes. More than 65 percent of the full-time faculty have earned the doctoral degree in their field of study. While the student-faculty ratio is 14:1, over the past five years the average class size has ranged from 13 to 17.

Student Government

The Indianapolis Student Government (ISG) consists of students elected to officer positions plus student representatives from each class, chosen for a one-year term in an annual student body election. ISG's main focus is to pass resolutions regarding student concerns.

Admission Requirements

Applicants for admission must be high school graduates or have a GED certificate and are expected to have taken a college-preparatory curriculum in high school. Applicants for regular admission should have completed a minimum of 4 years of English (literature, composition, and grammar), 2 years of mathematics (algebra and geometry), 2 years of laboratory science (biology and chemistry), 2 years of social science (U.S. history, government, and economics), and 2 years of any foreign language. In addition, applicants for full-time admission without restrictions should rank in the upper half of their class and have either a combined SAT I score of at least 920 or an ACT composite score of at least 20. Essays are not required for admission. For immediate consideration, transfer applicants should be in good academic standing at their original college and maintain a cumulative GPA of at least 2.0. An on-campus interview is recommended, anytime after the junior year of high school. To apply for admission, the Application for Admission, official high school transcript, official college transcript (if applicable), and official SAT I or ACT scores should be forwarded to the Office of Admissions.

Application and Information

All applications are reviewed on a rolling basis—an admission decision is made as soon as all documents are received, and notifications are mailed immediately thereafter. The deadline for applications is August 15 every year, but high school seniors should apply during the fall semester of their senior year for priority consideration.

Requests for appointments and information about the University should be directed to:

Director of Admissions
University of Indianapolis
1400 East Hanna Avenue
Indianapolis, Indiana 46227-3697
Telephone: 317-STUDENT
          317-788-3216
          800-232-8634 (toll-free)
Fax: 317-788-3300
E-mail: admissions@uindy.edu
World Wide Web: http://www.uindy.edu/

UNIVERSITY OF JUDAISM
College of Arts and Sciences
BEL AIR, CALIFORNIA

The University

Better known in the campus community as "the UJ," the University of Judaism's College of Arts and Sciences offers a thorough liberal arts education with a Jewish perspective. The unique balance of a mostly Jewish environment and rigorous nonsectarian academics has proven to be a highly successful combination, as evidenced by a ten-year placement rate into graduate schools that exceeds 90 percent. This success is due largely to the UJ's caring and accessible faculty of distinguished scholars who teach classes of typically 12–15 students and who emphasize interactive seminars more than impersonal lectures. Frequently, a spirited classroom discussion will continue in the hallways or cafeteria.

Accredited by the Western Association of Schools and Colleges, the school began in 1982 as Lee College at the University of Judaism. The University itself was founded in 1947 and also offers graduate degree programs in business, education, psychology, and rabbinics. The central institutional mission is to develop the future volunteer and professional leadership of the Jewish community, and to do so in an atmosphere of academic openness and intellectual excellence.

What particularly sets the UJ apart from other small, private, coed, liberal arts colleges is the Jewish life that flourishes on campus. Not only does the UJ have a kosher cafeteria and no classes on Jewish holidays, but celebrations of holidays such as Purim and Sukkot and weekly Shabbat activities foster a lively community environment that invites, but does not demand, participation.

Most undergraduates live on campus, enjoying spacious residence hall rooms, each with air conditioning, cable, phone jacks, and a large private bathroom. Residential-life features include a big screen TV lounge, fitness room, game lounge, kitchen commons, athletic facilities, and a coffeehouse. Activities range from a campus newspaper, choir, and literary magazine to political clubs, theater productions, musical ensembles, a radio station, and less structured favorites like mud football and midnight deli runs. The UJ also regularly hosts wider community events such as regional Hillel dances attended by hundreds of students from other Southern California colleges and universities.

A select fall entering class of about 50 students is drawn from thousands of inquiries representing every region and social segment of the U.S. and from numerous countries. Diversity is valued in admission selection, as are intellect, achievement, self-motivation, respect for Jewish values, and the eagerness to fully participate in a close campus community.

Location

Bel Air is one of the most desirable communities in Los Angeles. The University of Judaism is set on a 27-acre campus adjacent to both a quiet residential neighborhood and a rustic area that is great for hiking. Located on a hilltop, the setting offers panoramic views of the Santa Monica Mountains and San Fernando Valley. Within a 30-minute driving radius are the major resources of Southern California, from Hollywood and beaches to L.A.'s governmental, business, and religious centers. Within 10 minutes are such attractions as the Getty Museum, the Jewish-oriented Skirball Cultural Center, the Sherman Oaks Galleria shopping complex, and UCLA. Accordingly, UJ students access internships and community service projects just as readily as they venture to concerts, plays, movies, cafés, and sporting events. The campus itself is characterized by contemporary open-air architecture and grassy, tree-lined walkways.

Majors and Degrees

The College of Arts and Sciences confers the Bachelor of Arts degree. Standard academic majors include bioethics (premedicine, etc.), business, English and literature, Jewish studies, political science, and psychology. Established interdisciplinary majors include journalism, liberal studies (aimed at aspiring teachers), literature and politics, and U.S. public policy. Students may also design individualized majors or undertake a five-year program that extends the Bachelor of Arts in Business into a Master of Business Administration focused on nonprofit management.

Academic Program

The general education program consists of 70 credits. It is a blend of Jewish, Western and other world civilizations, communication, foreign language (usually Hebrew), and distribution requirements in math, science, arts, and computer study. The core curriculum is distinctive for its multidisciplinary approach, which draws on history, literature, philosophy, political science, and religion in its objective study of culture and civilization. There is no religious instruction required or expected.

Close faculty advisers assure graduation in four years for nearly every UJ undergraduate. The B.A. requires completion of 120 semester credits, including fulfillment of residency, general education, and major requirements. The number and pattern of major requirements vary by department. Fifteen elective credits must be taken outside the major. If concentrated in one field of upper-division study, elective courses may count as an academic minor. Residency requirements consist of 34 credits completed at the UJ, at least 15 of which are in the major.

Off-Campus Arrangements

Arranged individually to accommodate each UJ student's specific goal, study-abroad opportunities are abundant, typically occurring in the junior year. There is also a unique Freshman Year Abroad option for high school graduates who want a rich Israel immersion experience without delaying the start of their college education. This is done through Hadassah's Young Judaea Year Course in Israel, with academic oversight by the University of Judaism.

Those pursuing medically related studies through the innovative bioethics major regularly utilize the laboratories, staff, and other resources at nearby Cedars Sinai Medical Center. This partnership gives undergraduates an exceedingly rare opportunity for hands-on learning in a professional environment, using state-of-the-art equipment and techniques. It is an opportunity that also bolsters preparation for medical or other competitive graduate schools.

Academic Facilities

The campus library serves the University's wide range of academic disciplines with more than 100,000 volumes. It is most notable for holdings in Jewish culture and civilization. Some highlight collections include microfilm manuscripts of the Jewish Theological Seminary, all dissertations on Jewish subjects published in the U.S., and 5,000 rare Bibles, dating back as far as the sixteenth century. In addition, the Documentation Center houses archives of more than 1.5 million topically arranged articles relating to topics such as contemporary Jewish issues, Israel, the Middle East, Diaspora communities, and international affairs.

Adjacent to both the library and Documentation Center is the main Computer Center. It was significantly upgraded and enlarged in 1997 to meet the curricular, research, creative, and recreational needs of UJ students, including Internet and e-mail access. Both PC and Macintosh stations are abundant.

Campus arts facilities include studios for dance, music, and the visual arts. There is also a luxurious 475-seat theater, the home concert stage of the Los Angeles Philharmonic Chamber Music Society, with superb acoustics for plays, concerts, and speakers. Also notable is a scenic, terraced sculpture garden and a campus art gallery that offers exhibits by artists of local, national, and international renown as well as work by the University's own art students.

Costs

For the 2000–01 academic year, full-time tuition (12–18 units per semester) is $15,000. Room and board rates depend on the housing and meal plan selected; a double room and standard nineteen-meal-per-week plan cost $4000 per semester. Required student fees (registration, health services, etc.) amount to $530 per year. Incidental expenses, such as books, transportation, and personal expenses, vary from student to student but average $2000 per year.

Financial Aid

The aforementioned costs are eligible for coverage in a need-based financial aid package from the University of Judaism. And even those with low need or no need, but who are particularly strong candidates, may be awarded merit-based scholarships primarily through the UJ President's Scholars Program. These range in value from $5000 per year to full tuition and require an application by January 10.

The University of Judaism believes in need-blind admissions and commits major resources to seeing that genuine financial need is no barrier to attending. Therefore, any student who applies within deadlines (March 1 for the following fall) and who earns admission to the UJ receives an aid package that covers 100 percent of his or her need eligibility. This eligibility is determined by the nationally centralized needs analysis that is generated after the student submits a Free Application for Federal Student Aid (FAFSA). A brief supplemental UJ financial aid application is also required. Commencing in March, financial aid packages are offered within days of receiving all requested documentation.

In addition to its own tuition and housing grant allocations, UJ financial aid resources include Federal Pell Grants, Federal Supplemental Educational Opportunity Grants (FSEOG), Cal Grants, Federal Stafford Loans (subsidized and unsubsidized), the Federal PLUS Program, EXCEL Loans, and the Federal Work-Study Program (for campus jobs). More than 80 percent of UJ students receive financial aid.

Faculty

Nearly every full-time faculty member at the University of Judaism holds a doctorate degree from a highly esteemed university. Most are widely published and have received prestigious academic awards, yet their priority at the UJ is classroom teaching and personalized student advisement, much more so than outside research. UJ students and professors are usually on a first name basis.

Student Government

Through elected officers and volunteer committees, student government at the UJ plays a meaningful and frequently decisive role in everything from programming campus social activities to revising academic policies. Participation is open to all students regardless of major or class standing.

Admission Requirements

Admission to the College of Arts and Sciences at the University of Judaism is selective and individualized. Applicants are evaluated based on a combination of factors, including quality of preparatory curriculum, grades, SAT I or ACT scores, writing ability, academic references, quality of activities, character, and potential. An interview is recommended but not usually required. Freshman and transfer applications are welcome regardless of a candidate's religion, race, color, nationality, handicap, sex, or age. Applicants whose primary language is not English must submit a TOEFL. Students with 30 transferable college units may petition for a waiver of the SAT or ACT. Official transcripts of the entire secondary school and college record (if any) are mandatory.

A profile of a typical freshman is a B+ student who took a demanding preparatory track and scored in the mid-1100s on the SAT or mid-20s on the ACT while also exerting energy and leadership in significant outside activities, such as with youth groups, school publications, performing arts, or student government. Involvement in Jewish life is also common for must UJ students but not required or expected.

Early decision candidates must apply by November 15 and are notified by December 15. For regular fall admission, the priority application deadline for freshmen is January 31 (January 10 for President's Scholars Program applicants); for transfer students, it is April 15. Applications are accepted thereafter only if spaces are available. For spring admission, all candidates should apply by November 1. Regular fall admission notifications are issued as files are completed, starting in January.

Application and Information

For more information or other requests, students should contact:

Richard Scaffidi
Dean of Admissions
University of Judaism
15600 Mulholland Drive
Bel Air, California 90077-1599
Telephone: 310-476-9777
          888-UJ-FOR-ME (toll-free)
Fax: 310-471-1278
E-mail: admissions@uj.edu

A study break on the sunny UJ campus.

UNIVERSITY OF LA VERNE
LA VERNE, CALIFORNIA

The University
Founded in 1891, the University of La Verne is an independent university that emphasizes the liberal arts, the sciences, and career preparation. Faculty members and students are drawn from all segments of life and are reflective of the diverse nature of contemporary society. La Verne also has a special history of serving students who are the first in their families to attend college. The current undergraduate enrollment is about 1,200, and there are more than 200 faculty members. The University of La Verne prides itself on offering personalized education to students in small classes and excellent academic resources, such as the Wilson Library, which houses close to 200,000 volumes. Approximately one third of the students live on campus in residence halls, and roughly 80 percent receive some form of financial aid. The University of La Verne also has a generous merit scholarship program.

La Verne students are encouraged to think seriously about the world and its people through a core curriculum that promotes values, community service, lifelong learning, and diversity. The University also offers study through graduate and professional studies programs, the School of Continuing Education, and the College of Law. Bachelor's, master's, and doctoral degrees are offered in a variety of fields, including forty-eight liberal arts fields, educational leadership, jurisprudence, public administration, and psychology. The University is accredited by the Western Association of Schools and Colleges.

Students are motivated to involve themselves in the many athletic events, plays, concerts, art exhibitions, and student life activities on campus. Students are also involved in the campus newspaper, *La Verne Magazine*, the yearbook, literary publications, and the campus radio and television stations. La Verne teams participate in eleven intercollegiate men's sports and nine intercollegiate women's sports. Men's sports are baseball, basketball, cross-country, football, golf, soccer, swimming and diving, tennis, track and field, volleyball, and water polo. Women's sports are basketball, cross-country, soccer, softball, swimming and diving, tennis, track and field, volleyball, and water polo.

Location
The city of La Verne, located 35 miles east of Los Angeles, is a small residential community (population 32,000) in the heart of what was once a center of citrus culture. La Verne has become a city of change as the population in this and other Los Angeles suburbs has skyrocketed in the past few years. The city is close to all of southern California's cultural and entertainment centers and is only a short ride from beaches, mountains, and deserts.

Majors and Degrees
The University of La Verne offers the Bachelor of Arts and/or Bachelor of Science degree in accounting, art, behavioral science, biology, broadcasting, business administration, business economics, chemistry, child development, communications, criminology, diversified studies (education), English, environmental biology, environmental management, French, German, health-care management, history, human services, international business and languages, international studies, journalism, marketing, mathematics, music, organizational management, philosophy, physical education/athletic training, physics, political science, pre–health science, prelaw, psychology, public administration, radio, religion, social science, sociology, Spanish, television, and theater arts.

Academic Program
All undergraduate students are required to complete a minimum of 128 semester hours to qualify for graduation. The residence requirement is 32 semester hours. Each student must complete a minimum of 44 upper-division semester hours, with at least 24 upper-division hours being taken in the major field. A minimum of 16 semester hours at the upper-division level in the major must be taken through the University of La Verne.

The Campus Accelerated Program for Adults (CAPA) is a central campus program designed to answer the special needs of the working adult student. It stresses individualized academic counseling and offers the opportunity to complete a degree by taking classes in the evening and in Weekend College. Weekend College, which has been in operation since 1976, offers programs on Friday evening and Saturday.

Off-Campus Arrangements
It is possible for ULV students to obtain all of their education at off-campus locations through the School of Continuing Education. Twelve residence centers affiliated with the University provide educational opportunities for those seeking undergraduate degrees. Most, but not all, of the centers are located on military bases. Nea Makri in Greece; Naples, Italy; Sigonella, Sicily, Italy; Vandenberg Air Force Base, North Island Naval Air Station, and Point Mugu Missile Test Center in California; and Eielson Air Force Base and Elmendorf Air Force Base in Alaska are all sites of residence centers.

Programs of study leading to the B.S. in business administration, the B.S. in industrial science technology, the B.S. in public administration, and the B.S. in health-care management are offered at Professional Development Centers located at various industrial and hospital sites in California. At other sites in California, there are special programs leading to the B.A. in religion, the B.S. in vocational education, the B.S. in child development, and the B.A. in human sciences.

As a member of worldwide associations, La Verne can also offer students the opportunity to participate in a variety of structured programs abroad for the January Interterm, a semester, or a full year. In the Brethren College Abroad program, students may study in Germany, France, England, Spain, Ecuador, China, or Japan. Faculty-led excursions are offered to such places as Greece, the Pacific Rim countries, the Commonwealth of Independent States, Australia, Hawaii, and many other areas of the world.

Academic Facilities
Besides classrooms and administrative offices, the La Verne campus has laboratories for the physical and natural sciences, with instrumentation available to undergraduates that many universities are unable to offer even to graduate students. Language laboratories and a writing center provide assistance

for students who have problems with their writing. ULV also provides students with tutoring services through the Learning Enhancement Center, as well as an Honors Program for academically advanced students. A communications center, located in the Student Center, houses radio and television studios, where students can get hands-on experience with state-of-the-art broadcast-quality radio and television equipment. The University library houses 200,000 volumes. The law library has a collection of 70,000 volumes.

Costs

For 2000–01, the estimated cost of tuition for a full-time student is $16,800. (A student must take a minimum of 12 units per semester to attain full-time status.) Room and board fees are approximately $5650 per year. The total costs per year vary according to the room and meal plan chosen.

Financial Aid

In an attempt to bring a liberal arts education within the reach of qualified men and women, ULV makes financial assistance available in many ways. The primary consideration when awarding financial aid is the need of the student. The University provides aid through major federal and state financial aid programs. Academic scholarships, which are unrelated to financial need, are also offered. California State Grants are awarded to students on the basis of their grade point average. The amount of the grant is dependent upon computed financial need. ULV also awards many University-related scholarships that are based on both achievement and need. La Verne provides financial assistance for approximately 75 percent of its undergraduate student body.

Faculty

La Verne's faculty is composed of almost 300 men and women of high academic distinction, more than 80 percent of whom have earned a doctoral degree. The teaching faculty of ULV is primarily committed to the instruction of undergraduate students. The student-faculty ratio of 14:1 allows for personalized treatment of students. Upon enrollment, each student is assigned an adviser from his or her academic field.

Student Government

The Associated Students Federation (ASF) is headed by student leaders in a 12-person forum. The ASF forum establishes activities and maintains school policies. The ASF coordinates on-campus movies, sightseeing trips, concerts, presentations by guest performers and speakers, and other student activities.

Admission Requirements

Admission to the traditional undergraduate program for high school seniors and transfer students with fewer than 32 semester units is based on the application with personal essay, curriculum, academic record, SAT I or ACT scores, and two letters of recommendation.

Transfer students with 32 or more semester units must submit the application with personal essay, transcripts from all colleges attended, and two letters of recommendation. Transfer students are considered for admission with advanced standing. Credit is accepted for transferable courses completed with a grade of C- or higher.

Admission decisions are made without regard to race, national background, religion, or sex.

Application and Information

Students are encouraged to apply before February 1 for the following fall semester and by December 1 for the spring semester. However, the University does consider applications after the deadline as long as space is available.

For application forms or further information, students should contact:

Director of Admissions
University of La Verne
1950 Third Street
La Verne, California 91750
Telephone: 909-593-3511 Ext. 4026
              800-876-4858 (toll-free)
Fax: 909-392-2714
E-mail: admissions@ulv.edu
World Wide Web: http://www.ulv.edu

UNIVERSITY OF LOUISIANA AT LAFAYETTE
LAFAYETTE, LOUISIANA

The University

Founded in 1898, the University of Louisiana at Lafayette (UL Lafayette) is the second-largest university in Louisiana. Fundamentally an undergraduate institution, UL Lafayette is rapidly expanding its role in research and graduate instruction, offering Ph.D. degrees in cognitive science, computer engineering, computer science, English, environmental and evolutionary biology, Francophone studies, and mathematics. UL Lafayette also offers more than thirty master's degrees.

The current enrollment is about 17,000 men and women. The University has students from fifty U.S. states and possessions and from seventy-five countries; about 750 international students are enrolled. Almost one third of the students are 25 years of age or older.

Campus housing and off-campus apartments are available. Dormitory rooms are assigned on a first-come, first-served basis. It is suggested that an application for University housing be sent to the director of housing by March 1.

More than 200 different campus organizations, including seven sororities and fourteen fraternities, give students a range of extracurricular opportunities. UL Lafayette competes at the Division I-A level of NCAA athletics.

Location

UL Lafayette is situated in Lafayette, which has a mild climate and a population of 115,000. The city is administrative headquarters for many oil production, drilling, and service companies. The Lafayette area is the heart of Cajun country, an area of south-central Louisiana settled in the eighteenth century by French exiles from Nova Scotia. Since 1981, the Acadiana area has contributed more than $70 million in endowment funds for scholarships and other academic support.

Majors and Degrees

The University of Louisiana at Lafayette offers approximately 115 bachelor's degree programs and four associate degree programs through its nine undergraduate colleges. In addition to regional institutional accreditation, 97 percent of UL Lafayette's eligible undergraduate programs have achieved professional accreditation. The colleges and their programs are as follows: College of the Arts: architecture, interior design, industrial design, music (performance, piano pedagogy, jazz studies, music media, and theory-composition), performing arts (theater and choreography/dance), and visual arts (drawing, painting, sculpture, printmaking, media-film/video/animation, advertising design, ceramics, metal jewelry, photography, electronic art, and computer animation); College of Applied Life Sciences: agricultural education, apparel design and merchandising, child and family studies, dietetics, environmental/sustainable resources, family and consumer sciences education, hospitality management, pre–veterinary studies, and sustainable agriculture; College of Business Administration: accounting, business systems analysis and technology, economics, finance (insurance and risk management option), management, marketing, and professional land and resource management; College of Education: elementary education, kinesiology (including emphases in exercise science, health promotion and wellness, sports administration, and sports medicine/athletic training), music education (instrumental and vocal), secondary education (art, English, French, mathematics, general science/biology, social studies, Spanish, and speech), special education (mild/moderate elementary, mild/moderate secondary, early interventionist studies, and speech, language, and hearing specialist studies), and vocational education (agriculture, business, industrial arts, and vocational home economics); College of Engineering: chemical engineering, civil engineering, electrical engineering (computer engineering and telecommunications), industrial technology, mechanical engineering (CAD/CAM option), and petroleum engineering; College of Nursing and Allied Health Professions: nursing, dental hygiene, and emergency health science (associate degree); College of Liberal Arts: anthropology, criminal justice, English, history, interpersonal/public communication, mass communication (broadcast journalism and media advertising), modern languages (French, Francophone studies, and Spanish), philosophy, political science (prelaw option), psychology, public relations, sociology, and speech pathology/audiology; College of Sciences: biology, chemistry, computer science, geology, health information management, mathematics and statistics, microbiology, physics, resource biology and biodiversity, and preprofessional programs in dentistry, medicine, optometry, medical technology, pharmacy, and physical therapy; and College of General Studies: Bachelor of General Studies (associate degree option).

Academic Program

Bachelor's degree programs generally require the completion of at least 125 semester hours. That requirement includes a 42-hour core curriculum, which incorporates classes in English, communication, mathematics, science, literature, history, behavioral science, arts, and humanities. An active honors program offers advanced courses in many departments as well as special interdisciplinary honors courses. Highly motivated students can earn an honors degree by completing a quota of honors courses and by producing an honors thesis. Advanced placement is available by examinations given in about a dozen subject areas shortly before classes begin.

Off-Campus Arrangements

Study abroad for degree credit is available through UL Lafayette exchange agreements with the University of Guadalajara, Mexico; through the Université Sainte-Anne, Nova Scotia; through the UL Lafayette Summer School in Paris, France; and through programs in Northampton and Derby, England. Students may take a variety of undergraduate and graduate courses, which are taught by UL Lafayette faculty and geared to the surroundings. UL Lafayette is a member of the Codofil Consortium of Colleges and Universities, which sponsors an academic-year program at the Université d'Aix-Marseille in Aix-en-Provence, France, and the Université de l'État à Mons in Mons, Belgium. Financial aid is available. In addition, the French government offers teaching assistantships through which UL Lafayette students can teach English in France to finance their study at the Université du Maine le Mans.

UL Lafayette students can take graduate or undergraduate courses in marine biology through a summer field program sponsored by the Louisiana Universities Marine Consortium. Classes are held at field stations along the Louisiana coast.

Academic Facilities

Dupre Library houses more than 860,000 volumes, 5,949 periodicals, more than 2 million microforms, more than 5,200 recordings, and special photography and archive collections. Among these are the world's largest collection of French, Spanish, and British colonial records of Louisiana; the Women in Louisiana Collection; more than 1,500 photographs of the sugar industry; and archives of Acadian and Creole folklore and folklife.

E-mail, a personal Web page, Internet access, and standard applications such as word processing are available to students on a Sun client-server system. General campus access to this system is provided from 143 workstations located in two campus buildings, as well as from any terminal, PC, or Mac connected to the campus network. In addition, a PC lab in Dupre Library provides general access for common applications. Many academic departments also provide computer labs for use by their students. A recent student-funded initiative is funding PC labs in campus residence halls, along with a bank of Internet ports in the Student Union for owners of portable computers. Dial-up access is possible from off campus as well. UL Lafayette also runs an IBM 9672-R21, which is used for the online administrative database, online telephone registration, the library's online catalog, and academic applications. Additional information can be found on the UL Lafayette Web page listed below.

UL Lafayette is well provided with modern engineering equipment, including a highly sophisticated computer-aided design/manufacturing laboratory. The University's 600-acre farm laboratory includes a 30-acre pond for crawfish and catfish culture. Other facilities include two Van de Graaff accelerators, a modern electron microscopy laboratory, a television production laboratory with color video equipment, the Center for Greenhouse Research, an extensive herbarium, and two federal research facilities, the National Wetlands Research Center and the National Oceanic and Atmospheric Administration.

Costs

Tuition in 2000–01 for full-time undergraduate students who are Louisiana residents is $1010.25 per semester (for 12 or more hours). Out-of-state undergraduates pay costs of $3626.25 per semester. Books cost an estimated $350 per semester. A dormitory room and meals are about $1296 per semester. Other fees include occasional laboratory fees ($10–$50), a technology fee ($5 per credit, up to $60 per semester), the admissions fee ($20), and car registration. Children of alumni are granted in-state residency for fee purposes. All fees are subject to change and can be confirmed by the Registrar's Office.

Financial Aid

About 70 percent of UL Lafayette students receive financial aid of some kind. UL Lafayette participates in federal and state financial aid programs, such as the Federal Pell Grant, Federal Supplemental Educational Opportunity Grant (FSEOG), State Student Incentive Grant (SSIG), Tuition Opportunity Program for Students (TOPS), Nursing Loan, Federal Perkins Loan, Federal Work-Study, and Federal Stafford Student Loan programs. Financial need is assessed through the Free Application for Federal Student Aid (FAFSA), which is available through high school counselors and the UL Lafayette Financial Aid Office. On-campus jobs are based on financial need, and the community has many off-campus job opportunities. Assistance in securing an off-campus job is available through the Placement Office.

The University also has an excellent scholarship program. The application deadline is in January, but students are encouraged to apply earlier. UL Lafayette annually awards about $2.5 million in scholarships to academically gifted students.

Faculty

UL Lafayette places a high premium on its nationally competitive faculty. Its faculty includes MacArthur and McDonnell Fellowship winners, 7 endowed chairs, and 150 endowed professorships. This teaching-research–balanced faculty invites undergraduate students to participate in funded and ongoing research projects. Students consistently rate faculty members as highly caring.

The faculty is composed of approximately 555 full-time and 87 part-time members. Most graduate faculty members also teach undergraduate courses; graduate assistants teach freshman-level classes in some departments.

Student Government

An elected Student Government Association (SGA) represents student interests on campus and controls the disbursement of more than $70,000 in self-assessed student fees and oversees the allocation of almost $3 million for student activities. SGA provides legal consulting for students and funds a child development center and other services, homecoming, and various special events. It also disburses about $30,000 annually in scholarships.

UL Lafayette students are represented on almost all University committees. The UL Lafayette president makes himself available at a regular Monday afternoon meeting to answer students' questions and listen to problems. Student publications are independent of direct University control, although UL Lafayette provides an adviser for them.

Admission Requirements

UL Lafayette admits students regardless of race, sex, handicap, creed, or ethnic origin. Prospective students should send ACT or SAT I scores, a six-semester (minimum) high school transcript, and an admissions application (available on line at the Web site listed below) to the Director of Admissions.

All students must present a minimum ACT subscore of either a 17 in English (430 on the verbal portion of the SAT I) or a 19 in mathematics (460 on the quantitative portion of the SAT I) to qualify for regular admissions. Out-of-state students need a minimum ACT composite score of 17 (810 on the SAT I) and a 2.2 cumulative high school GPA. In-state students must present a combination of an ACT composite score and a high school cumulative GPA (on a 4.0 scale) of 18 and 2.0, 17 and 2.2, 16 and 2.4, or 15 and 2.6 or must present a 2.0 minimum GPA in 17½ units of core courses, including 4 units of English (composition and American, British, or world literature are suggested), 3 units of mathematics (algebra I, algebra II, geometry, trigonometry, calculus, or advanced math), 3 units of science (biology I is required, and biology II, chemistry, and physics are suggested), 3 units of social studies (American or world history are required, and civics, economics, geography, history, psychology, and sociology are suggested), and 4½ units of electives (½ unit of computer science or computer literacy, 1 unit of fine arts, 2 units of foreign language, and 1 unit of speech are suggested). Students who do not meet these requirements may apply for an admission exception. Up to 15 percent of the freshman class may be admitted as exceptions. Applications for admission exceptions are reviewed using criteria such as GPA, grade trends, class rank, special talents, school recommendations, extracurricular activities, leadership abilities, significant life/career experiences, and membership in an underrepresented group.

Transfer students must be eligible to attend the previous institution and must be eligible to enroll in regular freshman English and college algebra.

Application and Information

U.S. citizens should apply for admission at least thirty days prior to the beginning of classes, but earlier application is suggested. International students should apply at least ninety days before classes begin. The application fee is $20 for U.S. citizens and $30 for international students.

For more information, prospective students should contact:
Enrollment Services
University of Louisiana at Lafayette
P.O. Box 44652
Lafayette, Louisiana 70504

Telephone: 800-752-6553 (toll-free)
E-mail: enroll@louisiana.edu
World Wide Web: http://www.louisiana.edu

UNIVERSITY OF MAINE
ORONO, MAINE

The University

The University of Maine, the land-grant university and sea-grant college of the state of Maine, has a mission to provide teaching and public service and to carry out research for the state of Maine and the country. The University was established in 1865 as the Maine State College of Agriculture and the Mechanic Arts. When the institution opened its doors in 1868, it had 12 students and 2 faculty members. Today, as the University of Maine, it has 644 faculty members and 9,945 students who represent thirty-seven states and forty-nine countries. The University of Maine is a participant in the New England Regional Program sponsored by the New England Board of Higher Education.

The University of Maine is the flagship campus of the University of Maine System, which consists of six other independent institutions across the state. The college proper consists of 161 buildings on a 660-acre region of Maine's 5,500 acres of contiguous land. The campus is located in the midsection of the state and is 8 miles north of Bangor—the third-largest city in Maine—which is served daily by air and bus transportation. Campus living offers numerous housing situations, from apartment-style complexes for upperclass students and fraternity and sorority houses to a variety of residence halls. The University's campus overlooks the Stillwater River and is surrounded by forests and botanical gardens. Ivy-covered buildings and pathways shaded by evergreens and elms make it inviting and picturesque in all seasons.

The University has more than 120 student organizations, including honor and professional societies, fraternities, and sororities. Nine women's and eight men's intercollegiate NCAA Division I athletic programs are part of the campus community. Numerous intramural club sports give all students an opportunity to be physically active. Two gymnasiums, a field house, an indoor pool, a sports arena, a fitness center, and a new 10,000-seat athletic stadium are used for both NCAA Division I athletics and recreational sports. For students with creative interests, there are two theaters, an arts center, excellent music facilities, recital halls, and studios for dance and the visual arts. Community services include a daily newspaper, a radio station, a police and safety department, a fire department, and a health facility. Recently completed buildings include the Bryand Global Sciences Center, the Alfond Sports Stadium and Morse Center, and the Advanced Engineering Wood Composites Laboratory.

Location

The town of Orono is advantageously situated in central Maine, 240 miles north of Boston and 306 miles from Montreal. Within an easy drive of campus are many sites of great natural beauty, such as Acadia National Park, Mount Katahdin, and Baxter State Park, which offer a wide range of recreational opportunities. Within a 3-hour drive are several ski resorts, including Sugarloaf/USA and Sunday River.

Majors and Degrees

The University of Maine offers more than seventy 4-year baccalaureate degree programs through five colleges: the College of Business, Public Policy, and Health; the College of Education and Human Development; the College of Engineering; the College of Liberal Arts and Sciences; and the College of Natural Sciences, Forestry, and Agriculture. A Bachelor of University Studies degree for part-time evening adult learners is offered through the Division of Lifelong Learning.

Academic Program

The University of Maine is a year-round educational institution. The academic year is divided into two 15-week semesters, from early September to mid-May; a 3-week May term; a 3-week winter term; a summer session with 2- to 8-week sessions; and a summer field session. The University offers day as well as evening classes.

Each college sets its own graduation requirements in terms of grades and/or grade point average, as described in the University undergraduate catalog. All students in baccalaureate degree programs must also meet the University's general education requirements. They must receive passing grades in all required courses and earn the number of credit hours required by their program.

Each student is assigned an academic adviser whose role is to assist them in achieving their educational objectives and to guide them toward fulfillment of their program's requirements. Students may also utilize academic and personal counseling through the Division of Student Affairs.

Seniors who have achieved a grade point average of 3.7 or higher or who are in the top 5 percent in their college are graduated as summa cum laude; those with a GPA of 3.5 to 3.69 or who are in the top 10 percent of their college are graduated as magna cum laude; and those with a GPA of 3.3 to 3.49 or who are in the top 20 percent of their college are graduated as cum laude.

Qualified students who successfully complete the Honors Program offered by the University are graduated with Honors, High Honors, or Highest Honors. Honor society membership is extended to students who have achieved academic excellence. Today the campus has thirty societies, including Phi Beta Kappa, Phi Kappa Phi, Tau Beta Pi, Xi Sigma Pi, Kappa Delta Pi, Beta Gamma Sigma, and Alpha Zeta.

Military programs are available in Army and Naval/Marine ROTC.

Off-Campus Arrangements

At least forty departments of the University offer field-based learning programs, including internships, practicums, cooperative education programs, and field experience. Students are given academic credit and/or compensation for on-the-job experience in their major field.

The University of Maine offers a wide range of national and international student exchanges through the National Student Exchange (NSE), the Council on International Education Exchange (CIEE), the College Consortium for International Studies (CCIS), and the International Student Exchange Program (ISEP). The University also sponsors reciprocal exchanges between the University of Maine and such countries as Australia, France, Germany, and Japan.

The University sponsors a Junior Year Abroad Program in Salzburg, Austria, and administers an exchange program with University College, Galway, Ireland. The Canada Year program, coordinated by the University's Canadian-American Center, offers students the opportunity to study at various Canadian universities.

Academic Facilities

Fogler Library, located at the center of campus, was built in 1942, and an addition was completed in 1976. It is Maine's largest library collection and the eighteenth-largest library in New England. It contains 920,000 volumes and more than 2 million microforms, subscribes to 5,400 periodicals, and is a regional depository for more than 2 million government documents. Its departments include Reference Services, the Science and Engineering Center, Special Collections, the Learning Materials Center, Government Documents, and the Listening Center.

All departments on campus have the necessary laboratories and equipment to support student research. The most widely used facility is the Computer Center, which houses IBM, Digital, and Macintosh computers. Undergraduates have access to computer facilities through terminals located throughout the campus. For a fee, students can choose to connect to the University's computer system, which provides access to a variety of software programs and network services.

Among the other facilities on campus are art galleries, the only public observatory in the state, and a planetarium. The Maine Center for the Arts, built in 1986, includes the Hutchins Concert Hall (with a seating capacity of 1,628) and the Hudson Museum and William P. Palmer III Gallery for exhibition of the permanent collection of pre-Hispanic Mexican, Central American, and Native American artifacts. Renovated microbiology and biochemistry research and teaching facilities were completed in 1987. The innovative Donald P. Corbett Business Building was completed in 1993. The School of Performing Arts and the Class of 1944 Hall was completed in mid-1996.

Costs

Costs are adjusted annually by the University of Maine Board of Trustees. For the 2000–01 academic year, tuition for state residents is $135 per credit hour; for nonresident students, it is $384 per credit hour. (The average credit load for full-time students is 15 credit hours per semester or 30 credit hours for the academic year.) Nonresident students who qualify for the New England Regional Program pay the state resident tuition plus 50 percent. Required University fees ($714 per year for a full-time student) include the Comprehensive Fee, which provides a variety of health-care services and admission to cultural and recreational events. Books and supplies cost about $700 for the academic year. Room and board (nineteen meals per week) charges for the academic year are $5360. These costs are subject to change by legislative action.

Financial Aid

The University requires all financial aid applicants to file the Free Application for Federal Student Aid (FAFSA) with the College Scholarship Service. The form may be obtained from high school guidance offices. The deadline to apply for aid is March 1. The University believes awards of financial aid should be based upon financial need. Awards usually consist of a combination of several types of aid ranging from grants and scholarships to work-study jobs and student loans.

Faculty

The University of Maine has 644 full- and part-time faculty members and a student-faculty ratio of 15:1. A number of faculty members teach both graduate and undergraduate courses. Graduate students serve as teaching assistants in various departments. Faculty members are involved in teaching and research in their academic discipline and also serve as academic advisers to undergraduate students. In addition, they take an active part in the education of students outside the classroom through seminars, workshops, and discussion groups. A number of faculty members serve on the Student Advisory Committee, Student Conduct Committee, and other student organizations on campus and are involved in New Student Orientation and the Admissions Office's Open House programs.

Student Government

An elected president, vice president, and vice president of financial affairs direct and coordinate Student Government programs at the University of Maine. Student Government works closely with the Office of the Dean of Student Services and Community Life and appoints 200 student representatives to the various University committees. These committees are involved with residence hall programs, student discipline, athletics, and cultural activities on campus. The work of the executive budgetary committee of Student Government includes the budgeting of approximately $375,000 in student activity fees. Student Government comprises five governing boards and the General Student Senate.

Admission Requirements

The approval of candidates for admission is a selective process. The University is interested in students whose scholastic achievement, intellectual curiosity, and established study habits suggest promise of success in a comprehensive academic university environment. The evaluation of candidates is based on a review of their individual abilities, aptitudes, and interests. SAT I or ACT scores, along with grades and a counselor recommendation, are the major factors considered. In addition, students' school and community activities help the admissions staff to assess the diversity and background of the applicant pool.

The University recognizes advanced work completed in secondary schools by means of Advanced Placement tests. Also, students who demonstrate advanced knowledge may be exempted from certain courses and requirements if they pass examinations specially developed by the University's academic departments.

Application and Information

An application form, available from the Admissions Office or any Maine high school guidance office, should be submitted with the nonrefundable application fee. In addition, candidates are requested to submit official transcripts of their high school records along with counselor recommendations. Traditional age applicants are required to submit scores on either the SAT I or ACT.

Applications for admission to the University of Maine must be filed no later than two weeks prior to the start of classes for any semester. Confirmation deposits are due on May 1.

University of Maine
Office of Admission
5713 Chadbourne Hall
Orono, Maine 04469-5713

Telephone: 207-581-1561
Fax: 207-581-1213
E-mail: um-admit@maine.maine.edu
World Wide Web: http://www.umaine.edu/

UNIVERSITY OF MAINE AT FORT KENT
FORT KENT, MAINE

The University

The University of Maine at Fort Kent (UMFK) offers the combination of high-quality education and personalized attention today's students are looking for. UMFK's campus is not too large, so students are known to their professors by name. The favorable student-faculty ratio of 15:1 provides outstanding interaction. At the same time, the University is large enough to offer a wide variety of academic and extracurricular opportunities. The University's diverse student body includes individuals from small towns and big cities across the United States and Canada, as well as from Europe, Africa, South America, and Asia.

UMFK was founded in 1878 as the Madawaska Training School to educate teachers for what was known as the Madawaska Territory. Over the next century, the school evolved and refined its program into a comprehensive liberal–arts based institution. In 1970, it became part of the seven-campus University of Maine System.

University residence halls offer housing and meal service to the more than 950 full- and part-time UMFK students. Computer, cable TV, and phone hookups are provided in every room, and the halls also have lounges, game rooms, and free laundry facilities. Resident students and commuters alike participate in a variety of campus activities, including theatrical and musical performances, intercollegiate and intramural athletics, and numerous student organizations.

Location

The town of Fort Kent is situated on the banks of the Fish and St. John Rivers in an area originally settled by French-speaking Acadians from Maritime Canada. The St. John Valley community is noted as one of the country's few truly international, bilingual-bicultural regions, and the University of Maine at Fort Kent is known as a great place to learn and grow within that community.

The campus has convenient access to numerous areas of scenic natural beauty, as well as recreational opportunities, including ski areas and resorts, Baxter State Park, the Allagash Wilderness Waterway, and the Gaspé Peninsula in Canada's Quebec Province.

Majors and Degrees

The University of Maine at Fort Kent is a four-year baccalaureate-granting institution that offers the Bachelor of Arts in English and French; the Bachelor of Science in behavioral science, biology, business management, computer applications, education (K–12), environmental studies, nursing, social science field, and University studies; the Associate of Arts in general studies in bicultural studies, business, computer science, criminal justice, and human services; and the Associate of Science in forest technology.

Academic Program

Dedicated to providing a solid liberal arts education within programs designed to equip students for the twenty-first century, the University of Maine at Fort Kent divides the academic year into two 16-week semesters. Both day and evening classes run from early September through early May. Summer classes and workshops are also offered, beginning in May and usually ending in late July. All students, regardless of degree program and major, are required to complete a general education core curriculum and meet certain requirements for graduation. Each degree program and major also has a number of specific requirements that are described in the University catalog.

Entering freshmen are assigned an adviser who is a member of a special advising team devoted to ensuring the success of every student's first year at UMFK.

After the first year, students choose a faculty academic adviser in their field of study, who guides them toward completion of their program requirements.

Off-Campus Arrangements

UMFK offers opportunities for students to study abroad, including exchange programs with Canadian and European universities. A cooperative agreement between the University of Maine at Fort Kent and Université de Moncton-Edmundston Campus provides students with a unique opportunity for cross-registration at either campus. The French branch of the University of Moncton, is located only 22 miles from Fort Kent in Edmundston, New Brunswick. The universities celebrate the heritage of the original settlers of the Upper St. John River Valley.

Along with approximately 130 other public universities across the United States, the University of Maine at Fort Kent is a member of the National Student Exchange Program as well as the New England–Quebec and the New England–Nova Scotia Student Exchange Programs. These programs allow full-time students to pursue course work at other universities in the United States, Quebec, or Nova Scotia to satisfy part of the credit requirements for a degree at UMFK.

Bachelor of Science in environmental studies students also benefit from a cooperative program that allows them to spend a semester or a year studying at either the University of Maine at Presque Isle or the University of Maine at Machias. In addition, practical field experience is available to UMFK environmental studies students through an agreement with the National Audubon Expedition Institute. Through this program, students in good standing can spend a year on an excursion that takes them across the country and requires that they encounter and deal with an array of environmental issues.

Academic Facilities

Buildings on UMFK's 52-acre campus include the Cyr Hall classroom complex and computer laboratory, Fox Auditorium, the Sportscenter, Nowland Dining Hall, the residence halls, the Old Model School, and the Computer Center. In addition to its own collections, Blake Library provides students with a variety of available databases and electronic access to more than a million volumes in libraries of the University of Maine System. New construction and renovation projects for additional facilities are in the works.

The University also owns or has access to a number of facilities, including a 1,000-acre wood lot bordering St. Froid Lake, a biological park bordering the campus, the Fish and St. John Rivers, and a camp located in the Allagash Wilderness Waterway.

Costs

In 1999–2000, tuition was $3120 per year for Maine residents and $7590 per year for out-of-state students. Nonresident students who qualified for the New England Regional Program paid $4680 per year for tuition. Room and board costs for 1999–2000 were $4000 per year. Required University fees for new students were $284, which included application, matriculation, orientation, student activity, and technology fees. Tuition and fee figures listed are based on 15 credit hours per semester.

Financial Aid

The University of Maine at Fort Kent Office of Financial Aid administers scholarships, grants, loans, and work assistance to more than 80 percent of enrolled students. The University requires all applicants for financial aid to file the Free Application for Federal Student Aid (FAFSA), which is available from the UMFK Office of Financial Aid and from high school guidance offices. UMFK has a preferred filing date of March 15. Consideration is given at any time during the year; however, early application is recommended because awards depend on the availability of funds.

Faculty

Excellence has always been the goal of the 35-member UMFK faculty. Its members include accomplished scholars who hold the highest degree in their professional field. Faculty members are active in professional activities, research, and continuing education. Their top priority, however, is always teaching. Classes are generally small, and every faculty member teaches and advises students.

Student Government

UMFK has a long tradition of strong student government. The Student Senate, which represents all students, is a member of the University of Maine Organization of Student Governments.

Admission Requirements

Each applicant is considered on an individual basis by the UMFK Office of Admissions. Consideration is given to academic preparation, maturity, personal motivation, and goals. Particular attention is given to secondary school performance, especially in the junior and senior years. SAT I scores or ACT results are strongly recommended but not required.

Application and Information

Application for admission is made by completing a University of Maine System application form and submitting a nonrefundable fee of $25 to the UMFK Office of Admissions. The University follows a rolling admissions schedule and accepts applications at any time during the year. Students are usually accepted for entry in either September or January.

Applications and additional information are available from:

Office of Admissions
University of Maine at Fort Kent
25 Pleasant Street
Fort Kent, Maine 04743-1292

Telephone: 207-834-7600
           888-TRY-UMFK (879-8635)(toll-free)

Fax: 207-834-7609

E-mail: umfkadm@maine.maine.edu

World Wide Web: http://www.umfk.maine.edu

Students enjoy the close, family-like atmosphere that the University of Maine at Fort Kent provides. The low student-teacher ratio, personalized attention, and numerous campus events and activities all create the ideal setting for a top-quality learning and life experience.

UNIVERSITY OF MAINE AT MACHIAS
MACHIAS, MAINE

The University

The University of Maine at Machias (UMM) was incorporated by the state of Maine in 1909 and is a member of the University of Maine System. Of the approximately 1,000 undergraduate students attending UMM, about 75 percent are from the state of Maine, but many other states and countries are also represented. Approximately 50 percent of the full-time students live in University housing, which includes two large residence halls. The University of Maine at Machias has a total of nine buildings on a 42-acre campus located on a hill overlooking the town of Machias.

Location

The town of Machias, on the coast of Maine, has a population of 2,500. An additional 2,500 people live in the town of East Machias and surrounding areas. Machias is the business, educational, and political capital of Washington County. The town offers support services, shopping areas, churches of several denominations, and many outdoor recreational opportunities. The University acts as the meeting place of the county and offers most cultural events through the Maine State Commission on the Arts and Humanities. The University of Maine at Machias sees itself as having a responsibility to provide support to the community of which it is an integral part.

Majors and Degrees

The University of Maine at Machias awards Bachelor of Arts and Bachelor of Science degrees in behavioral science (concentrations in behavioral physiology, human services, and psychology), biology, business administration (concentrations in accounting, management, marketing, and office management), college studies (self-designed), education, English, environmental studies (concentrations in avian ecology, conservation biology and management, environmental education, environmental policy, and marine ecosystems), fine arts, history, interdisciplinary fine arts (a new program that combines music, theater, visual arts, and creative writing in a new twist to traditional arts programs), liberal arts, marine biology, and recreation management (concentrations in commercial recreation, environmental outdoor recreation, park management, recreation activity programming, sports and fitness management, and tourism/resort management).

Associate of Arts and Associate of Science degrees are offered in accounting, business technology, liberal arts, office management, recreation management, and small business management. An Associate of Arts degree is also offered for those who are undecided about a major.

The University offers an elementary education program, with supplements in early childhood and middle level education. Secondary education certification is offered in business, English, history, life science, and physical science.

Academic Program

Bachelor's degree candidates must complete at least 120 credit hours with a minimum cumulative grade point average of 2.0 and must also complete the core requirements in social sciences, business studies, humanities, fine arts, science/mathematics, and physical education. Associate degree candidates must complete at least 60 credit hours and must maintain a minimum grade point average of 2.0 while fulfilling the specific requirements of their major program.

Academic Facilities

All of the University's academic buildings are of modern construction and include a well-equipped science building with laboratories, a greenhouse, and marine studies aquariums and laboratories.

The newly completed Center for Lifelong Learning includes the Reynolds Center, a new aquatics center, a state-of-the-art fitness facility, racquetball/handball courts, an indoor equipment rental center, and a new bookstore with an Internet café. A conference center and a child-care center will be added to complete the final phases of the Center for Lifelong Learning.

Merrill Library provides a 24-hour study center for students, houses a collection of more than 85,000 volumes, and is linked to other libraries and educational resources throughout the state. A computer center with cross-campus networking and multiple computer labs enhances all of UMM's programs and gives access to the Internet and the World Wide Web. Individual computer access is also available in every residence hall room.

The on-campus radio station, WUMM, is run entirely by students. UMM's student resource center provides faculty and peer assistance as well as computer and audiovisual aids for all students. A variety of activities, from meetings to campus dances and other social events, can be accommodated in the student center. The performing arts center, a 358-seat amphitheater auditorium, is host to many campus and community meetings, seminars, festivals, and performing arts. It is the home of the Bad Little Falls Players and Stage Front: The Arts Downeast programs.

On Long Lake in Princeton, Maine, UMM maintains a 68-acre field site for use by recreation management, education, and environmental studies students. It is also available to all University organizations and personnel for leisure activities.

Costs

The basic expenses for the 1997–98 academic year (based on a 15-credit-hour load per semester) were $2940 per year for in-state tuition and $7200 per year for out-of-state tuition. UMM participates in the New England Regional Program, which allows reduced tuition ($4410 per year) for some out-of-state New England students. Room and board costs were $4075, fees were approximately $225, and most students averaged about $600 for books and school supplies.

Financial Aid

The University of Maine at Machias administers scholarships, loans, grants, work-study awards, and UMM scholarship aid. UMM has a Presidential Scholarship Program, a Distinguished Scholar Program, and a Leadership Scholarship Program for students who have excelled in academics and leadership. Awards are made on the basis of financial need, and students must submit the Free Application for Federal Student Aid (FAFSA) to the College Scholarship Service. March 1 is the University's financial aid priority deadline.

Faculty

The majority of UMM faculty members hold the highest degree in their professional field. The student-faculty ratio is approximately 14:1. All faculty members work as advisers and mentors to students within their areas of academic expertise. Usually on a first-name basis, faculty members develop a close relationship with students during their years of study at UMM and beyond.

Student Government

The University of Maine at Machias is a member of the University of Maine Organization of Student Governments and operates its own Student Senate.

Admission Requirements

Graduation from secondary school or a high school equivalency diploma (the result of passing scores on the General Educational Development test) is the basic requirement for admission. A recommended academic background for admission to baccalaureate programs includes 4 years of English, 3 years of mathematics, 2 laboratory sciences, 2 social sciences, a foreign language, and basic computer utilization. If a student is entering one of the business programs, consideration is given to business courses taken in high school, but college-preparatory English and math are still necessary. Scores on the SAT I or ACT are required for two-year liberal arts and business information systems majors and for all four-year majors. Students should rank in the top half of their high school class and have an overall average of at least B. Students applying for admission into one of the two-year business programs should complete college-preparatory English and mathematics courses in high school, have an overall C average or better, and graduate in the top two thirds of their senior class. The University of Maine at Machias does not discriminate on the basis of race, creed, color, sex, or national origin and is an Equal Opportunity/Affirmative Action employer.

Application and Information

Admission plans include early notification, regular decision, and early admission. UMM operates on a rolling admission system. Applicants for early notification should complete the application process by December 1. Candidates for regular decision should complete their applications as early as possible. Students may apply for early admission, through which they may be admitted directly into the University after completing three years of secondary school. Candidates for this program must have recommendations of support from their guidance counselor, principal, and/or high school board. Their high school grades should place them in the top 15 percent of their class. Transfer applicants should complete their applications by June 1 for the fall term or by December 1 for the spring term.

Applications and additional information may be obtained by contacting:

Director of Admissions
University of Maine at Machias
9 O'Brien Avenue
Machias, Maine 04654

Telephone: 207-255-1318
             888-468-6866 (toll-free)
Fax: 207-255-1363
E-mail: admissions@acad.umm.maine.edu
World Wide Web: http://www.umm.maine.edu

The newly constructed Center for Lifelong Learning at the University of Maine at Machias houses the Reynolds Athletic and Education Center, an enclosed aquatics center, a fully equipped fitness center, a bookstore, and an Internet café.

UNIVERSITY OF MARY HARDIN-BAYLOR
BELTON, TEXAS

The University

Chartered by the Republic of Texas in 1845, the University of Mary Hardin-Baylor (UMHB) is the oldest institution of higher learning offering continuous education in the state. UMHB is a Christ-centered, coeducational school affiliated with the Baptist General Convention of Texas and accredited by the Commission on Colleges of the Southern Association of Colleges and Schools, Texas Education Agency, Board of Nurse Examiners for the state of Texas, and the National League for Nursing Accrediting Commission. The University seeks the development of the whole person by providing opportunities that enable students to expand their horizons intellectually, physically, and spiritually. All students are required to attend chapel assembly programs for half of the semesters they spend at UMHB and to take two courses in religion. These are normally survey courses on the Old Testament and the New Testament.

There are numerous organizations on campus to provide the student with social and leadership opportunities. As a member of the NCAA Division III American Southwest Conference, the University's teams participate in men's intercollegiate baseball, basketball, cross-country, football, golf, soccer, and tennis and in women's intercollegiate basketball, cross-country, fast-pitch softball, golf, soccer, tennis, and volleyball.

Approximately one third of the University's full-time students live in the air-conditioned dormitories on campus. Most students live in double rooms. All room assignments are made by the University's housing office.

Total enrollment at the University is just over 2,500. Graduate students pursue the Master of Education degree, the Master of Arts degree in psychology, the Master of Business Administration degree, the Master of Health Services Management, the Master of Arts degree in counseling, or the Master of Science degree in information systems.

Location

The University is located in Belton, a quiet town of 15,000 people in the heart of central Texas. The nearby cities of Temple and Killeen have more than 150,000 residents combined. The Killeen-Temple area is the fastest-growing Standard Metropolitan Statistical Area in Texas.

Belton is on Interstate 35, approximately 150 miles south of the Dallas–Fort Worth metroplex and 60 miles north of Austin. Local topography varies from rolling plains to wooded hills. Two large lakes within a 15-minute drive of the campus and nearby golf courses provide many outdoor recreational opportunities.

Majors and Degrees

The University of Mary Hardin-Baylor offers course work leading to the Bachelor of Arts, Bachelor of Business Administration, Bachelor of Fine Arts, Bachelor of Professional Studies, Bachelor of Applied Science, Bachelor of Music, Bachelor of Science, Bachelor of Science in Nursing, and Bachelor of Social Work degrees.

Majors are offered in accounting, applied science, art, biology, business administration, chemistry, church music, communication, computer graphics design, computer information systems, computer science, computer studies, criminal justice, economics, elementary education, English, exercise and sports science, finance, history, information systems, management, marketing, mass communications/journalism, mathematics, medical technology, music education, music performance and pedagogy, nursing, performance studies, political science, professional studies, psychology, recreation, religion, secondary education, social work, sociology, Spanish, and technology and training. Minors are also offered in accounting, art, biology, business administration, chemistry, communication, computer information systems, computer studies, drama, economics, English, exercise and sports science, finance, French, generic special education, German, history, life-earth science, management, marketing, mass communication/journalism, mathematics, music, physical science, political science, psychology, reading, recreation, religion, sociology, and Spanish.

In addition to these undergraduate degrees, UMHB offers preprofessional programs, including predentistry, prelaw, premedical records administrator studies, premedicine, preoccupational therapy, preoptometry, prepharmacy, pre–physical therapy, pre–physician's assistant studies, and pre–veterinary studies.

Academic Program

The University of Mary Hardin-Baylor is a unique and energetic institution with an emphasis on Christian education. A relatively small student body means that students are able to receive considerable personal attention from instructors. The academic program stresses excellence in the humanities, the fine and professional arts, and the social and natural sciences.

All degrees involve a core of courses in English, religion, social science, mathematics, laboratory science or foreign language, humanities/fine arts, and physical education. The 63 to 65 hours of the core program serve as a base for expanding the student's understanding of the arts and sciences. Major fields of study require 24 to 38 semester hours of work, while minors require 18 to 24 semester hours.

Freshmen entering UMHB may receive credit for eligible scores on the Advanced Placement, ACT, or CLEP tests. There are also a number of courses for which the student may seek credit through departmental challenge examinations. During the junior year, a student may apply for acceptance into the University's honors program. This program consists of departmental honors courses, honors seminars, and a senior research project.

A program is offered for the high school student who has not yet graduated. Under the Select program, the University will admit to full-time status qualified students who have completed their junior year of high school and wish to forgo their senior year in order to begin study at the college level.

Academic Facilities

The newly remodeled Townsend Memorial Library serves as the base for UMHB students to involve themselves in various areas of research. This modern facility provides open stacks and has rare books and periodicals on microfiche to make material more readily available. The Computer Science Lab makes available a variety of computers and printers for students to use. Students in the Departments of Biology and Chemistry have the opportunity to work with research scientists on such projects as the Texas mammal collection and one of the state's most complete collections of both Texas freshwater and marine fish.

The University's Department of Chemistry allows undergraduates time to work with a nuclear magnetic resonance spectrometer, X-ray diffraction instrumentation, a computer programmed solely for chemistry-related research, and various spectrophotometers. This specialized equipment supports the ongoing research in which undergraduates may be involved.

The University's creative arts programs are housed in Presser Hall, which contains practice and rehearsal rooms and an acoustically perfect recital hall. Piano majors perform their recitals on the department's 9½-foot Steinway piano.

Costs

Tuition is $290 per semester hour for 2000–01. Room and board cost approximately $1850 per semester. Some courses also have a laboratory fee of $15 to $75. Private music lessons cost an additional $700 per semester for two 30-minute lessons each week.

Financial Aid

The University of Mary Hardin-Baylor is one of the most affordable private universities in the Southwest, with approximately 80 percent of its full-time undergraduate students receiving some kind of financial assistance. There are a number of aid programs funded by the University, including scholarships, grants, and student employment. In addition, the University participates in the Federal Perkins Loan, Federal Pell Grant, Federal Supplemental Educational Opportunity Grant, Federal Work-Study, Federal Stafford Student Loan, and Texas Hinson-Hazelwood Student Loan programs, as well as the Tuition Equalization Grant program for Texas students.

Faculty

The University of Mary Hardin-Baylor has an outstanding group of teaching professionals on its faculty. The instructors are not only well trained in their field but also take time to help their students grow professionally through close personal academic leadership and supervision. Most faculty members have earned doctoral degrees, and many continue to be involved in research. Because there are no graduate and teaching assistants, even freshmen have an opportunity to be taught by full-time professors and department heads, a privilege reserved for upperclass students on most larger campuses.

Student Government

The University's Student Government Association functions as a liaison between the University's administration and its students. The organization charters all other organizations on campus, recommends or elects students to certain standing committees, participates in student justice, and provides an open forum for discussion of common concerns.

Admission Requirements

Applicants are accepted if their composite ACT score is 19 or above or their SAT I score is 900 or above or if they graduate in the upper half of their senior class. Transfer applicants with more than 30 semester hours are accepted if their overall grade point average is 2.0 or higher. A certain number of students are accepted on scholastic probation. Students who are on scholastic suspension are not accepted.

The University of Mary Hardin-Baylor does not discriminate in any of its policies or programs on the basis of sex, physical handicap, or national or ethnic origin.

Application and Information

Candidates for admission to the University of Mary Hardin-Baylor must submit an application for admission, a $35 application fee, a high school transcript and/or a transcript from each college attended, and scores on the ACT or SAT I.

For application forms or further information, prospective students should contact:

UMHB Station Box 8004
University of Mary Hardin-Baylor
900 College Street
Belton, Texas 76513
Telephone: 254-295-8642
          800-727-UMHB (toll-free)
E-mail: stheodor@umhb.edu
World Wide Web: http://www.umhb.edu

Students from more than twenty-six states and twenty-two countries enjoy UMHB's scenic campus.

UNIVERSITY OF MARYLAND, BALTIMORE COUNTY
BALTIMORE, MARYLAND

The University

University of Maryland, Baltimore County (UMBC) students find out quickly that learning at an honors university takes place in many different ways and in a variety of settings. Students discover an environment with a strong undergraduate liberal arts and sciences focus. A mid-sized public research university, UMBC provides students with opportunities to get hands-on research experience through working with professors at the top of their fields. UMBC's academic reputation and industry partnerships help to place students in promising careers and leading graduate programs. In fact, one third of UMBC students immediately go on to graduate or professional schools.

Few universities, if any, can match UMBC for commitment to undergraduate education—or for undergraduate participation in real problem solving. The commitment shows in the University's resources and equipment. Undergraduate students have access to the latest technology in areas from geography to art history to chemistry. The International Media Center offers students multilingual word processing, worldwide databases, and satellite feeds from the International Channel, Deutsche Welle, and French, Russian, and Spanish stations. The Joint Center for Earth Systems Technology, set up by UMBC and the NASA/Goddard Space Flight Center, brings together professors and students from computer science, geography, environmental systems, and physics to study the earth's environmental changes. Students in UMBC's Imaging Research Center gain professional experience with companies such as the Discovery Channel, CNN, and PBS; students use the IRC's high-end equipment for applications, such as molecular imaging and three-dimensional cartography.

The campus climate is friendly and energetic. UMBC's nearly 9,000 undergraduates have enough ideas and interests to support more than 150 different student groups, including Greek organizations; recreational sports clubs, such as skydiving and crew; community outreach efforts, such as Habitat for Humanity; and campus events, including lectures, films, concerts, and plays. Friends get together frequently—all around campus and in UMBC's residence halls and garden-style apartments. Students enthusiastically follow UMBC NCAA Division I athletic teams, such as basketball, lacrosse, and soccer, attending games in the UMBC Stadium and Retriever Activities Center, which includes a new multipurpose gym, an auxiliary gym, a new weight room, and classrooms.

UMBC students are from forty-three states and seventy-one countries. UMBC's diverse undergraduate community includes 48 percent men and 52 percent women, 68 percent Caucasian, 15 percent African American, 13 percent Asian American, 2 percent Hispanic American, and 2 percent international students. Sixty-six percent of first-year students live on campus. A new residence hall is under construction and will be complete by summer 2000. Room layouts are based on a suite concept with a shared living room.

Location

Located a few miles south of Baltimore, UMBC is 15 minutes from downtown Baltimore and 45 minutes from Washington, D.C. Surrounded by business, government, and metropolitan centers, UMBC places students in co-ops and internships in more than 100 organizations each year in the Baltimore-Washington area and abroad. UMBC matches students with employers such as IBM, Computer Sciences Corporation, Silicon Graphics, the Smithsonian Institution, NASA, and the National Aquarium.

The Baltimore-Washington area is known for its music, sports, museums, restaurants, and historical traditions. Favorite student haunts include Fells Point, the Inner Harbor, Oriole Park at Camden Yards, Patapsco State Park, Annapolis, and Georgetown.

A 500-acre suburban Baltimore university, the UMBC campus includes more than thirty buildings enclosed by a 2-mile elliptical drive, with housing and dining facilities on one side and core facilities (classroom/lab buildings, a library, galleries, a student union, a bookstore, a gymnasium, an Olympic-size pool, and tennis courts) surrounding a central walkway.

Majors and Degrees

UMBC offers programs leading to Bachelor of Arts, Bachelor of Fine Arts, and Bachelor of Science degrees in the following areas: Africana studies, American studies, biochemistry and molecular biology, biological sciences, chemical and biochemical engineering, chemistry, computer engineering, computer science, dance, economics, emergency health services, English, geography and environmental systems, health science and policy, history, information systems, interdisciplinary studies, mathematics, mechanical engineering, modern languages and linguistics, music, philosophy, physics, political science, psychology, social work, sociology, theater, visual and performing arts, and visual arts. Students in the interdisciplinary studies program, working with faculty members, design their own course of study according to their specific educational and career goals.

UMBC offers preprofessional and allied health programs, including four-year predental, prelaw, premedical, pre-optometry, and pre–veterinary medicine programs, and two-year predental hygiene, premedical and research technology, prenursing, prepharmacy, pre–physical therapy, and diagnostic medical sonography programs.

Minor programs include Africana studies, American studies, anthropology, applied politics, art history and theory, biological sciences, computer science, dance, East Asian history, economics, emergency health services, environmental geography, geography, history, international affairs, international economics, Judaic studies, legal policy, mathematics, modern languages and linguistics, music, philosophy, physics, political science, political thought, psychology, public administration, religious studies, social welfare, sociology, theater, women's studies, and writing.

Academic Program

UMBC's academic calendar consists of fall and spring semesters, a session in January, and summer sessions ranging from six to eight weeks.

To receive a UMBC degree, students complete 120 to 128 credits plus two physical education courses. In addition to the requirements for the chosen major, a core of courses, called the general foundation requirements (GFR), provides a solid basis for a lifetime of learning. The GFR courses encompass four broad areas of human knowledge: humanities and fine arts, mathematics and natural sciences, social sciences, and languages and culture.

The UMBC Honors College is a special option for students seeking a community of like-minded people for whom the quest for knowledge is its own reward. Honors College students gain the enlightened perspective that comes with immersion in the liberal arts. Innovative approaches to study, unique internship options, and emphasis on independent research are among the hallmarks of the program. All Honors College students must take at least one honors course per semester; students choose from honors versions of core courses, special honors seminars, and plenty of other honors courses.

The Shriver Center links the resources of the campus to urgent social problems, particularly in the areas of education, criminal justice, health, the environment, and jobs, with special priority given to the needs of citizens with mental retardation. The Shriver Center places students in co-ops and internships at hundreds of businesses and organizations, organizes and manages community service projects that bring the resources of the University to people in need, and connects students to a wide range of social service projects.

Academic Facilities
UMBC's commitment to providing sufficient, modern academic and residential facilities has led to a number of construction projects on campus. The new Physics Building houses seminar rooms, computer labs, classroom space, and a telescope for atmospheric research and astronomical observation.

UMBC's landmark building, the Albin O. Kuhn Library and Gallery, rises seven stories over the UMBC campus. The library contains more than 750,000 books and bound volumes of journals, an extensive reference collection, 42,000 current journal subscriptions, 1,000 wired communication jacks to the World Wide Web, and 1.5 million other items, including slides, photographs, maps, musical scores, recordings, and microforms. Interlibrary loan services give UMBC students access to more than 16 million items across the country. Special Collections houses an extensive photography archive, the archives of the American Society for Microbiology, and several other collections. The gallery serves as a major exhibit resource for the campus and the region, displaying library holdings as well as art and artifacts from all over the world.

UMBC's modern engineering and computer science building contains several general access computer labs, which offer 360 PC workstations running Windows NT, 120 Silicon Graphics workstations, and 200 Power Macintosh workstations. The University computer services include a high-speed campus network, remote access capabilities, powerful networked multiprocessor systems for research, online information, e-mail accounts for all students, and directory services.

Costs
Estimated tuition and fees for 2000–01 are $5490 for Maryland residents and $10,258 for out-of-state students. Room and board costs vary; the average is $5809. Miscellaneous expenses, books, and transportation are approximately $1000 per year.

Financial Aid
As a member of the state university system, UMBC is able to keep costs relatively low. Approximately 55 percent of undergraduate students receive some financial aid in the form of grants, work-study, or loans. UMBC uses the Free Application for Federal Student Aid (FAFSA) to help determine students' financial need. Aid is awarded to qualified applicants on a first-come, first-served basis. In order for the applicant to be considered on time, the FAFSA report and all supporting documents must reach the UMBC Financial Aid Office by March 1. (Since aid is awarded only to admitted students, early application for admission is also important.)

A wide range of merit scholarships ranging from $5000 to $16,000 per year are awarded to students on the basis of academic or artistic merit. Well-qualified freshmen are automatically considered for general merit scholarships once they are admitted to the University. Special programs, such as the Humanities Scholars, the Artist Scholars, the Public Affairs Scholars, and the Meyerhoff Scholars, include an extracurricular travel or summer-study component. Candidates must be nominated by a high school official and undergo a rigorous selection and interview process.

Faculty
Many UMBC faculty members work at the frontiers of their disciplines, and they are eager to share their expertise with undergraduates. Because UMBC is a research university dedicated to undergraduate education, students have opportunities for research experience, instruction in state-of-the-art techniques, and introductions to prospective employers who partner with UMBC faculty members in research.

Leading faculty members, including deans and award-winning professors, teach entry-level classes. Often, classes are team-taught, bringing insights from different disciplines to bear on challenging questions. UMBC has 483 full-time and 314 part-time faculty members. Nearly 90 percent of the faculty hold doctorates or terminal degrees. The faculty-student ratio is 16:1.

Student Government
Elections are held each year for officers in UMBC's Student Government Association (SGA). The SGA represents the student body on a number of administrative committees, including the Undergraduate Council, the Library Committee, and the Student Health Advisory Committee.

Admission Requirements
In fall 1998, the average incoming freshman had a 3.35 cumulative GPA, ranked in the top quarter of his or her senior class, and had a combined SAT I score approaching 1200. Approximately 55 percent of freshman applicants are admitted each year. More than 20 percent enter with advanced credit, either through AP, I.B., or other college courses. Grades in academic courses and curriculum strength play an important part in the decision. An essay is also required.

Transfer students who present at least 28 semester hours of college-level work are admitted based on the strength of college success. A 2.5 cumulative average is recommended for full consideration.

Application and Information
Prospective freshmen are encouraged to submit applications by December 15 for full consideration for admission, campus housing, financial aid, and scholarships; the final deadline is March 15. Applicants may also be considered for spring admission by applying prior to December 15.

The deadline for transfer students is May 31 for fall admission and December 15 for spring admission, although earlier application is recommended for students seeking admission to special programs or wishing to be considered for campus housing, financial aid, or scholarships.

For further information, students or parents may contact:

Janice Doyle
Senior Director of Enrollment Services
Admissions
University of Maryland, Baltimore County
1000 Hilltop Circle
Baltimore, Maryland 21250

Telephone: 410-455-2291
Fax: 410-455-1094
World Wide Web: http://www.umbc.edu/undergrad

UMBC's chess team overwhelmingly defeated teams such as Harvard and Stanford and went on to claim first place at the 1999 Pan-American Intercollegiate Chess Team Championship—the "World Series" of college chess.

UNIVERSITY OF MARYLAND, COLLEGE PARK
COLLEGE PARK, MARYLAND

The University

Throughout its 145-year history, the University of Maryland has served as a premier public research university while dedicating itself to providing the highest quality undergraduate education. Designated as the state's flagship university, Maryland attracts the best students and faculty members from across the nation and around the world. Students enroll at Maryland for the reputation and quality of its academic programs, the outstanding and diverse opportunities both in and outside the classroom, and the success of its alumni.

Choosing from among more than 100 academic programs, 21,845 full-time and 2,872 part-time undergraduates are taught by a faculty of more than 1,900. Approximately 8,200 master's- and doctoral-level students are enrolled in the graduate school. About 75 percent of Maryland's undergraduates are state residents, with the remaining quarter coming from all fifty states, the District of Columbia, three territories, and 110 other countries. Maryland's diversity is one of its strongest assets, with 35 percent of students belonging to minority groups.

More than 8,000 undergraduates live on-campus. From traditional halls to apartments with kitchens and from single rooms to special-interest housing, students individualize their housing experience. Many students live near the campus in fraternity and sorority houses, apartments, and private homes. An extensive University shuttle bus system provides free transportation to neighboring communities in ten directions, allowing commuting students easy access to campus. Parking is readily available for both resident and commuter students.

The University sponsors more than 300 student clubs and organizations and hosts dozens of social, athletic, academic, and recreational activities each week. About 10 percent of students are members of twenty-five fraternities and twenty sororities. A full range of intramural and club sports use the University's campus recreation center, which houses indoor and outdoor swimming pools, free weights, fitness machines, courts, and a running track. Outdoor athletic facilities include an eighteen-hole golf course, a soccer/track complex, and playing fields. In addition, Maryland hosts teams in fifteen NCAA sports for both men and women, which compete in the Atlantic Coast Conference.

Location

Maryland students step off the campus and into one of the world's most vibrant centers of government, business, research, and culture. The University is located just minutes from the heart of Washington, D.C., and within half an hour of both Baltimore and Annapolis. Maryland's dynamic relationship with these cities gives students access to hands-on experience with government agencies, international corporations, trade associations, and foreign embassies. The Kennedy Center, NASA, the Smithsonian, the NIH, the Environmental Protection Agency, CNN, the National Archives, the FBI, and the *Washington Post* are just a few of the hundreds of places where Maryland students find opportunities for internships, research projects, and jobs. An on-campus Metrorail and MARC train station provide quick and easy public transportation to the entire Washington-Baltimore region. In addition, the city of College Park is a true college town, with dozens of restaurants, clubs, shops, and recreational activities designed for students.

Majors and Degrees

The University of Maryland offers one of the most comprehensive course selections available at any public or private institution. Programs leading to Bachelor of Arts and Bachelor of Science degrees include accounting, aerospace engineering, Afro-American studies, agricultural and resource economics, agricultural sciences, agronomy, American studies, animal sciences, anthropology, architecture, art education, art history and archaeology, art studio, astronomy, biochemistry, biological resources engineering, biological sciences, business and management, chemical engineering, chemistry, Chinese, civil and environmental engineering, classics, communication, computer engineering, computer science, criminology and criminal justice, dance, decision and information science, dietetics, early childhood education, economics, electrical engineering, elementary education, English, English education, environmental science and policy, family studies, finance, fire protection engineering, food science, foreign language education, French, geography, geology, Germanic studies, government and politics, health education, hearing and speech sciences, history, horticulture, human resources management, international business, Italian, Japanese, Jewish studies, journalism, kinesiology, landscape architecture, linguistics, logistics and transportation, marketing, materials sciences and engineering, mathematics, mathematics education, mechanical engineering, music, music education, natural resources management, nuclear engineering, nutritional science, operations and quality management, philosophy, physical education, physical sciences, physics, psychology, Romance languages, Russian, Russian area studies, science education, social studies education, sociology, Spanish, special education, speech education, theater, theater education, veterinary medicine, and women's studies. Preprofessional programs are also available in allied health, dentistry, law, medicine, nursing, pharmacy, and physical therapy.

Academic Program

Undergraduate education at Maryland aims to provide students with a sense of identity and purpose, a concern for others, a sense of responsibility for the quality of life around them, a continuing eagerness for knowledge and understanding, and a foundation for a lifetime of personal enrichment and success. Within a research setting such as Maryland's, undergraduate students take strong, interdisciplinary courses taught by renowned researchers and scholars.

Every undergraduate completes at least 120 credit hours to earn a degree, 46 of which are general education or CORE courses. The purpose of CORE is to help students achieve the intellectual integration and awareness they need to meet challenges in their personal, social, political, and professional lives. Although each program is unique, generally 30 to 36 credit hours are earned in the major field. Students may earn a double major, earn a certificate in a second area of study, and use AP and IB credit toward a degree.

University Honors offers the most academically talented students the opportunity to join a close-knit community of students and faculty members in small, challenging seminar courses and residential communities. College Park Scholars, an innovative living/learning program that is also designed for academically talented students, encourages students who share common intellectual interests to study and live together. Other special academic opportunities for undergraduates include First Year Focus, Gemstone, Humanities, Air Force ROTC, and a research assistant program.

The University operates on a semester system and offers two 6-week summer sessions and a three-week winter term. More than 3,000 undergraduate courses are taught at the University of Maryland.

Off-Campus Arrangements

Students at Maryland have the opportunity to formally study abroad for credit in Austria, Brazil, Canada, Costa Rica, Cuba, Denmark, England, France, Germany, Israel, Italy, Japan, Korea, Mexico, Spain, Sweden, and Vietnam. The National Student Exchange program allows students to study at one of more than 140 different U.S. colleges and universities for a semester or a year. Internships and cooperative education opportunities are plentiful in and around the nation's capital.

Academic Facilities

Encompassing 350 buildings on 1,500 acres, the University of Maryland houses dozens of research laboratories, performance venues, art galleries, and centers of study. Major academic and research facilities include the National Archives II, the Academy of Leadership, the Center for Agricultural Biotechnology, the Astronomy Observatory, the Center for Young Children, the Center of Entrepreneurship, the Engineering Wind Tunnel, the Fire and Rescue Institute, the Institute for Systems Research, the Performing Arts Center, the Space Systems Laboratory, and the Superconductivity Research Center.

A state-of-the-art computer science center and dozens of laboratories across campus hold more than 1,600 computer terminals for student use. All residence hall rooms have high-speed (10 MB) Ethernet connections to the Campus Data Network and to the Internet, World Wide Web, and e-mail. Seven campus libraries contain 2.8 million books, 5.4 million microfilm units, 166,000 audiovisual materials, and subscriptions to 30,000 periodicals.

Costs

For the 2000–01 academic year, undergraduate tuition and fees are $5136 for Maryland residents and $12,668 for out-of-state residents. Room and board costs are approximately $6300 for an academic year.

Financial Aid

An array of financial aid programs, including scholarships, grants, loans, and student employment opportunities, are available to undergraduates. To be considered for maximum need-based financial aid, students must submit the completed FAFSA to the FAFSA processor in time for receipt and acceptance by the University's February 15 priority financial aid deadline. The University proudly offers several merit scholarships for academically and creatively talented students; approximately $4 million per year is awarded. To be considered for most merit scholarships, an application for admission must be submitted by December 1. Last year, 68 percent of full-time students who applied for financial aid received it and were awarded an average of $7019.

Faculty

Maryland has a full-time teaching faculty of 1,389 and a part-time teaching faculty of 529 members. Eighty-nine percent hold a Ph.D. or terminal degree in their fields. Faculty honors recipients include Fulbright Scholars, Guggenheim Fellows, NSF Presidential Young Investigators, Sloan Fellows, and members of the National Academy of Sciences and the American Academy of Arts and Sciences. The average class size is 31; the student-faculty ratio is 14:1.

Student Government

Maryland students constitute a self-governing student body, of which every undergraduate is a member. The Student Government Association (SGA) is an integral part of the University's shared governance and regularly provides input and feedback to the University president, campus senate, and state legislature. Student leaders—both executive and legislative—are elected each fall in a multiparty election and are responsible for allocating more than $1 million to student organizations. The SGA also provides funding to a student legal aid office and student entertainment productions. In addition, the students are represented on the University System of Maryland Board of Regents by a student member.

Admission Requirements

The University of Maryland seeks to enroll students who demonstrate that they have potential for academic success and who, the University believes, will help build a talented, diverse, and interesting entering class. Admission to the University of Maryland is competitive. Each year nearly 20,000 applications are received for a fall freshman class of approximately 4,000. Transfer applications are received from approximately 7,500 students, of which Maryland enrolls 3,700 per year.

Academic potential of freshmen is assessed primarily by examination of high school course work and SAT I or ACT scores. All entering freshmen must have completed a minimum of 4 years of English; 3 years of social studies or history; 3 years of mathematics courses (4 years is recommended), including 2 years of algebra and 1 year of geometry; 2 years of a foreign language; and 2 years of science that involves laboratory work. Most successful applicants have also completed several honors and advanced courses during high school. Additional criteria reviewed include an essay, leadership and extracurricular activities, honors and awards, and counselor and teacher recommendations. Transfer students are assessed primarily by examination of previously completed college-level work.

According to the most recent profile of the enrolled freshmen class, the middle 50 percent have a combined SAT I score between 1150 and 1320, with an average high school GPA of 3.61.

Application and Information

Applications for fall freshman admission are due by February 15. Students are encouraged to apply by Maryland's priority application deadline of December 1 for best consideration for admission, merit-based scholarships, and invitation to University Honors or College Park Scholars. The spring freshman application deadline is November 1. Applications for fall transfer admission are due by July 1; for the spring semester, December 1. International students and students with any foreign academic records have earlier deadlines.

For application forms and further information about the University of Maryland, students should contact:

Office of Undergraduate Admissions
University of Maryland
College Park, Maryland 20742-5235
Telephone: 301-314-8385
              800-422-5867 (toll-free)
              301-314-9197 (TTY)
Fax: 301-314-9693
E-mail: um-admit@uga.umd.edu
World Wide Web: http://www.maryland.edu

UNIVERSITY OF MARYLAND EASTERN SHORE
PRINCESS ANNE, MARYLAND

The University

The University of Maryland Eastern Shore (UMES) is a land-grant, historically black college founded in 1886 as the Delaware Conference Academy. Since its beginning, the institution has had several name changes and governing bodies. It was Maryland State College from 1948 until 1970, when it became one of the five campuses that formed the University of Maryland. In 1988, it became a member of the eleven-campus University of Maryland System. UMES is approved by the state of Maryland and fully accredited by the Middle States Association of Colleges and Schools.

The campus is located on 700 acres of land. There are approximately 3,200 students enrolled; 93 percent are undergraduates. Students have various backgrounds and come from thirty states and a number of other countries. Fifty-five percent of the students live in on-campus housing. All students may keep cars on campus.

Graduate degree programs offered are as follows: Master of Arts in Teaching; Master of Education (M.Ed.) degree in guidance and counseling and in special education; Master of Science (M.S.) degree in agriculture and extension education, applied computer science, food and agricultural science, marine-estuarine-environmental sciences, technology education, and toxicology; Master of Physical Therapy (M.P.T.); and Doctor of Philosophy (Ph.D.) degree in marine/estuarine environmental sciences and toxocology.

Location

UMES is located in the small town of Princess Anne on the Eastern Shore of Maryland. The town dates back to 1733 and has many buildings and landmarks of historic interest. The quiet community environment is excellent for learning, yet it is only 3 hours by car from the abundant cultural and recreational facilities of Washington, D.C., and Baltimore, Maryland. The state's famous seaside resort, Ocean City, is only 1 hour from the campus. The campus is located 13 miles south of the town of Salisbury, which provides shopping and recreational facilities.

Majors and Degrees

The University of Maryland Eastern Shore awards the Bachelor of Arts (B.A.) and Bachelor of Science (B.S.) degrees in teaching and nonteaching programs in the following areas: accounting, agribusiness, agriculture, aviation sciences, art education, biology, business administration, chemistry, computer science, construction management technology, criminal justice, education, engineering technology, English, environmental science, general studies, human ecology, hotel and restaurant management, mathematics, music education, physician's assistant studies, rehabilitation services, and sociology. UMES offers teacher education programs in the following areas: specialty programs in art, music, and physical education for grades K–12 and special education for grades 1–8 and 6–12; secondary/middle school programs (grades 5–12) in biology, chemistry, English, mathematics, social science, and technology education; and secondary school programs (grades 7–12) in agriculture and business education. UMES offers a dual-degree program in sociology/social work in conjunction with Salisbury State University.

Teaching certification is offered in a number of the above areas at the secondary level.

UMES offers an engineering program in cooperation with the College of Engineering of the University of Maryland College Park and Salisbury State University.

UMES also offers two-year and four-year preprofessional programs in biology/dentistry, biology/medicine, biology/physical therapy, chemistry/medicine, dental hygiene, engineering, law, nursing, pharmacy, radiologic technology, and rehabilitation services/physical therapy.

Academic Program

The Bachelor of Arts or Bachelor of Science degree is awarded upon the completion of 120 hours of work. These credit hours are divided among general education requirements, core courses for the selected major, and electives. Students may receive credit by examination or through Advanced Placement tests.

UMES, in cooperation with the professional schools of the University of Maryland at Baltimore and the Virginia-Maryland Regional College of Veterinary Medicine, offers an honors program for students of promise and ability who can meet rigorous standards. The program includes preprofessional tracks in dental hygiene, dentistry, medicine, nursing, pharmacy, radiologic technology, social work, and veterinary medicine.

The University also offers a cooperative education program that gives students the opportunity to gain practical work experience in their major area while earning academic credit. Employment opportunities are located off campus.

An Individualized Admissions Program is offered to a limited number of students who do not meet the requirements for regular admission. Students are required to enroll in the University's precollege summer program (PACE).

UMES operates on a semester system and offers a five-week winter session and a regular summer session.

Academic Facilities

The UMES Frederick Douglass Library houses more than 177,000 books and periodicals, approximately 6,006 microforms, CD-ROMs, and other media within its expanded facility. It also has access to worldwide information via OCLC and Carl Systems Incorporated. The campus has a Student Development Center, which houses the Center for Basic and Communicative Skills and the Counseling Center. The Offices of Career Planning, Cooperative Education, and Student Activities are also located in this building.

Other facilities include the Ella Fitzgerald Performing Arts Center, the Richard A. Henson Education Center, the Art and Technology Center, a computer center, a number of laboratories in such areas as agriculture, biology, business education, chemistry, construction management, home economics, industrial arts, and physics, and a newly constructed health and physical education center.

Costs

For the 2000–01 academic year, tuition for Maryland residents is $3833. For out-of-state residents, tuition is $8443. Room and board costs are estimated at $4730. These costs do not include books, laboratory fees, or personal budgets.

Financial Aid

Financial aid consists of both federal and institutional programs. Federal programs consist of the Federal Pell Grant, Federal Supplemental Educational Opportunity Grant, and Federal Work-Study programs. Institutional programs consist of scholarships and departmental assistantships. To be considered for financial aid, students should apply as early in the year as possible since financial aid is generally awarded on the basis of need and in the order of application. The Free Application for Federal Student Aid (FAFSA) is required in addition to the institutional financial aid form. Merit scholarships are available.

Faculty

UMES has a faculty of 200 members (133 full-time and 67 part-time). Of tenured and tenure-track faculty members, 94 percent have terminal degrees. The average class size is 30 students. Students are assigned faculty advisers who help them to achieve degree goals by aiding in course selection and other academic matters.

Student Government

The University of Maryland believes strongly in student participation in its decision-making bodies. Two students from the eleven-campus system serve on the University's Board of Regents. The Student Government Association is the student-governing body on the UMES campus through which students promote the interests and welfare of the University community. Students are represented on the UMES Senate and all its committees and on the Student Judiciary Council, the Student Life Committee, and other student organizations through which students provide leadership.

Admission Requirements

Freshman applicants must have graduated from an accredited secondary school with a minimum 2.5 grade point average. Competitive scores must be earned on the SAT I or ACT. Students who did not graduate from a secondary school may be admitted on the basis of their GED test scores. Out-of-state students are admitted on a competitive basis.

Honors applicants, in addition to fulfilling regular admission requirements, must have a B average or better in academic subjects and three letters of recommendation and must have a special interview with the Honors Committee. Successful completion of the honors program facilitates admission to the professional schools of the University of Maryland in the city of Baltimore.

A limited number of students are admitted by exception. Students in this category are required to attend the University's precollege summer program (PACE).

Transfer students must have maintained a C average or better in all previous college work and must be in good academic standing.

Application and Information

To be considered for admission, all students must submit an application with a $25 nonrefundable application fee and SAT I or ACT scores. Applicants should request that their high school forward an official copy of their transcript directly to the Office of Admissions. Transfer students should submit official transcripts of all college work completed at all other institutions. Transfer students who have earned fewer than 12 credits of work at other colleges must submit their high school transcript as well.

Application material may be obtained by contacting:

Office of Admissions and Registrations
University of Maryland Eastern Shore
Princess Anne, Maryland 21853

Telephone: 410-651-6410
410-651-2200 (general information)
410-651-6178 (Recruitment Office)
World Wide Web: http://www.umes.umd.edu

UNIVERSITY OF MARYLAND UNIVERSITY COLLEGE
SCHWÄBISCH GMÜND, GERMANY

The University

The Schwäbisch Gmünd campus of the University of Maryland University College was established in 1992. The campus is the newest of the University System of Maryland (USM), which is one of the twelve largest public university systems in the United States and one of the most international universities in the world, serving 130,000 students in 700 programs at approximately 300 sites on five continents.

University of Maryland University College (UMUC) is one of eleven degree-granting institutions of USM. Since 1949, more than 1 million individuals have studied with UMUC in thirty different countries.

University of Maryland University College is accredited by the Commission on Higher Education of the Middle States Association of Colleges and Schools, a regional accrediting body recognized by the Commission on Recognition of Postsecondary Accreditation, and the United States Department of Education. Since courses taken at Schwäbisch Gmünd earn resident credit with the University of Maryland University College, the credits can be transferred to other accredited colleges and universities in the United States and elsewhere.

Students reside on campus where they enjoy a full American university experience in an international environment. Students live, study, dine, and relax with classmates from many different countries. They have the opportunity to share a residence hall room with someone from their own country or from another culture.

Currently, more than 200 students from approximately fifty nations are enrolled at UMUC/SG; 31 percent are U.S. citizens, 24 percent are German, and 45 percent are from around the globe.

Students can participate in a variety of extracurricular activities, including Student Senate, the campus newspaper, drama, athletic clubs (soccer and basketball), musicians forum, fine arts club, outdoors club, and numerous other special interest groups.

Location

Schwäbisch Gmünd is a beautiful medieval town of 65,000 inhabitants nestled in the scenic Swabian countryside, 30 minutes by car or train from Stuttgart. The town of Schwäbisch Gmünd has opened its heart to the University, and students are encouraged to explore local surroundings. The city has renamed the site of the campus "Universitätspark."

The campus is served by international airports in Stuttgart, Frankfurt, and Munich. Major European cultural and intellectual centers, including Prague, Strasbourg, Munich, Vienna, Salzburg, Zurich, and Heidelberg are within a few hours' drive. World-class ballet in Stuttgart, Oktoberfest in Munich, the architecture of Prague, theater in London, and the art museums of Paris are a few of the cultural opportunities awaiting students.

Majors and Degrees

At Schwäbisch Gmünd, University of Maryland University College offers a well-rounded curriculum leading to the American degrees of Bachelor of Arts (B.A.) or Bachelor of Science (B.S.). English is the language of instruction.

Students pursuing a B.A. or B.S. complete a curriculum of rigorous courses, including general education core course requirements and primary and secondary concentrations, as well as electives. German language and culture courses are optional but highly recommended.

Degree programs include business and management, computer studies, English, European studies, German language and literature, German studies, government and politics, history, international business management, international management studies, international relations, and psychology.

Academic Program

The University operates on a two-semester calendar, with classes starting in late August and mid-January; a three-week Maymester is offered following the spring semester. A minimum of 120 semester hours are required for all bachelor's degree programs.

There are fall and spring semester breaks, during which students are encouraged to travel throughout Europe. The University offers field studies trips as components of academic course work. Recent trips have offered students the ability to study in relax in Paris, Rome, Prague, and Vienna.

Academic Facilities

All residence halls are connected to the Internet. Students are not required to bring a computer to campus and have full access to on-campus labs. The campus is located at University Park, where all classrooms and student residence buildings are situated on the beautiful campus quad. Other buildings on campus include the Gutenberg Library, which holds 33,000 volumes and offers complete electronic access to the vast University System of Maryland libraries and houses the main computer lab, the Student Union (SUB), the Bistro (the cafeteria), a fitness facility, basketball and tennis courts, and the UniPark Theatre, which is open to the entire campus community for productions and concerts.

Costs

In 1999–2000, the tuition for a full-time student at UMUC-SG was approximately U.S.$11,000 (DM 21,000). Maryland resident tuition was approximately U.S.$7000. Room and board charges were approximately U.S.$4000 (DM 7940) based on a double room with full board.

Financial Aid

Financial assistance is awarded on the basis of financial need and academic merit. Approximately 50 percent of the students at Schwäbisch Gmünd receive financial aid in the form of a scholarship, grant, loan, and/or campus job. Unlike most undergraduate programs in American universities, UMUC/SG offers financial assistance to eligible students regardless of citizenship. Work-study funds are also available to both international and American students. Detailed information about financial assistance is available upon request.

Faculty

UMUC/SG has an international faculty and administration selected for dedication to multicultural education. There are no teaching assistants; all classes, which are small, are taught by faculty.

Student Government

There is an active Student Senate on campus.

Admission Requirements

Applications are considered on an equal basis for freshman admission, transfer admission, semester abroad, and year abroad. Completion of secondary education is required (U.S. high school diploma or equivalent).

The SAT I or ACT is required of applicants who graduate from an American high school and who have completed fewer than 12 semester hours of university-level work.

Students whose native language is not English or who graduated from a secondary school in which the primary language was not English must demonstrate language proficiency on the Test of English as a Foreign Language (TOEFL). International applicants should hold the equivalent of a U.S. high school diploma. Some European secondary school credentials, such as the German Abitur, British A-levels, and the International Baccalaureate (I.B.), may yield advanced standing at the freshman level (30 hours maximum) based on a course-by-course evaluation of official documentation of test results.

Application and Information

The admission application is available on the UMUC/SG Web site or by mail. Applicants are encouraged to submit their credentials as early as possible preceding the semester in which they wish to enroll. The fall 2001 semester deadline is August 1; the spring 2001 semester deadline is January 1. To enter Germany, visas are required for citizens of many countries. If a visa is necessary, several additional weeks are needed to complete the admission process; the length of time varies considerably. Applicants requiring visas are advised to submit applications and credentials well before the deadlines. (Visas are not required of citizens of the U.S. or the E.U.)

Applications are processed on a rolling basis. Applicants are notified of an admission decision once all required credentials have been received and a review has been completed.

Prospective students and parents are encouraged to make a campus visit whenever possible. Campus tours and information sessions are available Monday through Friday. There is an annual Open House program for prospective students and their parents each April.

A free videotape is available to prospective students and counselors upon request.

For further information, students should contact either of the following:

Office of Enrollment Management
University of Maryland University College
Universitätspark
73525 Schwäbisch Gmünd
Germany
Telephone: 49-7171-18070
Fax: 49-7171-1807320
E-mail: enroll@admin.sg.umuc.edu

U.S. Enrollment Management Office
Overseas Programs/SG
University of Maryland University College
3501 University Boulevard East, 3271J SFSC
Adelphi, Maryland 20783
Telephone: 301-985-7070
          800-955-4458 (toll-free)
Fax: 301-985-7075
E-mail: sginfo@umuc.edu
World Wide Web: http://www.sg.umuc.edu

UNIVERSITY OF MASSACHUSETTS AMHERST
AMHERST, MASSACHUSETTS

The University

The University of Massachusetts is a public, major research university, enrolling more than 18,200 undergraduates (about equally divided between men and women) and offering more than eighty bachelor's degree programs and six associate degree programs at the undergraduate level as well as seventy master's programs and fifty doctoral programs. The University's size enables it to offer a great diversity and choice of academic programs, housing arrangements, and extracurricular involvements. In addition, students can enroll with no extra charge in courses at Amherst, Hampshire, Mount Holyoke, and Smith Colleges through the Five College Consortium.

While 75 percent of the undergraduates are Massachusetts residents, students come from all around the country and the world. More than 10,000 students are housed (in either coed or single-sex accommodations) in forty-two residence halls in five different areas. Residence hall living is required in the freshman and sophomore years, unless a student is married, a veteran, or living at home with his or her parents. Many students choose to live in residence halls their entire four years. Campus social life revolves around the Five College area, the residence halls, more than 200 registered student organizations, and a Greek organization of fraternities and sororities. Many social-action, professional, and special interest groups are active in the community. The University participates in thirteen men's and fifteen women's intercollegiate varsity sports as a member of the Yankee Conference for football and other sports and of the Atlantic 10 Conference for basketball. The intramural program, one of the largest in the East, draws more than 10,000 participants annually.

Location

Situated on the Connecticut River in the Pioneer Valley of western Massachusetts, 20 miles north of Springfield, the campus of the University of Massachusetts Amherst consists of 1,463 acres of land and buildings. The *New York Times* calls Amherst one of the country's "Ten Best College Towns." The area offers the cultural and educational advantages of an urban environment while also enjoying a rural setting. Amherst is less than 100 miles from Boston, 150 miles from New York City, and only 30 miles from Vermont and New Hampshire. The Five College area in and around Amherst and Northampton offers an impressive array of cultural activity (film, dance, theater, music, and art) while also facilitating outdoor recreation, such as hiking, skiing, and camping in the Berkshire Hills and Vermont's Green Mountains. An extensive, free Five College bus service makes it easy for students to take advantage of academic and extracurricular activities at all five campuses.

Majors and Degrees

A two-year associate degree is offered in six majors in the Stockbridge School of Agriculture. A four-year bachelor's degree is offered in nine colleges or schools: Education, Engineering, Food and Natural Resources, Humanities and Fine Arts, Management, Natural Sciences and Mathematics, Nursing, Public Health and Health Sciences, and Social and Behavioral Sciences. Within many of these majors, a number of different programs, options, and concentrations are possible. A Bachelor's Degree with an Individualized Concentration (B.D.I.C.) is also available for upper-division students who wish to create their own faculty-advised major.

Academic Program

The academic calendar includes a fall and a spring semester separated by a monthlong vacation or winter session from Christmas to late January. Summer school is also available.

Students seeking a bachelor's degree must successfully complete a minimum of 120 credit hours (128 to 136 for engineering majors), including a core of required courses. Students also select a specific major, constituting specialized, intensive study in one discipline or in an approved interdisciplinary area. In addition, there are more than twenty nonmajor curricular programs (for example, aerospace studies, African studies, film studies, military science, and statistics). A variety of special academic programs are also offered: the Commonwealth College Honors Program, community service, area studies programs, legal studies, and women's studies. Learning Support Services, residential academic programs for first-year students, the Committee for the Collegiate Education of Black and Other Minority Students, the Bilingual Collegiate Program, the United Asia Learning Resource Center, the Native American Student Support Program, advising for undeclared majors, Diversity in Management Education Services for business majors, and the Minority Engineering Program provide other special academic opportunities. Options are available for honors study, independent study, credit by examination, and advanced placement. The Division of Continuing Education serves nonmatriculated students.

Off-Campus Arrangements

The Five College Consortium (Amherst, Hampshire, Mount Holyoke, and Smith colleges and the University of Massachusetts) permits students from the University of Massachusetts to study at and use the resources of any of the four other colleges in the area. A number of academic and cultural cooperative programs are also offered through the Five College Consortium.

A variety of programs facilitate study off campus. The Office of Internships coordinates credit-generating internships on national, state, and community levels. The International Programs Office assists students in arranging international study. The University Without Walls features off-campus study arrangements. In addition, specific departments sponsor clinical programs, international study, and internships as part of their individual curricular requirements or offerings. The University is a member of the National Student Exchange, which permits students to spend one to two semesters earning transferable credit at one of more than 150 institutions around the country.

Academic Facilities

The library system of the University of Massachusetts Amherst is composed of the twenty-eight-story W. E. B. Du Bois Library and several branch libraries. Holdings include more than 5 million books, periodicals, and other documents; more than 2 million of these items are in microformat. The Fine Arts Center, a working sculpture in itself, houses the fine arts departments (music, dance, art, and theater), several performance areas (including the main Concert Hall), galleries, and other fine arts facilities. Morrill Science Center, the Graduate Research Center, and several laboratories serve the sciences and applied sciences. The University operates a sophisticated computer laboratory and center with a variety of computers, microprocessors, and other equipment. Students have e-mail, online services, and Internet and World Wide Web access in computer labs, the library, residential halls, and several academic buildings.

Costs

Tuition and fees for 2000–01 are $5212 for in-state students and $13,365 for nonresident students. Room and board cost about $4790, depending on a student's choice of three meal plans. Kosher and vegetarian meals are available.

Financial Aid

Financial aid is based on need and is offered to students who cannot, through their own and/or their parents' reasonable efforts, meet the full cost of a college education. Aid consists of scholarships and grants, loans, and work-study employment. Students applying for financial aid are automatically considered for every University-administered program for which they are eligible. The basic financial aid application form required of all applicants is the Free Application for Federal Student Aid (FAFSA). The financial aid need-based resources available total more than $115 million for all types of aid. More than half of the students receive some support from the Financial Aid Office. Students should check with their guidance counselor for the most current financial aid information.

Faculty

More than 1,150 full-time, teaching faculty members compose a distinguished group committed to excellence in both teaching and scholarly research. About 94 percent of the full-time members hold the highest degree in their fields. Most faculty members not only teach and conduct research in their disciplines but also assist in the advising of students. Close interaction between students and faculty, both in and out of the classroom, is encouraged.

Student Government

Most University and student organizations rely on student participation in their decision-making processes. Selected in yearly campuswide elections, student government leaders and representatives participate in the decisions that shape students' educations and futures. The Student Senate is the legislative arm of the Student Government Association, and there is a Student Judiciary whose judges are appointed through the Student Senate and Area Governments. These area residential governments represent students regarding housing, social, cultural, and educational programs and issues. Students are also represented on many of the administrative decision-making bodies of the University, including the Board of Trustees.

Admission Requirements

All applicants must have a diploma from an accredited high school or a general equivalency diploma by the time they enroll at the University. The SAT I or ACT is also required, as is an essay. A college-preparatory high school background is recommended for entering freshmen. In fall 1999, entering freshmen averaged in the top 26 percent of their class. The middle 50 percent of their SAT I scores were 510 to 620 verbal and 520 to 620 math. Transfer students are considered after they have completed at least 12 credits of college work, although the most common entry level is after two years of satisfactory community or junior college study. Both high school grade point average (GPA) and SAT I or ACT test scores are the primary basis for determining admission to the University. Additional factors may be considered.

Application and Information

For application forms and further information, students should contact:

Office of Undergraduate Admissions
University Admissions Center
University of Massachusetts
Box 30120
Amherst, Massachusetts 01003-0120
Telephone: 413-545-0222
Fax: 413-545-4312
E-mail: mail@admissions.umass.edu
World Wide Web: http://www.umass.edu

The University of Massachusetts Amherst offers academic challenge, choice, and diversity in a quintessential New England college town.

UNIVERSITY OF MASSACHUSETTS BOSTON
BOSTON, MASSACHUSETTS

The University

The University of Massachusetts (UMass) Boston was founded in 1964 by the state legislature to provide the opportunity for superior undergraduate and graduate education at a moderate cost at a public urban campus located in the capital city of Boston. With more than 13,000 commuting students in its undergraduate, graduate, and continuing education programs, UMass Boston is the second-largest campus of the University of Massachusetts system. The University of Massachusetts Boston is a community of scholars who take pride in academic excellence, diversity, research, and service. The fabric of academic research and scholarship is tightly woven into the public and community service needs of Boston and the modern urban center.

UMass Boston enrolls a diversified student body that is representative of a wide variety of ages, ethnicities, academic interests, and life backgrounds. About one fifth are of traditional college age, 18 to 21; almost half are 22 to 29; and about one third are 30 and older. Three out of every 4 students are transfers. African- and Asian-American students make up about 25 percent of the total enrollment; about another 6 percent are Hispanic, and just over 1 percent are Native American.

More than seventy-five student organizations provide opportunities for cocurricular and extracurricular activities. University institutes provide scholarly research and public-service activities that focus on environmental issues, labor studies, gerontology, international programs, women in politics, the study of war and social consequences, and public policy. Further research is conducted on African-American, Asian, and Latino community issues, along with other concerns of the public interest that are particularly indigenous to urban areas.

The student body is composed of young, mature, and working adults, all of whom share a strong motivation to succeed academically and relate their classroom pursuits to their career aspirations. The University Advising Center provides comprehensive academic support, planning, and career advising services. A team of professional counselors provides personalized assistance to students in designing their course of study, utilizing tutorial and mentoring services, choosing a major and career path, and developing interviewing, resume writing, and job search skills.

Major new construction is being planned for a $50-million Campus Center that will centralize student services at the University.

Location

The University is located on a beautiful peninsula on Boston Harbor, just 3 miles south of downtown Boston, overlooking the bay and harbor islands. Three sides abut the ocean and afford magnificent views of the city and the Atlantic. The University's neighbors are the John F. Kennedy Presidential Library and the Massachusetts State Archives and Commonwealth Museum.

Located just a half mile off the Southeast Expressway (Interstate 93), the campus is easily accessible by motor vehicle and public transportation. The entrance to the campus is a seaside promenade drive. Two levels of underground parking are available at reasonable short- and long-term rates. A free shuttle bus runs every couple of minutes for the half-mile ride from the Metropolitan Boston Transit Authority's (MBTA) JFK/UMass "T" stop on the Red Line to the front door of the campus. Student discount "T" passes are available for frequent users.

The University wants students to be at home at UMass Boston. Many students commute from their home communities, while others utilize the free computerized Housing Referral Service for assistance with finding rental property and/or roommates.

Boston itself, with its worldwide standing as a cultural center and its well-earned reputation as America's favorite college town, offers UMass Boston students a wealth of resources for exploration and entertainment. Everything from Fenway Park and the FleetCenter to the Museum of Fine Arts is easily accessible from UMass Boston.

Majors and Degrees

Four undergraduate colleges award bachelor's degrees: the College of Arts and Sciences (thirty-seven majors, twenty-one programs of study, and eight special course groupings), the College of Management (ten concentrations), the College of Nursing (both a B.S.N. and an RN-B.S.N. accelerated program, as well as a program in human performance and fitness), and the College of Public and Community Service (twenty career concentrations). Premed, prelaw, and teacher-preparation programs are also offered, along with programs for honors study, credit by examination, and advanced placement. Students are encouraged to participate fully in designing their academic plan.

A joint Bachelor of Arts or Science/master's degree in business program is available for high academic achievers, as are a liberal arts and science degree with a minor in management and an engineering program.

Academic Program

The academic calendar runs from early September through the end of May. There are also a one-month optional winter session in January and summer school in June, July, and August. Matriculating students may choose to attend on a full- or part-time basis and may adjust their schedules from semester to semester. A minimum of 30 credits must be earned at UMass Boston as a residency requirement for graduation.

For the College of Arts and Sciences, 120 credits are required to graduate. The general education curriculum comprises three elements: the distribution requirement, the core curriculum requirement, and the writing requirement. In addition, requirements of the major must be fulfilled. The College offers an Honors Program and an Individual Major Program.

For the College of Management, the 120-credit undergraduate program leads to a B.S. degree in management. By fulfilling the general education, management, and elective course work requirements, graduates receive a liberal arts foundation and the theoretical, technical, and functional training to succeed in the business world.

The College of Nursing's B.S. program in nursing requires 123 credits, with a liberal arts foundation and intensive study of 63 credits in the principles and practices of nursing. The program in human performance and fitness prepares graduates for the technical aspects of a professional discipline with a foundation in liberal arts and an optional teacher training component.

The College of Public and Community Service is a nationally acclaimed model for competency-based education. The competency is the basic academic unit of the college. Unlike other programs, where students earn grades, a student earns competencies; a total of fifty are required across five distinct curriculum areas for graduation. A variety of learning options are available, including classroom study, self-directed and self-paced learning, and recognition for competence gained through prior learning and on-the-job training. Due to the nature of the program, recent high school graduates are usually not directly admissible unless they have considerable hands-on experience in the field.

Off-Campus Arrangements

The National Student Exchange Program offers UMass Boston students the opportunity to study at one of more than seventy participating colleges and universities in forty states at a cost comparable to what they pay to attend UMass Boston. The study-abroad program is available for students with a 3.0 GPA or better who seek international travel and academic experiences, as well as summer and winter session programs. UMass Boston also participates in the New England Regional Student Program and the Boston Five-College Exchange Program.

Cooperative Education and Internship Programs place students in work assignments related directly to their fields of study so that they may apply what they learn in the classroom to practical work settings. Under the Co-Op Program, students are placed in full-time paid positions for six-month work periods. Under the Internship Program, students are placed on a part-time basis, usually 15–20 hours per week, for the length of the semester or the summer months. Some internships are paid and some are on a volunteer basis. Both co-op and internship placements benefit students by combining relevant practical learning, valuable work experience, career awareness, resume enhancement, personal and professional growth, and, in many instances, opportunities for academic credit, good pay, and a permanent job after graduation.

Academic Facilities

The University's Healey Library holds a collection of more than 575,000 volumes and subscribes to more than 3,120 domestic and international journals and newspapers. UMass Boston is a member of the Boston Library Consortium.

The University's Computing Services provides students with seven-day-a-week access to desktop labs, with some 250 Dell Pentium III and Apple Macintosh G4 computers, as well as to other specialized, course-related facilities. A wide variety of information technology and data communications resources are available, with network connections in every office and classroom. The campus network is fiber-optic based, with ATM protocol. Computing Services houses equipment from Data General, Dell, Compaq, Sun, and Apple, and operating systems include NT, UNIX, Linux, Apple OS, and VMS.

The Kennedy Presidential Library is linked to the University by a variety of educational programs, enabling students to conduct research utilizing the more than 28 million pages of documents, 6.5 million feet of film, and more than 100,000 still photographs in the library's archives. Next door, the Archives of the Commonwealth of Massachusetts are a rich depository, covering more than 3½ centuries of Massachusetts history.

Costs

Annual tuition and fees for 1999–2000 were $4232 for Massachusetts residents studying full-time (12 or more credits) or $12,362 for out-of-state residents. Students enrolled part-time were charged according to the number of credits taken, with Massachusetts residents paying tuition of $71.50 per credit; out-of-state residents paid tuition of $406.50 per credit. Annual mandatory fees for in-state residents ranged from $557 for 3 credits to $2518 for 12 or more credits. Mandatory fees for out-of-state residents ranged from $571 to $2604.

Financial Aid

Financial aid is based on need and/or merit. Applicants complete the Free Application for Federal Student Aid (FAFSA), keeping in mind the priority deadline of March 1 for fall entrants and November 1 for spring entrants. Need-based aid is awarded to students who demonstrate financial need, as determined by federal methodology. Aid consists of grants, waivers, and self-help in the form of loans and work-study employment. An on-time applicant is automatically considered for every University-administered program for which they are eligible. Nearly 70 percent of the student body received some form of financial aid last year, totaling more than $40 million.

Faculty

UMass Boston is proud of its distinguished faculty of 861 members, more than 90 percent of whom have doctoral degrees. UMass Boston also has a student-faculty ratio of 15:1 and a small class size that averages 28 students. The faculty's top priority is teaching and advising students. Many of the faculty members also conduct research, publish materials, and participate in grant activities and professional organizations. Faculty members maintain office hours for students and make themselves accessible as mentors. The Faculty Council is the faculty governance body.

Student Government

The Undergraduate Student Senate is composed of elected members from the undergraduate colleges and programs and participates fully in matters related to the quality of student life and the allocation of the student activities trust fund. Students are also represented on numerous University- and college-based committees and councils that initiate major policy and procedural recommendations; they forward those recommendations to governance bodies and the administration for enactment.

Admission Requirements

All applicants must demonstrate that they have earned a diploma from an accredited high school or a general equivalency diploma by the time they matriculate at the University.

For freshman applicants, an official copy of the high school transcript is required, and a minimum of 16 college-preparatory academic units must have been taken (4 English, 3 mathematics, 2 social studies, 2 foreign languages, 3 sciences (2 with labs), and 2 electives). If the applicant has graduated from high school within the last three years, an official report of the SAT I or ACT score is also required. The mean SAT I score for recent freshman applicants was 1020. For nonnative English-speaking students who have been in the U.S. for fewer than four years, the TOEFL score report may also be submitted. For GED applicants, an official copy of the GED score report is required. All freshmen are required to submit two essays. Letters of recommendation are encouraged but not required.

All transfer applicants must submit two essays, and letters of recommendation are encouraged but not required. Transfer applicants are required to have at least a 2.0 grade point average for admission, although some programs require a 2.75 minimum GPA. All applications are evaluated on an individual basis, and all aspects of the application package are considered in the admission decision.

Application and Information

For an undergraduate viewbook and application for admission, students should contact:

Enrollment Information Service
University of Massachusetts Boston
100 Morrissey Boulevard
Boston, Massachusetts 02125-3393
Telephone: 617-287-6100
          617-287-6010 (TTY/TDD)
Fax: 617-287-5999
E-mail: enrollment.information@umb.edu
World Wide Web: http://www.umb.edu

UMass Boston is located on an easily accessible, picturesque peninsula, just 3 miles south of downtown Boston.

UNIVERSITY OF MASSACHUSETTS DARTMOUTH
NORTH DARTMOUTH, MASSACHUSETTS

The University

The University of Massachusetts Dartmouth traces its roots to 1895 when the Massachusetts legislature chartered the New Bedford Textile School and the Bradford Durfee Textile School in Fall River. As the region's economic base shifted from textiles to more diverse manufacturing and service industries, the program of the colleges changed. Courses were developed to respond to the needs of new generations of students, stimulated by the clear economic and social advantages of a well-educated citizenry. In 1962 Southeastern Massachusetts Technological Institute (SMTI) was created, and in 1969, out of a need and a clear demand for a comprehensive public university, SMTI became Southeastern Massachusetts University. Then, in 1988, the Swain School of Design was merged with the University's College of Visual and Performing Arts.

In 1991, a new University of Massachusetts system was created, which combined the Amherst and Boston campuses with the University of Lowell, Southeastern Massachusetts University, and the Medical Center in Worcester. Today, UMass Dartmouth provides educational programs, research, extension, and continuing education and cyber education in the liberal and creative arts and sciences and in the professions. A broad range of bachelor's and master's degrees and one program leading to a doctorate are offered. Graduate programs lead to the Master of Arts, Master of Business Administration, Master of Arts in Teaching, Master of Fine Arts, Master of Art Education, and Master of Science. A Ph.D. is offered in electrical engineering.

UMass Dartmouth enrolls approximately 5,500 students; 90 percent are from Massachusetts, with a growing number from other states and countries outside the United States. A residential campus with a variety of student organizations, athletic programs, cultural opportunities, and interest groups, the University fosters personal development, diversity, and responsible citizenship.

Location

Located in historic and scenic southeastern Massachusetts, which includes the nearby cities of Fall River and New Bedford and the Cape Cod region to the east, the campus is situated on 710 acres. The dramatic campus is the work of architect Paul Rudolph, former dean of the Yale University School of Art and Architecture. Metropolitan areas, with libraries, museums, theaters, and numerous educational institutions, are within an hour's drive: Boston to the north and Providence, Rhode Island, to the west. Recreational sites are minutes away and include beaches, hiking, and cultural and nightlife opportunities. New York City is four hours by car; the mountains of New Hampshire and Vermont are three to four hours away. Students can walk to homes and shops in the immediate area of the campus, while public transportation is available to nearby communities.

Majors and Degrees

There are five colleges within the University: College of Arts and Sciences (fifteen majors); Charlton College of Business (five majors); Engineering (eight majors); Nursing (one major); and Visual and Performing Arts (ten majors). In addition, honors programs, interdisciplinary studies, pre-law, pre-medical advising, and a number of different minors and options are available within various departments. The University offers the Bachelor of Arts, Bachelor of Fine Arts, Bachelor of Science, and Bachelor of Science in Nursing degrees at the undergraduate level.

Academic Programs

The University operates on a two-semester calendar with the fall semester beginning the first week of September and concluding in mid-December and the spring semester beginning in late January and concluding in late May. A five-week intersession is offered between semesters. Summer term courses are offered in June, July, and early August. Undergraduate students usually enroll in four or five courses each semester, and a typical course earns 3 credits. An undergraduate degree requires a minimum of 120 credits (there are a few majors which require 135 credits); a student can complete degree requirements for a specified major within a department or an approved interdepartmental major (30 credits). Students must also complete requirements according to the degree being sought.

Special learning opportunities include independent study, contract learning, and directed study; study abroad; study at a nearby university through cross-registration; and credit by examination. UMass Dartmouth is a member of SACHEM (Southeastern Association for Cooperation in Higher Education in Massachusetts), allowing for cross-registration at Bridgewater State College, Bristol Community College, Cape Cod Community College, Dean College, Massachusetts Maritime Academy, Massasoit Community College, Stonehill College, and Wheaton College. The University has formal exchange agreements with the University of Grenoble (France), the Lycée du Grésivaudan at Meylan and the Lycée Aristide Berges, Nottingham Trent University (England), the Baden-Württemberg Universities (Germany), Centro de Arte e Communiçãcao (Portugal), Nova Scotia College of Art and Design, the École Nationale Superieure des Industries Textiles, Université de Haute Alsace (France), and Minho University (Portugal). Students may also take initiative in finding other programs in addition to the exchange-agreement institutions.

The College of Engineering provides majors in any of the engineering fields to gain work experience through cooperative education or internships.

Academic Facilities

Computing is an integral part of the curriculum. All academic buildings, including student residences, are connected to a campuswide network. Computing clusters, located in the library and in most classroom buildings, support the classwork of students. More than 200 microcomputers (Apple Macintosh and IBM) or terminals are readily available. The network can be reached off campus by telephone modem. The University library supports all programs of instruction and research with more than 350,000 volumes, 2,000 periodicals, and 150,000 U.S. government publications. A large interlibrary loan network and delivery system makes millions of volumes available to the students. Each of the five colleges within the University is housed in academic facilities designed for its purposes with classrooms, laboratories, studies, galleries, faculty offices, and lounges.

Costs

In-state tuition and fees for 1999–2000 were $4200; non-Massachusetts resident tuition and fees were $11,700. Room and board expenses ranged from $5035 to $5457, depending on the meal plan chosen. Books and supplies cost approximately $700 a year depending on a student's courses. Specific fees may be assessed, depending on a student's course of study.

Financial Aid

Nearly all students are eligible for some type of financial aid. UMass Dartmouth awards financial aid based on federal, state, and institutional guidelines; students must submit the Free Application for Federal Student Aid (FAFSA). In determining need, the Financial Aid Services Office considers the total costs of attending the University (tuition, fees, books, room and board, the cost of commuting, and an allowance for living and personal expenses). The difference between total University cost and the estimate of expected family contribution is the amount that the financial aid staff considers to be financial need.

Faculty

The faculty, numbering 340 full-time members, is distributed over twenty-nine departments in the five colleges. More than two thirds of the faculty members have a Ph.D., with a significant number holding the terminal degree in their chosen discipline (e.g., business, fine arts, education). A student-faculty ratio of 15:1 ensures that classes are reasonably sized, with an average class size of 23 students. Faculty members are actively engaged in advising students, providing guidance throughout a student's academic career.

Student Government

The Student Senate is the governing body offering a forum for debate on matters of importance to the student body. The Student Judiciary, a system of courts or judicial agencies, provides students and organizations with the protection of due process in all disciplinary matters. A student is also elected to the University of Massachusetts Board of Trustees. Students serve on the Board of Governors, policy makers for the Campus Center; the Resident Hall Congress; and the Student Activities Board. Students are active, voting participants on policy-making committees that regulate both academic as well as social aspects of the University.

Admission Requirements

Admission is selective. Applicants are evaluated by both the general standards of the University and by the special standards of the academic areas that they request. In addition, the Board of Higher Education sets guidelines governing admissions standards for the University. Admission to some colleges or majors may be limited by spaces available. Students are admitted on a rolling basis with no set deadline. Qualified candidates will be accepted until the capacity has been reached in the program of choice. Each applicant's record is assessed on the basis of the depth and rigor of the secondary school program, rank in class and grade point average, SAT I or ACT results, college-level records for transfer applicants, and other appropriate measures. Students are invited to visit the University for a campus tour and a meeting with an admissions officer; interviews are not required.

The University realizes its commitment to equal access through standard, as well as alternative, admission programs. For College Now, the alternative program, applicants must meet at least one of three eligibility criteria: low income status, limited English background, or ethnic student of color status.

All applicants for freshman admission to the University are required to submit an application form with appropriate fee ($20 in-state and $40 out-of-state), a transcript of the secondary school record, SAT I or ACT results, and any other information that candidates consider important for the admissions committee to review. Transfer students, who comprise approximately one third of the new student population every year, are required to submit records for all college-level work completed in addition to the application form. The admission process is virtually the same for transfer candidates with primary emphasis on the student's previous college/university record.

Application and Information

Admissions is rolling except for early decision (freshman). The early decision deadline is November 15, with notification by December 15. All other decisions are made within three weeks of the completion of an application. For application forms and related information, students may call, write, or e-mail the admissions office.

Office of Admissions
UMass Dartmouth
285 Old Westport Road
North Dartmouth, Massachusetts 02747-2300
Telephone: 508-999-8605
Fax: 508-999-8755
E-mail: admissions@umassd.edu
World Wide Web: http://www.umassd.edu/

The size of UMass Dartmouth appeals to many students.

UNIVERSITY OF MASSACHUSETTS LOWELL
LOWELL, MASSACHUSETTS

The University

Throughout its 100-year history, the University of Massachusetts Lowell has excelled at providing innovative, responsive programs that meet both the needs of its students for a quality education and the needs of regional businesses for skilled practitioners and managers. Formed through the merger of a technical institute and a teacher's college, the University is now part of the five-campus University of Massachusetts system. The academic experience at UMass Lowell offers students comprehensive, broad-based programs characterized by a continuing effort to break down traditional barriers between disciplines and between the classroom and the "real world." Courses typically involve a practical component that can range from the political science team that competed nationally in a United Nations Model Assembly to the music business majors who went to a recording industry conference in California to the civil engineering students who helped the city of Lowell inventory and replace all its street signs. Faculty members are respected researchers who value their commitment to teaching and extend the learning experience beyond the classroom. Undergraduates participate in funded research and college policy committees, and senior faculty members are involved in student projects such as building and racing a solar-powered car. Strong links with local businesses, educational systems, and health-care providers benefit students through an increasing number of internships, part-time jobs, and grants. In short, students graduate with the hands-on experience and practical problem-solving skills employers are looking for.

The University's three campuses, spread over 100 acres on both sides of the Merrimack River, include classroom and laboratory buildings, two libraries, a student center, two gymnasiums, two dining halls, a Center for the Performing Arts, an art gallery, and numerous residence halls. In the next few years, a new campus center will be open and will provide additional social and recreational facilities. State-of-the-art laboratories include such special interest facilities as the six Sound Recording Technology Program studios, an interactive video lab (one of three in the country) that enables nursing students to simulate medical emergencies, and a manufacturing lab where engineering and management students team up to produce microelectronic components. The University's collaborative relationship with the city of Lowell has resulted in the completion of a nearby hockey arena and a baseball stadium on campus, both to be shared by UMass Lowell and professional teams.

UMass Lowell's 10,000 undergraduate students are ethnically, culturally, and economically diverse. Students are active in a wide variety of community service activities, including athletics-based programs for local high school students, the Adaptive Technology Program in which students create modified devices for the disabled, and volunteer work at local shelters and community programs. There are more than 100 campus organizations to choose from: academic, recreational, and special interest groups; the women's center; marching band; the student newspaper; an FM radio station; and the Off-Broadway Players. Campuswide events include University Week and Spring Carnival, and resident hall associations sponsor social and recreational events. The University sponsors twenty-two intercollegiate sports teams, including the nationally ranked Division I hockey team and an active recreational sports program. In conjunction with the five colleges, the Graduate School enrolls nearly 3,000 students in thirty master's degree and twelve doctoral programs.

Location

The University is located in Lowell, a city of 110,000 that has gained national attention by successfully leveraging its history, ethnic diversity, and entrepreneurial spirit to create a vital urban center. The site of a National Historical Park that honors the city as the birthplace of the industrial revolution, Lowell is also home to an acclaimed professional theater company, annual Kerouac and folk festivals, and museums that include the Museum of American Textile History and the Whistler House Museum. Located 26 miles from the cultural and educational riches of Boston and Cambridge, Lowell is also within an hour of ocean beaches and the lakes and mountains of New Hampshire via major highways and regional train and bus service.

Majors and Degrees

The College of Arts and Sciences offers baccalaureate programs in American studies, biological sciences, chemistry, computer science, criminal justice, economics, English, environmental studies, fine arts, graphic design, history, liberal arts, mathematics, modern languages, music, music business, philosophy, physics, political science, precertification for music education, psychology, sociology, and sound recording technology. Dual majors are permitted. Dual B.A./B.S. and B.S./M.S. degree programs are available in liberal arts, science, and engineering fields. Predental and premedical programs are available. The James B. Francis College of Engineering offers baccalaureate day programs in chemical, civil, electrical, mechanical, and plastics engineering. Baccalaureate technology programs include civil engineering technology, electronic engineering technology, and mechanical engineering technology. Engineering and engineering technology programs are accredited by the Engineering Accreditation Commission (EAC) and the Technology Accreditation Commission (TAC) of ABET. Combined bachelor's/master's programs, internships, and co-op opportunities are available in the College of Engineering. The College of Health Professions offers baccalaureate day programs in clinical laboratory sciences (NAACLS accredited), exercise physiology, health education, and nursing (NLNAC accredited). The College of Management offers baccalaureate day programs, all accredited by AACSB–The International Association for Management Education, in business administration (B.S.B.A., with concentrations in accounting, finance, management, management information systems, and marketing) and in industrial management (B.S.I.M.), in conjunction with the James B. Francis College of Engineering.

The University's Division of Continuing Studies and Corporate Education offers evening programs through the various colleges. Through the College of Arts and Sciences, baccalaureate programs in applied mathematics, criminal justice, informations systems and liberal arts are available. Through the College of Engineering, associate and baccalaureate degrees are offered in civil engineering technology, electronic engineering technology, and mechanical engineering technology. Through the College of Management, associate degree programs in accounting and management, and a baccalaureate degree in business administration are available. Certificate programs are offered in accounting, banking, computer-assisted manufacturing, computer proficiency, computer science, data/telecommunications, electrooptics, environmental technology, graphic design and digital imagery, hazardous waste management, Internet systems administration, land surveying, manufacturing technology, multimedia applications, nutrition, paralegal studies, plastics engineering technology, purchasing, quality assurance, security management, Spanish, technical writing, UNIX, wastewater treatment, water treatment, and Windows development programming.

Academic Program

The University operates on a calendar of two semesters, a condensed two-week intersession in January, and a summer term (with two sessions). Full-time undergraduates generally take five courses each semester. A minimum of 120 credits is required for baccalaureate degrees; the minimum credits required for professional degree programs are generally higher. A University core requirement is imposed for all baccalaureate curriculums. Majors require 30–60 credits. Elective course options vary widely according to the degree program and major area. Professional degree program options and requirements follow specific accreditation guidelines. Maximum curricular freedom is permitted in B.A. programs. The academic climate is serious and competitive and requires self-motivation. Approximately 50 percent of the undergraduates complete graduation requirements in four years.

Academic Facilities

The University has two comprehensive libraries with online capabilities that can be accessed from networked computers across the campus and from all dormitory rooms.

The University operates a state-of-the-art network facility that includes an OC-3 ATM backbone and 10/100 mbps switched technology to all desktops. Remote access via PPP or ISDN is also available. Clients to the network include more than 4,000 desktop and laboratory PCs with more than 100 servers. Applications on the network include e-mail, groupware, Microsoft Office products, cybereducation, interactive video, and numerous academic programming applications.

Costs

In order to maintain maximum affordability, the University's tuition will remain unchanged for the 2000–01 academic year. In 1999–2000, full-time undergraduate day tuition and fees for residents of Massachusetts were $4255 per year; for nonresidents of Massachusetts, $10,892 per year. Residence hall charges were $2910 per year. A full meal plan was $1926 per year. Accident insurance is covered by fees; major medical insurance is optional. Books and supplies are estimated at $400 to $600, depending upon the program. Undergraduate continuing education tuition was $175 per credit for on-campus courses and $200 per credit for off-campus and distance learning courses. (Quoted rates are subject to change.)

Financial Aid

The University is committed to making higher education accessible to all qualified students. The University participates in federal and state programs, assisting students through grants-in-aid, loans, employment opportunities, and scholarships. The amount of an award is determined by need, as indicated by the Free Application for Federal Student Aid (FAFSA), which should be filed by March 1. University scholarships are described in the undergraduate bulletin.

Faculty

The full-time resident faculty numbers 415. The part-time day faculty numbers 183. In addition, 193 part-time faculty members are employed in continuing education programs. Most faculty members teach and conduct research in their disciplines. Graduate teaching assistants also hold part-time instructional positions, particularly as discussion section leaders and laboratory teaching assistants.

Student Government

The Student Government Association and the Residence Hall Association provide opportunities in student government at the all-campus level. Leadership opportunities are provided in residence halls and student organizations. Students also participate in the disciplinary system and in most University committees.

Admission Requirements

All undergraduate day applicants must have a high school diploma or a general equivalency diploma and satisfactory SAT I scores. A minimum high school grade point average of 2.5 (on a 4.0 scale) is required, and the University places primary emphasis upon the high school record. Students whose high school average is below the required minimum may be considered for admission if they present SAT I verbal and mathematics scores that are higher than those specified for the admission of degree candidates by the college or program to which they wish to apply.

Transfer students are considered for fall- or spring-semester admissions. Transcripts of completed work must be on file prior to acceptance. Depending on the number of transfer credits and college GPA, transfer students who seek admission as matriculating day students may be asked to provide a high school record and SAT I scores.

Application and Information

For day programs, the University practices rolling admissions, which means that applications are evaluated as soon as they are complete. Entering freshmen are admitted for the fall or spring semester. For application forms and further information, students should contact the address listed below.

Office of Undergraduate Admissions
University of Massachusetts Lowell
883 Broadway Street
Room 110
Lowell, Massachusetts 01854-5104
Telephone: 978-934-3931
            800-410-4607 (toll-free)

The main administration building makes a convenient gathering spot between classes.

THE UNIVERSITY OF MEMPHIS
MEMPHIS, TENNESSEE

The University

Located on a beautifully landscaped campus in the heart of one of the South's largest and most progressive cities, the University of Memphis is the flagship institution of the State University and Community College System of Tennessee. Since its beginning in 1912, the University of Memphis has matured into a major public, urban university recognized regionally and nationally for its academic, research, and athletic programs. The University offers more than fifty undergraduate majors and more than seventy concentrations from which to choose.

The University campus comprises 1,160 acres at four sites. In addition to the main campus, the South Campus contains spacious living accommodations for married students, a research park, and outstanding varsity athletic training facilities. The University of Memphis also owns the Meeman Biological Field Station, a 623-acre tract used for biological and ecological studies. The Chucalissa Archaeological Museum in southwest Memphis is frequently used as a research and training facility in archaeology and anthropology.

The University of Memphis is an Equal Opportunity/Affirmative Action institution committed to the education of a non-racially identifiable student body. It has a total enrollment of 20,301 students, including more than 15,400 undergraduates, from almost every state and many other countries. Approximately 42 percent of University of Memphis students are between the ages of 18 and 22, and members of minority groups account for 37 percent of the enrollment.

Location

The greater Memphis area has a population of approximately 1 million, which makes the city the eighteenth largest in the country. Centrally located on the Mississippi River, Memphis is an active hub for business, agriculture, and the transportation industry. The city has the mid-South's largest medical center and offers many cultural and entertainment opportunities. Memphis has three large sports arenas: Liberty Bowl Memorial Stadium, the Mid-South Coliseum, and the Pyramid. Combined, these three stadiums attract major sports events and popular entertainers. With its many businesses, industries, and schools, Memphis provides students with employment opportunities in a variety of fields during and after their college careers.

Majors and Degrees

The College of Arts and Sciences comprises eighteen departments organized into three concentration groups: the humanities, the natural sciences, and the social sciences. Three degrees are offered: the Bachelor of Arts, the Bachelor of Science, and the Bachelor of Science in Chemistry. Majors include anthropology, biology, chemistry, computer science, criminology and criminal justice, economics, English, foreign languages, geography, geological sciences, history, international studies, mathematical sciences, microbiology and molecular cell sciences, philosophy, physics, political science, psychology, social work, and sociology.

The Fogelman College of Business and Economics offers programs of study leading to the Bachelor of Business Administration degree through nine areas: accountancy, decision sciences, economics, finance/insurance, an interdisciplinary program, management, management information systems, marketing, and real estate and business legal studies. Majors include accounting, business economics, finance, international business, logistics/marketing, management, management information systems, marketing management, production operations management, risk management and insurance, and sales. The programs of the College of Business and Economics are fully accredited by the AACSB–The International Association for Management Education.

The College of Communication and Fine Arts is made up of the Departments of Art, Communication, Journalism, Music, and Theatre and Dance. Major emphasis areas include art, art history, commercial music, communication, journalism, music, and theater. The College offers three undergraduate degrees: the Bachelor of Arts, the Bachelor of Fine Arts, and the Bachelor of Music.

The College of Education offers programs leading to the degree of Bachelor of Science in Education. The Departments of Consumer Science and Education, Human Movement Sciences and Education, and Instruction and Curriculum Leadership offer such majors as consumer science and education, exercise and sport science, human development and learning, integrative studies, special education, and sport and leisure studies. Preparation for teaching in secondary schools requires the baccalaureate degree in the chosen teaching field, followed by graduate study that culminates in the Master of Arts in Teaching (M.A.T.) degree.

The Herff College of Engineering is divided into the Departments of Civil Engineering, Electrical Engineering, Engineering Technology, and Mechanical Engineering. Each offers a choice of specialized four-year programs leading to a Bachelor of Science degree. Majors include architectural engineering, civil engineering, computer engineering, computer engineering technology, electrical engineering, electronics engineering technology, industrial and systems engineering, manufacturing engineering technology, and mechanical engineering.

The University College offers two nontraditional degrees: the Bachelor of Liberal Studies and the Bachelor of Professional Studies, for students with experience, talents, and interests served through personally designed, multidisciplinary programs. Examples of programs that have been developed include African-American studies, alcohol and drug abuse, American studies, aviation administration, biomedical illustration, commercial aviation, construction management services, fire administration, fire prevention technology, health services administration, human services, human services administration, Judaic studies, landscape design and horticulture studies, nonprofit development and administration, organizational leadership, paralegal studies, preschool and child-care administration, religion in society, services for the aging, technology management services, and women's studies.

The University of Memphis also offers specialized degree programs. A Bachelor of Science in Nursing degree is offered through the Loewenberg School of Nursing. Preprofessional training is offered for students who intend to enter law school or a college of dentistry, medicine, nursing, optometry, pharmacy, physical therapy, or veterinary medicine. The University also offers Air Force, Army, and Navy ROTC programs.

Academic Program

Many freshmen are advised through the Academic Counseling Unit of the Center for Student Development in preparation for formal enrollment in one of the degree-granting colleges. In addition to meeting the requirements for a specific degree, as established by the appropriate college or department, each student initially selects courses from broad offerings in the areas of communication skills, sciences, humanities, and social sciences, thereby ensuring the acquisition of breadth as well as depth of knowledge in various fields. A minimum of 132 semester hours, with a cumulative grade point average of 2.0 or higher, is required for most undergraduate degrees. A University-wide honors program is available for academically talented students. Student services that are normally available for day students are provided for evening and Saturday students through the Office of Student Information Services. Some entering freshmen will be assigned to their degree-granting college immediately for academic advising.

The academic year begins in late August and is divided into two semesters and a summer session. The summer session is divided into two terms of four to five weeks each, with an overlapping term of nine weeks.

Off-Campus Arrangements

The University of Memphis participates in both the International and National Student Exchange Programs, allowing students to study in other countries as well as in other states in the continental United States. The University also offers credit and noncredit courses at various locations throughout west Tennessee.

Academic Facilities

The University of Memphis' $26-million Ned R. McWherter Library provides one of the most electronically up-to-date information repositories within hundreds of miles. Students are able to tap into information stored in libraries around the world. Library collections contain more than 13 million items, which include monographs, periodical volumes, federal and state documents, maps, and manuscripts. The University also provides state-of-the-art computing facilities for student and faculty use, including Tiger LAN labs. A total of twenty-four labs with more than 600 PC and Macintosh workstations and seven "smart" classrooms complement the University's teaching and research activities. The Department of Theatre and Dance and the Department of Music, in their adjoining facilities, make an appreciable contribution to campus activities with their live drama and concert series, films, and programming over WUMR, the campus radio station.

Included among the many research facilities at the University of Memphis are the Center for Earthquake Research and Information, the Center for Electron Microscopy, the Federal Express Center for Cycle Time Research, the Ground Water Institute, and the Barbara K. Lipman Early Childhood School and Research Institutes.

The state of Tennessee has designated five Centers of Excellence at the University: the Center for applied Psychological Research, the Center for Research Initiatives and Strategies for the Communicatively Impaired, the Center for Research in Educational Policy, the Center for Excellence in Egyptian Art and Archaeology, and the Center for Earthquake Research and Information. In addition, the University houses twenty-four endowed Chairs of Excellence.

Costs

In 1999–2000, in-state students paid a maintenance fee of $1409 per semester for full-time study or $136 per semester hour for part-time study. Out-of-state students were assessed fees of $4039 per semester (full-time) or $366 per semester hour (part-time). On-campus residence hall rates range from $1950 to $3520 for an academic year. Full-time students pay an activity fee of $44 per semester, which is included in the above cost information.

Financial Aid

Financial assistance is provided through four basic sources: scholarships, grants, loans, and employment. Scholarships are offered through the Scholarship Office as well as through various academic, performance, and athletic departments. An application for admission is required to be considered for general and distinguished academic scholarship programs. Applicants for financial aid must submit the completed Free Application for Federal Student Aid (FAFSA) to the Financial Aid Office, which places the student under consideration for all financial aid programs. More than $70 million is awarded annually. The University operates two programs of student employment: the Federal Work-Study Program and a regular work program. The Tennessee Department of Employment Security maintains an office on campus to help students find off-campus employment.

Faculty

The University of Memphis has approximately 800 ranked faculty members. In addition, many adjunct professors are hired from the community to teach in their fields of expertise.

Student Government

The Student Government Association consists of officers, a senate, a cabinet, and a judiciary elected annually by the student body. Its goals are to present the opinions of the student body to the administration, to enact legislation beneficial to the students, and to promote a broad range of student activities.

Admission Requirements

The admission of entering freshmen is based on the transcript of a four-year course of study at an approved or accredited high school that includes prescribed units of English, mathematics, natural/physical sciences, U.S. history, social studies, foreign language, and visual/performing arts. Acceptable scores on the ACT or the SAT I are required. The General Educational Development test and high school equivalency diploma are accepted when applicable. Applicants must be at least 16 years old. First-time freshmen applicants are guaranteed admission with a cumulative high school GPA of at least 3.0, an ACT composite score of at least 20, or an SAT I composite score of at least 930.

The admission of transfer students is based on the applicant's quality point average, academic standing at a former institution, and scores on the approved admission tests.

Application and Information

Inquiries about admission and requests for information about any undergraduate college of the University should be addressed to the Office of Student Relations. Applications and supporting credentials must be submitted to the Office of Admissions at least thirty days before the beginning of the intended term of entry. While the established application deadlines are August 1 for the fall semester, December 1 for the spring semester, and May 1 for the summer session, early application is strongly encouraged to be considered for scholarship opportunities and to take advantage of early registration. Registration for fall classes occurs at New Student Orientation, which begins in June.

Prospective students are encouraged to visit the University for a campus tour, which can be arranged by contacting the Office of Student Relations.

Office of Student Relations and Orientation Services
159 Administration Building
The University of Memphis
Memphis, Tennessee 38152-3370
Telephone: 901-678-2169
800-669-2678 (toll-free)

The McWherter Library.

UNIVERSITY OF MINNESOTA, CROOKSTON
CROOKSTON, MINNESOTA

The University

Nationally recognized as a leader in information technology education, the University of Minnesota, Crookston (UMC), is part of the world-renowned University of Minnesota System. Founded in the late 1800s as a research station and then as a school of agriculture, UMC became a part of the University of Minnesota in 1965. Today, UMC is a four-year, public coeducational institution of 1,650 full- and part-time students.

Its focus on polytechnic education, commitment to technology, and overall high-quality programs have captured national attention. UMC earned a ranking in *U.S. News & World Report*'s 2000 listing of America's Best Colleges and received other national notice in publications such as the *Washington Post* and the *Atlanta Journal-Constitution*.

UMC is continuing to evolve to meet the educational demands of Minnesota and the world by developing a technology-rich, interactive living and learning community. UMC was one of the first campuses in the nation (1993) to begin issuing notebook computers to all full-time students. In addition, the entire campus is fully wired to the World Wide Web, with an Internet connection available at every classroom seat and in the library, the cafeteria, every study room, and every residence hall room. Students use their personal computers to gain access to and send information worldwide, write reports, analyze data, develop and deliver multimedia presentations, complete and turn in assignments, receive grade reports, and communicate with faculty members, friends, and family. UMC has become known nationally as the "Thinkpad University" and has emerged as one of the most technologically advanced campuses in the country.

UMC's mission of research and discovery, teaching and learning, and outreach and public service encompasses applied undergraduate instruction and research in agriculture; aviation; business; education management; environmental and natural resources; equine industries; health management; hotel, restaurant, and institutional management; information networking management; scientific and technical communication; sport and recreation management; and appropriate interdisciplinary studies (a complete program list can be found in the Majors and Degrees section).

UMC also is responding to the demands of life in the information age by offering a technologically advanced curriculum that prepares students for today's careers and also promotes an understanding of and appreciation for lifelong learning that prepares them for the careers of tomorrow.

UMC continues to keep its link to agriculture by offering several programs that reflect the technological advances of modern agriculture. Agriculture used to mean only animals and tractors, but the precision agriculture of today involves chemistry, biology, electronics, and business sciences.

Location

UMC's 237-acre scenic campus on the northern edge of Crookston combines the best of both worlds when it comes to location. It is situated in a small, safe community in the middle of one of the richest and most diversified agricultural regions in the world, the Red River Valley. At the same time, Crookston is a short drive away from a number of urban centers, such as Minneapolis–St. Paul, Duluth, Fargo, Grand Forks, and Winnipeg, Canada.

In addition, students live in a community that celebrates its diversity. Last year, a colorful mural was painted on a wall of a building near downtown that, according to newspaper accounts, "stands for the colors of life—the variety of people who live and work together in Crookston."

Majors and Degrees

A wide range of specialty programs are offered at UMC, many of which are available only at UMC and a handful of other institutions nationally.

Students can obtain a Bachelor of Science degree in accounting; agricultural aviation; agricultural education; agricultural industries sales and management; animal industries management (dairy management and meat animal management); applied studies; business management (management and marketing); early childhood education; equine industries management; food processing management; golf facilities and turf systems management; health management; hotel, restaurant, and institutional management; information networking management; natural resources (natural resources law enforcement, natural resource management, park management, and soil and water technology); plant industries management (agronomy and horticulture); scientific and technical communication; and sport and recreation management. A technical communication minor is also available.

Students can obtain a Bachelor of Applied Health or Bachelor of Manufacturing degree.

Two-year options are also available. Students can enroll in Associate in Applied Science degree programs in agricultural aviation; agricultural business; agronomy/soils; animal/dairy science; dietetic technician studies; equine science; horticulture; hotel, restaurant, and institutional management; information management; marketing and management; and natural resources. Associate in Science degree programs are available in agriculture and in business.

Academic Program

Students benefit from a personalized learning approach that centers on practical, real-world direct applications. The curriculum is learner driven, interactive, and supported with technology and involves collaboration among students, faculty members, and prospective employers. Students now enroll in classes at UMC on a semester calendar system.

With UMC's emphasis on technology, teaching methods are dramatically different. Students find a classroom environment that is completely connected to technology, allowing students and instructors to gain access to information and exchange information more effectively. That classroom environment also includes the latest in computer- and video-presentation technology that is available to instructors.

Communication between faculty members and students now includes the use of e-mail and the World Wide Web for such tasks as distributing a course syllabus, sending out assignments or worksheets that had previously been distributed as printed handouts, and turning in assignments to faculty members. In addition, students have 24-hour access to UMC's library holdings as well as to all of the information available on the World Wide Web through the personal computer each student is issued.

Off-Campus Arrangements

Through a number of programs available at other University of Minnesota campuses, UMC students can travel and study overseas. Students have the opportunity to study at sites around the world in such countries as Costa Rica, England, Japan, Sweden, and other European countries. Through the University of Minnesota System, students can take advantage of more than 170 study-abroad programs in sixty countries.

Academic Facilities

UMC is one of the most technologically advanced campuses in the country. Nearly 100 percent of campus classrooms have advanced faculty workstations, featuring overhead projection graphics cameras for still, video, and computer display.

The University's attractive grounds include thirty buildings, flower gardens that border a spacious mall, and a natural history area that contains virgin prairie land. UMC has many well-equipped special-purpose laboratories; an indoor animal science arena and equine stable; an enlarged library and learning resource center; a food service and hotel, restaurant, and institutional management building; a large indoor physical education and intercollegiate athletic facility; an outdoor recreational and athletic complex; an expanded student center; a $2.2-million environmental science facility that enables students to conduct undergraduate research in the areas of horticulture, botany, and agronomy; and a student housing apartment complex.

Costs

Tuition for 2000–01 is $3780 for residents. Room and board costs are $4046. Minnesota has a reciprocal agreement with South Dakota, North Dakota, and Wisconsin that allows students from those states to pay Minnesota resident tuition. Beyond these agreements, all U.S. and Canada residents pay UMC's in-state rate.

Financial Aid

Removing financial barriers to students' enrollment and success is the ultimate goal of UMC's financial aid program. UMC wishes to ensure that any qualified student who desires to pursue an education at UMC can obtain sufficient resources to do so. Accordingly, the University's Office of Admissions and Financial Aid administers a number of financial aid programs.

A number of need-based funding sources are available for new, incoming freshman students as well as for transfer students—whether part-time or full-time. UMC also offers a variety of merit-based scholarships.

For the need-based funding sources, a formula is used that factors the difference between UMC's estimate of what it will cost to attend UMC and the amount the federal and state governments expect students and their families to contribute to their education, based on information provided on the Free Application for Federal Student Aid (FAFSA).

The specialty merit-based scholarships range in awards from $300 to a maximum of full tuition. Many are renewable.

Faculty

UMC's faculty members bring a wide range of teaching and research expertise to the classroom. Faculty members are dedicated to teaching and also encourage students' involvement in undergraduate research, internships, and other out-of-classroom learning experiences. Students find a professor at the head of the class, not a teaching assistant.

Faculty members also pride themselves on building a true scholarly community at UMC. Because of the small class sizes, faculty-student interaction, both in and out of the classroom, is common. With a student-faculty ratio of 17:1, students are not anonymous at UMC.

Student Government

The Student Forum is the student government body that represents the interests of students at the University of Minnesota, Crookston. The Forum is the major source for expressing student opinion and initiating legislative action to promote and protect student interests. In addition, UMC's Office of Student Activities coordinates more than thirty student organizations that provide students with a chance to pursue their special interests, meet new people, and develop their potential for leadership, organization, and creativity.

Admission Requirements

Freshman students are eligible for traditional admission if they are in the upper half of their graduating class. Students may also be admitted with a composite score of 21 or above on the ACT. Students who do not meet either of these requirements are considered using a combination of high school rank, GPA, test scores, high school curriculum, and other indicators of academic potential.

Transfer students should consult with the transfer specialist in admissions for specific information.

UMC recommends a college-preparatory program that includes 4 years of English, 3 years of natural sciences, 3 years of mathematics, 2 years of social science, and 2 years of a second language.

Application and Information

Applying for admission to the University of Minnesota, Crookston, involves some important preliminary steps. Freshman students should send high school transcripts, submit an application fee and a completed application form, and submit results from the ACT. Transfer students must send college transcripts and submit an application fee and completed application form. The application priority deadline is March 1.

UMC has developed a helpful application guide called *Getting Started At UMC: Admissions Application Guide,* which is available for free by calling UMC's Office of Admissions and Financial Aid at the toll-free number listed below. Students can also visit UMC on the World Wide Web. Campus tours are available each weekday at 9 a.m., 10 a.m., and 1 p.m. Students are encouraged to call ahead two days before a planned visit.

For more information, students should contact:

Office of Admissions and Financial Aid
170 Owen Hall
University of Minnesota, Crookston
2900 University Avenue
Crookston, Minnesota 56716-5001
Telephone: 218-281-8569
           800-862-6466 (toll-free)
World Wide Web: http://www.crk.umn.edu

UMC is known nationally as the "Thinkpad University."

UNIVERSITY OF MISSOURI–KANSAS CITY
KANSAS CITY, MISSOURI

The University

The University of Missouri–Kansas City (UMKC) is a comprehensive, public, coed university. Beginning as the private University of Kansas City in 1933, the institution became part of the four-campus University of Missouri System in 1963.

UMKC is designated as the system's campus for the performing arts. In addition to this, UMKC is a research institution, currently a Carnegie Foundation Doctoral Level I institution.

UMKC's fall 1999 student population was just over 11,500; undergraduates are 59 percent of the total. Student diversity is a reality at UMKC. About 25 percent of students are international or are members of a minority group or have a special cultural/ethnic heritage.

UMKC offers more than 200 student organizations, including student government, academic societies, and fraternities and sororities.

Students may choose to live on campus in the residence hall or in UMKC's Twin Oaks apartments. However, most opt for the plentiful apartment complexes or areas that are within a 15- to 20-minute drive of the campus.

UMKC offers graduate degrees in nearly all of the undergraduate areas listed in the Majors and Degrees section, below.

Location

UMKC is located in the center of Kansas City's "cultural zone," a part of the city encompassing several museums, a premier research institute, a renowned technical and research library, and Kansas City's Country Club Plaza and Westport shopping and entertainment districts.

The University's Volker (main) campus is located on a 93-acre site lush with mature trees, gentle hills, and plenty of green space. UMKC also has a Hospital Hill campus located north of the main campus. UMKC's bus service connects the two campuses. Easy access is a Kansas City hallmark: in addition to a well-developed interstate highway system, Kansas City features more miles of tree-lined boulevards than Paris. (There are also more fountains than in any city outside of Rome.)

Majors and Degrees

The University of Missouri–Kansas City offers nationally accredited programs of study over a broad range of selected academic disciplines that lead to the Bachelor of Arts (B.A.); Bachelor of Science (B.S.); Bachelor of Business Administration (B.B.A.); Bachelor of Fine Arts (B.F.A.); Bachelor of Information Technology (B.I.T.); Bachelor of Music (B.M.); Bachelor of Liberal Arts (B.L.A.); accelerated Career Xpress degree programs, such as the Fast Track bachelor's in nursing; and combined baccalaureate/professional degrees, such as the six-year B.A./D.D.S. and B.A./M.D.

Degree programs and areas of emphasis within those programs are as follows: accounting (B.S.); American studies (B.A.); art (B.A.); art history (B.A.); biology (B.A., B.S.); business administration (B.B.A.); chemistry (B.A., B.S.); civil engineering (B.S.Ci.E., UMC program at UMKC); communications studies (B.A.); computer science telecommunications (B.A., B.S.), with emphases in software architecture (B.S.) and telecommunications networking (B.S.); criminal justice and criminology (B.A.); dance (B.F.A.); dental hygiene (B.S.D.H.), general and with emphases in clinical and classroom teaching; earth sciences (B.S.); economics (B.A.); electrical engineering (B.S.E.E., UMC program at UMKC); elementary education (B.A.); English (B.A.), with emphases in journalism and creative writing and secondary English education; environmental studies (B.A., B.S.), with emphases in chemistry (B.S.) or geosciences (B.S.); French (B.A.); geography (B.A., B.S.); geology (B.S.); German (B.A.); history (B.A.); information technology (B.I.T.); interdisciplinary studies (B.A., B.S.); Judaic studies (B.A.); liberal arts (B.L.A.); mathematics and statistics (B.A., B.S.); mechanical engineering (B.S.M.E., UMC program at UMKC); medical technology (B.S.); middle school education (B.A.); music (B.A.), with an emphasis in music therapy; music composition (B.M.), with an emphasis in music arranging; music education (B.M.E.), with emphases in choral, general, instrumental, and music therapy; music theory (B.M.); nursing (B.S.N.); performance (B.M.), general and with emphases in accordion, bassoon, cello, clarinet, flute, guitar, harpsichord, horn, jazz and studio music, oboe, organ, percussion, piano, piano pedagogy, saxophone, string bass, trombone, trumpet, tuba, viola, violin, and voice; philosophy (B.A.); physical education (B.A.), with emphases in teaching and nonteaching; physics (B.A., B.S.); political science (B.A.); psychology (B.A.); secondary education (B.A.), with emphases in art, English, foreign languages, general, mathematics, music, natural science, and social science; sociology (B.A.), with emphases in anthropology, deviant behavior, life course, and urban sociology; Spanish (B.A.); studio art (B.A.), with an emphasis in graphic design/photography; theater (B.A.); and urban affairs (B.A.).

Academic Program

Baccalaureate degrees require a minimum of 120 course credits and a common core of lower-division general education courses that may be selected from among several options in the arts, humanities, and social sciences and from the mathematical, physical, natural, and computer sciences.

Baccalaureate degree requirements are designed by the faculty for students seeking a broad background in either specific academic disciplines, the liberal arts, or interdisciplinary studies.

In many disciplines, individual programs of study can be designed for the student seeking employment immediately following graduation or for those preparing for graduate or professional education. In particular, the baccalaureate degree provides UMKC graduates a base of understanding across many disciplines.

The College of Arts and Sciences offers an honors program that admits students who rank in the top 10 percent of their high school class and place in the top 10 percent on the ACT.

Students ranking in the top 10 percent of their graduating class are graduated "with distinction." Students who complete the honors program receive their degrees with the designation "with honors."

UMKC's academic calendar offers fall (August-December) and winter (January-May) semesters as well as a summer session.

Off-Campus Arrangements

Study-abroad programs for students are available through numerous sources, including People to People International, the Missouri-London Program, Summer Study programs through the College of Arts and Sciences, and a variety of exchange agreements.

Academic Facilities

The UMKC library system, which includes its main library and libraries at the schools of dentistry, medicine, and law, holds more than 1.4 million volumes, more than 12,000 current serial subscriptions, and substantial collections of government documents, microfilms, sound recordings, and musical scores.

In addition to participating in a variety of local, state, and national library organizations, UMKC has close ties with the Linda Hall Library of Science and Technology, which is adjacent to UMKC's main campus.

Extensive academic computing facilities include a COMPAQ/DEC Alpha Cluster running OpenVMS, one of the highest performance superminicomputer installations in Missouri. A high-speed Internet connection gives users easy access to the World Wide Web, e-mail, library systems, data archives, bulletin boards, LISTSERVs, chats, and digests. Software, provided free of charge, connects home computers and student dormitory rooms to e-mail and the Internet. Students may have an account as long as they are enrolled in for-credit courses. Computer labs, with networked Mac and PC workstations, adaptive workstations, laser printers, and scanners, are located throughout campus. UMKC staff members support each lab. The labs include a wide variety of popular software as well as specialized software for the academic disciplines.

Costs

For fall 2000, the UMKC tuition is $136.80 per credit hour; other fees bring the typical total cost per hour to $159.25. The UMKC residence hall, a double occupancy room, and the University's Meal Plan A (average) cost $4865 for 2000–01. Off-campus expenses are room and board, $6390; transportation, $2610; medical and dental insurance, $1010; and personal expenses, $1630, for a total of $11,640.

Students who live in Kansas, Nebraska, Michigan, or Minnesota are eligible for the Midwest Student Exchange Program, which allows them to pay half the amount of standard out-of-state fees.

Financial Aid

In 1999, UMKC arranged for more than $81 million in financial assistance to 10,202 students—representing 76 percent of the student population. The Financial Aid Office administers some 500 aid sources. These include federal aid programs and academic scholarships, as well as benefit programs for veterans and their dependents.

There are two kinds of assistance offered: need-based (determined by family income and ability to pay according to a federal formula) and merit-based (determined by academic achievement, leadership, and special talents). Need-based programs include Federal Pell Grants, Federal Supplemental Educational Opportunity Grants, Federal Perkins Loans, Federal Direct Loans, and Federal Work-Study.

UMKC has extensive merit-based scholarship resources. Eligible freshmen can qualify for renewable scholarships of up to $3500. Merit-based scholarship programs also are available for transfer, minority, and nonresident students. No separate application is usually required; applications for admission are reviewed for eligibility.

To apply for financial aid, students must first apply for admission or readmission to UMKC. Students also must submit the Free Application for Federal Student Aid to the federal processor by March 1 of the year they intend to apply.

Faculty

UMKC has a faculty of 1,331, including 47 endowed chairs and professorships. More than 84 percent of full-time faculty members have a Ph.D. or the terminal degree in their field. Many have received designations of distinction or awards for teaching and scholarship. Fifteen have been named Curators' Professors or Distinguished Teaching Professors, the UM System's top faculty honors. More than 20 have received Fulbright scholarships. UMKC's student-teacher ratio is 9:1.

Student Government

The student governing body at UMKC is the Student Government Association (SGA) and comprises representatives from all academic units. In addition, each academic unit has a council to serve the needs of its students. Council and SGA elections are held annually.

Admission Requirements

UMKC is considered a selective institution, which means certain academic criteria must be met before official admission. Basic criteria for admission direct from high school for fall 2000 include 4 units of English, 4 units of math (algebra I or higher), 3 units of science (including one lab class), 3 units of social studies, 1 unit of fine arts, and 2 units of a single foreign language.

Previous academic success, extracurricular activity, and a specific talent or ability are other factors that are considered.

Students with a score of 24 or better on the ACT, or the SAT I equivalent, qualify for automatic admission.

About 65 percent of new undergraduate students at UMKC are transfers. Special policies are in place to ensure their success, including full transfer of course work from any other university in the UM System and articulation agreements with area community colleges.

Application and Information

A formal application for admission includes a complete Application for Admission (with nonrefundable application fee); high school class rank; official transcripts from previous higher education institutions, if any; and ACT scores (if fewer than 24 transferable college hours).

The ideal application deadlines for admission directly from high school are fall semester, April 1; winter semester, November 1; and summer session, May 1. Some UMKC academic units have earlier deadlines. Students are notified in writing regarding the status of their admission.

For an application, information, or to arrange a campus visit, students should contact:

    Office of Admissions
    University of Missouri–Kansas City
    5100 Rockhill Road
    Kansas City, Missouri 64110-2499
    Telephone: 816-235-1111
                  800-735-2966 (TT) (toll-free)
                  800-735-2466 (voice) (toll-free)
    Fax: 816-235-5544
    E-mail: admit@umkc.edu
    World Wide Web: http://www.umkc.edu

UMKC's campus is a tree-lined site of gently rolling hills located adjacent to Kansas City's Country Club Plaza district.

UNIVERSITY OF MISSOURI–ROLLA
ROLLA, MISSOURI

The University

Founded in 1870, the University of Missouri–Rolla (UMR), formerly the Missouri School of Mines and Metallurgy, has a proud history of preparing students for service and leadership. UMR is known nationally and internationally for the quality of its undergraduate education. In addition, it has achieved preeminence in selected areas of graduate engineering education and research. Providing a thorough grounding in the liberal arts, UMR offers all of its students a sense of the cultural context in which they, as modern scientists, live and work. UMR is the only university to ever win the Missouri Quality Award, which is patterned after the Malcolm Baldrige National Quality Award, established in 1987 to honor companies that provide exceptional customer service. Students are the acknowledged customers of this university, and UMR is aptly qualified to meet their individual needs.

The tradition of UMR is captured in its mission statement: "educating tomorrow's leaders." The mission is reflected in a national and international reputation for the high quality of undergraduate and graduate science and engineering programs. One of the most exciting of these programs is the "UMR PROMISE," which prepares students to make the most of postgraduation opportunities. UMR promises career opportunities after graduation, or the University will offer a one-year educational fee grant at UMR. The goal of this program is to help students achieve a balance of academic and cocurricular activities.

Students who enroll at UMR are looking for an outstanding education at a reasonable cost. UMR offers its students a solid technical background that is recognized throughout all types of industry. Many students are attracted to UMR because of its hands-on approach to education and the problem-solving nature of the educators. Several UMR labs are the only industry-level facilities on a college campus. Because UMR offers its students many opportunities for practical learning both in and out of the classroom, it has developed long-standing relationships with industry leaders and enjoys tremendous success in placing graduates after graduation.

With an approximate enrollment of 5,000, students are attracted to the University because it offers the affordability of a public institution yet retains a private college atmosphere and quality. Because UMR believes that an involved student will be more successful in life, it supports more than 200 cocurricular activities and organizations that range from professional honor societies to recreational clubs. UMR also participates in Division II men's and women's varsity sports and club contests with other colleges. UMR has a diverse student population; students represent forty-six states and thirty-four countries.

UMR recognizes the significant role that environment plays in a student's education. The University's residence halls are intended to provide students with a well-rounded, academically oriented, community living environment. Two residence hall complexes and three apartment complexes make up the different University housing communities, along with twenty fraternities and six sororities. Other facilities available to students include computer resource centers, meeting areas, game rooms, convenience stores, an indoor swimming pool, an indoor fitness center, an outdoor pool, various sporting facilities, and cafeterias. UMR also offers many cultural opportunities, including concerts, a performing arts series, the Remmers Special Artist/Lecturer Series, and special events.

In addition to undergraduate degrees, UMR offers Master of Science, Doctor of Philosophy, and Doctor of Engineering degrees.

Location

UMR is located in Rolla, Missouri, midway between St. Louis and Springfield and approximately 60 miles south of Jefferson City. Many students take advantage of recreational opportunities in the beautiful surrounding Ozark countryside. Within 15 minutes of campus, students may enjoy a host of recreational activities in the picturesque Mark Twain National Forest or National Scenic Riverways. Many students also enjoy weekend excursions to St. Louis, Springfield, Branson, or the Lake of the Ozarks. Campus groups loan camping, canoeing, and fishing equipment to students for nominal fees. Rolla offers shopping, swimming, movie theaters, live theater, coffeehouses, and restaurants, all within an easy walk from campus. Rolla was recently named "one of the best small towns in America" on the basis of educational facilities, low crime rate, and availability of health care. Rolla is a university town and is supportive of the University and its activities.

Majors and Degrees

UMR offers Bachelor of Science and Bachelor of Arts degrees. The University offers more degree programs in engineering than most universities in the country. Engineering degrees are offered in the aerospace, ceramic, chemical, civil, computer, electrical, geological, management, mechanical, metallurgical, mining, nuclear, and petroleum fields. Science degrees include biological sciences, chemistry, computer science, geology and geophysics, mathematics, and physics. Humanities and social science degrees include economics, English, history, management systems, philosophy, and psychology as well as a certificate program in secondary education. The humanities and social sciences also offer cooperative programs in business administration and political science. UMR also offers preprofessional programs in dentistry, law, medicine, nursing, pharmacy, and veterinary science.

Academic Program

The University is best known for outstanding education in engineering and science. The humanities programs, however, are also well established and acknowledged. There are two semesters each academic year as well as one summer session. A bachelor's degree is awarded upon successful completion of approximately 130 hours and fulfillment of various program and University requirements. UMR has many programs that provide academic support to students. The UM–Rolla Honors Academy recognizes outstanding students and applicants. Students who are selected for the academy receive research or teaching experience early in their college experience. Beginning in the freshman year, honors activities such as seminars and academic leadership courses challenge the best students on campus. The most prestigious undergraduate honor program, the Master Student Fellowship, makes it possible for students to earn both a bachelor's and a master's degree in ten semesters. In the graduate phase of the program, students receive stipends equivalent to graduate assistantships. UMR also offers a Freshman Engineering Program that provides support services in the areas of academic advising and career choice. Advanced credit may be earned through the following: Advanced Placement Program, CLEP, UM–Rolla Freshman Program, and the International Baccalaureate Program. UMR also offers the Transfer Assistance Program (TAP), which is designed for the student who would like to earn a UMR degree after attending two years at another institution. The Minority Engineering Program offers scholarships and is available to support and mentor students who are members of minority groups. The Women in Engineering Program offers special academic and financial support programs to female students. The University of Missouri–Rolla provides two weeklong summer programs for high school juniors: Introduction to Engineering and the Jackling Institute. Both programs allow students to experience college life through departmental demonstrations, discussions with faculty members and students, hands-on laboratory experiments, and campus living. Introduction to Engineering is sponsored by the School of Engineering and covers such fields as aerospace, chemical, civil, computer, electrical, and mechanical engineering. Jackling Institute is supported by the School of Mines and Metallurgy and covers ceramic, geological, metallurgical, mining, nuclear, and petroleum engineering as well as geology and geophysics. UMR also offers summer programs for members of minority groups. All summer program information can be found at http://www.umr.edu/admissions.

Off-Campus Arrangements

UMR supplements the traditional learning experience with practical knowledge. All students are encouraged to participate in cooperative programs or summer internships that help offset the expense of education while providing a valuable learning tool. These programs involve on-campus interviews, and students obtain professional experience that exposes them to job-related opportunities and helps them determine postgraduation goals. Students may also participate in a variety of study-abroad programs.

Academic Facilities

UMR is one of forty-seven leading engineering schools in America that make up the National Technological University. Courses conducted on the campuses of these universities are transmitted via satellite from TV-equipped college classrooms to students in various Fortune 500 companies across North America. The library is the primary learning resource center on campus. Its services and materials support and reinforce the campus' academic programs. The print collection includes more than 5,880 active periodical subscriptions. The library also maintains a strong collection of federal and state government publications. In this information age, technology plays an increasingly important role in the library's efforts to provide information quickly and to disseminate it broadly. The online public access catalog contains a record of all materials in the collection and links UMR to the other libraries in the University of Missouri System. A CD-ROM network distributes electronic databases campuswide 24 hours a day. State-of-the-art equipment and software in the multimedia center provide users with the capability to create presentations or study interactive instructional materials containing graphics, sound, and video. UMR has 77,449 square feet of classroom space and 315,514 square feet of laboratory facilities. Students have many opportunities to utilize research facilities that include the only packaging development research facility at a university. In addition, UMR offers two underground mines and two small quarries. Few universities have such facilities for instruction and research in mineral engineering. Students also have the opportunity to experience a supersonic blowdown wind tunnel, an acoustics laboratory, and an automatic control systems laboratory. The University offers the Rock Mechanics and Explosive Center, which is responsible for the High Pressure Waterjet Laboratory. The technology was utilized to create UMR Stonehenge, a partial reconstruction of the ancient megalith located in England. UMR also maintains a nuclear reactor on the campus that is used for education, research, and training.

Costs

Estimated educational freshman fees for the 2000–01 year are $4820 for in-state students and $12,440 for nonresident students. Room and board costs are estimated at $4795 for the 2000–01 academic year. Fee estimates are based on a typical freshman course load of 14 hours. In *U.S. News & World Report's 1999 America's Best Colleges Guidebook*, UMR tied for sixteenth among national universities for having the least debt load for graduates.

Financial Aid

Approximately 79 percent of all full-time students receive some form of financial assistance. The average annual amount of assistance received by a UMR student is $9730. Financial award packages include scholarships, grants, loans, and employment. More information is available by contacting UMR's Admission and Student Financial Assistance Office.

Faculty

Faculty members at UMR are a distinguished group committed to excelling in teaching and research. Ninety-eight percent of the full-time faculty members hold terminal degrees in their fields. Because of a 13:1 student-faculty ratio, faculty members are available for one-on-one student advisement and counseling. Because of UMR's size, most classes are taught by full-time faculty members; there is an average of 26 students per class.

Student Government

Student Council is the primary representative body of the students at UMR. It represents the interests of the student body by voicing student opinions on campus affairs to University administrators. The Student Council is composed of 100 elected delegates and 5 officers. Delegates represent recognized student organizations as well as members-at-large. In addition, many organizations have their own governing boards. These include residential halls, professional organizations, and interest groups.

Admission Requirements

Applicants who have completed the required core courses are admitted on the basis of their high school class rank and performance on standardized examinations (ACT or SAT I). Regular admission of first-time college students requires completion of at least 17 units of credit in the following: English, 4; mathematics, 4 (including algebra I or higher); science, 3; social studies, 3; fine arts, 1; and foreign language, 2. At UMR, 51 percent of students graduated in the top 10 percent of their class. The average ACT score is 28; the average SAT I score is 1270. Other admission criteria include extracurricular activity involving school or community service, talents, number and scope of college-preparatory courses taken, evidence of improvement in high school academic record, significant work experience, and supporting evidence attesting to one or more of the above in the form of an essay.

Application and Information

Applications for the fall semester should be submitted by July 1 (November 1 recommended), for the winter semester by December 1, and for the summer session by May 1. Applications must be received by February 1 (November 1 recommended) to be considered for scholarships. An application, $25 application fee, high school transcript, and one appropriate test score (ACT or SAT I) must be submitted. A personal statement is optional. Official high school or college transcripts should be sent directly from the current registrar's office to the Director of Admission and Student Financial Assistance. Students can join UMR's e-mail campaign by e-mailing go2umr@umr.edu. Prospective students may also find enrollment information and an online application at http://www.umr.edu/admissions.

All completed material should be sent to:

Director of Admission and Student Financial Assistance
University of Missouri–Rolla
102 Parker Hall, 1870 Miner Circle
Rolla, Missouri 65409-1060

Telephone: 800-522-0938 (toll-free)
E-mail: umrolla@umr.edu
World Wide Web: http://www.umr.edu

The University of Missouri–Rolla offers many opportunities for individual research at all levels of education.

UNIVERSITY OF MISSOURI–ST. LOUIS
ST. LOUIS, MISSOURI

The University

Helping students succeed is the mission of the University of Missouri–St. Louis. An exciting atmosphere of living and learning is apparent the moment people step foot on the University's beautifully landscaped, 250-acre campus in suburban St. Louis. More than 12,000 students, including 9,615 undergraduates, come to UM–St. Louis from forty states and eighty-five other countries.

Founded in 1963 as one of the four campuses of the University of Missouri, UM–St. Louis quickly grew to be the largest university in St. Louis and the third-largest in Missouri. UM–St. Louis offers students all the educational advantages and resources of a major urban research university with the personal attention of a small college; the average class size is 15 students.

Faculty members are nationally recognized experts in their fields, with 96 percent of tenured faculty holding a Ph.D. Classes are taught by professors, not graduate students or teaching assistants, to give students the utmost experience and knowledge.

UM–St. Louis offers eighty-six graduate and undergraduate degree programs in more than 100 instructional areas. Chemistry and political science are internationally recognized departments of eminence. Graduate and undergraduate degree programs are offered through the College of Arts and Sciences, the School of Business Administration, the Barnes College of Nursing, the School of Education, the Evening College, the Graduate School, the School of Optometry, and the Pierre Laclede Honors College. The Honors College is one of the fastest growing honors programs in the country and the only one with its own separate campus. UM–St. Louis also offers an innovative joint undergraduate degree in civil, electrical, and mechanical engineering in partnership with Washington University. A Bachelor of Fine Arts degree program started in 1996 in partnership with St. Louis Community College. The flexible curriculum offers numerous independent study options, certificate programs, and interdisciplinary studies.

Students get valuable real-world experience and a head start on their careers through internships and cooperative education programs with more than 400 St. Louis companies and organizations. Ninety-three percent of students graduating in the class of 1998 received job offers within six months of graduation.

UM–St. Louis has made a major investment in technology to provide some of the most technologically sophisticated classroom facilities in the U.S. Students are speeding through cyberspace with a new generation of computers, interactive media, and worldwide teleconferencing. This technology is integrated throughout the curriculum so all students, regardless of major, are on the cutting edge of advanced technology.

UM–St. Louis has three on-campus residence halls totaling 250 spaces. Student rooms are linked to the campus computer network, e-mail, the Internet, and the World Wide Web. University Meadows student apartments provide a choice of efficiency and two- and four-bedroom units that house a total of 500 students. Amenities include a clubhouse and pool. Mansion Hill Condominiums, located on a wooded estate next to campus, offers additional housing for 180 students.

UM–St. Louis is fully accredited by the North Central Association of Colleges and Schools. Additional accreditations include the AACSB–The International Association for Management Education, the National Council for Accreditation of Teacher Education, and the Missouri Department of Elementary and Secondary Education.

Location

UM–St. Louis occupies a beautiful suburban campus within easy reach of all the attractions of St. Louis, Missouri, a thriving metropolitan area with 2.2 million residents. The campus is served by two MetroLink stations, St. Louis's newest form of rapid transit, to provide direct access to Lambert St. Louis International Airport and the region's major cultural, sports, and entertainment attractions such as Cardinals baseball, Blues hockey, the St. Louis Rams, St. Louis Art Museum, St. Louis Zoo, St. Louis Symphony, Union Station, Laclede's Landing, and Forest Park. UM–St. Louis is the largest supplier of university-educated employees in the region, which ranks fifth nationally in the number of Fortune 100 headquarters.

Majors and Degrees

Undergraduate majors include accounting; anthropology; applied mathematics; art history and fine arts; behavioral sciences; biochemistry; biological sciences; biology; biotechnology; business administration, with areas of emphasis in finance, international business, logistics and operations management, management and organizational behavior, and marketing; chemistry; civil engineering; communication; computer science; criminology and criminal justice; early childhood education; economics; electrical engineering; elementary education; English; French; general studies; German; history; management information systems; mathematics; mechanical engineering; music; music education; nursing; optometry; philosophy; physical education; physics; political science; prelaw; premedicine; prepharmacy; pre-veterinary; psychology; public administration; secondary education; social work; sociology; Spanish; special education; studio art; and urban studies.

Academic Program

The University offers courses during fall and spring semesters, an 8-week summer session, and three 4-week sessions. All undergraduates take 33–39 semester hours of general education courses in English, mathematics, humanities, natural sciences, and social sciences. The bachelor's degree for most majors requires 120 credit hours. The bachelor's degree in electrical engineering requires 131 credit hours, and the bachelor's degree for civil and mechanical engineering requires 137 credit hours. Each degree program at UM–St. Louis has specific course requirements and may require a minimum grade point average.

Students enjoy a variety of educational experiences outside the classroom, including internships, cooperative education programs, study abroad and international exchange programs, and ROTC. Other opportunities include independent study options, accelerated-degree programs, advanced placement, English as a second language programs, tutorials and mentoring programs, organizations for African-American and international students, and specialized services for LCD students.

Off-Campus Arrangements

UM–St. Louis offers students extensive opportunities for study abroad through exchange programs in twenty-five countries worldwide. In the London Business Internship Program, for example, students spend a semester learning and working in London, one of the world's foremost financial centers. In addition, students may spend a year or a semester at one of 125 universities in the U.S. through the National Student Exchange Program.

Academic Facilities

Since the doors to the University first opened in 1963 on the grounds of the former Bellerive Country Club, UM–St. Louis has grown to include forty-four modern classroom buildings, research facilities, residence halls, student apartments, and an athletic complex. The $10-million Computer Center is one of the most technologically sophisticated classroom facilities in the U.S. The $10-million Molecular Electronics Center opened in 1996 to house expanded research and teaching in chemistry, physics, engineering, and physical sciences. The Anheuser-Busch Ecology Complex augments research activities of the biology department and the University's renowned International Center for Tropical Ecology in partnership with the Missouri Botanical Garden. In addition to spacious lecture halls and a 435-seat theater, the campus features extensive computer labs, multimedia facilities, radio station, Child Care Center, Community Optometry Clinic, and Eldercare Center.

The Mark Twain Athletic Complex features a state-of-the-art fitness center, weight room, indoor track, swimming pool, and basketball, volleyball, handball, and racquetball courts.

UM–St. Louis has three libraries: the main Thomas Jefferson Library, the Ward E. Barnes Education Library, and the Health Sciences Library. Library collections consist of 625,249 books, approximately 2 million microfilm titles, 2,903 periodicals, and extensive automated databases in both online and CD-ROM formats. In addition, the Western Historical Manuscript Collection contains primary source materials for research in history, the environment, politics, and social issues.

Costs

UM–St. Louis is a publicly supported, land-grant institution. The 1999–2000 educational fee for full-time, undergraduate Missouri residents was $3978 per year. The annual educational fee for full-time nonresident undergraduate students was $11,892.

Financial Aid

The primary function of the Student Financial Aid Office is to provide financial assistance to students who would otherwise be unable to attend UM–St. Louis. More than 66 percent of students receive some form of financial aid or scholarships. In the 1998–99 academic year, this aid exceeded $49 million. UM–St. Louis was one of the first universities nationally to participate in the Federal Direct Loan Program. Financial aid consists of a variety of scholarships, Federal Pell Grants, Federal Stafford Student Loans, work-study programs, Federal Perkins Loans, Federal Supplemental Educational Opportunity Grants, Federal Parent Loans for Undergraduate Students, and Missouri Student Grants. Some aid is available to qualified nonresident students through the National Access Award. Additional information may be obtained by contacting the Office of Financial Aid at 314-516-5526; e-mail: sfinaid@umslvma.umsl.edu; or World Wide Web at http://www.umsl.edu/services/finaid/.

Faculty

UM–St. Louis has 970 faculty members, including 11 Fulbright scholars. Ninety-six percent of tenured professors have a Ph.D. The student-faculty ratio is 10:1. Faculty members are noted researchers, scholars, authors, educators, and sought-after consultants to business, industry, government, and nonprofit groups. However, their principal mission is to teach. The vast majority of classes are taught by professors, not graduate students or teaching assistants.

Student Government

The Student Government Association welcomes participation by students. Additional student organizations include the Evening College Council, Panhellenic Council, University Program Board, and Residence Hall Council and the *Current* newspaper.

Admission Requirements

For first-time freshmen, selection for regular admission is based on high school class rank; ACT or SAT I scores; and required high school units. Applicants should submit an application, an official high school transcript, and appropriate test scores.

Students applying as transfer students who have fewer than 24 hours of college-level work should follow procedures for entering freshmen. Selection of students for regular admission is based on a minimum overall 2.0 grade point average (4.0 system) in all college-level courses at previous institutions. Students should submit an application and official transcripts from all colleges and universities attended.

Application and Information

The University of Missouri–St. Louis employs a rolling admission policy enabling students to start in any semester. A nonrefundable fee of $25 ($40 for international students) by check or money order made payable to University of Missouri must accompany all first-time applications for graduate and undergraduate student classifications.

Application forms and additional information are available by contacting:

Curtis Coonrod
Director of Admissions
Office of Admissions
144 Woods Hall
University of Missouri–St. Louis
8001 Natural Bridge Road
St. Louis, Missouri 63121-4499
Telephone: 314-516-5451
    888-GO-2-UMSL (toll-free in Missouri and in 618 area code in Illinois)
Fax: 314-516-5310
E-mail: admissions@umsl.edu
World Wide Web: http://www.umsl.edu

Students enjoy exciting opportunities for living and learning at UM–St. Louis.

UNIVERSITY OF MONTEVALLO
MONTEVALLO, ALABAMA

The University

The University was founded in 1896 when the town of Montevallo was selected to be the site of a state school. It became known as Alabama College, and, in 1969, the name was changed to the University of Montevallo (UM) to reflect the growth in both enrollment and academic programs.

Montevallo's "small college" experience features classes of reasonable size. The individual advising system is enhanced by an active Career Center. In addition, the University's emphasis on liberal arts is supported by a core curriculum with a comprehensive writing component. In order to achieve and maintain high-quality programs, UM is committed to the attainment of national accreditation for all of its undergraduate programs where such recognition is available and appropriate. Montevallo is accredited by the Commission on Colleges of the Southern Association of Colleges and Schools.

Located on a 160-acre campus, the University has redbrick walkways and tree-shaded lawns, with central portions of the campus designated as a National Historic District. The Olmsted brothers, landscape architects famous for designing New York's Central Park, Atlanta's Ponce de Leon Avenue Parks, and the Biltmore Estate near Asheville, North Carolina, also developed the first plan for the Montevallo campus. Their basic design ideas are still followed.

The University of Montevallo is a member of the Council of Public Liberal Arts Colleges (COPLAC). Montevallo is one of sixteen public liberal arts colleges and universities in the United States that are members of this alliance. As a member, Montevallo is dedicated to the education of undergraduates in the liberal arts tradition, the creation of teaching and learning communities, and the experience of access to undergraduate liberal arts education. The University has recently been recognized as a regional university by *U.S. News & World Report* in its "America's Best Colleges" publication and as a public institution that "has the advantage of a good private college at a fraction of the cost" in *Looking Beyond the Ivy League* by Loren Pope.

A variety of social and recreational opportunities are available. Campus activities, such as Greek-sponsored events, movies, theater productions, concerts, and athletic and other events, are regularly scheduled. Students may also participate in more than seventy campus organizations, including national fraternities and sororities, intramural athletics, clubs, and service and religious organizations. The University fields nine intercollegiate teams that compete in the Gulf South Conference and the NCAA Division II.

In fall 1999, the enrollment was 3,161, representing twenty-eight states and twenty other countries. The enrollment is approximately 65 percent women and 13 percent members of minority groups. In recent years, 71 percent of the freshmen have returned for the sophomore year. Of those who returned for the sophomore year, 64 percent graduated within five years.

Location

Located approximately 25 miles south of the metropolitan Birmingham area and with a population of 5,000, Montevallo offers students the advantage of living within walking distance of shops, restaurants, and banks. The location provides students with easy access to Birmingham, the state's largest metropolitan area, which offers many cultural, recreational, retail, and employment opportunities.

Majors and Degrees

UM's academic programs reflect its evolution from a school into a college and finally into a university with four colleges: the College of Arts & Sciences, Michael E. Stephens College of Business, College of Education, and College of Fine Arts. The following undergraduate degrees are granted: Bachelor of Arts, Bachelor of Business Administration, Bachelor of Fine Arts, Bachelor of Music, and Bachelor of Science.

The University offers programs in accounting, art, biology, chemistry, child and family studies, communication studies, dietetics, early childhood education, education of the hearing impaired, elementary education, English, family and consumer sciences, finance, French, history, interior design merchandising, kinesiology, language arts, management, marketing, mass communication, mathematics, music, political science, psychology, retail merchandising, social sciences, social work, sociology, Spanish, speech language pathology, and theater.

The five largest degree programs are art (B.A., B.F.A., B.S.), business (B.B.A.), communication science and disorders (B.S.), education (B.A., B.S.), and family and consumer sciences (B.A., B.S.). Also popular are biology (B.A., B.S.), English (B.A.), kinesiology (B.S.), mass communication (B.A., B.S.), and psychology (B.A., B.S.). Preprofessional studies in dentistry, engineering, law, medicine, nursing, pharmacy, and veterinary medicine are available. Air Force and Army ROTC programs are also available.

Academic Program

Montevallo's academic calendar consists of a fall semester, a spring semester, a May term, and a summer session with two 5-week terms. Students fulfill the core requirements in general education to qualify for undergraduate degrees. Courses in English, science, mathematics, the arts, and languages introduce students to a broad spectrum of knowledge and experiences designed to develop the mind, emotions, spirit, and body. The purposes of the programs are to enable students to participate as responsible and informed citizens, to become self-educating individuals, to work creatively and effectively, and to lead satisfying personal lives. A candidate for a degree must have a minimum of 130 semester hours of credit distributed according to curriculum requirements, 260 grade points, and a minimum cumulative grade point average of 2.0 (on a 4.0 scale) on all study attempted. Most students can earn a bachelor's degree in three years by attending six semesters and three summer sessions.

The popular University Honors Program is designed to provide intellectually talented students with specifically designed academic offerings, cocurricular activities, and recognition. CLEP, AP, IB, and military credit may be applied toward a degree.

Off-Campus Arrangements

The University's Stephens College of Business has sponsored student travel to Quebec City, Canada, and Europe for seminars and cultural activities. In addition, business majors may take advantage of student exchange agreements to study in Amsterdam, the Netherlands; Brussels, Belgium; Donetsk, the Ukraine; or Quebec City, Canada.

The University has offered international travel and summer-study programs each year since 1959. Students earn up to 8 semester hours for group study and travel experiences developed by the UM faculty. Montevallo is a member of the Marine Environmental Sciences Consortium, a public, nonprofit corporation dedicated to providing marine education, research, and service. Biology students with an emphasis in marine biology take courses at the Dauphin Island Sea Laboratory, Dauphin Island, Alabama.

There are 3-2 engineering programs with Auburn University, the University of Alabama, and the University of Alabama at Birmingham. These five-year dual-degree programs enable students to enroll at Montevallo for three years, then transfer to the School of Engineering of their choice. Upon successful completion of two years of engineering study, the student receives a Bachelor of Science in a specific area of engineering and a Bachelor of Science in mathematics from Montevallo.

The UM Career Center provides students and alumni with a wide range of programs and services related to career development issues and prepares candidates for entry into the world of work. Career counseling, career testing, employability training, posting of full-time and part-time jobs, job market information, internship information, graduate school information, employer files, on-campus interviews, and career fairs are offered by the UM Career Center. A career resource library is located on the premises.

Academic Facilities

The library has a collection that includes more than 250,000 books and subscribes to more than 2,400 journals in print, microform, and electronic versions. The library provides access to a wide variety of electronic databases, more than 20 of which are provided through the Alabama Virtual Library. Many of these databases include the full text of the materials retrieved. In 1999, the Music Library collection was incorporated into Carmichael Library. Other academic facilities available to students include computer labs in several programs, the Harbert Writing Center, and the Speech and Hearing Center, which provides assistance to students and the general public with hearing, language, or speech problems. Because Montevallo expects its students to graduate, not just enroll, many services are available to help them. One example is Student Support Services, a program funded by the U.S. Department of Education, which offers tutoring assistance in core curriculum courses, including mathematics. Another is Counseling Services, which provides individual counseling to any student.

Costs

For the 1999–2000 academic year, tuition was approximately $3150 for full-time, in-state students. Out-of-state tuition was approximately $6300 per year. Room and board charges were approximately $3500, the Student Government Association fee was $70, and the technology (computer services) fee was $70. Additional fees were charged for vehicle registration ($15), bowling classes ($20), and music lessons ($50 for private lessons and $42 for group lessons), and an optional health/wellness fee is $90.

Financial Aid

The University administers a comprehensive program of financial assistance. Federal, state, and University funds are combined to provide students with the scholarship, student employment, loan, and grant aid for which they qualify. Financial aid is meant to supplement students' resources and is not intended to be their only support. In 1999–2000, 72 percent of undergraduate students received some form of financial aid.

The awarding of need-based financial aid usually begins in May. The priority deadline is April 15. Students applying for federal financial aid or need-based scholarships should complete the Free Application for Federal Student Aid (FAFSA).

Every fall, the University publishes a brochure that includes information regarding available financial aid and scholarships. To request the brochure, students should contact the Student Financial Services Office, Station 6050, University of Montevallo, Montevallo, Alabama 35115-6000.

Faculty

Faculty members are committed to teaching, advising, research, and service. In 1999–2000, there were 136 full-time and 68 part-time members of the faculty. Of these, approximately 90 percent held terminal degrees in their respective fields. The student-faculty ratio is 16:1. Several campus surveys have revealed that students have found the faculty to be accessible and willing to help them succeed both inside and outside the classroom.

Student Government

Since 1916, the president and faculty have encouraged students to govern themselves in important areas of student life. The Student Government Association (SGA), whose motto is "students serving students," consists of an Executive Cabinet and Senate, elected annually by the student body. Each class and college, as well as commuters, adult returning students, graduate students, and international students, maintains representation in the Senate. In representing student interests and concerns, the SGA appoints students to various University interest committees and the Justice Council and publishes the *Fledgling*, a student handbook that contains pertinent information regarding student life. The SGA is also responsible for sponsoring the University Program Council (UPC), the Miss University of Montevallo Scholarship Pageant, College Night, and student publications.

Admission Requirements

Montevallo welcomes applications from those whose academic preparation, experience, and interests indicate a reasonable chance for success in a degree program. Applications are reviewed on an individual basis, and the University considers information from a variety of sources regarding a candidate's qualifications. Satisfactory scores on the ACT or the SAT I are required. International applicants are required to submit the results of the Test of English as a Foreign Language (TOEFL).

A freshman applicant must present a satisfactory high school transcript with a minimum of 16 academic credits from ninth grade through twelfth grade. The credits must include 4 in English, 4 in social studies, 2 in mathematics, 2 in science, and 4 in academic electives. A minimum grade point average of 2.0 on a 4.0 scale is required for regular admission. The University offers summer conditional admission for those who present marginal credentials, allowing limited numbers of students to enroll for the University's summer session(s) and to continue in the fall semester if summer grade point average requirements are met. Early admission and advanced placement are also available.

Students applying for transfer admission from accredited colleges and universities must have a minimum cumulative GPA of 2.0 on previous study attempted. A transfer student must be in good standing at the current or previous college.

Prospective students are encouraged to visit the campus. The Admissions Office is open on Monday, Wednesday, and Friday for interviews and tours by appointment at 10 a.m. and 1 p.m. Campus tours are available on Saturday at 10 a.m., with no appointment necessary.

Application and Information

The application deadline is August 1. All applications must be accompanied by the required $25 processing fee. Prospective students are encouraged to apply early to take advantage of scholarship and housing options. Once an applicant has submitted all required information, an admissions decision is made and notification is forwarded immediately.

For more information or an application packet, students should contact:

William C. Cannon Jr.
Director of Admissions
Station 6030 Palmer Hall
University of Montevallo
Montevallo, Alabama 35115-6000
Telephone: 205-665-6030
          800-292-4349 (toll-free)
E-mail: admissions@montevallo.edu
World Wide Web: http://www.montevallo.edu/

UNIVERSITY OF NEBRASKA–LINCOLN
LINCOLN, NEBRASKA

The University

Traditions, spirit, and pride play an important role at the University of Nebraska (NU). As soon students set foot on campus, they can feel it. It is in the faces of the 76,000 fans who pack Memorial Stadium on game days. It is also on the faces of students and teachers who make this big university a small, friendly place.

Established in 1869, the University of Nebraska opened its doors in 1871 with 20 students and one building. Since then, Nebraska has become a major university internationally known for excellence in teaching, research, and service to the community. For more than 130 years, students at the University of Nebraska have been challenged to pursue excellence and discover their own path to success in a stimulating academic environment. Students join more than 200,000 alumni who have made their mark as industry leaders in business, engineering, the arts, journalism, education, and the sciences. In addition to the undergraduate degree programs described below, NU offers 116 graduate degree programs.

The University of Nebraska is a major research university. NU is one of eighty-six universities nationwide to be granted the Carnegie Foundation's highest classification, Research University I. Nebraska has also been a member of the Association of American Universities since 1909; it is one of only sixty-two universities to claim this prestigious membership. This gives students an advantage. Classes are taught by faculty members who are experts in their fields, and students find a diverse variety of academic choices.

At Nebraska, technology is invented, and real-world problems are solved. Researchers and students at Nebraska have developed everything from a strain of grass that can survive with very little water to eggs that contain less cholesterol to a highway guard rail that helps stop the impact of a car crash.

NU's community is local and global. More than 18,000 undergraduate students from a wide range of ethnic, cultural, and economic backgrounds make their college home at Nebraska. Many students choose to live in one of NU's twelve residence halls, which provide a close-knit community and a support network for students within the larger campus community. Each residence hall has high-speed Internet access, cable television, air conditioning, and local phone service in every room and a resident assistant and health aid on every floor. Greek organizations at Nebraska offer interested students social, academic, community service, and campus living opportunities. There are fifteen sororities and twenty-four fraternities at NU. Rush information is mailed to students in the spring prior to enrollment.

Location

The University of Nebraska is located in the capital city of Lincoln, a community of more than 209,000 that combines a friendly college-town atmosphere with the entertainment and nightlife of a larger city. Lincoln boasts a thriving arts community with dozens of art galleries and the Lied Center for Performing Arts, which hosts major productions such as *Les Misérables* and *Cats* and performances by the Russian Ballet, Celine Dion, and cellist Yo-Yo Ma. Lincoln has more parks per capita than any other city in the U.S. and a growing network of bike paths that extend far beyond the city limits. There are sixteen golf courses, hundreds of restaurants, more than thirty movie screens, major shopping malls, and a restored downtown historic district complete with specialty shops, coffeehouses, and a dinner theater. Major metropolitan cities like Omaha, Kansas City, Chicago, and Denver are within a day's drive, and Lincoln is easily accessible by plane, train, and bus.

Majors and Degrees

The University of Nebraska–Lincoln offers 149 undergraduate majors, providing students with the opportunity to choose a challenging course of study and gain a solid background of fundamentals, critical thinking, and experience. With more than 80 percent of the classes under 40 students, there is a balance between lecture and lab and practice and theory, and the classes are taught by faculty members who are highly respected in their fields. Degree programs are distributed over the nine Colleges of Agricultural Sciences and Natural Resources, Architecture, Arts and Sciences, Business Administration, Engineering and Technology, Fine and Performing Arts, Human Resources and Family Sciences, Journalism and Mass Communications, and the Teachers College.

Academic Program

NU offers classes during the fall and spring semesters and during the summer sessions, which consist of a three-week presession, two 5-week sessions, and one 8-week session. Undergraduates must take a minimum of 12 hours to be full-time. Most undergraduate degree programs require 120 to 130 credit hours for graduation. Each degree program at NU has specific course requirements, and some require a minimum grade point average.

The University Honors Program provides motivated students with academic challenges, opportunities to learn from and do research with top faculty members, and a community of supportive peers. Students admitted to the highly selective J. D. Edwards Honors Program in Computer Science and Management become tomorrow's leaders in technology applications and solutions. Outside the classroom, students can participate in various experiences, including study abroad, internships, cooperative educational programs, ROTC, and research opportunities with faculty members. Students may also participate in tutoring and mentoring programs such as supplemental instruction, independent studies options, and English as a second language.

Off-Campus Arrangements

Students gain professional experience through an extensive internship and cooperative education program, connecting them to industry leaders in the U.S. government, NASA, General Motors, Microsoft, Gannet Newspapers, and Gallup. Through Nebraska's study-abroad programs, students can choose to study in one of more than fifty countries and at 140 universities. Financial aid often applies to study-abroad programs. Field courses are held at on-site locations to give students hands-on experience. Examples of popular courses include excavation of earth lodges at Fontenelle Forest and the study of parasitology specimens at Cedar Point Biological Station in western Nebraska.

Academic Facilities

NU is housed on 616 acres of land across two campuses, City Campus and East Campus. One of the University's newest facilities is the George W. Beadle Center for Genetics and Biomaterials Research. City Campus is also home to the nationally renowned Sheldon Memorial Art Gallery and Sculpture Garden, the Christlieb Collection of Western Art, and several other galleries. The Lied Center for Performing Arts draws big-name acts in contemporary entertainment, and the University of Nebraska State Museum boasts a world-class fossil collection. A number of specialized centers offer assistance to the state's citizens, including the Bureau of Business Research, the Food Processing Center, and the Technology Transfer Office, which expedites the movement of University-developed knowledge into real-world products and processes.

NU also offers students a variety of research libraries. Love Library is the main library located on City Campus and contains about half of the University's collection of 2.5 million volumes. C. Y. Thompson Library on East Campus and the various departmental libraries offer students excellent research facilities.

Costs

For the 1999–2000 academic year, in-state tuition and fees were approximately $3340 and out-of-state tuition and fees were approximately $7845 (based on a single, undergraduate student taking 15 credit hours per semester for two semesters). Room and board were approximately $4070 for a double room for two semesters. Books and supplies are estimated at $660.

Financial Aid

The University of Nebraska offers one of the most affordable high-quality educations in the country. It has one of the lowest total costs among Big 12, Big 10, and AAU institutions. In addition, about 65 percent of students at the University receive some type of scholarship or financial aid. Nebraska offers a wide range of scholarships based on academic achievement, leadership and involvement, and specific academic interests such as engineering, mathematics, computer science, business, and agricultural sciences. Last year approximately 1,216 students received freshmen scholarships worth more than $2.9 million. Full consideration for freshman scholarships is given to students whose admissions application materials are complete and on file in the Office of Admissions by January 15 (March 15 for transfer students). Fifty-seven percent of all applicants to Nebraska received need-based financial assistance last year in the form of grants, work-study, and student loans. Applications for these federal programs should be made by filing the Free Application for Federal Student Aid prior to March 1 preceding fall enrollment.

Faculty

Nebraska has a strong reputation for excellence in teaching. Highly respected in their fields, NU faculty members are active in industry and professional organizations, conduct research that leads to new discoveries, and constantly keep up with current trends and new thinking—and that is what they pass on to the students. The University of Nebraska has 1,531 faculty members, with more than 60 percent holding a doctoral degree. The student-faculty ratio is 15:1.

Student Government

The Association for Students at the University of Nebraska (ASUN) serves as the representative voice for NU students by gathering input from all students, advocating student concerns to the administration, and providing essential student services, ultimately working to improve the campus and enhance student life. The functions of ASUN are carried out by elected student senators representing each of the nine academic colleges, the division of general studies, graduate studies, and the professional schools.

Admission Requirements

In order to be eligible for assured admission to the University of Nebraska–Lincoln, students who graduated from high school after 1997 must have completed a set of 16 units of core courses, including 4 units of English, 4 of math, 3 of natural science, 3 of social science, and 2 of foreign language (1 unit = 1 high school year). In addition, students must have graduated in the upper half of their graduating class or earned a combined score of 950 or higher on the SAT I or a composite of 20 or higher on the ACT. Transfer students must also have a minimum 2.0 cumulative grade point average and at least a 2.0 GPA in their final semester of attendance at another postsecondary institution. Some academic programs may require higher test scores and class ranks than these minimums. Students are encouraged to apply for admission even if they do not meet one or more of the above requirements.

Application and Information

Students interested in applying for the fall semester should apply by the June 30 deadline, and those interested in applying for the spring semester should apply by December 15. Full consideration for scholarships is given to students whose admissions application materials are completed and received by January 15. A $25 application fee is required as are official transcripts from the student's high school and/or postsecondary institution and official ACT or SAT I scores. Students whose first language is not English should also send official TOEFL or MELAB scores.

To make arrangements to visit NU or to receive an application and admissions information, students should contact:

Office of Admissions
University of Nebraska–Lincoln
1410 Q Street
Lincoln, Nebraska 68588-0417
Telephone: 402-472-2023
           800-742-8800 (toll-free)
Fax: 402-472-0670
E-mail: nuhusker@unl.edu
World Wide Web: http://www.unl.edu/
                http://www.unl.edu/nuhusker/applying/
                application.html (to apply on line)

NU students look to the Student Union and Broyhill Fountain as gathering places for study groups, organization meetings, or spending time with friends.

UNIVERSITY OF NEVADA, LAS VEGAS
LAS VEGAS, NEVADA

The University

The University of Nevada, Las Vegas (UNLV), is recognized nationally as a comprehensive teaching and research university that provides students with an excellent education at a reasonable cost. UNLV has established an agenda for the next decade to make it a premier urban university. All UNLV programs are accredited by the Northwest Association of Schools and Colleges. Individual programs have further accreditation from professional accrediting organizations.

Since its founding in 1957, UNLV has seen dramatic growth in both its academic programs and its facilities. Nearly 155 undergraduate, master's, and doctoral degree programs are offered to more than 23,000 students. Eighty percent of UNLV's students are undergraduates, 79 percent are Nevada residents, 24 percent are minority students, and 4 percent are international students. The average class size is 20.

The University is located on a beautifully landscaped 335-acre campus. Classes are held in comfortable, well-equipped buildings that are showcases of modern architecture. Classroom, physics, and student services buildings opened in 1994, and an architecture building opened in 1997. Ground was broken for a $53-million library in early 1998. The William S. Boyd School of Law opened in fall 1998. The Lied Library opens in mid-2000.

UNLV's residential life program provides students with a secure, convenient place to live on the University campus. The modern residence halls are organized into suites of two rooms joined by a bathroom. Four students share a suite, with 2 per room. UNLV's dining facilities are excellent, providing students with quality, quantity, and choice.

More than 100 groups offer students an active social life, including intramural sports, Greek organizations, ethnic and religious clubs, a student newspaper, and campus radio and television stations. UNLV's Division of Student Services provides an array of advising, tutorial, and counseling services. Student Support Services provides textbooks on tape, interpreters for the deaf, lab assistants, and other services to students with disabilities.

Numerous concerts are performed throughout the year by UNLV's student music groups, choirs, dance companies, and ensembles. The Department of Theatre Arts also offers an excellent season of comedies, dramas, and musicals performed by students and community members, as well as performances by national professional touring companies. The student government sponsors lectures, films, concerts, and entertainment throughout the year.

Location

Las Vegas is located at the southern tip of Nevada in a desert valley surrounded by mountains. The Las Vegas metropolitan area is a rapidly growing community of more than 1 million residents with a strong sense of family and community pride. The surrounding area is one of the Southwest's most picturesque, offering residents outdoor recreation year-round. Within a 50-mile radius lie the shores of Lake Mead, Hoover Dam, and the Colorado River recreation area; the snow-skiing and hiking trails of 12,000-foot Mount Charleston; and a panoramic view of rugged rock mountains. Las Vegas has an average of 320 days of sunshine per year. The average daytime winter temperature is 60 degrees Fahrenheit. Summer daytime temperatures are usually more than 100 degrees Fahrenheit.

Majors and Degrees

Undergraduate programs are offered by the College of Business, College of Extended Studies, College of Education, Howard R. Hughes College of Engineering, College of Fine Arts, College of Health Sciences, William F. Harrah College of Hotel Administration, College of Liberal Arts, College of Science, and College of Urban Affairs.

Majors include accounting, anthropology, applied physics, architecture, art, art history, Asian studies, biology, chemistry, civil engineering, clinical lab sciences, communications studies, comprehensive medical imaging, computer engineering, computer science, construction management, criminal justice, culinary arts, dance, early childhood education, earth science, economics, electrical engineering, elementary education, English, environmental geology, environmental studies, film, finance, fitness management, French, geology, German, health-care administration, health education, health physics, history, hotel administration, interior architecture and design, international business, kinesiological sciences, landscape architecture, Latin American studies, liberal studies, linguistic studies, management, management information systems, marketing, mathematics, mechanical engineering, music, musical theater, nuclear medicine, nursing, philosophy, physical education, physics, political science, postsecondary/adult education, premedicine, psychology, radiologic technology, real estate, recreation, Romance languages, secondary education, senior adult theater, social work, sociology, Spanish, special education, sports injury management, theater arts, urban and regional planning, women's studies, and workforce education.

Academic Programs

The UNLV General Education Core requirement, which must be completed by all baccalaureate degree candidates, consists of courses in English composition and literature, logic, mathematics, computer science or statistics, U.S. and Nevada constitutions, social sciences, natural sciences, fine arts, and humanities. The balance of baccalaureate degree programs consists of college and departmental requirements. The number of credit hours required for baccalaureate degrees varies between 124 and 136, depending on the program of study. Numerous special academic opportunities are available, such as dual majors, dual baccalaureates, approved minors, internships, international studies, interdisciplinary programs, honors programs, and nontraditional credit (military credits, Advanced Placement, College-Level Examination Program, and correspondence credits).

The UNLV academic calendar has two semesters (fall and spring), each lasting approximately sixteen weeks. Three summer sessions are held from June through August.

Off-Campus Arrangements

International study programs are available throughout the year, with opportunities to spend one semester, one academic year, or a summer abroad. Academic credits earned in UNLV study-abroad programs are part of regular authorized course offerings. Students can make normal progress toward their UNLV degree while utilizing international resources and experiencing a different culture.

Academic Facilities

The James R. Dickinson Library houses a variety of collections and services in two buildings; there are more than a half-million books. The library houses more than a million other informational items. The campus has an excellent Curriculum Materials Library, which is used extensively by local school teachers and University students. The National Supercomputing Center for Energy and the Environment facilitates study of the engineering, socioeconomic, transportation, and social impacts of energy and hazardous waste management along with other appropriate studies. The center includes a Cray YMP 2/215 supercomputer and a Sun 4/490 front-end computer, ten color graphics workstations, and a Silicon Graphics workstation. There are four public computer labs on the UNLV campus with various types of equipment, including IBM PCs, Spool Printers, Gateways, NEC machines, Macintoshes, Image Writers, letter quality and laser printers, Apple II's, and DEC workstations.

Costs

For the 2000–01 academic year, average room and board costs are $2700 per semester, nonresident tuition is $3490 per semester, the per-credit-hour fee is $74 for nonresidents taking 7 or more credits, and books and supplies are estimated at $300 per semester. Graduates of schools in, or twelve-month residents of, approved counties may be charged reduced nonresident tuition. Approved counties are San Bernardino and Inyo counties in California. Residents of thirteen states (Alaska, Arizona, Colorado, Hawaii, Idaho, Montana, New Mexico, North Dakota, Oregon, South Dakota, Utah, Washington, and Wyoming) may enroll at reduced tuition rates through the Western Undergraduate Exchange Program. Children of alumni (bachelor's degree graduates only) may qualify for a reduction in nonresident tuition. Students who matriculate as nonresidents may be eligible for resident tuition upon fulfilling the university's twelve-month residency requirements.

Financial Aid

UNLV provides a variety of financial assistance to qualified students. Loans, grants, scholarships, and employment are all awarded to help students meet their educational expenses while attending UNLV. All students should explore every possible resource. A student's eligibility may be determined by financial need, scholastic achievement, special skills, or service. Prospective students may complete a financial aid application prior to or at the same time as the application for admission. The priority deadline for applying for scholarships is February 1. All paperwork for other forms of financial aid (loans, grants, and work-study) should also be submitted by February 1, but later submissions will be processed.

Faculty

More than 600 full-time instructional faculty members are involved in teaching, research, and community service. The scholars and scientists at UNLV are warm, caring people committed as much to excellence in teaching as they are to their research. In most colleges, a faculty adviser is assigned to each student to provide academic counseling through the undergraduate years. All levels of faculty are involved in undergraduate education. Graduate assistants have limited teaching and laboratory assignments. About 500 professional staff members and 700 state employees also serve students.

Student Government

All undergraduate students are automatically members of the Consolidated Students of the University of Nevada, Las Vegas (CSUN). CSUN is a self-governing body and is recognized by UNLV's faculty and the University and Community College System of Nevada. All officers are elected by the student body. CSUN has many boards and committees in which students are encouraged to get involved. CSUN provides students an opportunity to practice their communication skills and enrich their education both socially and academically.

Admission Requirements

Regular admission to UNLV is objectively based on a student's academic record and/or placement examination scores. The University does not limit the number of students that can be regularly admitted for any semester. An admitted student is placed in introductory English and mathematics according to his or her SAT I or ACT scores. The minimum grade point average (GPA) requirement for incoming freshmen from high school is 2.5. Completion of the following pre-college curriculum in high school is also required: 4 years of English; 3 years of algebra or higher-level mathematics; 3 years of natural science, with at least 2 years in a lab science; 3 years of social studies; and ½ year of computer literacy. Students who do not meet these requirements may still qualify for admission upon graduation from high school with a minimum GPA of 3.0 or a minimum GPA of 2.5 with an ACT composite score of 21 or higher or an SAT I combined score of 990 or higher. A student's cumulative, unweighted GPA is used for admission. Transfer admission is granted to a student who completes a minimum of 12 or more semester credits in transferable courses and earns a GPA of 2.0 or higher from a regionally accredited university or college. The applicant must be in good standing and eligible to return to the educational institution last attended.

An applicant who does not satisfy UNLV's minimum admission requirements may attend as a nonadmitted student or may request consideration for probationary admission by appealing to the University Admissions Committee.

Application and Information

Priority application deadlines are May 1 for the fall semester and November 1 for the spring semester. The nonrefundable application fee of $40 for domestic students and $95 for international students cannot be waived.

Catalogs are mailed first-class; the charge is determined by where it is sent.

To receive materials and information, students may contact:

Office of Admissions
University of Nevada, Las Vegas
Box 451021
4505 Maryland Parkway
Las Vegas, Nevada 89154-1021
Telephone: 702-895-3443 (admissions, tours, and immunizations)
Fax: 702-895-1118
Orientation: 702-895-4450
Main University number: 702-895-3011
Financial aid: 702-895-3424
UNLV events: 702-895-3131
World Wide Web: http://www.unlv.edu

UNIVERSITY OF NEVADA, RENO
RENO, NEVADA

The University

For the tenth straight year, the University of Nevada, Reno, has made the honor roll in the "America's Best Colleges" issue of *U.S. News & World Report*. Nevada was the state's only university named in the 1999 "National Universities" category—a superior group of 228 schools, including Harvard, Princeton, and Yale. This is further evidence of Nevada's growing reputation as one of the nation's best universities. The American Association of University Professors has given Nevada a Class 1 rating as a research institution. Funds for sponsored research, training, and public service totaled more than $80 million during fiscal year 1999 and are expected to top $110 million before the year 2003. Nevada's Reynolds School of Journalism has produced 5 Pulitzer Prize winners. According to the *Wall Street Journal*, Nevada's Mackay School of Mines is "said to be among the best half-dozen in the country." The Chemistry Department was ranked "very best" in its size in the U.S. and Canada by the National Science Foundation; the Geography Department, fifth in the U.S. in its size for undergraduate teaching; the Honors Program among the fifty-five best nationally in "a state's major university;" and the hydrologic sciences program, sixth nationally.

Accredited by the Northwest Association of Schools and Colleges, the University has 12,500 acres of field laboratories and research areas statewide. Nevada is internationally known for its research in earthquakes, fetal transplants, heap leach mining, remote sensing, and structural engineering. The University's Center for Environmental Sciences and Engineering prepares students for the growing demand for environmental scientists. Nevada is also known for having strong programs in agriculture, biochemistry, geriatrics, heart disease, theoretical chemistry, and speech pathology and audiology.

Students at Nevada may live in one of seven residence halls on campus or at one of ten fraternity and sorority houses nearby. Ten percent of students live on campus. They come from all seventeen Nevada counties, from all fifty states, and from more than sixty countries. For extracurricular activities, students may participate in more than 100 student organizations recognized by the Associated Students of the University of Nevada (ASUN). Support services include an active student services office that offers intensive orientation sessions for new students, academic advisement, counseling, tutoring, financial aid, a health service, and special programs. Nevada has upgraded Mackay Stadium, home to the Wolf Pack football team. Nevada, a member of the Western Athletic Conference, has seven men's and ten women's varsity sports teams.

A land-grant university that opened in 1874, Nevada has an enrollment of 12,532 students, which includes 4,005 men and 4,811 women undergraduates and a total of 3,132 graduate students. Degree programs at the University include seventy-four majors for an undergraduate degree, a Bachelor of General Studies program offered through the Division of Continuing Education, and sixty-four master's, thirty Ph.D., three Ed.D., and the M.D. and M.D./Ph.D. programs.

Location

The University is only four blocks from downtown Reno and serves as both an educational and cultural resource for the community. It is easily accessible from Interstate 80; the main Center Street entrance to campus is located one block north of the freeway.

Reno itself has one of the most attractive locations in the country. Situated in northern Nevada's Truckee Meadows at an elevation of 4,500 feet, it is on the eastern slope of the Sierra Nevada. The climate is cool and dry, and there are four distinct seasons. The area population is 311,000. Reno is only a 45-minute drive from scenic Lake Tahoe with its world-class skiing and limitless summer recreation, a 2-hour drive from Sacramento, and a 4-hour drive from San Francisco. Reno offers cultural events, including symphony, ballet, theater, and opera. Many University facilities, such as the Fleischmann Planetarium and Sheppard Fine Arts Gallery, are open to the public. The University also sponsors concerts, lectures, films, plays, and many other events for the community.

Majors and Degrees

Undergraduate degrees are awarded in the following academic units and majors: College of Agriculture: agricultural and applied economics, agricultural education, animal science, biochemistry, environmental and natural resource science, environmental policy analysis, and pre-veterinary science; College of Arts and Science: anthropology, art, biology, chemistry, English, fine arts, French, general studies, geography, German, history, international affairs, mathematics, music, music (applied), music education, philosophy, physics, political science, psychology, sociology, Spanish, speech communication, theater, and women's studies; College of Business Administration: accounting, computer information systems, economics, finance, gaming management, international business, logistics management, management, and marketing; College of Education: early childhood education (cooperative program), elementary education, elementary/special education, secondary education, and special education; College of Engineering: civil engineering, computer science, electrical engineering, engineering physics, environmental engineering, and mechanical engineering; College of Human and Community Sciences: criminal justice, general studies; health ecology; human development and family studies; human ecology; nursing, nutrition, and social work; Reynolds School of Journalism: journalism; School of Medicine: speech pathology; and Mackay School of Mines: chemical engineering, geological engineering, geology, geophysics, hydrogeology, metallurgical engineering, and mining engineering. Interdisciplinary undergraduate degrees are offered in interior design. The University also offers preparatory programs for law and medicine.

Academic Program

Students must complete a core curriculum of English, mathematics, natural sciences, social sciences, fine arts, Western traditions, capstone courses, and diversity, in addition to completing specific requirements for their degree. The number of credit hours required for graduation is typically 128–134. Credit by examination is available. The University also offers an honors program for exceptional students and an active Army ROTC program. The school calendar includes two 15-week semesters, beginning in August for the fall and January for the spring; an early summer minisession; and two 5-week summer sessions.

Off-Campus Arrangements

The University offers a number of study-abroad programs for credit, including the Basque Country in Spain, Australia, Chile, Costa Rica, Israel, Thailand, and several European sites. The University is also a member of the National Student Exchange Program, which gives undergraduates from Nevada an opportunity to study in other parts of the country. Similarly, the Western Interstate Commission for Higher Education (WICHE) provides grants to Nevada scholars to pursue disciplines not available in Nevada.

Academic Facilities

The library is the largest in Nevada, containing more than 970,000 volumes, 10,825 periodical subscriptions, 3.3 million microforms, and numerous electronic databases. There are a main library facility and four branch libraries that are located near the academic units they serve. The library is a member of the Research Libraries Information Network, a system shared by many other research libraries on the West Coast.

The historic brick buildings and tree-lined walkways remind many students and visitors of New England. The University's architectural integrity is being maintained as the campus expands. Within the past two years, the 255-acre campus has opened a $21-million, 110,000-square-foot College of Education Building and the $3.5-million DeLamare Library, which consolidated the collections of the mines and engineering libraries. The University is also anticipating the opening of its new $7-million Student Services Building by the beginning of the fall 2000 semester.

Costs

The per-credit cost for Nevada residents is $78 for 2000–01. Thus the total estimated cost for a student taking an average 15-credit load for two semesters is $2340. Out-of-state students pay $3490 tuition per semester in addition to per-credit fees. Students from certain California counties, however, are eligible for a reduction in out-of-state tuition under the University's "Good Neighbor" policy. The University of Nevada, Reno also participates in the Western Undergraduate Exchange (WUE) program that allows students from 12 western states (Alaska, Colorado, Hawaii, Idaho, Montana, New Mexico, North Dakota, Oregon, South Dakota, Utah, Washington, and Wyoming) to pay a reduced non-resident tuition. Fall 2000 WUE students pay $115 per credit and do not pay any additional out-of-state tuition. This reduced non-resident tuition is available to all programs of study. More information on these policies can be obtained by contacting the Registrar's Office. Though residence hall and meal plan fees vary, new students should budget about $5100 a year for room and board. Books and supplies are approximately $800 per year. Students should also budget extra money for personal needs and expenses.

Financial Aid

The University administers more than $38 million annually in grants, scholarships, student employment, and loans. To be eligible for financial aid, a student must be admitted into a degree program at the University.

To access all need-based programs, the Free Application for Federal Student Aid (FAFSA) must be filed with the federal processor as soon as possible after January 1 for the upcoming academic year. Early filers with the greatest financial need have the best opportunity for grant and work-study programs. The FAFSA can be filed on the Internet or in a paper format.

Applying for scholarships is a separate process. Incoming students must have a GPA of at least 3.0 to apply. The priority scholarship review date is October 15. The process typically begins in early December for the upcoming academic year. A completed admission application, test scores, and academic transcripts must be submitted by February 1 for the final scholarship deadline.

Faculty

In 1999–2000, the University had a total of 744 full-time and 89 part-time academic faculty members. Students benefit from studying at a school where approximately 94 percent of tenured faculty and 77 percent of full-time faculty hold the highest degrees attainable in their fields. Since the University of Nevada, Reno, is a land-grant institution, faculty members are expected to teach, conduct research, and provide public service to the state. The student-faculty ratio is 21:1.

Student Government

The ASUN government represents students in all University affairs. The ASUN Senate is composed of students from every school and college on campus. Students appointed by the ASUN president serve on University-wide committees and represent the students' viewpoint on all issues. ASUN recognizes more than 100 organizations, ranging from the advertising and international clubs to the peace and human rights group and the wildlife club. It also provides the financial support for concerts, lecture series, and picnics. Students participate in annual major events, such as Homecoming, Mackay Days, and Winter Carnival, sponsored by ASUN and the Greek organizations. ASUN also operates the campus bookstore.

Admission Requirements

To be admitted as a freshman, a potential student must be a graduate of an accredited high school and have an overall GPA of 2.5 or above. Early admission is available for high school seniors who take the ACT or SAT and have the scores sent directly to the admissions office. The state of Nevada also requires that all applicants have a diphtheria-tetanus shot in the last ten years and two doses of measles-mumps-rubella vaccine prior to admittance.

High school students should have taken a minimum of 4 years of English; 3 years of mathematics; 3 years of natural science, including 2 years in laboratory sciences; 3 years of social studies; and ½ year of computer literacy.

International students must have a minimum 3.0 GPA (B average) and a minimum score of 500 on the Test of English as a Foreign Language (TOEFL) or a recommendation from the Intensive English Language Center (IELC). They must also provide financial verification equivalent to tuition, fees, and living expenses for one academic year. For more information, students should contact International Outreach and Application Services/074, University of Nevada, Reno, Reno, Nevada 89557 U.S.A., call 775-784-6318, or visit the University's Web site at http://www.unr.edu/oiss.

Application and Information

Application for admission can be made at any time but should be completed no later than March 1 for the fall semester and November 1 for the spring semester. To apply, individuals must submit a completed application form, a nonrefundable $40 application fee, immunization records, an official transcript sent directly from the high school or each college the student attended, and ACT or SAT scores. Online applications are available at http://www.unr.edu/stsv/adm/howto.html. Students can register for classes by telephone or via the internet beginning in April for summer and fall semesters and November for spring semester.

For a campus tour and other information, students should contact:

Office for Prospective Students/110
University of Nevada, Reno
Reno, Nevada 89557-0002

Telephone: 775-784-4865
E-mail: asknevada@unr.edu
World Wide Web: http://www.unr.edu

UNIVERSITY OF NEW ENGLAND
BIDDEFORD AND PORTLAND, MAINE

The University

The University of New England (UNE) is a small, independent, coeducational university that offers a personalized education. It is composed of the Undergraduate College of Arts and Sciences, the College of Osteopathic Medicine, and the College of Health Professions. The College of Osteopathic Medicine grants the Doctor of Osteopathy degree. At the graduate level, the University confers the Master of Social Work, Master of Science in nurse anesthesia, Master of Science in Education, and Master of Science in physician assistant studies degrees.

The University has chosen as its primary fields of education the biological sciences and health (both mental and physical). Related programs in psychology, education, and business management are also important parts of the University's educational plan. The University of New England's philosophy of education and student life places emphasis on the quality of instruction and the practical application of academic material.

Each program includes the opportunity for learning in a community-based setting. Internships, co-ops, clinicals, and student teaching add up to the practical experience that allows students at UNE to apply the skills learned in the classroom to real job situations.

The University of New England has two campuses. The University Campus is located on the southern coast of Maine, in Biddeford, 90 miles north of Boston and 20 miles south of Portland, Maine's largest city. The campus has a total population of 2,400 students. UNE's Westbrook College Campus is located in Portland, Maine, and has a population of 399 students. As both campuses are geographically placed in areas that afford a high-quality lifestyle, it is only natural that the University of New England consistently engages itself in providing its students with high-quality programming and high-quality education.

The men and women who teach at the University of New England are an experienced group of people whose average age is 40. More than 85 percent have earned the highest degree in their field, and they bring to the University varied backgrounds as teachers and practitioners of their disciplines. They are highly competent, demanding, concerned, accessible, and willing to give individual attention to students. Most important, they have come to the University for many of the same reasons that prompt their students to attend. The match between what the faculty has to offer and what the students need and expect is the key to the rare educational environment at the University of New England. UNE's most recent accreditation report stated that "while many small institutions believe in individual attention, UNE does it."

The University encourages students to become involved in activities, clubs, and sports. Popular interests include scuba diving, skiing, hiking, biking, swimming, and photography. The University of New England offers a wide range of services on both campuses. Special features include a full health clinic, a dental hygiene clinic, a children's center that operates a kindergarten, career counseling, personal counseling, learning support services, and an extensive student leadership development program.

Both campuses offer a variety of cultural and social events. The Campus Center at the University Campus and the Finley Recreation Center on the Westbrook College Campus provide a setting for many recreational and sports activities. The University of New England Athletic Department operates an NCAA Division III varsity athletics program. Varsity sports for men are basketball, cross-country, golf, lacrosse, and soccer; varsity sports for women are basketball, cross-country, lacrosse, soccer, softball, and volleyball. Intramural teams in basketball, floor hockey, softball, skiing, and volleyball are popular.

On the University Campus in Biddeford, Decary Hall houses a cafeteria, classrooms, meeting rooms, and faculty and administrative offices. The University Health Center houses classrooms and the physical therapy clinic and also operates a community health clinic and the University's Sports Medicine Clinic. The Campus Center contains a fitness center, the campus bookstore, an indoor track, a gym, a pool, racquetball courts, a variety of multipurpose rooms, the student union, and administrative offices. The University maintains five dormitories on campus plus a graduate student housing park. Marcil Hall houses a variety of classrooms, faculty offices, and a facility for the physical therapy program. This past year, the University opened the $20-million Harold Alfond Center for Health Sciences.

On the University of New England's Westbrook College Campus, there are three residence halls and the Alexander Hall Student Union, which houses the dining hall, bookstore, the Wing Lounge, and a variety of meeting rooms. The Finley Recreation Center has a full gym and fitness facilities. Ludcke Auditorium, whose main structure was built in 1887, is home to concerts, plays, and a number of workshops and meetings.

Location

The University of New England's Westbrook College Campus is located in a quiet residential area just outside Portland, Maine. Portland is a vibrant city offering a great variety of entertainment options for the students. Portland's International Jetport allows easy access to the city, which is only a 2-hour drive north of Boston, Massachusetts. The University Campus is located on the banks of the Saco River and the shores of the Atlantic Ocean in Biddeford, Maine. This 540-acre campus is between the towns of Old Orchard Beach and Kennebunkport, 20 miles south of Portland, Maine, and 90 miles north of Boston, Massachusetts.

Majors and Degrees

The University Campus in Biddeford grants B.A. and B.S. degrees in the following programs: American studies, aquaculture and aquarium science, athletic training, biochemistry, biological sciences, elementary education, environmental science, environmental studies, exercise science, global studies, health services management, liberal studies (including a prelaw curriculum), marine biology, medical biology (predental, premed, and preveterinary), medical technology, a 3+2 prephysician assistant studies program, psychobiology, psychology and social relations, and sports and fitness management. There are five-year entry-level master's degree programs in occupational therapy and physical therapy. Also offered are certification programs in education. Individualized majors are also available.

The University of New England's Westbrook College Campus grants A.S., B.A., and B.S. degrees in the following majors: dental hygiene (A.S. and B.S.), early childhood education, nursing (A.D.N. and B.S.N.), and organizational leadership.

Academic Program

The University has chosen as its primary field of education the areas of the biological sciences and health care, human services, education, and business management. The core curriculum is so designed that all students are effectively exposed to the liberal arts, natural sciences, social sciences, and business, while concentrating on the development of their chosen career program.

A bachelor's degree is awarded upon successful completion of 120 credit hours and fulfillment of specific program and University requirements.

The University calendar consists of two semesters.

Off-Campus Arrangements

The University is committed to supplementing the traditional learning process with practical applications. All students are encouraged to participate in cooperative education programs, field placements, and practicums. These programs provide valuable learning situations and increase a student's exposure to job-related opportunities. These experiences are required by most majors for graduation. UNE is also a member of the International Student Exchange Program.

Academic Facilities

On the University Campus, Decary Hall houses classrooms, laboratories, and faculty and administrative offices. The Sanford E. Petts Health Center is home to the physical therapy clinic and the campus and community health clinic. The library (which houses 90,000 volumes and 700 periodicals) has been expanded to provide more library and classroom space. Marcil Hall houses classrooms, faculty offices, and the facility for the physical therapy program. The Harold Alfond Center for Health Sciences houses labs and classrooms for the University medical school, undergraduate health and life science programs, and graduate health programs.

On the University's Westbrook College Campus, Ludcke Auditorium is used for a variety of academic programs. Coleman Dental Hygiene Building houses classroom, clinic, and faculty space. The Blewett Science Center, home of UNE nursing programs, consists of science labs and classrooms, and Alumni Hall is a classroom facility. Proctor Hall is also a classroom building and is home to the Proctor Learning and Career Center. Josephine S. Abplanalp Library houses study space and computer terminals, along with an outstanding collection of books and periodicals and the Maine Women Writers Collection. The Children's Center is a day-care center and kindergarten and serves as a laboratory school for the early childhood education program.

Costs

The costs per academic year in 1999–2000 were tuition, $14,990; room and board, $6200; and fees, $510.

Financial Aid

In 1999–2000, approximately 90 percent of all full-time freshmen received some form of financial assistance. The average package was $10,200. Financial award packages include scholarships, grants, loans, and employment.

Faculty

The University has 100 full-time undergraduate faculty members, 85 percent of whom have the terminal degree in their field, and 40 part-time members, a number of whom have doctoral degrees and hold administrative positions.

Student Government

The Student Senate is a vital part of the student life at both campuses of the University of New England. The student government has its own funds, derived from the student fees. The organization covers student services and public relations.

Admission Requirements

The University welcomes applications from students who are seriously pursuing an education of high quality. Candidates can file their admission application after the completion of their junior year of high school. All applicants are considered on an individual basis.

Students applying for admission are expected to submit a completed application, a $40 nonrefundable application fee, transcripts of all academic work (high school and college), two letters of recommendation, and scores on either the ACT or SAT I. Students applying for admission should have completed a curriculum that includes English, mathematics, science, and social sciences. Those considering majors in the life or health sciences should show strength and preparation in mathematics and science. All prospective students are strongly encouraged to visit the campuses of the University of New England for an interview and tour. Interviews are held weekdays from 10 a.m. to 4 p.m. An appointment should be requested by letter or telephone.

Application and Information

Applications for the fall term are accepted until registration closes in September; those for the spring term are accepted through December. Students applying to the physical therapy program must do so by February 15.

For application information, students should contact:

Office of Admissions
University of New England
University Campus
Hills Beach Road
Biddeford, Maine 04005

Telephone: 207-283-0171
Fax: 207-286-3678
E-mail: admissions@mailbox.une.edu
World Wide Web: http://www.une.edu/

UNIVERSITY OF NEW HAVEN
WEST HAVEN, CONNECTICUT

The University

The University of New Haven is a private, coeducational university founded as a branch of Northeastern University in 1920. In 1926 it became an independent school and in 1958 expanded its programs to become a four-year college. The acquisition of the present campus in West Haven in 1960 promoted rapid expansion of facilities, faculty, and student body (the current enrollment includes 1,500 full-time undergraduates). The University offers excellent instruction in a great variety of academic disciplines, yet is small enough to accommodate individual programs and needs. Programs are constantly evolving to meet changing academic and career needs and the requirements of business, industry, and professional fields. The University's small class size fosters close student-faculty relationships.

The University operates a branch in New London. The main campus is located in West Haven on a hillside overlooking Long Island Sound, with a view of downtown New Haven. On the main campus are the main administration and classroom building; the School of Business; the School of Engineering and Applied Science; the School of Hotel, Restaurant, Tourism, and Dietetics Administration; the Graduate School; five residence halls; the library; the bookstore; the student center; the Computer Center; the psychology building; the College of Arts and Sciences; the School of Public Safety and Professional Studies; and the Admissions Building. The Charger Gymnasium and playing fields are located on the North Campus, two blocks from the main campus.

Intercollegiate varsity programs are offered in baseball, basketball, cross-country, football, lacrosse, soccer, softball, tennis, track, and volleyball. An extensive intramural program is also available for both men and women. Of the undergraduate day students, approximately 55 percent live on campus in the five residence halls. Two new coed residence halls house up to 200 freshmen, while three coed apartment complexes house primarily upperclass students. Apartments range from one to three bedrooms and hold 2 to 6 students. Approximately forty University clubs and organizations are open to interested students. Included are student chapters of professional societies, religious organizations, social groups, special interest clubs, student councils, cultural groups, and fraternities and sororities.

The Graduate School offers master's degrees in accounting; business administration; cellular and molecular biology; community psychology; computer and information science; criminal justice; education; electrical engineering; environmental engineering; environmental science; executive business administration; finance and financial services; fire science; forensic science; health-care administration; hospitality and tourism; human nutrition; industrial engineering; industrial hygiene; industrial/organizational psychology; industrial relations; mechanical engineering; occupational safety and health management; operations research; public administration; and taxation. Dual degrees are offered in business administration and industrial engineering and in business administration and public administration.

Location

West Haven is contiguous to New Haven. Within the city of New Haven are theaters, a coliseum that attracts star performers from the entertainment and sports worlds, a deepwater harbor and nearby beaches, fine restaurants, museums, and galleries. Numerous social and cultural programs are presented by the six colleges and universities in the area. New Haven is served by two airlines and major railroads, and its location at the junction of two interstate highways places the University of New Haven within easy driving distance of New York, Boston, Cape Cod, and the skiing areas of central and northern New England.

Majors and Degrees

The College of Arts and Sciences offers the Bachelor of Arts degree in art, chemistry, communication, economics, English, graphic design, history, interior design, liberal studies, mathematics, music and sound recording, music industry, political science, and psychology; the Bachelor of Science degree in applied mathematics, biology, biomedical computing, dental hygiene, environmental science, marine biology, medical technology, and music and sound recording; and the Associate of Science degree in biology, dental hygiene, general studies, graphic design, interior design, and journalism. The School of Business offers the Bachelor of Science degree in accounting, business administration, business economics, communication, finance, international business, management of sports industries, and marketing and the Associate of Science degree in business administration and communication. The School of Hotel, Restaurant, Tourism, and Dietetics Administration offers the Bachelor of Science in dietetics and hotel and restaurant management with a concentration in tourism administration as an option. An Associate of Science degree is available in hotel and restaurant management. The School of Engineering and Applied Science offers the Bachelor of Science degree in chemical engineering, chemistry, civil engineering, computer science, electrical engineering, general engineering, industrial engineering, and mechanical engineering and the Associate of Science degree in chemistry, civil engineering, computer science, electrical engineering, industrial engineering, and mechanical engineering. The School of Public Safety and Professional Studies offers the Bachelor of Science degree in air transportation management, arson investigation, criminal justice, fire protection engineering, fire science administration, fire science technology, forensic science, occupational safety and health administration, and occupational safety and health technology and the Associate of Science degree in aviation science, corrections, fire and occupational safety, law enforcement administration, and occupational safety and health.

Academic Program

As a suburban institution, the University of New Haven offers a broad range of programs in both liberal arts and professional areas. Professionalism is emphasized, and there are diverse opportunities for career-oriented internships, cooperative education, independent study, and industrial projects. Certain types of professional experience are required in a number of degree programs. The Center for Learning Resources offers a tutoring service that is open to all students. All tutoring is free, and students are accommodated by appointment or on a walk-in basis.

The undergraduate division operates on a 4-1-4 calendar. Credit is given for successful scores on the CLEP and Advanced Placement examinations. A University honors program provides outstanding study opportunities in most undergraduate disciplines. The residence requirement for all degrees is 30 credit hours.

The University of New Haven believes that all students studying for a bachelor's degree should develop a common set of skills; the University's goal is to prepare all graduates for the complex lives they will lead in a changing world. This can best be done through the University core curriculum, which consists of a minimum of eleven courses totaling 34 credits.

An available option at the University is cooperative education, an academic program that offers students the opportunity to combine career-oriented, paid, full-time work with their education. Students are also eligible to enroll in Air Force Reserve Officer Training Corps courses through a cooperative agreement with the University of Connecticut.

Academic Facilities

The Marvin K. Peterson Library contains more than 370,000 books, periodical volumes (including 1,320 current periodical titles), and government documents. It also includes more than 478,000 microforms of books, periodical volumes, and government documents. The University selects one third of available government publications. A large amount of material is stored and/or retrieved electronically via CD-ROM and on-line access. Modern research facilities include ten microreading stations and four microfilm reader-printers. Communication majors participate in sound workshops and study film production and radio broadcasting in well-equipped radio/television laboratories and studios. The School of Engineering and Applied Science is accredited by the Accreditation Board for Engineering and Technology and has the modern laboratories and equipment to support that accreditation. The College of Arts and Sciences has science laboratories, art studios, music rooms, a state-of-the-art sound recording studio, and laboratories for foreign language study, psychology, and reading. There are more than 140 computer terminals available to students on campus.

Costs

Tuition for the 2000–01 academic year, including the activity and health fees, is $15,520; room and board are $6960.

Financial Aid

The University of New Haven offers a comprehensive financial aid program that includes University resources as well as state, federal, and private aid programs. Approximately 70 percent of full-time undergraduate students receive some form of assistance. University students receive federal aid through the Federal Pell Grant, Federal Supplemental Educational Opportunity Grant, Federal Work-Study, Federal Perkins Loan, Federal Stafford Student Loan, and Federal PLUS loan programs. In addition to federal aid programs, the University administers programs sponsored by the state of Connecticut for Connecticut residents attending the University. Some students also qualify for financial aid from other states and from private companies, organizations, and foundations.

Faculty

It is a long-standing University policy that the faculty members teach a mix of undergraduate and graduate courses in order to preserve academic quality at all levels. There is no designated graduate faculty. Faculty members are selected and promoted primarily on the basis of teaching effectiveness, professional qualifications and performance, and contributions to the academic community. All classes are taught by faculty members; there are no teaching assistants. A few faculty members have administrative positions, but those who do continue to teach. There are 159 full-time and 432 part-time faculty members, making the student-faculty ratio 11:1. Eighty-eight percent of the faculty hold terminal degrees in their disciplines.

Student Government

The Day Student Government and the Evening Student Council supervise annual expenditures by undergraduate clubs and organizations, direct liaison committees and student courts, support student publications and the student-operated FM radio station, and schedule cultural and social events. Students are elected annually to the University's Board of Governors.

Admission Requirements

To be eligible for admission, the candidate must be a high school graduate or present evidence of equivalent preparation. Scores from the SAT I or the ACT are required. The admission decision is based on the student's overall high school record, rank in class, results of the SAT I or ACT, motivation, and extracurricular activities.

The prospective student is strongly encouraged to visit the campus for a personal interview and tour. Outstanding athletes with satisfactory academic qualifications are referred to members of the coaching staff for interviews. The admission staff conducts annual visits to high schools and two-year colleges on the East Coast. Out-of-state residents are considered for admission on the same basis as state residents.

Application and Information

To apply to the University, a student must submit the completed application form, a nonrefundable $25 fee, official records of all academic work completed, and results of the SAT I or ACT. International students are required to demonstrate proficiency in English as well as provide documentation of financial support. The University of New Haven does not discriminate on the basis of age, color, sex, religion, race, creed, national origin, or disability in admission or treatment of students, in administration or distribution of financial aid, or in recruitment or treatment of employees. The University is authorized under federal law to enroll nonimmigrant alien students who meet the University's academic and English proficiency standards. The admissions office employs a rolling admissions system.

For more information, students should contact:

Dean of Admissions
University of New Haven
300 Orange Avenue
West Haven, Connecticut 06516
Telephone: 203-932-7319
        800-DIAL-UNH (toll-free)
E-mail: adminfo@charger.newhaven.edu
World Wide Web: http://www.newhaven.edu

UNIVERSITY OF NEW ORLEANS
NEW ORLEANS, LOUISIANA

The University

The University of New Orleans (UNO) is part of the rich cultural tapestry of its hometown, which is one of the most extraordinary cities in the world. Established in 1956 to bring publicly supported higher education to the New Orleans area, UNO is fully accredited by the Commission on Colleges of the Southern Association of Colleges and Schools. With an enrollment of 16,000 (12,000 undergraduates and 4,000 graduate students), UNO offers both undergraduate and graduate degrees through the doctoral level. UNO derives its strength from its urban setting and strives to enhance the economic, social, and cultural amenities of New Orleans through its numerous research projects, outreach programs, and special cooperative agreements. The University of New Orleans attracts students from forty-eight states (10.6 percent) and eighty-one countries, with a majority of the students Louisiana residents (89.4 percent). The diverse student population (28 percent of students are members of ethnic minorities) provides an excellent opportunity for personal growth and understanding.

For students who are interested in on-campus housing, UNO offers three unique styles: Bienville Hall Dormitory, a coeducational residential hall for single students; Lafitte Village Apartments, a married student facility; and Privateer Place Apartments, UNO's newest addition to on-campus housing, which overlooks beautiful Lake Pontchartrain and includes a swimming pool and Jacuzzi. Campus dining facilities are conveniently located near all on-campus housing facilities and heavily populated student areas, with various hours of operation. Other student services include six on-campus computer labs that provide free Internet access, a learning resource center that offers additional tutoring services, student counseling services, an on-campus medical office and pharmacy, student legal counseling, and religious centers.

UNO has more than 100 active student organizations on campus, including academic, professional, Greek, social, political, and religious organizations. The newest addition to UNO's list of student organizations is the University pep band, the UNO Blue Zoo, which performs at all UNO home basketball games and other University-related events. The *Driftwood*, UNO's student newspaper, is published weekly, and the *Ellipsis*, a literary magazine, is published annually.

As a Division I member of the National Collegiate Athletic Association (NCAA), UNO fields men's teams in basketball, baseball, cross-country, golf, tennis, and track and field (indoor and outdoor) and women's teams in basketball, volleyball, cross-country, golf, tennis, and track and field (indoor and outdoor). UNO students can also participate in several recreational and intramural sports. Students entering the University in fall 2001 can expect to have access to a new 85,000-square-foot Wellness Center, which will feature a 12,000-square-foot cardiovascular, circuit, and free weight training room; an indoor jogging track; racquetball courts; outdoor sundeck; juice bar; and social lounge. In addition, UNO will increase the number of apartment units available on campus by constructing an addition to Privateer Place, the on-campus apartment complex.

Location

The University of New Orleans's 195-acre main campus is set in one of the most beautiful residential areas on the south shore of Lake Pontchartrain, only minutes from the fun and excitement of downtown New Orleans and the French Quarter. New Orleans is a cosmopolitan city, known for its great Southern hospitality and its unique tourist attractions. Renowned for its Creole and Cajun cuisine, Mardi Gras, and jazz music festivals, New Orleans culture offers a unique environment for students to grow, both socially and academically. Whether exploring the artsy Warehouse District or strolling down stately St. Charles Avenue, New Orleans has something for everyone, and the University of New Orleans is a part of it all.

Many of UNO's hotel, restaurant, and tourism administration majors find internships in the city's best hotels and restaurants. Naval architecture students have access to the nation's largest undergraduate program in naval architecture and marine engineering as well as to the UNO–Avondale Maritime Center. As New Orleans continues to attract computer technology–based businesses to what has been called "the Silicon Bayou," the UNO Research and Technology Park continues to expand, producing more than 8,000 new jobs. Computer science majors are able to network with potential employers in one of the fastest-growing computer technology markets in the country.

Majors and Degrees

Bachelor of Science degrees are offered in accounting; biological sciences; chemistry; civil and environmental engineering; computer science; economics; electrical engineering; finance; general business administration; general science; geology; geophysics; hotel, restaurant, and tourism administration; management; marketing; mathematics; mathematics education; mechanical engineering; naval architecture and marine engineering; physics; preprofessional programs; prenursing; pre-occupational therapy studies; pre-pharmacy; pre–physical therapy studies; pre–rehabilitation counseling; pre–respiratory therapy studies; pre–veterinary medicine; psychology; and science education.

Bachelor of Arts degrees are offered in anthropology; drama and communications, with drama options including acting, directing, and design and communications options including film, message design, radio, television, and video; economics; elementary education; English; English education; fine arts–history; fine arts–studio; foreign language education; French; geography; history; human performance and health promotion education; mathematics education; music (with options including instrumental, jazz studies, theory and composition, and vocal); music education; philosophy; political science; secondary education; social science education; sociology; and Spanish.

A four-year Bachelor of General Studies degree program is available for students who wish to design individual curricula. Credit programs in paralegal studies and medical coding are also offered.

Additional interdisciplinary minors are offered in interdisciplinary studies in hypermedia, Latin American studies, medical coding, print journalism, and women's studies.

Academic Program

All baccalaureate degree programs require a minimum of 128 semester hours with a minimum grade point average of 2.0 (C) in all work attempted in the college major. Also, all students must successfully complete an approved course demonstrating computer literacy. Other course requirements vary according to program. Programs leading to degrees with honors are offered in most academic majors. Credit for selected courses may be earned either through advanced-standing exams administered by the academic departments or through the College Board's Advanced Placement and College-Level Examination Program tests. College credit may also be gained for certain armed services and other nonacademic training. The academic year is composed of sixteen-week fall and spring semesters and three summer sessions.

Off-Campus Arrangements

The University of New Orleans Metropolitan College coordinates international study programs in Austria, Costa Rica, the Czech Republic, Ecuador, France, Honduras, and Italy. UNO's partnership with the University of Innsbruck, Austria, affords students an opportunity to participate in the largest international summer school of any American university in Europe. UNO also offers college-credit exchange programs in Brazil and Canada. Students may also attend another school within the continental United States via the National Student Exchange (NSE) for one semester or one year.

UNO also offers several off-campus facilities throughout the metropolitan New Orleans area, demonstrating UNO's commitment to community outreach. Off-campus locations offer both credit and noncredit courses, with hours varying from sunrise to evening and weekend classes.

Academic Facilities

The Earl K. Long Library's 1.5-million-volume collection includes approximately 12,000 journals, of which 3,800 are on current subscription. Microform holdings include microfilm, microcard, and microfiche formats; microtext readers and reader-printers are also available. Other facilities include individual study carrels, a music listening room, computer terminals connected to the Computer Research Center, a Kurzweil reader for the visually impaired, and photocopy services.

The Office of Educational Support Services includes a media resources center, which provides important media aids for the instructional staff in classroom presentations, and Television Resources, which coordinates a closed-circuit cable system and TV production studio. WWNO, the first public radio station in Louisiana, is located on the UNO campus.

The University's computer needs are served by a DEC VAX 7620 computer and associated peripheral equipment that provide the largest digital site in Louisiana. The campuswide LAN is one of the most comprehensive institution-based networks in the United States, with more than 700 access ports from all major buildings on campus.

The UNO Lee Circle Centre for the Arts includes the Ogden Museum, which houses the largest collection of Southern art in the world. The center also houses the National D-Day Museum, which includes the world's largest collection of World War II color film.

The 70,000-square-foot UNO Studio Center, located 20 minutes from the main campus, houses a professional-quality sound stage, including a 10,000-square-foot studio for University film projects. The UNO Studio Center is also available for professional film projects.

Costs

In 2000–01, combined undergraduate fees for full-time students for the fall and spring semesters are $2362 for Louisiana residents and $9406 for nonresidents; summer session fees for full-time students are $690 for Louisiana residents and $1240 for nonresidents. Residence hall and board fees total $3150 (double occupancy) for the fall and spring semesters. Costs of books and supplies total $800 per year. Additional charges include a $20 application fee, a $10 registration fee, field service and laboratory fees (usually $10 to $35) for some courses, a $50 car registration fee, a $30 late application fee, a $30 late registration fee, and a $5 per-credit-hour (maximum $75) technology fee. All fees are subject to change; they can be confirmed by calling the Office of Admissions.

Financial Aid

The Office of Student Financial Aid develops financial aid packages to assist students with their educational expenses. This package is usually a combination of grants, loans, student employment, and/or scholarships, which, along with family contribution, help to finance the student's education. To be eligible for most federal financial aid programs, students must enroll for at least 6 credit hours (half-time) in an eligible program (one that leads to a degree or certificate). Approximately 95 percent of all freshmen judged to have need were offered aid. The priority date for the financial aid application is May 1.

The University of New Orleans offers several academic scholarships. The deadline for filing an UNO scholarship application is January 15.

The University of New Orleans also offers scholarships in jazz studies, classical music, fine arts, drama and communications, and creative writing. These scholarships require either an audition or the submission of a portfolio or manuscript along with the scholarship application.

Faculty

UNO has 604 full-time and 309 part-time faculty members, most of whom participate in both graduate and undergraduate instruction and research activity. Graduate students serve as teaching assistants in laboratory courses under the close supervision of the faculty. Approximately 74 percent of the faculty hold doctorates, and the rest have at least a master's degree. Most full-time faculty members devote themselves exclusively to University-related pursuits and are integrally involved in student affairs through counseling, teaching, research, and social activities. The student-faculty ratio is 18:1.

Student Government

Every student enrolled at UNO is a member of the Student Government (SG).

Admission Requirements

Students seeking admission to the University of New Orleans should submit their application as early as possible in their senior year. Applicants must submit an official copy of their high school transcript indicating satisfactory completion of at least 17½ academic units. Of these units, 4 must be in English, 3 in mathematics, 3 in natural science (including biology I), 3 in social sciences (including American history), 2 in the same foreign language, ½ in computer science or literacy, and 2 additional units from the areas listed above or from advanced performing arts or fine arts/music. In addition, students must submit official copies of either their ACT or SAT I scores along with their application for admission.

Transfer students are required to submit an application and an official transcript from each institution previously attended. Transfer students must have a cumulative 2.0 GPA to be considered for admission. Students with fewer than 24 credit hours of college-level work must satisfy freshman requirements as well as transfer requirements.

Application and Information

The University of New Orleans has a rolling admissions policy, and students can expect to be notified about their application status two weeks after the Office of Admissions receives all required information. The application fee is $20. Priority deadlines for application are as follows: July 1 for the fall semester, November 15 for the spring semester, and May 1 for the summer semester. Deadlines for international students are June 1, October 1, and March 1, respectively.

Students should direct inquiries and application materials to:
    Office of Admissions
    University of New Orleans
    Lakefront 103 Administration Building
    New Orleans, Louisiana 70148
    Telephone: 504-280-6595
               800-256-5-UNO (toll-free)
    Fax: 504-280-5522
    E-mail: admissions@uno.edu
    World Wide Web: http://www.uno.edu

THE UNIVERSITY OF NORTH CAROLINA AT PEMBROKE
PEMBROKE, NORTH CAROLINA

The University

The University of North Carolina at Pembroke (UNCP), a constituent institution of the University of North Carolina, serves as a comprehensive university committed to academic excellence in a balanced program of teaching, research, and service. Combining the opportunities available at a large university with the personal attention characteristic of a small college, the University provides an intellectually challenging environment created by a faculty that is dedicated to effective teaching, to interactions with students, and to scholarship. Graduates are academically and personally prepared for rewarding careers, postgraduate education, and community leadership. UNCP was recently ranked number one in "overall quality of instruction" among the University of North Carolina schools, according to student surveys.

UNC Pembroke is a coeducational institution that enrolls approximately 3,100 students in undergraduate and graduate programs. Average class size is 25–30, and the student-faculty ratio is 16:1. Freshmen are guaranteed housing in one of the six residence halls on campus. UNC Pembroke offers more than sixty clubs and organizations, including fraternities and sororities, professional honor societies, and ethnic and religious groups. UNCP offers special programs, such as the North Carolina Teaching Fellows, Honors College, and Health Careers Programs, as well as various research and internship opportunities. UNCP students have the unique opportunity to work for the University's public television facility, WNCP-TV. Among the many programs broadcast to more than 660,000 homes is Action News 31, the only live, student-produced television news program in the state and one of only three in the nation. UNC Pembroke also has strong student ensembles in the performing and dramatic arts.

UNCP is a member of the Peach Belt Athletic Conference of the National Collegiate Athletic Association Division II and fields teams in men's and women's basketball, cross-country, and track; men's baseball, golf, soccer, and wrestling; and women's softball, tennis, and volleyball. The University also offers a full range of intramural sports programs.

Founded in 1887 to educate Native Americans, the University now serves a student body reflective of the rich cultural diversity of American society. *U.S. News & World Report* ranks UNCP second in campus diversity among Southern regional universities. As it stimulates interaction within and among its cultural groups, the University enables students to become informed, principled, and tolerant citizens with a global perspective. Drawing strength from its heritage, UNCP continues to expand its leadership role in enriching the intellectual, economic, social, and cultural life of the region, the state, and the nation.

Location

UNCP is located in the sandhills of North Carolina, an area famous for its temperate climate, natural scenic beauty, golf resorts, and Southern hospitality, in the historic town of Pembroke. Easily accessible from Interstate 95 and U.S. 74, North and South Carolina beaches are within a 1½-hour drive, and campus is within a 2-hour drive of the cities of the Research Triangle Park, Fayetteville, and Charlotte.

Majors and Degrees

UNC Pembroke offers a broad range of degrees and nationally accredited professional programs the bachelor's and master's levels. The University is organized into the College of Arts and Sciences, School of Mass Communications and Business, School of Education, and School of Graduate Studies. UNCP confers five undergraduate degrees: the Bachelor of Arts, Bachelor of Music, Bachelor of Science, Bachelor of Science in Nursing, and Bachelor of Social Work. Majors, minors, and/or concentrations are offered in African-American studies; American Indian studies; art (art education, arts management, studio art); biology (biology education, biomedical emphasis, botany, medical technology, molecular biology, zoology); business administration (accounting, applied science, economics, management); chemistry (physical science, science education); communicative arts (English, English education, theater arts); computer science; education (birth–kindergarten, elementary, middle grades, special education–learning disabilities and mental retardation); health, physical education, and recreation (community health education, health and physical education, physical education, recreational management/administration); history (American studies, social studies education); mass communications (broadcasting, journalism, public relations); mathematics (mathematics education, mathematics–computer science); music (elective studies in business/music industry option, music education); nursing (for registered nurses); philosophy and religion; political science (gerontology, international studies, prelaw, public policy and administration); psychology; social work and criminal justice; and sociology.

Preprofessional programs are offered in dentistry, law, medicine, optometry, pharmacy, public health, and veterinary medicine. A candidate for a degree in medical technology completes a three-year program at UNC Pembroke and an additional year at one of several cooperating hospitals. The student receives a Bachelor of Science in either biology or chemistry upon completion of the year's hospital work.

Academic Program

UNC Pembroke seeks to produce graduates with broad vision, who are sensitive to values, who recognize the complexity of social problems, and who will be contributing citizens with an international perspective and an appreciation for the achievements of diverse civilizations. To earn a degree, students must earn at least 120–128 semester hours of credit in a program of study. In addition to meeting all major program requirements, students seeking baccalaureate degrees are required to complete a 44-hour General Education program, which provides students with an understanding of the fundamental principles and contributions of a variety of disciplines. Moreover, the program fosters the ability to analyze and weigh evidence, exercise quantitative and scientific skills, make informed decisions, write and speak clearly, and think critically and creatively.

Academic Facilities

The Sampson-Livermore Library houses more than 200,000 books, 1,300 periodicals, and local historical materials and serves as the depository for selected state and federal documents. The School of Education's Education Center maintains a curriculum laboratory and test review resource center. The Department of English, Theatre, and Languages maintains a library of books, journals, and media resources for English education and foreign languages. Moreover, the Department of Music's library is home to various recordings and music scores by regional artists.

The Native American Resource Center offers a rich collection of authentic American Indian artifacts, handicrafts, and art as well as books, cassettes, record albums, and filmstrips about Native Americans, with emphasis on the Lumbee Indians of Robeson County. The center's exhibits include prehistoric tools and weapons, nineteenth-century household and farm equipment, and contemporary Indian art. Artifacts from Indian cultures of Canada and Central and South America as well as from other sections of the United States are also on display.

Each academic building houses at least one microcomputer laboratory. Additional computers are located in the Computer Center, the D. F. Lowry Building, and the Sampson-Livermore Library. The University's computer network is connected to LINC NET, a statewide data network, and the Internet, which provides worldwide computer access.

Costs

The 2000–01 estimated cost, including tuition, for in-state students residing on campus is $5300; out-of-state students residing on campus pay $13,200. In-state students not living on campus pay $1790, while out-of-state students not living on campus pay $9200. Costs are subject to change by the state legislature.

Financial Aid

UNC Pembroke makes every effort to assist students in securing the financial means necessary to attend the University. Aid is available to eligible students through scholarships, state and federal grants, loans, and college work-study. To apply for financial aid, students must complete the Free Application for Federal Student Aid (FAFSA), which is available from high school guidance offices. A variety of scholarships are available to students who demonstrate superior academic ability. Scholarships are awarded on the basis of personal and academic merit; some, however, are also based on financial need. The deadline for scholarship applications is December 1 if a student is applying for the spring and March 1 for the fall. Students applying for financial aid should complete the FAFSA by March 15.

Faculty

UNC Pembroke's teaching faculty numbers 154 full-time members, 80 percent of whom have doctoral or terminal degrees. The University has long valued personal attention within the classroom. With that in mind, all classes are taught by faculty members, not graduate assistants.

Student Government

The Student Government Association represents and safeguards the interests of the student body. Once a student enrolls at UNCP, he or she becomes a member of the SGA. Officers and class representatives are elected by the student body each spring. The Student Senate is the legislative branch and policymaking body of the SGA. The senate recommends policies and regulations necessary for the general welfare of the student body.

Admission Requirements

Applicants for freshman admission must provide evidence (high school transcript) of graduation from high school, satisfactory class rank and GPA, and scores from either the SAT I or the ACT. Students who graduated from high school in 1990 and after must present the following courses: 4 course units in English (the courses should emphasize grammar, composition, and literature); 3 course units in mathematics, including algebra I, algebra II, and geometry or a higher-level mathematics course for which algebra II is a prerequisite; 3 course units in science, including a life or biological science, a physical science, and a laboratory science; and 2 course units in social studies, including 1 unit in United States history. It is also recommended that students include two courses in one foreign language and that mathematics and a foreign language be taken in the senior year. If more than 24 transferable semester credit hours are presented, transfer students are evaluated for admission based on college work. Moreover, students must have at least a C average. For those students who have fewer than 24 semester credit hours, admissions decisions may be based on freshman criteria.

Application and Information

Applications should be submitted by December 1 for the spring semester and by July 15 for the fall semester. Students are encouraged to apply earlier if they wish to be considered for financial aid and scholarships. In addition, applications are accepted for both summer sessions. The deadlines are May 15 for summer session I and June 15 for summer session II. Applications and additional information are available from:

Director of Admissions
The University of North Carolina at Pembroke
One University Drive
P.O. Box 1510
Pembroke, North Carolina 28372-1510
Telephone: 910-521-6262
           800-949-UNCP (toll-free)
Fax: 910-521-6497
E-mail: admissions@papa.uncp.edu
World Wide Web: http://www.uncp.edu

UNIVERSITY OF NOTRE DAME
NOTRE DAME, INDIANA

The University

The University of Notre Dame, founded in 1842 by Rev. Edward F. Sorin, a priest of the Congregation of Holy Cross, is an independent, national Catholic university located adjacent to the city of South Bend, Indiana.

Admission to the University is highly competitive, with five applicants for each freshman class position. The number of students on campus who are members of minority groups has doubled in the past 10 years, and women, first admitted to undergraduate studies at Notre Dame in 1972, now account for 47 percent of undergraduate and overall enrollment.

The University is organized into four undergraduate colleges (the Colleges of Arts and Letters, Science, Engineering, and Business), the School of Architecture, the Law School, the Graduate School, five major research institutes, several centers and special programs, and the University library system. Fall 1999 enrollment was 10,654 students.

One indicator of the quality of Notre Dame's undergraduate programs is the success of its students in postbaccalaureate studies. The medical school acceptance rate of the University's preprofessional studies (premedicine) graduates is more than 70 percent, twice the national average. Notre Dame ranks eighteenth among private universities (first among Catholic institutions) in the number of doctorates earned by its undergraduate alumni—a record compiled over some 70 years.

The Graduate School, established in 1918, encompasses thirty-eight master's and twenty-four doctoral degree programs in and among twenty-seven University departments and institutes. While its graduate student body is small in comparison to many research institutions, Notre Dame nonetheless ranks among the nation's top fifty universities in the number of doctorates awarded annually.

The source of the University's academic strength is its faculty, which, since 1982, has seen the addition of more than 100 new members and the establishment of over sixty new endowed professorships.

At Notre Dame, education always has been linked to values, among them living in a community and volunteering in community service. Residence hall life (more than four out of five undergraduates live on campus) is both the hallmark of the Notre Dame experience and the wellspring of the University's rich tradition. A newer tradition, the University's Center for Social Concerns, serves as a catalyst for student volunteerism. Almost 80 percent of Notre Dame students engage in some form of voluntary community service during their years at the University, and at least 10 percent devote a year or more after graduation to serving the less fortunate in the U.S. and around the world.

Fighting Irish athletics are an important aspect of life at Notre Dame. Among college football teams, Notre Dame has compiled the highest winning percentage and the most national championships and Heisman Trophy winners. In recent years, Notre Dame also has developed one of the strongest overall athletic programs in the nation, with perennially powerful teams in women's basketball, cross-country, fencing, soccer, softball, swimming, tennis, and volleyball and men's baseball, cross-country, fencing, hockey, lacrosse, and tennis. In addition, Notre Dame ranks among the top three universities in the overall graduation rate of its student athletes.

Notre Dame consists of 1,250 tree-lined acres containing two lakes and 155 buildings (with an insured replacement value of more than $1.4 billion); the University is equally renowned for the quality of its physical plant and the beauty of its campus. Sacred Heart Basilica; the fourteen-story Hesburgh Library, with a 132-foot-high mural depicting Christ the Teacher; and the University's 120-year-old Main Building, with its famed Golden Dome, are among the most widely known university landmarks in the world.

Location

Centrally situated in the middle of the Midwest, Notre Dame is adjacent to the city of South Bend, Indiana, the center of a metropolitan area with a population of approximately 105,000. Downtown Chicago and its multiple cultural and entertainment options are just 90 miles by car or commuter railroad; the beautiful beaches of Lake Michigan are 30 miles to the west, and Indianapolis is 130 miles to the south. Other major Midwestern cities are within easy driving distance, and South Bend Regional Airport offers a variety of convenient airline options.

In addition to the many cultural, athletic, and recreational opportunities available at Notre Dame, the South Bend area includes the newly renovated Morris Performing Arts Center, the South Bend Regional Museum of Art, the Northern Indiana Historical Society Museum, the East Race Waterway, a minor-league professional baseball franchise, the College Football Hall of Fame, more than a dozen golf courses, and forty-five movie screens.

Majors and Degrees

The College of Arts and Letters offers Bachelor of Fine Arts degrees in art, art history, and design and Bachelor of Arts degrees in American studies; anthropology; classics (Greek and Latin); East Asian languages and literatures; economics; English; film, television, and theater; German and Russian languages and literatures; government and international studies; history; mathematics; medieval studies; music; philosophy; program of liberal studies; psychology; romance languages and literatures (French, Italian, and Spanish); sociology; and theology. The college also offers a variety of concentrations and special programs.

The College of Business offers Bachelor of Business degrees in accountancy, finance, management, management information systems, and marketing.

The College of Engineering offers Bachelor of Science degrees in aerospace and mechanical engineering, chemical engineering, civil engineering, computer engineering, computer science, electrical engineering, environmental geosciences, geological sciences, and mechanical engineering.

The College of Science offers Bachelor of Science degrees in biochemistry, biological sciences, chemistry, environmental sciences, mathematics, physics, preprofessional studies (premedicine), science-business, science-computing, and science-education.

The School of Architecture offers a five-year program of study that leads to the bachelor's degree and includes a required third year in Rome.

Academic Program

Graduate studies and research are vital and significant at Notre Dame, but it is the undergraduate teaching program for which the University is best known and most respected. The undergraduate program includes the four colleges, the School of Architecture, and the First Year of Studies. An innovative program in which all first-year students are enrolled, the First Year of Studies allows students to sample a wide variety of academic disciplines and provides them with a firm foundation for advancing into their major area of study. The program is one of the reasons that 93 percent of Notre Dame students earn their degree, a graduation rate bettered only by Harvard, Yale, Princeton, and Dartmouth.

The academic year is divided into two semesters, with the fall term beginning in late August and the spring term ending the first week in May. Students generally take five courses per semester.

Off-Campus Arrangements

Notre Dame has the largest proportion of students studying abroad of any major university in the U.S., according to a survey in the *Chronicle of Higher Education*. The far-flung international studies programs include semester and year-long opportunities in Jerusalem; London; Dublin; Rome; Cairo; Athens; the Caribbean; Mexico City; Angiers, France; Fremantle, Australia; Monterrey, Mexico; Nagoya, Japan; Salzburg and Innsbruck, Austria; Toledo, Spain; and Santiago, Chile. The University also offers a semester of classes and internships in Washington, D.C.

Academic Facilities

Notre Dame's teaching and research facilities are at once traditional and technologically advanced. DeBartolo Hall, an eighty-four-classroom learning center constructed in 1992 for all of the colleges, and the College of Business Administration complex, completed in 1995, offer the latest in computer and audiovisual teaching technology. A new environmental sciences center opened in 1998, and construction will begin soon on a $60-million undergraduate teaching center for the College of Science. One of the largest academic bookstores in higher education opened on campus in 1999, and a $35-million performing arts center is under construction. Hesburgh Library and nine other libraries on campus contain more than 2.5 million volumes. The University's residence hall computer network and 600 stations in eleven public clusters make Notre Dame one of the 100 Most Wired Colleges in the nation, according to *Yahoo! Internet Life* magazine.

Costs

Tuition and fees for the 2000–01 academic year are $23,860. Room, board, and telephone total $6040. Other expenses, including books, supplies, and transportation, are variable, depending on academic program, travel, and personal expenses.

Financial Aid

Notre Dame is committed to meeting a student's demonstrated financial need through a broad array of financial aid programs, including scholarships, grants, loans, and work. More than $27 million in institutional aid was administered for the 1999-2000 academic year. In addition, programs are available to students who do not demonstrate financial need, including financing options such as a monthly payment plan and student employment as well as federal and private student and parent loan programs. Approximately 75 percent of undergraduates receive aid from one or more financial aid programs. The Free Application for Federal Student Aid and the College Scholarship Service PROFILE together serve as the official applications for need-based financial assistance. Priority consideration is given to those students who complete the application process by February 15. The University subscribes to a need-blind admission policy.

Faculty

Notre Dame's teaching and research faculty numbers 706 members, with 336 additional regular faculty members in other categories, such as administrators, professional specialists, library staff members, and research fellows. In addition, there are 338 adjunct faculty members. All faculty members, including senior and chaired professors, teach undergraduate courses, and 97 percent hold a doctoral or terminal degree in their field. The student-faculty ratio is 12:1.

Student Government

The Student Union includes the student body president and vice president and their Cabinet, a Student Senate, and the Hall President's Council. The Campus Life Council, created by the University's Board of Trustees, is composed of students, faculty members, and administrators who recommend policy to the administration. There is also student representation on the Academic Council, the principal academic policy body of the University.

Students are assured freedom of inquiry, freedom of expression, and freedom of action within the regulations established by the University. In turn, the University community expects all students to be responsible in their social conduct so as to reflect favorably upon themselves and the institution.

Admission Requirements

Admission to the University of Notre Dame is highly competitive, and each application is evaluated on the following criteria: the high school record and rigor of curriculum, standardized testing (SAT I or ACT), extracurricular accomplishment and personal qualities, an essay and personal statement, and a teacher's evaluation. For the class of 2004, the middle 50 percent of admitted students ranked in the top 1 to 5 percent of their high school class and had SAT I combined scores of 1300 to 1430 and ACT composite scores of 29 to 32.

The University requires at least 16 units of full-credit high school work in solid academic subjects: English, mathematics, science, foreign language, and history/social science. Precalculus or calculus and chemistry and physics are required of all students who intend to concentrate in architecture, engineering, or science.

Those who wish to apply as transfer students must have at least one year at an accredited college, 27 semester hours of transferable credit, and a cumulative B (3.0) average.

Application and Information

First-year students may apply either early action or regular action. Early action candidates must submit applications by November 1, and decisions are mailed by mid-December. Regular action applicants must apply by January 9, and decisions are mailed by April 1. For transfer students, the application deadline is April 15 for fall admission. Applications are available through the Office of Undergraduate Admissions or on line via the University's Web site.

For additional information, students should contact:
University of Notre Dame
Office of Undergraduate Admissions
Main Building
Notre Dame, Indiana 46556
Telephone: 219-631-7505
Fax: 219-631-8865
E-mail: admissio.1@nd.edu
World Wide Web: http://www.nd.edu

UNIVERSITY OF OREGON
EUGENE, OREGON

The University

The University of Oregon (UO), a nationally and internationally recognized research university committed to liberal arts and sciences education and career preparation, is known as a rising star in the academic world. The UO is among the smallest public universities in the Association of American Universities—one of the most prestigious associations of colleges and universities in the world. In 1997, the UO was distinguished by *Yahoo! Internet Life* magazine and CAUSE as one of the nation's best-networked public universities and received one of only ten National Science Foundation Recognition Awards for the Integration of Research and Education for outstanding use of technology in education.

For fall 1999, 13,426 undergraduates enrolled at the UO. More than 30 percent of the student body is from outside the state of Oregon. Of the total number of students, 13 percent are members of minority groups, and 8 percent (nearly 1,400 students) are international students from eighty-two countries.

The UO offers students more than 250 different student organizations, including political and environmental groups, professional organizations, cultural heritage organizations, religious groups, and service programs. Intercollegiate competitions, club sports, and intramurals offer students several levels at which to participate in athletics. The University is a member of the PAC-10 Conference (NCAA Division I) and sponsors nine women's teams, including basketball, volleyball, and soccer, and seven men's teams, including football, tennis, and golf. The Oregon Ducks are a favorite with fans within the state and throughout the nation. The Outdoor Program takes advantage of the University's unique location and offers a host of wilderness adventures to students. In 1998, *Sports Afield* rated the UO the nation's best university for all-around outdoor activities. The University's School of Music hosts the internationally acclaimed Oregon Bach Festival and presents more than 250 concerts and recitals by visiting artists, faculty members, and students each year. Three theaters on campus offer a full range of productions produced by both faculty members and students. The University of Oregon is also home to a Museum of Natural History and a Museum of Art (UOMA). Recognized for its collections of Asian and Pacific Northwest art, UOMA is the largest art museum between Portland and Sacramento and is an educational resource to the University, the Willamette Valley, and the state of Oregon.

The UO's emphasis on "learning communities"—small, personalized teaching environments—has been a national model for undergraduate education. Students may choose from a number of special interest residence halls, including academics, creative arts, cross-cultural, health and fitness, international studies, and music halls. Freshmen are not required to live on campus, but most find the residence halls and their full-service dining halls convenient and economical.

Location

The 280-acre campus is located in the center of Eugene (population 126,500), a city known for its commitment to individuality, in the heart of the Willamette Valley. Both the Willamette and McKenzie Rivers run right through town, bordered by more than 250 miles of running trails and paved bike paths. Campus buildings date from 1876, when Deady Hall opened, to 1999, when renovation of the Recreation and Fitness Center and construction of the new William Knight School of Law building were completed. The Pacific Ocean is 1 hour west, and the Cascade Mountains are 1 hour east. Eugene is served by several major airlines and is on the main north-south Amtrak line, which runs between Seattle and San Diego.

Majors and Degrees

The University is organized into the College of Arts and Sciences and six professional schools and colleges (School of Architecture and Allied Arts, Lundquist College of Business, School of Law, College of Education, School of Journalism and Communication, and School of Music). The College of Arts and Sciences serves as a base for a liberal arts education and offers undergraduate majors in anthropology, Asian studies, biochemistry, biology, chemistry, Chinese, classical civilization, classics, comparative literature, computer and information science, economics, English, environmental science, environmental studies, ethnic studies, exercise and movement science, French, general science, geography, geological sciences, German, Greek, history, humanities, independent study, international studies, Italian, Japanese, Judaic studies, Latin, linguistics, mathematics, mathematics and computer science, philosophy, physics, political science, psychology, religious studies, Romance languages, Russian, sociology, Spanish, theater arts, and women's studies. Interdisciplinary undergraduate minors or certificates are available in computer information technology, European studies, folklore, German area studies, medieval studies, peace studies, Russian and East European studies, Scandinavian, second language acquisition and teaching, and Southeast Asian studies. Preparatory programs in the College of Arts and Sciences include business administration, dental hygiene, dentistry, engineering, forensic science, health sciences, law, library science, medical technology, medicine, nursing, occupational therapy, optometry, pharmacy, physical therapy, physician assistant studies, podiatry, social work, teacher education, and veterinary science.

The School of Architecture and Allied Arts features five-year professional degree programs in architecture, fine and applied arts, interior architecture, and landscape architecture as well as four-year degrees in art history and in planning, public policy and management. The Lundquist College of Business undergraduate program ranks in the top 2 percent of all public universities in the United States, offering majors in accounting and business administration with concentrations in entrepreneurship, finance, general business, management, and marketing. The School of Journalism and Communication is nationally accredited and offers majors in advertising, communication studies, electronic media production, journalism, magazine, news-editorial, and public relations. The School of Education offers a communication disorders and sciences major, an educational studies major, and preparation for teaching foreign languages, music, and special education. The School of Music offers degrees in dance, jazz studies, music, music composition, music education, music performance, and music theory.

Academic Program

Regardless of their major, students are required to complete general requirements. Students spend about one third of their academic careers on each of the general requirements, major requirements, and electives or requirements for completing a minor or a second major. The University is on a quarter system. One hundred eighty quarter credits are required for a Bachelor of Arts, Bachelor of Education, Bachelor of Music, or Bachelor of Science degree; 220 quarter credits are required for a Bachelor of Fine Arts (B.F.A.) or Bachelor of Landscape Architecture (B.L.A.) degree. The Bachelor of Interior Architecture (B.I.Arch.) degree requires 225 quarter credits, and the Bachelor of Architecture (B.Arch.) degree requires 231 quarter credits.

Small learning communities are available for new students: Freshman Interest Groups (FIGs) allow a small group of freshmen interested in the same academic area to share enrollment in three related courses. Freshman Seminars are small-group discussion courses taught by some of the University's most outstanding faculty members. Pathways are carefully designed one- or two-year groups of integrated courses that satisfy general education requirements, develop academic skills, and emulate a small-college experience. Open to all first-year students, Pathways offer the flexibility to choose a major while taking thematically linked courses. The Honors Track, the Oregon Institute of Marine Biology, International House, and the Honors Hall provide other learning communities.

Off-Campus Arrangements

The UO offers students more than seventy different overseas opportunities in Australia, Austria, Botswana, Cameroon, China, the Czech Republic, Denmark, Ecuador, England, Finland, France, Germany, Ghana, Greece, Hungary, India, Indonesia, Israel, Italy, Ivory Coast, Japan, Kenya, Madagascar, Mali, Mexico, Morocco, Norway, Poland, Russia, Scotland, Senegal, South Africa, South Korea, Spain, Sweden, Tanzania, Thailand, Uganda, Vietnam, Zanzibar, and Zimbabwe. Students may study up to a year at a university overseas, earning UO course credit. The University also participates in the National Student Exchange program, through which students may attend any of ninety-three colleges or universities in another state and pay that state's resident tuition.

Academic Facilities

The University of Oregon Library System consists of the Knight Library, law library, and four branch libraries (science, mathematics, architecture and allied arts, and map and aerial photography). The library system has more than 2 million volumes and subscribes to more than 18,000 journals.

University Computing provides central computing facilities and services, including the VMS cluster for interactive research and several instructional and open-access laboratories that provide connection to network resources. The Yamada Language Center is equipped with state-of-the-art computer-aided audio-visual equipment.

Costs

Resident undergraduate tuition for the 1999–2000 academic year was $3765 ($1255 per term), and nonresident undergraduate tuition was $13,152 ($4384 per term). On-campus residence halls, including room and board, cost approximately $5500 per academic year for multiple housing.

Financial Aid

Financial aid is available in the form of grants, loans, and/or work-study. To qualify, students must file the Free Application for Federal Student Aid (FAFSA). To be considered for financial aid at the UO, students must have applied for admission to the University and should indicate the UO as one of their first six choices. The UO awards financial aid based on individual need. Scholarships are awarded through the University, academic departments, and private sources. The general University scholarship application is due by February 1. For information on financial aid or scholarships and for applications, students should contact the Office of Student Financial Aid, 1278 University of Oregon, or call 800-760-6955 (toll-free).

For those seeking employment on or off campus, the Office of Student Employment provides several services, both for students who qualify for work-study and for those who do not qualify.

Faculty

Faculty members have won national awards for excellence in teaching and research and for making contributions to their fields of expertise. The UO has a student-teacher ratio of 18:1. Contact with faculty members is not limited to the classroom. A professor will act as an adviser to students, taking a personal interest in their educational progress.

Student Government

The Associated Students, University of Oregon (ASUO) administers a budget of $5.2 million, financing a broad range of academic, political, ethnic, religious, and recreational programs. The ASUO is part of the governing body of the University and also works as a lobbying organization at the state and national levels.

Admission Requirements

To be admitted to the University as a freshman, a student must complete the following high school course requirements: 4 years of English, 3 years of mathematics (including 1 year of algebra and two higher-level math courses), 3 years of social studies (including 1 year of U.S. history and 1 year of global studies), 2 years of science, and 2 years of a second language. In addition, freshman applicants must have a high school GPA of at least 3.0 (although alternative admission is possible for students whose cumulative GPA falls below 3.0), graduate from a standard or accredited high school, and submit SAT I or ACT scores. To be considered as a transfer, a student must have earned 36 or more quarter hours (24 semester hours) of college transfer credit and must have a GPA of at least 2.25 if an Oregon resident, 2.5 if a nonresident. Transfer students must also have completed one college-level English composition course and one college-level math course (with a prerequisite of intermediate algebra or above) with a grade of C– or better. Transfer applicants who do not meet regular admission requirements may be admitted on a special basis; for information, they should contact the Office of Admissions.

Application and Information

Applicants must submit an application with a $50 nonrefundable application fee, transcripts from each high school and/or college or university attended, and, for freshmen, SAT I or ACT scores. Students may apply any time after October 15 for the following academic year. The freshman application deadline is February 1. The transfer application deadline is May 15. Students planning to enter programs in architecture, fine and applied arts, interior architecture, landscape architecture, music, or the Clark Honors College should inquire directly to the appropriate department or to the Office of Admissions for early deadlines.

A campus visit is the best way to decide whether the University of Oregon is right for a student. For information and an application, students should write or call:

Office of Admissions
1217 University of Oregon
Eugene, Oregon 97403-1217
Telephone: 541-346-3201
        800-BE-A-DUCK (toll-free)
E-mail: uoadmit@oregon.uoregon.edu
World Wide Web: http://www.uoregon.edu

UNIVERSITY OF OTTAWA
OTTAWA, ONTARIO, CANADA

The University

In the heart of the national capital at the juncture of French and English Canada, the University of Ottawa has held a unique place on the Canadian academic map since its inception. Known as a meeting ground for two of the most prominent intellectual and scientific traditions in the world, it is the oldest and largest bilingual university in North America. Established by the Oblate Fathers as the College of Bytown in 1848, the institution was renamed College of Ottawa in 1861 and was elevated to university status by royal charter five years later. Following a major reorganization in 1965, the University became nondenominational and joined the ranks of Ontario's provincially funded institutions.

Over the years, the University has seen its distinct character and special mandate evolve in an increasingly multicultural milieu. Today, in what amounts to a small city within a city, almost 25,000 students from a variety of heritages study, live, and work together, surrounded by elements of both the English and French cultures.

In research, the University is an acknowledged leader in a variety of areas. Several breakthrough discoveries by University of Ottawa researchers have earned worldwide acclaim and recognition, such as the isolation and identification of the defective gene that causes myotonic muscular dystrophy. Other examples include the work done at the University of Ottawa Heart Institute at Ottawa Civic Hospital as well as at the Neuroscience Research Institute

Internationally, the University is involved in more than 100 bilateral agreements with governments, research institutes and universities throughout the world. Many of those agreements provide for exchanges that encourage faculty and student mobility and partnerships in a variety of academic pursuits.

Culturally, campus life is equally stimulating and diverse. The departments of music, theatre, and visual arts provide a variety of concerts, plays, and exhibitions. In addition, there are festivals, fairs, films, and public lectures of every description—many with an international flavor. Students can also take advantage of a full spectrum of interuniversity, intramural, and recreational sports activities, which round out a busy program that makes the University a lively and vibrant place. In addition, the University began construction of a state-of-the-art, multidimensional sports complex in September 1999 that is expected to open in September 2000.

The University of Ottawa offers undergraduate programs, professional programs requiring some undergraduate studies, and graduate programs leading to master's and doctoral degrees. Bachelor's degrees are offered in six threshold faculties: Administration, Arts, Engineering, Health Sciences, Sciences, and Social Sciences. The professional faculties are Education, Law, and Medicine. Through its Faculty of Graduate and Postdoctoral Studies, the University of Ottawa also offers masters and doctoral programs in most disciplines.

Location

The University of Ottawa is located on 70 acres of land in the center of Canada's capital, a thriving, bilingual metropolitan area of more than 1 million people, making it the fourth-largest city in Canada. The region is home to more than 100 foreign delegations and maintains an impressive list of world-class museums and attractions. In fact, Ottawa was recently voted the second-best metropolitan area in Canada in which to live and work.

Majors and Degrees

Most undergraduate programs take three or four years to complete. Regular three-year programs are available in administration, arts (general), and science (general). Regular four-year programs are available in the following disciplines: commerce (with options in accounting, entrepreneurial management, finance, human resource management, international management, management information systems, marketing, production–management science, and public policy and public management), engineering (chemical, civil, computer, electrical, mechanical, and software engineering), human kinetics, journalism (French only), mathematics/education, nursing, occupational therapy (French only), physiotherapy (French only), and science/education.

The University also offers three-year concentration programs in biochemistry, biology, Canadian studies, chemistry, classical studies, communication, computer science, criminology, economics, English, French, geography, geology, geology–physics, German, history, Italian, leisure studies, lettres françaises, linguistics, mathematics (arts or science), mathematics–science, medieval studies, music, philosophy, physics, physics–mathematics, political science, psychology (arts), religious studies, second language teaching, Slavic languages and literature, sociology, Spanish, theatre, visual arts, and women's studies. A second concentration is available in French as a second language.

Four-year honours programs are offered in accounting, biochemistry, biology, biopharmaceutical sciences, biotechnology, chemistry, classical studies, communication, computational chemistry, computational physics, computer science, criminology, economics, English, environmental science, environmental studies, French, geography, geology, geology–physics, history, Italian, Latin and English studies, leisure studies, linguistics, mathematics (arts or science), mathematics–science, music, philosophy, physics, physics–mathematics, physiology, political science (fourth year in French only), psychology (arts or science), religious studies, second language teaching, Slavic languages and literature, sociology (fourth year in French only), Spanish, theatre, translation, and visual arts (B.F.A.). Honours students can add a concentration to their degree by taking elective courses in any of these subject areas.

The University's professional programs are taught in the faculties of education, law, and medicine.

Certificate programs are available in arts administration, business administration, labour–management relations, public administration, and software technology.

Detailed information about specific program requirements can be found on the University's Web site, listed below.

Academic Programs

An important institution by Canadian standards, the University of Ottawa offers the diversity of degree programs that are usually only found at larger universities. In addition to a wide array of undergraduate programs, students can earn professional degrees in law, medicine and education. The fall and winter semesters run from September to December and from January to April, respectively. There is also a shorter spring/summer term.

Off-Campus Arrangements

The University of Ottawa has the second-largest cooperative program in Ontario. This allows students to gain valuable work experience while completing their studies. Some programs do not offer a co-op option but include discipline-related placements.

In addition, undergraduates can participate in international exchange programs that link the University with other institutions across Canada, the United States, and throughout the world. Students may choose to spend either a single term or an entire academic year at another university earning credits and experience that are applied to their University of Ottawa degree program. The available exchange programs include the Commonwealth Universities Study Abroad Consortium, Programs for North American and European Mobility, and the Canada-Taiwan Student Exchange Program.

Academic Facilities

The University of Ottawa has six libraries, including the Morisset Library for Arts and Sciences, libraries for health sciences, music, law, and education, and the Map Library. Their holdings include more than 4 million books, government documents, periodicals, newspapers, and microforms, as well as diverse audiovisual materials. University of Ottawa students also have access to the Carleton University library, the National Library, the National Archives, and the Library of Parliament. Students have access to 1,500 computer terminals across campus. The entire campus, including the library and residence halls, is connected to the Internet.

Costs

The 2000–01 tuition fee for Canadian citizens and permanent residents enrolled as full-time arts and science undergraduate students is Can$4031.16. The tuition fee for other programs is somewhat higher. The tuition fee for international students enrolled as full-time undergraduate students is Can$9271.16 (Can$10,321.16 for engineering and computer science). Residence costs for 2000–01 range from Can$2559 to Can$2979 (excluding meal plans). In addition, there are miscellaneous costs for course materials, books, supplies, and ancillary fees. There is also a Can$590.57 compulsory health insurance fee for international students. All fees are subject to change without notice.

Financial Aid

Financial aid is available to Canadian students who demonstrate a need for support in their pursuit of a post-secondary degree, often by applying to the financial aid program administered by the student's home province. Applications are available from high schools or from the University of Ottawa. The University offers a wide range of entrance and other scholarships and bursaries to Canadian students with excellent academic standing.

International students who seek financial aid or assistance have access to a limited number of bursaries at the University of Ottawa. They may also choose to contact the ministry of education in their home countries. The Canadian International Development Agency (CIDA), UNESCO, or other agencies may be a source of funding that is channelled through the ministry of education in the student's country of origin. Students from the United States may apply for a higher education loan through their local banking facility.

More information is available by visiting the financial aid and awards Web site at http://www.uottawa.ca/student or by calling 613-562-5810.

Faculty

The University of Ottawa is both a research and a teaching university, with approximately 1,400 full-time and part-time faculty members, approximately 96 percent of whom have obtained a Ph.D. degree. Many faculty members have received prestigious awards and recognition in their fields, both nationally and internationally.

Student Government

Undergraduate students are represented by the Student Federation of the University of Ottawa (SFUO). This governing body has an executive elected for a one-year term and is responsible for the administration of student affairs and interests on campus. In addition to representing student interests, the SFUO runs three businesses on campus, delegates the administration of some student affairs to federated bodies throughout the University's faculties and departments, and offers services to students.

Admission Requirements

To be considered for admission, the general admission requirements for Canadian applicants include an Ontario secondary school diploma and six Ontario Academic Courses (OACs) or the equivalent. Applicants also must meet the specific admission criteria of their program of choice. Information on the University's programs is sent to all Canadian secondary schools and colleges.

Admission requirements for international applicants vary according to the student's country of origin. Applicants may contact the University's Bureau for International Cooperation via e-mail (intl@uottawa.ca) or by visiting the University's Web site.

Application and Information

International applicants should submit their applications and all supporting documentation as soon as possible. Applications to the University of Ottawa are available from the Ontario Universities Application Centre (650 Woodlawn Road West, P.O. Box 1328, Guelph, Ontario, N1H 7P4, Canada). For fall entry, applications must be received by the Ontario Universities' Applications Centre and all supporting documentation must be received by the University's Admissions Office no later than June 1. For additional information about admissions, academic programs, or University visits and tours, students should contact:

InfoService
University of Ottawa
550 Cumberland Street
P.O. Box 450, Station A
Ottawa, Ontario K1N 6N5
Canada
Telephone: 613-562-5700
          877-UOTTAWA (toll-free)
          613-562-5317 (TTY)
Fax: 613-562-5323
E-mail: infoserv@uottawa.ca
World Wide Web: http://www.uottowa.ca

UNIVERSITY OF PITTSBURGH
PITTSBURGH, PENNSYLVANIA

The University

As a member of the Association of American Universities, the University of Pittsburgh is one of the foremost research institutions in the United States. In its third century, the University is committed to further enhancing its programs in teaching, research, and public service and to maintaining the stature and prestige of its schools, faculties, and graduates. At the center of the Pittsburgh campus is the Cathedral of Learning. This forty-two-story Gothic skyscraper, housing classrooms and administrative offices, is one of the tallest school buildings in the world. The current Pittsburgh campus enrollment is 26,162. Of that number, 17,168 are undergraduate students. The University provides a small-college, undergraduate education at its four regional campuses, located in western Pennsylvania in Bradford, Greensburg, Johnstown, and Titusville.

Location

Pittsburgh is consistently rated as one of the most livable cities in the United States. The city has a rich ethnic heritage, and many of its neighborhoods maintain their traditional characteristics. With nine Fortune 500 companies headquartered in the city, its corporate reputation provides a stimulating business climate, which enhances the quality of the many internship and career opportunities for students. Among the city's other attractions are concerts, folk and art festivals, professional sports (the Steelers, Pirates, and Penguins), the Pittsburgh Symphony, opera, theater, and ballet companies.

The University of Pittsburgh's 132-acre campus is located in the Oakland district, just 3 miles from downtown Pittsburgh. Oakland is noted for its parks, art galleries, museums, libraries, concert halls, and the internationally renowned botanical gardens of Phipps Conservatory. The city and the campus are easily accessible by car, bus, rail, and air, with limousine and taxi service to and from the campus readily available from the downtown train station and the suburban Pittsburgh International Airport.

Majors and Degrees

Bachelor of Science degrees are offered in accounting; applied mathematics; bioengineering, biological sciences; chemical engineering; chemistry; child development and child care; civil and environmental engineering; clinical dietetics and nutrition; computer engineering; computer science; ecology and evolution; economics; electrical engineering; emergency medicine; engineering physics; environmental geology; finance; general management; geology; health information management; health, physical, and recreation education–exercise science; health, physical, and recreation education–movement science; industrial engineering; information science; interdisciplinary studies; marketing; materials science and engineering; mathematics; mathematics-economics; mathematics-philosophy; mechanical engineering; medical technology; metallurgical engineering; microbiology; molecular biology; neuroscience; nursing; occupational therapy; physics; physics and astronomy; psychology; scientific computing; and statistics.

Bachelor of Arts degrees are offered in Africana studies, anthropology, architectural studies, Chinese, classics, communication science, economics, English literature, English writing, environmental studies, film studies, French, German, history, history and philosophy of science, history of art and architecture, interdisciplinary studies, Italian, Japanese, linguistics, mathematics-economics, mathematics-philosophy, music, philosophy, physics and astronomy, Polish, political science, politics and philosophy, religious studies, rhetoric and communication, Russian, social work, sociology, Spanish, studio arts, theater arts, and urban studies.

The College of General Studies offers the Bachelor of Science degree in dental hygiene, health services, liberal studies, and natural sciences area. Bachelor of Arts degrees are also available in administration of justice, humanities area, legal studies, liberal studies, media communications, public administration, and social sciences area.

A dual-major program is offered by the College of Arts and Sciences and the College of Business Administration. A joint-degree program is offered through the College of Arts and Sciences and the School of Engineering. A self-designed major is also available. Certificates are offered by the College of Arts and Sciences in children's literature, conceptual foundations of medicine, film studies, geographic information systems, German language, historic preservation, Jewish studies, medieval and Renaissance studies, professional translation, and women's studies. Certificates can be earned through the College of General Studies in communication, English writing, professional translation, statistical quality control, and women's studies. The School of Engineering offers a certificate in civil and environmental engineering and architectural studies, in energy resource utilization, and in international engineering studies. The School of Dental Medicine offers a certificate in dental hygiene. The University Center for International Studies offers certificates in Asian studies, East Asian studies, Latin American studies, Russian and East European studies, Russian studies, and West European studies.

Academic Program

The Pittsburgh campus includes sixteen schools that offer 285 degree programs. Eleven of these schools offer programs to undergraduate students. Admitting students at the freshman level are the College of Arts and Sciences, the College of Business Administration, the School of Engineering, and the School of Nursing. The Schools of Education, Information Sciences, Social Work, Health and Rehabilitation Sciences, and Pharmacy and the University Honors College admit students after they have completed specified entrance requirements. Many of the courses offered through the College of Arts and Sciences and the College of General Studies are offered in the evenings and on weekends, and some are offered off campus. Qualified entering freshmen may be conditionally accepted into the Pharm.D. program of the School of Pharmacy, with the provision that they successfully complete four terms of preprofessional study in the College of Arts and Sciences. The School of Dental Medicine offers the certificate program in dental hygiene.

The University offers many special programs, including external studies; independent study courses; and Air Force, Army, and Navy ROTC. Cross-registration with nine other Pittsburgh-area colleges and universities is also an option. The University calendar consists of three terms that run from August to December (fall term), January to April (spring term), and May to August (summer term). The fall and spring terms comprise the typical academic year. A number of summer sessions, which vary in length, are offered in the summer.

Qualified students may take honors classes through the University Honors College and may be considered for candidacy for the Bachelor of Philosophy degree. Students may design their own majors and combine degree programs with the assistance of an academic adviser. Undergraduate research and teaching assistantships are also available through the Honors College.

In the international dimension, students may earn certificates through the University Center for International Studies. Language majors and courses with an international focus are available throughout the various departments on campus. Extensive study-abroad options are available, as is a Semester at Sea on the world's only floating campus.

Academic Facilities

There are twenty-six University library collections on or near the Pittsburgh campus that contain approximately 7.6 million items (including microforms) and nearly 22,000 periodicals. PITTCAT is the University's online catalog, offering author, title, subject, and keyword access to materials in all University libraries.

Computing and network services are an integral part of the education and research missions of the University of Pittsburgh. The University was the first to integrate voice, data, and video on a fiber-optic distribution system. Six campus computing labs are equipped with more than 700 personal computers and workstations. There are many classrooms to which full-color, full-motion video can be delivered from remotely controlled videocassette recorders and various other devices. Each residence hall room is provided with network access, one port per student.

There are numerous educational opportunities for students in the University's six health sciences schools and through the UPMC Health System.

Costs

Tuition charges per year (two terms) for full-time undergraduates in 1999–2000 were as follows: College of Arts and Sciences, College of General Studies, School of Social Work, School of Education, and School of Dental Medicine, $6118 ($13,434 out-of-state); School of Engineering, $6568 ($14,712 out-of-state); School of Information Sciences, $6636 ($14,542 out-of-state); School of Nursing and School of Health and Rehabilitation Sciences, $7872 ($17,168 out-of-state); and College of Business Administration, $6910 ($15,178 out-of-state). Other costs were room and board, $5766; student health fee, $130; student activity fee, $120; computing and network services fee, $220; and security, safety, and transportation fee, $110.

Financial Aid

Approximately 70 percent of financial aid applicants receive financial aid. The application process is outlined in the Application for Undergraduate Admissions and Financial Aid. The filing deadline for freshmen is March 1; for transfers, May 1. Freshman applicants for the fall term who file a complete admissions application by January 15 of their senior year will automatically be considered for academic scholarships. These scholarships are based on high school performance, the degree of difficulty of the curriculum, class rank, and college entrance examination test results. Out of a freshman class of about 3,100, more than 700 scholarships are awarded, varying in amount from $1000 to full tuition, room, and board.

Faculty

The full-time faculty at the Pittsburgh campus totals 2,908 members. Of these, 2,618 hold doctorates. In addition to instruction, faculty members engage in a wide variety of research and sponsored programs, which totaled more than $304 million in the 1999 fiscal year.

Student Government

The Student Government Board is the official representative body of all undergraduates except those enrolled in the College of General Studies. In addition to maintaining standing committees, the board selects members of several governance units of the University. The College of General Studies Student Government Council advises members of the University community on matters of student interest and coordinates activities and services for the College's students.

Admission Requirements

All applicants for full-time study in the College of Arts and Sciences must have completed at least 15 academic units in an accredited secondary school by the beginning of the term in which they plan to enroll. The College of General Studies considers applicants who have satisfactorily passed the GED examination. The College of Arts and Sciences and all the schools of the University require SAT I or ACT scores. It is recommended that students take a challenging college-preparatory curriculum during each of their four years of high school. Transfer applicants are required to submit their high school transcript and a transcript from every college previously attended. Schools or programs may expect transfer applicants to have fulfilled various other academic requirements or to submit recommendations. Admission decisions are made after careful evaluation of each applicant's high school record, test scores, and personal qualifications.

Application and Information

For most freshman-entry and some transfer programs, the University follows a rolling admissions policy, that is, applications are reviewed on an individual basis by an Admissions Committee as they become complete. Qualified students are admitted until programs are filled and need not pay a tuition deposit until May 1, for fall term admission. Students should refer to the Transfer Application for Undergraduate Admissions and Financial Aid for upper-level division programs with deadlines, and note that freshman applicants desiring scholarship consideration for the fall term should apply by January 15. Applicants are encouraged to visit the campus. Small group information sessions, freshman and transfer interviews, open houses, and campus tours are offered on a regular basis.

For an application and more information, students should call or write:

Office of Admissions and Financial Aid
4227 Fifth Avenue
University of Pittsburgh
Pittsburgh, Pennsylvania 15213

Telephone: 412-624-PITT
E-mail: oafa+@pitt.edu
World Wide Web: http://www.pitt.edu/~oafa

The Cathedral of Learning, University of Pittsburgh.

UNIVERSITY OF PITTSBURGH AT BRADFORD
BRADFORD, PENNSYLVANIA

The University

The University of Pittsburgh at Bradford (Pitt-Bradford), Pennsylvania's Public Liberal Arts College, was founded in 1963. It is dedicated to providing students with a high-quality undergraduate education. Pitt-Bradford students enjoy the best of both worlds—a personalized undergraduate experience in a liberal arts college setting, coupled with the prestigious Pitt degree and the affiliation with an internationally recognized university. The University of Pittsburgh at Bradford is committed to preparing professionals in the liberal arts tradition.

Pitt-Bradford is noted for its dedicated and highly qualified faculty and staff, its strong academic and professional programs, and the attention it pays to students' individual needs. All of this leads to a prevailing sense of community. State-of-the-art computer equipment and modern facilities highlight the safe and friendly campus. In addition, the 1,200 Pitt-Bradford students have the distinct advantage of earning nationally recognized degrees at a cost that is less than that of 90 percent of private colleges nationwide.

Active learning is fostered through students' involvement in debates, discussions, individual and group research projects, computer-aided learning projects, art, field trips, drama, music, and a host of internships and independent study projects. On-campus apartment and town-house living provides a unique experience for students. Both types of living arrangements are complete with furnished rooms. Campus residents are required to participate in a board plan at the University dining hall. All students are guaranteed housing, and students are permitted to have cars on campus.

The T. L. McDowell Sports and Recreational Complex provides facilities for intercollegiate and intramural athletics as well as for a variety of recreational activities. A $9.3-million addition to the complex will be completed by 2001. Pitt-Bradford fields five men's and six women's NCAA Division III intercollegiate teams.

Location

The University of Pittsburgh at Bradford is located near the Allegheny National Forest in northwestern Pennsylvania. The 125-acre campus is 80 miles south of Buffalo and 160 miles northeast of Pittsburgh. The population of the Bradford region is approximately 22,000. Many national and international firms are located in Bradford, including Zippo Manufacturing and Dresser Manufacturing. Outdoor recreational opportunities such as hiking, camping, hunting, boating, fishing, and downhill and cross-country skiing are abundant. Pitt-Bradford is easily accessible by both air and ground transportation.

Majors and Degrees

Pitt-Bradford offers four-year majors in administration of justice, American studies, applied mathematics, biology, business management, chemistry, communications (radio and television), computer science, economics, English, geology and environmental science, history/political science, human relations, nursing, physical sciences, psychology, public relations, social sciences, sociology, sport and recreation management, sports medicine, and writing. Many of these majors prepare students for graduate study in dental medicine, law, medicine, optometry, physical therapy, and veterinary medicine. Students in a variety of majors can also choose to earn elementary or secondary education certification.

Occupational therapy and engineering (chemical, civil, computer, electrical, industrial, manufacturing, mechanical, and petroleum) are available at Pitt-Bradford for the first two years of study. The remainder of the program must be completed at the Pittsburgh campus.

Associate degrees are available in information systems and nursing (RN).

Pitt-Bradford offers a 3-4 program with the University of Pittsburgh School of Dental Medicine and the Pennsylvania College of Optometry, where students spend their first three years at Pitt-Bradford and spend the remaining four years at the appropriate graduate school.

Pitt-Bradford offers the first two years of preprofessional study for the doctorate in pharmacy. The final four years are completed at the Pittsburgh campus, where admission is competitive. Qualified high school seniors may be guaranteed admission to Pittsburgh's School of Pharmacy following successful completion of the preprofessional years at Pitt-Bradford.

Academic Program

Pitt-Bradford's academic programs are designed to prepare students for rewarding careers. The programs emphasize communications and critical-thinking skills and promote active learning through internships, field experiences, and collaborative faculty-student research. To earn a bachelor's degree, students must complete between 120 and 128 credit hours, depending on the program. To earn the associate degree, students must complete 60 to 70 credit hours.

In the business management program there is a strong teaching emphasis on real-world applications, and courses frequently involve cases drawn from actual business situations. Students may select a concentration in accounting, finance, international business, management information systems, or marketing. A new specialization in information technology is also available.

In the communication arts and humanities, Pitt-Bradford students in the communications, English, public relations, and writing programs gain experience by working on the staff of *The Source*, the student newspaper; participating in WDRQ, the college radio station; and publishing their works in *Baily's Beads*, the student literary magazine. Communication arts students utilize other excellent facilities on campus, including a television studio, an electronic newsroom, a radio room, and a video editing room with analog and digital technology.

Students interested in education may choose between elementary education and secondary education certification. Secondary education is available in biology, chemistry, earth and space science, English, general science, mathematics, social studies, and speech communication.

The mathematics, computer science, and engineering department provides numerous opportunities for Pitt-Bradford students. Students interested in mathematics may choose from secondary education, applied mathematics, and concentrations in actuarial science and physics. Computer science offers a variety of two-year and four-year programs, which are supported by the Pitt network and the computer science lab.

In the natural sciences, students may major in biology, chemistry, geology and environmental science, physical sciences, psychology, sport and recreation management, and sports medicine. These programs have outstanding success rates for students pursuing postgraduate studies in the medical, dental, and other health-related fields. Pitt-Bradford is also the home of the Allegheny Institute of Natural History.

Pitt-Bradford offers a variety of educational programs in nursing. The Associate of Science in Nursing (A.S.N.) is a two-year program. The Bachelor of Science in Nursing (RN-B.S.N. completion) is an additional two-year program that builds directly upon the A.S.N. degree. The School Nurse Certification is also available for registered nurses interested in caring for children of all ages in the school setting.

In the social sciences, students have a wide range of academic opportunities. The social science programs prepare students for careers in government and nonprofit organizations or, alternatively, for graduate study or law school. The administration of justice major allows students to pursue their interests in the American justice system, law, corrections, and the court system. The human relations program teaches behavioral sciences by combining course work in anthropology, psychology, and sociology.

Students who wish to pursue academic programs not completed at Pitt-Bradford may earn a maximum of 70 credits before relocating to another campus of the University. Students in arts and sciences are guaranteed relocation if they are in good academic standing. Engineering students must maintain a minimum quality point average of 2.5.

Academic Facilities

In addition to the T. Edward and Tullah Hanley Library on campus, Pitt-Bradford students have online access to the entire University of Pittsburgh library system, which includes nearly 4 million bound volumes, 3.8 million microform holdings, and 24,000 periodical subscriptions. Swarts Hall houses Pitt-Bradford's modern nursing laboratory, a writing lab, and O'Kain Auditorium, which is a 300-seat center for plays, concerts, and lectures. Fisher Hall, the science and computer science building, contains modern lab equipment and computer-aided learning centers.

Costs

For 2000–01, estimated tuition for full-time students per fifteen-week term is $3182 for Pennsylvania residents and $6988 for out-of-state students. Estimated nursing tuition is $4093 per term for Pennsylvania residents and $8928 for out-of-state students. Estimated room and board expenses are $2568 per term. Other costs include an activities fee of $60 per term, a freshman orientation fee of $90, and a computer fee of $110 per term. Books and supplies cost approximately $300 per term.

Financial Aid

Eighty-five percent of all Pitt-Bradford students receive some form of financial aid. A variety of loans, grants, scholarships, and work-study opportunities are awarded through the University. Applicants for all types of need-based financial aid must submit the Free Application for Federal Student Aid (FAFSA) by the March 1 priority deadline preceding the academic year for which assistance is requested. All Pennsylvania residents seeking aid will be considered for Pennsylvania Higher Education Assistance Agency (PHEAA) grants by completing the FAFSA. Out-of-state residents should check with their state agency for state grant requirements. Merit-based scholarships, awarded at entry, are based on academic achievement. Financial aid is also available through the University ROTC program. Veterans are encouraged to utilize VA educational benefits.

Faculty

Pitt-Bradford's 75 full-time faculty members hold doctorates and master's degrees from some of the most prestigious universities in the nation, including Cornell, Harvard, Stanford, and the University of Pittsburgh. Teaching is the primary activity of the faculty, and personal attention is emphasized in the classroom. Faculty members welcome the chance to meet with their students and know them by name. The student-faculty ratio is 15:1.

Student Government

The Student Government Association (SGA) plays an important role in college life. The SGA is responsible for chartering and funding more than thirty college clubs and organizations. The Student Activities Council branch of the SGA is responsible for scheduling diversified entertainment for Pitt-Bradford students throughout the year.

Admission Requirements

In reviewing applications, the Admissions Committee considers three primary factors in evaluating an applicant's ability to succeed in college work: the high school record, the results of standardized tests, and the high school's recommendations. In addition, personal qualifications, extracurricular activities, and potential to contribute to the college community may be taken into consideration.

Application and Information

Pitt-Bradford has a rolling admissions program, and students may apply at any time. All candidates are notified as soon as action is taken on their application.

Candidates for admission should complete and return the application with a nonrefundable $35 fee. Students must also submit an official copy of their high school record and scores from either the Scholastic Assessment Test (SAT I) or American College Testing's examination (ACT). In addition to fulfilling the above requirements, transfer applicants must submit all official college transcripts and must have a minimum cumulative grade point average of 2.0. The admissions office welcomes campus visits by students and their families; such visits help students arrive at a final decision about Pitt-Bradford. Interviews and tours are scheduled Monday through Friday, 9 a.m. to 3 p.m., and on selected Saturdays. Arrangements for these visits can be made by contacting the Office of Admissions.

For more information on the financial aid programs available, students should visit the Pitt-Bradford financial aid Web site, listed below, or contact the Financial Aid Office.

For application forms, catalogs, and further information, students should contact:

Office of Admissions
University of Pittsburgh at Bradford
300 Campus Drive
Bradford, Pennsylvania 16701-2898
Telephone: 814-362-7555
          800-872-1787 (toll-free)
World Wide Web: http://www.upb.pitt.edu

Pitt-Bradford: Pennsylvania's Public Liberal Arts College.

UNIVERSITY OF PITTSBURGH AT GREENSBURG
GREENSBURG, PENNSYLVANIA

The University

Established in 1963, the present campus is now home to a four-year, degree-granting, residential undergraduate college of the University of Pittsburgh. Accredited by the Middle States Association of Colleges and Schools, the University of Pittsburgh at Greensburg (UPG) offers seventeen baccalaureate degrees in both liberal arts and career-oriented programs. In addition to its bachelor's degree programs, UPG offers relocation options in baccalaureate programs that may be completed at other Pitt campuses after an initial year or two at Greensburg. The beautiful 217-acre streamside campus is situated in a wooded suburban location, once the setting of a private estate.

There are 1,304 full-time and 250 part-time students currently enrolled. The majority are Pennsylvania residents, but eight other states and several countries are also represented. There are more than 450 students living on campus.

In 1982, UPG acquired University Court (three apartment buildings) to house students on campus; each apartment in the complex accommodates 4 students. A Faculty Office Building was constructed in 1987. Both Chambers Hall (with a gymnasium, an indoor track, racquetball courts, dining facilities, offices, and a bookstore) and Robertshaw Hall (a residence hall) were completed in 1989. The McKenna Computer Center was doubled in size when it underwent major rebuilding in both 1989 and 1997. Millstein Library, a library and administration building, was completed in 1995. College Hall (a residence hall) opened in 1996.

Terra House, a residence for internationally minded students, and three newly constructed garden-style apartment buildings were first occupied in August 1999. Three additional garden-style apartment buildings are targeted for completion and occupancy in August 2001. Campus housing standards encompass private or semiprivate rooms and private or semiprivate baths. All residence facilities come equipped with basic cable service for television, microwave ovens (along with full-size ranges in all apartment units), refrigerators, local telephone service, and Pentium III computers (one computer for every 2 resident students), each connected through a high-speed Ethernet port to both the Internet and the University-wide network (Pittnet).

Location

UPG is located a little more than 2 miles southeast of the city of Greensburg (population 23,000) and about 35 miles southeast of Pittsburgh. Greensburg is the home of the Westmoreland Museum of Art, the Westmoreland Symphony Orchestra, and the Westmoreland Choral Society. Nearby recreational facilities include the Kirk Nevin Recreation Center (ice-skating, tennis, and swimming), Mt. Odin Park (golf), and Laurel Mountain, Seven Springs, and Hidden Valley (ski resorts).

Majors and Degrees

Four-year offerings include the following: the Bachelor of Arts degree in administration of justice (corrections and law enforcement options available), American studies, anthropology, communication, English literature, English writing (including creative writing, journalism, and public relations/advertising options), a humanities concentration, political science, a self-designed major, and a social science concentration; the Bachelor of Science degree in biological sciences (environmental science and preprofessional options available), business management, management/accounting, mathematics (applied), a natural science concentration, psychology, and a self-designed major. Four years of preparation are offered in such preprofessional areas as chiropractic, communication science (speech pathology and audiology), dental medicine, education, law, medicine, optometry, physical therapy, physician assistant studies, podiatry, and veterinary medicine. Two years of preparation for the University of Pittsburgh's upper-division programs in child development and child care, clinical dietetics and nutrition, health information management, occupational therapy, pharmacy, and social work are also available. Guaranteed/conditional admission is available to qualified students on the same basis as at the campus at Pittsburgh. The first year of all of the University of Pittsburgh School of Engineering programs can be completed at Greensburg. In addition, all four years of the Bachelor of Science in Information Science degree program may be completed under the auspices of the (Pittsburgh Campus–based) School of Information Sciences.

Academic Program

The entire degree program is designed to provide students with a sound program of general education, to give them the breadth of learning necessary in the modern world of specialized education, and to give them the depth of learning required for a vocation.

In addition to completing specific courses in their major, students must also complete general requirements. The total number of credits required for UPG's baccalaureate degree programs is 120 (126 for accounting and business management).

Students may earn credits toward graduation not only by taking and successfully finishing courses but also by taking a special examination. Each test for credit by examination must be arranged with the department teaching the course for which credit is desired. The examination must be in a specific course offered by the Greensburg campus.

The University of Pittsburgh at Greensburg, with the diversified backgrounds of its student population, utilizes the general examinations of CLEP as a means of evaluating adult candidates for advanced placement after admission to the college. The general examinations consist of five areas: English composition, humanities, social sciences, natural sciences, and mathematics.

Students who have participated in the Advanced Placement (AP) Program of the College Board may request consideration for college credit from UPG by having the Educational Testing Service forward their AP scores to the Office of Admissions.

The University calendar consists of three terms that run from August to December (fall term), January to April (spring term), and May to August (summer term). The fall and spring terms comprise the typical academic year. A number of shorter summer sessions run concurrently with the summer term.

Off-Campus Arrangements

Study abroad and Pitt's Semester at Sea programs afford interested students a wealth of educational and experiential possibilities. A wide range of local internships are designed to meld traditional academics with practical experience.

Academic Facilities

Originally situated in the center of town, the campus later moved and evolved around Lynch Hall (now an administration building but formerly the Tudor mansion of the original estate). Powers Hall (the second home of the library) was built in 1974 and underwent major reconstruction, enlargement, and conversion to classrooms in 1996.

The McKenna Computer Center provides all students with easy access to a wide range of local Windows, Macintosh, DOS, and UNIX applications through the high-speed University-wide Pittnet, through which students may also access the Internet and remote VMS and UNIX applications. Software packages include graphical Internet access tools, word processing, database, spreadsheet, graphics, statistics, CAD, communications, and courseware applications. The center also provides high-quality laser printing and color-scanning services.

The Millstein Library houses an expanding collection of more than 75,000 items, including books, microfilm, videotapes, records, and compact discs, and subscribes to more than 400 periodicals. Students are able to search PittCat, the University's online catalog, which has access to more than 3 million titles, and the University of Pittsburgh's Digital Library, which contains hundreds of databases on a variety of subjects. Access to the Internet is provided on all library devices through the University's computer system. Interlibrary loan service with other Pitt campuses is also available.

Smith Science Building was added in 1976 and underwent major renovations and enlargement in 1997. The building contains classrooms, the 270-seat Ferguson Theater, faculty offices, and labs for anthropology, biology, chemistry, physics, and engineering.

Additional building and renovations are planned for the future.

Costs

For the 1999–2000 academic year (two terms), full-time students who were Pennsylvania residents paid $6582 for tuition and general required fees; out-of-state residents paid $13,898. The 1999–2000 academic year room and board charges were $4830.

In 1999–2000, part-time students who were Pennsylvania residents paid $212 per credit; out-of-state students paid $459 per credit. General required fees for part-time students were $62 for each term of enrollment.

Financial Aid

About 80 percent of UPG's students receive some form of financial aid, including Federal Pell Grants, Federal Supplemental Educational Opportunity Grants, Federal Work-Study, Federal Perkins Loans, Federal Stafford Loans, Federal PLUS Loans, and Pennsylvania Higher Education Assistance Agency Grants. University Scholarships, based on financial need as well as academic achievement, are also available.

All applicants for financial aid must complete the Free Application for Federal Student Aid (FAFSA) and the UPG Financial Aid Application Supplement. They should also apply for a state grant according to the procedures established by their own state of residence.

Faculty

The faculty includes 99 members, 30 of whom teach part-time. Nine of the full-time faculty members are winners of the prestigious Chancellor's Outstanding Teaching Award. Most have earned their doctorate at one of a number of distinguished colleges and universities. They continue to author books, publish their work in journals, and present papers at national and international conferences.

Student Government

The Student Government Association (SGA) is composed of elected representatives from each class and provides students with an opportunity to participate in University planning and decision making. The SGA also serves as the principal forum for student views. The Activities Board similarly provides an opportunity for students to plan, promote, and produce a variety of educational, social, and recreational programs.

Admission Requirements

Applicants for full-time admission should have completed at least 15 units of credit in college-preparatory courses, taken in grades 9 through 12, including English, 4 units; algebra I; algebra II or geometry; history, 1 unit; laboratory science, 1 unit; and 7 additional units in any combination of those subject areas or a foreign language. Some students who have not completed 3 years of the same foreign language in high school may be required to take 1 year of a foreign language at UPG.

Students interested in engineering should have taken 2 years of algebra; ½ year of trigonometry; and 1 year each of plane geometry, chemistry, and physics.

Applicants for full-time admission must also submit the results of the SAT I or ACT (or request a waiver of this requirement).

Part-time admission is open to high school graduates or those who hold recognized equivalency certificates such as the GED.

Application and Information

An application fee of $35 must accompany the application. High school transcripts (as well as college transcripts for those who previously attended another postsecondary institution) must also be submitted. Full- or part-time admission is offered for the fall term (September through December), spring term (January through April), and summer term (May through August).

To obtain application materials or further information, students should call 724-836-9880. To arrange a meeting with an admissions officer and/or a tour appointment, students should call 724-836-9881.

For more information, students should contact:

Office of Admissions and Financial Aid
University of Pittsburgh at Greensburg
1150 Mt. Pleasant Road
Greensburg, Pennsylvania 15601-5860

Telephone: 724-836-9880
E-mail: upgadmit@pitt.edu
World Wide Web: http://www.pitt.edu/~upg/

View from center campus toward Millstein Library, one of the newest additions to the growing campus.

Peterson's Guide to Four-Year Colleges 2001   www.petersons.com   2807

UNIVERSITY OF PUGET SOUND
TACOMA, WASHINGTON

The University

Founded in 1888, the University of Puget Sound is an independent university committed to the liberal arts and sciences, superb teaching, and the recognition of each student as an individual. A nationally acclaimed teaching faculty, well-planned facilities, and a limited enrollment ensure excellence in education.

Puget Sound is one of only two independent colleges in Washington State to be granted a chapter by Phi Beta Kappa and is the only national liberal arts college in western Washington. A record number of Puget Sound graduates have been recipients of undergraduate and postgraduate honors, including Rhodes, National Science Foundation, Fulbright, Rotary, Watson, Phi Kappa Phi, Truman, Goldwater, Hertz, and National Endowment for the Humanities fellowships and scholarships.

In fall 1999, the University enrolled 2,600 students, with more than two thirds of the freshman class coming from outside the state of Washington. In addition, sixteen other countries were represented in the student body. Puget Sound is a 24-hour-a-day, seven-day-a-week residential community. Students live in eight residence halls, nine Greek-letter-society residences, and more than fifty University-owned houses on campus. Special theme houses and halls are available for students with common interests. The neighboring residential community provides many facilities for those who wish to live off campus. Approximately 30 percent of students belong to Greek letter organizations. State-of-the-art athletic facilities include Memorial Fieldhouse and Pamplin Fitness Center, Wallace Pool, Baker Stadium, an indoor climbing wall, and numerous varsity and intramural athletic fields.

Location

The campus is located in a quiet residential neighborhood in the historic North End of Tacoma. Thirty-five miles south of Seattle and easily accessible from Interstate 5, Tacoma is a dynamic city of 186,000 people. The University occupies thirty-eight buildings on a 97-acre parklike campus. The architecture is Tudor Gothic, with its distinctive red-brick pattern arches and porticoes. Located close to the shores of Puget Sound and a short distance from ski slopes and the Pacific Ocean, the University is also the center of much of Tacoma's cultural life. Tacoma also features Point Defiance Zoo and Aquarium, many parks, a public library system, museums, and hospitals.

Majors and Degrees

The University of Puget Sound offers more than fifty majors leading to the Bachelor of Arts, Bachelor of Science, and Bachelor of Music degrees. Academic majors are art, Asian studies, biology, business administration, chemistry, classics, communication, comparative sociology, computer science, computer science in business, economics, English, exercise science, foreign languages and literature (options in French, German, international affairs, and Spanish), geology, history, international political economy, mathematics, music, natural science, occupational therapy, philosophy, physics, politics and government, psychology, religion, and theater arts. The introduction of a special interdisciplinary major allows exceptional students the opportunity to pursue a degree in a recognized interdisciplinary or emergent field.

The University offers a dual-degree program in engineering, leading to a joint Bachelor of Arts/Bachelor of Science degree in engineering. A Bachelor of Engineering degree may also be earned. Students in this program complete prerequisites in chemistry, mathematics/computer science, and physics, then transfer to an accredited engineering school for course work in chemical, civil, electrical, environmental, mechanical, or petroleum engineering, among others. Affiliated schools are Washington University in St. Louis, Columbia University, Duke University, Boston University, and the University of Southern California. A six-year combination baccalaureate/master of physical therapy degree is offered, as is a five-year baccalaureate/master of arts in teaching (education) degree.

Academic Program

At the heart of the academic program is the core curriculum—eleven course groupings around which major and elective studies are arranged over a four-year period. The emphasis throughout a student's undergraduate education is on the acquisition of intellectual skills: the ability to express oneself clearly, both orally and in writing; the ability to reason quantitatively; and the ability to think logically, critically, and independently. By mastering the literature and techniques of a specific academic major, the student learns also to cultivate the unique power of his or her own mind and to respond vigorously, but humanely, to important social, moral, and intellectual challenges.

A particularly well designed curriculum for the freshman year and a model program of academic advising and career counseling enable each student to develop his or her own skills and interests in preparation for a lifetime of creative work and leisure. The highly successful and award-winning student orientation process—Prelude, Passages and Perspectives—is a nine-day program that allows new students to become involved in writing and thinking seminars, academic workshops, and a three-day excursion to the nearby Olympic Peninsula.

Courses are available in Japanese, Chinese, Greek, Latin, Latin American studies, African-American studies, environmental studies, and women studies, although majors are not offered in these areas.

The academic year is divided into two semesters, beginning in late August and mid-January, and a thirteen-week summer session (two miniterms). A normal academic load is 4 units (typically four courses) per semester. Each unit of credit is equivalent to 6 quarter hours or 4 semester hours. Thirty-two units are required for graduation.

Off-Campus Arrangements

The University of Puget Sound offers an outstanding selection of international opportunities for its students and operates or offers programs in forty-eight countries, including England, Scotland, Wales, Spain, France, Germany, Austria, China, Japan, Taiwan, Argentina, and Chile, among others. The Pacific Rim/Asia Study-Travel Program offers students an intense year of study and travel in six to eight Asian countries. A summer archaeological excavation in Israel rounds out the international opportunities at Puget Sound.

Puget Sound's location in one of the fastest-growing regions of the country places its internship program at the forefront of national liberal arts colleges. Opportunities for student research abound, as students may apply for summer research grants in the sciences, social sciences, and humanities.

Academic Facilities

Collins Memorial Library contains more than 465,000 volumes of books and periodicals plus a sizable collection of federal and Washington State government publications, maps, microforms, videotapes, cassettes, compact discs, and other media materials. These resources are strengthened through participation in Orbis, a consortium of thirteen baccalaureate–degree granting public and private institutions of higher education in Oregon and Washington, with combined holdings of 5,505,608 volumes. Among the other major academic facilities are Thompson Science Complex, Kittredge Art Gallery, the Concert Hall, Norton Clapp Theatre, Gordon D. Alcorn Arboretum, Lowry Wyatt Hall (completed in May 2000), and Slater Museum of Natural History.

Puget Sound, as a natural resource, provides students of environmental science and marine biology with a superb outdoor laboratory. A working relationship with Point Defiance Zoo and Aquarium, just minutes north of the campus, offers teaching and research opportunities in marine and biological sciences. Equipment and facilities in the Thompson Science Complex include a modern greenhouse; an observatory; an aquarium with a tidal cycle; a state-of-the-art genetics laboratory; a scanning electron microscope and a transmission electron microscope; ultraviolet, visible, fluorescence, infrared, and nuclear magnetic resonance spectrophotometric equipment; and a seismograph. Students also have access to human cadavers as learning tools. The University has special facilities for students of occupational and physical therapy, education, counseling, and psychology. The music building has twenty-two individual practice rooms.

All University residence halls and Greek houses are wired to provide students with instant access to Internet and e-mail accounts. In addition, 24-hour access to these services is available in computer labs on campus.

Costs

Tuition and required student fees are $21,270 and $155, respectively, for the 2000–01 academic year. Room and board costs are $5510. It is estimated that an additional $2750 per year is adequate for books, laundry, and other essentials, including travel to and from home.

Financial Aid

Eighty-five percent of the University's students receive financial aid in one or a combination of the following forms: scholarships, grants, low-interest loans, and part-time employment. Most financial aid is awarded on the basis of demonstrated financial need, as determined through analysis of the Free Application for Federal Student Aid (FAFSA). In addition, the University's Financial Aid Office administers a scholarship program based solely on academic merit: the Wyatt Trustee ($9000), the Trustee ($7000), President's ($5000), and Dean's ($3000) Scholarships. Each award is renewable annually. Many other talent awards are available in the arts, selected academic areas, forensics, and leadership. Admission decisions are made independent of financial need, and all students, regardless of family income, are encouraged to apply for financial aid.

Faculty

Members of the faculty work closely with individual students both in the classroom and in student-originated research projects within and across the disciplines. There are 211 full-time teaching faculty members. Ninety-eight percent of tenured faculty members hold a Ph.D. or an equivalent terminal degree. In agreement with Ted Taranovski, professor of history, the faculty feels that the University of Puget Sound is "an institution geared to human beings—small enough to give one a sense of community and yet large enough to provide an excellent academic curriculum; it is not an impersonal machine where people become cogs." In recent years, professors at the University have been recognized for their academic and teaching achievements through awards and distinctions, including the Graves Award in the Humanities and fellowships from various organizations, including the National Endowment for the Humanities, the American Council of Learned Societies, and the Danforth Foundation. Recently, the Carnegie Foundation for the Advancement of Teaching named history professor Mott Greene the Washington State Professor of the Year. Perhaps the best indicator of the faculty's expertise, however, lies in the comment made by a Puget Sound student: "The chance to get to know my professors has been one of the best experiences of my college education."

Student Government

Students find that participating in activities sponsored by the student government is an excellent way to learn outside the classroom and improve leadership abilities. Athletics include twenty-three varsity, various club, and numerous intramural teams. In addition, students are involved in numerous clubs and associations, such as forensics, theater, music, FM radio station, art and literary magazine, weekly newspaper, yearbook, Student Senate, religious groups, a variety of faculty and trustee committees, Black Student Union, Hui-O-Hawaii, Earth Activists, Understanding Sexuality, Asian Pacific American Student Union, Community for Hispanic Awareness, and Habitat for Humanity. Seventy-five percent of students participate in community service activities, one of the highest participation rates in the country.

Admission Requirements

Each applicant to the University of Puget Sound is considered individually and is admitted on the basis of his or her qualifications and achievements. In considering applicants for freshman admission, the Admission Committee evaluates the following: high school course selection, high school grade point average, rank in the graduating class (if available), SAT I or ACT scores, a counselor's and an academic teacher's recommendations, an essay, a recommended interview, and extracurricular activities. College credit is awarded to students who have earned scores of 4 or higher on Advanced Placement examinations. Credit for a score of 3 is available for selected examinations only. Credit is also available for the International Baccalaureate examinations.

Application and Information

Prospective freshmen may apply for admission anytime after the beginning of the senior year in high school. An admission decision is generally made on or before March 15. The application preference deadline is February 1. Students who have decided that Puget Sound is their first-choice college may choose one of two early decision plans. Early Decision I has a November 15 application deadline, with admission and tentative financial aid notification by December 15. Early Decision II has a December 15 application deadline, with admission and tentative financial aid notification by January 15. Transfer students are admitted in both semesters and for the summer session as well. Students applying for transfer admission should request the *Transfer Admission Guide*.

For more information about the University or for application materials, students should contact:

Peter M. Jones
Director of Admission
University of Puget Sound
1500 North Warner Street
Tacoma, Washington 98416-0062
Telephone: 253-879-3211
           800-396-7191 (toll-free)
E-mail: admission@ups.edu
World Wide Web: http://www.ups.edu

UNIVERSITY OF REDLANDS
REDLANDS, CALIFORNIA

The University

The University of Redlands has, for more than ninety years, offered its select student body a tradition of superior liberal education. While students may select from a variety of programs that prepare them for professional or graduate school, the heart and foundation of Redlands is in liberal studies. Its outstanding faculty, educated in the world's finest colleges and universities, provides students with extraordinary opportunities for learning and growth through excellent teaching and close, informal interaction. Intense intellectual activity is balanced by opportunities for quiet reflection, fun, and recreation.

The University enrolls approximately 1,800 students. Sixty-five percent of the freshman class comes from California and the remainder from forty-five other states and thirty-three countries. In addition to a strong academic program in the liberal arts, the sciences, preprofessional programs, and the arts, many extracurricular programs are available to the student, including forensics, music, drama, dance, and athletics. Internships are available for students in many academic programs. The School of Music and the Glenn Wallichs Theatre provide a rich selection of cultural events throughout the year. Prominent people are invited to the campus each year to give major addresses and participate in classes and public discussion groups, and many social functions are organized by the Student Life Office and individual residence halls. Additional social opportunities are provided for interested students by local nonresidential fraternities and sororities. A special counseling center provides services in the area of career and personal counseling.

Eighty-five percent of the students live on campus in residence halls that offer a variety of accommodations, including single sex, coed by separate wings, and coed by alternate suites.

The University of Redlands belongs to a select number of schools that have both National Merit Scholarship support and a chapter of Phi Beta Kappa, the nation's oldest and most prestigious academic honor society.

Master's programs are available at the University of Redlands in the fields of communicative disorders, education, management, and music.

Location

The University is located in the city of Redlands within the San Bernardino Valley. Overlooking the 130-acre campus are the two highest mountains in southern California, Mt. San Gorgonio and Mt. San Bernardino, each more than 10,000 feet high. Redlands has a population of 64,000 and is situated at an elevation of 1,500 feet. Metropolitan Los Angeles to the west and Palm Springs to the east are both about an hour's drive away by freeway.

Majors and Degrees

The B.A. degree is offered in the academic areas of art history, Asian studies, biology, business administration, communicative disorders, creative writing, economics, English literature, environmental studies, French, German, government, history, international relations, music, philosophy, professional writing, psychology, religion, sociology/anthropology, Spanish, and studio art. The B.S. degree is offered in accounting, biology, business management, chemistry, computer science, economics, environmental management, environmental science, mathematics, and physics. The professional degree of Bachelor of Music (B.M.) is offered by the School of Music. Primary and secondary credentials are granted by the Department of Education. Strong interdisciplinary programs in Latin American studies, prelaw, premedicine, race and ethnic studies, and women's studies are also available.

Academic Program

Academic majors are offered in the spirit of a liberal arts program with emphasis on developing the whole student. In addition to the standard academic program, international study programs, independent study, and an honors program are offered to provide greater diversity.

A liberal arts education, by definition, is an exposure to a wide variety of academic disciplines. Typically, such exposure carries no underlying theme but is distributed among broad categories such as the humanities, arts, social sciences, and natural sciences. The University of Redlands has never considered itself typical and, as a result, has developed an unusual approach to the implementation of its liberal arts philosophy by restructuring the general education requirements to provide a contemporary curriculum. This common experience emphasizes competence in writing, computing, problem solving, and creative skills, all of which are fundamental to a lifetime of learning and career development. In addition, the requirements include a first-year seminar, which integrates the academic program and close personal relationships between students and faculty. The overriding emphasis of this innovative curriculum is on a thorough investigation of human values as they affect the individual and society. An examination of the worth of the individual, respect for nature and life, free inquiry, and the understanding of other cultures are a few of the topics covered through various courses. It is hoped that this experience will broaden each student's understanding and will better equip the student to deal with our dynamic society.

The Johnston Center for Integrative Studies provides a nontraditional structure for a select group of highly motivated students. Johnston Center students are exempted from most of the academic structure of Redlands and instead negotiate their entire course of study with a faculty/peer committee. Drawing from the Redlands curriculum as well as from courses created each semester by the Johnston community, each student proposes an individually-designed general studies program and an area of concentration. Their course performance is evaluated in a narrative format rather than with letter grades. Johnston students live in the Johnston Complex, a living/learning community that includes student rooms, faculty offices, classrooms, and space for weekly community meetings. Students enrolled in the Johnston Center are expected to contribute to the life of the center's community.

The academic calendar divides the school year into a 4-1-4 plan providing a fall semester, interim, and a spring semester. The four classes taken in the fall semester are completed prior to the third Friday in December. The four-week interim in January offers a student the chance to pursue one subject in depth. Extensive off-campus opportunities, international travel, and independent study are available. The spring semester begins on the second Monday in February and runs through May.

Academic Facilities

The institution has extensive facilities for student use, including a modern library with 400,000 publications, Internet access, and online databases such as Dialog, ABI/Inform, PsychLit, ERIC Wilson Indecis, and Music Index. Additional facilities include the Glenn Wallichs Theatre, the Fletcher Jones Academic Computing Center, the Hunsaker University Center, the Peppers Art Center, and the Stauffer Center for Science and Mathematics. There are forty-two buildings on the 130-acre campus.

Costs

Tuition for 2000–01 is $20,260, and room and board costs are $7590.

Financial Aid

Recognizing that some worthy and capable students find it impossible to obtain a college education without financial assistance, the University has established a program of aid. Most aid is need-based, but no-need scholarships based on academic achievement in high school and/or college are available. Presidential Scholarships are also available, based on grades and test scores, as are Achievement Awards and Awards of Merit of up to full tuition for selected National Merit Finalists. Talent Awards, ranging from $500 to $2000 each, are available in art, creative writing, debate, and music.

Students seeking financial assistance should inquire through the Admissions Office when applying for admission. The Free Application for Federal Student Aid (FAFSA) should be submitted by February 15. FAFSA forms received after this date will be evaluated subject to the availability of funding. Forms may be obtained most conveniently from high school counselors' offices or college financial aid offices.

Faculty

The highly qualified full-time faculty numbers 136 men and women, 91 of whom hold doctorates or other terminal degrees in their field. The wide variety of academic backgrounds represented in the faculty provides students with an excellent opportunity to live and work in an atmosphere of intellectual inquiry. Academic advising is handled by the faculty, and all students are assigned an adviser in the area of their major interest.

Student Government

Authority and responsibility for student government is delegated to the Associated Students of the University by the president and the faculty to make possible genuine participation by students in the governance of the University. The organization is composed of all students in the college, and its officers are chosen by the student body. More than sixty positions of representation are open to students on faculty, administrative, trustee, and alumni committees. Among other activities and responsibilities, the student government finances and operates a student-union complex, on-campus bus system, radio station, information center, vending program, convocation series, and weekly newspaper.

Admission Requirements

Graduation from an accredited high school, or the equivalent, is necessary for admission. No set pattern of courses in high school is required, but applicants should have had 4 years of work in English and should have completed an academic program strongly emphasizing such studies as foreign language, science, mathematics (including algebra II), and social science. An average grade of at least B should have been maintained in the high school program. Applicants are requested to submit the results of the SAT I or the ACT. Standardized test scores are not required of transfers who bring 24 transferable units to the University.

Transfer students should have maintained a minimum 2.8 grade point average and may transfer up to 66 units of credit from a community college. There is a 30-unit residence requirement for transfers from other four-year institutions.

Application and Information

Applications are processed on a rolling basis. Those wishing to be considered for an academic or merit scholarship should apply by December 15. Those applying for need-based financial aid should apply by February 1. Transfer and late applicants should apply by March 1. Applications made after this date are considered on a space-available basis.

Further inquiry should be addressed to:

Dean of Admissions
University of Redlands
P.O. Box 3080
Redlands, California 92373-0999

Telephone: 800-455-5064 (toll-free)
Fax: 909-335-4089
E-mail: admissions@uor.edu
World Wide Web: http://www.redlands.edu

The University of Redlands stands out brilliantly against the majestic San Bernardino Mountains.

UNIVERSITY OF RHODE ISLAND
KINGSTON, RHODE ISLAND

The University

As a land-grant college since its founding in 1892, the University of Rhode Island emphasizes preparation for earning a living and for responsible citizenship, fosters research, and takes its expertise to the community in extension programs. The current undergraduate enrollment is about 10,700 men and women. The center of the spacious country campus is a quadrangle of handsome old granite buildings surrounded by other, newer academic buildings, student residence halls, and fraternity and sorority houses. On the plain below Kingston Hill are gymnasiums, athletic fields, tennis courts, a freshwater pond, agricultural fields, and greenhouses. There are nineteen residence halls on campus that offer a variety of living accommodations, including coeducational housing, all-freshman residence halls, several theme residence halls, and a "wellness dorm." Freshmen are guaranteed dormitory space if they meet the March 1 application deadline and send in their housing deposit by May 1. Three dining centers are operated by the University for the convenience of resident students. There are approximately 1,000 fraternity and sorority members living in nationally affiliated houses that are privately owned by alumni corporations. Some students commute from home, and about 2,000 students commute from houses or apartments in the beach areas known as "down-the-line." Approximately 45 percent of the undergraduate students come from outside Rhode Island.

Lectures, art programs, music and dance concerts, film programs, and theater presentations are available. An extensive program of intercollegiate and intramural athletics is offered and is sufficiently varied to provide an opportunity for every student to participate. The Tootell Physical Education Center and the Keaney Gymnasium provide excellent facilities, including three pools, three gymnasiums, three weight-training rooms, five handball courts, and a modern athletic training room. The Mackal Fieldhouse provides gymnasium space for a variety of recreational uses as well as an indoor track. In addition to a football stadium, there are twelve tennis courts, two softball diamonds, a baseball field, a lighted lacrosse/soccer field, a hockey field, and numerous practice fields for recreation and competition. A sailing pavilion and rowing facility are located off campus. The Memorial Union Building houses a wide variety of educational, social, cultural, and recreational services, including lounges, browsing rooms, study rooms, darkrooms, a student video center, a radio station, the campus newspaper, a games room, a craft center, a cafeteria, a snack bar, a restaurant, a ballroom, and a special events room.

Location

The University's 1,200-acre campus is located in the historic village of Kingston, 30 miles south of Providence in the northeastern metropolitan corridor between New York and Boston. Bus transportation is available from the campus to most locations in the area, including Wakefield, where the nearest shopping facilities are located. The Kingston Amtrak train station is 1 mile from campus, and the T. F. Greene Airport in Warwick, Rhode Island, is only about 25 miles from campus. The campus is only 6 miles from the ocean, and weekend ski trips are easily managed in the winter season.

Majors and Degrees

The College of Arts and Sciences offers the Bachelor of Arts, Bachelor of Science, Bachelor of Fine Arts, and Bachelor of Music degrees. The Bachelor of Arts degree is offered in African and African-American studies, anthropology, art history, art studio, biology, chemistry, classical studies, communication studies, comparative literature, economics, English, French, German, history, Italian, journalism, Latin American studies, mathematics, music, philosophy, physics, political science, psychology, public relations, sociology, Spanish, and women's studies. The Bachelor of Science degree is available in applied sociology, biological sciences, chemistry, chemistry and chemical oceanography, computer science, economics, environmental plant biology, marine biology, mathematics, physics, and physics and physical oceanography. The Bachelor of Fine Arts degree is offered in art and theater, and the Bachelor of Music degree is available in music education and music theory and composition.

The College of Business Administration offers the Bachelor of Science degree in accounting, finance, general business administration, international business, management, management information systems, and marketing.

The College of Engineering makes the Bachelor of Science degree available in biomedical, chemical, chemical and ocean, civil, computer, electrical, industrial, mechanical, and ocean engineering.

The College of the Environment and Life Sciences offers the Bachelor of Science degree in animal science and technology, aquaculture and fishery technology, clinical laboratory science, dietetics, environmental management, environmental plant biology, geology, geology and geological oceanography, marine affairs, marine resource development, microbiology, nutrition, resource economics and commerce, urban horticulture and turf management, water and soil science, and wildlife biology and management. The Bachelor of Landscape Architecture degree is awarded in landscape architecture.

The College of Human Science and Services offers the Bachelor of Science degree in communicative disorders, dental hygiene, elementary and secondary education, human development and family studies, human science and services, physical education, textile marketing, and textiles, fashion merchandising, and design.

The College of Nursing offers the Bachelor of Science degree in nursing.

The College of Pharmacy offers a six-year Doctor of Pharmacy degree.

Preprofessional preparation is available in dentistry, law, medicine, physical therapy, and veterinary studies.

Academic Program

All programs of study aim for a balance of the natural and social sciences, the humanities, and professional subjects. The courses and programs of study have been approved by national accrediting agencies and are accepted for credit by other approved institutions of higher education. All freshmen who enter the University to earn a bachelor's degree are first enrolled in University College; its advising program helps students choose a concentration and appropriate courses. A student must meet the curricular requirements of the college in which the degree is to be earned. As a general rule, 120 credits are required for a Bachelor of Arts degree and 130 for a Bachelor of Science degree, including the specified general education requirements. The University of Rhode Island operates on a two-semester calendar, with semesters beginning in September and January. Two 5-week summer sessions are also available. Advanced placement is granted to students who have passed a College Board Advanced

Placement examination with a grade of 3 or better. In addition, credit may be given for satisfactory scores on departmental proficiency examinations or College-Level Examination Program (CLEP) subject examinations. The University Honors Program offers bright and motivated students opportunities to broaden their intellectual development and to strengthen their preparation in their major fields of study.

Off-Campus Arrangements

The University Year for Action provides a full-time one- or two-semester internship for students interested in public service careers. The University has exchange agreements with universities in England, France, Germany, Japan, and Spain. Other off-campus study and exchange programs are also available.

Academic Facilities

The University library has more than 1 million bound volumes and 1.4 million titles on microform. Active research programs are carried on in all seven colleges, and many laboratories are available. The Graduate School of Oceanography, located on the Narragansett Bay Campus, provides undergraduates with a living research lab for science-related courses. The University houses a large collection of American historic textiles, a center for robotics research, a planetarium, the Watson House Museum, and an animal science farm.

Costs

The comprehensive cost for 2000–01 is estimated at $19,630 for out-of-state students and $11,188 for Rhode Islanders. This covered tuition, fees, and room and board. Books, travel, and personal expenses are not included in these figures. Laboratory fees are extra. The University participates in the cooperative plan of the New England Board of Higher Education, whereby students from other New England states are admitted to certain curricula at the University that are not offered in their own states. These students are charged in-state tuition plus a surcharge of 50 percent.

Financial Aid

To be considered for financial aid at the University, students must submit the Free Application for Federal Student Aid (FAFSA). The University's financial aid application must also be submitted. Although there is no deadline for applying, priority is given to applications received by March 1. Most students receive notification of decisions on or about April 1. Academic scholarships are available to incoming freshmen with superior academic credentials. Consideration for these scholarships is given to freshmen who apply by the December 15 early action deadline. For 1999–2000, 67 percent of new students who completed applications were awarded some form of aid. In addition, students have opportunities for employment through work-study programs that use federal, state, and institutional funds.

Faculty

The faculty consists of 648 full-time and 17 part-time members, or 1 professor for every 16 students. Eighty-eight percent of the full-time faculty members hold doctoral degrees. Faculty members serve both the graduate and undergraduate populations and have wide-ranging interests and responsibilities. In addition to teaching and research, they serve as advisers to the students in the University College and at the departmental and college levels.

Student Government

The Student Senate is a legislative body that represents the students to the administration and faculty and supervises extracurricular activities. It also distributes the activities tax funds among the various student organizations through its tax committee. Individual residence halls form their own governments. The Interfraternity Council supervises fraternity affairs, and the Panhellenic Association governs sorority life. The Commuter Association provides social and other assistance to commuter students.

Admission Requirements

Ideally, admission is a mutual selection process. It is hoped that those who seek admission will also be the kind of students sought by the University. Applicants are given individual consideration, but it is expected that all candidates will have completed at least 18 units of college-preparatory work; specific unit requirements vary for each of the seven colleges of the University. Academic achievement in a challenging high school program receives the strongest consideration in the review of an applicant's credentials. An audition is required to register for work toward the Bachelor of Music degree. All freshman candidates must submit a high school transcript and scores on the SAT I or the ACT examination, which should be taken no later than February 1 of the senior year. International students who are not immigrants must also complete an English proficiency test, administered by the U.S. Consulate, or the Test of English as a Foreign Language (TOEFL). Scores on equivalency examinations may be presented by applicants who have not been able to complete formal high school studies. Transfer students may enter in either semester and must submit transcripts of all previous work at both the high school and college levels. Early admission is available to high school juniors with superior records.

Students are selected primarily on the basis of academic competence and without regard to age, race, religion, color, sex, creed, national origin, handicap, or sexual orientation.

Visits to campus are encouraged, and interviews are recommended. Question-and-answer sessions are scheduled several afternoons per week in fall and winter. Students and parents are invited to participate in these meetings, which include a campus tour. Daily tours are provided for visitors, Monday to Saturday, while classes are in session. The Office of Admissions sends representatives to college fairs in Rhode Island and neighboring states throughout the year.

Application and Information

High school students are encouraged to submit applications early in their final year of preparatory study, as the University subscribes to a rolling admissions policy and reviews folders as soon as complete credentials have been submitted. The closing date for fall term freshman applications is March 1, and the deadline for transfer applications is May 1. Most decisions are reported in February, March, and April. The closing date for spring term applications is November 1. The early action deadline is December 15, and students receive notification by January 15. Requests for application forms and further information should be directed to:

Office of Admissions
Green Hall
University of Rhode Island
Kingston, Rhode Island 02881
Telephone: 401-874-7000
E-mail: uriadmit@uri.edu
World Wide Web: http://www.uri.edu/ugadmis

UNIVERSITY OF RIO GRANDE
RIO GRANDE, OHIO

The University

The University of Rio Grande, founded in 1876, is a private four-year institution in partnership with Rio Grande Community College, a two-year college supported by the state of Ohio. It is the only Ohio institution with a combined two- and four-year mission in higher education. Accredited by the North Central Association of Colleges and Schools, Rio Grande has a diverse population of approximately 2,000 students with an average age of 24 years.

Vibrant, progressive, and developing, the University of Rio Grande and Rio Grande Community College offer a stimulating learning environment combining the advantages of a small, rural community college with the colorful, challenging atmosphere of a university.

Rio students are diverse; they include traditional students in residence on a 170-acre campus as well as a growing population of nontraditional students who commute from Ohio and the contiguous states of West Virginia and Kentucky.

Rio Grande has created a student base that can be described as multicultural: some students travel from all over the nation and the world to study in one of the few fine woodworking programs in the nation. Rio Grande is particularly strong academically in education, business, and nursing programs. From two-year programs to four-year degrees and a unique master's program in classroom teaching, Rio Grande offers a comprehensive array of technical, professional, and liberal arts preparation.

The University is a member of the Mid-Ohio Conference and competes in men's baseball, basketball, cross-country, and soccer and women's basketball, softball, track, and volleyball. The University also has a complete intramural program. A variety of student activities, from Student Senate and fraternal life to a student-run newspaper, *Signals*, offer students a diverse out-of-classroom experience in the heart of Appalachia.

Athletic facilities include a sports center with indoor pool, fitness center, four racquetball courts, and varsity and multipurpose gymnasiums; baseball, softball, and soccer fields; a resilient all-weather track; sand volleyball courts; and four lighted tennis courts.

A graduate program is offered in the area of professional education with Master of Education degrees granted in the following areas of classroom teaching: fine arts, reading education K–12, learning disabilities, and mathematics.

Location

Rio Grande is located in southeastern Ohio, 12 miles from Gallipolis, a town along the Ohio River, and 75 miles from Columbus. The major airports that serve the area are in cities that include Columbus; Charleston, West Virginia (65 miles away); and Huntington, West Virginia (60 miles away). Canoeing and horseback riding in connection with the nearby Bob Evans Farms are recreational activities for many Rio students.

Majors and Degrees

The University of Rio Grande grants Bachelor of Science degrees with majors in accounting, American studies, art, art education, behavioral and social science comprehensive, biology, business education, business management, chemistry/physics, clinical laboratory sciences, communication, computer science, economics, elementary education, English, environmental science, fine arts, history, humanities, industrial technology, information technology, international business, marketing, mathematics, music, music education, nursing, physical education, preprofessional studies (engineering, law, medicine, and ministry), psychology, social science, social work, special education, sport and exercise studies, and theater.

The University also grants associate degrees in accounting, art, biology, business management, communication, computer operations, early childhood development, electronics technology, fine woodworking technology, general studies, health, history, manufacturing technology, mathematics, medical laboratory technology, microcomputer applications in business, nursing, office technology, plant maintenance technology, psychology, social services, sociology, and technical theater.

Academic Program

In addition to the specific curriculum required for their major or minor, candidates for the bachelor's degree are required to complete a core of general studies courses designed to expose students to the vast body of knowledge that exists beyond the declared major. This core covers communication, arts, sciences, mathematics, history, philosophy, and social sciences and provides students with a basic foundation of human learning.

Individualized majors are available for those students whose plans and goals differ from the University's established degree programs. These unique degree programs are individually designed through existing course work.

Many degrees require that students participate in extensive internships and practicum situations throughout the length of their program. The University believes that practical application is a major part of the learning process.

The University Honors Program offers talented and motivated students challenging opportunities for intellectual, academic, social, and ethical growth on both personal and societal levels. Freshman and sophomore students enroll in honors classes for general studies, while upperclass students focus on projects related to their field of study.

The University is set up on a quarter calendar, offering three full quarters (fall, winter, and spring) and a Summer Term that consists of two 5-week terms.

The University awards credit to students who have successfully completed the College-Level Examination Program, the Advanced Placement Program of the College Board, the ACT Proficiency Examination Program, Life Experience Credit, or locally administered proficiency tests, as well as credit for military service.

Academic Facilities

The University library currently contains 70,000 books, 784 periodicals, 1,750 recordings and other media, microcomputers for student use, tape recorders, and microfilm and microfiche and conducts an active interlibrary loan program. There are special collections in business management, art, science fiction, curriculum, juvenile literature, and government documents.

All classrooms and laboratories have been built or renovated in the last ten years.

Costs

The University of Rio Grande is one of the most distinctive institutions in America because it is the only private university that is subsidized by the state for a student's first two years of study. In addition, because of its dual role of private and public educational interests, tuition costs are lower than those at other private institutions. In-state students, therefore, enjoy an extremely low tuition rate for each of the first two years or until they complete 95 credit hours. Out-of-state students also benefit from this arrangement in that the University is able to keep their private rates extremely competitive because of this special contract with the state of Ohio. In 1999–2000, tuition rates for in-state entering students were $3000, and out-of-state students paid $8784. Room and board were set at $4800, but charges vary, depending on the board option selected by the student. These are annual rates; one third is due each quarter.

Financial Aid

The financial aid program combines merit-based assistance with traditional need-based assistance to further make the Rio experience an affordable one. More than 80 percent of all applicants for financial aid receive some form of assistance. The University administers federal and state programs, including the Federal Pell Grant, Federal Stafford Student Loan, Federal Perkins Loan, Federal PLUS loan, Federal Supplemental Educational Opportunity Grant, and the Ohio Instructional Grants programs. Campus employment is available, and a unique payment plan called the MAP Plan (Middle America Payment Plan) is available. To apply for assistance, students must complete the Free Application for Federal Student Aid (FAFSA) along with the institutional application for aid.

Faculty

Currently, the University has a full-time teaching faculty of 98 members. Approximately 60 percent of the full-time faculty members have doctoral or terminal degrees in their fields. All classes and labs are taught by faculty members, not by graduate students. Faculty members also serve as academic advisers to students and are involved in a variety of student activities. The student-faculty ratio is about 18:1, which fosters an excellent rapport between professors and students.

Student Government

Through various committees and organizations, particularly student senate, students have the opportunity to take part in determining scholastic, intellectual, recreational, social, and cultural activities. They have a voice and vote on every standing committee on campus.

Admission Requirements

The admission policy is formulated to implement the philosophy of the University, which implies that all who may profit from college-level education will be admitted. Admission is determined without regard to race, color, age, marital status, national or ethnic origin, socioeconomic status, political affiliation, religion, gender, or disability.

Applicants for admission are required to submit the following: ACT scores, an official secondary school record documenting satisfactory completion, official postsecondary transcripts, the official Admission Application, the application fee of $15, and the official medical record form. Other documentation and credentials may be required in certain admission categories. Students should consult the catalog.

Transfer students are evaluated with regard to the college-level work they have completed.

Application and Information

For more information, students should contact:

Director of Admissions
University of Rio Grande
Rio Grande, Ohio 45674
Telephone: 740-245-7208
               800-288-7246 (toll-free in Ohio)
Fax: 740-245-7260
E-mail: mabell@rio.edu
World Wide Web: http://www.rio.edu

Students on their way to class at the University of Rio Grande.

UNIVERSITY OF ROCHESTER
ROCHESTER, NEW YORK

The University

Founded in 1850, Rochester is now one of the leading private universities in the country, one of sixty-two members of the prestigious Association of American Universities, and one of nine members of the University Athletic Association, which is made up of national research institutions with similar academic and athletic philosophies. Including the University's Eastman School of Music, the University has a full-time enrollment of 4,100 undergraduates and 2,500 graduate students. Rochester's personal scale and the diversity of its colleges and professional schools permit both attention to the individual and unusual flexibility in planning undergraduate programs. Undergraduates may choose among courses in six colleges and professional schools: the College (Arts and Sciences and Engineering), the Simon School of Business Administration, the Warner School of Education and Human Development, the School of Medicine and Dentistry, the Eastman School of Music, and the School of Nursing.

Special opportunities include the Take Five program, which allows selected undergraduates a fifth year of courses that is tuition free; REMS, an eight-year combined bachelor's/medical degree; study abroad; Quest courses; a management certificate program; Senior Scholars Program; and Reach for Rochester employment programs that offer a national summer jobs program and paid internship experiences.

Located on a bend in the Genesee River, the 70-year-old River Campus is home to most undergraduates, who live in a variety of residence halls, fraternity houses, and special interest housing. Most of the original buildings have been recently renovated, and all residence halls are fully wired for computer access. Among the newest structures are Wilson Commons, recognized as one of the ten best student unions in the country; the multipurpose Robert B. Goergen Athletic Center; the Computer Studies Building; and Schlegel Hall (Business School). Students participate in more than 170 student organizations, including twenty-two varsity teams, thirty-six intramural and club sports, fourteen fraternities and nine sororities, performing arts groups, musical ensembles, a radio station, and the campus newspaper.

Location

With Lake Ontario on its northern border and the scenic Finger Lakes to the south, the Rochester area of more than a million people is located in an attractive setting that has been rated among the most livable in the United States. It offers a wide range of cultural and recreational opportunities that are provided by an unusual concentration of resources of the first order, including museums, parks, orchestras, a planetarium, theater companies, and professional sports teams.

Majors and Degrees

The University of Rochester offers a Bachelor of Arts program through the College, with majors in American Sign Language, anthropology, art history, biology, brain and cognitive sciences, chemistry, classics, cognitive science, comparative literature, computer science, economics, English, environmental studies, film studies, French, geological sciences, German, health and society, history, integrated sciences, interdepartmental studies, Japanese, linguistics, mathematics, mathematics/statistics, music, philosophy, physics, physics and astronomy, political science, psychology, religion, Russian, Russian studies, Spanish, statistics, studio arts, and women's studies. The College also offers certificate programs in actuarial studies, Asian studies, international relations, management studies, and Polish and Central European studies that complement traditional majors. Bachelor of Science programs are offered in the College with majors in applied mathematics, biological sciences (biochemistry, cell and developmental biology, ecology and evolutionary biology, microbiology, molecular genetics, or neuroscience), biology-geology, chemistry, computer science, environmental science, geological sciences, geomechanics, physics, and physics and astronomy. The School of Engineering and Applied Sciences offers Bachelor of Science programs in biomedical, chemical, computer, electrical, and mechanical engineering; geomechanics; optics; and engineering and applied sciences, an interdepartmental program with specializations in a variety of areas. A Bachelor of Arts program in engineering science and a certificate program in biomedical engineering are also offered. A Bachelor of Music degree is offered through the Eastman School, with majors in applied music, jazz studies and contemporary media, music composition, music education, and music theory. A Bachelor of Science degree is offered through the School of Nursing.

Additional programs include a 3-2 program offered through the William E. Simon Graduate School of Business Administration in which students earn both a B.A. or B.S. from the College and an M.B.A. from the Simon School in five years; 3-2 B.S./M.S. programs in mechanical engineering, chemical engineering, optics, materials science, electrical engineering, and applied mathematics; a 3-2 program leading to a B.A. or B.S. plus an M.S. in computer science; a 3-2 program in public policy analysis offered by the Department of Political Science, in which students earn both a B.A. or B.S. and an M.S. degree; a program leading to a B.A. or B.S. and an M.S. in public health; a 3-2 program leading to a B.A. in statistics and an M.S. in medical statistics; a 3-2 program leading to a B.A. in music and an M.A. in music education; and a 3-2 program in human development leading to a B.A. or B.S. in an undergraduate major and an M.S. in human development from the Warner School.

Academic Program

To receive a bachelor's degree, students should maintain a minimum average of C and complete thirty-two courses (thirty-two to thirty-six for the Bachelor of Science).

The distinctive Rochester Curriculum allows students to select their major from one of the three branches of learning (the humanities, the sciences, and the social sciences). In each of the two branches outside of their major, students then choose a "cluster" of three courses that lets them dig deeply in an area that particularly interests them. For most students, there are no other distribution requirements.

The Take Five program offers selected students the opportunity to take a tuition-free fifth year in order to pursue their varied interests.

The Quest program for first-year students offers the advantages of small classes, student/teacher collaboration, and original research. As a result, Quest courses teach first-year students how to learn, both as undergraduates and beyond.

Students may arrange independent study courses or pursue research in most departments. Those whose interests will not be fully realized through a traditional major, double major, or major/minor may design, with the assistance of faculty advisers, an interdepartmental concentration.

Undergraduates from any academic discipline may devote their senior year to a self-designed creative project in the form of scholarly research, a scientific experiment, or a literary or artistic work through the Senior Scholars Program.

Undergraduates enrolled in the College may enroll in classes, take private instruction, and participate in ensembles at the Eastman School of Music. A double-degree program leading to the Bachelor of Music degree from Eastman and a bachelor's degree from the College is also available.

The Rochester Early Medical Scholars (REMS) program is an eight-year B.A./B.S.-M.D. program for exceptionally talented undergraduates. Students enrolled in this program enter the University of Rochester with assurance of admission to the University's medical school upon completion of their undergraduate degree program.

The University's research centers include the Frederick Douglass Institute for African and African-American Studies, the Susan B. Anthony Center for Women's Leadership, the Center for Judaic Studies, the W. Allen Wallis Institute of Political Economy, the Center for Visual Science, the Sign Language Research Center, the Center for Polish and Central European Studies, and the Center for Optics Manufacturing.

The University's calendar provides two regular semesters.

Off-Campus Arrangements

Rochester offers full-year and semester-long study-abroad opportunities, as well as special summer and winter trips, through fifty different study-abroad programs. Semester and full-year destinations include Australia, Austria, Belgium, China, Egypt, France, Germany, Italy, Japan, Mexico, Poland, Russia, Spain, Sweden, and Taiwan. International internships are offered in Brussels, London, Paris, Bonn, and Madrid.

Academic Facilities

As one of the smallest Carnegie Research I universities in the nation, Rochester offers an environment that combines the extensive learning resources of a national university with the intensive personalized attention of a private college. Research opportunities for undergraduates are available in every field. Major research facilities include a comprehensive Medical Center; an extensive on-campus computer system; direct access to the CYBER 205 Supercomputer in Princeton, New Jersey; fifteen electron microscopes; a 12-trillion watt, 24-beam laser fusion laboratory; and a 3-million-volume library system, including the Eastman School's Sibley Music Library, the largest collection of any music school in the Western Hemisphere. The University is widely known as the nation's premier institution for the study of optics and is home to the Omega, the world's most powerful ultraviolet laser.

Costs

For 2000–01, approximate yearly expenses include tuition, $23,150; average room and board costs, $7740; and fees, $580. Expenses for books, travel, and personal items vary by student within a range of $1800 to $2300. Part-time study is offered on a per-course basis.

Financial Aid

The University offers a strong program of financial assistance, including academic merit scholarships, grants, loans, tuition payment plans, and part-time jobs. Applicants for financial aid should submit the PROFILE application and the Free Application for Federal Student Aid (FAFSA). Special awards include Bausch & Lomb Scholarships for top science and mathematics students, the Xerox Scholar Program for outstanding students in the humanities and/or social sciences, Kodak Young Leaders Scholarships, Rush Rhees Scholarships, National Merit and National Achievement Scholarships, grants to New York State residents and children of alumni, room and board grants to selected Naval ROTC scholars, Phi Theta Kappa Scholarships for transfer students, and Urban League and AHORA Scholarships. Special applications are not required for consideration for merit scholarships.

Faculty

Students work closely with a stimulating faculty of internationally renowned scholars, all of whom engage both in advanced research and in teaching at the undergraduate level. The University's faculty is held in particularly high regard by colleagues at sister institutions, and many of its departments are widely recognized as among the best in the country.

Student Government

All undergraduates are members of the Student Association, which has an annually elected president and a student Senate; there is also a Judicial Council, whose members are appointed by the Senate. The Student Association strives to coordinate student activities; protect academic freedom; improve students' cultural, social, and physical welfare; develop educational standards and facilities; and provide a forum for the expression of student views and interests.

Admission Requirements

The University of Rochester seeks to admit students who will take advantage of its resources, be strongly motivated to do their best, and contribute to the life of the University community. An applicant's character, extracurricular activities, job experience, academic accomplishments, and career goals are considered. About 57 percent of last year's enrolled students ranked in the top tenth of their secondary school classes. The middle 50 percent of enrolled freshmen scored between 1230 and 1410 on the SAT I and between 27 and 32 on the ACT.

The recommended application filing date for freshman applicants is January 15 for fall admission and November 1 for spring admission. An early decision plan is available. Transfer students are welcome for entrance in the fall and spring semesters, and applications are reviewed on a rolling basis. The University accepts the Common Application in addition to its own school application. An electronic online application is available from the Web site. Applicants for freshman admission are required to submit scores from either the SAT I or the ACT. SAT II examination results will be reviewed but are not required. Candidates for admission from lower-income groups are encouraged to investigate the Higher Education Opportunity Program (New York State residents only), which provides supportive services and financial aid.

The University of Rochester provides equal opportunity in admission regardless of sex, age, race, disability, color, creed, sexual orientation, and national or ethnic origin.

Application and Information

To obtain application forms and further information on admission and financial aid, students should contact:

Director of Admissions
University of Rochester
P.O. Box 270251
Rochester, New York 14627-0251
Telephone: 716-275-3221
        888-822-2256 (toll-free)
E-mail: admit@admissions.rochester.edu
World Wide Web: http://www.rochester.edu

Director of Admissions
Eastman School of Music
Rochester, New York 14604
Telephone: 716-274-1060

Rush Rhees Library on the University of Rochester's Eastman Quadrangle.

UNIVERSITY OF ST. FRANCIS
JOLIET, ILLINOIS

The University

Committed to the success of its students, the University of St. Francis (USF) offers a global perspective to its students, with strong career preparation, a liberal arts base, and the self-confidence to take on the world. More than 90 percent of USF graduates find a job in their chosen field or placement in graduate school within six months of graduation.

The University of St. Francis offers an intimate, personalized college experience, and students—residents, commuters, adult learners, and graduate students—benefit from an innovative student-centered approach. The University serves some 1,300 students at its Joliet campus, including approximately 200 nursing students. More than 3,000 students are served through programs offered off site at locations throughout the nation.

Some interesting facts about the University of St. Francis include the following: 60 percent of the University's science graduates are women, more than a third of all students are involved in volunteer programs, 50 percent of students are transfer students, the University has provided Illinois schools with more than 1,000 teachers, the average class size is 20, each student has an e-mail address, the University offers more than thirty student organizations, and prominent Chicago-based and national companies recruit on the campus each year.

More than sixty areas of undergraduate study are offered in the area of arts and sciences, business, computer science, education, and nursing. The University also offers undergraduate programs designed for adult learners, such as the Bachelor of Science in professional arts/applied organizational management and the B.S.N. Fast Track program for registered nurses.

Seven graduate programs are offered. Along with the M.S. in health services administration and the M.B.A., USF offers the M.S. in continuing education and training management, education, and nursing and the Master of Education with certification. A variety of continuing education and training programs in management and health-care are also offered.

Two of the University's programs are offered at locations nationwide: the Bachelor of Science in health arts, a degree-completion program for health-care professionals, and the Master of Science in health services administration. Online classes and complete programs, such as the M.B.A., are also offered.

The University of St. Francis is committed to teaching and to providing students with the challenges and support essential to meeting their potential. Small class sizes ensure that students get the individual attention and focus they need. The University's writing and math centers and tutoring programs provide an important support network. Programs for scholars, such as the Biology Fellows Program and various honor societies, provide challenging and relevant educational experiences beyond classroom learning. USF is at the forefront of technology, providing a variety of online research and experiences to its students.

The University of St. Francis is also committed to educating the student as a whole. A variety of student clubs and organizations are available, as are volunteer activities. Student Affairs sponsors many entertainment events as well as the Student Government Association.

Schola, the student choir, and *Loquitur*, the University's literary magazine, are popular activities. The University is also host to the annual Undergraduate Conference on English Language and Literature, which draws student presenters from prestigious colleges and universities throughout the nation.

Cultural musical events, which bring internationally and nationally acclaimed performers to the University, are sponsored through the Featured Performances series. Exhibits that bring the works of regionally recognized artists to the campus are planned.

During the past twenty years, USF teams have won fifty-one conference championships, have had fifty-eight national tournament appearances, and have won one national championship. USF has six sports programs for men and six programs for women as well as ten intramural programs.

Location

The University of St. Francis campus is on 16 acres, in the midst of a historic residential area known as Joliet's Cathedral area. The University is 35 miles southwest (about 45 minutes) of Chicago and easily accessible by major roadways and trains.

The University's College of Nursing building is located 10 minutes away from the main campus on Springfield Avenue, adjacent to Provena Saint Joseph Medical Center. The University also holds classes at a variety of health-care facilities throughout the nation.

Majors and Degrees

Undergraduate programs of study include accounting, actuarial science, advertising/public relations, American politics, applied organizational management, art, arts-advertising/public relations, arts-graphic design, arts-management, arts-marketing, biology, broadcasting, business, chemistry, commercial/public recreation, computer science, computer science/electronics, computer engineering, economics, elementary education, English, environmental science, finance, fine arts history, graphic design, history, human resource management, information science, international business, liberal studies, library science, literature, management, marketing, mass communications, mathematics, medical technology, music, natural science, nuclear medicine technology, nursing, philosophy, political science, predental, premedical, prepharmacy, pre–physical therapy, pre–veterinary medicine, psychology, public policy, radiation therapy, radiography, recreation administration, secondary education certification, social work, special education, studio art, technology management, theology, therapeutic recreation, visual arts, visual arts and education, and writing.

Academic Program

The University of St. Francis offers a comprehensive education designed to introduce the student to various modes and areas of inquiry. The core curriculum includes interdisciplinary courses taken in the freshman through junior years. The relationship of the major to the liberal education courses is addressed in a senior capstone experience in the major. For a baccalaureate degree, a student must earn 128 semester hours. Thirty-two semester hours must be earned at USF. In addition to the overall requirement of a 2.0 GPA, a student must achieve a grade of C or better in every course required of the major program. The University also offers Prior Learning Assessment (PLAP),

College Level Examination Program (CLEP), and advanced placement opportunities. Various honors and internship programs are available.

Academic Facilities

The University's oldest building, Tower Hall, is the focal point of activities, housing interactive learning classrooms, state-of-the-art laboratories, offices, two residence wings, dining facilities, the chapel, the bookstore, and the radio and television stations. St. Albert Hall is home to the Natural Science Learning Center and the University's main computing lab. Marian Hall is a residence hall housing 225 students, a residence wing for science students, lounges, a game room, computing lab, and Information Services offices.

The main campus includes the three-story library, which offers Internet access and houses the distance learning classroom. Online and off-campus students may fully utilize USF library services through the University's Web site. The Admissions Office is also on campus. The Recreation Center, with seating for 1,500, is a three-level facility that includes basketball, volleyball, and racquetball courts; a Nautilus training and exercise room; a conference room; and a classroom. The Moser Performing Arts Center houses an auditorium, art gallery, studio theater, and music and choir practice rooms as well as offices.

Saint Joseph College of Nursing and Allied Health is housed at a medical center complex, about 10 minutes from the Wilcox Street campus.

Costs

In 2000–01, tuition and fees for full-time students are $13,990; room and board are $5320. B.S.N. Fast Track tuition is $300 per credit hour.

Financial Aid

The University of St. Francis is committed to assisting students in obtaining a high-quality, private education. This commitment is evidenced by an average need-based financial aid package of more than $12,000 for freshman and transfer students. The University spends nearly $4 million in institutional aid and scholarships, in addition to nearly $6 million in federal and state assistance to enable students to attend USF. In order to apply for all forms of federal, state, and USF assistance, students must complete a financial aid application form. USF prefers that students complete the Free Application for Federal Student Aid (FAFSA).

Faculty

The University of St. Francis faculty is committed to teaching. The University has 65 full-time faculty members, more than half of whom have terminal degrees. Forty adjunct faculty members bring a variety of academic and professional experience to the classroom. Faculty advisers are an integral part of the USF experience.

The USF faculty is invested in the success of its students, both academically and personally. Nursing faculty members are strong clinicians. Their intense commitment to health-care and to patients ensures that students will be challenged academically and offered a personal, caring support system.

Admission Requirements

Although each applicant is considered individually, there are four general requirements for admission to the University of St. Francis: satisfactory ACT or SAT I scores; rank in the upper half of graduating class; at least 16 high school units in academic subjects or the equivalent of a high school diploma, including four units of English, two units of mathematics (algebra and geometry), two units of social studies, two units of science (one with lab), three units total with courses from two of three areas (foreign language, computer science, or music/art), and three units of electives; and satisfactory scores on the TOEFL from applicants for whom English is a second language.

High school students may apply for an early admission decision after the completion of their junior year. Prior to August 15, students should submit an application along with high school transcripts showing courses through the junior year. Early admission decisions are announced on August 15.

A $100 registration deposit is required thirty days after acceptance. This deposit is credited to the applicant's bill and is fully refundable until May 1 for students entering in the fall semester or January 1 for students entering in the spring semester.

Students attending other colleges may transfer to the University of St. Francis at any time during their academic careers. Students attending community colleges are not required to earn an associate degree to enter. The University has outstanding services for transfer students. Articulation agreements with community colleges ensure a smooth transition to USF.

Application and Information

Freshmen are admitted in the fall and spring. Students should take the ACT or SAT I and visit the campus for an interview by April 1. Entrance exams should be taken in the spring of the junior year or the fall of the senior year in high school. Applications, including a high school transcript and an application fee of $20, should be filed by August 15 for fall entry and December 1 for spring entry. Notification is on a rolling basis. Transfer students anticipating enrollment as a nursing major should submit an application for admission and have transcripts forwarded to the Center for Transfer and Adult Student from one year to one semester before their projected entry date.

For more information, contact

Vic Davolt, Director of Enrollment Management
University of St. Francis
500 Wilcox Street
Joliet, Illinois 60435
Telephone: 815-740-3400
　　　　　　800-735-7500 (toll-free)
E-mail: admissions@stfrancis.edu
World Wide Web: http://www.stfrancis.edu

Tower Hall, on the campus of the University of St. Francis.

UNIVERSITY OF ST. THOMAS
ST. PAUL, MINNESOTA

The University

The University of St. Thomas, founded in 1885, is a Catholic, independent, liberal arts university that emphasizes values-centered, career-oriented education. With 10,929 students, St. Thomas is Minnesota's largest independent college or university. Coeducational at the undergraduate level since 1977, St. Thomas welcomes students of all ages, nations, and religions and from a broad range of racial and financial backgrounds.

Fifty-four percent of its 5,399 undergraduates are women, as are 51 percent of its 5,530 graduate students. While more than 90 percent of St. Thomas undergraduate students hail from the Midwestern states, the University enrolls students from forty-six states and thirty-four countries. About 10 percent are people of color or from other countries; this figure represents more than three times the percentage of a decade ago. The Graduate School of Business is the fourth-largest school of its kind in the United States.

At the graduate level, St. Thomas offers thirty-eight master's, two education specialist, and five doctoral programs through its Graduate School of Applied Science and Engineering, the Graduate School of Arts and Sciences, the Graduate School of Business, the School of Education, the Graduate Department of Professional Psychology, the School of Social Work, and the Graduate School of Divinity.

About thirty campus and community outreach centers extend St. Thomas' presence in the region. They include the Center for Applied Math, Center for Applied Research, BeFriender Ministry, Campus Life-Care Center, Community Education Center, Conservatory of Music, Center for Economic Education, Center for Irish Studies, Luann Dummer Center for Women, Jay Phillips Center for Jewish-Christian Learning, Murray Institute, Center for Catholic Studies, Institute for Christian Social Thought and Management, Center for Senior Citizens' Education, Small Business Institute, and James Rogers Fox Communication Center. Centers associated with the Graduate School of Business include the Aspen Institute, Center for Entrepreneurship, Institute for Franchise Management, Institute for Venture Management, Small Business Development Center, FastTrac, Center for Health and Medical Affairs, Institute for Health Policy, Management Center, Minnesota Center for Corporate Responsibility, Center for Nonprofit Management, Center for Real Estate Education, and Institute for Creative Studies.

Murray-Herrick Campus Center is the center of student life. It contains the University's post office, bookstore, and dining facilities; student-life offices, such as Campus Ministry, Multicultural Student Services, and the Career and Counseling Center; and the student government, newspaper, yearbook, and club and student organization offices.

Approximately seventy-five clubs, sororities, fraternities, and professional and social groups thrive on campus. Students produce a weekly newspaper, the *Aquin;* the *Aquinas* yearbook; a literary magazine, *Summit Avenue Review;* and a television program, *Campus Scope.* Students with musical talent choose from about twenty vocal and instrumental groups. Numerous events, such as homecoming, keep the campus calendar full.

St. Thomas sponsors one of the most varied and extensive intramural sports programs among schools of its size in the country. In addition, twelve men's and eleven women's varsity teams compete in the Minnesota Intercollegiate Athletic Conference and the National Collegiate Athletic Association (NCAA) Division III. St. Thomas teams have won eight national titles over the past sixteen years. Club sports include Alpine skiing, crew, and lacrosse.

The centerpiece of St. Thomas' sports facilities is a physical education, athletics, and activities complex that includes the 2,200-seat Schoenecker Arena and Coughlan Field House, with an indoor track and basketball, racquetball, tennis, and volleyball courts. Two swimming pools, a 5,000-seat stadium, fitness and weight room facilities, and an Olympic-caliber track are among the varied facilities.

The historic Chapel of St. Thomas Aquinas houses the magnificent 2,787-pipe Gabriel Kney organ, a gift to the University in 1987. The Chapel of St. Thomas Aquinas and the recently renovated St. Mary's Chapel on the School of Divinity campus are the University's main worship centers. Masses are celebrated daily during the academic year, and a variety of ecumenical prayer services also are offered.

About half of the 1,867 students housed in eight campus residence halls are freshmen. An on-campus apartment residence for upperclass students opened in 1998. Date of application and class year are among the criteria considered for on-campus housing. Handicapped-accessible facilities are available.

Location

St. Thomas is located in St. Paul where the city's historic Summit Avenue meets the Mississippi River. While situated in a quiet, residential neighborhood, the 87-acre parklike campus is only minutes from the downtown areas of Minnesota's Twin Cities, St. Paul and Minneapolis. St. Thomas also offers classes at its downtown Minneapolis campus and at sites in Anoka and Chaska and at the Mall of America in Bloomington. St. Thomas' Daniel C. Gainey Conference Center is located in Owatonna.

The Twin Cities are known nationwide for their high quality of life. St. Paul is a winner of a "Most Livable City" award and home of the acclaimed Ordway Music Center for the Performing Arts and Science Museum of Minnesota; Minneapolis, the "City of Lakes," has the renowned Guthrie Theater, Walker Art Center, and Nicollet Mall. The cities also are home to scores of lakes, professional sports teams, and companies with worldwide reputations, such as 3M, Pillsbury, General Mills, and Medtronic.

Majors and Degrees

St. Thomas awards the Bachelor of Arts degree in seventy major fields, the Bachelor of Science degree in eight majors, and the Bachelor of Science in Mechanical Engineering (B.S.M.E.) degree. The majors available are actuarial science; art history; biology; business—accounting, business communication, entrepreneurship, financial management, general business management, human resources management, international business, leadership and management, marketing management, operations management, and real estate; Catholic studies; chemistry; classical civilization; classical languages; communication; community health education; criminal justice; East Asian studies; economics; education—communication arts and literature, elementary education, science and mathematics major for elementary education, science education, secondary education, and social studies education; engineering—mechanical; English; English—writing; environmental studies; French; geography; geology; German; health education; history; international studies; journalism and mass communication—advertising, broadcast journalism, media studies, print journalism, and public relations; justice and peace studies; Latin; literary studies; mathematics; music; music—business; music education; philosophy; physical education; physical education health promotion; physics; political science; psychology; psychology—behavioral neuroscience; quantitative methods and computer science; Russian; Russian and Central and East European studies; social sciences; social work; sociology; Spanish; theater; theology; and women's studies.

Students may take courses or choose a major field (if it is not offered by St. Thomas) through the Associated Colleges of the Twin Cities, a consortium of St. Thomas and four other nearby private colleges and universities. Free intercampus bus transportation and a common class schedule make access to other colleges convenient.

St. Thomas undergraduates may elect minors from fifty-five fields of study. Additional study and licensure programs are offered in Air Force, Army, and Navy ROTC; elementary and secondary school teacher licensure programs; individualized majors; middle school endorsements—broad area science; predentistry; pre-engineering; prelaw; premedicine; prepharmacy; pre–physical therapy; pre–veterinary medicine; social work licensure; and school social worker licensure programs.

Academic Program

The undergraduate program has two components: general education requirements in literature and writing, fine arts, social analysis, human diversity, historical studies, moral and philosophical reasoning, faith and the Catholic tradition, natural science and mathematical and quantitative reasoning, language and culture, health and fitness, and computer competency, and course requirements for completion of a major concentration. A total of 33 semester courses (132 semester credits) is required for a degree.

The University operates on a 4-1-4 calendar, with spring and fall semesters and a four-week January Term. St. Thomas also offers summer sessions.

Special programs include the Freshman Year Program, designed to promote student achievement in college; the Aquinas Scholars honors program; an independent reading program; study-abroad programs; internships; the Renaissance Program, which blends a liberal arts major with a business-related minor; and the School of Continuing Studies, the adult undergraduate evening and weekend division.

In most academic areas, credit is granted to students who have a score of 3 or higher on Advanced Placement examinations sponsored by the College Board. Students also may receive credit, with qualifying scores, through the College-Level Examination Program (CLEP). It is possible to earn credit for scores of 4 or higher on the International Baccalaureate Diploma examination in subjects included in the St. Thomas curriculum.

Academic Facilities

The University has eighty-three buildings on three campuses, with seventy-six on its main campus. The value of St. Thomas' physical plant is $125 million.

St. Thomas libraries house 441,321 volumes. The O'Shaughnessy-Frey Library Center opened in 1991 and seats 1,630 students, and the John Ireland Memorial Library seats 100. Access to more than 1 million volumes is provided through a consortium of local libraries via a computerized card catalog.

Three auditoriums and Foley Theater provide facilities for student theatrical performances as well as speakers, forums, and concerts. State-of-the-art equipment in the $37-million Frey Science and Engineering Center includes a Fourier-transform infrared spectrometer.

Students also have access to nearly 900 computer terminals throughout the campus—in the Learning Center, the Computing Center, residence halls, and departmental labs and at other locations. Students have access to the Internet and the campus e-mail network.

Costs

Tuition for the 2000–01 academic year is $17,088 for full-time students carrying 32 credits a year. The average room rate is $3211; the average board plan is $2196. Student fees (student activities and technology) are $225.

Financial Aid

Federal, state, and institutional aid programs are available for students who demonstrate need. More than 75 percent of St. Thomas undergraduate students receive some type of financial aid. St. Thomas awards scholarships to students who demonstrate strong academic potential and to students of color. The University's Student Employment Program offers on-campus employment opportunities on the basis of financial need; a limited number of non-need-based jobs also are available. For need-based financial aid consideration, students who have been accepted for admission must submit the Free Application for Federal Student Aid (FAFSA) form.

Faculty

St. Thomas' 745 faculty members make teaching their highest priority. Many involve students in their research efforts as well. Eighty-two percent of full-time St. Thomas faculty members have doctoral degrees. An undergraduate student-faculty ratio of approximately 17:1 allows for personal interaction between professors and students both inside and outside the classroom.

Student Government

The All College Council (ACC) is the main student government board at St. Thomas. It represents student views and interests in academic, financial, and social affairs. The ACC plans numerous campus events, provides a variety of student services, and communicates regularly with the University's administrators and the faculty. The ACC holds regular office hours and maintains an open-door policy.

Admission Requirements

Incoming freshmen should be in the top 40 percent of their high school class and have earned an ACT composite score of 20 or higher or an SAT I combined math and verbal score of 970 or higher. A grade point average of 2.3 or better in transferable credits is required of transfer students. A rolling admission system, which begins October 1, enables applicants to learn of their admission status within three weeks after their completed applications are reviewed. Deferred entrance may be arranged.

Application and Information

A completed application (including an essay or personal statement), a $30 nonrefundable application fee, an official high school transcript, and standardized test scores are required. Students may download an application from the Web site (listed below) or submit one electronically. High school seniors are encouraged to apply by the end of December. Transfer students are encouraged to contact the Office of Admissions for details.

For information and an application form, students should contact:

Office of Admissions
University of St. Thomas
Mail #32F-1
2115 Summit Avenue
St. Paul, Minnesota 55105-1096
Telephone: 651-962-6150
                800-328-6819 Ext. 2-6150 (toll-free)
Fax: 651-962-6160
E-mail: admissions@stthomas.edu
World Wide Web: http://www.stthomas.edu

UNIVERSITY OF ST. THOMAS
HOUSTON, TEXAS

The University

More than five decades ago, the Basilian Fathers founded the University of St. Thomas (UST), a liberal arts institution, as the first and only Catholic university in Houston. UST's philosophy is that reason and faith are partners, not competitors, in pursuing truth.

The University's commitment to the liberal arts tradition is based on a goal to educate the whole person. The University's liberal arts core curriculum is designed to broaden students' educational experiences. Each student has some choice in the liberal arts core, yet all students embrace knowledge in subjects that are essential to a liberal arts education, such as theology, philosophy, foreign language, literature, English, history, communication, natural and social sciences, fine and performing arts, and mathematics. A comprehensive understanding of truth grows from this body of knowledge and prepares students for life, for specific careers, and for leadership in society. UST combines a stimulating academic environment with the Basilian Fathers' belief that education is for life, not just for making a living.

Surrounding the academic mall, older homes that were centers of Houston's social life in the early 1900s today house various departments and classrooms. The Chapel of St. Basil is the most prominent and striking feature of the campus. Its stunning 24-karat gold leaf dome and 7-foot cross tower 70 feet above the academic quadrangle and dominate the campus; it provides a quiet place for prayer and reflection. The chapel's elegant design embodies the most contemporary architectural concepts to reinforce the University's ongoing mission with its students.

Many UST students take advantage of the opportunity to live on campus. Campus life offers a community for the students and gives them accessibility to faculty members, clubs, and organizations. On-campus housing includes the residence hall, University houses, and apartments.

The University is fully accredited by the Commission on Colleges of the Southern Association of Colleges and Schools.

Location

The University's beautiful tree-lined campus covers approximately fifteen city blocks and is conveniently located less than 10 minutes from downtown Houston and within walking distance of the city's major art galleries and museums. UST is nestled in a quiet residential area in Houston's Museum District and is close to everything that the city has to offer, including professional sports, restaurants, lakes, a ballet and symphony, malls, parks, opera, museums, and libraries. These cultural and social benefits of Houston add an exciting dimension to studying at the University of St. Thomas.

Majors and Degrees

The Bachelor of Arts degree is offered in biology, chemistry, communication, drama, economics, education, English, environmental studies, finance, fine arts, French, general studies, history, international studies, liberal arts, mathematics, music, music education, pastoral studies, philosophy, political science, psychology, Spanish, studio arts, and theology. Approved teacher preparation in elementary and secondary education is also available.

The Bachelor of Science degree is offered in chemistry and environmental science.

The Bachelor of Business Administration is offered in accounting, business administration, economics, finance, management information systems, and marketing.

Preprofessional programs at the University include allied health, dentistry, law, medicine, optometry, pharmacy, and veterinary science. Cooperative programs in engineering are available with the University of Houston, Texas A&M University, and the University of Notre Dame.

Academic Program

The University offers a broad and coherent undergraduate liberal arts core curriculum in philosophy, theology, the humanities, social sciences, mathematics, and science. Philosophy and theology provide an integrating framework for all undergraduate academic programs.

Through its strong commitment to the liberal arts, the University seeks to cultivate the life of the mind and impart knowledge to the student that will instill a love for truth and promote intellectual discipline. Undergraduates are encouraged to focus on this foundation for life and use it as a basis for careers that will serve the community.

The University observes a two-semester calendar, with semester examinations occurring before a monthlong Christmas break. An interim session and two summer sessions are also offered.

Off-Campus Arrangements

Students find UST's study-abroad program to be an outstanding opportunity to gain a firsthand look at cultures around the world. Each summer, UST students spend four weeks traveling to Merida, Mexico, to delve into the history and culture of the area and to explore Mayan ruins. UST also offers a program in England that provides students with a variety of summer and fall semester programs. Other study-abroad programs are available in Argentina, Australia, Brazil, China, Costa Rica, the Dominican Republic, France, Hungary, Japan, Poland, and Spain.

Academic Facilities

The Academic Mall, designed by renowned architect Philip Johnson, serves as the center of classroom activity on the UST campus. On the blocks surrounding the mall are various departmental houses. Houses that originally were the homes of some of Houston's leaders and founders now house faculty offices and classrooms as well as provide a social environment in which campus representatives and students hold meetings, study, or simply enjoy each other's company.

The main library, Doherty Library, has more than 190,000 volumes. There are an additional four departmental libraries on campus.

The Learning Resource Center gives students the resources they need to meet their educational challenges. The Writing Laboratory assists with writing assignments. Tutors for all classes are available at no cost on a one-time drop-in or continuing basis. Tutors help students start their papers, shape and organize their thoughts clearly, and revise strategically. The

Writing Laboratory has both Macintosh and PC-compatible computers. The Mathematics Help Center supports study in mathematics and statistics and offers calculus and algebra software for further tutoring assistance. Workshops to enhance study strategies, effective reading and writing, and computer use are also available at the center.

Costs

UST has received nine national recognitions since 1994 in *U.S. News & World Report's America's Best Colleges* and in *Money Guide: Best College Buys*. Tuition, fees, room, and board at UST are well below the national average for private schools and below the average cost for private colleges and universities in Texas. For full-time students, the estimated cost for tuition, books, and fees is $12,384 per year. The average room and board cost is $5326 per year.

Financial Aid

The University of St. Thomas recruits exceptional students who wish to be creatively and actively challenged in their education and who, in return, contributes to the quality of the University community with their talents and dedication to excellence. To support its mission of excellence, UST administers federal and state financial aid programs along with more than $3.5 million in merit-based scholarships each year. Many scholarships are valued between $26,500 and $53,000. Scholarships are awarded beginning in early fall; thus, early applications are encouraged. Scholarships can be applied to any session, including fall and spring semesters, intersession, and summer session, and to study-abroad programs. All applicants are strongly urged to complete both the FAFSA and the University's financial aid application in order to complement scholarships with state and/or federal funding. To qualify for University need-based scholarship consideration, completion of the FAFSA is required. Eligibility for financial aid is evaluated upon completion of a financial aid file. The priority deadline for financial aid consideration is March 1.

Faculty

UST's faculty is composed of both lay and religious faculty members. Eighty-seven percent of the full-time faculty members hold the highest degrees in their fields and have received degrees from more than 230 universities around the world. UST's Faculty/Student Research Program allows upper-level students to work one-on-one with faculty members in their fields of study.

Student Government

The main purpose of the Student Association is to provide a form of government to direct student life and activities. In order to accomplish this mission, the student leaders concentrate on increasing student involvement in campus organizations. Also, they are involved in the University's decision-making process by ensuring an effective communication network among the student organizations, by facilitating student involvement in the evaluation and change of educational standards and methods, and by contributing to the growth of the political, social, and educational consciousness of students. By procuring information from students, the Student Association passes resolutions that are indicative of the students' opinions on campus issues. All students are encouraged to become involved with the Student Association and to participate within the University committee structure. The Student Association is composed of 2 executive officers and 4 senators from each class, all of whom are elected by their peers. The Student Association's president meets with the University President on a monthly basis, and the Dean of Student Services serves as the Student Association's adviser, attending weekly student government meetings.

Admission Requirements

For admission consideration of freshman applicants, students must have graduated from an accredited high school with at least 16 academic units, including 4 in English, 2 in social studies (1 of which should be history), 3 in mathematics (algebra, geometry, trigonometry, or calculus), 2 in natural science, and 2 in foreign language. In addition, freshman applicants are required to submit a high school transcript and to take either the ACT or SAT; test scores either equal to or above the national average are normally expected. The General Educational Development (GED) test may serve as the high school transcript.

For admission consideration, transfer applicants must have a minimum GPA of 2.0 (on a 4.0 scale) and be in good academic standing at their former college. Transcripts must be submitted from every college previously attended. Transfer applicants who have completed fewer than 60 hours of college work must also submit high school transcripts and ACT or SAT scores.

All applicants must return a completed and signed application form, a nonrefundable $35 application fee, and an application essay. Applicants who are not citizens of the U.S. should request additional forms for international student admission. Resident aliens must have their alien registration cards copied by an admissions representative.

Application and Information

Early application is encouraged for admission, scholarship, and financial aid consideration. Students who are applying for financial aid are urged to submit all necessary forms and information prior to March 1. When all admissions records are on file and have been reviewed, the Admissions Committee notifies the student of its decision. After notification of acceptance, students must send a $200 housing deposit to the Office of Residence Life as soon as possible to hold a space.

For application forms and more information, students should contact:

Admissions Office
University of St. Thomas
3800 Montrose Boulevard
Houston, Texas 77006-4696
Telephone: 713-525-3500
          800-856-8565 (toll-free)
Fax: 713-525-3558
E-mail: admissions@stthom.edu
World Wide Web: http://www.stthom.edu

UNIVERSITY OF SAN DIEGO
SAN DIEGO, CALIFORNIA

The University
Known for its firm commitment to the liberal arts, the University of San Diego has created academic programs providing students with skills necessary to grow and advance personally and professionally. Beyond the traditional arts, sciences, and humanities, USD has developed some exceptional programs in business, engineering, marine science, international relations, and the health sciences. With a holistic philosophy, USD seeks to foster competence, international and cultural sensitivity, professional responsibility, and a spirit of volunteerism in each student. Both independent and Catholic, the University places a special emphasis on the exploration of human values.

The students who share in the life at USD and contribute to its growth are a diverse group representing all fifty states and more than fifty countries. There are currently 4,000 undergraduates out of a total University enrollment of 6,100 students. Fifty percent of USD's undergraduate students reside on campus, many in recently constructed facilities. The residence halls consist of traditional dormitories, suites, and apartment-style buildings. Several meal plans accommodate different schedules and tastes in food.

A friendly campus atmosphere, the opportunity for close rapport between faculty and students, and small classes that facilitate personal attention and faculty accessibility characterize the educational environment at the University of San Diego. Numerous campus activities are available to students, including social and cultural events, informal parties, special interest groups and clubs, and intercollegiate and intramural sports. The Recreation Department complements the academic experience at the University by offering students many opportunities to use their leisure time constructively and enjoyably. The Shiley Theatre is the center of many cultural activities on campus, including concerts, lectures, plays, and recitals. There are also more than sixty student-controlled clubs and organizations, including nationally affiliated fraternities and sororities, national honor societies, and service organizations.

Location
The 180-acre campus sits on a mesa commanding inspiring views of the Pacific Ocean, Mission Bay, San Diego harbor, and the surrounding mountains. USD is conveniently located minutes away from the cultural, recreational, business, and residential areas of San Diego, California's birthplace and second-largest city.

Located on the southern tip of California, San Diego offers a wide variety of recreational, business, science, art, and cultural activities. With an average daily temperature of 64 degrees in February and 76 degrees in August, the area is perfect for biking, jogging, tennis, softball, and all aquatic sports. In addition, San Diego is noted for an outstanding zoo, museums, Spanish missions, Sea World, and major sports programs. The proximity to Mexico provides an excellent opportunity for gaining firsthand insights into Mexican culture. The city of San Diego also offers educational advantages to students in the fields of social services, education, environmental and marine science, art, music, and archaeology. The International Airport, downtown, Mission Bay, and the Aquatic Center are just a few minutes from the campus.

Majors and Degrees
The University confers the Bachelor of Arts, Bachelor of Science, Bachelor of Business Administration, and Bachelor of Accountancy degrees. Undergraduate major programs are offered in accounting, anthropology, art, biology, business administration (with areas of emphasis in finance, management, and marketing), business economics, chemistry, communication studies, computer science, diversified liberal arts (education), economics, electrical engineering, English, environmental science, French, history, humanities, industrial engineering, international relations, Latino studies, marine science, mathematics, music, nursing (post-RN only), philosophy, physics, political science, psychology, religious studies, sociology, Spanish, and urban studies.

Teaching credential programs are available in bilingual/cross-cultural studies, counselor education, educational administration, elementary and secondary education, pupil personnel services, and special education.

Academic Program
The Freshman Preceptorial program begins each USD student's academic career with a combination of advising, orientation, and an introduction to college-level scholarship. The preceptor, instructing in a supportive, small-group environment, has frequent contact with each advisee and continues advising throughout the student's general education program. Once students declare a major, the responsibility of advising shifts to the department chairman, who provides guidance in regard to specialized and professional study. Several programs, such as those in marine science and international relations, combine multiple disciplines, and special advisers are assigned to these areas. All of USD's programs are built solidly on the liberal arts, developing critical thinking skills through an emphasis on fundamental disciplines, written and oral communication, and an understanding of the past. USD gives special attention to the exploration of human and spiritual values, the interrelations of knowledge, and the development of an international perspective.

The University operates on a 4-1-4 academic calendar. Normally, the student is in residence for eight semesters and completes approximately forty-four courses, completing a minimum of 124 units.

The honors program at the University gives promising students the opportunity for both independent academic research and intensive exchange of ideas with other honors students. Selection of students to the program is made primarily on the basis of past academic achievement. The program accepts 45 students per class and offers preceptorial and seminar course work.

College credit may be granted for Advanced Placement courses taken in secondary schools when the classes are completed with scores of 3, 4, or 5 on the appropriate Advanced Placement tests given by the College Board (a score of 4 or 5 must be attained for English credit).

A number of subject examinations of the College-Level Examination Program (CLEP) have been approved by the University faculty, and in certain specified areas students may qualify for college credit by satisfactory performance on the CLEP tests.

Off-Campus Arrangements

Students interested in studying abroad may enroll for a semester or year of study in Oxford, England; Florence, Italy; Toledo, Spain; Aix-en-Provence, Toulon, and Avignon, France; Freiburg, Germany; or Nanzan and Tokyo, Japan. The course of studies is basically tutorial, supplemented by theater attendance, travel, and cultural activities.

USD conducts a five-week summer session in Guadalajara, Mexico, in cooperation with several other American universities. The summer's experiences include concerts, lectures, and planned tours and excursions.

Academic Facilities

Named Alcalá Park after the Spanish university city of Alcalá de Henares, the campus is built in the style of the sixteenth-century Spanish Renaissance. Five important academic buildings have been constructed in recent years.

Copley Library, the hub of undergraduate academic life, houses a constantly growing collection of more than 300,000 volumes and more than 1,800 periodicals. Used by undergraduate students as well as by law students, USD's Legal Research Center contains the Law Library, which houses more than 253,000 volumes and microfiche. The University's Media Center is located in Maher Hall, and most of the University's academic services offices, the Educational Development Center, and the Academic Computing Center, as well as biology, mathematics, physics, and psychology research laboratories, are in Serra Hall.

The University Center, a two-story, 78,000-square-foot facility, serves as the hub of student life on campus. It offers students and faculty the use of music and study lounges, a game room, student organization offices, and a choice of five dining areas, including a grill, a deli, and a bakery.

Camino Hall is home to Shiley Theatre and also holds offices of the Fine Arts Department, soundproof practice rooms for music students, foreign language laboratories, and labs for chemistry. Founders Hall includes Founders Chapel and the Founders Art Gallery, which features exhibits by both professional and student artists.

Costs

Tuition is $19,020 for the 2000–01 academic year. Estimated residence costs, including room and board, average $6600 per year, depending on accommodations. Personal expenses, including books, are estimated at $2500.

Financial Aid

The primary purpose of the financial aid program at USD is to provide financial assistance to students who, without such aid, would be unable to attend the University. Each financial aid package is individually designed to meet a student's need, as indicated by the Free Application for Federal Student Aid (FAFSA) and the USD Financial Aid Application (USDFAA). Fifty percent of the students receive aid consisting of scholarships, grants, loans, and campus employment in packages ranging from $200 to $20,000 per academic year. A job placement center is available to students wishing to find off-campus employment. In addition, the University offers academic and leadership scholarships, which are not dependent on need. International students are not eligible for financial aid.

Faculty

The University of San Diego has a faculty of 274 full-time members and 252 part-time members. More than 97 percent of the faculty members hold earned doctorates, and all are committed to teaching as their primary responsibility. Only faculty members teach classes, and the members of the undergraduate and graduate faculty are the same. The undergraduate student–faculty ratio of 18:1 fosters small classes, personal instruction, and individual attention, as well as faculty involvement in academic advising and University activities.

Student Government

The officers of USD's Associated Students and the class senators, who together make up the central representative group of the undergraduate students, are responsible for overseeing campus activities and the distribution of student funds.

Admission Requirements

Admission is based upon evidence of the applicant's ability to achieve success—academically, socially, and personally—at the University of San Diego. The admission criteria are highly selective. Decisions are based on the following items: the student's high school record, satisfactory SAT I or ACT scores, a letter of academic recommendation, and an essay. Decisions are made by an admission committee, which reviews each application individually.

Applicants are expected to present a well-balanced secondary school program comprised of at least four academic subjects each year. Both the content of the program and the quality of the student's performance are considered.

The University normally admits transfer students who present a 3.0 or better grade point average if they were admissible to the University as freshmen. Candidates who were not eligible for admission to the University as freshmen must present at least 24 semester units of transferable academic college work with a 3.0 or better average for consideration.

The University welcomes international students who can demonstrate an ability to undertake college work with success in the United States. TOEFL and SAT I scores are required for their admission.

Arrangements for an admission informational seminar and a campus tour may be made through the Admissions Office. Students are selected without regard to race, religion, handicap, or national or ethnic origin.

Application and Information

Application for admission is made through the Undergraduate Admissions Office. Forms should be completed and filed, together with a transcript of credits, as early as possible and no later than January 5 for freshmen and March 1 for transfers. Upon receipt of all necessary materials, each application is reviewed. Candidates are notified of acceptance by April 15. USD observes the Candidates Reply Date (May 1) set by the College Board and requests accepted applicants to notify the University of their intentions by that date.

For additional information about the University of San Diego, students should contact:

Director of Undergraduate Admissions
University of San Diego
5998 Alcalá Park
San Diego, California 92110
Telephone: 619-260-4506
              800-248-4873 (toll-free)
Fax: 619-260-6836
World Wide Web: http://www.acusd.edu

UNIVERSITY OF SAN FRANCISCO
SAN FRANCISCO, CALIFORNIA

The University

From its beginnings as a one-room schoolhouse, founded in 1855 by the Jesuits, the University of San Francisco has developed into one of the largest Catholic universities on the West Coast. Throughout its growth, the University has maintained its small class size and low student-faculty ratio. For 144 years, USF has been committed to preparing students to improve the world in which they live. Jesuit education at USF focuses on individual attention to each student. Its programs in the arts, the sciences, business, education, nursing, and the law foster a love of learning grounded by the challenge to serve society.

The city of San Francisco is the USF student's laboratory. The histories of the city and its university are intertwined. A dynamic partnership between the city and the University creates countless opportunities for students to relate classroom theory to the realities of life now and into the twenty-first century. The 54-acre residential campus has 3,800 undergraduates. The student body consists of students from all fifty states and seventy-six countries. All freshman and sophomore students are required to live on campus, unless living with parents. Students have access not only to the University's facilities, such as libraries, gymnasiums, a health and recreation center with an Olympic-size swimming pool, a pub, a coffeehouse, and a games room, but also to all that the city of San Francisco has to offer, including the ballet, opera, museum exhibits, concerts, theater, and sports events. The University is located in a beautiful residential neighborhood.

Residence hall life is an opportunity for students to live with their peers in a pleasant, relaxed environment. The University of San Francisco has eight residence halls. Gillson Hall houses mainly freshmen and is coed. Hayes-Healy Hall is all female. Phelan Hall is for upperclassmen and is coed. The Lone Mountain Hall is for students who are over 21 and is also coed. Most rooms are double; however, some single rooms are available for upperclassmen. Each residence hall has laundry facilities, study/computer rooms, and television lounges.

There are many places to eat on campus and all are within easy walking distance of the residence halls and classrooms. The World Fare offers a food court–type dining environment. There are also two student-run coffeehouses, a fast-food restaurant, a pub called the Fog and Grog, an ice cream shop, a convenience store, and a bookstore.

USF undergraduates participate in more than fifty student-run associations, including sororities, honor societies, and social organizations such as the USF Surf Club and the USF Dons Club. Among these are the oldest continuously performing theater group west of the Mississippi River, an award-winning FM radio station, a weekly newspaper, and a literary magazine. One of the most active offices on campus is the Career Services Center, which helps students to select a career field and to learn about the work opportunities available to them as both students and graduates. The Koret Health and Recreation Center is an exciting addition to the USF campus. This on-campus complex provides facilities for exercise, racquetball, swimming, court games, and socializing.

Graduate programs are available in the arts and sciences, business, education, law, and nursing.

Location

The University of San Francisco is located on a beautiful 54-acre campus in a residential neighborhood. It is minutes from downtown San Francisco and the Pacific Ocean and just one block from the 1,000-acre Golden Gate Park. The advantages of an urban campus are numerous. Because of the diversity and geographical compactness of San Francisco, students find research facilities, opportunities for community involvement, and employment experiences that few cities can match.

Majors and Degrees

The University of San Francisco grants both B.A. and B.S. degrees. Majors available within the College of Arts and Sciences are biology, chemistry, communication arts (communication theory and mass media studies), computer science, economics, English, environmental science, exercise and sports science, fine arts and architecture, French, history, mathematics, performing arts, philosophy, physics, politics, psychology, psychology and religion, religious studies, sociology, Spanish, and theology. The McLaren College of Business offers degrees in accounting, finance, general business, hospitality management, international business, and marketing. The School of Nursing offers a four-year baccalaureate program in nursing for qualified high school graduates and for second-baccalaureate candidates. Teacher certification is available at the elementary or secondary level with the addition of a fifth year of study.

The USF Pre-Professional Health Committee serves to guide and recommend students to medical and dental professional health schools, as well as to schools for pharmacy, optometry, veterinary medicine, and podiatry. A student may complete the premedical or other prehealth science requirements as part of, or in addition to, the requirements of an academic major. The Pre-Professional Health Committee assists students with the application process, develops a professional file for each student, collects and mails recommendations to professional schools, conducts interviews in preparation for application, and endorses approved candidates via a committee letter of recommendation sent to all professional schools selected by the student.

USF offers a joint Bachelor of Fine Arts degree program with the San Francisco campus of the California College of Arts and Crafts. Students can major in architecture, drawing, fashion design, graphic design, illustration, industrial design, interior architecture, painting, or printmaking. This program gives students the best of both worlds: the traditional experience of a liberal arts university and a high-energy studio arts immersion.

Academic Program

The University of San Francisco is committed to providing students with the essentials of a well-rounded education. A baccalaureate degree is issued upon the successful completion of a 128-unit curriculum. The curriculum consists of 51 units of courses in general education chosen from six specified categories of knowledge, including a 9-unit block of basic skills courses, and 80–83 units that are divided between departmental major requirements and electives. An honors program is available for selected superior students seeking a strong academic challenge.

In an effort to encourage able high school students to move rapidly into the study of subjects now customarily reserved for colleges, the University of San Francisco honors the advanced placement of students, as certified by the College Board's Advanced Placement Program tests. The University also cooperates with the College-Level Examination Program (CLEP). Students intending to earn such credit must take CLEP examinations prior to their freshman course registration at the University.

The University of San Francisco offers a special program through the St. Ignatius Institute, which has an integrated core curriculum based on the great books of Western civilization and an emphasis upon the great works of Christianity. Any undergraduate student at the University, regardless of major, may take courses through the institute to meet general education requirements. The University offers Army ROTC. ROTC scholarships are available for qualified applicants as well as continuing students.

The academic year is based on the two-semester system. Summer sessions and a January intersession are also available.

Off-Campus Arrangements

The University of San Francisco sponsors numerous study-abroad programs including ones to Sophia University (Tokyo), Oxford (England), and Innsbruck (Austria), through USF's St. Ignatius Institute, and a program at Universidad Iberoamericana in Mexico City. USF is affiliated with Gonzaga University's study-abroad program in Florence (Italy) and with Loyola University of Chicago's program in Rome. USF is also an associate member of the Institute of European and Asian Studies, which offers programs in Durham and London, England; Paris, Dijon, and Nantes, France; Berlin and Freiburg, Germany; Vienna, Austria; Madrid and Salamanca, Spain; Milan, Italy; Tokyo and Nagoya, Japan; Moscow, Russia; Adelaide and Canberra, Australia; Beijing, China; and Singapore. Numerous other study-abroad opportunities are also available. USF will assist students in selecting a location, applying to programs, making financial arrangements, registering for academic credit, securing a passport and visa, and making travel plans.

A domestic student exchange program is also available with Fordham University in New York.

Academic Facilities

University of San Francisco students have access to Gleeson Library and its more than 700,000 volumes and to Harney Science Center, which houses the Computer Center, the Applied Math Laboratory, the Institute of Chemical Biology, and the Physics Research Laboratories. Cowell Hall, in addition to being the base for nursing classes and the Nursing Skills Laboratory, houses the Instructional Media Center, and Phelan Hall is the home of KDNS and KUSF, the University's AM and FM radio stations. McLaren Center, headquarters for the McLaren College of Business, houses an additional computer laboratory and special seminar rooms.

Costs

Tuition for the 1999–2000 school year was $17,710. Room and board were $7426 for the academic year. Books, fees, travel, and other expenses are about $2000 per year.

Financial Aid

A wide variety of scholarships, grants, loans, and work-study programs are available at the University. All students must submit the Free Application for Federal Student Aid (FAFSA). More than two thirds of all University students receive some type of financial aid. There are many on- and off-campus jobs available.

The University Scholars Program is available to new freshman applicants who have a minimum cumulative grade point average of 3.8 and a combined SAT I score of 1320 (neither portion below 500) or an ACT composite score of 30. Scholars are awarded a non-need-based scholarship that pays a significant percentage of the cost of tuition for four years of undergraduate study. To remain eligible, University Scholars are expected to maintain a GPA of 3.25. Eligible students are identified during the admission process and must apply under Early Action, which has a deadline of December 1.

Faculty

The University has a faculty of nearly 240 full-time and 350 part-time members; 91 percent of the full-time faculty members hold a doctoral degree. Approximately 250 faculty members are employed in the undergraduate divisions. The University of San Francisco tradition involves a close relationship between students and faculty members. This is reflected in the small size of classes, the low student-faculty ratio, and the faculty members' availability for counseling. Classes are not taught by student teachers or teachers' assistants.

Student Government

All undergraduates are members of the Associated Students of the University of San Francisco (ASUSF). The ASUSF government has three functions: to represent the official student viewpoint, to recommend policies, and to fund activities and services. It consists of three branches: the executive branch, the Student Senate, and the Student Court. The Senate is the central representative body of the undergraduate day students and oversees the spending of the $200,000-plus student budget.

Admission Requirements

The University seeks students who are sincerely interested in pursuing a well-rounded education. The admission process is selective, and each application is reviewed individually. To enhance the quality and diversity of its student body, the University of San Francisco encourages men and women of all races, nationalities, and religious beliefs to apply. Eligibility is based on the high school grade point average, the application essay, a personal recommendation, and satisfactory test scores. All applicants are required to take the SAT I or the ACT, and international applicants are required to take the TOEFL.

Application and Information

A completed application file consists of the application form, an essay, all academic transcripts, SAT I or ACT scores, and one letter of recommendation. For the fall semester, the application deadlines are December 1 for early action and February 1 for regular action.

Inquiries should be addressed to:

Office of Admissions
University of San Francisco
2130 Fulton Street
San Francisco, California 94117-1046
Telephone: 415-422-6563
        800-CALL-USF (toll-free outside California)
Fax: 415-422-2217
E-mail: admission@usfca.edu
World Wide Web: http://www.usfca.edu

Students gather on the Harney Plaza lawn between classes for further discussion and socializing.

UNIVERSITY OF SCRANTON
SCRANTON, PENNSYLVANIA

The University

At the University of Scranton, all of the programs and services provided are developed with the student in mind. The faculty and staff members and advisers are committed to offering students the best possible educational experience and opportunities both inside and outside the classroom. This balanced focus helps give students all of the tools and training necessary for a successful career and a lifetime of learning.

The University proudly shares in the 450-year-old tradition of Jesuit education—renowned for unparalleled quality that prepares young men and women to make a difference in their fields and in the world. Students are challenged to achieve their potential and to become concerned with the world around them. The University educates the whole person—intellectually, socially, physically, and spiritually. Students learn many disciplines as they master the professional preparation of their choosing.

As a university community, the University of Scranton is proud that more than 80 percent of the students who begin as freshmen remain to graduate. The national average is less than 50 percent. On average, 96 percent of graduates find employment or enter graduate/professional school within six months of graduation.

The University consistently places an average of 50 students per year into American schools of medicine, dentistry, optometry, podiatry, and veterinary medicine. On average, 40 of the University's students are accepted into law schools per year. Both rates continue to be significantly higher than the national averages. Since 1972, 97 students have received Fulbright fellowships and other prestigious international awards for postgraduate international study.

Because learning does not stop at the classroom door, the University provides opportunities to participate in an array of social, educational, wellness, and retreat activities. More than three fourths of students spend their weekends sharing in campus or community life.

Students participate in more than eighty clubs and organizations. Those who are interested in journalism or writing can become involved in *The Aquinas* (student newspaper), *Esprit* (literary journal), *Windhover* (yearbook), or Royal Network News (campus electronic news). Students can become active in the arts through the University Players, University Bands, and University Singers; develop as a leader through student government or explore politics with the Campus Democrats and College Republicans; or choose clubs that link to academic majors or that celebrate ethnic and cultural roots. They can experience the satisfaction of helping others through Students for Social Justice, Habitat for Humanity, and Collegiate Volunteers.

The University of Scranton continues a long and storied history of success in NCAA Division III athletics. Both the men's and women's basketball teams have won national championships. Ten men's and nine women's teams regularly compete for and win Middle Atlantic Conference (MAC) titles. In addition, the University offers numerous strong intramurals, recreational sports, and club sports, including crew, equestrian, rugby, skiing, track, and men's volleyball.

On the graduate level, students can earn the Master of Arts, Master of Business Administration, Master of Health Administration, and Master of Science degrees.

Location

Located in the city of Scranton (population: 80,000), the University of Scranton is within walking distance of internship and cultural opportunities. Students can intern at one of three hospitals within a mile of campus, law offices, and the *Scranton Times*, among others. Located two blocks from campus, the Courthouse Square hosts an Italian Festival and a St. Patrick's Day parade each year, along with entertainment and ethnic restaurants year-round. Students can also take advantage of hiking, skiing, camping, and concerts in the picturesque Pocono Mountains, which are only a short drive from campus.

The University of Scranton is about 2 hours from New York City, Syracuse, Philadelphia, and Danbury, Connecticut. Other cities are also easily accessible from Scranton. With an urban campus, the University of Scranton offers all of the opportunities of being in a city. Since there is no traffic through the heart of the campus, the University of Scranton has its own charm. One visit to the 50-acre campus is enough to show the friendliness and enthusiasm that is the cornerstone of the University of Scranton community. Students have a comfortable environment in which to study and to grow—a safe campus in one of the nation's safest cities.

Majors and Degrees

Majors are available in accounting, biochemistry, biology, biomathematics, biophysics, chemistry, chemistry/business, chemistry/computers, classical languages, communication, computer engineering, computer information systems, computer science, criminal justice, early childhood education, economics, electrical engineering, electronics/business, elementary education, English, enterprise management technology, environmental science, exercise science, finance, French, German, gerontology, health administration, history, human resources studies, human services, international business, international language/business, international studies, management, marketing, mathematics, medical technology, neuroscience, nursing, occupational therapy, operations management, philosophy, physical therapy, physics, political science, pre-engineering, psychology, secondary education, sociology, Spanish, special education, theater, and theology/religious studies.

These majors lead to Bachelor of Science and Bachelor of Arts degrees. In addition, physical therapy is offered as a five-year, direct-entry Master of Physical Therapy degree program that is open only to first-time freshmen.

Academic Program

The University has developed more than sixty programs of study to match students' interests and prepare them to meet the future with confidence. In addition to more than fifty academic majors, students can choose the highly successful prelaw and premedical programs. They can enhance study in a particular field through special concentrations, minors, double majors, bachelor's/master's degree combinations, ROTC, international study, internships, clinicals, research, and three programs of advanced study. The Special Jesuit Liberal Arts Program offers an exciting and challenging way for students to fill their general education requirements, culminating in a philosophy minor. The honors program provides honors tutorials and directed research in which students develop and present an honors thesis. The Business Leadership Program allows students to interact with established business leaders and develop a portfolio on effective leadership.

Academic Facilities

The University has put in place the physical resources necessary for young scholars to learn and grow. Recently, the University was named as one of the "100 Most Wired Colleges" by *Yahoo! Internet Life* magazine. The campuswide computer network supports communication and research both on campus and worldwide through the Internet. There are about a dozen microcomputer local area networks on campus, both IBM and Macintosh, extensively used for student access, training, and classes. Students can also access the University computer system in their dorm rooms. Laboratory facilities in the sciences and health sciences are modern and well equipped. One of the newest buildings, the Institute for Molecular

Biology and Medicine, is engaged in cutting-edge cancer research. The Weinberg Memorial Library, the largest resource center in northeastern Pennsylvania, provides students with the library research services necessary to support their classroom activities. The broadcast studios for WUSR-FM (99.5 MHz), a University-owned and -operated radio station that offers training and on-air experience to students, are in a new communications wing of St. Thomas Hall, along with the Office of Instructional Technology's television studio. The University undertook a significant investment over the last seventeen years to develop its facilities. The result is new and improved resources for learning, teaching, and research that rival those of any institution of its size.

Costs

Annual tuition for the 1999–2000 academic year was $17,540, with mandatory fees of $200. Room and board charges were $7710. Expenses for books, travel, and personal supplies are estimated at about $2000 for the year.

Financial Aid

A comprehensive financial aid and scholarship program assists approximately 80 percent of the full-time undergraduate body in the form of scholarships, grants, loans, and work-study opportunities. An aid package may consist of any or all of these sources, depending upon a student's individual circumstances. The average financial aid package for 1999–2000, exclusive of loans, was $13,900.

Both full and partial tuition academic scholarships are available. These are awarded on the basis of strong academic achievement, and extracurricular activities are considered. To be considered for academic scholarships, students need only to apply for admission; scholarships are need-blind and do not require any separate applications or interviews. The University also offers two special awards for minority students: the Claver Award, for students who have demonstrated financial need, and the Arrupe Scholarship, for high-achieving minority students.

To be considered for need-based aid, students must complete the Free Application for Federal Student Aid (FAFSA) and either the CSS PROFILE or the University's financial aid application. The priority filing deadline is February 15.

Faculty

Students come to the University of Scranton to learn; faculty members come to teach. Because teaching is enriched by serious research, the faculty members are also authors and scholars. Students in virtually any program can share in their professors' pursuit of knowledge through the successful Faculty/Student Research Program.

The faculty and staff members understand that education has to be personal in order for it to be effective. With an undergraduate enrollment of 3,500 students, the 250 full-time faculty members provide a student-to-faculty ratio of 14:1 and an average class size of 20. The University is known for delivering personal attention. Faculty members routinely join students for lunch in the Gunster Student Center and can be found alongside students in extracurricular activities.

Student Government

Students are elected and appointed to various committees, where they represent the entire student body. The Student Government plans all student activities, entertainment, and expenditures, working with class officers, club presidents, and the director of student activities. It also represents student opinion on various campus and community issues.

Just as the participation of students sets the tone for a large proportion of the University's achievements and daily affairs, student input is essential to its decision making. Students elected by the student body to serve on the University Senate. Others serve with department chairpersons and faculty members. Students also sit on various search committees, which recommend candidates for the principal administrative posts.

Admission Requirements

The University is an academic community that welcomes men and women of all races, national origins, and religious beliefs. It seeks students who have demonstrated the readiness to enter a challenging college program through their course selection and level, grades, class rank, and SAT I/ACT scores. Individual cases may vary, but it is recommended that a student complete a minimum of 4 years each of English and history/social sciences, 3 years each of mathematics and laboratory science, and 2 years of a foreign language. A minimum of 18 academic units is required for admission. Candidates for mathematics and science should have 4 units in both of these areas. In addition, physical therapy and occupational therapy students are required to submit documentation of experience in their field.

The University also pays special attention to students' involvement in activities, athletics, and service as well as work experience. In order for the University to get a better understanding of students as people, students are required to submit two letters of recommendation and an essay and are strongly encouraged to visit the campus for an informational interview or small-group presentation.

The University of Scranton welcomes transfer students from accredited two- and four-year colleges and universities. Transfer students are considered for physical therapy and occupational therapy programs only on a space-available basis. As a guideline for admission, transfer applicants must have a minimum average of 2.5 on a 4.0 scale for consideration. No transfer credit is given for grades below a 2.0.

Early admission, early action, advanced standing (through AP, CLEP, and college transfer credit), and deferred entrance are available.

Application and Information

Students seeking freshman admission to the University of Scranton must first complete the application form and then have an official copy of their high school transcript sent to the Admissions Office. Scores from the SAT I or ACT are also required. The Test of English as a Foreign Language (TOEFL) is a prerequisite for international students.

The University of Scranton offers an early action program, with a November 15 deadline. Students who apply early receive notification of admission by December 15. For students who choose not to apply for early action, the University operates on a rolling admissions basis, with an application deadline of March 1. The application deadline for the physical therapy program is November 15, with notification by January 15. The deadline for submission of class confirmation fees is May 1.

Transfer students should follow the same procedures as freshman applicants. In addition, they must submit an official transcript from all colleges previously attended. The deadline is July 1 for fall semester and December 15 for spring semester.

For further information, students may contact:

Director of Admissions
University of Scranton
800 Linden Street
Scranton, Pennsylvania 18510-4699

Telephone: 570-941-7540
             888-SCRANTON (toll-free)
Fax: 570-941-5928
E-mail: admissions@scranton.edu
World Wide Web: http://www.scranton.edu

The University Commons.

UNIVERSITY OF SOUTH CAROLINA
COLUMBIA, SOUTH CAROLINA

The University

The University of South Carolina's Columbia campus, founded in 1801 as South Carolina College, quickly achieved a reputation of academic excellence in the classical tradition and became one of the most distinguished colleges in the United States. Today's University of South Carolina continues this tradition of excellence.

The location of the campus is ideal for students participating in internships related to their majors or seeking part-time employment in the area. Columbia offers a wide variety of restaurants, entertainment, and shopping, all within walking distance of the campus. Columbia is also home to a philharmonic orchestra, a symphony, ballet and dance companies, theaters, and galleries.

Described as one of the most beautiful college campuses in America, the historic original campus is surrounded by restored nineteenth-century buildings and shaded by ancient oaks. Spreading out from the Horseshoe for more than thirty-five city blocks, the rest of the campus is composed of contemporary facilities in landscaped settings. Regularly scheduled or self-guided campus tours may be arranged through the University's Visitor Center.

Students live in a variety of residence halls, including a residential college. There are more than a dozen places to eat on campus, ranging from full-service cafeterias to salad bars and sandwich shops. A variety of meal plans may be purchased.

The more than 260 student organizations on campus offer a niche for any student interest from backpacking to politics, including fraternities, sororities, service, and honors organizations. There are also 120 intramural sports teams.

The University's varsity athletic teams, the Gamecocks and Lady Gamecocks, compete in Division I of the NCAA and play national schedules. The University of South Carolina is a member of the Southeastern Conference (SEC).

The Office of Disability Services assists physically challenged students with student orientation, registration, housing, library use, transportation, and classroom adaptation and provides sign language interpreters, readers and note takers, and personal, academic, and vocational counseling.

South Carolina has an all-campus enrollment of nearly 40,000. Of these, about 23,000 students are on the Columbia campus. About 78 percent are South Carolinians, while 22 percent represent the remaining forty-nine states and more than 100 other countries.

South Carolina is a comprehensive university that offers students more than seventy undergraduate majors ranging from traditional disciplines to technical and professional areas of study. There are a graduate school, schools of law and medicine, and advanced professional-degree programs. The University is fully accredited by the Southern Association of Colleges and Schools to award baccalaureate, master's, and doctoral degrees.

Highly motivated, exceptional students find a distinctive educational niche in the University's South Carolina Honors College—rated one of the best in the United States.

Of special note is the University 101 program ("The Student in the University"), which is designed to acquaint new students with the University and its academic resources. South Carolina's program is recognized as a model for other colleges and universities both in the United States and abroad.

Location

The University's main campus is located in downtown Columbia, South Carolina's capital, a Sunbelt city with a metropolitan population of about 500,000. Columbia is in the center of the state, a 3-hour drive from the scenic Blue Ridge Mountains or Myrtle Beach and the Grand Strand.

Majors and Degrees

Of the University of South Carolina's nineteen colleges and schools, thirteen offer the undergraduate degree.

The College of Hospitality, Retail, and Sport Management offers the Bachelor of Science degree in hotel, restaurant, and tourism administration; the Bachelor of Arts degree or the Bachelor of Science degree in interdisciplinary studies; the Bachelor of Science degree with a major in administrative information management; and programs of study leading to the Bachelor of Science degree with a major in retailing or sport administration.

The Darla Moore School of Business awards the Bachelor of Science in Business Administration degree in accounting, business economics, finance, insurance and risk management, management, management science, marketing, and real estate; the Bachelor of Science degree in business administration or economics; and the Master of Accountancy (or the Master of Taxation) degree in a five-year program.

The College of Criminal Justice offers the Bachelor of Science degree with a major in criminal justice.

The College of Education's undergraduate program awards the Bachelor of Arts degree and the Bachelor of Science degree in physical education in two tracks: certification in physical education and certification in athletic training; a degree with a concentration in school athletic coaching is also offered. All other teacher-preparation degrees are a combination of the baccalaureate and master's degrees, culminating in teacher certification.

The College of Engineering and Information Technology offers the Bachelor of Science degree in chemical engineering, civil and environmental engineering, computer engineering, electrical engineering, mechanical engineering, and computer science.

The School of the Environment provides an interdisciplinary curriculum and offers the environmental studies minor.

The College of Journalism and Mass Communications awards the Bachelor of Arts degree in journalism and mass communication in four programs of study: advertising/public relations and electronic and print media.

The College of Liberal Arts offers the Bachelor of Arts degree or, in some instances, the Bachelor of Science degree in African-American studies, anthropology, art education, art history, art studio, classical studies, contemporary European studies, economics, English, fine arts, French, geography, German, history, interdisciplinary studies, international studies, Italian,

Latin American studies, media arts, philosophy, political science, psychology, religious studies, sociology, Spanish, and theater, speech, and dance.

The School of Music awards the Bachelor of Arts degree (liberal arts with a major in music) and the Bachelor of Music degree in music performance, pedagogy, and composition; music theory and history; and music education.

The College of Nursing's undergraduate program offers the Bachelor of Science degree in nursing.

The College of Pharmacy awards the Doctor of Pharmacy (Pharm.D.) degree (a six-year entry-level degree) and the Bachelor of Science degree with a major in basic pharmaceutical science.

The School of Public Health offers an undergraduate program leading to the Bachelor of Science in Exercise Science degree.

The College of Science and Mathematics awards the Bachelor of Science degree in biology, chemistry, computer information systems, geology, geophysics, marine science, mathematics, physics, and statistics; the Bachelor of Science in Medical Technology degree; and the Bachelor of Science in Interdisciplinary Studies degree.

The South Carolina Honors College awards the *Baccalaureus Artium et Scientiae* degree, which allows honors students to pursue advanced study in several disciplines rather than in a single major. Students completing the Honors College's requirements, regardless of degree earned, are awarded that degree "with honors from South Carolina Honors College."

Academic Program

Completion of the baccalaureate degree requires acceptance from one of the schools or colleges granting undergraduate degrees, each of which has its own standards, prerequisites, and degree requirements. Minimum grade point average requirements for graduation vary depending upon the degree sought.

Off-Campus Arrangements

The University has study-abroad programs with more than fifty institutions in Europe, Africa, the Middle East, South America, and the Far East. Study for a semester or a year at another American university is also available. The National Student Exchange program allows students to study at any one of more than seventy-five U.S. college campuses for up to two semesters.

Academic Facilities

Thomas Cooper Library, the University's largest library, has holdings in excess of 7 million titles. The card catalog is accessible through a campuswide computer system.

The University's Koger Center for the Arts attracts nationally and internationally known performing artists. Adjacent to the center is the University's state-of-the-art School of Music building.

Other campus facilities include Drayton Hall's proscenium theater, Longstreet Theatre's arena stage, and Williams-Brice Stadium and the Carolina Coliseum, which feature top performers as well as Gamecock sports. Each of the University's colleges and schools has its own computer laboratories, computerized learning centers, and/or research laboratories.

Costs

For 2000–01, expenses for in-state students total approximately $9025 (including tuition and fees, room and board, and books and supplies). The total estimated expenses for out-of-state students are $15,375. These expenses are incurred by all full-time students living on campus. Students have additional expenses for personal and miscellaneous items.

Financial Aid

Nearly half of the University's students receive some type of financial assistance, including financial aid, loans, work-study opportunities, and/or scholarships. Applicants must complete the Free Application for Federal Student Aid (FAFSA) before they may be considered for financial aid. The FAFSA should be submitted to the processor four to six weeks prior to the University's April 15 deadline. Generally, students considered for scholarships rank in the top 10 percent of their high school class and score 1300 or better on the SAT I. Scholarships based upon merit and strong academic potential are available, with awards from $1500 to $9000 per year. Several of the University's departments also award scholarships to outstanding entering freshmen.

Faculty

There are 1,421 faculty members at the University, 89 percent of whom hold the Ph.D. or another terminal degree. Faculty members are engaged in teaching, research, student advising, and working with student organizations.

Student Government

The University's Student Government Association is large, with more than 300 students currently holding positions. There are 3 executive officers, an executive staff, a legislative branch, and a judicial system.

Admission Requirements

Freshman admission for fall 2001 is determined by a combination of high school records and SAT I or ACT scores. The following college-preparatory high school courses are required for admission to the University: 4 units of English (at least 2 must have strong grammar and composition components, at least 1 in English literature, and at least 1 in American literature); 4 units of academic electives (at least three different fields, selected from computer science, English, fine arts, foreign languages, humanities, laboratory science, mathematics above algebra II, or social sciences); 3 units of mathematics (including algebra I and II and geometry), although a higher-level mathematics course is strongly recommended (e.g., algebra III, trigonometry, precalculus, or calculus); 3 units of social studies (including 1 unit of United States history, although ½ unit of economics and ½ unit of government are strongly recommended); 3 units of laboratory science (2 units must be taken in two different fields, selected from among biology, chemistry, or physics, and the third unit may be from the same field as one of the first two units or from any laboratory science for which biology and/or chemistry is a prerequisite); 2 units of the same foreign language; and 1 unit of physical education or ROTC.

Application and Information

High school seniors applying for admission should do so during the fall of their senior year. Transfer students are advised to apply at least three months prior to the semester in which they plan to enter. The application fee is $35.

For additional information about the University, students may contact:

Office of Undergraduate Admissions
University of South Carolina
Columbia, South Carolina 29208
Telephone: 803-777-7700
              800-868-5USC (toll-free)
E-mail: admissions-ugrad@sc.edu
World Wide Web: http://www.sc.edu/admissions

UNIVERSITY OF SOUTHERN CALIFORNIA
LOS ANGELES, CALIFORNIA

UNIVERSITY OF SOUTHERN CALIFORNIA

The University

Los Angeles was a settlement of a few thousand people when the University of Southern California opened its doors in 1880. At the time, the University consisted of a single wooden building, 10 faculty members, and 53 students. Now the second-largest private university in the country, USC has an enrollment of approximately 28,000, half of whom are undergraduates, and is currently ranked ninth among private universities awarded federal funds for research. Equally committed to the liberal arts and the specialized education provided by its professional schools, the University stresses the blending of theory and practice in undergraduate education. The liberal arts offerings of the College of Letters, Arts, and Sciences are complemented by the curricula of USC's professional schools, which are the Schools of Architecture; Cinema-Television; Dentistry; Education; Engineering; Fine Arts; Gerontology; Law; Medicine; Music; Pharmacy; Policy, Planning and Development; Social Work; and Theatre, as well as the Graduate School, the Annenberg School for Communication, and the Marshall School of Business.

USC students come from all fifty states and more than 100 countries. The University's 450 clubs and organizations provide an outlet for the myriad interests and talents of the USC community. Among these are chapters of more than thirty honor societies, more than fifty academic organizations, twenty-six fraternities and twelve sororities, and more than thirty-five ethnic/cultural groups. Songfest, the all-University student-produced musical competition, is the largest event of its kind in the country; proceeds from the event benefit Troy Camp, the University-sponsored summer camp for inner-city children. The USC Student Volunteer Center coordinates more than 250 programs through which 8,000 students annually volunteer their services to the surrounding community. The intercollegiate athletics program has won more NCAA men's team championships, produced more Olympic athletes, and had more members receive NCAA postgraduate scholarships and fellowships than the intercollegiate sports program at any other school. USC also offers intramural competition in twenty-eight sports. Undergraduates are encouraged to live on or near the University Park campus, and two thirds of all undergraduates do so. Special student services include the Career Development Center, the Learning Center, the Student Health and Counseling Services, El Centro, Black Cultural and Student Affairs, and Asian Pacific American Student Services.

Location

USC's location in the heart of Los Angeles exposes undergraduates to the cultural, commercial, and political diversity of one of the world's great cosmopolitan centers. USC students have always taken advantage of the University's setting, obtaining internships with major corporations and new technology ventures and positions in federal, state, and city agencies; local galleries; museums; and the media. Across the street from USC in Exposition Park are three museums, including the California Museum of Science and Industry; a famous Rose Garden; and the Memorial Coliseum. Located nearby along the Figueroa Boulevard "Sports and Entertainment Corridor" are the Shrine Auditorium, frequent host to the Grammy and Oscar events; the enormous Los Angeles Convention Center; the Staples Arena, which hosts the Lakers, Kings, and Clippers and the 2000 Democratic Convention; and the Los Angeles Music Center, which offers plays and concerts.

Majors and Degrees

Bachelor's degrees are awarded in accounting, acting, aerospace engineering, African-American studies, American literature, American studies, anthropology, anthropology/linguistics, applied mechanics, architecture (five-year program), art history, Asian-American studies, astronomy, astrophysics, biological sciences, biomedical engineering, broadcast journalism, building science, business administration, business administration/cinema, chemical engineering, chemistry, Chicano/Latino studies, cinema-television: critical studies, cinema-television: production, civil engineering, classics, communication arts and sciences, comparative literature, computer engineering, computer science, construction engineering, creative writing, dental hygiene, dental science, design (theatrical), earth sciences, East Asian area studies, East Asian languages and cultures, economics, electrical engineering, English, environmental engineering, environmental studies, ethnic studies, exercise science, filmic writing, fine arts, French, gender studies, general studies (elementary teaching credential), geography, geological sciences, German, gerontology, Greek, health promotion and disease prevention studies, history, industrial and systems engineering, interdisciplinary studies, international relations, Italian, jazz studies, jazz studies (vocal), Judaic studies, landscape architecture, Latin, linguistics, literature and language, management and planning, mathematics, mechanical engineering, music, music composition, music composition (film scoring), music education, music industry, music performance (guitar, keyboards, strings, vocal arts, and winds/percussion), music recording, nursing, occupational therapy, petroleum engineering, philosophy, physical sciences, physics, physics/computer science, planning and development, political science, print journalism, psychobiology, psychology, public policy, public policy and management, public relations, religion, Russian, sociology, sociology/linguistics, Spanish, stage management, structural engineering, studio arts, technical direction, theater, urban applied anthropology, visual anthropology, and water resources engineering. Preprofessional emphases include business, dentistry, law, medicine, occupational therapy, pharmacy, physical therapy, physician assistant practice, planning, and teaching.

Academic Program

USC's academic program combines the educational values of a small private college with the vast resources of a major research university. Limited to 18 students, Freshman Seminars explore various topics of interest in contemporary scholarship and research, providing an intimate introduction to academic inquiry while encouraging the development of the advisory relationship between faculty and students. Undergraduates can participate in laboratory research as early as the freshman year in fields such as computer animation, photonics, robotics, and hypersonics or as early as the sophomore year in molecular and marine biology, neurobiology, polymer and organic chemistry, and theoretical and experimental physics. USC students are not restricted to courses offered in their majors but can register for courses in almost every field, and the total number of courses offered undergraduates exceeds 2,700. USC's curriculum and range of programs not only allows students to pursue double majors and interdisciplinary minors, but also makes such creative choices almost irresistible.

The fall semester runs from late August to December, and the spring semester runs from January to late April; summer sessions vary in length. Students normally enroll for 15 to 18 units per semester (or four classes). A total of 32 units of credit may be earned by examination.

Academic Facilities

USC's Doheny Memorial Library, seventeen specialized subject libraries, and three independent libraries have total holdings of more than 5.1 million books, documents, periodicals, and other materials. Among the specialized subject libraries are the Boeckmann Center for Iberian and Latin American Studies, the Arnold Schoenberg Institute Archives, the Roy P. Crocker Business Library, and the Hoose Philosophy Library. The central "information gateway library," wired from the ground up and located in the heart of USC's undergraduate residence halls, the Leavey Library features an assortment of work rooms, carrels and training rooms, and 300 computer workstations. Through Leavey's use of the latest network technologies, USC students have access to literally any printed or nonprinted information that is available on a computer network. There are studios, drafting rooms, photography and computer laboratories, a solar and wind-simulation laboratory, shop facilities, galleries, and theaters on campus, and the School of Cinema-Television has state-of-the-art production facilities. All of USC's freshman housing facilities and almost all undergraduate facilities have at least one Ethernet connection per student.

Costs

For 1999–2000, the estimated cost of attendance was $22,198 for tuition and fees, $7282 for room and board, and $600 per year for books and supplies.

Financial Aid

USC attempts to meet the full USC-determined financial need of all undergraduates who meet the established deadlines and requirements. More than 60 percent of the undergraduates receive some form of assistance. The University annually administers more than $160 million in undergraduate financial aid. Students interested in receiving financial aid must submit the Free Application for Federal Student Aid (FAFSA) and the Financial Aid PROFILE by January 31 to receive priority consideration for available funds. California residents must apply for Cal Grants when submitting the FAFSA. Those who submit their FAFSA and Financial Aid PROFILE forms by January 31 receive notification of their financial aid eligibility by April 1. Students may be asked to submit additional materials in support of their financial aid applications. USC offers scholarships ranging from several hundred dollars up to the full cost of tuition; many are based on academic performance, and some require students to submit separate scholarship applications.

Faculty

USC has 1,605 full-time and 976 part-time faculty members, with a faculty-student ratio of 1:15. The members of the faculty are equally committed to teaching and to scholarship. Faculty members make a purposeful effort to be involved in residential activities, creating a greater sense of community among faculty and students. North Complex Residential College, USC's newest faculty-in-residence housing option, houses 550 students who live in the same academic, social, and residential community throughout their years at USC. Faculty members also serve as advisers to student organizations and honors societies. All faculty members have scheduled office hours. Graduate students may serve as instructors for the discussion sections of some undergraduate courses that have a combined lecture-discussion format.

Student Government

Recognized by the administration as the official voice of the student body, the Student Senate is a student-elected representative body of 32 senators that provides a forum for the expression and advocacy of student concerns and is responsible for planning many of the events and programs held on campus.

Admission Requirements

USC admits students of diverse backgrounds, seeking a broad geographical and ethnic representation. Basic admission requirements are the same for all students, though some majors are more competitive or require special attributes. Talent is an important consideration for applicants to programs in such areas as architecture, cinema, drama, fine arts, journalism, and music. The University is an Equal Opportunity/Affirmative Action institution. Freshman admission is based on the high school record, class rank, SAT I or ACT scores, the secondary school report, the trend in grades and the strength of the academic program, and the quality of the writing samples. Letters of recommendation and interviews are welcomed, but not required. Sixteen yearlong courses, including at least thirteen in academic solids, are required of entering freshmen. The recommended pattern of academic course work for entrance is 4 years of English, 3 years of mathematics, 2 years of a single foreign language, 2 years of laboratory science, and 2 years of social science, plus 3 years of further study in any of the above areas or in acceptable electives. Students planning to study business, engineering, or any of the natural sciences or health professions should have taken 4 years of mathematics and as many science courses as possible. Transfer applicants with fewer than 30 semester units, or 45 quarter units, of satisfactory course work from a fully accredited college or university are evaluated on the basis of both high school and college work. Transfer applicants with more than 30 semester units, or 45 quarter units, of satisfactory course work from a fully accredited college or university are evaluated primarily on their college work but still must present high school records. Students may enter with advanced standing as the result of credit earned through the Advanced Placement or International Baccalaureate Higher Level examinations.

Application and Information

Students must apply by December 10 to be considered for available scholarships. The freshman application deadline is January 10, with notification by April 1. The deadline for transfer students wishing to enter in the fall is March 2. It should be noted that a few schools and departments have different deadlines. Applicants should refer to the USC Undergraduate Application for Admission for further information. For more information, application materials, and complete instructions, students should contact:

Office of Undergraduate Admission
University of Southern California
University Park
Los Angeles, California 90089-0911
Telephone: 213-740-1111
World Wide Web: http://www.usc.edu

UNIVERSITY OF SOUTHERN MAINE
PORTLAND, GORHAM, AND LEWISTON, MAINE

The University

Since its founding in 1878 as the Western Maine Normal School, the University of Southern Maine (USM) has become the only public, urban, comprehensive university in the state. Its mission is to provide excellence in higher education to talented and diverse students. The diverse student body, exceptional faculty, and three campus locations give USM a healthy learning atmosphere and a warm, open, and challenging environment. Individuals from as far away as Latin America, South Africa, Europe, and Asia are among the 10,645 students attending USM. The Portland and Gorham campuses enjoy full classroom facilities, library services, athletic facilities, and student centers. The Portland campus is the site of the Southworth Planetarium, which is ranked among the top ten small planetariums in the United States. Gorham is the major residential campus, with five residence halls housing nearly 1,200 students. There are tennis courts, cross-country ski trails, an art gallery, a gymnasium, a campus center, and year-round theater production. Two athletic facilities opened in 1997–98: an ice arena, featuring an Olympic-size ice rink (the only one of its kind in Maine) with seating for 750, and a field house, featuring a six-lane, 200-meter track; four tennis courts; basketball courts; and baseball and softball practice areas with seating for 750. Approximately 300 upperclass and graduate students are housed in Portland Hall in downtown Portland. USM's third campus is in the heart of the growing, vibrant communities of Lewiston and Auburn, located 35 miles north of Portland. The USM student body includes accomplished artists, musicians, writers, actors, and numerous all-American athletes. The athletic program is a vital part of the USM community and the greater Portland area. In addition to a full intramural program, USM currently fields intercollegiate athletic teams (NCAA Division III) for men in baseball, basketball, cross-country, ice hockey, indoor and outdoor track, lacrosse, soccer, and wrestling and for women in basketball, cross-country, field hockey, ice hockey, indoor and outdoor track, lacrosse, soccer, softball, and volleyball. Cheerleading, golf, sailing, and tennis are coeducational offerings. USM offers master's degrees in the areas of adult education, American and New England studies, applied immunology and molecular biology, business administration (M.B.A.), community planning and development, computer science, counseling, educational administration, educational leadership, health policy and management, industrial education, literacy education, nursing, occupational therapy, public policy and management, school psychology, special education, statistics, and teaching and learning; doctoral degrees are offered in law and public policy. The College of Education and Human Development also offers a postbaccalaureate fifth-year program leading to either elementary or secondary teacher certification.

Location

USM is located in greater Portland, a region with approximately 200,000 people that is the economic and cultural center of Maine. The campuses combine the diverse lifestyles of the sophisticated city of Portland on Casco Bay and the charming New England village of Gorham 10 miles inland. Greater Portland, as the hub of the southern Maine region, has experienced tremendous growth in recent years. Many of the state's major businesses and industries are located here, including banks, insurance firms, the state's largest medical center, health-related research companies, law firms, high-technology companies, and many government offices. The Lewiston/Auburn community is one of the fastest growing in the state and is well-known for its commitment to the arts.

Majors and Degrees

USM offers forty-four bachelor's degrees, three associate degrees, nineteen master's degrees, and two doctoral degrees through its College of Arts and Sciences, Lewiston-Auburn College, and six professional schools: the College of Education and Human Development, the School of Business, the School of Applied Science, the College of Nursing and Health Professions, the Muskie School of Public Service, and the School of Law. The College of Arts and Sciences is the heart of USM, comprising twenty-two academic departments. The College offers an associate degree in liberal arts and the following baccalaureate degrees (Bachelor of Arts degrees, except as noted): art (B.A. or B.F.A.), biology, chemistry/applied chemistry, communication, criminology, economics, English, environmental science and policy, French, geography-anthropology, geosciences, history, mathematics, music, music education, music performance (B.M.), philosophy, physics, political science, psychology, social work, sociology, and theater. Self-designed majors include biotechnology, classical studies, foreign languages, French studies, German studies, Hispanic studies, international studies, linguistics, media studies, and Russian studies. In addition, preprofessional study is offered in dentistry, law, medicine, and veterinary science.

The College of Education and Human Development offers an undergraduate teacher certification program, Teachers for Elementary and Middle Schools (TEAMS). It includes course work in an academic major that leads to a degree in a liberal arts field and a professional program of elementary teacher certification (K–8).

The School of Business offers Bachelor of Science (B.S.) degree programs in accounting and business administration, as well as an associate degree in business administration. These degrees provide the basis for careers in accounting, finance, banking, industry, government, and organizational management. The School of Applied Science offers B.S. degrees in applied technical leadership, computer science, electrical engineering, environmental safety and health, and industrial technology. The pre-engineering program provides introductory courses suitable for transfer elsewhere in any engineering discipline. B.S. degrees and teacher certification in technology education and applied technical education are also offered. The College of Nursing and Health Professions offers B.S. degrees in health sciences, nursing, sports medicine, and therapeutic recreation. An associate degree is also offered in therapeutic recreation. The sports medicine program includes three majors: athletic training, exercise specialist studies, and health fitness. The health sciences degree is available to those who have completed a two-year degree in a health field. Lewiston-Auburn College offers bachelor's degrees in arts and humanities, leadership and organizational studies, natural and applied science, and social and behavioral sciences. A B.A. degree in women's studies was introduced in 1998.

Academic Program

USM's educational programs are designed to meet the needs of a changing society. The curriculum offers a variety of courses in liberal arts that foster creative thinking and communication skills. Undergraduate education at USM is built around a strong, three-component core curriculum. The Basic Competence component develops a foundation of skills necessary for academic success, including the ability to write clearly, the ability to use quantitative information, and the ability to reason effectively. The Methods of Inquiry/Ways of Knowing component introduces the student to different disciplines: their subject matter, methods, and broader purposes. These include the fine arts, humanities, social sciences, and the natural sciences. The Interdisciplinary component seeks to counteract the fragmentation that results from academic specialization. Examples of interdisciplinary courses include Global Enlightenment; the Illuminated Autobiography; and Old and in the Way: Aging in America. The honors program provides an enriched undergraduate education to students who are outstanding in their ability, curiosity, creativity, and motivation. Approximately 30 to 40 students are admitted to the honors program each year. Students work closely with faculty members in a series of small seminar-type courses. Later, honors students participate in an advanced seminar and undertake a major independent research project under the direction of a faculty member. All honors program work stresses independent learning, original thinking, and the development of skills in research, writing, and oral expression. Speakers, seminars, discussion groups, artistic presentations, and social events are scheduled regularly at Honors House. The Russell Scholars Program, an innovative living and learning community, features collaborative teaching and learning, interdisciplinary courses, and a residential component. It includes a mentoring program, community service projects, and internships. In addition to the traditional and self-designed majors that are currently offered, motivated students may choose to design an academic program that is specifically suited to their personal career goals. In conjunction with a faculty committee, students have self-designed majors in areas related to organizational behavior, graphic design, public relations, medical technology, and broadcast journalism. USM's Cooperative Education Program provides students with opportunities to apply the knowledge they gain in the classroom.

Off-Campus Arrangements

USM offers study-abroad programs in cooperation with institutions in Austria, Canada, England, France, Ireland, Italy, the Netherlands, Scotland, Russia, China, and Japan. USM also participates in the National Student Exchange.

Academic Facilities

USM comprises more than 140 acres in Gorham, Portland, and Lewiston. The campus facilities include sixty-eight buildings with more than eighty classrooms and nearly sixty laboratories. The library's collection includes more than a million books, documents, journals, and microforms. Full reference, circulation, and interlibrary loan services are available at each location. An online catalog provides access to and remote borrowing from all University of Maine System libraries. Access to the Internet and other computerized indexes and databases is available at workstations in the library and remotely to authorized users. Special collections include the Jean Byers Sampson Center for Diversity in Maine and the renowned Osher Map Library. USM has a variety of computer resources available for student use. Networked microcomputers are available on the Portland, Gorham, and Lewiston-Auburn campuses. Internet access and e-mail services are available from any of the networked computers. Students who own computers can connect from their residence hall rooms. The computer science department offers UNIX on Digital/Compaq Alpha systems and Windows NT. Specialized Windows NT labs are also available for students in electrical engineering, environmental science and policy, geography, and geosciences. Music and foreign language departments have specialized Macintosh labs. Student microlab centers, staffed by student assistants, have been established on all three campuses. The labs have Windows- and Macintosh-compatible computers with many general purpose and course-specific software packages, including software for work processing, spreadsheets, mathematics/statistics, and databases.

Costs

Expenses for the 1999–2000 academic year were $121 per credit hour for in-state tuition, $4926 for room and board, $562 for fees, and about $750 for books and supplies. Out-of-state tuition was $337 per credit hour. USM also participates in the New England Regional Program, which allows reduced tuition for some out-of-state New England students. Tuition and fees are set annually.

Financial Aid

Lack of funds should not deter students from applying for admission to USM. During 1999–2000, more than $38 million was awarded to students through various financial aid programs, including grants, loans, and employment opportunities. More than 6,700 students received an average of $6500 in financial aid. USM also helped more than 4,700 students borrow more than $24 million in low-interest loans from commercial banks. The average loan was $4500. The Office of Student Financial Aid is available to help students explore funding sources outside USM. All students must complete the Free Application for Federal Student Aid (FAFSA). These forms are available from most high school guidance offices. For priority consideration, students are encouraged to apply by February 15.

Faculty

USM's dedicated faculty members represent a wide range of knowledge and expertise. They include Fulbright Fellows and authors of national note in every academic discipline. In the last ten years, more than 100 faculty members—all with doctoral degrees or the most advanced degrees appropriate to their disciplines—have been recruited from major institutions throughout the country. Faculty members are teachers who can communicate the excitement of learning and the joy of discovery to their students. USM does not employ graduate teaching assistants for undergraduate classes; labs and discussion groups are taught by faculty members themselves. The student-faculty ratio is approximately 13:1.

Student Government

A 21-member Senate, elected by undergraduates, is the principal governing body for student life. Students having problems in any aspect of university life have recourse through the Senate and the Student Grievance Committee.

Admission Requirements

Admission to USM is competitive and based primarily on the applicant's academic background, rigor of the high school program, and grades achieved. USM also considers SAT I or ACT scores, individual talents, and activities. Evaluations of transfer students emphasize their most recent college grades. USM recognizes that prospective students may come from differing academic backgrounds, some far removed from high school; therefore, USM has established different admission categories to accommodate the needs of various students. The admission staff can arrange tours of the campuses, provide information about academic programs, and discuss admission requirements. Industrial technology, technology education, environmental safety and health, and applied technical education/leadership programs require interviews prior to admission; music programs require an audition.

Application and Information

To apply to USM, students should submit a completed University of Maine System Application and a nonrefundable fee of $25. The application asks for details of their academic, extracurricular, and personal background and an essay on their interest in USM and the degree program to which they are applying. Admission is on a rolling basis (except for the nursing program); students should complete the application process by August 1 for the fall semester and December 1 for the spring semester, but priority deadlines are February 1 for fall and December 1 for spring. Nursing program applicants must apply by February 1 for fall semester admission. International students should submit a completed USM International Student Application by April 15 for fall and October 15 for spring. For more information, students should contact:

Director of Admissions
University of Southern Maine
37 College Avenue
Gorham, Maine 04038
Telephone: 207-780-5670
          207-780-5646 (TTY)
          800-800-4USM (toll-free)
E-mail: usmadm@usm.maine.edu
World Wide Web: http://www.usm.maine.edu

THE UNIVERSITY OF TAMPA
TAMPA, FLORIDA

The University

The University of Tampa is a private comprehensive university that offers challenging learning experiences in two colleges: the College of Liberal Arts and Sciences and the College of Business. Together, they offer hundreds of courses in more than sixty fields of study. In both colleges, students work with experts in their fields, and there is a shared belief in the value of a liberal arts–centered education, practical work experience, and the ability to communicate effectively, all of which are trademarks of a University of Tampa education.

Situated on a self-contained, beautiful, parklike campus on the Hillsborough River, the University is just two blocks from downtown Tampa. At the center of campus is Plant Hall, once a luxurious 511-room hotel for the rich and famous. Its ornate Victorian gingerbread and Moorish minarets, domes, and cupolas still remain a symbol of the city and one of the finest examples of Moorish architecture in the Western Hemisphere. Although Plant Hall receives most of the attention, the campus has other buildings, including a student center, a library, an art gallery, state-of-the-art science labs, a computer resource center, a television studio, a theater, six residence halls, and complete athletic facilities. Both coed and single-sex residence halls have mostly double rooms and suites with private baths. Representing fifty states and more than eighty countries, 3,300 students, including 2,300 full-time undergraduates, are enrolled at the University.

The environment outside the classroom is supportive, stimulating, and fun. Students choose from more than ninety student organizations, including honor societies, social clubs, fraternities, and sororities. The University of Tampa has one of the top NCAA Division II sports programs in the nation. Spartan athletes have won four national championships in recent years, three in baseball and one in soccer. Intercollegiate sports for men and women include basketball, crew, cross-country, soccer, and swimming. Men's baseball and golf and women's softball, tennis, and volleyball are also offered. All students may have cars on campus.

On the graduate level, the University offers the Master of Business Administration degree and the Master of Science in Nursing degree.

The University is accredited by the Southern Association of Colleges and Schools (SACS). The College of Business is accredited by AACSB–The International Association for Management Education.

Location

There is much more to Tampa's location than beautiful beaches and pleasant year-round temperatures. Home to 2.3 million people, Tampa Bay is one of the fastest-growing areas in the United States. The city is the commercial and cultural center of Florida's west coast.

Students attend concerts, art exhibitions, theater productions, dance performances, and special lectures on campus and nearby. Just across the river are the Museum of Art, the Ice Palace, the Performing Arts Center, the Convention Center, the Aquarium, and an outstanding public library. Busch Gardens is just a few miles from campus. Within 90 minutes are Disney World and Universal Studios in Orlando. Tampa International Airport conveniently connects students with every major city in the United States and around the globe.

Majors and Degrees

The University of Tampa offers bachelor's degrees in accounting, art, biochemistry, biology, chemistry, communication, computer graphics, computer information systems, criminology, economics, education, English, environmental science, exercise science and sport studies, finance, government and world affairs, graphic design, history, international business, liberal studies, management, marine science (biology and chemistry), marketing, mathematical programming, mathematics, music, nursing (RN required), performing arts, psychology, social sciences, sociology, Spanish, and writing. Certificate programs include art therapy, European studies, gerontology, and Latin American studies. Preprofessional programs include Allied Health, dentistry, law, medicine, and veterinary science. Minors and concentrations are offered in accounting, advertising, aerospace studies, business administration, computer information systems, dance/theater, economics, environmental science, exercise science and sports studies, finance, French, international studies, law and justice, marketing, military science, music, philosophy, physical education, recreation, sports management, sports medicine/athletic training, theater and speech, urban studies, and women's studies.

Academic Program

The curriculum is designed to give students a broad academic and cultural background as well as concentrated study in a major. Hundreds of internships are available in many areas of study. The Baccalaureate Experience begins with a special freshman seminar program designed to help students assess their skills and research their interests. Students may participate in a special Gateways orientation program during the freshman year. During the first two years, students pursue an integrated core program of thirteen courses consisting of two in English, one in math, one in computer science, two in natural sciences, three in social science, and three in humanities. Prior to graduation, students are also required to take three writing-intensive courses, one course that deals with non-Western/Third World concerns, and an international/global awareness course.

Transfer students who have an associate degree may be given full junior status. Students receive advanced placement by earning acceptable scores on Advanced Placement exams, the College-Level Examination Program tests, or by completing the International Baccalaureate Diploma. As much as one year's credit may be awarded.

For qualifying students, the University offers an Honors Program of expanded instruction and student research. The program features honors classes, honors floors in residence halls, a senior thesis, and study in London or at Oxford University.

From basic tutoring to graduate school placement test practice, the Academic Center for Excellence helps students stay on track academically. The Center is one of the few facilities internationally certified by the College Reading and Learning Association. The Saunders Writing Center also offers free tutorial assistance to students working on writing projects. Other academic support offices include the Academic Advising and Career Services Offices.

Army and Air Force ROTC programs are offered.

Off-Campus Arrangements

One-year study-abroad programs are available during the sophomore and junior years. Programs of shorter duration are also offered such as the Oxford Program in England; the Washington Center in Washington, D.C.; and the Model United Nations Program in Cambridge, Massachusetts.

Academic Facilities

The University has recently undertaken $70 million in construction and technology improvements. These include three new residence halls, a new student center, and the Sykes College of Business Building. A new high-speed computer network connects the entire campus. Every student has free access to the Internet and e-mail, either from their residence hall room or from one of the convenient computer labs located on campus.

The library is computerized and well equipped to meet the diversified needs of the students. It is also a depository for United States and state government publications.

The University has a fully equipped research vessel for marine science field research and is ideally located for marine research because of its proximity to the Gulf of Mexico, Tampa Bay, and numerous freshwater lakes, rivers, and cypress swamps. Other facilities include the Ferman Music Center, the Jaeb Computer Center, the Scarfone/Hartley art gallery, Falk Theatre, and the Walker Hall science wing. There are also a public-access cable television station and a radio station on campus.

Costs

The total estimated cost for the 2000–01 academic year, excluding summer sessions, is $21,702. This cost includes tuition and fees of $16,032 and average room and board costs of $5670. There is also a $30 application fee.

Financial Aid

A high-quality, private education at the University of Tampa is not as difficult to finance as students may think. Each family's situation is evaluated individually for need-based assistance. Academic achievements, leadership potential, athletic skills, and other special talents are recognized, regardless of need. Army and Air Force ROTC scholarships are also available. The Free Application for Federal Student Aid (FAFSA) is required to determine eligibility for need-based funds. Early estimates of aid are available October through January.

Faculty

UT faculty members hold degrees from the most prestigious universities. Ninety-five percent have Ph.D.'s, and many are Fulbright Scholars and recipients of teaching awards. All classes are taught by professors, not by graduate assistants. Faculty members prize the relationships they are able to fashion with students in classes where enrollment averages 19. The student-faculty ratio is 16:1. Faculty members also pursue scores of research projects each year, often with students as assistants. The College of Business provides cutting-edge opportunities for practical experience through its Centers for Ethics, Leadership, and Quality.

Student Government

Student Government is the principal avenue for student participation in campus governance. It also provides leadership and serves as the major coordinating body for more than ninety recognized student organizations, interest groups, fraternities and sororities, residence halls, and student productions. UT's student government was voted Florida's best in 1998 by *Florida Leader Magazine*.

Admission Requirements

Fifteen high school units are recommended from the following areas: 4 units in English, 2 units in college-preparatory mathematics, 2 units in science, 2 units in social studies, and 5 units of academic electives. A foreign language is not required, but 2 units are recommended. The results of the SAT I or the ACT are required. A personal essay and at least one recommendation from a high school counselor are requested.

Early admission may be granted to students who have completed 14 academic units by the end of their junior year and who have a minimum 3.0 average (on a 4.0 scale), good SAT I or ACT scores, and their counselor's or principal's recommendation. Transfer students should have an overall 2.0 average or better (on a 4.0 scale) for college or university work attempted. They must be in good academic and social standing with the institution of prior attendance.

All international students for whom English is not a native or first language should take the Test of English as a Foreign Language (TOEFL). For intensive English study, the American Language Academy is located on campus.

Applicants who fail to meet any one of the stated admission requirements may be considered on an individual basis by the Admissions Committee.

Application and Information

High school students may request an application after the end of their junior year.

Requests for application forms, catalogs, and other information should be directed to:

University of Tampa
Office of Admissions
401 West Kennedy Boulevard
Tampa, Florida 33606-1490

Telephone: 813-253-6211
           888-MINARET (toll-free)
Fax: 813-254-4955
E-mail: admissions@alpha.utampa.edu
World Wide Web: http://www.utampa.edu

The University of Tampa's Plant Hall was once a luxury hotel.

THE UNIVERSITY OF TENNESSEE AT MARTIN
MARTIN, TENNESSEE

The University

The University of Tennessee (UT) at Martin, located in rural northwestern Tennessee, is a primary campus of the University of Tennessee System and is the only public university in west Tennessee outside of Memphis. UT Martin traces its origin to Hall-Moody Institute, which was established by the Baptists of Martin in 1900. In 1927, the campus was acquired by the University of Tennessee and was known as UT Junior College until 1951, when it became a senior college known as the University of Tennessee Martin Branch. In 1967, it became known as the University of Tennessee at Martin.

UT Martin is especially proud of its 250-acre campus that features forty-six academic and support buildings and residence facilities. A 680-acre farm, which is adjacent to the campus, serves as a research unit of the University of Tennessee Agricultural Experiment Station. Residence facilities for 2,415 single students, as well as 256 apartments for married students and faculty members, are also located on campus.

In addition to being proud of its campus, UT Martin is also proud of its environment. The University offers a total collegiate experience through high-quality academics and student activities in a traditional residential college setting. The Martin community has been recognized as one of the safest college towns in the nation.

Degree programs in more than eighty specialized fields of study highlight a broad-based undergraduate program. Undergraduate programs constitute the core of the instructional effort and provide an educational experience that enables graduates to function effectively in a multicultural society while serving in their selected fields of study. Select graduate programs and preprofessional studies are also available.

UT Martin is a member of the Ohio Valley Conference (OVC) and competes in NCAA Division I competition in both men's and women's athletics. The UT Martin rodeo team, the only collegiate rodeo team in Tennessee, is a member of the National Intercollegiate Rodeo Association. Men's intercollegiate sports include baseball, basketball, football, golf, indoor and outdoor track, rifle, and tennis. Women compete at the intercollegiate level in basketball, cross-country, indoor and outdoor track, rifle, soccer, softball, tennis, and volleyball. Both men and women compete on the rodeo team.

Location

Martin is a small, friendly community located approximately 120 miles northeast of Memphis, 150 miles northwest of Nashville, and 200 miles southeast of St. Louis. A number of state recreation areas lie within a 50-mile radius of Martin, including scenic Reelfoot Lake, Kentucky Lake on the Tennessee River, the Land Between the Lakes Recreation Area, and Natchez Trace State Park. The Shiloh National Cemetery and Fort Donelson National Monument are also nearby.

Majors and Degrees

Baccalaureate degrees are offered in the Schools of Agriculture and Human Environment, Arts and Sciences, Business Administration, Education, and Engineering.

The majors, with areas of concentration in parentheses, include accounting, agriculture (agricultural business, agricultural science–professional education option, animal science, landscape science and management, plant and soil science), biology, chemistry, communications (broadcasting, news editorial, public relations), computer science, criminal justice, economics (finance, international business), human learning (preK–3, K–8, or 1–8 licensures), secondary licensure in biology, business, chemistry, earth and space science, economics, English, French, geography, government, history, mathematics, or Spanish; special education (K–12 or preschool/early childhood), engineering (civil, electrical, industrial, or mechanical), English, fine and performing arts (teaching option–art or studio option–art/design, dance, graphic design, or theater), French, geosciences (geography–travel and tourism, geology), health and human performance (K–12 licensure, athletic training, fitness management, sports management), health sciences (dental, medical, optometry, pharmacy), history, human environmental sciences (child, family, and consumer science education; dietetics; interior design/fashion merchandising), individualized concentrations, information systems (management information systems, office information systems), international studies, management, marketing, mathematics, music (instrumental, instrumental pedagogy, music education, performance-guitar, piano, piano pedagogy, voice), natural resources management (environmental management, park and recreation administration, soil and water conservation, wildlife biology), nursing, philosophy, political science (public administration), psychology, social work, sociology, and Spanish.

Preprofessional programs are offered in agricultural engineering, cytotechnology, dental hygiene, dentistry, forestry, health information management, medical technology, medicine, occupational therapy, optometry, pharmacy, physical therapy, and veterinary medicine.

Academic Program

The University of Tennessee at Martin has established an excellent reputation for high-quality undergraduate programs. An example is the University's Honors Programs, which are designed to allow outstanding students the opportunity to be challenged and motivated in their pursuit of an academic degree.

Honors programs at UT Martin consist of the University Scholars Program, Honors Seminar Program, Chancellor's Award Program, and Departmental Honors courses. Interdisciplinary inquiry and independent study and research characterize the various courses and activities that comprise the University Scholars Program. The Honors Seminar Program brings students and distinguished campus visitors (scholars, leaders, and artists) together in seminars and forums to discuss and examine issues and ideas. Departmental Honors courses are available in several areas, and students are admitted to these courses based on superior academic records and/or placement examinations.

Off-Campus Arrangements

UT Martin began a new extended-campus initiative in August 1999 by relocating the University's primary office of Extended Campus and Continuing Education from the Martin campus to the UT Agricultural Research Extension and Public Service Building in Jackson, Tennessee. The office oversees a growing number of extended-campus courses and programs in Jackson and across west Tennessee.

Academic Facilities

Academic programs, classes, and laboratories are housed in approximately half of the University's forty-six buildings, and a $9.7-million expansion of the 300,000-volume Paul Meek Library was completed in 1995. The library serves as a selective government documents repository and subscribes to approximately 1,500 periodicals in addition to more than 2,000 full-text online titles. The audiovisual section of the library includes a media viewing room with twenty-five carrels and two media classrooms with computer and video projection capabilities. This section also houses a 6,000-volume videotape collection. In addition to a student computer lab, a faculty multimedia lab, and an after-hours study area, the library features an Innovative Interfaces automation system that includes an Web-based, online catalog. A Special Collections area contains the papers of former governor Ned Ray McWherter and former congressman Ed Jones.

The Office of Computer Services, located in Crisp Hall, provides computing facilities and services for research, instruction, and administrative computing. Computer Services also operates a computer store to streamline the purchases of computers and to make it possible for students, faculty, and staff to receive the highest possible discounts. Computer laboratories, featuring both Windows-based and Apple Macintosh computers, are also located on campus. The campus is a node on the international Internet network and provides e-mail and World Wide Web access.

An internal fiber-optic network links all campus buildings, including residence hall rooms and University apartments, into the computer network.

UT Martin also has available two distance-learning classrooms on campus to handle compressed video teleconferencing, which is used to deliver UT Martin classes to off-campus sites. The University is also a part of the University of Tennessee's video network, which links all of the campuses in the UT system.

Costs

For the 1999–2000 academic year, full-time students who were Tennessee residents paid $1328 for tuition and fees, while full-time nonresidents paid $3958. Since students can take advantage of various monthly payment options and a variety of different plans, expenses for board were estimated at $884 per semester. Housing costs were $880 per semester. Costs for 2000–01 are subject to change.

Financial Aid

Financial assistance in the form of scholarships, grants, loans, and part-time employment is offered to students based on academic achievement and need. Funds for financial assistance are provided through federal and state programs as well as from private gifts to the University. The deadline for financial assistance applications, except Army ROTC scholarships, is March 1 for the academic year beginning the following fall semester. Students must complete the Application for Admissions and the Free Application for Federal Student Aid (FAFSA). The FAFSA form may be obtained from the Office of Student Financial Assistance and from most high school counselors' offices.

Faculty

Approximately 80 percent of the University's full-time faculty members hold a terminal degree in their particular disciplines.

Student Government

The Student Government Association (SGA), whose members are elected each spring, gives students a way of participating in the decision-making process. Student government provides student input to a variety of University-wide committees, works in conjunction with the Office of Student Life to provide campus entertainment, and helps students resolve problems. Another student group, the Student Activities Council (SAC), serves the campus by planning, promoting, and implementing social, cultural, intellectual, and recreational events for all members of the UT Martin community.

Admission Requirements

To be admitted to UT Martin, a student must be at least 16 years old and a graduate of an accredited high school. In addition, he or she must have an ACT composite score of at least 19 and a minimum cumulative high school grade point average of 2.25 on a 4.0 scale, or have an ACT composite score of at least 16 and a minimum cumulative high school grade point average of 2.6, or have a minimum score of 50 on the GED test.

Students must also have completed 4 units of English; 2 units of algebra; 1 unit of geometry, trigonometry, advanced mathematics, or calculus; 2 units of natural science, including at least one year of biology, chemistry, or physics; 1 unit of American history; 1 unit of European history, world history, or world geography; 2 units of a single foreign language; and 1 unit of visual and performing arts.

Application and Information

A completed application form, along with a $25 nonrefundable application fee (and a $100 refundable housing deposit, if applicable), must be filed with the Office of Admissions. In addition, first-time freshmen must also include a copy of ACT scores and their high school transcripts, and transfer students must have transcripts forwarded from each institution attended, including high school. Applications or additional information may be requested from:

Office of Admissions
The University of Tennessee at Martin
P.O. Box 918
Martin, Tennessee 38238
Telephone: 901-587-7020
           800-829-UTM1 (toll-free)
E-mail: jrayburn@utm.edu
World Wide Web: http://www.utm.edu

UT Martin is west Tennessee's public four-year university, with nationally recognized academic programs, innovative courses, and professional development opportunities designed for a new millennium.

THE UNIVERSITY OF TEXAS AT DALLAS
RICHARDSON, TEXAS

The University

Students at The University of Texas at Dallas (UT Dallas) enjoy many benefits, including apartment-style living, the comparatively low cost, moderate size, and accessibility to faculty members. The large concentration of high-technology companies nearby, the suburban setting, and the cultural and recreational opportunities of the Dallas metropolitan area provide further benefits. Students base their pride in UT Dallas on the high-quality academic programs, sense of community, and chance to shape University traditions and activities, which may not be available at larger campuses.

The UT Dallas freshman class regularly ranks first or second in terms of average SAT scores among students at Texas public universities. Last year, *Kiplinger's* recognized UT Dallas as one of the top 100 values in state universities based on cost, quality, retention, and financial aid. *U.S. News & World Report* ranked UT Dallas sixth in the nation among colleges whose students graduate with the least amount of debt.

UT Dallas students have excelled in national and international competition: the College Bowl team ranked fifth in the nation (first and second in Texas) in 1998, UTD's chess team won the 1999 National Collegiate Chess League Championship, the Odyssey of the Mind team placed first in its division in the 1999 world finals, and the debate team placed second in the National Select Sweepstakes.

The emphasis on academics dates back to the University's founding in 1969, when civic and industrial leaders Cecil Green, Erik Jonsson, and Eugene McDermott, the founders of Texas Instruments, gave the Southwest Center for Advanced Studies, a private research center, to the State of Texas. UT Dallas first offered doctoral and master's degrees before accepting junior and senior undergraduate students in 1975. In 1990, UT Dallas enrolled its first freshmen.

The University's research roots have grown into outstanding education and research programs from the freshman through Ph.D. level and provide benefits to qualified undergraduates: research opportunities with faculty members, employment at the many nearby high-technology companies, and academic programs offering fast-track master's degrees in which students may begin graduate studies in their senior year.

Beyond the classroom, UT Dallas students find an outstanding quality of life. Students live in apartments adjacent to the campus and find the prices competitive to that of dormitories on other campuses. The apartments provide students with their own living areas, kitchens, swimming pools, volleyball courts, and clubhouses. The University also has an Activities Center with basketball courts, a 25-meter pool, a fitness/weight room, racquetball and squash courts, locker rooms, and an auxiliary gym for indoor soccer. Students are active in more than ninety organizations, including educational, departmental, ethnic, honor, Greek, political, professional, recreational, religious, service, special interest, and student governance. Students also pursue music, theater, debate, and varsity sports and have a strong tradition of creating new organizations to meet their needs.

Location

UT Dallas is located on 500 acres in the Dallas suburb of Richardson and sits among one of the three largest concentrations of high-technology companies in the nation. The University has developed partnerships with many of those companies and others to provide employment opportunities for UT Dallas students, including co-op programs.

While the suburban setting offers a quieter setting for studying, the Dallas–Fort Worth area provides all the excitement of a major metropolitan complex, including movies, restaurants, the arts district, theater productions, museums, the symphony, theme parks, and professional sports teams.

Majors and Degrees

UT Dallas offers Bachelor of Arts and Bachelor of Science degrees in a wide range of academic programs. Majors include accounting, American studies, art and performance, arts and humanities, biology, biology–premedicine, business administration, chemistry, cognitive science, computer science, crime and justice studies, economics/finance, electrical engineering, gender studies, geography, geosciences, government/politics, historical studies, interdisciplinary studies, literary studies, mathematical sciences, neuroscience, physics, psychology, public administration, sociology, speech-language pathology and audiology, statistics, and telecommunications engineering.

Academic Program

Undergraduate education at UT Dallas is designed to acquaint students with knowledge of natural sciences, mathematics, arts, humanities, and social and behavioral sciences through a general education core of 42 semester credit hours; to provide depth in a major field of study; and to enhance depth of knowledge through courses outside students' majors and beyond the general education core. A total of at least 120 semester credit hours is required for graduation, with at least 51 junior- and senior-level semester credit hours.

Outstanding freshmen are eligible for admission to Collegium V, the UT Dallas honors program, featuring an enriched curriculum, special seminars, and research opportunities with faculty members.

Academic Facilities

UT Dallas has a well-equipped, modern campus with extensive research facilities, including student labs in natural sciences, engineering, computer science, and rhetoric. Students have access to Internet accounts and e-mail.

The Eugene McDermott Library houses a collection of 750,000 volumes and 1.65 million units of microform and provides access to a wide range of journals and newspapers through its Electronic Reference Center.

Costs

The cost of college varies from student to student even at the same university. The following costs are what a student might expect to pay for one year at UT Dallas, taking 14 semester credit hours in fall and spring semesters for a total of 28 semester credit hours.

For one year, Texas residents can expect total costs of $9000, including $3400 for tuition and fees, $750 for books, $2500 for housing, and $2350 for meals. Oklahoma residents can expect total costs of $9800 per year, while other nonresidents would pay approximately $15,000 per year. Personal and transportation costs vary with the individual, but a typical student can expect $1500 in miscellaneous expenses and $750 in transportation costs.

Students who are not Texas residents who earn a competitive scholarship of $1000 or more are eligible to pay the Texas resident tuition rate.

Financial Aid

The Academic Excellence Scholarship (AES) program offers a variety of generous awards to outstanding students. Scholarship programs range from $500 per semester (for eight semesters), to tuition, fees, and housing allowance for four years, to tuition and fees, housing allowance, and cash awards. Last year, approximately one third of the freshman class received these scholarships. In addition, UT Dallas is a sponsor of the National Merit Scholarship program.

The Financial Aid Office provides a comprehensive program of grants, need-based scholarships, loans, and job opportunities. To apply for need-based financial aid, students should complete the Free Application for Federal Student Aid (FAFSA), which is available from their high school counselors. To receive priority consideration for the fall semester, students should submit all financial aid application materials prior to May 1.

Faculty

UT Dallas has one of the best research faculties in the Southwest, and most of the undergraduate courses are taught by full-time faculty members, so students learn from leaders in their fields. UT Dallas has a total of 448 faculty members, with 240 of those being tenured or on tenure track. Students regularly praise the availability of faculty members to answer questions, give advice, and provide mentoring. Students often comment favorably on the availability of even the top administrators on campus. UT Dallas President Franklyn Jenifer holds office hours for students on Friday afternoons.

Student Government

Students play a critical role in shaping UT Dallas. Student Government Association leaders were instrumental in pushing for the recent expansion of the Student Union Building and construction of the University's new Activities Center. The University administration seeks student input on a wide range of issues, including fee structure, sports, recreation, entertainment, and other University programs affecting students.

Admission Requirements

The curriculum and the expectations of student performance at UT Dallas assume that entering freshmen have successfully completed a full, college-track high school curriculum, including language arts (4 units), mathematics (3.5 units), science (3 units of laboratory science, excluding physical science), social sciences (3 units), foreign language (2 units in a single foreign language), and fine arts (.5 units in music, art, or drama). In addition, students must demonstrate strong general verbal/quantitative aptitudes, as measured on national standardized tests (ACT or SAT I).

Students are automatically admitted to the University as first-time freshmen if they graduate in the top 10 percent of their class from an accredited Texas high school. Applications from all students not graduating from Texas high schools in the top 10 percent of their class are reviewed by the UT Dallas Admissions Committee, chaired by the Dean of Undergraduate Studies. These reviews give primary consideration to the applicant's scores on standardized tests and high school scholastic records, regarding both the type and nature of courses taken and the grades achieved in specific courses. Applicants may submit additional materials for the Admissions Committee to consider in evaluating their prospective success with a rigorous college curriculum in a challenging environment. Such material can document the applicant's achievements in work experiences, community service, extracurricular activities, and surmounting obstacles to pursue higher education. Letters of reference from high school teachers, counselors, supervisors, and activity leaders are appropriate in such instances. Students should refer to the UT Dallas catalog for further clarification.

Application and Information

To apply for admission to The University of Texas of Dallas, students should submit a completed application; two current high school transcripts sent directly from each school (two final high school transcripts that reflect graduation date, class rank, and national test scores must be sent upon graduation from high school); SAT I or ACT scores (if test scores are not on the high school transcript, they must be submitted by the testing agency); and a $25 nonrefundable application fee.

Permanent residents and U.S. citizens should submit applications, including all necessary supporting documents, prior to the following dates to ensure timely processing: fall semester, August 1; spring semester, December 1; and summer semester, May 1.

For further information, students should contact:
Barry Samsula
Director of Enrollment Services
The University of Texas at Dallas
P.O. Box 830688, CN12
Richardson, Texas 75083-0688
Telephone: 972-883-2270
　　　　　800-889-2443 (toll-free)
World Wide Web: http://www.utdallas.edu/

University of Texas at Dallas students enjoy apartment-style living.

UNIVERSITY OF THE ARTS
College of Art and Design
College of Performing Arts
College of Media and Communication
PHILADELPHIA, PENNSYLVANIA

The University

The only university in the nation devoted exclusively to education and training in design and the visual, media, and performing arts, the University of the Arts (UArts) is located in the heart of Philadelphia's professional arts community. Nearly 2,000 students from forty states and thirty countries are enrolled in the undergraduate and graduate programs. Composed of the College of Art and Design, the College of Performing Arts, and the newly formed College of Media and Communication, the University offers intensive concentration within a major field as well as creative challenges in multidisciplinary exploration. Founded in 1876, the Philadelphia College of Art and Design is one of the country's leading art colleges, with nationally renowned design, fine arts, and crafts departments. Since its founding in 1870 as the Philadelphia Musical Academy, the Philadelphia College of Performing Arts has expanded to include a School of Dance, with programs in ballet, modern, jazz, and tap, as well as a School of Theater Arts, with acting and musical theater. In 1996, the University inaugurated the College of Media and Communication to prepare students for new careers in emerging interdisciplinary fields, such as multimedia design, electronic communication, information architecture, computer-generated design, electronic arts and performance, and writing for film/TV.

The University sponsors a variety of activities and regular gallery and museum trips to New York City and Washington, D.C. One fourth of the students live in University housing, which provides coed apartment-style accommodations with complete kitchen and bath facilities and laundry rooms on the premises. Resident advisers live on each floor, and there is 24-hour security. Out-of-town freshmen are guaranteed housing if their contracts are received by June 1. A new on-campus student residence is now open; the University also assists students in finding off-campus residences.

Location

With the acquisition and total renovation of a seventeen-story, 220,000-square-foot building, the University campus now spans the Avenue of the Arts from South Street to Walnut Street, the business and cultural nerve center of Center City Philadelphia. Under construction next door to the University's historic Hamilton Hall is the city's magnificent Regional Performing Art Center; in the adjacent blocks are the famous Academy of Music, the new Wilma Theater, and the University's own Merriam Theater, which books touring Broadway shows for the general public and hosts UArts student performances. The area also has world-class museums (notably the Philadelphia Museum of Art and the Barnes Museum), galleries, music and dance facilities, superb restaurants, and retail stores. Of historic importance, but also modern and sophisticated, the city is at the same time a series of small, close-knit neighborhoods with verdant squares. Fairmount Park, the largest city park in the world, provides facilities for sports activities and picnicking. The University of the Arts has the reputation of being the safest campus in the city.

Majors and Degrees

In the art and design fields, the University confers the B.F.A. degree in animation, crafts, film, graphic design, illustration, painting and drawing, photography, printmaking, and sculpture and the B.S. degree in industrial design. It also offers a certificate program in art education and a concentration in art therapy. In the School of Music, the University confers the B.M. degree in composition; instrumental performance, with a jazz/contemporary focus; and vocal performance. The School of Dance offers B.F.A. degree programs in dance and dance education, and the School of Theater Arts offers B.F.A. degree programs in acting and musical theater, plus a concentration in stage combat. A two-year certificate is available in dance and music. The University also confers the B.F.A. degree in writing for film and television, a B.F.A. in multimedia, and a B.S. degree program in communication.

Academic Program

Students are attracted to UArts because of its dynamic, creative atmosphere. Whether majoring in dance, sculpture, graphic design or multimedia, they enjoy interacting with their talented peers in other disciplines. The Freshman Project, the culmination of the required first-year writing course in liberal arts, provides the first opportunity for freshmen to work with students in other majors on a cross-disciplinary creative project. Students are further encouraged, to the extent that their busy schedules allow, to take free elective courses outside their chosen major. All students take a total of 42 credits in liberal arts, which gives them substantial exposure to humanities, social science, and science and provides them with the historical and theoretical framework of their major field.

The freshman year in the College of Art and Design is devoted to the Foundation Program and is exploratory, allowing students to investigate various disciplines before deciding on a specific major. Students are assigned to small sections, each with a team of 3 instructors. In the fall, students take two-dimensional design, three-dimensional design, and drawing, and in the spring, they may substitute a Time and Motion course for one of these. General program requirements vary from department to department. At the end of the freshman year, students select a major in crafts, fine arts, graphic design, illustration, photo, film/TV, or animation, and they may add a concentration in art education or art therapy. A wide variety of internship experiences is available to qualified students. A minimum of 123 credits is required for graduation, including 18 credits in the Foundation Program, 42 credits in the major, 42 credits in liberal arts, 15 credits in electives (9 credits of which must be taken in a department other than the major), and 6 credits in other areas outside the major. Students may request credit by examination in liberal arts subjects and by portfolio examination in studio art subjects.

In the College of Performing Arts, the School of Music program stresses individualized training, with a performance emphasis. Students undergo intensive training in theory and musicianship. Private lessons are supplemented by master classes and ensemble work. In the School of Dance, two years of ballet, modern, and jazz dance are required before students choose a major in the junior year. Electives include improvisation repertory, partnering, Spanish dance, ethnic dance, character, and mime. The School of Theater Arts concentrates on developing the student's skill as an actor. In addition to the acting studio, requirements include courses in movement, stage combat, mime, and modern dance. In the College of Performing Arts, a minimum of 126 to 130 credits is required for graduation, 42 of which must be in liberal arts. Participation in the 17-credit MATPREP Program enables students to complete bachelor's and master's degrees in teaching music in five years. The University has close working relationships, including internships, with professional theater, dance, and music groups in Philadelphia and elsewhere. Students are also encouraged to seek professional roles.

The College of Media and Communication was inaugurated in 1996 in recognition of new artistic opportunities that have arisen due to advances in digital technology. In the College's first B.F.A. program, Writing for Film and Television, students learn to create original narrative prose and to adapt stories to different media through intensive creative writing experiences as well as through the study of mainstream and experimental literature, emphasizing the art of storytelling. The B.F.A. program in multimedia is designed to prepare students to work in fields in which close interaction among arts disciplines, digital fluency, collaboration, and effective communication are key components. Students learn to combine text, image, video, animation, and sound to educate, entertain, and communicate and explore concepts of interaction and communication design. The B.S. program in communication enables students to develop, in the first two years of this major, the conceptual understanding, creative problem-solving and technical skills, and story-telling ability required for effective communication in all media. After selecting a concentration in advertising, cyber journalism, or documentary production, students work in the studio and on location, both collaboratively and individually, on creative projects using primarily digital media. Internships in professional settings provide students in these programs with real-life experience in the field.

Academic Facilities

The University facilities are composed of numerous buildings, with studios, classrooms, galleries, theaters, lounges, cafes, dormitories, and administrative offices. The newly opened Terra Building considerably augments the University's academic space, providing seventeen floors of new studios, computer labs, classrooms, performing spaces, and TV and video production and recording studios. All design departments provide individual workstations for seniors and exhibition spaces that feature student and faculty work throughout the year. The University also maintains several public galleries, where students may exhibit their work along with curator-managed exhibitions of the work of distinguished guest artists. These include the Rosenwald-Wolf Gallery, the Arronson and Great Hall Galleries, and the Mednick Gallery. Student performances are held in the University's formal theaters, such as the 200-seat DanceTheatre, the historic 1,668-seat Merriam Theater, the black box theater, the music recital hall, the Arts Bank, and a 239-seat state-of-the-art theater and rehearsal hall, and in the many informal spaces on campus.

As part of a multimillion-dollar telecommunications project, the campus has installed a new multifunctional telephone system and a new campuswide data network, which provides Internet access for every computer attached to the network. Academic computing resources include more than twenty labs on Macintosh and PC platforms that are used for special applications, such as animation, digital imaging, 3-D modeling, multimedia, music, CAD, Web page design, and more, as well as some for word processing and general purposes. Several "smart" classrooms enable faculty members to use computer applications and Internet access in their presentations; smart studios allow students to function as they would in the professional world, with a computer in the studio or office.

Students work in a large number and variety of specialized facilities—both high technology and low—located throughout the campus that support the learning of their craft. Among these are the Typography Lab, the Borowsky Center for Publication Arts, digital video editing suites, photo/film/animation labs and darkrooms, a scanner lab, an SGI lab, a bronze foundry and plaster workshop, and crafts studios and workshops for ceramics, metals, wood, glassblowing, papermaking, and fibers. The performing arts facilities include a recording studio; music technology (MIDI) studios; editing suites; chamber music studios and practice rooms; computer labs; dance and movement studios, with barres, mirrors, and resilient floors; and acting studios.

The University's library facilities include the Albert M. Greenfield Library, which contains an extensive collection of books, journals, photographs, and videotapes devoted to the arts; a Picture Resource File; Special Collections, with special strengths in book arts and textiles; a slide library that has a collection of more than 140,000 slides of art works and historical images; and a music library that contains manuscripts, journals, scores, and listening and viewing facilities. The holdings include books and periodicals, music scores, mounted pictures, slides, music recorded in LP and CD formats, videocassettes, videodiscs, and multimedia formats.

Costs

Tuition for the 2000–01 academic year is $17,250 plus a general student fee of $600. Accommodations in 3- or 4-person apartment-style dormitory units range in cost from $4100 to $5350.

Financial Aid

More than 85 percent of the University's students received more than $17.1 million in scholarships and other financial aid in 1998–99. The University funds presidential scholarships based on artistic potential and academic achievement. Financial aid is also available on the basis of the applicant's demonstrated financial need. Applicants must submit the Free Application for Federal Student Aid (FAFSA). February 15 is the suggested filing date. The University administers the following federal, campus-based student assistance programs: Federal Perkins Loans, Federal Work-Study Program awards, and Federal Supplemental Educational Opportunity Grants. Applicants who wish to be considered for scholarships should complete applications for admission and financial aid prior to March 31. Families from many different income levels can qualify for some type of financial assistance. In addition, the University's location in a large, active city provides students with diverse opportunities for part-time employment.

Faculty

University faculty members are practicing professionals who are deeply committed to the development of their students. As active participants in the arts, they have successfully achieved recognition in their specific fields of study. It is this real-world experience that gives them the knowledge and understanding that are so vital in the training of young, emerging artists—not just professionally but also in terms of personal growth. The faculty consists of 325 full- and part-time members; the majority hold advanced degrees. The faculty-student ratio is approximately 1:9.

Student Government

The Student Congress is composed of representatives of the entire student body. Regulations governing student conduct (nonacademic) have been developed to maintain a viable and orderly institutional society, to protect and safeguard the common welfare of the student body, to provide leadership training, and to promote the best possible environment for professional growth and study.

Admission Requirements

Applicants must graduate from an accredited high school. Freshman applicants are required to submit scores on the SAT I or ACT. International applicants are required to submit scores on the Test of English as a Foreign Language (TOEFL); a minimum score of 500 is required. Early entrance and deferred entrance are possible. Transfer students may be given advanced standing.

Application and Information

In addition to submitting a portfolio or auditioning, applicants should submit their high school transcript, SAT I or ACT scores, one letter of recommendation, and a personal statement of purpose. The placement of transfer students is made after an evaluation of their portfolio or audition and a determination of their approved credits. The University of the Arts follows a system of rolling admission. All students are notified within two weeks of the receipt of all required materials. Students are encouraged to submit applications by March 15 for fall admission and December 1 for spring admission. For additional information, students should contact:

Office of Admission
University of the Arts
320 South Broad Street
Philadelphia, Pennsylvania 19102
Telephone: 215-717-6030
        800-616-ARTS (toll-free)
Fax: 215-717-6045
World Wide Web: http://www.uarts.edu

UNIVERSITY OF THE DISTRICT OF COLUMBIA
WASHINGTON, D.C.

The University

The University of the District of Columbia (UDC) is the only public institution of higher education in Washington, D.C. UDC was established in 1976 through the merger of Federal City College, Washington Technical Institute, and District of Columbia Teachers College. The University, through its predecessor institutions, has antecedents dating back more than 100 years. The University of the District of Columbia is the nation's first exclusively urban land-grant university. Certificate programs and associate, baccalaureate, and graduate degree programs are offered in academic, vocational, and technical areas.

The Van Ness Campus, located in the upper-northwest section of the city of Washington, D.C., accommodates facilities for University programs. The modern 21-acre campus includes a media center with the latest automated equipment; a 1,000-seat auditorium; an outdoor amphitheater; a physical activities center, which features a regulation-size swimming pool and a diving pool; outdoor tennis courts; handball courts; and an athletic field.

The University of the District of Columbia offers ten graduate degree programs. The following graduate degrees are offered in the College of Arts and Sciences: Master of Arts (M.A.) in early childhood education, in English composition and rhetoric, and in special education; Master of Science (M.S.) in clinical psychology, counseling, and speech and language pathology; and Master of Science in Teaching (M.S.T.) in mathematics. The School of Business and Public Administration offers the Master of Business Administration (M.B.A.) and the Master of Public Administration (M.P.A.). A minimum of 30 semester hours is required for the master's degree. The UDC David A. Clarke School of Law offers the J.D. degree, which requires a minimum of 90 semester hours.

The University of the District of Columbia is fully accredited by the Middle States Association of Colleges and Schools. The School of Law is provisionally accredited by the American Bar Association.

Location

Located in the capital of the United States, the University of the District of Columbia gives its students the opportunity to partake of the cultural, political, economic, and intellectual diversity that such a location provides. As an urban land-grant institution, the University takes an active part in the life of the Washington, D.C., community through outreach programs, such as the Institute of Gerontology and the Cooperative Extension Service. It also operates the Agricultural Experiment Station and the District of Columbia Water Resources Research Center as part of its land-grant mission.

Majors and Degrees

The University of the District of Columbia offers undergraduate degrees in both the College of Arts and Sciences and the College of Professional Studies.

In the College of Arts and Sciences, the following degrees are available: Bachelor of Arts (B.A.) in art, early childhood education, elementary education, English, French, history, mass media, political science, sociology/anthropology, Spanish, and theater arts; Bachelor of Music (B.M.); Bachelor of Science (B.S.) in biology, chemistry, environmental science, health education, mathematics, nutrition and food science, physics, psychology, and speech and language pathology; Associate of Arts (A.A.) in child development and nursery school education, graphic design, and music; and Associate of Applied Science (A.A.S.) in water quality and marine science.

The following degrees are offered in the College of Professional Studies: Bachelor of Architecture (B.Arch.); Bachelor of Arts (B.A.) in administration of justice, computer science, economics, and urban studies; Bachelor of Business Administration (B.B.A.) in accounting, business management, finance, marketing, and procurement and public contracting; Bachelor of Science (B.S.) in airway science, civil engineering, computer science, construction engineering technology, electrical engineering, electromechanical systems engineering technology, mechanical engineering, nursing, office administration, and printing management; Bachelor of Social Work (B.S.W.); Associate of Applied Science (A.A.S.) in administrative office management, architectural engineering technology, aviation maintenance technology, business technology, civil engineering technology, computer accounting technology, computer science technology, corrections administration, electronics engineering technology, law enforcement, legal assistant studies, medical radiography, mortuary science, nursing, printing technology, and respiratory therapy.

Academic Program

The requirement for a baccalaureate degree is the completion of a minimum of 120 semester hours, depending upon the academic program. A minimum of 60 semester hours is required for an associate degree.

Off-Campus Arrangements

Through its Division of Continuing Education, the University provides opportunities for federal and District of Columbia government employees to enroll in classes at their work sites. Under the terms of contracts and special arrangements with government agencies, the University provides opportunities for government employees to take undergraduate courses and participate in credit and noncredit short courses, workshops, and seminars.

In cooperation with the District of Columbia Department of Corrections, the University offers instruction to inmates at Lorton Correctional Complex, in Lorton, Virginia. Through its Servicemembers Opportunity College Program, the University gives members of the armed forces the opportunity to pursue educational goals and to receive maximum credit for educational experiences obtained in the military services.

Academic Facilities

The University offers students an opportunity for hands-on experience in a wide variety of disciplines, using modern, up-to-date equipment in many fields, including a printing laboratory equipped with computerized typesetting equipment and offset presses, computer laboratories, laboratories for the physical and life sciences, fine arts studios, music practice rooms, and media learning laboratories.

The University library collection consists of more than 500,000 books, approximately 19,000 audiovisual items, more than 600,000 volumes in microform, and more than 1,400 periodical subscriptions. The collection provides the latest technology, with Internet access for students' study, research, and enrichment.

Costs

The tuition for undergraduate residents of the District of Columbia is $75 per semester hour. For undergraduate nonresidents and international students, the tuition is $185 per semester hour. All students are charged the following mandatory fees: a $75 athletics fee, a $15 student activity fee, a $15 health service fee, and a $30 technology fee. There is a $35 fee for each laboratory course. Students without private health insurance are required to purchase health insurance through a group plan provided by contract to the University.

Law School tuition is $7000 for District of Columbia residents and $14,000 for non-residents. Health insurance and student fees are also required.

Financial Aid

The University's student aid program is designed to meet the needs of eligible students by providing grants, part-time employment, and loans. The amount of assistance awarded is governed by the availability of funds, a student's academic progress, and the amount of financial need. Generally, awards are made for the fall and spring terms; summer-session awards are made separately. Students can complete the Free Application for Federal Student Aid (FAFSA) to determine eligibility for all federal and institutional aid programs administered by the University's Office of Financial Aid. The application deadline is March 15.

Faculty

The University's faculty comprises nine departments in the College of Arts and Sciences, six departments in the College of Professional Studies, and the Learning Resources Division. There is no separate graduate faculty. Most faculty members who teach graduate courses also teach undergraduate courses. All faculty members serve as advisers or academic counselors.

Student Government

The Undergraduate Student Government Association, whose representatives are elected by the entire undergraduate student body, is responsible for planning, budgeting, and implementing all student activities except for intercollegiate athletics. The entire University student body also elects a voting member to the University's Board of Trustees each year.

Admission Requirements

The University of the District of Columbia exercises an open admissions policy. Proof of high school graduation or satisfactory completion of the General Educational Development (GED) test is required for admission. Because the University is a commuter institution, its student population is drawn mainly from the Washington metropolitan area. International applicants are considered on a competitive basis.

Applicants to the School of Law must take the Law School Admissions (LSAT) exam, complete applications for LSDAS and the School of Law, and submit two letters of recommendation. The law student population reflects undergraduate and graduate credentials from UDC and a variety of national institutions of higher learning. Transfer and visiting students are accepted each semester. First-year students commence study during the fall semester only.

Transfer applicants are admitted each semester. Admission is dependent upon the student's academic standing at the previous institution attended and his or her high school record, if applicable.

Application and Information

The application deadlines for U.S. citizens are June 14 for fall admission, November 15 for spring admission, and April 1 for summer admission. International students should apply by May 1 for fall admission and by September 15 for spring admission.

April 1 is the deadline for law school applications. Applications for financial aid may be filed upon admission to the School of Law. For additional information, students should contact the Office of Admissions at 202-274-7341 or on the Web at http://www.law.udc.edu.

For further information, students should contact:

Office of the Registrar
University of the District of Columbia
4200 Connecticut Avenue, NW
Washington, D.C. 20008
Telephone: 202-832-4888
World Wide Web: http://www.udc.edu

UNIVERSITY OF THE INCARNATE WORD
SAN ANTONIO, TEXAS

The University

Consistently rated among the top liberal arts colleges in the Southwest, the University of the Incarnate Word (UIW) welcomes the interest of prospective students seeking a challenging and diverse small Catholic college atmosphere. The University seeks students who value small classes, interaction with faculty members, and dynamic learning experiences. Founded in 1881 as Incarnate Word College by the Sisters of Charity of the Incarnate Word, the school achieved university status in 1996. The University has a population of 3,639 students, with 2,906 students seeking baccalaureate degrees in forty-three undergraduate programs and 734 students seeking degrees in sixteen graduate programs. Male students represent 40 percent of the population. The student body at the University of the Incarnate Word reflects the rich cultural diversity of south Texas—50 percent of students are Hispanic American, 33 percent are European American, 6 percent are African American, and 6 percent are international. Students at the University come from twenty-nine states and Puerto Rico as well as twenty-six other countries. Thirty percent of students reside on campus with housing options that include traditional dormitories, suites, and apartments. There are two dining facilities on campus, one of which is a full-service cafeteria. Its hours of operation are convenient to the campus population. There are more than thirty different clubs and organizations on campus, including fraternities and sororities, honors organizations, *The Logos* campus newspaper, a yearbook, and theater and musical ensembles.

The School of Graduate studies offers a Master of Arts (M.A.) in biology, communication arts, education, English, multidisciplinary studies, religious studies, and social gerontology; the Master of Arts in Administration (M.A.A.); the Master of Business Administration (M.B.A.); the Master of Education (M.Ed.) in physical education; the Master of Science in Nursing (M.S.N.); and the Master of Science (M.S.) in mathematics and nutrition. The Graduate School also offers a joint master's program in nursing and business (M.S.N./M.B.A.). In 1998, the University initiated its first doctoral programs, with concentrations in the three areas of organizational leadership, mathematics education, and international education and entrepreneurship.

The University of the Incarnate Word is fully accredited by the Southern Association of Colleges and Schools, Texas Education Agency, the Council of Baccalaureate and Higher Degree Programs of the National League for Nursing, the Committee on Accreditation of Allied Health Education (CAAHE), the American Dietetic Association, and the Joint Review Committee on Educational Programs in Nuclear Medicine. The University is affiliated with the American Association of Colleges for Teacher Education, Association of Collegiate Business Programs, Association of Texas Colleges and Universities, Association of Texas Graduate Schools, and the National Catholic Education Association.

The University of the Incarnate Word is an equal opportunity institution and an Affirmative Action employer.

Location

The University of the Incarnate Word is located in the Alamo Heights area of San Antonio—an area replete with artisans, studios, specialty shops, cafes, and coffeehouses. The 56-acre campus of rolling hills is filled with live oak and pecan trees and many varieties of blooming trees and flowers. In addition, the waters of the San Antonio River flow through the campus, originating from natural springs located nearby. Within easy walking distance are the Witte Museum, the San Antonio Zoo, Brackenridge Park, Sunken Garden Theatre, and San Antonio Botanical Gardens. San Antonio, the "City of Fiesta" and America's ninth-largest city, boasts an international reputation for beauty and excitement—the Alamo, Paseo de Rio (Riverwalk), historic missions, Market Square, Institute of Texan Cultures, Sea World of Texas, and Fiesta Texas are among its largest attractions. San Antonio is also home to five military bases, numerous cultural and civic groups, a symphony orchestra, the San Antonio Spurs (NBA), major concerts, and many festivals and celebrations. San Antonio International Airport and downtown San Antonio are just 10 minutes from the University and easily accessed via public transportation.

Majors and Degrees

The Bachelor of Arts (B.A.) degree is offered in art, communications arts, English, fashion management and design, fashion merchandising, history, interior environmental design, interdisciplinary studies, mathematics, music, music industry studies, philosophy, political science, psychology, religious studies, sociology, Spanish, and theater arts.

The Bachelor of Business Administration (B.B.A.) degree is offered in accounting, banking and finance, general business, hotel/restaurant management, international business, management, management information systems, marketing and merchandising management.

The Bachelor of Music (B.M.) is offered in applied music, music education, and music therapy.

The Bachelor of Science (B.S.) is offered in biology, chemistry, environmental science, medical technology, nuclear medicine technology, nutrition, and physical education. The Bachelor of Science in Nursing (B.S.N.) is also offered. Civil engineering with a concentration in environmental engineering is scheduled to be offered to incoming freshmen in fall 2000.

Teaching certification is available in all-level certification, early childhood education, elementary education, secondary education, and special education. Preprofessional preparation is available in dentistry, law, medicine, optometry, and veterinary science.

Academic Program

To receive any degree from the University of the Incarnate Word, a student must fulfill the requirements of the University's core curriculum in addition to course work specific to the major. The University of the Incarnate Word recognizes the core curriculum as the heart of the institution. Its mission of producing critical thinkers, effective communicators, ethical leaders, responsible citizens, and caring individuals is well demonstrated in the many successful graduates of the University. The core is composed of 64 hours of course work in rhetoric, literature and arts, foreign language, wellness development, mathematics and natural science, philosophy and religion, history and behavioral sciences, and computer literacy. Students must complete 45 hours of community service to receive their diploma.

The Bachelor of Arts degree entails 128 hours of specified course work; the Bachelor of Business Administration requires 133 hours; the Bachelor of Music specifies 137 hours; the Bachelor of Science in Nursing requires 136 hours; and the Bachelor of Science specifies 133 hours. Individual programs may vary in graduation requirements depending on the minor sought, teacher certification requirements, clinical requirements, and credits transferred.

Academic credit is granted to students who achieve a score of 3 or higher on the College Board Advanced Placement examination. The University routinely administers examinations in the College-Level Examination Program (CLEP) for credit purposes. The University operates on semester calendar with two summer sessions.

Off-Campus Arrangements

The School of Extended Studies operates extended education sites at four locations: Fort Sam Houston, Lackland A.F.B., Randolph A.F.B., and U.S.A.A. Corporation. The School's burgeoning Adult Degree Completion Program (ADCaP) assists working adults with college credit who seek to complete their bachelor's degree. Consortium agreements allow UIW students access to libraries at eight local colleges and universities. Additionally, students may cross register with three of these institutions for course work if necessary. The University of the Incarnate Word recognizes the importance of providing opportunities for students to gain employment experience in their major field before graduation. As a result UIW students are involved in numerous challenging and rewarding internship and cooperative education ventures in San Antonio as well as Austin; Dallas; Houston; Washington, D.C.; and Mexico City. A summer seminar program is available in Washington, D.C. Summer programs abroad include Mexico City, London, Madrid, Moscow, and Tokyo.

Academic Facilities

The library at the University houses 172,167 volumes and 1,145 periodical titles. Information systems currently available to students include CINAHL and HaPI for nursing majors; ERIC for education students; Compact Disclosure, ABI/INFORM, and NTDB for business majors; and OCLC online system, Info Trac, National Newspaper and Dissertation Abstract, Books in Print, Dialog, Dynix, and Internet for general student use. Also available are 39,073 audiovisual items, 113,145 items on microfiche, and 4,157 reels of microfilm. A $7-million expansion of the library was completed in October 1997. The University features a number of state-of-the-art computer facilities conveniently available to students. Most housing units are computer accessible. The Learning Assistance Center (LAC) underscores the University's commitment to student achievement. Study groups, tutors, and special services are coordinated through the LAC as well. The University's fine arts complex is among the most impressive in south Texas; it includes three theaters, including a downstage, art and music studios, and the Semmes Art Gallery.

Costs

For the 2000–01 academic year, full-time resident students pay $17,130 for tuition, room and board, books, and fees. Full-time students who commute to campus pay $12,470 for tuition.

Financial Aid

Approximately 64 percent of all UIW students receive financial assistance. The University awards Presidential/Academic, Performance/Visual Arts, and Athletic scholarships, none of which are need-based. Presidential/Academic scholarships are awarded based on high school grade point average and SAT/ACT test scores. All other forms of financial assistance are awarded based on financial need as determined by the Free Application for Federal Student Aid (FAFSA). Other federal/state/institutional financial assistance awarded includes the Federal Pell Grant, Federal Supplemental Educational Opportunity Grant, Texas Equalization Grant, UIW Grant, Federal Perkins Loan, Federal Subsidized and Unsubsidized Stafford Loans, Federal Parent Loan, Texas College Access Loan, Federal Work-Study, Texas Work-Study, and Institutional Employment.

Faculty

The University of the Incarnate Word prides itself on its more than 115-year tradition of teaching excellence. The University's 332 faculty members (128 full-time and 204 part-time) include scholars with a variety of backgrounds and experiences. Sixty-five percent of the full-time faculty members possess either a doctorate or terminal degree. Faculty members at the University insist on playing an active role in the students' learning process. Small class sizes facilitate the dialogue and interaction that faculty members and students enjoy most.

Student Government

The Student Government Association has a long and productive history at the University. Student representatives are included on every policy-making body, including the Board of Trustees. SGA initiatives include a number of forums each year on issues of student concern and workshop/seminars on events of significance (Black History Month, Women's History Month, Earth Day, and the annual Golden Harvest). SGA also approves funding allocations for student clubs and organizations. Elections are held in April of each year for president and executive officers and in September for individual representatives.

Admission Requirements

The University of the Incarnate Word actively recruits students who will enrich and be enriched by a small private selective Catholic liberal arts atmosphere. Applicants are evaluated using a number of criteria—GPA, course difficulty, class rank, SAT and/or ACT scores, letters of recommendation, extracurricular activities (including part-time work), and personal interview. Prospective students are strongly encouraged to visit the campus and interview with the Office of Admissions. Applicants with nontraditional or disadvantaged backgrounds are encouraged to apply. Prospective freshmen are advised to complete a minimum of 16 Carnegie units of work in high school, including 4 units of English, 2 units of mathematics, 2 units of natural science, 2 units of language, and 1 unit of the fine arts. Favorable consideration is given to students who enroll in courses at the honors or advanced placement (AP) level. High school graduates of less than two years of the entrance date must submit either SAT I or ACT test scores. Applicants must submit an official transcript of high school work completed or General Educational Development (GED) test scores. Students considering transferring to the University must submit official transcripts of all college-level work completed. Transfer students with fewer than 24 college credits attempted must submit official high school transcripts and ACT or SAT I scores as well. The University requires a minimum 2.5 cumulative GPA for consideration as a transfer student. It is recommended that international students apply no later than three months prior to the beginning of the intended semester of attendance. The Test of English as a Foreign Language (TOEFL) is required of international students. UIW offers an intensive summer English as a second language (ESL) institute for those who need to improve their competency skills.

Application and Information

Applications for admission are accepted on a rolling basis, although students are advised to submit them before April 1 as this is the priority deadline for financial assistance. A complete application file will be processed within one week. Application materials and further information on the University of the Incarnate Word may be obtained by contacting:

Director of Admissions
University of the Incarnate Word
4301 Broadway
San Antonio, Texas 78209
Telephone: 210-829-6005
          800-749-WORD (toll-free)
Fax: 210-829-3921
World Wide Web: http://www.uiw.edu

Blue skies and warm temperatures make for outdoor study sessions.

UNIVERSITY OF THE PACIFIC
STOCKTON, CALIFORNIA

The University

The University of the Pacific was established in 1851 as California's first chartered institution of higher education. The University's classic college environment combined with modern facilities provides students with the best of both worlds. An independent university known for the diversity of its academic programs and outstanding teaching faculty, Pacific has also acquired a reputation for educational innovation, as demonstrated by the development of its cooperative engineering program and its three-year professional programs in pharmacy and dentistry. The University, which draws its 3,000 undergraduate students from more than forty states and fifty countries, is located in a residential area of Stockton, and the architecture and landscaping of the 175-acre main campus provide an Ivy League setting.

The University of the Pacific is a residential university, offering on-campus housing in twelve residence halls, six fraternities, four sororities, and four apartment complexes (including a married student apartment complex). Approximately 50 percent of the students live in these facilities. Excellent support services are available to Pacific students to enhance their academic and personal development; these are offered through the Career and Internship Center, the Health Center, and the Counseling Center. Extracurricular activities include plays, concerts, speakers, and movies in one of four theater/auditoriums on campus; excellent athletic programs at the intercollegiate, intramural, and physical education levels; broadcasting (on KUOP-FM), journalism, and forensics; professional organizations and honor societies; and more than seventy special interest clubs. The McCaffrey Center (student union) houses a grocery store, a bookstore, a movie theater, a games area, two additional dining areas, and the Associated Students of the University of the Pacific (ASUOP) offices. Recreation and athletic facilities include three gyms; playing fields; tennis, volleyball, basketball, and racquetball courts; a 28,000-seat stadium; the 6,000-seat Spanos Center; an Olympic-size swimming pool; and a student fitness center.

The University's School of Dentistry is located in San Francisco, and Pacific's McGeorge School of Law is in Sacramento. Professional and graduate programs on the Stockton campus include the Doctor of Pharmacy (Pharm.D.) degree; master's and doctoral programs in a variety of areas in education; Master of Arts programs in communication, music therapy, psychology, and sport sciences; Master of Business Administration; Master of Science programs in biological sciences, chemistry, pharmaceutical sciences, physical therapy, and speech-language pathology; and Doctor of Philosophy programs in chemistry and pharmaceutical sciences.

Location

Stockton (population 250,000) is California's largest inland port. Situated between San Francisco and the Sierra Nevada, the area provides unlimited cultural and recreational opportunities within a short drive, including entertainment in San Francisco; skiing, camping, and backpacking in the Sierra Nevada; and waterskiing and boating in the San Joaquin Delta area. Stockton is served by Amtrak, bus lines, and three major freeways. Sacramento and Oakland International Airports are both within an hour drive from campus. The climate during the school year is pleasantly warm, with the rainy season generally restricted to the period between December and March. Summer temperatures are in the 80- and 90-degree ranges. Stockton has a diverse ethnic and economic background, offering opportunities for cultural enrichment and community service.

Majors and Degrees

The University of the Pacific offers the undergraduate degrees of Bachelor of Arts, Bachelor of Arts in Liberal Studies, Bachelor of Fine Arts, Bachelor of Music, Bachelor of Science, and Bachelor of Science in Engineering. Major areas are accounting, art, art history, arts and entertainment management, athletic training, biochemistry, biological sciences, business administration, chemistry, chemistry-biology, classics, communication, computer science, economics, education, engineering (civil, computer, electrical, management, and mechanical), engineering physics, English, entrepreneurship, finance, French, geology, geophysics, German, global economic relations, graphic design, history, international environmental policy, international management, international relations, international studies, Japanese, liberal studies, marketing, mathematics, music (education, history, management, performance, composition, and therapy), philosophy, physical sciences, physics, political science, psychology, religious studies, social science, sociology, Spanish, speech-language pathology, sport management, sports medicine, studio art, and theater arts.

Special programs include a five-year bachelor's/M.B.A. option; a six-year bachelor's/J.D. option; several predental/D.D.S. accelerated programs; a five-year engineering program, which incorporates twelve months of mandatory cooperative education work experience; a three-year professional pharmacy program leading to the Doctor of Pharmacy; a preliminary-teaching-credential program; an optional cooperative education program in the liberal arts; and preprofessional studies in dentistry, law, medicine, pharmacy, physical therapy, and other fields.

Academic Program

The University emphasizes a personal approach to education, featuring small classes and close working relationships between students and faculty members. The undergraduate academic programs are arranged through seven schools and colleges, each having its own distinctive features. Students enroll in one division but can take classes in the others and share common facilities. The College of the Pacific is a departmentally arranged liberal arts and sciences college, offering more than forty majors and preprofessional programs. Undergraduate professional divisions include the Conservatory of Music, the Eberhardt School of Business, the Benerd School of Education, the School of Engineering, and the School of International Studies. The School of Pharmacy and Health Sciences includes both undergraduate and first professional degree students. The Center for Professional and Continuing Education also offers special academic opportunities.

Each of the University's undergraduate divisions has its own academic requirements. However, the University emphasizes a commitment to the liberal arts and requires all students to have some exposure to the humanities, behavioral sciences, natural sciences, and social sciences through a University-wide general education program. Many freshmen enter the University without having decided on a major area of study, and they work extensively with their academic advisers before selecting a major. The liberal arts college allows a considerable amount of flexibility in the academic program, but the professional schools are more structured in their academic requirements. All divisions on the Stockton campus follow a semester calendar; however, the professional pharmacy program has three terms per year.

Off-Campus Arrangements

The University of the Pacific currently participates in more than 200 programs in seventy countries in Africa, Asia, Central and

South America, the Middle East, North America and the Caribbean, Oceania, and Western and Eastern Europe. Students may pursue interests as varied as art, business, or chemistry and may be allowed independent study, travel, and homestay opportunities. Pacific has arrangements for participation in study abroad through the Institute of European Studies, the International Student Exchange Program, and the School of International Training as well as through special arrangements with individual universities. In addition, students may participate in special programs at the United Nations in New York or may study the federal government in Washington, D.C., through agreements with Drew University and the American University, respectively.

Cooperative education and internships play important roles at the University. All School of Engineering students spend two 6-month periods off campus working in full-time paid co-op positions. Students enrolled in all other University divisions have the option of participating in part-time or full-time internships, arranged through the Career and Internship Center.

Academic Facilities

Excellent equipment and facilities are available to assist students in their academic work outside the classroom. The Stockton campus of the University of the Pacific maintains a main library with 400,000 volumes, 2,700 periodicals, 595,000 microform items, and 7,900 video and audio units. In addition, a science library is maintained by the School of Pharmacy and Health Sciences. Students have access to extensive computer facilities. Also available for students are the Educational Resource Center, language laboratories, the drama studio, music practice rooms, the music laboratory, and the student advising center.

Costs

For 2000–01, tuition and fees are $20,725, and room and board are $6378. It is estimated that an additional $2200 will cover books and personal expenses.

Financial Aid

The University of the Pacific encourages students to apply for financial aid from all sources, including local clubs and organizations, state and federal programs, and the University. It is the intention of the University, within the limits of its resources, to provide assistance to promising students who would not otherwise be able to attend. To this end, the University has developed a financial aid program that includes scholarships, grants, loans, and job opportunities. Financial aid awards from Pacific are based on a combination of financial need and/or academic achievement. In recent years, Pacific has significantly increased its merit-based scholarship programs and in 1997, became the first institution to provide matching scholarships to new students who receive a Cal Grant (California state gift aid). More than 75 percent of the student body receive some type of financial aid, and on-campus jobs are available through the Career and Internship Center. The priority date to apply for financial aid is February 15 for the fall semester.

Faculty

Of the 370 full-time faculty members on the Stockton campus, 86 percent have earned doctoral degrees or the highest degree in their field. The priority of Pacific's faculty is the education of individual students rather than research. The faculty members are actively engaged in classroom teaching and academic advising and also participate in numerous student social activities on campus. The faculty-student ratio is 1:15.

Student Government

The ASUOP, the student government organization, provides many services to the campus. The ASUOP president and Senate express the students' views as they work with the University administration. ASUOP operates a 250-seat movie theater, a grocery store, and an equipment-loan store. ASUOP Presents brings nationally known speakers to campus, and a very active social commission plans an extensive activities calendar that includes films, dances, and concerts on campus. Each school and college also has its own student association, all of them concerned with both academic and social activities. Students are included on committees reviewing academic affairs and the curriculum structure, evaluating courses and faculty members, and planning future facilities and programs.

Admission Requirements

The University of the Pacific seeks freshman applicants who have had strong college-preparatory backgrounds of four academic subjects each semester. A challenging secondary school program of 4 years of English, 4 years of social studies, 3 years of mathematics, 2 years of laboratory sciences, and 2 or more years of foreign language is highly recommended. Science students should include chemistry, physics, and higher mathematics. The University requires an official high school transcript, a counselor or teacher recommendation, SAT I or ACT scores, and a personal essay.

Application and Information

Out-of-state and international students are encouraged to apply, and approximately 450 transfer students and 700 freshmen enroll each year. Early Action (non-binding admission) is available for outstanding students who apply by December 15. Applications are accepted on a rolling basis, but applicants are encouraged to meet a February 15 priority date. All interested students are encouraged to arrange with the Office of Admissions to visit the campus. Further information may be obtained by contacting:

Office of Admissions
University of the Pacific
Stockton, California 95211
Telephone: 209-946-2211
          800-959-2867 (toll-free)
E-mail: admissions@uop.edu
World Wide Web: http://www.uop.edu

These students are meeting outside the Holt Memorial Library with the Robert Burns Tower in the background.

UNIVERSITY OF THE SCIENCES IN PHILADELPHIA
PHILADELPHIA, PENNSYLVANIA

The University

The University of the Sciences in Philadelphia (USP), formerly the Philadelphia College of Pharmacy and Science, was founded in 1821 as the Philadelphia College of Pharmacy, America's first college of pharmacy. The University of the Sciences in Philadelphia is located on a 30-acre campus in the academic section of historic Philadelphia known as University City. Besides USP, the University of Pennsylvania and Drexel University also call University City home. USP currently enrolls 2,025 undergraduate students in fifteen majors and 200 students in nine graduate programs. The campus consists of fourteen buildings, with a major campus expansion and renovation project planned to begin in 2000. The University offers a wide variety of cocurricular activities that include intercollegiate and intramural athletics; literary publications; social, professional, religious, and honors organizations; and musical and drama groups. USP competes athletically at the NAIA Division II and NCAA Division II levels, with men's teams in baseball, basketball, cross-country, golf, tennis, and rifle. Women's teams are available in basketball, cross-country, golf, softball, tennis, rifle, and volleyball.

Location

USP's location in the University City section of Philadelphia offers considerable advantage and appeal. It not only offers a wide variety of educational opportunities, but it also is a culturally, architecturally, and socially diverse community that caters to the local college student population. The University of the Sciences in Philadelphia is also actively involved with a number of local community organizations that are designed to foster improvement, development, and unity in the University City community. The Philadelphia metropolitan area is the home of more than forty other colleges and universities. USP students realize that Philadelphia and its immediate region provide unmatched levels of off-campus clinical and scientific opportunities, which are required in a number of programs. Within a short 20-minute trolley ride to the Center City area are the vast cultural, historical, and shopping attractions of the fifth-largest city in the United States.

Majors and Degrees

The University of the Sciences in Philadelphia includes three undergraduate colleges: the Philadelphia College of Pharmacy, which offers programs in pharmacy, pharmacology and toxicology, pharmaceutical technology, and pharmaceutical marketing and management; the College of Health Sciences, which offers programs in physical therapy, occupational therapy, physician assistant studies, and medical technology; and the College of Arts and Sciences, which offers majors in biochemistry, biology, biomedical writing, chemistry, environmental science, health psychology, microbiology, and pharmaceutical chemistry.

Academic Program

Four majors are offered in the Philadelphia College of Pharmacy: a six-year Doctor of Pharmacy (Pharm.D.) program and four-year B.S. degree programs in pharmacy and toxicology, pharmaceutical technology, and pharmaceutical marketing and management. In the Doctor of Pharmacy program, students are guaranteed a seat in the professional phase (years 3–6) as long as the preprofessional phase (years 1–2) is successfully completed and an acceptable academic record is maintained. The pharmacy program at USP is recognized worldwide and prepares students for the increasingly clinical nature of pharmacy practice.

Pharmacology and toxicology, pharmaceutical technology, and pharmaceutical marketing and management are unique B.S. degree programs that provide excellent career opportunities and address specific manpower needs within the pharmaceutical industry.

Four programs of study are available in the College of Health Sciences: physical therapy, occupational therapy, physician assistant studies, and medical technology. Both the physical therapy and occupational therapy programs are five-year, integrated undergraduate/professional degree programs that lead to the dual degrees of Bachelor of Science in health sciences and the Master of Physical Therapy (M.P.T.) or the Master of Occupational Therapy (M.O.T.), respectively. In both programs, students are admitted as freshmen and guaranteed a place in the professional phase, provided an acceptable academic record is maintained.

The physician assistant studies program at the University of the Sciences in Philadelphia is a five-year program that leads to the Bachelor of Science and Master of Science degrees in health science and is in partnership with the Philadelphia College of Osteopathic Medicine (PCOM). Students enrolled in the physician assistant studies program complete their preprofessional component (years 1–3) in the natural sciences, social sciences, and humanities at USP. The professional component of the program (years 4–5) is completed at PCOM.

Medical technology students at the University of the Sciences in Philadelphia receive an excellent three-year academic foundation in preparation for their fourth year, which is spent in a clinical setting at an approved hospital school of medical technology.

Eight different four-year Bachelor of Science degree programs are offered in the College of Arts and Sciences. They include biochemistry, biology, biomedical writing, chemistry, environmental science, health psychology, microbiology, and pharmaceutical chemistry. Health psychology B.S. students may elect to remain at USP for an additional year and qualify for the M.S. in health psychology program. The College of Arts and Sciences combines the expertise of an outstanding group of scientists, researchers, and educators with academic facilities not often found at an institution the size of USP. This combination creates an academic atmosphere of especially high quality.

The University of the Sciences in Philadelphia's strong tradition of excellence prepares graduates to enter postbaccalaureate degrees in medicine, dentistry, veterinary medicine, and other health professions. Traditionally, premed students choose to major in chemistry, biochemistry, biology, microbiology, or pharmacology and toxicology. The curricula in these and most of the other programs include the basic courses required for admission to medical school. Beginning with the first year, premed students receive individualized counseling by the Pre-Professional Advisor and their faculty adviser in selecting courses to meet their career goals.

An innovative Science Teacher Certification program is available for those students who are majoring in biology or chemistry and wish to pursue teaching careers. The areas of certification include biology, chemistry, general science, and environmental science.

Students may enroll at the University of the Sciences in the one-year Open Major program. Through a special orientation program, open majors are introduced to the various academic disciplines and career opportunities available to them. Open majors formally declare a major during the spring semester of the first year.

Academic Facilities

Classes and laboratory course work are conducted in seven academic buildings on the University of the Sciences in Philadelphia's campus, while the remaining buildings serve as residence halls or support-service facilities. USP houses more than eighty scientific laboratories and a sufficient number of computer terminals for student use. The Joseph W. England Library contains more than 80,000 volumes and 800 periodicals in addition to numerous electronic information programs.

Costs

Estimated tuition for the 2000–01 academic year is $14,800; room and board are anticipated to be $7000. Costs are subject to change.

Financial Aid

Currently, 90 percent of the undergraduates at USP receive financial assistance, amounting in the aggregate to more than $6 million. Types and sources of aid include Federal Perkins Loans; Health Professions Loans; Federal Work-Study Program; USP Merit Scholarships and Grants, student employment, and institutional loan funds; deferred tuition payment plans; student loans; and scholarships received from states, municipalities, and service clubs or other organizations. All applicants who seek financial assistance must complete the Free Application for Federal Student Aid (FAFSA). A number of academic scholarships and grants are awarded to first-year and transfer students each year. All applications are automatically reviewed for scholarship eligibility.

Faculty

There are 125 faculty members. Of these, 90 have doctoral degrees. All full-time faculty members teach undergraduates, and many also teach graduate students and conduct research. A total of 40 graduate assistants serve as laboratory aides.

Student Government

Student government is composed of representatives from all undergraduate classes and class officers. It takes an active part in governance by participation in faculty and administrative committees and sponsors a number of campus activities and functions.

Admission Requirements

The University of the Sciences in Philadelphia seeks students whose aptitudes and achievements are in the areas of science, mathematics, and humanities. Sixteen total high school credits are required and must include English (4 credits), mathematics (3 credits, including algebra I and II and plane geometry), and science (3 credits of laboratory science, including at least two of the following: biology, chemistry, and physics). Class rank, if provided by the applicant's high school, and grade point average are also considered in the admission decision process. Candidates are required to submit the results of their SAT and/or ACT examinations. Physical therapy and physician assistant studies applicants are required to complete and document a 20-hour volunteer/observation experience. Supplemental testing or an interview may be requested to clarify a specific aspect of a candidate's record. Applications for transfer are welcome, although the number of seats available each year are less than that for first-year students, since all students admitted to USP are admitted for the entire program length.

The University of the Sciences in Philadelphia does not discriminate in the administration of its educational policies, admission policies, scholarship and loan programs, or athletic and other University-administered programs on the basis of sex, age, handicap, race, creed, color, or national origin. All students are entitled to all of the rights, privileges, programs, and activities generally accorded or made available to students at the University. This institutional policy complies with the requirements of Title IX of the Education Amendments of 1972 (45 CRF 86), Section 504 of the Rehabilitation Act of 1973, and other applicable statutes and regulations.

Application and Information

An Admission Application Booklet may be obtained by calling the Admission Office. Each application must be accompanied by a nonrefundable $45 application fee. First-year applications for admission are considered until the entering class roster has been completed. USP follows a rolling admission policy, and applicants are notified of the admission decision after the University has received all required data. Students accepted into any of the programs have until May 1 to submit a nonrefundable deposit of $150 to hold a place in the class, although tuition deposits may be accepted in most programs after May 1. Applicants accepted after May 1 have two weeks to submit a tuition deposit.

Applicants for transfer to the physical therapy (January 1), pharmacy (January 15), occupational therapy (March 1), and physician assistant studies (March 15) programs must submit completed application documents by the dates indicated and are generally not subject to the rolling admission policy. Applications for transfer may be submitted after the filing deadline but are considered only after the applications that meet the deadline have been considered. Transfer applications for all other programs are reviewed on a rolling admission basis. Applicants who are accepted for transfer into the physical therapy, pharmacy, occupational therapy, and physician assistant studies programs are normally required to submit their tuition deposit before May 1. All other accepted transfer candidates have until May 1 to enroll.

Director of Admission
University of the Sciences in Philadelphia
600 South 43rd Street
Philadelphia, Pennsylvania 19104-4495
Telephone: 215-596-8810
          888-996-8747 (toll-free)
Fax: 215-596-8821
E-mail: admit@usip.edu
World Wide Web: http://www.usip.edu

UNIVERSITY OF THE VIRGIN ISLANDS
ST. THOMAS, U.S. VIRGIN ISLANDS

The University

The University of the Virgin Islands (UVI) was established by an act of the Virgin Islands legislature in 1962. UVI is the publicly supported university system of the U.S. Virgin Islands, serving the territory and the Caribbean. Originally the College of the Virgin Islands, the name was changed to University of the Virgin Islands in 1986 to better reflect the growth and diversification of its academic programs, community and regional service, and research.

The University is a comprehensive institution offering degrees in liberal arts and in professional programs to meet the higher education needs of the people of the Virgin Islands, the wider Caribbean, and the United States mainland. It is a major provider of the intellectual capital for development of the region through the integration of its teaching, research, and public service activities. The University offers undergraduate, graduate, and continuing education programs for responsible citizenship and productive, fulfilling careers. The University is a land-grant institution and a historically black university; therefore, it is committed to advancing knowledge through instruction, research, and public service, particularly in areas that contribute to understanding and resolving issues and problems unique to the Virgin Islands and the Caribbean.

The University's two campuses, on the islands of St. Croix and St. Thomas, are separated by 40 miles of Caribbean sea. The St. Croix campus has beautiful new residential facilities that provide housing for 102 students. The St. Thomas campus residence halls house 250 students.

UVI's 2,500 full-time, part-time, and graduate students come from the U.S. Virgin Islands, twenty-one states, and approximately fifteen other countries (mainly the nearby Caribbean island nations). As a small institution, UVI is able to ensure close contact among student, professors, and faculty advisers.

The University offers a wide range of extracurricular activities and events. Student publications include a literary magazine, a newspaper, and a yearbook. Musically talented students may be members of the Concert Band, the Jazz Ensemble, and the Concert Choir. Basketball, cricket, netball, soccer, tennis, and volleyball are included in the sports program. The University is acclaimed for the excellence of its dramatic productions.

Location

The Virgin Islands are located about 1,600 miles southeast of New York City and 1,200 miles east-southeast of Miami. The St. Thomas campus occupies 175 acres overlooking the Caribbean Sea and has its own beach and golf course. The St. Croix campus comprises 130 acres and includes the Virgin Islands Agricultural Experiment Station and Cooperative Extension Service. Both campuses have playing fields and outdoor athletic and recreational facilities, including basketball, volleyball, and tennis courts.

Majors and Degrees

UVI offers undergraduate degrees at the associate and baccalaureate levels. On the St. Thomas campus, B.A. degrees are offered in accounting, biology, business administration, elementary education, English, humanities, marine biology, mathematics, music education, psychology, social sciences, and vocational education. B.S. degrees may be earned in biology, chemistry, computer science, marine biology, mathematics, and nursing. A.A. degrees are awarded in accounting, business management, computer information systems, hotel/restaurant management, and police science and administration. The A.S. degree is awarded in physics.

On the St. Croix campus, B.A. programs are offered in accounting, business administration, and elementary education. B.S. degrees in computer science and mathematics are also available. The A.A. majors are accounting, business management, computer information systems, office systems, and police science and administration. The A.S. degree is awarded in nursing.

Academic Program

The University was founded as a liberal arts institution. For baccalaureate degrees, a minimum of 120 credits is required. An associate degree requires a minimum of 62 credits. To ensure a strong liberal arts background, all students must complete general education requirements. The successful completion of an English proficiency examination and a computer literacy examination are required for all degrees. The University operates on a semester system, with a six-week summer session.

University credit may be given for certain College Board Advanced Placement tests, the College-Level Examination Program, and the Proficiency Examination Program of American College Testing, Inc. Credit may be given for General Certificate of Education subjects passed at "A" level for students from British-oriented education systems.

Students have the opportunity to explore career options, serve as research assistants, and volunteer in the many research projects and public service activities conducted by professors and the research faculty. Areas of ongoing research related to small tropical island issues include marine biology, aquaculture, demography, hydrology, and geographic information systems.

Off-Campus Arrangements

The University is a member of the National Student Exchange (NSE) consortium. NSE enables students from member institutions to spend a year studying at UVI, and qualified UVI students may spend up to one year at one of the 161 institutions that participate in the NSE consortium. UVI also participates in the Caribbean Intercollegiate Exchange program, faculty and student exchanges with Emory University, a 3-2 engineering degree program with Columbia and Washington Universities, and a cooperative early medical school admissions program with Boston University. Qualified UVI students may be accepted provisionally into Boston University's medical school on completion of their sophomore year. Students attend Boston University during summer sessions and for their final year of undergraduate education, which is combined with the first year of medical school.

Academic Facilities

The collections of the University libraries total some 126,000 volumes and are developed collaboratively between campuses in support of academic programs. In addition, through membership in the Southeastern Library Network for interlibrary lending and through subscriptions to a variety of online databases, the libraries provide access to digital and traditional library resources worldwide. An extensive Caribbean collection is included among the libraries' holdings. Interested students can visit the libraries' Web page (http://libraries.uvi.edu) to review other resources and collections.

Telecommunications equipment facilitates communication between the two campuses and connects the University to the Internet. Voice mail, e-mail, audio, and video teleconferencing are utilized to bridge the distance between the islands and link the two campuses; distance-learning technology allows classes to be taught simultaneously on both campuses by video. Computers are available for students' use in the Freshman Center and in microcomputer laboratories on both campuses.

Facilities for laboratory courses in the sciences are available, as is a language laboratory. The Reichhold Center on the St. Thomas campus includes a 1,200-seat amphitheater and other facilities for the performing and visual arts. The new UVI Music Education Center houses music suites and a small theater.

Costs

Tuition for the 2000–01 academic year is $1365 per semester for residents of the Virgin Islands; for nonresidents, the equivalent figure is $4095. Students pay $128 for medical insurance, health service, student activity, and technology fees. Rooms on both campuses are $1250 per semester (single occupancy) and $1000 per semester (double occupancy). Board on the St. Thomas campus is $1915 per semester; on St. Croix, meals are purchased from the snack bar.

Financial Aid

Approximately 70 percent of the full-time undergraduate students receive financial aid. Available programs include federal and institutional scholarships, grants, loans, and work-study jobs. The Free Application for Federal Student Aid (FAFSA) is used to evaluate need. Financial aid applications should be submitted prior to March 1 for priority consideration. For further information, students should contact the Financial Aid Office.

Faculty

The University's teaching faculty comprises 180 highly qualified full-time and part-time members. Of the full-time members, 60 percent hold doctoral degrees in their disciplines. Faculty members come from diverse ethnic and cultural backgrounds, from the United States, the Virgin Islands, and a number of countries around the world. The faculty elects a member to the Board of Trustees annually.

Student Government

All members of the full-time student body are members of the Student Government Association. Officers elected by the student body serve as its voice within the University community. Students elect a representative to the Board of Trustees, alternating each year between the two campuses. In addition, students are members of most University standing committees, including the committees for academic standards, programs, and commencement.

Admission Requirements

A candidate for admission to the University must have earned a high school diploma or have achieved the equivalent of high school graduation (GED). The minimum acceptable high school grade point average is 2.0 on a 4.0 scale. All applicants must submit scores on either the SAT I or ACT. Transfer applicants must be in good academic and social standing and must have a minimum grade point average of 2.0 at previously attended institutions.

Application and Information

To complete the admission process, a student must submit a completed application form, a nonrefundable $20 application fee, high school and/or college transcripts, and SAT I or ACT scores. Students are admitted in both the fall and spring semesters. The application deadline for the fall semester is April 30 and for the spring semester, October 30. All required documents must be received by the deadline. Application forms and more detailed information can be obtained on line or from the Admissions Office.

Students should direct inquiries and applications to the St. Thomas campus to:

Director of Admissions and New Student Services
Admissions Office
University of the Virgin Islands
#2 John Brewers Bay
Charlotte Amalie, Virgin Islands 00802-9990
Telephone: 340-693-1150
E-mail: admissions@uvi.edu
World Wide Web: http://www.uvi.edu

Students should direct inquiries and applications to the St. Croix campus to:

Director of Admissions and Academic Services
Academic Services Office
University of the Virgin Islands
RR02, Box 10,000 Kingshill
St. Croix, Virgin Islands 00850
Telephone: 340-692-4158
World Wide Web: http://www.uvi.edu

The dormitories, viewed from the golf course, on the St. Thomas campus.

UNIVERSITY OF TULSA
TULSA, OKLAHOMA

The University

The University of Tulsa (TU) is Oklahoma's oldest private university. It was founded as a school for Indian girls in Muskogee, in Indian Territory, in 1894. The institution moved to Tulsa in 1907 and has grown into a fully accredited university that offers programs through the doctoral level. Traditionally committed to excellence in technical education, particularly in energy engineering and business administration, TU has also become well known for the study of the humanities, sciences, and law.

The current student body of 4,192 (2,924 undergraduates) is made up of students from forty-six states and more than sixty countries. More than thirty percent of the students are from outside Oklahoma. International and multicultural students make up approximately 28 percent of the student population. Campus life also encourages social and academic interaction between independent students and those belonging to the seven national fraternities and seven national sororities on campus. Many organizations, clubs, and societies, including Phi Beta Kappa, are available to accommodate special student interests. The Golden Hurricane athletic teams participate in NCAA Division I and the Western Athletic Conference (WAC). Student discounts are available for many cultural and social activities in Tulsa, and there are numerous opportunities on campus for students to meet and talk to nationally known speakers, artists, authors, and musicians.

In addition to the Greek housing, there are six residence halls and a state-of-the-art, on-campus apartment facility. A variety of room and board plans are available, including suites and single and double occupancy. All rooms are equipped with a telephone and Audix voice mailbox; cable television is available in all rooms. Off-campus apartments are also available at competitive rates. The Career Planning and Placement Office offers career guidance and coordinates employment interviews. More than 200 companies and firms visit the campus each year.

Location

The University of Tulsa is located in a quiet residential neighborhood just 3 miles from a thriving, renovated downtown business district. More than fifty major companies are headquartered in the city, making internships an important part of the educational process. Tulsa has more than 500,000 inhabitants. The city has such cultural assets as the Performing Arts Center, ballet theater, symphony, civic opera, two nationally renowned museums, and cultural festivals such as Reggaefest, Jazzfest, Mayfest, and Octoberfest. Many professional sports events are available in Tulsa, including baseball, golf, hockey, and tennis. An extensive riverpark development 3 miles from the campus has facilities for many activities, and there are numerous bicycle and jogging trails, along with an outdoor stage for concerts.

Majors and Degrees

The Henry Kendall College of Arts and Sciences grants the Bachelor of Arts or Bachelor of Science degree in anthropology, art, chemistry, communication, computer information systems, computer science, deaf education, economics, English, environmental policy, French, geology, history, law and society (an accelerated B.A./J.D. program), mathematics, music, musical theater, philosophy, physics, political science, psychology, sociology, Spanish, speech/language pathology, and theater. Students also have the opportunity to create their own designated area of concentration with the approval of the dean of the college. Preprofessional preparation is offered (dental, law, medical, veterinary medicine), and faculty advisers are available to assist students with course selection. Teacher certification at the elementary and secondary levels is available through the College of Arts and Sciences.

The College of Business Administration awards the Bachelor of Science degree in accounting, athletic training, economics, exercise and sports science, finance and real estate, international business and language, management, management information systems, marketing, nursing, and sports administration. In addition, the college offers minors in accounting, finance, international business, and management information systems. The Microsoft Corporation named the College of Business Administration as a recipient of the Innovators in Higher Education award for its site on the World Wide Web. TU was one of five colleges and universities in the nation to be selected for the award.

The College of Engineering and Applied Sciences offers the Bachelor of Science degree in biological sciences, chemical engineering, chemistry, computer science, electrical engineering, engineering physics, geosciences, mechanical engineering, and petroleum engineering. The college features state-of-the-art undergraduate research facilities. Over the last four years, 12 students were named recipients of the prestigious Barry M. Goldwater Scholarship, the nation's premier award for undergraduate students studying engineering, math, or science.

Academic Program

The goal of the undergraduate program is to produce well-rounded individuals who are knowledgeable in the liberal arts, academically astute, and technically proficient and who possess communication skills that will lead to success in their careers. All students are required to complete the University's general curriculum, which stresses creative writing and communication skills.

Candidates for graduation must complete at least 124 semester hours of course work, with more hours required of students majoring in engineering and business administration. This total includes the prescribed courses and electives in the general University curriculum and the work required in a major field of study, as determined by each college.

The University offers an honors program featuring innovative approaches to study within a traditional honors-program framework. Students in the program are involved in broadly based multidisciplinary study during their first two years and undertake more specialized work as upperclass students. Honors freshmen have the option to live in the Honors House.

Qualified students may be granted advanced standing or credit for successful scores on the tests of the Advanced Placement and College-Level Examination programs. CLEP credit is available in selected subject areas; passing scores are determined by individual departments. Students who complete the International Baccalaureate diploma with a score of 28 or above receive at least 30 college credits, the equivalent of one year in college.

The University of Tulsa operates on a semester calendar. The fall term begins in late August, the spring term in early January, and the summer session in mid-May.

Off-Campus Arrangements

The study-abroad program promotes cultural enrichment, language development, and personal growth through an organized, flexible program of international study. Tulsa is affiliated with the Institute of International Education in order to identify programs that meet its standards and expectations. In addition, seminars in international business organized by the College of Business Administration are held for three weeks each summer in Europe. An internship program in Washington, D.C., is also available. Students are encouraged to participate in off-campus study during their junior year.

Academic Facilities

The University of Tulsa's libraries (McFarlin Library and the Law Library) house more than 3.6 million items, including periodical subscriptions to scholarly and popular journals. McFarlin Library is the central facility for academic information resource services and was recently expanded to house a central computer lab of forty workstations. The library is open 96 hours a week, and the lab provides service 24 hours a day. McFarlin is a federal document depository that contains 500,000 government publications. Collections also include 2 million microforms. The library's graphic-based computer system, Innovative Interfaces (dubbed Farley), permits patrons within and beyond the library to access library holdings, the Internet, and the World Wide Web. The library subscribes to a broad array of electronic databases (indexes and full-text services) to 2,700 journals via 120 PCs. McFarlin is the campus trainer for computer software and the Internet. Special collections at McFarlin are internationally recognized and include rare books (125,000 volumes), literary and historical manuscripts from nineteenth and twentieth century authors, and Native American history—particularly Oklahoma's Five Civilized Tribes.

Keplinger Hall is the $15-million home to the College of Engineering and Applied Sciences. Modern and expansive equipment complement this facility.

The Mary K. Chapman Center for Communicative Disorders links the University to the community with its clinical facility and its curricula in education of the deaf and speech/language pathology. The Tulsa Center for the Study of Women's Literature offers concentrated studies in women's literature and in feminist literary critical theory. The Center for Educational Research and Evaluation conducts projects for educational and industrial groups, focusing on personnel evaluation, testing, and other related topics. The National Energy Law and Policy Institute researches energy law and policy development. The Petroleum and Energy Research Institute offers students the opportunity to participate in funded research projects. The Small Business Institute gives business majors an opportunity to work closely with the Tulsa business community in management counseling.

The Chapman Theatre is home to TU's symphony orchestra, concert band, wind ensemble, jazz workshop, modern choir, theater, and opera productions.

The Allen Chapman Activity Center is the University's student union. This $6-million facility features student organization offices, the Great Hall for lectures and entertainment, an art gallery, a fast-food facility, a cafeteria, a coffee shop, and the University bookstore.

The Donald W. Reynolds Center serves as the on-campus arena and convocation center. This $28-million state-of-the-art multipurpose facility is the home for several enhanced intercollegiate athletic programs, including men's and women's basketball and women's volleyball; cutting-edge facilities for video editing and strength training; and the state's only accredited academic program in athletic/sports medicine. The Reynolds Center supports and enhances student commencement activities, career fairs, student-sponsored concerts, cultural festivals, student intramural competitions, classroom instruction, and campus-related community events. The center is the nation's first collegiate arena to provide the latest in permanent two-way fiber-based communication links to the broadcast community through Venue-net, a technology that is the standard for professional sports in North America.

In 1998, the University of Tulsa completed its New Century Campaign by raising $108.5 million. The funds are being used to keep the University on the cutting edge of undergraduate instruction through faculty enhancement, electronic classrooms and laboratories, and renovation of facilities. The University is currently developing a 30-acre sports and recreation complex that will include a student fitness facility, an indoor/outdoor competition tennis center, an NCAA track and field, NCAA soccer and softball fields, multiuse recreational fields, and a student apartment complex.

Other recent improvements include the implementation of programs supporting and enriching the residential campus experience. These programs include freshman orientation trips, student leadership development initiatives, and several themed community options, including the First-Year Experience Hall; the Women in Science, Engineering, and Math Floor; and a Global Exploration and Language House.

Costs

In 2000–01, the estimated cost for students residing on campus is $18,060, including $13,400 in tuition and $4660 for room and board. In addition, expenses for books average around $1200 per year.

Financial Aid

Last year, aid totaling more than $30 million was disbursed to more than 75 percent of the University's students, with the average award for 1999 being approximately $14,000. Academic, athletic, and performance scholarships are available, as well as federally funded grants, loans, and Federal Work-Study awards. The University of Tulsa participates in the National Merit and National Achievement Scholarship Corporation's Finalist program, and the National Hispanic Scholar program. TU offers full tuition, room, and board scholarships for National Merit Finalists and full tuition scholarships for National Achievement Finalists and National Hispanic Scholars. Presidential and University Scholarships are also awarded to qualified students. Performance scholarships are available in music and theater. Applicants for aid should submit the Free Application for Federal Student Aid (FAFSA) and the TU Financial Aid Application by March 1 for priority consideration.

Faculty

The University has 310 full-time and 109 part-time faculty members, with 96 percent having earned the highest degree in their field of study. The faculty is primarily a teaching faculty, although most of its members are also involved in funded research or publishing activities. Many faculty members serve as student advisers. The faculty includes a number of distinguished scholars, with sixteen $1-million endowed chairs having been created since 1980. Faculty members are encouraged to participate in activities with students, and many serve as sponsors for student interest groups. TU's student-faculty ratio is 11:1.

Student Government

All full-time students are members of the Student Association, which consists of legislative, executive, and judicial branches. Regular elections are held for representatives from each college, who appropriate nearly $170,000 annually. The executive cabinet's main function is to arrange the programs of the speakers, artists, and events on campus that are sponsored by the Student Association.

Admission Requirements

The University of Tulsa seeks students whose academic background indicates potential for success in the University's competitive environment. Performance in high school college-preparatory subjects and scores on the SAT I or ACT are the primary criteria considered in the admission evaluation. The counselor recommendation and information about applicants' extracurricular activities and job experience are also considered. Campus visits and interviews are highly recommended but not required.

Application and Information

The University of Tulsa operates on a rolling admission policy. Highly qualified freshman applicants can apply and receive an admission decision during the fall semester of their senior year in high school. An application, accompanied by a six-semester secondary school transcript, ACT or SAT I scores, and a guidance counselor's recommendation, should be submitted when applying for admission. Completed applications should be sent to the Office of Admission.

For additional information, students should contact:

John C. Corso
Dean of Admission
University of Tulsa
600 South College Avenue
Tulsa, Oklahoma 74104-3189
Telephone: 918-631-2307 (in Tulsa)
                800-331-3050 (toll-free)
Fax: 918-631-5003
E-mail: admission@utulsa.edu
World Wide Web: http://www.utulsa.edu

UNIVERSITY OF VERMONT
BURLINGTON, VERMONT

The University

The University of Vermont, or UVM (from the Latin name Universitas Viridis Montis, which means University of the Green Mountains), is in its third century of educational excellence.

Founded in 1791, the University of Vermont is the fifth-oldest university in New England (after Harvard, Yale, Dartmouth, and Brown) and among the twenty oldest institutions of higher learning in the nation. UVM was one of the first universities to earn a chapter of Phi Beta Kappa and, in 1875, became the first to admit women to this national honor society.

A comprehensive research university, UVM enrolls students from a variety of geographical, social, economic, ethnic, and personal backgrounds. The University of Vermont deliberately seeks students with such diverse backgrounds, with approximately 40 percent of the student population coming from Vermont and 60 percent drawn from throughout the United States and around the world. Each of the 7,400 undergraduate students contributes his or her unique experiences to enrich this diverse campus community.

UVM is composed of eight undergraduate colleges and schools: the College of Agriculture and Life Sciences, the College of Arts and Sciences, the College of Education and Social Services, the College of Engineering and Mathematics, the School of Allied Health Sciences, the School of Business Administration, the School of Natural Resources, and the School of Nursing.

In addition there are the Graduate College and the College of Medicine. The Graduate College offers seventy-one master's degree programs and twenty doctoral programs in a variety of fields, including agriculture, business, education, engineering, foreign languages, health sciences, natural resources, physical and biological sciences, psychology, and social sciences. A Master of Physical Therapy program is offered.

In the first two years, students are required to live in one of the twenty-six residence halls, with options including small and large housing complexes, and historic older buildings as well as modern residence halls. Many students opt for theme-based housing.

Nearly 100 student organizations are currently recognized by the Student Government Association (equivalent to the student government). These include a broad range of academic, media-based, and recreational options, as well as arts, religious, cultural, and political organizations.

UVM fields thirteen men's and fourteen women's NCAA Division I athletic teams. More than thirty-seven intramural and club sports are available to all UVM undergraduates.

Location

UVM is located in Burlington, Vermont, a city of approximately 40,000. The University's main campus sits on a hill nestled between Lake Champlain and the Green Mountains. Because of the natural beauty of its surrounding area and its many sporting and entertainment opportunities, Burlington has been named one of the nation's "Big Ten" college towns by Edward B. Fiske in his book *The Best Buys in College Education.*

Majors and Degrees

The University of Vermont offers more than ninety undergraduate majors leading to Bachelor of Arts, Bachelor of Science, and Associate in Science degrees.

The College of Agriculture and Life Sciences offers the following majors: animal sciences, biochemical science, biological sciences, botany, community development and applied economics, dietetics, environmental science, environmental studies, family and consumer sciences education, microbiology, molecular genetics, nutrition and food sciences, plant and soil science, self-designed, undeclared, and urban forestry and landscape horticulture.

The College of Arts and Sciences offers the following majors: anthropology, art history, biology (B.A. and B.S. options), botany, chemistry (B.A. and B.S. options), classical civilization, communication science, computer science, economics, English, environmental sciences, environmental studies, French, geography, geology (B.A. and B.S. options), German, Greek, history, individually designed, international studies (Asian studies, Canadian studies, European studies, Latin America, and Russia/Eastern Europe options), Latin, mathematics, music (B.A. and B.Mus. options), philosophy, physics (B.A. and B.S. options), political science, psychology, religion, Russian, sociology, Spanish, studio art, theater, undeclared, women's studies, and zoology (B.A. and B.S options).

The College of Education and Social Services offers the following majors: art (B.S.A.E), early childhood education (P–3 and preschool; P–3 leads to the B.S.ED.), elementary education (K–6 and reading options leading to the B.S.ED), environmental studies, human development and family studies, music education (B.S.M.S), physical education, secondary education (English, language, mathematics, science, social science, and theater/communication options leading to the B.S.ED.), self-designed majors, social work, and undeclared.

The College of Engineering and Mathematics offers the following majors: civil engineering (B.S.C.E.), computer science (B.S.C.S.), electrical engineering (B.S.E.E.), engineering management (B.S.E.M.), mathematics (B.S.M.), mechanical engineering (B.S.M.E.), statistics (B.S.M.), and undeclared.

The School of Business Administration offers the business administration major (B.S.B.A.). During their senior year, business administration majors must complete one of the following concentrations: accounting, entrepreneurship, finance, human resource management, international management, management and the environment, management information systems, marketing, production and operations management, or a self-designed concentration.

The School of Natural Resources offers the following majors leading to the B.S. degree: environmental science, environmental studies, forestry, natural resources, recreation management, resource economics, undeclared, and wildlife and fisheries biology.

The School of Allied Health Sciences offers an Associate in Science degree major in dental hygiene. The School of Allied Health Sciences offers the following Bachelor of Science degree majors: biomedical technology, medical laboratory science, nuclear medicine technology, and radiation therapy.

The School of Nursing offers the professional nursing major. Graduates of this Bachelor of Science degree program are eligible for registered nurse (RN) licensure.

An accelerated B.S./D.V.M program with Tufts School of Veterinary Medicine and a B.A./J.D. program with Vermont Law

School are available. The University also offers curricula and advising for predental, prelaw, premedical, and pre–veterinary students.

Academic Program

The University's academic calendar consists of two semesters (fall and spring), with extensive summer courses also available. Students are classified based on progress toward meeting degree requirements in terms of credit hours earned as follows: first year, fewer than 27 credit hours; sophomore, 27 to fewer than 57 credit hours; junior, 57 to fewer than 87 credit hours; senior, 87 or more credit hours. A total of 122 credit hours are needed for graduation for most bachelor's programs at UVM. The number varies, however; some programs, such as those in the College of Engineering and Mathematics, require as many as 130 credit hours. The Associate in Science program in the School of Allied Health Sciences requires 60 credit hours.

General requirements are designed by the specific departments within the colleges and schools. In addition to the course requirements of the particular curriculum, students must also fulfill the general requirements in physical education and complete a course in race and culture. Academic advising is facilitated through faculty members who are assigned to incoming students. These faculty members assist the student with academic planning and course registration. A student remains under the guidance of this adviser until a major has been selected, at which time a department adviser is assigned.

Off-Campus Arrangements

The University offers an array of study-abroad programs in several countries through the Office of International Educational Services as well as in conjunction with other colleges and universities.

Academic Facilities

Facilities at the University of Vermont include state-of-the-art laboratories, computer services, and other educational resources. Main Campus, with its red brick buildings and classic architecture, has the stately look of a historic university, while Redstone and East campuses have a more contemporary feel, with modern buildings and views of the mountains and of Lake Champlain.

Bailey-Howe Library, the largest library in Vermont, contains more than 1.7 million books, serial back files, and government documents; 1.7 million microforms; 20,000 serial subscriptions; significant manuscripts and archival materials; and graphic, cartographic, audio, and film materials. There are also a medical library and a library for chemistry and physics.

University computing facilities are accessible to all students and include microcomputer labs housing Macintosh and DOS/Windows systems. All labs are networked, allowing access to UVM's host systems as well as national and international resources on the Internet. Network connections are also widely available in residence halls and individual rooms.

Costs

Tuition and fees for the 1999–2000 school year were $19,252 for out-of-state students and $8044 for Vermont residents. Room and board were at $5628. Miscellaneous personal expenses, including books and supplies, are in addition to these costs.

Financial Aid

More than half of UVM's students receive financial assistance. Awards are based on need as determined by the Free Application for Federal Student Aid (FAFSA) and the University's financial aid application. An applicant's financial aid award may include University and federal grant funds, on-campus employment, and student loans.

Financial assistance has no bearing on admission to the University.

Faculty

The University's student-faculty ratio of 14:1 enables faculty members to be accessible to students. UVM's faculty is composed of very distinguished scholars, 89 percent of whom hold a terminal degree in their specific field of interest.

Student Government

The Student Government Association, the primary student governing organization, assumes responsibility for voicing student concerns and interest in the political activities of the University community. It recognizes and funds more than 100 student organizations.

Admission Requirements

Prospective first-year students must present at least 16 high school units, including a minimum of 4 years of English, 3 years of mathematics, 3 years of social sciences, 2 years of the same foreign language, and 2 years of natural or physical science, including at least 1 year of lab science. In addition to the required and recommended courses, the overall strength and challenge of a student's course load is important.

Qualification for admission is determined on the basis of secondary school record, rank in graduating class, recommendations, writing ability, strength of preparation in the area chosen as a major, and scores on the SAT I. The ACT examination may be submitted in place of the SAT I.

Admission for nonresident students is competitive. Forty-seven percent of admitted students rank in the top 25 percent of their graduating class.

Transfer students must meet all entrance requirements mentioned above. Candidates must send an official transcript from each postsecondary school attended. SAT I and ACT results are not required for transfers.

Application and Information

Applications and supporting materials for first-year fall admission should be completed and on file by January 15 (November 1 for early action and early decision). Transfer students seeking fall admission should apply by April 1. First-year and transfer students seeking admission for spring semester should apply by November 1. The nonrefundable application fee is $45.

The University welcomes applications from all interested students regardless of race, religion, age, handicap, nationality, or sex. Prospective first-year and transfer students interested in applying for admission in either January or September can receive application forms by contacting:

Admissions Office
The University of Vermont
194 South Prospect Street
Burlington, Vermont 05401-3596
Telephone: 802-656-3370
Fax: 802-656-8611
E-mail: admissions@uvm.edu
World Wide Web: http://www.uvm.edu

UNIVERSITY OF WEST FLORIDA
PENSACOLA, FLORIDA

The University

One of the ten state universities of Florida, the University of West Florida enrolls approximately 8,000 students in its Colleges of Arts and Sciences, Business, and Professional Studies. The University of West Florida, which opened in fall 1967, is located on a 1,600-acre nature preserve 10 miles north of downtown Pensacola. The University's facilities, valued at more than $81 million, have been designed to complement the natural beauty of the site.

The University currently enrolls students from forty-seven states and sixty countries. Students and professors enjoy a relationship that is more common at a small, private college. Nearly 700 freshmen began their studies at UWF last year. The middle 50 percent statistics for the class are as follows: high school grade point average ranged from 2.7 to 3.8; SAT I total score ranged from 970 to 1180; and ACT composite ranged from 20 to 26.

In addition to its undergraduate programs, UWF also offers the master's degree in twenty-nine areas of study and specialist and Ed.D. degrees in education.

UWF operates centers in downtown Pensacola and at Eglin Air Force Base, a branch campus in Fort Walton Beach (in conjunction with a local community college), and a Navy program office at Naval Air Station Pensacola. In addition, UWF owns 152 acres of beachfront property on nearby Santa Rosa Island, adjacent to the Gulf Islands National Seashore. Available for both recreation and research, this property provides special opportunities for students pursuing degrees in marine biology and coastal studies.

The University of West Florida is a member of the NCAA Division II. Men's sports include baseball, basketball, cross-country, golf, soccer, and tennis. Women's sports include basketball, cross-country, soccer, softball, tennis, and volleyball. Students also participate in more than nineteen intramural sports and twenty club sports. The Program Council and the Residence Hall Advisory Council provide activities and events open to the entire campus community. The University serves as host to six national fraternities and five national sororities; 110 professional, academic, and religious organizations are open to UWF students.

A natatorium housing an Olympic-size pool adjoins the Field House, center for indoor sports and large-group activities and events. Varsity soccer fields, tennis courts, handball and racquetball courts, jogging trails, picnic areas, and sites for canoeing are available on campus. Varsity baseball and softball fields and a lighted track complete the UWF sports complex. Sailing and waterskiing facilities are nearby, and campus nature trails attract thousands of visitors annually.

Students may choose to live on or off campus in 1,200 spaces. Residents may choose from low-rise residence halls, student apartments, and a new residence hall scheduled to open in fall 2000 that will provide 300 new spaces.

UWF offers privatized housing located on campus. These two- or four-bedroom residence halls offer apartment-style living equipped with modern conveniences. There are also various apartment complexes conveniently located just beyond the campus.

Location

Students and visitors alike delight in the beauty of the campus, which is nestled in the rolling hills outside Pensacola, Florida. Wide verandas, massive moss-draped oaks, and spacious lawns capture the traditional charm and grace of the South, while modern architecture and state-of-the-art facilities blend in naturally among loblolly pines and meandering walkways.

Only minutes from the campus gate are the emerald waters and white beaches of the Gulf of Mexico and the Gulf Islands National Seashore, one of the nation's most beautiful beaches. The Pensacola area attracts vacationers from all around the country to its historic Seville Square, golf tournaments, sailing regattas, restaurants on the bay, and a variety of art and music festivals. WUWF, the University's public radio station, produces a monthly live program, Gulf Coast RadioLive. UWF is 3½ hours from New Orleans, 1 hour from Mobile, 3 hours from Tallahassee, and 5 hours from Atlanta.

Majors and Degrees

The University of West Florida awards the bachelor's degree in forty-four undergraduate programs with many areas of specialization. Undergraduate majors are available in the College of Arts and Sciences in anthropology, art, biology, chemistry, communication arts, computer information systems, computer science, English, environmental studies, fine arts, history, interdisciplinary humanities studies, interdisciplinary science, international studies, leisure studies, marine biology, mathematics, medical technology, music, nursing (an RN is required for admission), philosophy, physics, pre-engineering, preprofessional studies, psychology, social sciences (interdisciplinary), sociology, studio art, and theater as well as joint electrical engineering and computer engineering programs with the University of Florida.

Undergraduate majors in the College of Business include accounting, economics, finance, management, management information systems, and marketing. The College of Business is accredited by the AACSB–The International Association for Management Education.

The College of Professional Studies, which includes education programs that are accredited by the National Council for Accreditation of Teacher Education (NCATE), offers professional training and majors leading to bachelor's degrees in the following areas: criminal justice; elementary education; engineering technology; health education; health, leisure, and sports; legal administration; middle school education; military science; political science; prekindergarten/primary education; prelaw; social work; special education (emotionally handicapped, mentally handicapped, learning disabled); sports science; and vocational education. There are specialist programs in educational leadership and in curriculum and instruction and a doctoral program in curriculum and instruction.

Academic Program

A general curriculum is required for entering freshmen and for transfer students without an Associate in Arts degree from a Florida public community college. General studies provide students with a broad foundation in the liberal arts, science, and career and life planning. The academic skills of reading, writing, discourse, critical inquiry, logical thinking, and mathematical reasoning are central elements of the core curriculum.

Students of high ability may enter an honors program offering intensive instruction in a more individualized setting. Cooperative education programs are available in nearly every field, allowing UWF students to get a head start on their careers while paying for their education. Army and Air Force ROTC programs and scholarships are also available.

Off-Campus Arrangements

The Office of International Education and Programs arranges more than twenty study-abroad and student exchange programs on every continent except Antarctica. Participants may study in Austria, Canada, England, Finland, France, Germany, Japan, Mexico, the Netherlands, and Portugal.

Academic Facilities

The main campus consists of more than 100 buildings. Most prominent of these is the five-floor John C. Pace Library, which houses a collection of more than 2.1 million bound volumes and micropieces. Interconnected through computer linkages with state and national libraries for research purposes, the UWF library contains one of the finest special collections about the Gulf Coast area. Some of the items in this collection date back to the fourteenth century, and there are also a manuscript letter signed by Thomas Jefferson, books autographed by Albert Einstein, and materials carried aboard the space shuttle by UWF alumni.

Excellent science and technology laboratories for preprofessional majors, extensive video and film equipment, desktop publishing labs, an AP wire service, and an impressive computer science facility also support students' scholarly endeavors. Microcomputers, minicomputers, a diverse inventory of software, a real-time laboratory, modem linkages to residence halls, and 24-hour-a-day access to the computer center all are available to students in every field of study. Other major facilities include a Center for Fine and Performing Arts, a College of Professional Studies Complex, a Student Services Complex, and a newly renovated Commons.

Expansion and renovation continue to enhance the main campus. Phase one of a multibuilding science complex opened in 1997. Ongoing renovations of the Commons in 1998 featured a new bookstore, post office, and snack bar. An archaeology building and museum opened in 1999.

Costs

For fall 2000, tuition is $76.45 per credit for Florida residents and $309.40 per credit for out-of-state students. Room and board costs total $4532. The cost of books is estimated at $706. Transportation and personal expenses vary according to students' individual needs.

Financial Aid

About 45 percent of UWF students receive some form of financial aid and scholarships. UWF is committed to meeting a student's financial need. Aid is awarded on a first-come, first-served basis.

The Scholarship Program for outstanding freshmen allows students to receive early scholarship commitments as soon as they have decided to enroll in UWF. The John C. Pace Jr. scholarships are awarded to meritorious freshmen, transfers with A.A. degrees from Florida's community colleges, and minority students. Awards range from $1000 to $4000 per year. Special scholarships for members of minority groups, National Achievement Scholars, and students with talent in the arts are all awarded through this program. Non-Florida tuition grants are awarded to outstanding freshmen and transfer students. These awards reduce the amount of out-of-state fees.

Faculty

Faculty members at the University of West Florida include published authors, scientists engaged in a wide range of research projects, and journalists skilled in advertising and filmmaking. Eighty-one percent of the faculty hold doctoral degrees from major institutions throughout the United States.

Student Government

The Student Government Association is authorized to represent the student body in all matters concerning student life. The basic purposes of the student government are to provide students with an opportunity to participate in the decision-making process of the University; to review, evaluate, and allocate all student activity and service fee monies as allowed by state law (annually, some $1 million is allocated by students); to consider and make recommendations on all phases of student life; and to serve as the principal forum for discussion of matters of broad concern to the students.

Admission Requirements

The University of West Florida admits freshman applicants based on high school GPA, completion of college-preparatory courses, and test scores (either the ACT or the SAT I is accepted). Special consideration is given to applicants with special talents. College-preparatory courses should include 4 years of English; 3 each of math, social science, and natural science; 2 of the same foreign language; and 4 academic electives.

Transfer applicants with fewer than 60 hours are required to submit SAT I or ACT test scores and official transcripts from both the college(s) and the high school attended. Students transferring with 60 hours or more must submit their college transcript(s) only.

Application and Information

Students are encouraged to apply early in order to allow time for receipt of transcripts and to receive full consideration for financial aid and scholarships. Admissions decisions are made on a rolling basis. The University encourages visits to its beautiful campus and offers tours Monday, Wednesday, and Friday at 1 p.m. Students can visit the University of West Florida's home page via the Internet at the World Wide Web address listed below. Among the available features are the catalog, Saturday Open House dates, applications for admission, and the course guide for the current term. The live-data schedule includes up-to-date information on class availability, time, location, and instructor as well as a listing of courses taught through the Internet.

Additional information and application materials may be obtained by writing or calling:

Office of Admissions
University of West Florida
11000 University Parkway
Pensacola, Florida 32514-5750
Telephone: 850-474-2230
E-mail: admissions@uwf.edu
World Wide Web: http://www.uwf.edu

The UWF Sailing Club goes out for a day of sun and recreation on Pensacola Bay.

UNIVERSITY OF WEST LOS ANGELES
School of Paralegal Studies
LOS ANGELES, CALIFORNIA

The University and The School

For the past quarter-century, men and women seeking a quality education in paralegal studies have made the University of West Los Angeles's School of Paralegal Studies their first choice. Not only is UWLA accredited by the Western Association of Schools and Colleges (WASC), but the School of Paralegal Studies has also been approved since 1975 by the American Bar Association as a paralegal school that meets the ABA's rigorous standards. The School of Paralegal Studies is one of two schools that comprise the University of West Los Angeles; the School of Law (which offers the J.D. degree) is fully accredited by the Committee of Bar Examiners of the State Bar of California.

The philosophy and purpose that led to UWLA's founding in 1966 as a nonprofit private educational institution remain the essence of its mission today: to offer quality programs in legal education at a moderate cost to men and women from diverse backgrounds, especially those who must study part-time. At UWLA's School of Paralegal Studies, students may earn their Bachelor of Science degree with a major in paralegal studies by completing a variety of challenging and interesting courses that are offered on a flexible schedule of evening classes.

For people who have already earned their baccalaureate or associate degrees or at least 60 college semester units, the School offers the Paralegal Specialist Certificate Program, which enables students to obtain career training in as little as two to three terms (thirty to forty-five weeks). For people who have earned at least 30 semester units of college-level general education, the School offers a 45-unit Legal Assistant Certificate Program. UWLA is not a traditional four-year collegiate institution; all entering students in the B.S. degree/Legal Assistant Certificate program are college sophomores or juniors who have earned transferable credits elsewhere. The School prides itself on offering working adults an excellent opportunity to conveniently complete their college degrees in a field of study that is not only academically enriching but also career-relevant. As part of the B.S. degree program, students may earn the Legal Assistant Certificate, which is awarded upon completion of the courses required in the major, along with two paralegal specialist certificates.

Students at UWLA come from a variety of backgrounds and commute to campus from throughout the southern California area. Since UWLA's campus serves a small student population (approximately 100 students are enrolled in the School of Paralegal Studies in any one term, with 250 students in the School of Law), students can expect and get personal attention from academic counselors, registrars, internship coordinators, faculty members, and deans. Study skills workshops, student tutoring, and other enrichment programs are part of the regular student services offered by the School, all of which are designed to help students achieve their fullest potential.

The School of Paralegal Studies has been on the cutting edge of paralegal education for several decades. The School offers specializations in such diverse areas as real estate law, probate law, litigation, corporations, and criminal law.

The School has an active placement service, headed by the Placement Counselor, who assists graduating students and alumni with finding employment in the legal community. The counselor continually seeks new job source contacts.

The School remains committed to its goal of offering quality paralegal education to those men and women who know the value of an academically rewarding yet practical education, and it remains equally committed to helping its alumni who are employed as paralegals, staff advocates, legal managers, mediators, and legal assistants meet their personal and career goals.

The School has, at present, a student body composed of about 70 percent women and 30 percent men. Many students are in their thirties, but ages range from 22 to 62. The student body has students from various racial and ethnic backgrounds, including African American, Asian–Pacific Islander, Latino/Latina, Caucasian, and Native American.

Graduates are eligible to join the Paralegal Alumni Association (PAA), which is one of the strongest and most active paralegal alumni groups in the country; it offers annual continuing education seminars and other social events.

Location

The University of West Los Angeles is located on a 4.5-acre campus, northeast of the Los Angeles International Airport. Freeways make the campus convenient to all parts of the Los Angeles basin. The campus is situated approximately 3 miles from the Pacific Ocean to the west and 1 mile from the San Diego Freeway to the east. It offers convenient on-site parking without charge. The University's long-standing reputation as an excellent paralegal training institution makes it possible for students to consider internship and employment opportunities throughout the entire southern California legal community and beyond.

Majors and Degrees

The School of Paralegal Studies offers the B.S. degree in one major, paralegal studies, along with the opportunity to specialize in one of several areas, including real estate law, litigation, corporations, criminal law, and probate law. The School also offers certificate programs leading to the Paralegal Specialist Certificate and the Legal Assistant Certificate. Exceptional students may earn such commendations as Dean's List or graduation with honors.

Academic Program

Almost all courses are 3-credit units, with a total of 24 to 45 units required for the certificate in paralegal studies. For the Bachelor of Science degree, 6 additional units of upper-division general education are required at UWLA, for a total of 51 units (seventeen courses). All students must complete a required set of core courses, including legal theory and ethics, legal research and writing, and selected areas of substantive law. Students are given a choice of specialization courses such as real estate law and litigation, which cover both substantive and procedural law. Students are able to choose several courses from a variety of electives, including entertainment law, bankruptcy, immigration, law office administration, and computers and the law.

Substantive classes such as contracts and torts provide students with a strong foundation in the principles of common law and positive law. Students learn legal concepts through a combination of learning methods, including class discussions, case briefing exercises, research projects, and lectures. Each course is designed to give students the opportunity to integrate theoretical legal concepts with practical legal experience. As students progress in their course of study, they have a chance to research and write everything from legal memoranda to corporate resolutions to motions to the court. In addition, the School gives students the opportunity to design a course of study in an area of their choice via the Independent Study course, with a faculty member as a partner in that educational endeavor. The School offers a few courses on a credit-by-examination basis. With the thorough education that UWLA provides, students complete their degrees and/or certificates at

UWLA with a high degree of conceptual and practical legal knowledge that enables them to successfully compete in the workplace.

So that students can reach their educational goals as quickly as they wish, the School's academic calendar is offered on a trimester basis, with a flexible schedule of evening classes offered each term. The fall trimester is from September to December, the winter trimester is from January to mid-April, and the spring trimester is from May to early August.

Academic Facilities

The University is proud of its Kelton Law Library, a full-service law library with a complete collection of federal and state materials in addition to access to computerized legal research databases, including LEXIS and WESTLAW. The library offers materials on CD-ROM, videotape, and microfiche and includes a Computer Learning Lab with learning tutorials and various software used in legal work. Students have access to word processing computers and printers in the library. Study group meeting rooms and a periodical reading room are available to students as needed. A fully equipped computer lab provides students with access to the legal software commonly found in law offices today.

Costs

In the 1999–2000 academic year, tuition was $210 per unit; it is expected that this amount will be slightly higher in the future. Fees charged include small amounts for computer use and library use. Books and materials costs range from approximately $25 to $100 per course. UWLA does not provide housing for students.

Financial Aid

The Financial Aid Office assists students in finding resources to finance their education at UWLA. The governmental financial aid programs available to students attending UWLA's School of Paralegal Studies include Federal Pell Grants, Federal Supplemental Educational Opportunity Grants (FSEOG), Federal Work-Study (FWS), the Bureau of Indian Affairs Grant (BIA), Federal Stafford Student Loans, and benefits available through government sources to veterans of the U.S. armed forces. To apply for financial assistance, applicants must file a Free Application for Federal Student Aid (FAFSA), which is available from UWLA's Financial Aid Office, any college financial aid office, or any high school guidance office. Although applications are accepted throughout the year, students are encouraged to apply by March 2 of the calendar year for which aid is being requested if they want consideration for California State Grants/Fellowships for the academic year beginning in July or September.

A number of scholarships, some funded by alumni of the School, are available to students. Each year the School offers a program of scholarships (covering tuition for one or more courses) to qualified students. Specific information about scholarship criteria is available from the School.

Faculty

The School prides itself on its faculty, which includes a full-time professor as well as about 20 adjunct professors who are lawyers or paralegals bringing the "real world" of current legal practice into the classroom. Since class size is often small, teachers need not rely solely on lecture methods to convey information. Teachers are committed to sharing with students the academic challenges found in learning the law and the practical necessities found in the daily legal work faced by most paralegals. The faculty reflects the same diverse communities as the student body; teachers come from different age groups, racial and ethnic backgrounds, and academic backgrounds from collegiate and law school institutions throughout the country. The School is a member of the American Association for Paralegal Education (AAfPE), which helps to keep the faculty apprised of national trends in paralegal education and practice.

Student Government

All enrolled students are members of the Paralegal Student Body Association (PSBA), which is the student government for the School of Paralegal Studies. It is administered by its Executive Board, which consists of representatives elected by the student body each fall term. The board acts as the student voice in University affairs, including representation at meetings of the University's Board of Trustees. The PSBA occasionally engages in cooperative efforts with the Student Bar Association of UWLA's School of Law.

Admission Requirements

Admission to the various programs is based on educational level and a minimum GPA of 2.0. A student may be admitted with 30 semester units of college-level general education, 60 semester units of college-level courses, an A.A./A.S. degree, and/or a B.A./B.S. degree. The School's admissions policy is designed to enable all qualified applicants to feel welcome to study at UWLA.

Application and Information

Applicants must complete an application (which asks for a short writing sample) and submit that application, along with the $45 application fee, to the School's Admissions Office. Official academic transcripts of all college work completed prior to application must be sent directly to UWLA from every institution that the applicant has attended. No letters of recommendation are required.

Applications are accepted on a rolling basis and may be submitted at any time throughout the calendar year; accepted students may enroll in the next available term. Applications for the fall trimester should be submitted by August; for the winter trimester, by December; and for the spring trimester, by early April. Students are notified of admissions decisions promptly once all transcripts have been received. Applicants are encouraged to make an appointment to meet with the Admissions Counselor (telephone: 310-342-5287) to discuss their individual questions and concerns.

Interested persons may request an application and information from:

The School of Paralegal Studies
The University of West Los Angeles
1155 West Arbor Vitae Street
Inglewood, California 90301-2902

Telephone: 310-342-5208
Fax: 310-342-5296
World Wide Web: http://www.uwla.edu

The Kelton Law Library.

UNIVERSITY OF WINDSOR
WINDSOR, ONTARIO, CANADA

The University

The University of Windsor appeals to students who are seeking a respected institution with innovative programs, supportive faculty and staff, and a friendly community atmosphere conducive to living and learning.

The University of Windsor evolved from Assumption College, founded in 1847 as a Roman Catholic boys' school. Today, it is a publicly funded, comprehensive teaching and research institution that offers more than 130 fully accredited undergraduate, graduate, cooperative, and professional degree programs to more than 11,000 students. Yet one of its strongest attractions remains its traditional sense of community.

Windsor programs are offered by four academic colleges: Arts and Human Sciences; Engineering and Science; Business Administration, Education and Law; and Graduate Studies and Research. In addition to programs in the full range of basic scholarly disciplines in the arts and sciences, many professional programs are also offered, including law, education, computer science, engineering, and kinesiology. There are also three affiliated colleges: Assumption University (Roman Catholic), Canterbury College (Anglican), and Iona College (United), which provide spiritual and personal support.

The University of Windsor has forged innovative partnerships with business and industry. Among these are the University of Windsor/Chrysler Canada Ltd. Automotive Research and Development Centre, which is unique in North America; the London Life Great Lakes Environmental Research Centre; and the NSERC/Ford/University of Windsor Industrial Research Chair in Light Metals Casting.

Almost half of Windsor's students hail from outside the local area, including every Canadian province and fifty-five countries. About 55 percent of its students are women. Seven on-campus residences house about 1,400 students each year. About 50 percent of residence space is reserved for first-year students. An off-campus housing list is also available. Seven food service outlets are available with a range of hours to service student needs.

The CAW Student Centre is home to several food outlets, the Pub, a photocopying centre, student government offices, a health centre and pharmacy, the student newspaper and radio station, and a campus information service.

Athletic facilities include the St. Denis Centre, which has an indoor and outdoor track, weight rooms, saunas, indoor pool, and tennis courts, and the state-of-the-art Green Shield of Canada Sports Therapy Clinic. Men's and women's teams compete in nine varsity sports, and more than thirty recreational activities are available, from aerobics to Ultimate Frisbee.

A wide variety of student clubs and associations are sponsored by three student governments that represent full-time undergraduates, part-time undergraduates, and graduate and professional students. In addition to these student organizations, the University, through its Division of Student Affairs, provides student-oriented services, such as a first-year orientation (Head Start Program), peer support, study-skills seminars, tutors, academic writing seminars, cooperative education applications and placements, special needs accommodations, and a range of international student services, such as providing guidance on visa renewal and immigration regulations.

Location

The tree-lined campus of the University of Windsor comprises 55 hectares in the midst of Windsor, Ontario. The city of Windsor, a friendly community of 200,000, is on the same latitude as Rome and northern California. Its winters are moderate and summers are pleasant. Windsor sits on the Canada-U.S. border in the modern, high-technology manufacturing heartland of North America. This unique location means that Windsor students have opportunities for international study, research, and work experiences that no other university in Canada can match. Windsor's convenient public transit system provides bus service every 15 minutes to the University. Windsor is a community with an international flavour, great restaurants and pubs, and a vibrant arts and entertainment scene, which includes a symphony orchestra, art gallery, light opera, theatres, and dance companies. Just across the border in Michigan (5 minutes by bridge or tunnel), professional baseball, hockey, basketball, and football teams play; major concerts are held; and world-class international museums and cultural events beckon.

Majors and Degrees

The Bachelor of Applied Science (B.A.Sc.) degree is offered in engineering (civil, electrical, environmental, industrial and manufacturing systems, mechanical, and mechanical with options). The Bachelor of Arts (B.A.) is offered in anthropology, art history, Asian studies, Canadian studies, classical civilizations, communication studies, creative writing, criminology, drama, drama in education, economics, English, environmental resource management, family and social relations, French, geography, history, international relations and development studies, labour studies, language and logic, liberal and professional studies, mathematics and statistics, modern languages (German, Italian, Spanish), multicultural studies, philosophy, planning, political science, psychology, sociology, visual arts, and women's studies.

The Bachelor of Commerce (B.Comm.) degree is offered in business administration, business administration and economics, and honours business administration and computer science.

The Bachelor of Computer Science (B.C.S.) and Bachelor of Science (B.Sc.) degrees are offered in programs such as software development, computer information systems, and media design (in combination with visual arts and communication studies).

A Bachelor of Education (B.Ed.) degree, a one-year postdegree program, is offered at the primary/junior, junior/intermediate, and intermediate/senior levels.

The Bachelor of Fine Arts (B.F.A.) degree is offered in acting, music theatre, and visual arts. The Bachelor of Human Kinetics (B.H.K.) degree is offered in leisure and sport management and in movement science.

A Bachelor of Laws (LL.B.) degree is offered.

The Bachelor of Music (B.Mus.) degree is offered in individualized, performance, and school music. The Bachelor of Musical Arts (B.M.A.) and Bachelor of Music Therapy (B.Mus.Th.) degrees are also offered.

Bachelor of Science (B.Sc.) degrees are offered in biochemistry, biological sciences, chemistry, computer science, environmental biology, environmental geology, environmental resource management, environmental science, general science, general science and medical laboratory technology, geology, mathematics and statistics, physical geography, and physics. The Bachelor of Science in Nursing (B.Sc.N.) degree is also offered.

Other degree programs include the Bachelor of Public Administration (B.P.A.) and Bachelor of Social Work (B.S.W.).

Cooperative Education Programs, combining work experience and academic study, are offered in many areas of study, including business, computer science, engineering, environmental biology, environmental geology, geology, leisure and sport management, and movement science.

Academic Program

The University of Windsor academic year runs from September until April, with accelerated courses offered in May–June (intersession) and July–August (summer session). New students are invited to attend the University's Head Start Orientation Program, held each year in July.

The University of Windsor offers three-year Bachelor of Arts and Bachelor of Science degrees, which require 30 semester credits. It also offers four-year degree programs that require 40 semester credits and lead to the B.A., B.Sc., B.Comm., B.A.Sc., B.S.W., B.P.A., B.Mus.Th., B.F.A., B.H.K., and B.Sc.N. degrees. Requirements for graduation vary by degree. Details can be found on the University of Windsor's Web site (listed below).

Off-Campus Arrangements

Windsor has exchange programs with universities in different countries around the world, including Bangladesh, Chile, Cuba, France, Germany, Guyana, Holland, India, Italy, Japan, Jordan, Mexico, Spain, Sweden, and the United States.

Academic Facilities

The Leddy Library and Paul Martin Law Library house more than 2.3 million books and resources on-site. Students also have access to several campus computer labs with workstations featuring Pentium processors, with consultants always on hand. A number of residence rooms offer Internet access. The Multi-media Learning and Language Laboratory is the only one of its kind in Canada and is able to combine both audio and video learning through audio transmissions, video clips, images, and numeric or textual databases. The Lebel Art Gallery holds several shows each year, and the University Players stage more than fifty performances each season.

Costs

The 1999–2000 tuition fees per semester for Canadian citizens and permanent residents enrolled as full-time undergraduate students in most programs were Can$1850. Full-time international students in most programs paid fees each semester of Can$4800. The fee for full-time study for U.S. students in most programs per year was $3800 (U.S.). Residence and food services fees for each semester were approximately Can$2500 (double occupancy). Ancillary fees were approximately Can$200 per semester. Costs of books and course materials vary with the area of study but average about Can$100 per semester course taken.

Financial Aid

The University of Windsor provides more than Can$4 million in scholarships, awards, and bursaries awarded annually to undergraduate students. First-year students with an admission average of at least 80 percent may be eligible for an Entrance Scholarship that ranges from Can$500 to Can$1000 for one year to awards valued at up to Can$12,000 over four years. More than 750 entrance bursaries valued at Can$1000 are available to first-year students who demonstrate financial need based on family and/or personal income. Provincial financial aid programs are available to Canadian students in need. In addition, more than 1,000 campus jobs are available through the Ontario Work Study Plan. Interested students should refer to the *University of Windsor Undergraduate Calendar* for a comprehensive listing of all financial aid, or check the University's Web site (listed below).

Faculty

The University of Windsor, a teaching and research institution, has 440 full-time faculty members and librarians and hundreds of sessionals. Faculty and professional student advisers are willing counsellors for students, providing both advice and encouragement.

Student Government

Students at the University of Windsor are represented by three student government bodies: University of Windsor Students' Alliance (UWSA), Organization of Part-time University Students (OPUS), and Society of Graduate and Professional Students (SGPS). Each group provides an advocacy function on three levels: on behalf of individuals, through serving on University committees, and by interacting with outside groups. UWSA is also responsible for the CAW Student Centre, the Pub, and the Used Book Store, as well as services such as *The Lance* student newspaper and CJAM radio. SGPS also operates the Grad House pub.

Admission Requirements

For Ontario Secondary School graduates, basic requirements include the OSSD and six Ontario Academic Courses (OACs), which include OAC English 1. Each University of Windsor student must meet general admission requirements as well as any specific requirements demanded by their program of choice. All programs have minimum admission averages that may change.

Students from the United States must present scholastic records indicating good preparation and the ability to undertake a University degree program. Graduates of accredited high schools normally qualify for admission if the cumulative high school grade point average is 2.75 (B-) or above. Each applicant must present scores from either the ACT or the SAT I. Advanced Placement Examinations in certain prerequisite subjects also may be required. Highly qualified applicants from the United States will be given final acceptance after the first-term marks of the final year of high school have been received if the applicant meets the admission requirements at that time and providing the graduation certificate is present.

Admission for International Students to an undergraduate program is based on specific academic prerequisites. In some cases, satisfactory scores on such tests as the GMAT are necessary. For applicants whose native language is not English, a satisfactory score on an English proficiency test is required. To study in Windsor, Canada's immigration department requires a Student Authorization card.

Application and Information

For applications, students should contact:
Ontario Universities' Application Centre
650 Woodlawn Road West
P.O. Box 1328
Guelph, Ontario N1H 7P4
Canada
   or
University of Windsor
Office of Liaison and Applicant Services
Telephone: 800-864-2860 (toll-free)
Fax: 519-971-3653
E-mail: liaison@uwindsor.ca
World Wide Web: http://www.uwindsor.ca

UNIVERSITY OF WISCONSIN–GREEN BAY
GREEN BAY, WISCONSIN

The University

The University of Wisconsin–Green Bay (UW–Green Bay) is a comprehensive regional university with exceptional new facilities, a dynamic atmosphere, and a fresh approach to student learning.

UW–Green Bay is a midsize public university with 5,500 students. About one third of the student body resides on campus. Most students are from Wisconsin and other Midwest states, but the University enrolls individuals from thirty states and about three dozen other countries.

Founded in 1965, the campus is among the most modern and attractive in the highly respected, tradition-rich University of Wisconsin System. The setting is safe, scenic, and comfortable, with wooded trails, a nine-hole golf course, and a million-dollar view of the bay.

UW–Green Bay is heavily invested in state-of-the-art academic facilities and special amenities for students. A high-tech classroom building opens next year. Also new is a reconfigured computer network. The eight-story Cofrin Library is regarded among the finest in the state. Other features include an expanded University Union; attractive on-campus housing with single rooms, private baths, and apartment-style options; and newly dedicated student space in the University's Weidner Center—a major performing arts center that is regarded as one of the nation's best new concert halls. Students find a rich array of clubs, organizations, and leisure-time options, including a highly successful NCAA Division I sports program and performances by big-name entertainers at the Weidner Center.

The University prides itself on the Green Bay Idea—an innovative approach to learning, with personal attention from professors and interdisciplinary, problem-solving experience for students. Senior faculty members lead advanced and entry-level courses. They emphasize critical thinking and problem solving as essential skills for the Knowledge Age and a lifetime of learning.

Location

UW–Green Bay is located on the suburban, northeast edge of Green Bay, Wisconsin. Famous for the Packers and NFL football, the city is also known as a center of industry and commerce, with manufacturing, transportation, health care, and insurance as the most important sectors of the economy. No other American community of its size (metropolitan population of 250,000) has as many Forbes 500 firms. Green Bay is home to a developing entertainment district and excellent museums, parks, theaters, and sports-related facilities. It is the gateway to a favorite vacation destination in the scenic Door Peninsula, with its forested bluffs, historic harbors, and Lake Michigan beaches.

The campus is less than 2 hours north of Milwaukee and about 5 hours east of Minnesota's Twin Cities via the interstate highway. Green Bay's airport provides direct service to Chicago, Minneapolis, Detroit, and other major cities.

Majors and Degrees

UW–Green Bay grants Bachelor of Arts and Bachelor of Science degrees in seventeen interdisciplinary majors and eighteen disciplinary majors. Professional programs in nursing completion and social work award the B.S.N. and B.S.W., respectively. The disciplinary program in music awards the B.M. degree. A two-year associate degree is available. Undergraduate certificate programs are offered in international studies, English as a second language, military science, and athletic coaching. The University has preprofessional programs in nearly twenty fields, including dentistry, engineering, law, medicine, and pharmacy.

Interdisciplinary majors are as follows: business administration, with emphases in finance, management, and marketing; communication and the arts, with emphases in environmental design and integrated communications; communication processes, with emphases in electronic media, linguistics/teaching ESL, organizational communication, photography, print journalism, and public relations; education, with preparation in early childhood/elementary through secondary teaching; environmental policy and planning, with emphases in public policy and planning; environmental science, with emphases in ecology and biological resources management and physical systems: technology and management; human biology, with emphases in cytotechnology, exercise science, general human biology, health science, and nutritional science/dietetics; human development, with general, family, and preclinical/precounseling studies emphases; humanistic studies; individual major; information sciences; interdisciplinary studies; public administration, with emphases in public and nonprofit management and public policy; social change and development, with emphases in American social issues, global studies, law and social change, and women's studies; and urban and regional studies.

Disciplinary majors are as follows: accounting; art, with emphases in studio art, art education, and art management; biology, with emphases in plant biology, animal biology, cell/molecular biology, and field biology and ecology; chemistry; computer science; earth science; economics; English, with an emphasis in creative writing; French; German; history; mathematics, with emphases in math and statistics; music, with emphases in music education, performance, applied music, jazz studies, music history and literature, and music and business; philosophy; political science; psychology; Spanish; and theater, with emphases in performance, design/technical theater, theater studies, and musical theater.

The following areas are only available as minors: American Indian studies, anthropology, geography, physics, sociology, and women's studies.

Academic Program

The principal component of the Green Bay Idea is an emphasis on interdisciplinary—or multiple-subject—fields of study. Interdisciplinary majors apply knowledge from several subjects or disciplines to one field of study. As an example, an environmental science major will apply biology, chemistry, mathematics, botany, and other disciplines to the broader study of environmental issues. Every student completes either an interdisciplinary major or a disciplinary major, coupled with an interdisciplinary minor. The general education program includes course work in the natural sciences, social sciences, humanities, fine arts, and other cultures.

The interdisciplinary approach demands that students learn to examine things from many perspectives and work effectively with those from other fields. Students then pursue hands-on learning through internships, research, and team projects.

Off-Campus Arrangements

Formal exchange agreements exist with several universities abroad, and UW–Green Bay students have participated recently in formal exchange and language-immersion programs in Denmark, Guatemala, Germany, Mexico, the Netherlands, and Spain. Students can arrange to study almost anywhere through the University's links to international exchange networks. Those interested in two- to four-week excursions can join study tours of countries such as China, Peru, Switzerland, and Australia. UW–Green Bay participates in the National Student Exchange, which facilitates out-of-state study for a semester or year at universities and colleges across the United States.

Academic Facilities

A high-tech $17-million classroom building is slated to open next year. The David A. Cofrin Library remains the physical and symbolic heart of the modern campus. Central computing laboratories for students are located near the library and are open nearly 100 hours per week. A newly reconfigured information technology network positions the University among the state's leaders in terms of access and capabilities for student and faculty member users. Special computer labs serve academic programs such as business, graphic arts, geography, music, and psychology. The Weidner Center for the Performing Arts hosts major Broadway musicals, large orchestras, dance companies, and pop performers. The center features academic studios and provides master classes with acclaimed visiting artists as well as opportunities for internships and paid employment in the entertainment field. Students use the 2,000-seat hall for music, theater, and dance performances. Outdoors, science students enjoy field experiences on the 270-acre campus arboretum and University-managed nature preserves along the Lake Michigan shoreline.

Costs

Estimated 2000–01 tuition and fees for full-time students are $3200 for Wisconsin residents and $10,500 for nonresidents. Minnesota residents pay University of Minnesota tuition rates. Room and board averages $3600 for the academic year. Estimated expenses for books, supplies, and personal items are $600 per year.

Financial Aid

Financial aid awards are based on need and use the Free Application for Federal Student Aid (FAFSA), with an April 15 priority date. Academic and athletic scholarships are available. Using all typical aid programs, the University provides more than $17 million to more than 60 percent of its enrolling students. More than 1,000 students typically find part-time employment on campus. The community offers a wide variety of work opportunities for students.

Faculty

UW–Green Bay has about 180 full-time faculty members. Ad hoc, or part-time, instructors push the full-time-equivalent count to more than 200. There are few, if any, teaching assistants. Senior professors teach courses for freshmen and sophomores as well as upper-level courses. They engage in interesting and varied research but have teaching and advising students as their primary focus. Of full-time tenured and tenure-track faculty members, 97 percent hold the Ph.D. or other terminal degree.

Student Government

Elected and volunteer leadership opportunities exist through the Student Government Association (SGA). Members of the SGA leadership team serve as liaisons to the administration, serve on campuswide committees, and advise on issues of student concern. The Good Times Programming Board arranges social, cultural, recreational, and educational programming for students, with recent Hollywood blockbusters and college classics in the popular film series and acts including comedians, hypnotists, and up-and-coming bands, on the concert calendar. More than ninety clubs and organizations focus on special interests. These range from the weekly student newspaper to environmental, service, sports, and cultural groups.

Admission Requirements

Basic admission criteria are graduation from high school, completion of 17 prescribed academic high school units, class rank in upper 45 percent, or, if the student's school does not rank graduates, a minimum GPA of 2.75 plus a minimum ACT composite score of 23. Other applicants are considered on the basis of test scores, recommendations, special talent, and personal statement. Transfer student admission is based on completion of at least 15 acceptable credits with a GPA of at least 2.25. Both ACT and SAT I test scores are accepted. Applications may be submitted by paper form or electronically. Electronic applications are available on the University's Web site (http://apply.wisconsin.edu/).

Application and Information

Admission decisions are made on a rolling basis; early application is recommended.

For more information, students should contact:

Pam Harvey-Jacobs
Office of Admissions and Orientation
University of Wisconsin–Green Bay
2420 Nicolet Drive
Green Bay, Wisconsin 54311-7001
Telephone: 920-465-2111
Fax: 920-465-5754
E-mail: uwgb@uwgb.edu
World Wide Web: http://www.uwgb.edu

Comfortable and new on-campus housing, every room with a private bath, is a popular feature of UW–Green Bay.

UNIVERSITY OF WYOMING
LARAMIE, WYOMING

The University

More than any other institution of its kind, the University of Wyoming (UW) is a reflection of the state it serves. The broad range of outstanding academic programs mirrors the broad expanse of the dynamic Wyoming landscape. Its research goals, which benefit Wyoming and the world, are as lofty as the Snowy Range Mountains or the Grand Tetons.

Wyoming's people have been most influential in shaping the University. The distance between places, the beauty of the terrain, and the interdependence of neighbors have created a people who care about the land and who care about each other. In UW, an institution of higher learning has been developed that combines the academic ambitions of the nation's finest universities with a deep love for the state and a tremendous regard for the values of Wyoming's people. That has been UW's philosophy since it was founded in 1886 while Wyoming was still a territory and four years from statehood.

From the beginning, the land-grant mission has been to provide high-quality undergraduate and graduate education, research, and service. UW has remained true to the goal of serving the educational needs of students today and preparing them for a complex world tomorrow while preserving Wyoming's rich Western heritage.

Unique among the fifty states, Wyoming has only one university, which enjoys tremendous statewide support. More than 11,250 students from all parts of the U.S. and sixty other countries attend UW classes in Laramie and at sites around the state. UW offers bachelor's, master's, and doctoral degrees in six undergraduate colleges, including the Doctor of Pharmacy in the College of Health Sciences. In the Colleges of Agriculture, Arts and Sciences, Business, Education, Engineering, and Health Sciences, students gain a broad range of classroom, laboratory, and cocurricular experiences that are the educational building blocks for a successful career or graduate study. Undergraduate education is a high priority at UW. The brightest and best of the faculty members teach undergraduate classes.

More than 160 clubs and organizations are recognized by the University, including fourteen national fraternities and sororities. UW competes in Western Athletic Conference Division I NCAA athletics in fifteen men's and women's sports.

Campus recreational facilities include two indoor swimming pools, racquetball and tennis courts, an eighteen-hole golf course, an indoor climbing wall, weight rooms, rifle and archery ranges, indoor and outdoor tracks, softball and baseball fields, and a hockey rink. The student union hosts a variety of facilities, including a bowling alley and games room as well as meeting rooms and restaurants.

The University houses 2,400 students in six residence halls. Living environments include coed or single-sex floors, special interest floors, honors floors, and other academic environments.

Location

UW's 785-acre campus is located in Laramie, a small city of 30,000 in southeastern Wyoming. Laramie is conveniently located 50 miles west of Wyoming's capital, Cheyenne, and 130 miles northwest of Denver, Colorado. Laramie sits between two mountain ranges and offers outstanding outdoor recreation. The campus and the community mesh into a friendly and supportive university town.

Majors and Degrees

The University of Wyoming opened its doors in September 1887, with one building, 5 professors, 2 tutors, and 42 students. Programs of study available to those first students included philosophy, arts, literature, and science. Today, UW offers eighty-eight undergraduate programs and seventy graduate and professional degree programs within the Colleges of Agriculture, Arts and Sciences, Business, Education, Engineering, Health Sciences, and Law and the Graduate School. The College of Agriculture offers agricultural business, agricultural communications, agroecology, animal and veterinary sciences, family and consumer sciences (with options in child and family studies, human nutrition and food, and textiles and merchandising), microbiology, molecular biology, and rangeland ecology and watershed management. The College Arts and Sciences offers degrees in the biological sciences—biology, botany, physiology, psychology, wildlife and fisheries biology and management, and zoology; in the fine arts—art, music, music education (instrumental and vocal), music performance, music theory and composition, and theater and dance; in the humanities—English, English/theater, French, German, philosophy, Russian, and Spanish; interdisciplinary majors in criminal justice, American studies, humanities/fine arts, international studies, natural science/mathematics, self-designed major, social science, and women's studies; in the mathematical sciences—applied mathematics, computer science, management information systems (with options in accounting, business, and computer science), mathematics, and statistics; in physical science—astronomy/astrophysics, chemistry, environmental geology/geohydrology, geology, and physics; and in social sciences—anthropology, communication, economics, geography, history, journalism, political economy, political science, recreation and park administration, and sociology. The College of Business offers accounting, business administration, economics, finance, management, and marketing. In the College of Education, degrees may be earned in distributive education, elementary and special education, elementary education, secondary education, special education, trades and industrial education, and vocational agriculture. The College of Engineering offers degrees in architectural engineering, chemical engineering (with options in petroleum engineering and environmental engineering), civil engineering, electrical engineering (with options in bioengineering and computer engineering), and mechanical engineering. The College of Health Sciences offers dental hygiene, health education (with options in teaching and health behavior promotion), nursing, physical education (with options in teaching and exercise and sport science), and speech, language, and hearing sciences. UW also offers preprofessional programs in dentistry, forestry, law, medicine, occupational therapy, optometry, physical therapy, and veterinary medicine.

Academic Program

UW's commitment to student success is underscored by the large number of courses offered each semester, ensuring that students have an opportunity to graduate in four years in most majors.

UW's University Studies program requires all UW students to complete a set of common education requirements before receiving degrees. Reflecting UW's commitment to providing an education for complete living, the program is designed to develop the basic skills students need in areas such as writing and problem solving and to acquaint them with the realities of a global society.

The academic calendar consists of two semesters and a complete summer session. Baccalaureate programs require 128 to 164 credit hours of course work. The University Honors Program provides distinctive learning experiences for a select group of students who show promise of academic excellence at the university level. The Senior Research Project is the hallmark of this program and prepares students for graduate and professional school. Freshman interest groups offer clustered classes and common living areas that allow participants to develop close relationships with other students who share common interests.

Off-Campus Arrangements

Education at the University of Wyoming is not confined to the buildings that comprise the main campus in Laramie. Bringing educational opportunities to students in all twenty-three Wyoming counties continues to be a top University priority. Since UW's inception, courses have been taught throughout the state using the leading technology of the day. Today, courses are taught through video technology that allows professors in Laramie and students in communities throughout Wyoming to hear and see each other in classrooms hundreds of miles apart.

Selected undergraduate and graduate programs are also extended to Wyoming communities through traditional independent-study approaches, face-to-face instruction, and correspondence.

Study abroad and National Student Exchange opportunities are available to students in all academic programs.

Academic Facilities

While UW's faculty, staff, and students are what make the University truly exceptional, the main campus and its modern facilities support their efforts.

The attractive Laramie campus extends over 785 acres and includes eighty major buildings. There is a pleasant mix of modern and traditional structures, many constructed of native Wyoming sandstone. Campus wildlife habitats—bird nesting sites, animal feeders, and native wildflowers—add to the physical beauty of the campus and provide a natural laboratory for wildlife students.

The University Libraries' collections number more than 1.1 million volumes. The William Robertson Coe Library houses general reference, humanities, social science, and education and medical materials, as well as government documents and maps. Other libraries in the UW system are the Science Library, the Geology Library, the Film Library and Audio Visual Services, the Learning Resources Center, and the Rocky Mountain Herbarium Research Collection. The Hebard collection and other collections are housed in the American Heritage Center and the George W. Hopper Law Library. There are also branch libraries off campus: one at the UW/Casper College Center and one at the National Park Service Research Center Collection in Jackson.

An additional 21 million volumes are available through the Colorado Alliance of Research Libraries (CARL) network, a worldwide consortium of universities. CARL is one of many services provided through the University's campus information technology system that also gives students, staff, and faculty access to high-speed computers for instruction, research, and worldwide communication.

Costs

The University of Wyoming's tuition and fees were $7684 for nonresident students and $2416 for Wyoming residents in 1999–2000. The cost of room and board in the UW residence halls for one year was $4446. Other expenses for the year were estimated at $600 for books and supplies and $1500 for personal expenses.

Financial Aid

More than 72 percent of all UW students receive financial assistance to attend the University. A total of $41 million is available to UW students in the form of scholarships, grants, loans, and work-study. The UW Application for Financial Aid and Scholarships and the Free Application for Federal Student Aid (FAFSA) must be submitted for consideration for need-based assistance. Most scholarships are awarded based on merit rather than financial need. UW participates in the Western Undergraduate Exchange program.

Faculty

More than 600 professors have come to teach at UW from among the world's most respected colleges and universities. Recognized nationally and internationally as experts in their fields, they are deeply committed to the success of their students. UW's professors have as their primary responsibility the education of undergraduate students. Fewer than 10 percent of all credit hours are taught by graduate assistants. Many of the most accomplished professors teach first-year courses, enabling students to begin a mentoring process from the first day of class. Because Wyoming maintains a low student-faculty ratio that allows for individual instruction and attention, the professors truly get to know their students. This relationship transcends teaching to include academic advising and inclusion of undergraduates in cutting-edge research projects. Nearly 98 percent of all UW instructors hold a Ph.D. or the equivalent degree in their chosen fields.

Student Government

UW students play a significant role in the governance of the University. The Associated Students of the University of Wyoming considers legislation that touches on all aspects of student life. The student body president sits as an ex officio member of the University Board of Trustees.

Admission Requirements

A variety of factors are used to determine eligibility for admission to UW. Students who are high school graduates with fewer than 30 transferable college credit hours must have taken and passed thirteen core courses (4 years of English, 3 years of mathematics, 3 years of science, and 3 years of cultural context). A minimum grade point average of 2.75 and an ACT score of 20 or an SAT I score of 960 are also required. Admission with conditions is available to students who do not meet these standards, but who have a minimum 2.25 grade point average and an ACT composite score of 20 or an SAT I score of 960.

Application and Information

To be considered for admission, students must submit a completed UW application for admission, an official high school transcript, ACT or SAT I scores, and the $30 application fee. The priority deadline for financial aid is March 1.

UW encourages all prospective students and their parents to visit the campus. For more information or to schedule a campus tour, students should contact:

Admission Office
University of Wyoming
Box 3435
Laramie, Wyoming 82071-3435
Telephone: 307-766-5160
    800-DIAL-WYO (342-5996) (toll-free)
E-mail: undergraduate.admissions@uwyo.edu
World Wide Web: http://www.uwyo.edu/

Historic Old Main was built in 1886.

URBANA UNIVERSITY
URBANA, OHIO

The University

Founded in 1850, Urbana University's tree-covered campus is located on 128 acres, and its facilities offer a picturesque blend of modern and traditional architecture. The twenty-two buildings on campus range from Bailey Hall, an ivy-covered structure built in 1851, to the University Community Center, housing a 3,500-seat gymnasium, indoor swimming pool, racquetball courts, weight room, lounge areas, bookstore, and classrooms.

Urbana University is accredited by the Commission on Institutions of Higher Education of the North Central Association of Colleges and Schools and approved by the State of Ohio Department of Education.

The institution is a member of the National Association of Intercollegiate Athletics and the Mid-Ohio Conference (both men and women). Intercollegiate competition is offered in baseball, basketball, football, golf, and soccer for men and in basketball, golf, soccer, softball, and volleyball for women. A variety of activities are offered for student enrichment, including art exhibits, a film series, a theater club, concerts, and guest speakers. Students may also participate in the student newspaper, yearbook, or any of the many other clubs and organizations.

There are 1,109 students enrolled at Urbana, 562 men and 547 women.

Location

Urbana is a city of 12,000 people, located in west-central Ohio. While offering the security of a small-town community, Urbana is located near two major Ohio cities, Columbus (40 miles east) and Dayton (35 miles southwest). Major airports in these cities offer worldwide service. Three major interstate highways are within a 40-mile radius of Urbana.

Majors and Degrees

Urbana University offers four-year baccalaureate degrees through the Divisions of Business, Education and Allied Programs, Humanities and Social Sciences, and Mathematics and Sciences. Majors are available in business administration with an emphasis in accounting, computer systems and applications, general management, human resources management, or marketing; communications; comprehensive science with an emphasis in biology or chemistry; criminal justice; education with elementary, middle school, or secondary certification; English; liberal studies with an emphasis in humanities or social science; philosophy and religion; psychology; sociology; sports medicine; and sports science with an emphasis in sports management or lifetime fitness. Urbana University offers preprofessional programs in dentistry, law, and medicine. Students have the option of designing their own major with the approval of 2 faculty members and the dean of academic affairs. Two-year Associate of Arts degrees are offered in business administration and liberal studies.

Academic Program

Bachelor's degree candidates must complete 126 credit hours with a minimum quality point average of 2.0. Students must also demonstrate competence in mathematics, writing, reading comprehension, and speech through testing or by successfully completing specified course offerings. All students must fulfill core curriculum requirements and requirements of an authorized major before graduation. Candidates for the Associate in Arts degree must complete stated requirements in the business administration or liberal studies areas and must maintain at least a 2.0 average. Transfer students must earn a minimum of 30 credit hours in residence at Urbana University to be considered for a degree.

The academic year at the University consists of two 16-week semesters, beginning in August and January. In addition, classes are offered during the 8-week summer session. Evening classes are offered for students who wish to accelerate their degree programs or attend part-time.

Off-Campus Arrangements

Urbana University offers several off-campus degree programs in central and southwest Ohio. These programs enable individuals to attend college who might not otherwise be able to do so. Students enrolled in any of the off-campus programs work toward the same degrees as do on-campus students. Off-campus programs are located in Bellefontaine, Dayton, and Piqua.

The University is a member of the Southwestern Ohio Council for Higher Education (SOCHE), which has twenty-four members. Among the benefits of SOCHE is a cross-registration plan, under which Urbana students may register at no additional charge for courses at other member institutions. SOCHE membership enables Urbana University to maintain a small-college atmosphere while offering students many of the specialized benefits of larger universities.

Academic Facilities

Urbana University offers an intimate, family-like atmosphere in which to learn and prosper. The campus is home to a variety of architectural styles, ranging from historic Barclay and Bailey Halls to the latest addition of a math/science building. This complex houses state-of-the-art science and computer laboratories, several classrooms, and a 125-seat lecture hall.

Costs

Urbana University is a competitively priced private institution. Tuition for the 2000–01 academic year is $11,388. Board is $2900, and there is no charge for residence halls.

Financial Aid

Urbana University administers aid from a number of federal and state aid programs, including Federal Pell Grants, Ohio Instructional Grants, and Federal Perkins Loans. The University also offers grants on the basis of academic achievement, athletic ability, and financial need. An academic competition is held every February for 1 full, 4 three-quarter, and 7 half scholarships.

Faculty

Thirty-six well-qualified instructors make up the full-time University faculty. More than 70 percent have a Ph.D., and most have extensive practical experience in their academic area. The faculty is dedicated to the philosophy that education is a two-way experience in which students and faculty members grow together. A faculty-student ratio of 1:14 encourages a small and creative classroom atmosphere.

Student Government

The Student Government Association is composed of 8 to 12 members who represent the commuter, resident, minority, and international student bodies on campus. Its function is to ensure student representation in all forms of policymaking at the University, to assist in the allocation of student activity funds, and to provide a functional and positive reference source for the student body.

Admission Requirements

The Admissions and Academic Standards Committee considers a variety of elements in evaluating an application for admission. Individual achievement and involvement outside the classroom are weighed, as are the application, high school record, and SAT I or ACT scores. Applicants are encouraged to apply early in their senior year, although there is no stated deadline. While requirements for admission are flexible, applicants usually have taken 4 years of English, 3 years of mathematics, 3 years of science, and 3 years of humanities courses during secondary school.

Transfer admission requirements are structured to allow easy transition to Urbana University programs. Transfer students are expected to have maintained a GPA of at least 2.0.

Application and Information

Students seeking admission must submit a completed application form, an official copy of the secondary school transcript, official copies of college transcripts (if applicable), and SAT I or ACT scores. To obtain an admission and financial aid application form or additional information, students are encouraged to contact:

Office of Admissions
Urbana University
579 College Way
Urbana, Ohio 43078
Telephone: 937-484-1356
              800-7URBANA (toll-free in Ohio)
Fax: 937-484-1389
E-mail: admiss@urbana.edu

Students entering the library are greeted by the Latin phrase that translates to "Now it is possible intellectually to enter into the mysteries of faith."

URSINUS COLLEGE
COLLEGEVILLE, PENNSYLVANIA

The College

The cornerstones of the Ursinus College liberal arts program are self-reliance and responsibility, developed through an emphasis on independent achievement. The program is coherent, cumulative, and comprehensive, as all students are required to complete an Independent Learning Experience, which includes an internship, independent research, study abroad, or student teaching. The Ursinus Program does not stop at the classroom door but touches every area of students' lives. As one of 240 colleges granted a chapter of the national academic honor society Phi Beta Kappa, Ursinus College joins together some of the very best students and professors in the nation in a safe, beautiful setting that features outstanding facilities. Three out of 4 students go on to graduate study at some point after graduating from Ursinus. Students develop the habits of mind to become doctors, attorneys, college professors, high school teachers, artists, scientific researchers, writers, and corporate leaders. The College ranks seventeenth in the nation in the percentage of its graduates who have attended medical school. Historically, 90 percent of those who apply to medical, dental, and veterinary schools gain acceptance. College graduates also have a law school admissions record better than 90 percent. Among Ursinus' 11,000 living alumni are 1972 Nobel laureate, Gerald Edelman; NASA Magellan Mission Director, James F. Scott III; Chancellor of the Jewish Theological Seminary of New York, Ismar Schorsch; Ambassador and architect of the Camp David Peace Accord, Hermann F. Eilts; Sam Keen, author of *Fire in the Belly: On Being a Man* and other major books; United States Ambassador to Sierra Leone, Joseph H. Melrose Jr.; Geoff Bloom, president and CEO of Wolverine Worldwide Incorporated; and pediatric AIDS researcher Loretta P. Finnegan.

Since its founding in 1869, Ursinus has combined a residential experience with an uncompromising drive toward academic quality. Ursinus students are intelligent, motivated, and academically curious, as demonstrated by their excellence in advanced college-preparatory high school programs and cocurricular activities. The student body at Ursinus numbers 1,250, with equal numbers of men and women. Ursinus receives 2,000 applications each year and enrolls 360 students each fall. Forty-two percent of those enrolled in fall 1999 were ranked in the top 10 percent in their high schools, 142 were elected to the National Honor Society, 83 were captains of varsity sports, 15 were valedictorians or salutatorians, and 7 are National Merit Scholars. Sixteen percent of the entering class is composed of members of minority groups, and 5 percent of the class is composed of international students. The student body comes from twenty-eight states and fifteen other countries.

The Ursinus College graduating class of 1999 achieved exceptional results. Twenty-eight students published research papers, 156 gave presentations of their research and internship results are conferences, and 20 received grants and fellowships to graduate schools. Graduates of the class of 1999 attend twenty-five graduate schools, twelve law schools, fourteen medical schools, two dental schools, three veterinary schools, and five graduate schools of physical therapy.

Ursinus provides a variety of cocurricular outlets for students. The nationally recognized Berman Museum of Art, which features the collection of Philip and Muriel Berman, is open to the public. Their collection of American art is one of the finest in the world. Changing exhibits range from sixth-century B.C. excavations from Jerusalem to the hyperrealistic contemporary sculpture of Marc Sijan. Zack's Snack Bar is located in the recently renovated Wismer Center, which also houses the Ursinus Book Store, game room, television lounge, dance and movie facilities, and the Student Activities, Student Government Association (SGA), and Campus Activities Board (CAB) offices. The Residential Village, comprised of twenty-five renovated Victorian homes, complements the campus culture.

Ursinus students may live in these houses or in one of the residence halls. Six of the homes are special interest houses: Unity House, Musser International House, Service Learning House, Wellness House, the Java Trench (coffeehouse), and Biology House. Ursinus students, 93 percent of whom live on campus, enjoy their involvement in College activities. Willing to assume leadership roles, all students participate in at least one of the seventy-five special interest clubs and organizations, honorary academic societies, theater and musical programs, service opportunities, and preprofessional advisory groups. Publications include the weekly *Grizzly* newspaper and the *Lantern* literary magazine. The Literary Society meets weekly. The College offers fraternities and sororities and an extensive athletic program, including Division III intercollegiate varsity sports, Division I women's field hockey, junior varsity sports, and club and intramural activities.

Location

Ursinus is located in the town of Collegeville, which lies 25 miles northwest of Philadelphia along the Route 422 corridor. Its location offers both the charm of a small-town community surrounded by farmland and the convenience of restaurants, theaters, shops, and cultural and sports events in Philadelphia and nearby communities. Interests of all kinds can be explored within a 50-mile radius of the College. There are opportunities to ski in the mountains of the Poconos, hike and camp in French Creek State Park, shop in the famous King of Prussia malls, and relive history in Valley Forge National Park and the historic district of Philadelphia. The College is situated 100 miles from New York City. The recent relocation of three major pharmaceutical companies to the immediate area provides research opportunities for students.

Majors and Degrees

Ursinus offers undergraduate degrees in arts and sciences. The Bachelor of Arts (B.A.) is awarded to students with majors in anthropology/sociology, classical studies, communication arts, economics and business administration, English, environmental studies, French, German, history, international relations, philosophy and religion, politics, and Spanish. The Bachelor of Science (B.S.) is awarded to students with majors in biochemistry, biology, chemistry, computer science, exercise and sports science, mathematics, physics, and psychology. In addition, interdisciplinary majors may be arranged. The College offers a cooperative 3-2 engineering program. Secondary teaching certification is offered in many areas.

Academic Program

Ursinus is committed to undergraduate liberal education and requires students to select among choices in a core curriculum, with a minimum of 128 credits for the bachelor's degree. While completing departmental requirements in one of the major fields, students may add one or more minors. All students are required to complete an internship, an independent research project, a study-abroad program, or a student teaching experience. The College operates on a semester calendar. The fall term begins in late January and ends in mid-May. The College offers funded summer research opportunities with its aggressive undergraduate research scholars program.

Off-Campus Arrangements

Ursinus believes that students in all fields can be transformed by contact with other cultures, so it has created both national and international academic, research, and volunteered internship programs that turn the College into a global gateway. Ursinus offers a broad and diverse set of opportunities for off-campus study. Examples of national programs are the Howard University Semester and the Washington, D.C., Semester. Ursinus also sponsors international study programs to Australia, Costa Rica, England, France, Germany, Ireland, Japan, Mexico, New Zealand, Scotland and Senegal. Ursinus works with the Council on International Education Exchange to provide international experiences to various sites, including Argentina, Belgium, the Czech Republic, Ghana, Hungary, Indonesia, the Netherlands, Poland, Russia, and Tunisia.

Academic Facilities

Myrin Library's open-stack structure houses 185,000 volumes, 155,000 microforms, 17,500 audiovisual materials, and 900 current periodical subscriptions and is a selective depository for U.S. and Pennsylvania state government documents. All materials are accessible through a state-of-the-art Windows-based online computer catalog. Students also have access to more than 3.7 million volumes through the Tri-State College Library Cooperative. Ursinus distributes IBM ThinkPad laptop computers to all entering students, so all students have 24-hour access to the full range of computer applications, e-mail, and the Internet. All student residences are fully networked for computers, cable television, and personal telephones. Pfhaler Hall of Science has recently reopened after a $15-million renovation and addition. Within Pfhaler Hall, the Musser Lecture Hall features the latest in videoconferencing and audiovisual technology, the observatory features excellent high-resolution telescopes, and the laboratories are designed for faculty and student collaborative research. The F. W. Olin Academic Building is the home of all departments in the humanities and contains a 320-seat lecture hall, classrooms, seminar rooms, two microcomputer centers, the Writing Center, and faculty offices and research space. The International Learning Center, also in Olin Hall, provides computer, video, and satellite technology to practice languages. Bomberger Hall provides classrooms for many courses in the social sciences. Thomas Hall houses the psychology and biology departments and provides recently renovated facilities for independent student laboratory research as well as regular course work. Major pieces of scientific instrumentation include infrared spectrometers, a flow cytometer, liquid chromatographs, and a scanning electron microscope. Ritter Center for the Dramatic Arts houses a 260-seat theater with flexible staging, a television studio, and various auxiliary rooms. Helfferich Hall offers a swimming pool, studio, and a fully mirrored weight room with hydra equipment. In fall 2000 Ursinus plans to open the Lewes Field House, which features a four-lane indoor track and indoor tennis courts. Outdoor sports facilities include eight tennis courts, an all-weather track and steeplechase pit, and nine oversized athletics fields for intramural and intercollegiate sports.

Costs

The comprehensive cost for the 1999–2000 academic year for entering first-year students is $29,600. The cost includes $23,460 for tuition (which includes the IBM ThinkPad laptop computer) and $6140 for room and board.

Financial Aid

Approximately 85 percent of Ursinus students receive financial aid in the form of scholarships, grants, loans, campus employment, and state or federal aid. Eligibility for need-based financial aid is determined by the Ursinus Office of Financial Services using the Free Application for Federal Student Aid (FAFSA) and the CSS PROFILE. Approximately half of the College's students work part-time on campus each year. Merit- and talent-based scholarships, which are awarded regardless of need, include a number of awards of up to $12,500 as well as full tuition awards for National Merit Scholars. The FAFSA and PROFILE should reach the College Scholarship Service by February 15, which is the College's preferred filing date. No student is denied admission because of financial need. Ursinus College guarantees to meet the CSS PROFILE need of early decision admitted students.

Faculty

The focus of the College's 135 full- and part-time professors and instructors is on teaching students. All faculty members are also involved in research and writing. Ninety percent of the full-time faculty members have earned doctorates or the highest degree in their fields, and all members are encouraged to explore their fields of study through faculty development grants, leaves, and sabbaticals. The student-faculty ratio is 12:1. Most faculty members serve as academic advisers, and many serve as advisers to academically oriented clubs and interest groups.

Student Government

Through the Ursinus Student Government Association (USGA), students have responsibility in all essential areas of campus governance. Through the USGA committees, students may participate in the development of the academic, residential, and extracurricular life of the College. Great emphasis is placed on fostering responsibility in campus life.

Admissions Requirements

Applicants for admission to Ursinus must be graduates of an accredited high school and present a minimum of 16 academic credits starting in the ninth grade. Candidates for admission are required to submit SAT I or ACT scores. Students who have achieved top 10 percent ranking in their high schools or who have achieved a GPA of 3.5 or better at high schools that do not rank have the option of waiving their standardized test scores. For fall 1999, the middle 50 percent of combined SAT I scores earned by students entering Ursinus ranged from 1080 to 1275. SAT II Subject Tests are recommended but not required. Ursinus also recognizes the Advanced Placement Program of the College Board for college credit. All applicants are encouraged to arrange for a personal interview on campus, and merit scholarship applicants are required to have an on-campus interview.

Application and Information

Ursinus College accepts the Common Application. Candidates are asked to send a completed application accompanied by the nonrefundable $30 application fee no later than February 15. Candidates who wish to be considered for early decision must submit an application and complete their credentials prior to January 15. Ursinus College also has an early admission program for outstanding high school juniors; such students should contact the Office of Admissions for further information. Academic program brochures and application forms may be obtained by contacting:

Office of Admissions
Ursinus College
P.O. Box 1000
Collegeville, Pennsylvania 19426
Telephone: 610-409-3200
Fax: 610-409-3662
World Wide Web: http://www.ursinus.edu

UTICA COLLEGE
of Syracuse University
UTICA, NEW YORK

The College

Founded in 1946 as a college of Syracuse University, Utica College has a liberal educational philosophy and an informal, personal atmosphere. On the modern 138-acre campus on the southwestern edge of the medium-sized city of Utica, New York, students enjoy a close personal relationship with the faculty and staff. The student body (with a full-time enrollment in fall 1999 of 597 men and 1,011 women) is diverse, made up of men and women from many socioeconomic backgrounds. They represent a wide variety of ethnic groups, older students, veterans, and handicapped persons. Most students live on campus in five residence hall complexes and in one apartment-style complex. While students come from all parts of the United States and several other countries, most come from New York, New England, and the Middle Atlantic States.

The College is accredited by the Middle States Association of Colleges and Schools, and, where appropriate, certain programs are accredited by specific discipline-oriented accrediting organizations. Special student services are offered by the College in the areas of academic, personal, and career counseling, health, and international-student advising. There are more than eighty campus organizations devoted to individual interests, from service and social fraternities and sororities to cultural activities; from major-related clubs to sports groups; from student government to professional group affiliations. The Department of Athletics offers eight men's and ten women's intercollegiate sports programs and four club sports. In addition, there is a complete system of intramural and recreational sports.

Strebel Student Center is the social and recreational center of the campus. It houses Strebel Auditorium, the site of theatrical presentations; the Student Health Center; the bookstore; the Student Activities Office; a computer lounge; the dining hall; the Pioneer Cafe, a meeting and eating place; and offices for student clubs, the student newspaper, and the student radio station. Burrstone House and Conference Center contains meeting rooms, banquet halls, and entertainment space for the College community. The physical education complex includes a gymnasium, a minigym, racquetball courts, fitness and dance rooms, and a swimming pool. Other facilities include the Newman Center (for religious activities).

Location

Utica, with a population of 70,000, is the major city of the western Mohawk River valley. It is located 90 miles west of Albany and 50 miles east of Syracuse. The Munson-Williams-Proctor Institute, just a few minutes from campus, is an internationally known arts center, featuring an extraordinary museum of art and a school of art as well as a performing arts program. The Stanley Performing Arts Center in downtown Utica is home to the Broadway Theatre League, the Great Artists Series, the Utica Symphony Orchestra, and other major theatrical and musical productions. Other attractions include the F. X. Matt Brewery and the Utica Zoo. The city's park system includes the Val Bialas municipal ski slopes and ice-skating rink just a mile from the campus, public tennis courts, swimming pools, and public athletic fields. Excellent golfing, swimming, boating, fishing, hiking, camping, and shopping facilities surround the city. Utica is served by a major airport, a train station, and bus lines. City buses make regular stops on campus, providing easy access to the Utica area.

Majors and Degrees

Utica College offers the B.A. degree from Syracuse University in communication arts, economics, English, history, international studies, journalism studies, mathematics, philosophy, political science, social studies, and sociology and anthropology. The Syracuse University B.S. degree is offered in accounting (private and CPA), biology, business administration, business-economics, chemistry, computer science, criminal justice, criminal justice–economic crime investigation, liberal studies, nursing, occupational therapy, physical therapy, psychology–child life, public relations, public relations/journalism studies, and therapeutic recreation. The B.A. or the B.S. degree may be earned in physics and psychology.

Preprofessional programs include dentistry, law, medicine, pharmacy, and veterinary medicine. Special programs are available in elementary education, English as a second language (ESL), gerontology, joint medical degree, liberal arts–engineering, and secondary education. Students may minor in anthropology, business administration, chemistry, communication arts, computer science, English language, film studies, French, gender studies, gerontology, government, history, literature, mathematics, music, philosophy, psychology, sociology, Spanish, theater, and writing.

Academic Program

Students may either enter the College without a declared major or enter directly into one of thirty-one degree programs. To assist students in planning their programs of study and declaring a major, the Office of Academic Support assigns a faculty adviser to each student. In many instances, it is possible for a student to elect a dual major. Students who have not decided on a major are assigned special advisers. Accelerated programs, independent study, cooperative education, field placements, and internships are offered.

To earn a bachelor's degree, a student must complete a minimum of 120 to 128 credits, satisfy major and major-related requirements, and complete any special program requirements. All Utica College students, regardless of their major, must complete a liberal arts core program as part of the degree requirements and submit a satisfactory writing portfolio.

Utica College operates on a semester system, with the day and evening fall term beginning in late August and ending shortly before Christmas and the day and evening spring term beginning in late January and continuing until early May. A summer program also offers both day and evening sessions. Utica College offers the Higher Education Opportunity Program (HEOP), the Collegiate Science and Technology Entry Program (CSTEP), and a Summer Institute, which serves as an academic bridge between high school and college. Students enrolled in the fall Freshman Year Initiative receive guidance in the transition to college life while earning academic credit.

Off-Campus Arrangements

Utica College students are eligible to participate in the Division of International Programs offered through Syracuse University. This arrangement allows Utica College students to study abroad in France, Italy, and Spain, among other countries. Students are encouraged to complete internships and field placements to gain professional experience with businesses and organizations as well as College credit. Utica College's Cooperative Education Program allows students to earn money while gaining professional experience.

Academic Facilities

The Frank E. Gannett Memorial Library collection consists of 176,849 volumes, 1,268 serial subscriptions, and a microfilm collection of 62,087 units. The library is fully automated and shares a local system with Mid-York Library System. It also is a member of OCLC, a bibliographic database through which it is possible to locate and borrow interlibrary loan items from local, regional, national, and international libraries. The lower level of the building houses a Media Center, computer labs, and rooms for music and fine arts. Utica College hosts musical recitals, receptions, and special events in the Library Concourse, which contains the Edith Barrett Art Gallery and an atrium. Four buildings house classrooms, laboratories, and faculty offices: Hubbard Hall, the Administration Building, Gordon Science Center, and Rocco F. DePerno Hall. The academic buildings house eight computer laboratories for student use, including IBM-compatible and Apple Macintosh computers, as well as an Academic Support Services Center, Mathematics and Science Center, and Writing Center.

Costs

For 2000–01, tuition is $16,884. Room and board costs, based on a double room and a fourteen-meal plan, are $6660 annually. There is a student activities fee of $110 and a technology fee of $150. Books and supplies average $680 per year.

Financial Aid

The College is recognized as a best buy in education and works to control costs and keep its education affordable. The average financial aid package for 1999–2000 freshmen was $17,761. About two thirds of that aid came from grants and a third from loans and/or jobs. Approximately 92 percent of the freshmen received a financial aid package. At the same time, the College awarded numerous merit scholarships to students with outstanding grades and test scores.

Almost every federal and state financial aid program is available through Utica College. Students apply for institutional and governmental financial aid by filing the required financial aid forms by February 15. In addition, Utica College offers three different deferred-payment programs that spread out payments over the academic year.

Faculty

The faculty is a diverse group of academicians who can best be described as energetic and accomplished. While most of the 111 full-time faculty members hold advanced degrees, 92 percent have the terminal degree in their field—usually the Ph.D. While many faculty members are involved in research, the primary concern of the faculty is undergraduate education. All faculty members teach classes, providing constant direct contact between faculty and students. Class sizes average 15 to 20, and the student-faculty ratio is 14:1. All faculty members are involved in assisting students with their major areas of academic planning.

Student Government

One of the strongest traditions of the College is student participation in all of the College's affairs. Students participate in campus governing bodies and policymaking groups, extending the learning experience beyond the classroom. Students, faculty, and staff participate in the College Council, which gives each group a representative voice in governance of all College affairs—academic, social, cultural, administrative, and regulatory. Students also serve on all standing committees of the College.

Admission Requirements

Utica College admits students who can best benefit from the educational opportunities the College offers. The Admission Committee gives each application individual attention, and the prospect of a student's success at Utica College is measured primarily by an evaluation of past academic performance, scholastic ability, and personal characteristics. Freshman applicants must have completed 16 academic units, including four years of English. Students should follow a college-preparatory program, including 3 units of mathematics, 3 units of science, 2 units of foreign language, and 3 units of social studies.

Application and Information

Students may apply for fall, spring, or summer admission. Materials required include a completed Utica College application form, official high school or college transcripts, and a $35 application fee. Utica College prefers, but does not require, SAT I or ACT scores. A personal interview for all applicants is strongly suggested. Occupational therapy and physical therapy applicants must submit SAT I or ACT scores, a clinical recommendation, and a personal statement. International students must complete the international student application form. The application fee is waived for students who apply to HEOP or CSTEP. The College conducts a rolling admissions program (except for those applying for occupational therapy, physical therapy, or joint medical degree programs, or for academic merit scholarships, for whom the application deadline is January 15).

Inquiries should be sent to:

Director of Admissions
Utica College of Syracuse University
1600 Burrstone Road
Utica, New York 13502-4892
Telephone: 315-792-3006
         800-782-8884 (toll-free)
E-mail: admiss@utica.ucsu.edu
World Wide Web: http://www.ucsu.edu

The Frank E. Gannett Memorial Library on the campus of Utica College of Syracuse University.

VALPARAISO UNIVERSITY
VALPARAISO, INDIANA

The University

Valparaiso University (VU or Valpo) was founded in 1859 by citizens of Valparaiso, Indiana, but its recent history dates from 1925, when it was purchased by the Lutheran University Association. VU is one of the nation's largest Lutheran-affiliated universities, yet it remains independent and is open to individuals of all faiths. The University's 3,700 students represent most states and more than forty countries; 66 percent come from outside of Indiana. Valparaiso University is a residential community in which activities outside the classroom form an important part of campus life; more than 66 percent of its students live on campus. Approximately 100 extracurricular and cocurricular programs are open to all, including the campus radio station, Pre-Medical Society, International Student Association, and various NCAA Division I intercollegiate and intramural sports teams for men and women. Approximately 35 percent of the students are members of the eight national fraternities and seven national sororities at the University. Both in and out of the classroom, students and professors operate under a student-initiated honor code in which integrity is assumed to be the norm. When violations do occur, they are handled by peers through a student-composed Honor Council or a Student Court. Because of these structures and the whole philosophy of the University, relationships among students, faculty, and administration can be unusually free and open.

Major divisions at Valpo are the Colleges of Arts and Sciences, Business Administration, Engineering, and Nursing; Christ College (the honors college); the School of Law; and the Graduate Division.

Location

The University is located in Valparaiso, a community of 26,000 in northwest Indiana. Certain campus organizations and activities include citizens of the community, and the Town/Gown Committee meets regularly to further the established relationship. Valparaiso is located only 15 miles south of the Indiana Dunes National Lakeshore on Lake Michigan, which, in addition to being a famous recreational area, is perhaps the finest ecological laboratory in the nation. Chicago, with its many theaters, museums, restaurants, and cultural and sports events, is less than an hour away. Air service is available from Chicago's O'Hare and Midway international airports. In addition, South Bend's Michiana Regional Airport and Gary Airport are less than an hour away.

Majors and Degrees

Valparaiso University offers the following undergraduate degrees: Associate in Science, Bachelor of Arts, Bachelor of Music, Bachelor of Music Education, Bachelor of Science, Bachelor of Science in Accounting, Bachelor of Science in Business Administration, Bachelor of Science in Civil Engineering, Bachelor of Science in Education, Bachelor of Science in Electrical Engineering, Bachelor of Science in Fine Arts, Bachelor of Science in Mechanical Engineering, Bachelor of Science in Nursing, Bachelor of Science in Physical Education, and Bachelor of Social Work. The B.A. or B.S. degree may be earned in American studies, art, astronomy, athletic training, biology, broadcast meteorology, chemistry, Chinese and Japanese studies, classics, communication, computer science, criminology, economics, English, environmental science, exercise science, French, geography, geology, German, history, humanities, international economics and cultural affairs, international service, mathematics, meteorology, modern European studies, music, music enterprises, music performance, philosophy, physics, political science, pre–medical sciences, pre–seminary studies, psychology, sociology, Spanish, sports management, theater and television arts, and theology.

Academic Program

Valparaiso University has a long tradition of combining professional colleges with a strong commitment to the values and broadening experiences of the liberal arts. The University helps students of varied interests and objectives to clarify their goals and explore new possibilities. Programs are structured to provide a solid base for exploration in various fields, while offering students the freedom to develop depth in a specific interest. This philosophy is extended through the upper division, where students have three options in completing a degree: an individual plan of study involving the major and complementary courses from related fields of study, the election of a second academic major in addition to the first, or a special minor in connection with the major. Career planning is aided through the professional programs and the University's Career Center. Many students also gain professional work experience in their chosen field before graduation by participating in the cooperative education program and internships.

Valparaiso operates on the semester system; the fall semester begins in late August and ends before Christmas, and the spring semester starts in early January and ends during the second week in May. Valpo also has two summer terms that further extend opportunities for study on campus or at various off-campus locations.

The University participates in the Advanced Placement Program, the College-Level Examination Program, and the International Baccalaureate Program. In addition, Valparaiso provides its own placement testing in several academic areas.

All departments of the University offer opportunities for honors work through independent study, seminars, and research. Christ College, the honors college of Valparaiso, has a well-established but continuously evolving program designed to challenge gifted students. Christ College students enroll concurrently in any other VU college.

Off-Campus Arrangements

Valparaiso University sponsors study-abroad programs in Reutlingen and Tübingen, Germany; Puebla, Mexico; Paris, France; Hangzhou, China; Granada, Spain; and London and Cambridge, England. Valparaiso also sponsors semester-long study opportunities at two universities in Japan, one in Namibia, and another in Greece. VU students may study at other overseas locations through Valparaiso's membership in the Central States College Association. In addition, Valpo grants credit for the following cooperative programs: Urban Studies Semester (Chicago), Urban Affairs Semester and Washington Semester (Washington, D.C.), and United Nations Semester (New York City).

Academic Facilities

The Henry F. Moellering Memorial Library contains more than 568,949 volumes and more than 1.6 million microforms and receives 13,984 subscriptions. This library and the library of the School of Law operate with open stacks and are available to undergraduate and graduate students. Galileo, Valpo's online catalog, provides direct access to the collections. The University is also an Army Map Service depository for a special collection of 75,000 maps. The Neils Science Center houses an astronomical observatory, a greenhouse, a subcritical nuclear reactor, and other facilities that have earned the University a citation from the Atomic Energy Commission for having a model undergraduate physics laboratory.

Costs

Tuition for the 2000–01 academic year at Valparaiso University is $17,100, room is $2970, and board is $2152. General fees are $536. The total cost of tuition, room, board, and fees is $22,758. Students spend $1700 per year for books, supplies, and such miscellaneous expenses as laundry and travel.

Financial Aid

Eighty-five percent of Valparaiso's students receive financial aid totaling more than $30 million. The University attempts to make up the difference between the cost of attending Valparaiso and the amount a family can afford, as determined by the Free Application for Federal Student Aid (FAFSA). Valpo aid is available in the form of scholarships, grants, loans, and campus employment, and often the aid is a package of these awards. Students are also encouraged to apply for the federal government's Federal Pell Grant, Federal Perkins Loan, and Federal Supplemental Educational Opportunity Grant, state scholarships where applicable, and the various private grants and scholarships that are available. Early application is recommended for VU assistance, since the awarding of aid begins in February of the year of enrollment.

Faculty

Valparaiso's 368 faculty members share a common interest—teaching in ways that encourage students and faculty members to get to know one another. The majority are full-time, and a considerable number serve as advisers to the various academic and social organizations on campus. There are no graduate teaching assistants at Valpo. More than 87 percent of the professors have terminal degrees, and this figure reaches 100 percent in some departments. Each department has a full advising system to help students in course and program selection.

Student Government

Students and faculty members alike are involved in the internal governance of the institution. House Councils in each of the residence halls are composed of representatives elected by the residents. Each council makes decisions and sets standards within the rules established by the University. Students in the living units and off-campus students elect representatives to the Student Senate (composed entirely of students) and the University Senate (made up of an equal number of representatives from the student body, faculty, and administration). The functions of these two separate bodies cover most phases of student life.

Admission Requirements

Valparaiso admits candidates who exhibit the potential for academic success at the University. The freshman retention rate is 87 percent, reflecting in part the high quality of the admission program. Qualified students are admitted without regard to race, color, gender, disability, national origin, or ancestry. The credentials of each applicant are individually and personally evaluated, and consideration is given not only to ACT or SAT I scores, grade point average, and rank in class but also to grades and trends in the student's record, the nature of the high school and the program followed, outside interests, and recommendations. A campus visit and an interview with an admission counselor are recommended but not required. Students who have taken the ACT or SAT I in their junior year and have submitted their high school transcripts, complete through the eleventh grade, may be considered for admission.

Application and Information

An applicant must complete a formal University admission application or the Common Application to be considered for admission. In addition, VU requires a high school transcript (complete through the junior year), ACT or SAT I scores, and college transcripts (when applicable). Valpo's nonbinding early action option allows applicants to submit their applications no later than November 1 and to receive the admission decision by December 1. Regular admission notification begins on a rolling basis after December 1. For scholarship consideration, January 15 is the deadline for submitting a completed admission application.

Information and application forms for admission and financial aid may be obtained from:

Office of Admissions
Valparaiso University
Valparaiso, Indiana 46383-6493
Telephone: 219-464-5011
        888-GO-VALPO (toll-free)
Fax: 219-464-6898
E-mail: undergrad_admissions@valpo.edu
World Wide Web: http://www.valpo.edu

Valparaiso's Chapel of the Resurrection, one of the world's largest college chapels, stands at the center of the University's campus.

VANDERBILT UNIVERSITY
NASHVILLE, TENNESSEE

The University

When Commodore Cornelius Vanderbilt gave a million dollars to build and endow Vanderbilt University in 1873, he did so with the wish that it would "contribute to strengthening the ties which should exist between all sections of our common country." Today, Vanderbilt enrolls America's most talented students and challenges them daily to expand their intellectual horizons and to free their imaginations. Dialogue, service, the Honor Code, the search for knowledge, and personal fulfillment are all hallmarks of a Vanderbilt education.

Vanderbilt is a medium-sized university that includes four undergraduate schools and eight graduate and professional schools. Each year, more than 1,500 freshmen join the University, bringing the total undergraduate population to approximately 5,900 students. The total enrollment at Vanderbilt is 10,300.

Known for the Southern splendor of its residential 300-acre campus, Vanderbilt provides a variety of housing options for its undergraduates, 87 percent of whom live on campus all four years. One of its unique housing options is the McTyeire International House, designed for students interested in a range of foreign languages, such as Chinese, French, German, Japanese, and Spanish. Other options include traditional dormitories, apartments, and suites. Only six officers are allowed to live in each of the fraternity and sorority houses.

The newly expanded Sarratt Student Center houses a cinema, a pub, game and music-listening rooms, meeting rooms, an art gallery, craft and darkroom facilities, and an FM radio station. Facilities at the Student Recreation Center include gymnasiums, handball courts, an indoor swimming pool, racquetball courts, a climbing wall, an indoor suspended track, and a weight room. Other facilities include indoor and outdoor tennis courts, baseball and softball diamonds, and a sand volleyball court.

Location

Vanderbilt University is located approximately 3 miles west of downtown Nashville, the capital of Tennessee. As the music industry's "third coast," Nashville is a vibrant, growing city of 1 million residents. The greater Nashville area is also home to eighty-one parks and more than 30,000 acres of lakes. Three interstate highways intersect the city, and its international airport is served by eighteen airlines.

Majors and Degrees

The B.A., B.S., B.E., or B.M. degree is offered in anthropology, biology, biomedical engineering, chemical engineering, chemistry, child development, civil engineering, classical studies, cognitive studies, computer engineering, computer science, early childhood education, economics, electrical engineering, elementary education, engineering science, English, fine arts, French, geology, German, history, human and organizational development, mathematics, mechanical engineering, molecular biology, musical arts, music composition/theory, music performance, neuroscience, philosophy, physics and astronomy, political science, Portuguese, psychology, religious studies, secondary education, sociology, Spanish, special education, and theater. African-American studies, American and Southern studies, communication studies, East Asian studies, European studies, Latin American and Iberian studies, neuroscience, public policy studies, Russian and european studies, and urban studies may be pursued as interdisciplinary majors. Examples of individually designed majors include film studies, medieval studies, Slavic studies, and women's studies.

Academic Program

Students apply directly to one of four undergraduate schools: the College of Arts and Science, the School of Engineering, Peabody College (education and human development), or the Blair School of Music. Vanderbilt University operates on a two-semester calendar, and classes begin in late August. First-semester examinations take place prior to the winter holidays, and the second semester ends in early May. A variety of courses are offered during two summer sessions.

The College of Arts and Science provides many opportunities to experience a wide range of academic disciplines and subjects. Within the requirements of the College Program in Liberal Education (CPLE), students refine their skills in writing, mathematics, foreign language, the humanities, natural sciences, social sciences, history, and culture.

The Blair School of Music offers the Bachelor of Music in composition/theory, musical arts, and performance. Instruction is available in every instrument of the orchestra as well as piano, organ, saxophone, guitar, and voice. The curriculum combines intensive musical training with liberal arts studies. Approximately one third of a student's work is outside of music. The school also offers a liberal arts major, two minors, and a wide variety of courses, private instruction, and performing organizations for nonmajors.

The School of Engineering offers a century-long tradition of educating engineers for practice in industry, government, consulting, teaching, and research. In addition to technical courses, each student's program must include course work in English, the humanities, and the social sciences.

Peabody College offers degree programs leading to teacher certification and to careers in other areas of education, child development, cognitive studies, and human and organizational development. The degree reflects a strong liberal arts foundation on which is built a solid program of professional courses. All undergraduates must complete requirements in communication, the humanities, mathematics, the natural sciences, and the social sciences. Students have many field experiences throughout the four years.

Off-Campus Arrangements

Overseas study programs allow students to immerse themselves in the languages and cultures of other countries. Programs are offered in Argentina, Australia, Brazil, Chile, China, the Dominican Republic, England, France, Germany, Israel, Italy, Japan, Russia, and Spain. Vanderbilt students receive direct credit for their courses, and the cost of tuition for most of the programs is the same as for study on campus in Nashville.

Academic Facilities

Students and faculty members take advantage of Vanderbilt's extensive library resources, obtaining easy access to books, periodicals, documents, microforms, and reference materials. The Jean and Alexander Heard Library is supported by nine major resource centers, which include special collections, University Archives, and more than 2.3 million volumes.

Costs

The costs for 1999–2000 were tuition, $22,990; room and board, $8032 (average); books and supplies, $830 (average); and the student activity fee and recreation fee, $608. All costs are subject to change for 2000–01.

Financial Aid

About 55 percent of the University's undergraduate students receive some type of financial aid. Need-based aid is awarded according to the evaluation of the College Scholarship Service's PROFILE and the FAFSA. Vanderbilt provides assistance through Federal Pell Grants, Federal Supplemental Educational Opportunity Grants, state grants, University scholarships, Federal Stafford Student Loans, institutional loans, Federal Perkins Loans, and Federal Work-Study employment. Information on these and other programs can be obtained from the Office of Student Financial Aid, 2309 West End Avenue, Vanderbilt University, Nashville, Tennessee 37203-1725. A limited number of honor scholarships based on academic merit or, at the Blair School of Music, on performance audition are available. In addition, the Ingram Scholarship Program is designed for students who have shown exemplary initiative in community service. The Fred Russell-Grantland Rice Scholarship is awarded to a College of Arts and Science applicant who has demonstrated superior skills in sportswriting.

Faculty

Vanderbilt has a full-time faculty of 1,779 and a part-time faculty of more than 300. All undergraduate faculty members, many of whom hold awards for distinguished scholarship, are required to teach undergraduates. A low student-faculty ratio of 8:1 provides for close working relationships between students and professors who are recognized nationally and worldwide for their research. The average class size is 19.

Student Government

The SGA provides students with an opportunity to participate actively in maintaining the high quality of life on campus. It works with many of the more than 250 student organizations to bring nationally prominent speakers to campus. A vital part of life at Vanderbilt is the honor system, which is governed entirely by students through representatives on the Honor Council. Each year a senior is selected as a Young Alumni Trustee of the University's Board of Trust.

Admission Requirements

Vanderbilt seeks students with high standards of scholarship and character. Admission is based on a thorough review of academic and personal credentials.

Students must submit a minimum of 15 academic units at the secondary level, although most admitted students present 20 or more academic units. Applicants to the College of Arts and Science and the Blair School of Music must present a minimum of 2 years of a foreign language and applicants to the School of Engineering, a minimum of 4 units of mathematics. The Admissions Committee evaluates each student's secondary school academic record, extracurricular involvement, counselor and teacher recommendations, and personal characteristics. Students must also submit scores from either the SAT I or ACT. Applicants are encouraged to submit scores from three SAT II: Subject Tests (including Writing and Math I, IC, or IIC) for class placement. Applicants to the Blair School of Music must also audition on their primary instrument. A personal audition is preferred, but a cassette tape of high quality is usually acceptable for applicants who live more than 400 miles from Nashville. All applicants for the musical arts program may audition by tape.

Campus visits are strongly recommended. Prospective students should call in advance of their visit for information about group information sessions, campus tours, overnight accommodations, and opportunities to attend classes.

Application and Information

Students whose first choice is Vanderbilt may apply under the early decision plan. Applications and all supporting materials must be submitted by November 1 for Early Decision I and by January 7 for Early Decision II; notification is made by December 15 for Early Decision I and by February 15 for Early Decision II. The deadline for applying under the regular decision plan is January 7. Personal auditions are scheduled in December, January, and February at the Blair School of Music. Students are informed of the admission decision by April 1. Students seeking transfer admission must submit an application and all supporting materials no later than February 1 for fall semester admission and no later than November 15 for spring semester admission.

Office of Undergraduate Admissions
Vanderbilt University
2305 West End Avenue
Nashville, Tennessee 37203-1727
Telephone: 615-322-2561
        800-288-0432 (toll-free)
E-mail: admissions@vanderbilt.edu
World Wide Web: http://www.vanderbilt.edu/Admissions

VANDERCOOK COLLEGE OF MUSIC
CHICAGO, ILLINOIS

The College
VanderCook College of Music traces its roots back to Hale A. VanderCook, who opened his VanderCook Cornet School in 1909. Since the College's inception as a professional school for training music teachers in the late 1920s, its history has closely paralleled that of the music education movement in this country. VanderCook has consistently produced graduates who achieve recognition in the music education field.

VanderCook College is unusual and colorful, yet thoroughly practical. It is the only degree-granting institution in the United States that is solely dedicated to the career preparation of music educators. Its success lies both in the singleness of purpose and in the enthusiastic recommendations given by its graduates.

While VanderCook students train thoroughly in all facets of music, they excel in music education, including the teaching skills that are distinct from general musicianship. A remarkable 90 percent of graduates make their careers in the field of music education. VanderCook places 95 to 100 percent of its graduates in music education positions each year.

The College is small and selective. The student body has 81 undergraduate and 140 graduate students. The size of the student body contributes to the helpful and familylike atmosphere of the school.

VanderCook College of Music is accredited by the National Association of Schools of Music, the North Central Association of Colleges and Schools, and the Illinois Board of Higher Education.

VanderCook also offers a Master of Music Education degree and a Master of Music Education degree with certification.

Location
The College is located 3 miles south of the Loop on the Illinois Institute of Technology campus in Chicago, close to the heart of the city's magnificent musical and cultural centers. VanderCook students have the opportunity to hear the world-renowned Chicago Symphony Orchestra, the Lyric Opera, and many other musical performers. Public transportation is easily accessible. The city of Chicago is an important extension of the VanderCook campus.

Majors and Degrees
VanderCook College of Music offers music education as its only major. Students completing the appropriate course of study are awarded the Bachelor of Music Education.

Academic Program
VanderCook College of Music trains students in a musical discipline and in general academic areas. The curriculum is practical, emphasizing the proven fundamentals of music education. Each instrumental family is covered completely in two playing techniques courses. Students are given thorough performance and teaching knowledge of seventeen band and orchestral instruments. Vocal majors explore traditional vocal literature as well as the literature and teaching methods of jazz and show choirs and the choreography that is vital in those groups.

The academic year, which begins in the fall, is based on a semester system. Students may enter in either fall or spring. (Summer terms are for graduate students only.)

Academic Facilities
The College is housed in a modern, two-story structure. The physical plant contains classrooms, an academic library, a music library, a listening laboratory, practice rooms, a recital hall, a conference room, an instrument-repair laboratory, and various offices. VanderCook's Electronic Music Center contains computer workstations and MIDI hardware that use the latest in music software. In addition, VanderCook students have complete access to the student services provided by the Illinois Institute of Technology.

Costs
Tuition in 1999–2000 was $10,300. Room and board were $5250, and fees were $370.

Financial Aid
Each student is considered on an individual basis for financial aid. Merit-based scholarships are given for musical talent and are based on competitive auditions and academic achievement. Illinois residents may apply for the Monetary Award Program. Federal Stafford Student Loans are also available. Scholarships are renewable based on musical growth and participation as well as the student's cumulative grade point average.

Faculty
At VanderCook College of Music, all undergraduate classes are taught by either full-time or part-time faculty members who have many years of in-depth, practical experience in the field of music education to share with their students. Faculty members are dedicated to giving individual instruction, made possible by a 1:11 faculty-student ratio, which may be unavailable at a larger institution. All classes are taught by faculty members, not graduate students.

Admission Requirements

VanderCook College of Music seeks musically proficient students who have demonstrated talent and who desire to become fine music educators.

Candidates for admission must submit an application and essay along with high school transcripts and ACT or SAT I scores. Following the application, students should schedule an audition and interview with the Director of Admissions. If an on-campus audition is not possible, an audition tape can be submitted.

Transfer students must submit both high school and college transcripts. International students must submit TOEFL scores. All applicants are required to have three letters of reference.

Application and Information

Applications are accepted up to four weeks prior to the beginning of a term, subject to the availability of space.

Application forms, a current catalog, and additional information may be obtained by contacting:

George Pierard, Director of Admissions
VanderCook College of Music
3140 South Federal Street
Chicago, Illinois 60616-3731
Telephone: 312-225-6288
         800-448-2655 (toll-free)

VANGUARD UNIVERSITY OF SOUTHERN CALIFORNIA

COSTA MESA, CALIFORNIA

The University

Vanguard University (VU) (formerly Southern California College) is a Christian comprehensive university that offers a four-year Bachelor of Arts degree in eighteen majors; a four-year Bachelor of Science degree in four majors; Master of Arts degrees in religion, education, and psychology; and a Master of Theological Studies degree. Founded in 1920, VU is owned by the Southern California District of the Assemblies of God. Regional accreditation and membership in the Western Association of Schools and Colleges were granted in 1964. In 1967, the University received recognition and approval of its teaching credential program from the California State Board of Education. VU is the largest liberal arts college in the charismatic tradition west of the Rockies.

Vanguard University is committed to an education of high quality that integrates the Christian faith with learning and living. VU believes that the pursuit of intellectual achievement is not a threat to faith. Faith provides a foundation in which history, science, and the human condition can be more clearly understood.

One of the important features of VU is the deep concern for preparing the student "to live as a Christian." The student is seen as a whole person, seeking growth and maturity in daily living. This concern is reflected in the specific areas of values, decision making, relationships, world view, and integrity.

With 1,440 students, VU is large enough to be diverse and challenging but small enough to be a caring Christian community. Students come from more than twenty denominational backgrounds, every region of the United States, and many countries. A high percentage of those who apply for graduate school after graduation are accepted. Because of VU's fine reputation and proximity to major business centers where internships and work experience are available, those who do not attend graduate school usually find jobs soon after graduation.

Extracurricular activities range from intramural sports, such as basketball, broomball, flag football, floor hockey, Ping-Pong, racquetball, softball, and volleyball, to organizations such as Agora, Business Club, Campus Women's Association, Christian Outreach, Club Volleyball, College Democrats, College Republicans, Cultural Life, Delta Kappa, Dorm Council, Evangelicals for Orthodoxy, International Students, Sociology Club, and Surf Club. In addition, students can participate in such activities as cheerleading and can work on the newspaper and yearbook staffs. Vanguard University also participates in an intercollegiate athletics program for men and women that includes competition in baseball, basketball, cross-country, soccer, softball, tennis, track and field, and volleyball. The Athletics Department is affiliated with the Golden State Athletic Conference and the National Association of Intercollegiate Athletics (Division I).

Four residence halls and an apartment complex create the special blend of residence life at VU. Married students can live in on-campus apartments, while single students share with a roommate in any of these facilities. It is comfortable to have a home right on campus, but what makes residence life really important is the constant variety of people and experiences that provide opportunities for personal growth and the foundation of lasting relationships.

Location

Vanguard University is located 40 miles southeast of Los Angeles in Costa Mesa, California, 5 minutes from Newport Beach. VU lies in the heart of Orange County's cultural, commercial, and recreational opportunities. Due to their proximity to Los Angeles, students can avail themselves of the concerts, theaters, libraries, museums, and other cultural amenities for which the city is famous.

Just minutes from the campus and accessible by a number of freeways are miles of beautiful beaches, parks, and other recreation areas. Ski slopes are only 90 minutes away.

VU's prime location offers students a variety of possibilities for employment—in offices and in production and service industries as well. VU students have an excellent reputation as workers within the community.

Majors and Degrees

Vanguard University offers the Bachelor of Arts (B.A.) degree in the following fields of study: accounting, business administration, communication (public address, television and film), cultural anthropology, English, finance, history and political science, international business, liberal studies (education), management, management of information systems, marketing, music, psychology, religion (biblical studies, Christian formation and discipleship studies, intercultural and urban studies, pastoral leadership studies, youth leadership studies), social science, sociology, Spanish, and theater. Teaching credentials are offered in the following areas: single subject (secondary education) in English, life science, mathematics, music, physical education, physical science, and social science; and multiple subject (elementary education).

VU offers the Bachelor of Science (B.S.) degree in biology, chemistry, exercise and sports science (pre–physical therapy/athletic training, sports science, teaching/coaching), and mathematics.

Academic Program

Vanguard University offers an exceptional academic program. Because of the relatively small size of the University, a personal touch is added to classroom instruction. VU is a teaching university. There are no graduate assistants teaching courses. Because of this, there is a special, close working relationship between faculty members and students.

Because the University is committed to a liberal arts education, each student is required to take 55 credits in general education classes, including studies in humanities and fine arts, natural sciences and mathematics, religion, social science, and professional studies. This serves to provide the student with a well-balanced education. A minimum of 124 credits is required for graduation.

Students are encouraged to take a practicum or internship to gain practical experience in their particular field. Because of VU's advantageous southern California location, the opportunities for internships in nearly any professional field are virtually limitless. Also, VU offers a number of courses that include travel to other parts of the country and, sometimes, the world. An attempt is made to expand educational opportunities beyond mere classroom lectures.

The academic year is run on a semester system, one in the fall and one in the spring. Summer sessions are also offered.

Academic Facilities

All VU students have access to personal computers for reports, research, and writing assignments. The Communication Department works with state-of-the-art broadcasting equipment and other departments strive to give students the best available equipment and experience. On-campus facilities include a library; a theater; exercise/physiology, archaeology, psychology, computer, music, and science labs; and television and film facilities. Every room in every facility has access to the computer network.

Costs

For 2000–01, annual costs total $18,838 ($13,230 for tuition, $5060 for room and board, and $548 for fees). Part-time tuition is $514 per unit. Students spend an average of $648 on books and supplies, $549 for transportation, and $1215 for personal expenses.

Financial Aid

VU has put together a financial aid program that coordinates federal, state, and institutional aid to enable students to pursue a liberal arts education. The program includes the Federal Pell Grant, the Federal Supplemental Educational Opportunity Grant, the Federal Perkins Loan, California Grant A and B, the California Stafford Loan, and various VU grants and scholarships. First-time freshmen who have a grade point average of 3.0 or higher are eligible for academic scholarships of up to $5000 per year. A total of $10 million in financial aid is awarded annually to qualified VU students. In order to receive any financial assistance, a student must first apply for admission. The priority deadline for the financial aid application (FAFSA) is March 2. Campus jobs make it possible for many students to earn varying amounts and involve a number of job categories. In addition to the campus employment program, growing industrial centers in Costa Mesa, Irvine, and Newport Beach afford students excellent job opportunities.

Faculty

Over the years, students have repeatedly named VU's faculty as the University's greatest asset. There are 52 full-time teaching faculty members and 115 part-time members, all of whom are highly qualified. Seventy-nine percent of the full-time teaching faculty members have doctoral degrees. With a student-faculty ratio of 16:1, faculty members take an active part in the education of the students, both in and out of the classroom.

Student Government

The Associated Student Body (ASB), consisting of the entire student body, is an organization designed to carry on various student activities. The business of the association is managed by an ASB Council chosen by the students and representing the several areas of student activity. The ASB Council serves as a liaison between students, administration, and faculty and provides a means for the discussion and solution of student problems. The Dean of Students serves as adviser to the ASB Council.

Admission Requirements

Vanguard University practices selective admission and encourages applications from Christian students who desire an education that integrates the Christian faith with learning and living, provides intellectual challenge and growth, and encourages spiritual commitment. The University, therefore, reviews applicants' academic records, moral character, and willingness to comply with the standards and values of the University. All applicants are evaluated without regard to race, gender, age, political affiliation, national origin, or disabling conditions.

The average freshman enters VU with a high school grade point average of 3.36. A minimum GPA of 2.5 is required for freshmen. Transfer students are required to have at least a 2.0 GPA. A limited number of students who do not meet these GPA minimum requirements are admitted on a "provisional" standing. Applicants are required to provide a high school transcript, two character references, and SAT I or ACT scores in addition to the application form.

Application and Information

Admission decisions are made on a rolling basis; applications received earliest in the year are considered first. The application deadline is July 31 for the fall semester and December 31 for the spring semester.

For further information, students should contact:

Undergraduate Admissions Office
Vanguard University
55 Fair Drive
Costa Mesa, California 92626
Telephone: 714-556-3610 Ext. 217
        800-722-6279 (toll-free)
World Wide Web: http://www.vanguard.edu

Students establish lifetime friendships with people who share their faith and challenge their minds at Vanguard University.

VASSAR COLLEGE
POUGHKEEPSIE, NEW YORK

The College

Vassar is a coeducational, independent, residential undergraduate college of liberal arts and sciences. Founded in 1861, Vassar's original purpose was to provide for women the same high-quality education afforded only to men at the leading institutions of the day. Since its founding, Vassar has been both a pioneer and a leader in American higher education. Becoming fully coeducational in 1969, Vassar today offers its students a distinctive education that features a high level of academic rigor, a strong sense of equality between the sexes, a willingness to experiment, a dedication to the values of the liberal arts and sciences, and a commitment to the development of leadership.

Vassar's 2,250 students come from all fifty states and more than thirty countries. Vassar seeks a high level of ethnic, geographic, religious, and socioeconomic diversity in its student body, believing strongly that students with different backgrounds and experiences can play an important role in the overall educational purpose of the College. Students of color make up approximately 23 percent of the student body, while about 5 percent are international students. Firmly convinced of the advantages of a residential college setting, Vassar provides a variety of housing options to its students, and 98 percent of students live on campus. Housing is guaranteed for all students.

Students enjoy an active extracurricular, social, and cultural life at Vassar. There are more than 100 student clubs and organizations, including a weekly newspaper and nearly a dozen other student publications; political, religious, and personal affinity groups; a student-run FM radio station; theater, music, and dance performance groups; a volunteer network; debate; student government; an outing club; and dozens of other such activities. There are no fraternities or sororities. A pub and nonalcoholic café showcases local talent, while nationally known speakers, writers, and performers appear on campus throughout the year. A strong Division III athletic program features twenty-two varsity teams, eleven for men and eleven for women. Baseball is exclusive to men, as is field hockey to women; both sexes compete in basketball, crew, cross-country, fencing, lacrosse, soccer, squash, swimming and diving, tennis, and volleyball. Club sports include riding, rugby, sailing, skiing, and track. The College also supports a vigorous and popular intramural program.

Maintained as an arboretum with more than 200 varieties of trees, Vassar's landscaped 1,000-acre campus contains more than 100 buildings, including the College Center, the libraries, three theaters, a music recital hall, studio art facilities, two observatories, three science buildings, the computer center, the Frances Lehman Loeb Art Center, an environmental station, two athletic facilities, residence halls, and extensive classroom space.

Location

Vassar is located in a residential area 3 miles from the center of Poughkeepsie, New York, a city with an area population of approximately 100,000 people. Situated in the historic and beautiful mid-Hudson River Valley, the College offers its students easy access to New York City, about 75 miles to the south and served by extensive commuter rail connections, and to nearby outdoor recreational opportunities, including climbing, hiking, skiing, and camping at the region's many state parks, lakes, and mountainous regions. Students make extensive use of the city of Poughkeepsie and surrounding communities for internship and volunteer options in business, the arts, social service agencies, health facilities, and legal or political organizations.

Majors and Degrees

Vassar College grants the Bachelor of Arts degree to undergraduates. Departmental programs include anthropology, art, biology, chemistry, classics, computer science, drama and film, economics, education, English, French, geology and geography, German, Hispanic studies (Spanish), history, Italian, mathematics, music, philosophy, physical education and dance, physics and astronomy, political science, psychology, religion, Russian, and sociology. Interdepartmental programs include biochemistry, biopsychology, geography-anthropology, Latin American studies, medieval and Renaissance studies, and Victorian studies. Multidisciplinary programs include Africana studies; American culture; Asian studies; cognitive science; environmental studies; international studies; Jewish studies; science, technology, and society; urban studies; and women's studies. Students interested in engineering can complete a five-year dual-degree program with Dartmouth College.

Academic Program

Vassar's academic program is notable for its flexibility and breadth. No core curriculum exists, and students are given both great freedom and significant responsibility in shaping their own education. Students must select a major by the end of the sophomore year, but beyond the major they must fulfill only three additional specific requirements: a freshman course, a quantitative course, and a foreign language sequence. Freshman courses, offered across the curriculum, feature small, discussion-based classes, which usually serve as introductions to their disciplines and stress the effective expression of ideas in both written and oral work. By the end of the second year, all students must take one course that demands a significant amount of quantitative analysis, chosen from a broad array of options in the sciences, mathematics, computing, and the social sciences. Finally, all students must demonstrate intermediate proficiency in a foreign language, either by completing course work in one of the many languages taught at the College or by achieving sufficiently high scores on Advanced Placement or SAT II language tests.

Off-Campus Arrangements

33 percent of Vassar's students spend at least one semester studying away from campus and earn full academic credit. Many students choose to study at one of the programs sponsored by Vassar in England, France, Germany, Ireland, Italy, Morocco, or Spain. Those meeting major and GPA requirements may also join approved programs offered by other colleges in additional countries. Vassar students have studied at more than 100 sites in Africa, Asia, Australia, Europe, and the Americas, usually during their junior year. Domestically, students may elect to study at another institution through the Twelve College Exchange, a consortium of Northeastern liberal arts colleges, or through a variety of other exchange arrangements.

Academic Facilities

The libraries at Vassar offer holdings of almost 1 million volumes, 4,000 periodicals, and 350,000 microforms, as well as access to sophisticated databases and research networks. Extensive special collections are also offered by the art and music departments. These resources are augmented by an extensive campuswide computing network linking all student rooms and faculty offices via a fiber-optic network and providing access to the Internet. Computer clusters, strictly for student use, are located in every residence hall, the College Center, the library, the computer center, and most academic buildings. Three theaters, a concert hall, and extensive practice facilities provide space for performance opportunities in drama, music, and dance. The Frances Lehman Loeb Art Center, completed in 1993, houses one of the oldest and most extensive college art collections in the country, including more than 12,500 paintings, sculptures, prints, drawings, and photographs. Each of the physical science departments (biology, chemistry, geology, and physics-astronomy) has its own building with classrooms, offices, laboratory space, and modern equipment for study and research. The adjacent Vassar farm provides a 550-acre ecological field station for use by students in related disciplines. In astronomy, students use the campus observatory, completed in 1996, which houses three telescopes, including a 32-inch instrument, which is the largest at any college in the Northeast.

Costs

In 2000–01, costs include $24,610 for tuition, $330 for required fees, and $6940 for room and board. Books and personal expenses generally range from $1200 to $1500, and travel expenses vary.

Financial Aid

Bright and academically talented students are encouraged to apply to Vassar regardless of their personal financial circumstances. The College awards financial assistance to nearly 60 percent of the student body, and all aid is awarded solely on the basis of demonstrated financial need. In 1999–2000, students received $23 million in assistance, including Vassar College scholarships, federal and state funds, student loans, and campus employment.

To apply for financial aid, students should submit Vassar's Preliminary Application for Financial Aid and also must register during the fall of their senior year with the College Scholarship Service Financial Aid PROFILE service to obtain the appropriate forms. Both the PROFILE and the Free Application for Federal Student Aid (FAFSA) must be filed according to the schedule annually distributed with Vassar's application for admission. Financial aid award letters are sent within several days of admission decisions.

Faculty

More than 225 men and women comprise Vassar's outstanding faculty. More than 95 percent hold the doctorate or equivalent terminal degree in their fields. All faculty members teach undergraduates, and all are required to meet high standards for excellence in both teaching and research. The student-faculty ratio is 10:1, and the average class size is 16. Vassar professors have won virtually every external prize and grant for teaching and research, and many are nationally recognized as authorities in their disciplines. A majority of the faculty members live on campus or in the immediate neighborhood; 1 or 2 faculty members, often with their families, live in each residence hall as house fellows.

Student Government

Much of the on-campus cultural and social environment at Vassar is student-created. The Vassar Student Association (VSA) oversees the allocation of operating funds for campus organizations and events, sponsors elections for student leadership positions, and maintains standing committees for governance activities. Students serve on important campus committees with faculty members and contribute to the formation of college priorities.

Admission Requirements

Admission to Vassar is highly selective: in 1999–2000, 4,800 students applied for 630 places in the entering class. The primary criterion is academic ability, as evidenced by both high achievement in a demanding secondary school program and demonstrated intellectual curiosity. Standardized test results are also considered, and all candidates must submit results of the SAT I and three SAT II Subject Tests or the ACT. Nonnative speakers of English should also submit results of the TOEFL.

The Admission Committee also seeks evidence of leadership and talent, as demonstrated through participation in activities in the candidate's school, community, or personal endeavors. Motivation, potential, and personal strengths—as revealed primarily in essays and recommendations—are also weighed in the admission process.

Candidates are encouraged to visit the Vassar campus for a tour and group information session, which are offered weekdays year-round and on most Saturday mornings in the fall. Personal interviews are not required, but applicants may usually arrange an interview with alumni representatives by checking the appropriate space on the application form.

Application and Information

Applications for regular decision admission are due by January 1. Applicants are notified by April 1, and candidates must respond by May 1. Early decision, intended for those students who have concluded that Vassar is a clear first choice, has two possible submission deadlines: November 15 or January 1. Candidates who use the first deadline are notified by December 15, and those electing the second option hear from the College by early February. If accepted, early decision candidates must withdraw all other applications and submit the enrollment deposit to Vassar.

Transfer applications are accepted for both the fall and spring terms. The deadline for submission of transfer applications for midyear admission is November 15, with notification by mid-December. Candidates for transfer admission for the fall term must apply by April 1, with notification usually coming in early May.

Students should direct requests for additional information to:

Director of Admission
Office of Admission - Box 10
Vassar College
124 Raymond Avenue
Poughkeepsie, New York 12604-0010
Telephone: 845-437-7300
           800-827-7270 (toll-free)
Fax: 845-437-7063
E-mail: admissions@vassar.edu
World Wide Web: http://www.vassar.edu

VERMONT TECHNICAL COLLEGE
RANDOLPH CENTER, VERMONT

The College

Situated in a hilltop village near the heart of the Green Mountains, Vermont Technical College, founded in 1866, is the only technical college in the Vermont State Colleges system. Most of the 1,145 students enrolled come from Vermont and the other New England states.

Through its certificate, associate, and bachelor's degree programs in engineering technology and applied science, the College provides students with a broad-based practical education. As a result, VTC graduates are prepared to work effectively in a variety of positions that support the activities of engineers, scientists, and other professionals. A major advantage of the VTC education is that it gives students the skills and knowledge to go right into their careers or continue their education. For students interested in pursuing the bachelor's degree, VTC offers "two-plus-two" programs leading to the Bachelor of Science degree. The College also has articulation agreements with a number of top four-year institutions, including the University of Vermont, Northeastern University, Norwich University, Rochester Institute of Technology, SUNY Institute of Technology, the University of New Hampshire, and the College of Agriculture and Life Sciences at Cornell University. Since 1982, 98 percent of each year's graduates have been placed in jobs or continued their education. Of those taking jobs, 90 percent were working in fields directly related to their VTC degree.

There are twenty-two major buildings on the 544-acre campus, including a Student Health and Physical Education facility with a double-court gymnasium, a six-lane indoor pool, and two racquetball courts. The four residence halls can house 515 students. Every student room has connections for direct access to the campuswide computer network, telephone service, and cable TV lines.

Campus life at VTC also includes sports, recreation, social events, and community service learning opportunities. The Student Life Office arranges weekly activities and social events and provides students with support and counseling. There are more than thirty student clubs, from radio station WVTC-FM to the yearbook and student chapters of professional organizations. There is also an on-campus ski hill and a fitness center.

Students enthusiastically participate in the College's seven varsity and twenty-five intramural sports for men and women. The men's basketball team won the Northern New England Small College Conference championship tournament in 1991 and 1995, the men's soccer team won in 1992, the men's volleyball team won in 1992, 1993, 1994, and 1995, and the women's softball team won in 1994. The men's baseball team won the NNESCC championship in 1998 and 1999. VTC also competes in the National Small College Athletic Association (NSCAA) and advanced to its national men's championship tournaments in baseball (1995) and soccer (1998 and 1999). The women's volleyball team took the 1995 NSCAA regional championship and competed in the national championship tournament.

Location

VTC's location is rural but far from isolated (exit 4 of Interstate 89 is just a mile away). For day-to-day needs, the nearby village of Randolph offers a variety of shops and restaurants as well as a movie theater, a bowling alley, and the Chandler Music Hall. For special shopping and events, Burlington and Montpelier, Vermont, and Hanover, New Hampshire, are within an hour's drive. Boston and Montreal are just 3 hours away. There is convenient bus service from Randolph, and Amtrak's "Vermonter" stops in Randolph twice daily.

Students enjoy the variety of recreational activities available to them in Vermont. Some of the top ski resorts in the East are less than an hour from campus. Students can also hike on the Appalachian Trail, canoe on numerous lakes and rivers, camp in the Green Mountain National Forest, and bike on the miles of country roads.

Majors and Degrees

VTC offers five programs leading to the Associate in Engineering degree: civil and environmental engineering technology, computer engineering technology, electrical and electronics engineering technology, mechanical engineering technology, and rehabilitation engineering technology. There are opportunities for dual majors in several areas.

Programs leading to the Associate in Applied Science degree are accounting, agribusiness management technology, architectural and building engineering technology, automotive technology, biotechnology, business technology and management, construction practice and management, dairy farm management technology, landscape development and ornamental horticulture, plastics engineering technology, small-business management, and veterinary technology.

The Bachelor of Science degree is offered in architectural engineering technology, computer engineering technology, and electromechanical engineering technology. These are two-plus-two programs that accept graduates of VTC's two-year programs in related fields or transfer students from equivalent curricula at other accredited institutions.

Students interested in nursing may enroll in the nursing programs offered by VTC in Bennington, Brattleboro, or Colchester, Vermont, and on VTC's main campus. These programs lead to a certificate in practical nursing and to the Associate in Science in Nursing degree.

VTC also offers three-year options in selected associate degree programs for those students whose math, science, or English skills need some strengthening.

Academic Program

Whether preparing for an associate or a bachelor's degree program, VTC's students receive a rigorous broad-based education centered on a core curriculum that includes both technical and general education electives. The number of credits required for graduation ranges from 65 to 72 for the associate degree and from 130 to 139 for the bachelor's degree, depending on the program. Honors courses are offered in all engineering technology programs. Most degree programs also offer project courses, in which students work as teams on real-world applications in their fields of study.

The College is accredited by the New England Association of Schools and Colleges. In addition, the following degree programs are accredited by the Technology Accreditation Commission of the Accreditation Board for Engineering and Technology, Inc. (TAC of ABET): architectural and building engineering technology, architectural engineering technology, civil and environmental engineering technology, computer engineering technology, electrical and electronics engineering technology, and mechanical engineering technology. The veterinary technology program is accredited by the American

Veterinary Medical Association as a program for educating veterinary technicians. Practical nursing programs are approved by the Vermont Board of Nursing and accredited by the National League for Nursing Accrediting Commission (NLNAC). The associate degree program in nursing is approved by the Vermont Board of Nursing.

Academic Facilities

VTC students learn in modern laboratories with state-of-the-art equipment. Hartness Library houses some 57,000 books, 400 journal subscriptions, and hundreds of videocassettes and audiocassettes. The library's Web page (http://www.vtc.vsc.edu/library) provides 24-hour-a-day, seven-day-a-week access to the catalog of the Vermont State Colleges and links to various indexes, databases, and other Internet resources. Pentium-class PCs in the library connect to the campus network and the Internet. Facilities housed in the three major academic buildings include one 13-station and three 21-station computer-aided drafting and design labs; five 21-station general academic computing labs; an eight-station electrical/electronics lab; recently renovated mechanical labs, which include computer-numerically-controlled equipment and computer-aided manufacturing software; state-of-the-art veterinary technology facilities, including a twelve-station lab area, a radiography suite and darkroom, and a surgery suite; a biotechnology lab with instrumentation typical of the most modern research labs; a nursing lab with a dedicated computer room and nursing station; two civil engineering labs; architectural drafting studios; a campuswide microcomputer network with Internet access; four instrumented electronics labs; a fully equipped automotive technology center with the latest in computerized diagnostics; and a rehabilitation engineering technology laboratory with assistive technology such as voice-recognition computer software and twelve computer stations.

Agriculture students gain practical experience at the College's dairy facility. A main freestall barn houses a milking herd of 90 registered Holsteins. Students have the opportunity to participate in all aspects of the farm's management. Veterinary technology students work with several species of domestic animals in the livestock facility on the farm.

The Judd Support Center houses most of the College's academic support services. Students visit Judd to sign up for tutoring, meet with counselors to discuss personal or academic issues, or visit the career/transfer center to update their resumes and explore career options and internship opportunities. Disabilities services, where students with a disability can find out about classroom accommodations or assistive technology, is also located in Judd. In Conant Hall are the Learning Center, which offers drop-in and scheduled tutoring, supplemental instruction, study groups, and review sessions; and the General Education Department's Writing and Communication Center, which provides help with reading, writing, oral presentations, and study skills.

Costs

Tuition for 1999–2000 was $4956 per year for Vermont residents and $10,020 for out-of-state students. The yearly room rate was $3108, and the meal plan was $2190 per year. Other required annual fees totaled $684. An additional $353 health insurance fee is required of students not covered by another medical plan. Many of VTC's programs are available at reduced tuition to New England students through the New England Regional Student Program, sponsored by the New England Board of Higher Education.

Financial Aid

About 75 percent of VTC's students receive financial aid from federal, state, and campus-based sources. There are a growing number of institutional scholarships available, including the VTC Scholars Program, as well as work-study opportunities.

Prospective students seeking aid must file the Free Application for Federal Student Aid (FAFSA). Some state agencies may require additional information. Students are urged to apply for financial aid by the March 1 priority deadline so awards may be announced by May. However, applications are reviewed on a rolling basis after March 1 until available funds are exhausted. The VTC Web site provides more financial aid information.

Faculty

The College's excellence in instruction is a direct result of the quality of the faculty at VTC. The 65 full-time faculty members bring to the College a special blend of industrial experience and teaching expertise. Almost all have advanced degrees. Students are assured individual attention as a result of the 11:1 student-faculty ratio.

Student Government

The Associated Students of Vermont Technical College (ASVTC) is composed of elected student officers and volunteers representing residence halls and commuting students. ASVTC acts as liaison between the students and administration, advances students' interests, and promotes social activities.

Admission Requirements

Each applicant receives individual consideration for admission based on receipt and review of the official secondary school transcript, letters of recommendation, proof of high school graduation or a high school equivalency diploma, and SAT I scores. A personal interview is required only in the veterinary technology program, although an interview and campus visit are strongly recommended for all applicants.

Because of the technical nature of the curriculum, applicants should have a strong math and science aptitude.

Application and Information

VTC follows a rolling admission policy, but timely application is recommended. Applicants are notified of their status within two weeks of receipt of their completed application and supporting documents. For more information on Vermont Technical College, students should contact:

Director of Admissions
Vermont Technical College
Randolph Center, Vermont 05061
Telephone: 802-728-1000
          800-442-VTC-1 (toll-free)
E-mail: admissions@vtc.vsc.edu
World Wide Web: http://www.vtc.vsc.edu

The high-tech campus of Vermont Technical College is situated in a scenic New England village in the heart of Vermont.

VILLA JULIE COLLEGE
STEVENSON, MARYLAND

The College

Villa Julie College is a private institution dedicated to educating its 2,000 students in a personal atmosphere using state-of-the-art technology while being mindful of the significance of a strong liberal arts education. Individual attention by faculty members, extensive career preparation gained through real-world training, and an ideal location just north of Baltimore, Maryland, make the College truly unique. At Villa Julie, professors are more than just instructors; they are friends who promote intellectual growth and curiosity. By bringing years of professional experience into the classroom, the faculty members truly enhance the quality of learning. With a student-faculty ratio of 13:1, it is easy to understand why students often site the congenial rapport with faculty members as one of the College's strong points.

Villa Julie's dedication to leading the region and the nation in computer education is evidenced by the cutting-edge technology featured across the curriculum. Information systems classes are a mainstay within the curriculum, ensuring that each graduate is prepared to be a technological leader in his or her chosen field. State-of-the-art hardware and software exist in all of the College's computer labs, which have a 4:1 student-computer ratio. The entire computing network is fiber-optically linked to offer users access to the Internet and an opportunity to dial in and link up from their off-site PCs through modems.

Career and graduate school preparation and placement are the capstones of the Villa Julie education. Unlike most other colleges and universities, Villa Julie prepares its students for the postgraduate world, not just for graduation. Student interaction with the College's career development officers begins in the freshman year with skills and interest assessment workshops and culminates senior year with corporate on-campus employee recruitment. A comprehensive cooperative-education and internship program allows interested students to gain valuable experience at renowned companies such as Black and Decker, Procter and Gamble, Ernst and Young, Baltimore Gas and Electric (BGE), and the Zurich Group. Typically, 99 percent of the graduates who seek full-time employment accept permanent positions within six months of graduation. Approximately 8 percent of the graduates attend graduate/professional schools immediately following graduation.

Villa Julie's students are afforded the opportunity to reside in a college-supervised off-campus apartment complex 4½ miles from the main campus. This refreshing alternative to the traditionally crowded college-dormitory lifestyle places 4 students together in a spacious two-bedroom fully furnished apartment. A free shuttle is provided to transport students between the apartments and the college campus.

The cocurricular education gained by Villa Julie students through involvement in more than forty clubs and organizations, multiple honor societies, intramural sports, and NCAA Division III athletics is often as fulfilling as their classroom experiences. A few of the College's more popular organizations include the Student Government Association, the Drama Society, the Environmental Club, the Wilderness Leadership Society, the Community Service Corps, and *The Villager*, the campus newspaper. The Villa Julie Mustangs compete at the NCAA Division III level and are members of the Eastern Collegiate Athletic Conference. The following sports are offered: men's and women's basketball, cross-country, golf, lacrosse, soccer, tennis, and track and field; men's baseball and club volleyball; and women's field hockey, softball, and volleyball. Intramural sports are also available.

Villa Julie College's Master of Science in advanced information technologies provides students with the technical knowledge required to help organizations achieve a competitive advantage in an increasingly global, technology-driven, and information-rich marketplace. The degree program accomplishes this by providing students not only with the knowledge about a wide variety of technologies and their architectures, but also with an understanding of how technologies can be integrated. Unlike other programs that focus on learning one or more specific technologies or on the management of technologies, this program addresses the most important business issue—the integration of the full range of information technologies within an organization from both the strategic and operational perspective.

Location

Villa Julie's 60-acre wooded campus lies in one of Baltimore's upscale neighborhoods, Greenspring Valley. While being surrounded by horse farms and estate homes, the College is just 12 miles from downtown Baltimore. This location offers the student body the advantages of a quiet and peaceful learning atmosphere with the immediate availability of urban life. A variety of museums, theaters, historical sites of interest, and professional, semiprofessional, and intercollegiate sporting events are offered in the metropolitan area. A number of neighboring colleges and universities help round out the students' social opportunities.

Majors and Degrees

Villa Julie College awards master's, bachelor's, and associate degrees.

Bachelor's degrees in biology, biotechnology, business systems, chemistry, computer information systems, English language and literature, interdisciplinary studies, liberal arts and technology, nursing, paralegal studies, psychology, and visual communication design are offered. These degrees encompass the following fields of study: accounting, administrative sciences, art, business, business communication, business information systems, computer accounting, early childhood education teacher certification, economics, elementary education teacher certification, environmental technology, film, financial management, history, human resources, information systems, international business, marketing, mathematics, microbiology, military science (Army ROTC), nursing, paralegal studies, predentistry, prelaw, premedicine, prepharmacy, pre–physical therapy, preveterinary science, RN to B.S., science, social sciences, theater, video, and writing.

The associate degree can be obtained in accounting, art, arts and sciences, business administration, chemical laboratory technology, child development, communication arts (video, television, theater), computer information systems, court reporter studies, general studies, medical laboratory technology, and paralegal studies.

Academic Program

The College is committed to providing a solid basis in the liberal arts within every curriculum. Therefore, all students are required to complete courses that will help them develop an understanding of their cultural heritage, an appreciation of the arts and the humanities, the ability to easily and effectively communicate orally and in writing, an understanding of society and how it functions, a knowledge of scientific methods and an interpretation of the natural world, and the ability to reflect, to reason, and to handle quantitative knowledge.

Through courses in the major fields, students gain knowledge and a greater understanding of the subject area while gaining competency in applying the content and methods of inquiry to daily life. Students in all academic disciplines are also required to study subjects that enhance the knowledge acquired in their major and that relate technology to their field. The College's goal is to offer a synthesis of the liberal arts, current technology, and a major field that provide an education that prepares the student for gainful employment, for successful graduate study, and for productive involvement in today's world.

Academic Facilities

A recent expansion allows the College to utilize more than 100,000 square feet of new facilities, which include a 400-seat theater, multiple state-of-the-art computer labs and classrooms, video and graphic studios and suites, a student union, and an athletic complex. In addition, Knott Hall, one of the College's primary academic facilities, houses a number of multidimensional classrooms, computer labs, science labs, a lecture auditorium, faculty offices, and small study areas. Renovations to the College's old student center were completed in August 1998 and added a new science wing that houses classrooms, laboratories, cold-storage facilities, a greenhouse, and independent research sites. Each classroom and laboratory throughout the campus is capable of state-of-the-art multimedia projection and computer-assisted learning. In the College's Learning Center, students of all academic capabilities can gain educational assistance and advice from faculty members. The College's library boasts an extensive collection of more than 100,000 printed volumes, periodicals, video and audio tapes, microfilm and microfiche selections, and an interlibrary loan consortium. Complementing this collection is a highly automated system, which provides the library's catalog and the full-text editions of a number of periodicals and newspapers on CD-ROM. In addition to the electronic databases it owns, the library has access to thousands of outside databases such as WESTLAW, Dialog, Dow Jones News Retrieval, and the Internet. Through these databases, individuals can access information immediately from anywhere in the world. The Inscape Theater is home to the College's drama and video departments, which boast ownership of AVID and ADOBE, highly advanced digitized computer editing systems.

Costs

Villa Julie's cost is very reasonable. For the 1999–2000 academic year, tuition for full-time students was $10,250. Part-time tuition and fees were $305 per credit hour, plus a $30 registration fee per semester. The expense for off-campus housing is $3650 per year. The general service fee was $424, and the technology fee was $306.

Financial Aid

Villa Julie College offers financial assistance to qualified students in the form of scholarships, grants, loans, student employment, and a special payment plan. Villa Julie prides itself on the variety of scholarships it offers to incoming freshmen. In 1999, approximately 80 percent of the College's students received some financial assistance, and 47 percent of the freshmen entering the College in the fall received a Villa Julie Scholarship. Villa Julie College participates in all major federal financial aid programs as well as all Maryland state programs. Student applicants are required to file the Free Application for Federal Student Aid (FAFSA) and Villa Julie's Institutional Aid Application. The priority deadline for filing both forms is March 1. To be considered for the Villa Julie College Key Scholarship, the College's full-tuition award, students must file the Villa Julie Institutional Aid Application by January 15. This form must be filed by February 15 for all other scholarships.

Faculty

The faculty at Villa Julie College, which numbers more than 200, is first and foremost a teaching faculty. The College's 13:1 student-teacher ratio demonstrates the institutional emphasis on a personalized education. While a majority of the faculty members have the doctoral or terminal degree offered in their field, a significant number are widely published. In addition, the majority are concurrently employed as professional specialists in their fields.

Student Government

The Student Government Association (SGA) facilitates an environment that encourages students to express their thoughts and opinions concerning Villa Julie College, its policies, and sponsored activities. The SGA serves as the principal governing body of all campus clubs and activities. Through SGA events, students develop and learn the importance of time management skills and interpersonal relations. In conjunction with the Office of Campus Life, the Student Government Association organizes an array of campuswide events that promote the social aspects of college life such as cookouts, bonfires, flag and powderpuff football games, formal dances, bull and oyster roasts, and homecoming. Each student at Villa Julie is welcome and encouraged to participate in all SGA functions.

Admission Requirements

Applications for admission to Villa Julie College are reviewed on a rolling basis. Candidates are evaluated according to their academic qualifications and personal character. The successful completion of a four-year college-preparatory program is the basis for success at Villa Julie. Therefore, a candidate's high school record receives the greatest weight in the Admissions Committee's decision. Other important factors include performance on standardized tests (SAT I or ACT), feedback provided on the Secondary School Report and Recommendation Form, student-produced writing samples, and the admissions interview. Admission to the College is determined without regard for race, color, sex, religion, national or ethnic origin, or handicap. The College complies with all applicable laws and federal regulations regarding discrimination and accessibility on the condition of handicap, age, veteran status, or otherwise.

Application and Information

Applications for admission should be received by March 1 for fall semester entry and November 1 for spring semester entry. Applications received after these dates are reviewed on a space-available basis. Students applying to the College as freshmen must submit official high school transcripts, standardized test scores, the Secondary School Report and Recommendation Form, a typewritten writing sample, and a $25 nonrefundable application fee. In addition, each applicant must complete an admissions interview. Transfer students must submit all of the above credentials in addition to official transcripts from all colleges or universities they have attended.

For further information, scholarship deadlines, and application forms, students should contact:

Office of Admissions
Villa Julie College
1525 Greenspring Valley Road
Stevenson, Maryland 21153-0641
Telephone: 410-486-7001
        877-GO-TO-VJC (877-468-6852) (toll-free)
Fax: 410-602-6600
E-mail: admissions@vjc.edu
World Wide Web: http://www.vjc.edu

VILLANOVA UNIVERSITY
VILLANOVA, PENNSYLVANIA

The University
Since 1842, Villanova University has been under the direction of the Order of St. Augustine, better known as the "Augustinians," one of the oldest religious teaching orders of the Roman Catholic Church. The University's 254-acre campus is located 12 miles west of downtown Philadelphia in an attractive residential area. There are approximately 10,000 men and women currently enrolled; 6,000 are undergraduates.

Campus life encompasses a wide range of activities and groups. The Campus Activities Team provides a full schedule of films, concerts, and social events throughout the year. Special interest organizations are available in many areas; these include publications, music, theater, professional societies, fraternities and sororities, cultural and political groups, and volunteer organizations.

Location
Philadelphia, America's fifth-largest city, offers unparalleled opportunities to supplement campus life with cultural, recreational, and social service activities. The city offers professional sports in the form of the basketball 76ers, the football Eagles, the hockey Flyers, and the baseball Phillies. Philadelphia is the home of the world-renowned Philadelphia Orchestra and also the location of a wealth of museums, theaters, galleries, and historic attractions.

Majors and Degrees
Villanova University grants the Bachelor of Arts degree in the following majors: art history, classical studies, communication, economics, English, French, general arts (concentrations in Africana studies, Arab and Islamic studies, criminal justice, elementary education in cooperation with Rosemont College, ethics, Irish studies, Latin American studies, peace and justice, Russian area studies, and women's studies), geography, German, history, honors, human services, philosophy, political science, psychology, sociology, Spanish, and theology. Instruction in Arabic, Chinese, Italian, Japanese, and Russian is also available. The Bachelor of Science is awarded in the following majors: astronomy and astrophysics, biology, chemistry (concentration in biochemistry), comprehensive science (concentrations in biological chemistry and geography), computer science, honors, information science, mathematics, physics, and secondary education. Also offered are the following professional degrees: D.M.D. (seven-year Doctor of Medical Dentistry program in conjunction with the University of Pennsylvania), M.D. (seven-year Doctor of Medicine program with a six-year option in conjunction with MCP Hahnemann University), optometry (seven-year Doctor of Optometry program in conjunction with the Philadelphia College of Optometry), and physical therapy (six-year Master of Science program in conjunction with Thomas Jefferson University College of Health Professions). The College of Commerce and Finance grants the Bachelor of Science degree in accountancy, business administration, and economics. The degree program in business administration has majors in finance, management, and marketing. The management major offers a concentration in international business. The College of Engineering offers degrees in chemical, civil, computer, electrical, and mechanical engineering. The College of Nursing grants a Bachelor of Science in Nursing degree. Villanova grants the Associate of Arts in liberal arts and the Associate of Science in natural science.

Academic Program
The principal aim of the College of Liberal Arts and Sciences is to assist persons in educating themselves. To achieve this, the College offers a traditional liberal arts and sciences curriculum with a great deal of flexibility built into it, including a Humanities Core Seminar Program with class sizes of 10 to 15 students. Both general and specialized courses are provided. Stress is laid on critical thinking and effective communication. Accordingly, hundreds of theoretical and practical courses are offered in the arts, the humanities, and the physical and social sciences. Required components of the curriculum include ethics, fine arts, and courses designed to develop students' writing abilities. The multimillion-dollar St. Augustine Center for the Liberal Arts brings together the College's faculty members and students for seminars.

Emphasizing the analytical approach to business, the curriculum in the College of Commerce and Finance combines broad educational foundation courses with in-depth study of major functional fields of business and business processes, such as accounting information systems, financial flows and markets, management, and the impact of economic variables upon business and social issues. Foundation courses aim at developing proficiency in oral and written communications, the ability to apply the tools of quantitative analysis to the solution of business problems, and awareness of and sensitivity to moral values and law, the need for social responsibility, and the exercise of conscience.

In the first two years of the College of Engineering curriculum, work concentrates on such basic areas as chemistry, engineering science, mathematics, and physics, while in the last two years engineering analysis and design are stressed. Courses in the humanities are included in each engineering curriculum to make the young engineer more fully aware of social responsibilities and better able to consider nontechnical factors in the engineering decision-making process. Students learn the theoretical foundations of the engineering field through lectures and discussions, which are integrated with extensive hands-on laboratory and computer experience. Individual and group design projects utilize state-of-the-art equipment and instrumentation.

The College of Nursing curriculum consists of academic and professional study, including laboratory and health-agency experience under the guidance of qualified faculty members. Clinical facilities are selected on the basis of the educational objectives of the curriculum. The program provides clinical experiences beginning in the sophomore year in a variety of settings, including medical centers, community hospitals, and community health agencies. The curriculum builds upon a strong foundation of liberal arts and physical and behavioral sciences.

Naval and Marine ROTC programs are available for men and women on campus, Air Force ROTC through St. Joseph's University, and Army ROTC through Widener University on campus.

Off-Campus Arrangements

The Office of International Studies assists undergraduates in studying overseas in Africa, Asia, Europe, Latin America, and the Middle East for a summer, semester, or full academic year. All overseas programs must be affiliated with an overseas four-year college or university, have overseas faculty members, and provide bicultural experiences such as homestays. Students usually study overseas in their sophomore or junior year. Villanova's summer programs support language studies and area studies in such locales as Bethlehem (Palestine), Cádiz (Spain), Dijon (France), Galway (Ireland), Heidelberg (Germany), Siena (Italy), Urbino (Italy), and Valparaiso (Chile). Villanova also has special relations with Bethlehem University and Birzeit University (Palestine), University of Cádiz (Spain), University College of Galway (Ireland), University of Glasgow (Scotland), Lorenzo de Medici Institute (Italy), University of Urbino (Italy), and Victoria University of Manchester (England). Nursing majors may complete a year at King's College, London. College of Commerce and Finance students can spend a year at University Lille-ESPEME (France). College of Liberal Arts and Sciences students may spend a year studying at Queen Mary Westfield College, London, or Universidad Popular Autonóma del Estado de Puebla (Mexico).

The College of Liberal Arts and Sciences offers an Internship Program in which students work during the summer, fall, or spring terms of the junior or senior year. The internships are departmentally related, and students obtain from 3 to 15 credits for the experience. Part-time and full-time work experience is available in the Delaware Valley as well as New York City and Washington, D.C., which offers access to business, political, professional, and media leaders. The Colleges of Engineering and of Commerce and Finance also offer internship programs.

Academic Facilities

The Falvey Memorial Library provides resources and facilities for study and research by undergraduate students, graduate students, faculty members, and visiting scholars. The library's total seating capacity is 1,200. Its holdings include more than 800,000 volumes, 5,400 serial subscriptions, and more than a million microform items.

Costs

Tuition costs, including fees, averaged $20,500 for the 1999–2000 academic year. Room and board costs for the full academic year averaged $7850. Expenses for books, travel, and personal supplies are estimated at $1000 for the year.

Financial Aid

Financial assistance is granted on the basis of need. The aid applicant must file the Free Application for Federal Student Aid (FAFSA) no later than February 15, with the request that the results be sent to the Villanova University Office of Financial Assistance. These forms may be obtained from the applicant's guidance office. The family's income tax return for the previous year and Villanova's institutional financial aid application should be sent to Villanova's Office of Financial Assistance by March 15. Academic and athletic merit scholarships are also available.

Faculty

Villanova has 490 full-time and 319 part-time faculty members. The undergraduate and graduate faculty are the same. Of the faculty members, 93 percent hold doctorates or the equivalent. The student-faculty ratio is 13:1.

Student Government

The Student Government of Villanova is a representative body of all students. Its purpose is to provide a channel of communication between students and the University, to promote student legislation, and to assist in concerns involving students and the Villanova community. The Student Government performs the double role of providing student representation in the formulation of University policies and of expanding student services. Student senators provide input on matters of policy as voting members of the University Senate and its committees.

Admission Requirements

The basic criteria for admission are the applicant's high school record and class standing, scores on the SAT I or ACT, an essay, and extracurricular activities. Applicants must be graduates of approved secondary schools and must present units of study as prescribed for the various curricula of the University.

Application and Information

The deadline for receipt of the application by the Office of University Admission is January 7. The deadline for early action is December 1. The health affiliation programs' deadline is November 15. Applications should be sent to:

Office of University Admission
Villanova University
800 Lancaster Avenue
Villanova, Pennsylvania 19085-1672
Telephone: 610-519-4000
          800-338-7927 (toll-free)
Fax: 610-519-6450
E-mail: jvanblun@email.villanova.edu
World Wide Web: http://www.vill.edu

St. Thomas of Villanova Church.

VIRGINIA COMMONWEALTH UNIVERSITY
RICHMOND, VIRGINIA

The University

Virginia Commonwealth University was created in 1968 by an act of the General Assembly that combined the Richmond Professional Institute and the Medical College of Virginia. However, VCU uses the founding date of 1838, the year in which the Medical College of Virginia was created. VCU is one of three comprehensive universities in Virginia. On the graduate level, the University offers the M.A., M.Acc., M.B.A., M.F.A., M.A.E., M.Ed., M.H.A., M.M., M.M.Ed., M.P.A., M.P.H., M.S., M.S.N.A., M.S.O.T., M.S.W., M.T., M.Tax., M.I.S., M.U.R.P., D.D.S., M.D., Pharm.D., D.M.D., D.H.A., D.B.A., and Ph.D. degrees. Undergraduate and graduate programs are offered in more than 175 fields.

VCU is a diverse metropolitan university that has a major educational, cultural, and economic impact on the Richmond community. VCU is administratively and structurally composed of two campuses, the Academic (west) Campus and the Medical College of Virginia (east) Campus, operating as one institution. The two campuses provide distinct locations for learning. The Academic Campus, located in the historic Fan District, combines hand-paved streets and Victorian town houses with spacious, contemporary classroom facilities. It houses the following colleges and schools: Arts, Business, Education, Engineering, Humanities and Sciences, Social Work, the School of Graduate Studies, and the Division of University Outreach. The Medical College of Virginia Campus is located in the business section of Richmond, 1½ miles east of the Academic Campus. At this campus are the Divisions of Allied Health Professions, Dentistry, Medicine, Nursing, and Pharmacy. Each campus has several buildings listed on either the Virginia or National Historic Landmarks registers. Free shuttle service between the campuses is provided by the University.

Of the 23,451 men and women at VCU, 15,824 are undergraduates. More than 59 percent of the 2,460 freshmen reside in University residence facilities, which include modern high-rise buildings and stylish town houses. Approximately 170 student organizations exist on campus, reflecting the diverse social, political, religious, and academic interests of the student body. Campus life is active, and there are numerous social and athletic events scheduled through these groups. VCU also has one of the largest evening schools in the nation.

VCU offers postbaccalaureate certificate programs leading to undergraduate certificates in accounting, computer science, environmental studies, information systems, real estate and urban land development, statistics, and therapeutic recreation (second undergraduate degree, 30 hours).

Location

VCU is located in the city of Richmond, the state capital and focal point for Virginia's political, cultural, and social events. It is within a 1-hour drive of Williamsburg and within a 2-hour drive of the Blue Ridge Mountains, Virginia Beach, and Washington, D.C. Founded in 1607, Richmond is home to many historic sites. It also offers theater, concerts, symphony performances, ballet, art museums, shopping, athletics, and recreational opportunities. The University extends into the life of the city, and students participate in many activities in the University and Richmond communities.

Majors and Degrees

Virginia Commonwealth University awards B.A., B.F.A., B.G.S., B.M., B.M.Ed., B.S., and B.S.W. degrees. The undergraduate majors are accounting; advertising; art; art history; biology; biomedical engineering; business administration; chemical engineering; chemistry; clinical laboratory sciences; communication art and design; comparative literature; computer science; crafts (ceramics, fabric design, fiberwork, furniture design, glassworking, jewelry, metalsmithing, and woodworking); criminal justice (corrections, juvenile justice, law enforcement, and legal studies); dance and choreography; dental hygiene; economics; education (art, early childhood, health and physical middle school, music, secondary, special, and theater education); electrical engineering; electronic media (broadcasting); English; fashion design and illustration; fashion merchandising; finance; finance/insurance and risk management; French; German; history; human resource management/industrial relations; information systems; interior design; management; marketing; mass communications; mathematical sciences (applied mathematics, computing science, mathematics, operations research, and statistics); mechanical engineering; music (performance/jazz studies and composition); news editing; nontraditional studies; nursing; occupational therapy; office administration; painting and printmaking; pharmacy; philosophy; physical therapy; physics; political science; predentistry studies; prelaw studies; premedicine studies; preoptometry studies; preveterinary studies; psychology; public relations; radiological sciences (nuclear medicine, radiation therapy, and radiological technology); real estate and urban land development; recreation, parks, and tourism; religious studies; science; sculpture; social work; sociology and anthropology; Spanish; theater (performance and design/technical); and urban studies and planning. Selected study plans resulting in double majors and/or minors are available to students who wish to intensify their academic backgrounds in more than one area of study. A number of major programs offer students an opportunity to specialize within their major. Extensive pre-health sciences programs are also offered.

Undergraduate studies in elementary, middle school, secondary, and special education are part of a five-year program leading to a combination of a B.A. or B.S. and a Master of Arts in Teaching. Students must apply to the upper-division graduate program once they have junior status. Undergraduate study in physical therapy is part of a six-year program leading to the master's degree. Students apply to the graduate portion after completing the pre-physical therapy program. Undergraduate study in pharmacy leads to the Pharm.D.

Academic Program

The numerous schools that exist within the University allow students to take courses in many different disciplines. The requirements for a bachelor's degree vary from 120 to 137 semester hours, according to the major program. Advanced placement, early admission, early decision, honors programs, and credit by examination are available. An eight-year medical program, an eight-year dental program, as well as guaranteed admission to graduate programs in basic health sciences and programs in business (four-year programs leading to the master's degree) are available to superior freshmen. VCU operates on a traditional semester calendar, and numerous summer sessions are offered. Cooperative education and internships are available in most majors.

Off-Campus Arrangements

VCU sponsors various travel/study-abroad programs for students interested in gaining exposure to other cultures and languages.

Academic Facilities

A large number of support facilities and programs supplement the various academic offerings at VCU. These include animal laboratories and a workshop, math tutorial labs, well-equipped labs for the sciences, language labs, the Foreign Language Bank for those needing translating services, the Psychological Services Center, the Management Center, the Computer Center, the Center for Public Affairs, the Correctional Training and Evaluation Center, the Reading Center, the Teachers' Media Workshop, the University Child Study Center, the Cancer Center, the Poison Control Center, four teaching hospitals, two theaters, a music center, a ceramics and sculpture workshop, art studios, a graphics lab, an audiovisual lab, and a photography studio with complete darkroom facilities. The Anderson Gallery, a University-owned art museum, is located on the Academic Campus. The University is also the location of Virginia's Highway Safety Training Center and a new Biotechnology Research Park.

Costs

Academic-year expenses for undergraduate students in 2000–01 are estimated at $3587 for in-state tuition and fees or $13,041 for nonresident tuition and fees. Room and board are estimated at $4839.

Financial Aid

University financial aid programs serve approximately 67 percent of the student body. The University participates in all federal and state grant, loan, and work-study programs. The University also sponsors a major academic scholarship program whose awards are based upon academic merit rather than need. Normally, students encounter few problems finding part-time employment on campus or in the community. To apply for assistance, students are required to complete the Free Application for Federal Student Aid (FAFSA). The FAFSA must be mailed before March 15 to meet the University deadline. Further information may be obtained by contacting the Financial Aid Department at 901 West Franklin Street, P.O. Box 843537, Richmond, Virginia 23284-2527.

Faculty

Eighty-nine percent of VCU faculty members hold the highest degree in their professional field. Faculty members work with students in developing academic programs, supervise independent study programs, and assist with academic advising.

Student Government

The student government at Virginia Commonwealth University consists of a body of 33 senators representing both schools. Each of the senators serves on at least one of seven subcommittees. Elections are held during spring preregistration. The student government provides programs and services to the University community and gives students the opportunity to get involved with the governance of the institution.

Admission Requirements

Admission to programs on the Academic Campus requires graduation from an accredited secondary school (or a high school equivalency diploma) with a minimum of 20 unit requirements, which must include 4 units in English, 3 units in history, social sciences, or government, 3 units in mathematics (including at least 2 units in algebra I, geometry, and algebra II), and 2 units in science (1 unit in a laboratory science). Two units of foreign language are strongly recommended. Additional units in mathematics and other academically challenging areas of study are also recommended. The Advanced Studies diploma is preferred. Applicants are evaluated on the basis of their academic record in high school, class standing, SAT I or ACT scores, extracurricular activities, and suitability of preparation for the intended major. Transfer students with at least 30 semester hours or 45 quarter hours of undergraduate credit are admitted on the basis of their accumulated college credits.

Admission to programs on the Medical College of Virginia Campus requires from two to four years of undergraduate study. Each school and program has specified academic requirements. VCU does not discriminate on the basis of race, religious beliefs, disability, veteran's status, age, gender, or national origin and is an Equal Opportunity/Affirmative Action employer.

Application and Information

The processing of applications for the spring and fall semesters begins in October. Applicants are considered when all necessary documents have been received, and they are notified by April 1 if the application file is complete by February 1. Applicants interested in being considered under the early decision plan must apply before November 1 and are notified by December 1. Applicants interested in the eight-year medical program must apply by December 15. The necessary materials include the official application form, a $25 nonrefundable application fee, official high school transcripts, indicating class rank and grade point average, and scores on the SAT I (the VCU code number is 475570) or ACT (the VCU code number is 474379). Those applying to the School of the Arts must submit the VCU Arts Admissions Packet, and those intending to major in theater, dance, or music must audition or interview. Transfer applicants who have earned fewer than 30 semester hours or 45 quarter hours of credit must also meet freshman guidelines and submit those documents required of freshmen (including SAT I or ACT scores if the candidates are under 22 years of age) in addition to official transcripts from all institutions attended. The transfer application deadline is June 1 but may vary for health science programs.

Applications and additional information may be obtained by contacting:

Office of Undergraduate Admissions
Virginia Commonwealth University
821 West Franklin Street
P.O. Box 842526
Richmond, Virginia 23284-2526
Telephone: 804-828-1222
           800-841-3638 (toll-free)
E-mail: ugrad@vcu.edu
World Wide Web: http://www.vcu.edu

The state-of-the-art, multipurpose Siegel center is the newest of three recreational facilities on the Academic Campus of Virginia Commonwealth University.

VIRGINIA INTERMONT COLLEGE
BRISTOL, VIRGINIA

The College

Virginia Intermont College (VIC) was founded in 1884 and is a four-year, fully accredited, private institution for men and women. There are 828 students currently enrolled. Virginia Intermont is affiliated with the Baptist General Association of Virginia, but it is open to any qualified applicant regardless of sex, creed, race, handicap, or national origin. Students represent more than thirty states, several countries, and some twenty religious faiths.

The Fine Arts and Humanities programs at the College offer opportunities to see and hear renowned lecturers, poets, musicians, writers, artists, and performing groups. These cultural activities are offered for inspiration, education, and entertainment.

The student activities program provides dances, parties, picnics, camping trips, ski weekends, concerts, coffeehouse entertainment, tours, and modern and classic films. There are five colleges within a 25-mile radius, and students from area colleges participate in many of these events.

The nationally recognized equestrian program leads a quality list of successful athletic offerings at VIC. As a member of the Tennessee-Virginia Athletic Conference (TVAC), which is in affiliation with the National Association of Intercollegiate Athletics (NAIA), the athletic programs include men's and women's baseball, basketball, soccer, softball, and tennis. Student-athletes are seen on campus as an integral part of the community. VIC is extremely proud of its student–athlete's accomplishments in the classroom as well as in athletic competition.

Location

The name Intermont, meaning "among the mountains," is descriptive of the setting of the College. Virginia Intermont is located in Bristol, Virginia, one of the Tri-Cities, the other two of which are Johnson City and Kingsport, Tennessee. The campus is located on I-81 between Roanoke and Knoxville, only eight blocks from the heart of downtown Bristol and 2 miles from the Bristol Mall.

Majors and Degrees

The Bachelor of Arts degree is offered in art, business (business education, management, marketing, and office technology), dance, English, equine studies, history/political science, liberal arts, paralegal studies, performing arts (dance, music, musical theater, and theater), photography, physical education, religion, social work (B.S.W. degree), and teacher education (art K–12, biology 6–12, business 6–12, English 6–12, history/political science 6–12, interdisciplinary K–6, and physical education K–12).

The Bachelor of Science degree is offered in biology, business management, computer information management, medical technology, psychology, and sports management.

The Associate in Arts degree is offered in allied health, general studies, and graphic design.

Minors are offered in accounting/economics, biology, business, chemistry, computer applications/technology, dance, English, environmental management, equine-assisted growth and development, equine studies, gerontology, history, music, organizational marketing, photography, political science, psychology, religion, sociology, sports medicine, and theater arts.

Academic Program

The academic year is divided into two semesters, running from August through December and from January through May. There are a three-week May term and a six-week summer term available.

The core curriculum is made up of visual and performing arts, English, literature, math, biology or physical science, world civilization, computer fundamentals, economics or political science, psychology or sociology, philosophy or religion, physical education, and public speaking. All first-time freshmen are required to take College 101, a semester-long orientation course.

Many departments offer minicourses on weekends. These offer students the opportunity to learn new techniques in horsemanship, art, or photography as well as meet writers of national prominence.

Academic Facilities

Virginia Intermont's campus has a blend of modern and historic buildings. In addition to the traditional labs and classrooms there are ballet studios, the Trayer Theatre, the Fine Arts Gallery, art studios, and photography labs, all available for instruction and student use, as are an indoor swimming pool and the tennis courts. Equine courses are taught at the Riding Center, which is made up of two indoor rings, one outdoor ring, and stables for eighty horses, located 10 minutes from campus on 136 acres. A recent addition to the Virginia Intermont campus is the Virginia Hutton Blevins Art Complex, dedicated in November 1998, which houses sculpture, drawing, and painting studios; classrooms and offices; and gallery and storage space. A new student fitness center was completed in April 1999.

Harrison-Jones Memorial Hall contains a 982-person capacity auditorium and chapel, dressing rooms, a prayer room, reception areas, and an apartment for visitor use.

Costs

Tuition for the 2000–01 year is $11,150. For the residential student, room and board are $4950. There is a $120 general fee and $150 technical fee. Additional fees are charged for riding classes, ballet classes, science laboratories, and other special classes.

Financial Aid

Ninety percent of all students attending the College receive financial aid. Virginia Intermont makes aid available through the Federal Pell Grant, Federal Supplemental Educational Opportunity Grant, Federal Perkins Loan, and Federal Work-Study programs. All Virginia residents are eligible to receive a grant. Residents of Georgia, Rhode Island, Vermont, Pennsylvania, and Washington, D.C., should also apply for state-based aid. A number of scholarships are available for those who do not qualify for federal aid, such as honor scholarships, the Tri-Cities Scholarship, and the Whitehead Award. Loans at low interest rates are available from the Virginia Intermont College Loan Association, the Federal Stafford Student Loan Program, the

Keesee Educational Loan Fund, and the Pickett and Hatcher Loan Fund. Benefits are available for veterans and veterans' dependents.

An academic scholarship program has been implemented for students with grade point averages from 2.5 to 4.0. Scholarships range from $500 to full tuition, based on the student's qualifications.

Faculty

The student-faculty ratio at Virginia Intermont is 12:1. There are 66 full-time and regular part-time faculty members, who play an active part in advising students regarding scheduling and campus activities; the close student-faculty relationship allowed by the small size of the campus fosters interaction between the two groups.

Student Government

The Student Government Association (SGA) is the organization chiefly responsible for formulating and enforcing the regulations governing student life. The SGA has as its stated purpose "to represent and to further the best interests of the student body, to secure cooperation between different organizations, and to promote responsibility, self-control, and loyalty among the students."

Admission Requirements

Applicants must be graduates of an accredited high school, with at least a C average, who have taken a minimum of 15 units (4 units of English, 2 units of college-preparatory math, 2 units of social science, 1 unit of laboratory science, and 6 units of other electives). Students may also be admitted under the early admission plan after their junior year in high school. Applicants who have a GED diploma, those who have satisfactorily completed 24 semester hours of college work, or those seeking admission as special (non-degree-seeking) students are also considered.

Transfer students are welcome. Transfer credit is subject to approval by the academic dean before the student's acceptance by the College, and a cumulative grade average of C or better must be attained before admission to the upper division. Virginia Intermont requires that the final 30 semester hours toward degree requirements be earned at the College.

Application and Information

Applicants should submit an application, a high school transcript, SAT I or ACT scores, transcripts of previous college work (if applicable), and the nonrefundable $15 application fee.

For an application and financial aid information, students should contact:

Director of Admissions
Box D-460
Virginia Intermont College
1013 Moore Street
Bristol, Virginia 24201-4298
Telephone: 540-669-6101
        800-451-1-VIC (toll-free)
World Wide Web: http://www.vic.edu

Virginia Intermont College's close-knit community is a great place to make friends.

VIRGINIA MILITARY INSTITUTE
LEXINGTON, VIRGINIA

The Institute

The Virginia Military Institute, a four-year undergraduate college founded in 1839, combines the studies of a full college curriculum within a framework of military discipline that emphasizes the qualities of honor, integrity, and responsibility. After 157 years of preparing young men for future leadership roles, VMI has made the transition to coeducation, successfully assimilating women into the Corps of Cadets while maintaining those elements of the VMI experience that have formed the backbone of the Institute's traditions. The Institute graduated its first women in May 1999.

VMI's 1,250 cadets pursue B.A. or B.S. degrees in fourteen disciplines in the general fields of engineering, science, and liberal arts. Undergirding all aspects of cadet life is the VMI Honor Code, to which all cadets subscribe. VMI's unique educational system produces leaders in every field of endeavor: business, industry, public service, education, the professions, and the military. Approximately 18 percent of VMI graduates make the armed forces a career. VMI alumni have distinguished themselves in every American conflict since the Mexican War, including 500 alumni who served in Operations Desert Storm and Desert Shield.

The measure of the success of any college rests with the achievements of its alumni, and VMI graduates get a jump on their career paths: VMI ranks first among Virginia colleges in job placement upon graduation (according to the State Council of Higher Education in Virginia, 1998). Over the past twelve years, an average of 97 percent of VMI graduates seeking employment, armed forces commissions, or graduate/professional school admission have obtained their goals by October following graduation. The same source also shows that VMI graduates are ready to serve in their communities, as these young men and women also rank first in the state for the perception that the curriculum prepared them for responsible citizenship. Finally, VMI alums show gratitude to their alma mater with monetary gifts to perpetuate the system that provided them with such a unique education; the VMI Foundation, Inc., the Institute's private fundraising arm, has an endowment of more than $280 million and ranks first in the nation in endowment per student among public colleges and universities (according to the National Association of College and University Business Officers, 1999).

The Corps of Cadets is composed of young men and women who represent forty-six states and twenty-two countries. The Cadet Barracks, a National Historic Landmark where all cadets live, is the focus in the complex of buildings that encompasses the campus. In addition to academic facilities, there is a main cadet activities building and a structure connected to the barracks that contains numerous offices for cadet organizations. Other campus facilities include a mess hall, an assembly hall and chapel, a gymnasium, a football stadium, a multipurpose auditorium housing basketball facilities, an outdoor track, and a field house for indoor track and field events. On the perimeter are other athletic, physical, and military training facilities. VMI places great emphasis on strengthening the body as well as the mind. Programs ensure physical well-being not only for those engaged in the sixteen intercollegiate athletic teams fielded by VMI but also for those participating in club sports and in a wide range of intramural athletics. Other activities are limited only by the imagination and interests of the cadets. VMI offers participation in more than fifty clubs and organizations.

Few, if any, schools in the nation can claim that approximately one third of their student body participates in intercollegiate athletics. VMI fields sixteen teams (thirteen for men and three for women) at the NCAA Division I level. Such is the importance of a sound, broad-based intercollegiate program to the Institute. Each year, VMI's Keydet Club raises in excess of $1 million for athletic scholarships, with approximately 180 cadets receiving athletic grants-in-aid in all sixteen sports.

One of the Institute's oldest traditions is the system of orientation and instruction applied to new cadets by old cadets. Regardless of background or prior training, every cadet in his/her first year at VMI is a "Rat" and must live under the "Rat System." Cadets refer to classmates as "Brother Rat," and the friendships formed in this association are enduring.

Location

Lexington, home of both VMI and Washington and Lee University, is in Rockbridge County at the southern end of the Shenandoah Valley between the Blue Ridge and Allegheny mountains. It is an area rich in history and natural beauty, and the city's recently restored downtown area has become a popular center of tourism. A crossroads for two centuries, U.S. Highways 11 (north-south) and 60 (east-west) have their junction in the center of downtown Lexington, just a few blocks from VMI. Interstate Highways 81 and 64 intersect only minutes from the downtown area. Air service to VMI is available via the Roanoke Regional Airport, less than an hour from Lexington.

Majors and Degrees

Believing that excellence is best maintained at a small college by limiting the number of majors, VMI offers the baccalaureate degree in fourteen curricula. Bachelor of Science degrees are awarded in chemistry, civil engineering, computer science, electrical engineering, mechanical engineering, and physics. Bachelor of Arts degrees are conferred in economics and business, English, history, international studies, modern languages (pending approval by the State Council of Higher Education in Virginia), and psychology. In biology and mathematics, either a B.A. or B.S. can be earned. The choice between a course of study leading to a Bachelor of Arts and a Bachelor of Science degree is made before the cadet enters VMI, but transfer from one major field of study to another is permitted.

Academic Program

VMI's demanding academic program reflects the established needs and the emerging trends of a constantly changing society on the local, regional, national, and international levels. The Institute's rapidly developing international program includes student and faculty member exchanges with fourteen international academies and universities, seven internships, and numerous semester-abroad opportunities. VMI is classified as Liberal Arts Baccalaureate I by the Carnegie classification system, along with many of the nation's prestigious liberal arts colleges. Though best known for its engineering programs, 52 percent of its graduates major in liberal arts fields. Approximately 30 percent of the cadets major in one of the three engineering branches (civil, electrical, or mechanical), while economics/business and history are the two most popular majors. The 2000 edition of *U.S. News & World Report's* "America's Best Colleges" ranks VMI as one of the nation's top twenty non-Ph.D.-degree-granting institutions. In the firm conviction that education in the true sense is the disciplining of the individual as well as the mind, qualities of strong character become ingrained as they are made a basic part of cadet life. At VMI, the military atmosphere contributes to the Institute's philosophy of a broad and sound education.

In addition to the everyday military lifestyle, all cadets participate in one of the Reserve Officers' Training Corps

(ROTC) programs—Army, Air Force, or Naval/Marine Corps—maintained by the Department of Defense. Commissions in the armed forces are encouraged but not mandatory. Approximately 35 percent of each graduating class receives a commission.

Academic Facilities

Twenty-two major buildings are located on 134 acres in the main area of VMI, which is designated a National Historic District. Among the academic facilities is Preston Library, which houses an open-shelf collection of some 260,000 volumes, in addition to microfilm, microcards, and periodicals. The facilities for the liberal arts curricula, including their special departmental libraries, are located in a single building, Scott Shipp Hall, which is currently undergoing a $10.4-million face-lift. A number of separate buildings house the classrooms and laboratories of the engineering curricula and computer science, biology, chemistry, ROTC, and physics and mathematics curricula. The physics department has X-ray and nuclear physics laboratories and operates both an observatory and a planetarium. The George C. Marshall Research Museum is also located on the VMI post. In keeping with the age of technology, every cadet's room is wired for the Internet, 200 PCs are available in computer labs throughout the campus, and plug-ins for laptops can be accessed from a special study area in the barracks and in Preston Library.

Costs

Charges at VMI, based on a cadet's classification as a Virginia or an out-of-state resident, cover almost all direct expenses, including not only tuition, board (twenty-one meals per week), room, and fees but also uniforms, laundry, normal medical care, and even haircuts—virtually all expenses for the academic year except books and transportation. For 1999–2000, total annual charges for Virginia residents were $10,390. For non-Virginia residents, the costs were $19,830. Consideration of net costs for the four years of enrollment should take into account ROTC pay and allowances to qualified ROTC cadets, which total up to $10,000 for the four-year period.

Financial Aid

Persons interested in financial assistance should write to the director of financial aid. Although aid is generally awarded on the basis of financial need, numerous scholarships are also awarded for academic and athletic excellence and as room and board supplements for ROTC scholarship recipients.

Faculty

The Institute's small size permits a close relationship among instructors, cadets, and faculty advisers. The primary emphasis of the faculty is on teaching, but many members engage in research projects in which cadets often assist. Ninety-three percent of the full-time faculty members hold doctoral or terminal degrees. The cadet-faculty ratio is 12:1.

Student Government

VMI has both a regimental and class system of government. The regimental system oversees accountability and ceremonial functions, and both systems govern cadet appearance and conduct. The regiment of the Corps of Cadets is divided into two battalions, four companies each, plus a band company.

Each class at VMI is a close-knit unit within itself, and, although Institute regulations govern the discipline of cadets, a large measure of supervision rests with cadets themselves through a class system that administers standards of the Corps and privileges accorded the classes.

The heart of student government is an honor system as old as VMI itself, a system that is a cadet's application of principles of honor to all aspects of daily life. Some of the rules are written, others are not, but all are based on the code that cadets do not lie, cheat, or steal nor tolerate those who do. An honor court elected by the Corps enforces the rules of the honor system.

Admission Requirements

Applicants must be unmarried, 16 to 22 years of age, physically fit for enrollment in ROTC, and graduates of an accredited secondary school with 16 or more academic units. Recommended courses include English, 4; social studies, 3; laboratory sciences, 3; foreign language, 3; mathematics, 3 (including 2 years of algebra and 1 of geometry); and electives, 2. A one-year age waiver may be granted for an applicant who has served an active duty in the armed forces or if other circumstances dictate a waiver. Transfer students are accepted, but two years of residency at VMI are required. Other qualifications include rank in the top half of the senior class (significance of rank depends on class size and other factors), above-average scores on the College Board's SAT I or American College Testing's ACT, and satisfactory character recommendations. The average GPA of incoming freshmen is approximately 3.1. Extracurricular activities are viewed as desirable indications of leadership and character traits. Standards are applied without regard to gender, race, nationality, or religion, and all factors are weighed in the final determination of the applicant's qualifications.

Application and Information

An application may be submitted anytime between September 1 and April 1 of the senior year in high school and should be accompanied by a nonrefundable $25 application fee, a transcript of the school record for grades 9 through the last completed semester, and SAT I or ACT scores. Visits to the Institute are highly recommended.

Interested students should contact:

Director of Admissions
Virginia Military Institute
Lexington, Virginia 24450

Telephone: 540-464-7211
　　　　　800-767-4207 (toll-free)
Fax: 540-464-7746
E-mail: admissions@vmi.edu
World Wide Web: http://www.vmi.edu

VMI Barracks, a National Historic Landmark and home to the VMI Corps of Cadets.

VIRGINIA UNION UNIVERSITY
RICHMOND, VIRGINIA

The University

A pioneer in higher education, Virginia Union University (VUU) is a private institution that has inspired academic excellence and leadership development for 134 years. The University was founded in 1865, when few educational opportunities were available to black students. Established under the auspices of the Baptist Church, VUU now offers students of every race and economic group the opportunity to acquire knowledge and skills within a quality academic program. VUU consistently produces graduates who succeed in a variety of fields and hold positions of leadership throughout the country and world, including U.S. congressmen, physicians and scientists, attorneys and judges, ministers, state legislators, professional athletes, educators, business executives, 21 college presidents, and the first elected African-American governor in the United States.

VUU and its graduate Samuel DeWitt Proctor School of Theology are accredited by the Southern Association of Colleges and Schools. The social work program is accredited by the Council on Social Work Education. The Sydney Lewis School of Business is accredited by the Association of Collegiate Business Schools and Programs. VUU is a charter member of The College Fund.

To complement academic life, there are eight nationally chartered Greek organizations as well as more than thirty student clubs and interest groups on campus, including the University Choir, Accounting Club, Student Government Association, the VUU Players, Criminal Justice Society, Student Admissions Team, Biology Club, *The Informer*, the Library Club, and Student Life Committee. Social and cultural events include the Coronation Ball, Homecoming Week, the Annual Winter Concert, Visiting Lecture Series, Convocation, chapel services, and Black History Month. An increasing number of VUU students take advantage of internship opportunities in government, businesses, corporations, institutions, and agencies throughout metropolitan Richmond.

Intercollegiate and intramural athletics are an important part of VUU campus life. The Panthers participate in the Central Intercollegiate Athletic Association (CIAA), NCAA Division II. Men's and women's sports include basketball, cross-country, football, golf, softball, tennis, track and field, and volleyball. The men's basketball team is the first to win the CIAA tournament title four years running (1992–95); the team won this title again in 1998.

Location

VUU is located in Richmond, the capital of Virginia, a city of great historical interest with a mild, healthful climate. The city provides many cultural advantages: numerous museums, libraries, and educational institutions as well as a concert series, stock and dinner theaters, and professional sports. It is served by a network of superhighways, bus lines, and airlines. Colonial Williamsburg is only an hour's drive away, Washington, D.C., is an easy 2-hour drive away, and many beaches and parks are easily accessible.

Majors and Degrees

Virginia Union University offers the Bachelor of Science degree in accounting, biology, biology education, business administration (with concentrations in finance, human resource management, management, management information systems, and marketing), business education, chemistry, chemistry education, criminal justice, criminology, engineering, mathematics, and mathematics education. The Bachelor of Arts degree is offered in art, English, English education, exceptional education, history and political science, history education, interdisciplinary studies, journalism, music (including commercial music), music education, psychology, psychology education, religious studies, sociology, and speech and drama. Students also can earn the Bachelor of Social Work degree.

Virginia Union University offers a 3-2 dual-degree program in engineering in cooperation with Howard University, the University of Iowa, Virginia Commonwealth University, and the University of Michigan and a 3-3 dual-degree program in law with St. John's University in New York. Students spend three years at VUU, then two (engineering) or three (law) years at one of the other institutions. Bachelor's degrees are awarded by both institutions.

Academic Program

Candidates for the Bachelor of Arts or Bachelor of Science degree must complete a minimum of 124 semester hours, with a grade point average of 2.0 or better and, in addition, must earn a C or better in each course in the major and related areas. Students must demonstrate competence on examinations in their major and in an English essay taken during their junior or senior year. Any student enrolled for 12 or more semester hours is considered a full-time student.

All full-time students admitted as freshmen or sophomores enter into the General Program. Through this program, students are provided with a strong liberal arts background in mathematics, the natural and social sciences, the humanities (including religion), and foreign languages. The University invites its best students to join the Honors Program, which emphasizes General Honors courses for freshmen and sophomores and independent work and theses for upperclass students.

The state-approved teacher education program offers a student the opportunity to major in one of fifteen approved areas. Graduates prepared as teachers at Virginia Union meet the requirements for teaching certificates in thirty-two states and the District of Columbia.

Qualified high school seniors living within commuting distance of VUU may take 3 to 9 semester hours of college courses. The University also offers a six-week summer session designed to establish the necessary qualifications for college admission.

Off-Campus Arrangements

A cooperative education program permits students to alternate full-time study at the University with full-time paid employment in business, industry, government, or social service agencies.

Academic Facilities

The L. Douglas Wilder Library and Learning Resources Center houses approximately 147,600 volumes and 311 periodical subscriptions, 850 electronically available full-text periodicals, 66,400 periodicals in microform, 14,000 linear feet of manuscripts, and 1,000 audiovisual resources; electronic index systems (such as Infotrac, ERIC, WilsonDisc, Proquest, Dow Jones News/Retrieval Service, Newsbank, African American Biographical Database, and Easynet on line); Internet access; and the papers and memorabilia of the nation's first elected African-American governor, L. Douglas Wilder (VUU '51). A section of the renowned Schomberg Collection on Afro-American Culture and History at the New York Public Library is reproduced in the Microfilm Research Center.

White Hall, which houses the Department of Fine Arts, includes two galleries of rare African art: The Sellman Collection and the Kriegman Collection of African and Oceanic Art.

Students in the Criminology and Criminal Justice Program study in a living laboratory environment, the city of Richmond's Police Training Academy, which houses this academic department. The facility is a monument to this unprecedented partnership between Virginia Union and the city.

The University recently completed state-of-the-art language laboratory and science computer laboratory facilities and renovated Martin E. Gray Hall for teacher education, psychology, sociology, and social work.

Costs

For residential students, the fee for the 1999–2000 academic year, consisting of fall and spring semesters, was $13,830. This charge includes the room deposit, tuition, room, board, and activity and health fees. Day students are required to pay tuition and fees of $9580 for the academic year. Figures are not available yet for the 2000–01 academic year.

Financial Aid

All degree candidates are eligible to apply for financial assistance. Grants and scholarships ranging from $200 to $4000 per year are awarded on a first-come, first-served basis. Federal Perkins Loans may be obtained. Full scholarships are also awarded for academic or athletic achievement. Through the Federal Work-Study Program, a student can earn up to $1500 in an academic year by working on campus not more than 15 hours a week. Applicants should contact the director of financial aid at Virginia Union University for additional information.

Faculty

Students often name VUU's international and multiracial faculty as the University's top advantage. The size of the faculty allows for a personalized approach with students, as reflected by the favorable student-faculty ratio of 16:1. The commitment of faculty members is demonstrated by their willingness to help students through extra tutoring, their efforts to build rapport by inviting discussion groups into their homes, and their continual updating of courses.

Student Government

The Student Government Association recognizes the suggestions of each student and acts as the voice of student opinion. The University pays serious attention to this voice, which helps it to keep its programs moving in a relevant direction.

Admission Requirements

Superior students as well as those students who, despite cultural deprivation and limited finances, show the necessary potential are actively sought throughout the country. Freshman applicants should take the SAT I no earlier than March of the junior year and no later than March of the senior year. An applicant's high school guidance counselor should send a certified academic record showing units, grades, and rank in the graduating class. Transfer students should request that a complete transcript of their college academic program be sent to VUU's Office of Admissions. The status of the transferring student and the validation of transferred credits are determined after a semester's attendance. Students who have earned satisfactory scores on the General Educational Development test or a comparable test administered by a recognized examining agency are in a good position to be considered for admission. A personal interview is not necessary for admission, but prospective students are encouraged to visit the campus.

Application and Information

Prospective students are urged to apply early, no later than June 15 for the fall semester, December 1 for the spring semester, or May 1 for the summer session. A student seeking admission should contact the Office of Admissions for an application form. The completed application and a $25 fee should be returned to the Office of Admissions. Notification concerning admission is sent to the student as soon as possible after all records are evaluated.

Gil M. Powell
Director of Admissions
Virginia Union University
1500 North Lombardy Street
Richmond, Virginia 23220

Telephone: 800-368-3227 (toll-free)
E-mail: gpowell@vuu.edu
World Wide Web: http://www.admissions@vuu.edu

Virginia Union's mix of traditional and contemporary architectural styles is representative of the University's blending of classical studies with experiential learning opportunities.

VIRGINIA WESLEYAN COLLEGE
NORFOLK/VIRGINIA BEACH, VIRGINIA

The College

Virginia Wesleyan College is a community of scholars who strongly believe that education is the key to achieving life's goals and that the environment in which learning takes place makes all the difference in reaching these goals. The expansive 300-acre campus of this coeducational four-year college of liberal arts and sciences is designed to provide every opportunity to live and learn in an energetic, value-centered academic climate. Affiliated with the United Methodist Church and accredited by the Commission on Colleges of the Southern Association of Colleges and Schools, the College maintains a diverse student body and a low student-faculty ratio.

Students come to Virginia Wesleyan from more than thirty states and twenty countries and indicate that they are attracted to the College primarily because of its size, the high quality of its academic program, its location, and its friendly atmosphere.

Virginia Wesleyan seeks to attract students who can take advantage of the College's commitment to innovation, relevance, and involvement. Students who desire a strong, individualized academic program, who want the opportunity to study matters of concern to them in a key East Coast area, who have the ability to assume responsibility for their education, and who want to be involved with their colleagues and professors in creating a vital educational experience find a receptive environment.

Students at Virginia Wesleyan may choose from more than sixty-five on-campus extracurricular activities. Prospective students are encouraged to contact the Office of Admissions or visit the College Web site for further information about clubs, organizations, and sports that exist at the College.

Location

Located in one of the fastest-growing metropolitan areas in the country, Virginia Wesleyan extends its boundaries from the Norfolk/Virginia Beach area to cities and countries around the world. Students attend classes on the quiet, spacious, and wooded campus and practice the theoretical in domestic and international businesses and organizations located in the five cities of the Tidewater region. Possibilities for internships are almost endless, as are cultural and recreational opportunities. Virginia Wesleyan has several partners in education in the surrounding areas, including Norfolk Southern Corporation, the North Atlantic Treaty Organization (NATO) Atlantic Command, the Chesapeake Bay Foundation, and the Red Cross. Students can benefit by connecting with these partners during their four years at the College and apply what they have learned in the classroom.

The College is just 15 minutes west of the Virginia Beach resort area and 10 minutes east of downtown Norfolk, a center of trade and commerce. Historic Jamestown and Colonial Williamsburg are 45 minutes away, the state capital at Richmond is 2 hours from the campus, and Washington, D.C., is just a 3-hour drive.

Majors and Degrees

A Bachelor of Arts degree is awarded in the following fields: accounting, American studies, art, art education, biology, business, chemistry, communications, computer science, criminal justice, economics, elementary education, English, French, German, history, human services, international studies, journalism, management, mathematics, middle school education, modern foreign languages, music, music education, philosophy, political science, psychology, recreation/leisure studies, religious studies, secondary education, social ecology, sociology, and theater. The College offers preprofessional programs in dentistry, law, medicine, the ministry, pharmacology, physical therapy, teaching, and veterinary science, as well as preparation for graduate school in other major fields of study. A state-approved teacher education program leads to certification for teaching in elementary, middle, and secondary schools.

Academic Program

The College offers a liberal arts curriculum that is designed to allow students considerable freedom in planning their own program yet also ensures that they acquire not only the breadth of knowledge traditionally emphasized in a liberal education but also a sound foundation in a specific field.

A challenging honors program, in which students compete for full scholarships, is offered each year.

The academic calendar is on the 4-1-4 plan, featuring a one-course term in January when students can take special-topic courses, traditional and interdisciplinary courses, and travel-study courses in the United States and abroad. They can also participate in off-campus internships, field study programs, independent study, and senior projects. The College offers study-abroad programs in a number of countries.

A personalized faculty and peer advising system is the cornerstone of the College's transition programs. Freshman Seminar assists students in adjusting to college life, and the Senior Integrative Experience helps students progress to life after graduation. The College also offers services ranging from tutoring to individualized programs for students with special needs through the Learning Resources Center.

Academic Facilities

The Henry Clay Hofheimer II Library is an imposing building of modern design that appropriately sits at the center of the campus. This award-winning building has a growing collection of more than 110,000 volumes. The science building has well-equipped laboratories, classrooms, and a computer center serving the needs of the College's academic offerings in biology, chemistry, computer science, mathematics, and physics. Additional facilities include the Fine Arts Center and Hofheimer Laboratory Theatre, the Campus Dining Center, the Center for the Humanities, Monumental Chapel, academic villages I, II, and III, and Cunningham Gymnasium. Recent additions to the campus include a state-of-the-art academic center and an administration building. The College is currently building an $18.5-million student center. The expected date of completion is fall 2001.

Costs

College fees for 2000–01 total $20,800. This figure includes tuition and room and board. Approximately $450 to $650 pays for a student's books if he or she buys them new.

Financial Aid

The College believes that no student who wishes to attend Virginia Wesleyan College should be denied the opportunity because of limited financial resources. The director of financial aid is available to counsel students and their families regarding financial planning. In cases of demonstrated financial need, students may qualify for grants, low-interest loans, and work-study. Financial need is determined by an analysis of the Free Application for Federal Student Aid (FAFSA). March 1 is the mailing deadline for applying for financial assistance. The College also offers merit scholarships, without regard to need, to entering students with outstanding academic records. Scholarships ranging from $4000 to full comprehensive fees (over four years) are awarded to students based on their test scores, academic record, interviews, and essays. Leadership Scholarships from $4000 to $24,000 are available to students with demonstrated leadership abilities as evidenced through community service, extracurricular participation, and volunteerism. Special deadlines may apply. Students who think they may qualify should contact the Office of Admissions and Financial Aid.

Faculty

At the heart of any educational program are the persons who teach. The College has purposely recruited faculty members who have a primary interest in and commitment to classroom teaching. All together, the faculty have earned degrees from more than eighty separate colleges and universities. The richness of this educational experience is inevitably felt in their influence at Virginia Wesleyan.

Student Government

The Student Association offers every full-time student the opportunity to take full advantage of the College governance for academic, cocurricular, and administrative affairs. The Student Association provides an effective means to participate in all areas of student life. Student government is merely one of the more than sixty-five on-campus extracurricular activities from which students may choose.

Admission Requirements

The College places primary emphasis on the applicant's secondary school record, scores on the SAT I or ACT, the secondary school counselor's recommendation, personal characteristics, and evidence of leadership and involvement in extracurricular activities. Admission to the College is competitive. Admission decisions are made on a rolling basis.

In administering its admission policies, educational policies, financial aid programs, athletics, and other College programs and policies, Virginia Wesleyan does not discriminate on the basis of race, color, religion, national or ethnic origin, handicap, or sex.

Application and Information

Additional information can be obtained by contacting:

Office of Admissions and Financial Aid
Virginia Wesleyan College
1584 Wesleyan Drive
Norfolk/Virginia Beach, Virginia 23502-5599
Telephone: 757-455-3208
                 800-737-8684 (toll-free)
Fax: 757-461-5238
E-mail: admissions@vwc.edu
World Wide Web: http://www.vwc.edu

Students enjoy the moderate climate and safe environment year-round.

VITERBO UNIVERSITY
LA CROSSE, WISCONSIN

The University

Viterbo University is a four-year liberal arts university with a strong curriculum and a tradition of personalized instruction. Although the University was founded more than a century ago by the Franciscan Sisters of Perpetual Adoration, the student body of 1,800 men and women represents a variety of faiths and denominations. Viterbo excels in providing students with a rigorous and challenging educational experience, combined with a warm, nurturing environment for learning. The University is fully accredited by the American Dietetic Association, National Association of Schools of Music, National Council for Accreditation of Teacher Education, National League for Nursing Accrediting Commission, North Central Association of Colleges and Schools, the Wisconsin State Board of Nursing, and the American Chemical Society.

Students have many opportunities to participate in activities outside the classroom. Viterbo offers a program of NAIA Division II intercollegiate competition for both men and women. The women's program includes basketball, soccer, softball, and volleyball; the men's program consists of baseball, basketball, and soccer. There are intramural sports for relaxation and exercise. Viterbo has outdoor tennis courts on campus. In addition to enjoying special events and year-round campuswide events, students can join a number of special interest clubs, participate in student government, and get involved with the student newspaper, the *Lumen,* or the fine arts publication, *Touchstone.*

Students at Viterbo are encouraged to explore new experiences that may not be related to their field of study but help enrich their university experience. Students direct and perform in student-written plays, exhibit their work in the art gallery, and plan campus events such as Survival Weekend and Courtyard Carnival. In addition, there are student-sponsored films, live entertainment, theme dances, and other purely social functions occurring throughout the year.

Although Viterbo has a long history and tradition, many of the facilities on campus are new. The student union, which contains a complete university bookstore, the Crossroads Café, and a game room, provides a sunlit place for students to socialize and relax. The University also has a 100,000-volume-capacity library; a modern Student Activity Center with racquetball courts and fully equipped weight and fitness rooms; and a magnificent Fine Arts Center that each year hosts such internationally acclaimed entertainers as Ray Charles, Bill Cosby, and the Houston Symphony Orchestra, among others. Throughout the academic year, students find opportunities to attend a wide variety of concerts, plays, artists' receptions, and exhibits. The Fine Arts Center contains a spacious main theater, recital hall, experimental theater, art gallery, photography darkroom, fine arts library, and private practice rooms for music students.

Career Services and Internships provides a full range of resources for career planning, job placement, and graduate studies. It also helps students to draft resumes, sharpen interview skills, and provide important connections with professionals who can help graduates find the inside track for jobs. The Campus Ministry Center, Damiano House, is available for study, meetings, prayer, and relaxation. Campus ministers are available to students of every religious denomination to assist in their personal growth, to provide counsel, or even to help prepare for marriage. The student counseling office and student health office, staffed by professional personnel, are located in the student residence complex. In addition, one of the area's largest hospitals, the Franciscan Skemp Medical Center, part of the Mayo Health System, is located less than a block away.

Master's degree programs are available. Significant numbers of Master of Arts in Education and Master of Science in Nursing degrees are conferred annually.

Viterbo has four on-campus dormitory units, two of which are apartment complexes that offer apartment-style living. Dormitory life offers security, convenience, and easy access to campus facilities. Private telephones, laundry and kitchen facilities, snack bars, and private study rooms are a few of the homelike amenities available.

Location

Viterbo is located in La Crosse, Wisconsin, which was voted "Number One Small City in America" for its scenic setting, low crime rate, and year-round recreational and cultural activities. The campus lies between the Mississippi River to the west and high scenic bluffs to the east. La Crosse has sailing, swimming, canoeing, sandy beaches, and hiking trails that wind up through the high bluffs. With Mount La Crosse nearby, winter skiing, both downhill and cross-country, is a popular outdoor pastime. Downtown La Crosse has stores, theaters, art galleries, and fine restaurants, all located within easy walking distance of the Viterbo campus.

Majors and Degrees

There are thirty-eight majors and twenty-six minors offered. Viterbo University awards the Bachelor of Arts degree with majors in biology, chemistry, English, ministry, religious studies, sociology, Spanish, studio art, and theater. Students can also earn the degrees of Bachelor of Art Education, Bachelor of Integrated Studies, and Bachelor of Liberal Studies. Bachelor of Music majors are available in applied music performance, music education, and music pedagogy. Bachelor of Fine Arts degrees are conferred in arts administration, graphic design, music theater, studio art, and theater.

Bachelor of Science degrees are offered in biology, broad-field social studies, chemistry, computer information systems education, criminal justice, English, interdepartmental biology/chemistry, mathematics, organizational management, psychology, religious studies, social work, sociology, and theater education. Students may also earn Bachelor of Business Administration degrees with specialization in accounting, computer information systems, health-care administration, human resource development, management, and marketing. Bachelor of Science in Education degrees are available in elementary, middle, or secondary education. In addition, Viterbo confers Bachelor of Science degrees in nursing and Bachelor of Science degrees in community–medical dietetics. There is a wide range of preprofessional programs available, including chemical engineering, dentistry, law, medicine, and veterinary science.

Academic Program

Viterbo offers both an excellent and well-rounded educational foundation and specialized career training to prepare students for a changing world. There are programs in the arts, business, education, health sciences, humanities, and sciences. A minimum of 128 credits is required for graduation. Viterbo has a consistently high job placement rate for graduating seniors (95 percent) plus a career planning and internship program that gives students an opportunity to work in positions related to their field of interest. Viterbo makes available excellent career-testing, employment-preparation, and career-planning services for all its students.

Academic Facilities

Viterbo has a variety of academic facilities. The Learning Center offers free tutorial assistance in specific courses as well as general assistance with the basic skills necessary for academic success. The Learning Center has audiovisual equipment for use with self-instructional materials and a highly trained staff available to accommodate all the academic and personal needs of students. The Viterbo Media Center provides a setting for individual study with audiovisual aids. There is also a small facility where instructional materials such as color slides, transparencies, and graphic materials can be produced for a nominal fee.

At Viterbo, the student-computer ratio is 1:7. Students receive Web-based e-mail accounts that are accessible anywhere on campus or off, making it easier for students to communicate with family, friends, and professors. In addition to the holdings of the expanded University library, Viterbo students have access to the Health Sciences Library at Franciscan Skemp Medical Center, which serves the medical, dental, and nursing staffs. The Brophy Nursing Center, across the street from the medical center, is the center for health sciences. It contains laboratories, lecture and seminar rooms, and a student lounge and study. Murphy Center is the central administrative complex for the University and contains the media center, computer center, science labs, and classrooms.

Costs

Tuition for the 2000–01 academic year is $12,770. Other fees total $280. Room and board are $4530. Viterbo estimates that an additional $450 is needed to cover the cost of books and personal expenses.

Financial Aid

More than 90 percent of all Viterbo students receive financial aid for educational costs. Some type of financial aid package is guaranteed to students who apply before the March 15 deadline. In addition to numerous scholarships and need-based grants, there are student loan programs as well as a generous offering of student work-study jobs on campus for up to 20 hours a week during the regular academic year and 40 hours a week during the summer.

Faculty

Viterbo has 92 full-time faculty members and 65 part-time faculty members. The faculty is primarily a teaching faculty, although many continue their own research while teaching. Faculty members also serve as advisers to students majoring in their field of study. Of the 92 full-time faculty members, almost half hold either a Ph.D. or another terminal degree in their field. The student-faculty ratio is 14:1, and the small, intimate classes provide a supportive atmosphere for personal growth and development.

Student Government

Viterbo students are represented in the University plan of governance through the Student Representative Assembly (SRA). There are student class representatives as well as a student activities board that plans and coordinates student-life events on campus. Students are represented on the University planning committee, the curriculum development committee, and the committee for athletics and recreation. One student representative is involved with admission and recruitment, and 3 sit on the financial aid and scholarship committee. There is also a student publications board representative and 4 students on the University reconciliation board.

Viterbo planning bodies are very open to student representation. Students are encouraged to participate in every realm of University affairs, and SRA representatives are an important component of every major group or committee on campus.

Admission Requirements

Admission to Viterbo University is moderately difficult. Students generally rank in the top half of their assessed class—that is, in the top half of the ACT or SAT I score range or the top half of their high school class. The University recommends 3 years of high school mathematics and science and some study of a foreign language. Transfer students must have a minimum 2.0 grade point average. Although members of minority groups currently represent only 4 percent of the student body, the University is actively seeking to achieve a larger representation. In some cases, such as in the fine arts, a candidate's special talents are taken into consideration by the admission office. Recruitment is primarily through school visits and high school fairs. An on-campus interview is not required except in special cases.

Application and Information

To apply, students must submit an application, high school transcripts, and ACT or SAT I scores. The deadline for an application for the fall semester is August 15. The priority deadline for students seeking financial assistance is March 15. Students can expect to be notified within two weeks of application.

For further information, students are encouraged to contact:

Dr. Roland Nelson, Director of Admissions
Viterbo University
815 South 9th Street
La Crosse, Wisconsin 54601
Telephone: 608-796-3010
        800-848-3726 (800-VITERBO) (toll-free)
Fax: 608-796-3020
E-mail: admission@viterbo.edu
World Wide Web: http://www.viterbo.edu

VOORHEES COLLEGE
DENMARK, SOUTH CAROLINA

The College

Voorhees College was established in 1897 by a young black woman, Elizabeth Evelyn Wright. A former student of Booker T. Washington, Miss Wright, at 23, dreamed the seemingly impossible dream of starting a school for African-American youth in Denmark, South Carolina. The College's historic mission was to provide educational opportunities for young blacks in rural Bamberg County.

Today, Voorhees College, with an enrollment of almost 800 students, has evolved into a four-year liberal arts college with full accreditation by the Southern Association of Colleges and Schools. It is affiliated with the Episcopal Church and the College Fund/UNCF. The mission of the College remains the same—to educate the minds, hearts, and spirits of young African-American men and women.

Voorhees students participate in a variety of College-sponsored activities, including four national fraternities and four national sororities; two campus publications; theater and drama productions; intramural sports; ethnic, political, and religious organizations; honor, service, and leadership societies; the Voorhees College Concert Choir; the Student Government Association; and special interest groups.

The Voorhees College Tigers participate in the Eastern Intercollegiate Athletic Conference of the NAIA Division I in men's baseball, women's softball and volleyball, and men's and women's basketball and cross-country.

The College's buildings represent a pleasant combination of turn-of-the-century and contemporary architecture. Eight of the campus buildings comprise a Historic District and are listed on the National Register of Historic Places. The significance of the district lies not only in the building styles but also in the fact that many of the buildings were built solely by students at the school. The most recent addition to the campus is the Leonard E. Dawson Health and Human Resources Center, which houses a 2,200-seat arena, a student center, a snack bar, a swimming pool, a weight room, a dance studio, classrooms, and offices. In addition, a Humanities, Education and Fine Arts Center housing an art studio, a music hall, practice rooms, classrooms, faculty offices, and a model teacher education lab, is open. A track and field complex has also been completed.

Location

Situated in the midlands of South Carolina, Voorhees is located 1½ miles from the town of Denmark, South Carolina, on a well-landscaped 350-acre campus. Denmark is the home of approximately 4,500 residents. The campus is accessible by bus, train, and airline. The College's closest metropolitan neighbor is Columbia, the state's capital and largest city, which is approximately 50 miles north. The historic seaport of Charleston is 86 miles to the east of the campus.

Majors and Degrees

The Bachelor of Science (B.S.) and Bachelor of Arts (B.A.) degrees are awarded in accounting, biology, business administration, computer science, criminal justice, early childhood education, elementary education, English, English education, health and recreation, mathematics, mathematics education, organizational management, physical education, political science, and sociology. The degree in organizational management can only be earned through the Voorhees College Management Institute.

Preprofessional programs in engineering, law, medicine, and nursing are also available. Voorhees offers two joint degree programs—one in engineering with Clemson University and one in law with St. John's University in New York.

Academic Program

A student must satisfactorily complete a minimum of 122 semester hours of course work with a minimum cumulative grade point average of 2.0 (on a 4.0 scale) to be eligible for a Voorhees College bachelor's degree. Fifty-five semester hours of General Education Requirements are required of all students, regardless of their major(s). The College does not require a minor for graduation.

The College has established special programs to meet the academic needs and interests of its students: The Honors Program, The Academic Achievement Center, The Cooperative Education Program, and a ROTC program held in cooperation with South Carolina State University.

The College operates on a two-semester calendar, consisting of a fall semester and a spring semester, each lasting sixteen weeks. The fall semester begins in August and ends in mid-December; the spring semester begins in early January and ends in early May, with a nine-day spring break at Easter. The College's summer session consists of one 6-week term. During the fall and spring semesters, the normal class load ranges from 15 to 19 hours; for the summer session, 9 hours is the maximum.

Academic Facilities

Twenty-three buildings are located on the campus and are used for classrooms, faculty offices, administrative offices, student services, academic support programs, and cultural, recreational, and religious activities as well as residential living.

The Wright-Potts Library is a contemporary two-story facility located in the center of the campus. It contains more than 100,000 volumes supplemented by 431 periodicals. The collection also includes newspaper subscriptions, phonograph records, microfiche, tape cassettes, filmstrips, and video tapes.

The Academic Computing Center consists of three computer laboratories—two PC labs and one Macintosh lab. The College is fully networked and on line.

Costs

For the 1999–2000 academic year, tuition and fees were $5860, room charges were $1860 and board charges were $1330. The total cost for a full-time residential student was $9050. Fees are subject to change each year.

Financial Aid

Voorhees College's financial aid program includes College, state, and federal grants, scholarships, and loans. Students eligible for financial aid must be accepted for admission to Voorhees and apply in a timely manner. Parents are encouraged to file the appropriate tax forms early. Residents of the state of South Carolina are encouraged to file early for the South Carolina Tuition Grant. The application deadline for new freshmen is June 30. Approximately 97 percent of Voorhees students receive some form of financial assistance.

Faculty

The College's faculty is composed of 34 full-time faculty members and a number of part-time and adjunct faculty members who serve the College's Evening and Saturday College. Sixty-eight percent of the faculty members have earned doctorates. The faculty is in compliance with the accrediting body's criteria for scholarly preparation. The student-faculty ratio is 17:1.

Student Government

The Student Government Association is the official governing body of the Voorhees College student body. It is organized and operates under a constitution and bylaws outlined in the *Student Handbook*. Student representation is included on many standing committees of the College.

Admission Requirements

Voorhees College values diversity among its student body and encourages applications from qualified students who come from a wide variety of cultural and socioeconomic backgrounds. The College accepts students who have graduated from accredited high schools or passed the GED. Admission is open to all students who are interested in and can benefit from the College's program offerings. Transfer students are accepted if they are in good academic standing with the last college in which they were enrolled. Scores on the SAT I or ACT are strongly recommended for all new students.

Qualified applicants are admitted without regard to race, color, creed, national origin, sex, or physical handicap.

Application and Information

Voorhees College operates on a rolling admissions policy; therefore, students are accepted until the last day of the registration period. The application for admission, along with a $25 nonrefundable fee, should be accompanied by official high school and/or college transcripts, SAT I and/or ACT scores, two letters of recommendation, a transfer confidential form (transfer students only), and a medical form.

For additional information, students are encouraged to contact:

Director of Admissions and Records
Voorhees College
Mass Hall, Room 102
P.O. Box 678
Denmark, South Carolina 29042-0678
Telephone: 803-703-7111
        800-446-6250 (toll-free)
Fax: 803-793-1117
E-mail: elfphi@voorhees.edu
World Wide Web: http://www.voorhees.edu

WAGNER COLLEGE
STATEN ISLAND, NEW YORK

The College

Wagner College is a four-year residential college with a strong tradition in the liberal arts. This structure is fairly standard among established colleges, but Wagner only starts there. Wagner's proximity to Manhattan (a free 25-minute ferry ride away) enlarges the campus and the opportunities available to students. Wagner students make the connection to New York City's resources beginning in the fall of their freshman year. During their first semester, freshmen are involved in field experiences that are related to two of their academic courses. Upperclass mentorships and internships are available to Wagner students in many of Manhattan's most prestigious companies and cultural organizations during the entire year. The College's large and supportive alumni base in the greater New York area makes identifying an internship or a job after graduation much more possible at Wagner than at institutions located in rural, distant settings. At Wagner, they take "learning by doing" to new heights.

Wagner enrolls approximately 1,650 undergraduate and 350 graduate students from throughout the United States and twenty other countries. Students choose Wagner because it offers superb access to exceptional professional and cultural opportunities within a traditional college setting.

About 70 percent of Wagner undergraduates live on campus. The College has three residence halls overlooking New York Harbor. Wagner has a full array of activities and social events, many of which are planned by the student-life staff. These activities include clubs, twelve fraternities and sororities, concerts, trips, and athletics. The College has outstanding athletic programs, including NCAA Division I standing in seventeen areas, a variety of intramural sports, and an excellent coaching staff.

In addition to undergraduate programs, Wagner offers master's degree programs in business administration (M.B.A.), education, microbiology, and nursing.

Location

Wagner's location offers students the best of both worlds. Living on a wooded, countrylike campus 35 minutes from Manhattan has distinct advantages. The 105-acre campus overlooks New York Harbor and the spectacular Manhattan skyline. Students enjoy living in the beautiful Grymes Hill section of Staten Island and the proximity to the resources of Manhattan, which are easily accessible by bus, ferry, or car. Wagner has much to offer students who want the benefits of an education in New York City but who also wish to pursue their studies in a classic suburban college setting.

Majors and Degrees

Wagner College offers the Bachelor of Arts, Bachelor of Science, and Bachelor of Science in Education. Undergraduate majors and fields of concentration are in accounting, art, arts administration, biology, business administration, chemistry, computer applications, elementary education, English, family studies/social work, foreign languages (French, German, and Spanish), history, international affairs, mathematics, microbiology, music, nursing, philosophy, physician assistant studies, physics, political science, psychology, public policy and administration, religious studies, sociology and anthropology, and theater.

Academic Program

Wagner's undergraduate program is designed to provide a broad education in the liberal arts and in-depth study in one major subject. At Wagner, students can study in thirty-two majors, twenty-four minors, and eight professional programs. As part of the requirements for graduation, students must also complete three Learning Communities (LC): one in their freshman year, one in either sophomore or junior year, and the final in the senior year. At Wagner, Learning Communities consist of three courses that are linked by a simple theme and share a common set of students. The LCs are directly linked to field experiences based on the theme of the Learning Community. Freshman spend time throughout the semester at the designated site observing the organization, its practices, and its dynamics. Seniors are involved in a full-semester internship at an organization connected to their major field of study.

Each candidate is required to complete 36 units for the baccalaureate degree. Students must elect a major as part of their studies, and each student is further required to demonstrate proficiency in spoken and written English. All students in both the freshman and senior years will be involved in on-site experiences linked to interdisciplinary course work. The academic year is divided into the fall semester (September to December) and the spring semester (January to May). Students may also enroll in one of several summer sessions.

Wagner College provides advanced placement and advanced credit standing in general subjects for entering and current students who qualify. Qualification is determined by means of the Advanced Placement examinations.

Off-Campus Arrangements

Wagner College is a member of the prestigious Institute for the International Education of Students program (IES), which is the nation's oldest and most selective study-abroad program. Interested and qualified Wagner students may choose among semester, summer, and vacation study-abroad programs in such diverse urban-based centers as Beijing, Berlin, Canberra, Dublin, LaPlata, London, Madrid, Paris, Tokyo, and Vienna. Classes are taught through a combination approach in which U.S. students take classes designed expressly for them as well as classes run by universities located within the host city, integrating the U.S. students with students from that nation.

Academic Facilities

In addition to its mainframe computer lab, Wagner maintains a student laboratory for learning the professional applications of personal computer technology. Equipped with current generation IBM Pentium PCs, Mac and UNIX labs, the Spiro Center offers training in word processing and business/financial programs, including database management and financial spreadsheets. Other applications include scientific research methods and computer-aided design. Internet, e-mail, and voice mail are provided free to all students and can be accessed in all residence hall rooms, classrooms, and offices throughout the College.

Wagner's recently updated science center includes two electron microscopes and a fully functioning planetarium. College facilities also include a theater, art gallery, language laboratory, and a new sports and fitness center.

The Horrmann Library houses approximately 310,000 bound volumes as well as 1,000 titles in its periodical collection. The library is a member of the New York Metropolitan Reference and Research Library Agency, which provides access to more than 25 million volumes in the area.

Costs
Tuition for the 1999–2000 academic year was $18,000. Room and board for the academic year were $6500.

Financial Aid
More than 70 percent of Wagner students receive some kind of financial aid. In addition to the availability of state and federal aid programs, the College itself is a source of more than $8 million in student aid each year. Counselors are available to assist in completing the Financial Aid Form.

Faculty
Because of its commitment to academic excellence, Wagner has always drawn gifted faculty. Ninety-five percent of the full-time teachers hold a doctoral degree or the equivalent in their field. Many have published books and articles, and a large number have a combination of in-depth experience and academic qualifications. The faculty member-student relationship is a close one based on mutual respect. Because faculty members are concerned about their students' intellectual and personal growth, they participate in all areas of College life. All faculty members regard New York City as an incomparable resource for course work and field experience. The student-faculty ratio is 14:1.

Student Government
The Wagner College Student Government is democratically elected by the undergraduate student body. The government has legislative and judicial responsibilities. Students have numerous opportunities for involvement in organizations, special interest groups, and committees. Activities and events are planned by students with the assistance of the director of student activities.

Admission Requirements
Admission to Wagner is based primarily on academic ability. The admission committee also considers personal qualities that, in the College's view, enable a student to take maximum advantage of what Wagner has to offer and to contribute to the quality of campus life.

The applicant is assessed on the basis of high school achievement, class rank, and recommendations of the guidance counselor or academic teacher. In addition, the student's citizenship record (participation in extracurricular, community, or religious activities) and character record (including information derived from the recommendations) are reviewed. A personal interview is optional. Scores on the SAT I or ACT are required, and SAT II: Subject Tests are recommended. None of these factors is considered in isolation; all are weighed together so that a clear picture of the applicant and his or her chances for success at Wagner emerge.

Students considering Wagner should have completed a minimum of 18 units in the following academic areas: English, 4; history, 3; mathematics, 3; foreign language, 2; and science, 2. Four additional units from the following list of electives are recommended: art, 1; computer science, 1; foreign language, 2–4; history, 1–3; mathematics, 1–3; music, 1–2; natural sciences, 1–3; religion, 1; and social studies, 1–2.

Application and Information
Application should be made early in the senior year of high school. In addition to the completed application form and the nonrefundable fee, students are responsible for forwarding a secondary school transcript, two letters of recommendation, and SAT I or ACT scores to the Admissions Office. The early decision application deadline is December 1.

Candidates are urged, whenever possible, to make an appointment with the Admissions Office to visit the campus and discuss their plans and goals with a member of the admission staff. They are also encouraged to talk with currently enrolled Wagner students. Arrangements can be made for candidates to meet with faculty members in departments of particular interest.

Further information may be obtained by contacting:
Angelo Araimo
Dean of Admissions
Wagner College
1 Campus Road
Staten Island, New York 10301
Telephone: 718-390-3411
              800-221-1010 (toll-free outside New York)
Fax: 718-390-3105
E-mail: admissions@wagner.edu
World Wide Web: http://www.wagner.edu

Wagner students on the Oval in front of Main Hall.

WALSH UNIVERSITY
NORTH CANTON, OHIO

The University

Walsh University was founded in 1958 by the Brothers of Christian Instruction and is one of northeastern Ohio's finest liberal arts and sciences universities. As a coeducational and Catholic institution of higher education, Walsh emphasizes values-based education with an international perspective in the Judeo-Christian tradition. With approximately 1,600 students and 125 faculty members of full-time, part-time, and adjunct status, the University promotes academic excellence, a diverse community, and close student-faculty interaction. Its tree-lined campus encompasses ten separate buildings and 100 acres.

Students of Walsh pursue studies within more than forty academic majors and four graduate degree programs, all of which emphasize critical thinking, effective communication, and spiritual growth. Approximately 30 percent of Walsh's students are nontraditional; many are international. The traditional student population approaches 1,000, most of whom reside in four modern residence halls on campus.

Active and involved with campus and community life, Walsh students give back to others through various service projects both on and off campus with student organizations that help them cultivate leadership skills. Walsh encourages students to participate in intramural and intercollegiate athletics, including football, and academic clubs such as the Business Club, the Pre-Law Society, the student newspaper, and the forensics team.

Walsh University is accredited by the North Central Association of Colleges and Schools and is a member of the Ohio College Association, the National Association of Independent Colleges and Universities, and the Association of Catholic Colleges and Universities.

Location

Walsh University is conveniently located and easily accessible—only three miles from Ohio Interstate 77—in North Canton, a pleasant residential suburban area near Canton. Canton itself, which is about five miles from the Walsh campus, is a city of about 84,000 that offers a wide array of cultural, recreational, and athletic activities. Home of the Professional Football Hall of Fame and the President McKinley National Memorial, the city also has a symphony orchestra, an art institute, a civic opera, a theater guild, and ballet. A number of major manufacturers are headquartered in Stark County, including the Hoover Company, the Timken Company, and Diebold, Inc.

Just 20 miles north of campus is Akron, and Cleveland is within an hour's drive. The Akron-Canton Regional Airport, just north of campus on Interstate 77, serves the Canton-Stark County area, as do Amtrack trains and Greyhound buses.

Majors and Degrees

Walsh University offers business administration, general liberal arts, honors, international studies, preprofessional studies, and teacher preparation programs. It awards the Bachelor of Arts and Bachelor of Sciences degrees in accounting (general and specialized CPA tracks); biology; chemistry; clinical laboratory science; communication; comprehensive science; computer science; corporate communications; early childhood, elementary, comprehensive secondary, secondary, and special education; English; finance; French; general business; history; Latin American business studies; management; marketing; mathematics; nursing; pastoral ministry; philosophy/theology; physical education; political science; psychology; sociology; and Spanish. In addition, Walsh offers the Associate of Arts degree in accounting, finance, human services, liberal arts, management, and marketing.

Walsh offers preprofessional programs in dentistry, law, medicine, natural resources, physical therapy, podiatry, and veterinary science. Each is developed within the context of a regular academic major so that, for example, students enrolled in the University's B.S./M.A. program can earn a bachelor's degree in behavioral science and a master's degree in counseling and human development in 5½ years. Under an affiliation with Case Western Reserve University (CWRU) Walsh's program in dentistry leads to a B.S. from Walsh and a D.D.S. from CWRU.

Academic Program

The University promotes six basic values through its academic program: respect for self, others, and the environment; hospitality; service; integrity; an ethical approach to decision making; and excellence in the teaching-learning process.

Designed for academically gifted students, the honors program offers students the challenges they demand to achieve academic excellence. Honors students take advantage of such offerings as special seminars, independent studies, internships, and research projects.

The University's broad liberal arts base supports all its academic programs. About half of a student's program of study is within the liberal arts. The University's core curriculum is composed of an interdisciplinary foundation course and thematic clusters of courses. In the first, students learn the rigors of interdisciplinary study by examining different topics from a range of perspectives, such as art, literature, science, and technology. Clusters of courses include five coordinated elective courses that center on themes such as Shaping Civilization or the Environment. These courses help students examine how an issue is shaped by many factors.

The rest of a student's academic program is comprised of courses within a major field of study and elective courses. Major course work constitutes one fourth of a student's studies and helps students prepare for their careers. Elective courses, which constitute the remaining fourth of a student's program of study, enable students to develop personal interests, take more courses within their major field, or take additional core courses. The University encourages students to give careful thought to selecting a program of study and a major. Students can wait until the beginning of the junior year to choose their major and still complete all requirements to finish their program in four years. While many students select a double major as a way to improve their career opportunities after graduation, the design of individual programs requires consultation with a faculty adviser and a department head. To earn a bachelor's degree, students must successfully complete 130 semester hours.

The University's Intensive Degree Experience for Adult Learners (I.D.E.A.L.) program is an academic program targeted toward working adults who have earned college credits and who wish to earn their bachelor's degrees in an accelerated format. Classes are scheduled on nights and weekends to accommodate busy schedules. By taking these classes and earning credits for both past college work and for life experiences, I.D.E.A.L. students complete work for bachelor's degrees at a quicker pace than students in traditionally designed college programs.

Academic Facilities

The Walsh library has 130,000 volumes, 750 current periodical subscriptions on paper, 400 current full-text periodical subscriptions on CD-ROM, and a substantial microfilm and audiovisual collection. Online databases include those provided by OCLC, and specialized databases include Dialog, CompuServe, FirstSearch, PRISM, ProQuest, and EPIC.

Faculty

Walsh University fosters close working relationships between the faculty members and students. Beyond classroom teaching, faculty members serve as student counselors and tutors and take on roles as advisers for student organizations on campus. Composed of those with full-time, part-time, and adjunct appointments, the Walsh faculty numbers approximately 125; the majority of full-time faculty members hold terminal degrees in their fields.

Student Government

The Walsh University Student Government provides capable, responsible student government; fosters student involvement in the governance of the University; serves as a forum of student opinion; and functions as a liaison between students, administration, and faculty and staff members. It is composed of executive, legislative, and judicial branches, and among its many responsibilities is to plan student activities and campus community projects with the student affairs staff.

Costs

Tuition and fees for the academic year are $12,500 ($405 per credit hour), plus an $11 per-credit-hour general fee. Room and board charges are $5600 per year. Books and personal expenses cost an estimated $500 to $700 for the year. The University reserves the right to change the cost structure without notice.

Financial Aid

The primary purpose of Walsh University's aid program is to assist deserving students who cannot otherwise meet the costs of a college education. Financial aid takes the form of scholarships, work-study awards, grants, or loans, depending upon the resources available. The University offers a number of scholarships that range from $1500 to full-tuition to deserving students, and the Walsh Alumni Association offers a host of scholarships as well. State and federal grants and loans are available to students, along with the University's work-study program, which offers work that is compatible with students' academic loads. Financial aid is awarded for one year and is renewable in subsequent years if the student shows a continuing need and maintains a creditable academic record.

Applicants for admission may apply for financial aid by submitting the Free Application for Federal Student Aid (FAFSA) and the University's financial aid form. To allow for timely notification of financial aid awards, the University recommends that the FAFSA be mailed by March 15 in order to receive full analysis by May 1. Prospective students may obtain a FAFSA from their high school guidance counselors or from the University's financial aid office. The Walsh financial aid form is available from both the financial aid and admissions offices of the University.

Admissions Requirements

Students seeking admission to Walsh University must submit scores from the SAT I or ACT. A rolling admission policy is in effect, and students may enter at the beginning of each semester.

Walsh grants credit for college-level work completed in high school and for credits earned through the College-Level Examination Program, and qualified high school juniors and seniors may enroll in courses for college credit under the University's post-secondary enrollment program. The University seeks a diverse student body and welcomes transfer students.

Application and Information

Early application is recommended. In addition to SAT I or ACT scores, a transcript of high school grades and a completed admission application form are required.

Interested students are encouraged to contact:

Brett Freshour
Dean of Enrollment Management
Walsh University
2020 Easton Street N.W.
North Canton, Ohio 44720-3396

Fax: 330-490-7165
E-mail: admissions@alex.walsh.edu
World Wide Web: http://www.walsh.edu

Walsh University bases its education on three core values: excellence, integrity, and service.

WARNER PACIFIC COLLEGE
PORTLAND, OREGON

The College

Warner Pacific College promotes excellence in its students and offers them an individualized education in a Christian context. To uphold this mission, the academic program provides experiences that integrate knowledge, attitude, and faith with meaningful relationships. The concept of a Christian liberal arts education does not discount the importance of practical experience or the need to translate theory into practice. In fact, as a Christ-centered college, Warner Pacific emphasizes careers and lifelong learning with faculty and staff members and administrators who seek to prepare men and women for Kingdom service in the next millennium. And unlike many colleges, Warner Pacific's graduates are distinguished not only by their academic prowess but also by their exemplary character, a quality much sought after by prospective employers.

Since its founding in 1937, Warner Pacific has developed a full range of liberal arts curricula. Today, more than twenty-three fields of undergraduate study are offered as well as a certificate in family life education and a Master of Religion degree program.

Students are challenged in the classroom and encouraged to develop leadership skills by participating in on-campus activities and completing internships with organizations scattered throughout the Portland metropolitan area. Applying theory to real life maximizes the learning experience. Stemming from the College's belief in the value of hands-on application and accountability, Warner Pacific impresses upon students the importance of a lifelong commitment to service, which is modeled after the life and teachings of Jesus Christ. Consequently, Warner students tutor young children, visit the elderly, work with the homeless, and participate in many other worthwhile projects. In addition, numerous study-abroad opportunities are available through Warner Pacific and the Coalition for Christian Colleges and Universities.

Life on the Warner Pacific campus reverberates with activity, including residence life events aimed at building community, intramurals, drama, the yearbook, online student newspaper, and music. Warner Pacific is a member of the National Association of Intercollegiate Athletics and the Cascade Collegiate Conference as well as the National Christian College Athletic Association. Women's sports include basketball, cross-country, and volleyball. Men compete in basketball, cross-country, and soccer. By becoming involved in the Warner Pacific community, students develop friendships that often last a lifetime.

Traditional residence hall and apartment living provide an incomparable experience to 272 students. Total enrollment exceeds 700 students, representing seventeen states, eight nations, and twenty-seven denominations.

Location

Warner Pacific's central location in the Pacific Northwest provides students with access to impressive natural wonders. Snow-capped mountains, rugged coastlines, and vast wilderness and park areas offer ample opportunities for skiing, biking, hiking, rock climbing, and walking. Besides the attraction of the surrounding scenery, Warner Pacific's prime location, just 15 minutes outside of the thriving Portland metropolitan area, affords students the opportunity to partake of flourishing centers of technology, commerce, and the arts. As a result, exciting internships abound. In addition, students enjoy gallery openings, the theater, dining in unusual restaurants, and attending concerts. Reliable bus and light-rail systems allow students to take full advantage of all the Pacific Northwest has to offer.

Majors and Degrees

Warner Pacific offers two associate degrees and two bachelor's degrees. The Associate of Arts (A.A.) degree is offered in Christian education, general studies, and youth ministries. The Associate of Science (A.S.) degree is offered in health sciences, mathematics, and social sciences. The Bachelor of Arts (B.A.) degree is offered in American studies, English, history, liberal studies, music and youth ministries, music ministries, music studies, music theory/composition, and religion and Christian ministries. The Bachelor of Science (B.S.) degree is offered in administration of nonprofit organizations, biological science (preprofessional), business administration, developmental psychology, general science, health and human kinetics, human development, human development and family studies, music/business, music education, physical science, social science, and social work. A 2-2 degree program in nursing (guaranteed admittance) is offered in conjunction with Walla Walla College's Portland Adventist Hospital School of Nursing. Individualized majors, double majors, and several minor concentrations are also available.

Warner Pacific is accredited for teacher education and training through the Oregon State Teachers Standards and Practices Commission. The curriculum builds up a broad liberal arts foundation toward specialization in a chosen field while serving the Christian mission of the College. Extended field-based practicums are an integral part of the program. Education certification programs that prepare teachers for careers in public and private schools are available in the following areas: biology, grades 5–12; early childhood/elementary education (age 3–grade 8); elementary/middle school education, grades 3–10; language arts, grades 5–12; math, grades 5–9; music, grades K–12; reading, grades K–12; and social studies, grades 5–12. A cooperative program with the University of Portland leads to certification in handicapped learner studies.

Academic Program

In order to promote Christian excellence and an individualized education, students take courses in three categories: core studies, a major area of study, and elective credits. In general, each of these categories requires a third of a student's total program. A minor may be chosen as part of the elective program.

Course work to complete a bachelor's degree is available during the summer semester. In addition, the Degree Completion Program makes it possible for qualified adult learners to earn a Bachelor of Science in business administration or human development within a nontraditional course design and evening schedule.

The College operates on a semester calendar. The core studies requirement includes a minimum of 42 semester hours in communications, humanities, religion, mathematics, laboratory science, social science, the fine arts, and physical education/health. The major area of study requires completion of certain courses as specified in the College catalog. The remainder of the 124 semester hours may be earned through elective course work and/or a minor concentration.

Off-Campus Arrangements

Through the Oregon Independent Colleges Association, Warner Pacific has cooperative relationships with all of the private colleges and universities in the state. In addition, Warner accepts the completed Oregon Transfer Degree and the Clark College (Vancouver, Washington) A.A. degree as fulfillment of general education core requirements, with the exception of two religion and two upper-division humanities courses. ROTC programs are available in cooperation with the University of Portland; study opportunities and laboratory access at the Oregon Health Sciences University in Portland are readily available. The College participates in a consortium of colleges that maintains the Malheur (eastern Oregon) High Desert Study Center and is a member of the Coalition for Christian Colleges and Universities, which provides study opportunities in Oxford, England; Cairo, Egypt; Israel; Russia; Latin America; Los Angeles, California; Washington, D.C.; Au Sable, Michigan; and Colorado Springs, Colorado.

Academic Facilities

The Otto F. Linn Library provides study areas and housing for a collection of nearly 53,000 books and 450 periodicals. Access to a much larger collection is obtained through OPALL, a computer network that links the College with major public and university collections in Oregon and across the United States. Two biology, one physics, and two chemistry labs and an electron microscope are available. A performing arts auditorium and a small lecture/performance hall feature concerts and dramatic productions. There is a student computer lab as well as modem access in every student residence.

Costs

Annual costs for the 2000–01 academic year are tuition (12 to 18 credits per semester), $14,410; room and board (fifteen-meal plan, double room), $4600; books (estimated) $600; and miscellaneous personal expenses, $1500.

Financial Aid

Warner Pacific believes that any student who demonstrates the ability and motivation to learn should have access to Christian higher education; therefore, the staff is committed to helping parents and students find the necessary financial resources through federal and state assistance, personal and federally insured loans, private scholarships and programs, institutional assistance, and parental and student contributions. More than 90 percent of Warner students receive some type of aid, whether institutional or otherwise. In order to determine the amount of assistance a student qualifies for, the Financial Aid Office should receive a completed Free Application for Federal Student Aid (FAFSA) by April 15. The College manages nearly $2 million in institutional assistance each year in the form of competitive academic merit scholarships and fellowships, talent grants in music, international student fellowships, assistance designed to enhance ethnic diversity on campus, various types of church-related assistance (including a $2500 tuition discount to members of the Church of God, which is headquartered in Anderson, Indiana), and awards for dependents of alumni. The scholarship/fellowship priority application deadline is March 15. Students may be eligible to work on campus and are assisted in locating employment off campus.

Faculty

The 40 full-time and 14 part-time faculty members are solid academicians who are committed to excellence. These scholars bring their expertise, seasoned professional records, and commitment to the art of teaching to Warner Pacific. Students thrive under the tutelage of these ardent supporters. The student-faculty ratio is 14:1. All faculty members and most administrators teach; the undergraduate and graduate religion faculties teach in both programs. Faculty members also serve as academic advisers, and many are advisers to student organizations and clubs.

Student Government

Democratic self-government is seen as essential to the development of maturity and is a strategic part of the educational mission of the College; for this reason, student life is largely self-governed. The Student Council is the executive body of the Associated Students of Warner Pacific College; it operates under its own grant of powers from the Board of Trustees and creates policy that contributes to the governance of student life and activities. The council develops and coordinates an active social and spiritual agenda to meet the needs of all students.

Admission Requirements

Each applicant is considered on the basis of standard admission factors with an emphasis on the personal references submitted. The College seeks students who have the ability to pursue a course of study that emphasizes academic achievement, an openness to learning and teaching that is integrated with the Christian faith, and a willingness to live a disciplined life in accord with Christian principles and community practice (this includes agreeing to live within a Lifestyle Agreement that governs the social and ethical life of the campus). Graduation from an accredited high school (or the test equivalent) is required for admission to Warner Pacific College. A strong college-preparatory program is recommended. A minimum GPA of 2.5 in academic subjects, along with a combined SAT I score of at least 875, an ACT composite score of at least 18, or a Washington Pre-College Test score of at least 86, is required. The GPA of first-year students averages 3.28. The average combined SAT I score is 1021, and the average composite ACT score is 22. Students graduating from high school with a GPA of less than 2.5 may be considered for provisional admission. Transfer students make up a significant percentage of new students. Warner has transfer agreements with many community colleges, including all public two-year institutions in Oregon.

Application and Information

The College has a rolling admission policy; May 1 is the priority date for fall freshman applications. The following must be supplied in order for a student to be considered for admission: the application (including the application form, the Lifestyle Agreement, the personal essay, and a $25 nonrefundable fee), two references, an official transcript from high school and each college/university attended, and official scores on the SAT I, ACT, or other tests. Applicants can expect official notification of acceptance status within fifteen days of receipt of all required materials. Requests for further information and all forms should be addressed to:

Rick Johnsen, Director of Admissions
Warner Pacific College
2219 Southeast 68th Avenue
Portland, Oregon 97215
Telephone: 503-517-1020
               800-582-7885 (toll-free)
Fax: 503-517-1352
E-mail: admiss@warnerpacific.edu
World Wide Web: http://www.warnerpacific.edu

WARREN WILSON COLLEGE
ASHEVILLE, NORTH CAROLINA

The College

Since its founding in 1894, Warren Wilson College has educated students with a unique triad of a strong liberal arts program, work for the College, and service to those in need, which makes Warren Wilson unlike any other college. Its 750 students come from forty-two states and twenty-five countries, creating a diverse and vibrant academic community.

The academic program features a first-rate faculty that does all of the teaching and frequently participates in research with students. The average class size is small, and discussion is an important part of teaching. Fifteen majors are offered, with a commitment to quality in each program. Art, English, economics and business administration, education, biology, the nationally recognized environmental studies program, and outdoor leadership are the most popular majors.

Students at Warren Wilson are integral to the day-to-day operation of the College. Each student works 15 hours a week at a job that is essential to running the school. This experience helps build student confidence (students learn that there is no job they cannot learn to do) and a strong sense of community at the College. Many juniors and seniors have work assignments that coincide with their major. Students receive a work fellowship in the amount of $2472 each year for the work they do.

Service is also integral to the College's way of thinking. Warren Wilson is one of only a few colleges in the country that require student participation in community service for graduation. Service is offered to a wide range of individuals and agencies, nationally and abroad. Students must provide at least 20 hours of service each year to someone off campus.

The 1,100-acre campus includes a 300-acre working farm, 600 acres of forest, 25 miles of hiking trails, and a white-water kayaking course. The campus and the area are havens for outdoor activities, such as white-water sports, hiking, camping, mountain biking, and rock climbing.

Ninety-three percent of the students and 70 percent of the faculty members live on campus. The College offers intercollegiate basketball, cross-country, soccer, and swimming for men and women. White-water sports, softball, and cross-country are offered as club sports. The College also offers intramural sports, a wellness program, and a wide range of other activities.

Location

Warren Wilson is just outside the city of Asheville, North Carolina, in the heart of the Blue Ridge Mountains. Asheville, a city of nearly 100,000 people, is considered one of the most livable cities in the United States and was selected by the National League of Cities as the All-America City for 1998.

Surrounded by more than 1 million acres of national forest, Asheville is located in an ideal setting, presenting views of outstanding beauty throughout all four seasons. In the spring and summer, variations in altitude together with warm southern sun favor native vegetation: dogwood, wildflowers, rhododendron, mountain laurel, and azaleas cover the mountains. The arresting beauty of the autumn colors attracts photographers, artists, and sports enthusiasts from the world over. During the winter, natural snow is enhanced by machine-made snow, producing excellent downhill skiing.

A short drive from the Warren Wilson College campus are Great Smoky Mountains National Park, Pisgah National Forest, and the Blue Ridge Parkway, offering panoramic views, excellent camping facilities, and a perfect setting for class field trips.

Majors and Degrees

The bachelor's degree is awarded in art, biology, chemistry, economics and business administration, education (K–6 and secondary), English, environmental studies, history and political science, humanities, human services, integrative studies, mathematics and computer science, outdoor leadership, psychology, and social work.

Academic Program

The goal of the degree program at Warren Wilson College is the completion of three well-designed areas of study. First, students are expected to complete a core of required courses based on the theme "ways of knowing." A student earns 4 credits in each of the ten core areas. Second, students must develop a strength in one or more disciplines. A minimum of 128 semester hours is required for the baccalaureate degree, including the core plus major hours. Finally, a student must demonstrate the ability to work effectively with others by participation in a work-and-service program.

There is a required freshman seminar designed to provide new students the opportunity to explore various fields. A senior seminar, designed as a capstone experience, is required, as is a senior letter to evaluate the student's college experiences.

All Warren Wilson students must demonstrate competence in writing and mathematics either through testing or by completing core courses.

Each semester in the academic calendar is broken into two 8-week terms. A student traditionally takes only two courses per term (3 or 4 credit hours per course).

There are two honors programs at Warren Wilson. One is in English and the other is in the Division of Natural Sciences, where honors can be earned in biology, chemistry, environmental studies, and mathematics.

Off-Campus Arrangements

In addition to academics, work, and service, all qualified students are afforded the opportunity to study abroad. The College heavily subsidizes the cost for a cross-cultural international experience taken during the junior year or summer.

Academic Facilities

The Martha Ellison Library houses a collection of 100,000 books and 450 periodicals. It provides written records in all areas of the college curriculum and contributes to the cultural enrichment of students. The library is open and served by librarians and student assistants 75 hours each week. The building provides open access to books and periodicals during these hours. Individual carrels, lounge areas, and microfilm readers and printers are available, and there are IBM and Macintosh computers that students may use as word processors or for other prescribed purposes, including access to the Internet.

Computerized literature searching is available. The Martha Ellison Library is a teaching library, providing extensive and continuing bibliographic services, including courses, for the entire student body. Any resource materials not owned by the library may be acquired through interlibrary loan.

The campus arts complex includes the modern Kittredge Theatre; the Kittredge Music Wing, housing classrooms, studios, and a performance area; the Holden Arts Center, with a gallery, classrooms, studios, and a lecture hall; and an outdoor amphitheater. Instruction and performance events also take place in the chapel and the Craftshop/Ceramics Studio.

Costs

Total costs for the 2000–01 school year are $19,019. From this, the student's Work Program Fellowship of $2472 is deducted, leaving an actual cost of $16,547 for each student before any other aid.

Financial Aid

Warren Wilson offers a comprehensive financial aid program that seeks to enroll students from all economic backgrounds. This is accomplished through a combination of work, loans, grants, entitlements, and scholarships to students who complete their file prior to May. Students and their families should file the FAFSA and the Warren Wilson Financial Aid Application to be considered for all possible funds.

Faculty

The teaching faculty consists of 57 full-time members. Of these, 81 percent hold doctoral degrees. All classes and labs are taught by faculty members, not graduate students. Faculty members—1 for every 13 students—are available after class, during regular office hours, and often in their homes.

Student Government

The student body is involved in the democratic decision-making process of the College. A wide variety of leadership positions, elected and appointed, are open to students. Campuswide elections provide opportunities for student involvement in Student Caucus, Judicial Board, Social Regulations Committee, other College advisory committees, and the Cabinet. Student Caucus, the representative voice of the student body, is also responsible for appointing students to positions on approximately fifteen other campus committees ranging from Admissions to Library to Buildings and Grounds.

Admission Requirements

Admission to Warren Wilson College is based on both the personal and the academic qualifications of the applicant.

The selection criteria are devised to choose a student body with high standards of scholarship and personal goals and a willingness to provide community service.

Each candidate for admission must present an academic transcript from a secondary school. The transcript must show at least 12 academic units (a unit is one year's study in one subject). At least 4 years of English, 2 years of algebra, 1 year of geometry, 2 years of laboratory science, and 1 year of history are recommended for admission. Performance during high school is the best predictor of success in college. Therefore, great emphasis is placed upon the high school record. Grade trends can be very important.

Applicants must submit a recommendation from their high school counselor and scores from the SAT I or ACT. Students are also required to submit a personal essay.

Transfer students must present both high school and college transcripts. Transfer applicants must be in good standing with the college last attended and should also have a minimum 2.75 cumulative grade point average. At least one school year in residence at Warren Wilson is required for a transfer student to be eligible for a degree from Warren Wilson College.

There is no fee to apply for admission to Warren Wilson College.

Application and Information

An application form and further information may be obtained by contacting:

Office of Admission
Warren Wilson College
701 Warren Wilson Road
Asheville, North Carolina 28815-9000

Telephone: 800-934-3536 (toll-free)
E-mail: admit@warren-wilson.edu
World Wide Web: http://www.warren-wilson.edu

Warren Wilson College's Valley Home.

WARTBURG COLLEGE
WAVERLY, IOWA

The College

A college of the Evangelical Lutheran Church in America, Wartburg challenges and nurtures students for lives of leadership and service as a spirited expression of their faith and learning. Its enrollment of 1,546 includes students from thirty states and thirty countries. More than a third of Wartburg's first-year students graduated in the top 10 percent of their high school class. The campus is 85 percent residential, and living accommodations range from traditional residence halls to small manor units and 4-, 6-, or 8-person suites.

Wartburg students are active in more than 100 campus organizations, including honor societies, interest groups, and department-related clubs. The Wartburg Choir, Castle Singers, and Wind Ensemble make annual concert tours in the United States and travel abroad every fourth year during the College's one-month May Term. The annual Christmas with Wartburg production attracts more than 6,400 people to performances in Waverly, Cedar Falls, and Des Moines, Iowa. The Wartburg Community Symphony presents a five-concert season. Student publications include a weekly newspaper, a daily information bulletin, a yearbook, and a literary magazine. Students also manage a campus radio station and produce programs for the College's local cable television access channel. The Artist Series brings renowned performing artists to the campus, and a convocation series presents lectures by nationally and internationally recognized speakers. The Art Gallery features touring exhibitions and the work of prominent regional artists. Wartburg is a member of Division III of the National Collegiate Athletic Association. Its seventeen men's and women's athletic teams compete in the Iowa Intercollegiate Athletic Conference and regularly earn conference championships and national rankings. The Physical Education Center provides recreational facilities that include an indoor track, handball and racquetball courts, a weight room, a sauna, and an area that accommodates four basketball courts or five tennis courts.

The College's name honors the Wartburg Castle, a landmark in Eisenach, Germany, where Martin Luther sought refuge during the stormy days of the Reformation.

Wartburg welcomes students of all faiths and offers many avenues for worship, study, fellowship, service, and outreach. A chapel serves as a center for worship and a home for the College's active campus ministry program. Chapel services are scheduled three times a week, and a midweek Eucharist and Sunday morning service provide a variety of worship formats.

The Pathways Center, Writing Center, Career Development Center, and Student Health and Wellness Center provide student support services. Special advisers work with international and minority students.

The College is accredited by the North Central Association of Colleges and Schools. Specific programs are accredited by the National Association of Schools of Music, National Association for Music Therapy, Council on Social Work Education, and National Council for the Accreditation of Teacher Education.

Location

Waverly, a northeast Iowa community of 9,000 residents, is recognized statewide for its progressive businesses and industries. Its quiet neighborhoods, low crime rate, clean air, and friendly atmosphere contribute to a high quality of life. Scenic parks along the Cedar River, shopping areas, restaurants, a hospital, medical clinics, dental offices, and many churches are within walking distance. Students find part-time jobs and internships in Waverly, and local residents attend campus events and support College programs. The Waterloo–Cedar Falls metropolitan area (population 109,000) is 20 minutes from Waverly.

Majors and Degrees

The heart of education at Wartburg College is a four-year liberal arts curriculum that leads to one of five baccalaureate degrees. The Bachelor of Arts degree signifies study in the liberal arts with a concentration of courses in a major. The Bachelor of Music degree adds an extended concentration of work in musical performance. The Bachelor of Music Education degree prepares students to teach music or major in music therapy. The Bachelor of Applied Arts and Bachelor of Applied Science degrees combine liberal arts studies with a technical background.

Departmental majors are offered in accounting, applied music, art, biochemistry, biology, business administration (finance, international business, management, and marketing), chemistry, communication arts (electronic media, journalism, public relations), communication design, computer information systems, computer science, economics, education (Christian day school, early childhood, elementary, and secondary), English, fitness management, French, German, international relations, history, mathematics, music education (instrumental or vocal), music ministry, music performance, music theory, music therapy, philosophy, physical education, physics, political science, psychology, religion (camping ministry, parish education, urban ministry, and youth and family ministry), social work, sociology, Spanish, visual arts management, and writing.

Minors are offered in most academic departments and in four interdisciplinary programs: environmental studies, intercultural certification, leadership certification, and women's studies.

Wartburg offers cooperative programs and preprofessional advisement in architecture, dentistry, engineering, law, medical technology, medicine, nursing, occupational therapy, optometry, pharmacy, physical therapy, and veterinary medicine.

Certificate programs, designed for those already in a vocational setting, are available in accounting, computer information systems, and management.

Academic Program

Academic studies are divided into three relatively equal parts. A third of the classwork is taken through the Wartburg Plan—general education courses divided into foundational, area, and integrative studies. The second third of work is devoted to a major field of study, consisting of a prescribed group of courses that offer depth of knowledge in a discipline. The final third consists of elective courses, which students may choose from any academic area.

The College's 4-4-1 calendar culminates in the one-month May Term, when students concentrate on one course. May Term classes travel within Iowa, across the country, and abroad.

The Pathways Center, a comprehensive advising program, provides a one-stop resource for guiding students from high school to college and beyond. Career Services offers a four-year plan to assist students in assessing their skills, deciding on a career path, pursuing internships in their chosen field, and obtaining employment. For the past six years, 97 percent or more of Wartburg's spring graduates have found jobs or have been accepted into graduate school within seven months of graduation.

Wartburg encourages and fosters academic excellence through close faculty-student relationships and an integrated approach that combines the liberal arts with an emphasis on leadership education and global and multicultural studies. The library, Computer Center, and Writing Center provide support for academic programs. The student-faculty ratio is 14:1.

The College recognizes credit through Advanced Placement examinations, the College-Level Examination Program, DANTES, Departmental Challenge Examinations, and work at other institutions. It also awards credit for experiential learning.

Off-Campus Arrangements

Wartburg West in Denver, Colorado, places students in internships or field experiences related to their majors or in community service organizations. They also take academic courses dealing with religion and urban issues. The Washington Center Program allows students to participate in an academic internship program in Washington, D.C. International exchange programs with Bonn University and Jena University in Germany and International Christian University in Japan enable students to study abroad. French, German, and Spanish majors spend significant time studying abroad. Through the Venture Education Program, cultural immersion experiences are available in Australia, Brazil, China, England, France, Germany, Ghana, Guyana, Indonesia, Jamaica, Mexico, Palestine, Spain, Tanzania, and Turkey. Academic travel and on-site course work are offered each May Term, and students may enroll in internships during any term.

Academic Facilities

The Robert and Sally Vogel Library, opened in September 1999, is designed to accommodate all types of learning from individual research to group projects and faculty-student interaction. It houses books, periodicals, and reference materials as well as extensive electronic resources. The Classroom Technology Center is the home for the social sciences department and provides state-of-the-art technology for teaching and learning. Students have access to more than 200 Macintosh and PC-compatible microcomputers in five open-access and five departmental computing clusters throughout the campus. Each facility is connected to the campuswide network, and students can access file servers to distribute assignments, read Usenet news, use e-mail, and browse Internet resources on the World Wide Web. Becker Hall of Science contains instructional and research laboratories, lecture rooms, a symbolic computation laboratory, a 200-seat auditorium, a greenhouse, and a planetarium. The Fine Arts Center provides spacious rehearsal and recital halls, sixteen music studios, twenty-two practice rooms, a music therapy wing, art studios, and an art gallery. Its 21-workstation Presser Music Technology Classroom is equipped with keyboard/synthesizers and Macintosh computers for music theory, composition, and ear training classes. McElroy Communication Arts Center includes a journalism laboratory with Macintosh computers, a television studio with video capabilities, and a television control room equipped with TV production and digital editing equipment. The College radio station has two on-air production studios, digital audio editing, and computer-controlled programming, and broadcasts over the Internet. Whitehouse Business Center has specially designed classroom facilities for accounting, business, marketing, and economics classes.

Costs

For the 2000–01 academic year, tuition is $15,510, room is $2100, board is $2300, and fees are $255, for a total cost of $20,165.

Financial Aid

Wartburg supports the concept of a socially, culturally, and economically diverse student body, believing that contact with others from various backgrounds better prepares them for contemporary life. The College admits applicants on the basis of academic and personal promise, not the ability to pay. More than 97 percent of students receive financial aid in the form of scholarships, grants, loans, and employment. Merit-based academic and music scholarships are awarded to qualified students. The College allocates more than $8 million annually from its own resources for student aid. The application deadline for financial aid is May 1.

Faculty

The 93 full-time and 49 part-time faculty members form a close living-learning community with students and serve as academic advisers. Sixty-five percent of the full-time faculty hold an earned doctoral degree, and 85 percent hold the highest degree in their discipline. Although the emphasis is on teaching, the College provides faculty research and development opportunities. A sabbatical program permits professors to spend a term or a year on a growth project. Endowed chairs are held in communication arts, global and multicultural studies, and leadership.

Student Government

The Student Senate provides a student voice on campus issues. Its 35 members are selected annually. The Senate selects students to serve on a number of faculty-student committees dealing with all aspects of campus life. Senate members represent student interests to the faculty, administration, and Board of Regents.

Admission Requirements

Applicants are considered according to their potential for academic success, based upon high school rank, breadth and depth of previous study, test scores on the ACT or SAT I, an academic recommendation, and a personal interview with an admission representative. The recommended high school background is 4 years of English, 3 years of mathematics (algebra I and advanced courses), 3 years of science, 2 years of social science, 2 years of foreign language, and 1 year of computer study. Transfer students and international students should contact the Admissions Office to determine any special admission requirements.

Application and Information

A rolling admission policy is used, and applicants may apply at any time. The Wartburg College application for admission, the $20 application fee, one academic recommendation from a teacher, ACT or SAT I scores, and official copies of high school and college transcripts should be sent to the Admissions Office. The application fee is waived for students who make an official campus visit.

Doug Bowman, Director of Admission
Wartburg College
222 9th Street, NW
P.O. Box 1003
Waverly, Iowa 50677
Telephone: 319-352-8264
                800-772-2085 (toll-free)
Fax: 319-352-8579

Wartburg's Old Main, renovated in 1986, is listed on the National Register of Historic Places and houses the education and social work departments.

WASHINGTON & JEFFERSON COLLEGE
WASHINGTON, PENNSYLVANIA

The College

Founded in 1781, Washington & Jefferson College (W&J) is the eleventh-oldest college in the nation and the oldest college west of the Allegheny Mountains. It is an independent, coeducational, liberal arts college, located in Washington, Pennsylvania, 26 miles southwest of Pittsburgh. The current enrollment is 1,145 (584 men and 561 women), including representatives from twenty-four states and eight territories and other countries. As the student body is relatively small, students and faculty members are able to maintain close personal relationships both inside and outside the classroom. All students, except married students and those within commuting distance, live in campus housing. The ten fraternities and four sororities on campus are factors in social activities; 58 percent of the students who are eligible join each year. W&J is concerned with the full development of each student. Academic pursuits are considered most important, but the opportunities for each student to develop socially, culturally, and physically are abundant.

The College is accredited by the Middle States Association of Colleges and Schools, and its chemistry program is approved by the American Chemical Society. A chapter of Phi Beta Kappa, the national honor society that promotes scholarship among students and graduates of American colleges, has been active at the College since 1937.

Location

Washington, Pennsylvania, has a population of 20,000. Students at W&J have all the advantages of living in a small city, but Pittsburgh's libraries, concert halls, art galleries, and sports centers are less than 30 miles away. The southern Pennsylvania area also offers hiking, fishing, rafting, kayaking, canoeing, climbing, camping, and skiing.

Majors and Degrees

Washington & Jefferson College offers the B.A. degree in accounting, art, art education, biology, business administration, chemistry, economics, English, foreign languages (French, German, and Spanish), history, mathematics, philosophy, physics, political science, psychology, and sociology. An interdisciplinary major in industrial chemistry and management is available. Cooperative programs are offered in engineering (3-2) in cooperation with Case Western Reserve University or Washington University, in optometry (3-4) in cooperation with the Pennsylvania College of Optometry, in podiatric medicine (3-4) in cooperation with the Pennsylvania College of Podiatry and the Ohio College of Podiatric Medicine, and in pre–physical therapy (3-4) in cooperation with Allegheny University of the Health Sciences.

Preprofessional programs are offered in a variety of areas, including biochemistry, dentistry, entrepreneurial studies, human resource management, law, medicine, physical therapy, and veterinary medicine. Courses leading to secondary school teaching certification are offered in combination with a number of major areas. A thematic major program allows students the opportunity to specialize in areas of interest outside of the traditional curriculum by arranging a course load to meet their individual needs.

Academic Program

The College utilizes a 4-1-4 curriculum calendar, with the academic year divided into three distinct sessions: fall (September through December), intersession (January), and spring (February through May). The 4-1-4 also denotes the number of courses that a student carries throughout the year: four courses are taken in both the fall and spring sessions, and one is taken during the intersession. This accounts for nine courses each academic year, or the total of thirty-six courses, required for graduation in a four-year period.

Academic freedom and individual consideration characterize the curriculum at W&J. Specific courses required of all students include one course in freshman English, two courses in physical education, and the Freshman Forum, a course required for all freshmen. All students must complete a curriculum that includes a certain number of courses distributed among cultural and intellectual traditions, fine arts, languages and literature, sciences and mathematics, and social sciences. Students may concentrate on one major area or may double major in two different areas. Majors should be declared no later than the beginning of the junior year. To satisfy major requirements, a minimum of eight to ten courses must be taken in the major field, allowing the student a choice of twelve to fourteen electives. Students may use the January intersession in a variety of ways: they may elect to remain on campus and take a course, attend another college, study abroad, develop an independent study project, or intern in a career area.

Advising is an important component of W&J's preprofessional and major programs. Student mentors are assigned to all entering freshmen. Students select their academic advisers from the faculty members in their major departments. Students with a preprofessional interest are also advised through the various committees and faculty members who are able to provide information concerning career possibilities, graduate school, and academic course work. Advising is also available to aid the student who is undecided about the choice of a major discipline. Peer counseling is available for students interested in advice from other students in the College community.

Off-Campus Arrangements

Students may take advantage of the Junior Year Abroad program, or they may study in another country during the January intersession. Recently, W&J students have studied in London and Paris and in Australia, Egypt, Germany, Greece, Holland, Italy, Kenya, Mexico, the People's Republic of China, Russia, and Spain. The College sponsors courses in the United States in such diverse areas as New York City, Hawaii, Texas, and the Florida Everglades. Qualified students may participate in the Washington Semester at American University in Washington, D.C., during which they work with students from across the country on topics of current interest, interview experts and others active in shaping legislative policy, attend seminars with top government officials, and observe the processes of government firsthand. Independent study, study at other institutions, and a variety of internships are also available during the intersession. A cooperative exchange program with Royal Holloway and Bedford New College of the University of London is available.

Academic Facilities

Washington & Jefferson's facilities include thirty-four buildings, the newest being the Campus Center, which opened in 1993. The College library is an open-stack, two-story, air-conditioned building. A recently installed computer system allows campuswide access to the library's catalog of holdings. Research facilities and equipment at the College include a language laboratory, a full range of spectrometers, an isolator laboratory, an X-ray diffraction unit, a digital calorimeter, gas chromatography equipment, a neutron howitzer, an analog computer, a differential thermoanalyzer, an atomic absorption unit, a Gauss polygraph, a refrigerated centrifuge, a UV-visible flame spectrophotometer, Kirlian photography equipment used in the study of ESP, and a neuropsychology laboratory with stereotaxic equipment and a polygraph. The campus network is accessible from students' rooms and off campus. There are 350 computers available for student use in computer labs, academic buildings, classrooms, and science labs, where there is a student-to-computer ratio of 3:1. Student accounts provide access to the academic computer, file servers, the Internet, library services, e-mail, and online services. The College's overall student-to-computer ratio is 2:1.

Costs

For 1999–2000, the cost of an academic year at W&J was $23,750, with $18,675 allotted for tuition, $2410 for room, $2340 for board, and a $325 student service and activity fee. All fees are subject to change annually.

Financial Aid

Approximately 75 percent of W&J's student body receive some type of aid, such as a grant, loan, or work-study award. Aid is based on financial need, demonstrated ability, and the contribution the student will be able to make to the College community. Federal funds are available through the Federal Pell Grant, Federal Perkins Loan, Federal Stafford Student Loan, and Federal Work-Study programs. Veterans are eligible for assistance under the G.I. bill. A tuition payment plan is available through American Management Services (AMS). Aid is offered for a one-year period but is renewable as long as the student meets annual application deadlines, maintains good academic standing, and demonstrates financial need.

Washington & Jefferson College awards a variety of scholarships on the basis of academic merit. Accepted applicants are reviewed for eligibility. The qualifications include a minimum B+ average, a minimum combined score of 1000 on the SAT I or a minimum composite score of 23 on the ACT, a high class rank, and demonstrated abilities outside the classroom. On-campus interviews are recommended for potential scholarship candidates. Selection notification begins April 1. Scholarships may be renewed subject to annual academic performance.

All applicants for financial aid must file a Free Application for Federal Student Aid (FAFSA). The priority filing date for prospective freshmen is February 15. For further information about all forms of aid, students should contact the Office of Financial Aid.

Faculty

There are 88 full-time faculty members at W&J; the student–teaching faculty ratio is 12:1. Eighty-nine percent of faculty members hold a doctorate or the terminal degree in their field, and their primary concerns are their students and teaching. All faculty members are available for counseling, and they take a serious interest in the welfare of the students.

Student Government

Student government is a strong and vigorous organization at W&J. Students are regarded as mature individuals capable of governing themselves while furthering the best interests of the College community. Elected officials lead the student body in campus life programs, including the coordination of activities, legislation, student regulations, and distribution of funds to the various student organizations.

Admission Requirements

The breadth and depth of academic and extracurricular interests and achievements, academic background, personal character, and recommendations from a guidance counselor or principal are evaluated together with standardized test scores to determine a student's qualifications for admission. Applicants must complete at least 15 units of college-preparatory courses at an accredited secondary school, including 3 units of college-preparatory English, 3 units of college-preparatory mathematics, 2 units of a foreign language, and 1 unit of history, social science, or natural science. All applicants are required to complete an essay and to take either the SAT I: Reasoning Test and three SAT II: Subject Tests, one of which should be the Writing Test, or the ACT.

Early admission is available for qualified high school students who wish to begin college after their junior year. Academically qualified international students are encouraged to apply and should submit SAT I or ACT scores for evaluation by the Admission Committee. Students whose native language is not English should submit TOEFL scores in lieu of SAT I or ACT scores.

A personal interview, while not required, is strongly recommended for the prospective student. An applicant who wishes to visit the College should make an appointment with the Office of Admission; arrangements for an interview should be made in advance. Students who are unable to visit the College may arrange an interview with a College representative who visits high schools in various cities throughout the year, or they may have an interview with an alumni admission representative in their area.

Washington & Jefferson College does not discriminate in its educational programs, activities, or employment on the basis of race, color, religion, sex, age, disability, national origin, or any other legally protected status. Inquiries may be directed to the Affirmative Action Officer, Washington & Jefferson College, 60 South Lincoln Street, Washington, Pennsylvania 15301-4801; telephone: 724-223-6010.

Application and Information

An application for admission and additional information about Washington & Jefferson College, the major programs, and financial aid may be requested from the Office of Admission. Applicants should request that their SAT I or ACT scores, high school transcripts, and letters of recommendation be sent to the College. Transfer students are required to submit an official high school transcript, an official transcript of all previous college credits, and a certificate of honorable dismissal from each institution previously attended. A nonrefundable application fee of $25 must accompany the application for admission. Early decision applicants must submit an application by November 1 of their senior year. All other applications should be submitted by March 1 of the senior year for March 15 notification. The deadline for fall transfer applications is August 15.

For further information, students should contact:

Dean of Enrollment
Washington & Jefferson College
60 South Lincoln Street
Washington, Pennsylvania 15301
Telephone: 724-223-6025
         888-WANDJAY (toll-free)
Fax: 724-223-6534
E-mail: admission@washjeff.edu
World Wide Web: http://www.washjeff.edu

WASHINGTON AND LEE UNIVERSITY
LEXINGTON, VIRGINIA

The University

Founded in 1749, Washington and Lee University is a private, coeducational college devoted at the undergraduate level to providing educational excellence in the humanities, liberal arts and sciences, and business and commerce. The University includes a nationally prominent School of Law, which offers the Juris Doctor degree. Washington and Lee is small by choice and has an undergraduate enrollment limited to about 1,700 by means of a selective admission process. It is the University's purpose to bring together exceptionally able faculty members who are wholly committed to teaching at the undergraduate level and a student body of unusual achievement, motivation, personal integrity, and promise. The University devotes all its resources to the development of the student's capacity to understand and to use his or her training and talents wisely and productively.

As the ninth-oldest institution of higher learning in the United States, Washington and Lee is rich in history and tradition. George Washington made the first significant gift to the endowment—$50,000 in 1796—and Robert E. Lee served as president from the end of the Civil War until his death in 1870. As important as Washington's gift was to the financially pressed college, it was Lee's presidency that led to the transformation of the institution from a classical academy of limited influence into an educationally aggressive college of national stature. Under Lee's guidance, programs in law, engineering, and commerce were added; Lee also planned the first college-level curriculum in journalism in the nation. When he died in 1870, Lee was buried on the campus in the chapel built under his supervision; his family is buried there with him.

Clearly, tradition plays an important part in campus life, and it is precisely because of this heritage that students and faculty alike recognize a keen responsibility to fulfill the complex roles of a modern educational institution. Close student-teacher associations are fostered in an atmosphere that stresses individuality and integrity. Among the many characteristics that serve to distinguish Washington and Lee is the University's ability to provide a remarkably comprehensive academic program with more than 900 different courses offered in more than forty major areas while still retaining a faculty-student ratio of 1:10.

First- and second-year undergraduates are required to live on campus. Afterward, students make their own living arrangements; there are currently dormitory facilities with space for approximately 200 upperclass students, another 100 live in the on-campus Woods Creek apartments, and 450 others live in one of four theme houses, one of fifteen fraternity houses, or one of five sorority houses. Many who do not live in University housing rent apartments or share houses in the city or surrounding countryside.

All freshmen are required to take meals in the University's dining hall.

Location

Washington and Lee is situated on the edge of Lexington, a historic town of more than 7,000 year-round residents. Both Washington and Lee and neighboring Virginia Military Institute contribute to make Lexington a surprisingly cosmopolitan small town, which offers many opportunities, particularly of a cultural or artistic nature, that are generally found only in much larger cities. Indeed, Washington and Lee students have the best of both worlds, for the campus is only a few minutes' walk from open country perfectly suited for outdoor activities ranging from skiing in winter to swimming or tubing in warm weather. More than a dozen other colleges, including the University of Virginia, are within easy driving distance. Their proximity ensures that many social, athletic, and cultural opportunities are available to Washington and Lee students.

Majors and Degrees

Washington and Lee offers the Bachelor of Arts degree with majors in archaeology and anthropology, art history, biology, chemistry, classics, cognitive studies, computer science, East Asian studies, economics, English, environmental studies in geology, forestry and environmental studies, French, geology, German language, German literature, history, independent work, journalism, mathematics, medieval and Renaissance studies, music, natural sciences and mathematics, philosophy, physics, physics-engineering, politics, psychology, public policy, religion, Romance languages, Russian studies, sociology and anthropology, Spanish, studio art, and theater. The Bachelor of Science degree is offered with majors in biology, chemistry, chemistry-engineering, computer science, geology, independent work, mathematics, natural sciences and mathematics, neuroscience, physics, physics-engineering, and psychology. In addition, the University offers the Bachelor of Science degree with special attainments in chemistry and the Bachelor of Science degree with special attainments in commerce with majors in business administration or business administration and accounting.

Academic Program

Washington and Lee is dedicated to providing its students with a strong liberal arts education. The goals of this education include both breadth of knowledge (general education) and competence in a specialized discipline or field of knowledge (the major). Of the 121 credits required for an undergraduate degree, between 30 and 50 must be in the student's major. In addition, students are expected to fulfill the general education requirements of proficiency in English composition; proficiency in a foreign language through the intermediate level; 6 credits in literature; 12 credits in fine arts, history, philosophy, or religion; 10 credits in sciences and mathematics; and 9 credits in social sciences.

Among the many special opportunities for students are the Robert E. Lee Research Program, under which students work on an individual basis with professors on substantial research projects; an honors program, which encourages independent work; a cooperative engineering program, which offers combined-degree plans with two other universities; a series of exchange programs with institutions of higher learning in Japan, the People's Republic of China, and England; and a comprehensive study-abroad plan during the six-week spring term, a major feature of Washington and Lee's 4-4-2 academic calendar.

Academic Facilities

The historic front campus consists of about 50 acres, and the principal academic buildings are clustered on a mall. The

James G. Leyburn Library (1979) is designed to hold 500,000 volumes. The journalism and mass communications department is housed in Reid Hall, which contains a computerized newsroom and studios for student-operated FM radio and cable television stations. A new natural science facility, which includes Parmly and Howe Halls, opened in 1997. DuPont Hall is used primarily by the music and art departments, and Tucker, Robinson, Newcomb, and Payne Halls accommodate the humanities. Washington Hall, the central and oldest building, is an administrative building. The Williams School of Commerce, Economics, and Politics is housed in a renovated building. The School of Law is located in Sydney Lewis Hall, one of the nation's best-designed law school buildings. More information about student life and the academic program can be found on the University's Web site (listed below).

Costs

The tuition fee for the 2000–01 academic year is $17,790. The cost of a room averages $2600 a year. Meals in the University's dining hall are $3025 for the year and approximately the same at the various fraternity houses. A student activities fee of $175 is required of each student.

Financial Aid

Washington and Lee annually administers close to $5 million in University grants and scholarships. Types of aid in addition to University funds include the Federal Pell Grant, Federal Stafford Student Loan, Federal PLUS loan, Federal Supplemental Educational Opportunity Grant, Federal Perkins Loan, and Federal Work-Study programs and various state grant programs. Almost half of the student body receives some form of assistance. Candidates must make formal application for aid and must submit completed copies of the Washington and Lee Application for Financial Aid, the Free Application for Federal Student Aid, and a copy of their parents' federal income tax return for the most recent tax year. Generally, financial aid packages include a grant, a low-interest loan, and a work-study opportunity. In addition, the University offers a series of honor scholarships, up to the total cost of tuition, on a competitive basis to the most promising students. Honor scholarships require a separate application. Information may be obtained by writing to the Office of Financial Aid.

Faculty

The Washington and Lee faculty is composed of outstanding men and women of considerable scholarly achievement. More than 90 percent have the Ph.D. degree. Most are active researchers, creative writers, or creative or performing artists. And yet, the members of the Washington and Lee faculty are, first and foremost, teachers; the classroom is their first priority. A typical class at Washington and Lee has only 15 students. A quarter of all classes have fewer than 8 students. A student-faculty ratio of 10:1 results in close relationships between the students and their professors both in and out of the classroom.

Student Government

The Washington and Lee student government has authority to administer all student-related activities, and students are represented on every policymaking faculty committee. The Student Judicial Council, composed of representatives from the student body, has jurisdiction over all noncurricular student affairs. The student government also administers the century-old Honor System. The operating assumption to which all students subscribe as members of the Washington and Lee community is that they will be trustworthy and will expect trustworthiness of their fellow students. In a recent survey of the University's alumni, the Honor System was deemed second only to the quality of the faculty as the most important element of the Washington and Lee experience.

Admission Requirements

To be considered for admission, a student must have completed at least 16 units in college-preparatory subjects. At least 14 of these 16 units should be in English, foreign language, mathematics, history, the social sciences, and the natural sciences. Specific requirements are 4 units in English, 3 in mathematics, 2 in foreign language, 1 in a natural science (beyond general science), and 1 in history. All applicants must take either the Scholastic Assessment Test (SAT I) or American College Testing's ACT. In either case, three SAT II Subject Tests are required, one of which must be the Writing Test.

Washington and Lee is highly selective, and completion of the minimum requirements outlined above does not guarantee acceptance. Most successful candidates exceed the minimum in almost all areas and present secondary school and testing records reflecting aptitude and high achievement.

Application and Information

Brochures describing all aspects of Washington and Lee are available from the Office of Admissions, which also makes application materials available to prospective students. The deadline for applying is January 15; applicants are notified of the University's decision in early April. The application fee is $40. A nonreturnable tuition deposit of $350 together with a $150 room reservation fee and security deposit is required by May 1. Under the early decision plan, prospective students whose first choice is Washington and Lee may apply by December 1 and be notified of the admission decision by December 22. Although not required for admission, applicants are strongly encouraged to have an interview with a member of the admission staff or with an alumnus representative of the Alumni Admissions Program. Admission decisions are based on both objective criteria (class standing and SAT or ACT scores) and subjective data (including recommendations and school and community involvement).

For more information, students should contact:

Office of Admissions
Washington and Lee University
Lexington, Virginia 24450-0303
Telephone: 540-463-8710
E-mail: admissions@wlu.edu
World Wide Web: http://www.wlu.edu

WASHINGTON COLLEGE
CHESTERTOWN, MARYLAND

The College
Founded in 1782, Washington College is the tenth-oldest college in the United States. George Washington, for whom the College was named, was an early benefactor and member of the College's Board of Visitors and Governors. Today, the College is one of the few nationally recognized selective liberal arts institutions with an enrollment of fewer than 1,200 students. The intimacy of a small-college environment, the tradition of a challenging liberal arts curriculum, and the relaxed informality characteristic of the Chesapeake Bay region continue to exert their influence on the College and all who come to it.

The current enrollment is more than 1,100 men and women. Although most students come from the Northeast, international students and students from other regions of the country are enrolled in numbers sufficient to add geographic diversity to the student body. Eighty percent of all students live in residences located on the 120-acre campus; special interest housing is available for students interested in science, foreign languages, international studies, creative arts, and Greek organizations.

The College enjoys a high participation rate in intramural sports, in the performing arts, and in student publications, community service clubs, recreational activities, and social organizations. The Division III intercollegiate program offers fifteen varsity sports, including baseball, basketball, lacrosse, rowing, soccer, swimming, and tennis for men and basketball, field hockey, lacrosse, rowing, softball, swimming, tennis, and volleyball for women.

Location
Chestertown, a community of 4,000 people, is a popular port-of-call for Chesapeake Bay boaters, outdoors enthusiasts, and tourists on day trips from nearby Philadelphia, Baltimore, and Washington, D.C. The center of this eighteenth-century river town, with its historic district, shops, and restaurants, is a 5-minute walk from campus. The "town-gown" relationship is excellent.

Majors and Degrees
The Bachelor of Arts is awarded in American studies, art, business management, drama, economics, English, environmental studies, French, German, history, humanities, international studies, mathematics, music, philosophy, political science, psychology, sociology, and Spanish. The Bachelor of Science is awarded in biology, chemistry, and physics.

Washington College also offers a certification program in secondary education. Preprofessional programs in dentistry, medicine, or veterinary medicine may be developed within a major in the natural sciences; a preprofessional program in law is also available. A 3-2 dual-degree program in engineering with the University of Maryland and a 3-2 dual-degree program in nursing with Johns Hopkins University are also offered.

Academic Program
The College's four-course plan is intended to broaden and deepen a student's education by providing for the intensive study of a limited number of subjects and by encouraging individual responsibility for learning. General education requirements include two freshman seminars, two sophomore seminars, and eight semester courses chosen from the following categories: social science, natural science, the humanities, and formal studies (mathematics, computer science, music theory, logic, and foreign languages). Candidates for a degree must satisfactorily complete thirty-two semester courses and must fulfill the senior obligation (for example, a comprehensive examination or thesis).

Washington College offers a nationally renowned creative writing program and awards the prestigious Sophie Kerr Prize every year to the graduating senior who shows the most promise for a career in literary endeavors.

Successful scores (4 or 5) on Advanced Placement examinations can provide exemption from distribution requirements. With the aid of a faculty adviser, students can construct their own major fields of study in some areas or pursue independent study for course credit.

Off-Campus Arrangements
Students receive academic credit for a variety of off-campus programs. A study abroad program is offered at twenty-five sites worldwide, including sites in England, France, Spain, Germany, Scotland, Mexico, and Japan. In addition, subject to faculty approval, students can spend a year abroad at a university of their choice. The College participates in the Washington Semester at American University. Political science majors can also intern with the Maryland State Legislature in Annapolis, the state's capital. A clinical practicum in psychology and field experience in social work are also available.

Academic Facilities
The library, which has 200,000 volumes, more than 800 current periodical subscriptions, and extensive microfilm holdings, benefits from an efficient interlibrary loan system and an online card catalog. Well-equipped science laboratories allow for independent research, and a DATA General computer system and microcomputer network are readily available to interested students. The Gibson Fine Arts Center houses a 600-seat theater/auditorium that has complete facilities for study and performance in music and drama. Full facilities for art majors are located in the Constance S. Larrabee Creative Art Center.

Costs
Tuition for 1999–2000 was $19,750 and room and board were $5740, making a total of $25,940. Expenses, including books and transportation, usually range from $600 to $1000 annually.

Financial Aid
Washington College offers financial assistance to approximately 80 percent of its student body. Awards are based on need and academic performance. Financial aid includes scholarships, grants, loans, and jobs. The College participates in the Federal Perkins Loan Program, the Federal Stafford Student Loan Program, and the Federal Work-Study program. Federal Pell Grants and Federal Supplemental Educational Opportunity Grants are applicable to Washington College. In addition, financial assistance from the Maryland scholarship program and other state programs can be applied to expenses at the College.

Members of the National Honor Society and Cum Laude Society who are admitted to Washington College are awarded $40,000 academic scholarships ($10,000 annually for four years). Other academic scholarships ranging in value from $2500 to $10,000 are offered without regard to financial need.

To be eligible for financial assistance, applicants should file the FAFSA by February 15. An application for admission, with all supporting credentials, should be received by February 15 to establish eligibility. Students interested in Federal Pell Grant assistance or in-state scholarship programs must apply directly to the program concerned.

Faculty
Ninety-eight percent of the more than 70 full-time faculty members hold either a doctoral degree or a terminal degree in

their discipline. Faculty members engage in professional research and publication but emphasize teaching. Along with performing their classroom duties, faculty members serve as advisers to individuals and student groups. No classes are taught by graduate assistants. Faculty participation in student and College affairs reflects the strong sense of community that characterizes Washington College.

Student Government

The Student Government Association (SGA) is a significant part of the College community. In addition to coordinating social activities, the SGA plays an active role in academic affairs. Students elected by the SGA are voting members of College committees and attend faculty and board meetings.

Admission Requirements

High school students should complete a college-preparatory program, including a minimum of 4 years of English, 4 of social studies, 3 of mathematics, 3 of science, and 2 of a foreign language. SAT I or ACT scores and two teacher recommendations are also required. While interviews are not required for admission, interested students are encouraged to visit the campus. Both interviews and campus tours are available by appointment on weekdays throughout the year and on selected Saturdays during the fall semester.

Members of the College admission staff visit high schools throughout the United States, seeking above-average students with solid academic backgrounds. There are no quotas based on sex, and there are no religious, geographic, or ethnic restrictions. Indeed, the College seeks the most diverse student body possible, realizing that such diversity is an important aspect of the academic community.

Transfer students are accepted with or without the A.A. degree, and applicants with above-average records are encouraged to apply.

Application and Information

The application, a $40 fee, the high school transcript (and college transcript, for transfer applicants), scores on the SAT I or ACT, and two teacher recommendations are required. Applications for early decision must be received by November 15, and candidates are notified of the admission decision by December 15. For regular admission, forms must be submitted prior to February 15. Regular-decision candidates are notified of the admission decision on a rolling basis between January 15 and April 1. Applicants for financial assistance must complete the procedures outlined under Financial Aid.

Further information and application forms are available from:

Office of Admissions
Washington College
300 Washington Avenue
Chestertown, Maryland 21620-1197

Telephone: 410-778-7700
               800-422-1782 (toll-free)
E-mail: adm.off@washcoll.edu
World Wide Web: http://www.washcoll.edu

Casey Academic Center at Washington College.

WASHINGTON UNIVERSITY IN ST. LOUIS
ST. LOUIS, MISSOURI

The University

Washington University in St. Louis is a nationally ranked independent, coeducational university renowned for academic excellence. Washington comprises the College of Arts & Sciences and professional Schools of Architecture, Art, Business, Engineering and Applied Science, Law, Medicine (which includes occupational and physical therapy), and Social Work. A medium-sized major research university with 5,600 full-time undergraduates (plus 5,000 graduate students), the University offers students the complete academic resources and extracurricular opportunities of a larger university plus the friendliness and support of a small community.

Students come to Washington because of high-quality academic programs coupled with flexibility, opportunities, and encouragement for students to discover and develop their potential. Eighty-four percent of graduates enter graduate or professional school within seven years of graduation. The students are also diverse; 26 percent of undergraduates are multicultural and/or international. Students come from all fifty states and from eighty-six countries; 87 percent come from outside of Missouri, and 54 percent come from more than 500 miles away.

Although students are deeply involved in their studies, they find time to get involved in nearly 200 campus organizations. Two thirds participate in volunteer activities, three fourths participate in club or intramural sports, and one fourth join Greek organizations. Washington is an NCAA Division III school with eighteen varsity sports for men and women and is a founding member of the University Athletic Association.

Freshmen from outside St. Louis are required to live in the residence halls. Seventy-seven percent of undergraduates live in University-owned or -operated housing. Of the 23 percent who do not, most live within a 15-minute walk or can take a short, free shuttle ride. Ten on-campus residential colleges are located on the "South 40." A center of activity for its 3,750 residents, the South 40 houses meeting, recreation, and game rooms; music practice rooms; computing and laundry facilities; intramural fields; basketball and sand volleyball courts; and a video store and hair salon. Wohl Center houses dining facilities as well as student mailboxes, shops, and a coffeehouse, which features live music, comedy acts, and movies.

Special student services include counseling, health, and educational services and assistance for those with disabilities.

Location

Located in a suburban setting 7 miles from downtown St. Louis, Washington is surrounded by distinct areas, including University City and its eclectic shopping district, "The Loop"; the historic homes of Clayton, the county's financial and business center; and Forest Park, home of the zoo, the science center, and art and history museums, which are all free of charge. St. Louis offers cultural events and professional sport teams, including the Super Bowl Champion Rams. It is easy to get to attractions around the area by foot, bike, shuttle, car, bus, or MetroLink, the city's light rail system.

Majors and Degrees

Washington confers the baccalaureate degree through major programs in five of its schools. The School of Architecture offers a program in architecture. The School of Art offers programs in ceramics, fashion design, painting, photography, printmaking and illustration, sculpture, and visual communications (advertising design, graphic design, and illustration). The College of Arts & Sciences offers programs in African and Afro-American studies, anthropology, Arabic, archaeology, art history, biochemistry, biology, chemistry, Chinese, classics/ancient studies, comparative literature, dance, drama, earth and planetary sciences, East Asian studies, economics, education, educational studies, English, environmental studies, European studies, film and media studies, French, German, Hebrew (modern), history, international studies, Italian, Japanese, Jewish and Near Eastern studies, Latin American studies, linguistic studies, literature and history, mathematics, medieval and Renaissance studies, music, performing arts, Persian, philosophy, physics, political economy, political science, psychology, religious studies, Russian, Russian studies, social thought and analysis, Spanish, and women's studies. The School of Business offers programs in accounting; business, economics, and the law; finance; international business; management; marketing; operations and manufacturing management; and organization and human resources. The School of Engineering and Applied Science offers programs in biological and engineering sciences, biomedical engineering, chemical engineering, civil engineering, computer engineering, computer science, electrical engineering, mechanical engineering, physics, robotics, and systems science and engineering. Preprofessional advising programs that are available include business, dentistry, law, medicine, occupational therapy, physical therapy, social work, and veterinary medicine.

Academic Program

Studying across disciplines and taking advantage of myriad courses offered by the five undergraduate schools is a distinguishing feature of a Washington education. Students may pursue minors, double majors, two undergraduate degrees, and joint undergraduate/graduate degrees. Academic advisers work closely with students on course selection, majors, and research and internship opportunities.

Some students who receive a grade of 4 or 5 on AP examinations are often able to enter the University with college credits. Although requirements vary, each academic division requires proficiency in English composition.

The University's average undergraduate class size is 18. The College of Arts & Sciences offers three programs of small-group classes available exclusively to first-year students. The undergraduate student-faculty ratio is 7:1.

The University observes a two-semester academic year calendar.

Off-Campus Arrangements

St. Louis gives students numerous opportunities to participate in paid and unpaid internships.

Washington offers several formats for international study; this helps students choose programs to match their academic interests and personal goals. Currently, students are studying in seventeen countries in summer and yearlong programs. Others participate in study/internship programs where they study for one semester in another country and then work in a semester-long internship.

Academic Facilities

Ranked among the top private universities that receive federal support for research and development, Washington offers undergraduates incomparable opportunities to participate in research in all disciplines.

The thirteen departmental libraries on campus and the main branch, Olin Library, house more than 3.3 million volumes and 15,000 periodicals. From within the libraries, the many computer centers, and the students' rooms on campus, undergraduates can access databases such as the internationally recognized WU archive, World Window, and other information on the Internet. Most residence halls have computer centers that are open 24 hours a day with computing consultants available for help.

The Gallery of Art is one of the oldest university art museums in the U.S. Its permanent collection includes nineteenth-century American art and modern works by European and American artists. Edison Theatre is a professional theater on campus and attracts students, faculty, and St. Louis residents for drama, dance, and music performances by local, national, and international artists.

Costs

Tuition for the 2000–01 school year is $24,500, the student activities fee is $245, and average room and board costs are $7724. Additional costs for books and supplies vary with the course of study.

Financial Aid

Approximately 60 percent of Washington undergraduates receive some form of financial assistance. Students applying for financial aid scholarships should complete the Financial Aid PROFILE provided by the College Scholarship Service and the Free Application for Federal Student Aid (FAFSA). Both the PROFILE registration form and the FAFSA are available in high school guidance offices. The deadline to apply for need-based aid is February 15.

Washington is a leader in creating innovative, flexible payment plans. The University also offers a variety of academic scholarships and fellowships. High school seniors may compete for four-year Army ROTC scholarship awards.

Faculty

There are a total of 2,567 faculty members at Washington. Virtually all classes are taught by professors, not by graduate teaching assistants; the same faculty members teach graduate and undergraduate courses. Many have been awarded the highest honors in their disciplines. Because of Washington's relatively small size, students are encouraged to work with faculty members outside the classroom. Undergraduates participate in projects that range from laboratory research at the School of Medicine to graphic design in the School of Art's "Create Studio."

Student Government

There are two student governing bodies. The Congress of the South 40 governs the residential colleges, while the Student Union serves all undergraduates. Student representatives serve on the University's Board of Trustees and on steering committees for campus events. Student leaders administer an activities fund of almost $1 million.

Admission Requirements

Washington students have challenged themselves academically and personally during their high school years; most graduated in the top portion of their high school classes. Most applicants have taken advantage of honors, AP, and I.B. courses. Most candidates' transcripts include 4 years of English and mathematics (study of calculus is recommended for students interested in architecture, business, engineering, and the sciences), 3 to 4 years of history or social science and laboratory science (study in chemistry and physics is recommended for students interested in engineering), and at least 2 years of a foreign language. For students who plan to study the sciences, the University recommends study in chemistry and physics. Other important admission considerations are grades and class rank, counselor and teacher recommendations, an essay, extracurricular and community activities, and standardized test scores.

International and transfer students should contact the Office of Undergraduate Admissions for application information.

Application and Information

Freshman application deadlines are as follows: Early Decision I—November 15 with a December 15 notification; Early Decision II—January 1 with a January 15 notification; and regular decision—January 15 with an April 1 notification. Transfer student application deadlines are June 1 for the following fall semester and November 15 for the following spring semester.

For additional information, students should contact:

Office of Undergraduate Admissions
Washington University in St. Louis
Campus Box 1089
One Brookings Drive
St. Louis, Missouri 63130-4899
Telephone: 314-935-6000
          800-638-0700 (toll-free)
Fax: 314-935-4290
E-mail: admissions@wustl.edu
World Wide Web: http://admissions.wustl.edu

Robert S. Brookings Hall, located on the Hilltop Campus, exemplifies Washington University in St. Louis's collegiate Gothic architecture.

WAYNESBURG COLLEGE
WAYNESBURG, PENNSYLVANIA

The College

Waynesburg is a private, coeducational Christian college affiliated with the Presbyterian Church (U.S.A.). The College serves more than 1,500 students on a picturesque campus 1 hour from Pittsburgh. Waynesburg College offers students a broad knowledge that is required for global citizenship, a structured approach to personal and social development, and leadership opportunities in service to others.

Unique to Waynesburg College is its Service Learning Project. This special program offers Waynesburg students the opportunity to earn college credit and experience relationships with others beyond the classroom as they develop a sense of social responsibility and community service. The College is the only institution in Pennsylvania to host the Bonner Scholars Program, a leadership-through-service opportunity funded by the Bonner Foundation of Princeton, New Jersey.

The College has implemented a campus master plan, including a new Stover Campus Center for student activities, a Fine Arts Center, and a Performing Arts Center. Student publications, such as the newspaper, yearbook, and poetry magazine, provide outlets for aspiring journalists. The College has a drama group, a mixed chorus, a marching band, a pep band, an ensemble, and the well-known Lamplighters singing group. The VIP Forum and the Christ and Culture Lecture Series bring nationally prominent speakers to the campus annually. The Student Activities Board sponsors concerts, dances, comedy clubs, and various excursions. The College owns and operates its own radio station, WCYJ-FM, where students can hold positions in broadcasting and management. The College also has a mobile television unit and a closed-circuit television studio available for student use. In addition, students may become involved in organizations such as the Christian Fellowship, the Newman Club, and the Fellowship of Christian Athletes.

Waynesburg College offers a variety of intercollegiate varsity sports for men and women. Men compete in baseball, basketball, football, golf, soccer, tennis, and wrestling. Women compete on basketball, cross-country, golf, soccer, softball, tennis, and volleyball teams. In addition, Waynesburg offers an extensive intramural program. Skiing is a popular winter sport, and seven fine resorts are within an hour of Waynesburg. Students may also take an active part in organizing hiking, bicycling, and canoeing trips.

At the graduate level, the College offers a program leading to the Executive Master of Business Administration (M.B.A.) degree. All candidates for the M.B.A. are enrolled in 36 credit hours of instruction. The M.B.A. includes a criminal justice track.

Location

The College is located 50 miles south of Pittsburgh in the community of Waynesburg, which has a population of 12,000. The campus, just two blocks from the Waynesburg business district, is adjacent to a park with more than 12 acres of lawn and shade trees.

Majors and Degrees

Students can choose their major from more than forty areas of study, and preprofessional training is given in dentistry, law, medicine, and physical therapy. There are also preprofessional programs in dentistry, law, medicine, and veterinary medicine. The Bachelor of Arts (B.A.) degree is offered in art administration, communication, criminal justice administration, education, English, history, psychology, and social science. The Bachelor of Science (B.S.) degree is offered in athletic training, biology, chemistry, computer science, environmental science, forensic science, marine biology, mathematics, and medical technology. The Bachelor of Science in Nursing (B.S.N.) degree is offered in nursing. The Bachelor of Science in Business Administration (B.S.B.A.) degree is offered in accounting, finance, health services management, management, marketing, and small-business management. Certification in secondary and elementary education is available. The prelaw program is a 3-3 program in conjunction with Duquesne University School of Law.

Waynesburg College, in conjunction with Florida Institute of Technology, offers a combined curriculum of study that leads to the degree of Bachelor of Science in marine biology. The Bachelor of Science program requires three full years of undergraduate work at Waynesburg College, followed by an academic year at the Florida Institute of Technology in Melbourne, Florida.

Waynesburg College, in conjunction with several cooperating university schools of engineering, offers programs in chemical engineering, civil engineering, electrical engineering, engineering and public policy, mechanical engineering, systems science and engineering, and others. These provide for completion of the chemistry, mathematics/computer science, physics, and liberal arts course work in a small-campus environment where students receive the close personal attention that can be of critical importance to a beginning college student in such a competitive field. After completing the three-year program at Waynesburg College and upon recommendation by its Engineering Advisory Committee, the student applies for admission and, if accepted, moves directly into the program at the cooperating university of his or her choice for the last two years of engineering course work. Upon successful completion of those courses, the student receives a Bachelor of Science degree from Waynesburg College and a Bachelor of Science in engineering from the cooperating university.

In conjunction with approved schools of medical technology, Waynesburg offers a combined curriculum leading to the degree of Bachelor of Science from Waynesburg College and certification by the Registry of Medical Technologists. Students in the medical technology program complete a three-year program at Waynesburg, then complete a twelve-month training program in an approved school of medical technology.

The Associate in Science (A.S.) degree in business administration is offered in a two-year course of study with concentrations in accounting, finance, management, and marketing. An Associate in Arts (A.A.) degree in general studies and an A.S. in computer science are also offered.

The College offers fast-track programs in nursing and an accelerated business degree program. The programs are designed for the adult student with previous college credit.

Academic Program

All candidates for a baccalaureate degree complete a core of liberal arts courses that provides them with a broad background in the sciences, humanities, and arts. This core curriculum offers students a general approach, flexibility in terms of course selection, and time for the pursuit of special interests. In all major fields, at least 124 semester hours of work are required to obtain a baccalaureate degree. In addition, students are required to complete 30 hours of volunteer service before graduation. All candidates for the associate degree must complete a total of 60 semester hours of work.

Students may elect to take a total of 12 semester hours on a pass/fail basis in areas other than their major or correlated field.

The College recognizes and grants credit for scores at or above the 60th percentile on the general examination portion of the

College-Level Examination Program. Three semester hours of credit for each of the five tests, or a maximum of 15 semester hours, may be awarded to fully matriculated students. In addition, the College grants academic credit and/or advanced placement to students who have scored 3 or above on the Advanced Placement tests of the College Board.

Waynesburg College offers several summer sessions, as well as evening and summer-evening classes. The regular academic year is divided into two semesters, with a four-week break (mid-December to mid-January) between terms.

Off-Campus Arrangements

Internships are available in the areas of accounting, business, chemistry, communications, criminal justice, economics, English, history, political science, psychology, public service administration, small-business management, and sociology.

Several opportunities for study abroad in Austria, Costa Rica, Egypt, England, Israel, Kenya, Korea, Russia, and the Ukraine are available for interested students. One such opportunity, the Vira I. Heinz Study Travel Award, is awarded annually for summer travel and study to a woman who has completed her junior year at the College.

Academic Facilities

Every student receives an e-mail account to access the resources of both the campus network and the Internet in classrooms, labs, and resident halls. Labs are open during convenient hours in all classroom buildings. Lab assistants are available to help students with a variety of software applications for PCs or Macintoshes. The 100,000-volume Eberly Library provides online access to major university and public libraries, in addition to electronic cataloging of its own collection. Online access is also provided to abstracts and full-text versions of many periodicals. As an innovative leader in distance learning, the College maintains several video conference rooms that connect classes on campus to classes around the region.

Costs

For the 2000–01 year, tuition is $11,670. The activity fee for student organizations, publications, and athletic events is $280. The estimated annual cost for resident students who do not live on campus is $11,950. Room and board costs are $4620 per year. The estimated cost for resident students who live on campus is $16,770. These figures do not include travel, books, and incidental expenses.

Financial Aid

Waynesburg College strives to make its education affordable for all students. More than 90 percent of the students attending the College during the 1999–2000 academic year received some form of financial assistance. All students are encouraged to apply for financial aid even if they feel they may be ineligible. The College offers assistance/awards from federal, state, private, and College sources. Assistance may include scholarships, grants, work-study employment, and loans. Most financial aid awards are based upon financial need, which is calculated by subtracting the expected family contribution (EFC) from the cost of education. The EFC is calculated by the Department of Education, which uses the information that the family provides on the federal need analysis application. To apply for any form of aid, students must complete the Free Application for Federal Student Aid (FAFSA). The priority deadline for all students is March 15; financial aid applications received after the deadline will be processed on a rolling basis. For financial aid forms and information, students should contact the Financial Aid Office at 724-852-3208.

The College awards several honor scholarships for achievement and potential. The full tuition, room, and board Waynesburg College Ohio Honors Scholarship is given annually to 2 Ohio high school students interested in a career in the sciences or mathematics. The A. B. Miller Scholarship is awarded to students with a minimum 3.75 cumulative high school GPA and with 1200 or higher on the SAT I or 27 or higher on the ACT. It is also awarded to class valedictorians or salutatorians. The Presidential Honor Scholarship is a $4500 annual award. This award requires a high school GPA of 3.75. The Waynesburg Honor Scholarship is a $2000 annual award, and it requires an overall average of 3.5. The Waynesburg Achievement Award is a $1000 annual award with a GPA requirement of 3.2. All honor scholarships are renewable for up to four years if the student maintains the required grade point average. The Waynesburg College Alumni Council Scholarship is a $1000 annual award, and the Waynesburg College Leadership Award is a $1000 to $1600 annual award. The Bonner Scholars Program, which is supported by the Corella and Bertram F. Bonner Foundation, Inc., provides annual awards of $1950 to $3050 to students who have demonstrated a previous commitment and indicate a future commitment to community service.

Faculty

More than 60 percent of the liberal arts faculty have earned doctoral degrees. Each faculty member has demonstrated that teaching is his or her primary concern. At the same time, many faculty members have written scholarly articles and taken part in research and study projects. The student-faculty ratio is 16:1.

Student Government

The Student Senate consists of 7 officers elected by the student body. The president of the Student Senate also appoints student representatives to all major College committees, including a representative to the monthly faculty meetings.

Admission Requirements

In judging the qualifications of applicants, the Committee on Admissions adheres to the following requirements: graduation from an accredited high school, satisfactory grade point average and class rank in high school, and ACT or SAT I scores.

Students desiring to transfer to Waynesburg College should submit a formal application for admission and official high school and college transcripts to the director of admissions. Waynesburg welcomes transfer applications, and the evaluation program is flexible. Each course is evaluated individually, and all courses for which students have earned a grade of C or above may be accepted for transfer from a regionally accredited institution if they are similar to those courses offered at Waynesburg. Each year, transfer applicants are accepted from community and junior colleges, as well as from other four-year institutions.

Waynesburg College admits students of any race, color, sex, religion, or national or ethnic origin, does not discriminate on the basis of sex in the educational programs or activities that it operates, and is in compliance with Title IX of the Education Amendments of 1972. In compliance with Section 504 of the Rehabilitation Act of 1973, Waynesburg College does not discriminate on the basis of handicap in admission or access to its programs or activities.

Application and Information

Waynesburg operates on a rolling admission program and admits qualified applicants as soon as their application is complete. An enrollment deposit ($150 for resident students, $75 for commuting students) is required on the date stipulated in the acceptance letter. One half of this deposit is refunded if the College is notified of withdrawal according to the schedule published in the *Waynesburg College Catalogue*.

The Admissions Office welcomes telephone calls and campus visits from 8:30 a.m. to 4:30 p.m., Monday through Friday. Saturday morning interviews are available by appointment. College literature, such as catalogs, application forms, and financial aid information, may be obtained by contacting:

Director of Admissions
Waynesburg College
Waynesburg, Pennsylvania 15370
Telephone: 724-852-3248
          800-225-7393 (toll-free)
World Wide Web: http://waynesburg.edu/

WEBBER COLLEGE
BABSON PARK, FLORIDA

The College

Webber College was founded in 1927 by Roger Babson, who was an internationally known economist in the early 1900s. The four-year independent coeducational college is located on a beautiful 110-acre campus along the shoreline of Lake Caloosa, 45 minutes from Disney World, Cypress Gardens, and many other attractions. Webber is accredited by the Southern Association of Colleges and Schools. Built on a strong tradition that sets it apart, the College exemplifies integrity, high standards, and achievement. Webber College provides an environment that encourages success through academic excellence and hard work. About 240 men and 200 women are enrolled as undergraduates at Webber. Fifty-five percent of them are from Florida; the other 45 percent represent eleven states and forty-five different countries.

Webber College's off-campus internship programs provide a real-world business environment for Webber students. Field trips also supplement students' business education.

Webber College also offers a Master of Business Administration (M.B.A.) program and a Master of Accounting program.

The College offers intercollegiate sports in basketball, cross-country, golf, soccer, and tennis for men and in basketball, cross-country, soccer, softball, tennis, and volleyball for women. A cheerleading squad supports the intercollegiate athletic program. Intramural athletics are also available for all students. The College's physical education complex includes two gymnasiums, a weight room with Universal machines, a soccer field, an Olympic-size (junior size) swimming pool, and tennis courts. Windsurfing, canoeing, and sailing are also enjoyed by Webber students. Among the wide variety of social organizations and clubs are a national fraternity, a glee club, a student government association, an international club, Green Key ambassadors, a culture club, a travel-hospitality club, and athletic boosters. These groups and many others help to sponsor the various social functions at the College.

Location

The town of Babson Park, a very small rural residential community, is located in the heart of Florida's citrus country near a chain of freshwater lakes. The area has a relaxed and friendly atmosphere. Babson Park is conveniently near many major recreational facilities and national tourist attractions in central Florida.

Majors and Degrees

Webber College offers bachelor's and associate degrees in business administration, with ten different areas of concentration—accounting, finance, general business, global business, hotel and restaurant management, international travel and tourism, management, marketing, pre-law, and sport and club management.

Academic Program

The school operates on the semester system with two 15-week semesters, a 6-week Summer Term A, and a 6-week Summer Term B. The College requires the completion of 61 credit hours for the Associate of Science degree and 122 credit hours for the Bachelor of Science degree with a minimum grade point average of 2.0. The average course load is 15 hours per semester. Students in the Bachelor of Science degree program are required to complete 30 hours in the area of concentration, 30 hours in the business core, 41 hours in the general education core, and 21 hours of tailored electives. Students in the Associate of Science degree program are required to complete 21 hours in the business core, 19 hours in the general education core, and 21 hours in the area of concentration and tailored electives. All students must complete the last 30 credit hours at Webber College to receive a degree. Credit is awarded for successful scores on Advanced Placement (AP) tests and College-Level Examination Program (CLEP) general tests.

Off-Campus Arrangements

A study-abroad program for students working toward a bachelor's degree is offered for one or two semesters in Barcelona, Spain.

The hotel/restaurant and retailing departments have arrangements with major hotels and restaurants in the Orlando area and major retail stores, in state and out of state, for internship programs.

The finance department places student interns in various financial institutions and financial departments of local corporations. The International Travel and Tourism field placement gives students on-the-job experience in the travel industry.

Other off-campus experiences include elective courses in which students observe and analyze business operations and functions of local companies and present their findings in a project format comparable to a professional business consultant's.

The departmental field trip is an opportunity for students in all eight areas of concentration to travel abroad during a summer semester and to discover business techniques in an international environment.

Academic Facilities

The Roger Babson Learning Center, located in the central part of the campus, is a modern and comprehensive small-college library facility. The collection currently contains about 35,500 volumes, an assortment of audiovisual materials, and a CD-ROM computer program for reference materials. The library houses computers for student use.

The computer resources center is a data processing center and teaching facility whose microcomputers offer the latest modern technology for developing student excellence in business, communication, and creativity.

Costs

In 2000–01, the annual fee, which includes tuition, room and board, the student activities fee, and insurance, is $12,045. For commuting students, the annual fee is $9900. These figures are subject to change. The College estimates that $600 is adequate for books and supplies. Laboratory fees are additional.

Financial Aid

The Student Financial Aid Department offers students its counsel and assistance in meeting their educational expenses. Aid is awarded on the basis of an applicant's need, academic performance, and promise. Approximately 70 percent of the students at Webber College receive financial assistance. To demonstrate need, applicants are required to file the Free Application for Federal Student Aid (FAFSA). Various types of aid, such as scholarships, grants, loans, and Federal Work-Study awards, are used to meet student needs. A limited number of no-need scholarships are available; these awards are based on academic performance, on community and college service, or on athletic ability in basketball, tennis, volleyball, golf, soccer, softball, and cross-country. Applicants for aid must reapply each year. Webber College participates in the Federal Perkins Loan, Federal Supplemental Educational Opportunity Grant, and Federal Work-Study programs. All applicants are expected to apply for any entitlement grant for which they are eligible, such as the Federal Pell Grant; Florida residents must apply for a Florida Student Assistance Grant and the Florida Tuition Voucher Program. Federal Stafford Student Loans are also available. Financial aid applicants should submit their requests and forms before April 1 in order to be eligible for certain financial aid programs.

Faculty

More than 60 percent of Webber's full-time faculty members hold doctoral degrees. The faculty-student ratio is 1:14, and all students are assigned a faculty adviser. All faculty members have posted office hours and are available for consultation and advising. Many of Webber's faculty members have a minimum of five years' actual professional work experience in their area of specialization in addition to their years of classroom teaching. This combination of applied and classroom work experience gives them an unusual ability to relate to the needs and concerns of their students.

Student Government

The Student Government Association, the chief governing body on Webber's campus, is composed of elected student representatives and a faculty adviser and deals with nonacademic areas of student life. The association serves as an advisory and coordinating body for student organizations and involves students in campus policy and actions. Representatives from various student organizations serve on the Student Government Association, as do members elected from the College community.

Admission Requirements

Applicants must have graduated from an accredited high school with a minimum of 4 years of English and 3 years of mathematics and preparation in seven other academic subjects. Most accepted candidates rank in the top 50 percent of their high school class. Scores on the SAT I or ACT are required for admission. International applicants must submit scores on the Test of English as a Foreign Language (TOEFL).

Early admission is possible for promising high school juniors who have test scores near the top 15th percentile statewide or nationally, a minimum 3.0 grade point average (on a 4.0 scale), a strong recommendation from their counselor or principal, and a letter of permission from their parents or guardian. A campus interview with the Dean of Student Development is required.

Applications from transfer students are welcome, as are those from students resuming their education or adult students who have delayed their entrance to college. Transfer students must be in good standing at their former institution.

Applicants who fail to meet regular admission requirements may be considered on an individual basis by the Admissions Committee for conditional acceptance. An interview is strongly recommended for all applicants.

Application and Information

An application is ready for consideration by the Admissions Committee when it has been received with a $35 application fee, the required test scores and references, and transcripts from each school attended. The College uses a system of rolling admissions. It is recommended that applications be submitted as early as possible, since on-campus housing is limited. (Freshmen are required to live in the dormitory unless they reside with a parent, guardian, or spouse.)

For application forms, catalogs, and additional information, students should contact:

Director of Admissions
Webber College
1201 Alternate 27 South
P.O. Box 96
Babson Park, Florida 33827-9990
Telephone: 863-638-1431
E-mail: admissions@webber.edu
World Wide Web: http://www.webber.edu

Students take a break between classes at Webber College.

WEBB INSTITUTE
GLEN COVE, NEW YORK

The Institute

Webb Institute was founded in 1889 to provide an opportunity for worthy young students to obtain an education in the "art and science of designing ships and their propulsion systems." The Institute has followed this basic objective to the present, and its graduates are active throughout the United States in the ship design, ship construction, yacht design, and marine operations industries and in appropriate government offices.

The 26-acre campus is the former estate of Herbert L. Pratt and lies on Long Island Sound. Because of the Institute's small size and intensive academic program, varsity sports are limited. However, Webb participates in intercollegiate baseball, basketball, sailing, soccer, tennis, and volleyball, for which ample facilities are provided. The campus has a gymnasium, tennis courts, playing fields, and a beach. Golf and swimming facilities are available nearby.

Webb Institute maintains an enrollment ranging from 80 to 90 men and women, all of whom live on campus. Webb students must be U.S. citizens.

Location

Glen Cove is a city of about 25,000 residents and is located on Long Island's North Shore about an hour from the center of New York City. Convenient train service from Glen Cove to New York brings the variety of cultural, educational, and recreational activities available in the city within easy reach of Webb students.

Majors and Degrees

Webb Institute offers an engineering program in ship design, which involves both naval architecture and marine engineering. The undergraduate degree awarded is the Bachelor of Science in Naval Architecture and Marine Engineering.

Academic Program

The engineering program in ship design consists of fundamental foundation courses in mathematics, science, and engineering sciences, capped by extensive professional design courses. A coherent program in humanities supplements the technical program to round out undergraduate education.

In addition, students have a two-month cooperative-job experience each year in the U.S. marine and maritime industry. During this period, freshmen work as helper mechanics in shipyards, sophomores obtain seagoing experience aboard ship, and juniors and seniors work as engineering assistants in design and technical offices of various marine firms. This important part of the program provides excellent articulation of the educational and career experiences. Innovative engineering ideas are encouraged in the thesis required during the last year. The program is fully accredited. Graduates are well equipped to pursue postgraduate studies.

Semesters run from late August to mid-December and from late February to late June. January and February are winter work periods, and the period from late June to late August is vacation.

Academic Facilities

Full laboratory support is provided for chemistry, physics, metallurgy, and the various engineering courses. A ship model testing tank is available for ship and boat hull studies. Computer facilities are provided on campus. The Livingston Library contains extensive holdings in naval architecture, marine engineering, and general engineering, as well as collections in literature, arts, social sciences, and music.

Costs

All students admitted to Webb are accepted on a tuition- and fee-free basis (full scholarship). Room and board costs are $6250 in 2000–01. About $700 per year is required for books and supplies. A $150 room deposit fee is payable on entry and refunded, less any breakage costs, on departure. The Student Organization requires a $40 deposit on entry, also refundable on departure.

Financial Aid

As stated, a full scholarship covering tuition and fees is awarded to all accepted candidates. The winter work co-op in industry provides income for the student that significantly assists in other expenses. Supplementary aid opportunities are available through the Federal Pell Grant, Federal Stafford Student Loans, and in-house grant programs. Students requiring financial assistance must submit the Free Application for Federal Student Aid (FAFSA) after March 31 but not later than July 1 of the year of entry.

Faculty

Webb Institute has a highly qualified faculty. Many members possess engineering licenses and engage in sponsored research programs, consult for commercial firms, and research and write technical papers. Classes are limited to 25 students, and the student-faculty ratio is 7:1. Each student is assigned a faculty adviser, and consultation with individual faculty members is encouraged.

Student Government

The Student Organization is highly active in student administrative, social, and educational affairs. It is supplemented by an Honor Council and honor system. Together, these entities provide students with a high degree of responsibility for ordering and conducting student life.

Admission Requirements

Admission to Webb is highly competitive. The qualifying requirements for admission are graduation from high school with a B+ (85) or better average in 16 credits of basic high school subjects. Admission selections are based on high school standing (generally in the upper 10 percent) and scores on the College Board's SAT I and Subject Tests in Mathematics (Level I or II), Physics or Chemistry, and the Writing Test. The final selection follows a personal interview conducted at Webb or at a location convenient to the applicant. The entering class is usually restricted to 25 freshmen.

All application papers must be submitted by February 15, and all required College Board tests must be taken before that date. Advanced placement is not given in any of the course offerings. Campus visits by interested students are strongly recommended; prior appointments must be made. An early decision plan is available for qualified candidates.

Webb Institute does not discriminate in admission in the areas of gender, race, or religion. Academic qualities and career motivation are the only criteria.

Application and Information

A catalog and application forms are available upon request.

William G. Murray
Director of Admissions
Webb Institute
Glen Cove, New York 11542
Telephone: 516-671-2213
E-mail: admissions@webb-institute.edu
World Wide Web: http://www.webb-institute.edu

The academic facilities of Webb Institute are located on Long Island Sound in the former residence of Herbert L. Pratt.

WEBSTER UNIVERSITY
ST. LOUIS, MISSOURI

The University

Founded in 1915, Webster University is a coeducational liberal arts institution that has been termed innovative and international. However, it is traditional in offering a substantial basis for advanced study in academic and professional specialties. The student population at Webster is as diverse as the University's programs and represents a wide range of cultures and backgrounds. There are approximately 1,800 full-time students enrolled from forty-one states and thirty countries. Webster students are self-motivated and show a desire to design their own academic programs and extracurricular activities and to assume responsibility for them. Webster encourages and supports individual development in students' social and recreational activities as well as in their academic programs. An apartment-style student housing complex opened in 1998.

There are many opportunities for creative development through clubs, cultural societies, and other organizations as well as through campus publications and the student government. Webster offers intercollegiate athletics in men's and women's basketball, soccer, and tennis; men's baseball and golf; and women's cross-country, softball, swimming, and volleyball. Webster University also sponsors a broad spectrum of cultural events. The Loretto-Hilton Center for the Performing Arts is a focus of theatrical and musical activity for the St. Louis community as well as for Webster University students. It houses the Repertory Theatre of St. Louis, the Webster University Symphony, the Opera Theatre of St. Louis, and the major lecture series presented by the University.

At the graduate level, Webster offers the Master of Arts, Master of Arts in Teaching, Master of Business Administration, Master of Music, and Doctor of Applied Management degrees.

Location

Webster's 47-acre campus is located in the St. Louis suburb of Webster Groves, which is a wooded residential area that serves as a cultural center for the St. Louis area. The University is 13 miles southwest of the Gateway Arch, the Mississippi riverfront, and Laclede's Landing and 4 miles south of Forest Park, a 1,400-acre area with 35 acres of lakes and ponds. Located in the park are the St. Louis Zoo, St. Louis Art Museum, Municipal Opera, and the St. Louis Science Center. Webster is 30 minutes from Lambert International Airport, Six Flags over Mid-America, Busch Memorial Stadium (home of the St. Louis Cardinals), and the TWA Dome (home of the NFL Rams). The St. Louis Blues hockey and St. Louis Ambush indoor soccer games can be viewed in the nearby Kiel Center.

Majors and Degrees

At the undergraduate level, Webster awards the Bachelor of Arts, Bachelor of Business Administration, Bachelor of Fine Arts, Bachelor of Music, Bachelor of Music Education, and Bachelor of Science. Majors include accounting, advertising and marketing communications, American studies, anthropology, art, audio production, biology, broadcast journalism, business administration, ceramics, choral music, computer science, creative writing, dance, early childhood education, economics, elementary education, English, film, French, general science, German, global journalism, graphic design, health-care administration, history, human resource management, instrumental music, interactive media, international business, international relations, jazz studies, journalism, legal studies, management, marketing, mathematics, media communications, media literacy, musical theater, music performance, music technology, music theory/composition, oral communications, painting, philosophy, photography, political science, printmaking, psychology, public relations, religion, scriptwriting, sculpture, social science, sociology, Spanish, special education, theater arts, video production, and vocal performance.

A student may also construct an individualized area of concentration. Webster offers courses leading to Missouri state teacher certification. Webster also offers an accelerated B.A./M.A. option to qualified students in certain areas.

Academic Program

It is the University's objective to offer a liberal arts education that prepares students for a wide variety of occupations by teaching skills that can be applied in many fields. Webster's flexible program allows a student to pursue defined career goals within the context of a broader liberal arts curriculum. Students must successfully complete 128 credit hours for a bachelor's degree; a minimum of 30 of these hours must be earned directly from Webster. Specific requirements for an area of concentration or major and general education requirements must also be fulfilled.

The undergraduate studies program offers more than seventy programs of study. Webster's curriculum requires specific courses within the major field of study. Outside the major field, students have the opportunity to integrate all course work by electing those courses that they believe will best develop and fulfill individual goals and objectives. Courses are carefully evaluated and chosen during preregistration in consultation with the student's academic adviser, a member of Webster's faculty. This system, combined with Webster's 16:1 student-faculty ratio, provides students with the personalized attention and close interaction that encourage both academic growth and personal development.

Webster's combined B.A./M.A. program, requiring 152 credit hours, enables students with outstanding academic records to complete both a bachelor's degree and a master's degree through an accelerated program. A carefully designed course of study integrates upper-level undergraduate work with initial graduate courses, reducing by 12 credit hours the total time required for both degrees.

Transfer credit may be granted for college-level work completed with a grade of C or better at another accredited institution, satisfactory performance on CLEP and Advanced Placement examinations, and participation in International Baccalaureate, military, and in-service training programs. The University grants credit for qualified experiential learning. Students may register for individualized learning options, including independent study, fieldwork, internships, and semester sabbatical experiences (on-the-job apprenticeships in the community).

The University observes a two-semester, sixteen-week calendar; the first semester ends before the Christmas break. Many courses are offered in eight-week terms—two each semester and one during the summer.

Off-Campus Arrangements

Undergraduate students may choose to study abroad or earn a degree in economics, management, international relations, psychology, or computer studies at one of Webster's European campuses in Geneva, Switzerland; Vienna, Austria; Leiden, the Netherlands; and London, England. Study opportunities are also available at Webster's campus in Thailand. In addition, the foreign language department grants credit for individualized programs of study abroad. Local off-campus opportunities include practicums in social service agencies, the media, state and local government agencies, and St. Louis–area businesses and industries. Students may also arrange sabbatical study leaves.

Academic Facilities

Webster's library, shared with Eden Theological Seminary, has a combined collection of more than 250,000 volumes and also contains more than 100,000 records, slides, filmstrips, microfilms, microfiche, and 16-mm films. PASSPORTS, the library's integrated research system, provides 24-hour access to full-text databases via the Internet. The Leif J. Sverdrup Business/ Technology Complex contains the Grant Business and Management Center, a state-of-the-art media center, the mathematics and computer science departments, microcomputer labs, and lounges. The Loretto-Hilton Center for the Performing Arts houses dance and theater practice and performance facilities and provides a home for the repertory company. The Music Building includes classrooms, practice rooms, and a recital hall, and it houses the only Archifoon in the United States. The Visual Arts Building houses the art department's drawing, painting, printmaking, ceramics, sculpture, and graphic design studios along with one of several galleries. The Pearson House is home to the English and philosophy departments. The H. Sam Priest Center for International Studies houses the University's foreign language and history/political science departments.

Costs

For 1999–2000, the general fees at Webster University for one academic year were $12,150 for tuition, $5400 for room and board, and $800 for books and supplies. Tuition for theater conservatory students was $15,190. All out-of-town freshmen are required to take room and board contracts. The fee for private music lessons varies. Students in art and media should expect to pay approximately $200 in fees and supplies. All fees are subject to change; the Office of Undergraduate Admission can provide up-to-date information.

Financial Aid

Webster University has a strong financial aid and scholarship program to meet the needs of students as demonstrated on the Free Application for Federal Student Aid (FAFSA). In the academic year 1999–2000, Webster administered more than $8.5 million in financial aid. Sources of aid include Webster University scholarships, Webster University grants, federal and state grants, loans, and work-study funds. The average financial aid package in 1999–2000 was $11,000. Applications for financial aid or scholarships can be considered only after admission to the University. The deadline for scholarship applications is April 1; application forms are available from the Office of Undergraduate Admission.

Faculty

Webster University places great importance upon having a strong teaching faculty supported by a strong adjunct faculty of well-trained practitioners. The full-time faculty numbers approximately 140, and 70 percent hold the highest degree in their field. The adjunct faculty, including actors in residence and professional musicians who teach part-time, numbers approximately 300. Most of the musicians are regular members of the nationally acclaimed St. Louis Symphony Orchestra. Actors in residence are members of the Repertory Theatre of St. Louis, which is housed at Webster University.

Student Government

The Student Government Association is a student governing organization composed of 15 members elected by the undergraduate student body. The organization is the main vehicle for communication between the students and other members of the University community, including the faculty and the administration. It is also responsible for budgeting and distributing student activities funds.

Admission Requirements

Webster University actively seeks a diverse student body and admits students on an individual basis. Applicants most likely to be accepted are in the top 50 percent of their graduating class, have a cumulative grade point average of at least a B, and have an ACT composite score of 21 or above and/or a combined SAT score of at least 1000. All applicants are considered without regard to race, color, sex, religion, or national origin. Freshman and transfer applications are accepted for fall, spring, and summer enrollment.

Transfer students must submit credentials from all college-level work attempted. In general, Webster grants credit for any college-level work in which the student received a grade of C or better. As a general rule, only 64 hours can be transferred from junior colleges. Transfer students who have completed less than one year of college-level work must also submit high school transcripts.

Applicants from abroad must submit official secondary school and/or college transcripts and the Declaration of Finances Form of the College Scholarship Service. All students accepted from abroad are assigned to appropriate ESL (English as a second language) classes based upon the results of a standardized placement test administered prior to enrollment.

Although personal interviews and campus visits are not required, they are encouraged. Students who wish to major in art, dance, music, or theater arts are required to audition or present a portfolio for acceptance into the program.

Application and Information

Early application is encouraged. All students applying to Webster must submit an application with a $25 nonrefundable application fee. Freshmen must submit high school transcripts or GED scores and SAT I or ACT scores. Webster operates on a rolling admission policy. As soon as all credentials are received, students are notified of the decision of the Admission Committee. Accepted freshmen should file a letter of intent within thirty days and a $100 tuition deposit (refundable until May 1). The hours of the Webster University undergraduate admission office are 7:30 a.m. to 5:30 p.m., Monday through Thursday; 7:30 to 4:30 p.m. on Friday.

Application packets are available from:

Office of Undergraduate Admission
Webster University
470 East Lockwood
St. Louis, Missouri 63119-3194

Telephone: 314-968-6991
        800-75-ENROLL (toll-free)
World Wide Web: http://www.webster.edu

Leif J. Sverdrup Business/Technology Complex.

WELLESLEY COLLEGE
WELLESLEY, MASSACHUSETTS

The College

Wellesley College is an independent, residential liberal arts college for women with an enrollment of 2,300 students. Situated on a 500-acre campus 12 miles west of Boston, Wellesley is a college for the serious student with high expectations for her personal and professional life. Students at the College come from across the U.S., from around the world, and from many different cultures and backgrounds. They have prepared for Wellesley at hundreds of different secondary schools.

Most students live in residence halls on campus—each hall is its own community within the larger Wellesley community. Residents may gather for informal talks over dinner. Residences also sponsor social events, guest lecturers, dinners with faculty members, and guests-in-residence.

Wellesley's Sports Center includes an eight-lane, 25-meter/25-yard swimming pool and separate diving well; a volleyball arena; badminton, squash, and racquetball courts; fencing/dance/exercise studios; weight machine and free-weights rooms; and an athletic training area. The field house has a basketball arena, indoor tennis courts, a 200-meter track, and a cardiovascular machine area. Outdoor sports facilities include a boathouse for canoes, sailboats, and crew shells and a swimming beach, both located on the campus's Lake Waban. Wellesley also maintains a nine-hole golf course, twenty-four tennis courts, and field hockey, lacrosse, and soccer fields.

Many extracurricular activities are often held in the Schneider College Center, which is used by all members of the College community. Throughout the year, distinguished artists, musicians, lecturers, and public figures are invited to the campus, and their presentations are free of charge. There are no sororities, but there are several academic societies, including two historically black public service organizations. Ethos, the black student association on campus, is housed in Harambee House and brings speakers as well as artistic and cultural events to the College throughout the year. Alianza, the organization primarily for international Hispanic and Latin American students, and Mezcla, the organization for Hispanic/Latina students, were formed by students from these groups at Wellesley to promote their feelings of solidarity and to enrich the College community through cultural offerings. These two groups collaborate closely. Members of Alianza and Mezcla are also involved in communities off campus, especially in the Spanish-speaking communities of Boston. The Asian Student Union, an umbrella organization for many clubs, sponsors films, seminars, and workshops on campus as well as social and cultural events with other colleges in the Boston area. The Slater International Center provides a meeting place where international students at Wellesley can relax and share common experiences.

Location

The College is located in the town of Wellesley, a suburban community of more than 27,000 people, with many shops, restaurants, and bookstores. Its proximity to Boston allows students to take advantage of the vast array of opportunities there, which include volunteer work and internships in government or social agencies; performances given by the Boston Ballet or the Boston Symphony; sports events, such as Boston Celtics, Bruins, and Red Sox games; and visits to the Museum of Fine Arts, the Museum of Science, or the many historic sites. Within metropolitan Boston, there are approximately 250,000 college and university students and many major educational institutions. The campus is only a short distance from New England winter sports areas as well as from the Atlantic coast and Cape Cod beaches.

Majors and Degrees

Wellesley College grants the B.A. and offers majors in humanities: art history, Chinese, English, French, German, Greek, Italian, Japanese, Latin, music, Russian, Spanish, and studio art; in social sciences: Africana studies, anthropology, economics, history, philosophy, political science, psychology, religion, sociology, and women's studies; and in science and mathematics: astronomy, biological sciences, chemistry, computer science, geology, mathematics, and physics. The nineteen interdepartmental majors are American studies, architecture, biological chemistry, Chinese studies, classical and Near Eastern archaeology, classical civilization, cognitive science, comparative literature, French cultural studies, German studies, international relations, Italian culture, Japanese studies, Jewish studies, language studies, Latin American studies, medieval/Renaissance studies, neuroscience, and Russian area studies. Students may also design individual majors, such as environmental science, peace and justice studies, theater studies, and urban studies.

Academic Program

Each candidate is required to complete 32 credits of academic work with a C average or better. Nine credits must be taken in the following general areas: language and literature; visual arts, music, video, film, and theater; social and behavioral analysis; epistemology and cognition; ethics, religion, and moral philosophy; historical studies; natural and physical science; and mathematical modeling and problem solving in the natural sciences, mathematics, and computer science. Proficiency in one foreign language is required, as are courses in writing and quantitative reasoning. Students must also complete a one-course multicultural requirement designed to allow the student to see a people, culture, or society through its own eyes. Wellesley offers a thorough background for students preparing to attend medical school or law school. Medical school acceptance rates generally range from 64 percent to 74 percent; acceptance to law school is approximately 80 percent. Between 25 and 30 percent of Wellesley's graduates continue directly on to graduate school.

The Elisabeth Kaiser Davis Degree Program at Wellesley welcomes women who are beyond the traditional undergraduate age to complete a B.A. degree on a part-time or full-time basis. The program takes into account the special needs of adult students regarding admission, advising, orientation, housing, and financial aid. Postbaccalaureate study at Wellesley is for men and women who have a bachelor's degree and wish to complete further undergraduate work for a specific purpose. Many students take courses to prepare for medical school or other graduate programs. Those interested in these programs should contact the Board of Admission.

Off-Campus Arrangements

Wellesley has cross-registration programs with MIT, Babson, and Brandeis. Through the Twelve College Exchange program, students may live and study for a semester or a full academic year at any of the member institutions (Amherst, Bowdoin, Connecticut College, Dartmouth, Mount Holyoke, Smith, Trinity, Vassar, Wesleyan, Wheaton, and Williams). Students may also attend the National Theater Institute at the Eugene O'Neill Theater Center, which is accredited by Connecticut College, and the Williams–Mystic Seaport Program in Maritime Studies. In addition, there are exchanges with Spelman College, a predominantly black liberal arts college for women in Atlanta, Georgia, and with Mills College in Oakland, California.

Approximately 30 percent of the junior class studies abroad each year for either a semester or a year. Students attend programs sponsored by other colleges and universities or those sponsored by Wellesley. At present, Wellesley runs programs in Aix-en-Provence, France; Konstanz, Germany; and Oaxaca, Mexico. Wellesley is a consortium member for programs in Spain, Italy, and Japan and offers exchange programs with institutions in the United Kingdom, Japan, Argentina, and Korea. The Washington Internship Program provides 18 to 20 juniors with an opportunity to spend the summer in Washington, D.C., working within the federal government, within Congress, at public interest organizations, and at cultural and scientific institutions.

Academic Facilities

The College library contains more than 1.3 million volumes and more than 2,500 periodical subscriptions, government documents, and audiovisual holdings. Special collections include rare books and manuscripts, book arts, and English and American poetry. Departmental libraries focus on art, astronomy, music, and science. Access to a broad range of electronic reference and full-text resources is provided through the library's World Wide Web site. Wellesley is the only undergraduate institution in the Boston Library Consortium, an association of major research and academic libraries devoted to sharing resources. The Knapp Media and Technology Center consolidates course support services, media services, and language laboratory facilities. Providing access to the most current instructional technology, the center is a facility where students, the faculty, and staff members can collaborate in interactive learning and on creating multimedia projects. Technology is an integral part of every student's life at Wellesley. The campus network provides a wealth of research opportunities on campus and through the Internet. E-mail and electronic bulletin boards are important extensions of both social and academic communication. Courses use technology for activities as diverse as reviewing art history slides and interacting with animated simulations of biological and chemical processes. Every student has network access in her dorm room. In addition, there are shared clusters of PCs and Macintoshes in every residence.

The Jewett Arts Center houses extensive facilities for the art and music departments, including a concert hall, student galleries, two libraries, and art studios and music practice rooms. The Davis Museum and Cultural Center, located in a separate building, houses exhibition galleries, an art collection of 5,000 works, a print room, a study gallery/seminar room, a café, and a cinema. The Science Center houses laboratories, classrooms, and offices for eight scientific disciplines; a vivarium; a science library of more than 105,000 volumes; and shared support facilities. The completely up-to-date instrumentation available for undergraduate use includes an X-ray diffractometer, spectrometers (nuclear magnetic resonance, mass, Mössbauer, UV, and IR), electron microscopes, and argon and dye lasers. An expansion and renovation project of the Science Center made available several laboratories (molecular biology, cognitive learning, laser, electronics, and optics) and other facilities. The Whitin Observatory includes 24-inch, 12-inch, and 6-inch telescopes, as well as a library, classrooms, and auxiliary instruments. The greenhouses contain two research houses and one of the largest teaching collections of plants in the Northeast, including specimens that range from temperate to tropical species. Botanical facilities include growth chambers with temperature, light, and humidity control as well as extensive botanical gardens and an arboretum.

Costs

For 2000–01, costs are $23,718 for tuition and $7480 for room and board. The student activity fee is $156, and the facilities fee is $300. Wellesley estimates that an additional $1800 per year is adequate for books, laundry, and other essentials, exclusive of travel to and from home.

Financial Aid

Approximately 50 percent of Wellesley students receive financial aid through the College. Usually aid consists of a combination of grants and loans, as well as student employment during the academic year. In addition, other students receive outside scholarships and grants, and many work on or off campus through the Student Employment Office. The decision to admit a student is made independently of her financial need. Full need, as determined by Wellesley's standards and policies, is met through the financial aid package.

Faculty

Instruction by faculty members of all ranks is available to all students. Currently, there are 230 full-time and 102 part-time faculty members; 98 percent of full-time tenure-track faculty members hold the doctoral degree or final degree in their field, and 54 percent of tenured faculty members are women. The faculty consists of scholars actively involved in research and writing; however, teaching is a major priority, and students find their professors to be easily accessible.

Student Government

Students, through election to the College Government Senate and through voting representation on College committees, share responsibility in the decision-making processes of the College. Students serve on committees of the Board of Trustees, on the Board of Admission, and on important departmental committees. Students regulate their lives in the residence halls through House Council and manage student activity funds used to support more than 130 student organizations. The honor system is a strong tradition at Wellesley, permitting self-scheduled examinations, take-home tests, and a lack of stringent social regulations.

Admission Requirements

Admission to Wellesley is competitive. Prospective applicants should have a strong secondary school record and are advised to take the most academically challenging course of study available to them. Students entering Wellesley normally have completed four years of college-preparatory studies in secondary school. However, Wellesley also considers applications from students who plan to complete only three years of high school and who demonstrate academic strength and social and personal maturity. Good preparation includes training in clear and coherent writing and in interpreting literature, in the principles of mathematics, and in history; experience in at least two laboratory sciences; and competence in at least one foreign language—ancient or modern—usually achieved through four years of study. College credit may be given to students who have taken Advanced Placement examinations. Wellesley participates in an early decision plan. Transfer students are admitted in both semesters. The ACT or SAT I and three SAT II Subject Tests, one of which must be the Writing Test, are required for admission. An interview is strongly recommended. The Test of English as a Foreign Language (TOEFL) or the SAT II: English Language Proficiency Test (ELPT) is highly recommended of all international students when English is not their first language.

Application and Information

For more information about Wellesley College, students should contact:

Dean of Admission
Wellesley College
106 Central Street
Wellesley, Massachusetts 02481
Telephone: 781-283-2270
Fax: 781-283-3678
World Wide Web: http://www.wellesley.edu/Admission/

WELLS COLLEGE
AURORA, NEW YORK

The College

Wells College, founded in 1868, is proud to be the second institution in the country to award the baccalaureate degree to women. Its founder, Henry Wells, who built his fortune with the creation of the Wells Fargo Express, believed that women would play a vital role in the future of America.

What truly distinguishes Wells from other colleges and universities is that it dares to be small. With an enrollment of 404 students, Wells students do not sit quietly among rows of neatly lined desks; instead, they join their classmates and professors around seminar tables where they are expected to contribute their ideas. Wells faculty members are graduates of many of the country's top universities, and 100 percent hold a Ph.D. or equivalent degree. They are widely published and respected in their fields, but teaching is their first priority.

Academic opportunities include independent and interdisciplinary study, internships, and study-abroad programs. In addition, a campus newspaper, several musical and drama groups, a literary magazine and book arts center, environmental and political organizations, and other organizations provide important opportunities for student involvement. A full program of cultural events, symposia, and lectures enhances the academic and social life of the College.

Students interested in athletics may participate on intercollegiate teams in field hockey, lacrosse, soccer, swimming, and tennis. There are also a number of intramural opportunities, including basketball, soccer, swimming, tennis, and volleyball. Athletic facilities include indoor and outdoor tennis courts, a gymnasium, a weight room, a nine-hole golf course, and a campus boathouse and dock used in teaching sailing, canoeing, lifeguarding, and outdoor survival skills.

Location

The village of Aurora is located on the eastern shore of Cayuga Lake in the Finger Lakes resort region of upstate New York. Aurora is in the center of an area well-known for its concentration of prestigious private colleges, including Cornell University, Ithaca College, Hobart and William Smith College, Colgate University, Hamilton College, and Syracuse University. Wells College is within a 60-mile radius of five colleges and universities with a total enrollment of more than 50,000 students. Aurora is 25 miles from Ithaca, 60 miles from Syracuse, and 60 miles from Rochester.

Majors and Degrees

Wells College offers the Bachelor of Arts degree with concentrations in African-American studies, American cultures, anthropology/cross-cultural studies, art history, biochemistry and molecular biology, biology, chemistry, computer science, creative writing, economics, English, environmental policies and values, environmental sciences, ethics and philosophy, French, German, government and politics, history, human nature and values, international studies, literature, management, mathematics, music, physics, psychology, religious studies, sociology, Spanish, studio art, theater and dance, and women's studies. In consultation with the dean and faculty, students may design their own concentrations and majors. In addition, Wells offers programs that lead to provisional certification in elementary and secondary education, as well as preprofessional programs in business, engineering, law, medicine, and veterinary science.

The College offers dual-degree programs in engineering with Case Western Reserve University, Clarkson University, Columbia University, Cornell University, and Washington University, as well as dual-degree M.B.A. and M.P.H. programs with the University of Rochester. Wells also offers a dual-degree 3-4 program with the College of Veterinary Medicine of Cornell University, which leads to the D.V.M. degree. In the dual-degree programs, the student earns both her B.A. from Wells College and the professional degree from the affiliated university within five years, with the exception of the D.V.M. program, which takes seven years.

Academic Program

The academic philosophy at Wells is firmly rooted in the liberal arts. The College is organized into four academic divisions: the humanities, natural and mathematical sciences, social sciences, and the arts, but faculty members in all divisions work together to produce a curriculum that recognizes connections between subject areas and fits many pieces together, just as they fit together in life.

Students take two multidisciplinary courses during their first year that have an emphasis on the scope and breadth of human inquiry and creative synthesis necessary for leadership in a wide range of areas. Wells 101, Approaches to the Liberal Arts, is a shared experience for first-year students in the fall that incorporates a multidisciplinary approach to familiarize students with the liberal arts. Writing, critical thinking, discussion, collaborative learning, respect for diversity, and attendance at campus cultural events are integral to the course. Wells 102, the first-year seminar, consists of various topics that continue to develop writing and other skills that are important to students in their academic careers.

Wells students are traditionally required to complete a thesis or project during the senior year. While the core curriculum provides a shared academic experience for students, the senior thesis provides a student with the opportunity to complete a thoughtful, in-depth analysis of a topic of the student's choosing.

Off-Campus Arrangements

Wells College students may spend January intersession, a semester, or even a year in another setting abroad or in the United States. Wells sponsors or is affiliated with programs in the following cities and countries: Copenhagen, Denmark; Paris, Grenoble, and St. Victor Lacoste, France; Berlin, Bonn, and Heidelberg, Germany; Florence and Rome, Italy; Puebla, Mexico; Dakar, Senegal; Seville, Spain; and London, Bath, and York, United Kingdom. Students may pursue global study in science through the School for Field Studies in Africa, Australia, the Caribbean, and Hawaii. The Washington Semester at American University in Washington, D.C., is a popular option for those students interested in communication, economics, or government. Wells also offers an independent cross-registration with Cornell University and Ithaca College.

Academic Facilities

The Louis Jefferson Long Library has received numerous awards for its architectural design. It has an open-stack collection of more than 248,130 volumes, 412 periodicals, and 13,383 microfilms. The library is a member of the South Central

Research Library Council and the New York State Interlibrary Loan Network. Facilities include an online computer center, individual study carrels, seminar and group-study rooms, and an art gallery. There are department libraries in art, economics, English, mathematics, music, philosophy, and the sciences located throughout campus. The Barler Hall of Music houses a recital hall with superb acoustics, vocal and instrumental practice rooms, a music library, and a listening laboratory. Facilities for printmaking, painting, ceramics, sculpture, and photography are located in the Campbell Arts Building. The Cleveland Hall of Languages contains modern equipment for learning foreign languages. The Zabriskie Science Building houses modern laboratories for chemistry, biology, and physics, as well as a computer laboratory, library, darkroom, and greenhouse. The art history and history departments are located in Morgan Hall. In addition to the seminar rooms and art history library, Morgan has an extensive slide library and small art gallery. Macmillan Hall has classrooms, faculty and administrative offices, several computer laboratories, and department libraries. The east wing of Macmillan houses the Margaret Phipps Auditorium, a theater facility used for theater arts instruction, concerts, lectures, and dramatic productions.

Costs

Tuition fees for the students in 1999–2000 were $11,850; room and board were $6100, and fees were $450. Tuition is guaranteed for four years of enrollment at Wells.

Financial Aid

Approximately 85 percent of Wells students receive financial aid packaged in the form of grants, scholarships, and loans.

Faculty

Wells College has 55 faculty members, 100 percent of the full-time undergraduate faculty members hold Ph.D. or terminal degrees. Fifty percent of the faculty members are women. The first priority of the faculty members is teaching, although they do receive recognition for scholarship in their respective fields.

Student Government

The student body is self-governing through the Collegiate Association. The three main governing bodies of the association are the Student-Faculty Administration Board, the Collegiate Council, and the Community Court. Students serve on faculty committees that make decisions concerning administrative and curricular matters.

Admission Requirements

Wells College students come from diverse geographic and socioeconomic backgrounds. To provide the foundation for study at Wells, each candidate for admission is expected to complete a solid college-preparatory program during her four years of secondary school. The College recommends a program of study that includes 4 years of English grammar, composition, and literature; 2 years of history; 3 years of a foreign language; 3 years of mathematics, with emphasis on basic algebraic, geometric, and trigonometric concepts and deductive reasoning; and 2 years of laboratory science. Scores from the SAT I or the ACT are required, and a personal interview is strongly encouraged.

Application and Information

Applications should be received early in the senior year of high school and not later than March 1 of the year in which entrance is desired. Applications from early decision and early action candidates must be received by December 15.

Transfer applications are reviewed on a rolling basis. Transfer students are eligible for merit scholarships and financial aid.

A campus visit is highly recommended for prospective students. Typically, the visit includes a guided tour of the Wells College campus and facilities, overnight accommodations in the residence halls, a personal interview, and the option of attending classes. Appointments with faculty members and financial aid representatives are also available.

For more information about Wells College or to schedule a campus visit, students should contact:

Admissions Office
Wells College
Aurora, New York 13026
Telephone: 800-952-9355 (toll-free)
E-mail: admissions@wells.edu

Students enjoy a close-knit college evironment at Wells.

WENTWORTH INSTITUTE OF TECHNOLOGY
BOSTON, MASSACHUSETTS

The Institute

Wentworth Institute of Technology was founded in 1904 to provide education in the mechanical arts. Today, it is one of the nation's leading technical institutes, offering study in a variety of disciplines. Wentworth has a current undergraduate day enrollment of 3,225 men and women and graduates more engineering technicians and technologists each year than any other college in the United States. The technical education acquired at Wentworth enables graduates to assume creative and responsible careers in business and industry. Wentworth is located on a 35-acre campus on Huntington Avenue in Boston.

Wentworth provides dormitory and suite-style residence halls on campus for men and women. Students residing in the residence halls are on a full meal plan. Upperclass students have the option of living in on-campus apartments. Students residing in the apartments may prepare their own meals. A cafeteria and a snack bar are available for those wishing to purchase their meals.

Career counseling and placement assistance are available to all alumni and to students who have completed at least one semester of study at the Institute. While many graduates of Wentworth are employed in the Boston area, alumni have secured positions throughout the United States and abroad.

Location

Boston is the educational center of New England. It is a city of charm, tradition, and elegance—a major center of art, science, music, history, medicine, and education. Wentworth is situated near the heart of Boston and is surrounded by institutions that provide the cultural advantages for which the city is famous. The Museum of Fine Arts, with its store of art treasures, is diagonally across the street, and admission is free to any student with a Wentworth ID card. Symphony Hall is just a few blocks away. The Harvard Medical School, the New England Conservatory of Music, Emmanuel College, Simmons College, Massachusetts College of Pharmacy and Allied Health Sciences, the Massachusetts College of Art, Roxbury Community College, and Northeastern University are among the many educational institutions within a few blocks of the campus.

Majors and Degrees

Wentworth Institute of Technology is a technical college of great diversity. Degree programs are offered in the fields of architecture, computer science, design, engineering, engineering technology, and management of technology.

Specifically, bachelor's degrees are awarded in the following majors: the Bachelor of Architecture; the Bachelor of Science in architectural engineering technology, civil engineering technology, computer engineering technology, computer science, construction engineering technology, construction management, electromechanical engineering, electronic engineering technology, environmental engineering, facilities planning and management, industrial design, interior design, management of technology, manufacturing engineering technology, and mechanical engineering technology. Baccalaureate degrees in architecture and interior design are designated as first professional degrees. Completion of a Wentworth baccalaureate degree requires four or five years, depending on the program.

Associate in Applied Science degrees can be earned in most majors that grant bachelor's degrees at Wentworth. Although students must apply and be admitted to a four- or five-year bachelor's degree program, they may elect to leave with an associate degree after two years. The STEP program is designed for international students and permanent residents who need to strengthen their English skills before completing their studies in one of Wentworth's bachelor's degree programs.

Academic Program

At Wentworth Institute of Technology, college-level study in technological fundamentals and principles is combined with appropriate laboratory, field, and studio experience. Students apply theory to practical problems, and they acquire skills and techniques by using, operating, and controlling equipment and instruments particular to their area of specialization. In addition, study in the social sciences and humanities provides a balanced understanding of the world in which graduates work. Wentworth's programs of study are more practical than theoretical in approach, and the Institute's academic requirements demand extensive time and effort.

During the first two years of study in a degree program at Wentworth, students lay the foundation for more advanced study in the third and fourth (and fifth, where applicable) years. While nearly all majors allow continuous study from the freshman through the senior year, the architecture major requires a petition for readmission to the baccalaureate program during the sophomore year.

All bachelor's degree programs are conducted as cooperative (co-op) education programs: upon entering their third year, students alternate semesters of academic study at Wentworth with semester-long periods of employment in industry. Two semesters of co-op employment are required; one additional (summer) semester of co-op is optional. Both students and the companies that hire them are enthusiastic about the co-op program and agree that it is a mutually valuable experience.

Academic Facilities

Wentworth's twenty-seven buildings house classrooms, laboratories, studios, administrative offices, and other facilities. Modern Beatty Hall houses the Alumni Library, computer center, classrooms, dining areas, and office space. State-of-the-art laboratories, such as the Richard H. Lufkin Technology Center and the Davis Center for Advanced Graphics and Interactive Learning, are situated throughout the campus.

Costs

For 1999–2000, tuition was $12,450, books and supplies were approximately $1000, and room and board were about $6500 (this figure varies according to accommodation).

Financial Aid

Scholarships are available to students who demonstrate need and academic promise. Merit scholarships are also available. Wentworth also provides federal and state financial assistance, such as Federal Pell and Federal Supplemental Educational Opportunity Grants, Federal Perkins Loans, Federal Work-Study awards, Gilbert Matching Grants, and Massachusetts No-Interest Loans to students with financial need in accordance with federal and state guidelines.

Wentworth participates in the Federal Direct Lending program.

As a result, students are eligible to borrow under the Federal Direct Stafford Loan program and parents may borrow under the Federal Direct PLUS program. Individuals participating in these programs borrow money directly from the federal government rather than through lending institutions.

In addition to these need-based programs, Wentworth also participates in the MEFA loan program sponsored by the Massachusetts Educational Financing Authority. Wentworth offers several payment options through payment plans and alternative loan financing.

To apply for financial aid, new students should complete the Free Application for Federal Student Aid (FAFSA) by March 1. Applications received after this date will be considered as funds allow.

Faculty

Wentworth's faculty includes 115 full-time and 124 part-time members. The primary responsibility of every faculty member is teaching. Although professors may engage in some research and related work, student development remains the central mission of Wentworth's faculty. Upon entering Wentworth, every student is assigned a faculty adviser. The student-faculty ratio is 24:1.

Student Government

Wentworth's Student Government performs an essential function as the official representative of the student body. Its purposes are to receive and express student opinion, to advance the best interests of the student body with the administration and faculty and with other institutions and associations, to support all extracurricular activities of the student body, and to serve as a bond between the student body and the faculty to foster mutual cooperation and understanding. The Student Government is made up of elected representatives from each class section and the officers elected by the student body at large. The Student Government sponsors social functions and student organizations and serves as an advocate for student concerns.

Admission Requirements

Applicants must be graduates of secondary schools (or have passed the GED test) and must meet specific entrance requirements. All programs require four years of English, a laboratory science, and mathematics through algebra II in a college-preparatory program. Both the architectural engineering technology and Bachelor of Architecture programs require a course in basic drafting. All programs require the submission of SAT I scores. International students and transfers are welcome.

Application and Information

Students are admitted to Wentworth for September and January enrollment. The priority application deadline for the fall semester is May 1; for the spring, the deadline is December 1. Notification of admission is made on a rolling basis. An application form, an application fee of $30, transcripts from the secondary school and any colleges previously attended, and SAT I scores should be sent to:

Admissions Office
Wentworth Institute of Technology
550 Huntington Avenue
Boston, Massachusetts 02115

Telephone: 617-989-4000
              800-556-0610 (toll-free)
Fax: 617-989-4010
E-mail: admissions@wit.edu
World Wide Web: http://www.wit.edu

Wentworth Hall.

WESLEYAN COLLEGE
MACON, GEORGIA

The College

Wesleyan College, chartered in 1836, has the distinction of being the world's first college chartered to grant degrees to women. Today, Wesleyan is regarded as one of the nation's finest colleges and remains dedicated to the education of women.

Wesleyan is a four-year, Methodist-related, liberal arts college. Enrollment is limited to fewer than 1,000 students. This is done primarily to support a learner-based curriculum that limits classes to no more than 20 students and to provide opportunities for meaningful participation in the life of the college community. Wesleyan's student body has been cited among the nation's most diverse and includes students from more than twenty-five states and a dozen other countries.

The College is located on a beautiful 200-acre wooded campus. The Georgian-style brick buildings include two new student apartment buildings. All residential halls have been recently renovated and offer single rooms and suites. A new multipurpose athletic facility has just been completed and includes a fitness center, an equestrian center, tennis courts, and soccer and softball fields. Among other recreational facilities are a gymnasium with a heated pool and a lake with a jogging trail. Student services include an orientation for incoming students, an on-campus health center, an academic center, and career planning and placement services.

Most of the extracurricular activities of Wesleyan's students are coordinated through Activity Councils. The Campus Activities Board plans concert-dance weekends, mixers with nearby colleges, fashion shows, holiday trips, and special dinners. The Student Recreation Council coordinates competitive activities in basketball, soccer, softball, swimming, and individual sports. Wesleyan is a member of the National Collegiate Athletic Association (NCAA) Division III. There are intercollegiate basketball, equestrian, soccer, softball, tennis, and volleyball teams. The Council on Religious Concerns encourages religious life on campus and sponsors activities that involve students with community life. Students help in local institutions such as the Georgia Academy for the Blind, the Methodist Children's Home, and neighborhood schools and churches. They also participate in interest clubs, student publications, performing arts groups, honor societies, and professional fraternities. A number of College traditions are perpetuated by spirited but friendly competition among the four classes.

Wesleyan offers the Master of Arts degree in middle-level science and middle-level mathematics and in early childhood education.

Location

Wesleyan is located in a suburb of the beautiful, historic city of Macon, Georgia, the third-largest city in the state. Macon is the cultural, educational, medical, and economic leader of middle Georgia. Five coeducational institutions are within a 60-mile radius of the Wesleyan campus. Located at the junction of U.S. Highways I-75 and I-16, Macon is easily accessible by public and private transportation. Metropolitan Atlanta is about an hour's drive to the north, and the Wesleyan campus lies within an easy morning's drive of the Georgia, Florida, and South Carolina beaches and the mountains of north Georgia. The city of Macon offers varied entertainment and many cultural opportunities, including the Georgia Music and Athletic Halls of Fame. Visits by nationally and internationally acclaimed speakers and a series of popular and classical concerts are held on the Wesleyan campus each year, as are special events associated with Macon's renowned Cherry Blossom Festival.

Majors and Degrees

Wesleyan College offers twenty-one areas of study leading to the Bachelor of Arts (A.B.) degree. The Bachelor of Arts is offered in American studies, art history, biology, business administration (concentration in accounting or management), chemistry, communication, education (early childhood, middle grades, and secondary), English, history, history/political science, humanities, international business, international relations, mathematics, music (performance emphasis—piano, organ, and voice), philosophy, psychology, religion, Spanish, and studio art. In addition to these majors, the following academic concentrations are offered as minors: African studies, computer science, economics, French, German, neuroscience, physics, theater, and women's studies. Self-designed interdisciplinary majors are also available

There are preprofessional programs in dentistry, engineering, law, medicine, and veterinary medicine. Students may elect to pursue their academic or professional interests through a double major, a major in combination with a minor program of studies, an interdisciplinary major, or an independently developed program of studies.

Wesleyan offers a dual-degree program in engineering in cooperation with Georgia Institute of Technology, Auburn University, and Mercer University. Three years of study at Wesleyan and two years of study at Georgia Tech, Auburn, or Mercer lead to an A.B. degree from Wesleyan and a B.S. degree from the other institution.

Academic Program

The College's goal is to prepare students for a lifetime of learning and change. Each major program contains general education requirements for breadth of learning and major field requirements for career and/or graduate school preparation. All degree programs require the completion of 120 semester hours with a cumulative average of C (2.0) or better.

Wesleyan provides a challenging academic environment coupled with individualized attention. Each student is assisted by a faculty adviser, a preprofessional or career adviser, and a peer counselor in the selection of academic and internship experiences that lead to intellectual and career fulfillment. All classes are offered in a seminar style, with an emphasis on interactive or participatory learning. Each student has a research or internship experience.

Through Wesleyan's Computer Focus Program, each entering full-time student is required to purchase a personal computer, for which the College offers special financing options. The ability to utilize information technology toward the enhancement of learning and career preparation is central to the academic program. The networked campus is connected to the Internet, which gives each student access to a world of information from her dorm room.

Credit by examination and exemption from required courses are possible with acceptable scores on the Advanced Placement (AP), International Baccalaureate (I.B.), and College-Level Examination Program (CLEP) tests or acceptable grades in high school–college joint enrollment courses. Students may also exempt courses by taking departmental examinations. Thirty semester hours of credit is the maximum a student can receive by exemption through AP, I.B., CLEP, or departmental exams.

The College operates on an early semester plan. First-semester classes begin August 23, 2000, and end December 15, 2000. The second semester begins January 8, 2001, and ends with graduation on May 2, 2001. There are an optional May term and two summer school sessions.

Off-Campus Arrangements

Through Wesleyan's International Study Abroad and Exchange Program, students can study abroad for one full year, one semester, a May term, or a summer session. Through cooperative agreements with the Institute for the International Education of Students (IES) and National Student Exchange (NSE), students may study abroad in Australia, China, France, Germany, Great Britain, Japan, Spain, and other countries. In addition, Wesleyan has direct exchange agreements with Sofia University (Bulgaria), Sookmyung Women's University (South Korea), International Christian University (Japan), Westminster College (England), and Ulyanovsk State University (Russia).

Off-campus opportunities in Macon are available through the Internship Program, which places students with area businesses, community agencies, health organizations, arts groups, and the media. Summer internships can be arranged through the Governor's Intern Program, in a student's hometown, and in other locations. Academic credit given for off-campus experiences varies.

Academic Facilities

Willet Memorial Library has more than 139,000 volumes and subscribes to 603 periodicals. There are 26,030 items in microform and 6,500 tapes and records. (Wesleyan's membership in three consortia allows students access to the holdings of fifty libraries through interlibrary loan.) The library has informal study areas, individual carrels, a language lab, seminar rooms, and a listening room. The Georgia Room houses 4,500 rare volumes and treasures of Americana. The Porter Fine Arts Building serves as a cultural center for the campus and community. It houses the music and theater departments, and, in addition to classrooms, offices, and studios, it contains two art galleries and a studio theater. Its Porter Auditorium has a seating capacity of 1,200 and contains one of the largest pipe organs in the Southeast. Taylor Hall houses laboratories and classrooms for science and math. This building includes state-of-the-art laboratory equipment, a computer lab, and an electronic classroom. Tate Hall contains classrooms for the Humanities, Social Science, and Education divisions. The art department is located in a 10,000-square-foot building designed exclusively for teaching the studio arts. Construction on the new Munroe Science Center begins in summer 2000.

Costs

Tuition for 2000–01 is $15,450. Room and board cost $7150. There are student activity ($250), technology ($300), and wellness ($500) fees. Students should keep in mind the additional cost of books, supplies, travel, and personal expenses.

Financial Aid

Students seeking financial assistance are required to submit the Free Application for Federal Student Aid (FAFSA). This form may be obtained from a high school counselor or from Wesleyan. Any student who demonstrates financial need is qualified for some type of assistance.

Wesleyan offers no-need scholarships to incoming first-year students on the basis of academic ability, leadership, or special talents. These scholarships range from $1000 to full tuition, room, and board. Transfer fellowships are available based on cumulative grade point average and hours earned. Minimum requirements are a 3.0 GPA and 30 semester hours or 45 quarter hours.

Wesleyan participates in the Federal Perkins Loan, Federal Pell Grant, Federal Supplemental Educational Opportunity Grant, Federal Work-Study, and Federal Family Education Loan programs. Residents of Georgia may apply for the Georgia State Tuition Equalization Grant and Hope Grant, which provide up to $4000 a year to a student who attends a private college in the state and has at least a B average. Georgia Student Incentive Grants are also available, as are certain loans, other scholarships, and part-time employment. Approximately 90 percent of Wesleyan's students receive financial assistance through scholarships, talent awards, grants, loans, part-time employment, or Georgia State Tuition Equalization Grants.

Faculty

The academic program at Wesleyan is guided by an exceptionally able, dedicated, and caring faculty. There are 48 full-time faculty members; 100 percent have earned doctoral or terminal degrees. The student-faculty ratio is 11:1. No courses are taught by graduate assistants. Faculty members serve as academic advisers and help students plan their academic program. Many professors participate in extracurricular activities with students on campus.

Student Government

Wesleyan's Student Government Association, through an agreement with the president and faculty of the College, governs the student body with emphasis on responsibility and freedom. An honor tradition, based upon the concept that individual freedom is a right founded on responsibility, is inherent in campus life. Violations of student government regulations are handled through a system of judicial processes with a system for appeals.

Admission Requirements

Applicants to Wesleyan must submit a completed application with a $30 application fee, official academic transcripts, official SAT I or ACT scores, an evaluation written by an English teacher, a recommendation from a guidance counselor or principal, and an essay. The completion of a minimum of 16 academic course units in a secondary school is required. Wesleyan feels that a campus visit is extremely beneficial, and visitors can be full participants in campus activities. An interview is strongly recommended. Candidates for early admission must complete twelve academic courses, and an interview is required of them. Applications from transfer and international students are welcome. Credit for work below a grade of C cannot be transferred, and a minimum score of 550 on the Test of English as Foreign Language (TOEFL) is required of international students. Wesleyan accepts qualified students without regard to race, religion, national or ethnic origin, age, or handicap.

Application and Information

Admission to Wesleyan is selective. The application deadline is November 1 for early decision, December 15 for early action, and March 1 for regular decision (final priority deadline).

For additional information or to request an application form, students should contact:

Dean of Admissions
Wesleyan College
4760 Forsyth Road
Macon, Georgia 31210-4299
Telephone: 912-757-5206
 800-447-6610 (toll-free)
World Wide Web: http://www.wesleyancollege.edu

Wesleyan has the distinction of being the world's first college chartered to grant degrees to women.

WESLEYAN UNIVERSITY
MIDDLETOWN, CONNECTICUT

The University

Wesleyan University, established in 1831, is a small, private, nonsectarian university of liberal arts and sciences for men and women. It is among the most selective in the country. Wesleyan combines the welcoming, noncompetitive atmosphere of a small school with the research facilities, instructional caliber, and faculty of a much larger university.

The University's curriculum offers more than 960 courses in more than forty majors and several nonmajor fields of study. Opportunities exist for independent study, double majors, tutorials, original undergraduate research in the sciences and humanities, graduate-level research in the sciences and music, off-campus study projects, international and ethnographic study, and individual instruction in the performing arts with nationally recognized artists. Wesleyan has a full-time graduate enrollment of about 150.

Wesleyan has a long-standing tradition of bringing together people of different social, racial, ethnic, and geographic backgrounds. Students of color make up 28 percent of the class of 2002: 11 percent African American, 11 percent Asian or Asian/Pacific American, and 6 percent Latino. Among undergraduates, forty-three states and twenty countries are represented. Of the 2,700 undergraduates, roughly 50 percent are men and 50 percent are women.

Student-sponsored activities form the core of Wesleyan's social life. The more than 175 student organizations at Wesleyan cover a range of interests. Seventy-five percent of the students are involved in community service. Athletics at the varsity, intramural, and club level are well-supported and popular. Some features of the state-of-the-art Freeman Athletic Center are a 50-meter pool and diving area, outdoor tracks, a skating arena, tennis courts, indoor tracks, games courts, and weight-training facilities. Wesleyan participates in Division III sports, with varsity teams in baseball (men only), basketball, crew, cross-country, field hockey (women only), football (men only), golf, ice hockey, indoor track, lacrosse, soccer, softball (women only), squash, swimming, tennis, track and field, volleyball (women only), and wrestling.

Location

Middletown is more than the stereotypical New England "college town." Middletown is a small manufacturing and service-industry city of about 45,000 residents that is situated along the Connecticut River midway between Hartford and New Haven. New York City and Boston are each 2 hours away. People of color make up about 20 percent of the city's population.

Majors and Degrees

Wesleyan University grants only one undergraduate degree, the Bachelor of Arts. Major programs are in the following disciplines: African-American studies, American studies, anthropology, art, art history and architectural history, astronomy, biology, chemistry, classical studies (classical civilization), College of Letters, College of Social Studies, dance, earth and environmental sciences, East Asian studies, economics, English, film studies, German studies, government, history, Latin American studies, mathematics and computer science, mathematics-economics, medieval studies, molecular biology and biochemistry, music, neuroscience and behavior, philosophy, physics, psychology, religion, Romance languages and literatures (French literature, French studies, Italian studies, Romance literatures, Spanish literature), Russian language and literature (Russian and Eastern Europe studies), science in society, sociology, studio arts, theater, University Major (individualized), and women's studies. Nonmajor courses or study programs also offered include archaeology, Asian languages and literatures (Chinese and Japanese), Certificate in Environmental Studies, Certificate in International Relations, Hebrew, and physical education.

Academic Program

Utilizing an open and flexible curriculum with no required courses or core curriculum, intellectual independence, the acquisition of critical thinking skills, and the ability to master and link distinct fields of learning are the goals of a Wesleyan education. Students at Wesleyan are encouraged to see themselves as scholars and to participate in the exchange of ideas. They form working relationships with professors who serve as intellectual role models. Wesleyan is academically demanding but surprisingly noncompetitive. Students readily find their niche in the classroom, in campus life, and in the wider community of Middletown, Connecticut.

Off-Campus Arrangements

Wesleyan conducts its own foreign study programs in Paris, Jerusalem, and Regensburg, Germany. The University also cosponsors programs in China, Japan, Spain, and England. Students may participate in approximately 150 programs all over the world, and nearly 50 percent of students spend at least one semester abroad. Wesleyan students have won more Watson Fellowships for international study than students at any other college or university. Students also study elsewhere in the U.S. through such programs as the Twelve College Exchange and the Historically Black Colleges Exchange.

Academic Facilities

The 120-acre campus maintains outstanding facilities. The Science Center has sophisticated research laboratories and opportunities to work with faculty members and graduate students in all the physical sciences and physics. The Center for the Arts incorporates a 400-seat theater and extensive studio space, the Davison Arts Center's museum-quality collection of prints and photographs, and The World Music Hall, for teaching and performance of the music and dance of non-Western traditions. Other facilities include the Van Vleck Observatory, with the second-largest telescope in New England; the Science Library and Olin Memorial Library, which catalog more than 1 million volumes; and the Mansfield Freeman Center for East Asian Studies.

Extensive investments in telecommunications and computing have provided network connections in all residence halls and voice mail for all students. Undergraduates may access the Internet and World Wide Web using personal computers in their rooms or from public terminals available in various computing laboratories. Other computing resources include e-mail and World Wide Web servers, mainframes and minicomputers, a new electronic portfolio, and extensive departmental computing resources across campus. Wesleyan is a member of NSFnet, a national supercomputer network.

Costs

Tuition and required fees for 2000–01 are $26,095, room and board cost $6630, and books and miscellaneous expenses average $1770, for a total student expense budget of $34,495.

Financial Aid

Approximately 50 percent of all enrolled students receive need-based financial aid. Wesleyan admits students without knowledge of their financial situation and offers financial aid to every admitted student who requires it. There are, however, a small number of scholarships for international students.

Faculty

Wesleyan has more than 325 faculty members; 285 conduct full-time instruction, to create a student-faculty ratio of approximately 11:1. Every faculty member teaches and is required to meet high standards for both teaching and research.

Passionate teaching is a key element of the Wesleyan experience. Wesleyan's faculty is unusually productive and includes a Pulitzer Prize winner, a MacArthur ("genius grant") Fellow, and numerous recipients of Rockefeller, Guggenheim, and other national prizes for teaching and research. The faculty members' involvement in research brings innovation and depth to their teaching. Thirty percent are women, and 10 percent are persons of color.

Student Government

The Wesleyan Student Assembly (WSA) holds elections for class officers and controls funding for student-sponsored activities. Students participate in important campus committees along with faculty members, and the Student Judicial Board has jurisdiction in complaints against students accused of violating community health and safety. The rules of conduct that apply at Wesleyan are fully described in *The Blue Book*. The Wesleyan Honor System used to protect academic integrity among students is more than 100 years old.

Admission Requirements

Wesleyan's Office of Admission evaluates prospective students according to their academic achievement, their intellectual curiosity, their extracurricular achievements, and those human qualities that improve the life of the University community.

About 65 percent of students rank in the top tenth of their secondary school classes; median SAT I scores are 680 verbal and 670 math. Interviews are not required as part of the admission process, but Wesleyan recommends that students arrange an interview on campus or with a local alumnus(a) if possible. The common application is accepted.

Application and Information

For more information, students should contact:

Office of Admission
Wesleyan University
Middletown, Connecticut 06459

Telephone: 860-685-3000
E-mail: admissions@wesleyan.edu
World Wide Web: http://www.admiss.wesleyan.edu

WESLEY COLLEGE
DOVER, DELAWARE

The College

Wesley College, the oldest private college in Delaware, is a fully accredited, coeducational, comprehensive liberal arts institution.

Nestled in a quiet, historic residential community, Wesley College is United Methodist Church–affiliated with an enrollment of 1,732 full- and part-time students, mostly representing the Mid-Atlantic region. Average class size ranges from 20 to 35 students.

Approximately 60 percent of students reside on campus in modern, well-equipped residence halls. All residence halls are subdivided into residential societies, each of which schedules its own social activities and events throughout the year. Housing assignments take students' interests and other personal characteristics into consideration whenever possible. All dormitory rooms are intranet accessible.

Wesley has many special interest groups in which students become involved. These include environmental education, drama, music, business activities, the Student Wesley Christian Association, the College newspaper, the radio station, cultural and lecture series, and many other College-sponsored activities. The physical education program at Wesley emphasizes the carry-over value of athletics as well as the importance of physical development to the individual. Men have intercollegiate teams in baseball, basketball, cheerleading, cross-country, football, golf, lacrosse, soccer, and tennis. Women compete with other varsity teams in basketball, cheerleading, cross-country, field hockey, golf, lacrosse, soccer, softball, and tennis. A well-organized intramural program offers a wide choice of sports, including basketball, cross-country, flag football, soccer, softball, tennis, and volleyball. Seven out of 10 students are active in at least one intramural activity. Wesley is a member of NCAA Division III and the Pennsylvania Athletic Conference.

The mission of the College is to be a premier institution for helping students gain the knowledge, skills, and moral and ethical attitudes necessary to achieve their personal goals and contribute to the welfare of their communities in a global society. The College endeavors to impart a desire for lifelong learning and an enhanced capacity for critical and creative thinking so that students can reap the rewards of intellectual growth and professional effectiveness. As a college in a covenant relationship with the United Methodist Church and founded upon Christian principles, Wesley strives to realize a holistic campus environment of common purpose, caring, tolerance, inclusiveness, responsibility, and service that is the heart of community.

In addition to its undergraduate degrees, Wesley College awards the Master of Science in Nursing (M.S.N.) degree, three Master of Education degrees, the Master of Business Administration (M.B.A.) degree, and the Master of Science degree in environmental science.

Location

Dover is the capital of the country's first state and has approximately 35,000 residents. New York City, Baltimore, Philadelphia, and Washington, D.C., are within a 2- to 3-hour drive of the campus. The College is located within Dover's major residential community, with stores and banks within easy walking distance and malls a short commute. Dover has a number of fine eating establishments as well as fast-order restaurants. Seafood is a specialty in Dover because of the city's proximity to the Delaware and Chesapeake Bays and to the Atlantic Ocean. Dover is served by two major bus lines, with stops near the campus. In addition, the famous Delaware beaches are within a 45-minute drive of the campus.

Many students become involved in local activities, including volunteer work at private and public agencies. On campus volunteer activities include a new, unique three-way partnership between a state-funded charter school (Campus Community School), the Wesley Boys and Girls Club, and the College. The area churches welcome Wesley students. Students are employed in many community businesses through the cooperative-education program at Wesley or simply work in part-time jobs to earn extra money. Many Dover residents attend Wesley as part-time students and use the College's facilities on a regular basis.

Majors and Degrees

Bachelor of Arts and Bachelor of Science degrees are awarded in accounting, American studies, biology, business administration (international business, management, and marketing), communications, education (elementary K–4, elementary 5–8, and physical education K–12), English, environmental science, history, international studies, liberal studies, medical technology, paralegal studies, physical education (exercise science, sports management, and sports medicine), political science, and psychology.

A limited number of associate degrees are available in nursing (RN) and other liberal arts programs.

Academic Program

The comprehensive academic calendar year consists of two semesters and a double summer session. Winterim sessions are available in England and France, offering unique opportunities for travel and study.

Bachelor's degree candidates begin with the foundation core curriculum, which emphasizes an overarching theme of the individual in a global community. The centerpiece of the core is the series' four interdisciplinary Wesley seminars, one to be taken each year of the four years of undergraduate study. Interdisciplinary threads bind the core curriculum and the major prorams into a purposeful design. These threads are critical thinking, communication across disciplines, technological literacy, multicultural awareness, aesthetic appreciation, and ethical sensibility. The core provides a distinctive undergraduate experience for students, establishes coherent links between the curricular and cocurricular programs, and provides community service options beyond the College campus.

Academic Facilities

The Robert H. Parker Library contains a collection of more than 80,000 hardbound volumes and more than 500 academic journals and periodicals. In addition, Wesley is part of KentNet, a consortium of Dover area libraries. Through the consortium, more than 474,000 volumes are accessible to Wesley students at facilities within a mile of the campus. Computers located in the library are connected to the College's campuswide network and have the capability to access the library's CD-ROM network.

Individual and group instruction on the use of information resources, including the World Wide Web, is provided by the library staff. The library also carries a collection of videotape titles, which are available for individual and group viewing.

Access to new communications technology is provided through facilities equipped for production of on-campus broadcasts or taped distribution. The multimedia lab allows students to create and print electronic messages.

Costs

For 2000–01, Wesley's tuition and fees are $12,019 per year. Room and board are $5194 per year. Books and supplies total approximately $600 per year.

Financial Aid

Financial aid is available in the form of endowed scholarships, federal scholarships, grants, work-study programs, and loans. Approximately 85 percent of Wesley students receive financial aid. Wesley uses the Free Application for Federal Student Aid (FAFSA). For maximum consideration, students and their families are urged to complete and send their FAFSA as early in the new year as possible. Financial aid awards must be confirmed by the student within fifteen days of notification.

The Wesley Scholars Program recognizes the institution's top academic undergraduate students. Selection for this program is very competitive and deadlines are adhered to. A Wesley Scholars application must be submitted for consideration by March 1. Numerous merit scholarships are also awarded. Application for these awards is not required.

Faculty

Wesley College emphasizes teaching. More than 80 percent of faculty members hold a doctoral or other terminal degree in their subject area and attend workshops and conferences to keep abreast of current activities in their fields. Most faculty members serve as academic advisers to students. All have regularly scheduled office hours and are available for student conferences on a daily basis.

Student Government

Student leadership develops through various agencies of College governance. Student representatives work in close cooperation with faculty members and administrators.

Admission Requirements

Many factors are considered in the selection of a Wesley student. The most important are the applicant's secondary school courses and grades, along with the required SAT I or ACT scores. On-campus interviews are strongly recommended. Secondary school recommendations are also important. International students are welcome and are encouraged to apply by January 1 for the following fall semester. Admission decisions are made without regard to race, religion, color, age, gender, handicap, or national origin.

Applicants should have 16 secondary school units in English, social studies, laboratory science, mathematics, and electives. The submission of SAT I or ACT scores is required.

Wesley offers an early decision plan for qualified candidates who have completed their junior year of secondary school. Early acceptance and deferred entrance are also available. Wesley's admission staff visits more than 600 secondary schools in the Middle Atlantic and New England regions each year.

Students, parents, and counselors are welcome to contact the Office of Admissions for information.

Wesley College reserves the right to change some or all rates, policies, or courses when necessary, without prior notice.

Application and Information

The College follows a rolling admission policy. Secondary school records should be attached to the Wesley College application form.

To schedule an admission interview and tour, students should call the Office of Admissions (telephone number listed below). A College prospectus, application form, and financial aid information are available by contacting:

Arthur T. Jacobs
Director of Admissions
Wesley College
120 North State Street
Dover, Delaware 19901
Telephone: 302-736-2400
           800-937-5398 (toll-free)
E-mail: admissions@mail.wesley.edu
World Wide Web: http://www.wesley.edu

A student relaxes in the beautiful surroundings of Wesley College.

WEST CHESTER UNIVERSITY OF PENNSYLVANIA
WEST CHESTER, PENNSYLVANIA

The University

West Chester University (WCU) is the second largest of the fourteen institutions in the Pennsylvania State System of Higher Education and the third-largest university in the Philadelphia metropolitan area. Officially founded in 1871, the University traces its heritage to the West Chester Academy, which existed from 1812 to 1869. The University's 391-acre campus has well-maintained facilities, including eight modern residence halls and garden-style apartments. In keeping with West Chester's rich heritage, the University's Quadrangle buildings, part of the original campus, are on the National Register of Historic Places.

While the University attracts the majority of its students from Pennsylvania, New Jersey, and Delaware, it also enrolls many students from other areas across the United States and from more than fifty countries. The undergraduate enrollment is 8,224 men and women full-time and 1,557 part-time.

Each year, the University community schedules an impressive series of events, including programs with well-known musicians, authors, political figures, and others. Numerous campus groups in music, theater, athletics, and other activities, as well as clubs, fraternities, sororities, service organizations, and honor societies, provide students with the opportunity to participate in a full range of programs. The University offers twenty-three intercollegiate sports and thirteen club sports for men and women. In addition to the facilities in the health and physical education complex, the University has a field house and a gymnasium for varsity sports.

Location

The University is located in West Chester, a community in southeastern Pennsylvania that is strategically located at the center of the mid-Atlantic corridor. The seat of Chester County government for almost two centuries, West Chester retains much of its historical charm in its buildings and unspoiled countryside, yet it offers the twentieth-century advantages of a town in the heart of an expanding economic area. West Chester is just 25 miles west of Philadelphia and 17 miles north of Wilmington, Delaware, putting the libraries, museums, and other cultural and historical resources of both cities within easy reach. It is also only 2 hours from New York City and 3 hours from Washington, D.C.

Majors and Degrees

The Bachelor of Arts is offered in American studies, anthropology, anthropology-sociology, art, biology, communication studies, communicative disorders, comparative literature, economics, foreign languages (French, German, Latin, Russian, and Spanish), geography, history, liberal studies, literature, mathematics, mathematics–computer science, philosophy, philosophy-religion, political science, political science–international relations, political science–public administration, psychology, social work, sociology, theater arts, and women's studies.

The Bachelor of Science is offered in accounting, athletic training, biology, biology (cell and molecular, clinical microbiology, and ecology), chemistry, chemistry-biology, chemistry-geology, clinical chemistry, computer and information sciences, criminal justice, earth science, economics, finance, forensic chemistry, health and physical education, health education, health sciences, liberal studies, management, marketing, pharmaceutical product development, physics, physics (pre-engineering), public health, public health (environmental and nutrition).

The Bachelor of Science in Nursing, the Bachelor of Fine Arts (studio arts), and the Bachelor of Music (general, instrumental, keyboard, music education, and vocal) degrees are also offered.

The Bachelor of Science in Education degree is offered in early childhood education; elementary education; health and physical education; health education; music education; secondary education in the areas of biology, chemistry, communications, comprehensive social studies (anthropology, geography, history, political science, psychology, and sociology), earth-space science, English, foreign languages (French, German, Latin, Russian, and Spanish), history, mathematics, and physics; and special education.

Preprofessional studies are available in law, medicine, and theology. In cooperation with the Pennsylvania State University, West Chester University offers a 3-2 dual-degree program combining liberal arts, physics, and engineering. Also available are early admission assurance programs with the Allegheny University of the Health Sciences Medical College of Pennsylvania, School of Medicine; West Chester University/Pennsylvania State University, College of Medicine; and the Philadelphia College of Osteopathic Medicine. The University provides special admission opportunities and scholarships to the Widener University School of Law–Harrisburg Campus.

Certification programs are available in health and physical education teacher certification, driver education and safe living, and outdoor recreation pursuits.

Interdisciplinary areas of study with transcript recognition include ethnic studies, Latin American studies, Russian studies, and women's studies. Minors are available in most majors and in several interdisciplinary areas.

Academic Program

West Chester University is a comprehensive, multipurpose institution now in its second century. The University comprises the College of Arts and Sciences, the School of Business and Public Affairs, the School of Education, the School of Health Sciences, and the School of Music. It operates on a two-semester basis; summer sessions are available.

An honors program is available to qualified students for both upper and lower division study; internships and field experiences, self-designed majors, and independent study are also offered. A variety of credit-by-examination programs are available.

Off-Campus Arrangements

Through the Junior-Year-Abroad program, students may spend one or more semesters at the University of Ghana, Ghana; University of Edinburgh, Scotland, University of Wales, Swansea; Leeds University, England; American College in London, England; and Paul Valery University, France. West Chester also sponsors a number of annual courses, which include study abroad during spring, summer, and winter breaks.

West Chester University participates in the National Student Exchange Program, in which students spend up to a year at any one of seventy member schools across the United States, broadening their cultural and academic horizons. Automatic transfer of credit is arranged.

Academic Facilities

The Francis Harvey Green Library houses more than 500,000 volumes, more than 2,500 periodicals, and a micromedia collection with more than 350,000 titles. Services include interlibrary loans, reference advice, computerized online literature searching, and the availability of CD-ROM databases.

The University's extensive state-of-the-art computer facilities include the IBM ES/9221 mainframe and more than 400 IBM and Apple workstations that are available to students. The University has Braille printers, translators, and speech synthesizers for its visually impaired students. Students can use the computing facilities 16 hours a day.

The Boucher Science Center offers modern multimedia lecture halls, extensive laboratories, and study areas where students can work together. Boucher Science Center is connected to the Schmucker Science Center, which houses a fully equipped observatory and planetarium. The center's extensive laboratories have such instrumentation as automated spectrophotometers, electron analytical equipment, atomic absorption spectrometers, and a variety of chromatographs, including gas chromatographs–mass spectrometers.

The campus includes a 100-acre natural area for environmental studies; speech and hearing and reading clinics; two theaters; music facilities, with practice, rehearsal, and listening rooms; and a large, modern health and physical education complex that houses a gymnasium, a natatorium with two pool areas and a diving well, dance studios, research laboratories, physical therapy rooms, saunas, and a health resource center.

Costs

West Chester University provides education of fine quality at an affordable cost. Full-time undergraduate students who are legal residents of Pennsylvania paid $3618 per year for tuition for 12 to 18 semester hours in 1999–2000. For semester hours more than 18 or fewer than 12, the cost was $150 per semester hour. Out-of-state students were charged $9046 per year for 12–18 semester hours and $377 per semester hour for hours more than 18 or fewer than 12. Room and board were $4636 per year for on-campus residents. Student fees were $804 per year. (Costs are determined by the state and are subject to change.)

Financial Aid

The financial aid available to students includes work-study programs, grants, loans, special awards, and scholarships. A limited number of Merit Scholarships are awarded based on the student's academic standing and accomplishments in high school. Students who qualify will be invited to apply. About 71 percent of all full-time undergraduate students receive some form of aid.

Faculty

West Chester University has a faculty of more than 700 members. The majority hold doctoral degrees, and many are engaged in research and serve as consultants in their field of expertise. The student-faculty ratio is 17:1.

Student Government

The Student Governmental Association represents all students on the West Chester campus. In addition, the Residence Hall Association represents resident students, and the Off Campus Student Association represents commuting students.

Admission Requirements

Applicants to West Chester University are evaluated on the basis of scholarship, character, and potential for achievement. The requirements for admission include graduation from an approved secondary school and satisfactory standardized test scores (SAT I, ACT, or TOEFL acceptable), or a General Educational Development (GED) certificate from an approved agency. Certain selective programs require an interview for admission. Admission options include early admission, transfer, entry to earn a second baccalaureate degree, and special admission programs for the educationally and/or financially disadvantaged. Students may receive advanced placement or credit through scores on Advanced Placement (AP) tests and College-Level Examination Program (CLEP) subject examinations.

West Chester University is an Equal Opportunity/Affirmative Action institution and is committed to providing barrier-free facilities for persons with impaired mobility.

Application and Information

Students are admitted for the fall or spring semester. Applicants for the fall semester are urged to begin the application procedure at the start of their senior year of secondary school. Applicants for the spring semester should apply by December 1. International students are encouraged to apply by May 1 for the fall semester and August 1 for the spring semester. The University operates on a modified rolling admission policy; applicants with the best qualifications are given priority, and their applications are processed expeditiously. Students are encouraged to visit WCU's campus. To arrange a visit or to attend an information session, students may call the Office of Admissions; for updated information or directions, they may check the University's World Wide Web site.

Additional information and required forms are available from:

Office of Admissions
Emil H. Messikomer Hall
West Chester University of Pennsylvania
100 West Rosedale Avenue
West Chester, Pennsylvania 19383
Telephone: 610-436-3411
          877-355-2165 (toll-free)
E-mail: ugadmiss@wcupa.edu
World Wide Web: http://www.wcupa.edu

Class is held on the academic quad during a beautiful spring day.

WESTERN CAROLINA UNIVERSITY
CULLOWHEE, NORTH CAROLINA

The University

Excellent teaching is a strength and personal touch makes a difference at Western Carolina University (WCU), the first public university in North Carolina to require that freshmen bring computers to campus. WCU prepares students well for careers and lives in the technological age. Equally committed to providing personal attention and guidance to each student, WCU places strong emphasis on teaching and creating a learning environment in which students are central. Founded in 1889, WCU is a campus of the University of North Carolina, one of the strongest academic university systems in the nation. Support for new master's degrees in accounting, nursing, and physical therapy; funding for an intercollegiate women's soccer team; preparation for a $28-million fine and performing arts center; a campuswide computer network; and millions of dollars in renovation funds are some of the recent benefits of WCU's affiliation. While most classes are held at the main campus in Cullowhee, WCU conducts a variety of programs at western North Carolina sites, including the University of North Carolina Center in Asheville and the Cherokee Center in Cherokee. A distance learning and teleconference center provides noncredit, continuing education, and other programs to hundreds of participants each year. The Research and Graduate School offers twelve master's degrees in more than fifty areas, the doctorate in educational leadership, and the educational specialist degree.

Location

WCU is located in Cullowhee, North Carolina, 52 miles west of Asheville. Scenic vistas, clear white-water streams, and dense forests abound in the southern Appalachian Mountain region. The climate is mild, with four distinct seasons. The nearby Blue Ridge and Great Smoky Mountains attract millions of tourists each year to take part in recreational activities, including snow skiing, whitewater rafting, canoeing, kayaking, mountain biking, camping, and hiking. Major southeast cities such as Charlotte, North Carolina; Knoxville, Tennessee; Atlanta, Georgia; and Greenville, South Carolina, are within a 2 to 3-hour drive of the campus. WCU's 265-acre campus offers all the amenities of a small town: classroom buildings, eleven residence halls, two full-service cafeterias, two food courts, fast-food restaurants, health services, a bank, a computer store, a bookstore, a library, a fitness center, two indoor swimming pools, tennis courts, a golf driving range, a jogging trail, a quarter-mile track, intramural fields, a dance club, and ample parking that allows freshmen to bring cars to campus.

Majors and Degrees

WCU offers 120 majors and areas of concentration to undergraduates through four colleges: Applied Sciences, Arts and Sciences, Business, and Education and Allied Professions. The Honors College offers extra academic challenge and social opportunities in an optional residential setting for high-achieving, qualified students. For undergraduates, WCU offers the Bachelor of Arts (B.A.), Bachelor of Science (B.S.), Bachelor of Science in Education, Bachelor of Fine Arts (B.F.A.), Bachelor of Science in Business Administration, and Bachelor of Science in Nursing (B.S.N.) degrees in the following majors: accounting, anthropology, art, art education, biology, birth–kindergarten, business administration and law, chemistry, child and family relations, clinical laboratory sciences, communication, communication disorders, computer information systems, computer science, criminal justice, economics, electronics engineering technology, elementary education, emergency medical care, English, English education, environmental health, family and consumer science, finance, French, French education, geography, geography-planning, geology, German, German education, health information management, health services management, history, hospitality management, industrial distribution, industrial technology, interior design, international business, management, manufacturing engineering technology, marketing, mathematics, mathematics education, middle grades education, music, music education, natural resources management, nursing, nutrition and dietetics, parks and recreation management, philosophy, physical education, physics, political science, psychology, recreational therapy, science education, social sciences, social sciences education, social work, sociology, Spanish, Spanish education, special education, special studies, speech and theater arts, sport management, and theater. WCU's preprofessional programs (pre-engineering, preforestry, prelaw, premedicine, prepharmacy, and pre–veterinary medicine) prepare students well for admission to professional schools with tailor-made academic programs, small classes, undergraduate research, internships, and individual counseling. Students who participate in the International Baccalaureate (I.B.) or Advanced Placement (AP) programs in high school may receive college credit from WCU in as many as thirty areas.

Academic Program

WCU is on the way to being designated a National Merit University. In the past four years, 19 students who are National Merit Finalists have enrolled and begun working toward degrees. These top students may qualify for the WCU Meritorious Award, which provides in-state tuition, fees, room and board, and a computer for eight semesters. The Honors College offers extra academic and social opportunities for qualified students who want to make the best of their college experience. One of the few honors programs in the state to offer students a residential option, the college is among the few nationwide to award graduates with a special honors diploma. Each spring, students are invited to present research findings in the WCU Undergraduate Research Symposium. The best projects proceed to national conventions, where WCU students consistently win top honors. To help freshmen ease into college life, WCU offers the Freshman Emphasis and the Learning Communities programs. Both provide a residential option, extra help from professors, peer mentors, academic support, and an instant social network. WCU undergraduates begin their college studies with the General Education Program, 41 semester hours of course work in written and oral communication, mathematics, computer literacy, leisure and fitness, social sciences, physical and biological sciences, humanities, comparative cultures, and the human past. Usually completed within the first two years, the general education requirement is the liberal arts part of every major. To earn a bachelor's degree, students must successfully complete between 120 and 128 semester hours of credit, or about forty courses. Students are encouraged to select a major—an academic area of focus—by their second year that determines course selections for the junior and senior years and often a career path. Students who are undecided about a major can get help from a variety of sources, including professors, personal academic advisers, and career counselors.

Off-Campus Arrangements

WCU offers a wide array of study-abroad experiences. Students take advantage of opportunities such as studying the criminal justice and education systems in England, international business law in the Netherlands, hospitality management in China, and language and culture in Mexico. WCU is a member of the National Student Exchange, which means that students can pay WCU tuition and take courses on other U.S. and international campuses. Closer to home, WCU students in natural resources management and the sciences routinely conduct field work at off-campus field stations in the nearby Pisgah and Nantahala National Forests and in the Great Smoky Mountains National Park, where WCU students are participating in a vast scientific inventory of all of the park's living organisms. Education, nursing, geography, and other fields offer off-campus internships and opportunities for hands-on learning as well.

Academic Facilities

WCU lends its resources—cultural, financial, and informational—to the western North Carolina region, sustaining and enhancing the lives and livelihoods of businesses, families, individuals, schools, and local governments. WCU fulfills part of this commitment through galleries, museums, theaters, music halls, and centers such as the Center for Mathematics and Science Education, Computer Center, Coulter Faculty Center, Developmental Evaluation Center, Highlands Biological Station, International Programs and Services, Mountain Aquacultural Research Center, Mountain Heritage Museum, Mountain Resource Center, North Carolina Center for the Advancement of Teaching, Hunter Library's Special Collections, Reading Center, Speech and Hearing Center, and the Distance Learning and Teleconference Center. WCU is home to two of the largest facilities in western North Carolina. The 8,000-seat Ramsey Regional Activity Center attracts nationally known speakers, major concerts, theater and television productions, banquets, receptions, and conferences, as well as WCU athletic events. A major research facility, Hunter Library contains more than 500,000 books and bound periodicals and provides access to ninety databases and the Internet.

Costs

At WCU, financial aid begins with reasonable costs for every student. The out-of-state tuition is lower than the resident costs in many states. Undergraduates are able to forego the high cost of textbooks through the book rental plan. Students can expect to pay these annual expenses for 1999–2000: in-state tuition, $918, or out-of-state tuition, $8188; room, $1540 (double occupancy); board, $1370–$1840; book expenses, $145 rental fee; and required fees, $974.50. Fees are set by the North Carolina Legislature and are subject to change.

Financial Aid

Thirty-eight percent of WCU freshmen receive some form of financial aid, which includes grants, loans, scholarships, and student employment. Entering students who are interested in applying for financial aid must complete the Free Application for Federal Student Aid (FAFSA) as soon as possible after January 1. Since the most attractive sources of assistance are limited, applicants are encouraged to complete the FAFSA by the University priority deadline of March 31. WCU awards three types of financial aid: scholarships and grants, which do not have to be repaid; long-term and low-interest loans; and employment. University and departmental merit scholarships, such as the Excellence Award, Founder's Scholarship, Valedictorian Scholarship, and Western Meritorious Award for National Merit Finalists, are also available to qualified students. The North Carolina Teaching Fellows Program at WCU provides full tuition and other expenses for eight semesters to qualified North Carolina residents who agree to teach in the state for a specified period upon graduation.

Faculty

Full-time faculty members number 324 and hold degrees from major colleges and universities. Eighty-three percent have doctoral or terminal degrees. The student-faculty ratio is 16:1. As a result, WCU faculty members know their students as well as they do their subjects. They spend time with students outside of class, meeting for informal study groups, organized trips, and individual counseling sessions. While they conduct research, write books, publish in professional journals, and belong to state and national professional organizations, WCU faculty members love to teach.

Student Government

WCU strongly supports active student participation in campus leadership through groups such as the Student Government Association (SGA), Resident Student Association, Student Media Board, fraternities and sororities, and student advisory councils. The SGA promotes students' interests while serving as a liaison between students and the administration. The SGA governs through the executive, legislative, and judicial branches. The SGA president is an ex officio member of the WCU Board of Trustees and a member of the Association of Student Governments, which serves the sixteen campuses of the University of North Carolina. The SGA coordinates the disbursement of student activity fees to some sixty campus organizations. Each year, WCU students receive a copy of the Student Handbook, which lists student organizations and includes the Student Bill of Rights and Code of Conduct. The recently adopted *Greek Life: A Plan for Excellence* was written by a committee of students, faculty members, and administrators; it defines the relationship between WCU and its fraternities and sororities.

Admission Requirements

Western Carolina University seeks students with proven academic performance and solid academic potential. National Merit Finalists, high school valedictorians, and students in the top 10 percent of their high school classes are strongly encouraged to apply for merit scholarships. Admission decisions for incoming freshmen are based on the strength of the applicants' credentials, including high school course work, grades, class rank, and standardized test scores (SAT or ACT). Required courses include 4 units of English; algebra I, algebra II, and geometry or an advanced math course for which algebra II is a prerequisite; one physical science, one biological science, and a third laboratory science; and U.S. history and one additional social science course. Two units of one foreign language are strongly recommended. On-campus interviews and letters of recommendation are not required but are useful for students who wish to appeal an admission decision. College courses and grades are used to determine the eligibility of transfer students and freshmen with dual enrollment credit. As a member of the University of North Carolina, Western cannot exceed an out-of-state enrollment of 18 percent.

Application and Information

Western is on rolling admission, which means that the earlier students apply, the better their chances for admission and the sooner they are notified of a decision. Early application with partial transcripts is encouraged, but final admission is deferred until full application materials and transcripts are received. Students are usually notified of a decision within three to four weeks of submitting all required admissions materials. All required materials must be received no later than thirty days prior to the term for which a student is making application. Application forms and additional information are available from:

Philip Cauley, Associate Director of Admissions
242 H. F. Robinson Building
Western Carolina University
Cullowhee, North Carolina 28723
Telephone: 800-928-2369 (toll-free) or 828-227-7317
Fax: 828-227-7319
E-mail: admiss@wcu.edu
World Wide Web: http://www.wcu.edu

An opening celebration welcomes students each fall to Western Carolina University.

WESTERN ILLINOIS UNIVERSITY
MACOMB, ILLINOIS

The University

The campus of Western Illinois University (WIU) extends over 1,464 acres and includes fifty-two buildings. The residence halls on campus provide for a variety of lifestyles and house more than half of the 12,934 students at the University. Single and double rooms, study floors, nonsmoking rooms, and academic major areas are just a few examples of residence options. The University Union is the center of campus activities and includes a food court, a bookstore, bowling alleys, an ice-cream parlor, meeting rooms, an area for billiards, and lounge areas. More than 250 student organizations offer a variety of cocurricular activities to supplement formal classroom education. Cultural programs reflecting both local and national interests are on the calendar several evenings each week.

Intercollegiate and intramural athletic programs are available for both women and men. The campus has three swimming pools, a nine-hole golf course, tennis courts, assorted activity fields, and a Campus Recreation Center, which is open evenings and weekends for student enjoyment.

There are 10,434 undergraduate students currently enrolled. Although the majority of students are from Illinois, forty-five other states and forty-five countries are represented in the student body.

Career placement services are offered to graduating students and graduates. Nearly 93 percent of the graduates who register with the job placement office are placed in desirable positions. Health services are available through the Beu Health Center, which is located in the center of the campus and is staffed and in operation at all times when the University is in regular session.

Location

Macomb, a community of 20,000 people, is located in the heart of the western Illinois farmland about 240 miles southwest of Chicago. Amtrak offers daily service to and from Chicago. Bus service is available, and the Macomb Municipal Airport provides facilities and services for charter and private planes. The community serves a large rural area as a center for shopping, health services, industry and employment, and recreation. Most religions are represented in the immediate area. Argyle State Park, which is located about 9 miles from the campus, provides opportunities for boating, fishing, camping, and picnicking.

Majors and Degrees

Western Illinois University offers the following undergraduate degree programs: Bachelor of Arts, Bachelor of Business, Bachelor of Fine Arts, Bachelor of Science, Bachelor of Science in Education, and Bachelor of Social Work. Major programs of study include accountancy, agriculture (agricultural business, agricultural science),* art,* bilingual/bicultural education,* biology (botany, microbiology, zoology),* board of trustees, broadcasting, chemistry,* clinical laboratory science, communication, communication sciences and disorders,* computer science (business), economics, elementary education (early childhood education),* English (literature and language),* family and consumer sciences (fashion merchandising, food service/lodging management, foods/nutrition/dietetics), finance, French,* geography,* geology, health education and promotion, health services management, history,* human resource management, individual studies, information management, instructional technology and telecommunications, journalism, law enforcement and justice administration, management, manufacturing engineering technology, marketing (marketing management, supply chain management), mathematics,* music (applied music, music business, music therapy),* philosophy, physical education (athletic training, fitness instruction),* physics,* political science,* psychology,* recreation/park/tourism administration, social work, sociology, Spanish,* special education,* and theater. Those programs followed by * offer teacher certification.

Thirteen preprofessional programs are offered to prepare students for professional study at other universities: agricultural engineering, architecture, chemical engineering, dentistry, engineering, forestry, law, medicine, nursing, optometry, pharmacy, physical therapy, and veterinary medicine. The majority of students in the premedicine program have attended medical school at Southern Illinois University, the University of Illinois, and Loyola University. In addition, dual-degree programs are available in dentistry and engineering in cooperation with the College of Dentistry of the University of Illinois at Chicago and the College of Engineering of the University of Illinois at Urbana-Champaign.

Academic Program

It is the philosophy of the University that a broad general education should be an integral part of every degree program. Thus, approximately one third of the degree requirements involve study and the development of fundamental skills in the arts and sciences. The remainder of the program is devoted to either a comprehensive major or a major/minor plus general electives. Credit is awarded for acceptable scores on CLEP general and subject examinations and on the College Board's Advanced Placement examinations in English, foreign languages, history, and mathematics. Proficiency examinations are administered on campus through specific departments. Special educational opportunities for students with high aptitude and superior ability are offered in all colleges at WIU through the honors program. Western Illinois University is on the semester system; the fall semester closes before the Christmas holidays and the spring semester closes in mid-May. Two 4-week summer sessions run concurrently with one 8-week summer session from mid-June to early August.

Western offers a four-year and a two-year program in the study of military science through Army ROTC. Successful completion of the program and requirements for the baccalaureate degree leads to a commission as a second lieutenant in the Army.

Off-Campus Arrangements

WIU's program in clinical laboratory science includes three years of study on campus followed by twelve months at an approved school of medical technology. Students enrolled in a teacher education program spend one term off campus as supervised student teachers in cooperating public schools. Off-campus internships or field experiences are available in the following majors: accountancy; agriculture; art; biology; broadcasting; chemistry; communication sciences and disorders; computer science; economics; English; family and consumer sciences; finance; French; geography; geology; health education and promotion; history; human resource management; individual studies; information management; instructional technology and telecommunications; law enforcement and justice administration; manufacturing engineering technology; mathematics; music; physical education; physics; political science; psychology; recreation, park, and tourism administration; social work; and sociology.

One-year and one-semester study-abroad programs are available in Australia, Canada, England, France, Germany, Japan, Mexico, Spain, and any one of a hundred other locations worldwide. Students electing to participate in a study-abroad program earn credit toward their undergraduate degree program while enrolled in a university abroad.

Academic Facilities

Western's University Library has six floors of library materials, with shelving space for 1 million volumes and seating for 2,500 readers. It has a regional research center in special collections, four on-campus specialized branch libraries, an extensive legal reference collection, depository status with the Illinois and U.S. governments, and access to the ILLINET online network, which provides a catalog of WIU's library holdings and those of 800 other libraries.

Major computer facilities staffed by trained personnel are strategically located across the campus in residence halls and academic buildings. Laboratory facilities containing state-of-the-art equipment provide students with current technological hands-on experience in their discipline of study. A research station west of campus on the Mississippi River, a field campus south of campus, and a 300-acre farm north of campus provide nearby instructional facilities for students enrolled in agriculture, biology, and recreation, park, and tourism administration courses. Three theaters and an art gallery provide performing arts students with a rich variety of local, regional, national, and international cultural and artistic opportunities. WIU's off-campus undergraduate center in Moline, Illinois, offers area residents and placebound students the opportunity to enroll in undergraduate course work in several disciplines and complete degree requirements in ten different majors.

Costs

Western ensures that a student's college years are a good investment with its guaranteed four-year rate for tuition, fees, and room and board. All new undergraduate students entering the University are automatically included in the plan, which freezes the per-hour rate that a student pays for a four-year period, so costs stay the same each year as long as the student maintains continuous enrollment at Western.

New students enrolling for the 2000–01 academic year pay the following annual guaranteed rates (based on an average class load of 15 semester hours): $2812.50 for tuition ($93.75 per credit hour), $923.70 for fees, $2698 for a double room, and $1808 for the basic a la carte board rate. Out-of-state tuition is assessed at two times the rate of in-state tuition.

Financial Aid

During the 1998–99 academic year, 9,653 WIU undergraduate students received financial aid from funds totaling $47 million. Financial aid is available through state and federal programs for full- or part-time WIU students. Students should use the Free Application for Federal Student Aid (FAFSA) to apply for the following state and federal programs: Federal Pell Grant, Federal Supplemental Educational Opportunity Grant, Federal Perkins Loan, Federal Stafford Student Loan, Federal Work-Study Program, and Illinois Monetary Award Program (MAP). Students should begin the process by completing their federal income tax return as early as possible to provide accurate information on the FAFSA and then filing the FAFSA as soon as possible after January 1. Many student jobs are available in areas such as secretarial work, food service, and building and grounds maintenance. WIU awards talent grants and academic scholarships. Talent grants are offered in men's and women's athletics, music, art, theater, agriculture, student services, and debate. More than 1,000 students annually receive scholarships through the WIU Foundation. The majority of scholarships reward high academic potential and achievement, while others consider hometown, academic interest, or financial need. To receive an application for WIU scholarship opportunities, students should contact the WIU Scholarship Office.

Faculty

Seventy-four percent of the 672 faculty members have doctorates or the highest degree in their fields. The student-faculty ratio is 15:1, and the average class has 25 students. The faculty is responsible for 95 percent of the total student credit hours earned at the undergraduate level, with graduate teaching assistants contributing the remaining 5 percent. As a group, full professors devote approximately 90 percent of their professional responsibilities to undergraduate instruction. Publication and research are encouraged, and many of the faculty members have received federal and other grants, fellowships, and awards.

Student Government

Students are actively involved in University affairs through elected representatives to the Student Government Association. As students at a public institution, these representatives also frequently become involved in the legislative process through lobbying efforts in the state capital.

Admission Requirements

Students applying as freshmen are admitted if they have a minimum ACT composite score of 22 (or an equivalent SAT I score) and a minimum of a 2.2 GPA (on a 4.0 scale) or if they rank in the upper 40 percent of their high school graduating class and achieve a minimum ACT composite score of 18 (or an equivalent SAT I score) and a minimum of a 2.2 GPA (on a 4.0 scale). Students must also have completed 4 years of English; 3 years each of math, science, and social sciences; and 2 years of electives. Transfer students who have earned 24 semester hours of college credit are considered on the basis of college performance only. These students must have a cumulative average of at least C for all hours attempted and must have been in good standing at the last school attended. Students who have earned fewer than 24 semester hours of college credit must meet the freshman admission requirements, have a cumulative average of at least C in all college hours attempted, and be in good standing at the last college attended. All documents required for admission must be sent directly from the reporting institution to the Admissions Office at Western.

Application and Information

Application forms and admission materials may be secured by contacting:

Admissions Office
Sherman Hall 115
Western Illinois University
1 University Circle
Macomb, Illinois 61455-1390

Telephone: 309-298-3157
         877-PICKWIU (toll-free)
World Wide Web: http://www.wiu.edu

Sherman Hall, the main administration building.

WESTERN MARYLAND COLLEGE
WESTMINSTER, MARYLAND

The College

Western Maryland College (WMC) provides an ideal location for learning that brings together students from twenty-three states and nineteen countries. Its picturesque campus, including a nine-hole golf course, is situated on a hilltop in historic Westminster, just a short drive from two of the nation's major metropolitan centers, Baltimore and Washington, D.C. Western Maryland was one of the first coeducational colleges in the nation and has been both innovative and independent since its founding in 1867.

The tradition of liberal arts studies rests comfortably at Western Maryland, which has exemplary teaching, both at the undergraduate and graduate levels, as its central mission. Faculty members are engaged in research and professional writing, are involved at the highest levels of their respective professions, and are sought after as consultants in many spheres, but their primary mission is teaching. The enrollment of 1,600 undergraduates enables WMC to care about students in a personal way, to provide individual guidance, and to be responsive to the needs of students. Graduates leave Western Maryland enriched not just because of their classwork, but also because of their meaningful interactions with one another.

A flexible liberal arts curriculum stresses the ability to think critically and creatively, to act humanely and responsibly, and to be expressive. WMC is fully accredited by the Middle States Association of Colleges and Secondary Schools and is listed as one of the selective national liberal arts colleges by the Carnegie Foundation for the Advancement of Teaching. WMC is internationally recognized for its graduate program in training teachers for the deaf.

Location

Thirty miles northwest of Baltimore's Inner Harbor and 56 miles north of Washington, D.C., Western Maryland College overlooks historic Westminster, Maryland, Carroll County's largest town and county seat. Within walking distance are gift boutiques, book and music stores, art galleries, and restaurants that line one of America's longest main streets. Both nearby metropolitan cities offer students opportunities for learning and leisure—art and history museums, internships on Capitol Hill, Baltimore Orioles and Ravens games, and bayside seafood and nightlife.

Majors and Degrees

The educational programs serve students who enter with firm choices of majors or career ambitions and students who are undecided. All students take a least 30 percent of their course work in the liberal arts: humanities, natural sciences and mathematics, and social sciences. The Bachelor of Arts degree is offered in twenty-three major areas of study: art, art history, biology, business administration, chemistry, communication, economics, English, exercise science and physical education, French, German, history, mathematics, music, philosophy, physics, political science, psychology, religious studies, social work, sociology, Spanish, and theater arts. Students may choose a dual major or design their own major if their academic interests and goals take them beyond an existing program. In addition, most departments offer minor programs or particular courses to help students focus on or achieve specific goals.

The College also offers certification programs in social work and in elementary and secondary education (Maryland certification includes reciprocity with more than thirty-five other states), 3-2 programs in engineering and forestry, and professional programs in dentistry, law, medicine, the ministry, and museum studies. The College also offers an Army ROTC program.

Academic Program

WMC's flexible curriculum enables students to acquire a broad base of knowledge in the areas of humanities, natural sciences and mathematics, and social sciences and to pursue in-depth learning in one or more of the sixty fields of study. The program links wide-ranging educational experiences with strong career preparation through an extensive internship program. A total of 128 credit hours is required for graduation.

First-year–student seminars provide students with a unique opportunity to become better prepared for many facets of college life. Limited to 15 students, these courses on a variety of topics emphasize important skills—writing, oral presentation, study skills, critical thinking, and time management.

Faculty advisers offer guidance across the curriculum and work closely with their advisees as they make decisions about course and major selections and planning strategies. Students may also request help from the Center for Career Services, which offers vocational testing, counseling, and guidance.

During the College's January Term, a three-week term between the fall and spring semesters, students and faculty members are encouraged to explore new areas and expand their intellectual horizons. Students choose from the specially designed (unconventional) courses that are offered, often at special locations. Some students take advantage of January Term for independent off-campus study or to join one of the popular international study tours.

Off-Campus Arrangements

Through its WMC–Budapest campus, the College offers an easy option for students to study abroad. WMC also offers opportunities for off-campus study through American University's Washington Semester and Drew University's Semester on the United Nations and Semester on the European Community. Many overseas study programs are available.

Academic Facilities

Among the forty buildings on the 160-acre campus are the Hoover Library, with access to materials from rare books to CD-ROMs to e-mail and Internet accounts and an audiovisual media and microcomputing center; Hill Hall, featuring the Writing Center and multimedia presentation classrooms; Peterson Hall, which offers a modern photography lab, a graphic arts computer classroom, and an art gallery for the College's permanent collection and visiting exhibitions; and Alumni Hall, home to the performing arts and summer repertory Theatre-on-the-Hill program. A new $13-million state-of-the-art biology and chemistry laboratory building opened in fall 1999.

Costs

WMC keeps its fees within the reach of students coming from families with moderate incomes while offering a liberal arts education of outstanding value. Tuition charges are comprehensive and include Student Health Service fees and Student Activities fees. Tuition for 2000–01 is $19,600, room and board are $5350, and personal expenses (including books and transportation) are estimated at $600 per year.

Financial Aid

WMC supports a program of financial aid to eligible students on the basis of both need and merit. Nearly 80 percent of WMC students receive financial assistance. Students who have been accepted by the College and can demonstrate financial need as required by the federal government may be eligible for assistance in the form of scholarships, grants, loans, and opportunities for student employment. Typically an award is a package of these four resources, tailored to the student's needs.

Academic scholarships covering partial to full tuition are available for qualified students based on their academic record, SAT I or ACT scores, and extracurricular involvement. First-year students should apply by February 1; transfer scholarships are competitive, and preference is given to students who apply before March 15. The College also offers partial and full ROTC scholarships.

To apply, students should file the Free Application for Federal Student Aid (FAFSA) with the federal processor and apply for admission to WMC. Students also must submit a WMC financial aid application, which is available upon request.

Faculty

Faculty members—90 full-time professors, 95 percent of whom hold the most advanced degrees in their fields—devote themselves to classroom, lab, and studio teaching. Many conduct research; most involve students in their work. Professors teach a maximum of three courses each semester, allowing them ample time to spend with students outside of the classroom, helping them plan academic programs, arrange internships, and prepare for careers. An average class size of 20 students encourages discussion, and learning is collaborative rather than competitive. WMC's president, provost, dean of students, and financial vice president all teach undergraduate courses. Faculty members also serve as advisers to many student organizations.

Student Government

All students are automatically members of the Student Government Assembly (SGA), which is the student body's central governing and coordinating organization. It consists of two main parts: the Executive Council, elected by the student body at large, and the Senate, composed of representatives from the classes. Students hold full voting membership on most policy-making College committees, serving with faculty members, administrative staff members, and trustees in dealing with concerns such as the curriculum, academic policy, athletics, calendar, schedule, admissions, and financial aid.

Admission Requirements

WMC welcomes applications from men and women who desire the lifelong personal and professional benefits of a liberal arts education and who eagerly enter the partnerships necessary to achieve it. The College annually enrolls 400–500 first-year students, including international students and students beyond traditional college age. In addition, the College welcomes applications from students wishing to transfer from community colleges and other four-year colleges and universities.

Prospective applicants should have a broad secondary school program, including 4 years of English, 3 years of social studies, 3 years of a foreign language, 3 years of work in laboratory sciences (biology and chemistry), and 3 years of mathematics. In addition to the school record, WMC evaluates the potential academic success of each applicant by considering SAT I or ACT scores, class rank, application essay, recommendations, and participation in nonacademic activities. Each year, about 20 percent of new students transfer to WMC from two- and four-year colleges and universities. Transfer students must have a minimum GPA of 2.5 in college course work and submit an official transcript.

Personal interviews and campus tours are strongly recommended and are available Monday through Friday at 10:30 a.m. and 2 p.m. and on Saturdays by appointment. The College regularly holds open houses that include formal and informal presentations on academic programs, student life, financial assistance, and other topics.

WMC seeks diversity in its student population and does not discriminate in the recruitment, admission, and employment of students and faculty and staff members in the operation of any of its educational programs and activities as defined by law.

Application and Information

Deadlines for receiving completed applications are December 1 for early action, February 1 for academic scholarship consideration, and March 15 for regular admission. Applications from transfer students are accepted through the summer. Complete applications, along with a $40 nonrefundable application fee, should be sent to:

M. Martha O'Connell, Dean of Admissions
Western Maryland College
2 College Hill
Westminster, Maryland 21157-4390
Telephone: 410-857-2230
          800-638-5005 (Voice/TDD) (toll-free)
E-mail: admissio@wmdc.edu
World Wide Web: http://www.wmdc.edu

The brick pathways that front Hoover Library are a campus focal point.

WESTERN MICHIGAN UNIVERSITY
KALAMAZOO, MICHIGAN

The University

Western Michigan University is one of the nation's leading midsized universities, making a difference in the world through a commitment to academic excellence and public service. *U.S. News & World Report* has ranked the University "in the major leagues of American higher education" as one of the country's 229 top national universities. WMU is one of only ninety-one public universities in the nation—and only four in Michigan—to have a chapter of Phi Beta Kappa, the nation's premier honor society.

WMU is counted among Michigan's top four universities in both size and the complexity and variety of its offerings. Yet WMU ranks ninth among the state's fifteen public universities in tuition and required fees and is listed in *America's 100 Best College Buys*. Its student-faculty ratio is a comfortable 16:1. Only ninety-five of its 4,000 classes have more than 100 students.

With 27,744 students, WMU is the fourth-largest university in Michigan and among the nation's sixty largest universities. Members of minority groups represent 6 percent of total enrollment; international students represent 11 percent. About 6,300 students live in twenty-two residence halls that provide a variety of living arrangements.

Founded in 1903, WMU has seven degree-granting colleges—Arts and Sciences, Aviation, the Haworth College of Business, Education, Engineering and Applied Sciences, Fine Arts, and Health and Human Services—as well as the Graduate College and Lee Honors College. The University offers 254 academic programs, more than 160 of them at the undergraduate level.

Major factors in WMU's success include promotion of out-of-class learning and creation of cutting-edge instructional facilities. More than $320 million has been spent on new buildings and state-of-the-art equipment over the past decade, including $50 million in modern student recreation facilities.

The University has 400 registered student organizations that enhance the out-of-class experience of its students, including a wide range of Greek-letter, academic, honorary, and professional organizations. In addition, WMU provides an atmosphere of cultural richness. Its strong commitment to diversity and equal opportunity helps attract faculty, staff, and students of all ages, backgrounds, and nationalities from all fifty states and nearly 100 nations.

Cultural events at Miller Auditorium, acclaimed arts programs, and NCAA Division I-A Mid-American Conference and Central Collegiate Hockey Association sports teams add variety and vitality to campus life. Men's varsity sports include baseball, basketball, cross-country, football, ice hockey, soccer, tennis, and track. Women's varsity sports include basketball, cross-country, gymnastics, soccer, softball, tennis, track, and volleyball. There also are many intramural and club sports.

Location

Kalamazoo is the fifth-largest city in Michigan, with a countywide population exceeding 280,000 residents. The campus is located midway between Detroit and Chicago, 2½ hours from each city. Commercial transportation includes train, bus, and airline services. The Kalamazoo community offers a wide array of lively entertainment: sports, such as professional baseball and hockey; music, from jazz to heavy metal; intimate comedy clubs; and dining, from fast food to international cuisine. West Michigan is home to many thriving businesses, industries, and Fortune 500 companies, including Haworth Inc., Pharmacia & Upjohn Inc., and Kellogg Co.—each offering internship possibilities. Kalamazoo is just 45 minutes from Lake Michigan beaches and only 3 to 4 hours from northern Michigan's ski country. Excellent local skiing is only 30 minutes from the campus.

Majors and Degrees

WMU offers bachelor's degree programs in these fields: accountancy, administrative systems, advertising and promotion, aeronautical engineering, African studies, American studies, anthropology, art, art history, art teaching, Asian studies, automotive engineering technology, aviation flight science, aviation maintenance and technology–advanced technology, aviation maintenance and technology–maintenance management, aviation science and administration, biochemistry, biology, biomedical sciences, Black Americana studies, broadcast and cable production, business-oriented chemistry, chemical engineering, chemistry, communication studies, community health (education), computer engineering, computer information systems, computer science, computer science–theory and analysis, construction engineering and management, criminal justice, dance, dietetics (education), earth science, economics, electrical engineering, elementary education, elementary education–music, engineering graphics and design technology, engineering management technology, English, environmental studies, European studies, exercise science (education), family studies (education), finance, food marketing, food service administration (education), French, general business, general engineering, geography, geology, geophysics, gerontology, German, graphic design, health education teaching, history, home economics education, human resource management, hydrogeology, industrial design, industrial engineering, industrial technology (education), integrated supply management, interior design (education), interpersonal communication, journalism, Latin, Latin American studies, management, manufacturing engineering, manufacturing engineering technology, marketing, materials engineering, mathematics, mechanical engineering, media studies, music, music composition, music education, music history, music–jazz studies, music performance, music theater performance, music theory, music therapy, nursing, occupational therapy, organizational communication, paper engineering, paper science, philosophy, physical education–teacher/coach, physics, political science, political science in public administration, prearchitecture, pre–business administration, predentistry, prelaw, premedicine, printing, psychology, public administration, public history, public relations, recreation (education), religion, Russian and East European studies, sales and business marketing, secondary education (biology, business, chemistry, earth science, English, French, geography, German, history, Latin, marketing, mathematics, physics, political science, and Spanish), social work, sociology, Spanish, special education–emotionally impaired, special education–mentally impaired, special education–visually impaired, speech pathology and audiology, statistics, student-planned major, technology and design (education), telecommunications management, textile and apparel studies (education), theater, theater education, tourism and travel, travel instruction, and women's studies.

Academic Program

WMU offers undergraduate students a rich blend of academic majors and minors, as well as its general education program. This program assures that students graduate with proficiencies and perspectives they need to succeed in the next century. The

University Curriculum Program is for students who are undecided about a major and wish to explore WMU's academic offerings. Last fall, more than 2,100 students enrolled in the University Curriculum Program, which won a national award for outstanding academic advising. The Lee Honors College provides undergraduates with a unique living/learning environment offering the intimacy of a small college with the resources of a major university.

Off-Campus Arrangements

A host of U.S. business-industry partnerships, as well as exchange agreements with universities around the world, provide countless training and research opportunities for graduate and undergraduate students alike. WMU has linkages with more than forty universities and agencies in more than twenty countries. The University provides assistance to students seeking internships in their chosen fields of study.

Academic Facilities

The University Libraries, with the fourth-largest holdings in Michigan, and the University Computing Center together provide campuswide access to worldwide information resources, comparable with the best universities in the Midwest. Work has been completed on a $45.3-million expansion project, which includes a new Science Research Pavilion that combines teaching and research in exciting new ways. The Gilmore Theatre Complex offers four varied performance spaces, including the Multi-Form Theatre.

Costs

WMU is committed to keeping costs as low as possible to assure that all qualified students have access to the University. WMU's tuition and fees are among the lowest in the state. Costs for 1999–2000 were tuition and fees, $3944; room and board, $4831; and books and supplies, $760. Personal and travel expenses vary based on individual factors.

Financial Aid

Last year, nearly 18,000 students received financial assistance totaling more than $116 million. There are three basic types of financial aid: merit-based programs, need-based programs, and student employment.

Merit-based programs include the Medallion Scholarship and the Cultural Diversity Scholarship Programs, the University's two most honored scholarships for entering freshmen. Awards range from $4800 to $32,000 over four years. Other scholarships and awards include the Army ROTC awards, Michigan National Guard awards, the Award for National Merit Scholarships, and many other sponsored and departmental scholarships for new and currently enrolled students. Merit-based scholarships also are available to community college transfer students, ranging in value from $1000 to $6000.

Need-based loans, grants, college work-study, and other aid options are provided for students who demonstrate particular financial need. To be considered, students should complete the Free Application for Federal Student Aid.

The student employment option reflects research indicating that students who work part-time are more likely to graduate than students who do not work at all. About 40 percent of WMU's students work while in school, and more than 2,000 jobs are offered through the college work-study program.

WMU provides a tuition payment plan through Academic Management Services (AMS) and Tuition Management Systems. This allows parents and students to pay college costs in monthly installments. No interest is charged for these services, which may be renewed annually for $45. Students should contact AMS at 800-556-6684 or Tuition Management Systems at 800-722-4867 for more information.

Faculty

WMU's commitment to academic excellence means that many of its 868 full-time and 466 part-time faculty members conduct research. Tenured professors teach freshman-level courses, and full-time faculty members teach three quarters of all classes. Almost 92 percent of WMU faculty members have earned a doctorate or other terminal degree in their fields.

Student Government

Governance structures include the Western Student Association and its Student Senate and the Residence Hall Association. Each provides students with a wide variety of opportunities for leadership.

Admission Requirements

Admission to the University is based on a combination of factors, including grade point average, ACT scores, number and kinds of college-prep courses, and trend of grades. In addition, students must meet specific course requirements that include 4 years of English; 3 years of mathematics, including intermediate algebra; 3 years of social sciences; and 2 years of biological/physical sciences. Students who do not meet these requirements but are otherwise admissible may still be admitted to WMU and take the necessary courses as University-level work for credit during their first year.

Transfer students with a minimum of 26 transferable hours (39 quarter hours) at the time of application and a GPA of at least 2.0 (C average) will be considered for admission. Trend of the most recent grades also will be taken into account. Applicants with fewer than 26 transferable hours (39 quarter hours) at the time of application also must submit a high school transcript. In such cases, admission will be based on both college and high school records. For more information, students can request the Transfer Brochure from the Office of Admissions and Orientation.

Application and Information

For an application or additional information, students should contact:

Office of Admissions and Orientation
Western Michigan University
1201 Oliver Street
Kalamazoo, Michigan 49008-5720
Telephone: 616-387-2000
        800-400-4WMU (toll-free)
World Wide Web: http://www.wmich.edu

This imposing clock tower joins Waldo Library, on the right, with the University Computing Center.

WESTERN MONTANA COLLEGE OF THE UNIVERSITY OF MONTANA
DILLON, MONTANA

The College

Western Montana College of The University of Montana is a small, public, four-year college originally established in 1893 in beautiful southwestern Montana. Western nurtures scholarship, creativity, lifelong learning, and high standards. The intimate size of Western's campus provides accessibility to all aspects of academic and extracurricular life.

Currently enrolling an average of 1,100 students, Western specializes in providing individual attention, personalized caring and commitment, and hands-on classroom experiences using state-of-the-art technology. All classes are taught by professors, not graduate students, and the average class size is 20 or fewer. The 34-acre campus is small, friendly, and beautiful, and the sixteen major buildings are easily accessible.

Athletics are an important part of campus life at Western Montana College. One in every 5 Western students participates in a sport. Western is affiliated with the National Association of Intercollegiate Athletics and participates in the Frontier Conference. Varsity sports are offered for women in basketball, rodeo, golf, and volleyball. Men compete in basketball, football, golf, and rodeo.

Western is affiliated with The University of Montana, which also has four-year campuses in Missoula and Butte and a two-year campus in Helena.

Location

Located at the southwestern tip of Big Sky Country, the quiet and safe town of Dillon is home to Western. Dillon has a population of 5,000. The town has numerous restaurants, a hospital, a movie theater, and a host of local merchants. Dillon is the seat of Beaverhead County, Montana's largest county. The 3.3-million-acre Beaverhead–Deer Lodge National Forest is known for its seasonal outdoor recreational opportunities. Fishing, hunting, boating, downhill and cross-country skiing, backpacking, horseback riding, and camping are all available within an hour's drive. The area is also rich in Western history. The region's weather is mild in the winter and cool in the summer, with average daily high temperatures of 35 and 76 degrees, respectively. Annual precipitation averages 10 inches. Rich farmland, rugged mountains, and wide expanses of the old frontier surround Dillon, yet major Montana and Idaho cities are easily accessible by interstate highway.

Majors and Degrees

More than half of Western's students enter the field of teacher education. Western offers the following degrees and majors: Bachelor of Science in elementary education; Bachelor of Science in secondary education, with majors in art K–12, biology, business education, chemistry, English, general science, history, industrial arts technology, mathematics, music K–12, physical education and health K–12 (offers emphasis in athletic coaching), physical science, and social science (some of these majors require a minor); Bachelor of Applied Science; Bachelor of Arts in arts, business and communications, environmental sciences, literature and writing, and social science; general Associate of Arts and Associate of Science provide a two-year degree with a full general education curriculum. Other two-year degrees include the Associate of Applied Science in business (with options in business management, information processing, human resource management, and office systems technology), computer layout and design, early childhood education, and tourism and recreation.

Minors are offered in all major areas in addition to chemistry, computer science, drama, early childhood education, earth science, library K–12, reading K–12, and special education. Preprofessional programs may be planned to meet the needs of the individual students.

Academic Program

Each graduate of any associate or baccalaureate degree is expected to have demonstrated competency in both oral and written communication as applied to the particular major and minor fields. The foundation of the general education requirements is oral and written communication. Between 35 and 40 general education credits are required for all four-year degree programs.

The baccalaureate degree is conferred upon completion of the proper curriculum, with a minimum of 120 semester credits and with an overall (institutional plus transfer) scholastic average of at least 2.0. Some baccalaureate degrees may require a higher cumulative grade point average.

The Bachelor of Arts requires completion of a cooperative education/internship or a senior project/thesis.

The Western Montana College of The University of Montana Honors Program is designed to offer enrichment and challenge to a small number of students who are chosen to participate. Classes in the Honors Program are thematically based interdisciplinary seminars that emphasize independent research. Students who successfully complete a sequence of honors classes throughout their college career are designated Honors Graduates. Some honors classes may be substituted for general education requirements.

Western operates on the semester system. Each academic year has two semesters during the fall and spring, four-week courses during May interim, and four- and six-week courses during the summer.

Continuing education offers evening and weekend workshops throughout the academic year.

Academic Facilities

The compact campus is guarded by Old Main Hall, built in 1895. The historic, architecturally impressive building houses many faculty offices, newly renovated classrooms, and an art gallery/museum. The library (60,000 books, 19,500 microform titles, 500 periodicals, and 500 records, tapes, and CDs) is the focal point for academics at Western. The library houses a telecommunications lab with PCs, modems, and printers that allow access to the Internet, databases, and utilities. An audiovisual laboratory is also available.

The microcomputer center maintains more than seventy-five IBM and Apple computers exclusively for student use. Computers are also located in the residence halls, Learning Center, office-simulation center, library, and math/science center. Each individual room in the newly renovated residence halls is equipped with computer hookups and networked to the campus computer system. The Learning Center provides students with individualized programs to assist in reading, writing, math, or science. The Early Childhood Education Center offers day care to both on-campus and community children, which provides opportunities for hands-on experience for students in related majors.

Costs

Western Montana College of The University of Montana prides itself on providing an outstanding education for a relatively low cost. For the 1999–2000 academic year, state resident tuition and fees were $2700; nonresident tuition and fees were $7200. Board and a double room were $3500. Books and supplies are estimated at $600. Living expenses, including estimated costs of phone, personal transportation, and other miscellaneous expenses, are estimated to be $2000. Residents of states participating in the WICHE/WUE program (Alaska, Arizona, Colorado, Hawaii, Idaho, Nevada, New Mexico, North Dakota, Oregon, South Dakota, Utah, Washington, and Wyoming) pay approximately 150 percent of Montana-resident tuition and fees. Eligibility for WUE is through an application process and selection based on merit.

Financial Aid

More than 60 percent of Western students receive some form of financial assistance while working toward a degree. The more than $2.5 million awarded includes scholarships, grants, loans, and work-study opportunities. Applicants must submit the Free Application for Federal Student Aid and the Western Montana College Financial Aid Application by March 1. Job opportunities are available both on campus and in the Dillon community.

Faculty

Fifty resident, full-time faculty members teach at Western. No courses are taught by graduate assistants. Nearly 75 percent of faculty members hold terminal degrees. The faculty-student ratio of 1:18 allows considerable interaction and personal attention. All faculty members, including part-time, are academic advisers for students. In addition, faculty members participate actively in student-oriented activities, serve as advisers to student clubs, and conduct extracurricular workshops and field trips.

Student Government

All students registered at Western are members of the Associated Students of Western Montana College (ASWMC). ASWMC is governed by officers elected each spring. The president serves as a member of the Administrative Council. The ASWMC Activities Board is responsible for organizing a balanced calendar of social, recreational, educational, and cultural programs appropriate to the goals and needs of the campus community. Funding is allocated annually by the Student Senate from student activity fees.

Admission Requirements

All applicants must file an application for admission with a nonrefundable $30 fee. Freshmen must submit their high school record (posting date of graduation and rank in class) and scores from either the ACT or SAT I. Transfer applicants must submit official transcripts from each college or university attended. Transfer applicants who have earned fewer than 12 postsecondary quarter or semester credits must also submit an official high school transcript and standardized test scores.

Graduates of fully accredited high schools are eligible for admission as first-time undergraduate students, provided they have a minimum score of 20 on the ACT or 960 on the SAT I, have at least a 2.5 high school grade point average, or rank in the upper half of their graduating class and have completed the prescribed college-preparatory curriculum. Freshman applicants' college-preparatory program must include 4 years of English, 3 years of mathematics (2 years of algebra and 1 of geometry), 3 years of social studies, 2 years of a laboratory science, and 2 years of electives chosen from foreign language, computer science, visual or performing arts, or vocational education.

Transfer students normally are required to have a minimum cumulative grade point average of 2.0, based on a 4.0 system, for all college work attempted.

Application and Information

Western has a rolling admission policy. Students are informed of acceptance two weeks after their admission files have been completed. The Admissions and New Student Services Office is open Monday through Friday, 8 a.m. to 5 p.m. Visitors are welcome to contact the office to schedule a campus tour, obtain admission materials, or meet with an admissions representative. Prospective students are invited to see Western during the campus visitation programs: "Dawg Days," held each fall, and "Showtime," held the first weekend in March. For further information, students should contact:

Admissions and New Student Services
Western Montana College of The University of Montana
710 South Atlantic
Dillon, Montana 59725-3598

Telephone: 800-WMC-MONT (toll-free)
  406-683-7331
Fax: 406-683-7493
E-mail: admissions@wmc.edu
World Wide Web: http://www.wmc.edu

Western Montana College's Old Main Hall is one of the most architecturally notable of all buildings on Montana campuses.

WESTERN NEW ENGLAND COLLEGE
SPRINGFIELD, MASSACHUSETTS

The College

The history of Western New England College dates from 1919; in that year, Northeastern University established a Springfield Division, which in 1951 became known as Western New England College. From its inception, Western New England has sought to provide students with a strong professional and liberal arts education. The College offers thirty-two undergraduate majors in the Schools of Arts and Sciences, Business, and Engineering. Western New England College offers a unique program combining undergraduate and graduate courses, as well as eight graduate degrees. A Juris Doctor program is also available. The College also assists many part-time students with an Office of Continuing Education.

Students who enroll at Western New England College seek a solid liberal education with the goal of entering a profession or graduate school upon completion of their studies at the College. The average age of undergraduate students is 20 years, and 57 percent of the undergraduates are men. There are about 1,950 full-time undergraduates, and the total College enrollment is approximately 5,150. Currently, 53 percent of the students come from out of state; 1 percent are from other countries; and approximately 72 percent of students live on campus.

The Campus Activities Board has specific responsibility for lecture programs, concerts, the performing arts, and traditional events such as Homecoming, Family Weekend, and Spring Week. There are athletic programs at the varsity and intramural levels. Varsity sports are played at the NCAA Division III level. Men's sports include baseball, basketball, cross-country, football, golf, ice hockey, lacrosse, soccer, tennis, and wrestling. Women's sports include basketball, cross-country, field hockey, lacrosse, soccer, softball, swimming, tennis, and volleyball. Non-NCAA participation sports include men's and women's bowling and martial arts. Students live in residence halls varying in type from the traditional to a suite-style arrangement. Students may also reside in garden-style apartments located on campus.

The Alumni Healthful Living Center is among the finest collegiate health and recreation facilities. The 158,000-square-foot Center houses all of the College's physical education classes and provides a wide array of recreational and sports opportunities for students.

Graduate degrees offered by the College are the Master of Business Administration (One-Year Weekend Program also available) and the Master of Science in accounting, criminal justice administration, information systems, electrical engineering, mechanical engineering, and engineering management. A Juris Doctor program is also offered.

Location

The College is located in a residential section of Springfield, Massachusetts, about 4 miles from the city's downtown area. Because Springfield is a city of 157,000 people, there are a variety of social, cultural, and athletic activities from which to choose. Some of the city's special features are City Stage, a professional theater; the Quadrangle, a complex of museums; the Basketball Hall of Fame; the Springfield Falcons hockey team; a professional men's basketball team; the Eastern States Exposition; and activities, shows, and concerts held in the Springfield Civic Center and Symphony Hall.

Majors and Degrees

Western New England College offers the following areas of study at the baccalaureate degree level: in the School of Arts and Sciences—American studies, biology, chemistry, computer science, criminal justice, economics, English (communication or literature concentration), environmental science, government, history, international studies, mathematical sciences, prepharmacy (Doctor of Pharmacy degree program offered in conjunction with the Massachusetts College of Pharmacy and Health Sciences), pre–physician assistant studies (the Master of Physician Assistant Studies program is offered in conjunction with the Massachusetts College of Pharmacy and Health Sciences), psychology, social work, and sociology; in the School of Business—accounting, computer information systems, finance, general business, international business, management, marketing, marketing communication/advertising, and sport management; and in the School of Engineering—biomedical engineering (options in electrical, life sciences, and mechanical), electrical engineering (options in computer and electrical), industrial engineering (options in manufacturing and systems), and mechanical engineering (options in manufacturing and mechanical).

Western New England College also offers academic programs in elementary education and secondary education. The College's 3 + 3 Law Program offers students an opportunity to earn their bachelor's degree and a Juris Doctor degree from Western New England College School of Law in six years rather than seven. The College also offers preprofessional studies in law and medicine.

Academic Program

Five courses are usually taken each semester. Specific departmental degree requirements are stated in the College Catalogue.

Western New England College participates in the College Board's Advanced Placement (AP) Program and College-Level Examination Program (CLEP). Successful completion of these programs may result in the earning of academic credit and the waiving of certain courses.

The College operates on a two-semester calendar.

Academic Facilities

The Western New England campus contains nineteen major buildings and is situated on 215 acres. Classes are held in five classroom-laboratory buildings, which contain more than sixty-five classrooms. The D'Amour Library contains 119,000 volumes and is currently receiving 266 periodicals, with access to more than 5,000 titles via the Internet. The College is committed to providing students with access to a wide range of computing hardware and software. Students are expected to learn and use current computing technology in their courses for accessing materials, doing research, writing assignments, submitting work, and communicating with faculty members and peers. The College has a campuswide network linking all buildings to hundreds of PCs in public areas, including the Churchill Hall Lab, the D'Amour Library, the Writing and Math Centers, the Accounting Lab, the School of Law, and the Engineering Labs. All registered students have Internet e-mail accounts. In addition, each semester more than 20 faculty members and several hundred students use a special software package, customized for Western New England College, to provide safe and secure file transport between faculty members, students, campus organizations, and informal groups. All College residence hall rooms are wired for Internet access. In addition, the School of Engineering has a large number of microcomputers, graphic plotters, and other peripherals used to support the laboratory programs.

Costs

Tuition for the 2000–01 academic year is $14,354. The comprehensive room and board fee is $7050. Other fees and expenses are approximately $1150.

Financial Aid

Western New England College offers an extensive financial assistance program in the form of merit and need-based scholarships, loans, grants, and on-campus employment. Applicants for financial aid must submit the Free Application for Federal Student Aid (FAFSA), the Western New England College application for financial aid, and a copy of the federal income tax form 1040. In 1999–2000, approximately 76 percent of the students at WNEC received financial assistance; the average award was $9,909.

Faculty

The ratio of students to faculty members is 17:1. The average class size is 20, and students have ample opportunity to meet with faculty members outside of class.

Student Government

The Student Senate is the official voice of full-time students and is composed of 2 representatives from each class; representatives from the Schools of Arts and Sciences, Business, and Engineering; and representatives from the commuter and resident student groups. The Student Senate serves as the liaison among the students, the faculty, and the administration of the College.

Admission Requirements

Western New England College seeks students who wish to acquire a professional and liberal education at a small New England college in a suburban setting. Applicants must have graduated from an approved secondary school or have obtained a general equivalency diploma. The college-preparatory units should include a minimum of 4 units of English, 2 units of mathematics, 1 unit of laboratory science, and 1 unit of U.S. history. Applicants who wish to major in chemistry, computer science, environmental science, or mathematics are required to present 3 units of mathematics. Prospective majors in biology, chemistry, and environmental science are required to present 1 unit of chemistry; in addition, it is recommended that chemistry and environmental science majors have 1 unit of physics. Prospective majors in prepharmacy and pre–physician assistant studies are required to present 3 units of mathematics, including algebra I and II and geometry. These students are also required to present 2 units of laboratory science, including biology and chemistry; physics with a laboratory and precalculus are both recommended. Prospective engineering students must present 1 unit of physics or 1 unit of chemistry (preferably both) as well as 4 units of mathematics. Prospective business majors must present 3 units of mathematics. Freshman applicants are required to submit scores on the SAT I or ACT. International applicants should take the Test of English as a Foreign Language (TOEFL) and have their scores forwarded to the Admissions Office.

Application and Information

The College follows a rolling admission policy for all programs except for pre–physician assistant studies; there is no specific deadline for application. The priority deadline for pre–physician assistant studies is February 1. However, students are encouraged to apply early in order to receive complete consideration for admission, financial aid, and housing. In addition to the application form, the following must be sent: SAT I or ACT scores, a recommendation from the student's counselor or teacher, and an official secondary school transcript. Transfer applicants should include official transcripts of any college work. Notification of acceptance begins in late fall.

For complete admission information, students should contact:

Admissions Office
Western New England College
1215 Wilbraham Road
Springfield, Massachusetts 01119
Telephone: 413-782-1321
           800-325-1122 Ext. 1321 (toll-free)
Fax: 413-782-1777
E-mail: ugradmis@wnec.edu
World Wide Web: http://www.wnec.edu

Students enjoy the beautiful and spacious Western New England College campus.

WESTERN OREGON UNIVERSITY
MONMOUTH, OREGON

The University

In the early 1850s, hardy pioneers crossed the Oregon Trail to found a church and school in the Willamette Valley. Monmouth University opened with a handful of students in 1856. Today, Western Oregon University (WOU) serves more than 4,515 undergraduate and graduate students. In its rich 143-year history, the school has evolved from a private institution into a public liberal arts university. WOU's dedication to teacher preparation has stood the test of time, while the institution has also responded to the changing needs of its students and community with programs in the liberal arts and sciences. Graduate-level programs include a Master of Arts in Teaching, a Master of Science in Education, and a Master of Arts/Master of Science in correctional administration. The University houses a Regional Center on Deafness and offers graduate programs in rehabilitation and deaf education. There are also endorsements available in special education programs at the graduate level.

Of the students attending Western Oregon University, 89 percent are from Oregon. About 87 international students and 432 students of color attend the institution. The University continues to benefit from the diversity of its students' personal experiences, educational goals, and professional aspirations. Extracurricular opportunities abound on WOU's campus. Students stay active in more than sixty clubs, including academic organizations, cultural clubs, honor societies, performing arts groups, religious organizations, service organizations, sports clubs, and student media.

On-campus attractions include several art galleries, main-stage productions in Rice Auditorium, ensemble performances, a Spring Dance Concert, and student-directed plays. The Edgar H. Smith Fine Arts series draws sellout crowds every year. The Multicultural Student Union also sponsors events year-round, including a powwow during Native American Month, an African-American celebration, and a Cinco de Mayo celebration. Currently, six men's and seven women's athletic teams compete each year in the NCAA Division II. Approximately 500 students also participate in intramurals on campus each term. A swimming pool, track, and weight room, as well as playing fields, basketball courts, racquetball courts, and tennis courts, are available for student use.

Western Oregon University requires first-year students to live on campus, where convenient, affordable living; personal support from Resident Assistants; and opportunities for friendship and leadership find common ground. Freshmen share a room with another student and share a common bathroom with the students on their floor. Some returning students continue living in the residence halls, while others seek housing in Monmouth or in nearby communities. Students are welcome to bring their cars to campus.

Location

Western Oregon University is located in Monmouth, Oregon, a community of 8,000 that lies in the heart of the Willamette Valley. With its relaxed pace, friendly community, and pride in hometown values, Monmouth offers students all the benefits of small-town living. Monmouth is also a "dry" town; the sale of alcoholic beverages is prohibited within city limits.

Summers in Monmouth are sunny and warm, while the winters bring cool temperatures and frequent rains, keeping the area lush and green. Paths around the campus provide scenic spots for walking, biking, running, and roller blading, and views of the colorful landscape and Mt. Jefferson can be seen on a clear day. The campus itself offers a beautiful, parklike atmosphere.

The University is just minutes west of the capital city, Salem, and offers quick access to Portland, Corvallis, and Eugene. The Oregon coast and Cascade Mountains are also within easy reach, allowing students to enjoy some of the state's best recreational opportunities.

Students and local residents share a common interest in preserving the quality of life in Monmouth. They often combine their energy, resources, and enthusiasm to support the University's educational, artistic, cultural, and athletic activities.

Majors and Degrees

In the College of Education, students can earn a bachelor's degree in education and interdisciplinary studies, with authorizations at the early childhood, elementary, middle, and high school levels. For middle and high school authorizations, the following endorsements are available: biology, English/language arts, foreign language, health, integrated science, mathematics, physical education, and social sciences. Licensed teachers can pursue endorsements in bilingual/ESOL, deaf education, media/information technology, and reading. A bachelor's degree in American Sign Language/English Interpretation is also offered. Admission into the College of Education is competitive.

The College of Liberal Arts and Sciences offers bachelor's degrees in art, the arts, biology, business, chemistry, chemistry (forensic option), community crime prevention, computer science, computer science/math, contemporary music, corrections, dance, economics, English, fire services administration (upper-division transfer program), geography, history, humanities, interdisciplinary studies, international studies, law enforcement, mathematics, music, natural science, philosophy, political science, psychology, public policy and administration, social science, sociology, Spanish, speech communication, and theater arts. Undergraduate minors are offered in most of the programs listed above, as well as in anthropology, environmental studies, French, gender studies, German, Latin American studies, legal studies, military science, philosophy, and physics.

Preprofessional course work is available for students pursuing careers in dentistry, dental hygiene, journalism, law, medical technology, medicine, nursing, occupational/physical therapy, optometry, pharmacy, physician assistant studies, podiatry, and veterinary medicine.

Academic Program

The undergraduate program at Western Oregon University includes the following components: the Liberal Arts Core Curriculum (LACC), a major, a minor, and electives. The University operates on a quarter system, and students must earn 192 credits to graduate. The LACC includes courses in writing, speech, creative arts, humanities, science, social science, and others. This general education sequence benefits all students, particularly those who are undecided, by exposing them to possible majors.

While they are trying to select a major, students may visit with staff members in the Central Advising Office. Those who have declared a major will be assigned an adviser in their department.

The Honors Program invites students to accept new challenges and requires completion of a senior-year thesis based on independent research. For information or an application, students may call 503-838-8224.

The University houses a Regional Center on Deafness with a major in ASL/EI.

Off-Campus Arrangements

A strong belief that colleges and universities must prepare students to live and work in a global society is the underlying philosophy of Western Oregon University's International Exchange Programs. Currently, students have opportunities to earn college credit while studying in such countries as Australia, Austria, China, Ecuador, England, France, Germany, Greece, Ireland, Italy, Japan, Mexico, New Zealand, Scotland, South Korea, Spain, and Thailand. The University continues to expand its partnerships with colleges and universities around the world.

Academic Facilities

More than 182,000 books, 1,800 magazines, 654,000 microfilms, and 106,400 government documents are available at Western Oregon University's library. Combined resources in the Oregon University System and in Orbis (a multilibrary consortium) are available to students and faculty. Electronic resources provide access to WOLF (WOU's online catalog), numerous online indexes for journals covering all disciplines, full-text newspapers, and the Internet, including the World Wide Web.

In the Academic Computing Resource Center, students have access to a drop-in computer laboratory equipped with seventy computers and free laser printing. Every student can have an e-mail address as well.

Costs

Resident undergraduate tuition for the 1999–2000 school year was $3276. Undergraduate tuition for nonresidents was $10,293. Tuition rates increase an average of 4 percent each year. Residence hall rates vary, depending on the living environment and the meal plan a student chooses. In 1999–2000, a double room in the residence halls cost $5004, including a meal plan.

Financial Aid

The University distributed $21 million in financial aid in 1999–2000, and more than 66 percent of students received a package. To be considered for loans, grants, and work-study, students must submit the Free Application for Federal Student Aid (FAFSA), indicating Western Oregon University as one of their college choices. Students should mail the FAFSA by February 1 to receive maximum consideration. In addition, they need to have applied for admission to WOU. For more information, students may call 503-838-8475 V/TTY.

By completing WOU's General Scholarship Application, students can be considered for numerous awards, including Oregon Laurels and Presidential Scholarships. The deadline is March 1. Academic departments sponsor additional scholarships for which students may apply. Finally, the Diversity Achievement Scholarship enables WOU to award renewable scholarships to Oregon residents who meet specific eligibility requirements.

Work-study opportunities and part-time work positions are advertised through the Student Employment office, which is located in the Financial Aid Office.

Faculty

At Western Oregon University, students have the opportunity to develop close working relationships with their professors. While faculty members are engaged in research and scholarly activities, teaching remains a true priority. There are 150 full-time and 118 adjunct/part-time faculty members; 97 percent of the full-time faculty members hold doctoral/terminal degrees in their fields. The student-to-faculty ratio is approximately 17:1.

Student Government

The Associated Students of Western Oregon University (ASWOU) serves as the voice of the student population. Student leaders implement policies, make budget recommendations, and organize Homecoming, dances, and concerts. They also work with the Oregon Student Association to support voter registration, increases in financial aid, and other important issues in higher education. The Incidental Fee Committee allocates nearly $1 million each year to such areas as athletics, ASWOU, child care, interpreting, student media, Student Leadership and Activities, and the Werner University Center. Elected, appointed, and volunteer positions are available, allowing students to gain valuable leadership experience and to contribute significantly to the institution.

Admission Requirements

To be admitted as a freshman, a student must graduate from a standard or accredited high school, have at least a 2.75 cumulative GPA, submit SAT I or ACT scores, and complete fourteen subject requirements: 4 years of English; 3 years of math, including algebra II or its equivalent or higher; 3 years of social studies, including 1 year of U.S. history, 1 year of global studies, and 1 year of social studies electives; 2 years of science, including 1 year of a lab science; and 2 years of the same foreign language at the high school level. A student may also elect to take two quarters or semesters of the same foreign language at the collegiate level. (American Sign Language is acceptable in meeting the foreign language requirement at the high school level only.) The language requirement may also be met by satisfactory performance on an approved assessment of foreign language knowledge and/or proficiency. For details on how to satisfy the requirement via knowledge assessment or proficiency, the Office of Admissions should be contacted. Those graduating prior to 1997 are exempted from the foreign language requirement. Students who do not meet the high school graduation, GPA, or subject requirements should contact the Office of Admissions to discuss admission alternatives.

To be admitted as a transfer, a student must have completed 24 or more transferable college-level quarter hour credits (16 semester hours) and have a cumulative GPA of at least 2.0 in all college-level work attempted. All transfer students who graduated from high school in 1997 or later must meet the following foreign language requirement: two years of a foreign language in the same language at the high school level or two quarters or semesters of the same language at the collegiate level. Students who do not meet this requirement should contact the Office of Admissions. Transfer applicants who have between 12 and 23 transferable quarter hour credits must meet all freshman admission requirements and have a GPA of at least 2.0 in all college-level course work.

Western Oregon University offers a special admission process for students who do not meet regular admission requirements, alternatives, or exceptions.

Application and Information

To apply for admission, students must submit a completed application, a $50 nonrefundable application fee, and official transcripts from each high school and/or college or university attended. Freshmen must also send either their SAT I or ACT scores. WOU operates on rolling admissions.

For additional information or to schedule a campus visit, students may call or write:

Office of Admissions
Western Oregon University
Monmouth, Oregon 97361
Telephone: 503-838-8211 V/TTY
          877-877-1593 (toll-free)
Fax: 503-838-8067
E-mail: wolfgram@wou.edu
World Wide Web: http://www.wou.edu/studentaffairs/admissions

WESTERN STATE COLLEGE OF COLORADO
GUNNISON, COLORADO

The College

Western State College of Colorado is an exemplary undergraduate college of liberal arts and sciences with compatible professional disciplines. Committed to excellence in undergraduate education, Western provides a focused range of studies that takes advantage of its rural mountain location. The residential campus gives students the opportunity to become actively engaged in campus life.

The fact that Western State College is located in an Alpine valley high in Colorado's Rocky Mountains—set at an elevation of 7,735 feet, higher than any other four-year college in the nation—influences the nature of the College and the faculty members and students it attracts. For example, many academic disciplines seek to take advantage of what has been called "the greatest natural outdoor laboratory in the country." Especially benefited by an environment in which more than 80 percent of the land is controlled by the National Forest Service, the National Park Service, and other state and federal agencies are the disciplines of biology, geology, other environmental sciences, still and video photography, art, and recreation.

The environment and reputation of the College attract approximately 2,500 students from all over the world. Typically, more than forty-eight states and about fifteen other nations are represented. Approximately 65 percent of the students come from Colorado, with about 40 percent of those from the Denver metropolitan area. Approximately one half of the students live on campus in dormitories and apartments. The campus includes forty-two buildings on 231 landscaped acres, plus 280 adjoining undeveloped acres and the 1,200 acres of "W" Mountain, located across the valley.

Much of the students' social life is centered on the campus. Honorary societies for many academic disciplines are active, as are about sixty other special interest clubs and organizations. Included are groups formed around common interests in religion, academic fraternities and sororities, and outdoor and indoor recreation. Especially prominent on campus are the student media: the campus newspaper, television station, literary magazine, and FM radio station. Highly respected throughout the state is the WSC Mountain Rescue Team, which is frequently called upon to assist official agencies. It is one of the only nationally certified college-based rescue team. The intercollegiate athletic program includes eleven teams, which are affiliated with the NCAA Division II. Men's sports include basketball, cross-country, football, indoor and outdoor track and field, and wrestling. Women compete in basketball, cross-country, indoor and outdoor track and field, and volleyball. Both men and women field national-caliber Nordic and Alpine ski teams, which compete in the NCAA Division I. In addition, the students have organized club-level teams that represent the College in intercollegiate competition in men's and women's soccer, as well as men's baseball, ice hockey, lacrosse, rugby, and volleyball. Other opportunities for athletic involvement come through an exceptionally active intramural program, which involves about 75 percent of WSC students. One source of special pride is that so many Western athletes earn academic all-district and All-America honors.

Location

Western is located on the eastern edge of Gunnison, a community of approximately 7,000 people dedicated to serving the three primary industries of the area: education and other public service activities, summer and winter tourism, and ranching. An analysis of the 1980 census published in *USA Today* identified Gunnison County as the eighth–best-educated community in the nation (in terms of years of education per capita). For summer activities, thousands of tourists visit the area to fish, golf, climb, boat, windsurf, photograph the scenery, and just enjoy the cool climate. The many mountain trails make hiking and biking very popular. In the winter, skiing and other winter sports, such as snowshoeing, snowmobiling, winter camping, and ice fishing attract many more tourists. Two major ski areas are nearby: Crested Butte is 31 miles and Monarch is 45 miles from the campus. The state's largest body of water, Blue Mesa Reservoir, is 9 miles from town. Many Western students find employment in the community and at the ski areas. They also find internship opportunities and other ways to become involved in community life. Local churches welcome student and faculty involvement. The major political parties, which usually have College faculty members as their local leaders, actively solicit student involvement. One reason that the College and the local community enjoy such a pleasant symbiosis lies in the fact that more than 900 alumni of Western continue to live in the valley.

Majors and Degrees

Western State College of Colorado confers the Bachelor of Arts degree in accounting, anthropology, art, biology, business administration, chemistry, communication and theater, economics, education, English, geography, history, kinesiology, mathematics, music, physics, political science, psychology, recreation, sociology, and Spanish. Minors are offered in all of these disciplines and in computer science, environmental studies, geology, headwaters regional studies, journalism, prelaw, and small business. Students desiring certification as teachers or school administrators at the elementary level or secondary level pursue academic majors in other disciplines while taking the required courses in professional education. Western State College also confers the Bachelor of Fine Arts degree in art.

Within the academic majors, students may gain preprofessional preparation for dentistry, engineering, law, law enforcement, medicine, nursing, optometry, osteopathy, pharmacy, physical therapy, theology, veterinary medicine, and other professions.

While successful students may gain admission to specialized programs at any major university, Western has guaranteed-transfer agreements with Colorado State University in the following areas: chemical engineering; fishery biology; forest biology; forest management; forestry and natural resources; human nutrition, dietetics, or nutrition/fitness; landscape architecture; mechanical, electrical, or civil engineering; natural resources management; range ecology; range/forest management; watershed sciences; wildlife biology; and wood science and technology.

Academic Program

The faculty of Western is committed to the delivery of a curriculum that requires students to (1) demonstrate mastery of basic skills; (2) engage in breadth of study, integrate knowledge from a variety of fields, and apply what is studied to life; (3) study one discipline or group of disciplines deeply enough to prepare for professional employment and/or future study; and (4) demonstrate leadership and self-discipline. To graduate, students must complete a minimum of 120 semester hours of credit. Successful completion of a core curriculum of interdisciplinary studies and of a concentrated course of study in a selected academic major are also required.

To facilitate the transfer of junior college students, Western has developed detailed agreements with all of the two-year colleges in Colorado. The agreements guarantee that students who carefully follow the prescribed courses of study will fit into Western's upper-level programs; these students are able to graduate on schedule with none of the conflicts often encountered in the transfer process. These agreements relate to almost all disciplines. For example, students who have undertaken programs of study at the junior college level in accounting, art, business, communications, hotel and resort management, mathematics, the natural and social sciences, and ski-area operations are readily accommodated into Western baccalaureate programs.

Academic Facilities

Academic facilities at the College include well-equipped classrooms, three auditoriums (a traditional theater, a theater-in-the-round, and a recital hall), an art gallery, television and radio studios, laboratories for the natural sciences, botany laboratories, a biofeedback laboratory for psychology, and a darkroom. Students have direct access to the College's VAX 8500 computer through terminals located in various centers throughout the campus or through student-owned modems. As many as 125 stand-alone microcomputers—IBM-compatible, Apple, and Zenith—are also available for academic use.

The spacious library contains more than 110,000 volumes; more than half a million government documents, microforms, and audiovisual materials; and more than 825 carefully selected periodicals. Computerized access to all local and regional library holdings is available. The library also provides a supervised place for late-evening study and has a staff professionally and personally committed to providing the best possible service.

Costs

Tuition for the 1999–2000 academic year was $1516 for residents of Colorado. Nonresident tuition was $7028. Fees totaled $692. Room and board costs were about $5190. The College maintains an excellent accident-and-health insurance plan. The plan covers the expense of illness and injury subject to certain exclusions. The cost of the insurance for one calendar year was $650. The average cost of books and supplies is $500 per year. Students involved in classes that require auxiliary supplies and equipment are charged a fee that usually averages $14 per class. (These figures are subject to change in 2000–01.)

Financial Aid

Sufficient financial assistance is available to enable diligent and deserving students to complete their education. At Western, this assistance takes many forms, including state, federal, and institutional scholarships; grants; loans; and opportunities for employment on campus. Interested students should write to the Office of Financial Aid for a booklet that provides essential and up-to-date information. An extraordinary opportunity for qualified students comes through the Foundation Scholarship program funded by the Western State College Foundation.

Faculty

The faculty of Western comprises 120 full-time and 18 part-time teachers. While many do independent research in support of their teaching and some publish the results of their work, the primary basis of their employment is teaching and advising students and assisting with extracurricular student activities. Approximately 80 percent of the faculty members hold doctorates in their fields.

Student Government

The Student Government Association assumes responsibility through its Student Senate for representing student interests in numerous ways. The Senate assigns student members to important College committees; organizes most extracurricular activities, such as concerts, speakers, movies, club programs, and student media; and participates directly in the processes of budgeting and administering almost half a million dollars in student fees. The students also elect a Student Trustee, who sits as a member of the Board of Trustees for the Consortium of State Colleges.

Admission Requirements

Each prospective student at Western is considered individually. Admission is based on both academic and personal attributes that match the outstanding opportunities for study, recreation, and personal involvement at Western. Applicants for admission to the College should have graduated from an accredited high school or passed the GED with a minimum score of 50. Of the total secondary school units, it is recommended that at least 10 be chosen from the academic fields of English, foreign languages, mathematics, science, and social sciences, including no fewer than 3 units of English. In addition, students should have a GPA of at least 2.5, rank in the upper two thirds of their high school graduating class, and earn a combined score of 950 or higher on the SAT I or a composite score of 20 or higher on the ACT. Prospective transfer students must have earned a minimum 2.0 GPA in at least 12 academic credit hours. Those not meeting this criteria are considered on an individual basis.

Application and Information

Applications for admission to Western may be submitted after the student has completed his or her junior year. The application form should be submitted with previous college and/or high school transcripts, SAT I or ACT scores, and a $25 fee. Transfer students with 30 undergraduate credit hours need only submit their college transcripts, the application, and the fee. While not required, a campus visit is strongly recommended. The application form identifies the required information and materials.

Timothy Albers
Director of Admissions
Western State College of Colorado
Gunnison, Colorado 81231

Telephone: 800-876-5309 (toll-free)
World Wide Web: http://www.western.edu

WESTMINSTER CHOIR COLLEGE OF RIDER UNIVERSITY
PRINCETON, NEW JERSEY

The College

Home of the famous Westminster Symphonic Choir, Westminster Choir College integrates music study with professional choral performances conducted in concert with major symphony orchestras. Westminster Choir College offers outstanding music training in a stimulating yet friendly learning environment. Westminster appeals to students who seek excellent musical training and substantial performance experience to become well-rounded career musicians. The College attracts talented musicians from around the world for superb training and practical experience as performers, composers, conductors, teachers, and church musicians.

As a world-renowned music conservatory within Rider University, Westminster provides the advantages of a small, private college with the breadth of curriculum and recreational opportunities of a comprehensive liberal arts university. The Westminster student body is diverse and multicultural (23 percent are members of minority groups and 19 percent are international students) yet totals more than 400 students.

All Westminster students perform in professional concerts each year. The 200-voice Westminster Symphonic Choir sings and records on a regular basis with the New York Philharmonic and the Philadelphia Orchestra under world-class conductors in Lincoln Center, Carnegie Hall, and the Philadelphia Academy of Music. The Westminster Symphonic Choir has performed and recorded with conductors, including Bernstein, Ormandy, Masur, Toscanini, Walter, Leinsdorf, Mehta, Ozawa, and Muti. In 1995, the New York Philharmonic recorded their performance of the Brahms *Requiem* with the Westminster Symphonic Choir. Students may also perform in six additional choirs, including the Westminster Choir (Choir-in-Residence at the Spoleto Festival U.S.A.), the Westminster Singers, Chapel Choir, Westminster Concert Bell Choir, Jubilee Singers (performing music of the Afro-American heritage), and schola cantorum. The Westminster choirs tour nationally and internationally. Westminster also offers students opportunities to perform in ensembles with pianists, organists, and the Westminster Conservatory Community Orchestra. Young composers' works are showcased on campus and in community concerts.

All Westminster classes are taught by faculty members; no classes are taught by graduate students. The student-faculty ratio of 7:1 creates an intimate and supportive learning environment.

Westminster's distinguished alumni include the winner of the 1994 Metropolitan Opera National Competition; professors at Rice, Notre Dame, Manhattan School of Music, and the Cincinnati Conservatory of Music; performers with the Metropolitan Opera, the New York City Opera, and the Chicago Lyric Opera; and leading music ministers and teachers worldwide.

Westminster's scenic 23-acre campus, ideally situated in picturesque Princeton within walking distance of Princeton's Palmer Square, is an outstanding atmosphere for living, performing, and learning. Westminster's campus centers around elegant Williamson Hall in the original Georgian quadrangle, providing an intimate setting for recitals and chamber ensembles. The College also has a Student Activities Center that houses the student newspaper, other organizations, the dining commons, and the College bookstore.

Rider University offers all of its students many extracurricular activities, including opportunities to participate in theatrical productions, intramural athletics, and intercollegiate athletic teams in several sports. NCAA Division I sports include baseball, basketball, lacrosse, soccer, swimming, volleyball, and wrestling.

At the graduate level, Westminster offers programs leading to the Master of Music degree in choral conducting, sacred music, composition, music education, piano accompanying and vocal coaching, and piano, organ, and voice performance. Westminster is accredited by the National Association of Schools of Music (NASM) and the Middle States Association of Colleges and Schools. Its undergraduate music education program is accredited by the National Association of State Directors of Teacher Education and Certification (NASDTEC), which facilitates transferring teaching certificates from participating states.

Location

Located in the culturally rich town of Princeton, New Jersey, Westminster is a 40-minute train ride from the cosmopolitan cultural centers of New York City and Philadelphia, offering Westminster students a wealth of educational and recreational activities. Princeton University, a short walk from Westminster, offers lectures, art exhibits, recitals, and concerts. Through a cooperative agreement, Westminster students may enroll in courses at Princeton University and use the University's athletic and recreational facilities. Near the Westminster campus, the Tony Award–winning McCarter Theatre stages several major productions each year and hosts guest artists and musical performers.

Majors and Degrees

Westminster grants the Bachelor of Music degree, with majors in sacred music, music education, organ performance, piano (with emphases in performance, accompanying, and pedagogy), theory and composition, and voice performance, and the Bachelor of Arts degree in music, with concentrations in varied fields, including arts administration, psychology/sociology, religion/philosophy, and theater and literature. Individualized majors may also be arranged within the B.A. in music degree program. Cross-registration with Princeton University, Princeton Theological Seminary, Princeton Ballet School, and Rider University further enhances academic offerings for Westminster undergraduates. Rider University offers a full spectrum of liberal arts and science degrees.

Academic Program

In addition to course work in their major and minor areas, students take courses in arts and sciences, including foreign languages, English, mathematics, computer science, and world cultures. Course work may be supplemented by internships, fieldwork, and independent study. Approximately 80 percent of Westminster students are employed in sacred music positions in the region as choir directors, organists, and soloists. The Westminster Career Development Office provides specialized career services for musicians.

Westminster Choir College follows a two-semester calendar. Academic courses and music workshops are also available in the summer session and in special weekend workshops throughout the year.

Off-Campus Arrangements

Internships are available in theater, arts administration, sacred music, and piano pedagogy. Students may also teach music lessons at the Westminster Conservatory and teach music in public and private schools through the music education fieldwork program. Qualified students may apply for a semester or year abroad.

Academic Facilities

Westminster Choir College performance facilities include the Fine Arts Theatre (550 seats), Bristol Hall (350 seats), Williamson Hall (100 seats), Scheide Hall (100 seats), and the

Playhouse/Opera Theatre (300 seats). Stately Bristol Hall, housing a 50-rank Aeolian-Skinner organ, a 16-rank Fisk organ, a 14-rank Noack organ, and a 9-foot Steinway grand piano, is a large recital facility for student, faculty, and guest performers. Nestled among the trees, the Playhouse/Opera Theatre offers a stage and two Steinway grand pianos. Beyond Bristol Chapel, Scheide Recital Hall showcases a 44-rank Casavant organ. Westminster offers practice rooms in each of its three residence halls and has more than 120 pianos and 21 pipe organs, including practice organs by Flentrop, Holtkamp, Schantz, Moller, and Noack.

Talbott Library/Learning Center houses 55,000 books and microforms, plus 23,000 music scores and 160 periodical titles. The Performance Collection contains 6,000 titles in multiple copies for student study, class assignments, student teaching, and church choirs. A single-copy reference file of 45,000 individual octavos is the largest collection of its type in the United States. Voice students use a state-of-the-art voice laboratory, an invaluable resource for vocal pedagogy, for the scientific study of the vocal mechanism and singing. The Piano Department has a fully equipped piano laboratory in which an entire class of students can be instructed simultaneously. The Media Center contains more than 9,000 recordings and videos, with facilities for student playback. The Music Education Resource Collection contains 1,000 textbooks, recordings, filmstrips, charts, and resource materials in addition to listening equipment and an electronic piano. The library also houses a state-of-the-art electronic music computer laboratory with fifteen Kurzweil synthesizers, sixteen Macintosh Power PCs running Finale and Performer, a multimedia center with CD-ROM and laser disc, computers customized for music theory and sight-singing programs, and 100 music fundamental programs.

Westminster students may also consult the comprehensive collections of the Rider and Princeton university libraries. Westminster students use the campus academic computing laboratory, containing a combination of Macintosh and IBM computers, printers, and scanners for word processing, spreadsheets, database, draw and paint, desktop publishing, and multimedia applications and general academic computing needs. Additional computer laboratories at Rider with connections to the University mainframe are also available.

Costs

Westminster's tuition and fees are $17,180 per academic year. The complete cost of tuition and room and board in a campus residence hall (double occupancy) is $24,560. Tuition for part-time students is $625 per credit. Special program-related fees include $245 for senior student teaching.

Financial Aid

Westminster provides substantial financial aid awards to its students. All accepted students who complete the Free Application for Federal Student Aid (FAFSA) are automatically evaluated for financial aid. Students who have been accepted and have submitted the FAFSA before March 1 receive priority consideration for financial aid awards. Those accepted and applying for aid after the March priority deadline are considered for the remaining funds. Financial aid awards include scholarships for talent and academic merit plus state scholarships, Federal Pell Grants, Tuition Aid Grants, Federal Supplemental Educational Opportunity Grants, Distinguished and Garden State Scholars Program, and Educational Opportunity Program awards.

Faculty

Westminster has a teaching faculty of 72. Faculty members are all distinguished performers and scholars. Leonard Bernstein described Joseph Flummerfelt, Principal Conductor and Artistic Director, as the "greatest choral conductor in the world." Joan Lippincott, Professor of Organ and internationally known recitalist, is University Organist at Princeton University. Composers-in-Residence include Daniel Pinkham, Morten Lauridsen, and Libby Larson. Master classes have included such noted artists as Marilyn Horne and Claude Frank.

Student Government

Through student government, Westminster students have the opportunity to participate in determining cultural, recreational, and policy issues. The Joint Committee on Academic and Student Life, consisting of students, faculty members, and administrators, makes policy recommendations about academic and student life.

Admission Requirements

Westminster accepts applicants based on indicators of musical talent and academic achievement. Audition scores, high school grade point average, SAT I or ACT test scores, and recommendations are all considered in determining the applicant's potential for academic and musical achievement at the college level. Early admission is available for outstanding students after completion of the junior year.

Transfer students are evaluated on the basis of their audition score and their academic record in college in addition to the above criteria. Transfer credits are evaluated after enrollment. Freshmen and transfer applicants are considered on a continuous basis. An audition, high school transcripts, two letters of recommendation, and SAT I or ACT test scores (for first-time freshmen who are not international students), and an interview for some majors are required. An essay, a minimum 3.0 grade point average, 3 years of high school math and science, and 3 years of high school foreign language are recommended. Auditions are held five times per year on campus. Taped auditions are permitted when distance is prohibitive. All international students are required to submit TOEFL scores with their application, in addition to the criteria listed within the application packet.

Application and Information

For admissions information, students should contact:

Matthew T. Kadlubowski
Director of Admissions
Westminster Choir College
101 Walnut Lane
Princeton, New Jersey 08542-3899
Telephone: 609-921-7144
     800-96-CHOIR (toll-free)
Fax: 609-921-2538
E-mail: wccadmission@rider.edu
World Wide Web: http://westminster.rider.edu

The development of sound vocal technique is enhanced by individual and small-group instruction with artist faculty members who are also active performers.

WESTMINSTER COLLEGE
FULTON, MISSOURI

The College

Founded in 1851, Westminster is a private, coeducational, liberal arts and sciences college that has a proven record of preparing its graduates for promising careers in business, public service, and professional service. Westminster College currently enrolls approximately 700 students, and 40 percent of these students come from outside Missouri. States strongly represented are Oklahoma, Arkansas, Texas, Kansas, and Illinois. Facilities include the Hunter Activity Center, which houses a gymnasium, an indoor running track, racquetball courts, student mailboxes, a recreation room, student activity offices, and the campus grill. The expanded Priest Athletic Complex includes varsity and practice facilities for soccer, softball, and football. The Wetterau Field Sports Facility includes athletic offices, varsity locker rooms, training rooms, and a varsity weight room. Placement after graduation is given high priority at Westminster. Whether students plan to enter the professional world immediately or pursue a graduate program, they are given encouragement, advice, and guidance in preparing for life after Westminster. Included in the placement effort is an important linking of current students with graduates who are now in influential positions in society. In addition, Westminster's formalized internship program is designed to extend the student's learning opportunities beyond the traditional classroom setting into professional work environments.

The Green Lecture Series, a distinguished series on economic, social, and international affairs, was established in 1936 as a memorial to John Findley Green, an 1884 Westminster graduate. The roster of past speakers includes former Presidents Bush, Reagan, and Truman; former British Prime Minister Edward Heath; former CIA Director William Casey; former U.S. Ambassador to Russia Robert S. Strauss; former President of the Soviet Union Mikhail Gorbachev; and Nobel laureate Lech Walesa, former President of Poland. The 1996 Green Lecture, presented by Lady Margaret Thatcher, commemorated the 50th anniversary of Winston Churchill's "Iron Curtain" address held in the historic Westminster Gym.

Westminster College uses as its chapel a seventeenth-century English church, which was dismantled in London and rebuilt on the campus. The lower level of the church houses the Winston Churchill Memorial and Library, which contains memorabilia of Sir Winston Churchill and World War II. The church, originally designed by Sir Christopher Wren, is a national landmark that attracts approximately 30,000 visitors annually.

Location

Fulton is a safe, historic community of approximately 10,000 people, situated in the rolling hills and trees of central Missouri. Westminster is located a little more than an hour north of the Lake of the Ozarks, a beautiful recreational area. Within 25 minutes to the west is Columbia, a college town of more than 70,000 people. Just to the south of Fulton is Jefferson City, Missouri's state capital. Kansas City is 2½ hours west, and St. Louis is located 2 hours east on Interstate 70.

Majors and Degrees

Westminster grants the Bachelor of Arts degree in the following major fields: accounting, anthropology, biology, business administration, chemistry, computer science, economics, elementary education, English, environmental studies, French, history, international business, international studies, management information systems, mathematics, middle school education, philosophy, physical education, physics, political science, psychology, religion, secondary education, sociology, and Spanish.

Preprofessional tracks are offered in athletic training, dentistry, law, medicine, and therapy. An individualized five-year engineering program is available to Westminster students. This program allows students to attend Westminster for three years and Washington University in St. Louis for two, resulting in a Bachelor of Arts degree from Westminster and a Bachelor of Science degree from Washington University.

Students who wish to design their own academic majors may do so through the self-designed major, which brings together an interdisciplinary committee of faculty members to serve as advisers. Examples include advertising, communications, hospital management, public administration, and sports management.

Academic Program

Westminster is a selective college with an innovative curriculum based on the liberal arts that emphasizes breadth as well as depth. The College's general education program reflects a commitment to liberal learning in the arts and sciences and to providing its students with opportunities to explore the aesthetic, cultural, ethical, historical, scientific, and social contexts in which they will live, work, and learn in the twenty-first century. Requirements for the baccalaureate degree are usually completed in four years. Students must satisfy general course requirements as well as departmental requirements in courses outside of their major. Academic advisers guide all students through the four years of their enrollment. The Westminster Seminar Program is designed to bridge the gap between high school and college and introduce students to campus facilities, resources, faculty members, and other students. The program begins one week prior to the start of classes and continues for the remainder of the semester for all first-year students. The professor of this class in turn becomes the students' adviser until the students declare majors.

Westminster operates on a traditional two-semester calendar. An optional three-week term is available after the spring semester for special travel and field study courses or internships.

Off-Campus Arrangements

The College's Center for Off-Campus and International Programs assists students seeking overseas study opportunities or pursuing exchange opportunities with sister institutions. Westminster participates in the Institutes of European and Asian Studies, which provide twenty campuses throughout the world for Westminster students to spend a semester or a year studying abroad. The College's strong historical relationship with England has led to several educational opportunities, including the Westminster Semester in England with the University of Sunderland and exchange programs with Queen Mary and Westfield College and the University of East Anglia School of English and American Studies, which allows 3 students a year to study in Norwich, located 2 hours from London. Other overseas exchange programs are available at Kansai Gaidai University (Osaka, Japan) and with L'Ecole Supérieure des Sciences Commerciales (ESSCA: School for Business Study) in Angers, France, allows French majors the opportunity to study abroad in a French-speaking environment. Other off-campus programs include the United Nations Semester, the Washington Semester, and the Chicago Urban Studies Semester.

Academic Facilities

The Coulter Science Center provides space for modern classrooms and laboratories for biology, chemistry, mathematics, and physics. Most other classes meet in Newnham Hall and Westminster Hall. Reeves Library includes ample space for study and research, with a recent addition housing four computer classrooms, a language lab, multimedia classrooms and facilities, additional computers, and student workstations. Students also have computer connections available in all residence halls and fraternity rooms, allowing 24-hour access to computers and the Internet.

Costs

The basic cost for the 1999–2000 academic year was $19,320 for tuition, room, board, and the student activity fee. The College estimates that students should allow $2400 annually for books, supplies, and personal expenses.

Financial Aid

More than 90 percent of the College's students receive assistance through scholarships, grants, loans, or employment. Federal aid programs include the Federal Pell Grant, Federal Supplemental Educational Opportunity Grant, Federal Perkins Loan, and Federal Work-Study programs. To determine eligibility for need-based aid, students should complete the Free Application for Federal Student Aid (FAFSA) anytime after January 1.

A merit-based aid program recognizes and rewards outstanding students. Academic scholarships, ranging from $2000 to full tuition, are awarded and based on grades and test scores. Students who have actively participated in leadership roles in their high school, church, or community may be recognized with a Leadership Scholarship.

Faculty

The 61 faculty members are part of a unique learning environment where students and teachers work together to discover answers to the complex problems faced in and out of the classroom and, in the process, establish life-long relationships. Approximately 80 percent of the distinguished faculty members hold the doctorate or equivalent terminal degree, many are published authors, and others are engaged in advanced research and scholarly study. Although faculty members are involved in research and writing, they primarily constitute a teaching faculty whose main concern is the education of the undergraduate student.

Student Government

The Westminster College Student Government Association is composed of all students of the College. Its officers are elected by the entire student body. The Student Government Association serves the interests of the individual student and student groups and sponsors and supports activities and events on their behalf. The activity fee charged each student gives the Student Government Association a sizable budget to carry out such programs as intramurals, community relations, publications, entertainment, and other special events.

Admission Requirements

Each application is considered individually by the dean of admissions and the Admissions Committee, which evaluates a number of factors, including courses taken in secondary school, a counselor's recommendation, test scores (either ACT or SAT I), grade point average, essay, and activities. Generally, applicants should rank in the upper half of their graduating class. Transfer students must submit a high school transcript and a transcript from each college previously attended. There is also an early admission program for qualified high school juniors.

Application and Information

To apply to Westminster College a student should submit the application for admission, along with an official copy of the secondary school transcript, test scores on either the ACT or SAT I, and a recommendation from a high school official. The College operates on a rolling admissions calendar. While there is no application deadline, students are encouraged to apply early.

Westminster College does not discriminate on the basis of race, sex, color, national or ethnic origin, or physical handicap in the administration of its educational policies, admissions policies, scholarship and loan programs, or other school-administered programs.

For further information regarding admissions, financial assistance, academic programs, and campus visits, students should write or call:

Office of Enrollment Services (Admissions and Financial Aid)
Westminster College
501 Westminster Avenue
Fulton, Missouri 65251-9906
Telephone: 573-592-5251
              800-475-3361 (toll-free)
Fax: 573-592-5255
E-mail: admissions@jaynet.wcmo.edu

The monumental sculpture "Breakthrough" incorporates eight sections of the Berlin Wall and commemorates the collapse of the Iron Curtain and the end of the Cold War.

WESTMINSTER COLLEGE
NEW WILMINGTON, PENNSYLVANIA

The College

Westminster College, an independent, coeducational liberal arts college related to the Presbyterian Church (U.S.A.), was founded in 1852. Westminster's liberal arts foundation thrives in a caring environment supported by an integrative curriculum featuring state-of-the-art technology and opportunities for involvement to prepare students for a diverse world. Westminster College is annually recognized among the nation's best liberal arts colleges by *U.S. News & World Report* and as one of the nation's best college buys by *Money*. Nearly 1,500 students benefit from individualized attention from dedicated faculty members while choosing from forty majors and nearly 100 campus organizations on the New Wilmington, Pennsylvania, campus. The College provides many programs to augment the academic and social life of the academic community, including lectures, dramatic productions, art exhibitions, concerts, symposia, dances, films, and other activities. Students may choose to participate in a wide variety of groups and activities, such as dramatics, publications, volunteer and social service teams, athletics, religious groups, musical groups, radio and television stations, fraternities and sororities, honoraries, and special interest groups.

A natatorium and physical education and fitness center are included among Westminster's major buildings, and athletics are carefully integrated into the overall educational program. A full range of intercollegiate and intramural sports for men and women gives each student the opportunity to participate at the level of his or her interest and ability. Westminster students compete in sixteen varsity sports as Division III members of the NCAA. Westminster has been called the most successful football program at any level, based on its six national championships and eleven undefeated seasons, and the men's basketball team has had more wins than any other program in NAIA history. Nearly 99 percent of student athletes who letter in a varsity sport graduate.

Location

Westminster is located in New Wilmington, a small residential town in western Pennsylvania. The campus is surrounded by wooded hills, Amish farmlands, scenic country roads, and streams. The town is not far from several large cities. It is 60 miles north of Pittsburgh, 80 miles south of Erie, and 85 miles southeast of Cleveland. New Castle is 9 miles to the south, and Youngstown, Ohio, is 17 miles to the west. The College is within a few miles of I-79, I-80, and the Ohio and Pennsylvania turnpikes. Nearby cities provide transportation to all points by bus, and transportation is available from the Pittsburgh and Youngstown airports.

Majors and Degrees

Westminster College grants three undergraduate degrees: the Bachelor of Arts, the Bachelor of Science, and the Bachelor of Music. The choice of major field can be made from the following: accounting, art, biology, broadcast communications, business administration (finance, health-care administration, human resource management, management, and marketing), chemistry, Christian education, church music, computer science, economics, elementary education, English, financial economics, French, German, history, Latin, mathematics, molecular biology/biotechnology, music, music—applied, music composition, music education, philosophy, physics, political science, psychology, religion, sociology (criminal justice), Spanish, and theater. Interdisciplinary majors are available in computer information systems, environmental science, intercultural studies, international business, international politics, management science, organizational behavior, and public relations. Preprofessional programs are offered in dentistry, law, medicine, the ministry, and veterinary medicine. A 3-2 engineering program is offered in cooperation with Pennsylvania State University, Case Western Reserve University, and Washington University in St. Louis.

Secondary education certification with a major in an academic discipline is offered.

Academic Program

The liberal arts degree offered by Westminster College reflects the diversity and depth of the classical education and the practicality of its application. Good writing and speaking skills are emphasized, and science and philosophy become a part of life at Westminster.

Course requirements for graduation vary according to the major fields, but all-College requirements include courses in writing, communication, religion, computer science, foreign language, and physical education as well as courses from categories covering the humanities, fine arts, social sciences, natural sciences, and literature. Double majors, minors, and individual interdisciplinary programs are possible.

Westminster operates on a two-term academic year. The fall term runs from September through December, and the spring term runs from January through May.

Every four years since 1936, in conjunction with the Presidential election year, Westminster has held a Mock National Political Convention (for the party out of office) in which more than three fourths of the students have participated, naming their own "candidate."

Off-Campus Arrangements

Westminster engages in several cooperative programs with other colleges and institutions to provide students with opportunities for in-depth study off campus. Among these is a program at Berea College in Kentucky, in which students study the culture of southern Appalachia. Westminster also offers a Washington Semester in the nation's capital and a Sea Semester in conjunction with Boston University. In addition, it is possible to spend a semester or year studying in France, Germany, Spain, and other countries.

Academic Facilities

McGill Library and the J. S. Mack Science Library contain more than 220,000 volumes and receive about 970 periodicals per year. These library collections are supplemented through the College's membership in the Library Consortium and two computerized networks (one regional and the other national), which provide the best services possible through interlibrary loans and other library activities.

Westminster's campus extends more than 300 acres and has more than twenty major buildings. The facilities include classrooms, a 300-seat theater, a 1,750-seat auditorium, radio and TV stations, and an outdoor environmental-science field laboratory. The Hoyt Science Resource Center contains modern science areas, including electron microscopes and an X-ray defractor, expanded computer science facilities, and a planetarium.

Costs

Westminster College is one of the most affordable national liberal arts colleges in Pennsylvania and is annually listed as one of America's best college buys. For the academic year 2000–01, tuition and fees are $16,985, and room and board are $4735, bringing the total cost for the year to $21,720.

Financial Aid

About 80 percent of Westminster's students receive some sort of financial aid. Scholarships, Federal Stafford Student Loans, grants, and campus employment are offered to students who have financial need. The student's eligibility for financial aid is determined by the Free Application for Federal Student Aid form. Also, non-need scholarships of up to 50 percent of tuition are awarded to students of high academic ability; these are renewable each year if the student maintains good academic standing. Activity grants in music, theater, and sports are also available. Information is available through the Dean of Admissions or Director of Financial Aid.

Faculty

There are 99 full-time faculty members at Westminster College, 92 percent of whom hold earned doctorates or the highest terminal degree in their field. The student-faculty ratio is 15:1. The faculty members are characterized by their interest in and concern for their students.

Student Government

All students, by virtue of their undergraduate registration and payment of fees, are members of the Student Government Association. The Student Senate, the central representative and legislative organization of the Student Government Association, recognizes student organizations, allocates money appropriated by the Board of Trustees, and carries out other responsibilities. In cooperation with the staff of the Dean of Student Affairs, the student senators, through the Campus Programming Committee, plan an extensive student activities program.

Admission Requirements

Students admitted to the College should have received a high school diploma and should have completed a college-preparatory program of study in secondary school, consisting of a minimum of 16 units (including at least 4 units of English, 2 units of a foreign language, 3 units of mathematics, and 2 units each of science and social studies). Each new applicant is required to take the SAT I or the ACT, preferably during the junior year of high school or early in the senior year.

Application and Information

A completed application with the $20 application fee may be submitted anytime after the student's junior year in secondary school. The student should also see that the required SAT I or ACT scores and a high school transcript are sent to the College. The transcript should include grades from the ninth grade through the eleventh grade.

For application forms and further information, students should contact:

Dean of Admissions
Westminster College
New Wilmington, Pennsylvania 16172
Telephone: 800-942-8033 (toll-free)
E-mail: admis@westminster.edu

Students get their feet wet at Westminster College.

WESTMINSTER COLLEGE
SALT LAKE CITY, UTAH

The College

Westminster College is the only independent, private, liberal arts college in Utah. Westminster has been a vital part of the Intermountain West's history and educational heritage since 1875.

The current student body of 2,300 is characterized by diversity as well as a spirit of community. Students come from twenty-eight states and twenty-three countries. Most are attracted to the College because of its small size and the personal attention students receive, its prime location in a moderately large urban area close to mountain skiing and recreation areas, and its relatively modest tuition and fees.

The College is located in a quiet residential area about 10 minutes southeast of downtown Salt Lake City. On-campus housing consists of residence halls for both men and women, which can accommodate 360 students. Off-campus rental housing (apartments and homes) is readily available in the neighborhood.

Student activities include student government, campus publications, choir, intramural sports, honorary societies, the campus ministry council, the ski club, and a variety of special interest groups, including aviation, nursing, science, education, pre-med, and computer science.

Westminster College offers intercollegiate basketball and soccer for men and basketball and volleyball for women.

Student services include academic advising, career planning and placement, internships, personal counseling, tutoring, and testing.

Location

Salt Lake City, home of the 2002 Winter Olympics, is a metropolitan area of approximately 1.3 million people. It is located in a valley (elevation 4,700 feet) between two rugged mountain ranges. Salt Lake City has an international airport and good rail service. Downtown Salt Lake City is easily accessible to students by bus, car, or bicycle. Attractions in the downtown area include professional sports events, ballet, theater, concerts, and shopping to suit all tastes.

The area has four pleasant seasons, with limited amounts of rain and snow in the valley and moderate temperatures. The Wasatch Mountains, bordering the Salt Lake Valley on the east, have what has been called "the greatest snow on earth." These mountains are ideal for the winter sports enthusiast as well as those who enjoy hiking, biking, and camping.

Majors and Degrees

Westminster College offers Bachelor of Arts and Bachelor of Science degrees in the following areas: accounting, art, aviation, biology, chemistry, communication, computer science, economics, education (early childhood, elementary, secondary, and special education), English, finance, history, human resource management, information resource management, international business, management (business), marketing, mathematics, nursing, philosophy, physics, political studies, preprofessional programs (dentistry, law, medicine, veterinary medicine, and 3-2 engineering), psychology, social science, sociology, and special education.

Course work leading to an academic minor is available in the following additional areas: environmental studies, French, music, religion, Spanish, and speech and theater arts.

Academic Program

Each student must complete at least 124 semester credit hours to receive a bachelor's degree. Of this amount, approximately 40 hours consist of liberal arts education core requirements common to all students regardless of major. Credit-hour requirements vary widely among majors, but all students are exposed to liberal arts concepts as well as practical, career-oriented experiences.

Credit is awarded for successful scores on Advanced Placement and CLEP examinations.

Students can participate in the Reserve Officers' Training Corps programs of the U.S. Air Force, U.S. Army, and U.S. Navy through cooperative programs at the University of Utah.

The College has a 4-4-1 calendar, consisting of two 15-week semesters followed by a one-month May Term. There is also a summer session.

Off-Campus Arrangements

Westminster students may participate in travel/study trips (for credit) during May Term and the summer session. Students can also make individual arrangements for international study by advisement from the College's International Studies Chair and the Career Resource Center and through a cooperative agreement with the Foreign Study Office at the University of Utah.

Academic Facilities

Westminster's campus has six major classroom buildings, a science laboratory building, student computer terminal room, fine arts building, a nursing laboratory, and a separate building for classes in wheel-thrown and hand-built pottery. A new multilevel, 47,000-square-foot, $15-million library opened in fall 1997.

Costs

Tuition and fees for 2000–01 are $13,730 for the academic year for a full-time student (registering for 12 to 16 semester hours). This figure includes costs for the fall semester, spring semester, and May Term. Room and board are $4570 for the same period. Books and supplies are estimated at $900 per year.

Financial Aid

Ninety six percent of freshmen at Westminster receive financial aid, averaging approximately $9000 each year per student. Aid programs include need-based institutional grants and need-based federal aid programs, such as grants, loans, and employment (Federal Work-Study). The Free Application for Federal Student Aid is the only form required for new students. Students wishing to apply for federal aid programs should plan to submit applications by early April, although there is no set deadline for federal aid applications.

Merit-based scholarships are available to incoming freshmen

and transfer students as well as to continuing students, thanks to a generous endowment program and institutional aid program. Every full-time student admitted to Westminster is automatically considered for merit-based scholarships awarded by the College, which are based on GPA from previous academic (high school or college) course work. More than $6.6 million was awarded in institutional scholarships in 1998–99.

Faculty

With 100 full-time and a number of part-time faculty members, the student-faculty ratio is 17:1. All faculty members teach; no research faculty positions exist. Graduate students do not teach. Many full-time faculty members are actively involved as advisers and sponsors of campus-based student activities. Approximately 80 percent of the faculty members hold terminal degrees.

Student Government

The official student governing body is the Associated Students of Westminster College (ASWC), which controls all student activities and organizations and provides funding and authorization for them. The ASWC is made up of three branches: the Executive Cabinet, the Legislative Assembly, and the Judiciary Branch. The three branches function in similar fashion to the federal government system. The president of the ASWC is considered chief spokesperson for the student body and has access to all chief administrators of the College.

Admission Requirements

Individual applications are reviewed on the basis of a student's potential for success at Westminster. Academic preparation, which includes both course work and grades, is most important. Also important to the review committee are items such as entrance exams (ACT or SAT I), recommendations, and extracurricular activities. A campus visit to meet with an academic counselor is recommended, as it helps complete the picture for both the prospective student and the college.

Transfer students must have earned at least a 2.5 cumulative GPA in previous college work.

International students must have at least a 3.0 GPA in non–U.S. high school or college work and a TOEFL score of at least 550 (or equivalent).

Application and Information

To apply for admission, a student must submit an application for admission, application fee, and official transcripts of previous high school and/or college classwork. Freshman applicants must submit ACT or SAT I scores. Applicants are notified of their admission status within two weeks of receipt of all required materials. All admission decisions are made on a rolling basis, and applications are processed until the date of class registration. New applicants are accepted for the start of all sessions.

For application forms and additional information, students should contact:

Office of Admissions
Westminster College
1840 South 1300 East
Salt Lake City, Utah 84105
Telephone: 801-832-2200
              800-748-4753 (toll-free)
E-mail: admispub@wcslc.edu
World Wide Web: http://www.wcslc.edu

Westminster College blends educational tradition with the spirit of the West.

WESTMONT COLLEGE
SANTA BARBARA, CALIFORNIA

The College

Westmont stands among the preeminent Christian liberal arts colleges in the United States. Students develop a heightened appreciation for their cultural and religious heritage, the ability to direct their continuing self-development and learning, the competence to function as leaders and servants in society, a foundation for entering or receiving advanced training in a profession or career, and confidence in the authority of Scripture. Residence life, athletics, off-campus programs, and opportunities for local and international Christian service also contribute to balanced personal and spiritual development. Alumni enter a wide variety of professions and vocations and pursue professional-, master's-, and doctoral-level programs at the world's finest research universities, including UCLA, Stanford, Harvard, Yale, Princeton, the University of Chicago, Cambridge, and many others.

Although its 1,200 students come to Westmont from the majority of states and many countries throughout the world, the highest percentage come from California. Approximately 60 percent are women, 40 percent are men, 16 percent are from minority groups, and 1 percent are international students. Ninety percent of the students live in the five residence halls on campus or the apartment complex off campus.

As a member of the National Association of Intercollegiate Athletics and the Golden State Athletic Conference, Westmont provides intercollegiate sports for men and women in basketball, cross-country, soccer, tennis, and track and field. Men also compete in baseball, club rugby, club soccer, and club volleyball, and women also compete in volleyball and club lacrosse. The intramural program offers a wide variety of activities as well. There are numerous clubs and organizations, including a student newspaper, literary magazine, yearbook, radio station, choral and music ensembles, a multicultural club, political organizations, theater productions, community service organizations, and Christian service, mission, and outreach programs. The Ruth Kerr Memorial Student Center (1983) houses the main campus dining facilities. Two integral components of the Westmont experience are the Chapel-Convocation Program and the Leadership Program. The Chapel Program, which students are required to attend three days a week, provides a wide variety of speakers and programs to inspire and challenge students to continue growing in their relationship with Jesus Christ. The Leadership Program is committed to training leaders to facilitate positive global changes.

Location

Ruth Kerr, president of the Kerr Manufacturing Company, was one of the founders of Westmont College. She led in opening the first campus in Los Angeles in 1937 and in moving the College to Santa Barbara in 1945. Westmont is located on a 133-acre campus, rich with pine, oak, and eucalyptus trees, in Montecito, an estate area of Santa Barbara nestled between the Pacific Ocean and the Santa Ynez Mountains. Students enjoy the beach and the mountain trails most of the year. Santa Barbara has a wealth of history and culture, and theaters, libraries, concerts, and lectures are just minutes from the campus. The College operates regularly scheduled shuttles to and from the campus to various parts of the city.

Majors and Degrees

Westmont College awards the Bachelor of Arts (B.A.) and Bachelor of Science (B.S.) degrees in twenty-six liberal-arts majors. These include alternative major, art, biology, chemistry, communication studies, computer science, economics and business, education, engineering physics, English, English–modern languages, French, history, kinesiology and physical education, mathematics, music, neuroscience, philosophy, physics, political science, psychology, religious studies, social science, sociology and anthropology, Spanish, and theater arts. The College is approved by the California Commission for Teacher Preparation and Licensing to offer a teacher-preparation program enabling students to qualify for either the single-subject or the multiple-subject credential. Preprofessional programs include athletic training, dentistry, engineering, law, medicine, the ministry and missionary studies, optometry, pharmacy, physical therapy, and veterinary studies. A 3-2 program combining liberal arts and engineering is offered in cooperation with Stanford University; the University of Southern California; the University of California, Santa Barbara; Boston University; Washington University (St. Louis); and other institutions having accredited schools of engineering.

Academic Program

Westmont's academic program is designed to give students broad exposure to the humanities and social and natural sciences as well as in-depth study of a major field or fields. In many academic departments, students may also gain up to 18 units for approved internships and practicums. The College's academic calendar consists of two 16-week semesters and an optional six-week Mayterm. Westmont students must successfully complete 124 semester units of credit to earn a baccalaureate degree. The general education requirements total a maximum of 64 units and consist of 16 units of religious studies, 8 units in interdisciplinary studies, 4 units of English composition, 8 units of a foreign language (unless the student had 2 years of the same language in high school), 4 units of physical education, and 28 units in distribution requirements. Students are encouraged to complete these in their first two years and complete their major units (36–66) and elective units during their last two years. Students have the option of taking a double major or a major and a minor.

Westmont grants up to 32 units of advanced placement and/or credit to students who earn scores of 4 or 5 on the Advanced Placement tests and to those earning a score of 5, 6, or 7 on the higher level of the International Baccalaureate exam. Credit is given for College-Level Examination Program (CLEP) scores of 500 or above on the CLEP general tests and 50 or above on the subject matter tests, provided that the student has not already completed introductory college courses in those test areas. CLEP credit is awarded for elective units only. Westmont offers honors study/directed study, honors classes, and in-course honors and hosts six national honor societies (Omicron Delta Kappa, Phi Kappa Phi, Phi Sigma Tau, Psi Chi, Sigma Delta Pi, and Sigma Tau Delta). An Army ROTC program is available through the University of California, Santa Barbara.

Off-Campus Arrangements

Off-campus programs include the Europe Semester, which is offered each fall and provides the broadest geographical scope, with extended stays in Athens, Florence, Jerusalem, London, Paris, and Rome. The England Semester, offered every other year, combines travel and residential study in the British Isles for students of literature. Semesters in France and Spain offer French and Spanish majors the opportunity to study these languages in their home countries, as does the Latin American Studies Program, which combines the study of Spanish culture and language in Belize, Chile, Costa Rica, and Honduras. Similar programs are offered at Jerusalem University College in Israel; Daystar University in Nairobi, Kenya; the Middle East Studies Program at the American University in Cairo, Egypt; and in the Russian Studies Program in Moscow, Nizhni Novgorod, and St. Petersburg (through Westmont's membership in the Coalition for Christian Colleges and Universities). Participants in the International Business Institute program visit the major economic and political capitals of Europe and Asia. The Westmont Economics/Business Program in Asia introduces students to the diverse economic growth in the Pacific Rim. The East Asia Program addresses contemporary world issues in China, Japan, and Taiwan. An additional summer program in Asia offers students an opportunity to study life and culture in Sri Lanka.

Domestic off-campus programs include the San Francisco Urban Program, which studies modern American urban society and offers urban internships; the Washington Semester, highlighting national political processes and incorporating internships in national, international, and economic policy, justice, and journalism; a semester at Bethune-Cookman, a historically black college in Florida; the Consortium Visitor Program, enabling students to study at any of the Christian College Consortium's twelve other member colleges; and other programs sponsored by the Coalition for Christian Colleges and Universities.

Academic Facilities

The tri-level Roger John Voskuyl Library is the academic center of Westmont. The library holds 164,274 catalogued items (35,000 bound periodicals, 121,329 reference and general items, and 7,945 media items), 717 print periodical subscriptions, and 2,494 online periodical subscriptions as well as seven classrooms; audiovisual equipment; math, language, and computer laboratories; and three IBM RS-6000 computers, which are used for instructional purposes. Forty-seven lab computers are connected to the mainframe for student use. Westmont has a 10Base T Ethernet network with a fiber-optic backbone, operating at ten MB/second. There are Ethernet connections in every office and dorm room and in many classrooms. The entire network has access to e-mail and the Internet through a T-1 line. A total of 100 terminals are available throughout the College for student use. The network accommodates IBM-compatible, Macintosh, and RISC/UNIX microcomputers. The library features an after-hours study room, a rare book archives room, and dozens of individual carrels and lockable study cubicles for faculty members and students, and houses the Writer's Corner and offices for the Director of First-Year Students and the Career and Life Planning department.

The Reynolds Art Gallery features art studios and a classroom. Students and professional artists exhibit their work year-round in the gallery. Porter Theatre contains state-of-the-art equipment for dramatic productions and concerts.

The George Carroll Observatory contains a 6-inch refracting telescope and a 16½-inch reflecting telescope, the largest in Santa Barbara. The Mericos H. Whittier Science Building houses the College's science program and equipment, including an ultracentrifuge, a liquid scintillation counter for measuring radioactivity, physiographic units and other equipment for advanced physiological studies, low-pressure liquid chromatography equipment, sophisticated environmental instrumentation, atomic absorption spectrophotometers, Fourier-transform NMR spectrometers, infrared and ultraviolet-visible spectrophotometers, gas and high-performance liquid chromatographs, and gamma-ray spectrometers.

Costs

Tuition and fees for 2000–01 are $20,964, and room and board for the academic year are $7068. The cost of books, personal expenses, and transportation is estimated at $2754. Private weekly music instruction is about $485 for fourteen weeks.

Financial Aid

Westmont has a strong financial aid program, so no student should hesitate to apply for lack of financial resources. Eighty-two percent of Westmont's students receive some form of financial assistance; the average amount of aid awarded exceeds $13,000 per year. Included in the program are President's, Provost's, and Westmont Scholarships that range from $3000 to $8000. These merit scholarships are awarded to students who have demonstrated high academic achievement. Westmont also gives awards to students who demonstrate strength in art, music, theater arts, and athletics. After submitting the Free Application for Federal Student Aid (FAFSA), students may be eligible for generous state grants, aid from federal programs, institutional grants, loans, and work-study programs, based on financial needs.

Faculty

One of the highest priorities at Westmont is the attraction and retention of outstanding Christian teachers and scholars. The College's professors are dedicated to the integration of faith and learning, while also being actively involved in the lives of students. There are 85 full-time and 54 part-time faculty members. The student-faculty ratio is 14:1; the average class size is 20. Eighty-nine percent of the full-time faculty members have their doctoral degree. Westmont's faculty members are committed to teaching at the undergraduate level, and they have additional advising responsibilities with either incoming first-year students or students in their major. A Director of First-Year Students is responsible for the advising and orientation of new students. Although teaching is their primary scholarly activity, many faculty members engage in research, write books, and publish articles in leading journals and periodicals.

Student Government

The Westmont College Student Association (WCSA) is an entirely self-governing body. Students elect their own WCSA representatives, who are then responsible for organizing social, cultural, and educational activities. They actively participate in and are voting members on almost all faculty committees, while also allocating the student budget to various clubs and organizations. Christian Concerns, another student-managed organization, is responsible for organizing on- and off-campus ministries and mission opportunities.

Admission Requirements

Westmont attracts high school graduates who, in most cases, have at least a B+ average in academic subject areas, rank near the top of their high school class, have followed a college-preparatory curriculum, present acceptable SAT I or ACT scores, and would benefit from and contribute to the goals and mission of Westmont. International students must submit TOEFL scores (minimum: 560, paper-based; 220, computer-based). Other factors considered are personal areas covered by the application (activities, leadership, motivation), and the quality of written response. Students are encouraged but not required to have an interview, and letters of recommendation can enhance an applicant's file.

For transfer students from an accredited two- or four-year college or university or a Bible college or university that is accredited by the American Association of Bible Colleges, the evaluation is based on achievement in solid, transferable course work, an assessment of the personal areas covered by the application (as stated above), and the quality of the written responses. High school records must be submitted if the applicant has completed fewer than 24 college-level credits at the time of application.

Application and Information

Entrance to Westmont is possible at the beginning of either the fall or spring semester. Westmont offers an early action plan. High school seniors interested in applying for early action must submit the application by December 1; notifications will be mailed on January 15. The priority deadline for regular decision is March 1; notifications are mailed on March 15. Students will continue to be admitted as files are completed until the class has been filled. There is an application fee of $40. Applications may be submitted online via Westmont's Web site (listed below) or through other online application services, such as Peterson's CollegeQuest, XAP, CollegeLink, College Edge, U.S. News, or APPLY! The Admissions Office encourages applicants to complete the application process as early as possible.

Visitors are welcome at any time. Campus visitors can stay overnight in the residence halls, attend classes and chapel, speak with professors or coaches, have a music audition, share a portfolio with the art department, and have meals with Westmont students. Several Preview Day events are planned each semester.

For further information regarding admissions, students should contact:

Dean of Admissions
Westmont College
955 La Paz Road
Santa Barbara, California 93108
Telephone: 800-777-9011 (toll-free)
Fax: 805-565-6234
E-mail: admissions@westmont.edu
World Wide Web: http://www.westmont.edu/

WEST VIRGINIA UNIVERSITY INSTITUTE OF TECHNOLOGY
MONTGOMERY, WEST VIRGINIA

The University and the Institute

West Virginia University Institute of Technology has experienced a number of significant changes since it began as a preparatory school extension of West Virginia University in 1895. It began offering bachelor's degrees in engineering in 1952. Since 1961, the number of students has tripled to the current enrollment of more than 2,500, and the number of academic buildings has similarly increased from six to twenty. Students from more than twenty states and fifteen countries create a cosmopolitan population. Approximately one third of the full-time students live in the three dormitories on the 200-acre campus, which is located in the mountains of West Virginia. There are numerous social, athletic, and cultural activities on campus through which students can satisfy personal interests. Five national social fraternities and two sororities have chapters at Tech.

Location

Montgomery, West Virginia, is a small town of about 2,500 residents, just 28 miles southeast of Charleston, the state capital. Interstate Highways 64, 77, and 79 all run within 30 miles of the campus, and U.S. Route 60, a major east-west artery, runs immediately adjacent to the campus. Hawks Nest State Park, with its aerial tram to the bottom of the New River canyon, is located 30 miles from the campus. The New River, considered by many authoritative geologists to be the second-oldest river in the world, is a challenge to enthusiasts of white-water rafting, and the New River Gorge Bridge is the largest arch bridge east of the Mississippi. Tech is also conveniently located near Snowshoe Mountain, Silver Creek, and Winter Place Ski Lodge, three popular snow-skiing areas.

Majors and Degrees

Tech offers the Bachelor of Arts, Bachelor of Science, Associate in Science, and Associate of Applied Science degrees. The Bachelor of Arts degree is available in history and government. Bachelor of Science degrees are offered in accounting; biology; business management; chemical, civil, electrical, and mechanical engineering; chemistry; computer science; electronic, industrial, and engineering technology; health services administration; industrial relations and human resources; management information systems; mathematics; nursing; printing management; public service administration; and technology management. Two-year Associate in Science degrees are offered in business technology (emphases in accounting, banking, business supervision, and computer information systems), dental hygiene, engineering technologies (civil, drafting and design, electrical, and mechanical), general studies, office administration (emphases in executive, legal, and medical secretarial studies), printing, respiratory care technology, and surgical technology. A two-year Associate of Applied Science degree is offered in automotive service technology. A one-year certificate program is offered in office technology.

Academic Program

Tech is organized into three major divisions: the Leonard C. Nelson College of Engineering; the College of Business, Humanities, and Sciences; and the Community and Technical College. The baccalaureate and associate degrees offered by Tech prepare students for careers in areas where today's job market has many openings. Although it is the only institute of technology in West Virginia, Tech realizes that leaders in all fields should have training in the liberal arts, and it has programs in business, the humanities, and the social sciences as well as two-year programs in several engineering technologies and other career-oriented areas. All students are required to take core courses in the liberal arts and sciences.

In addition to being earned in a traditional program, the Bachelor of Arts degree may also be earned through the Regents Program, which has been designed for adults who wish to complete their college studies. This program offers them an opportunity to gain credits toward the degree for work and life experience.

To earn a bachelor's degree, students must complete a minimum of 128 semester hours. To earn an associate degree, students must complete a minimum of 64 semester hours.

Tech has a two-semester calendar. The first semester begins in August and ends in December; the second begins in January and ends in May. Limited summer course offerings are available.

Off-Campus Arrangements

An optional five-year cooperative education program is open to students majoring in several fields. More than 100 students are placed each year in approximately fifty private and public businesses. The co-op student's second, third, and fourth years provide four semesters of study and five periods of work, while the freshman and senior years are spent on campus.

Academic Facilities

Tech's twenty academic buildings range from Old Main, built in 1896 and renovated in 1958, to Orndorff Hall, which houses modern science laboratories, classrooms, and offices. The $5-million Vining Library holds more than 520,000 volumes, including microtext, and houses the Center for Instructional Technology, which provides the latest in teaching innovations and instructional methodologies for use by both faculty and students.

Costs

For 1999–2000, costs for tuition and fees per semester were $1323 for West Virginia residents and $3229 for out-of-state students plus an additional $54 for engineering students. Room costs were $1045 per semester; board costs totaled $979 for a fifteen-meal plan and $1195 for a nineteen-meal plan. Students should expect to spend approximately $250 each semester for books.

Financial Aid

Tech offers a wide range of financial aid resources, including privately and federally funded loans, Federal Pell Grants, Federal Supplemental Educational Opportunity Grants, Federal Work-Study Program awards, privately funded scholarships for both academic and special talent, and West Virginia Higher Education Grant Program awards. The student's parents or guardians are required to submit the Free Application for Federal Student Aid (FAFSA) to the Pennsylvania Higher Education Assistance Agency for processing and eventual receipt of the need analysis report by Tech for determination of eligibility. Applications for financial aid, both from incoming freshmen and from enrolled students, should be submitted to WVU Tech's Office of Student Financial Aid by April 1 in order to receive consideration for the next academic year.

Faculty

Faculty members at Tech are well prepared both academically and professionally to teach the institution's career-oriented curricula. Faculty members come from all over the United States and from several other countries, and most have had considerable practical experience in their field. In the Leonard C. Nelson College of Engineering alone, nearly 90 percent of the faculty have earned doctorates. The student-faculty ratio is 18:1. Faculty members work with students in developing academic programs, and they assist in personal counseling, although Tech also has professional counselors on the staff to help students with their problems.

Student Government

The Student Government Association (SGA) at Tech consists of students elected in campuswide referendums that are held each fall and spring. One of the SGA's most important functions is to develop a budget on which to base the student activity fees that fund the many diverse student activities and organizations on campus.

Admission Requirements

Applicants who are residents of West Virginia must graduate from an accredited high school or pass the GED test and must take the ACT and have test scores sent to the Institute directly from American College Testing, Inc. Out-of-state residents must graduate from an accredited high school or pass the GED test, rank in the upper three fourths of their graduating class or attain a standard composite score of at least 17 on the ACT (SAT I combined score of at least 820), and have their scores sent to the Institute directly from American College Testing, Inc., or the Educational Testing Service. Scores are used for placement and counseling purposes, and no other test may be substituted.

Admission to the college does not necessarily admit a student to all programs. Prerequisites apply for admission to certain curricula, as follows: for engineering, 2 units of algebra, 1 unit of plane geometry, 1 unit of advanced math, a minimum 3.0 GPA, and a math ACT score of at least 21; for engineering technology, 1 unit of algebra, 1 unit of plane geometry, and ½ unit of trigonometry. If a student lacks one or more of these prerequisites, he or she will be given an opportunity to enroll in pretechnology mathematics courses. Allied health–nursing candidates need 2 units of algebra and 2 units of laboratory science, 1 unit of which must be in chemistry. Dental hygiene candidates need 1 unit of algebra, 1 unit of biology, and 1 unit of chemistry. Because of the limited enrollment in allied health programs, candidates for these areas are selected by a special committee. Students with high school averages of B or better and/or ACT composite scores of 20 (SAT I combined score of 950) or higher are given priority by the admission committee.

Application and Information

Students are encouraged to apply by January. Applications are processed on a rolling decision basis. Students with a B average or better are notified of the admission decision upon receipt of their sixth-semester high school transcript and ACT or SAT I scores. All other students are notified upon receipt of their seventh-semester or final transcript and ACT or SAT I scores.

Applications for admission and requests for further information should be addressed to:

Director of Admissions
West Virginia University Institute of Technology
Montgomery, West Virginia 25136

Telephone: 888-554-TECH (toll-free)
E-mail: wvutech@wvit.wvnet.edu

Old Main.

WEST VIRGINIA WESLEYAN COLLEGE
BUCKHANNON, WEST VIRGINIA

The College

Founded by the United Methodist Church in 1890, West Virginia Wesleyan College welcomes students of all geographic, religious, and ethnic backgrounds. The College assures high-quality education with a personal touch and serves as the "home among the hills" for all students. The four-year liberal arts program encourages students to develop an understanding of their own individuality, a commitment to the surrounding community, and an involvement in curricular and cocurricular resources. The Christian ideals upon which the College was established prepare students to lead respected lives in work, leisure, and service to all humankind.

Wesleyan is accredited by the North Central Association of Colleges and Schools and approved by the University Senate of the United Methodist Church. The nursing program is accredited by the National League for Nursing Accrediting Commission, the teacher education program is accredited by the National Council for Accreditation of Teacher Education (NCATE), the music program is accredited by the National Association of Schools of Music, and the athletic training program is accredited by the Commission on Accreditation of Allied Health Education Programs (CAAHEP).

Wesleyan's more than 1,500 students originate from thirty-six states and twenty-nine countries. Forty-five percent of the student body come from West Virginia and 55 percent are out-of-state students. Approximately 10 percent of the students are minority or international students. Eighty-five percent reside on campus in a variety of housing options, including residence halls, apartments, and substance-free housing. Housing is guaranteed for four years of undergraduate study in one of ten residence units

Campus dining is provided seven days a week in the French A. See Dining Center, where meals are provided by a contracted professional catering service. All students residing on campus are required to board on campus; students living off campus have the option of boarding on campus.

The dynamic student life program offers more than seventy clubs and organizations in which students may participate. Some of the cocurricular activities that the majority of students take part in are student governance clubs, the campus radio station, the newspaper and yearbook clubs, six fraternities and five sororities, seventeen NCAA Division II sports teams, intramurals, Christian Life Council, regionally renowned performing arts groups, comprehensive community service opportunities, and the Campus Activities Board, which schedules nightly weekend entertainment. Wesleyan's location allows students to enjoy endless opportunities for outdoor adventure, such as whitewater rafting, hiking, mountain biking, downhill skiing, camping, and caving.

Among the many services available to students is an advising and career center, which helps students with job placement, class scheduling, internship opportunities, and study abroad. The center also provides special tests, such as the LSAT, GRE, or GMAT, to prepare graduates for professional schools. A Counseling and Wellness Center allows students to receive personal and educational guidance as well as health services through the Health Center. The Student Academic Support Services provides learning resources for all students as well as specific services for students with diagnosed learning differences.

The Freshman Seminar Program eases the transition from high school to college by providing faculty advising and student mentoring for the first semester. The program begins at orientation and helps students become acclimated to the Wesleyan community.

In partnership with IBM, all students receive a ThinkPad laptop computer for all four years of undergraduate study. Students use the computer in classrooms as well as the residence halls. The campus fiber-optic system allows for rapid Internet and e-mail access from all academic buildings and residence hall rooms.

Location

Situated in the foothills of the Allegheny Mountains, Wesleyan's 100-acre campus is located in the historic city of Buckhannon, West Virginia. Buckhannon has been included in Norman Crampton's book, *The Top 100 Best Small Towns in America*, a Random House publication. Students are drawn to this picturesque and friendly setting and the many restaurants, social events, and outdoor adventures available within a short distance from campus.

Majors and Degrees

The College awards four undergraduate academic degrees: the Bachelor of Arts in art (art education, ceramics, graphic design, and painting and drawing), chemistry, Christian education and church leadership, communication studies, dramatic arts, economics, education (elementary, secondary, and combined elementary/secondary), English (literature, teaching, and writing), environmental science, history, international studies, music (applied and theory), philosophy, physics, political science, psychology, public relations, religion, and sociology; the Bachelor of Music Education; the Bachelor of Science in accounting, athletic training, biology, business administration, chemistry, computer information science, computer science, engineering physics, environmental science, management, marketing, mathematics, and physical education; and the Bachelor of Science in Nursing.

Preprofessional programs are offered in dentistry, law, medicine, ministry, optometry, pharmacy, physical therapy, and veterinary medicine. The degrees are determined by the content of the student's program.

Academic Program

Students are required to complete 120 credit hours of course work to become eligible for graduation. Approximately one third of those hours are taken in a student's major, one third in the general studies curriculum requirement, and one third in electives. The general studies and elective courses are taken to develop and enhance a student's worldview. These classes range from contemporary issues to humanities and can be taken along with courses within the individual's major concentration throughout the four years.

The 4-1-4 academic calendar is another feature at Wesleyan. During the optional January Term, students can focus on one class for the whole term, either as part of their major concentration or to fulfill a general studies or elective requirement. These classes may be taken on campus, but there are also opportunities for study abroad.

The honors program is offered for superior students who meet the specific requirements and are willing to commit themselves to a rigorous and enriching program that affirms the highest ideals of a liberal arts institution. Challenging classes and cultural outings are an integral part of the honors program and are offered throughout the academic year.

Off-Campus Arrangements

Wesleyan encourages students to look beyond the traditional classroom and expand their education. For this reason, study abroad is highly encouraged and is an important part of the students' experience. In the past, students have studied in such countries as Australia, Bulgaria, England, Ireland, Spain, and Wales, but there are a number of other countries students have the option of attending. In addition, work experience internships are required for many majors and highly encourage for others. Internships are available locally as well as in such cities as Washington, D.C.; New York City; Pittsburgh; and other cities around the globe. These off-campus opportunities can be taken for a complete semester or during the January Term.

Academic Facilities

Wesleyan's twenty-three buildings, including ten modern residence hall units, house some of the most impressive facilities in the region. The Annie Merner Pfeiffer Library is a "wireless" environment and a spacious facility that contains more than 105,000 volumes, 700 periodicals, and 10,000 media materials. More than 220 million resources worldwide can be accessed online or through a number of CD-ROM databases beyond Wesleyan. Located in the center of campus is Wesley Chapel, the largest sanctuary in West Virginia, and Martin Religious Center. The chapel serves as the focal point of many campus activities, including religious and cultural events. The hub of the campus, Benedum Campus and Community Center, is an impressive building that houses a convenience store, bookstore, swimming pool, student development offices, study lounges, and a cabaret-style restaurant, the Cat's Claw. The Rockefeller Health and Physical Education Center includes a main gymnasium that seats 3,700 spectators, an intramural gymnasium, weight and nautilus training rooms, and an indoor astroturfed training area. Other vital buildings include Christopher Hall of Science, which has state-of-the-art science equipment; Middleton Hall, which houses admission and financial planning offices as well as the Nursing Department; and the Lynch-Raine Administration Building.

Costs

The 2000–01 costs at Wesleyan are $16,800 for tuition, $4350 for room and board, and $1250 for student fees, which include a student activity fee and technology fee. These costs do not include books, travel, clothing, medical insurance, or other personal expenses. Wesleyan offers an interest-free monthly payment plan during the academic year.

Financial Aid

Wesleyan awards financial aid on the basis of scholastic achievements, special talents and abilities, and financial need. A number of scholarships are available, including awards for academics, athletics, community service, leadership, and performing and visual arts. Student employment is available in most areas of the College community, financed through a blend of institutional and federal funds. Students may apply for low-cost federal loans. Students should file the Free Application for Federal Student Aid by February 15. The institutional code number is 003830. Wesleyan also offers an early estimator financial aid service to assist with the costs of a Wesleyan education. Currently, more than 85 percent of all Wesleyan students receive some kind of financial assistance.

Faculty

The faculty at Wesleyan has a primary goal of teaching and advising. More than 80 percent of the full-time faculty members hold the highest degree in their respective fields. With a 15:1 student-faculty ratio, classes are small, and personal attention is evident in most departments. Not only are faculty members teachers and advisers, but they are also mentors and friends.

Student Government

The Community Council, one of the first college-based community governing bodies in the country, is structured to encourage and promote student participation. The 4 peer-elected officers are elected by their respective classes or representative student organizations. Community Council meets weekly, along with faculty, administration, and staff members, and is recognized as the driving force behind many issues on campus.

Admission Requirements

Wesleyan seeks students who have proven academic credentials combined with achievements and talents that would enhance the quality of life on campus. Students are selected by the Office of Admission on the basis of their high school transcripts, college entrance exam results, letters of recommendation, campus interviews, and other supporting information. All applicants must take the SAT or ACT and submit secondary school transcripts from all schools attended along with the application for admission. Candidates are considered on an individual basis without regard to race, religion, geographic origin, or handicap. Essays and campus interviews are strongly encouraged and may be required in certain instances. Advanced Placement credit and International Baccalaureate courses are accepted.

Application and Information

A completed application form must be submitted along with a nonrefundable $25 application fee anytime after the junior year or during the senior year of high school. Early decision applicants must have their completed application file, including high school transcripts and SAT/ACT scores, submitted to the Office of Admission by December 1. Admission offers are made on a rolling admission basis, which enables students to receive notification of the admission decision shortly after all their credentials have been received. The regular application deadline is March 1. Financial aid candidates should complete the Free Application for Federal Student Aid as early as possible. Interviews, campus tours, faculty and staff appointments, and class visits are encouraged and may be made through the Office of Admission.

Requests for an application form, viewbook, and other information should be addressed to:

Office of Admission
West Virginia Wesleyan College
59 College Avenue
Buckhannon, West Virginia 26201
Telephone: 304-473-8510
               800-722-9933 (toll-free)
E-mail: admission@wvwc.edu
World Wide Web: http://www.wvwc.edu

The Benedum Campus and Community Center is the hub of student life—both inside and out.

WHEATON COLLEGE
WHEATON, ILLINOIS

The College

Wheaton College's 140-year history demonstrates the benefits of stable leadership in private Christian higher education: it has had only 7 presidents since it was founded in 1860. Interdenominational and international in constituency, the student body of about 2,300 undergraduates (including 180 students in the Conservatory of Music) and 350 graduate students represents all fifty states, some forty countries, and about forty religious denominations. Eighty percent of the students come from outside Illinois.

In addition to its undergraduate programs, Wheaton College offers the Master of Arts in Teaching (M.A.T.) degree and the Master of Arts (M.A.) degree in clinical psychology, educational ministries, evangelism, missions/intercultural studies, and theological studies, as well as a Doctor of Psychology degree. Two certificate programs—Advanced Biblical Studies and Teaching English as a Second Language—are available.

The student activity calendar includes concerts of all kinds, Chicago outings, films, theater productions, athletic contests, and banquets. The Office of Christian Outreach provides areas for student ministry in Missions, Christian Service Council Ministries, and World Christian Fellowship. The Men's Glee Club, the Women's Chorale, the Concert Choir, the Symphony Orchestra, the Wind Ensemble, and the Gospel Choir, open by audition to all Wheaton students, give concerts throughout the Chicago area and make annual tours to other sections of the United States and to Canada. Radio broadcasting experience is provided by WETN, the campus FM radio station.

Wheaton is a member of NCAA Division III. Intercollegiate sports include baseball, basketball, cross-country, football, golf, soccer, softball, swimming, tennis, track, volleyball, and wrestling. In addition, the College has a well-developed club sports program, including cheerleading, crew, drill team, equestrian, ice hockey, lacrosse, tae kwon do, and ultimate frisbee, as well as fifteen intramural sports. The Chrouser Fitness Center offers a 35-meter pool and an exercise physiology laboratory.

Through efforts of the student body, the College publishes the *Record*, a weekly newspaper; *Kodon*, the College literary magazine; and *The Tower* yearbook. An additional thirty clubs and organizations round out the cocurricular offerings.

Location

Wheaton's 80-acre campus is located in a residential suburb (population 50,000) 25 miles west of Chicago. The educational and cultural features of the Chicago metropolitan area are readily available to students. The Wheaton area is the home of more than forty Christian organizations.

Majors and Degrees

Wheaton grants the Bachelor of Arts and Bachelor of Science degrees and, through the Wheaton Conservatory of Music, the Bachelor of Music and Bachelor of Music Education degrees.

The following majors are available in the arts and sciences: ancient languages, anthropology, archaeology, art, biblical studies, biology, business/economics, chemistry, Christian education, communications, computer science/math, economics, education, English, environmental science, geological studies, history, interdisciplinary studies, kinesiology, mathematics, modern languages (French, German, and Spanish), music, philosophy, physical science, physics, political science, psychology, religious studies, social science, and sociology. Also, 3-2 programs are available in engineering and nursing, as is a five-year cooperative engineering program with Illinois Institute of Technology.

The Wheaton Conservatory of Music offers majors in music composition, music education, music history–literature, music performance, and music with elective studies in an outside field. Students seeking these professional music degrees normally begin their programs as freshmen.

An on-campus program in military science leads to a commission in the U.S. Army at graduation. In addition to the majors offered, Wheaton has programs leading to teacher certification and to athletic training certification as well as programs preparing students for careers in business, health professions, law, and ministry.

Academic Program

Wheaton is a pervasively Christian college at which faculty and students work together, both inside and outside the classroom, to apply Christian principles and values to the needs and problems of the individual and society. The vigorous search for knowledge and wisdom in any area of human activity is based on the belief that all truth is God's truth. The academic curriculum combines with the extensive cocurriculum of artistic, athletic, religious, service, and social activities to achieve a lively interaction of Christian faith, learning, and living. Because of the College's strong commitment to developing effective servant/leaders for the church and society worldwide, the educational emphasis in all degree programs is on the whole person and the overall Wheaton experience.

To meet the requirements of all baccalaureate degrees, students must complete a minimum of 124 semester hours, 36 of which must be in the upper division, and have at least a C (2.0) average overall.

The major field is selected sometime during the second year of general education courses taken to meet competency and area requirements. Students must demonstrate competence (either by examination or by taking prescribed courses) in foreign language, mathematics, speech, and writing. All students must complete area requirements in art, biblical studies, foreign language, history, kinesiology, literature, music, natural science, philosophy, and social science. A student may be granted advanced placement or college credit on the basis of examination (SAT II or AP). The number of credits granted and the level of placement are determined by the registrar and the chairman of the department in which the course is taught.

The College operates on a semester academic calendar, beginning in late August and ending in early May. An eight-week summer term is also offered.

Off-Campus Arrangements

Wheaton College offers a variety of off-campus opportunities to enhance students' programs of study. The High Road program is a rugged wilderness education experience available to entering freshmen at the College's Honey Rock Camp in northern Wisconsin. The Human Needs and Global Resources (HNGR)

Program focuses on responses to human needs from a multidisciplinary perspective. It offers a concentration of courses leading to a six- to twelve-month internship overseas, followed by a seminar on campus. By participating in this program, students can earn up to 12 hours of credit. A similar program in urban studies is focused on U.S. cities.

Other special summer programs for credit include field study at the Wheaton College Science Station in the Black Hills of South Dakota; working with youth at Honey Rock Camp; interdisciplinary study in East Asia; the study of English literature in England; language study in France, Germany, and Spain; the Wheaton-in-the-Holy-Lands Program, involving biblical and archaeological studies; and an international study program based in England and the Netherlands, offering courses in economics, political science, and psychology.

Wheaton is a member of the Christian College Coalition, based in Washington, D.C. Coalition activities increase students' learning opportunities by bringing special programs to campus and by providing off-campus study. Off-campus programs include American Studies in Washington, D.C., Latin American Studies in Costa Rica, Middle East Studies in Cairo, and the Los Angeles Film Studies Center. In addition, Wheaton's membership in the Christian College Consortium allows students a semester of study at one of the other twelve consortium colleges.

Cooperative programs in social science are available at American and Drew universities, and students may participate in a European seminar conducted by Gordon College.

Academic Facilities

Wheaton's combined libraries have a collection of more than 700,000 items and belong to LIBRAS, an association of fourteen suburban liberal arts college libraries, and the Chicago Area Theological Library Association. The Peter Stam Music Library holds more than 9,500 recordings, 8,000 scores, and 425 titles in music education. The Wade Center is a special collection of the books and papers of 7 British authors, including C. S. Lewis and J. R. R. Tolkien.

The Billy Graham Center, a research and study center, houses a museum, a library, and archives, all focused on evangelism and world missions.

Adams Hall houses an art gallery and studios, and Arena Theater is home to several theater productions each year.

Specialized laboratory facilities and modern equipment are available for general and advanced work in various science departments and for individual student research projects. Numerous microcomputers, as well as larger types of data processing equipment, are readily available for student use.

Costs

Tuition for the 2000–01 year is $15,540; room and board for the year are $5260.

Financial Aid

Most Wheaton College financial aid is allocated on the basis of need as demonstrated by information supplied on the Free Application for Federal Student Aid (FAFSA) and the CSS Profile. Students from Alaska, Illinois, Pennsylvania, Rhode Island, and Vermont are expected to apply for state grants or scholarships along with their application for Wheaton College aid.

Substantial student aid is available in the form of grants, loans, and work-study opportunities provided by government and College resources. The average aid package is more than $10,000. The Career Development Center provides free service to help students secure part-time jobs.

Faculty

The approximately 160 Wheaton faculty members, of whom about 86 percent hold earned doctorates, come from a variety of colleges and universities in the United States and abroad. As active Christians, they are interested in the spiritual and intellectual development of their students. The faculty members' primary commitment as educators and advisers is enriched by their considerable research, publishing, and artistic performance activities. All undergraduate courses are taught by faculty members.

To ensure a rich range of perspectives and expertise, every department at Wheaton has at least 3 full-time professors, and most have 5 to 10. The student-faculty ratio is 15:1.

Student Government

Student Government ensures a student voice in institutional affairs and provides a wide range of opportunities to develop leadership abilities. Student Leadership Workshops, the apportionment of student fees, and the official representation of the student body are some of the activities under the direction of the Student Government. The College Union, an all-student organization, plans and directs cultural, social, and recreational activities.

Admission Requirements

Wheaton is a selective college that seeks to enroll students who evidence a vital Christian experience, high moral character, personal integrity, social concern, strong academic ability and motivation, and the desire to pursue Christian higher education as defined in the aims and objectives of the College. These qualities are evaluated by consideration of each applicant's academic record, autobiographical essays, test scores, recommendations, interview, and participation in extracurricular activities. For students applying to the Conservatory of Music, strong consideration is given to the evaluation of the required audition.

Applicants must have a high school diploma or the equivalent and, at the time of graduation, should have completed a college-preparatory curriculum with a minimum of 18 acceptable units. Of the 18 units, 15 must be in English, foreign language, mathematics, science, and social studies. No units are granted for health and such courses as band, choir, driver's education, and physical education, but a maximum of 3 units for vocational subjects is allowed.

Satisfactory scores on the SAT I or on the ACT examination are required of all applicants to the freshman class. The middle 50 percent range of scores for those admitted is 27–31 (ACT) and 1280–1420 (SAT I).

Application and Information

An application packet, complete with detailed instructions and requirements, can be obtained from the Admissions Office. For early action (non-binding), students seeking admission in the fall term should apply to the College by November 1. All other applications for undergraduate admission in the fall should be received by January 15. The final deadline for Conservatory of Music applications is March 1.

Further information is available from:

Admissions Office
Wheaton College
Wheaton, Illinois 60187
Telephone: 630-752-5005
          800-222-2419 (toll-free)
E-mail: admissions@wheaton.edu
      music@wheaton.edu
World Wide Web: http://www.wheaton.edu

WHEATON COLLEGE
NORTON, MASSACHUSETTS

The College
Wheaton College is an independent liberal arts college of approximately 1,500 women and men. Founded as a seminary for women in 1834, Wheaton was chartered as a college in 1912 and enrolled its first coeducational class in 1988. Students come from forty states and thirty countries. Nearly all students live on campus in both single-sex and coed student-run dormitories.

The vitality of this classic liberal arts college grows out of each student's involvement in the social and academic life of the campus. There are many extracurricular activities and organizations, including intercollegiate and intramural sports such as baseball, basketball, cross-country, field hockey, lacrosse, soccer, softball, synchronized swimming, tennis, and track; musical groups such as the Whims, Wheatones, Gentleman Callers, and chamber music ensembles; the Modern Dance Group; the Black Students Association; the Student Government Association; the Christian Fellowship; Hillel; the International Students Association; the Asian Student Association; and the newspaper, yearbook, campus radio station, and literary magazine. Wheaton also has a chapter of Phi Beta Kappa. A number of lecture series are offered, and concerts, plays, films, colloquia, art exhibits, and social events are scheduled regularly. Through the Filene Center for Work and Learning, hundreds of students annually undertake career exploration internships, field placements, and community service positions in local towns, as well as in Boston, Providence, and overseas. This out-of-classroom learning is documented through the Filene Center, where all students maintain their experiential transcript, the Wheaton Work and Public Service Record. The Filene Center also provides a full range of career services, graduate and professional school counseling, alumnae networks, and databases of part-time and summer job opportunities.

Location
The 385-acre campus with eighty-five buildings is in the countrylike surroundings of Norton. The newest additions to the campus include two 50-person residence halls; a multipurpose athletics facility, which includes a fieldhouse, a pool, and a gymnasium; and Sidell Baseball Stadium. Norton is located 30 minutes from Providence and 45 minutes from Boston. Throughout the week, Wheaton provides access by means of vans to public transportation to Boston and by bus to Boston directly on the weekends. The College is also situated within an hour's drive of the beautiful beaches of Cape Cod, Massachusetts, and Newport, Rhode Island. The Tweeter Center for Performing Arts is located 2½ miles away.

Majors and Degrees
Wheaton College grants the Bachelor of Arts degree with formal majors in American studies, anthropology, art (history and studio), Asian studies, biochemistry, biology, chemistry, classical civilization, classics (Greek and Latin), computer science, economics, economics-mathematics, English (literature and writing), English dramatic literature, environmental science, French, German, Hispanic studies, history, international relations, mathematics, mathematics and computer science, music, philosophy, physics, physics and astronomy, political science, psychobiology, psychology, religion, Russian, Russian studies, sociology, theater, and women's studies. Students may also create their own interdepartmental majors.

Five-year dual-degree programs are available in engineering with Thayer School of Engineering (Dartmouth), George Washington University and Worcester Polytechnic Institute, in business and management with Clark University and the University of Rochester, in religion with Andover-Newton Theological School, in optometry with the New England School of Optometry, in communications with Emerson College, and in fine arts with the School of the Museum of Fine Arts in Boston.

Academic Program
A general education curriculum continues Wheaton's tradition of commitment to the liberal arts, while responding to changing student needs and changing human knowledge. Common-topic freshman seminars provide an exceptional opportunity for students to exchange ideas with each other and with faculty members. Each student must also complete the equivalent of two semesters of physical education. A minimum of thirty-two semester courses with an average of at least C is required for graduation. All students are also required to complete one evaluated out-of-classroom experience through a reflective learning model administered by the Filene Center for Work and Learning.

Course credit is granted through the Advanced Placement Program or the College-Level Examination Program on an individual basis. Independent studies, research, and fieldwork are available to students for academic credit.

In addition to major department offerings, courses may be taken in astronomy, computer science, drama, education, family studies, film, and linguistics.

Off-Campus Arrangements
Wheaton participates in the Twelve-College Exchange Program, whose other members include Amherst, Bowdoin, Connecticut College, Dartmouth, Mount Holyoke, Smith, Trinity, Vassar, Wellesley, Wesleyan, and Williams. Locally, Wheaton students may cross-register for courses at Brown University and other colleges in the Southeastern Association for Cooperation in Higher Education in Massachusetts (SACHEM).

Wheaton students may study government or economics during a semester in Washington, D.C., sponsored by American University, explore marine ecology at the Marine Biological Laboratory at Woods Hole, or participate in a semester-long program in American maritime studies, sponsored by Williams College at Mystic Seaport. The National Theater Institute Program offers selected students the opportunity to spend a semester at the Eugene O'Neill Theater Center in Waterford, Connecticut. Students may also participate in the Salt Center for Documentary Field Studies in Portland, Maine.

International study is available through any one of several approved Junior Year Abroad programs, for which the College grants credit. Wheaton sponsors its own programs as part of a consortium in Cordoba, Spain, and Rehovot, Israel. Part or all of the junior year may also be spent at universities in Belgium, China, France, Germany, Great Britain, Greece, India, Israel, Italy, Japan, Kenya, Spain, Switzerland, Thailand, and the Latin American republics. Through a program affiliation, many of the College's study-abroad opportunities include the opportunity to combine university study with related internships with multinational corporations, foreign governments, art galleries, museums, advertising agencies, and much more. In addition, the College sponsors faculty-led summer and January-term programs in Belize, Ecuador, Kenya, and Thailand.

A Career Exploration Internship Program allows students to work from one to four weeks in a professional field of interest during the January break. More than 600 internship positions are listed with the Filene Center for Work and Learning; housing is often provided in various locations by Wheaton graduates.

Academic Facilities

Wheaton's library has 371,071 volumes, 2,252 current periodicals and newspapers, 72,277 microfilm units, and 8,093 records and tapes; a Women's Information Center; and a College Archives/Special Collections area. Wheaton participates in library consortia, which provide direct access to three local college libraries and computer access to collections throughout the country. Automated services include indexes on CD-ROM, online searching of remote databases, and a fully integrated system containing the Wheaton Library catalog, acquisitions, and circulation information. The Library also supports the academic program through bibliographic instruction sessions, including participation in the First-Year Seminars.

The Science Center has fully equipped laboratories for both faculty and student research and two greenhouses. Other facilities include the Balfour-Hood Student Center; the Watson Fine Arts Center with a proscenium theater, a "black box" theater, art studios, and a gallery; a laboratory nursery school; and the Academic Computing Center. The Academic Computing Center offers students access to more than eighty-five Macintosh and PC computers as well as multimedia equipment, scanners, and laser printers. The center also operates a number of other classrooms around campus with permanent computer and digital projection equipment. All academic and administrative buildings and all dormitories are part of a campuswide network. Students are offered accounts for e-mail and Internet access.

Costs

The comprehensive fee for 2000–01 is $31,370, which consists of tuition, $24,225; room, $3650; board, $3270; and a student activities fee, $225.

Financial Aid

Students who demonstrate financial need normally receive a combination of grants, loans, and opportunities for employment on campus. The decision to award financial aid is made independently of the admission decision. Students applying for financial aid must complete the Free Application for Federal Student Aid (FAFSA) and the Financial Aid PROFILE by February 1. Sixty-eight percent of Wheaton's students receive some form of financial aid.

Faculty

The student-faculty ratio is 13:1. Ninety-eight percent of the faculty members hold the Ph.D. degree. Professors are very accessible to students, act as academic advisers, and often become involved with student activities.

Student Government

The Student Government Association, an active and influential organization, includes all members of the Wheaton community. Students are invited to attend faculty meetings and serve as voting members on most faculty committees. Rules are minimal, based on student self-government and an honor system stressing individual honor and responsibility.

Admission Requirements

Wheaton does not prescribe rigid entrance requirements, but most entering students have had 4 years of English, 3 or 4 years of mathematics, 4 or 5 years of one or two languages, 2 years of social studies, and 2 or 3 years of science. However, these guidelines are not to be taken as requirements. Applications are reviewed on an individual basis, and the academic achievement, the challenge of the curriculum, evaluations by teachers and counselors, and the extracurricular contributions of each candidate are all taken into account.

The submission of standardized test results is optional for the purposes of admission. Those who wish their scores to be considered should arrange for official score reports to be sent from the appropriate testing agency directly to the Wheaton Office of Admission. Reports must be received no later than the application deadline for the corresponding decision plan. Unofficial test scores (i.e., those reported on high school transcripts) are not considered. A personal interview is expected for all applicants.

Transfer students are admitted to the freshman, sophomore, and junior classes each year. Transfer applicants must have maintained a promising record and must be eligible for honorable dismissal from the college they are attending. A transfer student must attend Wheaton at least two years in order to receive a degree from the College. Students who wish to enter in the spring semester must apply by November 15. An early action plan is available for students who apply by February 1 for the fall semester; the regular decision deadline is April 1.

Application and Information

Students who consider Wheaton their first choice may apply for an early decision by November 15. Decisions are mailed by December 15. An early action plan is also available for students who apply by December 15. Decisions are mailed by February 1. The deadline for regular-decision applicants is February 1; notification for these students is made during the first week of April.

For more information, students are encouraged to contact:

Dean of Admission and Student Aid
Wheaton College
Norton, Massachusetts 02766
Telephone: 508-286-8251
           800-394-6003 (toll-free)
E-mail: admission@wheatonma.edu
World Wide Web: http://www.wheatonma.edu

Park Hall, the administration building (left), and Mary Lyon Hall, a classroom building (right), are among the handsome facilities on Wheaton College's extensive 300-acre campus.

WHEELING JESUIT UNIVERSITY
WHEELING, WEST VIRGINIA

The University

Wheeling Jesuit University, founded in 1954, is the youngest of America's twenty-eight Jesuit colleges and the only one that has been coeducational from the beginning. The University aims to develop men and women who think clearly and act wisely, with courage, competence, and compassion. Students have the advantage of a world-recognized Jesuit education on a scale where personal student-faculty interaction occurs daily. Although Catholic in affiliation, Wheeling Jesuit University welcomes students of all faiths. Of the 1,159 undergraduate students, approximately 65 percent are Catholic. Students come from twenty-nine states, with the majority from the East and Midwest. International students come from twenty-one different countries.

Wheeling Jesuit University is accredited by the North Central Association of Colleges and Schools, and its programs in the respective areas are accredited by the National League for Nursing and the AMA Committee on Allied Health Education and Accreditation.

The campus has fifteen modern buildings spread out over 65 acres of rolling hillside. Residential housing is available to all students who wish to live on campus, and 80 percent of the students enrolled take advantage of this. The dining hall and snack bar are operated by the Sodexho-Marriott Corporation, and a rathskeller is operated by the students. Student organizations and clubs offer an array of cultural and social activities, including dramatics, a University newspaper and magazine, cinema, concerts, and community services. Intercollegiate sports include men's and women's basketball, cross-country, golf, soccer, swimming, and track and field; men's lacrosse; and women's volleyball. Club and intramural sports include basketball, football, ice hockey, lacrosse, rugby, softball, tennis, and volleyball. The Health Recreation Center features a 2,200-seat gymnasium, a jogging track, racquetball courts, and a six-lane swimming pool.

In addition to the undergraduate degree programs shown below, the University offers a six-year program leading to a master's degree in physical therapy.

Location

Wheeling, one of the country's most livable and safe small cities, has a population of approximately 50,000 and is easily accessible by interstate highways. The University is a 1-hour drive from the international airport in Pittsburgh, Pennsylvania, and a 2-hour drive from Columbus, Ohio. Many recreational and cultural facilities are available, including 1,500-acre Oglebay Park and 250-acre Wheeling Park. Excellent local recreational areas provide opportunities for camping, golf, hiking, skiing, swimming, and other activities.

Majors and Degrees

The Bachelor of Arts degree is granted in criminal justice, French, history, international studies, liberal studies (elementary education), literature, philosophy, political and economic philosophy, political science, professional writing, psychology, Romance languages, Spanish, and theology. The Bachelor of Science degree is awarded in accounting, biology, chemistry, computer science, environmental studies, international business, management, marketing, mathematics, nuclear medicine technology, nursing, physics, product design and development, and respiratory therapy. Independent majors may be arranged. Preprofessional programs in dentistry, law, medicine, pharmacy, physical therapy, and veterinary medicine are also available. A teacher preparation program provides teaching certification in many subjects. This program prepares students to teach grades kindergarten through 12.

For especially able students, a five-year program has been developed that enables them to earn a bachelor's degree in one of the liberal arts above and also, after the fifth year, a Master in Business Administration degree. A 3-2 engineering program is offered in conjunction with Case Western Reserve University.

A special program called "Hunting for a Future" (HUNT) is available to help entering students who are undecided about a major.

Academic Program

Wheeling Jesuit University combines preprofessional majors with those in traditional arts and sciences. A strong background in the liberal arts is provided to all students through a required general studies core curriculum. A minimum of 120 credit hours completed with an average of 2.0 or better is required for graduation. The Laut Honors Program for students of exceptional ability is a sequence of honors courses, an independent project or thesis, a special senior seminar, and a January cross-cultural experience. In 1998–99, the program involved approximately 50 students.

Off-Campus Arrangements

Students may study abroad through programs offered in conjunction with two Jesuit "sister schools": Loyola University Chicago (Rome Center for Liberal Arts) and Loyola Marymount University of Los Angeles (St. Gallen Graduate School of Business, Switzerland). Additional study-abroad opportunities in Argentina, Austria, Belgium, Egypt, England, France, Germany, Italy, Jamaica, Japan, Poland, and Spain are available in cooperation with American University or the Pennsylvania Consortium for International Education.

Academic Facilities

Since 1993, more than $50 million has been spent at Wheeling Jesuit University on new facilities designed for student use. The main classroom building, Donahue Hall, was totally renovated in 1987, and a new computer/science building is planned for late 2001. The library is electronically integrated with the entire campus by fiber-optic cable, which permits students in the residence halls to interact with all units of the University. The Erma Ora Byrd Center for Educational Technologies is a NASA building that houses the Classroom of the Future Program, with its high-tech teaching and research rooms that serve as the cornerstone for the teacher education programs. The Robert C. Byrd National Technology Transfer Center inspired the Technical Innovation Program, which consists of a major in product design and development and a minor in technology.

Costs

Tuition and fees in 1999–2000 were $15,210. Room and board costs were $5200. Books and supplies cost approximately $300 to $600, and personal expenses average $600 per year.

Financial Aid

Wheeling Jesuit University assists students who have financial need with financial award packages that include loans, grants, work-study jobs, and scholarships. In 1999–2000, 92 percent of full-day students received some form of aid. The average assistance level to those receiving aid was more than $14,775. Federal aid available includes Federal Perkins Loans, Federal Pell Grants, Federal Work-Study awards, Federal Supplemental Educational Opportunity Grants, and Federal Direct Student Loans. West Virginia and Pennsylvania state grants can be used at Wheeling Jesuit University by eligible students. The University also provides need-based grants from institutional funds.

Scholarships based solely on academic ability are also awarded by the University. These scholarships range from $500 to $5000 per year. Two full-tuition and six half-tuition scholarships are awarded on a competitive basis to entering Laut Honors Program students. National Merit Semifinalists receive half-tuition scholarships. All academic scholarships are renewable each year if a grade average of B or better is maintained. Athletic scholarships are awarded to men and women in various intercollegiate sports. Competitive choral, music ministry, and Christian leadership scholarships are also awarded.

For further information on scholarships or financial aid, applicants should contact the Financial Aid Department at Wheeling Jesuit University. The FAFSA should be filed by March 1.

Faculty

An energetic, diversified faculty (73 percent of whose members have doctoral or other terminal degrees) has a strong voice in the policies of the institution through a faculty council and other standing committees. All 82 full-time faculty members are professional teachers; no teaching is done by graduate assistants. About 10 percent of the faculty members are Jesuits. Faculty members and students interact outside the classroom through activities, dining, intramural sports, and informal gatherings. The student-faculty ratio is 12:1. Academic advising is done by the faculty.

Student Government

Students participate fully in formulating the policies of the University through the Student Government and residence hall governments and as voting or auditing participants on virtually all faculty-administration committees of the University. Students plan and control the entire student activity budget.

Admission Requirements

Wheeling Jesuit University is a democratic institution where all students are accepted on the same basis, regardless of sex, race, creed, or color. The Committee on Admissions selects students best qualified to complete the required program of studies. Applicants are considered for admission if they have successfully completed a high school course of study and have achieved reasonable success on either the SAT I or the ACT. For transfer students, transcripts are required from colleges previously attended.

Application and Information

There is a rolling admissions policy. Students receive notification of the admissions decision shortly after all their academic credentials have been received by the Admissions Office.

For more information, students should contact:

Office of Admissions
Wheeling Jesuit University
Wheeling, West Virginia 26003
Telephone: 304-243-2359
                800-624-6992 (toll-free)
Fax: 304-243-2397
E-mail: admiss@wju.edu
World Wide Web: http://www.wju.edu

Wheeling Jesuit University's main classroom building, Donahue Hall.

WHEELOCK COLLEGE
BOSTON, MASSACHUSETTS

The College

Wheelock College prepares students for careers that enrich the lives of children and families. Founded in 1888, Wheelock has consistently produced progressive and highly respected professionals for such fields as elementary education, preschool and kindergarten teaching, special education, day care, social work, and child life work. The 650 undergraduate women and men at Wheelock come from throughout the United States and from several countries. Beginning in their freshman year, students benefit from close contact with outstanding faculty and from direct fieldwork with children and families.

Wheelock's campus is beautifully kept, and the atmosphere is warm and friendly. Classes are small, and professors are known by their first names. Comfortable dormitories provide housing and many social activities for those who wish to live on campus. The College Center, with its wide-screen TV, snack bar, and often-used dance floor, is an attraction for the entire Wheelock community and for many students from neighboring schools. Wheelock students enjoy more than thirty-five clubs and organizations and actively participate in a variety of varsity and intramural sports. The College sponsors many cultural and theatrical events as well as such traditional activities as Family Weekend, the Sophomore-Senior Banquet, and Black History Month.

Location

Bordering Boston and suburban Brookline, Wheelock is ideally located across from Longwood Park and only a few blocks from the Museum of Fine Arts, several world-renowned hospitals, and many other institutions of higher learning. Students can walk to the shops and restaurants in Coolidge Corner or cheer for the Red Sox in nearby Fenway Park. They can discover the unmatched cultural and historical richness of downtown Boston, only a short subway ride away. They can walk the Freedom Trail, attend concerts and plays, or meet friends from other colleges for a day of fun at Faneuil Hall. The entire Boston area provides Wheelock students with exciting opportunities for extracurricular enjoyment and for their practical fieldwork with children and families.

Majors and Degrees

At Wheelock, students pursue one of three professional directions: teaching, child life, or social work. Within teaching, there are two separate areas of concentration: early childhood care and education focuses on the comprehensive care and education of children from birth to 8 years old. Elementary education prepares students to become teachers of children in grades 1–6. Students may pursue special education in the elementary education program. The child life program explores the emotional and psychological needs of hospitalized children and their families and prepares students to work as child life specialists with medical teams in hospitals or clinics. Students interested in teaching or in child life major in one of four liberal arts areas: human development, the arts, the humanities, or mathematics/science. These multidisciplinary majors are designed to form a strong foundation for professional studies and for lifelong learning. Social work majors prepare to work in social service agencies, state agencies, and schools to advocate for and support children and their families. Graduates of Wheelock receive the Bachelor of Arts, the Bachelor of Science, or the Bachelor of Social Work degree.

Academic Program

The focus of study at Wheelock is education and human services. Faculty members stress the importance of combining liberal arts, professional studies, and hands-on experience. Students begin work with children and families in their freshman year as part of a required course entitled Children and Their Environments. Practical work continues in the sophomore year through a course called Human Growth and Development, which involves theory and fieldwork. Juniors and seniors participate in supervised field experiences and student teaching in a variety of settings—elementary schools, day-care centers, nursery schools, museums, hospitals, social service agencies, and clinics—in urban and suburban locations. Professional courses provide preparation for field experience and support to students during their fieldwork. By combining the appropriate courses and field experience, Wheelock graduates are eligible for certification as early childhood, elementary school, or special needs teachers.

Off-Campus Arrangements

Students are encouraged to engage in independent study in an area of specific academic interest. In some academic programs, students may elect to study off campus.

Wheelock College is a member of the Colleges of the Fenway, a collaboration among Emmanuel College, Massachusetts College of Art, Massachusetts College of Pharmacy and Allied Health Sciences, Simmons College, Wentworth Institute of Technology, and Wheelock College. Each college maintains its unique identity, while providing students with access to academic programs and student services on all five campuses. Wheelock students can cross-register for courses and participate in social and extracurricular activities at any of the other institutions.

Academic Facilities

Wheelock's innovative Resource Center has a fully equipped workshop and holds a large collection of commercially manufactured, scrap, and natural materials for students to use in the creation of projects and original curriculum tools. Wheelock's library contains 94,703 volumes, providing reference and study facilities, collections in liberal arts areas, and extensive resources in children's literature and curriculum materials. The College also has extensive art studios with facilities for work in ceramics, weaving, and photography. One of the largest and best-equipped stages in Boston is found in the Lucy Wheelock Auditorium and Activities Building. The Activities Building also houses science and music classrooms, the gymnasium, a 700-seat auditorium, the Little Theatre, a music listening room, and an art gallery. All classrooms at Wheelock are equipped with dataports for Internet access and teacher workstations for integrating technology into the classroom. In addition, all students have Internet capabilities in their rooms.

Costs

In 2000–01, tuition is $17,410, and room and board are $6945, for a total of $24,355. A reasonable estimate for books and supplies is $400 per year and for personal expenses, $800, exclusive of travel to and from school.

Financial Aid

Wheelock provides financial aid for all applicants who demonstrate need. Currently, about 80 percent of the student body receives financial aid, usually in a combination of grants, loans, and work. Wheelock participates in the Federal Stafford Student Loan, Federal Perkins Loan, Federal Supplemental Educational Opportunity Grant, Federal Pell Grant, and Federal Work-Study programs. The College uses its own funds to provide additional grants, loans, and employment. The Financial Aid Office must receive the Free Application for Federal Student Aid (FAFSA) and the Financial Aid PROFILE processed by the College Scholarship Service and the Verification Worksheet by March 1 for students who plan to enter in September or by December 1 for midyear students.

Faculty

All of Wheelock's faculty members, many of whom are nationally recognized for their research, are actively engaged in classroom teaching. Faculty members also serve as academic advisers, as fieldwork supervisors, and, often, as advisers for student organizations. A student-faculty ratio of only 11:1 allows Wheelock professors to work closely with students both in and out of the classroom.

Student Government

The student government organization is the principal undergraduate governing body on campus. Its members are elected in the spring from the residence halls and from the day student population. The board meets weekly, often with the vice president for student development and the president of the College, to discuss issues of concern to the student body. In addition, each residence hall has its own governing body and makes its own policies and regulations. Through the Commuter Organization, commuting students participate in most aspects of student life. Students sit on many of the administrative committees of the College, including the Board of Trustees.

Admission Requirements

Wheelock seeks and admits women and men of all ages, from a variety of racial, geographic, ethnic, and economic backgrounds, who have the potential for creative, effective work with young children. Each admission decision is made after careful consideration of an applicant's academic record, interview, SAT I scores, written essay, recommendations, and work experience and involvement with children. On-campus interviews are highly recommended and can be arranged by mail or telephone. A telephone interview can be arranged for those students who are unable to visit the campus. The College has Open Houses in October and November for prospective students.

Application and Information

A complete Wheelock application consists of the Wheelock application form with a writing sample, one work and one academic recommendation, the school transcript, SAT I scores, and an application fee. The Admissions Committee is glad to review additional information that the candidate feels would be helpful to the committee in making the admission decision. Early decision applications are due on December 1, regular freshman applications on March 1, and transfer applications on April 15. Applicants can expect to hear from the Admissions Office by January 1 for early decision and within one month after regular applications are completed.

For more information about Wheelock, students should contact:

Lynne E. Dailey
Dean of Admissions
Wheelock College
200 The Riverway
Boston, Massachusetts 02215-4176
Telephone: 617-879-2206
              800-734-5212 (toll-free)
E-mail: undergrad@wheelock.edu
World Wide Web: http://www.wheelock.edu

Fieldwork in schools, hospitals, and social services settings is one of the focal points of education at Wheelock.

WHITE PINES COLLEGE
CHESTER, NEW HAMPSHIRE

The College

White Pines College offers students a foundation in the liberal and fine arts and a thorough professional preparation for careers in the commercial arts. The College offers programs of study in various professional majors, including art and illustration, graphic design and media arts, photography, and professional writing, as well as an associate degree in liberal studies. The programs are complementary. Students specialize in one area but also gain experience and knowledge in the intersections among art/illustration, design, photography, and the written word.

The low faculty-student ratio; artist/writer-in-residence programs; a robust program of guest lectures, exhibitions, art contests and shows, and internships; and relationships with professional associations complement and strengthen the College's offerings. The College's aim is to provide all students with the education, knowledge, skills, and experiences they need to become both thoughtful citizens and successful professionals.

Students at White Pines College find that the tranquil setting of the campus provides them with the kind of environment that is essential for creative inspiration. Yet the College is close to Manchester, Portsmouth, and Boston—cities that are rich in history and culture. Students travel frequently to these cities to work at internship sites, visit galleries and museums, and attend a diverse assortment of artistic performances.

The College is a private, coeducational, nonsectarian institution. White Pines College is accredited to award the Associate in Arts degree and the Bachelor of Arts degree by the Postsecondary Education Commission of the State of New Hampshire. It is accredited to award the Associate in Arts degree by the New England Association of Schools and Colleges, and it is in application to award the Bachelor of Arts degree; this application is currently under review.

White Pines College has a small enrollment of approximately 150 students. The average age of students is 19, although the age of students ranges from 17 to 55. Many of these students are residential, but a number of students choose to enroll as commuters. All resident students are full-time, but commuters may choose to enroll on a full-time or part-time basis. The classroom student-teacher ratio is very low, approximately 8:1, which allows for a great deal of personalized instruction. The College believes that this sort of interaction is critical given the arts focus of the institution.

There are three residence halls on the White Pines College campus. These buildings are single-sex residence halls with lounge areas, laundry facilities, and various recreational amenities. They are conveniently located near all of the academic and studio facilities.

The White Pines College Dining Commons provides meals for students, faculty and staff members, and visitors. Breakfast, lunch, and dinner are served in this facility seven days a week during the academic year and for portions of the summer session, as well.

Extracurricular programs at White Pines College are designed to enhance and enrich the learning experience, and students are expected to be active members of the campus community, both in and out of the classroom.

Location

White Pines College offers the aspiring artist a natural setting that nurtures both artistic and intellectual development. The campus is situated on 85 acres in the center of Chester, New Hampshire, a classic rural town near Manchester. The campus buildings are a mixture of restored eighteenth-century houses and new buildings that preserve the feel of Colonial New England while providing modern conveniences and spaces appropriate for classroom learning and artistic creation. Many of the houses in the vicinity of the College are beautifully maintained antique homes from the Colonial, Federal, and Victorian periods. The town square, only a few hundred yards from the White Pines campus, comprises a classic white Colonial church, the Town Hall, and a general store.

Majors and Degrees

White Pines College offers majors in art and illustration, graphic design and media arts, photography, and professional writing as well as an interdisciplinary arts option. The College also offers an Associate in Arts major in liberal studies.

Academic Program

The arts foundation courses at White Pines College introduce students to the majors offered and provide the concepts, vocabularies, and insight that are essential preparation for further study. Foundation courses emphasize verbal, visual, technical, and written skills. The foundation curriculum is carefully sequenced to provide varied and complementary courses that interact with other foundation courses as well as with the liberal arts component of the curriculum.

Close acquaintance with the liberal arts sharpens students' oral and written communication skills; it provides them with opportunities to explore historical, social, and scientific contexts and concepts; and it develops an appreciation of ideas and experiences that form the basis of all human endeavors. The liberal arts component of a White Pines College education begins by establishing a foundation in English composition, art history, and the humanities. Students then move on to explore three traditional and challenging areas of study—the sciences, the social sciences, and history—and explore the liberal arts in greater depth by choosing from a variety of course offerings, some of them at the upper level.

In the White Pines curriculum, courses in the liberal arts, fine arts, and commercial arts are integrated throughout the undergraduate experience with opportunities to learn from and interact with working professionals. The College's internship program and career planning resources prepare students to enter their chosen professional field with the appropriate knowledge, skills, experience, and preparation to succeed.

The programs leading to the Bachelor of Arts degree require a minimum of 120 credits; the Associate in Arts degree in liberal studies requires a minimum of 60 credits.

White Pines College follows a traditional academic calendar of two semesters. Summer-session courses are optional. Fall semester generally begins at the end of August; spring semester begins in early January.

Academic Facilities

At White Pines College, office, classroom, and living spaces on campus are relatively compact and create a comfortable environment for highly personalized interaction. The largest classroom holds no more than 40 persons, and classes at the College rarely exceed 15 students.

The Photography Studio is located in Douglas Barn and includes a darkroom with multiple workstations for black-and-white and color printing. Separate studio areas are provided. In the exhibit areas, each student has the opportunity to have photography selected for display for the benefit and enjoyment of fellow students and the community.

Wadleigh Library provides academic research support for the programs offered on campus. The facility has been designed so that it can accommodate twice the number of volumes currently in the collection. The library also provides individual study carrels, study space in the reference and other areas, meeting spaces for study groups, a computer design laboratory, and a small auditorium for lectures and presentations. Networked personal computers for student use also are located in Wadleigh Library.

The Graphic Design and Media Arts computer classroom provides Macintosh computers for graphic design, digital imaging, and advertising classes, using state-of-the-art software such as Quark Xpress and Adobe Photoshop. In addition, Wadleigh Library houses a number of personal computers and printers specifically for student use. These machines are equipped with current releases of word-processing software (Microsoft Word and Office 97).

Each student is permitted to have one car on campus, and free parking is provided. The College provides occasional transportation to Manchester, Portsmouth, and Boston and to recreational sites.

Costs

In 2000–01, tuition for full-time students is $10,100. Room and board (double room) are $5500. Tuition per credit hour for full-time students, part-time students (8 to 11 credits per semester), and study-abroad students is $340. Semester charges include a bookstore deposit for nonphotography majors of $350, a bookstore deposit for photography majors of $650, a semester service fee of $125, and a freshman orientation fee of $90.

Financial Aid

White Pines College is dedicated to helping its students determine the best possible means for financing their education and offers advice to students and their families regardless of income level. White Pines makes every effort possible to assist students who wish to attend, through its programs of need- and merit-based financial assistance. These programs consist of loans, grants, work, and scholarships. The College offers opportunities through federal financial aid programs (Federal Pell Grants, FSEOG, Federal Perkins Loans, Federal Stafford Student Loans, Federal Work-Study, and Federal PLUS loans) and institutional financial aid programs. The College administers an attractive institutional scholarship program, offering scholarships ranging from $3000 to full tuition for up to four years of study.

Faculty

There are 8 full-time faculty members at White Pines College and 12 part-time faculty members. Faculty members participate in advising students in curriculum and career planning and act in supervisory capacities for internships.

Student Government

The Student Government, in consultation with the Director of Student Life, plans and schedules activities and events for the academic year. The campus calendar offers numerous events, including dramatic performances, ski trips, art and photography exhibits, dances, music recitals, film screenings and discussions, and lectures and discussion groups concerning important social and political issues.

Admission Requirements

White Pines College is a small college by design and enrolls small classes of highly talented women and men in its Bachelor of Arts and Associate in Arts programs. Applicants for admission to either program are judged by many criteria, including academic performance and potential; artistic achievements and potential; extracurricular accomplishments and activities; communication skills, both written and verbal; standardized test scores (SAT I or ACT); energy and determination; and quality of character.

Standardized tests, such as the SAT I or ACT, are recommended but not required. The College admits freshmen and transfer students and seeks a diverse student body.

Freshman admissions procedures involve submission of a completed application form; providing official copies of transcripts from all secondary schools and colleges or universities attended; submitting three letters of recommendation and the required personal statement (additional writing samples may be included); forwarding SAT I or ACT scores, if available; submitting the $25 application fee; and participating in an interview with an Admissions Office representative. The interview may take place in person or via telephone.

Application and Information

White Pines College operates on a rolling admissions policy, meaning that decisions are made on applications as they become complete. There is no application deadline; however, students are encouraged to submit applications no later than May 1 for fall admission and no later than December 15 for spring admission.

For more information, students should contact:

Director of Admissions
White Pines College
40 Chester Street
Chester, New Hampshire 03036
Telephone: 603-887-4401
          800-974-6372 (toll-free)
World Wide Web: http://www.Whitepines.edu

WHITMAN COLLEGE
WALLA WALLA, WASHINGTON

The College
Challenging its students to excel in the sciences, the humanities, the arts, and the social sciences, Whitman College combines the educational values of the best liberal arts colleges of the East with the outdoor frankness and vigor of the Pacific Northwest. Since 1859, men and women have chosen this private, independent college because of its commitment to undergraduate education. With just 1,300 students and an average class size of 14, Whitman encourages students to be active participants in their own education. In 1913, the College led the nation by requiring all undergraduates to successfully complete a comprehensive examination in the major field of study. The installation of a chapter of Phi Beta Kappa in 1919, the first in the Northwest, marked the general recognition of the high quality of Whitman's curriculum and the standards of teaching and learning that distinguish the College. More than 60 percent of Whitman's students enroll in a graduate program of some type within five years of earning their undergraduate degree.

The current enrollment includes students from forty states and thirty countries. A residential college, Whitman has approximately 75 percent of its students residing on campus. A variety of residence hall living options are available, including coeducational housing, apartment-style housing, twelve special interest houses, four fraternity houses, and an all-women's residence hall that houses, among others, the members of five sororities. Freshmen and sophomores must live on campus and may indicate a preference for a particular residence hall. Whitman has an intensely active student body. The College offers more than 100 interest groups and clubs and has a nationally recognized debate team, a highly acclaimed theater program, and a music department that includes sixteen musical groups and produces an opera every other year. The College fields twenty varsity teams (ten for men and ten for women) and offers ten club sports and twelve intramural activities.

Location
Whitman is located in Walla Walla, a historic community of 30,000, nestled in the foothills of the Blue Mountains of southeastern Washington. With rich natural terrain at its doorstep, outdoor activities abound. These include cross-country and downhill skiing, backpacking, hiking, kayaking, rafting, and rock-climbing. The Walla Walla Valley has four distinct seasons and a dry, sunny climate. Whitman imports a wide array of cultural activities to campus, including concerts, art exhibits, forums, internationally renowned speakers and performers, and cinema arts films. Students also perform with the community symphony, browse in the area's seventeen art galleries, and act in the community theater.

Majors and Degrees
Whitman College confers the B.A. degree with departmental majors in anthropology, art (history and studio), biology, chemistry, economics, English, foreign languages and literatures (French, German, or Spanish), geology, history, mathematics, music, philosophy, physics, politics, psychology, sociology, and theater. Combined or interdepartmental major study programs are offered in Asian studies, astronomy-geology, biology-geology, chemistry-biology, chemistry-geology, economics-mathematics, environmental studies (emphasis in biology, chemistry, economics, geology, physics, politics, or sociology), geology-physics, mathematics-computer science, mathematics-physics, and physics-astronomy. Minor study options are available in each of the departmental programs, as well as American ethnic studies, Chinese, classics, computer science, education, environmental studies, gender studies, Japanese, physical education, religion, rhetoric and public address, sports medicine, sports studies/recreation and athletics, and studies in world literature. Students with special interests may develop combined or interdepartmental major programs, subject to faculty approval. Students may also study to earn a teaching certificate. Whitman offers outstanding cooperative programs in engineering with Caltech, Columbia, Duke, University of Washington, and Washington University in St. Louis; in environmental management or forestry with Duke; in law with Columbia School of Law; in international studies and international business with the Monterey Institute of International Studies; in education with the Bank Street College of Education; and in computer science and oceanography with the University of Washington.

Academic Program
Whitman's primary goal is to provide an atmosphere in which students can learn how to learn. At the heart of Whitman's academic curriculum is the general studies program, through which students learn how to develop intellectual skills, reason, read critically and write effectively, understand humanity's cultural and historical roots, fashion standards for judgment of basic values, and lead others. The required general studies program consists of a freshman core and distribution requirements. The freshman core is an interdisciplinary seminar with extensive reading, writing, and discussion. To satisfy the distribution requirement, students complete at least 6 semester credits in six of the following areas: descriptive science; fine arts; history and literature; language, writing, and rhetoric; philosophy and religion; physical science and mathematics; and social science. Every candidate for a bachelor's degree must complete at least 124 credits in appropriate courses with acceptable grades. Honors programs are available for qualified students. Whitman helps fund student research, and approximately 125 students present professional-level research at the College's Annual Undergraduate Conference. Advanced placement and a maximum of 8 semester credits in each subject area are allowed for scores of 5 and 4 on the College Board's Advanced Placement tests. (The economics, English, and history departments accept only a score of 5.) Whitman observes a two-semester calendar with a three-day student-run interim program in early January.

Off-Campus Arrangements
Whitman is noted for its strong study-abroad and domestic off-campus study programs. Each year, approximately 40 percent of the junior class studies in programs in thirty overseas locations. In addition to academic course work, many students pursue internships for credit or research opportunities. The College is formally affiliated with the Institute for the International Education of Students, which has programs in Australia, Austria, England, France, Germany, Italy, and Spain. The School for Field Studies has opportunities in Australia, Canada, the Caribbean, Costa Rica, East Anglia, Kenya, and Mexico. Students may also study at the Universities of Manchester and York in England; St. Andrews University in Scotland; Doshisha University in Kyoto, Japan; and the University of Otago in Dunedin, New Zealand and at programs in Argentina, China, Costa Rica, Greece, Hungary, Italy, Ireland, Japan, Mexico, Spain, Sri Lanka, Taiwan, and Zimbabwe. Each year, 4 Whitman students or graduates are selected to teach English to university students in Kunming or Xi'an in the People's Republic of China. The College offers urban-semester study and internships in Chicago, Philadelphia, and Washington, D.C. Students may participate in one of more than 300 science research internships available through the College.

Academic Facilities
To enhance Whitman's learning environment, students have access to exceptional facilities and technological and cultural

resources. The recently expanded 24-hour Penrose Memorial Library houses more than 320,000 volumes, 550,000 government documents, and 2,000 subscriptions. In addition, the ORBIS network provides access to approximately 3.5 million volumes that can be delivered to Whitman in three or fewer days. Olin Hall of Humanities and Fine Arts features an audiovisual center, extensive art studios, foreign language labs, and the Donald Sheehan Art Gallery; another addition houses the computing equipment and is the center for the campuswide fiber-optic network. The student-computer ratio is 14:1. Maxey Hall, the center for the social sciences, includes a natural history and anthropology laboratory, a 350-seat auditorium, and animal demonstration labs. The Hall of Science houses a sophisticated physics lecture-demonstration hall and laboratory and support facilities for two electron microscopes. The hall also contains laboratories for botany, ecology, vertebrate biology, physiology and developmental biology, and biochemistry and genetics; preparation and display areas for the herbarium and the preserved animal collections; a planetarium; a seismograph; and large, well-equipped student research laboratories. The Frances Geiger Hunter Conservatory, which houses communication arts and technology facilities, includes videoconferencing facilities and multimedia labs. Whitman operates an observatory located several miles from campus as well as a 27-acre mountain property serving as an environmental studies field station. The Hall of Music houses an acoustically perfect performance hall and more than twenty-five practice rooms. Other major facilities are the Harper Joy Theatre, a 315-seat drama center, and Cordiner Hall, a 1,400-seat concert auditorium that features a 3,000-pipe Holtkamp organ. In the next two years, Whitman will have a new campus center and a new wing to its Science Building.

Costs

Tuition and fees for 2000–01 are $21,550. Room and board are $6090. The estimated cost of books, supplies, and incidentals is $1000. Associated student body fees are $192.

Financial Aid

Financial aid offers are usually a combination of scholarship and grant aid, low-interest loans, and employment opportunities. In 1999–2000, Whitman provided almost $15 million to 85 percent of its students. Sixty percent of Whitman students qualified for need-based aid. About half of the students are employed part-time on campus. Whitman also has an extensive achievement scholarship program that rewards students with exceptional academic records. Awards range from $4000 to $8000 and are renewable for four years. Special awards are also available for students with exceptional academic achievement or talent in art, music, debate, theater, and leadership. To apply for financial aid, students must submit the Free Application for Federal Student Aid (FAFSA) and the CSS PROFILE form. Early decision candidates should apply for financial aid by January 5; regular admission and transfer admission candidates must apply by February 1. Spring semester candidates must apply by December 1.

Faculty

Whitman College's faculty is composed of men and women selected, retained, and promoted chiefly for their demonstrated effectiveness as teachers as well as for their leadership in their fields. Ninety-three percent of the faculty hold a doctoral degree, and virtually all serve as academic advisers. The student-faculty ratio is 10:1. Recognized nationally for faculty accessibility, Whitman offers personal attention outside the classroom that differentiates its education from others. At Whitman, students collaborate with professors on research projects, compete with them on the athletics field, serve with them on College committees, and dine with them in their homes. In the past five years, Whitman faculty members have distinguished themselves by receiving awards, honors, and fellowships from the National Institute of Mental Health, National Endowment for the Humanities, Battelle Research Institute, Washington State Arts Commission, Burlington Northern Foundation, Department of Health and Human Services, and Department of Energy.

Student Government

The College encourages students to participate and to take leadership roles in self-governing campus organizations. The largest of these is the Associated Students of Whitman College (ASWC), of which every student is a member. The ASWC acts through an elected student congress and executive council and is responsible for the *Pioneer* (the weekly student newspaper), choral contest, homecoming, Renaissance Faire, radio station KWCW-FM, Interim, and many concerts, presenters, and social events.

Admission Requirements

Whitman is a highly selective college that seeks academic excellence and diversity within its student body. Competition for admission is keen; 64 percent of entering freshmen rank in the top 10 percent of their high school class. The Admission Committee looks for evidence of demonstrated intellectual achievement, motivation, creativity, responsibility, and maturity. The middle 50 percent of the class that entered Whitman in 1999 scored in the following ranges on the SAT I: 610 to 710 verbal and 600 to 700 math. The minimum TOEFL scores for international students are 220 on the computer-based test and 560 on the paper test; the minimum ELPT score was 960. The following pattern of high school subjects is recommended: 4 years of English, 4 of mathematics, 3 of laboratory science, 2 of history or social science, and 2 of foreign language. Students who have decided early in their senior year that Whitman is their first choice are encouraged to apply for admission under the Early Decision Plan.

Application and Information

The application deadlines and notification dates for admission to Whitman are as follows: early decision candidates apply by November 15 or January 1 and receive notification of admission in December or January; regular admission and transfer candidates for the fall semester apply by February 1 and receive notification by April 1; spring semester candidates apply by December 1 and receive notification by December 15. Freshman candidates are required to submit the following credentials: the Common Application (for selective colleges), School Report Form, secondary school transcript, test scores (SAT I or ACT), Personal Supplement (Whitman's own form), a teacher recommendation, and an application fee of $45. International applicants must also submit a TOEFL, ELPT, or APIEL score and the College Board's International Student Financial Aid Application and Certification. For more information, students should contact:

Office of Admission
Whitman College
515 Boyer Avenue
Walla Walla, Washington 99362-2046

Telephone: 509-527-5176
Fax: 509-527-4967
E-mail: admission@whitman.edu
World Wide Web: http://www.whitman.edu

Flag football brings fans to Ankeny Field.

WHITTIER COLLEGE
WHITTIER, CALIFORNIA

The College

Whittier is a small, selective liberal arts college devoted to helping people lead productive, fulfilling lives by giving them the skills and abilities to make a difference. Whittier was founded in 1887 by the Religious Society of Friends, also known as the Quakers. Though the school is now religiously independent, it still cherishes the values its founders placed on honesty, integrity, tolerance, love for learning, and decision by consensus. At Whittier, every person matters, and matters equally.

Whittier is recognized as one of the most diverse liberal arts colleges in America. Of its 1,300 undergraduates, more than a third are from outside of California and almost half are members of minority groups. Approximately one third of incoming freshmen are the first in their families to go to college. Whittier delivers a traditional liberal arts education adapted to the needs of a new generation and encourages students to adapt their education still further by finding new ways to solve the world's problems.

The National Endowment for the Humanities has designated the Whittier curriculum as a national model for small colleges. The education is organized around active and interactive learning that involves discussion and participation as much as formal lectures. Students can choose between the Liberal Education Program, which emphasizes combining the insights of different disciplines, and the Whittier Scholars Program, which allows students to design individualized degree programs. Whittier believes that giving students a hand in their own education is the best way to prepare them for taking control of their lives after graduation.

Whittier is among a select group of colleges and universities that offer a residential Faculty Masters Program modeled on Cambridge and Oxford. Senior faculty members and their families live on campus with the students in spacious homes designed especially for programming and entertaining. By living and learning together, students and faculty members at Whittier are able to take education beyond the classroom and apply it to life.

More than seventy clubs and organizations are active on campus. There are twenty-two varsity sports for men and women at the NCAA Division III level; a comprehensive intramural and club sports program; a newspaper; academic, ethnic, and religious organizations; and nine societies, similar to traditional fraternities and sororities.

The College is fully accredited. Whittier confers the Juris Doctor through its School of Law, which is accredited by the American Bar Association, the Association of American Law Schools, the California State Bar of Examiners, and the Western Association of Schools and Colleges.

Location

Los Angeles borders but does not invade the sunny atmosphere of the 95-acre campus. The College is nestled in the La Puente hills in a classic, Midwestern-style town. Two blocks from campus, students enjoy the restaurants and shops of tree-shaded Uptown Whittier. Los Angeles's downtown financial district, museums, and libraries are within a half hour's drive, and southern California's beaches, deserts, and mountains are not much farther.

Majors and Degrees

Whittier College grants the Bachelor of Arts degree with fields of concentration in art, biochemistry, biology, business administration, chemistry, economics, English, French, history, mathematics, music, philosophy, physical education and recreation, physics, political science, psychology, religious studies, social work, sociology, Spanish, and theater arts. The education department offers six teaching credentials. Interdisciplinary studies are offered in anthropology, child development, comparative cultures, environmental science, international studies, and mathematics–business administration; others may be individually designed through the Whittier Scholars Program. Centered on the liberal arts, the Whittier curriculum offers career-related programs to prepare students for future professional and postgraduate work. Preprofessional programs are offered in such areas as athletic training, dentistry, education, engineering, law, medicine, optometry, pharmacy, physical therapy, social work, and veterinary science.

A 3-2 program in liberal arts and engineering is offered in cooperation with Washington University in St. Louis, Boston University, Case Western Reserve, and the Universities of Minnesota and Southern California.

Academic Program

The unusual flexibility of the Whittier curriculum permits substantial academic freedom combined with personal responsibility. The curriculum features team-taught and paired courses, natural arenas for heated discussion and mind-opening challenges. The College recognizes, encourages, and responds to different learning patterns by providing classroom, independent, field, and foreign studies. The academic calendar is essentially a 4-1-4 arrangement, consisting of two 15-week terms—in the fall and spring—separated by a 4-week January term. Opportunities for experiential learning and exploration into special areas are available.

The College requires that students complete 120 semester credits for graduation. The standard degree program requires that a student complete liberal education offerings for a total of 41 credits in seven areas. In addition, all students must complete a 30-credit-hour major and fulfill the College's writing requirement.

For students who prefer more participation in the planning of their academic program and want to have a larger voice in their curriculum, the College offers the Whittier Scholars Program. Under the guidance of a faculty mentor or adviser, each student develops an educational program that culminates in a senior project. Each student assumes personal responsibility for developing his or her educational program.

Students may obtain credit through Advanced Placement tests and International Baccalaureate Diploma examinations. Class honors and honors at commencement are also awarded in recognition of academic achievement. Approximately 30 percent of Whittier's graduates go directly to graduate and professional schools, while many more pursue graduate work after beginning their careers.

Off-Campus Arrangements

Whittier's College-in-Copenhagen, Denmark, is now in its fortieth year as a study-abroad program. Students who take part in this program during the fall term are taught in English, live with Danish families, and travel extensively throughout Europe. Programs for credit are available at more than sixty universities in eighteen countries throughout the world through a consortium agreement with the University of Miami. Credit is also available through the SITA consortium in India. Students may also make arrangements to study in programs sponsored by other institutions in approximately eighty countries across the globe.

Academic Facilities

The Wardman Library has facilities for 400 people and contains more than 225,000 volumes, 1,350 periodicals, special collections, and microprint materials. It is supplemented by a special science library. The Whittier College Media Center adds new dimensions to teaching and learning through such services as closed-circuit television, audiovisual equipment, and extensive collections of audiotapes, videotapes, and films. The John Stauffer Science Center has classrooms, laboratories, and equipment for the natural sciences. It houses the Keck Image Processing Center, a botanical center, an electron microscope, and the Nobert Erteszek Student Computer Center, which contains a Digital UNIX Alphaserver and 150 Apple and IBM computers.

The Broadoaks School, a teaching center and laboratory preschool for young children, is a major resource for the early childhood development program.

The Shannon Center for the Performing Arts provides a state-of-the-art setting for the many concerts and main-stage productions produced by the faculty and students each year. The arts are further enhanced through separate facilities for studio art and the Peasley Center of Music, which provides a location for group and individual instruction in musical performance and theory. The 3,000-seat Harris Amphitheatre is the site of outdoor theatrical and musical productions, academic convocations, and commencement ceremonies.

Costs

The annual cost in 1999–2000 for tuition was $19,830; fees, $400; room and board, $6730 (average); books, $650; incidental expenses, $1360; and transportation, $580. The estimated total cost for all students was $29,550. All basic charges may be paid in installments.

Financial Aid

Three types of programs exist to help students pursue a Whittier College education: scholarships, which recognize outstanding academic achievement, leadership, service, or talent; financing plans, which assist families that pay the costs themselves; and need-based aid, for families that need help in order to meet costs. Academic Merit Scholarships range from $2000 up to full tuition, and financial need is not a consideration in granting these awards. The priority filing date for need-based aid is February 15.

Faculty

The focus of the College is on undergraduate education. There are two graduate programs, in education and law. In the College, there are 93 full-time faculty members, and 93 percent of them hold the terminal degree. In the Law School, all of the 27 full-time faculty members hold the terminal degree.

Faculty members consider undergraduate teaching and advising to be their highest priority, and there is not a separate graduate faculty. An annual teaching excellence award is given, and all full-time faculty members serve as mentors to students as part of the award-winning student advisement program. In six of the past seven years, faculty members have received advising excellence awards from the National Academic Advising Association.

A distinctive feature of faculty involvement in student life is the Faculty Masters Program, wherein faculty families live on campus in beautiful, spacious homes and offer intellectually and culturally stimulating programs several times each week. Most other faculty members live in proximity to the campus and host classes or other student activities in their homes.

In addition to their uncommon commitment to high-quality undergraduate teaching, Whittier faculty members are nationally and internationally recognized scholars, publishing important books and winning prestigious, competitive awards, such as NSF and NEH fellowships and the Graves award. The student-faculty ratio of about 13:1 ensures small classes. The College attracts many guest faculty, including those in the Woodrow Wilson National Fellowship Foundation Visiting Fellows Program.

Student Government

Students elect their own representatives to student government and, through them, control their own government and budget. Through a president, council of representatives, and committee system, they share responsibility for planning all social and cultural activities. Students largely govern their own nonacademic lives as well, including residence hall living. They actively participate and vote on most committees of the faculty, and their representatives attend regular faculty meetings. The College is governed by consensus.

Admission Requirements

Whittier seeks students with sound academic promise, motivation, and strong personal qualifications. The admission committee makes its decision through an assessment of individual qualities, talents, and interests as well as by the more common standards of measurement. Transfers from junior and community colleges as well as from other colleges or universities are considered. A careful evaluation is made of each applicant's academic record, course of study, personal recommendations, and school activities. A personal interview, while not required, is strongly recommended. At the time of admission, most freshman candidates have had 4 years of English, 3 or 4 years of mathematics, 2 or 3 years of social studies, 2 or 3 years of one foreign language, and 2 or 3 years of laboratory science. Honors, international baccalaureate, and advanced placement courses add further strength to an applicant's record.

Application and Information

Entrance to Whittier is possible during the fall for freshman applicants and fall or spring for transfer applicants. The priority deadline for applicants for fall is February 1. Early action candidates should submit complete applications by December 1.

For further information about admission and Whittier College, students should contact:

Office of Admission
Whittier College
13406 East Philadelphia Avenue
P.O. Box 634
Whittier, California 90608-0634
Telephone: 562-907-4238
Fax: 562-907-4870
E-mail: admission@whittier.edu
World Wide Web: http://www.whittier.edu

WHITWORTH COLLEGE
SPOKANE, WASHINGTON

The College

Whitworth College is a private, Christian liberal arts college affiliated with the Presbyterian Church (U.S.A.). Whitworth's mission is to provide its diverse student body an education of the mind and the heart, equipping its graduates to honor God, follow Christ, and serve humanity. This mission is carried out by a community of Christian scholars committed to teaching excellence and the integration of faith and learning.

The campus has forty buildings, mostly of red brick, which border the parklike Loop, including the Harriet Cheney Cowles Memorial Library, Cowles Memorial Auditorium, Schumacher Health Center, and Dixon Hall. The Seeley Mudd Chapel, located at the heart of the campus, has an expanded worship area, seminar rooms, and staff offices. The Whitworth Fieldhouse and Aquatic Center has a 25-meter, six-lane pool with a movable bulkhead and a 15-foot diving pool. The campus center, which houses the bookstore, post office, snack bar, and student media, student government offices, and a 450-seat dining hall, was completed in August 1998.

The College's 1,500 full-time undergraduate students come from thirty-one states and twenty-six countries. Nearly 65 percent of the full-time undergraduate students live on campus in eight residential areas that range from traditional dormitory buildings to cottage-size minidorms. Residence life is considered an essential part of a student's growth process, and living groups are encouraged, with the help of trained residence staff, to design their own living environments. Peer leaders in each residence hall include resident assistants, health coordinators, resident chaplains, cultural diversity advocates, and career information advisers.

Also serving the personal development of each student are the chaplain's and Student Life offices. Religious life on campus is centered on midweek chapel; Hosanna, a singing praise service; and Thursday evening Compline, a quiet contemplative gathering. Bible studies, discussion groups, and opportunities for service also originate in the office of the chaplain. A twice-weekly Forum, when the entire campus community gathers to hear a speaker or a program on a challenging, thought-provoking topic, provides a view of events from an off-campus perspective. The Student Life Program assists all students in adjusting to college life and defining individual goals by providing counseling, tutoring, services for international students and members of minority groups, job placement, career planning, and aptitude testing.

Whitworth College holds membership in the NCAA Division III and is a member of the Northwest Conference of Independent Colleges. Varsity teams for men compete in baseball, basketball, cross-country, football, soccer, swimming, tennis, and track and field. Women's teams compete in basketball, cross-country, soccer, softball, swimming, tennis, track and field, and volleyball. A broad intramural program, as well as club sports, offers athletic competition to everyone on campus, including faculty members and staff, and fitness evaluation services are available to all. Whitworth believes that physical development is an essential element in each student's pursuit of personal wholeness.

Location

Whitworth College is located just 15 minutes from downtown Spokane on a scenic, wooded 200-acre site, surrounded by quiet suburban residential areas. Spokane, a metropolitan area with a population of 355,000, is surrounded by an extraordinary recreation area, containing thousands of acres of state and national forests, four major ski resorts, and more than seventy-five lakes within an hour's drive. The city is the commercial and cultural center for more than a million people, and the size of this market area is reflected in the excellence of Spokane's many facilities and services, hospitals, shopping centers, and transportation.

Majors and Degrees

Whitworth awards Bachelor of Arts and Bachelor of Science degrees. Majors are available in accounting, American studies, art, arts administration, biology, business management, chemistry, communication, computer science, economics, education (elementary and secondary certification programs, with academic department emphases), English, French, history, international business, international political economy, international studies, journalism, mathematics, music (applied, education, or special emphasis), nursing, peace studies, philosophy, physical education, physics, political science, psychology, religion, sociology, Spanish, speech communication, sports medicine, and theater arts.

Preprofessional programs are offered in dentistry, engineering (3-2), law, medical technology, medicine, ministry, occupational therapy, pharmacy, physical therapy, and veterinary medicine.

Academic Program

Whitworth's liberal arts philosophy is embodied in its curriculum, which is designed to lead students beyond content to competence. Within a Christian environment, students are encouraged to prepare for their future by developing responsibility, confidence, maturity, and initiative along with academic skills. The College believes that academic growth occurs best in concert with personal and spiritual growth, and it has focused attention equally on both areas of development.

To earn a bachelor's degree, students must complete 130 semester hours, including courses that fulfill both major and general graduation requirements. In addition to attaining depth in a major field, each student acquires the breadth of a liberal arts education through the interdisciplinary core studies, which emphasize the integrated nature of knowledge.

The College's 4-1-4 calendar provides time for intensive study in a single subject during the month of January, often in an off-campus setting.

Off-Campus Arrangements

January terms and full semesters of off-campus study are available to encourage students to relate their education to real-life environments. Urban studies in San Francisco; international studies in Europe, Latin America, South Africa, and the Middle East; music studies in Rome and Munich; and rural studies in various locales are offered to augment classroom learning. Students are not sent to these lands or areas to travel as tourists; they are accompanied by faculty members who guide their research and studies and join them in experiencing the culture to the greatest degree possible.

Exchange-student arrangements are available with colleges and universities in Germany, Hong Kong, Japan, Korea, Mexico, the People's Republic of China, and Thailand.

Cooperative education/internship opportunities are available for Whitworth students in Spokane or in almost any area of the country. For instance, political studies majors routinely intern in Washington, D.C. The co-op/internship program enables students to gain some actual experience and build contacts in a chosen field prior to graduation. A January-term internship often leads to declaring a major, a modification of a career goal, or, just as often, a job opportunity.

Academic Facilities

With its state-of-the-art information retrieval technology and a capacity exceeding 250,000 volumes, the Harriet Cheney Cowles Memorial Library provides students and faculty members with a superb research facility. The library's computerized card catalogs and databases also provide access to the holdings of other libraries in the region and across the country. In addition, the library is home to three computer labs, six group study rooms, climate-controlled archives, a music library, a curriculum lab for teacher education, audiovisual services, and a Writing Center.

The Whitworth Music Building has the most advanced facilities available for music education. Laboratories for chemistry, physics, and biology are maintained in the Eric Johnston Science Center. A generous grant from the National Science Foundation will provide funds to upgrade these laboratories. The Fine Arts building contains studios for drawing, painting, and pottery and houses the John Koehler Gallery, which is used for student shows. The Dr. James P. Evans Sports Medicine Center includes a complete hydrotherapy center, ultrasound equipment, and a variety of ergometers and isokinetic machines.

Costs

Tuition for the 2000–01 academic year is $16,700, room and board are $5500, and fees are $224. Books and personal expenses are about $2400.

Financial Aid

Whitworth College has a comprehensive aid program for more than 85 percent of its students. The Free Application for Federal Student Aid (FAFSA) is used to determine a student's financial need for awarding grants, scholarships, loans, and work-study. Academic scholarships and fine arts talent awards are available to exceptional students regardless of their demonstrated need. Student employment, under the Federal Work-Study Program, is available on campus for up to 20 hours per week through the Student Employment Office, which provides placement assistance for off-campus jobs as well. The following non-need-based federal loan programs are available to Whitworth students and their families: the Federal Unsubsidized Stafford Loan and the Federal PLUS loan for parents.

Faculty

The Whitworth faculty is made up of 86 full-time professors, 60 of whom have earned either a Ph.D. or the terminal degree in their field. These scholars have chosen to devote themselves to teaching undergraduates. They come from a variety of Christian denominations but are united in their enthusiasm for the Christian faith and its central role in one's life choices. Because the College has a student-faculty ratio of 16:1, professors are accessible and interested in each student's progress and problems.

Student Government

A full-time student activities coordinator works with the elected members of the Associated Students of Whitworth College and the appointed student managers to plan and carry out College activities, which range from Homecoming festivities to mountain climbs to political lobbying. Student government is responsible for most of the social programs on campus. Individual students are full-fledged members, along with faculty members, of various councils that formulate major campus policies.

Admission Requirements

Whitworth selects its students from those applicants who, by reason of their academic achievement, measured aptitudes, and academic interests, demonstrate their ability to succeed at a liberal arts college. Generally, 4 years of English; 3 years each of history, science (including lab science), and mathematics; and 2 years of a foreign language constitute a competitive college-preparatory program for a high school applicant. Transfer students are also welcome to apply; Whitworth grants junior standing and a waiver of most general graduation requirements to students who have earned an approved Associate of Arts degree at any Washington community college.

Application and Information

High-achieving students who have decided that Whitworth College is their first choice are eligible to apply for early action. The early action application deadline is November 30. For regular admission, the deadline is March 1. Campus visits are recommended from September through May while classes are in session.

Application for admission may be made by submitting a completed Whitworth application form, an evaluation by the student's high school counselor or principal, a current transcript of high school work, and ACT or SAT I scores.

For further information and for application forms, prospective students should contact:

Office of Admissions
Whitworth College
West 300 Hawthorne Road
Spokane, Washington 99251-0106

Telephone: 509-777-3212
           800-533-4668 (toll-free)
E-mail: admission@whitworth.edu
World Wide Web: http://www.whitworth.edu

Whitworth students represent twenty-nine states and twenty-four countries.

WIDENER UNIVERSITY
CHESTER, PENNSYLVANIA

The University

Widener University is a multicampus, comprehensive, nationally and internationally recognized teaching institution located in and accredited by both the commonwealth of Pennsylvania and the state of Delaware. The University offers more than sixty majors and more than ninety-five programs of study leading to the associate, baccalaureate, master's, and doctoral degrees. There are currently 7,500 students, including 1,850 graduate students, 2,250 full-time undergraduate students, of whom 1300 are residential students, and 1,700 evening undergraduate students. Wilmington, Delaware, and Harrisburg, Pennsylvania, are also the sites of the Widener University School of Law where 1,700 students are enrolled.

Learning doesn't end in the classroom. Widener offers both diversity and excellent quality in its extracurricular activities. More than eighty student organizations are recognized on the Widener campus, including student government, musical groups, honor societies, fraternities, sororities, academic and professional associations, publications, social and recreational clubs, and an FM radio station, recording studio, and TV production studio. Widener offers eleven intercollegiate sports for women and eleven for men as well as six intramural sports. Traditional residence halls, apartments, and theme houses are available. Housing is guaranteed for all four years.

Expanded and renovated in 1997, University Center houses student and faculty dining rooms, a convenience store, TV lounge, post office, bookstore, a bank branch, and a fitness center. Academic Center North and Cottee Hall are the newest academic buildings, constructed in 1988 and 1993, respectively. ACN houses the School of Hospitality Management and the Scott Center for Computing Technology. Cottee houses facilities for the graduate-level physical therapy program. The Schwartz Physical Education Center is a modern, all-weather facility that features an athletic stadium.

Location

Located in Delaware County, Pennsylvania, Widener's main campus is easily accessible from I-95, I-476, and the Philadelphia Airport and is an easy commute from southern New Jersey or Wilmington, Delaware. The University is only 15 minutes from historic Philadelphia, 2 hours from either New York City or Washington, D.C., and 1½ hours from Baltimore or the New Jersey beaches.

Majors and Degrees

Widener offers the degrees of Bachelor of Arts and Bachelor of Science in the following fields: accounting, anthropology, behavioral science, biology, chemistry, communication studies, computer science, criminal justice, economics, education, engineering, English, environmental science, government and politics, history, hospitality management, humanities, international business, international relations, management, mathematics, modern languages, nursing, physics, political economy, psychology, science administration, science education, social work, sociology, and sport management. Preprofessional programs include chiropractic, dentistry, law, medicine, occupational therapy, optometry, osteopathy, podiatry, physical therapy, and veterinary medicine.

Dual majors may also be taken in many areas, and a multidisciplinary (open) major may be created by any degree-seeking candidate in consultation with a faculty adviser. Freshmen who are undecided about a major may elect the Exploratory Studies program during the first year. In addition, options exist in the School of Business Administration and in the School of Engineering for accelerated programs leading to combined undergraduate and either M.B.A. or Master in Engineering degrees.

The Center for Education offers two options for students seeking certification in elementary and/or early childhood education: the bachelor's degree in elementary and/or early childhood education or the bachelor's degree in an academic major with certification. Multiple secondary certifications include bilingual education, biology, chemistry, earth/space science, English, French, general science, math, physics, social studies, and Spanish.

Academic Program

The distribution of required courses and the quantitative requirements are set by the various undergraduate units (the College of Arts and Sciences, the School of Engineering, the School of Human Service Professions, the School of Business Administration, the School of Hospitality Management, and the School of Nursing). All students are required to complete a minimum of 12 semester hours in each of the three areas of humanities, social science, and science/technology. (A semester hour consists of 1 hour per week in the classroom each semester or 2 to 3 hours per week in laboratory or fieldwork each semester.) An overall academic average of at least 2.0 is required for graduation. In addition to satisfying all other requirements for any degree, a candidate must complete in residence at Widener the final 45 semester hours required for that degree.

High school students who participate in the Advanced Placement (AP) Program of the College Board and earn a score of 3 or better on specific AP examinations receive degree credit for the subject or subjects concerned upon submission of the examination results. Any student may earn up to 23 semester hours of credit through successful scores on the general examinations of the College-Level Examination Program (CLEP). To receive credit, the student must have accumulated no prior credits in the subject area of the specific general examination. No credit is given for the general examination in English. Credit may also be earned through any of the seventeen CLEP subject examinations that correspond to Widener University courses. There is no limit to the number of credits a student may earn through the CLEP subject examinations. However, the final 45 credits for any undergraduate degree must be completed at Widener University.

Widener operates on a two-semester calendar. The first semester begins in early September and ends before Christmas; the second semester runs from mid-January to early May. The summer sessions include one presession of three weeks and two regular sessions of five weeks each, providing fully accredited courses in economics and management, engineering, the humanities, the physical sciences, and the social sciences.

Off-Campus Arrangements

Optional four-year cooperative education programs are offered in engineering and business. These programs are designed to augment the curricula with two periods of full-time, off-campus work experience (totaling twelve months of employment), while enabling the student to earn a bachelor's degree within the normal four-year period. Off-campus field experience is also offered in such areas of study as community psychology and social work.

Academic Facilities

The focal point of the main campus is Wolfgram Memorial Library, which currently houses more than 238,000 volumes of bound books and journals. There are also 575,000 volumes in the library of the Widener University School of Law. Other facilities include Kirkbride Hall, a four-story science/engineering laboratory building; Kapelski Learning Center, a modern classroom facility; and Alumni Auditorium, built with funds donated by the Alumni Association, housing the Burt Mustin Memorial Theatre, a 400-seat, air-conditioned auditorium for dramatics, lectures, movies, and mass meetings.

Costs

Tuition for the 2000–01 academic year for most students is $17,950. The cost of room and board ranges from $6750 to $7900.

Families who wish to spread the payment of tuition over an eight-month period may take advantage of the Widener Payment Plan through the Business Office.

Financial Aid

The goal of Widener's financial aid program is to make sure that every qualified student who wants to attend the University has the financial resources to do so. Widener University offers both need-based and merit-based financial aid, and currently 70 percent of the student body is receiving some form of financial assistance. Financial aid consists of scholarships, grants, loans, and employment, which may be offered to students singly or in various combinations. Special merit scholarships are available to incoming students of exceptional academic ability or achievement, including awards of 60 percent tuition with SAT I scores of at least 1250 and a minimum GPA of 3.8, 45 percent tuition with SAT I scores of at least 1100 and a minimum GPA of 3.5, 35 percent tuition with SAT I scores of at least 1050 and a minimum GPA of 3.3, and 30 percent tuition with SAT I scores of at least 1000 and a minimum GPA of 3.0.

Students who submit an application for financial aid are considered for aid under all programs for which they are eligible. Financial aid applicants are notified of their aid in the spring prior to their enrollment at the University. Students are required to file either the Free Application for Federal Student Aid (FAFSA) or the Pennsylvania Higher Education Assistance Agency form. The priority deadline is April 1.

Faculty

The University faculty of 313 members is drawn from leading national and international graduate schools. Doctoral and terminal degrees are held by 91 percent of the faculty members. The student-faculty ratio is 12:1, and the average class size is 27.

Student Government

The Student Government Association (SGA) coordinates student activities and exercises legislative, executive, and judicial authority. Participation in the daily life of the institution via student government is a facet of the total collegiate experience, and students are encouraged to become active in the SGA.

Admission Requirements

Admission to Widener is competitive and is based primarily upon the quality of the high school record. Recommendations, extracurricular involvement, personal essay, and the pattern of test scores are also weighed in the decision.

To apply for admission, students should submit a completed application with the $30 application fee; have their current high school forward a transcript of their academic records; send a copy of their SAT I or ACT scores; and ask their high school counselor to complete and return the high school recommendation form. Scores on SAT II: Subject Tests are recommended but not required. An interview is highly recommended but not required.

Students from twenty-six states and forty other countries are attending Widener; 46 percent ranked in the top quarter of their high school graduating class, 92 percent in the top half. Their mean combined SAT I score was 1015, and 80 percent scored between 940 and 1060.

Application and Information

The University uses a rolling admission system, and applicants are notified of the decision as soon as their application is complete. Most students apply by February of their senior year in high school. Qualified students applying after March 1 are offered admission on a space-available basis.

Transfer applicants are encouraged to apply and are also admitted on a rolling basis.

For further information or an appointment, students should contact:

Widener University
Office of Admissions
One University Place
Chester, Pennsylvania 19013-5792
Telephone: 610-499-4126
E-mail: admissions.office@widener.edu
World Wide Web: http://www.widener.edu

WILBERFORCE UNIVERSITY
WILBERFORCE, OHIO

The University

Currently, more than 800 students are enrolled at Wilberforce University, allowing for a 12:1 student-teacher ratio. The student body is diverse, with a number of students coming from Ohio, Michigan, Illinois, Indiana, New York, Pennsylvania, California, and Georgia. International students come from Africa, Canada, the Caribbean, and the British West Indies.

The experiences that students have outside the classroom are important elements of campus life. Wilberforce University is committed to the development of students. Social life and academic achievement are integral aspects of the educational experience. Activities include scholarly forums, service learning/volunteering, poetry readings, travel to nearby colleges and communities, plays, movies, and local sporting events.

Departmental clubs and social organizations enable students to concentrate on particular areas of study, career fields, and academic honors. Eight chapters of national Greek-letter fraternities and sororities offer service, social activities, and opportunities for lasting friendship. Other outlets include the Student Government Association, national honor societies, the campus newspaper, the yearbook staff, the campus radio station, the Debate Club, the Engineering and Computer Science Club, the Business and Economics Club, Students in Free Enterprise, the National Association of Black Accountants, the National Student Business League, the University Concert Choir, the Gospel Chorus, the Jazz Band, the Black Male Coalition, the International Student Club, the University Jazzers and Cheerleaders, and Black Women United.

Wilberforce University's athletic programs (NAIA Division I) include men's and women's basketball, cross-country, golf, and track and field. Wilberforce University is a member of the American MidEast Conference. The intramural program offers basketball, flag football, soccer, softball, and tennis.

The North Central Association of Colleges and Universities accredits Wilberforce University.

Location

The University is situated in southwestern Ohio in the city of Wilberforce, offering tranquility and proximity to major urban areas and their cultural opportunities. Dayton is just 20 miles away; Cincinnati and Columbus are within an hour's drive. Xenia, with a population of 25,000, is 3 miles from campus, and Springfield, a metropolitan area of 100,000, is 15 miles away. Southwestern Ohio is a region that has major cultural attractions, ballets, theaters, and museums. The National Afro-American Museum is located on the old campus of Wilberforce University. Near the campus are John Bryan State Park, the Clarence Brown Reservoir, and the Glen Helen wilderness area. The famed King's Island Amusement Park is less than an hour's drive from campus.

Majors and Degrees

Wilberforce University awards the Bachelor of Arts and Bachelor of Science degrees. Majors are offered in accounting, biology/premed, broadcast media, business economics, chemistry, communications, finance, fine arts, health services administration, liberal arts, literature, management, marketing, mass media, mathematics, music (composition, theory, and voice), philosophy and religion, political science/prelaw, psychology, print journalism, rehabilitation services, secondary education, social work, sociology, and theater. Bachelor of Science degrees in engineering or computer science can by earned in computer engineering, computer information systems, computer science, electrical engineering, and engineering physics. Wilberforce University also offers dual-degree programs (3-2) in aerospace, architectural, and nuclear engineering in conjunction with the University of Cincinnati and in chemical, civil, electrical, and mechanical engineering in cooperation with the University of Dayton. Upon completion, students receive degrees in comprehensive science or mathematics and engineering or computer science. Additional courses are offered in Caribbean studies and the Black Heritage Series.

Academic Program

To receive a bachelor's degree, students must complete at least 128 semester hours with an overall grade point average of no less than 2.0. At least 30 semester hours must be completed in residence during the senior year. Graduation prerequisites also include the satisfactory completion of a program of core requirements. Advanced standing may be granted through successful scores on College-Level Examination Program (CLEP) general and subject tests and Advanced Placement (AP) examinations. All students must demonstrate competence in writing by passing the Junior Level Competency Test, become computer literate by enrolling in a required computer literacy course, and successfully complete two cooperative education experiences. Army and Air Force ROTC programs are offered through nearby Central State and Wright State universities.

Wilberforce follows a semester schedule. The fall semester begins in mid-August and ends in mid-December. The spring semester begins in mid-January and ends in mid-May. There are no summer sessions.

Off-Campus Arrangements

Wilberforce University is a member of the Southwestern Ohio Council of Higher Education (SOCHE), an eighteen-college consortium. Membership enables Wilberforce students to cross-register for courses and use the library facilities of any of the other seventeen institutions.

Academic Facilities

The University library, with more than 63,000 volumes, 350 periodicals, and 300 microfilm titles, operates seven days a week. The modern classroom building, like all of the facilities on the main campus, is air conditioned. It contains a radio station, a state-of-the-art computer center, numerous classrooms, and the reading, writing, math, and speech laboratories.

Costs

Wilberforce University is a competitively priced, private liberal arts university. Students are able to gain all the benefits of a high-quality liberal arts education at an affordable cost. Wilberforce University is affiliated and supported by grants the African Methodist Episcopal Church. The University is also a member institution of the United Negro College Fund (UNCF). Grants from the government, foundations, corporations, alumni, and other friends of the University help to keep the cost affordable. Student living on campus find each room equipped with a Pentium computer, which provides each student with online access, e-mail, research, and the Internet. Provisions for this service are included in the general fees.

Student dormitories and housing have been renovated and new buildings have been built for the 2000–01 school year. Students who live on campus must apply for housing upon being admitted. Admitted students planning to attend the University must submit a $360 enrollment fee by June 1 for the fall semester and December 15 for the spring semester.

Financial Aid

Loans, grants, and scholarships are available and are awarded on the basis of need. Ninety-five percent of the enrolled students receive some form of financial assistance. Eligible students can receive federal funds, such as Federal Pell Grants, Federal Supplemental Educational Opportunity Grants, Federal Work-Study employment, Federal Perkins Loans, and Federal Stafford Student Loans. State grants are also available for residents of Ohio, Pennsylvania, and Washington, D.C.

The priority deadline to file for financial aid for the fall semester is April 30; the final deadline is June 1. The deadline for the spring semester is November 15. All students should use the Free Application for Federal Student Aid (FAFSA) in applying for aid. The University also requires the completion of its financial aid application. All students must provide proof of income through copies of income tax returns or related documents. All financial aid is awarded on a rolling basis.

Faculty

There are 55 full-time and 25 part-time faculty members at Wilberforce University. All have advanced degrees, and 53 percent have a Ph.D. or the terminal degree in their field. The student-faculty ratio is 12:1. Since the University has primarily a teaching faculty, each student is ensured personalized attention.

Student Government

Leadership opportunities are provided through the Student Government Association (SGA), class offices, committees, and residence halls. The SGA is the main voice and political force of the student body. The members are elected by students to serve as student representatives to the Board of Trustees or as officers in their respective classes. Student representation on faculty-staff committees ensures vital input regarding recommendations and changes in academic, student life, and University-wide policies.

Admission Requirements

Wilberforce University is a selective university that operates on a rolling admissions basis. Students applying for admission must have at least a 2.0 (C) grade point average with a strong showing in the college-preparatory areas and must have completed 15 acceptable units of study, including 4 units of English, 2 to 3 units of mathematics (including algebra), 2 to 3 units of science (including one laboratory science), and 2 units of social studies (including U.S. history). ACT or SAT scores are required for evaluation purposes. An interview is not required but is helpful, and it can be conducted either in person or by telephone. Early decision and early admission are also available.

Wilberforce actively recruits students from throughout the continental United States and other countries, as well as those who want to transfer from community and junior colleges or other four-year institutions. Wilberforce University has articulation agreements with several community colleges throughout the United States. Students are able to transfer credits from associate degree programs to the University and continue pursuing their bachelor's degree. Additional information can be requested from the Office of Admissions.

Applicants should arrange to have an official copy of their high school transcript or evidence of an equivalent level of academic attainment, such as the GED, sent to the admissions office. Ohio students must show proof of passing the Ninth Grade Proficiency Test. Applicants must also submit two recommendations (one from a counselor and one from a teacher) and an essay. In addition to high school transcripts, transfer students should provide copies of transcripts from any college or university attended.

Application and Information

New students are accepted for each semester. Applications for admission in the fall semester must be submitted by July 1. The application deadline for the spring semester is November 15. Applications are accepted anytime after the junior year is completed in high school.

For additional information or application materials, students should contact:

Office of Admissions
Wilberforce University
Wilberforce, Ohio 45384
Telephone: 937-376-2911
          800-367-8568 (toll-free)
          800-367-8565 (toll-free, Student
             Financial Services and Scholarships)
World Wide Web: http://www.wilberforce.edu

WILFRID LAURIER UNIVERSITY
WATERLOO, ONTARIO, CANADA

The University

From its origins in 1911 as a Lutheran seminary, publicly funded Wilfrid Laurier University has grown into one of Canada's finest smaller universities. In its annual ranking of all Canadian universities, *Maclean's* magazine consistently rates Laurier among the country's best in terms of quality, innovation, "best overall" institution, and the quality of its student body.

Laurier, which is named after Canada's first French-Canadian prime minister, has 6,000 full-time undergraduate students and 500 full-time graduate students studying in five academic faculties: Arts, Science, Business and Economics, Music, and the graduate School of Social Work. In Arts and Science, Laurier has particular strengths in psychology, archeology, geography and environmental studies, biology, and computing, and Laurier's renowned music and business programs attract students from around the world. English is the language of instruction.

Laurier students often say they appreciate the University's strong sense of community, its relatively small size and friendly atmosphere, the accessibility of its professors, and the active campus life. Many also appreciate Laurier's cooperative education programs, which alternate terms of study with paid work terms; the on-campus residences; excellent recreation facilities; and the University's active career placement service.

Laurier guarantees a space in a residence for any first-year student who requests it.

In 1999, Laurier opened a new campus in Brantford, Ontario, which offers a multidisciplinary general B.A. degree.

Location

Wilfrid Laurier University is located in Waterloo, Ontario, a small city of 90,000 that conjoins with the city of Kitchener for a combined population of more than 270,000. The area's first European settlers were Mennonites from Pennsylvania, and the horse-and-buggy Mennonite culture is still alive in the surrounding small communities. Kitchener-Waterloo is a thriving community that is home to several insurance companies, two universities, a community college, and numerous cutting-edge software and high-technology manufacturing corporations. Kitchener-Waterloo is about 65 miles west of Toronto and 120 miles from Niagara Falls and Buffalo. Detroit is a 3-hour drive away. There is regular bus service to Toronto and passenger train service to Toronto and Chicago.

Kitchener-Waterloo is home to a fine professional orchestra, and it hosts the largest Bavarian festival in North America—Oktoberfest—for ten days each fall. The famous Stratford Shakespearean Festival is less than 1 hour away, and neighboring towns and villages offer such delights as the Elmira Maple Syrup Festival in the spring and the Wellesley Apple Butter and Cheese Festival in the fall. The sandy beaches of Lake Huron and Lake Erie are just 2 hours away.

Majors and Degrees

Wilfrid Laurier University offers general (three-year) degrees in arts and science (B.A. and B.Sc.) and honors (four-year) degrees in arts, business administration, music, music therapy, and science (B.A., B.B.A., B.Mus., B.Mus.Th., and B.Sc.) as well as diplomas in business and music. There is also a five-year cooperative honors computing and business program, which awards graduates an honors B.Sc. and an honors B.B.A. Many graduate programs are also offered. Laurier's Web site (listed on the reverse of this page) has further details.

The majors offered for a general B.A. are anthropology, archeology, biology, Canadian studies, classical studies, communication studies, computing, development and international studies, economics, English, film studies, fine arts, French, geography, German, Greek, history, kinesiology and physical education, Latin, mathematics, philosophy, political science, psychology, religion and culture, sociology, Spanish, theatre, and women's studies. General B.Sc. degrees are offered in biology, chemistry, computing, mathematics, physical geography, and physics. Honors B.A. programs are offered in anthropology, archeology, biology, classical studies, economics, English language and literature, environmental studies, French, German, Greek, history, kinesiology and physical education, Latin, mathematics, music, philosophy, political science, psychology, religion and culture, sociology, sociology and social anthropology, and Spanish. Honors B.Sc. degrees are offered in biology, biology and chemistry, biology and mathematics, biology and psychology, chemistry, chemistry and mathematics, computing and computer electronics, geography, kinesiology and physical education, mathematics, and psychology. Both the Bachelor of Business Administration and the Bachelor of Music degrees are offered only at the honors (four-year) level.

Academic Program

Wilfrid Laurier University's academic year runs from September to April, although some courses are also offered in the spring (May and June) and summer (July and August) terms. Laurier also offers many courses through distance education, some of them Web-based.

Off-Campus Arrangements

Laurier believes strongly in the value of multicultural experience. The University has exchange programs in place with universities in Australia, Austria, England, France, Germany, Japan, Mexico, the Netherlands, Quebec, South Africa, Sweden, and Taiwan. Through the World University Service of Canada, exchanges are also available at institutions in Africa, Asia, and Latin America. In addition, Laurier's archeology program conducts digs in Jordan and Ontario.

Academic Facilities

Laurier's library is linked to the libraries of the University of Waterloo and the University of Guelph, giving Laurier students access to a wealth of research material. CD-ROM and Internet-based materials are also accessible. All Laurier students have an e-mail address and can access the Internet and numerous word processing and other programs from within the many computer labs located throughout the University.

On-campus services to students include a bookstore, a writing center, a special needs office, University chaplains, musical and theatrical productions, health services, career services, dozens of clubs, competitive and recreational sports, and fitness facilities in the Laurier Athletic Complex.

Costs

Tuition for two terms in 1999–2000 (usually 5 credits) was $7000. Health insurance was $579 for a year. Other fees, depending on the program of study, may apply; students should consult Laurier's calendar or Web site for details. Residence accommodation varied from $1210 to $1848 per term. The University meal plan, required for students living in one of the University's dormitory-style residences, was $1339 per term. All costs are expressed in Canadian dollars. Updated costs can be found on Laurier's Web site, which is listed below.

Financial Aid

Students studying at Laurier on a student visa can apply for in-course scholarships and bursaries. A few scholarships are available for incoming visa students. Ontario universities do not offer athletic scholarships.

Faculty

About 90 percent of Laurier's faculty members have Ph.D.'s. In some fields, music and accounting in particular, instructors are hired based on their professional qualifications rather than advanced academic standing. Regardless, Laurier places a strong emphasis on quality teaching while also encouraging faculty members to pursue original research. Numerous Laurier professors have won provincial and national awards for their teaching. Laurier faculty members also publish their work in many scholarly journals and are quite successful in competing for national research grants.

Student Government

Laurier's administration has a warm working relationship with the University's students, who are represented by the Wilfrid Laurier University Students' Union (WLUSU) and the Wilfrid Laurier University Graduate Student Association. WLUSU owns the Fred Nichols Campus Center, a major building on the Laurier campus; runs several enterprises, including a restaurant and pub; and also coordinates the numerous student clubs and associations on campus. Student representatives sit on both the University's Senate and Board of Governors, and the Dean of Students' Office is jointly funded by the University and the students.

Admission Requirements

Applicants who have completed U.S. grade 12 with superior academic standing and a minimum combined SAT I score of 1000 and who can meet the specific requirements of the faculty being applied to are considered for admission to the first year of a degree program. Otherwise, applicants must present acceptable final standing in U.S. grade 12 and 24 semester hours at an accredited college or university in courses from the humanities, social sciences, and natural sciences.

Application and Information

Applications for fall entry should be received by April 30, with all supporting documentation submitted by June 30.

For more information about Laurier, interested students should contact:

Admissions—Office of the Registrar
Wilfrid Laurier University
75 University Avenue West
Waterloo, Ontario N2L 3C5
Canada
Telephone: 519-884-0710 Ext. 3351
Fax: 519-884-8826
E-mail: admissions@mach1.wlu.ca
World Wide Web: http://www.wlu.ca

The Quadrangle at Wilfrid Laurier University.

WILKES UNIVERSITY
WILKES-BARRE, PENNSYLVANIA

The University

Located at the foot of the Pocono Mountains, along the shore of the Susquehanna River and within walking distance of downtown Wilkes-Barre, Pennsylvania, Wilkes University is a private, comprehensive institution with more than 1,600 undergraduate students. The University is structured into the College of Arts, Sciences and Professional Studies; the Nesbitt School of Pharmacy; and University College (for undecided students). Wilkes offers a broad range of bachelor's and master's programs in the humanities, social and natural sciences, business administration, nursing, and education as well as a Doctor of Pharmacy degree.

The Wilkes campus features a parklike quadrangle surrounded by modern classroom buildings and historic nineteenth-century mansions that have been restored as student residences and academic buildings. Campus facilities include a sports and conference center, an outdoor athletic complex and field house, a state-of-the-art science classroom building, a modern academic classroom/office building, and a performing arts center. A student union with a food court, a bookstore, entertainment rooms, a bank, a post office, and a nightclub opened in 1999.

Hands-on learning, small classes, and strong student-professor relationships are the hallmarks of the Wilkes experience. Programs are designed to prepare students with a well-rounded liberal arts foundation that cultivates independent thinking and gives students the credentials necessary for entrance into graduate and professional schools and professional life. Academic advising integrated with career planning is stressed, and hands-on experiences are provided in laboratory, internship, and cooperative education settings. Free tutorial services are available to all students as well.

The University is accredited by the Middle States Association of Colleges and Schools and has specialized accreditation in the sciences, engineering, nursing, education, and business. Wilkes students graduate with the confidence and competence they need to succeed professionally and with the knowledge required to participate as enlightened members of society. More than 99 percent are employed or attending graduate/professional school within six months of receiving their degrees.

Residential alternatives range from traditional single-sex residence halls to coeducational facilities in nineteenth-century mansions. First-year students applying prior to May 1 are guaranteed housing. Campus housing is available for all four years. Architecturally, residence halls vary from modern, multi-floor buildings to mansions listed on the National Register of Historic Places. Medical and dental care, department stores, specialty shops, and other services are available within three blocks of campus. A large number of nearby churches and synagogues welcome students' participation in worship.

At Wilkes University, student activities complement academic life. Intercollegiate athletics encompass thirteen Division III sports, and an active and varied intramural program is offered. Nearly seventy clubs and organizations recognize student achievement and provide opportunities for leadership development, professional growth, and community service. The student-run Programming Board schedules movies and performances by comedians, musicians, and other entertainers, while other organizations sponsor dinner dances, block parties, and special events. Wilkes students are active community volunteers, participating in numerous local and national service projects each year.

Master's degrees are awarded in business administration, education, electrical engineering, and nursing. The University also offers a six-year program leading to the Doctor of Pharmacy degree. A Master of Science is also offered.

Location

The county seat of Luzerne County, Wilkes-Barre is a medium-sized city of 50,000 in the midst of a metropolitan area of 400,000. A wide range of recreational facilities are minutes away, including the Lackawanna County Multi-Purpose Stadium (home of the Wilkes-Barre/Scranton Red Barons Triple A baseball team); a new arena, which serves as home for the Wilkes-Barre/Scranton Penguins hockey team, an area convention center, and civic arena; the Pocono Mountain ski resorts; numerous golf courses; state parks; outdoor tennis courts; and Pocono Downs harness racing.

Located in downtown Wilkes-Barre, the F. M. Kirby Center of Performing Arts features symphony, ballet, theatrical, and musical performances. Other area cultural offerings include art galleries, ethnic and community festivals, and numerous libraries and museums. The city is also approximately 2 hours from the cultural resources of both New York City and Philadelphia.

The area's economic strength derives in part from its transportation resources. Wilkes-Barre is in proximity to the intersection of Interstates 80, 81, and 476 and within 3 to 6 hours of major markets such as Washington, D.C.; Baltimore; and Boston. The Wilkes-Barre/Scranton International Airport enables travelers to arrive at most domestic destinations via one-stop or nonstop flights.

Majors and Degrees

Wilkes University offers Bachelor of Arts, Bachelor of Business Administration, Bachelor of Science, and Bachelor of Music degrees. Majors include accounting, biochemistry, biology, business administration (concentrations in banking and finance, entrepreneurship, health services administration, management and industrial relations, and marketing), chemistry, communications (concentrations in journalism, organizational communication, rhetoric and public communication, and telecommunications), computer information systems, computer science, earth and environmental sciences, electrical engineering, elementary and secondary education (both with certification), engineering management, English (concentrations in literature and writing), environmental engineering, foreign language and literature (French and Spanish), history, international studies, mathematics, mechanical engineering, medical technology, music, nursing, philosophy, political science, psychology, sociology, and theater arts. Individualized studies are also available, and students may participate in the Air Force ROTC program.

Premedical and pre-law preparation are particularly strong programs. In addition to the University's prepharmacy program, other preprofessional programs are available in dentistry, optometry, and veterinary science. The University offers affiliated programs in medicine with the Philadelphia College of Osteopathic Medicine and the Penn State–Hershey Medical Center, in optometry with the Pennsylvania College of Optometry and the State University of New York (SUNY) College of Optometry, in podiatry with the Pennsylvania College of Podiatry, in occupational and physical therapy with Temple University, and in medicine and physical therapy with MCP Hahnemann University.

Academic Program

Through a rigorous curriculum that emphasizes hands-on experience and training, Wilkes helps students to prepare in all majors to adapt to a technologically and socially evolving world. To graduate, students are required to complete a core curriculum and must complete from 120 to 136 credits, depending upon their major field. Graduates demonstrate mastery of the fundamental intellectual skills as well as the essential concepts and techniques of their field. Wilkes also teaches students responsibility and independence by expecting and encouraging active participation in the classroom and laboratory.

The University operates on a dual-semester calendar, with optional summer sessions and a January intersession. Advanced Placement test credits are accepted.

Off-Campus Arrangements

An extensive cooperative education program is available to all students, with credit applicable in most major fields. Many government offices and private businesses in northeastern Pennsylvania, as well as in New York City, Philadelphia, Harrisburg, and Washington, D.C., employ Wilkes students. The study-abroad adviser works with interested students, placing them in the situation best suited to their academic pursuits. Most recently, students have attended programs in Austria, England, the Dominican Republic, France, and Germany.

Academic Facilities

The Eugene S. Farley Library has more than 220,000 volumes of books and bound journals, 1,100 current journal and newspaper subscriptions, database searches, and 700,000 microforms. Complete laboratory facilities are available for biology, chemistry, earth and environmental sciences, engineering, nursing, pharmacy, and psychology. Student-produced programming is broadcast from WCLH-FM, the University's 2,000-watt radio station, and transmitted from a professional-quality television studio via a local cable provider. Numerous PC and Macintosh microcomputers are available for student use, with an overall student-computer ratio of 5:1. The Sordoni Art Gallery is professionally equipped and staffed and produces exhibits each year by regionally, nationally, and internationally known artists. The Dorothy Dickson Darte Center for the Performing Arts contains a fully equipped 500-seat theater for the presentation of plays, concerts, ballet, and other performances and lectures. Adjoining the center are studios, practice and rehearsal rooms, and faculty offices for the Department of Visual and Performing Arts. A new classroom/office building accommodates extensive computer facilities, psychology research laboratories, and modern classrooms with the newest audiovisual equipment. The University also operates a state-of-the-art distance learning facility that allows global conferencing and study using Internet and videoconferencing technology.

Costs

For the 2000–01 academic year, tuition is $16,275 per year, and room and board is $7385. General, activity, and technology fees total $700 per year. Books cost approximately $500 per year.

Financial Aid

Financial aid is available to those students who demonstrate quality academic ability and/or financial need, as verified by the Free Application for Federal Student Aid (FAFSA). Merit-based and need-based aid is available from Wilkes University for qualified students. Scholarships ranging from $6000 per year to full tuition are available to students solely on the basis of academic ability. Approximately 90 percent of the student body receive some type of financial assistance, including scholarships, grants, loans, and work-study awards.

Faculty

Wilkes University has a nationally recruited full-time faculty of 120 members, approximately 94 percent of whom have earned Ph.D.'s or terminal degrees in their chosen field. Faculty evaluation criteria emphasize teaching excellence and effective advising, while recognizing continued scholarly activities. The student-faculty ratio is 14:1.

Student Government

An active student government provides a structure for student participation in University governance and student discipline. The Inter-Residence Council and Commuter Council coordinate extracurricular activities for on-campus and commuter students.

Admission Requirements

Admission to Wilkes University is traditional. SAT I and/or ACT scores are required. In cases where a student has taken the examination more than once, scores from the highest testing in each category are used in the evaluation process. Applicants for the freshman class should either have completed or be in the process of completing a college-preparatory course of study, including 3 to 4 years of mathematics, social studies, science, and English. Additional courses should be elected in academic subjects according to individual interests. Acceptable electives include foreign language and computing, among others. Students who have not followed this pattern may still qualify for admission if there is other strong evidence of preparation for college work. Letters of recommendation and SAT II Subject Test scores are not required but may be submitted. Students intending to major in engineering, mathematics, or medical technology should have completed algebra I and II, geometry, and trigonometry prior to enrollment. Students intending to major in nursing should have completed courses in biology and chemistry. An audition is required for all prospective music and theater arts students. Transfer students must submit a transcript from every college previously attended. All students are admitted to the University and not to specific departments, with the exception of the professional Nesbitt School of Pharmacy. Students individually receive academic advisement at the time of registration and throughout their enrollment.

Wilkes University is an Equal Opportunity/Affirmative Action institution. No applicant shall be denied admission to the University because of race, color, gender, religion, national or ethnic origin, sexual orientation, or handicap.

Application and Information

Applications for admission should be completed early in the senior year of secondary school and sent to the Dean of Enrollment Services. Applications are reviewed after all of the student's credentials have been received. The review of applications generally begins on September 1, and notification of the University's decision reaches the student two to four weeks after the application file is complete.

Dean of Enrollment Services
Office of Admission
Wilkes University
P.O. Box 111
Wilkes-Barre, Pennsylvania 18766
Telephone: 800-945-5378 Ext. 4400 (toll-free)
570-408-4400

WILLIAM JEWELL COLLEGE
LIBERTY, MISSOURI

The College

The architecture of the William Jewell College campus has a classic Colonial American style, with a collection of red brick, ivy-covered, hilltop buildings overlooking the Kansas City skyline 12 miles away. Founded in 1849 in cooperation with the Baptists of Missouri, William Jewell was among the first four-year men's colleges west of the Mississippi River. In 1921, it became coeducational. The College prepares students for leadership by challenging them to achieve their highest level of excellence and to embrace a spirit of service. The quadrangle of six buildings located "on the hill" forms the nucleus of campus life. The Mabee Center for Physical Education, Greene Stadium, Brown Hall, and the Pillsbury Music Center are adjacent. The White Science Center provides state-of-the-art facilities for the departments of biology, chemistry, computer studies, mathematics, and physics. Seven modern residence halls are all within walking distance of the quadrangle. The 1,200 men and women attending William Jewell College are drawn from twenty-eight states and thirteen countries. More than fifteen denominations are represented. Most students live on campus. Participation in extracurricular activities is encouraged as a valuable extension of academic work. Students may choose to involve themselves in music, forensics, religious programs, athletics, departmental honoraries, sororities and fraternities, and many other activities and groups. The nationally recognized Fine Arts Program provides opportunities for students to enjoy such performers as Luciano Pavarotti, Kiri Te Kanawa, and Marilyn Horne or to attend performances by such professional companies as the Houston Ballet, the Royal Shakespeare Company, and the Alvin Ailey Dance Theatre.

Location

Liberty, Missouri, is located 15 minutes north of downtown Kansas City, Missouri. The College's location provides a quiet campus of surpassing beauty, ideal for study and contemplation, and easy access to the social and cultural advantages of a city of 1.6 million people. Liberty, which has a population of 25,000, is near the Kansas City International Airport (20 minutes), an Amtrak station (20 minutes), and bus stations (15 minutes).

Majors and Degrees

William Jewell College offers four-year programs that lead to Bachelor of Arts and Bachelor of Science degrees. The Bachelor of Arts degree is granted in art, biochemistry, biology, British studies, business administration, chemistry, communication, computer science, economics, education, engineering, English, French, history, international business, international relations, Japanese area studies, mathematics, music, philosophy, physics, political science, psychology, religion, and Spanish. The Bachelor of Science degree is conferred in accounting, business administration, education, information systems, mathematics (with data processing emphasis), medical technology, music, and nursing.

Academic Program

William Jewell College is an institution dedicated to preparing a new generation of leaders through a distinctive liberal arts curriculum that embraces the whole individual. The Jewell curriculum allows students to make connections between liberal arts and the professions, service and career accomplishments, and the campus and the complex world beyond. Under College guidelines, students may choose or design their area of concentration (major) in accordance with their own interests, abilities, and objectives. The area of concentration is worked out in consultation with each student's personal adviser and normally consists of six to ten courses (24 to 40 semester hours). Students who want an added challenge of academic excellence may do independent study in the honors program and seek graduation with honors or achievement. A small number of highly motivated students may plan from one to four semesters of their college career in unconventional patterns that will help them meet their educational goals. William Jewell College's commitment to liberal arts education is expressed in degree requirements that guarantee breadth of education as well as specialization in a major. A general education curriculum aims to prepare students to be vital, contributing, and successful citizens of a global community. Students study the traditional disciplines as they arise from and are relevant to the search to understand the meaning of "the responsible self" in modern society. The curriculum offers students a learning experience that builds through three stages: an introductory/skills level, an intermediate interdisciplinary level, and an advanced capstone level. A small number of intellectually outstanding students are admitted each year to the Oxbridge Honors Program, which is supported by a multimillion-dollar gift from the Hall Family Foundation. An Oxbridge student may pursue a major in English language and literature, history, history of ideas (an interdisciplinary major in the great books of the Western intellectual tradition), institutions and policy (philosophy, economics, and political science), music, or science (molecular biology) under a tutorial system of directed study and examinations adapted from the traditional method of the Universities of Oxford and Cambridge. Oxbridge tutorial majors spend the junior year in either Oxford or Cambridge. Students who are 23 years of age or older find the New Horizons Program at William Jewell geared to their specific needs. Those students entering college for the first time or after several years of absence find support services readily available. Special information on applying for admission, scholarships and grants, academic advising, challenge examination procedures, and other concerns may be secured by contacting the Admission Office. Students at William Jewell College may be granted advanced placement with or without credit through the Advanced Placement Program and College-Level Examination Program tests of the College Board, through the International Baccalaureate Program, and through departmental examinations.

Off-Campus Arrangements

Each student is encouraged to pursue an off-campus field experience. Advisers assist students in developing a program that relates to their educational goals. Typical programs involve study-abroad programs, work-study programs in the inner city, social or religious service, vocational internships, or study at another college. Programs may be formally structured classwork or independent study. In addition, students may participate in the United Nations Semester of Drew University and the Washington Semester of American University. Nearly 20 percent of the students participate in an overseas study opportunity. William Jewell has relationships with universities and study programs around the world and is distinguished by its ties to England. The College offers three programs in Oxford and Cambridge for honors students: a year of study at Homerton College (Cambridge) or at the Centre for Medieval and Renaissance Studies (affiliated with Keble College, Oxford) or either a semester or a year of study with the Oxford Overseas Study Course in Oxford. Harlaxton College, near Grantham, England, offers a full academic program for one semester of study, including an interdisciplinary course in British studies, which is required of all students. Two specialized programs of study in England connect overseas study with William Jewell's preprofessional programs. The nursing program at Harlaxton allows junior nursing majors to learn about the British National

Health Service, while the British Teacher Education Program affords elementary education majors the chance to observe interdisciplinary, thematic teaching in British primary schools. The College also has strong ties to Asia. An exchange program with Seinan Gakuin University in Fukuoka, Japan, allows William Jewell students to earn a Japanese area studies major for their year of study. Each year, several William Jewell students may enroll at Hong Kong Baptist University, an English-language university with strong programs in business and many other academic areas. Other English-language programs are located in Australia; Vienna, Austria; Freiburg, Germany; and Milan, Italy. Foreign language programs are offered in France, Germany, Mexico, and Spain, including a summer program in Córdoba led by William Jewell faculty members.

Academic Facilities

The Charles F. Curry Library houses 255,875 bound volumes, 865 current journals, 5,075 records, 3,406 tape recordings, 196,911 units of microtext, and 12,900 units of media (filmstrips, motion pictures, slides, and videotapes). The library also has several special collections. The Learning Resource Center provides audiovisual services for the entire campus. William Jewell is a member of the Kansas City Library Consortium, an association of area colleges with an online public access catalog database that provides Jewell students with access to more than 2.5 million volumes. Jewell Hall, which is listed on the National Register of Historic Places, served as a hospital for Union soldiers during the Civil War. Construction began on the building in 1849 and was completed in 1853. Jewell Hall has been completely renovated and remains one of the College's primary classroom buildings.

Costs

For the 2000–01 academic year, tuition and fees are $6900, and room and board are $4250. The estimated cost of books, travel, and personal expenses is $3300.

Financial Aid

Academic scholarships ranging from $500 to full tuition are awarded annually to qualified students. Activity and athletic scholarships are also available. William Jewell College participates in the Missouri Student Grant Program and in the Federal Pell Grant, Federal Supplemental Educational Opportunity Grant, Federal Work-Study, and Federal Perkins Loan programs. Students seeking financial assistance are encouraged to submit the Free Application for Federal Student Aid (FAFSA), designating William Jewell as a school choice. Applicants must apply for assistance before March 15 and must be accepted for admission before assistance can be awarded. Awards are often in the form of a package, which may include a combination of federal, state, and College funds.

Faculty

The faculty is a group of professionals highly qualified in their respective academic disciplines. All hold master's degrees; 3 of every 5 hold doctoral degrees. It is a teaching faculty; the entire energy of the faculty is spent in undergraduate instruction rather than in graduate teaching or research. From their freshman year, students are under the instruction of full professors, never under the instruction of graduate students or graduate assistants. All faculty members are designated "teacher-adviser," because the personal advisory relationship with students is an important part of the educational experience at William Jewell College. Each student is assigned an academic adviser who takes a personal interest in assisting the student to plan an academic program to meet specific goals. The majority of the faculty are full-time members who are totally committed to the academic and personal growth of students. Most faculty members live close to campus, and many are closely involved with student activities and cocurricular programs.

Student Government

The Student Senate provides a forum for student opinion on many diverse issues and serves as a working link among the students, faculty, administration, and Board of Trustees. Students sit on all major faculty committees, and the Student Senate president sits in the College president's Administrative Cabinet meetings. The College is receptive to student ideas, and dialogue is encouraged.

Admission Requirements

Admission to William Jewell College is competitive. The College encourages applications from students who are serious about enrolling in a coeducational liberal arts college and who have indicated through their secondary school record that they are sufficiently mature to profit from and contribute to the College. William Jewell actively encourages geographic and cultural diversity on the campus. To be considered for admission, students are asked to submit ACT or SAT I scores, a copy of the secondary school record, and two recommendations, one academic and one personal. Preference is given to graduates of an accredited high school who have had 17 units of high school credits, as follows: English, 4; mathematics, 4; science, 3; social studies, 3; foreign language, 2; fine arts, 1; and additional units in the areas above. Individual consideration is given to veterans and other mature applicants who may not meet all requirements. Transfer students are welcome, and credit is granted for work comparable to that offered at William Jewell College. Each candidate for admission should have a personal interview with a member of the admission staff. This interview may be arranged at the student's school or home or at a time when the student may be visiting the campus.

Application and Information

An applicant for admission may complete the William Jewell application form or the Common Application form. William Jewell processes applications for the fall semester under three plans. For early action, the application deadline is November 15 and the notification date is December 1. For scholarship priority, the application deadline is January 31 and the notification date is February 15. For regular decision, the application deadline is March 15 and the notification date is April 1. All applications received and completed after March 15 are reviewed on a space-available basis; notification begins after April 1. The application fee is $25.

For additional information, interested students should contact:

Dean of Enrollment
William Jewell College
500 College Hill
Liberty, Missouri 64068
Telephone: 816-781-7700 Ext. 5137
              800-753-7009 (toll-free)
Fax: 816-415-5027
E-mail: admission@william.jewell.edu
World Wide Web: http://www.jewell.edu

White Science Center (on the left) stands near the gateway to William Jewell College in Liberty, Missouri. The $7.5-million structure houses laboratories and classroom facilities for biology, chemistry, physics, and computer sciences.

WILLIAM PATERSON UNIVERSITY OF NEW JERSEY
WAYNE, NEW JERSEY

The University

Since its founding in 1855, William Paterson University has grown into a comprehensive state institution whose programs reflect the area's need for challenging, affordable educational options. Ideally midsized (the total enrollment is 9,758, of whom 8,133 are degree-seeking undergraduates), William Paterson offers a wider variety of academic programs than smaller universities, yet provides students with a more personalized atmosphere than larger institutions. Once the site of the family estate of Garret Hobart, the twenty-fourth vice president of the United States, William Paterson's 320-acre spacious campus, which has wooded areas and waterfalls, offers an environment in which students may develop both intellectually and socially. Although the majority of the University's students come from the New Jersey and New York vicinity, some international and out-of-state students enroll each year. Twenty-four percent of the undergraduates reside on campus in residence halls or apartment-style facilities, which accommodate 1,987 students. In general, on-campus housing is offered on a first-come, first-served basis.

Social, cultural, and recreational activities complement the academic programs. Cultural events take place throughout the year, featuring both William Paterson's own talent and renowned professional artists. Among the programs are concerts presenting jazz, classical, and contemporary music; theater productions; gallery exhibits; and a distinguished-lecturer series. The most popular spot for social activities is the Student Center, which contains an art gallery, a performing arts lounge, a game room, an ATM, a bookstore, and several auxiliary dining areas. The Student Activities Programming Board helps the more than fifty clubs and organizations to develop diverse activities for the entire student body. William Paterson has twenty-six social fraternities and sororities and eleven honor societies. The student newspaper, the *Beacon*, serves as a voice for the entire campus community. Students staff the campus radio station (WPSC) and the television station (WPC-TV), which develops a number of widely distributed television programs for local and statewide cable networks. The Rec Center serves as the focal point for physical recreation. In addition to the main courts, which accommodate badminton, basketball, indoor tennis, and volleyball, the 4,000-seat facility has racquetball courts, an exercise room, saunas, and Jacuzzis. The University has eighteen intercollegiate sports teams, nine for men and nine for women, including successful NCAA teams in men's baseball and women's softball. In addition, bowling, horseback riding, and ice hockey are organized as club sports. The University has an Olympic-size indoor pool, outdoor tennis courts, and a lighted athletics field complex.

Location

William Paterson University is located in northern New Jersey in the busy suburban town of Wayne. Several major recreational and cultural centers are nearby. New York City is just 20 miles to the east, the seacoast is an hour's drive south, skiing is 30 miles north, and the Meadowlands Sports Complex is a half-hour drive away.

Majors and Degrees

William Paterson University grants four undergraduate degrees—the B.A., B.S., B.F.A., and B.M.—and offers degree programs through its five colleges: Arts and Communication, Business, Education, Humanities and Social Sciences, and Science and Health.

The Bachelor of Arts degree is awarded in African, African-American, and Caribbean studies; anthropology; art; communication; English; French; geography; history; mathematics; music; philosophy; political science; psychology; sociology; Spanish; special education; and women's studies. The Bachelor of Science degree is conferred in accounting, applied chemistry, biology, biotechnology, business administration, community health/school health education, computer science, environmental science, nursing, and physical education. The Bachelor of Fine Arts degree in fine arts and the Bachelor of Music degree in music are also offered.

Certification is available in elementary, secondary, and special education. Preprofessional programs in communication disorders, dentistry, engineering, law, medicine, and veterinary medicine are arranged at the request of students.

Academic Program

Students must complete a minimum of 128 credits to earn a baccalaureate degree. Degree programs include a 60-credit general education requirement, 30–60 credits in a major, and 20–40 in elective courses. (In specialized degree programs, such as the B.F.A. and the B.M., general education and major course requirements may differ.) Students uncertain of which career path to follow may take advantage of advisement and counseling programs. In addition, the general education requirements enable students to take up to 60 credits before declaring a major, so that they can acquire a basic understanding of all major fields of knowledge before having to choose a specific area. Diagnostic testing and career seminars, provided by the Career Development Office, also ensure that students receive the guidance necessary to make wise course selections and career decisions.

William Paterson offers a variety of special programs. Honors programs are designed for those ambitious and well-qualified students who want to add a challenging dimension to their major. Currently, there are seven honors programs—in biopsychology, cognitive sciences, humanities, life science and environmental ethics, music, nursing, and performance studies. Students who have completed the premedical program in the College of Science and Health have consistently been accepted by American medical schools during the last ten years.

Students who successfully complete Advanced Placement tests and/or College-Level Examination Program tests may receive credit for acceptable scores. In addition, credit may be awarded for military training and experience.

William Paterson University operates on a two-semester and two-summer-session system.

Off-Campus Arrangements

William Paterson offers a special opportunity for off-campus study. Semester Abroad, a 15-credit program, is open to sophomores and juniors who wish to study for a semester at selected institutions in Australia, Denmark, Great Britain, Greece, Israel, Spain, and other countries around the world.

Academic Facilities

Situated on a 320-acre campus set among rolling hills, William Paterson's facilities are easily accessible, promote interaction among students, and encourage participation by all students in the various academic, cultural, and recreational programs. In completing a $10.4-million construction project, the University has expanded the Sarah Byrd Askew Library's bound collection by 33 percent and increased the seating capacity by 100 percent. The library contains a comprehensive collection of 320,000 books, 13,000 audiovisual items, 1,600 periodicals, a large microprint collection of dissertations, and a complete file of Educational Research Information Center (ERIC) materials.

The library's special-collections room houses rare and out-of-print items on New Jersey and valuable editions of literary works. Supporting William Paterson's varied cultural and artistic offerings are the Ben Shahn Center for Visual Arts, which contains art galleries, studios, and classrooms, and the Shea Center for Performing Arts, which contains a 940-seat theater as well as band, choral, and orchestra practice rooms and classrooms.

Hobart Hall, a state-of-the-art communication facility, is designed to educate communication majors in the most contemporary communication technology, including teleconferences. The facility houses two broadcast-quality TV studios, a multipurpose computer lab, a film studio, an FCC-licensed FM radio station, an uplink and four downlink satellite dishes, a cable system linking 95 percent of the buildings on campus, and a computerized telephone system for voice and data transmission. Also, William Paterson is finalizing the process of creating fiber-optic links throughout the campus.

A two-story academic building, the Atrium, which contains a writing center, multimedia language lab, tutorial center, and computing support facilities, was completed in 1996.

Among the other academic resources are extensive computer facilities, a filmmaking laboratory, professionally equipped color television studios, a child-care center, a nursing instructional center, a language lab, and a speech and hearing clinic. William Paterson University has dual accreditation from the American Speech-Language-Hearing Association for its speech and hearing clinic and its graduate program in communication disorders. The science research facilities contain two electron microscopes and various specialized labs.

Costs

Annual tuition (including fees) for the 2000–01 academic year is $4690 for full-time (12 credits or more) students who are New Jersey residents and $7360 for full-time nonresident students. Room and board cost approximately $5800 per year. All charges are subject to change per the Board of Trustees.

Financial Aid

Financial aid is available through a number of federal and state grant, loan, scholarship, and work-study programs. To apply for need-based aid, students must file the Free Application for Federal Student Aid (FAFSA) with the United States Department of Education by the priority date of April 1.

Both the University and the Alumni Association award a number of competitive scholarships, based solely on academic merit, to entering freshmen. They are the Scholarships for Academic Excellence, scholarships for African-American and Hispanic students, and Trustee and Presidential Scholarships. Academic Achievement Scholarships are awarded only on a competitive basis to continuing students.

Faculty

William Paterson's 342 full-time and 425 part-time faculty members bring to the classroom a valuable blend of accomplished scholarship and practical, applied experience. Faculty members assist students with curriculum and career planning, which engenders open, personal communication between the students and faculty.

Through a formal reciprocal exchange relationship with various institutions worldwide, and through the Fulbright Scholarship Program, William Paterson University often receives visiting international scholars.

Student Government

The Student Government Association (SGA), of which all full-time and part-time students are automatically members, has become an influential voice in University decision making. Elected officers and various committees convey students' perspectives to the administration and advance their causes. The SGA is also responsible for chartering more than fifty campus organizations and allocating student activity fees among them.

Admission Requirements

Admission to William Paterson University is competitive. Admissions decisions for entering freshmen are based on a complete review of the students' academic record (course of study, grades, and rank) as well as the results of the SAT I or ACT. Applicants are considered eligible if they have taken a minimum of 16 Carnegie units and have demonstrated strong academic ability. The students' secondary school record must show the following courses: English, 4 years (composition and literature); mathematics, 3 years (algebra I and II and geometry); laboratory science, 2 years (biology, chemistry, or physics); social science, 2 years (American history, world history, or political science); and additional college-preparatory subjects, 5 units (advanced mathematics, literature, foreign language, or social sciences). In addition, students selecting a major in art or music (except musical studies) must submit a portfolio for review by the Art Department or must audition for the Music Department.

Transfer students must present at least 12 college-level credits with a minimum 2.0 grade point average (GPA); computer science, nursing, and special education majors, as well as teacher certification program applicants, must have a minimum 2.5 GPA. Applicants with fewer than 12 college credits must submit a high school transcript. Application review will be completed only upon receipt of official transcripts from high schools and especially colleges and universities. Unofficial transcripts or transcripts sent by students will not be used for admissions.

Application and Information

Application forms and transcripts from candidates for freshman status must be received by May 1 for fall admission and November 1 for spring admission. Transfer students, readmitted students, and students seeking a second bachelor's degree must submit their materials by May 1 and November 1 for fall and spring entry, respectively. However, the University closes the application process earlier when the number of new and continuing students strains its ability to provide effective programs and services. A $35 application fee is required. Applications are reviewed on a rolling basis. Campus tours are available during the fall and spring semesters on weekdays by appointment when classes are in session.

For additional information and application forms for admission or scholarships, students should contact:

Office of Admissions
William Paterson University of New Jersey
Wayne, New Jersey 07470
Telephone: 973-720-2125
 877-WPU-EXCEL (toll-free)
World Wide Web: http://www.wpunj.edu

William Paterson University's hilltop suburban campus offers an environment where students may develop both intellectually and socially.

WILLIAM PENN UNIVERSITY
OSKALOOSA, IOWA

The University

A world of opportunities is available at William Penn University in Oskaloosa, Iowa. From excellent academic programs and a caring faculty to extracurricular activities and athletics to internships and exciting career prospects, William Penn University challenges students to explore all of these opportunities.

One hundred twenty-six years ago, members of the Society of Friends (Quakers) had a vision for the future. The Quaker values of integrity, simplicity, compassion, ethical practice, acceptance, tolerance, and service continue to be the framework for the quality of education that William Penn University provides to students today. The recent change to university status reflects the rapid growth of the campus locations in Oskaloosa, Des Moines, and Ames, Iowa, and encompasses the two colleges—the College for Working Adults and the College for Arts, Sciences, and Professional Studies.

Opportunities abound for students to get involved at William Penn University, including student government, campus ministry, departmental clubs and organizations, intramural athletics, and music activities. After-class activities include regular movie nights, Y nights, and Saturday night dances. Special events like the Halloween decorating contest, Christmas caroling, late-night bowling, campus beautification, community-campus nights, and snow-skiing outings provide students with study breaks.

William Penn University has a strong tradition of excellence in college athletics. As a member of the Iowa Intercollegiate Athletic Conference (NCAA Division III), William Penn has won a national championship, regional championships, and conference championships in both men's and women's athletics. Men compete in baseball, basketball, cross-country, football, golf, soccer, tennis, track, and wrestling. Women compete in basketball, cross-country, golf, soccer, softball, tennis, track, and volleyball.

More than 1,200 students attend William Penn University, with forty-one states and several countries represented. Twelve undergraduate majors with twenty-two areas of emphasis are offered on a semester-system calendar. Twelve major buildings, including a women's residence hall and two coed residence halls, are centered on the 40-acre campus. A new townhouse residence facility for upperclassmen will be completed in August 2000. Many student activities are held in the Atkins Memorial Union, gymnasium, and fitness center. The George Daily Auditorium, a community auditorium two blocks from the campus, is a 696-seat, state-of-the-art facility that is the site of many University functions.

Location

Located in the rolling hills of southeast Iowa, William Penn University lies on the north edge of Oskaloosa, Iowa. Oskaloosa was established as a small mining center in the early 1800s. It has since grown to more than 12,000 people but still retains a small-town atmosphere.

In the summer, the community band performs in the bandstand every Thursday night. At Christmas, thousands of tiny white lights brighten the city square and bandstand. A variety of city activities are planned—Sweet Corn Days in July, Oskyfest in October, a lighted Christmas parade in December, and Art on the Square in June.

The area also has parks and playgrounds, lighted ballparks, tennis courts, movie theaters, a bowling alley, a roller-skating rink, the YMCA-YWCA Center, and fitness centers. Hiking, boating, fishing, swimming, and camping are conveniently nearby at Lake Keomah State Park, Red Rock Lake, and Lake Rathbun.

Majors and Degrees

William Penn University awards the Bachelor of Arts degree in accounting; applied computer science, with emphases in business, communication, engineering, and mathematics; biology, with emphases in bioprocess technology, environmental studies, preprofessional studies, and science education; business management; communication studies, with emphases in English, journalism and electronic media, and public relations; elementary education, with endorsements in health (K–6), reading, and special education (K–6); history/government; industrial technology, with emphases in engineering technology, industrial management, and technology; mechanical engineering; psychology, with emphases in general psychology and human services; physical education, with emphases in sports administration and wellness and recreation; secondary teaching, with endorsements in athletic coaching authorization, business-general, driver and safety education, English/language arts, health (7–12), industrial technology, mathematics, natural science, physical education (K–12), special education (7–12), and social science; and sociology, with emphases in criminology and general sociology. The College for Working Adults awards the Bachelor of Arts in Business degree.

Academic Program

William Penn University, accredited by the Commission on Institutions of Higher Education of the North Central Association of Colleges and Schools, offers two full semesters, a May term, and two 5-week summer sessions every academic year. The academic program is based on four foundational concepts: leadership, ethical practice, lifelong learning, and commitment to service. These concepts are emphasized throughout the University experience. The Leadership Core, William Penn University's general education requirement, has been named by the John Templeton Foundation to the Honor Roll for Character Building Colleges. It was one of thirty-five colleges in the nation cited for exemplary programming in leadership. Majors consist of at least 30 hours in the student's area of concentration and must be completed with a cumulative GPA of at least 2.0 (on a 4.0 scale).

William Penn's teacher education program offers a major in elementary education and twenty secondary endorsements, including coaching, driver and safety education, industrial technology, reading, and special education (multicategorical). William Penn is one of only two institutions in the state to offer certification for industrial technology teachers and the only private institution in the state to offer the four-year major in industrial technology.

Academic Facilities

Wilcox Library currently holds nearly 75,000 volumes plus sound recordings, microforms, CD-ROM databases, and audio-visual materials. The library subscribes to more than 400 periodicals and to numerous online electronic databases. The

Quaker Collection, an extensive holding of Quaker monographs, photographs, and other materials, is also part of Wilcox Library. In addition, the Academic Success Center and the Jones Mid-East Collection are located in the library.

William Penn's computer facilities contain up-to-date equipment. Networked Macintosh and IBM-compatible microcomputers are available in the computer lab and connect students with e-mail and the Internet. Students also have access to the University's Hewlett-Packard 3000 superminicomputer through terminals located in the computer lab. Knowledgeable lab assistants are always on duty in the computer lab to answer questions and help students understand the computers and software. The dorms are part of the campus' local-area network, and students with their own computers can access the Internet directly from their rooms for a small, one-time connection fee.

Ware Recital Hall, a 140-seat auditorium in McGrew Fine Arts Center, is the setting for many recitals, concerts, and lectures. Special speakers give talks in Penn 400, a 255-seat auditorium that was renovated in 1987.

Most classes are held in Penn Hall, which was built in 1917. This building stands in the center of Penn's 40-acre campus.

Costs

Full-time tuition for 2000–01 is $12,400. The room fee is $1620. Board is $2520.

Financial Aid

To help admitted students meet their expenses, William Penn University has established a very strong financial aid program. Its goal is to provide assistance to students who have strong scholastic backgrounds, special abilities or talents, or financial need. Currently, more than 98 percent of the University's students receive financial assistance in some form.

Two types of financial assistance are available: merit-based scholarships and awards and need-based assistance. Merit-based scholarships and awards are based on academic achievement or on a student's special ability or talent, without consideration of financial need. William Penn University offers several merit-based scholarships and awards, including the Presidential Scholarship (tuition, fees, and books) for valedictorians and salutatorians at accredited high schools, the William Penn Academic Scholarship (up to $8000 per year), the Humanities Scholarship, the Music Scholarship, and other institutional grants and scholarships. Need-based assistance is based on the financial help a student needs to attend William Penn University and is available in three forms: grants, campus employment, and loans.

Students must apply for financial assistance each year by completing the Free Application for Federal Student Aid (FAFSA).

Faculty

William Penn University's faculty is made up of 40 full-time and 20 part-time members. The emphasis at William Penn is on teaching, but students are often able to become involved and work with faculty members on individual research projects. Faculty members are encouraged to get to know students both in the classroom and through cocurricular activities. The faculty-student ratio is 1:14.

Student Government

The Student Government Association (SGA) serves as the governing organization for all students and student organizations. The SGA, led by the student body president, is very active in planning campus activities and events, including Homecoming and Parents' Weekend. The student body is represented by the student body president at all Board of Trustees meetings, and students are a part of many campus committees.

Admission Requirements

Students from accredited high schools and college transfers are considered for admission to William Penn University based on their grade point average, class rank, ACT or SAT I scores, and likelihood of academic success. William Penn University has a rolling admissions policy.

Application and Information

Applications are accepted on a rolling basis and are reviewed as soon as they are complete. Students should send a completed application, the $20 application fee, official copies of all high school and/or college transcripts or the GED score, and ACT or SAT I results to the Office of Admissions.

International students should submit TOEFL scores along with an international student application and a statement of financial support. An ESL program is available for students seeking to improve their English skills.

Campus tours and information sessions are available throughout the week.

To obtain additional information, students are encouraged to contact:

Mary Boyd
Director of Admissions
William Penn University
201 Trueblood Avenue
Oskaloosa, Iowa 52577
Telephone: 515-673-1012
                800-779-7366 (toll-free)
E-mail: admissions@wmpenn.edu
World Wide Web: http://www.wmpenn.edu

At William Penn University, students are taught to run toward a successful future.

WILLIAM WOODS UNIVERSITY
FULTON, MISSOURI

The University

As an independent, selective, coeducational institution, William Woods University (WWU) serves a total enrollment of 1,300 students and offers degrees in forty-one undergraduate and graduate majors in both traditional and nontraditional settings. Chartered in 1870 as an all-female institution serving young women orphaned by the Civil War, the school moved to its Fulton, Missouri, location in 1890, changing its name to Daughter's College of the Christian Church. By the turn of the twentieth century, the school adopted the William Woods College name and began offering undergraduate programs. In 1962, William Woods officially became a four-year liberal arts college, and in 1993, William Woods became a university, awarding graduate degrees. In 1997, the University became a fully coeducational institution.

The diverse student body of William Woods University consists of 905 undergraduate and 413 graduate students from thirty-three states and nineteen other countries. Eighty percent of the students live in the thirteen residence halls on campus.

More than 30,000 students from five nearby colleges and universities offer William Woods students abundant social opportunities in Fulton and the surrounding area. William Woods has more than forty clubs and four national fraternal organizations. Students have the opportunity to participate in a wide range of extracurricular activities. Intercollegiate sports include men's baseball, golf, soccer, and volleyball and women's basketball, golf, soccer, softball, tennis, and volleyball.

Architectural planning has begun for a new 25,000-square-foot addition to the Helen Stephens Sports Complex to increase the academic and recreational opportunities available to the students. The new building, slated to open in fall 2001, will provide additional space for the sports medicine program as well as physical education and recreation. The current Helen Stephens Sports Complex houses a 45-foot by 75-foot swimming pool, a gymnasium, classrooms, a weight room, and a whirlpool and sauna. The University's Weider Fitness Center also contains a large number of pieces of aerobic fitness equipment for student use.

The on-campus Equine Center includes four stables, two indoor arenas, an outdoor arena, a blacksmith's shop, and a 30-acre cross-country course. The McNutt Student Center, a multipurpose geodesic domed structure, houses the student activities center and the admission office, as well as a 1,251-seat auditorium.

The University's graduate and adult studies division offers programs leading to the Master of Business Administration, Master of Education Administration, Master of Curriculum and Instruction, and Master of Equestrian Education.

Location

The beautiful 170-acre William Woods campus is located in Fulton, Missouri, a historic community of 12,000. William Woods students enjoy the charm and safety that a small town offers, along with the cultural and recreational facilities of nearby cities and educational institutions. Columbia, home of the University of Missouri and its 25,000 students, is 25 miles west. Fulton sits midway between Kansas City and St. Louis and is a scenic hour's drive north of mid-Missouri's premier recreational area, the Lake of the Ozarks.

Majors and Degrees

William Woods University offers programs leading to the Bachelor of Arts, Bachelor of Science, Bachelor of Social Work, and Bachelor of Fine Arts degrees. Majors and minors include accounting, art, athletic training, biology, business administration, computer and information science, early childhood education, elementary education, English, equestrian science, equine administration, French, graphic design, history, interdisciplinary studies, international studies, interpreting, Japanese, journalism/mass communication, juvenile justice, management, marketing, mathematics, middle school education, music, paralegal studies, philosophy, physical education, physical science, political and legal studies, psychology, secondary education, social work, sociology, Spanish, special education, sports medicine, theater, and unified science.

Academic Program

At William Woods, students are encouraged to develop a comprehensive, global vision of the world. The workplace is expanding globally, and so must a student's education. Academic programs are designed to prepare the graduate for an active role in a profession or graduate study as well as in society. William Woods purposely remains a small university because it wishes to emphasize the recognition of each student as an individual and to provide the advantages of small classes. The University encourages a close relationship between students, professors, and faculty advisers.

A minimum of 122 credit hours is required for the baccalaureate degree; these include both departmental and general education requirements. The University requires all students to complete a core of common studies. These courses include English, communications, mathematics, fine and performing arts, humanities, history, cultural diversity, natural science, and behavioral/social science. In addition, students gain practical experience through internships offered in many programs of study. WWU is one of only ten schools in the country to offer a four-year degree in American Sign Language (ASL) interpreting.

The University grants advanced placement and appropriate credit to qualified students on the basis of College Board Advanced Placement examinations, advanced-placement high school courses, CLEP scores, community college courses, International Baccalaureate, or other supporting evidence of superior scholarship and accomplishments. William Woods also offers accelerated and independent study for advanced students. In addition, the Century Scholars program offered by William Woods is a three-year baccalaureate degree program that may be selected by qualified students.

Off-Campus Arrangements

William Woods participates in exchange agreements with five other regional institutions, providing many academic and cocurricular opportunities. Through cooperative agreements and direct affiliations with institutions abroad, opportunities for fully accredited study abroad are available to qualified students. Approved programs currently are available through the following organizations: American Institute for Foreign Study, Council International Education, and Beaver College. Direct affiliation programs are available at the following institutions: Regent's College in London, Espiritu Santo University in Ecuador, Altai State University in Russia, and Nagoya Women's University in Japan.

Academic Facilities

The William Woods University Library contains more than 122,000 printed volumes, more than 4,000 journal titles in printed and full-text electronic form, and thousands of nonprint items, including videos, CD-ROMs, and computer software. A separate law library is located within the library building. WWU is a charter member of MOBIUS, a statewide consortium of academic libraries that provides online patron-initiated borrowing to WWU students and faculty members from all participating libraries in Missouri. WWU has eight computer labs for instructional and student use. The library, all classroom buildings, and all residence halls have direct connections to the Internet through the campus network. Distance education students also have access to electronic library resources from remote sites.

The Burton Business and Economics Building, a three-level structure of 35,000 square feet, houses the Division of Business and the Departments of Legal Studies and Interpreting/American Sign Language. A model courtroom provides space for mock trials. The campus also has a new 40,000-square-foot Center for the Arts, which houses the Division of Visual, Performing and Communication Arts. Built with a glassed-in main foyer and sculpture garden, the facility contains a performance theater, a television studio, an art gallery for exhibitions, foundry and kilns, and computer labs, as well as numerous classrooms dedicated to studio art, jewelry, sculpture, printing, graphic design, photography, ceramics, music, weaving, and other activities.

Costs

Resident student fees for the 2000–01 academic year are as follows: tuition and fees, $13,200; and room and board, $5600. The application fee is $25. Since the 1997–98 academic year, students who graduate from William Woods University and who have been enrolled continuously as full-time students receive a reimbursement of all tuition increases that occur during their enrollment at WWU.

Financial Aid

In 1998–99, approximately 85 percent of the University's students received some form of financial assistance. William Woods participates in the Federal Pell Grant, Federal Supplemental Educational Opportunity Grant, Missouri Grant, Federal Perkins Loan, Federal Stafford Student Loan, and Federal Work-Study programs. Parents of students applying for need-based assistance are required to file the Free Application for Federal Student Aid (FAFSA). In addition to providing awards for achievement in art, athletics, equestrian science, and performing arts, William Woods also offers academic scholarships based on class rank and ACT or SAT I scores. Scholarships are offered to students graduating first in their class as well as to those students who have achieved National Merit Finalist status. William Woods has designed a new scholarship intended to make the University more affordable and, at the same time, to encourage and reward campus and community involvement that makes a complete, well-rounded liberal arts background. This new $5000 LEAD (Leading, Educating and Developing) scholarship is available to any student, regardless of financial need, who agrees to make a commitment to campus and community involvement. Information, instructions about applying, and necessary forms are available in the Student Financial Services Office or on the University's Web site, listed below.

Faculty

William Woods has 50 full-time and 31 part-time faculty members; no classes are taught by graduate students. Students enjoy the relaxed and informal atmosphere of small classes conducted by a diverse teaching faculty; the student-faculty ratio is 8:1. Most of the professors are experienced professionals, and 48 percent hold Ph.D.'s or other terminal degrees. The faculty's enthusiasm and dedication to students are among the University's greatest assets.

Student Government

Self-government is a tradition at William Woods. The Campus Government Association (CGA) has administrative, legislative, and judicial authority in student affairs. One unusual feature of the student government is the appointment of a Commission on Student Life every two years. Through this commission, student members review campus policies and propose changes that reflect the wishes of current students.

Admission Requirements

The Enrollment Council at William Woods considers each application individually. The council reviews an applicant's high school courses, grades, activities, performance on the SAT I or ACT, rank in class, and personal references. Early admission and early acceptance policies exist at William Woods. Transfer students who have cumulative grade point averages of C (2.5) or above are eligible for acceptance. Admission counselors will arrange visits for prospective students and their parents. The Office of Admission also arranges campus tours and interviews during the regular school terms and summer months.

William Woods University welcomes qualified students of any race, color, gender, and national or ethnic origin and those who are physically or mentally handicapped, according to the definition in Section 504 of the Rehabilitation Act of 1973.

Application and Information

To apply for admission, students should submit a current application with a $25 application fee, authorize their high school to send an academic transcript to William Woods, and request that SAT I or ACT scores be sent to the University. Students are accepted on a rolling admission basis after all necessary credentials have been received. While there is no deadline for applying, the University encourages students to apply as early as possible since William Woods limits enrollment to 750 students in the residential program. For an application form, financial assistance information, and brochures, students should contact:

Mary Hawk
Dean of Admission
William Woods University
200 West Twelfth Street
Fulton, Missouri 65251-1098
Telephone: 573-592-4221
        800-995-3159 (toll-free)
E-mail: admissions@iris.wmwoods.edu
World Wide Web: http://www.williamwoods.edu

William Woods is located on a self-contained, 170-acre campus.

WILMINGTON COLLEGE
NEW CASTLE, DELAWARE

The College
Wilmington College, founded in 1967, is a private career-oriented institution offering undergraduate and graduate degrees. The College is accredited by the Middle States Association of Colleges and Schools. The educational programs are designed to help students of varied academic backgrounds achieve their potential in a small-college environment where individual attention plays an important part in the academic and personal growth of each student. The current enrollment is 6,000 men and women. The student body consists of a combination of recent high school graduates and returning adult students who wish to upgrade their educational levels and enhance their learning capabilities.

At the graduate level, master's degrees are offered in business, community counseling, education, and nursing. A doctoral program in education is also offered.

A variety of extracurricular activities provide channels for students' special interests. The College is a member of both the National Association of Intercollegiate Athletics (NAIA) and the National Collegiate Athletic Association (NCAA). Wilmington College offers intercollegiate teams for baseball and basketball for men and basketball, softball, and volleyball for women. Intramural sports for men and women are provided during the fall and spring semesters.

The College sponsors extracurricular events and group activities, the most popular of which are the Aviation Club, the Psychology Club, and the student yearbook.

Location
Wilmington College's main campus is located near the historic town of New Castle, approximately 6 miles from the city of Wilmington. New Castle is filled with museums, buildings, and other sites of interest dating back to before the Revolutionary War. To serve the educational needs of Delaware's population, Wilmington College offers many of its programs at five other convenient locations—Dover Air Force Base, Silver Lake Complex, Georgetown, the Wilmington Graduate Center, and a site at Rehoboth Beach.

Majors and Degrees
Wilmington College offers an Associate of Arts degree in general studies and an Associate of Science degree in early childhood education. The College confers the Bachelor of Arts degree in behavioral science and the Bachelor of Science degree in accounting, aviation maintenance management, aviation management, business management, communication technologies operation and maintenance, criminal justice, elementary education, finance, human resources management, interactive multimedia design and communication, Internet and networking design and technology, nursing (RNs only), and sports management.

Academic Program
The academic program of the College has been developed to provide a personal approach to career education. Each student is assigned an academic adviser to assist with curriculum and career development. Representatives from business, industry, health care, and education serve as adjunct faculty. They work closely with faculty members to design practical experiences and special interest courses to meet student needs. A personalized education and a well-trained faculty give students the skills that will make them competitive in the job market. Wilmington College offers programs on a year-round basis that are designed to fit a student's schedule. Courses at the New Castle campus are offered both during the day and in the evening. In addition to the traditional fifteen-week semester, many courses are offered in a seven-week accelerated format and a weekend format. The fall semester begins in September and ends before Christmas. The spring semester begins in January and ends in April. The summer sessions are offered in the seven-week accelerated format during the months of May, June, July, and August.

Academic Facilities
The College's seventeen buildings house classrooms, offices, the bookstore, a radio station and TV studio, computer labs, the gymnasium, and the Wilmington College Cafe. The latest addition to the campus is a 70,000-square-foot building that will house the library, classrooms, faculty offices, and state-of-the-art labs for nursing, communication, and the sciences.

The Wilmington College Library houses a collection of more than 142,000 bound volumes and subscribes to more than 500 periodicals. Also available in the library are microcomputers, electronic links to other libraries, and a growing collection of software programs and nonprint media for student use.

Costs
For the 2000–01 academic year, tuition is $624 per 3-credit course at the New Castle campus. The registration fee is $25 per term, and the graduation fee is $25. For certain courses, there may be additional laboratory fees. These fees are provided in the appropriate registration program.

Tuition at various Wilmington College sites varies. For current costs, students should contact the site of attendance.

Financial Aid
The purpose of the financial aid program at Wilmington College is to supplement the resources of the students and their family in order to give needy students the opportunity to obtain a college education. Applicants for financial aid are urged to apply early, since funds are limited. Financial aid is generally awarded in a combination of loan, grant, and employment. The major student financial aid programs in which the College participates are Federal Pell Grants, Federal Supplemental Educational Opportunity Grants, Federal Work-Study, and Federal Stafford Student Loans. Delaware students may be eligible for assistance from the Delaware Postsecondary Scholarship Fund Program. Academic, service, and athletics scholarships are also available.

Applicants for aid should request the necessary application forms from the Financial Aid Office. Awards are not made until a student has been officially accepted by the College. For further information, students should contact the financial aid officer at the College.

Faculty
There are 460 full- and part-time faculty members at Wilmington College who offer personalized attention to each student. Full-time professors, as well as adjunct faculty members from busi-

ness, industry, health care, and education serve as faculty advisers in diversified career fields. The student-faculty ratio is 22:1.

Student Government

The Student Government sponsors many activities throughout the academic year. There are day trips to New York City, Philadelphia, and the Inner Harbor at Baltimore. There are discounted dinner theater tickets and an annual ski trip.

The Student Government is also a way for students to become involved in campus activities and to bring new events to campus.

Admission Requirements

Wilmington College welcomes applications from men and women of all ages and of every race, color, and creed who, in its judgment, show promise of academic achievement regardless of past performance. The College seeks a diversified student body and encourages the submission of applications from students of widely differing backgrounds, aptitudes, and interests, including career-minded adults who wish to upgrade their skills or complete a degree program.

In addition to considering an applicant's academic record, the Admissions Committee relies heavily upon the recommendation of the student's guidance counselor or principal as to the applicant's desire to attend Wilmington College and ability to benefit from the programs and services offered. The College recognizes the effect of determination and motivation on students' performance in college and is eager to give them a chance to prove themselves.

Candidates must be graduates of an accredited high school or have successfully completed a General Educational Development (GED) program. SAT I scores are preferred and are taken into consideration for admission to the College, but they are not required. Applications are reviewed and accepted on a continuous basis. Freshmen are admitted to the fall, spring, and summer sessions.

Application and Information

Applications for admission, along with a $25 application fee and all other required materials, should be submitted no later than one month prior to the beginning of a semester. The College uses a rolling admission plan, and applicants are notified of the admission decision within three weeks of the receipt of all materials.

Requests for additional information and for application forms should be directed to:

Dean of Admissions
Wilmington College
320 DuPont Highway
New Castle, Delaware 19720-6491
Telephone: 302-328-9407
E-mail: inquire@wilmcoll.edu

The Pratt Student Center.

WILSON COLLEGE
CHAMBERSBURG, PENNSYLVANIA

The College
Wilson College, founded in 1869, is a distinctive liberal arts college that prepares students for rewarding lives and careers, leadership roles in a global society, social responsibility, and a lifetime of learning. Students from twenty-one different states and nine countries join a cooperative learning community that embraces educational opportunities both inside and outside of the classroom.

The College is committed to the education and advancement of women. Programs in the College for Women celebrate, reflect upon, and critique women's contributions to society and offer women unique opportunities to grow in intellect, self-confidence, leadership abilities, and feeling of self-worth in their chosen roles. Offerings in the College for Continuing Education draw upon the strengths of the Women's College while recognizing the needs of older adults, both women and men. The total College full-time-equivalent enrollment is 900, with a full-time-equivalent enrollment of 350 in the College for Women.

Within Wilson's intentionally small, close-knit community, built upon shared governance under an Honor Principle, students learn by direct participation and initiative to maintain a lifestyle based on mutual trust, empathetic understanding, and respect for others and for the natural world.

Wilson's Residential Women with Children Program provides on-campus residential housing year-round to single mothers and their children so that the mother can pursue a bachelor's degree full-time. Providing appropriate housing in which both mothers and children can succeed is another way in which Wilson College is providing today's women with the tools to become academically, financially, and personally successful.

Location
Wilson College is located in a residential neighborhood of historic Chambersburg (population about 20,000) in Franklin County. It is located in the scenic Cumberland Valley at the intersection of Interstate 81 and U.S. Route 30, approximately 50 miles southwest of Harrisburg, Pennsylvania, and 90 miles northwest of Washington, D.C., and Baltimore, Maryland.

Majors and Degrees
Wilson offers programs leading to the Bachelor of Arts or Bachelor of Science degree. Majors are available in the following fields: accounting, behavioral sciences (psychology and sociology), biology, business and economics (economics, international business, management, management information systems, and marketing), chemistry, education (elementary and secondary), English, environmental studies (ecological perspectives, natural and sustainable systems, and social systems), equestrian studies (equestrian management and equine management), equine facilitated therapeutics, exercise and sports science, fine arts (art history and studio art), French, history and political science (history, international relations, and political science), international studies, legal studies, mass communications, mathematics, philosophy and religion, psychobiology, Spanish, and veterinary medical technology. Special majors may be designed to develop a specific focus through the integration of several disciplines.

Preprofessional programs include law, medicine, and veterinary medicine.

Minors are available in archaeology, art history, athletic coaching, biology, business, chemistry, computer science, dance, economics, English, entrepreneurship and small business management, environmental studies, French, German, historic preservation, history, Latin, management information systems, mass communications, mathematics, music, peace studies, philosophy/religion literature, political science, psychology, social ethics, sociology, Spanish, studio art, and women's studies.

Academic Program
The Bachelor of Arts and the Bachelor of Science degrees require the successful completion of a minimum of thirty-six courses, at least eighteen of which must be outside any single discipline. All students follow a liberal studies curriculum that includes a first-year seminar; foundational courses in writing, foreign language, computer studies, quantitative skills, and physical activity and wellness; and transdisciplinary studies courses in art and literature, environmental studies, multicultural studies, natural science, and women's studies. Students have the opportunity to pursue specialized interests through independent studies, advanced study or research, and internships in professional settings.

The Wilson College calendar includes two semesters and the January term. First-semester final examinations come before the winter vacation. The January term is often used for internships, independent studies, field experiences, special courses at other institutions, and travel.

Off-Campus Arrangements
Opportunities for off-campus study, including study abroad and other special programs, are available to qualified students under several plans. Through programs offered by other institutions, Wilson women may make arrangements for study abroad, usually during the junior year, or for study at the United Nations and in Washington, D.C. In addition, internships, independent studies, and other field experiences may be arranged for the summer, for regular semesters, or for the January Term Off-Campus.

Academic Facilities
Wilson's library contains about 165,000 volumes, as well as microfilm holdings and periodicals. In addition to its own collection, the College has ready access to the resources of libraries throughout the world. Academic facilities include student research laboratories, veterinary medical technology laboratories, X-ray and surgical facilities, an electron microscope, a nuclear resonance spectrometer, computer facilities, a learning resource center, and a unique Center for Environmental Education and Sustainable Living. Personal computers are available to students in residence halls and academic buildings.

The fine arts department houses a gallery and individual studios for painting and graphics as well as an art annex with ceramics, sculpture, and printmaking facilities.

Costs

The cost for a full-time student in residence at Wilson College in 2000–01 is $20,225, including $13,569 for tuition, $6306 for room and board, and $350 for fees. All costs and fees are subject to change.

Financial Aid

Approximately 90 percent of the students at Wilson benefit from a strong financial aid program that provides assistance through a combination of grants, loans, and student employment. Awards are based on financial need, which is determined from information provided through the Free Application for Federal Student Aid (FAFSA) form. A brochure describing the financial aid program is available from the Office of Admissions.

Merit scholarships are awarded on a competitive basis to incoming freshmen and transfer students. Awards are made for full tuition (Sarah Wilson Scholarship), three-quarter tuition (Trustee Scholarship), and half tuition (Presidential Scholarship). In order to be considered, applicants must have combined SAT scores of 1200 or higher (or a 27 ACT composite) and have a minimum 3.3 cumulative average. In addition, transfer students should have a minimum GPA of 3.0 in all previously completed college course work. Recipients must be enrolled full time, i.e., at least four courses per semester.

The Phoenix Scholarship Program is automatically awarded to accepted students whose GPA is above 3.0 on a 4.0 scale, whose class ranking is in the top 30 percent, and/or who have scored above 1000 on the SAT I. Phoenix awards range from $2000 to $6000.

Faculty

The faculty at Wilson is organized in three divisions: Humanities, Sciences, and Social Sciences. This structure facilitates communication among the disciplines and encourages the development of interdisciplinary courses. There are 36 full-time and 34 part-time faculty members. Of the full-time faculty, 72 percent have doctorates or other terminal degrees in their fields; 56 percent are women. The student-faculty ratio of 10:1 allows for small classes and close working relationships. Primarily concerned with their role as teachers, Wilson's faculty members are responsive to students' needs and interests, while pursuing their own interests in research, publishing, or artistic achievement.

Student Government

Every student at Wilson is a member of the Wilson College Government Association. Senators chosen from each residence hall represent their constituents in all areas of College government. Students also serve on faculty committees and on committees of the Board of Trustees.

Admission Requirements

Wilson admits students of any race, color, religion, national or ethnic origin, or geographical location. Neither the number of applications from a single school or region nor the need for financial aid is considered in the admission process. The recommended secondary program should include 4 years of English, 4 years of social studies, 3 years of mathematics, 2 years of lab science, and 2 years of a foreign language. The Admissions Committee also carefully considers applicants whose credentials vary from this pattern. In addition, early admission is available to well-qualified students who wish to enter college after three years of secondary school.

The Admissions Committee acts upon an application after receiving all required documents. These include the candidate's application, an essay, an official secondary school transcript, and SAT I or ACT scores. Transfer students must also submit an official college transcript. International students from non-English-speaking countries are required to submit results from the TOEFL.

Application and Information

Applications are welcome for both the fall and spring semesters. Wilson College uses a rolling admission plan, which enables the Admissions Committee to act upon a candidate's application as soon as possible after it is completed. Although there are no deadlines for application, candidates are encouraged to apply as early as possible.

For further information and application forms, students should contact:

M. Edgerton Deuel II
Director of Admissions
Wilson College
1015 Philadelphia Avenue
Chambersburg, Pennsylvania 17201-1285
Telephone: 717-262-2002
        800-421-8402 (toll-free)
E-mail: admissions@wilson.edu

The library at Wilson College.

WINGATE UNIVERSITY
WINGATE, NORTH CAROLINA

The University

Wingate University was founded in 1896 and offers an excellent educational experience in a traditional environment. Students are respected, and there is concern for the individual. Wingate enrolls both resident and commuting students, and students come from more than twenty-nine states and several countries. There are 1,300 men and women currently enrolled. There are residence halls for men and for women and six honors apartment buildings on the North Campus. Four hundred additional units of on-campus student apartments are currently under construction and will be in use in fall 2000. Most housing is air conditioned.

Social life at Wingate University includes a full schedule of activities planned by the Student Government Association (SGA) and the Activities Program Board of the Dickson-Palmer Student Center. There are more than thirty-five clubs on campus, including the Christian Student Union. An active Greek system includes three national fraternities and two national sororities. For men, Wingate University participates in NCAA Division II intercollegiate baseball, basketball, cross-country, football, golf, lacrosse, soccer, and tennis. For women, NCAA Division II intercollegiate basketball, cross-country, golf, soccer, softball, swimming, tennis, and volleyball are available. An active year-round intramural program is also carried on at Wingate. The Cannon Athletic Complex opened in 1986; it houses a basketball arena, an Olympic-size indoor pool, racquetball courts, and physical fitness facilities, including a second full-size gym.

Austin Memorial Auditorium seats 1,100 and serves as a cultural center for the University and the area. Each year, the University Lyceum Series brings outstanding programs to the campus. The Dickson-Palmer Student Center houses the campus store, game rooms, a lounge, a fitness center, the Klondike Grill, the campus post office, a social hall, facilities for student organizations, and other multipurpose rooms. New on-campus student apartments are scheduled for completion during summer 2000 and house approximately 400 students. A new $8.3-million Fine Arts Center and a $3.5-million football stadium and field house were dedicated and used for the first time during the 1998–99 academic year.

Wingate University is affiliated with the Baptist State Convention of North Carolina and is accredited by the Southern Association of Colleges and Schools, NCATE, the North Carolina Department of Public Instruction, and the Association of Collegiate Business Schools and Programs (ACBSP).

The School of Education and the School of Business and Economics offer master's degrees.

Location

Nestled halfway between the North Carolina mountains and seashore, Wingate's location offers unlimited opportunities for students. Wingate University is in Wingate, North Carolina, 4 miles from Monroe (population 25,000) and just 20 miles east of Metropolitan Charlotte. Many venues, including Ovens Auditorium, Blumenthal Arts Center, Carolina Panthers Stadium (Ericsson Stadium), Blockbuster Pavilion, the Charlotte Motor Speedway, Independence Arena, and the Charlotte Coliseum, sites of cultural and sports events, are accessible in 45 minutes or less.

Majors and Degrees

Wingate University offers five undergraduate degrees: Bachelor of Arts, Bachelor of Science, Bachelor of Music Education, Bachelor of Fine Arts, and Bachelor of Liberal Studies. Majors are offered in accounting; American studies; art, with concentrations in computer graphics, 2-D studio art, and 3-D studio art; athletic training/sports medicine; biology; business administration, with concentrations in finance, management, management information systems, and marketing; business mathematics; chemistry; chemistry business; communication studies, with concentrations in broadcast journalism, media arts, organizational communications, public relations, and speech; economics; education, with concentrations in art (K–12), elementary (K–6), middle grades (6–9), music (K–12), physical (K–12), reading (K–12), and secondary (9–12 in biology/chemistry, English, history, and mathematics); English; environmental biology; general studies; history; human services; mathematics, with a concentration in computer science; music, with concentrations in business, communications, and performance; parks and recreation administration; philosophy; religious studies; sociology; Spanish; and sport management. Preprofessional programs are offered in dentistry, law, medicine, ministerial, pharmacy, and veterinary medicine.

Academic Program

All students are required to complete core education courses in the humanities, the fine arts, foreign language, mathematics, the sciences, and the social sciences. Students then choose from a variety of majors—planned programs of study. In addition, they may select a concentration (minimum requirement of 18 hours) from one of thirty-two academic areas. Concentrations are optional in all programs except intermediate education, which has a built-in requirement. Almost all programs offer a component of independent study if a student desires it.

Wingate has an honors program for its most qualified students.

All students are given the opportunity to receive credit through International Baccalaureate, Advanced Placement, the College-Level Examination Program (CLEP), or departmental examinations.

The Freshman Experience Program helps freshmen successfully adjust to college and explore career opportunities, academic issues, and social issues. The program is taught by faculty advisers with the assistance of peer advisers.

The duPont Summer Research Program teams top students and faculty members in studies in a broad range of topics.

Other important aspects of the University's overall program are academic advising, career planning, and placement services. The liberal arts emphasis at Wingate is ensured through the Lyceum Events Series. Students must attend forty of these events (which include arts, religious, political, dramatic, musical, literary, and other entertaining and cultural events) during their four years at Wingate.

Wingate's calendar year includes a fall semester, a spring semester, a May term, and two 4-week summer sessions.

Off-Campus Arrangements

More than 25 years ago, Wingate pioneered an annual program of international study called W'International. This program offers all qualifying juniors an international study experience at virtually no cost above regular tuition and fees. Students who complete both the W'International seminar (weekly sessions during the fall semester preceding the trip) and the travel component with a Wingate University professor receive 2 hours of credit. In addition, a semester-long international program in London allows students to live in London and complete a full semester's work there under the tutelage of Wingate professors. Wingate also has student exchange agreements with universities in Mexico City and Hong Kong.

More than 55 percent of Wingate graduates have studied abroad at least once during their four years at Wingate.

Academic Facilities

The Ethel K. Smith Library is the heart of academic life on campus. The large air-conditioned building, enlarged and remodeled in 1992, is equipped with study tables and carrels and has more than 110,000 volumes, 500 periodicals, 300,000 titles on microfiche and CD-ROM, and a special collection of children's literature. Wingate was the first independent college in North Carolina to install the Integrated On-line Catalog and Circulation System, which greatly assists students' research projects. The library recently added twenty-five new Pentium PC terminals and several high-speed printers, which provide students with access to the Internet and the World Wide Web, as well as virtual library access to more than 2,000 full-text online journals and 6,000 indexes.

The Academic Resources Center, which opened in 1992, houses all campus tutorial programs and student support services, including LSAT and GRE review programs.

The new $8.3-million George A. Batte, Jr. Fine Arts Center, which opened in spring 1999, houses a 550-seat theater, a 175-seat recital hall, a secure art gallery, music practice rooms, music classrooms, and performance areas.

The Computing Center directs both the administrative and academic systems for the whole campus. In addition, microcomputer labs are available for student use in several campus locations. All PCs in the computer labs provide direct access to the library's online system. These facilities are open long hours to accommodate student needs.

Costs

The basic charge for tuition and general fees in 2000–01 is $13,050. Room and board cost $5200. There is no additional charge for out-of-state residents.

Financial Aid

Approximately 85 percent of the students at Wingate University receive financial aid. Students must apply each year by filing the Free Application for Federal Student Aid. Students are expected to file by April 15.

Wingate offers generous merit-based academic, athletic, and music scholarships to excellent students who qualify. There are also scholarships for transfer students. Additional aid for students comes from Federal Pell Grants, Federal Supplemental Educational Opportunity Grants, North Carolina Contract Grants, and North Carolina Student Incentive Grants. Federal Stafford Student Loans are available, if needed. Most aid packages are renewable each undergraduate year, assuming students' family circumstances remain about the same. A convenient monthly payment plan is also available. Jobs in the library, the student center, the cafeteria, and other areas are available; earnings are paid directly to the students.

Faculty

The University has 86 full-time faculty members. More than 84 percent of these hold earned doctorates or terminal degrees. Faculty emphasis is on teaching, and the majority of the faculty members serve as academic advisers. The average class size is 20 students, and all classes are taught by professors, not by graduate assistants. Student-faculty dialogue is encouraged, and the student-faculty ratio is kept low (less than 13:1) to stimulate interaction between the two groups. The duPont Summer Research Program provides an opportunity for faculty members and students to collaborate on independent research in their fields of interest.

Student Government

Students are actively involved in institutional government. Student Government Association members are elected in campuswide elections, and the SGA has authority in matters relating to student discipline and the campus honor code. Campus rules reflect North Carolina laws and the Christian heritage of Wingate University. Student government also plays an active role in planning campus activities. Students serve as voting members of each University Assembly committee that deals directly with student life.

Admission Requirements

Freshman applicants should be qualified graduates of an accredited high school. Freshman applicants are considered on the basis of class rank, high school average, curriculum, and test scores (SAT I or ACT).

Transfer students are encouraged to apply. To qualify for admission, they must be academically eligible to return to their previous institution, have a minimum 2.0 GPA, and must provide official transcripts of all previous work.

Campus interviews are strongly encouraged but not required.

Application and Information

When students are applying for admission, the following must be sent in and must be complete: the application and $25 processing fee, transcripts of all work attempted, SAT I or ACT scores, and two letters of recommendation. Applications for freshman admission should be sent in as soon as possible during the senior year of high school. Wingate uses a rolling admission policy. In most cases, students are notified of the admission decision within two weeks after their application file has been completed. Wingate University is operated on a nondiscriminatory basis. Online applications are available on the Wingate Web site (see below).

Application materials should be sent to:
Dean of Admissions
Wingate University
Wingate, North Carolina 28174
Telephone: 704-233-8200
        800-755-5550 (toll-free)
Fax: 704-233-8110
E-mail: admit@wingate.edu
World Wide Web: http://www.wingate.edu

The Stegall Administration Building at Wingate University.

WINTHROP UNIVERSITY
ROCK HILL, SOUTH CAROLINA

The University

Winthrop University, founded in 1886, has been an educational leader in South Carolina for more than a century. Originally a training school for teachers, the school has grown into a national-caliber comprehensive teaching university committed to being a model of excellence in public higher education. Winthrop's distinctive mission is to offer challenging academic programs to a high-achieving, culturally diverse, and socially responsible student body of more than 5,800 students. Forty-one states and thirty-eight other countries are represented in Winthrop's undergraduate and graduate population.

The University offers a total of seventy-two undergraduate and forty-nine graduate degree programs through the four academic divisions: the College of Arts and Sciences, the College of Business Administration, the College of Education, and the College of Visual and Performing Arts.

In 1997, Winthrop achieved its goal of 100 percent national accreditation of eligible academic programs, distinguishing the University as the only comprehensive teaching school among senior colleges and universities in the state to reach that level of accreditation. Winthrop also joined an elite group of only seventeen universities and colleges nationwide with accreditations by the National Associations of Schools of Art and Design, Dance, Music, and Theatre, establishing the University as a regional center for the arts.

Some of the most significant educational experiences at Winthrop occur outside the classroom as students actively participate in the life of the campus. More than 100 campus organizations offer outlets for special interests or talents and provide opportunities to hone leadership skills and build confidence and interpersonal skills. In addition, students enjoy recreational sports and NCAA Division I intercollegiate competition in men's and women's basketball, cross-country, golf, indoor and outdoor track, and tennis; women's softball and volleyball; and men's baseball and soccer.

Winthrop's students also benefit from Dinkins Student Union (DSU), the University's activities board. Ranked as one of the top five programming boards in the nation for the past five years, DSU schedules a broad array of fun and interesting entertainment, including bands, comedians, lecturers, and novelty acts for student enjoyment.

Upon graduation, Winthrop students successfully continue their education in prestigious graduate and professional programs or enter a wide variety of positions in the arts, business, education, medicine, government, law, or other professions.

Location

Winthrop's beautiful, tree-lined campus is included on the National Register of Historic Places. The 100-acre main campus, complemented by a 450-acre athletics and recreational area, including a lake and coliseum, provides an ideal collegiate setting. Winthrop's location in Rock Hill, South Carolina, offers the friendly atmosphere of a college town while attractions such as professional sports and entertainment are only 30 minutes away in Charlotte, North Carolina.

Majors and Degrees

At the undergraduate level, the University offers academic programs leading to the Bachelor of Arts, the Bachelor of Fine Arts, the Bachelor of Music, the Bachelor of Music Education, the Bachelor of Science, and the Bachelor of Social Work.

Majors offered leading to the B.A. include art; art history; dance; English; general communication disorders; history; integrated marketing communication; mass communication: broadcast and journalism; mathematics; modern languages: French and Spanish; music; philosophy and religion; political science; psychology; public administration; sociology, criminology; theater: design/technical, and performance.

The B.F.A. in art is offered with the following concentrations: ceramics, general studio, graphic design, interior design, painting, photography, printmaking, and sculpture. The Bachelor of Music in performance and the Bachelor of Music Education with options in choral and instrumental music are also offered.

Majors leading to the B.S. include biology, medical technology; business administration with options in accounting, computer information systems, economics, entrepreneurship, finance, general business, health service management, management, and marketing; chemistry; computer science; early childhood education; elementary education; family and consumer sciences; human nutrition, dietetics, food systems management; integrated marketing communication; mathematics, statistics; physical education, fitness/wellness; science communication; special education: mild disabilities, severe disabilities; and sport management.

Teacher training programs leading to state certification are available in the fields of art, biology, chemistry, dance, early childhood education, elementary education, English, history, mathematics, modern languages, music, physical education, political science, sociology, special education, and theater.

Academic Program

The University is accredited by the Commission on Colleges of the Southern Association of Colleges and Schools (1866 Southern Lane, Decatur, Georgia 30033-4097; telephone: 404-697-4501) to award bachelor's, master's, and specialist's degrees. Additional national accreditation of individual programs sets the University apart from its peers and assures Winthrop students of a top-notch curriculum taught by qualified faculty members using the best available resources.

A strong liberal arts core provides the foundation for Winthrop's undergraduate and graduate degree programs offered in the four academic divisions: the Colleges of Arts and Sciences, Business, Education, and Visual and Performing Arts. A minimum of 124 credits is required for a baccalaureate degree, with a specified number of general education, major-specific, and elective hours for each degree.

Special student programs include the Honors Program; the Critical Issues Symposium for freshmen; cooperative education and internships; PACE for academically gifted African-American students; New Start for adult learners; Leadership Winthrop; and Peer Mentoring, a first-year support program.

Off-Campus Arrangements

Winthrop students can experience the excitement of studying abroad at a number of institutions in countries such as Australia, China, Germany, Russia, and Spain. In addition, Winthrop also participates in the National Student Exchange Program, which allows Winthrop students to study for up to one year at one of more than 130 colleges and universities throughout the United States while paying Winthrop's tuition.

Academic Facilities

The faculty members and collections of the Dacus Library are an integral part of the University's instructional program. The Dacus On-line Catalog system provides easy access to the library's collections. The library's holdings total more than

500,000 volumes and volume-equivalents, which are supplemented by resources available through the national interlibrary loan program.

Winthrop's academic computing department supports the instructional and research functions of the University. Students have access to diverse computing resources, including more than fifteen computer laboratories that support PC, Macintosh, and UNIX systems for open-access and instructional needs. All campus buildings and residence halls are connected to the campus network and the Internet. Students are provided with consolidated computing services, including Web-based e-mail, central server storage space, and personal Web pages. The Academic Computing Center also provides computer access and Braille printing services to visually impaired students.

The Writing Center, Math Lab, and Language Lab facilities assist students who want to improve skills in specific areas. Multimedia classrooms and distance learning facilities provide an added dimension to classroom instruction.

The University also maintains several versatile performing spaces. Byrnes Auditorium, which seats 3,500; the recently renovated 216-seat Frances May Barnes Recital Hall; and Tillman Auditorium, with a capacity of 700, are excellent facilities that are widely used for a variety of activities in the Winthrop community. In addition, Johnson Hall, which includes a 331-seat proscenium theater, a 100-seat studio theater, an actor's studio, and two dance studios, provides a comfortable home for the Department of Theatre and Dance. Johnson also houses the Department of Mass Communication and is equipped with broadcast facilities, including a student-operated radio station; editing booths; and equipment for its broadcasting and journalism students. Winthrop Galleries in the Rutledge Building includes two professional exhibition spaces, and a student gallery in McLaurin provides space for art design students to show their work.

Costs

For 1999–2000, the annual tuition cost for full-time South Carolina residents was $4106. Out-of-state tuition was $7414. Room and board costs for all students for a double-occupancy room and a meal plan of twenty-one meals per week totaled $4022.

Financial Aid

At Winthrop, 65 percent of all students receive some form of financial assistance. The University offers a variety of scholarships to high-achieving freshmen with strong high school records and SAT or ACT scores. The scholarships range from $1500 to full tuition and meals. The completed admissions application also serves as the application for academic scholarships. Additional scholarships are available to talented students in the visual and performing arts as well as in all of Winthrop's sixteen intercollegiate sports. Winthrop's financial aid packages, which are processed in the Financial Resource Center, can include grants, loans, or student employment. Students should complete the Free Application for Federal Student Aid (FAFSA) and the Winthrop institutional aid form as soon as possible after January 1 of their senior year. Families often take advantage of the Winthrop Payment Plan, which divides each semester's costs into four convenient payments. For more information, please contact the Financial Resource Center at 803-323-2189 or by e-mail at wufrc@winthrop.edu.

Faculty

Effective, quality teaching is the number one priority of Winthrop's faculty members, who include renowned scholars, researchers, and creative artists. All classes are taught by faculty members, and class size typically ranges from 15 to 30 students, fostering close personal contact between student and teacher. Of the 290 full-time faculty members, 82 percent hold the highest degree in their field. With a student-faculty ratio of 15:1, Winthrop faculty members are able to take a personal interest in the individual needs and development of every student.

Student Government

The Student Government Association (SGA) includes all Winthrop students and is a primary means for students to become involved in campus activities and policy making. Comprised of three branches (executive, judicial, and legislative), the association deals with important student issues such as student activities, judicial affairs, club and organizational allocations and charters, and campus safety.

Admission Requirements

Winthrop carefully reviews each applicant on an individual basis and the admissions process is designed to determine the right match between high-achieving students and the distinctive educational opportunities offered at Winthrop. Freshman applications are evaluated primarily by using high school performance, including class rank; level of course work; completion of high school prerequisites; standardized test scores (SAT or ACT); and guidance counselor recommendation. Other criteria, including letters of recommendation, essay or personal statement, and extracurricular activities, will be considered if presented.

Transfer applicants who have completed 30 semester hours/45 quarter hours or more of course work at an institution that is accredited by the commission on colleges of a regional accrediting agency must present a cumulative grade point ratio of at least 2.0 on a 4.0 scale. Applicants with fewer than 30 semester hours/45 quarter hours are additionally evaluated on their high school academic record and standardized test scores. Applicants who have been out of high school for five or more years are not required to submit standardized test scores.

Application and Information

The following admission credentials should be submitted by applicants: a completed application for admission, the $35 application fee, an official high school transcript or graduate equivalency diploma, and official results of the SAT I or ACT. Transfer applicants must submit transcripts from all colleges previously attended. Application deadlines are May 1 for fall enrollment and January 1 for spring enrollment. Applications are reviewed on a rolling basis. To be considered for academic scholarships, students should submit their completed admissions application by January 15.

For more information, students should contact:

Office of Admissions
Winthrop University
Rock Hill, South Carolina 29733
Telephone: 803-323-2191
          800-763-0230 (toll-free)
E-mail: admissions@winthrop.edu
World Wide Web: http://www.winthrop.edu

Built in 1894, Tillman Hall is the main administration building for Winthrop University. An excellent example of the Romanesque architecture popular in the 1890s, Tillman was placed on the National Register of Historic Places in 1977.

WOFFORD COLLEGE
SPARTANBURG, SOUTH CAROLINA

The College

"The way I was encouraged to learn and develop as an individual—that's what I prize most about my education." So says David Bresenham, a graduate of Wofford College and Harvard Law School, who is now pursuing a career in the Hollywood entertainment industry. This emphasis on bringing out the best in each student has been the College's hallmark for almost 150 years and is largely responsible for Wofford's reputation as a leader among liberal arts colleges. In fact—along with Davidson, Duke, Furman, and Wake Forest—Wofford is one of only five independent colleges and universities in the Carolinas with a Phi Beta Kappa chapter.

Today, the College's reputation for excellence and innovation is still growing. The Wofford community is particularly excited about breaking ground for an expanded and updated $14-million science center that will incorporate the latest teaching technology; it will open the doors to innovation in undergraduate scientific research. The new facility will open in late 2000.

The Richardson Physical Activities Building opened in 1995. It provides opportunities for recreation and fitness and allows the campus to serve as the summer training site for the Carolina Panthers of the National Football League. A member of the Southern Conference, Wofford is the smallest college in the nation with a Division I football program. Scholarships are available in eight sports each for men and women.

National fraternities and sororities are chartered on campus and a little more than half of the men and women belong to these social organizations. Fraternities and sororities have on-campus lodges, but members live in residence halls and eat with other students in the College dining hall.

Wofford is proud of its continuing relationship with the United Methodist Church, but several other denominations sponsor campus ministries and there is no requirement to participate in religious services or activities.

The Wofford experience is residential. Most students are between the ages of 18 and 22, attend classes full-time, and live on campus in modern residence halls, many of which offer suites with private areas for study and sleep. Enrollment is 1,100 students, of whom about 53 percent are men and 47 percent are women. African Americans and other persons of color make up about 12 percent of the student body. The majority of Wofford students come from South Carolina, but thirty other states and three other nations are represented. In the 1990s, first-year student retention averaged about 90 percent, and four-year graduation rates approach 80 percent of each entering class.

Location

For many years, Spartanburg has been "the crossroads of the New South." Because I-85 and I-26 cross near the city, Charlotte, Atlanta, the Appalachian ski slopes, and South Carolina's famous beach resorts are all within a 2- or 3-hour drive. The Greenville-Spartanburg airport, about 30 minutes from the campus, is served by several major airlines.

A recent article in the *Los Angeles Times* called Spartanburg County the heart of "the South Carolina boom belt." Much of this excitement is due to the opening of the new North American home of BMW, which is located in western Spartanburg County. Dozens of other international companies operate in the area. Wofford students can arrange summer internships at a number of these corporations, including Milliken & Company, which is internationally known for its research and management innovations.

Spartanburg and neighboring Greenville offer lively entertainment and shopping opportunities. WestGate, one of South Carolina's largest shopping malls, is located about 10 minutes away. Spartanburg Memorial Auditorium is adjacent to the Wofford campus, and the proposed Spartanburg Renaissance project is expected to bring a first-class hotel and conference center to a site only three blocks from the College's main entrance.

Majors and Degrees

Wofford students earn Bachelor of Arts and Bachelor of Science degrees; no graduate programs are offered. Majors are offered in accounting, art history, biology, business economics, chemistry, computer science, economics, English, finance, French, German, government, history, humanities, intercultural studies, intercultural studies for business, mathematics, philosophy, physics, psychology, religion, sociology, and Spanish.

Wofford is a good place to prepare for graduate studies or professional education in schools of business, dentistry, law, medicine, and theology. About 30 percent of Wofford's seniors immediately continue their studies, and more than 10 percent of the alumni have chosen careers in medicine or other health-care fields.

Wofford encourages double majors, particularly if a student seeks to develop real proficiency in a second language or has completed Advanced Placement courses in high school. The curriculum also allows time to take courses in Army ROTC, computational science, education for secondary school teacher's certification, fine arts (art, creative writing, music, and theater), geology, Latin American studies, and physical education.

Academic Program

Wofford's strongest commitment is to graduate leaders—men and women who have moral values and civic consciences. Providing learning opportunities away from the campus is essential to meeting that goal.

In a 1999 study by the Institute of International Education, Wofford was third in the nation in the percentage of its students who earned academic credit outside of the United States. Wofford is associated with several international education organizations, and a member of the foreign language faculty serves as the director of programs abroad.

A Presidential International Scholar is chosen each year to undertake a yearlong all-expenses-paid tour to study a particular problem of global importance. Topics have included the relationship between religion and economic progress and historic preservation around the world.

The College operates on a 4-1-4 academic calendar. The Interim is conducted during four weeks in January between the fall and spring semesters. During this time, students work on only one project. Interim projects fall under four basic headings: seminars built around a topic of special interest to a member of the faculty; career-oriented internships or "externships," which are particularly popular for prelaw, premedical, and preministerial students; travel/study projects, many of which take students out of the United States; and faculty-directed independent research/study projects that usually involve about 10 percent of the student body.

While Wofford does not offer majors in the fine arts, students enjoy music and drama as cocurricular activities. Audiences enjoy three or four productions each year by the Wofford Theatre Workshop in the well-equipped Tony White Theater, and choir and glee club concerts are popular both on campus and in the community. The Wofford arts scene is further enhanced by the World Films Series and visits by well-known writers.

Academic Facilities

The Franklin W. Olin Building is equipped with academic and administrative computers, which provide round-the-clock access to the Internet. In 1999, Wofford was recognized as one of *Yahoo! Internet Life* magazine's top 100 Wired Colleges because of its fully integrated campuswide technology network.

The Sandor Teszler Library houses more than 253,000 volumes and microforms. It is open 96 hours per week.

Foreign language instruction features the latest interactive laboratory equipment as well as a satellite earth station for monitoring telecasts from abroad. The eighty-seat teaching theater in the Olin Building is fully equipped to teach advanced students the art of simultaneous translation.

Costs

The comprehensive fee for the 1999–2000 academic year was $21,990. This included $16,975 for tuition and fees and $5015 for room and board. These figures are close to the national average for four-year independent colleges. Wofford has been cited several times for its management efficiency by *U.S. News & World Report* and is included on several lists of "Best Buys in College Education."

Financial Aid

In 1999–2000, the Wofford financial aid office distributed more than $14.1 million in scholarships, grants, work-study, and guaranteed loans. About 55 percent of the students qualified for financial aid based on need. Many changes are expected in government financial aid programs over the next several years. Deserving students who qualify for financial aid should call or write the financial aid office to obtain a current handbook.

The Wofford Scholars Program offers exceptionally qualified students the opportunity to compete for academic scholarships, some of which are worth more than $80,000 over a four-year period. Interested students should contact their high school guidance counselor or the Wofford Admissions Office.

The Bonner Scholars Program, established in 1991, enables about 80 Wofford students to partially finance their education by working as volunteers in human service agencies and after-school mentoring programs.

March 15 is the deadline for financial aid applications for the fall semester. After this date, applications are considered, but funds normally are very limited.

Faculty

The faculty-student ratio (full-time equivalent) at Wofford is 1:14, and more than half of the classes enroll fewer than 20 students. Of the 71 full-time teaching faculty members, 92 percent have earned a Ph.D. or equivalent doctoral degree.

Student Government

Campus life at Wofford is a spontaneous creation of faculty, staff, and students, rather than something artificially programmed by administrators. There are only a few basic rules at Wofford, but self-discipline, respect for others, and involvement in different activities are stressed. The Campus Union and Judicial Commission, composed of elected student delegates, serve as coordinating bodies for campus life.

Admission Requirements

Wofford College admits men and women of good character who demonstrate the potential for successful academic work. Wofford seeks students from diverse racial, cultural, economic, and geographic backgrounds. Typical Wofford freshmen have completed an honors or advanced-placement secondary school curriculum. About half of them rank in the top 10 percent of their high school class. Prospective students must submit scores on either the ACT or SAT I. SAT I scores in the middle two quartiles of the class range from 540–610 verbal and 540–650 math.

Transfer students are admitted each year and are evaluated individually on the basis of their previous college-level work and other qualifications. Transfer students must complete at least 30 hours at Wofford to receive a degree.

Application and Information

The deadline for admission for the fall term is the preceding February 1, with a notification date of March 15. Early decision and early action options are available; students can request a College viewbook or visit Wofford's Web site, listed below.

To obtain more information about Wofford College or the admissions process, students should contact:

The Admissions Office
Wofford College
429 North Church Street
Spartanburg, South Carolina 29303-3663

Telephone: 864-597-4130
E-mail: admissions@wofford.edu
World Wide Web: http://www.wofford.edu

The Franklin W. Olin Building, the Academic Technology Center.

WOODBURY UNIVERSITY
BURBANK, CALIFORNIA

The University

Woodbury University offers students practical, applied education; high academic standards; and small classes. The University is an accredited, independent, nonprofit, coeducational, nonsectarian institution.

Students attend Woodbury because of its specialization in the areas of architecture, business, computers, professional design, and arts and sciences. Also offered is a Master of Business Administration program. The carefully designed curricula at Woodbury give students hands-on experience in their majors in addition to an effective general education. Woodbury maintains small classes to ensure individual student attention.

The University presents a variety of opportunities for all students to join cultural, social, and professional organizations, both on and off campus. The Office of Student Services at Woodbury helps meet students' needs through career planning and job placement workshops; educational, cultural, social, and recreational programs; the sponsorship of various student groups; and special services for international students. The career services office provides Woodbury students and alumni with lifetime employment assistance.

Woodbury's 22-acre campus in Burbank provides students with such on-campus amenities as a swimming pool, gymnasium, residence halls, an athletic field, and food services, all situated on beautifully landscaped grounds.

Founded in 1884, Woodbury's primary mission is to provide programs requisite for success and leadership and to encourage each person's creativity. The University is accredited by the Senior Commission of the Western Association of Schools and Colleges and is approved by the Postsecondary Commission, California Department of Education. The Interior Design Program is accredited by the Foundation for Interior Design Education Research. The Architecture Program is accredited by the National Architectural Accrediting Board.

Location

The Los Angeles metropolitan area serves not only as a business, financial, and design center but also as one of the great shipping centers of the world. The University is closely linked to these resources and commercial communities, which provide students with a firsthand laboratory in which to study the professional positions they have set as their goals.

The campus location offers students beaches, mountains, and deserts within a 90-minute drive. Art, history, and science museums; professional sporting events; and world-class entertainment are local attractions students can enjoy.

Majors and Degrees

The Bachelor of Science degree is offered in accounting, animation arts, business and management, communications, computer information systems, fashion design, fashion marketing, graphic design and multimedia, history and politics, humanities, marketing, and psychology and management. In addition, the Bachelor of Architecture and Bachelor of Interior Architecture degrees are offered.

Academic Program

The academic programs at Woodbury are designed to provide students with the higher education necessary for success and leadership in their chosen fields. The principal emphasis is on relevance of subject matter and personalized instruction, complemented by a strong focus on general education. The academic calendar is based on the semester system. The number of elective units varies depending on the major.

To encourage the achievement of academic excellence, Woodbury University recognizes students who demonstrate the initiative and sense of responsibility to excel. Such superior performance is recognized with special awards.

Academic Facilities

The University library houses a collection of books, magazines, technical reports, trade journals, and reading materials carefully selected to meet fully the curricular needs of students. Microfilm reader-printers, film printers, and copying machines are available, as are special library services, including reference materials on line and on CD-ROM.

Special design facilities provide for the needs of students majoring in animation arts, architecture, fashion design, graphic design and multimedia, and interior design. Included are darkrooms, design studios, a critique and presentation area, and display areas.

Computer facilities include IBM PC compatibles with Internet access, Macintoshes, and a terminal lab for student access to two Digital VAX 4200 systems. The facility includes classrooms and laboratories with terminals and printers exclusively for student use. Woodbury is one of only a few universities in the country that provides a multimedia notebook computer to every full-time freshman.

Costs

Tuition for full-time study (two semesters) for 1999–2000 was $17,361 for the Bachelor of Science program and $18,239 for the Bachelor of Architecture program. The cost of room and board (ten meals per week) was $6000 for 1999–2000. Estimated expenses for a year (two semesters) were approximately $650 for books and supplies, $560 for transportation, and $1495 for personal expenses.

Financial Aid

Assisting students who lack adequate financial resources to attend Woodbury is a primary concern of the University. Various sources of financial aid are available to help meet education costs. Eligible students generally are awarded a financial aid package consisting of a combination of available funds.

Financial aid for eligible U.S. citizens and permanent residents includes Federal Pell Grants, California Grants A and B for California residents, Federal Family Educational Loans, veterans' educational benefits, Federal Supplemental Educational Opportunity Grants, Federal Work-Study awards, Federal Perkins Loans, local scholarships, and Woodbury grants. The University offers financial aid and counseling, as well as part-time employment and full-time placement services. Classes are scheduled to permit students to work part-time, usually in the area of their major interest, so that they may not only meet financial needs but also gain excellent experience.

Faculty

Students benefit from faculty members who are both experts and practitioners in their fields. A student-faculty ratio of 18:1

allows students to work individually with advisers and instructors to structure their course selections, arrange internships, and plan for the future.

Student Government

The student government at Woodbury, known as the Associated Student Government (ASG), represents the entire student body. The ASG consists of 11 undergraduate students who serve as members of the governing board. These students are elected each spring for a year's term. The purpose of the organization is to promote educational advancement, to further intercultural relations, to enhance cooperation among students, and to serve the best interests of the students of Woodbury University.

Admission Requirements

The Admissions Committee evaluates each application on an individual basis. Academic course load and achievement have a significant impact on the admission decision, and interviews are strongly recommended. Each applicant must submit a completed application form and fee or fee waiver, official transcripts from all schools attended, two letters of recommendation, and an answer to one of three essay questions. Students applying to the animation arts major are also required to submit a portfolio. SAT I or ACT scores are required for all freshman applicants and transfer applicants with fewer than 30 semester or 45 quarter units.

Application and Information

Applications are accepted throughout the year for entrance in the fall, spring, and summer terms. Freshman applicants are encouraged to apply before the priority date, March 1. The priority application deadline for transfer students is April 15. Students should direct all materials and inquiries to the Office of Admission at the address below.

Office of Admission
Woodbury University
7500 Glenoaks Boulevard
Burbank, California 91510-7846
Telephone: 818-767-0888, ext. 221
              800-784-WOOD (toll-free)
E-mail: admissions@vaxb.woodbury.edu
World Wide Web: http://www.woodbury.edu

The Woodbury University Los Angeles Times Library.

WORCESTER STATE COLLEGE
WORCESTER, MASSACHUSETTS

The College

Founded in 1874, Worcester State College has a long, impressive record of teacher education. Traditionally, the College has been a gateway to a more fulfilling life for those who would not otherwise have been able to pursue higher education—immigrants, women, nontraditional students, minorities, retirees and elders, and returning veterans. Worcester State's commitment to that mission is as strong today as it was in 1874. Worcester State College has developed into a comprehensive liberal arts institution with more than 4,800 undergraduates and 800 graduate and professional students and a full-time faculty of 150. A wide range of four-year degree programs are offered, as are a number of graduate programs leading to master's degrees. A new emphasis on allied health and biotechnology programs will lead the College into the twenty-first century.

Worcester State College is located on 58 acres on the outskirts of New England's second-largest city and consists of seven major complexes: the Administration Building, the Sullivan Academic Center, the Learning Resource Center, the Gymnasium, the Student Center, Dowden Hall, and Chandler Village (in 2000, the College will complete construction on the Science and Technology Building). The Student Center provides cultural, social, and personal growth and opportunities and offers many services and conveniences for students. The center serves as the "hearthstone" of the campus community.

The College's athletic department provides numerous opportunities for all students to participate in intercollegiate and intramural athletics. Varsity sports for men are baseball, basketball, cross-country, football, golf, hockey, soccer, tennis, and track (indoor and outdoor). Varsity sports for women are basketball, cross-country, field hockey, soccer, softball, tennis, track (indoor and outdoor), and volleyball. Club sports include men's and women's crew and equitation. Other extracurricular offerings include numerous clubs and organizations, lectures, films, arts and crafts exhibits, performing artists, dances, and charter travel service. Students operate their own weekly newspaper, TV station (closed-circuit), and daily radio station (WSCW). The College also has its own Web site. Services of the professionally staffed Career Development and Counseling Center are available to students, as is the Academic Success Center. Students also have access to the center's library of information on careers and graduate schools.

Location

Through a shuttle service, students have easy access to Worcester, which is called the "Heart of New England" because of its location at the geographic center of the six-state region. Rich in history, the city has a population of 170,000 and is about 40 miles west of Boston; 45 miles north of Providence, Rhode Island; and 60 miles northeast of Hartford, Connecticut. More than 700,000 people live less than an hour's drive from the city. The Worcester Art Museum is one of the finest in the country. The Higgins Armory Museum has the greatest collection of armor east of the Mississippi. Other cultural benefits are provided by the Worcester Science Center and the American Antiquarian Society. The Worcester Centrum and Convention Center has a seating capacity of 15,500 and hosts a variety of national sports and entertainment events and exhibits. The Worcester Music Festival, an annual event since 1858, attracts nationally and internationally known performers. The city's parks total 1,290 acres, and there are seven city beaches. Boating and fishing are available in Worcester.

Majors and Degrees

Worcester State College confers the Bachelor of Arts, Bachelor of Science, and Bachelor of Science in Education degrees. Majors are offered in biology, biotechnology, business administration, chemistry, communication disorders, communications, computer science, economics, education, English, geography, health studies, history, mathematics, natural science, nursing (a four-year program and an upper-division program for RNs), occupational therapy, psychology, sociology, Spanish, and urban studies. Minors are available in art, biology, business administration, chemistry, communication disorders, communications, community health, computer science, economics, English, French, geography, health studies, history, mathematics, Middle East studies, music, natural science, philosophy, physics, political science, psychology, sociology, Spanish, theater, and urban studies. Provisional certification programs are offered in early childhood, elementary, and middle school–secondary education.

Academic Program

The academic year is divided into two semesters, the first beginning in early September and ending in late December and the second beginning in mid-January and ending in late May. The College offers a strong futuristic focus in health and biomedical sciences while continuing its traditional commitment to liberal arts and sciences, business, and teacher education. Volunteer internships, which can be undertaken for college credit, are available in business and social service agencies, in biomedical and biotechnology firms, and in government and the media. Internships are available locally as well as in Washington, D.C., and at Disney World.

Off-Campus Arrangements

Each semester, full-time students at Worcester State may take one course free of charge on a space-available basis at any of the other institutions in the Colleges of Worcester Consortium. Members of the consortium are Anna Maria College, Assumption College, Becker College, Clark University, College of the Holy Cross, Quinsigamond Community College, Tufts University School of Veterinary Medicine, the University of Massachusetts Medical Center, Worcester Polytechnic Institute, and Worcester State College. Because Worcester State is one of nine state colleges participating in the College Academic Program Sharing (CAPS) program, students may study for a semester or a year at another of the state colleges. Worcester State College has joint admissions agreements with Quinsigamond Community College and Mount Wachusett Community College and has articulation agreements with several other two-year colleges.

Full-time students at Worcester State may spend one semester abroad at Worcester College in Worcester, England, or at the University of Puerto Rico in Cayey as part of a student exchange program. In addition, opportunities to study abroad in any one of more than twenty different countries are open to students from any public institution of higher education in Massachusetts under the auspices of the Massachusetts Council for International Education, which is headquartered at the University of Massachusetts Amherst.

Academic Facilities

The Sullivan Academic Center houses classrooms, science laboratories, a communication disorders clinic, a greenhouse, administrative and faculty offices, and the Learning Assistance Center, which offers tutoring in several subject areas. The Administration Building houses administrative and faculty offices, classrooms, psychology and science laboratories, and a nursing clinic. In addition to its fitness and athletic facilities, the Gymnasium Building includes general classrooms, art studios, and occupational therapy laboratories.

The Learning Resources Center (LRC) houses the library, a comfortable place for study and research, with more than 142,000 volumes and approximately 1,000 current periodicals. A CD-ROM network electronically provides ready access to several resources. The library is part of a joint effort of fifteen academic, public, and special-collection libraries that share advanced technologies in library and information sciences. In addition, the building houses the Media Center, which provides student access to television, radio, and film production facilities. The LRC also houses a complex of modern telecommunications and electronic learning facilities. Among these are a writing classroom, a math lab, and several labs for use in computer science classes. In addition, a bank of computers is available for general use by members of the campus community. The College supports both PC's and Macintoshes. All labs are networked and are tied to the campus fiber-optic network; this provides students with Internet connections and access to the World Wide Web. Additional computer labs are located in the various academic departments to afford the opportunity to integrate computer technology throughout the curriculum.

The Academic Success Center, located in the Student Center, is dedicated to fostering a healthy academic climate on campus. The Success Center operates the orientation program and is also responsible for academic advising, counseling, minority affairs, career services, disability services, and international student services. In addition, the Learning Assistance Center provides individual tutoring services designed to increase student academic effectiveness.

Costs

Tuition for full-time study in 1999–2000 was $2495 for in-state residents and $8395 for out-of-state students. Yearly fees were $1345, and the cost of books and supplies averaged $500. Campus housing costs were $4140 for the year, plus an additional $270. A technical access charge and board were $1330. All costs are subject to change.

Financial Aid

Students at Worcester State College may apply for all forms of federal, state, and institutional grant and loan assistance by submitting prior to March 1 a Free Application for Federal Student Aid (FAFSA) and a Worcester State College Financial Aid Application. In addition to need-based financial aid and academic scholarships, the College also offers a tuition payment plan. Academic scholarships, offered to promising freshmen at the time of their acceptance, are also available to upperclass students who demonstrate scholarly excellence.

Faculty

There are 150 full-time faculty members, of whom more than 64 percent hold earned doctorates. With the student-faculty ratio of 18:1, there is ample opportunity for interaction between students and faculty members. Upon matriculation and declaration of a major, each student is assigned a faculty adviser, who assists him or her in developing an educational program. The major adviser also guides students throughout their years at the College.

Student Government

The Student Government Association (SGA) is the representative body of the undergraduate student population. Its goals include advocacy of student concerns and rights, involvement in academic and administrative policy decisions, and facilitation of communications between administration, faculty members, staff, and students. Payment of the activity fee entitles any undergraduate student to participate in the Association through selection of representation, involvement in legislative and administrative meetings, seeking of elected office, appointment to institutional committees, and involvement in other activities of the Association.

The SGA annually elects a student representative to sit as a voting member of the College's Board of Trustees.

Admission Requirements

The College admits applicants who have demonstrated strong academic ability. Acceptance of high school seniors and those who have graduated within the past two years is determined by the high school transcript, academic units, and a minimum grade point average (GPA) of 3.0. This GPA is recalculated using only college-preparatory course work. Applicants with GPAs below 3.0 may be considered for admission by using a sliding scale that includes the GPA and total SAT I scores. A total SAT I score of 890 is the minimum for applicants in this category. For those students whose primary language is not English, a TOEFL score of 550 or higher is required. Additional standards for admission are a minimum of sixteen college-preparatory courses taken in the following subject areas: English (four), mathematics (three), natural science (three), social science (two), foreign language (two), and elective courses (two) from these same disciplines, as well as computer science, visual/performing arts, and humanities.

Worcester State College also welcomes applications from transfer students. In order to be eligible, students must meet one of the following sets of criteria: 12 or more transferable college credits and a 2.5 college GPA; 13 to 23 transferable college credits, a 2.0 college GPA, and a high school transcript that meets the admission standards for freshman applicants; or 24 or more transferable college credits and a 2.0 college GPA. Transfer applicants should arrange to have all college transcripts as well as a final high school transcript sent directly to the Admissions Office.

Although admission interviews are not required, applicants are urged to visit the College during scheduled information sessions, campus tours, or to seek information from the offices concerned with academic advising, athletics, financial aid, housing, and student activities. For information on campus tours or open campus events, students should contact the Admissions Office.

Application and Information

The application deadline for the January semester is November 15. The application priority deadline for September is June 1. Applications received after this date will be reviewed on the basis of vacancies. High school candidates are strongly encouraged to apply after the first marking period of the senior year. Applicants are notified of admission decisions on a rolling basis. Letters of notification are forwarded starting in early November for the spring semester and mid-January for the fall semester.

Candidates to either the occupational therapy or nursing programs must submit their applications by January 30; notifications are forwarded in early March.

International students are strongly encouraged to apply for the September semester with a priority deadline of May 1. Translations from a professional evaluating agency in the United States must be provided for all international transcripts. Candidates must also submit results of the SAT I (or a TOEFL score if English is not the primary language) and an affidavit of financial support.

Application forms may be obtained by contacting:

Beth Axelson, Associate Director of Admissions
Admissions Office
Worcester State College
486 Chandler Street
Worcester, Massachusetts 01602
Telephone: 508-929-8040
Fax: 508-929-8183
E-mail: admissions@worcester.edu
World Wide Web: http://www.worc.mass.edu

WRIGHT STATE UNIVERSITY
DAYTON, OHIO

The University

Wright State University (WSU) is an easily accessible campus that supports a diverse student body of more than 16,000 students. Wright State offers bachelor's degrees in more than 100 undergraduate majors as well as thirty-two master's degree programs and three doctoral programs. The University continues to grow and mature as an institution, while striving to maintain an innovative spirit between its faculty members and students and programs and research. Wright State is currently ranked third in research funding among Ohio's thirteen state universities and colleges.

The growing reputation of Wright State has attracted students from throughout Ohio as well as thirty-three other states and fifty-eight countries. The creation of additional on-campus housing for students has increased the opportunity for students from across Ohio and other states to attend Wright State. Currently, the University has modern suite-style residence halls and apartments for more than 2,500 students. More than 50 percent of new freshmen live on campus. A variety of coeducational living environments, including alcohol- and smoke-free environments, are available.

State-of-the-art computer facilities are located in each academic building and the University library. All residence hall rooms have Internet access, and 24-hour computer labs are located in each of the residence halls. Many classrooms have advanced audiovisual equipment, which has increased the use of technology for instructional purposes by faculty members.

Wright State is a comprehensive University in terms of both academic programs and extracurricular activities. There are more than 130 student clubs, organizations, and activities that provide opportunities for students to meet new people, explore different cultures, and gain leadership skills. Recreational facilities are located in the Student Union, the Nutter Center, and the residence halls. Adding excitement and energy to campus life, Wright State's varsity athletics teams compete at the NCAA Division I level through the Midwestern Collegiate Conference.

Wright State has a particularly active Disability Services program and encourages disabled students to participate in all facets of University life. WSU's facilities have been designed to remove architectural barriers and permit more effective and independent use of the facilities. Applicants who require supportive services should arrange for an interview with the Office of Disability Services at least three months prior to enrollment.

Location

The 557-acre main campus, surrounded by a lush biological preserve, is located in a Miami Valley suburban community 12 miles northeast of Dayton, Ohio. The Miami Valley area has a tradition of innovation and is rich in industry and research, including nearby Wright Patterson Air Force Base. The University has convenient highway access and is less than a 2-hour drive from Cincinnati and Columbus. Wright State University Lake Campus is located in Celina, Ohio, approximately 70 miles northwest of Dayton. The Lake Campus is on the shore of beautiful Grand Lake St. Marys.

Majors and Degrees

Fully accredited by the North Central Association of Colleges and Schools, Wright State's main campus grants the Bachelor of Arts, Bachelor of Fine Arts, Bachelor of Music, Bachelor of Science, Bachelor of Science in Business, Bachelor of Science in Computer Engineering, Bachelor of Science in Education, Bachelor of Science in Engineering, Bachelor of Science in Medical Technology, and Bachelor of Science in Nursing. Majors and programs of study include College of Business and Administration—accountancy, business economics, finance, financial services, human resource management, international business management, management information systems, marketing, and operations management; College of Education and Human Services—business (comprehensive), early childhood education, middle childhood education, physical education, and rehabilitation services; College of Engineering and Computer Science—biomedical engineering, computer engineering, computer science, electrical engineering, engineering physics, industrial and systems engineering, materials science and engineering, and mechanical engineering; College of Liberal Arts—acting, anthropology, art, art history, classical humanities, communication, dance, design technology, economics, English, French, geography, German, Greek, history, international studies, Latin, mass communications, motion pictures, motion picture history/theory/criticism, motion picture production, music, music composition, music education, music history, music history and literature, music performance, music theory, organizational communications, philosophy, political science, religion, selected studies, social and industrial communication, social work, sociology, Spanish, theater arts management, theater design/technology, theater studies, and urban studies; and College of Science and Mathematics—biological sciences, chemistry, environmental health sciences, geology, mathematics, medical technology, physics, psychology, and science education. The College of Nursing and Health offers the Bachelor of Science in Nursing.

Wright State grants the Associate of Arts, Associate of Applied Business, Associate of Applied Science, and the Associate of Science through the Lake campus.

The Wright State University Lake Campus in Celina, Ohio, offers associate degrees with course work in the following fields of study: accounting technology, biological sciences, business and administration, business management technology, chemistry, community/rehabilitation services, electronics engineering technology, English, geography, history, industrial engineering technology, management information systems, mathematics, mechanical drafting/design engineering technology, mechanical engineering technology, office information systems (executive, legal, and medical secretarial studies and word processing), psychology, social work, and sociology.

Academic Program

University College serves as the academic home of many first-year students. It can help students determine and achieve their academic and career goals. Academic advisers in University College provide students with assistance in scheduling courses and meeting entry requirements for their major. All students, regardless of their intended major, must complete a core group of general education requirements.

Students who complete advanced-placement course work while in high school may be granted University credit on the basis of their examination scores. Wright State University accepts credits from accredited institutions earned through dual-enrollment programs, such as Ohio's Post Secondary Enrollment Program.

The University honors program creates a learning environment that students can expect to find at a small liberal arts college rather than within a large university. Honors students benefit from small, discussion-centered courses with experienced faculty members; opportunities for leadership in the Student Honors Association and the Mid-East Honor Association;

self-directed research with faculty members; and honors housing. Admission to the honors program is based on ACT and SAT scores, high school grade point average, and class rank. Upon admission to the University, eligible students will be sent an application for the honors program.

Other academic programs of note include Air Force and Army ROTC and adult education programs.

Off-Campus Arrangements

Wright State's membership in the Southwestern Ohio Council for Higher Education enables full-time students to take courses at many area colleges and universities at Wright State's tuition rates. Wright State students can gain hands-on experience through cooperative education and internships. Student who have attained sophomore standing can work with the Office of Career Services and faculty members in their major to find co-op and internship opportunities. Many majors include courses that require students to work with community agencies, businesses, and industries to solve real-world problems.

Wright State students who desire an international experience can spend a quarter or more overseas in one of more than twenty countries or travel with a group of Wright State students and faculty members to Brazil or Japan during the summer.

Academic Facilities

Major academic buildings on the main campus include the Creative Arts Center, the Paul Lawrence Dunbar Library, the Telecommunications Center, four main classroom buildings, the Brehm Laboratory, the Bio-Science Building, the Russ Engineering Center, the Mathematical and Microbiological Sciences Building, the Health Sciences Building, the Medical Sciences Building, the Rike Hall Business Administration Building, the Student Union, and University Hall. Other facilities are available in downtown Dayton and Celina. Wright State students also have access to the libraries of all the institutions in the Southwestern Ohio Council for Higher Education. The combined library holdings total more than a million volumes.

Costs

For 1999–2000, tuition and fees for Ohio residents were $1379 per quarter. Tuition and fees for out-of-state students were $2758 per quarter. Room and board were $1684 per quarter, and additional expenses, including books and supplies, were approximately $900 per year.

Financial Aid

Three forms of financial aid are available: grants and scholarships, which do not require repayment; long-term and short-term loans, which must be repaid; and part-time student employment. Students applying for financial aid must complete both the WSU financial aid application and the Free Application for Federal Student Aid (FAFSA). Sixty-five percent of Wright State's students receive financial aid. University scholarships, based solely on academic ability, are awarded each fall. A special scholarship application must be filed, and additional credentials such as letters of recommendation may be required. Further details concerning financial aid and scholarship programs are available through the Office of Financial Aid.

Faculty

WSU's faculty has 670 full-time and 22 part-time members. About 80 percent hold the highest degrees in their fields. More than 75 percent of classes have less than 50 students.

Student Government

The Student Government Association is the representative body for Wright State students. Leaders and representatives are elected by the entire student body. Its members participate in the University Senate, which is composed of faculty members, administration, and student representatives. It deals with academic regulations, curriculum changes, and other matters of University-wide policy.

Admission Requirements

Ohio students who have graduated from an accredited high school with a college-preparatory curriculum, a minimum 2.0 grade point average (on a 4.0 scale), and a minimum ACT composite score of 18 or a minimum SAT I combined score of 840 are eligible to enter Wright State. Applications from students not meeting these requirements or from students holding a state-approved high school equivalency certificate will be reviewed on an individual basis. Out-of-state students must have a minimum GPA of 2.5 and an ACT score of 20 or an SAT score of 960. Students applying as freshmen should submit a WSU application form, a nonrefundable $30 application fee, a copy of their high school transcript, a College-Preparatory Curriculum Completion Form, and ACT or SAT I scores.

The transfer policy among the University's academic divisions varies and depends on the number of transfer hours applicants have acquired and their cumulative grade point average. The Office of Admissions can provide specific requirements for each college. Transfer applicants must submit official transcripts from each college and university attended and must have at least a 2.0 GPA for admission to the University. The appropriate college of the University will determine how a student's credit is to be applied to the Wright State academic credit requirements.

Application and Information

Application deadlines vary depending on the quarter for which a student is applying. In general, students should submit the completed application and appropriate fee, transcripts, and test scores (where applicable) as soon as possible to ensure a good selection of courses. International students and others with questions about exceptional circumstances should contact the Office of Admissions.

Cathy Davis
Director of Admissions
E 148 Student Union
Wright State University
Dayton, Ohio 45435
Telephone: 937-775-5700
        800-247-1770 (toll-free)
E-mail: admissions@wright.edu
World Wide Web: http://www.wright.edu

The Student Union includes a fitness center with aerobic and weight training equipment, a small gymnasium, and a pool for open recreation activities.

XAVIER UNIVERSITY
CINCINNATI, OHIO

The University

Founded in 1831, Xavier University is the fourth oldest of the twenty-eight Jesuit colleges and universities in the United States. There are approximately 4,000 undergraduate students attending Xavier during the day, and the total University enrollment is 6,400. Coeducational in all divisions, the University has students from more than thirty-five states and forty-two countries. Students may choose from more than sixty undergraduate majors in three colleges and can later pursue graduate degrees in eleven areas. Xavier is nationally recognized for providing a high-quality personalized education rooted in the Catholic Jesuit tradition. Major University divisions are the Colleges of Arts and Sciences, Business Administration, and Social Sciences; the Center for Adult and Part-time Students; and the Graduate School.

Location

Xavier is located on 125 acres in a residential section of Cincinnati. Noted for its beautiful suburbs and parks, the city also has a reputation as a cultural center because of its museums, zoo, art academy, operatic performances, theater, and nationally renowned symphony orchestra. In addition, Cincinnati has been named America's most livable city and one of the top ten cities for work and family life. Students can see major-league professional teams in action in several sports, and there are facilities for a variety of recreational activities.

Majors and Degrees

Xavier's College of Arts and Sciences awards the Bachelor of Arts or Bachelor of Science degree in applied science (chemistry or physics/engineering), art, biology, chemical science, chemistry, classics, communication arts, computer science, English, history, mathematics, medical technology, modern languages, music, natural science (preprofessional programs in dentistry, medicine, and veterinary studies), philosophy, physics, pre–mortuary science, and theology. Students studying the preprofessional programs in the natural sciences are assisted with entrance into a health career or medical school by the preprofessional health advising office. Xavier also offers an associate degree in radiologic technology.

The Williams College of Business awards the Bachelor of Science in Business Administration degree in accounting, economics, entrepreneurial studies, finance, general business, human resources, information systems, management, and marketing. Cooperative education (co-op) opportunities are offered to qualified students.

Majors and areas of study offered through Xavier's College of Social Sciences include athletic training, criminal justice, economics, education (early childhood, middle childhood, secondary, Montessori, and special education), international affairs, nursing, occupational therapy, political science, psychology, social work, sociology, and sports management/sports marketing.

Xavier offers a preprofessional program in law. Students in the program are free to select any major of interest to them. The prelaw adviser assists students in their course selection and preparation for law school.

A two-year preprofessional program in pharmacy is also offered, preparing students for entrance into a school of pharmacy. Students who decide not to go on in pharmacy may continue at Xavier for a four-year degree in science.

Xavier offers pre-engineering programs in conjunction with the University of Cincinnati. In addition, an environmental management program is offered in conjunction with Duke University. After spending three years at Xavier in biology and two years at Duke in environmental management, students graduate with a Bachelor of Science in applied biology from Xavier and either a Master of Environmental Management or a Master of Forestry from Duke.

Students may select minor areas of study in art history, biology, business, chemistry, classical studies, communication arts, computer science, corrections, criminal justice, economics, education (Montessori and secondary), English, environmental studies, French, German, Greek, history, information technology, international affairs, international studies, jazz, Latin, Latin American studies, mathematics, music, peace studies, performance studies, philosophy, physics, political science, psychology, Spanish, studio art, theology, and women and minorities studies. The Center for Adult and Part-time Students serves those who wish to continue their education but are not in a position to attend regular daytime classes. In addition to the bachelor's degrees, the division offers two-year associate degree programs in a number of fields.

Academic Program

The academic year consists of two semesters, and summer courses are available. While the number of semester hours required for graduation varies with the program chosen, a minimum of 120 hours are required for a degree. A student must fulfill the required semester hours in a major as well as the basic requirements of the core curriculum. With an emphasis on liberal arts education, the curriculum serves to prepare the individual for a full and purposeful life as well as for a career. The student must complete a designated number of hours in the humanities, mathematics, philosophy, sciences, social sciences, and theology, and considerable freedom is permitted in the selection of courses in these areas.

Special programs include the Honors Bachelor of Arts degree program, the University Scholars Program, and programs in peace and justice and in women's and minority studies. The four-year program in international affairs provides students with the fundamentals of international relations through classwork, internships, and study abroad.

Off-Campus Arrangements

Sixteen area colleges, including Xavier, have formed the Greater Cincinnati Consortium of Colleges and Universities through which all students at member colleges may take courses not available at their home institution. Xavier encourages full-time students to take advantage of this opportunity for curriculum enrichment through cross-registration. In addition, students who wish to spend a year abroad as part of their undergraduate education have a number of possibilities open to them through the Xavier Study-Abroad Program. The Fredin Memorial Scholarship is awarded annually to an outstanding student for a year of study at the Sorbonne in Paris.

Academic Facilities

The McDonald Memorial Library supports all of the University's programs and offers extensive opportunities for print and computerized research, including online and CD-ROM resources. The University Center hosts seminars, workshops, and many extracurricular programs. The University Theatre is used by the communication arts department as well as for many University functions. Xavier's own radio and TV stations, WVXU-FM and XUTV, are a great resource for communication arts students. The television studio has full-color production capabilities. The $8.8-million Science Center project provides a modern science facility that serves the needs of today's students. The center comprises a physics building and renovated buildings for the biology and chemistry departments.

Costs

Tuition and fees at Xavier for 2000–01 are $7840 per semester, while room and board costs average $3225 per semester, depending on accommodations. Books and supplies cost approximately $500 per semester. (Costs are subject to change.)

Financial Aid

The Financial Aid Office has adequate funds to meet the demonstrated financial need of students from families in all income categories. Academic scholarships, which are competitive and renewable, are divided into five categories. The Trustee, Presidential, and Honor scholarships are awarded each year on the basis of students' academic qualifications. Ten 4-year, non-need, full-tuition St. Francis Xavier Scholarships are awarded annually to students of superior academic ability and extracurricular involvement. The Xavier Service Fellowships are awarded on the basis of academic merit and out-of-class service to school, church, or community. These awards pay full tuition, room, and board and provide a book allowance. In addition, Xavier offers departmental scholarships, music and art scholarships, performing arts grants, minority awards, and ROTC scholarships. The University also participates in the following federally sponsored aid programs: the Federal Perkins Loan, Federal Pell Grant, Federal Supplemental Educational Opportunity Grant, Federal Work-Study, and Federal Stafford Student Loan programs. Residents of Ohio may qualify for assistance under the Ohio Instructional Grant Program. In order to be considered for financial aid, one must complete the Free Application for Federal Student Aid (FAFSA).

Faculty

The faculty for all divisions numbers 439 members, of whom 244 are full-time. There are no teaching assistants, and graduate students do not teach. More than 80 percent of the faculty members hold doctoral degrees. Of Xavier's faculty members, 10 percent are Jesuits. The student-faculty ratio is 17:1 and the average class size is 22 students. Academic, vocational, and personal counseling and counseling for veterans are readily available. The University has always enjoyed a reputation for good rapport and excellent personal relationships between faculty members and students.

Student Government

The Student Government is the principal agency of student participation in University governance and is devoted to improving the quality of student life. Students choose from more than 100 different academic clubs, social organizations, and intramural group teams. The Student Senate, the main governing organization of the student body, is composed of 16 elected members. Xavier students sit on numerous University committees. A new student center will open in fall 2001.

Admission Requirements

Xavier is open to qualified men and women regardless of religion, race, color, handicap, or national origin. Students who have demonstrated past academic achievement and who show promise and aptitude for successful performance at Xavier are encouraged to apply for admission. A student's potential for success in college studies is judged by the high school average, rank in class, aptitude test scores (ACT or SAT I), and recommendations. Of these, the high school record is the most important factor. An applicant must present a minimum of 15 high school units, consisting of 4 in English, 3 in mathematics, 2 in social science, 2 in a natural science, 2 in a foreign language, and 2 in electives. An interview is strongly recommended.

Transfer students in good academic standing are invited to apply to Xavier. Transfer students must submit transcripts from their high schools and each college attended. Admission decisions are made on a rolling basis within two to four weeks of the date an application is received.

Application and Information

To be considered for admission, a student must submit the application form with the $25 application fee; the official high school transcript sent by the school with a teacher recommendation; and scores on the SAT I or ACT, which may be included on the high school record. Students are strongly encouraged to apply by the March 15 priority deadline.

An application and additional information may be obtained by contacting:

Office of Admission
Xavier University
3800 Victory Parkway
Cincinnati, Ohio 45207-5311
Telephone: 513-745-3301
          800-344-4698 Ext. 3301 (toll-free)
E-mail: xuadmit@xu.edu
World Wide Web: www.xu.edu

Xavier University's academic mall.

YORK COLLEGE
OF THE CITY UNIVERSITY OF NEW YORK
JAMAICA, NEW YORK

The College

Founded in 1966, York College offers a distinctive educational experience within the City University of New York (CUNY) system. This small, modernized institution embodies the essential qualities of a major university: a strong liberal arts foundation, a distinguished faculty, preprofessional programs, and career planning. At the same time, students are offered the intimacy, individualized attention, and sense of community unavailable at larger universities.

More than fifty student organizations, representing various academic and ethnic interests and including student publications, welcome student participation. Students participate in intercollegiate and intramural athletics and a variety of recreational activities.

In 1986, York College opened a new facility in Jamaica, New York, constituting the academic core of its new campus. The structure—which includes an interior mall that covers four levels and is topped by a glass skylight—houses up-to-date laboratory, computer, and library facilities. It provides an excellent academic and social environment for York College students. Work was completed on an athletic and physical education complex, as well as on a performing arts center with a 1,500-seat theater, in 1990.

Location

Centrally located in Queens, New York, York College is accessible by car, bus, subway, and the Long Island Rail Road. Easy access to the rest of Queens and New York City enables York College students to engage in extensive community service as a part of their curriculum. The College is 4 miles from John F. Kennedy Airport.

Majors and Degrees

York College awards Bachelor of Arts and Bachelor of Science degrees in the following liberal arts and career-oriented majors: accounting, Afro-American studies, anthropology, art history, biology, biotechnology, business administration, chemistry, community health, economics, education (bilingual, early childhood, and elementary), English, environmental health science, French, geology, gerontology, health education, health promotion management, history, information systems management, marketing, mathematics, medical technology, movement science (nonteaching physical education), music, nursing, occupational therapy, philosophy, physical education (teaching), physics, political science, psychology, social work, sociology, Spanish, speech, and studio art.

Many majors have an integral cooperative education component that enables students in the junior and senior years to alternate semesters between school and paid internships.

Academic Program

The curriculum at York College is designed to give students a firm and broad base in the liberal arts as well as to permit specialization in a career or professional area. The required liberal arts core includes courses in the humanities, social sciences, and natural sciences, and selections may be made from a range of courses. At least 120 credits are required to earn a bachelor's degree. Students should refer to the College's current catalog for the credit requirements for each major.

Cooperative education is designed to give students practical work experience to supplement the theoretical work in the classroom. Three job placements are made, giving students a range of opportunities. Upon graduation, students are better prepared for the labor market, have significant job experience and references, and are well equipped to seek employment in their field.

York College has an ongoing commitment to its community, and community service is an integral part of many of the academic programs. Students in the areas of community health, education, gerontology, health promotion management, occupational therapy, physical education, political science, psychology, and social work have the opportunity to become involved in community service fieldwork and internships. They gain valuable experience while making a contribution to the community.

Academic Facilities

York College's modern facility on Guy R. Brewer Boulevard and Liberty Avenue provides extensive science and computer laboratories, a large library, and up-to-date education technology. Music majors studying electronic music and jazz have access to a computer music studio that has microcomputers, digital synthesizers, MIDI interfaces, sound sampling systems, and multitrack tape recorders. The Computer Graphics Lab of York College is the most modern graphics lab in the City University system. In this advanced facility, students can display three-dimensional scientific figures, create graphic business charts and presentations, develop desktop publishing skills, or utilize computer-aided design in other disciplines and fields of study. Students interested in media and the communication arts have access to a fully equipped television production studio, including audio production. There are also a theater complex and a physical education facility that includes an Olympic-size swimming pool, an athletic field, tennis and handball courts, a health promotion center, a health promotion lab, and biofeedback facilities.

Costs

For 2000–01, the cost of tuition for newly enrolled full-time students is $3200 per year for in-state residents and $6800 per year for newly enrolled out-of-state residents. The student activity fee is $91.70 per year. Room and board are not available at York College. Tuition is subject to change.

Financial Aid

Financial aid is available for qualified students on the basis of need through state and federal aid programs. For full consideration, applicants should file the City University of New York Application for Federal State Student Aid (CUNY AFSSA). Applications for the fall semester should be submitted by the preceding June.

Faculty

More than 85 percent of the full-time faculty members hold a doctoral degree. The faculty is dedicated to scholarship, research, and high-quality teaching. Faculty members work closely with students to provide the academic and intellectual support necessary for the students' successful development.

Student Government

The student government, composed of elected student representatives, is responsible for the allocation of money for student activities. Members of the student government serve on College-wide committees that decide College policy.

Admission Requirements

Admission is based upon the applicant's academic average and academic units. Classwork and SAT I or ACT scores may be considered in the admission decision. Admission is centrally processed by the City University of New York and directly at the Office of Admissions of York College.

Application and Information

Applicants to the freshman class are admitted on a monthly basis starting in February for the fall semester; transfer applicants are admitted starting in April. The application fee is $40 for freshmen and $50 for transfer students. Application forms may be obtained by contacting the Admissions Office at the address below.

For further information, students should contact:

Admissions Office
York College of the
   City University of New York
Jamaica, New York 11451

Telephone: 718-262-2165
Fax: 718-262-2601
Email: admissions@york.cuny.edu
World Wide Web: http://www.york.cuny.edu

On the campus of York College of the City University of New York.

YORK UNIVERSITY
TORONTO, ONTARIO, CANADA

The University
Since it was founded in 1959, York University has developed a national and international reputation for innovation and excellence in scholarship, teaching, and research. York offers undergraduate and graduate degrees in the humanities and social sciences, business, environmental studies, fine arts, pure and applied science, social work, education, and law and is home to twenty leading research centres. There are just under 40,000 students at York, making it the third-largest university in Canada. Because of its size, York can offer a wide range of opportunities and services for its students. The University is made up of two very different campuses, so students can choose the learning environment that suits them best. The York Campus, in Toronto's north end, is a modern learning environment with extensive facilities, including a bookstore, thirty-six restaurants, a retail mall, an athletics complex, on-campus housing, and hundreds of on-campus events and cultural activities. The Glendon Campus, in midtown Toronto, is a small liberal arts college with a close-knit community where classes are taught in English and French. Students do not need to be fluent in French to attend Glendon; although it helps to have studied French through the twelfth grade, students can come to Glendon without any knowledge of French.

Location
York University is located in Toronto, Canada's largest city and main financial centre. Named one of the world's best cities in which to live by *Fortune* magazine, Toronto is known for friendliness and safety. As one of the world's most multicultural cities, Toronto has theater, music, and restaurants from all over the globe. From art galleries and museums to restaurants and major-league sports, Toronto has all of the elements of a world-class city. Toronto is convenient—it is a 1-hour flight from New York City, Boston, Chicago, or Detroit and a 90-minute drive from the Canadian-U.S. border at Buffalo, New York.

Majors and Degrees
The Bachelor of Arts (daytime studies, York campus) is offered in African studies, anthropology, applied mathematics, business and society, Canadian studies, classical studies (includes Greek and Latin), classics, computer science, coordinated business, creative writing, East Asian studies, economics, economics and business, English, French studies, geography, German studies, global political studies, health and society, history, humanities, individualized studies, information technology, kinesiology and health science, labour studies, languages/literatures and linguistics (includes courses in Chinese, German, Hebrew, Italian, Japanese, Russian, and Spanish), Latin American and Caribbean studies, law and society, mass communications, mathematics, mathematics for commerce, philosophy, political science, psychology, public policy and administration, religious studies, science/technology/culture and society, social and political thought, sociology, statistics, urban studies, and women's studies. Joint programs with some Ontario community colleges are available in communication arts, early childhood education, gerontology, and rehabilitation services. The Bachelor of Business Administration is offered in accounting, economics, entrepreneurship and family business, finance, management science/information systems, marketing, organizational behaviour and industrial relations, and strategic management. An International Bachelor of Business Administration is also offered. The Bachelor of Environmental Studies is offered in environmental policy and action; global development, peace, and justice; human settlement and population; and nature, technology, and society. The Faculty of Fine Arts offers the Bachelor of Design as well as the Bachelor of Fine Arts (B.F.A.) and the Bachelor of Arts (B.A.) in the following programs: cultural studies (B.A. only), dance (B.F.A. only), film and video, music, theater, and visual arts (includes art history, drawing, media arts, painting, photography, printmaking, and sculpture). The Bachelor of Arts at the Glendon Campus (courses taught in English and/or French) is offered in business economics, Canadian studies, computer science, drama studies, economics, English, environmental and health sciences, études françaises, Hispanic studies, history, information technology, international studies, linguistics and language studies, mathematics, mathematics for commerce, multidisciplinary studies, philosophy, political science, psychology, sociology, translation, and women's studies. A joint program with Seneca College is available in early childhood education. Certificates are available in intercultural studies, refugee and migration studies, Spanish/English and English/Spanish translation, teaching English as an international language, and technical and professional writing. The Bachelor of Science is offered in applied mathematics, astronomy, atmospheric chemistry, biology, chemistry, computer science, earth and atmospheric science, environmental science, geography, kinesiology and health science, mathematics, physics, psychology, space and communication sciences, and statistics. A joint program with Seneca College is available in rehabilitation services. Atkinson College offers the following degrees, primarily in the evening: Bachelor of Administrative Studies (accounting,* business research,* general management,* health administration,* human resource management,* information technology, and marketing), Bachelor of Arts (business economics, Canadian studies, classical studies, conservation and environmental studies, computer science, economics, English, fine arts (including creative arts and cultural expression, film, music, theater, and visual arts), geography, history, humanities, liberal studies, mathematics, philosophy, political science, psychology, public administration and management, public service studies,* science and technology studies, social science, sociology, urban studies, and women's studies), Bachelor of Science (computer science, general science mathematics, and psychology), Bachelor of Science in Nursing, and Bachelor of Social Work. The Bachelor of Education (concurrent) is offered in primary-junior (junior kindergarten–grade 6), junior-intermediate (grades 4–10), and intermediate-senior (grades 7–final year of high school) levels. The Bachelor of Education (consecutive) is offered in primary-junior (junior kindergarten–grade 6), junior-intermediate (grades 4–10, with options in computer science, English, environmental science, fine arts dance, fine arts drama, fine arts music, fine arts visual arts, French as a second language, geography, history, mathematics, physical education, religious studies, and science general), and intermediate-senior (grades 7–final year of high school, with options in computer science, economics, English, environmental science, fine arts dance, fine arts drama, fine arts music, fine arts visual arts, French as a second language, geography, history, individual and society, mathematics, physical education, political science, religious studies, science biology, science chemistry, science general,** science physics, and Spanish). York's Osgoode Hall law school offers a Bachelor of Laws. An asterisk (*) indicates that a program is available through distance education. The program with the double asterisk (**) is not available at the intermediate-senior level to students who select biology, chemistry, or physics as a teaching subject.

Academic Program
Students can begin their studies at York in September (all programs), January (Faculty of Arts and Atkinson), or May (Atkinson, Faculty of Pure and Applied Science, and Glendon). Students can study on a full- or part-time basis during the day or evening. All undergraduate and professional degrees have specific requirements that students are required to complete prior to graduating. All undergraduate students at York complete up to a maximum of four general education courses to round out their degree programs. Detailed information on

program requirements can be found in the University calendars on York's Web site, which is listed below.

Off-Campus Arrangements

York offers more than 100 exchange and study-abroad opportunities in thirty-five countries around the world. All undergraduate students can take part in an academic exchange for one year or semester if they are in an honors program, have completed two years of study, maintained at least an overall B average, and, in some cases, have proficiency in the host country's language.

Academic Facilities

York offers students five libraries with a total collection of more than 4.4 million items, including 2.2 million books as well as maps, films, videos, archives, sound recordings, and compact disks. There are visual arts studios, three theaters, two art galleries, state-of-the-art science laboratories, and an observatory with two telescopes. York students have access to a wide range of computer facilities, including forty-two computer labs and 1,900 workstations. All students receive free e-mail and Internet access. To help students succeed in their studies, there are academic tutors, advisers to help with course selection, and an extensive learning disabilities program. Students whose first language is not English can get extra help at the English as a Second Language Tutoring Centre and take ESL courses that count toward their degrees. Those who need to improve their English to attend university can take intensive ESL courses at the York University English Language Institute before starting a regular degree program.

Costs

For the 1999–2000 academic year, tuition fees for a full-time student were approximately Can$4445 for Canadian citizens and permanent residents or Can$10,800 for international students. Room and board, including a meal plan that costs Can$1800, cost approximately Can$4650 for a double room (students living in residence must purchase a meal plan). Course materials, books, and supplies generally average approximately Can$800. International students must also pay a Can$690 health insurance fee. All fees are subject to change.

Financial Aid

York offers entrance scholarships to undergraduate candidates with excellent academic grades. These scholarships range in value from Can$500 to Can$6000. The scholarships are for first-year study only and are not renewable. Applicants are considered for scholarships at the time of admission. International candidates can compete for the prestigious Global Leader of Tomorrow Award, worth Can$10,500 and renewable for up to four years of undergraduate study as long as excellent grades are maintained. An application for this award is necessary. Once at York, international students are eligible for continuing student scholarships worth up to Can$2500 based on their performance in York courses. U.S. citizens may be eligible to receive U.S. federal funding to study at York (York's FAFSA code is 007679). All full-time international students may work part-time on campus. For details, students should contact the Office of International Admissions.

Faculty

York's professors are known internationally for excellence and innovation in teaching and research. In the past six years, two York professors have been named Canadian Professor of the Year by the Council for the Advancement and Support of Education. More than 50 York faculty members have received provincial and national awards for teaching excellence. Ninety-four percent of York's 3,000 professors hold Ph.D.'s, and 88 percent of all first-year courses are taught by tenured professors—the highest percentage of any university in Canada.

Student Government

There are sixteen recognized student governments at York. Most are located within the residential colleges and faculties. There is also a central student government, the York Federation of Students, which offers many services, including a health plan, a course evaluation guide, International Identity Cards, and Student Saver Cards. York University students also have representation on the Board of Governors, Senate, Faculty Councils, Council of Masters, and other advisory committees.

Admission Requirements

York is a selective university; therefore, only those candidates who show potential for academic success are considered for admission. Some programs that are very limited in enrolment may require a higher average and specific preparation in certain subject areas. As a guideline, students from the U.S. educational system should present a minimum overall B average on academic high school work. This is considered along with a combined score of at least 1100 on the SAT I or a composite score of at least 24 on the ACT exam. York's CEEB Code is 0894.

Application and Information

Applications are available from the Office of International Admissions or on line at http://www.yorku.ca/admissions. Students applying to other Ontario universities in addition to York may use the common application available on line at http://www.ouac.on.ca or from the Ontario Universities' Application Centre (650 Woodlawn Road West; P.O. Box 1328; Guelph, Ontario N1H 7P4, Canada). All undergraduate programs begin in September. Some programs also start in January or May. The early deadline for September entry is February 1; the final deadline is June 1. International applicants are strongly encouraged to apply by February 1, especially for fine arts and the Schulich School of Business. November 1 is the deadline for the January term, March 1 for the May term.

For additional information about admissions, academic programs, or University visits and tours, students should contact:

Office of International Admissions
York University
4700 Keele Street
Toronto, Ontario M3J 1P3
Canada
Telephone: 416-736-5825
Fax: 416-650-8195
E-mail: intlenq@yorku.ca
World Wide Web: http://www.yorku.ca

Vari Hall, the focal point of the York campus.

YOUNGSTOWN STATE UNIVERSITY
YOUNGSTOWN, OHIO

The University

Located on a spectacular 140-acre campus near downtown Youngstown, Ohio, Youngstown State University (YSU) offers its students a comprehensive selection of major programs backed by a strong tradition of teaching and scholarship. YSU's diverse student body of more than 12,200 and a student-faculty ratio of 20:1 provide the personal contact associated with a smaller institution, and its connection to the Ohio state system of higher education enables it to draw on the vast resources of that system. The average class size is 26 for lectures and 13 for labs.

Youngstown State seeks to offer its students a vital living and learning environment with a relatively small, cohesive campus and a wealth of curricular and cocurricular activities. Attractive residence halls house close to 1,000 students and include a special residential honors facility. Student activities abound, with more than 140 student organizations, including social sororities and fraternities and opportunities for participation in theater, performing groups, student publications, intramural and intercollegiate athletics, and activity planning.

Youngstown State University competes in NCAA athletics. In the past decade, it has captured four Division I-AA national football championships. During the same decade, the women's basketball team won four Mid-Continent Conference titles and played two years in the NCAA tournament. The University fields ten women's and seven men's intercollegiate Division I teams. Fitness and recreational facilities are free to all YSU students in the Beeghly Physical Education Center and the Stambaugh Sports Complex, including track, tennis, swimming, racquetball, basketball, handball, Nautilus, aerobic conditioning, and free-weights.

Of the more than 12,500 students at YSU, 11,025 are undergraduates. Multicultural students number 1,286, and international students hail from fifty-five countries. Students benefit from a wide range of student services: complete tutorial assistance in all subject areas, with special centers for writing, reading, and mathematics; counseling and health services; career testing, planning, and placement; special programs for multicultural, women, and nontraditional students (those older than 25); and an orientation program that includes mentoring by faculty and staff members and upperclass students.

The University seeks a balance between teaching, service, and scholarly activity that serves both its students and the larger community of scholars. The University is committed to keeping its doors open to all who seek higher education and equally committed to giving students every opportunity to enrich their minds, develop their creativity and problem-solving abilities, and become informed, conscientious citizens of the world.

Location

Youngstown is at the center of a metropolitan area of 600,000, located 60 miles from both Pittsburgh and Cleveland. The campus is within easy driving or walking distance of restaurants, shopping centers, museums, and parks. The University is a major contributor to the city's cultural and recreational vitality, each year presenting hundreds of concerts, exhibits, lectures, performances, and athletic contests. The city offers an outstanding symphony orchestra, three community theaters, a vital arts community, and unlimited recreational options provided by 2,500-acre Mill Creek Park. YSU students can take advantage of close ties to area businesses for internships and work co-op programs, which provide valuable on-the-job experience.

Majors and Degrees

The College of Arts and Sciences offers majors in Africana studies, American studies, anthropology, biology, chemistry, combined science, computer information systems, computer science, earth science, economics, English, environmental studies, French, geography, geology, German, history, Italian, Latin, mathematics, office information systems, philosophy, physics/astronomy, political science, professional writing and editing, psychology, religious studies, Russian, social studies, sociology, and Spanish.

The Beeghly College of Education offers majors in counseling, early and middle childhood education, educational administration, educational leadership, gifted and talented educational specialist studies, secondary education (with specialized teaching fields), and special education.

The Rayen College of Engineering and Technology offers majors in chemical engineering, civil engineering, civil engineering technology, drafting and design technology, electrical engineering, electrical engineering technology, industrial engineering, mechanical engineering, and mechanical engineering technology.

The College of Fine and Performing Arts offers majors in art, art history, music/history and literature, music/music education, music/performance, music/theory and composition, telecommunication studies, and theater.

The Bifonte College of Health and Human Services offers majors in allied health, community health, criminal justice, dental hygiene, dietetic technology, emergency medical technology, exercise science, family and consumer sciences education, food and nutrition, histotechnology, home economics services, hospitality management, medical assisting technology, medical laboratory technology, medical technology, merchandising (fashion and interiors), military science, nursing, nursing home administration, physical education, physical therapy, police science and corrections, prekindergarten, respiratory care, social service technology, and social work.

The Williamson College of Business Administration offers majors in accounting, advertising and public relations, advertising art, finance, general administration, labor studies, management, marketing, marketing/fashion retail, marketing/industrial, marketing management, marketing management technology, marketing/retailing, marketing/shopping center, and public administration. Associate degrees are offered with concentrations in accounting, finance, management, and marketing.

Interdisciplinary minors are offered in American studies, environmental science, journalism, linguistics, peace and conflict studies, and women's studies.

Students may also enroll for a combined B.S./M.D. program with the Northeastern Ohio Universities College of Medicine. Each student successfully completing this program is awarded the Bachelor of Science degree from Youngstown State University and the M.D. degree from the College of Medicine.

Academic Program

YSU is distinct among universities in that it is one of a few comprehensive metropolitan institutions that provide associate, baccalaureate, and graduate instruction and continuing education in one location. Currently, the University offers a broad curriculum in the School of Graduate Studies and six colleges: Arts and Sciences, Education, Engineering and Technology, Fine and Performing Arts, Health and Human Services, and Business Administration. The spirit of cooperation among departments and colleges permits students to pursue interdisciplinary majors and minors, to major in one department or college and minor in another, or to pursue double majors. Youngstown State University provides for a broad-based education through a core curriculum of at least 46 quarter hours in the areas of humanities, social studies, and science and mathematics. In addition to fulfilling this general education requirement, each student must complete the major and/or minor requirements in order to meet the minimum 186 quarter hours required for the baccalaureate degree.

Conversion of associate degree credits into baccalaureate programs is possible within the University. Transfer and dual-admission agreements with two-year institutions and community colleges provide opportunities for transfer into baccalaureate programs at Youngstown State.

The Individualized Curriculum Program is available to students whose needs are not met by existing conventional programs. Students may design curricula to suit their particular needs, allowing alternative paths for earning the undergraduate degrees currently offered.

Off-Campus Arrangements

YSU offers cooperative/internship education programs in which students participate in both classroom and experiential study via employment in a government, industry, or business setting. Opportunities for international studies for academic credit are available in several majors.

Academic Facilities

Maag Library houses more than a half-million books and more than 200,000 government documents and subscribes to more than 3,100 periodicals and scholarly journals. Online research services provide access to all state university libraries in Ohio and a wide range of other information sources. The library's resources are augmented by the Curriculum Resource Center in the College of Education. A Multimedia Center, housed in Maag Library, offers research materials in a variety of formats.

Comprehensive computing facilities are readily available to students throughout the campus. Scientific laboratories at YSU are fully outfitted with up-to-date instructional and research equipment. Studios and performance halls in the College of Fine and Performing Arts have been recently renovated for acoustic excellence, and the McDonough Museum of Art is an innovative exhibit space for student and faculty work.

Costs

Tuition and fees for an Ohio resident for 2000–01 are $3994 for full-time freshmen and sophomores and $4162 for full-time juniors and seniors. For students residing in certain counties in New York, West Virginia, and western Pennsylvania, the out-of-state tuition surcharge is reduced, making the total cost $5938 for full-time freshmen and sophomores and $6106 for full-time juniors and seniors. The charge for University housing, including meals, is $4800 per year. The University estimates books and supplies at $860 per year and on-campus parking at $78 per semester. Some laboratory and computer classes entail a la fee, ranging from $20 to $40. All fees and charges are subject to change.

Financial Aid

Financial aid is awarded in four basic forms: scholarships, grants, loans, and on-campus employment. Depending on the student's computed financial need, the award may include a package of any or all of these components in varying amounts. Financial aid applications should be submitted to the University by March 1 for fall-quarter assistance and must be resubmitted each year.

About 75 percent of Youngstown State students receive some form of financial aid through a comprehensive program that includes need-based and performance-based aid. The average award in 1999–2000 was $3778 per student receiving aid. Youngstown State prides itself on an exemplary scholarship program that rewards academic performance and promise. The University Scholars program was instituted in 1992–93 to provide full-cost scholarships for 160 high-achieving students. Numerous other scholarships are available under a wide range of criteria.

Faculty

YSU's faculty has 406 full-time and 380 part-time members. About 80 percent of full-time faculty members hold the highest degree in their fields. Since small classes are the norm at YSU, faculty members and students enjoy many opportunities for informal interaction.

Student Government

Student Government exercises the power to conduct student elections, to recommend student representatives to serve on joint faculty-student committees, and to supervise programs funded from its operating budget. Members are elected by the student body to executive positions and to the legislative branch in proportion to the enrollment in each college. Student Government nominates students for two gubernatorial appointments to the University Board of Trustees.

Admission Requirements

Ohio residents and residents of Mercer and Lawrence Counties in Pennsylvania must have graduated from high school with a state-approved diploma or passed the test of General Educational Development (GED). Nonresidents must have graduated in the upper two thirds of their high school class, have a minimum ACT composite score of 17, have a minimum combined recentered SAT I score of 820, or have passed the GED test. Transfer applicants must have earned at least a 2.0 accumulated point average and be in good standing at the last institution attended.

Application and Information

Application deadlines vary depending on the semester and the program for which a student is applying. Under the EARLY registration program, students who are admitted by February 15 become eligible for advance advisement and registration in fall classes. Applications must be accompanied by a nonrefundable fee. For more information and an application, students should contact:

Undergraduate Recruitment and Admissions
Youngstown State University
One University Plaza
Youngstown, Ohio 44555
Telephone: 330-742-2000
           330-742-1564 (TTY/TDD)
           877-468-6978 (toll-free)
Fax: 330-742-3674
E-mail: enroll@ysu.edu
World Wide Web: http://www.ysu.edu

The fountain area is representative of YSU's award-winning landscaping and is a favorite gathering spot for students.

An Alphabetically Arranged Index to Colleges and Universities by Name Can Be Located on Page 1105.

NOTES

NOTES

NOTES

Peterson's unplugged

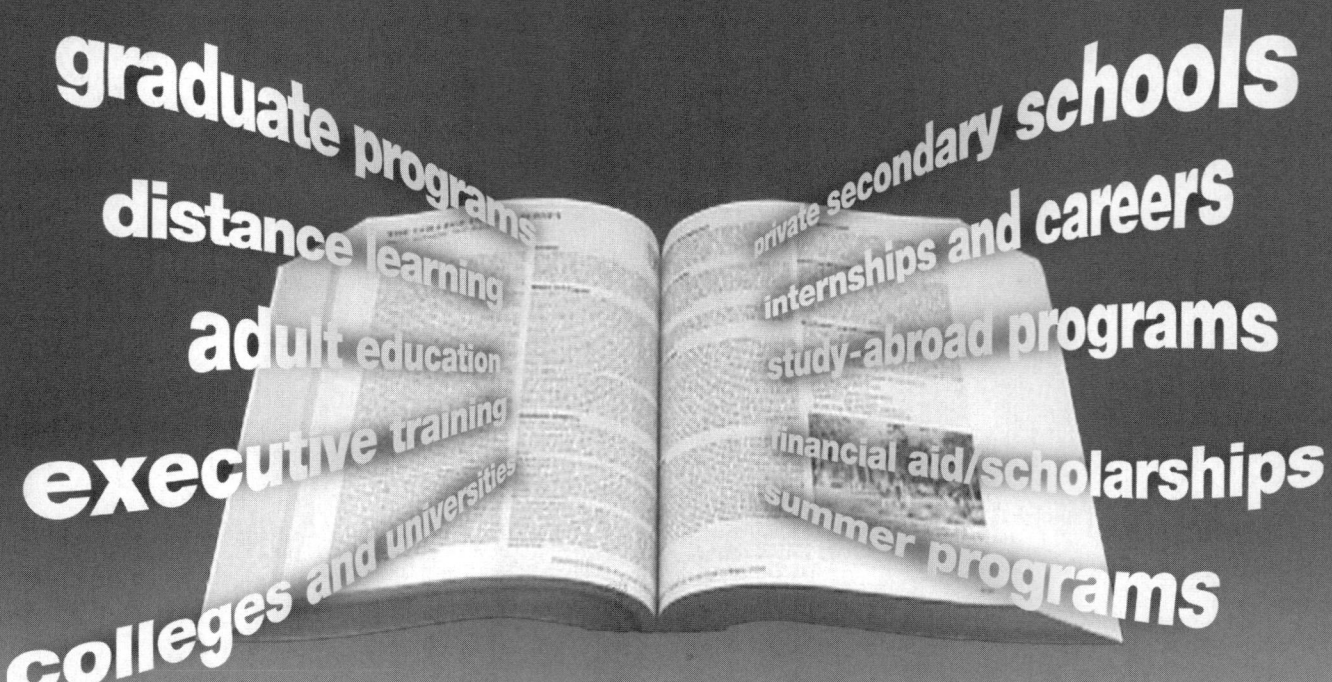

graduate programs
distance learning
adult education
executive training
colleges and universities
private secondary schools
internships and careers
study-abroad programs
financial aid/scholarships
summer programs

Peterson's quality on every page!

For more than three decades, we've offered a complete selection of books to guide you in all of your educational endeavors. You can find our vast collection of titles at your local bookstore or online at **petersons.com**.

High school student headed for college?

Busy professional interested in distance learning?

Parent searching for the perfect private school or summer camp?

Human resource manager looking for executive education programs?

AOL Keyword: Petersons
Phone: 800-338-3282

NOTES

Virtually anything is possible @ petersons.com

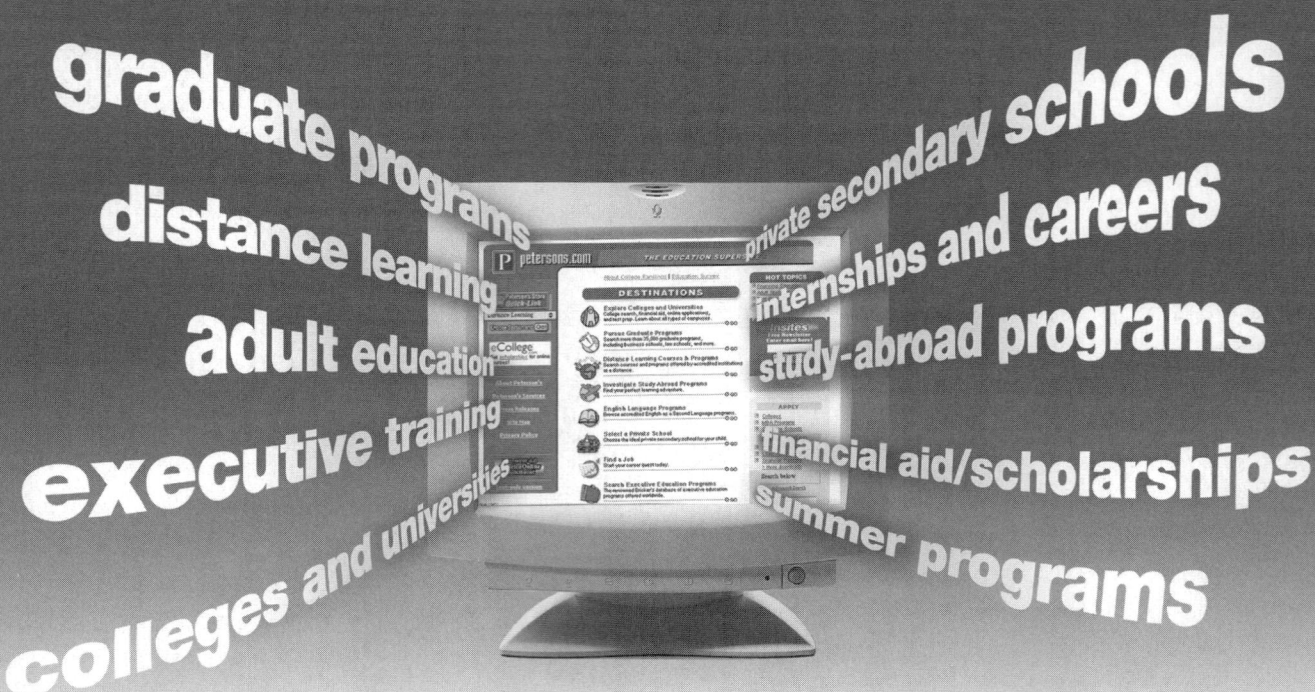

graduate programs
distance learning
adult education
executive training
colleges and universities
private secondary schools
internships and careers
study-abroad programs
financial aid/scholarships
summer programs

Peterson's quality with every click!

Whether you're a high school student headed for college or a busy professional interested in distance learning, you'll find all of the tools you need literally right at your fingertips!

Petersons.com is your ultimate online adviser, connecting you with "virtually any" educational or career need.

Visit us today at **petersons.com**
AOL Keyword: Petersons

Count on us to show you how to:

Apply to more than 1,200 colleges online

Finance the education of your dreams

Find a summer camp for your child

Make important career choices

Earn a degree online

Search executive education programs

Peterson's
Thomson Learning™

NOTES

PETERSON'S and eCollege.com Scholarship Fund

eCollege.com *www.ecollege.com/scholarships*

It's Simple Economics.

There are two things every student can use more of—time and money. You know that online distance learning saves you time, but what about money? That's where eCollege.com comes in. We're offering up to $2,000,000 in scholarships for students who want to utilize the power and convenience of the Internet as they pursue their degree or certificate. eCollege.com partners with schools across the country—from leading universities to local community colleges—to provide the highest quality educational technology and services. Visit www.ecollege.com/scholarships to see if there is a scholarship that's right for you.

www.ecollege.com/scholarships

NOTES

COLLEGE PARENTS OF AMERICA

College Parents of America (CPA) is the only national membership association dedicated to helping parents prepare for and put their students through college easily, economically, and safely. CPA is a resource, an adviser, and an advocate working on behalf of the millions of parents throughout the United States with current or future college students.

CPA guides families from the time they begin saving and preparing their students for college all the way through graduation. CPA provides new information on savings strategies, financial aid, tax savings, and other ways to help pay for college; advises college parents on the individual opportunities and challenges they will encounter during their students' college years; and serves as an advocate and voice on Capitol Hill, in state capitals, and on the nation's campuses. During the 1998 national budget debate, for example, CPA promoted tax credits and deductions for college expenses and continues to work to expand tax reductions for college costs.

CPA keeps members informed through its newsletter, The College Parent Advisor, which features advice from guest experts on timely issues; through its interactive Web site (**ww.collegeparents.org**); and through a toll-free member hotline.

CPA also collaborates on initiatives to inform and assist parents and their students, such as:

- **Advancing Personal Financial Knowledge** through "Money Talks," an educational program cosponsored by MasterCard International that helps parents teach their children good money management skills;

- **Combating Alcohol Abuse on Campus** in a partnership initiative with the U.S. Department of Education's Higher Education Center for Alcohol and Other Drug Prevention that advises parents on how to talk with their students about alcohol;

- **Fighting Financial Aid Scams** by alerting parents to the steps to avoid them in a partnership effort with the Federal Trade Commission.

In addition, CPA offers families special discounts on college-related products and services.

College Parents of America's members include parents, grandparents, colleges, universities, corporations, associations, and other organizations. To join, send in the enclosed tear-out card for a special discount on membership, call toll-free **888-256-4627** for automated information, or visit **www.collegeparents.org** on the Internet.

College Parents of America,
700 Thirteenth Street, NW, Suite 950,
Washington, DC 20005
(202) 661-2170